PUBLIC LIBRARY CORE COLLECTION:

NONFICTION

FIFTEENTH EDITION

CORE COLLECTION SERIES

Formerly
STANDARD CATALOG SERIES

CHRISTI SHOWMAN FARRAR, GENERAL EDITOR

CHILDREN'S CORE COLLECTION

MIDDLE AND JUNIOR HIGH CORE COLLECTION

SENIOR HIGH CORE COLLECTION

PUBLIC LIBRARY CORE COLLECTION: NONFICTION

FICTION CORE COLLECTION

PUBLIC LIBRARY CORE COLLECTION: NONFICTION

A Selection Guide to Reference Books
and
Adult Nonfiction

FIFTEENTH EDITION

Former title:

Public Library Catalog

EDITED BY

NEAL WYATT

KENDAL SPIRES

AND

GABRIELA TOTH

H. W. Wilson
A Division of EBSCO Information Services
Ipswich, Massachusetts
2015
GREY HOUSE PUBLISHING

ISBN 978-1-61925-473-2
ebook ISBN: 978-0-8242-1445-6

Abridged Dewey Decimal Classification and Relative Index, Edition 15 is © 2004-2012 OCLC Online Computer Library Center, Inc. Used with Permission. DDC, Dewey, Dewey Decimal Classification, and WebDewey are registered trademarks of OCLC.

Public Library Core Collection, 2015, published by Grey House Publishing, Inc., Amenia, NY, under exclusive license from EBSCO Information Systems, Inc.

A catalog record for this title is available from the Library of Congress.

PRINTED IN CANADA

CONTENTS

PREFACE

PUBLIC LIBRARY CORE COLLECTION: NONFICTION, formerly entitled Public Library Catalog, is a list of recommended reference and nonfiction books for adults, in classified order. The Core Collections are also available in electronic format via EBSCO*host,* updated weekly.

What's new in this edition?

Each new edition of PUBLIC LIBRARY CORE COLLECTION: NONFICTION is a mixture of the old and the new. Older titles, some in updated versions, are included if they remain the best titles in their field. Newer titles reflect new topics of interest and new interpretations of traditional knowledge. This edition of the Core Collection features general revisions to most subject areas.

History

The first of several installments of the "Standard Catalog" for the general library was published in 1918. It was called STANDARD CATALOG: SOCIOLOGY SECTION. Additional installments were issued over the next fourteen years, covering Biography; Fiction; Fine Arts; History and Travel; Science and Useful Arts; Literature and Philology; and Philosophy, Religion and General Works. Finally, a fully integrated first edition of the STANDARD CATALOG FOR PUBLIC LIBRARIES was assembled and published in 1934. The contents were displayed in classified order, according to the Dewey Decimal Classification. The name was changed to PUBLIC LIBRARY CATALOG with the publication of the fifth edition in 1969, and then to PUBLIC LIBRARY CORE COLLECTION: NONFICTION with the thirteenth edition in 2008.

Although a Fiction Section was issued in 1923, followed by supplements in 1928 and 1931, fiction was omitted from the first edition of the complete Catalog in 1934. A new expanded edition of the Fiction Section was published as FICTION CATALOG in 1942. In its preface that Catalog was referred to as "a companion volume to the Standard Catalog for Public Libraries." This complementary relationship has continued to the present. PUBLIC LIBRARY CORE COLLECTION: NONFICTION has always listed works of literary criticism and literary history and books about literary technique.

Scope and Purpose

This volume lists nonfiction books published in the United States, or published in other countries and distributed in the United States. It excludes non-print materials; periodicals; non-English items (with the exception of dictionaries), and works of an ephemeral nature. All books were in print at the time of listing. Original paperback editions are included. Entries for hardcover editions provide information about the availability of paperback reprints where possible. This volume comprises over 12,000 book titles with multiple subject access.

The Core Collection is intended to serve the needs of public and undergraduate libraries and stand as a basic or "opening day" collection. The newer titles help in identifying areas in a collection that can be updated or strengthened. Retention of useful material from the previous edition enables the librarian to make informed decisions about weeding a collection. With its classified arrangement, complete bibliographical data, and descriptive and critical annotations, the Core Collection provides useful information for the acquisitions librarian, the reference librarian, and the cataloger. Entries provide information about the availability of electronic versions of books listed.

Preparation

Books included in this edition were selected by experienced librarians representing public library systems and academic libraries across the United States who also act as a committee of advisors on library policy and trends. The names of participating librarians and their affiliations are listed in the Acknowledgments.

Organization

The Core Collection is organized into two parts: the Classified Collection; and an Author, Title, and Subject Index.

Part 1. Classified Collection. This is arranged according to the Dewey Decimal Classification. Within classes, arrangement is by main entry, with complete bibliographical and cataloging information given for each book. The classified arrangement, along with the descriptive and critical annotations, provides a useful guide to book selection. Entries include such information as price and ISBN to facilitate acquisitions.

Part 2. Author, Title, and Subject Index. This is a comprehensive key to the Classified List with entries for authors, titles, and subjects.

ACKNOWLEDGMENTS

H. W. Wilson and EBSCO Information Services express special gratitude to the following librarians who both advised the company in editorial matters and assisted in the selection of titles for this Core Collection:

Advisory Board

James E. Bobick
Author and Consultant
Pittsburgh, Pennsylvania

Gail de Vos
University of Alberta
Edmonton, Alberta, Canada

Mary Griffin
Omaha Public Library
Omaha, Nebraska

Steven Jablonski
Skokie Public Library
Skokie, Illinois

Brett W. Lear
Martin County Library
System
Stuart, Florida

John J. Meier
Penn State University
University Park, Pennsylvania

Mary Rasner
Library Consultant
Melrose, Massachusetts

DIRECTIONS FOR USE OF THE CORE COLLECTION

USES OF THE COLLECTION

PUBLIC LIBRARY CORE COLLECTION: NONFICTION is designed to serve a number of purposes:

As an aid in purchasing. The Core Collection is designed to assist in the selection and ordering of titles. Annotations are provided for each title along with information concerning the publisher, ISBN, price, and availability. Since Part 1, Classified Collection, is arranged according to the Dewey Decimal Classification, the Core Collection may be used to identify parts of the library collection that should be updated or strengthened. In evaluating the suitability of a work each library will want to consider the special character of the community it serves.

As an aid to the reader's advisor. The work of the reader's advisor is furthered by the information about sequels and companion volumes and the descriptive and critical annotations in the Classified Collection, and by the subject access in the Index.

As an aid in verification of information. For this purpose full bibliographical data are provided in the Classified Collection. Entries also include recommended subject headings based on *Sears List of Subject Headings* and a suggested classification derived from the *Abridged Dewey Decimal Classification and Relative Index*. Notes describe editions available, awards, publication history, and other titles in the series.

As an aid in collection maintenance. Information about titles available on a subject facilitates decisions to rebind, replace, or discard items. If a book has been deleted from the Core Collection in this edition because it is no longer in print, that deletion is not intended as a sign that the book is no longer valuable or that it should necessarily be weeded from the collection.

As an instructional aid. The Core Collection is useful in courses that deal with literature and book selection for public libraries.

ORGANIZATION

The Core Collection consists of two parts: a Classified Collection, and an Author, Title, and Subject Index.

Part 1. Classified Collection

The Classified Collection is arranged with nonfiction books first, classified according to the Dewey Decimal Classification in numerical order from 000 to 999. Individual biographies are classed at 92 and precede the 920s (collective biography). The information supplied for each book includes bibliographic description, suggested subject headings, an annotation, and frequently, an evaluation from a notable source.

An Outline of Classification, which serves as a table of contents for the Classified Collection, is reproduced following this section. It should be noted that many topics can be classified in more than one discipline. If a particular title is not found where it might be expected, the Index should be consulted to determine if it is classified elsewhere.

Within classes, works are arranged alphabetically under main entry, usually the author. Works of individual biography are arranged alphabetically under the biography's subject.

Each listing consists of a full bibliographical description. Prices, which are always subject to change, have been obtained from the publisher, when available, and are as current as possible. Entries include recommended subject headings derived from the *Sears List of Subject Headings*, a suggested classification number from the *Abridged Dewey Decimal Classification and Relative Index*, a brief description of the contents, and, whenever possible, an evaluation from a quoted source. The following is an example of a typical entry and a description of its components:

Roach, Mary, 1959-
★ **Stiff**; the curious lives of human cadavers.
Norton 2003 303 p il $23.95; pa $13.95   **611**
1. Dead 2. Dissection 3. Human experimentation in medicine
ISBN 0-393-05093-9; 0-393-32482-6 pa
LC 2002-152908
The author "explains how surgeons and doctors use cadavers donated for research purposes to help the living, and also examines potential new variations on how we bury the dead." Libr J
"For those who are interested in the fields of medicine or forensics and are aware of some of the procedures, this book makes excellent reading." SLJ
Includes bibliographical references

The star at the beginning of the entry indicates that this is a "most highly recommended" title. The name of the author, Mary Roach, is given in conformity with *Anglo-American Cataloguing Rules*, 2nd edition, 2002 revision. The title of the book is *Stiff: the curious lives of human cadavers*. The book was published by Norton in 2003.

The book has 303 pages and contains illustrations. It is published in hardcover and paperback, and sells for $23.95 and $13.95, respectively. (Prices given were current when the Collection went to press.)

At the end of the last line of type in the body entry is 611 in boldface type. This is the classification number or category derived from the fifteenth edition of the *Abridged Dewey Decimal Classification*.

The numbered terms "1. Dead 2. Dissection 3. Human experimentation in medicine" are recommended subject headings for this book based on *Sears List of Subject Headings*.

The ISBN (International Standard Book Number) is included to facilitate ordering. The Library of Congress control number is provided when available.

Following are three notes supplying additional information about the book. The first is a description of the book's content, in this case, an excerpt from *Library Journal*. The second is a critical note from *School Library Journal*. Such annotations are useful in evaluating books for selection and in determining which of several books on the same subject is best suited for the individual reader. The final note describes special features, such as a bibliography, if applicable. Notes are also made to describe sequels and companion volumes, editions available, awards, and publication history.

Part 2. Author, Title, and Subject Index

The Index is a single alphabetical list of all the books entered in the Core Collection. Each book is entered under author; title (if distinctive); and subject. The classification number, displayed in boldface type, is the key to the location of the main entry for the book in the Classified Collection.

Appropriate added entries are made for joint authors and editors. "See" references are made from forms of names or subjects that are not used as headings. "See also" references are made to related or more specific headings.

The following are examples of Index entries for the book cited above:

Author	**Roach, Mary, 1959-**	
	Stiff	**611**
Title	**Stiff.** Roach, M.	**611**
Subject	**DEAD**	
	Roach, M. Stiff.	**611**

Standards Used

Anglo-American Cataloguing Rules, 2nd ed., 2002 revision, 2005 update. Chicago: American Library Association, 2005.

Bristow, Barbara A. and Christi Showman Farrar, eds. *Sears List of Subject Headings*. 21st ed. Ipswich, MA: The H. W. Wilson Company, 2014.

Dewey, Melvil. *Abridged Dewey Decimal Classification and Relative Index*. 15th ed. Edited by Joan S. Mitchell, et al. Dublin, Ohio: OCLC, 2012.

OUTLINE OF CLASSIFICATION

Reproduced below is the Second Summary of the Dewey Decimal Classification. * As Part 1 of this Core Collection is arranged according to this classification, the outline will serve as a table of contents for it. Please note, however, that the inclusion of this outline is not to be considered a substitute for consulting the Dewey Decimal Classification itself.

* Reproduced from Edition 15 of the Abridged Dewey Decimal Classification and Relative Index, published in 2012, by permission of OCLC Online Computer Library Center, Inc., owner of copyright.

000   COMPUTER SCIENCE, KNOWLEDGE & SYSTEMS

001.1   Intellectual life

Levine, Lawrence W.

The **opening** of the American mind; canons, culture, and history. Beacon Press 1996 xxiv, 212p hardcover o.p. pa $18   **001.1**
  1. Higher education 2. Multiculturalism 3. United States -- Intellectual life
  ISBN 0-8070-3119-4 pa

LC 96-33866

The author "examines the current critique of higher education, the major debates over the curriculum and the canon over two centuries, and changes in the perceptions of the national culture. . . . Levine insists that there is no stable canon of writers; that universities have always mirrored dominant cultural attitudes toward gender, race, and ethnicity; and that diversity, pluralism, and multiculturalism have been present throughout American history." Choice

"Levine's presentation is eloquent, eminently reasonable, and gratifyingly optimistic." Booklist

Includes bibliographical references

001.4   Research; statistical methods

Feldman, Burton

The **Nobel** Prize; a history of genius, controversy, and prestige. Arcade Pub. 2000 489p il $29.95; pa $15.95   **001.4**
  1. Nobel Prizes
  ISBN 1-55970-537-X; 1-55970-592-2 pa

LC 00-42002

The author provides a "history of the prizes awarded in the sciences, literature, social sciences, and humankind's . . . peace efforts. This is the first comprehensive critical history of the prizes to appear, and it's very good." Libr J

Includes bibliographical references

MacLeod, Don

How to find out anything; from extreme Google searches to scouring government documents, a guide to uncovering anything about everyone and everything. Don MacLeod. 1st ed. Prentice Hall Press 2012 x, 256 p.p (pbk.) $20   **001.4**
  1. Research 2. Internet searching 3. Information resources 4. Research -- Methodology 5. Electronic information resources   6.   Electronic information resource searching
  ISBN 0735204675; 9780735204676

LC 2012010974

In this book, "researcher Don MacLeod explains how to find what you're looking for quickly, efficiently, and accurately--and how to avoid the most common mistakes of the Google Age. . . . [The author] shows you how to unveil nearly anything about anyone. From top CEO's salaries to police records, . . . researching for a term paper or digging up dirt on an ex, the advice in this book arms you with the sleuthing skills to tackle any mystery." (Publisher's note)

Tufte, Edward R.

The **visual** display of quantitative information; 2nd ed; Graphics Press 2001 197p il $40   **001.4**
  1. Statistics -- Graphic methods
  ISBN 0-9613921-4-2

LC 2001-271866

First published 1983

This book focuses "on statistical graphics, charts, tables. Theory and practice in the design of data graphics, 250 illustrations of the best (and a few of the worst) statistical graphics, with . . . analysis of how to display data for precise, effective, quick analysis." Publisher's note

001.9   Controversial knowledge

Bullard, Thomas E.

The **myth** and mystery of UFOs. University Press of Kansas 2010 417p il $35   **001.9**
  1. Unidentified flying objects
  ISBN 978-0-7006-1729-6; 0-7006-1729-9

LC 2010-26289

"Bullard is well known in the UFO community because he leaves the door open that there may be some basis in reality behind UFO stories while also contending that the UFO field is fertile ground for rumor and legend. His bibliography is impressive, and the book is a full account of UFO sightings and the development of 'Ufology.' He concludes that there is enough evidence to suggest that UFOs deserve a place in academic inquiry, with more scientific research needed. . . . Those interested in the UFO phenomenon will find tons of interesting material to ponder and a different way of looking at it." Libr J

Includes bibliographical references

Shermer, Michael

Why people believe weird things; pseudoscience, superstition, and other confusions of our time.

foreword by Stephen Jay Gould. rev and expanded;
Freeman, W.H. 2002 xxvi, 349p il pa $16   **001.9**
   1. Science 2. Parapsychology 3. Belief and doubt
   ISBN 0-8050-7089-3

                           LC 2002-68784
   First published 1997
   The author "explores the very human reasons people
find otherworldly phenomena, conspiracy theories, and
cults so appealing. In . . . [the] chapter, 'Why Smart People
Believe in Weird Things' he takes on science luminaries
like physicist Frank Tippler and others, who hide their
spiritual beliefs behind the trappings of science." Publisher's note
   Includes bibliographical references

001.944   Monsters and related phenomena

Kaplan, Matt
   Medusa's gaze and vampire's bite; the science
of monsters. Matt Kaplan. Scribner 2012 244 p.
(hardcover : alk. paper) $26   **001.944**
   1. Zombies 2. Vampires 3. Anthropology 4. Cyclopes
(Greek mythology) 5. Monsters -- History 6. Animals,
Mythical -- History 7. Dangerous animals -- Folklore
-- History
   ISBN 1451667981; 9781451667981; 9781451667998;
9781451668001

                           LC 2012016553
   In this book, journalist "[Matt] Kaplan sheds light on
why people fear monsters, from the Calydonian Boar depicted on ancient Greek friezes to the creatures of films like
Alien and Jurassic Park. He uses science and anthropology
to make educated guesses about how figures like cyclops,
zombies, vampires, and dragons worked their way into humanity's collective imagination." (Library Journal)

Prothero, Donald R., 1954-
   Abominable science! origins of the Yeti, Nessie,
and other famous cryptids. Daniel Loxton and Donald R. Prothero. Columbia University Press 2013
432 p. (cloth : alk. paper) $29.95   **001.944**
   1. Cryptozoology 2. Pseudoscience 3. Mythical
animals
   ISBN 0231153201; 9780231153201

                           LC 2013008424
   In this book, "after examining the nature of science and
pseudoscience and their relation to cryptozoology, [Daniel]
Loxton and [Donald R.] Prothero take on Bigfoot; the Yeti . .
.; the Loch Ness monster . . . [and] the Congo dinosaur. They
conclude with an analysis of the psychology behind the persistent belief in paranormal phenomena . . . and consider . .
. the challenge it poses to clear and critical thinking in our
increasingly complex world." (Publisher's note)
   Includes bibliographical references and index

002   The book

Basbanes, Nicholas A.
   Patience & fortitude; a roving chronicle of book
people, book places, and book culture. HarperCollins
Pubs. 2001 636p il hardcover o.p. pa $19.95 **002**
   1. Libraries 2. Book collecting 3. Books and reading
   ISBN 0-06-019695-5; 0-06-051446-9 pa

                           LC 2001-16935
   "Basbanes's fund of stories will delight readers who
value books for more than just a good story, have a yen for
second-hand books plucked from dusty shops or look to
book catalogs for suspense and excitement." Publ Wkly
   Includes bibliographical references

Buzbee, Lewis
   The **yellow** -lighted bookshop; a memoir, a history. Graywolf Press 2006 216p $17   **002**
   1. Booksellers and bookselling
   ISBN 1-55597-450-3

                           LC 2005-938151
   The author "tells the story of his lifelong obsession [with
books], from his elementary school Weekly Reader orders
to his first jobs clerking in bookstores and his short career
as a publisher's rep. Woven into these personal essays is a
tangential discourse on the history of bookmaking and bookselling, from the ancient Romans and Chinese to the modern
era." Publ Wkly
   This "is a tribute to those who crave the cozy confines of
a bookshop." Booklist

Darnton, Robert
   The **case** for books; past, present, and future.
PublicAffairs 2009 218p il $23.95   **002**
   1. Books and reading -- History
   ISBN 978-1-58648-826-0
   "These essays bring balance and a refreshing perspective
to the nervous predictions over the future of print." Libr J
   Includes bibliographical references

002.07   Education, research, related topics

Lansky, Aaron
   Outwitting history; the amazing adventures of
a man who rescued a million Yiddish books. Algonquin Books of Chapel Hill 2004 316p   **002.07**
   1. Book collecting 2. Yiddish language 3. National
Yiddish Book Center
   ISBN 1-56512-429-4

                           LC 2004-51587
   "Part memoir and part history, this is the . . . tale of how
Lansky retrieved thousands of books from dumpsters and
abandoned buildings across America. He also rescued books
from the aftermath of the 1994 terrorist bombing of the Jewish Community Center in Buenos Aires and went to Havana
to save the few remaining Yiddish books of a vestigial Jewish community there." Libr J
   "The book is a testimony to [Lansky's] love of Judaism and literature and his desire to make a difference in the
world." Publ Wkly
   Includes bibliographical references

003 Systems

Taleb, Nassim Nicholas

The **black** swan; the impact of the highly improbable. [by] Nassim Nicholas Taleb. 2nd ed; Random House Trade Paperbacks 2010 xxxiii, 444p il pa $17 **003**

1. Forecasting
ISBN 0-8129-7381-X; 978-0-8129-7381-5
LC 2010-292618

First published 2007

Examines the role of the unexpected, discussing why improbable events are not anticipated or understood properly, and how humans rationalize the black swan phenomenon to make it appear less random.

The author "is really a philosopher in a businessman's clothing and his irreverent writing style, with its frequent first-person asides and tangential musings that go on for pages, actually helps make heavy intellectual discussions more accessible." Risk Management

Includes bibliographical references

004 Computer science; computer programming, programs, data; special computer methods

Dyson, George

Turing's cathedral; the origins of the digital universe. George Dyson. Pantheon Books 2012 xxii, 401 p.p (hardback) $29.95 **004**

1. Symbolic logic 2. Computers -- History 3. Mathematics -- History 4. Computer science -- History 5. Turing, Alan Mathison, 1912-1954 6. Turing machines 7. Computable functions 8. Random access memory
ISBN 9780375422775
LC 2011030265

In this book, "science historian George Dyson shines light on the critical period when computers came into being. He begins with British mathematician Alan Turing's . . . 1936 description of a machine designed to resolve a problem in mathematical logic. . . . Dyson focuses on US efforts, when . . . a group of engineers, scientists and mathematicians, gathered together by Hungarian-American polymath John von Neumann . . . bent their minds to the making of the IAS machine." (New Scientist)

Includes bibliographical references and index

How Computers Work; by Ron White ; illustrated by Tim Downs. 10th ed Que 2014 432 p. pbk $39.99 **004**

1. Personal computers
ISBN 9780789749840; 078974984X

First published 1993 by Ziff-Davis Press. Frequently revised

An "illustrated guide to the world of PCs and technology. In this . . . edition, you'll find detailed information not just about every last component of hardware found inside your PC, but also . . . explanations about home networking, the Internet, PC security, and even how cell phone networks operate." (Publisher's note)

Isaacson, Walter

★ The **innovators**; how a group of inventors, hackers, geniuses, and geeks created the digital revolution. Walter Isaacson. Simon & Schuster 2014 560 p. **004**

1. Computer scientists 2. Internet -- History 3. Computers -- History 4. Computer science -- History
ISBN 9781476708690; 9781476708706
LC 2014021391

This book, by Walter Isaacson, is the "story of the people who created the computer and the Internet. . . . [He] begins with Ada Lovelace, Lord Byron's daughter, who pioneered computer programming in the 1840s. He explores the fascinating personalities that created our current digital revolution, such as Vannevar Bush, Alan Turing, John von Neumann, J.C.R. Licklider, Doug Engelbart, Robert Noyce, Bill Gates, Steve Wozniak, Steve Jobs, Tim Berners-Lee, and Larry Page." (Publisher's note)

Markoff, John

What the dormouse said-- how the sixties counterculture shaped the personal computer industry. Viking Penguin 2005 xxiii, 310p il $25.95; pa $16 **004**

1. Counter culture 2. Computers and civilization 3. Computers -- History
ISBN 0-670-03382-0; 0-14-303676-9 pa
LC 2004-61181

"This book is a rare treat and a must-read for everyone who has had the pleasure of using the mysterious friend called the PC." Choice

Includes bibliographical references

Vamosi, Robert

When gadgets betray us; the dark side of our infatuation with new technologies. Basic Books 2011 222p **004**

1. Computer crimes 2. Computer security 3. Electronic apparatus and appliances 4. Software failures 5. Computers -- Health aspects 6. Computers -- Social aspects
ISBN 978-0-465-01958-8
LC 2010-43829

"The book is about hardware hacking and new kinds of identity fraud." (Publisher's note) Index.

"Read this, and you'll never again ignore the default security settings on accounts or your devices again. Gadget geeks and lay readers would benefit from Vamosi's information." Libr J

Includes bibliographical references

004.092 Computer scientists

Ping Fu

Bend, not break; a life in two worlds. Ping Fu with MeiMei Fox. Portfolio/Penguin 2013 288 p. $27.95 **004.092**

1. Resilience (Personality trait) 2. Geomagic (Firm) 3. Young women -- China -- Biography 4. Chinese American women -- Biography 5. Businesswomen

3

-- United States -- Biography 6. Entrepreneurship --
United States -- Biography 7. Nanjing hang kong hang
tian da xue -- Biography 8. Political refugees -- United
States -- Biography 9. Women computer scientists
-- United States -- Biography 10. China -- History --
Cultural Revolution, 1966-1976 -- Personal narratives
ISBN 1591845521; 9781591845522

LC 2012035389

This book, by Ping Fu with MeiMei Fox, is the autobiography of a Chinese immigrant. "Born on the eve of China's
Cultural Revolution, Ping . . . grew up fighting hunger . . .
and shielding her younger sister from the teenagers in Mao's
Red Guard. At twenty-five, she found her way to the United
States." This book "depicts a journey from . . . the dogmatic anticapitalism of Mao's China to the high-stakes, take-
no-prisoners world of technology start-ups in the United
States." (Publisher's note)

004.1   General works on specific types of computers

Johnson, George

A **shortcut** through time; the path to a quantum
computer. Knopf 2003 204p il hardcover o.p. pa
$13   **004.1**
    1. Computers 2. Quantum theory
    ISBN 0-375-41193-3; 0-375-72618-7 pa

LC 2002-73013

The author "communicates some of the propositions offered by theorists about the virtually unlimited computing
power that may follow certain practical triumphs that are not
quite in sight." N Y Times Book Rev

"Johnson has presented the fascinating science of quantum computing and its future development in a down-to-
earth style." Libr J

Includes bibliographical references

004.16   Personal computers

Mueller, Scott

★ **Upgrading** and repairing PCs; by Scott Mueller. 14th ed. QUE 2013 xix, 1605 p.p ill. (hardcover) $59.99   **004.16**
    1. Microcomputers -- Upgrading 2. Microcomputers
    -- Maintenance and repair
    ISBN 0789750007; 9780789750006

LC 2001099514

This book is the 21st edition of Scott Mueller's guide
to personal computer hardware. It offers "information on
troubleshooting and fixing problems, adding hardware, op-
timizing performance, and building new PCs." There is also
"coverage of the newest hardware innovations and maintenance techniques" as of 2013. (Publisher's note)

004.67   Wide-area networks

Boyd, Danah

It's complicated; the social lives of networked
teens. Danah Boyd. Yale University Press 2014 296
p. (clothbound : alk. paper) $25   **004.67**
    1. Teenagers 2. Internet and teenagers 3. Online social
    networks 4. Information technology -- Social aspects
    5. Teenagers -- Social life and customs -- 21st century
    ISBN 0300166311; 9780300166316

LC 2013031950

Author Danah Boyd "uncovers some of the major myths
regarding teens' use of social media. She explores tropes
about identity, privacy, safety, danger, and bullying. Ultimately, Boyd argues that society fails young people when
paternalism and protectionism hinder teenagers' ability to
become informed, thoughtful, and engaged citizens through
their online interactions. Yet despite an environment of
rampant fear-mongering, Boyd finds that teens often find
ways to engage and to develop a sense of identity." (Publisher's note)

"This groundbreaking survey of the online social habits
and realities of American teens, based on extensive fieldwork, also serves as an important corrective to numerous
persistent, widely held notions about young people, public
life, and the Internet...Boyd discusses bullying, media literacy, and social inequality; debunks the pervasiveness of
online predation; addresses problematic assumptions behind the term digital native; defends Wikipedia as a great
educational tool that makes transparent the evolution of
knowledge; and astutely points out that the technology may
be new, but teens, as always, simply want to socialize, be
known, spend time with friends, and participate in public
life... Exciting, challenging, and liberating; this title is essential reading for adults with any interest in or control over
teens." (Library Journal)

Includes bibliographical references and index

Lessig, Lawrence

The **future** of ideas; the fate of the commons
in a connected world. Random House 2001 352p
hardcover o.p. pa $15   **004.67**
    1. Internet 2. Copyright 3. Information society
    ISBN 0-375-72644-6 pa

LC 2001-31968

The author "argues that as the Internet faces the challenges of intellectual property laws, it should not become so
controlled that it discourages innovation and creativity in the
digital world." Libr J

"Some of Lessig's sweeping proposals are sure to spark
a lively debate, but his well-reasoned, clearly written argument is powerful." Publ Wkly

Moreno, Megan

Sex, drugs 'n Facebook; a parents' toolkit for
promoting healthy Internet use. by Megan A. Moreno. Hunter House Inc. 2013 268 p. (trade paper)
$17.95   **004.67**
    1. Social media 2. Internet and teenagers 3. Parenting
    4. Online etiquette
    ISBN 0897936590; 9780897936590; 9780897936606

LC 2012048533

In this book, author Megan Moreno presents "a guide to help [parents] teach your kids about balance and boundaries in their internet and media use and the skills they need to thrive online. This guide provides a clear toolkit for teaching our young people how to avoid the dangers of the internet while taking advantage of its full potential." (Publisher's note)

Includes bibliographical references and index

Obee, Jennifer

Social networking; the ultimate teen guide. Jenna Obee. Scarecrow Press 2012 258 p.   **004.67**
1. Social networking 2. Internet and teenagers 3. Online social networks
ISBN 0810881209; 9780810881204; 9780810881211
LC 2011049875

This book by Jennifer Obee "helps young adults make the most of their online experience, giving them a complete understanding of social networking while also addressing online safety. . . . Author Jennifer Obee helps teens navigate through the challenging intricacies of social networks, covering such topics as: Facebook . . . Youtube . . . [and] Twitter." The book includes "quotes from teenagers about their favorite sites and personal stories." (Publisher's note)

Includes bibliographical references and index

Steyer, James P.

Talking back to Facebook; a common sense guide to raising kids in the digital age. James P. Steyer ; with a foreword by Chelsea Clinton. Scribner 2012 206 p. (hardcover : alk. paper) $25   **004.67**
1. Social media 2. Child rearing 3. Internet and children 4. Facebook (Electronic resource) 5. Internet and children -- Safety measures
ISBN 1451658117; 9781451657340; 9781451657357; 9781451658118
LC 2012007165

This book looks at raising children in the digital age. It "begins by examining how technology affects a growing child's brain ('mental brownouts'), the relationship problems that are exploited by e-communication, how the 'impulse-enabling nature of social media platforms, coupled with the vulnerable and inexperienced social and emotional development of many young people, can be combustible,' and the alarming loss of privacy for digital natives." (Library Journal)

Includes bibliographical references (p. 189-198) and index

Stryker, Cole

Hacking the Future; Privacy, Identity, and Anonymity on the Web. Cole Stryker. Penguin Group USA 2012 255 p. (hardcover) $25.95   **004.67**
1. Right of privacy 2. Internet -- Social aspects
ISBN 1590209745; 9781590209745

This book, by Cole Stryker, offers "a broad look at how anonymity influences politics, activism, religion, and art. Stryker presents a strong defense of anonymity and explores some of the tools and organizations relating to this issue, especially as it has evolved with the ubiquity of the Internet." (Publisher's note)

"A multilayered and well-reasoned retort against all those who would seek to erase anonymity from the Web... The author explores the rich history of anonymity in politics, literature and culture, while also debunking the notion that only troublemakers fear revealing their identities to the world... One of the most well-informed examinations of the Internet available today." Kirkus

004.678   Internet

Arora, Pankaj

To the cloud; cloud powering an enterprise. Pankaj Arora, Raj Biyani, Salil Dave. McGraw Hill 2012 xx, 119 p.p ill. $30   **004.678**
1. Cloud computing 2. Business planning 3. Web services 4. Information technology -- Management 5. Business enterprises -- Data processing
ISBN 007179221X; 9780071792219
LC 2011277377

This book looks at cloud computing. This guide "lays out a four-step framework, leveraging the experience and best practices of Microsoft's own IT group. The book delivers end-to-end business and technology guidance, describing how to analyze application portfolios to identify good cloud candidates, choose the right cloud models, consider architecture and security, and understand how shifting operations to the cloud affects budgeting and staffing." (Publisher's note)

Includes bibliographical references and index

005   Computer programming, programs, data

Campbell-Kelly, Martin

From airline reservations to Sonic the Hedgehog; a history of the software industry. MIT Press 2003 372p il (History of computing) $42.50; pa $16.95   **005**
1. Computer software industry
ISBN 0-262-03303-8; 0-262-53262-X pa
LC 2002-75351

The author presents a "history of the software industry from the 1950s to 1995. Dividing the business into three sectors (software contracting, corporate software precuts, and mass-market software products), he examines the key products and players in each. . . . The result is a well-rounded look at the software industry from a business perspective." Libr J

Includes bibliographical references

Davis, Mark

Digital assassination; protecting your reputation, brand, or business against online attacks. by Richard Torrenzano and Mark Davis. 1st ed. St. Martin's Press 2011 viii, 289 p.p (hardcover) $25.99   **005**
1. Reputation 2. Public opinion 3. Internet -- Security measures
ISBN 0312617917; 9780312617912
LC 2011025849

In this book, authors [Richard] Torrenzano . . . and [Mark] Davis . . . discuss how various Internet tools are being used by digital maligners to harm reputations and perform character assassinations. The authors explain how anyone can tap into social media . . . to mount an electronic onslaught, severely altering the digital reputation of a person or a company. They argue that the dark side of human behavior, not technology, is the driving factor behind this phenomenon." (Library Journal)

Includes bibliographical references and index.

005.082   Data encryption

Olson, Parmy

We are Anonymous; inside the hacker world of Lulzsec, Anonymous, and the global cyber insurgency. Parmy Olson. Little, Brown and Co. 2012 xi, 498 p.p $26.99   **005.082**
1. Hacktivism 2. Lulzsec (Group) 3. Computer hackers 4. Anonymous (Group)
ISBN 0316213543; 9780316213547

LC 2012936919

This book by Parmy Olson presents an "account of the hacker collective Anonymous and its splinter group, Lulz-Sec. . . . A nebulous group of hackers and Internet activists . . . [Anonymous] not only took down the Scientology website, but went on to attack other targets, including the anti-gay Westboro Baptist Church and the Tunisian government. . . . . [LulzSec] attacked companies just for the sake of publicly embarrassing them for laughs." (Kirkus Reviews)

Includes bibliographical references and index.

006.3   Artificial intelligence

Baker, Stephen

Final Jeopardy; man vs. machine and the quest to know everything. Houghton Mifflin Harcourt 2011 268p $24   **006.3**
1. Database management 2. Artificial intelligence 3. Watson (Computer) 4. Jeopardy (Television program) 5. Natural language processing (Computer science)
ISBN 978-0-547-48316-0; 0-547-48316-3

LC 2010051653

"In February 2011, the world watched as a computer named Watson handily beat the two greatest Jeopardy champions of all time. The contest was reminiscent of when IBM's Deep Blue defeated chess grandmaster Garry Kasparov, but Jeopardy was a much more difficult game for a computer to master. Although Baker . . . reviews the match in his last chapter, his primary focus here is on the compelling story of Watson's creation and education. . . . This is a thought-provoking view of one of IBM's major contributions to the computing field." Libr J

Includes bibliographical references

006.7   Multimedia systems

Solomon, Laura

The **librarian's** nitty-gritty guide to social media; Laura Solomon. ALA Editions, an imprint

of the American Library Association 2013 224 p. $52   **006.7**
1. Librarians 2. Social media 3. Online social networks -- Library applications
ISBN 0838911609; 9780838911600

LC 2012027302

Here, Laura Solomon offers a guide for the use of social media by libraries. The book "provides case studies of libraries that have excelled with their marketing efforts." She offers an "analysis of what success is and how to measure it to gain support from stakeholders." Also provided are "detailed sample postings that not only give suggestions for libraries to model but also examine unsuccessful posts and explain what makes them less than desirable." (Library Journal)

Includes bibliographical references and index

Stone, Biz

Things a little bird told me; confessions of the creative mind. Biz Stone. Grand Central Publishing 2014 240 p. illustrations (hardback) $26   **006.7**
1. Businesspeople 2. Internet industry 3. Twitter (Web site) 4. Success in business 5. Twitter 6. Online social networks -- United States 7. Entrepreneurship -- United States -- Anecdotes
ISBN 1455528714; 9781455528714

LC 2013047280

In this book, Biz Stone "discusses the power of creativity and how to harness it, through stories from his remarkable life and career. . . . Biz tells fascinating, pivotal, and personal stories from his early life and his careers at Google and Twitter, sharing his knowledge about the nature and importance of ingenuity today. . . . Biz also addresses failure, the value of vulnerability, ambition, and corporate culture." (Publisher's note)

"Readers will enjoy the tales of the ups and downs of Silicon Valley among major players, from Google to Apple to Facebook, as well as the insightful advice that can be applied to any career or enterprise." Booklist

Tortorella, Neil

Starting your career as a freelance web designer. Allworth Press 2011 251p il pa $19.95   **006.7**
1. Vocational guidance 2. Web sites -- Design
ISBN 978-1-58115-859-5

LC 2011019292

"This is not a book about how to design websites; it is about managing the financial, legal, and business realities of being a freelance web designer. . . . Part One deals with the fundamentals of being a freelancer, including analyzing one's abilities and talents, formulating a business plan, understanding taxes and insurance, and finding trusted business advisers. In Part Two, Tortorella discusses the necessary proficiencies of the portfolio, proposals, project management, and marketing. . . . Tortorella's contribution is the nuts-and-bolts handbook for success in the field of freelance web design and will find a ready audience with the fledgling right-brain designer or the college student considering web design as a career." Libr J

Includes bibliographical references

011 Bibliographies and catalogs

American reference books annual 2014, volume 45; edited by Shannon Graff Hysell. Libraries Unlimited 2014 574 p $155 **011**
1. Reference books -- Bibliography 2. Libraries -- Collection development
ISBN 9781610695480
Annual. First published 1970

This book "provides librarians with insightful, critical reviews of all reference resources released in 2013 as well as some from 2012 and 2014. Highlighting both the positive and negative aspects of each resource, users will be able to make informed decisions about which new resources are most appropriate for their collection and their patrons' needs." (Publisher's note)

"Each issue covers the reference book output (including reprints) of the previous year (i.e., the 1970 volume covers 1969 publications). Offers descriptive and evaluative notes (many of them signed by contributors), with references to selected reviews. Limited to titles in English. Classed arrangement; author-subject-title index." Guide to Ref Books. 11th edition

Ellington, Elisabeth

A **year** of reading; a month-by-month guide to classics and crowd-pleasers for you and your book group. by H. Elisabeth Ellington and Jane Freimiller. Sourcebooks 2002 314p pa $14.95 **011**
1. Best books 2. Books and reading
ISBN 1-57071-935-7

LC 2002-6926

"Five titles designated as crowd pleasers, classics, challenges, memoirs, or potluck options are provided for each month. . . . There are brief descriptions of each book, thought-provoking discussion questions, information about the authors, video and Internet resources, and lists of related readings. Literary discussion groups will welcome this invaluable resource." Booklist

Guide to reference books; edited by Robert Balay; associate editor, Vee Friesner Carrington; with special editorial assistance by Murray S. Martin. 11th ed; American Lib. Assn. 1996 xxvii, 2020p $275 **011**
1. Reference books 2. Reference books -- Bibliography
ISBN 0-8389-0669-9

LC 95-26322

First published 1902

Nearly 16,000 entries provide details on general reference works and on reference books in the humanities, social and behavioral sciences, history and area studies, and science, technology, and medicine. Electronic resources are included

Includes bibliographical references

Pearl, Nancy

Book lust; recommended reading for every mood, moment, and reason. Sasquatch Books 2003 287p pa $16.95 **011**
1. Best books 2. Books and reading
ISBN 1-57061-381-8

LC 2003-45796

Pearl's "recommendations are arranged under an alphabetical, subjective, but certainly comprehensive system of categories, which range from 'Academic Mysteries' to 'World War II Nonfiction' and from 'First Novels' to 'Three-Hanky Readers.' Within each category, Pearl's commentaries are concise and sound. A book difficult to put down and easy to be guided by." Booklist

★ **Recommended** reference books for small and medium-sized libraries and media centers, Vol. 34; volume 34 Shannon Graff Hysell, associate editor. Libraries Unlimited 2014 301 p. $75 **011**
1. Reference books 2. Reference books -- Reviews 3. Reference books -- Bibliography
ISBN 9781610695510
Annual. First published 1981

"This volume presents the top 550 reviews from the latest edition of American Reference Books Annual (ARBA) to give collection development librarians working in small to medium-sized libraries the best information for choosing new titles for their libraries. Overviewing the breadth of reference products (both print and online) that became available in 2013, all of the titles . . . have price points that will appeal to libraries on a budget." (Publisher's note)

Includes "books, e-books, free websites, and pay sites. These are broken down into major subject headings and minor ones within the major." VOYA

Reference sources for small and medium-sized libraries; Jack O'Gorman, editor. 7th ed; American Library Association 2008 329p pa $88 **011**
1. Reference books 2. Reference books -- Bibliography
ISBN 0-8389-0943-4; 978-0-8389-0943-0

LC 2007-40026

First published 1969 with title: Reference books for small and medium-sized libraries

"Intended as a guide for college and large secondary school libraries as well as for public libraries. Items are grouped in subject categories and further subdivided by type of reference source or other suitable subdivision. Sections were prepared by individual compilers or teams of compilers. Good annotations; coverage of various subject fields is unusually even for a work of this kind; index of names and titles." Guide to Ref Books. 11th edition

Includes bibliographical references

Saricks, Joyce G.

Read on--audiobooks; reading lists for every taste. Libraries Unlimited 2011 145p (Read on series) pa $30 **011**
1. Audiobooks -- Catalogs 2. Libraries -- Special collections -- Audiobooks
ISBN 978-1-59158-804-7 pa; 978-1-59158-807-8 ebook

LC 2010051372

"More than 300 selections, fiction and nonfiction, are grouped into five chapters according to their primary appeal: language (including voice), mood, story, characters, or setting. Within each category, titles are listed by shared themes, such as full-cast readings or armchair travel. . . . All libraries that circulate audiobooks should shelve this guide alongside." Booklist

Includes bibliographical references

011.6 General bibliographies and catalogs of works for young people and people with disabilities; for specific types of libraries

Rosow, La Vergne
★ **Accessing** the classics; great reads for adults, teens, and English language learners. Libraries Unlimited 2006 301p pa $40 **011.6**
1. Best books 2. Reading -- Remedial teaching
ISBN 1-56308-891-6; 978-1-56308-891-9
LC 2005-30838

"This collection of annotated titles aims at providing resources for anyone who works with inexperienced or low-literacy teenagers or adults." Voice Youth Advocates

"The intended audience is wide-ranging and includes anyone who wishes to foster language and literacy skills. Essential reading." Booklist

Includes bibliographical references

Safford, Barbara Ripp
Guide to reference materials for school library media centers; 6th ed; Libraries Unlimited 2010 236p $60 **011.6**
1. Instructional materials centers 2. School libraries -- Catalogs 3. Reference books -- Bibliography
ISBN 978-1-59158-277-9; 1-59158-277-6
LC 2009-51190

First edition by Christine Gehrt Wynar published 1973 with title: Guide to reference books for school media centers

"This volume has been updated to include web-based reference offerings as well as listings of older sources, provided that their content is still valid. . . . This title profiles resources recommended for use by school librarians for collection management, readers' advisory, teaching, general reference materials, the social sciences and humanities, and science and technology. This volume is an excellent starting point for new school librarians, as well as for those who are building a library from scratch." SLJ

Includes bibliographical references

016 Bibliographies and catalogs of works on specific subjects

Adamson, Lynda G.
Notable women in American history; a guide to recommended biographies and autobiographies. Greenwood Press 1999 450p $52.95 **016**
1. Reference books 2. Women -- Biography --
Dictionaries
ISBN 0-313-29584-0
LC 98-55350

Companion volume to Notable women in world history

This volume "concentrates on women who made contributions to U.S. history from the colonial period through 1998. The 500 women covered were born in America or became naturalized citizens; had a full-length biography or autobiography published since 1970; and, in the case of twentieth-century actors, authors, and poets, have been recognized by their peers." Booklist

Notable women in world history; a guide to recommended biographies and autobiographies. Greenwood Press 1998 401p $52.95 **016**
1. Reference books 2. Women -- Biography --
Dictionaries
ISBN 0-313-29818-1
LC 97-33136

"The entries are arranged alphabetically by last name with appropriate cross-references for alternative designations. Each contains the woman's name, key dates, occupation or avocation, and birthplace. A short biographical sketch about parents, education, general achievement, and recognition or awards follows. Women of all time periods are included. . . . Because it includes only those born outside the U.S., it complements sources on American women. Notable Women in World History is a useful addition to academic, public, and high-school libraries. It would be especially useful for women's studies collections." Booklist

All music guide to classical music; the definitive guide to classical music. edited by Chris Woodstra, Gerald Brennan, Allen Schrott. Backbeat Books 2005 1607p $34.95 **016**
1. Music -- Discography
ISBN 0-87930-865-6
LC 2005-23988

"The 1500 A-to-Z entries include established composers, performers, and ensembles of every style and era. . . . The final 25 pages are devoted to one-page discussions of form in classical music, historical periods (ten divisions), and genres such as ballet, film music, and opera. . . . This is an excellent resource for both classical novices and aficionados. There is simply no other single volume on the market as inclusive." Libr J

American foreign relations since 1600; a guide to the literature. Robert L. Beisner, editor. 2nd ed; ABC-CLIO 2003 2v set $255 **016**
1. Reference books 2. United States -- Foreign relations -- Bibliography
ISBN 1-57607-080-8
LC 2003-8684

First published 1983 under the editorship of Richard Dean Burns with title: Guide to American foreign relations since 1700

"The arrangement is essentially chronological, with the first of 32 chapters covering reference works and bibliographies and the second chapter, overviews and synthesis. Individual chapter editors . . . include journal articles, essays in collections, and dissertations. . . . Each chapter begins with a brief statement of the editor's selection criteria. Works in related specialties are listed for their influence on foreign relations, including Native American relations, gender and ethnic issues, and religious groups. . . . This is an excellent book; imaginative users will find ways to apply these listings to a wide variety of projects." Libr J

Includes bibliographical references

Bleiler, Richard

★ **Reference** and research guide to mystery and detective fiction; [by] Richard J. Bleiler. 2nd ed; Libraries Unlimited 2003 828p (Reference sources in the humanities series) $78 **016**

1. Reference books 2. Mystery fiction -- Bibliography
ISBN 1-56308-924-6

LC 2003-58905

First published 1999 with title: Reference guide to mystery and detective fiction

"Separate chapters cover sources as diverse as maps and atlases, writers' associations and awards, character indexes, calendars, and quotations in addition to guides, encyclopedias, and dictionaries." Choice

Includes bibliographical references

Bosman, Ellen

Gay, lesbian, bisexual, and transgendered literature; a genre guide. [by] Ellen Bosman and John P. Bradford; edited by Robert B. Marks Ridinger. Libraries Unlimited 2008 422p (Genreflecting advisory series) $60 **016**

1. Homosexuality in literature
ISBN 978-1-59158-194-9; 1-59158-194-X

LC 2007-49022

"This addition to the Genreflecting Advisory Series fills a gap, focusing on popular literature with gay, lesbian, bisexual, and transgendered characters, themes, or authors. The first three chapters provide an excellent introduction and history of GLBT literature along with a discussion of collection develop-ment and readers'-advisory issues . . . An excellent tool for readers' advisory, as well as an outstanding reference on an important type of literature, this guide is highly recommended for public and academic libraries with GLBT collections." Booklist

Includes bibliographical references

Bouricius, Ann

The **romance** readers' advisory; the librarian's guide to love in the stacks. American Lib. Assn. 2000 107p pa $56 **016**

1. Reference books 2. Love stories -- Bibliography 3. Love stories -- History and criticism
ISBN 0-8389-0779-2

LC 99-57295

The author provides "information about the highly popular romance genre and its diverse subgenres; addresses key issues regarding the establishment of a romance collection; and, in a series of reading lists, recommends outstanding romances of all flavors for avid fans and new converts." Booklist

Burgess, Michael

Reference guide to science fiction, fantasy, and horror; [by] Michael Burgess, Lisa R. Bartle. 2nd ed; Libraries Unlimited 2002 605p (Reference sources in the humanities series) $75 **016**

1. Reference books 2. Science fiction -- Bibliography
ISBN 1-56308-548-8

LC 2002-151707

First published 1992

A guide to "amateur and professional reference materials in the related fields of science fiction, fantasy, and horror. . . . The book is divided into 32 sections . . . including 'Encyclopedias and Dictionaries,' 'Magazine and Anthology Indexes,' 'Subject Bibliographies,' 'Character Dictionaries and Author Cyclopedias,' and 'Film and Television Catalogs.' . . . Complete bibliographic citations are followed by literature and readable annotations that vary from a brief note to three or four lengthy paragraphs. The annotations consist of description and succinct analysis of the strengths and weaknesses of each item. . . . 'Major On-Line Resources,' is a particularly valuable examination of 20 Web sites." Booklist

Includes bibliographical references

Burt, Daniel S.

The **biography** book; a reader's guide to nonfiction, fictional, and film biographies of the 500 most fascinating individuals of all time. Oryx Press 2001 629p $83.95 **016**

1. Reference books 2. Biography -- Bibliography
ISBN 1-57356-256-4

LC 00-10116

This "book provides annotated bibliographies of works on international historical figures. Entries are arranged alphabetically by person and begin with a paragraph on the individual's life and significance. Each entry contains a birth and death date, and recommended autobiographical and biographical studies. Primary sources include letters, memoirs, diaries, interviews, etc. Biographical novels, fictional portraits, films, documentaries, and theatrical performances are also identified. . . . A wonderful resource for students, biography lovers, and librarians." SLJ

Includes bibliographical references

Fonseca, Anthony J.

Hooked on horror III; a guide to reading interests. [by] Anthony J. Fonseca and June Michele Pulliam. Libraries Unlimited 2009 xxiii, 515p (Genreflecting advisory series) $62 **016**

1. Horror films 2. Reference books 3. Horror fiction -- Bibliography
ISBN 978-1-59158-540-4

LC 2008-45518

First published 1999 with title: Hooked on horror

This book "provides annotations of horror books published between 2003 and 2008, including collections, anthologies, and series." Voice Youth Advocates

Includes bibliographical references

Frolund, Tina

Genrefied classics; a guide to reading interests in classical literature. Libraries Unlimited 2007 xxiv, 365p (Genreflecting advisory series) $45   **016**

    1. Reference books 2. Fiction -- Bibliography
    ISBN 1-59158-172-9; 978-1-59158-172-7

                LC 2006-33740

"By identifying the genre characteristics of more than 400 classic fiction works, and organizing titles according to these features, this guide helps readers find the type of books they enjoy." Publisher's note

Includes bibliographical references

Herald, Diana Tixier

Fluent in fantasy; the next generation. [by] Diana Tixier Herald and Bonnie Kunzel. Libraries Unlimited 2008 312p (Genreflecting advisory series) $52   **016**

    1. Reference books 2. Fantasy fiction -- Bibliography
    ISBN 978-1-59158-198-7; 1-59158-198-2

                LC 2007-28840

First published 1999

"More than 2,000 titles are arranged by author in 14 thematic chapters, including 'Epic Fantasy,' 'Arthurian Legend,' and 'Time Travel Romance.'. . . An essential collection development and readers'-advisory tool." Booklist

Includes bibliographical references

★ **Genreflecting**; a guide to popular reading interests. edited by Wayne A. Wiegand. Libraries Unlimited 2013 622 p. (Genreflecting advisory series) (Hardcopy : acid-free paper) $75   **016**

    1. Reference books 2. Books and reading 3. Reading interests 4. Fiction -- Bibliography 5. Fiction genres -- Bibliography 6. English fiction -- Stories, plots, etc 7. American fiction -- Stories, plots, etc 8. Popular literature -- Stories, plots, etc
    ISBN 9781598848403; 1598848402

                LC 2012051480

First published 1982 under the authorship of Betty Rosenberg

This book for librarians on popular reading interests features "chapters devoted to each major genre with an overview of the genre's characteristics and appeal elements followed by definitions of popular subgenres, lists of benchmark titles, reader favorites, book-group selections, and resources for further investigation. Parts I and 2 focus on readers'-advisory services in the public library for the novice. . . . The chapters on the genres, found in part 3, are the series' stock-in-trade." (Booklist)

Includes bibliographical references

★ **Strictly** science fiction; a guide to reading interests. [by] Diana Tixier Herald, Bonnie Kunzel. Libraries Unlimited 2002 xxii, 297p (Genreflecting advisory series) $55   **016**

    1. Reference books 2. Science fiction -- Bibliography 3. Science fiction -- History and criticism
    ISBN 1-56308-893-2

                LC 2002-3186

"Good indexing, by author, title, subject, and character name, along with chapters devoted to books written for children and young adults and genre-blended books (such as science fiction/ romance or science fiction/mystery), sets this reference apart." Libr J

Includes bibliographical references

Hollands, Neil

Read on . . . fantasy fiction; reading lists for every taste. Libraries Unlimited 2007 210p (Read on series) pa $30   **016**

    1. Reference books 2. Fantasy fiction -- Bibliography
    ISBN 978-1-59158-330-1; 1-59158-330-6

                LC 2007-7841

"Librarians who do readers advisory for teens or adults will wonder how they ever got along without this funny, opinionated, wide-angle guide." SLJ

Husband, Janet

Sequels; an annotated guide to novels in series. [by] Janet G. Husband & Jonathan F. Husband. 4th ed; American Library Association 2009 782p pa $95   **016**

    1. Reference books 2. Fiction -- Bibliography
    ISBN 978-0-8389-0967-6

                LC 2009-16426

First published 1982

"A selective, annotated list of the best, most enduring, and most popular novels in series. Short stories and children's books are excluded; classics, mysteries, and science fiction are included. Each work is listed in the best current edition, in the preferred order for reading. Arranged by author, with a title and subject index." Ref Sources for Small & Medium-sized Libr. 5th edition

Includes bibliographical references

Johnson, Sarah L.

Historical fiction II; a guide to the genre. Libraries Unlimited 2009 738p (Genreflecting advisory series) $65   **016**

    1. Reference books 2. Historical fiction -- Bibliography
    ISBN 978-1-59158-624-1

                LC 2008-45537

"Johnson has updated her outstanding Historical Fiction: A Guide to the Genre (2005) by covering historical fiction from 2004 through mid-2008 and adding such new features as ISBNs for each book and keyword descriptors after each annotation. . . . This volume continues rather than replaces the earlier work, adding more than 2,700 new titles." Booklist

Includes bibliographical references

Montgomery, Denise L.

Ottemiller's index to plays in collections; an author and title index to plays appearing in collections published since 1900. Scarecrow Press, Inc. 2011 xlix, 781 p.p   **016**

    1. Drama -- Indexes
    ISBN 9780810877207; 9780810877214

                LC 2010053010

"Returning after some 20 years, this volume (7th ed., 1988) remains the classic index to plays in collections and anthologies... Plays are indexed by title, author, and anthology title. Montgomery adds more than 2,300 new authors and 3,593 new plays, expanding the work's focus to include works from 103 countries and making works by women and LGBT authors more discoverable." Choice

Morris, Vanessa Irvin

The **readers'** advisory guide to street literature; Vanessa Irvin Morris ; foreword by Teri Woods. American Library Association 2012 xxiii, 138 p.p ill. (alk. paper) $48.00 **016**
1. Readers' advisory services 2. Urban fiction -- Bibliography 3. Urban fiction -- History and criticism 4. Fiction in libraries 5. Street life -- Fiction -- Bibliography 6. Urban fiction, American -- Bibliography 7. Readers' advisory services -- United States 8. Young adult fiction, American -- Bibliography 9. Urban fiction, American -- History and criticism
ISBN 0838911102; 9780838911105

LC 2011029685

In this book, author Vanessa Irvin "Morris presents a[n] . . . overview of the genre [of street literature]. From exploring the genre's roots . . . to articulating the appeal of the books, this . . . volume covers unique . . . material. For example, there is an entire chapter on teen-friendly street lit as well as material on collection development. Appendixes include a list of publishers and unannotated book lists." (Booklist)

Includes bibliographical references (p. 113-130) and index

Pearl, Nancy

Now read this; a guide to mainstream fiction, 1978-1998. [by] Nancy Pearl, with the assistance of Martha Knappe and Chris Higashi; foreword by Joyce S. Saricks. Libraries Unlimited 1999 432p $65 **016**
1. Best books 2. Reference books 3. Fiction -- Bibliography
ISBN 1-56308-659-X

LC 99-15280

Annotated list of 1000 books categorized by setting, story, characterization, or language
Includes bibliographical references

Now read this II; a guide to mainstream fiction, 1990-2001. Libraries Unlimited 2002 300p il $55 **016**
1. Best books 2. Reference books 3. Fiction -- Bibliography
ISBN 1-56308-867-3

LC 2002-274079

This is an annotated list of 500 books categorized by setting, story, characterization, or language. "New features include a YA designation for selected titles, a section on fiction trends, and two appendixes, one on genre bridges (books that share elements with genre fiction) and one on book groups.

Like others in the Genreflecting series, this work is a truly useful tool." Booklist

★ **Now** read this III; a guide to mainstream fiction. [by] Nancy Pearl and Sarah Statz Cords. Libraries Unlimited 2010 xxiii, 405p $60 **016**
1. Best books 2. Reference books 3. Fiction -- Bibliography
ISBN 978-1-59158-570-1

LC 2009-49898

An annotated list of over 500 books categorized by setting, story, characterization, or language. "This volume covers books published since 2002, with heavy emphasis on the last three years. Appendixes provide bridges to other genres, book award information, further resources, and advice for book groups, and everything is thoroughly indexed by author, title, and subject." Booklist

Includes bibliographical references

Printed sources; a guide to published genealogical records. edited by Kory L. Meyerink. Ancestry 1998 840p $49.95 **016**
1. Reference books 2. Genealogy -- Bibliography 3. United States -- History -- Bibliography
ISBN 0-916489-70-1

LC 98-10852

The book opens with an "introductory chapter that highlights categories of research, the evaluation of records, interlibrary loan, and even the Dewey Decimal system. Editor Meyerink then divides the book into four sections encompassing background information (how-to-books, atlases), finding aids, printed original records, and compiled records (family histories, periodicals)." Libr J

Ramsdell, Kristin, 1940-

Romance fiction; a guide to the genre. Kristin Ramsdell. Libraries Unlimited 2012 xxii, 719 p.p (hardcopy : acid-free paper) $55 **016**
1. Romances 2. Book selection 3. Romance literature 4. Love stories -- Bibliography 5. Love stories -- History and criticism
ISBN 159158177X; 9781591581772; 9781610692359

LC 2011045879

Author Kristin Ramsdell explains in the preface that "this volume is actually the second edition of her 'Happily Ever After: A Guide to Reading Interests in Romance Fiction', published . . . in 1987. . . . [The book discusses] the definition and appeal of romance and contain[s] general information about advising readers and building collections, [while also looking at] subgenres of romance, from contemporary to ethnic/multicultural." (Booklist)

Includes bibliographical references and indexes.

Riechel, Rosemarie

Easy information sources for ESL, adult learners, & new readers. Neal-Schuman Publishers 2009 285p pa $65 **016**
1. Libraries -- Special collections 2. English as a second language -- Bibliography 3. High interest-low vocabulary books -- Bibliography
ISBN 978-1-55570-650-0; 1-55570-650-9

LC 2008-40028

"This work is aimed at educators and librarians working with adults whose English is poor. Advice on ways to use children's nonfiction for adults; reference interview strategies; book selection, placement, and utilization; collection development; and readers' advisory enables this work to not only suggest sources but also offer new ways of serving this growing and diverse population." Booklist

Includes bibliographical references

Roche, Rick

Read on-- biography; reading lists for every taste. Rick Roche. Libraries Unlimited 2012 xvi, 163 p.p (hardcopy : alk. paper) $30　　　　**016**
1. Autobiography 2. Book selection 3. Biography -- Bibliography 4. Autobiography -- Bibliography
ISBN 1598847015; 1610691792; 9781598847017; 9781610691796

LC 2011046293

In this book, author Rick Roche "focuses on life stories written in the third person, with subjects ranging from individuals who lived in ancient times to the present-day, hailed from myriad nations, and gained fame in diverse fields. The contents are organized in order to facilitate identification of read-alikes and easy selection of titles according to appeal features such as character, story, language, setting, and mood.

Includes bibliographical references and indexes.

Thompson, Jason

★ **Manga** : the complete guide. Ballantine Books/Del Rey Manga 2007 592p il pa $19.95 **016**
1. Reference books 2. Manga -- Bibliography 3. Graphic novels -- Bibliography
ISBN 978-0-345-48590-8

Former manga editor at Viz, Thompson reviews more than 900 manga titles that have been translated and published in the U.S. This book includes only original manga series published in Japan and then translated into English for U.S. publication. Titles include series that are no longer in print. The book also includes sidebar discussions on the many genres included in manga, including the age and genre divisions and such topics as otaku (hard-core fans), underground manga, and more. Separate sections cover yaoi and gay manga, and adult manga (often called hentai). It also includes an artist index. Each review includes a description of the series, how many volumes it has, an age rating, and content indicators.

Trott, Barry

Read on . . . crime fiction; reading lists for every taste. Libraries Unlimited 2008 146p (Read on series) pa $30　　　　**016**
1. Reference books 2. Mystery fiction -- Bibliography
ISBN 978-1-59158-373-8

LC 2007-33858

The author organizes recommended crime fiction titles by "five 'appeal characteristics' commonly employed by RA professionals: story, character, setting, mood, and language. Under these broad categories, he offers an assortment of creatively titled reading lists ('Serf and Turf: Medieval Mysteries') that illustrate aspects of one of the appeal factors. Arrows designate one title per list selected as a good starting

point for that category. . . . Both readers' advisors and crime-fiction fans will find all sorts of inventive ways to use this book, including, of course, compiling their own lists of titles or categories that should have been represented." Booklist

016.33　Economics--bibliographies

Ernsthausen, David G.

★ **Strauss's** handbook of business information; a guide for librarians, students, and researchers. Rita W. Moss and David G. Ernsthausen. 2nd ed; Libraries Unlimited 2012 xix, 399 p.p il (acid-free paper) $100　　　　**016.33**
1. Business 2. Reference books 3. Business -- Databases -- Handbooks, manuals, etc 4. Government publications -- United States -- Handbooks, manuals, etc 5. Business -- Reference books -- Bibliography -- Handbooks, manuals, etc 6. Business -- Electronic information resources -- Handbooks, manuals, etc 7. Business information services -- United States -- Handbooks, manuals, etc
ISBN 1598848070; 1610692365; 9781598848076; 9781610692366

LC 2011041547

First edition by Diane Wheeler Strauss published 1988 with title: Handbook of business information

This business information handbook by Diane Wheeler Straus "is divided into two main parts. The first seven chapters cover business information according to the formats in which it is made available. The second part of the book covers specific topics within the area of business. Included are chapters on marketing; money, credit, and banking; and the many aspects of investment ranging from stocks through bonds, mutual funds, and futures and options." (Publisher's note)

This edition "first covers 'formats': directories, periodicals, loose-leaf services, government information services, and electronic sources. References are then organized by 'fields': banking, marketing, accounting, stocks and bonds, etc. Graphics include screen shots of e-sources." Libr J

Includes bibliographical references and indexes.

016.6　Bibliographies of technology (Applied sciences)

Covert, Jack

★ The **100** best business books of all time; what they say, why they matter, and how they can help you. [by] Jack Covert and Todd Sattersten. Portfolio 2009 335p il $25.95　　　　**016.6**
1. Best books 2. Business -- Bibliography
ISBN 978-1-59184-240-8

LC 2008-36664

"Covert and Sattersten operate 800-CEO-READ, a specialty business-book retailer. Out of the countless business books they have read every year for a quarter century, they have culled 100 of the best and presented them in review format. . . . This list and the fine reviews are proof positive that business books can offer a rich treasure of stories and inspiration." Booklist

Includes bibliographical references

020 Library and information sciences

★ **Core** technology competencies for librarians and library staff; a LITA guide. Susan M. Thompson, editor. Neal-Schuman Publishers 2009 248p il pa $65   **020**
1. Library education 2. Information technology 3. Technological innovations 4. Librarians -- In-service training
ISBN 978-1-55570-660-9

LC 2008-46174

In this book, "a coterie of experts identify competencies for technology specialists and describe several competency implementation programs. Useful for everyone from the systems librarian to the 'lone information technology librarian.'" Am Libr

Includes bibliographical references

Gleick, James

The **information**. Pantheon Books 2011 526p il $29.95   **020**
1. Information science
ISBN 978-0-375-42372-7; 0-375-42372-9

LC 2010-23221

"As he traces the evolution of intertwined ideas, [Gleick] provides vivid portraits of [Claude] Shannon and other pioneers of our Information Age, including Charles Babbage, whose unbuilt 19th-century 'Analytical Engine' anticipated modern computers, and Alan Turing, whose machines helped the Allies crack German codes during World War II." Wall Street J

Includes bibliographical references

Johnson, Marilyn

★ **This** book is overdue! how librarians and cybrarians can save us all. Harper 2010 272p $24.99   **020**
1. Librarians 2. Library science
ISBN 978-0-06-143160-9; 0-06-143160-5

LC 2010-07860

"In an information age full of Google-powered searches, free-by-Bittorrent media downloads and Wiki-powered knowledge databases, the librarian may seem like an antiquated concept. . . . [The author] is here to reverse that notion with a topical, witty study of the vital ways modern librarians uphold their traditional roles as educators, archivists, and curators of a community legacy. . . . Johnson's wry report is a must-read for anyone who's used a library in the past quarter century." Publ Wkly

Includes bibliographical references

Kroski, Ellusa

Web 2.0 for librarians and information professionals. Neal-Schuman Publishers 2008 209p il pa $75   **020**
1. Web 2.0 2. Web 2.0 -- Library applications
ISBN 978-1-55570-614-2; 1-55570-614-2

LC 2007-43249

"Whether you are just beginning the journey in the transformation of the Web or want to begin implementing this exciting tool in your library, this outstanding resource will take the mystery out of these concepts and be an excellent addition to your reference section." Libr Media Connect

Includes glossary and bibliographical references

Lankes, R. David

The **atlas** of new librarianship. MIT Press; Association of College & Research Libraries 2011 408p il $55   **020**
1. Library science 2. Libraries and community 3. Librarianship
ISBN 978-0-262-01509-7

LC 2010-22788

The author initiates a "conversation about librarianship and its future. He builds this conversation using an atlas, or topical mapping, to engage librarians in exploring their profession, their mission, and their future. . . . Grounding the atlas in the why of librarianship, Lankes argues that libraries serve not only as repositories providing access to information but as fertile ground for actively using collections, resources, and information to create knowledge and foster learning via ongoing conversations with our communities. He invites librarians to expand librarianship beyond the support of information seeking, access, and literacy and toward participation in and co-ownership of a community's knowledge-creation processes. . . . Essential for all librarians." Libr J

Includes bibliographical references.

Library mashups; exploring new ways to deliver library data. edited by Nicole C. Engard. Information Today, Inc. 2009 334p il map pa $39.50   **020**
1. Internet resources 2. Web sites -- Design
ISBN 978-1-57387-372-7

LC 2009-25999

"Editor Engard assembles 21 articles from 25 international contributors to focus on mashups within the library environment. Readers with little knowledge of mashups will find chapters such as 'What Is a Mashup?' and 'Behind the Scenes: Some Technical Details on Mashups' especially helpful. Other portions of this book cover topics such as mashups in library Web sites, mashups of catalog data, and mashups and media (e.g., photos)." Booklist

Includes bibliographical references

What Do I Read Next? A Reader's Guide to Current Genre Fiction. Gale Cengage Learning. Gale Cengage Learning 2012 738 p. (hardcover) $254   **020**
1. Book selection 2. Books and reading
ISBN 1414461372; 9781414461373

This volume is a book selection guide. It uses similarities in various books to help "readers to independently choose titles of interest published in the last year. Each entry describes a separate book, listing everything readers need to know to make selections. Arranged by author within six genre sections, detailed entries provide" information about the title, publisher, series, and temporal and geographical setting. (Publisher's note)

Woodward, Jeannette

The **transformed** library; e-books, expertise, and evolution. Jeannette Woodward. ALA Editions, an imprint of the American Library Association 2013 131 p. $55   **020**

1. Libraries 2. Technological innovations 3. Libraries and society 4. Libraries -- Forecasting 5. Libraries and the Internet 6. Library science -- Philosophy 7. Libraries -- Aims and objectives 8. Libraries -- Information technology 9. Libraries and electronic publishing 10. Librarians -- Effect of technological innovations on
ISBN 0838911641; 9780838911648
           LC 2012023767

In this book, Jeannette Woodward considers: are "librarians and libraries facing oblivion as some prognosticators claim? Woodward outlines the technological forces that have coalesced to 'threaten' the future of libraries including financial constraints, digital books, ebook-publisher approaches to libraries, outsourcing, downsizing library space, and librarians' reaction to perceived threats." (Library Journal)
Includes bibliographical references and index

020.9   History, geographic treatment, biography

The **21st-century** black librarian in America; issues and challenges. edited by Andrew P. Jackson (Sekou Molefi Baako), Julius Jefferson Jr., Akilah Nosakhere. Scarecrow Press 2012 xxii, 277 p.p (hardcover) $80   **020.9**

1. Library science 2. African American librarians 3. African Americans and libraries
ISBN 0810882450; 9780810882454
           LC 2011042051

BCALA Literary Award: Outstanding Contribution to Publishing Citation (2013)

This book is a "collection of 48 essays by Black librarians and library supporters [that] identifies racism as one of many challenges of the new century." Topics covered include "poorly equipped school libraries and the need to preserve the school library, a call to action to all librarians to make the shift to new and innovative models of public education, . . . racism in the history of library and information science, and challenges that have plagued librarianship for decades." (Publisher's note)

"With 47 chapters and eight parts, this wide-ranging collection offers a varied and prolific assortment of essays related to black librarianship in America. . . . The 21st Century Black Librarian in America is highly recommended for collections concerned with diversity in librarianship, the history of the field of librarianship, the education of library profes-

sionals, and activism in the profession." College & Research Libraries (C&RL)
Includes bibliographical references and index.

Wright, Alex

Cataloging the world; Paul Otlet and the birth of the information age. Alex Wright. Oxford University Press 2014 360 p. (acid-free paper) $27.95   **020.9**

1. Bibliographers -- Biography 2. Bibliographic control -- History 3. Documentation 4. Mundaneum -- History 5. Universal bibliography 6. Classification -- Books 7. World Wide Web -- History 8. Information organization -- History 9. Bibliographers -- Belgium -- Biography
ISBN 0199931410; 9780199931415
           LC 2013035233

"In 'Cataloging the World,' Alex Wright introduces us to a figure who stands out in the long line of thinkers and idealists who devoted themselves to the task. Beginning in the late nineteenth century, Paul Otlet, a librarian by training, worked at expanding the potential of the catalog card, the world's first information chip." (Publisher's note)

"Wright ends his illuminating story in the present, where Otlet's thoughts about the connection of information to knowledge, and knowledge to insight, are still urgent." Kirkus
Includes bibliographical references and index

020.92   Information scientists

Defending professionalism; a resource for librarians, information specialists, knowledge managers, and archivists. Bill Crowley, editor. Libraries Unlimited, an imprint of ABC-CLIO, LLC 2012 235 p. (paperback) $50.00   **020.92**

1. Librarians 2. Professional ethics 3. Information scientists 4. Library education 5. Libraries and society 6. Archivists -- Training of 7. Knowledge workers -- Training of 8. Archivists -- Professional ethics 9. Librarians -- Professional ethics 10. Information scientists -- Training of 11. Knowledge workers -- Professional ethics 12. Information scientists -- Professional ethics
ISBN 1598848690; 9781598848694
           LC 2012006410

This book, edited by Bill Crowley, offers "arguments and approaches for combating library and information deprofessionalization. . . . Composed of 14 chapters written by contemporary practitioners," the book "provides managers, funding authorities, educators, and practitioners with practical, political, and theoretical reasons why it is in their self-interest to employ professionally educated personnel." (Publisher's note)
Includes bibliographical references and index

Hanagarne, Josh

The **world's** strongest librarian; a memoir of Tourette's, faith, strength, and the power of family. Joshua Hanagarne. Gotham Books 2013 288 p. (hardcover) $26   **020.92**

1. Tourette syndrome 2. Public libraries -- Utah -- Salt Lake City 3. Librarians -- Utah -- Salt Lake City --

Biography
ISBN 1592407870; 9781592407873

LC 2012037713

This memoir, by Josh Hanagarne, is the story of a Mormon with Tourette Syndrome. "By the time [Josh Hanagarne] was twenty, . . . his Tourette's tics escalated to nightmarish levels. Determined to conquer his affliction, Josh underwent everything from quack remedies to lethargy-inducing drug regimes. . . . At last, an eccentric, autistic strongman . . . taught Josh how to 'throttle' his tics into submission through strength-training." (Publisher's note)

021.2   Relationships with the community

Brookover, Sophie

Pop goes the library; using pop culture to connect with your whole community. [by] Sophie Brookover and Elizabeth Burns. Information Today, Inc. 2008 298p il pa $39.50   **021.2**
1. Libraries and community 2. Libraries -- Special collections -- Popular culture
ISBN 978-1-57387-336-9

LC 2008-19509

"This work defines how popular culture can contribute to any library. . . . The authors explore what popular culture is and, more importantly, what it is not. Also examined are what it means to create a popular-culture collection and how to use popular culture to generate staff and public support. . . . This book is required reading." Booklist
Includes bibliographical references

Hill, Chrystie

Inside, outside, and online; building your library community. foreword by Steven Cohen. American Library Association 2009 175p pa $48   **021.2**
1. Libraries and community 2. Library administration 3. Libraries -- Evaluation
ISBN 978-0-8389-0987-4; 0-8389-0987-6

LC 2008-52520

In this "how-to manual, author Hill makes a . . . case for community building as an essential form of service in public libraries, both for their survival and relevance and also for the needs of those Americans who find themselves 'bowling alone.' She outlines five steps in the process she recommends public libraries follow to build communities: assess, deliver, engage, iterate, and sustain." Booklist
Includes bibliographical references

Librarians as community partners; an outreach handbook. edited by Carol Smallwood. American Library Association 2010 204p pa $55   **021.2**
1. Cultural programs 2. Libraries and community 3. Libraries -- Public relations
ISBN 978-0-8389-1006-1

LC 2009-20359

"Thirty-seven public, school, and academic librarians here share 'how we did outreach good' and produce a joyful collection. . . . Beyond a bounty of ideas are practical suggestions and examples that can be used for the library to approach organizations, groups, and governmental entities for grant applications. While the creative is foremost, the financial and efficient are also addressed with the essential details of who did what, how it was funded, and the nature of follow-up. . . . Even the smallest library with a handful of staff could benefit from this book." Libr J
Includes bibliographical references

021.7   Promotion of libraries, archives, information centers

Marketing your library; tips and tools that work. edited by Carol Smallwood, Vera Gubnitskaia and Kerol Harrod ; foreword by Michael Germano. McFarland & Company, Inc., Publishers 2012 ix, 221 p.p ill. (softcover : acid-free paper) $55.00   **021.7**
1. Libraries -- Marketing 2. Libraries -- Public relations
ISBN 0786465433; 9780786465439

LC 2012004460

This book, edited by Carol Smallwood, Vera Gubnitskaia, and Kerol Harrod, presents "how-to case studies from practicing public, school, academic, and special librarians" intended to help librarians "improve brand management, campaign organization, community outreach, media interaction, social media, and event planning and implementation." (Publisher's note)
Includes bibliographical references and index

Schall, Lucy

Teen talkback with interactive booktalks! Lucy Schall. Libraries Unlimited, an imprint of ABC-CLIO, LLC 2013 xviii, 305 p.p (hardcopy) $45   **021.7**
1. Reading 2. Book talks 3. Young adult literature 4. Young adults' libraries 5. Fiction genres -- Bibliography 6. Reading promotion -- United States 7. Teenagers -- Books and reading -- United States
ISBN 1610692896; 9781610692892

LC 2013000241

This book, by Lucy Schall, "is . . . a resource, supplying ready-to-use, interactive booktalks and curriculum connections for more than 100 recently published young adult books. This . . . book is . . . [a] tool for motivating teens to read. It shows how to make booktalks interactive and get teens participating in the presentation, rather than passively listening. Book selections include titles published from 2008 to 2012 organized in seven categories." (Publisher's note)

"Although mostly fiction, there are some nonfiction choices included and the balance of newer titles is respectable. Due to the plethora of topics, detail in descriptions, and variety of related works listed, librarians will be able to locate books for the pickiest of readers." Lib Med Con
Includes bibliographical references and index

Thenell, Jan

The **library's** crisis communications planner; a PR guide for handling every emergency. American Library Association 2004 77p il pa $25   **021.7**
1. Libraries -- Public relations
ISBN 0-8389-0870-5

LC 2004-10891

Offering "advice, firsthand experience, scenarios, and guidelines for communicating effectively before, during, and after a crisis or crisis-producing events, ... [the author's] guide is a ready-made workshop on how to establish and maintain relationships with the media, including how to write a press release, how to keep all staff informed and aware of what to do when an emergency occurs, and how to make sure library board members and other community stakeholders are notified and/or involved. Whether or not you have a public relations office or officer, this slim volume is a must for your professional shelf." Libr J

Includes bibliographical references

022   Administration of physical plant

Petroski, Henry
The **book** on the bookshelf. Knopf 1999 290p $26   **022**
1. Books 2. Libraries 3. Bookbinding
ISBN 0-375-40649-2
LC 99-14336

The author discusses the formatting and housing of books throughout history

"The charm of this book lies in the way that it helps us take a fresh look at an old, long-familiar object. . . . This survey of the subject is probably definitive." Christ Sci Monit

Includes bibliographical references

023   Personnel management (Human resource management)

Giesecke, Joan
★ **Fundamentals** of library supervision; [by] Joan Giesecke and Beth McNeil. 2nd ed.; American Library Association 2010 189p il (ALA fundamentals series) pa $55   **023**
1. Personnel management 2. Libraries -- Administration
ISBN 978-0-8389-1016-0
LC 2009-28890

First published 2005

"The authors give advice on how to build relationships with bosses, peers, and reports; establish good communication skills; create a healthy work climate; motivate others; and build a team. . . . Each chapter includes a succinct bibliography, allowing the new manager to continue his or her education—especially useful for more complex topics like project management." Libr J

Includes bibliographical references

Stanley, Mary J.
Managing library employees; a how-to-do-it manual. Neal-Schuman Publishers 2008 247p il (How-to-do-it manuals for libraries) pa $59.95 **023**
1. Personnel management 2. Libraries -- Handbooks, manuals, etc.
ISBN 978-1-55570-628-9; 1-55570-628-2
LC 2007-51961

"Oriented to librarians who do not have a human resources department in the library, Managing Library Employees is for the nonexpert trying to come to terms with managing a library's largest expenditure and asset—its employees. The chapters are divided into subtopics posed as questions. . . . The chapters also provide information on writing an effective job description, designing a disciplinary procedure, and identifying potential issues that might lead to a lawsuit. . . . This useful guide for everyday situations should be on any library director or manager's professional reference shelf." Booklist

Includes bibliographical references

Tucker, Dennis C.
Crash course in library supervision; meeting the key players. [by] Dennis C. Tucker and Shelley Elizabeth Mosley. Libraries Unlimited 2008 139p il (Crash course series) pa $30   **023**
1. Libraries -- Administration
ISBN 978-1-59158-564-0; 1-59158-564-3
LC 2007-30131

This book "covers the basics for new public library administrators, with an emphasis on interpersonal relations. . . . The book should prove valuable to all new library administrators." Booklist

Includes bibliographical references

025   Operations of libraries, archives, information centers

Bolan, Kimberly
Technology made simple; an improvement guide for small and medium libraries. [by] Kimberly Bolan and Robert Cullin. American Library Association 2007 213p il $40   **025**
1. Information technology 2. Libraries -- Automation
ISBN 0-8389-0920-5; 978-0-8389-0920-1
LC 2006-13191

The authors present an "overview of basic public library technologies. . . . Using examples from a plethora of small- and medium-sized libraries to illustrate how such specific issues as self-check, hiring for attitude, tech policies, staff and public training, and formal planning can be approached as doable and nonthreatening to the non-specialist, this guide is an excellent demonstration of how order can make big issues approchable. . . . Libraries should purchase it for their staff collections but also make reading and implementing various suggestions part of their work plans." Voice Youth Advocates

Includes bibliographical references

Burke, John J., 1875-1936
Neal -Schuman library technology companion; a basic guide for library staff. [by] John J. Burke. 3rd ed.; Neal-Schuman Publishers 2009 279p il **025**
1. Information technology 2. Technological innovations 3. Libraries -- Automation
ISBN 978-1-55570-676-0
LC 2009-23646

First published 2001

"Separated into five parts, the work begins with a discussion of the basics, followed by descriptions of the tools, such as computers and networks. Next addressed are how to put technology to work and how to build and maintain the technology environment. The final chapter talks about future trends. . . . [This is] a valuable reference manual for practicing librarians and textbook for a library-school course. The work addresses all aspects of librarianship and technology—teaching, security, databases, social networking, and more." Booklist

Includes bibliographical references

Cohn, John M.

The **complete** library technology planner; a guidebook with sample technology plans and RFPs on CD-ROM. [by] John M. Cohn and Ann L. Kelsey; with a foreword by Keith Michael Fiels. Neal-Schuman Publishers 2010 xxiv, 163p il pa $99.95 **025**

1. Information technology 2. Planning, Library 3. Libraries -- Automation 4. Automation of library processes -- Handbooks, manuals, etc.

ISBN 978-1-55570-681-4; 1-55570-681-9

LC 2009-41008

"This book provides a comprehensive wealth of information for libraries in need of creating or updating a technology plan. Whether your goal is to introduce an integrated library system (ILS) or transfer from an existing system to a new one, Cohn and Kelsey make clear the strategic planning process involved and provide the tools needed to create a plan, including how to meet funding requirements, implement the plan, and evaluate its success. The accompanying CD-ROM contains 38 sample technology plans and requests for proposals (RFPs) that have been collected from 32 different libraries." Libr J

Includes bibliographical references

Kovacs, Diane K.

The **Kovacs** guide to electronic library collection development; essential core subject collections, selection criteria, and guidelines. 2nd ed; Neal-Schuman Publishers 2009 xxiii, 303p il pa $150 **025**

1. Digital libraries

ISBN 978-1-55570-664-7; 1-55570-664-9

LC 2009-27772

First published 2004; written by Diane K. Kovacs and Kara L. Robinson.

"Chapters cover general collection guidelines and licensing basics; especially useful are individual sections citing specific Web sites for e-collection sources in ready reference, business, medicine, biology, engineering, physical and earth sciences, and the social sciences and humanities. Kovacs . . . is a very diligent researcher, and her latest title again offers librarians much useful information. " Booklist

Includes bibliographical references

More technology for the rest of us; a second primer on computing for the non-IT librarian. Nancy Courtney, editor. Libraries Unlimited 2010 172p il pa $50 **025**

1. Digital libraries. 2. Digital preservation. 3. Libraries and the Internet. 4. Libraries -- Information technology.

5. Libraries -- Technological innovations.

ISBN 978-1-59158-939-6 pa; 1-59158-939-8 pa; 978-1-59158-941-9 ebook; 1-59158-941-X ebook

LC 2009051166

Continuation of Technology for the rest of us (2005)

"11 chapters provide readings on technology topics of interest to today's librarian. Each chapter, authored by a different practicing librarian, describes how the specific technology works and addresses its current and potential use in the library. . . . This book is a one-stop resource for gaining a basic overview of topics such as Web services, digital data preservation and curation, cloud computing, learning management systems, content management systems, metadata repurposing using XSLT, and more." Booklist

Includes bibliographical references

Pearl, Nancy

More book lust; recommended reading for every mood, moment, and reason. Sasquatch Books 2005 286p pa $16.95 **025**

1. Best books 2. Books and reading

ISBN 1-57061-435-0

LC 2004-66292

Sequel to: Book lust (2003)

The author presents a list of "books she or someone else really enjoyed reading, presented in more than 100 lists covering a delightful range of topics, from the biographical or geographical (Winston Churchill, Africa) to favorite writers categorized as 'too good to miss'. . . . If you're clueless about what to read next, you'll find something to pique your interest here." Publ Wkly

Includes bibliographical references

Pulliam, June Michele

Read on . . . horror fiction; [by] June Michele Pulliam and Anthony J. Fonseca. Libraries Unlimited 2006 xvii, 182 p (Read on series) **025**

1. Reference books 2. Horror tales -- Bibliography. 3. Fiction in libraries -- United States. 4. Horror tales, American -- Bibliography. 5. Readers' advisory services -- United States. 6. Public libraries -- United States -- Book lists.

ISBN 1-59158-176-1; 978-1-59158-176-5 (pbk. : alk. paper)

LC 2006012719

Includes bibliographical references and index..

025.04 Information storage and retrieval systems

Dornfest, Rael

Google hacks; [by] Rael Dornfest, Paul Bausch, and Tara Calishain. 3rd ed.; O'Reilly 2006 xxxii, 510p il $24.99 **025.04**

1. Google (Web site) 2. Internet searching

ISBN 0-596-52706-3; 978-0-596-52706-8

LC 2006-285771

First published 2003 under the authorship of Tara Calishain and Rael Dornfest

This guide to the search engine Google gives instructions on how to use such tools as Google Earth, Google Maps,

Google Blog Search, Video Search, and Music Search, as well as different ways of using Google products, such as using Google to keep track of new blog posts and building customized Google maps.

Includes bibliographical references

Gale directory of databases. Gale Res. 2008 2v in 4 parts set $585   **025.04**
   1. Reference books 2. Information systems -- Directories
   ISBN 978-0-7876-9755-6; 0-7876-9755-9

Annual. First published 1993. Formed by the merger of Directory of online databases, Directory of portable databases, and Computer-readable databases

"Descriptive entries include such details as producer name and contact information, summary of content, database language, geographic coverage, year first available, time span, updating, availability, rates, and more." Publisher's note

Jaeger, Paul T.

★ **Public** libraries and internet service roles; measuring and maximizing Internet services. [by] Charles R. McClure and Paul T. Jaeger. American Library Association 2009 112p il map $65 **025.04**
   1. Internet 2. Public libraries 3. Libraries and the Internet 4. Internet -- Public libraries 5. Librarianship -- Social aspects 6. Public libraries -- Social aspects 7. Public libraries -- Aims and objectives
   ISBN 978-0-8389-3576-7; 0-8389-3576-1
                          LC 2008-26622

The authors "summarize the existing research on the meanings of social roles and expectations of public libraries and the results of studies detailing those roles and expectations in relation to the Internet. . . . Their book raises our awareness of some very critical issues and is required reading for anyone who cares about public libraries." Booklist

Includes bibliographical references

Norlin, Elaina

Usability testing for library websites; a hands-on guide. [by] Elaina Norlin, CM! Winters. American Lib. Assn. 2002 69p il pa $35   **025.04**
   1. Web sites
   ISBN 0-8389-3511-7
                          LC 2001-33817

"Four goals are explored in improving library sites: usefulness, effectiveness, learn-ability, and user satisfaction. . . . Steps for recruitment of a testing team, development of sample questions and tasks, and evaluation of results are included." SLJ

Includes bibliographical references

Pariser, Eli

The **filter** bubble; what the Internet is hiding from you. Penguin Press 2011 294p $25.95 **025.04**
   1. Internet 2. World Wide Web 3. Information systems 4. Semantic Web 5. Invisible Web 6. Internet -- Censorship 7. Information organization
   ISBN 978-1-59420-300-8; 1-59420-300-8
                      LC 2011010403

The author examines "the personalization of search-engine results. . . . He is most concerned with its political and social implications, and particularly with what he believes to be its high toll on serendipitous discovery." (N Y Times Book Rev) Index.

"The distinction between citizen and consumer forms the core of [this book] . . . . Are we consumers whose role in society is primarily to purchase and use products, or are we citizens who make informed decisions in an attempt to make life better for ourselves and the world? The Internet, as Eli Pariser convincingly argues in the book, is hurtling toward a consumer model, existing primarily to sell people stuff at the expense of everything else. Pariser is focused on the 'personalization' model, as well as the 'filter bubble' that the gives the book its name. The biggest companies on the Internet, specifically Google and Facebook, are changing the Internet to match users' specific interests, habits, and purchasing preferences, often without us even knowing we're getting personalized content. Pariser isn't simply a disgruntled anticapitalist, though—he lays out the societal and cognitive reasons this particular form of personalization is threatening, using anecdotes, data, philosophy, and social as well as cognitive psychology." A V Club

Includes bibliographical references

Seife, Charles

Virtual unreality; just because the Internet told you, how do you know it's true? Charles Seife. Viking 2014 256 p. $26.95   **025.04**
   1. Internet 2. Information literacy 3. Information resources 4. Internet literacy 5. Internet -- Safety measures 6. Internet fraud -- Prevention 7. Computer network resources -- Evaluation 8. Electronic information resource literacy
   ISBN 0670026085; 9780670026081
                      LC 2013047849

This book, by Charles Seife, "explains how to separate fact from fantasy in the digital world. . . . Digital information is a powerful tool that spreads unbelievably rapidly . . ., even when that information is actually a lie. . . . Charles Seife uses the skepticism, wit, and sharp facility for analysis . . . to take us deep into the Internet information jungle and cut a path through the trickery, fakery, and cyber skullduggery that the online world enables." (Publisher's note)

"Intense and incisive, Seife's exposé of potent tricks on the mesmerizing, overpowering Internet makes us very wary about anything that cannot be verified with our own eyes." Pub Wkly

Includes bibliographical references and index

025.042   World Wide Web

Hock, Randolph

The **Extreme** Searcher's Internet Handbook; A Guide for the Serious Searcher. by Randolph Hock. 3rd ed.; Information Today, Inc. 2013 xxi, 315 p.p ill. ; (paperback) $24.95   **025.042**
   1. Internet research 2. Internet searching 3. Web search engines
   ISBN 1937290026; 9781937290023
                      LC 2012039960

This book by Randolph Hock presents a "guide for anyone who conducts research on the internet—including librarians, teachers, students, business professionals, and writers. This fully revised handbook details what users must know to take full advantage of internet search tools and resources. From the latest online tools to the new and enhanced services offered by standbys such as Google, the major search engines and their myriad of possibilities are thoroughly discussed." (Publisher's note)

Peltier-Davis, Cheryl Ann

The **cybrarian's** web; an A-Z guide to 101 free Web 2.0 tools and other resources. Cheryl Ann Peltier-Davis. Information Today, Inc. 2011 xxv, 486 p.p ill. (pbk.) $49.50 **025.042**
1. Web 2.0 2. Library science 3. Library services 4. Web sites -- Directories 5. Libraries and the Internet 6. Free computer software -- Computer network resources
ISBN 1573874272; 9781573874274

LC 2011035916
This book, by Cheryl Ann Peltier-Davis, offers a "field guide to the best of free Web 2.0 tools and their practical applications in libraries and information centers. Designed for info[rmation] pro[fessionals] who want to use the latest tech tools to connect, collaborate, and create, you'll find resources to help . . . [l]aunch a local news & events blog[,] . . . [c]reate a virtual reference desk[,] . . . [p]roduce & stream live video[, and more]." (Publisher's note)
"If you are looking for a definitive resource on Web 2.0, then The Cybrarian's Web should be high up on your list." Booklist
Includes bibliographical references and index

025.06 Information storage and retrieval systems devoted to specific subjects

Bolles, Mark Emery

What color is your parachute? guide to job-hunting online. Mark Emery Bolles and Richard Nelson Bolles. Ten Speed Press 2011 186 p. (paperback) $12.99 **025.06**
1. Web sites -- Directories 2. Job hunting -- Internet resources 3. Web sites -- United States -- Directories 4. Job hunting -- United States -- Computer network resources
ISBN 1607740338; 9781607740339

LC 2010051035
This book, by Mark Emery Bolles and Richard N. Bolles, is a companion to the authors' vocational guidance and job-hunting guide, focusing on use of the Internet. "The [book] shows you how to quickly find the data that will be most helpful . . . , how to identify . . . the places where you will most enjoy working, how to leverage the power of social networking sites, and how to use your Internet time most effectively, avoiding the common pitfalls and setting you up for success." (Publisher's note)
Includes bibliographical references (p. 177-179) and indexes

025.1 Administration

Gerding, Stephanie K.

Winning grants; a how-to-do-it manual for librarians with multimedia tutorials and grant development tools. [by] Pamela H. MacKellar and Stephanie K. Gerding. Neal-Schuman Publishers 2010 xxi, 242p il (How-to-do-it manuals for librarians) **025.1**
1. Fund raising 2. Grants-in-aid
ISBN 978-1-55570-700-2

LC 2010017965
First published 2006 with title: Grants for libraries
"This great all-around resource should be a staple for those just entering the challenging world of grant seeking and for the well-rounded library collection." Libr J
Includes bibliographical references

Johnson, Doug

★ The **indispensable** librarian; surviving and thriving in school libraries in the information age. Doug Johnson ; illustrations by Brady Johnson. Linworth, an imprint of ABC-CLIO, LLC 2013 xix, 207 p.p illustrations (pbk.) $40 **025.1**
1. Librarians 2. School libraries 3. School librarians -- United States 4. School libraries -- United States -- Administration
ISBN 161069239X; 9781610692397

LC 2012051394
This book, by Doug A. Johnson, "defines and clarifies the role of the school library media specialist in a technologically enhanced school, providing relevant examples and useful advice on a variety of topics; and underscores the importance of strong management skills, especially regarding collaborative planning and communications. The book is written especially for K-12 school librarians, both new and experienced, and is also suitable for pre-service librarians as a textbook." (Publisher's note)
"Johnson offers both theory and practical suggestions on ways to embed [librarians] and [their] jobs into the fabric of a school's culture and curriculum." Lib Med Con
Includes bibliographical references and index

Landau, Herbert B.

The **small** public library survival guide; thriving on less. American Library Association 2008 159p pa $42 **025.1**
1. Library finance 2. Public libraries 3. Libraries and community
ISBN 978-0-8389-3575-0; 0-8389-3575-3

LC 2008-7425
This "volume covers many topics of interest to staff in small public libraries. Written in a conversational, accessible style, information is presented in short chapters with relevant examples and sample documents. . . . Covering topics from low-budget programming to building 'noncash support from the community,' this text has something for almost everyone involved in the operations of a small public library. . . . Easy and enjoyable to read." Voice Youth Advocates
Includes bibliographical references

Larson, Jeanette C.

★ The **public** library policy writer; a guidebook with model policies on CD-ROM. [by] Jeanette C. Larson and Herman L. Totten. Neal-Schuman Publishers 2008 xxi, 280p $75 **025.1**

1. Public libraries 2. Libraries -- Administration

ISBN 978-1-55570-603-6; 1-55570-603-7

LC 2008-17622

"This guidebook is written mainly for small to medium-sized library directors who need to analyze current policies, revise or update those still in use, and develop new ones. The book is organized by administrative and service areas such as employment practices, staff and patron conduct, use of materials, collection development, and access to facilities... . This practical tool should be useful to administrators, staff, and library boards." Booklist

Includes bibliographical references

Laughlin, Sara

The **quality** library; a guide to staff-driven improvement, better efficiency, and happier customers. [by] Sara Laughlin and Ray W. Wilson. American Library Association 2008 144p il pa $55 **025.1**

1. Customer services 2. Management 3. Planning, Library 4. Libraries -- Management 5. Total quality management 6. Libraries -- Administration

ISBN 0-8389-0952-3; 978-0-8389-0952-2

LC 2007-30710

"Building on an earlier publication, The Library's Continuous Improvement Fieldbook: 29 Ready-to-Use Tools . . . Laughlin and Wilson have created a manual for administrators and employees who want to improve their libraries by improving their processes. . . . This can be a useful guide for libraries whose governing bodies are looking for business-like solutions and for managers who want to heed input from those who do the job." Booklist

Includes bibliographical references

MacKellar, Pamela H.

Writing successful technology grant proposals; a LITA guide. Pamela H. MacKellar. Neal-Schuman Publishers, Inc. 2012 xviii, 227 p.p (alk. paper) $70.00 **025.1**

1. Information technology 2. Libraries -- Administration 3. Proposal writing for grants 4. Proposal writing for grants -- United States 5. Libraries -- Automation -- United States -- Finance 6. Proposal writing in library science -- United States 7. Libraries -- Information technology -- United States -- Finance

ISBN 1555707637; 9781555707637

LC 2011046318

This book, by Pamela H. MacKellar, offers instruction on grant writing. "[H]ow can you write a successful grant proposal? . . . This comprehensive book on grants for libraries focuses on technology, . . . specific sources and resources for technology grants, . . . and technology project success stories so you get real life examples of how others like you made their libraries stronger through technology grants." (Publisher's note)

Includes bibliographical references and index

Mosley, Pixey Anne

The **challenge** of library management; leading with emotional engagement. by Wyoma vanDuinkerken and Pixey Anne Mosley. American Library Association 2011 169 p. $52 **025.1**

1. Personnel management 2. Libraries -- Administration 3. Leadership 4. Organizational change -- Management 5. Library administration -- Problems, exercises, etc

ISBN 0838911021; 9780838911020

LC 2011011349

This book, by Wyoma vanDuinkerken and Pixey Anne Moseley, is designed to show library managers how to "engage library staff in the process and encourage their active participation, navigate successfully through common types of change, such as space planning, departmental reorganization, and changes in work responsibilities, [and] draw on concepts from psychology, communication, empowerment, planning, and evaluation to minimize friction." (Publisher's note)

"The information they provide mostly concerns dealing with employees in order to ensure an effective and successful change initiative in a library setting...While the authors tailor the advice to librarians by using example specific to libraries, the advice could be applied to any organizational setting. All in all, the suggestions contained here are helpful when planning change in a library. Each chapter concludes with a list of key ideas to keep in mind and questions for reflection.—" (VOYA)

Includes bibliographical references (p. 155-163) and index

Our new public, a changing clientele; bewildering issues or new challenges for managing libraries? edited by James R. Kennedy, Lisa Vardaman, and Gerard B. McCabe. Libraries Unlimited 2008 305p (Libraries Unlimited library management collection) $45 **025.1**

1. Libraries and students 2. Libraries -- Administration

ISBN 978-1-59158-407-0

LC 2007-35907

"Several chapters in this . . . title discuss the milennials—children of the baby boomers—and digital natives and how they have already had an impact on library service... . Each chapter offers practical advice based on experiences, and each includes a list of references. Library managers and those aspiring to be managers will find help in providing services for a younger demographic." Booklist

Includes bibliographical references

Smith, G. Stevenson

Cost control for nonprofits in crisis; G. Stevenson Smith. American Library Association 2011 viii, 133 p.p ill. (pbk. : alk. paper) $75.00 **025.1**

1. Finance 2. Financial crises 3. Nonprofit organizations 4. Libraries -- Cost control 5. Libraries -- Cost effectiveness 6. Library finance -- United States 7. Nonprofit organizations -- Cost control 8. Library administration -- Decision making 9. Nonprofit organizations -- Cost effectiveness 10. Nonprofit organizations -- United States -- Finance 11. Nonprofit

organizations -- Management -- Decision making
ISBN 083891098X; 9780838910986

LC 2011025285

Author G. Stevenson Smith's book provides financial advice and tips. "Libraries, like many other cultural institutions such as museums, art councils, and theater groups, are looking for answers to the pressing problem of financial stability, and ultimately survival . . . [Smith's book] helps managers and directors tackle the harsh realities before them . . . [He] offers [t]echniques for determining the most cost-effective methods of providing services to clients and patrons of nonprofit cultural institutions." (Publisher's note)
Includes bibliographical references and index

025.17 Administration of collections of special materials

√**Managing** Electronic Resources; a LITA Guide. Edited by Ryan O. Weir. ALA TechSource, an imprint of the American Library Assoc. 2012 xii, 179 p.p (pbk.) $65 **025.17**
1. Digital libraries 2. Libraries -- Collection development 3. Electronic reference services (Libraries) 4. Electronic information resources -- Management 5. Libraries -- Special collections -- Electronic information resources
ISBN 155570767X; 9781555707675

LC 2012015102

In this book, Ryan O. Weir presents a "guide to developing and maintaining electronic library collections. Topics include evaluation, selection, and cataloging of electronic resources; strategies for contract negotiation; how to gather and interpret data about electronic resource use; . . . and staffing for electronic collections, as well as projections about how electronic resources will continue to evolve and impact libraries in the future." (Voice of Youth Advocates)
Includes bibliographical references and index

★ **No** shelf required; e-books in libraries. edited by Sue Polanka. American Library Association 2011 182p pa $65 **025.17**
1. Electronic books
ISBN 978-0-83891-054-2

LC 2010-14045

"Following a chapter on e-book history are chapters discussing e-books and students' learning; e-books in school, public, and academic libraries; and e-book acquisitions and management. . . . An essential guide to a topic of high importance." Booklist
Includes bibliographical references

025.2 Acquisitions and collection development

Alabaster, Carol

Developing an outstanding core collection; a guide for libraries. 2nd ed; American Library Association 2010 191p il pa $60 **025.2**
1. Best books 2. Reference books 3. Libraries -- Collection development 4. Public libraries -- Collection

development
ISBN 978-0-8389-1040-5

LC 2009-40342

First published 2002

The author suggests "that the general public needs materials beyond current best-sellers and ready-reference works; that those materials should be high-quality, enduring pieces; and that librarians are the best persons to decide what constitutes appropriate core collections for their communities. . . . [She also] addresses the technological changes that drastically affect reading habits and our ability to satisfy the needs of 'the people's university.' . . . [This book is] required reading for all those charged with the task of adult collection development." Booklist
Includes bibliographical references

Baker, Nicholson

√ **Double** fold; libraries and the assault on paper. Random House 2001 370p il hardcover o.p. pa $14 **025.2**
1. Paper 2. Libraries -- Special collections 3. Library resources -- Conservation and restoration
ISBN 0-375-72621-7 pa

LC 00-59171

Baker criticizes libraries for discarding books, magazines and newspapers and disputes the arguments for doing so "that libraries are running out of space, and that paper, because of its acid content, is rapidly turning to dust. . . . What the Library of Congress spends in a year on microfilming would, (according to Baker), buy a storage facility 'the size of a Home Depot, which would hold a century of newsprint.' . . . Librarians, he says, 'have lied to us shamelessly about the extent of paper's fragility, and they continue to lie about it.'" N Y Times Book Rev
Includes bibliographical references

Brenner, Robin E.

√ ★ **Understanding** manga and anime. Libraries Unlimited 2007 335p il pa $40 **025.2**
1. Anime 2. Manga -- Study and teaching 3. Libraries -- Collection development 4. Libraries -- Special collections -- Graphic novels
ISBN 978-1-59158-332-5; 1-59158-332-2

LC 2007-9773

The author "provides thorough explanations of manga and anime vocabulary, potential censorship issues because of cultural disparities, and typical Manga conventions. . . . No professional collection could possibly be complete without this all-inclusive and exceptional work." Voice Youth Advocates

√**Building** and managing e-book collections; a how-to-do-it manual for librarians. edited by Richard Kaplan. Neal-Schuman 2012 xv, 197 p.p (pbk. : alk. paper) $75 **025.2**
1. Libraries -- Collection development 2. Libraries and electronic publishing 3. Libraries -- Special Collections -- Electronic books 4. Electronic books 5. Libraries -- Special collections -- Electronic books
ISBN 1555707769; 9781555707767

LC 2012018143

This book on library collections of e-books, edited by Richard B. Kaplan, focuses on "collection development issues, including the selection process and development policies, the use of approval plans, patron-driven acquisition, and practical solutions for creating your e-book collection policies. Chapters on budgeting and licensing cover ownership versus leasing models . . . on digital rights management, and strategies for success in retention, access, and budgeting." (Publisher's note)

Includes bibliographical references and index

Charles, John A.

The **mystery** readers' advisory; the librarian's clues to murder and mayhem. [by] John Charles, Joanna Morrison, [and] Candace Clark. American Library Association 2002 227p (ALA readers' advisory series) pa $45   **025.2**

    1. Reference books 2. Reference services (Libraries) 3. Mystery fiction -- Bibliography
    ISBN 0-8389-0811-X; 978-0-8389-0811-2
           LC 01-45083

"Covering everything a librarian would need to know to successfully build and promote a mystery collection, the authors include chapters on weeding and marketing the collection, with a great section on how to do a readers' advisory interview. . . . The text is peppered with authors and titles to know and plenty of plot teasers to fill your reading list. There are thorough discussions of the different subgenres, from police procedural to romantic suspense and other genre blends. . . . The lists of mystery periodicals, reference sources, and Web sites are well-rounded and up-to-date." Voice Youth Advocates

Includes bibliographical references

Foerstel, Herbert N.

    ★ **Banned** in the U.S.A; a reference guide to book censorship in schools and public libraries. rev and expanded ed; Greenwood Press 2002 xxvii, 296p $54.95   **025.2**

    1. Censorship 2. Books -- Censorship 3. Libraries -- Censorship 4. Censorship -- United States 5. Book selection -- United States 6. Textbooks -- Censorship -- United States 7. Public schools -- Censorship -- United States 8. Public libraries -- Censorship -- United States 9. Public libraries -- Book selection -- United States
    ISBN 0-313-31166-8
           LC 2001-55620

First published 1994

"Librarians and teachers need this book, but patrons who want to better understand the threats to their First Amendment rights should be led to it as well." SLJ

Includes bibliographical references

Gallaway, Beth

    ★ **Game** on! gaming at the library. Neal-Schuman Publishers 2009 306p il pa $55   **025.2**

    1. Video games 2. Video games and children 3. Video games and teenagers 4. Multimedia library services 5. Electronic games -- Collections 6. Libraries -- Special collections
    ISBN 1-55570-595-2; 978-1-55570-595-4
           LC 2009-14110

"An essential guide for any librarian who plans on embracing the video-game phenomenon, or at the very least, understanding it. . . . [The chapters] are well organized and contain an abundance of practical information. The sections on selection, collection, and circulation of video games include relevant advice on policy, cataloging, marketing, storage, and displays. . . . The annotated list of video games for a core collection is wonderful for selection purposes." SLJ

Includes bibliographical references

Goldsmith, Francisca

The **readers'** advisory guide to graphic novels. American Library Association 2010 124p (ALA readers' advisory series) pa $45   **025.2**

    1. Graphic novels -- Bibliography 2. Libraries -- Special collections -- Graphic novels
    ISBN 978-0-8389-1008-5; 0-8389-1008-4
           LC 2009-25239

"After dispelling the two main myths that ghettoize graphic novels—they are just for adolescents and they are far less complex than texts without pictures—Goldsmith emphasizes that GNs are a format and not a genre. She suggests active and passive ways to offer readers' advisory (RA) from face-to-face encounters with patrons to book displays and book groups and offers guidance on helping established GN readers to find new titles they might enjoy. . . . All in all it is a valuable and quite readable resource that belongs in every library's professional collection." Voice Youth Advocates

Includes glossary and bibliographical references

Graphic novels beyond the basics; insights and issues for libraries. Martha Cornog and Timothy Perper, editors. Libraries Unlimited 2009 xxx, 281p il pa $45   **025.2**

    1. Graphic novels -- History and criticism 2. Comic books, strips, etc. -- History and criticism 3. Libraries -- Special collections -- Graphic novels
    ISBN 978-1-59158-478-0; 1-59158-478-7
           LC 2009-16189

Editors Cornog and Perper have collected essays by experts Robin Brenner, Francisca Goldsmith, Trina Robbins, Michael R. Lavin, Gilles Poitras, Lorena O'English, Michael Niederhausen, Erin Byrne, and Cornog herself, all about graphic novels in libraries. Topics covered range from the appeal of superheroes to manga, the appeal of comics to women and girls, anime, independent comics, dealing with challenges to the material, and more. Appendices provide resource information on African American-interest graphic novels, Latino-Interest graphic novels, LGBT-interest graphic novels, religious-themed graphic novels, a bibliography of books about graphic novels in libraries, and online resources.

"Whether you are serious about the genre, interested in the history, or looking for ammunition, this book should be on your shelf. The wealth of knowledge and research that went into these essays is impressive, and reading this book will put you on the road to becoming an expert." Libr Media Connect

Includes bibliographical references

★ **Intellectual** freedom manual; 8th ed; American Library Association 2010 xxii, 439 p.p **025.2**
1. Intellectual freedom -- United States -- Handbooks, manuals, etc. 2. Libraries -- Censorship -- United States -- Handbooks, manuals, etc.
ISBN 0838935907; 9780838935903
LC 2010016157
"All libraries should have a copy of this book to use when writing or revising policies; indispensable." Libr J

Laguardia, Cheryl
Marketing your library's electronic resources; a how-to-do-it manual. Marie R. Kennedy, Cheryl LaGuardia. Neal-Schuman, an imprint of the American Library Association 2013 177 p. (How-to-do-it manuals) $60 **025.2**
1. Library resources 2. Libraries -- Collection development 3. Libraries -- Special Collections -- Electronic books 4. Libraries -- Marketing 5. Electronic information resources -- Marketing 6. Libraries -- United States -- Marketing -- Case studies 7. Libraries -- Special collections -- Electronic information resources
ISBN 1555708897; 9781555708894
LC 2012028267
This book, by Marie R. Kennedy and Cheryl LaGuardia, "guides readers through every step of developing, implementing, and evaluating plans to market [a library's] e-resources in an approachable and user-friendly way. . . . Their book includes four complete programs from both public and academic libraries [and] a step-by-step organization guide, with a variety of feedback and assessment forms which can be used as models." (Publisher's note)
"Every library needs to know how to educate its patrons about these resources, and this book provides a well-organized, uncomplicated plan for doing so." VOYA
Includes bibliographical references and index

Pinnell-Stephens, June
★ **Protecting** intellectual freedom in your public library; scenarios from the front lines. June Pinnell-Stephens for the Office for Intellectual Freedom. American Library Association 2012 xi, 148 p.p (pbk. : alk. paper) $50.00 **025.2**
1. Censorship 2. Library science 3. Public libraries 4. Intellectual freedom 5. Intellectual freedom -- United States 6. Public libraries -- Censorship -- United States 7. Public libraries -- Censorship -- United States -- Case studies
ISBN 0838935834; 9780838935835
LC 2011029691
This book, by June Pinnell-Stephens, offers a guide to intellectual freedom concerns and rights as relating to public library administration. "When confronted with challenges like censorship and policy disputes, public librarians and paraprofessionals need reliable how-to guidance. . . . [T]his book provides . . . analysis of how IF plays out in the world of public libraries . . . and advice on how to effectively handle intellectual freedom challenges." (Publisher's note)
Includes bibliographical references and index.

Rethinking collection development and management; Becky Albitz, Christine Avery, and Diane

Zabel, editors. Libraries Unlimited 2014 xiv, 394 p.p (pbk. : acid-free paper) $60 **025.2**
1. Acquisitions (Libraries) 2. Collection management (Libraries) 3. Collection development (Libraries) 4. Library materials -- Conservation and restoration
ISBN 1610693051; 9781610693059
LC 2013038447
"This collection of thought-provoking essays . . . covers theory, research, and best practices in collection development, examining how it has evolved, identifying how some librarians are creatively responding to these changes, and predicting what is coming next." Publisher's note
Includes bibliographical references and index

Serchay, David S.
The **librarian's** guide to graphic novels for adults. Neal-Schuman Publishers 2010 320p il $65 **025.2**
1. Graphic novels -- Collections 2. Graphic novels -- Administration 3. Libraries -- Special collections -- Graphic novels
ISBN 978-1-55570-662-3
LC 2009-41011
"This book will inspire librarians—and others—with little knowledge of graphic novels (GNs) for adults to pick one up and see what all the buzz is about. Serchay puts forth a complete guide that will enable any librarian, whether a GN novice or seasoned fan, to establish a brand-new collection, fully understanding what GNs are, where to purchase them, how to catalog them, and how to review, promote, and maintain the new collection." Libr J
Includes bibliographical references

Singer, Carol A.
Fundamentals of Managing Reference Collections; Carol A. Singer. American Library Association 2012 xii, 167 p.p (pbk.) $60 **025.2**
1. Reference books 2. Libraries -- Special collections 3. Electronic reference services (Libraries) 4. Reference books -- United States 5. Electronic reference sources -- United States 6. Libraries -- Special collections -- Reference sources 7. Collection management (Libraries) -- United States -- Case studies
ISBN 0838911536; 9780838911532
LC 2011044446
Author Carol A. "Singer's book offers information and insight on best practices for reference collection management, no matter the size, and shows why managing without a plan is a recipe for clutter and confusion." Singer discusses "the importance of collection development policies, and how to effectively involve others in the decision-making process," in addition to "new insights into selecting reference materials" and "strategies for collection maintenance." (Publisher's note)
Includes bibliographical references and index

White, Andrew C.
★ **E** -metrics for library and information professionals; how to use data for managing and evaluating

electronic resource collections. Neal-Schuman Publishers 2006 249p il pa $75   **025.2**
   1. Digital libraries
   ISBN 1-55570-514-6
                    LC 2004-54678

"Designed to introduce readers to e-metrics ('the measurements of the use and activity of networked information'), this book is made up of 10 chapters that are divided among three major sections. Part 1 supplies a definition of e-metrics, explores their use in libraries, and discusses vendor-supplied electronic data reports. Part 2 explains why libraries need e-metrics, focusing on how they can be used for public relations, collection management, and library administration. Part 3 offers ways that libraries can build local e-metrics. Chapters cover the capturing and processing of statistics, infrastructure and technical requirements, and staffing needs. With its coherent structure, well-articulated language, and illustrative material (tables, figures, and examples), this book has much to recommend it." Booklist
   Includes bibliographical references

025.3   Bibliographic analysis and control

Maxwell, Robert L.
   FRBR; a guide for the perplexed. American Library Association 2008 151p il pa $50   **025.3**
   1. FRBR (Conceptual model)
   ISBN 978-0-8389-0950-8; 0-8389-0950-7
                    LC 2007-27845

This book explains "Functional Requirements for Bibliographic Records (FRBR), an evolving conceptual model developed to assist users in navigating library catalogs to find the information they want and need. Maxwell . . . explains and illustrates the FRBR model, details why the document and model are important for the future of information organization, and explains what a catalog based on FRBR principles might look like. He also briefly illustrates the use of Functional Requirements for Authority Data (FRAD)." Booklist
   Includes bibliographic references

Mitchell, Anne M.
   ★ **Cataloging** and organizing digital resources; a how-to-do-it manual for librarians. Neal-Schuman Publishers 2005 219p il (How-to-do-it manuals for librarians) pa $75   **025.3**
   1. Cataloging 2. Reference books 3. Digital libraries 4. Information systems
   ISBN 1-55570-521-9
                    LC 2005-903

This "volume addresses the ways a library can manage electronic collections. The goal is to provide an overview of management concerns and issues regarding bibliographic control in an online environment and to suggest tools that are available. The 10 chapters address such topics as development of digital libraries, organization of work flow, alternatives to cataloging, cataloging rules and records, online monographs and serials, integration of resources, and trends. Each chapter offers an introduction; guidelines, instructions, or strategies; and a summary and references. The writing is clear, with plentiful examples that include figures and titles." Booklist

Oliver, Chris
   ★ **Introducing** RDA; a guide to the basics. Chris Oliver. American Library Association 2010 vii, 117 p.p ill. (paperback) $45   **025.3**
   1. Cataloging 2. Resource description and access -- Handbooks, manuals, etc. 3. Cataloging -- Standards 4. Descriptive cataloging -- Standards
   ISBN 083893594X; 9780838935941
                    LC 2010021719

This book looks at Resource Description and Access (RDA), the cataloging standard that's replacing Anglo-American Cataloguing Rules (AACR). "Through numerous examples, [Chris] Oliver compares and contrasts RDA and AACR. He also discusses RDA background and its connection to the Functional Requirements for Bibliographic Records (FRBR) and Functional Requirements for Authority Data (FRAD) models and international standards." (Library Journal)
   This is "a useful guide that provides a clear explanation of what RDA is all about. . . . Highly recommended for novice and experienced catalogers." Libr J
   Includes bibliographical references (p. 105-109) and index.

025.32   Descriptive cataloging

Maxwell, Robert L.
   Maxwell's handbook for RDA, resource description & access; explaining and illustrating RDA: resource description and access using MARC21. Robert L. Maxwell. ALA Editions, an imprint of the American Library Association 2013 x, 900 p.p (pbk. : alk. paper) $98   **025.32**
   1. Cataloging 2. Resource description and access -- Handbooks, manuals, etc. 3. Resource description & access -- Handbooks, manuals, etc 4. Descriptive cataloging -- Standards -- Handbooks, manuals, etc
   ISBN 0838911722; 9780838911723
                    LC 2013035124

In this book, "cataloging expert Robert Maxwell brings his trademark practical commentary to bear on the new, unified cataloging standard. Designed to interpret and explain RDA: Resource Description and Access, this handbook illustrates and applies the new cataloging rules in the MARC21 environment for every type of information format." (Publisher's note)
   "Through full and numerous cataloging examples, the author covers FRBR (functional requirements for bibliographic records) basics and how to record the attributes for entities such as manifestations, items, persons, corporate bodies, places, expressions, and works. The examples are not limited to just the print format but also include electronic materials, music, series, and maps." LJ
   Includes bibliographical references and index

025.4   Subject analysis and control

Dewey, Melvil
  ★ **Dewey** decimal classification and relative index; devised by Melvil Dewey. ed 22; OCLC 2003 4v set $375   **025.4**
  1. Dewey Decimal Classification
  ISBN 0-910608-70-9
                                                 LC 2003-50872
  First published anonymously in 1876

Library of Congress/Cataloging Policy and Support Office
✓ **Library** of Congress subject headings; prepared by the Policy and Standards Division, Library Services. 31st ed; Library of Congress 2009 5v **025.4**
  1. Subject headings
  Annual. Variant title: Subject headings used in the dictionary catalogs of the Library of Congress. Issued previously by the Subject Cataloging Division and later by the Office for Subject Cataloging Policy
  This work contains the headings and cross-references established and applied by the Library of Congress.

  ★ **Sears** list of subject headings; Joseph Miller, editor; Susan McCarthy, associate editor. 20th ed; H.W. Wilson Co. 2010 liii, 847p $150   **025.4**
  1. Reference books 2. Subject headings
  ISBN 978-0-8242-1105-9; 0-8242-1105-7
                                                 LC 2010-5731
  First published 1923 with title: List of subject headings for small libraries, by Minnie Earl Sears
  "The Sears List of Subject Headings delivers a core list of key headings, together with patterns and examples to guide the cataloger in creating additional headings as required. It features: agreement with the Dewey Decimal Classification system to ensure that subject headings conform with library standards; [a] thesaurus-like format; accompanying list of canceled and replacement headings; and legends within the list that identify earlier forms of headings; scope notes accompanying . . . headings where clarification of the specialized use of a term may be required." Publisher's note
  Includes bibliographical references

025.5   Services for users

Buker, Derek M.
  The **science** -fiction and fantasy readers' advisory; the librarian's guide to cyborgs, aliens, and sorcerers. American Lib. Assn. 2002 230p (ALA readers' advisory series) pa $50   **025.5**
  1. Reference books 2. Reference services (Libraries) 3. Fantasy fiction -- Bibliography 4. Science fiction -- Bibliography
  ISBN 0-8389-0831-4; 978-0-8389-0831-0
                                                 LC 2002-1494
  A "well-organized, humorous guide to providing readers' advisory to customers wanting science fiction or fantasy recommendations. . . . The book is divided into two parts, one dealing with science fiction and one with fantasy, and

further divides these genres into their many subgenres, providing short annotated lists of recommended titles as well as longer lists without annotations. . . . What this guide does best is demonstrate the wide scope of science fiction and fantasy literature; it gives many suggestions and recommendations across this broad range." SLJ
  Includes bibliographical references

Cords, Sarah Statz
  The **real** story; a guide to nonfiction reading interests. edited by Robert Burgin. Libraries Unlimited 2006 xxxii, 460p (Genreflecting advisory series) $55   **025.5**
  1. Books and reading 2. Reference services (Libraries)
  ISBN 1-59158-283-0
                                                 LC 2006-3712
  The author "describes more than 555 popular nonfiction titles published over the last 15 years, along with classic titles such as Truman Capote's In Cold Blood. . . . Cords has identified 11 broad categories based on subjects, genres, and appeal factors. Among the categories are 'Biography,' 'Travel,' 'True Adventure,' and 'True Crime.' . . . A must-read for any librarian who recommends popular reading titles, it belongs at the reference and readers'-advisory desks of most libraries." Booklist
  Includes bibliographical references

  ★ **Crash** course in readers' advisory; Cynthia Orr. Libraries Unlimited 2015 125 p. (paperback) $45   **025.5**
  1. Readers' advisory services
  ISBN 1610698258; 9781610698252
                                                 LC 2014027064
  Includes bibliographical references and index

Evans, G. Edward
  Introduction to library public services; [by] G. Edward Evans and Thomas L. Carter. 7th ed; Libraries Unlimited 2009 401p il (Library and information science text series) $65; pa $50   **025.5**
  1. Library services 2. Library circulation 3. Reference services (Libraries)
  ISBN 978-1-59158-596-1; 978-1-59158-595-4 pa
                                                 LC 2008-37445
  First published 1972 under the authorship of Marty Bloomberg with title: Introduction to public services for library technicians
  "Each chapter covers the role, purpose, and philosophy related to major functional areas of public service, including points to ponder, forms and flowcharts, review questions and suggested readings." Publisher's note

Ford, Charlotte
  Crash course in reference. Libraries Unlimited 2008 143p il (Crash course)   **025.5**
  1. Reference books 2. Reference services (Libraries) 3. Reference services -- Handbooks, manuals, etc.
  ISBN 978-1-59158-463-6
                                                 LC 2007-52948
  "A basic explanation of reference services for those with little formal LIS training working in small rural libraries or others who have been working in other areas and wish to

brush up on their skills, this author provides an introduction to reference services including search strategies." Publisher's note

Includes bibliographical references

Hernon, Peter

Assessing service quality; satisfying the expectations of library customers. [by] Peter Hernon + Ellen Altman. 2nd ed; American Library Association 2010 206p il pa $65   **025.5**
1. Library services 2. Libraries -- Public relations
ISBN 978-0-8389-1021-4; 0-8389-1021-1
LC 2009-40332

First published 1998

The authors "concentrate on how to assess service quality and customer satisfaction. Here they suggest . . . ways to think about library services, clarify the distinction between service quality and customer satisfaction, present strategies for developing a customer service plan, identify procedures to measure service quality and satisfaction, and . . . challenge conventional thinking about these powerful principles. . . . Kudos to these authors for providing an essential resource for librarians who understand that folks who walk into their libraries are not patrons but customers." Libr J

Includes bibliographical references

Jerrard, Jane

★ **Crisis** in employment; a librarian's guide to helping job seekers. foreword by Denise Davis. American Library Association 2009 66p il pa $40   **025.5**
1. Unemployment 2. Libraries and community 3. Reference services (Libraries) 4. Vocational guidance -- Information services
ISBN 978-0-8389-1013-9
LC 2009-16684

This "special report provides suggestions for providing low-cost assistance to job-seeking unemployed library users. With examples from various public libraries, the report offers advice for planning, how to get the most out of resources at hand, dealing with the need for additional computers, suggestions for community partnerships, and how to best assist users who need to become computer literate for a successful job search." Libr J

Includes bibliographical references

Kern, M. Kathleen

★ **Virtual** reference best practices; tailoring services to your library. American Library Association 2009 148p il pa $50   **025.5**
1. Reference services (Libraries)
ISBN 978-0-8389-0975-1
LC 2008-15379

The author "offers advice and assistance for libraries considering VR. . . . Kern's guidebook includes useful forms and exercises for every aspect of the VR process from a market assessment of the library's community served to an evaluation of the service. . . . Even those [libraries] which already offer virtual reference will find assistance and suggestions to improve their services." Voice Youth Advocates

Includes bibliographical references

Moyer, Jessica E.

The **readers'** advisory handbook; edited by Jessica E. Moyer and Kaite Mediatore Stover. American Library Association 2010 220p (ALA readers' advisory series) pa $55   **025.5**
1. Best books 2. Reference services (Libraries)
ISBN 978-0-8389-1042-9
LC 2009-45793

"This great generalist title offers guidelines not only on readers' advisory (RA) but on related matters of collection development and marketing books to different reading audiences. . . . [The authors] gather information and instruction from 15 contributing public and school librarians on self-education, managing and improving groups of selectors, making quick but thorough evaluations of different types of materials, writing reviews, and working with book groups as well as other kinds of programming." Libr J

Includes bibliographical references

Research -based readers' advisory; with contributions by Amanda Blau and others. American Library Association 2008 278p (ALA readers' advisory series) pa $50   **025.5**
1. Reference services (Libraries)
ISBN 978-0-8389-0959-1; 0-8389-0959-0
LC 2007-49421

"Following a survey of the current state of RA, 11 chapters cover topics such as 'Nonfiction Readers and Nonfiction Advisory,' 'Romance and Genre Readers,' and 'Tools for Readers' Advisory.' Each chapter begins with a 'Research View,' in which Moyer summarizes the latest literature. Following the 'Research View' is a 'Librarian's View,' in which an impressive array of contributors talk about practical applications." Booklist

Includes bibliographical references

Mulac, Carolyn M.

Fundamentals of reference; Carolyn M. Mulac. American Library Association 2012 xii., 131 p.p (pbk. : alk. paper) $52   **025.5**
1. Reference services (Libraries) 2. Reference books -- Bibliography 3. Electronic reference services (Libraries) 4. Internet in library reference services
ISBN 0838910874; 9780838910870
LC 2012010058

Author Carolyn M. Mulac's book offers an "introduction to reference sources and services for a variety of readers, from library staff members who are asked to work in the reference department to managers and others who wish to familiarize themselves with this important area of librarianship." Mulac "presents an overview of the basic tools and techniques of reference work, including" reference services and reference sources. (Publisher's note)

Includes bibliographical references and index

Nilsen, Kirsti

Conducting the reference interview; a how-to-do-it manual for librarians. [by] Catherine Sheldrick Ross, Kirsti Nilsen, and Marie L. Radford. 2nd ed;

Neal-Schuman Publishers Inc. 2009 290p il (How-to-do-it manuals for librarians) pa $75   **025.5**

   1. Reference services (Libraries) 2. Reference interview 3. Reference services -- Automation 4. Electronic reference services (Libraries)

   ISBN 978-1-55570-655-5

                                   LC 2009-17660

  First published 2002

  This book aims to teach librarians how "to understand the needs of public, academic and special library users across any virtual setting—email, text messaging, social networking websites—as well as in traditional and face-to-face models of communication." Publisher's note

  Includes bibliographical references

Saricks, Joyce G.

  The **readers'** advisory guide to genre fiction. American Lib. Assn. 2001 460p (ALA readers' advisory series) pa $38   **025.5**

   1. Reference books 2. Reference services (Libraries) 3. Fiction -- Bibliography

   ISBN 0-8389-0803-9; 978-0-8389-0803-7

                                   LC 2001-22750

  The author explores popular fiction genres. "Each genre, from adventure to literary fiction, is given its own chapter in which the genre is defined, its characteristics and appeal to its fans are described, key authors and subgenres are discussed, the preparation needed to work with readers is detailed, and tips on the readers' advisory interview are offered." Voice Youth Advocates

  Includes bibliographical references

  ★ **Readers'** advisory service in the public library; 3rd ed; American Library Association 2005 211p il pa $38   **025.5**

   1. Public libraries 2. Reference services (Libraries)

   ISBN 0-8389-0897-7

                                   LC 2004-29271

  First published 1989

  In this guide to readers' advisory, "online tools for identifying and evaluating titles to suggest to today's new adult leisure readers are described, in addition to . . . tried-and-true print sources. The value of personal reading suggestions from staff and patrons is addressed. Topics for discussion and techniques for marketing good reading material are offered. . . . A priority for all libraries involved in readers' advisory." Booklist

  Includes bibliographical references

Spratford, Becky Siegel

  The **horror** readers' advisory; the librarian's guide to vampires, killer tomatoes, and haunted houses. [by] Becky Siegel Spratford [and] Tammy Hennigh Clausen. American Library Association 2004 161p il (ALA readers' advisory series) pa $36 **025.5**

   1. Reference services (Libraries) 2. Horror fiction -- History and criticism

   ISBN 0-8389-0871-3

                                   LC 2003-25530

  This is a "guide to horror fiction, explaining its appeal and advising on how librarians unfamiliar with the genre can broaden their own knowledge and build a viable collec-

tion. The text briefly outlines the characteristics of the main categories, or subgenres, including the usual monsters and occult creatures; extreme suspense of all types; hauntings and possession; and a section on classic works of horror, along with tips for interviewing readers of each subgenre. . . . [This] small, helpful book will be a boon to readers' advisors needing fresh meat for horror fans." Libr J

  Includes bibliographical references

Virtual reference service; from competencies to assessment. edited by R. David Lankes . . . [et al.] Neal-Schuman Publishers 2008 206p il (Virtual reference desk series) $75   **025.5**

   1. Reference services (Libraries)

   ISBN 978-1-55570-528-2

                                   LC 2007-24104

  "Featuring essays from the 2005 7th Annual Virtual Reference Desk Conference, this book focuses on the evolving aspects of virtual reference theory, research, and practice. . . . The topics explored include the implementation and expansion of virtual reference programs, and the training and assessment that is necessary to ensure the success of these services. . . . This is a valuable resource for library practitioners involved with reference services." Am Ref Books Annu, 2008

  Includes bibliographical references

Wichman, Emily T.

  Librarian's guide to passive programming; easy and affordable activities for all ages. Emily T. Wichman. Libraries Unlimited Inc. 2012 xvii, 152 p.p ill. (pbk. : acid-free paper) $40   **025.5**

   1. Librarians 2. Library finance 3. Library services 4. Libraries -- Activity programs -- United States

   ISBN 159884895X; 9781598848953; 9781598848960

                                   LC 2011045419

  In her book, author Emily T. Wichman discusses library budget cuts, and how "librarians are seeking new ways to stretch their programming dollars and maximize staff resources. Passive programming allows libraries to inexpensively showcase their services while inviting visitors of all ages to enjoy the value that libraries bring to the community." (Publisher's note)

  Includes bibliographical references and index.

Wyatt, Neal

  The **readers'** advisory guide to nonfiction. American Library Association 2007 318p (ALA reader's advisory series) pa $48   **025.5**

   1. Public libraries 2. Reference services (Libraries)

   ISBN 978-0-8389-0936-2; 0-8389-0936-1

                                   LC 2006-102318

  Wyatt "focuses on eight popular categories: history, true crime, true adventure, science, memoir, food/cooking, travel, and sports. Within each, she explains the scope, popularity, style, major authors and works, and the subject's position in readers' advisory interviews. Wyatt addresses who is reading nonfiction and why, while providing RAs with the tools and language to incorporate nonfiction into discussions that point readers to what to read next. . . . [This] guide includes nonfiction bibliography, key authors, benchmark books with annotations, and core collections." Publisher's note

Includes bibliographical references

025.7   Physical preparation for storage and use

Lavender, Kenneth

★ **Book** repair; a how-to-do-it manual. Kenneth Lavender. 2nd ed; Neal-Schuman Publishers Inc. 2011 xiv, 265 p.p il (How-to-do-it manuals for libraries) (alk. paper) $80   **025.7**

1. Librarians 2. Paperback books 3. Bookbinding -- Repairing -- Handbooks, manuals, etc 4. Books -- Conservation and restoration -- Handbooks, manuals, etc
ISBN 1555707475; 1555707483; 9781555707477; 9781555707484

LC 2011022636

First published 1992

Author Kenneth Lavender provides a "step-by-step manual . . . on basic book repair techniques and sound preservation practices . . . [which] offers illustrated sections on cleaning, mending, hinge and spine repair, strengthening paperbacks, and more. . . . A full discussion of when and how to make repairs is provided, as is a discussion of alternative conservation practices that will enable each librarian to develop procedures appropriate to his or her library." (Publisher's note)

"Covering both basic book repair techniques and . . . conservation practices, this . . . manual offers illustrated sections on cleaning, mending, hinge and spine repair, strengthening paperbacks, [etc.]. . . . Chapters cover: wet and water-damaged books; mold and mildew; repair of book linings and pamphlet bindings; using acid-free materials to repair damaged books; lining paper objects; affordable repair tools and supplies. . . . A full discussion of when and how to make repairs, and alternative conservation practices that enable each librarian to develop procedures appropriate to his or her library are also provided." Publisher's note

Includes bibliographical references and index.

Schechter, Abraham A.

Basic book repair methods; illustrated by the author. Libraries Unlimited 1999 102p il pa $37 **025.7**

1. Books -- Conservation and restoration
ISBN 1-56308-700-6

LC 98-50950

Photographs accompany step-by-step instructions for common preservation techniques, from the cleaning of pages and their readhesion, to case reattachment and rebacking.

Includes bibliographical references

025.8   Maintenance and preservation of collections

Halsted, Deborah D.

★ **Disaster** planning; a how-to-do-it manual for librarians with planning templates on CD-ROM.

Neal-Schuman Publishers 2005 xx, 247p il (How-to-do-it manuals for librarians) pa $85   **025.8**

1. Disaster relief 2. Accidents -- Prevention 3. Library resources -- Conservation and restoration
ISBN 1-55570-486-7

LC 2003-65152

"Step-by-step instructions discuss creating a working disaster team, establishing a communications strategy, identifying relief and recovery agencies, developing response plans, and examining issues of cutting-edge library security. . . . This valuable resource is an important addition to most professional collections." Booklist

Includes bibliographical references

Kahn, Miriam B.

Disaster response and planning for libraries; Miriam B. Kahn. 2nd ed; American Library Association 2012 158 p. bibl il (paperback) $60.00 **025.8**

1. Libraries -- Safety measures 2. Disaster response and recovery 3. Library resources -- Conservation and restoration 4. Libraries -- Safety measures -- Planning 5. Library materials -- Conservation and restoration 6. Library materials -- Conservation and restoration -- Planning
ISBN 083891151X; 9780838911518

LC 2011043703

This book by Miriam B. Kahn presents a "step-by-step, how-to guide for preparing and responding to all types of library disasters." It includes "guidance for creating protocols and response plans tailored to your own institution . . . pointers for handling . . . library materials when damaged . . . information on preparing for technology recovery . . . [and] reproducible checklists and forms." (Publisher's note)

Includes bibliographical references (pages 143-154) and index

026   Specific kinds of institutions

★ **Directory** of special libraries and information centers, [2008] a guide to more than 35,000 special libraries, research libraries, information centers, archives, and data centers maintained by government agencies . . . Matthew Miskelly, content project editor. 34th ed.; Thompson/Gale 2008 3v set $1260   **026**

1. Reference books 2. Special libraries -- Directories
ISBN 978-0-7876-9679-5; 0-7876-9679-X

Annual. First published 1963. Volume one is kept up to date by mid-year supplementary volume (v3)

"Volume 1, in three parts, provides . . . contact and descriptive information on more than 35,800 subject-specific resource collections maintained by various government agencies, businesses, publishers, educational and nonprofit organizations, and associations around the world. . . . Volume 2, Geographic and Personnel Indexes, provides access to profiled libraries by geographic region, as well as by the professional staff that are cited in each listing." Publisher's note

027   General libraries, archives, information centers

★ **American** library directory 2008-2009; 61st ed; Information Today 2008 2v set $299.95   **027**
1. Reference books 2. Libraries -- Directories
ISBN 978-1-57387-320-8; 1-57387-320-9
Annual. First published 1923 by Bowker
"Includes U.S. and Canadian public, academic, and special libraries arranged by state or province, city, and institution. Gives personnel and statistical data, subject interests, and special collections." Ref Sources for Small & Medium-sized Libr. 6th edition

Ryback, Timothy W.
Hitler's private library; the books that shaped his life. Alfred A. Knopf 2008 xx, 278p il map $25.95   **027**
1. Heads of state 2. Nazi leaders 3. Germany -- History -- 1933-1945
ISBN 978-1-4000-4204-3; 1-4000-4204-6
LC 2008-22010
"Thanks to [Ryback's] imaginative research—and his willingness to investigate a very creepy subject—we come closer to one of the most elusive men ever to shape world history." New Repub
Includes bibliographical references

027.4   Public libraries

Butler, Patricia M.
Joint libraries; models that work. Claire B. Gunnels, Susan E. Green, and Patricia M. Butler. American Library Association 2012 220 p. $60.00   **027.4**
1. Public libraries 2. Academic libraries 3. Library cooperation 4. Joint-use libraries -- United States
ISBN 0838911382; 9780838911389
LC 2011044057
This book provides a "look at joint library models, including the determining factors that lead to increased success and issues that may lead to project failures. This title includes a brief discussion of the history behind school library joint partnerships; however, the authors primarily focus on joint academic/public libraries, giving concrete examples from their own experiences as well as information from examples of multi-use libraries across the country." (Voice of Youth Advocates)
Includes bibliographical references and index.

Matthews, Joseph R.
Scorecards for results; a guide for developing a library balanced scorecard. Libraries Unlimited 2008 112p pa $45   **027.4**
1. Public libraries 2. Libraries -- Administration
ISBN 978-1-59158-698-2
LC 2008-3689
"A balanced scorecard (BSC) is 'a process and culture for choosing, using, and revising measures' to help libraries focus on the success of their mission. . . . [The author] has developed a BSC workbook for public libraries. . . . Indi-

vidual chapters here detail the six steps in developing and using a balanced scorecard, with sample vision statements, strategic themes, and performance measures." Libr J
Includes bibliographical references

McCook, Kathleen de la Peña
★ **Introduction** to public librarianship. Neal-Schuman Publishers 2004 406p il   **027.4**
1. Public libraries 2. Public librarianship 3. Public libraries -- United States
ISBN 1-55570-475-1
LC 2004-46012
"The book is a necessary addition to all professional collections, not to collect dust, but to become respectfully dog-eared and coffee-stained through repeated use." Florida Libraries
Includes bibliographical references

027.5   Government libraries

Conaway, James
America's library; the story of the Library of Congress, 1800-2000. foreword by James Billington; introduction by Edmund Morris. Yale Univ. Press 2000 226p il $48   **027.5**
1. Library of Congress
ISBN 978-0-300-08308-8; 0-300-08308-4
LC 99-58751
This history of the Library of Congress is organized "around that tiny, hardy band of men and women who have used both political acumen and intellectual vision to build the library's collections and establish those services that make the LC library to both Congress and nation. Richly supplemented with photographs, this history reaches out to touch all who love libraries." Booklist
Includes bibliographical references

027.6   Libraries for special groups and organizations

Moller, Sharon Chickering
Library service to Spanish speaking patrons; a practical guide. Libraries Unlimited 2001 207p pa $30   **027.6**
1. Public libraries 2. Libraries and Hispanic Americans
ISBN 1-56308-719-7
LC 00-45090
"Intended to stimulate discussion among library service planners and to offer counsel to service providers, this book should become required reading in any jurisdiction with an underserved Latino population." Voice Youth Advocates
Includes bibliographical references

Roberts, Ann
Crash course in library services to people with disabilities; [by] Ann Roberts and Richard J. Smith.

Libraries Unlimited 2010 158p (Crash course series) pa $30   **027.6**
1. Libraries and people with disabilities
ISBN 978-1-59158-767-5

LC 2009-23985

"Librarians who are striving to fill the information needs of people with different mental and physical challenges will find that this title answers many of their questions. . . . Among the topics that are discussed are the implications of the Americans with Disabilities Act; marketing, programs, and services; assistive technologies; and the particular needs of older adults and people with mental and physical disabilities." Booklist

Includes bibliographical references

027.62   Libraries for specific age groups

Braafladt, Keith
Technology and literacy; 21st century library programming for children and teens. by Jennifer Nelson and Keith Braafladt. American Library Association 2012 129 p. (alk. paper) $50.00   **027.62**
1. Library services 2. Literacy programs 3. Literature and technology 4. Children's libraries -- Activity programs 5. Scratch (Computer program language) 6. Computer literacy -- Study and teaching 7. Technological literacy -- Study and teaching 8. Young adults' libraries -- Activity programs
ISBN 0838911080; 9780838911082

LC 2011035104

This book by Jennifer Nelson presents a "guide for creating and implementing technology-based programming in public libraries. . . . Beginning chapters explain and present a plan for offering such programs, providing steps on how to execute them. . . . The author explains the value of this type of programming and the process involved with adoption, and covers planning, gathering support from both administration and staff, marketing . . . managing time, etc." (School Library Journal)

Includes bibliographical references and index.

Brown, Amy
Let's start the music; programming for primary grades. Amy Brown. ALA Editions, an imprint of the American Library Association 2013 184 p. $45   **027.62**
1. Music -- Study and teaching 2. Children's libraries -- Activity programs 3. Music -- Instruction and study -- United States 4. School libraries -- Activity programs -- United States
ISBN 0838911668; 9780838911662

LC 2013010871

In this book, author Amy Brown "explores several benefits of integrating music into story and literacy programs, then outlines simple strategies for all children's staff to feature more music and instruments in their events. Brown shares 13 themed programs, ranging from sing-alongs and animals to fairy tales and food, and each theme includes an extensive list of books, songs, an activity, and an instrument craft." (School Library Journal)

Includes bibliographical references and index

Del Negro, Janice M.
Folktales aloud; practical advice for playful storytelling. Janice M. Del Negro. American Library Association 2014 212 p. (alk. paper) $47   **027.62**
1. Fairy tales 2. Storytelling 3. Children's libraries -- Activity programs 4. Elementary school libraries -- Activity programs
ISBN 0838911358; 9780838911358

LC 2013028036

This book, by Janice M. Del Negro, "aims to show that storytelling is still vital in librarianship and throughout the greater community. . . . The text provides useful information for novice and seasoned storytellers alike while engaging the reader with its conversational tone. The chapters are broken down by audience age . . . and include information about audience needs and wants, stories, and resource information." (Booklist)

Includes bibliographical references and index

Eagle, MK
★ **Answering** teens' tough questions; a YALSA guide. mk Eagle. Neal-Schuman, an imprint of the American Library Association 2012 x, 125 p.p $49.95   **027.62**
1. Librarians 2. Library services 3. Teenagers -- Attitudes 4. Teenagers -- United States -- Attitudes 5. Libraries and teenagers -- United States 6. Young adults' libraries -- United States 7. Teenagers -- Services for -- United States 8. Teenagers -- United States -- Social conditions 9. Young adult services librarians -- United States -- Attitudes
ISBN 1555707947; 9781555707941

LC 2012015104

Author mk Eagle presents a book that "offers any librarian a quick primer on talking with young adults about the tough and often controversial topics of sex, drugs, alcohol, and violence." It provides "quick overviews on the issues themselves as well as tips for navigating these waters with teens. . . . . Chapters include sex, sexuality, homelessness, tattoos and piercings, dating violence, abuse, drugs and alcohol, emotional and mental health, and the juvenile justice system." (Publisher's note)

Includes bibliographical references and index

Fiore, Carole D.
★ **Fiore's** summer library reading program handbook. Neal-Schuman Publishers 2005 xxiii, 312p pa $65   **027.62**
1. Books and reading 2. Children's libraries
ISBN 1-55570-513-8

LC 2004-31104

"This research-laden handbook . . . serves as a 'comprehensive program-planning and implementation tool' for public libraries seeking to revamp, revise, or develop a summer library reading program. . . . This is an invaluable resource, both for its concrete guidance and its abstract exploration of the meaning of summer library programs." Bull Cent Child Books

Includes bibliographical references

Flowers, Sarah

Evaluating teen services and programs; Sarah Flowers. Neal-Schuman, an imprint of the American Library Association 2012 xv, 119 p.p (pbk.) $49.95   **027.62**
1. Library services 2. Young adults' libraries 3. Libraries -- United States 4. Libraries and teenagers -- United States 5. Young adults' libraries -- Evaluation -- United States
ISBN 1555707939; 9781555707934

LC 2012015105

Author Sarah Flowers presents "a guide that provides basic information to help teen/youth services librarians, library directors, library school students studying teen services, and middle/high school librarians examine all aspects of their teen programs and services to determine where improvement is needed. Find out what you need to develop goals and objectives for evaluation, and learn how to collect the data that will give you a realistic picture of your library's strengths and weaknesses." (Publisher's note)

Includes bibliographical references and index

Pattee, Amy S.

Developing library collections for today's young adults; Amy S. Pattee. The Scarecrow Press, Inc. 2013 267 p. (cloth) $55   **027.62**
1. Multimedia 2. Library services 3. Young adults' libraries 4. Libraries -- Special collections 5. Libraries and teenagers -- United States 6. Multimedia library services -- United States
ISBN 0810887347; 9780810887343

LC 2013018596

This book, by Amy S. Pattee, "features policies that deal expressly with materials that respect the intellecual freedom of young library patrons. It emphasizes the importance of everything from needs assessment to collection development, encouraging librarians to consider informational, recreational, and curricular needs and interests as the library staff select material on behalf of young adults." (Publisher's note)

"The book's greatest asset is that it manages to be extremely specific and thorough without becoming overwhelming." VOYA

Includes bibliographical references and index

Sweeney, Jennifer

Literacy; a way out for at-risk youth. Jennifer Sweeney. Libraries Unlimited 2012 xx, 133 pagesp (pbk. : acid-free paper) $40.00   **027.62**
1. Literacy 2. Prison librarians 3. Juvenile delinquents -- Books and reading 4. Prison libraries -- United States 5. Literacy programs -- United States 6. Juvenile corrections -- United States 7. Libraries and prisons -- United States 8. Literacy -- Social aspects -- United States 9. Juvenile delinquents -- Education -- United States 10. Libraries and juvenile delinquents -- United States 11. Problem youth -- Books and reading -- United States 12. Juvenile delinquents -- Rehabilitation -- United States 13. Juvenile delinquents -- Books and reading -- United States
ISBN 9781598846744; 9781598846751; 1598846744

LC 2011042804

This looks at corrections librarianship, focusing on juvenile institutions. The book "provides librarians in juvenile detention facilities with tools to face their unique challenges, such as collaborating with corrections staff and encouraging youth to maintain their connection to the library after release." (Barnes and Noble)

Includes bibliographical references and index.

Vaillancourt, Renee J.

Bare bones young adult services; tips for public library generalists. American Lib. Assn. 2000 142p il pa $33   **027.62**
1. Public libraries 2. Young adults' libraries 3. Libraries and students
ISBN 0-8389-3497-8

LC 99-35643

The author "provides guidelines for forming Teen Advisory Boards and focus groups, dealing with unruly adolescent patrons, providing homework support, as well as some basic programming ideas. She also discusses collection development and suggests resources that specialize in reviewing teen-level materials." SLJ

Includes bibliographical references

028   Reading and use of other information media

Basbanes, Nicholas A.

★ **Every** book its reader; the power of the printed word to stir the world. HarperCollins 2005 360p il $29.95; pa $15.95   **028**
1. Best books 2. Books and reading
ISBN 0-06-059323-7; 978-0-06-059323-0; 0-06-059324-5 pa; 978-0-06-059324-7 pa

LC 2005-46164

The author "focuses on peoples' reading habits and on the books they have read, both obscure and renowned, as well as on the importance of particular books in specific contexts. Basbanes begins by interviewing some of the best-read people alive, among them David McCullough, Harold Bloom, Helen Vendler, and Elaine Pagels; he also mentions a wide variety of contemporary and historical personages. The loosely related stories are often inspirational, making this an engrossing read." Libr J

Includes bibliographical references

The **CIA** World Factbook 2014; Central Intelligence Agency. W W Norton & Co Inc 2013 960 p. (paperback) $16.95   **028**
1. Almanacs 2. Geopolitics 3. Population -- Statistics
ISBN 1626360731; 9781626360730

This book, updated for 2014, "offers complete and up-to-date information on the world's nations. This . . . guide is packed with detailed information on the politics, populations, military expenditures, and economics of 2014." Included are "detailed maps," "statistics on the population of each country, with details on literacy rates, HIV prevalence, and age structure," and "information on each country's climate and natural hazards." (Publisher's note)

Dirda, Michael

Book by book; notes on reading and life. Henry Holt 2006 170p $17 **028**

1. Best books 2. Books and reading
ISBN 978-0-8050-7877-0; 0-8050-7877-0

LC 2005-55451

The author "writes a guide to reading and its life lessons ranging widely and pithily through the universal themes of learning, school, work, love, childhood and spiritual guidance. Dirda's message is simple: if reading is to be life enhancing, we need to focus our attention on books that are rewarding. . . . For those who enjoy books about reading, and for all those seeking to encourage others to read, Dirda's brief yet suggestive book will inspire." Publ Wkly

Hooper, Brad

The **short** story readers' advisory; a guide for librarians. American Lib. Assn. 2000 135p pa $32 **028**

1. Short stories -- History and criticism
ISBN 0-8389-0782-2

LC 99-85751

This work contains over 200 critical essays covering short story authors past and present. A step-by-step guide on how to interview readers in order to match their tastes with appropriate stories is included.

Includes bibliographical references

Maatta, Stephanie L.

A **few** good books; using contemporary readers' advisory strategies to connect readers with books. Neal-Schuman Publishers 2010 xix, 387p pa $69.95 **028**

1. Reference services (Libraries) 2. Books and reading -- History
ISBN 978-1-55570-669-2; 1-55570-669-X

LC 2009-40999

"Chapter topics begin with a history of reading, from cuneiform to electronic books, and a summary of reading theories. Discussions and examples of the new communication technologies such as blogs, wikis, podcasting, social cataloging Web sites, and social networks used to engage readers and 'enhance the reading experience' follow. Three chapters focus on readers advisory strategies, including one on special populations, and five chapters present an analysis of the various genres." Libr Media Connect

"This comprehensive and up-to-date guide is a treasure trove of practical advice and resources that will help make the RA experience even more effective and enjoyable." Libr J

Includes bibliographical references

Ross, Catherine Sheldrick

★ **Reading** matters; what the research reveals about reading, libraries, and community. by Catherine Sheldrick Ross, Lynne E.F. McKechnie, and Paulette M. Rothbauer. Libraries Unlimited 2006 p. cm. **028**

1. Books and reading. 2. Reading interests. 3. Reading promotion. 4. Popular literature. 5. Libraries and community. 6. Reading -- Social aspects. 7. Public services (Libraries)
ISBN 1-59158-066-8 (pbk. : alk. paper)

LC 2005030839

Includes bibliographical references and index..

028.1   Reviews

Naidoo, Jamie Campbell

★ **Rainbow** family collections; selecting and using children's books with lesbian, gay, bisexual, transgender, and queer content. Jamie Campbell Naidoo. Libraries Unlimited, an imprint of ABC-CLIO, LLC 2012 xvii, 260 p.p ill. (hardback) $50 **028.1**

1. Libraries and sexual minorities 2. Sexual minorities in literature 3. Libraries and sexual minorities -- United States 4. Libraries -- Special collections -- Sexual minorities 5. Sexual minorities -- Juvenile literature -- Bibliography 6. Children's libraries -- Collection development -- United States 7. Children's libraries -- Services to minorities -- United States 8. Children of sexual minority parents -- Books and reading -- United States
ISBN 1598849603; 9781598849608

LC 2012008362

This book by Jamie Campbell Naidoo "highlight[s] titles for children from infancy to age 11" featuring lesbian, gay, bisexual, transgender, and queer content. It "supplies a synopsis of the title's content, lists awards it has received, cites professional reviews, and provides suggestions for librarians considering acquisition. The book also provides a brief historical overview of LGBTQ children's literature along with the major book awards for this genre." (Publisher's note)

Includes bibliographical references and index

Szymborska, Wislawa

Nonrequired reading; prose pieces. translated from the Polish by Clare Cavanagh. Harcourt 2002 233p $24 **028.1**

1. Books and reading
ISBN 0-15-100660-1

LC 2002-2440

The Nobel laureate's "essays are musings with unexpected twists on topics as diverse as Korean fairy tales, paleontology and the hygiene of the nobility." N Y Times Book Rev

"The skillful simplicity and lyric quality of these essays make them distinctive. With her poet's gift for compression, Szymborska captures large concepts and brilliantly reduces them to pithy, two-page essays." Libr J

Includes bibliographical references

028.5   Reading and use of other information media by young people

Allyn, Pam

What to read when; the books and stories to read with your child, and all the best times to read them. Avery 2009 318p pa $16.95 **028.5**

1. Children -- Books and reading
ISBN 978-1-58333-334-1

LC 2008-54501

The author "provides many ways to promote a love of reading to children and offers top-ten lists of reasons to read to kids that incorporate practical, easy-to-use tips to encourage literacy from a young age. . . . This is an indispensable guide to choosing age-appropriate books for children. Allyn provides a list of more than 300 titles on 50 themes including such issues as adoption, feelings about school, sharing, and coping with illness. This valuable resource for children's librarians, educators, and parents is highly recommended." Libr J

The **Cambridge** guide to children's books in English; [edited by] Victor Watson; advisory editors, Elizabeth L. Keyser, Juliet Partridge, Morag Styles. Cambridge Univ. Press 2001 814p il $75 **028.5**
1. Reference books 2. Children's literature -- Encyclopedias
ISBN 0-521-55064-5

LC 00-65163

This reference provides an "overview of historic and contemporary children's books published in English. The entries include authors, illustrators, and significant works primarily from Britain, the US, Canada, Australia, New Zealand, India, and Africa. . . . Major themes, such as fairy tales, fantasy, folktales, legends, mythology, and young adult fiction, are covered as well as less-expected entries on topics such as bias, the bush, disability, ecology, and nudity in children's books. Nonbook media are also covered by entries on animated cartoons, comics, superheroes, and television for children." Choice
Includes bibliographical references

Helbig, Alethea
Dictionary of American young adult fiction, 1997-2001; books of recognized merit. {by} Alethea K. Helbig and Agnes Regan Perkins. Greenwood Press 2004 xxii, 558p $75 **028.5**
1. Best books 2. Reference books 3. Youth -- Books and reading 4. Young adult literature -- Dictionaries 5. Young adult literature -- Bio-bibliography
ISBN 0-313-32430-1

LC 2003-56804

"The 290 books included {in this volume} have been recognized by one or more of the following: Alex Award, ALA Best Books for Young Adults, Booklist, NYPL, and the Michael L. Printz Award. Approximately 60 of the listed books are adult books considered appropriate for young adults by the award committees. The 741 entries, which include books, their authors, major characters, and settings, are listed alphabetically and range in length from a couple of paragraphs to a bit more than a page. Book entries describe plot, themes, and characters, as well as relevant literary awards, while author entries consist of a brief biography and bibliography. . . . {The information is collected} usefully for selectors of young adult fiction, reader's advisers, teachers, and libraries supporting young adult fiction teaching." Libr J
Includes bibliographical references

Keane, Nancy J.
101 great, ready-to-use book lists for teens; Nancy J. Keane. Libraries Unlimited, an imprint of ABC-CLIO, LLC 2012 xiv, 263 p.p (paperback) $40; (ebook) $40 **028.5**
1. Book selection 2. Books and reading 3. Young adult literature -- Bibliography 4. High school libraries

-- Book lists 5. Young adults' libraries -- Book lists 6. Teenagers -- Books and reading -- United States
ISBN 1610691342; 9781610691345; 9781610691352

LC 2011051428

This book offers a "compilation of YA [Young Adult] materials . . . published prior to August 2011. The book is divided . . . into themed lists such as 'Genres,' 'Readalikes,' and 'Teaching Literary Elements.' The themes . . . include . . . topics such as 'Romance,' 'Autism & Asperger's Syndrome,' 'Different Belief Systems,' and 'Crossing the Border.' Each entry includes the title, author, publisher, publication date, page numbers, an annotation, Lexile level when available, and interest level by grade or age range." (School Library Journal)
"This is a useful resource for new librarians and may also be helpful to seasoned librarians. The emphasis is on books published within the last ten years, but some older titles are included." Lib Med Con
Includes bibliographical references and index

030 General encyclopedic works

The **World** Almanac and Book of Facts 2015; edited by Sarah Janssen. Simon & Schuster 2014 1008 p. $13.99 **030**
1. Almanacs 2. Geography 3. Popular culture
ISBN 1600571905; 9781600571909
Annual. First published 1868. Publisher varies
"This is the most comprehensive and well-known of almanacs. . . . Contains a chronology of the year's events, consumer information, historical anniversaries, annual climatological data, and forecasts. Color section has flags and maps. Includes detailed index." N Y Public Libr Book of How & Where to Look It Up

031 General encyclopedic works in specific languages and language families

Jacobs, A. J.
The **know** -it-all; one man's humble quest to become the smartest person in the world. Simon & Schuster 2004 386p $25 **031**
1. Encyclopaedia Britannica
ISBN 0-7432-5060-5

LC 2004-48233

This "book stems from the author's herculean effort to read every volume of the majestic Encyclopaedia Britannica. . . . Jacobs turns his quest for intellectual enlightenment into alphabetically ordered, humorous ruminations on all persons and events of his life. . . . Plenty of good fun pours out of this prose." Booklist
Includes bibliographical references

Lih, Andrew
The **Wikipedia** revolution; how a bunch of nobodies created the world's greatest encyclopedia. Hyperion 2009 246p il map $24.99 **031**
1. User generated content 2. Electronic encyclopedias
ISBN 978-1-4013-0371-6

LC 2008-51137

"Wikipedia is a revolutionary phenomenon, changing fundamentally the landscape of networked collaboration, e-learning, and, as librarians know all too well, mediated information provision. Depicted here is a Wikipedia insider's narrative of the development of Wikipedia. . . . [Lih] characterizes this revolution as only partly technological. The real revolution is social-an apt point when one considers the philosophical underpinnings of this resource, the articles' neutral point of view, while remaining a free resource anyone can use and distribute." Libr J

Includes bibliographical references

★ The **new** encyclopaedia Britannica; 15th ed.; Encyclopædia Britannica 2009 32v il map apply to publisher for price   **031**
1. Reference books 2. Encyclopedias and dictionaries
ISBN 978-1-59339-837-8

First published 1768 in England; in the United States 1902. Now published with the editorial advice of the University of Chicago. First published with current title with the fifteenth edition in 1974. Frequently revised

"In three sections: Propaedia, or outline of knowledge; Macropaedia, with longer in-depth articles covering major topics; and Micropaedia, with shorter A-to-Z ready reference entries. Britannica's reputation as the basic encyclopedia for all libraries and reference collections is based on the writing and knowledge of thousands of expert contributors and consultants. Updated between major editions by the Britannica Book of the Year." NY Public Libr Book of How & Where to Look It Up

Includes bibliographical references

031.02   Books of miscellaneous facts

Famous first facts, international edition; a record of first happenings, discoveries, and inventions in world history. {edited by} Steven Anzovin & Janet Podell. Wilson, H.W. 2000 837p $140   **031.02**
1. Reference books 2. Encyclopedias and dictionaries
ISBN 0-8242-0958-3

LC 99-86869

This work "contains more than 5000 firsts from hundreds of countries and ranging in time from 3.5 billion years ago (the age of the oldest continental land discovered) to 2001 (the scheduled date of completion of the first building over 1500 feet tall). . . . {It} groups related entries under broad subject categories (arranged alphabetically) and sub-categories. Within each category or sub-category, entries are arranged chronologically." Publisher's note

Kane, Joseph Nathan

Famous first facts; a record of first happenings, discoveries, and inventions in American history. [by] Joseph Nathan Kane, Steven Anzovin, & Janet Podell. 6th ed.; Wilson, H.W. 2006 1307p il $185 **031.02**
1. Reference books 2. Encyclopedias and dictionaries
3. United States -- History -- Dictionaries
ISBN 978-0-8242-1065-6; 0-8242-1065-4

LC 2006-3096

First published 1933

Over 7500 entries cover first occurences in American history, organized into 16 chapters each divided into sections. Sections are alphabetically organized, and individual entries are organized chronologically within each section. Includes five indexes: subject index, index by years, index by days, index to personal names, and geographical index

"Besides serving as an essential ready-reference source, the book is also fun to read out loud to colleagues—when was bubble gum first manufactured in the U.S.? When was the spray can introduced?" Booklist

The **New** York Public Library desk reference; 4th ed; Hyperion 2002 999p il maps $34.95   **031.02**
1. Reference books 2. Encyclopedias and dictionaries
ISBN 0-7868-6846-5

LC 2002-27480

First published 1989 by Webster's New World

Divided into chapters, this reference features charts, tables, lists, and illustrations providing information in such categories as signs and symbols, mathematics and science basics, the arts, grammar and punctuation, etiquette, personal finance, first aid, and household tips.

Includes bibliographical references

051   General serial publications in specific languages and language families

Meyerowitz, Rick

Drunk stoned brilliant dead; the writers and artists who made the National Lampoon insanely great. Abrams 2010 319p il $40   **051**
1. Satire 2. American wit and humor 3. National lampoon (Periodical)
ISBN 978-0-8109-8848-4; 0-8109-8848-8

This is the "first Lampoon book that celebrates the wild, eye-intoxicating diversity of its illustrations, photography, cartoons, comic strips, graphics—parodies of everything from matchbooks to Marvel Comics to modern art. In toto this volume is a testament to the dazzling design expertise of its formative art directors, Michael Gross and David Kaestle. Rick Meyerowitz, a charter member of the Lampoon crew . . . , has in effect edited a magnificent 320-page issue of the magazine that reprints much of its finest work. And in brief, funny, and for once malice-free memoirs from its principals, the collection evokes the sparkling camaraderie that drove it. If you grew up with the Lampoon, this book is a trip down memory lane like no other; if not, it will demonstrate that the much-maligned 70s could produce humor that has never been surpassed." Vanity Fair

060.4   Special topics of general organizations

Encyclopedia of Associations; An Associations Unlimited Reference. 53 edition Gale / Cengage Learning 2014 3700 p. 3v $1084   **060.4**
1. Reference books
ISBN 1414477988; 9781414477985
Annual

A "comprehensive source for detailed information on nonprofit American membership organizations of national scope. Every entry offers a wealth of valuable data, typically including the organization's complete name, address and phone number together with the primary official's name and title; fax number, when available; founding date, purpose, activities and dues; national and international conferences; and more." Publisher's note

Robert, Henry M.

Robert's rules of order newly revised; Henry M. Robert III, Daniel H. Honemann, and Thomas J. Balch ; with the assistance of Daniel E. Seabold and Shmuel Gerber. 11th ed Da Capo Press 2011 lii, 716 p.p $18.95   **060.4**
  1. Parliamentary practice
  ISBN 030682020X; 9780306820205; 9780306820212
                     LC 2011932260

"The eleventh edition has been thoroughly revised to address common inquiries and incorporate new rules, interpretations, and procedures made necessary by the evolution of parliamentary procedure, including new material relating to electronic communication and electronic meetings." Publisher's note

Webster's New World Robert's rules of order; simplified and applied. by Robert McConnell Productions. 3rd ed Houghton Mifflin Harcourt 2014 xxii, 388p $11.95   **060.4**
  1. Parliamentary practice
  ISBN 0764563998; 9780544236035

"Organized so users can find what they need quickly and easily, this revised edition includes an entire new chapter on proper procedure for conducting homeowners' associations." Publisher's note

061   General organizations

The Foundation Directory 2014; 36th ed Foundation Center 2014 2976 p. ill. $215   **061**
  1. Reference books 2. Endowments -- Directories
  ISBN 1595424733; 9781595424730
  Annual. First published 1960 by Russell Sage. Replaces American foundations and their fields

"Provides detailed information concerning independent, corporate, community, and private foundations with assets of at least $2 million or annual giving of at least $200,000. Geographical arrangement. Entries give date founded; names of officers, contact, and donors; foundation type; financial data; fields of interest; types of support; limitations; application information; and number of staff. Six indexes: Donors, officers, and trustees; Geographic; Types of support; Subject; Foundations new to edition; Foundations name index." Guide to Ref Books. 11th edition

069   Museology (Museum science)

★ Museums of the world; [editors: Nikolaus Himmler, Ruth Lochar, Hildegard Toma] 15th rev. and enl. ed; K.G. Saur 2008 2v il set $749 **069**
  1. Reference books 2. Museums -- Directories
  ISBN 978-3-598-20695-5; 3-598-20695-X
  First published 1973. Periodically revised

This set "covers more than 54,500 museums in 202 countries, listed hierarchically by country and place, and within places alphabetically by name. A separate chapter records some 500 museum associations in 132 countries." Publisher's note

070   Documentary media, educational media, news media; journalism; publishing

Angell, Roger

Let me finish. Harcourt 2006 302p $25   **070**
  1. Authors 2. Sportswriters 3. Short story writers
  ISBN 0-15-101350-0; 978-0-15-101350-0
                   LC 2005-33067

This is a collection of autobiographical essays from the New Yorker columnist. "The topics of the individual essays range from baseball in the 1930s (Gehrig and Ruth in Yankee Stadium, Mel Ott and Bill Terry at the Polo Grounds) to friends, family, and colleagues at the New Yorker, where Angell, now in his eighties, has worked for 40 years and where his mother, Katherine, and stepfather, E. B. White, worked before him." Booklist

"The assembled pieces add up to a fine memoir." Publ Wkly

Bragg, Rick

★ All over but the shoutin' Pantheon Bks. 1997 xxii, 329p hardcover o.p. pa $14   **070**
  1. Authors 2. Journalists 3. Memoirists
  ISBN 0-679-44258-8; 0-679-77402-5 pa
                   LC 97-9918

"Honest, unsentimental, and so elegantly spare it nearly hurts to read, this memoir by Pulitzer Prize-winning journalist Bragg recounts a dirt-poor childhood in Alabama and the debt he owes his mother." Libr J

Brokaw, Tom

A long way from home; growing up in the American heartland. Random House 2002 272p $24.95; pa $12.95   **070**
  1. Journalists 2. Television news anchors
  ISBN 0-375-50763-9; 0-375-75935-2 pa
                 LC 2002-31865

"Peppered with photographs . . . this tribute to an idyllic childhood should please Brokaw's loyal fans." Publ Wkly

Cronkite, Walter, 1916-2009

A reporter's life. Knopf 1997 384p il $26.95; pa $15   **070**
  1. Radio reporters 2. Television news anchors
  ISBN 0-394-57879-1; 0-345-41103-X pa
                 LC 96-21053

Cronkite's "memoir is a short course on the flow of events in the second half of this century—events the world knows more about because of Walter Cronkite's work, and some of which might not have happened without it." N Y Times Book Rev

Gabler, Neal

Winchell; gossip, power, and the culture of celebrity. Knopf 1994 681p il hardcover o.p. pa $17   **070**
1. Television personalities 2. Columnists 3. Radio personalities 4. Political commentators
ISBN 0-679-76439-9 pa
     LC 93-44259
"At the peak of his career during the 1930s and 1940s, Walter Winchell was America's most powerful and feared journalist; when he died in 1972, he had been long forgotten. Gabler's biography brings back to life the man credited with inventing the gossip column and with creating today's celebrity culture." Libr J
Includes bibliographical references

Hainey, Michael

After visiting friends; a son's story. Michael Hainey. 1st Scribner hardcover ed. Scribner 2013 320 p. ill. (hardcover) $26   **070**
1. Mysterious deaths 2. Father-son relationship 3. Journalists -- United States -- Biography
ISBN 1451676565; 9781451676563; 9781451676617
     LC 2012039168
In this memoir, Michael Hainey "reconstructs the few years he recalls with his father and painstakingly searches for clues that might help him understand his father's death," which occurred with Hainey was six. "When he turns 35, Hainey sets off on a quest to interview as many of his father's friends as will talk to him, to review all the published details of his father's death, and to discover what his father was really like," ultimately discovering a long-held secret about his family. (Publishers Weekly)
"This is a beautifully written exploration of family bonds and the secrets that may test them." Booklist

Kovach, Bill

Blur; how to know what's true in the age of information overload. [by] Bill Kovach and Tom Rosenstiel. Bloomsbury 2010 227p $26   **070**
1. Journalism -- Objectivity
ISBN 978-1-59691-565-7
     LC 2010-19766
"Kovach and Rosenstiel combine journalism and civics in this valuable and insightful resource to help Americans adapt to an era that demands that readers become their own editors and news aggregators." Booklist
Includes bibliographical references

Levy, Edmond

Making a winning short; how to write, direct, edit, and produce a short film. Holt & Co. 1994 290p pa $17   **070**
1. Motion pictures -- Production and direction
ISBN 0-8050-2680-0
     LC 94-6621

"Using examples from his own career, Levy . . . explains all aspects of creating a short film, from the development of the idea to what food and drink to provide for actors and crew. After Levy's easy-to-follow lessons are finished, he offers a list of film festivals that accept short films, titles of short films that he believes to be some of the finest examples of the genre, and a reading list. . . . A worthy addition to all performing arts collections." Libr J

O'Faolain, Nuala

Are you somebody; the accidental memoir of a Dublin woman. Holt & Co. 1998 215p hardcover o.p. pa $13   **070**
1. Authors 2. Novelists 3. Columnists 4. Memoirists
ISBN 0-8050-5664-4 pa
     LC 97-29725
First published 1996 in Ireland
This is a "moving and painfully honest memoir." Libr J

★ Reporting Iraq; an oral history of the war by the journalists who covered it. edited by Mike Hoyt, John Palattella, and the staff of the Columbia Journalism Review. Melville House 2007 191p il pa $21.95   **070**
1. Reporters and reporting 2. Iraq War, 2003- -- Personal narratives
ISBN 978-1-93363-334-3; 1-93363-334-4
"44 reporters casually and directly discuss all angles of the War in Iraq, including their own shock, fear and incomprehension, in this compilation of interviews conducted by The Columbia Journalism Review. . . . This vital, breathtaking collection may be the closest contemporary reporting gets to cutting through the fog of war." Publ Wkly

Ross, Lillian

Here but not here; a love story. Counterpoint 2001 240p il pa $15   **070**
1. Journalists 2. Magazine editors 3. Authors, American 4. New Yorker (Periodical)
ISBN 1-582-43110-8; 978-1-582-43110-9
     LC 00-65948
First published 1998 by Random House
"Ross writes directly and with great feeling about her years with Shawn. . . . It is a remarkable and very moving love story, composed like most great love stories of both passion and regret." Booklist

Schorr, Daniel

Staying tuned; a life in journalism. Pocket Bks. 2001 354p il hardcover o.p. pa $14   **070**
1. Television reporters 2. Political commentators
ISBN 0-671-02088-9 pa
     LC 2001-21014
Schorr tells of his life as a reporter for CBS, CNN and National Public Radio.
"Schorr's memoir is as much an inside look at the famous world figures of the latter half of the twentieth century as it is the story of one man's life and career." Booklist

Thompson, Hunter S.

★ Fear and loathing in America; the brutal odyssey of an outlaw journalist, 1968-1976. foreword by

David Halberstam; edited by Douglas Brinkley. Simon & Schuster 2000 xxv, 756p il $30; pa $15 **070**
1. Authors 2. Novelists 3. Journalists 4. Satirists 5. Columnists 6. Nonfiction writers
ISBN 0-684-87315-X; 0-684-87316-8 pa
LC 00-47012
"During the period covered in this collection, Thompson was a vital, deliriously erratic force in journalism, covering the turbulent 1968 Democratic National Convention in Chicago, the 1968 election of Richard M. Nixon, the 1972 campaign, Watergate, the falls of Nixon and Saigon." N Y Times Book Rev

070.1 Documentary media, educational media, news media

Henderson, Harry
Power of the news media. Facts on File 2004 316p il (Library in a book) $45 **070.1**
1. Press 2. Broadcast journalism
ISBN 0-8160-4768-5
LC 2003-18900
The author's "format—breaking topics into quick-hit subsections—makes it an ideal source for students researching a particular aspect of news media. . . . Every American should have a working knowledge of the topic, and this book is a recommended resource." Voice Youth Advocates
Includes bibliographical references

Wenger, Debora Halpern
Advancing the story; broadcast journalism in a multimedia world. [by] Debora Halpern Wenger and Deborah Potter. 2nd ed.; CQ Press 2011 xxxi, 380p il pa $36.95 **070.1**
1. Broadcast journalism
ISBN 978-1-60871-714-9
LC 2010049469
First published 2008
"While stressing basics of good journalism with emphasis on attention to detail, [the] authors explain how technology has changed the approach to content preparation among those invested in the Internet and integrated technology." Journalism and Mass Communication Educator [review of 2008 edition]
Includes bibliographical references

070.4 Journalism

Boykoff, Maxwell T.
Who speaks for the climate? making sense of media reporting on climate change. Maxwell T. Boykoff. Cambridge University Press 2011 xii, 228 p.p ill. (pbk.) $29.99 **070.4**
1. Climate change in mass media 2. Climate change -- Public opinion 3. Mass media and the environment 4. Climatic changes -- Public opinion 5. Global warming -- Prevention -- Public opinion
ISBN 0521115841; 052113305X; 9780521115841;

9780521133050
LC 2011026308
It was the author's intent to answer the question "'Who -- through media traction -- become[s] authorized to make sense of, translate and speak on behalf of climate change?' . . . The author . . . draws from social theory, polling results, and a deep interdisciplinary pool of climate-related research . . . [to] deliver a . . . picture of the heterogeneous dimensions of supranational climate -- and anti-science -- rhetoric that constructs public (mis)understanding on climate change." (Science Communication)
Includes bibliographical references and index.

Colvin, Marie, 1957-2012
On the Front Line; the collected journalism of Marie Colvin. by Marie Colvin. Harpercollins 2013 560 p. $19.99 **070.4**
1. War news 2. Journaling 3. Journalists 4. History, Modern -- 1989- 5. War victims -- Anecdotes 6. Women war correspondents 7. Atrocities -- History -- 20th century
ISBN 0007487967; 9780007487967
LC 2012551759
This book, winner of the Orwell Special Prize, is a collection of the late 'Sunday Times' war correspondent Marie Colvin's work. It "includes her various interviews with Yasser Arafat and Colonel Gadaffi; reports from East Timor in 1999 where she shamed the UN into protecting its refugees; accounts of her terrifying escape from the Russian army in Chechnya; and reports from the strongholds of the Sri Lankan Tamil Tigers where she was hit by shrapnel, leaving her blind in one eye." (Publisher's note)

Cronkite, Walter, 1916-2009
Cronkite's war; his World War II letters home. Walter Cronkite IV and Maurice Isserman. National Geographic Society 2013 xxxiv, 318 p.p ill., map (hardcover) $28 **070.4**
1. Letters 2. World War, 1939-1945 -- Journalists 3. Love-letters -- United States 4. United Press 5. World War, 1939-1945 -- Campaigns -- Europe 6. World War, 1939-1945 -- Aerial operations, American 7. War correspondents -- United States -- Correspondence 8. World War, 1939-1945 -- Journalists -- Correspondence 9. World War, 1939-1945 -- England -- London -- Anecdotes
ISBN 1426210191; 9781426210198
LC 2012045334
This book presents a selection of letters that journalist Walter Cronkite sent to his wife Betsy in Kansas City while he was in London, England reporting on World War II. These letters, "which barely mention any dangers the journalist faced, are mostly from England in the period 1943-45. They detail the daily routines of a journalist in wartime: arranging meetings, writing stories under deadline, dealing with military censors, struggling to travel anywhere, shortages and rationing of everything." (Library Journal)
Includes bibliographical references (pages 313-314) and index.

Friedlander, Edward Jay

Feature writing for newspapers and magazines; the pursuit of excellence. [by] Edward Jay Friedlander, John Lee. 6th ed.; Pearson/A&B 2008 334p pa $86.80   **070.4**
1. Journalism
ISBN 0-205-48466-2; 978-0-205-48466-9
        LC 2007-20885
First published 1988
Through suggestions and examples this guide for the novice writer provides tips from Pulitzer Prize-winning journalists and other magazine and newspaper feature writers.

Fuller, Jack

What is happening to news; the information explosion and the crisis in journalism. The University of Chicago Press 2010 214p $25   **070.4**
1. Journalism 2. Information society 3. Journalistic ethics 4. Journalism -- United States
ISBN 0-226-26898-5; 978-0-226-26898-9; 978-0-226-26899-6 ebook
        LC 2009039090
"This worthy addition to the journalism bookshelf will stand the test of time." Choice
Includes bibliographical references

Johnson, Marilyn

★ The **dead** beat; lost souls, lucky stiffs, and the perverse pleasures of obituaries. HarperCollins 2006 244p il $24.95   **070.4**
1. Obituaries
ISBN 0-06-075875-9
        LC 2005-52817
"Johnson handles her offbeat topic with an appropriate level of humor, while still respecting the gravity of mortality." Publ Wkly
Includes bibliographical references

Reporting Vietnam. Library of Am. 1998 2v il maps v1-v2 ea $35; v2 pa $17.95   **070.4**
1. Vietnam War, 1961-1975 2. Reporters and reporting
ISBN 1-88301-158-2 v1; 1-88301-159-0 v2; 1-88301-190-6 v2 pa
        LC 98-12267
This collection includes "newspaper, magazine, book excerpts, and one TV commentary, Walter Cronkite's post-Tet report concluding that the United States should quickly negotiate its way out." Commonweal
"This book will help readers understand better what it was like to live through that tumultuous period of American history." Publ Wkly
Includes bibliographical references

Strayed, Cheryl

Tiny beautiful things; advice on love and life from Dear Sugar. Cheryl Strayed. Vintage Books 2012 xi, 353 p.p (pbk.) $14.95   **070.4**
1. Advice columns 2. Conduct of life 3. Conduct of life -- Miscellanea
ISBN 0307949338; 9780307949325; 9780307949332
        LC 2012007154

This book by internet advice columnist Cheryl Strayed "presents verbatim letters and their detailed published replies." (Kirkus Reviews) "In many ways, it is a portrait of Strayed herself: she describes her estranged father, her . . . first marriage, her relationship with her current husband . . . and her . . . mother, who died suddenly while Strayed was in college. She answers queries on subjects ranging from professional jealousy to leaving a loved partner." (Library Journal)

Tobin, James

Reporting America at war; an oral history. compiled by Michelle Ferrari with commentary by James Tobin. Hyperion 2003 241p il $23.95   **070.4**
1. War 2. Reporters and reporting
ISBN 1-401-30072-3
        LC 2003-49966
"Beginning with Edward R. Morrow's live reports during the London blitz and ending with an epilogue on the second war in Iraq, this oral history contains transcripts of interviews with 11 top correspondents. Murrow is one of three deceased reporters included (the others are Martha Gellhorn and Homer Bigart), along with Walter Cronkite, Andy Rooney, Frank Gibney, Malcolm Browne, David Halberstam, Morley Safer, Ward Just, Gloria Emerson, Chris Hedges and Christiane Amanpour. . . . Tobin's introductions and transitional and informational interpolations within the transcripts hold this informative volume together." Publ Wkly
Includes bibliographical references

Tobin, James E.

Ernie Pyle's war; America's eyewitness to World War II. Free Press 1997 312p il pa $15   **070.4**
1. Journalists 2. World War, 1939-1945 3. Biography, Individual
ISBN 0-684-83642-4; 0-7432-8476-3 pa; 978-0-7432-8476-9 pa
        LC 97-6165
This is a biography of the World War II correspondent who "followed the troops from North Africa to Italy to Normandy and then across the Pacific to Okinawa, where he was killed." (Choice) Index.
"Living and working among the troops he so vividly chronicled, Pyle offered a unique insider's perspective of the harsh reality experienced by the common soldier during World War II. . . . A respectful and insightful biography of a giant among journalists." Booklist
Includes bibliographical references

070.409   History, geographic treatment, biography

Brinkley, Douglas

★ **Cronkite**; Douglas Brinkley. Harper, an imprint of HarperCollins Publishers 2012 xi, 819 p.p (hardback) $34.99   **070.409**
1. Television broadcasting of news 2. Journalists -- United States -- Biography 3. Television journalists -- United States -- Biography
ISBN 0061374261; 9780061374265
        LC 2011051467

This book, by Douglas Brinkley, is a biography of Walter Cronkite. "For decades, Walter Cronkite was known as 'the most trusted man in America'. . . . Brinkley traces Cronkite's story from his roots in Missouri and Texas through the Great Depression, . . . to World War II [and later]. . . . [H]e covered presidential elections, the space program, Vietnam, and the first televised broadcasts of the Olympic Games, as both a reporter and later as an anchor for the evening news." (Publisher's note)

070.449   Journalism--Specific subjects

Deford, Frank

Over time; my life as a sportswriter. Frank Deford. Atlantic Monthly Press 2012 354 p. $25   **070.449**
1. Autobiographies 2. Sports journalism
ISBN 0802120156; 9780802120151

In this autobiography sportswriter Frank Deford describes how he "joined 'Sports Illustrated' in 1962. . . . In 1990, he was Editor-in-Chief of 'The National Sports Daily,' one of the most ambitious--and ill-fated--projects in the history of American print journalism. But then, he's endured: writing ten novels, winning an Emmy . . . , [and reading] commentary on NPR's 'Morning Edition.'" (Publisher's note)

Starkman, Dean

The **best** business writing 2012; edited by Dean Starkman et. al. Columbia University Press 2012 439 p. $18.95   **070.449**
1. Business 2. Businesspeople
ISBN 0231160739; 9780231160735

This anthology of business writing for the year 2012 presents "the year's well-known and crucial-to-know developments in business and finance." It is divided into thematic sections, such as bad business behavior; the financial system and its discontents; trends in global markets; the relationship between politics and money; big-picture practices; and news from the corporate world." (Publisher's note)
Includes bibliographical references and index.

070.5   Publishing

2009 guide to literary agents; 18th annual ed.; Writer's Digest 2008 362p il pa $27.99   **070.5**
1. Reference books 2. Authors and publishers -- Directories
ISBN 978-1-58297-548-1; 1-58297-548-5
Annual. Supersedes in part Guide to literary agents & art/photo reps

"An invaluable tool for writers in search of an agent, this guide is indexed by agency, agent, format, subject, and geographic location. Submission procedures, fees, contracts and what to ask a prospective agent are covered." Libr J

2013 Writer's market; edited by Robert Lee Brewer. Writer's Digest Books 2012 921 p. (paperback) $29.99   **070.5**
1. Authors 2. Publishers and publishing
ISBN 1599635933; 9781599635934

This book "details thousands of publishing opportunities for writers, including listings for book publishers, consumer and trade magazines, contests and awards, and literary agents. These listings include contact and submission information to help writers get their work published." (Publisher's note)

★ **American** book trade directory 2008-2009; 54th ed; Information Today 2008 1850p $299.95   **070.5**
1. Book industry 2. Book collecting 3. Reference books 4. Publishers and publishing -- Directories
ISBN 978-1-57387-317-8; 1-57387-317-9
Annual. First published 1915 by Bowker with title: American book trade manual

"Includes lists of booksellers, wholesalers, and publishers in the United States, with related information on the book trade in Canada, the United Kingdom, and Ireland. Bookstores are arranged under state and city with speciality of each noted. Separate lists include exporters, importers, and dealers in foreign books. Index of retailers and wholesalers in the United States and Canada." Ref Sources for Small & Medium-sized LIbr. 6th edition

★ The **Columbia** guide to digital publishing; edited by William E. Kasdorf. Columbia Univ. Press 2003 lxi, 750p $65; pa $34.95   **070.5**
1. Electronic publishing
ISBN 0-231-12498-8; 0-231-12499-6 pa
LC 2002-41462

This volume begins with an introductory chapter on "the role of digital publishing in various facets of the publishing industry. . . . Other chapters address topics such as: the technical infrastructure, mark-up, content management, digital rights management, e-books, archiving issues, legal issues, accessibility, and international issues." The Indexer
Includes bibliographical references

Crawford, Walt

The **librarian's** guide to micropublishing; helping patrons and communities use free and low-cost publishing tools to tell their stories. Walt Crawford. Information Today, Inc. 2012 ix, 172 p.p $49.50   **070.5**
1. Librarians 2. Self-publishing 3. Publishers and publishing -- Handbooks, manuals, etc. 4. Desktop publishing 5. On-demand publications 6. Libraries and publishing 7. Libraries -- Publishing -- Computer programs
ISBN 1573874302; 9781573874304
LC 2011044882

In this book, "Walt Crawford explains the how, what, and why of libraries and community micropublishing. He details the use of no-cost/low-cost publishing tools Lulu and CreateSpace and equips librarians to guide their patrons in the production of quality print books. He offers step-by-step instructions for using MS Word to design and edit manuscripts that can be printed in flexible quantities via on-demand technology." (Publisher's note)

Includes bibliographical references (pages 159-161) and index

Germano, William P.

Getting it published; a guide for scholars and anyone else serious about serious books. {by} William Germano. University of Chicago Press 2001 197p (Chicago guides to writing, editing, and publishing) $35; pa $15   **070.5**

1. Authors and publishers 2. Publishers and publishing
ISBN 0-226-28843-9; 0-226-28844-7 pa
       LC 00-46715

The author "deconstructs and demystifies what publishers and editors actually do and what authors should look for in finding the right house for their subject and in putting the right words in their contract. He also does a lot of hand-holding through the review process and the production of the manuscript." Booklist

Includes bibliographical references (p. 193) and index

Graham, Katharine, 1917-2001

Personal history. Knopf 1997 642p il pa $15.95; $35   **070.5**

1. Authors 2. Journalists 3. Memoirists 4. Washington post 5. Newspaper executives 6. Biography, Individual
ISBN 0-375-70104-4 pa; 0-394-58585-2
       LC 96-49638

This is a memoir by the publisher of the Washington Post. Index.

"Throughout this easy-to-read story, Graham writes about her personal life and the lives of others, ranging from presidents to household help, with sympathy and grace." Libr J

Herman, Jeff

Jeff Herman's guide to book publishers, editors, & literary agents 2008; who they are! what they want! how to win them over! 18th ed.; Three Dog Press; Distributed to the book trade by Watson-Guptill 2008 991p $29.95   **070.5**

1. Authors and publishers 2. Publishers and publishing
ISBN 978-0-9772682-2-1; 0-9772682-2-5

Annual. First published 1992 by Prima Pub. with title: Insider's guide to book editors, publishers, and literary agents. Variant title: Writer's guide to book editors, publishers, and literary agents

Herman provides "portraits of more than 100 agents plus tips on writing query letters and nonfiction book proposals, dealing with rejections, ghostwriting, and self-publishing. With an excellent glossary and sample author-agent and collaboration agreements." Libr J

Includes bibliographical references

International literary market place 2009. Information Today 2008 1800p pa $259   **070.5**

1. Reference books 2. Publishers and publishing -- Directories
ISBN 978-1-57387-325-3; 1-57387-325-X

Annual. First published 1965 by Bowker

This directory of the international book publishing industry covers over 180 countries worldwide and profiles "more than 15,000 book-related concerns around the globe, including . . . 10,500 publishers and literary agents; 1,100 major booksellers and book clubs; 1,500 major libraries and library associations . . . and thousands of other book-related concerns—including trade organizations, distributors, dealers, literary associations, trade publications, book trade events, and other resources . . . organized in a country-by-country format." Publisher's note

Kachka, Boris

Hothouse; the art of survival and the survival of art at America's most celebrated publishing house, Farrar, Straus, & Giroux. Boris Kachka. Simon & Schuster 2013 400 p. illustrations (some color) (hardcover) $28   **070.5**

1. Publishers and publishing -- History -- 20th century 3. Farrar, Straus, and Giroux -- History 4. Authors and publishers -- New York (State) -- New York -- History -- 20th century 5. Publishers and publishing -- New York (State) -- New York -- History -- 20th century
ISBN 1451691890; 9781451691894; 9781451691917
       LC 2013003199

In this book on Farrar, Straus, & Giroux, author Boris Kachka "chronicles the midsized independent publishing house whose mission of bringing high culture to the mass market set the tone for postwar American letters. . . . Threading through Kachka's . . . narrative is an epochal shift in the industry: from the old FSG, with its . . . febrile literary passions, to the new era of bland media conglomerates." (Publishers Weekly)

"Entertaining, accessible, smart, and thought-provoking, this is a book very much in tune with the lost literary milieu it recreates." Pub Wkly

Includes bibliographical references and index

Literary market place 2009. Bowker 2008 2v pa $309   **070.5**

1. Reference books 2. Publishers and publishing -- Directories
ISBN 978-1-57387-329-1; 1-57387-329-2

Annual. First published 1940. In 1972 absorbed Names & numbers. Subtitle varies

"Directory of U.S. and Canadian book publishers and related businesses such as book clubs, literary agents, translators, and manufacturers. Gives names of executives and addresses, telephone numbers, and fields of specialization for each publishing company." N Y Public Libr Book of How & Where to Look It Up

Nasaw, David

The **chief** : the life of William Randolph Hearst. Houghton Mifflin 2000 687p il $35; pa $16 **070.5**

1. Newspaper editors 2. Newspaper executives
ISBN 0-395-82759-0; 0-618-15446-9 pa
       LC 99-462122

"Few publishers have loomed as large in their lifetimes, or cast as long a shadow after death, as William Randolph Hearst. . . . Nasaw's judicious and comprehensive biography

sensibly seeks to understand its subject, not to judge him."
New Yorker

Includes bibliographical references

Neuburger, Emily K.
Minders of make-believe; idealists, entrepreneurs, and the shaping of American children's literature. Houghton Mifflin Co. 2008 402p $28 **070.5**

1. Publishers and publishing 2. Children -- Books and reading 3. Children's literature -- History and criticism
ISBN 978-0-395-67407-9; 0-395-67407-7

LC 2008-00589

"Marcus' approach and tone are always, and irresistibly, well informed, sensible, and intelligent. . . . It is hard to imagine any issue that he has overlooked, and the resulting book is, in word, indispensable." Booklist

Includes bibliographical references

No shelf required 2; use and management of electronic books. edited by Sue Polanka. American Library Association 2012 xiv, 254 p.p ill. (alk. paper) $65 **070.5**

1. Electronic books 2. Library resources 3. Electronic publishing 4. Libraries and electronic publishing 5. Libraries -- Special collections -- Electronic books
ISBN 0838911455; 9780838911457

LC 2011040497

This book "brings together a variety of professionals to share their expertise about e-books with librarians and publishers. Providing forward-thinking ideas while remaining grounded in practical information that can be implemented in all kinds of libraries, the topics explored include an introduction to e-books . . . and an overview of their history and development . . . e-book technology . . . why e-books are good for learning, and how librarians can market them." (Publisher's note)

Includes bibliographical references and index

Pettegree, Andrew
The **book** in the Renaissance. Yale University Press 2010 421p il $40 **070.5**

1. Printing 2. Renaissance 3. Book industry 4. Reformation -- Europe 5. Europe -- History -- 1492-1789 6. Books -- Europe -- History -- 1400-1600 7. Printing -- Europe -- History -- 16th century 8. Book industries and trade -- Europe -- History -- 16th century
ISBN 978-0-300-11009-8; 0-300-11009-X

LC 2009-26513

The author's "treatment is both thorough and engaging, ably situating the social, economic, and historical within the stories of individuals involved." Libr J

Includes bibliographical references

Poynter, Dan
★ The **self** -publishing manual; how to write, print and sell your own book. 16th ed; Para Pub. 2007 463p pa $19.95 **070.5**

1. Publishers and publishing
ISBN 978-1-568601-42-7; 1-568601-42-5
First published 1979. Periodically revised

"Poynter gives the basics for producing a commercially successful manuscript, taking the reader step-by-step

through printing a book, determining its value, promoting and advertising, fulfilling orders, and coping with being published. There are appendixes on printers, professional organizations, and fulfillment warehouses." Libr J

The **Publish**-it-yourself handbook; [literary tradition and how to] edited by Bill Henderson. 25th anniversary ed.; Pushcart Press 1998 346p il pa $18 **070.5**

1. Publishers and publishing
ISBN 1-888-88903-9
First published 1973. Periodically revised

An anthology of articles about how to publish without the assistance of commercial or vanity publishers.

Publishers, distributors & wholesalers of the United States 2009. Bowker 2008 2v set $475 **070.5**

1. Reference books 2. Publishers and publishing -- Directories
ISBN 978-0-8352-4966-9

Annual. First published 1979 with title: Publishers and distributors of the United States

This directory provides information on "more than 150,000 U.S. publishers, wholesalers, distributors, software firms, audiocassette producers, museum and association imprints, and trade organizations that publish." Publisher's note

Rose, M. J.
How to publish and promote online; {by} M. J. Rose and Angela Adair-Hoy. St. Martin's Griffin 2001 266p pa $13.95 **070.5**

1. Publishers and publishing 2. Authorship -- Internet resources
ISBN 0-312-27191-3

LC 00-45833

The authors "provide encouragement and tips for aspiring authors hoping to publish their works electronically." Booklist

Shepard, Stephen B.
Deadlines and disruption; the turbulent road from print to digital. by Stephen Shepard. McGraw-Hill 2012 304 p. (hardback) $28 **070.5**

1. Journalism 2. Online journalism 3. Journalism -- Technological innovations 4. Newspaper publishing -- Technological innovations
ISBN 0071802649; 9780071802642

LC 2012016577

This book is "[Stephen B.] Shepard's story of his life in print journalism, and a . . . look at the way journalism is evolving due to electronic media, social networking, and the ability of anyone with a computer and an opinion to make him- or herself heard. Is journalism dying? Not according to Shepard. It's changing, yes, but in some respects it's also improving." (Booklist)

Suber, Peter

Open access; Peter Suber. MIT Press 2012 xii, 242 p.p (paperback) $12.95 **070.5**

1. Open access publishing
ISBN 0262517639; 9780262517638

LC 2011038297

This book, by Peter Suber, is part of the "MIT Press Essential Knowledge" series. "The Internet lets us share perfect copies of our work with a worldwide audience at virtually no cost. . . . In this concise introduction, . . . Suber tells us what open access is and isn't, how it benefits authors and readers of research, how we pay for it, how it avoids copyright problems, how it has moved from the periphery to the mainstream, and what its future may hold." Publisher's note

Includes bibliographical references (p. [177]-221) and index

070.5092 Publishers--biography

Seaver, Richard

The **tender** hour of twilight; Paris in the '50s, New York in the '60s : a memoir of publishing's golden age. Richard Seaver ; edited by Jeannette Seaver. Farrar, Straus and Giroux 2012 xxi, 457 p.p (alk. paper) $35 **070.5092**

1. Translators -- United States -- Biography 2. Book editors -- United States -- Biography 3. Publishers and publishing -- United States -- Biography
ISBN 0374273782; 9780374273781

LC 2011024951

"[T]he first part of . . . [Richard Seaver's] memoir is about Paris in the Fifties and the adventure of publishing [Samuel] Beckett among others, [while] the second part is about Grove Press in New York, where he became one of the early editors of an enterprise financed and led by Barney Rosset. It's a story of Grove's long battles with censorship, with which Seaver was closely involved. . . . [One] censorship problem was encountered with Henry Miller's 'Tropic of Cancer,' about which Rosset had written an essay and which was banned in almost every country in the world. . . . [In addition,] Seaver's memoir testifies to Beckett's patience in dealing with collaborators, even if he held them to the highest standards." (New York Review of Books)

070.92   Biography regardless of area, region, place

Bogus, Carl T.

★ **Buckley**; William F. Buckley Jr. and the rise of American Conservatism. Carl T. Bogus. Bloomsbury 2011 416 p. $30.00 **070.92**

1. Conservatism -- United States -- History 2. United States -- Politics and government 3. Journalists -- United States -- Biography 4. Conservatism -- United States -- Biography
ISBN 1596915803; 9781596915800

LC 2011012734

This book is not only a biography of publisher William F. Buckley; it also looks at "the story of the conservative movement's origins" in the U.S. during the 20th century. Author Carl T. Bogus "explains the competing philosophies of different conservative sects—Burkean conservatism, libertarianism, Ayn Rand's objectivism." (Library Journal)

Includes bibliographical references and index.

Koppel, Ted

Off camera; private thoughts made public. Knopf 2000 320p hardcover o.p. pa $14 **070.92**

1. Television moderators 2. Television news anchors
ISBN 0-375-72708-6 pa

LC 00-34919

The television journalist of Nightline presents a daily diary for 1999 chronicling "the controversial events from the century's last year, such as the Clinton impeachment trial and the Columbine High School shootings. . . . The subtitle of the book may lead some readers to expect a bit of muckraking, but they will be disappointed. . . . Yet one does not get the sense that Koppel is restraining himself or hiding anything, merely that this is a person who lives his life with integrity so that his private thoughts are full of the same." Libr J

Levy, Bernard Henri

★ **Who** killed Daniel Pearl? Melville House Pub 2003 454p $25.95; pa $16.95 **070.92**

1. Homicide 2. Kidnapping 3. Journalists
ISBN 0-9718659-4-9; 0-9749609-4-2 pa

LC 2003-13576

Levy reports on "the murder of the Wall Street Journal correspondent Daniel Pearl. . . . [He] follows the trail of the kidnappers to the highest reaches of Osama bin Laden's Al Qaeda and Pakistan's Inter-Services Intelligence agency, and to the links he claims exist between them." N Y Times Book Rev

Martinez, Domingo

★ The **boy** kings of Texas; a memoir. Domingo Martinez. Lyons Press 2012 xii, 443 p.p ill. (pbk.) $16.95 **070.92**

1. Americanization 2. Journalists -- United States -- Biography 5. Mexican Americans -- Texas, South -- Biography
ISBN 0762779195; 9780762779192

LC 2012018732

National Book Awards Finalist (2012)

This memoir by Domingo Martinez "recounts the story of a border-town family in Brownsville, Texas in the 1980's, as each member of the family desperately tries to assimilate and escape life on the border to become 'real' Americans, even at the expense of their shared family history." (Publisher's note)

O'Faolain, Nuala

Almost there; the onward journey of a Dublin woman. Riverhead Bks. 2003 275p $24.95; pa $14 **070.92**

1. Authors 2. Novelists 3. Ireland 4. Columnists 5. Memoirists
ISBN 1-57322-241-0; 1-57322-374-3 pa

LC 2002-36722

In this autobiography the author "reveals the emotional damage she still suffers from being raised in a large family by an alcoholic mother and a remote father." Booklist

This "is a thought-provoking work that differs markedly from the self-serving memoirs we frequently see." Libr J

Pearl, Mariane

★ A **mighty** heart; the brave life and death of my husband, Danny Pearl. [by] Mariane Pearl, with Sarah Crichton. Scribner 2003 278p $25; pa $13 **070.92**

1. Journalists

ISBN 0-7432-4442-7; 0-7432-6237-9 pa

LC 2003-60143

"On January 23, 2002, Danny Pearl, the South Asia bureau chief of the Wall Street Journal stationed in Pakistan, left his Karachi home to go to some meetings. It was the last time his wife, fellow journalist Mariane, saw him alive. . . . This memoir, written by his widow, begins the morning of his abduction and takes us through the confirmation of his abduction, the efforts to free him, and his assassination. . . . Plenty of words have been written about the Pearl abduction, but these are by far the most personal and most poignant." Booklist

Politkovskaya, Anna, 1958-2006

Is journalism worth dying for? translated by Arch Tait. Melville House 2011 468 p. [8] p. of plates **070.92**

1. Journalism 2. Russia (Federation) -- Politics and government -- 1991-

ISBN 978-1-935554-40-0 pa; 1-935554-40-9 pa

LC 2011922469

'This book is written by "Anna Politkovskaya [who] won international fame for her courageous reporting. . . . Beginning with a brief introduction by the author about her pariah status, the book contains essays that characterize . . . Politkovskaya more fully than she allowed in her other books. From deeply personal statements about the nature of journalism, to . . . reports from Chechnya, to . . . pieces of memoir, to, finally, the first translation of the series of investigative reports that Politkovskaya was working on at the time of her murder—pieces many believe led to her assassination." (Publisher's note)

Includes Index

Thompson, Hunter S., 1937-2005

The **kingdom** of fear; loathsome secrets of a star-crossed child in the final days of the American century. Simon & Schuster 2003 xx, 354p il hardcover o.p. pa $16 **070.92**

1. Authors 2. Novelists 3. Journalists 4. Satirists 5. Columnists 6. Nonfiction writers

ISBN 0-684-87323-0; 978-0-684-87324-4; 0-684-87324-9 pa

LC 2002-191228

In this book the American journalist writes about his life and career experiences

"Just as Thompson paved his own way in writing about politics, sports, news and culture throughout the 1960s and '70s, he now offers an autobiography that is typically unorthodox in style but still revealing previously unknown

facts about its subject. Wavering between the uproarious and the lunatic, it's vintage Thompson through and through." Publ Wkly

071 Geographic treatment of journalism and newspapers

Baker, Nicholson

The **World** on Sunday; graphic art in Joseph Pulitzer's newspaper (1898-1911) [by] Nicholson Baker and Margaret Brentano. Bulfinch Press 2005 131p il $50 **071**

1. New York world (Newspaper)

ISBN 0-8212-6193-2

LC 2005-00224

This book collects 85 examples of graphic art from the Sunday edition of the New York World

This volume "offers a kaleidoscopic tour through, an ebullient moment in American history when the country was emerging from the shadowy gaslight age and bursting into the glare of the modern. It is a big, lush, coffee-table-size book suffused with gaiety and the optimism of an age blissfully unaware of darknesses soon to come. . . . The World on Sunday is the result of a heroic piece of cultural preservation." N Y Rev Books

Burns, Eric

Infamous scribblers; the founding fathers and the rowdy beginnings of American journalism. Public Affairs 2006 467p hardcover o.p. pa $15.95 **071**

1. Journalism 2. Newspapers -- United States

ISBN 978-1-58648-334-0; 1-58648-334-X; 978-1-58648-428-6 pa; 1-58648-428-1 pa

LC 2005-53542

The author "explores the role newspapers played in the founding of the country." Libr J

"From the sniping feuds among Boston's first papers to sex scandals involving Alexander Hamilton and Thomas Jefferson, the snappy patter gives clear indication of how much Burns . . . relishes telling his story." Publ Wkly

Includes bibliographical references

Campbell, W. Joseph

Getting it wrong; ten of the greatest misreported stories in American journalism. University of California Press 2010 269p il $60; pa $24.95 **071**

1. Journalistic ethics 2. Journalism -- Objectivity

ISBN 0-520-25566-6; 0-520-26209-3 pa; 978-0-520-25566-1; 978-0-520-26209-6 pa

LC 2009047705

This "provocative book provides a wealth of case studies in the complexity of journalism and history. It reinforces the truism that journalists, authors and book reviewers alike should all be more skeptical—and definitely more humble." Am Journalism Rev

Includes bibliographical references

Ellison, Sarah

War at the Wall Street journal; inside the struggle to control an American business empire. Houghton Mifflin Harcourt 2010 274p $27   **071**

1. Wall Street journal 2. Dow Jones & Co., Inc.

ISBN 978-0-547-15243-1; 0-547-15243-4

LC 2009-46266

"Sarah Ellison has written a definitive, indeed cinematic, account of the News Corporation's conquest and occupation of this venerable business publication, and of the subterranean battle of motives and moods in the Bancroft family psychodrama." N Y Times Book Rev

Includes bibliographical references

McChesney, Robert Waterman, 1952-

The **death** and life of American journalism; the media revolution that will begin the world again. [by] Robert W. McChesney, John Nichols. Nation Books 2010 352p il $26.95   **071**

1. Journalism

ISBN 978-1-56858-605-2; 1-56858-605-1

LC 2010-282015

The author provides "a compelling blueprint for rejuvenating meaningful journalism in the US. This is really two books in one. First, it is an immensely readable history of—and insightful deconstruction of myths surrounding—freedom of the press and a cogent analysis of how press freedom was narrowly redefined in the 20th century to protect the business of newspapering from government interference. Second, it is a visionary manifesto for government subsidy of American journalism, a 'massive public intervention to produce a public good.'" Choice

Includes bibliographical references

McMillian, John

Smoking typewriters; the Sixties underground press and the rise of alternative media in America. [by] John McMillian. Oxford University Press 2011 277p il $27.95   **071**

1. Radicalism 2. Alternative press

ISBN 978-0-19-531992-7

LC 2010-26243

The book "argues that for young people seeking to engender new forms of culture and politics, alternative newspapers of the era held a singular power to embody principles of participatory democracy, radical journalism, and youth empowerment—and in the process reflected, reinforced, and peddled some of the period's most representative values. Thus 'Smoking Typewriters' offers a[n] . . . argument that the underground press was one of the New Left's most important counterinstitutions. The book combines institutional history, social and cultural analysis, and fresh retellings of both major and lesser-known episodes within the underground press to offer a kaleidoscopic narrative of colorful story lines and revolving, idiosyncratic characters." (Journal of American History)

This is a "readable, richly detailed study of the hundreds of anti-establishment 1960s newspapers—from the Los Angeles Free Press to Rag (Austin, Texas) and The Paper (East Lansing, Mich.)—that 'educated, politicized and built communities among disaffected youths in every region of the country.' . . . A welcome book on the '60s—a nostal-

gia trip for those who were there and a vivid work of history for anyone curious about the journalism that jolted a decade." Kirkus

Includes bibliographical references

The **New** new journalism; conversations with America's best nonfiction writers on their craft. [edited and with an introduction by] Robert S. Boynton. Vintage Books 2005 xxxiv, 456p pa $13.95 **071**

1. Journalism

ISBN 1-400-03356-X

LC 2004-57161

The author "offers interviews with 19 writers who detail how and why they produce their work. . . . A fascinating book that makes the reader want to go out and get every book the writers have written as well as those mentioned as sources of inspiration." Booklist

Includes bibliographical references

Ostertag, Bob

People's movements, people's press; the journalism of social justice movements. Beacon Press 2006 232p il $23.95   **071**

1. Social movements 2. Alternative press

ISBN 0-8070-6164-6; 978-0-8070-6164-0

LC 2005-31735

The author "focuses on five social movements—abolition, women's suffrage, gay and lesbian liberation, veterans against the Vietnam War, and environmentalism—and examines the resulting journalism in the context of each. He argues that the press played an integral part in the development and effectiveness of each movement and explores . . . the interplay among the publications, the movements, and society." Libr J

"Readers interested in the intersection of the media and social movements will appreciate this insightful book." Booklist

Includes bibliographical references

Ritchie, Donald A.

Reporting from Washington; the history of the Washington press corps. Oxford University Press 2005 390p il $30   **071**

1. Reporters and reporting 2. Journalism -- Objectivity 3. Press -- Government policy

ISBN 0-19-517861-0

LC 2004-18892

The author "focuses on the period from 1932, when the rising influence of radio and FDR's aggressive politicking broke the dominance of newspapers, until 2001, when the terrorist attacks on the U.S. refocused attention on the government and the press. . . . Ritchie presents a rich perspective on the people who write the first draft of history, investigating and then breaking the Teapot Dome and Watergate scandals, among others." Booklist

Includes bibliographical references

Written into history; Pulitzer Prize reporting of the twentieth century from the New York times. edited and with an introduction by Anthony Lewis.

Times Bks. 2001 xxv, 355p hardcover o.p. pa $17 **071**
1. Journalism 2. Pulitzer Prizes
ISBN 0-8050-6849-X; 0-8050-7178-4 pa
LC 2001-35555
"For anyone interested in recent history or journalism at its best, this book will prove worthwhile." Publ Wkly

071.3 Journalism--United States

Carpini, Michael X. Delli

After broadcast news; media regimes, democracy, and the new information environment. Bruce A. Williams, Michael X. Delli Carpini. Cambridge University Press 2011 xii, 361 p.p (paperback) $32.99 **071.3**
1. Mass media 2. Online journalism 3. Broadcast journalism 4. Democracy -- United States 5. Press and politics -- United States 6. Mass media -- Political aspects -- United States 7. Popular culture -- Political aspects -- United States 8. Broadcast journalism -- Political aspects -- United States
ISBN 0521279836; 9780521279833; 9781107010314
LC 2011009191
This book posits that the "new media environment has challenged the role of professional journalists as the primary source of politically relevant information" and "puts this challenge into historical context, arguing that it is the latest of several critical moments, driven by economic, political, cultural, and technological changes, in which the relationship among citizens, political elites, and the media has been contested." (Publisher's note)
Includes bibliographical references and index.

080 General collections

Adler, Mortimer J.

How to think about the great ideas; from the great books of Western civilization. {by} Mortimer J. Adler; edited by Max Weismann. Open Court 2000 xxiv, 530p pa $24.95 **080**
1. Great books of the Western world
ISBN 0-8126-9412-0
LC 99-45251
This volume contains the transcripts of 52 half-hour segments of Adler's 1953-1954 television program The great ideas
"The book showcases Adler's ideas about all the big categories—truth, beauty, freedom, love, sex, art, justice, rationality, humankind's nature, Darwinism, government." Publ Wkly

Andrews, Robert

Famous lines; a Columbia dictionary of familiar quotations. Columbia Univ. Press 1997 xxiii, 625p $38.95 **080**
1. Quotations 2. Reference books
ISBN 0-231-10218-6
LC 96-43879

This work "contains more than 6,000 witticisms, enduring observations, and incendiary statements from all kinds of people from antiquity to yesterday. Besides identifying the source, Andrews . . . provides details of the first publication, specific chapter and scene, and even the character speaking. Besides quotes from Shakespeare and Oscar Wilde, readers will find fascinating quotes from Monty Python, Gloria Steinem, and maybe your favorite author, for example, Agatha Christie. The more than 500 subject headings include homelessness, AIDS, sexual harassment, murder, and war." Booklist
Includes bibliographical references

Elder, Robert K.

Last words of the executed; with a foreword by Studs Terkel. The University of Chicago Press 2010 301p ebook $22.50; $22.50 **080**
1. Capital punishment 2. Death -- Quotations
ISBN 978-0-226-20269-3 ebook; 978-0-226-20268-6
LC 2009-38402
"Whatever side in the argument [over the death penalty] one habitually takes, this book is recommended reading, so that in addition to learning how we put people to death, one can also put to the test the firmness of one's convictions." N Y Rev Books
Includes bibliographical references

081 General collections in specific languages and language families

McPhee, John A.

Irons in the fire; {by} John McPhee. Farrar, Straus & Giroux 1997 215p $22; pa $14 **081**
ISBN 0-374-17726-0; 0-374-52545-5 pa
LC 96-32358
"John McPhee's essays are proof that the kind of journalism that can effortlessly put a topic into perfect perspective will never go out of style." N Y Times Book Rev

Pauling, Linus C.

Linus Pauling in his own words; selections from his writings, speeches, and interviews. edited by Barbara Marinacci; introduction by Linus Pauling. Simon & Schuster 1995 320p hardcover o.p. pa $20 **081**
1. Chemists 2. College teachers 3. Writers on science 4. Nobel laureates for peace 5. Nobel laureates for chemistry
ISBN 0-6848-1387-4 ps
LC 95-31123
This book "attempts to follow the life and career of Dr. Pauling through his own writings, interspersed with narrative by the editor. The book succeeds wonderfully. Linus Pauling is unique among modern scientists, both for winning two Nobel Prizes and for his political and social views. Through his writings, the breadth and depth of his work become clear to the reader." Sci Books Films
Includes bibliographical references

082   General collections in English

Brown, Craig

✓ **Hello** goodbye hello; a circle of 101 remarkable meetings. Craig Brown. Simon & Schuster 2012 xxi, 356 p.p (hardcover) $26.95   **082**

1. Fame 2. Celebrities 3. Interpersonal relations 4. Celebrities -- Humor 5. Celebrities -- Quotations

ISBN 145168360X; 9781451683608; 9781451684520

LC 2012003987

This book, by Craig Brown, "is a daisy chain of 101 . . . true encounters. . . . Who could imagine such unlikely--but true--encounters as these: Martha Graham meets Madonna, . . . Frank Lloyd Wright meets Marilyn Monroe, . . . [and] Harpo Marx meets George Bernard Shaw. . . . [The author] shows how the celebrated and gifted . . . got along famously or disastrously or indifferently with one another." (Publisher's note)

Includes bibliographical references (p. 335-356).

Quotations for all occasions; compiled by Catherine Frank. Columbia Univ. Press 2000 260p $55; pa $18.95   **082**

1. Quotations

ISBN 0-231-11290-4; 0-231-11291-2 pa

LC 00-24048

This title "organizes its 1500-plus quotes into three sections that cover 150 different occasions. 'Every Year' contains quotes for such annual events as holidays, birthdays, days of the week, and seasons, while 'Occasionally' encompasses quotes for less frequent events, like going back to school, breaking up, quitting smoking, and school reunions. The final section is for 'Once in a Lifetime' experiences, such as turning 16, getting a first car, menopause, and retirement." Libr J

Includes bibliographical references

✓ ★ The **Yale** book of quotations; edited by Fred R. Shapiro; foreword by Joseph Epstein. Yale University Press 2006 1104p $50   **082**

1. Quotations

ISBN 978-0-300-10798-2; 0-300-10798-6

LC 2006-12317

The more than 12,000 "range over literature, history, popular culture, sports, computers, science, politics, law, and the social sciences, and although American quotations are emphasized, the book's scope is global. The authors represented are as diverse as William Shakespeare, John Lennon, Jack Dempsey, both Presidents Bush, J.K. Rowling, Rita Mae Brown, Confucius, Warren Buffet, and Deng Xiaoping. The entries are arranged by author, then chronologically and alphabetically by source title within the same year. A significant effort was made to trace the first published occurrence of a quotation, and whenever possible the wording is taken from the original source. . . . Electronic products such as the Times Digital Archive, JSTOR, Proquest Historical Newspapers and American Periodical Series, LexisNexis, Newspaperarchive.com, Questia, Eighteenth Century Collections Online, and Literature Online were all used." Libr J

098   Prohibited works, forgeries, hoaxes

✓ **Bosmajian, Haig A.**

★ **Burning** books; [by] Haig Bosmajian. McFarland 2006 233p $39.95   **098**

1. Book burning

ISBN 0-7864-2208-4; 978-0-7864-2208-1

LC 2005-35201

"This work provides a detailed account of book burning worldwide over the past 2000 years. The book burners are identified, along with the works they deliberately set aflame." Publisher's note

Includes bibliographical references

Katsoulis, Melissa

Literary hoaxes; an eye-opening history of famous frauds. Skyhorse Pub. 2009 328p $22.95 **098**

1. Literary forgeries

ISBN 978-1-60239-794-1

LC 2009-30421

The author describes "several notorious literary frauds, tracing the art of the Big Lie from Dionysius the Renegade, who wrote a fake Sophocles play that insulted his Stoic teachers, to more modern publishing pranks." Publ Wkly

"The book is by no means comprehensive, nor does it intend to be, but it is an excellent and informative survey of a fascinating and often newsworthy subject." Booklist

100   PHILOSOPHY

100   Philosophy, parapsychology and occultism, psychology

✓ **Blackburn, Simon, 1944-**

Think : a compelling introduction to philosophy. Oxford Univ. Press 1999 312p $25   **100**

1. Philosophy

ISBN 0-19-210024-6

LC 00-265266

The author explores such areas as knowledge, mind, free will, identity, God, goodness and justice. "His method is to introduce what other philosophers—primarily Plato, Descartes, Locke, Berkeley, Leibniz, Hume, and Kant—have had to say about these themes. . . . Readers new to the subject could very well be captivated." Libr J

Includes bibliographical references

Ferry, Luc

A **brief** history of thought; Luc Ferry ; translated by Theo Cuffe. HarperPerennial 2012 304p.   **100**

1. Philosophy 2. Christianity 3. Postmodernism 4. Existentialism

ISBN 9780062074249

This book "offers a thematic introduction to continental philosophy constructed around the biggest questions: how can we lead a meaningful life knowing that we will die but without the consolation of religion? . . . The author's episodic treatment starts with the Stoic concept of man as a fragment of a harmonious cosmos, moves on to Descartes,

Rousseau, and Kant and their establishment of philosophy based on reason and individual freedom, climaxes with Nietzsche's demolition of modernist certitudes-a stance he finds both thrilling and unsatisfying--and ponders the abiding need to embrace a world we must ultimately lose." (Publishers Weekly)

Pigliucci, Massimo

Answers for Aristotle; how science and philosophy can lead us to a more meaningful life. Massimo Pigliucci. Basic Books 2012 312 p. (hardcover) $27.99; (ebook) $27.99 **100**
1. Philosophy 2. Science -- Philosophy 3. Life 4. Ethics 5. Science 6. Conduct of life
ISBN 0465021387; 9780465021383; 9780465032808
LC 2012013186

In this book, philosopher Massimo Pigliucci examines the "connections between science and philosophy." He "begins with 'sci-phi,' the 'idea that philosophy and science can be combined to give us the best possible knowledge about the world and how to act within it.'" He also "links Aristotle's observations on the striving for moral and physical happiness against the desire for immediate gratification with recent research on weight loss, demonstrating the physical limits of most treatments." (Publishers Weekly)
Includes bibliographical references and index

Rorty, Amelie Oksenberg

★ The **many** faces of philosophy; reflections from Plato to Arendt. edited by Amélie Oksenberg Rorty. Oxford Univ. Press 2003 xxix, 512p $40; pa $24.95 **100**
1. Philosophy
ISBN 0-19-513402-8; 0-19-517655-3 pa
LC 2002-30342

This is a collection of "self-reflective musings by canonical Western philosophers, culled from letters, prefaces, memoirs, political tracts, and replies to critics. . . . No single-volume collection of philosophical autobiographies spans the entire history of philosophy as this one does." Choice
Includes bibliographical references

Russell, Bertrand

★ The **problems** of philosophy. Hackett Pub. Co 1990 167p (Hackett classics) $27.95; pa $8.95 **100**
1. Philosophy
ISBN 978-0-87220-099-9; 0-87220-099-X; 978-0-87220-098-2 pa; 0-87220-098-1 pa
LC 90-81389

First published 1912 by Holt
The author discusses: appearance and reality, matter, idealism, theories of knowledge, universals, intuition, and truth
"The work is concise, free from technical terms and perfectly clear to the general reader with no prior knowledge of the subject." Booklist
Includes bibliographical references

103 Dictionaries, encyclopedias, concordances of philosophy

Blackburn, Simon, 1944-

The **Oxford** dictionary of philosophy; 2nd ed.; Oxford University Press 2005 407p il $45 **103**
1. Reference books 2. Philosophy -- Dictionaries
ISBN 0-19-861014-9; 978-0-19-861014-4
LC 2006-271895

First published 1994
This dictionary "contains over 2,500 entries, including biographies of nearly 500 influential philosophers. The dictionary provides . . . coverage of not only Western philosophical traditions, but also themes from Chinese, Indian, Islamic, and Jewish philosophy." Publisher's note
Includes bibliographical references

★ The **Cambridge** dictionary of philosophy; edited by Robert Audi. 2nd ed; Cambridge Univ. Press 1999 xxxv, 1001p il hardcover o.p. pa $32.99 **103**
1. Reference books 2. Philosophy -- Dictionaries
ISBN 0-521-63136-X; 0-521-63722-8 pa
LC 99-12920

First published 1995
This work contains some 4,400 entries including 50 on major contemporary philosophers. Wide coverage of Western philosophy as well as non-Western and non-European philosophers is included. The rapidly growing fields of philosophy of mind and applied ethics are also covered

★ **Encyclopedia** of philosophy; Donald M. Borchert, editor in chief. 2nd ed; Macmillan Reference USA 2005 10v il set $995 **103**
1. Reference books 2. Philosophy -- Encyclopedias
ISBN 0-02-865780-2
LC 2005-18573

First published 1967 in eight volumes under the editorship of Paul Edwards
For a fuller review, see: Booklist, June 1 & 15, 2006
"Among the many topics covered are African, Islamic, Jewish, Russian, Chinese, and Buddhist philosophies; bioethics and biomedical ethics; art and aesthetics; epistemology; metaphysics; peace and war; social and political philosophy; the Holocaust; feminist thought; and much more. Additionally, . . . [it] also features 1,000 biographical entries on major figures in philosophical thought throughout history." Publisher's note
Includes bibliographical references

★ The **Oxford** companion to philosophy; edited by Ted Honderich. 2nd ed., new ed; Oxford University Press 2005 1056p il $60 **103**
1. Reference books 2. Philosophy -- Encyclopedias
ISBN 0-19-926479-1
LC 2005-275452

First published 1995
"Including more than 2200 alphabetically arranged entries from nearly 300 contributors, . . . [this book] provides an encyclopedic view of philosophy's past and present, its ideas, disputes (the editor himself contributes an article on unlikely philosophical propositions), and key figures, living

and dead. . . . This title makes an excellent companion for standard multivolume subject encyclopedias." SLJ

Includes bibliographical references

109   History and collected biography

Durant, William James

★ The **story** of philosophy; the lives and opinions of the great philosophers. by Will Durant. [2nd ed]; Simon & Schuster 1933 412p hardcover o.p. pa $15   **109**

1. Philosophers 2. Philosophy -- History

ISBN 0-671-69500-2; 0-671-20159-X pa

First published 1926

A selective account of western thinkers from Socrates and Kant to Schopenhauer and Dewey.

Includes bibliographical references

King, Peter J.

★ **One** hundred philosophers; the life and work of the world's greatest thinkers. Barron's Educ. Ser. 2004 192p il pa $19.95   **109**

1. Philosophers

ISBN 0-7641-2791-8

LC 2003-110643

The author "has done a masterful job in presenting the life and work of what he calls 'the world's greatest thinkers.' . . . The concise and clearly written description of the thinker's life and ideas are just what a student or a layperson needs to gather an overview of the thinker's life and intellectual contributions." Am Ref Books Annu, 2005

Includes bibliographical references

Russell, Bertrand

A **history** of Western philosophy; and its connection with political and social circumstances from the earliest times to the present day. Simon & Schuster 1945 xxiii, 895p hardcover o.p. pa $25   **109**

1. Science -- History 2. Philosophy -- History

ISBN 0-671-31400-9; 0-671-20158-1 pa

Originally designed and partly delivered as lectures at the Barnes Foundation in Pennsylvania

"My purpose is to exhibit philosophy as an integral part of social and political life; not as the isolated speculations of remarkable individuals." Preface

Solomon, Robert C.

A **passion** for wisdom; a very brief history of philosophy. {by} Robert C. Solomon, Kathleen M. Higgins. Oxford Univ. Press 1997 137p hardcover o.p. pa $12.95   **109**

1. Philosophy -- History

ISBN 0-19-511209-1 pa

LC 96-42034

The authors "provide a multicultural account of philosophical thought and developments across nearly 4000 years. The volume is necessarily simplified but not simplistic, and the thoughts themselves are given precedent over the biographies of the thinkers." SLJ

Includes bibliographical references

World philosophers and their works; editor, John K. Roth; managing editor, Christina J. Moose; project editor, Rowena Wildin. Salem Press 2000 3v il set $331   **109**

1. Philosophers

ISBN 0-89356-878-3

LC 99-55143

The editor "presents substantial entries that for 226 philosophers give brief biographies, justify the inclusion of each thinker, list their most important works, analyze their lifework, and locate them within the context of philosophy." Choice

Includes bibliographical references

111   Ontology

Barrow, John D.

The **book** of nothing; vacuums, voids, and the latest ideas about the origins of the universe. Pantheon Bks. 2001 361p il hardcover o.p. pa $15 **111**

1. Zero (The number) 2. Science -- History

ISBN 0-375-72609-8 pa

LC 00-58894

This volume traces the concept of nothing "from a Babylonian place holder, a Mayan decoration in the empty space where no number fell and an Indian dot signifying all the current aspects of zero, to one of the most essential elements in mathematics, physics and cosmology." Publ Wkly

The **infinite** book; a short guide to the boundless, timeless, and endless. Pantheon Books 2005 328p il $26   **111**

1. Infinite

ISBN 0-375-42227-7

LC 2004-60206

First published 2004 in the United Kingdom

The author "approaches the subject [of infinity] from the viewpoints of mathematics, physics, and scientific cosmology and also delves into philosophers' and theologians' reflections concerning infinity. . . . Well suited to a general audience, this book requires no specialized knowledge of mathematics or science." Libr J

Includes bibliographical references

Eco, Umberto

History of beauty; translated by Alastair McEwen. Rizzoli Int. Pubs. 2004 438p il $40   **111**

1. Aesthetics 2. Arts -- Philosophy

ISBN 0-8478-2646-5

Published in the United Kingdom with title: On beauty: a history of a western idea

The editor "traces the protean subject of beauty in art, literature, philosophy, the mass media, and other humanities from ancient times to the present, setting forth various Western cultural aesthetic ideals ranging from ancient Greek to modern American. . . . This is not a quick, one-time coffee-table read but a nearly flawless presentation of the history of a fascinating and elusive idea that will delight and enlighten general readers as well as scholars." Libr J

Includes bibliographical references

Encyclopedia of aesthetics; editor in chief, Michael Kelly. Oxford Univ. Press 1998 4v set $495 **111**
1. Reference books 2. Aesthetics -- Encyclopedias
ISBN 0-19-511307-1

LC 98-18741

"Drawing from experts in the areas of philosophy, art, history, psychology, feminist theory, legal theory, and many more, the encyclopedia presents 600 signed essays alphabetically arranged. Most entries include a headnote clarifying the topic. Entries range from the philosophical essay on ugliness, to the more reality-based article on the impact of AIDS on the arts. Comprehensive coverage includes key figures, concepts, periods, theories, and movements in the history of aesthetics." Am Libr

Heidegger, Martin
★ **Being** and time; translated by John Macquarrie & Edward Robinson. Harper & Row 1962 589p hardcover o.p. pa $19.99 **111**
1. Ontology 2. Phenomenology
ISBN 0-06-063850-8; 0-06-157559-3 pa
Original German edition, 1927

"All of Heidegger's work revolves around the essential inquiry: what is the nature of being? In his most important book, . . . he distinguishes between two types of being: human existence (Dasein) and nonhuman presence (Vorhandensein)." Reader's Ency. 4th edition
Includes bibliographical references

On **ugliness**; edited byUmberto Eco; translated by Alastair McEwen. Rizzoli 2007 455p il $45 **111**
1. Aesthetics 2. Arts -- Philosophy
ISBN 978-0-8478-2986-6; 0-8478-2986-3

LC 2007-930249

In this "collection of images and written excerpts from ancient times to the present, all woven together with a provocative commentary and translated by Alastair McEwen, . . . [the editor] asks: Is repulsiveness, too, in the eye of the beholder? And what do we learn about that beholder when we delve into his aversions? Selecting stark visual images of gore, deformity, moral turpitude and malice, and quotations from sources ranging from Plato to radical feminists, Eco unfurls a taxonomy of ugliness. As gross-out contests go, it's both absorbing and highbrow." N Y Times Book Rev
Includes bibliographical references

Watson, Lyall
Dark nature; a natural history of evil. HarperCollins Pubs. 1996 318p hardcover o.p. pa $19 **111**
1. Human beings 2. Good and evil 3. Biology -- Philosophy
ISBN 0-06-092790-9 pa

LC 96-1663

First published 1995 in the United Kingdom

The author "ranges through philosophy, psychology, anthropology, history, ecology and especially biology.... Watson believes that aggression is in our genes and examines such phenomena as war, rape and murder as manifestations of that aggression. But while he firmly believes that humans are made up of both good and evil and that natural selection is completely amoral, he is sanguine about humans as the world's first ethical animals with the capability of making moral decisions." Publ Wkly
Includes bibliographical references

113   Cosmology (Philosophy of nature)

Holt, Jim
Why does the world exist? an existential detective story. Jim Holt. 1st ed. Liveright Pub. Corp. 2012 vi, 309 p.p ill. (hardcover) $27.95 **113**
1. Cosmology
ISBN 0871404095; 9780871404091; 9780871403599

LC 2012015177

It was the author's intent to answer the question "'why is there something rather than nothing?'" Author Jim Holt explores "the claims of evolutionary biology, neuropsychology, theoretical physics, natural religion theology, contemporary mysticism, and militant atheism. . . . He interviews several philosophers and scientists currently engaged in answering the question." (Library Journal)
Includes bibliographical references and index.

Teilhard de Chardin, Pierre
★ The **phenomenon** of man; with an introduction by Julian Huxley. Harper & Row 1959 318p hardcover o.p. pa $14.95 **113**
1. Universe 2. Evolution 3. Human beings
ISBN 0-06-090495-X pa
Original French edition, 1955; this translation by Bernard Wall

The author integrates scientific findings with the tenets of Christian faith in this study of human evolution and destiny

Whitehead, Alfred North
★ **Process** and reality; an essay in cosmology. corrected ed; Free Press 1978 xxxi, 413p hardcover o.p. pa $18.95 **113**
1. Universe 2. Science -- Philosophy
ISBN 0-02-934570-7 pa

LC 77-90011

First published 1929

This book presents a condensed scheme of cosmological ideas developed by confrontation with various topics of experience. The aesthetic, moral and religious interests are thus brought into relation with those elements of knowledge which have their origin in natural science
Includes bibliographical references

Wilson, Edward O.
★ **In** search of nature. Island Press 1996 214p il $22; pa $15 **113**
1. Human beings 2. Sociobiology 3. Human ecology 4. Philosophy of nature 5. Biological diversity
ISBN 1-55963-215-1; 1-55963-216-X pa

LC 96-11226

"A compilation of a dozen journal articles and book chapters published between 1975 and 1993, this collection is grouped into three thematic sections dealing with the importance of the preservation of biodiversity to our physical and emotional well-being, the deep-seated interconnectedness of animal nature and human nature . . . and the underlying genetic basis of human social behavior." Libr J

"Concerned people of all ages should enjoy the reasoning provided by the dedicated scientific writing presented in this attractive book." Sci Books Films

Includes bibliographical references

115 Time

Gorst, Martin

★ **Measuring** eternity; the search for the beginning of time. Broadway Bks. 2002 338p il $23.95; pa $13.95 **115**
1. Time
ISBN 0-7679-0827-9; 0-7679-0844-9 pa
LC 2001-37556

"For the most part Gorst avoids retrospective judgments on what now seem to be spectacular errors of calculation. Instead, he peppers his account with snippets and asides that bring the protagonists to life and make the story of time surprisingly easy to trace." New Sci

Includes bibliographical references

121 Epistemology (Theory of knowledge)

Blackburn, Simon, 1944-

★ **Truth**; a guide. Simon Blackburn. Oxford University Press 2005 xxi, 238p $25 **121**
1. Truth
ISBN 0-19-516824-0
LC 2004-19800

The author "wants to help readers attain a philosophical understanding of the concept of 'truth.' . . . Blackburn reviews what philosophers, writers, novelists, scientists, and disparate thinkers have had to say about it, including Plato, Francis Bacon, Voltaire, Locke, Hume, Wittgenstein, William James, Rorty, and Nietzsche." Libr J

This book "traverses a broad terrain, exploring many points of the map of human knowledge and thinkers of all stripes." N Y Times Book Rev

Includes bibliographical references

Dennett, Daniel Clement, 1942-

Intuition Pumps and Other Tools for Thinking; Daniel C. Dennett. W W Norton & Co Inc 2013 512 p. $28.95 **121**
1. Thought experiments 2. Thought and thinking 3. Philosophy -- Miscellanea
ISBN 0393082067; 9780393082067
LC 2013000930

In this book, "opening with . . . [a] tutorial on argumentative strategies from reductio ad absurdum to Occam's Razor to rhetorical questions, [Daniel C.] Dennett expounds his ideas through a series of 'intuition pumps,' his term for the hypothetical scenarios philosophers contrive to explore difficult concepts." These include "conceiving of the body as a robotic survival vehicle for the genes, or the brain as a clueless man trapped in a sealed chamber." (Publishers Weekly)

Includes bibliographical references and index

Hecht, Jennifer Michael

Doubt : a history; the great doubters and their legacy of innovation, from Socrates and Jesus to Thomas Jefferson and Emily Dickinson. HarperSanFrancisco 2003 xxi, 551p il $27.95; pa $16.95 **121**
1. Belief and doubt
ISBN 0-06-009772-8; 0-06-009795-7 pa
LC 2004-266061

The author's "brief but splendid study of the great Renaissance skeptic Montaigne is alone worth the price of the book. Hecht's warm prose, lucid insights, and impeccable research combine for a lively, thoughtful, and first-rate study of a neglected idea." Libr J

Locke, John, 1632-1704

An **essay** concerning human understanding; edited by Roger Woolhouse. Penguin Books 1997 xxvii, 784p pa $17 **121**
1. Theory of knowledge 2. Thought and thinking
ISBN 0-14-043482-8
LC 98-175907

This essay first published 1690, deals "with the nature and scope of human knowledge. Its basic premise is the empirical origin of ideas, which can be described as the raw material with which the mind works. Locke's essay contributed greatly to the growth of 18th-century empiricism." Reader's Ency. 4th edition

Includes bibliographical references

Sartre, Jean Paul, 1905-1980

★ **Truth** and existence; original text established and annotated by Arlette Elkaïm-Sartre; translated by Adrian van den Hoven; edited and with an introduction by Ronald Aronson. University of Chicago Press 1992 xlix, 94p hardcover o.p. pa $11 **121**
1. Theory of knowledge
ISBN 0-226-73523-0 pa
LC 92-5889

Written in 1948; original French edition, 1989

This book "presents Sartre's ontology of truth in terms of his characteristic key moral questions of freedom, action, and bad faith. Here is Sartre the existentialist at his most original and most provocative." Univ Press Books for Public and Second Sch Libr

Includes bibliographical references

Wilson, Edward O., 1929-

Consilience; the unity of knowledge. Knopf 1998 332p $27.50; pa $15 **121**
1. Philosophy 2. Theory of knowledge 3. Science -- Philosophy
ISBN 0-679-45077-7; 0-679-76867-X pa
LC 97-2816

The author's "extraordinarily clear, evocative imagery and elegant sentences make us see how a consilient world of knowledge might look. . . . Wilson's book of faith in the dream of reason and objective knowledge is a tour de force." Publ Wkly

Includes bibliographical references

128   Humankind

Abram, David

The **spell** of the sensuous; perception and language in a more-than-human world. Pantheon Bks. 1996 326p hardcover o.p. pa $14.95   **128**
  1. Perception 2. Mind and body 3. Philosophy of nature 4. Language and languages
  ISBN 0-679-77639-7 pa

LC 95-31466

This book grew out of Abram's "explorations of magic and sorcery in indigenous cultures and the relationship between magic and the natural world. Where he leads the reader after this is tough to summarize: Edmund Husserl, Maurice Merleau-Ponty, Balinese sorcerers, origins of the alphabet, Kant, Newton. Word by word this is readable and connected to a fascinating thesis: that our perceptions grew from the natural world around us, and we can 'return to our senses' and be reinvigorated, reformed, by the experience." Libr J
Includes bibliographical references

Bloom, Howard

The **Lucifer** principle; a scientific expedition into the forces of history. Atlantic Monthly Press 1995 466p hardcover o.p. pa $16   **128**
  1. Culture 2. Evolution 3. Human beings 4. Good and evil 5. Modern civilization 6. History -- Philosophy
  ISBN 0-87113-664-3 pa

LC 94-11464

The 'Lucifer principle' is the author's "theory that evil—which manifests in violence, destructiveness and war—is woven into our biological fabric. . . . [In this study] Bloom applies the ideas of sociobiology, ethology and the 'killer ape' school of anthropology to the broad canvas of history." Publ Wkly
"A disturbing book, but its broad generalities wear down the sharp edges of its arguments, leaving something that becomes food for thought rather than reason to despair." Booklist
Includes bibliographical references

Cannadine, David, 1950-

The **undivided** past; humanity beyond our differences. by David Cannadine. 1st ed. Alfred A. Knopf 2013 352 p. (hardcover) $26.95   **128**
  1. Sociology 2. Human behavior 3. World history
  ISBN 0307269078; 9780307269072

LC 2012029278

This book is David Cannadine's "examination of the fundamental ways in which humanity divides itself. While these all stem from an innate 'us vs. them' mentality, Cannadine takes the investigation a step further, looking at how we think of ourselves in terms of religion, class, nation, race, gender, and civilization. . . . He points out that . . . a wide variety of factors can create numerous factions and differences within any grouping." (Publishers Weekly)
Includes bibliographical references and index

Christian, Brian

The **most** human human; what talking with computers teaches us about what it means to be alive. Doubleday 2011 303p $27.95; ebook $13.99 **128**
  1. Human beings 2. Artificial intelligence
  ISBN 978-0-385-53306-5; 978-0-385-53307-2 ebook

LC 2010-48572

"In a fast-paced, witty, and thoroughly winning style, Christian documents his experience in the 2009 Turing Test, a competition in which judges engage in five-minute instant-message conversations with unidentified partners, and must then decide whether each interlocutor was a human or a machine. . . . This fabulous book demonstrates that we are capable of experiencing and sharing far deeper thoughts than even the best computers—and that too often we fail to achieve the highest level of humanness." Publ Wkly

Devlin, Keith J.

Goodbye, Descartes; the end of logic and the search for a new cosmology of the mind. Wiley 1997 301p hardcover o.p. pa $14.95   **128**
  1. Logic 2. Authors 3. Linguistics 4. Mind and body 5. Artificial intelligence 6. Essayists 7. Linguists 8. Dissenters 9. Social critics 10. College teachers 11. Nonfiction writers 12. Writers on politics
  ISBN 0-471-14216-6; 0-471-25186-0 pa

LC 96-25493

"Devlin traces the history of logic, particularly mathematical logic, over two-plus millennia and the shorter history of Chomsky's Cartesian linguistics to explain why at least some 'mathematicians and scientists have come to realize that the truly difficult problems of the information age . . . concern ourselves—what it is to think, to reason, and to engage in conversation.'" Booklist
"An excellent book that should be read by everyone who has ever wondered how we communicate with one another but find it so frustrating to interact with computers." Libr J
Includes bibliographical references

Frayn, Michael

The **human** touch; our part in the creation of a universe. Metropolitan Books 2007 505p $32.50   **128**
  1. Cosmology 2. Science -- Philosophy
  ISBN 978-0-8050-8148-0; 0-8050-8148-8

LC 2006-48204

First published 2006 in the United Kingdom
"Beginning with a description of the continual 'traffic' between humans and the universe, Frayn shapes a cohesive introduction to philosophy that includes elements of science, determinism, physics, mathematics, psychology, linguistics, and epistemology." Libr J
Includes bibliographical references

Irvine, William Braxton

On desire; why we want what we want. [by] William B. Irvine. Oxford University Press 2005 322p $24   **128**
  1. Desire
  ISBN 0-19-518862-4

LC 2005-05938

The author "explains how desire–really a multitude of desires, uninvited and unannounced–manifests itself, how it can be identified and parsed, and how it can be mastered in a way that offers the best chance at self-fulfillment. He uses modern psychology to delineate desire but then shows how the world's great religions–here mainly Christianity and Buddhism, but also Hinduism, Islam, and Judaism–address this phenomenon. He advocates no particular approach, admitting instead that different tacks probably work for different people. And he never lets the reader think that mastering desire will be easy. This is that rare book that should appeal to a wide range of readers without necessarily trying to do so." Booklist

Louv, Richard, 1949-

The **nature** principle; human restoration and the end of nature-deficit disorder. Algonquin Books of Chapel Hill 2011 317p $24.95 **128**
1. Nature 2. Environmental influence on humans 3. Nature -- Psychological aspects
ISBN 9781565125810; 1565125819
LC 2011-3626

This book argues for the importance of fulfilling the "need to be outdoors" for adults. Author Richard Louv "believes that seven nature-based precepts can reshape our lives, including balancing technology with nature; achieving a mind/body/nature connection; incorporating biophilic design in our homes, communities and workplaces; and giving natural history more importance. . . . He affirms and expands on how nature is essential for our mental and physical health--and our very souls." (Christian Century)

An "exploration of nature's significance in our lives and what role it will play in the future. . . . [Louv discusses] seven precepts of natural power, introducing such concepts as the 'purposeful place,' where natural history is as highly valued as human history. While the author comes across as a bit self-obsessed and the book is written to suburban and urban audiences, his writing style is clear and raises many valid points. . . . Louv heartily exhorts readers to become more engaged in the world around them, as citizen naturalists out to discover their own bioregions. Taking time to find and create an everyday Eden is not only beneficial to the individual, but to the community as a whole." Kirkus

Includes bibliographical references and index.

★ The **Oxford** companion to the mind; edited by Richard L. Gregory. 2nd ed; Oxford University Press 2005 1004p il $75 **128**
1. Reference books 2. Psychology -- Dictionaries
ISBN 0-19-866224-6
LC 2004-275127

First published 1987

This "is one of those texts one wishes for enough hours in the day to read from cover to cover. . . . For those interested in the mind, this is a wonderful reference and a resource for learning more about themselves." Sci Books Films

This book "contains over 1000 alphabetically arranged entries on all aspects of the mind, including topics in neurophysiology, communication, psychology, and philosophy, as well as people relevant to the field." Libr J

Terkel, Studs, 1912-2008

Will the circle be unbroken? reflections on death, rebirth, and a hunger for faith. New Press (NY) 2001 xxiv, 407p $25.95 **128**
1. Death 2. Faith
ISBN 1-56584-692-3

"Terkel talks to 60 people about their encounters with death. His subjects range from emergency room doctors and paramedics to public figures such as author Kurt Vonnegut and guitarist Doc Watson. A stirring celebration of life and exploration of death." Booklist

Trachtenberg, Peter

The **book** of calamities; five questions about suffering and its meaning. Little, Brown 2008 450p $23.99 **128**
1. Suffering
ISBN 978-0-316-15879-4; 0-316-15879-8
LC 2008-13351

This book "succeeds because it asks the right questions, calls on the experience of articulate witnesses and—through skillful narrative and trenchant observation—beguiles the reader into facing heartbreaking reality." Publ Wkly

Includes bibliographical references

Wilson, Edward O., 1929-

The **Meaning** of Human Existence; by Edward O. Wilson. W.W. Norton & Co Inc. 2014 207 p. $23.95 **128**
1. Human beings 2. Meaning (Philosophy)
ISBN 0871401002; 9780871401007
LC 2014016707

In this book, author Edward O. Wilson, "bridges science and philosophy to create a twenty-first-century treatise on human existence. Once criticized for his over-reliance on genetics, Wilson unfurls here his most expansive and advanced theories on human behavior, recognizing that, even though the human and the spider evolved similarly, the poet's sonnet is wholly different from the spider's web." (Publisher's note)

"Wilson's suggested solutions to our paradoxical predicaments are firmly rooted in science and finely crafted with tonic common sense, unusual directness, and no small measure of valor." Booklist

130 Parapsychology and occultism

Dolnick, Barrie

Luck; understanding luck and improving the odds. [by] Barrie Dolnick and Anthony H. Davidson. Harmony Books 2007 236p $19.95 **130**
1. Chance 2. Superstition
ISBN 978-0-307-34750-3; 0-307-34750-8
LC 2007-13235

This "mini reference examines the concept of luck throughout history as observed by a variety of religious sects and practiced in many cultures. The authors help readers develop a personal-luck profile and detail how to apply astrology, numerology, and even herbology toward increasing the odds in one's favor. A practical section on gambling advises readers how to play cards, dice, or the roulette wheel with caution." Libr J

Includes bibliographical references

Goodman, Linda

Linda Goodman's star signs; the secret codes of the universe: forgotten rainbows and forgotten melodies of ancient wisdom. St. Martin's Press 1987 xli, 477p il hardcover o.p. pa $17.95 **130**

1. Astrology 2. Occultism 3. Parapsychology 4. New Age movement

ISBN 0-312-19203-7 pa

LC 87-28375

"Goodman explains numerology, lexigrams (secret codes of words, names, and titles), the power of sound, and the power of color. . . . Along with explanations of karma and other modes of spiritual growth, she interweaves her own experiences with avatars and gurus, as well as common folk who are on their own spiritual path." Booklist

133.1 Apparitions

Aykroyd, Peter

A **history** of ghosts; the true story of seances, mediums, ghosts, and ghostbusters. by Peter H. Aykroyd; with Angela Narth; foreword by Dan Aykroyd. Rodale 2009 237p il $25.99 **133.1**

1. Ghosts 2. Spiritualism

ISBN 978-1-60529-875-7; 1-60529-875-1

LC 2009-18360

The author's "grandfather was a spiritualist: he believed the human personality survives after bodily death, and practiced regular communication with ghosts—much of which he documented in journals. Aykroyd broadens the discussion with historical figures like Sir Arthur Conan Doyle, creator of Sherlock Holmes, who joined the Society of Psychical Research three weeks after his father's death. . . . This is a smart consideration of the paranormal and a curious artifact of the Aykroyd legacy." Publ Wkly

Includes bibliographical references

Brown, Alan

Haunted Georgia; ghosts and strange phenomena of the Peach State. Stackpole Books 2008 138p il pa $10.95 **133.1**

1. Ghosts 2. Georgia

ISBN 978-0-8117-3443-1; 0-8117-3443-9

LC 2007-25887

"This collection draws from the state's historic past, with stories of phantom pirates from the coast and restless Civil War spirits from Sherman's March and Andersonville Prison. Unusual creatures, such as the devilish Wog of Winder and the monstrous Hogzilla of River Oak Plantation, make appearances. There's also the fatal pillar in Augusta, the haunted orphanage in Savannah, the ghost of Mary MacRae

searching for her lost love on St. Simon's Island, and dozens more." Publisher's note

Includes bibliographical references

Haunted Kentucky; ghosts and strange phenomena of the Bluegrass State. illustrated by Alan Brown. Stackpole Books 2009 120p il pa $10.95 **133.1**

1. Ghosts 2. Kentucky

ISBN 978-0-8117-3584-1; 0-8117-3584-2

LC 2009-3415

"This volume includes stories about the headless ghost of Old Fort Herrod, the vanishing hitchhiker of Meshack Road, the Great Meat Storm of 1876, and the sinister witch's grave at Pilot's Knob Cemetery. A host of strange creatures also wander the state, among them Goat Man, Lizard Man, and the Herrington Lake Monster." Publisher's note

Includes bibliographical references

Haunted South Carolina; ghosts and strange phenomena of the Palmetto State. illustrations by Marc Radle. Stackpole Books 2010 115p il pa $10.95 **133.1**

1. Ghosts 2. South Carolina

ISBN 978-0-8117-3635-0; 0-8117-3635-0

LC 2009-32601

"The stories of phantoms from the Indian conflicts, the American Revolution, and the Civil War still wandering the landscape of South Carolina are recounted here. Other strange phenomena include Messie the Lake Murray Monster, the trinocular Third Eye Man, the halfheaded Lost Cadet, the Ghost Hound of Goshen, and the bloodsucking Boo Hag." Publisher's note

Includes bibliographical references

Haunted Tennessee; ghosts and strange phenomena of the volunteer state. illustrations by Heather Adel Wiggins. Stackpole Books 2009 138p il pa $10.95 **133.1**

1. Ghosts 2. Tennessee

ISBN 978-0-8117-3540-7; 0-8117-3540-0

LC 2008-40678

"Readers will encounter the spirits of the Battle of Shiloh, the Fiddlin' Snake Man of Johnson County, Andrew Jackson at the Hermitage, Hank Williams at Ryman Auditorium, and Elvis Presley at Graceland. Strange creatures are also featured, including Bigfoot, the famed Wampus Cat, and the legendary Bell Witch." Publisher's note

Includes bibliographical references

Haunted Texas; ghosts and strange phenomena of the Lone Star State. illustrations by Heather Adel Wiggins. Stackpole Books 2008 122p il pa $10.95 **133.1**

1. Ghosts 2. Texas

ISBN 978-0-8117-3500-1; 0-8117-3500-1

LC 2007-48786

"This collection, drawn from the deserts of the west to the beaches of the Gulf Shore, includes eerie tales of the spirits that haunt the Alamo, Old Rip the horned toad, UFO sightings in north Texas, the never-ending ride of El Muerto, the ghost on board the USS Lexington, and the watchful specter of Miss Bettie at Galveston's Ashton Villa." Publisher's note

Includes bibliographical references

Farnsworth, Cheri

Haunted Connecticut; ghosts and strange phenomena of the Constitution State. by Cheri Revai. Stackpole Books 2006 119p il pa $10.95   **133.1**

1. Ghosts 2. Connecticut

ISBN 978-0-8117-3296-3; 0-8117-3296-7

LC 2006-9390

"Stories of supernatural occurrences in Connecticut, including the curse on Dudleytown, the spirit of Hanna Cranna who causes car crashes in Monroe, the phantom black dog of Meriden, buried-alive Midnight Mary, the lost village of Bara-Hack, and . . . more." Publisher's note

Includes bibliographical references

Haunted Hudson Valley; ghosts and strange phenomena of New York's Sleepy Hollow country. illustrations by Marc Radle. Stackpole Books 2010 121p il pa $10.95   **133.1**

1. Ghosts 2. Hudson River (N.Y. and N.J.)

ISBN 978-0-8117-3621-3; 0-8117-3621-0

LC 2009-40866

"'The whole neighborhood abounds with local tales, haunted spots, and twilight superstitions,' wrote Washington Irving in the 1820s. This part of New York, straddling the Hudson River from New York City to Albany, is still rife with stories of the paranormal, including a temperance reformer who haunts the Bull's Head Inn, a floating ball of fire at the College of Saint Rose, the ghost girl of the Bardavon Opera House in Poughkeepsie, the spirits of West Point, UFOs at Indian Point 3 nuclear power plant, and the phantoms of Smalley's Inn in Carmel." Publisher's note

Includes bibliographical references

Haunted Massachusetts; ghosts and strange phenomena of the Bay State. [by] Cheri Revai, illustrations by Heather Adel Wiggins. Stackpole Books 2005 119p il pa $10.95   **133.1**

1. Ghosts 2. Massachusetts

ISBN 978-0-8117-3221-5; 0-8117-3221-5

LC 2004-25254

A "look at unexplained phenomena in Massachusetts, including the wandering spirit of lost child Lucy Keyes, the monkey-like Dover Demon, the ghost that leaves tips at Stone's Public Tavern, hauntings in Lizzie Borden's house, the Black Flash phantom in Provincetown, and . . . more." Publisher's note

Includes bibliographical references

Haunted New York; ghosts and strange phenomena of the Empire State. [by] Cheri Revai; illustrations by Heather Adel Wiggins. Stackpole Books 2005 117p il pa $10.95   **133.1**

1. Ghosts 2. New York (State)

ISBN 978-0-8117-3249-9; 0-8117-3249-5

LC 2005-9365

A "look at supernatural phenomena in New York, including the ghost of a British soldier at Fort Ontario, Champ the Lake Champlain monster, the haunted castle of Captain

Beardslee, spirits in Manhattan's oldest house, the alien abduction at the Brooklyn Bridge, and many more." Publisher's note

Includes bibliographical references

Haunted New York City; ghosts and strange phenomena of the Big Apple. [by] Cheri Revai; illustrations by Heather Adel Wiggins. Stackpole Books 2008 120p il pa $10.95   **133.1**

1. Ghosts 2. New York (N.Y.)

ISBN 978-0-8117-3471-4; 0-8117-3471-4

LC 2007-25890

"Stories of the paranormal from the five boroughs are compiled in this volume, including the phantom searching for lost gold in the Parrish House in the Bronx, the demonic flying Coney Island Monster in Brooklyn, the haunted St. Paul's Chapel in Manhattan, the raving ghost of Mount Olivet Cemetery in Queens, the restless spirits that peer from the windows of the Kreischer Mansion in Staten Island, and many others." Publisher's note

Includes bibliographical references

Godfrey, Linda S.

Haunted Wisconsin; ghosts and strange phenomena of the badger state. Stackpole Books 2010 122p il pa $10.95   **133.1**

1. Ghosts 2. Wisconsin

ISBN 978-0-8117-3636-7; 0-8117-3636-9

LC 2010-914

"Readers will encounter Kenosha's Headless Nun, the Man Bat of Lacrosse, Rocky the Rock Lake Monster, and John Dillinger's phantom. They will explore Aztalan's ancient mounds, the ghostly bars and taverns of Madison and Milwaukee, and the creepy town of Caryville, one of the most haunted places in America." Publisher's note

Includes bibliographical references

Guiley, Rosemary Ellen

★ The **encyclopedia** of ghosts and spirits; foreword by Troy Taylor. 3rd ed; Facts on File 2007 564p il $75   **133.1**

1. Reference books 2. Ghosts -- Encyclopedias

ISBN 978-0-8160-6737-4; 0-8160-6737-6

LC 2006-103302

First published 1992

This work examines famous hauntings, historical personages and happenings, and various legends and myths about ghosts and spirits throughout the world. Recent events, new findings about old myths and updated information on major figures in the field are covered.

"Believers and skeptics alike seeking information on various phenomena will find this book useful." Booklist

Includes bibliographical references

Martinelli, Patricia A.

Haunted Delaware; ghosts and strange phenomena of the First State. illustrations by Heather Adel Wiggins. Stackpole Books 2006 119p il pa $10.95   **133.1**

1. Ghosts 2. Delaware

ISBN 978-0-8117-3297-0; 0-8117-3297-5

LC 2005-29805

"Tales of unexplained phenomena in Delaware, including the evil murderess Patty Cannon, the judge who was buried twice, the vengeful phantom dog of Frederica, the wizard of Belltown who sold his soul to the Devil, the Girl of the Dunes waiting on her lost love, and . . . more. Includes information on ghost tours in the region." Publisher's note

Includes bibliographical references

Haunted New Jersey; ghosts and strange phenomena of the Garden State. [by] Patricia A. Martinelli and Charles A. Stansfield, Jr. Stackpole Books 2004 120p il pa $10.95   **133.1**

1. Ghosts 2. New Jersey

ISBN 978-0-8117-3156-0; 0-8117-3156-1

LC 2003-23431

This is a "look at unexplained phenomena in New Jersey, featuring information on ghost tours in the state." Publisher's note

Includes bibliographical references

Nesbitt, Mark

Haunted Pennsylvania; ghosts and strange phenomena of the Keystone State. [by] Mark Nesbitt and Patty A. Wilson; illustrations by Heather Adel Wiggins. Stackpole Books 2006 133p il pa $10.95   **133.1**

1. Ghosts 2. Pennsylvania

ISBN 978-0-8117-3298-7; 0-8117-3298-3

LC 2006-10129

"A collection of . . . stories, including the Civil War ghosts of Gettysburg, spirits at John Brown's tannery, the fiddling ghost of Potter County, hauntings at the Eastern State Penitentiary, the mysterious indelible handprint, and many more." Publisher's note

Includes bibliographical references

Norman, Michael

Haunted America; {by} Michael Norman and Beth Scott. TOR Bks. 1994 411p maps hardcover o.p. pa $7.99   **133.1**

1. Ghosts

ISBN 0-8125-5054-4 pa

LC 94-28984

"This collection of chilling tales of the supernatural includes at least one story from each state and from the English-speaking Canadian provinces. The stories recount sightings of ghostly apparitions and mysterious happenings, and their history and evolution is documented." Libr J

Includes bibliographical references

Okonowicz, Ed

Haunted Maryland; ghosts and strange phenomena of the Old Line State. illustrations by Heather Adel Wiggins. Stackpole Books 2007 137p il pa $10.95   **133.1**

1. Ghosts 2. Maryland

ISBN 978-0-8117-3409-7; 0-8117-3409-9

LC 2006-102022

"Tales of unexplained phenomena in Maryland, including the bleeding stone of White House Farm, the vengeful ghost of Bigg Lizz, the Chesapeake sea monster fondly

known as Chessie, America's most haunted lighthouse, the mysterious 'Toaster' who visits Edgar Allan Poe's grave, and . . . more." Publisher's note

Includes bibliographical references

Ramsland, Katherine M., 1953-

Ghost; investigating the other side. {by} Katherine Ramsland. St. Martin's Press 2001 322p il $25.95; pa $6.99   **133.1**

1. Ghosts

ISBN 0-312-26164-0; 0-312-98373-5 pa

LC 2001-41725

"Although prepared to dismiss many so-called paranormal occurrences in favor of natural explanations, {the author} nevertheless encounters, experiences, and investigates a variety of inexplicable visual, photographic, and verbal manifestations. Both skeptics and believers will be intrigued by this first-person exploration of ghostly visitations." Booklist

Includes bibliographical references

Stansfield, Charles A.

Haunted Arizona; ghosts and strange phenomena of the Grand Canyon State. [by] Charles A. Stansfield, Jr.; illustrations by Marc Radle. Stackpole Books 2010 138p il pa $10.95   **133.1**

1. Ghosts 2. Arizona

ISBN 978-0-8117-3620-6; 0-8117-3620-2

LC 2009-33322

"Tales in this volume include the spirits of Tombstone, the ghost train of Curly Bill, the mysterious appearances of the Blue Lady, and the phantoms that crossed the Atlantic to haunt London Bridge." Publisher's note

Includes bibliographical references

Haunted Jersey shore; ghosts and strange phenomena of the Garden State coast. [by] Charles A. Stansfield, Jr.; illustrations by Heather Adel Wiggins. Stackpole Books 2006 115p il pa $10.95   **133.1**

1. Ghosts 2. New Jersey

ISBN 978-0-8117-3267-3; 0-8117-3267-3

LC 2005-19596

A "look into the haunted history of the New Jersey coastline, with tales of pirates and treasure, loves lost at sea, Civil War ghosts, and monsters and other strange beings that lurk in the countryside." Publisher's note

Includes bibliographical references

Haunted Maine; ghosts and strange phenomena of the Pine Tree State. [by] Charles A. Stansfield, Jr. Stackpole Books 2007 117p il pa $10.95   **133.1**

1. Ghosts 2. Maine

ISBN 978-0-8117-3373-1; 0-8117-3373-4

LC 2006-18546

A "look at spooky legends and stories of the paranormal, including the guardian spirit of Portland Head Light, the preacher and the cats from Hell, the ghost of Marie Antoinette, the ghost who toasts independence, and the logger who befriended the Devil." Publisher's note

Includes bibliographical references

Haunted northern California; ghosts and strange phenomena of the Golden State. [by] Charles A. Stansfield, Jr.; illustrations by Heather Adel Wiggins. Stackpole Books 2009 136p il pa $10.95   **133.1**
1. Ghosts 2. California
ISBN 978-0-8117-3586-5; 0-8117-3586-9

LC 2009-3157

"This region includes the North and Central coasts, the Santa Clara and Sacramento valleys, the East Bay, and the Northern Sierra, where readers will experience strange encounters at Alcatraz, in the abandoned town of Bodie, and aboard the aircraft carrier Hornet. Also included are stories of the legendary Bear Man, Native American ghost dancers, and the spirits of novelist Jack London, the bandit Black Bart, and the ill-fated Donner party." Publisher's note

Includes bibliographical references

Haunted Ohio; ghosts and strange phenomena of the Buckeye State. [by] Charles A. Stansfield Jr.; illustrations by Heather Adel Wiggins. Stackpole Books 2008 102p il pa $10.95   **133.1**
1. Ghosts 2. Ohio
ISBN 978-0-8117-3472-1; 0-8117-3472-2

LC 2007-37709

"From across the plains to the metropolitan centers of Cleveland, Columbus, and Cincinnati come a variety of stories and legends, including the phantom in Dayton's Woodland Cemetery who perches atop his tombstone, the pitiful spirits of the Millfield miners, the fearsome ghost of boatman Mike Fink, and many more." Publisher's note

Includes bibliographical references

Haunted Southern California; ghosts and strange phenomena of the Golden State. Stackpole Books 2009 118p il pa $10.95   **133.1**
1. Ghosts 2. California
ISBN 978-0-8117-3539-1; 0-8117-3539-7

LC 2008-30857

"This region includes the Central Coast, the San Joaquin Valley, and metropolitan Los Angeles and San Diego, where readers will encounter the spirits of gold prospectors, cowboys, Spanish padres, and movie stars, as well as the phantom camels of Fort Tejon, the shape-shifting witch of Tulare, underwater UFOs, ghosts aboard the Queen Mary, and the tragic specter of Marilyn Monroe." Publisher's note

Includes bibliographical references

Haunted Vermont; ghosts and strange phenomena of the Green Mountain State. [by] Charles A. Stansfield, Jr.; illustrations by Heather Adel Wiggins. Stackpole Books 2007 115p il pa $10.95   **133.1**
1. Ghosts 2. Vermont
ISBN 978-0-8117-3399-1; 0-8117-3399-8

LC 2006-34011

"A collection of . . . stories from the Green Mountain state, including the Barre Vampire, the Thetford Horror, the

spirit of Robert Lincoln, the ghostly sentries of Bennington Monument, and many others." Publisher's note

Includes bibliographical references

Taylor, L. B.
Haunted Virginia; ghosts and strange phenomena of the Old Dominion. [by] L.B. Taylor, Jr. Stackpole Books 2009 120p il pa $10.95   **133.1**
1. Ghosts 2. Virginia
ISBN 978-0-8117-3541-4; 0-8117-3541-9

LC 2008-35174

"This volume includes stories on the female stranger of Gadsby's Tavern in Alexandria, the mysterious stone showers in Newport, the ghost hound of the Blue Ridge, Mad Lucy of Williamsburg, and the spirits of native sons Thomas Jefferson, Robert E. Lee, and Edgar Allan Poe." Publisher's note

Includes bibliographical references

Taylor, Troy
Haunted Illinois; ghosts and strange phenomena of the prairie state. illustrations by Heather Adel Wiggins. Stackpole Books 2008 140p il pa $10.95   **133.1**
1. Ghosts 2. Illinois
ISBN 978-0-8117-3499-8; 0-8117-3499-4

LC 2007-40206

"This volume explores the supernatural side of the Prairie State, with stories on the horrors of an old slave house, the numerous spirits of Alton's McPike Mansion, the cemetery where the dead walk, the Spring Valley Vampire, the ghosts of the Bartonville Asylum, Chicago's famous Resurrection Mary, and the spirit world of Abraham Lincoln." Publisher's note

Includes bibliographical references

Thuma, Cynthia
Haunted Florida; ghosts and strange phenomena of the Sunshine State. [by] Cynthia Thuma and Catherine Lower; illustrations by Heather Adel Wiggins. Stackpole Books 2008 101p il pa $10.95   **133.1**
1. Ghosts 2. Florida
ISBN 978-0-8117-3498-1; 0-8117-3498-6

LC 2007-40121

"This compilation of supernatural tales shows Florida to be a state rife with eerie occurences and ghostly denizens. Stories include the spirit of Uncle Charlie at Fernandina Beach's Palace Saloon, the infamous Chupacabras of south Florida, a count's strange obsession with his dead wife, and the mysterious Skunk Ape of Collier County." Publisher's note

Includes bibliographical references

Wilson, Patty A.
Haunted North Carolina; ghosts and strange phenomena of the Tar Heel State. illustrations by Heather Adel Wiggins. Stackpole Books 2009 138p il pa $10.95   **133.1**
1. Ghosts 2. North Carolina
ISBN 978-0-8117-3585-8; 0-8117-3585-0

LC 2009-19333

"Readers will encounter the spirit of infant Virginia Dare in the form of a white deer, shipwreck survivors guided by ghosts to safety, a Halifax County reverend's encounter with the Devil, phantom marauders at Hannah's Creek Swamp, the spirit who directed his will from the grave, hauntings in the State Capitol, and mysterious figures at Devil's Stairs." Publisher's note

Includes bibliographical references

Haunted West Virginia; ghosts & strange phenomena of the mountain state. illustrations by Heather Adel Wiggins. Stackpole Books 2007 138p il pa $10.95 **133.1**

1. Ghosts 2. West Virginia
ISBN 978-0-8117-3400-4; 0-8117-3400-5

LC 2007-347

"Stories of supernatural occurences in West Virginia, including the restless spirits of Harpers Ferry, the legendary Mothman of Point Pleasant, the ghosts of Twistabout Ridge, the phantom hitchhikers on the West Virginia Turnpike, and . . . more." Publisher's note

Includes bibliographical references

133.3092 Divinatory arts

Gerson, Stéphane

Nostradamus; how an obscure Renaissance astrologer became the modern prophet of doom. Stephane Gerson. St. Martins Press 2012 368 p. (hardcover) $29.99 **133.3092**

1. Prophecies 2. Prophecies (Occultism) 3. Twentieth century -- Forecasts
ISBN 0312613687; 9780312613686

LC 2012031001

In this book, "historian Stéphane Gerson takes readers on a journey back in time to explore the life and afterlife of Michel de Nostredame, the astrologer whose 'Prophecies' have been interpreted, adopted by successive media, and eventually transformed into the Gospel of Doom for the modern age. . . . Gerson shows that Nostradamus . . . tells us more about our past and our present than about our future." (Publisher's note)

133.4   Demonology and witchcraft

Adler, Margot

Drawing down the moon; witches, Druids, goddess-worshippers, and other pagans in America. [Rev and updated ed]; Penguin Books 2006 646p il pa $18 **133.4**

1. Paganism 2. Witchcraft
ISBN 0-14-303819-2; 978-0-14-303819-1

LC 2006-43786

First published 1979 by Viking

A survey of goddess worship and witchcraft movements discussing their basic philosophies and practices

"Despite its clear anti-Judaic and anti-Christian bias, this book is recommended for general and college audiences in-terested in religion, the occult, and modern social phenomena." Choice {review of 1979 edition}

Includes bibliographical references

Carlson, Laurie M.

A **fever** in Salem; a new interpretation of the New England witch trials. Dee, I.R. 1999 197p hardcover o.p. pa $14.95 **133.4**

1. Witchcraft 2. Salem (Mass.) -- History
ISBN 1-56663-253-6; 1-56663-309-5 pa

LC 99-27520

In this reading of the New England witch trials, Carlson argues that "the 'possessed' of Salem, and perhaps of many other places where witchcraft was suspected, were in thrall not to devilry but to a mysterious disease of the brain, encephalitis lethargica, popularly known as sleeping sickness." New Yorker

"Carlson's compelling narrative begs for assessment by medical experts. A valuable purchase for libraries seeking more than a basic summary of the witch trials." Libr J

Includes bibliographical references

Guiley, Rosemary Ellen

The **encyclopedia** of demons and demonology; foreword by John Zaffis. Facts On File 2009 302p il $82.50; pa $24.95 **133.4**

1. Reference books 2. Demonology -- Encyclopedias
ISBN 978-0-8160-7314-6; 0-8160-7314-7; 978-0-8160-7315-3 pa; 0-8160-7315-5 pa

LC 2008-52488

"This encyclopedia delineates beliefs about demons and demonology. The text emerges from an exploration of the darker aspects of folklore, myths, culture, and religion, covering major issues, people, and events in a historical and phenomenological perspective. Its over 400 A-to-Z entries cover topics such as demons in different cultures and religious traditions, possession, exorcism, and demon types. . . . Clear, concise, and balanced, this will attract a range of non-scholarly audiences, especially those interested in the occult, paranormal, folklore, myths, and religion. A solid addition to public libraries." Libr J

Includes bibliographical references

The **encyclopedia** of witches, witchcraft, and Wicca; 3rd ed; Facts On File 2008 436p il $85; pa $24.95 **133.4**

1. Reference books 2. Witchcraft -- Encyclopedias
ISBN 978-0-8160-7103-6; 0-8160-7103-9; 978-0-8160-7104-3 pa; 0-8160-7104-7 pa

LC 2008-8917

First published 1989 with title: The encyclopedia of witches and witchcraft

"Spanning centuries and continents, the book defines 480 of witchcraft's and wizardry's major historical events, figures, tools, sites, symbols, and abstract terms. The highly engaging, alphabetically organized entries run several paragraphs in length and deftly clarify a term's etymology as well as its spiritual, historical, or spell-making significance." Libr J

Includes bibliographical references

Hutton, Ronald

The **triumph** of the moon; a history of modern pagan witchcraft. Oxford Univ. Press 1999 486p $55.50; pa $17.95   **133.4**

   1. Witchcraft 2. Neopaganism
   ISBN 0-19-820744-1; 0-19-285449-6 pa

LC 99-31586

This "history of paganism in 19th- and 20th-century Britain centers on Wicca, the system of witchcraft Gerald B. Gardner introduced to a startled public in the 1950s. . . . Hutton's exceptional work is by far the most scholarly, comprehensive and judicious analysis of the subject yet published." Publ Wkly

Includes bibliographical references

Karlsen, Carol F.

★ The **devil** in the shape of a woman; witchcraft in colonial New England. Norton 1987 360p hardcover o.p. pa $16.95   **133.4**

   1. Witchcraft 2. New England -- History -- 1600-1775, Colonial period
   ISBN 0-393-02478-4; 0-393-31759-5 pa

LC 87-16615

The author presents a "social history of witchcraft in Puritan New England (1620-1725). She unearths detailed evidence which demonstrates that prosecuted and accused witches generally were older, married women who had violated the religious and/or economic Puritan social hierarchy. . . . A well-written, provocative addition to the . . . scholarship on New England witchcraft." Libr J

Includes bibliographical references

Levack, Brian P.

The **Devil** within; possession and exorcism in the Christian West. by Brian Levack. Yale University Press 2013 360 p. (cl : alk. paper) $35   **133.4**

   1. Exorcism 2. Europe -- Religion 3. Demoniac possession 4. Exorcism -- Europe -- History 5. Demoniac possession -- Europe -- History
   ISBN 0300114729; 9780300114720

LC 2012042933

This book "focuses on possession and exorcism in the Reformation period, but also reaches back to the fifteenth century and forward to our own times. . . . Challenging the commonly held belief that possession signals physical or mental illness, the author argues that demoniacs and exorcists--consciously or not--are following their various religious cultures, and their performances can only be understood in those contexts." (Publisher's note)

"In this riveting, readable study, Levack . . . offers readers a comprehensive view of reports of demon possession and efforts to rid victims of it." Pub Wkly

Robisheaux, Thomas

The **last** witch of Langenburg; murder in a German village. [by] Thomas Robisheaux. W. W. Norton & Co. 2009 427p il map   **133.4**

   1. Homicide 2. Witchcraft 3. Murder -- Germany -- History 4. Germany -- History -- 1517-1740 5. Witchcraft -- Germany -- History
   ISBN 0-393-06551-0; 9780393065510

LC 2008-43052

This "account of one of Europe's last witch panics draws on court documents, eyewitness testimonies, and an early autopsy report to chronicle the 1672 trial of Anna Schmeig and her family, who were accused of sorcery when a neighbor girl died after eating one of Anna's butter cakes." (Publisher's note) Bibliography. Index.

The author "gives us the story of one of the last witch hunts in Europe. In 1672, in a German village, a young woman who had just given birth to her second child died after eating a Shrovetide cake made by her neighbor. Stories of witches poisoning innocents were common in the Franconia region. The neighbor was arrested, and the entire family charged with witchcraft. You can't beat a witch hunt for drama. Every childhood nightmare is called to mind—the dark forest on the edge of town, the inaccessibility of God and, worse, our own friends and family. Forget memoir; this is nonfiction." Seattle Times

Includes bibliographical references

133.5   Astrology

Goodman, Linda

Linda Goodman's sun signs. Taplinger 1968 xxiii, 549p $29.95   **133.5**

   1. Zodiac 2. Astrology
   ISBN 0-8008-4900-0

The author tells how to identify and deal with people according to their astrological signs

"This book is part astrology, part psychology, and always entertaining." Libr J

Lewis, James R.

★ The **astrology** book; the encyclopedia of heavenly influences. 2nd ed; Visible Ink Press 2003 928p il pa $24.95   **133.5**

   1. Reference books 2. Astrology -- Encyclopedias
   ISBN 1-57859-144-9

First published 1994 by Gale Res. with title: The astrology encyclopedia

"Although aimed at the believer, Lewis' work may be confidently consulted by the skeptic seeking basic information about astrology." Booklist

Miller, Susan

Planets and possibilities; explore the worlds beyond your sun sign. Warner Bks. 2001 418p il $30; pa $15.95   **133.5**

   1. Astrology
   ISBN 0-446-52434-4; 0-446-67806-6 pa

The author provides "character analysis of each sign. The cosmic gifts, relationship trends, financial tendencies, and career tendencies associated with each sign are all described in detail. The mythology of each sign is included as well, nicely rounding out the book." Libr J

Snodgrass, Mary Ellen

Signs of the zodiac; a reference guide to historical, mythological, and cultural associations. illustrat-

ed by Raymond Miller Barrett, Jr. Greenwood Press
1997 243p il $46.95 **133.5**
1. Zodiac 2. Astrology
ISBN 0-313-30276-6

LC 97-5598

"After brief descriptions of zodiacal variants from other
parts of the world, plus chapters on the historical foundations
of astrology and its pervasiveness in the arts and sciences,
Snodgrass treats each sign to a full workover: major stars in
each, mythological background and symbology, commonly
accepted character traits of those born under its influence,
and thumbnail biographies of select prominent people who
exemplify those traits." SLJ

Includes bibliographical references

133.6 Palmistry

Reid, Lori
The **art** of hand reading. DK Pub. 1996 120p il
hardcover o.p. pa $15 **133.6**
1. Palmistry
ISBN 0-7894-4837-8 pa

LC 96-15506

This volume uses color photographs of hands and hand-
prints to analyze all the significant lines, mounts, and markings on hands. It shows how the different areas of the palm
reveal the balance between instinctive desires and powers of
intellect and reason

133.8 Psychic phenomena

Bader, Christopher D.
Paranormal America; ghost encounters, UFO
sightings, Bigfoot hunts, and other curiosities in
religion and culture. [by] Christopher D. Bader, F.
Carson Mencken, and Joseph O. Baker. New York
University Press 2010 264p il $70; pa $20 **133.8**
1. Parapsychology 2. Curiosities and wonders
ISBN 978-0-8147-9134-9; 978-0-8147-9135-6 pa;
978-0-8147-8642-0 ebook

LC 2010-16525

Authors "Christopher D. Bader, F. Carson Mencken, and
Joseph O. Baker take their readers on a . . . journey into 'the
world of people who devote themselves to the "quest"' for
contact with angels, aliens, and other unusual beings. . . . To
flesh out the findings of the 2005 Baylor Religion Survey, a
national random sample of American religious beliefs (two
of the authors were principle investigators), and to understand who is attracted to paranormal beliefs, Bader, Menck-
en, and Baker accompany bigfoot hunters into the woods
and listen to stories about alien abductions and ghostly apparitions. . . . By drawing on both the Baylor survey and
qualitative research, these three sociologists conclude that
'the paranormal is normal' and challenge the stereotype that
those drawn to the paranormal come from the margins of
society." (Journal of American History)

The authors "examine America's belief in paranormal
phenomena inside and outside of mainstream religion—
from UFOs and Bigfoot to speaking in tongues and guardian angels. They look at how belief affects lives, examining

common stereotypes faced by believers and considering
whether belief in a mainstream religion makes one likely to
ascribe to more otherworldly occurrences. . . . While this academic work showcases an astounding amount of research,
the quick pacing and engaging language keep it from being
a dry report of BRS findings. It is accessible to any reader
with an interest in the convergence of paranormal beliefs and
religion." Libr J

Includes bibliographical references

Clegg, Brian
Extra Sensory; The Science and Pseudoscience
of Telepathy and Other Powers of the Mind. Brian
Clegg. St. Martin's Press 2013 320 p. (hardcover)
$25.99 **133.8**
1. Parapsychology 2. Extrasensory perception
ISBN 1250019060; 9781250019066

LC 2013004038

This book, by Brian Clegg, "look[s] at the untapped abilities of human beings, from ESP to Telekenesis and other
real life sciences that are currently being studied today. . . . Is
there any solid evidence to back up these talents, or are they
nothing more than fantasy? . . . By looking at possible physical mechanisms for ESP and taking in the best scientific evidence, the reader can discover if this is all wishful thinking
and deception, or a fascinating reality." (Publisher's note)

Sheldrake, Rupert
Dogs that know when their owners are coming
home; and other unexplained powers of animals.
Crown 1999 352p il hardcover o.p. pa $14 **133.8**
1. Pets 2. Extrasensory perception
ISBN 0-609-80533-9 pa

LC 99-25439

"The author reports the results of five years of extensive research as he followed up on anecdotal accounts from
pet owners on the homing abilities of lost pets, animals that
show premonitions of earthquakes or epileptic seizures, and
the fact that animals anticipate the arrival home of their
owners." Booklist

Includes bibliographical references

The **sense** of being stared at; and other aspects of
the extended mind. Crown 2003 369p il hardcover
o.p. pa $13.95 **133.8**
1. Extrasensory perception
ISBN 1-4000-5129-0 pa

LC 2002-9943

"A most unusual book—fascinating, scientifically
sound, and fun to read—it posits that ESP and 'other aspects
of the extended mind' are not paranormal but natural functions. Every library should make room on its shelves for this
one." Libr J

Includes bibliographical references

133.9   Spiritualism

Blum, Deborah

   Ghost hunters; William James and the search for scientific proof of life after death. Penguin Press 2006 370p $25.95; pa $15   **133.9**
   1. Philosophers 2. Spiritualism 3. Psychologists 4. Parapsychology 5. Writers on science
   ISBN 1-59420-090-4; 978-1-59420-090-8; 0-14-303895-8 pa; 978-0-14-303895-5 pa

                 LC 2006-44948

   In this book, the author examines the Victorian era conflict between science and religion "by reviewing the history of the British Society for Psychical Research and its U.S. counterpart, the American Society for Psychical Research, both of which aimed to find scientific proof of the existence of the supernatural. . . . Her clearly written presentation of the history, frauds, and personalities involved in this unique slice of Victorian life is recommended for all history of science collections." Libr J
   Includes bibliographical references

Moody, Raymond A.

   ★ **Life** after life; the investigation of a phenomenon--survival of bodily death. [by] Raymond A. Moody, Jr.; with a new preface by Melvin Morse and a foreword by Elizabeth Kübler-Ross. HarperSanFrancisco 2001 xxviii, 175p pa $14   **133.9**
   1. Death 2. Future life 3. Near-death experiences
   ISBN 0-06-251739-2

                 LC 00-46156

   First published 1975 by MBB Inc.
   The author "investigates more than one hundred case studies of people who experienced 'clinical death' and were subsequently revived." Publisher's note

Roach, Mary, 1959-

   ★ **Spook**; science tackles the afterlife. Norton 2005 311p il   **133.9**
   1. Future life 2. Religion and science 3. Soul 4. Death
   ISBN 0393059626

                 LC 2005-14450

   The author investigates a range of theories and beliefs about the soul's migration after death.
   "Roach perfectly balances her skepticism and her boundless curiosity with a sincere desire to know. . . . She is an original who can enliven any subject with wit, keen reporting and a sly intelligence." Publ Wkly
   Includes bibliographical references

141   Idealism and related systems and doctrines

Berlin, Isaiah

   The **roots** of romanticism; edited by Henry Hardy. Princeton Univ. Press 1999 171p (A.W. Mellon lectures in the fine arts) pa $19.95   **141**
   1. Romanticism 2. Arts -- Philosophy
   ISBN 0-691-00713-6; 978-0-691-08662-0 pa; 0-691-08662-0 pa

                 LC 98-41657

   This is an edited transcript of the lectures "and the supporting bibliographic notes from which Berlin worked on his idea of romanticism. . . . Arguing that the concept flows from late 18th-century German thought and society, Berlin addresses romanticism's effect on the Enlightenment, the roles played by Hamann, Herder, and other early Romanticists in the codification of the movement, the more distilled approaches of Kant and Schiller, and romanticism's lingering effects on Western intellectual posture. . . . An excellent resource for both beginning researcher and seasoned scholar." Libr J
   Includes bibliographical references

   ★ The **essential** transcendentalists; edited and introduced by Richard G. Geldard. J.P. Tarcher/Penguin 2005 265p pa $15.95   **141**
   1. Transcendentalism
   ISBN 1-58542-434-X

                 LC 2005-44016

   This study "is divided into three main sections. . . . The first is 'Primary Texts,' with selections from the writings of Sampson Reed, James Marsh, Amos Alcott (father of Louisa May), and Ralph Waldo Emerson. The second, 'Individual Voices,' introduces selections from Frederic Hedge, Margaret Fuller, and Henry David Thoreau. The last is 'The Transcendental Heritage,' which features the works of Walt Whitman, Emily Dickinson, Wallace Stevens, Loren Eiseley, and Annie Dillard. This is a highly informed, elegantly written, fascinating story told through commentary, historical overview, and selections from classic works. It belongs in all libraries." Libr J
   Includes bibliographical references

142   Critical philosophy

Barrett, William

   ★ **Irrational** man; a study in existential philosophy. Doubleday 1958 278p hardcover o.p. pa $12.95   **142**
   1. Existentialism
   ISBN 0-385-03138-6 pa
   This discussion of existentialism traces its origins and analyzes the contributions of chief exponents of existentialist thought—Nietzsche, Kierkegaard, Heidegger and Sartre

   Existentialism from Dostoevsky to Sartre; rev and expanded; New Am. Lib. 1975 384p pa $15.95   **142**
   1. Poets 2. Authors 3. Novelists 4. Dramatists 5. Theologians 6. Philosophers 7. Existentialism 8. Essayists 9. Biographers 10. Nonfiction writers 11. Short story writers 12. Writers on religion 13. Nobel laureates for literature
   ISBN 0-452-00930-8
   First published 1956 by World Pub.
   This book contains selections from the basic writings of Dostoevsky, Kierkegaard, Nietzsche, Rilke, Ortega y Gasset, Jaspers, Heidegger, Sartre and Camus.

Sartre, Jean Paul, 1905-1980

★ **Being** and nothingness; an essay on phenomenological ontology. translated and with an introduction by Hazel E. Barnes. Philosophical Lib. 1956 638p **142**

1. Existentialism

Original French edition, 1943

This is "Sartre's major attempt to systematize his theoretical analysis of the human condition and human consciousness which underlies 'Existentialism.'" Reader's Ency. 4th edition

Existentialism and human emotions. Philosophical Library: Distributed to the Book trade by Citadel Press 1957 96p pa $9.95 **142**

1. Existentialism

ISBN 0-8065-0902-3 pa

"The section on 'Existentialism' is taken from the book of that name; translated by Bernard Frechtman; all other selections are from 'Being and nothingness' translated by Hazel E. Barnes"

146 Naturalism and related systems and doctrines

Dennett, Daniel Clement

Darwin's dangerous idea; evolution and the meanings of life. {by} Daniel C. Dennett. Simon & Schuster 1995 586p il hardcover o.p. pa $16 **146**

1. Authors 2. Evolution 3. Geologists 4. Mathematicians 5. Natural selection 6. Paleontologists 7. College teachers 8. Writers on science

ISBN 0-684-82471-X pa

LC 94-49158

"Current controversies associated with the origin of life, sociobiology, punctuated equilibrium, the evolution of culture and language, and evolutionary ethics are investigated rigorously within the context of Darwinian science and philosophy. Dennett challenges the ideas of several imminent scientists, including Roger Penrose and Stephen Jay Gould, who, Dennett asserts, tend to limit the power or implications of Darwin's dangerous ideas." Libr J

Includes bibliographical references

150 Psychology

Colman, Andrew M.

★ A **dictionary** of psychology; 2nd ed; Oxford University Press 2006 861p il $45; pa $17.95 **150**

1. Reference books 2. Psychology -- Dictionaries

ISBN 978-0-19-280632-1; 0-19-280632-7; 978-0-19-861035-9 pa; 0-19-861035-1 pa

LC 2005-31810

First published 2001

"This work defines the most common as well as the most important issues facing psychology today.... [The book features] over 11,000 cross-referenced entries, covering everything from anxiety and cognitive impairment to hypolexia (another name for dyslexia) and postpartum depression....

For professionals and students of psychology, this is a good place to start their research." SLJ

Includes bibliographical references

Cordon, Luis A.

★ **Popular** psychology; an encyclopedia. Greenwood Press 2005 274p il $75 **150**

1. Reference books 2. Psychology -- Encyclopedias

ISBN 0-313-32457-3

LC 2004-17426

This book "provides a concise guide for anyone seeking to understand the true scientific nature of psychology." Libr Media Connect

Includes bibliographical references

The **Gale** encyclopedia of psychology; Bonnie R. Strickland, executive editor. 2nd ed; Gale Group 2001 701p il $191.50 **150**

1. Reference books 2. Psychology -- Encyclopedias

ISBN 0-7876-4786-1

LC 00-34736

First published 1996

Coverage includes noteworthy people, movements, theories, and important case studies and experiments. The articles, ranging from 25 to 1,500 words examine such diverse topics as abnormal psychology, bipolar disorder, Sigmund Freud and insomnia

Includes bibliographical references

Glasser, William

Choice theory; a new psychology of personal freedom. HarperCollins Pubs. 1998 340p il $24; pa $13.95 **150**

1. Psychology

ISBN 0-06-019109-0; 0-06-093014-4 pa

LC 97-36025

"Choice theory helps its users avoid confrontation and ask pertinent questions. It sees conscious or unconscious desire for external control as the main problem in the four major personal relationships: husband-wife, parent-child, teacher-student, and manager-worker.... Combining choice theory and reality therapy in his practice, Glasser has been able to shorten the durations of his treatment programs substantially. As he presents them here, his theories and approaches can be applied in education and business as well as for self-help." Booklist

Kubler-Ross, Elisabeth

The **wheel** of life; a memoir of living and dying. Scribner 1997 286p il hardcover o.p. pa $13 **150**

1. Psychiatrists 2. College teachers 3. Writers on medicine

ISBN 0-684-84631-4 pa

LC 97-6435

In this autobiography "Kübler-Ross describes her growing-up years in Switzerland as one of a set of triplet sisters, her fight to become a doctor, and later, the even stronger opposition she met when she began her research on death and dying. Despite the weightiness inherent in working with and writing about mortality, the book has a light, almost airy feel to it, which goes along with the author's central theme that death is merely a transformation." Booklist

Salem health; psychology & mental health. editor, Nancy A. Piotrowski. Salem Press 2010 5v il set $495   **150**
1. Reference books 2. Psychology -- Encyclopedias
ISBN 978-1-58765-556-2

First published 1993 with title: Survey of social science, Psychology series. Previous edition published with title: Magill's encyclopedia of social science: psychology

"The well-written, well-researched, concise text offers an easily accessible collection of information." Choice

Includes bibliographical references

150.19   Systems, schools, viewpoints

Bettelheim, Bruno
Freud and man's soul. Knopf 1983 111p hardcover o.p. pa $9   **150.19**
1. Psychoanalysis 2. Psychoanalysts 3. Writers on medicine
ISBN 0-394-71036-3 pa

LC 82-47809

The author argues that Freud was a great humanist and that mistranslation of his work has lead American psychoanalysis astray

Freud, Sigmund
★ The **basic** writings of Sigmund Freud; translated and edited by A.A. Brill. Modern Lib. 1995 973p $24.95   **150.19**
1. Dreams 2. Psychoanalysis
ISBN 0-679-60166-X

LC 95-13411

A reissue of the 1938 edition

"Freud's findings and, even more, the way he presents them to us give us the confidence that this demanding and potentially dangerous voyage of self-discovery will result in our becoming more fully human, so that we may no longer be enslaaved without knowing it to the dark forces that reside in us." Bruno Bettelheim

★ The **Freud** reader; edited by Peter Gay. Norton 1989 832p hardcover o.p. pa $21.95   **150.19**
1. Psychoanalysis
ISBN 0-393-31403-0 pa

LC 89-2949

This "work includes some 50 of Freud's texts, organized chronologically with headnotes. The selections range from case studies and theoretical discussions about dreams, anxiety and anal eroticism to essays on lay analysis and religion as humankind's obsessional neurosis." Libr J

Includes bibliographical references

Fromm, Erich
On being human; foreword by Rainer Funk. Continuum 1994 180p hardcover o.p. pa $29.95 **150.19**
1. Humanism 2. Psychoanalysis 3. Social psychology
ISBN 0-8264-0576-2; 0-8264-1005-7 pa

LC 93-9243

This volume includes the author's writings on humanism, social psychology, and psychoanalysis from the 1960s,

based on Fromm's lectures, works written for specific occasions, and manuscripts intended as books.

Includes bibliographical references

Gay, Peter
A **Godless** Jew; Freud, atheism, and the making of psychoanalysis. Yale Univ. Press 1987 182p hardcover o.p. pa $17   **150.19**
1. Atheism 2. Psychoanalysis 3. Psychoanalysts 4. Writers on medicine
ISBN 0-300-04008-3; 0-300-04608-1 pa

LC 87-8267

The author "reviews the various claims for the Jewishness of psychoanalysis and finds them to be wholly without merit. Paradoxically, he argues that Freud's position as an outsider—an atheist and Jew—enabled him to pierce the taboo topics of sexuality and the unconscious which led to his momentous discoveries." Publ Wkly

Includes bibliographical references

Hayman, Ronald
A **life** of Jung. Norton 2001 xxi, 522p il hardcover o.p. pa $18.95   **150.19**
1. Psychiatrists 2. Psychologists 3. Writers on medicine
ISBN 0-393-32322-6 pa

LC 00-54802

First published 1999 in the United Kingdom

"One of the many strengths of this candid and discerning biography is that Hayman enlists . . . provocative, alarming material to build a careful, nuanced portrait of his subject that neither excuses nor excoriates his actions and words." Publ Wkly

Includes bibliographical references

Jung, C. G. (Carl Gustav), 1875-1961
★ The **basic** writings of C. G. Jung; edited with an introduction by Violet Staub de Laszlo. Modern Lib. 1993 xxxiii, 691p $21.95   **150.19**
1. Psychoanalysis
ISBN 0-679-60071-X

LC 93-17801

This is a reissue of the 1959 edition

This volume contains excerpts from Symbols of transformation, On the nature of the psyche, Relations between the ego and the unconscious, Psychological types, Psychology of the transference, and Psychology and religion. It also includes Archetypes of the collective unconscious, Psychological aspects of the mother archetype, On the nature of dreams, On the psychogenesis of schizophrenia, Introduction to the religious and psychological problems of alchemy, and Marriage as a psychological relationship.

Includes bibliographical references

The **essential** Jung; selected and introduced by Anthony Storr. Princeton Univ. Press 1983 447p hardcover o.p. pa $18.95   **150.19**
1. Psychoanalysis
ISBN 0-691-02935-0 pa

LC 82-61441

Storr's "selections from Jung's writings are lucid and accessible; linked by skillful explanatory passages, they provide both interested laypersons and students with a perspective on Jung." Libr J

Includes bibliographical references

★ **Man** and his symbols; {by} Carl G. Jung {et al.} Doubleday 1964 320p il $30; pa $7.99 **150.19**
1. Self 2. Dreams 3. Symbolism 4. Psychology 5. Art -- Psychology
ISBN 0-385-05221-9; 0-440-35183-9 pa

"The basic ideas of Jungian psychology are presented in popular language in six essays by Dr. Jung and {four} of his pupils; these are correlated to dreams and symbols and are shown in their archetypal relationships to ancient myths, present-day thought and art." Libr J

Includes bibliographical references

Memories, dreams, reflections; recorded and edited by Aniela Jaffé; translated from the German by Richard and Clara Winston. rev ed; Vintage Bks. 1989 430p pa $14 **150.19**
1. Psychiatrists 2. Psychologists 3. Writers on medicine
ISBN 0-679-72395-1

LC 88-37040

First published 1963 by Pantheon Bks.

"This volume of recollections reveals the intellectual and spiritual development of an eminent Swiss psychologist and psychiatrist while only touching upon the outward events of his long and productive life. . . . An important, firsthand document for readers who wish to understand this seminal writer and thinker." Booklist

Includes bibliographical references

The **portable** Jung; edited with an introduction by Joseph Campbell; translated by R. F. C. Hull. Viking 1971 xli, 659p hardcover o.p. pa $17 **150.19**
1. Psychoanalysis
ISBN 0-14-015070-6 pa

A collection of writings spanning the career of the pioneering psychoanalyst. Includes a chronology and bibliography.

May, Rollo
★ The **discovery** of being; writings in existential psychology. Norton 1983 192p hardcover o.p. **150.19**
1. Psychotherapy 2. Existentialism

LC 83-4282

The author "provides the reader with principles of his existential psychotherapy; delineates his view of the cultural-historical context that gave rise to both psychoanalysis and existentialism; and sets forth what he considers to be the contributions to therapy of an existential approach." Choice

Includes bibliographical references

Rogers, Carl R.
A **way** of being. Houghton Mifflin 1980 395p hardcover o.p. pa $15 **150.19**
1. Humanism 2. Psychology
ISBN 0-395-75530-1 pa

LC 80-20275

The author offers a "collection of papers, talks, autobiographical sketches and vignettes of patients' experiences in workshops and therapy." Publ Wkly

"This is a book rich in theoretical insights and experiential sharing, and full of invigorating optimism." Libr J

Includes bibliographical references

Skinner, B. F.
★ **About** behaviorism. Knopf 1974 256p hardcover o.p. pa $12 **150.19**
1. Behaviorism
ISBN 0-394-71618-3 pa

The author defines, analyzes and defends the science of behaviorism with chapters exploring the causes of behavior, operant behavior, verbal behavior, thinking, causes and reasons, knowledge, emotion and self

Includes bibliographical references

Thurschwell, Pamela
Sigmund Freud; 2nd ed.; Routledge 2009 162p (Routledge critical thinkers) $95; pa $22.95 **150.19**
1. Psychoanalysis 2. Psychoanalysts 3. Writers on medicine
ISBN 978-0-415-47368-2; 978-0-415-47369-9 pa

First published 2000

"The book contains chapters on early theories, interpretation, sexuality, case histories, maps of the mind, society and religion, and psychoanalysis's aftermath, including feminist criticism and a remarkable summary of Jacques Lacan's role." Booklist [review of 2000 edition]

Includes bibliographical references

150.9 History, geographic treatment, biography

Kagan, Jerome
An **argument** for mind. Yale University Press 2006 287p $27.50; pa $17 **150.9**
1. Psychology -- History
ISBN 978-0-300-11337-2; 0-300-11337-4; 978-0-300-12603-7 pa; 0-300-12603-4 pa

LC 2005-33441

The author "gives an overview of his theories and research on human development as well as the history of the field of psychology in the last half century." Libr J

"Jerome Kagan writes elegantly, with humor . . . and with profound intellectual depth and range." Sci Books Films

Includes bibliographical references

152.1 Sensory perception

Ackerman, Diane, 1948-
A **natural** history of the senses. Random House 1990 331p hardcover o.p. pa $14.95 **152.1**
1. Senses and sensation
ISBN 0-394-57335-8; 978-0-679-73566-3 pa; 0-679-73566-6 pa

LC 89-43416

"Ackerman celebrates the senses by examining their biological bases and the various and bizarre ways we have come to indulge them. Her catalog of the senses is itself a sensuous journey, with prose rich in imagery and rhythm. Ackerman's book is a provocative and entertaining treat whose details will bestir the reader's imagination." Libr J

Includes bibliographic references

Herz, Rachel S.

The **scent** of desire; discovering our enigmatic sense of smell. [by] Rachel Herz. William Morrow 2007 xxi, 266p $24.95; pa $13.95   **152.1**

1. Smell

ISBN 978-0-06-082537-9; 0-06-082537-5; 978-0-06-082538-6 pa; 0-06-082538-3 pa

LC 2007-33563

The author argues that the sense of smell "is vital to our well being—so important to mental and physical health that its loss can drive some people to suicide. Herz explores the relationships between scent, emotion and behavior, emphasizing that scent is an important component of sexual attraction and thus crucial for the survival of our species." Publ Wkly

"This is one of those all-too-rare books that is involving, well written, and solidly grounded in research." Libr J

Includes bibliographical references

152.14   Visual perception

Hoffman, Donald D.

Visual intelligence; how we create what we see. Norton 1998 294p il hardcover o.p. pa $17.95   **152.14**

1. Vision 2. Perception

ISBN 0-393-31967-9 pa

LC 98-6181

The author "argues that the brain, via the eyes, doesn't see what is 'really' in a scene being viewed but rather constructs one image from 'countless possible interpretations' from the scene gathered at the retina." Booklist

This book offers "wit, insight and charm. . . . An outstanding example of creative popular science." Publ Wkly

Includes bibliographical references

152.3   Movements and motor functions

Provine, Robert R.

Curious behavior; yawning, laughing, hiccupping, and beyond. Robert R. Provine. Harvard University Press 2012 288 p. (alk. paper) $24.95 **152.3**

1. Hiccups 2. Sneezing 3. Human body 4. Human behavior 5. Human biology 6. Neuropsychology 7. Evolutionary psychology

ISBN 0674048512; 9780674048515

LC 2012007754

This book by author Robert R. Provine is "about many instinctive behaviors. . . which science has overlooked. Provine 'redresses historic debts' by focusing on such bodily behaviors as 'Farting and Belching.' Tickling, for example, may tap into a neural mechanism for distinguishing ourselves from others. . . . Contagious yawns--affecting 55% of those

watching yawn videos--may reflect how our brains replicate observed behavior to create empathy." (Publishers Weekly)

Includes bibliographical references

152.4   Emotions

Ackerman, Diane, 1948-

A **natural** history of love. Random House 1994 xxiii, 358p hardcover o.p. pa $14   **152.4**

1. Love 2. Sexual behavior

ISBN 0-679-76183-7 pa

LC 94-171385

Companion volume to A natural history of the senses

"Ackerman sets out on her exploration by reviewing the lessons provided across time by such lovers as Antony and Cleopatra, Orpheus and Eurydice, Dido and Aeneas, Abelard and Heloise and Romeo and Juliet. During this journey, she explores the neurophysiology of love. . . . With dazzling poetic charm and insight, she uses history, literature, science, psychology, and personal experience as tools to illuminate the vigor and vehemence of the thrilling, devastating, and comforting phenomenon of love." Libr J

Bloom, Paul

How pleasure works; the new science of why we like what we like. W. W. Norton 2010 280p il $26.95   **152.4**

1. Pleasure

ISBN 0-393-06632-0; 978-0-393-06632-6

LC 2010-05803

Refuting the "explanation of pleasure as a simple sensory response, Bloom . . . [argues] that pleasure is grounded in our beliefs about the deeper nature or essence of a given thing." (Publisher's note) Index.

Bloom "presents essentialism as a weighty determinant of our pleasures. . . . [He] probes the history of sentimental objects, the contact and context that give them meaning; how we hope that qualities of the things we eat will pervade us; the ways in which we are attracted to the process of making art and storytelling; and the strange case of giving and receiving pain. A heartening, well-developed argument." Kirkus

Includes bibliographical references

Clark, Taylor

Nerve; poise under pressure, serenity under stress, and the brave new science of fear and cool. Little, Brown and Company 2011 310p $25.99; ebook $12.99   **152.4**

1. Fear 2. Anxiety

ISBN 978-0-316-04289-5; 978-0-316-12686-1 ebook

LC 2010-38835

The author interviews and tells "the stories of numerous individuals, exploring how they react to fear, stress, and extreme pressure. He compares the way those who seem immune to stress and fear approach difficult situations with that of the larger general population, who tend to respond instinctively in ways that actually increase negative emotions." Libr J

"A compassionate psychological page-turner." Kirkus

Includes bibliographical references

Damasio, Antonio R.

Looking for Spinoza; joy, sorrow, and the feeling rain. {by} Antonio Damasio. Harcourt 2003 355p il $28; pa $15   **152.4**
1. Authors 2. Emotions 3. Philosophers 4. Essayists 5. Writers on religion
ISBN 0-15-100557-5; 0-15-602871-9 pa
LC 2002-11347

This is a "discussion of the difference between emotions (of the body) and feelings (of the mind), various sites in the brain that trigger these states, and the . . . synthesis of the homeostatic process, memory, sensory input, imagination, and foresight that links the unconscious to consciousness and feelings to reasoning." Booklist

Includes bibliographical references

De Waal, Frans

The age of empathy; nature's lessons for a kinder society. with drawings by the author. Harmony Books 2009 291p il   **152.4**
1. Empathy 2. Animal behavior
ISBN 0-307-40776-4; 978-0-307-40776-4

The author "examines what he calls the behavioral 'glue' of primate societies: empathy, sympathy, a sense of fair play, and trust. In tracing the origins and evolution of empathy, de Waal points out that our ability to take another's perspective is an automatic impulse with a long evolutionary history in the mammalian line. . . . This insightful work . . . will appeal to a wide variety of general readers interested in the links between human evolution and animal behavior."

The author "examines what he calls the behavioral 'glue' of primate societies: empathy, sympathy, a sense of fair play, and trust. In tracing the origins and evolution of empathy, de Waal points out that our ability to take another's perspective is an automatic impulse with a long evolutionary history in the mammalian line. . . . This insightful work . . . will appeal to a wide variety of general readers interested in the links between human evolution and animal behavior." Libr J

Includes bibliographical references

Fromm, Erich

★ The art of loving; Centennial ed; Continuum 2000 130p $18.95   **152.4**
1. Love
ISBN 0-8264-1260-2
LC 00-21030

A reissue of the title first published 1956
"An astonishingly simple presentation of an abstract subject." Booklist

Gardner, Daniel

The science of fear; why we fear the things we shouldn't-- and put ourselves in greater danger. Dutton 2008 339p $24.95   **152.4**
1. Fear
ISBN 978-0-525-95062-2; 0-525-95062-1
LC 2008-03024

Gardner "analyses everything from the media's predilection for irrational scare stories to the cynical use of fear by politicians pushing a particular agenda. . . . [He] never falls into the trap of becoming frustrated and embittered by the waste and needless worry that he is documenting. A per-

sonal anecdote about an unwise foray into a Nigerian slum in search of a stolen wallet disposes of the idea that the author is immune to the foibles he describes. What could easily have been a catalogue of misgovernance and stupidity instead becomes a cheery corrective to modern paranoia," Economist

Includes bibliographical references

Gilligan, Carol

★ The birth of pleasure. Knopf 2002 253p $24; pa $13   **152.4**
1. Love 2. Interpersonal relations
ISBN 0-679-44037-2; 0-679-75943-3 pa
LC 2001-50329

The author examines "why love between a man and a woman is so often burdened by a history of loss and how it can be freed and opened to the pursuit of happiness. Tracing a lineage from Greek mythology to our own most intimate relationships, she asks why we relive tragic stories of loss and betrayal; drawing on her own research, she offers a radical new map of love." Publisher's note

Gilligan's "mastery of literary sources and her intelligent but nonacademic writing style make this an enjoyable, challenging work." Publ Wkly

Includes bibliographical references

Goleman, Daniel

★ Emotional intelligence; 10th anniversary ed.; Bantam Books 2006 xxiv, 358p il $29; pa $18   **152.4**
1. Emotions 2. Marriage 3. Medicine 4. Intellect 5. Parenting 6. Temperament 7. Industrial relations 8. Emotionally disturbed children 9. Education -- Curricula
ISBN 978-0-553-80491-1; 0-553-80491-X; 978-0-553-38371-3 pa; 0-553-38371-X pa
LC 2006-283929

First published 1995

The author explains "how to develop our emotional intelligence in ways that can improve our relationships, our parenting, our classrooms, and our workplaces. Goleman assures us that our temperaments may be determined by neurochemistry, but they can be altered." Booklist

Includes bibliographical references

Jamison, Kay R.

Exuberance; the passion for life. by Kay Redfield Jamison. Knopf 2004 405p il $24.95 **152.4**
1. Happiness
ISBN 0-375-40144-X
LC 2004-46561

The author "examines the contagious nature of exuberance, which she defines as 'a psychological state characterized by high mood and high energy,' offering diverse examples that range from John Muir and FDR to Mary Poppins and Peter Pan. Having in mind the simply put idea that 'those who are exuberant act,' the author details the energetic efforts of scientists, naturalists, politicians and even her meteorologist father." Publ Wkly

Includes bibliographical references

Jeffers, Susan J.

Feel the fear--and do it anyway; [by] Susan Jeffers. Ballantine Books 2007 214p il pa $13.95 **152.4**
1. Fear
ISBN 978-0-345-48742-1

LC 2007-271292

First published 1987 by Harcourt Brace Jovanovich
"By mixing positive thinking with situational exercises that examine basic fear responses, psychologist Jeffers shows that fear is what you make of it and that in most cases it is unfounded." Libr J
Includes bibliographical references

Lerner, Harriet Goldhor

★ The **dance** of anger; a woman's guide to changing the patterns of intimate relationships. [by] Harriet Lerner. Perennial Currents 2005 239p il pa $13.95   **152.4**
1. Anger 2. Women -- Psychology
ISBN 0-06-074104-X

LC 2004-60074

First published 1985
The author examines the ways women express anger, as well as how women's anger is viewed by society and throughout history.
Includes bibliographical references

Levy, Alexander

The **orphaned** adult; understanding and coping with grief and change after the death of our parents. Perseus Bks. 1999 190p hardcover o.p. pa $15.95   **152.4**
1. Death 2. Bereavement 3. Loss (Psychology)
ISBN 0-7382-0361-0 pa

LC 99-64773

"Incorporating his own personal experience with the accounts of others who have lost their parents, psychologist Levy examines this profound life-changing event with compassion and understanding." Libr J

Lewis, Thomas

★ A **general** theory of love; [by] Thomas Lewis, Fari Amini, Richard Lannon. Random House 2000 274p il hardcover o.p. pa $13   **152.4**
1. Love
ISBN 0-375-70922-3 pa

LC 99-49930

The authors "aim to help physicians treat patients by showing how the many and varied aspects of love, including the lack and the warping of it, affect patients' problems and strengths and by discussing what must, therefore, be involved in treating patients." Booklist
Includes bibliographical references

Nettle, Daniel

Happiness; the science behind your smile. Oxford University Press 2005 216p il $21; pa $13.95   **152.4**
1. Happiness
ISBN 0-19-280558-4; 978-0-19-280558-4; 0-19-

280559-2 pa; 978-0-19-280559-1 pa

LC 2004-30585

The author discusses "why the study of happiness is important; how to define happiness from a scientific perspective; why making more money will not make one any happier; why some people seem more adept than others at being happy; and what Prozac and other drugs have to do with happiness." Choice
"With absolute clarity and admirable brevity, Nettle explores the pursuit of happiness and, happily, makes good sense of it all." Publ Wkly
Includes bibliographical references

Orloff, Judith

Emotional freedom; liberate yourself from negative emotions and transform your life. Harmony Books 2009 401p $24.95   **152.4**
1. Emotions 2. Self-realization
ISBN 978-0-307-33818-1

LC 2008-21482

"In Part 1, Orloff presents four components of emotion—biology, energy, spirituality, and psychology—and provides a 20-question assessment to highlight individuals' strengths and weaknesses. . . . Orloff divides Part 2 into seven chapters, each devoted to a difficult negative emotion. Throughout, Orloff details how one can use the four components of emotion to transform negative emotions into positive ones and become a more centered and emotionally healthy person. . . . This well-written book is full of good advice for anyone who wants to take more control of his or her emotional life." Libr J

Tavris, Carol

Anger; the misunderstood emotion. rev ed; Simon & Schuster 1989 383p pa $14   **152.4**
1. Anger
ISBN 0-671-67523-0

LC 89-33129

First published 1983
The author contends that anger is a complex, socially learned response that is not necessarily cathartic
Includes bibliographical references

153   Conscious mental processes and intelligence

Baars, Bernard J.

In the theater of consciousness; the workspace of the mind. Oxford Univ. Press 1997 193p il $35; pa $14.95   **153**
1. Intellect 2. Consciousness 3. Theory of knowledge
ISBN 0-19-510265-7; 0-19-514703-0 pa

LC 96-10379

The author "does a masterful job of explicating the issues and distinctions related to consciousness providing representative charts, graphs, and figures to relate both theory and data. . . . A most accessible and up-to-date introduction to current ideas about consciousness, and a valuable work for general readers." Choice
Includes bibliographical references

Brain rules; 12 principles for surviving and thriving at work, home, and school. John Medina. 2nd ed. Pear Press 2014 288 p. illustrations pbk $15.95   **153**
1. Perception 2. Senses and sensation 3. Human information processing
ISBN 9780983263371

"Dr. John Medina, a molecular biologist, shares his life-long interest in how the brain sciences might influence the way we teach our children and the way we work. In each chapter, he describes a brain rule--what scientists know for sure about how our brains work--and then offers transformative ideas for our daily lives." Publisher's note

Carter, Rita
  ★ **Exploring** consciousness. University of Calif. Press 2002 320p il $34.95   **153**
1. Consciousness
ISBN 0-520-23737-4
LC 2002-25900

This work explores the nature, origins, and purpose of consciousness from philosophical, scientific, and experiential perspectives

"A treasure trove of fact, argument and opinion, doing an excellent job of conveying both research and controversies. The general reader will find it filled with stimulating material." New Sci
Includes bibliographical references

Damasio, Antonio R.
  The **feeling** of what happens; body and emotion in the making of consciousness. Harcourt Brace & Co. 1999 386p il $28; pa $15   **153**
1. Emotions 2. Consciousness
ISBN 0-15-100369-6; 0-15-601075-5 pa
LC 99-26357

The author contends "that consciousness arises from our ability to map relations between the self and others through our emotions. This bold attempt to mend the classical breach between emotion and reason is all the more compelling for its poetic expression." Publ Wkly
Includes bibliographical references

Eagleman, David
  Incognito; the brains behind the mind. Pantheon 2011 290p il $26.95   **153**
1. Brain 2. Subconsciousness
ISBN 978-0-307-37733-3
LC 2010053184

"Eagleman's main theme is that what one calls 'me,' the conscious mind, is only the tip of the iceberg, and that most of the interesting and important things the brain does are inaccessible to the brain's 'owner.' . . . What Eagleman does is explain the idea to the neophyte through discussion of dozens of fascinating, engaging examples. . . . Eagleman's prose is vivid and, more important, accessible." Choice
Includes bibliographical references

Edelman, Shimon
  ★ The **happiness** of pursuit; what neuroscience can teach us about the good life. Shimon Edelman. Basic Books 2012 x, 237 p.p   **153**
1. Happiness 2. Perception 3. Psychology 4. Thought

and thinking 5. Ego 6. Self 7. Thinking 8. Cognition 9. Mind-Body Relations, Metaphysical
ISBN 0465022243; 9780465022243
LC 2011039326

This book by psychologist Shimon Edelman "offers a fundamental understanding of pleasure and joy via the brain. Using the concept of the mind as a computing device, he unpacks how the human brain is highly active, involved in patterned networks, and constantly learning from experience. As our brains predict the future through pursuit of experience, we are rewarded both in real time and in the long run. Essentially, as Edelman discovers, it's the journey, rather than the destination, that matters." (Publisher's note)
Includes bibliographical references and index.

Hallinan, Joseph T.
  Why we make mistakes; how we look without seeing, forget things in seconds, and are all pretty sure we are way above average. Broadway Books 2009 283p $24.95   **153**
1. Errors 2. Failure (Psychology)
ISBN 978-0-7679-2805-2; 0-7679-2805-9
LC 2008-30818

"Hallinan examines 13 pitfalls that make us vulnerable to mistakes: 'we look but don't always see,' 'we like things tidy' and 'we don't constrain ourselves' among them. Each chapter takes on a different drawback, packing in an impressive range of intriguing and practical real-world examples. . . . He also looks at the serious consequences of multitasking and data overload on what is at best a two or three-track mind." Publ Wkly
Includes bibliographical references

Hofstadter, Douglas R.
  I am a strange loop. Basic Books 2007 412p il 26.95   **153**
1. Self 2. Consciousness
ISBN 978-0-465-03078-1; 0-465-03078-5
The author's model of self is neither "spiritual—he's not a religious man—nor is it locked into the cold neurological materialism of cellular mechanics. . . . [The book] scales some lofty conceptual heights, but it remains very personal, and it's deeply colored by the facts of Hofstadter's later life." Time
bibliography: p. 377-82

Kandel, Eric R.
  ★ **In** search of memory; the emergence of a new science of mind. W. W. Norton & Company 2006 510p il $29.95   **153**
1. Memory 2. Nervous system 3. Neuroscientists 4. College teachers 5. Nobel laureates for physiology or medicine
ISBN 0-393-05863-8; 978-0-393-05863-5
LC 2005-28565

The author "recounts his own revolutionary research in establishing the molecular chemistry of short-term memory and the cellular dynamics of long-term memory, highlighting particularly the potential of his findings for the treatment of Alzheimer's and other mental disorders. But even as he outlines the biomechanics of memory, Kandel shares his personal reminiscences of the years during which he unraveled those mysteries. . . . An autobiography of exceptional substance." Booklist

Includes bibliographical references

Karpf, Anne

The **human** voice; how this extraordinary instrument reveals essential clues about who we are. Bloomsbury 2006 399p $24.95   **153**

ISBN 1-58234-299-7; 978-1-58234-299-3

LC 2006-9698

"Beginning with a description of how the voice actually works, [the author argues for] . . . its vital role in the bonding of mothers and children, and eventually in all social interaction." Publisher's note

This "book is packed with information . . . backed up by prolific references to relevant research." Times Lit Suppl

Includes bibliographical references

Pinker, Steven

How the mind works. Norton 1997 660p il hardcover o.p. pa $18.95   **153**

1. Brain 2. Emotions 3. Evolution 4. Intellect 5. Reasoning 6. Psychology 7. Natural selection

ISBN 978-0-393-33477-7 pa

LC 97-1855

Pinker "has a gift for making enormously complicated mechanisms—and human foibles—accessible." Publ Wkly

Includes bibliographical references

Rosenbaum, David A., 1952-

It's a jungle in there; how competition and cooperation in the brain shape the mind. David A. Rosenbaum. Oxford University Press 2014 272 p. ill. $29.95   **153**

1. Cognitive psychology 2. Competition (Psychology) 3. Brain 4. Neuropsychology

ISBN 0199829772; 9780199829774

LC 2013028959

In this book, author David A. Rosenbaum "argues that the overarching theory of biology, Darwin's theory, should be the overarching theory of cognitive psychology, the science of mental functioning. He explores this new and intriguing idea by showing how neural elements compete and cooperate in a kind of inner jungle, where only the fittest survive. Competition within your brain does as much to shape who you are as the physical and figurative competition you face externally." (Publisher's note)

"Tying the vicissitudes of psychology to any one principle, even loosely, is bold, but Rosenbaum's careful prose will ignite thoughtful debate." Pub Wkly

Includes bibliographical references and index

Sagan, Carl, 1934-1996

The **dragons** of Eden; speculations on the evolution of human intelligence. Random House 1977 263p il hardcover o.p. pa $7.50   **153**

1. Brain 2. Genetics 3. Intellect

ISBN 0-345-34629-7 pa

LC 76-53472

In this study of human intellect "Sagan is principally preoccupied with the neocortex, with its left hemisphere, responsible for language and logic, a right hemisphere in charge of intuition and spatial dimension, and a corpus callosum that mediates and synthesizes the two." Atl Mon

Includes bibliographical references

Schulz, Kathryn

Being wrong; adventures in the margin of error. Ecco 2010 405p il $26.99; pa $20.99   **153**

1. Errors 2. Decision making 3. Error 4. Expertise 5. Fallibility 6. Errors -- Psychological aspects

ISBN 0-06-117604-4; 0-06-199793-5 pa; 978-0-06-117604-3; 978-0-06-199793-8 pa

Schulz explores "why we find it so gratifying to be right and so maddening to be mistaken, and how this attitude toward error corrodes relationships—whether between family members, colleagues, neighbors, or nations. Along the way, she takes us on a . . . tour of human fallibility, from wrongful convictions to no-fault divorce; medical mistakes to misadventures at sea; failed prophecies to false memories; 'I told you so!' to 'Mistakes were made.' Drawing on thinkers such as Augustine, Darwin, Freud, Gertrude Stein, Alan Greenspan, and Groucho Marx, she proposes a new way of looking at wrongness. In this view, error is both a given and a gift—one that can transform our worldviews, our relationships, and ourselves." (Publisher's note) Index.

The author discusses "how we make mistakes, how we behave when we find we have been wrong, and how our errors change us. . . . Schulz writes with such lucidity and wit that her philosophical enquiry becomes a page-turner." Publ Wkly

Includes bibliographical references

153.1   Memory and learning

Foer, Joshua

Moonwalking with Einstein; the art and science of remembering everything. Penguin Press 2011 307p $26.95   **153.1**

1. Memory 2. Memory disorders -- Treatment

ISBN 978-1-59420-229-2

LC 2010-30265

"Mr. Foer writes in these pages with fresh enthusiasm. His narrative is smart and funny and . . . it's informed by a humanism that enables its author to place the mysteries of the brain within a larger philosophical and cultural context." N Y Times (Late N Y Ed)

Includes bibliographical references

Goldman, Bob

Brain fitness; anti-aging strategies for achieving super mind power. {by} Robert M. Goldman with Ronald Klatz and Lisa Berger. Doubleday 1999 333p il hardcover o.p. pa $14.95   **153.1**

1. Aging 2. Memory 3. Stress (Physiology)

ISBN 0-385-48869-6 pa

LC 98-18785

This is an "exploration of techniques—mental workouts, memory training, physical exercises, and nutrition and dietary supplements—that readers can use to maximize their concentration, memory, imagination, energy, intelligence, and creativity while decreasing fatigue and stress and preventing Alzheimer's disease and other brain diseases." Libr J

Includes bibliographical references

Malone, Michael S.

The **guardian** of all things; the epic story of human memory. Michael S. Malone. St. Martin's Press 2012 xii, 290 p.p (hardcover) $25.99 **153.1**

1. Memory 2. Civilization 3. Technology and civilization 4. Civilization -- History

ISBN 0312620314; 9780312620318; 9781250014924

LC 2012010246

This book by Michael S. Malone is an "exploration of the history of memory and human civilization. . . . [The book] is a sweeping scientific history that takes us on a 10,000-year-old journey replete with incredible ideas, inventions, and transformations. From cave drawings to oral histories to libraries to the internet, 'The Guardian of All Things' is the history of how humans have relentlessly pursued new ways to preserve and manage memory, both within the human brain and as a series of inventions external to it." (Publisher's note)

Includes bibliographical references and index.

Schacter, Daniel L.

Searching for memory; the brain, the mind, and the past. Basic Bks. 1996 398p il hardcover o.p. pa $17.50 **153.1**

1. Brain 2. Memory

ISBN 0-465-07552-5 pa

LC 96-19521

"This is an excellent book on an important topic: it is exceptionally well written; its examples of defects in memory are fascinating, as are the theories based on them; and its arguments are illustrated with opposite pictures, reproduced from works by many modern artists, and passages from novels." N Y Times Book Rev

Includes bibliographical references

The **seven** sins of memory; how the mind forgets and remembers. Houghton Mifflin 2001 272p il hardcover o.p. **153.1**

1. Memory 2. Memory disorders 3. Recollection (Psychology)

ISBN 0-618-04019-6; 0-618-21919-6 pa

LC 00-53885

Schacter discusses "the 'different ways in which memory can get us into trouble.' . . . We forget things over time (transience). We often forget where we put our house keys because we were preoccupied with something else (absent-mindedness). We can't remember someone's name (blocking). We mistake an idealized version of our past for a real recollection (misattribution) or claim an 'implanted' memory as our own when it has been suggested by someone else (suggestibility). Our memories are often . . . influenced by our current beliefs (bias). In some cases, we obsessively remember traumatic or painful events that we'd much rather forget (persistence)." (N Y Times Book Rev) Index.

The author discusses "the curious processes of memory by classifying its malfunctions into seven categories: transience, absent-mindedness, blocking, misattribution, suggestibility, bias, and persistence. Schacter illustrates each of these 'sins' with examples of routine misfortunes common to all." Libr J

Includes bibliographical references

153.3 Imagination, imagery, creativity

Csikszentmihalyi, Mihaly

Creativity; flow and the psychology of discovery and invention. HarperCollins Pubs. 1996 456p hardcover o.p. pa $15 **153.3**

1. Creative ability 2. Creative thinking

ISBN 0-06-092820-4 pa

LC 96-4116

"Utilizing the interviews garnered from 91 respondents (ranging from philosopher Mortimer Adler to biologist Edward O. Wilson to politician Eugene McCarthy), the author . . . demonstrates the processes that these acknowledged creative thinkers and doers go through and the characteristics that make them stand out. . . . Csikszentmihalyi also deals with creativity and aging and ways to enhance one's own personal creativity." Libr J

Includes bibliographical references

Gawain, Shakti

★ **Creative** visualization; use the power of your imagination to create what you want in your life. 30th anniversary ed.; Nataraj Pub./New World Library 2008 175p $25; pa $12.95 **153.3**

1. Imagination 2. Self-realization

ISBN 978-1-577-31636-7; 1-577-31636-3; 978-1-577-31229-1 pa; 1-577-31229-5 pa

LC 2008-14400

First published 1978 by Whatever Pub.

"The author asserts that people can achieve an ideal existence simply through mental visualization." Libr J

Includes bibliographical references

May, Rollo

The **courage** to create. Norton 1975 143p hardcover o.p. pa $11.95 **153.3**

1. Courage 2. Consciousness 3. Creative ability

ISBN 0-393-31106-6 pa

The author argues that creativity is an act of encounter and draws on examples from literature, art, and psychoanalysis

Includes bibliographical references

153.35 Creativity

Bissell, Tom

Magic hours; essays on creators and creation. Tom Bissell. Believer Books 2012 301 p. **153.35**

1. Arts 2. American essays 3. Creative ability 4. Cultural critique

ISBN 1936365766; 9781936365760

In this book of essays, "essayist Tom Bissell explores the highs and lows of the creative process. He takes us from the set of 'The Big Bang Theory' to the first novel of Ernest Hemingway to the final work of David Foster Wallace; from the films of Werner Herzog to the film of Tommy Wiseau to the editorial meeting in which Paula Fox's work was re-launched into the world. . . . These essays represent ten years of Bissell's . . . writing on every aspect of creation--be it Iraq War documentaries or video-game character voices." (Publisher's note)

153.4   Thought, thinking, reasoning, intuition, value, judgment

Berdik, Chris

Mind over mind; the surprising power of placebos, expectations, and assumptions. Chris Berdik. Current Hardcover 2012 272 p. (hardback) $26.95   **153.4**
1. Perception 2. Mind and body 3. Expectation (Psychology) 4. Cognitive psychology 5. Thought and thinking
ISBN 1591845092; 9781591845096
                   LC 2012019144
This book, by Chris Berdik, "offers a . . . look at the frontiers of expectations research, revealing how our brains work in the future tense and how our assumptions . . . bend reality. We learn how placebo calories can fill us up, . . . how fake surgery can sometimes work better than real surgery, and how imaginary power can be corrupting. . . . Their influence seems based on illusion, even trickery, but they can create their own reality, for good or for ill." (Publisher's note)
Includes bibliographical references and index

Dobelli, Rolf

The **art** of thinking clearly; Rolf Dobelli ; translated by Nicky Griffin. HarperBusiness 2013 384 p. (hardcover) $25.99   **153.4**
1. Decision making 2. Thought and thinking 3. Cognition 4. Reasoning (Psychology) 5. Errors -- Psychological aspects
ISBN 0062219707; 9780062219688
                   LC 2013003934
This book, by Rolf Dobelli, is a "look at human psychology and reasoning--essential reading for anyone who wants to avoid 'cognitive errors' and make better choices in all aspects of their lives. . . . [It offers] examples of cognitive biases, simple errors we all make in our day-to-day thinking. But by knowing what they are and how to spot them, we can avoid them and make better decisions." (Publisher's note)

Gladwell, Malcolm

Blink : the power of thinking without thinking. Little, Brown and Co 2005 277p il $25.95   **153.4**
1. Intuition 2. Decision making
ISBN 0-316-17232-4
                   LC 2004-13916
Gladwell "has a dazzling ability to find commonality in disparate fields of study. . . . Each case study is satisfying, and Gladwell imparts his own evident pleasure in delving into a wide range of fields and seeking an underlying truth." Publ Wkly
Includes bibliographical references

Herbert, Wray

On second thought; outsmarting your mind's hard-wired habits. Crown Publishers 2010 289p $25   **153.4**
1. Thought and thinking
ISBN 0-307-46163-7; 978-0-307-46163-6
                   LC 2010-03073
"The brain is like a dual processor, [Herbert] argues—one part is logical, deliberate, and cautious, while the other is much older and primitive. The latter is the heuristic brain—fast, impressionistic, and sometimes irrational. After years of evolution, the brain has become hardwired with mental shortcuts that help us quickly navigate our daily lives. However, they can also distort our thinking and lead to poor decision making. . . . Heuristics are neither good nor bad—the trick, Herbert says, is in recognizing when to question an instant response." Libr J

Kahneman, Daniel, 1934-

Thinking, fast and slow; Daniel Kahneman. Farrar, Straus and Giroux 2011 499p. ill.   **153.4**
1. Intuition 2. Reasoning 3. Decision making 4. Thought and thinking
ISBN 0374275637; 9780374275631
                   LC 2011027143
In this book, author Daniel Kahneman examines "the mind and explains the two systems that drive the way we think. System 1 is fast, intuitive, and emotional; System 2 is slower, more deliberative, and more logical. Kahneman exposes the . . . capabilities--and also the faults and biases--of fast thinking, and reveals the pervasive influence of intuitive impressions on our thoughts and behavior." (Publisher's note)
Includes bibliographical references (p. 447-481) and index.

Konnikova, Maria, 1987-

Mastermind; how to think like Sherlock Holmes. Maria Konnikova. Viking Adult 2013 273 p. (hardback) $26.95   **153.4**
1. Perception 2. Holmes, Sherlock (Fictional character) 3. Logic 4. Reasoning
ISBN 0670026573; 9780670026579
                   LC 2012035455
In this book, psychologist Maria Konnikova "examines [fictional character Sherlock] Holmes's powers of perception and problem solving through the lens of her discipline. The book is part literary analysis and part self-help guide, teaching readers how to sharpen the ways they observe the world, store and retrieve memories, and make decisions." (Scientific American)

Miller, G. Wayne

Top Brain, Bottom Brain; Surprising Insights into How You Think. Stephen M. Kosslyn, Ph.D. and G. Wayne Miller. Simon & Schuster 2013 224 p. $25   **153.4**
1. Brain 2. Personality 3. Thought and thinking 4. Cognition 5. Cognitive psychology 6. Cognitive neuroscience
ISBN 1451645104; 9781451645101
                   LC 2013024491

Authors Stephen Kosslyn and G. Wayne Miller "offer a novel way to learn about how each of us thinks. For the past fifty years, popular culture has led us to believe in the left brain vs. right brain theory of personality types. It would be an illuminating theory if it did not have one major drawback: It is simply not supported by science. In contrast, the Top Brain, Bottom Brain theory is based on solid research that has stayed within the confines of labs all over the world." (Publisher's note)

"[T]his study is an invigorating thought-experiment on reassembling the brain's dynamic parts." Pub Wkly

Includes bibliographical references and index

Shermer, Michael

The **believing** brain; from ghosts and gods to politics and conspiracies--how we construct beliefs and reinforce them as truths. Times Books 2011 385p il $28 **153.4**
1. Belief and doubt 2. Theory of knowledge 3. Knowledge, Theory of 4. Cognitive neuroscience
ISBN 9780805091250; 0805091254

LC 2010-30706

This book discusses the science of the human brain in relation to belief formation. "[T]he book is clearly less about the examples than about the theory Shermer uses to explain them all. . . . Shermer's theory looks like this: The human mind is inherently a 'belief engine'; we perceive endless bits of information, and we must posit beliefs as ways of organizing and making sense of them. . . . Having found a possible explanation, we then seek confirming evidence and deepenings of the patterns and agents we believe we have discerned. The result, Shermer claims, is that we live much of the time in 'belief-dependent realism,' which is to say that our beliefs are shaping what we see in the world, rather than the world shaping our beliefs. . . . Shermer also believes in a dividing line between benign or helpful beliefs and malignant ones (like religion)." (Commonweal)

"A timely, reasoned reflection on the nature of belief, offering a levelheaded corrective to the divisiveness of extreme partisanship." Kirkus

Includes bibliographical references and index.

Trivers, Robert

The **folly** of fools; the logic of deceit and self-deception in human life. Robert Trivers. Basic Books 2011 xvi, 397 p.p $28 **153.4**
1. Deception 2. Evolution 3. Psychology 4. Self-deception 5. Deception -- Social aspects 6. Deception -- Psychological aspects
ISBN 0465027555; 9780465027552; 9780465028054

LC 2011028453

The author "argues that self-deception evolved in the service of deceit--the better to fool others. We do it for biological reasons--in order to help us survive and procreate. From viruses mimicking host behavior to humans misremembering (sometimes intentionally) the details of a quarrel, science has proven that the deceptive one can always outwit the masses. But we undertake this deception at our own peril." (Publisher's note)

Includes bibliographical references (p. 355-383) and index

Watts, Duncan J.

Everything is obvious; once you know the answer. Crown Business 2011 335p il $26 **153.4**
1. Reasoning 2. Thought and thinking 3. Common sense
ISBN 978-0-385-53168-9; 0-385-53168-0

LC 2010031550

It was the author's intent to demonstrate that "while what we mean when we say 'common sense' may seem to most people like, well, common sense, it is in reality a series of complex social rules, a priori assumptions, and inaccurate instinctive responses. . . . He taps into everything from marketing (a field relying heavily on sociological concepts) to Artificial Intelligence, methodically unpacking assumptions and revealing the hidden intricacies of what we call obvious." (Publishers Weekly)

The author posits "that common sense is a shockingly unreliable guide to truth and yet we rely on it virtually to the exclusion of other methods of reasoning. Mr. Watts, a former sociology professor and physicist who is now a researcher for Yahoo, has written a fascinating book that ranges through psychology, economics, marketing and the science of social networks. He is especially interested in the mistakes we make when we reason about how people influence one another—such as our tendency to think of groups in terms of representative or important members rather than as whole entities. . . . The enterprise of prediction-making is another casualty of the limits of common sense. Mr. Watts suggests that the entire field of business strategy suffers from a delusion that the future can be forecast with enough numerical precision to enable accurate planning. One solution he endorses is a systematic process of imagining detailed alternative narratives of the future." Wall Street J

Includes bibliographical references

153.6 Communication

Pease, Allan

The **definitive** book of body language; [by] Allan & Barbara Pease. Bantam Books 2006 386p il $23 **153.6**
1. Nonverbal communication
ISBN 0-553-80472-3; 978-0-553-80472-0

LC 2006-42657

"The authors examine each component of body language." Publisher's note

"The book is amply and wittily illustrated with celebrity photographs. . . . This is a fascinating book." N Y Times Book Rev

Includes bibliographical references

153.7 Perceptual processes

Chabris, Christopher

The **invisible** gorilla; and other ways our intuitions deceive us. [by] Christopher Chabris and Daniel Simons. Crown 2010 306p $27; pa $14 **153.7**
1. Memory 2. Perception 3. Thought and thinking
ISBN 978-0-307-45965-7; 0-307-45965-9; 978-0-307-45966-4 pa; 0-307-45966-7 pa

LC 2009-45325

The authors "won a 2004 Ig Nobel Prize for their widely reported 'gorilla experiment,' which showed that when people focus on one thing, it's easy to overlook other things—even a woman in a gorilla suit. . . . [In this book,] they explore this habit of 'inattentional blindness' and other common ways in which we distort our perception of reality. Their readable book offers surprising insights into just how clueless we are about how our minds work and how we experience the world." Kirkus

Includes bibliographical references

Ellard, Colin

★ **You** are here; why we can find our way to the moon but get lost in the mall. Doubleday 2009 328p il map $25 **153.7**
1. Direction sense 2. Space perception
ISBN 978-0-385-52806-1; 0-385-52806-X
LC 2009-07822

Ellard argues that in the modern age the human sense of navigation and direction has diminished greatly.

"If you're looking for an eye-opening, if somewhat embarrassing, book to help understand why you keep getting lost when you know you shouldn't and what you can do about it well, here you are." Booklist

Includes bibliographical references

Goleman, Daniel

Focus; the hidden driver of excellence. Daniel Goleman. Harper 2013 320 p. $28.99 **153.7**
1. Attention 2. Self-control 3. Thought and thinking
ISBN 0062114867; 9780062114860
LC 2013007290

Author Daniel Goleman's book "delves into the science of attention in all its varieties, presenting a long overdue discussion of this little-noticed and under-rated mental asset. In an era of unstoppable distractions, Goleman persuasively argues that now more than ever we must learn to sharpen focus if we are to survive in a complex world." (Publisher's note)

Greenspan, Stanley I.

The **first** idea; how symbols, language, and intelligence evolved from our early primate ancestors to modern humans. [by] Stanley I. Greenspan, Stuart G. Shanker. 1st Da Capo Press ed; Da Capo Press 2004 504p $25 **153.7**
1. Evolution 2. Theory of knowledge
ISBN 0-7382-0680-6
LC 2004-10658

"This book should appeal most to readers working in psychology and child development, but its revolutionary ideas no doubt will lead to lively and well-publicized debates." Publ Wkly

Includes bibliographical references

Klein, Stefan

The **secret** pulse of time; making sense of life's scarcest commodity. translated by Shelley Frisch. Marlowe & Co. 2007 xxi, 343p il $25 **153.7**
1. Time 2. Perception 3. Time management
ISBN 978-1-6009-4017-0; 1-6009-4017-X
Original German edition, 2006

"Sure to give readers fresh perspective on their everyday lives, Klein's concepts are well illustrated in copious examples from literature and popular culture, and Frisch's fluid, flawless translation makes his text as captivating as it is enlightening." Publ Wkly

Includes bibliographical references

Zimbardo, Philip G.

The **time** paradox; the new psychology of time that will change your life. [by] Philip Zimbardo and John Boyd. Free Press 2008 358p il $27 **153.7**
1. Time perception
ISBN 978-1-4165-4198-1; 1-4165-4198-5
LC 2008-2149

This is an "investigation of how attitudes toward time affect every aspect of human life. The authors help readers determine their personal time zone before revealing how to 'reclaim yesterday, enjoy today, and master tomorrow.' Balance never seemed so attainable." Libr J

Includes bibliographical references

153.753 Time and rhythm perception

Hammond, Claudia

Time Warped. HarperCollins 2013 342 p. (paperback) $14.99 **153.753**
1. Time 2. Time perception
ISBN 0062225200; 9780062225207
LC 2012452877

It was the author Claudia Hammond's intent to explore "time, and how we perceive it" and to answer the questions "why does time seem to pass faster as we grow older? Or fly when we are having fun? How come we humans, possibly uniquely, have an ability to travel mentally through time? . . . She describes the . . . experiments psychologists have devised to explore how our brains construct--and warp--time."(New Scientist)

153.8 Will (Volition)

Akst, Daniel

We have met the enemy; self-control in an age of excess. Penguin Press 2011 303p $26.95 **153.8**
1. Self-control 2. Supply and demand
ISBN 978-1-59420-281-0
LC 2010-28525

"Akst combines the disciplines of history, philosophy, psychology, economics, and literature in examining this phenomenon and inspires readers to view self-control in a positive light. Essential for all people concerned with their own overindulgences and with the future of society in general." Libr J

Includes bibliographical references

Cialdini, Robert B.

★ **Influence** : the psychology of persuasion; Rev. ed.; 1st Collins business essentials ed; Collins 2007 320p il pa $17.95   **153.8**

1. Persuasion (Psychology)
ISBN 0-06-124189-X; 978-0-06-124189-5
First published 1984

The author "explains the psychology of why people say 'yes'—and how to apply these understandings." Publisher's note

Includes bibliographical references

Dennett, Daniel Clement

Freedom evolves; {by} Daniel C. Dennett. Viking 2003 347p il $24.95; pa $17   **153.8**

1. Decision making 2. Free will and determinism
ISBN 0-670-03186-0; 0-14-200384-0 pa
LC 2002-28085

"Drawing on evolutionary biology, neuroscience, economic game theory, philosophy and Richard Dawkins's meme, the author argues that there is indeed such a thing as free will, but it 'is not a preexisting feature of our existence, like the law of gravity.' . . . This book comprises a kind of toolbox of intellectual exercises favoring cultural evolution, the idea that culture, morality and freedom are as much a result of evolution by natural selection as our physical and genetic attributes. Yet genetic determinism, he argues, does not imply inevitability, as his critics may claim, nor does it cancel out the soul. . . . Dennett clearly relishes pushing other scientists' buttons. Though natural selection itself is still a subject of controversy, the author . . . most certainly is in the vanguard of the philosophy of science." Publ Wkly

Includes bibliographical references

Dutton, Kevin

Split -second persuasion; the ancient art and new science of changing minds. Houghton Mifflin Harcourt 2011 296p il $26   **153.8**

1. Persuasion (Psychology)
ISBN 978-0-15-101279-4
LC 2010-5739

First published 2010 in the United Kingdom

"This is a well-researched, wide-ranging treatise on the psychology of persuasion. The first section reviews research from an impressive variety of disciplines, from neuroscience to the biological and social sciences. The second section focuses on the author's main theme—split-second persuasion—a powerful 'superstrain' of persuasion that occurs quickly. Written for a less-experienced audience, the book is clear and nontechnical." Choice

Includes bibliographical references

Iyengar, Sheena

The **art** of choosing. Twelve 2010 329p il $25.99   **153.8**

1. Decision making 2. Choice (Psychology)
ISBN 978-0-446-50410-2; 0-446-50410-6
LC 2009-37664

"In 'The Art of Choosing,' a broad and fascinating survey of current research on the subject, Iyengar stitches together personal anecdotes, examples from popular culture, and scientific evidence to explain the complex calculus that goes into

our everyday choices, from picking our favorite soda to choosing our medical insurance. She also writes about the ways in which her blindness — Iyengar lost her sight as a teenager — has given her a unique perspective on the subject." Salon

Lehrer, Jonah

How we decide. Houghton Mifflin Harcourt 2009 302p $25   **153.8**

1. Decision making
ISBN 978-0-618-62011-1; 0-618-62011-7
LC 2008036769

This is an "exploration of the brain's inner workings during the decision-making process." Kirkus

"Lehrer is a delight to read, and this is a fascinating book . . . that will help everyone better understand themselves and their decision making." Publ Wkly

Includes bibliographical references

Levine, Robert

The **power** of persuasion; how we're bought and sold. Wiley 2003 278p hardcover o.p. pa $14.95 **153.8**

1. Interpersonal relations 2. Persuasion (Psychology)
ISBN 0-471-26634-5; 0-471-76317-9 pa
LC 2002-9952

The author "opens by demonstrating that all of us . . . can be persuaded under the right circumstances. He goes on to study financial manipulation and the use of the sense of obligation . . . and then proceeds to a nuts-and-bolts analysis of salesmanship by describing what he learned and did (and had done to him) as an automobile salesman. . . . Inevitably, he moves to cults, the Moonies and the ultimate persuasion horror story, Jonestown." Publ Wkly

Includes bibliographical references

Partnoy, Frank

Wait; the art and science of delay. Frank Partnoy. PublicAffairs 2012 xii, 290 p.p   **153.8**

1. Patience 2. Decision making 3. Thought and thinking 4. Procrastination
ISBN 1610390040; 9781610390040; 9781610390057
LC 2012010970

In this book, Frank Partnoy "weaves together findings from hundreds of scientific studies and interviews with wide-ranging experts to craft a picture of effective decision-making that runs counter to our . . . fast-paced world. Even as technology exerts new pressures to speed up our lives, it turns out that the choices we make . . . benefit profoundly from delay. As this . . . book reveals, taking control of time and slowing down our responses yields better results in almost every arena of life." (Publisher's note)

Includes bibliographical references and index.

153.9   Intelligence and aptitudes

Beilock, Sian L.

Choke; what the secrets of the brain reveal about getting it right when you have to. Free Press 2010 294p il $26; ebook $12.99   **153.9**

1. Success 2. Failure (Psychology)
ISBN 978-1-4165-9617-2; 978-1-4391-0962-5 ebook
LC 2010-10595

"A star golfer misses a critical putt; a brilliant student fails to ace a test; a savvy salesperson blows a key presentation. Each of these people has suffered the same bump in mental processing: They have just choked under pressure. . . . By studying how the brain works when we are doing our best — and when we choke — Beilock has formulated practical ideas about how to overcome performance lapses at critical moments." Science Daily

Bloom, Harold

 Genius; a mosaic of one hundred exemplary creative minds. Warner Bks. 2002 814p il $35.95; pa $19.95   **153.9**

 1. Genius 2. Authors 3. Literature -- History and criticism

 ISBN 0-446-52717-3; 0-446-69129-1 pa

             LC 2002-16808

 "Although the book is a delight to read, its real value lies in the author's ability to provoke the reader into thinking about literature, genius, and related topics. No similar work discusses literary genius in this way or covers this many writers." Libr J

 Includes bibliographical references

Gould, Stephen Jay, 1941-2002

 The **mismeasure** of man; rev & expanded ed; Norton 1996 444p il hardcover o.p. pa $15.95 **153.9**

 1. Intelligence tests 2. Ability -- Testing

 ISBN 0-393-31425-1 pa

             LC 95-44442

 First published 1981

 The author examines the history of various scientific methods used to measure intelligence. He demonstrates how the research was used to perpetuate the myth of the intellectual superiority of the white male

 Includes bibliographical references

Kurzweil, Ray, 1948-

 ★ The **singularity** is near; when humans transcend biology. [by] Ray Kurzweil. Viking 2005 652p il $29.95; pa $18   **153.9**

 1. Robots 2. Genetics 3. Evolution 4. Nanotechnology

 ISBN 0-670-03384-7; 0-14-303788-9 pa

             LC 2004-61231

 The book provides an "argument that a sudden acceleration in the growth of knowledge is about to make immortality technologically feasible. . . . A part of the argument concerns the transformation the human body will undergo as a result of the explosive increase of knowledge he believes is imminent.

 Nanotechnology will enable the design of nanobots . . . that will 'have myriad roles within the human body, including reversing human aging (to the extent that this task will not already have been completed through biotechnology, such as genetic engineering).' . . . But this will still not be immortality, and perfecting the human body is a phase in a much larger transformation. . . . 'Ultimately, the entire universe will become saturated with our intelligence.'" (New York Review of Books)

 "Anyone can grasp Mr. Kurzweil's main idea: that mankind's technological knowledge has been snowballing, with dizzying prospects for the future. The basics are clearly ex-

pressed. But for those more knowledgeable and inquisitive, the author argues his case in fascinating detail." N Y Times (Late N Y Ed)

 Includes bibliographical references

Murdoch, Stephen

 IQ; a smart history of a failed idea. J. Wiley and Sons 2007 269p $24.95   **153.9**

 1. Intelligence tests

 ISBN 978-0-471-69977-4; 0-471-69977-2

             LC 2006-32488

 The author "traces now ubiquitous but still controversial attempts to measure intelligence to its origins in the late 19th and early 20th centuries. . . . This is a thoughtful overview and a welcome reminder of the dangers of relying on such standardized tests." Publ Wkly

 Includes bibliographical references

Stanovich, Keith E.

 What intelligence tests miss; the psychology of rational thought. Yale University Press 2009 308p il $30   **153.9**

 1. Intelligence tests 2. Thought and thinking

 ISBN 978-0-300-12385-2; 0-300-12385-X

             LC 2008-37325

 Stanovich "argues that IQ tests measure cognitive efficiency but not the degree to which subjects make rational decisions. He explains that individuals with high IQs are as likely as others to go for quick, easy answers, adopt beliefs that preclude rational thinking, or be unaware of the rules of chance and probability—a concept Stanovich terms dysrationalia. . . . This is an important book for much the same reason that Daniel Goleman's bestselling Emotional Intelligence has proven so useful: it is based on sound evidence and allows for better prediction and education for success." Libr J

 Includes bibliographical references

154.2   The subconscious

Kandel, Eric R., 1929-

 The **age** of insight; the quest to understand the unconscious in art, mind, and brain : from Vienna 1900 to the present. Eric R. Kandel. Random House 2011 636 p.   **154.2**

 1. Intellect 2. Perception 3. Subconsciousness 4. Art -- Psychological aspects 5. Subconsciousness in art

 ISBN 9781400068715; 9781588369307

             LC 2011025274

 This book examines "the interplay among art, psychology and brain science." It focuses on "Austrian artists Gustav Klimt, Oskar Kokoschka and Egon Schiele, each of whom was profoundly influenced by Sigmund Freud and by the emerging scientific approach to medicine in their day. Kandel describes the psychological and biological insights reflected in their paintings, as well as the neuroscience behind how the beholder perceives the paintings." (Scientific American)

Mlodinow, Leonard

Subliminal; how your unconscious mind rules your behavior. Leonard Mlodinow. Pantheon Books 2012 viii, 260 p.p ill. (hardcover) $25.95 **154.2**
1. Human behavior 2. Decision making 3. Subconsciousness 4. Applied psychology
ISBN 9780307378217; 0307378217

LC 2011048098

In this book about the unconscious, physicist Leonard "Mlodinow runs through study after study and some . . . real-life examples to reveal how subliminal processing controls our sensory systems, creates and distorts memories and guides our intuitions about people. . . . He is pragmatic about how completely it leads us astray and the near-impossibility of overriding it, but he . . . acknowledg[es] how lost he would be without it." (New Scientist)

Includes bibliographical references and index

Tallis, Frank

Hidden minds; a history of the unconscious. Arcade Pub. 2002 194p $25.95 **154.2**
1. Subconsciousness
ISBN 1-55970-643-0

LC 2002-74566

The author "presents the history of the unconscious from Leibniz to Pierre Janet and Freud to current experimentation, and he emphasizes that the unconscious is now at the heart of neuroscience. He describes historic medical and scientific advances and the individuals who made them, and he draws on Coleridge, DeQuincey, Moss Hart, and other writers to show how the literate public viewed the unconscious at various times." Booklist

"Highly readable and possessing a surprising degree of depth, this book manages to be both entertaining and informative." Libr J

Includes bibliographical references

Vedantam, Shankar

The hidden brain; how our unconscious minds elect presidents, control markets, wage wars, and save our lives. Spiegel & Grau 2009 270p $26; pa $16 **154.2**
1. Perception 2. Subconsciousness 3. Motivation (Psychology)
ISBN 978-0-385-52521-3; 0-385-52521-4; 978-0-385-52522-0 pa; 0-385-52522-2 pa

LC 2009-19717

"Vedantam theorizes that there's a hidden world in our heads filled with unconscious biases, often small, hidden errors in thinking that manipulate our attitudes and actions without our knowing it. Autonomy is a myth, he says, because knowledge and rational intention are not responsible for our choices. This thesis is not news— since Freud, psychologists have taken the unconscious into account—but Vedanta argues that if we are influenced sometimes, then why not all the time, whether we're launching a romance or a genocide." Publ Wkly

"A tour into dark realms of the psyche by a personable guide." Kirkus

Includes bibliographical references

154.6 Sleep phenomena

Freud, Sigmund

★ Interpretation of dreams; translated by Joyce Crick; edited with an introduction by Ritchie Robinson. Oxford University Press 2008 514p il (Oxford world's classics) pa $14.95 **154.6**
1. Dreams 2. Psychoanalysis
ISBN 978-0-19-953758-7; 0-19-953758-5

Original German edition, 1900; first English translation published 1913

Groundbreaking analysis of dreams as manifestations of suppressed unconscious desires

Lewis, James R.

★ The dream encyclopedia; [by] James R. Lewis and Evelyn Dorothy Oliver. 2nd ed.; Visible Ink Press 2009 xxi, 410p il pa $24.95 **154.6**
1. Reference books 2. Dreams -- Encyclopedias
ISBN 978-1-57859-216-6

LC 2009-5132

First published 1995 by Gale Res.

This "reference examines more than 250 dream-related topics, from art to history to science, including how factors such as self-healing, ESP, literature, religion, sex, cognition and memory, and medical conditions can all have an effect on dreams. Dream symbolism and interpretation is examined in historical, cultural, and psychological detail." Publisher's note

Includes bibliographical references

155 Differential and developmental psychology

Bailey, Rebecca Anne

Easy to love, difficult to discipline; the 7 basic skills for turning conflict into cooperation. {by} Becky A. Bailey. Morrow 2000 285p hardcover o.p. pa $12.95 **155**
1. Parenting 2. Child rearing
ISBN 0-06-000775-3 pa

LC 99-44313

"Bailey contends that the difficult but rewarding task of guiding children's behavior starts only when parents are able to discipline themselves and become models of self-control. . . . Bailey's underlying message is positive and hopeful, supported with humorous anecdotes and helpful solutions." Publ Wkly

Includes bibliographical references

Kagan, Jerome

The human spark; the science of human development. Jerome Kagan. Basic Books 2013 352 p. (hardcover) $28.99 **155**
1. Psychology 2. Child development 3. Child psychology
ISBN 0465029825; 9780465029822

LC 2012047558

In this book, developmental psychologist Jerome Kagan points out that "a great deal of what we 'know' about human development isn't firmly anchored in empirical science.

He aims to correct that by encouraging readers to question received knowledge . . . and he does so by presenting [a] . . . discussion of the epistemology of psychology, alongside . . . critiques of the methodologies used in psychological research and the social applications of misinterpreted findings." (Publishers Weekly)

Includes bibliographical references and index

155.2   Individual psychology

Cain, Susan

Quiet; the power of introverts in a world that can't stop talking. Susan Cain. Crown Publishers 2012 x, 333 p.p   **155.2**

1. Introversion 2. Interpersonal relations 3. Introversion and extroversion 4. Introverts 5. Extraversion
ISBN 9780307352149; 9780307452207

LC 2010053204

It was the author's intent to discuss "the one-third to one-half of the population who are introverts. She defines the term broadly, including 'solitude-seeking' and 'contemplative,' but also 'sensitive,' 'humble,' and 'risk-averse.' Such individuals, she claims . . . are "'disproportionately represented among the ranks of the spectacularly creative.' Yet the American school and workplace make it difficult for those who draw strength from solitary musing by overemphasizing teamwork. . . . She notes [that] introverts can negotiate as well as, or better than, alpha males and females because they can take a firm stand 'without inflaming [their] counterpart's ego.' Cain provides tips to parents and teachers of children who are introverted or seem socially awkward and isolated. She suggests, for instance, exposing them gradually to new experiences that are otherwise overstimulating." (Publishers Weekly)

Includes bibliographical references (p. [277]-323) and index

Csikszentmihalyi, Mihaly

★ **Flow** : the psychology of optimal experience. Harper Perennial 2008 303p pa $14.95   **155.2**

1. Attention 2. Happiness 3. Applied psychology
ISBN 978-0-06-133920-2; 0-06-133920-2
First published 1990

This book offers a discussion of "'flow,' a field of behavioral science examining connections between satisfaction and daily activities. [According to the author], a flow state ensues when one is engaged in self-controlled, goal-related, meaningful actions. . . . This thoroughly researched study is an intriguing look at the age-old problem of the pursuit of happiness and how, through conscious effort, we may more easily attain it." Libr J

Dimitrius, Jo-Ellan

Reading people; how to understand people and predict their behavior--anytime, anyplace. {by} Jo-Ellan Dimitrius and Mark Mazzarella. Random House 1998 281p hardcover o.p. pa $14.95 **155.2**

1. Personality 2. Nonverbal communication
ISBN 0-345-42587-1 pa

LC 98-4934

"Dimitrius shares the people-reading techniques she developed over 15 years as a jury consultant. In so doing, she provides a wealth of tips and strategies for ferreting out people's real viewpoints, motives and character traits." Publ Wkly

Ehrenreich, Barbara

★ **Bright** -sided; how the relentless promotion of positive thinking has undermined America. Metropolitan Books/Henry Holt and Co. 2009 235p $23   **155.2**

1. Success 2. Optimism 3. Happiness 4. Self-confidence
ISBN 978-0-8050-8749-9; 0-8050-8749-4

LC 2009-23588

The author "explains the ongoing appeal of positive thinking as a consequence of alienation. Positive thinking, she argues, . . . is an ideology that sustains economic inequality by isolating individuals from brute facts." Bookforum

"The author's tough-minded and convincing broadside raises troubling questions about many aspects of contemporary American life. . . . Bright, incisive, provocative thinking." Kirkus

Includes bibliographical references

Gladwell, Malcolm, 1963-

David and Goliath; underdogs, misfits, and the art of battling giants. Malcolm Gladwell. Little, Brown & Co. 2013 304 p. illustrations (hardcover) $29   **155.2**

1. Success 2. Self-help techniques 3. Opportunity 4. Motivation (Psychology) 5. Struggle -- Psychological aspects
ISBN 9780316204361; 0316204366; 9780316239851

LC 2013941807

In this book, author Malcolm Gladwell "examines and challenges our concepts of 'advantage' and 'disadvantage' in a way that may seem intuitive to some and surprising to others. Beginning with the classic tale of David and Goliath and moving through history with figures such as Lawrence of Arabia and Martin Luther King Jr., Gladwell shows how, time and again, players labeled 'underdog' use that status to their advantage and prevail through the elements of cunning and surprise." (Booklist)

"Gladwell rewards readers with moving stories, surprising insights and consistently provocative ideas." Kirkus

Includes bibliographical references and index

Hamer, Dean H.

Living with our genes; why they matter more than you think. {by} Dean Hamer and Peter Copeland. Doubleday 1998 355p hardcover o.p. pa $14.95   **155.2**

1. Personality 2. Temperament 3. Behavior genetics
ISBN 0-385-48584-0 pa

LC 97-29818

"The authors devote chapters to the most compelling of human behaviors and conditions: sex, worry, anger, thrill-seeking, addiction, intelligence, eating and aging. They explore the biochemistry underlying the characteristics in question, and ask how much of that biochemistry is under genetic control. . . . This thought-provoking book's explanations of how our genes 'express' themselves is sure to capture the imaginations of readers." Publ Wkly

Includes bibliographical references

Harris, Judith Rich

No two alike; human nature and human individuality. W.W. Norton & Co. 2006 322p il $26.95 **155.2**

1. Personality 2. Individuality

ISBN 0-393-05948-0

LC 2005-25837

The author "tackles a question that has long been a mystery: Why do identical twins who grow up together—same genes, reared by the same parents—differ in personality?" Publisher's note

"Harris makes behavioral genetics and evolutionary psychology enjoyable and accessible to general readers as well as scholars." Libr J

Includes bibliographical references

Helgoe, Laurie A.

Introvert power; why your inner life is your hidden strength. [by] Laurie Helgoe. Sourcebooks 2008 xxiv, 256p il pa $15.95 **155.2**

1. Introversion and extroversion

ISBN 978-1-4022-1117-1; 1-4022-1117-1

LC 2008-4967

Shows readers how to use introversion not as a weakness but as a source of power.

"The author's voice is vivid and engaging, and she skillfully draws real-life examples of awkward scenarios introverts find themselves in when forced to play a role in society or the workplace. Readers will find much insight, as well as a comforting sense of being understood and validated." Publ Wkly

Includes bibliographical references

Hood, Bruce

The self illusion; how the social brain creates identity. Bruce Hood. Oxford University Press 2012 xvii, 349 p.p ill. (trade : alk. paper) $29.95 **155.2**

1. Self 2. Brain 3. Theory of knowledge 4. Cognition

ISBN 019989759X; 9780199897599

LC 2011047151

This book presents an "account of . . . developments in psychology and neuroscience that are helping to substantiate theories of selfhood positing that there is no concrete identity at the core of our being, and that our sense of self is an illusion spun from narratives we construct about our lives." It "explor[es] subjects such as free will, the unconscious, [and] the role of (false) memories in building identity." (New Scientist)

Includes bibliographical references (p. 297-341) and index.

Keltner, Dacher

Born to be good; the science of a meaningful life. W. W. Norton & Co. 2009 336p il $25.95 **155.2**

1. Altruism 2. Cooperation 3. Helping behavior 4. Interpersonal relations

ISBN 978-0-393-06512-1

LC 2008-42492

This book argues "that humans are not hardwired to lead lives that are 'nasty, brutish, and short.' . . . [Keltner investigates why humans have] evolved positive emotions like gratitude, amusement, awe, and compassion that promote ethical action and are the fabric of cooperative societies." Publisher's note

"A landmark book in the science of emotion and its implications for ethics and human universals, this is essential for all libraries." Libr J

Includes bibliographical references

Lunden, Joan

Wake -up calls; making the most out of every day. McGraw-Hill 2000 230p il $19.95; pa $12 **155.2**

1. Conduct of life 2. Self-realization

ISBN 0-07-136126-X; 0-07-137970-3 pa

A collection of aphorisms and life principles the author feels may inspire readers faced with stress, change, and adversity

Includes bibliographical references

Myers, Isabel Briggs

Gifts differing; understanding personality type. [by] Isabel Briggs Myers with Peter B. Myers. Davies-Black Pub 1995 228p il pa $16.95 **155.2**

1. Personality

ISBN 0-89106-074-X

LC 95-4184

First published 1980 by Consulting Psychologists Press

This is a guide to the 16 personality types distinguished in the Myers-Briggs Type Indicator.

Includes bibliographical references

Pinker, Steven

The blank slate; the denial of human nature in modern intellectual life. Viking 2002 509p $27.95; pa $16 **155.2**

1. Nature and nurture

ISBN 0-670-03151-8; 0-14-2003344 pa

LC 2002-22719

The author "attacks the notion that an infant's mind is a blank slate, arguing instead that human beings have an inherited universal structure shaped by the demands made upon the species for survival, albeit with plenty of room for cultural and individual variation." Publ Wkly

Includes bibliographical references

Seligman, Martin E. P.

★ Learned optimism; how to change your mind and your life. Vintage Books 2006 319p pa $14.95 **155.2**

1. Self-perception 2. Adjustment (Psychology)

ISBN 1-4000-7839-3; 978-1-4000-7839-4

LC 2006-277713

First published 1991

Seligman "has written a lively, very accessible book. . . . Presented for lay readers, this book can be highly recommended to professionals as well for its lucid and informative introduction to cognitive therapy and its approach to issues of mood and depression." Libr J

Includes bibliographical references

Shenk, David

The **genius** in all of us; why everything you've been told about genetics, talent, and IQ is wrong. Doubleday 2010 302p il $26.95   **155.2**

1. Ability 2. Heredity 3. Intellect

ISBN 978-0-385-52365-3; 0-385-52365-3

LC 2009-18376

Shenk "tells engaging stories, lucidly explains complex research and offers fresh insights into the nature of exceptional performance. . . . [This is] deeply interesting and important book." N Y Times Book Rev

Includes bibliographical references

Triandis, Harry C.

Fooling ourselves; self-deception in politics, religion, and terrorism. Harry C. Triandis. Praeger Publishers 2009 xxvi, 246p (alk. paper) $49.95 **155.2**

1. Deception 2. Psychology 3. Social psychology 4. Psychology of religion

ISBN 9780313364389; 0313364389

LC 2008033679

In this book, author Harry C. "Triandis shows how and why self-deception takes place, and its subtle and profound effects on our everyday lives. Self-deception occurs because we often see the world the way we would like it to be, rather than the way it is. Our brains so long for things the way we want them, we might not even be aware we are fooling ourselves. . . . Across cultures and around the world, self-deception is a phenomenon that has subtle and profound effects on everyday life, explains Triandis, . . . former president of the International Association of Cross-Cultural Psychology. In this work, he not only explains how and why self-deceptions occur in three areas - politics, religion, and terrorism - but also how to recognize and reduce the frequency of fooling ourselves." (Publisher's note)

Includes bibliographical references (p. [209]-235) and indexes.

Weber, Robert J.

The **created** self; reinventing body, persona, spirit. Norton 2000 350p il hardcover o.p. pa $14.95   **155.2**

1. Self 2. Psychology

ISBN 0-393-32121-5 pa

LC 99-37480

The author contends that "having a self enables the individual to pursue creative endeavors, which though often adaptive from an evolutionary standpoint, actually extend beyond what can be explained in terms of biological, reproductive aims. Using the model of the self developed by William James . . . Weber attempts to show that the self is a constantly developing, 'unitary system', consisting of bodily awareness, persona and spirit, over which the individual has control." Publ Wkly

Includes bibliographical references

Young-Eisendrath, Polly

The **self** -esteem trap; raising confident and compassionate kids in an age of self-importance. Little, Brown 2008 248p $25.99   **155.2**

1. Self-esteem 2. Child psychology

ISBN 978-0-316-01311-6; 0-316-01311-0

LC 2008-2224

The author argues that "those born between 1970 and 2000 (Gen Me-ers) . . . are a vastly discontented group who find their lives unsatisfying and feel entitled to success owing to an overestimation of what the world will bring. She views this as a cultural problem begun in the 1980s when the collapse of the traditional parental hierarchy coincided with a hyperfocus on self-esteem. . . . This is well written, accessible, soundly researched, and beautifully insightful." Libr J

Includes bibliographical references

155.3   Sex psychology; psychology of people by gender or sex, by sexual orientation

Eldredge, Niles

★ **Why** we do it; rethinking sex and the selfish gene. Norton 2004 269p il $24.95   **155.3**

1. Evolution 2. Sociobiology 3. Sex (Biology)

ISBN 0-393-05082-3

LC 2003-27564

The author "believes that sociobiologists like Richard Dawkins and E.O. Wilson are dead wrong in their explanation of life as a mechanism by which 'selfish genes' try to propagate and ensure their own survival. Explaining that life as we know it combines two drives, one economic and one reproductive, Eldredge writes that 'the drive to eat and simply stay alive' is as fundamental as the drive to reproduce." Publ Wkly

"This book, while written for the lay reader, is appropriate for a scientific audience as well. It could be used as supplementary reading in college courses in animal behavior." Sci Books & Films

Lerner, Harriet Goldhor

The **dance** of deception; pretending and truthtelling in women's lives. HarperCollins Pubs. 1993 254p hardcover o.p.   **155.3**

1. Truthfulness and falsehood 2. Women -- Psychology

LC 92-53376

"Patriarchal culture teaches women to pretend and sometimes deceive, Lerner says, and in her study of the role this dissembling plays in women's lives, she shows how 'pretending reflects deep prohibitions, real and imagined, against a more direct and forthright assertion of self.' . . . She acknowledges that truth telling is not easy, yet her discussion of the many ways women lie and how lying affects them clearly shows the benefits of honesty and makes her prescription appealing." Booklist

Includes bibliographical references

Pincott, J.

Do gentlemen really prefer blondes? bodies, behavior and brains: the science behind sex, love, and attraction. [by] Jena Pincott. Delacorte Press 2008 351p il $20 **155.3**

1. Dating (Social customs) 2. Sexual behavior
ISBN 978-0-385-34215-5; 0-385-34215-2

LC 2008-23933

"This book puts together a tremendous amount of potentially useful information in a well-written, entertaining, and easy-to-understand format." Libr J

The author "argues that desire is strongly rooted in evolutionary biases and consults a variety of studies . . . to reveal the extent to which hormones dictate human behavior." Publ Wkly

Includes bibliographical references

Riggle, Ellen D. B.

A **positive** view of LGBTQ; Ellen D.B. Riggle and Sharon S. Rostosky. Rowman & Littlefield 2011 193p. **155.3**

1. Homosexuality 2. Gender identity 3. Sexual minorities 4. Positive psychology
ISBN 9781442212817; 9781442212831

LC 2011027007

The book explores "the strengths and benefits of Lesbian, Gay, Bisexual, Transgender, and Queer (LGTBQ) identities. . . . Focusing on how LGTBQ-identified individuals can cultivate a sense of well-being and a personal identity that allows them to flourish in all areas of life, the authors explore a variety of themes. Through personal stories from people with a variety of backgrounds and gender and sexual identities, readers will learn more about expressing gender and sexuality; creating strong and intimate relationships; exploring unique perspectives on empathy, compassion, and social justice; belonging to communities and acting as role models and mentors; and, enjoying the benefits of living an authentic life." (Publisher's note)

Includes bibliographical references and index.

155.4   Psychology of specific ages

Barnet, Ann B.

The **youngest** minds; parenting and genes in the development of intellect and emotion. {by} Ann B. Barnet and Richard J. Barnet. Simon & Schuster 1998 352p il hardcover o.p. pa $22.95 **155.4**

1. Child psychology 2. Child development
ISBN 978-0-684-85440-3; 0-684-85440-6

LC 98-13450

The authors debate "the relative importance of genetics vs. environment in shaping human personality. Explaining recent work in language acquisition and emotional development . . . they provide an accessisble summary of our current state of knowledge of brain development and chemistry while placing significantly greater emphasis on the role played by environmental factors." Publ Wkly

Includes bibliographical references

Brazelton, T. Berry

The **irreducible** needs of children; what every child must have to grow, learn, and flourish. {by} T.

Berry Brazelton, Stanley I. Greenspan. Perseus Bks. 2000 xx, 228p hardcover o.p. pa $14 **155.4**

1. Child rearing 2. Child psychology 3. Child development
ISBN 0-7382-0516-8 pa

LC 2001-2290

This is "a practical, well-organized volume, of value to parents, physicians, teachers, sociologists, and others who wish to improve children's lives locally and globally." Booklist

Includes bibliographical references

★ **To** listen to a child; understanding the normal problems of growing up. photographs by B.A. King. Addison-Wesley 1984 184p il hardcover o.p. **155.4**

1. Child psychology 2. Child development 3. Parent-child relationship 4. Emotionally disturbed children 5. Children -- Health and hygiene

LC 84-6174

"Brazelton's sensible, authoritative, clear approach provides parents with the kinds of information they need to relax over the long pull, and to understand and cope with day-to-day difficulties." Publ Wkly

Elkind, David

★ The **power** of play; how spontaneous, imaginative activities lead to happier, healthier children. Da Capo Lifelong 2007 240p $24 **155.4**

1. Play
ISBN 0-7382-1053-6; 978-0-7382-1053-7

LC 2006-35592

"Prescribing the trinity of play, love, and work, . . . [the author] shows how the integration of these elements at various stages of development, from infancy to adolescence, leads to happier, well-adjusted individuals with a greater potential for academic success. Elkind will connect with parents when he reveals that 'Toys R Not Us' and argues that less is more; that children should use toys for inspiration, not distraction." Libr J

Includes bibliographical references

Gopnik, Alison

The **scientist** in the crib; minds, brains, and how children learn. [by] Alison Gopnik, Andrew N. Meltzoff, Patricia K. Kuhl. Morrow 1999 279p hardcover o.p. pa $14 **155.4**

1. Child development 2. Psychology of learning
ISBN 0-688-17788-3 pa

LC 99-24247

The authors examine "how children learn to understand and use language, control their emotions and arouse the emotions of others, and establish relationships. . . . Prospective and actual parents stand to learn much that may be helpful to them and their children from this lively book." Booklist

Includes bibliographical references

Harris, Paul L.

Trusting what you're told; how children learn from others. Paul L. Harris. Belknap Press of Har-

vard University Press 2012 253 p. (alk. paper)
$26.95   **155.4**
   1. Child psychology 2. Psychology of learning 3.
Children 4. Learning, Psychology of
ISBN 0674065727; 9780674065727

                      LC 2011046701

This book by Paul L. Harris focuses on the ways in
which children learn and "begins by reminding us of a basic
truth: Most of what we know we learned from others. . . .
[The book] opens a window into the moral reasoning of elementary school vegetarians, the preschooler's ability to distinguish historical narrative from fiction, and the six-year-
old's nuanced stance toward magic. . . . We are biologically
designed to learn from one another, Harris demonstrates."
(Publisher's note)

Includes bibliographical references (p. [222]-241)
and index

Linn, Susan

The **case** for make believe; saving play in a
commercialized world. New Press 2008 258p
$24.95   **155.4**
   1. Play 2. Imagination 3. Advertising and children
ISBN 978-1-56584-970-9; 1-56584-970-1

                      LC 2007-42435

"Puppeteer and therapist Linn draws on years of work
at Boston Children's Hospital to make a thoughtful case for
creative play. She distinguishes between children who are
familiar with concepts of imagination and make-believe versus those who know only how to play with manufactured
toys linked to media campaigns or within the constructs of
rule-driven environments. . . . None of this will be news to
most parents, but Linn seeks to discover what it means for
children to no longer spend time pretending to be someone
or somewhere else. Her research is comprehensive, her firsthand knowledge is impressive, and her examples are damning in their conclusions." Booklist

Includes bibliographical references

Louv, Richard

Last child in the woods; saving our children from
nature-deficit disorder. Algonquin Books of Chapel
Hill 2005 323p $24.95   **155.4**
   1. Child psychology 2. Environmental influence on
humans
ISBN 1-56512-391-3

                      LC 2004-66034

"Louv's book is a call to action, full of warnings—but
also full of ideas for change." Publ Wkly

Includes bibliographical references

Piaget, Jean

★ The **moral** judgment of the child; {translated
by Marjorie Gabain} Free Press 1948 418p hardcover o.p. pa $15   **155.4**
   1. Ethics 2. Human behavior 3. Child psychology
ISBN 0-684-83330-1 pa
Original French edition, 1932

Piaget studies, not the moral behavior of children, but
their ideas about right and wrong, the rules of a game, adult
authority, and cooperation and justice

Segal, Nancy L.

Entwined lives; twins and what they tell us about
human behavior. Plume 2000 396p il pa $16 **155.4**
   1. Twins
ISBN 0-452-28057-5; 978-0-452-28057-1

                      LC 99-59376

First published 1999 by Dutton

"This elegantly written study cogently distills and makes
available to the general reader a wealth of research from the
fields of behavioral genetics, evolutionary psychology and
social science." Publ Wkly

Includes bibliographical references

★ **Indivisible** by two; lives of extraordinary
twins. Harvard University Press 2005 280p il
$24.95   **155.4**
   1. Twins
ISBN 0-674-01933-4; 978-0-674-01933-1

                      LC 2005-45979

The author "makes use of a particularly powerful research method for answering . . . vexing questions about
why our own and other people's lives turn out the way they
do. Segal studies twins—identical, that is, from a single fertilized egg, and fraternal, from two eggs fertilized by different sperm—as well as pseudotwins, children of the same
age who are raised together. She does so with a passion that
derives in part from the fact that she is a fraternal twin herself." N Y Rev Books

White, Burton L.

The **new** first three years of life; 20th anniversary ed; Fireside Bks. 1995 384p il pa $14 **155.4**
   1. Child psychology 2. Infants -- Development
ISBN 0-684-80419-0

                      LC 95-18297

First published 1975 with title: The first three years
of life

"White describes the seven developmental phases of the
first three years of life. He provides parents with a comprehensive treasury of techniques for enhancing development
and establishing discipline that are refreshingly straight-for-
ward and based on real-world experience." Publ Wkly

155.44   Children by status and relationships

Wright, Lawrence

Twins; and what they tell us about who we are.
Wiley 1997 202p $22.95; pa $14.95   **155.44**
   1. Twins
ISBN 0-471-25220-4; 0-471-29644-9 pa

                      LC 97-38827

"Wright presents the conflicting, and often confounding results from twin studies done primarily over the last
50 years. . . . The book serves up questions such as: 'Do our
genes determine our personality?' 'How much, if any, effect
do parents have on the personalities of their children?'." SLJ

"Wright does an admirable job of sorting through the
differing research in a well-reasoned, clearheaded manner."
Publ Wkly

Includes bibliographical references

155.45   Exceptional children; children by social and economic levels, by ethnic or national group

Winner, Ellen
Gifted children; myths and realities. Basic Bks. 1996 449p il hardcover o.p. pa $21   **155.45**
1. Gifted children
ISBN 0-465-01759-2 pa
LC 95-49279

This study considers the following questions "are gifted children gifted in all subject areas? Are artistically gifted children gifted or talented? Does giftedness depend on IQ? What role do environment and biology play in giftedness? Are gifted children psychological and social misfits? In her analyses, Winner cites and explains a broad range of recent research, including extensive notes and references with each chapter. She then offers her recommendations for dealing with gifted children in America's educational systems." Libr J

155.5   Psychology of young people twelve to twenty

Siegel, Daniel J.
Brainstorm; the power and purpose of the teenage brain. Daniel J. Siegel, M.D. Jeremy P. Tarcher/ Penguin 2013 336 p. ill $27.95   **155.5**
1. Adolescent psychology 2. Brain 3. Cognition in adolescence
ISBN 158542935X; 9781585429356
LC 2013029724

This book, by Daniel J. Siegel, "illuminates how brain development impacts teenagers' behavior and relationships. Drawing on important new research in the field of interpersonal neurobiology, he explores exciting ways in which understanding how the teenage brain functions can help parents make what is in fact an incredibly positive period of growth, change, and experimentation in their children's lives less lonely and distressing on both sides of the generational divide." (Publisher's note)

"Smart advice . . . on providing the most supportive and brain-healthy environment during the tumultuous years of adolescence." Kirkus

155.6   Psychology of adults

Ackerman, Diane, 1948-
Deep play; illustrations by Peter Sis. Random House 1999 235p il hardcover o.p. pa $13   **155.6**
1. Play -- Psychological aspects
ISBN 0-679-77135-2 pa
LC 98-35067

The author contends that "deep play, 'ecstatic' play, transcends practical concerns and grants us passage to the sacred and the holy. Art is deep play, so is religion, the contemplation of nature, and playing sports; in short, pursuits that are all-consuming and inspire feelings of awe and a profound sense of connection with the universe. By turns anecdotal and philosophic, Ackerman vividly recounts her own 'deep play' experiences." Booklist
Includes bibliographical references

Engel, Beverly
The nice girl syndrome; stop being manipulated and abused--and start standing up for yourself. John Wiley & Sons 2008 245p $24.95   **155.6**
1. Self-esteem 2. Conduct of life 3. Self-confidence 4. Women -- Psychology
ISBN 978-0-470-17938-3; 0-470-17938-4
LC 2008-8382

The author argues "that while society superficially rewards nice girls, they suffer deeply in their intimate and work relationships by losing personal power and parading inauthentic selves. . . . Most useful for its thorough treatment for how 'nice girls' are socialized and for Engel's concise antidote (the four 'Power C's': confidence, competence, conviction and courage) this book will challenge, entertain and empower its readers." Publ Wkly
Includes bibliographical references

Friday, Nancy
My mother/my self; the daughter's search for identity. Delta Trade Paperbacks 1997 425p pa $17   **155.6**
1. Mothers 2. Mother-daughter relationship 3. Women -- Psychology
ISBN 0-385-32015-9; 978-0-385-32015-3
LC 98-115632

First published 1977 by Delacorte Press
The author explores the psychological aspects of the mother-daughter relationship.
Includes bibliographical references

Lerner, Harriet Goldhor
The dance of intimacy; a woman's guide to courageous acts of change in key relationships. Harper & Row 1989 255p hardcover o.p. pa $14   **155.6**
1. Interpersonal relations 2. Women -- Psychology
ISBN 0-06-091646-X pa
LC 88-45519

The author explains "how to operate more effectively in key relationships—whether it be with a distant or unfaithful spouse, a depressed sister, a difficult mother, an alcoholic father, an uncommitted lover, a dying parent, or a family member that we have written off." Publisher's note
Includes bibliographical references

Levinson, Daniel J.
The seasons of a man's life; by Daniel J. Levinson {et al.} Knopf 1978 363p hardcover o.p. pa $15   **155.6**
1. Middle age 2. Men -- Psychology
ISBN 0-394-533901-0 pa
LC 77-20978

The Levinson theory divides a man's "life cycle into five overlapping eras. . . . Each era is marked by periods of stability during which life structures are built. These stable periods alternate with transition periods during which life structures change." Saturday Rev

Includes bibliographical references

The **seasons** of a woman's life; in collaboration with Judy D. Levinson. Knopf 1996 438p hardcover o.p. pa $23　　　　　　　　**155.6**

1. Middle age 2. Women -- Psychology

ISBN 0-345-31174-4 pa

LC 95-20893

"This work asks whether there is a human life cycle and a process of adult growth similar to the process of child development, and how gender affects the lives of individual women and women in general. The Levinson team interviewed 15 homemakers, 15 women with corporate-financial careers, and 15 women with academic careers. Their stories are the core of Levinson's book." Booklist

Includes bibliographical references

155.67　People in late adulthood

Alford, Henry

How to live; a search for wisdom from old people (while they are still on this earth) Twelve 2009 262p $23.99　　　　　　　　**155.67**

1. Aging 2. Elderly

ISBN 978-0-446-19603-1; 0-446-19603-7

LC 2008-15576

The author "embarks on a quest to find wisdom. Alford notes that Benjamin Franklin helped pen the Constitution at age 81 and Michelangelo completed the Pietà at 91. Who better to consult than septuagenarians, octogenarians, and nonagenarians? He interviews well-known figures—literary critic Harold Bloom, comedian Phyllis Diller, spiritual leader Ram Dass, and playwright Edward Albee—as well as lesser-known yet equally captivating people. . . . Alford is a master of turns of phrase, diction, dialog, and technique. Essential reading." Libr J

155.7　Evolutionary psychology

Clark, William R.

Are we hardwired? the role of genes in human behavior. by William R. Clark & Michael Grunstein. Oxford Univ. Press 2000 322p il hardcover o.p. pa $24.95　　　　　　　　**155.7**

1. Behavior genetics

ISBN 0-19-513826-0; 978-0-19-517800-5 pa; 0-19-517800-9 pa

LC 99-54699

The authors offer an "overview of the current evidence supporting genetic causes for general behavioral tendencies, such as aggression, consumption, sexual preferences, and, most controversial, intelligence. Case studies of identical twins separated as infants provide some of the most compelling proofs." Libr J

Includes bibliographical references

Maestripieri, Dario

Games primates play; an undercover investigation of the evolution and economics of human relationships. Dario Maestripieri. Basic Books 2012 xviii, 302 p.p (hardcover : alk. paper) : $27.99 **155.7**

1. Evolution 2. Interpersonal relations 3. Behavior evolution 4. Control (Psychology) 5. Primates -- Behavior 6. Dominance (Psychology)

ISBN 046502078X; 9780465020782

LC 2011045523

In this book, "[Dario] Maestripieri argues that human behaviour, like our anatomy, can be explained by looking at our biology. Natural selection strongly shaped our social behaviour, and the same pressures faced by our ancestors would also have influenced our closest living relatives--other primates. . . . In economic terms, he argues that we choose mates who enhance our material interests--but only so long as the benefits outweigh the costs." (New Scientist)

Includes bibliographical references (p. 277-295) and index

Ridley, Matt

The **agile** gene; how nature turns on nurture. Perennial 2004 326p pa $13.99　　　　　　　　**155.7**

1. Genetics 2. Nature and nurture

ISBN 978-0-06-000679-2; 0-06-000679-X

First published 2003 with title: Nature via nurture

"In February 2001 it was announced that the human genome contains not 100,000 genes, as originally postulated, but only 30,000. This . . . revision led some scientists to conclude that there are simply not enough human genes to account for all the different ways people behave: we must be made by nurture, not nature. . . . [Ridley argues that] nurture depends on genes, too, and genes need nurture. Genes not only predetermine the broad structure of the brain, they also absorb formative experiences, react to social cues, and even run memory. They are consequences as well as causes of the will." Publisher's note

Includes bibliographical references

155.8　Ethnopsychology and national psychology

Levi-Strauss, Claude

★ The **savage** mind. University of Chicago Press 1966 290p il (Nature of human society series) hardcover o.p. pa $18　　　　　　　　**155.8**

1. Anthropology 2. Ethnopsychology

ISBN 0-226-47484-4 pa

Original French edition, 1962

"An anthropological study of the nature of thought, concepts and systems as they occur in various cultures." Chicago Public Libr

Includes bibliographical references

155.9   Environmental psychology

Attig, Thomas

The **heart** of grief; death and the search for lasting love. Oxford Univ. Press 2000 xx, 289p hardcover o.p. pa $15.95   **155.9**
   1. Death 2. Bereavement 3. Loss (Psychology)
   ISBN 0-19-511873-1; 0-19-515625-0 pa

LC 99-49842

"The pain of loss can be overcome, says Attig . . . by survivors who keep alive in their hearts their love for the departed. He repeats his message in each of some 50 brief chapters, using numerous anecdotes gleaned from his experiences as a counselor to explain how he has helped people cope with the loss of loved ones." Publ Wkly

"A reassuring and useful book for those grieving or counseling those who grieve." Libr J

Benson, Herbert

★ The **relaxation** response; by Herbert Benson, with Miriam Z. Klipper. Updated & expanded [ed.]; Quill 2001 liv, 179p il pa $13.99   **155.9**
   1. Rest 2. Stress (Physiology) 3. Stress (Psychology)
   ISBN 0-380-81595-8

LC 2003-269877

First published 1975 by Morrow

This guide to relieving stress is "recommended for patients suffering from heart conditions, hypertension, chronic pain, and other ailments. A classic." Libr J

Includes bibliographical references

Berns, Nancy

★ **Closure**; the rush to end grief and what it costs us. Temple University Press 2011 213p $75.50; pa $24.95; ebook $24.95   **155.9**
   1. Bereavement 2. Loss (Psychology)
   ISBN 1-43990-576-2; 1-43990-577-0 pa; 1-43990-578-9 ebook; 978-1-43990-576-0; 978-1-43990-577-7 pa; 978-1-43990-578-4 ebook

LC 2011002611

"'Closure' as a signifier for the end of grief has come into wide use, and Berns, who experienced a profound loss when she gave birth to a stillborn son, is here to reinforce what most of us intuitively know: feeling bad about losing a loved one never really ends. By commodifying the concept of closure in order to sell products and services, however, society has put pressure on us to conform to the prevailing 'feeling rules,' suggesting that disappointment, loss, and grief can and should come to an arbitrary end. . . . Berns wisely counsels us to find other language and perspectives for living with grief, and this lucid debunking of the current use of the word 'closure' is a breath of fresh air, recommended for both general readers and specialists." Libr J

Includes bibliographical references

Brehony, Kathleen A.

After the darkest hour; how suffering begins the journey to wisdom. {by} Kathleen Brehony. Holt & Co. 2000 274p il hardcover o.p. pa $14   **155.9**
   1. Suffering 2. Adjustment (Psychology)
   ISBN 0-8050-6436-2 pa

LC 00-29577

"Brehony provides stories and anecdotes throughout the book of people both known and unknown who have gotten through traumatic situations and have learned something from them. . . . Peppered throughout with inspirational quotations, this book teeters on the brink of self-help sentiment, but it succeeds where others might fail in its practicality." Booklist

Includes bibliographical references

Buchholz, Ester Schaler

The **call** of solitude; alonetime in a world of attachment. Simon & Schuster 1997 365p hardcover o.p. pa $22   **155.9**
   1. Solitude
   ISBN 0-684-87280-3 pa

LC 97-20698

"Buchholz's wide-ranging discussion, slanted toward professionals but accessible to interested general readers, may overreach on occasion, but she is often convincing in her timely and provocative advocacy of 'alonetime.'" Publ Wkly

Includes bibliographical references

Dresser, Norine

Saying goodbye to someone you love; your journey through end-of-life and grief. [by] Norine Dresser, Fredda Wasserman. DemosHealth Pub. 2010 210p pa $16.95   **155.9**
   1. Death 2. Bereavement
   ISBN 978-1-932603-85-9

LC 2010-2096

The authors "draw from their experience as hospice workers to illustrate how people have brought up the subject of death with the dying, made end-of-life decisions, and planned (or not held) a funeral service. Dresser and Wasserman not only offer comfort and companionship but provide practical suggestions for conversation starters, ideas for memorials, and a whole section on handling the grief of children. Essential for anyone experiencing end-of-life issues." Libr J

Includes bibliographical references

Edelman, Hope

Motherless daughters; the legacy of loss. 2nd ed; Da Capo Press 2006 pa $15.95   **155.9**
   1. Bereavement 2. Loss (Psychology) 3. Mother-daughter relationship
   ISBN 978-0-7382-1026-1

LC 2005-33840

First published 1994 by Addison-Wesley

"Writing of her own experiences of losing her mother when she was 17, and the grief of hundreds of women she interviewed who lost their mothers through death, abandonment or another form of separation . . . . Edelman marshals a wealth of anecdotal evidence, supplemented with psychological research about bereavement, that indicates that one's longing for a mother never disappears." Publ Wkly

Includes bibliographical references

Motherless mothers; how mother loss shapes the parents we become. HarperCollins 2006 xxxiii, 410p hardcover o.p. pa $14.95   **155.9**
   1. Parenting 2. Bereavement 3. Loss (Psychology) 4.

Mother-daughter relationship

ISBN 0-06-053246-7 pa; 978-0-06-053246-8 pa

LC 2005-52812

In this follow-up to Motherless daughters, the author describes "how the loss of a mother to death or abandonment can affect the ways women raise their own children." Publisher's note

Edelman "presents emotionally charged concepts in clear, memorable terms (e.g., reaching the 'neon number' of a mother's age of death) to encourage frank, cathartic discussion." Publ Wkly

Includes bibliographical references

Emswiler, Mary Ann

Guiding your child through grief; {by} Mary Ann Emswiler and James P. Emswiler. Bantam Bks. 2000 286p il pa $13.95   155.9

1. Death 2. Bereavement 3. Child rearing

ISBN 0-553-38025-7

LC 00-23645

"Thoroughly researched and bolstered with the wisdom of bereavement experts nationwide, this fine guide does those working through the loss of loved ones an enormous service. It should rank amongst the first line of defense and support for those facing a death in the family." Publ Wkly

Includes bibliographical references

Gilbert, Sandra M.

★ Death's door; modern dying and the ways we grieve. Norton 2006 580p il $29.95; pa $17.95   155.9

1. Death 2. Bereavement

ISBN 0-393-05131-5; 978-0-393-05131-5; 0-393-32969-0 pa; 978-0-393-32969-8 pa

LC 2004-65430

"Those who have experienced the death of a loved one will recognize themselves in this meticulously researched, comprehensively organized, and exceptionally caring examination of society's attitudes about mortality and mourning." Booklist

Includes bibliographical references

Gonzales, Laurence

Surviving survival; the art and science of resilience. Laurence Gonzales. W.W. Norton 2012 272 p. (hardcover) $26.95   155.9

1. Psychology 2. Brain -- Physiology 3. Adjustment (Psychology) 4. Resourcefulness 5. Resilience (Personality trait) 6. Disasters -- Psychological aspects

ISBN 0393083187; 9780393083187

LC 2012015592

This book examines "the mental processes that enable us to cope with the trauma that often sets in during and after a challenge to our survival. . . . [Laurence] Gonzales narrates . . . tales, not all of them elective; his survivors are those who have suffered war and terrorism as well as falls off mountains and into choppy surf." The book includes "explanations of the science behind . . . how the amygdala works. . . . One characteristic of success, writes Gonzales, is the ability to step outside oneself to help others." (Kirkus Reviews)

Includes bibliographical references and index

Gosling, Sam

Snoop; what your stuff says about you. Basic Books 2008 263p il map $25   155.9

1. Materialism 2. Social psychology

ISBN 978-0-465-02781-1; 0-465-02781-4

LC 2007-52071

"Unlike many current books on behaviour, Snoop does not contain a single brain scan or discussion of neural activity. Instead, it adopts a shamelessly social approach, focusing on how people behave in the real world rather than in a brain scanner, and presents explanations at the level of individual personalities and social interactions. It works, not least because it has the huge advantage of being exclusively concerned with the one topic that most people find endlessly fascinating: themselves." New Sci

Includes bibliographical references

Karr-Morse, Robin

Scared sick; Robin Karr-Morse with Meredith S. Wiley. Basic Books 2012 xvii, 301p   155.9

1. Mothers 2. Diseases 3. Parenting 4. Child psychology 5. Child development 6. Psychic trauma

ISBN 9780465013548; 9780465028122

LC 2011029405

This book presents an "investigation of the importance of attachment between baby and caretaker—usually the mother—in setting the path to physical and mental health. . . . [The authors] write that without that bond, there is danger that a baby will be stressed, triggering the hypothalamus-pituitary-adrenal axis and flooding the baby's developing nervous system with flight-or-fight hormones. The baby, unable to flee or fight, may succumb to trauma, defined as being frozen in fear. Such trauma is the root of being 'scared sick': suffering ills that may not appear until later in life. Among many others, these can include autism, Alzheimer's, addiction, ADHD, schizophrenia, PTSD, suicide, chronic pain, obesity, heart disease, diabetes and cancer." (Kirkus)

Includes bibliographical references and index.

Kingma, Daphne Rose

The ten things to do when your life falls apart; an emotional and spiritual handbook. New World Library 2010 xxiv, 214p pa $14.95   155.9

1. Suffering 2. Adjustment (Psychology)

ISBN 978-1-57731-698-5

LC 2010-1049

The author "writes for readers whose lives are being wrenched apart by sudden job loss, the death of a loved one, financial ruin, or a dire medical diagnosis. When any of these things happens, either separately or simultaneously, Kingma offers a list of ten ways whereby readers can eventually learn that their difficulties have meaning and purpose. . . . For those lost in the turbulence of life, Kingma offers a genuine hand through." Libr J

Kosko, Bart

★ Noise. Viking 2006 252p il $24.95   155.9

1. Noise

ISBN 0-670-03495-9; 978-0-670-03495-6

LC 2006-44708

The author "discusses the science and subjectivity of noise, achieving a high 'wow' factor in a highly entertaining disclosure of surprising facts and concepts." Booklist

Includes bibliographical references

Kubler-Ross, Elisabeth

★ **On** children and death. Macmillan 1983 279p hardcover o.p. pa $12   **155.9**
1. Death 2. Child psychology
ISBN 0-684-83939-3 pa

LC 83-11252

A look at how one copes with a child's death by disease, accident or murder

Includes bibliographical references

★ **On** death and dying. Scribner Classics 1997 286p il $23; pa $13   **155.9**
1. Death 2. Terminal care
ISBN 0-684-84223-8; 0-684-83938-5 pa

LC 97-177294

A reissue of the title first published 1969 by Macmillan

A look at the psychological, sociological and theological issues faced by the terminally ill and their caregivers

Includes bibliographical references

Lazare, Aaron

On apology. Oxford University Press 2004 306p $24; pa $13.95   **155.9**
1. Apologizing
ISBN 0-19-517343-0; 0-19-518911-6 pa

LC 2004-43470

"Among the topics covered in this . . . book are the growing importance of apologies (the 'apology phenomenon'), how apologies heal, why people do not apologize, and apology and forgiveness." Sci Books Films

"Everybody on earth could benefit from this small but essential book." Publ Wkly

Includes bibliographical references

Pastoureau, Michel

Black; the history of a color. translated from the French by Jody Gladding. Princeton University Press 2009 210p il $35   **155.9**
1. Black
ISBN 978-0-691-13930-2; 0-691-13930-X

LC 2008-25145

"This handsome, strikingly designed, richly illustrated book traces the history of the color black in Europe. . . . [The author] takes special care to define what the universe of color might have been for earlier societies, and carefully follows black's changing social status from archetypical color of darkness, death, and monastic virtue to preferred color of royalty and Romantic melancholy. . . . This book is well researched, skillfully written, and a pleasure to read." Choice

Includes bibliographical references

Prochnik, George

In pursuit of silence; listening for meaning in a world of noise. Doubleday 2010 342p $26   **155.9**
1. Noise 2. Silence
ISBN 978-0-385-52888-7; 0-385-52888-4

LC 2009-41991

"Prochnik's quest for the many meanings of silence takes him on an adventure of profound listening. A Trappist monk says that silence offers a 'radical confrontation with ourselves'; anti-noise policymakers in Europe explain noise-mapping projects; and deaf students reveal unexpected ways of observing space and light. To understand silence, one must understand noise as well, and Prochnik, an advocate for quiet, takes himself to a car-audio competition where boom-car enthusiasts compete in decibel production. He investigates the unexpected paradoxes at the heart of our relationship with sound: we create noise in order to soundproof ourselves, and we create noise by clamoring for silence. There is a difference between mere noise control and genuine silence, and Prochnik makes an eloquent case for the latter, whether in the form of personal contemplation or communal spaces of tranquillity." New Yorker

Includes bibliographical references.

Ripley, Amanda

The **unthinkable**; who survives when disaster strikes and why. Crown Publishers 2008 xx, 266p il $24.95   **155.9**
1. Disasters 2. Disaster relief 3. Survival skills
ISBN 978-0-307-35289-7

LC 2007-40315

Ripley "offers an elementary discussion of disaster and survival, drawing on both survivors' personal accounts and scientific studies that reveal how the human brain functions under duress. She shows how individuals and groups react when such disasters as shipwrecks, fires, terrorist attacks, and tsunamis occur, detailing the traits survivors demonstrate that help them respond effectively. . . . Offering tips on how we can boost our odds, her self-help approach to survival will attract readers." Libr J

Includes bibliographical references

Sife, Wallace

The **loss** of a pet; 3rd ed; Howell Book House 2005 260p il pa $14.99   **155.9**
1. Pets 2. Death 3. Bereavement
ISBN 0-7645-7930-4

LC 2005-12603

First published 1993

The author "addresses the pet owner whose grief at a pet's death is largely misunderstood or even ridiculed by friends, associates and society in general. . . . Sife is to be commended for offering information that is not only compassionate but concise, wide-ranging and, above all, practical." Publ Wkly {review of 1993 edition}

Wickersham, Joan

The **suicide** index; putting my father's death in order. Harcourt 2008 316p $25; pa $14.95   **155.9**
1. Suicide 2. Father-daughter relationship
ISBN 978-0-1510-1490-3; 0-1510-1490-6; 978-0-1560-3380-0 pa; 0-1560-3380-1 pa

LC 2007-29299

"Wickersham's memoir unravels the twisted branches of family ties in the aftermath of her father's suicide as she attempts to answer the question, Why did he do it? . . . Wickersham's effort is worth the read. . . . This book is beautifully written and haunts the reader long after it's closed. Recommended." Libr J

Zimbardo, Philip

The **Lucifer** effect; understanding how good people turn evil. [by] Philip Zimbardo. Random House 2007 xx, 551p il $27.95 **155.9**
1. Good and evil 2. Social psychology 3. Good and evil -- Psychological aspects
ISBN 1-4000-6411-2; 978-1-4000-6411-3

LC 2006-50388

"What makes good people do bad things? How can moral people be seduced to act immorally? Where is the line separating good from evil, and who is in danger of crossing it? . . . [Zimbardo argues that] situational forces and group dynamics can work in concert to make monsters out of decent men and women. . . . [Zimbardo describes his] Stanford Prison Experiment, . . . in which a group of college-student volunteers was randomly divided into 'guards' and 'inmates' and then placed in a mock prison environment. . . . Ordinary college students were transformed into either brutal, sadistic guards or emotionally broken prisoners." (Publisher's note) Index.

The author "masterminded the famous Stanford Prison Experiment, in which college students randomly assigned to be guards or inmates found themselves enacting sadistic abuse or abject submissiveness. In this penetrating investigation, he revisits . . . the SPE study and applies it to historical examples of injustice and atrocity, especially the Abu Ghraib outrages by the U.S. military. . . . Combining a dense but readable and often engrossing exposition of social psychology research with an impassioned moral seriousness, Zimbardo challenges readers to look beyond glib denunciations of evil-doers and ponder our collective responsibility for the world's ills." Publ Wkly

Includes bibliographical references

156   Comparative psychology

Fouts, Roger

Next of kin; what chimpanzees have taught me about who we are. {by} Roger Fouts with Stephen Tukel Mills; introduction by Jane Goodall. Morrow 1997 420p il hardcover o.p. pa $14 **156**
1. Chimpanzees 2. Animal communication
ISBN 0-380-72822-2 pa

LC 97-15144

This is an account of a study known as Project Washoe where a female chimpanzee was taught American Sign Language

"What makes this book an exceptional popularization of scientific research is the authors' ability to charm with a fascinating story while also teaching why the story is so fascinating." Booklist

Includes bibliographical references

Miller, Peter

The **smart** swarm; how understanding flocks, schools, and colonies can make us better at communicating, decision making, and getting things done. Avery 2010 xx, 283p $26 **156**
1. Human behavior 2. Animal behavior 3. Decision making
ISBN 978-1-58333-390-7

LC 2009-48619

The author "examines hives, mounds, colonies, and swarms, whose complex systems of engagement and collective decision making have catalyzed innovations in engineering and can suggest solutions to such problems as climate change. . . . Miller informs, engages, entertains, and even surprises in this thought-provoking study of problem making and problem solving, and through the comparison of human and insect scenarios, shows how social cues and signals can either bring about social cooperation or destruction." Publ Wkly

Includes bibliographical references

Peterson, Dale

The **moral** lives of animals. Bloomsbury Press 2010 342p **156**
1. Ethics 2. Animal behavior 3. Animal intelligence 4. Moral motivation 5. Animal psychology
ISBN 978-1-59691-424-7

LC 2010024662

Peterson "examines the moral behavior observed in animals and argues that human beings are not the only species to live by the principles of cooperation, kindness, and empathy." (Publisher's note) Bibliography. Index.

The author "develops his thoughts on how morality evolved in mammals, including humans. He initially concentrates on where morality comes from, covering basic concepts, linguistic bias, definitions of morality, and a theory of morality's structure. Rules of morality follow with topics such as authority, violence, sex, possession, and communication. . . . Although written for a general audience, this book challenges readers to absorb new information in an area unfamiliar to most. It is definitely worth the effort and is highly recommended for high school-age readers and up." Libr J

Includes bibliographical references

Suddendorf, Thomas

The **gap**; the science of what separates us from other animals. Thomas Suddendorf. Basic Books 2013 368 p. (hardcover) $29.99 **156**
1. Human beings 2. Comparative psychology 3. Psychology 4. Psychology, Comparative
ISBN 0465030149; 9780465030149

LC 2013017538

Author Thomas Suddendorf "provides a definitive account of the mental qualities that separate humans from other animals. Drawing on . . . research on apes, children, and human evolution, he surveys the abilities most often cited as uniquely human--language, intelligence, morality, culture, theory of mind--and finds that two traits account for most of the ways in which our minds appear so distinct: [the] ability to imagine . . .and our insatiable drive to link our minds together." (Publisher's note)

"A reader-friendly examination of the great gap that exists between human beings and the rest of the animal world and an explanation of how our minds came to be unique." Kirkus

Includes bibliographical references and index

Waal, Frans de

Our inner ape; a leading primatologist explains why we are who we are. photographs by the author. Riverhead Books 2005 274p il $24.95 **156**

1. Human behavior 2. Comparative psychology 3. Primates -- Behavior

ISBN 1-57322-312-3

LC 2005-42768

This book compares human "social behavior with that of two species of apes: chimpanzees and bonobos." N Y Times Book Rev

"Readers might be surprised at how much these apes and their stories resonate with their own lives, and may well be left with an urge to spend a few hours watching primates themselves at the local zoo." Publ Wkly

Includes bibliographical references

158 Applied psychology

Achor, Shawn

Before happiness; the 5 hidden keys to achieving success, spreading happiness, and sustaining positive change. by Shawn Achor. Crown Business 2013 256 p. (hc : alk. paper) $26 **158**

1. Happiness 2. Change (Psychology) 3. Success 4. Positive psychology

ISBN 0770436730; 9780770436735

LC 2013022564

In this book, "a happiness researcher investigates why some people can embrace positivity while others are mired in pessimism. Expanding on the theories he presented in 'The Happiness Advantage' . . . [Shawn] Achor now turns his attention to the question of how people learn to accept the possibility of happiness. . . . Happiness . . . is not the same as blind optimism but rather the ability to focus on the positive aspects of a situation while not becoming overwhelmed by the challenges." (Kirkus Reviews)

Includes bibliographical references and index

The **best** within us; positive psychology perspectives on Eudaimonia. edited by Alan S. Waterman. American Psychological Association 2013 xv, 303 p.p $69.95 **158**

1. Philosophy 2. Positive psychology 3. Happiness 4. Well-being

ISBN 1433812614; 9781433812613

LC 2012030170

This book, edited by Alan S. Waterman, "assembles a panel of distinguished scholars whose work has been central to understanding positive aspects of psychological functioning. Together, the chapters explore the many ways in which the philosophic concept of eudaimonia is being employed in psychology. Eudaimonia is defined in this volume as flourishing, realization of potentials reflecting the true self, and happiness that comes from the pursuit of virtue/excellence." (Publisher's note)

Includes bibliographical references and index

Bloomfield, Harold H.

Making peace with your past; the six essential steps to enjoying a great future. {by} Harold H. Bloomfield with Philip Goldberg. HarperCollins Pubs. 2000 269p hardcover o.p. pa $13 **158**

1. Self-realization 2. Applied psychology

ISBN 0-06-093314-3 pa

LC 99-89719

The author "addresses the syndrome Freud called 'repetition compulsion'—humans' tendency to re-create what they have not worked through. . . . With revealing exercises, Bloomfield shows readers how to rediscover 'the passion to live {their} highest destiny.'" Libr J

Includes bibliographical references

Burns, David D.

Feeling good; the new mood therapy. preface by Aaron T. Beck. Rev and updated; Avon Bks. 1999 xxxii, 706p il pa $15 **158**

1. Psychotherapy 2. Depression (Psychology)

ISBN 0-380-73176-2

LC 99-461798

First published 1980

"The author reports on results of treating depression (from mild blues to serious cases) with 'cognitive thinking.' . . . The therapy involves fighting automatic responses to disappointments by intelligent thinking that can put one's shortcomings into perspective." Publ Wkly {review of 1980 edition}

"The author . . . writes simply, clearly, and without any jargon; better yet, he has a sense of compassion and a sense of humor, and is aware of his own limitations." Libr J {review of 1980 edition}

Includes bibliographical references

Canfield, Jack

The **success** principles; how to get from where you are to where you want to be. by Jack Canfield with Janet Switzer. HarperCollins Publishers 2005 xxxiii, 473p il $24.95 **158**

1. Success

ISBN 0-06-059488-8

LC 2004-54259

A self-improvement guide for business professionals, teachers, students, parents, or anyone interested in promoting themselves within today's success-oriented culture shares sixty-four principles on how to reach desired goals

The author "has an easy style and talks directly to readers, responding to potential 'what ifs' and 'buts' with encouragement and sound advice. The book's layout is superb—small paragraphs are punctuated by italicized quotes, questions for self-study, and several appropriate cartoons." Libr J

Includes bibliographical references

Carnegie, Dale

★ **How** to win friends and influence people; editorial consultant, Dorothy Carnegie, editorial as-

sistance, Arthur R. Pell. Pocket Books 1982 276p
pa $6.99   **158**
1. Success 2. Applied psychology
ISBN 0-671-72365-0; 978-0-671-72365-1

LC 94-176452

First published 1936 by Simon & Schuster

"This grandfather of all people-skills books was first
published in 1937. It was an overnight hit, eventually selling 15 million copies. . . . [It] emphasizes fundamental techniques for handling people without making them feel manipulated. . . . Carnegie illustrates his points with anecdotes
of historical figures, leaders of the business world, and everyday folks." Joan Price [This text refers to an out of print
or unavailable edition of this title.]

An examination of the psychology of business and
social success.

Includes bibliographical references

Covey, Stephen R.
★ The **7** habits of highly effective people; restoring the character ethic. [Rev. ed.]; Free Press
2004 372p il $26; pa $15.95   **158**
1. Success 2. Conduct of life
ISBN 0-7432-7245-5; 0-7432-6951-9 pa

LC 2004-57494

First published 1989

The author describes seven habits designed to help people solve personal and professional problems.

The **8th** habit; from effectiveness to greatness.
Free Press 2004 408p il $26   **158**
1. Success 2. Self-realization
ISBN 0-684-84665-9

LC 2004-56371

"The original seven habits of highly successful people
are still relevant, but Covey . . . says that the new Informa-
tion/Knowledge Worker Age, exemplified by the Internet,
calls for an eighth habit to achieve personal and organizational excellence: 'Find your voice and inspire others to find
theirs.' . . . The bulk of the book details how, after finding
your own voice, you can inspire others and create a workplace where people feel engaged." Publ Wkly

"Though conceived for individuals, Covey's book will
be of tremendous importance to organizations and businesses." Libr J

Includes bibliographical references

First things first; to live, to love, to learn, to leave
a legacy. {by} Stephen R. Covey, A. Roger Merrill,
Rebecca R. Merrill. Simon & Schuster 1994 360p il
hardcover o.p. pa $14   **158**
1. Conduct of life 2. Time management
ISBN 0-684-80203-1 pa

LC 94-2305

The authors "offer a 'principle-centered' approach to
time management that emphasizes what 'represents our
vision, values, principles, mission, conscience, direction—
what we feel is important and how we lead our lives.' The
authors argue that central to our lives are 'four needs and
capacities—to live, to love, to learn, to leave a legacy.' The
ideas here are not only clearly explained but are reinforced

by scenarios from the authors' lives and self-directed activities for the reader." Libr J

Includes bibliographical references

Dyer, Wayne W.
★ The **power** of intention; learning to co-cre-
ate your world your way. Hay House 2004 259p
$24.95; pa $14.95   **158**
1. Intentionalism
ISBN 1-401-90215-4; 1-401-90216-2 pa

LC 2003-14622

The author argues that "there are seven faces, or energy
fields, of intention: creativity, kindness, love, beauty, expansion, abundance and receptivity. Drawing on a variety of
spiritual traditions and gurus, Dyer . . . describes how to sur-
mount the barriers that may get in the way of connecting to
this power, such as negative thinking, relying on the opinion
of others or retaining a controlling ego." Publ Wkly

Foster, Rick
How we choose to be happy; the 9 choices of
extremely happy people--their secrets, their stories.
Rev; Berkley Publishing Group 2004 xxi, 228p pa
$14.95   **158**
1. Happiness
ISBN 978-0-399-52990-0; 0-399-52990-X

First published 1999

The authors "interviewed happy people from all walks of
life, from the United States to Eastern Europe. The resulting
personal stories, writing exercises, and quotes together inform and instruct the reader in the nine principles discovered
by the authors in their travels." Libr J

Gegax, Tom
Winning in the game of life; self-coaching secrets for success. RH Publishing 2003 318p pa
$14   **158**
1. Success 2. Self-realization
ISBN 978-0-9740675-0-6; 0-9740675-0-4

First published 1999 by Harmony Bks.

"For Gegax, creating a winning life plan requires defining a mission and taking steps that balances career, friends,
community, and family into an integrated whole." Booklist

Gilbert, Daniel
★ **Stumbling** on happiness; [by] Daniel Gilbert.
Alfred A. Knopf 2006 277p il   **158**
1. Happiness
ISBN 1-4000-4266-6; 1-4000-7742-7 pa; 978-1-
4000-4266-1; 978-1-4000-7742-7 pa

LC 2005044459

This book argues that "events that we anticipate will give
us joy make us less happy than we think; things that fill us
with dread will make us less unhappy, for less long, than we
anticipate." (N Y Times Book Rev) Index.

"The book is a sly, irresistible romp down, or through,
memory lane—past, present, and future. It is not only
wildly entertaining but also hilarious . . . and yet full of
startling insight, imaginative conclusions, and even bits of
wisdom." Booklist

Includes bibliographical references

Goleman, Daniel

★ **Social** intelligence; the new science of human relationships. Bantam Books 2006 403p il $28; pa $14 **158**

1. Emotions 2. Intellect
ISBN 0-553-80352-2; 978-0-553-80352-5; 0-553-38449-X pa; 978-0-553-38449-9 pa

LC 2006-45971

The author "argues for a new social model of intelligence drawn from the emerging field of social neuroscience. . . . Goleman illuminates new theories about attachment, bonding, and the making and remaking of memory as he examines how our brains are wired for altruism, compassion, concern and rapport." Publ Wkly

Includes bibliographical references

Hay, Louise L.

You can heal your life. Hay House 1987 226p pa $14.95 **158**

1. Mind and body 2. Health self-care 3. Self-realization 4. Holistic medicine
ISBN 0-937611-01-8

LC 88-200391

First published 1984

The author's "key message in this . . . work is: 'If we are willing to do the mental work, almost anything can be healed.' Louise explains how limiting beliefs and ideas are often the cause of illness." Publisher's note

Includes bibliographical references

Hodgkinson, Tom

How to be idle. HarperCollins Publishers 2005 286p il $18.95 **158**

1. Conduct of life
ISBN 0-06-077968-3

LC 2004-59932

The author "presents 24 essays defending life's idle pleasures, which are, he says, vilified by our modern society. He meditates on sleeping in, fishing, smoking and drinking, and even waxes poetic about the hangover. The whole book is soaked with nostalgia for the turn-of-the-century English gentleman's lifestyle; Hodgkinson defends his arguments by quoting Jerome K. Jerome, G.K. Chesterton and, of course, that icon of British foppery, Oscar Wilde." Publ Wkly

Includes bibliographical references

Klauser, Henriette Anne

Write it down, make it happen; knowing what you want--and getting it! Scribner 2000 250p hardcover o.p. pa $12 **158**

1. Applied psychology
ISBN 0-684-85002-8 pa

LC 99-43551

The author "instructs her readers to write down their most extravagant wishes and, merely by the act of recording them, make them come true. . . . Her technique is intended to clarify goals, increase self-confidence, and dispel self-doubt, and she describes how it has dramatically improved her life and the lives of her friends and acquaintances." Libr J

Includes bibliographical references

May, Rollo

★ **Freedom** and destiny. Norton 1981 275p hardcover o.p. pa $14 **158**

1. Fate and fatalism 2. Applied psychology 3. Free will and determinism
ISBN 0-393-31842-7 pa

LC 81-4009

This book examines "the continuing tension in our lives between the possibilities freedom offers and the various limitations imposed upon us by our particular fate or destiny." America

Includes bibliographical references

McGraw, Phillip C.

Life strategies; doing what works, doing what matters. Hyperion 1999 282p il $21.95; pa $13.95 **158**

1. Success
ISBN 0-7868-6548-2; 0-7868-8459-2 pa

LC 98-46748

"McGraw claims that people in dire situations have serious problems, including denial and choosing initial assumptions without testing them for accuracy. To create a life strategy that works, McGraw lays out his ten 'Life Laws' along with checklists and 18 assignments." Libr J

Michels, Barry, 1954-

The tools; transform your problems into courage, confidence, and creativity. Phil Stutz and Barry Michels. 1st ed. Spiegel & Grau 2012 271 p. ill. (alk. paper) $25 **158**

1. Applied psychology 2. Change (Psychology) 3. Self-help techniques 4. Self-actualization (Psychology)
ISBN 067964444X; 9780679644446; 9780679644453

LC 2011044717

In this book, "psychiatrist [Phil] Stutz and psychotherapist [Barry] Michels promote a rapid and streamlined method of self-improvement. Michels . . . teaches readers to end procrastination and negativity by tapping into higher forces. . . . [T]he authors' techniques are designed to access intense intrapersonal areas. The 'Inner Authority' tool, for example, involves imagining the Jungian Shadow to reach greater self-expression." (Publishers Weekly)

Miller, Caroline Adams

★ **Creating** your best life; the ultimate life list guide. [by] Caroline Adams Miller and Dr. Michael B. Frisch. Sterling Pub. 2009 276p il $19.95; pa $14.95 **158**

1. Success 2. Happiness
ISBN 978-1-4027-6259-8; 1-4027-6259-3; 978-1-4027-7998-5 pa; 1-4027-7998-4 pa

LC 2010-275766

"Instead of making New Year's resolutions, it may be more beneficial to assemble a goal-setting list. So believe positive psychologist/life coach Miller and clinical psychologist Frisch . . . who have put together dozens of interactive exercises and assessments to guide readers in self-discovery and life-list creation. Whether or not readers follow through with every assignment, they will undoubtedly be inspired to think about goals and live more consciously and productively." Libr J

Includes bibliographical references

Myers, Betsy
 Take the lead; motivate, inspire, and bring out the best in yourself and everyone around you. [by] Betsy Myers with John David Mann. Atria 2011 240p $25; ebook $11.99   **158**
  1. Leadership 2. Motivation (Psychology)
  ISBN 978-1-4391-6067-1; 978-1-4391-6395-5 ebook
                                                LC 2011015072

Myers "look at characteristics and traits that enable individuals to motivate, inspire, and influence individuals and groups. [She] explores what constitutes successful modern leadership, focusing on qualities of emotional intelligence, which she maintains are as essential to leadership effectiveness as more tactical management abilities. The author organizes the book around seven leadership traits: authenticity, connection, respect, clarity, willingness to collaborate, an openness to continuous learning, and the courage to do the right thing. . . . Written in an intelligent but conversational and approachable tone, this inspirational primer is a perfect read for anyone seeking to understand, develop, or unleash his or her genuine leadership potential." Publ Wkly

Includes bibliographical references

The **Oxford** handbook of happiness; edited by Susan A. David, Ilona Boniwell, and Amanda Conley Ayers. Oxford University Press 2013 xxx, 1097 p.p (Oxford library of psychology) (hbk.) $225   **158**
  1. Happiness 2. Philosophy 3. Psychology 4. Joy 5. Well-being 6. Satisfaction
  ISBN 019955725X; 9780199557257
                                                LC 2012538502

This book, edited by Susan David, Ilona Boniwell, and Amanda Conley Ayers, "focus[es] on psychological, philosophical, evolutionary, economic and spiritual approaches to happiness; happiness in society, education, organisations and relationships; and the assessment and development of happiness. Readers will find information on psychological constructs such as resilience, flow, and emotional intelligence." (Publisher's note)

Includes bibliographical references and indexes

Peck, M. Scott
 Further along the road less traveled; the unending journey toward spiritual growth: the edited lectures. Simon & Schuster 1993 255p hardcover o.p. pa $14   **158**
  1. Spiritual life 2. Self-realization 3. Applied psychology
  ISBN 0-684-84723-X pa
                                                LC 93-31322

The author "discusses 'growing up'—becoming self-aware, working through cycles of blame and toward wholesale forgiveness—and then the self-examination we each

must undergo in order to groom ourselves for the most important step of all: the search for God." Booklist

 ★ The **road** less traveled; a new psychology of love, traditional values, and spiritual growth. 25th anniversary ed; Simon & Schuster 2002 315p $22.95   **158**
  1. Love 2. Applied psychology
  ISBN 0-7432-3825-7
                                                LC 2002-75858

A reissue of the title first published 1978

This book attempts to bring together "psychology and religion. It is divided into four areas—discipline, love, religion and growth, and grace—and within each Peck tackles the . . . struggle between stagnation and progress which goes on in all of us throughout our lives." Libr J

 The **road** less traveled and beyond; spiritual growth in an age of anxiety. Simon & Schuster 1997 314p $23; pa $14   **158**
  1. Self-realization 2. Applied psychology
  ISBN 0-684-81314-9; 0-684-83561-4 pa
                                                LC 96-43391

In this volume Peck "continues his journey through the existential conflicts and baffling paradoxes on the meandering road of personal development. . . . Through copious detailed references from his previous books, he allows readers unfamiliar with them to understand and enjoy the present work, which completes his Road trilogy." Publ Wkly

Prager, Dennis
 Happiness is a serious problem; a human nature repair manual. ReganBooks 1998 179p hardcover o.p. pa $13   **158**
  1. Happiness
  ISBN 0-06-098735-1 pa
                                                LC 97-35404

The author "uses the pursuit of happiness as a central motif but generally instructs in the modern art of self-improvement. The 31 short chapters . . . are cogent, complete, and preach a nonreligious yet morally guided moderation that should appeal across a wide range of patron groups." Libr J

Richardson, Brenda Lane
 What mama couldn't tell us about love; healing the emotional legacy of slavery; celebrating our light. {by} Brenda Lane Richardson and Brenda Wade. HarperCollins Pubs. 1999 xxviii, 241p hardcover o.p. pa $13.95   **158**
  1. Love 2. African American women 3. Women -- Psychology
  ISBN 0-06-09379-9 pa
                                                LC 99-12127

The authors present a "self-help guide on relationships and intimacy for African American women. What makes this work unique is that it makes the direct connection between slavery and emotional health. . . . The resource sections on assistance for individual or group work, mental health organizations, and sisterly support are valuable additions." Booklist

Includes bibliographical references

Robbins, Tony

Unlimited power; the new science of personal achievement. [by] Anthony Robbins. 1st Fireside ed.; Simon & Schuster 1997 425p il pa $15   **158**
1. Success 2. Applied psychology
ISBN 0-684-84577-6

LC 97-35403
First published 1986

The author offers advice and techniques for achieving personal and professional success using neurolinguistic programming (NLP).

Salzberg, Sharon

Real happiness; learn the power of meditation: a 28-day program. Workman Publishing 2011 208p pa $14.99   **158**
1. Meditation
ISBN 978-0-7611-5925-4

LC 2010-52087
The author "provides a 28-day program for incorporating meditation into one's life. Written for beginners, the book explains breathing and sitting techniques, the science behind the practice, and 12 guided meditations. Interspersed throughout are FAQs from Salzberg's students regarding their difficulties with the practice. The accompanying CD includes nine meditations to guide readers through breathing, walking, emotional, and loving-kindness exercises. This is one of the best guides for anyone interested in exploring meditation or mindfulness." Libr J

Includes bibliographical references

Schwartz, David Joseph

★ The **magic** of thinking big; 1st Fireside ed.; Simon & Schuster 1987 192p pa $14.95   **158**
1. Success
ISBN 0-671-64678-8

LC 87-8516
First published 1959 by Prentice-Hall

In this motivational book, the author presents a "program for getting the most out of your job, your marriage and family life, and your community." Publisher's note

Siegel, Bernie S.

Prescriptions for living; inspirational lessons for a joyful, loving life. HarperCollins Pubs. 1998 xxiv, 210p hardcover o.p. pa $14   **158**
1. Spiritual life 2. Self-realization
ISBN 0-06-092936-7 pa

LC 98-39059
"Among the topics Siegel covers are how to find peace of mind; how to love, encourage, and forgive other people as well as yourself; and how to thrive in bad times and survive the good times. For those ready to be uplifted by the soothing repetition of time-tested homilies, Siegel delivers the goods." Booklist

Stone, Douglas

Difficult conversations; how to discuss what matters most. {by} Douglas Stone, Bruce Patton, Sheila Heen. Viking 1999 xxi, 250p il hardcover o.p. pa $14   **158**
1. Communication 2. Interpersonal relations
ISBN 0-14-028852-X pa

LC 98-33346
The authors "blend a daunting array of disciplines into highly readable and practical advice." Booklist

Tolle, Eckhart

A **new** earth; awakening to your life's purpose. Dutton/Penguin Group 2005 315p $24.95   **158**
1. Spiritual life 2. Self-realization
ISBN 978-0-525-94802-5; 0-525-94802-3

LC 2005-23358
"According to Tolle, . . . humans are on the verge of creating a new world by a personal transformation that shifts our attention away from our ever-expanding egos." Publ Wkly

Includes bibliographical references

The **power** of now; a guide to spiritual enlightenment. New World Library 1999 193p $22.95; pa $14   **158**
1. Spiritual life 2. Self-realization
ISBN 978-1-57731-152-2; 1-57731-152-3; 978-1-57731-480-6 pa; 1-57731-480-8 pa

LC 99-42366
First published 1997 in Canada

"The author describes his transition from despair to self-realization soon after his 29th birthday. Tolle took another ten years to understand this transformation, during which time he evolved a philosophy that has parallels in Buddhism, relaxation techniques, and meditation theory. . . In The Power of Now he shows readers how to recognize themselves as the creators of their own pain, and how to have a pain-free existence by living fully in the present." Publisher's note

Ury, William

Getting past no; negotiating with difficult people. {by} William L. Ury. Bantam Bks. 1991 161p hardcover o.p. pa $14.95   **158**
1. Negotiation
ISBN 0-553-37131-2 pa

LC 91-10101
"Ury presents a five-step agenda to deal successfully with opponents, be they unruly teenagers, labor leaders, terrorists or international politicians. Strategies focus on self-discipline, or tactics for defusing the adversary's attacks, and suggestions for developing options designed to lead to a mutually satisfactory agreement." Publ Wkly

Includes bibliographical references

Viscott, David S.

Emotional resilience; simple truths for dealing with the unfinished business of your past. by David

Viscott. Harmony Bks. 1996 358p il hardcover o.p. pa $15   **158**

1. Human behavior 2. Attitude (Psychology)
ISBN 0-517-88825-4 pa

LC 96-407

The author outlines his 10 step self help program. "His method, which includes truth telling, acceptance of self and others, letting go of the past and of false expectations, and taking responsibility for one's life, is for those trapped in emotionally confining situations, whether personal relationships, educational impasses, or financial situations." Booklist

158.1   Personal improvement and analysis

Ban Breathnach, Sarah

A **man's** journey to simple abundance; [by] Sarah Ban Breathnach and friends; edited by Michael Segell. Scribner 2000 448p $22   **158.1**

1. Men 2. Conduct of life
ISBN 0-7432-0061-6

LC 00-45012

"A collection of 50-plus pieces on men's experiences. . . . The book's sections cover family, emotional and moral concerns, men's roles and obligations, success and failure, amusements and obsessions, and the deepest values in life. . . . Contributors include respected novelists (Rick Bass, Jim Harrison, Reynolds Price), journalists (Roy Blount, Harold Evans), pop-culture figures (Sting, director Garry Marshall), and representatives of religious and spiritual movements." Booklist

Includes bibliographical references

★ The **power** of habit; by Charles Duhigg. Random House 2012 xx, 371 p.p   **158.1**

1. Business planning 2. Change (Psychology) 3. Habit -- Social aspects
ISBN 9780679603856; 9781400069286

LC 2011029545

In this book, "science writer Charles Duhigg explores the reasons why we find it so hard to change ingrained behaviour. . . . [H]abits usually start with a simple sensory cue . . . which sets up a craving in the brain's reward centres. This yearning overrides the regions involved in self-control. . . . From nail-biting to alcoholism, Duhigg offers . . . insights into the triggers that set people on a downward spiral, and proven ways to fight those urges. . . . Habitual behaviours can propagate through an organisation or society, he argues, offering convincing anecdotes that cover everything from the success of Starbucks to the civil rights movement. . . . [Duhigg examines the] way advertising hijacks your brain's reward centres to set off a new, irresistible habit." (New Scientist)

Includes bibliographical references and index

Viorst, Judith

Imperfect control; our lifelong struggles with power and surrender. Simon & Schuster 1998 446p hardcover o.p. pa $14   **158.1**

1. Psychology
ISBN 0-684-84814-7 pa

LC 97-37302

"Referring to the works of social scientists, psychologists, and philosophers as well as literary examples and personal experiences, Viorst shows how issues of power and surrender confront and affect us throughout our lives. . . . Her book is very readable, with traces of the author's special brand of humor woven throughout." Libr J

Includes bibliographical references

158.2   Interpersonal relations

Goodman, Ellen

I know just what you mean; the power of friendship in women's lives. {by} Ellen Goodman, Patricia O'Brien. Simon & Schuster 2000 300p il $25; pa $14   **158.2**

1. Friendship 2. Women -- Psychology
ISBN 0-684-84287-4; 0-7432-0171-X pa

LC 00-24859

Goodman and O'Brien "examine their friendship of more than 25 years and a host of other friendships among women, famous and unknown." Booklist

"Heavy on insight and light on psychological jargon, this book is an intelligent, observant read." Publ Wkly

Grant, Adam

Give and take; a revolutionary approach to success. Adam M. Grant. Viking 2013 320 p. $27.95   **158.2**

1. Success 2. Social networking 3. Success in business 4. Interpersonal relations
ISBN 0670026557; 9780670026555

LC 2012039995

This book, by Adam M. Grant, focuses on the topic of success. Grant "shows how one of America's best networkers developed his connections, why the creative genius behind one of the most popular shows in television history toiled for years in anonymity, how a basketball executive responsible for multiple draft busts transformed his franchise into a winner, and how we could have anticipated Enron's demise four years before the company collapsed." (Publisher's note)

Includes bibliographical references and index

Hallowell, Edward M.

Connect. Pantheon Bks. 1999 xx, 328p hardcover o.p. pa $13.95   **158.2**

1. Quality of life 2. Interpersonal relations
ISBN 0-7434-0621-4 pa

LC 99-13082

The author "urges readers to 'make time for connectedness,' which he alternately defines as having person-to-person interaction or being involved with something greater than oneself." Libr J

Stengel, Richard

You're too kind; a brief history of flattery. Simon & Schuster 2000 315p $25; pa $14   **158.2**

1. Flattery 2. Flattery -- History
ISBN 0-684-85491-0; 0-684-85492-9 pa

Stengel presents a history of flattery, from ancient Egypt to the present. Index.

"Charting the uses of flattery and the social contexts in which it is used from biblical times to the present, Stengel . . . illustrates that more than mere praise, flattery is praise with a motive, be it benign or grasping. . . . Enjoyable and informative." Libr J

Includes bibliographical references

160   Philosophical logic

Copi, Irving M.
★ **Introduction** to logic; [by] Irving M. Copi, Carl Cohen. 13th ed; Pearson/Prentice-Hall 2008 670p il $104   **160**
1. Logic
ISBN 978-0-13-614139-6; 0-13-614139-0
LC 2007-41752

First published 1953. Periodically revised
This introduction to logic covers language, fallacies, definitions, categories, arguments, deduction, probability and other areas of logical inquiry such as thought and reasoning
Includes bibliographical references

169   Analogy

Hofstadter, Douglas
✓ **Surfaces** and essences; Analogy As the Fuel and Fire of Thinking. Douglas Hofstadter, Emmanuel Sander. Basic Books 2013 608 p. (hardcover) $35   **169**
1. Analogy 2. Thought and thinking
ISBN 0465018475; 9780465018475
LC 2013932688

This book, by Douglas Hofstadter and Emmanuel Sander, "put[s] forth a highly novel perspective on cognition. We are constantly faced with a swirling and intermingling multitude of ill-defined situations. Our brain's job is to try to make sense of this unpredictable, swarming chaos of stimuli. How does it do so? The ceaseless hail of input triggers analogies galore, helping us to pinpoint the essence of what is going on." (Publisher's note)

170   Ethics (Moral philosophy)

Aristotle, 384-322 B.C.
✓ ★ **Nicomachean** ethics; translation (with historical introduction) by Christopher Rowe; philosophical introduction and commentary by Sarah Broadie. Oxford University Press 2002 468p pa $29.95 **170**
1. Ethics
ISBN 978-0-19-875271-4; 0-19-875271-7
LC 2002-283430

According to Aristotle's ethical treatises, "happiness is the goal of life. Pleasure, fame, and wealth, however, will not bring one the highest happiness, which is achieved only through the contemplation of philosophic truth, because it exercises man's peculiar virtue, the rational principle." Reader's Ency. 3d edition
Includes bibliographical references

Carter, Stephen L.
✓ **Integrity**. Basic Bks. 1996 277p hardcover o.p. pa $14   **170**
1. Ethics 2. Conduct of life
ISBN 0-06-092807-7 pa
LC 95-44538

The author seeks to define "integrity in both personal and political terms. . . . Mr. Carter divides true integrity into three parts: discernment, steadfastness and forthrightness. Anyone who wants to act with integrity must first think hard about what is right and wrong. . . . Once the right course of action suggests itself, it should be acted upon, even if doing so is risky or unpleasant. . . . People of integrity, finally, are willing to defend what they do in public." N Y Times Book Rev
Includes bibliographical references

Coles, Robert
✓ ★ **Lives** of moral leadership. Random House 2000 247p hardcover o.p. pa $13.95 **170**
1. Ethics 2. Leadership 3. Conduct of life
ISBN 0-375-75835-6 pa
LC 00-27858

Drawing on interviews he conducted over the past four decades with public and private figures, Coles reflects on the meaning of moral leadership in the United States

Comte-Sponville, Andre
✓ A **small** treatise on the great virtues; the uses of philosophy in everyday life. translated by Catherine Temerson. Metropolitan Bks. 2001 352p $27.50; pa $16   **170**
1. Ethics
ISBN 0-8050-4555-4; 0-8050-4556-2 pa
LC 2001-30299

Original French edition, 1995
"His subject demands a sober seriousness, but Comte-Sponville still manages to avoid taking himself too seriously: humility makes it into his litany of virtues, as does humor. A laudable renewal of the ancient quest for ethical wisdom." Booklist
Includes bibliographical references

Edelman, Marian Wright
✓ The **measure** of our success; a letter to my children and yours. HarperPerennial 1993 97p pa $10   **170**
1. Ethics 2. Child rearing 3. Human behavior 4. United States -- Moral conditions
ISBN 0-06-097546-6; 978-0-06-097546-3
LC 92-54846

First published 1992 by Beacon Press
The author presents her "beliefs on child rearing and moral values. . . . She includes a personal letter to her three sons, who were born into a family with a shared African American and Jewish heritage, and offers 25 lessons, or 'road maps', for life." Libr J

Encyclopedia of applied ethics. Academic Press 1998 4v set $790   **170**
1. Reference books 2. Ethics -- Encyclopedias
ISBN 0-12-227065-7
LC 97-74395

"Arranged in an A-Z format, the set describes 282 topics in 5000- to 6000-word articles. Coverage includes most of the 'hot topics' of our day from abortion and adoption to zoos. Typical of the broad coverage, 'Aids in the Developing World' includes a glossary description of clinical research, a discussion of sex education, and comments on resource allocation." Libr J

Encyclopedia of ethics; edited by Lawrence C. Becker and Charlotte B. Becker. 2nd ed; Routledge 2001 3v set $370   **170**
1. Reference books 2. Ethics -- Encyclopedias
ISBN 0-415-93672-1

LC 2001-19657
First published 1992 by Garland
"The coverage of ethical theory as pursued among English-speaking philosophers remains the scope of this set. Entries are listed in word-by-word alphabetical order. A list of entries gives a convenient overview of headwords and see references. A subject index provides a guide to subjects discussed in the text of the entries, including persons; and a citation index provides an author-by-author listing of writers, and some editors, cited in the bibliographies of all 581 entries." Booklist
Includes bibliographical references and index

★ **Ethics;** edited by John K. Roth. Rev. ed.; Salem Press 2005 3v set $331   **170**
1. Reference books 2. Ethics -- Encyclopedias
ISBN 1-58765-170-X

LC 2004-21797
First published 1994
For a fuller review, see: Booklist, June 1 & 15, 2005
The aim of this set is "to provide accessible entry points for those grappling with ethical issues and concerns. The 1000-plus articles cover people, events, organizations, trends, and issues. . . . This well-organized, highly useful work will be popular with researchers and general readers." SLJ
Includes bibliographical references

Fleming, Thomas
The **morality** of everyday life; rediscovering an ancient alternative to the liberal tradition. University of Missouri Press 2004 270p $44.95   **170**
1. Ethics
ISBN 0-8262-1509-2

LC 2003-23962
"Writing much more accessibly and knowledgeably than most modern, professional philosophers, Fleming revivifies the body of thought with which civilization was created and without which it is disintegrating." Booklist
Includes bibliographical references

Gaines, Patrice
Moments of grace; meeting the challenge to change. Crown 1997 206p hardcover o.p. pa $15   **170**
1. Conversion 2. Conduct of life
ISBN 0-609-80171-6 pa

LC 96-25404
Companion volume to Laughing in the dark (1994)

"Gaines manifests an intelligent and mellow wisdom. She treats her own insight into her travails as spiritual awakenings, or gifts from God. Without preaching or cheerleading, she points out the powerful, life-changing lessons available in her experiences and in those of others." Publ Wkly

Global values 101; a short course. edited by Kate Holbrook . . . [et al.] Beacon Press 2006 276p pa $14   **170**
1. Social values
ISBN 0-8070-0305-0

LC 2005-13091
"For Personal Choice and Global Transformation, the exceedingly popular and controversial Harvard undergraduate religion course that spawned this book, . . . [the editors] invited about a dozen people—'from janitors to billionaires, from professors to corporate CEOs to nuns'—to their class each semester to answer tough, well-informed questions posed by their students. Transcripts of 16 of those conversations comprise this timely, thought-provoking volume that opens with historian Howard Zinn and closes with independent journalist Amy Goodman." Libr J
Includes bibliographical references

Gottlieb, Daniel
Learning from the heart; lessons on living, loving, and listening. Sterling Pub. 2008 170p $17.95   **170**
1. Conduct of life
ISBN 978-1-4027-4999-5; 1-4027-4999-6

LC 2007-35100
"Having rebuilt his life after an accident that left him a quadriplegic in his thirties, . . . [the author] here shares his observations on what makes us human. . . . An uplifting book abounding with encouragement for daily living; recommended for public libraries." Libr J

Greene, Joshua
Moral tribes; emotion, reason, and the gap between us and them. by Joshua D. Greene. Penguin Press 2013 432 p. $29.95   **170**
1. Ethics 2. Emotions 3. Social psychology 4. Civilization
ISBN 1594202605; 9781594202605

LC 2013007775
In this book, "[Joshua] Greene, a philosopher and scientist, draws on research in psychology and neuroscience to explore the roots of morality, particularly the tragedy of commonsense morality, when people of different races, religions, ethnic groups, and nationalities share the same sense of morality but apply it from different perspectives in whose differences lie the roots of conflict. Us-versus-them conflicts date back to tribal life." (Booklist)
Includes bibliographical references (pages 388-403) and index

Haidt, Jonathan
The **happiness** hypothesis; finding modern truth in ancient wisdom. Basic Books 2005 297p il $26; pa $15.95   **170**
1. Happiness
ISBN 978-0-465-02801-6; 0-465-02801-2; 978-0-465-

02802-3 pa; 0-465-02802-0 pa

LC 2005-21163

"Using the wisdom culled from the world's greatest civilizations as a foundation, social psychologist Haidt comes to terms with 10 Great Ideas, viewing them through a contemporary filter to learn which of their lessons may still apply to modern lives. . . . Fascinating stuff, accessibly expressed." Booklist

Includes bibliographical references

Hauser, Marc D.

★ **Moral** minds; how nature designed our universal sense of right and wrong. Ecco 2006 489p il $27.95 **170**

1. Ethics

ISBN 978-0-06-078070-8; 0-06-078070-3

LC 2006-41324

"Hauser has picked a subject that philosophers have vented about since philosophy began, and knows it. He explores Kant and Hume and Rawls in some detail and uses their insights to characterize different aspects of the human mental apparatus that can become involved in moral judgments. But while he pays respects to these thinkers of the past, he does not kowtow to them." Humanist

Includes bibliographical references

Kalman, Maira

And the pursuit of happiness. Penguin Group 2010 471p il $29.95 **170**

1. Democracy 2. Happiness 3. United States -- Description and travel

ISBN 978-1-59420-267-4

"First published as an illustrated, 12-part blog in the New York Times, artist-author Kalman's . . . meditation on democracy is now available in a single volume. Despite its original episodic publication, the book coheres beautifully in terms of both artistic unity and the careful evolution of its overarching theme. Each chapter—beginning with the January inauguration of Barack Obama, an event that was the catalyst for the book—represents a month of Kalman's yearlong quest, which included visits to both coasts. Thus, the month of February is devoted to her loving celebration of Abraham Lincoln; March to 'the essence of democracy, the town meeting'; and so on to December, which concerns George Washington and, finally, a tender and loving evocation of happiness itself. Kalman's art and its wonderful interaction with her hand-lettered text is every bit as idiosyncratic as her approach to her subject, and the result is an achievement that evokes her widely praised picture books for children." Booklist

Kübler-Ross, Elisabeth

★ **Life** lessons; two experts on death and dying teach us about the mysteries of life and living. [by] Elisabeth Kübler-Ross and David Kessler. Scribner 2000 224p $24; pa $13 **170**

1. Death 2. Conduct of life

ISBN 0-684-87074-6; 0-684-87075-4 pa

LC 00-57387

"As in each of their previous individual works, the authors provide useful and accessible information." Libr J

Martin, Mike W.

Happiness and the good life; Mike W. Martin. Oxford University Press 2012 xiii, 230 p.p **170**

1. Happiness 2. Philosophy 3. Conduct of life 4. Well-being

ISBN 0199845212; 9780199845217

LC 2011019584

Author Mike W. Martin "connects the meaning of happiness with the philosophical notion of 'the good life.' Defining happiness as loving one's life and valuing it in ways manifested by ample enjoyment and a deep sense of meaning, Martin explores the ways in which happiness interacts with all other dimensions of good lives--in particular with moral decency and goodness, authenticity, mental health, self-fulfillment, and meaningfulness." (Publisher's note)

Includes bibliographical references (p. 211-224) and index

McCullough, David

You Are Not Special; And Other Encouragements. David G. McCullough. HarperCollins 2014 352 p. illustrations $21.99 **170**

1. Commencements 2. High school students

ISBN 006225734X; 9780062257345

"In 'You Are (Not) Special,' [author David] McCullough elaborates on his now-famous speech exploring how, for what purpose, and for whose sake, we're raising our kids. With wry, affectionate humor, McCullough takes on hovering parents, ineffectual schools, professional college prep, electronic distractions, club sports, and generally the manifestations, and the applications and consequences of privilege." (Publisher's note)

"The author tackles big issues, such as gender and race, with searching sincerity, open-heartedness, and a deft, light touch." Kirkus

McMahon, Darrin M.

★ **Happiness**; a history. Atlantic Monthly Press 2005 544p il $27.50 **170**

1. Happiness

ISBN 0-8711-3886-7

LC 2005-48009

Utilizing different types of sources including "art and architecture, music and theology, literature and myth . . . [the author] traces the transformation of the concept of happiness through more than 2000 years of Western thought. . . . Filled with ample and provoking commentary, this work keeps the reader engaged and makes valuable contributions to the concept of happiness with each successive chapter." Libr J

Includes bibliographical references

Reader's Digest Association

Everyday greatness; inspiration for a meaningful life. insights and commentary by Steven R. Covey; compiled by David K. Hatch. Rutledge Hill Press 2006 445p $24.99 **170**

1. Conduct of life

ISBN 978-1-4016-0241-3; 1-4016-0241-X

LC 2006-19786

"The stories, which the authors have gleaned from Reader's Digest, illustrate 21 principles such as integrity, gratitude, respect, and perseverance. Covey provides commentary, reflections, and further insights on how readers can apply each principle to their own lives in today's world. Truly inspiring." Libr J

Includes bibliographical references

Schoch, Richard W.

The **secrets** of happiness; three thousand years of searching for the good life. Scribner 2006 243p $23; pa $13.95   **170**

1. Happiness

ISBN 978-0-7432-9292-4; 0-7432-9292-8; 978-0-7432-9293-1 pa; 0-7432-9293-6 pa

                    LC 2006-44375

"The essence of happiness, Schoch believes, is not simply feeling good—a state some today consider an entitlement. Rather, it lies in one's quest to create a better world. First highlighting the Greek philosopher Epicurus, the Roman Stoic Seneca and medieval Islamic scholar Abu Hamid al-Ghazali, Schoch explains that although these three thinkers had very different experiences, they were united in their search for a more fulfilling life under sometimes adverse conditions. Schoch then explores the ideas found in eight sacred and secular traditions, including Buddhism, Hinduism, Christianity and Epicureanism. . . . Schoch writes in an informed, lively style and his nonjudgmental stance will appeal to many who seek not easy self-help but to wrestle with issues of meaning and values." Publ Wkly

Includes bibliographical references

This I believe; the personal philosophies of remarkable men and women. edited by Jay Allison and Dan Gediman, with John Gregory and Viki Merrick; photographs by Nubar Alexanian. H. Holt 2006 xxi, 281p il $23   **170**

1. Conduct of life 2. Belief and doubt

ISBN 0-8050-8087-2; 978-0-8050-8087-2

                    LC 2006-43522

This collection of essays from a popular radio series "draws transcripts from both the original series and its newer version, including some remarkable statements from the likes of dancer/choreographer Martha Graham, autistic academic Temple Grandin, writer and physicist Alan Lightman, novelist and social critic Thomas Mann, economic historian Arnold Toynbee, and feminist writer Rebecca West. Astonishing to hear and astonishing to read and reread, this work is a wonderful addition to any library." Libr J

This I believe II; more personal philosophies of remarkable men and women. edited by Jay Allison and Dan Gediman; with John Gregory and Viki Merrick; additional editing by Emily Botein . . . [et al.] Henry Holt 2008 268p $23   **170**

1. Conduct of life 2. Belief and doubt

ISBN 978-0-8050-8768-0; 0-8050-8768-0

                    LC 2008-10110

"Many [of these essays] will leave you breathless. And those that don't astonish may simply humble you." Christ Sci Monit

Tutu, Desmond, 1931-

Made for goodness; and why this makes all the difference. [by] Desmond M. Tutu and Mpho

A. Tutu; edited by Douglas C. Abrams. HarperOne 2010 206p $25.99   **170**

1. Good and evil 2. Religious life 3. Conduct of life 4. Christian life

ISBN 978-0-06-170659-2

                    LC 2010-3774

In this book, the South African archbishop and his daughter, an Anglican priest, present their spiritual vision of hope for humanity.

"The book is founded on the broad notion that we are created with the freedom to choose good or evil but also incline fundamentally to the good. . . . A crucially important book from the Nobel Peace Prize winner; a witness to our tumultuous times." Libr J

Wolfe, Alan

Moral freedom; the impossible idea that defines the way we live now. Norton 2001 256p hardcover o.p. pa $14.95   **170**

1. Ethics 2. Values 3. Public opinion 4. United States -- Moral conditions

ISBN 0-393-04843-8; 0-393-32302-1 pa

                    LC 00-51969

"Wolfe here discusses the results of a national public opinion poll he helped design on American beliefs about values, which he supplemented with detailed interviews of people from eight different U.S. communities. These ranged widely, from the Castro district of San Francisco to San Antonio." Libr J

Includes bibliographical references

171   Ethical systems

Moeller, Hans-Georg

The **moral** fool; a comparative case for amorality. Columbia University Press 2009 212p   **171**

1. Social ethics 2. Social values 3. Moral conditions

ISBN 9780231145084; 9780231145091

                    LC 2008050513

"This engaging and often difficult study is a well-conceived critique of ethical and moral thinking from an amoral perspective or standpoint. . . . Throughout this study Moeller considers controversial ethical and moral problems from his amoral perspective: civil rights, abortion, religious and just wars, capital punishment, ethnic cleansing, segregation, sexual orientation, political purges, and more. . . . The author's amoral slant on these subjects is difficult to contest; this is a landmark study that anyone who champions ethics and morality must confront. Very highly recommended." Libr J

Includes bibliographical references

Rand, Ayn

★ The **virtue** of selfishness; a new concept of egoism. with additional articles by Nathaniel Branden. Centennial ed; Signet/New American Library 2005 173p pa $7.99   **171**

1. Egoism 2. Objectivism (Philosophy)

ISBN 0-451-16393-1

First published 1964

The author "sets forth the moral principles of Objectivism, the philosophy that holds man's life—the life proper to a rational being—as the standard of moral values and regards altruism as incompatible with man's nature, with the creative requirements of his survival, and with a free society." Publisher's note

172   Applied ethics

Ignatieff, Michael

The **lesser** evil; political ethics in an age of terror. Princeton University Press 2004 212p (The Gifford lectures) $29.95; pa $16.95   **172**

1. Terrorism 2. Political ethics
ISBN 0-691-11751-9; 0-691-12393-4 pa

The author "presents an overview of how democracies have dealt with terrorist movements in the past and how they might best approach the terrorist threat today. . . . This should be required reading for all informed citizens as we face an uncertain future." Libr J

Includes bibliographical references

Sandel, Michael J., 1953-

Justice; what's the right thing to do? Farrar, Straus & Giroux 2009 308p $25; pa $15   **172**

1. Ethics 2. Values 3. Justice
ISBN 0-374-18065-2; 0-374-53250-8 pa; 978-0-374-18065-2; 978-0-374-53250-5 pa

LC 2009-25438

This book is based on a course the author teaches at Harvard University. It is a companion to a series on public television. Sandel examines various philosophical approaches to justice and seeks to show how they relate to contemporary political debates on such issues as same-sex marriage, reparations for slavery, surrogate motherhood and immigration reform. Index.

"The author has a talent for making the difficult—Kant's 'categorical imperative' or Rawls's 'difference principle'—readily comprehensible, and his relentless, though never oppressive, reason shines throughout the narrative. Sparkling commentary from the professor we all wish we had." Kirkus

Includes bibliographical references

174   Occupational ethics

Callahan, David

The **cheating** culture; why more Americans are doing wrong to get ahead. Harcourt 2004 353p $26; pa $14   **174**

1. Social ethics 2. Business ethics
ISBN 0-15-101018-8; 0-15-603005-5 pa

LC 2003-15529

"If all business school students could be required to read one book, this should be it." Choice

Includes bibliographical references

Clones and clones; facts and fantasies about human cloning. edited by Martha C. Nussbaum and Cass R. Sunstein. Norton 1998 351p $26.95; pa $15.95   **174**

1. Cloning 2. Bioethics 3. Reproductive technology
ISBN 0-393-04648-6; 0-393-32001-4 pa

LC 97-51781

This is a collection of essays and short stories on cloning. The contributors include Richard Dawkins; Eric A. Posner and Richard A. Posner; Andrea Dworkin; William N. Estridge and Edward Stein; and Richard A. Epstein

"The spectrum of authors and their varying perspectives in fact and fiction are assets to anyone who hopes to understand this broad issue and its vast cultural implications." Publ Wkly

Includes bibliographical references

Conway, Erik M.

Merchants of doubt; how a handful of scientists obscured the truth on issues from tobacco smoke to global warming. [by] Naomi Oreskes and Erik M. Conway. Bloomsbury Press 2010 355p $27   **174**

1. Science -- Ethical aspects
ISBN 978-1-59691-610-4; 1-59691-610-9

LC 2009-43183

"A well-documented, pulls-no-punches account of how science works and how political motives can hijack the process by which scientific information is disseminated to the public." Kirkus

Includes bibliographical references

Covey, Stephen M. R.

★ **Smart** trust; creating prosperity, energy and joy in a low-trust world. Stephen M.R. Covey and Greg Link ; with Rebecca R. Merrill. Free Press 2012 xxiii, 296 p.p $27   **174**

1. Trust 2. Ethics 3. Business ethics 4. Organizational behavior 5. Leadership -- Moral and ethical aspects
ISBN 1451651457; 9781451651454; 9781451651478

LC 2011039458

It was the authors' intent to demonstrate that "the biggest impediment to global economic health is not the economics of the financial crisis but the loss of trust the crisis caused. . . . The authors make the case for the importance of trust and then teach readers how to trust in an untrustworthy world: by coupling the universal innate propensity to trust with a high level of critical analysis." (Library Journal)

Includes bibliographical references and index.

★ **Encyclopedia** of bioethics; Stephen G. Post, editor in chief. 3rd ed; Macmillan Reference USA 2003 5v set $595   **174**

1. Reference books 2. Bioethics -- Encyclopedias 3. Medical ethics -- Encyclopedias
ISBN 0-02-865774-8

LC 2003-15694

"This new edition of a classic work, which addresses timely issues such as same-sex marriages and direct advertising of prescription drugs, belongs in all academic libraries and all but the smallest public libraries. It is an outstanding resource for students, professionals, and the interested public." Booklist

Includes bibliographical references

The **Ethics** of organ transplants; the current debate. edited by Arthur L. Caplan and Daniel H. Coelho. Prometheus Bks. 1998 350p il pa $20   **174**

1. Medical ethics 2. Transplantation of organs, tissues, etc.

ISBN 1-57392-224-2

LC 98-31722

The editors "have selected 35 articles that are representative of the ethical issues surrounding organ transplantation. . . . In many cases, the editors have selected companion articles that illustrate contrasting viewpoints on a particular issue." Libr J

Includes bibliographical references

Fox, Michael W.

Beyond evolution; the genetically altered future of plants, animals, the earth--humans. Lyons Press 1999 256p $24.95   **174**

1. Bioethics 2. Genetic engineering

ISBN 1-55821-901-3

LC 99-12866

The author "argues that biotechnology—coupled with industrial, chemical-based agriculture—will only accelerate the adverse environmental and consumer-health consequences of factory farming." Publ Wkly

Includes bibliographical references

Gentile, Mary C.

Giving voice to values; how to speak your mind when you know what's right. Yale University Press 2010 xliv, 273p $26   **174**

1. Values 2. Leadership 3. Business ethics

ISBN 978-0-300-16118-2

LC 2010011905

The author sets "out to tackle the 'ethics in business' conundrum. . . . [She] explores not only why we sometimes do not act alongside our values, but also how employees can do just that, while still advancing their careers." Risk Management

Gentile "offers a powerful action-oriented manifesto for living with integrity, fighting for one's convictions, and building a more ethical workplace." Publ Wkly

Includes bibliographical references

Hawthorne, Fran

Ethical chic; the inside story of the companies we think we love. by Fran Hawthorne. Beacon Press 2012 xxvi, 181 p.p (alk. paper) $25.95   **174**

1. Corporate culture 2. Social responsibility of business 3. Brand loyalty -- United States -- Case studies 4. Business ethics -- United States -- Case studies 5. Corporate image -- United States -- Case studies 6. Social responsibility of business -- United States -- Case studies 7. Corporations -- Moral and ethical aspects -- United States -- Case studies

ISBN 0807000949; 9780807000946

LC 2011048739

In this book, journalist Fran Hawthorne "evaluates six companies (Tom's of Maine, Timberland, Starbucks, Apple, Trader Joe's, and American Apparel) that have built brands around goodness . . . . In reviewing the impact of these companies on the environment, treatment of workers, and public service, Hawthorne's methodology is mainly qualitative, based on interviews with company representatives, union leaders, and staff at various watchdog organizations." (Publishers Weekly)

Includes bibliographical references

Lutz, Tom

Doing nothing; a history of loafers, loungers, slackers and bums in America. Farrar, Straus and Giroux 2006 384p $25   **174**

1. Conduct of life

ISBN 0-8654-7650-0; 978-0-8654-76

LC 2005-27230

"With layabouts such as Theodore Dreiser, the Beats, and our epoch's own Anna Nicole Simpson on offer, cultural-history mavens won't be able to pass Lutz up." Booklist

Mackey, John, 1953-

Conscious capitalism; liberating the heroic spirit of business. John Mackey & Raj Sisodia. Harvard Business Review Press 2013 344 p. (hardcover) $27   **174**

1. Capitalism -- Ethical aspects 2. Social responsibility of business 3. Social values 4. Business ethics 5. Corporations -- Moral and ethical aspects

ISBN 1422144208; 9781422144206

LC 2012025305

"In this book, Whole Foods Market cofounder John Mackey and professor and Conscious Capitalism, Inc. cofounder Raj Sisodia argue for the inherent good of both business and capitalism. Featuring some of today's best-known companies, they illustrate how these two forces can--and do--work most powerfully to create value for all stakeholders: including customers, employees, suppliers, investors, society, and the environment." (Publisher's note)

Includes bibliographical references

Munson, Ronald

★ **Raising** the dead; organ transplants, ethics, and society. Oxford Univ. Press 2002 288p $55; pa $19.95   **174**

1. Medical ethics 2. Transplantation of organs, tissues, etc.

ISBN 0-19-513299-8; 0-19-517801-7 pa

LC 2001-36119

This examination of the "variety of ethical issues surrounding organ transplantation . . . discusses the definition of death, methods for obtaining organs, recipient selection, xenotransplantation, and stem cell research." Libr J

"Lucid and compelling writing on a much-debated topic." Booklist

Includes bibliographical references

Preer, Jean

Library ethics; [by] Jean Preer. Libraries Unlimited 2008 255p il pa $45   **174**

1. Ethics 2. Librarians -- Ethics 3. Librarians -- Professional ethics 4. Library science -- Moral and ethical aspects

ISBN 978-1-59158-636-4

LC 2008-21122

"This title takes an inclusive look at why library ethics are needed in the 21st century. This highly practical, substantial, and carefully planned resource is designed to help information professionals figure out their professional values and where they stand when faced with ethical dilemmas. . . . New practitioners entering the field would be wise to use this book as their first professional bible. Those already in the library profession may find this title to be a good refresher." Libr Media Connect

Includes bibliographical references

Ruggie, John

Just Business; Multinational Corporations and Human Rights. John Gerard Ruggie. W W Norton & Co Inc 2013 304 p. $23.95 **174**
1. Human rights 2. Business ethics 3. Business enterprises 4. International business enterprises -- Moral and ethical aspects
ISBN 0393062880; 9780393062885

LC 2012047820

Author John Gerard Ruggie focuses on human rights in the business world. "Ruggie demonstrates how, to solve a seemingly unsolvable problem, he had to abandon many widespread and long-held understandings about the relationships between businesses, governments, rights, and law. . . . He also takes us through the journey of assembling the right type of team, of witnessing the severity of the problem firsthand, and of pressing through the many obstacles such a daunting endeavor faced." (Publisher's note)

Includes bibliographical references and index

United States/President's Council on Bioethics

★ Human cloning and human dignity; the report of the President's Council on bioethics. with a foreword by Leon R. Kass, chairman. PublicAffairs 2002 350p il pa $14 **174**
1. Cloning 2. Bioethics
ISBN 1-58648-176-2

This "report focuses on three major issues: cloning to produce children (reproductive uses), cloning for biomedical research (therapeutic uses), and various public policies that could be enacted. The council members were divided on their recommendations regarding human cloning, so both a majority and a minority opinion are presented here." Libr J

Includes bibliographical references

Wilmut, Ian

★ The second creation; Dolly and the age of biological control. [by] Ian Wilmut, Keith Campbell and Colin Tudge. Harvard University Press 2001 360p il pa $16.95 **174**
1. Cloning
ISBN 978-0-674-00586-0

First published 2000 by Farrar, Straus & Giroux

The scientists responsible for cloning the ewe Dolly "tell the full story of how they did it. . . . To demystify cloning (now called nuclear transfer by experts), the authors trace the history of cell biology and embryology, the linked sciences that made it possible, explaining in lucid terms the fundamental principles that brought Dolly and her successors to life." Booklist

174.2 Medical and health professions

Caplan, Arthur L.

Smart mice, not-so-smart people; an interesting and amusing guide to bioethics. Rowman & Littlefield 2006 210p $21.95; pa $14.95 **174.2**
1. Medical ethics
ISBN 978-0-7425-4171-9; 0-7425-4171-1; 978-0-7425-4172-6 pa; 0-7425-4172-X pa

LC 2006-14275

The author discusses "issues at the center of the new genetics, cloning in the laboratory and in the media, stem cell research, experiments on human subjects, blood donation and organ transplantation, and healthcare delivery." Publisher's note

Elliott, Carl

White coat, black hat; adventures on the dark side of medicine. Beacon Press 2010 224p $24.95 **174.2**
1. Drug industry 2. Medical ethics 3. Medicine -- United States 4. Medical ethics -- United States 5. Drugs -- Effectiveness -- Evaluation 6. Conflict of interests -- United States 7. Pharmaceutical industry -- United States
ISBN 978-0-8070-6142-8

LC 201006119

The author argues that "over the past twenty-five years, the practice of medicine has been subverted by the business of medicine, sacrificing old-style doctoring to fit the values of consumer capitalism. In this . . . narrative, physician and moral philosopher Carl Elliott traces the evolutionary path of this new direction in health care." (Publisher's note) Index.

Elliott "examines the part played by the pharmaceutical industry in constructing 'a medical system in which deception is often not just tolerated but rewarded.' While some abuses—including the use of subjects to test drugs without informed consent—are not new, these practices continue despite the existence of regulatory institutional-review boards set up by Congress, because these too have now become profit centers. Elliott writes that pharmaceutical companies hire PR specialists who not only supply educational materials to promote products, they also train medical professionals to be 'opinion leaders' and even write papers in their name." Kirkus

Includes bibliographical references

Scott, Christopher Thomas

Stem cell now; from the experiment that shook the world to the new politics of life. [by] Christopher Thomas Scott; foreword by Donald Kennedy. Pi Press 2006 243p il $24.95 **174.2**
1. Stem cell research
ISBN 0-13-173798-8; 978-0-13-173798-3

LC 2005-23266

In addition to discussing the political and ethical implications of stem cell research, the author "outlines the many types of stem cells and how they hold promise for biomedical applications, particularly for people with Parkinson's, spinal cord injuries, and other conditions with great unmet medical needs." Libr J

"This book is illuminating reading for everyone who wants to understand a hot-button topic that will dominate the

political, medical and religious arenas for years to come."
Publ Wkly

Includes bibliographical references

Tucker, Todd

★ The **great** starvation experiment; the heroic men who starved so that millions could live. Free Press 2006 270p il $26   **174.2**
1. Starvation 2. Human experimentation in medicine 3. Centenarians 4. Physiologists 5. College teachers
ISBN 0-7432-7030-4; 978-0-7432-7030-4

LC 2006-278255

"As WWII neared an end, 36 idealistic conscientious objectors, members of the Civilian Public Service, volunteered to be systematically starved. The project, headed by Dr. Ancel Keys, was designed to develop an understanding of the physiology and psychology of starvation and to provide strategies to manage the mass starvation that might follow the war's end in Europe. Tucker . . . provides a fascinating and moving history of the experiment, centering on the lives and experiences of the volunteers and the formidable obstacles they overcame." Publ Wkly

Includes bibliographical references and index

Washington, Harriet A.

★ **Medical** apartheid; the dark history of medical experimentation on Black Americans from colonial times to the present. Doubleday 2006 501p il hardcover o.p. pa $17   **174.2**
1. Human experimentation in medicine 2. African Americans -- Health and hygiene
ISBN 0-385-50993-6; 978-0-385-50993-0; 0-7679-1547-X pa; 978-0-7679-1547-2 pa

LC 2005-51873

The author offers a "history of medical experimentation on and mistreatment of black Americans in this stunning work, which is both broad in scope and well documented." Booklist

Includes bibliographical references

176   Ethics of sex and reproduction

Corvino, John

What's wrong with homosexuality? John Corvino. Oxford University Press 2013 192 p. (Philosophy in action) (hardcover) $22.95   **176**
1. Same-sex marriage 2. Homosexuality -- Moral and ethical aspects 3. Same-sex marriage -- Moral and ethical aspects
ISBN 0199856311; 9780199856312

LC 2012027319

This book, by John Corvino, "address[es] the standard objections to homosexuality and offering insight into the culture wars more generally. Is homosexuality unnatural? Does the Bible condemn it? Are people born gay (and should it matter either way)? Corvino approaches such questions . . . [and] makes a fresh case for moral engagement, forcefully rejecting the idea that morality is a 'private matter.'" (Publisher's note)

Includes bibliographical references and index.

Freitas, Donna

The **end** of sex; how hookup culture is leaving a generation unhappy, sexually unfulfilled, and confused about intimacy. Donna Freitas. Basic Books 2013 240 p. (pbk. : alk. paper) $25.99   **176**
1. Sex -- Psychological aspects 2. College students -- Sexual behavior 3. Sexual ethics 4. Intimacy (Psychology) 5. Dating (Social customs) 6. Youth -- Sexual behavior
ISBN 0465002153; 9780465002153

LC 2012042226

This book is an "attack on the casual-sex culture at American universities, which is marked not by free love, but by pressure to have as much sex with as little emotional connection as possible (and often while drunk). Through interviews and demographic surveys, [Donna] Freitas constructs an anthropological survey on what hooking up and dating (or its absence) look like on campuses today. She lays out convincing arguments against this harmful kind of sexual culture." (Publishers Weekly)

Includes bibliographical references

Green, Ronald Michael

Babies by design; the ethics of genetic choice. Yale University Press 2007 279p il hardcover o.p. pa $19   **176**
1. Medical genetics 2. Genetic engineering 3. Reproductive technology
ISBN 978-0-300-12546-7; 0-300-12546-1; 978-0-300-14308-9 pa; 0-300-14308-7 pa

LC 2007-19927

"By providing examples, contextualizing issues within the framework of stories in popular fiction, and presenting a balanced view of the topics, the author allows the reader to fully explore the issues embedded in the scientific transformation created by the genomic revolution." Sci Books Films

Includes bibliographical references

Mundy, Liza

Everything conceivable; how assisted reproduction is changing men, women, and the world. Alfred A. Knopf 2007 xx, 406p $26.95   **176**
1. Reproductive technology
ISBN 978-1-4000-4428-3; 1-4000-4428-6

LC 2006-51432

The author "opens a mind-boggling Pandora's box to issues that surely give us pause. This book is destined to become a bible for those seeking to examine the many ways of making babies and the complex questions that result." Dallas Morning News

Includes bibliographical references

Stock, Gregory

Redesigning humans; our inevitable genetic future. Houghton Mifflin 2002 277p $24; pa $14 **176**
1. Genetics 2. Genetic engineering 3. Reproductive technology
ISBN 0-618-06026-X; 0-618-34083-1 pa

LC 2001-51890

The author gives an "overview of the new biotechnology that will allow scientists to delay aging and to insert genes that enhance physical and cognitive performance, combat disease or improve looks into embryos. Stock thoughtfully weighs the ethical dilemmas such advances present, arguing that the real threat is not frivolous abuse of technology but the fact that we don't know the long-term effects of these genetic changes." Publ Wkly

Includes bibliographical references and index

Wilmut, Ian

✓ ★ **After** Dolly; the uses and misuses of human cloning. Norton 2006 335p il $24.95; pa $15.95 **176**

1. Cloning 2. Reproductive technology
ISBN 0-393-06066-7; 978-0-393-06066-9; 0-393-33026-5 pa; 978-0-393-33026-7 pa

LC 2006-2030

In this "account of the program that eventuated in Dolly, ... [Wilmut] covers a variety of the social, medical, and scientific implications of cloning.... Wilmut, aided by science writer Highfield, well explains potentially confusing issues, in the end making a strong enough case to convince us that Dolly neither lived nor died in vain." Booklist

Includes bibliographical references

177 Ethics of social relations

Ariely, Dan

✓ The **honest** truth about dishonesty; how we lie to everyone---especially ourselves. Dan Ariely. 1st ed. Harper 2012 xiii, 285 p.p (hardback) $26.99 **177**

1. Honesty 2. Deception 3. Truthfulness and falsehood
ISBN 0062183591; 9780062183590; 9780062183613

LC 2012015990

This book "explains the psychological and economic factors that drive people to lie and cheat." Author Dan Ariely "explores the rational cost-benefit forces that propel dishonesty, such as the amount of money to be gained, the probability of being caught, and conflicts of interest. To illustrate his argument, Ariely cites examples ranging from the Enron scandal to Ponzi schemes to owning fake designer bags." (Library Journal)

Includes bibliographical references (pages 267-273) and index.

Armstrong, Karen

Twelve steps to a compassionate life. Alfred A. Knopf 2010 222p $22.95; ebook $11.99 **177**

1. Compassion 2. Twelve-step programs
ISBN 978-0-307-59559-1; 978-0-307-59563-8 ebook

LC 2010-36870

The author offers "guidelines for a spiritual practice designed to make humanity a kinder and saner species.... [Armstrong] worked with 'leading thinkers from a variety of major faiths' to compose a Charter for Compassion, which calls for the restoration of 'compassion to the heart of religious and moral life' in a 'dangerously polarized' world. Not content with merely stating lofty goals, however, Armstrong ... now tells the full and profound story of altruism throughout human history." Booklist

"Armstrong weaves together the teachings of diverse religions in a graceful, approachable manner. A commendable effort well-executed." Kirkus

Includes bibliographical references

Campbell, Jeremy

✓ The **liar's** tale; a history of falsehood. Norton 2001 363p $26.95; pa $15.95 **177**

1. Truthfulness and falsehood
ISBN 0-393-02559-4; 0-393-32361-7 pa

LC 2001-30286

Campbell discusses lying in history and in the writings of "philosophers and thinkers from the ancient Greeks to Darwin, Nietzsche, Marx, and Freud, down to ... {the} postmodern deconstructionists." Christ Sci Monit

"This challenging romp through the underbelly of intellectual history ... is fascinating and troublesome." NY Times Book Rev

Includes bibliographical references

★ **Count** on me; tales of sisterhoods and fierce friendships. by Las Comadres para las Americas. Atria Books 2012 272 p. $16.00 **177**

1. Essays 2. Hispanic American women 3. Female friendship -- Fiction 4. Social networks -- America 5. Female friendship -- America 6. Las Comadres para las Americas 7. Social networks -- United States 8. Female friendship -- United States 9. Hispanic American women -- Biography 10. Hispanic American women -- Social conditions 11. Hispanic American women -- Social life and customs
ISBN 1451642016; 9781451642018

LC 2012015552

This book is "[a]n anthology celebrating sisterhood and the special bonds that connect Latinas from diverse backgrounds.... The stories in this collection [nearly] all deal with the topic of female friendship.... Several of the pieces deal with the relationship between a Latina author and a cherished teacher who became a lifelong 'comadre,' a Spanish word to describe complex relationships between women." (Kirkus)

Sullivan, Evelin E.

✓ The **concise** book of lying; {by} Evelin Sullivan. Farrar, Straus & Giroux 2001 334p il $25; pa $15 **177**

1. Truthfulness and falsehood
ISBN 0-374-12868-5; 0-312-42047-1 pa

LC 2001-18760

The author discusses lying in history and literature. She examines what impels people to lie and what the results of lying might be

"Anyone interested in the history and philosophy of human nature will appreciate this compelling and cleverly written volume." Libr J

Includes bibliographical references

179   Other ethical norms

Baur, Gene

  Farm Sanctuary; changing hearts and minds about animals and food. Simon & Schuster 2008 286p il $25   **179**

  1. Animal welfare 2. Livestock industry

  ISBN 978-0-7432-9158-3; 0-7432-9158-1

                     LC 2008-297873

  A founder of an organization dedicated to promoting the compassionate treatment of animals and combating factory farming addresses the ethics of breeding animals for food, exposing inhumane practices utilized by typical food-production companies.

  "Baur's report is not for the faint of heart, but it is critical reading for anyone willing to ask about the origin of their food, and readers are rewarded with tales of animals who have been saved, and the surprising things that have been learned about farm animals from close observation of their habits. A life-altering read." Booklist

  Includes bibliographical references

Beers, Diane L.

  ★ **For** the prevention of cruelty; the history and legacy of animal rights activism in the United States. Swallow Press/Ohio University Press 2006 312p il $34.95; $19.95   **179**

  1. Animal rights movement

  ISBN 0-8040-1086-2; 978-0-8040-1086-3; 0-8040-1087-0 pa; 978-0-8040-1087-0 pa

                     LC 2006-4294

  This "study of the animal advocacy movement in the U.S. since the ASPCA's founding in 1866 fills a glaring historical gap with exceptional style, accuracy and insight." Publ Wkly

  Includes bibliographical references

Blum, Deborah

  The **monkey** wars. Oxford Univ. Press 1994 306p hardcover o.p. pa $19.95   **179**

  1. Animal rights 2. Animal experimentation

  ISBN 0-19-510109-X pa

                     LC 94-12439

  "The 'wars' between scientific researchers and animal-rights activists have several aspects: fanaticism, propaganda, pragmatism, and idealism. Blum has written a beautifully balanced account of the major individuals and organizations involved. She points out the different shades of belief and approaches in the conflict and shows how these have developed over the years." Booklist

  Includes bibliographical references

Coetzee, J. M.

  The **lives** of animals; {by} J.M. Coetzee; {reflections by} Marjorie Garber {et al.}; edited and introduced by Amy Gutmann. Princeton Univ. Press 1999 127p (University Center for Human Values series) $29.95; pa $13.95   **179**

  1. Animal rights 2. Animal welfare

  ISBN 0-691-00443-9; 0-691-07089-X pa

                     LC 98-39591

  "This hybrid collection of fiction and essays is a provocative version of Socratic philosophy. It begins with a story about a Doris Lessing-like author who visits her conflicted son and his antagonistic wife while lecturing at the university where they teach. The mother's hobbyhorse, that Animals R Us, embarrasses the academic couple, and her suggestion that they are like Nazis because they eat meat infuriates them. Other distinguished academics carry on this dialogue in playful fiction and sober commentary, in which the most eloquent part may be the descriptions of communication with animals." New Yorker

  Includes bibliographical references

  Encyclopedia of animal rights and animal welfare; edited by Marc Bekoff; foreword by Jane Goodall. 2nd ed.; Greenwood Press 2010 2v il set $165   **179**

  1. Reference books 2. Animal rights -- Encyclopedias 3. Animal welfare -- Encyclopedias

  ISBN 978-0-313-35255-3; 0-313-35255-0

                    LC 2009-22275

  First published 1998

  "This encyclopedia shows why both animal rights and animal welfare matter around the world. . . . More than 200 entries are included that cover 50 or so topics ranging from activism, animal welfare, anthrozoology, companion animals, and law and animals to pain, stress, and suffering; sports; and animal and wildlife ethics." Libr J

  Includes bibliographical references

Fox, Michael W.

  Inhumane society; the American way of exploiting animals. introduction by Cleveland Amory. St. Martin's Press 1990 268p hardcover o.p. pa $18.95   **179**

  1. Animal welfare

  ISBN 0-312-30213-4 pa

                    LC 89-70299

  The author "looks at the exploitative and inhumane treatment of domestic, agriculture, and laboratory animals." Booklist

  This book "is very readable and takes a strong stance while presenting a creditably balanced treatment of the issues." Libr J

  Includes bibliographical references

Greek, C. Ray

  Sacred cows and golden geese; the human cost of experiments on animals. {by} C. Ray Greek and Jean Swingle Greek; foreword by Jane Goodall. Continuum 2000 256p $24.95; pa $18.95   **179**

  1. Animal experimentation

  ISBN 0-8264-1226-2; 0-8264-1402-8 pa

                    LC 99-57157

  This "covers the history of animal experimentation, legislation that promulgates it, the real cost to humans, and alternatives. It is a well-written, if disturbing, book." Libr J

  Includes bibliographical references

Hall, Stephen S.

Wisdom; from philosophy to neuroscience. Alfred A. Knopf 2010 333p $27.95 **179**

1. Decision making 2. Neuropsychology
ISBN 978-0-307-26910-2; 0-307-26910-2

LC 2009-27438

"Those searching for easy tips on achieving wisdom will not find them here, but diligent readers will be rewarded. A steady stream of insights into the psychology and neurological mechanisms of wise decision-makingand the researchers uncovering them." Kirkus

Magill, R. Jay

Sincerity; how a moral ideal born five hundred years ago inspired religious wars, modern art, hipster chic, and the curious notion that we all have something to say (no matter how dull) R. Jay Magill, Jr. W. W. Norton & Co. Inc. 2012 272 p. (hardcover) $25.95 **179**

1. Catholic Church 2. Christian heresies 3. Doctrinal theology 4. Sincerity
ISBN 0393080986; 9780393080988

LC 2012010360

Author R. Jay Magill "examines sincerity from a variety of perspectives--religious, philosophical, political, sociological, artistic--as Western culture has alternately feared sincerity, embraced it, or denied the very possibility of it. . . . Sincerity and irony, rather than polar opposites, are complementary correctives, with the latter exposing the hypocrisies within professions of the former. The author . . . traces the early equation of sincerity with heresy as a challenge to the dogmatic authority of the Catholic Church." (Kirkus Reviews)

Includes bibliographical references and index.

McCain, John S., 1936-

Why courage matters; the way to a braver life. [by] John McCain with Mark Salter. Random House 2004 209p il $16.95 **179**

1. Courage
ISBN 1-400-06030-3

LC 2003-58626

Senator McCain tells his favorite stories of courage. "In offering anecdotes of individuals whose actions embody the rarity of true courage, his well-drawn examples range from Navajo leaders to Colorado River explorers to Jewish freedom fighter Hannah Senesh and Burmese dissident and Nobel Peace Prize-recipient Aung San Suu Kyi. He reflects on the wellsprings of courage, defining it as conscious self-sacrifice 'for the sake of others or to uphold a virtue,' encompassing actions that may be spurred by honor, outrage, a sense of duty, one's conscience, or moral obligation." SLJ

Miller, William Ian

Faking it. Cambridge University Press 2003 290p $42; pa $18.99 **179**

1. Social role 2. Identity (Psychology)
ISBN 0-521-83018-4; 0-521-61370-1 pa

LC 2003-43750

"In this refreshing book, Miller . . . considers the human propensity for fraudulence and the correlative fear of being found out. He makes us laugh as he describes trying to wing it in his class on property law or eyeing an attractive woman a few pews up during prayer, and he entertains us with stories of adults who overestimate their sexual prowess and children who find out that saying 'please' doesn't buy them what they were told it would." Libr J

Includes bibliographical references

Rudacille, Deborah

★ The scalpel and the butterfly; the conflict between animal research and animal protection. University of California Press 2001 389p pa $21.95 **179**

1. Animal welfare 2. Animal experimentation
ISBN 978-0-520-23154-2; 0-520-23154-6

LC 2001-27339

First published 2000 by Farrar, Straus & Giroux with subtitle: the war between animal research and animal protection

The author gives a "history of the conflict between anti-vivisectionists and research scientists. She begins with French physician Claude Bernard. . . . Rudacille then documents the rise of the animal welfare movement in Britain and the United States and legislation designed to govern the use of animals in research. . . . The author also discusses the Nazi 'science' of eugenics and explores the ethical implications of such new scientific developments as xenotransplantation." Libr J

Includes bibliographical references

Shevelow, Kathryn

For the love of animals; the rise of the animal protection movement. Henry Holt and Co. 2008 352p il $27.50 **179**

1. Animal rights movement
ISBN 978-0-8050-8090-2; 0-8050-8090-2

LC 2007-47353

The author "documents the history of animal cruelty and the slow, controversial and much maligned rise of the animal protection movement in 17th and 18th-century England. . . . This is a fascinating, often disturbing and frequently funny book, a must read for anyone concerned with the treatment of animals and a call to action for the next generation of animal rights activists." Publ Wkly

Includes bibliographical references

Tillich, Paul

★ The courage to be; with an introduction by Peter J. Gomes. 2nd ed; Yale Univ. Press 2000 197p (Yale Nota bene) pa $12.95 **179**

1. Anxiety 2. Courage 3. Ontology 4. Existentialism
ISBN 0-300-08471-4

LC 00-102364

First published 1952

The author offers advice on how to conquer the anxiety caused by the loss of meaning in one's life

Tutu, Desmond, 1931-

The book of forgiving; the fourfold path for healing ourselves and our world. Desmond Tutu and Mpho A. Tutu ; edited by Douglas C. Abrams. HarperOne 2014 240 p. ill $25.99 **179**

1. Forgiveness 2. Reconciliation
ISBN 0062203568; 9780062203564; 9780062203571

LC 2013033890

In this book, Desmond Tutu and his daughter Mpho "lay out the simple but profound truths about the significance of forgiveness, how it works, why everyone needs to know how to grant it and receive it, and why granting forgiveness is the greatest gift we can give to ourselves when we have been wronged." (Publisher's note)

"The book is almost entirely practical in focus, geared toward helping people come to grips with issues of anger, grief and loss. It includes meditations, rituals and journal exercises after each chapter." Kirkus

Includes bibliographical references

Wise, Steven M.

★ **Drawing** the line; science and the case for animal rights. Perseus Bks. 2002 322p $26; pa $18 **179**

1. Animal rights

ISBN 0-7382-0340-8; 0-7382-0810-8 pa

Wise "sets out to determine whether animals ranging from dolphins to his family dog . . . have mental abilities meriting {legal} protection. . . . The key to granting any of them rights, Wise argues, is whether they possess 'practical autonomy'—desires and the ability to act to satisfy them." Christ Sci Monit

Includes bibliographical references

179.7 Respect and disrespect for human life

Durkheim, Emile

★ **Suicide,** a study in sociology; translated by John A. Spaulding and George Simpson; edited with an introduction by George Simpson. Free Press 1951 405p maps hardcover o.p. pa $18.95 **179.7**

1. Suicide

ISBN 0-684-83632-7 pa

Original French edition, 1897

Durkheim's "Suicide is a major sociological classic, one that is still read today, not so much for its data, which are limited and out-of-date, but for the brilliance of his analysis of suicide rates and other data that had been initially obtained for administrative rather than scientific purposes." Reader's Adviser

Includes bibliographical references

Filene, Peter G.

In the arms of others; a cultural history of the right-to-die in America. Dee, I.R. 1998 282p il hardcover o.p. pa $15.95 **179.7**

1. Sick 2. Euthanasia 3. Right to die

ISBN 1-56663-268-4 pa

LC 97-42583

"A fine general overview of the right-to-die question." Libr J

Includes bibliographical references

Humphry, Derek

★ **Final** exit; the practicalities of self-deliverance and assisted sucide for the dying. 3rd ed; Delta Trade Paperbacks 2002 xxviii, 220p pa $13.95 **179.7**

1. Suicide 2. Right to die

ISBN 0-385-33653-5

LC 2002-19403

First published 1991 by Hemlock Society

This offers information about how to commit suicide for the terminally ill and about the legality and ethics of assisted suicide and euthanasia

Includes bibliographical references

Kiernan, Stephen P.

★ **Last** rights; rescuing the end of life from the medical system. St. Martin's Press 2006 301p $25.95 **179.7**

1. Death 2. Terminal care

ISBN 978-0-312-34224-1; 0-312-34224-1

LC 2006-47449

"Anyone who has stood helplessly by as physicians insisted that a battery of tests and interventions could prolong the life of a loved one, only to see those expensive efforts fail, is certain to be moved by Kiernan's presentation." Booklist

Includes bibliographical references

Marcus, Eric

Why suicide? answers to 200 of the most frequently asked questions about suicide, attempted suicide, and assisted suicide. HarperSanFrancisco 1996 240p pa $14 **179.7**

1. Suicide

ISBN 0-06-251166-1

LC 95-33431

The author's "questions range from 'Does everyone have thoughts of suicide?' to 'What are the arguments against legalizing doctor-assisted suicide?' His responses reflect not only a knowledgeable and well-informed consideration of suicidology but also empathetic treatment. The typical response aims to educate by giving factual information and/or practical advice as well as to console by providing personal stories from suicide survivors." Libr J

Includes bibliographical references

McKhann, Charles F.

A **time** to die; the place for physician assistance. Yale Univ. Press 1999 268p $42; pa $19 **179.7**

1. Euthanasia

ISBN 0-300-07631-2; 0-300-08698-9 pa

LC 98-22193

The author "believes that physician-assisted suicide is not only desirable but inevitable. Humanity is divided in two parts, he says: those who have seen a loved one die a miserable death and those who have not. . . . McKhann argues level-headedly about patients, doctors, and laws." Booklist

Includes bibliographical references and index

Peck, M. Scott

Denial of the soul; spiritual and medical perspectives on euthanasia and mortality. Harmony Bks. 1997 242p hardcover o.p. pa $19   **179.7**
1. Death 2. Suicide 3. Euthanasia 4. Right to die 5. Medical ethics
ISBN 0-609-80134-1 pa

LC 97-157271

The author "argues against, with very few exceptions, euthanasia and physician-assisted suicide on demand." Publ Wkly

"Peck is a wonderful writer, engaging, intelligent, and full of stories from his long psychiatric practice; as usual, he takes on big issues with seriousness, sensitivity, and balance." Libr J

Wanzer, Sidney H.

★ **To** die well; your right to comfort, calm, and choice in the last days of life. Da Capo 2007 209p $24; pa $15   **179.7**
1. Euthanasia 2. Right to die 3. Terminal care -- Ethical aspects
ISBN 0-7382-1083-8; 978-0-7382-1083-4; 0-7382-1163-X pa; 978-0-7382-1163-3 pa

The authors present "what individuals can do to achieve a peaceful death for themselves and their loved ones. Using a combination of patient stories and their own expert discussions, the authors describe the legal rights of terminally ill patients to end their medical care. They also address the controversial issue of hastening the death of terminally ill patients. . . . More useful than the many other recent books on death and dying, this influential volume should be on the shelves of every public and university library." Libr J

Wiesenthal, Simon

★ The **sunflower**; on the possibilities and limits of forgiveness. [by] Simon Wiesenthal; with a symposium edited by Harry James Cargas and Bonny V. Fetterman. rev and expanded ed, 2nd pa. ed; Schocken Books 1998 289p pa $14   **179.7**
1. Forgiveness 2. Holocaust, 1933-1945 -- Personal narratives
ISBN 0-8052-1060-1

LC 99-198049

Original French edition, 1969

"The responses to the author's question are as varied as their authors. The mystery of evil and atonement remain, and the reader is left challenged on these most basic issues of meaning in human life." Publ Wkly

Yount, Lisa

★ **Right** to die and euthanasia; rev ed; Facts on File 2007 312p il (Library in a book) $45   **179.7**
1. Euthanasia 2. Right to die
ISBN 978-0-8160-6275-1

LC 2006-33424

First published 2000 with title: Physician-assisted suicide and euthanasia

This reference source contains an overview of the subjects, a chronology of significant events (including the Terri Schiavo case), biographical information on important figures, a glossary of terms, and an annotated bibliography.

Includes glossary and bibliographical references

180   History, geographic treatment, biography

Gottlieb, Anthony

The **dream** of reason; a history of western philosophy from the Greeks to the Renaissance. Norton 2000 468p $27.95; pa $17.95   **180**
1. Philosophy -- History
ISBN 0-393-04951-5; 0-393-32365-X pa

LC 00-49012

"This book is the first installment of . . . a survey in two volumes of the whole of Western philosophy, from its origins in Greece in the sixth century B.C. to the present day." N Y Times Book Rev

"This eloquent book offers a lively chronicle of the evolution of Western philosophy." Publ Wkly

Includes bibliographical references

181   Eastern philosophy

Buber, Martin

★ **I** and thou; translated by Ronald Gregor Smith. Scribner 2000 126p $22; pa $11   **181**
1. God 2. Ontology 3. Jewish philosophy
ISBN 0-7432-0133-7; 0-7432-0133-7 pa

Original German edition, 1923; first published in English 1958

In this book, the author "conceived the individual as in permanent relationship with all forms of life, finding his fulfillment in the reciprocity of the relationship—the 'Thou' being God." Reader's Adviser

Confucius

★ The **Analects**; [by] Confucius; translated by Arthur Waley; with an introduction by Sarah Allan. Knopf 2000 xxxi, 257p $19   **181**
1. Chinese ethics 2. Chinese philosophy
ISBN 0-375-41204-2

LC 00-53460

This translation first published 1938 in the United Kingdom

"One of the Chinese 'Four Books.' A brief, unsystematic collection of fragmentary writings attributed to Confucius and his school. . . . It is one of the most influential works in the history of Chinese thought." Reader's Ency

Includes bibliographical references

183   Sophistic, Socratic, related Greek philosophies

Kreeft, Peter

★ **Philosophy** 101 by Socrates; an introduction to philosophy via Plato's apology : forty things philosophy is according to history's first and wisest

philosopher. by Peter Kreeft. St. Augustines Press 2012 149 p. $12   **183**
1. Teaching 2. Philosophers 3. History -- Philosophy 4. Philosophy -- Introductions
ISBN 0898709253; 158731830X; 9781587318306
LC 2001098029

Author Peter "Kreeft uses the dialogues of Socrates in this book to help the reader grow in that love of wisdom. He says that no master of the art of philosophizing has ever been more simple, clear, and accessible to beginners as Socrates. He focuses on Plato's dialogues, the Apology of Socrates, as a model partner for the reader to dialogue with. Kreeft calls it 'the Magna Carta of philosophy,' a timeless classic that is 'a portable classroom.'" (Publisher's note)

Stone, I. F. (Isidor Feinstein), 1907-1989
The **trial** of Socrates. Anchor Bks. 1989 282p pa $14.95   **183**
1. Philosophers
ISBN 0-385-26032-6; 978-0-385-26032-9
First published 1988 by Little, Brown

The author attempts "to show that Athens was totally committed to free speech and did not normally place any check on it, and, therefore, that the trial of Socrates was a singular aberration which might be explicable, if finally not justifiable." Commentary
Includes bibliographical references

Waterfield, Robin
Why Socrates died; dispelling the myths. W. W. Norton & Co. 2009 253p il map $27.95   **183**
1. Trials 2. Hellenism 3. Philosophers 4. Philosophy, Ancient
ISBN 978-0-393-06527-5
LC 2009-4317

This "account of the trial and execution of the philosopher draws on Greek sources to separate truth from myth, . . . [arguing for] Socrates' character as a deeply moral thinker whose convictions strongly contrasted those of his former student, Alcibaides." (Publishers note)

The author "sets out to explain why Socrates died: he discusses his trial, but also offers an informed and well-written account of classical Athenian history." Times Higher Ed
Includes bibliographical references

184   Platonic philosophy

Hare, R. M.
Plato. Oxford Univ. Press 1982 82p (Past masters series) hardcover o.p. pa $9.95   **184**
1. Authors 2. Philosophers 3. Essayists
ISBN 0-19-287585-X pa
LC 83-159441

The author examines the chief Platonic concepts in their political and intellectual contexts
Includes bibliographical references

185   Aristotelian philosophy

Adler, Mortimer J.
Aristotle for everybody; difficult thought made easy. Macmillan 1978 206p hardcover o.p. pa $13   **185**
1. Philosophers 2. Writers on science
ISBN 0-684-83823-0 pa
LC 78-853

Adler traces "in the simplest language and with occasional modern analogues, the logic and growth of Aristotle's basic doctrines." Publ Wkly
Includes bibliographical references

Shields, Christopher John
Aristotle; Christopher Shields. Routledge, Taylor & Francis Group 2014 xviii, 505 pagesp (Routledge philosophers) (hardback : alk. paper) $160; (pbk. : alk. paper) $32.95   **185**
1. Values 2. Virtue 3. Philosophers 4. Ancient philosophy
ISBN 9780415622486; 9780415622493
LC 2013021013

This book, by Christopher John Shields, "introduces the whole of Aristotle's philosophy, showing . . . much of his thinking on the nature of the soul and the mind, ethics, politics, and the arts. Beginning with a brief biography, Shields carefully explains the fundamental elements of Aristotle's thought. . . . Subsequently he discusses Aristotle's metaphysics, the theory of categories, logical theory, and his conception of the human being as a composite of soul and body." (Publisher's note)
Includes bibliographical references and index

187   Epicurean philosophy

Lucretius Carus, Titus
On the nature of things: De rerum natura; [by] Lucretius; edited and translated by Anthony M. Esolen. Johns Hopkins Univ. Press 1995 296p pa $25   **187**
1. Poetry -- By individual authors
ISBN 978-0-8018-5055-4; 0-8018-5055-X
LC 94-25165

"Writing in the waning days of the Roman Republic—as Rome's politics grew individualistic and treacherous, its high-life wanton, its piety introspective and morbid—Lucretius sets forth a rational and materialistic view of the world which offers a retreat into a quiet community of wisdom and friendship." Publisher's note

188   Stoic philosophy

Marcus Aurelius
★ **Meditations**; a new translation, with an introduction, by Gregory Hays. Modern Lib. 2002 lvii, 191p $19.95   **188**
1. Ethics 2. Stoics
ISBN 0-679-64260-9
LC 2001-57947

"An emperor and Stoic philosopher records his thoughts as he struggles for composure and order in the face of national disaster." Good Read

189   Medieval western philosophy

Davies, Brian

The **thought** of Thomas Aquinas. Oxford Univ. Press 1992 391p hardcover o.p. pa $44.95   **189**
1. Saints 2. Theologians 3. Doctrinal theology
ISBN 0-19-826753-3 pa

LC 91-35671

"Davies aims to cover the whole programme of the Summa in 370 pages. This necessarily means that, though his writing is admirably clear and never cryptic, much of what he says is extremely concise, and some topics get less airing than others." Times Lit Suppl
Includes bibliographical references

The **Renaissance** philosophy of man; {by} Petrarca {and others}; selections in translation, edited by Ernst Cassirer, Paul Oskar Kristeller, John Herman Randall, Jr. University of Chicago Press 1948 405p hardcover o.p. pa $17.50   **189**
1. Poets 2. Authors 3. Philosophers 4. Medieval philosophy 5. Writers on science
ISBN 0-226-09604-1 pa

This book provides English translations from selected writings of six early Italian Renaissance philosophers from about the middle of the fourteenth century to the end of the sixteenth. Francesco Petrarca, Lorenzo Valla, Marsilio Ficino, Giovanni Pico della Mirandola, Pietro Pomponazzi, and Juan Luis Vives are represented. An introduction accompanies each of the translations
Includes bibliographical references

Rubenstein, Richard E.

Aristotle's children; how Christians, Muslims, and Jews rediscovered ancient wisdom and illuminated the Dark Ages. Harcourt 2003 368p $27 **189**
1. Philosophers 2. Medieval philosophy 3. Writers on science
ISBN 0-15-100720-9

LC 2003-6582

"Although the book purports to trace Aristotle's influence on Christianity, Islam and Judaism, it devotes more attention to Christianity. Even so, Rubenstein's lively prose, his lucid insights and his crystal-clear historical analyses make this a first-rate study in the history of ideas." Publ Wkly
Includes bibliographical references

Thomas Aquinas

Selected writings; edited and translated with an introduction and notes by Ralph McInerny. Penguin Bks. 1998 xxxviii, 841p pa $14.95   **189**
ISBN 0-14-043632-4

Arranged chronologically, this collection of theological and philosophical writings brings together sermons, com-

mentaries, responses to criticism and lengthy extracts from the Summa theologia.
Includes bibliographical references

190   Modern western and other noneastern philosophy

Berlin, Isaiah

The **sense** of reality; studies in ideas and their history. edited by Henry Hardy; with an introduction by Patrick Gardiner. Farrar, Straus & Giroux 1997 xx, 278p hardcover o.p. pa $13   **190**
1. Poets 2. Authors 3. Communism 4. Novelists 5. Socialism 6. Dramatists 7. Nationalism 8. Philosophers 9. Essayists 10. Social activists 11. Short story writers 12. History -- Philosophy 13. Nobel laureates for literature 14. Russian literature -- History and criticism
ISBN 0-374-52569-2 pa

LC 96-39829

First published 1996 in the United Kingdom

Berlin maintains that "the great goods of human life are diverse and conflicting. . . . Values like self-realization and social cohesion, economic progress and settled communities cannot always be made compatible. Sometimes we must choose between them. In the nine seminal essays collected in 'The Sense of Reality' ranging over such diverse subjects as the Romantic movement, Marxism, Kant's influence on nationalism and the thought of Rabindranath Tagore, Berlin argues with rare wisdom and passion that every such choice entails a loss." N Y Times Book Rev
Includes bibliographical references

★ The **Columbia** history of Western philosophy; edited by Richard H. Popkin. Columbia Univ. Press 1999 xxvi, 836p $64.50   **190**
1. Philosophy -- History
ISBN 0-231-10128-7

LC 98-15219

This is an overview "of Western philosophy, from the pre-Socratics to 20th-century philosophy, both analytic and continental." Libr J

"This survey's coverage of medieval Islamic, Jewish, and Christian philosophy is particularly strong." Choice
Includes bibliographical references

Critchley, Simon

The **book** of dead philosophers. Vintage Books 2009 xxxviii, 265p il pa $15.95   **190**
1. Death 2. Philosophers
ISBN 978-0-307-39043-1

LC 2008-47719

"A primer on just about every notable philosophical figure in history, this book challenges readers to learn from the philosophers' conduct in life and the circumstances of their deaths. . . . It is a witty and generous gift that will leave readers perhaps a little less afraid of death and more appreciative of life." Publ Wkly
Includes bibliographical references (p. 286-98)

Gay, Peter

The **rise** of modern paganism. Norton 1995 xviii, 555, xvp (The Enlightenment: an interpretation) pa $19.95   **190**

1. Enlightenment 2. Modern philosophy 3. Europe -- Intellectual life

ISBN 0-393-31302-6

First published 1966 by Knopf

Voume one of a two volume series examining the ideas, experiences and impact of leading Enlightenment figures in 18th century Europe and America.

Includes bibliographical references

The **science** of freedom. Norton 1996 xx, 705, xviiip (The Enlightenment: an interpretation) pa $19.95   **190**

1. Enlightenment 2. Modern philosophy 3. Europe -- Intellectual life

ISBN 0-393-31366-2

First published 1969

Volume two of a two-volume series examining the ideas, experiences and impact of leading Enlightenment figures in 18th century Europe and America.

Himmelfarb, Gertrude

The **moral** imagination; from Edmund Burke to Lionel Trilling. Ivan R. Dee 2006 259p $26   **190**

1. Modern philosophy 2. Political science

ISBN 1-56663-624-8

LC 2005-19838

The author "specializes in Victorian Britain and profiles some of its leading writers and statesmen, along with philosophical forerunners and descendants, to probe the complexities of two centuries of conservative thought. . . . Himmelfarb's stylish blend of literary criticism and intellectual history yields a stimulating reappraisal of a multifaceted and influential worldview." Publ Wkly

Includes bibliographical references

The **roads** to modernity; the British, French, and American enlightenments. Knopf 2004 284p $25   **190**

1. Enlightenment 2. Europe -- Intellectual life 3. United States -- Intellectual life

ISBN 1-400-04236-4

LC 2003-60576

"This is a book with important ideological implications that deserves to be read and debated across the political spectrum." Publ Wkly

Includes bibliographical references

Magee, Bryan

The **story** of philosophy. DK Pub. 1998 240p il hardcover o.p. pa $20   **190**

1. Philosophy

ISBN 0-7894-3511-X; 0-7894-7994-X pa

LC 98-3780

This "illustrated volume converts two-and-a-half millennia of Western philosophy into a colorful parade of provocative figures—from Heraclitus to Heidegger—who have enlarged the boundaries of thought." Booklist

"Writing with a clear and lively style, Magee provides an excellent introduction to the topic." SLJ

Includes bibliographical references

Miller, Jim

Examined lives; [by] James Miller. Farrar, Straus and Giroux 2011 422p ill. $28   **190**

1. Biography 2. Philosophers 3. Conduct of life 4. Biography, Collective 5. Philosophers -- Biography 6. Philosophy -- Psychological aspects

ISBN 978-0-374-15085-3

LC 201014385

This book, a "New York Times" Notable Book for 2011, looks at the lives of "12 philosophers: Socrates, Plato, Diogenes the Cynic, . . . Aristotle, Seneca, Augustine, Montaigne, Descartes, Rousseau, Kant, Emerson and Nietzsche. In each case, he explores the life selectively, looking for 'crux' points and investigating how ideas of the philosophical life have changed. Few readers will be astounded to learn that philosophers make as much of a mess of their lives as anyone else. But [James] Miller . . . shows us philosophers becoming ever more inclined to reflect on these failings, and suggests that this makes their lives more rather than less studying." (N Y Times)

Includes bibliographical references

Nadler, Steven M.

The **best** of all possible worlds; a story of philosophers, God, and evil. [by] Steven Nadler. Farrar, Straus and Giroux 2008 300p $25   **190**

1. God 2. Theologians 3. Philosophers 4. Good and evil 5. Mathematicians 6. Modern philosophy 7. Essayists

ISBN 978-0-374-22998-6; 0-374-22998-8

LC 2008-29143

This book "is written simply and clearly, without condescension, flashiness or oversimplification. But it's a demanding book nonetheless, and you need to pay attention. You'll be amply rewarded if you do." Washington Post Book World

Includes bibliographical references

The **Oxford** history of Western philosophy; edited by Anthony Kenny. Oxford Univ. Press 1994 407p il maps hardcover o.p. pa $15   **190**

1. Philosophy -- History

ISBN 0-19-824278-6; 0-19-289329-7 pa

LC 94-9858

This volume covers "the ancients, the medievals, continental philosophers like Hegel, Nietzsche, and Sartre, and the English analyticals (Bentham and Mill), followed by a survey of political philosophies." Booklist

"The illustrations have been wisely chosen to show the constant play between art and idea. Some familiarity with analytic philosophy would be useful to gain the most from the text, but this is a significant addition to the literature." Libr J

Includes bibliographical references

Sedgwick, Peter

★ **Descartes** to Derrida; an introduction to European philosophy. Blackwell 2001 310p $76.95; pa $33.95 **190**

1. Modern philosophy
ISBN 0-631-20142-4; 0-631-20143-2 pa

LC 00-57917

"This critical survey of issues in European philosophy offers . . . accounts of crucial texts by important thinkers. Sedgwick draws key ideas from these sources, analysing the various relationships between them and linking them to central themes in philosophical enquiry, such as the nature of subjectivity, reason and experience, anti-humanism and the nature of language." Publisher's note

"This book should take a place as one of the key texts in humanities programs throughout the English-speaking world." Choice

Includes bibliographical references

191   Philosophy of United States and Canada

Dewey, John

★ The **philosophy** of John Dewey; edited with an introduction and commentary by John J. McDermott. University of Chicago Press 1981 2v in 1 pa $25 **191**

1. Philosophers 2. Psychologists 3. Writers on science
ISBN 0-226-14401-1

LC 80-39766

First published 1973 in two volumes by Putnam

A digest of extracts from the American philosopher's most important works

Includes bibliographical references

Rand, Ayn

The **voice** of reason; essays in objectivist thought; edited and with an introduction by Leonard Peikoff; and with additional essays by Leonard Peikoff and Peter Schwartz. New Am. Lib. 1989 353p hardcover o.p. pa $18 **191**

1. American philosophy 2. Objectivism (Philosophy)
ISBN 0-45-300634-5; 0-45-201046-2 pa

LC 88-18192

The late author opposed liberalism and championed "capitalism, self-interest, and objective reality against collectivism, altruism, and mysticism. . . . These lectures, newspaper columns, and magazine articles are entirely characteristic of her—surprisingly emotional and dogmatic for a professed rationalist. Additional essays by editor Peikoff and disciple Peter Schwartz are of a piece." Booklist

Includes bibliographical references

Romano, Carlin

America the philosophical; Carlin Romano. Knopf 2012 672 p. **191**

1. American philosophy 2. Philosophy -- Social aspects 3. Popular culture -- United States 4. United States -- Intellectual life 5. Philosophy -- United States
ISBN 0679434704; 9780679434702

LC 2011034753

This book offers a "diagnosis of the condition of philosophical thinking in America today. . . . [Carlin Romano] realizes that philosophy has traditionally been the ballpark for white men to play in, so he . . . add[s] to the team some prominent women, African Americans, Native Americans, gays and others. But he begins with the famous white men (William James, George Santayana, John Dewey et al.) and looks at key figures later on--John Rawls and Richard Rorty among them." (Kirkus)

Includes bibliographical references (p. [611]-639) and index

192   Philosophy of British Isles

Edmonds, David

Wittgenstein's poker; the story of a ten-minute argument between two great philosophers. {by} David Edmonds and John Eidinow. Ecco Press 2001 340p il $24; pa $13.95 **192**

1. Philosophers 2. Logicians 3. Nonfiction writers
ISBN 0-06-621244-8; 0-06-093664-9 pa

LC 2002-276301

"On the Cambridge University campus in 1946, two of the twentieth-century's most notable philosophers, Ludwig Wittgenstein and Karl Popper, squared off in an intense 10-minute clash rumored to have culminated with Wittgenstein brandishing a red-hot poker. The authors explain what the fight was about and how it reflects the development of philosophy. Ivory-tower drama at its crackling best." Booklist

Includes bibliographical references (p. {317}-327) and index

193   Philosophy of Germany and Austria

Hegel, Georg Wilhelm Friedrich, 1770-1831

★ The **philosophy** of Hegel; edited with an introduction by Carl J. Friedrich. Modern Lib. 1954 552p pa $10.75 **193**

ISBN 0-07-553655-2 pa

Contents: The philosophy of history; The history of philosophy; The science of logic; Philosophy of right and law, or natural law and political science outlines; Lectures on aesthetics; The phenomenology of the spirit (1807); Political essays; Bibliography

Kant, Immanuel

★ **Basic** writings of Kant; edited and with an introduction by Allen W. Wood. Modern Lib. 2001 xxv, 478p pa $15.95 **193**

1. Philosophy
ISBN 0-375-75733-3

LC 2001-18303

First Modern Library edition published 1949 with title: The philosophy of Kant

This volume presents the essential works of the philosopher including "selected excerpts from his most frequently taught essays and book-length publications, including 'Critique of Pure Reason, Critique of Judgment,' and 'Eternal Peace.'" Publisher's note

★ **Critique** of pure reason; translated by Marcus Weigelt. Rev ed; Penguin 2003 lxxvi, 708p (Penguin classics) pa $20 **193**

1. Reason 2. Theory of knowledge
ISBN 978-0-14-044747-7; 0-14-044747-4
Original German edition, 1781

In this philosophical work Kant "attempted to define the possibility and limits of our knowledge. He denied that we can ever know how the world 'really' is. However, he tried to show that science nevertheless has a sort of universal validity, insofar as it consists of sense experience, which comes from the world, coupled with the mind, which orders this sense experience according to the 'categories of the understanding' and the intuitions of space and time." Reader's Ency. 4th edition

Krell, David Farrell

Basic writings; from Being and time (1927) to The task of thinking (1964) edited, with general introduction and introductions to each selection by David Farrell Krell. rev and expanded ed; HarperSanFrancisco 1993 452p pa $17.95 **193**

ISBN 0-06-063763-3

LC 91-58187

This anthology first published 1977 by Harper & Row
Includes bibliographical references

Nietzsche, Friedrich Wilhelm, 1844-1900

★ **Basic** writings of Nietzsche; introduction by Peter Gay; translated and edited, with commentaries, by Walter Kaufmann. Modern Lib. 2000 xxiv, 862p pa $14.95 **193**

ISBN 0-679-78339-3

LC 00-64578

First Modern Library edition published 1968

"Gathers the complete texts of five of Nietzsche's most important works, from his first book to his last: The Birth of Tragedy, Beyond Good and Evil; On the Genealogy of Morals; The Case of Wagner; and Ecce Homo. . . . Included also are seventy-five aphorisms, selections from Nietzsche's correspondence, and variants from drafts for Ecce Homo." Publisher's note

The **portable** Nietzsche; selected and translated, with an introduction, prefaces, and notes, by Walter Kaufmann. Viking 1954 687p hardcover o.p. pa $17 **193**

ISBN 0-14-015062-5 pa

Includes the complete texts of Thus spake Zarathustra, Twilight of the idols, The antichrist, and Nietzsche contra Wagner. Selections from other works, notes and letters complete the volume

★ **Thus** spoke Zarathustra; a book for everyone and nobody. [by] Friedrich Nietzsche; translated with an introduction and notes by Graham Parkes. Oxford University Press 2005 xliii, 335p (Oxford world's classics) pa $14.95 **193**

ISBN 0-19-280583-5

LC 2005-19431

Written between 1883-1892

A philosophical narrative in which Nietzsche "transforms the ancient Persian philosopher Zarathustra . . . into a mouthpiece for his own views. Nietzsche develops his doctrine of the 'Ubermensch' in a prophetic, quasi-biblical style. Nietzsche's Zarathustra announces the death of God, and preaches a new 'faithfulness to the earth,' which includes a new respect for the body . . . and attentiveness to this world rather than the next. He also attacks pity and virtue as weapons of weakness." Reader's Ency. 4th edition

Includes bibliographical references

The **will** to power; a new translation by Walter Kaufmann and R. J. Hollingdale; edited with commentary by Walter Kaufmann; with facsimiles of the original manuscript. Random House 1967 xxxii, 576p hardcover o.p. pa $16 **193**

ISBN 0-394-70437-1 pa

Ratner-Rosenhagen, Jennifer

American Nietzsche; a history of an icon and his ideas. Jennifer Ratner-Rosenhagen. University of Chicago Press 2012 452 p. ill. $30.00 **193**

1. American philosophy 2. United States -- Civilization -- Foreign influences 3. Philosophy, American 4. United States -- Intellectual life 5. United States -- Civilization -- German influences

ISBN 0226705811; 9780226705811

LC 2011011189

This book, by Jennifer Ratner-Rosenhagen, presents an "examination of [philosopher Friedrich Nietzsche's] influence on America . . . [and] how his philosophy helped challenge and influence the ideas of a diverse group of Americans. She looks at why each group or individual was drawn to Nietzsche's attack on universal truths and morality, and how they used his writings to support and develop their own philosophy, belief system, or cause." (Library Journal)

"Ratner-Rosenhagen's skillful combining of historical research and philosophical analysis in a way that is both accessible and informative makes this book a pleasure to read." LJ

Includes bibliographical references and index

Safranski, Rudiger

Nietzsche; a philosophical biography. translated by Shelley Frisch. Norton 2001 409p $29.95; pa $18.95 **193**

1. Authors 2. Philosophers 3. Essayists
ISBN 0-393-05008-4; 0-393-32380-3 pa

LC 2001-52130

This is a biography "of the life and thought of the nineteenth-century German philosopher Friedrich Nietzche." (Publisher's note) Chronology. Bibliography. Index.

"With brilliant insights and impressive scholarship, Safranski . . . here makes a major contribution to understanding and appreciating the lasting significance of Friedrich Nietzsche." Libr J

Includes bibliographical references

Sherratt, Yvonne

Hitler's philosophers; Yvonne Sherratt. Yale University Press 2012 328 p. (hardcover) $35 **193**
1. Political philosophy 2. Philosophers -- Germany 3. Philosophy, German -- 20th century 4. Philosophers -- Germany -- History -- 20th century
ISBN 0300151934; 9780300151930

LC 2012026930

This book, by Yvonne Sherratt, explores the philosophical policy of Adolf Hitler. The author presents "evidence back to the 1920s of Hitler's vulgarization of noble thinkers of the past. . . . She reveals how philosophers of the 1930s eagerly collaborated to lend the Nazi regime a cloak of respectability. . . . And while these eminent men sanctioned slaughter, Semitic thinkers like Walter Benjamin and opponents like Kurt Huber were hunted down or murdered." (Publisher's note)

Solomon, Robert C.

What Nietzsche really said; {by} Robert C. Solomon and Kathleen M. Higgins. Schocken Bks. 2000 263p hardcover o.p. pa $13 **193**
1. Authors 2. Philosophers 3. Essayists
ISBN 0-8052-1094-6 pa

LC 99-33796

The authors offer an "overview of Friedrich Nietzsche's life, thought, and influence. . . . Particularly helpful are their brief annotations of Nietzsche's 14 books and short analyses of the thinkers who influenced him." Libr J

Includes bibliographical references

194 Philosophy of France

Gray, Francine du Plessix

Simone Weil. Viking 2001 248p il (Penguin lives series) $19.95 **194**
1. Essayists 2. Political and social philosophers
ISBN 0-670-89998-4

LC 00-51367

The author "recounts the chronology of Weil's short life, all the while interweaving Weil's emerging political, philosophical, and spiritual ideas into the biographical narrative." Libr J

"Part intellectual primer and part case study, this slim, sympathetic biography makes us question whether we value Weil's thinking despite the example of her punishing, courageous, profoundly exasperating life, or because of it." New Yorker

Includes bibliographical references

196 Philosophy of Spain and Portugal

Ortega y Gasset, Jose

What is philosophy? translated from the Spanish by Mildred Adams. Norton 1961 252p hardcover o.p. pa $10.95 **196**
1. Philosophy
ISBN 0-393-00126-1 pa

This volume by the influential Spanish philosopher, essayist and critic "consists of a series of lectures begun in 1929 at the University of Madrid. Interrupted when the University was closed as a result of political troubles, they were resumed in a Madrid theatre. Part of the lectures had been given earlier in Buenos Aires." N Y Times Book Rev

200 RELIGION

200 Religion

Armstrong, Karen

A **history** of God; the 4000 year quest of Judaism, Christianity, and Islam. Knopf 1993 xxiii, 460p maps hardcover o.p. pa $15.95 **200**
1. God 2. Islam 3. Judaism 4. Christianity
ISBN 0-345-38456-3 pa

LC 92-38318

This is a study of ideas and experiences of God in Judaism, Christianity and Islam from Abraham to the twentieth century

"Public librarians should be aware that conservative readers may be offended by this book, and even religious scholars may find Armstrong's rather one-sided 'death of God' optimism about humanity a bit passé. Otherwise, this is an excellent and informative book." Libr J

Bowker, John

World religions; contributing consultants: David Bowker [et al.] DK Pub. 1997 200p il maps $35; pa $16.95 **200**
1. Religion 2. Religions
ISBN 0-7894-1439-2; 0-7566-1772-3 pa

LC 96-38277

Each chapter begins with an "introduction and is followed by one-or-two page sections that explain the basic tenets of the faith, symbols, events, people, buildings, works of art, and the differences and similarities to other religions. Hinduism, Buddhism, Judaism, Christianity, and Islam are included as are Jainism, Sikhism, Chinese and Japanese religions, and Native religions." SLJ

Chittister, Joan

The **gift** of years; growing older gracefully. BlueBridge 2008 222p $19.95 **200**
1. Elderly 2. Aging -- Religious aspects
ISBN 978-1-933346-10-6; 1-933346-10-8

LC 2008-00332

"This collection of inspirational reflections, 'not meant to be read in one sitting, or even in order, but one topic at a time,' abounds in gentle insights and arresting aphorisms." Publ Wkly

Includes bibliographical references

Dawkins, Richard, 1941-

★ The **God** delusion. Houghton Mifflin Co. 2006 406p $27; pa $15.95 **200**
1. God 2. Atheism 3. Religion
ISBN 978-0-618-68000-9; 0-618-68000-4; 978-0-618-

91824-9 pa; 0-618-91824-8 pa

LC 2006-15506

"Both fans of Dawkins and his many opponents will want to read this book." Libr J

Includes bibliographical references

De Botton, Alain, 1969-

Religion for atheists; Alain de Botton. Pantheon Books 2012 320p. ill. **200**

1. Atheism 2. Religious life 3. Conduct of life 4. Religion -- Philosophy 5. Atheists

ISBN 9780307379108

LC 2011021286

It was the author's intent to demonstrate "that the supernatural claims of religion are entirely false--but that it still has some very important things to teach the secular world." The author "suggests . . . that we look to religion for insights into how to, among other concerns, build a sense of community, make our relationships last, overcome feelings of envy and inadequacy, inspire travel and reconnect with the natural world." (Publisher's note)

Dennett, Daniel Clement

Breaking the spell; religion as a natural phenomenon. [by] Daniel C. Dennett. Viking 2006 448p il $25.95 **200**

1. Religion

ISBN 0-670-03472-X

LC 2005-42415

This book examines the "question of why we believe in God and how religion shapes our lives and our future. . . . [Dennett] contends that the 'belief in belief' has fogged any attempt to rationally consider the existence of God and the relationship between divinity and human need." Publisher's note

"A book certain to spark heated controversy." Booklist

Includes bibliographical references

Dreyfus, Hubert L., 1929-

All things shining; reading the Western classics to find meaning in a secular age. [by] Hubert Dreyfus and Sean Dorrance Kelly. Free Press 2011 254p $26; ebook $12.99 **200**

1. Religion 2. Religions 3. Meaning (Philosophy)

ISBN 978-1-4165-9615-8; 1-4165-9615-1; 978-1-4391-0170-4 ebook; 1-4391-0170-1 ebook

LC 2010021750

This book contains "readings of authors including Homer, Dante, Descartes and Kant, as well as the novelists Herman Melville and David Foster Wallace." (N Y Times (Late N Y Ed)) Index.

"A provocative, illuminating and inspirational exhortation to 'Ask not why the gods have abandoned you, but why you have abandoned the gods.'" Kirkus

Includes bibliographical references

The **encyclopedia** of cults, sects, and new religions; {edited by} James R. Lewis. 2nd ed; Prometheus Bks. 2002 951p il $180 **200**

1. Cults 2. Reference books 3. Sects -- Encyclopedias

4. United States -- Religion -- Encyclopedias

ISBN 1-57392-888-7

LC 2002-19180

First published 1998

This reference contains "information on approximately 1,000 religious groups, ranging from small churches with less than a hundred members (Chishti Order of America) to organizations such as the Assemblies of God that number in the millions. Most entries are relatively short. The more controversial religions, as well as religious groups that have had a high profile lately, receive more lengthy treatments. Also included are entries on broader religious movements such as the New Age and the Charismatic Movement. . . . Each article outlines the history of the group, its founders and leaders, its main teachings, and an approximate number of followers or congregations. The explanations are clearly written, interesting and understandable, without too much scholarly jargon." Booklist

Includes bibliographical references

★ **Encyclopedia** of religion; Lindsay Jones, editor in chief. 2nd ed; Macmillan Reference USA 2005 15v il set $1295 **200**

1. Reference books 2. Religions -- Encyclopedias

ISBN 0-02-865733-0

LC 2004-17052

First published 1987 in 16 volumes

"Treats theoretical (e.g., doctrines, myths, theologies, ethics), practical (e.g., cults, sacraments, meditations), and sociological (e.g., religious groups, ecclesiastical forms) aspects of religion; includes extensive coverage of non-Western religions. Signed articles by some 1,400 contributors worldwide end with bibliographies. Many composite entries treat two or more related topics. . . . Has quickly become the standard work." Guide to Ref Books. 11th edition [review of 1993 edition]

Includes bibliographical references

★ **Encyclopedia** of religious rites, rituals, and festivals; Frank A. Salamone, editor. Routledge 2004 487p il (Routledge encyclopedias of religion and society) $150 **200**

1. Reference books 2. Rites and ceremonies 3. Religions -- Encyclopedias

ISBN 0-415-94180-6

LC 2003-20389

"Articles describing types of practices common to many cultures treat such topics as death rituals, hunting rituals, puberty rites, and sport and ritual. Specific occasions that involve ceremonies include Divali, Easter, Ramadan, and Yom Kippur. Some practices like cannibalism, haircutting rituals, and snake handling are described in separate articles." SLJ

"The entries can be understood by readers unfamiliar with the topics covered, but the work is suitable for all levels of scholars." Choice

Includes bibliographical references

Hall, Timothy L.

★ **American** religious leaders. Facts on File 2003 430p il (American biographies) $65 **200**
1. Religious biography 2. United States -- Religion
ISBN 0-8160-4534-8

LC 2002-2454

"This is a perfect source for fast, basic information for anyone who wishes a two-minute reading synopsis on an American religious leader. It should be within arms reach of any reference librarian working an information desk or a telephone." Am Ref Books Annu, 2003
Includes bibliographical references

Hexham, Irving

Understanding world religions. Zondervan 2011 512p il map $39.99; ebook $30.99 **200**
1. Religions
ISBN 978-0-310-25944-2; 0-310-25944-4; 978-0-310-31448-6 ebook; 0-310-31448-8 ebook

LC 2010013103

This "world religions text explores various religions under the broad categories of African Religions, the Yogic Traditions (including Buddhism), and the Abrahamic traditions." Publisher's note
Includes bibliographical references

Hitchens, Christopher

God is not great; how religion poisons everything. Twelve 2007 307p $24.99 **200**
1. Atheism 2. Religion
ISBN 978-0-44657-980-3; 0-44657-980-7

LC 2006-23039

In this work Hitchens catalogs "the major arguments against religion, which he deems a pernicious force. First, he writes, faith misrepresents the origin of the cosmos as well as that of humanity; second, it fosters servility, solipsism, and sexual repression; and, third, it is based on wishful thinking. Hitchens spares no targets in this manifesto, criticizing both Western and Eastern faiths." Libr J
Includes bibliographical references

Hutchison, William R.

Religious pluralism in America; the contentious history of a founding ideal. Yale University Press 2003 262p $32.50; pa $18 **200**
1. United States -- Religion
ISBN 0-300-09813-8; 0-300-10516-9 pa

LC 2002-151893

The author "illuminates the cultural transformations that enabled twentieth-century Americans to embrace belatedly the religious diversity that emerged in the nineteenth-century influx of Catholic and Jewish immigrants and in the rise of new American-born faiths such as Mormonism and Transcendentalism. . . . Though he acknowledges the concerns of critics worried about the moral balkanization of a society lacking shared religious premises, Hutchison hails America's new religious pluralism as a great achievement. A balanced and informative narrative." Booklist
Includes bibliographical references

King, Barbara J.

Evolving God; a provocative view on the origins of religion. Doubleday 2007 262p il $24.95 **200**
1. Religion 2. Social change
ISBN 978-0-385-51104-9; 0-385-51104-3

LC 2006-270101

The author "contends that religion, conceived as a system not of beliefs but of actions, not as theology but as worship, is a consequence of primate evolution. . . . In conclusion, she weighs the popular debate over evolution, noting high skepticism about human evolution and high belief in God, and questions the compulsion to choose either evolution or belief. Anyone who recognizes that compulsion, internal or external, may profit from reading this brilliant book." Booklist
Includes bibliographical references

Messadie, Gerald

A **history** of the devil; translated from the French by Marc Romano. Kodansha Int. 1996 377p hardcover o.p. pa $16 **200**
1. Devil 2. Demonology
ISBN 1-56836-198-X pa

LC 95-4949

"Using a comparative and phenomenological approach, the author traces the idea of the Devil from ancient Greece and India to contemporary Western culture. What emerges from Messadie's explorations is that the Devil is a very recent concept, arising primarily out of Zoroastrianism in Persia in the sixth century B.C." Publ Wkly
"Messadie's highly engaging and provocative cultural history is essential for most libraries." Libr J
Includes bibliographical references

Minois, Georges

The **atheist's** Bible; the most dangerous book that never existed. Georges Minois ; translated by Lys Ann Weiss. The University of Chicago Press 2012 249 p. map (cloth : alk. paper) $30 **200**
1. Atheism -- History 2. De tribus impostoribus 3. Rationalism -- History
ISBN 0226530299; 9780226530291

LC 2012011212

This book by Georges Minois, translated by Lys Ann Weiss, explains that "in 1239, Pope Gregory IX accused Frederick II, the Holy Roman Emperor, of . . . [writing] a supremely blasphemous book--'De tribus impostoribus,' or the 'Treatise of the Three Impostors'--in which Frederick denounced Moses, Jesus, and Muhammad as impostors. . . . Minois tracks the course of the book from its origins in 1239 to its most salient episodes in the seventeenth and eighteenth centuries." (Publisher's note)
Includes bibliographical references and index

National Geographic concise history of world religions; an illustrated time line. edited by Tim Cooke. National Geographic 2011 352 p. col. ill. (hardcover) $40.00 **200**
1. Ethics 2. World history 3. Religious institutions 4. Religions -- Encyclopedias 5. Religion -- History -- Chronology 6. Religions 7. Religion and ethics 8.

Religions -- History
ISBN 1426206984; 9781426206986

LC 2011276808

This book "continues the 'Concise History' series with [a] . . . take on major religions and lesser-known faiths of all times and nations." It offers a "global perspective on the history of faith in the Americas, Europe, Asia and Oceania, and Africa and the Middle East. . . . 50 feature essays explore in detail the origins, development and influence of faith." (Publisher's Note)

Includes bibliographical references (p. 343-344) and index

Prothero, Stephen R.

God is not one; the eight rival religions that run the world--and why their differences matter. [by] Stephen Prothero. HarperOne 2010 388p $26.99; ebook $9.99 **200**
1. Religions
ISBN 978-0-06-157127-5; 0-06-157127-X; 978-0-06-199120-2 ebook; 0-06-199120-1 ebook

LC 2009053372

Prothero argues that each of the major world religions have different worldviews and approaches to spiritual questions. The book contains chapters on Islam (the way of submission); Christianity (the way of salvation); Confucianism (the way of propriety); Hinduism (the way of devotion); Buddhism (the way of awakening); Yoruba religion (the way of connection); Judaism (the way of exile and return); Daoism (the way of flourishing); Atheism (the way of reason).

"Provocative, thoughtful, fiercely intelligent and, for both believing and nonbelieving, formal and informal students of religion, a must-read." Booklist

Includes bibliographical references

Religious literacy; what every American needs to know--and doesn't. [by] Stephen Prothero. HarperSanFrancisco 2007 296p $24.95 **200**
1. Religions
ISBN 978-0-06-084670-1; 0-06-084670-4

LC 2006-41310

"In this book, the author combines a lively history of the rise and fall of American religious literacy with a set of proposed remedies based on his hope that 'the Fall into religious ignorance is reversible.' He also includes a useful multicultural glossary of religious definitions and allusions, in which religious illiterates can find the prodigal son, the promised land, the Quakers and the Koran." Washington Post Book World

Includes bibliographical references

Religions of the world; a comprehensive encyclopedia of beliefs and practices. J. Gordon Melton, Martin Baumann, editors; Todd M. Johnson, world religious statistics; Donald Wiebe, introduction. 2nd ed.; ABC-CLIO 2010 6v il map set $595 **200**
1. Reference books 2. Religions -- Encyclopedias
ISBN 978-1-59884-203-6; 978-1-59884-204-3 ebook

LC 2010-29403

First published 2002

"Entries include profiles on religion in the world's smallest countries (the Vatican and San Marino), profiles on religion in recently established or disputed countries (Kosovo and Nagorno-Karabakh), as well as profiles on religion in some of the world's most remote places (Antarctica and Easter Island)." Publisher's note

"With its currency and particular emphasis, this work warrants the attention of virtually every academic and pubic library." Booklist

Includes bibliographical references

Turner, Alice K.

The **history** of hell. Harcourt Brace & Co. 1993 275p il hardcover o.p. pa $22 **200**
1. Hell
ISBN 0-15-600137-3 pa

LC 93-9909

"Belief in a hell or some sort of afterlife has been intrinsic to the religions of the world ever since the first stories were shared aloud and incised in clay tablets. Turner's richly illustrated history surveys the myriad forms hell has taken in the West from Sumer to Rome and beyond." Booklist

Weber, Eugen

Apocalypses; prophesies, cults, and millennial beliefs through the ages. [by] Eugen Weber. Harvard Univ. Press 1999 294p $27.50; pa $16.95 **200**
1. Millennium 2. End of the world
ISBN 0-674-04080-5; 0-674-00395-0 pa

LC 99-18001

"Weber traces millennial beliefs as professed through the ages. From ancient and pre-Christian times to the present day, humankind has had an unshakable belief that the end is at hand. . . . Weber has an excellent grasp of his subject, an accessible style, and an understated sense of humor." Booklist

Includes bibliographical references

Williams, Juan

This far by faith; stories from the African-American religious experience. [by] Juan Williams and Quinton Dixie. Morrow 2003 326p il hardcover o.p. pa $15.95 **200**
1. African Americans -- History 2. African Americans -- Religion
ISBN 0-06-018863-4; 0-06-093424-7 pa

LC 2002-71884

This study of African American worship "interweaves stories of individual spiritual journeys and accounts of church leaders and religious movements. The authors . . . [aim to] link blacks' faith to their ongoing fight for equality." Christ Sci Monit

"Brief topical articles and captioned illustrations supplement the main text, creating a balanced, readable, and nuanced introduction to the power of faith to sustain the African American community." Libr J

200.1 Systems, scientific principles, psychology of religion

Barrett, Justin L.

Born believers; the science of children's religious belief. Justin L. Barrett. Free Press 2012 x, 302 p.p **200.1**
1. Belief and doubt 2. Child psychology 3. Faith -- Psychology 4. Children -- Religious life 5. God 6. Psychology, Religious
ISBN 1439196540; 9781439196540

LC 2011039581

In this book, "the author looks at cross-cultural studies of children conducted by experts in the 'cognitive science of religion.' The studies indicate that, from an early age, humans know the difference between inanimate objects and 'agents'--people or forces that can move or make things move. As they develop, children are prone to see agents as powerful forces unlike humans. By four or five, kids see a purpose, not only in objects, but also in creatures, rocks, rivers and mountains. . . . In the second part of the book, the author indicts atheism by arguing that if one accepts natural selection then one cannot reject the natural religion of childhood--it must have survival value." (Kirkus)

Includes bibliographical references and index

200.8 Groups of people

Circling faith; Southern women on spirituality. edited by Wendy Reed and Jennifer Horne. University of Alabama Press 2012 xiv, 230 p.p (trade cloth) $29.95 **200.8**
1. Women -- Religious life -- Southern states 2. Spirituality 3. Women authors -- Religious life 4. Southern women -- Religious life
ISBN 0817317678; 0817357017; 0817386084; 9780817317676; 9780817357016; 9780817386085

LC 2011034803

This book, edited by Wendy Reed and Jennifer Horne, "is a collection of essays by southern women that encompasses spirituality and the experience of winding through the religiously charged environment of the American South. . . . These essays showcase the large spectrum of spirituality that abides in the South, as well as the equally large spectrum of individual women who hold these faiths." (Publisher's note)

200.9 History, geographic treatment, biography

Almond, Gabriel Abraham

★ **Strong** religion; the rise of fundamentalisms around the world. {by} Gabriel A. Almond, R. Scott Appleby, and Emmanuel Sivan. University of Chicago Press 2003 281p il $49; pa $19 **200.9**
1. Religious fundamentalism
ISBN 0-226-01497-5; 0-226-01498-3 pa

LC 2002-13665

This "may be the single most cogent sociohistorical analysis of the modern religious phenomenon called funda-

mentalism. . . . This foundational work is essential for academic and major public libraries." Libr J

Includes bibliographical references

Armstrong, Karen

★ The **battle** for God; fundamentalism in Judaism, Christianity, and Islam. Knopf 2000 442p $29.95; pa $15.95 **200.9**
1. Judaism 2. Islamic fundamentalism 3. Christian fundamentalism 4. Religious fundamentalism 5. Israel -- History
ISBN 0-679-43597-2; 0-345-39169-1 pa

LC 99-34022

This is a "study of fundamentalism among Jews (in Israel), Christians (American Protestants), and Muslims (Sunni Egyptians and Shiite Iranians). Armstrong argues that all strains of fundamentalism, despite their differences, are fearful defenses against modernity. . . . The author is sympathetic to the human need for spiritual meaning, but she points out that the intellectual flaws of fundamentalist beliefs are customarily accompanied by paranoia, anger, and aggression—which, in turn, frequently betray the message of the faith." New Yorker

Includes bibliographical references

★ The **great** transformation; the beginning of our religious traditions. Knopf 2006 469p il map $30 **200.9**
1. Religion -- History
ISBN 0-375-41317-0

LC 2005-47536

"This could very possibly be one of the greatest intellectual histories ever written." Libr J

Includes bibliographical references

Balmer, Randall Herbert

Religion in twentieth century America; {by} Randall Balmer. Oxford Univ. Press 2001 142p il (Religion in American life) $28 **200.9**
1. United States -- Religion
ISBN 0-19-511295-4

LC 00-60674

"This title is accessible and reliable, brief and lively, and makes a fine addition to most libraries." SLJ

Includes bibliographical references

Believer, beware; first person dispatches from the margins of faith. selected by Jeff Sharlet, Peter Manseau, and the editors of Killing the Buddha. Beacon Press 2009 263p pa $16 **200.9**
1. Faith 2. United States -- Religion
ISBN 978-0-8070-7739-9; 0-8070-7739-9

LC 2008-47403

"The editors are among the smart, candid, and insightful authors whose personal narratives form the book's 35 brief chapters. The selections represent a wide range of experiences from cheating on bar mitzvah prep to discovering hunger as spiritual food in a Ramadan fast, from sabotaging Bible camp to stumbling upon barbershop theology. Contributions reflect the scope of religious diversity, including orthodox Judaism, Roman Catholicism, Islam, Zen Buddhism and even a meditation on agnosticism. Some are funny, others heartbreaking, and some are simply revelatory." Publ Wkly

Includes bibliographical references

Butler, Jon

Religion in American life; a short history. [by] Jon Butler, Grant Wacker, and Randall Balmer. Updated ed.; Oxford University Press 2008 496p il pa $19.95   **200.9**
1. United States -- Religion
ISBN 978-0-19-533329-9; 0-19-533329-2

LC 2007-24915

First published 2002

This volume begins by describing the state of religious affairs in the old and new worlds. The survey continues with a look at the religious landscape of 19th-century America and concludes with an examination of current religious beliefs and practices.

Includes bibliographical references (p. 437-463)

★ The **Cambridge** illustrated history of religions; edited by John Bowker. Cambridge Univ. Press 2002 336p il (Cambridge illustrated history) $40   **200.9**
1. Religions
ISBN 0-521-81037-X

LC 2001-37866

"The major religions get thoroughgoing treatment, with short introductions also given to the Zoroastrianism; the religions of Greece, Rome, Egypt, and Mesopotamia; aboriginal religions; and new religious movements. . . . Christianity receives a separate chapter as well as substantial treatment in chapters on Chinese, Korean, and Japanese religions. . . . This volume presents a large amount of information in an engaging way, offering much scholarly insight for the lay reader." Libr J

Includes bibliographical references

Controversial New Religions; edited by James R. Lewis and Jesper Aa. Petersen. 2nd Edition Oxford University Press 2014 480 p. pa. $35 **200.9**
1. Cults 2. Religion
ISBN 9780199315314

LC 2013049363

"This volume collects papers on those specific New Religious Movements (NRMS) that have generated the most scholarly attention. With few exceptions, these organizations are also the controversial groups that have attracted the attention of the mass media, often because they have been involved in, or accused of, violent or anti-social activities. Among the movements . . . profiled are such groups as the Branch Davidians, Heaven's Gate, Aum Shinrikyo, Solar Temple, Scientology, and Falun Gong." (Publisher's note)

★ **Eastern** religions; origins, beliefs, practices, holy texts, sacred places. general editor, Michael D. Coogan; [contributors] Vasudha Narayanan . . . [et al.] Oxford University Press 2005 552p il $35; pa $19.95   **200.9**
1. Shinto 2. Taoism 3. Buddhism 4. Hinduism 5. Confucianism 6. East Asia -- Religion 7. South Asia

-- Religion
ISBN 0-19-522190-7; 978-0-19-522190-9; 0-19-522191-5 pa; 978-0-19-522191-6 pa

LC 2004-30376

This is an introduction "to major South Asian and East Asian religious traditions. Four expert authors introduce Hinduism, Buddhism, Taoism, Confucianism, and Shinto. To aid comparison, each article has parallel sections on origins and historical development, aspects of the divine, sacred texts, sacred persons, ethical principles, sacred space, sacred time, death and the afterlife, and society and religion. The clear, crisp prose avoids academic jargon without losing the complexity and richness of the traditions being examined." Libr J

Includes bibliographical references

★ **Encyclopedia** of fundamentalism; Brenda E. Brasher, editor. Routledge 2001 558p il (Religion and society) $125   **200.9**
1. Religious fundamentalism
ISBN 0-415-92244-5

LC 2001-19951

This reference covers "fundamentalism, from definition, history, and beliefs to movements and churches, significant individuals, and expressions in various world religions. Creationism, fascism, rock music, and the Taliban are a sample of the topics covered. The contributors provide clear, readable explanations. . . . This beautifully laid-out work is the one to have." Libr J

Includes bibliographical references

Kugel, James L.

In the valley of the shadow; on the foundations of religious belief (and their connection to a certain, fleeting state of mind) Free Press 2011 237p **200.9**
1. Hebraists 2. College teachers 3. Cancer -- Religious aspects
ISBN 978-1-4391-3009-4; 978-1-4391-3010-0 pa; 978-1-4391-5055-9 ebook

LC 2010-28086

The author invites readers to witness the exploration on religion that he undertook after being diagnosed with an aggressive, and likely fatal, form of cancer.

"Written with eloquence suitable to a scholar of Biblical poetry, Kugel's memoir-cum-meditation will appeal to thoughtful Jewish and non-Jewish readers alike." Libr J

Includes bibliographical references

Leon, Luis D.

Religion and American cultures; an encyclopedia of traditions, diversity, and popular expressions. Gary Laderman and Luis León, editors; foreword by Amanda Porterfield. ABC-CLIO 2003 3v set $285   **200.9**
1. Reference books 2. United States -- Religion -- Encyclopedias
ISBN 1-57607-238-X

LC 2003-8644

"This resource explores the various ways Americans approach religion. Its first volume features chapters on ethnic groups and sectarian beliefs, the second comprises essay entries on distinct practices, and the third collects primary documents. Cotton Mather, Shirley MacLaine, and Elijah Muhammad are represented, along with such pivotal documents as The Maryland TolerationAct and the American Indian Religious Freedom Act." Libr J

Includes bibliographical references

Melton, J. Gordon

★ **Melton's** encyclopedia of American religions; [by] J. Gordon Melton; James Beverley, associate editor; Constance Jones, assistant editor; Pamela S. Nadell, assistant editor; foreword by Rodney Stark. 8th ed.; Gale, Cengage Learning 2009 xxvi, 1386p il map $380   **200.9**
   1. Reference books 2. Sects -- Encyclopedias 3. United States -- Religion -- Encyclopedias
   ISBN 978-0-7876-9696-2

LC 2008-37465

First published 1978 by McGrath Publishing Company with title: Encyclopedia of American religions

This encyclopedia features "coverage on more than 2,300 North American religious groups in the U.S. and Canada—from Adventists to Zen Buddhists. Information on these groups is presented in two . . . . sections. These sections contain essays and directory listings that describe the historical development of religious families and give . . . information about each group within those families, including, when available, rubrics for membership figures, educational facilities and periodicals." Publisher's note

Includes bibliographical references

Moore, R. Laurence

Selling God; American religion in the marketplace of culture. Oxford Univ. Press 1994 317p hardcover o.p. pa $19.95   **200.9**
   1. United States -- Religion
   ISBN 0-19-509838-2 pa

LC 93-19624

"Moore traces the history of marketing techniques in American religion. The first amendment ban on state religion necessitated a competitive approach. Moore asserts that religion 'had to sell itself not only in the competitive church market, but also in a general market of other cultural commodities.'" Libr J

The author "is balanced and nonpedantic, treating religion as a cultural element of history." N Y Times Book Rev

Includes bibliographical references

Naipaul, V. S.

The **masque** of Africa; glimpses of African belief. Alfred A. Knopf 2010 241p $26.95; ebook $26.95   **200.9**
   1. Africa -- Religion 2. Africa -- Description and travel
   ISBN 978-0-307-27073-3; 0-307-27073-4; 978-0-307-59449-5 ebook; 0-307-59449-1 ebook

LC 2010-01256

This is a "book for outsiders, for those who may never visit Africa or may know it only superficially. But it is also a book in which Africans themselves may find something to learn. Naipaul is a difficult, imperfect narrator who does not care to be liked, but he is an honest one and doesn't dissemble. Somehow, by the end of it all, and despite his best efforts, I have grown to like him." Observer (London)

Queen, Edward L.

Encyclopedia of American religious history; [by] Edward L. Queen II, Stephen R. Prothero, and Gardiner H. Shattuck, Jr.; foreword by Martin E. Marty, editorial adviser; book producer, Marie A. Cantlon. 3rd ed.; Facts On File 2009 3v il (Facts on File library of American history) set $250   **200.9**
   1. Reference books 2. United States -- Religion -- Encyclopedias
   ISBN 978-0-8160-6660-5

LC 2007-52350

First published 1995

This reference source presents over 800 articles examining different religions, religious leaders, events, and other topics that helped shape the history of religion in America. The coverage extends from Puritan America to the moral majority.

Includes bibliographical references

Wolfe, Alan

The **transformation** of American religion; how we actually live our faith. Free Press 2003 309p $26   **200.9**
   1. United States -- Religion
   ISBN 0-7432-2839-1

LC 2003-44870

The author "examines the ways that American religion has been so transformed over the past five decades that it is no longer recognizable. He explores every facet of American religion—worship, fellowship, doctrine, tradition, morality, sin, witness and identity—as he investigates the fading of practices or beliefs that once dominated." Publ Wkly

"This provocative book is a must-read for a wide variety of readers." Choice

Includes bibliographical references

200.92 Biography

Ostman, Cami

Beyond belief; the secret lives of women in extreme religions. edited by Susan Tive & Cami Ostman. Seal Press 2013 313 p. $16   **200.92**
   1. Women -- Religious life 2. Religious fundamentalism 3. Women and religion 4. Patriarchy -- Religious aspects 5. Religion -- Controversial literature
   ISBN 1580054420; 9781580054423

LC 2012041943

This book presents "a collection of . . . personal stories written by women of varying ages, races, and religious backgrounds who share one commonality: they've all experienced and rejected extreme religions. Covering a wide range of religious communities--including Evangelical, Catholic, Jewish, Mormon, Muslim . . . and Jehovah's Witness--the stories in Beyond Belief reveal how these women became involved . . . and why they came to the decision to eventually abandon their faiths." (Publisher's note)

201   Specific aspects of religion

Armstrong, Karen, 1944-

★ **Fields** of Blood; Religion and the History of Violence. by Karen Armstrong. Random House Inc 2014. 496 p. $30   **201**

1. Violence -- Religious aspects
ISBN 0307957047; 9780307957047

This book, by Karen Armstrong, is an "exploration of religion and the history of human violence. . . . While many historians have looked at violence in connection with particular religious manifestations (jihad in Islam or Christianity's Crusades), Armstrong looks at each faith--not only Christianity and Islam, but also Buddhism, Hinduism, Confucianism, Daoism, and Judaism--in its totality over time." (Publisher's note)

Includes bibliographic references, notes, and index

Barr, Stephen M.

★ **Modern** physics and ancient faith. University of Notre Dame Press 2003 312p il hardcover o.p. pa $18   **201**

1. Physics 2. Religion and science
ISBN 0-268-03471-0; 978-0-268-02198-6 pa; 0-268-02198-8 pa

LC 2002-151565

"Neither religiously sectarian nor technically daunting, this is a book that invites the widest range of readers to ponder the deepest kind of questions." Booklist

The author "argues that the great discoveries of modern physics are more compatible with the central teachings of Christianity and Judaism about God, the cosmos, and the human soul than with the atheistic viewpoint of scientific materialism." Publ Wkly

Includes bibliographical references

Campbell, David E., 1971-

American grace; how religion divides and unites us. [by] Robert D. Putnam [and] David E. Campbell, with the assistance of Shaylyn Romney Garrett. Simon & Schuster 2010 673p il map $30   **201**

1. United States -- Religion 2. Religion -- Social aspects 3. United States -- Religion -- 1960- 4. Religion and sociology -- United States
ISBN 978-1-4165-6671-7; 1-4165-6671-6

LC 2010-27838

The book examines "the place of religion in contemporary American society. Relying on a 2006-2007 survey of their own, but also employing an array of other survey data and monographic studies, Robert D. Putnam and David E. Campbell give a[n] . . . account of . . . the religious demography of the United States and offer . . . views on how religion has shaped contemporary American social and political values and identities." (Journal of American History)

"An essential resource for anyone trying to understand twenty-first-century America." Booklist

Includes bibliographical references

Campbell, Joseph

Creative mythology. Arkana 1991 730p (The masks of God) pa $18   **201**

1. Mythology in literature
ISBN 978-0-14-019440-1; 0-14-019440-1
First published 1968 by Viking

"This volume explores the whole inner story of modern culture since the Dark Ages, treating modern man's unique position as the creator of his own mythology." Publisher's note

Includes bibliographical references

Occidental mythology. Arkana 1991 564p (The masks of God) pa $18   **201**

1. Mythology
ISBN 978-0-14-019441-8; 0-14-019441-X
First published 1964 by Viking

"A systematic . . . comparison of the themes that underlie the art, worship, and literature of the Western world." Publisher's note

Includes bibliographical references

Oriental mythology. Arkana 1991 561p (The masks of God) pa $18   **201**

1. Oriental mythology
ISBN 978-0-14-019442-5; 0-14-019442-8
First published 1962 by Viking

"An exploration of Eastern mythology as it developed into the distinctive religions of Egypt, India, China, and Japan." Publisher's note

Includes bibliographical references

★ The **power** of myth; [by] Joseph Campbell, with Bill Moyers; Betty Sue Flowers, editor. Doubleday 1988 231p il hardcover o.p. pa $29.95   **201**

1. Mythology 2. Religious art 3. Spiritual life
ISBN 0-385-24773-7; 0-385-24774-5

LC 88-4218

This companion to a public television series records conversations between Campbell and Bill Moyers. Campbell reflects on themes and symbols from world religions and mythologies and explores their relevance for his own spiritual journey.

"Campbell is the hero on his own voyage of discovery. This well-bound book on lovely paper with helpful illustrations from art is highly recommended for all libraries." Choice

Primitive mythology. Arkana 1991 504p (The masks of God) pa $18   **201**

1. Mythology
ISBN 978-0-14-019443-2; 0-14-019443-6
First published 1959 by Viking

The author "discusses the primitive roots of mythology, examining them in light of . . . discoveries in archaeology, anthropology, and psychology." Publisher's note

Includes bibliographical references

Coles, Robert

The **secular** mind. Princeton Univ. Press 1999
189p $45; pa $15.95 **201**
1. Secularism 2. Religion and science
ISBN 0-691-05805-9; 0-691-08862-4 pa
LC 98-39388
"This is a potent and powerful work readers will think
about and return to again and again." Publ Wkly

Consolmagno, Guy

God's mechanics; how scientists and engineers
make sense of religion. Jossey-Bass 2007 245p
$24.95 **201**
1. Religion and science
ISBN 978-0-7879-9466-2; 0-7879-9466-9
LC 2007-19067
"Combining personal memoir with conversations within
the techie world, Consolmagno describes questions about
the universe and the meaning of life that attract techies
into religious belief and practice, concluding that 'techies
are not looking for proof. They're looking for confidence.'"
Publ Wkly

Davis, Kenneth C.

Don't know much about mythology; everything
you need to know about the greatest stories in human
history but never learned. HarperCollins Publishers
2005 545p $26.95; pa $14.95 **201**
1. Mythology
ISBN 0-06-019460-X; 978-0-06-019460-4; 0-06-
093257-0 pa; 978-0-06-093257-2 pa
LC 2005-43341
The author "examines the myths created by societies
ranging from Egypt, Greece and Rome to Africa, India and
the Americas, proceeding . . . by way of question and answer as he surveys each mythmaking culture. . . . His survey
provides a superb starting point for entering the world of
mythology." Publ Wkly
Includes bibliographical references

Deloria, Vine

Evolution, creationism, and other modern myths;
a critical inquiry. [by] Vine Deloria, Jr. Fulcrum
2002 274p $24.95; pa $18.95 **201**
1. Evolution 2. Creationism 3. Religion and science
ISBN 1-55591-159-5; 1-55591-458-6 pa
LC 2002-8171
The author "argues that both sides in the evolution-ver-
sus-creationism debate are wrong. . . . This intellectual duel
finds only mistaken orthodoxies in the field, for creationism
has no scientific basis, but evolution is far from proven. . . .
Certain to be controversial, likely to outrage the faithful of
both camps, and a stunning good read." Booklist
Includes bibliographical references

★ **Encyclopedia** of science and religion; J. Wentzel
Vrede van Huyssteen, editor in chief. Macmillan
Ref. 2003 2v set $280 **201**
1. Reference books 2. Religion and science --

Encyclopedias
ISBN 0-02-865704-7
LC 2002-152471
"Thousands of books have been written about the relationship between science and religion, but few can be characterized as reference resources. This two-volume set helps
fill that niche with more than 400 scholarly articles written
by experts from around the world." Libr J
Includes bibliographical references

Frank, Adam

The **constant** fire; beyond the science vs. religion debate. University of California Press 2009
288p $24.95 **201**
1. Religion and science
ISBN 978-0-520-25412-1; 0-520-25412-0
LC 2008-25402
Frank "attempts to move past the antagonisms between
religious fundamentalists and the New Atheists. Instead of
debating the Bible or arguing about the existence of evil, he
turns to thinkers like William James, Rudolf Otto and Mir-
cea Eliade for ideas about experience, the sacred, the sublime and hierophanies, manifestations of the sacred in the
physical world." Nation
"An elegant reimagining of the relationship between science and spirituality. . . . Challenges the assumption that science and religion are implacable foes." Chron Higher Educ
Includes bibliographical references (p. 269-281)
and index

Glucklich, Ariel

Dying for heaven; holy pleasure and suicide
bombers--why the best qualities of religion are also
its most dangerous. HarperCollins 2009 345p
$25.99 **201**
1. Suicide bombers 2. Terrorism -- Religious aspects
ISBN 978-0-06-143081-7
LC 2009-5174
"Extremely well written, and at times quite funny . . .
this book is an absolute necessity for a public seeking to understand religious nuance and zealotry; it deserves careful
attention and a broad readership." Libr J
Includes bibliographical references

Haidt, Jonathan

The **righteous** mind; why good people are divided by politics and religion. Jonathan Haidt. Pantheon
Books 2012 419 p. $28.95 **201**
1. Social values 2. Social psychology 3. Political
psychology 4. Psychology of religion 5. Ethics
-- Psychological aspects 6. Ethics 7. Psychology,
Religious
ISBN 9780307377906
LC 2011032036
"The core of the book [by Jonathan Haidt] is an attempt
at a Darwinian explanation of morality, contending that moral behavior emerges from a natural process of competition
among human groups. . . . A part of 'The Righteous Mind'
is a . . . critique of . . . [a] primitive type of rationalism. . . .
Much of his book is an attempt to apply the findings of evo-

lutionary psychology to the political gridlock that . . . exists in the United States." (New Republic)

Includes bibliographical references and index.

The **History** of science and religion in the western tradition; an encyclopedia. Gary B. Ferngren, general editor; Edward J. Larson, Darrel W. Amundsen, co-editors; Anne-Marie E. Nakhla, assistant editor. Garland 2000 xxi, 586p (Garland reference library of the humanities) $195 **201**
1. Religion and science
ISBN 0-8153-1656-9

LC 00-25153

This is a collection of articles "grouped under ten headings covering everything from the relationship of science and religion to the approaches taken by specific religious traditions, from alchemy to chemistry to materialism to spiritualism. Ferngren . . . and his coeditors take the stand that the historical relationship between science and religion follows a complex model rather than the popularly understood model of unalterable conflict. The result is a work, well worth reading through or browsing, that is filled with respect for the roles and methodologies of both religion and science." Libr J

Includes bibliographical references and index

Jordan, Michael

Dictionary of gods and goddesses; 2nd ed; Facts on File 2004 402p il (Facts on File library of religion and mythology) $45 **201**
1. Reference books 2. Gods and goddesses -- Dictionaries
ISBN 0-8160-5923-3

LC 2004-13028

First published 1993

The author's "alphabetical list includes gods and goddesses from a variety of religions. Each entry provides a brief description with cross-references where appropriate; some supply translations of the names. Longer entries include origin, dates of observance, synonyms, geographic location of the cult center, art references by type (e.g., stone carvings), and literary sources. . . . This [is] a usable, well-written resource for short descriptions of cross-cultural deities." Choice

Includes bibliographical references

Karabell, Zachary

Peace be upon you; the story of Muslim, Christian, and Jewish coexistence. Random House 2007 343p map $26.95 **201**
1. Interfaith relations 2. Christianity and other religions 3. Islam -- Relations 4. Judaism -- Relations
ISBN 978-1-4000-4368-2; 1-4000-4368-9

LC 2006-31501

"Countering the tendency to focus on crusaides, jihads, and pogroms, Karabell highlights epochs of interfaith toleration and cooperation, insisting that such harmony reflects the pacific doctrine central to the Abrahamic faiths." Booklist

"This outstanding book . . . combines in a single volume centuries of interaction among the three great monotheistic religions." Choice

Includes bibliographical references (p. 317-326)

Kimball, Charles

When religion becomes lethal; the explosive mix of politics and religion in Judaism, Christianity, and Islam. Jossey-Bass 2011 254p $27.95; ebook $14.99 **201**
1. Islam and politics 2. Religion and politics 3. Religious fundamentalism 4. Christianity and politics 5. Judaism and politics
ISBN 978-0-470-58190-2; 0-470-58190-5; 978-1-1180-3056-1 ebook

LC 2010052515

The author "begins with a careful overview of how, in sacred text and history, religion and politics interact in Judaism, Christianity, and Islam. He then examines the constructive and destructive ways adherents of the faiths have interpreted and acted on their traditions in the public square, focusing specifically on Israel, the U.S., Iraq, and Iran." Sojourners

Includes bibliographical references (p. 229-232)

Leeming, David Adams

A **dictionary** of Asian mythology; [by] David Leeming. Oxford Univ. Press 2001 232p $39.95; pa $29 **201**
1. Reference books 2. Asian mythology -- Dictionaries 3. Asia -- Religion -- Dictionaries
ISBN 0-19-512052-3; 0-19-512053-1 pa

LC 00-62389

"This concise dictionary references the mythologies of India, China, Tibet, Central and Southeast Asia, and Japan. The authoritative text is clearly written, thorough in coverage, and stylistically distinguished." Libr J

Includes bibliographical references

★ The **Oxford** companion to world mythology. Oxford University Press 2006 xxxvii, 469p $65 **201**
1. Reference books 2. Mythology -- Dictionaries
ISBN 0-19-515669-2

LC 2005-14216

"This volume presents approximately 2,000 concise entries in dictionary format. Leeming, . . . in an attempt to be 'inclusive and reasonably comprehensive,' ranges far outside the Western tradition to cover figures and folklore from Africa, Asia, and the Americas, as well as from the sacred narratives of religions. . . . Approximately 100 black-and-white illustrations, along with a few color plates, provide examples of artistic renderings of various myths. . . . This work should find a place in any general reference collection." Choice

Includes bibliographical references

Mercatante, Anthony S.

The **Facts** on File encyclopedia of world mythology and legend; [by] Anthony S. Mercatante & James R. Dow. 3rd ed; Facts On File 2008 2v il (Facts on File library of religion and mythology) set $150 **201**
1. Reference books 2. Mythology -- Encyclopedias
ISBN 978-0-8160-7311-5

LC 2007-51965

First published 1988

"Jammed with information and filled with both impressive scholarship and entertaining tidbits . . . it is highly recommended for all libraries." Libr J

Includes bibliographical references

Niebuhr, Gustav

Beyond tolerance; searching for interfaith understanding in America. Viking 2008 xxxviii, 218p $25.95   **201**

1. Religious tolerance 2. Interfaith relations
ISBN 978-0-670-01956-4; 0-670-01956-9

LC 2007-40479

"Niebuhr brings his reporter's eye for detail to this work, which he populates with people and organizations who strive to find religious meaning in our diverse lives. This is no dry, academic exposition. Written for a general audience, it is also valuable for scholars wishing to see an America many might have thought was calcifying into an insular continent, worshipping hard gods or God." Libr J

Includes bibliographical references (p. 208-212)

Nussbaum, Martha Craven, 1947-

★ The **new** religious intolerance; overcoming the politics of fear in an anxious age. Martha C. Nussbaum. Belknap Press of Harvard University Press 2012 xiii, 285 p.p (hbk. : alk. paper) $26.95   **201**

1. Freedom of religion 2. Religious tolerance 3. Islamophobia -- United States 4. Religious discrimination 5. Fear -- Religious aspects
ISBN 0674065905; 9780674065901

LC 2011051712

In this book Martha C. Nussbaum "enters the debate on anti-Muslim discrimination. . . . She invites us to examine disputes about women's use of the burka and the construction of an Islamic-initiated 'multifaith community center' near New York's Ground Zero. The author's argument for tolerant accommodation falls within the 'Socratic and Christian/Kantian' commitment to live an examined life in relations with religious minorities." (Library Journal)

Includes bibliographical references (p. 247-267) and index

Robinson, Marilynne, 1943-

Absence of mind; the dispelling of inwardness from the modern myth of the self. Yale University Press 2010 158p (Terry lectures)   **201**

1. Modern philosophy 2. Religion and science 3. Thought and thinking 4. Philosophy, Modern
ISBN 0-300-14518-7; 978-0-300-14518-2

LC 2009044020

"From Freud to Steven Pinker, much of what passes for scientific writing in the modern period, [Robinson] argues, is scientific in name only. Real science is forever searching after truth. Parascience, by contrast, is dogmatic, forever pretending it is in the 'clutch of certitudes.'" (Bookforum) Index.

"The title refers to what Robinson argues is missing from modern thought: the mind, the individual subjective experience of perception and reflection. Science, she says, has leapt from biology, theory and real science to 'parascientific' statements of faith. . . . Parascience, Robinson says, grew out of 19th century positivism. She discusses Auguste Comte as an early progenitor of parascience, moves to Freud, whose ideas have been largely discredited but whose influence remains prevalent, and then to contemporary parascience writers like Richard Dawkins, Daniel Dennett and E. O. Wilson. All of them, she says, use the language of science to claim legitimacy for their inconsistent, nonscientific statements of faith about what it means to be human. . . . Beneath the complex philosophical argument, Robinson makes a profound defence of the Imago Dei and of love. This book resounds with wisdom, passion and prophetic anger." Christian Week

Includes bibliographical references

Stark, Rodney

For the glory of God; how monotheism led to reformations, science, witch-hunts, and the end of slavery. Princeton Univ. Press 2003 488p il $45; pa $18.95   **201**

1. Slavery 2. Monotheism 3. Witchcraft 4. Reformation 5. Religion and science
ISBN 0-691-11436-6; 0-691-11950-3 pa

LC 2002-31746

A "provocative volume—lucid and tightly reasoned." Booklist

Includes bibliographical references and index

One true God; historical consequences of monotheism. Princeton Univ. Press 2001 319p il $47.50; pa $19.95   **201**

1. God 2. Monotheism
ISBN 0-691-08923-X; 0-691-11500-1 pa

LC 2001-21128

Stark seeks "a theoretical understanding of monotheism that will be . . . 'sociologically useful.' . . . Stark's theory has monotheism—the belief that there is just one God, just one giver of supernatural blessings and curses—as its object. He wants to explain monotheism's origins and development, to show its main effects upon the behavior and attitudes of social groups, and to account for the fact that monotheists are sometimes aggressively intolerant of those who do not share their beliefs and at other times civilly forebearing." Commonweal

Includes bibliographical references and index

Stedman, Chris

Faitheist; how an atheist found common ground with the religious. Chris Stedman. Beacon Press 2012 191 p. (hardcover : alk. paper) $22.95   **201**

1. Faith 2. Atheism 3. Spiritual biography 4. Dialogue -- Religious aspects
ISBN 0807014397; 9780807014394

LC 2012022520

This book is an "account of a gay man's experiences growing away from God and into a thoughtful and humane atheist." Author Chris Stedman moved away from his Evangelical Christian faith but "still sought to understand religion, both intellectually and through community interfaith work. The more he delved into the deeper questions of religion and morality, the more he saw the commonalities he shared with men and women of faith." (Kirkus)

Includes bibliographical references

201.65 Religion and science

Sacks, Jonathan

★ The **great** partnership; science, religion, and the search for meaning. Jonathan Sacks. Schocken Books 2011 x, 370 p.p $28.95 **201.65**

1. Faith 2. Religion and science
ISBN 0805243011; 9780805243017

LC 2012006601

In this book Jonathan Sacks "argues not only that science and religion are compatible, but that they complement each other--and that the world needs both. . . . [According to Sacks,] Science teaches us where we come from. Religion explains to us why we are here. Science is the search for explanation. Religion is the search for meaning. We need scientific explanation to understand nature. We need meaning to understand human behavior." (Publisher's note)

Includes bibliographical references

203 Public worship and other practices

Davidson, Linda Kay

Pilgrimage : from the Ganges to Graceland: an encyclopedia; [by] Linda Kay Davidson and David M. Gitlitz. ABC-CLIO 2002 2v il maps set $185 **203**

1. Pilgrims and pilgrimages
ISBN 1-57607-004-2

LC 2002-10119

"Defining a pilgrimage site by 'its ability to attract a transient population of devotees,' this . . . encyclopedia surveys the world's major destinations, from Delphi to Stonewall Inn. Entries are alphabetical and in addition to the sites also profile prominent figures, belief systems, activities, and institutions." Libr J

"This splendid encyclopedia is a delight to read and pleasing to view." Booklist

Includes bibliographical references and index

★ **How** to be a perfect stranger; the essential religious etiquette handbook. edited by Stuart M. Matlins & Arthur J. Magida. 5th ed.; SkyLight Paths Pub. 2011 402p pa $19.99 **203**

1. Etiquette 2. Rites and ceremonies
ISBN 978-1-59473-294-2

LC 2010-31668

First published 1996-1997 in two volumes by Jewish Lights Pub.

This guide "provides brief overviews of many religions: services, life-cycle events, home celebrations. It explains rituals so that those unfamiliar with them will know what to expect, how to dress, whether to bring a gift, and so on. It also has a glossary, explains various religious calendars, and lists religious festivals." Booklist

Manseau, Peter

Rag and bone; a journey among the world's holy dead. Henry Holt and Co. 2009 243p il $25 **203**

1. Relics
ISBN 978-0-8050-8652-2; 0-8050-8652-8

LC 2008-39465

"Manseau embarks on a global odyssey in search of the 'dismembered toes, splinters of shinbone, stolen bits of hair, burned remnants of an anonymous rib cage, and other odds and ends' belonging to saints and other sacred figures. The result is an entertaining, sometimes affecting inquiry into man's yearning for spiritual transcendence through the worship of holy relics, real or otherwise—from the Shroud of Turin . . . to more obscure bits of clothing and body parts. The book could have been ghoulish, but Manseau's irreverent approach and enthusiasm keep the tone surprisingly light." N Y Times Book Rev

204 Religious experience, life, practice

Colegate, Isabel

A pelican in the wilderness; hermits and solitaries. Counterpoint 2002 284p il hardcover o.p. pa $15.95 **204**

1. Hermits 2. Solitude
ISBN 1-58243-121-3; 1-58243-238-4 pa

LC 2001-47242

This "is a study of the soul that wants to be alone and knows how to do it; frequently met (so to say) in religion, the urge is also found in celebrities (J.D. Salinger, Howard Hughes)." N Y Times Book Rev

Coles, Robert

★ The **spiritual** life of children. Houghton Mifflin 1990 358p il hardcover o.p. pa $14 **204**

1. Children -- Religious life
ISBN 0-395-59923-7 pa

LC 90-40097

"One of the delights of his presentation is the combination of the children's searching comments and the struggle the author makes to hear beyond his own conceptions." J Youth Serv Libr

Includes bibliographical references

Lundberg, C. David

Unifying truths of the world's religions; practical principles for living and loving in peace. Heavenlight Press 2010 426p pa $18.95 **204**

1. Religions 2. Truth -- Religious aspects
ISBN 978-0-979-63082-8

This book presents a list of 33 inspirational principles that appear in the sacred texts of different eastern and western religions.

205 Religious ethics

De Waal, Frans

The **Bonobo** and the Atheist; In Search of Humanism Among the Primates. Frans de Waal ; with

drawings by the author. W W Norton & Co Inc 2013
304 p. (hardcover) $27.95 **205**
1. Ethics 2. Evolution 3. Primates -- Behavior
ISBN 0393073777; 9780393073775

LC 72010399

In this book, author "Frans de Waal argues that human
morality . . . does not begin and end with religion but is in
fact a product of evolution. . . . He delivers . . . evidence for
the seeds of ethical behavior in primate societies that further
cements the case for the biological origins of human fairness. . . . In doing so, de Waal explores for the first time the
implications of his work for our understanding of modern
religion." (Publisher's note)

209   Sects and reform movements

★ **Belief** beyond boundaries; Wicca, Celtic spirituality and the new age. edited by Joanne Pearson.
Ashgate 2002 339p il maps (Religion today)
$94.95; pa $29.95 **209**
1. Cults
ISBN 0-7546-0744-5; 0-7546-0820-4 pa

LC 2001-53654

This volume "explores 'religions' or forms of spirituality that tend to be marginal to the mainstream of British and
North American religious expression. The book examines
how alternative spiritualities traditionally classed as 'New
Age' or new religious movements have grown exponentially
in recent years. It progresses to detailed examination of Paganism, Celtic spirituality, Wicca, witchcraft, North American indigenous religion and New Age, considering the impact of the rise of science on religion and the emergence of
new categories of spirituality." Publisher's note

"Though somewhat academic in tone, this is a solid
overview of several New Age spiritual movements." Libr J
Includes bibliographical references

210   Philosophy and theory of religion

Huxley, Aldous
★ The **perennial** philosophy. Harper & Row
1945 312p hardcover o.p. pa $14 **210**
1. Philosophy and religion 2. Religion -- Philosophy
ISBN 0-06-057058-X pa
An anthology of and commentary on Chinese, Latin,
Greek, Catholic and Protestant mysticism
Includes bibliographical references

James, William
★ The **varieties** of religious experience; a study
in human nature. introduction by Reinhold Niebuhr.
Simon & Schuster 2004 398p pa $15 **210**
1. Mysticism 2. Conversion 3. Psychology 4. New
Thought 5. Religious life 6. Spiritual healing 7.
Religion -- Philosophy
ISBN 978-0-7432-5787-9; 0-7432-5787-1

LC 2004-42870

First published 1902 by Longman

"Based on material James had collected on the psychology and philosophy of religion for lectures at the University
of Edinburgh in 1901 and 1902. The varieties of religious
experience contains numerous descriptions of religious
states of consciousness, which James presented from a pragmatic point of view." HarperCollins Reader's Ency of Am
Lit. 2nd edition
Includes bibliographical references

211   Concepts of God

Armstrong, Karen
The **case** for God. Knopf 2009 406p $27.95 **211**
1. God 2. Apologetics 3. Christian life 4. Religious
life
ISBN 978-0-307-26918-8

LC 2009-14044

"'Magisterial' is the adjective of choice to describe Armstrong's work; her usual confident sweep across times and
cultures rises above the 'answer-the-atheists' tired angle to
make a passionate footnoted argument for the human need
for a God." Publ Wkly
Includes bibliographical references

Berlinerblau, Jacques
How to be secular; a call to arms for religious
freedom. Jacques Berlinerblau. Houghton Mifflin
Harcourt 2012 xxix, 306 p.p $26.00 **211**
1. Humanism 2. Freedom of religion 3. Christianity --
United States 4. United States -- Religion 5. Secularism
-- United States 6. Church and state -- United States 7.
Freedom of religion -- United States
ISBN 0547473346; 9780547473345

LC 2012014226

Author Jacques Berlinerblau looks at secularism. "Arguing that the revival of religion in the United States since the
1970s has led to the ascent of the Christian Right and the
crackup of secularism, the author cites examples of ways in
which traditional boundaries have been breached, including
the creation of the White House Office of Faith-based and
Neighborhood Partnerships and frequent threats by elected
officials to establish Christianity as the national religion."
(Kirkus)
Includes bibliographical references (p. [212]-290)
and index

Jacoby, Susan
Freethinkers : a history of American secularism. Metropolitan Books 2004 417p il $27.50; pa
$16 **211**
1. Secularism
ISBN 0-8050-7442-2; 0-8050-7776-6 pa

LC 2003-59294

"Enlightening, invigorating, and responsibly yet passionately argued, Jacoby's unparalleled history of American
secularism offers a much needed perspective on today's
most urgent social issues." Booklist
Includes bibliographical references

Niose, David

Nonbeliever nation; the rise of secular Americans. David Niose. Palgrave Macmillan 2012 262 p. (hardcover) $27   **211**
1. Secularism -- United States 2. Religion and politics -- United States 3. Culture conflict -- United States
ISBN 023033895X; 9780230338951
           LC 2011049323

This book, by David Niose, explores trends in non-religious observance in the United States. "Nearly one in five Americans are nonbelievers . . . and they are flexing their muscles like never before. . . . From gay marriage to education policy to contentious church-state battles . . . [the author] shows how . . . secular Americans . . . are mobilizing and forming groups all over the country . . . to challenge the exaltation of religion in American politics and public life." (Publisher's note)

Russell, Sharman Apt

Standing in the light; my life as a pantheist. Basic Books 2008 306p map $25; pa $16.95   **211**
1. Authors 2. Novelists 3. Pantheism 4. College teachers 5. Children's authors 6. Nonfiction writers
ISBN 978-0-465-00517-8; 0-465-00517-9; 978-0-465-01380-7 pa; 0-465-01380-5 pa
           LC 2008-03958

"This quietly arresting book . . . offers a braided narrative, weaving Russell's own spiritual autobiography with a thoughtfully selected intellectual history of pantheism and accounts of forays into the natural world, as she endeavors to work with other civic-minded folk to preserve the native habitat of their homes in New Mexico's Gila River Valley. Gradually, generously, and in fits and starts—rather like her own quest—Russell's encounter with an indifferent cosmos grows slyly compelling." Bookforum

Includes bibliographical references

212   Existence of God, ways of knowing God, attributes of God

Overman, Dean L.

A **case** for the existence of God. Rowman & Littlefield 2008 xxxii, 229p $24.95   **212**
1. God 2. Religion and science
ISBN 978-0-7425-6312-4; 0-7425-6312-X
           LC 2008-21731

"Drawing on modern cosmology and information theory, Overman exposes fallacies that have infested skeptics' thinking since Hume and Kant. Clearer reasoning establishes an astonishing harmony between quantum physics and religious orthodoxy, so providing a credible defense for free will and moral judgment. Still, readers looking for certainty will not find it here: Overman acknowledges that the believer must make a leap of faith. . . . The intensely personal character of spiritual conversion emerges in the lives of the nine remarkable believers—including St. Augustine and Pascal, Dostoyevsky and Weil—whose testimonies resonate with passionate conviction. A book for readers willing to wrestle with the largest questions." Booklist

Includes bibliographical references

215   Science and religion

Ecklund, Elaine Howard

Science vs. religion; what scientists really think. Oxford University Press 2010 228p $27.95   **215**
1. Religion and science 2. Scientists -- Attitudes 3. Universities and colleges -- United States -- Faculty
ISBN 978-0-19-539298-2; 0-19-539298-1
           LC 2009-34731

Ecklund's "outstanding research, articulately presented, and judicious recommendations make this a valuable work for all who care about the subject of science and religion." Libr J

Includes bibliographical references

Hagerty, Barbara Bradley

Fingerprints of God; the search for the science of spirituality. Riverhead Books 2009 323p $26.95   **215**
1. Religion and science
ISBN 978-1-59448-877-1
           LC 2009-3921

The author attempts to answer "questions about the science of spiritual experience. Along the way she tells the story of her own intriguing spiritual evolution. . . . Throughout the book, one is struck by the humility Hagerty brings to her subject—something lacking in many contemporary debates over the meaning of faith and the existence of God—and her skepticism about the science offered up as proof of spiritual experience. . . . Hagerty's engaging book poses a provocative challenge to anyone who has ever wondered where faith comes from, and what it can do for—and to—us." Washington Post Book World

Includes bibliographical references

220   Bible

Jacobs, A. J.

The **year** of living biblically; one man's humble quest to follow the Bible as literally as possible. A.J. Jacobs. Simon & Schuster 2007 388p ill. (pbk.) $16; (hbk.) $25   **220**
1. Bible 2. Authors 3. Religion 4. Humorists 5. Autobiographies 6. Bible -- Criticism
ISBN 9780743291484; 9780743291477; 0743291476
           LC 200709573

It was the author's intent to "follow the more than 800 rules found in the Hebrew Bible" and to chronicle the experience. "Jacobs spends 388 days investigating how a 21st-century New Yorker can live the lifestyle outlined in the Old Testament. Repeatedly, he tries to follow literal meanings only to find that he has misinterpreted the ritual, moral, agricultural, and sacrificial laws. For example, he throws pebbles at a man in Central Park, intending to replicate a stoning, but after consulting with his team of religious advisers discovers that in biblical times, stoning actually meant pushing the victim off a cliff. . . . He concludes that people today practice 'cafeteria religion,' picking and choosing which rules to follow." (Library Journal)

"Throughout his journey, Jacobs comes across as a generous and thoughtful (and, yes, slightly neurotic) participant observer, lacing his story with absurdly funny cultural commentary as well as nuanced insights into the impossible task of biblical literalism." Publ Wkly

Includes bibliographical references (p. [343]-348) and index.

★ The **Oxford** illustrated history of the Bible; edited by John Rogerson. Oxford Univ. Press 2001 395p il $40 **220**
    1. Bible -- History
    ISBN 0-19-860118-2
                  LC 2001-272513
This volume offers an "overview of the origins of the Bible we know (consisting of the Old and New Testaments and the Apocrypha), the transmission and translation of the texts, and the historical and contemporary interpretation and influence of the Bible. Enhancing this overview are numerous color and black-and-white illustrations." Libr J

Includes bibliographical references

Pelikan, Jaroslav Jan
  ★ **Whose** Bible is it? a history of the Scriptures through the ages. [by] Jaroslav Pelikan. Viking 2004 274p il $24.95 **220**
    1. Bible -- History
    ISBN 0-670-03385-5
                  LC 2004-58049
The author "offers a masterly overview of [the] complex development of the Bible over the ages. . . . This engaging, concise, and highly readable work demonstrates that the most influential book in Western civilization has always held different meanings for different peoples." Christ Sci Monit

Includes bibliographical references

220.3 Encyclopedias and topical dictionaries

Abingdon Press
  The **New** Interpreter's dictionary of the Bible; [edited by Katharine Doob Sakenfeld et al.] Abingdon Press 2009 5v il map set $400 **220.3**
    1. Reference books 2. Bible -- Encyclopedias
    ISBN 978-0-687-33346-2
First published 1962-1976 under the editorship of George A. Buttrick with title: The Interpreter's dictionary of the Bible

"A scholarly encyclopedic dictionary designed for the preacher, scholar, student, teacher, and general reader, referring to both the King James Version and the Revised Standard Version, to the Apocrypha, the Pseudepigrapha, the Dead Sea Scrolls, and other ancient manuscripts. . . . Important for modern biblical study." Guide to Ref Books. 11th edition

Includes bibliographical references

Eerdmans dictionary of the Bible; David Noel Freedman, editor-in-chief; Allen C. Myers, associate editor; Astrid B. Beck, managing editor. Eerdmans 2000 xxxiii, 1425p il maps $45 **220.3**
    1. Reference books 2. Bible (as subject) -- Dictionaries
    ISBN 0-8028-2400-5
                  LC 00-56124

This "dictionary contains nearly 5,000 alphabetically ordered articles by 600 biblical scholars on the books, persons, places and significant terms found in the Bible." America

"Up-to-date, comprehensive, and well written, the EDB is highly recommended." Libr J

Includes bibliographical references

The **Oxford** encyclopedia of the books of the Bible; Michael D. Coogan, editor in chief. Oxford University Press 2011 2 v. ill., maps **220.3**
    1. Bible -- Encyclopedias
    ISBN 9780195377378; 0195377370
                  LC 2011013649
This reference book provides "overviews of scholarship on some of the most important topics of study in the field of biblical studies. The 'Encyclopedia' contains almost 120 . . . entries, ranging in length from 500 to 10,000 words, on each of the canonical books of the Bible, major apocryphal books of the New and Old Testaments, important noncanonical texts, and thematic essays on topics such as canonicity, textual criticism, and translation. 'Books of the Bible' has . . . cross-references to other . . . points of interest within the Encyclopedia, and . . . lists of abbreviations and an index. . . . Illustrations of various types supplement the text. . . . Bibliographies for all entries [are also included]." (Publisher's note)

Includes bibliographical references and index.

Oxford University Press
  The **Oxford** companion to the Bible; edited by Bruce M. Metzger, Michael D. Coogan. Oxford Univ. Press 1993 xxi, 874p il map $70 **220.3**
    1. Reference books 2. Bible (as subject) -- Dictionaries
    ISBN 0-19-504645-5
                  LC 93-19315
"The many contributors read as a veritable who's who among biblical scholars. Although this companion is not meant to be an exhaustive reference, it is a highly reliable guide." Booklist

Society of Biblical Literature
  The **HarperCollins** Bible dictionary; general editor, Paul J. Achtemeier; associate editors, Roger S. Boraas {et al.} with the Society of Biblical Literature. HarperSanFrancisco 1996 xxiv, 1256p il $47.95 **220.3**
    1. Reference books 2. Bible -- Dictionaries
    ISBN 0-06-060037-3
                  LC 96-25424
First published 1985 with title: Harper's Bible dictionary

This volume features a "two-column format, with 16 single-column articles interspersed throughout (including 'Art in the Biblical Period,' 'Jesus Christ,' and 'The temple'), and it is well illustrated. Many of the longer articles include a brief bibliography. . . . Though not a flawless work (e.g., the article 'Manasseh' treats only the 14th king of Judah but neither the patriarch nor the tribe of Israel that also bear the name), it is outstanding in terms of scholarship and writing." Libr J

Zondervan illustrated Bible dictionary; [edited by] J.D. Douglas and Merrill C. Tenney; revised by

Moises Silva. Zondervan 2011 1571 p. col. ill., maps $29.99   **220.3**
1. Bible -- Dictionaries
ISBN 9780310229834

LC 2010034210

This reference book "provides a visual . . . journey for anyone interested in learning more about the world of the Bible. Through the articles, sidebars, charts, maps, and full-color images included in this volume, the text of the Old and New Testaments [is enhanced]. . . . As a condensation of the Zondervan Pictorial Encyclopedia of the Bible, the information contained within this reference work is . . . biblically sound. The material is based completely on the NIV [New International Version] and cross-referenced to the King James Version, and it contains over 7,200 entries, 500 full-color photographs, charts, and illustrations, 75 full-color maps, and a Scripture index." (Publisher's note)
Includes bibliographical references.

220.4   Texts, versions, translations

Daniell, David
The **Bible** in English. Yale University Press 2003 xx, 899p $40   **220.4**
1. Bible -- History 2. Bible -- Versions
ISBN 0-300-09930-4

LC 2002-153177

"This book is a vibrant history of the more than 350 English translations of the Bible and what they meant to their translators, readers, and times. The fascinating story ranges from the translations of William Tyndale (who was martyred in 1536 for his work), to Coverdale's translation, the Geneva Bibles, the King James Bible, and the many American translations in the twentieth century." Univ Press Books for Public and Second Sch Libr, 2004
Includes bibliographical references

220.5   Modern versions and translations

Bible
The **HarperCollins** study Bible; New Revised Standard Version, including the Apocraphal/Deutero-canonical books with concordance. general editor, revised edition, Harold W. Attridge; general editor, original edition, Wayne A. Meeks; associate editors, Jouette M. Bassler [et al.] with the Society of Biblical Literature. Fully rev and updated; HarperSanFrancisco 2006 lxvi, 2204p il map $44.95   **220.5**
ISBN 978-0-06-078685-4; 0-06-078685-X

LC 2007-277226

First published 1993
"This edition of the Bible—newly annotated by the Society of Biblical Studies—is definitely for a wide audience. It is interdenominational, incorporates the latest in

biblical scholarship, and is sensitive to unnecessary gender specificity." Booklist

★ The **new** Jerusalem Bible; [general editor: Henry Wansbrough] Doubleday 1985 2108p map $45; pa $29.95   **220.5**
ISBN 0-385-14264-1; 978-0-385-14264-9; 0-385-24833-4 pa; 978-0-385-24833-4 pa

LC 85-16070

First published in this format 1966 with title: The Jerusalem Bible
"Derives from the French version edited at the Dominican Ecole Biblique de Jerusalem and known as 'La Bible de Jerusalem.' The introductions and notes are 'a direct translation from the French, though revised and brought up to date in some places' but translation of the Biblical text goes back to the original languages." Guide to Ref Books. 11th edition

The **Oxford** study Bible; Revised English Bible with the Apocrypha. edited by M. Jack Suggs, Katharine Doob Sakenfeld, James R. Mueller. Oxford University Press 1992 xxviii, 199, 1597p map hardcover o.p. pa $34.99   **220.5**
ISBN 0-19-529001-1; 0-19-529000-3 pa

LC 92-137886

A revised edition of The new English Bible, published 1970
An annotated version of the Revised English Bible. "This volume combines a cultural guide to the biblical world and an annotated Bible. Its notes feature the reflections of Protestant, Roman Catholic, and Jewish scholars." Publisher's note

★ The **Bible**: Authorized King James Version; with an introduction and notes by Robert Carroll and Stephen Prickett. Oxford University Press 2008 lxxiv, 1039, 248, 445p il map (Oxford world's classics) pa $18.95   **220.5**
ISBN 978-0-19-953594-1

LC 2008-273825

This Oxford World's Classics version first published 1997
The authorized or King James Version originally published 1611.
Includes bibliographical references

Bloom, Harold, 1930-
The **shadow** of a great rock; a literary appreciation of the King James Bible. Yale University Press 2011 311p $28   **220.5**
1. Bible -- English -- Authorized
ISBN 978-0-300-16683-5; 0-300-16683-4

LC 2011003148

This book "is Harold Bloom's . . . tribute to the strength of [the King James Bible]. . . . Like Shakespeare, Bloom writes, the Bible 'represents the fullness of life and can give you more life.' . . . Bloom's literary appreciation turns out to be a wrestling with religious questions as well. . . . For Bloom, the Tanakh is above all a story of great personalities, the most memorable of them being Jacob, Joseph, and David. . . . But the transcendent personality . . . is that of God himself. Bloom describes God as 'an outrageous fellow,' and cautions that 'we cannot know his nature because it is not nature.' He is the strangest, most transgressive character ever created, and therefore more disturbing than anything in Shakespeare or Dostoyevsky." (Yale Review)

"Bloom approaches the King James Bible seeking not religious truth but literary beauty. And he marvels at how much he finds, particularly given the undistinguished committee who—under royal commission—completed this landmark translation of scripture 400 years ago. As a linguistically sophisticated scholar, Bloom moves adroitly between the KJB and the earlier translations of Tyndale and Coverdale, expressing astonishment at how often the KJB translators, despite their missteps, improve on the work of their talented predecessors." Booklist

Bragg, Melvyn

The **book** of books; the radical impact of the King James Bible, 1611-2011. Counterpoint 2011 370p il $28 **220.5**

1. Bible -- English -- Authorized

ISBN 978-1-58243-781-1; 1-58243-781-5

LC 2011-12432

"Bragg pays eloquent homage to the literary grandeur of the scriptures that shaped his own outlook. But this heartfelt and far-reaching tribute makes its special mark in tracing the links between the KJB and revolutions in science, politics and society, from the savants of the Royal Society to Abolitionists and Martin Luther King." Independent (UK)

Includes bibliographical references

Brake, Donald L.

A **visual** history of the English Bible; the tumultuous tale of the world's bestselling book. Baker Books 2008 349p il $29.99 **220.5**

1. Bible -- History

ISBN 978-0-8010-1316-4

LC 2008-5492

"In 16 chapters, . . . [the author] employs a descriptive narrative chronological method that treats major issues (e.g., the seven rules for translation), the versions of the Bible (e.g., Geneva, King James, and Douay-Rhemes), and translators (e.g., John Wycliff, William Tyndale, and Myles Coverdale)." Libr J

"Refreshingly readable and lavishly illustrated, this volume is essential to anyone wanting to understand the Bible and its hazardous progress through the ages." Publ Wkly

Includes bibliographical references

Cruden, Alexander

★ **Cruden's** Complete concordance; with index to proper names and their meanings. edited by A.D. Adams, C.H. Irwin, S.A. Waters. Zondervan Pub. House 1968 803p (Zondervan classic reference series) $24.99; pa $8.99 **220.5**

1. Bible -- Concordances

ISBN 0-310-22920-0; 0-310-48971-7 pa

First edition 1737. Frequently revised

"The special value of this title is that Cruden provides an index to the Apocrypha. Note that some reprints of the work omit the Apocrypha in the concordance." Ref Sources for Small & Medium-sized Libr. 5th edition

Ferrell, Lori Anne

The **Bible** and the people. Yale University Press 2008 273p il map $32.50 **220.5**

1. Bible -- History

ISBN 978-0-300-11424-9

LC 2008-26769

"The Christian Bible is not only a physical object but also a delivery system for spiritual and secular ideas, according to cultural historian Ferrell. . . . Examining the English Bible collection at the Huntington Library, Ferrell discusses these Bibles' historical, political, and social impact on Christian belief and practice in Great Britain and America from the Middle Ages to the present. . . . Written for a general audience, this is an engaging and accessible overview of the history of the English Bible." Libr J

Includes bibliographical references

★ The **New** American Bible; translated from the original languages with critical use of all the ancient sources including the revised Psalms and the revised New Testament. authorized by the Board of Trustees of the Confraternity of Christian Doctrine and approved by the Administrative Committee Board of the National Conference of Catholic Bishops and the United States Catholic Conference. Oxford University Press 2006 xxiii, 1514p $39.99 **220.5**

ISBN 978-0-19-528904-6; 0-19-528904-8

First published 1970 by Kenedy

"Roman Catholic version based on modern English translations; replaces the Douay edition." N Y Public Libr Book of How & Where to Look It Up

Strong, James

The **strongest** Strong's exhaustive concordance of the Bible; 21st century ed, fully rev and corrected by John R. Kohlenberger III and James A. Swanson; Zondervan 2001 1742p maps $34.99 **220.5**

1. Bible -- Concordances

ISBN 0-310-23343-7

LC 2001-26577

A version of Strong's exhaustive concordance of the Bible originally published 1894

"Kohlenberger has teamed with James A. Swanson to produce a volume that cross-indexes a . . . database with exhaustive Hebrew and Greek dictionaries and adds Nave's Topical Bible Reference System (essentially a Bible dictionary with subjects, persons, places, and biblical books in alphabetic order). . . . Charts plot the chronology of events in the Old and New Testament, miracles and parables of Jesus, and messianic prophecies. There is a harmony (parallels) of gospel stories, lists of biblical kings, weights and measures, Old Testament feasts, sacred days, sacrifices, and the major social concerns of the Mosaic Covenant. There is also a chart of the Hebrew Calendar. The work is based on the King James Version of the Bible and is generally conservative." Am Ref Books Annu, 2003

220.6 Interpretation and criticism (Exegesis)

Beal, Timothy

The **rise** and fall of the Bible; the unexpected history of an accidental book. [by] Timothy Beal. Houghton Mifflin Harcourt 2011 244p il $25 **220.6**

1. Bible -- Criticism

ISBN 978-0-15-101358-6

LC 2010-5734

"The author's attempt to reclaim a sense of the Bible as a rich source of history and spiritual depth is refreshing given today's mass-marketing of scripture. The narrative is well-written and engaging." Kirkus

Includes bibliographical references

Bowker, John

The **complete** Bible handbook; an illustrated companion. DK Pub. 1998 544p il maps $39.95; pa $25 **220.6**

1. Bible -- Commentaries

ISBN 0-7894-3568-3; 0-7894-8154-5 pa

LC 98-4478

In this volume "every book of the Bible (including Jewish Apocrypha) has its own entry, and there are supplementary entries on specific stories, theological concerns, history (Routes of the Exodus), or background (Gods and Goddesses of the Ancient Near East). In his introduction, Bowker presents a well-balanced summary of the Bible as a piece of literature and as scripture in our time and in history. . . . One of the book's strengths is its abundance of pictures." Voice Youth Advocates

Includes bibliographical references

Manser, Martin H.

Critical companion to the Bible; a literary reference. [by] Martin H. Manser; associate editors, David Barratt, Pieter J. Lalleman, Julius Steinberg. Facts On File, Inc. 2009 488p il (Facts on File library of world literature) $75 **220.6**

1. Bible as literature 2. Bible -- Criticism

ISBN 978-0-8160-7065-7

LC 2008-29257

"This reference provides an excellent introduction to not only just the literary but also the theological studies of the Bible through the ages." Booklist

Includes bibliographical references

The **Oxford** encyclopedia of biblical interpretation; Steven McKenzie, editor in chief. Oxford University Press 2013 1164 p. (set : alk. paper) $395 **220.6**

1. Bible -- Encyclopedias 2. Bible -- Hermeneutics -- Encyclopedias 3. Bible -- Criticism, interpretation, etc. -- Encyclopedias

ISBN 0199832269; 9780199832262; 9780199993352; 9780199993369

LC 2012041156

This encyclopedia, edited by Steven McKenzie, provides "detailed, comprehensive treatments of the latest approaches to and methods for interpretation of the Bible written by expert practitioners. It will provide a single source for authoritative reference overviews of scholarship on some of the most important topics of study in the field of biblical studies." (Publisher's note)

"[M]ost entries are understandable by lay readers and undergraduate students familiar with basic approaches to biblical interpretation. The inclusion of modern scholarship and recent developments in the field sets this work apart from other general Bible encyclopedias." LJ

Wray, T. J.

What the Bible really tells us; the essential guide to biblical literacy. Rowman & Littlefield Publishers 2011 249p $24.95; ebook $23.99 **220.6**

1. Bible -- Criticism

ISBN 978-0-7425-6253-0; 978-1-4422-1293-0 ebook

LC 2011011778

"Wray devotes a couple of introductory chapters to the biblical world and the tools and methods scholars use in their exegetical work. But her intention is to get people reading the Bible, not to offer an academic, verse-by-verse commentary. Subsequent chapters, therefore, explore what the Bible says about such issues as wealth, heaven, hell, sex, and the environment, dispelling many commonly held assumptions and pointing out where disagreements in interpretation lie along the way. Wray succeeds in sharing the wisdom of the Bible by making it accessible, interesting, and fun." Booklist

Includes bibliographical references

220.7 Commentaries

Oxford Bible commentary; edited by John Barton and John Muddiman. Oxford Univ. Press 2001 xxv, 1386p maps $79.95 **220.7**

1. Bible -- Commentaries

ISBN 0-19-875500-7

LC 2001-21139

"An international, interfaith group of scholars is responsible for this rich, far-reaching commentary, which is most profitably studied alongside a copy of the New Revised Standard Version upon which it is based." Choice

Includes bibliographical references

Society of Biblical Literature

★ The **HarperCollins** Bible commentary; general editor, James L. Mays; associate editors, Joseph Blenkinsopp {et al.}; with the Society of Biblical Literature. rev ed; HarperSanFrancisco 2000 xxvi, 1203p il $49.50 **220.7**

1. Bible -- Commentaries

ISBN 0-06-065548-8

LC 00-20818

First published 1988 with title: Harper's Bible commentary

This work is "outstanding in terms of scholarship and writing." Libr J

Includes bibliographical references

220.8 Nonreligious subjects treated in Bible

Knust, Jennifer Wright

★ **Unprotected** texts; the Bible's surprising contradictions about sex and desire. HarperOne 2010 343p $25.99; ebook $20.99 **220.8**

1. Sexual behavior 2. Bible -- Criticism
ISBN 978-0-06-172558-6; 978-0-06-201082-7 ebook

"Knust's impressive and highly readable analysis of Old and New Testament Bible stories explores mores of ancient cultures, which supported prostitution and polygamy along with slavery and patriarchy. In doing so, she makes a convincing case for religious leaders and others to take greater care and responsibility in extracting wisdom needed for healing contemporary society. . . . For those wanting to understand the Bible as a chronicle of human conduct for achieving the goals of survival, peace, and fulfillment, this is a treasure." Booklist

Includes bibliographical references

Murphy, Cullen

The **Word** according to Eve; women and the Bible in ancient times and our own. Houghton Mifflin 1998 302p $24; pa $14 **220.8**

1. Feminism 2. Women in the Bible 3. Bible -- Criticism
ISBN 0-395-70113-9; 0-618-00192-1 pa

LC 98-18015

This is an examination of feminist Biblical scholarship. Murphy "divides his study into Old Testament scholarship and New Testament and early church history." N Y Times Book Rev

Includes bibliographical references

220.9 Geography, history, chronology, persons of Bible lands in Bible times

Currie, Robin

The **letter** and the scroll; what archaeology tells us about the Bible. [by] Robin Currie and Stephen Hyslop. National Geographic 2009 335p il map $40 **220.9**

1. Bible -- Antiquities
ISBN 978-1-4262-0514-9

LC 2009-8572

"This gorgeous book . . . covering the people and events of the Bible, placed into their archaeological context, will delight and inform those who are interested in the Bible from a religious, cultural, or historical perspective. . . . [The book] investigates a variety of topics—such as cities, languages, luxury goods, wars, taxes, writings, and ancient art— through artifacts and archaeological evidence to provide an extensive background for the reader." Libr J

Includes bibliographical references

Freund, Richard A.

Digging through the Bible; understanding biblical people, places, and controversies through archae-ology. Rowman & Littlefield 2008 381p il map $44.95 **220.9**

1. Bible -- Antiquities
ISBN 978-0-7425-4644-8; 0-7425-4644-6

LC 2008-18594

"It is often the work of biblical literalists to find harmonies and agreements in the scriptural record. Others seek, and celebrate, the differing views of the biblical writers. Freund . . . has put together a masterful and eminently readable study of these differences, not to resolve them, but rather to explore the rich traditions that produced these writings. In an invaluable introductory chapter, he leads the reader through the world of biblical archeology, examining the methods of textual criticism and historical research. He then explores the biblical and archeological foundations for our understandings of such notables as Abraham, David, Jesus, Mary and many others." Publ Wkly

Includes bibliographical references

Kee, Howard Clark

The **Cambridge** companion to the Bible; Bruce Chilton, general editor; Howard Clark Kee . . . [et al.] 2nd ed; Cambridge University Press 2008 724p il $100; pa $34.99 **220.9**

1. Bible -- History of Biblical events
ISBN 978-0-521-86997-3; 978-0-521-69140-6 pa

LC 2008-270190

First published 1997

"This is an excellent, single-volume resource for serious students of the Bible. . . . The text is generally accessible; extensive maps and illustrations add to its popular appeal." Booklist [review of 1997 edition]

Includes bibliographical references

Oxford Bible atlas; edited by Adrian Curtis. 4th ed.; Oxford University Press 2007 229p il map $35 **220.9**

1. Reference books 2. Bible -- Geography
ISBN 0-19-100158-9; 978-0-19-100158-1

First published 1962

This atlas includes "81 full-color illustrations as well as 27 maps—e.g., of Jerusalem and the Holy Land, the Middle East and the eastern Mediterranean lands—all with terrain modeling. The text is divided into four main sections: 'The Setting,' 'The Hebrew Bible,' 'The New Testament,' and 'Archaeology in Bible Lands.'. . . [This is] a handsome background resource for Bible study." Libr J

Includes bibliographical references

The **Oxford** history of the biblical world; edited by Michael D. Coogan. Oxford Univ. Press 1998 643p il maps $60; pa $19.95 **220.9**

1. Ancient civilization 2. Bible -- History of biblical events
ISBN 0-19-508707-0; 0-19-513937-2 pa

LC 98-16042

"Organized chronologically, the essays explore the many cultures of ancient Canaan, Israel, Judea, and Palestine from 10,000 B.C.E. to the rise of Islam in the seventh century C.E. Illustrations, maps, charts, chronologies, and bibliographies enhance the uniformly well-written essays. But the strengths of the work are its currency and breadth of coverage and perspective." Libr J

Includes bibliographical references

Tischler, Nancy M.

Men and women of the Bible; a readers guide. Greenwood Press 2002 267p il $59.95   **220.9**

1. Bible -- Biography
ISBN 0-313-31714-3

LC 2002-75347

This resource provides "information on 100 biblical characters and their cultural significance in Western civilization. . . . Entries are arranged alphabetically from Aaron to Zephaniah, concisely written, and adhere to a uniform pattern. Subjects are listed by name with the addition of etymological information. A synopsis of the relevant biblical story follows, utilizing the King James version of the Bible. . . . The author also includes information on each person as a character in later works, including Western literature, legend, and painting." Booklist

Includes bibliographical references

221   Old Testament (Tanakh)

Bible. O.T.

★ **Tanakh**; a new translation of the Holy Scriptures according to the traditional Hebrew text. Jewish Publ. Soc. 1985 xxvi, 1624p $35; pa $22   **221**

ISBN 0-8276-0252-9; 0-8276-0366-5 pa

LC 85-10006

This volume represents a "collaboration between rabbis from the Orthodox, Conservative, and Reform branches of Judaism, and scholars in Semitic languages and biblical studies. The translators relied on the Hebrew tenth-century Masoretic text that is Judaism's standard. The Torah, Prophets, and Writings are here in a single volume." Publisher's note

Friedman, Matti

The **Aleppo** Codex; a true story of obsession, faith, and the pursuit of an ancient Bible. Matti Friedman. Algonquin Books of Chapel Hill 2012 298 p.   **221**

1. Syria 2. Manuscripts 3. Aleppo Codex -- History
ISBN 1616200405; 9781616200404

LC 2012002327

2013 Sophie Brody Medal Winner

This book by Matti Friedman "unveils the journey of a sacred text—the tenth-century annotated bible known as the Aleppo Codex—from its hiding place in a Syrian synagogue to the newly founded state of Israel. Based on . . . independent research . . . the book proposes a new theory of what happened when the codex left Aleppo, Syria, in the late 1940s and eventually surfaced in Jerusalem, mysteriously incomplete. . . . Along the way, he raises critical questions about who owns historical treasures and the role of myth and legend in the creation of a nation." (Publisher's note)

Includes bibliographical references.

The **Jewish** Bible. The Jewish Publication Society 2008 291p il map (JPS guide) pa $22   **221**

1. Bible -- O.T. -- Introductions
ISBN 978-0-8276-0851-1; 0-8276-0851-9

LC 2008-10794

"One in a series of concise reference books on different aspects of Judaism, this includes a history of the Jewish scriptures, translations through the centuries, how to read the Bible, summaries of each book, and an extensive glossary." Univ Press Books for Public and Second Sch Libr, 2009

Includes bibliographical references

Kugel, James L.

How to read the Bible; a guide to scripture, then and now. Free Press 2007 819p il map $35   **221**

1. Bible -- O.T. -- Criticism
ISBN 978-0-7432-3586-0; 0-7432-3586-X

LC 2007-23466

"Kugel has written a wonderful book, one that lays bare the worlds both of modem biblical scholarship and of ancient biblical interpretation with wit and erudition." Commentary

Includes bibliographical references

Telushkin, Joseph

Biblical literacy; the most important people, events, and ideas of the Hebrew Bible. Morrow 1997 xxviii, 628p $29.95   **221**

1. Jewish ethics 2. Bible -- O.T. -- Criticism
ISBN 0-688-14297-4

LC 97-6645

"Biblical truths that many a reader may have glossed over before stand out, thanks to this superb book, and, more important, misunderstandings are cleared up and previously mistranslated words correctly rendered." Booklist

Includes bibliographical references

222   Historical books of Old Testament

Armstrong, Karen

In the beginning; a new interpretation of Genesis. Knopf 1996 195p hardcover o.p. pa $14   **222**

1. Bible -- O.T. -- Genesis -- Criticism
ISBN 0-345-40604-4 pa

LC 96-26170

Armstrong "interprets selected accounts of Genesis using an archetypal approach to literature so as to offer insights into the problematic nature of human religion, especially the problems of separation between humans and God. . . . The text of Genesis (NRSV) makes up a third of the book's volume." Libr J

Includes bibliographical references

Baden, Joel

The **historical** David; the real life of an invented hero. Joel Baden. HarperOne 2013 320 p. $26.99   **222**

1. Bible. Old Testament
ISBN 0062188313; 9780062188311; 9780062188373

LC 2013011646

Author Joel Baden "offers a controversial look at the history of King David, the founder of the nation of Israel whose bloodline leads to Jesus, challenging prevailing popular beliefs about his legend. Baden makes clear that the biblical account of David is an attempt to shape the events of his life politically and theologically.He explores the events that lie behind the David story, events that are grounded in the context of the ancient Near East and continue to inform modern Israel." (Publisher's note)

Bible. O.T. Genesis

The **book** of Genesis; illustrated by R. Crumb. W.W. Norton 2009 un il map $24.95 **222**
1. Graphic novels
ISBN 978-0-393-06102-4; 0-393-06102-7
LC 2009-14303
An illustrated adaptation of the entire book of Genesis, providing the biblical accounts of the Creation, Adam and Eve, Cain and Abel, Noah and the ark, the Tower of Babel, and other people and events.

"This is the Bible that distressed 19th-century English philanthropist and man of letters Thomas Bowdler: not stories for sweet-faced kiddies, but sex and blood. . . . We could not expect less from the patriarch of underground comix—themselves notorious for sex and violence and deals gone sour. Indeed, Crumb's muscular, detailed black-and-white seems ideally suited to Old Testament scuffles and seaminess." Libr J

Bible. O.T. Pentateuch

The **book** of J; translated from the Hebrew by David Rosenberg; interpreted by Harold Bloom. Vintage Books 1991 340p pa $12 **222**
1. Bible -- O.T. -- Criticism
ISBN 0-679-73624-7; 978-0-679-73624-0
First published 1990 by Grove Weidenfeld
This volume "contains three works: David Rosenberg's translation of those parts of the Pentateuch that have been attributed to the J Writer (most of Genesis and Exodus, parts of Numbers and Deuteronomy), Bloom's introduction, and, following the translation, his [commentary]." Voice Lit Suppl

The **five** books of Moses; Genesis, Exodus, Leviticus, Numbers, Deuteronomy. a new translation with introductions, notes, and commentary by Everett Fox. Schocken Bks. 1995 xxxi, 1024p hardcover o.p. pa $27.50 **222**
1. Bible. Pentateuch -- Commentaries.
ISBN 0-8052-1119-5 pa
LC 95-10143
Fox's "introductions propose and outline a literary structure for each book, his commentary {addresses} . . . thematic and structural characteristics of the text, {and} his . . . notes point out linguistic features and cruxes and the interpretive issues that surround them." N Y Times Book Rev
This translation "captures the beautiful, majestic, and dynamic character of biblical Hebrew. . . . An essential purchase for all libraries." Libr J

★ The **Torah** : the five books of Moses; a new translation of the Holy Scriptures according to the Masoretic text; first section. Jewish Publication Society 1963 393p $20; pa $15 **222**
ISBN 0-8276-0015-1; 0-8276-0680-X pa
This "translation of Genesis, Exodus, Leviticus, Numbers, and Deuteronomy was prepared . . . to present a version of the Bible that takes into account modern insights and knowledge of ancient times. . . . Of chief value to persons of the Jewish religion but of interest to Bible scholars of any religion." Booklist

The **contemporary** Torah; a gender-sensitive adaptation of the JPS translation. revising editor, David E.S. Stein; consulting editors, Adele Berlin, Ellen Frankel, and Carol L. Meyers. Jewish Publication Society 2006 xlii, 412p $28 **222**
ISBN 0-8276-0796-2; 978-0-8276-0796-5
LC 2006-40608
A modern adaptation of the Jewish Publication Society's translation of the Torah. "In places where the ancient audience probably would not have construed gender as pertinent to the text's plain sense, the editors changed words into gender-neutral terms; where gender was probably understood to be at stake, they left the text as originally translated, or even introduced gendered language where none existed before. They made these changes regardless of whether words referred to God, angels, or human beings." Publisher's note

Dershowitz, Alan M.

The **Genesis** of justice; ten stories of biblical injustice that led to the Ten Commandments and modern law. Warner Bks. 2000 273p $28; pa $14.95 222
1. Justice 2. Bible -- O.T. -- Genesis -- Criticism
ISBN 0-446-52479-4; 0-446-67677-2 pa
LC 99-50220
"For believers of all faiths, as well as nonbelievers, this is an outstanding work." Libr J
Includes bibliographical references

Feiler, Bruce S.

Abraham; a journey to the heart of three faiths. [by] Bruce Feiler. Morrow 2002 224p $23.95; pa $12.95 **222**
1. Prophets 2. Biblical characters
ISBN 0-380-97776-1; 0-06-052509-6 pa
LC 2002-70309
"Feiler explores how Christian, Judaic, and Islamic understandings of Abraham, a patriarch to all three faiths, express interfaith disagreements. On the way to a passionate, prayerful argument for interfaith peace, Feiler mixes theological meditation, adventurous travelogue, and sly wit." Booklist

Hazony, David

The **Ten** commandments; how our most ancient moral text can renew modern life. Scribner 2010 288p $26; ebook $12.99 **222**
1. Ten commandments -- Criticism
ISBN 978-1-4165-6235-1; 978-1-4165-62511 ebook
LC 2009-43129
The author "uses the biblical text as a point of departure for 10 wide-ranging essays, examining each command-

ment as a contribution to constructing the good society. . . . Hazony has succeeded in extending the Ten Commandments to an impressive vision of how to attain the good society." Publ Wkly

Includes bibliographical references

Kass, Leon

The **beginning** of wisdom; reading Genesis. {by} Leon R. Kass. Free Press 2003 576p $35 **222**

1. Bible -- O.T. -- Genesis -- Criticism

ISBN 0-7432-4299-8

LC 2002-45593

The author "sees Genesis as a text that offers wisdom about the nature of man and how we ought to live, while it also calls for interpretation, reflection, and judgment. . . . Kass presents many enlightening insights, the result of his attempts to understand the text on its own terms and relating it to contemporary concerns, especially tradition and parenthood. While not everyone will agree with his interpretations, which tend to the conservative, Kass offers much to be pondered by thoughtful readers, both academics and, especially, educated laypeople." Libr J

Includes bibliographical references

Klinghoffer, David

The **discovery** of God; Abraham and the birth of monotheism. Doubleday 2003 348p map $26; pa $14.95 **222**

1. Prophets 2. Monotheism 3. Biblical characters 4. Bible -- O.T. -- History of Biblical events

ISBN 0-385-49973-6; 0-385-49974-4 pa

LC 2002-31566

This book "makes no attempt to prove the historical accuracy of the stories from Genesis, but rather advances an impassioned argument for their relevance." Natl Rev

Includes bibliographical references

McKenzie, Steven L.

King David; a biography. Oxford Univ. Press 2000 232p il maps $41.50 **222**

1. Kings

ISBN 0-19-513273-4

LC 99-44315

McKenzie "views David as a ruthless, brutal usurper who would be well at home among many modern-day rulers. . . . Much of this portrait is inevitably speculation, and it is likely to outrage David's defenders . Still, given the limitations of written sources, McKenzie effectively coats his assertions with a veneer of credibility." Booklist

Includes bibliographical references

Moyers, Bill

Genesis : a living conversation. Doubleday 1996 361p il hardcover o.p. pa $22.95 **222**

1. Bible -- O.T. -- Genesis -- Criticism

ISBN 0-385-49043-7 pa

LC 96-15318

Companion volume to the PBS series led by Bill Moyers in which writers and religious thinkers discussed episodes from the first book of the Bible. Among the participants are Burton Visotzky, a rabbi who initiated the conversations which gave rise to the series, "Elaine Pagels, Karen

Armstrong, . . . John Barth, and Oscar Hijuelos. The book is divided by biblical tale (Adam and Eve, Cain and Abel, the blinding of Isaac) with five or six of the participants discussing the moral, literary, and personal meanings of the stories." Booklist

223   Poetic books of Old Testament

Kushner, Harold S., 1935-

The **book** of Job; when bad things happened to a good person. Harold S. Kushner. Nextbook : Schocken 2012 201 p. $24 **223**

1. God 2. Suffering -- Religious aspects 3. Bible. O.T. Job -- Commentaries 4. Suffering -- Religious aspects -- Judaism

ISBN 0805242929; 9780805242928

LC 2011051531

This book by Harold S. Kushner presents a "guide to that most fascinating of biblical texts, the book of Job, and what it can teach us about living in a troubled world. Kushner examines the questions raised by Job's experience, questions that have challenged wisdom seekers and worshippers for centuries. What kind of God permits such bad things to happen to good people? Why does God test loyal followers? Can a truly good God be all-powerful?" (Publisher's note)

225   New Testament

Borg, Marcus J.

Evolution of the Word; reading the New Testament in the order it was written. Marcus J. Borg. 1st ed. HarperOne 2012 viii, 608 p.p $29.99 **225**

1. Bible. New Testament 2. Bible. N.T. -- Chronology 3. Bible. N.T. -- Criticism, interpretation, etc

ISBN 9780062082121; 0062082108; 9780062082107

LC 2012001947

This New Testament with commentary, edited by Marcus J. Borg, changes "the order of the New Testament, . . . putting the books in . . . the order in which they were written. By doing so, [he] allows us to read these documents in their historical context. . . . Borg offers . . . introductions for each book so that as we read through these biblical documents . . . we see afresh what concerns and pressures shaped this movement as it evolved into a new religion." (Publisher's note)

Includes bibliographical references.

Brown, Raymond Edward

An **introduction** to the New Testament; by Raymond E. Brown. Yale University Press 1997 xxxviii, 878p map (Anchor Bible reference library) $55 **225**

1. Bible -- N.T. -- Criticism

ISBN 978-0-300-14016-3; 0-300-14016-9

A reissue of the title first published 1997 by Doubleday

Brown's book "culminates his life's work and synthesizes the best of his generation's historical-critical scholarship clearly and cogently for beginners and advanced students alike." N Y Times Book Rev

Wilson, A. N.

Paul : the mind of the Apostle. Norton 1997
273p hardcover o.p. pa $16.95 **225**
1. Saints 2. Apostles 3. Writers on religion
ISBN 0-393-31760-9 pa

LC 96-47834

"Wilson's insights fascinate and provoke. Even as rich
and incisive a portrait as this one cannot provide a complete understanding of Paul or the turbulent time in which
he lived, but readers will come away seeing the enigmatic
apostle as an imaginative transformer who shaped a worldwide religious movement." Booklist

Includes bibliographical references

225.9 Geography, history, chronology, persons of New Testament lands in New Testament times

Murphy-O'Connor, J.

Paul; a critical life. {by} Jerome Murphy-
O'Connor. Clarendon Press 1996 416p maps hardcover o.p. pa $21 **225.9**
1. Saints 2. Apostles 3. Writers on religion
ISBN 01-9-285342-2 pa

LC 95-49173

"This is likely to become the standard work on Paul's
life for the next generation and is warmly recommended as
such." Choice

Includes bibliographical references

Ruden, Sarah

Paul among the people; the Apostle reinterpreted
and reimagined in his own time. Pantheon Books
2010 214p $25; ebook $25 **225.9**
1. Saints 2. Apostles 3. Writers on religion 4. Bible
-- N.T. -- Epistles of Paul -- Criticism
ISBN 978-0-375-42501-1; 978-0-307-37902-3 ebook

LC 2009-20969

"In 'reimagining' Paul with the aid of her intimate
knowledge of classical literature, Ruden hasn't only helped
us to better understand him and his message in the context
of his time (as indispensable as that service is). She has also
brought Paul to us, to our time. . . . In an uncanny way, her
book is animated by the apostle's style: his urgency, his argumentative agility, his bluntness, his exasperation, his vision of great felicity." Natl Rev

Includes bibliographical references

226 Gospels and Acts

Bonhoeffer, Dietrich

The cost of discipleship; containing material not
previously translated. rev and unabridged ed; Macmillan 1959 hardcover o.p. pa $12 **226**
1. Sermon on the mount 2. Bible -- N.T. -- Gospels
-- Criticism
ISBN 0-684-81500-1 pa
Original German edition, 1937. This edition translated
by R. H. Fuller with some revision by Irmgard Booth

The first part of the book "is an exposition of the conception of discipleship that is to be found in the Synoptic Gospels, together with an interpretation of the Sermon on the
Mount. The second part consists of Bonhoeffer's attempt to
show how the terminology used by the evangelists has been
translated into the language of the Church of the Apostle
Paul." Magill. Masterpieces of Christ Lit in Summary Form

Chilton, Bruce

Mary Magdalene; a biography. Doubleday 2005
220p map $23.95 **226**
1. Saints
ISBN 0-385-51317-8

LC 2005-45446

Through an "examination of available texts (canonical gospels, the most important noncanonical gospels, and
other early Christian writings) and sober speculation, Chilton traces [Mary Magdalene's] . . . relationship to Jesus and
claims that it was she who taught Jesus the power of vision,
anointing, and touch and the disciples that Jesus had overcome death; without her, according to Chilton, resurrection
might never have become a central Christian teaching. He
also traces her later legend, the ambivalence of Gnosticism
toward her, her medieval cult and denigration, and 20th-
century reassessments." Libr J

Kloppenborg, John S.

Q, the earliest Gospel; an introduction to the
original stories and sayings of Jesus. Westminster
John Knox Press 2008 170p il pa $19.95 **226**
1. Q hypothesis (Synoptics criticism)
ISBN 978-0-664-23222-1; 0-664-23222-1

LC 2008-8394

The author is an "authority on the Q Gospel, a 'sayings
gospel' that is thought to be a source (from the German
Quelle for source) for the Gospels of Matthew and Luke.
No copy of Q has been found, but scholars have recreated
it through analysis of the three synoptic Gospels, looking
for common elements and focusing on the sayings of Jesus.
This book is a succinct introduction to Q, addressing questions about its composition and importance. . . . A complete
reconstruction of Q is included as well as notes and a bibliography." Libr J

Wroe, Ann

Pontius Pilate. Modern Library 2000 412p $26;
pa $14.95 **226**
1. Government officials 2. Colonial administrators
ISBN 0-375-50305-6; 0-375-75397-4 pa

LC 99-43000

First published 1999 in the United Kingdom with title:
Pilate: the biography of an invented man
"As long as readers don't take this as accurate history but
enjoy it as a well-written, imaginative, and creative portrait
of Pilate and his times, the book serves a useful purpose."
Libr J

Includes bibliographical references

226.3 Mark

Bible. N.T. Gospels

The **three** Gospels; {by} Reynolds Price. Scribner 1996 288p $23; pa $13 **226.3**
ISBN 0-684-80336-4; 0-684-83281-X pa

LC 95-39948

"Of the four canonical Gospels, Mr. Price has chosen to translate the two that seem to him to express the strongest differing yet complementary perceptions of the life of Jesus—Mark and John. To these he has appended a third text, roughly the same length as each of the other two, which he calls 'An Honest Account of a Memorable Life: An Apocryphal Gospel.' . . . {The author also includes} a general preface, mainly devoted to the problems of translating New Testament Greek, and . . . prefatory interpretive essays for Mark and John and an explanatory introduction to the modern Apocryphal Gospel." N Y Times Book Rev

"Although there is so much to appreciate in these commentaries and in the translated texts, the best part of the book . . . is left to last: Price's own joyously written account of Jesus' life." Booklist

227 Epistles

Borg, Marcus J.

The **first** Paul; reclaiming the radical visionary behind the Church's conservative icon. [by] Marcus J. Borg, John Dominic Crossan. HarperOne 2009 230p $24.99; pa $13.99 **227**
1. Saints 2. Apostles 3. Writers on religion 4. Bible -- N.T. -- Epistles of Paul -- Criticism
ISBN 978-0-06-143072-5; 0-06-143072-2; 978-0-06-143073-2 pa; 0-06-143073-0 pa

LC 2009-004881

"The great epistolary apostle is revealed as neither anti-Semitic, anti-sex, nor misogynist, but a preacher of social and political equality." Booklist
Includes bibliographical references

228

Pagels, Elaine H., 1943-

Revelations; visions, prophecy, and politics in the book of Revelation. Elaine Pagels. Viking 2012 ix, 246 p.p **228**
1. Revelation 2. Eschatology 3. Bible. New Testament 4. Religion and politics -- History 5. Bible. N.T. Revelation -- Criticism, interpretation, etc.
ISBN 0670023345; 9780670023349

LC 2011037551

This book presents an interpretation of the Book of Revelation from the Christian Bible, touching on its narrative, themes, and historical background. "[Elaine] Pagels . . . shows that Revelation, far from being meant as a hallucinatory prophecy, is actually a coded account of events that were happening at the time John was writing." The author determines that based on historical conflicts between Jewish and Gentile followers of Jesus Christ, the "Revelation is essentially an anti-Christian polemic." (New Yorker)
Includes bibliographical references (p. 179-225) and index

229 Apocrypha, pseudepigrapha, intertestamental works

Bible. O.T. Apocrypha

★ The **Apocrypha**; new revised standard version. Cambridge University Press 1993 262p pa $14.99 **229**
ISBN 978-0-521-50776-9; 0-521-50776-6

"These books form part of the sacred literature of the Alexandrian Jews. . . . Some of them form an historical link between the Old and New Testament, others have a linguistic value in connexion with the Hellenistic phraseology of the latter. The narratives of Apocrypha are partly historical records, and partly allegorical." Oxford Univ. Press

Pagels, Elaine H.

★ **Beyond** belief; the secret Gospel of Thomas. {by} Elaine Pagels. Random House 2003 241p $26.95 **229**
1. Christianity 2. Gospel of Thomas 3. Bible -- N.T. -- John -- Criticism
ISBN 0-375-50156-8

LC 2002-36840

"Even those who possess only a nodding acquaintance with Gnostic writings will find themselves stimulated by the author's arguments and perhaps transformed by her conclusions. A fresh and exciting work of theology and spirituality." Booklist
Includes bibliographical references

230 Christianity

Holifield, E. Brooks

★ **Theology** in America; Christian thought from the age of the Puritans to the Civil War. Yale University Press 2003 617p hardcover o.p. pa $23 **230**
1. Doctrinal theology
ISBN 0-300-09574-0; 978-0-300-10765-4 pa; 0-300-10765-X pa

LC 2003-42289

"In this majestic achievement, Holifield . . . provides a first-rate, richly evocative and unrivaled history of theology in America. . . . This masterfully narrated, splendid book will become the definitive study of the development of American theology." Publ Wkly
Includes bibliographical references

Kung, Hans

Great Christian thinkers. Continuum 1994 235p hardcover o.p. pa $19.95 **230**
1. Saints 2. Bishops 3. Apostles 4. Theology 5. Theologians 6. Philosophers 7. Social reformers 8.

Religious leaders 9. Writers on religion
ISBN 0-8264-0848-6 pa

LC 94-883

The author "attempts a new approach to the introduction-to-theology genre by critically tracing the developing thought of key, usually 'paradigm-shifting,' theologians (Paul, Origen, Augustine, Aquinas, Luther, Schleiermacher, and Karl Barth) in relation to their social, intellectual, and religious environment. He explores the significance of their life and work for the Christian world in an interesting, quite understandable manner." Libr J

Includes bibliographical references

Lewis, C. S.

★ **Mere** Christianity; a revised and amplified edition, with a new introduction, of the three books, Broadcast talks, Christian behaviour, and Beyond personality. HarperSanFrancisco 2001 xx, 227p $19.95; pa $10 **230**

1. Christian philosophy
ISBN 0-06-065288-8; 0-06-065292-6 pa

LC 00-49862

First published 1952

This omnibus edition includes most of C. S. Lewis' writings on Christian theology and moral philosophy

Includes bibliographical references

Oxford companion to Christian thought; edited by Adrian Hastings {et al.} Oxford Univ. Press 2000 xxviii, 777p $75 **230**

1. Reference books 2. Theology -- Dictionaries
ISBN 0-19-860024-0

LC 2001-267818

This volume focuses "on the movement of ideas among Christians. The articles (more than 500) by 268 scholars (mostly British) range in length from half a column . . . to seven pages. . . . They broadly cover the themes . . . persons . . . places . . . and historical periods . . . that characterize Christian thought." Choice

Includes bibliographical references

Teilhard de Chardin, Pierre

★ The **divine** milieu; an essay on the interior life. Harper & Row 1960 144p hardcover o.p. pa $14 **230**

1. Christian philosophy
ISBN 978-0-06-093725-6 pa; 0-06-093725-4 pa
Original French edition, 1957

In this book Father de Chardin describes his spiritual philosophy

231   Christian doctrinal theology

Cairns, Scott

The **end** of suffering; finding purpose in pain. Paraclete Press 2009 126p pa $15.99 **231**

1. Suffering
ISBN 978-1-55725-563-1; 1-55725-563-6

LC 2009-18728

The author "offers a profoundly touching and deeply considered treatment of the notion of suffering, especially grief, in a Christian's life. For Cairns, suffering is not about the presence of evil; instead, it provides occasions where God can be known more intimately. . . . Eloquent in its simplicity, Cairns's brief book is a superb treatment of the thorny issues of suffering and grief." Libr J

Includes bibliographical references

231.7   Relation to the world

Humes, Edward

Monkey girl; evolution, education, religion, and the battle for America's soul. HarperCollins Publishers 2007 380p $25.95 **231.7**

1. Evolution 2. Creationism
ISBN 978-0-06-088548-9; 0-06-088548-3

LC 2006-50263

Humes "may be the most successful so far in making a complicated issue accessible and in putting human faces on both sides of the evolution divide. Clearly based on exhaustive reporting that takes the reader from the hard benches of a Harrisburg, Pa., federal district courtroom to the kitchen tables of Dover families whose children were taunted as 'monkey girls,' Humes' fast-moving, richly detailed book reads like a suspense novel." Chicago Tribune

Lewis, C. S.

Miracles; a preliminary study. HarperSanFrancisco 2001 294p pa $13.95 **231.7**

1. Miracles
ISBN 0-06-065301-9; 978-0-06-065301-9

LC 00-49863

First published 1947 by Macmillan

"Mr. Lewis casts his net fairly wide and, under the guise of a book on miracles, offers a rational justification both of theism and of doctrinal Christianity." Times Lit Suppl

Miller, Kenneth R.

Finding Darwin's God; a scientist's search for common ground between God and evolution. Cliff St. Bks. 1999 338p il hardcover o.p. **231.7**

1. Evolution 2. Religion and science 3. Evolution (Biology) 4. Evolution (Biology) -- Religious aspects -- Christianity
ISBN 0-06-017593-1; 0-06-123350-1 pa

LC 99016754

This work seeks to establish that "evolution is scientifically true. Miller, a practicing Roman Catholic, attempts to demonstrate that it is also compatible with a belief in God." (Christ Sci Monit) Index.

The author "explains the difference between evolution as validated scientific fact and as an evolving theory. He illustrates his contentions with examples from astronomy, geology, physics and molecular biology, confronting the illogic of creationists with persuasive reasons based on the known physical properties of the universe. . . . Then standing firmly on Darwinian ground, he turns to take on, with equal vigor, his outspoken colleagues in science who espouse a materialistic, agnostic or atheistic vision of reality." Publ Wkly

Includes bibliographical references

Scott, Robert A.

Miracle cures; saints, pilgrimage, and the healing powers of belief. University of California Press 2010 xxix, 235p il map $24.95; ebook $20   **231.7**
    1. Psychophysiology 2. Spiritual healing 3. Placebo (Medicine) 4. Middle Ages -- History 5. Miracles -- Christianity 6. Health -- Psychological aspects
    ISBN 978-0-520-26275-1; 978-0-520-94620-0 ebook
                    LC 2009-37269
    The author "illuminates the Christian practice of pilgrimages to healing shrines from medieval to contemporary times. He also explores the contemporary phenomenon of 'virtual pilgrimage' on the Internet as a foil to the practice of physical pilgrimage. The author carefully weaves detailed textual and historiographic work with the latest social scientific findings on pain, and environmental and behavioral factors that promote health and shape the experience of illness. . . . Readers at all levels should enjoy this engaging but sophisticated book." Choice
    Includes bibliographical references

Wintz, Jack

Will I see my dog in heaven? God's saving love for the whole family of creation. Paraclete Press 2009 153p pa $14.99   **231.7**
    1. Future life 2. Animals -- Religious aspects
    ISBN 978-1-55725-568-6
                    LC 2009-259
    The author, a Franciscan friar, argues that "God's promise of a new creation at the end of time extends to the animal companions we have known and loved in this life. . . . Strongly recommended." Libr J
    Includes bibliographical references

Woodward, Kenneth L.

The **book** of miracles; the meaning of the miracle stories in Christianity, Judaism, Buddhism, Hinduism, Islam. Simon & Schuster 2000 429p hardcover o.p. pa $16   **231.7**
    1. Miracles
    ISBN 0-7432-0029-2 pa
                    LC 99-88083
    "A great resource for studies in comparative religions and interfaith dialog." Libr J
    Includes bibliographical references

232   Jesus Christ and his family

Blum, Edward J.

★ The **color** of Christ; the Son of God and the saga of race in America. Edward J. Blum and Paul Harvey. University of North Carolina Press 2012 340 p. ill. $32.5   **232**
    1. Racism 2. African Americans -- Religion 3. United States -- Church history 4. Racism -- United States 5. Indians of North America -- Religion 6. Racism -- Religious aspects -- Christianity
    ISBN 0807835722; 9780807835722
                    LC 2012004088

    This book, by Edward J. Blum and Paul Harvey, discusses Christianity and racism in the U.S., discussing "how, in a country founded by Puritans who destroyed depictions of Jesus, Americans came to believe in the whiteness of Christ. Some envisioned a white Christ who would sanctify the exploitation of Native Americans and African Americans and bless imperial expansion. Many others gazed at a messiah, not necessarily white, who was willing and able to confront white supremacy." (Publisher's note)
    Includes bibliographical references (p. [283]-325) and index

Gordon, Mary, 1949-

Reading Jesus; a writer's encounter with the Gospels. Pantheon Books 2009 205p $24.95   **232**
    1. Bible -- N.T. -- Gospels -- Criticism 2. Jesus Christ
    ISBN 978-0-375-42457-1
                    LC 2009-04975
    Gordon "examines her faith by closely reading, in a kind of literary lectio divina (sacred reading), the four Christian gospels that recount the life of Christ. The accounts by evangelists Matthew, Mark, Luke and John of the life of Jesus have a common subject and amazingly different treatments. Gordon tackles the power and puzzle of the Christian gospels with measure and imagination, providing welcome relief for those left cold by scholarly or fundamentalist parsing." Publ Wkly

Vermes, Geza

The **changing** faces of Jesus. Viking 2001 324p map hardcover o.p. pa $15.86   **232**
    1. Jesus Christ
    ISBN 0-14-026524-4 pa
                    LC 00-43897
    "Vermes's vast knowledge of first century Judaism ensures that this work will become one of the most important works in historical Jesus studies, and his readable style makes it useful for both public and academic library patrons." Libr J
    Includes bibliographical references

232.9   Family and life of Jesus

Aslan, Reza, 1972-

Zealot; The Life and Times of Jesus of Nazareth. Reza Aslan. Random House Inc 2014 336 p. $27   **232.9**
    1. Church history
    ISBN 140006922X; 9780679603535; 9781400069224
                    LC 2013941682
    In this book on Jesus of Nazareth, author Reza Aslan argues "that Jesus was a Jewish zealot, a rebel against Rome and the Romans' local agents. . . . Jesus never intended to found a church, much less a new religion. He was loyal to the law of Moses as he interpreted. Jesus opposed not only the Roman overlords . . . but also their representatives in Palestine: 'the Temple priests, the wealthy Jewish aristocracy, the Herodian elite.'" (New York Times)
    Includes bibliographical references (pages [273]-282) and index

Benedict XVI, Pope, 1927-

Jesus of Nazareth. part two; Holy week, from the entrance into Jerusalem to the Resurrection. by Joseph Ratzinger, Pope Benedict XVI. Ignatius Press 2011 362p $24.95   **232.9**
    1. Holy Week 2. Biography, Individual 3. Bible -- N.T. -- Gospels -- Criticism 4. Bible -- N.T. -- Gospels -- Criticism, interpretation, etc.
    ISBN 978-1-58617-500-9; 1-58617-500-9

This is "the second volume in [the author's] 'Jesus of Nazareth' series. . . . [This book] is a worthy contribution to the field not only because it was written by a pope, but also because it combines solid scholarship with deep spirituality. As such it joins the Jesus of history to the Christ of faith in an accessible narrative. This volume explores the drama of Holy Week. . . . The focus is on the meaning of the events, with a strong reiteration of recent church teaching against imputing guilt for Jesus' death to the Jews of that time or now." Publ Wkly

Bock, Darrell L.

Who is Jesus? linking the historical Jesus with the Christ of faith. Darrell L. Bock. Howard Books 2012 238 p. $15.99   **232.9**
    ISBN 1439190682; 9781439190685

LC 2012001352
In this book, author Darrell L. Bock "insists that qualified historians have created a series of objective and reasonable rules . . . [that] must be followed by Jesus historians. Comparing the biblical text with what is known about the historical context in which Jesus lived can help sort out the many . . . misunderstandings that have arisen over the years. After listing 10 relevant rules for Jesus scholars, Bock then examines the scriptural accounts." (Publishers Weekly)
Includes bibliographical references.

Chilton, Bruce

Rabbi Jesus; an intimate biography. Doubleday 2000 xxii, 330p il maps hardcover o.p. pa $14.95   **232.9**
    ISBN 0-385-49793-8 pa

LC 00-31548
The author presents a "wonderfully fresh presentation of the implications of Jesus's being a Jewish male living in the context of first-century Judaism." Libr J
Includes bibliographical references

Fredriksen, Paula

Jesus of Nazareth, King of the Jews; a Jewish life and the emergence of Christianity. Knopf 1999 327p hardcover o.p. pa $14   **232.9**
    ISBN 0-679-76746-0 pa

LC 99-31054
"To Fredriksen, Jesus was an observant Jew immersed in a context bounded by Galilee and Jerusalem. He was crucified as an imperial Roman deterrent to unruly inhabitants of a region prone to rebellion, and the emergence of Christianity is a work of creative theological reinterpretation as much as of historical memory." Booklist
Includes bibliographical references

Girzone, Joseph F.

A **portrait** of Jesus. Doubleday 1998 179p il hardcover o.p. pa $11.95   **232.9**
    1. Christian life
    ISBN 0-385-48477-1 pa

LC 98-15618
The author "gives a simple narrative account of Jesus' life, envisioning facets of the person reflected in the gospel stories." Libr J
"This is popular liberal Catholic theology, more filled with forgiveness and fellowship than shaming and hierarchy. Many a non-Catholic and even non-Christian may embrace it, too." Booklist

Meier, John P.

A **marginal** Jew; rethinking the historical Jesus. Doubleday 1991 3v maps (Anchor Bible reference library) v1 $45; v2 $42.50; v3 $45   **232.9**
    ISBN 0-385-26425-9 v1; 0-385-46992-6 v2; 0-385-46993-4 v3

LC 91-10538
The first three volumes in a projected series of four devoted to an examination of the historical Jesus and his Jewish environment
The author "summarizes the first two volumes of A Marginal Jew and forecasts the next while meticulously documenting his understanding of the relations between the historical Jesus, his historical companions, and his historical competitors—Pharisees, Sadduccees, Essenes, and others. . . . The only thing common about Meier's project is fascination with the character of Jesus. Those who share that will find this dense, academic work worth their effort." Booklist {review of volume 3}
Includes bibliographical references

Pelikan, Jaroslav Jan

The **illustrated** Jesus through the centuries. Yale Univ. Press 1997 254p il $25   **232.9**
    ISBN 0-300-07268-6

LC 97-7360
Companion volume to Mary through the centuries
In this revision of Jesus through the centuries (1985) the author "has abridged the text and turns to illustrations to convey his interpretations. . . . Very beautiful and very appealing for the general reader, this edition by no means replaces the scholarship and documentation of the first; those notations and references are missing in the illustrated edition. However, the illustrations enhance this interesting and insightful text." Libr J

Wilson, A. N.

Jesus. Norton 1992 269p $22.95   **232.9**
    ISBN 0-393-03087-3

LC 92-37046
The author attempts to understand Jesus as a historical figure and ethical teacher within the context of first-century Judaism
Includes bibliographical references

232.91   Mary, mother of Jesus

Pelikan, Jaroslav Jan

  Mary through the centuries; her place in the history of culture. Yale Univ. Press 1996 267p il $40; pa $14.95   **232.91**

  1. Saints

  ISBN 0-300-06951-0; 0-300-07661-4 pa

                      LC 96-24726

Companion volume to The illustrated Jesus through the centuries

  "Although volumes have been written about the Virgin Mary from a wide variety of perspectives, it is rare to find a scholarly work that is easily accessible to the general, educated reader." Choice

  Includes bibliographical references

233   Humankind

Jacobs, Alan

  Original sin; a cultural history. HarperOne 2008 286p $24.95; pa $14.99   **233**

  1. Sin

  ISBN 978-0-06-078340-2; 0-06-078340-0; 978-0-06-087257-1 pa; 0-06-087257-8 pa

                      LC 2008-06582

This is "a playful, wide-ranging, erudite meditation on the nagging question of whether human beings enter the world predisposed to evil and sinfulness. . . . Original Sin has a great deal to offer both the general reader and those already well versed in this most controversial of theological arenas." America

  Includes bibliographical references

Kierkegaard, Søren, 1813-1855

  The **concept** of anxiety; a simple psychologically oriented deliberation in view of the dogmatic problem of hereditary sin. Soren Kierkegaard ; edited and translated with introduction and notes by Alastair Hannay. Liveright Publishing Corporation 2014 288 p. (hardcover) $27.95   **233**

  1. Sin 2. Psychology of religion 3. Anxiety -- Religious aspects -- Christianity

  ISBN 0871407191; 9780871407191

                      LC 2013037399

In this book, author Soren Kierkegaard "describes the nature and forms of anxiety, placing the domain of anxiety within the mental-emotional states of human existence that precede the qualitative leap of faith to the spiritual state of Christianity. It is through anxiety that the self becomes aware of its dialectical relation between the finite and the infinite, the temporal and the eternal." (Publisher's note)

  "Almost as valuable as the translation is Hannay's introduction in which he provides the background necessary to grapple with Kierkegaard and a heartfelt argument for the value of studying this fountainhead of existentialism in general and Anxiety in particular." LJ

  Includes bibliographical references

235   Spiritual beings

McCarthy, David Matzko

  Sharing God's Good Company; A Theology of the Communion of Saints. David Matzko McCarthy. W.B. Eerdmans Pub. Co. 2012 viii, 174 p.p (pbk. : alk. paper) $28   **235**

  1. Christian saints 2. Christian saints -- Biography -- History and criticism

  ISBN 080286709X; 9780802867094

                      LC 2011049265

This book by David Matzko McCarthy "explores the role and significance of the saints in Christians' lives today. While examining the lives of specific saints like Martin de Porres, Thérèse de Lisieux, and Mother Teresa, McCarthy especially focuses on such topics as the veneration of martyrs, realism and hagiography, science and miracles, images and pilgrimage, and why the saints continue to captivate Christians and inspire devotion." (Publisher's note)

  Includes bibliographical references and index.

Pagels, Elaine H.

  The **origin** of Satan; {by} Elaine Pagels. Random House 1995 214p hardcover o.p. pa $12 **235**

  1. Devil 2. Bible -- N.T. -- Gospels -- Criticism

  ISBN 0-679-73118-0 pa

                      LC 95-7983

Pagels "shows herself to be a masterful guide through the risk-laden complexities of biblical studies." Publ Wkly

  Includes bibliographical references

Woodward, Kenneth L.

  Making saints; how the Catholic Church determines who becomes a saint, who doesn't, and why. Simon & Schuster 1990 461p il hardcover o.p. pa $21.50   **235**

  1. Catholic Church 2. Christian saints

  ISBN 0-684-81530-3 pa

                      LC 90-10117

A study of the politics and procedures of the modern process of canonization in the Roman Catholic church

  This is "the most comprehensive, critical and up-to-date look at saint making so far written." N Y Times Book Rev

  Includes bibliographical references

Wray, T. J.

  The **birth** of Satan; tracing the devil's biblical roots. [by] T.J. Wray, Gregory Mobley. Palgrave Macmillan 2005 211p $24.95   **235**

  1. Devil

  ISBN 1-4039-6933-7

                      LC 2005-43046

The authors find Satan's "origins in a biblical character and in early Jewish and Christian writings outside of the scriptures. They try to understand why we as a species strive to feel fearful, why being frightened—vicariously, at least—is so appealing. . . . A thoughtful, informative examination." Booklist

  Includes bibliographical references

236 Eschatology

Brown, Samuel Morris
In heaven as it is on earth; Samuel Morris Brown. Oxford University Press 2012 xii, 392 p illustrations **236**
1. Death 2. Church of Jesus Christ of Latter-day Saints -- History
ISBN 9780199793570

LC 2011002848
'This book examines Mormonism "through the lens of founder Joseph Smith's profound preoccupation with the specter of death. Revisiting historical documents and scripture from this . . . perspective, Brown offers . . . insight into the origin and meaning of some of Mormonism's earliest beliefs and practices. The world of early Mormonism was besieged by death--infant mortality, violence, and disease were rampant. A prolonged battle with typhoid fever, punctuated by painful surgeries including a threatened leg amputation, and the sudden loss of his beloved brother Alvin cast a long shadow over Smith's own life. Smith embraced and was deeply influenced by the culture of 'holy dying'--with its emphasis on deathbed salvation, melodramatic bereavement, and belief in the Providential nature of untimely death--that sought to cope with the widespread mortality of the period." (Publisher's note)
Includes bibliographical references and index

Eire, Carlos M. N.
A very brief history of eternity; [by] Carlos Eire. Princeton University Press 2010 268p il $24.95; ebook $24.95 **236**
1. Eternity 2. Western civilization
ISBN 978-0-691-13357-7; 978-1-4008-3187-6 ebook
LC 2009-22951
The author's "skill at engaging readers conceals the rigorous, thoughtful research and methodology that went into this volume. . . . This thought-provoking book is sure to be a classic." Choice
Includes bibliographical references

Miller, Lisa
Heaven; our 2000-year-old fascination with the afterlife. Harper 2010 331p $25.99 **236**
1. Heaven 2. United States -- Religion
ISBN 978-0-06-055475-0; 0-06-055475-4
LC 2009-26063
In this "sweeping historical and literary geography of heaven . . . [Miller] talks to priests, a Dominican monk, Muslim clerics, rabbis, and professors (and even visits a psychic, who channels a balding Ed Asner look-alike — no one she knows, though she racks her brain). She doesn't ignore pop culture, either, touching on everything from The Lovely Bones to the hugely popular Left Behind series. . . . But once she has finished reporting and researching, Miller's book loses its hard journalistic edge and becomes something else: a memoir. Her own qualms about faith have danced around the edges of the story, but finally they come front and center. What Miller ultimately concludes may surprise you. It certainly surprised her." Entertainment Wkly

Spong, John Shelby
Eternal life; a new vision: beyond religion, beyond theism, beyond heaven and hell. Harper One 2009 xx, 268p $24.99 **236**
1. Death 2. Eternity 3. Future life
ISBN 978-0-06-076206-3
LC 2008-51443
The author "recalls gaining his first awareness of death, that of a pet when he was three, and with it the devastating lesson that when something or someone dies, they disappear forever. . . . He discusses the self-consciousness involved in the adoption of religion to cope with the finality of death." Booklist
This book "offers new insights into religion's big questions about life and death, making an invaluable contribution to both religious scholarship and faithful exploration." Publ Wkly
Includes bibliographical references

Wright, N. T.
Surprised by hope; rethinking heaven, the resurrection, and the mission of the church. HarperOne 2008 332p $24.95 **236**
1. Hope 2. Eschatology 3. Future life
ISBN 978-0-06-155182-6; 0-06-155182-1
"Readers will need a Bible handy to appreciate this work fully, as Wright prefers to cite rather than print Scripture. His prose, deep but not murky, is lightened by glints of humor. For any library serving patrons who are willing to think a bit about religion." Libr J
Includes bibliographical references

239 Apologetics and polemics

Augustine, Saint, Bishop of Hippo
Concerning the city of God against the pagans; [by] St. Augustine ; translated by Henry Bettenson ; with a new introduction by G.R. Evans. Penguin Books 2003 lxxi, 1097p (Penguin classics) pa $16 **239**
1. Apologetics
ISBN 978-0-14-044894-8; 0-14-044894-2
LC 2004-269353
This translation first published 1972
"Written as an eloquent defence of the faith at a time when the Roman Empire was on the brink of collapse, it examines the ancient pagan religions of Rome, the arguments of the Greek philosophers and the revelations of the Bible. Pointing the way forward to a citizenship that transcends worldly politics and will last for eternity, City of God represents a dramatic turning point in the unfolding of Christian doctrine. The new introduction by Gill Evans examines the text in the light of contemporary Greek and Roman thought and political change." Publisher's note
Includes bibliographical references

Keller, Timothy J.

The **reason** for God; belief in an age of skepticism. Dutton 2008 293p $24.95   **239**

1. Faith 2. Skepticism 3. Apologetics

ISBN 978-0-525-95049-3; 0-525-95049-4

LC 2007-43745

"Using literature, philosophy, and pop culture, the author gives . . . reasons for a strong belief in God. . . . [The author] presents a religious view without being overly critical of the secular side presented in other books. . . . This book presents a valid, well-written, and well-researched argument." Libr J

241   Christian ethics

Anderson, Gary A.

Sin; a history. Yale University Press 2009 253p $30; pa $20   **241**

1. Sin 2. Sin -- Christianity 3. Sin -- Biblical teaching

ISBN 978-0-300-14989-0; 0-300-14989-1; 978-0-300-16809-9 pa; 0-300-16809-8 pa

LC 2009012342

This book "is a significant contribution both to scriptural interpretation and to theology proper, and an object lesson in how to do both well. . . . The richness and precision of Anderson's engagement with the texts he treats cannot be adequately conveyed in a short review, which is why you should read his book." Commonweal

Includes bibliographical references

Chapman, Gary D.

Love as a way of life; seven keys to transforming every aspect of your life. [by] Gary Chapman. Doubleday 2008 239p $19.95; pa $13.95   **241**

1. Love -- Religious aspects 2. Interpersonal relations -- Religious aspects

ISBN 978-0-385-51858-1; 0-385-51858-7; 978-1-4000-7259-0 pa; 1-4000-7259-X pa

LC 2007-50546

"All self-help books run the risk of cliché, but Chapman manages to make tried-and-true material feel fresh through carefully chosen examples from his pastoral counseling practice and his own life. . . . Although Christian faith provides the scaffolding for his program and a concluding chapter makes the need for God's help explicit, Chapman's judicious counsel can be implemented by people of many religious traditions." Publ Wkly

Includes bibliographical references

Davis, Will

Enough; finding more by living with less. Will Davis, Jr. Revell 2012 232 p. (pbk.) $13.99   **241**

1. Simplicity 2. Christian life 3. Conduct of life 4. Simplicity -- Religious aspects -- Christianity 5. Contentment -- Religious aspects -- Christianity

ISBN 0800720024; 9780800720025

LC 2012003547

This Christian book, by Will Davis Jr., "challenges readers to discover the peace that comes through contentment with what we have and have compassion for those in need. Through . . . statistics, scriptural insight, and real-life stories,

Davis gently leads readers to consider living with less in order to do more for the kingdom." (Publisher's note)

Includes bibliographical references (p. 231-232)

Pagels, Elaine H.

Adam, Eve, and the serpent. Random House 1988 xxviii, 189p hardcover o.p. pa $12   **241**

1. Sexual behavior 2. Bible -- O.T. -- Criticism

ISBN 0-679-72232-7 pa

LC 87-43227

"Pagels writes with a rare combination of formidable knowledge and easy fluency. The old controversies she discusses become, in her hands, matters of immediate interest." Economist

Includes bibliographical references

Price, Reynolds

A serious way of wondering; the ethics of Jesus imagined. Scribner 2003 146p hardcover o.p. pa $14.95   **241**

1. Christian ethics

ISBN 0-7432-3008-6; 0-7432-3009-4 pa

LC 2003-41506

"In three . . . apocryphal gospel stories, Price's Jesus engages in conversations about homosexuality, suicide and the plight of women in male-dominated societies. . . . Elegant and passionate, Price's provocative parables provide no simple answers to the saccharine question 'What would Jesus do?' Rather, they compel us to imagine creatively our engagements with Jesus' teachings and the impact of those teachings on our lives." Publ Wkly

Includes bibliographical references

Segal, Alan F.

Sinning in the Hebrew Bible; how the worst stories speak for its truth. Alan F. Segal. Columbia University Press 2012 286 p. (hardcover) $89.50; (paperback) $29.50; (ebook) $28.99   **241**

1. Sin 2. Bible. Old Testament 3. Sin -- Biblical teaching 4. Bible. O.T. -- Criticism, interpretation, etc

ISBN 0231159277; 9780231159265; 9780231159272; 9780231504348

LC 2011046083

This book, by Alan F. Segal, explores how "stories of rape, murder, adultery, and conquest raise crucial issues in the Hebrew Bible, and their interpretation helps societies form their religious and moral beliefs. . . . Rereading these stories in their different forms and varying contexts, Alan F. Segal demonstrates the significance of sinning throughout history and today. . . . Segal ultimately positions the Hebrew Bible as a foundational moral text and a history book." (Publisher's note)

Includes bibliographical references and index

242   Devotional literature

Augustine, Saint, Bishop of Hippo

Confessions; translated with an introduction and notes by Henry Chadwick. Oxford University Press

1998 xxviii, 311p (Oxford world's classics) pa $7.95 **242**

ISBN 978-0-19-283372-3; 0-19-283372-3

"These confessions were written at the end of the fourth century by the most distinguished of the Latin fathers as a revelation of his spiritual experience. They have been a source of religious inspiration through the centuries." Pratt Alcove

Includes bibliographical references

King, Martin Luther, Jr., 1929-1968

Thou, dear God; Martin Luther King, Jr. ; foreword by the Julius R. Scruggs ; edited and introduced by Lewis V. Baldwin. Beacon Press 2012 245 p. **242**

1. Prayers

ISBN 9780807086032

LC 2011031431

This book "is the first and only collection of sixty-eight prayers by Martin Luther King, Jr. Arranged thematically in six parts--with prayers for spiritual guidance, special occasions, times of adversity, times of trial, uncertain times, and social justice--Baptist minister and King scholar Lewis Baldwin introduces the book and each section with short essays. Included are both personal and public prayers King recited as a seminarian, graduate student, preacher, pastor, and, finally, civil rights leader, along with a special section that reveals the biblical sources that most inspired King. Collectively they illustrate how King turned to private prayer for his own spiritual fulfillment and to public prayer as a way to move, inspire, and reaffirm a quest for peace and social justice." (Publisher's note)

Includes bibliographical references (p. 239-245).

Rennebohm, Craig

Souls in the hands of a tender God; stories of the search for home and healing on the streets. [by] Craig Rennebohm with David Paul. Beacon Press 2008 208p $23.95; pa $18 **242**

1. Mental illness 2. Spiritual healing 3. Mental health -- Religious aspects

ISBN 978-0-8070-0042-7; 0-8070-0042-6; 978-0-8070-0043-4 pa; 0-8070-0043-4 pa

LC 2007-31506

"For decades Rennebohm, a Protestant pastor, has walked the streets of Seattle, making contact with mentally ill homeless people and slowly drawing them into 'circles of care' so they can find safe housing, receive medical and psychological help and rejoin the human community. In this collaboration with Paul, Rennebohm interweaves themes of the Spirit working in desperate lives, the unshakable dignity of human souls and the necessity of companionship for healing as he vividly portrays the lost people he encounters. . . . As well as a guide to how others can help be healing presences to the mentally ill, this hopeful book is a meditation on faith in a broken world." Publ Wkly

Includes bibliographical references

Thomas à Kempis

The imitation of Christ; {by} Thomas à Kempis. Vintage Books 1998 xliii, 242p pa $12.95 **242**

ISBN 978-0-375-70018-7; 0-375-70018-8

This devotional classic originally written in Latin in the 15th century "traces in four books the gradual progress of the soul to Christian perfection, its detachment from the world, and its union with God." Oxford Companion to Engl Lit. Concise edition

Ugolino, di Monte Santa Maria

The little flowers of St. Francis of Assisi; written by Ugolino di Monte Santa Maria; edited by and adapted from a translation by W. Heywood; with a new preface by Madeleine L'Engle. Vintage Books 1998 xxxviii, 120p (Vintage spiritual classics) pa $13 **242**

1. Saints 2. Writers on religion

ISBN 978-0-375-70020-0; 0-375-70020-X

LC 97-48815

This translation first published 1906 in the United Kingdom

These "simple anecdotes exemplify St. Francis' love of nature, man and of God." Bookman's Manual

Includes bibliographical references

248   Christian experience, practice, life

Brizendine, Judy

Stunned by grief; remapping your life when loss changes everything. BennettKnepp Publishing 2011 274p il pa $18.95 **248**

1. Bereavement 2. Loss (Psychology) 3. Spiritual healing 4. Adjustment (Psychology)

ISBN 978-0-9831688-1-2

"A former market analyst and interior designer, . . . [the author] found her world turned upside down when her husband died. She uses her own experience combined with the advice of psychologists, grief counselors, the Bible, and fellow mourners to provide a sort of roadmap for the unwelcome journey of grief. In bite-size pieces, she covers the progression of grief, the intrinsic anger and guilt felt in the process, and the possibility of dealing with and planning a new future. . . . This book will comfort and support anyone new to grief and will serve as a companion in times of loneliness. Realistic, practical, and highly recommended." Libr J

Includes bibliographical references

Lewis, C. S. (Clive Staples), 1898-1963

Letters to Malcolm: chiefly on prayer. 1964 124p hardcover o.p. pa $13 **248**

1. Prayer 2. Christian life

ISBN 978-0-15-602766-3

The author's "reflections on prayer are here set down in the form of thoughtful and engaging letters to his friend Malcolm." Cincinnati Public Libr

★ The Screwtape letters; with, Screwtape proposes a toast. HarperSanFrancisco 2001 209p $22.95; pa $11.95 **248**

1. Satire 2. Christian life

ISBN 0-06-065289-6; 0-06-065293-4 pa

LC 00-49860

The Screwtape letters first published 1943 by Macmillan; this combined edition first published 1961 by Macmillan

"A popular work on Christian moral and theological problems. . . . It is in the form of a series of letters in which a devil, Screwtape, advises his nephew, Wormwood, on how to deal with his human 'patients.'" Reader's Ency. 4th edition

Lucado, Max

Fearless; imagine your life without fear. Thomas Nelson 2009 221p $24.99   **248**

1. Fear -- Religious aspects
ISBN 978-0-8499-2139-1

LC 2009-707

The author offers a faith-based primer on how to live without fear.

"Skillful as a surgeon, . . . [Lucado] discerns and identifies the cancer of fear that touches every human being, and with like precision speaks healing words that cut right the heart. While there exists no fast fix or simple cure for the fear-bound individual, Lucado's tempered counsel and faith-driven remedies will offer day-by-day spiritual medicine of the most potent kind." Publ Wkly

Includes bibliographical references

Peale, Norman Vincent

★ The **power** of positive living. Fawcett Columbine 1996 224p pa $13.95   **248**

1. Success 2. Applied psychology 3. Pastoral psychology
ISBN 0-449-91166-7; 978-0-449-91166-2

LC 96096721

First published 1952 by Prentice-Hall

In this volume "Peale strings together dozens of personal success stories ('success' is always materialistic) that make readers feel good. Believing (in yourself, others, values, God) is all-important, and the stories of wealthy business executives who made it on their own grab center stage." Libr J

Zondervan dictionary of Christian spirituality; Glen G. Scorgie, general editor; consulting editors: Simon Chan, Gordon T. Smith, James D. Smith III. Zondervan 2011 852p $39.99   **248**

1. Reference books 2. Christianity -- Dictionaries
ISBN 978-0-310-29066-7

LC 2010037314

"The first section presents six to seven-page entries on topics such as spiritual theology, human personhood, education and spiritual formation, and liturgical spirituality. Also included are articles describing the history of Christian spirituality from 100 C.E. to the present. Each article is followed by a bibliography and a further-reading list. The second section is a dictionary with entries on a broad variety of subjects: biblical figures, popes, mystics, saints, philosophers, spiritual leaders, and educators, as well as concepts and areas of concern including poverty, humanism, suffering, vows, the Kingdom of God, and peace." Libr J

Includes bibliographical references

248.2   Religious experience

Armstrong, Karen

Visions of God; four medieval mystics and their writings. Bantam Bks. 1994 228p pa $19   **248.2**

1. Authors 2. Hermits 3. Mysticism 4. Mystics 5. Writers on religion
ISBN 0-553-35199-0

LC 94-20217

"The collection is eminently readable and should serve to make these important sources more accessible to a general audience. The selections are arranged chronologically, but Armstrong's reflections also place them in a 'developmental sequence.'" Booklist

Includes bibliographical references

Downing, David C.

Into the region of awe; mysticism in C. S. Lewis. InterVarsity Press 2005 207p $17   **248.2**

1. Authors 2. Mysticism 3. Novelists 4. Theologians 5. Essayists 6. Satirists 7. Literary critics 8. Children's authors
ISBN 0-8308-3284-X; 978-0-8308-3284-2

LC 2004-29844

This is a "book on the writer/thinker's complex attitudes toward mysticism and mystical experience. Downing is keenly responsible in his approach to Lewis's biography and background and candid about Lewis's reservations about mysticism in his own theology; the author's affection for his subject ably informs this sensitive reading of Lewis's life and writings." Libr J

Includes bibliographical references

248.4   Christian life and practice

Carter, Jimmy, 1924-

Living faith. Times Bks. 1996 256p hardcover o.p. pa $13   **248.4**

1. Governors 2. Presidents 3. Nobel laureates for peace 4. Presidents -- United States
ISBN 0-8129-3034-7 pa

LC 96-20993

In this "spiritual autobiography, the former president . . . traces the growth and development of his faith through his career in the Navy and various political offices, and through his work with Habitat for Humanity (which builds housing for poor Americans) and the Carter Center (an international peacemaking organization). Carter also discusses the impact that Soren Kierkegaard and Reinhold Niebuhr have had on his life." Publ Wkly

Sources of strength; meditations on scripture for a living faith. Times Bks. 1997 252p hardcover o.p. pa $14.99   **248.4**

1. Christian life 2. Bible -- Meditations
ISBN 0-8129-3236-6 pa

LC 97-27501

Companion volume to Living faith

This "is a collection of 52 brief Bible lessons—one for each week of the year—written by former president Jimmy Carter. All were used in adult Sunday school classes he taught himself. Carter's lessons are open-minded and so-cially progressive while remaining unapologetically conservative and Christian theologically. . . . The lessons are grouped in nine categories, such as 'What We Believe' and 'Christians in the World,' but each lesson stands well on its own." Libr J

Chittister, Joan

Following the path; the search for a life of passion, purpose, and joy. Image 2012 188 p. $18.00 **248.4**

1. Self-help techniques
ISBN 030795398X; 9780307953988

This book considers "the questions 'What am I supposed to do with my life?' and 'How do I know when I've found my purpose?' [which] can seem endless and overwhelming. . . . [Author] Sister Joan [Chittister] brings the insights of her years of teaching and contemplation to bear on this issue." She examin[es] . . . spiritual calling and gifts, change and discernment." (Publisher's note) This book "is meant to give someone in the process of making a life decision at any age—in early adulthood, at the point of middle-age change and later, when we find ourselves at the crossroads without a name—some ideas against which to pit their own minds, their own circumstances." (Author's note)

Girzone, Joseph F.

Never alone; a personal way to God. Doubleday 1994 115p il hardcover o.p. pa $10.95 **248.4**

1. Spiritual life
ISBN 0-3854-7683-3 pa

LC 93-38725

Girzone's "empathy for the loneliness and insecurity of being human guides readers toward a more satisfying religious experience than that provided by organized religions, which he continues to criticize for not sufficiently following the living message of Jesus' life." Booklist

Heim, Tami

@stickyjesus; how to live out your faith online. Toni Birdsong, Tami Heim. Abingdon Press 2012 224 p. **248.4**

1. Christian life 2. Computer literacy 3. Online social networks 4. Internet -- Social aspects 5. Christian life -- Meditations
ISBN 1426741898; 9781426741890

LC 2011044377

This book instructs Christian readers in incorporating technology, computers, and the Internet into their faith. The book "is a fusion of discipleship, faith sharing, marketing, and a Get Started 101 on Twitter, Facebook and blogging. '@stickyJesus' . . . challenges Christ followers to regain [their] God-given dominion on earth, which includes the Internet. With knowledge, skills, and Holy Spirit guidance, [the authors] encourage believers to dig in and learn how to navigate this online world. . . . The book also includes personal testimonies. . . . These are real people and ministries (about a dozen) making a difference because they walk, talk and connect differently online." (Publisher's Note)

Includes bibliographical references.

Jakes, T. D., 1957-

Instinct; the power to unleash your inborn drive. T.D. Jakes. Faith Words 2014 271 p. (hardcover) $25 **248.4**

1. Spiritual life 2. Self-help techniques 3. Instinct 4. Christian life
ISBN 1455554049; 9781455554041

LC 2014007406

In this book, author T. D. Jakes "outlines how to rediscover your natural aptitudes and re-claim the wisdom of your past experiences." He claims that "Knowing when to close a deal, when to take a risk, and when to listen to your heart will become possible when you're in touch with the instincts that God gave you." (Publisher's note)

"This positive book encourages readers to get in touch with their instincts, trust them, and rely on them." Pub Wkly

Martin, James

The **Jesuit** guide to almost everything; a spirituality for real life. HarperOne 2010 420p il $26.99; ebook $11.99 **248.4**

1. Saints 2. Priests 3. Spiritual life 4. Catholic Church 5. Religious leaders 6. Writers on religion
ISBN 978-0-06-143268-2; 978-0-06-198140-1 ebook

LC 2009030505

"In this digestible account of all things Jesuit, James Martin, S.J., encapsulates the uniquely Ignatian concept of spirituality. Translating the essence of the Jesuit philosophy into layman's terms, he uses both traditional stories and personal anecdotes to vividly illustrate the Jesuit approach to God, friendship, social justice, decision-making, prayer, simplicity, obedience, and self-actualization. Martin's engaging, intimate tone will appeal to anyone interested in understanding the history, the efficacy, and the universality of the Jesuit mission and way of life." Booklist

Includes bibliographical references

Nouwen, Henri

Discernment; reading the signs of daily life. Henri J. M. Nouwen, with Michael J. Christensen and Rebecca J. Laird. HarperOne 2013 xxix, 223 p.p (hc) $25.99 **248.4**

1. Theology 2. Christian life 3. Christian ethics 4. Discernment (Christian theology)
ISBN 9780061686153; 0061686158; 9780061686160

LC 2013004593

This book "features the wisdom that spiritual leader and counselor Henri J. M. Nouwen brought to the essential question asked by every Christian and seeker: What should I do with my life? Nouwen emphasizes listening to the Word of God--in our hearts, in the Bible, in the community of faith, and in the voice of the poor as a way to discern God's plan." (Publisher's note)

Includes bibliographical references

Riess, Jana

Flunking sainthood; a year of breaking the Sabbath, forgetting to pray, and still loving my neighbor. Paraclete Press 2011 179p pa $16.99 **248.4**

1. Success 2. Christian life 3. Spiritual life 4. Failure

(Psychology)
ISBN 978-1-55725-660-7

LC 2011022595

The author "intended to devote an entire year ('a year-long experiment') to mastering 12 different spiritual challenges, including praying at fixed times during the day, exhibiting gratitude, observing the Sabbath, practicing hospitality according to the rules set by St. Benedict, abstaining from eating meat, and amply demonstrating her generosity. But nothing turned out as planned. . . . Although her spiritual quest falls far short, she can still proffer spiritual lessons. Anyone who has failed to live up to expectations, which means most everyone, will love this book." Booklist

Includes bibliographical references

248.8   Guides to Christian life for specific groups of people

Hendey, Lisa M.

A **book** of saints for Catholic moms; 52 companions for your heart, mind, body, and soul. Lisa M. Hendey. Ave Maria Press 2011 xiv, 334 p.p ill.   **248.8**
1. Prayers 2. Catholics 3. Motherhood 4. Christian saints 5. Devotional exercises 6. Mothers -- Prayers and devotions 7. Catholic Church -- Prayers and devotions 8. Christian saints -- Prayers and devotions
ISBN 1594712735; 9781594712739

LC 2011025284

In this book, Lisa M. Hende "familiarizes readers with saints — one for each week of the year — who are relevant to nearly every aspect of a Catholic mother's life, divided into categories of heart, mind, body and soul. She offers related Scripture verses for the week as well as practical suggestions and activities. . . . [The book covers] topics such as 'overflowing mounds of dirty laundry' or serious issues such as mental illness and single parenthood. . . . Hendey . . . details the saints' trials and triumphs that . . . people struggle with the same intrinsic issues today. Although many of the individual saints are patrons to various groups or issues . . . Hendey . . . relat[es] each saint's legacy to common dilemmas faced by mothers." (Our Sunday Visitor)

252   Texts of sermons

American sermons; the pilgrims to Martin Luther King, Jr. Library of Am. 1999 939p $40   **252**
1. Sermons
ISBN 1-88301-165-5

LC 98-34295

"To peruse this work is to become reacquainted with the literary eloquence of our distant and recent past and to observe what has happened to rhetoric itself over the centuries." N Y Times Book Rev

Includes bibliographical references

King, Martin Luther, Jr., 1929-1968
★ **Strength** to love; foreword by Coretta Scott King. Fortress 2010 168p il pa $20   **252**
1. Sermons
ISBN 978-0-8006-9740-2

First published 1963 by Harper & Row
A collection of sermons addressing social injustice and racism.
Includes bibliographical references

253   Pastoral office and work (Pastoral theology)

McKibben, Bill
Eaarth; making a life on a tough new planet. Times Books 2010 253p $24   **253**
1. Environmental degradation 2. Human influence on nature 3. Greenhouse effect 4. Climate -- Environmental aspects
ISBN 978-0-8050-9056-7; 0-8050-9056-8

LC 2009-30040

The author "demonstrates how global warming has already occurred and is irreversible. He describes a new 'Eaarth,' where the cumulative effects of the release of carbon dioxide in the atmosphere have already changed the planet. . . . McKibben envisions a future in which humanity transitions from unfettered growth and a dependence on external markets for sustenance and fossil-fuel-driven energy, to smaller, self-contained communities, growing food locally and generating sustainable distributed electricity. An absolute must-read." Kirkus

Includes bibliographical references

255   Religious congregations and orders

Norris, Kathleen
The **cloister** walk. Riverhead Bks. 1996 384p hardcover o.p. pa $12.95   **255**
1. Spiritual life 2. Monasticism and religious orders 3. Catholic Church -- Liturgy
ISBN 1-57322-584-3 pa

LC 96-863

Companion volume to Dakota: a spiritual geography (1993)

The author relates her experiences as a lay oblate at St. John's Abbey, a Benedictine monastery in Collegeville, Minnesota. The narrative is arranged chronologically according to the rhythm of the Catholic liturgical calendar

"Kathleen Norris knows about faith. She also knows a lot about doubt. . . . As a married Protestant woman, Norris appears to be an improbable candidate to live in a community of celibate men. Yet as she 'walks' with the Benedictine monks, spending days in continual reading, prayer, and singing, she gains new perspectives on their life and her own." Christ Sci Monit

261.2   Christianity and other systems of belief

Carroll, James
Constantine's sword; the church and the Jews: a history. Houghton Mifflin 2001 756p $28; pa $16   **261.2**
1. Judaism 2. Christianity and other religions 3.

Catholic Church -- Relations -- Judaism
ISBN 0-395-77927-8; 0-6142-1908-0 pa

LC 00-61329

"This magisterial work will satisfy Jewish and Christians readers alike, challenging both to a renewed conversation with one another." Publ Wkly

Includes bibliographical references

Kertzer, David I.

The **Popes** against the Jews; the Vatican's role in the rise of modern anti-semitism. Knopf 2001 355p $27.95; pa $15 **261.2**

1. Antisemitism 2. Catholic Church -- Relations -- Judaism

ISBN 0-375-40623-9; 0-375-70605-4 pa

LC 2001-33728

"This is a devastating indictment, and fair-minded critics will find flaws in Kertzer's methodology and sweeping conclusions. Nevertheless, he has opened a window that should be opened." Booklist

Includes bibliographical references

261.5 Christianity and secular disciplines

Barbour, Ian G.

When science meets religion; enemies, strangers, or partners? HarperSanFrancisco 2000 205p pa $16.95 **261.5**

1. Religion and science

ISBN 0-06-060381-X

LC 99-55579

The author "guides readers through a four-fold typology of the science/religion relationship—Conflict, Independence, Dialogue and Integration. . . . Barbour's own sympathies are markedly on the side of dialogue and integration, but he makes an unusually sucessful effort to represent other perspectives in a fair light." Publ Wkly

Includes bibliographical references

Grant, Edward

★ **Science** and religion, 400 B.C. to A.D. 1550; from Aristotle to Copernicus. Greenwood Press 2004 xxvi, 307p il (Greenwood guides to science and religion) $67.95 **261.5**

1. Religion and science

ISBN 0-313-32858-7

LC 2004-17429

"With this new book, grounded in five decades of active scholarship, Edward Grant provides a synthetic account of the relationship between science and religion from Greek antiquity to the beginnings of the Scientific Revolution. Intended as an introduction for the general reader, the book successfully argues its central point–namely, that contrary to popular belief today, the medieval Church promoted scientific thought, which in turn profoundly influenced theological understanding. . . . Grant's book, along with the eight primary documents it provides, is an introduction students and teachers will welcome." Journal of the History of Science in Society

Includes bibliographical references

Noble, David F.

The **religion** of technology; the divinity of man and the spirit of invention. Knopf 1997 273p hardcover o.p. pa $14.95 **261.5**

1. God 2. Religion and science 3. Technology and civilization

ISBN 0-14-027916-4 pa

LC 96-48019

"Covering a period of a thousand years, Noble traces the evolution of the Western idea of technological development from the ninth century, when, {he argues}, the useful arts became connected to the concept of redemption, up to the twentieth, when humans began to exercise God-like knowledge and powers." Publisher's note

"This is a dense, fascinating study of technology and Christianity." Libr J

Includes bibliographical references

Olson, Richard

★ **Science** and religion, 1450-1900; from Copernicus to Darwin. [by] Richard G. Olson. Greenwood Press 2004 292p il (Greenwood guides to science and religion) $65 **261.5**

1. Religion and science

ISBN 0-313-32694-0

LC 2004-47501

The issues discussed "should be especially helpful to those who are interested in the historical background to current science-religion issues being debated in the United States." Sci Books Films

Includes bibliographical references

261.7 Christianity and political affairs

Dionne, E. J., 1952-

Souled out; reclaiming faith and politics after the religious right. Princeton University Press 2008 251p $24.95; pa $17.95 **261.7**

1. Christianity and politics 2. Christian conservatism 3. Christian fundamentalism 4. Religious right -- United States 5. Right and left (Political science) 6. Christianity and politics -- United States

ISBN 0691134588; 0691143293; 9780691134581; 9780691143293

LC 2007-45172

This book argues that "the era of the Religious Right— and the crude exploitation of faith for political advantage— is over." (Publisher's note) Index.

This "is an astute and important review of the intersection of faith and public policy." America

Includes bibliographical references

Zagorin, Perez

How the idea of religious toleration came to the West. Princeton University Press 2003 371p il hardcover o.p. pa $24.95 **261.7**

1. Religious tolerance

ISBN 0-691-09270-2; 978-0-691-12142-0; 0-691-12142-7 pa

LC 2002-42565

The author discusses "a time when both the Catholic Church and the main new Protestant denominations embraced a policy of endorsing religious persecution, coercing unity, and, with the state's help, mercilessly crushing dissent and heresy. This position had its roots in certain intellectual and religious traditions, which Zagorin trace before showing how out of the same traditions came the beginnings of pluralism in the West. . . . His book—which ranges from England through the Netherlands, the post-1685 Huguenot Diaspora, and the American colonies—also exposes a close connection between toleration and religious freedom." Publisher's note

"A deeply scholarly but ultimately engaging argument for the origins of religious toleration in Western culture since the Enlightenment." Libr J

Includes bibliographical references

261.8 Christianity and socioeconomic problems

Chu, Jeff, 1977-

Does Jesus Really Love Me? A Gay Christian's Pilgrimage in Search of God in America. by Jeff Chu. HarperCollins 2013 368 p. $26.99   **261.8**
1. Gay men 2. Christianity 3. Homosexuality -- United States 4. Christian gays -- United States 5. Homosexuality -- Religious aspects -- Christianity
ISBN 0062049739; 9780062049735
LC 2013464818
Lambda Literary Awards Finalist (2014)
This book, by Jeff Chu, "is part memoir and part investigative analysis that explores the explosive and confusing intersection of faith, politics, and sexuality in Christian America. . . . From Brooklyn to Nashville to California, from Westboro Baptist Church and their 'God Hates Fags' protest signs, to the pioneering Episcopalian bishop Mary Glasspool--who proclaims a message of liberation and divine love, Chu captures spiritual snapshots of Christian America." (Publisher's note)
"[T]he book brings complexity and humanity to a discourse often lacking in both." Pub Wkly

D'Antonio, Michael

★ **Mortal** Sins; Sex, Crime, and the Era of Catholic Scandal. Michael D'Antonio. St. Martin's Press 2013 416 p. $26.99   **261.8**
1. Child sexual abuse by clergy 2. Catholic Church -- Clergy -- Sexual behavior 3. Catholic Church -- Discipline 4. Catholic Church -- United States
ISBN 0312594895; 9780312594893
LC 2013003725
This book presents a "history of the Catholic Church's 'most severe crisis since the Reformation': the revelations of endemic sexual abuse of minors by priests in the United States and Europe. . . . In 1984, American priest Thomas Doyle learned of a lawsuit brought by parents of a victim, and was deeply troubled. . . . Along with plaintiffs' attorney Jeffrey Anderson, Doyle and a few others worked tirelessly to get the church, the media, and the public to pay attention." (Publishers Weekly)

Martin, William C.

With God on our side; the rise of the religious right in America. {by} William Martin. Broadway Bks. 1996 418p il $27.50; pa $15   **261.8**
1. Conservatism 2. Religion and politics 3. Religious fundamentalism 4. Christianity and politics 5. Evangelists 6. Inspirational writers 7. Christian Coalition (Organization)
ISBN 0-553-06745-1; 0-553-06749-4 pa
LC 96-2919
"Unlike some companion volumes to television documentaries, Martin's well-written, superbly organized work stands on its own. . . . {It} is required reading for anyone seeking to understand the rise of the Religious Right. . . . Nothing has been published that can match Martin's book in sweep and substance." Christ Century

Includes bibliographical references

262 Ecclesiology

Chaves, Mark

Ordaining women; culture and conflict in religious organizations. Harvard Univ. Press 1997 237p hardcover o.p. pa $18.50   **262**
1. Christian sociology 2. Ordination of women 3. Women in Christianity 4. United States -- Church history
ISBN 0-674-64146-9 pa
LC 97-12518
The author provides a "study of the 19th- and 20th-century ordination policies and practices of many Christian groups in the United States, including the Roman Catholic Church." Libr J

Includes bibliographical references

Meyers, Robin R.

Saving Jesus from the church; how to stop worshiping Christ and start following Jesus. HarperOne 2009 243p $24.99   **262**
1. Christianity 2. Christian life
ISBN 978-0-06-156821-3; 0-06-156821-X
LC 2008-51766
"In a progressive rather than negatively critical mode, in strong contrast to much of Far Right Protestantism, . . . [the author] suggests with typical elegance that a recovery of true Christianity emphasizes compassion over condemnation, blessing over sin, and equity over individual prosperity. Highly recommended." Libr J

Includes bibliographical references

Reese, Thomas J.

Inside the Vatican; the politics and organization of the Catholic Church. Harvard Univ. Press 1996 317p il $30; pa $16.95   **262**
1. Popes 2. Papacy 3. Catholic Church 4. Vatican City
ISBN 0-674-93260-9; 0-679-93261-7 pa
LC 96-26641
The author examines "the internal workings of the Vatican both as city-state and the headquarters of the Roman

Catholic Church. . . . With its wealth of information, historical background, and analysis, Reese's work should be an important addition for a variety of libraries." Libr J

Includes bibliographical references

Wills, Garry, 1934-

Papal sin; structures of deceit. Doubleday 2000 326p **262**

1. Papacy 2. Catholic Church

ISBN 0-385-49410-6; 0-385-49411-4 pa

LC 99-54851

In Part I—"'Historical Dishonesties'—{Wills claims that the Catholic} hierarchy has persistently lied . . . about what the church did and did not do during the Holocaust. Part 2—'Doctrinal Dishonesties'—argues that recent popes . . . have cared more about retaining their grip on authority than about the needs of those whom they claim to serve. In the last two parts of the book—'The Honesty Issue' and 'The Splendor of Truth'—Wills writes about his heroes: Lord Acton, Cardinal Newman and St. Augustine. He offers them as exemplars to whom the church might turn." (N Y Times Book Rev) Index.

The author "argues that the Church is not merely the clergy but the whole body of believers. His examination of papal policies on such topics as the Holocaust, clerical celibacy, and the role of women finds that the Church has often distorted history and Scripture in the attempt to bolster its authority. There's an undertone of grief to this rationally argued book, which ends with a wistful vision of the Church as it might be." New Yorker

Includes bibliographical references

262.001   Philosophy and theory

Meyers, Robin

The **underground** church; reclaiming the subversive way of Jesus. Robin Meyers. 1st ed. Jossey-Bass 2012 xiv, 266 p.p (cloth) $24.95   **262.001**

1. Christianity 2. Church history

ISBN 1118061594; 9781118061596

LC 2011039903

In this book, "[Robin] Meyers . . . offers a number of subversive ideas . . . reminding readers that Jesus came to feed the hungry, wage nonviolence, and generally afflict the comfortable in his day. . . . Hospitality is a cardinal Christian virtue. So is nonviolence, but it's so hard that most fail at a practice that demands discipline and sacrifice. Meyers calls for other practices . . .including low or no-interest money-lending and tithing." (Publishers Weekly)

Includes bibliographical references.

264   Public worship

Episcopal Church/Book of common prayer

★ The **Book** of common prayer and administration of the sacraments and other rites and ceremonies of the church; together with the Psalter or Psalms of David according to the use of the Episcopal Church.

Church Hymnal Corp, Seabury Press 1979 1001p pew ed., black $19   **264**

ISBN 0-89869-081-1

LC 81-204603

The official liturgy of the Episcopal Church.

Lucatero, Heliodoro

★ The **living** Mass; changes to the Roman missal and how we worship. Liguori 2011 64p il pa $4.99   **264**

1. Catholic Church -- Liturgy

ISBN 978-0-7648-2007-6

This book seeks to answer questions about the changes made to the Roman Missal "as well as to give some insight into the history of the development of the Roman Missal from early Church times, through the Middle Ages, through the different Church councils, and up to the present day. A comparison of each change features old and new text side-by-side with the changes highlighted in bold type." Publisher's note

Includes bibliographical references

270   History, geographic treatment, biography of Christianity; Church history; Christian denominations and sects

The Bloomsbury Guide to Christian Spirituality. Bloomsbury Academic 2012 356 p. $49.95 **270**

1. Spiritual life 2. Christianity -- Encyclopedias

ISBN 1441184848; 9781441184849

This book is a "single-volume orientation to Christian spirituality. . . . Topics are . . . inclusive (sources, traditions, practices, dialogue with other faiths, contemporary issues). Three indexes (biblical citations, names, subjects) enable rapid searches through the text. The 30-plus contributors include world-class scholars Bernard McGinn, Richard Rohr, Benedicta Ward, and coeditor [Richard] Woods." (Choice)

Chidester, David

Christianity; a global history. HarperSanFrancisco 2000 627p il hardcover o.p. pa $21.95 **270**

1. Christianity 2. Church history

ISBN 0-06-251708-2; 0-06-251770-8 pa

LC 00-37006

"Highly recommended for religion and history collections looking for a work that anchors modern sensibilities to ancient ideas." Libr J

Includes bibliographical references

Cox, Harvey Gallagher

The **future** of faith; [by] Harvey Cox. HarperOne 2009 245p $24.99   **270**

1. Holy Spirit 2. Christianity

ISBN 978-0-06-175552-1; 0-06-175552-4

LC 2008-54429

Presents an interpretation of why Christian beliefs and dogma are giving way to new grassroots movements rooted in social justice and spiritual experience.

This "spirited portrait of our religious landscape challenges us to think in new ways about faith." Publ Wkly

Includes bibliographical references

Craughwell, Thomas J.

Saints behaving badly; the cutthroats, crooks, trollops, con men, and devil-worshippers who became saints. Doubleday 2006 190p $15.95   **270**

1. Christian saints

ISBN 0-385-51720-3; 978-0-385-51720-1

LC 2006-299594

The author presents a "review of 32 less-than-perfect saints, among them St. Olga, St. Mary of Egypt, and Thomas a Becket. Relying on a wide range of sources—including his own expertise—he writes concise and informative profiles of these holy people that chronicle their respective rises to sainthood and end with what inspired them to abandon their wicked ways." Libr J

Includes bibliographical references

Jenkins, Philip

Jesus wars; how four patriarchs, three queens, and two emperors decided what Christians would believe for the next 1,500 years. HarperOne 2010 328p map $26.99   **270**

1. Doctrinal theology 2. Councils and synods 3. Christian civilization 4. Church history -- 30-600, Early church

ISBN 978-0-06-176894-1

The author focuses "not only on the theological definitions of the nature of Christ, promulgated by various Christian political and ecclesiastical leaders from the fourth through the seventh centuries, but also on the political machinations, violent persecutions, and scheming that made 'wars' of these debates. . . . In showing general readers how he finds fresh ideas and the resurrections of past teachings invigorating to religious studies, Jenkins provides an accessible book, and one with mild suspense and intrigue." Libr J

Includes bibliographical references and index

★ The **lost** history of Christianity; the thousand-year golden age of the church in the Middle East, Africa, and Asia--and how it died. HarperOne 2008 315p map $26.95   **270**

1. Christian civilization 2. Church history -- 30-600, Early church

ISBN 978-0-06-147280-0; 0-06-147280-8

A lost history revealing that, for centuries, Christianity's center was actually in the Middle East, Asia, and Africa, with significant communities extending as far as China.

"This is an important counterweight to previous histories that have focused almost exclusively on Christianity in the West." Publ Wkly

Includes bibliographical references

The **new** faces of Christianity; believing the Bible in the global south. Oxford University Press 2006 252p $26   **270**

1. Forecasting 2. Christianity

ISBN 978-0-19-530065-9; 0-19-530065-3

LC 2006-15490

Jenkins explores the growth of Christianity in Africa, Asia and Latin America.

"Those interested in religious trends across the globe, the Muslim-Christian friction, and world politics will benefit from this resource." Libr J

Includes bibliographical references

MacCulloch, Diarmaid

★ **Christianity**; the first three thousand years. Viking 2010 1161p il map $45   **270**

1. Church history

ISBN 978-0-670-02126-0; 0-670-02126-1

LC 2009-40184

First published 2009 in the United Kingdom

"It is difficult to imagine a more comprehensive and surprisingly accessible volume on the subject than MacCulloch's. . . . Want a refresher on the rise of the papacy? It is here. On Charlemagne and Carolingians? That is here, too. On the Fourth Crusade and its aftermath? Look no farther." N Y Times Book Rev

Includes bibliographical references

Martin, James

My life with the saints. Loyola Press 2006 411p $22.95   **270**

1. Christian saints

ISBN 0-8294-2001-0

LC 2005-28466

The author "relates how he discovered various 'saints' and how each has affected his life. . . . Despite a theme built on a particular facet of Catholic belief, Martin's animated style and wide-ranging experiences make this a book readers of diverse backgrounds will enjoy." Publ Wkly

Includes bibliographical references

Tickle, Phyllis

The **great** emergence; how Christianity is changing and why. Baker Books 2008 172p il $17.99 **270**

1. Christianity

ISBN 0-8010-1313-5; 978-0-8010-1313-3

LC 2008-21706

The author "examines a phenomenon she refers to as the Great Emergence, a once-every-500-years trend within Christianity, in which a new and 'more vital' form of the religion emerges. She believes such a development is happening now." Booklist

"This is a must-read for anyone seeking to understand the face and future of Christianity." Publ Wkly

Includes bibliographical references

270.09   Areas, regions, places in general; biography

McBrien, Richard P.

Lives of the saints; from Mary and Francis of Assisi to John XXIII and Mother Teresa. HarperSanFrancisco 2001 xxiii, 646p il hardcover o.p. pa $19.95   **270.09**

1. Christian saints

ISBN 0-06-123283-1 pa

LC 00-53933

"This work goes beyond the Roman Catholic Church's list of saints to include those of the Orthodox, Anglican, and Lutheran churches. Concise and well-researched biographical sketches are arranged by feast days, with access provided by indexes for saints, personal names, and subjects. Complementing the biographies are thoughtful essays on the history of saints, their place in religious history, and canonization; a series of seven tables on feast days, patron saints, iconography, and papal canonization." Libr J

Includes bibliographical references

270.1   Historical periods

Encyclopedia of early Christianity; edited by Everett Ferguson. 2nd ed; Garland 1997 2v il maps (Garland reference library of the humanities) set $245; pa set $55   **270.1**
1. Reference books 2. Christianity -- Encyclopedias
ISBN 0-8153-1663-1; 0-8153-3319-6 pa

LC 96-36865

First published 1990
"Covers persons, places, doctrines, practices, art, liturgy, heresies, and schisms from the time of Jesus to approximately 600 CE. Articles by . . . specialists include bibliographies and cross-references. Extensive subject index. Intended for general readers, students, and professionals in fields outside religion who want information concerning early Christianity." Guide to Ref Books. 11th edition {entry for 1990 edition}

Riley, Gregory J.
The **river** of God; a new history of Christian origins. HarperSanFrancisco 2001 252p hardcover o.p. pa $14.95   **270.1**
1. Church history -- 30-600, Early church
ISBN 0-06-066979-9; 0-06-066980-2 pa

LC 2001-16888

"This volume will become one of the most important books on the subject." Libr J
Includes bibliographical references

Voices of early Christianity; documents from the origins of Christianity. Kevin W. Kaatz, editor. Greenwood 2013 xxii, 277 p.p (Voices of an era) (hardcopy : alk. paper) $100   **270.1**
1. Christianity 2. Religion -- History 3. Women in Christianity 4. Church history -- Primitive and early church, ca. 30-600 -- Sources
ISBN 1598849522; 9781598849523

LC 2012041162

The "editor's intention with this book is to teach about early Christianity using primary-source documents, with the title also offering a treatise on how to evaluate and think critically about primary sources." Topics include "'Early Christian Life,' 'The Church,' 'Early Christian Women,' 'Conflicts of the Early Church,' 'Persecution,' and 'Church and Politics.'" (Library Journal)
Includes bibliographical references (pages 255-264) and index

270.2   Period of ecumenical councils, 325-787

Brown, Peter
Through the eye of a needle; wealth, the fall of Rome, and the making of Christianity in the West, 350-550 AD. Peter Brown. Princeton University Press 2012 759 p.   **270.2**
1. Rome -- History 2. Church history -- 30-600, Early church 3. Wealth -- Religious aspects -- Christianity 4. Rome -- History -- Empire, 284-476 5. Wealth -- Religious aspects -- Christianity -- History 6. Church history -- Primitive and early church, ca. 30-600
ISBN 069115290X; 9780691152905

LC 2011045697

This book, by Peter Brown, is a history "of the vexing problem of wealth in Christianity in the waning days of the Roman Empire. . . . Peter Brown examines the rise of the church through the lens of money and the challenges it posed to an institution that espoused the virtue of poverty and called avarice the root of all evil, . . . challeng[ing] the widely held notion that Christianity's growing wealth sapped Rome of its ability to resist the barbarian invasions." (Publisher's note)
Includes bibliographical references and index

Wills, Garry, 1934-
Saint Augustine. Viking 1999 xx, 152p (Penguin lives series) $19.95   **270.2**
1. Saints 2. Bishops 3. Theologians 4. Philosophers 5. Writers on religion
ISBN 0-670-88610-6

LC 98-50317

Wills begins "by addressing centuries of misconceptions. Though his admiration for the saint is occasionally tainted by defensiveness, his account of Augustine's search for a faith and a philosophy engages our sympathy. He also conveys the turbulence of the era, when the Roman Empire was beleaguered by barbarians and the Catholic Church by heretics, and shows how Augustine's responses to the troubles of his time have shaped Christianity down to our own." New Yorker
Includes bibliographical references

270.6   Period of Reformation and Counter-Reformation, 1517-1648

MacCulloch, Diarmaid
The **Reformation**; a house divided. Viking 2004 xxiv, 792p il map $34.95; pa $18   **270.6**
1. Reformation
ISBN 0-670-03296-4; 0-14-303538-X pa

LC 2003-61607

First published 2003 in the United Kingdom
The author "has produced the definitive survey for this generation. . . . This well-written book is a joy to read, with new facts and interpretations on nearly every page." Libr J
Includes bibliographical references

271   Religious congregations and orders in church history

Butcher, Carmen Acevedo

Man of blessing; a life of St. Benedict. Paraclete Press 2006 180p map $21.95 **271**

1. Monks 2. Saints 3. Writers on religion
ISBN 1-55725-485-0; 978-1-55725-485-6

LC 2005-35827

This is the "story of the life of St. Benedict of Nursia, who founded Western monasticism in the sixth century and later became the patron saint of Europe. . . . The book's readability will make it easy for patrons to escape into late Roman culture and find peace in a monastic simplicity." Libr J

Includes bibliographical references

Johnson, Mary

An **unquenchable** thirst; Mary Johnson. Spiegel & Grau 2011 xv, 526p.p **271**

1. Nuns 2. Teachers 3. Autobiographies 4. Orators 5. Memoirists 6. Missionaries
ISBN 9780385527477; 9781588369864 (ebook); 9780385527484

LC 2010038858

This book presents a "memoir of one woman's experience in Mother Teresa's order, the Missionaries of Charity. . . . As she progressed in the order and became Sister Donata, the issues she faced became darker: a sexually predatory subordinate, theological disputes, an increasingly rigid system of rules and regulations and a love affair with a priest. Throughout the book, the author describes her interactions with Mother Teresa, but she does not try to pass off their relationship as especially close. . . . As it became increasingly clear to [Mary] Johnson that the Missionaries of Charity's vision and management were diverging from her own beliefs and values, she struggled with her place in the order and eventually made the decision to leave after two decades of service." (Kirkus)

Merton, Thomas

Intimate Merton; his life from his journals. edited by Patrick Hart and Jonathan Montaldo. HarperSanFrancisco 1999 374p il hardcover o.p. pa $16 **271**

1. Monks 2. Poets 3. Authors 4. Nonfiction writers 5. Writers on religion
ISBN 0-06-251629-9 pa

LC 99-33239

"This is a one-volume condensation of Merton's journals, which have been published over the last few years; its seven chapters correspond to the seven volumes of Merton's complete journals. . . . {The editors} have maintained all of Merton's central themes—including controversial ones, like the relationship with the nurse identified as 'M.' and Merton's doubts about his vocation." Libr J

Spink, Kathryn

Mother Teresa; a complete authorized biography. HarperSanFrancisco 1997 306p il hardcover o.p. pa $15.95 **271**

1. Nuns 2. Missionaries 3. Missions -- India 4.

Missionaries of Charity 5. Nobel laureates for peace
ISBN 0-06-251553-5 pa

LC 97-41349

"Spink's biography benefits from her own 18-year involvement with the work of the Missionaries of Charity Order as well as from the intimate relationship she developed over the years with Mother Teresa. . . . A final chapter in the book provides glimpses of Mother Teresa's affection for Princess Diana, a brief description of Mother Teresa's funeral and a short account of the election of Sister Nirmal as her successor." Publ Wkly

271.791

Haag, Michael

The **Tragedy** of the Templars; The Rise and Fall of the Crusader States. Michael Haag. HarperCollins 2013 384 p. $16.99 **271.791**

1. Crusades 2. Templars -- History
ISBN 0062059750; 9780062059758

In this book, Michael Haag provides an "account of the Crusades, including the history of the Crusader states—known as Outremer—established by the Franks after the First Crusade. He . . . examines the Crusades from both the Christian and Muslim perspectives, drawing from contemporary chronicles, church records, and correspondence by Templars. Haag covers the motivations for the Crusades, why both Muslims and Christians wanted control of the Holy Land, and how the Templars were established." (Library Journal)

272   Persecutions in general church history

Kamen, Henry

The **Spanish** Inquisition; a historical revision. Yale Univ. Press 1998 369p il $45; pa $14.80 **272**

1. Inquisition 2. Antisemitism 3. Jews -- Spain 4. Spain -- History
ISBN 0-300-07522-7; 0-300-07880-3 pa

LC 97-32451

First published 1965 in the United Kingdom; first United States edition 1966 by New Am. Lib.

In this revision of his 1965 study, the author "restates his original argument. . . . He reaffirms his contention that an all-powerful, torture-mad Inquisition is largely a 19th-century myth. In its place he portrays a poor, understaffed institution whose scattered tribunals had only a limited reach and whose methods were more humane than those of most secular courts. . . . As for the Inquisition's much-vaunted role as Big Brother and its responsibility for intellectual decline, Kamen rejects this hypothesis out of hand. . . . {He} also dismisses the notion that the Inquisition enjoyed widespread popular support." N Y Times Book Rev

Includes bibliographical references

Perez, Joseph

★ The **Spanish** Inquisition; a history. trans. by Janet Lloyd. Yale University Press 2005 248p $26; pa $17   **272**

1. Inquisition 2. Spain -- History
ISBN 0-300-10790-0; 0-300-11982-8 pa

LC 2004-114614

The author "tells the history of the Spanish Inquisition from its medieval beginnings to its nineteenth-century ending. . . . He explores the inner workings of its councils, and shows how its officers, inquisitors, and leaders lived and worked." Univ Press Books for Public and Second Sch Libr, 2006

Includes bibliographical references

275 Christianity in Asia

Liao Yiwu

God is red; the secret story of how Christianity survived and flourished in Communist China. Liao Yiwu ; translated by Wen Huang. HarperOne 2011 231 p. $25.99   **275**

1. Persecution 2. Communism -- China 3. Christianity -- China 4. China -- Church history -- 21st century 5. China -- Church history -- 20th century 6. Communism and Christianity -- China -- History -- 20th century 7. Communism and Christianity -- China -- History -- 21st century
ISBN 0062078461; 9780062078469; 9780062078483

LC 2010051154

"The author examines Christianity, which survived under China's Cultural Revolution despite attempts to eradicate it as a 'lackey of the imperialists.' . . . In an attempt to understand why a foreign religion gained such popularity, Liao interviews a wide range of Chinese Christians, from an elderly nun who witnessed both the closing and eventual reopening of her church by the Communist regime, to a missionary doctor treating impoverished villagers in lieu of working in a government-run hospital, to a dying tailor who finds meaning in his recent conversion to the faith. . . . Will appeal to both Christian and secular readers interested in the cultural realities of China's Great Leap Forward." Kirkus

277 Christianity in North America

Barth, Kelly

My almost certainly real imaginary Jesus; a memoir. Kelly Barth. Arktoi Books 2012 229 p. (alk. paper) $17.95   **277**

1. Lesbians' writings 2. Christian biography 3. Christian biography -- United States 4. Lesbians -- United States -- Biography
ISBN 0980040752; 9780980040753

LC 2012006480

Author Kelly Barth presents a memoir and discusses being Christian and gay. The book focuses on young homosexuals "venturing into the very heart of enemy territory and the church's false promises of altar calls and sexual cures. . . . Barth particularly addresses the disconnect between the radical and very human Jesus of history and the church's supernatural savior. She asks the question to all in the closet--both closet Christians and closet homosexuals: Which is more difficult, admitting to being Christian or admitting to being gay?" (Publisher's note)

Includes bibliographical references and index

Bawer, Bruce

Stealing Jesus; how fundamentalism betrays Christianity. Crown 1997 340p hardcover o.p. pa $14   **277**

1. Christianity 2. Christian fundamentalism 3. United States -- Church history
ISBN 0-609-80222-4 pa

LC 97-20111

The author "contends that fundamentalist Christianity, what he calls the 'Church of Law,' has been preaching a message of wrath and judgment to modern American culture that Bawer believes is incompatible with Jesus' message of love. . . . [His] graceful prose and lucid insights make this a must-read book for anyone concerned with the relationship of Christianity to contemporary American culture." Publ Wkly

Boyle, Gregory J.

Tattoos on the heart; the power of boundless compassion. [by] Gregory Boyle. Free Press 2010 217p $25; pa $14; ebook $11.99   **277**

1. Church work 2. Christian life
ISBN 978-1-4391-5302-4; 1-4391-5302-7; 978-1-4391-5315-4 pa; 1-4391-5315-9 pa; 978-1-4391-7177-6 ebook; 1-4391-7177-7 ebook

LC 2009-32970

"Jesuit priest Boyle recounts his two decades of working with 'homies' in Los Angeles County, which contains 1,100 gangs with nearly 86,000 members. Boyle's Homeboy Industries is the largest gang intervention program in the country, offering job training, tattoo removal, and employment to members of enemy gangs." Publ Wkly

Dochuk, Darren

From Bible belt to sunbelt; plain-folk religion, grassroots politics, and the rise of evangelical conservatism. W.W. Norton 2011 520p il   **277**

1. Conservatism 2. Evangelicalism 3. California 4. Evangelicalism -- Southern California 5. Christianity and politics -- Evangelicalism 6. California -- Church history -- 20th century 7. Conservatism -- Religious aspects -- Christianity -- History -- 20th century
ISBN 0393066827; 9780393066821

LC 2010032740

"A five-decade history of the evangelical movement in southern California [argues that] . . . the influx of migrants from the Bible Belt during the Great Depression ultimately led to the rise of the New Right and modern conservatism in the late twentieth century." (Publisher's note) Bibliography. Index.

"Well-written and documented, a supremely helpful guide in sorting out how we arrived at that odd state of affairs." Kirkus

Includes bibliographical references and index

Luhrmann, T. M. (Tanya M.), 1959-

When God talks back; understanding the American evangelical relationship with God. by T.M. Luhrmann. Alfred A. Knopf 2012 464 p. **277**
1. Prayer 2. God -- Christianity 3. Psychology of religion 4. Evangelicalism -- United States 5. United States -- Church history 6. Evangelicalism -- Psychology -- Case studies 7. Vineyard Christian Fellowship -- Case studies
ISBN 9780307264794

LC 2011040116

The book provides an "analysis of evangelical communities in America. [Author T. M.] Luhrmann . . . entered the Vineyard Christian Fellowship openly . . . and she was both welcome and eventually somewhat transformed. . . . She sketches the history of the Vineyard. . . . As the title suggests, the author devotes much of her discussion to the conversation between believers and their God, a conversation facilitated by specific techniques of prayer." (Kirkus Reviews)
Includes bibliographical references and index

Marty, Martin E.

Pilgrims in their own land; 500 years of religion in America. Penguin Books 1985 500p il pa $18 **277**
1. United States -- Religion 2. United States -- Church history
ISBN 0-14-008268-9; 978-0-14-008268-5

LC 85-3596

First published 1984 by Little, Brown
This book examines "the force of religion in the United States since colonial times. Marty considers not only the religious beliefs and rituals brought to America by the various European settlers, but also those of native Americans. The clashes between Protestant, Catholic, Judaic, and other religious groups are perceived in light of their influence upon the development of this nation up to the present." Booklist
Includes bibliographical references

280 Denominations and sects of Christian church

Atwood, Craig D.

★ **Handbook** of denominations in the United States; [by] Craig D. Atwood, Frank S. Mead, Samuel S. Hill. 13th ed.; Abingdon Press 2010 416p il $24 **280**
1. Sects 2. United States -- Religion
ISBN 978-1-4267-0048-4; 1-4267-0048-2

LC 2010-07092

First published 1951. Periodically revised
"History and present structure of Christian religious bodies in the United States. Reports on doctrines of different churches. Includes bibliography and index." NY Public Libr Book of How & Where to Look It Up
Includes bibliographical references

★ The **encyclopedia** of Protestantism; Hans Hillerbrand, editor. Routledge 2004 4v set $695 **280**
1. Reference books 2. Protestantism -- Encyclopedias
ISBN 0-415-92472-3

LC 2003-11582

"Nearly 500 contributors provide descriptions and explanations of matters of theology, culture, eminent lives, material artifacts, and comparative religions; the A-to-Z entries range from 'Apocalypticism' to 'Latin America,' 'Pilgrim's Progress,' and 'Women Clergy.' . . . [This work] is an excellent resource to engage in the exploration of humanities, policy issues, and concerns beyond the specifically religious while also providing deep analyses of theological matters." Libr J
Includes bibliographical references

282 Roman Catholic Church

★ **2013** Our Sunday Visitor Catholic almanac; edited by Gregory Erlandson and Matthew E. Bunson. Our Sunday Visitor Pub. Division 2012 640 p. (paperback) $32.95 **282**
1. Almanacs 2. Catholic Church
ISBN 1612786073; 9781612786070

This almanac is an "annual, comprehensive guide to the Catholic Church." The book "is arranged by subject, providing . . . information on the year in review, doctrine of the Catholic Church, dates and events in Catholic history, and the life of the Church in the world." Topics include canon law, a glossary of Catholic terms, the church calendar, scripture, saints, sacraments, and church history. (Publisher's note)

Allen, John L., 1965-

The **Catholic** church; what everyone needs to know. by John L. Allen. Oxford University Press 2013 298 p. (What Everyone Needs to Know) $16.95 **282**
1. Catholic Church -- History 2. Catholic Church -- Doctrines
ISBN 0199975108; 9780199975105; 9780199975112

LC 2012038594

In this book, author John L. Allen, Jr, "one of the world's leading authorities on the Vatican, offers an authoritative and accessible guide to the past, present, and future of the Church. The Catholic Church remains by far the largest branch of the worldwide Christian family, and is growing at a remarkable clip. Yet the Church has also been rocked by a series of scandals related to the sexual abuse of minors by clergy, and, even more devastating, the cover-up by the Church hierarchy." (Publisher's note)

Buckley, William F. (William Frank), 1925-2008

Nearer, my God; an autobiography of faith. Harcourt Brace & Co. 1998 xx, 313p il pa $14 **282**
1. Authors 2. Novelists 3. Columnists 4. Magazine editors
ISBN 0-15-600618-9

LC 98-16194

First published 1997 by Doubleday
"As we might expect, Nearer My God is rich in anecdote, witty, and animated by what Buckley refers to as his 'polemical inclinations.'. . . But what gives it unity as a book, and not just a loose collection of pieces bound in cloth, is the warmth and the depth of Buckley's faith, at once complex and many-sided." Christ Today

Buttiglione, Rocco
Karol Wojtyla; the thought of the man who became Pope John Paul II. translated by Paolo Guietti and Francesca Murphy. Eerdmans 1997 384p $35 **282**
1. Popes
ISBN 0-8028-3848-0
LC 97-23188
Original Italian edition, 1982
The author traces the Pope's "intellectual development, offering a critique of his literary works and a detailed analysis of how he was influenced by Thomism and phenomenology, which he sought to reconcile while emphasizing individual freedom of conscience. . . . Recommended for general collections for its broad sweep complementary to other biographies on the pope." Libr J

Carroll, James
Toward a new Catholic Church; the promise of reform. Houghton Mifflin 2002 130p pa $8.95 **282**
1. Catholic Church
ISBN 0-618-31337-0
LC 2002-27262
The author "has a reform agenda . . . consisting of five proposals: expand the faithful's biblical literacy in sophistication and depth; purge the church's political pretensions and behavior; reformulate Christology to emphasize Jesus as revelator rather than savior; run the church democratically; and repent of anti-Semitism, sexism, homophobia, and other ills by admitting the church has sinned. . . . An important statement." Booklist
Includes bibliographical references

Collins, Paul
The modern Inquisition; seven prominent Catholics and their struggles with the Vatican. Overlook Press 2002 260p $29.95 **282**
1. Catholic Church
ISBN 1-58567-270-X
LC 2002-25223
This work is an "assessment of the Roman Catholic Church's treatment of its theologians who reflect contrary views from those of the Congregation for the Doctrine of the Faith (CDF). . . . In eight passionately written essays, {Collins} considers the lives, work, and trials of several priests and sisters whose ideas were reviewed by the CDF. . . . Among them Hans Kung, Lavinia Byrne, Charles Curran, Jeannine Gramick and Robert Nugent, Tissa Balusaria, and the author himself." Libr J
Includes bibliographical references

Duffy, Eamon
Saints & sinners; a history of the popes. 3rd ed.; Yale Nota Bene/Yale University Press 2006 474p il pa $22 **282**
1. Papacy 2. Catholic Church -- History
ISBN 978-0-300-11597-0
First published 1997
This illustrated volume is a companion piece to a six-part television series of the same name. The book offers an overview of the 2,000-year history of the papacy.
Includes bibliographical references

Gillis, Chester
Roman Catholicism in America. Columbia Univ. Press 1999 365p il (Columbia contemporary American religion series) $60; pa $20.50 **282**
1. United States -- Church history 2. Catholic Church -- United States
ISBN 0-231-10870-2; 0-231-10871-0 pa
LC 99-17945
This is "an excellent survey." Libr J
Includes bibliographical references

Guiley, Rosemary Ellen
The encyclopedia of saints. Facts on File 2001 419p il $82.50; pa $24.95 **282**
1. Reference books 2. Christian saints -- Dictionaries
ISBN 0-8160-4133-4; 0-8160-4134-2 pa
LC 00-69176
This volume offers "accounts of the lives and experiences of more than 400 principal saints, from early martyrs such as Lucy of Syracuse to recently canonized saints such as Katherine Drexel. Entries provide a biographical overview, a record of the saint's religious journeys and mystical experiences, a discussion of personal philosophies and important theological influences, as well as his or her patronage, feast days and popular role within the Church." Publisher's note

The HarperCollins encyclopedia of Catholicism; general editor, Richard P. McBrien; associate editors, Harold W. Attridge {et al.} HarperSanFrancisco 1995 xxxviii, 1349p il maps $47.50 **282**
1. Reference books 2. Catholic Church -- Encyclopedias
ISBN 0-06-065338-8
LC 94-39972
"This encyclopedic dictionary contains 4700 entries by 277 experts. . . . Broad-ranging topics in Catholic theology, history, culture, art, canon law, literature, etc., are replete with cross references, photos, maps, tables, diagrams, and charts." Libr J

John Paul
Crossing the threshold of hope; edited by Vittorio Messori. Knopf 1994 244p hardcover o.p. pa $15 **282**
1. Faith 2. Apologetics 3. Christian life 4. Catholic Church
ISBN 0-679-76561-1 pa
LC 94-78675
In this book the Pope responds to written questions by an Italian Catholic journalist originally planned for a television interview which never took place. The questions addressed include: what is the papacy?; when and how should one pray?; is there proof of God's existence?; is Jesus the Son of God?; why is there so much evil in the world?; why does God tolerate suffering?; is only Rome right?; and what are human rights?
"This is a book to be read for insights, perspectives, connections, formulations that spark meditation and enrich our understanding." Commonweal

Kung, Hans

The **Catholic** Church; a short history. translated by John Bowden. Modern Lib. 2001 xxv, 221p (Modern Library chronicles) $19.95; pa $9.95 **282**
1. Catholic Church
ISBN 0-679-64092-4; 0-8129-6762-3 pa
LC 00-67568

The author "presents a summary of the major persons and movements that have formed the Catholic Church from its beginnings to the present." Libr J

"About as good a brief presentation of the 'liberal' view of church history as anyone could reasonably expect." Booklist

Maxwell-Stuart, P. G.

Chronicle of the popes; the reign-by-reign record of the papacy from St. Peter to the present. Thames & Hudson 1997 240p il maps $34.95 **282**
1. Papacy 2. Catholic Church -- History
ISBN 0-500-01798-0
LC 97-60230

This survey examines the lives and deeds of the 264 popes from St. Peter to John Paul II

This history of the papacy "provides a good selection of illustrations with a lightweight text." N Y Times Book Rev
Includes bibliographical references

Medwick, Cathleen

Teresa of Avila; the progress of a soul. Knopf 1999 282p hardcover o.p. pa $12.95 **282**
1. Nuns 2. Saints 3. Authors 4. Christian saints 5. Mystics 6. Memoirists 7. Writers on religion
ISBN 0-385-50129-3 pa
LC 99-18921

In this biography of the sixteenth-century Spanish nun, "Medwick traces Teresa's early years, her entrance into the genteel life of the Convent of the Incarnation in Avila, her second conversion as a person of prayer, and her subsequent trials as a founder of reformed monasteries of women under the austere rule of Mount Carmel." Commonweal
Includes bibliographical references

★ **New** Catholic encyclopedia; prepared by an editorial staff at the Catholic University of America. 2nd ed; Gale Group 2003 15v il maps set $1,981 **282**
1. Reference books 2. Catholic Church -- Encyclopedias
ISBN 978-0-7876-4004-0; 0-7876-4004-2
LC 2002-924

First published 1967 as an update to the Catholic encyclopedia. Kept up-to-date by yearly supplements

This encyclopedia "covers the history of the eastern churches, the churches of the Protestant Reformation, and other ecclesial communities as well as the Christian roots based in ancient Israel and Judaism. No comprehensive resource on Catholicism can be complete without touching on other world religions as well, including Islam, Buddhism, and Hinduism. This resource provides entries not only on the doctrine, organization, and history of the church, but also on the people, institutions, and social changes that have affected the church over the years. Arranged alphabetically, the entries run in length from half a page to several pages

in length. All entries provide the name of the contributor and a bibliography. Cross-references to related articles are located throughout the work. Adding to the usefulness of the set are more than 3,000 black-and-white photographs, maps, and charts that complement the scholarly articles." Am Ref Books Annu, 2003

★ The **Official** Catholic directory 2008. National Register Pub. 2008 2109p $335 **282**
1. Reference books 2. Catholic Church -- Directories
ISBN 978-0-87217-550-1; 0-87217-550-1
Annual. First published 1886. Title and publisher vary

"Contains a large amount of useful and detailed directory, institutional, and statistical information about the organization, clergy, churches, missions, schools, religious orders, etc., of the Catholic church in the U.S. and its possessions. Coverage varies." Guide to Ref Books. 11th edition

Steinfels, Peter

A **people** adrift; the crisis of the Roman Catholic Church in America. Simon & Schuster 2003 xxi, 392p hardcover o.p. pa $15 **282**
1. Catholic Church -- United States
ISBN 0-684-83663-7; 0-7432-6144-5 pa
LC 2003-54208

"Steinfels sounds a call for a reasoned common ground that respects the richness of tradition and also reflects the reality of the practices and needs of more than 60 million American Catholics, rather than the agendas of any number of the small but vocal groups within Catholicism. This book will be hailed by many, and with good reason." Publ Wkly
Includes bibliographical references

Wills, Garry, 1934-

Why I am a Catholic. Houghton Mifflin 2002 390p $26; pa $14 **282**
1. Papacy 2. Catholic Church
ISBN 0-618-13429-8; 0-618-38048-5 pa
LC 2002-283644

The author "begins with a very personal, though brief, look at his life as a Catholic, which includes time spent as a Jesuit novice, then proceeds with a detailed defense of his views on the church and its papacy. He concludes with an explanation of the Apostles' Creed, which he regards as the true foundation of his faith." Publ Wkly
Includes bibliographical references

282.03   Roman Catholic Church--dictionaries

Collinge, William J.

★ **Historical** dictionary of Catholicism; William J. Collinge. 2nd ed. Scarecrow Press 2012 xxvii, 593 p.p (hardcover : alk. paper) $95 **282.03**
1. Church history -- Dictionaries 2. Catholic Church -- Dictionaries
ISBN 0810857553; 9780810857551; 9780810879799
LC 2011035077

Author William J. Collinge discusses "theology, doctrines, and worship of the religion [in his book]. He covers the entire Catholic tradition from the time of Jesus to the present, including the periods before the present division of

Christianity into Roman Catholic, Eastern Orthodox, and Protestant. Collinge has also included entries on heretical, schismatic, and dissident movements within Catholicism, and he covers the relation of Catholicism to other Christian traditions, to the major non-Christian religions, and to Western cultural and philosophical traditions." (Publisher's note)

Includes bibliographical references (p. 507-586) and index.

283   Anglican churches

Winner, Lauren F.

Still; Lauren F. Winner. HarperOne 2012 256p. **283**

1. Faith 2. Divorce 3. Bereavement 4. Depression (Psychology)

ISBN 978-0-06-176811-8; 9780061768118

LC 2011017200

In this book, "the author explores her emotional landscape as she struggles to move beyond the depression that plagues her following her mother's death and her own divorce. [She e]xamin[es] feelings of grief, failure, and doubt that she never expected to encounter after her conversion from Judaism to Christianity. . . . Narrative accounts of visiting her mother's grave; 'the failed cool-professor moment;' infiltrating a synagogue, in costume, to participate in Purim; and a church visit that results in her holding hands with 'one of the people from whom Jesus would have cast a demon' all provide a . . . window into a seeker trying to find equilibrium in a stage of faith and life that is neither beginning nor end, but, she fears, 'an extended sojourn into the spiritual equivalent of middle school.'" (Publishers Weekly)

286   Baptist, Restoration movement, Adventist churches

Zichterman, Jocelyn R.

I fired God; my life inside--and escape from--the secret world of the independent fundamental Baptist cult. Jocelyn Zichterman. St. Martin's Press 2013 293 p. (hardcover) $25.99 **286**

1. Christian fundamentalism 2. Independent Fundamental Churches of America 3. Abused children -- Religious life 4. Baptists -- Controversial literature 5. Baptists -- United States -- Biography 6. Psychological abuse victims -- Religious life 7. Psychological abuse -- Religious aspects -- Christianity

ISBN 1250026261; 9781250026262

LC 2012042119

Author Jocelyn R. Zichterman was "raised in the secret world of the Independent Fundamental Baptist (IFB) church." Here, she "aims here to shed light on a faith that is largely unknown in mainstream America although it has hundreds of thousands of followers. The IFB movement grew out of the Doctrine of Separation conceptualized by Bob Jones . . . , teaching believers to separate from other faiths, including other Christian sects, to avoid being secularized and compromising the true faith." (Library Journal)

Includes bibliographical references (pages [279]-293)

287   Methodist churches; churches related to Methodism

Shaver, Lisa J.

Beyond the pulpit; women's rhetorical roles in the antebellum religious press. Lisa J. Shaver. University of Pittsburgh Press 2012 x, 169 p.p (pbk. : alk. paper) $24.95 **287**

1. Periodicals 2. Methodist Church 3. Women -- Religious life 4. Women -- United States -- History 5. United States -- Church history -- 19th century 6. Women and journalism -- United States -- History -- 19th century 7. Women in the Methodist Church -- United States -- History -- 19th century 8. Methodist Church -- United States -- Periodicals -- History -- 19th century 9. Methodist women -- Press coverage -- United States -- History -- 19th century 10. Methodist women -- Religious life -- United States -- History -- 19th century

ISBN 0822961695; 9780822961697

LC 2011039632

This book, by Lisa J. Shaver, examines the history of Methodist women. "In the formative years of the Methodist Church in the United States, women played significant roles. . . . Although women's participation helped the church to become the nation's largest denomination by the mid-nineteenth century, their official roles diminished during that time. . . . Shaver examines Methodist periodicals as a rhetorical space to which women turned to find, and make, self-meaning." (Publisher's note)

Includes bibliographical references and index.

Tomkins, Stephen

★ **John** Wesley; a biography. Eerdmans 2003 208p pa $20 **287**

1. Theologians 2. Methodist Church 3. Evangelists 4. Writers on religion

ISBN 0-8028-2499-4

LC 2003-54328

In this biography of the founder of the Methodist religion "Tomkins presents a keenly engaging portrait of a great man full of contradictoriness. Wesley insisted he was loyal to the Church of England yet consented to his followers setting up establishments and engaging in practices that flouted Anglican authority. . . . He altered the face of Christianity in the West by inspiring modern evangelicalism and Pentecostalism. A fascinating figure, fascinatingly limned." Booklist

Includes bibliographical references

289   Other denominations and sects

Stein, Stephen J.

The **Shaker** experience in America; a history of the United Society of Believers. Yale Univ. Press 1992 xx, 554p il $65; pa $21 **289**

1. Shakers

ISBN 0-300-05139-5; 0-300-05933-7 pa

LC 91-30836

A historical look at the evolution of Shakerism focusing on the movement's cultural values, religion and artifacts

Includes bibliographical references

289.3   Latter-Day Saints (Mormons)

Abanes, Richard

★ **One** nation under gods; a history of the Mormon Church. Four Walls Eight Windows 2002 xxv, 651p il $32; pa $22   **289.3**

1. Church of Jesus Christ of Latter-day Saints
ISBN 1-56858-219-6; 1-56858-283-8 pa

LC 2001-40430

The author "explains what Mormons believe, as well as how Mormonism came to be the religion that it is today. . . . [He also discusses the] origins of Mormonism, the socioeconomic factors that contributed to its growth, its ongoing political agenda, and its religious teachings." Publisher's note

"This well-researched and readable history will be of interest to anyone seeking an objective Mormon history." Libr J

Includes bibliographical references

Beam, Alex

American crucifixion; the murder of Joseph Smith and the fate of the Mormon church. Alex Beam. PublicAffairs 2014 352 p. illustrations, maps (hardcover) $26.99   **289.3**

1. Mormons 2. Church of Jesus Christ of Latter-day Saints -- History
ISBN 1610393139; 9781610393133; 9781610393140

LC 2014004063

This book, by Alex Beam, focuses on "founding prophet of Mormonism, Joseph Smith. . . . Beam tells how Smith went from charismatic leader to public enemy: How his most seismic revelation--the doctrine of polygamy--created a rift among his people; how that schism turned to violence; and how, ultimately, Smith could not escape the consequences of his ambition and pride . . . Smith's brutal assassination propelled the Mormons to colonize the American West." (Publisher's note)

"Beam offers a captivating saga of Smith's rise and fall and of a colorful cast of characters who contributed to the internal politics and rivalries that led to Smith's death and drove the Mormons forward to their destiny." Booklist

Includes bibliographical references and index

Book of Mormon

★ The **Book** of Mormon; another testament of Jesus Christ. [translated by Joseph Smith, Jr.] Doubleday 2004 586p $24.95   **289.3**

1. Mormons 2. Church of Jesus Christ of Latter-day Saints
ISBN 0-385-51316-X

LC 2004-51982

First published 1830

"Based on golden plates which Joseph Smith claimed were revealed to him, and which he unearthed from Cumorah Hill, New York, this book is roughly similar in structure to the Bible. . . . Emphasized are the doctrines of pre-existence, perfection, the afterlife, and Christ's second coming." Haydn. Thesaurus of Book Dig

Bushman, Richard L.

Joseph Smith and the beginnings of Mormonism. University of Ill. Press 1984 262p maps hardcover o.p. pa $16.95   **289.3**

1. Church of Jesus Christ of Latter-day Saints 2. Mormon leaders
ISBN 0-252-06012-1 pa

LC 84-2451

The author surveys the historical background of the Mormon church with particular emphasis on the spiritual growth of its founder, Joseph Smith

"Resulting from many years of careful research and reflections, this book will stand for decades as a major contribution in the field." Choice

Includes bibliographical references

Mormonism; a very short introduction. [by] Richard Lyman Bushman. Oxford University Press 2008 130p il (Very short introductions) pa $11.95   **289.3**

1. Church of Jesus Christ of Latter-day Saints
ISBN 978-0-19-531030-6

LC 2007-44444

This book "explains who Mormons are: what they believe and how they live their lives . . . [and] ranges from the history of the Church of Jesus Christ of Latter-day Saints to the contentious issues of contemporary Mormonism." Publisher's note

This is an "outstanding, reliable overview of Mormon history and beliefs." Libr J

Includes bibliographical references (p. 121-123)

Givens, Terryl

By the hand of Mormon; the American scripture that launched a new world religion. [by] Terryl L. Givens. Oxford Univ. Press 2002 230p il maps hardcover o.p. pa $16.95   **289.3**

1. Book of Mormon
ISBN 0-19-513818-X; 0-19-516888-7 pa

LC 2001-53118

The author "investigates the history and theology of the Book of Mormon, which he calls 'perhaps the most religiously influential, hotly contested, and, in the secular press at least, intellectually under-investigated book in America.' Givens persuasively demonstrates how the Book of Mormon was trumpeted by early Latter-day Saints more for the fact of its existence . . . than for its content per se." Publ Wkly

Includes bibliographical references

Gutjahr, Paul C.

The **Book** of Mormon; a biography. Paul C. Gutjahr. Princeton University Press 2012 xix, 255 p.p   **289.3**

1. Mormons 2. Sacred books 3. Church of Jesus Christ of Latter-day Saints -- History 4. Book of Mormon -- History 5. Book of Mormon -- Criticism, interpretation, etc
ISBN 9780691144801

LC 2011044063

This book presents a history of the Book of Mormon. "[Paul C.] Gutjahr recounts the life of Joseph Smith, whose status as the prophet of the Church of Jesus Christ of Latter-Day Saints rests upon his claim that he translated the Book of Mormon from ancient gold plates delivered to him by an angel.

. . . Undeterred by skeptics' allegations of fraud, a small army of missionaries have made the book a powerful proselytizing tool, attracting millions . . . to their faith." (Booklist)

Includes bibliographical references (pages 209-246) and index

Hardy, Grant

★ **Understanding** the Book of Mormon; a reader's guide. Oxford University Press 2010 336p $29.95   **289.3**

1. Book of Mormon -- Criticism
ISBN 978-0-19-973170-1

       LC 2009-26675

In this analysis of the Book of Mormon's narrative structure, the author describes the work's "characters, events, and ideas, as he explores the story and its messages. He identifies the book's literary techniques, such as characterization, embedded documents, allusions, and parallel narratives." Publisher's note

Includes bibliographical references

Krakauer, Jon

Under the banner of heaven; a story of violent faith. Doubleday 2003 xxxii, 665p map $26; pa $14.95   **289.3**

1. Church of Jesus Christ of Latter-day Saints
ISBN 0-385-50951-0; 1-4000-3280-6 pa

       LC 2003-43824

"In 1984, Brenda Lafferty and her baby daughter Erica were found murdered in their Utah home, victims of a 'removal revelation' that her Mormon brother-in-law had supposedly received from God. Krakauer . . . aims to explain why and how this crime happened by recounting the history of Mormonism from its conception by Joseph Smith in the 19th century and tracing the origins of its extremist sects through to the present day." Libr J

Includes bibliographical references

Ostling, Richard N.

Mormon America; the power and the promise. [by] Richard N. Ostling and Joan K. Ostling. Rev. ed.; HarperOne 2007 xxvi, 469p il map pa $17.95 **289.3**

1. Church of Jesus Christ of Latter-day Saints
ISBN 978-0-06-143295-8

       LC 2008-275419

First published 1999

"This thorough, thoughtful treatment of LDS beliefs and practices, written by non-Mormons, is a boon to members and interested lay readers alike." Libr J

Includes bibliographical references

289.5   Church of Christ, Scientist (Christian Science)

Eddy, Mary Baker

★ **Science** and health, with key to the Scriptures; Trustees under the will of Mary Baker G. Eddy. Christian Science Pub. Soc. 2000 pa $9.95   **289.5**

1. Christian Science
ISBN 978-0-87952-259-9; 0-87952-259-3

First published 1875

This work is the foundation of the Christian Science religion, setting forth Mrs. Baker's interpretations of the Holy Scriptures and the method of healing. It has not been revised since her death in 1910.

Fraser, Caroline

God's perfect child; living and dying in the Christian Science Church. Metropolitan Bks. 1999 561p il hardcover o.p. pa $16   **289.5**

1. Christian Science 2. Writers on religion 3. Christian Science leaders
ISBN 0-8050-4431-0 pa

       LC 99-17535

This "history traces the roots of the Christian Science church to nineteenth-century Calvinism, Emersonian self-reliance, and the remarkable life of its grandiose, anxiety-ridden founder, Mary Baker Eddy. . . . A work of compelling skepticism and scholarship." New Yorker

Includes bibliographical references

Gill, Gillian

Mary Baker Eddy. Perseus Bks. 1998 xxxv, 713p il hardcover o.p. pa $24   **289.5**

1. Christian Science 2. Writers on religion 3. Christian Science leaders
ISBN 0-7382-0227-4 pa

       LC 98-86397

This "biography of Christian Science's founder offers detailed depictions of her early years of obscurity, her multiple marriages, the controversies she endured, and the inspiration that sustained her." Libr J

Includes bibliographical references

Schoepflin, Rennie B.

Christian Science on trial; religious healing in America. Johns Hopkins Univ. Press 2002 301p il (Medicine, science, and religion in historical context) $39.95   **289.5**

1. Christian Science
ISBN 0-8018-7057-7

       LC 2001-8512

"A historical examination of Christian Science's evolution during the late 19th and early 20th centuries and the faith's struggle for existence and respectability in the midst of organized American medicine's efforts to curtail its influence." Libr J

Includes bibliographical references and index

289.6   Society of Friends (Quakers)

Hamm, Thomas D.

★ The **Quakers** in America. Columbia Univ. Press 2003 293p il (Columbia contemporary American religion series) $48.50; pa $27   **289.6**

1. Society of Friends
ISBN 0-231-12362-0; 0-231-12363-9 pa

       LC 2002-41422

The author provides an "introduction to Quaker origins abroad, their influences on American politics and culture, as well as their beliefs and traditions as they are played out on American soil. Though this is a serious history with a glossary, chronology, and 40 pages of notes, cartoons and anecdotes leaven the text. For both public and academic libraries." Libr J

Includes bibliographical references

289.7 Mennonite churches

Hostetler, John A.

Amish society; 4th ed; Johns Hopkins Univ. Press 1993 435p il maps hardcover o.p. pa $20   **289.7**
1. Amish
ISBN 0-8018-4441-X; 0-8018-4442-8

LC 92-19304

First published 1963
This book discusses the sectarian origins of the Amish, immigration history, family and community life, population trends, farming practices, technological innovations, education, medicine and the effects of government regulation.

Includes bibliographical references

Kraybill, Donald B.

Concise encyclopedia of Amish, Brethren, Hutterites, and Mennonites; Donald B. Kraybill. Johns Hopkins University Press 2010 302p ill., maps   **289.7**
1. Amish 2. Mennonites 3. Hutterian Brethren
ISBN 9780801896576; 0801896576

LC 2009046015

In this book author "[Donald B.] Kraybill [provides an] . . . overview of the beliefs and cultural practices of Amish, Brethren, Hutterites, and Mennonites in North America. Found throughout Canada, Central America, Mexico, and the United States, these religious communities include more than 200 different groups with 800,000 members in 17 countries. Through 340 short entries, Kraybill offers readers information on a wide range of topics related to religious views and social practices. With . . . consideration of how these diverse communities are related, this compact reference provides a . . . synopsis of these groups in the twenty-first century." (Publisher's note)

Includes bibliographical references   (p. 259-285) and index.

★ **On** the backroad to heaven; Old Order Hutterites, Mennonites, Amish, and Brethren. {by} Donald B. Kraybill, Carl F. Bowman. Johns Hopkins Univ. Press 2001 330p il maps (Center books in Anabaptist studies) $57; pa $16.95   **289.7**
1. Amish 2. Mennonites 3. Hutterian Brethren
ISBN 0-8018-6565-4; 0-8018-7089-5 pa

LC 00-10406

"This look at the history, similarities and differences between four groups of Old Order faithful in North America—Hutterites, Mennonites, Amish and Brethren—is fasci-

nating. . . . A book that, in one volume, tackles history, sociology and future trends—and does it well." Christ Century

Includes bibliographical references

The riddle of Amish culture; rev ed; Johns Hopkins Univ. Press 2001 397p il maps (Center books in Anabaptist studies) $65; pa $16.95   **289.7**
1. Amish
ISBN 0-8018-6771-1; 0-8018-6772-X pa

LC 00-13054

First published 1989
The author examines the history and culture of the Amish, discussing such topics as the social structure of Amish society, rites of redemption and purification, recreation and social gatherings, work, technology, public relations, and social change

Includes bibliographical references and index

Mackall, Joe

Plain secrets; an outsider among the Amish. Beacon Press 2007 xxxiv, 208p $24.95; pa $13   **289.7**
1. Amish
ISBN 0-80701-064-2; 978-0-80701-064-8; 0-80701-065-0 pa; 978-0-80701-065-5 pa

LC 2007-924329

"This is a loving portrait, warts and all, of an often-misunderstood people." Booklist

Includes bibliographical references

289.9 Denominations and sects not provided for elsewhere

Holden, Andrew

★ **Jehovah's** Witnesses; portrait of a contemporary religious movement. Routledge 2002 206p $80; pa $23.95   **289.9**
1. Jehovah's Witnesses
ISBN 0-415-26609-2; 0-415-26610-6 pa

LC 2001-45726

"This ethnographic study, academic in tone and British in orientation, offers several chapters of general information about the faith and analyzes its relationship to the wider society." Libr J

Includes bibliographical references

292 Classical religion (Greek and Roman religion)

Graves, Robert

★ The **Greek** myths; Combined ed; Penguin Books 1992 782p pa $19.95   **292**
1. Classical mythology
ISBN 0-14-017199-1
First published 1955
A collection of the author's interpretations of Greek myths based on anthropological and archaeological findings

★ The **Oxford** dictionary of classical myth and religion; edited by Simon Price and Emily Kearns. Oxford University Press 2003 599p maps $39.95; pa $17.95 **292**

1. Reference books 2. Classical mythology -- Dictionaries

ISBN 0-19-280288-7; 0-19-280289-5 pa

LC 2004-298013

"Instead of separating mythology and Judeo-Christian religion into separate references, this work covers all religious life in the ancient Greco-Roman world. The result is a generally accessible and academically current compendium of information on gods and holy beings, religious practices, festivals, sacred sites, myths, authors, and texts of the period. The reader will find not only Athena and Zeus but also Jesus Christ and St. Augustine, Mani and Zoroaster." Libr J

294   Religions of Indic origin

Dalrymple, William

Nine lives; in search of the sacred in modern India. A.A. Knopf 2010 275p il map $26.95 **294**

1. India -- Religion

ISBN 978-0-307-27282-9; 0-307-27282-6

LC 2010-06362

First published 2009 in the United Kingdom

"Throughout the book, Dalrymple showcases his knowledge of the breadth of India and his fearless willingness to penetrate its sometimes unsavory nooks and crannies, rendering this a truly heartfelt work for readers craving a deeper connection to India and its rich spiritual heritage. A remarkable feat of journalism." Kirkus

Includes bibliographical references

Iyengar, B. K. S.

Light on life; the yoga journey to wholeness, inner peace, and ultimate freedom. [by] B.K.S. Iyengar, with John J. Evans and Douglas Abrams. Rodale 2005 xxii, 282p il $24.95; pa $15.95 **294**

1. Yoga

ISBN 1-59486-248-6; 978-1-59486-248-9; 1-59486-524-8 pa

LC 2005-15700

The author "expounds the philosophy of yoga—its metaphysics, of which yoga poses, or asanas, represent the physical component. . . . Not the book with which to begin the yoga journey, it is highly recommended for those advanced on the path and interested in learning from a master of flexibility and wisdom." Publ Wkly

294.3   Buddhism

Armstrong, Karen

Buddha. Viking 2001 xxix, 205p map (Penguin lives series) hardcover o.p. pa $13 **294.3**

1. Philosophers 2. Buddhist leaders

ISBN 0-670-89193-2; 0-14-303436-7 pa

LC 00-43808

"Armstrong interprets the mythologized story of the Buddha's abandonment of his life of comfort and privilege; commitment to practicing advanced forms of yoga and near-

ly fatal asceticism; enlightenment beneath a bodhi tree; and 45 years of wandering and teaching until his death in 483. And as she does so, she lucidly explains his revelations and influence." Booklist

Includes bibliographical references

Bernstein, Richard

Ultimate journey; retracing the path of an ancient Buddhist monk who crossed Asia in search of enlightenment. Knopf 2001 352p il maps hardcover o.p. pa $14 **294.3**

1. Buddhism 2. Buddhist monks

ISBN 0-679-78157-9 pa

LC 2001-267521

"In 629, a Buddhist monk named Hsuan Tsang set out from China, crossing Asia in search of Buddhist truth. Bernstein . . . decided to retrace the monk's journey over the silk road to Pakistan and India and back to China. In this entertaining and well-written account, more travel literature than religious study, he juxtaposes his account of Hsuan Tsang's experiences with descriptions of his own trials." Libr J

Includes bibliographical references

Bstan-'dzin-rgya-mtsho, Dalai Lama XIV, 1935-

★ **How** to be compassionate; a handbook for creating inner peace and a happier world. [by] His Holiness the Dalai Lama; translated from oral teachings and edited by Jeffrey Hopkins. Atria Books 2011 xi, 147 p.p $14 **294.3**

1. Buddhism 2. Compassion 3. Religious life

ISBN 1451623917; 9781451623901; 9781451623925

LC 2011281813

In this book, the Tibetan Buddhist spiritual leader the Dalai Lama demonstrates that "the surest path to true happiness lies in being intimately concerned with the welfare of others," or "in compassion." (Publisher's note) The author "works . . . from the Buddhist places (awareness, nonattachment) to speak to general readers about habits that make for unhappiness (anger, for one) and the attitudes that increase contentment." (Library Journal)

"Light on politics and even lighter on the more abstruse points of Tibetan Buddhism, this is a fine and accessible book for the everyday reader." Libr J

Includes bibliographical references (p. [145]-147)

Violence and compassion; {by} the Dalai Lama and Jean-Claude Carrière. Doubleday 1996 248p hardcover o.p. pa $11.50 **294.3**

1. Buddhism

ISBN 0-385-50144-7 pa

LC 95-30694

"This book records the conversation that screenwriter Carrière . . . held with the Dalai Lama, the exiled leader of Tibetan Buddhism, in 1993. The topics covered range from exile and reincarnation to education and science." Libr J

"This is a rich and invigorating volume, full of ponderable wisdom." Booklist

Chödrön, Pema

How to meditate; a practical guide to making friends with your mind. Pema Chodron. Sounds True 2013 viii, 175 p.p $19.95   **294.3**
1. Buddhism 2. Meditation
ISBN 1604079339; 9781604079333
LC 2012046126

In this book, by Pema Chödrön, the author, an "American-born Tibetan Buddhist nun . . . , explores in-depth what she considers the essentials for an evolving practice [of meditation] that helps you live in a wholehearted way. . . . Meditation, Pema explains, gives us a golden key to address this yearning. This comprehensive guide shows readers how to honestly meet and openly relate with the mind to embrace the fullness of our experience." (Publisher's note)

"At all times Chodron is careful not to overwhelm readers or make meditation feel like an Everest expedition, and she features her own practice as an example of challenges and successes." LJ

Crane, George

Bones of the master; a Buddhist monk's search for the lost heart of China. Bantam Bks. 2000 293p il maps hardcover o.p. pa $14.95   **294.3**
1. Buddhism 2. Mongolia 3. Buddhist monks
ISBN 0-553-37908-9 pa
LC 99-37868

This is an account of the friendship between Crane and Tsung Tsai, a Buddhist monk, and their journey to Mongolia to bury the bones of the monk's teacher

"Crane chronicles their perilous and miraculous adventures, the beauty of Mongolia's wilderness of wind and sand, and Tsung Tsai's transcendent determination with uncommon clarity, wit, vitality, and love." Booklist

Johnson, Tim

Tragedy in crimson; how the Dalai Lama conquered the world but lost the battle with China. Nation Books 2011 333p map pa $26.99   **294.3**
1. Buddhist leaders 2. Political leaders 3. Nobel laureates for peace 4. China -- Politics and government 5. Tibet (China) -- Description and travel
ISBN 978-1-56858-601-4
LC 2010-37497

"A current, objective, basic primer on the Free Tibet movement and the Dalai Lama was sorely needed, and . . . [the author] has provided exactly that." Natl Rev
Includes bibliographical references

Keown, Damien

★ A **dictionary** of Buddhism; contributors, Stephen Hodge, Charles Jones, Paoli Tinti. Oxford Univ. Press 2003 357p il maps hardcover o.p. pa $15.95   **294.3**
1. Buddhism
ISBN 0-19-860560-9; 978-0-19-280062-6 pa; 0-19-280062-0 pa
LC 2003-276701

This dictionary covers Buddhist terms, biography, scriptures, important places and includes discussions of ethical issues and other matters

"The entries are short . . . but such accessibility is the very reason why this should be on the bookshelf of every student of Buddhism." Publ Wkly

Kerouac, Jack

Some of the dharma. Viking 1997 419p hardcover o.p. pa $20   **294.3**
1. Buddhism
ISBN 0-14-028707-8 pa
LC 97-12870

"Begun in December 1951 as a notebook for his Buddhist studies, this work records Kerouac's reactions to a variety of Buddhist texts. Over the course of five years, it grew to include poems, prayers, dialogs, meditations, and notes on his reading, as well as commentary on family, friends, and meaningful concerns in his life. . . . Long anticipated by Kerouac scholars, this major work belongs in all literature collections." Libr J

Olson, Carl

Historical dictionary of Buddhism. Scarecrow Press 2009 xxix, 327p il map (Historical dictionaries of religions, philosophies, and movements) $105; ebook $105   **294.3**
1. Reference books 2. Buddhism -- Dictionaries
ISBN 978-0-8108-5771-1; 0-8108-5771-5; 978-0-8108-6317-0 ebook; 0-8108-6317-0 ebook
LC 2009-7383

First published 1993 under the authorship of Charles S. Prebish

This dictionary covers "Buddhist concepts, significant figures, movements, schools, places, activities, and periods. . . . [It also features] a chronology, an introductory essay, a bibliography, and over 700 cross-referenced dictionary entries." Publisher's note
Includes bibliographical references

Sogyal

The Tibetan book of living and dying; edited by Patrick Gaffney and Andrew Harvey. rev and updated ed; HarperSanFrancisco 2002 441p il $28.95; pa $17.95   **294.3**
1. Death 2. Buddhism
ISBN 0-06-250793-1; 0-06-250834-2 pa
LC 2002-523084

First published 1992

The author "is well qualified to pass on his tradition. He does this beautifully, in limpid prose free of the scholastic list making that deadens many Tibetan Buddhist primers." N Y Times Book Rev {review of 1992 edition}
Includes bibliographical references (p. 415-418) and index

Sutin, Lawrence

★ **All** is change; the two-thousand year journey of Buddhism to the West. Little, Brown 2006 403p il $25.99   **294.3**
1. Buddhism
ISBN 978-0-316-74156-9; 0-316-74156-6
LC 2006-40824

"Greeks and Buddhists in India found common metaphysical ground 2,000 years ago, and Sutin also documents parallels between Buddist and Gnostic teachings in this vital study of a remarkable spiritual migration." Booklist

Includes bibliographical references

Suzuki, Daisetz Teitaro

★ **Manual** of Zen Buddhism. Grove Press 1960 192p il pa $13   **294.3**

1. Buddhist art 2. Zen Buddhism

ISBN 0-8021-3065-8

Fisrt published 1950 in the United Kingdom

In this volume, D. T. Suzuki has brought together some of Zen Buddhism's original sources. Included are the sutras or sermons of the Buddha: the gathas or hymns; the philosophical puzzles known as koan; and the dharanis or invocations to expel evil spirits. In addition to the written selections there are reproductions of Buddhist drawings and paintings, including religious statues found in Zen temples

Thondup, Tulku

Enlightened journey; Buddhist practice as daily life. edited by Harold Talbott. Shambhala Publs. 1995 268p pa $16.95   **294.3**

1. Buddhism

ISBN 1-57062-021-0

LC 94-36154

This is an "exposition on one of the more important sects of Tibetan Buddhism. As such, it comprises 15 talks and articles by Thondup, {a} leader and teacher of the Nyingma school of Tibetan Buddhism. His purpose here is to show how daily life can become the basis of Buddhist spiritual training, and each talk is an introduction to various aspects of Buddhism, covering such topics as meditation as a means to arouse compassion and the importance of suffering to reach enlightenment." Libr J

Includes bibliographical references

Thurman, Robert A. F.

Why the Dalai Lama matters; his act of truth as the solution for China, Tibet, and the world. [by] Robert Thurman. Beyond Words Pub. 2008 xxiv, 231p il map $23   **294.3**

1. Buddhism 2. Tibet (China) 3. Buddhist leaders 4. Political leaders 5. Nobel laureates for peace

ISBN 978-1-58270-220-9; 1-58270-220-9

LC 2008-8529

The author presents an "introduction to Buddhism and the Tibetan concept of the Dalai Lama before focusing on the current 'living embodiment of the Buddha'—a man born as Tenzin Gyatso—the 14th Dalai Lama. Thurman sympathetically renders his lifelong friend as a 'simple Buddhist monk,' a teacher, philosopher, scientist and the political representative of the Tibetan people. . . . The book concludes with a five-step plan to broker peace between Tibet and China—an agenda simultaneously pragmatic and idealistic, demonstrating truly the talent and power of faith." Publ Wkly

Includes bibliographical references

Watts, Alan

The **way** of Zen. Vintage Books 1999 236p il pa $13.95   **294.3**

1. Zen Buddhism

ISBN 0-375-70510-4

First published 1957 by Pantheon Bks.

This is an historical and cultural survey of Zen, tracing its origins in Indian and Chinese thought. The author describes the Zen way of living and its techniques for overcoming the mind's conflict between symbolic thought and actual experience.

Includes bibliographical references

294.5   Hinduism

Doniger, Wendy

On Hinduism; Wendy Doniger. Oxford University Press, USA 2014 680 p. (hardback : alk. paper) $39.95   **294.5**

1. Hinduism

ISBN 0199360073; 9780199360079

LC 2013038952

Includes bibliographical references (pages 627-648) and index

This book of essays, by Wendy Doniger, is about Hinduism. "The essays contemplate the nature of Hinduism; Hindu concepts of divinity; attitudes concerning gender, control, and desire; the question of reality and illusion; and the impermanent and the eternal in the two great Sanskrit epics, the 'Ramayana' and the 'Mahabharata.' . . . Doniger concludes with . . . autobiographical essays in which she reflects on . . . the influence of Hinduism on her own philosophy of life." (Publisher's note)

"This book assumes some basic knowledge of the subject, but [Doniger's] writing is clear and direct and will be intelligible to readers unacquainted with the technicalities of Hindu doctrine and literature." LJ

Goldberg, Philip

American Veda; from Emerson and the Beatles to yoga and meditation: how Indian spirituality changed the West. Doubleday Religion 2010 398p il ebook $26; $26   **294.5**

1. Yoga 2. Vedanta 3. Hinduism 4. United States -- Religion

ISBN 978-0-307-71961-4 ebook; 978-0-385-52134-5

LC 2010-11040

"From meditating movie stars, scandalous gurus, and psychedelic drugs to genuine spiritual breakthroughs and devotion to helping others, Goldberg's history of 'American Veda' takes measure of a powerful, if underappreciated, force." Booklist

Includes bibliographical references

Mahabharata/Bhagavadgita

★ **Bhagavad** Gita; a new translation. [translated by] Stephen Mitchell. Harmony Bks. 2000 223p hardcover o.p. pa $13.95   **294.5**

ISBN 0-609-60550-X; 0-609-81034-0 pa

LC 00-28286

"An eighteen-part discussion between the god Krishna, an avatar of Vishnu appearing as a charioteer, and Arjuna, a warrior about to enter battle, on the nature and meaning of life. Sometimes called the New Testament of Hinduism, it is an interpolation in the great Hindu epic the Mahabharata." Reader's Ency. 4th edition

Sivananda Yoga Vedanta Center (London, England)

Yoga mind & body. DK Pub. 2008 168p il pa $15   **294.5**

1. Yoga
ISBN 978-0-7566-3674-6

LC 2008-489063

First published 1996

"This guide stresses the five points of exercise, breathing, meditation, diet, and relaxation for improved health and happiness. In addition to basic yoga poses, Yoga Mind & Body provides meditation tools, stress relief exercises, and recipes for healthful nutrition." Publisher's note

294.6   Sikhism

Singh, Patwant

The **Sikhs**. Knopf 2000 276p il hardcover o.p. pa $14   **294.6**

1. Sikhs
ISBN 0-375-40728-6; 0-385-50206-0 pa

LC 99-31807

The author "traces Sikh history from its origins in the 15th century through Indira Gandhi's 1984 storming of the Golden Temple. . . . Sikhs, he argues, have for centuries been an embattled people because their culture and religion defy the predominant religions in the region, as well as the Indian caste system with its ruling elite." Publ Wkly

Includes bibliographical references

296   Judaism

The **Cambridge** history of Judaism; v1 edited by W.D. Davies [and] Louis Finkelstein. Cambridge Univ. Press 1984 461p v1 il maps $194   **296**

1. Judaism -- History
ISBN 0-521-21880-2

LC 77-85704

"The first of . . . four volumes on the history of the Jews from the destruction of the Temple in 586 BC to the closure of the Mishnah in AD 250, the work deals not solely with Judaism . . . but with the entire material history of the Jews in the Land of Israel as well as in Babylonia and Egypt." Choice

Includes bibliographical references

Encyclopaedia Judaica; Fred Skolnik, editor-in-chief; Michael Berenbaum, executive editor. 2nd ed; Macmillan Reference USA in association with the Keter Pub. House 2007 22v il map   **296**

1. Jews 2. Judaism 3. Reference books 4. Judaism

-- Encyclopedias
ISBN 0-02-865928-7; 978-0-02-865928-2

LC 2006020426

First published 1972 in 16 volumes
ALA RUSA Dartmouth Medal (2007)

This "is a welcome addition to reference collections. By documenting the modern Jewish experience while retaining links with its rich past, it provides users with information about all aspects of Jewish religion and culture." Booklist

Includes bibliographical references

Freedman, Samuel G.

Jew vs. Jew; the struggle for the soul of American Jewry. Simon & Schuster 2000 397p $26; pa $14   **296**

1. Judaism 2. Jews -- United States
ISBN 0-684-85944-0; 0-684-85945-9 pa

LC 00-33907

The author "describes the paradoxical situation faced by today's American Jews, living in a country where religious freedom has yielded unreconcilable devisiveness. . . . This is a helpful guide for anyone seeking an understanding of intra-Jewish conflicts in contemporary America." Libr J

Includes bibliographical references

Kushner, Harold S., 1935-

To life! a celebration of Jewish being and thinking. Warner Books 1994 304p pa $14.99   **296**

1. Judaism
ISBN 0-446-67002-2; 978-0-446-67002-9

LC 94-25828

First published 1993 by Little, Brown

The author discusses the meaning of Jewish customs and ceremonies and the purpose of prayer. Antisemitism, Jewish-Christian relations, and the importance of Israel to contemporary Jews are also examined.

"This is a very easy book to read, to discuss, even to argue about, and Kushner's celebration is everything his many readers could have hoped it would be." Booklist

★ The **New** encyclopedia of Judaism; editor-in-chief, Geoffrey Wigoder; coeditors, Fred Skolnik & Shmuel Himelstein. New York Univ. Press 2002 856p il $79.95   **296**

1. Reference books 2. Judaism -- Dictionaries
ISBN 0-8147-9388-6

LC 2002-16614

First published 1989 with title: The Encyclopedia of Judaism

This reference "seeks to present a balanced picture, offering current thinking among scholars in Reform, Conservative, and Orthodox movements and a roster of contributors hailing from Israel, England, and the United States. While the scholarship is solid, the material is readily accessible to a popular audience, and the work is magnificently illustrated." Libr J

Includes bibliographical references

★ The **Oxford** dictionary of the Jewish religion; editor in chief, Adele Berlin. 2nd ed. Oxford

University Press 2011 xxiv, 934 p.p (hardcover) $195 **296**

1. Judaism -- Dictionaries 2. Judaism -- Encyclopedias
ISBN 0199730040; 9780199730049; 9780199759279
LC 2010035774

This book, by Maxine Grossman, edited by Adele Berlin, presents an updated, second edition of its original 1997 publication. It "focuses on recent and changing rituals in the Jewish community. . . . Nearly 200 internationally renowned scholars have created a new edition that incorporates updated bibliographies, biographies of 20th-century individuals who have shaped the recent thought and history of Judaism, and an index with alternate spellings of Hebrew terms." (Publisher's note)

Includes bibliographical references and index.

Reader's guide to Judaism; editor, Michael Terry. Fitzroy Dearborn Pubs. 2000 718p (Reader's guide) $135 **296**

1. Reference books 2. Judaism -- Encyclopedias
ISBN 1-57958-139-0
LC 2001-274119

This "work covers over 400 topics, including interfaith relations, historical periods, philosophical and mystical movements, important figures, and more. Preceding each essay is a bibliography of five to ten English-language titles. . . . Written by librarians and scholars . . . these 1000 to 2000-word essays include a descriptive and often analytical overview of each book. . . . This is an excellent tool for building Judaica collections in public and academic libraries." Libr J

Includes bibliographical references

Robinson, George

Essential Judaism; a complete guide to beliefs, customs and rituals. Pocket Bks. 2000 xxi, 644p hardcover o.p. pa $20 **296**

1. Judaism
ISBN 0-671-03480-4; 0-671-03481-2 pa
LC 99-55288

This book "attempts to provide the essentials of Judaism for novices, outsiders and those who, like Robinson, rediscovered their heritage as adults. It's an excellent introductory resource, vast but accessibly organized." Publ Wkly

Includes bibliographical references

Sarna, Jonathan D.

★ **American** Judaism; a history. Yale University Press 2004 xx, 490p il $35 **296**

1. Judaism 2. Jews -- United States
ISBN 0-300-10197-X
LC 2003-14464

"This comprehensive and insightful study of the American Jewish experience is much more than just a record of events. It is an account of how people shaped events: establishing and maintaining communities, responding to challenges, and working for change. It is compelling reading for Jews and non-Jews alike." Booklist

Includes bibliographical references

Wouk, Herman

This is my God: the Jewish way of life. Little, Brown 1987 345p hardcover o.p. pa $16.95 **296**

1. Judaism
ISBN 0-316-95514-0 pa
LC 87-3245

First published 1959 by Doubleday

The author, an orthodox Jew, writes a personal declaration of faith. He explains holy days, fasts, and presents the historical background of Judaism.

Includes bibliographical references

296.09 History, geographic treatment, biography

The **Cambridge** history of Judaism; v3 edited by William Horbury, John Sturdy and W.D. Davies. Cambridge Univ. Press 1999 1254p v3 il maps $190 **296.09**

1. Judaism -- History
ISBN 0-521-24377-7

This third volume of a four-volume history "contains thirty-two essays on aspects of Judaism in the early Roman period, primarily the period between Pompey and Vespasian but often ranging into the rabbinic period." J Relig

Includes bibliographical references

Cole, Peter

★ **Sacred** trash; [by] Adina Hoffman & Peter Cole. Nextbook : Schocken 2011 283p. ill., ports. **296.09**

1. Manuscripts 2. Jews -- History 3. Cultural property 4. Cairo Genizah 5. Judaism -- History -- Sources
ISBN 978-0-8052-4258-4; 0-8052-4258-9
LC 201016751

Sophie Brody Award (2012)

This is an account of the discovery, about 120 years ago, of a cache of documents in the storeroom of a synagogue in Cairo. The cache, referred to as a geniza, includes "letters, wills, bills of lading, prayers, marriage contracts and writs of divorce, Bibles, money orders, court depositions, business inventories, leases, magic charms and receipts." (N Y Times Book Rev)

Includes bibliographical references.

296.1 Sources

Abegg, Martin G.

The **Dead** Sea scrolls; a new translation. [by] Michael O. Wise, Martin G. Abegg Jr., and Edward M. Cook. Rev ed; HarperSanFrancisco 2005 662p pa $24.95 **296.1**

ISBN 0-06-076662-X
LC 2005-46285

First published 1996

This translation captures "the nuances of the Hebrew, and sometimes the Greek, of the scrolls, many of which are merely fragments. Also contained here is a thorough introduction to the history of the discovery of the scrolls and a

theory about the community that produced the scrolls."
Publ Wkly

"An engaging necessity for updating Dead Sea Scrolls collections." Booklist

Includes bibliographical references

The **Encyclopedia** of the Dead Sea scrolls; {edited by} Lawrence H. Schiffman and James C. VanderKam. Oxford Univ. Press 2000 2v set $295   **296.1**
1. Dead Sea scrolls
ISBN 0-19-508450-0

LC 99-55300

"In addition to individual texts, coverage extends to the archeological sites themselves; important historical figures (Moses) and groups (Essenes, Pharisees) as they are represented in the scrolls; scholars important to Dead Sea scroll research . . . and methods employed both to date and to preserve these ancient documents." Booklist

Golb, Norman

Who wrote the Dead Sea scrolls? the search for the secret of Qumran. Scribner 1995 446p il maps hardcover o.p. pa $22   **296.1**
1. Dead Sea scrolls 2. Judaism -- History
ISBN 0-684-80692-4 pa

LC 94-23295

"This is an archival book that should be considered for any collection dealing with the Dead Sea Scrolls. It is well written and can be read by the interested person as well as by the professional scholar." Choice

Includes bibliographical references

Schiffman, Lawrence H.

Reclaiming the Dead Sea scrolls; the history of Judaism, the background of Christianity, the lost library of Qumran. with a foreword by Chaim Potok. Jewish Publ. Soc. 1994 xxvii, 529p il maps   **296.1**
1. Dead Sea scrolls 2. Judaism -- History

LC 94-26489

Schiffman provides a "description and evaluation of the scrolls, the archeology of Qumran (the site near the Dead Sea from which the scrolls originated), the history and nature of the Jewish community that lived at Qumran and the setting of the scrolls in Jewish history and thought from the second century B.C. through the first century A.D." N Y Times Book Rev

Includes bibliographical references

Shanks, Hershel

The **mystery** and meaning of the Dead Sea scrolls. Random House 1998 xxi, 246p il maps hardcover o.p. pa $14   **296.1**
1. Dead Sea scrolls
ISBN 0-679-78089-0 pa

LC 97-29391

"Shanks looks at the key questions surrounding the Dead Sea Scrolls (who wrote them, what they say, and what they mean vis-à-vis Judaism and Christianity) and gives readers the most up-to-date information along with his own best

guesses about what it all means, easily incorporating many divergent theories." Booklist

Includes bibliographical references

296.3   Theology, ethics, views of social issues

Kushner, Harold S., 1935-

★ **When** bad things happen to good people; with a new preface by the author. 20th anniversary ed; Schocken Bks. 2001 202p $21   **296.3**
1. Suffering 2. Providence and government of God
ISBN 0-8052-4193-0

LC 2001-531062

A reissue of the title first published 1981

"A bright and happy infant, Rabbi Kushner's first-born son gradually succumbed to progeria, 'rapid aging': he never grew beyond three feet tall, looked like a hairless, wizened old man, and died in his teens. This book is his father's attempt to make sense out of his son's fate, his own pain, and the pain of others enduring undeserved misfortunes." Libr J

Telushkin, Joseph

Jewish wisdom; ethical, spiritual, and historical lessons from the great works and thinkers. {by} Rabbi Joseph Telushkin. Morrow 1994 xxiv, 663p $26   **296.3**
1. Judaism 2. Jewish ethics
ISBN 0-688-12958-7

LC 94-9186

"Organized by subject, this is a collection of teachings and quotations from the Talmud, the Bible, rabbinical commentaries, and ancient and modern religious and secular writings. Writers include Elie Wiesel, Isaac Bashevis Singer, Hebrew poet Hayim Bialik, Cynthia Ozick, Emile Zola, Albert Einstein, Bruno Bettelheim, Gertrude Stein, Irving Howe, and Maimonides. . . . Jews—and even non-Jews—will find the book a treasure." Booklist

Includes bibliographical references

296.4   Traditions, rites, public services

Axelrod, Matt

Your guide to the Jewish holidays; from shofar to Seder. cantor Matt Axelrod. Jason Aronson 2013 214 p. (cloth : alk. paper) $30   **296.4**
1. Jewish holidays 2. Fasts and feasts -- Judaism
ISBN 0765709899; 9780765709899; 9780765709905

LC 2013033886

This book, by cantor Matt Axelrod, "takes a . . . look at the 11 most important Jewish holidays. Instead of simply explaining that Jews are obligated to observe in a certain way because of a biblical text, Axelrod shows where each holiday, along with its rituals, came from in a historical context. He provides a humorous retelling of the biblical passages relating to the holiday, explorations of rituals associated with each holiday, and descriptions of traditional foods." (Publisher's note)

Bolsta, Hyla Shifra

The **illuminated** Kaddish; interpretations of the Mourner's Prayer. paintings, calligraphy, and interpretations by Hyla Shifra Bolsta. KTAV Pub. House, Inc. 2012 108 p. col. ill. $27.50 **296.4**
1. Prayer 2. Judaism -- Customs and practices 3. Illumination of books and manuscripts 4. Kaddish 5. Judaism -- Liturgy -- Texts 6. Jewish illumination of books and manuscripts
ISBN 1602801916; 9781602801912
LC 2011033483
This book from author and illustrator Hyla Bolsta is an illuminated version of the Kaddish, "a prayer recited as part of the funeral rites of a Jewish believer." Here, "she connects the words throughout by a motif of leaves and branches from the tree of life." The prayer "is a kind of perennial puzzle . . . . Why praise God, in the words of Ezekiel, rather than mourn the death? Bolsta's scholarship, insights, and art suggest some answers." (Library Journal)
Includes bibliographical references

Eisenberg, Ronald L.

★ The **JPS** guide to Jewish traditions; [by] Ron Eisenberg. The Jewish Publication Society 2004 xxiii, 806p $40 **296.4**
1. Reference books 2. Judaism -- Encyclopedias
ISBN 0-8276-0760-1
LC 2004-6399
This "work covers the major elements of Jewish life, including life-cycle events (birth, bar and bat mitzvah, marriage, divorce, parenting, and death), the Sabbath and holidays, the synagogue, prayer, and the Bible and Jewish literature. . . . The author has done a masterful job in distilling the major beliefs and practices of a 3,000-year-old religion into lively and informative prose and in creating an accessible, essential reference work." Booklist
Includes bibliographical references

Goldman, Ari L.

Being Jewish; the spiritual and cultural practice of Judaism today. Simon & Schuster 2000 286p $25 **296.4**
1. Jewish holidays 2. Judaism -- Customs and practices
ISBN 0-684-82389-6
LC 00-44047
"An excellent resource." Booklist
Includes bibliographical references

★ **New** American Haggadah; edited by Jonathan Safran Foer ; with a new translation by Nathan Englander ; designed by Oded Ezer ; commentaries by Nathaniel Deutsch ("House of Study") ... [et al.] ; timeline created by Mia Sara Bruch. Little, Brown & Co. 2012 149 p. ill. $29.99 **296.4**
1. Seder 2. Prayers 3. Jews -- History 4. Rites and ceremonies 5. Haggadah 6. Haggadot -- Texts 7. Seder -- Liturgy -- Texts 8. Judaism -- Liturgy -- Texts
ISBN 0316069868; 9780316069861
LC 2011040637
Author Jonathan Foer retells a major story in Jewish history. "Read each year around the seder table, the Haggadah

recounts through prayer, song, and ritual the extraordinary story of Exodus, when Moses led the Israelites out of slavery in Egypt to wander the desert for forty years before reaching the Promised Land. . . . [This prayer book includes] commentary by major Jewish writers and thinkers [including] Jeffrey Goldberg, Lemony Snicket, Rebecca Newberger Goldstein, and Nathaniel Deutsch." (Publisher's note)

Shulevitz, Judith

The **Sabbath** world; glimpses of a different order of time. Random House 2010 246p $26 **296.4**
1. Sabbath 2. Rest -- Religious aspects 3. Time -- Religious aspects
ISBN 978-1-4000-6200-3; 1-4000-6200-4
LC 2009-26417
"In personal terms, and without sanctimony, [the author] explores the history of the Sabbath, its philosophical foundations, its consolations, its purposes, and, in doing so, writes a swift, penetrating book intent on shattering the habits of mindless workaholism and the inability to recognize the blessings of rest, reflection, spirit, and family." New Yorker

Wieseltier, Leon

Kaddish. Knopf 1998 588p $27.50; pa $16 **296.4**
1. Funeral rites and ceremonies 2. Kaddish 3. Judaism -- Customs and practices
ISBN 0-375-40389-2; 0-375-70362-4 pa
LC 98-15881
"When his father died in 1996 . . . Wieseltier began to observe the Jewish rituals of the traditional year of mourning. His own mourning led him to an in-depth study of the history and meaning of Kaddish in Judaism. Wieseltier provides a work of history, philosophy and spiritual memoir that demonstrates how the practice of religion meets the needs of a troubled soul." Publ Wkly

296.7 Religious experience, life, practice

Diamant, Anita

Pitching my tent; on marriage, motherhood, friendship, and other leaps of faith. Scribner 2003 223p hardcover o.p. pa $15 **296.7**
1. Jewish women
ISBN 0-7432-4616-0; 0-7432-4617-9 pa
LC 2003-45440
"This collection of short essays, culled primarily from the Boston Globe Sunday Magazine and then reworked, . . . [are] organized around such themes as love and marriage, child rearing, friendship and living a religious life. . . . The book's strength lies in its woman-to-woman conversational tone, especially in the opening section about married life and its dark side. . . . These morsels will make a tasty snack for Diamant's admirers." Publ Wkly

Isaacs, Ronald H.

★ **Kosher** living; it's more than just the food. [by] Ron Isaacs. Jossey-Bass 2005 xlvii, 286p $22.95   **296.7**
    1. Judaism -- Customs and practices
    ISBN 0-7879-7642-3
                 LC 2004-26727

"The book not only covers the expected Jewish topics— circumcision, marriage, prayer, Shabbat, synagogue behavior and more—but also . . . [items] such as employer-employee relations, shopping and even war. . . . This resource offers timeless wisdom through a contemporary lens." Publ Wkly

Includes bibliographical references

Kushner, Harold S., 1935-

How good do we have to be? a new understanding of guilt and forgiveness. Little, Brown 1996 181p hardcover o.p. pa $11.95   **296.7**
    1. Guilt 2. Good and evil 3. Bible -- O.T. -- Genesis -- Criticism
    ISBN 0-316-51933-2 pa
                 LC 95-25350

The author "here retells the Genesis story of . . . {Adam and Eve to argue} that the imperfections of humankind do not merit the loss of God's love, nor should they foster the guilt and anxiety that they often do in a society driven by a misguided attachment to perfection. . . . {Kushner sees} acceptance and forgiveness as a means of overcoming the insidious consequences of a preoccupation with perfection." Libr J

"This is one psychological self-help book that deserves the popularity it is likely to achieve." Booklist

Who needs God; [by] Harold Kushner. Fireside 2002 212p pa $14   **296.7**
    1. God -- Judaism
    ISBN 0-7432-3477-4
    First published 1989 by Summit Bks.

The author "believes that 'human life has meaning . . . but only in religious terms.' According to this crucial realization, it is religion that connects us to God and community." Libr J

Levy, Naomi

To begin again; a journey toward comfort, strength, and faith in difficult times. Knopf 1998 267p hardcover o.p. pa $12.95   **296.7**
    1. Bereavement 2. Judaism -- Customs and practices
    ISBN 0-345-41383-0 pa
                 LC 98-16024

The author "offers a progressive Jewish approach to coping with life's darker moments. Having faced the murder of her father when she was 15, Levy joined the first class of women to study at the Jewish Theological Seminary. Drawing on her own suffering and her experience as a rabbi, she constructs a map for personal renewal." Publ Wkly

"A wise and practical guide for readers of any religious persuasion." Libr J

Reuben, Steven Carr

★ **Becoming** Jewish; the challenges, rewards, and paths to conversion. [by] Steven Carr Reuben and Jennifer S. Hanin; [foreword by Bab Saget] Rowman & Littlefield Publishers 2011 256p $22.95; ebook $22.95   **296.7**
    1. Conversion 2. Converts to Judaism
    ISBN 978-1-4422-0848-3; 978-1-4422-0849-0 ebook
                 LC 2011014083

"The authors explain such details as finding the right denomination, choosing a rabbi, selecting a Hebrew name, and the need to learn Hebrew. They also discuss Jewish culture and beliefs, holidays, and traditions. Chapters on telling family and friends about the decision to convert, raising Jewish children, kabbalah, anti-Semitism, and Israel help those converting understand important issues. . . . Written in a casual, friendly style with good humor and warmth, this accessible guide will help anyone considering conversion to Judaism." Booklist

297   Islam, Babism, Bahai Faith

Armstrong, Karen

★ **Islam**; a short history. Modern Lib. 2000 xxxiv, 222p maps $19.95; pa $11.95   **297**
    1. Islam
    ISBN 0-679-64040-1; 0-8129-6618-X pa
                 LC 00-25285

This history of the Islamic faith focuses on the religion's attitude toward politics

The author "does an admirable job of presenting Islamic history from an objective, unbiased point of view." Libr J

Includes bibliographical references

Muhammad; a prophet for our time. Atlas Books/HarperCollins Publishers 2006 249p map (Eminent lives) $21.95; pa $14.95   **297**
    1. Islam 2. Prophets 3. Islamic leaders 4. Writers on religion
    ISBN 0-06-059897-2; 978-0-06-059897-6; 0-06-115577-2 pa; 978-0-06-115577-2 pa
                 LC 2006-45864

First published 1991 in the United Kingdom with subtitle: A Western attempt to understand Islam; Original American edition published 1992 with subtitle: A biography of the prophet

This is a biography of the founder of Islam.

"Readers of these pages cannot escape the genius of Muhammad and his aim for peace and compassion among nations and among Muslims themselves. . . . Recommended for all libraries." Libr J

Includes bibliographical references

Aslan, Reza

★ **No** god but God; the origins, evolution, and future of Islam. Random House 2005 xxiv, 310p $25.95; pa $14.95   **297**
    1. Islam
    ISBN 1-4000-6213-6; 0-8129-7189-2 pa
                 LC 2004-54053

"Beginning with an exploration of the religious climate in the years before the Prophet's Revelation, Aslan traces the story of Islam from the Prophet's life and the so-called golden age of the first four caliphs all the way through European colonization and subsequent independence. . . . This is an excellent overview that doubles as an impassioned call to reform." Booklist

Includes bibliographical references

Bawer, Bruce

Surrender; appeasing Islam, sacrificing freedom. Doubleday 2009 321p $24.95   **297**

    1. Freedom of speech 2. Islam -- Relations

    ISBN 978-0-385-52398-1; 0-385-52398-X

                         LC 2008-35743

"Bawer files a hefty brief of case reports on Muslim campaigns against free speech, primarily in western Europe but also in Canada and the U.S. Official infatuation with political correctness (PC), the determination that no one ever be offended, and multiculturalism, the dogma that all cultural perspectives are equally and universally valid, undergird what Bawer believes amounts to a surrender of Western liberal traditions. What may seal the fate of free speech, he argues, are the apparent inabilities of Western ruling elites to be offended by Muslims rioting, threatening by fatwa, and murdering non-Muslims . . . and to assert the priority of Western liberal values in the West. . . . Sublimely literate and rational, Bawer is no crank, however angry he gets." Booklist

Includes bibliographical references

Ben Jelloun, Tahar

Islam explained. New Press (NY) 2002 120p hardcover o.p.   pa $13.95   **297**

    1. Islam

    ISBN 1-56584-781-4; 1-56584-897-7 pa

                         LC 2002-30500

"Cast in the form of an extended conversation between Ben Jelloun and his young daughter. . . . Father and child discuss the history of Islam, what it means to be a Muslim today, the challenges facing the Islamic world, and terrorism. . . Its openness and emotional honesty, particularly when discussing the tragedy of 9/11, make it a valuable addition to a growing public discourse. As an introduction to the religion, it is spotty, but as a liberal Muslim voice of reconciliation, heartbreak, and compassion, it is priceless." Booklist

Campo, Juan Eduardo

Encyclopedia of Islam; [by] Juan E. Campo. Facts On File 2008 750p il map (Encyclopedia of world religions) $85   **297**

    1. Reference books 2. Islam -- Encyclopedias

    ISBN 978-0-8160-5454-1; 0-8160-5454-1

                        LC 2008-5621

"In about 600 A-to-Z entries, this encyclopedic guide explores the terms, concepts, personalities, historical events, and institutions that helped shape the history of this religion and the way it is practiced today." Publisher's note

Includes bibliographical references

Ernst, Carl W.

Following Muhammad; rethinking Islam in the contemporary world. University of North Carolina Press 2003 244p il (Islamic civilization & Muslim networks) $24.95; pa $16.95   **297**

    1. Islam

    ISBN 0-8078-2837-8; 0-8078-5577-4 pa

                        LC 2003-11162

The author "informs readers of the roles played by colonialism, Christian missionary efforts, and Western conceptions of just what 'religion' is, all in relation to American conceptions of Islam." Libr J

Includes bibliographical references

Esposito, John L., 1940-

Islam; the straight path. Rev. 3rd ed., updated with new epilogue; Oxford University Press 2005 304p map pa $39.95   **297**

    1. Islam

    ISBN 0-19-518266-9

                        LC 2004-61688

    First published 1988

This "survey text introduces the faith, belief, and practice of Islam from its earliest origins up to its contemporary resurgence." Publisher's note

Includes bibliographical references

What everyone needs to know about Islam. Oxford Univ. Press 2002 204p $18.95   **297**

    1. Islam

    ISBN 0-19-515713-3

                        LC 2002-8387

In question-and-answer format the author presents information on a variety of aspects of Islam. The "format allows readers to skip ahead to areas that interest them, including hot-button issues such as 'Why are Muslims so violent?' or 'Why do Muslim women wear veils and long garments?' In his answers, which are anywhere from a paragraph to several pages long, Esposito elegantly educates the reader through what the Qur'an says, how Muslims are influenced by their local cultures, and how the unique politics of Islamic countries affects Muslims' views." Publ Wkly

Includes bibliographical references

Fuller, Graham E., 1937-

A **world** without Islam. Little, Brown and Co. 2010 328p $25.99   **297**

    1. East and West 2. Islamic civilization 3. Islam -- History 4. Islam -- Relations

    ISBN 978-0-316-04119-5; 978-0-316-07201-4 ebook

                        LC 2009-54078

"A cogent argument demonstrating that a knowledgeable awareness of the rich dynamics that drive societies will better help diffuse tensions." Kirkus

Includes bibliographical references

Gardell, Mattias

In the name of Elijah Muhammad; Louis Farrakhan and the Nation of Islam. Duke Univ. Press 1996

482p (C. Eric Lincoln series on the black experience)
$59.95; pa $23.95 **297**
1. Black Muslims 2. Black Muslim leaders 3. Civil
rights activists
ISBN 0-8223-1852-0; 0-8223-1845-8 pa

LC 96-22666

"Some will appreciate the author's brief critical airing
of claims of pre-Columbian Africans in America and accounts of Muslims and the slave trade, but he is at his best
when focusing on the leaders and on the changing theology
of the Nation of Islam (NOI) and similar African American
groups in the 20th-century US. The book is balanced and
well researched." Choice

Includes bibliographical references

Gordon, Matthew

Understanding Islam; origins, beliefs, practices,
holy texts, sacred places. [by] Matthew S. Gordon.
Sterling Pub. Co. 2010 112p pa $9.95 **297**
1. Islam
ISBN 978-1-90748-616-6

LC 2010-2376

First published 2001 by Facts on File

This "exploration of Islam's history, beliefs, and practices . . . [addresses] issues such as political Islam, Islam and
Israel, and Islamic fundamentalism." Publisher's note

Includes bibliographical references

Grieve, Paul

★ A **brief** guide to Islam; history, faith and politics: the complete introduction. Carroll & Graf 2006
433p il map pa $13.95 **297**
1. Islam
ISBN 0-7867-1804-8; 978-0-7867-1804-7

LC 2006-282191

The author "starts his book with a look at the similarities and differences among the three major world religions:
Judaism, Christianity, and Islam. From there, he explores the
history of Islam and the foundations of the culture that grew
out of the Islamic faith." Libr J

"If you read only one book about Islam this year, this
should be it." Publ Wkly

Griswold, Eliza

The **tenth** parallel; dispatches from the fault line
between Christianity and Islam. Farrar, Straus and
Giroux 2010 317p il map $27; ebook $12.99 **297**
1. Christianity and other religions 2. Islam -- Relations
-- Christianity
ISBN 978-0-374-27318-7; 0-374-27318-9; 978-1-
4299-7966-5 ebook; 1-4299-7966-6 ebook

LC 2010-1480

This "is a beautifully written book, full of arresting
stories woven around a provocative issue—whether fundamentalism leads to violence—which Griswold investigates
through individual lives rather than caricatures or abstractions." N Y Times Book Rev

Includes bibliographical references

Hazleton, Lesley

After the prophet; the epic story of the Shia-
Sunni split in Islam. Doubleday 2009 239p map
$26.95 **297**
1. Shi'ah 2. Sunnis 3. Prophets 4. Imams 5. Caliphs
6. Islamic leaders 7. Islam -- History 8. Writers on
religion 9. Spouses of prominent persons
ISBN 978-0-385-52393-6

LC 2009-6498

"In June 632, the founder of Islam died without having
clearly designated a successor. It seemed obvious to some
that Muhammad's first cousin, Ali, who occupied the place
of a son in the prophet's circle, would assume leadership.
But Aisha, Muhammad's favorite, youngest, and most forceful wife, favored her father, and others backed Muhammad's
greatest warrior. Ali would succeed, but not until 25 years
later. Thus began the turmoil that eventuated in the bisection
of Muslims into Sunni and Shia and that Hazleton describes
in a new masterpiece of a kind of history seldom seen these
days, in which the telling of a complicated, eventful story
takes precedence over constant quotation of documents and
squabbling with other historians." Booklist

Includes bibliographical references

Islam in der Gegenwart./English.

★ **Islam** in the world today; a handbook of politics, religion, culture, and society. edited by Werner
Ende and Udo Steinbach. Cornell University Press
2010 1114p il $85 **297**
1. Islamic civilization 2. Islam -- History
ISBN 978-0-8014-4571-2

LC 2009-39910

First published 1989 in Germany

This is "one of the most authoritative works on Islam in
the modern world. . . . The volume is divided into three parts;
the first is a historical overview of the Islamic world from its
beginnings in the seventh century to the present, including
a description of the different sects and movements of Islam
and their influence in the world today. The second, and most
extensive, section discusses the political role of Islam in the
modern world, Islamic economics, social systems, and law.
. . . The final section describes Islamic culture and civilization, including art, literature, and architecture, and their
intersection with the West." Libr J

Includes bibliographical references

Johnson, Ian

A **mosque** in Munich; Nazis, the CIA, and the
Muslim brotherhood in the West. Houghton Mifflin
Harcourt 2010 318p $27 **297**
1. Mosques 2. Cold war 3. Islam and politics 4. Islamic
fundamentalism 5. Cold War 6. Munich (Germany)
7. Mosques -- Germany 8. Islamic Brotherhood 9.
Islamic fundamentalism -- Germany 10. United States
-- Central Intelligence Agency
ISBN 978-0-15-101418-7; 0-15-101418-3

LC 2009-35285

"Mr. Johnson brings to life a previously overlooked episode in the Muslim Brotherhood's story and thus in the story
of Islamism as a whole: How a radical European beachhead
came to be established in Munich. It should be said that the
story takes some confusing turns; even alert readers may

find themselves flipping to the list of characters at the back of the book, or to the index, to help them follow the narrative. But many of the details are astonishing and the larger implications for our own time disturbing." Wall Street J

Includes bibliographical references

Karsh, Efraim

Islamic imperialism; a history. Yale University Press 2006 276p map $30   **297**

1. Jihad 2. Imperialism 3. Islam and politics
ISBN 0-300-10603-3

LC 2005-34836

The author "surveys for a general audience the region's Islamic political past. Parallel to his narrative, Karsh frequently contrasts the universalistic proclamations of Islam with cycles of imperial consolidation and fragmentation. After recounting the Prophet Muhammad's religio-political establishment of Islam, and the discord about his legacy that continues today, Karsh narrates the battles over Muhammad's caliphate that eventuated in the Umayyad and Abbasid Empires. Karsh's commentary often looks forward to contemporary ideologues of Islam who ransack history to justify grievances. . . . An informative foundation for further exploration of Islamic history." Libr J

Kepel, Gilles

Jihad; the trail of political Islam. translated by Anthony F. Roberts. Harvard Univ. Press 2002 454p $33.95; pa $15.95   **297**

1. Islam and politics
ISBN 0-674-00877-4; 0-674-01090-6 pa

LC 2002-17181

Original French edition, 2000

"Kepel argues that the terrorism seen today throughout the world results from the failure of Islamic fundamentalism and not its success. . . . Fascinating despite its copious detail." Booklist

Lewis, Bernard, 1916-

★ The **crisis** of Islam; holy war and unholy terror. Modern Library 2003 xxxii, 184p map hardcover o.p. pa $13.95   **297**

1. Islam and politics 2. Islamic fundamentalism 3. Terrorism -- Religious aspects
ISBN 0-679-64281-1; 0-8129-6785-2 pa

LC 2002-45219

"Written in an easily accessible style, this analysis provides a digestible overview for Westerners still asking why." Booklist

Includes bibliographical references

The **Many** faces of Islam; perspectives on a resurgent civilization. Nissim Rejwan {editor} University Press of Fla. 2000 282p $55   **297**

1. Islam 2. Islamic countries -- Politics and government
ISBN 0-8130-1807-2

LC 00-32587

The editor offers "perspectives on modern Islamic culture and religious practice. Seeking to dispel the perception that Islamic fundmentalism and extremism represent Islam in its entirety, Rejwan surveys the issues and provides numerous excerpts from modern writers and scholars, Muslim

and non-Muslim, summarizing the many problems and dilemmas facing contemporary Muslims." Univ. Press Books for Public and Second Sch Libr, 2001

Naipaul, V. S.

Beyond belief; Islamic excursions among the converted peoples. Random House 1998 408p hardcover o.p. pa $15   **297**

1. Islam 2. Islamic countries -- Description
ISBN 0-375-70648-8 pa

LC 97-37350

"Retracing a voyage he made in 1979, the novelist and essayist journeys through Indonesia, Iran, Pakistan and Malaya, using Islam as a window on the animism, nationalism, capitalism and other isms he encounters there." N Y Times Book Rev

Nasr, Seyyed Hossein

Islam : religion, history, and civilization. HarperSanFrancisco 2002 xx, 198p pa $12.95   **297**

1. Islam 2. Islamic civilization
ISBN 0-06-050714-4

LC 2002-32810

This introduction to the world of Islam explores the following topics: What is Islam?; The doctrines and beliefs of Islam; Islamic practices and institutions; The history of Islam; Schools of Islamic thought; Islam in the contemporary world; Islam and other religions; The spiritual and religious significance of Islam

"Provides compelling analysis of contemporary Islam and its conflicts without overwhelming the reader with information." Booklist

Includes bibliographical references

Nasr, Vali

★ The **Shia** revival; how conflicts within Islam will shape the future. Norton 2006 287p map $25.95   **297**

1. Shi'ah 2. Islam and politics
ISBN 0-393-06211-2; 978-0-393-06211-3

LC 2006-12361

This "is a historical account of sectarian conflicts in the Muslim world, and how the future rests in finding a peaceful solution to the ancient rivalries between the Shias and the Sunnis." Publisher's note

"So enlightening and perspective altering that no one concerned about the Middle East should miss reading it." Booklist

Includes bibliographical references

★ The **Oxford** dictionary of Islam; John L. Esposito, editor in chief. Oxford Univ. Press 2003 359p hardcover o.p. pa $18.95   **297**

1. Reference books 2. Islam -- Dictionaries
ISBN 0-19-512558-4; 0-19-512559-2 pa

LC 2002-30261

"Aimed at general readers with little knowledge of Islam, the dictionary focuses on 19th- and 20th-century topics, including many social, religious, and political aspects of modern Islam. Entries include hot topics (e.g., al-Qaeda, Osama Bin Laden, Afghanistan), various religious and political sects (Nation of Islam, Sevener Shiis, the Philippines'

Moro National Liberation Front), and muslim views on a variety of issues (abortion, suicide, science, the treatment of women). Entries arranged alphabetically, use standard transliterations. Cross-references are listed at the end of entries, and attempts are made to link Arabic and English terms." Choice

"This is an excellent resource for ready-reference collections in any library." Libr J

Includes bibliographical references

The **Oxford** history of Islam; {edited by} John Esposito. Oxford Univ. Press 1999 749p il map $49.95   **297**
1. Islam
ISBN 0-19-510799-3

LC 99-13219

"Contributors treat, among other things, Muslim history, law, and society; art and architecture; and regional differences. Chapters on the 'Globalization of Islam' and 'Contemporary Islam' are particularly relevant to current events. . . . An ideal one-volume source." Libr J

Includes bibliographical references

Zafar, Harris, 1979-
Demystifying Islam; tackling the tough questions. Harris Zafar. Rowman & Littlefied 2014 218 p. map (cloth : alk. paper) $35   **297**
1. Islamophobia 2. Islam -- Relations 3. Islam 4. Islam -- Doctrines
ISBN 1442223278; 9781442223271; 9781442223288

LC 2014004827

This book, by Harris Zafar, asks questions such as "What really is Shariah law? How is a Muslim to understand Jihad? Does Islam oppose Western values such as free speech or freedom of religion? What place do women have according to Islam? . . . Author Harris Zafar . . . is forthright about issues where Muslims disagree, and he digs into history through vast research and scholarship to track the origins of differing beliefs." (Publisher's note)

"This book is less of a spiritual introduction than it is a cultural one, and an excellent starting point for people navigating interfaith relationships or working to improve understanding and representation in organizations and public discussion." Pub Wkly

Includes bibliographical referencees and index

297.09   History, geographic treatment, biography

Abdul Rauf, Feisal, 1948-
Moving the mountain; beyond ground zero to a new vision of Islam in America. Feisal Abdul Rauf. Free Press 2012 xiv, 225 p.p (hardcover) $24 **297.09**
1. Islamic law 2. Religious tolerance 3. Muslims -- United States 4. Islam -- United States
ISBN 1451656009; 9781451656008

LC 2011050797

Author Feisal Abdul Rauf "offers a . . . comparative study of the 'People of the Book,' focusing partly on the similarities between the three Abrahamic faiths. . . . Rauf delves into the 'bogeyman' of Shariah law, comparing it to the U.S. Constitution." He also discusses "Islam since 9/11" and his time as "imam of the al-Farah Mosque in New York City." (Kirkus Reviews)

Includes bibliographical references

Nasr, Amir Ahmad
My Isl@m; how fundamentalism stole my mind-and doubt freed my soul. Amir Ahmad Nasr. St. Martin's Press 2013 304 p.   **297.09**
1. Belief and doubt 2. Internet and religion 3. Islamic fundamentalism 4. Muslims -- Malaysia -- Biography
ISBN 9781250016485; 9781250016799

LC 2013004044

The author, "a Sudanese blogger . . . blends memoir with political thought and activism in his book, a distillation of his last few years blogging about Islam and the Muslim world. [Amir Ahmad] Nasr, who grew up in Qatar and Malaysia, recounts his early religious education. . . . . The book . . . follows his journey out of a simplistic understanding of Islam, through rationalism and semi-atheism, towards a conversion to Sufism, the mystical school of Islam." (Publishers Weekly)

297.092   Biography

All-American; 45 American men on being Muslim. edited by Wajahat Ali & Zahra T. Suratwala ; foreword by Congressman Keith Ellison. White Cloud Press 2012 xiv, 256 p.p ill. (pbk.) $16.95   **297.092**
1. Muslims -- United States 2. Muslim men -- United States 3. Muslim men -- United States -- Biography
ISBN 1935952595; 9781935952596

LC 2012014744

"In this second book in the 'I Speak For Myself' series," edited by Wajahat Ali, "American Muslim men speak out on their lives and how their Muslim beliefs play out in private and on the public stage. Contributors include high profile figures in the American Muslim community, representing a new generation that is making a profound impact inside and outside the Muslim world." (Publisher's note)

Smith, Jane Idleman
Islam in America; {by} Jane I. Smith. Columbia Univ. Press 1999 251p il (Columbia contemporary American religion series) $60; pa $20.50 **297.092**
1. Islam
ISBN 0-231-10966-0; 0-231-10967-9 pa

LC 98-31943

The author discusses "the basic tenets of the Muslim faith, surveys the history of Islam in this country, and profiles the lifestyles, religious practices, and worldviews of American Muslims. Sections of the book cover the role of women in American Islam, raising and educating children, the use of products acceptable to Muslims, appropriate dress and behavior, concerns about prejudice and unfair treatment, and other issues related to life in {America}." Univ Press Books for Public and Second Sch Libr, 2001

Includes bibliographical references

297.1 Islam

★ The **meaning** of the glorious Koran; an explanatory translation by Marmaduke Pickthall; with an introduction by William Montgomery Watt. A.A. Knopf 1992 xxiv, 693p il $22   **297.1**
1. Qur'an
ISBN 0-679-41736-2; 978-0-679-41736-1
LC 92-52928
This translation first published 1930
"The sacred scripture of Islam, regarded by Muslims as the Word of God, and except in sura I.—which is a prayer to God—and some few passages in which Muhammad or the angels speak in the first person, the speaker throughout is God." Ency Britannica

The **Qur'an**; English translation and parallel Arabic text. translated, with an introduction and notes, by M.A.S. Abdel Haleem. Oxford University Press 2010 xxxix, 624 p.p maps (hardcover) $45   **297.1**
1. Qur'an
ISBN 019957071X; 9780199570713
LC 2010281328
This book, by M. A. S. Abdel Haleem, offers an English translation of the Qur'an with Arab text presented in parallel. "This translation is written in contemporary language . . ., set page-for-page against the most widespread traditional calligraphic Arabic text. . . . Furthermore, Haleem includes notes that explain geographical, historical, and personal allusions as well as an index in which Qur'anic material is arranged into topics for easy reference." (Publisher's note)
"Because the Koran stresses its Arabic nature, devout Muslims believe that only an Arabic version is the actual Koran and insist that its translation cannot be more than an approximate interpretation. . . Yet anyone wishing to understand Islamic civilization and global affairs may find this Koran very useful. . . . Highly recommended." LJ
Includes bibliographical references and index

The **Qur'an**: an encyclopedia; edited by Oliver Leaman. Taylor & Francis Group 2006 xxvii, 771p $280; pa $45   **297.1**
1. Reference books 2. Koran -- Encyclopedias
ISBN 0-415-32639-7; 978-0-415-32639-1; 0-415-77529-9 pa; 978-0-415-32639-1 pa
"The objective of this encyclopedia is to fill a gap between general introductions and more technical works and provide the non-specialist with a resource covering all aspects of the text and its reception." Booklist
Includes bibliographical references

Wagner, Walter H.
Opening the Qur'an; introducing Islam's holy book. University of Notre Dame Press 2008 547p $45   **297.1**
1. Qur'an -- Criticism
ISBN 978-0-268-04415-2; 0-268-04415-5
LC 2008-27221
"The Qu'ran is difficult for non-Muslims to understand. The author, a Biblical scholar and religious historian, seeks to make the Qu'ran more accessible. He describes the histor-ical and theological context. He explains specific passages and specific topics (such as the place of women; justice and jihad; and the hereafter)." Univ Press Books for Public and Second Sch Libr, 2009
This "work makes an important contribution to the contemporary Muslim-Christian conversation." Catholic Hist Rev
Includes bibliographical references

297.4 Sufism (Islamic mysticism)

Ernst, Carl W.
The **Shambhala** guide to Sufism. Shambhala Publs. 1997 xxi, 264p il pa $18.95   **297.4**
1. Sufism
ISBN 1-57062-180-2
LC 97-10189
This guide to Sufism "covers its beginnings, its basic philosophies, and its place in Islam." Libr J
Includes bibliographical references

297.6 Islamic leaders and organization

Hazleton, Lesley, 1945-
The **First** Muslim; The Story of Muhammad. Lesley Hazleton. Riverhead Hardcover 2013 320 p. map (hardcover) $27.95   **297.6**
1. Islam -- History
ISBN 1594487286; 9781594487286
LC 2012038501
This book, by Lesley Hazleton, offers a biography of the Prophet Muhammad. "Muhammad's was a life of almost unparalleled historical importance; yet for all the iconic power of his name, the intensely dramatic story of the prophet of Islam is not well known. . . . Hazleton's account follows the arc of Muhammad's rise from powerlessness to power, from anonymity to renown, from insignificance to lasting significance." (Publisher's note)
Includes bibliographical references (p. [299]-310) and index.

297.8 Islamic sects and reform movements

Evanzz, Karl
The **messenger** : the rise and fall of Elijah Muhammad. Pantheon Bks. 1999 667p hardcover o.p. pa $18   **297.8**
1. Black Muslim leaders 2. Civil rights activists
ISBN 0-679-77406-8 pa
LC 99-11826
A "critical biography of one of America's leading black nationalists of the 20th century. One of the founders of the Nation of Islam (NOI), Muhammad helped convert thousands of African Americans to the religion popularly known as the Black Muslims. Evanzz concludes that Muhammad was essentially a con man who used his considerable powers of persuasion to get rich and seduce women. Especially

fascinating is Evanzz's extensive use of FBI files to make his case." Libr J

Includes bibliographical references

Levinsohn, Florence Hamlish

Looking for Farrakhan. Dee, I.R. 1997 305p $25   **297.8**

1. Black Muslims 2. Black Muslim leaders

ISBN 1-56663-157-2

LC 97-11335

Levinsohn's "biography, which reflects on the black experience and how it changed young Eugene Walcott into Louis Farrakhan, leader of the Nation of Islam, attempts to make sense of this prominent figure in American politics." Libr J

299   Religions not provided for elsewhere

★ The **Gnostic** Bible; edited by Willis Barnstone and Marvin Meyer. Rev. ed.; Shambhala 2009 881p pa $29.95   **299**

1. Gnosticism

ISBN 978-1-59030-631-4; 1-59030-631-7

LC 2008-36431

First published 2003

"The book provides Gnostic texts from their Jewish origins, into early Christianities, on into the medieval world. Though it concentrates on the early Jewish-Christian matrix of early Gnosticism, the collection . . . manifests the breadth and depth of Gnostic variations in neo-Platonist, Manichean, Mandean, Islam, and Cathar movements." Choice

Includes bibliographical references

Pagels, Elaine H.

★ The **Gnostic** Gospels; by Elaine Pagels. Random House 1979 xxxvi, 182p hardcover o.p. pa $12   **299**

1. Gnosticism

ISBN 0-679-72453-2 pa

LC 79-4764

An examination of the origins of early Christianity based on Gnostic texts rediscovered in the 20th century.

Pagels "writes for the layman, which is refreshing, and she does so lucidly, which is a challenge, especially when 'gnosticism' was regarded by its own adherents to be for the initiated only." Christ Sci Monit

Includes bibliographical references

Reitman, Janet

★ **Inside** Scientology. Houghton Mifflin Harcourt 2011 xx, 444p $28   **299**

1. Scientology 2. United States -- Religion

ISBN 978-0-618-88302-8; 0-618-88302-9

LC 2010-49837

An expose "culled from hundreds of interviews with active Scientologists and defectors alike. Reitman brings an almost clinical detachment to the religion's story, from its birth in the sci-fi imagination of founder L. Ron Hubbard to its current Hollywood heyday. Her revelations—including abuse allegations against church leader David Miscavige and

details about the organization's aggressive courtship of Tom Cruise—come with impressive backup." Entertaiment Wkly

Includes bibliographical references

Wilkinson, Richard H.

★ The **complete** gods and goddesses of ancient Egypt. Thames & Hudson 2003 256p il $39.95 **299**

1. Egyptian mythology 2. Gods and goddesses 3. Egypt -- Religion

ISBN 0-500-05120-8

LC 2002-110321

"Wilkinson's gorgeously illustrated book adds new dimension to popular literature on ancient Egypt. . . . And once readers open the book to look at the pictures, they well may stay to read the well-organized, comprehensive, clearly written text." Booklist

Includes bibliographical references

Wright, Lawrence

★ **Going** Clear; Scientology, Hollywood, and the Prison of Belief. Lawrence Wright. Random House Inc 2013 xiii, 430 p.p ill. $28.95   **299**

1. Cults 2. Scientology 3. Scientology. 4. Scientology --Doctrines.

ISBN 0307700666; 9780307700667

LC 2012532009

This book from Pulitzer Prize winner Lawrence Wright looks at the Church of Scientology. It begins "with the life of L. Ron Hubbard, a manic-depressive, wannabe naval hero, sci-fi writer and self-styled shaman" whose book "Dianetics" "laid the groundwork for a 'religion' where 'thetans' (souls) are stymied by 'engrams,' self-destructive suggestive impulses lodged in the brain." The Church's connections to the U.S. entertainment industry and its behavior toward outsiders are examined. (Kirkus Reviews)

Includes bibliographical references (p. [373]-418) and index.

299.5   Religions of East and Southeast Asian origin

I ching

★ The **classic** of changes; a new translation of the I Ching as interpreted by Wang Bi. translated by Richard John Lynn. Columbia Univ. Press 1994 602p (Translations from the Asian classics) $27.95; pa $17.95   **299.5**

1. Divination

ISBN 0-231-08294-0; 0-231-08295-9 pa

LC 93-43999

"Most available editions of the I Ching are based on the James Legge translation, a work produced over 140 years ago and characterized by romanticized and idiomatic Victorian English. Although not more accurate or revealing than the Legge, this new translation is welcome because of its crisp usage of modern-day English." Libr J

Lao-tzu

★ **Tao** te ching; the new translation from Tao te ching: the definitive edition. translation by Jona-

than Star. Jeremy P. Tarcher/Penguin 2008 103p pa
$10 **299.5**

ISBN 978-1-58542-618-8

LC 2007-44948

This translation first published 2001 with title: Tao te ching: the definitive edition

"Chinese Taoist text attributed to Lao Tzu, supposedly an elder contemporary of Confucius (551?-479 BC). . . . A brief work in eighty-one-paragraphs in both verse and prose, it probably dates from the 4th or 3rd century BC, although some believe it may be as early as the 6th century BC. Because of its concise, poetic language, its meaning is subject to many interpretations. It is generally agreed that it is both a mystical book about union with the absolute, and a political handbook on how to rule and survive in chaotic times." Reader's Ency. 4th edition

Yang Lihui

★ **Handbook** of Chinese mythology; [by] Lihui Yang and Deming An, with Jessica Anderson Turner. ABC-CLIO 2005 293p il (Handbooks of world mythology) $75 **299.5**

1. Asian mythology

ISBN 1-57607-806-X

LC 2005-13851

"This volume provides useful information to the reader. The authors' credibility and in-depth scholarship offer a rare opportunity to experience Chinese mythology through Chinese eyes." Booklist

Includes bibliographical references

299.6 Religions originating among Black Africans and people of Black African descent

Chevannes, Barry

Rastafari : roots and ideology. Syracuse Univ. Press 1994 298p (Utopianism and communitarianism) hardcover o.p. pa $19.95 **299.6**

1. Rastafari movement 2. Jamaica -- Religion

ISBN 0-8156-0296-0 pa

LC 94-18608

"Vital for students of African American religions and Caribbean religions, but also of interest to anthropologists, sociologists, and historians." Choice

Includes bibliographical references

★ The **Encyclopedia** of African and African-American religions; Stephen D. Glazier, editor. Routledge 2000 xx, 452p il maps $150 **299.6**

1. Reference books 2. Blacks -- Religion 3. African Americans -- Religion -- Encyclopedias

ISBN 0-415-92245-3

LC 00-59136

"This encyclopedia is a good starting point for understanding the complex interrelationships among African, African American, and European religious beliefs, practices, and traditions in a global context." Libr J

299.7 Religions of North American native origin

Castaneda, Carlos

The **teachings** of Don Juan; a Yaqui way of knowledge. University of Calif. Press 1968 196p $32.50; pa $16.95 **299.7**

1. Mystics 2. Yaqui Indians -- Religion

ISBN 0-520-21755-1; 0-520-21757-8 pa

"This book is the record of a young anthropologist's experiences as the apprentice of a [Yaqui] Indian sorcerer. Over a period of four years, Mr. Castaneda paid intermittant visits to Don Juan, first in Arizona, then in Sonora, Mexico." N Y Times Book Rev

Other titles about Don Juan are:

The active side of infinity (1999)

The art of dreaming (1993)

The eagle's gift (1981)

The fire from within (1984)

Journey to Ixtlan (1972)

Magical passes (1998)

The power of silence (1987)

The second ring of power (1977)

A separate reality (1971)

Tales of power (1974)

Nabokov, Peter

Where the lightning strikes; the lives of American Indian sacred places. Viking 2005 350p hardcover o.p. pa $17 **299.7**

1. Sacred space 2. Native Americans -- Religion

ISBN 0-670-03432-0; 0-14-303881-8 pa

LC 2005-42227

The author presents "16 'biographies of place,' each of a habitat illustrating the bond between North American Indian cultures and their environment perpetuated by myths, legends, and rituals. . . . The author's careful documentation of unbroken reverence for these sacred places powerfully illuminates Native American attachment to the earth itself." Booklist

Includes bibliographical references

Popol vuh

Popol vuh; the Mayan book of the dawn of life. translated by Dennis Tedlock; with commentary based on the ancient knowledge of the modern Quiché Maya. rev ed; Simon & Schuster 1996 388p il maps pa $15 **299.7**

1. Mayas -- Religion 2. Native Americans -- Religion

ISBN 0-684-81845-0

LC 95-46822

A modern translation of the 16th century Mayan holy book

"Tedlock's translation splendidly combines scholarship, imagination, and literary sensitivity. His photographs (derived from field work in Guatemala) vividly illustrate the text, and the notes (based on his collaboration with a contemporary Quiché shaman) fascinate and inform." Libr J

Includes bibliographical references

300 SOCIAL SCIENCES, SOCIOLOGY & ANTHROPOLOGY

300   Social sciences

Isserman, Maurice

The **other** American: the life of Michael Harrington. PublicAffairs 2000 449p $28.50; pa $14   **300**

1. Authors 2. Social critics 3. College teachers 4. Nonfiction writers 5. Writers on politics 6. Political scientists 7. Inspirational writers

ISBN 1-89162-030-4; 1-58648-036-7 pa

LC 99-56654

This biography of the leftist social critic and author of the influential The other America (1962) is "also a veritable Zagat's guide through the left sectarian factions of the last three-quarters of the 20th century." N Y Times Book Rev

Includes bibliographical references

Oxford University Press

★ **Dictionary** of the social sciences; edited by Craig Calhoun. Oxford Univ. Press 2002 563p $75   **300**

1. Reference books 2. Social sciences -- Dictionaries

ISBN 0-19-512371-9

LC 00-68151

This dictionary provides "definitions of key terms, offering entries that also discuss the intellectual issues behind the terms' usage. The entries cover all the social sciences except for law, education, and public administration. . . . Some 275 biographies are included." Libr J

Includes bibliographical references

Rosenblatt, Roger

★ **Kayak** morning; Roger Rosenblatt. Ecco 2012 160p.   **300**

1. Grief 2. Autobiographies 3. Kayaks and kayaking

ISBN 9780062084033

In this memoir, the author questions "why [he] cannot come to terms with his grief [over the death of his 38-year-old daughter] two and a half years later. As [Roger] Rosenblatt, a writer and professor of English and writing at Stony Brook University, takes up kayaking near his home in Quogue on Long Island, he begins to contemplate his connection to nature and his place in it by observing the sea. The kayak becomes a metaphorical conveyance as he floats from one topic to the next . . . everything from life versus death to personal memories and classical literature. . . . The piece . . . combines short vignettes, poetic verses, snippets of conversations and meaningful quotations." (Publishers Weekly)

301   Sociology and anthropology

Best, Joel

Stat -spotting; a field guide to identifying dubious data. University of California Press 2008 132p il $19.95   **301**

1. Statistics

ISBN 978-0-520-25746-7; 0-520-25746-4

LC 2008-17175

This "is an easily digestible guide to understanding how simple miscalculations, botched translations and inappropriate graphics misled the American public. This concise book helps readers understand how politicians and the media twist statistics to match the goals of their agenda. Author Joel Best describes how things like bloating figures by misplacing a decimal point or using enlarged graphics to visually distract readers from analyzing the data objectively. If you want a better understanding of the reality behind those charts and graphs you see in books, on television and in the media then you need to read this book." Univ Press Books for Public and Second Sch Libr, 2009

Includes bibliographical references

Encyclopedia of sociology; Edgar F. Borgatta, editor-in-chief, Rhonda Montgomery, managing editor. 2nd ed; Macmillan Ref. USA 2000 5v set $575   **301**

1. Reference books 2. Sociology -- Encyclopedias

ISBN 0-02-864853-6

LC 00-28402

First published 1992

This set includes about 400 articles covering all fields and subfields of sociology: social psychology, social demography, social anthropology, social history, social geography, social ecology, certain branches of political science, political economy, and sociolinguistics. More recent studies include affirmative action, alernative lifestyles, genocide, information society, sexually transmitted diseases and terrorism

Includes bibliographical references

Required reading;   sociology's most influential books.   edited by Dan Clawson.   University of Mass. Press 1998 221p hardcover o.p. pa $17.95   **301**

1. Best books 2. Reference books 3. Sociology -- Bibliography

ISBN 1-55849-153-8 pa

LC 98-11944

This volume "identifies and discusses 17 of the 'most influential' books in sociology written during the last 25 years. . . . The power of this book lies in reconsiderations by eminent sociologists of important titles in light of a quarter of a century's worth of political, social, and economic change." Libr J

Includes bibliographical references

Taussig, Michael

I swear I saw this; drawings in fieldwork notebooks, namely my own. Michael Taussig. The University of Chicago Press 2011 173 p. (hardcover : alk. paper) $48.00   **301**

1. Travel writing 2. Theory of knowledge 3. Illustration of books 4. Anthropology -- Methodology 5. Anthropology -- Fieldwork 6. Anthropological illustration

ISBN 0226789829; 0226789837; 9780226789828; 9780226789835

LC 2011025411

This book offers "anthropologist Michael Taussig's reflections on the fieldwork notebooks he kept through forty years of travels in Colombia. Taking as a starting point a drawing he made in Medellin in 2006--as well as its caption, 'I swear I saw this'--Taussig considers the fieldwork notebook as a type of modernist literature and the place where writers and other creators first work out the imaginative logic of discovery." (Publisher's note)

Includes bibliographical references (p. 165-170) and index

√ **World** of sociology; Joseph M. Palmisano, editor. Gale Group 2001 2v il set $160   **301**
   1. Reference books 2. Sociology -- Encyclopedias
   ISBN 0-7876-4965-1

         LC 00-48399

This is a "subject-specific guide to concepts, theories, discoveries, pioneers, issues and ethical questions associated with sociology. It includes approximately 1,000-1,500 alphabetically arranged topical essays, definitions and biographies." Publisher's note

Includes bibliographical references

302   Specific topics in sociology and anthropology

Eldridge, Lawrence Allen
   Chronicles of a Two-Front War; Civil Rights and Vietnam in the African American Press. by Lawerence Allen Eldridge. Univ of Missouri Pr 2012 352 p. (hardcover) $45.00   **302**
   1. Vietnam War, 1961-1975 2. African Americans -- History
   ISBN 082621939X; 9780826219398

The book by author Lawerence Allen Eldridge "examine[s] coverage of the Vietnam War by black news publications, from the Gulf of Tonkin incident in August 1964 to the final withdrawal of American ground forces in the spring of 1973 and the fall of Saigon in the spring of 1975. Eldridge reveals how the black press not only reported the war but also weighed its significance in the context of the civil rights movement." (Publisher's note)

Gladwell, Malcolm, 1963-
√ **Outliers**; the story of success. Little, Brown and Co. 2008 309p $27.99   **302**
   1. Success
   ISBN 978-0-316-01792-3; 0-316-01792-2

         LC 2008-32824

Gladwell's "subject is success — an 'outlier' is a superachiever, like Bill Gates or the four Beatles, and Gladwell wants to know what sets these titans apart. It's not mere talent, he insists, offering up instead one thrilling, exquisitely unfurled counterargument after another. . . . There are both brilliant yarns and life lessons here: Outliers is riveting science, self-help, and entertainment, all in one book." Entertainment Wkly

Includes bibliographical references

√ The **tipping** point; how little things can make a big difference. Malcolm Gladwell. Little, Brown 2000 viii, 279 p $27.99   **302**
   1. Causation 2. Social psychology 3. Contagion

(Social psychology)
   ISBN 0316316962; 9780316316965

         LC 99047576

It was the author's intent to demonstrate "that ideas, products, messages and behaviors 'spread just like viruses do.' . . . [Malcolm Gladwell] follows the growth of 'word-of-mouth epidemics' triggered with the help of three pivotal types. These are Connectors, sociable personalities who bring people together; Mavens, who like to pass along knowledge; and Salesmen, adept at persuading the unenlightened. (Paul Revere, for example, was a Maven and a Connector). . . . [The book] offers a smorgasbord of . . . snippets summarizing research on topics such as conversational patterns, infants' crib talk, judging other people's character, cheating habits in schoolchildren, memory sharing among families or couples, and the dehumanizing effects of prisons." (Publishers Weekly)

Includes bibliographical references and index.

302.2   Communication

Biedermann, Hans
   ★ **Dictionary** of symbolism; cultural icons and the meanings behind them. translated by James Hulbert. Meridan Book 1994 465p il pa $25   **302.2**
   1. Reference books 2. Signs and symbols
   ISBN 0-452-01118-3

         LC 93-30616

Original German edition, 1989

This dictionary "incorporates symbols that originated in Asia, Africa, Europe and the 'New World'. There are almost 600 entries from mythology, fairy tale, psychology, religion, and sociology, plus historical and legendary figures. With 2000 black-and-white illustrations, the book is highly attractive. The symbols are accompanied by thorough interpretations based on various sources." SLJ

Includes bibliographical references

McLuhan, Marshall, 1911-1980
√ The **global** village; transformations in world life and media in the 21st century. [by] Marshall McLuhan and Bruce R. Powers. Oxford Univ. Press 1989 220p il (Communication and society) hardcover o.p. pa $14.95   **302.2**
   1. Mass media 2. Technology and civilization
   ISBN 0-19-507910-8 pa

         LC 88-22718

This book "was written, according to Powers, between 1974 and 1980 . . . and 'put together' between 1976 and 1984. McLuhan's thesis has always been that electronic technologies have been altering and reconstituting people in ways they don't understand and causing them to lose their private identities. This book probes the same theme from different angles, but with the same McLuhanesque all-over-the-place reasoning." Libr J

Includes bibliographical references

Tannen, Deborah

You just don't understand; women and men in conversation. Quill 2001 342p pa $13.95   **302.2**

1. Conversation 2. Sex differences (Psychology)

ISBN 978-0-06-095962-3; 0-06-095962-2

First published 1990 by Morrow

"Aside from the vivid examples and lively prose, what makes this book particularly engaging is that the author makes linguistics . . . interesting and usable." N Y Times Book Rev

Includes bibliographical references

302.23   Media (Means of communication)

Clark, Lynn Schofield

The **parent** app; understanding families in the digital age. Lynn Schofield Clark. Oxford University Press 2013 xx, 299 p.p (alk. paper) $29.95 **302.23**

1. Digital media and families 2. Parent and child 3. Internet and families 4. Internet -- Social aspects

ISBN 0199899614; 9780199899616

LC 2012006687

This book by Lynn Schofield Clark provides families with "strategies for coping with the dilemmas of digital and mobile media in modern life. . . . Clark set about interviewing scores of mothers and fathers, identifying not only their various approaches, but how they differ according to family income. Clark tackles a host of issues, such as family communication, online predators, cyber bullying, sexting, gamer drop-outs, helicopter parenting, . . . and much more." (Publisher's note)

Includes bibliographical references (p. 275-291) and index

Durham, M. Gigi

The **Lolita** effect; the media sexualization of young girls and what we can do about it. [by] M. Gigi Durham, Ph.D. Overlook Press 2008 320p $24.95; pa $14.95   **302.23**

1. Body image 2. Mass media 3. Girls -- Sexual behavior 4. United States -- Social conditions

ISBN 978-1-5902-00636; 1-5902-0063-2; 978-1-5902-0215-9 pa; 1-5902-0215-5 pa

In this "exploration of the media's exploitation of girls, Durham exposes the links between destructive teenage self-images and the popular, highly sexed, and negative representations of girls in magazines, television programs, and movies. . . . [Her] provocative and erudite study of the demeaning way society views girls serves to both alarm and educate; consider it required reading for parents and their daughters." Booklist

Includes bibliographical references

Gladstone, Brooke

★ The **influencing** machine; Brooke Gladstone on the media. illustrated by Josh Neufeld; with additional penciling by Randy Jones and Susann Ferris-Jones. W. W. Norton 2011 xxii, 170p ill. (chiefly col.) (hbk.) $23.95; (hbk.) $16.95   **302.23**

1. Journalism 2. Mass media 3. Broadcast journalism

4. Comic books, strips, etc. 5. Graphic novels 6. Journalism -- Graphic novels 7. Broadcast journalism -- Graphic novels

ISBN 0393077799; 9780393077797

LC 2011009820

This work of graphic nonfiction explores the "history of media's influence. . . . [F]rom the 'Acta Diurna' posted in ancient Rome to the outcries over President Adams's Alien and Sedition Acts and McCarthy's Red Scare, [Brooke] Gladstone traces not only the birth of the press, but also its various muzzles. The press will not always stay silent, as she illustrates with Daniel Ellsberg and the Pentagon Papers. . . . Yet government opacity still abounds, and Gladstone pointedly wonders if secrecy really makes us safer. . . . Gladstone points to seven key biases that cognizant media consumers should worry about: commercial, bad news, status quo, access, visual, narrative, and fairness. These dovetail . . . into a . . . discussion of war journalism." (Publishers Weekly)

"Gladstone's is an indispensible guide to our ever-evolving media landscape that's brought vividly to life." Publ Wkly

Includes bibliographical references (p. 163-170).

Gonzalez, Juan, 1969-

News for all the people; Juan Gonzalez and Joseph Torres. Verso 2011 432p $29.95   **302.23**

1. Mass media 2. United States -- Race relations

ISBN 978-1-84467-687-3

This book "provide[s] a history of the development of 'the American system of news,' with emphasis on the government's role . . . and . . . construct[s] an account of the struggle across the 'fundamental fault-line' of race and ethnicity that shaped both mainstream and dissident media. . . . The stories of Hispanic, Native-American, African-American, and Asian-American journalists risking lives and well-being to raise their voices, constitute the true heart of this book. Some of the pioneers' names are reasonably familiar, . . . [b]ut there are dozens of others rescued from obscurity, ranging from Joaquín de Lisa and Joseph Antonio Boniquet, founders in 1809 of 'El Mensajero' of New Orleans, to Ruben Salazar of Los Angeles, assassinated while covering a riot in 1970." (Columbia Journalism Review)

Includes bibliographical references

Jones, Gerard

Killing monsters; why children need fantasy, super heroes, and make-believe violence. foreword by Lynn Ponton. Basic Bks. 2002 261p $25; pa $15   **302.23**

1. Fantasy 2. Children 3. Violence 4. Mass media

ISBN 0-465-03695-3; 0-465-03696-1 pa

LC 2001-52667

The author "argues that violent video games, movies, music and comics provide a safe fantasy world within which children learn to become familiar with and control the frightening emotions of anger, violence and sexuality." Publ Wkly

"Although not an academic, the author has done his homework. He presents his case convincingly, and the concluding notes provide support." SLJ

Includes bibliographical references (p. 233-250) and index

McChesney, Robert Waterman, 1952-

Digital disconnect; how capitalism is turning the Internet against democracy. Robert W. McChesney. The New Press 2013 320 p. (hardcover) $27.95 **302.23**

1. Democracy 2. Capitalism 3. Internet -- Political aspects

ISBN 1595588671; 9781595588678

LC 2012035748

This book, by Robert W. McChesney, "address[es] the relationship between economic power and the digital world. . . . McChesney . . . argues that the sharp decline in the enforcement of antitrust violations, the increase in patents on digital technology . . . and other policies have made the internet a place of numbing commercialism. . . . Robert McChesney . . . urg[es] us to reclaim the democratizing potential of the digital revolution while we still can." (Publisher's note)

Includes bibliographical references and index

Palfrey, John

Born digital; understanding the first generation of digital natives. [by] John Palfrey and Urs Gasser. Basic Books 2008 375p $25.95 **302.23**

1. Information society 2. Internet and children 3. Information technology 4. Internet and teenagers 5. Internet -- Social aspects

ISBN 9780465005154

LC 2008-21538

The authors "document the myriad ways downloading, text-messaging, Massively Multiplayer Online Games-playing, YouTube-watching youth are transforming society. Energetic, expert, and forward-looking, the authors serve as envoys between the generations, addressing issues that worry parents and educators, from privacy and safety concerns to the quality of digital information, the psychological and physical effects of information overload and excessive on-line time, and legal and ethical issues, all the while stressing the need for digital literacy and critical thinking." Booklist

Includes bibliographical references

Postman, Neil

Amusing ourselves to death; public discourse in the age of show business. Viking 1985 184p hardcover o.p. pa $14 **302.23**

1. Mass media 2. Television broadcasting 3. United States -- Civilization

ISBN 0-14-009438-5 pa

LC 85-5335

The author argues that the constant exposure to television has contributed to a decline in America's intellectual life.

"A sustained, withering and thought-provoking attack on television and what it is doing to us." Publ Wkly

Includes bibliographical references

Standage, Tom

Writing on the wall; Social Media - the First 2,000 Years. Tom Standage. St. Martin's Press 2013 288 p. illustrations $26 **302.23**

1. Social media -- History 2. Social networking -- History

ISBN 1620402831; 9781620402832

In this book, author Tom Standage "draws comparisons between modern social media and the forms of communication and information dissemination used over 2,000 years to show how, in fact, 'History retweets itself.' Examples include ancient Roman graffiti that bears a strong resemblance to a Facebook status update . . . and Martin Luther's 95 theses, perhaps the first document to go viral." (Publishers Weekly)

"Standage offers historical perspective on such concerns about evolving social media as faddishness, coarsening of discourse, distraction from serious work, and erosion of social skills." Booklist

Includes bibliographical references and index

Understanding media; the extensions of man. by Marshall McLuhan; edited by W. Terrence Gordon. Critical ed.; Gingko Press 2003 611p ill.; **302.23**

1. Mass media 2. Mass media -- United States -- History

ISBN 1584230738

LC 2003012174

"Terms and phrases such as "the global village" and "the medium is the message" are ow part of the lexicon, and McLuhan's theories continue to challenge our sensibilities and our assumptions about how and what we communicate." (Publisher's Note)

Includes bibliographical references (p. 569-574) and index..

Zuckerman, Ethan

Rewire; digital cosmopolitans in the age of connection. Ethan Zuckerman. W W Norton & Co Inc 2013 288 p. (hardcover) $26.95 **302.23**

1. Internet 2. Cosmopolitanism 3. Internet -- Social aspects 4. Social media

ISBN 0393082830; 9780393082838

LC 2013007124

This book is a reflection "on what it means to be a citizen of the world in the Internet age," where Ethan Zuckerman "declares that, far from aspiring to full engagement with others around the world, we seek to connect with people who share our values, nationality, gender, and race. . . . He argues that we all possess the capacity to build networks that 'rewire' our world with a better sense of interdependence." (Publishers Weekly)

Includes bibliographical references and index

302.3   Social interaction within groups

King, Larry

How to talk to anyone, anytime, anywhere; the secrets of good communication. [by] Larry King with Bill Gilbert. Crown 1994 220p hardcover o.p. pa $12.95 **302.3**

1. Conversation 2. Communication

ISBN 0-517-88453-4 pa

LC 94-31458

King "shows you how to break the ice with strangers, what to say at a wedding or a funeral, and how to sell yourself to a prospective employer—or interview a prospective employee. He gives his secrets for how to survive if you have to appear on radio or television, and how to recover from making a blooper." Publisher's note

O'Connor, Rory

Friends, followers, and the future; how social media are changing politics, threatening big brands, and killing traditional media. Rory O'Connor. City Lights Books 2012 285 p. (pbk.) $15.95   **302.3**
1. Mass media 2. Communication 3. Social networking 4. Social media 5. Social media -- Economic aspects 6. Social media -- Political aspects
ISBN 0872865568; 9780872865563
LC 2012005506

This book, by Rory O'Connor, offers "a look at how social media are transforming our world. . . . O'Connor explains the trends and explores what tech visionaries, media makers, political advisers, and businesspeople are saying about the meteoric rise of the various social networks of friends and followers, and what they bode for our future." (Publisher's note)

Sciolino, Elaine

La seduction; how the French play the game of life. Times Books/Henry Holt 2011 338p il   **302.3**
1. Seduction 2. Sex customs -- France -- History 3. France -- Social life and customs
ISBN 0-8050-9115-7; 9780805091151
LC 2010049572

According to the author, "seduction plays a crucial role in how the French relate to one another—not just in romantic relationships but also in how they conduct business, enjoy food and drink, define style, engage in intellectual debate, elect politicians, and project power around the world. While sexual repartee and conquest remain at the heart of seduction, for the French seduction has become a philosophy of life, even an ideology, that can confuse outsiders. In [this book, Sciolino looks at] . . . how seduction works in all areas, analyzing its limits as well as its power." (Publisher's note)

The author "deals with the subtle and cultural ways seduction shapes all aspects of French life. She takes a broad approach and writes less about the sexual associations of the word and more about the pleasure game the French play in order to 'attract or influence, to win over, even if just for fun.' Ms. Sciolino's pedigree as a commentator on things French is first class. She was a student in France in 1969 and returned to live and work there as a correspondent for Newsweek, then later as the Bureau Chief of The New York Times in Paris, and now as a correspondent for the paper. She finds French life permeated with the seduction factor, and in a journalistic fashion looks at it in an array of fields, including politics, foreign affairs, literature, history, film, advertising, beauty, scent, fashion, entertaining, food and wine, and sex, and makes her mostly French victims unveil some rules and secrets." Daily Beast
Includes bibliographical references

302.34   Social interaction in primary groups

Agatston, Patricia W.

Cyberbullying; bullying in the digital age. Robin M. Kowalski, Susan P. Limber, and Patricia W. Ag-

atston. Wiley-Blackwell 2012 xi, 282 p.p (pbk.) $24.95   **302.34**
1. Social media 2. Cyberbullying 3. School children 4. Computers and children 5. Bullying
ISBN 1444334816; 9781444334814; 9781444334807
LC 2011046026

In this book, "psychologists explore the reality of cyberbullies. . . . Advances in social media, email, instant messaging, and cell phones . . . have moved bullying from a schoolyard fear to a constant threat. The second edition of 'Cyberbullying' offers the most current information on this constantly-evolving issue and outlines the unique concerns and challenges it raises for children, parents, and educators." (Publisher's note)
Includes bibliographical references and index

Bazelon, Emily

★ **Sticks** and stones; defeating the culture of bullying and rediscovering the power of character and empathy. by Emily Bazelon. Random House 2013 viii, 386 p.p ill. (hardcover) $27   **302.34**
1. Bullies 2. Adolescence 3. Social media 4. Bullying in schools 5. Bullying -- Prevention 6. Bullying in schools -- Prevention
ISBN 0812992806; 9780679644002; 9780812992809
LC 2012022773

This book, by Emily Bazelon, discusses teen culture in the U.S., focusing on bullying. "Being a teenager has never been easy, but in recent years, with the rise of the Internet and social media, it has become exponentially more challenging. . . . Bazelon defines what bullying is and, just as important, what it is not. She explores when intervention is essential and when kids should be given the freedom to fend for themselves. She also dispels persistent myths." (Publisher's note)

"While less prescriptive than other books on the topic, very useful FAQs are included, as are resource lists for readers. Masterfully written, Bazelon's book will increase understanding, awareness, and action." Pub Wkly
Includes bibliographical references and index

Strauss, Susan L.

★ **Sexual** harassment and bullying; a guide to keeping kids safe and holding schools accountable. Susan L. Strauss. Rowman & Littlefield Publishers 2012 290 p. (cloth : alk. paper) $34.95   **302.34**
1. Bullies 2. Social media 3. Sexual harassment 4. Bullying 5. Bullying -- Prevention 6. Sexual harassment in education 7. Sexual harassment -- Prevention
ISBN 1442201622; 9781442201620
LC 2011031731

In this book, "[Susan L.] Strauss draws on her experiences as consultant, former high-school teacher, and parent of a child who was sexually harassed to advise parents, teachers, and other adults on how to protect children" from bullying and harassment. She gives definitions of bullying and harassment, "offers a particular focus on the kind of harassment of gay, bisexual, and transgendered students," and examines "how social media . . . have ramped up bullying and harassment." (Booklist)
Includes bibliographical references and index.

Whitson, Signe

8 keys to end bullying; strategies for parents & schools. Signe Whitson ; foreword by Babette Rothschild. W.W. Norton & Co Inc. 2014 240 p. (8 keys to mental health series) (pbk.) $19.95   **302.34**
1. Bullies 2. Classroom management 3. Bullying -- Prevention 4. Aggressiveness in children 5. Bullying in schools -- Prevention
ISBN 0393709280; 9780393709285

LC 2014001241

This book by Signe Whitson discusses how "social media bullying . . . has given the widespread problem a new dimension. While no magic cure-all exists, adults can learn . . . techniques that can make a huge difference in the lives of kids. In 8 core strategies, this book lays them out, from establishing meaningful connections with kids to creating a positive school climate, addressing cyberbullying, building social emotional competence, . . . and much more." (Publisher's note)

"Complete with example scenarios, exercises for readers, and sample responses, the author does a convincing job of helping adults feel empowered to address this important issue." LJ

Includes bibliographical references and index

302.5   Relation of individual to society

Olds, Jacqueline

The **lonely** American; drifting apart in the twenty-first century. [by] Jacqueline Olds and Richard S. Schwartz. Beacon Press 2008 228p $24.95   **302.5**
1. Loneliness 2. Loneliness -- United States 3. Social isolation -- United States
ISBN 978-0-8070-0034-2; 0-8070-0034-5

LC 2008-19339

The authors "paint a tragic picture of a nation of individual units—families, couples and, increasingly, single people—that have all but ceased to function as a society. While the authors focus largely on the psychological impact of all this isolation, they also explain its physical toll on Americans and their world. Not only is social isolation an indicator for substance abuse, violent crime and early death, it is also linked to greater consumption of consumer goods. . . . In keeping with their profession as psychoanalysts, Olds and Schwartz maintain a kind and caring tone throughout The Lonely American, neither scolding nor scoffing at the nation of individuals Americans have become" PopMatters

Includes bibliographical references and index.

303.3   Coordination and control

Century, Douglas

Making a difference; stories of vision and courage from America's leaders. Chesley "Sully" Sullenberger, with Douglas Century. 1st ed. HarperCollins 2012 x, 318 p.p (hbk.) $26.99   **303.3**
1. Leadership 2. Leadership -- United States -- Case studies
ISBN 0061924709; 9780061924705; 9780061924712;

9780062101365; 9780062128317

LC 2011045074

Author Chesley Sullenberger tells his own story and the story of "first officer Jeff Skiles . . . [as] advocates and champions for aviation safety and the profession of airline pilots. . . . [He also looks at] three-time World Series-winning baseball manager Tony La Russa; Admiral Thad Allen, who brought innovative methods . . . to deal . . . with the aftermath of Hurricane Katrina; Gene Kranz, the NASA Flight Director who . . . brought Apollo 13 and its crew safely home; and Michelle Rhee, who was brought in to overhaul the Washington, D.C., school system." (Kirkus Reviews)

Corning, Peter

The **fair** society; [by] Peter Corning. University of Chicago Press 2011 237p $27.50   **303.3**
1. Fairness 2. Basic needs 3. Social ethics 4. Social policy 5. Social justice 6. Social contract
ISBN 978-0-226-11627-3; 0-226-11627-1

LC 2010021771

It was the author's intent to demonstrate "that human nature has evolved in such a way as to create a natural revulsion to [unfair situations] . . . He recounts various evolutionary arguments for the notion that our hunter-gatherer ancestors possessed a deep sense of fairness and developed 'a pattern of egalitarian sharing' in which 'dominance behaviors were actively resisted by coalitions of other group members.' . . . Corning endeavors to show that the capitalist system as currently practiced in the United States and elsewhere is manifestly unfair. . . . he proposes a new type of society founded on a biosocial contract, which he describes as a 'truly voluntary bargain among various (empowered) stakeholders over how the benefits and obligations in a society are to be apportioned among the members' that is 'grounded in our growing understanding of human nature and the basic purpose of a human society.'"(American Scientist)

"Corning argues that both capitalism and socialism fail the fairness test—both in theory and in practice—and he calls for a new social contract based on three complementary fairness principles: equality in relation to our basic needs, equity (or merit) in relation to our personal efforts and accomplishments, and reciprocity—an obligation for everyone to contribute a fair share in return for the benefits they receive from society. Corning also proposes a set of transformative economic and political reforms that would move us toward the ideal of what he terms a Fair Society, including full employment and a 'basic needs guarantee' for all of our people, a shift in our economic system toward stakeholder (versus shareholder) capitalism, a strong effort to promote cooperative, not-for-profit community development and, not least, a lifelong community service ethic that would include a year or two of national service for all who are able to do so." Politics and Life Sciences

Includes bibliographical references

Huxley, Aldous

★ **Brave** new world revisited. Harper & Row 1958 147p hardcover o.p. pa $11.95   **303.3**
1. Culture 2. Propaganda 3. Brainwashing 4. Totalitarianism
ISBN 0-06-089852-6 pa

In response to his 1932 novel Brave new world "Huxley reconsiders his prophecies and fears that some of these may be coming true much sooner than he thought." Oxford Companion to Engl Lit. 5th edition

Nader, Ralph

Told you so; the big book of weekly columns. by Ralph Nader. Seven Stories Press 2013 xv, 520 p.p (pbk.) $29.95 **303.3**

> 1. Social problems 2. United States -- Social conditions 3. Social justice -- United States 4. Corporate power -- United States 5. United States -- Social policy -- 21st century 6. United States -- Economic policy -- 21st century 7. United States -- Social conditions -- 21st century 8. United States -- Politics and government -- 21st century
> ISBN 1609804740; 9781609804749

> LC 2013001625

Author Ralph Nader "presents a panoramic portrait of the problems confronting our society and provides examples of the many actions an organized citizenry could and should take to create a more just and environmentally sustainable world. Drawing on decades of experience, Nader's columns document the consequences of concentrated corporate power; threats to our food, water and air; the corrosive effect of commercialism on our children; the dismantling of worker rights; and the attacks on our civil rights." (Publisher's note)

> Includes index

✓ **Naím, Moisés, 1952-**

The **end** of power; from boardrooms to battlefields and churches to states, why being in charge isn't what it used to be. Moisés Naím. Basic Books, a member of the Perseus Books Group 2013 xiii, 306 p.p (hardcover) $27.99 **303.3**

> 1. Power (Social sciences) 2. Organization
> ISBN 0465031560; 9780465031566

> LC 2012049642

This book, by Moises Naim, explores "the struggle between once-dominant megaplayers and the new micropowers challenging them in every field of human endeavor. . . . Naim . . . covers the seismic changes underway in business, religion, education, within families, and in all matters of war and peace. . . . Those in power retain it by erecting powerful barriers . . . [and] insurgent forces dismantle those barriers more quickly and easily than ever." (Publisher's note)

> Includes bibliographical references and index

✓ **Rosenberg, Tina**

Join the club; how peer pressure can transform the world. W.W. Norton & Company 2011 xxiv, 402p $25.95 **303.3**

> 1. Peer pressure 2. Social change 3. Social groups
> ISBN 978-0-393-06858-0

> LC 2010-52146

The author "examines how creative thinking and critical analysis of group dynamics turned some of India's lowest caste women into successful entrepreneurs and village leaders, how a group of ragtag Serbian students used street theater to topple a repressive dictator, and why a suburban Chicago megachurch finds its doctrine best disseminated one dinner table at a time. This social cure, Rosenberg posits, has the power to channel herd mentality into forces that can bring about positive changes for at-risk individuals, wheth-

er they are battling AIDS in South Africa or drug abuse in South Carolina." Booklist

> "A solid, sweeping examination of peer pressure as a force for social change." Kirkus

> Includes bibliographical references

Surowiecki, James

✓ The **wisdom** of crowds; why the many are smarter than the few and how collective wisdom shapes business, economies, societies and nations. Doubleday 2004 xxi, 296p $24.95; pa $14 **303.3**

> 1. Crowds 2. Social psychology
> ISBN 0-385-50386-5; 0-385-72170-6 pa

> LC 2003-70095

The author "analyzes the concept of collective wisdom and applies it to various areas of the social sciences, including economics and politics. . . . This work is an intriguing study of collective intelligence and how it works in contemporary society." Libr J

> Includes bibliographical references

✓ **Wills, Garry, 1934-**

Certain trumpets; the call of leaders. Simon & Schuster 1994 336p il hardcover o.p. pa $16 **303.3**

> 1. Leadership -- Case studies. 2. Social participation -- Case studies. 3. Power (Social sciences) -- Case studies.
> ISBN 0-671-65702-X; 978-0-684-80138-4 pa; 0-684-80138-8 pa

> LC 94-6526

The author "has chosen 16 figures who exemplify a distinctive leadership type—for example, military (Napoleon), charismatic (King David), saintly (Catholic worker activist Dorothy Day). Each leader is contrasted with an 'anti-type' who, in Wills's judgment, failed to capitalize on strengths similar to those of his or her successful counterpart. . . . Wills pairs Martha Graham with Madonna, Socrates with Ludwig Wittgenstein, Eleanor Roosevelt with Nancy Reagan in a wise, witty, entertaining look at the psychology of leaders and their followers." Publ Wkly

> Includes bibliographical references

303.34 Leadership

✓ **Kellerman, Barbara**

The **end** of leadership. Harper Business 2012 256 p. $27.99 **303.34**

> 1. Leadership 2. Social change
> ISBN 0062069160; 9780062069160

Here, Barbara Kellerman "details vast societal changes that have demeaned and downgraded leaders and altered the relationship between leaders and followers. The Internet and other advances in communication technology brought more information, encouraged greater self-expression and expanded connection. With information available instantly to everyone, followers (citizens, employees, stockholders) learned of their leaders' faults and began questioning their authority." (Kirkus)

303.4   Social change

Baker, Stephen

The **numerati**. Houghton Mifflin Co. 2008 244p
$26   **303.4**

1. Data processing 2. Mathematical models
ISBN 978-0-618-78460-8; 0-618-78460-8

LC 2008-17830

The author "spotlights a new breed of entrepreneurial
mathematicians (the numerati) engaged in harnessing the
avalanche of private data individuals provide when they use
a credit card, donate to a cause, surf the Internet—or even
make a phone call. . . . An intriguing but disquieting look at
a not too distant future when our thoughts will remain private, but computers will disclose our tastes, opinions, habits
and quirks to curious parties, not all of whom have our best
interests at heart." Publ Wkly

Includes bibliographical references

Barash, David P.

Homo mysterious; evolutionary puzzles of human nature. David P. Barash. Oxford University Press
2012 329 p. (hardback : alk. paper) $27.95   **303.4**

1. Evolution 2. Human beings 3. Sociobiology 4. Sex
(Biology) 5. Human evolution 6. Social evolution 7.
Evolution (Biology)
ISBN 0199751943; 9780199751945

LC 2011044302

This book, by David P. Barash, examines "evolutionary
questions about the human condition . . . [such as] why do
women have orgasms; why does menopause exist; why do
men have shorter average life spans than women; what's the
evolutionary reason for homosexuality, the arts, and religion. . . . He shows how tentative scientific explanations are
and the critical role hypothesis testing plays in our understanding of the world." (Publishers Weekly)

Includes bibliographical references and index.

Carr, Nicholas

The **big** switch; rewiring the world, from Edison
to Google. W. W. Norton & Company 2008 278p
$25.95; pa $16.95   **303.4**

1. Internet 2. Information technology 3. Technological
innovations 4. Computers and civilization
ISBN 978-0-393-06228-1; 0-393-06228-7; 978-0-393-
33394-7 pa; 0-393-33394-9 pa

LC 2007-38084

The author "examines the future of the Internet, which
he says may one day completely replace the desktop PC as
all computing services are delivered over the Net as a utility, the Internet morphing into one giant 'World Wide Computer.'" Booklist

Includes bibliographical references

Diamond, Jared M.

★ **Guns**, germs, and steel; the fates of human
societies. [by] Jared Diamond. Norton 2005 518p
il map $24.95   **303.4**

1. Ethnology 2. Food supply 3. Social change 4.
Technology and civilization 5. Environmental influence

on humans
ISBN 0-393-06131-0; 978-0-393-06131-4

LC 2005-284261

First published 1997

"This book poses a simple but profound question about
the distribution of wealth and power in the modern world:
'Why weren't Native Americans, Africans, and Aboriginal
Australians the ones who decimated, subjugated, or extermi-
nated Europeans and Asians?'. . . To explore the discrepan-
cies in technological and cultural development he looks not
at peoples but at places, and at the natural resources available to different indigenous populations since 11,000 B.C.
The scope and the explanatory power of this book are astounding." New Yorker [review of 1997 edition]

Includes bibliographical references

Ferris, Timothy

The **science** of liberty; democracy, reason and
the laws of nature. Harper 2010 368p $26.99 **303.4**

1. Democracy 2. Science and civilization 3. Science
-- History
ISBN 978-0-06-078150-7; 0-06-078150-5

LC 2009-27505

The author "argues that science and the rise of 'science
societies' are the fundamental drivers of liberty and democracy. . . . Ferris traces the dual scientific and democratic
revolutions from their Renaissance, Enlightenment, and
early modern origins to the titanic twentieth-century battles
between the liberal democracies and their fascist and communist rivals. Ferris also explores the scientific orientation
of the United States' founders, such as Thomas Jefferson and
Benjamin Franklin, and its relevance to their constitutional
thinking and their noble 'experiment' of a new nation. The
Science of Liberty is sweeping and provocative, even if
many may still doubt that science can extinguish prejudices,
parochialisms, and illiberal impulses." Foreign Affairs

Includes bibliographical references

Gore, Albert, 1948-

The **future**; six drivers of global change. Al
Gore. Random House 2013 xxxi, 558 p.p (hard-
back) $30   **303.4**

1. Forecasting 2. Climate change 3. World history
-- 21st century 4. Globalization 5. Social change 6.
Technological innovations 7. Global environmental
change 8. Economic history -- 21st century
ISBN 0812992946; 9780812992946

LC 2012039890

This book, by Al Gore, offers an "assessment of six critical drivers of global change in the decades to come. . . . Al
Gore surveys . . . ever-increasing economic globalization .
. ., worldwide digital communications, . . . the balance of
global political, economic, and military power . . . , unsustainable growth in consumption, pollution flows, and depletion of the planet's strategic resources . . . , [and] genomic,
biotechnology, neuroscience, and life sciences revolutions."
(Publisher's note)

"Gore's strengths lie in his passion for the subject and in
his ability to take the long view by putting current events and
trends in historical context," PubWkly

Includes bibliographical references (pages 379-387)
and index

Heath, Chip

Switch; how to change things when change is hard. [by] Chip Heath and Dan Heath. Broadway Books 2010 305p $26; pa $15.95; ebook $11.99   **303.4**
1. Change (Psychology)
ISBN 978-0-385-52875-7; 978-0-307-74235-3 pa; 978-0-307-59016-9 ebook
LC 2009-27814

The authors "analyze what must be addressed if societal, organizational, and personal habits and practices are to be instilled with new ideas. They draw upon numerous behavioral studies, business case studies, and hypothetical examples to illustrate their principles." Libr J

This book "offers many insights about human behavior and psychology that marketing professionals, communications experts, and public-policy makes might all appreciate." Futurist

Includes bibliographical references

Hessler, Peter

Country driving; a journey through China from farm to factory. Harper 2010 438p map $27.99   **303.4**
1. Highway transportation 2. Journalists 3. China -- Description and travel 4. Transportation, Automotive -- China
ISBN 0-06-180409-6; 978-0-06-180409-0
LC 2009-27502

In 2001, Peter Hessler, the Beijing correspondent for The New Yorker, acquired his Chinese driver's license. For the next seven years, he traveled the country, tracking how the automobile and improved roads were transforming China. . . . Country Driving begins with Hessler's 7,000-mile trip across northern China, following the Great Wall, from the East China Sea to the Tibetan plateau. He investigates a historically important rural region being abandoned, as young people migrate to jobs in the southeast. Next Hessler spends six years in Sancha, a small farming village in the mountains north of Beijing, which changes dramatically after the local road is paved and the capital's auto boom brings new tourism. Finally, he turns his attention to urban China, researching development . . . in Lishui, a small southeastern city where officials hope that a new government-built expressway will transform a farm region into a major industrial center. (Publisher's note)

"Full of exotic detail, solid reporting, and ironic observation, Country Driving offers a personal snapshot of the world's second superpower hurtling through the 21st century." Boston Globe

Includes bibliographical references

Hoffman, Abbie

The best of Abbie Hoffman; foreword by Norman Mailer; edited by Dan Simon with the author. Four Walls Eight Windows 1989 421p il hardcover o.p. pa $18.95   **303.4**
1. Radicalism 2. United States -- Civilization
ISBN 0-941423-27-1; 0-941423-42-5 pa
LC 89-23585

This volume contains selections from Revolution for the hell of it, Woodstock Nation, Steal this book, and New writings.

Ladd, Brian

Autophobia; love and hate in the automotive age. University of Chicago Press 2008 227p il $22.50   **303.4**
1. Automobiles 2. Environmental degradation 3. Automobiles -- Social aspects 4. Transportation, Automotive -- United States
ISBN 0-226-46741-4; 978-0-226-46741-2
LC 2008-14520

This is "a look at the car and its critics." (N Y Times Book Rev) Index.

Ladd "documents a century of expanding U.S. reliance on vehicles powered by oil, most of which has to be imported. He frames his analysis in familiar concepts: the automotive industry as employer, urban migration from cities by families relying on automobiles for transportation, traffic/congestion/roadways, and damage to the environment from burning fossil fuels. . . . [The author shows] how the car is completely woven into the fabric of our cultural and economic history. As such, he writes, we have accepted the dark side of the automobile—pollution, congestion, high energy costs, and accidental loss of life—in exchange for personal mobility." Libr J

Includes bibliographical references

Lanier, Jaron

★ You are not a gadget; a manifesto. Alfred A. Knopf 2010 209p $24.95   **303.4**
1. Information technology 2. Technological innovations 3. Technology and civilization 4. Web sites -- Design 5. Digital media -- Social aspects 6. Information technology -- Social aspects 7. Technological innovations -- Social aspects
ISBN 0-307-26964-7; 978-0-307-26964-5
LC 2009-20298

The author, an artist and computer scientist, offers an examination of the way the World Wide Web "is transforming our lives. . . . [He maintains that] the web's first designers made crucial choices (such as making one's presence anonymous) that have had enormous—and often unintended—consequences. What's more, these designs quickly became 'locked in,' a permanent part of the web's very structure. Lanier discusses the technical and cultural problems that [he believes] can grow out of poorly considered digital design and warns that our financial markets and sites like Wikipedia, Facebook, and Twitter are elevating the 'wisdom' of mobs and computer algorithms over the intelligence and judgment of individuals. . . . [Lanier argues that] a new humanistic technology is necessary." (Publisher's note)

"In the nineteen-eighties, Lanier belonged to what he calls a 'merry band' of Internet pioneers who believed that the digital revolution would mean a groundswell of creativity. But, he argues in this manifesto, around the turn of this century the dream was hijacked by 'digital Maoists,' who value the crowd above the individual. Their influence, he writes, has led to an online culture of mashups, 'pervasive anonymity' (which encourages bullying and moblike behavior), open access (so that individual ownership is devalued or lost), and social-networking sites that reduce 'the deep meaning of personhood.' He fears that these characteristics are perilously close to 'lock-in': becoming permanent features of the Web. Lanier's detractors have accused him of Ludditism, but his argument will make intuitive sense to anyone concerned with questions of propriety, responsibility, and authenticity." New Yorker

Linden, Eugene

The **ragged** edge of the world; encounters at the frontier where modernity, wildlands, and indigenous peoples meet. Viking 2011 260p $26.95 **303.4**
1. Ethnology
ISBN 978-0-670-02251-9
LC 2010043578

"Traveling to the rain forests of Borneo and to the Amazon, the Antarctic, and Africa, Linden provides firsthand accounts of cargo cults in New Guinea, practices of Pygmy tribes in Africa, and conservation efforts in Cuba—some of which show positive responses to deforestation and loss of habitat for wildlife, while others reveal the downward spiral to extinction for rain forests and many animal species. He highlights cultural extinction as much as environmental devastation to habitats. . . . Linden provides an original look at globalization and its impact on various cultures and species throughout the world. Anyone interested in global environmental issues will find this book informative." Libr J

Otto, Shawn

Fool me twice; fighting the assault on science in America. [by] Shawn Lawrence Otto. Rodale 2011 376p $25.99 **303.4**
1. Learning and scholarship 2. Science -- United States 3. Science -- Study and teaching 4. United States -- Intellectual life
ISBN 978-1-60529-217-5; 1-60529-217-6
LC 2011033902

The author "explores the devaluation of science in America. His exhaustively researched text explains the three-pronged attack on science: how right-wing Christian fervor discredits evolution; how post-modernism and cultural sensitivity makes people believe that objective truth doesn't exist; and how corporations discredit scientists in order to further economic agendas. . . . The accessible book will inform scientists about what has happened to their field, provide an overview for laypeople, and allow educators to equip themselves to address these issues for the next generation and reverse this troubling trend." Publ Wkly
Includes bibliographical references

Pagel, Mark

Wired for culture; origins of the human social mind. Mark Pagel. W. W. Norton & Company 2012 416 p. **303.4**
1. Culture 2. Evolution 3. Social change 4. Social sciences 5. Language and languages 6. Human evolution 7. Social evolution 8. Evolution (Biology) 9. Evolutionary genetics
ISBN 0393065871; 9780393065879
LC 2011044465

This book "frames cultural development in the language of Richard Dawkins's selfish gene theory. . . . Dawkins . . . coined the term 'meme' as the cultural analogue of a gene.

[Mark] Pagel . . . [argues that m]emes . . . have built vehicles around themselves made up of groups of people. . . . [He] explores the implications of the emerging consensus across . . . religion, the arts and economics, . . . consciousness, deception, conflict and thevery idea of truth." (New Scientist)
Includes bibliographical references and index

Pipher, Mary

The **green** boat; reviving ourselves in our capsized culture. Mary Pipher. Riverhead Books 2013 240 p. $16 **303.4**
1. Environmental movement 2. Culture shock 3. Adjustment (Psychology) 4. Social change -- Psychological aspects 5. Social problems -- Psychological aspects
ISBN 1594485852; 9781594485855
LC 2012043406

Here, Mary Pipher offers an "approach to acknowledging the global environmental crisis." She "explains, the overwhelming amount of information about the desperate state of our planet leads to stress, avoiding discussion, willful ignorance, and outright denial. . . . Piper distinguishes between 'distractionable intelligence,' which makes us feel helpless, and 'actionable intelligence,' which combines information with suggestions for addressing problems." (Publishers Weekly)

The **Radical** reader; a documentary history of the American radical tradition. edited by Timothy Patrick McCarthy and John McMillian; foreword by Eric Foner. New Press 2003 688p $65; lib bdg $21.95 **303.4**
1. Radicalism
ISBN 1-56584-827-6; 1-56584-682-6 lib bdg
LC 2002-41051

"By bringing many hard-to-find documents under one cover, this anthology will excite readers in discussing why radicals from all walks of life have made progressive ideals meaningful to Americans. Recommended for college, high school, and public libraries." Libr J
Includes bibliographical references

Reeves, Byron

Total engagement; using games and virtual worlds to change the way people work and businesses compete. [by] Byron Reeves [and] J. Leighton Read. Harvard Business Press 2009 274p $29.95 **303.4**
1. Play 2. Work 3. Games 4. Group relations training
ISBN 978-1-4221-4657-6; 1-4221-4657-X
LC 2009-35808

The authors "discuss how game design can be a great interface for office work. They describe how using avatars (virtual personal characters) and online games can increase employee engagement and productivity and facilitate team building, collaboration, and leadership skills. They anticipate online games changing how people will work, and they view virtual-world work interfaces as inevitable and definitive." Choice
Includes bibliographical references

Shirky, Clay

Cognitive surplus; creativity and generosity in a connected age. Penguin Press 2010 242p $25.95 **303.4**

1. Social networking 2. Information society 3. Social media 4. Mass media -- Social aspects

ISBN 1-59420-253-2; 978-1-59420-253-7

LC 2009-53882

This is an "inquiry into what we might join together to do instead if we weren't watching TV." (N Y Times Book Rev) Index.

Shirky "argues that new technology is making it possible for people to collaborate in ways that have the potential to change society. By 'cognitive surplus,' the author refers to the free time of the world's educated citizenry, which amounts to more than one trillion hours per year. . . . [He] discusses the many factors that have given rise to social media and suggests the conditions that will best allow voluntary groups to take advantage of the world's aggregate free time to benefit society. . . . [Shirky] may be overly optimistic about the possible benefits of social media, but he makes clear their growing global importance. An informed look at the social impact of the Internet." Kirkus

Includes bibliographical references

Solnit, Rebecca

A **paradise** built in hell; the extraordinary communities that arise in disasters. Viking 2009 353p $27.95 **303.4**

1. Disasters

ISBN 978-0-670-02107-9; 0-670-02107-5

LC 2009-04101

"An engaging book, full of fascinating detail, 'Paradise' especially deserves a close reading by political leaders at every level, as well as the news media who cover disasters." Christ Sci Monit

Includes bibliographical references

Tapscott, Don, 1947-

Macrowikinomics; rebooting business and the world. [by] Don Tapscott and Anthony D. Williams. Portfolio/Penguin 2010 424p $27.95 **303.4**

1. Information technology 2. Online social networks 3. Technological innovations

ISBN 978-1-59184-356-6

LC 2010023338

The authors "present a new framework for understanding social and economic innovations applicable to the spectrum of industries under which people utilize emerging Web applications to foster a more economically, socially, and ecologically sustainable world. . . . [This book] addresses an important issue and is good preparation for an epoch of staggering technological leaps." Choice

Includes bibliographical references

Toffler, Alvin

★ **Future** shock. Bantam Books 1990 561p pa $7.99 **303.4**

1. Family 2. Children 3. Democracy 4. Education 5. Social change 6. Adaptation (Biology) 7. Interpersonal relations 8. Technology and civilization 9. Modern civilization -- 1950-

ISBN 978-0-553-27737-1; 0-553-27737-5

First published 1970 by Random House

According to the author, "future shock is 'the dizzying disorientation brought on by the premature arrival of the future.' . . . Toffler outlines some interesting strategies for survival, writing in a clear popular style." Publ Wkly

Includes bibliographical references

Turkle, Sherry

Alone together. Basic Books 2011 360p $28.95 **303.4**

1. Information technology 2. Interpersonal relations 3. Human-computer interaction 4. Information technology -- Social aspects

ISBN 978-0-465-01021-9; 0-465-01021-0

LC 2010-30614

This book "is the third in a trilogy, part of a project [author Sherry Turkle] . . . has been working on since she joined MIT in 1976 and noticed that the people there were using the language of psychology to talk about their machines. . . . Turkle picks out the contradictions of the networked life that everyone has now come to take for granted, but adolescents especially: the desire for attention and the desire to hide, constantly online but dreading the exposure of a phone call. . . . Turkle argues that people risk impairing the quality of their thought and communication by so often resorting to media designed only for short, simplified messages." (London Review of Books)

"Turkle argues that people are increasingly functioning without face-to-face contact. For all the talk of convenience and connection derived from texting, e-mailing, and social networking, Turkle reaffirms that what humans still instinctively need is each other, and she encounters dissatisfaction and alienation among users. . . . Turkle's prescient book makes a strong case that what was meant to be a way to facilitate communications has pushed people closer to their machines and further away from each other." Publ Wkly

Includes bibliographical references

Werth, Barry

Banquet at Delmonico's; how evolution conquered Gilded Age America. Random House 2009 xxxi, 362p $27 **303.4**

1. Evolution 2. Philosophers 3. Social Darwinism 4. United States -- Social conditions

ISBN 978-1-4000-6778-7; 1-4000-6778-2

LC 2008-16567

"Werth effortlessly brings each eccentric character to life through colorful details and well-chosen anecdotes, while taking us on a whirlwind tour of Gilded Age politics and society. Banquet at Delmonico's crackles with energy and wit." N Y Times Book Rev

Includes bibliographical references

303.48   Causes of change

Diamandis, Peter, 1961-

Abundance; the future is better than you think. Peter H. Diamandis and Steven Kotler. Simon & Schuster 2012 p. cm.   **303.48**

1. Population 2. Food supply 3. Natural resources 4. Technological forecasting 5. Technology -- Social aspects 6. Technological innovations -- Forecasting
ISBN 1451614217; 9781451614213

LC 2011039926

Author Peter H. Diamandis reports that abundance can establish "hard targets for change and lays out a strategic roadmap for governments, industry and entrepreneurs, giving us plenty of reason for optimism. Examining human need by category--water, food, energy, healthcare, education, freedom--Diamandis . . . introduce[s] dozens of innovators making great strides in each area: Larry Page, Steven Hawking, Dean Kamen, Daniel Kahneman, Elon Musk, Bill Joy, Stewart Brand, Jeff Skoll, Ray Kurzweil, Ratan Tata, Craig Venter, among many, many others." (Amazon)

Encyclopedia of mathematics and society; Sarah J. Greenwald , Jill E. Thomley, [editors] Salem Press 2012 3 v. (xxxi, 1191 p.)p   **303.48**

1. Mathematics -- History 2. Mathematics -- Encyclopedias 3. Mathematics -- Social aspects
ISBN 1587658445; 1587658453; 1587658461; 158765847X; 9781587658440; 9781587658457; 9781587658464; 9781587658471

LC 2011021856

This encyclopedia of mathematics "focus[es] on how the basic concepts of figures relate to everyday life. As the editors phrase it, the purpose of these compact volumes is to 'weave multilayered connections between society, history, people, applications, and mathematics.' . . . [T]opics covered include 'Cooking,' 'Earthquakes,' 'Mathematics and Religion,' and 'Skydiving.' While some purely mathematical principles are discussed, they are always placed in relation to the larger context of human affairs, such as in the essay 'Algebra in Society.' Pieces open with boldface headword(s), a classification of the subject matter, and a one-line summary of the material to follow. A short bibliography and cross-references follow." (Libr J)

Includes bibliographical references and index

Freeberg, Ernest

The **Age** of Edison; Electric Light and the Invention of Modern America. Ernest Freeberg. Penguin Group USA 2013 368 p. ill. (hardcover) $27.95   **303.48**

1. Electric lighting 2. Technological innovations -- History 3. Electric lighting -- United States -- History 4. Technological innovations -- United States -- History 5. Technological innovations -- Social aspects -- United States -- History
ISBN 1594204268; 9781594204265

LC 2012039513

This book, by Ernest Freeberg, discusses the social impact of the invention of electricity, as part of the "Penguin History of American Life" series. It "places the story of Edison's invention in the context of a technological revolution that transformed America and Europe. . . . Edison and his fellow inventors emerged from a culture shaped by . . . a lively popular press that took an interest in science and technology, and an American patent system that encouraged innovation." (Publisher's note)

Includes bibliographical references (pages 317-341) and index

Guest, Robert

Borderless economics; Chinese sea turtles, Indian fridges, and the new fruits of global capitalism. Robert Guest. Palgrave Macmillan 2011 256 p. $27.00   **303.48**

1. Wealth 2. Economics 3. Business networks 4. Diffusion of innovations 5. Immigrants -- United States 6. Globalization -- Economic aspects
ISBN 0230113826; 9780230113824

LC 2011022135

This book offers a "survey of the global impact of the 215 million people who live outside their countries of origin." Author Robert Guest "contends that the three percent (and growing) part of the world's population that is migrating is disproportionately contributing to the creation of international wealth, both in the sense of financial assets and the development of new technological and economic capabilities." (Kirkus)

Includes bibliographical references and index.

Johnson, Steven, 1968-

Future perfect; the case for progress in a networked age. Steven Johnson. Riverhead Books 2012 xxxvii, 231 p.p (alk. paper) $26.95   **303.48**

1. Progress 2. Social change 3. Information networks 4. Technology and civilization 5. Information technology -- Social aspects 6. Social networks
ISBN 1594488207; 9781594488207

LC 2012026086

This book by Steven Johnson "makes the case that a new model of political change is on the rise, transforming everything from local governments to classrooms, from protest movements to health care . . . . -- influenced by the success and interconnectedness of the Internet, but not dependent on high-tech solutions. . . . Johnson explores this new vision of progress through a series of . . . narratives: from the 'miracle on the Hudson' to the planning of the French railway system." (Publisher's note)

Includes bibliographical references and index

Kotler, Steven

Abundance; the future is better than you think. Peter H. Diamandis and Steven Kotler. Free Press 2012 386 p. $26.99   **303.48**

1. Social problems 2. Technology and civilization 3. Technological innovations -- Forecasting 4. Technological forecasting 5. Technology -- Social aspects
ISBN 9781451614213; 1451614217

LC 2011039926

This book discusses technological innovations, looking at how they could help in "finding solutions for world problems, from poverty and disease to climate change and pollution. . . . Peter Diamandis, founder of the X Prize Foundation, and journalist Steven Kotler argue that innovation can provide 9 billion people with a world of plenty. . . . [Lowell Wood envisions a] toilet that would burn faeces to evaporate urine, thus preventing water pollution while generating surplus energy that could power cellphones and lights. . . . "Abundance" extols the potential of 3D printers to make almost any kind of product at home." (New Scientist)

Includes bibliographical references (p. [305]-356) and index

Kunstler, James Howard

Too much magic; wishful thinking, technology, and the fate of the nation. James Howard Kunstler. Atlantic Monthly Press 2012 245 p. (hardcover) $25.00   **303.48**

    1. Technological innovations   2. Technology and civilization 3. United States -- Economic conditions

ISBN 080212030X; 9780802120304

In this book, James Howard Kunstler "recount[s] the evidence supporting his predictions about our radically altered future. . . . The dangerously stressed systems that underpin the society we've known since World War II -- 'agriculture, commerce, manufacturing, transport, finance, the oil-gas-coal industry, the electric grid' -- are too large, too complex and too expensive to sustain any longer." (Kirkus Reviews)

Moreno, Jonathan D.

The **body** politic; Jonathan D. Moreno. Bellevue Literary Press 2011 207p.   **303.48**

    1. Science 2. Abortion 3. Eugenics 4. United States 5. Stem cell research

ISBN 9781934137383 pa; 1934137383 pa

                   LC 2011026354

In this book, a "Kirkus Reviews" Best Book of the Year, the author uses the term "'biopolitics,' popularized by [philosopher] Michel Foucault . . . to describe historical and current debates over issues ranging from abortion and health care to stem cells and genetically modified organisms. . . . [He] unpacks . . . distrust of technology, on both the political right and left. . . . Both extremes place 'human dignity' as central to their trepidation toward technology, but they have starkly contrasting ideas of what such a concept embodies. The far-left greens fear the effects of technology on social justice, while the neoconservatives are more concerned with technology as a source of alienation from what makes us truly human. . . . Ultimately, Moreno shows that the disarming features of modern biology reflect those of all science as a human endeavor." (washingtonindependentreveiwofbooks.com)

Includes bibliographical references and index.

Morozov, Evgeny

The **net** delusion; Evgeny Morozov. Public Affairs 2011 xvii, 409 p.p   **303.48**

    1. Democracy 2. Freedom of information 3. Internet -- Political aspects 4. Iran -- Politics and government 5. Internet -- Social aspects

ISBN 978-1-58648-874-1; 1-58648-874-0

                   LC 2010039066

This book challenges "[t]he idea that the internet was fomenting revolution and promoting democracy in Iran . . . [and the] belief that communications technology, and the

internet in particular, is inherently pro-democratic. In this gleefully iconoclastic book, Evgeny Morozov takes a stand against this "cyber-utopian" view, arguing that the internet can be just as effective at sustaining authoritarian regimes. By assuming that the internet is always pro-democratic, he says, Western policymakers are operating with a 'voluntary intellectual handicap' that makes it harder rather than easier to promote democracy. . . . He starts with the events in Iran, which illustrate his argument in microcosm. . . . Mr Morozov catalogues many similar examples of the internet being used with similarly pacifying consequences today, as authoritarian regimes make an implicit deal with their populations: help yourselves to pirated films, silly video clips and online pornography, but stay away from politics." (Economist)

Includes bibliographical references and index.

Rushkoff, Douglas

Present Shock; When Everything Happens Now. Douglas Rushkoff. Penguin Group USA 2013 vii, 296 p.p (hardcover) $26.95   **303.48**

    1. Conduct of life 2. Mass media -- Social aspects 3. Information technology -- Social aspects 4. Technology -- Philosophy 5. Technology -- Social aspects

ISBN 1591844762; 9781591844761

                   LC 2012039915

This book, by Douglas Rushkoff, explains how 21st-century society has "created technologies that would help connect us faster, gather news, map the planet, compile knowledge, and connect with anyone, at anytime. . . . And the dissonance between our digital selves and our analog bodies has thrown us into a new state of anxiety: present shock." (Publisher's note)

Includes bibliographical references and index

Silver, Brian L.

The **ascent** of science. Oxford Univ. Press 1998 534p il hardcover o.p. pa $53   **303.48**

    1. Thought and thinking 2. Science -- History 3. Science -- Philosophy

ISBN 0-19-513427-3

                   LC 97-15430

The author discusses a "variety of topics, from Pythagorean musings and lodestones to quantum mechanical puzzles and DNA structures. Yes, chaos theory and cosmology are included too. All this is sandwiched between interesting references to historical matters, philosophical positions, some controversies, and to Shakespeare, Shelley, and Shaw also. A book commendable for its breadth, depth, and vision." Choice

Includes bibliographical references

Steiner-Adair, Catherine

The **Big** Disconnect; Protecting Childhood and Family Relationships in the Digital Age. HarperCollins 2013 384 p. $26.99   **303.48**

    1. Parenting 2. Parent-child relationship 3. Internet -- Social aspects

ISBN 0062082426; 9780062082428

"Parents text relentlessly or worship the computer screen, while children learn more from social media than from school. The result? Distorted family dynamics and children unable to develop sustaining relationships. Advice from a clinical psychologist." (Library Journal)

Tenner, Edward

Our own devices; How Technology Remakes Humanity. Alfred A. Knopf 2004 336p hardcover o.p. pa $14.95; pa $18   **303.48**
1. Technological innovations 2. Technology and civilization
ISBN 0-375-70707-7 pa; 9780375707070
                    LC 2002-40694
"For a work that covers such a broad topic, this book is a page-turner, largely due to its clear prose and the author's approach to the material. While not lavishly illustrated, there seems to be a picture every time one is needed to illustrate the technology being discussed." SLJ
Includes bibliographical references

Thompson, Clive

Smarter Than You Think; How Technology Is Changing Our Minds for the Better. Clive Thompson. Penguin Group USA 2013 352 p. $27.95   **303.48**
1. Internet -- Social aspects 2. Technological innovations -- Social aspects 3. Social media 4. Thought and thinking 5. Internet -- Psychological aspects 6. Information technology -- Social aspects 7. Information technology -- Psychological aspects
ISBN 1594204454; 9781594204456
                    LC 2013017155
In this book "about the advent of technology and its influence on humans, journalist [Clive] Thompson . . . admits that we often allow ourselves to be used by facets of new technologies and that we must exercise caution to avoid this; yet, he demonstrates, digital tools can have a huge positive impact on us, for they provide us with infinite memory, the ability to discover connections . . . previously unknown to us, and new and abundant avenues for communication and publishing." (Publishers Weekly)
Includes bibliographical references and index

Venter, J. Craig, 1946-

Life at the Speed of Light; From the Double Helix to the Dawn of Digital Life. by J. Craig Venter. Penguin Group USA 2013 240 p. $26.95   **303.48**
1. Genomes 2. Genomics 3. Artificial life 4. Biology -- Philosophy 5. Science -- Social aspects
ISBN 0670025402; 9780670025404
                    LC 2013017049
In this book author J. Craig Venter "presents a fascinating and authoritative study of [synthetic genomics]—detailing its origins, current challenges and controversies, and projected effects on our lives. This scientific frontier provides an opportunity to ponder anew the age-old question 'What is life?' and examine what we really mean by 'playing God.'" (Publisher's note)
Includes bibliographical references and index

Weinberger, David

Too big to know; rethinking knowledge now that the facts aren't the facts, experts are everywhere, and the smartest person in the room is the room. David

Weinberger. Basic Books 2011 xiv, 231 p.p (alk. paper) $25.99   **303.48**
1. Internet 2. Theory of knowledge 3. Information technology 4. Knowledge, Sociology of 5. Internet -- Social aspects 6. Information technology -- Social aspects
ISBN 0465021425; 9780465021420; 9780465028139
                    LC 2011034727
It was the author's intent to demonstrate "that the collaborative, hyperlinked, instant nature of the Internet has fundamentally altered the way humans relate with knowledge. . . . The democratizing of knowledge is not without its dangers. Bad information has equal access to the common well with good information, and is just as viral. But crowdsourced and refereed resources like Wikipedia give [David] Weinberger hope." (Kirkus Reviews)
Includes bibliographical references (p. 199-218) and index.

303.483   Development of science and technology

Johnson, Clay

The information diet; Clay A. Johnson. 1st ed. O'Reilly Media 2012 ix, 150p.p   **303.483**
1. Conduct of life 2. Information society
ISBN 9781449304683; 1449304680
                    LC 2011410787
This book examines how humans have "become gluttons for texts, instant messages, emails, RSS feeds, downloads, videos, status updates, and tweets. We're all battling a storm of distractions, buffeted with notifications and tempted by tasty tidbits of information. And just as too much junk food can lead to obesity, too much junk information can lead to cluelessness. 'The Information Diet' shows you how to thrive in this information glut--what to look for, what to avoid, and how to be selective. In the process, author Clay Johnson explains the role information has played throughout history, and why following his prescribed diet is essential for everyone who strives to be smart, productive, and sane." (Publisher's note)
Includes bibliographical references.

Nature engaged; science in practice from the Renaissance to the present. edited by Mario Biagioli and Jessica Riskin. Palgrave Macmillan 2012 xi, 301 p.p (Palgrave studies in cultural and intellectual history) (hbk.) $85   **303.483**
1. Essays 2. Science -- History 3. Science and civilization 4. Science -- Social aspects
ISBN 023010276X; 9780230102767
                    LC 2012474431
Mario Biagioli and Jessica Riskin have compiled a "collection of essays composed by leading scholars from around the world. . . . The essays address a wide scope of historical subjects, from astronomy to technology, and from cartography to cosmography, with each entry focusing on a particular cultural or social aspect of the subject." (Choice)
Includes bibliographical references and index

303.49   Social forecasts

Kaku, Michio

Physics of the future; how science will shape human destiny and our daily lives by the year 2100. Doubleday 2011 389p il $28.95; ebook $12.99   **303.49**

1. Science 2. Forecasting 3. Science -- Social aspects 4. Science -- History -- 21st century

ISBN 978-0-385-53080-4; 978-0-385-53081-1 ebook

LC 2010-26569

"The book's lively, user-friendly style should appeal equally to fans of science fiction and popular science." Booklist

Includes bibliographical references

303.6   Conflict and conflict resolution

Camus, Albert

The **rebel**; an essay on man in revolt. with a foreword by Sir Herbert Read; a revised and complete translation of L'homme révolté by Anthony Bower. Vintage Bks. 1991 306p pa $12   **303.6**

1. Authors 2. Nihilism 3. Novelists 4. Revolutions 5. Philosophers 6. Essayists 7. Memoirists 8. Revolutionaries 9. Short story writers 10. Writers on politics 11. Political and social philosophers

ISBN 0-679-73384-1

LC 91-50022

Original French edition, 1951; this translation first published 1956 by Knopf

The author describes how the theories of philosophers have been used with disastrous effect by political leaders from the French Revolution through the nihilist revolutions of Russia and the governments of Lenin, Hitler and Stalin. The conclusion calls for a return to a political philosophy having as its aim the happiness and development of living human beings

Carr, Caleb

The **lessons** of terror; a history of warfare against civilians: why it has always failed and why it will fail again. Random House 2002 272p hardcover o.p. pa $12.95   **303.6**

1. Terrorism

ISBN 0-375-76074-1 pa

LC 2002-280604

The author argues "that terrorism must be viewed in terms of 'military history, rather than political science or sociology,' and that the refusal to label terrorists as soldiers, rather than criminals, is a mistake. . . . This often fascinating, accessible tome skillfully contends that the terrorizing of civilians has a long and controversial history but, as an inferior method, is prone to failure." Publ Wkly

Includes bibliographical references

Dershowitz, Alan M.

Why terrorism works; understanding the threat, responding to the challenge. Yale Univ. Press 2002 271p $24.95; pa $16   **303.6**

1. Terrorism

ISBN 0-300-09766-2; 0-300-10153-8 pa

LC 2002-6387

The author "argues forcefully that the attacks of September 11 were largely of our own doing—the international community, Dershowitz says, repeatedly rewards terrorists with appeasement and legitimization, refusing to take the necessary steps to curtail attacks. . . . These penetrating arguments force readers to consider how we got to September 11, how far we are willing to pursue terrorists and how much freedom we are willing to give up for our security." Publ Wkly

Includes bibliographical references

Herbst, Philip

Talking terrorism; a dictionary of the loaded language of political violence. Greenwood Press 2003 220p $49.95   **303.6**

1. Reference books 2. Terrorism -- Dictionaries

ISBN 0-313-32486-7

LC 2003-44071

"This is a dictionary with a social and political objective: to explore how supposedly civilized people, groups, and governments the world over use language to provide a moral justification for violence. . . .The 150 A-to-Z entries range from one half to several pages in length and include definitions, an examination of the charged use of a term both historically and in the present, and . . . cross references." Libr J

"This work is original, refreshing, and insightful. It attempts to discern the why of terrorism and political violence from the perspective of language." Choice

Includes bibliographical references

Morris, Ian

War! What is it good for? conflict and the progress of civilization from primates to robots. Ian Morris. Farrar Straus & Giroux 2014 512 p. illustrations, maps (hardback) $30   **303.6**

1. War 2. Military history 3. War and civilization 4. War and society

ISBN 0374286000; 9780374286002

LC 2013038722

This book, by Ian Morris, "tells the gruesome . . . story of fifteen thousand years of war, going beyond the battles and brutality to reveal what war has really done to and for the world. . . . War, and war alone, has created bigger, more complex societies, ruled by governments that have stamped out internal violence. Strangely enough, killing has made the world safer, and the safety it has produced has allowed people to make the world richer too." (Publisher's note)

"A profoundly uncomfortable but provocative argument that 'productive war' promotes greater safety, a decrease in violence and economic growth." Kirkus

Includes bibliographical references and index

Sontag, Susan, 1933-2004

Regarding the pain of others. Farrar, Straus & Giroux 2003 131p hardcover o.p. pa $12   **303.6**
    1. Violence 2. Atrocities 3. Photojournalism 4. War photography 5. Documentary photography
    ISBN 978-0-312-42219-6

                  LC 2002-192527
    Companion volume to On photography (1977)
    "All libraries, regardless of type, size, or demographics, should own this book." Libr J

304   Factors affecting social behavior

Sagan, Carl, 1934-1996

Shadows of forgotten ancestors; a search for who we are. {by} Carl Sagan, Ann Druyan. Random House 1992 505p hardcover o.p. pa $15.95   **304**
    1. Evolution 2. Life -- Origin
    ISBN 0-345-38472-5 pa

                  LC 92-50155
    "Despite a preference for the overly dramatic phrase at the expense of scientific clarity, the argument is coherent throughout." Libr J
    Includes bibliographical references

304.2   Human ecology

Cerveny, Randall S.

Weather's greatest mysteries solved! [by] Randy Cerveny. Prometheus Books 2009 328p il map $26.98   **304.2**
    1. Climate
    ISBN 978-1-59102-720-1; 1-59102-720-9

                  LC 2009-04493
    The author discusses "the investigative process, theories, and the techniques of weather and climate research. Presenting the issues as unsolved mysteries, he engages readers and explains how science is conducted. Each short chapter contains a fictional vignette personalizing a weather or climate-related mystery." Choice
    Includes bibliographical references

Diamond, Jared M.

★ **Collapse** : how societies choose to fail or succeed. Viking 2005 575p il $29.95; pa $17   **304.2**
    1. Social change 2. Environmental policy
    ISBN 0-670-03337-5; 0-14-303655-6 pa

                  LC 2004-57152
    The author "examines storied examples of human economic and social collapse, and even extinction, including Easter Island, classical Mayan civilization and the Greenland Norse. He explores patterns of population growth, overfarming, overgrazing and overhunting, often abetted by drought, cold, rigid social mores and warfare, that lead inexorably to vicious circles of deforestation, erosion and starvation prompted by the disappearance of plant and animal food sources. . . . Readers will find his book an enthralling,

and disturbing, reminder of the indissoluble links that bind humans to nature." Publ Wkly
    Includes bibliographical references

Flannery, Tim, 1956-

An **explorer's** notebook; essays on life, history and climate. Tim Flannery. Atlantic Monthly Press 2014 284 p. illustrations (hardcover) $26   **304.2**
    1. Essays 2. Scientists 3. Human ecology 4. Human beings -- Effect of climate on 5. Human beings -- Effect of environment on
    ISBN 9780802122315; 0802122310
    Includes bibliographical references
    "With its selection of . . . essays and articles written over the past 25 years, 'An Explorer's Notebook' charts the evolution of a young scientist doing fieldwork in remote locations to the major thinker who has changed the way we think about global warming. In over thirty pieces, [author Tim] Flannery writes about his journeys in the jungles of New Guinea and Indonesia, about the extraordinary people he met and the species he discovered." (Publisher's note)
    "Flannery offers readers insight into his extraordinary career through selected essays he wrote about his own work as well as about the books that have shaped his thinking." Kirkus

Gessner, David

My green manifesto; down the Charles River in pursuit of a new environmentalism. David Gessner. 1st ed.; Milkweed Editions 2011 225 p. $15 **304.2**
    1. Environmentalists 2. Canoes and canoeing 3. Environmental movement 4. Environmental protection 5. Charles River (Mass.) -- Description and travel 6. Environmentalism 7. Environmentalism -- Massachusetts -- Charles River 8. Environmental protection -- Massachusetts -- Charles River
    ISBN 9781571313249 pa

                  LC 2011012994
    In this book, the author "canoes down Boston's Charles River with Dan Driscoll, an upbeat, pot-smoking, environmental planner, who has spent nearly 20 years fighting to revitalize the once famously polluted river. . . . [David] Gessner sets out to find a new environmentalism, something 'that is a part of [his] everyday life, not running roughshod over it.' For Gessner, environmentalism begins with a connection to a particular place. . . . And while his friend's fight to bring a bit of the natural world back to the banks of the Charles may not account for much in the long run, Gessner believes that committing to a lifelong environmental fight is an act of personal fulfillment." (Publishers Wkly)
    Includes bibliographical references.

Gilding, Paul

The **great** disruption; why the climate crisis will bring on the end of shopping and the birth of a new world. Bloomsbury Press 2011 292p $25   **304.2**
    1. Human ecology 2. Social change 3. Economic development
    ISBN 978-1-60819-223-6

                  LC 2010-35843
    "Gilding's confidence in our ability to transform disaster into a 'happiness economy' may astonish readers, but the

book provides a refreshing, provocative alternative to the recent spate of gloom-and-doom climate-change studies." Publ Wkly

Includes bibliographical references

Hertsgaard, Mark

Hot; living through the next fifty years on earth. Houghton Mifflin Harcourt 2011 339p $25   **304.2**

1. Greenhouse effect 2. Climate -- Environmental aspects

ISBN 978-0-618-82612-4; 0-618-82612-2

LC 2010-12416

"The author notes that we have entered the 'second era of global warming.' Even if greenhouse-gas emissions ceased today, the consequences would continue for hundreds of years. Consequently, the author persuasively argues that we need to begin adapting to those changes, which does not mean that mitigating global warming is no longer important; in fact, it grows more urgent every day. . . . Starkly clear and of utmost importance. " Kirkus

Includes bibliographical references

Jensen, Derrick

What we leave behind; [by] Derrick Jensen and Aric McBay. Seven Stories Press 2009 453p pa $24.95   **304.2**

1. Pollution 2. Refuse and refuse disposal

ISBN 978-1-58322-867-8

LC 2008-47287

Jensen and McBay argue that "the global industrial system . . . produces massive amounts of unsustainable and toxic wastes. . . . The authors focus on some of these harmful products, discuss reasons why our culture produces so much waste, and explain why individual action is insufficient to solve our enormous problems. . . . This compelling book has a refreshing style, at once very personal and very passionate. It is also thorough, with historical, scientific, statistical, and anecdotal evidence filtered through a lot of anger and some quirky humor." Libr J

Includes bibliographical references

McPhee, John A.

The control of nature. Farrar, Straus & Giroux 1989 272p $17.95; pa $12   **304.2**

1. Environmental protection 2. Human influence on nature

ISBN 0-374-12890-1; 0-374-52259-6 pa

LC 89-1052

The three essays which make up this book first appeared in the New Yorker. They describe "efforts to pit human ingenuity against the might of Mother Nature . . . in the lower Mississippi Valley, on the volcanic islands of Iceland, and in the canyons of Los Angeles's San Gabriel mountains. In each case, {McPhee argues}, people risk their lives and incur colossal expense to live in places where geology and weather say they have no business to be." Libr J

Owen, David, 1955-

Green metropolis; why living smaller, living closer, and driving less are the keys to sustainability. Riverhead Books 2009 357p $25.95   **304.2**

1. Human ecology 2. Urban ecology 3. Sustainable

architecture 4. Green technology 5. Urban ecology -- Social aspects

ISBN 1-59448-882-7; 978-1-59448-882-5

LC 2009-17116

Owen argues "that Manhattan, Hong Kong and large, old European cities are inherently greener than less densely populated places because a higher percentage of their inhabitants walk, bike and use mass transit than drive; they share infrastructure and civic services more efficiently; they live in smaller spaces and use less energy to heat their homes." (N Y Times Book Rev) Index.

This is "a compelling analysis of the world's environmental predicament that upends orthodox opinion and points the way to practical solutions." Publ Wkly

Includes bibliographical references

Smith, Laurence C.

The world in 2050; four forces shaping civilization's northern future. Dutton 2010 322p il map $26.95   **304.2**

1. Forecasting 2. Climate -- Environmental aspects

ISBN 978-0-525-95181-0

LC 2010-29553

This "thought experiment predicts that four 'megatrends'—more people, fewer resources, globalization, and climate change—will utterly transform the world in the next 40 years." Mother Jones

"Smith demonstrates the breadth of geography and emerges as a champion of the discipline. His engaging style and understandable prose will appeal to a wide range of readers interested in social and environmental sciences." Libr J

Includes bibliographical references

Weisman, Alan

Countdown; Our Last, Best Hope for a Future on Earth? Alan Weisman. Little, Brown and Co. 2013 528 p. $28   **304.2**

1. Population 2. Sustainability 3. Overpopulation 4. Population ecology 5. Nature -- Effect of human beings on

ISBN 0316097756; 9780316097758

LC 2013017113

In this book, author Alan Weisman "visits an extraordinary range of the world's cultures, religions, nationalities, tribes, and political systems to learn what in their beliefs, histories, liturgies, or current circumstances might suggest that sometimes it's in their own best interest to limit their growth. [He] reveals what may be the fastest, most acceptable, practical, and affordable way of returning our planet and our presence on it to balance." (Publisher's note)

"Provocative and sobering, this vividly reported book raises profound concerns about our future." Pub Wkly

Includes bibliographical references (pages 442-496) and index

Wohlforth, Charles

The fate of nature; rediscovering our ability to rescue the earth. Thomas Dunne Books/St. Martin's Press 2010 434p map $27.99   **304.2**

1. Human ecology 2. Environmental protection 3. Conservation of natural resources 4. Natural history

-- Alaska
ISBN 978-0-312-37737-3; 0-312-37737-1
LC 2009-45779
The author "considers the consequences of Captain John Cook's hasty visit to the gulf in 1778, the Russian conquest of coastal Alaska, . . . the crash of the herring fisheries, and the cruel fates of the region's indigenous peoples. But Wohlforth believes that our 'consuming nature' is balanced by the impulse to understand and cherish the living world, which is borne out in his compelling profiles of whale biologist Eva Saulitis; Geerat Vermeij, a blind evolutionary scientist who discovered an arms race among crustaceans; and various environmental heroes. . . . By analyzing competition and evolution, culture and economics, habits of living and of mind, science and suffering, Wohlforth brings a truly ecological perspective to the global debate over how to protect the biosphere." Booklist
Includes bibliographical references

304.5   Genetic factors

Taylor, Shelley E.
The **tending** instinct; how nurturing is essential for who we are and how we live. Times Bks. 2002 290p $25; pa $16   **304.5**
1. Sociobiology 2. Stress (Psychology) 3. Sex differences (Psychology)
ISBN 0-8050-6837-6; 0-8050-7289-6 pa
LC 2002-19879
The author "launched a series of innovative experiments that led her to believe that humans are biologically wired to nurture. She thus devised no less than a whole new psychology of women, presented in this accessible and well-grounded work." Libr J
Includes bibliographical references

304.6   Population

Encyclopedia of the U.S. Census; from the constitution to the American community survey. editors, Margo J. Anderson, Constance F. Citro, and Joseph J. Salvo. 2nd ed. CQ Press 2013 456 p. Hardcover $195   **304.6**
1. United States -- Census -- Encyclopedias
ISBN 9781608710256
LC 2011036339
"The Encyclopedia of the U.S. Census, Second Edition" updates and expands a critically-acclaimed resource for the history, politics, content, procedures and uses of the decennial census of the American population. The new edition highlights changes in the Census Bureau's data collection and dissemination practices for the 2010 enumeration, including the use of a short-form questionnaire for the actual population count, and the release in late 2010 of the American Community Survey (ACS) 5-year data set based on rolling samples of the U.S. population and gathered using the long-form questionnaire. The second edition also comprehensively covers the fallout from the 2000 census and recent issues affecting the administration of the 2010 count." (Publisher's Note)

The alphabetically arranged articles "explain the history, methodology, and results of U.S. censuses since 1790... Maps, tables, and charts show how the composition of the population has changed, where the center of population has moved over time, and how the address lists and census tracts are developed." Booklist
Includes bibliographical references and index
Encyclopedia of the United States census

Farley, Reynolds
★ The **American** people; Census 2000. [edited by] Reynolds Farley and John Haaga. Russell Sage 2005 456p il map $35   **304.6**
1. United States -- Census 2. United States -- Population
ISBN 0-8715-4273-0
LC 2005-50433
This book "is more than just a compilation of tables and charts of raw census data. It is an interpretative guide to understanding the demographic breakdown of American society. Chapters include: 'Gender Inequalities', 'Cohorts and Socioeconomic Progress' and 'The Lives and Times of the Baby Boomers'. Editors Farley and Haaga show trends in American culture that will not be found anywhere else." Univ Press Books for Public and Second Sch Libr, 2006
Includes bibliographical references

Hitchens, Christopher, 1949-2011
★ **Mortality**; Christopher Hitchens. 1st ed. Twelve 2012 160 p. (hardcover) $22.99; (paperback) $14.99; (ebook) $21.80   **304.6**
1. Terminally ill 2. Cancer -- Patients 3. Cancer -- Chemotherapy 4. Death 5. Mortality 6. Authors, American -- Biography 7. Terminally ill -- United States -- Biography 8. Cancer -- Patients -- United States -- Biography
ISBN 1455502758; 9781455502752; 9781455523474; 9781742695198
LC 2012014024
This memoir chronicles the decline of cultural critic Christopher Hitchens during the later stages of esophageal cancer. Here, he "shares his thoughts about his suffering, the etiquette of illness and wellness, and religion." He talks about the battle metaphors doctors and friends use to describe his illness and his feelings about the loss of his voice from the treatment. (Publishers Weekly)

Peake, Riley
Mapping Census 2010; the geography of American change. Riley Peake. Esri Press 2012 1 atlas (xiv, 90 p.)p (pbk.) $18.95   **304.6**
1. Minorities 2. United States -- Census 3. United States -- Population 4. United States -- Census, 23rd, 2010 -- Maps 5. United States -- Population -- Statistics -- Maps 6. Minorities -- United States -- Population -- Statistics -- Maps
ISBN 1589483197; 9781589483194
LC 2012288678
Author Riley Peake's book "is an atlas of the American people--who we are, and where we are. Using the latest census data and geographic information system (GIS) technology, this atlas examines how our unique population is moving and changing. These large, full-color maps illustrate

population density, age, and racial and ethnic composition with clarity." (Publisher's note)

Includes bibliographical references

304.8   Movement of people

✓ **Urrea, Luis Alberto**

★ The **devil's** highway; a true story. Luis Alberto Urrea. Little, Brown 2004 xii, 239p (pbk.) $13.99   **304.8**

1. Illegal aliens 2. Mexico -- Immigration and emigration 3. United States -- Immigration and emigration 4. Illegal aliens -- Crimes against -- Mexican-American Border Region

ISBN 9780316746717; 9780316010801

LC 2003058930

This book "tracks the paths" of "26 Mexican men" who in 2001 "scrambled across the border into an area of the Arizona desert known as the Devil's highway. Only 12 made it safely across. . . . Their enemies were many: the U.S. Border Patrol ('La Migra'); gung-ho gringo vigilantes bent on taking the law into their own hands; the Mexican Federales; rattlesnakes; severe hypothermia and the remorseless sun. . . . But while many point to the group's smugglers . . . as the prime villains of the tragedy, [Luis Alberto] Urrea unloads on . . . 'the politics of stupidity that rules both sides of the border.' Mexican and U.S. border policy is backward, Urrea finds, and it does little to stem the flow of immigrants. Since the policy results in Mexicans making the crossing in increasingly forbidding areas, it contributes to the conditions that kill those who attempt it." (Publishers Weekly)

305   Groups of people

★ **After** the storm; black intellectuals explore the meaning of Hurricane Katrina. edited by David Dante Troutt. New Press 2006 xxvii, 164p il $22.95   **305**

1. Hurricane Katrina, 2005 2. African Americans -- Social conditions

ISBN 978-1-59558-116-7; 1-59558-116-2

LC 2006-8883

The contributors "assess why Katrina was handled as it was (and still is), how inevitable future crises should be handled differently, and how redevelopment of New Orleans should occur. Angry, learned, focused, readable, essential." Libr J

Includes bibliographical references

✓ **Azam Zanganeh, Lila**

My sister, guard your veil; my brother guard, your eyes; uncensored Iranian voices. Lila Azam Zanganeh, editor. Beacon Press 2006 132p il pa $12   **305**

1. Women -- Iran 2. Iran -- Social conditions

ISBN 0-8070-0463-4; 978-0-8070-0463-0

LC 2005-27496

"In the first anthology of its kind, Lila Azam Zanganeh argues that although Iran looms large in the American imagi-

nation, it is grossly misunderstood - seen either as the third pillar of Bush's infamous "axis of evil" or as a nation teeming with youths clamoring for revolution.

This collection showcases the real scope and complexity of Iran through the work of a stellar group of contributors'"including Azar Nafisi and with original art by Marjane Satrapi. Their collective goal is to counter the many existing cultural and political cliches about Iran"

This "volume features frank interviews with an array of reputable Iranians intellectuals, artists, and writers, some of whom live in exile. Their compelling personal experiences, views, and opinions answer some persistent questions about the lives of ordinary people in Iran and challenge established myths and stereotypes....This volume opens a window on the irrepressible talents, aspirations, and energy of Iranians both at home and abroad, despite their adverse conditions" MultiCult Rev

✓ **Baldwin, Neil**

★ **Henry** Ford and the Jews; the mass production of hate. PublicAffairs 2001 416p il $27.50; pa $16   **305**

1. Antisemitism 2. Philanthropists 3. Automobile industry 4. Automobile executives 5. Jews -- United States

ISBN 1-891620-52-5; 1-58648-163-0 pa

LC 2001-41679

"Baldwin reveals the complex tale of how 'Heinrich' Ford promoted a virulent brand of antisemitism, disseminating his point of view through a privately-published newspaper, The Dearborn Independent—and how the Jewish American community responded with alarm and courage." Publisher's note

"The strength of this biography lies in context: by emphasizing Ford's background, influences and the world around the auto manufacturer, Baldwin . . . brings a fresh approach to what has long been known about one of America's most famous anti-Semites." Publ Wkly

Includes bibliographical references

✓ **Bergner, Daniel**

★ **What** Do Women Want? Adventures in the Science of Female Desire. Daniel Burgner. HarperCollins 2013 224 p. (hardcover) $25.99   **305**

1. Women -- Sexual behavior 2. Sex -- Psychological aspects

ISBN 0061906085; 9780061906084

This book, by Daniel Bergner, "disseminates the latest scientific research and paints an unprecedented portrait of female lust: the triggers, the fantasies, the mind-body connection (and disconnection), the reasons behind the loss of libido, and, most revelatory, that this loss is not inevitable. . . . While debunking the myths popularized by evolutionary psychology, Bergner also looks at the future of female sexuality." (Publisher's note)

"Stylishly written and cogently organized, making it easy and rewarding for lay readers to understand and appreciate some fairly complex science." Kirkus

Gates, Henry Louis

The **African** -American century; how Black Americans have shaped our country. {by} Henry Louis Gates, Jr. and Cornel West. Free Press 2000 414p il hardcover o.p. pa $16 **305**
1. African Americans -- Biography 2. African Americans -- Intellectual life
ISBN 0-684-86414-2; 0-684-86415-0 pa

LC 00-63596

"Gates and West have listed and written biographies of their choices of the 100 most important and influential [African Americans] of the . . . twentieth century. In their opinion the subjects that they have selected have made significant impacts and contributions to American society. . . . The entries are arranged by decade and by the person's period of prominence in society, 1900-1909 through 1990-1999. Profiles include Madame C.J. Walker, Langston Hughes, Carter G. Woodson, Paul Robeson, Thurgood Marshall, and Colin Powell." MultiCult Rev

Includes bibliographical references

Hrabowski, Freeman A.

Overcoming the odds; raising academically successful African American young women. {by} Freeman A. Hrabowski III {et al.} Oxford Univ. Press 2002 272p $25 **305**
1. African American women 2. African Americans -- Education
ISBN 0-19-512642-4

LC 2001-32152

Companion volume to Beating the odds; raising academically successful African American males (1998)

This volume "focuses on young black women overcoming the stereotypical image: high-school dropout, unwed mother, welfare recipient. Based on interviews with students and parents, the book answers the question, What does it take to succeed academically?" Booklist

Includes bibliographical references

Reef, Catherine

Working in America. Facts On File 2007 xxviii, 484p il map (American experience) $80 **305**
1. Labor -- United States
ISBN 978-0-8160-6239-3; 0-8160-6239-0

LC 2006-31191

First published 2000

"Each chapter begins with a . . . narrative that chronicles the experience of workers in the United States—from factory workers, cowboys, seamstresses, and newsboys to truck drivers, migrant farm workers, computer programmers, and genetic engineers. Chronologies of important events follow, along with eyewitness testimonies on the experience of working in a wide range of professions and trades—from Thomas Jefferson, Malcolm X, Samuel Gompers, Charlotte Perkins Gilman, Jesse Jackson, Cesar Chavez, and Jane Addams, as well as a wide range of American workers." Publisher's note

Includes bibliographical references

Rubin, Richard

Confederacy of silence; a true tale of the new old South. Atria Bks. 2002 438p $26; pa $14 **305**
1. Mississippi -- Race relations
ISBN 0-671-03666-1; 0-671-03667-X pa

LC 2002-510321

"Rubin's memoir exposes the racial polarity of the Delta in clear, effective prose." Publ Wkly

305.23 Young people

Canada, Geoffrey

Fist, stick, knife, gun; a personal history of violence in America. Beacon Press 1995 179p pa $13 **305.23**
1. Children 2. Violence 3. New York (N.Y.) -- Social conditions
ISBN 0-8070-0422-7; 978-0-8070-0423-4 pa; 0-8070-0423-5 pa

LC 94-41357

"This is a graphic adaptation of famous activist and educator Canada's work of the same name. It explores his Bronx, NY, childhood and foray into increasingly violent activity. The use of violence as self-protection in a rough neighborhood and the introduction of guns into the mix make for a profound reflection on inner-city violence." (Library Journal)

"A more powerful depiction of the tragic life of urban children and a more compelling plea to end 'America's war against itself' cannot be imagined." Publ Wkly

Coles, Robert

Children of crisis; selections from the Pulitzer Prize-winning five-volume Children of crisis series; with a new introduction by the author. Little, Brown 2003 714p il pa $22.95 **305.23**
1. Children with social disabilities 2. Children -- United States
ISBN 9780316151023

LC 2003-47522

These are selections of Coles' social study of "African American children caught in the throes of the South's racial integration; the young children of impoverished sharecroppers, migrant workers, and mountaineers in Appalachia; children whose families were transformed by the migration from South to North, from rural to urban communities; Latino, Native American, and Eskimo children in the poorest communities of the American West; the children of America's wealthiest families, wrestling with the burden of their own privilege." Publisher's note

Konner, Melvin

The **evolution** of childhood. Belknap Press of Harvard University Press 2010 943p $39.95 **305.23**
1. Children 2. Evolution 3. Child development 4. Emotions in children 5. Human evolution 6. Children -- Anthropometry
ISBN 978-0-674-04566-8; 0-674-04566-1

LC 2009050775

It was the author's intent "to describe 'the foundations of psychosocial growth' in an evolutionary context. A goal of the book is to provide the basis for understanding the modification of that biological heritage in interaction with the environment. . . . [Melvin] Konner's focus is on how 'the laws and facts of biology underlie normally developing social behavior' . . . [The book] is divided into five broad sections: evolution (focused on the phylogenetic origins of childhood), maturation (the genetic, physiological, and anatomical bases of psychosocial growth), socialization ('the evolving social context of ontogeny'), enculturation (the transmission and evolution of culture), and a conclusion. Between each of the first four major parts of the book, there is a transition essay." (Current Anthropology)

This book "explores the biological evolution of human behavior and specifically the behavior of children. Melvin Konner . . . weaves a compelling web of theories and studies across a remarkable array of disciplines, from experimental genetics to ethnology. He ranges back to the earliest, egg-laying mammals, discusses topics as seemingly modern as cross-gender identity conflicts, and draws on scientific work examining all manner of species with which humans share distinct characteristics. . . . To read this book is to be in the company of a helpful and hopeful teacher who is eager to share what he's found." Atl Mon

Includes bibliographical references

Kozol, Jonathan, 1936-

Ordinary resurrections; children in the years of hope. Harper Perennial 2001 388p pa $14 **305.23**
1. Children 2. Bronx (New York, N.Y.) -- Social conditions
ISBN 978-0-06-095645-5; 0-06-095645-3
First published 2000 by Crown

"Kozol tells of his continued visits with the children who attend the afterschool program at St. Ann's Episcopal Church in the racially segregated, impoverished South Bronx." SLJ

Includes bibliographical references

Mintz, Steven

★ **Huck's** raft; a history of American childhood. Belknap Press of Harvard University Press 2004 445p il $29.95 **305.23**
1. Children -- United States
ISBN 0-674-01508-8
LC 2004-42220

The author "revisits the treatment of children from the Puritan era up to the edge of the millennium, . . . showing that we have alternately vilified our offspring . . . and glorified them. . . . In addition, the roles children have assumed in the workforce have fluctuated with the needs of the era—economic expansion led to harsh child labor, while its aftermath, prosperity, led to an interest in child welfare. . . . Mintz's thorough yet accessibly written study delves into the external forces that have shaped the lives of our young while also probing the internal developments in their collective consciousness." Libr J

Includes bibliographical references

Orenstein, Peggy

Cinderella ate my daughter; dispatches from the frontlines of the new girlie-girl culture. HarperCollins 2011 244p $25.99 **305.23**
1. Mother-daughter relationship 2. Femininity 3. Girls -- Psychology 4. Mothers and daughters
ISBN 0061711527; 9780061711527
LC 2010-28724

Orenstein examines aspects and manifestations of sexualized girlhood such as child beauty pageants and Disney Princess dolls. Bibliography. Index.

The author "finds today's pink and princess-obsessed girl culture grating when it threatens to lure her own young daughter, Daisy. In her quest to determine whether princess mania is merely a passing phase or a more sinister marketing plot with long-term negative impact, Orenstein travels to Disneyland, American Girl Place, the American International Toy Fair; visits a children's beauty pageant; attends a Miley Cyrus concert; tools around the Internet; and interviews parents, historians, psychologists, marketers, and others. . . . With insight and biting humor, the author explores her own conflicting feelings as a mother as she protects her offspring and probes the roots and tendrils of the girlie-girl movement." Publ Wkly

Includes bibliographical references

Orme, Nicholas

Medieval children. Yale Univ. Press 2001 387p il $39.95; pa $19.95 **305.23**
1. Middle Ages 2. Children -- History
ISBN 0-300-08541-9; 0-300-09754-9 pa
LC 2001-26172

This is an "examination of the daily lives of medieval children from diverse classes and backgrounds. . . . Orme's exacting research gives the book weight, and his affectionate, eloquent prose carries its immediate manner from history to sociology to philosophy and back again." Booklist

Includes bibliographical references

Shachtman, Tom

★ **Rumspringa**; to be or not to be Amish. North Point Press 2006 286p hardcover o.p. pa $16 **305.23**
1. Amish 2. Teenagers -- Religious life
ISBN 0-86547-687-X; 978-0-86547-687-5; 0-86547-742-6 pa; 978-0-86547-742-1 pa
LC 2006-4329

"Rumspringa is Tom Shachtman's celebrated look at a little-known Amish coming-of-age ritual, the rumspringa--the period of "running around" that begins for their youth at age sixteen. During this time, Amish youth are allowed to live outside the bounds of their faith, experimenting with alcohol, premarital sex, revealing clothes, telephones, drugs, and wild parties. By allowing such broad freedoms, their parents hope they will learn enough to help them make the most important decision of their lives--whether to be baptized as Christians, join the church, and forever give up worldly ways, or to remain in the world." (Publisher's note)

"Shachtman is like a maestro, masterfully conducting an orchestra of history, anthropology, psychology, sociology, and journalism together in a harmonious and evocative symphony of all things Amish." Christ Sci Monit

Includes bibliographical references

Simmons, Rachel

★ **Odd** girl out; the hidden culture of aggression in girls. Revised and updated Harcourt 2011 296p pa $15 **305.23**

1. Girls 2. Aggressiveness (Psychology) 3. Girls -- Psychology 4. Aggressiveness in children
ISBN 9780547520193

LC 2001-6864

"In this updated edition, educator and bullying expert Rachel Simmons gives girls, parents, and educators proven and innovative strategies for navigating social dynamics in person and online, as well as brand new classroom initiatives and step-by-step parental suggestions for dealing with conventional bullying. With up-to-the-minute research and real-life stories, Odd Girl Out continues to be the definitive resource on the most pressing social issues facing girls today." (Publisher's note)

"Why are girls inclined to relational rather than physical aggression? Simmons contends that girls are socialized into a psychological double bind. They are told that they must be good, nice and quiet and that they should value close and intimate relationships. . . . According to Simmons, girls fear that an expression of conflict will damage their relationships. . . . Trapped in a constraining, stereotypical gender role, some girls craft ways of expressing their anger covertly. . . . Odd Girl Out explores this grim side of girlhood with {stories} . . . about girls hurting other girls." (Women's Rev Books) Index.

Includes bibliographical references

305.235 Young people twelve to twenty

Flanagan, Caitlin

Girl land; Caitlin Flanagan. Little, Brown and Co. 2012 209 p. **305.235**

1. Girls 2. Adolescence 3. American essays 4. Teenage girls -- Psychology 5. Teenage girls -- United States
ISBN 9780316065986

LC 2011024934

The book discusses "[t]he transition from girl to woman [which according to the author] is an experience that has changed radically over the generations: everything from how a girl learns about her period to how she expects to be treated by boys and men. Girls today observe these passages very differently, and yet the landmarks themselves have remained remarkably constant-proof, [Caitlin] Flanagan believes, of their significance. In a world where protections of girls' privacy and personal freedom seem to disappear every day, the ultimate challenge modern parents face is finding a way to defend both." (Publisher's note)

Includes bibliographical references

Hine, Thomas

The **rise** and fall of the American teenager. Bard 1999 322p $24; pa $14; prebind $23.99 **305.235**

1. Teenagers 2. Adolescence
ISBN 0-380-97358-8; 0-380-72853-2 pa; 9781439573587

LC 99-24381

In this social history Hine "writes about ways the culture has affected what teenage has meant for youth and how youth have been perceived, as in World War II when teenagers readily took on roles supporting the war effort. Interesting, enjoyable, and multifaceted, Hine's work defies pigeonholing by covering anthropology, psychology, communications, and sociology." Libr J

Includes bibliographical references

305.24 Adults

Sheehy, Gail

New passages; mapping your life across time. Random House 1995 xxv, 498p hardcover o.p. pa $15.95 **305.24**

1. Aging 2. Adulthood 3. Middle age 4. Socialization 5. United States -- Social conditions
ISBN 0-345-40445-9 pa

LC 94-43996

Companion volume to Passages (1976)

This work is "grounded in the economic and psychological realities that make adult life so complex today. The major themes of this book are accurate and important." N Y Times Book Rev

Includes bibliographical references

Taylor, D. J.

Bright young people; the lost generation of London's jazz age. Farrar, Straus and Giroux 2009 361p il $27 **305.24**

1. Bohemianism 2. Great Britain -- Social life and customs
ISBN 978-0-374-11683-5; 0-374-11683-0

LC 2008-31366

First published 2007 in the United Kingdom

The author "chronicles the doings of London's gilded youth in the Roaring Twenties. Even if you think you know a lot (or enough) about them; even if you've read the acerbic novels of the early Evelyn Waugh or plowed your way through Anthony Powell's A Dance to the Music of Time, there's bound to be material here you haven't seen or heard of." Washington Post Book World

Includes bibliographical references

305.26 People in late adulthood

Carter, Jimmy, 1924-

The **virtues** of aging. Ballantine Pub. Group 1998 140p (Library of contemporary thought) hardcover o.p. pa $11.95 **305.26**

1. Aging
ISBN 0-345-42826-9; 0-345-42592-8 pa

LC 98-25298

"At age 56, Jimmy Carter 'involuntarily retired' when he was defeated for a second term as president by Ronald Reagan in 1980. . . . Carter sketches how he and Rosalynn created new careers and new lives for themselves—as authors, educators, and senior family members and as a couple growing old together. He adds statistics about the aging population, makes suggestions for healthy living, and defines successful aging." Libr J

Friedan, Betty, 1921-2006

The **fountain** of age. Simon & Schuster 1993 671p hardcover o.p. pa $26.95   **305.26**
1. Old age 2. Women -- United States
ISBN 0-671-89853-1 pa

LC 93-4090

The author "challenges our culture's pessimistic attitude toward aging. Friedan argues that we should view the years after 60 as a new stage of development, rather than as a time of decline and disease." Libr J

"Betty Friedan's metaphorical fountain of age spouts research, observation, conjecture, evangelical fervor, revolutionary rhetoric, and denial. The result is a pool of optimism in which the mother of the woman's movement examines the unlifted face of age and finds it lovable." New Repub

Includes bibliographical references

Jacoby, Susan

Never say die; the myth and marketing of the new old age. Pantheon Books 2011 332p $27.95 **305.26**
1. Aging 2. Elderly 3. Old age 4. Aged -- United States
ISBN 978-0-307-37794-4; 0-307-37794-6

LC 2010-17123

In this book, author "Susan Jacoby turns an . . . eye on the marketers of longevity--pharmaceutical companies, lifestyle gurus, and scientific businessmen who suggest that there will soon be a 'cure' for the 'disease' of aging. She separates wishful hype from realistic hope. . . . Finally, Jacoby raises the fundamental question of whether living longer is a desirable thing unless it means living better, and she considers the profound moral and ethical concerns raised by increasing longevity." (Publisher's note)

This is a "critique of the myth that a radically new old age—unmarred by physical or mental deterioration, financial problems, or intimate loneliness—awaits the huge baby boom generation." Publisher's note

Includes bibliographical references

Lawrence-Lightfoot, Sara

The **third** chapter; passion, risk, and adventure in the 25 years after 50. Farrar, Straus and Giroux 2009 260p $25   **305.26**
1. Aging 2. Old age 3. Elderly -- United States
ISBN 978-0-374-27549-5; 0-374-27549-1

LC 2008-29147

"New opportunities for creativity and self-fulfillment await men and women between the ages of 50 and 75. . . . [The author] coins the term 'Third Chapter' to describe the rich possibilities as illustrated in her extended interviews with 40 well-educated, affluent Americans. Founding her thesis on classic formulations of life-stage development, particularly that of Erik Erikson, the author offers a wide range of models for people who feel burned out, restless or dissatisfied with their lives, describing how each of her subjects became 'a different person.' . . . Readers feeling that something is missing from their lives, that there is some-

thing more they can contribute, will find this book a helpful guide." Publ Wkly

Includes bibliographical references

Pillemer, Karl A.

30 lessons for living; tried and true advice from the wisest Americans. [by] Karl Pillemer. Hudson Street Press 2011 271p $25.95   **305.26**
1. Aging 2. Old age 3. Happiness 4. Conduct of life 5. Elderly -- United States
ISBN 978-1-59463-084-2

LC 2011017113

"Who better to teach lessons on living . . . than the thousands of Americans over the age of 65 who have successfully navigated the territories of marriage, career, money, and aging? By conducting innumerable interviews, Pillemer found that their advice upends contemporary wisdom: they suggest marrying a person like oneself, choosing a career for intrinsic rewards, and spending more time with one's children. The author skillfully weaves a prevailing theme (e.g., parenting, aging fearlessly) with self-disclosing statements from interviewees to create a compelling, inspirational book. One of the best of its kind. " Libr J

Includes bibliographical references

305.31   Men

Bly, Robert

★ **Iron** John; a book about men. DaCapo Press 2004 268p pa $15   **305.31**
1. Men -- Psychology
ISBN 0-306-81376-9

LC 2004-56137

First published 1990 by Addison-Wesley

"Drawing vitally upon such diverse sources as ancient mythology, classic literature (including his own poetry), anthropology, psychology, and even the responses of the real-life men who have participated in his seminars ('gatherings'), Bly staunchly redefines male identity, emphasizing the importance of what he calls 'warrior energy' and all its positive implications." Booklist

Includes bibliographical references.

Bordo, Susan

The **male** body; a new look at men in public and in private. Farrar, Straus & Giroux 1999 358p il hardcover o.p. pa $16   **305.31**
1. Men 2. Gay men 3. Sexual harassment 4. Personal appearance
ISBN 0-374-52732-6 pa

LC 99-25386

"Bordo sets out to map the ambivalent attitudes that exist in the American cultural imagination toward male bodies and, in particular, toward the penis and its 'symbolic double,' the phallus. . . . Part memoir, part elegy, this feminist guided tour of the male body concludes with real hope for improved relations between the sexes." Publ Wkly

Includes bibliographical references

305.310973   Men -- United States

Vaillant, George E.

Triumphs of experience; the men of the Harvard Grant Study. George E. Vaillant. Belknap Press of Harvard University Press 2012 457 p. (alk. paper) $27.95   **305.310973**
1. Aging 2. Elderly men 3. Longitudinal studies 4. Men -- United States -- Longitudinal studies 5. Aging -- Social aspects -- United States -- Longitudinal studies 6. Aging -- Psychological aspects -- United States -- Longitudinal studies
ISBN 0674059824; 9780674059825
                                        LC 2012028519
This book, by George E. Vaillant, profiles "the longest longitudinal study of human development ever undertaken. . . . Begun in 1938, the Grant Study of Adult Development charted the physical and emotional health of over 200 men, starting with their undergraduate days. . . . Now George Vaillant follows the men into their nineties, documenting for the first time what it is like to flourish far beyond conventional retirement." (Publisher's note)
Includes bibliographical references and index

305.38   Specific groups of men

McCall, Nathan

Makes me wanna holler; a young black man in America. Random House 1994 404p hardcover o.p. pa $14.95   **305.38**
1. Journalists 2. Essayists 3. Memoirists 4. African Americans -- Biography
ISBN 0-679-74070-8 pa
                                        LC 93-30654
The author relates the "story of his rise from poverty to success as a journalist at the Washington Post. He uses graphic language, blunt descriptions, honest expression, introspection, and careful observation to describe his early years in Portsmouth, Virginia, as a young black male, the recipient of a 12-year prison sentence for armed robbery, whose life was dangerously out of control. Insensitivity, alienation, racial hatred, drugs (especially crack), guns, rape, robbery, the black American as an endangered species—McCall covers it all in a depressing yet spellbinding documentary." Libr J

305.4   Women

Adovasio, J. M.

The **invisible** sex; uncovering the true roles of women in prehistory. by J .M. Adovasio, Olga Soffer & Jake Page. Collins 2007 320p il map $26.95   **305.4**
1. Gender role 2. Prehistoric peoples 3. Sex role
ISBN 978-0-06-117091-1; 0-06-117091-7
                                        LC 2006-50582
In this study of prehistoric culture, the authors argue "that women invented all kinds of critical materials, including the clothing necessary for life in colder climates, the ropes used to make rafts that enabled long-distance travel by water, and nets used for communal hunting. Even more important, women played a central role in the development of language and social life—in short, in our becoming human." Publisher's note
Includes bibliographical references (p. 283-290)

Badkhen, Anna

★ The **world** is a carpet; four seasons in an Afghan village. Anna Badkhen. Riverhead Hardcover 2013 288 p. (hardback) $26.95   **305.4**
1. Nomads 2. Afghanistan 3. Carpets -- Afghanistan 4. Weaving -- Afghanistan 5. Women weavers -- Afghanistan 6. Rugs, Oriental -- Afghanistan 7. Afghanistan -- Social life and customs 8. Women -- Afghanistan -- Social conditions -- 21st century
ISBN 1594488320; 9781594488320
                                        LC 2013003827
This book relates the year author Anna Badkhen spent in a "Balkh village in northern Afghanistan that could not be found on the map, where the illiterate Turkoman women fashioned the most exquisite rugs in the world." She chronicles "the hard lives of the inhabitant survivors," who deal with opium addiction, poverty, and colonizers. (Kirkus Reviews)

Beauvoir, Simone de

★ The **second** sex; translated and edited by H. M. Parshley; with an introduction by Margaret Crosland. Knopf 1993 lv, 786p $23; pa $17   **305.4**
1. Women
ISBN 0-679-42016-9; 0-679-72451-6 pa
                                        LC 92-54303
Original French edition, 1949; this translation first published 1953
This "thorough analysis of women's secondary status in society, became a classic of feminist literature." Reader's Ency. 3d edition

Bitchfest; ten years of cultural criticism from the pages of Bitch magazine. edited by Lisa Jervis and Andi Zeisler. Farrar, Straus & Giroux 2006 372p pa $16   **305.4**
1. Feminism 2. Popular culture -- United States
ISBN 978-0-374-11343-8 pa; 0-374-11343-2 pa
                                        LC 2005-36156
"This work represents an alternating mix of the most hilarious, alarming, and unexpected essays from Bitch magazine's first ten years. . . . Readers new to this feminist quarterly will find the articles, almost without exception, original, intelligent, and well written. This compilation has staying power." Libr J
Includes bibliographical references

Collins, Gail

America's women; four hundred years of dolls, drudges, helpmates, and heroines. Morrow 2003 556p il $27.95; pa $15.95   **305.4**
1. Women -- United States -- History
ISBN 0-06-018510-4; 0-06-122722-6 pa
                                        LC 2003-51011

This is a history of American women from colonial times to the present

"Collins elegantly and eruditely celebrates the hard-won victories, overwhelming obstacles, and selfless contributions of a captivating array of influential women." Booklist

Includes bibliographical references

When everything changed; the amazing journey of American women from 1960 to the present. Little, Brown and Co. 2009 471p il $27.99   **305.4**
1. Women -- United States -- History
ISBN 978-0-316-05954-1; 0-316-05954-4

LC 2008-54933

"Collins can be deadly serious and great fun to read at the same time. A revelatory book for readers of both sexes, and sure to become required reading for any American women's-studies course." Kirkus

Includes bibliographical references

★ The **Columbia** documentary history of American women since 1941; edited by Harriet Sigerman. Columbia University Press 2003 690p $94; pa $34.50   **305.4**
1. Feminism 2. Women's rights 3. Women -- United States -- History -- Sources
ISBN 0-231-11698-5; 0-231-11699-3 pa

LC 2002-41395

This collection of public and private primary sources includes such topics as employment opportunities, "the ideas and changes brought about by the women's movement, the challenges to and defense of reproductive rights, the backlash against feminism in the name of family values, and new visions for women's lives in the twenty-first century." Publisher's note

Includes bibliographical references

The **essential** feminist reader; edited and with an introduction by Estelle B. Freedman. Modern Library 2007 472p pa $17.95   **305.4**
1. Feminism
ISBN 0-8129-7460-3; 978-0-8129-7460-7

This collection of writings by feminist authors "features primary source material from around the globe, including short works of fiction and drama, political manifestos, and the work of less well-known writers." Publisher's note

Includes bibliographical references

Fleet, Carole Brody

Widows wear stilettos; a practical and emotional guide for the young widow. by Carole Brody Fleet with Syd Harriet. New Horizon Press 2009 223p pa $14.95   **305.4**
1. Widows
ISBN 978-0-88282-339-3; 0-88282-339-6

A guide for women who have "experienced the loss of a partner at a young age. Fleet's presentation is frank and interspersed with bits of honest humor. The text is easy to read, with charts and tips sprinkled throughout. Fleet, with psychotherapist Harriet, provides information on how to organize details such as funeral arrangements, wills, social security, and insurance at a time when organization is the last thing a new widow may want to face. She discusses emo-

tional, physical, and spiritual health and finishes by focusing on living the rest of your life. This is a book about hope, and women will want to read it and share it with others, regardless of marital status or age." Libr J

Friedan, Betty, 1921-2006

★ The **feminine** mystique; with a new introduction. Norton 1997 xlviii, 452p hardcover o.p. pa $15.95   **305.4**
1. Feminism 2. Women -- United States
ISBN 0-393-32257-2 pa

LC 97-8877

A reissue of the title first published 1963

An "analysis of the dilemma facing the educated American woman; the post-war emphasis on the feminine image of the role as wife and mother has caused the American woman to lose her identity, says the author." Cincinnati Public Libr

Includes bibliographical references

Greer, Germaine

The **madwoman's** underclothes; essays and occasional writings. Atlantic Monthly Press 1987 xxvii, 305p hardcover o.p. pa $12.95   **305.4**
1. Feminism 2. Women -- Social conditions
ISBN 0-87113-308-3 pa

LC 87-11475

First published 1986 in the United Kingdom

A collection of the British feminist's nonfiction writings spanning her career from the 1960s to the 1980s.

Grunwald, Lisa

★ **Women's** letters; America from the Revolutionary War to the present. edited by Lisa Grunwald & Stephen J. Adler. Dial Press 2005 824p il hardcover o.p. pa $18; pa $18   **305.4**
1. Women -- United States -- History -- Sources
ISBN 9780385335560; 0-385-33553-9; 0-385-33556-3 pa

LC 2005-41446

"This is a delightful collection of belles letters in the most literal sense of the term." Publ Wkly

Includes bibliographical references

No small courage; a history of women in the United States. edited by Nancy Cott. Oxford Univ. Press 2000 646p il maps hardcover o.p. pa $21.95   **305.4**
1. Women -- United States -- History
ISBN 0-19-513946-1; 978-0-19-517323-9 pa; 0-19-517323-6 pa

LC 00-21130

"By examining the flow of American history as it has affected women {the authors} illuminate aspects of the past that have often been neglected." Booklist

Includes bibliographical references

Rodriguez, Deborah

Kabul Beauty School; an American woman goes behind the veil. Random House 2007 275p $24.95; pa $14.95   **305.4**
1. Beauty shops 2. Women -- Afghanistan 3. Kabul

Beauty School (Afghanistan)

ISBN 978-1-4000-6559-2; 1-4000-6559-3; 978-0-8129-7673-1 pa; 0-8129-7673-8 pa

LC 2006-50384

"Rodriguez's experiences will delight readers as she recounts such tales as two friends acting as 'parents' and negotiating a dowry for her marriage to an Afghan man or her students puzzling over a donation of a carton of thongs. Most of all, they will share her admiration for Afghan women's survival and triumph in chaotic times." SLJ

Schnall, Marianne

What will it take to make a woman president? conversations about women, leadership, and power. by Marianne Schnall. Seal Press 2013 384 p. $17   **305.4**

1. Women politicians 2. Gender and politics 3. Presidential candidates -- United States 4. Women -- United States -- Attitudes 5. Women -- United States -- Interviews 6. Politicians -- United States -- Attitudes 7. Women political activists -- United States 8. Women presidential candidates -- United States

ISBN 158005496X; 9781580054966

LC 2013031218

Amelia Bloomer Project (2014)

This book, by Marianne Schnall, "features interviews with politicians, public officials, thought leaders, writers, artists, and activists in an attempt to discover the obstacles that have held women back and what needs to change in order to elect a woman into the White House. With insights and personal anecdotes . . . , this book addresses timely, provocative issues involving women, politics, and power." (Publisher's note)

"Through far-ranging conversations, Schnall gained insight into factors contributing to the country's failure to elect a woman to its highest office and sought advice as to how we can not only better prepare for the next presidential election but create a world in which today's young women feel empowered to break out of stereotypical roles. The good news is that there is universal agreement among those profiled that the country will, indeed, elect a woman president. The more disconcerting message is that there is still much work to do in order to achieve true gender parity." (Booklist)

Ulrich, Laurel

Well -behaved women seldom make history; [by] Laurel Thatcher Ulrich. Alfred A. Knopf 2007 xxxiv, 284p il $24   **305.4**

1. Poets 2. Authors 3. Feminism 4. Novelists 5. Suffragists 6. Women in literature 7. Essayists 8. Biographers 9. Women -- History 10. Short story writers

ISBN 978-1-4000-4159-6; 1-4000-4159-6

LC 2006-100581

The author "uses 'three classic works in Western feminism' as a springboard for examining the theme of 'bad' behavior. . . . [They are] Christine de Pizan's 'Book of the City of Ladies,' written in 1405; Elizabeth Cady Stanton's 'Eighty Years and More,' published in 1898; and 'A Room of One's Own' [1929], based on two lectures Virginia Woolf gave in 1928." N Y Times Book Rev

This book "is by no means jargon-ridden or academic in tone. Ulrich's style is plain and direct, agreeable but without frills, and she moves efficiently right along. The book is a pleasure to read." Washington Post Book World

Includes bibliographical references

Wolf, Naomi

The **beauty** myth; how images of beauty are used against women. Perennial 2002 348p pa $14.95   **305.4**

1. Women 2. Gender role 3. Personal appearance 4. Sex role

ISBN 0-06-051218-0

LC 2002-72516

First published 1991 by Morrow

The author "presents a provocative and persuasive account of the pervasiveness of the beauty ideal in all facets of Western culture." Libr J

Includes bibliographical references

Xinran

Message from an unknown Chinese mother; stories of loss and love. translated from Chinese by Nicky Harman. Scribner 2011 xxvii, 239p $25; ebook $11.99   **305.4**

1. Mothers 2. Children -- China 3. China -- Social conditions

ISBN 978-1-4516-1089-5; 978-1-4516-1095-6 ebook

First published 2010 in the United Kingdom

The author "collects the heartbreaking stories of Chinese women forced to give up their baby girls because of the one-child-only policy or feudal traditions that prefer boys, in an oral history written for those abandoned daughters. . . . This is a brutally honest book written for those relinquished children, so that they will know how much their birth mothers loved them and how—in the words of one mother who gave up her daughter—'they paid for that love with an endless stream of bitter tears.'" Publ Wkly

Zeitz, Joshua

Flapper; a madcap story of sex, style, celebrity, and the women who made America modern. Crown Publishers 2006 338p il $24.95   **305.4**

1. Women -- United States 2. Popular culture -- United States 3. United States -- History -- 1919-1933

ISBN 1-4000-8053-3; 978-1-4000-8053-3

LC 2005-24297

"An essential exploration of the women Zeitz deems 'the first thoroughly modern American[s].'" Booklist

Includes bibliographical references

305.42   Social role and status of women

Armstrong, Jennifer Keishin

Sexy feminism; a girl's guide to love, success, and style. Jennifer Keishin Armstrong and Heather Wood Rudúlph. Mariner Books 2013 xxii, 228 p.p (paperback) $15.95   **305.42**

1. Feminism 2. Self-realization 3. Women -- Social

conditions 4. Success 5. Self-realization in women
ISBN 0547738307; 9780547738307

LC 2012040351

This book, by Jennifer Keishin Armstrong and Heather Wood Rudulph, discusses feminism in the 21st century. "For many young women the radicalism of the Second Wave is unappealing, and the . . . Third Wave feels out of date. . . . [This book offers] an inclusive, approachable kind of feminism--miniskirts, lip gloss, and waxing permitted. Covering a range of topics from body issues and workplace gender politics to fashion, dating, and sex." (Publisher's note)

Includes bibliographical references (p. [217]-228).

Brownmiller, Susan

In our time; memoir of a revolution. Dial Press (NY) 1999 360p hardcover o.p. pa $15.95 **305.42**
1. Feminism 2. Women's movement
ISBN 0-385-31831-6 pa

LC 99-39344

This book focuses on the women's movement between 1967 and 1977

"A riveting blend of eyewitness accounts and keen analysis, this is history at its most vital and a stirring testament to our ability to come together to combat social injustice, no matter how deeply entrenched it has become." Booklist

Coontz, Stephanie

A **strange** stirring; the Feminine mystique and American women at the dawn of the 1960s. Stephanie Coontz. Basic Books 2011 xxiii, 222 p.p **305.42**
1. Authors 2. Feminism 3. Feminism -- United States -- History -- 20th century 4. Women -- United States -- Social conditions -- 20th century
ISBN 0465002005; 9780465002009

LC 2010022163

The book "documents the circumstances of middle-class American women in the early 1960s and the impact of Betty Friedan's The Feminine Mystique (1963). Stephanie Coontz makes it clear that although Friedan, and many observers since, have exaggerated the book's role in launching the second wave of the feminist movement, thousands of women were profoundly affected by it. . . . [Stephanie] Coontz begins with a stark look at the circumstances facing women in the early 1960s, including legal discrimination and widely held cultural beliefs about women's nature and proper role. . . . The book ends with a chapter on the circumstances of women today. Despite the gains of the feminist movement, gender expectations still limit women's possibilities." (Journal of American History)

Includes bibliographical references (p. 191-208) and index

Richardson, Sarah

The **political** worlds of women; gender and politics in nineteenth century Britain. by Sarah Richardson. Routledge 2013 252 p. (Routledge research in gender and history) (hbk) $125 **305.42**
1. Gender and politics 2. Women -- Political activity 3. Great Britain -- Politics and government -- 19th century 4. Feminism -- Great Britain -- History -- 19th century 5. Women -- Great Britain -- Social conditions -- 19th century 6. Women -- Political activity -- Great Britain -- History -- 19th century
ISBN 0415825660; 9780415825665

LC 2012041942

Author Sarah Richardson discussed British politics in between 1800-1870. "By adopting a broader interpretation of political participation, the author identifies how middle-class women were able to contribute to political affairs in the nineteenth century. This volume examines female engagement in both traditional and unconventional political arenas, including female sociability, salons, child-rearing and education, health, consumption, religious reform and nationalism." (Publisher's note)

Includes bibliographical references and index

Rosin, Hanna

The **end** of men; and the rise of women. Hanna Rosin. Riverhead Books 2012 310 p. (hbk.) $27.95 **305.42**
1. Women -- History 2. Man-woman relationship 3. Feminism 4. Women -- Social conditions -- 21st century 5. Women -- Economic conditions -- 21st century
ISBN 1594488045; 9781594488047

LC 2012018005

This book by Hanna Rosin is a "portrait of women, men, and power in a transformed world. Men have been the dominant sex since, well, the dawn of mankind. . . . [But] this unprecedented moment, by almost every measure, women are no longer gaining on men: They have pulled decisively ahead. Rosin reveals how this new state of affairs is radically shifting the power dynamics between men and women at every level of society, with profound implications for marriage, sex, children, work, and more." (Publisher's note)

Includes bibliographical references and index.

Spar, Debora L.

Wonder Women; Sex, Power, and the Quest for Perfection. Sarah Crichton Books 2013 320 p. $27 **305.42**
1. Feminism 2. Women -- Social conditions
ISBN 0374298750; 9780374298753

This book "addresses the state of feminism and suggests that, despite historic gains in education, the workforce, and equal rights, American women suffer under 'an excruciating set of mutually exclusive expectations' resulting, paradoxically, from the proliferation of options that feminism made possible." Debora L. Spar "traces how the movement's 'expansive and revolutionary' political goals have evolved into a set of 'vast and towering expectations' that trouble women at every stage of their lives." (Publishers Weekly)

Steinem, Gloria

Moving beyond words. Simon & Schuster 1994 319p hardcover o.p. pa $19.95 **305.42**
1. Feminism
ISBN 0-671-51052-5 pa

LC 94-4839

"Ms. Steinem's enduring contribution to the women's movement has been her ability to popularize feminist issues to a wide and often wary audience." N Y Times Book Rev
Includes bibliographical references

✓ **Outrageous** acts and everyday rebellions; 2nd ed; Holt & Co. 1995 xxii, 406p pa $17   **305.42**
1. Feminism
ISBN 0-8050-4202-4

LC 95-31711
First published 1983
In addition to material addressing specific feminist issues, this collection includes personal accounts of political leaders and noted women.
Includes bibliographical references

The unfinished revolution; voices from the global fight for women's rights. edited by Minky Worden. Seven Stories Press 2012 xviii, 361 p.p col. ill. (paperback) $25.95   **305.42**
1. Human rights 2. Women's rights
ISBN 1609803876; 9781609803872

LC 2011052738
This book edited by Minky Worden is a collection of "essays assessing the progress of worldwide rights for women and girls since the UN's human rights conferences in the 1990s. The ongoing global struggle consists of three distinct spheres: economic issues (human trafficking, property rights); violence against women and their health rights (including genital mutilation); and harmful traditions (religious clothing restraints, so-called honor crimes)." (Booklist)
Includes bibliographical references and index

Wolf, Naomi
✓ **Vagina**; A New Biography. Naomi Wolf. HarperCollins 2012 xii, 381 p., [8] p. of platesp ill. $27.99   **305.42**
1. Vagina 2. Femininity 3. Nervous system 4. Reproductive system 5. Women -- Sexual behavior
ISBN 0061989169; 9780061989162

LC 2012454997
This book by Naomi Wolf "explores the effect of new neurobiological discoveries on our understanding of female sexuality. When the author began noticing . . . diminished sexual response at age 46, she visited a gynecologist, who diagnosed her with an impacted pelvic nerve. . . . Wolf set out to document the mind-body link with the goal of informing women of the crucial role that neurology plays not only in their sex lives, but also in . . . their creativity and sense of well-being." (Kirkus Reviews)
Includes bibliographical references (p. [335]-365) and index.

305.42   Social role and status of women

Miller, Cathleen
Champion of choice; the life and legacy of women's advocate Nafis Sadik. Cathleen Miller. University of Nebraska Press 2013 536 p. (hardcover) $34.95   **305.42**
1. Population control 2. Family planning -- Developing countries 3. Women physicians -- Pakistan -- Biography 4. Reproductive rights -- Developing countries 5. Women social reformers -- Pakistan -- Biography 6. Women's health services -- Developing countries
ISBN 080321104X; 9780803211049

LC 2012035075
This book is a biography of Dr. Nafis Sadik, who changed the world for women through her work on population control. The book "follows the improbable path of the Pakistani Sadik through partition, medical school, her early work in local population control and her efforts for the U.N. Population Fund, which she directed for 13 years." (Kirkus)
Includes bibliographical references and index

Moran, Caitlin
✓ ★ **How** to be a woman; Caitlin Moran. Harper Perennial 2011 305 p. (pbk.) $15.99   **305.42**
1. Feminism 2. Women -- Great Britain 3. Journalists -- England -- Biography 4. Women journalists -- England -- Biography 5. Women -- Great Britain -- Social conditions -- Humor
ISBN 0062124293; 9780062124296

LC 2012372347
Originally published: London : Ebury Press, 2011.
This book is "part memoir, part postmodern feminist rant" from British TV critic Caitlin Moran. "Moran's journey into womanhood begins on her 13th birthday when boys throw rocks at her 182-pound body, and her only friend, her sister Caz, hands her a homemade card reminding her to please turn 18 or die soon so Caz can inherit her bedroom." Moran "embarrasses herself often enough to become an authority on how to masturbate; name one's breasts; and forgo a Brazilian bikini wax." (Publishers Weekly)

305.48   Specific groups of women

Mah, Adeline Yen
✓ **Falling** leaves; a true story of an unwanted Chinese daughter. Wiley 1998 278p il $22.95 **305.48**
1. Physicians 2. China -- Social life and customs
ISBN 0-471-24742-1

LC 97-40144
First published 1997 in the United Kingdom with title: Falling leaves return to their roots
"Although the focus of this memoir is the author's struggle to be loved by a family that treated her cruelly, it is more notable for its portrait of the domestic affairs of an immensely wealthy, Westernized Chinese family in Shanghai as the city evolved under the harsh strictures of Mao and Deng. . . . In recounting this painful tale, Yen Mah's unadorned prose is powerful, her insights keen and her portrait of her family devastating." Publ Wkly

Scroggins, Deborah
✓ **Wanted** women; faith, lies, and the war on terror: the lives of Ayaan Hirsi Ali and Aafia Siddiqui. by Deborah Scroggins. Harper 2011 p. cm.   **305.48**
1. Feminism 2. Terrorism 3. Muslim women 4.

Women political activists 5. Muslim women -- Social conditions 6. Muslim women -- Political activity
ISBN 9780060898977

LC 2011022153

This book explores the topics of "militant Islam, Muslim women's rights, and the war on terror--brought into focus through two lives on opposite sides: activist Ayaan Hirsi Ali and religious extremist Aafia Siddiqui. . . . Ayaan Hirsi Ali, a Somali-born former member of the Dutch Parliament and the author of the international bestseller 'Infidel,' was raised as a Muslim fundamentalist in Kenya. A feminist, political analyst, writer, and fierce critic of her former religion, she champions the West in what she insists must be a war against Islam. . . . Aafia Siddiqui, a native of Pakistan, moved to the United States to pursue a doctorate in neuroscience. A decade later, she returned to Pakistan, where her involvement with al-Qaeda, including her marriage to one of the 9/11 plotters, led the CIA to regard her as one of the most dangerous terrorists in the world." (Publisher's note)

305.5 People by social and economic levels

Boo, Katherine

★ **Behind** the beautiful forevers; Katherine Boo. Random House 2012 xxii, 256 p.p   **305.5**
  1. Poverty 2. Bombay (India) 3. Political corruption 4. Creative nonfiction 5. Urban poor -- India -- Bombay 6. Urban poor -- India -- Mumbai
  ISBN 1400067553; 9780679645504; 9781400067558

LC 2011019555

This book examines "the stark lives of the inhabitants of Annawadi, a slum across from Mumbai's Sahar Airport, to reveal the . . . inequality and urban poverty still endemic in India's democracy. Using recorded and videotaped conversations, interviews, documents, and the assistance of interlocutors, [Katherine] Boo profiles the lives of some of the slum dwellers from November 2007 to March 2011. . . . [Boo] claims she witnessed most of the events described in the book." (Library Journal)

Brooks, David

The **social** animal; the hidden sources of love, character, and achievement. Random House 2011 424p $27; ebook $13.99   **305.5**
  1. Character 2. Social status 3. Elite (Social sciences)
  ISBN 978-1-4000-6760-2; 1-4000-6760-X; 978-0-679-60393-1 ebook; 0-679-60393-X ebook

LC 2010045785

"Brooks offers fictional characters Harold and Erica to illustrate how humans communicate, are educated, and succeed—or don't. Synthesizing research on human unconsciousness, Brooks meshes sociology, psychology, and economics to show how character is formed and how we strive for happiness and success. . . . [The author] offers a new look at the assumptions we make about life and a close, deep examination of the failure of social and economic policies that do not take into account the complexities of human behavior, treating us as if we were totally rational and guided by our thoughts rather than some combination of intellect and emotion." Booklist

Includes bibliographical references

Ehrenreich, Barbara, 1941-

★ **Nickel** and dimed; on (not) getting by in America. Metropolitan Bks. 2001 221p hardcover o.p. pa $15   **305.5**
  1. Poverty 2. Minimum wage 3. Labor -- United States
  ISBN 0-8050-6388-9; 0-8050-8838-5 pa

LC 00-52514

This is an exposé "of such abstractions as 'living wage' and 'affordable housing.' Ehrenreich worked, for a month at a time, at 'unskilled' jobs—as a waitress and chambermaid in Florida, a housecleaner and nursing-home aide in Maine, a Wal-Mart clerk in Minnesota—to report on how people survive on wages of six or seven dollars an hour." New Yorker

"No real answers to the problem but a compelling sketch of its reality and pervasiveness." Libr J

Epstein, Joseph, 1937-

Snobbery; The American Version. Houghton Mifflin 2002 274p $25; pa $14   **305.5**
  1. Snobs and snobbishness 2. Social status -- United States 3. Snobs and snobbishness -- United States
  ISBN 0-395-94417-1; 0-618-34073-4 pa

LC 2001-51623

Epstein tracks the evolution of intellectual and cultural snobbery in the United States. He suggests that the traditional snobbery associated with the class system has given way in recent decades to a more complex phenomenon based on taste. Index.

"Every bracing page is a mirror in which readers can't help but recognize themselves, and each offers a quotable quip . . . and much to think about." Booklist

Includes bibliographical references

Freeland, Chrystia

Plutocrats; the rise of the new global super-rich and the fall of everyone else. Chrystia Freeland. Penguin Press 2012 xv, 330 p.p $27.95   **305.5**
  1. Rich 2. Elite (Social sciences) 3. Power (Social sciences) 4. Poor 5. Rich people -- Conduct of life
  ISBN 1594204098; 9781594204098

LC 2012015119

This book, by Chrystia Freeland, offers an "examination of wealth disparity, income inequality, and the new global elite. . . . In the last few decades what it means to be rich has changed dramatically. . . . The wealthiest 0.1 percent . . . are outpacing the rest of us at break-neck speed. . . . [The book] demonstrates how social upheavals generated by the first Gilded Age may pale in comparison to what is in store for us." (Publisher's note)

Includes bibliographical references and index

Freeland, Chrystia, 1968-

Plutocrats; the rise of the new global super-rich and the fall of everyone else. Chrystia Freeland. Penguin Press 2012 p. cm.   **305.5**
  1. Poor 2. Rich people -- Conduct of life
  ISBN 9781594204098

LC 2012015119

This book, by Chrystia Freeland, offers an "examination of wealth disparity, income inequality, and the new global elite. . . . In the last few decades what it means to be rich has changed dramatically. . . . The wealthiest 0.1 percent . . . are outpacing the rest of us at break-neck speed. . . . [The book] demonstrates how social upheavals generated by the first Gilded Age may pale in comparison to what is in store for us." (Publisher's note)

Freeman, Joshua Benjamin

Working -class New York; life and labor since World War II. [by] Joshua B. Freeman. New Press (NY) 2000 409p il $35; pa $19.95   **305.5**
    1. Labor unions 2. Working class 3. New York (N.Y.) -- Social conditions
    ISBN 1-56584-575-7; 1-56584-712-1 pa
                                            LC 99-87940
"Freeman charts the postwar rise and eventual fall of Manhattan working-class life and culture. . . . Strong narrative drive, attention to detail and historical insight make this a superb addition to studies of postwar culture, urbanology and labor history." Publ Wkly
    Includes bibliographical references

Hayes, Christopher

Twilight of the elites; America after meritocracy. Christopher Hayes. Crown Publishers 2012 292 p.   **305.5**
    1. Equality 2. Leadership 3. Elite (Social sciences) 4. United States -- Politics and government -- 21st century 5. Power (Social sciences) 6. Corporate power -- United States 7. Business and politics -- United States 8. United States -- Social conditions -- 21st century 9. United States -- Economic conditions -- 21st century
    ISBN 9780307720450; 9780307720474
                                            LC 2012002435
This book looks at the meritocracy and income inequality in the U.S. since the 1960s. Combining "political analysis, . . . social commentary, . . . and . . . historical understanding, 'Twilight of Elites' describes how the society we have come to inhabit -- utterly forgiving at the top and relentlessly punitive at the bottom -- produces leaders who are out of touch with the people they have been trusted to govern." (Publisher's note)
    Includes bibliographical references and index.

Hedges, Chris

Days of destruction, days of revolt; Chris Hedges and Joe Sacco. Nation Books 2012 xv, 302 p.p ill. (hardback) $28   **305.5**
    1. Camden (N.J.) 2. Social conflict 3. Poor -- United States 4. Pine Ridge Indian Reservation (S.D.) 5. Mines and mineral resources -- United States 6. Crime -- United States 7. Social classes -- United States 8. United States -- Social conditions -- 20th century
    ISBN 1568586434; 9781568586434; 9781568587103
                                            LC 2012004701
This book by Chris Hedges and Joe Sacco examines the impact of capitalism in America's society through a "tour of some of the worst places in America: the Pine Ridge reservation in South Dakota, which paces the nation in drug abuse, alcoholism, and teen suicide rates; Camden, NJ, one of the country's poorest and most dangerous cities; Welch, WV, where coal companies have relentlessly mined both human and natural resources; and Immokalee, FL, where

migrant farm workers toil in virtual slavery." (Columbia Journalism Review)
    Includes bibliographical references (p. 287-291) and index

Jadhav, Narendra

    ★ **Untouchables**; my family's triumphant journey out of the caste system in modern India. Scribner 2005 307p $26   **305.5**
    1. Caste 2. India -- Social conditions
    ISBN 0-7432-7079-7
                                            LC 2005-44166
Original Indian edition, 1993; first published in English 2003 by Viking with title: Outcaste, a memoir
"This moving story of perseverance from a sector of India rarely represented to American readers will be a standard text on Indian and Dalit themes for years to come." Libr J

Laskas, Jeanne Marie, 1958-

    ★ **Hidden** America; from coal miners to cowboys, an extraordinary exploration of the unseen people who make this country work. Jeanne Marie Laskas. Penguin Group USA 2012 318 p.   **305.5**
    1. United States -- Description and travel 2. United States -- Social conditions -- 1980- 3. Working class -- United States -- Biography 4. Working class -- United States -- Social conditions
    ISBN 0399159002; 9780399159008
                                            LC 2012025457
Author Jeanne Marie Laskas presents a book "about the people who make our lives run every day--and yet we barely think of them. Laskas spent weeks in an Ohio coal mine and on an Alaskan oil rig; in a Maine migrant labor camp, a Texas beef ranch, the air traffic control tower at New York's La-Guardia Airport, a California landfill, an Arizona gun shop, the cab of a long-haul truck in Iowa, and the stadium of the Cincinnati Ben-Gals cheerleaders." (Publisher's note)

LeBlanc, Adrian Nicole

Random family; love, drugs, trouble, and coming of age in the Bronx. Scribner 2003 408p $25 **305.5**
    1. Poor -- New York (N.Y.) 2. Youth -- New York (N.Y.) 3. Bronx (New York, N.Y.) -- Social conditions
    ISBN 0-684-86387-1
                                            LC 2002-26673
"This is a slice-of-life chronicle of black and Puerto Rican teens in the South Bronx during the 1980s. Looking for excitement, prosperity, love, sex, connection, and family, they instead find drugs, abuse, babies, and prison—a continuation of the home life they had hoped to escape." Libr J
    "A painstaking feat of reporting and empathy that resulted from 10 years of hanging out with a hard-pressed, loosely defined family in the Bronx." N Y Times Book Rev

Maharidge, Dale

Someplace like America; tales from the new Great Depression. photographs by Michael S. Williamson; with a foreword by Bruce Springsteen. University of California Press 2011 244p il $29.95   **305.5**
    1. Poverty 2. Unemployed 3. Working class 4. United States -- Social conditions 5. United States -- Economic

conditions
ISBN 978-0-520-26247-8; 0-520-26247-6

LC 2010-53750

"Maharidge and Williamson continue their heartfelt chronicle of the travails facing America's poor and homeless in this follow-up to the 1995 Journey to Nowhere. Presenting new stories from today's 'Great Depression' and updating their accounts of those impoverished during the recession of the '80s and the supposed boom years of the '90s, this book evokes the Depression-era collaboration of Walker Evans and James Agee. . . . At the core of the narrative are the individuals who've found themselves dispossessed, hopping freight trains to look for work, waiting in food bank lines, huddling in shanties hand-built from scraps and billboard tarps, and mourning the closings of the steel mills where they once worked. Williamson's gritty photographs—of blind storefronts, abandoned lots choked with weeds, faces lined with dirt and worry, stalwart families, and squatters hunched over meager campfires—are an equally eloquent testimonial." Publ Wkly

Includes bibliographical references.

Painter, Nell Irvin

★ **Sojourner** Truth; a life, a symbol. Norton 1996 370p il hardcover o.p. pa $15.95   **305.5**
1. Feminism 2. Abolitionists 3. Memoirists 4. African American women -- Biography
ISBN 0-393-02739-2; 0-393-31708-0 pa

LC 95-47595

"Sojourner Truth's remarkable career as a powerful, impassioned speaker and advocate of abolitionism and women's rights spanned more than 30 years. Painter . . . traces Truth's life and legacy using a variety of sources, including her many photographs." Libr J

"Painter persuasively offers us the real woman behind the myth." Publ Wkly

Includes bibliographical references

Rothkopf, David

Superclass; the global power elite and the world they are making. [by] David Rothkopf. Farrar, Straus and Giroux 2008 400p   **305.5**
1. Elite (Social sciences) 2. Power (Social sciences)
ISBN 978-0-374-27210-4

LC 2007-36569

The author examines a small population with a large amount of global influence. Index.

"Neither hand-wringing nor worshipful, this book delivers an unsettling account of what the immense and growing power of this superclass bodes for the future." Publ Wkly

Includes bibliographical references (p. 235-355)

Smith, Douglas

Former people; the final days of the Russian aristocracy. Douglas Smith. 1st ed. Farrar, Straus and Giroux 2012 xvii, 464 pages, 32 unnumbered pages of platesp illustrations, maps (hardcover : alk. paper) $30.00   **305.5**
1. Communism 2. Russia -- History 3. Nobility -- Russia 4. Aristocracy (Social class) -- Soviet Union 5. Aristocracy (Social class) -- Russia -- History -- 20th century
ISBN 0374157618; 9780374157616

LC 2012003819

This book "examines the . . . 'fate of the nobility in the decades following the Russian Revolution,' when they were sometimes given the Orwellian title 'former people.' The author of several books on Russia . . . , [Douglas] Smith focuses on three generations of two families: the Sheremetsevs of St. Petersburg and the Golitsyns of Moscow." (Publishers Weekly)

Includes bibliographical references (pages 416-435) and index.

Stiglitz, Joseph E., 1943-

★ The **price** of inequality; how today's divided society endangers our future. Joseph E. Stiglitz. W.W. Norton & Co. 2012 xxxi, 414 p.p (hbk.) $27.95   **305.5**
1. Wealth 2. Finance -- United States 3. Equality -- United States 4. Global Financial Crisis, 2008-2009 5. United States -- Social conditions -- 21st century 6. United States -- Economic conditions -- 21st century 7. Income distribution -- Social aspects -- United States
ISBN 0393088693; 9780393088694

LC 2012014811

In this book, author Joseph E. Stiglitz "insists that increasing inequality in the United States stems from a breakdown of the country's political and economic systems." Stiglitz suggests that "inequality is a by-product of the ability to exploit consumers through monopoly power. . . . He shows that the consequences include a monopolistic redistribution powerful enough to have caused massive distortions in the U.S. financial system." (Kirkus Reviews)

Includes bibliographical references and index.

Veblen, Thorstein

★ The **theory** of the leisure class; edited with an introduction and notes by Martha Banta. Oxford University Press 2007 (Oxford world's classics) pa $15.95   **305.5**
1. Social classes
ISBN 978-0-19-280684-0; 0-19-280684-X

LC 2007-8544

First published 1899 by Macmillan

In this economic treatise, "Veblen held that the feudal subdivision of classes had continued into modern times, the lords employing themselves uselessly . . . while the lower classes labored at industrial pursuits to support the whole of society. The leisure class, Veblen said, justifies itself solely by practicing 'conspicuous leisure and conspicuous consumption'; he defined waste as any activity not contributing to material productivity." Benet Reader's Ency. 4th edition

Wyman, Mark

Hoboes; bindlestiffs, fruit tramps, and the harvesting of the West. Hill and Wang 2010 336p il map $28   **305.5**
1. Tramps 2. Migrant labor 3. West (U.S.) -- History
ISBN 978-0-8090-3021-7

LC 2009-20834

"A vigorous, well-written multicultural history of the West as it really was." Kirkus

Includes bibliographical references

Zubok, Vladislav

Zhivago's children; the last Russian intelligentsia. [by] Vladislav Zubok. Belknap Press of Harvard University Press 2009 453p il $35   **305.5**
1. Soviet Union -- History 2. Socialism -- Soviet Union 3. Intellectuals -- Soviet Union 4. Soviet Union -- Intellectual life 5. Soviet Union -- History -- 1953-1985 6. Intellectuals -- Soviet Union -- History
ISBN 978-0-674-03344-3; 0-674-03344-2

LC 2008-53107

This "is a thorough, scholarly examination of a vital era in Russian history whose themes of human rights, freedom and dissent will resonate among experts and lay readers alike." Washington Post

Includes bibliographical references

305.8   Ethnic and national groups

The **African** American almanac; Christopher A. Brooks, editor; foreword by Benjamin Jealous. 11th ed; Gale Cengage Learning 2011 1601p il map $297   **305.8**
1. Reference books 2. African Americans
ISBN 978-1-4144-4547-2

First edition under the editorship of Harry A. Ploski published 1967 by Bellwether with title: The Negro almanac. Periodically revised. Editors vary

"Reference covering the cultural and political history of Black Americans. Includes generous amount of statistical information and biographies of Black Americans, both historical and contemporary." N Y Public Libr. Book of How & Where to Look It Up

American Jewish Historical Society

American Jewish history; edited by Jeffrey S. Gurock. Routledge 1998 8v in 13 set $1,705 **305.8**
1. Jews -- United States -- History
ISBN 0-415-91933-9

"This set is a compilation of 211 articles . . . chosen to relate the history of American Jews to that of other Americans or to that of Jews all over the world. . . . The wide range of issues discussed in the set includes anti-Semitism among the suffragettes, Jewish-black relations, the role of synagogue sisterhoods, and the political and cultural impact of Zionism. American Jewish History is a unique source." Booklist

Bayoumi, Moustafa

How does it feel to be a problem? being young and Arab in America. Penguin Press 2008 290p pa $15; $24.95   **305.8**
1. Arab American youth 2. Young men -- Psychology 3. Young men -- United States 4. Race awareness -- United States 5. United States -- Race relations 6. Arab Americans -- Ethnic identity 7. Arab Americans -- Social conditions 8. Brooklyn (New York, N.Y.) --

Ethnic relations
ISBN 978-0-14-311541-0 pa; 978-1-59420-176-9

LC 2007-49272

This book is based on interviews with seven young Arab Americans who live in Brooklyn. It "evaluates their daily encounters with such factors as prejudice, the Christian faith, and their relationships with friends and family members in the Middle East." (Publisher's note)

The author "wondered how younger generations of Arab Americans were faring in a post-9/11 U.S. against the backdrop of fear and suspicion. By focusing on the lives of seven young people living in Brooklyn, Bayoumi offers a revealing portrait of life for people who are often scrutinized but seldom heard from." Booklist

Includes bibliographical references

Beckerman, Gal

When they come for us we'll be gone; the epic struggle to save Soviet Jewry. Houghton Mifflin Harcourt 2010 598p il $30   **305.8**
1. Jews -- Russia 2. Jews -- Persecutions 3. Jews -- Soviet Union -- History 4. Soviet Union -- Ethnic relations 5. Soviet Union -- Social conditions 6. Jews -- Persecutions -- Soviet Union 7. Jews -- Soviet Union -- Politics and government 8. Soviet Union -- Emigration and immigration -- Government policy
ISBN 0-618-57309-7; 978-0-618-57309-7

LC 2010-05735

"At the end of World War II, nearly three million Jews were trapped inside the Soviet Union. They lived a paradox: unwanted by a repressive Stalinist state yet forbidden to leave. Those who tried were followed by the KGB, often denied jobs and higher education, even forced into menial labor or imprisoned simply for studying Hebrew or gathering with other Jews. When They Come for Us, We'll Be Gone is the astonishing and inspiring account of their rescue. It is one of the great exodus stories of modern times." (Publisher's Note)

"Beckerman tells a complex tale set in the United States, Israel and the Soviet Union. Some of the most potent historical forces of the century shaped the departure of 1.3 million Jews from the Soviet Union: the Holocaust, assimilation, the human rights movements, the birth of Israel and the Cold War. . . . The author is gifted at weaving this very human and very political tale together. He lays out how this struggle intersected with other movements, including the drive for democracy in the Soviet Union and the fight for civil rights in the United States. All the while, he keeps the reader mindful of Cold War politics. Beckerman also teases out the Jewish role in the rise of U.S. neoconservatism, tracking such figures as Richard Perle and Paul Wolfowitz as they learn the political trade." Cleveland Plain Dealer

Includes bibliographical references

Berlin, Ira

The **making** of African America; the four great migrations. Viking 2010 304p $27.95   **305.8**
1. Internal migration 2. African Americans -- History 3. Slave trade -- United States 4. African Americans -- Migrations -- History 5. United States -- Immigration and emigration 6. Migration, Internal -- United States

-- History

ISBN 978-0-670-02137-6; 0-670-02137-7

LC 2009-28366

"This . . . book proposes a new framework for African American history. Breaking with what he calls the 'master narrative' that frames the subject as an ongoing struggle for freedom and equality, Ira Berlin argues that the experience of relocation and the formation of new communities in new contexts have been pivotal in the making and remaking of African American society. . . . Based on secondary sources, this . . . book briskly narrates four hundred years of history, highlighting the 'four great migrations.' . . . 'The Making of African America' aims to show how migrations reorganized culture and social life. Each of his four major relocations yields a new African America." (Journal of American History)

"Berlin's neat synthesis offers the sharp insights and provocative commentary of one of the foremost historians of black America. Essential for library collections, general readers, and scholars of African American history." Libr J

Includes bibliographical references

Bishop, Bill

The **big** sort; why the clustering of like-minded America is tearing us apart. with Robert G. Cushing. Houghton Mifflin 2008 370p il map $25   **305.8**

1. Minorities -- United States 2. Regionalism -- United States 3. Segregation -- United States 4. Regionalism -- Political aspects 5. Social conflict -- United States 6. Political culture -- United States 7. United States -- Social conditions -- 1980- 8. United States -- Politics and government -- 1989-

ISBN 0-618-68935-4; 978-0-618-68935-4

LC 2007-43907

This volume originated in a series of articles written by journalist Bill Bishop and sociologist Robert Cushing, contending that "Americans have been sorting themselves over the past three decades into . . . homogeneous communities, not by region or by red state or blue state, but by city and even neighborhood." (Publisher's note) Index.

"Bishop's argument is meticulously researched—surveys and polls proliferate—and his reach is broad. . . . [The] portrait of our 'post materialistic' society will . . . generate chatter [and] the idea is catchy." Publ Wkly

Includes bibliographical references

Biss, Eula

Notes from no man's land; American essays. Graywolf Press 2009 230p   **305.8**

1. Poets 2. Authors 3. Essayists 4. Group identity -- United States 5. United States -- Race relations 6. United States -- Description and travel

ISBN 1-55597-518-6; 978-1-55597-518-0

LC 20080935599

"This essay collection won the 2008 Graywolf Press Nonfiction Prize." (Libr J)

"These essays are about many things, but the theme of race runs through them all. They are not 'about' race, however, not in the way essays are usually 'about' something. Instead of presenting her opening gambits and using the body of the essay to support her initial points, Biss finds her jumping-off point and examines her observations and experiences. Although her juxtapositions are occasionally forced, it is impossible to remain unmoved by Biss's work." Libr J

Blackmon, Douglas A.

Slavery by another name; the re-enslavement of Black people in America from the Civil War to World War II. Doubleday 2008 466p il $29.95; pa $16.95   **305.8**

1. Slavery -- United States 2. United States -- Race relations 3. African Americans -- Civil rights

ISBN 978-0-385-50625-0; 0-385-50625-2; 978-0-385-72270-4 pa; 0-385-72270-2 pa

LC 2007-34500

The author "gives a groundbreaking and disturbing account of a sordid chapter in American history—the lease (essentially the sale) of convicts to commercial interests between the end of the 19th century and well into the 20th. . . . [The] book reveals in devastating detail the legal and commercial forces that created this neoslavery along with deeply moving and totally appalling personal testimonies of survivors." Publ Wkly

Includes bibliographical references (p. 444-459)

Chang, Iris

★ The **Chinese** in America; a narrative history. Viking 2003 496p il hardcover o.p. pa $16   **305.8**

1. Chinese Americans -- History

ISBN 0-670-03123-2; 0-14-200417-0 pa

LC 2002-44858

The author recounts "the immigration of Chinese people to the U.S. from the early nineteenth century to the end of the twentieth. . . . Chang threads personal stories of individuals she came across in her research into her book, making it a much more human account. . . . This is history at its most dramatic and relevant." Booklist

Includes bibliographical references

Chesler, Phyllis

The **new** anti-semitism; the current crisis and what we must do about it. Jossey-Bass 2003 307p $24.95; pa $15.95   **305.8**

1. Antisemitism 2. Israel-Arab conflicts

ISBN 0-7879-6851-X; 0-7879-7803-5 pa

LC 2003-6448

The author "addresses what she sees as a re-emergence of virulent anti-Jewish hatred cloaked in 'political correctness,' closely linked to anti-American attitudes, sustained by many liberal feminists, intellectuals and Jewish leftists, acted upon by Islamic terrorists and jihadists, and fueled by a 'demonization of Jews' in the media. One of the main thrusts of Chesler's argument is that in our contemporary world anti-Zionism is nearly inseparable from anti-Semitism, and that while there are valid criticisms to be made of Israeli policies—for instance, she sees the West Bank settlements as an impediment to peace—many of these critiques are, she contends, rooted in a profound and socially accepted anti-Semitism." Publ Wkly

Includes bibliographical references

Curtis, Edward E., 1970-

✓ **Muslims** in America; a short history. Oxford University Press 2009 144p il (Religion in American life) pa $12.95   **305.8**

1. Muslims 2. Ethnic relations 3. Islam -- History 4. Muslims -- United States 5. Islam -- United States -- History 6. Muslims -- United States -- History 7. United States -- Religious life and customs
ISBN 978-0-19-536756-0

LC 2008-47566

The author "has authored a fine and succinct history that spans centuries. . . . Although geared toward non-Muslims, American Muslims would also learn a great deal from reading about their own history. . . . [Readers] will undoubtedly be intrigued by Curtis's compelling little read." Publ Wkly

Includes bibliographical references

Diner, Hasia R.

A **time** for gathering; the second migration, 1820-1880. Johns Hopkins Univ. Press 1992 313p il (Jewish people in America) hardcover o.p. pa $20.95   **305.8**

1. Jews -- United States -- History
ISBN 0-8018-4344-8; 0-8018-5121-1 pa

LC 91-45368

This second volume in a five-volume history of American Jewry focuses on the German-speaking Jewish immigrants who came to the United States in the nineteenth century.

Includes bibliographical references

Diouf, Sylviane A.

Slavery's exiles; the story of the American Maroons. Sylviane A. Diouf. New York University Press 2014 384 p. illustrations, maps (hardback) $29.95   **305.8**

1. Fugitive slaves 2. Southern States -- Race relations 3. United States -- Race relations -- History 4. Maroons -- Southern States -- History
ISBN 081472437X; 9780814724378; 9780814760284

LC 2013029821

In this book, author Sylvaine A. Diouf "reconstructs the lives of blacks who sought freedom and self-determination on the margins of an American slave society. Whether newly arrived from Africa or already acculturated to the demands of servitude, whether they fled to the hinterlands to live in secluded swamps or in the mountains, or to the borderlands, close by farms, plantations or towns, the maroons ran away intending to stay away, seeking autonomy even at the price of unspeakable danger." (Kirkus Reviews)

"By applying a geographical approach to her study, Diouf enlightens slavery scholarship with a new story of how runaway slaves could challenge the traditional roles established for black men and women, while at the same time forging a cultural identity that was uniquely their own." Choice

Includes bibliographical references and index

Du Bois, W. E. B. (William Edward Burghardt), 1868-1963

★ The **souls** of Black folk; edited with an introduction and notes by Brent Hayes Edwards. Oxford University Press 2007 xxxvi, 223p il (Oxford world's classics) pa $12.95   **305.8**

1. African Americans
ISBN 978-0-19-280678-9; 0-19-280678-5

LC 2006-35193

First published 1903 by McClurg

"A collection of fifteen essays and sketches by W.E.B. Du Bois. In it he describes the lives of African American farmers, sketches the role of music in their churches, details the history of the Freedman's Bureau, discusses the career of Booker T. Washington, and advocates a commitment to higher education for the most talented African American youth." Benet's Reader's Ency of Am Lit

Includes bibliographical references

Encyclopedia of Muslim-American history; edited by Edward E. Curtis, IV. Facts on File 2010 628p 2v il (Facts on File library of American history) set $195   **305.8**

1. Reference books 2. Muslims -- United States 3. Muslims -- United States -- Encyclopedias
ISBN 978-0-8160-7575-1; 978-1-4381-3040-8 ebook

LC 2009-24875

The editor "has assembled a fascinating and timely resource detailing the history and contributions of Muslim Americans in the United States. More than 300 articles, written by scholars, historians, and experts in Islam and American history, outline the long legacy and impact that Muslim Americans have had since their earliest arrival on slave ships in the 18th century. . . . A necessary and timely resource to remind us of the vital contributions that Muslim Americans have made to our culture and society since its founding." Libr J

Includes bibliographical references

Everett, Daniel Leonard

✓ **Don't** sleep, there are snakes; life and language in the Amazonian jungle. [by] Daniel L. Everett. Pantheon Books 2008 283p il $26.95   **305.8**

1. Pirahã Indians 2. Amazon River valley -- Languages
ISBN 978-0-375-42502-8; 0-375-42502-0

LC 2008-16306

The author "has crafted a fascinating account of his 30 years of linguistics work among the Pirahã (pronounced pee-da-HAN) Indians, a tribal group living along the Maici and Marmelos Rivers in a remote area of western Brazil. . . . With a clear, detail-rich writing style, Everett provides evocative ethnographic descriptions of Pirahã life and culture as well as perceptive linguistic analysis." Libr J

Includes bibliographical references

Faber, Eli

A **time** for planting; the first migration, 1654-1820. Johns Hopkins Univ. Press 1992 188p il (Jewish people in America) hardcover o.p. pa $14.95   **305.8**

1. Jews -- United States -- History
ISBN 0-8018-4343-X; 0-8018-5120-3 pa

LC 91-45341

This is the initial volume in a five-volume series tracing the history of Jews in the United States from the seventeenth century to the period following World War II. It focuses on the Sephardic Jews who settled in New Amsterdam, Newport, Rhode Island, Philadelphia, Charleston and other colonial towns.

Includes bibliographical references

Family affair; what It means to be African American today. [edited by] Gil L. Robertson IV. Bolden 2009 407p pa $16   **305.8**

1. African Americans -- Race identity

ISBN 978-1932841-35-0; 1-932841-35-0

LC 2008-45716

"This thoughtful collection of short essays, addressing a wide range of issues and emotions facing African Americans, should become a well-thumbed nightstand fixture." Publ Wkly

Feingold, Henry L.

A **time** for searching; entering the mainstream, 1920-1945. Johns Hopkins Univ. Press 1992 338p il (Jewish people in America) hardcover o.p. pa $21.95   **305.8**

1. Jews -- United States -- History

ISBN 0-8018-4346-4; 0-8018-5123-8 pa

LC 91-45367

This fourth volume in The Jewish People in America series addresses the period from the end of World War I to World War II. The author discusses "the emergence of anti-Semitism, second-generation Jewish acculturation and secularization, political behavior, and Zionism, . . . aiming to explain the disarray of the American Jewish community during the Holocaust." Libr J

Includes bibliographical references

Flavell, Julie

When London was capital of America. Yale University Press 2010 305p il map $32.50   **305.8**

1. Americans -- England 2. London (England) -- History 3. Americans -- England -- London 4. Great Britain -- History -- 1714-1837 5. London (England) -- Intellectual life 6. Americans -- England -- London -- History 7. London (England) -- History -- 18th century 8. London (England) -- Intellectual life -- 18th century

ISBN 978-0-300-13739-2; 0-300-13739-7

LC 2009-53163

"Beautifully reimagining a city that was a distant but integral part of American life, Flavell's book is essential reading for anyone interested in the colonial period." N Y Times Book Rev

Includes bibliographical references

Franklin, John Hope

★ **From** slavery to freedom; a history of African Americans. [by] John Hope Franklin, Evelyn Higginbotham. 9th ed.; McGraw-Hill 2010 xxv, 710p il map $100.63   **305.8**

1. Slavery -- United States 2. African Americans -- History

ISBN 978-0-07-296378-6; 0-07-296378-6

LC 2009-42935

First published 1947

A survey of African-Americans history from slavery to the present.

Includes bibliographical references

★ **Freedom** on my mind; the Columbia documentary history of the African American experience. Manning Marable, general editor; Nishani Frazier and John McMillian, assistant editors. Columbia University Press 2003 734p $80   **305.8**

1. African Americans -- History -- Sources

ISBN 0-231-10890-7

LC 2003-51605

This "anthology features the works of noteworthy figures of African American history and culture . . . and provides a tapestry of personal correspondence, excerpts from slave narratives and autobiographies, leaflets, speeches, oral histories and interviews, political manifestos, song lyrics, and important statements of black institutions and organizations. . . . A necessary text of readings for both introductory and advanced African American studies courses." Choice

Includes bibliographical references

Gates, Henry Louis

In search of our roots; how 19 extraordinary African Americans reclaimed their past. Crown Publishers 2008 438p il map $27.50   **305.8**

1. Genealogy 2. African Americans

ISBN 978-0-307-38240-5

LC 2008-11860

The author combines "historical research with DNA analysis to recreate the family trees of African-American celebrities like Oprah Winfrey and Quincy Jones, as well as intellectuals, authors, comedians, musicians and athletes." Publ Wkly

"Bright, inquisitive take on the multifarious murky stories and relationships that make up the history of a dispossessed people." Kirkus

Includes bibliographical references

Life upon these shores; looking at African American history, 1513-2008. Knopf 2011 487p il $50   **305.8**

1. African Americans -- History 2. United States -- Civilization

ISBN 978-0-307-59342-9

LC 2011014277

"With nearly 900 illustrations (formal portraits, news photos, historic lithographs, broadsides, flyers, posters, newspaper clippings, advertisements) complemented by a succinct but informing text, Harvard professor Gates (Black in Latin America) provides a visual sojourn through African-American history, a generally upbeat march from Juan Garrido, accompanying Cortés in 1519, to Barack Obama taking the presidential oath in 2008. Gathered in this chronologically arranged compendium, with its focus on the accomplishments and moments of achievement in the African-American community, is a wealth of materials about the historical, political, social, literary, and scientific events influencing American social and political culture." Publ Wkly

Includes bibliographical references

Gibbon, Piers

Tribe; endangered peoples around the world. [by] Piers Gibbon with Jane Houston. Firefly Books 2010 192p il $45 **305.8**
1. Ethnology 2. Acculturation
ISBN 978-1-55407-742-7; 1-55407-742-7
LC 2011-380573

Presents the cultures, beliefs, and societal patterns of over two hundred indigenous peoples and describes their degrees of integration with other societies and the integrity of their indigenous identities. Contains some images of nudity.

This is "a wonderful compendium of diversity and a useful platform for thought, providing an opportunity to pose questions to ourselves. . . . It reminds us that there is so much that we still don't know, so much more to the world than we see in our homes and high streets; that the world is wondrous and precious and has an innate value that must be both defended and empowered if it is to survive." Geographical

Includes bibliographical references

Goodman, Jordan

The **devil** and Mr. Casement; one man's battle for human rights in South America's heart of darkness. Farrar, Straus and Giroux 2010 322p il map $30 **305.8**
1. Spies 2. Diplomats 3. Atrocities 4. Human rights 5. Peru -- History 6. Revolutionaries 7. Native Americans -- South America
ISBN 978-0-374-13840-0; 0-374-13840-0
LC 2009-29528

"An incisive rendering of an important episode in the ongoing battle for the rights of individuals." Kirkus

Includes bibliographical references

Griffin, John Howard

★ **Black** like me; the definitive Griffin estate edition, corrected from original manuscripts. foreword by Studs Terkel; with historic photographs by Don Rutledge; and an afterword by Robert Bonazzi. 2nd Wings Press ed., with index; Wings Press 2006 243p il $29.95 **305.8**
1. Prejudices 2. African Americans -- Southern States
ISBN 978-0-930324-73-5

First published 1961 by Houghton Mifflin

The author, "who is white, a Catholic, and a Texan, conceived and carried out the unusual notion of blackening his skin with a newly developed pigment drug and traveling through the Deep South as a Negro. This book, part of which appeared in the Negro magazine Sepia, is a journal account of that experience." New Yorker

Includes bibliographical references

Gross, Ariela J.

What blood won't tell; a history of race on trial in America. [by] Ariela J. Gross. Harvard University Press 2008 368p pa. $21; $29.95 **305.8**
1. Minorities 2. Race discrimination 3. United States -- Race relations 4. Race discrimination -- Laws and regulations 5. Minorities -- Legal status, laws, etc. -- United States 6. Race discrimination -- Law and legislation -- United States
ISBN 9780674047983; 978-0-674-03130-2; 0-674-03130-X
LC 2008011271

This book examines "the legal fight of nonwhite citizens not to be counted as black under the . . . 'one drop' rule of racial categorization—a stigma that could lock them out of all sorts of social benefits, from business contracts to rights of inheritance and land ownership." Bookforum

Includes bibliographical references

Gross, Jan Tomasz

Fear : anti-semitism in Poland after Auschwitz; an essay in historical interpretation. [by] Jan T. Gross. Random House 2005 303p il $25.95 **305.8**
1. Antisemitism 2. Jews -- Poland 3. Holocaust, 1933-1945 4. Jews -- Persecutions
ISBN 0-375-50924-0; 978-0-375-50924-7
LC 2005-52913

The author describes "how surviving Polish Jews, having escaped the fate of 90 percent of their community—three million people—returned to their homeland to be vilified, terrorized and, in some 1,500 instances, murdered, sometimes in ways as bestial as anything the Nazis had devised." N Y Times Book Rev

"This is a masterful work that sheds necessary light on a tragic and often-ignored aspect of postwar history." Booklist

Includes bibliographical references

Hahn, Steven

A **nation** under our feet; Black political struggles in the rural South, from slavery to the great migration. Steven Hahn. Belknap Press of Harvard University Press 2003 610p il $35; pa $18.95 **305.8**
1. Southern States -- Race relations 2. African Americans -- Political activity
ISBN 0-674-01169-4; 0-674-01765-X pa
LC 2003-45326

The author "examines the development of African American political culture during its formative years in the last half of the 19th century, arguing that African Americans actively shaped their own political identity during this critical time period in an often overlooked comprehensive grassroots movement." Choice

This book "is one of the most important works in American social history to appear in recent years." Nation

Includes bibliographical references

Heap, Chad

Slumming; sexual and racial encounters in American nightlife, 1885-1940. [by] Chad Heap. University of Chicago Press 2009 420p il map $35 **305.8**
1. Sexual behavior 2. United States -- Race relations 3. Chicago (Ill.) -- Social life and customs 4. New York (N.Y.) -- Social life and customs
ISBN 0-226-32243-2; 978-0-226-32243-8
LC 2007-10881

"From its appearance as a 'fashionable dissipation' centered on the immigrant and working-class districts of 1880s New York through its spread to Chicago and into the 1930s nightspots frequented by lesbians and gay men, Slumming charts the development of this popular pastime, demonstrating how its moralizing origins were soon outstripped by the artistic, racial, and sexual adventuring that typified Jazz-Age America. Vividly recreating the allure of storied neighborhoods such as Greenwich Village and Bronzeville, with their bohemian tearooms, rent parties, and 'black and tan' cabarets, Heap plumbs the complicated mix of curiosity and desire that drew respectable white urbanites to venture into previously off-limits locales." Bookmarks

Includes bibliographical references

Hendrickson, Paul

Sons of Mississippi; a story of race and its legacy. Knopf 2003 343p il map $26; pa $15   **305.8**
1. Police brutality 2. Mississippi -- Race relations 3. African Americans -- Mississippi
ISBN 0-375-40461-9; 0-375-70425-6 pa
LC 2002-29857

"The number of telling quotes, interviews with friends and family, primary and secondary sources, allusions to art and history, and gut reactions Hendrickson offers are what really make the book. . . . He repeatedly comes up with electric interview material, and deftly places these men within the defining events of their times, when 'a 100-year-old way of life was cracking beneath them.'" Publ Wkly

Includes bibliographical references

Hill, Anita, 1956-

Reimagining equality; stories of gender, race, and finding home. Beacon Press 2011 xxiv, 195p $25.95   **305.8**
1. African American women 2. African Americans -- Housing 3. Houses -- Buying and selling 4. African Americans -- Social conditions
ISBN 978-0-8070-1437-0
LC 2011020232

The author "addresses the prime mortgage debacle, specifically how 'owning a home, and thus acquiring this piece of the American Dream has become increasingly difficult for people of color and single women,' and presents an indictment of subprime and predatory lending." Publ Wkly

Includes bibliographical references

Johnson, Walter

River of dark dreams; slavery and empire in the cotton kingdom. Walter Johnson. The Belknap Press of Harvard University Press 2013 560 p. (hardcover) $35   **305.8**
1. Cotton manufacture 2. Slavery -- United States 3. Mississippi River Valley -- History 4. Slavery -- Mississippi River Valley -- History -- 19th century 5. Mississippi River Valley -- Commerce -- History -- 19th century 6. Cotton growing -- Mississippi River Valley -- History -- 19th century 7. Mississippi River Valley -- Race relations -- History -- 19th century
ISBN 0674045556; 9780674045552
LC 2012030065

This book, by Walter Johnson, explores how "when Jefferson acquired the Louisiana Territory, he envisioned an 'empire for liberty' populated by self-sufficient white farmers . . . , [but] was transformed instead into a booming capitalist economy . . . dependent on the coerced labor of slaves. [The book] places the Cotton Kingdom at the center of

worldwide webs of exchange and exploitation that extended across oceans and drove an insatiable hunger for new lands." (Publisher's note)

Includes bibliographical references and index

Jones, Jacqueline

A **dreadful** deceit; the myth of race from the colonial era to Obama's America. Jacqueline Jones. Basic Books 2013 400 p. (hardback) $29.99 **305.8**
1. African Americans 2. United States -- Race relations -- History 3. Race -- Philosophy 4. African Americans -- Biography 5. Race awareness -- United States -- History 6. African Americans -- Race identity -- History
ISBN 0465036708; 9780465036707
LC 2013031130

"In 'A Dreadful Deceit,' . . . historian Jacqueline Jones traces the lives of [six] African Americans to illustrate the strange history of 'race' in America. In truth, Jones shows, race does not exist, and the very factors that we think of as determining it--a person's heritage or skin color--are mere pretexts for the brutalization of powerless people by the powerful." (Publisher's note)

Includes bibliographical references and index

Letters from Black America; edited by Pamela Newkirk. Farrar, Straus, and Giroux 2009 372p il $30   **305.8**
1. African Americans -- Social conditions 2. American letters -- African American authors
ISBN 978-0-374-10109-1; 0-374-10109-4
LC 2008-41265

"This anthology features the writings of individuals who range from highly celebrated to barely literate and presents stories that are of vital historical importance and touchingly personal. Newkirk divides the letters by topic—covering family, courtship and romance, politics and social justice, education and scholarship, war, art and culture, and the African diaspora—and offers concise introductions to each. . . . While this unique collection of letters represents a frank depiction of the black experience, the great achievement is that these writings often go far beyond race and class to simply tell the story of the human experience in America." Libr J

Includes bibliographical references

Lukas, J. Anthony

Common ground; a turbulent decade in the lives of three American families. Knopf 1985 659p il maps hardcover o.p. pa $18   **305.8**
1. School integration 2. Busing (School integration) 3. Boston (Mass.) -- Race relations
ISBN 0-394-74616-3 pa
LC 85-127

"By focusing on three families—one of them welfare black, one upper-middle-class white and one working-class Irish—a veteran journalist recreates the school-busing struggles of Boston in the 1970s, and delineates . . . the moral complexities of caste and class in America." Newsday

Malek, Alia

A **country** called Amreeka; Arab roots, American stories. Free Press 2009 305p il $25   **305.8**
1. Immigrants -- United States 2. Arab Americans --

Social conditions
ISBN 978-1-4165-8972-3

LC 2008-55091

"In this superb snapshot of the Americans of Arab-speaking descent, individuals with roots in Jordan, Yemen, the Palestinian territories and Lebanon share their stories and demonstrate the extent to which, even as they play football, work assembly lines and hold public office, they remain shut out of the national narrative. With a remarkable ability to capture her subjects' voices, . . . [the author] sketches illuminating responses to her question: 'What does American history look and feel like in the eyes and skin of Arab Americans?'" Publ Wkly

Includes bibliographical references

McWhorter, John H.

Losing the race; self-sabotage in Black America. [with a new afterword by the author] Perennial 2001 299p pa $13.95 **305.8**
1. African Americans -- Education 2. African Americans -- Social conditions
ISBN 978-0-06-093593-1; 0-06-093593-6

LC 2001-24092

First published 2000 by Free Press

McWhorter discusses what he sees as "a cult of anti-intellectualism 'that has infected black America. . . . He concluded [black students] were held back by three defeatist thought patterns': the Cult of Victimology, which leads blacks to blame their problems on racism; the Cult of Separatism, which makes blacks think that whatever whites do, they should do the opposite; and the Cult of Anti-Intellectualism, which holds that scholastic excellence is a white thing." Time

Includes bibliographical references

Minutaglio, Bill

In search of the blues; a journey to the soul of Black Texas. foreword by Linda Jones. University of Texas Press 2010 167p il (Southwestern writers collection series) $50; pa $24.95 **305.8**
1. Blues music 2. African Americans -- Texas 3. Texas -- Social life and customs
ISBN 978-0-292-72247-7; 0-292-72247-8; 978-0-292-72289-7 pa; 0-292-72289-3 pa

LC 2009-44161

This volume includes "profiles of football coach Ray Rhodes and rumors of a lynched ancestor in Mexia, and of Fahim Minkah, a former Black Panther once considered the most dangerous black militant in the Dallas area — who now devotes his life to ridding neighborhoods of drug dealers. . . . There are portraits of neighborhoods, streets and clubs and, of course, blues musicians such as T-Bone Walker, Lightnin' Hopkins and Buckwheat Zydeco, all painted with Minutaglio's closely-observed, deeply reported and beautifully written prose. . . . [This is] not only a celebration of the blues, black culture and black Texans but a celebration of extraordinary journalism and writing." San Antonio Express-News

Monterrey, Manuel

Americanos; Latino life in the United States. [by] Edward James Olmos, Lea Ybarra, Manuel Monterrey; preface by Edward James Olmos; introduction by Carlos Fuentes. Little, Brown 1999 176p il $39; pa $25 **305.8**
1. Latinos (U.S.) 2. Hispanic Americans
ISBN 0-316-64914-7; 0-316-64909-0 pa

LC 98-51930

This work includes essays, poetry, and commentary in English and Spanish by such authors as Carlos Fuentes and Maya Angelou and over 200 photographs of Latin Americans from many parts of the United States.

"This is a beautiful, vibrant . . . book; it may also be one of the more socially important books to appear in some time." Booklist

Morley, Jefferson

Snow -storm in August; Washington City, Francis Scott Key, and the forgotten race riot of 1835. Jefferson Morley. 1st ed. Nan A. Talese/Doubleday 2012 xii, 334 p.p ill., map (ebook) $85.00; (paperback) $16.00; (hardcover) $28.95 **305.8**
1. Riots -- United States 2. Washington (D.C.) -- History 3. United States -- Race relations -- History 4. Washington (D.C.) -- History -- 19th century 5. Trials (Attempted murder) -- Washington (D.C.) 6. Slavery -- Washington (D.C.) -- History -- 19th century 7. Race riots -- Washington (D.C.) -- History -- 19th century 8. Washington (D.C.) -- Race relations -- History -- 19th century 9. Free African Americans -- Washington (D.C.) -- History -- 19th century
ISBN 9780385533386; 9780307477484; 9780385533379; 0385533373

LC 2011042032

This book is an "account of the 1835 Washington, DC, race riot that spotlighted the increasingly tense and complex relations among whites, free blacks, and slaves in the nation's capital. White rioters, enraged by freedom-seeking slave Arthur Bowen's attempted murder of his owner, took out their animosity on free blacks such as successful restaurateur and ex-slave Beverly Snow." (Library Journal)

Includes bibliographical references (p. 307-319) and index.

Murray, Charles, 1943-

Coming apart; Charles Murray. Crown Forum 2012 407 p. **305.8**
1. Equality 2. Social conflict 3. Social classes -- United States 4. Social mobility -- United States 5. United States -- Social conditions -- 1980- 6. Whites -- United States -- Social conditions 7. United States -- Economic conditions -- 1945- 8. Whites -- United States -- Economic conditions 9. United States -- Social conditions -- 1960-1980
ISBN 0307453421; 9780307453426; 9780307453440

LC 2011501987

This book argues "that a new upper class and a new lower class have diverged so far in core behaviors and values that they barely recognize their underlying American kinship." It argues that "[t]he top and bottom of white America increasingly live in different cultures, . . . with the powerful upper class living in enclaves surrounded by their own kind, ignorant about life in mainstream America, and the lower class suffering from erosions of family and community life." (Publisher's note)

"Though it provides much to argue with, the book is a timely investigation into a worsening class divide no one can afford to ignore." (Publishers Weekly)

Includes bibliographical references and index

Nagel, Joane

American Indian ethnic renewal; Red power and the resurgence of identity and culture. Oxford Univ. Press 1996 298p il hardcover o.p. pa $21.95 **305.8**
    1. Native Americans
    ISBN 0-19-512063-9 pa

                    LC 94-23948

The author "argues that American Indian political activism, especially the Red Power movement of the 1970s, was directly responsible for both a cultural renaissance among Indian peoples and major changes in federal Indian policy." Libr J

Includes bibliographical references

Packard, Jerrold M.

American nightmare; the history of Jim Crow. St. Martin's Press 2002 291p $24.95; pa $14.95 **305.8**
    1. African Americans -- Segregation 2. Southern States -- Race relations
    ISBN 0-312-26122-5; 0-312-30241-X pa

                    LC 2001-41960

"American Nightmare examines and explains Jim Crow from its beginnings to its end: how it came into being, how it was lived, how it was justified, and how, at long last, it was overcome only a few short decades ago. Most importantly, this book reveals how a nation founded on principles of equality and freedom came to enact as law a pervasive system of inequality and virtual slavery." (Publisher's Note)

"This is a clear, concise, historical narrative of a draconian reality." Publ Wkly

Includes bibliographical references (p. {275}-280) and index

Painter, Nell Irvin

The **history** of White people. W.W. Norton 2010 496p il map $27.95 **305.8**
    1. Whites 2. United States -- Race relations
    ISBN 978-0-393-04934-3; 0-393-04934-5

                    LC 2009-34515

The author "examines the history of 'whiteness' as a racial category and rhetorical weapon: who is considered to be 'white,' who is not, what such distinctions mean, and how notions of whiteness have morphed over time in response to shifting demographics, aesthetic tastes, and political exigencies. . . . Painter's narrative succeeds as an engaging and sophisticated intellectual history, as well as an eloquent reminder of the fluidity (and perhaps futility) of racial categories." Booklist

Includes bibliographical references

Reed, Ishmael

Another day at the front; dispatches from the race war. Basic Bks. 2002 xliv, 189p $24; pa $14.95 **305.8**
    1. Racism 2. United States -- Race relations 3. African

Americans -- Civil rights
    ISBN 0-465-06891-X; 0-465-06892-8 pa

                    LC 2002-10563

The author "gathers a series of original and revamped essays from recent years on a variety of topics, from the Confederate flag to NPR, with the underlying theme that African Americans have been living in a police state for the past 300 years. These brief essays, written in Reed's lively hit-and-run style, are certainly provocative, particularly as he jabs at many well-known critics both black and white." Libr J

Roberts, Dorothy

Fatal invention; how science, politics, and big business re-create race in the twenty-first century. New Press 2011 388p $29.95 **305.8**
    1. Race 2. Physical anthropology 3. Genomics 4. Human population genetics
    ISBN 9781595584953; 1595584951

                    LC 2011012830

In this book, "legal scholar and social critic Dorothy Roberts argues that America is once again at the brink of a virulent outbreak of classifying population by race. By searching for differences at the molecular level, a new race-based science is obscuring racism in our society and legitimizing state brutality against communities of color at a time when America claims to be post-racial." (Publisher's note)

The author "examines the development and contemporary consequences of 'race as a political system,' bringing science, law, commerce, and race ideologies, virtual thickets of controversy, under one canopy. . . . Roberts is consistently lucid. Her book is alarming but not alarmist, controversial but evidential, impassioned but rational." Publ Wkly

Includes bibliographical references and index.

Robinson, Eugene

Disintegration; the splintering of Black America. Doubleday 2010 254p $24.95 **305.8**
    1. United States -- Race relations 2. African Americans -- Race identity 3. United States -- Social conditions 4. African Americans -- Social conditions 5. African Americans -- Economic conditions
    ISBN 978-0-385-52654-8; 0-385-52654-7

                    LC 2010-20405

"This book will have great appeal to African Americans and others concerned about issues of race and equality." Libr J

Includes bibliographical references

Sabar, Ariel

My father's paradise; a son's search for his Jewish past in Kurdish Iraq. Algonquin Books of Chapel Hill 2008 332p il map $25.95 **305.8**
    1. Sephardim 2. Linguists 3. Jews -- Iraq 4. College teachers
    ISBN 978-1-56512-490-5; 1-56512-490-1

                    LC 2008-24811

Sabar writes about his father's early life as a Sephardic Jew in Iraq and his father's authorship of a dictionary of Neo-Aramaic.

This "is an engaging account of a wonderful, enlightening journey, a voyage with the power to move readers deeply even as it stretches across differences of culture, family, and memory." Christ Sci Monit

Includes bibliographical references

Shapiro, Edward S.

A **time** for healing; American Jewry since World War II. Johns Hopkins Univ. Press 1992 313p il (Jewish people in America) hardcover o.p. pa $14.95 **305.8**

1. Jews -- United States -- History

ISBN 0-8018-4347-2; 0-8018-5124-6 pa

LC 91-38385

This volume is the fifth and last in The Jewish People in America, a series sponsored by the American Jewish Historical Society. "This history of American Jewry after 1945 has two broad themes. One is the rapid social and economic mobility of American Jews. . . . The other major theme is the adaptation of Jews to unprecedented conditions of affluence and freedom." Preface

Includes bibliographical references

Sharfstein, Daniel J.

The **invisible** line; three American families and the secret journey from black to white. Penguin Press 2011 396p il $27.95 **305.8**

1. Race awareness 2. Racially mixed people 3. Race awareness -- United States 4. United States -- Race relations 5. Racially mixed people -- United States 6. Race -- Social aspects -- United States 7. Miscegenation -- United States -- History

ISBN 978-1-59420-282-7; 1-59420-282-6

LC 2010-29647

"This popular history makes vivid use of primary documents to reconstruct the sagas of three families who crossed the color line from black to white. They negotiated this transition by means of legal challenges and such racial categories as 'Melungeons' and 'Black Dutch,' or simply by staying quiet when neighbors made assumptions based on cues of class and complexion. . . . This is an important reconsideration of the porousness of racial categories . . . and also a powerful evocation of the peril and insecurity that blacks faced both before and after the Civil War." New Yorker

Includes bibliographical references

Slate, Nico

Colored cosmopolitanism; the shared struggle for freedom in the United States and India. Nico Slate. Harvard University Press 2012 321 p. (alk. paper) $39.95 **305.8**

1. Race awareness 2. Race relations 3. Human rights advocacy 4. Racism -- India -- History 5. India -- Race relations -- History 6. Racism -- United States -- History 7. India -- Relations -- United States 8. United States -- Relations -- India 9. United States -- Race relations -- History 10. African Americans -- Civil rights -- History 11. Minorities -- Civil rights -- India -- History 12. African Americans -- Relations with East Indians

ISBN 0674059670; 9780674059672

LC 2011013395

In this book, professor "[Nico] Slate . . . details the links between human rights activists in the two countries in this . . . history. From the late 19th to the mid-20th century, Indi-

ans and African-Americans found common ground in their fights against colonialism on one side of the world and racism on the other, creating a 'colored cosmopolitanism' that brought together—people of color—in a shared pact to up-end oppression." (Publishers Weekly)

Includes bibliographical references and index.

Sokol, Jason

★ **There** goes my everything; white Southerners in the age of civil rights, 1945-1975. Knopf 2006 433p il $27.95 **305.8**

1. African Americans -- Civil rights 2. Southern States -- Race relations

ISBN 0-307-26356-8; 978-0-307-26356-8

LC 2005-44488

This book "explores the complexities of white attitudes in the South during the civil rights era." N Y Times Book Rev

"This chronicle of the destruction of the white Southern hierarchy belongs in all libraries, public and academic." Libr J

Includes bibliographical references

Sorin, Gerald

A **time** for building; the third migration, 1880-1920. Johns Hopkins Univ. Press 1992 306p il (Jewish people in America) hardcover o.p. pa $14.95 **305.8**

1. Jews -- United States -- History

ISBN 0-8018-4345-6; 0-8018-5122-X pa

LC 91-40700

This volume, the third in The Jewish People in America, a series sponsored by the American Jewish Historical Society, focuses on Eastern European Jewish immigration to the United States between 1880 and 1920.

Includes bibliographical references

Thorpe, Helen

Just like us; the true story of four Mexican girls coming of age in America. Scribner 2009 387p $27.99 **305.8**

1. Illegal aliens 2. Mexican Americans 3. Hispanic American women

ISBN 978-1-4165-3893-6

LC 2009-22722

The author "chronicles the coming-of-age of four Mexican American teenagers in Colorado. The young women struggle to reconcile an elusive American dream with the irony of their situations—only two of them have immigration papers, an invisible distinction that sets them at odds with one another and with the nation they consider home." Atl Mon

"Thorpe does a masterful job of exploring issues of class, race, and culture in the American amalgam through the lives of four young Mexican women." Booklist

Those who forget the past; the question of anti-Semitism. edited and with an introduction by Ron Rosenbaum; afterword by Cynthia Ozick. Ran-

dom House Trade Paperbacks 2004 lxix, 649p
pa $16.95　　　　　　　　　　　　　**305.8**
1. Antisemitism
ISBN 0-8129-7203-1

LC 2003-65542

This "anthology comprises nearly 50 short contemporary essays by sociologists, literary figures, critics, educators, philosophers, and others. . . . This volume not only provides historical background from which to investigate the global comeback of 'the oldest hatred' but looks at artifacts of its resurgence." Libr J

"This is an important and vital contribution to efforts to comprehend what is new and what is the same in this ancient virus of ignorance and hatred." Booklist

Includes bibliographical references

Walker, Clarence Earl

Mongrel nation; the America begotten by Thomas Jefferson and Sally Hemings. [by] Clarence E. Walker. University of Virginia Press 2008 128p $22.95　　　　　　　　　　　　**305.8**
1. Slaves 2. Architects 3. Presidents 4. Vicepresidents 5. Racially mixed people 6. Essayists 7. Mistresses 8. United States -- Race relations 9. African Americans -- Race identity
ISBN 978-0-8139-2777-0; 0-8139-2777-3; 978-0-8139-2778-7 pa; 0-8139-2778-1 pa

LC 2008-24042

The author "uses the contradictions between Jefferson's writings on race and his 38-year relationship with his slave Sally Hemings as a prism through which to view the complexities of American race relations. . . Walker maintains that unless the nation can fully recognize the Jefferson-Hemings relationship, it can never have a true sense of its identity." Booklist

Includes bibliographical references

Wilson, Jennifer

Running away to home; our family's journey to Croatia in search of who we are, where we came from, and what really matters. St. Martin's Press 2011 320p il $25.99; ebook $12.99　　**305.8**
1. Croatia -- Description and travel 2. Croatia -- Social life and customs
ISBN 978-0-312-59895-2; 978-1-4299-8908-4 ebook

LC 2011024841

"Travel writer Wilson, her architect husband, and their two small children spent a family sabbatical in Mrkopalj, Croatia, an unlikely destination for most folks but the birthplace of Wilson's great-grandparents. Wilson and family arrived in the village speaking little Croatian but soon became part of the community. She relates how they explored the area, tracked down distant relatives, and became immersed in the traditions of daily life. . . . This thoughtful, amusing tale reads like a novel and will have wide appeal." Libr J

Womack, Ytasha

Post Black; how a new generation is redefining African American identity. [by] Ytasha L. Womack; foreword by Derek T. Dingle. Lawrence Hill Books 2010 206p il pa $16.95　　　　　　**305.8**
1. African Americans -- Race identity 2. African

Americans -- Social conditions
ISBN 978-1-55652-805-7; 1-55652-805-1

LC 2009-29619

This is "an engaging and ambitious discussion of African American identity in the 21st century." Publ Wkly

Includes bibliographical references

Woodward, C. Vann

The **strange** career of Jim Crow; 3rd rev ed; Oxford Univ. Press 1974 233p hardcover o.p. pa $17.95　　　　　　　　　　　　**305.8**
1. African Americans -- Segregation
ISBN 0-19-514690-5 pa

First published 1955

An account of segregation in the South which analyzes events from 1877 to the Nixon administration.

Includes bibliographical references

Zeskind, Leonard

Blood and politics; the history of the white nationalist movement from the margins to the mainstream. Farrar, Straus and Giroux 2009 xxiv, 645p $37.50　　　　　　　　　　　　**305.8**
1. Racism 2. White supremacy movements 3. Nationalism -- United States 4. United States -- Race relations 5. United States -- Politics and government -- 1945-
ISBN 0-374-10903-6; 978-0-374-10903-5

LC 2008-46131

"Zeskind's rigorously researched and eloquent book is a definitive history of white nationalism and contains alarming warnings for a resurgence in racist politics." Publ Wkly

Includes bibliographical references

Thompson, Tracy

★ The **new** mind of the South; an unconventional portrait for the twenty-first century. Tracy Thompson. 1st Simon & Schuster hc. ed. Simon & Schuster 2013 263 p. (hardcover) $26　　　**305.800**
1. Group identity -- Southern States 2. Southern States -- Race relations 3. Southern States -- Civilization -- 21st century
ISBN 1439158037; 9781439158036; 9781439160138

LC 2012021581

This book, by Tracy Thompson, explores the culture of the American South. "Thompson spent years traveling through the region and discovered a South both amazingly similar and radically different from the land she knew as a child. . . . Drawing on mountains of data, interviews, and a whole new set of historic archives, Thompson upends stereotypes and fallacies to reveal the true heart of the South today--a region still misunderstood by outsiders and even by its own people." (Publisher's note)

Includes bibliographical references and index

305.868　Spanish Americans

The **Hispanic** databook; detailed profiles of states and 782 places with Hispanic population, including 23 ethnic backgrounds from Argentinean to

Venezuelan, with rankings and comparisons of states, counties and places. David Garoogian, senior editor. 3rd ed. Grey House Pub. 2013 xxiii, 1707 p.p col. ill., col. maps. (paperback) $165   **305.868**
1. Hispanic Americans -- Encyclopedias 2. United States -- Social conditions -- Statistics 3. Hispanic Americans -- Population -- Statistics
ISBN 1619250047; 9781619250048
                                        LC 2012376274
This book, edited by David Garoogian, "takes a detailed look at [Hispanic Americans] . . . by examining data on national, state, county, and place (city, town, etc.) levels.It contains profiles on 782 places with the highest concentrations of Hispanic/Latino population, comprising 23 ethnic backgrounds from Argentinean to Venezuelan, and includes 26 statistical topics, including Homeownership, Income, Language Spoke at Home, Jobs, Rent, and Poverty." (Publisher's note)

Morales, Ed
Living in Spanglish; the search for a new Latino identity in America. St. Martin's Press 2002 310p $25.95; pa $14.95   **305.868**
1. Latinos (U.S.) 2. Racially mixed people 3. Hispanic Americans 4. United States -- Ethnic relations
ISBN 0-312-26232-9; 0-312-31000-5 pa
                                        LC 2001-48867
"To the author, Spanglish isn't just . . . {an} increasingly common linguistic mélange. . . . It is the breakdown of the either/or of a black/white worldview through the inevitable mingling of race and culture. . . . The author meditates on his own coming to terms with Latino identity as well as positing the larger point that 'We have spent the last several centuries preparing for our role as the first wholly postmodern culture.'. . . His ideas are provocative and engaging." Booklist

305.892   Semites

City of promises; a history of the Jews of New York. general editor, Deborah Dash Moore. New York University Press 2012 3 v. (1108 p.) (boxed set : alk. paper) $99   **305.892**
1. Jews -- New York (N.Y.) -- History 2. New York (N.Y.) -- Ethnic relations 3. Jews -- New York (State) -- New York
ISBN 0814717314; 9780814717318; 9780814729328; 9780814745212; 9780814776322; 9780814776926
                                        LC 2012003246
This "three-volume history, overseen by [Deborah Dash] Moore provides . . . [an] overview of the role that Jews have played in the history and success of the Big Apple. . . . The series "traces the history of New York Jews back to the first Dutch Jews who settled in the New Amsterdam colony . . . show[s] how the influx of immigrant Jews from Europe changed the city . . . [and] examines a range of . . . issues, including . . . Jewish feminism." (Kirkus Reviews)
Includes bibliographical references and index

Goldhagen, Daniel Jonah
The Devil That Never Dies; The Rise and Threat of Global Antisemitism. Daniel Jonah Goldhagen. Little, Brown and Co. 2013 432 p. $30   **305.892**
1. Antisemitism 2. Globalization -- Social aspects 3. Antisemitism -- History -- 20th century 4. Antisemitism -- History -- 21st century
ISBN 031609787X; 9780316097871
                                        LC 2013941806
In this book, by Daniel Jonah Goldhagen, "reveals the unprecedented, global form of [antisemitism]; its strategic use by states; its powerful appeal to individuals and groups; and how technology has fueled the flames that had been smoldering prior to the millennium." (Publisher's note)
"Goldhagen . . . comes out swinging in this frontal assault on anti-Semitism and its practitioners . . . . A frightening photograph of a mutable demon so many fail to recognize and continue to embrace." Kirkus
Includes bibliographical references (pages 460-472) and index

Nirenberg, David
Anti -Judaism; the Western tradition. David Nirenberg. W. W. Norton & Company 2013 624 p. (hardcover) $35   **305.892**
1. Judaism 2. Philosophy 3. Jewish philosophy 4. Jewish civilization 5. Antisemitism -- Europe -- History 6. Europe, Western -- Ethnic relations 7. Civilization, Western -- Jewish influences
ISBN 0393058247; 9780393058246
                                        LC 2012031082
This book is a "history tracing how the engagement with 'Jewish questions' have shaped 3,000 years of Western thought. [David] Nirenberg . . . fashions a . . . study of how writers and thinkers from Jesus to Marx to Edward Said have recycled ideas about Jews and Jewishness in creating their own constructions of reality." (Kirkus)
Includes bibliographical references and index

Smith, Helmut Walser
The butcher's tale; murder and anti-semitism in a German town. Norton 2002 270p il maps $25.95; pa $14.95   **305.892**
1. Homicide 2. Antisemitism 3. Germany -- Ethnic relations
ISBN 0-393-05098-X; 0-393-32505-9 pa
                                        LC 2002-22883
The author "does a masterful job exploring the history of the blood libel . . . as well as of community and how people band together to bring about great good or in the case of Konitz genuine evil. . . . Although classed by the publisher as history/Judaica, this powerful volume will also appeal to true-crime readers and anyone interested in the dynamics that can turn a peaceful community into a place of hatred and violence." Publ Wkly
Includes bibliographical references

Wasserstein, Bernard
On the eve; the Jews of Europe before the Second World War. Bernard Wasserstein. Simon & Schuster 2012 xxi, 552 p.p   **305.892**
1. Antisemitism 2. Jews -- Europe 3. Jews -- History

4. Jews -- Social conditions 5. World War, 1939-1945 -- Causes 6. Jews -- Europe -- History -- 20th century 7. Jews -- Persecutions -- Europe -- History -- 20th century
ISBN 1416594272; 9781416594277; 9781416594284; 9781439101698

LC 2011020529

This book by Bernard Wasserstein "presents a[n] . . . interpretation of the collapse of European Jewish civilization even before the Nazi onslaught." Wasserstein "focuses not on the anti-Semites but on the Jews . . . refut[ing] the common misconception that they were unaware of the gathering forces of their enemies. . . . It explores their hopes, anxieties, and ambitions, their family ties, social relations, and intellectual creativity." (Publisher's note)

Includes bibliographical references and index.

305.896   Africans and people of African descent

Du Bois, W. E. B. (William Edward Burghardt), 1868-1963

The **Oxford** W. E. B. Du Bois reader; edited by Eric J. Sundquist. Oxford Univ. Press 1996 680p pa $34.95   **305.896**
1. African Americans 2. United States -- Race relations
ISBN 0-19-509178-7

LC 95-21307

This reader covers Du Bois's "writing career, from the 1890s through the early 1960s. The volume selects key essays and longer works that portray the range of Du Bois's thought on such subjects as African American culture, the politics and sociology of American race relations, art and music, black leadership, gender and women's rights, Pan-Africanism and anti-colonialism, and Communism in the U.S. and abroad." Publisher's note

Includes bibliographical references

Gates, Henry Louis

The **future** of the race; by Henry Louis Gates, Jr. and Cornel West. Knopf 1996 196p hardcover o.p. pa $12.95   **305.896**
1. Authors 2. Novelists 3. Historians 4. Editors 5. Essayists 6. Sociologists 7. Nonfiction writers 8. Civil rights activists 9. United States -- Race relations 10. African Americans -- Intellectual life 11. African Americans -- Social conditions
ISBN 0-679-44405-X; 0-679-76378-3 pa

LC 96-14450

"Gates and West explore the challenge of W.E.B. Du-Bois's famous essay 'The Talented Tenth' and consider the future of African American society in light of it. . . . The authors examine the responsibility of the successful and talented black middle and upper classes to uplift the impoverished. . . . The text includes DuBois's 'The Talented Tenth' and, reprinted for the first time, his 1948 critique of it." Libr J

Includes bibliographical references

Hébrard, Jean M.

Freedom papers; an Atlantic odyssey in the age of emancipation. Rebecca J. Scott and Jean M. Hébrard. Harvard University Press 2012 259 p.   **305.896**
1. Freedom 2. Slavery 3. Biography 4. Blacks -- Atlantic Ocean Region -- Social conditions 5. Creoles -- Atlantic Ocean Region -- Social conditions
ISBN 0674047745; 9780674047747

LC 2011038130

This book, by Rebecca J. Scott and Jean M. Hébrard, received the 2012 Albert J. Beveridge Award and the 2012 James A. Rawley Prize in Atlantic History. The book "follows the Tinchants as each generation tries to use the power and legitimacy of documents to help secure freedom and respect. The strategies they used to overcome the constraints of slavery, war, and colonialism suggest the contours of the lives of people of color across the Atlantic world during this turbulent epoch." (Publisher's note)

Includes bibliographical references and index

Kelly, Joseph

America's longest siege; Charleston, slavery, and the slow march toward Civil War. by Joseph Kelly. Overlook Duckworth 2013 384 p. ill., maps (hardcover) $28.95   **305.896**
1. Slavery -- United States 2. Charleston (S.C.) -- History -- Siege, 1863 3. Charleston (S.C.) -- History -- 1775-1865 4. Charleston (S.C.) -- Race relations -- History 5. Slaves -- South Carolina -- Charleston -- History 6. Slavery -- South Carolina -- Charleston -- History 7. African Americans -- South Carolina -- Charleston -- Social conditions
ISBN 159020719X; 9781590207192

LC 2013015841

In this book, Joseph Kelly "examines the great ideological dispute [around slavery] that underpinned the Civil War by focusing on [Charleston, South Carolina's] long-running internal conflict regarding its moral distaste for and economic addiction to slave labor (Charleston was a major port for incoming slaves)." Kelly "traces the development of the town's views on slavery while simultaneously relating attempts to break down or bulwark the institution." (Publishers Weekly)

Includes bibliographical references and index.

King, Gilbert

★ **Devil** in the grove; Thurgood Marshall, the Groveland Boys, and the dawn of a new America. Gilbert King. Harper 2012 x, 434 p.p ill.   **305.896**
1. Civil rights 2. Florida -- Race relations 3. United States -- History -- 1945-1953 4. Rape -- Florida -- Groveland 5. African Americans -- Civil rights 6. Groveland (Fla.) -- Race relations 7. National Association for the Advancement of Colored People 8. Discrimination in criminal justice administration -- Florida -- Groveland
ISBN 9780061792267; 9780061792281; 9780062097712

LC 2011033757

Pulitzer Prize: General Nonfiction (2013)

This book presents an "account of Thurgood Marshall's role as a prominent civil rights attorney in challenging racist 'justice' in the South. . . . Principally . . . the 1949 arrest and unjust prosecution of four young black men, designated 'the Groveland Boys.' In this case, Marshall and the NAACP pursued every legal remedy to save the lives of these young men falsely accused of rape by a white woman, whose preposterous story went unquestioned by authorities. At great personal risk, Marshall tenaciously challenged the hegemony of McCall, eventually bringing to an end the racist reign of terror in Lake County and drawing it and its underlying mentality to national attention." (Libr J)

Includes bibliographical references (p. [413]-416) and index.

Loury, Glenn C.
The **anatomy** of racial inequality. Harvard Univ. Press 2001 226p il (W.E.B. Du Bois lectures) $22.95   **305.896**
1. United States -- Race relations 2. African Americans -- Social conditions 3. African Americans -- Economic conditions
ISBN 0-674-00625-9

LC 2001-39192
"Loury argues that the image white Americans have of black Americans as less than full citizens influences policy far more than who African-Americans actually are. Although much of Loury's argument is theoretical . . . he grapples eloquently and vigorously with such concrete examples as affirmative action, arguments about racial IQ differences and racial profiling." Publ Wkly
Includes bibliographical references

Raboteau, Emily
Searching for Zion; The Quest for Home in the African Diaspora. by Emily Raboteau. Atlantic Monthly Press 2013 320 p. $25   **305.896**
1. Home 2. Blacks
ISBN 0802120032; 9780802120038
This book by Emily Raboteau focuses on "black communities that left home in search of a Promised Land. . . . On her ten-year journey back in time and around the globe, through the Bush years and into the age of Obama, Raboteau wanders to Jamaica, Ethiopia, Ghana, and the American South to explore the complex and contradictory perspectives of Black Zionists." (Publisher's note)

★ **Remembering** Jim Crow; African Americans tell about life in the segregated South. edited by William H. Chafe [et al.] New Press (NY) 2001 xxxv, 346p il $55; pa $16.95   **305.896**
1. African Americans -- Segregation 2. Southern States -- Race relations 3. African Americans -- Southern States
ISBN 1-56584-697-4; 1-56584-778-4 pa

LC 2001-31224
Companion volume to Remembering slavery
This work offers "views into the thoughts, activities, and anxieties of black Americans. . . . Included are two one-hour CDs of the radio documentary produced by American Radio Works, a transcript of the audio program, 50 rare segregation-era photographs, biographical information, and sugges-

tions for further reading. This [is a] superb primary source." Libr J
Includes bibliographical references

305.897   North American native peoples

Burns, Mike
★ The **only** one living to tell; the autobiography of a Yavapai Indian. Mike Burns ; edited by Gregory McNamee. University of Arizona Press 2012 179 p. (pbk. : alk. paper) $17.95   **305.897**
1. Yavapai Indians -- History 2. Yavapai Indians -- Biography
ISBN 0816501203; 9780816501205

LC 2011046513
This book is an autobiography of Mike Burns edited by Gregory McNamee. "Mike Burns--born Hoomothya--was around eight years old in 1872 when the US military murdered his family and as many as seventy-six other Yavapai men, women, and children in the Skeleton Cave Massacre in Arizona. One of only a few young survivors, he was adopted by an army captain and ended up serving as a scout in the US army and adventuring in the West." (Publisher's note)
Includes bibliographical references.

Fenn, Elizabeth A.
Encounters at the heart of the world; a history of the mandan people. Elizabeth A. Fenn. Hill and Wang, a division of Farrar, Straus and Giroux 2014 480 p. illustrations, maps (hardback) $35 **305.897**
1. Mandan Indians 2. Native Americans -- History
ISBN 0809042398; 9780809042395

LC 2013032994
This book, by Elizabeth A. Fenn, tells the "history of the tribe that once thrived on the upper Missouri River in present-day North Dakota. . . . Peaking at a population of 12,000 by 1500, and still a vital presence when Lewis and Clark visited in 1804, the Mandans were besieged by a 'daunting succession of challenges,' including Norway rats that decimated their corn stores, two waves of smallpox, whooping cough, and cholera, reducing their numbers to 300 by 1838." (Booklist)
"A nonpolemical, engaging study of a once-thriving Indian nation of the American heartland whose origins and demise tell us much about ourselves." Kirkus
Includes bibliographical references and index

Wohlforth, Charles
The **whale** and the supercomputer; on the northern front of climate change. 1st ed; North Point Press 2004 322p $25; pa $14   **305.897**
1. Inuit 2. Climate 3. Arctic regions
ISBN 0-86547-659-4; 0-86547-714-0 pa

LC 2003-19448
"While the book's main focus is on climate change in the Arctic, . . . [the author includes] discussions of the worldview of the Inupiat in contrast to that of Western scientists, the conflict between rural and urban culture, the philosophy of science, and the machinations surrounding funding for science. Wohlforth writes beautifully, managing to wax

philosophical while providing detailed notes for those skeptical of the points he makes." Sci Books Films

Includes bibliographical references

305.9   People by occupation and miscellaneous social statuses; people with disabilities and illnesses, gifted people

Martinez, Ruben

★ The **new** Americans; photographs by Joseph Rodríguez. New Press 2004 251p il $25   **305.9**
1. United States -- Immigration and emigration
ISBN 1-565-84792-X

LC 2003-70621

"Masterfully evoking such diverse settings as a Palestinian wedding in Chicago, a raucous ball game in Guatemala City and a torpid migrant trailer camp in California, Martinez's writing is clear-eyed and incisive—and sometimes heartbreaking and hilarious." Publ Wkly

Includes bibliographical references

Nugent, Benjamin

American nerd; the story of my people. Scribner 2008 224p $20   **305.9**
1. Gifted children 2. Creative ability 3. Popular culture -- United States
ISBN 978-0-7432-8801-9; 0-7432-8801-7

A study of the nerd in American popular culture and throughout history discussed in such contexts as the rise of online gaming, the science fiction club, ethnicity, Asperger's syndrome, autism, and high school and college debating.

"In a lighthearted, often laugh-out-loud manner, Nugent challenges us to reexamine our long-held belief of what it means to be a nerd and to reposition the nerd as, if not an American hero, at least an American antihero. Great fun and remarkably insightful between the laughs." Booklist

Pipher, Mary Bray

The **middle** of everywhere; the world's refugees come to our town. {by} Mary Pipher. Harcourt 2002 xxv, 390p $25; pa $14; $23.95   **305.9**
1. Refugees
ISBN 0-15-100600-8; 0-15-602737-2 pa; 9781439560235

LC 2001-5863

"In cities all over the country, refugees arrive daily. Lost Boys from Sudan, survivors from Kosovo, families fleeing Afghanistan and Vietnam: they come with nothing but the desire to experience the American dream. Their endurance in the face of tragedy and their ability to hold on to the virtues of family, love, and joy are a lesson for Americans. Their stories will make you laugh and weep--and give you a deeper understanding of the wider world in which we live. The Middle of Everywhere moves beyond the headlines into the homes of refugees from around the world. Working as a cultural broker, teacher, and therapist, Mary Pipher has once again opened our eyes--and our hearts--to those with whom we share the future." (Publisher's Note)

The author "writes in rich, empathetic language and with a keen, observant eye for detail and nuance." Publ Wkly

Includes bibliographical references

Shannon, Lisa

A **thousand** sisters; my journey into the worst place on earth to be a woman. [by] Lisa J. Shannon; foreword by Zainab Salbi. Seal Press 2010 335p il $24.95   **305.9**
1. Women -- Congo (Republic)
ISBN 978-1-58005-296-2

LC 2009-25391

"Shannon presents images of the uncensored horror stories that, to many Congolese, have become regrettably routine: Congo's vile colonial history and the Rwandan genocide spillover that has caused the murders of more than five million Congolese people; children forced to kill and rape in their own communities; daily child deaths from easily curable illnesses; grisly murders of men and children in front of their wives and mothers; families burned alive inside their homes; women who must choose between rape and watching their children starve. . . . Juxtaposing brutality with beauty, Shannon's direct prose is a stirring reminder that these horrors are real and ongoing. An alarming and inspiring message that will hopefully spur much-needed action." Kirkus

Includes bibliographical references

Stephenson, Michael

The **last** full measure; how soldiers die in battle. Michael Stephenson. Crown Publishers 2012 xvi, 464 p.p $28.00; $28.00   **305.9**
1. Ordnance 2. Soldiers 3. Weapons -- History 4. Military art and science -- History 5. Military history 6. Battle casualties -- History
ISBN 0307395847; 0307952770; 9780307395849; 9780307952776

LC 2011005874

In this book, "[Michael] Stephenson . . . provides . . . descriptions of the ways in which soldiers have died in battle throughout history. Arranged chronologically, the book begins with analyses of ancient weapons and armor, and the deaths and destruction they caused, and then proceeds through history to discuss modern warfare. The physical and psychological effects of weapons are constant themes." (Library Journal)

Includes bibliographical references (p. [441]-452) and index

306   Culture and institutions

Ault, James M.

Spirit and flesh; life in a fundamentalist Baptist church. Knopf 2004 435p $27.95   **306**
1. Christian fundamentalism
ISBN 0-375-40242-X

LC 2003-65650

"In an attempt to understand the growing influence of the Christian Right . . . [the author] spent three years inside the world of a Massachusetts fundamentalist church he encountered while studying a variety of new-right groups. He observed—and where possible participated in—the daily lives of the members of a church he calls Shawmut River. His book takes us into worship services, home Bible studies, youth events, men's prayer breakfasts and Saturday work groups, after-Sunday-service family dinners, and bitter conflicts leading to a church split." Publisher's note

This "is a mix of ethnography and spiritual autobiography that deserves a hearing from fundamentalism's cultured despisers." N Y Times Book Rev

Carter, Jimmy, 1924-

Our endangered values; America's moral crisis. Simon & Schuster 2005 212p $25 **306**
1. Social values 2. Church and state 3. Christianity and politics 4. United States -- Moral conditions 5. United States -- Politics and government -- 2001-
ISBN 0-7432-8457-7

LC 2005-54051

"This book is an eloquent personal testament that deserves a wide readership, regardless of political affiliation." Libr J

Cult pop culture; how the fringe became mainstream. Bob Batchelor, editor. Praeger 2012 3 v. 736 p. (set : alk. paper) $163.00 **306**
1. Sports 2. Music industry 3. Motion pictures 4. Popular culture 5. United States -- Social life and customs 6. Subculture -- United States 7. Popular culture -- United States 8. National characteristics, American
ISBN 0313357803; 0313357811; 031335782X; 0313357838; 0313357846; 0313357854; 0313358044; 0313358052; 9780313357800; 9780313357817; 9780313357824; 9780313357831; 9780313357848; 9780313357855; 9780313358043; 9780313358050

LC 2011027591

This book "offers 60 essays on people and subjects of pop-culture fascination. This is a study not only of individual pop phenomena and obsession, but also of American culture. A pop-culture time line covering 1900 to 2011 precedes the articles in Volume 1, which cover film and TV, while the other volumes address music and literature, industries, events, and sports." Topics covered include "Elvis, Star Wars, comic books" and "hair bands, book clubs," and "antiques." (Library Journal)
Includes bibliographical references and index.

De Grazia, Victoria

Irresistible empire; America's advance through twentieth-century Europe. Belknap Press of Harvard University Press 2005 586p il $29.95 **306**
1. Consumption (Economics) 2. Europe -- Foreign relations -- United States 3. United States -- Foreign relations -- Europe
ISBN 0-674-01672-6

LC 2004-59943

The author "contends that U.S. companies—and consumerism—have been making inroads in Europe for the past hundred years. She argues that an early, and major, U.S. innovation treated foreign territories as extensions of domestic markets. . . . De Grazia writes clearly, giving an uncommon perspective on the ways and means by which the U.S. and Europe drew close after WWII." Publ Wkly
Includes bibliographical references

Flanders, Judith

Inside the Victorian home; a portrait of domestic life in Victorian England. W.W. Norton 2004 xxviii, 499p il $34.95 **306**
1. Great Britain -- History -- 19th century 2. Great Britain -- Social life and customs
ISBN 0-393-05209-5

LC 2003-27693

First published 2003 in the United Kingdom with title: The Victorian house

"Room by room, Flanders walks us through the typical home of upper-middle-class Britain, explaining its use, its décor, the habits of occupants, and more. The result is a genteel yet absorbing and thoroughly researched book. . . . Fearsomely entertaining and yet a wonderful addition to academic literature, this book is sure to become a classic." Libr J
Includes bibliographical references

Gioia, Ted

The **birth** (and death) of the cool. Speck Press 2009 256p $25 **306**
1. Lifestyles 2. Jazz musicians 3. Popular culture -- United States
ISBN 978-1-933108-31-5

LC 2009-18827

"Describing 'cool' as a set of 'beliefs, values, and behavior patterns' rooted in the personal and musical styles of Bix Beiderbecke, Lester Young and Miles Davis (with a healthy dose of Bugs Bunny), Gioia argues that while their ironic detachment once held sway, earnestness has made its way back on top. His narrative history of cool hits intriguing touchstones, such as Lee Strasberg and Frank Sinatra, while a time line appendix provides even more cultural referents—for the new sincerity as well, culminating with the arrival of Susan Boyle and Twitter." Publ Wkly
Includes bibliographical references

Lasch, Christopher

The **revolt** of the elites; and the betrayal of democracy. Norton 1995 276p $22; pa $14.95 **306**
1. Democracy 2. Elite (Social sciences) 3. United States -- Social conditions
ISBN 0-393-03699-5; 0-393-31371-9 pa

LC 94-37270

Lasch "argues that democracy today is threatened not by the masses, as José Ortega y Gasset (The Revolt of the Masses) had said, but by the elites. These elites—mobile and increasingly global in outlook—refuse to accept limits or ties to nation and place. Lasch contends that, as they isolate themselves in their networks and enclaves, they abandon the middle class, divide the nation, and betray the idea of a democracy for all America's citizens." Publisher's note
Includes bibliographical references

Marzollo, Jean

Fathers & babies; how babies grow and what they need from you from birth to 18 months. illus-

trated by Irene Trivas. HarperPerennial 1993 235p
il pa $13.95   **306**
> 1. Father-child relationship 2. Infants -- Care
> ISBN 0-06-096908-3
>
>   LC 92-53386

Marzollo covers "infant development from the physical
and social to the intellectual, psychological and creative. . .
. Her book provides step-by-step instructions on fixing bottles, bathing and feeding, changing a diaper, toilet training,
helping a child develop langauge skills, and disciplining the
older baby." Libr J

Mead, Margaret

    ★ **Coming** of age in Samoa; a psychological
study of primitive youth for Western civilisation.
foreword by Franz Boas. Morrow 1928 297p il
hardcover o.p. pa $14   **306**
> 1. Adolescence 2. Sex differences (Psychology) 3.
> Samoan Islands -- Social life and customs
> ISBN 0-688-05033-6 pa

An anthropological study of adolescent Samoan girls

Shadid, Anthony

    ★ **House** of stone; a memoir of home, family,
and a lost Middle East. Anthony Shadid. Houghton
Mifflin Harcourt 2012 xviii, 311 p.p (hardback)
$26   **306**
> 1. Family life 2. Arab Americans 3. Houses
> -- Remodeling 4. Families -- Lebanon 5. Home --
> Lebanon -- History 6. Middle East -- Social conditions
> 7. Lebanon -- Emigration and immigration -- Social
> aspects
> ISBN 0547134665; 9780547134666
>
>   LC 2011036906

National Book Awards Finalist (2012)

    This memoir offers the following: "an Arab-American
story of immigrant roots; an evocation of Lebanon and its
anguished history; a lament for a vanishing Middle East; an
exploration of the meaning of home. . . . The story of [the]
. . . effort [of rebuilding a house in Marjayoun, Lebanon,]
forms the frame of the book, with each stage of building in-
tercut by tales of [Anthony] Shadid's globe-straddling family across four generations." (New York Review of Books)

Talbot, David

    Season of the witch; enchantment, terror, and
deliverance in the City of Love. David Talbot. Free
Press 2012 xvii, 452 p.p   **306**
> 1. Counter culture 2. Social problems 3. San Francisco
> (Calif.) -- History 4. Political culture -- San Francisco
> (Calif.) 5. San Francisco (Calif.) -- Biography 6. San
> Francisco (Calif.) -- History -- 20th century 7. San
> Francisco (Calif.) -- Social conditions -- 20th century 8.
> San Francisco (Calif.) -- Social life and customs -- 20th
> century 9. Social change -- California -- San Francisco
> -- History -- 20th century 10. Counterculture --
> California -- San Francisco -- History -- 20th century 11.
> Social problems -- California -- San Francisco -- History
> -- 20th century 12. Culture conflict -- California -- San
> Francisco -- History -- 20th century 13. Political culture
> -- California -- San Francisco -- History -- 20th century
> 14. City and town life -- California -- San Francisco --

History -- 20th century
> ISBN 1439108218; 9781439108215
>
>   LC 2011032082

In this book, author David Talbot "recounts the . . . story
of San Francisco in the turbulent years between 1967 and
1982. . . . The cool gray city of love was the epicenter of the
1960s cultural revolution. But by the early 1970s, San Francisco's ecstatic experiment came crashing down from its
starry heights. The city was rocked by savage murder sprees,
mysterious terror campaigns, political assassinations, street
riots, and finally a terrifying sexual epidemic. . . . David Talbot takes us deep into the riveting story of his city's ascent,
decline, and heroic recovery. He draws intimate portraits of
San Francisco's legendary demons and saviors. . . . He reveals how the city emerged from the trials of this period with
a new brand of 'San Francisco values.'" (Publisher's note)

    Includes bibliographical references, discography, film-
ographies, and index.

Underhill, Paco

    The **call** of the mall; a walking tour through the
crossroads of our shopping culture. Simon & Schuster 2004 227p hardcover o.p. pa $14   **306**
> 1. Consumers 2. Consumption (Economics) 3.
> Shopping centers and malls
> ISBN 0-7432-3591-6; 0-7432-3592-4 pa
>
>   LC 2003-64960

The author takes readers on a "tour of a typical Saturday
at a large, regional mall. He examines the routes there, the
shopping center itself, the stores, food, entertainment, ambience. and the customers. He shows why the mall is the way
it is and how it could be improved. He provides insight into
how the stores are arranged, how they display merchandise.
and the different ways that men and women respond to this
environment." SLJ

Wann, David

    The **new** normal; an agenda for responsible liv-
ing. St. Martin's Griffin 2011 274p il pa $14.99 **306**
> 1. Lifestyles 2. Social values 3. Conduct of life 4.
> Quality of life
> ISBN 978-0-312-57543-4
>
>   LC 2010-37913

"Wann pulls from the disciplines of biology, anthropology, history, and psychology to make his case that the current
paradigm of bigger and more is not working. He proposes
the 'Era of Emerging Restoration,' in which healthy families, communities, and ecosystems are the best measures of
wealth. . . . This is one of the best approaches to promoting a
sustainable world." Libr J

    Includes bibliographical references

306.01   Culture -- philosophy

Pickett, Kate

    The **spirit** level; why greater equality makes so-
cieties stronger. Richard Wilkinson and Kate Pickett.
Bloomsbury Press 2010 xv, 330 p.p il (hardcover :
alk. paper) $28   **306.01**
> 1. Equality 2. Social policy 3. Social classes 4.

Quality of life 5. Social mobility
ISBN 1608193411; 9781608193417; 9781608190362; 1608190366

LC 2009030428

First published in Great Britain by Allen Lane, 2009

It was the authors' intent to "rank the quality of life in twenty-three countries, mainly European,, but with Singapore, Israel, and the United States also on the list. To evaluate the well-being of each society, Richard Wilkinson and Kate Pickett use indices ranging from obesity and incarceration rates to teenage births and the feelings people have about their fellow countrymen. They then relate these variables to how income is distributed in each society.... Linking social indicators to economic disparities, the authors conclude that 'reducing inequality is the best way of improving the quality of the social environment.'" (New York Review of Books)

"Large inequalities of income in a society have often been regarded as divisive and corrosive, and it is common knowledge that in rich societies the poor have shorter lives and suffer more from almost every social problem. This . . . book, based on thirty years' research, argues that more unequal societies are bad for almost everyone within them—the well-off as well as the poor." (Publisher's note) Index.

The authors "make an eloquent case that the income gap between a nation's richest and poorest is the most powerful indicator of a functioning and healthy society. . . . Felicitous prose and fascinating findings make this essential reading." Publ Wkly

Includes bibliographical references (p. 27-1297) and index.

306.2   Cultural institutions

Freeman, Joanne B.

Affairs of honor; national politics in the new republic. Yale Univ. Press 2001 xxiv, 376p $29.95; pa $16.95   **306.2**
1. United States -- Politics and government -- 1783-1865
ISBN 0-300-08877-9; 0-300-09755-7 pa

LC 2001-915

"Freeman's prose is lively, and she balances entertaining narrative with sharp analysis." Publ Wkly

Includes bibliographical references (p. 347-364) and index

Goldwag, Arthur

The **new** hate; a history of fear and loathing on the populist right. Arthur Goldwag. Pantheon Books 2012 368 p. $27.95   **306.2**
1. Conspiracies 2. Radicalism -- United States 3. Conservatism -- United States -- History 4. United States -- Politics and government 5. United States -- Ethnic relations -- History 6. Politics and culture -- United States 7. Right-wing extremists -- United States 8. Hate groups -- Political aspects -- United States 9. Conspiracy theories -- Political aspects -- United States
ISBN 0307379698; 9780307379696

LC 2011028589

The author "[Arthur] Goldwag ... delivers an ... history of organized hate groups and their role in U.S. politics. Less

about prejudice than America's 'relentless quest for scapegoats,' he traces the American conspiratorial tradition from colonial times--where the Puritans feared Jesuit conspiracies as much as Indian ambushes--to the present, covering the movements and vitriolic commentary against the Masons, Catholics, Jews, Communists, and Muslims. . . . Goldwag combines his research with contemporary analysis to explain what conspiracy theories all have in common and to show how the new hate is the same as the old, though it's now 'hiding in plain sight.'" (Publishers Wkly)

Includes bibliographical references and index

Maddow, Rachel, 1973-

Drift; the unmooring of American military power. Rachel Maddow. Crown 2012 275 p.   **306.2**
1. Militarism -- United States 2. United States -- Military policy 2. United States -- Foreign relations -- 1989- 3. United States -- Politics and government -- 1989- 4. United States -- Armed Forces -- Appropriations and expenditures
ISBN 9780307460981; 9780307461001

LC 2012000998

The author "examines how the country has lost control of its national-security policy. The author holds Dick Cheney . . . responsible, . . . associating . . . [him] with the presidential prerogative of war-making powers. . . . American forces are now accompanied by . . . private contractors who perform functions that used to be reserved to the military, without either accountability or military control. . . . She grounds her argument in the Founding Fathers' debates about going to war." (Kirkus Reviews)

Includes bibliographical references and index

306.3   Economic institutions

Annis, Barbara

Work with me; the 8 blind spots between men and women in business. Barbara Annis and John Gray. Palgrave Macmillan 2013 272 p. (hardcover) $27   **306.3**
1. Gender role 2. Work environment 3. Business communication 4. Men -- Attitudes 5. Women -- Attitudes 6. Interpersonal relations 7. Communication in organizations 8. Sex discrimination in employment 9. Sex role in the work environment
ISBN 023034190X; 9780230341906

LC 2012044297

This book, by Barbara Annis and John Gray, seeks "to resolve the most stressful and confusing challenges facing men and women at work. Annis and Gray reveal . . . the Eight Gender Blind Spots, the false assumptions and opinions men and women have of each other, and in many ways, believe of themselves. Through research, science, and stories, Annis and Gray expose the blind spots that cause our misunderstandings, miscommunications, mistrust, resentment, and frustrations at work." (Publisher's note)

DeWolf, Thomas Norman

Gather at the table; the healing journey of a daughter of slavery and a son of the slave trade. Thomas Norman DeWolf and Sharon Leslie Morgan ;

foreword by Joy Angela DeGruy. Beacon Press 2012 xvii, 212 p.p (hbk. : alk. paper) $25.95   **306.3**
1. Slavery -- United States 2. United States -- Race relations 3. Slavery -- United States -- History
ISBN 0807014419; 9780807014417

LC 2012009318

In this book by Thomas Norman DeWolf and Sharon Morgan "two people--a black woman and a white man--confront the legacy of slavery and racism head-on. . . . [DeWolf and Morgan] visit[ed] ancestral towns, courthouses, cemeteries, plantations, antebellum mansions, and historic sites. They spent time with one another's families and friends and engaged in deep conversations about how the lingering trauma of slavery shaped their lives." (Publisher's note)

Includes bibliographical references (p. 210-212)

Enslaved women in America; an encyclopedia. Daina Ramey Berry, editor in chief, with Deleso A. Alford, senior editor. Greenwood 2012 xxix, 381 p.p (hard copy : alk. paper) $89.00   **306.3**
1. Slavery -- United States -- History -- Encyclopedias 2. Women slaves -- United States -- History -- Encyclopedias
ISBN 0313349088; 0313349096; 9780313349089; 9780313349096

LC 2011053291

This book "updates readers on research about enslaved women. [Daina Ramey] Berry's introduction serves as a short explanation of this area of research, which has lagged behind investigations of the history of male bondmen. Alphabetical and topical lists of entries open the volume. Each of the more than 100 entries, most of which are one to five pages in length, includes See also references and a suggested reading list. All aspects of the daily life of bondwomen are covered." (Library Journal)

Includes bibliographical references and index.

Fukuyama, Francis
Trust; the social virtues and the creation of prosperity. Free Press 1995 458p hardcover o.p. pa $16   **306.3**
1. Economics 2. International economic relations
ISBN 0-684-82525-2 pa

LC 95-19320

The author "compares how selected modern economies organize themselves, and he argues that these same societies depend on 'civil society' and the creation and maintenance of 'social capital' for their vitality and economic success. By social capital he means the set of intermediate institutions, such as businesses, unions, and voluntary organizations (churches, charities, clubs) that facilitate trust beyond the more traditional family oriented structures to socialize people into their culture and transmit both knowledge and values. . . . Fukuyama proposes that natural cultural laws are important determinants of a nation's wealth. This stimulating, well-documented volume will be widely read and discussed." Choice

Includes bibliographical references

Nathans, Sydney
To free a family; Sydney Nathans. Harvard University Press 2012 330 p. [20] p of plates, ill, maps   **306.3**
1. Family 2. Fugitive slaves 3. United States -- History -- 1783-1865 4. Cambridge (Mass.) -- Biography 5. Orange County (N.C.) -- Biography 6. Fugitive slaves -- Northeastern States -- Biography 7. Women slaves -- North Carolina -- Orange County -- Biography 8. African American women -- Massachusetts -- Cambridge -- Biography 9. Family reunions -- Massachusetts -- Cambridge -- History -- 19th century
ISBN 9780674062122

LC 2011023122

This book "tells the . . . story of Mary Walker, who in August 1848 fled her owner for refuge in the North and spent the next seventeen years trying to recover her family. . . . This story is anchored in two . . . collections of letters and diaries, that of her former North Carolina slaveholders and that of the northern family--Susan and Peter Lesley--who protected and employed her." (Publisher's note)

Includes bibliographical references and index

Postma, Johannes
The **Atlantic** slave trade. Greenwood Press 2003 xxii, 177p map (Greenwood guides to historic events, 1500-1900) $45   **306.3**
1. Slave trade
ISBN 0-313-31862-X

LC 2002-35338

The author "covers the entire Atlantic slave trade era, from the 1400s to the final abolition of chattel slavery in the New World in 1888. The focus is on Africa and the entire New World. While he describes the many horrors of the Middle Passage, he also examines how the slave trade contributed to the development of the modern international economy. The last chapters discuss the efforts to abolish the slave trade and its legacy." SLJ

Includes bibliographical references

Williams, Heather Andrea
Help me to find my people; the African American search for family lost in slavery. by Heather Andrea Williams. University of North Carolina Press 2012 251 p. ill. (cloth : alk. paper) $30   **306.3**
1. Archives 2. Family reunions 3. Slave narratives 4. African American families -- History 5. Slavery -- Social aspects -- United States -- History 6. Slaves -- Family relationships -- United States -- History
ISBN 0807835544; 9780807835548

LC 2011050216

Author "Heather Andrea Williams uses slave narratives, letters, interviews, public records, and diaries to guide readers back to devastating moments of family separation during slavery when people were sold away from parents, siblings, spouses, and children. . . . [She tells the] stories of separation and the long, usually unsuccessful journeys toward reunification. . . . Williams follows those who were separated, chronicles their searches, and documents the rare experience of reunion." (Publisher's note)

Includes bibliographical references and index

Yano, Christine R.

Pink globalization; Hello Kitty's trek across the Pacific. by Christine R. Yano. Duke University Press 2013 336 p. (cloth : alk. paper) $89.95 **306.3**

1. Globalization 2. Japan -- Economic conditions 3. Japan -- Social life and customs 4. Exports -- Japan 5. Japan -- Commerce 6. Character merchandising 7. Hello Kitty (Fictitious character)

ISBN 0822353512; 9780822353515; 9780822353638

LC 2013005285

Author Christine R. Yano "examines the creation and rise of Hello Kitty as a part of Japanese Cute-Cool culture. Yano argues that the international popularity of Hello Kitty is one aspect of what she calls pink globalization—the spread of goods and images labeled cute (kawaii) from Japan to other parts of the industrial world. The concept of pink globalization connects the expansion of Japanese companies to overseas markets, the enhanced distribution of Japanese products, and the rise of Japan's national cool." (Publisher's note)

Includes bibliographical references and index

306.4 Specific aspects of culture

Amidon, Stephen

Something like the gods; a cultural history of the athlete from Achilles to Lebron. Stephen Amidon. St. Martin's Press 2012 240 p. (hardback) $24.99 **306.4**

1. Athletes 2. Gladiators 3. Olympic athletes 4. Knights and knighthood 5. Athletes -- History 6. Sports -- Social aspects -- History

ISBN 1609611233; 9781609611231

LC 2012002365

In this book, Stephen Amidon examines the history of athletes and their perceived prowess. "From the shamanistic athletic rituals of Paleolithic hunters to the exploits of today's millionaire sports superstars, athletes have fascinated and transfixed us for centuries. . . . Amidon explores this universalist nature of the athlete, including the godlike efforts of the Greek warriors of the ancient Olympics; the tragic heroics of the Roman gladiator; and the romantic image of the jousting knight errant to the civilized amateur ideal of the Victorian era." (Kirkus Reviews)

Burr, Ty

Gods like us; on movie stardom and modern fame. Ty Burr. Pantheon 2012 448 p. (hardback) $28.95 **306.4**

1. Motion pictures -- History and criticism 2. Fame -- Social aspects -- United States 3. Popular culture -- United States -- History

ISBN 0307377660; 9780307377661

LC 2012000618

This book is a "history of stardom from the early days of silent film through the contemporary world of YouTube. [Ty] Burr . . . traces the rise of Hollywood legends, television stars, and musicians ranging from Mary Pickford, Lucille Ball, and Marlon Brando to Tom Cruise and Michael Jackson. He analyzes their roles both onscreen and off, their

symbolic significance, and how they have inspired both the adoration and the envy of their audiences." (Library Journal)

Includes bibliographical references and index.

Chidester, Brian

Pop surf culture; music, design, film, and fashion from the Bohemian surf boom. [by] Brian Chidester and Domenic Priore; forewords by Kathy Zukerman (aka Gidget) and Billy Al Bengston (aka Moondoggie) Santa Monica Press 2008 271p il $39.95 **306.4**

1. Surfing 2. Popular culture -- United States

ISBN 978-1-59580-035-0; 1-59580-035-2

LC 2008-01803

"Throughout, the authors have the good sense to realize that the power of the surfing story is as much in the showing—the rich visual panorama—as in the telling. No walls of narrative here; every page is crowded with images of the corresponding period. . . . More than a catalog of beach-blanket movies or a survey of surf music, it connects the historical dots between the surf culture we experienced domestically, the economic culture that made it marketable, and the foreign cultures that made it possible in the first place." PopMatters

Includes bibliographical references

Ekirch, A. Roger

★ At day's close; night in times past. Norton 2005 447p il $25.95 **306.4**

1. Night

ISBN 0-393-05089-0

LC 2005-2784

"This history finds Ekirch reminding us of how preindustrial Westerners lived during the nocturnal hours, when most were plunged into almost total darkness. . . . A rich weave of citation and archival evidence, Ekirch's narrative is rooted in the material realities of the past, evoking a bygone world of extreme physicality and preindustrial survival stratagems." Publ Wkly

Includes bibliographical references

Elliott, Carl

Better than well; American medicine meets the American dream. foreword by Peter D. Kramer. Norton 2003 xxi, 357p $26.95; pa $14.95 **306.4**

1. Self-perception 2. Social medicine 3. American national characteristics

ISBN 0-393-05201-X; 0-393-32565-2 pa

LC 2002-15947

This is an "engaging and provocative book. . . . As Elliott considers Americans' yearning for self-improvement and fulfillment, he takes readers on a refreshingly quirky journey, its twists and turns dotted with cultural and literary references." Christ Sci Monit

Includes bibliographical references

Fadiman, Anne

★ The spirit catches you and you fall down; a Hmong child, her American doctors, and the collision of two cultures. Anne Fadiman. Farrar, Straus & Giroux 1997 xi, 339p $25; (pbk.) $15 **306.4**

1. Epilepsy 2. Medical care 3. Culture conflict

4. Hmong (Asian people) 5. Epilepsy in children 6. Hmong Americans -- Medicine 7. Intercultural communication 8. Hmong American children -- Medical care -- California 9. Transcultural medical care -- California -- Case studies
ISBN 0374267812; 9780374533403

LC 97005175

Los Angeles Times Book Prizes: Current Interest (1997), National Book Critics Circle Award: General Nonfiction (1997)

This book presents an "anthropological exploration of the Hmong population in Merced County, California. Following the case of Lia (a Hmong child with a progressive and unpredictable form of epilepsy), Fadiman maps out the controversies raised by the collision between Western medicine and holistic healing traditions of Hmong immigrants. Unable to enter the Laotian forest to find herbs for Lia that will 'fix her spirit,' her family becomes resigned to the Merced County emergency system, which has little understanding of Hmong animist traditions. [Anne] Fadiman reveals the rigidity and weaknesses of these two ethnographically separated cultures." (Library Journal)

Includes bibliographical references (p. [311]-324) and index.

Gross, Michael

✓ **Starstruck** : when a fan gets close to fame; [by] Michael Joseph Gross. Bloomsbury 2005 239p $23.95; pa $14.95   **306.4**
1. Fans 2. Celebrities 3. Popular culture
ISBN 1-58234-316-0; 1-59691-094-1 pa

LC 2004-30339

The author "interviews fans, collectors, celebrities and publicists in an effort to paint a broad portrait of changing celebrity culture. . . . Gross's writing is honest and humane, and his book is an entertaining look at modern celebrity culture." Publ Wkly

Leonard, Annie

✓ The **story** of stuff; how our obsession with stuff is trashing the planet, our communities, and our health--and a vision for change. [by] Annie Leonard with Ariane Conrad. Free Press 2010 xxxiv, 317p il $26   **306.4**
1. Material culture 2. Consumption (Economics)
ISBN 978-1-4391-2566-3

LC 2009-42207

"Leonard explains that our consumer goods undergo extraction, production, distribution, consumption, and disposal processes that are trashing the planet, diminishing our resources, exploiting workers, and contributing to high levels of disease and death. She advocates an international cooperative effort to develop domestic and international policies and laws that will reverse our planet's ecological decline and leave a sustainable world for future generations." LJ

"Leonard explains that our consumer goods undergo extraction, production, distribution, consumption, and disposal processes that are trashing the planet, diminishing our resources, exploiting workers, and contributing to high levels of disease and death. She advocates an international cooperative effort to develop domestic and international policies and laws that will reverse our planet's ecological decline and leave a sustainable world for future generations. . . . An important work for consumers of all ages." Libr J

Levine, Mark

✓ **Heavy** metal Islam; rock, resistance, and the struggle for the soul of Islam. Three Rivers Press 2008 296p il pa $13.95   **306.4**
1. Heavy metal (Music) 2. Music -- Islamic countries
ISBN 978-0-307-35339-9; 0-307-35339-7

LC 2008-02801

This is "a deeply felt, informed volume that's both hopeful and emotionally honest. . . . Anyone—regardless of musical preference—who wants an eye-level glimpse into the Middle East should pick up Heavy Metal Islam. Headbanging optional." Paste

Includes bibliographical references

McGonigal, Jane

✓ **Reality** is broken; why games make us better and how they can change the world. Penguin Press 2011 388p il   **306.4**
1. Computer games -- Social aspects
ISBN 1594202850; 9781594202858

LC 2010029619

McGonigal argues "that videogames are increasingly fulfilling genuine human needs. . . . [She also argues that] we can use the lessons of game design to fix what is wrong with the real world." (Publisher's note) Index.

"If the world of gaming seems alien to you, this book will crack it wide open. For experienced gamers, it will likely inspire you to play or even invent better, more meaningful games. Despite her expertise, McGonigal's book is never overly technical, and as with a good computer game, anyone, regardless of gaming experience, is likely to get sucked in." New Sci

Includes bibliographical references

Pollan, Michael

✓ The **botany** of desire; Michael Pollan. Random House 2001 xxv, 271 p.p $24.95; pa $13.95 **306.4**
1. Apples 2. Tulips 3. Potatoes 4. Marijuana 5. Economic botany 6. Human-plant relationships
ISBN 0-375-50129-0; 0-375-76039-3 pa; 9780375760396; 9780375501296

LC 00066479

In this book, author "Michael Pollan . . . demonstrates how people and domesticated plants have formed a similarly reciprocal relationship. He . . . links four fundamental human desires--sweetness, beauty, intoxication, and control--with the plants that satisfy them: the apple, the tulip, marijuana, and the potato. In telling the stories of four familiar species, Pollan illustrates how the plants have evolved to satisfy humankind's most basic yearnings. And just as we've benefited from these plants, we have also done well by them. So who is really domesticating whom?" (Publisher's note)

"Pollan intertwines history, anecdote, and revelation as he investigates the connection between four plants that have thrived under human care—apples, tulips, marijuana, and potatoes—and the four human desires they satisfy in return: sweetness, beauty, intoxication, and control. . . . Pollan's dynamic, intelligent, and intrepid parsing of the wondrous dialogue between plants and humans is positively paradigm-altering." Booklist

Includes bibliographical references and index.

Robinson, Jo

Eating on the wild side; the missing link to optimum health. Jo Robinson ; illustrations by Andie Styner. Little Brown & Co 2013 416 p. ill. $16 **306.4**

1. Nutrition 2. Natural foods

ISBN 0316227935; 9780316227933; 9780316227940

LC 2013934815

IACP Cookbook Award (2014)

This book, by Jo Robinson. discusses how "ever since farmers first planted seeds . . . , humans have been destroying the nutritional value of their fruits and vegetables. Unwittingly, we've been selecting plants that are high in starch and sugar and low in vitamins, minerals, fiber, and antioxidants." Robinson "reveals the solution--choosing modern varieties that approach the nutritional content of wild plants but that also please the modern palate." (Publisher's note)

Rose, Frank

The art of immersion; how the digital generation is remaking Hollywood, Madison Avenue, and the way we tell stories. W.W. Norton & Co. 2011 354p $26.95 **306.4**

1. Internet marketing 2. Internet entertainment 3. Internet -- Social aspects

ISBN 978-0-393-07601-1

LC 2010-38676

The author "theorizes that we are encountering a profound shift in the way we play, consume, and communicate. He explains that our experiences with television, movies, games, and advertisements are becoming increasingly more immersive and consumer-driven. . . . This engrossing study of how new media is reshaping the entertainment, advertising, and communication industries is an essential read for professionals in the fields of digital communications, marketing, and advertising, as well as for fans of gaming and pop culture." Libr J

Includes bibliographical references

Simons, Eric

The Secret Lives of Sports Fans; Eric Simons. Penguin Group USA 2013 320 p. (hardcover) $26.95 **306.4**

1. Social psychology 2. Sports spectators

ISBN 1590208641; 9781590208649

This book, by Eric Simons, explores how "sports fandom is either an aspect of a person's fundamental identity, or completely incomprehensible to those who aren't fans at all. What is happening in our brains and bodies when we feel strong emotion while watching a game? How do sports fans resemble political junkies, and why do we form such a strong attachment to a sports team?" (Publisher's note)

Trumble, Angus

The finger; a handbook. Farrar, Straus and Giroux 2010 300p il $28 **306.4**

1. Fingers

ISBN 978-0-374-15498-1; 0-374-15498-8

LC 2009-42220

Art historian Angus Trumble examines the finger from every possible angle. His inquiries into its representation in art take us from Buddhist statues in Kyoto to the ceiling of the Sistine Chapel, from cave art to Picasso's Guernica, from Van Dyck's and Rubens's winning ways with gloves to the longstanding French taste for tapering digits. But Trumble also asks . . . questions about the finger in general. Publisher's note

On the whole, The Finger is a deft, enjoyable and often provocative investigation into some overlooked and interrelated aspects of human experience. Washington Post

Includes bibliographical references

306.44 Language

Lepore, Jill

A is for American; letters and other characters in the newly United States. Knopf 2002 241p il $25; pa $13 **306.44**

1. Slaves 2. Artists 3. Painters 4. Inventors 5. Architects 6. Americanisms 7. Sociolinguistics 8. Artisans 9. Essayists 10. Metalworkers 11. Indian leaders 12. Lexicographers 13. Writers on law 14. Teachers of the deaf 15. Telecommunications executives 16. English language -- Social aspects

ISBN 0-375-40449-X; 0-375-70408-6 pa

LC 2001-38057

"Each man's story delivers a wealth of irony along with valuable history. . . . Some familiar accounts, some not well known, but all told with a fresh eye to their national significance." Booklist

Includes bibliographical references

306.46 Culture and institutions -- technology

Cukier, Kenneth

Big data; a revolution that will transform how we live, work, and think. Viktor Mayer-Schönberger and Kenneth Cukier. Houghton Mifflin Harcourt 2013 242 p. (hardcover) $27 **306.46**

1. Data processing 2. Information resources 3. Internet -- Social aspects 4. Social change 5. Big data -- Social aspects 6. Technological innovations -- Social aspects 7. Electronic information resources -- Social aspects

ISBN 0544002695; 9780544002692

LC 2012538859

This book, by Viktor Mayer-Schönberger and Kenneth Cukier, discusses Big Data "and the dramatic impact it will have on the economy, science, and society at large. . . . 'Big data' refers to our . . . ability to crunch vast collections of information, analyze it instantly, and draw sometimes profoundly surprising conclusions from it. This emerging science can translate myriad phenomena . . . into searchable form, and uses our increasing computing power to unearth epiphanies." (Publisher's note)

Includes bibliographical references (p. [217]-226) and index.

306.7   Sexual relations

Bader, Michael J.

Arousal, the secret logic of sexual fantasies. Thomas Dunne Bks./St. Martin's Press 2002 293p $23.95; pa $14.95   306.7
1. Sexual behavior
ISBN 0-312-26933-1; 0-312-30242-8 pa
LC 2001-51290

"Bader covers how arousal works, how fantasies assist in arousal, the role of fantasies in therapy, and the social meaning of fantasies. Throughout, he gives numerous case studies, examples, and sensible and compassionate conjectures about particular fantasies and the fantasizing process. Bader is a clear, graceful writer, and he makes his points with rare facility in a way useful to both lay people and therapeutic professionals." Libr J

Includes bibliographical references

Barash, David P.

The **myth** of monogamy; fidelity and infidelity in animals and people. [by] David P. Barash, Judith Eve Lipton. Freeman, W.H. 2001 227p $24.95; pa $15   306.7
1. Adultery 2. Marriage 3. Sexual behavior
ISBN 0-7167-4004-4; 0-8050-7136-9 pa

This is "guaranteed to entertain and may even pique thoughtful readers' interests." Sci Books Films

Includes bibliographical references

Bergner, Daniel

The **other** side of desire; four journeys into the far realms of lust and longing. Ecco 2009 208p $24.95   306.7
1. Compulsive behavior 2. Sexual behavior
ISBN 978-0-06-088556-4; 0-06-088556-4

The author "approaches deviance with a reporter's notepad. He selects four areas: foot fetishism, sadomasochism, pedophilia, and an obsession for amputees. In each case, he finds and follows a devotee. In the process, Bergner does what science cannot: He illuminates peculiar longings. His method is at first descriptive and finally poetic. The message of the book is in the interplay among personal narratives that prove alternately bizarre and mundane." Slate

Bernstein, Richard

The **East,** the West, and sex; a history of erotic encounters. Knopf 2009 325p il $27.95   306.7
1. Erotica 2. Orientalism 3. Asian national characteristics
ISBN 978-0-375-41409-1
LC 2008-55079

"This probing, absorbing and eclectic study critically challenges morally and politically correct interpretations of the Western sexual exploitation of the East." Publ Wkly

Includes bibliographical references

Kipnis, Laura

How to become a scandal; adventures in bad behavior. Metropolitan Books 2010 209p il $24 306.7
1. Scandals 2. Celebrities 3. Conduct of life 4. Deviant behavior
ISBN 978-0-8050-8979-0; 0-8050-8979-9
LC 2010-05036

The author "picks through the mortifying carnage of other people's lives, exploring why we both relish and condemn bad behavior. Divided in two parts, 'Downfalls' and 'Uproars,' this slight and easy-to-digest book covers four major popular-culture scandals of the last two decades. These include those of love-crazed, diaper-wearing astronaut Lisa Nowak; the dishonorable judge Sol Wachtler; whistle-blower Linda Tripp; and the 'overimaginative,' so-called memoirist James Frey. . . . Light and fun." Kirkus

Includes bibliographical references

Longing to tell; Black women talk about sexuality and intimacy. {compiled by} Tricia Rose. Farrar, Straus & Giroux 2003 415p $25; pa $15 306.7
1. African American women 2. Women -- Sexual behavior
ISBN 0-374-19061-5; 0-312-42372-1 pa
LC 2002-32541

"By letting the women speak for themselves and following the histories with a passionate afterword, Rose provides a collection that is as compelling as it is sorely needed." Publ Wkly

Includes bibliographical references

McConnachie, James

The **book** of love; the story of the Kamasutra. Metropolitan Books 2008 267p il $27.50; pa $17   306.7
1. Kamasutra 2. Sexual behavior
ISBN 978-0-8050-8818-2; 0-8050-8818-0; 978-0-8050-9019-2 pa; 0-8050-9019-3 pa
LC 2007-47172

"In an impressively researched, charming volume, McConnachie traces the Kamasutra's history from its creation by the third-century sage Vatsyayana as a guide to the good life for urbane dandies. . . . Since not a single posture is described, consider it G-rated." Booklist

Includes bibliographical references

The **Routledge** history of sex and the body; 1500 to the present. edited by Sarah Toulalan and Kate Fisher. Routledge 2013 xv, 579 p.p (The Routledge histories) (alk. paper) $195   306.7
1. Human body 2. Sex -- History 3. Sex -- Western countries -- History 4. Sexology -- Western countries -- History
ISBN 0203436865; 0415472377; 9780203436868; 9780415472371
LC 2012037890

This book, edited by Sarah Toulalan and Kate Fisher, "provides an overview of the main themes surrounding the history of sexuality from 1500 to the present day. Covering themes such as science, identity, the gaze, courtship, reproduction, sexual violence and the importance of race, the volume offers a comprehensive view of the history of sex and the body." (Publisher's note)

Includes bibliographical references (p. 533-561) and index

Shlain, Leonard

Sex, time, and power; how women's sexuality shaped human evolution. Viking 2003 xx, 420p il $25.95; pa $16 **306.7**
1. Evolution 2. Women -- Sexual behavior
ISBN 0-670-03233-6; 0-14-200467-7 pa
LC 2002-41186

The author "takes an evolutionary approach to solving the conundrums of misogyny and patriarchy, guiding his . . . readers through . . . speculations about the purpose of such seemingly impractical, even dangerous traits as bipedalism, menstruation, the perils of childbirth, and the helplessness of infants. . . . Lucid and compelling, Shlain asks startling and crucial questions about human nature and presents truly imaginative and mind-stretching answers." Booklist

Includes bibliographical references

Sugar in my bowl; real women write about real sex. edited by Erica Jong. Ecco 2011 238p il $21.99; ebook $9.99 **306.7**
1. Sex 2. Sexual behavior 3. Women -- Sexual behavior
ISBN 9780061875762; 0061875767; 9780062092205 ebook; 0062092200 ebook
LC 2011012689

In this book, "poet, novelist, and essayist . . . Erica Jong . . . offers us a provocative collection of essays about sex from some of the most respected female authors writing today." Contributors to the book, including "Gail Collins, Eve Ensler, Daphne Merken, Anne Roiphe, Liz Smith, Naomi Wolf, and Jennifer Weiner . . . speak openly about female desire—what provokes it and what satisfies it." (Publisher's note)

A "frank collection of personal essays, short fiction and cartoons celebrating female desire. The approaches to the still-taboo topic of feminine sexuality—at least, for women writers seeking approbation from the literary establishment—are, as Jong notes, 'as varied as sexuality itself' and as exuberantly diverse as the contributors themselves. They range from such emerging talents as Elisa Albert and J.A.K. Andres to such luminaries as Rebecca Walker, Eve Ensler, Susan Cheever, Anne Roiphe and Fay Weldon, and represent a multiethnic, multigenerational swath of some of the finest women writers in the United States. Most of the pieces deal with the perennial themes of sexual coming-of-age, social and religious sexual hang-ups and lusty obsessions for male bodies (as well as female ones). Some deal with lesser-discussed—but no less important—subjects like procreative sex and eroticism in old age. Still others fearlessly explore fetishism, childhood masturbation, kink, [and] sexual addiction." Kirkus

Wolf, Naomi

Promiscuities; the secret struggle for womanhood. Random House 1997 xxx, 286p hardcover o.p. pa $15 **306.7**
1. Girls -- Sexual behavior 2. Women -- Sexual behavior
ISBN 0-449-90764-3 pa
LC 96-46724

This "work centers on the way American culture of the late Sixties and Seventies created a generation of females torn between the need to express their sensuality and the desire to meet society's behavioral expectations. To illustrate her position, Wolf relies . . . on the coming-of-age experiences of herself, her friends, and acquaintances in her hometown, San Francisco." Libr J

"Wolf offers some astute and eminently realizable suggestions for a new approach to sexual education, even healing." Booklist

Includes bibliographical references

Yes means yes! visions of female sexual power & a world without rape. [by] Jaclyn Friedman & Jessica Valenti [editors]; foreword by Margaret Cho. Seal Press 2008 361p pa $16.95 **306.7**
1. Rape 2. Sexism 3. Gender role 4. Sex role 5. Women -- Sexual behavior
ISBN 978-1-58005-257-3; 1-58005-257-6
LC 2008-20989

The editors "present an extraordinary, eye-opening essay collection that focuses on the importance of sexual identity and ownership in the struggle against rape in the U.S., as well as a number of related issues, including sexual pleasure, self-esteem and the mixed societal messages that turn 'nice guys' bad." Publ Wkly

Includes bibliographical references

306.76   Sexual orientation, transgenderism, intersexuality

Blank, Hanne

Straight; the surprisingly short history of heterosexuality. Hanne Blank. Beacon Press 2012 xxvii, 228 p.p (hardcover : acid-free paper) $26.95 **306.76**
1. Homosexuality -- History 2. Heterosexuality -- History
ISBN 0807044431; 9780807044438
LC 2011031432

In this book, Hanne Blank "sets out to explore the changing views of marriage, heterosexuality, and conceptions of biological sex itself over the past 150 years, systematically exploring the history from scientific, philosophical, and sociological perspectives. . . . She argues that although sexual contact between men and women has existed since time immemorial, the word and idea of heterosexuality as an identity is a relatively recent invention." (Library Journal)

Includes bibliographical references and index

Bronski, Michael

★ A **queer** history of the United States. Beacon Press 2011 xx, 287p $27.95 **306.76**

1. Homosexuality -- United States -- History

ISBN 978-0-8070-4439-1

LC 2010-50225

"This enthralling history spans 500 years of evolving perspectives on sexuality in America—from the European setters' violent responses to the more fluid gender roles of Native Americans to how the birth control pill, which separated sex from reproduction, contributed to the cause of LGBT liberation. . . . A savvy political, legal, literary (and even fashion) history, Bronski's narrative is as intellectually rigorous as it is entertaining." Publ Wkly

You can tell just by looking; and 20 other myths about LGBT life and people. Michael Bronski, Ann Pellegrini, Michael Amico. Beacon Press 2013 208 p. (pbk.) $16 **306.76**

1. Bisexuality 2. Homosexuality 3. Gay liberation movement 4. Gays -- United States 5. Lesbians -- United States 6. Bisexuals -- United States 7. Gay liberation movement -- United States 8. Transgender people -- United States -- History

ISBN 0807042455; 9780807042458

LC 2013023146

Lambda Literary Awards Finalist (2014)

In this book, authors Michael Bronski, Ann Pellegrini, and Michael Amico "come together to unpack . . . myths about lesbian, gay, bisexual, and transgender people, culture, and life in America. [Some] myths . . . have been used to justify discrimination and oppression of LGBT people. Others . . . have been embraced by LGBT communities and their allies. In discussing and dispelling these myths—including gay-positive ones—the authors challenge readers to question their own beliefs." (Publisher's note)

Includes bibliographical references and index

Duberman, Martin B., 1930-

The **Martin** Duberman reader; the essential historical, biographical, and autobiographical writings. Martin Duberman. The New Press 2013 384 p. (paperback) $21.95 **306.76**

1. LGBT people 2. United States -- Social conditions 3. United States -- History 4. Gays -- United States -- History 5. Gay rights -- United States -- History 6. United States -- Politics and government

ISBN 1595586792; 9781595586797

LC 2012041856

This book, by Martin Duberman, offers a reader featuring essays and autobiographical writings of the LGBT scholar. "For the past fifty years, prize-winning historian Martin Duberman's groundbreaking writings have established him as one of our preeminent public intellectuals. Founder of the first graduate program in LGBT studies in the country, . . . Duberman is also an equally gifted playwright and essayist." (Publisher's note)

Eisner, Shiri

Bi; notes for a bisexual revolution. Shiri Eisner. Seal Press 2013 345 p. $16 **306.76**

1. Sex 2. Bisexuality

ISBN 1580054749; 9781580054744

LC 2012047200

Lambda Literary Awards Finalist (2014)

This book, by Shiri Eisner, offers a "comprehensive look at bisexual politics—from the issues surrounding biphobia/monosexism, feminism, and transgenderism to the practice of labeling those who identify as bi as either 'too bisexual' . . . or 'not bisexual enough'. . . . In this . . . book, feminist bisexual and genderqueer activist Shiri Eisner takes readers on a journey through the many aspects of the meanings and politics of bisexuality." (Publisher's note)

Faderman, Lillian

Gay L.A. a history of sexual outlaws, power politics, and lipstick lesbians. [by] Lillian Faderman and Stuart Timmons. Basic Books 2006 431p il $27.50 **306.76**

1. Homosexuality 2. Gay liberation movement 3. Los Angeles (Calif.)

ISBN 978-0-465-02288-5; 0-465-02288-X

LC 2006-23470

This history of lesbian and gay life in Los Angeles "stretches from the humane tolerance of pre-contact indigenous peoples, through the 20th-century crisis years of homophobia and AIDS and ultimately into the victories and setbacks in this century. . . . Full of fascinating anecdotes (including much on Hollywood), wise and fair analysis, and significant and inspiring examples of courageous resistance recaptured from the unwritten histories of the past, Gay L.A. deserves a prominent place in every library." Libr J

Includes bibliographical references

Fellows, Will

Gay bar; the fabulous, true story of a daring woman and her boys in the 1950s. [by] Will Fellows and Helen P. Branson; introduction by Blanche M. Baker. University of Wisconsin Press 2010 xx, 166p il $26.95; ebook $14.95 **306.76**

1. Gay men 2. Restaurants 3. Los Angeles (Calif.)

ISBN 978-0-299-24850-5; 978-0-299-24853-6 ebook

LC 2010011528

An expanded edition of the original 1957 publication Gay Bar by Helen P. Branson, interleaved with commentary and excerpts from letters and essays appearing in L.A. gay publications of the period

This is "the firsthand, contemporary account by a straight woman, Branson, who owned a gay bar in 1950s Los Angeles. . . . The book shows Branson to be a compassionate and astute observer of gay mores, now providing a rare primary source of gay life in an era from which such information is hard to obtain. Researchers will find material on the relationships between gay men and women, what gay parties were like, and the distinct house rules that Branson set up for patronage of her bar, among other topics. . . . General readers of memoir or LGBT lit, as well as historians, will find Gay Bar to be a charming, informative read." Libr J

Includes bibliographical references

Gambone, Philip

Travels in a gay nation; portraits of LGBTQ Americans. University of Wisconsin Press 2010 294p (Living out: gay and lesbian autobiographies) pa $26.95; ebook $16.95 **306.76**

1. Gay men 2. Lesbians 3. Transgender people 4. Bisexuals 5. Transgendered people

ISBN 978-0-299-23684-7 pa; 978-0-299-23683-0 ebook

LC 2009041591

"The 44 profiles here are of artists, writers, activists, politicians, and intellectuals. Gambone's interviewees are diverse in many ways (age, gender, race, background), but they are all people of noted accomplishment, the best-known probably being Dorothy Allison, Tammy Baldwin, Kate Clinton, Barney Frank, and George Takei, but at least half the names should be familiar to most LGBT readers. Gambone is a smart interviewer with a laid-back, engaging style, and he knows how to bring out the most interesting qualities of his subjects." Libr J

Hanhardt, Christina B.

Safe space; gay neighborhood history and the politics of violence. Christina B. Hanhardt. Duke University Press 2013 376 p. (Perverse modernities) (cloth : alk. paper) $94.95 **306.76**

1. Gay rights 2. LGBT people -- Civil rights 3. Gentrification -- United States 4. Community policing 5. Gay liberation movement

ISBN 0822354578; 9780822354574; 9780822354703

LC 2013013825

Lambda Awards Winner: LGBT Studies (2014)

In this book, part of the Perverse Modernities series, "Christina B. Hanhardt examines how LGBT calls for 'safe space' have been shaped by broader public safety initiatives that . . . have had devastating effects along race and class lines. Drawing on . . . research in New York City and San Francisco, Hanhardt traces the entwined histories of LGBT activism, urban development, and U.S. policy in relation to poverty and crime." (Publisher's note)

"Tracing the granular details of lesbian and gay activism against street violence, Hanhardt . . . challenges commonly accepted narratives about safe streets, LGBT identity, and intersections of visibility and vulnerability." Choice

Includes bibliographical references and index

Hirshman, Linda

Victory; the triumphant gay revolution. Linda Hirshman. Harper 2012 464 p. $27.99 **306.76**

1. Civil rights 2. LGBT people -- Legal status, laws, etc. 3. Gays -- Legal status, laws, etc. -- United States 4. United States -- Social conditions -- 21st century 5. Gay liberation movement -- United States -- History

ISBN 0061965502; 9780061965500

LC 2012406399

This book by Linda Hirshman discusses the "triumph of the gay-rights movement. Drawing on previous histories and more than 100 interviews, the author shows how the movement has been successful over the years in countering bigoted notions. . . . Hirshman . . . [presents] discussions of court cases and their attendant legal issues, and on occasion she offers perceptive comparisons between the gay-rights

movement and other, concurrent movements for equality." (Kirkus Reviews)

Includes bibliographical references (p. [357]-423) and index

Parkinson, R. B.

A little gay history; desire and diversity across the world. Richard Parkinson ; with contributions by Kate Smith and Max Carocci. Columbia University Press 2013 128 p. col. ill., map (pbk. : alk. paper) $19.95 **306.76**

1. Art 2. Homosexuality -- History

ISBN 023116663X; 9780231166638

LC 2013001699

Stonewall Book Awards: Nonfiction Honor Book (2014)

Author R.B. Parkinson presents answers to questions such as "When was the first chat line between men established? Who was the first 'lesbian'? Were ancient Greek men who had sex with each other necessarily 'gay' and what did Shakespeare think about crossdressing? . . . through close readings of art objects from the British Museum's far-ranging collection." (Publisher's note)

"This little gay history is a little terrific book. . . . Parkinson . . . explore[s] the subject of homosexual desire throughout history; he discusses artistic movements, ordinary material culture, facades of conventional life, warrior traditions, legal persecutions, and definitions of the sacred." (Library Journal)

Includes bibliographical references

Persistence; all ways butch and femme. [edited by] Ivan E. Coyote and Zena Sharman. Arsenal Pulp Press 2011 312 p. **306.76**

1. Gender role 2. Lesbians' writings 3. Lesbians -- Personal narratives 4. Lesbians -- Identity 5. Biography, Collective 6. Lesbians' writings, Canadian

ISBN 9781551523972 pa

LC 2010671168

In this book, honored as a Stonewall Honor Book by the American Library Association and Lambda Literary Award finalist, "[c]ontributors such as Jewelle Gomez ("The Gilda Stories"), Thea Hillman ("Intersex"), S. Bear Bergman ("Butch is a Noun"), Chandra Mayor ("All the Pretty Girls"), Amber Dawn ("Sub Rosa"), Anna Camilleri ("Brazen Femme"), Debra Anderson ("Code White"), Anne Fleming ("Anomaly"), Michael V. Smith ("Cumberland"), and Zoe Whittall ("Bottle Rocket Hearts") explore the parameters, history, and power of a multitude of butch and femme realities. . . . [The book] look[s] at what the words butch and femme can mean in today's ever-shifting gender landscape, with one eye on the past and the other on what is to come." (Publisher's note)

Robb, Graham

★ Strangers : homosexual love in the nineteenth century. W.W. Norton 2004 341p il $26.95; pa $15.95 **306.76**

1. Homosexuality

ISBN 0-393-02038-X; 0-393-32649-7 pa

LC 2003-66239

The author "has produced a brilliant work of social archaeology. . . . In excavating the long-buried lives of our gay great-great-granduncles and lesbian great-great-grandaunts, Robb has done more than make a major historical contribution. He has, as it were, provided their distant nieces and nephews, gay and straight, with a family tree that we have never had before." N Y Times Book Rev

Savage, Dan

✓ American Savage; insights, slights, and fights on faith, sex, love, and politics. by Dan Savage. Dutton 2013 320 p. (hardcover) $26.95   **306.76**

1. Sex 2. LGBT people 3. Gays -- United States 4. Gay men -- United States -- Biography
ISBN 0525954104; 9780525954101

LC 2013001374

This book by sex columnist and gay rights advocate Dan Savage presents a "collection of 17 new essays. . . . Savage introduces readers to his son's coming out as straight . . . . Sexual mores such as debates over monogamy and the closeted are grappled with. He also takes on conservative opponents . . . his Roman Catholic upbringing and his mother." (Library Journal)

Schwartz, John ✓

Oddly normal; one family's struggle to help their teenage son come to terms with his sexuality. John Schwartz. 1st ed. Gotham Books 2012 xiv, 290 p.p ill. (hardcover) $26   **306.76**

1. Gay teenagers 2. Parents of gays 3. Families 4. Parent and teenager
ISBN 1592407285; 9781592407286

LC 2012014369

Includes bibliographical references (p. 279-290).

This book by John Schwartz is a "memoir by the father of a gay teen. . . . After mustering the courage to come out to his classmates, [Shwartz's] thirteen-year-old son, Joe, was in the hospital following a failed suicide attempt. . . . 'Oddly Normal' is Schwartz's . . . attempt to address his family's own struggles within a culture that is changing fast, but not fast enough to help gay kids like Joe." (Publisher's note)

306.77   Sexual and related practices

Solomon, John

DSK; the scandal that brought down Dominique Strauss-Kahn. John Solomon. Thomas Dunne Books 2012 xi, 274 p.p (hardback) $25.99   **306.77**

1. Scandals 2. Sex crimes 3. Statesmen -- France -- Biography 4. Statesmen -- France 5. Sex scandals -- New York State -- New York
ISBN 1250012635; 9781250012630; 9781250012647

LC 2012009436

This book, by John Solomon, about the 2011 sex scandal surrounding French politician Dominique Strauss-Kahn "grew out of . . . an interview with Ms. [Nafi] Diallo published . . . shortly before the prosecutors dropped the case. His book [asserts that] . . . the prosecutors first rushed too quickly to judgment against Mr. Strauss-Kahn. . . . But when they then found that Ms. Diallo had told lies about her past in Guinea, . . . they rushed too fast in the other direction." (Economist)

"This is a fascinating examination of the roles of politics, race, class, social status, and egos in one of the decade's most sensational criminal cases." Booklist

306.8   Marriage and family

Because I said so; 33 mothers write about children, ✓ sex, men, aging, faith, race, and themselves. from the editors of Mothers who think Camille, Peri, & Kate Moses. HarperCollins 2005 xxi, 372p $24.95; pa $13.95   **306.8**

1. Mothers
ISBN 0-06-059878-6; 0-06-059879-4 pa

LC 2004-62007

Contributors to this collection of essays on modern motherhood include "writers such as Janet Fitch, Mariane Pearl, Mary Roach, Susan Straight, Margaret Talbot, Rosellen Brown, Beth Kephart, Ariel Gore, and Ana Castillo." Publisher's note

"Women will appreciate the humor and candor, and men will gain insight into the stunning challenges of motherhood." Booklist

Includes bibliographical references

Brower, Sam ✓

Prophet's prey; my seven-year investigation into Warren Jeffs and the Fundamentalist Church of Latter-Day Saints. [preface by Jon Krakauer] Bloomsbury USA 2011 323p il $27   **306.8**

1. Polygamy 2. Christian fundamentalism 3. Church of Jesus Christ of Latter-day Saints 4. Mormon leaders
ISBN 1-60819-275-X; 978-1-60819-275-5

"Private investigator Brower gives readers a firsthand look at the investigation that brought down prophet Warren Jeffs and the cultlike Fundamentalist Church of Jesus Christ of Latter Day Saints. . . . This compelling story of one man's crusade against a pedophile prophet will appeal to readers of current events and religious history as well as to crime fans." Libr J

Celani, David P.

Leaving home; the art of separating from your difficult family. Columbia University Press 2005 156p $24.95   **306.8**

1. Adult child abuse victims
ISBN 0-231-13476-2

LC 2004-51980

The author "explains how children in abusive or neglectful homes develop both wounded and hopeful selves and why they compulsively pick the worst possible mate or make self-destructive decisions. Full of compassion and encouragement, this book will prepare readers to leave home and to live a life free of interpersonal failures." Libr J

Includes bibliographical references

Garner, Abigail

★ **Families** like mine; children of gay parents tell it like it is. HarperCollins 2004 256p hardcover o.p. pa $13.95 **306.8**
> 1. Gay parents 2. Parent-child relationship
> ISBN 0-06-052757-9; 0-06-052758-7 pa
>> LC 2003-56975

The author "examines growing up in a queer household from every angle, using her own experiences and those of about fifty other adult children of LGBT parents." Voice Youth Advocates

This book "should quickly become a mainstay resource for many family service agencies and public libraries serving LGBT patrons." Booklist

Includes bibliographical references

Howey, Noelle

Dress codes of three girlhoods--my mother's, my father's, and mine. Picador 2002 332p $24; pa $14 **306.8**
> 1. Transsexualism 2. Parent-child relationship
> ISBN 0-312-26921-8; 0-312-42220-2 pa
>> LC 2001-59060

This is a "look back at how teenager Howey and her mother struggled with her father's transformation from a bad-tempered dad to a loving transgendered woman." Libr J

"Howey manages to entertain, console, and enlighten readers. The book is impossible to ignore, and impossible to put down." SLJ

Maybe baby; 28 writers tell the truth about skepticism, infertility, baby lust, childlessness, ambivalence, and how they made the biggest decisions of their lives. edited by Lori Leibovich; foreword by Anne Lamott. HarperCollins 2006 266p $24.95; pa $13.95 **306.8**
> 1. Parenting 2. Pregnancy 3. Childlessness
> ISBN 0-06-073781-6; 978-0-06-073781-8; 0-06-073782-4 pa; 978-0-06-073782-5 pa
>> LC 2005-52686

"This work, an outgrowth of a Salon.com series that ran in 2003, considers one of modern life's great issues: parenthood. Divided into three sections ('No,' 'Maybe,' and 'Yes'), the 28 essays personalize the choices found in broader society today. . . . These superbly written essays are recommended for all libraries, especially gender studies and sociology collections." Libr J

Phillips, Kathy J.

The **moon** in the water; reflections on an aging parent. Vanderbilt University Press 2008 139p il $19.95 **306.8**
> 1. Caregivers 2. Aging parents 3. Parent-child relationship
> ISBN 978-0-8265-1586-5; 0-8265-1586-X
>> LC 2007-26255

"By turns witty, compassionate, wise, and intensely personal, Phillips's book is perfect for our 'sandwich generation,' facing the care of elderly parents and trying to continue spiritual journeys even in the face of the end." Libr J

Includes bibliographical references

Ray, Barbara E.

Not quite adults; why 20-somethings are choosing a slower path to adulthood, and why it's good for everyone. [by] Rick Settersten and Barbara E. Ray. 1st ed. Delacorte Press 2010 xxiii, 239 p.p (paperback) $15.00 **306.8**
> 1. Adulthood 2. Youth -- Education 3. Youth -- Employment 4. Youth -- United States
> ISBN 0553807404; 9780440339793; 9780553807400
>> LC 2010027109

This authors of this book "document the many ways that touch points of adulthood . . . are happening years later for people currently in their twenties and thirties than for their parents and grandparents" as well as "the vast disparity of resources and opportunities . . . between 'swimmers,' as the authors term college-educated youth with strong family support and wide social networks, and 'treaders,' a larger group of young people suffering chronic, generational resource deficits." (Library Journal)

"Drawing on eight years of data and more than 500 interviews with young people between 18 and 34, Richard Settersten and Barbara Ray dismantle the common belief that this generation has been coddled into laziness. Rather, these young adults have come of age at a particularly merciless moment. . . . 'Not Quite Adults' offers a valuable portrait of the diverging destinies of young people today." Economist

Includes bibliographical references

Scott, Laura S.

Two is enough; a couple's guide to living childless by choice. Seal Press 2009 254p pa $16.95 **306.8**
> 1. Childlessness
> ISBN 978-1-58005-263-4
>> LC 2009-4841

The author discusses "people choosing to forgo having children. She bases her observations on an extensive survey, exploring the decision-making process that relates not only to the ramifications of this decision but also to living a childless life in a pronatal world. Scott discusses this emotionally wrought topic in a measured, neutral tone that will appeal to those making these decisions and their extended families." Libr J

Includes bibliographical references

Vickery, Amanda

Behind closed doors; at home in Georgian England. Yale University Press 2009 382p il $45 **306.8**
> 1. Social status -- England 2. Households -- England -- History 3. Social control -- England -- History 4. Great Britain -- History -- 1714-1837 5. Great Britain -- Social life and customs 6. England -- Social conditions -- 18th century 7. Material culture -- Great Britain -- History 8. Sex role -- England -- History -- 18th century
> ISBN 0-300-15453-4; 978-0-300-15453-5
>> LC 2009-18592

Vickery concentrates on the "life stories of the bachelors and spinsters, wives, widows and divorcees who occupied the buildings [of England under the Georges] ." (Hist Today) Bibliography. Index.

"Vickery's greatest achievement is to upend the notion that the home was divided into separate spheres in which men were responsible for brick and stone while women ruled over domestic life. Instead, Vickery brilliantly shows that these boundaries were fluid and mutable. . . . [This work] demonstrates that rigorous academic work can also be nosy, gossipy and utterly engaging." N Y Times Book Rev

Includes bibliographical references

Warner, Judith

★ **Perfect** madness; motherhood in the age of anxiety. Riverhead Books 2005 327p $23.95; pa $15   **306.8**

1. Mothers 2. Dual-career families
ISBN 1-573-22304-2; 1-594-48170-9 pa

LC 2004-56615

"Writing from the perspective of her first few years of motherhood spent in France and her subsequent return to the U.S., Warner ponders the cultural factors driving the madness of pursuing perfect motherhood and the toll it is taking on American women." Booklist

Includes bibliographical references

306.81   Marriage and marital status

Klinenberg, Eric

Going solo; the extraordinary rise and surprising appeal of living alone. Eric Klinenberg. Penguin Press 2012 273 p.   **306.81**

1. Housing 2. Social psychology 3. Youth -- United States 4. Single people -- United States 5. Living alone -- United States 6. Single people -- United States -- Psychology
ISBN 9781594203220

LC 2011031522

This book explores why more than 50 percent of American adults are single--and why the usually prefer to live that way. . . . The author examines both ends of the age spectrum in an attempt to understand the social implication of this trend. He finds that among relatively affluent young adults in the 25-to-34 age bracket, living solo is seen as a rite of passage into adulthood--a period allowing more sexual freedom, a chance to explore relationships without commitment and a major focus on career building. A similar increase in solitary living is becoming the norm among the elderly. . . . [Eric] Klinenberg suggests that public support is needed to provide affordable, urban assisted-living facilities in which the elderly can maintain their independence for as long as possible. (Kirkus)

Includes bibliographical references and index

Roiphe, Anne Richardson

Married; a fine predicament. {by} Anne Roiphe. Basic Bks. 2002 285p $25; pa $14.95   **306.81**

1. Marriage
ISBN 0-465-07066-3; 0-465-07067-1 pa

LC 2002-3506

The author writes "about how marriage and women's lives have changed since the 1950s, and about constants in human nature and the beleaguered but not yet improved upon institution of marriage. . . . Roiphe's rumination is a bit indulgent and soft with hearsay, yet it is timely, clever, candid, generous, and free of sentiment or trivialization." Booklist

306.85   Family

Barry, Dave, 1947-

You can date boys when you're forty; Dave Barry on parenting and other topics he knows very little about. Dave Barry. G.P. Putnam's Sons 2014 240 p. illustrations (hardback) $26.95   **306.85**

1. Family life 2. Wit and humor 3. Parenting -- Humor 4. Family -- Humor
ISBN 0399165940; 9780399165948

LC 2013037714

This book, by humorist Dave Barry "includes nine never-before-published essays. . . Though not only about parenting (Viagra commercials, horseback riding, cremation and grammar are just a few of the topics addressed), Barry . . . [focuses on] describing his role as the 65-year-old dad of a 13-year-old daughter." (Publishers Weekly)

"A mishmash, but even those who don't have children and have never lived in Miami or searched for a Wi-Fi connection in the Israeli desert will appreciate Barry's lighthearted absurdity." Kirkus

Hochschild, Arlie Russell

The **outsourced** self; intimate life in market times. Arlie Russell Hochschild. Metropolitan Books 2012 300 p. ill.   **306.85**

1. Sociology 2. Outsourcing 3. Free enterprise 4. Family -- Economic aspects 5. Families -- Economic aspects -- United States -- History 6. Interpersonal relations and culture -- United States -- History
ISBN 080508889X; 9780805088892

LC 2011044135

In this book, "sociologist [Arlie Russell] Hochschild . . . compares Turner, Maine--the self-sufficient farming village where she spent summers as a child--with the global marketplace, where" outsourcing is common. Some of "Hochschild's . . . chapters center on surrogate motherhood. . . . Hochschild makes the . . . observation that many pressing for a greater expansion of the free market, gutting of regulations, and cuts in social services are the same people who call for stronger family values, perhaps unaware of the way the market distorts them." (Publishers Weekly)

Includes bibliographical references and index.

Winik, Marion

The **lunch** -box chronicles; notes from the parenting underground. Pantheon Bks. 1998 229p hardcover o.p. pa $15   **306.85**

1. Parenting 2. Single parent family
ISBN 0-375-70170-2 pa

LC 97-26753

The author "covers death, bedtime stories, sexuality, God, team sports for geeks and other topics in this collection of personal essays on raising children." N Y Times Book Rev

"Winik brings together in winning fashion her decidedly nonmainstream attitude, laugh-out-loud humor, and refreshing candor." Booklist

306.87   Intrafamily relationships

Duron, Lori

Raising my rainbow; adventures in raising a slightly effeminate, possibly gay, totally fabulous son. Lori Duron. Crown Trade 2013 224 p. $15 **306.87**
    1. LGBT youth 2. Gender role 3. Parent-child relationship 4. Child rearing 5. Child psychology
    ISBN 0770437729; 9780770437725

                     LC 2012042444

Stonewall Book Award: Israel Fishman Non-Fiction Award (2014)

This book, by Lori Duron, is the author's "account of her and her family's adventures of distress and happiness raising a gender-creative son. . . . C.J. is gender variant or gender nonconforming, . . . whatever the term, Lori has a boy who likes girl stuff. . . . He floats on the gender-variation spectrum from super-macho-masculine on the left all the way to super-girly-feminine on the right." (Publisher's note)

"In Duron's story, parents will find support for a 'love them, not change them' style of parenting, optimism about the outcomes for their gender-creative children, sympathy for the difficulties of parenting, and an affirmation of the appropriateness and necessity for fierce advocacy." Pub Wkly

Tannen, Deborah

I only say this because I love you; how the way we talk can make or break family relationships throughout our lives. Random House 2001 xxvii, 336p hardcover o.p. pa $15.95 **306.87**
    1. Family 2. Communication
    ISBN 0-345-40752-0 pa

                     LC 00-68851

"With lively prose and genuine concern for people, Tannen brings linguistic concepts—metamessage, re-framing, indirect request—to bear on dozens of situations to help lay readers strenghten family ties." Libr J

Includes bibliographical references

306.872   Spousal relationship

Yalom, Marilyn

A **history** of the wife. HarperCollins Pubs. 2001 441p il hardcover o.p. pa $14.95 **306.872**
    1. Marriage 2. Women -- History
    ISBN 0-06-093156-6 pa

                     LC 00-58153

Yalom "has apparently written the first truly comprehensive history of the Western female spousal experience; indeed, there are precious few long views of either marriage or the family to which this book can be compared." Libr J

306.874   Parent-child relationship

Block, Shira

When Your Parent Moves in; Every Adult Child's Guide to Living With an Aging Parent. [by] David Horgan and Shira Block. 1st ed. Adams Media Corp 2009 xxi, 233 p.p (paperback) $12.95 **306.874**
    1. Aging parents 2. Shared housing 3. Parent-child relationship
    ISBN 1605500127; 9781605500126

This book on deciding whether and how to share one's home with an aging parent is focused on "help[ing] readers make the best possible decision for their individual situations. . . . Chapter 1 offers an overview of the signals that a parent might need a change in lifestyle and living arrangements. . . . Each subsequent chapter deals with a specific issue. The chapters present two scenarios that illustrate the challenges faced when dealing with this issue." (Adaptation & Aging)

Chua, Amy

Battle hymn of the tiger mother. Penguin Press 2011 237p il **306.874**
    1. Mothers 2. Parenting 3. Child rearing 4. Memoirists 5. Law teachers 6. College teachers 7. Mothers and daughters 8. Chinese American families
    ISBN 9781594202841; 1594202842; 9780143120582

                     LC 2010029623

It was the author's "stated intent . . . to present the differences between Western and Chinese parenting styles by sharing experiences with her own children. . . . As the daughter of Chinese immigrants, she is poised to contrast the two disparate styles, even as she points out that being a 'Chinese Mother' . . . is more a state of mind than a genetic trait. . . . She insists that Western children are no happier than Chinese ones." (Booklist)

Includes bibliographical references

Crews, Kambri

Burn down the ground; a memoir. Kambri Crews. Villard 2012 xiv, 334 p.p **306.874**
    1. Deaf 2. Fathers 3. Domestic violence 4. Adult child abuse victims -- Biography 5. Texas -- Biography 6. Children of deaf parents -- Biography
    ISBN 0345516028; 9780345516022

                     LC 2011040828

The author provides an "account of her dysfunctional childhood and the father who both charmed and victimized her family. As the hearing child of two deaf adults, Crews grew up between worlds. . . . But not long after they moved from their tin-shed shelter into a mobile home, Crews began to see evidence of domestic abuse that took the form of mysterious bruises on her mother's face and inexplicably cruel behavior in her brother. Her home life continued to show signs of ugly undercurrents, yet only silence prevailed, and the author threw herself into school and a full-time job. . . . At age 31, she received the shattering news that her father had stabbed his girlfriend." (Kirkus)

Cusk, Rachel

A **life's** work; on becoming a mother. Picador 2002 213p $22; pa $13 **306.874**
    1. Mothers 2. Parenting
    ISBN 0-312-26987-0; 0-312-31130-3 pa

                     LC 2001-54894

First published 2001 in the United Kingdom

"This is not a happy guide; instead, it is a penetrating, sometimes joyful and amusing, sometimes frightening and disturbing look at pregnancy and motherhood." Booklist

DeGarmo, John

The **foster** parenting manual; a practical guide to creating a loving, safe and stable home. John DeGarmo ; foreword by Mary Perdue. Jessica Kingsley Publishers 2013 160 p. $17.95   **306.874**
1. Parenting 2. Foster children 3. Foster home care 4. Foster parents
ISBN 184905956X; 9781849059565
LC 2013012292

This book, by John Degarmo, "is a comprehensive guide offering proven, friendly advice for novice and experienced parents alike. . . . He describes what to expect from the process, how to access help and how to ensure the best care for your child. He tackles thorny issues such as children's use of the Internet and social media, managing contact with birth parents and how to support your child at school." (Publisher's note)

"DeGarmo includes both big-picture ideas about child development and nuts-and-bolts considerations for fostering, such as how often a caseworker must visit a home, what foster families are reimbursed for, and what training is required." LJ

Includes bibliographical references (page 142-154) and index

Gallagher, Shaun

Experimenting with babies; 50 amazing science projects you can perform on your kid. by Shaun Gallagher. Perigee Book 2013 224 p. (pbk.) $16   **306.874**
1. Infants 2. Science -- Experiments 3. Parent and child
ISBN 0399162461; 9780399162466
LC 2013021018

This book, by Shaun Gallagher, "shows you how to re-create landmark scientific studies on cognitive, motor, language, and behavioral development—using your [infant] as the research subject. Simple [and] engaging, . . . each project sheds light on how your baby is acquiring new skills--everything from recognizing faces, voices, and shapes to understanding new words, learning to walk, and even distinguishing between right and wrong." (Publisher's note)

"This is a unique work that presents an enjoyable and intelligent look at child development." LJ

Includes bibliographical references

Holroyd, Michael

A **book** of secrets; Michael Holroyd. Farrar, Straus and Giroux 2011 xiv, 258p.p ill.   **306.874**
1. Essays 2. Biography 3. Illegitimacy 4. Gifted women 5. Women -- Biography 6. Biography, Collective
ISBN 0-374-11558-3; 978-0-374-11558-6 0-374-11558-3
LC 2011003839

In this book, a "Publisher's Weekly" Best Nonfiction title for 2011, author "[Michael] Holroyd brings a company of unknown women into the light. From Alice Keppel, the mis-tress of both the second Lord Grimthorpe and the Prince of Wales; to Eve Fairfax, a muse of Auguste Rodin; to the novelist Violet Trefusis, the lover of Vita Sackville-West--these women are always on the periphery of the respectable world. Also on the margins is the . . . biographer, who on occasion turns an . . . eye upon himself as part of his investigations in the maze of biography." (Publisher's note)

Includes bibliographical references and index.

Livingston, Patricia

But dad! a survival guide for single fathers of tween and teen daughters. Gretchen Gross and Patricia Livingston. Rowman & Littlefield Publishers 2012 192 p.   **306.874**
1. Parenting 2. Unmarried fathers 3. Girls -- Health and hygiene 4. Father-daughter relationship 5. Teenage girls 6. Single fathers 7. Fathers and daughters
ISBN 9781442212671; 9781442212688
LC 2011044670

This book offers a guide to being a single "father to a tween or teenage daughter. . . . Whether rendered a one-man show by divorce, death, or deployment, single fathers face a slew of unique challenges when parenting adolescent girls. They must navigate issues like menstruation, female social development (including the great, dreaded D-word: Dating), the establishment of positive male role models, and more subtle issues, like negotiating new forms of father-daughter physical contact. In addition to these dad-and-daughter topics, the book also contains . . . information on general parenting areas, such as fiscal responsibility and setting boundaries." (Publishers Weekly)

McConville, Brigid

On Becoming a Mother; Welcoming Your New Baby and Your New Life With Wisdom from Around the World. Brigid McConville. Pgw 2014 304 p. illustrations $16.99   **306.874**
1. Infants 2. Mother-child relationship
ISBN 1780743890; 9781780743899
Includes index

This book by Brigid McConville discusses mothering practices around the world, "From the Mexican rebozo used to rock the belly and ease back pain during pregnancy to the Bengali practice of taking off a woman's bangles to help her visualize a speedy labor, . . . from the proverbs printed on the kangas used to carry East African newborns to the Japanese ritual where Sumo wrestlers are asked to make infants cry." (Publisher's note)

"The American baby shower, Islamic naming ceremonies, and first birthdays in Korea sit comfortably next to each other in this global celebration of motherhood." Pub Wkly

Newman, Katherine S., 1953-

The **accordion** family; boomerang kids, anxious parents, and the private toll of global competition. Katherine S. Newman. Beacon Press 2012 xxiii, 261 p.p charts $25.95   **306.874**
1. Parent-child relationship 2. Globalization -- Economic aspects 3. Adult children living with parents 4. Parent and adult child 5. Competition, International

6. Adult children -- Family relationships
ISBN 0807007439; 9780807007433

LC 2011027846

This book "examines the proliferation of 'accordion families,'" in which children continue to live with their parents late into their 20s and 30s. . . . [Katherine] Newman's inquiry takes her around the world to examine how family structures are responding to societal changes. She examines how high unemployment rates, the rise of short-term employment, staggered birth rates, longer life expectancies, and the high cost of living have affected the younger generation's transition to adulthood." (Publishers Weekly)

Includes bibliographical references and index

Pipher, Mary Bray

Another country; navigating the emotional terrain of our elders. [by] Mary Pipher. Riverhead Bks. 1999 xx, 328p hardcover o.p. pa $13.95 **306.874**
1. Aging parents 2. Parent-child relationship
ISBN 1-57322-784-6 pa

LC 98-31877

The author is interested in studying "the aging process in order to promote meaningful connections between the generations and more cultural support for pursuing them. . . . Pipher describes strategies for dealing with illness, physical decline, the death of a husband or wife and the emotional problems that arise for both the elderly and their families. . . . One of the strengths of this excellent study is that Pipher includes examples of troubled as well as rewarding marital and parent/child relationships." Publ Wkly

Sandler, Lauren

One and only; the freedom of having an only child, and the joy of being one. Lauren Sandler. Simon & Schuster 2013 224 p. $24.99 **306.874**
1. Parenting 2. Only child 3. Families 4. Family size
ISBN 1451626959; 9781451626957

LC 2013000707

Author Lauren Sandier, an only child, considers only children. "Though she says this is not a memoir, her personal story is woven throughout, beginning with her mother's decision to have one child and ending with the author's apparent decision not to have a second child . . . The focus of the book, however, is on dissecting the research surrounding the myth of the lonely, selfish, maladjusted only child." (Publishers Weekly)

Includes bibliographical references

Taffel, Ron

The **second** family; how adolescent power is challenging the American family. [by] Ron Taffel with Melinda Blau. St. Martin's Press 2001 204p $23.95; pa $12.95 **306.874**
1. Parenting 2. Teenagers 3. Popular culture
ISBN 0-312-26137-3; 0-312-28493-4 pa

LC 00-45993

In this work the author "tracks adolescents' defection from the 'first family' (Mom, Dad, and siblings) for the 'second family' (the peer group and pop culture). This is not, he argues, an angry or rebellious culture but a comfort-seeking one—be it with sex, drugs, recreation, body sculpture, and consumer items." Libr J

This book is "required reading for anyone interacting with adolescents today." Voice Youth Advocates

When I first held you; 22 critically acclaimed writers talk about the triumphs, challenges, and transformative experience of fatherhood. edited by Brian Gresko ; introduction by Darin Strauss. Berkley Books 2014 304 p. $15 **306.874**
1. Fatherhood 2. Authors -- Family life 3. Fathers
ISBN 0425269248; 9780425269244

LC 2013050514

In this book, edited by Brian Gresko, "22 of today's masterful writers get straight to the heart of modern fatherhood. . . . From making that ultimate decision to have a kid to making it through the birth to tangling with a toddler mid-tantrum, and eventually letting a teen loose in the world, these fathers explore every facet of fatherhood and show how being a father changed the way they saw the world--and themselves." (Publisher's note)

"This impressive collection deeply probes both the exterior and interior changes that come with fatherhood." Pub Wkly

306.88 Alteration of family arrangements

Aikman, Becky

Saturday night widows; the adventures of six friends remaking their lives. Becky Aikman. Crown 2013 337 p. $26 **306.88**
1. Widows 2. Self-help groups 3. Widowhood
ISBN 0307590437; 9780307590435

LC 2012021057

This book, by Becky Aikman, profiles "six marriages, six heartbreaks, [and] one shared beginning. . . . In this . . . memoir, she explores surprising new discoveries about how people experience grief and transcend loss and, following her own remarriage, forms a group with five other young widows to test these unconventional ideas. Together, these friends summon the humor, resilience, and striving spirit essential for anyone overcoming adversity." (Publisher's note)

306.89 Separation and divorce

Green, Janice

Divorce after 50; your guide to the unique legal & financial challenges. Nolo 2010 370p pa $29.99 **306.89**
1. Divorce -- Law and legislation
ISBN 978-1-4133-1081-8; 1-4133-1081-8

LC 2009-21435

The author "explores the special legal, monetary, and emotional burdens of a marital split that occurs after age 50. She covers how to select and work with an attorney, the choice of legal mechanisms for terminating a marriage, and how to work out a fair division of marital property. . . . This book fills a gap on the self-help divorce shelf. Essential for public libraries." Libr J

Moffett, Kay

Not your mother's divorce; a practical, girl-friend-to-girlfriend guide to surviving the end of an early marriage. [by] Kay Moffett and Sarah Touborg. Broadway Bks. 2003 259p pa $12.95 **306.89**

1. Divorce
ISBN 0-7679-1350-7

LC 2003-58531

The authors "help young divorcées tackle both legal and emotional problems. . . . Overwhelming issues like mutual photographs, wedding rings, and family, as well as legal counsel, mediators, and even Internet divorce, are discussed with authority and sensitivity. The authors realize that each person is different and comes out her relationship with a different set of circumstances, so they also provide many personal stories—including their own." Libr J

Wallerstein, Judith S.

Second chances; men, women, and children a decade after divorce. [by] Judith S. Wallerstein and Sandra Blakeslee. Houghton Mifflin 2004 329p il pa $14 **306.89**

1. Divorce 2. Children of divorced parents
ISBN 0-618-44689-3; 978-0-618-44689-6

LC 2004-273131

First published 1989 by Ticknor & Fields

In 1971 the author "began a study of 131 children and adolescents from 60 families and their divorcing parents, in Marin County, California. . . . The researchers reinterviewed all family members 18 months later, again 5 years after divorce, and again 10 years after divorce. . . . 'Second Chances' is Ms. Wallerstein's account of the course and consequences of divorce for these parents and children." N Y Times Book Rev

Includes bibliographical references

306.9 Institutions pertaining to death

Encyclopedia of death and dying; edited by Glennys Howarth and Oliver Leaman. Routledge 2001 xxii, 534p il $140 **306.9**

1. Reference books 2. Death -- Encyclopedias
ISBN 0-415-18825-3

LC 2001-19234

"This work will enrich all academic and public library collections." Libr J

Includes bibliographical references and index

Handbook of death & dying; Clifton D. Bryant, editor in chief. Sage Publications 2003 2v il set $350 **306.9**

1. Death
ISBN 0-7619-2514-7

LC 2003-14864

This is "a collection of 103 comprehensive essays clustered in 10 general areas. . . . In the first volume the section 'Death in the Cultural Context' treats issues in confronting death, with essays on fear of death, death in popular culture, spiritualism, and more. The 12 essays that make up 'Death in the Social Context' consider topics such as trends in mortality, accidental death, and terrorism. Suicide, capital punishment, euthanasia, and the hospice movement are among other topics in the first volume. The second volume deals with the response to death. . . . The substantive essays are generally between 9 to 15 pages, with extensive bibliographies." Booklist

Lovejoy, Bess

Rest in pieces; the curious fates of famous corpses. Bess Lovejoy. Simon & Schuster 2013 xviii, 329 p.p ill. (hardcover) $22 **306.9**

1. Dead -- Miscellanea 2. Celebrities -- Biography 3. Celebrities -- Death -- Miscellanea 4. Celebrities -- Biography -- Miscellanea
ISBN 1451654987; 9781451654981

LC 2012034706

This book, by Bess Lovejoy, discusses how "the famous deceased have been stolen, burned, sold, pickled, frozen, stuffed, impersonated, and even filed away in a lawyer's office. . . . From Mozart to Hitler, [the book] . . . connects the lives of the famous dead to the hilarious and horrifying adventures of their corpses, and traces the evolution of cultural attitudes toward death." (Publisher's note)

Includes bibliographical references and index

Schechter, Harold

The **whole** death catalog; a lively guide to the bitter end. Ballantine Books 2009 304p il pa $18 **306.9**

1. Death
ISBN 978-0-345-49964-6

LC 2009-13779

The author "offers readers a scholarly yet wildly hilarious romp through the cultural history of death and dying. It is not only rollicking entertainment but also provides a wealth of practical and historical information about death." Libr J

Includes bibliographical references

307 Communities

Wilkerson, Isabel

★ The **warmth** of other suns; the epic story of America's great migration. Random House 2010 622p $30; ebook $30 **307**

1. Internal migration 2. African Americans -- History 3. African Americans -- Migrations -- History -- 20th century
ISBN 978-0-679-44432-9; 0-679-44432-7; 978-0-679-60407-5 ebook; 0-679-60407-3 ebook

LC 2009-49753

This book focuses on "the Great Migration (1910-1970)--the six-million-strong African American flights from the U.S. South." Author Isabel Wilkerson "seeks to tell the 'larger emotional truths' of the Migration in such ways that spotlight 'people's interior lives and motivations.' . . . Wilkerson contends that this movement was more than a demographic shift, but an action of then-unparalleled collective black agency: [I]t was the first big step the nation's servant class ever took without asking.'" (Contemporary Sociology)

An "account of the Great Migration, the 55-year stretch (1915–70) during which 6 million black Americans fled the Jim Crow South. Wilkerson, a Pulitzer Prize-winning journalist, uses the journeys of three of them — a Mississippi sharecropper, a Louisiana doctor, and a Florida laborer — to etch an indelible and compulsively readable portrait of race, class, and politics in 20th-century America. History is rarely distilled so finely." Entertainment Wkly

Includes bibliographical references

307.1 Planning and development

Binelli, Mark

Detroit City is the place to be; the afterlife of an American metropolis. Mark Binelli. Metropolitan Books 2012 318 p. (hardback) $28   **307.1**
1. Detroit (Mich.) 2. City planning -- Michigan -- Detroit 3. Cities and towns -- Michigan -- Detroit
ISBN 0805092293; 9780805092295

LC 2012016123

This book by Mark Binelli describes how the 21st century economic crisis in Detroit, Michigan, "has managed to do the unthinkable: turn the end of days into a laboratory for the future. Urban planners, land speculators, neopastoral agriculturalists, and utopian environmentalists--all have been drawn to Detroit's baroquely decaying, nothing-left-to-lose frontier. . . . We glimpse a longshot future Detroit that . . . could be the boldest reimagining of a post-industrial city in our new century." (Publisher's note)

Qin Shao

Shanghai gone; domicide and defiance in a Chinese megacity. by Qin Shao. Rowman & Littlefield Publishers, Inc. 2013 326 p. (State and society in East Asia) (cloth : alkaline paper) $79   **307.1**
1. Demonstrations 2. Shanghai (China) 3. City and town life 4. Shanghai (China) -- Social conditions 5. City planning -- China -- Shanghai -- History 6. Social change -- China -- Shanghai -- History 7. Protest movements -- China -- Shanghai -- History 8. City and town life -- China -- Shanghai -- History
ISBN 1442211318; 9781442211315; 9781442211322

LC 2012030732

This book, by Qin Shao, applies "the concept of domicide—the eradication of a home against the will of its dwellers—to the sweeping destruction of neighborhoods, families, and life patterns to make way for the new Shanghai. Here we find the holdouts and protesters, men and women who have stubbornly resisted domicide and demanded justice." (Publisher's note)

Includes bibliographical references and index

Seidman, Karl F.

Coming home to New Orleans; neighborhood rebuilding after Katrina. Karl F. Seidman. Oxford University Press 2013 xvii, 383 p.p (cloth : alk. paper) $35   **307.1**
1. Urban renewal 2. New Orleans (La.) 3. Community development 4. Hurricane Katrina, 2005 -- Social aspects 5. City planning -- Louisiana -- New Orleans -- Citizen participation 6. Urban renewal -- Louisiana

-- New Orleans -- Citizen participation 7. Economic development -- Louisiana -- New Orleans -- Citizen participation 8. Community development -- Louisiana -- New Orleans -- Citizen participation 9. Neighborhood planning -- Louisiana -- New Orleans -- Citizen participation
ISBN 0199945519; 9780199945511; 9780199945528

LC 2012033086

Author Karl F. Seidman's book addresses "neighborhood-scale recovery and the role of grassroots efforts in rebuilding New Orleans" after Hurricane Katrina. The book "provides a concise history of the recovery planning and implementation process with a new account of how the city government worked to build capacity to undertake rebuilding projects on a massive scale." (Publisher's note)

Includes bibliographical references and index

307.24 Communities -- movement from rural to urban communities

Saunders, Doug

Arrival city; Doug Saunders. Pantheon Books 2010 356p. ill.   **307.24**
1. Urbanization 2. Globalization 3. Internal migration 4. Cities and towns -- Growth
ISBN 9780375425493

LC 2010029651

In this book, the author examines "global urbanization. He concentrates on the slums and satellite communities that act as portals from villages to cities and, in turn, revitalize village economies. . . . Citing the statistical relationship between urbanization and falling poverty rates, as well as historical precedents like Paris, . . . Saunders insists urban migration means improvement overall, and that the arrival city serves as a springboard for the integration of new populations. While the picture of urbanization veers from gloomier forecasts by analysts like Mike Davis (Planet of Slums), it does so by eschewing direct questioning of the global economic system driving much of this migration." (Publishers Weekly)

Includes bibliographical references (p. 325-343) and index.

307.7 Specific kinds of communities

Carr, Patrick J.

Hollowing out the middle; the rural brain drain and what it means for America. [by] Patrick J. Carr and Maria J. Kefalas. Beacon Press 2009 239p map $26.95; pa $16   **307.7**
1. Youth -- United States 2. Cities and towns -- United States 3. Cities and towns -- Middle Western States 4. Youth -- United States -- Social conditions 5. United States -- Rural conditions -- 20th century 6. Brain drain -- United States -- History -- 20th century
ISBN 978-0-8070-4238-0; 978-0-8070-0614-6 pa

LC 2009-10392

"In 2001, with funding from the MacArthur Foundation, sociologists Patrick J. Carr and Maria J. Kefalas moved to Iowa to understand the rural brain drain and the exodus of young people from America's countryside. Articles and books - notably Richard Florida's "The Rise of the Creative Class" celebrate the migration of highly productive and creative workers to key cities. But what happens to the towns that they desert, and to the people who are left behind?" (Publisher's Note)

"Whatever the future may hold, the authors alert readers to this major change with clarity and compassion." Publ Wkly

Includes bibliographical references

Grandin, Greg

Fordlandia; the rise and fall of Henry Ford's forgotten jungle city. Metropolitan Books 2009 416p il map **307.7**

1. Plantations 2. Philanthropists 3. Ford Motor Co. 4. Automobile executives 5. Planned communities -- Brazil 6. Fordlandia Plantation (Brazil)

ISBN 0-8050-8236-0; 978-0-8050-8236-4

LC 2008049642

National Book Award Finalists (2009)

This is an account of Henry Ford's attempt to recreate small-town America in the . . . Amazon. In 1927, Ford . . . bought a tract of land twice the size of Delaware in the Brazilian Amazon. . . . Ford's early success in imposing time clocks and square dances on the jungle soon collapsed, as indigenous workers . . . turned the place into a . . . tropical boomtown. (Publisher's note) Index.

Grandin's account is an epic tale of a clash between cultures, values, man, and nature. Booklist

Includes bibliographical references

Green, Hardy

The **company** town; the industrial Edens and Satanic mills that shaped the American economy. Basic Books 2010 248p il $26.95 **307.7**

1. Cities and towns 2. Industrial relations 3. Industries -- United States 4. Industries -- United States -- History 5. Company towns -- United States -- History 6. Industrial relations -- United States -- History

ISBN 978-0-465-01826-0

LC 2010-13434

"The book provides a valuable perspective on a well-worn history, detailing the heinous, lofty, and occasionally absurd ways companies have tried to shape their workers' lives beyond factory walls." Publ Wkly

Includes bibliographical references

Mumford, Lewis

The **city** in history; its origins, its transformation, and its prospects. Harcourt Brace & World 1961 657p il hardcover o.p. pa $29 **307.7**

1. City and town life 2. Civilization -- History 3. Cities and towns -- History

ISBN 0-15-618035-9 pa

More than a history of the forms and functions of the city throughout the ages, this is a portrait of the development of

man as a religious, a political, an economic, a cultural, and a sexual being

Includes bibliographical references

The **culture** of cities. Greenwood Press 1981 586p il lib bdg $57.95 **307.7**

1. City planning 2. Cities and towns 3. Regional planning

ISBN 0-313-22746-2

LC 80-23130

First published 1938 by Harcourt Brace & Co.

Traces the growth of cities from medieval times to the twentieth century

Includes bibliographical references

Wilson, David Sloan

The **neighborhood** project; using evolution to improve my city, one block at a time. Little, Brown and Company 2011 432p $25.99; ebook $12.99 **307.7**

1. Cities and towns -- Growth 2. Cities and towns -- Civic improvement

ISBN 978-0-316-03767-9; 978-0-316-17525-8 ebook

LC 2011002752

"Although the book meanders—Wilson gives a vivid, in-depth description of several scientific studies, and offers a biography for each scientist he cites—the tangents are mostly pleasurable and provide more evidence for how lives, like ideas, intersect in fascinating ways." Publ Wkly

Includes bibliographical references

307.76   Urban communities

Made in Australia; The Future of Australian Cities. Richard Weller, Julian Bolleter. University of Western Australia Press 2013 328 p. $49.95 **307.76**

1. Australia 2. Population 3. Cities and towns 4. Architecture -- Australia 5. City planning -- Australia 6. Australia -- Social conditions 7. Australia -- Economic conditions 8. Cities and towns -- Australia -- Growth

ISBN 1742584926; 9781742584928

LC 2012537482

In this book, Richard Weller and Julian Bolleter set "the stage for the growth of eight Australian cities and their respective infrastructures." Then they "examine population trends and resource needs for each metropolitan area through 2056. They consider geographical and resource limitations on each city, along with specific population growth estimates, in a . . . discussion of options available to these cities if they are to adequately support the needs of a growing population." (Choice)

Includes bibliographical references

Smith, P. D.

★ **City**; a guidebook for the urban age. P.D. Smith. Bloomsbury 2012 383 p. **307.76**

1. Civilization 2. Urban sociology 3. Cities and towns -- HIstory 4. City and town life -- History 5. City life -- History 6. Cities and towns -- History 7. Sociology,

Urban -- History

ISBN 1608196763; 9781608196760

LC 2011051430

This book is an "illustrated guide to 7,000 years of urban life for an age when more than half of the world's population lives in cities. From the earliest Sumerian city of Eridu to the wired eco-cities of the future, [P.D.] Smith embarks on a multicentury tour highlighting urban history, customs, infrastructure, architecture, language, markets, crime, parks, cemeteries, transportation, food, and leisure activities across cultures. He . . . provid[es] panoramic yet focused views of a particular subject, such as . . . the development of language from cuneiform script to 16th-century street speech and its effect on cockney, to the new London dialect of the 21st century, Jafaican." (Publishers Weekly)

Includes bibliographical references and index

Suburban Nation: The Rise of Sprawl and the Decline of the American Dream; the rise of sprawl and the decline of the American Dream. Andres Duany, Elizabeth Plater-Zyberk, and Jeff Speck. 10th anniversary ed. North Point Press 2010 294 p. pa. $20 **307.76**

1. Suburbs 2. Urbanization 3. City planning 4. Urban renewal 5. Suburbs -- United States 6. Urban policy -- United States 7. Urbanization -- United States 8. Community development, Urban -- United States

ISBN 9780865477506

LC 2011292714

"For a decade, Suburban Nation has given voice to a growing movement in North America to put an end to suburban sprawl and replace the last century's automobile-based settlement patterns with a return to more traditional planning. Founders of the Congress for the New Urbanism, Andres Duany and Elizabeth Plater-Zyberk are at the forefront of the movement... A lively lament about the failures of postwar planning, this is also that rare book that offers solutions..." (San Francisco Chronicle)

This tenth anniversary edition includes a new preface by the authors.

"In this culmination of a 20-year crusade against suburban sprawl, the husband-and-wife architectural firm of Duany and Plater-Zyberk (DPZ) presents its manifesto for city planning. Armed with studies and statistics, the authors fault unchecked suburban growth for sapping vitality from urban centers, depleting natural resources, and breeding an alienated, enslaved automobile citizenry. Their solution is to reconsider pre-World War II methods of mixed-use planning and pedestrian-centered, environmentally sensitive design... Suburban Nation synthesizes decades of theory and experience, providing practical advice and stratagems for officials, activists, developers, and anyone else determined to say "no" to sprawl." (Library Journal)

310 Collections of general statistics

★ The **Europa** world year book 2014; 55th ed. Europa Publications 2014 2v **310**

1. Statistics 2. Reference books 3. Political science

ISBN 978-1857437140

Annual. First published 1959 with title: The Europa year book

"The best annual directory of the nations of the world. For each country it includes demographic and economic statistics, and facts about constitution and government, political parties, press, trade and industry, publishers, etc. Also incorporates a substantive section with listings and information about international organizations." Ref Sources for Small & Medium-sized Libr. 6th edition

"The best annual directory of the nations of the world. For each country it includes demographic and economic statistics, and facts about constitution and government, political parties, press, trade and industry, publishers, etc. Also incorporates a substantive section with listings and information about international organizations." Ref Sources for Small & Medium-sized Libr. 6th edition

317 General statistics of North America

★ Proquest Statistical Abstract of the United States 2013; ProQuest LLC. 1st ed. Rowman & Littlefield Pub Inc 2012 xvi, 1025 p.p (hardcover) $179 **317**

1. Almanacs 2. United States -- Census

ISBN 159888591X; 9781598885910

This almanac, published by ProQuest, offers statistical summaries of Census data and socio-demographic information of the United States as of 2013. This annually compiled work "is the best-known statistical reference publication in the country. . . . As a carefully selected collection of statistics on the social, political, and economic conditions of the United States, it is a snapshot of America and its people." (Publisher's note)

320 Political science (Politics and government)

Aristotle

Politics. Oxford University Press 1998 480p (Oxford world's classics) pa $12.95 **320**

1. Political science

ISBN 978-0-19-283393-8

"Discussion of public affairs by the most eminent of the Greek philosophers in terms applicable to many of the problems of modern political science." Pratt Alcove

Brookhiser, Richard

What would the Founders do? our questions, their answers. Basic Books 2006 261p $26 **320**

1. Statesmen -- United States 2. Presidents -- United States 3. United States -- Politics and government -- 2001-

ISBN 0-465-00819-4; 978-0-465-00819-3

The author "uses the Founders' written and oral statements to imagine their thoughts concerning contemporary issues ranging from stem cells and terrorism to censorship and gay marriage. The short answers he gives for each question can be serious or witty and are often infused with interesting historical facts." Libr J

Includes bibliographical references

Fukuyama, Francis

The **origins** of political order; from prehuman times to the French Revolution. Farrar, Straus and Giroux 2011 585p $35   **320**

1. Democracy 2. State, The 3. Comparative government
ISBN 978-0-374-22734-0; 0-374-22734-9

LC 2010-38534

Includes bibliographical references

Kaplan, Robert D.

Warrior politics; why leadership demands a pagan ethos. Random House 2002 xxii, 198p $22.95; pa $12   **320**

1. Leadership 2. Political ethics 3. International relations
ISBN 0-375-50563-6; 0-375-72627-6 pa

LC 2001-31862

"Integrating classic and contemporary scholarship, the author argues that the ills of the twentieth century are 'less unique than we think' and draws parallels between the complacency of Rome at its height and that of the U.S." Booklist

"This is a provocative, smart and polemical work that will stimulate lively discussion." Publ Wkly

Includes bibliographical references

Nathan, John

Japan unbound; a volatile nation's quest for pride and purpose. Houghton Mifflin 2004 271p $25   **320**

1. Japan -- Civilization
ISBN 0-618-13894-3

LC 2003-60559

The author "explores the dynamics of cultural continuity and change in Japan driven in part by economic stagnation. . . . The author also confronts the reader with the links between a loss of personal pride and purpose as a result of economic uncertainty, and the search for a new basis of pride and purpose in the form of heightened nationalism. . . . This book is a must for general and specialized library collections." Choice

Includes bibliographical references

Paine, Thomas

★ **Rights** of man; and, Common sense. Knopf 1994 lii, 306p $19   **320**

1. Political science 2. France -- History -- 1789-1799, Revolution 3. United States -- Politics and government -- 1775-1783, Revolution
ISBN 0-679-43314-7

LC 94-5989

This volume combines Rights of man with Common sense which was "published anonymously at Philadelphia (Jan. 10, 1776). . . . Over 100,000 copies were sold by the end of March, and it is generally considered the most important literary influence on the movement for independence." Oxford Companion to Am Lit. 5th edition

Includes bibliographical references

Purdy, Jedediah

A **tolerable** anarchy; rebels, reactionaries, and the making of American freedom. Alfred A. Knopf 2009 294p $23.95   **320**

1. Freedom 2. American national characteristics 3. United States -- Politics and government
ISBN 978-1-4000-4447-4; 1-4000-4447-2

LC 2008-49552

"The author discusses the various ways in which notions of 'freedom' have animated Americans since the eighteenth century and, in doing so, explores the notion that Americans' complicated and sometimes reluctant approaches to public responsibility may be a function of a lack of consensus about what it means to be free." Booklist

"Purdy's thesis is a work in progress by an inventive mind in evolution, a didactic and synoptic tour of American thoughts on freedom." N Y Times Book Rev

Includes bibliographical references

Unger, Miles J.

Machiavelli; a biography. Miles J. Unger. 1st Simon & Schuster hc. ed. Simon & Schuster 2011 x, 400 p.p ill. (some col.) , map (hardcover) $28 **320**

1. Authors 2. Statesmen 3. Dramatists 4. Philosophers 5. Authors, Italian -- Biography 6. Statesmen -- Italy -- Biography 7. Intellectuals -- Italy -- Biography 8. Italy -- History -- 1492-1559 -- Biography 9. Political scientists -- Italy -- Biography 10. Florence (Italy) -- History -- 1421-1737 -- Biography
ISBN 1416556281; 9781416556282

LC 2010054130

This book is Miles J. Unger's biography of Machiavelli. "Unger utilizes Machiavelli's correspondence to present a complex portrait, showing his subject in the varied public roles he played: civil servant, diplomat, political philosopher, and playwright. All of Machiavelli's writings are discussed and analyzed here." (Library Journal)

Includes bibliographical references (p. [353]-386) and index.

★ The **United** States government internet directory; edited by Shana Hertz Hattis. Bernan Press 2014 600 p. pa $72   **320**

1. Reference books 2. Web sites -- Directories 3. Internet resources -- Directories 4. Government information -- Directories
ISBN ; 1598887157; 9781598887150

LC 2010237279

Annual. First published 2004 with title: The United States government Internet manual. Published in 2009 with title: E-government and web directory

This directory "contains more than 2,000 Web site records, organized into 20 subject-themed chapters; provides descriptions and URLs for each site; . . . includes information about the sponsoring agency; notes the useful or unique aspects of the site; lists some of the major government publications hosted on the site; evaluates the most important and frequently sought sites; provides a roster of congressional members with members' Web sites includes a one-page 'Quick Guide' to the major federal agencies and the leading online library, data source, and finding aid sites; [and] highlights the Freedom of Information Act Web pages to access U.S. federal executive agency records." Publisher's note

Washington Information Directory 2014-2015. Congressional Quarterly, Inc. 2014 983 p. il. Hardcover $195 **320**
1. Reference books 2. Washington (D.C.) -- Directories
ISBN 9781483347929
Annual. First published 1975/76
"This substantial and user-friendly guide . . . [is] a vital resource for navigating Washington's intricate bureaucratic web." Libr J

320.01 Philosophy and theory

Leo Strauss's defense of the philosophic life; reading "What is political philosophy?" edited by Rafael Major. University of Chicago Press 2013 222 p. (cloth : alkaline paper) $85 **320.01**
1. Political philosophy
ISBN 0226924203; 0226924211; 9780226924205; 9780226924212
LC 2012020623
This book, edited by Rafael Major, "addresses almost every major theme in [Leo Strauss] life's work and is often viewed as a defense of his overall philosophic approach. Included are treatments of Strauss's esoteric method of reading, his critique of behavioral political science, and his views on classical political philosophy. Key thinkers whose work Strauss responded to are also analyzed in depth: Plato, Al-Farabi, Maimonides, Hobbes, and Locke." (Publisher's note)
Includes bibliographical references and index

The politics book; Big ideas simply explained. edited by Rebecca Warren and Kate Johnsen ; illustrated by James Graham. 1st American ed. DK Pub. 2013 352 p. ill. (some col.) (Big ideas simply explained) (hardcover) $25.00 **320.01**
1. Political philosophy
ISBN 1465402144; 9781465402141
LC 2012533724
This book, part of the Big Ideas Simply Explained series, looks at political philosophy. "More than 100 political philosophers, among them Confucius, Plato, Machiavelli, Mary Wollstonecraft, Karl Marx, Ito Hirobumi, Emiliano Zapata, Jomo Kenyatta, and Mao Zedong, are covered in seven chronological sections ranging from 'Ancient Political Thought' to 'Postwar Politics.'" (Library Journal)

Ryan, Alan
On politics; a history of political thought from Herodotus to the present. Alan Ryan. W. W. Norton & Co. 2012 1114 p. (hardcover) $75 **320.01**
1. Political science 2. Political philosophy 3. Political scientists -- History 4. Political science -- Philosophy -- History
ISBN 1846147794; 9780871404657; 9781846147791
LC 2012012351

This is a two-volume work that looks at the "history of political theory." The first volume covers writings "from Herodotus through Aristotle, the ancient Roman theorists of law, St. Augustine and the medievals, right up to Machiavelli." The second volume "covers the turn of the 17th century to the present. Starting with Thomas Hobbes, whom Ryan regards as the father of our modern conceptions of politics, the book ranges through Locke, Rousseau, Hegel, and Marx." (Publishers Weekly)
Includes bibliographical references and index

320.092 Biography

Jaume, Lucien
Tocqueville; the aristocratic sources of liberty. Lucien Jaume ; translated by Arthur Goldhammer. Princeton University Press 2013 356 p. (hardcover) $35 **320.092**
1. Political science 2. France -- Politics and government -- 1815-1914 3. Democracy -- Philosophy 4. Historians -- France -- Biography 5. Political science -- France -- History -- 19th century
ISBN 0691152047; 9780691152042
LC 2012032469
This book, by Lucien Jaume, focuses on "Alexis de Tocqueville . . . , the young French aristocrat who came to early America and, enthralled by what he saw, proceeded to write an American book explaining democratic America to itself. . . . Jaume provides a . . . new interpretation of Tocqueville's book as well as a fresh intellectual and psychological portrait of the author." (Publisher's note)
Includes bibliographical references and index

Judt, Tony, 1948-2010
Thinking the twentieth century; Tony Judt, with Timothy Snyder. Penguin 2012 414 p. **320.092**
1. Historians 2. Jews -- History 3. Political science 4. Philosophy -- History 5. United States -- Politics and government -- 20th century 6. College teachers 7. Nonfiction writers 8. History -- Philosophy
ISBN 9781594203237
LC 2011031473
"The book is a history of twentieth-century thought. It begins with . . . [author Tony Judt's] reflections on Jewish idealism and Jewish suffering in Europe and ends with a devastating account of the failure of American politics in the post-cold war world. It is also an intellectual autobiography. . . . [Topics include] the argument . . . for a one-state solution in Israel . . . [and] Friedrich Hayek's ideas about economics and state planning." (New York Review of Books)
Includes bibliographical references

320.1 The state

Cicero, Marcus Tullius, 106-43 B.C.
The **republic;** and, The laws; [by] Cicero; translated by Niall Rudd; with an introduction and notes by Jonathan Powell and Niall Rudd. Oxford Univer-

sity Press 1998 xliii, 242p (Oxford world's classics)
pa $12.95   **320.1**
1. State, The 2. Political science 3. Rome -- History
ISBN 978-0-19-283236-8; 0-19-283236-0

LC 97-23394

"Cicero's The Republic is an impassioned plea for responsible government written just before the civil war that ended the Roman Republic in a dialogue following Plato. Drawing on Greek political theory, the work embodies the mature reflections of a Roman ex-consul on the nature of political organization, on justice in society, and on the qualities needed in a statesman. Its sequel, The Laws , expounds the influential doctrine of Natural Law, which applies to all mankind, and sets out an ideal code for a reformed Roman Republic, already half in the realm of utopia." Publisher's note

Includes bibliographical references

Hobbes, Thomas

★ **Leviathan**; edited with an introduction and notes by J.C.A. Gaskin. Oxford University Press 2008 lv, 508p (Oxford world's classics) pa $9.95   **320.1**
1. State, The 2. Political science
ISBN 978-0-19-953728-0

First published 1651

"A treatise on the origin and ends of government. . . . This work, a defense of secular monarchy, written while the Puritan Commonwealth ruled England, contains Hobbes's famous theory of the sovereign state." Benet's Reader's Ency. 4th edition

Machiavelli, Niccolo

★ The **prince**. Knopf 1992 xxxi, 190p (Everyman's library) $16   **320.1**
1. Political ethics 2. Political science
ISBN 0-679-41044-9

LC 91-53225

Written in 1513

"A handbook of advice on the acquisition, use, and maintenance of political power, dedicated to Lorenzo de Medici." Haydn. Thesaurus of Book Dig

Rousseau, Jean-Jacques

★ The **social** contract; translated by Maurice Cranston. Penguin Books 2006 167p pa $10 **320.1**
1. Political science
ISBN 978-0-14-303749-1; 0-14-303749-8

LC 2006-43772

First published 1762

"A treatise on the origins and organization of government and the rights of citizens. Rousseau's thesis states that, since no man has any natural authority over another, the social contract, freely entered into, creates natural reciprocal obligations between citizens." Benet's Reader's Ency. 4th edition

Includes bibliographical references

Runciman, David

Political hypocrisy; the mask of power, from Hobbes to Orwell and beyond. Princeton University Press 2008 272p il $29.95   **320.1**
1. Political ethics
ISBN 978-0-691-12931-0; 0-691-12931-2

LC 2007-46793

"A very intelligent, subtle, and learned guide to the classics and to the preeminent historical examples of hypocrisy from Mandeville and Hobbes, to Jefferson and the Victorians." Times Lit Suppl

Includes bibliographical references (p. 245-258)

320.4   Structure and functions of government

Han, Lori Cox

Handbook to American democracy; Lori Cox Han and Tomislav Han. Facts On File 2011 224 p.   **320.4**
1. United States -- History 2. Democracy -- United States -- History 3. United States -- Politics and government 4. United States -- Politics and government -- Handbooks, manuals, etc
ISBN 0816078548; 9780816078547

LC 2011005185

The authors "address the foundations of American democracy and the three branches of American government. The books introduce offices, history, and issues in eight chapters each (e.g., 'The Founding Fathers and the American Revolution,' 'How Congress Is Organized,' and 'Vice Presidents, Presidential Advisers, and America's First Ladies'). The material is complemented by black-and-white photos and sidebars on legal cases, laws and legislation, statistics, maps, biographies of major figures such as Henry VIII, and other primary materials, and chapters close with a summary. . . . [The volumes] each include an individual glossary, index, selected bibliography, and table of contents." (Libr J)

Includes bibliographical references and index

320.5   Political ideologies

Allitt, Patrick

★ The **conservatives**; ideas and personalities throughout American history. Yale University Press 2009 325p $35   **320.5**
1. Conservatism 2. United States -- Politics and government
ISBN 978-0-300-11894-0; 0-300-11894-5

LC 2008-42559

"From present-day questions of taxation and big government, Allitt traces conservative principles to the earliest days of the republic. . . . Cutting across the stereotypes of present-day conservatism, this nuanced, thoughtful history should educate the unaffiliated and help the disillusioned recover." Publ Wkly

Includes bibliographical references

Brown, Archie

★ The **rise** and fall of communism. Ecco 2009
720p il map $35.99   **320.5**
   1. Communism
   ISBN 0-06-113879-7; 978-0-06-113879-9
Brown has crafted a readable and judicious account
of Communist history, from its theoretical beginnings in
19th-century Europe to its practical collapse at the end of
the 1980s, that is both controversial and commonsensical.
. . . Given the immense sweep of time, ideology and geography he strives to cover in 600-odd pagesas Brown observes, almost every one of his chapters could be a book
on its ownThe Rise and Fall of Communism is a work of
considerable delicacy and nuance. Salon
   Includes bibliographical references

Ezekiel, Raphael S.

The **racist** mind; portraits of American Neo-Na-
zis and Klansmen. Viking 1995 xxxv, 330p hardcover o.p. pa $20   **320.5**
   1. Racism 2. Ku Klux Klan 3. White supremacy
movements 4. White Aryan Resistance 5. United
States -- Race relations
   ISBN 0-14-023449-7 pa
                    LC 94-45177
"White supremacy groups are examined in this brutally
honest portrait of hate and fear, based on personal interviews and interactions. A disturbingly provocative look at
the frightening ignorance existing in the 1990s." Booklist
   Includes bibliographical references

Potter, Will

Green is the new red. City Lights Books 2011
301 p.   **320.5**
   1. Ecoterrorism 2. Political activists 3. Environmental
movement
   ISBN 9780872865389
                  LC 2010053209
It was the author's intent to demonstrate that "the U.S.
government is using post-9/11 anti-terrorism resources to
target environmentalists and animal rights activists. . . .
Tracing funds from animal-exploiting corporations to Congress and the passing of the big business-friendly Animal
Enterprise Terrorism Act, Potter reports on an increased usage of the terrorism enhancement in court cases. . . . [Will]
Potter warns of the crumbling of the 'legal wall separating
"terrorist" from "dissident" or "undesirable" and concludes
his account with a call to action and a decry of the injustice
that results in the "terrorist" label being put on those who
threaten American corporate interests." (Publishers weekly)
   Includes bibliographical references and index.

320.50973   Political ideologies -- United States

Self, Robert O.

All in the family; the realignment of American
democracy since the 1960s. Robert O. Self. Hill and
Wang 2012 528 p. (alk. paper) $30.00 **320.50973**
   1. United States -- History 2. United States -- Social
conditions 3. United States -- Politics and government
4. United States -- Social conditions -- 1945- 5.

Families -- Political aspects -- United States 6. United
States -- Politics and government -- 1989- 7. Social
values -- Political aspects -- United States 8. United
States -- Politics and government -- 1945-1989
   ISBN 0809095025; 9780809095025
                  LC 2011051271
In this book, Professor Robert O. Self "attempts to make
sense of the shift in American politics and social movements from 1964 through 2004, from the 'center-left social
welfare polity' of the mid-20th century to the 'center-right
free market system' of the 21st century. There's a heavy
focus on gender and sexuality, covering everything from
the women's movement to abortion and antifeminism."
(Publishers Weekly)

320.51   Liberalism

Brennan, Jason

Libertarianism; what everyone needs to know.
by Jason Brennan. Oxford University Press 2012
xvi, 213 p.p (hardback) $74; (pbk.) $16.95 **320.51**
   1. Libertarianism 2. Republican Party (U.S.) 3.
Libertarianism -- United States 4. United States --
Politics and government
   ISBN 0199933898; 019993391X; 9780199933891;
9780199933914
                  LC 2012020049
Author Jason Brennan "offers a nuanced portrait of
libertarianism, proceeding through a series of questions to
illuminate the essential elements of libertarianism and the
problems the philosophy addresses, including such topics as
the Value of Liberty, Human Nature and Ethics, Economic
Liberty, Civil Rights, Social Justice and the Poor, Government and Democracy, and Contemporary Politics." (Publisher's note)
   Includes bibliographical references (p. [191]-198)
and index

Carville, James

★ It's the middle class, stupid! James Carville
and Stan Greenberg. Blue Rider Press 2012 321 p.
$26.95   **320.51**
   1. Middle class 2. Equality -- United States 3. United
States -- Social conditions 4. Politics, Practical -- United
States 5. United States -- Politics and government --
2009- 6. United States -- Politics and government --
2001-2009
   ISBN 0399160396; 9780399160394
                  LC 2012018191
In this book, "[James] Carville . . . and [Stan] Greenberg
offer a plea to save America's floundering middle class. . . .
The authors outline a grim cycle of 'institutionalize inequality,' declining wages, reduced benefits, and skyrocketing
higher education prices, all of which that are blocking middle class children from top educations and, later on, career
benefits." (Publishers Weekly)
   Includes bibliographical references.

320.6   Policy making

Collins, Gail

As Texas goes; how the Lone Star State hijacked the American agenda. Gail Collins. Liveright Pub. Corporation 2012 267 p.   **320.6**

1. Texas -- History 2. Social policy -- Texas 3. Economic policy -- Texas 4. Texas -- Politics and government 5. Texas -- Social policy 6. Texas -- Economic policy 7. Texas -- Politics and government -- 1951-
ISBN 0871404079; 9780871404077

LC 2012007794

This book is a "study of Texas's government and its discontents. New York Times columnist [Gail] Collins . . . argues . . . [that Texas] is a disastrous model of public policy that inspired the Republican Party's national platform: a rickety economic boom based on insecure, poverty-level jobs and massive state incentives to corporations; financial deregulation that led to banking meltdowns; a raft of ill-advised education nostrums." (Publishers Weekly)

Includes bibliographical references and index

320.973   Politics -- United States

Bawer, Bruce

The **victims'** revolution; the rise of identity studies and the closing of the liberal mind. Bruce Bawer. Broadside Books 2012 378 p.   **320.973**

1. Humanities 2. Group identity 3. Learning and scholarship 4. United States -- Intellectual life 5. Identity politics -- United States 6. Group identity -- Political aspects -- United States
ISBN 0061807370; 9780061807374

LC 2012032311

This book, by Bruce Bawer, offers a "critique of the identity-based revolution that has transformed American campuses." In "the 1960s and '70s, . . . a new generation of scholar-activists rejected traditional humanism in favor of a radical ideology that denied esthetic merit and objective truth. . . . Bawer concludes that . . . these programs ha[ve] impoverished our thought [and] confused our politics . . . with politically correct mush." (Publisher's note)

Includes bibliographical references and index

Edwards, Mickey

The **parties** versus the people; how to turn Republicans and Democrats into Americans. Mickey Edwards. Yale University Press 2012 xxiii, 208 p.p (hardcover) $25   **320.973**

1. Democratic Party (U.S.) 2. Republican Party (U.S.) 3. United States -- Politics and government 4. Democracy -- United States 5. Political parties -- United States 6. Two-party systems -- United States 7. Divided government -- United States 8. Polarization (Social sciences) -- United States
ISBN 0300184565; 9780300184563

LC 2012013008

This book, by Mickey Edwards, "identifies exactly how [the American] . . . political and governing systems reward intransigence, discourage compromise, and undermine our democracy. He then describes exactly what must be done

to banish the negative effects of partisan warfare from our political system. . . . He offers graphic examples of how this problem has intensified and reveals how political battles have become nothing more than conflicts between party machines." (Publisher's note)

Includes bibliographical references (p. 187-192) and index.

321.8   Democratic government

Dobson, William J.

The **dictator's** learning curve; inside the global battle for democracy. by William J. Dobson. Doubleday 2012 341p. $28.95   **321.8**

1. Democracy 2. Dictators 3. Dictatorship 4. Democratization
ISBN 0385533357; 9780385533355

LC 2011050286

This book presents a "study of how heavy-handed repression by authoritarian regimes has given way to more subtle forms of control. Despite some reassuring advances in democracy over the last 40 years. . . . [William J.] Dobson sees a pernicious, no-less-repressive shift in the tactics of autocrats still hanging on. . . . Dobson travels around the globe, from Malaysia to Venezuela, chronicling his encounters with both camps." (Kirkus Reviews)

Includes bibliographical references and index

321.9   Authoritarian government

Arendt, Hannah

★ **Origins** of totalitarianism; new ed with added prefaces; Harcourt Brace Jovanovich 1973 xliii, 527p pa $19   **321.9**

1. Imperialism 2. Antisemitism 3. Totalitarianism
ISBN 0-15-670153-7
First published 1951 in the United Kingdom with title: The burden of our time

In this book, the author documents her "belief that Nazism and Communism had their roots in the anti-Semitism and imperialism of the 19th century." Benet's Reader's Ency. 4th edition

Includes bibliographical references

Paxton, Robert O.

★ The **anatomy** of fascism; [by] Robert Paxton. Knopf 2004 321p $26; pa $15   **321.9**

1. Fascism
ISBN 1-4000-4094-9; 1-4000-3391-8 pa

LC 2004-100489

"While there are countless studies on fascism, readers will be hard pressed to find anything more in-depth from a scholar with Paxton's credentials." Libr J

Includes bibliographical references

322 Relation of the state to organized groups and their members

Buruma, Ian

Taming the gods; religion and democracy on three continents. Princeton University Press 2010 142p $19.95 **322**

1. Democracy 2. Church and state 3. China -- Religion 4. Japan -- Religion 5. Europe -- Religion 6. Religion and state 7. United States -- Religion 8. Democracy -- Religious aspects

ISBN 978-0-691-13489-5; 0-691-13489-8

LC 2009-31550

The author "tackles the vexing issue of the religious challenge to liberal democracy.... Buruma is that rare bird equally at home not only in Europe and America, but also in East and West. He devotes a chapter to Europe and America, one to China and Japan, and a third to Europe again, but this time focused on its confrontation with Islam. Throughout all, Buruma sounds a recurrent note: the toxicity of blending religion and politics, whether when religion usurps the mantle of politics or politics usurps that of religion." Globe and Mail

Includes bibliographical references

Power, Inc. the epic rivalry between big business and government-- and the reckoning that lies ahead. David Rothkopf. Farrar, Straus and Giroux 2011 436 p. **322**

1. Capitalism 2. Industrial policy 3. Economics -- History 4. Business and politics 5. Big business 6. Capitalism -- Political aspects

ISBN 9780374151287

LC 2011036672

In this book, "[David] Rothkopf . . . uses . . . examples . . . to show the massive influence big business wields in our world and claims that our current economic struggles are not new but, rather, have their roots in history. The rivalry between public and private power has existed for centuries, and, Rothkopf argues, must be managed to achieve a balance that will work for the future. He examines the watershed years of 1288, 1648, 1776, and 1848 to illustrate the common threads of this struggle through history. Whether it is the Treaty of Westphalia, the Industrial Revolution, or the fall of communism, Rothkopf puts an economic spin on historic events and times of change. (Libr J)

Includes bibliographical references and index

Preston, Andrew

Sword of the spirit, shield of faith; religion in American war and diplomacy. by Andrew Preston. Alfred A. Knopf 2012 815 p. **322**

1. Protestantism 2. Military policy -- United States 3. United States -- Foreign relations 4. Religion and politics -- United States 5. International relations -- Religious aspects 6. United States -- Military policy -- Religious aspects 7. United States -- Foreign relations -- Religious aspects 8. United States -- History, Military -- Religious aspects 9. Religion and international relations -- United States -- History

ISBN 9781400043231

LC 2011035138

It was the author's intention to provide an "examination of the consistent application of the founding religious principles to American foreign policy, from the colonists' sense of a Protestant exceptionalism to President Obama's 'Good Niebuhr Policy.' . . . [Author Andrew] Preston explores this fascinating paradox of a nation founded on freedom of religion yet exhibiting, in its relations with the wider world, a profound belief in a Judeo-Christian sense of 'exceptional virtue.'" (Kirkus Reviews)

Includes bibliographical references and index

Tobin, Jacqueline

★ From Midnight to Dawn; the last tracks of the underground railroad. [by] Jacqueline Tobin with Hettie Jones. Doubleday 2006 272p il hardcover o.p. pa $14 **322**

1. Abolitionists 2. Underground railroad 3. Slavery -- United States

ISBN 978-0-385-51431-6; 0-385-51431-X; 978-1-4000-7936-0 pa; 1-4000-7936-5 pa

LC 2006-46304

"There's an enlightening portrait of Josiah Henson (the model for Stowe's Uncle Tom) as a political activist, a fascinating look at the pioneering journalist and early feminist Mary Ann Shadd and an intriguing section on the deep 'Canadian connection to Harpers Ferry,' as John Brown meets with the fugitives in Chatham. Accessible and fluidly written, the book will appeal to general readers." Publ Wkly

Includes bibliographical references

Winters, Michael Sean

God's right hand; Michael Sean Winters. HarperOne 2012 384p. **322**

1. Religion and politics 2. Christianity -- United States 3. Fundamentalism 4. Moral Majority, Inc 5. Religious right -- United States 6. Church and state -- United States 7. United States -- Moral conditions 8. United States -- Social conditions 9. Christianity and politics -- United States 10. Baptists -- United States -- Clergy -- Biography

ISBN 9780061970672

LC 2011031293

The book offers a "biography of the . . . conservative pastor who reshaped the landscape of American politics- -Jerry Falwell. . . . He was a man of strong views--and he knew that those views were shared by millions of Americans who were disengaged with public life. Falwell led them into the public square, articulated a coherent rationale for their involvement with politics, and made them the largest and most organized constituency in the contemporary Republican Party." (Publisher's note)

322.4 Political action groups

Chalmers, David Mark

Hooded Americanism: the history of the Ku Klux Klan; 3rd ed; Duke Univ. Press 1987 477p il hardcover o.p. pa $24.95 **322.4**

1. Ku Klux Klan

ISBN 0-8223-0772-3 pa

LC 86-29133

First published 1965 by Doubleday; this is a reissue of the 1981 edition published by Watts

This book recounts the history of the Klan. It describes the sociological and psychological forces behind the Klan, and sets forth its dogmas

"The book is written in a breezy, journalistic style. . . . Especially instructive and sobering is Chalmers' account of the role of the Klan in politics." J Am Hist

Includes bibliographical references

Conner, Claire

Wrapped in the flag; a personal history of America's radical right. Claire Conner. Beacon Press 2013 264 p. (alk. paper) $25.95   **322.4**
1. Conservatism 2. John Birch Society 3. United States -- Politics and government -- 1945-1989 4. Right-wing extremists -- United States -- History -- 20th century 5. Right and left (Political science) -- United States -- History -- 20th century
ISBN 080707750X; 9780807077504

                 LC 2012049353

This book provides an insider's view of the John Birch Society (JBS), "the most radical right-wing organization of the Cold War era." It "describes the seeming paranoia and questionable logic of the most devoted JBS members. [Claire] Conner provides . . . descriptions of many of the eccentric JBS leaders, including founder Robert Welch. . . . She describes her evolution from a fervently pro-life organizer to a somewhat disillusioned woman who is more" pro-choice. (Library Journal)

Includes bibliographical references and index

Esposito, John L.

Unholy war; terror in the name of Islam. Oxford Univ. Press 2002 196p hardcover o.p. pa $15.95   **322.4**
1. Islam and politics 2. Terrorism -- Religious aspects 3. United States -- Foreign opinion
ISBN 0-19-515435-5; 0-19-516886-0 pa

                 LC 2001-58009

The author "explains the teachings of Islam—the Quran, the example of the Prophet, Islamic law—about jihad or holy war, the use of violence, and terrorism. He chronicles the rise of extremist groups and examines their frightening worldview and tactics." Publisher's note

Includes bibliographical references

Gandhi, Mahatma

★ **Gandhi** on non-violence; selected texts from Mohandas K. Gandhi's Non-violence in peace and war. edited with an introduction by Thomas Merton; preface by Mark Kurlansky. New Directions 2007 101p pa $13.95   **322.4**
1. Passive resistance 2. India -- Politics and government
ISBN 978-0-8112-1686-9

                 LC 2007-32262

First published 1965

In an introductory essay Merton "considers Gandhi's ideas, not in relation to their Indian context, but in terms of their applicability to all men's lives. Brief quotations from Gandhi's writings make up most of the book." Asia: a Guide to Paperbacks

Includes bibliographical references

Hamilton, Neil A.

Rebels and renegades; a chronology of social and political dissent in the United States. Routledge 2002 361p il $100; pa. $48.95   **322.4**
1. Radicalism 2. Right and left (Political science)
ISBN 0-415-93639-X; 9780415869386

                 LC 2002-8916

The author "examines the historical role that radicals and reactionaries have played in shaping American society and culture. Arranged in nine chapters, the book features a chronological format that begins in 1620 with the Pilgrims and ends with the September 11, 2001 terrorist attacks. Each chapter opens with an overview of the time period, and individual entries consist of one- or two-page descriptions of radicals, their activities, and their impact." Libr J

Includes bibliographical references

Ronson, Jon

Them : adventures with extremists. Simon & Schuster 2002 330p $24; pa $13   **322.4**
1. Radicalism 2. Conspiracies
ISBN 0-7432-2707-7; 0-7432-3321-2 pa

                 LC 2001-47411

First published 2001 in the United Kingdom

This book "is at times funny, other times unsettling, but always astonishing. So difficult to accept are Ronson's narratives that any conclusions must be left up to the reader." Booklist

323   Civil and political rights

Arsenault, Raymond

★ **Freedom** riders; 1961 and the struggle for racial justice. Oxford University Press 2006 690p il map (Pivotal moments in American history) $32.50   **323**
1. Congress of Racial Equality 2. Segregation in transportation 3. African Americans -- Segregation 4. African Americans -- Civil rights 5. Southern States -- Race relations 6. Civil rights -- Constitutional history 7. Civil rights movements -- Southern States 8. Civil rights workers -- Southern states -- History 9. African Americans -- Segregation -- Southern States 10. Civil rights activists -- Southern States -- History 11. Segregation in transportation -- Southern States -- History 12. Civil rights workers -- United States -- History -- 20th century 13. African Americans -- Civil rights -- Southern States -- History -- 20th century
ISBN 0-19-513674-8; 978-0-19-513674-6

                 LC 2005-18108

This is a history of the "six months [in 1961] in which black and white volunteers descended on the South to challenge segregated travel." N Y Times (Late N Y Ed)

Includes bibliographical references

Berry, Mary Frances

My face is black is true; Callie House and the struggle for ex-slave reparations. Knopf 2006 314p il $26.95; pa $14.95 **323**

1. Needleworkers 2. Laundry workers 3. Social activists 4. African Americans -- Reparations 5. African American women -- Biography

ISBN 1-4000-4003-5 Knopf; 0-307-27705-4 pa, Vintage; 978-0-307-27705-3 pa, Vintage

LC 2004-51330

The author "unearths the intriguing story of Callie House (1861–1928), a Tennessee washerwoman and seamstress become activist, and the organization she led, the National Ex-Slave Mutual Relief, Bounty and Pension Association. . . . Students and scholars of African-American history, as well as those engaged in the current reparations debates, will be deeply informed by the rise and fall of the Ex-Slave Association." Publ Wkly

Includes bibliographical references

Brinkley, Douglas

Rosa Parks. Viking 2000 246p (Penguin lives series) hardcover o.p. pa $13 **323**

1. Civil rights activists 2. African Americans -- Civil rights 3. African American women -- Biography

ISBN 0-670-89160-6; 0-14-303600-9 pa

LC 00-35916

"Rosa Parks' story takes readers from rural Alabama to the Montgomery Industrial School for Girls, marriage to barber Raymond Parks, quiet activism in the '30s and '40s, a first experience of integration at the Highlander Folk School, arrest in 1955 and the bus boycott, a move to Detroit, and more than 20 years on the staff of Rep. John Conyers (D-Mich.)." Booklist

Includes bibliographical references

Cleaver, Eldridge

Target zero; a life in writing. edited by Kathleen Cleaver; foreword by Henry Louis Gates, Jr.; afterword by Cecil Brown. Palgrave Macmillan 2005 xxvi, 336p $27.95; pa $16.95 **323**

1. Dissenters 2. Memoirists 3. Civil rights activists

ISBN 978-1-4039-6237-9; 1-4039-6237-5; 978-1-4039-7657-4 pa; 1-4039-7657-0 pa

LC 2005-51252

"The book's four parts chart Cleaver's life trhough his essays, short stories, letters, interviews, and poems, many previously unpublished. . . . This well-crafted reader . . . is a rich experience." Choice

"The book's four parts chart Cleaver's life trhough his essays, short stories, letters, interviews, and poems, many previously unpublished. . . . This well-crafted reader . . . is a rich experience." Choice

Includes bibliographical references

Cotton, Dorothy

If your back's not bent; the role of the Citizenship Education Program in the civil rights movement. Dorothy F. Cotton. Atria Books 2012 xxi, 323 p.p ill. (hardcover) $25 **323**

1. Civil rights -- United States -- History 2. Citizenship Education Program -- History 3. African American women educators -- Biography 4. Southern Christian Leadership Conference -- History 5. African American women civil rights workers -- Biography 6. United States -- Race relations -- History -- 20th century 7. African Americans -- Civil rights -- History -- 20th century 8. Civil rights movements -- United States -- History -- 20th century

ISBN 0743296834; 9780743296830; 9780743296847; 9781439187425

LC 2012004463

This book looks at the "Citizen Education Program (CEP), an adult grassroots training program directed by Dorothy Cotton" during the Civil Rights Movement era. The book "recounts the accomplishments and the drama of this training that was largely ignored by the media" and "describes who participated and how they were transformed . . . from victims to active citizens, and how they transformed their communities and ultimately the country into a place of greater freedom and justice for all." (Publisher's note)

Dershowitz, Alan M.

★ Rights from wrongs; a secular theory of the origins of rights. Basic Books 2004 261p $24 **323**

1. Civil rights 2. Human rights

ISBN 0-465-01713-4

LC 2004-20006

The author "asserts that human rights derive from the world's experience with 'wrongs,' i.e., injustice. Only after seeing genocide, for example, did the notion develop that this was a violation of human rights. Dershowitz . . . has a rare ability to develop complex ideas in readable prose. . . . Whether conservative or liberal, absolutist or relativist, readers will find areas of disagreement, but most will concur that a talented and creative legal mind is at work." Publ Wkly

Includes bibliographical references

Dyson, Michael Eric

I may not get there with you: the true Martin Luther King, Jr. Free Press 2000 404p $25; pa $15 **323**

1. Clergy 2. Nonfiction writers 3. Civil rights activists 4. Nobel laureates for peace 5. African Americans -- Biography 6. African Americans -- Civil rights

ISBN 0-684-86776-1; 0-684-83037-X pa

LC 99-40478

Dyson "believes that the ministry fostered King's rhetorical gifts but also encouraged his authoritarian personality. We learn much about his flaws, and about conflict, dissent, and generational differences within the black community, as Dyson insists that King, properly understood, remains a controversial figure." New Yorker

Includes bibliographical references

Hartman, Saidiya V.

★ Lose your mother; a journey along the Atlantic slave route. [by] Saidiya Hartman. Farrar, Straus and Giroux 2007 270p il $25; pa $14 **323**

1. Slave trade 2. Ghana -- Description and travel

ISBN 978-0-374-27082-7; 0-374-27082-1; 978-0-374-53115-7 pa; 0-374-53115-3 pa

LC 2006-29407

This "is a groundbreaking book for its ability to combine autobiography, history, and politics in an unprecedented style. . . . Hartman's book is not just to be read by historians of slavery or the Atlantic World, but by all of those who desire to write of the past." Rev Am Hist

Includes bibliographical references

Human rights in our own backyard; injustice and resistance in the United States. edited by William T. Armaline, Davita Silfen Glasberg, and Bandana Purkayastha. 1st ed. University of Pennsylvania Press 2011 xiv, 325 p.p (hardcover : alk. paper) $59.95 **323**

1. Social justice 2. Human rights -- United States 3. United States -- Social conditions 4. Human rights -- Government policy -- United States

ISBN 0812243609; 9780812243604

LC 2011024455

In this book, edited by William T. Armaline, Davita Silfen Glasberg, and Bandana Purkayastha, "the contributors . . . argue that many of the greatest immediate and structural threats to human rights, and some of the most significant efforts to realize human rights in practice, can be found in" the United States. The book asks, "[h]ow do people in the U.S. address human rights issues? What strategies have they adopted, and how successful have they been?" (Publisher's note)

Includes bibliographical references and index

King, Martin Luther, Jr., 1929-1968

The **autobiography** of Martin Luther King, Jr; edited by Clayborne Carson. Warner Bks. 1998 400p il $25; pa $15.95 **323**

1. Clergy 2. Nonfiction writers 3. Civil rights activists 4. Nobel laureates for peace 5. African Americans -- Biography 6. African Americans -- Civil rights

ISBN 0-446-52412-3; 0-446-67650-0 pa

LC 98-35704

"Carson, director of Martin Luther King Jr. Papers Project, brings together selections from King's writings, speeches, and recordings to create this fascinating 'autobiography' of the famed civil rights leader and Nobel Peace Prize winner. The writings trace King's struggles with religion, philosophy, and the racial politics of the U.S." Booklist

Includes bibliographical references

Kotz, Nick

★ **Judgment** days; Lyndon Baines Johnson, Martin Luther King, Jr., and the laws that changed America. Houghton Mifflin 2005 522p $26 **323**

1. Clergy 2. Presidents 3. Vice-presidents 4. Senators 5. Nonfiction writers 6. Members of Congress 7. Civil rights activists 8. Civil Rights Act of 1964 9. Nobel laureates for peace 10. Voting Rights Act of 1965 11. United States -- Race relations 12. United States -- Politics and government -- 1961-1974

ISBN 0-618-08825-3

LC 2004-59852

This is a "narrative of how President Johnson and King temporarily overcame their mutual suspicion to battle successfully for the Civil Rights Acts of 1964 and 1968 and the 1965 Voting Rights Act. . . . This book is an informed politi-

cal investigation of these two civil rights warriors and the cause for which they fought and, in King's case, died." Libr J

Lourie, Richard

Sakharov; a biography. University Press of New England 2002 465p il $35 **323**

1. Physicists 2. Dissenters 3. Nobel laureates for peace 4. Political and social philosophers

ISBN 1-58465-207-1

LC 2001-5246

A biography "of Andrei Sakharov, the nuclear physicist who developed into an authentic apostle of humanity and democracy in the former Soviet Union." N Y Times Book Rev

"Utilizing newly accessible KGB files as well as Sakharov's personal correspondence, Lourie provides a revealing portrait of an extraordinary man to whom the world owes a great debt." Booklist

Includes bibliographical references

Schulz, William F.

In our own best interest; how defending human rights benefits us all. foreword by Mary Robinson. Beacon Press 2001 235p $25; pa $15 **323**

1. Human rights

ISBN 0-8070-0226-7; 0-8070-0227-5 pa

LC 2001-392

According to the author, "defending human rights pays off not only in terms of justice, but also in ways that can include greater economic growth, a more protected environment, better public health, and a generally less violent world." America

Includes bibliographical references (p. {203}-224) and index

Shipler, David K.

The **rights** of the people; how our search for safety invades our liberties. Alfred A. Knopf 2011 366p $27.95; ebook $13.99 **323**

1. Civil rights 2. Law enforcement 3. Rule of law -- United States 4. Civil rights -- United States

ISBN 978-1-4000-4362-0; 978-0-307-59550-8 ebook

LC 2010-34255

The book "offers provocative real-life accounts of how privacy has been sacrificed in the modern era. The outlines of some of the stories he tells are familiar, such as the arrest of Brandon Mayfield, a Muslim lawyer in Portland, Oregon, whose fingerprint the FBI erroneously 'matched' to fingerprints from the Madrid train bombing in 2004. . . . [David K.] Shipler's goal is not to reformulate legal doctrine but to show us, through the experience of Americans subject to intrusive police tactics, where existing doctrine has left us; we live in a world where a federal judge can resignedly say, as Shipler quotes US District Judge Paul Friedman, 'I don't think that there's much left of the Fourth Amendment in criminal law.' As Shipler . . . illustrates, the dual wars on drugs and terror have brought us to this point. Time and again, constitutional law has bent to the imperatives of the state in conflict." (New York Review of Books)

"Identifying five periods in American history when the Bill of Rights has been under particular assault, Shipler . . . argues that we are in the middle of a sixth, a post-9/11 era in which our liberties are once again endangered. .

. . A timely call for vigilance, for insisting on the protections the Framers provided against an always overreaching government." Kirkus

Includes bibliographical references

Sugrue, Thomas J.

Sweet land of liberty; the forgotten struggle for civil rights in the North. Random House 2008 xxviii, 688p il $35   323

1. United States -- Race relations 2. African Americans -- Civil rights

ISBN 978-0-679-64303-6; 0-679-64303-6

LC 2008-2081

The author "shows that black exclusion, poverty, and racial violence permeated America on both sides of the Mason-Dixon Line. . . . This splendid read brims with insights broadening and deepening understanding of the black-white mold of modern America. Highly recommended and essential for collections on U.S. history, social movements, race relations, or civil rights." Libr J

Includes bibliographical references

Theoharis, Jeanne

The **rebellious** life of Mrs. Rosa Parks; Jeanne Theoharis. Beacon Press 2012 360 p. (hardcover : alk. paper) $27.95   323.092

1. Montgomery (Ala.) -- Biography 2. Montgomery (Ala.) -- Race relations 3. Civil rights workers -- Alabama -- Montgomery -- Biography 4. African American women civil rights workers -- Alabama -- Montgomery -- Biography 5. Segregation in transportation -- Alabama -- Montgomery -- History -- 20th century 6. African Americans -- Civil rights -- Alabama -- Montgomery -- History -- 20th century

ISBN 0807050474; 9780807050477; 9780807050484

LC 2012031992

This book by Jeanne Theoharis is a "political biography of Rosa Parks [that] examines her six decades of activism, challenging perceptions of her as an accidental actor in the civil rights movement. . . . [Theoharis] shows readers how this civil rights movement radical sought--for more than a half a century--to expose and eradicate the American racial-caste system in jobs, schools, public services, and criminal justice." (Publisher's note)

Includes bibliographical references and index

323.1   Civil and political rights of nondominant groups

Boyd, Herb

★ We shall overcome; a living history of the civil rights struggle told in words, pictures and the voices of the participants. Sourcebooks 2004 272p il $45   323.1

1. African Americans -- Civil rights

ISBN 1-402-20213-X

LC 2004-12509

"Through text, images, and actual recordings (found on 2 CDs), Boyd . . . presents some of the major events in the Civil Rights Movement, including the murder of Em-

mett Till, the march on Washington, and the life and death of Martin Luther King Jr." Libr J

Includes bibliographical references

Branch, Taylor, 1947-

★ **Pillar** of fire; America in the King years, 1963-65. Simon & Schuster 1998 746p il hardcover o.p.   323.1

1. Clergy 2. Nonfiction writers 3. Civil rights activists 4. Nobel laureates for peace 5. African Americans -- Civil rights 6. United States -- History -- 1961-1969 7. United States -- History -- 1961-1974 8. Afro-Americans -- Civil rights -- History -- 20th century

ISBN 0-684-84809-0 pa

LC 97-46076

"Branch began telling the story of the civil rights movement in his . . . Parting the Waters: America in the King Years, 1954-63. Here he picks up where he left off, narrating the history of the years 1963-65, when the movement won . . . the Civil Rights Act of 1964 and the Voting Rights Act of 1965." (Commonweal) Bibliography. Index.

"Branch's research is impeccable and his knowledge of his material solid. . . . The book is significant for marshaling so much information, particularly the profiles of all the many individuals involved in the race issues of that time." Booklist

Includes bibliographical references

The **economic** civil rights movement; African Americans and the struggle for economic power. edited by Michael Ezra. Routledge 2013 vi, 213 p.p (Routledge studies in African American history) (hbk) $125   323.1

1. Income gap -- United States 2. African Americans -- Civil rights 3. African Americans -- Economic conditions 4. Income distribution -- United States 5. Civil rights movements -- United States 6. Equality -- Economic aspects -- United States

ISBN 0415537363; 9780415537360

LC 2012051038

Editor Michael Ezra presents "thirteen original essays that analyze the significance of economic power to the black freedom struggle by exploring how African Americans fought for increased economic autonomy in an attempt to improve the quality of their lives. It covers a wide range of campaigns ranging from the World War II era through the civil rights and black power movements and beyond." (Publisher's note)

Includes bibliographical references and index

Egerton, John

Speak now against the day; the generation before the civil rights movement in the South. University of North Carolina Press 1995 704p il pa $27.50 323.1

1. African Americans -- Civil rights 2. Southern States -- Race relations

ISBN 0-8078-4557-4; 978-0-8078-4557-8

First published 1994 by Knopf

This "book is a stunning achievement: a sprawling, engrossing, deeply moving account." N Y Times Book Rev

Includes bibliographical references

Euchner, Charles C.

Nobody turn me around; a people's history of the 1963 march on Washington. Beacon Press 2010 226p $26.95 **323.1**

1. Civil rights demonstrations 2. Washington (D.C.) 3. African Americans -- Civil rights

ISBN 978-0-8070-0059-5

LC 2009-46943

Draws on the oral histories of more than one hundred participants to provide a behind-the-scenes look at the historic 1963 March on Washington that culminated in Martin Luther King Jr.'s "I Have a Dream" speech.

"A sweeping, comprehensive look at a pivotal march in American history." Booklist

Includes bibliographical references

The **Eyes** on the prize civil rights reader; documents, speeches, and firsthand accounts from the black freedom struggle, 1954-1990. general editors, Clayborne Carson {et al.} Penguin Bks. 1991 764p pa $18 **323.1**

1. United States -- Race relations 2. African Americans -- Civil rights

ISBN 0-14-015403-5

LC 91-9507

First published 1987 with title: Eyes on the prize: America's civil rights years, a reader and guide

"An anthology of primary material important in the historiography of this country's civil rights movement. . . . Not simply for reference use, this compilation makes provocative cover-to-cover reading and is extremely worthy of consideration by every library." Booklist

Includes bibliographical references

Greenhaw, Wayne

Fighting the devil in Dixie; how civil rights activists took on the Ku Klux Klan in Alabama. Lawrence Hill Books 2011 316p il $26.95 **323.1**

1. Ku Klux Klan (1915-) 2. Alabama -- Race relations 3. African Americans -- Civil rights

ISBN 978-1-56976-345-2

LC 2010-30114

"Greenhaw takes readers on a journey behind the scenes of the civil rights struggle in Alabama. Tapping into his personal experiences growing up in segregated south Alabama and his connections to those on both sides of the struggle, he weaves the story of individuals, both black and white, who worked at the local level to banish segregation from their home state." Libr J

"The author skillfully weaves a rich historical tapestry from his deeply engaged, firsthand observations. Impressively captures stark, stunning history in the making." Kirkus

Includes bibliographical references

Guinier, Lani

The **miner's** canary; enlisting race, resisting power, transforming democracy. {by} Lani Guinier and Gerald Torres. Harvard Univ. Press 2002 392p $28.95; pa $16.95 **323.1**

1. Minorities 2. United States -- Race relations 3.

United States -- Politics and government

ISBN 0-674-00469-8; 0-674-01084-1 pa

LC 2001-39629

"Guinier and Torres call for the building of grass-roots, cross-racial coalitions to remake . . . structures of power by fostering public participation in politics and reforming the process of democracy." Publisher's note

The authors "grapple intelligently and with passionate wit with such explosive topics as racial profiling and the elusiveness of racial identification and identity . . . making this one of the most provocative and challenging books on race produced in years." Publ Wkly

Includes bibliographical references

Halberstam, David

★ The **children**. Fawcett Books 1999 783p il pa $18.95 **323.1**

1. Clergy 2. Mayors 3. Educators 4. Physicians 5. Psychiatrists 6. Songwriters 7. College teachers 8. Social activists 9. Members of Congress 10. School administrators 11. Civil rights activists 12. Local government officials 13. United States -- Race relations 14. African Americans -- Civil rights

ISBN 978-0-449-00439-5; 0-449-00439-2

First published 1998 by Random House

This is a "recreation of the early days of the civil rights movement. . . . The author focuses on a small group of young African Americans who attended the Reverend James Lawson's workshop for nonviolent demonstrators in Nashville in 1959, then went on to play active roles in the movement. . . . A masterful achievement in reporting, research and understanding." Publ Wkly

Includes bibliographical references

Joseph, Peniel E.

Dark days, bright nights; from Black power to Barack Obama. BasicCivitas Books 2010 277p $26 **323.1**

1. Lawyers 2. Presidents 3. Black power 4. Senators 5. State legislators 6. Black Muslim leaders 7. Civil rights activists 8. Nobel laureates for peace 9. African Americans -- Civil rights

ISBN 978-0-465-01366-1; 0-465-01366-X

LC 2009-37946

This is a "discussion of black power's successes and its contributions to the civil rights movement. . . . Joseph examines two paths to black social justice—'black power' and the pulpit-driven civil rights movement—which popular history has traditionally pitted in opposition. . . . [This] book is a vivid and welcome recasting of the history—and the myriad interpretations—of the movement." Booklist

Includes bibliographical references

★ **Waiting** 'til the midnight hour; a narrative history of Black power in America. Henry Holt and Co. 2006 399p il hardcover o.p. pa $17 **323.1**

1. Black power 2. African Americans -- Civil rights

ISBN 978-0-8050-7539-7; 0-8050-7539-9; 978-0-8050-8335-4 pa; 0-8050-8335-9 pa

LC 2005-46765

"Rather than simply detailing the history of radical organizations, Joseph . . . also profiles several famous leaders and uses their stories to spearhead a discussion of the intellectual and practical history of Black Power as a political movement. . . . Enthusiastically recommended for public and academic libraries." Libr J

Includes bibliographical references

Katznelson, Ira

★ **When** affirmative action was white; an untold history of racial inequality in twentieth-century America. W.W. Norton 2005 238p pa $16.95; $25.95 **323.1**

1. Race discrimination 2. Affirmative action programs 3. African Americans -- Economic conditions
ISBN 9780393328516; 0-393-05213-3

LC 2004-24359

The author "offers history and analysis demonstrating that the national social welfare programs of 60 and 70 years ago—e.g., Social Security, labor laws that created collective bargaining for unions, and the GI Bill—in fact gave affirmative economic opportunities to whites at the expense of racial minorities, particularly blacks." Libr J

"Katznelson offers a penetrating . . . analysis, supported by vivid examples and statistics." N Y Times Book Rev

Includes bibliographical references

King, Martin Luther, Jr., 1929-1968

★ A **testament** of hope; the essential writings of Martin Luther King, Jr. edited by James Melvin Washington. Harper & Row 1986 xxvi, 676p hardcover o.p. pa $23.95 **323.1**

1. United States -- Race relations 2. African Americans -- Civil rights
ISBN 0-06-250931-4; 0-06-064691-8 pa

LC 85-45370

"King's most important writings are gathered together in one source. The arrangement is topical: philosophy, sermons and public addresses, essays, interviews and excerpts of his books. The material within each of these categories is arranged chronologically. Included are Dr. King's writings on nonviolence, integration and politics." SLJ

Includes bibliographical references

Where do we go from here; chaos or community? [by] Martin Luther King, Jr.; [foreword by Coretta Scott King; introduction by Vincent Harding] Beacon Press 2010 xxiv, 223p (King legacy series) $24.95; pa $14 **323.1**

1. Racism 2. United States -- Race relations 3. African Americans -- Civil rights
ISBN 978-0-8070-0076-2; 978-0-8070-0067-0 pa

LC 2009035950

First published 1967 by Harper & Row

The author reaffirms his belief in the power of nonviolence to achieve full citizenship for black people in America and defines his attitude toward the Black Power movement and the white backlash.

Includes bibliographical references

Why we can't wait; [by] Martin Luther King, Jr. Harper & Row 1964 178p il hardcover o.p. pa $6.95 **323.1**

1. African Americans -- Civil rights 2. Birmingham (Ala.) -- Race relations
ISBN 0-06-012395-8; 0-451-52753-4 pa

The author first reviews the background of the 1963 civil rights demands. He then describes the strategy of the Birmingham campaign and outlines future action

Lewis, Andrew B.

The **shadows** of youth; the remarkable journey of the civil rights generation. Hill and Wang 2009 356p $28 **323.1**

1. Political activists 2. African Americans -- Biography 3. United States -- Race relations 4. African Americans -- Civil rights 5. Student Nonviolent Coordinating Committee
ISBN 978-0-8090-8598-9; 0-8090-8598-4

LC 2009-9980

The author "offers an engaging look at some of the major figures in the budding civil rights movement: John Lewis, son of a poor tenant cotton farmer; Marion Barry, ambitious son of poor southern parents; Diane Nash, from a middle-class Chicago family; Stokely Carmichael, who learned black culture from his Caribbean roots and politics from a leftist friend; and Julian Bond, born of black privilege. Lewis chronicles the coming together of these young people, and others, in the formation of the Student Nonviolent Coordinating Committee." Booklist

Includes bibliographical references (p. 329-335)

Litwack, Leon F.

How free is free? The long death of Jim Crow. Harvard University Press 2009 187p (Nathan I. Huggins lectures) $18.95 **323.1**

1. African Americans -- Segregation 2. African Americans -- Civil rights 3. Southern States -- Race relations 4. African Americans -- Southern States
ISBN 978-0-674-03152-4

LC 2008-36468

"An interesting analysis of the dynamics of race and class and how they continue to affect progress." Booklist

Includes bibliographical references

McGuire, Danielle L.

At the dark end of the street; Black women, rape, and resistance: a new history of the civil rights movement, from Rosa Parks to the rise of Black Power. Alfred A. Knopf 2010 324p il $27.95; e-book $27.95 **323.1**

1. Rape 2. African American women 3. African Americans -- Civil rights 4. Southern States -- Race relations 5. African American women -- Violence against 6. Rape -- Political aspects -- Southern States 7. Southern States -- Race relations -- History -- 20th century 8. African American women -- Civil rights -- History -- 20th century 9. Civil rights movements -- Southern States -- History -- 20th century
ISBN 978-0-307-26906-5; 978-0-307-59447-1 e-book

LC 2010-12072

"McGuire restores to memory the courageous black women who dared seek legal remedy, when black women and their families faced particular hazards for doing so. McGuire brings the reader through a dark time via a painful but somehow gratifying passage in this compelling, carefully documented work." Publ Wkly

Includes bibliographical references and index

Prucha, Francis Paul

The **great** father; the United States government and the American Indians. University of Neb. Press 1984 2v il hardcover o.p. pa $60   323.1

1. Native Americans -- Government relations
ISBN 0-8032-8734-8 pa

LC 83-16837

"Beginning with the American Revolution and continuing to 1980, Prucha . . . brilliantly chronicles the history of relations between the federal government and Native Americans, in a work that belongs in all public and academic libraries." Libr J

Includes bibliographical references

★ **Reporting** civil rights. Library of Am. 2003 2v ea $40   323.1

1. Journalism 2. United States -- Race relations 3. African Americans -- Civil rights
ISBN 1-931082-28-6 v1; 1-931082-29-4 v2

LC 2002-27459

"An important anthology for readers interested in the history of the civil rights movement." Booklist

Spagna, Ana Maria

Test ride on the Sunnyland bus; a daughter's civil rights journey. University of Nebraska Press 2010 270p il (River teeth literary nonfiction prize) pa $19.95   323.1

1. Boycotts 2. Civil rights activists 3. Florida -- Race relations 4. African Americans -- Civil rights
ISBN 978-0-8032-1712-6

LC 2009034320

This book "chronicles the story of an American family against the backdrop of one of the civil rights movement's lesser-known stories. In January 1957, Joseph Spagna and five other young men waited to board a city bus called the Sunnyland in Tallahassee, Florida. Their plan was simple but dangerous: ride the bus together—three blacks and three whites—get arrested, and take their case to the U.S. Supreme Court. Fifty years later Ana Maria Spagna sets off on a journey to understand what happened and why." Publisher's note

Sullivan, Patricia

Lift every voice; the NAACP and the making of the Civil Rights Movement. New Press 2009 514p il $26.95   323.1

1. African Americans -- Civil rights 2. Civil rights -- United States -- History -- 20th century 3. National Association for the Advancement of Colored People 4. United States -- Race relations -- History -- 20th century 5. African Americans -- Civil rights -- History -- 20th century
ISBN 978-1-59558-446-5

LC 2009-9473

This is an "examination of the NAACP's growth and influence, from its inception in 1909 to the present." Index.

The author "delivers a solidly researched examination of the organization's growth and influence, leaving us with a

vital account of 100 years of foundational civil rights activism." Publ Wkly

Includes bibliographical references

Voices in our blood; America's best on the civil rights movement. edited by Jon Meacham. Random House 2001 561p hardcover o.p. pa $16.95   323.1

1. United States -- Race relations 2. African Americans -- Civil rights
ISBN 0-375-75881-X pa

LC 00-41474

A "collection of acclaimed 'voices' narrating the environment, origin, and progress of the Civil Rights movement, as told by reporters, artists, novelists, historians, and authors such as Maya Angelou, Eudora Welty, James Baldwin, Richard Wright, Willie Morris, Robert Penn Warren, Alice Walker, Murray Kempton, E. B. White, William Faulkner, Ralph Ellison, and Rebecca West." Libr J

Wallace, Anthony F. C.

The **long** bitter trail; Andrew Jackson and the Indians. consulting editor, Eric Foner. Hill & Wang 1993 143p maps (Critical issue series) hardcover o.p. pa $11   323.1

1. Generals 2. Presidents 3. Native Americans -- Government relations
ISBN 0-8090-1552-8 pa

LC 92-32609

A "retelling of the story of the Trail of Tears. This refers to the forced removal in the 1830s of thousands of Indians, particularly the Cherokee and the Choctaw, from the American east to west of the Mississippi River. The author expands his focus to examine the relocation of numerous Indian groups. Central to the story is Andrew Jackson, who assumed the presidency confronted with a government divided over the question of Indian removal and who soon became one of its major proponents." Publ Wkly

Watson, Bruce

Freedom summer; the savage season that made Mississippi burn and made America a democracy. Viking 2010 369p il $27.95   323.1

1. African Americans -- Suffrage 2. Mississippi -- Race relations 3. African Americans -- Civil rights 4. Student Nonviolent Coordinating Committee
ISBN 978-0-670-02170-3

LC 2009-47211

This book "combines a political overview of the Mississippi civil rights struggle in the summer of 1964 with more than 50 personal accounts from those who were there, both the famous (including Sidney Poitier, Pete Seeger, John Lewis, Stokely Carmichael) and the lesser known, including the more than 200 volunteer students from the North who lived and worked with local residents and taught in the Freedom Schools in converted shacks and church basements. . . . The personal interviews, some from people telling their stories for the first time, make gripping drama, as they recount the standoffs, the struggle for voter registration, the reign of terror that encompassed church burnings and murders." Booklist

Includes bibliographical references

Williams, Juan

Eyes on the prize: America's civil rights years, 1954-1965; [by] Juan Williams with the Eyes on the prize production team; introduction by Julian Bond. Viking 1987 300p il hardcover o.p. pa $20 **323.1**
>   1. United States -- Race relations 2. African Americans -- Civil rights
>   ISBN 0-670-81412-1; 0-14-009653-1 pa
>
>   LC 86-40271

"This companion volume to the PBS TV series of the same name is an . . . account of black America's struggle for social and political equality, covering the civil rights battle from the landmark Brown v. Board of Education decision in 1954 to the Selma protest marches, and Voting Rights Act of 1965." Libr J

"Highly recommended both as a socio-historical document and as a heartfelt, poignant remembrance of a movement and its activists." Booklist

Includes bibliographical references

323.11 Ethnic and national groups

Brysac, Shareen Blair

Pax ethnica; where and how diversity succeeds. Karl E. Meyer and Shareen Blair Brysac. PublicAffairs 2012 xxiii, 270 p.p (hardcover) $28.99 **323.11**
>   1. Peace 2. Ethnic relations 3. Multiculturalism 4. Cultural pluralism 5. Ethnic conflict
>   ISBN 1586488295; 9781586488291; 9781610390484
>
>   LC 2011042959

This book by Karl E. Meyer and Shareen Blair Brysac presents a "tour of five societies -- where people of diverse ethnicities, races, and religions live together in peace. . . . [Meyer and Brysac] undertook a two-year exploration of oases of civility, places notable for minimal violence, rising life-expectancy, high literacy, and pragmatic compromises on cultural rights. . . . They document ways and means that have proven successful in defusing ethnic tensions." (Publisher's note)

Includes bibliographical references and index

Hoxie, Frederick E.

This Indian country; American Indian political activists and the place they made. Frederick E. Hoxie. Penguin Press 2012 467 p. $32.95 **323.11**
>   1. Native Americans -- History 2. Native American political activists 3. Native Americans -- Politics and government 4. United States -- Race relations 5. United States -- Politics and government 6. Indian activists -- United States -- History 7. Political activists -- United States -- History 8. Indians of North America -- Politics and government
>   ISBN 1594203652; 9781594203657
>
>   LC 2012009287

This book by Frederick E. Hoxie "profiles eight Native American lawyers, lobbyists, writers, and politicians who 'chose to oppose the oppressions of the United States with words and ideas rather than violence.'" These include 'mid-19th-century leader William Potter Ross . . . who negotiated with the Union Pacific Railroad over its claims to tribal lands . . . and writer Vine Deloria Jr., who . . . argued

that U.S. policies should forward Indian self-governance." (Publishers Weekly)

Includes bibliographical references and index.

Rieder, Jonathan

Gospel of freedom; Martin Luther King, Jr.'s letter from Birmingham Jail and the struggle that changed a nation. Jonathan Rieder. St. Martin's Press 2013 240 p. illustrations $25 **323.11**
>   1. Nonviolence 2. African Americans -- Civil rights 3. Birmingham (Ala.) -- Race relations 4. African Americans -- Civil rights -- Alabama -- Birmingham 5. Civil disobedience -- Alabama -- Birmingham -- History -- 20th century 6. Civil rights movements -- Alabama -- Birmingham -- History -- 20th century
>   ISBN 1620400588; 9781620400586
>
>   LC 2012044387

This book, by Jonathan Rieder, focuses on "[t]he letter that Martin Luther King Jr. penned from a Birmingham, Alabama, jail 50 years ago. . . . The letter was King's impassioned response to eight white Birmingham clergymen who had appealed to him for moderation. Here Rieder first discusses the events that led to King's arrest, then addresses the letter's importance during the civil rights struggle." (Library Journal)

"Rieder's trenchant comments approach the letter on historical and literary grounds but also as a way to better understand the often elusive King. Several chapters offer a close analysis of the letter, while later chapters trace the impact it had on subsequent events." Booklist

Includes bibliographical references and index

323.1196 Blacks (African origin)--civil and human rights

Kantrowitz, Stephen

More than freedom; fighting for black citizenship in a white republic, 1829-1889. Stephen Kantrowitz. Penguin Press 2012 514 p. **323.1196**
>   1. Abolitionists 2. Slaves -- Emancipation 3. Reconstruction (1865-1876) 4. African Americans -- Civil rights 5. United States -- History -- 1861-1865, Civil War 6. Boston Region (Mass.) -- Race relations -- History -- 19th century 7. African Americans -- Civil rights -- Massachusetts -- Boston Region -- History -- 19th century
>   ISBN 1594203423; 9781594203428
>
>   LC 2011044724

This book by Stephen Kantrowitz provides a "narrative account of the long struggle of Northern activists-both black and white, famous and obscure-to establish African Americans as free citizens, from abolitionism through the Civil War, Reconstruction, and its demise. . . . [Kantrowitz] chronicles this epic struggle through the lived experiences of black and white activists in and around Boston. . . . [T]heir goals and achievements went far beyond emancipation." (Publisher's note)

Includes bibliographical references (p. [442]-499) and index

Kelley, Kitty

Let Freedom Ring; Stanley Tretick's Iconic Images of the March on Washington. Kitty Kelly. St. Martin's Press 2013 176 p. $24.99   **323.1196**

1. Civil rights demonstrations -- United States -- Pictorial works 2. March on Washington for Jobs and Freedom (1963 : Washington, D.C.) 3. Documentary photography 4. Photographers -- United States 5. African Americans -- Civil rights -- History -- 20th century -- Pictorial works 6. March on Washington for Jobs and Freedom (1963 : Washington, D.C.) -- Pictorial works 7. Civil rights demonstrations -- Washington (D.C.) -- History -- 20th century -- Pictorial works
ISBN 1250021464; 9781250021465

LC 2013009956

This book presents photographs of the 1963 "March on Washington to urge passage of the civil rights bill." It includes "never-before-published photographs of the historic march as well as the events that led up to it. [Photographer Stanley] Tretick . . . documents the rising hopes and tensions as blacks and whites pressed for equity and obstructionists fought their efforts. . . . [Kitty] Kelley provides narrative background and context." (Booklist)

Includes bibliographical references and index

Marshall, James P.

Student activism and civil rights in Mississippi; protest politics and the struggle for racial justice, 1960-1965. James P. Marshall. Louisiana State University Press 2013 xxvi, 300 p.p (cloth : alk. paper) $45   **323.1196**

1. Mississippi 2. Activism -- United States -- History 3. Civil rights -- United States -- History 4. Mississippi Freedom Democratic Party 5. Mississippi -- Politics and government -- 1951- 6. Student movements -- Mississippi -- History -- 20th century 7. Civil rights movements -- Mississippi -- History -- 20th century 8. African Americans -- Civil rights -- Mississippi -- History -- 20th century 9. African Americans -- Mississippi -- Politics and government -- 20th century 10. College students -- Political activity -- Mississippi -- History -- 20th century 11. African American college students -- Political activity -- Mississippi -- History -- 20th century
ISBN 0807149845; 9780807149843; 9780807149850; 9780807149867; 9780807149874

LC 2012026512

In this book, author James P. Marshall "tells the complete story of the quest for civil rights in Mississippi. Using a voluminous array of sources as well as his own memories, Marshall weaves together an astonishing account of student protestors and local activists who risked their lives for equality, standing between southern resistance and federal inaction." (Publisher's note)

"Independent scholar Marshall delineates with precision the different factions and controversies within the civil rights community . . . An outstanding work." Choice

Includes bibliographical references (p. 261-290) and index

323.3 Civil and political rights of other social groups

Goss, Kristin A.

The **paradox** of gender equality; how American women's groups gained and lost their public voice. Kristin A. Goss. University of Michigan Press 2013 xiii, 240 p.p (CAWP series in gender and American politics) (cloth : alk. paper) $70   **323.3**

1. Women -- Political activity 2. Women in politics -- United States 3. Democracy -- United States 4. Women's rights -- United States 5. Women -- Suffrage -- United States 6. Political participation -- United States 7. Women -- Political activity -- United States
ISBN 047211851X; 9780472028733; 9780472118519

LC 2012025918

In this "study of congressional testimony, [Kristin A.] Goss" explores "women's collective participation in American political and public life from the end of the Civil War to the start of the 21st century. Goss provides a multifaceted history of the continuous nature of women's collective activism, criticizing former scholarship that asserts that women's engagement in participatory democracy occurred in waves." (Choice)

Includes bibliographical references and index

Lampo, David

A **fundamental** freedom; why Republicans, conservatives, and Libertarians should support gay rights. David Lampo. Rowman & Littlefield Publishers 2012 195 p.   **323.3**

1. Freedom 2. Political parties 3. Civil rights -- United States 4. Gay rights -- United States 5. Homophobia -- United States 6. Conservatism -- United States 7. Libertarianism -- United States 8. Republican Party (U.S. : 1854-) 9. Christianity and politics -- United States 10. Homosexuality -- Moral and ethical aspects 11. United States -- Politics and government -- 2009-
ISBN 1442215712; 9781442215719; 9781442215733

LC 2011048982

Author "David Lampo makes the case that support for gay rights will provide long-term political benefits for the GOP and the conservative movement. He argues that an anti-gay agenda succinctly exposes the hypocrisy of those who talk of limited government and individual rights but ignore both when it comes to gay rights and other personal freedom issues . . . He also presents a variety of polling data that show that rank-and-file Republicans, including many Tea Party supporters, are far more supportive of gay rights than commonly presumed." (Amazon)

Walters, Suzanna Danuta

The **tolerance** trap; how God, genes, and good intentions are sabotaging gay equality. Suzanna Danuta Walters. NYU Press 2014 336 p. (Intersections : transdisciplinary perspectives on gender studies and sexualities) (hardback) $29.95   **323.3**

1. Toleration 2. LGBT people -- Civil rights 3. Equality 4. Tolerance 5. Gay rights
ISBN 0814770576; 9780814770573

LC 2013045557

"In 'The Tolerance Trap,' Suzanna Walters takes on received wisdom about gay identities and gay rights, arguing that we are not 'almost there,' but on the contrary have settled for a watered-down goal of tolerance and acceptance rather than a robust claim to full civil rights. . . . A sharp and . . . cultural critique, this book . . . argues that a too-soon declaration of victory short-circuits full equality and deprives us all of . . . full integration." (Publisher's note)

"An enlightening examination of identity and the quest for 'deep freedom' by a largely misunderstood and marginalized group." Kirkus

Includes bibliographical references and index

323.4 Specific civil rights; limitation and suspension of civil rights

Conroy, John

Unspeakable acts, ordinary people; the dynamics of torture. University of California Press 2001
304p pa $19.95   **323.4**
1. Torture 2. Persecution 3. Police brutality 4. Israel 5. Northern Ireland
ISBN 0-520-23039-6

LC 2001-33218

First published 2000 by Knopf

The author "interviews torturers, torture victims, and government officials from such diverse locations as Israel, Northern Ireland, and a Chicago police interrogation room, focusing on how torture is performed and why." Booklist

Includes bibliographical references

McCoy, Alfred W.

★ A **question** of torture; CIA interrogation from the Cold War to the War on Terror. Metropolitan Books 2006 290p il (The American empire project)
$25; pa $15   **323.4**
1. Torture 2. Intelligence service -- United States 3. United States -- Central Intelligence Agency
ISBN 978-0-8050-8041-4; 0-8050-8041-4; 978-0-8050-8248-7 pa; 0-8050-8248-4 pa

LC 2005-51124

The author "shows how, since 1950, the CIA and various nations have augmented traditional physical torture with psychological abuse techniques of 'sensory disorientation' and 'self-inflicted pain,' which he documents with some gruesome first-person accounts by victims and with stories of doctors who conducted horrific experiments." Libr J

Includes bibliographical references

323.44 Freedom of action (Liberty)

Fischer, David Hackett

Liberty and freedom. Oxford University Press 2004 851p il (America, a cultural history)
$50   **323.44**
1. Freedom 2. American national characteristics 3. Liberty -- History 4. United States -- History 5.

National characteristics, American
ISBN 0-19-516253-6

LC 2004-5197

"This book studies American ideas of liberty and freedom as visions of an open society, through the symbols they have inspired from the Revolutionary era through 9/11." (Publisher's note) Index.

This "beautifully illustrated book shifts subtly from a rich graphic survey, incorporating painting, flags and sculpture, to a broader chronicle of the many ways Americans have articulated their most cherished ideals." Publ Wkly

Includes bibliographical references

Foner, Eric, 1943-

The **story** of American freedom. Norton 1998
422p il hardcover o.p. pa $16.95   **323.44**
1. Freedom 2. Cold war 3. Conservatism 4. Labor movement 5. Slavery -- United States 6. United States -- History 7. Women -- Social conditions 8. African Americans -- Civil rights 9. United States -- Economic conditions -- 1933-1945
ISBN 0-393-31962-8 pa

LC 98-3290

Foner offers a "survey of the various meanings—political, economic, personal, moral—that Americans have attached to freedom from the Revolution until today." Commentary

"The book's strongest claim to distinction lies . . . in its succinct, information-packed, wonderfully readable account of the twists and turns in 20th-century American history." N Y Times Book Rev

Includes bibliographical references

Stone, Geoffrey R.

★ **Perilous** times; free speech in wartime from the Sedition Act of 1798 to the war on terrorism. Norton 2004 xx, 730p il $35   **323.44**
1. Freedom of speech
ISBN 0-393-05880-8

LC 2004-17871

The author "delivers rich material in an engaging, character-based narrative. Stone offers deep insight into rhetorical history and the men and women who made it—resisters like Clement Vallandingham, Emma Goldman, Fred Korematsu and Daniel Ellsberg; presidents faced with wartime dilemmas; and the prosecutors, defenders and Supreme Court justices who shaped our understanding of the First Amendment today." Publ Wkly

Includes bibliographical references

323.6 Citizenship and related topics

Ellis, Richard

To the flag; the unlikely history of the Pledge of Allegiance. [by] Richard J. Ellis. University Press of Kansas 2005 297p il hardcover o.p. pa $15.95   **323.6**
1. Pledge of Allegiance
ISBN 0-7006-1372-2; 0-7006-1521-0 pa

LC 2004-23110

The author provides an "account not only of the pledge's 19th century beginnings, but also of its recent use as a political tool. A must read for political junkies of any age!" Univ Press Books for Public and Second Sch Libr, 2006

324   The political process

Larson, Edward J.

A **magnificent** catastrophe; the tumultuous election of 1800, America's first presidential campaign. Free Press 2007 335p il $27   **324**

1. Statesmen 2. Architects 3. Presidents 4. Vice-presidents 5. Essayists 6. Secretaries of the treasury 7. Presidents -- United States -- Election -- 1800 8. United States -- Politics and government -- 1783-1809
ISBN 978-0-7432-9316-7; 0-7432-9316-9
LC 2007-16017

The author "recreates the dramatic presidential race of 1800, which, Larson says, stamped American democracy with its distinctive partisan character as Republicans and Federalists battled for the presidency. . . . [This is] an invaluable study of a crucial chapter in the lives of the founding fathers—and of the nation." Publ Wkly
Includes bibliographical references

Schoen, Douglas E.

The **power** of the vote; electing presidents, overthrowing dictators, and promoting democracy around the world. William Morrow 2007 396p pa $25.95   **324**

1. Democratic Party (U.S.) 2. Political consultants 3. United States -- Politics and government
ISBN 978-0-06-123188-9; 0-06-123188-6
LC 2006-52877

The author presents an account of his work as a politcal strategist.
Includes bibliographical references

Traister, Rebecca

Big girls don't cry; the election that changed everything for American women. Free Press 2010 336p $26   **324**

1. Mayors 2. Lawyers 3. Feminism 4. Governors 5. Senators 6. Secretaries of state 7. Spouses of presidents 8. Hospital administrators 9. Presidential candidates 10. Women -- Political activity 11. Women in politics -- United States 12. Presidents -- United States -- Election -- 2008
ISBN 978-1-4391-5028-3; 1-4391-5028-1
LC 2010-09631

This is "a passionate, visionary and very personal account of the cultural ferment that accompanied the election of '08." N Y Times Book Rev
Includes bibliographical references

Weatherford, Doris

Women in American politics; history and milestones. Doris Weatherford. CQ Press 2012 575 p. ill. $250   **324**

1. Women politicians 2. Women political activists

3. Women -- Political activity 4. Women in politics -- United States 5. United States -- Politics and government 6. Women -- Political activity -- United States -- History
ISBN 1608710076; 9781608710072
LC 2011044100

This book presents a "history of American women in politics. . . . Coverage begins with the women's suffrage movement and concludes with a state-by-state guide to women who have held or currently hold public office. Other chapters address such topics as political parties, interest groups, and political action committees. Each chapter begins with an overview followed by a chronologically arranged, detailed analysis and concludes with profiles of pertinent women." (Library Journal)

"There are no current print publications with a similar scope that are equally comprehensive, as easy to use, or as clearly written." Booklist
Includes bibliographical references and indexes

324.2   Political parties

McGerr, Michael E.

A **fierce** discontent; the rise and fall of the Progressive movement in America, 1870-1920. [by] Michael McGerr. Oxford University Press 2005 395p pa $19.95   **324.2**

1. Progressivism (United States politics)
ISBN 978-0-19-518365-8; 0-19-518365-7
LC 2004-30592

First published 2003 by the Free Press

The author "examines the social, cultural and political currents of a movement that, through its early successes and ultimate failure, has defined today's 'disappointing' political climate. . . . In three parts, McGerr illuminates the origins of Progressive thought, the movement's meteoric ascent in American life and its descent into 'the Red scare, race riots, strikes and inflation,' positing that the Progressive vision of remaking America in its own middle-class image eventually sparked a backlash that persists to this day. . . . Simply put, this is history at its best." Publ Wkly
Includes bibliographical references

McGregor, Richard

The **Party**; the secret world of China's communist rulers. Harper 2010 302p il map   **324.2**

1. Communism -- China 2. Communist Party (China) 3. Economic policy -- China 4. China -- Politics and government
ISBN 9780061708770; 9780061998089

McGregor "examines China's Communist Party, with a focus on the large role it has played in the nation's competition with the United States." (Publisher's note) Index.

"An astute, well-crafted work that should be enormously useful in understanding China's role in the world." Kirkus
Includes bibliographical references

324.273   Parties of United States

Gillespie, J. David

Challengers to duopoly; why third parties matter in American two-party politics. J. David Gillespie. University of South Carolina Press 2012 xiii, 290 p.p (pbk) $24.95   **324.273**

1. United States -- Politics and government 2. Third parties (United States politics) -- History 3. Political participation -- United States -- History
ISBN 1611170141; 9781611170139; 9781611170146
LC 2011046340

Includes bibliographical references and index

Gould, Lewis L.

★ **Grand** Old Party; a history of the Republicans. Random House 2003 597p il $35   **324.273**

1. Republican Party (U.S.)
ISBN 0-375-50741-8
LC 2003-46604

This is an "account of the Grand Old Party that spans its earliest days under Abraham Lincoln to its conservative bent today. Much of the book documents the shifts of its platform. . . . Gould also discusses the leadership qualities, farsighted policies, conservative federal spending, and willingness to provide social programs at the cost of future generations of four Republican presidents—Lincoln, Theodore Roosevelt, Eisenhower, and Reagan." Libr J

Includes bibliographical references

Lofgren, Mike

The **party** is over; how Republicans went crazy, Democrats became useless, and the middle class got shafted. Mike Lofgren. Viking 2012 p. cm. **324.273**

1. Democratic Party (U.S.) 2. Republican Party (U.S.) 3. United States -- Politics and government 4. Democratic Party (U.S.) -- History -- 20th century 5. Democratic Party (U.S.) -- History -- 21st century 6. Republican Party (U.S. : 1854-) -- History -- 20th century 7. Republican Party (U.S. : 1854-) -- History -- 21st century 8. Political parties -- United States -- History -- 20th century 9. Political parties -- United States -- History -- 21st century
ISBN 9780670026265
LC 2012014990

This New York Times bestselling book, by Mike Lofgren, criticizes 21st-century American politics. "There was a time, not so very long ago, when perfectly rational people ran the Republican Party. So how did the party of Lincoln become the party of lunatics? That is what this book aims to answer. Fear not, the [Democrats] come in for their share of tough talk--they are zombies, a party of the living dead." (Publisher's note)

Includes bibliographical references and index

324.5   Nominating candidates

Congressional Quarterly, Inc.

National party conventions, 1831-2008. CQ Press 2010 375p il pa $65   **324.5**

1. Political parties 2. Political conventions
ISBN 978-1-60426-540-8
LC 2009040264

First published 1995 with title: National party conventions, 1831¿1992

This volume offers information about Republican and Democratic Party national conventions including sites, delegates, chief officers and keynote speakers, party organization and rules, credential fights, platform fights, ballots, and candidates.

Includes bibliographical references

324.6   Election systems and procedures; suffrage

Benenson, Bob

Elections A to Z; Dave Tarr, Bob Benenson. 4th ed. SAGE Publications 2012 xxxvii, 793 p.p ill. (cloth) $125   **324.6**

1. Suffrage 2. Elections 3. United States -- Politics and government 4. Elections -- United States -- Encyclopedias
ISBN 0872897699; 9780872897694
LC 2012008921

This book is a "resource on the history and process of U.S. national elections" that has been updated to include articles on the Tea Party political movement and "the Supreme Court's 2010 Citizens United decision. The approximately 225 alphabetically arranged articles cover topics from 'Absentee Voting' and 'Electoral Behavior' to 'Beauty Contest' and 'Scandals'; they also offer separate entries on black, women's, and youth suffrage." (School Library Journal)

Includes bibliographical references (p. 731-733) and index

Congressional Quarterly, Inc.

Guide to U.S. elections; 6th ed.; CQ Press 2010 2v il map set $420   **324.6**

1. Reference books 2. Elections -- United States -- Statistics
ISBN 978-1-60426-536-1
LC 2009-33938

First published 1975 with title: Congressional Quarterly's guide to U.S. elections

This is a compilation of data drawn from different sources on gubernatorial, congressional, and presidential elections.

"The clearly written, analytical essays . . . focus on key issues such as reapportionment and redistricting, campaign finance, political party development, party conventions, politics and war, the electoral process, and the ethnic and gender composition of Congress. . . . It is an important resource for students and researchers needing historical or contemporary election data and analysis." Choice

Includes bibliographical references

★ **Presidential** elections 1789-2008. CQ Press 2010 295p il map pa $65   **324.6**
1. Presidents -- United States -- Election
ISBN 978-1-60426-541-5

LC 2009-40267

First published 1995 with title: Presidential elections, 1789¿1992

This book offers information about the electoral college, electoral votes and popular votes in each presidential election, voter turnout, primary returns, and Democratic and Republican Party conventions.

Includes bibliographical references

Dudden, Faye E.

Fighting chance; the struggle over woman suffrage and Black suffrage in Reconstruction America. Oxford University Press 2011 287p il $34.95 **324.6**
1. Reconstruction (1865-1876) 2. Women -- Suffrage 3. African Americans -- Suffrage
ISBN 978-0-19-977263-6; 0-19-977263-0

LC 2010053188

"Likely to be a classic study, it is recommended for all readers in American studies and Reconstruction history." Libr J

Includes bibliographical references

Rubin, Aviel D.

Brave new ballot; the battle to safeguard democracy in the age of electronic voting. Morgan Road Books 2006 280p $24.95   **324.6**
1. Voting machines
ISBN 0-7679-2210-7; 978-0-7679-2210-4

LC 2006-41917

The author "found himself at center stage of the debate surrounding the safety and security of electronic voting when he and his grad students exposed serious failings in the code in electronic voting machines manufactured by Diebold. . . . Rubin thoroughly analyzes the vulnerabilities of electronic voting and offers an absorbing account of how his involvement in the e-voting controversy affected his life and career, in what he describes as a scenario from a bad Hollywood script. In this highly accessible book, Rubin offers readers a look at the weaknesses of electronic voting systems and the need for paper records." Booklist

Includes bibliographical references

324.7   Conduct of election campaigns

Greenberg, Stanley B.

Dispatches from the war room; in the trenches with five extraordinary leaders. Thomas Dunne Books/St. Martin's Press 2009 501p il $29.95 **324.7**
1. Generals 2. Diplomats 3. Governors 4. Leadership 5. Presidents 6. World politics 7. Prime ministers 8. Political prisoners 9. Cabinet members 10. Political leaders 11. Military officials 12. Members of Parliament 13. Human rights activists 14. Nobel

laureates for peace
ISBN 978-0-312-35152-6; 0-312-35152-6

LC 2008-29884

"While there is plenty of talk about focus groups and polling numbers, Greenberg doesn't get bogged down in jargon, and the strength of the book lies in his insider perspective on the leaders who helped shape this century." Publ Wkly

Includes bibliographical references

Harding, James

Alpha dogs; the Americans who turned political spin into a global business. Farrar, Straus, and Giroux 2008 252p $25; pa $15   **324.7**
1. Politics 2. Public relations 3. Sawyer-Miller Group
ISBN 978-0-374-10367-5; 0-374-10367-4; 978-0-374-53175-1 pa; 0-374-53175-7 pa

LC 2007-47953

"Harding draws on over 200 interviews to reconstruct the behind-the-scenes history of the Sawyer Miller Group's meteoric rise to power and influence, offering an intimate look at the firm's involvement in global politics. . . . This fascinating book vividly renders political history with clear insight and rich detail." Publ Wkly

Includes bibliographical references

324.9   History and geographic treatment of elections

Dershowitz, Alan M.

Supreme injustice; how the high court hijacked election 2000. Oxford Univ. Press 2001 275p il hardcover o.p. pa $14.95   **324.9**
1. Governors 2. Presidents 3. Vice-presidents 4. Conservationists 5. Senators 6. Baseball executives 7. Members of Congress 8. Children of presidents 9. Presidential candidates 10. Nobel laureates for peace 11. Energy industry executives 12. Presidents -- United States -- Election -- 2000
ISBN 0-19-514827-4; 0-19-515807-5 pa

LC 2001-32193

"This well-reasoned and controversial book asks central questions about American democracy and the role of citizens and courts in our society." Libr J

Includes bibliographical references

Karabell, Zachary

The **last** campaign; how Harry Truman won the 1948 election. Knopf 2000 308p hardcover o.p. pa $14   **324.9**
1. Governors 2. Presidents 3. Vice-presidents 4. Senators 5. District attorneys 6. Presidential candidates 7. Presidents -- United States -- Election -- 1948
ISBN 0-375-70077-3 pa

LC 99-28567

This is an account of the presidential campaign which pitted Truman against Dewey.

"The author is strongest discussing the impact of the press, polls, and radio and describing the importance of the convention, which was then 'a mix of high politics, low politics and entertainment.'" Libr J

Includes bibliographical references

Lipsitz, Keena

Competitive elections and the American voter; Keena Lipsitz. University of Pennsylvania Press 2011 x, 249 p.p (hardcover : alk. paper) $49.95 **324.9**

1. Rhetoric 2. Democracy 3. Political parties 4. Political science 5. United States -- Politics and government 6. Elections -- United States 7. Political campaigns -- United States

ISBN 081224334X; 9780812243345

LC 2010053741

This book, by Keena Lipsitz, "argues that highly contested electoral battles create an environment that allows citizens to make more enlightened decisions. The first book to use democratic theory to evaluate the quality of campaign rhetoric, [it] offers a[n] . . . overview of political contests at different levels of government. Lipsitz draws on a range of contemporary democratic theories . . . [and] reminds us that we avoid political controversy and conflict at our peril." (Publisher's note)

Includes bibliographical references and index.

Morris, Roy

Fraud of the century; Rutherford B. Hayes, Samuel Tilden, and the stolen election of 1876. {by} Roy Morris, Jr. Simon & Schuster 2003 311p il hardcover o.p. pa $14 **324.9**

1. Lawyers 2. Generals 3. Governors 4. Presidents 5. Political corruption 6. Political leaders 7. Presidential candidates 8. Presidents -- United States -- Election

ISBN 0-7432-2386-1; 978-0-7432-5552-3; 0-7432-5552-6 pa

LC 2002-36507

"Morris has an eye for detail and a lively writing style that make this highly detailed, first-rate work of history read more like a whodunnit than a historical examination." Libr J

Includes bibliographical references (p. 287-296) and index

324.973   Elections -- United States

Halperin, Mark

★ **Double** Down; Game Change 2012. Mark Halperin, John Heilemann. Penguin Group USA 2013 499 p. ill. (hardback) $29.95 **324.973**

1. Presidents -- United States -- Election -- 2012 2. Presidential candidates -- United States 3. United States -- Politics and government -- 2009- 4. Political campaigns -- United States -- History -- 21st century

ISBN 1594204403; 9781594204401

LC 2013431166

This book by Mark Halperin and John Heileman chronicles the 2012 U.S. Presidential election. "Their focus is always on the candidates with the most buzz among not just voters, but the Washington, D.C., cognoscenti." Candidates profiled include Barack Obama, Mitt Romney, Jon Huntsman, Newt Gingrich, and Chris Christie. (Kirkus Reviews)

"The well-connected authors have worked their sources thoroughly to give readers a warts-and-all look at what went on behind the scenes." Booklist

Popkin, Samuel L.

The **candidate**; what it takes to win, and hold the White House. Samuel L. Popkin. Oxford University Press 2012 viii, 350 p.p (hardcover) $27.95 **324.973**

1. Presidents -- United States -- Election 2. Presidential candidates -- United States 3. Presidents -- United States -- Election -- History 4. Presidential candidates -- United States -- History 5. Presidential candidates -- United States -- Case studies

ISBN 9780199922079

LC 2012006845

In this book, Samuel L. Popkin "analyzes what it takes to win [a political] campaign. . . . Based on detailed analyses of the winners--and losers--of the last 60 years of presidential campaigns, Popkin explains how challengers get to the White House, how incumbents stay there for a second term, and how successors hold power for their party." (Publisher's note)

Includes bibliographical references and index

325   International migration and colonization

Cannato, Vincent J.

American passage; the history of Ellis Island. [by] Vincent J. Cannato. Harper 2009 487p il $27.99 **325**

1. Immigrants -- United States 2. Ellis Island (N.J. and N.Y.) 3. Ellis Island Immigration Station 4. Immigrants -- United States -- History 5. United States -- Immigration and emigration 6. United States -- Emigration and immigration -- History

ISBN 978-0-06-074273-7; 0-06-074273-9

LC 2008-52245

"The author reaches back to the island's beginnings in the early 19th century, when, then named Gibbet Island, it served as a venue for hanging convicted pirates. Cannato then chronicles the many different people—immigrants, immigration officials, politicians and others—who made Ellis Island what it was in the early 20th century. . . . Ambitious in scope and rooted in solid storytelling." Kirkus

Includes bibliographical references

Conrad, Sebastian

German colonialism; a short history. Sebastian Conrad ; translated by Sorcha O'Hagan. Cambridge University Press 2012 xii, 233 p.p **325**

1. Europe -- Colonies 2. Reformation -- Germany 3. Germany -- Colonies -- History 4. Germany -- Foreign relations -- 1871-1918

ISBN 1107400473; 9781107008144; 9781107400474

LC 2011025088

This book, by Sebastian Conrad, focuses on "the expansion of the [German colonial] empire from its origins in the acquisition of substantial territories in present day Togo, Cameroon, Namibia and Tanzania to new settlements in East Asia and the Pacific and reveals the colonialist culture which permeated the German nation and its politics." (Publisher's note)

Includes bibliographical references and index

Daniels, Roger

Coming to America; a history of immigration and ethnicity in American life. 2nd ed; Perennial 2002 515p il map pa $17.95   **325**

1. Minorities 2. United States -- Immigration and emigration

ISBN 0-06-050577-X

LC 2002-72436

First published 1990

"After discussing the topic of immigration in general and sociological theories of why people migrate between countries, Daniel discusses each racial or national group that came to the United States during the various eras of the nation's history." SLJ {review of 1990 edition}

Includes bibliographical references

Handlin, Oscar

The **uprooted**; 2nd ed; Little, Brown 1973 333p hardcover o.p. pa $18.99   **325**

1. Acculturation 2. United States -- Immigration and emigration

ISBN 0-316-34313-7 pa

First published 1951

This account of the American immigrant experience and the acculturation process describes employment, religion, ghetto life, benevolent societies, boss politics, family life, and social alienation

Yans-McLaughlin, Virginia

Ellis Island and the peopling of America; the official guide. [by] Virginia Yans-McLaughlin and Marjorie Lightman, with the Statue of Liberty-Ellis Island Foundation. New Press (NY) 1997 209p il maps pa $19.95; $28.95   **325**

1. Ellis Island Immigration Station 2. United States -- Immigration and emigration

ISBN 1-56584-364-9; 9781439504628

LC 96-54713

Photographs, time lines, charts and historical documents from the Ellis Island Museum accompany a text that places immigration policy in its historical context.

326   Slavery and emancipation

Berlin, Ira

Generations of captivity; a history of African-American slaves. Belknap Press 2003 374p maps $29.95; pa $16.95   **326**

1. Slavery -- United States

ISBN 0-674-01061-2; 0-674-01624-6 pa

LC 2002-28142

"Berlin has given us a moving, insightful account of slavery in the United States. Readers will not soon forget the story he has told, nor should they." N Y Times Book Rev

Includes bibliographical references and index

Blight, David W.

A **slave** no more; two men who escaped to freedom: including their own narratives of emancipation. Harcourt 2007 307p il map   **326**

1. Slaves 2. Diarists 3. Slavery -- United States 4. African Americans -- Biography

ISBN 978-0-15-101232-9; 0-15-101232-6

LC 2007-14467

"Required reading for scholars or even casual students, this signal [sic] contribution is essential for any collection on slavery, emancipation, or African American or U.S. history and literature." Libr J

Includes bibliographical references

DeWolf, Thomas Norman

Inheriting the trade; a Northern family confronts its legacy as the largest slave-trading dynasty in U.S. history. Beacon Press 2008 262p $24.95; pa $16   **326**

1. Slave trade 2. Slave traders 3. Biography, Individual 4. Slavery -- United States 5. Local government officials 6. County government officials 7. Slave trade -- Cuba -- History 8. Slave trade -- New England -- History 9. Slave trade -- West Africa -- History

ISBN 978-0-8070-7281-3; 0-8070-7281-8; 978-0-8070-7282-0 pa; 0-8070-7282-6 pa

LC 2007-19708

"A companion book to the PBS documentary POV: Traces of the Trade, this is the memoir of the DeWolfe family's learning and acknowledgement of their legacy in the African slave trade of American history. The family retraces the slave trade journey from the North, through Africa and the Caribbean, to the South. This story chronicles their journey, how they dealt with the shame of the family's past, and how slavery in the United States has contributed to racism in the world today." Univ Press Books for Public and Second Sch Libr, 2009

Includes bibliographical references

Douglass, Frederick, 1818-1895

★ **Frederick** Douglass: selected speeches and writings; edited by Philip S. Foner; abridged and adapted by Yuval Taylor. Hill Bks. 1999 789p hardcover o.p. pa $32.95   **326**

1. Speeches, addresses, etc., American 2. African Americans -- Civil rights -- History -- 19th century 3. Slaves -- United States -- Social conditions -- 19th century 4. Antislavery movements -- United States -- History -- 19th century

ISBN 1-55652-352-1 pa

LC 99-23180

Based on Foner's five-volume The life and writings of Frederick Douglass (1950-1975), this volume "covers Douglass' speeches and writings over a 54-year period. The breadth and depth of his focus and concerns reflected in more than 2,000 speeches, editorials, articles, and letters provide a wellspring of knowledge about the man and his intellect." Booklist

Includes bibliographical references

Gallay, Alan

The **Indian** slave trade; the rise of the English empire in the American South, 1670-1717. Yale Univ. Press 2002 444p maps $35; pa $18 **326**

1. Slave trade 2. Native Americans -- Southern States

ISBN 0-300-08754-3; 0-300-10193-7 pa

LC 2001-5270

"Powerfully argued and densely detailed. . . . Gallay's stunning and engrossing work, aimed especially at advanced students and scholars, seems to spur a renewed debate on the origins and meaning of racial slavery." Choice

Includes bibliographical references and index

Hochschild, Adam

★ **Bury** the chains; prophets, slaves, and rebels in the first human rights crusade. Houghton Mifflin 2005 468p il $26.95 **326**

1. Slavery

ISBN 0-618-10469-0

LC 2004-54091

This is an account of the "methods, and motivations behind the cause officially launched in 1787 that culminated by 1838 in the formal end of forced labor in the British Empire." Libr J

The author "brings drama and incredible research to this thrilling look at the little-celebrated abolition movement in Britain and its reverberations throughout modern democracies." Booklist

Includes bibliographical references

Horton, James Oliver

★ **Slavery** and the making of America; [by] James Oliver Horton [and] Lois E. Horton. Oxford University Press 2004 254p il maps $35; pa $18.95 **326**

1. Slavery -- United States 2. African Americans -- History

ISBN 0-19-517903-X; 0-19-530451-9 pa

LC 2004-13617

The authors "explore the economic, social, and cultural implications of the enslavement of Africans in America, from the selection of slaves from certain regions of Africa to harvest the newly introduced rice crops of the Carolinas to the incentive of freedom offered on both sides of the American Revolution and Civil War to induce the assistance of slaves." Booklist

"The oft-told tale is made fresh through up-to-date slavery scholarship, the extensive use of slave narratives and archival photos and, especially, a focus on individual experience." Publ Wkly

Johnson, Walter

Soul by soul; life inside the antebellum slave market. Harvard Univ. Press 1999 283p il $28.50; pa $15.95 **326**

1. Slave trade 2. Slavery -- United States 3. New Orleans (La.) -- Race relations

ISBN 0-674-82148-3; 0-674-00539-2 pa

LC 99-46696

This is an examination of the antebellum slave market. "Using slave narratives, court records, planters' letters, and more, Johnson enters the slave pens and showrooms of the New Orleans slave market to observe how slavery turned men and women into merchandise and how slaves resisted such efforts to steal their humanity." Libr J

Includes bibliographical references and index

Jordan, Don

White cargo; the forgotten history of Britain's white slaves in America. [by] Don Jordan and Michael Walsh. New York University Press 2008 320p il map hardcover o.p. pa $20 **326**

1. Contract labor 2. Slavery -- History 3. Great Britain -- Social conditions 4. United States -- History -- 1600-1775, Colonial period

ISBN 978-0-8147-4272-3; 0-8147-4296-3; 978-0-8147-4296-9 pa; 0-8147-4296-3 pa

LC 2007-37976

First published 2007 in the United Kingdom

This "is a colorful series of portraits of villains and victims, exploiters and exploited, rendered with bemused outrage." Choice

Includes bibliographical references

Rediker, Marcus

★ The **Amistad** rebellion; an Atlantic odyssey of slavery and freedom. Marcus Rediker. Viking 2012 288 p. $27.95 **326**

1. Slave revolts 2. Slavery -- United States 3. Amistad (Schooner) 4. Slave trade -- America -- History 5. Slave insurrections -- United States 6. Antislavery movements -- United States 7. Sierra Leoneans -- United States -- History -- 19th century

ISBN 0670025046; 9780670025046

LC 2012014810

In this book, Marcus Rediker "reframes the story [of the Spanish slave schooner Armistad] to show how a small group of courageous men fought and won an epic battle against Spanish and American slaveholders and their governments. He reaches back to Africa to find the rebels' roots, narrates their cataclysmic transatlantic journey, and unfolds a prison story . . . featuring . . . portraits of the Africans, their captors, and their abolitionist allies." (Publisher's note)

Includes bibliographical references and index

Remembering slavery; African Americans talk about their personal experiences of slavery and emancipation. edited by Ira Berlin, Marc Favreau, and Steven F. Miller. New Press (NY) 1998 355p hardcover o.p. pa $16.95 **326**

1. Slavery -- United States 2. African Americans -- History -- Sources

ISBN 1-56584-587-0 pa

This "book-and-tapes collection of slave narratives, drawn from slave narratives and audio recordings of former slaves collected by the Federal Writers' Project (FWP) during the 1930s and 1940s (some of which have been remastered and included in two 60-minute cassettes with the book), brings slavery to life as few recent books have done." Libr J

Includes bibliographical references

White, Shane

★ The **sounds** of slavery; discovering African American history through songs, sermons, and speech. [by] Shane White and Graham White. Beacon Press 2005 xxii, 241p hardcover o.p. pa $17   **326**

     1. Plantation life 2. Slavery -- United States 3. African Americans -- History

     ISBN 0-8070-5026-1; 0-8070-5027-X pa

                          LC 2004-21447

     "Drawing on WPA interviews with former slaves, slave narratives, and other historical documents from the 1700s through the 1850s, the authors provide the context for the field calls, work songs, sermons, and other sounds and utterances of slaves on American plantations. The authors also focus on recollections of the wails of slaves being whipped, the barking of hounds hunting down runaways, and the keening of women losing their children to the slave block. The combination of the CD and the book brings vibrancy and texture to a complex history that has been long neglected." Booklist

     Includes discography and bibliographical references

Wills, Garry, 1934-

'**Negro** president' Jefferson and the slave power. Houghton Mifflin 2003 274p il $25; pa $14   **326**

     1. Architects 2. Presidents 3. Vice-presidents 4. Essayists 5. Slavery -- United States 6. United States -- Politics and government -- 1783-1865

     ISBN 0-618-34398-9; 0-618-48537-6 pa

                          LC 2003-56710

     The author "argues that the Constitution's three-fifths clause for slave 'representation' in Congress and the Electoral College gave slaveholders the edge in winning most presidential elections, controlling the federal government, and maintaining slavery by throttling personal liberties. Jefferson, Madison, Jackson, and other slaveholders became 'Negro' Presidents because of the three-fifths clause, claimed their political opponents, including the Federalists." Libr J

     "Wills makes a valuable contribution to our understanding of Jefferson and the new American nation." Choice

     Includes bibliographical references

Winch, Julie

A **gentleman** of color: the life of James Forten. Oxford Univ. Press 2002 501p il hardcover o.p. pa $18.95   **326**

     1. Abolitionists 2. Philanthropists 3. Sailmakers 4. African Americans -- Biography

     ISBN 0-19-508691-0; 0-19-516340-0 pa

                          LC 2001-36215

     The author "has done a masterful job of researching and piecing together Forten's life. . . . But the strength of the book—aside from rediscovering Forten—is the careful and often surprising research into the complexity of African-American life in the 18th and early 19th centuries." Publ Wkly

     Includes bibliographical references

327   International relations

Bobbitt, Philip

The **shield** of Achilles; war, peace, and the course of history. Knopf 2002 xxxii, 919p $40; pa $19.95   **327**

     1. War 2. Peace 3. State, The 4. International relations

     ISBN 0-375-41292-1; 0-385-72138-2 pa

                          LC 2001-38085

     In this volume, Bobbitt presents "a history of diplomacy from 1500 to 1990; a theory of the history of the state; [and] an analysis of globalization. As he moves from the past into our current embrace of free-market ideology, Bobbitt introduces what he calls the 'market-state'—a new kind of government. . . . In the new 'market-state,' citizens transcend terrestrial borders and adhere to economic allegiances, rendered ever more fluid by the Internet." Christ Sci Monit

     "This work will be a valuable and intriguing look at where we have been and where we might be going." Booklist

     Includes bibliographical references

Burk, Kathleen

Old world, new world; Great Britain and America from the beginning. Atlantic Monthly Press 2008 830p il map $35   **327**

     1. Great Britain -- Foreign relations -- United States 2. United States -- Foreign relations -- Great Britain

     ISBN 978-0-87113-971-9

     First published 2007 in the United Kingdom

     This is "the most reliable, lucidly narrated and generous history of the mutual entanglement of Britain and America we are likely to have for some time." Times Lit Suppl

     Includes bibliographical references

Crist, David

★ The **twilight** war; the secret history of America's thirty-year conflict with Iran. David Crist. Penguin Press 2012 638 p., [16] p. of platesp ill., maps $36.00   **327**

     1. Iran -- History -- 1979- 2. United States -- Foreign relations -- Iran 3. Espionage, Iranian -- History 4. Espionage, American -- History 5. Iran -- Foreign relations -- United States 6. United States. Central Intelligence Agency 7. Iran -- Military relations -- United States 8. United States -- Military relations -- Iran

     ISBN 1594203415; 9781594203411

                          LC 2011050573

     This book by David Crist presents an "account of American-Iranian hostilities since the 1979 revolution. . . . Crist makes the case that the United States is already enmeshed in a hidden war with Iran that has raged unacknowledged for decades. This shadow war is characterized by espionage, assassination plots, and frequent eruptions of open hostilities, and exacerbated by egregious missteps and blunders by both sides." (Publishers Weekly)

     Includes bibliographical references (p. [576]-623) and index

Feingold, Russ, 1953-

While America sleeps; Russ Feingold. Crown Publishers 2011 viii, 304 p col. ill., maps **327**

1. International relations 2. United States -- Foreign relations 3. September 11 terrorist attacks, 2001 4. United States -- Politics and government 5. September 11 Terrorist Attacks, 2001 -- Influence 6. Political culture -- United States -- History -- 21st century 7. Progressivism (United States politics) -- History -- 21st century 8. Terrorism -- Government policy -- United States -- History -- 21st century

ISBN 9780307952523; 9780307952547

LC 2011051735

In this book, former U.S. Senator Russ "Feingold revisits the U.S. reaction in the wake of the [September 2001 terrorist] attacks, which set off an 'unfortunate trend' in soured international relations that is only presently being arrested under President Obama. While Feingold graciously allows former President Bush accolades for his initial words of resolve and restraint after 9/11, he grew increasingly alarmed by the hysterical fear gripping Washington, and cast the lone vote against the Patriot Act. . . . In the post-9/11 Risk game, as he calls it, Feingold urged the government not to lose sight of other important strategic spots like Yemen, Indonesia and Somalia. . . . [H]e first urged the troop withdrawal from Iraq in 2005. . . . He has been a vocal proponent for 'restoring the rule of law' to the presidency and of Obama's health-care legislation." (Kirkus)

Includes bibliographical references and index

Gaddis, John Lewis, 1941-

George F. Kennan; An American Life. John Lewis Gaddis. Penguin Press 2011 xi, 784p.p 16 p. of plates **327**

1. Cold war 2. Diplomats 3. Historians 4. World Politics -- 1945-1989 5. Cold War -- Diplomatic history 6. United States -- Foreign Relations 7. Ambassadors -- United States -- Biography

ISBN 1594203121; 9781594203121

LC 2011021786

Pulitzer Prize: Biography or Autobiography (2012)
National Book Critics Circle Award: Biography (2011)

The book presents a biography of U.S. statesman George F. Kennan, which the author composed using "Kennan's . . . diary, . . . the 300-plus boxes of other papers by Kennan now open for research at Princeton, . . . interviews with the former diplomat and his associates, . . . [and] family papers still in the possession of Kennan's daughter." The author "sides largely with Kennan's critics . . . in the heated debate over Kennan's advocacy in 1957-1958 for US 'disengagement' from the cold war in Europe." (New York Review of Books)

Includes bibliographical references and index.

Gates, Robert M.

From the shadows; the ultimate insider's story of five presidents and how they won the Cold War. Simon & Schuster 1996 604p il hardcover o.p. pa $16 **327**

1. Cold war 2. Soviet Union -- Foreign relations -- United States 3. United States -- Foreign relations --

Soviet Union

ISBN 0-684-83497-9 pa

LC 95-51704

"Gates chronicles the demise of Communism in Eastern Europe and the Soviet Union from the . . . perspective of someone who served during the Nixon through Bush administrations." Libr J

This is an "often entertaining, frequently self-serving but always thoughtful account of the United States' long effort to contain the Soviet Union." N Y Times Book Rev

Includes bibliographical references

Gelb, Leslie H.

Power rules; how common sense can rescue American foreign policy. Harper 2009 334p **327**

1. Power (Social sciences) 2. International relations 3. National security -- United States 4. United States -- Foreign relations 5. Power (Social sciences) -- United States

ISBN 0-06-171454-2; 978-0-06-171454-2

LC 2008-51977

According to Leslie Gelb, "Washington risks losing the essential lifeblood of its national security—its power—unless American leaders relearn the lessons of how to use that power. . . . [The author argues that] America's future power must be based on the principle of mutual indispensability: Washington is the indispensable leader because it alone can galvanize coalitions to solve major international problems (and all nations know this), while other key nations are indispensable partners in getting the job done. The reality is this: succeed together or fail apart." (Publisher's note) Index.

This book "is filled with gritty, shrewd, specific advice on foreign policy ends and means. . . . Gelb's ruminations are welcome and stimulating." N Y Times Book Rev

Includes bibliographical references

Gerges, Fawaz

Obama and the Middle East; the end of America's moment? Fawaz Gerges. Palgrave Macmillan 2011 292 p. **327**

1. International relations 2. Middle East -- Politics and government 3. United States -- Foreign relations -- Middle East

ISBN 0230113818; 9780230113817

LC 2011019900

This book by Fawaz A. Gerges provides an "assessment of Obama's current foreign policy. . . . Gerges . . . reaches back to the post-World War II era to explain the issues that have challenged the Obama administration and examines the president's responses, from his negotiations with Israel and Palestine to his drawdown from Afghanistan and withdrawal from Iraq" as well as Obama's response to the Arab Spring. "Gerges' conclusion is [that] the United States is near the end of its moment in the Middle East." (Publisher's note)

Includes bibliographical references.

Gutman, Roy

How we missed the story; Osama bin Laden, the Taliban, and the hijacking of Afghanistan. United States Institute of Peace 2008 321p map $26 **327**

1. Terrorism 2. Terrorists 3. September 11 terrorist attacks, 2001 4. Taliban 5. Afghanistan -- Foreign

relations -- United States 6. United States -- Foreign relations -- Afghanistan

ISBN 978-1-60127-024-5; 1-60127-024-0

LC 2007-32944

This "is a powerfully well-researched work that will have lasting value. It is unique in providing as detailed an analysis of the politics and personalities in Afghanistan (and Pakistan) as it does for those in Washington, DC and merging the two into a single stream. Specialists on either of these two foreign cultures will find much to learn from his interviews and new documentation. More general readers will be attracted by [Gutman's] clear exposition of a very complex situation, one that is populated by larger than life personalities." Middle East J

Includes bibliographical references

Hart, Gary

The **fourth** power; a grand strategy for the United States in the 21st Century. Oxford University Press 2004 187p $22 **327**

1. World politics -- 1991- 2. Military policy -- United States 3. United States -- Foreign relations

ISBN 0-19-517683-9

LC 2004-1444

The author "fears that containment of communism has been supplanted by a blatant strategy of empire as the basis of American foreign policy. . . . As an alternative, Hart promotes a foreign policy designed to advance the 'fourth power'—that is, the power of core American values, including representative government and individual liberty. . . . Hart states his case with eloquence and generally sound reasoning, and his assertions deserve to be seriously considered." Booklist

Herring, George C., 1936-

From colony to superpower; U.S. foreign relations since 1776. Oxford University Press 2008 1035p il map (Oxford history of the United States) $35; pa. $24.95 **327**

1. United States -- Foreign relations

ISBN 978-0-19-507822-0; 0-19-507822-5; 9780199765539

LC 2008-07996

This is a "chronicle of American foreign relations from the nation's founding to the present." Publisher's note

The author "recaptures a quarter-millennium of American foreign policy with fluidity and felicity." N Y Times Book Rev

Includes bibliographical references (p. 965-995)

Jacques, Martin

When China rules the world; the end of the western world and the birth of a new global order. Penguin Press 2009 xxv, 550p il map $29.95 **327**

1. Globalization 2. Forecasting 3. China -- History 4. China -- Foreign relations 5. China -- Economic conditions 6. China -- Foreign economic relations

ISBN 1-59420-185-4; 978-1-59420-185-1

LC 2009-27298

The author contends "that we are moving into an era of contested modernity. The central player in this new world will be China. . . . Although clearly influenced by the west,

its extraordinary size and history mean that it will remain highly distinct, and as it exercises its rapidly growing power it will change much more than the world's geopolitics. The nation-state as we understand it will no longer be globally dominant, and the Westphalian state-system will be transformed; ideas of race will be redrawn." (Publisher's note)

This "comprehensive and richly detailed analysis will be an indispensable resource for anyone who wants to understand contemporary China." New Statesman

Includes bibliographical references

Kagan, Robert

★ **Dangerous** nation. Knopf 2006 527p $30 **327**

1. United States -- Foreign relations 2. United States -- Territorial expansion

ISBN 0-375-41105-4

LC 2006-45264

The author argues "that Americans have been increasing their global power and influence steadily for the past four centuries. . . . He focuses on the Declaration of Independence as the document that firmly established the American conviction that the inalienable rights of all mankind transcended territorial borders and blood ties. American nationalism, he [aims to] show, was always internationalist at its core." Publisher's note

This "is a first-rate work of history, based on prodigious reading and enlivened by a powerful prose style." Economist

Includes bibliographical references

Kaplan, Robert D., 1952-

Monsoon; the Indian Ocean and the future of American power. Random House 2010 366p map $28 **327**

1. National security -- United States 2. Indian Ocean region -- Strategic aspects 3. National security -- Indian Ocean region 4. Indian Ocean region -- Foreign relations -- United States 5. United States -- Foreign relations -- Indian Ocean region

ISBN 1-4000-6746-4; 978-1-4000-6746-6

LC 2009-49752

This is an "examination of the Indian Ocean region and the countries known as 'Monsoon Asia.'" (Publisher's note) Glossary. Index.

"The book's political and economic focus and forecasts are smart and brim with apercus on the intersection of power, politics, and resource consumption (especially water), and give full weight to the impact of colonialism. An ambitious and prescient study equally at ease analyzing the work of the Indian poet Rabindranath Tagore, the finer points of the Indian state of Gujarat's flirtation with fascism, and the economic impact of the Asian tsunami on Indonesia." Publ Wkly

Includes bibliographical references

Kinzer, Stephen

All the Shah's men; an American coup and the roots of Middle East terror. John Wiley & Sons 2003 258p il map hardcover o.p. pa $14.95 **327**

1. Prime ministers 2. Iran -- Politics and government 3.

United States -- Foreign relations -- Iran
ISBN 0-471-26517-9; 0-471-67878-3 pa
LC 2003-9968

The author "has reconstructed the CIA's 1953 overthrow of the elected leader of Iran, Mohammad Mossadegh, who was wildly popular at home for having nationalized his country's oil industry. The coup ushered in the long and brutal dictatorship of Mohammad Reza Shah, widely seen as a U.S. puppet and himself overthrown by the Islamic revolution of 1979." Publ Wkly

"This comprehensive . . . account of the nationalization of the Anglo-Iranian Oil Company under the leadership of Mohammad Mossadegh in 1951 . . . is a valuable and informative work." Choice

Includes bibliographical references

Mann, Jim

About face; a history of America's curious relationship with China, from Nixon to Clinton. Knopf 1999 433p il $30; pa $16   327
1. Actors 2. Diplomats 3. Governors 4. Presidents 5. Vice-presidents 6. Senators 7. College teachers 8. Nonfiction writers 9. Members of Congress 10. Writers on politics 11. Secretaries of state 12. Parents of presidents 13. Presidential advisers 14. United Nations officials 15. Nobel laureates for peace 16. International relations specialists 17. China -- Foreign relations -- United States 18. United States -- Foreign relations -- China
ISBN 0-679-45053-X; 0-679-76861-0 pa
LC 98-6285

"Mann's descriptions of the behind-the-scenes jockeying among U.S. policy makers—the micropolitics behind the geopolitics—are so entertaining that his book will appeal to readers beyond foreign policy junkies." Publ Wkly

Includes bibliographical references

Moynihan, Daniel Patrick

On the law of nations. Harvard Univ. Press 1990 211p $37; pa $10.95   327
1. International law 2. United States -- Foreign relations
ISBN 0-674-63575-2; 0-674-63576-0 pa
LC 90-33227

"In the seven essays in this volume, Moynihan traces U.S. attitudes toward international law from the American Revolution to the current administration, and he makes a powerful argument for a return to the conventions of international behavior set out by Woodrow Wilson and the United Nations." Libr J

Schoultz, Lars

That infernal little Cuban republic; the United States and the Cuban Revolution. University of North Carolina Press 2009 745p map   327
1. Cuba -- History 2. Cuba -- Politics and government -- 1959- 3. United States -- Foreign relations -- Cuba 4. Cuba -- Foreign relations -- United States
ISBN 0-8078-3260-X; 978-0-8078-3260-8
LC 2008036714

This is a "history of US-Cuba relations since World War II." (Nation) Index.

"This is a gripping, expertly told story of one of the most complicated foreign policy relationship in the western hemisphere." Publ Wkly

Includes bibliographical references

Talbott, Strobe

The Russia hand; a memoir of presidential diplomacy. Random House 2002 478p il $29.95; pa $15.95   327
1. Governors 2. Presidents 3. Russia -- Foreign relations -- United States 4. United States -- Foreign relations -- Russia
ISBN 0-375-50714-0; 0-8129-6846-8 pa
LC 2001-48843

Talbott writes of his experiences as "President Bill Clinton's top adviser and operative for relations with the former Soviet Union. . . . 'The Russia Hand' recounts the major and minor crises over issues like the expansion of NATO, the removal of missiles from Ukraine, Western military action against the Bosnian Serbs, the . . . confrontation over Kosovo, the question of antimissile defense." N Y Times (Late N Y Ed)

Includes bibliographical references

Tuchman, Barbara Wertheim

★ Stilwell and the American experience in China, 1911-45; [by] Barbara W. Tuchman. Grove Press 2001 621p map pa $20   327
1. Generals 2. Presidents 3. Sino-Japanese Conflict, 1937-1945 4. World War, 1939-1945 -- China 5. China -- Foreign relations -- United States 6. United States -- Foreign relations -- China
ISBN 0-8021-3852-7; 978-0-8021-3852-1
LC 2001-40154

First published 1970 by Macmillian

Using the career of General "Vinegar Joe" Stilwell as a vehicle, this is a history of America's relations with China from the end of the Manchu Empire to the rise of Mao Tsetung.

Includes bibliographical references

Unger, Craig

House of Bush, house of Saud; the secret relationship between the world's two most powerful dynasties. Scribner 2004 356p il $26; pa $15   327
1. September 11 terrorist attacks, 2001 2. Political leaders 3. Saudi Arabia -- Kings and rulers
ISBN 0-7432-5337-X; 0-7432-5339-6 pa
LC 2004-274217

The author "pieces together the highly unusual and close personal and financial relationships between the Bush family and the ruling family of Saudi Arabia—and questions the implications for Bush's preparedness, or possible lack thereof, for September 11. . . . Unger also questions whether the Bush grew so complacent about the Saudis that his administration ignored then White House terrorism czar Richard Clarke's repeated warnings and recommendations about the Saudis and al-Qaeda." Publ Wkly

Includes bibliographical references

Westad, Odd Arne

Restless empire; China and the world since 1750. Odd Arne Westad. Basic Books 2012 ix, 515 p.p maps　　　**327**

1. China -- Foreign relations -- History 2. China -- Foreign relations -- 1949- 3. China -- Foreign relations -- 1644-1912 4. China -- Foreign relations -- 1912-1949
ISBN 0465019331; 9780465019335; 9780465029365
LC 2012021635

This book by Odd Arne Westad "traces China's complex foreign affairs over the past 250 years, identifying the forces that will determine the country's path in the decades to come. . . . Since the height of the Qing Empire in the eighteenth century, China's interactions--and confrontations--with foreign powers have caused its worldview to fluctuate wildly between extremes of dominance and subjugation, emulation and defiance." (Publisher's note)

Includes bibliographical references (p. 479-499) and index

Wise, David

Tiger trap; America's secret spy war with China. Houghton Mifflin Harcourt 2011 292p il $28　　**327**

1. Intelligence service 2. Chinese espionage 3. Intelligence service -- China 4. United States -- Federal Bureau of Investigation
ISBN 978-0-547-55310-8; 0-547-553102
LC 2010-42025

"For decades during the Cold War, the most captivating spy-vs.-spy battle was the one waged between Moscow and Washington. With the rise of China, a new player has entered the game. These days, it seems, not a month goes by without an intelligence case involving alleged Chinese spies stealing American industrial secrets, or reports that China tried to pay an American to join the CIA, or Chinese hackers (perhaps from the government) breaking into the Gmail accounts of U.S. officials and human rights activists. Move over U.S.S.R., China is America's espionage enemy No. 1. . . . Wise is a master of page-turning nonfiction, and from that perspective 'Tiger Trap' doesn't disappoint. His book paints a sobering, sometimes pathetic picture of American law enforcement and counterintelligence forces that appear woefully incapable of coping with the challenge from China. Some of the cases Wise details seem right out of the Keystone Kops." Washington Post

Includes bibliographical references

327.1　Foreign policy and specific topics in international relations

Abrams, Irwin

The **Nobel** Peace Prize and the laureates; an illustrated biographical history, 1901-2001. Centennial ed; Science Hist. Publs. 2001 350p il pa $35; pa $35　　　**327.1**

1. Nobel Prizes 2. Reference books 3. Biography -- Dictionaries
ISBN 9780881354577; 0-88135-388-4
LC 2001-49554

First published 1988 by G.K. Hall & Co.

This reference work "provides a biography with bibliographic references (and a photograph) of each individual winner of the Nobel Peace Prize from its inception in 1901 through the 2001 award. . . . The introductory material and all the biographical entries are concise, well-written, meet high academic standards, and are enjoyable as well." Choice

Includes bibliographical references

Brzezinski, Zbigniew, 1928-

Strategic vision; America and the crisis of global power. Zbigniew Brzezinski. Basic Books 2012 viii, 208 p.p (hbk.) $26　　　**327.1**

1. Economic development 2. World politics -- 1991- 3. Balance of power -- Forecasting 4. World politics -- 21st century -- Forecasting 5. Geopolitics -- History -- 21st century -- Forecasting 6. International relations -- History -- 21st century -- Forecasting 7. United States -- Foreign relations -- 21st century -- Forecasting
ISBN 046502954X; 0465029558; 9780465029549; 9780465029556
LC 2011033312

This book, by Zbigniew Brzezinski, "argues that without an America that is economically vital, socially appealing, responsibly powerful, and capable of sustaining an intelligent foreign engagement, the geopolitical prospects for the West could become increasingly grave. The ongoing changes in the distribution of global power and mounting global strife make it all the more essential that America does not retreat into an ignorant garrison-state mentality or wallow in cultural hedonism." (Publisher's note)

"Jimmy Carter's national security advisor offers an astute, elegant appraisal of the waning of America's "global appeal" and the severe consequences of the shifting of power from West to East." Kirkus

Includes bibliographical references (p. 195-196) and index

Emmott, Bill

Rivals; how the power struggle between China, India and Japan will shape our next decade. Harcourt 2008 342p il map $26; pa $15.95　　　**327.1**

1. Balance of power 2. International relations 3. China -- Foreign economic relations 4. India -- Foreign economic relations 5. Japan -- Foreign economic relations
ISBN 978-0-15-101503-0; 0-15-101503-1; 978-0-15-603362-6 pa; 0-15-603362-3 pa
LC 2007-52804

"Former Economist editor Emmott discusses foreign relations among China, India, and Japan, as seen through the lens of economics. . . . Examining each country in turn, Emmott reviews reforms that have spurred the torrid economic pace or, in Japan's case, overcome depression in the 1990s. The strains created by phenomenal growth, both internationally in competition for raw materials and domestically in politics, bear on the author's main concern: the possibility of war between these nations. . . . Factoring in the influence of the U.S. and ultimately proposing nine policies to help ensure peace, Emmott displays an informative grip and strategic fluency benefiting those tracking trends in Asian economics and politics." Booklist

Includes bibliographical references

Rhodes, Richard

The **twilight** of the bombs; recent challenges, new dangers, and the prospects for a world without nuclear weapons. Alfred A. Knopf 2010 366p il $27.95 **327.1**

1. Arms race 2. Arms control 3. Nuclear weapons
ISBN 978-0-307-26754-2; 0-307-26754-7

LC 2010-03901

"Rhodes documents events from the end of the Cold War to 2003 that, he believes, point toward the feasibility of eradicating nuclear weapons. He chronicles the underpublicized drama of the era: the efforts to contain the spread of nuclear weapons after the Soviet Union's collapse, the nuclear disarmament of South Africa, the fallout from India's and Pakistan's nuclear tests, and the negotiations with North Korea over its nuclear ambitions. In Rhodes's telling, big personalities clash and cooperate, jokes and epiphanies punctuate the debate, and offbeat details energize the narrative." Washington Post

Includes bibliographical references

Schlesinger, Arthur M. (Arthur Meier), 1917-2007

★ **War** and the American presidency; [by] Arthur M. Schlesinger, Jr. W. W. Norton 2004 160p **327.1**

1. Iraq War, 2003-2011 2. Governors 3. Presidents 4. Iraq War, 2003- 5. Baseball executives 6. Children of presidents 7. Democracy -- United States 8. Energy industry executives 9. United States -- Foreign relations 10. War and emergency powers -- United States
ISBN 0393060020; 0393327698

LC 200409872

This book by Arthur M. Schlesinger Jr. "offers a 21st-century . . . examination of the revolution in foreign policy that defines the US response to the terrorist attacks of 2001. Schlesinger places the Bush Doctrine and the war against Iraq in historical context, tracing the evolution of presidential power and US national security doctrine from the early presidencies to the Bush presidency." (Choice: Current Reviews for Academic Libraries)

This book "explores the war in Iraq, the presidency, and the future of democracy." Publisher's note

Taubman, Philip

The **partnership**; by Philip Taubman. Harper 2012 xviii, 478 p.p **327.1**

1. Strategy 2. Nuclear weapons 3. Terrorism -- Prevention 4. Nuclear weapons -- Government policy -- United States -- History -- 20th century
ISBN 9780061744006; 9780061744075

LC 2011028258

This book tells the story of "five men--all members of the Cold War brain trust behind the U.S. nuclear arsenal--[who] have come together to combat . . . [the] threat [of nuclear terrorism], leading a movement that is shaking the nuclear establishment and challenging the United States and other nations to reconsider their strategic policies. . . . [The book] tells the . . . story of their campaign to reduce the threat of a nuclear attack and, ultimately, eliminate nuclear weapons altogether. It is a . . . look at these men--Henry Kissinger, George Shultz, Sam Nunn, William Perry, and the renowned Stanford physicist Sidney Drell--the origins of

their unlikely joint effort, and their dealings with President Obama and other world leaders." (Publisher's note)

327.12 Espionage and subversion

Andrew, Christopher M.

Defend the realm; the authorized history of MI5. [by] Christopher Andrew. Alfred A. Knopf 2009 xxii, 1032p il $40 **327.12**

1. Great Britain -- MI5 2. Intelligence service -- Great Britain
ISBN 978-0-307-26363-6; 0-307-26363-0

LC 2009-25463

"This unique publication is definitive and fascinating. Definitive because, after decades of ill-informed or partial accounts this book fully defines and describes its subject; no future writer can ignore it. Fascinating because the fluent clarity of Andrew's narrative, his eye for colourful individual detail and the sheer interest of his subjects. . . . This book is essential reading for anyone with even the slightest interest in intelligence in the modern period." Spectator

Includes bibliographical references

Bamford, James

The **shadow** factory; the ultra-secret NSA from 9/11 to the eavesdropping on America. Doubleday 2008 395p $27.95 **327.12**

1. Intelligence service 2. Electronic surveillance 3. United States -- National Security Agency 4. United States -- Politics and government -- 2001-
ISBN 978-0-385-52132-1; 0-385-52132-4

LC 2008-26448

Bamford argues that "the NSA's failure to detect the presence of two of the 9/11 hijackers inside the United States led the NSA to abandon its long-held policy of spying only on enemies outside the country. Instead, after 9/11 it turned its almost limitless ability to listen in on friend and foe alike over to the Bush Administration to use as a weapon in the war on terror. . . . Bamford details how the agency has conducted domestic surveillance without court approval." Publisher's note

The book is "full of technical details and insider politics for those who follow such things, but Bamford's overarching theme is the grand scale of the threat to privacy." San Francisco Chron

Includes bibliographical references

Dorril, Stephen

MI6; inside the covert world of Her Majesty's secret intelligence service. Free Press 2000 907p $40; pa $22 **327.12**

1. Great Britain -- MI6 2. Intelligence service -- Great Britain
ISBN 0-7432-0379-8; 0-7432-1778-0 pa

LC 00-29385

This study of the British secret intelligence service "focuses on the years since World War II, when MI6 was dedicated to winning the cold war. . . . The book is invaluable for readers who want to separate spy fact from spy fiction." Booklist

Garton Ash, Timothy

The **file**; a personal history. Random House 1997 262p hardcover o.p. pa $14   **327.12**

1. Authors 2. Essayists 3. Historians 4. Nonfiction writers 5. Secret service -- Germany (East) 6. Intelligence service -- Germany (East) 7. Germany (East) -- Ministerium für Staatssicherheit

ISBN 0-679-77785-7 pa

"For much of 1980, while working on a doctorate in history, Garton Ash lived in East Berlin. . . . He became an object of interest to East Germany's . . . secret police known by the acronym Stasi. In The File, Garton Ash, now 42, tries to reconstruct that year . . . by comparing his private notes from the period with what he found in Stasi's newly opened records. Going further, he located and interviewed some of the informers and bureaucrats who had spied on him." (Time)

"The author went to Berlin to study in 1978 and soon came under the scrutiny of the Stasi, the notorious East German secret police. In 1993, Garton Ash had the opportunity to examine the secret file kept on him. Comparing the file reports with his private diary of the time, he finds distortions, fabrications, and surprising omissions in the file. . . . This work makes an important contribution to the literature of the new Europe." Libr J

Greenwald, Glenn, 1967-

★ **No** place to hide; Edward Snowden, the NSA, and the U.S. surveillance state. Glenn Greenwald. Henry Holt & Co. 2014 320 p. illustrations (hardcover) $27   **327.12**

1. Whistle blowing 2. Intelligence service -- United States

ISBN 162779073X; 9781627790734; 9781627790741

LC 2014932888

This book tells how "In May 2013, [author] Glenn Greenwald set out for Hong Kong to meet an anonymous source who claimed to have astonishing evidence of pervasive government spying. . . . That source turned out to be the 29-year-old NSA contractor Edward Snowden, and his revelations about the agency's widespread, systemic overreach proved to be some of the most explosive and consequential news in recent history." (Publisher's note)

"In his analysis, the author breaks down the dense NSA subject matter and uses excerpts and slides from the documents to illustrate his points, making this work readable for even those unfamiliar with the technical concepts." LJ

Includes bibliographical references and index

Grose, Peter

Operation Rollback; America's secret war behind the Iron Curtain. Houghton Mifflin 2000 256p il map $25; pa $15   **327.12**

1. Authors 2. Cold war 3. Diplomats 4. Historians 5. Centenarians 6. Nonfiction writers 7. Soviet Union -- Foreign relations -- United States 8. United States -- Foreign relations -- Soviet Union

ISBN 0-395-51606-4; 0-618-15458-2 pa

LC 99-89830

"Thorough, thought-provoking and entertaining, this is a work that casts considerable light on a topic that has long lingered in the shadows." Publ Wkly

Includes bibliographical references

Gup, Ted

Book of honor; covert lives and classified deaths at the CIA. Doubleday 2000 390p il hardcover o.p. pa $15   **327.12**

1. Spies 2. United States -- Central Intelligence Agency

ISBN 0-385-49541-2 pa

LC 99-89017

This exposé "reveals the names—and personal stories—of some three dozen CIA agents who died in the line of duty and whose identities have been kept secret—sometimes for decades. . . . Gup's sleuthing is a remarkable coup, full of high-level intrigue, cover-ups and drama." Publ Wkly

Hamrick, S. J.

Deceiving the deceivers; Kim Philby, Donald Maclean & Guy Burgess. Yale University Press 2004 297p $29.95   **327.12**

1. Spies 2. Diplomats 3. Espionage 4. Memoirists

ISBN 0-300-10416-2; 978-0-300-10416-5

LC 2004-53695

In this "analysis of one of the most famous Cold War espionage cases, Hamrick . . . asserts that British Intelligence had identified Donald Maclean as a Soviet agent earlier than the accepted date of spring 1951. . . . {Hamilton's} subversive recasting of the Philby-Maclean-Burgess case will fascinate and challenge all those interested in Cold War history." Publ Wkly

Includes bibliographical references

Haynes, John Earl

Spies; the rise and fall of the KGB in America. [by] John Earl Haynes, Harvey Klehr, and Alexander Vassiliev; with translations by Philip Redko and Steven Shabad. Yale University Press 2009 liii, 650p il $35; pa $24   **327.12**

1. Spies 2. Russian espionage 3. KGB

ISBN 978-0-300-12390-6; 0-300-12390-6; 978-0-300-16438-1 pa; 0-300-16438-6 pa

LC 2008-45628

This history of Soviet espionage in the United States "offers a remarkable portrait of the KGB's efforts—drawn largely from the KGB's own files. This achievement is possible only because Alexander Vassiliev, a former KGB agent, was allowed extensive access to the raw espionage files for two years in the mid-1990s. . . . Spies is chockablock with poignant individual tales." Newsweek

Includes bibliographical references

Venona; decoding Soviet espionage in America. [by] John Earl Haynes and Harvey Klehr. Yale Univ. Press 1999 487p $35; pa $14.95   **327.12**

1. Lawyers 2. Diplomats 3. Russian espionage 4. Communist Party (U.S.) 5. Communism -- United States

ISBN 0-300-07771-8; 0-300-08462-5 pa

LC 98-51464

"The Venona Project, a U.S. secret revealed only in 1995, decrypted Soviet intelligence's wartime cable traffic. . . . The authors systematically recount Venona's references to approximately 350 Soviet spies in U.S. government and industry—some of them highly placed, most notoriously Alger Hiss. . . . Venona may open a fundamental revision of U.S. history." Booklist

Herrington, Stuart A.
Traitors among us; inside the spy catcher's world. Harcourt 2000 409p il pa $14   **327.12**
1. Spies 2. Soldiers 3. Russian espionage 4. Berlin (Germany) 5. Intelligence service -- United States
ISBN 0-15-601117-4
LC 00-38893
First published 1999 by Presidio Press
"Herrington, former head of the U.S. Army Counterintelligence Unit . . . offers a fascinating view of life as a spy catcher in West Berlin during the height of the Cold War. His description of the search for and capture of Clyde Conrad and James Hall . . . (who for 13 years handed over America's secret war plans to the Soviets) surpasses any spy fiction." Libr J

Laird, Thomas
Into Tibet; the CIA's first atomic spy and his secret expedition to Lhasa. Grove Press 2002 364p il $26; pa $15   **327.12**
1. American espionage 2. Tibet (China) 3. China -- Foreign relations -- United States 4. United States -- Foreign relations -- China
ISBN 0-8021-1714-7; 0-8021-3999-X pa
LC 2001-58459
The author "traces the story of two CIA agents, Douglas Mackiernan and Frank Bessac, sent on an intelligence expedition to Tibet in 1949-1950. . . . Focusing on the heart-stopping details of the expedition itself, Laird gives the now familiar story of callous CIA manipulation an absorbing twist." Publ Wkly
Includes bibliographical references

Macintyre, Ben, 1963-
A **Spy** Among Friends; Kim Philby and the Great Betrayal. Ben Macintyre. Crown Publishers 2014 384 p. illustrations, portraits $27   **327.12**
1. Spies 2. Betrayal 3. Spies -- Great Britain -- Biography 4. Espionage, Soviet -- Great Britain -- History
ISBN 0804136637; 9780804136631
LC 2014003296
This book by Ben MacIntyre describes how "even as the web of suspicion closed around him, and [spy Kim] Philby was driven to greater lies to protect his cover, his two friends never abandoned him--until it was too late. The stunning truth of his betrayal would have devastating consequences on the two men who thought they knew him best, and on the intelligence services he left crippled in his wake." (Publisher's note)
"A tale of espionage, alcoholism, bad manners and the chivalrous code of spies--the real world of James Bond, that is, as played out by clerks and not superheroes." Kirkus
Includes bibliographical references (pages 309-359)

and index

Richelson, Jeffrey
The **wizards** of Langley; inside the CIA's Directorate of Science and Technology. {by} Jeffrey T. Richelson. Westview Press 2001 386p il hardcover o.p. pa $17   **327.12**
1. United States -- Central Intelligence Agency -- Directorate of Science and Technology
ISBN 0-8133-4059-4 pa
The author "provides a richly detailed account of the agency's work." Libr J

Stafford, David
Spies beneath Berlin. Overlook Press 2003 211p il $24.95; pa $15.95   **327.12**
1. Cold war 2. Espionage 3. KGB 4. United States -- Central Intelligence Agency
ISBN 1-58567-361-7; 1-58567-549-0 pa
LC 2002-34628
This is the "story of the secret tunnel beneath the Russian sector of Berlin that existed for more than a year in the mid-1950s and enabled the British and Americans to tap into all area Russian telephone conversations. But this amazing intelligence achievement was complicated by another development: the KGB knew about the tunnel through the traitorous activities of its undercover agent, George Blake, but could not reveal that they knew for fear that they might compromise the invaluable Blake. . . . What a great story! And Stafford tells it exceedingly well in sprightly prose. This book belongs in all collections that cover Cold War espionage." Libr J
Includes bibliographical references

Taubman, Philip
Secret empire; Eisenhower, the CIA, and the hidden story of America's space espionage. Simon & Schuster 2003 xx, 441p il $27; pa $15   **327.12**
1. Cold war 2. Aerial reconnaissance 3. United States -- Central Intelligence Agency
ISBN 0-684-85699-9; 0-684-85700-6 pa
LC 2002-42937
"This book functions marvelously as a history of science, detailing the research, engineering and policy decisions behind the U2 and Corona, but it's also an excellent social history of the Cold War in the 1950s and early '60s. It's a page-turner as well." Publ Wkly
Includes bibliographical references

Trulock, Notra
Code name Kindred Spirit; inside the Chinese nuclear espionage scandal. Encounter Bks. 2002 xxi, 385p il $26.95   **327.12**
1. Spies 2. Computer scientists 3. Los Alamos National Laboratory -- Security measures
ISBN 1-89355-451-1
LC 2002-67856
Trulock was the head of the Department of Energy's "intelligence office during the investigation into whether Los Alamos scientist Wen Ho Lee had given nuclear warhead secrets to China. . . . This detailed account reveals that the spy hunt didn't focus solely on Lee, or even on Los Alamos.

. . . While he denies knowledge as to whether Lee 'did it,' the author drops hints that Lee and his wife may have been double agents. . . . He provides a unique look into the American intelligence community and an unsettling perspective on the lax attitude toward national security." Publ Wkly

Includes bibliographical references

Vise, David A.

The **bureau** and the mole; the unmasking of Robert Philip Hanssen, the most dangerous double agent in FBI history. Atlantic Monthly Press 2002 272p il $25; pa $14   **327.12**

1. Spies 2. Espionage 3. FBI agents 4. United States -- Federal Bureau of Investigation

ISBN 0-87113-834-4; 0-8021-3951-5 pa

LC 2001-53872

"In February 2001, FBI special agent Bob Hanssen was arrested as a double agent for Russian intelligence in what turned out to be the biggest sellout of U.S. national security secrets in the long history of the bureau. . . . {The author} details how Hanssen did it and how he got caught." Booklist

Includes bibliographical references

Weinstein, Allen

The **haunted** wood; Soviet espionage in America--the Stalin era. {by} Allen Weinstein, Alexander Vassiliev. Random House 1999 xxviii, 402p il hardcover o.p. pa $23   **327.12**

1. Spies 2. Russian espionage 3. United States -- History -- 1933-1945

ISBN 0-375-75536-5 pa

LC 98-11801

"This is a relentlessly powerful book and an eye-operner for all readers." Libr J

Includes bibliographical references

Wise, David

Cassidy's run; the secret spy war over nerve gas. Random House 2000 228p il hardcover o.p. pa $15   **327.12**

1. Spies 2. Russian espionage 3. United States -- Federal Bureau of Investigation

ISBN 0-8129-9263-6 pa

LC 99-15802

The "reconstruction of a hitherto unknown counterespionage case. Joseph Cassidy's double life began in August 1959. . . . For 20 years Cassidy, a master sergeant, worked for the United States during the day and pretended to work for the Soviet Union at night. . . . The F.B.I. decided to use this double agent to undermine the Soviet chemical weapons industry." N Y Times Book Rev

Spy : the inside story of how the FBI's Robert Hanssen betrayed America. Random House 2002 309p $24.95; pa $13.95   **327.12**

1. Spies 2. Espionage 3. FBI agents 4. United States -- Federal Bureau of Investigation

ISBN 0-375-50745-0; 0-375-75894-1 pa

LC 2002-31867

"A relentless reporter and true expert on the world of spying, Wise recounts Hanssen's story and the hunt to catch him in precise, if sometimes overwhelming detail." N Y Times Book Rev

327.120973   Espionage and subversion -- United States

Sulick, Michael J.

Spying in America; espionage from the Revolutionary War to the dawn of the Cold War. Michael J. Sulick. Georgetown University Press 2012 xiii, 320 p.p. ill. (hardcover) $26.95   **327.120973**

1. Intelligence service 2. Military intelligence 3. Spies -- United States 4. Spies -- United States -- History 5. Spies -- United States -- Biography 6. Espionage -- United States -- History 7. Espionage -- United States -- Case studies 8. Military intelligence -- United States -- History 9. Spies -- Communist countries -- History -- 20th century 10. Espionage, German -- United States -- History -- 20th century 11. United States -- History -- Civil War, 1861-1865 -- Secret service

ISBN 1589019261; 9781589019263

LC 2011052068

This book, by Michael J. Sulick, explores the history of espionage against the United States. "Since the birth of our country, nations large and small, from Russia and China to Ghana and Ecuador, have stolen the most precious secrets of the United States. . . . [The book] presents a history of more than thirty espionage cases inside the United States . . . from the American Revolution, through the Civil War and two World Wars, to the atomic age of the Manhattan Project." (Publisher's note)

Includes bibliographical references (p. 293-302) and index

327.1273 CIA (Intelligence agency)

Woods, Randall

★ **Shadow** warrior; William Egan Colby and the CIA. Randall B. Woods. Basic Books 2013 576 p. (hbk. : alk. paper) $29.99   **327.1273**

1. United States. Central Intelligence Agency 2. Intelligence officers -- United States -- Biography 3. World War, 1939-1945 -- Secret service -- United States 4. Vietnam War, 1961-1975 -- Secret service -- United States

ISBN 0465021948; 9780465021949; 9780465037889

LC 2012040332

This book by Randall B. Woods presents a biography of "World War II commando, Cold War spy, and CIA director under presidents [Richard] Nixon and [Gerald] Ford, William Egan Colby. Drawing on multiple new sources, including interviews with members of Colby's family, Woods has crafted a . . . biography of one of the most fascinating and controversial figures of the twentieth century." (Publisher's note)

Includes bibliographical references and index

327.2 Diplomacy

Kissinger, Henry, 1923-
Diplomacy. Simon & Schuster 1994 912p il maps hardcover o.p. pa $22 **327.2**
1. Cold war 2. Emperors 3. Diplomacy 4. United States -- Foreign relations
ISBN 0-671-51099-1 pa

LC 93-44001

"This is an important contribution to the theoretical literature on foreign affairs and will also serve quite ably as a one-volume synthesis of modern diplomatic history. All libraries should have this impressive book." Libr J

Includes bibliographical references

327.73 Foreign relations -- United States

Bass, Gary Jonathan, 1969-
The **Blood** telegram; Nixon, Kissinger, and a forgotten genocide. by Gary J. Bass. Alfred A. Knopf 2013 528 p. $30 **327.73**
1. Bangladesh 2. Nixon, Richard M. (Richard Milhous), 1913-1994 3. Genocide -- Bangladesh 4. United States -- Foreign relations -- 1969-1974 5. South Asia -- Foreign relations -- United States 6. United States -- Foreign relations -- South Asia 7. Bangladesh -- History -- Revolution, 1971 -- Atrocities
ISBN 0307700208; 9780307700209

LC 2013014788

This book by Gary J. Bass examines "humanitarian crisis that propelled the creation of Bangladesh." Particular focus is given to how "[Richard] Nixon's deep distrust of India--which he viewed as an ungovernable cauldron of Soviet-leaning liberals, lefties and hippies--and his longtime support of the military in Pakistan disastrously steered his and [Henry] Kissinger's resolve not to stay the hand of Gen. Agha Mohammad Yahya Khan against a dissenting East Pakistan in March 1971." (Kirkus Reviews)

Includes bibliographical references and index

Haass, Richard N., 1951-
Foreign policy begins at home; the case for putting America's house in order. by Richard Haass. Basic Books 2013 viii, 195 p.p (hardcover) $25.99 **327.73**
1. Economic policy -- United States 2. United States -- Foreign relations 3. World politics 4. International relations 5. Security, International 6. United States -- Politics and government
ISBN 0465057985; 9780465057986

LC 2012049203

Here, Richard N. Haass focuses on "domestic economic policy as the foundation of U.S. power. He notes the current national budget debates, which, he says, result from systemic changes in the U.S. economy and in international geoeconomic realities that impact our national security." He explores the post-Cold War world, the effects of 9/11 and the 2008 global financial crisis, and discusses a "more discriminating and pragmatic foreign policy that is supported by a more disciplined domestic policy." (Library Journal)

Includes bibliographical references (pages 169-183) and index.

Leverett, Flynt
Going to Tehran; why the United States must come to terms with the Islamic Republic of Iran. Flynt Leverett and Hillary Mann Leverett. Henry Holt & Co 2013 496 p. (hardback) $32 **327.73**
1. Nuclear weapons 2. Iran -- Foreign relations -- United States 3. United States -- Foreign relations -- Iran 4. United States -- Foreign relations -- 2001-
ISBN 0805094199; 9780805094190

LC 2012036700

This book offers an "analysis of the Islamic Republic's policies, intentions, and capabilities," focusing particularly on Iran's developing nuclear capabilities. The authors "call for a reset in relations and substantial engagement rather than saber-rattling and sanctions" and "accuse the American government of 'shameless duplicity.'" (Publishers Weekly)

Morris, Seymour
Supreme Commander; MacArthur's Triumph in Japan. by Seymour Morris Jr. HarperCollins 2014 368 p. illustrations $26.99 **327.73**
1. World War, 1939-1945 -- Peace 2. Japan -- History -- 1945-1952, Allied occupation
ISBN 0062287931; 9780062287939

LC 2013498721

Includes bibliographical references and index

In this book, author Seymour Morris Jr. "combines political history, military biography, and business management to tell the story of General Douglas MacArthur's tremendous success in rebuilding Japan after World War II. . . . As the uniquely titled Supreme Commander for the Allied Powers, he was charged with transforming a defeated, militarist empire into a beacon of peace and democracy." (Publisher's note)

"A well-crafted history of an underappreciated aspect of MacArthur's career." LJ

Nasr, Vali
The **dispensable** nation; American foreign policy in retreat. Vali Nasr. Doubleday 2013 336 p. $28.95 **327.73**
1. Political science 2. United States -- Foreign relations 3. Middle East -- Foreign relations -- United States 4. United States -- Foreign relations -- Middle East 5. Islamic countries -- Foreign relations -- United States 6. United States -- Foreign relations -- Islamic countries
ISBN 038553647X; 9780385536479

LC 2012043100

In this book, author Vali Nasr "questions America's . . . choice to engage less and matter less in the world. Nasr makes a compelling case that behind specific flawed decisions lurked a desire by the White House to pivot away from the complex problems of the Muslim world. Drawing on his . . . expertise in Middle East affairs and firsthand experience in diplomacy, Nasr demonstrates why turning our backs is dangerous and, what's more, sells short American power." (Publisher's note)

Includes bibliographical references (pages 259-283) and index

Rice, Condoleezza, 1954-

No higher honor; A Memoir of My Years in Washington. Condoleezza Rice. Random House Inc. 2011 xviii, 766 p.p illustrations, maps $35   **327.73**
1. War on Terrorism, 2001-2009 2. Stateswomen -- United States -- Biography 3. United States. Dept. of State -- Biography 7. National Security Council (U.S.) -- Biography 4. United States -- Foreign relations -- 2001-2009 5. Women cabinet officers -- United States -- Biography
ISBN 030758786X; 9780307587862; 9780307952479
LC 2011534059

Author Condoleezza Rice "takes the reader into secret negotiating rooms where the fates of Israel, the Palestinian Authority, and Lebanon often hung in the balance, and it draws back the curtain on how frighteningly close all-out war loomed . . . [in response to] the September 11, 2001, terrorist attacks . . . [and] in clashes involving Pakistan-India and Russia-Georgia, and in East Africa." (Publisher's note)

328   The legislative process

Barone, Michael

The **almanac** of American politics 2012; Michael Barone, Chuck McCutcheon. University of Chicago Press 2011 xviii, 1838 p.p (hardcover) $110; (paperback) $85.00   **328**
1. Almanacs 2. United States -- Politics and government -- 2001-
ISBN 0226038076; 0226038084; 9780226038070; 9780226038087
LC 2011929193

This book, by Michael Barone and Chuck McCutcheon, is a 2012 edition almanac on U.S. politics. It "includes profiles of every member of Congress and every governor. It offers in-depth and completely up-to-date narrative profiles of all 50 states and 435 House districts, covering everything from economics to history to, of course, politics." (Publisher's note)

Congressional Quarterly, Inc.

★ **Congress** A to Z; 5th ed.; CQ Press 2008 xxxiv, 704p il map (CQ's American government A to Z series) $85   **328**
1. Reference books 2. United States -- Congress
ISBN 978-0-87289-558-4
LC 2008-11284

First published 1988
This work provides information on the structure and work of Congress in some 340 alphabetical entries.
Includes bibliographical references

Congress and the Nation; a review of government and politics in the postwar years. Congressional Quarterly 1965   **328**
1. Legislation 2. United States -- Congress 3. United States -- Politics and government -- 20th century

"Overview and detailed coverage of presidential, legislative, and political events in every major subject area." N Y Public Libr Book of How & Where to Look It Up

★ **CQ's** politics in America, 2010; the 111th Congress. by Congressional Quarterly staff; Chuck McCutcheon and Christina L. Lyons, editors. Congressional Quarterly, Inc. 2009 xxvi, 1214p il $125; pa $89   **328**
1. Reference books 2. United States -- Congress 3. Elections -- United States
ISBN 978-1-60426-602-3; 978-1-60426-603-0 pa
Biennial. First published 1981
Provides an analysis of every lawmaker in the 111th Congress, including biographical data, contact information, election results, and committee assignments.
"An outstanding, highly detailed guide to contemporary politics." Libr J

★ **Guide** to Congress; 6th ed.; CQ Press 2008 2v il map set $350   **328**
1. United States -- Congress
ISBN 978-0-8728-9295-8
LC 2007-33245

First published 1971 with title: Congressional Quarterly's guide to the Congress of the United States
"To really understand Congress, there is nothing better than these large volumes." Booklist
Includes bibliographical references

Crespino, Joseph

★ **Strom** Thurmond's America; Joseph Crespino. Hill and Wang 2012 x, 404 p.p ill.   **328**
1. Southern States -- Race relations 2. Southern States -- Politics and government 3. Legislators -- United States -- Biography 4. Politicians -- South Carolina -- Biography 5. United States. Congress. Senate -- Biography 6. South Carolina -- Politics and government -- 1951- 7. Southern States -- Politics and government -- 1951- 8. South Carolina -- Politics and government -- 1865-1950 9. Southern States -- Politics and government -- 1865-1950
ISBN 0809094800; 9780809094806
LC 2011048025

This book, by Joseph Crespino, is a biography of the mid-20th century American Senator Strom Thurmond, "one of the South's last race-baiting demagogues and as a national power broker who, along with Barry Goldwater and Ronald Reagan, was a major figure in modern conservative politics. . . . Crespino's . . . portrait reveals that Thurmond was, in fact, both a segregationist and a Sunbelt conservative." (Publisher's note)
Includes bibliographical references and index

Hamilton, Lee H.

How Congress works and why you should care. Indiana University Press 2004 156p $29.95; pa $14.95   **328**
1. United States -- Congress
ISBN 0-253-34425-5; 0-253-21695-8 pa
LC 2003-17926

This "primer details the history of Congress, its importance and some of the critical actions it has taken. . . . Hamilton also describes the 'complicated and untidy' process by which Congress really works and why we 'need more people who know how to practice the art of politics.' . . . Parents should send this primer off with their kids to college." Publ Wkly

Includes bibliographical references

Kaiser, Robert Greeley

So damn much money; the triumph of lobbying and the corrosion of American government. [by] Robert G. Kaiser. Knopf 2009 398p il $27.95 **328**

1. Lobbying 2. Political corruption 3. Lobbyists 4. United States -- Congress

ISBN 978-0-307-26654-5; 0-307-26654-0

LC 2008-33862

"Lobbying, Kaiser writes, is a business of 'huge numbers and vague standards,' forever reorienting itself in an effort to skate just inside the limits of legality. Kaiser follows the career of Gerald S. J. Cassidy, a kid from a poor family who became a lawyer for migrant workers, an aide to George McGovern, and, latterly, a lobbyist for universities, cranberries, defense contractors, and Taiwan. Cassidy pioneered the use of earmarks, fought to save the Seawolf submarine, and took congressmen to N.C.A.A. Final Four games. . . . Kaiser's account dwells less on blatant corruption than on what is perfectly, depressingly legal." New Yorker

Includes bibliographical references

Official Congressional directory, 2009-2010; 111th Congress convened January 6, 2009. Joint Committee on Printing, United States Congress. U.S. Government Printing Office 2009 xxiv, 1207p map $55; pa $45 **328**

1. Reference books 2. United States -- Congress -- Directories

ISBN 978-0-16-083728-9; 978-0-16-083727-2 pa

Biennial

"Covers biographical information, committee assignments of members of Congress, and officers of Congress." N Y Public Libr Book of How & Where to Look It Up

Remini, Robert Vincent

Daniel Webster; the man and his time. {by} Robert V. Remini. Norton 1997 796p il $26; pa $14 **328**

1. Lawyers 2. Statesmen 3. Secretaries of state 4. United States -- Politics and government -- 1815-1861

ISBN 0-393-04552-8; 0-375-72715-9 pa

LC 97-24371

This work explores the life and times of the influential politician and statesman of antebellum America

"Remini tends to exaggerate Webster's personal peccadilloes, but it cannot be said that he underestimates his subject's importance to American political culture. For Remini, Webster's muscular nationalism, embroidered with Lincoln's democratic eloquence, provided the foundation for a strong and enduring union." Choice

Includes bibliographical references

Robert C. Byrd Center for Legislative Studies

Congress investigates; a critical and documentary history. edited by Roger A. Bruns, David L. Hostetter, Raymond W. Smock; Robert C. Byrd Center for Legislative Studies. Rev. ed; Facts on File 2011 2v il (Facts on File library of American history) set $195 **328**

1. Reference books 2. Governmental investigations -- United States

ISBN 978-0-8160-7679-6; 978-1-4381-3545-8 ebook

LC 2010020268

First published 1975

The editors "have gathered here information on congressional investigations from the Colonial period to the 21st century. The entries, written by U.S. historians and archivists, each offer an overview, chronology, documents, excerpts from congressional committee reports and testimony, and a bibliography; many also include black-and-white illustrations, photographs, or political cartoons. They cover well-known events such as the Teapot Dome scandal, the burning of Washington in 1814, the Hurricane Katrina inquiry of 2005–06, and several lesser-known happenings—General St. Clair's defeat of 1792–93 and the Pujo Committee on the 'Money Trust,' for example. . . . This well-researched and richly detailed resource provides an excellent overview of major congressional investigations and will be a quality addition to a high school, public, or undergraduate academic library." Libr J

Includes bibliographical references

Stathis, Stephen W.

Landmark debates in Congress; from the Declaration of independence to the war in Iraq. CQ Press 2009 514p il map $145 **328**

1. Reference books 2. American speeches 3. Parliamentary practice 4. United States -- Congress -- History 5. United States -- Politics and government -- Sources

ISBN 978-0-87289-976-6; 0-87289-976-4

LC 2008-41380

"Presenting excerpts of speeches delivered in the House of Representatives and the Senate, this volume seeks to give readers 'a window into how Congress, seemingly constituting a cross-section of society, has wrestled with some of the most thorny questions facing American democracy.' Such monumental issues as war, slavery, impeachment of the President, amendments to the Constitution, and other bones of contention illuminate the legislative process. . . . A depiction of real people struggling to solve real problems, this book helps to humanize 'the marble men'—and women—of our national legislative body." Libr J

Includes bibliographical references

Treese, Joel D.

Biographical directory of the American Congress, 1774-1996; the Continental Congress, September 5, 1774, to October 21, 1788, and the Congress of the United States, from the First through the 104th Congress, March 4, 1789, to January 3, 1997. CQ Staff Directories 1997 2108p il $295 **328**

1. Reference books 2. United States -- Congress 3.

United States -- Biography -- Dictionaries

ISBN 0-87289-124-0

First published 1869 with title: Dictionary of the United States congress

This directory provides brief biographies of members of Congress from the Continental Congress through the 104th Congress. Each entry includes date and place of birth, education and employment, some entries also give additional biographical references

This is "an indispensable reference tool for students and scholars of U.S. history and politics. . . . It is the most comprehensive biographical source on congressional members." Am Ref Books Annu, 1998

328.2   Initiative and referendum

Broder, David S.

Democracy derailed; initiative campaigns and the power of money. Harcourt 2000 260p map hardcover o.p. pa $14   **328.2**

     1. Democracy 2. Referendum 3. United States -- Politics and government

     ISBN 0-15-601410-6 pa

                  LC 99-54190

"The initiative process, available in half the states and hundreds of cities, allows for the placement on election ballots of legislative proposals that emanate directly from sources outside the legislative branch of government. . . . {The author explores how} lawyers, campaign consultants, signature-gathering firms, and other players sell their services to affluent interest groups or wealthy individuals who mask private policy and business agendas under the guise of political reform." Libr J

     Includes bibliographical references

328.73   Legislative process -- United States

Arenberg, Richard A.

Defending the filibuster; the soul of the senate. Richard A. Arenberg and Robert B. Dove ; foreword by Senator Mark Udall and Senator Ted Kaufman. Indiana University Press 2012 xviii, 261 p.p (hardcover) $35; (ebook) $29.99   **328.73**

     1. Filibustering 2. United States. Congress. Senate 3. Filibusters (Political science) -- United States 4. United States. Congress. Senate -- Freedom of debate

     ISBN 0253001919; 9780253001917; 9780253006981

               LC 2012025529

This book offers a defense of the filibuster legal tactic. The authors "demystify the arcane rules and customs that make possible the filibuster and related tactics like holds and 'filling the amendment tree,' and they explain why perennial reform suggestions like requiring old-fashioned marathon speaking filibusters or ratcheting cloture majorities will not work. Finally, they offer some modest suggestions for reform while adamantly defending the underlying right" to the filibuster. (Kirkus)

     Includes bibliographical references (p. [231]-247) and index.

Baker, Richard A.

The **American** Senate; an insider's history. Neil MacNeil and Richard A. Baker. Oxford University Press, Inc. 2013 472 p. (hardcover) $29.95 **328.73**

     1. United States. Congress. Senate -- History

     ISBN 0195367618; 9780195367614

               LC 2012046807

This book by Richard A. Baker and Neil MacNeil "explore[s] the [U.S.] Senate's historical evolution with one eye on persistent structural pressures and the other on recent transformations. Here, for example, are the Senate's struggles with the presidency--from George Washington's first, disastrous visit . . . through now-forgotten conflicts with Presidents Garfield and Cleveland, to current war powers disputes. The authors also explore the Senate's potent investigative power." (Publisher's note)

     Includes bibliographical references and index.

Snowe, Olympia J. (Olympia Jean), 1947-

Fighting for common ground; how we can fix the stalemate in Congress. by Olympia Snowe. 1st ed. Weinstein Books 2013 viii, 302 p.p ill. (hardcover) $26.00 **328.73**

     1. United States. Congress 2. United States. Congress. Senate -- Biography 3. Women legislators -- United States -- Biography 4. United States -- Politics and government -- 20th century 5. United States -- Politics and government -- 21st century

     ISBN 1602862176; 9781602862173

               LC 2012533873

In this book, former Senator Olympia Snowe "details the cost to the American public of a Congress so polarized that it passes record low numbers of laws and can't agree on a budget. Snowe offers an insider's view of how Congress came to by so dysfunctional, including a behind-the-scenes look at her role in working with both sides to get President Obama's health-care bill passed. She recounts her personal history" as well, discussing being an orphan and her widowhood. (Booklist)

330   Economics

Acemoglu, Daron

Why nations fail; the origins of power, prosperity and poverty. Daron Acemoglu and James A. Robinson. Crown Publishers 2012 529 p. ill., map $30   **330**

     1. Nations 2. Economic conditions 3. Poverty -- Developing countries 4. Economics -- Political aspects 5. Revolutions -- Economic aspects 6. Developing countries -- Social policy 7. Economic history -- Political aspects 8. Developing countries -- Economic policy 9. Economic development -- Developing countries

     ISBN 0307719219; 9780307719218

               LC 2011023538

This book attempts to answer the question "'Why Nations Fail.' . . . [The authors] favour . . . an approach rooted solely in institutional economics, which studies the impact of political environments on economic outcomes. . . . They offer [the following] . . . diagnosis: some governments get it wrong on purpose. . . . Inclusive institutions protect individual rights and encourage investment and effort. Where inclusive governments emerge, great wealth follows." (Economist)

"The authors make what could be a weighty topic both engaging and accessible. It will appeal not only to students of economics and political science but also to anyone looking to gain insight into the current state of our global economy, its origins, and the kind of transformations that might level the playing field." LJ

Includes bibliographical references (p. [465]-509) and index

Adler, Moshe

Economics for the rest of us; debunking the science that makes life dismal. New Press 2009 217p il $24.95; ebook $24.95   330
1. Income 2. Economics 3. Salaries, wages, etc.
ISBN 978-1-59558-101-3; 978-1-59558-527-1 ebook
LC 2009-24968

"Only occasionally relying on graphs or tables, Adler provides an accessible summary of quite complex debates in economic theory." Choice

Includes bibliographical references

Dubner, Stephen J., 1963-

★ **Freakonomics**; a rogue economist explores the hidden side of everything. [by] Steven D. Levitt and Stephen J. Dubner. William Morrow 2005 242p hardcover o.p. pa $15.99   330
1. Economics 2. Economics -- Sociological aspects 3. Economics -- Psychological aspects
ISBN 0-06-073132-X; 0-06-073133-8 pa
LC 2004-65478

The authors "evaluate intriguing questions such as 'What do Schoolteachers and Sumo Wrestlers Have in Common?' 'How is the Ku Klux Klan Like a Group of Real Estate Agents?' 'Where Have All the Criminals Gone?' and 'What Makes a Perfect Parent?'... This excellent, readable book will enlighten many library patrons." Booklist

Includes bibliographical references

Encyclopedia of Business Information Sources; edited by Virgil L. Burton. Gale / Cengage Learning 2013 1210 p. (paperback) $657   330
1. Businesspeople 2. Business -- Encyclopedias
ISBN 1414478119; 9781414478111

The 23rd edition of this book, edited by Virgil L. Burton, offers "a bibliographic guide to citations covering over 1,100 subjects of interest to business personnel." It "includes abstracts and indexes, almanacs and yearbooks, bibliographies, online databases, research centers and institutes and much more." (Publisher's note)

Ferguson, Niall

★ The **ascent** of money; a financial history of the world. Penguin Press 2008 441p $29.95   330
1. Money 2. International finance 3. Economics -- History
ISBN 978-1-59420-192-9; 1-59420-192-7

The author "presents the history of money within these contexts: the rise of money and the history of credit, and the histories of the bond market, the stock market, insurance,

the real-estate market, and international finance. There is an ease to his prose that leaves this complicated subject interesting to and approachable by any general reader." Booklist

Includes bibliographical references

Headquarters USA 2012; A Directory of Contact Information for Headquarters and Other Central Offices of Major Businesses & Organizations in the United States and in Canada. edited by Julia Leeper. 34th ed. Omnigraphics Inc 2012 2866 p. $216   330
1. Business enterprises 2. Nonprofit organizations
ISBN 1934228524; 9781934228524

This book, edited by Julia Leeper, covers "the headquarters of the largest and most important businesses in the United States and Canada, . . . [which] includes a wide range of non-profit organizations, professional associations, government agencies and offices, educational and cultural institutions, and business leaders and other notable individuals. . . . Listings include fax numbers and web site addresses, and . . . stock symbols and exchanges are provided for companies whose stock is traded on the NASDAQ, New York, or American Stock Exchange." (Publisher's note)

Levitt, Steven D.

Superfreakonomics; global cooling, patriotic prostitutes, and why suicide bombers should buy life insurance. [by] Steven D. Levitt & Stephen J. Dubner. William Morrow 2009 270p $29.99; pa $15.99; ebook $9.99   330
1. Economics
ISBN 978-0-06-088957-9; 0-06-088957-8; 978-0-06-088958-6 pa; 0-06-088958-6 pa; 978-0-06-195993-6 ebook; 0-06-195993-6 ebook
LC 2009035852

Sequel to Freakonomics (2005)

The authors "assert that the unifying principle in the various topics they address is people responding to incentives in ways that are not necessarily predictable or manifest. Major themes are explored using a wide range of examples, e.g., life and death issues, terrorism, altruism, medical care, crime, and the environment. . . . Levitt and Dubner succeed in applying economic analysis to timely topics with stimulation, wit, and humor. Best of all, their book will appeal to a broad segment of the population." Choice

Includes bibliographical references

Oxford University Press

The **Oxford** encyclopedia of economic history; Joel Mokyr, editor in chief. Oxford University Press 2003 5v set $695   330
1. Reference books 2. Economic history -- Encyclopedias
ISBN 0-19-510507-9
LC 2003-8992

This encyclopedia includes "over 900 contributions from 800 scholars to explore key concepts of economics, firms and individuals, institutions, countries, and cities. Although scholarly in tone, this volume is an excellent starting point for those wishing to trace ideas and industries across chronological boundaries." Libr J

Includes bibliographical references and index

Sowell, Thomas

Basic economics; a common sense guide to the economy. 4th ed.; Basic Books 2011 689p $39.95   **330**

1. Economics
ISBN 978-0-465-02252-6
First published 2000

Thomas Sowell explains the principles of economics in plain jargon for the general public, answering questions like: Why are homeless people sleeping on the sidewalks of New York in the winter, when the abandoned apartment buildings have four times as many dwelling units as there are homeless people in the city? Why did Russians have to import food to feed people in Moscow, when Russia itself had vast amounts of some of the richest farmland in Europe?

"Sowell's volume does a fantastic job in cultivating the reader's 'economic imagination.'" Choice

★ The **Statesman's** Yearbook 2014; The Politics, Cultures and Economies of the World. edited by Barry Turner. 150th ed. Palgrave Macmillan 2013 1608 p. (hardcover) $325   **330**

1. Almanacs 2. Geopolitics
ISBN 0230377696; 9780230377691

This reference book "presents a political, economic and social account of every country of the world together with facts and analysis. The 2014 edition includes revised and updated biographical profiles of all current leaders," "revised economic overviews for every country," and a "chronology of key political events from April 2010 to March 2011." (Publisher's note)

Taylor, Timothy

The **instant** economist; Timothy Taylor. Plume 2012 x, 260p.p ill. pa $16   **330**

1. Economics
ISBN 978-0-452-29752-4

LC 2011033416

This book provides an introduction to "[e]conomics [which] isn't just about numbers: It's about politics, psychology, history, and so much more. We are all economists-when we work, save for the future, invest, pay taxes, and buy our groceries. Yet many of us feel lost when the subject arises. . . . Timothy Taylor tackles all the key questions and hot topics of both microeconomics and macroeconomics, including: Why do budget deficits matter? What exactly does the Federal Reserve do? Does globalization take jobs away from American workers? Why is health insurance so costly?" (Publisher's note)

Includes bibliographical references

Wheelan, Charles J.

★ **Naked** economics; {by} Charles Wheelan; foreword by Burton G. Malkiel. Norton 2002 xxii, 260p $25.95; pa $15.95   **330**

1. Finance 2. Economics 3. Financial services industry
ISBN 0-393-04982-5; 0-393-32486-9 pa

LC 2002-23580

This is an introduction to economics. Index.

The author explains the essentials of economics, defining "terms like GDP and inflation, explaining how they work and what the short- and long-term impact might be. . . . This

is a thoughtful, well-written introduction to economics, with the author projecting a genuine excitement for his material." Libr J

Includes bibliographical references

330.1   Systems, schools, theories

Appleby, Joyce

The **relentless** revolution; a history of capitalism. [by] Joyce Appleby. W.W. Norton 2010 494p $29.95   **330.1**

1. Capitalism -- History 2. Economic conditions 3. Economic history
ISBN 978-0-393-06894-8; 0-393-06894-3

LC 2009-35676

"Whether masterfully discussing the significance of agricultural progress that made capitalism possible, or touching lightly on the impact of Amazon and e-mail, Appleby offers consistently illuminating commentary. A useful introduction to a vast, complex topic." Kirkus

Includes bibliographical references

Heilbroner, Robert L.

★ The **worldly** philosophers; the lives, times, and ideas of the great economic thinkers. Rev. 7th ed.; Simon & Schuster 1999 365p pa $16   **330.1**

1. Authors 2. Utopias 3. Economics 4. Capitalism 5. Economists 6. Depressions 7. Imperialism 8. Journalists 9. Social critics 10. Nonfiction writers 11. Patrons of the arts 12. Writers on politics 13. Political and social philosophers
ISBN 0-684-86214-X

LC 99-14050

First published 1953

The author traces the story of economics and the great economists from Adam Smith, Malthus, Ricardo, the Utopians, Marx, Veblen and Keynes to those working with the problems of our contemporary world

Includes bibliographical references

Keynes, John Maynard, 1883-1946

★ The **general** theory of employment, interest and money. Harcourt Brace & Co. 1936 403p hardcover o.p. pa $15   **330.1**

1. Money 2. Economics 3. Interest (Economics)
ISBN 0-15-634711-3 pa

This work "revolutionized economic theory by showing how unemployment could occur 'involuntarily'. For 30 years after the Second World War governments of western nations pursued 'Keynesian' full-employment policies." Oxford Companion to Engl Lit. 5th edition

Marx, Karl, 1818-1883

★ **Capital** : an abridged edition; edited with an introduction and notes by David McLellan. Oxford University Press 2008 xxxii, 499p (Oxford world's classics) pa $16.95   **330.1**

1. Capital 2. Economics
ISBN 978-0-19-953570-5

LC 2008-274361

Abridged edition first published 1995

This abridged edition of Marx's three-volume "denunciation of mid-Victorian capitalist society . . . offers virtually all of Volume 1, which Marx himself published in 1867; excerpts from a . . . translation of 'The Result of the Immediate Process Production'; and a selection of key chapters from Volume 3, which Engels published in 1895." Publisher's note

Patel, Raj

The **value** of nothing; how to reshape market society and redefine democracy. Picador 2010 250p pa $14 **330.1**
1. Democracy 2. Economic policy 3. Free enterprise
ISBN 978-0-312-42924-9

LC 2009-41546

The author "lays bare the social, political, and environmental damage caused by free markets and the commoditization of every facet of any market society. . . . Patel debunks the myth that markets are the perfect form of social organization, effectively arguing that the tyranny they exert can and must be replaced by strategies benefiting all humanity and ensuring our very survival. This work is written calmly and sensibly enough that it could change some readers' minds, although it will leave free-market apologists spluttering. Highly recommended." Libr J

Includes bibliographical references

Sandel, Michael J., 1953-

What money can't buy; the moral limits of markets. Michael J. Sandel. Farrar Straus & Giroux 2012 244 p. **330.1**
1. Capitalism 2. Business ethics 3. Free enterprise 4. Economics -- Philosophy
ISBN 0374203032; 9780374203030

LC 2011052182

In this book author Michael J. Sandel "takes on . . . the . . . ethical questions . . . Is there something wrong with a world in which everything is for sale? If so, how can we prevent market values from reaching into spheres of life where they don't belong? What are the moral limits of markets? In recent decades, market values have crowded out nonmarket norms in almost every aspect of life—medicine, education, government, law, art, sports, even family life and personal relations. Without quite realizing it, Sandel argues, we have drifted from having a market economy to being a market society. . . . What is the proper role of markets in a democratic society—and how can we protect the moral and civic goods that markets don't honor and that money can't buy?" (Publisher's note)

Includes bibliographical references and index

Smith, Adam, 1723-1790

★ The **wealth** of nations; introduction by Robert Reich; edited, with notes, marginal summary, and enlarged index by Edwin Cannan. Modern Library 2000 xxvi, 1154p pa $15.95 **330.1**
1. Economics
ISBN 0-679-78336-9; 978-0-679-78336-7

LC 00-64573

First published 1776

This treatise "is the first comprehensive treatment of the whole subject of political economy, and is remarkable for its breadth of view. . . . In it, the author presents an attack on the mercantile system, and an advocacy of freedom of commerce and industry." Oxford Companion to Engl Lit. 6th edition

Includes bibliographical references

330.12 Systems

Burgin, Angus

The **great** persuasion; reinventing free markets since the Depression. Angus Burgin. Harvard University Press 2012 303 p. (hardcover) $29.95 **330.12**
1. Free enterprise 2. Economic policy -- United States -- History 3. United States -- Economic conditions -- 20th century 4. Capitalism 5. Economic policy
ISBN 0674058135; 9780674058132

LC 2012015061

This book, by Angus Burgin, explores the history of free market capitalism in the U.S. It "traces the evolution of postwar economic thought. . . . Conservatives often point to Friedrich Hayek as the most influential defender of the free market. By examining the work of such organizations as the Mont Pèlerin Society, . . . Burgin reveals that Hayek and his colleagues were deeply conflicted about many of the enduring problems of capitalism." (Publisher's note)

Includes bibliographical references and index

McMillan, John

Reinventing the bazaar; a natural history of markets. Norton 2002 278p $25.95; pa $15.95 **330.12**
1. Capitalism
ISBN 0-393-05021-1; 0-393-32371-4 pa

LC 2002-521

The author "examines how markets in ancient times evolved and shows how countries experimented with markets, some successfully and some not. . . . He takes a refreshingly commonsense approach to his subject, doesn't talk down to his readers, and refrains from excessive economic jargon." Libr J

Includes bibliographical references

Soto, Hernando de

The **mystery** of capital; why captitalism triumphs in the West and fails everywhere else. Basic Bks. 2000 276p il $27.50; pa $17 **330.12**
1. Capitalism
ISBN 0-465-01614-6; 0-465-01615-4 pa

LC 00-34301

The author contends that "the poor do not really 'own' the property they work, because they are not registered as owning it, and because of this, they cannot turn it into capital. . . . The market is restricted and the growth of wealth retarded. His solution is simple: give the poor title to the property they own de facto, and their countries will become capital rich." N Y Times Book Rev

330.9   Economic situation and conditions

Bartiromo, Maria

The **weekend** that changed Wall Street; an eyewitness account. [by] Maria Bartiromo, with Catherine Whitney. Portfolio Penguin 2010 232p $26.95   **330.9**

1. Bank failures 2. Global Financial Crisis, 2008-2009
ISBN 978-1-59184-351-1

LC 2010026892

"Bartiromo lays out the facts of the Lehman Brothers downfall using both her own account and those of the most powerful people on Wall Street. . . . The most fascinating aspects of . . . [this book] were not so much the details of the collapse . . . but the book's early focus on the lavish lives of those involved in the Wall Street game; Bartiromo details the parties they threw, the apartments they owned that resembled art galleries and the confidence they exuded, which came across not only in their business conversations, but also in the casual talks between the author and her trusting subjects. " Risk Management

Includes bibliographical references

The **best** business writing 2013; edited by Dean Starkman, Martha M. Hamilton, Ryan Chittum, and Felix Salmon. Columbia University Press 2013 568 p. (Columbia Journalism Review books) (pbk. : alk. paper) $18.95   **330.9**

1. Journalism 2. Business writing 3. Business 4. Businesspeople 5. Business enterprises -- Corrupt practices
ISBN 0231160755; 9780231160759

LC 2012047913

This book, edited by Dean Starkman, Martha M. Hamilton, Ryan Chittum, and Felix Salmon, is a collection of the "most engaging or rigorous business writing" of 2013. It "showcases content from diverse sources, including newspapers, magazines, and blogs." Several articles "scrutinize the recent economic downturn." (Publishers Weekly)

De Graaf, John

What's the economy for, anyway? why it's time to stop chasing growth and start pursuing happiness. [by] John de Graaf and David K. Batker; foreword by James Gustave Speth. Bloomsbury Press 2011 292p il $25   **330.9**

1. Happiness 2. Economic development 3. United States -- Economic conditions
ISBN 978-1-60819-510-7; 1-60819-510-4

LC 2011017438

De Graaf and Batker "examine new ways to think about economic processes, specifically as they relate to human happiness and well-being. The authors show that the indicators of performance developed during World War II—the 'Gross National Product'—have become both obscurantist and counterproductive. They argue that human purposes and needs ought to provide the basis for much more broadly based measures of performance, which would consider what is the greatest good and benefit for the greatest number of people over the longest period of time. . . . An entertaining

presentation of important ideas and information about how lives could be improved." Kirkus

Includes bibliographical references

The **economists'** voice 2.0; the financial crisis, health care reform, and more. editors, Aaron S. Edlin, Joseph E. Stiglitz ; coeditors, Bradford De-Long ... [et al]. Columbia University Press 2012 viii, 270 p.p ill. (cloth : alk. paper) $27.95 **330.9**

1. Medical policy -- United States 2. Economic policy -- United States 3. United States -- Economic conditions 4. Economics -- United States 5. United States -- Economic policy -- 2009- 6. United States -- Economic conditions -- 2009-
ISBN 0231160143; 9780231160148

LC 2011047626

"This collection," edited by Aaron S. Edlin and Joseph E. Stiglitz, "contains thirty-two essays written by academics, economists, presidential advisors, legal specialists, researchers, consultants, and policy makers. They tackle the plain economics and architecture of health care reform, its implications for society and the future of the health insurance industry, and the value of the health insurance subsidies and exchanges built into the law." (Publisher's note)

Includes bibliographical references and index.

Epping, Randy Charles

The **21st** century economy; a beginner's guide: with 101 easy-to-learn tools for surviving and thriving in the new global marketplace. Vintage Books 2009 316p pa $14.95   **330.9**

1. Globalization 2. Economic conditions 3. International trade 4. International finance
ISBN 978-0-307-38790-5

LC 2008-41554

This is an "explanation of the workings of our modern economy and hundreds of terms, such as subprime debt, CDO, IMF, money supply, and discount rate. . . . [The author] is able to explain the global economy in language that most readers will find both understandable and interesting." Libr J

Friedman, Jeffrey

Engineering the financial crisis; systemic risk and the failure of regulation. Jeffrey Friedman and Wladimir Kraus. University of Pennsylvania Press 2011 x, 212 p.p   **330.9**

1. Cooperative banks 2. Banks and banking -- United States 3. Global Financial Crisis, 2008-2009 4. Basel II (2004) 5. Basle Accord (1988) 6. Economics -- Political aspects 7. Bank capital -- Law and legislation 8. Banks and banking -- Risk management 9. Financial crises -- United States -- History -- 21st century
ISBN 0812243579; 9780812243574

LC 2011024456

Author Jeffrey Friedman discusses "the Basel Accords, a set of international standards for banking supervision and regulation . . . [The book looks at the] role that bank capital requirements and other government regulations played in the recent financial crisis . . . [The author argues] that by encouraging banks to invest in highly rated mortgage-backed bonds, the Basel Accords created an overconcentration of risk in the banking industry." (Publisher's note)

Includes bibliographical references (p. [175]-200) and index

Huffington, Arianna

Third World America; how our politicians are abandoning the middle class and betraying the American dream. Crown Publishers 2010 276p $23.99; ebook $9.99 **330.9**

1. Social policy -- United States 2. Economic policy -- United States 3. United States -- Politics and government -- 2001-

ISBN 978-0-307-71982-9; 978-0-307-71997-3 ebook

LC 2010-26871

The author "argues that overspending on war at the expense of domestic issues and the alarming decline of the middle class are troubling signals that the U.S. is losing its economic, political, and social stability—a stability that has always been maintained by the middle class. . . . An engaging analysis of troubling economic and political trends." Booklist

Krugman, Paul R., 1953-

★ End this depression now! Paul Krugman. W.W. Norton & Co. 2012 xii, 259 p.p ill. $24.95 **330.9**

1. Recessions 2. Unemployment 3. Economic policy -- United States 4. United States -- Economic conditions 5. United States -- Economic policy -- 21st century 6. Recessions -- United States -- History -- 21st century 7. Unemployment -- United States -- History -- 21st century 8. Financial crises -- United States -- History -- 21st century

ISBN 0393088774; 9780393088779

LC 2012009067

This book, by Nobel Prize-winning economist Paul Krugman, discusses the U.S. Great Recession of 2008 and following. It asks why "'nations rich in resources, talent, and knowledge--all the ingredients for prosperity and a decent standard of living for all--remain in a state of intense pain.' . . . How did we get stuck in what now can only be called a depression? And above all, how do we free ourselves?" (Publisher's note)

"Krugman's forceful jargon-free criticisms and solutions directed at a general audience are a thoughtful contribution to both economic and political discourse in this election year. Highly recommended for a broad readership." LJ

Lanchester, John

★ I.O.U. why everyone owes everyone and no one can pay. Simon & Schuster 2010 260p $25 **330.9**

1. Economic conditions 2. International finance 3. Global Financial Crisis, 2008-2009

ISBN 978-1-4391-6984-1; 1-4391-6984-5

LC 2009-36465

This book is "equal parts history, economic primer, and social commentary—that manages to be, by turns, acidic, frightening, and sharply funny." Entertainment Wkly

Includes bibliographical references

Lewis, Michael

The big short; inside the doomsday machine. W.W. Norton 2010 266p **330.9**

1. Financial crises 2. Global Financial Crisis, 2008-2009 3. Financial crises -- United States 4. United States -- Economic conditions 5. United States -- Economic conditions -- 2001-2009

ISBN 0-393-07223-1; 0-393-33882-7 pa; 978-0-393-07223-5; 978-0-393-33882-9 pa

LC 201004804

This is a study of the financial crisis that began in 2008. Michael Lewis, the author of Liar's Poker (1989) contends that "the roots of the meltdown of 2008 can be found in the 1980s, . . . when complex financial products like mortgage derivatives were developed." (N Y Times (Late N Y Ed))

"'The Big Short' manages to give us the truest picture yet of what went wrong on Wall Street—and why. At times, it reads like a morality play, at other times like a modern-day farce. But as with any good play, its value lies in the way it reveals character and motive and explores the cultural context in which the plot unfolds." Washington Post

Liveris, Andrew

Make it in America; the case for re-inventing the economy. Wiley 2011 xxi, 208p il $24.95; ebook $16.99 **330.9**

1. Manufactures 2. Economic forecasting 3. Industrial policy -- United States 4. United States -- Economic conditions

ISBN 978-0-470-93022-9; 0-470-93022-5; 9781118019405 ebook

LC 2010045654

The author "calls for a national strategy to revive manufacturing. We need manufacturing jobs, he says, if we are to keep a growing population busy and start paying off our debts to the rest of the world." Wall Street J

Includes bibliographical references

Madrick, Jeffrey G.

Age of greed; the triumph of finance and the decline of America, 1970 to the present. [by] Jeff Madrick. Alfred A. Knopf 2011 464p il $30; ebook $14.99 **330.9**

1. Wealth 2. Financial crises 3. Capitalists and financiers 4. Wealth -- Moral and ethical aspects 5. Financial crises -- United States -- History 6. United States -- Economic policy -- 2001-2009 7. United States -- Economic policy -- 20th century 8. United States -- Politics and government -- 20th century 9. United States -- Politics and government -- 21st century

ISBN 978-1-4000-4171-8; 978-0-307-59671-0 ebook

LC 2011003399

This book "is a fascinating and deeply disturbing tale of hypocrisy, corruption, and insatiable greed. But more than that, it's a much-needed reminder of just how we got into the mess we're in—a reminder that is greatly needed when we are still being told that greed is good." New York Rev Books

Includes bibliographical references

Martínez, Rubén

Desert America; boom and bust in the new Old West. Rubén Martínez. Metropolitan Books/ Henry Holt and Company 2012 333 p. $28.00 **330.9**
1. Poverty 2. West (U.S.) 3. Drugs and crime 4. Immigrants -- United States 5. New Mexico -- Race relations 6. New Mexico -- Social conditions -- 21st century 7. New Mexico -- Economic conditions -- 21st century
ISBN 0805079777; 9780805079777
LC 2011040587
"In this first-person report . . . [Rubén] Martínez . . . sojourns in the more remote regions of the Southwest . . . and finds the front line of a battle over the American past and future. . . . Martínez does his best to immerse himself in a largely Latino community that is extremely aware of outsiders, weighing the stark realities of his neighbors' lives while musing on disparities and dislocations teaching back hundreds of years." (Publishers Weekly)

McLean, Bethany

All the devils are here; the hidden history of the financial crisis. [by] Bethany McLean and Joe Nocera. Portfolio/Penguin 2010 380p il $32.95 **330.9**
1. Mortgages 2. International finance 3. Global Financial Crisis, 2008-2009 4. Mortgage-backed securities 5. Financial crises -- United States
ISBN 978-1-59184-363-4; 1-59184-363-4
LC 2010-32893
This is an "account of the late financial meltdown, when, in the words of one analyst, 'we went from a collective belief in soundness to a collective belief in insolvency.' . . . Hard-hitting reporting and fluent writing bring the utter devastation of the Great Recession to life." Kirkus
Includes bibliographical references

Paulson, Henry M.

★ **On** the brink; inside the race to stop the collapse of the global financial system. Business Plus 2010 478p il $28.99 **330.9**
1. Global Financial Crisis, 2008-2009 2. Economic policy -- United States
ISBN 978-0-446-56193-8; 0-446-56193-2
LC 2009-939043
"This is the ultimate insider's account of the crisis, and, owing to its evenhanded tone and penetrating insights into government actions, it will also remain an important contribution to the historical record of the crisis, essential reading for everyone interested in knowing what happened." Libr J

Perino, Michael A.

The **hellhound** of Wall Street; how Ferdinand Pecora's investigation of the Great Crash forever changed American finance. [by] Michael Perino. Penguin Press 2010 341p il $27.95 **330.9**
1. Judges 2. Lawyers 3. Stock exchanges 4. Financial crises 5. Stock market crash, 1929 6. Regulatory agency officials
ISBN 978-1-59420-272-8
LC 2010-19157
The author "recounts the 1933 investigation into Wall Street abuses by the Senate Committee on Banking and Cur-

rency, focusing on the 10-day interrogation by chief counsel Ferdinand Pecora of executives of National City Bank (precursor to Citigroup). . . . Perino's book is a trenchant, entertaining study of the New Deal's heroic beginnings, one with obvious relevance to latter-day efforts to rein in Wall Street's excesses." Publ Wkly
Includes bibliographical references

Piscione, Deborah Perry

Secrets of Silicon Valley; what everyone else can learn from the innovation capital of the world. Deborah Perry Piscione. Palgrave Macmillan 2013 256 p. (hardcover) $27 **330.9**
1. High technology industry 2. Santa Clara Valley (Santa Clara County, Calif.) -- Economic conditions 3. Technological innovations -- California -- Santa Clara County 4. High technology industries -- California -- Santa Clara County
ISBN 0230342116; 9780230342118
LC 2012038481
This book, by Deborah Perry Piscione, explores the economics of Silicon Valley. "While the global economy languishes, one place just keeps growing . . . : Silicon Valley. . . . Piscione takes us inside this vibrant ecosystem where meritocracy rules the day. She explores Silicon Valley's exceptionally risk-tolerant culture, and why it thrives despite the many laws that make California one of the worst states in the union for business." (Publisher's note)

Rajan, Raghuram G., 1963-

Fault lines; how hidden fractures still threaten the world economy. Princeton University Press 2010 260p **330.9**
1. Global Financial Crisis, 2008-2009 2. Economic history -- 21st century 3. United States -- Social conditions 4. United States -- Economic conditions 5. Income distribution -- United States -- History 6. United States -- Social conditions -- 21st century 7. United States -- Economic conditions -- 21st century
ISBN 9780691146836; 9780691152639; 9781400834211
LC 2010-6031
Some have blamed global financial crisis of 2008-2009 on "bankers who took irrational risks and left the rest of us to foot the bill. . . . Rajan argues that serious flaws in the economy are also to blame, and warns that a potentially more devastating crisis awaits us if they aren't fixed. Rajan [aims to] show how the individual choices that collectively brought about the economic meltdown—made by bankers, government officials, and ordinary homeowners—were rational responses to a flawed global financial order in which the incentives to take on risk are . . . out of step with the dangers those risks pose. He traces [what he views as] the deepening fault lines in a world overly dependent on the indebted American consumer to power global economic growth and stave off global downturns. He [argues that] . . . America's growing inequality and thin social safety net create tremendous political pressure to encourage easy credit and keep job creation robust, no matter what the consequences to the economy's long-term health; and . . . [that] the U.S. financial sector, with its skewed incentives, is the critical but unstable link between an overstimulated America and an

underconsuming world. . . . . He outlines the hard choices [he believes] we need to make to ensure a more stable world economy and restore lasting prosperity." (Publisher's note) Bibliography. Index.

The author "explains the financial market panic of 2008 and argues that the weaknesses or fault lines in the world economy that led to financial collapse and recession persist. . . . Economists who can challenge their peers while remaining accessible to the general reader are rare, but Rajan belongs to this elite group. No short summary can do justice to this well-written, insightful, and nuanced study." Choice

Includes bibliographical references

Reich, Robert B.

Aftershock; the next economy and America's future. Alfred A. Knopf 2010 174p il $25; ebook $11.99 **330.9**

1. United States -- Economic policy 2. United States -- Social conditions 3. United States -- Economic conditions 4. United States -- Social conditions -- Forecasting

ISBN 978-0-307-59281-1; 0-307-59281-2; 978-0-307-59452-5 ebook

LC 2010-04134

Reich "argues that America will not have a sustained economic recovery until the middle class has more buying power. In this call for reform, the author writes that the increasing concentration of wealth among a small percentage of Americans was the main culprit in the destabilization of the U.S. economy in 2008. . . . Lucid and cogent." Kirkus

Includes bibliographical references

Sachs, Jeffrey, 1954-

The **price** of civilization; reawakening American virtue and prosperity. Random House 2011 324p il $27; ebook $12.99 **330.9**

1. Economic policy -- United States 2. United States -- Economic policy -- 2009- 3. Environmental responsibility -- United States 4. United States -- Economic conditions -- 2009- 5. Social responsibility of business -- United States 6. United States -- Economic conditions -- 21st century 7. United States -- Politics and government -- 21st century

ISBN 9781400068418; 140006841X; 9780679605027 ebook; 0679605029 ebook

LC 2011014631

The author "explores the economic, political, social, and psychological roots of the U.S.'s 30-year journey 'from decades of consensus and high achievement to an era of deep division and growing crisis.' He indicts America's elites for abandoning social responsibility, politicians for giving up on solving problems, the media for distraction and hyper-commercialization, and citizens for surrendering to that distraction. He urges mindfulness, clear goals for political reform, and significant tax changes, and he suggests that the millennial generation will lead the way to a restoration of the nation's highest aspirations" Booklist

Includes bibliographical references (p. [277]-307) and index.

Sorkin, Andrew Ross

★ **Too** big to fail; the inside story of how Wall Street and Washington fought to save the financial system from crisis--and themselves. Viking 2009 xx, 600p il $32.95; pa $18 **330.9**

1. Financial crises 2. Global Financial Crisis, 2008-2009

ISBN 978-0-670-02125-3; 0-670-02125-3; 978-0-14-311824-4 pa; 0-14-311824-2 pa

LC 2009-36494

This is an account of the recent financial crisis.

"Sorkin boasts of the hours spent interviewing, emailing, inspecting telephone call logs, billing time sheets and even expense reports [for this book], and his reward is the fullest and most convincing account of the Lehman debacle. Conversations are reconstructed, and an air of authenticity created by the accumulation of thousands of small facts." Times Lit Suppl

Includes bibliographical references

330.91 Areas, regions, places in general

Sharma, Ruchir

★ **Breakout** nations; in pursuit of the next economic miracles. Ruchir Sharma. W.W. Norton & Co. 2012 x, 292 p.p $26.95 **330.91**

1. Economic development 2. Economic forecasting 3. Developing countries -- Economic conditions 4. Economic history -- 21st century

ISBN 0393080269; 9780393080261

LC 2012005810

This book, by Ruchir Sharma, examines how "[a]fter a decade of rapid growth, the world's most celebrated emerging markets are poised to slow down. . . . To identify the economic stars of the future we should abandon the habit of extrapolating from the recent past and lumping wildly diverse countries together. . . . What emerges is a clear picture of the shifting balance of global economic power and how it plays out for emerging nations and for the West." (Publisher's note)

Includes bibliographical references and index.

330.973 Economic conditions -- United States

Barlett, Donald L.

The **betrayal** of the American dream; Donald L. Barlett and James B. Steele. 1st ed. PublicAffairs 2012 xxi, 289 p.p ill. (hardcover) $26.99; (ebook) $26.99 **330.973**

1. Middle class -- United States 2. Economic policy -- United States 3. United States -- Economic conditions 4. United States -- Economic policy -- 2009- 5. United States -- Economic conditions -- 2009- 6. Middle class -- United States -- Economic conditions -- 21st century 7. Working class -- United States -- Economic conditions -- 21st century

ISBN 1586489690; 9781586489694; 9781586489700

LC 2012012879

In this book, authors Donald L. Barlett and James B. Steele "maintain that the deficit is less the result of government programs than plummeting tax revenue from the rich. . . . The authors' solutions include: Revise the tax code so corporations and the rich pay more than the middle class instead of less, discard the clueless ideology of free trade . . . re-regulate disastrously unregulated areas, and enforce current laws equally instead of giving the influential a free pass." (Kirkus Reviews)

Includes bibliographical references and index.

Blinder, Alan S.

After the music stopped; the financial crisis, the response, and the work ahead. Alan S. Blinder. Penguin Press 2013 xix, 476 p.p ill. (hardcover) $29.95   **330.973**
1. Global Financial Crisis, 2008-2009 2. United States -- Economic conditions 3. Finance -- United States 4. Financial crises -- United States 5. United States -- Economic policy -- 2009- 6. United States -- Economic conditions -- 2009-
ISBN 1594205302; 9781594205309
       LC 2012031025

In this book, "[Alan S.] Blinder, a corporate executive and former vice chairman of the Federal Reserve, sets out to tell the American people what happened during the financial crisis of 2007-09. He explains the events that are still reverberating in the U.S. and globally and will challenge public policy for years." (Booklist)

Includes bibliographical references (p. [455]-462) and index.

Ferguson, Charles

Predator nation; corporate criminals, political corruption, and the hijacking of America. Charles Ferguson. Crown Business 2012 vii, 369 p.p ill. $27.00   **330.973**
1. Securities fraud 2. Elite (Social sciences) 3. Wall Street (New York, N.Y.) 4. Manufacturing industries -- United States 5. Equality -- United States 6. United States -- Economic policy 7. Financial crises -- United States 8. Banks and banking -- United States 9. Global Financial Crisis, 2008-2009 10. United States -- Politics and government 11. United States -- Economic conditions -- 2009-
ISBN 030795255X; 9780307952554
       LC 2011052366

In this book, "author Charles H. Ferguson . . . explains how a predator elite took over the country, step by step, and he exposes the networks of academic, financial, and political influence, in all recent administrations, that prepared the predators' path to conquest." Topics include the decline of the manufacturing industry, fraud in the finance industry, and income inequality in the U.S. (Publisher's note)

Includes bibliographical references (p. 333-349) and index

Lind, Michael, 1962-

Land of promise; an economic history of the United States. by Michael Lind. Broadside Books 2012 586 p. (hardback) $29.99   **330.973**
1. United States -- History 2. Technological innovations

-- History 3. United States -- Economic conditions
ISBN 0061834807; 9780061834806; 9780061834813
       LC 2011047794

Author Michael Lind presents an "account of how a weak collection of former British colonies became an industrial, financial, and military colossus. From the eighteenth to the twenty-first centuries, the American economy has been transformed by wave after wave of emerging technology: the steam engine, electricity, the internal combustion engine, computer technology." Lind "demonstrates that Americans, since the earliest days of the republic, have reinvented the American economy--and have the power to do so again." (Publisher's note)

McCraw, Thomas K., 1940-2012

★ The **founders** and finance; how Hamilton, Gallatin, and other immigrants forged a new economy. Thomas K. McCraw. Belknap Press of Harvard University Press 2012 485 p. (hardcover) $35 **330.973**
1. Fiscal policy -- United States -- History 2. United States -- Economic policy 3. United States -- History -- 1783-1865 4. Finance, Public -- United States -- History 5. Monetary policy -- United States -- History 6. United States. Dept. of the Treasury -- History 7. United States -- History -- Revolution, 1775-1783 8. United States -- Politics and government -- 1783-1865
ISBN 0674066928; 9780674066922
       LC 2012014006

This book, by Thomas K. McCraw, shows how "analyzes the skills and worldliness of Alexander Hamilton . . . , Albert Gallatin . . . , and other immigrant founders who guided the [United States] to prosperity. . . . Innovations designed by Hamilton, Gallatin, and other immigrants enabled the United States to control its debts, to pay for the Louisiana Purchase of 1803, and . . . preserve[] the nation's hard-won independence from Britain." (Publisher's note)

"McCraw is a talented storyteller. His highly readable and fascinating work portrays the brilliance of Hamilton and Gallatin against the difficulty of their time and is strongly recommended to all readers interested in American and financial history." LJ

Includes bibliographical references and index

331   Economics of labor, finance, land, energy

Crawford, Matthew B.

Shop class as soulcraft; an inquiry into the value of work. Penguin Press 2009 246p il $25.95   **331**
1. Work
ISBN 978-1-59420-223-0
       LC 2009-1789

The author "extols the value of making and fixing things in this masterful paean to what he calls 'manual competence,' the ability to work with one's hands. . . . With wit and humor, the author deftly mixes the details of his own experience as a tradesman and then proprietor of a motorcycle repair shop with more philosophical considerations." Publ Wkly

Includes bibliographical references

De Botton, Alain, 1969-

The **pleasures** and sorrows of work. Pantheon Books 2009 326p il $26 **331**

1. Labor 2. Work -- Social aspects

ISBN 978-0-375-42444-1

LC 2008-46060

In this study of the workplace, the author visits "the under-charted worlds of the office, the factory, the fishing fleet and the logistics centre. . . . [He discusses such questions about work as]: Why do we do it? What makes it pleasurable? What is its meaning? And why do we daily exhaust not only ourselves but also the planet?" (Publisher's note)

"De Botton's sprightly mix of reportage and rumination expands beyond the workplace to investigate the broader meaning of life." Publ Wkly

Lichtenstein, Nelson

State of the Union: a century of American labor. Princeton Univ. Press 2002 336p il (Politics and society in twentieth-century America) hardcover o.p. pa $18.95 **331**

1. Labor unions 2. Labor -- United States

ISBN 0-691-11654-7 pa

LC 2001-36863

The author "analyzes the history of the labor movement from the 1930's to the present in the context of U.S. economics, politics, and democracy and from this he formulates ideas about where labor may find opportunities in this new century." Libr J

Includes bibliographical references

Murolo, Priscilla

From the folks who brought you the weekend; a short, illustrated history of labor in the United States. {by} Priscilla Murolo and A.B. Chitty; illustrations by Joe Sacco. New Press (NY) 2001 xx, 364p hardcover o.p. pa $17.95 **331**

1. Working class 2. Labor movement 3. Labor -- United States

ISBN 1-56584-776-8 pa

LC 2001-30978

"Brandishing little-known facts, the authors reshape common views of social history." Publ Wkly

Includes bibliographical references

Murray, R. Emmett

★ The **lexicon** of labor; more than 500 key terms, biographical sketches, and historical insights concerning labor in America. Rev. and updated ed.; New Press 2010 235p pa $16.95 **331**

1. Reference books 2. Labor -- United States -- Dictionaries

ISBN 978-1-59558-226-3

LC 2010-8276

First published 1998

This is an "encyclopedia of 500 entries for terms, concepts, people, legislation, places, and events in U.S. labor history." Booklist

This is an "encyclopedia of 500 entries for terms, concepts, people, legislation, places, and events in U.S. labor history." Booklist

Includes bibliographical references

331.1 Labor force and market

Damp, Dennis V.

★ The **book** of U.S. government jobs; where they are, what's available, and how to complete a Federal resume. 11th ed.; Bookhaven Press 2011 308p il pa $27.95 **331.1**

1. Civil service -- United States

ISBN 978-0-943641-29-4

LC 2011903343

First published 1986

This is "an essential guide to securing well-paying federal positions. [Its] . . . 11 chapters offer highly detailed instruction on where to locate and how to apply for federal jobs. Featuring tips for interview and exam performance, the accessible text presents instructive narratives and helpful sidebar hints. . . . Other chapters clarify the qualifications necessary for securing positions with the police, the postal service, and the homeland security administration." Libr J

Includes bibliographical references

Taylor, Nick

★ **American** -made; the enduring legacy of the WPA: when FDR put the nation to work. Bantam Books 2008 630p il $27 **331.1**

1. New Deal, 1933-1939 2. United States -- Works Progress Administration

ISBN 978-0-553-80235-1; 0-553-80235-6

LC 2007-34563

"Lavishly illustrated, the book also has a list of New Deal organizations, a partial list of construction projects, a New Deal chronology, and endnotes. It will be a boon to all 20th-century history collections." Libr J

Includes bibliographical references

Woodward, Bob, 1943-

Maestro : Greenspan's Fed and the American boom. Simon & Schuster 2000 270p il $25; pa $14 **331.1**

1. Economists 2. Bankers 3. Government officials 4. Presidential advisers 5. Regulatory agency officials 6. Monetary policy -- United States 7. Board of Governors of the Federal Reserve System 8. Federal Reserve System (U.S.) -- Board of Governors 9. Monetary policy -- United States -- History -- 20th century

ISBN 0-7432-0412-3; 0-7432-0562-6 pa

LC 00-52627

Woodward discusses the influence exerted over the American economy by the chairman of the Federal Reserve Board, Alan Greenspan. Index.

"In a surprisingly short book, Woodward lucidly explains the axes of intellectual and political disagreement over monetary policy, productivity growth, irrational exuberance and more, shedding new light on major conflicts of the Greenspan era and demystifying this most political of ostensibly technical institutions." N Y Times Book Rev

Includes bibliographical references

331.10973   Labor force and market -- United States

Bittle, Scott

Where did the jobs go-- and how do we get them back? your guided tour to America's employment crisis. Scott Bittle and Jean Johnson. WilliamMorrow 2012 xix, 342 p.p (paperback) $16.99   **331.10973**

1. Employment 2. Unemployment 3. United States -- Economic conditions 4. Unemployment -- United States 5. Unemployment -- Government policy -- United States

ISBN 0061715662; 9780061715662

LC 2012371737

This book by Scott Bittle and Jean Johnson presents a "discussion and study guide on unemployment. . . . The authors provide a[n] . . . analysis of the many problems caused by the unemployment crisis, as well as possible solutions. . . . The authors . . . provide a[n] . . . historical discussion of the 1930s Depression and FDR's WPA program, as well as estimates of the financial costs of possible solutions and the ramifications for other sectors of American society." (Kirkus Reviews)

Includes bibliographical references (p. [302]-342)

331.12   Labor market

Occupational outlook handbook 2013-2014. Skyhorse Pub. 2012 vi, 889 p.p (paperback) $16.95   **331.12**

1. Occupations 2. Vocational guidance

ISBN 1616086181; 9781616086183

This book, written by the U.S. Department of Labor, "is designed to provide valuable, up-to-date assistance to individuals making decisions about their futures. Accompanying each profession are descriptions of the nature of the work, working environment, job outlook training, and the required education, as well as job earnings, related occupations, and additional information sources." (Publisher's note)

331.13   Discrimination in employment, labor shortages, unemployment

Snyder, Don J.

The **cliff** walk; a memoir of a lost job and a life found. Little, Brown 1997 265p $23.95; pa $12.95   **331.13**

1. Authors 2. Carpenters 3. College teachers

ISBN 0-316-80308-1; 0-316-80348-0 pa

LC 96-51163

"When the author is fired by Colgate University, he never doubts that his brilliance and charm will soon gain him entrance to a new ivory tower. Instead, he is forced to move his family of five to Maine in the off season. With his

pride and his checking account steadily eroding, he concocts wild schemes—stealing golf balls from a nearby course with his son, and secretly contemplating selling his unborn child. Finally, Snyder gives his last seventeen hundred dollars to a dying woman so she can take her children to Disney World. This dire act propels him into a real job—building a house—and toward a vision of self that depends more on strength than on prestige." New Yorker

331.2   Conditions of employment

Lowenstein, Roger

While America aged; how pension debts ruined General Motors, stopped the NYC subways, bankrupted San Diego, and loom as the next financial crisis. Penguin Press 2008 274p $25.95   **331.2**

1. Pensions 2. Retirement income

ISBN 978-1-594-20167-7; 1-59420-167-6

LC 2007-42508

This book chronicles three "pension cases: the collapse of the over-obligated General Motors, the pension strike that haulted New York City's subways, . . . [and the bankrupting of] the city of San Diego." Publisher's note

"A chilling anatomy of one bad decision followed by another—and another." Kirkus

Includes bibliographical references

Schultz, Ellen

Retirement heist; how companies plunder and profit from the nest eggs of American workers. [by] Ellen E. Schultz. Portfolio/Penguin 2011 245p $26.95   **331.2**

1. Pensions 2. Corporations 3. Life insurance

ISBN 978-1-59184-333-7; 1-59184-333-2

LC 2011015064

"Readers are no stranger to the grumblings of their corporate overlords: Pensions are untenable; health-care costs too high; retiree benefits hurt competitiveness. But according to . . . Schultz, employee pensions actually make money for corporations, and the funds diverted from them help feather the beds of multimillionaire executives. She exposes all this and more in a rapid-fire narrative. Individual stories of retired men and women (some with more than 40 years of service) robbed of their nest eggs put a human face on the proceedings. . . . Essential reading for anyone who works for a living." Kirkus

Includes bibliographical references

Shulman, Beth

The **betrayal** of work; how low-wage jobs fail 30 million Americans and their families. New Press (NY) 2003 255p $25.95   **331.2**

1. Work 2. Minimum wage 3. Labor -- United States 4. United States -- Economic conditions

ISBN 1-56584-733-4

LC 2003-43413

The author "analyzes one of the downsides of the 'new economy': the large number of American jobs that pay poverty-level wages, have few or no benefits, and create child-care nightmares." Libr J

Includes bibliographical references

Terkel, Studs, 1912-2008

Working; people talk about what they do all day and how they feel about what they do. The New Press 1997 589p pa $16.95 **331.2**

1. Work 2. Labor -- United States 3. United States -- Social conditions

ISBN 978-1-56584-342-4; 1-56584-342-8

First published 1974 by Pantheon Bks.

Based on interviews, this study describes the working lives and feelings of people engaged in occupations ranging from interstate truck driver to stockbroker to bookbinder to corporation president.

This "is not a dry, academic treatise but a sensitive portrayal of the experience of working, with all its pain, tension, frustrations, and occasional satisfactions." Best Sellers

331.25 Other conditions of employment

Chertavian, Gerald.

A Year Up; how a pioneering program that teaches young adults real skills for real jobs- - with real success. Gerald Chertavian. Viking 2012 viii, 358 p.p **331.25**

1. Youth -- Employment 2. Year Up (Organization) 4. Internship programs -- United States 3. Occupational training -- United States 4. Internship programs -- New York (State) 5. Young adults -- Employment -- United States 6. Poor youth -- Employment -- New York (State) 7. Young adults -- Vocational education -- United States 8. Poor youth -- Vocational education -- New York (State)

ISBN 9780670023776

LC 2012000606

This book is an "account of the origins and growth of Year Up, a groundbreaking employment program. Year Up founder and [chief executive officer] [Gerald] Chertavian debuts with this memoir about his nationwide program, which is aimed at 'closing the ever-widening Opportunity Divide in this country.'" (Kirkus)

331.3 Labor force by personal attributes

Fideler, Elizabeth F.

Men still at work; professionals over sixty and on the job. Elizabeth F. Fideler. Rowman & Littlefield Pub Inc. 2014 232 p. (cloth : alk. paper) $36 **331.3**

1. Age and employment 2. Elderly men -- Employment 3. Retirement age -- United States 4. Age and employment -- United States 5. Professional employees -- United States 6. Older men -- Employment -- United States

ISBN 1442222751; 9781442222755

LC 2013040402

This book, by Elizabeth F. Fideler, "explores the reasons why many men are continuing to work well beyond the traditional retirement age. In today's challenging economy, they are the second-fastest growing group of workers (just behind older women). Filled with profiles of older working men, . . . [it] explores thorny issues such as masculinity and

the 'need to provide,' as well as economic issues, job satisfaction, and more." (Publisher's note)

"Overall, an engaging, accessible overview of what the future holds for many younger men who will undoubtedly work into their 60s ... and beyond." Choice

Includes bibliographical references and index

Levine, Marvin J.

Children for hire; the perils of child labor in the United States. Praeger Pubs. 2003 233p $49.95 **331.3**

1. Child labor 2. Youth -- Employment 3. Teenagers -- Employment

ISBN 1-56720-433-3

LC 2002-29767

The author defines the problem of child labor and "analyzes the working conditions of people under 18, the legal context for their employment and exploitation, and the impact of such labor upon the education and development of America's young people. An important work about a hidden social problem." Libr J

Includes bibliographical references

331.4 Women workers

Berebitsky, Julie

Sex and the office; a history of gender, power, and desire. Julie Berebitsky. Yale University Press 2012 x, 359 p.p (cloth : alk. paper) $38 **331.4**

1. Sexual harassment 2. Sex in the workplace 3. Women employees -- United States -- History 4. Sex role -- United States -- History -- 20th century 5. Women -- Employment -- United States -- History -- 20th century

ISBN 0300118996; 9780300118995

LC 2011026337

This book by Julie Berebitsky "explores how Americans' attitudes toward sexuality and gender in the office have changed since the 1860s. . . . Berebitsky recounts the actual experiences of female and male office workers; draws on archival sources . . . and explores how popular sources--including cartoons, advertisements, advice guides, and a wide array of fictional accounts--have represented wanted and unwelcome romantic and sexual advances." (Publisher's note)

Includes bibliographical references and index

Chang, Leslie T.

Factory girls; from village to city in a changing China. Spiegel & Grau 2008 420p map $26; pa $16 **331.4**

1. Migrant labor 2. Manufacturing industries 3. Women -- China

ISBN 978-0-385-52017-1; 0-385-52017-4; 978-0-385-52018-8 pa; 0-385-52018-2 pa

LC 2008-12880

This "is an exceptionally vivid and compassionate depiction of the day-to-day dramas, and the fears and aspirations, of the real people who are powering China's economic boom." N Y Times Book Rev

Includes bibliographical references

Featherstone, Liza

Selling women short; the landmark battle for workers' rights at Wal-Mart. Basic Bks. 2004 282p $25   **331.4**

1. Sex discrimination 2. Wal-Mart Stores, Inc.
ISBN 0-465-02315-0

LC 2004-10298

Using an "investigation of the class action suit Dukes v. Wal-Mart Stores, Inc. and . . . interviews with female workers, Featherstone indicts Wal-Mart for low wages, discriminatory policies and sexist practices. . . . This is a clearly written and compelling book." Publ Wkly

Includes bibliographical references

Fideler, Elizabeth F.

Women still at work; professionals over sixty and on the job. Elizabeth S. Fideler. Rowman & Littlefield Publishers 2012 vii, 209 p.p (cloth : alk. paper) $37.50; (ebook) $36.99   **331.4**

1. Age and employment 2. Elderly women -- Employment 3. Age and employment -- United States 4. Older women -- Employment -- United States
ISBN 144221550X; 9781442215504; 9781442215528

LC 2012017802

In this book on older women in the workforce, Elizabeth F. Fideler "tells the everyday stories of hard-working women and the reasons they're still on the job, with a focus on women in the professional workforce. . . . Their stories showcase some of the key themes women choose to stay at work -- including job satisfaction, diminishing retirement savings, the need to support children or parents longer in life, exercising the hard-won right to work, and more." (Publisher's note)

Includes bibliographical references.

Kessler-Harris, Alice

★ **Out** to work; a history of wage-earning women in the United States. 20th anniversary ed; Oxford Univ. Press 2003 414p il pa $19.95   **331.4**

1. Women -- Employment -- History
ISBN 0-19-515709-5

LC 2003-267644

First published 1982

"This work remains a landmark in the field of analyzing the history of women's work in the United States from Colonial times to the Reagan era." Libr J

Includes bibliographical references

Povich, Lynn

★ The **good** girls revolt; how the women of Newsweek sued their bosses and changed the workplace. Lynn Povich. PublicAffairs 2012 xx, 249 p.p (hardcover) $25.99   **331.4**

1. Sexism 2. Women journalists 3. Sex discrimination in employment 4. Sex discrimination -- Law and legislation 5. Newsweek 6. Women journalists -- United States 7. Sex discrimination in employment -- United States 8. Sex role in the work environment -- United States
ISBN 161039173X; 9781610391733; 9781610391740

LC 2012006936

Amelia Bloomer Project (2014)

This book by Lynn Povich explains how, in 1970, "forty-six 'Newsweek' women charged the magazine with discrimination in hiring and promotion. It was the first female class action lawsuit--the first by women journalists--and it inspired other women in the media to quickly follow suit. . . . 'The Good Girls Revolt' also explores why changes in the law didn't solve everything. Through the lives of young female journalists at Newsweek today, Lynn Povich shows what has--and hasn't--changed in the workplace." (Publisher's note)

Includes bibliographical references and index.

Ryckman, Pamela

Stiletto network; inside the women's power circles that are changing the face of business. Pamela Ryckman. American Management Association 2013 256 p. (hardcover) $22.95   **331.4**

1. Women executives 2. Women -- Social conditions 3. Businesswomen 4. Business networks 5. Strategic alliances 6. Women in the professions
ISBN 0814432530; 9780814432532

LC 2012051563

This book by Pamela Ryckman looks at the "female heads of industry [who] are the forerunners of a radical shift in power. It's about what happens when bright, extraordinary women, from captains of industry to aspiring entrepreneurs, come together to celebrate and unwind, debate and compare notes. It's about how they mine their collective intelligence to realize their dreams or champion a cause, . . . how they join forces to ensure each woman gets what she needs." (Publisher's note)

331.5   Workers by personal attributes other than age

Browne, John

The **Glass** Closet; Why Coming Out Is Good Business. John Browne. HarperCollins Publishers 2014 240 p. $27.99   **331.5**

1. LGBT people 2. Businesspeople 3. Autobiographies
ISBN 0062316974; 9780062316974

1st U.S. edition

"Part memoir and part social criticism, 'The Glass Closet' addresses the issue of homophobia that still pervades corporations around the world and underscores the immense challenges faced by LGBT employees. . . . In 'The Glass Closet,' Lord John Browne . . . seeks to unsettle business leaders by exposing the culture of homophobia that remains rampant in corporations around the world, and which prevents employees from showing their authentic selves." (Publisher's note)

"Brown's rhetoric is businesslike and a little dry but also to the point, supported by research, and culturally significant. He has taken pains to provide strikingly honest personal narratives and uses them to put a face on the problems at hand.—" Booklist

Includes bibliographical references (p. 203-234) and index

331.6　Workers by ethnic and national origin

Bacon, David

Illegal people; how globalization creates migration and criminalizes immigrants. Beacon Press 2008 261p $25.95; pa $18　**331.6**
1. Labor policy 2. Globalization 3. Migrant labor 4. Illegal aliens
ISBN 978-0-8070-4226-7; 978-0-8070-4230-4 pa
LC 2008-15394
The author "follows the lives of undocumented workers at the Westin Suite Hotel in California and a Smithfield meatpacking plant in North Carolina, who travel back and forth from Mexico to the U.S. He examines the economic and social forces in both countries that lure workers to a market where they can earn higher wages but are vulnerable to exploitation. . . . A fascinating look at trade and immigration policies and the people directly affected by them." Booklist
Includes bibliographical references

Breslin, Jimmy

The **short** sweet dream of Eduardo Gutierrez. Crown 2002 213p hardcover o.p. pa $12　**331.6**
1. Construction workers
ISBN 1-400-04682-3 pa
LC 2001-47283
"A true-life account of an illegal Mexican immigrant who died on a New York construction site, and of the dreary lives and modest ambitions common to Mexicans in this country." N Y Times Book Rev

331.7　Labor by industry and occupation

Farr, J. Michael

★ **100** fastest-growing careers; your complete guidebook to major jobs with the most growth and openings. [by] Michael Farr. 11th ed.; JIST Works 2010 402p il (Top careers series) pa $17.95　**331.7**
1. Occupations 2. Vocational guidance
ISBN 978-1-5935-7783-4
Biennial. First published 1997 to replace America's 50 fastest growing jobs
This volume "provides information about pay, outlook, education, and skills needed to obtain some of the most promising jobs in the world of work." Publisher's note
Includes bibliographical references

Ferguson Publishing

The **top** 100; the fastest growing careers for the 21st century. 5th ed.; Ferguson 2011 388p $75; pa $19.95　**331.7**
1. Occupations 2. Vocational guidance
ISBN 978-0-8160-8367-1; 0-8160-8367-3; 978-0-8160-8359-6 pa; 0-8160-8359-2 pa; 978-1-4381-3767-4 ebook; 1-4381-3767-2 ebook
LC 2011004455
First published 1998
This book provides information "on jobs projected to experience the fastest growth, the greatest opportunity, and the best earnings through 2018, according to statistics from the U.S. Department of Labor. . . . Each job article describes the job duties; required education, training, and skills; expected earnings; and . . . more." Publisher's note

Fisher, James Terence

On the Irish waterfront; the crusader, the movie, and the soul of the port of New York. [by] James T. Fisher. Cornell University Press 2009 370p il map (Cushwa Center studies of Catholicism in Twentieth-century America) $29.95　**331.7**
1. Stevedores 2. Irish Americans 3. Catholic Church -- Missions 4. New York Harbor (N.Y. and N.J.) 5. On the waterfront (Motion picture)
ISBN 978-0-8014-4804-1; 0-8014-4804-2
LC 2009-13058
The author presents a "history of the New York-New Jersey waterfront depicted in Elia Kazan's Oscar-winning 1954 film, On the Waterfront. Fischer's impeccable research delves into the real-life stories behind the characters, particularly Pete Corridan, the crusading Catholic priest who tried to reform the longshoremen's union and the recently deceased Bud Schulberg, who adapted Malcolm Johnson's 1949 Pulitzer Prize-winning 'Crime on the Waterfront' newspaper series for the screen. . . . This engaging narrative is essential reading for both labor historians and cinema buffs, plus anyone studying the waterfront, working-class and immigrant history, anticommunism, blacklisting, and the House Un-American Activities Committee." Libr J
Includes bibliographical references

J.G. Ferguson Publishing Company

★ **Encyclopedia** of careers and vocational guidance; 15th ed.; Ferguson 2010 5v il set $249.95　**331.7**
1. Reference books 2. Occupations -- Encyclopedias 3. Vocational guidance -- Encyclopedias
ISBN 978-0-8160-8313-8; 0-8160-8313-4
LC 2010-17724
First published 1967
"These five volumes contain more than 700 . . . [articles] on careers in nearly 100 industries. Each three to five-page entry provides a concise and engaging profile of fields like accounting, animal care, computers, the environment, publishing, sales, and the visual arts. Included in each job entry are an overview, a history, a description, requirements, employers, advancement, earnings, work environment, outlook, and more." Libr J [review of 2008 edition]
Includes bibliographical references

Nagle, Robin

Picking up; on the streets and behind the trucks with the sanitation workers of New York City. Robin Nagle. Farrar, Straus and Giroux 2013 x, 280 p., [8] p. of platesp ill., map (hardcover) $28　**331.7**
1. Municipal officials and employees 2. Refuse and refuse disposal -- New York (N.Y.) 3. Sanitation workers -- New York (State) -- New York
ISBN 0689825528; 9780374299293
LC 2012028941
In this book, "Robin Nagle introduces us to the men and women of New York City's Department of Sanitation and makes clear why this small army of uniformed workers is

the most important labor force on the streets. Seeking to understand every aspect of the Department's mission, Nagle accompanied crews on their routes, questioned supervisors and commissioners, and listened to story after story about blizzards, hazardous wastes, and the insults of everyday New Yorkers." (Publisher's note)

Includes bibliographical references and index

331.702   Choice of vocation

McKenna, Amy

Nontraditional   careers for women and men; more than 30 great jobs for women and men with apprenticeships through phds. by Andrew Morkes and Amy McKenna. College & Career Press 2012 280 p. $19.95   **331.702**

1. Occupations 2. Professions 3. Vocational guidance 4. Men -- Employment -- United States -- Juvenile literature 5. Vocational guidance -- United States -- Juvenile literature 6. Women -- Employment -- United States -- Juvenile literature

ISBN 0974525197; 9780974525198

LC 2011046915

This book about nontraditional employment with an emphasis on gender "is chock-full of career articles encompassing a wide variety of fields. Each career article includes salary information, skills needed, minimum education level, employment outlook, information about the career, certification and licensing information, tips for getting a job in this career, and industry resources." (Voice of Youth Advocates)

331.763   Agricultural workers -- economics

Higgs, Catherine

Chocolate islands; cocoa, slavery, and colonial Africa. Catherine Higgs. Ohio University Press 2012 xv, 230 p.p (pb : alk. paper) $26.95   **331.763**

1. Cacao growers 2. Slavery -- History 3. Sao Tome and Principe -- History 4. Cadbury Brothers -- History 5. Slavery -- Sao Tome and Principe -- History 6. Cacao -- Harvesting -- Moral and ethical aspects 7. Forced labor -- Sao Tome and Principe -- History 8. Portugal -- Colonies -- Africa -- Administration 9. Cacao growers -- Sao Tome and Principe -- History 10. Cacao -- Harvesting -- Sao Tome and Principe -- History

ISBN 0821420062; 9780821420065; 9780821444221

LC 2012009341

In this book, "Catherine Higgs traces the early-twentieth-century journey of the Englishman Joseph Burtt to the Portuguese colony of São Tomé and Príncipe -- the chocolate islands -- through Angola and Mozambique, and finally to British Southern Africa. Burtt had been hired by the chocolate firm Cadbury Brothers Limited to determine if the cocoa it was buying from the islands had been harvested by slave laborers forcibly recruited from Angola." (Publishers Weekly)

Includes bibliographical references (p. 175-223) and index

331.8   Labor unions, labor-management bargaining and disputes

Dray, Philip

There is power in a union; the epic story of labor in America. Doubleday 2010 772p il $35; ebook $35   **331.8**

1. Labor movement 2. Industrialization 3. Labor unions -- United States 4. United States -- Social conditions 5. Labor unions -- United States -- History 6. Labor movement -- United States -- History 7. Industrialization -- United States -- History

ISBN 978-0-385-52629-6; 0-385-52629-6; 978-0-385-53360-7 ebook

LC 201002357

This is a "narrative history of American labor. . . . From the textile mills of Lowell, Massachusetts . . . to the triumph of unions in the twentieth century and their waning influence today, the contest between labor and capital for their share of American bounty has shaped our national experience. Philip Dray's ambition is to show us the vital accomplishments of organized labor in that time and illuminate its central role in our social, political, economic, and cultural evolution." (Publisher's note) Bibliography. Index.

The author "follows organized labor from the struggles of early 19th-century female textile workers to the present-day retreat of organized labor following the failed 1981 air traffic controllers' strike. . . . Packed with vivid characters and dramatic scenes, Dray's fine recap of a neglected but vital tradition has much to say about labor's current straits." Publ Wkly

Includes bibliographical references

Dubofsky, Melvyn

★ **Labor** in America; a history. [by] Melvyn Dubofsky, Foster Rhea Dulles. 7th ed; Harlan Davidson 2005 472p il pa $34.95   **331.8**

1. Labor unions 2. Working class 3. Labor -- United States

ISBN 978-0-88295-998-6; 0-88295-998-0

LC 2003-13265

First published 1949 by Crowell under the authorship of Foster Rhea Dulles. Periodically revised

A study of the social and political impact of the American labor movement since colonial times

Includes bibliographical references

★ **Historical** encyclopedia of American labor; edited by Robert Weir and James P. Hanlan. Greenwood Press 2003 2v set $175   **331.8**

1. Reference books 2. Labor movement -- Encyclopedias 3. Labor -- United States -- Encyclopedias

ISBN 0-313-31840-9

LC 2003-52847

This "encyclopedia includes approximately 400 entries designed for the general researcher, students, and lay readers interested in learning more about such topics as unions, union leaders, union history, important laws and court cases, and labor terminology. An appendix contains excerpts from over 50 primary documents." Libr J

Includes bibliographical references

Shaw, Randy

Beyond the fields; Cesar Chavez, the UFW, and the struggle for justice in the 21st century. University of California Press 2008 347p il **331.8**
1. Social action 2. Agricultural laborers 3. Labor leaders 4. United Farm Workers of America 5. Social justice -- United States 6. Social action -- United States -- History -- 20th century
ISBN 0520251075; 0520268040; 9780520251076; 9780520268043

LC 2008-31252

This book explores the impact of César Chávez and the United Farm Workers "on 21st-century social justice movements. Beyond the Fields [aims to show] . . . how Chávez and the UFW's imprint can be found in the modern reshaping of the American labor movement, the building of Latino political power, the transformation of Los Angeles and California politics, the fight for environmental justice, and the . . . movement for immigrant rights. [According to the author], many of the ideas, tactics, and strategies that Chávez and the UFW initiated or revived—including the boycott, the fast, clergy-labor partnerships and door-to-door voter outreach— are now so commonplace that their roots in the farmworkers' movement [are] forgotten. . . . UFW volunteers and staff were dedicated to furthering economic justice, and many devoted their post-UFW lives to working for social change." (Publisher's note) Index.

"Shaw's book is the product of extensive research, and it's invaluable for anyone interested in the evolution of unionization over the past forty years." Washington Monthly
Includes bibliographical references and index

St. James encyclopedia of labor history worldwide; major events in labor history and their impact. with introductions by Willie Thompson and Daniel Nelson; Neil Schlager, editor; produced by Schlager Groups. St. James Press 2003 2v set $260 **331.8**
1. Reference books 2. Labor movement -- Encyclopedias
ISBN 1-558-62542-9

LC 2003-294

"This reference promises to fill an important niche for larger public and academic libraries." Libr J

Stepan-Norris, Judith

Left out; Reds and America's industrial unions. [by] Judith Stepan-Norris, Maurice Zeitlin. Cambridge Univ. Press 2002 375p $75; pa $27 **331.8**
1. Labor -- United States 2. Labor unions -- United States
ISBN 0-521-79212-6; 0-521-79840-X pa

LC 2001-37655

"In 1947, ten 'Communist-dominated unions' were expelled from the CIO. The mythology that developed is that these unions sacrificed the interests of the American worker to the foreign policy dictates of the Statlin-era Soviet Union. The authors, both sociologists, use statistical analysis of contracts to argue that these unions actually had the most democracy, the most pro-labor contracts, and the best track record in fighting for gender and racial equality in the labor movement." Libr J

Includes bibliographical references

Zieger, Robert H.

American workers, American unions; the twentieth century. {by} Robert H. Zieger & Gilbert J. Gall. 3rd ed; Johns Hopkins Univ. Press 2002 292p (The American moment) pa $17.95 **331.8**
1. Labor unions 2. Labor -- United States
ISBN 0-8018-7078-X

LC 2002-3250

First published 1986

"This standard work of American labor history from the Gilded Age onward has been updated to almost the present, with the last paragraph discussing September 11. Zieger's strength lies in his striving for a balanced survey." Libr J
Includes bibliographical references

331.88 Labor unions (Trade unions)

Gorn, Elliott J.

Mother Jones; the most dangerous woman in America. Hill & Wang 2001 408p il hardcover o.p. pa $14 **331.88**
1. Centenarians 2. Labor leaders
ISBN 0-8090-7094-4 pa

LC 00-44997

This is a biography of union organizer and labor leader Mary Harris Jones, known more popularly as Mother Jones
Gorn "has successfully separated fact from myth . . . situating Jones's story within a wider cultural frame." Publ Wkly
Includes bibliographical references

331.880973 Labor unions (trade unions) -- United States

Labor rising; the past and future of working people in America. edited by Richard A. Greenwald, Daniel Katz. New Press, The 2012 318 p. (paperback) $20.95 **331.880973**
1. Working class 2. Labor economics 3. Labor movement -- History 4. Working class -- United States -- History 5. Labor movement -- United States -- History
ISBN 1595585184; 9781595585189

LC 2012001464

Editors Daniel Katz and Richard A. Greenwald present a "volume [that] provides readers with an understanding of the history that is directly relevant to the economic and political crises working people face today, and points the way to a revitalized twenty-first-century labor movement. With original contributions from leading labor historians, social critics, and activists," the book "makes crucial connections between the past and present, and then looks forward, asking how we might imagine a different future for all Americans." (Publisher's note)

332   Financial economics

Gasparino, Charles

The **sellout**; how three decades of Wall Street greed and government mismanagement destroyed the global financial system. Harper Business 2009 553p $27.99   **332**

1. Wall Street (New York, N.Y.) 2. Global Financial Crisis, 2008-2009

ISBN 978-0-06-169716-6; 0-06-169716-8

LC 2009-28097

"Of all the books documenting the financial crisis . . . The Sellout tells it better than most. Filled with very little of the boring, complex financial jargon that comprises many books of the genre, this tome makes for a surprisingly entertaining and easy read." Risk Management

Includes bibliographical references

Guyer, C. Stephen

On the Money Journal; C. Stephen Guyer's Guide for How You Acquire, Borrow, Protect, Move, Watch, Play With, Go to Jail For, and Have Fun With Our Most Popular Commodity. by Stephen Guyer. Parsifal Press 2007 215 p. (paperback) $18.95 **332**

1. Personal finance 2. Finance -- United States

ISBN 0977940500; 9780977940509

Author Stephen Guyer's book "is the financial column [for] C-level executives. . . . Published monthly by American Cities Business Journals, [it] . . . is a . . . [offers a] look at the stuff that makes the world go 'round. . . . [The book serves as a] guide for how you can acquire, borrow, protect, move, watch, play with, go to jail for, and have fun with, our most popular commodity-Money!" (Publisher's note)

Mayer, Robert

Quick cash; the story of the loan shark. Northern Illinois University Press 2010 293p $35   **332**

1. Loans 2. Usury

ISBN 978-0-8758-0430-9; 0-8758-0430-6

LC 2010014718

This book "traces high-interest lending from the late 19th century through the latest financial crisis. While the book focuses on Chicago, it does reference lending practices throughout the South and New York City. Chapters delve into the social issues of the early 20th century that created a market for these high-interest loans, the various government policies that tried to regulate the lenders, and the legal and economic changes that gave rise to the current methods of payday lending since the 1980s. . . . [The author] has created an original and multidisciplinary look at subprime lending in the United States that is accessible to a wide variety of readers, including students and professionals." Libr J

Includes bibliographical references

Piketty, Thomas, 1971-

Capital in the twenty-first century; Thomas Piketty ; translated by Arthur Goldhammer. The Belknap Press of Harvard University Press 2014 696 p. illustrations (alk. paper) $39.95   **332**

1. Equality 2. Economic forecasting 3. Economic development -- History 4. Wealth 5. Capital 6. Labor economics 7. Income distribution

ISBN 067443000X; 9780674430006

LC 2013036024

"In 'Capital in the Twenty-First Century,' Thomas Piketty analyzes a unique collection of data from twenty countries, ranging as far back as the eighteenth century, to uncover key economic and social patterns. . . . Piketty shows that modern economic growth and the diffusion of knowledge have allowed us to avoid inequalities on the apocalyptic scale predicted by Karl Marx. . . . Political action has curbed dangerous inequalities in the past, Piketty says, and may do so again." (Publisher's note)

Shows "that plain language can be put to work explaining the most complex of ideas, foremost among them the fact that economic inequality is at an all-time high--and is only bound to grow worse." Kirkus

Includes bibliographical references and index

332.024   Personal finance

Armstrong, Frank

The **retirement** challenge--will you sink or swim? a complete, do-it-yourself toolkit to navigate your financial future. FT Press 2009 266p il pa $21.99   **332.024**

1. Retirement 2. Personal finance

ISBN 0-13-236132-9; 978-0-13-236132-3

LC 2008-29134

"With a companion web site (www.sink-swim.com), this planning guide takes readers through the steps: determining retirement age, setting up retirement funds, forecasting financial needs, and much, much more." Libr J

Bradford, Stacey L.

The **Wall** Street Journal: financial guidebook for new parents. Three Rivers Press 2009 196p il pa $14.95   **332.024**

1. Parents 2. Personal finance

ISBN 978-0-307-40707-8; 0-307-40707-1

LC 2008-50657

The author "presents a relevant and witty overview of the awesome task facing new parents—affording their kids. She covers all the major issues, including child tax credits, the Family and Medical Leave Act of 1993, flexible spending accounts, and 529 plans; even wills, trusts, and disability insurance are considered." Libr J

D'Agnese, Joseph

The **money** book for freelancers, part-time, and the self-employed; the only personal finance system for people with not-so-regular jobs. [by] Joseph D'Agnese & Denise Kiernan. Three Rivers Press 2010 306p il pa $15   **332.024**

1. Self-employed 2. Personal finance

ISBN 978-0-307-45366-2; 0-307-45366-9

LC 2009-31596

"The authors describe how one can maximize financial security without compromising success by addressing debts, taxes, emergency funds, and retirement savings using their 'Freelance Finance System.' They preach commonsense ideas such as accountability and restraint but also describe plenty of clever ways to make one's money go further. . . . Developed from the personal experiences of the authors, this book is fun and relevant. . . . Recommended for anyone who is self-employed now or is facing a new work-life situation." Libr J

Economides, Annette, 1961-

The **moneysmart** family system; teaching financial independence to children of every age. Steve Economides, Annette Economides. Thomas Nelson 2012 272 p. $16.99   **332.024**
1. Child rearing 2. Personal finance 3. Household budgets 4. Finance, Personal 5. Families -- Economic aspects 6. Children -- Finance, Personal
ISBN 1400202841; 9781400202843
LC 2012941594

This book, by Steve and Annette Economides, teaches how to "raise financially responsible kids of any age in a society filled with consumerism." The "Economides raised their five kids while spending 77 percent less than the USDA predicted. And the money they did spend was also used to train their children to become financially independent." Their "system will show you how to teach your children to manage money and have a good attitude while they're learning." (Publisher''s note)

Glink, Ilyce R.

50 simple things you can do to improve your personal finances; how to spend less, save more, and make the most of what you have. Three Rivers Press (NY) 2001 222p pa $14   **332.024**
1. Personal finance
ISBN 0-8129-2742-7
LC 00-66675

The author gives advice on such topics as personal budgets and savings, credit and debt, investments, insurance, taxes, marriage, partnerships and children, and retirement planning.

Hirshman, Susan L.

Does this make my assets look fat? a woman's guide to finding financial empowerment and success. St. Martin's Press 2010 302p il $24.99; ebook $11.99   **332.024**
1. Investments 2. Personal finance 3. Women -- United States
ISBN 978-0-312-38553-8; 0-312-38553-6; 978-1-4299-5006-0 ebook; 1-4299-5006-4 ebook
LC 2010-21668

"Comparing getting one's financial house in order to dieting, Hirshman . . . presents chapters on assessing personal finance fitness and gives comprehensive definitions and explanations of, as well as practical suggestions on, various investment strategies." Libr J

Jason, Julie

★ The **AARP** Retirement Survival Guide; how to make smart financial decisions in good times and bad. Sterling Pub. Co. 2009 340p pa $14.95 **332.024**
1. Pensions 2. Personal finance 3. Retirement income
ISBN 978-1-4027-4341-2
LC 2008-20577

This guide to retirement "includes a solid grounding in the basics (such as the infamous What's your number? discussion), careful outlines of how to approach retirement income products as well as the stock market, and approaches to taxes and to potential advisors." Booklist
Includes bibliographical references

Kessel, Brent

It's not about the money; unlock your money type to achieve spiritual and financial abundance. HarperOne 2008 xxi, 299p il $24.95; pa $14.99 **332.024**
1. Money 2. Self-perception 3. Personal finance 4. Applied psychology
ISBN 978-0-06-123406-4; 978-0-06-123405-7 pa
LC 2007-18380

The author "offers 'holistic financial advice' in this Buddhist-influenced . . . [book] promising both a better financial strategy and greater fulfillment and happiness. . . . Readers interested in an Eastern-influenced approach will find useful advice on how to think about money, as well as insight into what makes us tick." Publ Wkly
Includes bibliographical references

Kiyosaki, Robert T., 1947-

Why "A" Students Work for "C" Students and Why "B" Students Work for the Government; Rich Dad's Guide to Financial Education for Parents. Robert T. Kiyosaki. Perseus Distribution Services 2013 453 p. (paperback) $16.95 **332.024**
1. Creative ability 2. Education -- Aims and objectives
ISBN 1612680763; 9781612680767

In this book, Robert T. Kiyosaki "expands on his belief that the school system was created to churn out . . . 'A Students' who read well, memorize well and test well . . . and not the creative thinkers . . . who grow up to be the innovators and creators of new ideas, businesses, applications and products. The book urges parents . . . to . . . focus, instead, on concepts, ideas, and helping their child find their true genius, their special gift." (Publisher's note)

Kobliner, Beth

Get a financial life; personal finance in your twenties and thirties. Beth Kobliner. 3rd ed. Simon & Schuster 2009 336 p. $16 **332.024**
1. Debt 2. Money 3. Housing 4. Personal finance 5. Finance, Personal 6. Young adults -- Finance, Personal
ISBN 0743264363; 9780743264365
LC 2008046645

Author Beth Kobliner "focuses exclusively on what you need to know when you're just starting to pay serious attention to money matters. . . . [The book offers] solutions and cutting edge tools in this brave new world of financial madness. . . . [It] covers everything a young person needs to know to get on the path to long-lasting financial security . .

. from debt and housing issues to banking, investing, taxes, and insurance." (bethkobliner.com)

Includes bibliographical references and index

McNaughton, Deborah

The **essential** credit repair handbook; [a quick and handy guide for anyone who wants to get and stay out of debt] Career Press 2011 224p pa $14.99   **332.024**

1. Debt 2. Consumer credit 3. Personal finance
ISBN 978-1-60163-160-2 pa; 1-60163-160-X pa; 978-1-60163-666-9 ebook; 1-60163-666-0 ebook

LC 2011010730

This book discusses "how to: dispute late payments, charge-offs, and collection accounts; rebuild your life after a bankruptcy, foreclosure, or short sale; re-establish your credit in spite of a bad credit report; set new financial goals; [and] understand the latest credit card laws and regulations. . . . [This is a] guide for people who are getting over bankruptcy, foreclosure, short sale, or any financial hardship affecting their credit and are looking to rebuild or re-establish their credit." Publisher's note

Includes bibliographical references

Miller, Mark

The **hard** times guide to retirement security; practical strategies for money, work, and living. Wiley 2010 223p il pa $16.95; ebook $11.99 **332.024**

1. Retirement income
ISBN 978-1-57660-362-8 pa; 978-0-470-90834-1 ebook

LC 2010-14478

This guide to retirement after the financial crisis touches upon "issues such as insuring against the risk of outliving your assets, recalibrating damaged retirement portfolios, managing the risk of health-care expenses in retirement, and career strategies for workers who are 50 years old and up." Publisher's note

Orman, Suze

The **money** class; learn to create your new American dream. Spiegel & Grau 2011 281p $26; ebook $13.99   **332.024**

1. Wealth 2. Personal finance
ISBN 978-1-4000-6973-6; 978-0-679-60470-9 ebook

LC 2011-1394

"Organized into nine 'classes,' with each class/chapter further divided into related lessons, . . . [this book is] upbeat and no-nonsense, offering lessons on family matters, homeownership, saving for college, emergencies, retirement, and more. Orman firmly guides readers when dealing with parenting issues or underwater mortgages. . . . After finishing Orman's book, and completing her exercises, readers will have a very clear sense of how they can achieve what she has rechristened the 'New American Dream.'" Publ Wkly

Pepper, Carol

The **seven** pearls of financial wisdom; a woman's guide to enjoying wealth and power. Carol Pepper and Camilla Webster. 1st ed. St. Martin's Press

2012 viii, 338 p.p (hardcover) $25.99; (paperback) $19.99   **332.024**

1. Businesswomen 2. Life cycle, Human 3. Women -- Personal finance 4. New business enterprises 5. Women -- Finance, Personal 6. Investments -- Psychological aspects
ISBN 0312641664; 1250008328; 9780312641665; 9781250008329; 9781250035486

LC 2012010250

"The goal of wealth-management adviser [Carol] Pepper and financial journalist [Camilla] Webster is to assist with common issues that arise in women's financial lives and to turn those issues into assets. . . . They discuss romance, children, crises ranging from health problems to natural disasters, leadership, wealth accrual, leaving a legacy, and mapping out a path to financial security. . . . Women are encouraged to start their own businesses, invest wisely . . . and live well." (Library Journal)

Includes bibliographical references and index.

Pond, Jonathan D.

Grow your money! 101 easy tips to plan, save, and invest. Collins 2008 xlv, 352p $26.95 **332.024**

1. Investments 2. Public finance 3. Retirement income
ISBN 978-0-06-112140-1; 0-06-112140-1

LC 2007-24071

The author offers "investment and financial definitions, debt-management strategies, retirement and home-ownership considerations, tax tips, and more, enabling lay readers to understand these seemingly daunting and complex issues." Libr J

Quinn, Jane Bryant

Making the most of your money now; the classic bestseller. Completely rev. for the new economy; Simon & Schuster hardcover ed.; Simon & Schuster 2010 1242p $35   **332.024**

1. Investments 2. Personal finance
ISBN 978-0-7432-6996-4; 0-7432-6996-9

LC 2009-32610

First published 1991 with title: Making the most of your money

This guide includes information about investing, buying a home, life and health insurance, retirement planning, checklists for life changes, finding a financial advisor, and financing college.

"This is an excellent primer, especially for those new to managing their money." Libr J

Romans, Christine

How to speak money; the language and knowledge you need now. Ali Velshi and Christine Romans. John Wiley & Sons 2012 xviii, 190 p.p   **332.024**

1. Money 2. Personal finance 3. Economics -- Terminology 4. Finance, Personal
ISBN 9781118114957

LC 2011033518

In this book about personal finance, "[a]uthors and CNN financial experts Ali Velshi and Christine Romans speak the global language of money. . . . Speaking money affects every area of your life. It's more than simply your savings or the investments you may have. It involves the way you think about money, the way you teach your children about it, and the way you were taught about it yourself. It's about the way you spend it, save it, invest it, use it, need it and want it. The book will . . . [cover] the male and female spending and investing disparity, . . . emerging international economies, . . . [the] hurdle of student debt, . . . [and explain] how to plan appropriately for retirement." (Publisher's note)

Includes bibliographical references (p. 179-180) and index

Schwab-Pomerantz, Carrie

It pays to talk; how to have the essential conversations with your family about money and investing. [by] Carrie Schwab-Pomerantz and Charles R. Schwab. Crown Business 2003 386p il hardcover o.p. pa $14   **332.024**
1. Investments 2. Personal finance
ISBN 0-609-61028-7; 1-4000-4960-1 pa
LC 2002-5994

The authors "share their insights on money, investing and the conversations that need to accompany these. Their focus is on the importance of conducting different lifestage conversations (e.g., how to financially approach being single, getting married, raising children, helping parents), and this . . . primer provides one-stop shopping for the many phases of financial understanding and planning. . . . This educational volume provides a useful framework that a family can refer to when approaching those often difficult but necessary conversations about finances." Publ Wkly

Includes bibliographical references

Solin, Daniel R.

The **smartest** retirement book you'll ever read. Penguin Group 2009 255p $21.95   **332.024**
1. Investments 2. Personal finance 3. Retirement income
ISBN 978-0-399-53520-8
LC 2009014075

The author "offers short chapters on a variety of retirement subjects, each concluding with a pithy summarization. . . [It is] clearly written and easy to understand, tackling such topics as stocks, bonds, annuities, pensions, and cash withdrawal strategies." Libr J

Includes bibliographical references

Tobias, Andrew P.

★ The **only** investment guide you'll ever need; [by] Andrew Tobias. Completely updated and rev.; Houghton Mifflin Harcourt 2011 306p il pa $14.95   **332.024**
1. Investments 2. Personal finance
ISBN 978-0-547-44725-4
LC 2010-41533

First published 1978

This book offers advice on such topics as personal investments, tax strategies, life insurance, stock market trading, college funds, real estate, and inheritance.

Includes bibliographical references

Walsh, Peter

Lighten up; love what you have, have what you need, be happier with less. Free Press 2011 288p $26; pa $15; ebook $12.99   **332.024**
1. Happiness 2. Conduct of life 3. Personal finance
ISBN 978-1-4391-5514-1; 978-1-4391-5515-8 pa; 978-1-4391-6008-4 ebook
LC 2010030244

The author "coaches readers in dealing with psychological clutter tied to money and finances so they can live thrifty lives that are also liberating, pleasurable, and rewarding. . . . At the crux of this book are three audits designed to instigate life changes: a financial audit combined with assessments of the physical junk filling our homes and the emotional junk causing tension in our lives. Throughout, Walsh challenges readers to face not just the physical clutter overwhelming their homes but also the psychological underpinnings to their habits and attitudes, to confront family members, and to establish tough boundaries within the limits of their family's means. . . . Motivated readers will find plenty of helpful tips to jump-start their self-transformations." Publ Wkly

Weltman, Barbara

★ **J.K.** Lasser's guide for tough times; tax and financial solutions to see you through. John Wiley 2009 224p pa $18.95   **332.024**
1. Taxation 2. Income tax 3. Investments 4. Personal finance
ISBN 978-0-470-40232-0; 0-470-40232-6
LC 2008-32269

"Besides tax and financial advice for coping with a down economy, Weltman examines steps being taken by the federal government (mortgage relief, stimulus packages) to ease the recession." Libr J

Yeager, Jeff

The **cheapskate** next door; the surprising secrets of Americans living happily below their means. Broadway Books 2010 231p pa $12.99; ebook $12.99   **332.024**
1. Personal finance
ISBN 978-0-7679-3132-8 pa; 978-0-307-59247-7 ebook
LC 2009-42287

The author offers a "lesson on living happily well below your means. Interviewing a variety of self-professed cheapskates, he finds—despite a diversity of lifestyles, backgrounds, and beliefs—common practices and philosophies when it came to money. . . . He presents their tips on frugal living in grocery shopping, entertainment, and sensible parenting." Publ Wkly

"The amazing fact about this book is that in addition to his instructions making perfect sense, like no other book of its kind, this one can be read simply for the humor of the author's prose." Booklist

The **ultimate** cheapskate's road map to true riches; a practical (and fun) guide to enjoying life

more by spending less. Broadway Books 2008 241p
pa $12.95   **332.024**
1. Personal finance
ISBN 978-0-7679-2695-9; 0-7679-2695-1

LC 2007-34883

"From 'cheapskate shops' to inexpensive hobbies (e.g.,
bird watching), this lighthearted but practical 'road map'
shows how to save up your money." Libr J

332.1 Banks

Ahamed, Liaquat
 Lords of finance; the bankers who broke the
world. Penguin Press 2009 564p il $32.95   **332.1**
1. Capitalists and financiers
ISBN 978-1-59420-182-0

LC 2008-44512

This is a "history of the lead-up to the Great Depression
as seen through the careers of the West's principal bankers."
Kirkus
"A grand, sweeping narrative of immense scope and
power." N Y Times Book Rev
Includes bibliographical references

Farrell, Greg
 Crash of the titans; greed, hubris, the fall of Merrill Lynch, and the near-collapse of Bank of America.
Crown Business 2010 471p $27; pa $17; ebook
$12.99   **332.1**
1. Bank failures 2. Corporate mergers and acquisitions
3. Bank of America NA 4. Merrill Lynch & Co., Inc.
ISBN 978-0-307-71786-3; 978-0-307-71787-0 pa;
978-0-307-71788-7 ebook

LC 2010485623

This is an account of the decline of Merrill Lynch & Co.
and Bank of America Corp. The author claims that "at the
moment they should have been minding their balance sheets,
. . . many of the financial industry's masters of the universe
were preoccupied with their bonuses, expense accounts, and
office renovations." Businessweek
Includes bibliographical references

Johnson, Simon
 13 bankers; the Wall Street takeover and the next
financial meltdown. [by] Simon Johnson and James
Kwak. Pantheon Books 2010 304p il $26.95; pa
$15.95; ebook $11.99   **332.1**
1. Bank failures 2. Financial crises 3. Finance --
United States 4. Banks and banking -- United States
ISBN 978-0-307-37905-4; 0-307-37905-1; 978-0-307-
47660-9 pa; 0-307-47660-X pa; 978-0-307-37922-1
ebook

LC 2010-00168

Johnson and Kwak examine not only how Wall Street's
ideology, wealth, and political power among policy makers
in Washington led to the financial debacle of 2008, but also
what the lessons learned portend for the future.
"The book is a thoughtful, stimulating read on a topic of
much ongoing debate and concern." Choice
Includes bibliographical references

Meltzer, Allan H.
 ★ A **history** of the Federal Reserve; v1 with a
foreword by Alan Greenspan. University of Chicago
Press 2002 800p v1 $75; pa $25   **332.1**
1. Federal Reserve banks 2. Federal Reserve System
(U.S.) -- Board of Governors
ISBN 0-226-51999-6; 0-226-52000-5 pa

LC 2002-72007

The author "provides a definitive history of the U.S.
Federal Reserve from its founding in 1913 to its establishment as a separate, independent entity in 1951. Using meeting minutes, correspondence, and internal Federal Reserve
documents, he traces the reasons behind Federal Reserves
policy decisions, highlights the impact that individuals and
events had on the Fed, and examines the Fed's influence on
international affairs. . . . This well-written and thoroughgoing account is recommended for academic, business, and
public libraries." Libr J
Includes bibliographical references

Overtveldt, Johan van
 Bernanke's test; Ben Bernanke, Alan Greens-
pan, and the drama of the central banker. Agate 2009
287p il $26   **332.1**
1. Economists 2. Bankers 3. Government officials 4.
Presidential advisers 5. Regulatory agency officials 6.
Economic policy -- United States 7. Monetary policy
-- United States 8. Banks and banking -- United States
9. Federal Reserve System (U.S.) -- Board of Governors
ISBN 978-1-932841-37-4; 1-932841-37-7

LC 2008-45741

"An examination of the challenges facing Fed chair Ben
Bernanke as he addresses the problems affecting the U.S.
economy inherited from his predecessor, Alan Greenspan, .
. . [with] a historical look at how other central bankers have
dealt with similar crises." Publisher's note
"Anyone who wants to understand the role of the Fed
in the current crisis will find this an accessible primer."
Publ Wkly
Includes bibliographical references

Parks, Tim
 Medici money; banking, metaphysics, and art
in fifteenth-century Florence. W. W. Norton & Co.
2005 273p il map (Enterprise) $22.95   **332.1**
1. Banks and banking 2. Bankers 3. Political leaders
4. Florence (Italy) -- History
ISBN 0-393-05827-1

LC 2004-30516

This is an "account of the fabled Medici dynasty of Renaissance Florence spanning 1397-1494." Booklist
"The general reader will learn from this book a great
deal about the era, and those who bestrode it, without getting bogged down in excessive scholarly detail." Natl Rev
Includes bibliographical references

Rockefeller, David
 Memoirs. Random House 2002 517p $35; pa
$17.95   **332.1**
1. Philanthropists 2. Bankers 3. Chase Manhattan

Bank, N.A.
ISBN 0-679-40588-7; 0-8129-6973-1 pa

LC 2002-24800

"This autobiography by the youngest son of John D. Rockefeller Jr. and Abby Aldrich Rockefeller is also a history of 20th-century America and its influence in the world order." Libr J

"Rockefeller's style is restrained and self-deprecating; the account of his attempts to modernize and globalize Chase makes for excellent business history, and his sketch of his complicated relationship with his brother is especially convincing." New Yorker

Wessel, David

★ In Fed we trust; Ben Bernanke's war on the great panic. Crown Business 2009 323p $26.99   **332.1**

1. Economists 2. Banks and banking 3. Global Financial Crisis, 2008-2009 4. Government officials 5. Regulatory agency officials 6. Monetary policy -- United States 7. Federal Reserve System (U.S.) -- Board of Governors
ISBN 978-0-307-45968-8; 0-307-45968-3

LC 2009-289789

This book reviews events of 2008 as the U. S. government attempted to stave off financial panic.

The author "has written a gripping blow-by-blow account of how the top brass at the Federal Reserve and Treasury flailed against financial collapse. . . . [The story] is a thrilling one, deftly told by a veteran journalist with access to those involved. Mr Wessel has an eye for enlivening detail, . . . and he has a knack for making finance accessible to the layman without boring the specialist." Economist

Includes bibliographical references

332.3   Credit and loan institutions

Grind, Kirsten

The lost bank; the story of Washington Mutual--the biggest bank failure in American history. Kirsten Grind. Simon & Schuster 2012 389 p.   **332.3**

1. Bank failures 2. Financial crises 3. Washington Mutual, Inc. 4. Savings and loan associations 5. Banks and banking -- United States 6. Washington Mutual, Inc 7. Bank failures -- United States -- History 8. Banks and banking -- Washington (State) -- Seattle -- History 9. Savings and loan association failures -- United States -- History 10. Savings and loan associations -- Washington (State) -- Seattle -- History
ISBN 1451617925; 9781451617924; 9781451617931; 9781451617948

LC 2011048587

In this book, "reporter [Kirsten] Grind chronicles the rise of Washington Mutual from a sleepy Seattle-based thrift to America's biggest savings and loan bank, its reckless plunge into the can't-lose subprime mortgage market, and its 2008 failure. . . . [The book includes] personalities like Kerry Killinger, WaMu's . . . CEO, and Jamie Dimon, the . . . JPMorgan leader who swallowed WaMu, . . . [as well as the] WaMu salespeople. . . . Grind pens a . . . guide to the delusions and frauds powering the debacle, from Fed chief

Alan Greenspan's . . . economic forecasts down to the falsified documents that put people with no income, assets, or perhaps even pulses into mortgages they could never repay." (Publishers Weekly)

Includes bibliographical references.

332.4   Money

Rickards, James

Currency wars; the making of the next global crisis. Portfolio/Penguin 2011 288p $26.95   **332.4**

1. Monetary policy 2. Financial crises 3. Foreign exchange
ISBN 978-1-59184-449-5

LC 2011026906

The author "tells us we are in a new currency war that could destroy faith in the U.S. dollar; he examines that war through the lens of economic policy, national security, and historical precedent. As a national security issue, he tells a fascinating story of his involvement with the Pentagon and other agencies in designing and participating in a war game using currencies and capital markets, instead of ships and planes, to gain early warning of attacks on the U.S. dollar. . . . He presents a compelling case for his views and offers thought-provoking information for library patrons. This is a must-read book." Booklist

Includes bibliographical references

332.6   Investment

Bernstein, William

The four pillars of investing; lessons for building a winning portfolio. [by] William J. Bernstein. McGraw Hill 2010 331p il $30   **332.6**

1. Investments
ISBN 978-0-07-174705-9
First published 2002

The author discusses "the four pillars—the theory of investing, the history of investing, the psychology of investing, and the business of investing. . . . Using humor, Bernstein advises readers to employ sound tenets of investing to manage risk while building a foundation of assests for the long term." Libr J

Includes bibliographical references

The investor's manifesto; preparing for prosperity, Armageddon, and everything in between. [by] William J. Bernstein. Wiley 2010 xxii, 201p il $24.95; ebook $24.95   **332.6**

1. Stocks 2. Securities 3. Investments
ISBN 978-0-470-50514-4; 978-0-470-55807-2 ebook

LC 2009-20116

"Touching on lessons from the dot.com and 2008 market sell-offs, . . . [the author] discusses market and investor psychology, asset allocation, the unpredictability of returns, how to keep costs low, and, ultimately, how to avoid dying poor." Libr J

Includes bibliographical references

Boeckh, J. Anthony

The **great** reflation; how investors can profit from the new world of money. John Wiley & Sons 2010 xxii, 314p il $34.95   **332.6**

1. Investments 2. Business cycles 3. Financial crises 4. Personal finance

ISBN 978-0-470-53877-7

LC 2009-54227

"After laying out the post-2008 state of the U.S. economy and the inflation/deflation dangers as the Federal Reserve attempts to stimulate activity in the shadow of massive debt deleveraging, economist Boeckh then presents various investing scenarios." Libr J

Includes bibliographical references

Bogle, John C., 1929-

The **clash** of the cultures; investment vs. speculation. John C. Bogle. John Wiley & Sons 2012 xxv, 353 p.p ill. (hardcover) $29.95; (ebook) $29.95; (ebook) $40.00   **332.6**

1. Investments 2. Speculation 3. Mutual funds 4. Capital gains

ISBN 9781118122778; 9781118224748 pdf; 9781118414378

LC 2012026770

This book, by John C. Bogle, explores how "speculation has come to dominate investment. . . . Over the course of his sixty-year career in the mutual fund industry, Vanguard Group founder John C. Bogle has witnessed . . . the prudent, value-adding culture of long-term investment . . . crowded out by an aggressive, value-destroying culture of short-term speculation. . . . [This book] urges a return to the common sense principles of long-term investing." (Publisher's note)

Includes bibliographical references and index.

Buffett, Mary

Warren Buffett and the art of stock arbitrage; proven strategies for arbitrage and other special investment situations. [by] Mary Buffett & David Clark. Scribner 2010 153p $25; ebook $11.99   **332.6**

1. Investments 2. Financiers

ISBN 978-1-4391-9882-7; 978-1-4516-0645-4 ebook

LC 2011280299

Analyzes Buffett's techniques for arbitrage and special situations investing and offers step-by-step instructions on how to take advantage of such events as spin-offs, liquidations, recapitalizations, and tender offers.

"The writing is concise and straightforward, the examples are current and clear, and there are simple formulas on how to determine risk in both arbitrage and valuing liquidations." Libr J

Includes glossary

Cohan, William D.

Money and power; how Goldman Sachs came to rule the world. Doubleday 2011 658p $30.50; ebook $14.99   **332.6**

1. Securities 2. Investments 3. Banks and banking 4. Goldman Sachs & Co. 5. Goldman Sachs Group, Inc.

ISBN 978-0-385-52384-4; 978-0-385-53497-0 ebook

This is a history of the New York-based banking and investment firm from its founding in 1869 to the present.

"The book offers the best analysis yet of Goldman's increasingly tangled web of conflicts. . . . The writing is crisp and the research meticulous, drawing on reams of documents made publicly available by congressional committees and the Financial Crisis Inquiry Commission." Economist

Includes bibliographical references

Cortese, Amy

Locavesting; the revolution in local investing and how to profit from it. John Wiley 2011 252p $22.95; ebook $10.99   **332.6**

1. Investments 2. Small business 3. Community development

ISBN 978-0-470-91138-9; 978-1-1180-8578-3 ebook

LC 2011005647

"With the recent crash of the financial markets, many investors are looking for new places to put their money. At the same time, many small businesses are finding it ever more difficult to get credit. Cortese . . . covers this current confluence, providing examples of how investing in local small businesses can be beneficial to all parties. . . . Various types of funding methods are discussed, including cooperatives, credit unions, local stock exchanges, community development funds, public venture capital, and raising money through social networking. . . . Timely and easy to read, this is a nice introduction to something many of us have never considered. A good choice for public libraries and fruitful reading for small businesses and investors." Libr J

Includes bibliographical references

Cramer, James J.

Confessions of a street addict. Simon & Schuster 2002 339p $26; pa $14   **332.6**

1. Stocks 2. Wall Street (New York, N.Y.)

ISBN 0-7432-2487-6; 0-7432-2488-4 pa

LC 2002-22902

The author "recounts his turbulent dual career as hedge fund manager and media pundit. . . . This is a lively, informative portrait of the highest levels of finance and media in the last decade." Publ Wkly

Downes, John

★ **Finance** and investment handbook; [by] John Downes, Jordan Elliot Goodman. 8th ed.; Barron's Educational Series 2010 1152p il $39.99   **332.6**

1. Investments 2. Personal finance

ISBN 978-0-7641-6269-5; 0-7641-6269-1

LC 2010-31548

First published 1986 with title: Barron's finance & investment handbook. Periodically revised

This "volume presents a financial dictionary with definitions of more than 5,000 terms, an analysis of . . . investment opportunities, guidelines for non-experts on what to look for when reading corporate reports and financial news sources, . . . [a] directory of hundreds of publicly traded corporations in the United States and Canada, and a directory listing the names and addresses of brokerage houses, mutual funds families, banks, . . . information on federal and state regulators, and other major financial institutions." Publisher's note

Includes bibliographical references

Fox, Justin

★ The **myth** of the rational market; a history of risk, reward, and delusion on Wall Street. Harper Business 2009 382p $27.99; pa $16.99 **332.6**
1. Economics 2. Wall Street (New York, N.Y.) 3. Economics -- History 4. Economics -- Psychological aspects 5. Rational expectations (Economic theory)
ISBN 0-06-059899-9; 0-06-059903-0 pa; 978-0-06-059899-0; 978-0-06-059903-4 pa

LC 2008-52718

This book chronicles "the rise and fall of the efficient market theory.... The theory holds that the market is always right, and that the decisions of millions of rational investors, all acting on information to outsmart one another, always provide the best judge of a stock's value." (Publisher's note) Index.

"A must-read for anyone interested in the markets, our economy or government, this dense but spellbinding work brings modern finance and economics to life." Publ Wkly
Includes bibliographical references

Hagstrom, Robert G.

The **Warren** Buffett way; 2nd ed; John Wiley 2005 xxiii, 245p il $24.95; pa $14.95 **332.6**
1. Investments 2. Financiers
ISBN 0-471-64811-6; 0-471-74367-4 pa

LC 2004-13841

First published 1994

This edition "encompasses Buffett's numerous investments and accomplishments over the past ten years, as well as the timeless and highly successful investment strategies and techniques he has always used to come out a market winner." Publisher's note
Includes bibliographical references

Hudson, Michael

The **monster**; how a gang of predatory lenders and Wall Street bankers fleeced America--and spawned a global crisis. [by] Michael W. Hudson. Times Books 2010 365p $26; ebook $12.99 **332.6**
1. Mortgages 2. Global Financial Crisis, 2008-2009 3. Banks and banking -- Corrupt practices
ISBN 978-0-8050-9046-8; 978-1-4299-4004-7 ebook

LC 2010-3223

The author "exposes the source of the so-called toxic subprime mortgages that led to the 2008 financial crisis. He picks his way through a warren of mortgage brokers and lending companies that sat just outside banking regulations in the years following the savings and loan crisis. The book concentrates on the practices of mortgage lenders FAMCO and Ameriquest Mortgage, at one point the largest U.S. subprime lender. . . . This is essential reading for anyone concerned with the mortgage crisis." Libr J
Includes bibliographical references

Kelly, Kate

Street fighters; the last 72 hours of Bear Stearns, the toughest firm on Wall Street. Portfolio 2009 247p hardcover o.p. pa $16 **332.6**
1. Investments 2. Wall Street (New York, N.Y.) 3. Bear, Stearns & Co. Inc.
ISBN 978-1-5918-4273-6; 1-5918-4273-5; 978-1-5918-4318-4 pa; 1-5918-4318-9 pa

LC 2009-07694

This is an account of the collapse of the Bear Stearns investment bank in March 2008.

"Enlivened by graphic descriptions of executive disarray and cameo profiles of scrambling financiers as they come to appreciate the magnitude of the disaster they unleashed . . . this riveting account puts the ensuing worldwide financial crises in stark perspective." Publ Wkly
Includes bibliographical references

Lewis, Michael

Flash boys; a Wall Street revolt. Michael Lewis. W.W. Norton & Co Inc. 2014 288 p. (hardcover : alk. paper) $27.95 **332.6**
1. Financial services industry 2. Wall Street (New York, N.Y.) 3. Business -- Corrupt practices 4. Stockbrokers -- United States 5. Finance -- United States -- History -- 21st century
ISBN 0393244660; 9780393244663

LC 2014003208

Written by Michael Lewis, "'Flash Boys' is about a small group of Wall Street guys who figure out that the U.S. stock market has been rigged for the benefit of insiders and that, post-financial crisis, the markets have become not more free but less, and more controlled by the big Wall Street banks. Working at different firms, they come to this realization separately; but after they discover one another, the flash boys band together and set out to reform the financial markets." (Publisher's note)

An "engrossing true-life morality play that unmasks the devil in the details of high finance." Pub Wkly
Includes bibliographical references and index

Lowenstein, Roger

The **end** of Wall Street. Penguin Press 2010 xxv, 339p $27.95 **332.6**
1. Wall Street (New York, N.Y.) 2. Global Financial Crisis, 2008-2009
ISBN 978-1-59420-239-1; 1-59420-239-7

LC 2009-50864

Lowenstein "examines the past three years of economic collapse, chronicling actions and inactions from dozens of villains and a few heroes. . . . [He] identifies more than 100 key players, almost all of them middle-aged white males from Wall Street, private mortgage companies, law firms, federal government agencies and the U.S. Congress. The narrative consistently demonstrates how almost all of those who could have halted the coming recession by employing common sense instead decided that the housing market would never collapse." Kirkus
Includes bibliographical references

Lutnick, Howard

On top of the world; Cantor Fitzgerald and 9/11: a story of loss and renewal. {by} Howard Lutnick and Tom Barbash. HarperCollins Pubs. 2002 282p il $25.95; pa $14.95 **332.6**
1. September 11 terrorist attacks, 2001 2. Cantor Fitzgerald LP 3. World Trade Center (New York, N.Y.)
ISBN 0-06-051029-3; 0-06-051030-7 pa

LC 2002-27550

The bond-trading firm Cantor Fitzgerald lost 658 employees on September 11, 2001. "'On Top of the World' sets out to tell the story of Cantor Fitzgerald's tragedy, and its survival, largely from its chairman's point of view; the book is interspersed with ... passages in {Howard} Lutnick's own voice." N Y Times Book Rev

Mahar, Maggie

★ **Bull!** : a history of the boom, 1982-1999; what drove the breakneck market--and what every investor needs to know about financial cycles. HarperBusiness 2003 xxii, 486p il $27.95; pa $16.95 **332.6**
1. Business cycles 2. Wall Street (New York, N.Y.)
ISBN 0-06-056413-X; 0-06-056414-8 pa

LC 2003-51131

This is a "history of the 1982-99 bull market in U.S. stocks. {The author} explains that this bull market got its initial impetus from both the undervaluation of equities during the 1970s and the end of the Cold War. . . . Mahar concludes by summarizing how investors who haven't seen a bear market for 17 years might plan their investing strategies. Mahar takes complicated topics and explains them clearly for the average reader. Her exceptional book is most highly recommended to even the smallest public or academic library." Libr J
Includes bibliographical references

Malkiel, Burton Gordon, 1932-

★ A **random** walk down Wall Street; the time-tested strategy for successful investing. [by] Burton G. Malkiel. Rev. ed.; W.W. Norton & Co. 2011 445p il $29.95 **332.6**
1. Stocks 2. Investments
ISBN 978-0-393-08143-5

LC 2010-41866

First published 1973
The author argues "that it is extremely rare for an individual investor to consistently beat the stock-market averages. Investors are better off buying and holding an index fund than attempting to buy and sell individual securities or actively managed mutual funds. . . . This readable investment guide for individuals offers information on the full range of new investment products available, the results of current research by academics and other marketplace professionals, and a section on investment strategies for retired investors or those anticipating retirement. This excellent book offers important information for individual investors and is a valuable resource for library patrons." Booklist

McGee, Suzanne

Chasing Goldman Sachs; how the masters of the universe melted Wall Street down--and why they'll take us to the brink again. Crown Publishers 2010 398p $27; ebook $13.99 **332.6**
1. Banks and banking 2. Global Financial Crisis, 2008-2009 3. Goldman Sachs & Co.
ISBN 978-0-307-46011-0; 0-307-46011-8; 978-0-307-46012-7 ebook

LC 2009-53440

This " is an exceptionally lucid, well-written account of how and why the financial system broke down." Washington Post
Includes bibliographical references

Tett, Gillian

Fool's gold; how the bold dream of a small tribe at J.P. Morgan was corrupted by Wall Street greed and unleashed a catastrophe. Free Press 2009 293p $26; pa $16 **332.6**
1. Investments 2. Wall Street (New York, N.Y.)
ISBN 978-1-4165-9857-2; 1-4165-9857-X; 978-1-4391-0013-4 pa; 1-4391-0013-6 pa

LC 2009-5127

Traces the relationship between a team of JP Morgan banking gurus and the current financial crisis, documenting their invention of a bold variety of allegedly risk-free investments that sparked a frenzy in the banking world and may have directly contributed to the market crash.

Tett "deploys a remarkable sense of pacing, generating real suspense over rapidly inflating debt on bank balance sheets; by the time Lehman Brothers fails, the book has become a bonafide page-turner. . . . Tett's explosive, illuminating narrative is the one to read for anyone confused by the present financial mess." Publ Wkly
Includes bibliographical references

332.601 Philosophy and theory

Dreman, David

Contrarian investment strategies; the psychological edge. David Dreman. Free Press 2012 viii, 481 p.p $30 **332.601**
1. Profit 2. Stocks 3. Stock exchanges 4. Investment analysis 5. Investments -- Psychological aspects
ISBN 0743297962; 9780743297967

LC 2011023716

Author David Dreman discusses "new findings in psychology that explain why the stock market is inescapably given to bubbles, panics, and periods of high volatility. He also shows how we can use these findings to reliably profit from market errors, crash-proof our portfolios, and earn market-beating long-term returns. . . . [The book] shows why the 'best' stocks are consistently overvalued while the so-called worst, contrarian stocks are undervalued, and [Dreman] lays out his proven and simple rules for avoiding the pitfalls and spotting the bargains." (Publisher's note)
Includes bibliographical references and index.

332.63 Specific forms of investment

Siegel, Jeremy J.

Stocks for the long run; the definitive guide to financial market returns & long-term investment strategies. Jeremy J. Siegel. Fifth edition McGraw-Hill Education 2014 422 p illustrations $40 **332.63**
1. Stocks 2. Rate of return
ISBN 9780071800518 ; 0071800514

LC 2013037218

First published 1994 by Irwin
This book, by Jeremy J. Siegel, "answers all the important questions of today: How did the crisis alter the financial markets and the future of stock returns? What are the sources of long-term economic growth? How does the Fed really im-

pact investing decisions? Should you hedge against currency instability?" (Publisher's note)

"New material encompasses the causes and consequences of the 2008-09 financial crises. . . . The writing is so lucid that lay investors can readily comprehend the concepts." Choice

Includes bibliographical references and index

Weatherall, James Owen

The **physics** of Wall Street; a brief history of predicting the unpredictable. James Owen Weatherall. Houghton Mifflin Harcourt 2013 304 p. $27 **332.63**

1. Finance 2. Physics 3. Securities -- United States 4. Wall Street (New York, N.Y.)

ISBN 0547317271; 9780547317274

LC 2012017323

In this book, professor "[James Owen] Weatherall looks at the role played by physicists and their ideas in financial markets, and argues . . . that their contributions should be more widely used and recognized. Himself a physicist, philosopher, and mathematician, Weatherall suggests that the profession's essential contribution to finance is to develop models of how financial markets operate using insights from science." (Publishers Weekly)

Includes bibliographical references and index

332.66 Investment banks

Smith, Greg

Why I left Goldman Sachs; a Wall street story. Greg Smith. Business Plus 2012 276 p. (hardcover) $27.99 **332.66**

1. Financial institutions

ISBN 1455527475; 9781455527472; 9781455527489; 9781455527496; 9781619696013

LC 2012945268

This book by Greg Smith "shows the evolution of Wall Street into an industry riddled with conflicts of interest and a profit-at-all-costs mentality. . . . After conversations with nine Goldman Sachs partners over a twelve-month period proved fruitless, Smith came to believe that the only way the system would ever change was for an insider to finally speak out publicly. He walked away from his career [at Goldman Sachs] and took matters into his own hands. This is his story." (Publisher's note)

332.67 Investments in specific industries, in specific kinds of enterprise, by specific kinds of investors; international investment; investment guides

Nolan, Peter

Is China buying the world? Peter Nolan. Polity 2012 147 p. $19.95 **332.67**

1. International competition 2. China -- Economic conditions -- 1970-

ISBN 0745660789; 9780745660783

This book by Peter Nolan "probes behind the media rhetoric and shows that the idea that China is buying the

world is a myth. . . . Giant firms from high income countries with leading technologies and brands have greatly increased their investments in developing countries, with China at the forefront. . . . By contrast, Chinese firms have a negligible presence in the high-income countries." (Publisher's note)

332.7 Credit

Acharya, Viral V.

Guaranteed to fail; Fannie Mae, Freddie Mac, and the debacle of mortgage finance. [by] Viral V. Acharya [et al.] Princeton University Press 2011 232p il $24.95; ebook $24.95 **332.7**

1. Housing 2. Mortgages 3. Financial crises 4. Business failures 5. Fannie Mae 6. Federal Home Loan Mortgage Corporation

ISBN 978-0-691-15078-9; 978-1-4008-3809-7 ebook

LC 2011000247

"The authors of Guaranteed to Fail are specialists in applied financial and housing economics. They believe in the necessity of choosing among three options: should Fannie Mae and Freddie Mac exist? Should there be a private-public partnership of mortgage guarantees? Should government end housing subsidies? . . . The authors argue that overextension in housing came from the private sector, Congress, and government-sponsored enterprises." Choice

Includes bibliographical references

Andrews, Edmund L.

Busted; life inside the great mortgage meltdown. W. W. Norton 2009 220p $25.95 **332.7**

1. Mortgages 2. Real estate 3. Houses -- Buying and selling

ISBN 978-0-393-06794-1; 0-393-96794-7

LC 2009-09074

This is an "examination of the housing crisis, a story that turned personal when New York Times economics reporter Andrews got caught up in the housing bubble after falling in love with a woman and a house." Publ Wkly

Atwood, Margaret, 1939-

Payback; debt and the shadow side of wealth. House of Anansi Press 2008 230p (CBC Massey lectures) **332.7**

1. Debt 2. Wealth 3. Debt in literature 4. Debt -- Social aspects 5. Debt -- Moral and ethical aspects

ISBN 978-0-88784-800-1

This volume collects novelist Margaret Atwood's Massey Lectures, originally broadcast on the CBC. She investigates the "subject of debt, exploring debt as an ancient and central motif in religion, literature, and the structure of human societies." (Publisher's note) Bibliography. Index.

"Delivered with . . . [Atwood's] trademark wit and imagination, this is a meditation that challenges conventional thinking on one of the most morally pressing issues we face." Booklist

Includes bibliographical references

Howard, Timothy

The **mortgage** wars; inside Fannie Mae, big-money politics, and the collapse of the American

dream. Timothy Howard. McGraw-Hill 2013 304 p. (hardback) $30 **332.7**
1. Mortgages 2. Housing -- United States -- History 3. Federal National Mortgage Association 4. Mortgage loans -- United States 5. Subprime mortgage loans -- United States 6. Mortgage banks -- United States -- History
ISBN 0071821090; 9780071821094

LC 2013033450

In this book "former Fannie Mae CFO [Timothy] Howard lays bare . . . how the agency was undermined, and its executive leadership framed, by a confederation of political opponents. . . . His . . . account traces behind-the-scenes activity beginning around 1998. He describes a bipartisan league of free market ideologues, political hatchet men operating as financial regulators, and major business and corporate interests eager to privatize Fannie Mae's mortgage business for their own benefits." (Kirkus Reviews)

Leonard, Robin
★ **Credit** repair; by Robin Leonard and Attorney John Lamb. 9th ed.; Nolo 2009 268p il pa $24.99 **332.7**
1. Consumer credit
ISBN 978-1-4133-1019-1; 1-4133-1019-2

LC 2009-4833

First published 1996. Periodically revised
This book offers advice on assessing your debt situation, avoiding overspending, handling existing debts, cleaning your credit file, how credit reports are used, and building and maintaining good credit.
Includes bibliographical references

Morgenson, Gretchen
Reckless endangerment; how outsized ambition, greed, and corruption led to economic armageddon. [by] Gretchen Morgenson, Joshua Rosner. Times Books 2011 331p il $30; ebook $12.99 **332.7**
1. Mortgages 2. Financial crises 3. Global Financial Crisis, 2008-2009 4. Fannie Mae 5. Subprime mortgage loans 6. Financial crises -- United States -- 21st century
ISBN 978-0-8050-9120-5; 978-1-4299-6577-4 ebook

LC 2010047594

"A sobering account of some sordid recent history that's so clear and detailed that pros and novices will find its account rich and informative, and deeply depressing." Publ Wkly

Scurlock, James D.
Maxed out; hard times, easy credit, and the era of predatory lenders. Scribner 2007 248p il $24 **332.7**
1. Consumer credit 2. Debtor and creditor
ISBN 978-1-4165-3251-4; 1-4165-3251-X

LC 2006-51246

Scurlock presents a critique of the credit industry in the United States.
This is an "astute indictment of the credit industry. . . . Not all financial experts share Scurlock's pessimism about an indebted society. But he builds a persuasive case that deserves serious attention." Christ Sci Monit
Includes bibliographical references

333   Economics of land and energy

Clover, Charles
The **end** of the line; how overfishing is changing the world and what we eat. New Press 2006 386p $26.95 **333**
1. Commercial fishing
ISBN 978-1-59558-109-9; 1-59558-109-X

LC 2006-12058

First published 2004 in the United Kingdom
"Clover's hard-hitting approach will probably anger some, but his argument that we will soon run out of fish unless we take drastic measures . . . is persuasive." Publ Wkly
Includes bibliographical references

Renewable energy; sustainable concepts for the energy change. edited by Roland Wengenmayr and Thomas Bührke, translated by William D. Brewer. Wiley-VCH 2013 vi, 164 p.p $44.95 **333**
1. Energy policy 2. Energy development 3. Renewable energy resources 4. Renewable energy sources
ISBN 3527411879; 9783527411870

LC 2012540474

This book, edited by Roland Wengenmayr and Thomas Bührke, examines "changes in terms of energy sources. The increasing number of wind power plants, solar collectors and photovoltaic installations demonstrates perceptibly that many innovations for tapping renewable energy sources have matured: very few other technologies have developed so dynamically in the past years. Nearly all the chapters were written by professionals in the respective fields." (Publisher's note)
Includes bibliographical references and index

333.3   Private ownership of land

Haden, Jeff
★ The **complete** dictionary of real estate terms explained simply; what smart investors need to know. Atlantic Pub. Group 2006 286p pa $21.95 **333.3**
1. Reference books 2. Real estate -- Dictionaries
ISBN 978-0-910627-01-6; 0-910627-01-0

LC 2006-29746

"A licensed real estate broker defines over 2400 terms for potential home buyers and sellers." Libr J
Includes bibliographical references

Irwin, Robert
Tips & traps for negotiating real estate; 3rd ed.; McGraw-Hill 2010 246p (Tips & traps series) pa $17; ebook $17 **333.3**
1. Negotiation 2. Real estate business 3. Real estate investment 4. Houses -- Buying and selling
ISBN 978-0-07-175040-0 pa; 978-0-07-175088-2 ebook

LC 2010029971

First published 1995
This guide to negotiating real estate transactions covers "getting a better price in a down market; negotiating a quick sale; dealing with reluctant lenders; keeping the upper hand

when buying a foreclosed property; [and] talking a seller into financing your purchase." Publisher's note

Linklater, Andro

Owning the earth; the transforming history of land ownership. by Andro Linklater. Bloomsbury USA 2013 496 p. illustrations, maps (alk. paper) $30 **333.3**
1. Feudalism 2. Land tenure 3. Landlord and tenant 4. Land tenure -- History
ISBN 1620402890; 9781620402894
LC 2013011970

In this book, author Andro Linklater "focuses on the history of land ownership as driving human activity from the earliest ages and being the key to the creation of democracy. . . . Evolving from the collision of crown and chief barons that resulted in the Magna Carta, the impetus for owning land gained steam in the 1500s in England with the land revolution, which displaced subsistence farming via the feudal system in favor of a few rich owners profiting from the buying of land and increasing yields." (Kirkus Reviews)

"Many aspire to land ownership, taking the concept--that individuals may obtain a sliver of our planet as their own--for granted. Linklater's global study looks at land ownership--feudal, private, communal--through the lens of history and politics, rather than as merely a matter for economic study. The results are enlightening for our understanding not only of the past but of our future." (Library Journal)

Includes bibliographical references and index

333.7 Natural resources and energy

Duncan, Dayton

The **national** parks; America's best idea: an illustrated history. with a preface by Ken Burns; picture research by Susanna Steisel and Aileen Silverstone. Alfred A. Knopf 2009 403p il map $50 **333.7**
1. Nature conservation 2. United States -- Local history 3. National parks and reserves -- United States 4. United States -- National Park Service -- History
ISBN 978-0-307-26896-9
LC 2009-20880

The author delves "into the history of the park idea, from the first sighting by white men in 1851 of the valley that would become Yosemite and the creation of the world's first national park at Yellowstone in 1872, through the most recent additions to a system that now encompasses nearly four hundred sites and 84 million acres." Publisher's note

Includes bibliographical references

Encyclopedia of global resources; editor, Craig W. Allin. Salem Press 2010 4v il map set $395 **333.7**
1. Reference books 2. Natural resources -- Encyclopedias
ISBN 978-1-58765-644-6; 1-58765-644-2
LC 2010-1984

First published 1998 with title: Natural resources

"This four-volume set provides a wide variety of perspectives about Earth's natural resources and explains the interrelationships among resource exploitation, environmen-

talism, geology, and biology. Allin . . . presents 576 articles on resources such as oil and tar sands, nations from Argentina to Zimbabwe, government laws and conventions, and historical events. . . . [This encyclopedia] offers real value and sheds important light on where we derive our mineral and biological resources, how they are processed, what they are used for, and how they fit into the global economy." Libr J

Includes bibliographical references

Goleman, Daniel

Ecological intelligence; how knowing the hidden impacts of what we buy can change everything. Doubleday 2009 276p $26 **333.7**
1. Consumers 2. Industries 3. Environmental protection
ISBN 0-385-52782-9; 978-0-385-52782-8
LC 2008-41811

"Brimming with intriguing, useful, and galvanizing information, this is an exceptionally sharp, innovative, and realistic approach to raising the demand for environmentally safe merchandise." Booklist

Miller, Char

Gifford Pinchot and the making of modern environmentalism. Island Press (Washington, D.C.) 2001 458p il $28 **333.7**
1. Governors 2. Conservationists 3. Foresters
ISBN 1-55963-822-2
LC 2001-5665

"Charismatic, progressive, and controversial, Gifford Pinchot (1865-1946) established and directed the Forest Service under Theodore Roosevelt, lobbied hard for responsible logging practices, expressed prescient warnings about pollution, and called for sustainable energy. Miller's animated biography portrays Pinchot in all his fervor, and environmentalism in all its complexity." Booklist

Includes bibliographical references and index

Park, Chris

A **dictionary** of environment and conservation; by Chris Park. 2nd ed. Oxford University Press 2013 484 p. (Oxford paperback reference) (paperback) $21.95 **333.7**
1. Environment 2. Conservation of natural resources 3. Environmental sciences -- Dictionaries 4. Conservation of natural resources -- Dictionaries
ISBN 0199641668; 9780199641666
LC 2008006450

This book by Michael Allaby and Chris Park "provides over 9,000 alphabetically arranged entries on scientific and social aspects of the environment, including concise and authoritative information on key thinkers, treaties, movements, organizations, concepts, and theories. For the second edition, Allaby has added over 700 new entries, including 'aerial plankton,' 'cyclone collector,' 'oasis,' and 'supertramp.'" (Publisher's note)

"The second edition of this user-friendly title is updated with 800 new entries, expanding the work to more than 500 pages...Students will appreciate having access to this information in one convenient source. This affordable title is recommended for public and academic libraries." (Booklist)

Speth, James Gustave

The **bridge** at the end of the world; capitalism, the environment, and crossing from crisis to sustainability. Yale University Press 2008 295p il $28 **333.7**

1. Capitalism 2. Environmental policy
ISBN 978-0-300-13611-1; 0-300-13611-0

LC 2007-43584

This book "is a superb synthesis of the great economic questions of our time: how to reconcile markets with environmental sustainability; efficiency with equality; and trade and global openness with socially defensible standards of living." Am Prospect

Includes bibliographical references

Wilkins, Thurman

John Muir; apostle of nature. University of Okla. Press 1995 xxvii, 302p il maps (Oklahoma western biographies) hardcover o.p. pa $21.95 **333.7**

1. Authors 2. Naturalists 3. Writers on nature
ISBN 0-8061-2797-X pa

LC 95-11426

"Wilkins follows Muir from his Scottish boyhood, clouded by a harsh, fundamentalist father, to an adolescence of arduous farmwork in Wisconsin to a lifelong career of exploration and study of wildernesses, particularly those of the western U.S., and vividly relates some of Muir's more perilous adventures on cliffside and snowfield. . . . An affectionate, uncluttered tale of an American folk hero." Booklist

Includes bibliographical references

333.72 Conservation and protection

★ **American** earth; environmental writing since Thoreau. edited by Bill McKibben; foreword by Al Gore. Literary Classics of the United States 2008 1047p il (Library of America) $40 **333.72**

1. Nature conservation 2. Environmental movement 3. Environmental protection 4. Literature -- Collections
ISBN 978-1-59853-020-9; 1-59853-020-8

LC 2007-940683

This book "can be read as a survey of the literature of American environmentalism, but above all, it should be enjoyed for the sheer beauty of the writing." Publ Wkly

Includes bibliographical references

Beavan, Colin

No impact man; the adventures of a guilty liberal who attempts to save the planet, and the discoveries he makes about himself and our way of life in the process. Farrar, Straus, and Giroux 2009 274p $25; pa $15 **333.72**

1. Environmental protection
ISBN 978-0-374-22288-8; 0-374-22288-6; 978-0-312-42983-6 pa; 0-312-42983-5 pa

LC 2009-10188

"An inspiring, persuasive argument that individuals are not helpless in the battle against environmental degradation and global warming." Kirkus

Includes bibliographical references

Brinkley, Douglas

The **quiet** world; saving Alaska's wilderness kingdom, 1879-1960. Harper 2011 576p il map $29.99; ebook $23.99 **333.72**

1. Nature conservation 2. Environmental protection 3. Natural history -- Alaska
ISBN 978-0-06-200596-0; 978-0-06-203533-2 ebook

This book "brims over with information and insight, passion and insistence and some carelessness. In fact, it's a bit like Alaska itself: large, formidable, raw and ultimately unforgettable." Washington Post

Includes bibliographical references

Green volunteers; the world guide to voluntary work in nature conservation. editor, Fabio Ausenda. 7th ed; Green Volunteers; distributed by Universe Pub 2009 255p (We care guides) pa $16.95 **333.72**

1. Reference books 2. Volunteer work -- Directories 3. Nature conservation -- Directories
ISBN 978-88-89060-14-8; 88-89060-14-X

LC 2008-943207

First published 1999. Frequently revised

This book "lists over 200 projects worldwide for those who want to experience active conservation work as a volunteer. Projects are in a variety of habitats and countries, lasting from one week to one year or more. Projects involve volunteer work in wildlife rehabilitation centers, national parks, and protected areas, and general conservation work with a variety of animal species." Publisher's note

Kostigen, Thomas M.

The **green** book; the everyday guide to saving the planet one simple step at a time. Elizabeth Rogers and Thomas M. Kostigen; with a foreword by Cameron Diaz and William McDonough. Three Rivers Press 2007 xix, 201p $13.95 **333.72**

1. Environmental movement 2. Environmental protection 3. Environmentalism 4. Environmental protection -- Citizen participation
ISBN 9780307381354; 0307381358

LC 2007013222

It was the authors' intent to "address the fact that Americans endanger the balance of the ecosystem by the amount of waste we produce, the amount of water we use, and the amount of energy we consume." In order to influence readers' behavior, they present "observations and suggestions for living green" from "celebrities including Robert Redford, Ellen DeGeneres, Jennifer Aniston, Faith Hill, and Dale Earnhardt Jr." (Booklist) Topics include "ATM receipts . . . [t]urn[ing] off the tap while you brush your teeth . . . [and] voice-mail service for your home phone." (Publisher's notes)

Includes bibliographical references (p. [147]-197) and index..

McDaniel, Carl N.

Wisdom for a livable planet; the visionary work of Terri Swearingen, Dave Foreman, Wes Jackson, Helena Norberg-Hodge, Werner Fornos, Herman Daly, Stephen Schneider, and David Orr. Trin-

ity University Press 2005 277p hardcover o.p. pa
$17.95 **333.72**
   1. Environmental sciences
   ISBN 1-595-34008-4; 1-595-34009-2 pa
                LC 2004-19081
   The author personalizes "critical environmental issues
via profiles of eight 'visionaries' agitating for a more livable planet. . . . His subjects are prominent in the areas of
hazardous waste incineration, biodiversity, sustainable agriculture, appropriate technology, population control, rational
economic planning, climate concerns and environmental
education. . . . The stories of these eight ecological warriors
are profoundly appealing in that they show the diverse ways
that people can commit to a common cause." Publ Wkly
   Includes bibliographical references

McKibben, Bill, 1960-
   ★ The **Bill** McKibben reader; pieces from an
active life. Henry Holt 2008 442p pa $18 **333.72**
   1. Environmental protection
   ISBN 978-0-8050-7627-1 pa; 0-8050-7627-1 pa
                LC 2007-39609
   This is a "collection of essays gleaned from books and
periodicals published between 1982 and 2007. Most of the
44 essays come from a diverse array of magazines, including The New Yorker, Mother Jones, Outside, Gourmet, and
Christian Century. . . . Essays are loosely divided into categories that include consumerism, activism, the changing
planet, the meaning of community, and the sufficiency of
nature. . . . Readers new to McKibben will be entertained,
informed, and perhaps even inspired to make the positive
changes that McKibben desires for the world." Libr J

Nelson, Gaylord
   Beyond Earth Day; fulfilling the promise. [by]
Gaylord Nelson with Susan Campbell and Paul Woz-
niak; with a foreword by Robert Kennedy, Jr. Uni-
versity of Wisconsin Press 2002 xx, 201p il map
$26.95 **333.72**
   1. Earth Day 2. Environmental movement
   ISBN 0-299-18040-9
                LC 2002-2806
   "The Earth Day founder presents exceptionally lucid ex-
planations of a host of current ecoissues." Booklist
   Includes bibliographical references

333.73   Land

Biggers, Jeff
   Reckoning at Eagle Creek; the secret legacy of
coal in the heartland. Nation Books 2010 300p il
$26.95 **333.73**
   1. Coal mines and mining 2. Shawnee National Forest
region (Ill.)
   ISBN 978-1-56858-421-8; 1-56858-421-0
                LC 2009-32686
   Biggers "takes a look at coal and its role in the history
of southern Illinois as well as its human and environmental
costs. Biggers also tells a personal story as he chronicles the
saga of his family's strip-mined homestead in an area that

one day would be a part of the Shawnee National Forest. . . .
A lot of history is presented here in a personal style by a cultural historian with a keen eye. A valuable read for followers
of environmental history." Libr J
   Includes bibliographical references

333.79   Energy

Helm, Dieter
   The **carbon** crunch; how we're getting climate
change wrong--and how to fix it. Dieter Helm. Yale
University Press 2012 xiii, 273 p.p (hardcover)
$35 **333.79**
   1. Energy policy 2. Climate change 3. Renewable
energy resources 4. Energy conservation 5. Renewable
energy sources 6. Greenhouse gas mitigation 7.
Climatic changes -- Prevention
   ISBN 0300186592; 9780300186598
                LC 2012017386
   In this book Dieter Helm examines the economics of
climate change regulation policies, finding fault in "their
basic design. They have caused people to focus on the most
expensive ways of mitigating climate change, rather than
the cheapest, imposing high cost for little gain. . . .The
heart of Mr Helm's book is an examination of the economics of renewable energy" and wind energy in particular.
(Economist)
   Includes bibliographical references and index

Koerth-Baker, Maggie
   Before the lights go out; conquering the energy
crisis before it conquers us. Maggie Koerth-Baker.
John Wiley & Sons 2012 xii, 290 p.p $27.95 **333.79**
   1. Solar energy 2. Biomass energy 3. Climate
change 4. Energy policy -- United States 5. Energy
consumption -- United States 6. Energy development
-- United States 7. Energy conservation -- United States
8. Renewable energy sources -- United States
   ISBN 0470876255; 9780470876251
                LC 2011043334
   Author Maggie KoerthBaker tells "how our energy systems really work today, and what we'll have to do to keep
them working in the years to come. . . . [She discusses]
climate change, [solar farms,] and conversion efficiency.
. . . [KoerthBaker provides information on the future of]
economics and social incentives [and how they] will be the
things that build our new world." (maggiekb.com)
   Includes bibliographical references and index.

Levi, Michael
   Power surge; energy, opportunity, and the battle
for America's future. by Michael Levi. Oxford University Press 2013 260 p. (hardback : alk. paper)
$27.95 **333.79**
   1. Energy resources 2. Energy policy -- United States
3. Renewable energy -- United States 4. Energy
industries -- United States
   ISBN 0199986169; 9780199986163
                LC 2012043264
   In this book, author Michael Levi "takes on the big
claims made by both sides in the fight over American en-

ergy, showing what the changes underway mean for the United States and the world. Both unfolding revolutions in American energy offer big opportunities for the country to strengthen its economy, bolster its security, and protect the environment. Levi shows how to seize those with a new strategy that blends the best of old and new energy while avoiding the real dangers." (Publisher's note)

"Readers seeking to understand America's energy policies and prospects will welcome this even-handed, smart, and accessible book on a topic of incomparable economic importance." Pub Wkly

Includes bibliographical references and index

McGraw, Seamus

The **end** of country. Random House 2011 245p $26; ebook $13.99   **333.79**

1. Energy policy 2. Energy resources 3. Pennsylvania
ISBN 978-1-4000-6853-1; 978-0-679-60431-0 ebook
LC 2010035972

"In 2006, in a hardscrabble part of Pennsylvania that had long lost its allure as a farming and industrial area, geologists began investigating the Marcellus Shale. It turned out to be the richest deposit of natural gas ever discovered anywhere. When his widowed mother was approached about permitting natural-gas exploration on their farm, journalist McGraw had to weigh their need for money against the future prospects of the farmland. Chronicling the impact of the find on his mother and her neighbors, McGraw's research led to this impressively detailed, highly engaging look at issues of energy policy, economics, and sociology that arose when a bucolic town was suddenly faced with the 'traveling circus' of energy exploration. . . . A completely engaging look at how energy policy affected a quiet, rural town." Booklist

Muller, Richard A., 1944-

Energy for future presidents; the science behind the headlines. Richard A. Muller. W. W. Norton 2012 xvii, 350 p.p ill., maps (hardcover) $26.95   **333.79**

1. Energy resources 2. Energy development 3. Energy policy -- United States 4. Technology and state 5. Energy policy -- Social aspects 6. Power resources -- Social aspects
ISBN 0393081613; 9780393081619
LC 2012015586

This book, by Richard A. Muller, discusses U.S. energy policy. "The near-meltdown of Fukushima, the upheavals in the Middle East, the BP oil rig explosion, and the looming reality of global warming have reminded . . . all U.S. citizens that nothing has more impact on our lives than the supply of and demand for energy. Its procurement dominates our economy and foreign policy. . . . But the 'energy question' is more confusing, contentious, and complicated than ever before." (Publisher's note)

Includes bibliographical references and index

Newton, David E.

World energy crisis; a reference handbook. David E. Newton. ABC-CLIO 2013 xviii, 334 p.p ill.

(Contemporary world issues. Science, technology, and medicine) (hardcover) $58   **333.79**

1. Energy policy 2. Energy consumption 3. Energy conservation 4. Energy security 5. Energy industries 6. Energy development
ISBN 1610691474; 9781610691475; 9781610691482
LC 2012016975

This book, by David E. Newton, is part of the "Contemporary World Issues" reference series. It "provides a thorough investigation of . . . our current global energy situation, and what actions should be taken to prevent a crippling fuel-supply catastrophe in the future. The book presents a historical background for current energy problems that discusses the supply and consumption of various forms of energy at different periods of history." (Publisher's note)

Includes bibliographical references (p. 269-305) and index

Yergin, Daniel

The **quest**; energy, security and the remaking of the modern world. Penguin Press 2011 804p il map $37.95   **333.79**

1. Energy policy 2. Globalization 3. Energy resources 4. Money -- Political aspects 5. Power resources -- Political aspects
ISBN 978-1-59420-283-4; 1-59420-283-4
LC 2011013100

This book "combines four books. The first . . . provides global history of oil, natural gas, and nuclear power from 1991 to 2011. . . . The second part of 'The Quest' traces a path from the discovery of climate change as an esoteric interest of a few scientists in the nineteenth century to the introduction of 'new climate change policies . . . intended to make a profound transformation of the energy foundations that support the world economy.' . . . 'The Quest''s third part looks at nuclear and renewable alternatives to fossil fuels. . . . When Yergin looks to the future in his fourth book, he asks how the economic benefits from an average megawatt of power can be increased while at the same time reducing its negative effects on the environment and health." (New York Review of Books)

This book "is a masterly piece of work and, as a comprehensive guide to the world's great energy needs and dilemmas, it will be hard to beat." Economist

Includes bibliographical references

333.792   Primary forms of energy

Ferguson, Charles D.

Nuclear energy; what everyone needs to know. Charles D. Ferguson. Oxford University Press 2011 xvii, 222 p.p (What everyone needs to know) (hardback) $74   **333.792**

1. Nuclear energy 2. Nuclear power plants
ISBN 0199759456; 9780199759453; 9780199759460
LC 2010044449

In this book, "Charles D. Ferguson provides an authoritative account of the key facts about nuclear energy. What is the origin of nuclear energy? What countries use commercial nuclear power, and how much electricity do they obtain from it? How can future nuclear power plants be made safer? What can countries do to protect their nuclear facilities from military attacks? How hazardous is radioactive waste? Is nuclear energy a renewable energy source?" (Publisher's note)

"This compelling assembly of historical and scientific information deftly steps through the essential discoveries, definitions, and theory that led to the development of nuclear reactors and nuclear bombs. . . . [F]ollowing chapters . . . cover safety, climate change, nuclear proliferation concerns, security, and the politically charged options for disposal of radioactive waste." Choice

Includes bibliographical references and index

333.793   Secondary forms of energy

Couch, Julianne

Traveling the power line; from the Mojave Desert to the Bay of Fundy. Julianne Couch. University of Nebraska Press 2013 xx, 214 p.p (Our sustainable future) (paperback) $19.95   **333.793**
1. Electric power 2. Power resources -- United States 3. Electric power plants -- United States
ISBN 0803245068; 9780803245068

LC 2012035997

In this book, journalist Julianne Couch "chronicles her visits to nine electrical power stations across the country, examining the pros and cons of the fuel sources used at each site." She looks at sources including "wind, water, geothermal, solar and nuclear power. Between 2008 and 2010, Couch traveled . . . to talk to 'scientists, engineers, policy advocates, environmental activists, industry experts and the folks who work in or live around various sites of energy production.'" (Kirkus)

Includes bibliographical references (pages 213-216).

333.794   Renewable energy sources

Pernick, Ron

Clean Tech Nation; How the U.S. Can Lead in the New Global Economy. Ron Pernick. HarperCollins 2012 320 p. $29.99   **333.794**
1. Economic development 2. Sustainable development 3. Technological innovations 4. Economic policy -- United States
ISBN 0062088440; 9780062088444

This book, by Ron Pernick and Clint Wilder, discusses how "the United States risks losing out on the most critical opportunity for job creation and global economic leadership in the 21st century. . . . If the U.S. is to remain dominant, as it has in the earlier high-tech and Internet revolutions, it needs to supercharge efforts at every level--in federal, state, and city governments, and in schools, small businesses, and large companies." (Publisher's note)

333.8   Subsurface resources

Goodstein, David L.

Out of gas; the end of the age of oil. {by} David Goodstein. Norton 2004 140p il $21.95; pa $13.95   **333.8**
1. Petroleum
ISBN 0-393-05857-3; 0-393-32647-0 pa

LC 2003-10376

"Goodstein's predictions are based on a sophisticated understanding of physics and thermodynamics, and on a simple observation about natural resources." N Y Times Book Rev

Includes bibliographical references and index

Wilber, Tom

Under the surface; fracking, fortunes and the fate of the Marcellus Shale. Tom Wilber. Cornell University Press 2012 272 p. (cloth : alk. paper) $27.95   **333.8**
1. Natural gas 2. Shale gas industry 3. Hydraulic fracturing 4. Marcellus Shale 5. Shale gas industry -- Pennsylvania 6. Hydraulic fracturing -- Pennsylvania 7. Shale gas industry -- New York (State) 8. Hydraulic fracturing -- New York (State)
ISBN 0801450160; 9780801450167

LC 2011047166

This book by Tom Wilber is a "journalistic overview of shale gas development and the controversies surrounding it. . . . [Wilber] gives a voice to all constituencies, including farmers and landowners tempted by the prospects of wealth but wary of the consequences, policymakers struggling with divisive issues, and activists coordinating campaigns based on their visions of economic salvation and environmental ruin." (Publisher's note)

Includes bibliographical references and index.

333.91   Water and lands adjoining bodies of water

Dean, Cornelia

Against the tide; the battle for America's beaches. Columbia Univ. Press 1999 279p il $60; pa $18.95   **333.91**
1. Coasts 2. Beaches 3. Seashore ecology
ISBN 0-231-08418-8; 0-231-08419-6 pa

LC 98-50755

Dean discusses the ecology of American beaches and contends that they are threatened by coastal development and erosion

"This thoroughly researched and thoughtful book is destined to become a classic of environmental science writing." Libr J

Includes bibliographical references

Fishman, Charles

The **big** thirst; Charles Fishman. Free Press 2011 388p. ebook $12.99; $26.99   **333.91**
1. Water supply 2. Infrastructure (Economics) 3.

Water resources development
ISBN 978-1-4391-2493-2 ebook; 978-1-4391-0207-7
LC 2010033989

This book presents an "assessment of the current politics, economics, and culture of water." It was the author's intent to demonstrate "that the water we have now is all the water we will ever have and that our 'golden age' of 'abundant, safe, and cheap' water may soon end, thanks to deteriorating infrastructure, . . . rising urban populations, and climate change. Both 'water complacency' and 'water poverty' are rampant. . . . Among his many case studies are Las Vegas' water extravaganzas and India's lack of 24/7 water even in its booming cities, which keeps millions of girls out of school to collect and carry each day's water supply. . . . Fishman praises tap water, observes that water consciousness is 'infectious,' and declares that 'most water problems are, in fact, solvable'." (Booklist)

This is a "lively and invaluable assessment of the current politics, economics, and culture of water. Lyrical in his descriptions of the beauty and wonder of water, Fishman is rigorous when explaining that the water we have now is all the water we will ever have and that our 'golden age' of 'abundant, safe, and cheap' water may soon end, thanks to deteriorating infrastructure (7 billion gallons leak out of our water systems every day), rising urban populations, and climate change." Booklist

Includes bibliographical references and index.

Harden, Blaine

A **river** lost; the life and death of the Columbia. Norton 1996 271p maps $25; pa $14.95 **333.91**
1. Columbia River
ISBN 0-393-03936-6; 0-393-31690-4 pa
LC 95-38618

In this look at the development of Columbia River region, the author "examines the changes—sociological, environmental, economic and aesthetic—that the taming of this great river wrought. His wonderful account touches on the destruction of Native American cultures dependent on the river and its salmon, and on the near extinction of the salmon themselves. Also fairly portrayed are the people and industries currently dependent on both the managed river and massive government subsidies." Publ Wkly

Includes bibliographical references

Rothfeder, Jeffrey

Every drop for sale; our desperate battle over water in a world about to run out. Tarcher/Putnam 2001 205p hardcover o.p. pa $14.95 **333.91**
1. Water supply
ISBN 1-58542-114-6; 978-1-58542-367-5 pa;
1-58542-367-X pa
LC 2001-27903

"Like the drip of water on stone, Rothfeder's steady exposition of horrors will wear down any reader's doubts that water is the next flashpoint of global politics, human rights and health issues." Publ Wkly

Includes bibliographical references

Ward, Diane Raines

Water wars; drought, flood, folly, and the politics of thirst. Riverhead Bks. 2002 280p $24.95; pa $14 **333.91**
1. Water rights 2. Water supply 3. Hydraulic engineering
ISBN 1-57322-229-1; 1-57322-995-4 pa
LC 2002-21301

The author considers the problems of "droughts, pollution, population growth, and climate change—which threaten to make water . . . the cause of war within our lifetime. . . . {She} tells the stories of those working to solve them: hydrologists, politicians, engineers, and everyday people." Publisher's note

"Ward writes with the sensibilities and concerns of an environmentalist. But unexpectedly, delightfully, she's an environmentalist who loves the scale, ingenuity and power of engineering." N Y Times Book Rev

Includes bibliographical references and index

333.95   Biological resources

Barrow, Mark V.

Nature's ghosts; confronting extinction from the age of Jefferson to the age of ecology. [by] Mark V. Barrow, Jr. University of Chicago Press 2009 497p il $35 **333.95**
1. Biologists 2. Extinct animals 3. Endangered species 4. Wildlife conservation 5. Extinction (Biology) 6. Endangered species -- Law and legislation 7. Wildlife conservation -- United States -- History
ISBN 978-0-226-03814-8; 0-226-03814-9
LC 2008-49085

The author "retraces the history of the earliest European and North American naturalists, from those who refused to believe that species comprising a perfect, stable world could go extinct, to the acceptance of extinction at the hands of humans and the legal mechanisms created to halt it. . . . Professionals in ecology, conservation biology, and wildlife management and readers interested in natural history will find this book hard to put down." Choice

Includes bibliographical references

Chadwick, Douglas H.

The **company** we keep; America's endangered species. {by} Douglas H. Chadwick and Joel Sartore. National Geographic Soc. 1996 157p il hardcover o.p. pa $16 **333.95**
1. Endangered species 2. Wildlife conservation 3. Environmental policy -- United States
ISBN 0-7922-7132-7 pa
LC 96-18874

"The book is not built solely around the photographs. But the pictures are collectively a good storyteller. They're well-edited, and accompanied by maps and charts that help explain how man is threatening many species." Christ Sci Monit

Includes bibliographical references

Cousteau, Jacques Yves, 1910-1997

The **human,** the orchid, and the octopus; exploring and conserving our natural world. [by] Jacques Cousteau and Susan Schiefelbein. Bloomsbury 2007 305p hardcover o.p. pa $16 **333.95**
1. Oceanography 2. Nature conservation 3. Human influence on nature
ISBN 978-1-59691-417-9; 1-59691-417-3; 978-1-59691-418-6 pa; 1-59691-418-1 pa
LC 2007-18824
Original French edition, 1997
"Cousteau's reverence for life's miracles . . . shines through in this eloquent testimony on the importance of pursuing higher ideals, particularly the preservation of the oceans and the natural world for future generations." Publ Wkly
Includes bibliographical references

Ellis, Richard

Tuna; a love story. Alfred A. Knopf 2008 334p il $27.95; pa $16 **333.95**
1. Tuna 2. Commercial fishing 3. Endangered species
ISBN 978-0-307-26715-3; 0-307-26715-6; 978-0-307-38710-3 pa; 0-307-38710-0 pa
LC 2007-52253
"Ellis loves this fish. His rapt description of the physiology that makes tunas one of the fastest things in the ocean . . . lends emotional urgency to his account of the collapsing tuna fishery." Orion
Includes bibliographical references

Fraser, Caroline

Rewilding the world; dispatches from the conservation revolution. Metropolitan Books 2009 400p map $28.50 **333.95**
1. Ecology 2. Endangered species 3. Wildlife conservation
ISBN 978-0-8050-7826-8; 0-8050-7826-6
LC 2009-32989
"Heavily researched with endnotes for those looking for more information, this truly is an essential read for conservationists, biologists, and anyone interested in the natural world." Libr J
Includes bibliographical references

Goodall, Jane, 1934-

★ The **ten** trusts; what we must do to care for the animals we love. {by} Jane Goodall and Marc Bekoff. HarperSanFrancisco 2002 xx, 200p hardcover o.p. pa $14,95 **333.95**
1. Animal rights 2. Animal welfare 3. Wildlife conservation 4. Human influence on nature
ISBN 0-06-251757-0; 0-06-055611-0 pa
LC 2002-68717
"An accessible, compelling, and important exposé." Booklist
Includes bibliographical references

Greenberg, Paul

American catch; the fight for our local seafood. Paul Greenberg. The Penguin Press 2014 320 p. $26.95 **333.95**
1. Seafood industry -- United States 2. Commercial fishing -- United States 3. Fish trade 4. Local foods -- United States 5. Fishes -- Conservation -- United States
ISBN 1594204489; 9781594204487
LC 2014005395
In this book, author Paul Greenberg tells "the surprising story of why Americans stopped eating from their own waters. In 2005, the United States imported five billion pounds of seafood, nearly double what we imported twenty years earlier. . . . During that same period, our seafood exports quadrupled. 'American Catch' examines New York oysters, Gulf shrimp, and Alaskan salmon to reveal how it came to be that 91 percent of the seafood Americans eat is foreign." (Publisher's note)
Includes bibliographical references and index

Four fish; the future of the last wild food. Penguin Press 2010 284p $25.95 **333.95**
1. Tuna 2. Salmon 3. Codfish 4. Bass (Fish) 5. Fish culture 6. Commercial fishing
ISBN 978-1-59420-256-8
LC 2010-1276
"The narrative is grounded in common sense and anchored by first-rate, on-scene reporting from the Yukon and Mekong Rivers, Lake Bardawil in the Sinai Peninsula and the waters off the coasts of Long Island, Greece, Hawaii and the Shetland Islands. Hugely informative, sincere and infectiously curious and enthusiastic." Kirkus
Includes bibliographical references

Hoekstra, Jonathan M.

The **atlas** of global conservation; changes, challenges and opportunities to make a difference. [by] Jonathan Hoekstra ... [et al.]; edited by Jennifer L. Molnar. University of California Press 2010 234p il map $49.95 **333.95**
1. Atlases 2. Globalization 3. Reference books 4. Environmental protection 5. Conservation of natural resources
ISBN 978-0-520-26256-0
LC 2009-23617
"Focusing primarily on biomes and ecosystems, this valuable atlas promotes a deeper understanding of the challenges involved in preserving and maintaining these habitats and resources. Basically an analysis of the current state of the globe, the book highlights conservation challenges through chapters on habitats, species distributions, deforestation, global warming, coastal development, and pollution. . . . The book is unique and well done." Voice Youth Advocates
Includes bibliographical references

Horwitz, Joshua

War of the Whales; A True Story. by Joshua Horwitz. Simon & Schuster 2014 448 p. ill. (some col.), col. map $28 **333.95**
1. Whales 2. Military research 3. United States. Navy
ISBN 1451645015; 9781451645019

This book, by Joshua Horwitz, "is the gripping tale of a crusading attorney who stumbles on one of the US Navy's best-kept secrets: a submarine detection system that floods entire ocean basins with high-intensity sound--and drives whales onto beaches. As Joel Reynolds launches a legal fight to expose and challenge the Navy program, marine biologist Ken Balcomb witnesses a mysterious mass stranding of whales near his research station in the Bahamas." (Publisher's note)

"Based on years of interviews and research, Horwitz delivers a powerful, engrossing narrative that raises serious questions about the unchecked use of secrecy by the military to advance its institutional power." Kirkus

Kurlansky, Mark

Cod; a biography of the fish that changed the world. Penguin Bks. 1998 294p il pa $14 **333.95**
1. Codfish 2. Commercial fishing 3. Cooking -- Fish
ISBN 0-14-027501-0
LC 97-12165
First published 1997 by Walker & Co.
Kurlansky discusses the history of commercial cod fishing and the plight of the Atlantic fish and fisheries today as the cod faces extinction.
This book offers "maximum readability, plenty of handsome illustrations, and a 40-page appendix of superlatively annotated recipes." Booklist
Includes bibliographical references

Lebbin, Daniel J.

The **American** Bird Conservancy guide to bird conservation; [by] Daniel J. Lebbin, Michael J. Parr, and George H. Fenwick; with a foreword by Jonathan Franzen. University of Chicago Press 2010 446p il map $45; ebook $27 **333.95**
1. Wildlife conservation 2. Birds -- United States
ISBN 978-0-226-64727-2; 0-226-64727-7; 978-0-226-6472-6 ebook
LC 2010007646
The authors survey "the comprehensive status of bird conservation in the Americas, primarily focusing on North America. . . . 'WatchList Birds' provides accounts for 212 US birds—priority species for conservation—with a color plate, map, and text sections on distribution, threats, conservation, and action. 'Habitats' gives an overview of 12 major North American habitats (tundra, wetlands, grasslands, etc.) and includes several prime site descriptions within each, accompanied by the same features as the 'WatchList' accounts. The third major section, 'Threats,' includes sections such as 'Habitat Loss,' 'Pollution and Toxics,' and 'Climate Change,' and describes problems, solutions, and actions. . . . A beautiful production visually, the book is inviting as well as an unprecedented, rewarding conservation reference source." Choice
Includes glossary and bibliographical references

Life on earth; an encyclopedia of biodiversity, ecology, and evolution. edited by Niles Eldredge. ABC-CLIO 2002 2v set $185 **333.95**
1. Reference books 2. Biological diversity --

Encyclopedias
ISBN 1-57607-286-X
LC 2002-15852
"Four introductory essays outline the definition, importance, and preservation of biodiversity. Many of the 194 articles are about specific phyla or species . . . or important concepts. . . . Others address issues that will appeal to students and general readers. . . . Articles are clearly written, usually define specialized terms, and include bibliographies of books and popular and scholarly periodical articles." Booklist
Includes bibliographical references

McNamee, Thomas

The **return** of the wolf to Yellowstone. Holt & Co. 1997 354p il maps hardcover o.p. pa $15 **333.95**
1. Wolves 2. Endangered species 3. Yellowstone National Park
ISBN 0-8050-5792-7 pa
LC 96-39702
"An advocate for the reintroduction of the gray wolf to Yellowstone National Park, McNamee kept careful watch over the legal wrangling that accompanied this controversial endeavor, the challenges of its execution, and the complex questions it has raised, then recorded the entire story in this vivid day-by-day chronicle." Booklist
Includes bibliographical references

Mooallem, Jon

Wild ones; a sometimes dismaying, weirdly reassuring story about looking at people looking at animals in America. Jon Mooallem. The Penguin Press 2013 339 p. (hardcover) $27.95 **333.95**
1. Ecology 2. Human-animal relationship 3. Endangered species -- United States 4. Wildlife conservation -- United States 5. Endangered species -- United States -- Psychological aspects
ISBN 159420442X; 9781594204425
LC 2012047006
In this book, the "plights of polar bears, Lange's metalmark butterflies and whooping cranes frame [a] discussion of humankind's relations with the animal kingdom, the environment and itself." Author Jon Mooallem "contrasts the perilous circumstances threatening some species with the conflicts that arise among sentiment, commerce and environmental science." (Kirkus Reviews)
Includes bibliographical references and index

Orenstein, Ronald

Ivory, horn and blood; behind the elephant and rhinoceros poaching crisis. Ronald Orenstein. Firefly Books 2013 216 p. color illustrations $29.95 **333.95**
1. Ivory 2. Poaching 3. Elephants 4. Rhinoceros 5. Ivory industry -- Corrupt practices 6. Rhinoceroses -- Effect of poaching on 7. African elephant -- Effect of poaching on 8. Asiatic elephant -- Effect of poaching on 9. Rhinoceros horn industry -- Corrupt practices
ISBN 1770852271; 9781770852273
LC 2013427986
This book, by Ronald Orenstein, describes how "today a new ivory crisis has arisen, fuelled by internal wars in Africa and a growing market in the Far East. . . . Bands of militia

have crossed from one side of Africa to the other, slaughtering elephants with automatic weapons. A market surge in Vietnam and elsewhere has led to a growing criminal onslaught against the world's rhinoceroses. The situation, for both elephants and rhinos, is dire." (Publisher's note)

"Orenstein brings his considerable expertise to bear on this complex catastrophe, presenting all sides of some of the most polarizing issues." LJ

Includes bibliographical references (pages [194]-211) and index

Owens, Delia

The **eye** of the elephant; an epic adventure in the African wilderness. [by] Delia and Mark Owens. Houghton Mifflin 1992 305p il hardcover o.p. pa $16   **333.95**
  1. Elephants 2. Wildlife conservation
  ISBN 0-395-42381-3; 0-395-68090-5 pa

                    LC 92-17691

This is an account of the authors' efforts to save elephants in the Luangwa Valley of Zambia from poachers by involving and educating the local people.

This "is a provocative, disturbing, and eminently readable work." Nat Hist

Includes bibliographic references

Followed by Secrets of the savanna

★ **Sustaining** life; how human health depends on biodiversity. edited by Eric Chivian and Aaron Bernstein; Center for Health and the Global Environment Harvard Medical School; foreword by Edward O. Wilson; prologue by Kofi Annan. Oxford University Press 2008 542p il map $34.95   **333.95**
  1. Environmental health 2. Biological diversity
  ISBN 978-0-19-517509-7; 0-19-517509-3

                LC 2007-20609

"A collaborative survey of biodiversity issues written and/or reviewed for accuracy by more than 100 scientists, this volume is motivated by its UN sponsors' sense of the world populace's indifference to the consequences of environmental degradation. Conceiving that implicating human health with the health of other species may enlist its concern, the authors collectively warn that present extinction rates are abnormally high. Seven categories of endangered species stand in as portents of the dire effects to ecosystems when extinction occurs. . . . Abundantly illustrated, this is a valuable, urgent resource suited to any general-interest library." Booklist

Includes bibliographical references (p. 445-514)

Wilson, Edward O., 1929-

The **diversity** of life. Harvard Univ. Press 1992 424p il maps (Questions of science) $31.50 **333.95**
  1. Ecology 2. Nature conservation
  ISBN 0-674-21298-3

                LC 92-9018

"Identifying five natural events that have disrupted evolution and global diversity (climatic changes, meteorite strikes), Wilson maintains that the present sixth great extinc-

tion is being caused by human neglect and ignorance. This important book is highly recommended." Libr J

Includes bibliographical references

★ The **future** of life. Knopf 2002 xxiv, 229p il $22; pa $13   **333.95**
  1. Endangered species 2. Nature conservation
  ISBN 0-679-45078-5; 0-679-76811-4 pa

                LC 2001-38316

Wilson "proposes that there is yet time to avoid a grand planetary environmental crash provided we get serious, acknowledge a duty of stewardship and recognize an emotional affiliation . . . . with other kinds of life." NY Times Book Rev

A **window** on eternity; A Biologist's Walk Through Gorongosa National Park. Edward O. Wilson ; photographs by Piotr Naskrecki. Simon & Schuster 2014 228 p. col illustrations, color maps (hardback) $30   **333.95**
  1. Biodiversity 2. Nature conservation 3. Biodiversity -- Mozambique -- Parque Nacional da Gorongosa 4. Natural history -- Mozambique -- Parque Nacional da Gorongosa 5. Nature conservation -- Mozambique -- Parque Nacional da Gorongosa 6. Restoration ecology -- Mozambique -- Parque Nacional da Gorongosa 7. Parque Nacional da Gorongosa (Mozambique) -- Description and travel
  ISBN 1476747415; 9781476747415

                LC 2013032607

Author Edward O. Wilson presents a book of "prose and . . . photography about . . . Gorongosa National Park in Mozambique. . . . Wilson takes readers to the summit of Mount Gorongosa, sacred to the local people and the park's vital watershed. From the forests of the mountain he brings us to the deep gorges on the edge of the Rift Valley, previously unexplored by biologists, to search for new species and assess their ancient origins." (Publisher's note)

"Wilson . . . presents a lyrical ode to biodiversity within the framework of a memoir of his work in Mozambique's Gorongosa National Park, helping to rebuild it from the loss of nearly all of its megafauna as it was neglected, repurposed as a battleground, and destroyed by poachers during the 16-year civil war." Pub Wkly

335   Socialism and related systems

Avrich, Karen

Sasha and Emma; the anarchist odyssey of Alexander Berkman and Emma Goldman. Paul Avrich and Karen Avrich. Belknap Press of Harvard University Press 2012 x, 490 p.p (hbk. : alk. paper) $35   **335**
  1. Anarchism and anarchists 2. Anarchism -- United States -- History 3. Anarchists -- United States -- Biography
  ISBN 0674065980; 9780674065987

                LC 2012008659

This book, by Paul and Karen Avrich, is a biography of the anarchists, terrorists and political extremists Emma Goldman and Alexander Berkman. "Berkman shocked the country in 1892 with . . . the failed assassination of the industrialist Henry Clay Frick. . . . Through an attempted prison breakout, multiple bombing plots, and a dramatic deportation from America, these two unrelenting activists insisted on the improbable ideal of a socially just, self-governing utopia." (Publisher's note)

Includes bibliographical references and index.

Butterworth, Alex

The **world** that never was; a true story of dreamers, schemers, anarchists and secret agents. Pantheon Books 2010 482p il ebook $30.00; $30.00 **335**
1. Anarchism and anarchists 2. Anarchism -- History
ISBN 9780307379030; 9780375425110
LC 2009-48115

Butterworth "presents a history of anarchism from the 1871 Paris Commune to the 1905 Russian Revolution through stories of violent revolutionaries, the secret police who tracked them, and famous figures who played lesser-known roles." (Publisher's note) Index.

"A narrative taut with intrigue and freighted with contemporary significance." Booklist
Includes bibliographical references

Rudahl, Sharon

A **dangerous** woman; the graphic biography of Emma Goldman. The New Press 2007 115p il $17.95 **335**
1. Graphic novels 2. Biographical graphic novels 3. Essayists 4. Anarchists 5. Memoirists 6. Writers on politics 7. Family planning advocates 8. Anarchism and anarchists -- Graphic novels
ISBN 978-1-59558-064-1
LC 2007-15415

Emma Goldman was a revolutionary activist, speaker, writer, and feminist and anarchist. An immigrant to the U.S., she spoke out against inhumane working conditions, taught contraception, and opposed conscription for World War I. She founded the Free Speech League (a precursor to the ACLU), and the magazine Mother Earth. When she was deported to Russia just after the Bolshevik Revolution, she became disillusioned with the authoritarianism she found there, and she ended up supporting the fight against fascism in the Spanish Civil War. Rudahl based her graphic novel on Goldman's autobiography. The book includes nudity, sexual situations, and some violence.

335.4 Marxian systems

Marx, Karl, 1818-1883

★ The **Communist** manifesto; [by] Karl Marx and Friedrich Engels; with an introduction and notes by Gareth Stedman Jones. Penguin Books 2002 287p pa $7 **335.4**
1. Communism
ISBN 0-14-044757-1
First published 1848

This document "analyzes history in terms of class conflict, predicts the imminent overthrow of the ruling bourgeoisie by the oppressed proletariat, and envisions a resulting classless society in which personal property would be abolished. The 'Manifesto' calls upon the proletariat of the world to unite and strengthen itself for this final revolution." Benet's Reader's Ency 4th edition
Includes bibliographical references

Pipes, Richard

★ **Communism** : a history. Modern Lib. 2001 175p hardcover o.p. pa $10.95 **335.4**
1. Communism
ISBN 0-679-64050-9; 0-8129-6864-6 pa
LC 2001-275458

"As a brief, polemical diatribe . . . this short account of communism should provoke and instruct." Libr J
Includes bibliographical references

Priestland, David

The **red** flag; a history of communism. Grove Press 2009 xxvii, 675p il $30 **335.4**
1. Communism
ISBN 978-0-8021-1924-7

"Starting with the origins of communist ideology in the French Revolution, . . . [this book] presents an interesting analysis of Marx's thinking as being shaped as much by Romanticism as by the Enlightenment. Priestland also examines communist governments and movements in Africa, Asia, Europe and Latin America as well as the Soviet Union, and discusses the Nazi-Soviet pact as well as Stalin's ban on anti-fascist activity in Europe, concluding with a level-headed account of the communist collapse." New Statesman
Includes bibliographical references

Sperber, Jonathan

Karl Marx; a nineteenth-century life. Jonathan Sperber. W W Norton & Co Inc 2013 512 p. (hardcover) $35 **335.4**
1. Communists -- Germany -- Biography 2. Philosophers -- Germany -- Biography
ISBN 0871404672; 9780871404671
LC 2012044951

This book by Jonathan Sperber is a biography of "Karl Marx, the German philosopher and political firebrand turned London émigré journalist. . . . Sperber demonstrates that Marx had more in common with Robespierre than with twentieth-century Communists. Using the complete Marx and Engels database . . . Sperber juxtaposes the private man against the public agitator who helped foment the 1848-49 Revolution and whose incendiary books inflamed the dissident world of Europe." (Publisher's note)
Includes bibliographical references (p.   ) and index

Wheen, Francis

Karl Marx; a life. Norton 2000 431p il $27.95; pa $14.95 **335.4**
1. Communism 2. Writers on politics 3. Political and social philosophers
ISBN 0-393-04923-X; 0-393-32157-6 pa
LC 99-87466

First published 1999 in the United Kingdom

"Following Marx from his childhood in Trier, Germany, through his exile in London, Wheen . . . takes readers from hovel to grand house, from the International Working Man's

Association to Capital, from obscurity to notoriety and back again." Publ Wkly

Includes bibliographical references

336.2   Taxes

Burman, Leonard E.

Taxes in America; what everyone needs to know. Leonard E. Burman, Joel Slemrod. Oxford University Press 2013 280 p. (pbk. : alk. paper) $16.95 **336.2**

1. Taxation -- United States

ISBN 0199890269; 9780199890262; 9780199890279

LC 2012026106

In this book, Leonard E. Burman and Joel Slemrod provide an "explanation of how . . . [the U.S.] tax system works, how it affects people and businesses, and how it might be improved. They address such questions as how to recognize Fool's Gold tax reform plans. How much more tax could the IRS collect with better enforcement? How do tax burdens vary around the world? Why do corporations pay so little tax, even though they earn trillions of dollars every year?" (Publisher's note)

Includes bibliographical references and index

★ **J.K.** Lasser's your income tax 2009; prepared by the J.K. Lasser Tax Institute. Wiley 2008 xxviii, 816p il pa $18.95   **336.2**

1. Income tax

ISBN 978-0-470-28002-7; 0-470-28002-6

Annual. First published by Simon & Schuster. Began publication with 1936 issue. Title varies. Early issues prepared by J.K. Lasser

This "guide offers line-by-line instructions on filling out tax forms and what to do to prepare throught the year." Libr J

336.3   Public debt and expenditures

Johnson, Simon

White House burning; the founding fathers, our national debt, and why it matters to you. Simon Johnson, James Kwak. 1st ed. Pantheon Books 2012 352 p. ill. $26.95   **336.3**

1. Public debts -- United States 2. Deficit financing -- United States 3. United States -- Appropriations and expenditures 4. Debts, Public -- United States 5. Budget deficit -- United States 6. Government spending policy -- United States

ISBN 0307906965; 9780307906960

LC 2012000435

In this book, "[Simon] Johnson (Entrepreneurship and Management/MIT) and [James] Kwak (Univ. of Connecticut School of Law) . . . explain how the [U.S.] national debt began to grow, why it is willfully misrepresented by politicians and misunderstood by much of the citizenry and whether it is ever likely to cripple the richest nation in the world. . . . The authors . . . [also offer a] demonstration of the fallacy of likening government debt to the debt of an individual family." (Kirkus Reviews)

Includes bibliographical references (p. [241]-324) and index.

337   International economics

Friedman, Thomas L.

The **Lexus** and the olive tree; Updated and expanded ed; Farrar, Straus, Giroux 2000 xxi, 469p $30   **337**

1. Free trade 2. Business and politics 3. International economic relations 4. United States -- Foreign economic relations

ISBN 978-0-374-18552-7; 0-374-18552-2

LC 00-29411

First published 1999

Friedman "explains, with anecdotes as well as analyses, what the instant electronic global economy is and what it may take to live there." N Y Times Book Rev

Stiglitz, Joseph E.

Globalization and its discontents. Norton 2002 xxii, 282p $24.95; pa $15.95   **337**

1. Globalization 2. International finance 3. International economic relations 4. International Monetary Fund 5. Developing countries -- Economic conditions

ISBN 0-393-05124-2; 0-393-32439-7 pa

LC 2002-23148

"This smart, provocative study contributes significantly to the ongoing globalization debate." Publ Wkly

Includes bibliographical references

Zizek, Slavoj

First as tragedy, then as farce. Verso 2009 157p pa $12.95   **337**

1. Communism 2. Capitalism 3. Globalization

ISBN 978-1-84467-428-2

"An earnest and timely challenge, Zizek's critique of capitalism and repositioning of communist thought is both insightful and well-reasoned, and guaranteed to rile readers across the political and theoretical spectrum." Publ Wkly

Includes bibliographical references

338   Production

Clark, Taylor

Starbucked; a double tall tale of caffeine, commerce, and culture. Little, Brown 2007 297p $25.99   **338**

1. Coffeehouses 2. Coffee industry 3. Starbucks Corporation

ISBN 978-0-316-01348-2; 0-316-01348-X

LC 2007-13074

This "is a breezily written business yarn with plenty of big-picture punch." Christ Sci Monit

Includes bibliographical references

Cook, John

Our noise; the story of Merge Records, the indie label that got big and stayed small. [by] John Cook with Mac McCaughan and Laura Ballance. Algonquin Books of Chapel Hill 2009 289p il pa $18.95   **338**

1. Rock music -- History and criticism 2. Merge

Records (Chapel Hill, N.C.: Firm)
ISBN 978-1-56512-624-4; 1-56512-624-6

LC 2009-12495

This is "an oral history of Merge Records, featuring interviews from its founders (McCaughan and Ballance), its numerous signees (featuring members of Lambchop, Spoon, the Arcade Fire, and more), and various admirers and business partners (like Dischord Records founder/Fugazi frontman Ian MacKaye). Author John Cook alternates his chapters between recounting the history of the Merge label and then profiling one particular band. . . . For still being in the game after putting out two decades worth of classic albums . . . , it's obvious that Merge—with its success and its struggles—is still wanting nothing more than to make some peers of its own. In our rushed digital age of today, there's something profoundly sweet about such a simple sentiment." PopMatters

★ **Encyclopedia** of American business; general editor, W. Davis Folsom; associate editor, Stacia N. VanDyne. Rev. ed.; Facts On File 2011 2v (Facts on File library of American history) set $150 **338**

1. Reference books 2. Business -- Encyclopedias
ISBN 978-0-8160-8112-7

LC 2010-28372

First published 2004

"Five general areas of business are covered: accounting, banking, finance, marketing, and management. This encyclopedia focuses on the terms, concepts, and associations that one is most likely to encounter in business." Publisher's note

Includes bibliographical references

Schwantes, Carlos A.

The **West** the railroads made; [by] Carlos A. Schwantes, James P. Ronda. University of Washington Press in association with Washington State Historical Society and the John 2008 xx, 229p il map $39.95 **338**

1. West (U.S.) -- History 2. Railroads -- United States
ISBN 978-0-295-98769-9

LC 2007-29363

"Sprinkled throughout with marvelous reproductions of photos, maps, artwork and railroad memorabilia, this book highlights a fascinating era in our history. . . . A stunning work using well chosen archival resources to tell the story." Univ Press Books for Public and Second Sch Libr, 2009

Includes bibliographical references

338.0973   Production -- United States

Cox, Hank H.

American drive; how manufacturing will save our country. Richard E. Dauch with Hank H. Cox. St. Martin's Press 2012 xii, 334 p.p. ill. (chiefly col.) **338.0973**

1. Banks and banking 2. Automobile industry 3. United States -- Economic conditions 4. Job creation --

United States 5. Industrial management -- United States
ISBN 9781250010827; 9781250010834

LC 2012028235

Author Richard E. "Dauch narrates the story of AAM [American Axle and Manufacturing] against the backdrop of his nearly fifty years in the auto industry, from . . . foreign competition, government bailouts, battles with unions, and the recent Great Recession . . . [He provides] lessons on leadership, advanced product technology, communication, negotiation, and making profits in the most difficult times . . . [The book] transcends the auto industry and draws a blueprint for job creation, manufacturing competitiveness, economic growth, and excellence in America." (Amazon)

338.1   Specific kinds of industries

Ackerman-Leist, Philip

Rebuilding the foodshed; how to create local, sustainable, and secure food systems. Philip Ackerman-Leist. Post Carbon Institute""||"Chelsea Green Pub. 2013 360 p. (A community resilience guide) (paperback) $19.95 **338.1**

1. Local foods 2. Agriculture -- Government policy 3. Food supply 4. Food security
ISBN 1603584234; 9781603584234; 9781603584241

LC 2012043955

This book is about food policy. Farmer and professor Philip Ackerman-Leist "ruminates his way through the conundrums and possibilities of local food, demonstrating how words and their definitions can shed light on and transform our understanding of the rapidly evolving, often confusing, emotion-fraught questions of what people eat, where the food comes from, who has access to what, and how the answers to these questions affect the lives of eaters and growers." (Publishers Weekly)

Includes bibliographical references and index

Astyk, Sharon

A **nation** of farmers; defeating the food crisis on American soil. [by] Sharon Astyk & Aaron Newton. New Society Publishers 2009 392p il pa $19.95 **338.1**

1. Food relief 2. Food supply
ISBN 978-0-86571-623-0

LC 2009-483077

The authors "argue that it is both possible and necessary to stop the harm caused by industrial agriculture. They show how the food crisis is tied to the energy crisis, global warming, and resource depletion and conclude that worldwide food shortages are imminent. . . . This outstanding and well-written compendium of insights and recommendations, of fervent idealism and practical solutions, is highly recommended." Libr J

Includes bibliographical references

Berry, Wendell, 1934-

Citizenship papers. Shoemaker & Hoard 2003 189p $24; pa $15 **338.1**

1. Agriculture -- Government policy 2. Economic policy -- United States 3. Agriculture -- Environmental

aspects

ISBN 1-593-76000-0; 1-593-76037-X pa

LC 2003-13811

"Berry's recent essays may restate what he has said before—that agribusiness and the new globalism are inimical to human thriving—but they say it better, and through different immediate subjects, saliently including sound sheep raising and 9/11, than ever before." Booklist

The **essential** agrarian reader; the future of culture, community, and the land. edited by Norman Wirzba. University Press of Kentucky 2003 276p il $27 **338.1**
1. Human ecology 2. Agriculture -- Economic aspects 3. Agriculture -- Environmental aspects
ISBN 0-8131-2285-6

LC 2003-8808

"In this collection of . . . essays, farmers, philosophers, scientists, and environmentalists look at the ways in which industrial agriculture, unchecked consumerism, and the squandering of natural resources have caused great harm. . . . The contributors . . . are leaders in their fields, and have lucid, expressive writing styles. Highly recommended." Libr J
Includes bibliographical references

Hamilton, Lisa M.
Deeply rooted; unconventional farmers in the age of agribusiness. Counterpoint 2009 313p $25 **338.1**
1. Farmers
ISBN 978-1-5937-6180-6; 1-5937-6180-5

LC 2008-50526

Hamilton "profiles farmers and ranchers who believe that 'agriculture is not an industry' but, rather, 'a fundamental act that determines whether we as a society will live or die.'. . . Hamilton's in-depth portraits of independent farmers offer invaluable perspectives on American agriculture, past and present, while offering hope for a life-sustaining future." Booklist
Includes bibliographical references

Hesterman, Oran B.
Fair food; growing a healthy, sustainable food system for all. PublicAffairs 2011 302p il $24.99; ebook $9.99 **338.1**
1. Food supply 2. Food industry 3. Sustainable agriculture
ISBN 978-1-61039-006-4; 978-1-61039-007-1 ebook

LC 2010-53129

Hesterman "writes that our food system is broken and will not be able to continue supporting the world population for much longer. The author's deft explanation of our current cultivation and consumption of food should have families moving away from their supermarket aisles and into farmers' markets and community-supported agriculture programs. Hesterman urges much-needed change on the federal level, as well. . . . Guides and resources are included to help the average consumer source food locally, and the author also includes a breakdown of federal legislation and how it should be amended. A thorough, inspiring guide on how to restructure the food system for a long and healthy future, for consumers and legislators alike." Kirkus
Includes bibliographical references

Hewitt, Ben
The **town** that food saved; how one community found vitality in local food. Rodale 2009 234p $24.99 **338.1**
1. Food supply 2. Food industry 3. Entrepreneurship 4. Sustainable agriculture
ISBN 978-1-60529-686-9; 1-60529-686-4

LC 2009-34294

"Adroitly balancing professional neutrality with personal commitment, Hewitt engagingly examines this paradigm shift in the way a community feeds its citizens." Booklist

Peacock, Kathy Wilson
★ **Food** security; Kathy Wilson Peacock ; foreword by Mary K. Hendrickson. Facts On File 2011 344 p. (acid-free paper) $45.00 **338.1**
1. Scarcity 2. Nutrition 3. Food supply 4. Food supply -- Juvenile literature 5. Food security -- Juvenile literature 6. Food -- Safety measures -- Juvenile literature
ISBN 0816082030; 9780816082032

LC 2011018414

This reference book "examines problems related to the amount, accessibility, and nutritional quality of the human food supply. Set up by a foreword by rural sociologist Mary Hendrickson, this topically arranged volume features three sections: a substantial introduction to global food security, with comprehensive case studies from representative countries (Bangladesh, China, the Democratic Republic of Congo, Haiti, the U.S., and Yemen); primary source documents; and research tools. The introduction defines food security and elucidates related topics such as global food supplies, causes and effects of food shortfalls, the potential effects of climate change and the global water crisis on food production, international history of food insecurity, and counterstrategies." (Booklist)
Includes bibliographical references and index.

Stuart, Andrea
Sugar in the Blood; A Family's Story of Slavery and Empire. Andrea Stuart. Knopf 2013 xix, 353 p.p ill., maps, geneal. tables $27.95 **338.1**
1. Stuart family 2. Slavery -- History 3. Barbados -- History 4. Slavery -- Barbados -- History 5. Sugar trade -- Barbados -- History 6. Sugarcane industry -- Barbados -- History
ISBN 0307272834; 9780307272836

LC 2012034259

This book, by Andrea Stuart, is a family history and overview of slavery and the sugar industry. "In the late 1630s, . . . George Ashby . . . fell into the life of a sugar plantation owner by mere chance, but by the time he harvested his first crop, a revolution was fully under way. . . . Stuart uses her own family story--from the seventeenth century through the present--as the pivot for this . . . tale of migration, settlement, survival, slavery and the making of the Americas." (Publisher's note)
Includes bibliographical references (p. [335]-341) and index

338.2 Extraction of minerals

Burrough, Bryan

The **big** rich; the rise and fall of the greatest Texas oil fortunes. Penguin Press 2009 466p il $29.95; pa $16   **338.2**

1. Petroleum industry

ISBN 978-1-59420-199-8; 1-59420-199-4; 978-0-14-311682-0 pa; 0-14-311682-7 pa

LC 2008-27043

The author "details the multigenerational saga of the 'Big Four' Texas oil families of Roy Cullen, H.L. Hunt, Clint Murchison, and Sid Richardson, from the discovery of oil under Beaumont, TX, in 1901 to the demolition of the infamous Shamrock Hotel, the last bastion of oil-fueled Texas excess, in 1987." Libr J

"Full of schadenfreude and speculation—and solid, timely history too." Kirkus

Includes bibliographical references

House, Silas

Something's rising; Appalachians fighting mountaintop removal. [by] Silas House and Jason Howard; foreword by Lee Smith. University Press of Kentucky 2009 xiv, 306 p.p $27.95   **338.2**

1. Landscape protection 2. Coal mines and mining 3. Mountaintop mining 4. Environmentalism -- Appalachian Region, Southern 5. Appalachian Region, Southern -- Environmental conditions

ISBN 978-0-8131-2546-6; 0813125464; 9780813125466

LC 2008049846

The authors focus on "the long-growing mining crisis in Central Appalachia. Twelve Appalachians—among them a college student, former union organizers, community activists and the octogenarian 'mother of folk,' Jean Ritchey—provide firsthand accounts of a disappearing way of life, a vital ecology in rapid decline, an industry that refuses to take responsibility for the devastation it causes (blowing the tops off mountains is only the latest, most destructive technique), and a nation too hooked on cheap energy to help. . . . This important collection illuminates the ongoing betrayal of the American mining town." Publ Wkly

Includes bibliographical references (p. [287]-290) and index

LeCain, Timothy J.

Mass destruction; the men and giant mines that wired America and scarred the planet. Rutgers University Press 2009 273p il map $26.95   **338.2**

1. Mining engineering 2. Copper mines and mining 3. Mining engineers 4. Copper industry and trade -- History 5. Copper mines and mining -- Western States 6. Copper mines and mining -- Environmental aspects

ISBN 978-0-8135-4529-5; 0-8135-4529-3

LC 2008-35434

The author writes "about the history, the engineering challenges, the successes of production and resulting consumption, and the environmental consequences of open-pit copper mining, mainly in the first half of the 20th century. . . . This book provokes serious second thoughts about the future of the exploitation of nature's bounty, and it should appeal to a wide audience." Choice

Includes bibliographical references and index

Maass, Peter

Crude world; the violent twilight of oil. Alfred A. Knopf 2009 276p il $27   **338.2**

1. Petroleum industry

ISBN 978-1-4000-4169-5

LC 2009-12303

The author "traveled the globe to uncover the effects of what he calls the resource curse—the power of oil to cause environmental disaster, political corruption, and economic strife wherever it is discovered." Booklist

"An absorbing, relentlessly discouraging account of the disastrous effect of oil wealth on nearly everyone." Kirkus

Includes bibliographical references (p. 233-62)

Margonelli, Lisa

Oil on the brain; adventures from the pump to the pipeline. Doubleday 2007 324p hardcover o.p. pa $14.95   **338.2**

1. Petroleum industry

ISBN 0-385-51145-0; 978-0-385-51145-2; 0-7679-1697-2 pa; 978-0-7679-1697-4 pa

LC 2006-20789

Margonelli examines how oil travels from petroleum fields to neighborhood gas stations.

The author "adds something fresh to the discussion by eschewing the popular (but dreary) doomsday angle in favor of an 'adventures in . . .' approach. . . . By giving voice to the people who are the links in the global oil chain, Margonelli invites us to leapfrog all the rhetoric, dry statistics, and dire pronouncements about oil in order to truly understand it." Fast Company

Includes bibliographical references

Yergin, Daniel

★ The **prize**; the epic quest for oil, money & power. Free Press 2008 908p il map pa $22 **338.2**

1. World politics 2. Petroleum industry

ISBN 978-1-4391-1012-6; 1-4391-1012-3

LC 2009-291302

First published 1991

This is a "history of the oil industry, from the first oil well ever drilled (near Titusville, Pennsylvania, in 1859) to the Iraqi invasion of Kuwait. It recalls advances in technology, innovations in salesmanship, and wars and truces among corporations and nations." New Yorker

Includes bibliographical references

Zuckerman, Gregory

The **frackers**; the outrageous inside story of the new billionaire wildcatters. Gregory Zuckerman. Portfolio Penguin 2013 416 p. (hardback) $29.95   **338.2**

1. Energy resources 2. Shale gas industry 3. Hydraulic fracturing 4. Businesspeople -- United States -- Biography 5. Energy industries -- United States -- Biography 7. Petroleum industry and trade -- United

States -- Biography
ISBN 1591846455; 9781591846451

LC 2013037926

This book explores "one of America's biggest economic and scientific revolutions of recent decades: the tapping of abundant oil and natural gas reserves within our own borders using a technique called fracking. . . . Focusing on a half dozen 'wildcatters,' the ones who seek out potential drilling sites, Zuckerman takes us through their decades long drought while they refined the techniques of horizontal hydraulic drilling." (Publishers Weekly)

"[S]hows us the beneficial side of fracking and the potentially environmentally disastrous side, and lets us find our own ground to stand on. A lively, exciting, and definitely thought-provoking book." Booklist

Includes bibliographical references

338.3 Other extractive industries

Hilborn, Ray

Overfishing; what everyone needs to know. Ray Hilborn with Ulrike Hilborn. Oxford University Press 2012 xviii, 150 p.p (pbk. : alk. paper) $16.95 **338.3**
 1. Overfishing 2. Commercial fishing 3. Sustainable fisheries 4. Fisheries -- Environmental aspects
 ISBN 0199798141; 9780199798131; 9780199798148

LC 2011031308

This book by Ray and Ulrike Hilborn provides an "explanation of the broad issues associated with overfishing. Guiding readers through the scientific, political, economic, and ethical issues associated with harvesting fish from the ocean, it will provide answers to questions about which fisheries are sustainably managed and which are not. Overall, the authors present a hopeful view of the future of fisheries." (Publisher's note)

Includes bibliographical references (p. [131]-139) and index

338.4 Secondary industries and services

Almond, Steve

★ **Candyfreak** : a journey through the chocolate underbelly of America. Algonquin Books of Chapel Hill 2004 266p $21.95 **338.4**
 1. Candy 2. Authors 3. Chocolate 4. Humorists 5. Journalists 6. Short story writers
 ISBN 1-56512-421-9

LC 2003-70801

The author tells how candy "shaped his childhood and continues to define his life in ways large and small. . . . Once hundreds of American confectioners delivered regional favorites to consumers, but now the big three of candy—Hershey, Mars, and Nestlé—control the market. To find out what happened to those candies of yesteryear, Almond talks to candy collectors and historians and visits a few of the remaining independent candy companies. . . . Flavored with the author's amusingly tart sense of humor, Candyfreak is an intriguing chronicle of the passions that candy inspires and the pleasures it offers." Libr J

Includes bibliographical references

Avorn, Jerry

★ **Powerful** medicines; the benefits, risks, and costs of prescription drugs. Knopf 2004 448p $27.50 **338.4**
 1. Drugs 2. Drug industry
 ISBN 0-375-41483-5

LC 2003-66119

The author explains "the current American prescription-drug debacle, placing it within the larger context of overall medical cost concerns. He . . . discusses what often goes awry when overworked physicians can't keep abreast of voluminous research, when patients are underinformed about generic drug availability, and when profits provide the sole motivation for pharmaceutical research. . . . A comprehensive, interesting read." Booklist

Includes bibliographical references

Becker, Elizabeth

Overbooked; the exploding business of travel and tourism. Elizabeth Becker. Simon & Schuster 2013 464 p. (hardback) $28 **338.4**
 1. Travel 2. Cultural tourism 3. Tourism 4. Tourism -- Political aspects 5. Tourism -- Cross cultural studies 6. Tourism -- Moral and ethical aspects
 ISBN 1439160996; 9781439160992; 9781439161005

LC 2012032848

In this book, Elizabeth Becker explores the growing global tourism industry. She "travels widely, experiencing and analyzing 'the stealth industry of the twenty-first century,' which is proliferating across regions, cultures, and ecosystems, and developing in specialized niches like 'sex tourism,' 'dark tourism,' and 'heritage tourism.'" (Publishers Weekly)

Burhans, Dirk E.

Crunch! a history of the great American potato chip. [by] Dirk Burhans. University of Wisconsin Press 2008 203p il $26.95 **338.4**
 1. Potato chips
 ISBN 978-0-299-22770-8

LC 2008-11962

The author "presents a gastronomic and industrial history of the potato chip. Drawing from documents, material culture (packaging), and . . . interviews with potato farmers and chippers, the author touches on changes in farming, packaging, food processing, food regulation, antitrust regulation, industry associations, and lobbying, all through the story of this simple, beloved American snack." Choice

"A wonderfully readable history that spans popular culture, local history, agriculture, economics, business and biography. Pass the chips please!" Univ Press Books for Public and Second Sch Libr, 2009

Includes bibliographical references

Callahan, Daniel

Taming the beloved beast; how medical technology costs are destroying our health care system. Princeton University Press 2009 267p $29.95 **338.4**
 1. Medical technology 2. Medical care -- Costs
 ISBN 978-0-691-14236-4; 0-691-14236-X

LC 2009-1503

According to Callahan, . . . Americans want universal health care but are divided over how to obtain it. While bringing insightful ethical, social, political, and economic perspectives to this timely, well-documented discourse of the ballooning costs of American health care and Medicare, Callahan concentrates on the growing costs of medical technology, which, along with uncontrolled governmental health-care spending, threaten to drag this country into financial crisis. Libr J

Includes bibliographical references and index

Diaz, Tom

The **last** gun; how changes in the gun industry are killing Americans and what it will take to stop it. Tom Diaz. The New Press 2013 319 p. (hardcover) $26.95   **338.4**
1. Gun control 2. Firearms industry -- United States 3. Firearms ownership -- United States 4. Gun control -- United States 5. Firearms -- Law and legislation -- United States
ISBN 1595588302; 9781595588302

LC 2012047230

This book, by Tom Diaz, explores gun control in the U.S. "By any account, gun violence in the United States has reached epidemic proportions. . . . Tom Diaz presents a chilling, up-to-date survey of the changed landscape of gun manufacturing and marketing. [The book] explores how the gun industry and the nature of gun violence have changed . . . [and arguing] that now is the time for a renewed political effort to attack gun violence at its source--the guns themselves." (Publisher's note)

Includes bibliographical references (pages 255-319).

Fine, Doug

Too high to fail; cannabis and the new green economic revolution. Doug Fine. Gotham Books 2012 xlv, 314 p.p (hardcover) $28.00; (paperback) $16.00   **338.4**
1. Marijuana industry 2. Marijuana -- Economic aspects
ISBN 1592407099; 9781592407095; 9781592407613

LC 2012014437

It was author "[Doug] Fine's intention . . . to track one cloned female cannabis plant, later named Lucille, from the farmer who tended her to the first patient who inhaled her smoke. Along the way, the author explores the intertwined history of humans and cannabis, as well as potential future benefits of cannabis, including biofuel, textiles, foodstuffs, farming and substantial economic boosts for cash-strapped communities." (Kirkus Reviews)

Lewis, Michael

The **new** new thing; a Silicon Valley story. Norton 1999 268p $25.95   **338.4**
1. Computer software industry 2. Computer software executives
ISBN 0-393-04813-6

LC 99-43412

The author offers a "look at the life and career of Dr. Jim Clark, the eccentric but brilliant visionary who thus far has created three multi-billion-dollar ground-breaking enterprises—Silicon Graphics, Netscape, and Healtheon." Libr J

This "is a splendid, entirely satisfying book, intelligent and fun and revealing and troubling in the correct proportions, resolutely skeptical but not at all cynical, brimming with fabulous scenes as well as sharp analysis." NY Times Book Rev

McMillan, Tracie

★ The **American** way of eating; undercover at Walmart, Applebee's, farm fields, and the dinner table. Tracie McMillan. Scribner 2012 x, 319 p.p $25   **338.4**
1. Poverty 2. American cooking 3. Agriculture -- United States 4. Food industry -- United States 5. Cooking, American 6. Food supply -- United States 7. Food industry and trade -- United States 8. Food habits -- Economic aspects -- United States
ISBN 1439171955; 9781439171950; 9781439171974

LC 2012372266

This book by journalist Tracie McMillan discusses the economics of the food industry of the United States. "[S]he watched the debate about America's meals unfold, one that urges us to pay food's true cost—which is to say, pay more. So in 2009 McMillan embarked on a[n] . . . undercover journey to see what it takes to eat well in America. For nearly a year, she worked, ate, and lived alongside the working poor to examine how Americans eat when price matters." (Publisher's note)

"Full of personal stories of the daily struggle to put food of any kind on the table in today's economy, McMillan's book will force readers to question their own methods of purchasing and preparing food." Kirkus

Includes bibliographical references (p. 255-318)

Mitford, Jessica

★ The **American** way of death revisited. Knopf 1998 296p hardcover o.p. pa $14   **338.4**
1. Cremation 2. Undertakers and undertaking 3. Funeral rites and ceremonies
ISBN 0-679-77186-7 pa

LC 97-49349

First published 1963 by Simon & Schuster with title: The American way of death

"Very interesting, informative, and easy to read, this book is written with wit, solid information, and refreshing bluntness." Libr J

Noonan, Meg Lukens

The **coat** route; craft, luxury, and obsession on the trail of a $50,000 coat. Meg Lukens Noonan. Spiegel & Grau 2013 272 p. (alk. paper) $27 **338.4**
1. Luxuries 2. Men's clothing 3. Luxury 4. Custom-made clothing
ISBN 1400069939; 9781400069934

LC 2012042994

In this book, Meg Lukens Noonan follows the making of a $50,000 overcoat. The "journey begins in the Peruvian mountains with the elusive . . . vicuna (the animal that provides the fleece for the coat), and is followed by stops in Florence, to meet the creator of the coat's silk lining—enigmatic menswear designer Stefano Ricci; Yorkshire, where a textile mill spins vicuna fleece into yarn that Gary Eastwood's Pennine Weavers turns into cloth; and Birmingham, for hand-carved buffalo horn buttons." (Publishers Weekly)

Includes bibliographical references and index

Petersen, Melody

Our daily meds; how the pharmaceutical companies transformed themselves into slick marketing machines and hooked the nation on prescription drugs. Farrar, Straus and Giroux 2008 432p $26   **338.4**

1. Drug industry

ISBN 978-0-374-22827-9; 0-374-22827-2

LC 2008-2097

The author shows how corporate salesmanship has triumphed over science inside the biggest pharmaceutical companies and, in turn, how this promotion driven industry has taken over the practice of medicine and is changing American life.

"Petersen takes readers beyond glossy advertising and celebrity endorsements to glimpse the alarming dark side of the American pharmaceutical industry." Libr J

Includes bibliographical references (p. 409-412)

Rudacille, Deborah

Roots of steel; the boom and bust of an American mill town. Pantheon Books 2010 290p $27   **338.4**

1. Steel industry 2. Maryland -- History 3. United States -- Economic conditions

ISBN 9780375423680; 978-0-375-42368-0

LC 2009020962

"Rudacille has delivered a book that would do Studs Terkel proud, partaking of his oral-historical approach to the past at turns, imbued with his pro-labor spirit throughout. Required reading for activists and for those wondering where things went wrong for America's working people." Kirkus

Includes bibliographical references

Suisman, David

Selling sounds; the commercial revolution in American music. Harvard University Press 2009 356p il $29.95   **338.4**

1. Music industry 2. Music -- United States 3. Music trade -- United States 4. Music -- United States -- History and criticism

ISBN 0-674-03337-X; 978-0-674-03337-5

LC 2008-55620

"Suisman investigates the early decades of the popular music industry, from 1880 to 1930." (Nation) Index.

"A fascinating, well-written, richly detailed story of how music became a commodity in America. . . . [Suisman's] scholarship is amazingly wide-ranging." Washington Times

Includes bibliographical references

Tobbell, Dominique A.

Pills, power, and policy; the struggle for drug reform in Cold War America and its consequences. Dominique A. Tobbell. University of California Press"||"Millbank Memorial Fund 2012 xv, 294 p.p (pbk. : alk. paper) $26.95   **338.4**

1. Drugs 2. Industrial policy 3. Industrial relations -- United States 4. History, 20th Century -- United States 5. Drug Industry -- history 6.

Economics, Pharmaceutical -- United States 7. Drugs -- Research -- United States -- History -- 20th century 8. Pharmaceutical industry -- United States -- History -- 20th century

ISBN 0520271130; 0520271149; 9780520271135; 9780520271142

LC 2011014878

This book "offers a . . . history of how the American drug industry and key sectors of the medical profession came to be allies against pharmaceutical reform. It details the political strategies they have used to influence public opinion, shape legislative reform, and define the regulatory environment of prescription drugs." (Amazon.com)

Includes bibliographical references and index.

Vlasic, Bill

Once upon a car; the fall and resurrection of America's big three auto makers--GM, Ford, and Chrysler. William Morrow 2011 394p   **338.4**

1. Automobile industry 2. Chrysler Corp. 3. Ford Motor Co. 4. General Motors Corp.

ISBN 978-0-06-184562-8; 978-0-06-204222-4 ebook

LC 2011020572

The author "examines the perfect storm of overseas competition, economic downturn, rising gas prices, union pressures, legacy costs, and lumbering bureaucracy that brought the U.S. auto industry to its knees. He takes us into the boardrooms and inside the heads of such people as Rick Wagoner, former GM CEO, who was ousted by Steve Rattner; Obama's 'car czar,' Bill Ford Jr., great-grandson of Henry Ford and chairman of Ford Motor Company; and billionaire financier Kirk Kerkorian, who at different times held 10-percent stakes in both GM and Ford. This is an engrossing look at big business in crisis, forever changed but never willing to give up." Booklist

Includes bibliographical references

Washington, Harriet A.

Deadly monopolies; the shocking corporate takeover of life itself, and the consequences for your health and our medical future. Doubleday 2011 433p il $28.95; ebook $14.99   **338.4**

1. Drug industry 2. Medical ethics 3. Drugs -- Marketing

ISBN 978-0-385-52892-4; 978-0-385-53405-5 ebook

LC 2011013033

"Extensively documented with minimal scientific jargon, this book is recommended for any reader interested in the future of our health system." Libr J

Includes bibliographical references

338.5 General production economics

Galbraith, John Kenneth

★ The **great** crash, 1929; with a new introduction by the author; foreword by James K. Galbraith. Houghton Mifflin Co. 2009 206p pa $14.95 **338.5**

1. Great Depression, 1929-1939 2. United States -- Economic conditions -- 1919-1933

ISBN 978-0-547-24816-5

First published 1955

Beginning with the bull market of Coolidge and Hoover and continuing through the stock market crash, the author analyzes its causes and speculates about the chances of another crash.

Includes bibliographical references

Panic; the story of modern financial insanity. [edited by] Michael Lewis. W. W. Norton & Company 2009 391p il $27.95; pa $18.95   **338.5**
1. Financial crises
ISBN 978-0-393-06514-5; 978-0-393-33798-3 pa
LC 2008-39523

The editor "has compiled an anthology of articles related to five major financial crises in recent decades: the 1987 stock market crash, the Russian default, the Asian currency crisis, the Internet bubble and . . . the subprime mortgage collapse (the final article included is from January 2008). For each crisis, Lewis offers articles from journals, books, transcripts, and newspapers, all written immediately before, during, or after the event. . . . Timely and highly readable, this work includes in one accessible source two decades' worth of some of the best writing on the various crises and panics." Libr J

Reinhart, Carmen M., 1955-
   This time is different; eight centuries of financial folly. [by] Carmen M. Reinhart, Kenneth S. Rogoff. Princeton University Press 2009 xlv, 463p il $35   **338.5**
   1. Fiscal policy 2. Business cycles 3. Financial crises 4. International finance
   ISBN 978-0-691-14216-6; 0-691-14216-5
LC 2009-22616

The authors "have compiled an impressive database, which covers eight centuries of government debt defaults from around the world. They have also collected statistics on inflation rates from every country where information is available and on banking crises and international capital flows over the past couple of centuries. This lengthy historical study gives what they call a 'panoramic view' of the unending cycle of boom and bust, showing how claims that 'this time is different' are invariably proven wrong. . . . [This] is an important addition to the literature of financial history." Wall Street J

Includes bibliographical references (p. 400-433)

Shafir, Eldar
   Scarcity; why having too little means so much. Sendhil Mullainathan and Eldar Shafir. Times Books, Henry Holt and Company 2013 304 p. $28   **338.5**
   1. Scarcity 2. Decision making 3. Supply and demand
   ISBN 0805092641; 9780805092646
LC 2013004167

In this book, authors Sendhil Mullainathan and Eldar Shafir "discuss how scarcity affects our daily lives, recounting anecdotes of their own foibles and making . . . connections that bring this research alive. Their book provides a new way of understanding why the poor stay poor and the busy stay busy, and it reveals not only how scarcity leads us astray but also how individuals and organizations can better manage scarcity for greater satisfaction and success." (Publisher's note)

Includes bibliographical references and index

The value of a dollar; prices and incomes in the United States, 1860-2009. [edited] by Scott Derks. 4th ed; Grey House Pub. 2009 690p il $155   **338.5**
1. Prices 2. Reference books 3. Salaries, wages, etc. 4. Cost and standard of living
ISBN 978-1-59237-403-8
First published 1994

"Both great-grandparents and serious students in historical research will benefit from this book. It will be an especially valuable study to students of American history, economics, and even mathematics." Libr J

Includes bibliographical references

The value of a dollar: colonial era to the Civil War, 1600-1865; [edited by] Scott Derks and Tony Smith. Grey House Pub. 2005 436p il $155   **338.5**
1. Prices 2. Reference books 3. Salaries, wages, etc. 4. Cost and standard of living
ISBN 1-59237-094-2; 978-1-59237-094-8
LC 2006-275331

"This source is an engaging statistical summary that looks at the history of the American people through the eyes of everyday workers and consumers. The 265 years it covers are presented in six chronological chapters: '1600-1749: The Development of the Colonies,' '1750-1774: The Run up to the War of American Independence,' and so on, ending with the close of the Civil War in 1865. . . . [This book] will find a happy audience among students, researchers, and general browsers. It offers a fascinating and detailed look at early American history from the viewpoint of everyday people trying to make ends meet." Booklist

Includes bibliographical references

338.7   Business enterprises

Abrams, John
   Companies we keep; employee ownership and the business of community and place. foreword by William Greider. 2nd ed.; Chelsea Green Pub. Co. 2008 333p il pa $17.95   **338.7**
   1. Management 2. Business ethics 3. Employee ownership
   ISBN 978-1-60358-000-7
LC 2008-25075

First published 2005 with title: Company we keep

The author posits a "business model based on community, goodwill, craftsmanship, and not-so-big growth, outlining the steps he took to help his own firm become a 'more democratic, more responsible, more permanent kind of company.'" Libr J

Includes bibliographical references

Angwin, Julia

✓ **Stealing** MySpace; the battle to control the most popular website in America. Random House 2009 371p il $27 **338.7**

1. MySpace (Web site) 2. Electronic commerce
ISBN 978-1-4000-6694-0; 1-4000-6694-8

LC 2008-23504

"The author traces the development of MySpace, sorting out its convoluted journey to success." Booklist

"This engrossing look at how MySpace became a media powerhouse will find a solid audience of business history, technology and entrepreneurship readers." Publ Wkly

Includes bibliographical references

Arden, Lynie

✓ ★ The **work** -at-home sourcebook; 10th ed.; Live Oak Pubns 2009 400p il pa $19.95 **338.7**

1. Home-based business
ISBN 978-0-911781-20-5

First published 1987. Frequently revised

"Each entry in this helpful listing of firms that hire free-lancers and franchises that can be home-based includes contact information and advice on how to get one's foot in the door. The book also features directories of marketplaces for handicrafts and online certification programs." Libr J

Auletta, Ken

✓ **Googled**; the end of the world as we know it. Penguin Press 2009 384p $27.95 **338.7**

1. Internet industry 2. Internet searching 3. Web search engines 4. Computer scientists 5. Social responsibility of business 6. Google, Inc. 7. Internet executives 8. Information technology executives
ISBN 978-1-594-20235-3

LC 2009-24770

The author's "thorough reporting and declarative writing provide a crisp, informative read. . . . Auletta displays the skill of a responsible journalist in both researching and crafting this snapshot of today's technological landscape. " Christ Sci Monit

Includes bibliographical references

Breen, Bill

✓ **Brick** by brick; by David C. Robertson and Bill Breen. 1st ed. Crown Business 2013 xii, 305 p.p (hardcover) $26.00 **338.7**

1. LEGO toys 2. Toy industry 3. LEGO toys -- History 4. LEGO koncernen (Denmark) 5. Toy industry -- Denmark -- Management
ISBN 030795160X; 9780307951601

LC 2013004798

This book, written by David Robertson and Bill Breen, examines toy manufacturer LEGO. "it spotlights the company's disciplined approach to harnessing creativity and re-counts one of the most remarkable business transformations in recent memory." It "reveals how LEGO failed to keep pace with the revolutionary changes in kids' lives and began sliding into irrelevance. It took a new LEGO management team – faced with the growing rage for electronic toys, few barriers to entry, and ultra-demanding consumers – to . . . transform LEGO." (Publisher's note)

Brenner, Joel Glenn

✓ The **emperors** of chocolate; inside the secret world of Hershey and Mars. Random House 1999 366p il hardcover o.p. pa $14.95 **338.7**

1. Chocolate 2. Mars, Inc. 3. Hershey Foods Corp. 4. Food industry executives
ISBN 0-7679-0457-5 pa

LC 98-21610

"Brenner examines the candy industry, focusing on the rivalry between Hershey and Mars. Milton Hersey was and Forrest Mars is highly secretive and eccentric, and they both amassed huge fortunes. A wonderful inside look at success-ful businessmen." Booklist

Includes bibliographical references

Brinkley, Douglas

✓ ★ **Wheels** for the world; Henry Ford, his company, and a century of progress, 1903-2003. Viking 2003 xxii, 858p il $34.95; pa $18 **338.7**

1. Philanthropists 2. Automobile industry 3. Ford Motor Co. 4. Automobile executives
ISBN 0-670-03181-X; 0-14-200439-1 pa

LC 2003-33066

"Car lovers will appreciate this amazing account of the birth of the automobile industry, including funny anecdotes about the trusty Model T, the evolution of the V-8 engine, the artistic design of the Thunderbird, sophistication of the Lin-coln Continental, and popularity of the Mustang." Booklist

Includes bibliographical references

Bruck, Connie

✓ **When** Hollywood had a king; the reign of Lew Wasserman, who leveraged talent into power and in-fluence. Random House 2003 512p il hardcover o.p. pa $16.95 **338.7**

1. MCA Inc. 2. Talent agents 3. Motion picture executives
ISBN 0-375-50168-1; 978-0-8129-7217-7 pa; 0-8129-7217-1 pa

LC 2003-41418

"Those who are interested in comprehensive details about the inner workings of the entertainment industry—its history, business, customs, people, and gossip—will find this a fascinating read and a solid resource." Libr J

Includes bibliographical references

Burrows, Peter

✓ **Backfire** : Carly Fiorina's high-stakes battle for the soul of Hewlett-Packard. Wiley 2003 296p il $27.95 **338.7**

1. Computer industry 2. Hewlett-Packard Co. 3. Compaq Computer Corporation 4. Computer industry executives 5. Telecommunications executives
ISBN 0-471-26765-1

LC 2002-156443

This is an account "of the bitter boardroom fight that erupted after Hewlett-Packard announced plans to merge with Compaq in the late summer of 2001 . . . [with a focus on] the charismatic Carleton S. Fiorina, who became one of the highest-ranking women in American business in 1999 when she was tapped as the first outside chief executive of the Hewlett-Packard company. . . . [This] is a riveting, colorful, fast-paced account of the Compaq battle." N Y Times Book Rev

Includes bibliographical references

Casnocha, Ben

My start-up life; what a (very) young CEO learned on his journey through Silicon Valley. Ben Casnocha ; foreword by Marc Benioff. Jossey-Bass 2007 xiv, 189 p.p (cloth) $24.95 **338.7**

1. Entrepreneurship 2. New business enterprises 3. Computer software industry 4. Comcate (Firm) 5. Entrepreneurship -- United States 6. Computer software industry -- United States 7. Internet software industry -- United States 8. New business enterprises -- United States -- Management

ISBN 0787996130; 9780787996130

LC 2007007866

This book is written by "Ben Casnocha [who] discovered he was entrepreneur at age 12 and hasn't slowed down since. In this . . . instructive book, Ben dissects the entrepreneurship 'gene,' explaining that everyone has inherited it if they have an idea to make the world a better place. In Casnocha's case, he found a better way for city governments to communicate with constituents on the Web. Six years later, Comcate has dozens of municipal clients, a growing staff, and a record of excellence. This book is the story of his start-up, but also a conversation with his mentors, clients and fellow entrepreneurs about how to make a business idea work and how to have the time of your life trying." (Publisher's note)

Includes bibliographical references (p. 185-188).

Cohen, Rich

The **fish** that ate the whale; the life and times of America's banana king. Rich Cohen. Farrar, Straus and Giroux 2012 xiii, 270 p.p **338.7**

1. Biography 2. Businessmen 3. Business and politics 4. United Fruit Company -- Biography 5. Banana trade -- Louisiana -- New Orleans -- History 6. Jewish businesspeople -- Louisiana -- New Orleans -- Biography

ISBN 0374299277; 9780374299279

LC 2011041207

This biography describes the life of the 20th-century American fruit businessman Samuel Zemurray. "He worked as . . . a banana hauler, a dockside hustler, and a plantation owner. He battled and conquered the United Fruit Company, becoming a symbol of the best and worst of the United States. . . . Starting with nothing but a cart of freckled bananas, he built a sprawling empire . . . connected to the birth of modern American diplomacy, public relations, business, and war." (Publisher's note)

Includes bibliographical references.

Coll, Steve

★ **Private** empire; ExxonMobil and American power. Steve Coll. Penguin Press 2012 685 p. $36.00 **338.7**

1. Global warming 2. Petroleum industry 3. Iraq War, 2003-2011 4. Corporate mergers and acquisitions 5. Exxon Corporation 6. Exxon Mobil Corporation 7. Big business -- United States 8. Corporate power -- United States 9. Petroleum industry and trade -- Political

aspects -- United States

ISBN 1594203350; 9781594203350

LC 2011044722

In this book "two-time Pulitzer winner [Steve] Coll . . . demonstrates how the merger of Exxon and Mobil has allowed the company to wield more power and wealth than even the American government, in the manner of John D. Rockefeller. . . . The Exxon-Mobil merger in 1999 created a global behemoth and also provoked small wars at drilling spots where the poor and disenfranchised deeply resented the foreign workers on native soil and disrupted the extraction by violence and insurgency." (Kirkus Reviews)

Includes bibliographical references (p. [659]-664) and index

Harris, Blake J.

Console wars; Sega, Nintendo, and the battle that defined a generation. Blake J. Harris. It Books 2014 576 p. (hardback) $22.99 **338.7**

1. Video games 2. Video games -- History 3. Video games industry -- History 4. Electronic games industry -- History

ISBN 0062276719; 9780062276698; 9780062276704

LC 2013050668

This book, by Blake J. Harris, is a "behind-the-scenes business thriller that chronicles how Sega . . . took on the juggernaut Nintendo and revolutionized the video game industry. In 1990, Nintendo had a virtual monopoly on the video game industry. Sega, on the other hand, was just a faltering arcade company with big aspirations and even bigger personalities. But that would all change with the arrival of Tom Kalinske." (Publisher's note)

"Harris defines the players immediately, honing in on their most notable characteristics, and puts the reader in the thick of the meetings and deal-making with a confidence stemming from hundreds of interviews." Booklist

Kealing, Bob

Tupperware, unsealed; Brownie Wise, Earl Tupper, and the home party pioneers. University Press of Florida 2008 250p il $28 **338.7**

1. Containers 2. Sales personnel 3. Tupperware Corp. 4. Household products industry executives

ISBN 0-8130-3227-X; 978-0-8130-3227-6

LC 2007-47539

The author "explores the origins of the Tupperware industry as seen through the insightful genius of Brownie Wise, the impetus behind the home party craze that catapulted Tupperware revenues into the millions. . . . This work proves to be a valuable contribution to the growing body of literature that focuses on the individual contributions of women to US business and industry." Choice

Includes bibliographical references

Kirkpatrick, David

The **Facebook** effect; the inside story of the company that is connecting the world. Simon & Schuster 2010 372p il $26 **338.7**

1. Internet industry 2. Social networking 3. Online social networks 4. Facebook Inc. 5. Internet executives

6. Internet -- Social aspects
ISBN 978-1-4391-0211-4; 1-4391-0211-2

LC 2009-51983

The author was encouraged by Mark Zuckerberg, the founder and chief executive of Facebook.com, to write this book and was granted extensive access to him and his associates. Their cooperation has resulted in a mostly sympathetic at times, gushingly laudatory account of the company, though Mr. Kirkpatrick does not shy away from dissecting its missteps and successive disputes over privacy. He gives the reader a detailed understanding of how the company grew from a 2004 Harvard dorm-room project into the world's second-most-visited site after Google. N Y Times (Late NY Ed)

Includes bibliographical references

Knoedelseder, William

Bitter brew; the rise and fall of Anheuser-Busch and America's kings of beer. William Knoedelseder. HarperBusiness 2012 396 p. $27.99   **338.7**

1. Anheuser-Busch, inc. -- History 2. Beer industry -- United States -- History 3. Brewing industry -- United States -- History
ISBN 0062009265; 9780062009265

LC 2012026942

This book by William Knoedelseder is a history of the Anheuser-Busch beer company. It is a "saga of one of the wealthiest, longest-lasting, and most colorful family dynasties in the history of American commerce--a cautionary tale about prosperity, profligacy, hubris, and the blessings and dark consequences of success. . . . [The] narrative captures the Busch saga through five generations. At the same time, it weaves a broader story of American progress and decline over the past 150 years." (Publisher's note)

Krass, Peter

Carnegie. Wiley 2002 612p il $35; pa $19.95   **338.7**

1. Philanthropists 2. Metal industry executives
ISBN 0-471-38630-8; 0-471-46883-5 pa

LC 2002-10162

"From bobbin boy in a cotton mill to one of American history's most famous characters, Carnegie's life was one of contradictions. In his lifetime, Carnegie gave away a staggering $350 million, setting a standard for social conscience. Krass used original sources such as letters, diaries, and other writings by primary and peripheral characters in Carnegie's life to penetrate the public persona and show the man who crusaded for universal literacy and world peace." Booklist

Includes bibliographical references

Kurlansky, Mark, 1948-

Birdseye; the adventures of a curious man. Mark Kurlansky. Doubleday 2012 251 p.   **338.7**

1. Businessmen 2. Frozen foods 3. Inventors -- Biography 4. Food industry -- United States 5. Inventors -- United States -- Biography 6. Businessmen -- United States -- Biography 7. Frozen foods industry -- United States -- History
ISBN 0385527055; 9780385527057; 9780385535885

LC 2011044891

This book explains that "[t]here was far more to American inventor Clarence Birdseye (1886-1956) than met the eye; he was slight and cheerful but restlessly curious. He was drawn into a life of travel to remote parts of the continent in search of adventure and new experiences. He invented tools and processes, notably that which enabled quick freezing of foodstuffs and revolutionized culinary habits. Birdseye launched not just the frozen-vegetable company that bears his now-famous name but an entire industry. [Mark] Kurlansky, whose past works include the popular histories 'Salt' and 'Cod,' paints a complete picture of Birdseye's unusual career and accomplishments." (Libr J)

Includes bibliographical references and index

Lashinsky, Adam

Inside Apple; how America's most admired-and secretive-company really works. Adam Lashinsky. Business Plus 2012 223 p. $26.99   **338.7**

1. Business planning 2. Apple Inc. -- Management 3. Apple Computer, Inc 4. Corporate culture -- United States 5. Success in business -- United States 6. Computer industry -- United States -- Management
ISBN 145551215X; 9781455512157

LC 2011044773

In this book, "[Adam] Lashinsky . . . investigates the core of Apple before, during, and after the reign of the late Steve Jobs, not only to discover how the company works and if its success can be replicated, but also to speculate about Apple's future." He "outlines salient factors that concurrently contribute to Apple's success and deviate from standard business practice." (Publishers Weekly)

Levy, Steven

In the plex; how Google thinks, works, and shapes our lives. Simon & Schuster 2011 424p $26; ebook $12.99   **338.7**

1. Google (Web site) 2. Google, Inc.
ISBN 978-1-4165-9658-5; 1-4165-9658-5; 978-1-4165-9671-4 ebook; 1-4165-9671-2 ebook

LC 2010049964

The author presents a behind-the-scenes story of the Internet search engine company Google.

This is "the most comprehensive, intelligent and readable analysis of Google to date. Levy is particularly good on how those behind Google think and work. . . . [This work] teems with original insight into Google's most controversial affairs." New Sci

Includes bibliographical references

Lutz, Bob, 1932-

Car guys vs. bean counters; the battle for the soul of American business. [by] Bob Lutz. Portfolio/Penguin 2011 241p il $26.95   **338.7**

1. Automobile industry 2. Automobile executives 3. Corporate turnarounds 4. General Motors Corp. -- Bankruptcy 5. Automobile industry and trade -- United States -- Finance
ISBN 978-1-59184-400-6; 1-59184-400-2

LC 2011010720

The author "describes how he was pulled out of retirement to turn around a bankrupt General Motors in 2008, recounting how he transitioned the company away from office politics and penny pinching." Publisher's note

Macy, Beth

Factory man; how one furniture maker battled offshoring, stayed local - and helped save an American town. Beth Macy. Little, Brown and Co. 2014 464 p. illustrations (hardcover) $28   338.7
1. Outsourcing 2. Furniture making 3. American furniture
ISBN 0316231436; 9780316231411; 9780316231435; 9780316231565

LC 2014937343

"With over $500 million a year in sales, the Bassett Furniture Company was once the world's biggest wood furniture manufacturer. . . . But beginning in the 1980s, the Bassett company suffered from an influx of cheap Asian furniture as the first wave of imports struck, and ultimately moved nearly all its production to Asia. Only one man fought back: John Bassett III, a shrewd and determined third-generation factory man who used grit, tenacity, and will to compete against China and ultimately save his family's company." (Publisher's note)

"Macy's down-to-earth writing style and abundance of personal stories from manufacturing's beleaguered front lines make her work a stirring critique of globalization." Booklist
Includes bibliographical references (pages [415]-442) and index

Magner, Mike

Poisoned legacy; the human cost of BP's rise to power. Mike Magner. St. Martin's Press 2011 432 p. $18   338.7
1. Oil wells -- Blowouts 2. Oil spills -- Environmental aspects 3. Petroleum industry -- Ethical aspects 4. Offshore oil well drilling -- Safety measures 5. British Petroleum Company 6. Petroleum refineries -- Accidents -- United States 7. Petroleum workers -- Health and hygiene -- United States 8. Petroleum industry and trade -- Moral and ethical aspects
ISBN 9780312554941

LC 2010054461

In this book, an "exposé of the British oil giant," BP, "gives a comprehensive rundown of the [2010] Gulf oil well explosion and leak, and of the rushed scheduling, substandard engineering, skipped tests, and faulty equipment that precipitated that disaster. That's just the capstone of [Mike Magner's] detailed account of BP's misadventures in North America, which include a 2005 explosion at the company's Texas refinery that killed 15 people, a 200,000-gallon leak from a corroded Alaskan oil pipeline, a steady drip of workplace accidents, fatalities, and pollution violations and a drumbeat of callow apologies, lawsuits, fines, and criminal probes." (Publishers Wkly)
Includes bibliographical references (p. [381]-398) and index

Mazzeo, Tilar J.

The secret of Chanel No. 5; the intimate history of the world's most famous perfume. Harper 2010 281p il $25.99   338.7
1. Perfumes 2. Fashion designers 3. Perfumers 4.

Chanel (Firm) 5. Cosmetics industry executives
ISBN 978-0-06-179101-7; 0-06-179101-6

LC 2010-15284

This "'unauthorized biography of a scent' unearths the roots of the creation and fame of Coco Chanel's famous perfume. . . . Mazzeo's lush prose covers relevant aspects of Coco Chanel's life, from the stark beauty of the orphanage where she was raised to the glamour and luxury of her adulthood, to the scents that wove through her life and shaped the development of her signature perfume. However, the book never bogs down in the details—despite the extensive research showcased in the bibliography—and a smooth pacing keeps it moving along at a fast clip." Libr J
Includes bibliographical references

Micklethwait, John

The company; a short history of a revolutionary idea. [by] John Micklethwait and Adrian Wooldridge. Modern Library 2003 xxiii, 227p (Modern Library chronicles) hardcover o.p. pa $14.95   338.7
1. Corporations 2. Business enterprises
ISBN 0-679-64249-8; 0-8129-7287-2 pa

LC 2002-26429

In this history of the joint-stock company, Micklethwait and Wooldridge "trace its progress from Assyrian partnership agreements through the 16th- and 17th-century European 'charter companies' that opened trade with distant parts of the world, to today's multinationals. The authors' breadth of knowledge is impressive. They infuse their engaging prose with a wide range of cultural, historical and literary references, with quotes from poets to presidents. . . . Moreover, the authors argue that for all the change companies have engendered over time, their force has been for an aggregate good." Publ Wkly
Includes bibliographical references

Nalebuff, Barry, 1958-

Mission in a bottle; the honest guide to doing business differently--and succeeding. by Seth Goldman and Barry J. Naelbuff and illustrated by Sungyoon Choi. Crown Business 2013 288 p. $23   338.7
1. Entrepreneurship 2. Business enterprises 3. Graphic novels 4. Iced tea -- United States -- Comic books, strips, etc 5. Tea trade -- United States -- Comic books, strips, etc 6. Honest Tea (Firm) -- History -- Comic books, strips, etc 7. Soft drink industry -- United States -- Comic books, strips, etc
ISBN 0770437494; 9780770437497

LC 2013004799

Authors Seth Goldman and Barry Nalebuff, "cofounders of Honest Tea tell the engaging story of how they created and built a mission-driven business, offering a wealth of insights and advice to entrepreneurs, would-be entrepreneurs, and millions of Honest Tea drinkers about the challenges and hurdles of creating a successful business--and the importance of perseverance and creative problem-solving." (Publisher's note)

"[T]his candid portrait of leveraging resources to build a business from the ground up is a useful and cleverly conceptualized read." Pub Wkly

Orbanes, Philip

The **game** makers; the story of Parker Brothers from Tiddledy Winks to Trivial Pursuit. {by} Philip E. Orbanes. Harvard Business School Press 2003 272p il $29.95 **338.7**
    1. Parker Brothers (Firm)
    ISBN 1-591-39269-1
                      LC 2003-10768

This is a study of the Parker Brothers, who developed such games as Monopoly, Clue and Risk. The author contends that the games "reflect the American world view of the 20th century. Life is a ruthless struggle in which there are many losers, but it takes place within a framework of unbendable and fairminded rules." Economist
Includes bibliographical references

Saxon, A. H.

P. T. Barnum: the legend and the man. Columbia Univ. Press 1989 437p il hardcover o.p. pa $22.50 **338.7**
    1. Circus executives
    ISBN 0-231-05687-7 pa
                      LC 89-982

"Working primarily from Barnum's letters, business papers, family members' and associates' diaries, and legal documents, Saxon has pieced together a picture of the legendary circus owner. Saxon's detailed coverage of Barnum's life . . . is rich with anecdotes yet scholarly enough to please any researcher. Saxon succeeds admirably in capturing the essence of Barnum." Booklist
Includes bibliographical references

Spector, Robert

Amazon.com; get big fast. HarperBusiness 2000 xxii, 263p hardcover o.p. pa $16 **338.7**
    1. Internet 2. Booksellers and bookselling 3. Amazon. com Inc.
    ISBN 0-06-662042-2 pa
                      LC 99-87599

"Spector looks at a Seattle company that has turned retailing and customer service upside down. Online bookseller Amazon.com almost instantly became a part of America's popular culture, but Amazon.com has yet to turn a profit." Booklist
Includes bibliographical references

Stross, Randall

Planet Google; how one company's all-encompassing vision is transforming our lives. [by] Randall Stross. Free Press 2008 275p $26 **338.7**
    1. Google (Web site) 2. Internet searching 3. Google, Inc. 4. Internet industry 5. Web search engines 6. Information organization
    ISBN 1-41654-691-X; 978-1-41654-691-7
                      LC 2008-18788

New York Times columnist Randall Stross examines the internet search engine Google and the company that developed it. He contends that Google is "becoming as dominant a force on the Web as Microsoft became on the PC. . . . The more offerings Google adds, and the more ubiquitous a presence it becomes, [Stross argues], the more dependent its users become on its services and the more information

they contribute to its . . . collection of data." (Publisher's note) Index.
This is "an outstanding business history of Google from its humble beginnings through the dot-com era to current times." Libr J
Includes bibliographical references (p. 201-257)

Vaidhyanathan, Siva

The **Googlization** of everything; (and why we should worry) University of California Press 2011 265p $26.95; ebook $22 **338.7**
    1. Google (Web site) 2. Internet industry 3. Google, Inc. 4. Internet -- Social aspects
    ISBN 978-0-520-25882-2; 978-0-520-94869-3 ebook
                      LC 2010-27772

The author "shows how Google's methods of capturing, storing and filtering information are often elitist and increasingly invasive. . . . Citing some of the company's most controversial headlines, from the toddler who was captured naked in his grandmother's garden with Google Street View to the settlement between Google and the Author's Guild over copyrights, the author unmasks the monster behind the friendly interface with the suspense of a horror novel. An urgent reminder to look more closely at dangers that lurk in plain sight. " Kirkus
Includes bibliographical references

Vise, David A.

★ The **Google** story; [by] David A. Vise and Mark Malseed. Updated ed.; Delacorte Press 2008 330p il hardcover o.p. pa $15 **338.7**
    1. Computer scientists 2. Google, Inc. 3. Internet executives 4. Information technology executives
    ISBN 978-0-385-34272-8; 978-0-385-34273-5 pa
                      LC 2009-285529

First published 2005
The authors present a business history of the Internet search engine company, focusing particular attention on the story of founders Larry Page and Sergey Brin.

338.8   Combinations

Bown, Stephen R.

Merchant kings; when companies ruled the world, 1600-1900. [by] Stephen Bown. Thomas Dunne Books 2010 314p il map $26.99 **338.8**
    1. Merchants 2. Multinational corporations 3. Europe -- Commerce
    ISBN 978-0-312-61611-3
                      LC 2010-34783

The author "has produced a magnificent description of the six great companies, and their leaders, that dominated the 'Heroic Age of Commerce.' Bown demonstrates how the corporations served as stalking horses for kings and parliaments while enriching shareholders and the powerful managers themselves. . . . Bown presents a fascinating look at the men who exploited resources and native peoples while laying the foundations of empires." Publ Wkly
Includes bibliographical references

MacIntosh, Julie

Dethroning the king; the hostile takeover of Anheuser-Busch, an American icon. Wiley 2010 408p il $27.95   **338.8**

    1. Corporate mergers and acquisitions 2. Anheuser-Busch, Inc. 3. Beverage industry executives

    ISBN 978-0-470-59270-0

                        LC 2010-32279

"In a narrative that reads as fast as any fiction thriller, . . . MacIntosh details the 2008 takeover of the iconic Anheuser-Busch brewing company by Belgian corporation InBev, focusing particularly on the company's importance to the St. Louis region; its management, or lack thereof, by the Busch family (particularly the August Busches III and IV); and the broader unsettled economic climate of 2008." Libr J

Includes bibliographical references

338.973   Economic development -- United States

Speth, James Gustave, 1942-

  ★ **America** the possible; manifesto for a new economy. James Gustave Speth. Yale University Press 2012 249 p. (hardback) $30.00   **338.973**

    1. Economics 2. Democracy -- United States 3. United States -- Politics and government 4. Social justice -- United States 5. United States -- Economic policy 6. Environmental policy -- United States 7. Progressivism (United States politics)

    ISBN 0300180764; 9780300180763

                     LC 2012012170

The book, by author James Gustave Speth, "spells out the specific changes that are needed to move toward a new political economy--one in which the true priority is to sustain people and planet. Supported by a . . . "theory of change" that explains how system change can come to America, the book also presents a vision of political, social, and economic life in a renewed America. . . . In short, this is a book about the American future and the strong possibility that we . . . have it in ourselves to use our freedom and our democracy in powerful ways to create . . . a reborn America." (Publisher's note)

Includes bibliographical references and index

339.2   Distribution of income and wealth

Bernstein, William

  The **birth** of plenty; how the prosperity of the modern world was created. [by] William J. Bernstein. McGraw-Hill 2004 420p il $29.95   **339.2**

    1. Wealth 2. Quality of life 3. Economic conditions

    ISBN 0-07-142192-0

                   LC 2003-26155

The author "examines the four factors that fell into place to create a formula for human progress: property rights, scientific rationalism, capital markets, and transportation and communication. From the rise of common law to the invention of the steam engine, from the creation of currencies to shipbuilding, this is an in-depth history of the rise of prosperity." Booklist

Includes bibliographical references

Garson, Barbara

  Down the up escalator; how the 99 percent live in the Great Recession. Barbara Garson. Doubleday 2013 288 p. (hardcover) $26.95; (electronic) $80.85   **339.2**

    1. Employment 2. Global Financial Crisis, 2008-2009 3. United States -- Economic conditions 4. Equality -- United States -- History -- 21st century 5. Income distribution -- United States -- History -- 21st century

    ISBN 0385532741; 9780385532747; 9780385532754

                    LC 2012020359

This book, by Barbara Garson, explores how "the Great Recession has thrown huge economic challenges at almost all Americans save the super-affluent few. . . . Garson has interviewed an economically and geographically wide variety of Americans to show the painful waste in all this loss and insecurity, and describe how individuals are coping." (Publisher's note)

Milanovic, Branko

  The **haves** and the have-nots; a short and idiosyncratic history of global inequality. Basic Books 2010 258p il map $27.95   **339.2**

    1. Wealth 2. Poverty 3. Wealth -- History 4. Poverty -- History 5. Income distribution

    ISBN 0-465-01974-9; 978-0-465-01974-8

                    LC 2010-29295

The first essay in this book discusses "how economists think about income inequality within a country—in particular, how it is measured, and how it is related to a country's overall economic health. . . . In his second and third essays, Milanovic switches to . . . inequality around the world." (N Y Times Book Rev) Index.

"Students, practitioners, and anyone interested in economics and the issue of inequality would enjoy this." Libr J

Includes bibliographical references

Noah, Timothy

  The **great** divergence; America's growing inequality crisis and what we can do about it. Timothy Noah. Bloomsbury 2012 264 p.   **339.2**

    1. Wealth 2. Poverty 3. Equality 4. Economic policy -- United States 5. United States -- Economic conditions 6. Wealth -- United States 7. Poverty -- United States 8. Equality -- United States 9. United States -- Economic policy 10. Income distribution -- United States

    ISBN 9781608196333

                    LC 2011048447

This book examines the "political dimensions of the outrageous disparity in incomes that has developed since 1979. . . . [Timothy] Noah discusses the rise and fall of the trade-union movement and demonstrates that turning points in that movement were also turning points in the growth of income inequality. . . . Noah also calls out financial deregulation as a major offender, and he lists measures that he believes can help the situation." (Kirkus Reviews)

Ridley, Matt

The **rational** optimist; how prosperity evolves. Fourth Estate, Harper 2010 438p il $26.99 **339.2**

1. Reason 2. Wealth 3. Optimism
ISBN 978-0-06-145205-5

LC 2010-4907

The author posits that as long as civilization engages in exchange and specialization, we will be able to reinvent ourselves and responsibly use earthly resources ad infinitum. . . . Ridley puts current perceptions about violence, wealth, and the environment into historical perspective, reaching back thousands of years to advocate global free trade, smaller government, and the use of fossil fuels. He confidently takes on the experts, from modern sociologists who fret over the current level of violence in the world to environmentalists who disdain genetically modified crops. An ambitious and sunny paean to human ingenuity, this is an argument for why ambitious optimism is morally mandatory. Publ Wkly

Includes bibliographical references

339.4 Factors affecting income and wealth

Banerjee, Abhijit

Poor economics; a radical rethinking of the way to fight global poverty. [by] Abhijit V. Banerjee and Esther Duflo. PublicAffairs 2011 303p $26.99 **339.4**

1. Poverty 2. Foreign aid 3. Poverty -- Prevention 4. Economic assistance -- Developing countries
ISBN 978-1-58648-798-0; 1-58648-798-1

LC 2010-50938

This book "draws on a variety of evidence, not limiting itself to the results of randomised trials, as if they are the only route to truth. And the authors' interest is not confined to 'what works', but also to how and why it works. Indeed, Ms Duflo and Mr Banerjee, perhaps more than some of their disciples, are able theorists as well as thoroughgoing empiricists." Economist

Includes bibliographical references

Cohen, Lizabeth

A **consumer's** republic; the politics of mass consumption in postwar America. Knopf 2003 567p il $35; pa $16.95 **339.4**

1. Consumers 2. Consumption (Economics) 3. United States -- Social conditions
ISBN 0-375-40750-2; 0-375-70737-9 pa

LC 2002-141599

"Without question, this is a difficult, demanding, and dense book—but it is also a greatly significant contribution to business literature. . . . Cohen submits a copiously researched, brilliantly conceived, and ultimately quite instructive study of American economics since the Depression." Booklist

Includes bibliographical references

Gerth, Karl

As China goes, so goes the world; how Chinese consumers are transforming everything. Hill and Wang 2010 258p il $26; ebook $12.99 **339.4**

1. Consumers 2. Consumption (Economics) 3. China

-- Economic conditions
ISBN 978-0-8090-3429-1; 978-1-4299-6246-9 ebook

LC 2010-12647

"Interested in consumerism, Gerth delves into the effects individuals' purchasing preferences are producing on China." Booklist

"Nuanced, balanced and accessible—essential reading for anyone trying to make sense of China today." Kirkus

Includes bibliographical references

Miller, Geoffrey F.

Spent; sex, evolution, and consumer behavior. [by] Geoffrey Miller. Viking 2009 374p $26.95 **339.4**

1. Consumers 2. Consumption (Economics)
ISBN 978-0-670-02062-1; 0-670-02062-1

LC 2008-51554

"Since evolutionary psychology seeks to examine how natural selection acts on psychological and mental traits, Miller applies this knowledge to help us understand what actually motivates us to buy. He pokes fun at popular culture and at the things we buy and flaunt to inflate our self-esteem and try to make ourselves more attractive. Personality research can inform the study of consumer behavior, and Miller shows us how having a better understanding of our own personalities will help us avoid the pitfalls of runaway consumerism." Libr J

Includes bibliographical references

Novogratz, Jacqueline

The **blue** sweater; bridging the gap between rich and poor in an interconnected world. Jacqueline Novogratz. Rodale||"Distrib. to the trade by Macmillan 2009 x, 262 p.p $15.99 **339.4**

1. Globalization 2. Poverty -- Developing countries 3. Philanthropists -- Personal narratives 4. Domestic economic assistance -- Developing countries 5. Poverty 6. Charities 7. Microfinance 8. Economic assistance
ISBN 1594869154 (hardcover); 9781594869150 (hardcover)

LC 2008043621

This book, "[p]art coming-of-age story, part blueprint for effecting real change, . . . explores what it means to create meaningful solutions to global poverty and release human potential in an interconnected world. For [author] Jacqueline Novogratz it all started back home in Alexandria, Virginia, with the blue sweater . . . she outgrew . . . and gave . . . to Goodwill. Eleven years later in Africa, she spotted a young boy wearing that very sweater, with her name still on the tag inside. . . . Novogratz relates her experiences over two decades, first in Africa and later in India and Pakistan. She began as a banker and philanthropist, and now works as a venture capitalist, trying to effect real change in countries where the average citizen lives on less than $4 a day." (Publisher's note)

Rivlin, Gary

Broke, USA; from pawnshops to Poverty, Inc.: how the working poor became big business. Harper 2010 358p $26.99 **339.4**

1. Poor -- United States 2. United States -- Economic

conditions
ISBN 978-0-06-173321-5

LC 2010-2874

"A timely, important, and deeply disturbing look at the cycle of debt of the nation's most vulnerable." Publ Wkly

Includes bibliographical references

Roberts, James A.

Shiny objects; why we spend money we don't have in search of happiness we can't buy. James A. Roberts. HarperOne 2011 368 p. $25.99   **339.4**

1. Consumers 2. American dream 3. Consumption (Economics) -- United States 4. American Dream 5. Materialism -- United States

ISBN 0062093606; 9780062093608

LC 2010005086

In this book James A. Roberts "studies why Americans believe and behave as if possessions will induce, increase, and enhance happiness -- when, as studies show, materialism 'negatively correlate[s]' with well-being. He examines the psychological underpinnings of our desire to purchase -- even beyond our means. . . . Roberts offers a history of American consumerism, drawing parallels between different eras." (Publishers Weekly)

Includes bibliographical references.

Waldfogel, Joel

Scroogenomics; why you shouldn't buy presents for the holidays. Princeton University Press 2009 173p $9.95   **339.4**

1. Gifts 2. Consumption (Economics)

ISBN 9780691142647

LC 2009-6177

The author "assesses holiday gift giving through the lens of economic tenets such as opportunity costs and deadweight loss. The result is a short but engaging manifesto on the inefficiency of the tradition, concluding with several solutions to increase satisfaction for both givers and receivers." Libr J

Includes bibliographical references

339.5   Macroeconomic policy

Steil, Benn

The **battle** of Bretton Woods; John Maynard Keynes, Harry Dexter White, and the making of a new world order. Benn Steil. Princeton University Press 2013 472 p. (hardcover) $29.95   **339.5**

1. Economic conditions 2. World War, 1939-1945 3. Monetary policy -- History -- 20th century 4. International finance -- History -- 20th century

ISBN 0691149097; 9780691149097

LC 2012035709

Author Benn Steil, the director of international economics at the Council on Foreign Relations, "revisits the 1944 conference that created 'the new global monetary architecture' for the postwar world. As the American Army entered Rome and the Russians drove the Nazis out of Minsk, delegates from 44 Allied nations gathered in Bretton Woods, N.H., to hammer out the ground rules for international eco-

nomic equilibrium following the defeat of the Axis powers." (Kirkus Reviews)

Includes bibliographical references and index

340   Law

★ **Black's** law dictionary; Bryan A. Garner, editor in chief. 9th ed.; West 2009 xxxi, 1920p $80   **340**

1. Reference books 2. Law -- Dictionaries

ISBN 978-0-314-19949-2

LC 2009-459279

First published 1891 with title: A dictionary of law, under the authorship of Henry Campbell Black. Periodically revised to bring terms up to date

This law dictionary contains more than 45,000 terms, including archaic terms and references to statutes and cases.

Includes bibliographical references

Feinman, Jay M.

★ **Law** 101; 3rd ed.; Oxford University Press 2010 363p $27.95   **340**

1. Law -- United States

ISBN 978-0-19-539513-6

LC 2010-487303

First published 2000

This book "covers the main subjects taught in the first year of law school. Readers are introduced to every aspect of the legal system, from constitutional law and the litigation process to tort law, contract law, property law, and criminal law." Publisher's note

Legal systems of the world; a political, social, and cultural encyclopedia. edited by Herbert M. Kritzer. ABC-CLIO 2002 4v il maps set $385   **340**

1. Reference books 2. Law -- Encyclopedias

ISBN 1-57607-231-2

LC 2002-2659

"Written by an international team of more than 350 legal scholars, the more than 400 signed entries cover legal systems of countries from around the world, Australia, and the provinces of Canada; transnational systems (International Court of Justice); general systems (Islamlic law, indigenous, and folk legal systems); and key concepts. Each country profile includes a map with an inset of its location on the globe, general information about the country, its history, diagrams of its court structure, the evolution of its legal framework, its current structure, staffing or how judges are appointed, any specialized judicial bodies (i.e. military court), and the impact that the legal system has had on the country. Articles conclude with references and a bibliography. Academic and public libraries will find this source invaluable for comparative studies in legal and judicial systems."—"The Best of the Best Reference Sources." Am Libr

Includes bibliographical references

Nolo (Firm)

★ **Nolo's** encyclopedia of everyday law; answers to your most frequently asked legal questions.

by Shae Irving & Nolo editors. 8th ed.; Nolo 2011
494p pa $34.99 **340**
1. Law -- United States
ISBN 978-1-4133-1321-5 pa; 1-4133-1321-3 pa;
978-1-4133-1347-5 ebook; 1-4133-1347-7 ebook
LC 2010-31328
First published as a replacement of Nolo's everyday law
book. Frequently revised

This offers answers to frequently asked legal questions
about such topics as credit and debt, workplace rights, wills,
divorce, bankruptcy, social security, tenant's rights, child
custody and visitation, patents and trademarks, travel, partnerships, healthcare directives and powers of attorney.

Includes bibliographical references

Tucker, Virginia

Finding the answers to legal questions; a how-to-
do-it manual. [by] Virginia Tucker and Marc Lamp-
son. Neal-Schuman Publishers 2011 274p (How-to-
do-it manuals for libraries) pa $75 **340**
1. Law -- Research
ISBN 978-1-55570-718-7
LC 2010-36421

"Comprehensive and easily understood by the non-law-
yer, this book would be a useful addition to the reference
collections of public libraries." Catholic Library World

Includes bibliographical references

340.071   Law schools

Tamanaha, Brian Z.

Failing law schools; Brian Z. Tamanaha. The
University of Chicago Press 2012 xvi, 235 p.p
(cloth) $25.00 **340.071**
1. Debt 2. Lawyers -- United States 3. American Bar
Association 4. Law schools -- United States -- Finance
5. Law -- Study and teaching -- United States
ISBN 0226923614; 0226923622; 9780226923611;
9780226923628
LC 2012006829

In this book, Brian Z. Tamanaha "argues that ABA
[American Bar Association] accreditation was established to
keep out poor and immigrant students, 'U.S. News' doesn't
verify schools' self-reported numbers, most professors have
little or no experience practicing law, and schools artificially
inflate the employment numbers of their graduates. The result is that too many schools produce impossibly indebted
graduates who can't find work and, when they do, make legal services unaffordable." (Library Journal)

340.092   Biography

Burke, Dennis

Law man; Shon Hopwood with Dennis
Burke. Crown Publishers 2012 308 p. col. ill.
$25.00 **340.092**
1. Lawyers -- Biography 2. Prisoners -- Biography 3.

Jailhouse lawyers -- Nebraska -- Biography
ISBN 0307887839; 9780307887832; 9780307887856
LC 2011035313

This book, by Shon Hopwood with Dennis Burke, offers
a memoir of a man who reformed after being imprisoned
for bank robbery into a successful jailhouse lawyer. "By
the time Shon walked out of Pekin Prison he'd pulled off
a series of legal miracles, earned the undying gratitude of
numerous inmates, won the woman of his dreams, and built
a new life for himself far greater than anything he could have
imagined." (Publisher's note)

"Hopwood's prison memoir and long journey back into
society are told with brutal and riveting honesty." LJ

340.5   Legal systems

Miller, William Ian

Eye for an eye. Cambridge University Press
2005 266p $28; pa $19.99 **340.5**
1. Justice
ISBN 978-0-521-85680-5; 0-521-85680-9; 978-0-521-
70467-0 pa; 0-521-70467-7 pa
LC 2005-8077

"Analyzing the law of the talion—an eye for an eye,
tooth for a tooth—literally, William Ian Miller presents .
. . [a] meditation on the concept of 'pay back.'" Publisher's note

Includes bibliographical references

341.23   United Nations

Annan, Kofi A. (Kofi Atta), 1938-

Interventions; a life in war and peace. Kofi An-
nan with Nader Mousavizadeh. Penguin Press 2012
xiv, 383 p.p $36 **341.23**
1. Diplomats 2. World politics -- 1989- 3. United
Nations -- Biography 4. Statesmen -- Ghana --
Biography
ISBN 1594204209; 9781594204203
LC 2012008173

In this memoir, "with the assistance of . . . [Nader]
Mousavizadeh . . . , former United Nations Secretary-Gen-
eral [Kofi] Annan discusses the major benchmarks of his life
and career. The author, born in 1934, passes briefly over his
education and early career at the World Health Organization and U.N., where he worked until his retirement in 2006,
and moves rapidly into his main topic: the transformation of
U.N. Peacekeeping Operations since the late 1980s and early
'90s." (Kirkus Reviews)

Fasulo, Linda M.

★ An **insider's** guide to the UN; [by] Linda
Fasulo. 2nd ed; Yale University Press 2009 262p il
pa $17 **341.23**
1. United Nations
ISBN 978-0-300-14197-9; 0-300-14197-1
LC 2008-52231

First published 2003

This "guide to the United Nations surveys the world
body's programs and activities, and covers key issues in-

cluding human rights, climate change, counterterrorism, nuclear proliferation, peacekeeping, and UN reform. It also offers guidelines for setting up a Model UN." Publisher's note

Includes bibliographical references

Mires, Charlene

Capital of the world; the race to host the United Nations. Charlene Mires. New York University Press 2013 320 p. (hardcover) $29.95   **341.23**

1. United Nations   2. United States -- History   3. United Nations -- Headquarters   4. New York (N.Y.) -- Buildings, structures, etc

ISBN 0814707947; 9780814707944

LC 2012035350

In this book, Pulitzer Prize winner Charlene Mires "investigates a largely unexamined aspect of the birth of the United Nations: the attempt by many U.S. cities during the closing days of World War II to persuade it to base its headquarters in their respective communities. Mires has tracked down . . . archival sources and forgotten newspaper accounts, uncovering a . . . chronicle involving countless American politicians, foreign diplomats, and community promoters who participated." (Library Journal)

Includes bibliographical references and index

Moore, John Allphin

★ **Encyclopedia** of the United Nations; [by] John Allphin Moore, Jr., Jerry Pubantz. 2nd ed.; Facts On File 2008 2v il (Facts on File library of world history) set $125   **341.23**

1. United Nations 2. Reference books 3. International relations -- Encyclopedias

ISBN 978-0-8160-6913-2

LC 2007-29559

First published 2002

This set features entries on "the United Nations's institutions, procedures, policies, specialized agencies, historic personalities, initiatives, and involvement in world affairs. . . . The appendixes contain important UN documents, such as the Charter of the United Nations, the Universal Declaration of Human Rights, the Statute of the International Court of Justice, and the recent Security Council Resolution." Publisher's note

Includes bibliographical references

Osmanczyk, Edmund Jan

Encyclopedia of the United Nations and international agreements; [by] Jan Edmund Osmancyzk; edited and revised by Anthony Mango. 3rd ed; Routledge 2002 4v set $550   **341.23**

1. United Nations 2. Reference books 3. International relations -- Encyclopedias

ISBN 0-415-93920-8

LC 2002-10761

Original Polish edition, 1975; first English language edition 1985

"An alphabetically arranged treasure trove of information on the United Nations, its specialized agencies, and many intergovernmental and non-governmental organizations. This especially valuable resource for smaller collections includes the full or partial texts of some 3,000 international agreements, conventions, and treaties as well as

definitions of political, economic, military, geographical, and diplomatic terms. Analytical and agreements-conventions-treaties indexes." Ref Sources for Small & Medium-sized Libr. 6th edition [entry for 1990 edition]

Includes bibliographical references and index

341.5   Disputes and conflicts between states

Bass, Gary J.

Freedom's battle; the origins of humanitarian intervention. Alfred A. Knopf 2008 509p $35   **341.5**

1. Humanitarian intervention

ISBN 978-0-307-26648-4; 0-307-26648-6

LC 2007-52252

This "history of nineteenth-century campaigns to stop atrocities in Greece, Syria, and Bulgaria is a corrective to the idea that humanitarian interventions are a product of the 'dreamy interlude' between 1989 and 9/11. The compelling narrative, rich with accounts of parliamentary debate and battlefield confrontation, presents a world of familiar political and military concerns, from the pressure of nonstop media coverage to the importance of a clear exit strategy. Bass's thesis that humanitarianism long preceded the crises of Bosnia and Rwanda is persuasive." New Yorker

Includes bibliographical references

341.69   War crimes

Rashke, Richard

★ **Useful** Enemies; John Demanjuk and America's Open-Door Policy for Nazi War Criminals. Delphinium 2013 621 p. $29.95   **341.69**

1. War criminals 2. United States -- Immigration and emigration

ISBN 1883285518; 9781883285517

This book looks at John Demjanjuk, convicted of Nazi war crimes in 2011. Richard Rashke "uses Demjanjuk's story to explore the troubling implications of U.S. immigration patterns after WWII; the author contends that the United States knowingly accepted Nazis while simultaneously denying entry to Holocaust survivors, a trend motivated by a political agenda concerned with monitoring Europe in the postwar period and during the cold war." (Publishers Weekly)

342   Branches of law; laws, regulations, cases; law of specific jurisdictions, areas, socioeconomic regions

Amar, Akhil Reed

★ **America's** constitution; a biography. Random House 2005 657p il $29.95; pa $16.95   **342**

1. Constitutional history -- United States

ISBN 1-400-06262-4; 0-8129-7272-4 pa

LC 2004-61464

This is a "guide to the goals and meaning intended by those who drafted and ratified the original 1787 document and its 27 amendments." Economist

"Only rarely do you find a book that embodies scholarship at its most solid and invigorating; this is such a book." Publ Wkly

Includes bibliographical references

The annotated U.S. Constitution and Declaration of Independence; edited by Jack N. Rakove. Belknap Press 2009 354p il $24.95   342
1. United States -- Constitution 2. Constitutional law -- United States 3. Constitutional history -- United States 4. United States -- Declaration of Independence 5. United States -- Constitution -- 1st-10th amendments
ISBN 0-674-03606-9; 978-0-674-03606-2
LC 2009-22907
This is an explication of the Declaration of Independence, the Bill of Rights, and the Constitution. Bibliography.

The author "presents both the Declaration and the Constitution with carefully laid out annotation that's accessible to general readers as well as high school and college students. His extended introduction provides a readable and instructive analysis of how the writing of the Constitution progressed, especially on matters concerning representation, executive power, and creation of the amendments. His annotations often rely upon contemporary usage and meaning from the time of the Declaration of Independence and Constitution . . . and he compares such usage to other documents of the time." Libr J

Includes bibliographical references

Beeman, Richard
★ **Plain,** honest men; the making of the American Constitution. [by] Richard Beeman. Random House 2009 514p il $30   342
1. Constitutional history -- United States 2. United States -- Constitutional Convention (1787)
ISBN 978-1-4000-6570-7; 1-4000-6570-4
LC 2008-28841
"In a day-by-day narrative, Beeman dramatizes the Constitutional Convention in Philadelphia, paying particular attention to the characters of the delegates and the moods of their debates." Booklist

"Masterfully told American history for the scholar and general reader alike." Kirkus

Includes bibliographical references

Berkin, Carol
A **brilliant** solution; inventing the American Constitution. Harcourt 2002 310p $26; pa $14 **342**
1. Constitutional history -- United States 2. United States -- Constitutional Convention (1787) 3. United States -- Politics and government -- 1783-1809
ISBN 0-15-100948-1; 0-15-602872-7 pa
LC 2002-5648
This history of the 1787 Constitutional Convention "emphasizes the importance of the delegates' anxieties, showing how they insinuated themselves into some of the compromises, such as the equality of the states in the Senate. Shrewd at integrating biographical detail on the delegates into their debates, Berkin fares well in comparison with previous historians on the topic." Booklist

Bezanson, Randall P.
How free can the press be? University of Illinois Press 2003 258p (History of communication) $34.95   342
1. Freedom of speech
ISBN 0-252-02866-X
LC 2003-2148
The author "ponders the contradictions of a free press in this study of nine historical court cases involving free speech. He critically explores the thorny issues surrounding freedom of the press and the press's use of First Amendment protections. Drawing on selected Supreme Court and lower court cases to illustrate his argument, Bezanson articulates important legal questions pertaining to First Amendment rights." Libr J

Includes bibliographical references

Bray, Ilona M.
How to get a green card; by Ilona Bray and Loida Nicolas Lewis; updated by Ruby Lieberman. 9th ed; Nolo 2010 334p il pa $39.99   342
1. Aliens -- United States 2. United States -- Immigration and emigration
ISBN 978-1-4133-1103-7
First published 1993. Periodically revised
This guide covers different ways to get a green card, alternatives to a green card, fiancé and fiancée visas, visa lotteries, applying for refugee status and political asylum, and immigration applications.

★ **U.S.** immigration made easy; [by] Ilona Bray. 15th ed.; Nolo 2011 596p il pa $44.99   342
1. United States -- Immigration and emigration
ISBN 978-1-4133-1207-2
First published 1989 by Sheridan Chandler Co. under the authorship of Martha S. Siegel and Laurence A. Canter. Periodically revised
This guide "discusses immigration paperwork, green cards, and other types of temporary visas and when to involve a lawyer." Libr J

Breyer, Stephen G.
Active liberty; interpreting our democratic Constitution. [by] Stephen Breyer. Knopf 2005 161p $21   342
1. United States -- Supreme Court 2. Constitutional law -- United States
ISBN 0-307-26313-4
LC 2005-44242
The Supreme Court Justice presents his view on the Constitution of the United States.

"This will be essential reading at a possibly watershed moment for the Supreme Court." Publ Wkly

Includes bibliographical references

Davis, Thomas J.
Plessy v. Ferguson; Thomas J. Davis. Greenwood 2012 xx, 238 p.p (Landmarks of the American mosaic) (hardcover) $58   342
1. Segregation 2. United States -- Race relations -- History 3. Segregation -- Law and legislation -- United

States -- History 6. Segregation in transportation -- Law
and legislation -- Louisiana -- History
ISBN 0313391874; 9780313391873

LC 2012011735

This book, by Thomas J. Davis, discusses the U.S. Supreme Court case Plessy v. Ferguson as part of the "Landmarks of the American Mosaic" series. "Contrary to popular
misconceptions, Plessy v. Ferguson was not a simple case
of black vs. white separation, but rather a challenging and
complex protest for U.S. law to fully accept mixed ancestry
and multiculturalism." (Publisher's note)

Includes bibliographical references (p. 219-222)
and index.

The **Debate** on the Constitution; Federalist and Anti-
federalist speeches, articles, and letters during the
struggle over ratification. Library of Am. 1993
2v ea $35   **342**
1. Constitutional history -- United States 2. United
States -- Politics and government -- 1783-1809
ISBN 0-940450-42-9; 0-940450-64-X

LC 92-25449

In addition to the documents themselves, these volumes
contain "brief biographical notes on the various speakers
and writers, a chronology of key events in American independence and the establishment of the new governmental
system, notes on contemporary state constitutions, and notes
explicating the text of the reprinted documents." Christ
Sci Monit

Encyclopedia of the American Constitution; edited
by Leonard W. Levy and Kenneth L. Karst. 2nd
ed; Macmillan Ref. USA 2000 6v set $595 **342**
1. Reference books 2. Constitutional law -- United
States
ISBN 0-02-864880-3

LC 00-29203

First published 1986 in 4 volumes

This "reference contains approximately 3000 contributions from academics, lawyers, and judges concerning key
constitutional law cases and legislative developments relating to constitutional issues (e.g., abortion, welfare rights,
and affirmative action)." Libr J

Includes bibliographical referencess

★ **Encyclopedia** of the First Amendment; edited by
John R. Vile, David L. Hudson Jr., David Schultz.
CQ Press 2009 2v il set $275   **342**
1. Reference books 2. United States -- Constitution
-- 1st-10th amendments -- Encyclopedias
ISBN 978-0-87289-311-5; 0-87289-311-1

LC 2008-36077

This "is an excellent resource for anyone who wants to
learn more about broadcast regulation, the establishment of
religion clause, students' rights, or a myriad of other topics involving the First Amendment and its political, cultural,
and legal significance." Booklist

Includes bibliographical references

★ The **Federalist**; edited, with introduction and
notes, by Jacob E. Cooke. Wesleyan Univ. Press
1982 xxx, 672p pa $27.95   **342**
1. United States -- Constitution
ISBN 0-8195-6077-4

LC 82-2815

A reissue of the 1961 edition

"From 27 Oct. 1787 to 2 April 1788, 77 essays were
published in the semi-weekly 'Independent Journal' of New
York, entitled 'The Federalist,' and signed first 'A Citizen
of Nwe York' then 'Publius.' Eight more were added when
they were collected in book form {in 1789}. . . . They were
so acute and massively learned in their exposition of the true
intent of the Constitution, that even the courts have accepted
them as authoritative comments in doubtful cases; and they
are held by all the civilized world as among the noblest
storehouses of political philosophy in existence. A classic
textbook of political science." Ency Americana

Ford, Richard T.

Rights gone wrong; Richard Thompson Ford.
Farrar, Straus and Giroux 2011 272p.   **342**
1. Racism 2. Civil rights 3. Discrimination 4. United
States -- Social conditions
ISBN 9780374250355

LC 2011010705

It was the author's intent to demonstrate "that both the
progressive left and the colorblind right are guilty of the
same error: defining discrimination too abstractly and condemning it too categorically, with similarly perverse results.
According to Ford, the urge to condemn discrimination in all
its forms . . . has led people on the left and the right to reject
'reasonable, prudent and innocent distinctions.' It has also
led activists, judges and government officials to concentrate
on eliminating even trivial forms of discrimination at the expense of more effective means to social justice, like expanding economic opportunities for the poor." (N Y Times)

Includes bibliographical references and index.

Hennessey, Jonathan

The **United** States Constitution; a graphic adap-
tation. written by Jonathan Hennessey; art by Aaron
McConnell. Hill and Wang 2008 149p il $35; pa
$16.95   **342**
1. Graphic novels 2. United States -- Constitution
-- Graphic novels 3. Constitutional history -- United
States -- Graphic novels
ISBN 978-0-8090-9487-5; 0-8090-9487-8; 978-0-
8090-9470-7 pa; 0-8090-9470-3 pa

LC 2008-17927

The author and illustrator go "through the entire U. S.
Constitution, article by article, amendment by amendment,
explaining their meaning and implications—in comics format. Avoiding the didactic, the book succeeds in being both
consistently entertaining and illuminating." Publ Wkly

Includes bibliographical references

Maddex, Robert L.

The **U.S.** Constitution A to Z; 2nd ed.; CQ Press
2008 xxix, 736p il map (CQ's American government A to Z series) $85   **342**
1. Reference books 2. Constitutional law -- United

States -- Encyclopedias 3. Constitutional history -- United States -- Encyclopedias
ISBN 978-0-87289-764-9

LC 2008-21902

First published 2002

"Maddex offers over 200 articles about issues (abortion, gun control), legal concepts (due process, privacy), landmark cases (Roe v. Wade, Brown v. Board of Education) and people (John Adams, Thurgood Marshall) related to the Constitution. . . . The unique feature of this work is its collection of source materials. . . . It is an excellent, concise reference." Choice [review of 2002 edition]

Includes bibliographical references

Madison, James, 1751-1836

★ The **Constitutional** Convention; a narrative history from the notes of James Madison. [edited by] Edward J. Larson and Michael P. Winship. Modern Library 2005 229p pa $13.95 **342**

1. Constitutional history -- United States 2. United States -- Constitutional Convention (1787) 3. United States -- Politics and government -- Sources
ISBN 0-8129-7517-0

LC 2005-41649

"This book tells the convention's turbulent story in Madison's own words, drawn from the notes he took at the scene and giving us a daily blow-by-blow. . . . [The editors] steer readers through the fierce debates with helpful explanations and editorial asides, as well as a cogent epilogue, making this primary source far more than a tidy civics lesson." Publ Wkly

Includes bibliographical references

Maier, Pauline, 1938-2013

Ratification; the people debate the Constitution, 1787-1788. Simon & Schuster 2010 589p il map $30 **342**

1. Constitutional history -- United States
ISBN 978-0-684-86854-7; 0-684-86854-7

LC 2010-27709

In this book on the ratification of the U.S. Constitution, Pauline Maier explores "dynamics within the individual state ratification conventions" with a focus on "how the structure of debate within the individual state conventions affected the final votes in each state. Rather than demonstrate the inevitability of the Constitution's triumph, Maier . . . shows how remarkable the Federalist victory was." (Reviews in American History)

"On Sept. 17, 1787, the convention that had been sitting in Philadelphia for four months to design a new form of government for the United States adjourned, offering its handiwork to the nation. Almost a year later, on Sept. 13, 1788, Congress declared that the Constitution had been duly ratified, and prescribed the rules for the first presidential election the following year. . . . [This] book shows how America got from the first date to the second—and ultimately to today, since we still live with the same document, however modified." N Y Times Book Rev

Includes bibliographical references

Meyerson, Michael

Liberty's blueprint; how Madison and Hamilton wrote the Federalist Papers, defined the constitution, and made democracy safe for the world. [by] Michael I. Myerson. Basic Books 2008 309p $26.95 **342**

1. Constitutional law -- United States 2. Constitutional history -- United States
ISBN 978-0-465-00264-1; 0-465-00264-1

LC 2007-35376

Meyerson examines the history and contemporary relevance of The Federalist Papers, "the series of essays written by Alexander Hamilton and James Madison to explain the proposed Constitution to the American people and persuade them to ratify it." Publisher's note

"This fine book is the fullest and most insightful account we have of the collaboration between Alexander Hamilton and James Madison." J Am Hist

Includes bibliographical references

Noonan, John Thomas

Narrowing the nation's power: the Supreme Court sides with the states; {by} John T. Noonan, Jr. University of Calif. Press 2002 203p $34.95; pa $14.95 **342**

1. State governments 2. United States -- Supreme Court
ISBN 0-520-23574-6; 0-520-24068-5 pa

LC 2002-19473

"In this highly recommended work, the author convincingly sounds the alarm." Libr J

Includes bibliographical references

Nussbaum, Martha Craven

Liberty of conscience; in defense of America's tradition of religious equality. [by] Martha Nussbaum. Basic Books 2008 406p $28.95 **342**

1. Freedom of religion
ISBN 978-0-465-05164-9; 0-465-05164-2

LC 2007-38176

This "is a historical and conceptual study of the American tradition of religious freedom." (Publisher's note) Index.

The author "plumbs the historical, political, philosophical, and legal debates surrounding religious freedom." Booklist

The Oxford guide to United States Supreme Court decisions; edited by Kermit L. Hall, James W. Ely, Jr. 2nd ed.; Oxford University Press 2009 499p $35 **342**

1. Reference books 2. United States -- Supreme Court 3. Constitutional law -- United States
ISBN 978-0-19-537939-6

LC 2008-23763

First published 1999

The editors "assemble the scholarship of 161 field specialists, who summarize the Supreme Court's 440 most significant cases. Scholar-signed, multiparagraph entries are alphabetized by case name, include argued and decided dates, and detail vote divisions. The book closes with a glossary, an appendix containing the complete Constitution, a chronology of justices since 1789, and a list of presidential appointments. An outstanding single-volume reference." Libr J

Includes bibliographical references

Rabban, David M.

Free speech in its forgotten years. Cambridge Univ. Press 1997 404p il (Cambridge historical studies in American law and society) $60; pa $22   **342**

1. Freedom of speech 2. Constitutional law -- United States

ISBN 0-521-62013-9; 0-521-65537-4 pa

    LC 97-15281

The author "focuses on free speech issues between the Civil War and World War I. Through an impressive marshaling of controversies, cases, and litigants, he persuasively argues that libertarian radicalism and the Free Speech League . . . deserve much of the credit for pushing valuable First Amendment issues to the forefront of American social, political, and legal circles. . . . This enlightening work fills a void in First Amendment civil liberties studies." Libr J

Includes bibliographical references and index

Rehnquist, William H.

All the laws but one; civil liberties in wartime. Knopf 1998 254p il $27.50; pa $14   **342**

1. Civil rights 2. World War, 1914-1918 3. World War, 1939-1945 4. National security -- United States 5. United States -- History -- 1861-1865, Civil War 6. Japanese Americans -- Evacuation and relocation, 1942-1945

ISBN 0-679-44661-3; 0-679-76732-0 pa

    LC 98-12641

This is "Supreme Court Chief Justice Rehnquist's narrative of the conflict between civil liberties and military necessity. . . . Fully two-thirds of the book covers Civil War issues. . . . One chapter discusses World War I espionage and draft resistance cases; three, the World War II internment of Japanese Americans and the imposition of martial law in Hawaii. . . . Far from a complete survey of wartime civil liberties—reviewing only cases that reached the Supreme Court before 1950—this is nonetheless both enlightening and entertaining." Booklist

Includes bibliographical references

Schultz, David A.

Encyclopedia of the United States Constitution; [by] David Schultz. Facts On File 2009 2v il (Facts on File library of American history) set $150   **342**

1. Reference books 2. Constitutional law -- United States -- Encyclopedias

ISBN 978-0-8160-6763-3; 0-8160-6763-5

    LC 2008-23349

"This reference source can help high-school students, the general public, and other interested parties comprehend the fundamental concepts, evolutionary character, and historic people and events that have shaped the [Constitution.] . . . The alphabetically arranged entries cover terms, events, people, landmark cases, and issues that help explain the Constitution's history. The appendix provides the Declaration of Independence, the Articles of Confederation, the Constitution, and the Bill of Rights as well as 'Other Amendments

to the Constitution,' a 'U.S. Constitution Time Line,' and instructions on locating court cases." Booklist

Includes bibliographical references

Simon, James F.

What kind of nation; Thomas Jefferson, John Marshall, and the epic struggle to create a United States. Simon & Schuster 2002 348p $27.50; pa $14   **342**

1. Architects 2. Presidents 3. Executive power 4. Vice-presidents 5. Essayists 6. Biographers 7. Writers on law 8. Secretaries of state 9. Supreme Court justices 10. United States -- Supreme Court 11. Constitutional history -- United States 12. United States -- Politics and government -- 1783-1809

ISBN 0-684-84870-8; 0-684-84871-6 pa

    LC 2001-55027

The author "examines the decades of conflict between the states' rights views of Thomas Jefferson and the federalist beliefs of John Marshall." Publ Wkly

"Simon's enlivening account proves that writing about constitutional law needn't be the dry preserve of academics." Booklist

Includes bibliographical references

Strebeigh, Fred

Equal; women reshape American law. W.W. Norton 2009 582p $35   **342**

1. Trials 2. Women's rights 3. Women -- Law and legislation

ISBN 978-0-393-06555-8; 0-393-06555-3

    LC 2008-44463

"This book generates a genuine appreciation for the legal entrepreneurs who fought long and hard to make possible the careers of many a professional woman." Wilson Quarterly

Includes bibliographical references

United States Constitution

★ The **Constitution** of the United States of America; analysis and interpretation: analysis of cases decided by the Supreme Court of the United States to June 28, 2002. prepared by the Congressional Research Service, Library of Congress; Johnny H. Killian, George A. Costello, Kenneth R. Thomas, co-editors; David M. Ackerman, Henry Cohen, Robert Meltz, contributors. U.S. Govt. Ptg. Office 2004 xxii, 2608p $215   **342**

1. Constitutional law -- United States

ISBN 978-0-16-072379-7; 0-16-072379-5

    LC 2005-414932

First published 1953. Periodically revised and kept up to date by supplements

"Sometimes known by its short title, the Constitution Annotated provides commentary on every article, section, and clause of the basic instrument, as well as the amendments, with citations to selected United States Supreme Court decisions construing these provisions." Introd to U.S. Govt Info Sources. 5th edition

Includes bibliographical references

Vile, John R.

The **Constitutional** Convention of 1787; a comprehensive encyclopedia of America's founding. ABC-CLIO 2005 2v il set $185   **342**
1. Reference books 2. Constitutional law -- United States -- Encyclopedias 3. Constitutional history -- United States -- Encyclopedias
ISBN 1-85109-669-8

LC 2005-24214

This "resource covers the people, events, committees, ideology, and documents related to the drafting of the Constitution." SLJ

Includes bibliographical references

Encyclopedia of constitutional amendments, proposed amendments, and amending issues, 1789-2010; 3rd ed.; ABC-CLIO 2010 2v set $165   **342**
1. Reference books 2. Constitutional law -- United States -- Encyclopedias 3. Constitutional history -- United States -- Encyclopedias
ISBN 978-1-59884-316-3; 1-59884-316-8; 978-1-59884-317-0 ebook; 1-59884-317-6 ebook

LC 2010-2113

First published 1996, covering 1789-1995

The author "discusses the Constitution, its 27 ratified amendments, and the approximately 11,700 amendments proposed within the titular time frame to present 'a unique window into American history and politics.' The alphabetical format and detailed index make information access a breeze, and the six appendixes provide a reprint of the Constitution along with charts of the number of proposals by decade, key events, and names of individuals submitting the proposals." Libr J

Includes bibliographical references

Waldman, Steven

Founding faith; providence, politics, and the birth of religious freedom in America. Random House 2008 277p $26   **342**
1. Freedom of religion 2. United States -- Religion 3. Freedom of religion -- United States 4. United States -- Religion -- History 5. Founding Fathers of the United States -- Religious life
ISBN 1400064376; 9781400064373

LC 2007-21710

Walman examines the religious attitude of various founding fathers, focusing particularly on Benjamin Franklin, John Adams, George Wshington, Thomas Jefferson, and James Madison. He argues that "our nation's Founders forged a new approach to religious liberty, a revolutionary formula that promoted faith by leaving it alone. . . . [Waldman contends that] neither side in the culture war has accurately depicted the true origins of the First Amendment." (Publisher's note) Index.

This "is an excellent book about an important subject: the inescapable—but manageable—intersection of religious belief and public life. With a grasp of history and an understanding of the exigencies of the moment, Waldman finds a middle ground between those who think of the Founders as apostles in powdered wigs and those who assert, equally in-

accurately, that the Founders believed religion had no place in politics." Newsweek

Includes bibliographical references

Weiner, Mark Stuart

Black trials; citizenship from the beginnings of slavery to the end of caste. [by] Mark S. Weiner. Alfred A. Knopf 2004 421p $26.95; pa $16.95   **342**
1. Trials 2. African Americans -- Civil rights
ISBN 0-375-40981-5; 0-375-70884-7 pa

LC 2004-40860

The author "examines how court proceedings involving black people—and whites trying to assist them—have served as windows onto race relations and the power of whites over blacks in the U.S. from its earliest days. . . . This book is the best of its kind—a serious, deeply felt reflection on the weight of history on contemporary affairs." Publ Wkly

Includes bibliographical references

Wexler, Jay

Holy hullabaloos; a road trip to the battlegrounds of the church/state wars. Beacon Press 2009 251p pa $20   **342**
1. Freedom of religion 2. Church and state 3. Religious minorities 4. Church and state -- United States
ISBN 0-8070-0044-2; 978-0-8070-0044-1

LC 2008-47405

"This is a rare treat, a combination of thoughtful analysis and quirky humor that illuminates an issue that rarely elicits a laugh—and that is central to the American body politic." Publ Wkly

Includes bibliographical references

Wise, Steven M.

Though the heavens may fall; the landmark trial that led to the end of human slavery. Da Capo Press 2005 282p il $25; pa $17.95   **342**
1. Slaves 2. Trials 3. Slavery
ISBN 0-7382-0695-4; 0-306-81450-1 pa

LC 2004-25346

The author "has an eye for evocative detail and an interest in the trappings and procedures of an 18th-century courtroom that do as much to engage the reader as the drama of the trials themselves." N Y Times Book Rev

Includes bibliographical references

342.73   Constitutional law -- United States

Healy, Thomas

The **great** dissent; how Oliver Wendell Holmes changed his mind and changed the history of free speech in America. by Thomas Healy. Henry Holt and Company 2013 336 p. $28   **342.73**
1. Freedom of speech 2. United States. Constitution. 1st-10th amendments 3. Freedom of speech -- United States 4. Trials (Anarchy) -- New York (State) -- New York -- History -- 20th century
ISBN 0805094563; 9780805094565

LC 2012047539

Author Thomas Healy examines U.S. Supreme Court Justice Oliver Wendell Holmes' "1919 the court opinion that solidified free speech rights in American political doctrine. Holmes' change of heart has long been pondered by legal scholars and historians. Drawing on newly uncovered letters and memos, legal scholar Healy recounts Holmes' long, slow process of advocating for free speech at a time of great national turmoil." (Booklist)

Includes bibliographical references and index

Risen, Clay

The **bill** of the century; the epic battle for the Civil Rights Act. Clay Risen. Bloomsbury Press 2014 320 p. illustrations (hardback) $28   342.73
1. United States. Civil Rights Act of 1964 2. Civil rights -- United States -- History
ISBN 1608198243; 9781608198245

LC 2014004662

"Clay Risen shows [that] the battle for the Civil Rights Act was a . . . broad, epic struggle, a sweeping tale of unceasing grassroots activism, ringing speeches, backroom deal-making and finally, hand-to-hand legislative combat. The larger-than-life cast of characters ranges from Senate lions like Mike Mansfield and Strom Thurmond to NAACP lobbyist Charles Mitchell, called 'the 101st senator' for his Capitol Hill clout, and industrialist J. Irwin Miller, who helped mobilize a powerful religious coalition for the bill." (Publisher's note)

"A work of high academic quality written with a journalist's flair for telling a tale." Choice

Includes bibliographical references and index

Tribe, Laurence H., 1941-

Uncertain justice; the Roberts court and the constitution. Laurence Tribe, Joshua Matz. Henry Holt & Co. 2014 416 p. (hardback) $32   342.73
1. Roberts, John G., 1955- 2. United States. Supreme Court 3. Constitutional law -- United States 4. Constitutional law -- Social aspects -- United States
ISBN 0805099093; 9780805099096

LC 2014002845

This book, by Laurence Tribe and Joshua Matz, argues that "the Roberts Court is shaking the foundation of our nation's laws. . . . Tribe . . . and Matz dig deeply into the court's recent rulings, stepping beyond tired debates over judicial 'activism' to draw out hidden meanings and silent battles. The undercurrents they reveal suggest a strikingly different vision for the future of our country, one that is sure to be hotly debated." (Publisher's note)

"A well-researched, unsettling investigation of recent trends in the nation's highest court." Kirkus

Includes bibliographical references and index

342.7302   Constitutions -- United States

Raphael, Ray

Constitutional myths; what we get wrong and how to get it right. by Ray Raphael. The New Press 2013 xiii, 316 p.p (hardcover) $26.95   342.7302
1. Founding Fathers of the United States 2. Constitutional history -- United States 3. United States

-- History -- 1783-1815 4. Constitutional history -- United States -- 18th century
ISBN 1595588329; 9781595588326

LC 2012041849

This book on the U.S. Constitution is "more concerned with contextualizing the Founder Fathers than in interpreting them. One by one, [Ray] Raphael . . . addresses some of the more pervasive interpretations of the Constitution and the men who crafted it. . . .Through careful analysis of the 1787 Constitutional Convention, Raphael demonstrates that nothing about the Constitution is as simple as contemporary discourse makes it seem." (Publishers Weekly)

Includes bibliographical references and index.

342.7308   Gays -- Legal status, laws, etc. -- United States

Carpenter, Dale

Flagrant conduct; the story of Lawrence v. Texas: how a bedroom arrest decriminalized gay Americans. Dale Carpenter. W. W. Norton & Company 2012 xv, 345 p.p   342.7308
1. Gay rights -- United States 2. United States. Supreme Court 3. Right of privacy -- United States 4. Gay men -- Legal status, laws, etc. 5. Homosexuality -- Law and legislation -- Texas 6. Trials (Sodomy) -- Texas 7. Texas -- Trials, litigation, etc. 8. Gays -- Legal status, laws, etc. -- United States 9. Homosexuality -- Law and legislation -- Texas -- Criminal provisions
ISBN 0393062082; 9780393062083

LC 2011047245

This book looks at the "2003 landmark 'Lawrence v. Texas' Supreme Court case [which] established the right of homosexuals to engage in private sexual conduct. After setting the sociopolitical and legal scene, [Dale] Carpenter . . . describes the 1998 arrest of John Lawrence and Tyron Garner and the ensuing events as gay rights groups in Houston grasped the potential of the case as a national test. Chapters introduce participants, describe the so-called crime, compare differing accounts of the arrest, follow court events, and explain the stakes. Carpenter . . . discuss[es] legal strategies and Supreme Court arguments, and the elite lawyers and strategists of the defense team . . . in stark contrast to the ill-prepared Harris County district attorney." (Libr J)

Includes bibliographical references and index

342.80873 Customary law -- Latin America

Herneández, Tanya Katerí

Racial subordination in Latin America; the role of the state, customary law, and the new civil rights response. Tanya Katerí Hernández. Cambridge University Press 2013 viii, 247 p.p (hbk.) $90   342.80873
1. Race discrimination 2. Latin America -- Civilization 3. Civil rights -- Latin America 4. Customary law -- Latin America 5. Africans -- Legal status, laws, etc. -- Latin America 6. Race discrimination -- Law and

legislation -- Latin America
ISBN 1107024862; 9781107024861

LC 2012017768

This book, by Tanya Kateri Hernandez, "disrupts the traditional narrative of Latin America's legally benign racial past by comprehensively examining the existence of customary laws of racial regulation and the historic complicity of Latin American states in erecting and sustaining racial hierarchies. The book has a particular relevance for the contemporary U.S. racial context in which Jim Crow laws have long been abolished and a "post-racial" rhetoric undermines the commitment to racial equality laws." (Publisher's note)

Includes bibliographical references (pages 201-238) and index

343 Military, defense, public property, public finance, tax, commerce (trade), industrial law

Benedict, Jeff

Little pink house; a true story of defiance and courage. Grand Central Publishing 2009 397p il $26.99   **343**
1. Nurses 2. Eminent domain
ISBN 978-0-446-50862-9; 0-446-50862-4

LC 2008-17650

"Benedict has pieced together a fascinating narrative, using e-mail messages, planning documents, interviews and personal diaries to produce a sordid account of ruthless local politicians working hand-in-medical-glove with big business to drive hardworking Americans from their homes." N Y Times Book Rev

Fishman, Stephen

Working for yourself; law & taxes for independent contractors, freelancers & consultants. 8th ed.; Nolo 2011 360p pa $39.99   **343**
1. Self-employed
ISBN 978-1-4133-1331-4 pa; 978-1-4133-1357-4 ebook

LC 2010-38423

First published 1997 with title: Wage slave no more. Frequently revised

"There's a good chance having a side business will mean being an independent contractor, a freelancer, or a consultant. This thorough and well-organized volume will guide individuals through the legal and tax issues that come with the territory. From deciding on legal structures to drafting contracts to collecting payment from deadbeat clients, this is excellent information." Libr J

Includes bibliographical references

Witt, John Fabian

Lincoln's code; the laws of war in American history. John Fabian Witt. Free Press 2012 viii, 498 p., [16] p.p ill. (hbk.) $32   **343**
1. Law 2. War 3. United States -- History -- 1861-1865, Civil War 4. War -- United States -- History 5. War (International law) -- History 6. Military law -- United States -- History 7. United States -- History -- Civil War, 1861-1865 8. War and emergency legislation

-- United States -- History
ISBN 1416569839; 9781416569831

LC 2012006187

This book by author John Fabian Witt "reviews the background of U.S. laws of war. Witt . . . examines the laws of war in the 18th and 19th centuries from the French and Indian Wars to the Spanish American War. The focus is on the Civil War, where an entirely new rulebook on the laws of war was drafted by Franz Lieber and approved by President Lincoln." (Library Journal)

Includes bibliographical references (p. 401-470) and index

344 Labor, social service, education, cultural law

Ball, Howard, 1937-

At liberty to die; the battle for death with dignity in America. Howard Ball. New York University Press 2012 ix, 229 p.p (alk. paper) $30.00   **344**
1. Euthanasia 2. Brain death 3. Right to die -- Law and legislation 4. Euthanasia -- Law and legislation -- United States 5. Right to die -- Law and legislation -- United States 6. Assisted suicide -- Law and legislation -- United States
ISBN 081474527X; 0814769756; 0814791042; 9780814745274; 9780814769751; 9780814791042

LC 2011052258

In this book, political scientist Howard Ball offers a "legal history of the right to die in America. He starts with the case of Nancy Cruzan, who was left in a persistent vegetative state after a car accident, and the Supreme Court's ruling that the state had the right to require 'clear and convincing evidence' of Cruzan's intentions before removing her from life support. He then traces battles to legalize physician-assisted death (PAD) in Oregon, Washington State, Montana, Vermont, and Hawaii." (Library Journal)

Includes bibliographical references and index.

Hull, N. E. H.

★ **Roe** v. Wade; the abortion rights controversy in American history. [by] N.E.H. Hull and Peter Charles Hoffer. 2nd ed., rev. & expanded.; University Press of Kansas 2010 370p (Landmark law cases & American society) $39.95; pa $19.95   **344**
1. Roe v. Wade 2. District attorneys 3. Pro-choice activists 4. Abortion -- Law and legislation
ISBN 978-0-7006-1753-1; 0-7006-1753-1; 978-0-7006-1754-8 pa; 0-7006-1754-X pa

LC 2010-21294

First published 2001

Thsi book "highlights the abortion issue's historical background; highlights Roe v. Wade's core issues, essential personalities, and key precedents; tracks the case's path through the courts; clarifies the jurisprudence behind the court's ruling in Roe; and gauges its impact on American society and subsequent challenges to it in Webster v. Reproductive Services (1989) and Casey v. Planned Parenthood (1992). . . . [It includes] chapters covering abortion politics and legal battles in the post-9/11 era." Publisher's note

Includes bibliographical references

James, Vaughn E.

The **Alzheimer's** advisor; a caregiver's guide to dealing with the tough legal and practical issues. AMACOM - American Management Association 2009 300p pa $19.95 **344**

1. Caregivers 2. Alzheimer's disease 3. Medicine -- Law and legislation

ISBN 978-0-8144-0924-4; 0-8144-0924-5

LC 2008-20258

The author "deals with the often overlooked but difficult legal and financial responsibilities associated with caring for elders with memory loss and/or dementia." Libr J

Includes bibliographical references

Joel, Lewin G.

Every employee's guide to the law; what you need to know about your rights in the workplace--and what to do if they are violated. {by} Lewin G. Joel III. 3rd ed, rev and updated; Pantheon Bks. 2001 431p pa $16 **344**

1. Employees -- Civil rights 2. Labor -- Law and legislation

ISBN 0-375-71445-6

LC 2001-21501

First published 1993

The author offers legal advice on such subjects as employee interviews, wages, hours, health and safety, sexual harassment, privacy, discrimination, and benefits.

Lombardo, Paul A.

Three generations, no imbeciles; eugenics, the Supreme Court, and Buck v. Bell. Johns Hopkins University Press 2008 365p il **344**

1. Eugenics 2. Sterilization (Birth control) 3. People with mental disabilities 4. Buck v. Bell 5. Forced sterilization 6. Mentally handicapped 7. Constitutional history 8. Sterilization, Eugenic 9. Constitutional law -- United States 10. United States -- Supreme Court -- History 11. Insanity -- Jurisprudence -- United States 12. Eugenics -- United States -- History -- 20th century

ISBN 0-8018-9010-1; 978-0-8018-9010-9

LC 2008-6546

This book examines the case of Buck v. Bell, covering the events of the trial and the 1927 Supreme Court decision that upheld Virginia's 1924 Eugenical Sterilization Act, which called for compulsory sterilization of the "feeble-minded". Index.

The author "traces a seminal 1927 Supreme Court case arising from the attempt by authorities in Virginia to force the sterilization of a woman believed to be mentally and socially 'insufficient.'" Libr J

Includes bibliographical references

Matthews, Joseph L.

★ **Social** security, Medicare & government pensions; get the most out of your retirement & medical benefits. with Dorothy Matthews Berman. 16th ed.; Nolo 2011 482p pa $29.99 **344**

1. Medicare 2. Pensions 3. Social security

ISBN 978-1-4133-1327-7 pa; 1-4133-1327-2 pa;

978-1-4133-1353-6 ebook; 1-4133-1353-1 ebook

LC 2010-38404

First published 1983 with title: Sourcebook for older Americans. Frequently revised

This guide discusses such topics as how to claim social security benefits, social security disability, civil service and veterans benefits, and Medicare procedures.

Nather, David

★ The **new** health care system; everything you need to know. Thomas Dunne Books 2010 230p pa $12.99 **344**

1. Medicaid 2. Medicare 3. Health insurance 4. Medical care -- Government policy

ISBN 978-0-312-64934-0

In this "primer on health-care reform, . . . Nather explains how insurance works, what the big changes are, and when everything will happen. It's a conversational guide that tells readers how to sign up for Medicare, and what to do if they're uninsured, or if they work for a small business versus a large company. . . . Nather's book, which includes a useful glossary, provides an excellent snapshot of how the post-reform health-care system should work as it stands now." Booklist

Nourse, Victoria F.

In reckless hands; Skinner v. Oklahoma and the near-triumph of American eugenics. W.W. Norton & Company 2008 240p il map $24.95 **344**

1. Thieves 2. Eugenics 3. Prisoners 4. Sterilization (Birth control) 5. Sterilization, Eugenic 6. Constitutional law -- United States 7. Eugenics -- United States -- History -- 20th century

ISBN 978-0-393-06529-9; 0-393-06529-4

LC 2008-13140

The author "provides a legal history of the Supreme Court case that served to increase the recognition of individual rights, although it fell short of ending the practice and debate of eugenics in the US. . . . This book deserves attention from those interested in the history and politics of the legal system." Choice

Includes bibliographical references

Sack, Steven Mitchell

The **employee** rights handbook; effective legal strategies to protect your job from interview to pink slip. 3rd ed., rev. & enlarged ed.; Legal Strategies Publications 2010 620p $39.95 **344**

1. Employee rights 2. Labor -- Law and legislation

ISBN 978-0-9636306-7-4

LC 2010-926886

First published 1990 by Facts on File

The author "advises readers on topics from avoiding prehiring abuses and protecting on-the-job rights through postemployment litigation and finding and hiring a lawyer. . . . Readers looking for an all-in-one employee legal primer or layperson's quick reference should find this a useful tool." Libr J

Steingold, Fred

The **employer's** legal handbook; by Fred S. Steingold; edited by Alayna Schroeder. 9th ed.; Nolo 2009 374p pa $49.99 **344**

1. Labor -- Law and legislation
ISBN 978-1-4133-1023-8; 1-4133-1023-0

LC 2009-11075

First published 1994. Frequently revised

This guide for employers discusses "how to comply with the most recent workplace laws and regulations, run a safe and fair workplace and avoid lawsuits." Publisher's note

Includes bibliographical references

345 Criminal law

Bogira, Steve

Courtroom 302; a year behind the scenes in an American criminal courthouse. Knopf 2005 404p hardcover o.p. pa $16 **345**

1. Courts 2. Administration of criminal justice
ISBN 0-679-43252-3; 0-679-75206-4 pa

LC 2004-57636

Bogira provides "a balanced view of the realities of the day-to-day, assembly-line grind that marks so much of the process from arrest to final disposition. . . . The brilliance of Bogira's insights will lead many to hope that he will follow this debut with proposals to cure the many ills he has diagnosed." Publ Wkly

Includes bibliographical references

Boyle, Kevin

Arc of justice; a saga of race, rights, and murder in the Jazz Age. Holt & Co. 2004 415p il $26; pa $15 **345**

1. Physicians 2. Trials (Homicide) 3. Lawyers 4. Memoirists 5. Writers on law 6. Trials (Murder) 7. State legislators 8. African Americans -- Civil rights 9. Detroit (Mich.) -- Race relations 10. African Americans -- Michigan -- Detroit 11. African Americans -- Civil rights -- History -- 20th century
ISBN 0-8050-7145-8; 0-8050-7933-5 pa

LC 2004-47352

In 1925, Dr. Ossian Sweet, an African American, moved into an all-white neighborhood in Detroit with his wife, Gladys. Mobs attacked his home. He and his friends fired on the attackers in self-defense and a white man was killed. "The Sweets and the nine other men there that night were charged with first-degree murder. The case was a significant moment in the early civil rights movement. . . . {This is an} account of the incident and trial. . . . {Clarence Darrow} joined the defense team three months after the end of the Scopes trial." (N Y Times (Late N Y Ed)) Bibliography. Index.

Boyle "has brilliantly rescued from obscurity a fascinating chapter in American history that had profound implications for the rise of the Civil Rights movement." Publ Wkly

Includes bibliographical references

Colmez, Coralie

Math on trial; how numbers get used and abused in the courtroom. Leila Schneps and Coralie Colmez.

Basic Books 2013 xi, 256 p.p ill., ports. (hardcover) $26.99 **345**

1. Mathematics 2. Judicial error 3. Forensic sciences 4. Forensic statistics
ISBN 0465032923; 9780465032921

LC 2012040624

In this book, "Leila Schneps and Coralie Colmez describe ten trials spanning from the nineteenth century to today, in which mathematical arguments were used--and disastrously misused--as evidence. . . . Offering a fresh angle on cases from the nineteenth-century Dreyfus affair to the murder trial of Dutch nurse Lucia de Berk, Schneps and Colmez show how the improper application of mathematical concepts can mean the difference between walking free and life in prison." (Publisher's note)

Includes bibliographical references and index.

Dunne, Dominick

Justice; crimes, trials, and punishments. Crown 2001 337p hardcover o.p. pa $14 **345**

1. Trials
ISBN 0-609-80963-6 pa

LC 2001-28214

"Fascinating stuff, though less than complimentary about the American system of justice." Booklist

Feige, David

Indefensible; one lawyer's journey into the inferno of American justice. Little, Brown and Co. 2006 276p $24.95 **345**

1. Lawyers 2. Administration of criminal justice 3. Writers on law
ISBN 978-0-316-15623-3; 0-316-15623-X

LC 2006-1283

The author "takes us through a typically harrowing day as a public defender, dealing with arbitrary judges and clients who are often victims of the judicial system. . . . Feige skillfully shares his wisdom and his humanity and sheds light on a justice system that too often works irrationally." Publ Wkly

Geoghegan, Thomas

In America's court; how a civil lawyer who likes to settle stumbled into a criminal trial. New Press (NY) 2002 206p $23.95; pa $15.95 **345**

1. Administration of criminal justice
ISBN 1-56584-732-6; 1-56584-817-9 pa

LC 2002-20065

The author "describes participating in a criminal trial after arranging to assist in the defense of a young man accused of committing a felony murder. As the trial proceeds, he talks about his work as a civil lawyer, what it means to be a lawyer, and the issues lawyers face." Libr J

Hoffer, Peter Charles

The **Salem** witchcraft trials; a legal history. University Press of Kan. 1997 165p (Landmark

law cases & American society) hardcover o.p. pa
$12.95   **345**
 1. Trials 2. Salem (Mass.) -- History
 ISBN 0-7006-0858-3; 0-7006-0859-1 pa
                                        LC 97-19986
 "Hoffer discusses the legal nature of the charges of
witchcraft, the evidential and procedural characteristics of
the trials of the accused, and the roles and attitudes of the
ministers and magistrates who controlled the proceedings. .
. . Hoffer offers little that is new in terms of interpretation,
but he presents it well and in a manner easily grasped by the
general reader." Choice
 Includes bibliographical references

Kadri, Sadakat
 The **trial**; a history, from Socrates to O. J. Simpson. Random House 2005 459p il $29.95   **345**
 1. Trials
 ISBN 0-375-50550-4
                                      LC 2005-42925
 This "history of the trial from ancient times to the present provides . . . [a] history of the various forms and purposes of trials throughout Western civilization. . . . The result is
a magnificent book suitable for all sorts of people, from inquisitive high school students to blue-chip lawyers." Choice
 Includes bibliographical references

Lewis, Anthony
 Gideon's trumpet. Random House 1964 262p
hardcover o.p. pa $12.95   **345**
 1. Law -- United States 2. United States -- Supreme
Court
 ISBN 0-679-72312-9 pa
 An account of the case of a Florida man convicted of
burglary which brought about a historic decision of the Supreme Court decreeing that in all states a defendant is entitled to counsel.
 Includes bibliographical references

Lipstadt, Deborah E.
 The **Eichmann** trial. Nextbook/Schocken 2011
237p (Jewish encounters) $24.95   **345**
 1. War criminals 2. War crime trials 3. Nazi leaders
4. Holocaust, 1933-1945 5. Holocaust, Jewish (1939-
1945)
 ISBN 978-0-8052-4260-7; 0-8052-4260-0
                                      LC 2010-28620
 "Lipstadt has done a great service by untethering the trial
from [Hannah] Arendt's polarizing presence, recovering the
event as a gripping legal drama, as well as a hinge moment
in Israel's history and in the world's delayed awakening to
the magnitude of the Holocaust." N Y Times Book Rev
 Includes bibliographical references

Mack, Raneta Lawson
 A **layperson's** guide to criminal law. Greenwood
Press 1999 201p $69.95   **345**
 1. Criminal law
 ISBN 0-313-30556-0
                                       LC 98-53382
 This explanation of the basics of criminal law includes
numerous hypothetical situations that place some of the

more difficult concepts in an "everyday" context. An overview of the criminal trial process, from the arrest to the final
verdict is also provided
 Includes bibliographical references (p. {197}) and index

Malcolm, Janet
 Iphigenia in Forest Hills; anatomy of a murder
trial. Yale University Press 2011 155p $25   **345**
 1. Dentists 2. Trials (Homicide) 3. Murderers 4.
Internists 5. Murder victims 6. Trials (Murder) --
Queens (New York, N.Y.)
 ISBN 978-0-300-16746-7; 0-300-16746-6
                                      LC 2010-35851
 "Malcolm's book chronicles the fate of Mazoltuv Boruk-
hova, a 35-year-old doctor and a member of the Bukharan
Jewish sect who stands accused of hiring an assassin to kill
her ex-husband, Daniel Malakov. On the morning of Oct.
28, 2007, Malakov was shot to death in a park in Queens,
N.Y., in front of his and Borukhova's 4-year-old daughter. .
. . Malcolm shows us what happens when the abstract ideals
of the law are applied, as they always are, by human beings.
We meet one judge who, acting out of incompetence or malice, makes an inexplicable and terrible child-custody decision. Another proves less interested in serving justice than in
wrapping up proceedings in time for his Caribbean vacation.
A lawyer who, on the stand, appears to be 'intelligent and
well-spoken' turns out to be both negligent and delusional.
. . . All told, it's such a damning portrait of American jurisprudence that Malcolm scarcely need editorialize. As lawyers would say, res ipsa loquitur: the thing speaks for itself."
Boston Globe

Newton, Michael A.
 Enemy of the state; the trial and execution of
Saddam Hussein. [by] Michael A. Newton & Michael P. Scharf. St. Martin's Press 2008 305p il
$26.95   **345**
 1. Trials 2. Presidents
 ISBN 978-0-312-38556-9; 0-312-38556-0
                                      LC 2008-21087
 The authors "provided judicial assistance to the trial of
Saddam Hussein and other Ba'athists, including training
of judicial personnel, writing rules for the Iraqi Tribunal,
and observing the nine-month trial proceedings. Here, they
write of their experiences and provide perspective on the
trial, which began in October 2005, including gavel-to-gavel
coverage of the proceedings. . . . Their insiders' account is
directed toward general adult audiences and will effectively
aid them in understanding this crucial phase as Iraq struggles
toward its future." Libr J
 Includes bibliographical references

Rabinowitz, Dorothy
 ★ **No** crueler tyrannies; accusation, false witness, and other terrors of our times. Simon & Schuster 2003 239p (A Wall Street Journal book) $25; pa
$13   **345**
 1. Trials 2. Child sexual abuse
 ISBN 0-7432-2834-0; 0-7432-2840-5 pa
                                      LC 2002-44670
 This book "reexamines high-profile cases of the 1980s
and 1990s involving mass sexual abuse. Demonstrating that

overzealous prosecutors and indifferent courts led to the prosecution of many innocents, Rabinowitz provides . . . analyses of the major cases, especially those that involved child-care workers. . . . This gripping, well-written book about social injustice and public hysteria is recommended for social science and law collections." Libr J

Spence, Gerry

The **smoking** gun; day by day through a shocking murder trial with Gerry Spence: a true story. Scribner 2003 435p hardcover o.p. pa $7.99 **345**
1. Trials (Homicide)
ISBN 0-7432-4696-9; 978-0-7434-7052-0; 0-7434-7052-4

LC 2003-42722

"This disquieting book shows that the facts don't speak for themselves, innocence is rarely presumed and justice is far from a first priority in America's courtrooms. Spence is a gifted storyteller and his rhetorical skills are mesmerizing. The blizzards of argument and counterargument that would be tedious reading in less talented hands are neatly incorporated into this thrilling account of injustice barely averted." Publ Wkly

Temkin, Moshik, 1971-

The **Sacco** -Vanzetti Affair; America on trial. Yale University Press 2009 316p il $35 **345**
1. Trials (Homicide) 2. Sacco-Vanzetti case 3. Sacco-Vanzetti Trial, Dedham, Mass., 1921 4. Trials (Murder) -- Massachusetts -- Dedham 5. United States -- Foreign public opinion, European -- History
ISBN 978-0-300-12484-2; 0-300-12484-8

LC 2008-45606

This "study of the trial and appeals of these two condemned murderers and of the life and times of the country, which feared foreign contamination, surpasses all prior analyses of this subject in terms of scope, erudition, and objectivity. . . . This book discusses many fascinating elements of controversy, not least the long-term views held by Sacco and Vanzetti's defenders and accusers and how their participation in the search for justice was perceived by their peers." Libr J
Includes bibliographical references

Turow, Scott

★ **Ultimate** punishment; a lawyer's reflections on dealing with the death penalty. Farrar, Straus and Giroux 2003 164p $18 **345**
1. Capital punishment
ISBN 0-374-12873-1

LC 2003-7873

"In 2000 Governor George Ryan of Illinois declared a moratorium on executions. . . . Ryan established a commission to study the state's capital punishment system and propose reforms. In 2002 the commission issued its report. . . . Among the people Ryan appointed to the commission was Scott Turow, a . . . novelist and practicing attorney, with experience in death penalty cases. He was, at the time of his appointment, a self-described 'agnostic' on capital punishment. Ultimate Punishment is Turow's account of his struggle to resolve for himself the question, Should we retain the death penalty?" Christ Century
Includes bibliographical references

Walsh, John Evangelist

Moonlight; Abraham Lincoln and the Almanac trial. St. Martin's Press 2000 166p il $22.95 **345**
1. Trials 2. Lawyers 3. Presidents 4. State legislators 5. Members of Congress
ISBN 0-312-22922-4

LC 99-59606

This is "the story of how Abraham Lincoln secured the acquittal of murder suspect William 'Duff' Armstrong, the son of an old New Salem friend, by making use of an almanac to discredit a witness's description of the position of the moon on the night in question." Libr J
Includes bibliographical references

Watson, Bruce

★ **Sacco** and Vanzetti; the men, the murders and the judgment of mankind. Viking 2007 433p il $25.95; pa $16 **345**
1. Trials (Homicide) 2. Sacco-Vanzetti case 3. Anarchists
ISBN 978-0-670-06353-6; 0-670-06353-3; 978-0-14-3114284 pa; 0-14-311428-X pa

LC 2006-103092

The author "has written a well-researched page-turner. Highly recommended." Libr J
Includes bibliographical references

345.73   Criminal justice--law--United States

Beloof, Douglas E.

Victims' rights; a documentary and reference guide. Douglas E. Beloof. Greenwood 2012 xi, 313 p.p (hbk. : alk. paper) $100.00 **345.73**
1. Victims of crimes 2. Victims of crimes -- Legal status, laws, etc. 3. Victims of crimes -- Legal status, laws, etc. -- United States
ISBN 0313393451; 9780313393457; 9780313393464

LC 2011043292

This book by Douglas E. Beloof "traces the origins, evolution, and results of the victims' rights movement. It puts victims' rights in a legal, historical, and contemporary context, and . . . collects important victims' rights documents in a single volume." It "bring[s] together dozens of varied documents such as presidential task force reports and recommendations, Supreme Court cases, state constitutions, human rights reports, critical articles, and political documents." (Publisher's note)
Includes bibliographical references and index.

Houppert, Karen

Chasing Gideon; the elusive quest for poor people's justice. Karen Houppert. The New Press 2013 288 p. (hardcover) $26.95 **345.73**
1. Legal aid 2. Right to counsel 3. Right to counsel -- United States 4. Legal assistance to the poor -- United

States
ISBN 1595588698; 9781595588692

LC 2012047464

This book, by Karen Houppert, profiles public defense in U.S. law. "On March 18, 1963, . . . the U.S. Supreme Court unanimously ruled in Gideon v. Wainwright that all defendants facing significant jail time have the constitutional right to a free attorney if they cannot afford their own. . . . [The] book . . . chronicles the stories of people in all parts of the country who have relied on Gideon's promise." (Publisher's note)

Includes bibliographical references.

Mandery, Evan J.

A **wild** justice; the death and resurrection of capital punishment in America. Evan J. Mandery. W W Norton & Co Inc 2013 496 p. (hardcover) $29.95   **345.73**

1. Capital punishment -- United States 2. Constitutional law -- United States 3. Capital punishment -- United States. -- History -- 20th century
ISBN 0393239586; 9780393239584

LC 2013010126

In this book, Evan J. Mandery "traces the building momentum within the country and the court to question the legality of a punishment the Founding Fathers took for granted", the death penalty. He starts with "when the Supreme Court declined to accept the appeal of a 1963 rape case, [and] Justice Arthur Goldberg published an unusual dissent questioning the constitutionality of the death penalty." (Kirkus Reviews)

Includes bibliographical references and index

Smith, Clive Stafford

The **injustice** system; a murder in Miami and a trial gone wrong. Clive Stafford Smith. Viking 2012 xi, 352 p.p $27.95   **345.73**

1. Trials (Homicide) 2. Capital punishment -- United States 3. Administration of criminal justice -- United States 4. Trials (Murder) -- Florida 5. Criminal justice, Administration of -- United States
ISBN 0670023701; 9780670023707

LC 2012019068

This book presents an "account of a questionable 1989 death penalty case by the lawyer who tried to get it overturned. By the time [Clive Stafford] Smith . . . became involved in the case of Kris Maharaj . . . [he] had been convicted and sentenced to death in Miami for the murder of a former business partner and his son. . . . In the author's view, the case is a glaring, but by no means unique, example of massive flaws in the American criminal justice system." (Kirkus Reviews)

Includes bibliographical references and index

Strang, Dean A.

Worse than the devil; anarchists, Clarence Darrow, and justice in a time of terror. Dean A. Strang. The University of Wisconsin Press 2013 xviii, 268 p.p ill., map (paperback) $26.95   **345.73**

1. Trials 2. Judicial error 3. Anarchism and anarchists 4. Milwaukee (Wis.) -- History -- 20th century 5. Bay View (Milwaukee, Wis.) -- History -- 20th century 6.

Anarchists -- Wisconsin -- Milwaukee -- History -- 20th century 7. Trials (Riots) -- Wisconsin -- Milwaukee -- History -- 20th century 8. Italian Americans -- Wisconsin -- Milwaukee -- History -- 20th century 9. Judicial corruption -- Wisconsin -- Milwaukee -- History -- 20th century
ISBN 0299293947; 9780299293932; 9780299293949

LC 2012032689

This book, by Dean A. Strang, profiles how "in 1917 a bomb exploded in . . . Milwaukee. . . . Those responsible never were apprehended, but . . . all assumed that the perpetrators were Italian. Days later, eleven alleged Italian anarchists went to trial on unrelated charges involving a fracas that had occurred two months before. Against the backdrop of World War I . . . and . . . a prevailing hatred and fear of radical immigrants, the Italians had an unfair trial." (Publisher's note)

Includes bibliographical references and index

346   Private law

American Bar Association

★ The **American** Bar Association legal guide for small business; everything you need to know about small business, from start-up to employment to financing and selling. 2nd ed.; Random House Reference 2010 472p pa $16.99   **346**

1. Small business
ISBN 978-0-375-72303-2; 0-375-72303-X

LC 2009-49394

First published 2000
Topics covered "include legal forms of operating businesses, buying an existing business or a franchise, hiring and firing employees, managing temps and independent contractors, dealing with contracts and scams, taxes of all types, and, finally, closing, selling, or bequeathing the business." Libr J [review of 2000 edition]

Butler, Rebecca P.

★ **Copyright** for teachers & librarians in the 21st century. Neal-Schuman Publishers 2011 274p il pa $70   **346**

1. Copyright 2. Fair use (Copyright)
ISBN 978-1-55570-738-5

LC 2011012600

First published 2004 with title: Copyright for teachers and librarians

"Library educator Rebecca Butler explains fair use, public domain, documentation and licenses, permissions, violations and penalties, policies and ethics codes, citations, creation and ownership, how to register copyrights, and gives tips for staying out of trouble." Publisher's note

Includes bibliographical references

Elias, Stephen

Chapter 13 bankruptcy; keep your property & repay debts over time. [by] Stephen Elias &

Robin Leonard. 10th ed.; Nolo 2010 486p il pa
$39.99 **346**
   1. Bankruptcy
ISBN 978-1-4133-1069-6; 1-4133-1069-9
LC 2009-21416
First published 1995. Periodically revised
Answers questions about bankruptcy that range from
how to face the reality of being in debt and possible alternatives to filing procedures and strategies for rebuilding credit
after the process is complete.

★ The **foreclosure** survival guide; keep your
house or walk away with money in your pocket. 2nd
ed.; Nolo 2009 304p pa $24.99 **346**
   1. Foreclosure
ISBN 978-1-4133-1059-7; 1-4133-1059-1
LC 2009-11885
First published 2008. Frequently revised
"Elias explains how foreclosure works, what options
there may be for keeping a home when in default, and what
to do when that is not possible. He includes instruction on
negotiating a workout with a lender as well as chapters on
how to use bankruptcy to avoid foreclosure. . . . Straightforward and timely." Libr J

Encyclopedia of crime and punishment; edited
by David Levinson. Sage Publs. 2002 4v set
$600 **346**
   1. Reference books 2. Administration of criminal
justice 3. Crime -- Encyclopedias
ISBN 0-7619-2258-X
LC 2002-1220
"The 439 signed entries cover 13 major themes: crimes
and related behaviors, law and justice, policing, forensics,
corrections, victimology, punishment, social and cultural
context, international aspects, concepts and theories, research methods and information, organizations and institutions, and special populations. . . . {This is} easy to understand and useful for beginning research in the field of
criminal justice." Booklist
Includes bibliographical references

Fishman, Stephen
   The **public** domain; how to find & use copy-
right-free writings, music, art & more. 5th ed.; Nolo
2010 462p il map pa $39.99 **346**
   1. Copyright
ISBN 978-1-4133-1205-8; 1-4133-1205-5
LC 2009-39940
First published 2001. Frequently revised
This book offers "information about finding copyright-
free writings, music, art, photography, software, maps, databases, videos, and more." Publisher's note

Leonard, Robin
   ★ **Solve** your money troubles; debt, credit &
bankruptcy. by Robin Leonard & Margaret Reiter.
12th ed.; Nolo 2009 520p pa $24.99 **346**
   1. Credit 2. Debtor and creditor
ISBN 978-1-4133-1022-1; 1-4133-1022-2
LC 2009-10728

First published 1991 with title: Money troubles.
Frequently revised
This guide offers advice on how to manage debts, in-
cluding how to create a budget, negotiate with creditors, and
rebuild your credit.
Includes bibliographical references

Lessig, Lawrence
   Remix; making art and commerce thrive in the
hybrid economy. Penguin Press 2008 xxii, 327p
$25.95 **346**
   1. Copyright
ISBN 978-1-59420-172-1
LC 2008-32392
As Lessig "sees it, if intellectual-property law is left as
it is an entire generation will be criminalized. He argues that
the ways in which young people break copyright laws help
them to become the sort of people we want them to be—
creative and collaborative. Kids today are simply not going
to give up downloading music and using copyrighted material in YouTube videos: they belong to a culture for which
'remix' is 'the essential art.' Lessig's proposals for revising
copyright are compelling, because they rethink intellectual-
property rights without abandoning them." New Yorker
Includes bibliographical references

Pakroo, Peri
   ★ The **small** business start-up kit; by Peri H.
Pakroo; edited by Marcia Stewart. 6th ed.; Nolo
2010 352p pa $29.99 **346**
   1. Commercial law 2. Small business 3. Business
enterprises
ISBN 978-1-4133-1099-3; 1-4133-1099-0
LC 2009-37822
First published 2000. Frequently revised
"In addition to covering essential legal basics, . . . [the
author] advises on picking a business name and the best
location, drafting and using contracts, managing business
finances using technology, choosing the right business structure, and reaching customers using social media. . . . The
CD-ROM includes contact information for state agencies
that deal with businesses and taxes." Libr J

Pascoe, Peggy
   What comes naturally; miscegenation law and
the making of race in America. Oxford University
Press 2009 404p il map **346**
   1. Interracial marriage 2. Miscegenation -- United
States -- History 3. Interracial marriage -- United States
-- History 4. Racially mixed people -- Legal status,
laws, etc. -- United States
ISBN 0-19-509463-8; 978-0-19-509463-3
LC 2008-18035
"Peggy Pascoe's book, 'What Comes Naturally,' has
won five major book awards--two from the American His-
torical Association, two from the Organization of American
Historians, and one from the Law and Society Association;
it was also a finalist for another from the American Studies
Association. . . . It . . . [examines] laws banning interracial
marriage in the United States, . . . informed by sociological,
anthropological, and feminist theories of race-making, the

state, law, and the intersections of race, class, and gender." (Contemporary Sociology)

"This compelling history of the United States miscegenation law demonstrates its centrality to maintaining white supremacy in the century following the Civil War. Pascoe, broadening her focus beyond black-white relations, considers Western states' prohibition of marriage between whites and American Indians, Chinese, Japanese, and Filipinos, as well as blacks. She weaves a fascinating story out of significant court cases." New Yorker

Includes bibliographical references and index

Pressman, David

Patent it yourself; your step-by-step guide to filing at the U.S. Patent Office. 14th ed.; Nolo 2009 596p il pa $49.99 **346**
1. Patents 2. Inventions
ISBN 978-1-4133-1058-0; 1-4133-1058-3
LC 2009-11888
First published 1979. Periodically revised
This guide for the amateur inventor covers patent searching, filing and infringement.
Includes bibliographical references

Stim, Richard

Contracts; the essential business desk reference. Nolo 2011 477p (Nolo's quick reference series) pa $39.99; ebook $39.99 **346**
1. Contracts 2. Reference books
ISBN 978-1-4133-1281-2 pa; 1-4133-1281-0 pa; 978-1-4133-1289-8 ebook; 1-4133-1289-6 ebook
LC 2010-21161
The author "helps laypeople navigate the sometimes murky waters of contractual agreements. Stim dedicates sections to writing different types of contracts, a dictionary of terms found in contracts and similar legal documents, and how to enforce these agreements once they're made. The bulk of the book is an alphabetized list of terms related to legal words and concepts. There is also a well-thought-out section on statutes of limitations on contract claims by state as well as contract sample documents scattered throughout." Libr J

★ **Patent,** copyright & trademark; 11th ed.; Nolo 2010 636p il pa $44.99 **346**
1. Patents 2. Copyright 3. Trademarks
ISBN 978-1-4133-1200-3; 1-4133-1200-4
LC 2009-48208
First published 1996. Periodically revised
The author explains concepts, issues, and terms concerning intellectual property, discusses trade secrets, copyright, patent, and trademark law, and provides sample forms.
Includes bibliographical references

346.01 Persons and domestic relations

American Civil Liberties Union

★ The **rights** of women; the authoritative ACLU guide to women's rights. [by] Lenora M. Lapidus, Emily J. Martin, and Namita Luthra. 4th ed.; New York University 2009 412p (American Civil Liberties Union handbook) $75; pa $19 **346.01**
1. Women's rights 2. Women -- Law and legislation
ISBN 978-0-8147-5230-2; 0-8147-5230-6; 978-0-8147-5229-6 pa; 0-8147-5229-2 pa
LC 2008-47033
First published 1973 by Sunrise Books/Dutton
Topics covered include "employment, education, housing, and public accommodations. This handbook also examines the specific issues of trafficking, violence against women, welfare reform, and reproductive freedom." Publisher's note
Includes bibliographical references

Clifford, Denis

A **legal** guide for lesbian and gay couples; by Denis Clifford, Frederick Hertz, and Emily Doskow. 15th ed; Nolo 2010 333p pa $34.99 **346.01**
1. Gay couples -- Legal status, laws, etc.
ISBN 978-1-4133-1091-7; 1-4133-1091-5
LC 2009-37846
First published 1980 by Addison-Wesley under the authorship of Hayden Curry and Denis Clifford
This handbook addresses "legal issues with which gay and lesbian couples are certain to contend . . . [including] advice for GLBT parents and prospective parents. Moreover, it addresses other legal considerations such as finanical arrangements. Indispensable for gay and lesbian readers, as well as for attorneys who may lack familiarity in this area." Libr J
Includes bibliographical references

Doskow, Emily

★ **Nolo's** essential guide to divorce; 3rd ed.; Nolo 2010 496p il pa $24.99 **346.01**
1. Divorce -- Law and legislation
ISBN 978-1-4133-1255-3; 1-4133-1255-1
LC 2010-8698
First published 2006
The author "covers the before, during, and after of divorce, counseling readers on the types of divorces, how to make decisions about living arrangements and the division of property, and how custody decisions are made. She advocates minimizing conflict but includes sections on domestic violence and kidnapping if the worst happens. Appendixes contain state-to-state grounds for divorce and financial inventory forms." Libr J

Sember, Brette McWhorter

★ **Seniors'** rights; your legal guide to living life to the fullest. Sphinx Pub 2004 243p pa $19.95 **346.01**
1. Elderly -- Law and legislation
ISBN 1-572-48386-5
LC 2004-10704
"The author endeavors to help seniors understand their rights involving medical care, bank accounts, retirement accounts, housing, and discrimination. . . . The first step to protecting your rights, as she indicates, is understanding them, and this book will help seniors achieve that goal." Booklist

Sherman, Charles Edward

Make any divorce better! specific steps to make things smoother, faster, less painful, and save you a lot of money. [by] Ed Sherman; [foreword by Warren Farrell] Nolo Press Occidental 2008 177p il $24.95 **346.01**

1. Divorce -- Law and legislation
ISBN 978-0-944508-64-0; 0-944508-64-2

LC 2007-930632

First published 2003 with title: Divorce solutions

The author "offers an insider's guide to making divorce go smoothly, quickly, painlessly, and inexpensively, revealing how the law works against divorcing couples and showing how to beat the system. . . . His no-nonsense guide to the legalities and practicalities of divorce is highly recommended for all public libraries." Libr J

Women's legal guide; editor, Barbara R. Hauser with Julie A. Tigges. Fulcrum 1996 526p hardcover o.p. pa $22.95 **346.01**

1. Women -- Law and legislation
ISBN 1-55591-303-2 pa

LC 95-46893

"This is a collection of essays written by women attorneys for women who need legal information. Family- and health- related issues such as divorce, family violence, and reproductive rights are covered, as are business topics of particular concern to women. . . . Estate planning, sexual discrimination, dealing with disabilities, and the rights of lesbian women are considered as well. The writing is consistently clear, objective, and practical." Libr J

Includes bibliographical references

Woodhouse, Violet

★ **Divorce** & money; how to make the best financial decisions during divorce. with Dale Fetherling. 10th ed.; Nolo 2011 511p pa $34.99 **346.01**

1. Divorce -- Law and legislation
ISBN 978-1-4133-1314-7 pa; 1-4133-1314-0 pa; 978-1-4133-1337-6 ebook; 1-4133-1337-X ebook

LC 2010-31198

First published 1991. Periodically revised

A guide to financial problems that arise as a result of divorce proceedings.

Includes bibliographical references

346.0168 Same-sex marriage

Becker, Jo

★ **Forcing** the spring; inside the fight for marriage equality. Jo Becker. The Penguin Press 2014 480 p. illustrations (hardback) $29.95 **346.0168**

1. United States. Supreme Court 2. Same-sex marriage -- United States 3. California. Proposition 8 (2008) 4. Locus standi -- United States -- Cases 5. United States. Defense of Marriage Act 6. Same-sex marriage -- Law and legislation -- United States -- Cases
ISBN 1594204446; 9781594204449

LC 2014005342

Written by Jo Becker, this book offers an "account of five remarkable years in American civil rights history: when the United States experienced a tectonic shift on the issue of marriage equality. Beginning with the historical legal challenge of California's ban on same-sex marriage, Becker expands the scope to encompass all aspects of this momentous struggle, offering a . . . behind-the-scenes narrative." (Publisher's note)

"Becker's chronicle of a legal battle reveals deeper changes in the cultural and political landscape of a nation grappling with old prejudices and changing public opinion that continue to resonate." Booklist

Includes bibliographical references and index

346.04 Property

Crews, Kenneth D.

Copyright law for librarians and educators; creative strategies and practical solutions. with contributions from Dwayne K. Buttler . . . [et al.] 2nd ed; American Library Association 2012 xii, 192 p.p ill. (alk. paper) $57 **346.04**

1. Copyright 2. Sound recordings 3. Fair use (Copyright) 4. Copyright -- United States 5. Fair use (Copyright) -- United States 6. Teachers -- United States -- Handbooks, manuals, etc 7. Librarians -- United States -- Handbooks, manuals, etc
ISBN 0838910920; 9780838910924

LC 2011027604

First published 2000 with title: Copyright essentials for librarians and educators

Author Kenneth D. Crews' book "allows readers to get up to speed on current interpretations of the Digital Millennium Copyright Act from a librarian-educator viewpoint." It also "draws on cutting-edge case law in 18 discrete areas of copyright, including specialized and controversial music and sound recording issues. [This guide offers] information professionals . . . the tools they need to take control of their rights and responsibilities as copyright owners and users." (Publisher's note)

The author "addresses 18 areas of copyright in 5 parts. He begins with the scope of protectable works as well as works without copyright protection. Next, he discusses the rights of ownership, including duration and exceptions. He then explains fair use and its related guidelines. Part 4 focuses on the TEACH Act, Section 108, and responsibilities and liabilities. Lastly, Crews examines special issues such as the Digital Millennium Copyright Act." Booklist

Includes bibliographical references and index.

Decherney, Peter

Hollywood's copyright wars; from Edison to the internet. Peter Decherney. Columbia University Press 2012 287 p. (cloth : alk. paper) $34.50 **346.04**

1. Copyright 2. Motion picture industry 3. Television supplies industry 4. Copyright -- Motion pictures -- United States -- History 5. Copyright -- Broadcasting rights -- United States -- History
ISBN 0231159463; 9780231159463

LC 2011041745

This book by Peter Decherney "follows the struggle of the film, television, and digital media industries to influence and adapt to copyright law . . . beginning with Thomas Edison's aggressive patent and copyright disputes and concluding with recent lawsuits against YouTube and Universal. Decherney shows that the history of intellectual property in Hollywood has not always mirrored the evolution of the law. Many landmark decisions have barely changed the industry's behavior." (Publisher's note)

Includes bibliographical references and index

Elias, Stephen

★ **Trademark**; legal care for your business & product name. by Stephen Elias & Richard Stim. 9th ed.; Nolo 2010 448p il pa $39.99   **346.04**

    1. Trademarks

    ISBN 978-1-4133-1256-0; 1-4133-1256-X

               LC 2010-9267

First published 1992. Periodically revised

The authors explain "how to: choose a distinctive name or logo that others can't copy; search for other marks that might conflict with your own; register your mark with the U.S. Patent and Trademark Office; protect your marks from unauthorized use by others; resolve trademark disputes outside the courtroom; [and] create an Internet presence with an eye on trademark law." Publisher's note

Fishman, Stephen

★ **Copyright** handbook; what every writer needs to know. 10th ed.; Nolo 2008 527p il pa $39.99   **346.04**

    1. Copyright

    ISBN 978-1-4133-0893-8; 1-4133-0893-7

               LC 2008-7882

First published 1991. Frequently revised

"Designed as a practical handbook for writers and publishers. Includes a list of legal aid groups and sample forms." Guide to Ref Books. 11th edition

Includes bibliographical references

Gasaway, Laura N.

Copyright questions and answers for information professionals; from the columns of Against the Grain. by Laura N. Gasaway. Purdue University Press 2013 xiii, 284 p.p (paperback) $24.95; (ebook) $11.99; (ebook) $11.99   **346.04**

    1. Copyright 2. Fair use (Copyright) 3. Intellectual property 4. Copyright -- United States 5. Fair use (Copyright) -- United States 6. Photocopying -- Fair use(Copyright) -- United States

    ISBN 1557536392; 9781557536396; 9781612492537 pdf; 9781612492544

               LC 2012032276

Laura N. Gasaway's "book begins with a basic primer on copyright. Then each topical chapter (e.g., Licensing, Performance and Displays, Digitization, etc.) presents a short introduction to the issues involved, followed by related questions and answers. The author includes reference to the applicable section of the copyright law as well as to other laws dealing with the subject. All in all, there are answers to well over 300 questions concerning copyright, fair use, and related issues." (Library Journal)

Hyde, Lewis, 1945-

Common as air; revolution, art, and ownership. Farrar, Straus and Giroux 2010 306p $26   **346.04**

    1. Arts 2. Culture 3. Patents 4. Copyright 5. Intellectual property 6. Information commons

    ISBN 0-374-22313-0; 978-0-374-22313-7

               LC 2010-02388

Hyde argues against "efforts to close off sectors of knowledge so as to exploit them for private profit." (N Y Times Book Rev) Index.

This is "an eloquent and erudite plea for protecting our cultural patrimony from appropriation by commercial interests." N Y Times Book Rev

Includes bibliographical references

Hylton, Keith N.

Laws of creation; property rights in the world of ideas. by Ronald A. Cass and Keith N. Hylton. Harvard University Press 2013 275 p. $55   **346.04**

    1. Copyright 2. Intellectual property

    ISBN 9780674066458; 0674066456

               LC 2012011488

In this book authors Ronald A. Cass and Keith N. Hylton "look closely at the [intellectual property] doctrines that have been developed over many years in patent, copyright, trademark, and trade secret law. Over time, the authors show, a set of rules has emerged that supports wealth-creating innovation while generally avoiding overly expansive, growth-retarding licensing regimes." (Publisher's note)

Includes bibliographical references and index

Leamer, Laurence

The **price** of justice; a true story of two lawyers' epic battle against corruption and greed in coal country. Laurence Leamer. Times Books 2013 xii, 432 p.p (hardcover) $30.00   **346.04**

    1. Fair trial -- United States 2. Judges -- Recusal -- United States 3. Massey Energy (Firm) -- Trials, litigation, etc 4. Coal trade -- Corrupt practices -- West Virginia

    ISBN 9780805094718

               LC 2012041537

Includes bibliographical references and index.

Portman, Janet

★ **Every** tenant's legal guide; by Janet Portman and Marcia Stewart. 6th ed.; Nolo 2009 445p il pa $34.99   **346.04**

    1. Landlord and tenant

    ISBN 978-1-4133-1015-3; 1-4133-1015-X

               LC 2009-4832

First published 1997. Frequently revised

This guide explains how to find and inspect a home, negotiate clauses in a lease or rental agreement, understand rules on rent increases and late rent, get repairs and maintenance, protect privacy rights, fight discrimination, deal with environmental hazards, security deposits, evictions and legal procedures.

Russell, Carrie

Complete copyright for K-12 librarians and educators; Carrie Russell. American Library Association 2012 xi, 173 p.p ill. (chiefly col.) (alk. paper) $50   **346.04**

1. Copyright 2. Fair use (Copyright) 3. Segregation -- Law and legislation 4. Copyright -- United States 5. Fair use (Copyright) -- United States 6. Librarians -- Legal status, laws, etc. -- United States 7. School libraries -- Law and legislation -- United States

ISBN 0838910831; 9780838910832

LC 2012016674

This book by Carrie Russell "is designed as a resource for educators, offering guidance for providing material to students while carefully observing copyright law. The book offers detailed advice on distinctive issues of intellectual property in the school setting; explores scenarios often encountered by educators . . . and precisely defines 'fair use,' by showing readers exactly what's possible within the law." (Education Digest)

Includes bibliographical references and index

Stewart, Marcia

★ **Every** landlord's legal guide; by Marcia Stewart and Ralph Warner & Janet Portman. 10th ed.; Nolo 2010 462p pa $44.99   **346.04**

1. Landlord and tenant

ISBN 978-1-4133-1197-6; 1-4133-1197-0

LC 2009-39934

First published 1996. Frequently revised

This guide covers how to "screen and choosing tenants; prepare leases and rental agreements; collect and returning deposits; avoid discrimination charges; keep up with repairs and maintenance; hire the right property manager; minimize your liability; [and] deal with problem tenants." Publisher's note

Strauss, Steven D.

Landlord and tenant. Norton 1998 155p (Ask a lawyer) $25; pa $14   **346.04**

1. Landlord and tenant

ISBN 0-393-04585-4; 0-393-31730-7 pa

LC 97-33617

This book covers the legal rights and responsibilities of tenants and landlords including such topics as what to look for in an apartment or lease, how to evict tenants or avoid eviction, and how to break a lease

Wherry, Timothy Lee

★ **Intellectual** property; everything the digital-age librarian needs to know. American Library Association 2008 141p il $50   **346.04**

1. Patents 2. Copyright 3. Trademarks

ISBN 978-0-8389-0948-5; 0-8389-0948-5

LC 2007-13893

The author "explains the difference between patents, copyrights, and trademarks and when one would want to obtain any one or a combination of the three. He goes on to instruct readers on how technology has simplified the process of both searching and acquiring these three types of intellectual property protection. . . . This informative and necessary volume is a must have for any professional reference collection." Voice Youth Advocates

346.05 Inheritance, succession, fiduciary trusts, trustees

Clifford, Denis

★ **Make** your own living trust; 10th ed.; Nolo 2011 338p pa $39.99   **346.05**

1. Estate planning 2. Inheritance and succession

ISBN 978-1-4133-1316-1 pa; 1-4133-1316-7 pa; 978-1-4133-1344-4 ebook; 1-4133-1344-2 ebook

LC 2010-38422

First published 1993. Periodically revised

"Explains what trusts are, how they work, and who should use them. The CD provides a basic living trust, basic shared living trust, and AB living trust, plus other key forms." Publisher's note

★ **Plan** your estate; 10th ed; Nolo 2010 539p pa $44.99   **346.05**

1. Estate planning

ISBN 978-1-4133-1201-0

First published 1989. Periodically revised

This guide covers basic estate planning, probate avoidance, living wills, federal estate and gift taxes, trusts, durable powers of attorney, and more.

Shotwell, Barbara

Pass it on; a practical approach to the fears and facts of planning your estate. [by] Barbara Shotwell and Nancy R. Greenway. Hyperion 2000 286p il $22.95; pa $14.95   **346.05**

1. Estate planning

ISBN 0-7868-6580-6; 0-7868-8494-0 pa

LC 99-49481

The authors explain "the essential estate-planning documents, various kinds of trusts, retirement plans, business considerations, and the probate process. . . . The text is replete with cartoons, quotes, illustrative song titles, and anecdotes that add levity and accessibility without oversimplifying the treatment of the subject." Libr J

Strauss, Steven D.

Wills and trusts. Norton 1998 176p (Ask a lawyer) $25; pa $14   **346.05**

1. Wills 2. Estate planning

ISBN 0-393-04583-8; 0-393-31728-5 pa

LC 97-33619

"Strauss specializes in transforming the arcane and obtuse into everyman's lingo and comprehension." Booklist

346.07   Commercial law

Elias, Stephen

★ **How** to file for Chapter 7 bankruptcy; by Stephen Elias, Albin Renauer, & Robin Leonard. 16th ed.; Nolo 2009 555p il pa $39.99   **346.07**
1. Bankruptcy
ISBN 978-1-4133-1060-3; 1-4133-1060-5
           LC 2009-21419
First published 1989. Periodically revised. Variant title: How to file for bankruptcy
This guide offers advice on such topics as personal debt, property liability, asset protection, rebuilding credit, and filling out and filing forms.
Includes bibliographical references

346.73082   Banks (Finance) -- law -- United States

Kaiser, Robert G.

Act of Congress; how America's essential institution works, and how it doesn't. Robert G. Kaiser. 1st ed. Alfred A. Knopf 2013 xxvi, 417 p.p (hardcover) $27.95   **346.73082**
1. United States. Congress 2. United States. Dodd-Frank Wall Street Reform and Consumer Protection Act 3. Global Financial Crisis, 2008-2009 4. Financial services industry -- Law and legislation -- United States
ISBN 030770016X; 9780307700162
           LC 2012038245
In this book, journalist Robert G. Kaiser "chronicles the journey of the Dodd-Frank act, a complex package of banking and market regulations passed in 2011 that few voters paid attention to. . . . While the bill was moving through Congress, Kaiser had access to lawmakers of both parties and their staffs, executive-branch officials, and lobbyists; he finds the drama in arcane parliamentary procedure and paints . . . fly-on-the-wall scenes of legislative sausage making." (Publishers Weekly)
Includes bibliographical references (pages 391-400) and index.

347   Procedure and courts

Breyer, Stephen G., 1938-

Making our democracy work; a judge's view. [by] Stephen Breyer. Alfred A. Knopf 2010 270p il $26.95   **347**
1. United States -- Supreme Court 2. Judicial review -- United States 3. Separation of powers -- United States 4. United States -- Politics and government 5. Judicial review -- United States -- History 6. Political questions and judicial power -- United States
ISBN 0-307-26991-4; 978-0-307-26991-1
           LC 2010-16839
"Why does the public accept the Court's decisions as legitimate and follow them, even when those decisions are highly unpopular? What must the Court do to maintain the public's faith? How can the Court help make . . . democracy work? These are the questions that Justice Stephen Breyer [examines]." (Publisher's note) Index.
"A sitting Justice explains how the Supreme Court won the public trust and what it must do to keep it. Employing a succession of cases from Marbury v. Madison to Bush v. Gore, Breyer . . . offers a short, highly accessible course on the evolution of judicial review, the doctrine permitting the Court to invalidate laws conflicting with the Constitution. . . . Speaking out without talking down, Breyer renders a signal service to his fellow citizens." Kirkus
Includes bibliographical references

Faigman, David L.

Laboratory of justice; the Supreme Court's 200-year struggle to integrate science and the law. Times Books, Henry Holt 2004 417p $27.50; pa $17 **347**
1. Science -- Governmental policy 2. United States -- Supreme Court 3. Constitutional law -- United States
ISBN 0-8050-7274-8; 0-8050-7845-2 pa
           LC 2003-57049
"This insightful and accessible study throws light on how new ways of understanding the world produce new readings of our Constitution." Publ Wkly
Includes bibliographical references

Finkelman, Paul

★ **Landmark** decisions of the United States Supreme Court; [by] Paul Finkelman, Melvin I. Urofsky. 2nd ed.; CQ Press 2008 791p il $250   **347**
1. United States -- Supreme Court 2. Constitutional law -- United States
ISBN 978-0-87289-409-9
           LC 2007-42588
First published 2003
This "provides the historical context and constitutional perspective of more than 1,000 of the most important Supreme Court cases." Publisher's note
Includes bibliographical references

Friedman, Barry

The **will** of the people; how public opinion has influenced the Supreme Court and shaped the meaning of the Constitution. Farrar, Straus and Giroux 2009 614p   **347**
1. Public opinion 2. United States -- Supreme Court 3. Public opinion -- United States 4. United States -- Supreme Court -- Public opinion 5. Judicial process -- United States -- Public opinion
ISBN 0374220344; 0374532370 pa; 9780374220341; 9780374532376 pa
           LC 2008054247
This is an account of the relationship between popular opinion and the Supreme Court from the Declaration of Independence to the end of the Rehnquist court in 2005. (Publisher's note) Index.
This book is a thought-provoking and authoritative history of the Supreme Court's relationship to popular opinion. . . . Friedman's contribution to [the] discussion is the breadth and detail of his historical canvas, and it's a significant one. N Y Times Book Rev
Includes bibliographical references

★ **Great** American trials; Edward W. Knappman, editor; Stephen G. Christianson and Lisa Paddock, consulting legal editors. 2nd ed; Gale Group 2002 2v il set $170 **347**
1. Trials
ISBN 0-7876-4901-5
First published 1994
Featuring approximately 360 trials from the 1800s to the present, entries "cover the principals involved, the crime charged, the verdict and sentence, and the significance and impact of each trial." Publisher's note
Includes bibliographical references

Leiter, Richard A.
Landmark Supreme Court cases; the most influential decisions of the Supreme Court of the United States. [by] Gary Hartman, Roy M. Mersky, [and] Cindy Tate Slavinski. Facts on File 2004 594p (Facts on File library of American history) $70; pa $21.95 **347**
1. Law -- United States 2. United States -- Supreme Court
ISBN 0-8160-2452-9; 0-8160-6923-9 pa
LC 2003-57776
This is "an excellent source for beginning researchers. . . The discussion of the case's significance and its implications will be useful for students." SLJ
Includes bibliographical references

Marshall, Thurgood
Thurgood Marshall; his speeches, writings, arguments, opinions, and reminiscences. edited by Mark Tushnet; foreword by Randall Kennedy. Hill Bks. 2001 xxvi, 548p (Library of Black America) $40; pa $24.95 **347**
1. Lawyers 2. Solicitors general 3. Civil rights activists 4. Supreme Court justices 5. African Americans -- Biography 6. United States -- Supreme Court 7. African Americans -- Civil rights
ISBN 1-55652-385-8; 1-55652-386-6 pa
LC 2001-16793
"In a career ranging from his trial and appellate work for the NAACP to his tenure as an associate justice of the Court, Marshall wrought revolutionary changes in U.S. law and politics, and this collection of his legal briefs, writings, speeches, and judicial opinions, plus a never-before-published oral interview, gives us a superior analysis of the advocate, the democrat, the dissenter, and the unflagging fighter for equality." Libr J
Includes bibliographical references

O'Brien, David M.
Storm center; the Supreme Court in American politics. 8th ed; W.W. Norton 2008 xx, 458p il pa $29.85 **347**
1. United States -- Supreme Court
ISBN 978-0-393-93218-8; 0-393-93218-4
LC 2008-7373
First published 1986. Periodically revised
The author discusses "the day-to-day workings of the Court justices and their law clerks, how cases are accepted

for hearing, what negotiations and compromises go on, how case opinions get written—and what happens to American society when two conservative presidents, Reagan and Bush, appoint the majority of justices." Publisher's note
Includes bibliographical references

★ **The Oxford** companion to the Supreme Court of the United States; editor in chief, Kermit L. Hall; editors, James W. Ely, Jr., Joel B. Grossman. 2nd ed.; Oxford University Press 2005 xxv, 1239p il $65 **347**
1. Reference books 2. United States -- Supreme Court
ISBN 0-19-517661-8
LC 2004-29463
First published 1992
This encyclopedia includes over 1200 articles "on all aspects of the court's history, justices, operations, and cases. Over 300 experts contributed the entries, which vary in length; some have bibliographic references. The organization . . . [includes] alphabetical entries, portraits of the justices, cross-references, and indexes by both case name and topic." Choice

Shesol, Jeff
★ **Supreme** power; Franklin Roosevelt vs. the Supreme Court. W. W. Norton & Co. 2010 644p il $27.95 **347**
1. Governors 2. Presidents 3. People with disabilities 4. Philatelists 5. United States -- Supreme Court 6. United States -- Politics and government -- 20th century 7. Political questions and judicial power -- United States -- History
ISBN 978-0-393-06474-2; 0-393-06474-3
LC 2009-46365
The book examines the interaction between U.S. President Franklin Delano Roosevelt and the Supreme Court. "FDR took up the idea of expanding the number of justices on the Court. This was the famous 'court-packing plan.' The story of the plan and the . . . political battle over it . . . [is] told . . . by Jeff Shesol in his . . . [book] 'Supreme Power.' Shesol looks at the battle through the eyes of all the major players--FDR and his advisers, the congressional leadership that was handed the unappealing job of putting the plan into effect, the congressional opposition, the many politicians and interest groups that organized over the plan, and the justices themselves." (New York Review of Books)
This "is an impressive and engaging book—an excellent work of narrative history. It is deeply researched and beautifully written. Even readers who already know the outcome will find it hard not to feel the suspense that surrounded the battle, so successfully does Shesol recreate the atmosphere of this great controversy." N Y Times Book Rev
Includes bibliographical references

Smith, Jean Edward
John Marshall; definer of a nation. Holt & Co. 1996 736p il hardcover o.p. pa $22 **347**
1. Biographers 2. Writers on law 3. Secretaries of state 4. Supreme Court justices 5. United States -- Supreme Court
ISBN 0-8050-5510-X pa
LC 96-15072

"Mr. Smith's splendid biography deserves a large reader-ship mostly because it has recovered Marshall the man." N Y Times Book Rev

Includes bibliographical references

Toobin, Jeffrey R.

★ The **nine**; inside the secret world of the Supreme Court. [by] Jeffrey Toobin. Doubleday 2007 369p il $27.95   **347**
   1. United States -- Supreme Court
   ISBN 978-0-385-51640-2

                 LC 2007-20287

"Beautifully written, this is an essential purchase for all libraries interested in the contemporary Supreme Court." Libr J

Includes bibliographical references

Warner, Ralph E.

★ **Everybody's** guide to small claims court; by Ralph Warner. 13th ed.; Nolo 2010 480p pa $29.99   **347**
   1. Small claims court
   ISBN 978-1-4133-1102-0; 1-4133-1102-4

                 LC 2009-41947

First published 1980 by Addison-Wesley. Periodically revised

Presents resources and step-by-step instructions for defending one's case in small claims court, and discusses specific kinds of cases, such as motor vehicle repair and purchase, vehicle accident, and landlord-tenant cases.

Williams, Juan

Thurgood Marshall; American revolutionary. Times Bks. 1998 459p il hardcover o.p. pa $16 **347**
   1. Lawyers 2. Solicitors general 3. Civil rights activists 4. Supreme Court justices 5. African Americans -- Biography 6. United States -- Supreme Court 7. African Americans -- Civil rights
   ISBN 0-8129-3299-4 pa

                 LC 98-9735

"Williams presents Marshall as a revolutionary 'of grand vision,' but this well-rounded portrait of the man also addresses his vanities and warts, from his ascension to his deflation and subsequent redemption. This is a must read for all Americans concerned with the struggle for civil and individual rights." Booklist

Includes bibliographical references

347.73   Civil procedure and courts of the United States

Coyle, Marcia

★ The **Roberts** court; the struggle for the constitution. Marcia Coyle. Simon & Schuster 2013 352 p. (hardcover) $28   **347.73**
   1. Roberts, John G., 1955- 2. United States. Constitution 3. United States. Supreme Court 4. United States. Supreme Court -- History -- 21st century 5. Political questions and judicial power -- United States -- History

-- 21st century
   ISBN 1451627513; 9781451627510; 9781451627527; 9781451627534

                 LC 2012051637

In this book, author Marcia Coyle "reveals the fault lines in the conservative-dominated [U.S. Supreme] Court led by Chief Justice John Roberts Jr." It "captures four landmark decisions--concerning health care, money in elections, guns at home, and race in schools. Her analysis shows how dedicated conservative lawyers and groups are strategizing to find cases and crafting them to bring up the judicial road to the Supreme Court with an eye on a receptive conservative majority." (Publisher's note)

Includes bibliographical references and index

Gibson, Larry S.

Young Thurgood; the making of a Supreme Court Justice. by Larry S. Gibson. Prometheus Books 2012 413 p. (cloth : alk. paper) $28 **347.73**
   1. Judges -- United States -- Biography 2. United States. Supreme Court -- History 3. United States. Supreme Court -- Officials and employees
   ISBN 1616145714; 9781616145712

                 LC 2012027517

This book by Larry S. Gibson is a biography of U.S. Supreme Court Justice Thurgood Marshall. "He transformed the nation's legal landscape by challenging the racial segregation that had relegated millions to second-class citizenship. . . . Marshall's personality, attitudes, priorities, and work habits had crystallized during earlier years in Maryland. . . . [This book] is the first close examination of the formative period in Marshall's life." (Publisher's note)

Includes bibliographical references and index.

Jost, Kenneth

★ The **Supreme** Court A to Z; Kenneth Jost. 5th ed. CQ Press 2012 xvii, 668 p.p ill. (hardcover : alk. paper) $125.00   **347.73**
   1. United States. Supreme Court -- Biography 2. United States. Supreme Court -- Encyclopedias
   ISBN 1608717445; 9781608717446

                 LC 2012000642

This book by Kenneth Jost "offers . . . information about the Supreme Court, including its history, traditions, organization, dynamics, and personalities. The entries in The Supreme Court A to Z are arranged alphabetically and are . . . cross-referenced to related information. This volume also has a detailed index, reference materials on Supreme Court nominations, a seat chart of the justices, the U.S. Constitution, online sources of decisions, and a bibliography." (Publisher's note)

Includes bibliographical references (p. 617-630) and index.

Justices of the United States Supreme Court; their lives and major opinions. edited by Leon Friedman & Fred L. Israel. Facts On File 2013 1600 p. (hbk. alk. paper) $375   **347.73**
   1. Judges -- Biography 2. Judges -- United States -- Biography 3. United States. Supreme Court --

Biography
ISBN 0816070156; 9780816070152

LC 2009021252

This book by Leon Friedman and Fred L. Israel "examines the biographical facts of each Supreme Court justice's life, including his or her background in the law, the paths that led each one to the Supreme Court, and each justice's major decisions, as well as how these decisions reveal an underlying legal philosophy. All entries and their corresponding bibliographies have been thoroughly updated in this revised four-volume set." (Publisher's note)

Includes bibliographical references and index

Mersky, Roy M.

Landmark Supreme Court cases; the most influential decisions of the Supreme Court of the United States. Richard A. Leiter, Roy M. Mersky. 2nd ed. Facts on File 2012 3 v., xx, 1224 p.p (hardbound : alk. paper) $250.00   **347.73**
1. Civil rights 2. Freedom of speech 3. Freedom of the press 4. United States. Supreme Court 5. Law -- United States -- Cases 6. United States -- Supreme Court

ISBN 9780816069576; 0816069573

LC 2010048195

Authors Richard A. Leiter and Roy M. Mersky's book discusses landmark U.S. Supreme Court "cases on such issues as freedom of speech, freedom of the press, civil rights, labor unions, abortion, antitrust and competition, due process, search and seizure, executive privilege, and more. Organized chronologically by issue, each entry includes the case title and legal citation, year of decision, key issue, historical background, legal arguments, decision (majority and dissenting opinions), aftermath and significance, related cases, and recommended reading." (Publisher's note)

"The authors describe some 350 influential US Supreme Court decisions. Arranged by subjects such as abortion and taxation, the . . . entries include an abstract of the decision, . . . the case's history, summary of the arguments, the salient issues involved, its significance, related cases, and recommended readings including law journal articles." Choice

Includes bibliographical references and index.

O'Connor, Sandra Day, 1930-

★ **Out** of order; stories from the history of the Supreme Court. Sandra Day O'Connor. 1st ed. Random House Inc. 2013 xviii, 233 p.p ill. (hardcover) $26; (ebook) $78.00   **347.73**
1. Courts -- History 2. United States. Supreme Court 3. Law -- United States -- History 4. United States. Supreme Court -- History 5. United States. Supreme Court -- Anecdotes 6. Courts of last resort -- United States -- History 7. Courts of last resort -- United States -- Anecdotes

ISBN 0812993926; 9780812993929; 9780812993936

LC 2012025708

This book, by Sandra Day O'Connor, "the first woman to sit on the United States Supreme Court, . . . [discusses] the history and evolution of the highest court in the land. . . . [This book] sheds light on the centuries of change and upheaval that transformed the Supreme Court from its un-

certain beginnings into the . . . institution that thrives and endures today." (Publisher's note)

Includes bibliographical references and index

Sotomayor, Sonia, 1954-

★ **My** beloved world; Sonia Sotomayor. Knopf 2013 ix, 315 p., [16] p. of platesp ill. (hardback) $27.95   **347.73**
1. Hispanic American women 2. Hispanic American women -- Biography 3. Judges -- United States -- Biography 4. Hispanic American judges -- Biography 5. United States. Supreme Court -- Officials and employees -- Biography

ISBN 0307594882; 9780307594884

LC 2012031797

Author Sonia Sotomayor presents a biography as "the first Hispanic and third woman appointed to the United States Supreme Court . . . She determined to become a lawyer, . . . from valedictorian of her high school class to the highest honors at Princeton, Yale Law School, the New York County District Attorney's office, private practice, and appointment to the Federal District Court before the age of forty." (Publisher's note)

The Supreme Court justices; illustrated biographies, 1789-2012. edited by Clare Cushman, the Supreme Court Historical Society ; foreword by Chief Justice John G. Roberts, Jr. 3rd ed. CQ Press, an imprint of SAGE Publications 2013 xx, 562 p.p ill., ports. (hardcover) $135   **347.73**
1. Judges -- Biography 2. Judges -- United States -- Biography 3. United States. Supreme Court -- History 4. United States. Supreme Court -- Officials and employees -- Biography

ISBN 1608718328; 9781608718320

LC 2012031502

This book, edited by Clare Cushman, is "a single-volume reference profiling every Supreme Court justice from John Jay through Elena Kagan. An original essay on each justice paints a . . . picture of his or her individuality as shaped by family, education, pre-Court career, and the times in which he or she lived. Each biographical essay also presents the major issues on which the justice presided. Essays are arranged in the order of the justices' appointments." (Publisher's note)

"Written by leading constitutional scholars, the well-researched essays are arranged in chronological order of the justices' appointment to the Court. The volume includes a revised bibliography organized by individual justices, and a thorough index. . . . Recommended." Choice

Includes bibliographical references (pages 516-538) and index.

Toobin, Jeffrey

The **oath**; the Obama White House and the Supreme Court. Jeffrey Toobin. Doubleday 2012 viii, 325 p.p $28.95   **347.73**
1. Roberts, John G., 1955- 2. United States. Supreme Court 3. United States -- Politics and government -- 2009- 4. Constitutional history -- United States 5. United States. Supreme Court -- History -- 21st century 6. Political questions and judicial power -- United States

-- History -- 21st century
ISBN 0385527209; 9780385527200

LC 2012029205

This book by Jeffrey Toobin offers an "account of the current struggle over constitutional interpretation." It "interweaves three topics: the leading cases that illustrate the ambition of the [John] Roberts Court; the four appointments since 2006 ([John] Roberts, Samuel Alito, Sonia Sotomayor, and Elena Kagan) that have turned the court into an institution . . . divided between five committed Republicans and four committed Democrats; and . . . sketches of all the justices, including the three recent retirees (Sandra Day O'Connor, David Souter, and John Paul Stevens)." (Bookforum)

Includes bibliographical references and index.

Tushnet, Mark

In the balance; law and politics on the Roberts Court. Mark Tushnet. W W Norton & Co Inc 2013 352 p. (hardcover) $28.95   **347.73**
1. Judicial power 2. Roberts, John G., 1955- 3. United States. Supreme Court 4. Judges -- United States 5. Law -- Political aspects -- United States 6. Political questions and judicial power -- United States
ISBN 0393073440; 9780393073447

LC 2013012744

In this book, "constitutional law expert Mark Tushnet clarifies the lines of conflict and what is at stake on the Supreme Court as it hangs 'in the balance' between its conservatives and its liberals." He "cover[s] the legal philosophies that have informed decisions on major cases such as the Affordable Care Act, the political structures behind Court appointments, and the face-off between John Roberts and Elena Kagan for intellectual dominance of the Court." (Publisher's note)

Includes bibliographical references and index

348   Laws, regulations, cases

★ Major acts of Congress; Brian K. Landsberg, editor in chief. Macmillan Reference USA 2004 3v il set $290   **348**
1. Reference books 2. Law -- United States -- Encyclopedias
ISBN 0-02-865749-7

LC 2003-18747

This "will be a top-tier reference work for students and laypersons researching federal legislation." Booklist

Includes bibliographical references

Stathis, Stephen W.

Landmark legislation, 1774-2002; major U.S. acts and treaties. {by} Stephen Stathis. CQ Press 2003 22, 429p $130   **348**
1. Legislation
ISBN 1-56802-781-8

LC 2003-3531

"This well-organized volume will allow users to quickly find a description of important legislation and determine where they can locate the full text. . . . This will be a useful source for academic and public libraries." Booklist

Includes bibliographical references

★ U.S. laws, acts, and treaties; edited by Timothy L. Hall. Salem Press 2003 3v (Magill's choice) set $188   **348**
1. Law -- United States 2. United States -- Foreign relations -- Treaties
ISBN 1-58765-098-3

LC 2002-156063

This "is a collection of 433 major U.S. acts of Congress and U.S. treaties covering the time period from 1776 through 2002, beginning with the Declaration of Independence and ending with the Homeland Security Act. . . . The essays, chronically arranged and varying in length from 500 to 2,000 words, cover the historical origins and main provisions of each law or treaty. . . . This set presents a good coverage of landmark laws and treaties in a concise, easy-to-read, and easy-to-use work. It is geared toward high-school and undergraduate students but would also make a useful and functional reference tool for public libraries." Booklist

Includes bibliographical references

349   Law of specific jurisdictions, areas, socioeconomic regions, regional intergovernmental organizations

Clark, David Scott

The Oxford companion to American law; editor in chief, Kermit L. Hall; editors, David S. Clark {et al.} Oxford Univ. Press 2002 xxvi, 912p $75   **349**
1. Law -- United States
ISBN 0-19-508878-6

LC 2002-284010

The alphabetically arranged "entries consider how law, legal institutions, and court decisions are related to social demands and legal responses. . . . The volume also includes standard legal terms and key legal concepts, such as verdicts and venues, as well as biographical statements about leading individuals in the legal profession. . . . With a substantial breadth of information and analysis, this volume is accessible to every reader. All libraries will find it an invaluable reference source." Libr J

Includes bibliographical references

Friedman, Lawrence Meir

American law in the 20th century; {by} Lawrence M. Friedman. Yale Univ. Press 2002 722p $38   **349**
1. Law -- United States
ISBN 0-300-09137-0

LC 2001-3332

The author "examines the American legal system as an integral part of the larger society, both reflecting and causing changes therein. By adopting such a focus, the author makes his book accessible to readers who are not legal scholars." Booklist

Includes bibliographical references

★ Gale encyclopedia of American law; 3rd ed.; Gale/Cengage Learning 2011 14v il map set $1604   **349**
1. Reference books 2. Law -- United States --

Encyclopedias
ISBN 978-1-4144-3684-5; 1-4144-3684-X; 978-1-
4144-4302-7 ebook; 1-4144-4302-1 ebook

LC 2010-45527

First published 1983-1985 with title: The Guide to
American law. Previous edition published with title: West's
encyclopedia of American law

Explains legal terms and concepts in everyday language,
covering a wide variety of persons, entities, and events that
have shaped the U.S. legal system and influenced public perceptions of it.

Includes bibliographical references

★ **Gale** encyclopedia of everyday law; Jeffrey Wilson, editor. 2nd ed.; Thomson Gale 2006 2v set
$325   **349**
1. Law -- United States
ISBN 1-4144-0353-4

LC 2006-10071

First published 2003

This encyclopedia includes "descriptions of each issue's
historical background, covering important statutes and cases; profiles of various U.S. laws and regulations; details of
how laws and regulations vary from state to state, and; . . .
bibliographies, including print and Web resources and lists
of relevant organizations." Publisher's note

Includes bibliographical references

★ **National** survey of state laws; Richard A. Leiter, editor. 6th ed; Thomson Gale 2008 808p
$140   **349**
1. Law -- United States
ISBN 978-0-7876-9874-4; 0-7876-9874-1
Irregular. First published 1993

Summarizes state laws on 50 subjects, divided into
general legal categories: business and consumer, criminal,
education, employment, family, general civil, real estate,
and tax.

351   Public administration

Kettl, Donald F.
The **next** government of the United States; why
our institutions fail us and how to fix them. W. W.
Norton & Co. 2009 288p il $25.95   **351**
1. Administrative agencies 2. United States -- Politics
and government -- 2001-
ISBN 978-0-393-05112-4; 0-393-05112-9

LC 2008-38584

"Kettl's cogent and unbiased analysis of the failure
of government institutions posits that current challenges,
whether in health care or disaster response, have outgrown
the capacity of monolithic government agencies, even while
the size of government continues to swell. . . . He presents
a balanced and unpartisan analysis of the Hurricane Katrina
debacle, examining human error and generations of poor decision making as well as the intricacies of federalism and
the organizational complexity of government institutions."
Publ Wkly

Includes bibliographical references

Phillips, Kevin P.
Arrogant capital; Washington, Wall Street, and
the frustration of American politics. {by} Kevin Phillips. Little, Brown 1994 231p hardcover o.p. pa
$18.99   **351**
1. Political corruption 2. United States -- Politics and
government -- 20th century
ISBN 0-316-70602-7 pa

LC 94-10035

This book "suggests that Bill Clinton's early successes
and later failures were both symptoms of a deeper political and economic shift. That shift . . . is the collapse of the
capacity of the US economy to sustain growth in jobs and
income for the middle class. The 'arrogant capital' of Phillips's title means both Washington, DC, with its lobbyists
and warring interest groups, and the financial capital that
flows through brokerages and investment banks without creating an adequate base for middle-class employment." N Y
Rev Books

Phillips "makes a convincing case that voters see Washington as the enemy because they can't crack the interlock
between interest-group power and the political system." N Y
Times Book Rev

Includes bibliographical references

351.076   Review and exercise

Civil service arithmetic and vocabulary; [by] Joe
Krasowski . . . [et al.] 15th ed.; Arco/Thomson
Learning 2005 347p pa $14.95   **351.076**
1. Civil service -- Examinations
ISBN 0-7689-1697-6; 978-0-7689-1697-3
First published 1951. Periodically revised

Contains basic instructions for working every type of
math problem found on the exams. The vocabulary section
includes a review of vocabulary words, verbal analogies,
and sentence completion problems.

352.13   Administration of subordinate
jurisdictions

★ The **book** of the states; [compiled by] the Council
of State Governments. 2010 ed; Council of State
Governments 2010 627p il map $125   **352.13**
1. State governments
ISBN 978-0-87292-7667

Biennial, 1935-2001. Annual from 2002. Began
publication 1935

"In addition to general articles on various aspects of
state government, this source provides many statistical and
directory data, the principal state officials, and such information as the nickname, motto, flower, bird, song, and tree of
each state." Ref Sources for Small & Medium-sized Libr.
6th edition

★ **Counties** USA; a directory of United States counties. Darren L. Smith, managing editor. Omnigraphics 2006 840p il map $149   **352.13**
1. Reference books 2. County government 3. United

States -- Statistics
ISBN 978-0-7808-0821-8
First published 1997
This is "an excellent choice, offering multiple uses as a country directory, demographic source, and gazetteer." Choice [review of 2003 edition]

352.23   Chief executives

Encyclopedia of the U.S. presidency; a historical reference. edited by Nancy Beck Young. Facts On File 2013 6 v., 2500 p.p ill., maps (hardcover) $550   352.23
1. Presidents -- United States -- Encyclopedias 2. Presidents -- United States -- Encyclopedias, Juvenile 3. Presidents -- United States -- History -- Encyclopedias, Juvenile 4. United States -- Politics and government -- Encyclopedias, Juvenile
ISBN 0816067449; 9780816067442
                                        LC 2010020746
This six-volume set looks at the American presidency. The "opening volume includes 19 thematic essays dealing with various topics surrounding the history of the presidency including 'Origins of the Presidency,' 'Presidency and the Politics of Race,' and 'The Presidency and Popular Culture.' The ensuing volumes follow a chronological arrangement of individually signed entries covering from Washington to Obama." (Library Journal)
Includes bibliographical references and index

Fellow citizens; the Penguin book of U.S. presidential inaugural addresses. edited with an introduction and commentaries by Robert V. Remini and Terry Golway. Penguin Books 2008 476p $16   352.23
1. American speeches 2. Presidents -- United States -- Inaugural addresses
ISBN 978-0-14-311453-6; 0-14-311453-0
                                        LC 2008-19970
"Two distinguished historians round up every presidential inaugural address and preface it with commentary on the rhetoric and historical context of the discourse. . . . Reflecting the major events of American history, as well as a rhetorical evolution from prolixity to brevity, this . . . is a great resource." Booklist
Includes bibliographical references

Guide to the presidency and the executive branch; Michael Nelson, editor. 5th ed. CQ Press 2013 2 v. (xix, 2141 p.)p ill. (cloth : alk. paper) $425   352.23
1. Political science 2. Presidents -- United States
ISBN 9781608719068
                                        LC 2012023291
This two-volume guide is a source "for researchers seeking an understanding of those who have occupied the White House and on the institution of the U.S. presidency." Its chapters "explain the structure, powers, and operations of the office and the president's relationship with Congress and the Supreme Court." In this fifth edition, there is "coverage of the George W. Bush presidency, the 2008 election,

and the first 3 years of the presidency of Barack Obama." (Publisher's note)
Includes bibliographical references and index

My fellow citizens; the inaugural addresses of the presidents of the United States, 1789-2009. with an introduction by Arthur M. Schlesinger, Jr. and commentary by Fred L. Israel. Facts On File 2010 428p (Facts on File library of American history) $45   352.23
1. Presidents -- United States -- Inaugural addresses
ISBN 978-0-8160-8253-7; 0-8160-8253-7
                                        LC 2009-32184

First published 2007
"Features the original text of all 56 inaugural speeches, each with an explanatory essay." Publisher's note

Owen, Roger
The **rise** and fall of Arab presidents for life; Roger Owen. Harvard University Press 2012 xi, 248 p.p (alk. paper) $24.95   352.23
1. Dictators 2. Presidents -- Middle East 3. Middle East -- Politics and government 4. Monarchy -- Middle East 5. Monarchy -- Arab countries 6. Authoritarianism -- Middle East 7. Middle East -- Kings and rulers 8. Arab countries -- Kings and rulers 9. Authoritarianism -- Arab countries 10. Presidents -- Middle East -- History 11. Presidents -- Arab countries -- History 12. Middle East -- Politics and government -- 1945- 13. Arab countries -- Politics and government -- 1945-
ISBN 0674065832; 9780674065833
                                        LC 2011045764
This book, by Roger Owen, examines the political history of Arab political regimes in the 20th century. "Monarchical presidential regimes in the Arab world looked as though they would last indefinitely--until events in Tunisia and Egypt made clear their time was up. This . . . book [seeks] to lay bare the dynamics of a governmental system that largely defined the Arab Middle East in the twentieth century, and the popular opposition they engendered." (Publisher's note)
Includes bibliographical references (p. 217-226) and index

Raphael, Ray
Mr. president; how and why the founders created a chief executive. by Ray Raphael. Alfred A. Knopf 2012 324 p.   352.23
1. Executive power -- United States 2. Founding Fathers of the United States 3. Presidents -- United States -- Biography 4. Constitutional conventions -- United States 5. United States -- Politics and government -- 1783-1809 6. Presidents -- United States -- History -- 18th century
ISBN 9780307595270
                                        LC 2011033471
This book presents a "biography of the Constitutional Convention and the herculean task faced by the representatives. The author paints a picture of heroes--Edmund Randolph, George Mason, James Wilson and James Madison, among others--noting that the founders developed a government presupposing that George Washington would be the first chief executive. . . . In order to show how their views

evolved as they toiled, Raphael explores the founders' writings in chronological order." (Kirkus Reviews)

Includes bibliographical references (p. [289]-309) and index

State of the union; presidential rhetoric from Woodrow Wilson to George W. Bush. CQ Press 2007 1185p il $140   **352.23**
1. American speeches 2. Presidents -- United States -- Messages 3. Presidents -- United States -- Inaugural addresses 4. United States -- Politics and government -- Sources
ISBN 978-0-87289-433-4; 0-87289-433-9

LC 2006-35973

"This volume includes over 100 full-text addresses delivered by Presidents from 1913 to 2006 and comes complete with prefatory notes for context." Libr J
Includes bibliographical references

352.3   Executive management

Moynihan, Daniel Patrick, 1927-2003
√ **Secrecy**; the American experience. {by} Daniel Patrick Moynihan; introduction by Richard Gid Powers. Yale Univ. Press 1998 262p il $38; pa $16   **352.3**
1. Executive power 2. National security -- United States
ISBN 0-300-07756-4; 0-300-08079-4 pa

LC 98-8144

"Using his background as chairman of the bipartisan Commission on Protecting and Reducing Government Secrecy, Moynihan provides a fascinating account of the development of secrecy as a mode of regulation for the U.S. government since World War I: how it was born, how world events shaped it, how it has adversely affected momentous political decisions—dropping the bomb on Hiroshima, the Bay of Pigs fiasco, the Iran-contra affair—and how it has eluded efforts to curtail or end it." America
Includes bibliographical references

352.4   Financial administration and budgets

Kramer, Mattea
√ ★ A **people's** guide to the federal budget; National Priorities Project ; written by Mattea Kramer ... [et al.] ; foreword by Barbara Ehrenreich ; afterword by Josh Silver. Interlink Books 2012 219 p. (pbk.) $15.00   **352.4**
1. Budget -- United States 2. United States. Congress 3. United States -- Appropriations and expenditures 4. Fiscal policy -- United States 5. Budget deficits -- United States 6. Government spending policy -- United States
ISBN 1566568870; 9781566568876

LC 2012007930

This book focuses on U.S. fiscal policy, government spending, and the federal budget. It "addresses such issues as discretionary and mandatory spending; how the federal government creates a budget; where the money comes from

and goes; and the federal debt. . . . Other important priorities include construction of roads and highways, law enforcement, and veterans' assistance." (Booklist)
Includes bibliographical references.

353   Specific fields of public administration

Gentry, Curt
√ **J.** Edgar Hoover; the man and the secrets. Norton 1991 846p il hardcover o.p. pa $17.95   **353**
1. FBI officials 2. United States -- Federal Bureau of Investigation
ISBN 0-393-32128-2 pa

LC 90-30576

The author "has based his account of Hoover on more than 300 interviews and on access to previously classified FBI documents. . . . Gentry paints a portrait of Hoover as the 'indispensable man,' with many provocative revelations about his political dealings." Libr J
Includes bibliographical references

353.9   Public administration of safety, sanitation, waste control

Hilts, Philip J.
√ ★ **Protecting** America's health; the FDA, business, and one hundred years of regulation. University of North Carolina Press 2004 394p pa $19.95 **353.9**
1. Drug industry 2. Food adulteration and inspection 3. Food -- Law and legislation 4. United States -- Food and Drug Administration
ISBN 978-0-8078-5582-9; 0-8078-5582-0
First published 2003 by Knopf
"This fascinating look at the inside story reveals how disastrous unfettered capitalism would be without reasonable regulation." Booklist
Includes bibliographical references

355   Military science

★ **Amazons** to fighter pilots; a biographical dictionary of military women. Reina Pennington, editor; foreword by Gerhard Weinberg. Greenwood Press 2003 2v il set $175   **355**
1. Reference books 2. Women soldiers -- Biography -- Dictionaries
ISBN 0-313-29197-7

LC 2002-44777

"Entries profile over 300 remarkable women of the military, covering such groups as the Amazons, women in the Spanish Civil War, and Native Americans. . . . Additional tidbits—quotations, statistics, information on women and war—appear in sidebars throughout the text. Lists grouping entries by geographical regions, time periods, and branch of service serve as finding aids for researchers." Publisher's note

"This peerless work, situated at the nexus of military history and women's studies, is an essential companion to more male-biased biographical resources." Choice

Includes bibliographical references

Arnold, James R.

Jungle of snakes; a century of counterinsurgency warfare from the Philippines to Iraq. Bloomsbury Press 2009 291p map $28 **355**

1. Military history 2. Counterinsurgency
ISBN 978-1-59691-503-9; 1-59691-503-X

LC 2008-54018

The author "studies past insurgency responses to help clarify the U.S. efforts in Iraq. The author investigates four counterinsurgencies that either proved successful in putting down rebellion—the United States in the Philippines following war with Spain in 1898; the British response to the Malayan Emergency in 1948—or disastrous—the French invasion of Algeria in 1830; the U.S. quagmire in Vietnam—and offers lessons to be drawn from them. . . . A reasonably argued work that delivers needed insight and historical precedent to the current war debate." Kirkus

Includes bibliographical references

Axelrod, Alan

★ The **encyclopedia** of the American armed forces. Facts on File 2005 2v il (Facts on File library of American history) set $175 **355**

1. Reference books 2. United States -- Armed forces -- Encyclopedias
ISBN 0-8160-4700-6

LC 2004-20549

"The four sections each document a major branch of the United States military: Army, Navy, Marine Corps, and Air Force. Each branch has an initial list of entries, a list of branch-specific abbreviations and acronyms, and a short bibliography." Choice

Includes bibliographical references

Bacevich, Andrew J., 1947-

Washington rules; America's path to permanent war. [by] Andrew J. Bacevich. Metropolitan Books 2010 286p $25 **355**

1. Military policy -- United States 2. United States -- Foreign relations 3. United States -- Military policy -- Decision making 4. United States -- Foreign relations -- Decision making
ISBN 978-0-8050-9141-0; 0-8050-9141-6

LC 2010-06302

"From Harry S. Truman's presidency to today, Bacevich argues, Americans have trumpeted the credo that they alone must 'lead, save, liberate and ultimately transform the world.'" (N Y Times Book Rev) Index.

"The U.S. spends more on the military than the entire rest of the world combined and maintains 300,000 troops abroad in an 'empire of bases,' all part of a credo of global leadership and a consensus that the U.S. must maintain a state of semiwar. . . . [The author offers an] analysis of the assumptions behind the credo of global leadership and eternal military vigilance that has become increasingly expensive and unsustainable." Booklist

Includes bibliographical references

★ **Barron's** how to prepare for the ASVAB; Armed Services Vocational Aptitude Battery. compiled by the Editorial Department of Barron's Educational Series, Inc; edited by Terry L. Duran. 8th ed.; Barron's Educ. Ser. 2006 484p il pa $18.99 **355**

1. United States -- Armed forces -- Examinations
ISBN 0-7641-3281-4; 978-0-7641-3281-0

First published 1984. Frequently revised

This study guide includes practice examinations and a review of pertinent subject areas.

Belfiore, Michael

★ The **department** of mad scientists; how DARPA is remaking our world, from the Internet to artificial limbs. Smithsonian Books/Harper 2009 xxiii, 295p $26.99; ebook $12.99 **355**

1. Science -- Governmental policy 2. United States -- Advanced Research Projects Agency
ISBN 978-0-06-157793-2; 0-06-157793-6; 978-0-06-195937-0 ebook; 0-06-195937-5 ebook

LC 2009-18015

"Founded by Eisenhower in response to Sputnik and the Soviet space program, DARPA [Defense Advanced Research Projects Agency] mixes military officers with sneaker-wearing scientists, seeking paradigm-shifting ideas in varied fields—from energy, robotics, and rockets to peopleless operating rooms, driverless cars, and planes that can fly halfway around the world in just hours. DARPA gave birth to the Internet, GPS, and mind-controlled robotic arms. . . . Michael Belfiore was given unprecedented access to write this first-ever popular account of DARPA." Bookmarks

Includes bibliographical references

The **Book** of war; edited by John Keegan. Viking 1999 492p hardcover o.p. pa $17 **355**

1. Military history
ISBN 0-14-029655-7 pa

LC 99-42660

This is an "anthology of eyewitness and participant writing covering 25 centuries, from Thucydides' history of the Peloponnesian War to a small-unit engagement between British and Iraqi infantry in the Persian Gulf war." N Y Times Book Rev

Includes bibliographical references

Boot, Max

★ **War** made new; technology, warfare, and the course of history, 1500 to today. Gotham Books 2006 624p il map $24.95 **355**

1. Military history 2. Military art and science
ISBN 978-1-592-40222-9; 1-592-40222-4

LC 2006-15518

"Throughout, Boot provides a vivid and engaging mix of historical narrative and analysis, showing the bloody real-world results of abstract decisionmaking about the nature and degree of a country's military preparedness. His twelve case studies, stretching from the defeat of the Spanish Armada to the current situation in Iraq, point to a variety of disparate lessons but some themes that are surprisingly constant over time and space." Commentary

Buckley, Gail Lumet

★ **American** patriots; the story of Blacks in the military from the Revolution to Desert Storm. [by] Gail Buckley. Random House 2001 xxiv, 534p il hardcover o.p. pa $15.95 **355**

    1. African American soldiers 2. United States -- Race relations 3. United States -- Military history

    ISBN 0-375-50279-3; 0-375-76009-1 pa

                  LC 00-51825

This is an account "of blacks in the U.S. military, both at home and abroad, from the 1770s to the 1990s. . . . This readable, spirited story deserves a place in every U.S. history collection, as well as in the black or military collections." Libr J

    Includes bibliographical references

Carroll, James

House of war; the Pentagon and the disastrous rise of American power. Houghton Mifflin Co. 2006 657p il $30 **355**

    1. Military policy -- United States 2. United States -- Dept. of Defense 3. Pentagon (Arlington, Va.: Building)

    ISBN 0-618-18780-4; 978-0-618-18780-5

               LC 2005-24014

"Chronicling the ascent of America's military establishment from 1943 to the aftermath of 9/11, Carroll uses the Pentagon as a metaphor for a U.S. political culture that values military power over human rights and seeks to project U.S. influence and values abroad by force, if necessary, whether invited by other countries or not. . . . Certain to be a widely read and discussed book, this is worthy of space on the shelves of all libraries." Libr J

    Includes bibliographical references

Clausewitz, Carl von

★ **On** war; {by} Carl von Clausewitz; edited and translated by Michael Howard and Peter Paret; introductory essays by Peter Paret, Michael Howard and Bernard Brodie; with commentary by Bernard Brodie. Princeton Univ. Press 1976 717p $95; pa $26.95 **355**

    1. War 2. Military art and science

    ISBN 0-691-05657-9; 0-691-01854-5 pa

    Original German edition, 1833

"Drawing on the experiences of Frederick the Great and Napoleon, Clausewitz tried to analyze the workings of military genius by isolating the factors that decide success in war. His conclusions have remained generally applicable, and since his work contains a minimum of technical discussion, it has retained a wide appeal." Ency Britannica

Cohen, Eliot A.

Conquered into liberty. Free Press 2011 405p il map $30; ebook $14.99 **355**

    1. New York (State) -- History 2. United States -- Military history 3. United States -- History -- 1755-1763, French and Indian War

    ISBN 978-0-7432-4990-4; 978-1-4516-2733-6 ebook

              LC 2011023717

It was the author's intent to demonstrate "that there is more to the American military heritage than the U.S.'s conventional war-fighting and its European antecedents. We should expand the concept of 'American' to include pre-revolutionary times, and so include nearly 200 years of frontier fighting . . . . In . . . [an] examination of 18th-century warfare along the northeastern seaboard . . . Cohen sees two less-appreciated sources for the way Americans currently fight. First was the birth of a unique strain of raiding, ambushing, subversion, living off the land, ad hoc alliance-building with indigenous peoples, long-range reconnaissance, and patrolling behind enemy lines. Second, writes Cohen, was the very fact that these non-traditional tactics were rooted in the distinctiveness of colonial society. . . . Cohen believes that this legacy endures". (National Review)

This is "an engaging account of the wars fought on the 'Great Warpath.' These were the trails, especially around Lakes George and Champlain, which marked a kind of western border for early settlers. The author recounts the eight major battles in those successive campaigns. He includes two naval battles: Plattsburgh, during the War of 1812, and Valcour Island in 1776, both of which he presents as decisive but underrated contributions to securing the young republic from foreign threat. . . . A delightful-to-read piece of American history." Kirkus

    Includes bibliographical references

Daalder, Ivo H.

In the shadow of the Oval Office; profiles of the national security advisers and the presidents they served: from JFK to George W. Bush. [by] Ivo H. Daalder and I.M. Destler. Simon & Schuster 2009 386p $27 **355**

    1. National security -- United States 2. Presidents -- United States -- Staff 3. United States -- Special Assistant to the President for National Security Affairs

    ISBN 978-1-416-55319-9; 1-416-55319-3

              LC 2008-40699

"A revealing, unsettling look at how our presidents receive advice on foreign policy." Kirkus

    Includes bibliographical references

De Pauw, Linda Grant

Battle cries and lullabies; women in war from prehistory to the present. University of Okla. Press 1998 395p il hardcover o.p. pa $21.95 **355**

    1. Women soldiers 2. Military history 3. Women -- History

    ISBN 0-8061-3288-4 pa

              LC 98-21219

"Though the book never directly states its larger claims, the wealth of evidence it provides renders the controversy over women in combat almost quaint—their presence on and near the battlefield is ancient, inescapable and irreversible." Publ Wkly

    Includes bibliographical references

★ **Dictionary** of military terms; a guide to the language of warfare and military institutions. compiled by Trevor N. Dupuy {et al.} 2nd ed; Wilson, H.W. 2003 271p il $85 **355**

    1. Reference books 2. Military art and science --

Dictionaries
ISBN 0-8242-1025-5

LC 2002-32960

First published 1986

"This is a very readable book for the general reader and will make a great addition to public, academic, and some high-school libraries as well as being useful for military professionals." Booklist

Dictionary of wars; George Childs Kohn, editor. 3rd ed.; Facts on File 2006 692p il (Facts on File library of world history) $85; pa $22.95 **355**
1. Reference books 2. Military history -- Dictionaries
ISBN 0-8160-6577-2; 978-0-8160-6577-6; 0-8160-6578-0 pa; 978-0-8160-6578-3 pa

LC 2005-58936

First published 1986

"Entries include the dates of events and a brief summary of their causes, effects, and consequences. The straightforward writing style emphasizes basic facts rather than arguments justifying or opposing each conflict. This, along with the occasional cross-references and helpful and complete general and geographic indexes, makes the encyclopedia accessible to most students." SLJ

Dower, John W.
Cultures of war; Pearl Harbor, Hiroshima, 9-11, Iraq. New Press 2010 596p il $29.95 **355**
1. Iraq War, 2003-2011 2. War and civilization 3. World War, 1939-1945 4. September 11 terrorist attacks, 2001 5. Iraq War, 2003- 6. Military policy -- United States 7. United States -- Military policy 8. War and society -- United States 9. United States -- History, Military -- 20th century 10. United States -- History, Military -- 21st century
ISBN 978-0-393-06150-5; 0-393-06150-7

LC 2010-20395

The author "draws astute ironies between Pearl Harbor and 9/11 in terms of the overweening arrogance of military superpowers. The author moves back and forth between these two definitive eras in history, providing a brilliant examination of the willful self-delusion and selective reasoning involved in the highest levels of decision making—from Japan's spectacularly ill-advised bombing of Pearl Harbor to the Bush Administration's bundling of 'weapons of mass destruction' and Osama bin Laden as justification for invasion of Iraq. . . . An unrelenting, incisive, masterly comparative study." Kirkus

Includes bibliographical references and index.

★ **Encyclopedia** of American military history; Spencer C. Tucker, general editor; associate editors David Coffey, John C. Fredriksen, Justin D. Murphy. Facts on File 2003 3v il maps set $225 **355**
1. Reference books 2. United States -- Military history -- Encyclopedias
ISBN 0-8160-4355-8

LC 2002-29658

"More than 1,200 entries cover military leaders, wars, campaigns, battles, events, famous soldiers, military branches, key technological developments, overviews of weapons systems, and more. It covers the period from the colonial wars to the present, and gives special attention to the minorities and women who have contributed significantly to American military success." Publisher's note

Includes bibliographical references

The **encyclopedia** of Middle East wars; the United States in the Persian Gulf, Afghanistan, and Iraq conflicts. Spencer C. Tucker, editor; Priscilla Mary Roberts, editor, documents volume; foreword by Anthony C. Zinni. ABC-CLIO 2010 1887p 5v il map set $495 **355**
1. Reference books 2. Iraq War, 2003- -- Encyclopedias 3. Afghan War, 2001- -- Encyclopedias 4. Persian Gulf War, 1991 -- Encyclopedias 5. Middle East -- Military history -- Encyclopedias
ISBN 978-1-85109-947-4; 978-1-85109-948-1 ebook

LC 2010-33812

"An essential resource for anyone seeking detailed information and in-depth reading on U.S. actions and involvement in the Middle East region during the last 15 years." Libr J

Includes bibliographical references

France, John
Perilous glory; the rise of western military power. John France. Yale University Press 2011 ix, 448 p.p ill., maps $35 **355**
1. War -- History 2. War and civilization 3. Military art and science -- History 4. Military history
ISBN 0300120745; 9780300120745

LC 2011006437

In this book, "[John] France acknowledges the significance of democracy . . . and technology in the nineteenth-century transformation of warfare . . . . [but] argues . . . that the resulting rise of the 'Western' style of warfare to international significance was largely fortuitous, coinciding with the decline and stagnation of the Ottomans and the Mughals, inheritors of the previously dominant form of steppe warfare that had emerged from Eurasia in antiquity." (Times Literary Supplement)

Fredriksen, John C.
American military leaders; from colonial times to the present. ABC-CLIO 1999 2v il set $175 **355**
1. Soldiers -- United States 2. United States -- Military history
ISBN 1-57607-001-8

LC 99-27929

"Prominent men and women of the military are the scope of this reference work. Coverage includes the most famous of leaders such as Grant, Patton, and Schwarzkopf; but what makes the source so outstanding is its inclusion of forgotten leaders such as Native American Stand Watie, aviator Jackie Cochran, and army educator Alden Partridge. Biographies range from two to three pages, concluding with a bibliography. Photographs and illustrations are included, and both a subject index and a list of leaders organized by their military titles can be found at the end of volume two." Am Libr

Includes bibliographical references

Gaddis, John Lewis

✓ **Surprise,** security, and the American experience. Harvard University Press 2004 150p (Joanna Jackson Goldman memorial lecture on American civilization and government) $18.95 **355**

    1. National security -- United States 2. United States -- Foreign relations

    ISBN 0-674-01174-0

                    LC 2003-56935

    The author "argues that three salient elements of President Bush's security strategy—pre-emption, unilateralism and hegemony—have deep roots in America's history." N Y Times Book Rev

    "This compact, provocative history of an idea-in-action has the potential to alter the U.S.'s collective self-image." Publ Wkly

    Includes bibliographical references

Gordin, Michael D.

✓ **Red** cloud at dawn; Truman, Stalin, and the end of the atomic monopoly. Farrar, Straus and Giroux 2009 402p il map $27 **355**

    1. Arms race 2. Presidents 3. Heads of state 4. Nuclear weapons 5. Vice-presidents 6. Senators 7. Communist leaders 8. Political leaders 9. Nuclear weapons -- History 10. World politics -- 1945-1955 11. Arms race -- History -- 20th century 12. Soviet Union -- Foreign relations -- 1945-1991 13. United States -- Foreign relations -- 1945-1953 14. Soviet Union -- Foreign relations -- United States 15. United States -- Foreign relations -- Soviet Union

    ISBN 0-374-25682-9; 978-0-374-25682-1

                    LC 2009-01424

    Gordin examines the years from 1945 to 1949 "in which only the United States possessed atomic weapons." (N Y Times Book Rev) Index.

    The author "brings considerable scholarship to the subject of how the Soviets succeeded in building an atomic bomb. He weaves an impressively wide range of sources, including new material from ex-Soviet and western archives, into a brilliant narrative about the intelligence war." Hist Today

    Includes bibliographical references

Hagedorn, Ann

✓ The **invisible** soldiers; how America outsourced our security. Ann Hagedorn. Simon & Schuster 2014 352 p. $28 **355**

    1. Private military companies 2. National security -- United States 3. United States -- Military policy 4. United States -- Politics and government

    ISBN 1416598804; 9781416598800

                    LC 2014015007

    This book, by Ann Hagedorn, is "about the privatization of America's national security. . . . [P]rivate military and security companies (PMSCs) . . . are a bona-fide industry, an indispensable part of American foreign and military policy. PMSCs assist US forces in combat operations and replace them after the military withdraws from combat zones; they guard our embassies; they play key roles in US counterterrorism strategies; and Homeland Security depends on them." (Publisher's note)

    "A brisk, disturbing account that adds to the sense that liberties taken in the war on terror have created long-term liabilities for American society." Kirkus

    Includes bibliographical references and index

Hanson, Victor Davis

✓ The **father** of us all; war and history, ancient and modern. Bloomsbury 2010 259p $25 **355**

    1. War 2. Military history

    ISBN 978-1-60819-165-9; 1-60819-165-6

                    LC 2009-41714

    "This anthology brings together 13 of Hanson's essays and reviews, revised and re-edited. They have appeared over the past decade in periodicals from the American Spectator to the New York Times. Hanson's introductory generalization that war is a human enterprise that seems inseparable from the human condition structures such subjects as an eloquent answer to the question 'Why Study War?', a defense of the historicity of the film 300, about the Persian Wars, in a masterpiece of envelope pushing, and a comprehensive and dazzling analysis of why America fights as she does. . . . The pieces are well written, sometimes elegantly so, and closely reasoned." Publ Wkly

    Includes bibliographical references

    The **soul** of battle; from ancient times to the present day, how three great liberators vanquished tyranny. Anchor Books 2001 480p pa $16.95 **355**

    1. Generals 2. Military history 3. Memoirists 4. Army officers 5. Secretaries of war

    ISBN 0-385-72059-9; 978-0-385-72059-5

                    LC 00-63979

    First published 1999 by Free Press

    "Hanson narrates the success of three military campaigns-Epaminondas defeat of the Spartans in the fourth century B.C., Sherman's march through Georgia and the Carolinas during the Civil War, and Patton's race into Germany at the head of the Third Army in 1944-45. . . . In Hanson's view, the individual traits of spontaneity and creativity that are nourished in a free society are assets, not hindrances, in warfare." Booklist

    Includes bibliographical references

Hastings, Max

✓ **Warriors**; portraits from the battlefield. Knopf 2006 xxiii, 354p il maps $27.50 **355**

    1. Soldiers 2. Military history

    ISBN 1-4000-4441-3; 978-1-4000-4441-2

                    LC 2005-44302

    The author "selects memoirs and biographies about 15 combatants (one of them a woman) and distills accounts of their lives and trenchant observations about their personalities. . . . Filled with poignant psychological insight, Hastings' remarkable sketches will provoke greater-than-average demand from the military affairs readership." Booklist

    Includes bibliographical references

Hirshson, Stanley P.

General Patton: a soldier's life. HarperCollins Pubs. 2002 xxii, 826p il maps $34.95; pa $18.95   355

    1. Generals 2. Army officers
    ISBN 0-06-000982-9; 0-06-000983-7 pa
                                LC 2002-68881

The author attempts "to round out the unknown familial aspects of Patton's life and {provide a} . . . context for understanding the enigmatic commander. . . . Those interested in Patton will find Hirshson's book valuable reading." Libr J

The author attempts "to round out the unknown familial aspects of Patton's life and {provide a} . . . context for understanding the enigmatic commander. . . . Those interested in Patton will find Hirshson's book valuable reading." Libr J

    Includes bibliographical references

Karpin, Michael I.

The bomb in the basement; how Israel went nuclear and what that means for the world. [by] Michael Karpin. Simon & Schuster 2006 404p il map $26; pa $15   355

    1. Nuclear weapons 2. Israel -- Military history
    ISBN 0-7432-6594-7; 978-0-7432-6594-2; 0-7432-6595-5 pa; 978-0-7432-6595-9 pa
                                LC 2005-51689

"For all those interested in understanding how Israel's idealistic origins dovetail with its hawkish position in the game of nuclear deterrence and fraught relationship with other countries in the Middle East, this well-researched study is a must-read." Publ Wkly

    Includes bibliographical references

Kennett, Lee B.

Sherman; a soldier's life. [by] Lee Kennett. HarperCollins Pubs. 2001 426p il maps hardcover o.p. pa $14.95   355

    1. Generals 2. Memoirists 3. Secretaries of war 4. United States -- History -- 1861-1865, Civil War
    ISBN 0-06-093074-8 pa
                                LC 2001-16687

This is a "well-balanced analytical biography." Publ Wkly

    Includes bibliographical references

Kindsvatter, Peter S.

American soldiers; ground combat in the World Wars, Korea, and Vietnam. foreword by Russell F. Weigley. University Press of Kan. 2003 432p il (Modern war studies) $34.95   355

    1. Soldiers -- United States 2. United States -- Marine Corps 3. United States -- Army -- Infantry 4. United States -- Military history
    ISBN 0-7006-1229-7
                                LC 2002-12957

"Mining twentieth-century foot soldiers' memoirs and novels, Kindsvatter integrates this literature of personal experience into a generalized assessment of what combat was like and how men reacted to it. . . . Kindsvatter's illuminating work is about coping with . . . fear at the foxhole level, and it . . . powerfully conveys the psychology and military sociology of combat in the draft-era armies." Booklist

    Includes bibliographical references

Langewiesche, William

The atomic bazaar; the rise of the nuclear poor. Farrar, Straus and Giroux 2007 179p map $22   355

    1. Arms control 2. Nuclear weapons
    ISBN 978-0-374-10678-2; 0-374-10678-9
                              LC 2006-102539

"This is the story of the inexorable drift of nuclear weapons technology from the hands of the rich into the hands of the poor. As more unstable and undeveloped nations find ways of acquiring the ultimate arms, the stakes of state-sponsored nuclear activity have soared . . . . Even more disturbing is the likelihood of such weapons being manufactured and deployed by guerrilla non-state terrorists. Langewiesche also recounts the recent history of Abdul Qadeer Khan, the scientist at the forefront of nuclear development and trade in the Middle East." Publisher's note

"Langewiesche's bracing expose of nuclear criminality blasts away the ubiquitous misinformation usually attendant on this alarming subject." Booklist

Lipsky, David

Absolutely American; four years at West Point. Houghton Mifflin 2003 317p il $25   355

    1. United States Military Academy
    ISBN 0-618-09542-X
                              LC 2002-191339

"The book must have been extremely hard to organize. And yet it reads with a novelistic flow. . . . It turns out that how teenagers get turned into leaders is not a simple story, but it is wonderfully told in this book." N Y Times Book Rev

Magill's guide to military history; editor, John Powell; managing editor, Christina J. Moose; project editor, Rowena Wildin. Salem Press 2001 5v il set $473   355

    1. Reference books 2. Military history -- Dictionaries
    ISBN 0-89356-014-6
                              LC 00-66072

This "is a worldwide, illustrated, alphabetical survey of war, weapons, battles, civilizations, people and their place in military history, ancient times to the 21st century. Its 1,518 entries and over 300 thorough essays with keywords in boldface are all indexed by category in volume 5." Choice

    Includes bibliographical references

Nicholson, Alexander

Fighting to serve; behind the scenes in the war to repeal "don't ask, don't tell" Alexander Nicholson. Chicago Review Press 2012 288 p. $26.95   355

    1. Military policy -- United States 2. Don't ask, don't tell (Military policy) 3. Nicholson, Alexander 4. Servicemembers United (United States) 5. United States. Army -- Gays -- Biography 6. Gay military personnel -- United States -- Biography 7. Gay rights -- United States -- History -- 21st century 8. Gay military personnel -- Government policy -- United States
    ISBN 1613743726; 9781613743720
                              LC 2012021821

This book "provides an . . . account of the road to repeal the 'Don't Ask, Don't Tell' (DADT) law prohibiting the open service of" LGBT "military members." Author Alexander Nicholson "offer[s] commentary on a range of incidents: being personally forced out of the army by the DADT policy; meeting and persuading former chairman of the Joint Chiefs of Staff, Gen. John Shalikashvili, of the cause's benefits . . . ; leading and speaking at rallies; and coordinating directly with the White House." (Publishers Weekly)

Phillips, Charles
★ **Encyclopedia** of wars; [by] Charles Phillips and Alan Axelrod. Facts on File 2005 3v map (Facts on File library of world history) set $300 **355**
1. Reference books 2. Military history -- Encyclopedias
ISBN 0-8160-2851-6
LC 2003-28010
Phillips and Axelrod "have produced a very readable and . . . well-researched book that both scholars and history buffs will enjoy." Booklist
Includes bibliographical references

Rhodes, Richard
Arsenals of folly; the making of the nuclear arms race. Alfred A. Knopf 2007 386p il $28.95 **355**
1. Arms race 2. Nuclear weapons
ISBN 978-0-375-41413-8; 0-375-41413-4
LC 2007-17613
"This historical record, drawing upon many firsthand accounts and interviews, details pivotal events in world history and should be necessary reading for anyone interested in 20th-century history." Libr J
Includes bibliographical references

Rose, Gideon
How wars end; why we always fight the last battle: a history of American intervention from World War I to Afghanistan. Simon & Schuster 2010 413p $27 **355**
1. War 2. War -- Termination 3. Disengagement (Military science) 4. United States -- Military policy 5. United States -- Military history 6. Military planning -- United States
ISBN 978-1-4165-9053-8; 1-4165-9053-6
LC 2010-34817
"Surveying the settlements of America's wars since WWI, Rose analyzes reasons for the manner and substance of their conclusions. . . . Public spirited and accessible, Rose's presentation should impress anyone hoping for better management of war and peace by Washington." Booklist
Includes bibliographical references

Rosenbaum, Ron
How the end begins; the road to a nuclear World War III. Simon & Schuster 2011 304p $28; ebook $14.99 **355**
1. World War III 2. Nuclear warfare 3. Nuclear weapons
ISBN 978-1-4165-9421-5; 978-1-4391-9007-4 ebook
LC 2010-22474

This book "raises fundamental questions more acutely than dozens of other recent books on the nuclear problem. There is much to learn from it." N Y Times Book Rev
Includes bibliographical references

Ruggero, Ed
Duty first; West Point and the making of American leaders. HarperCollins Pubs. 2001 342p il $27.50; pa $14.95 **355**
1. Leadership 2. United States Military Academy
ISBN 0-06-019317-4; 0-06-093133-7 pa
LC 00-59775
In this report about the contemporary West Point experience, the author "tries to explain precisely what makes the United States Military Academy, better known as West Point, a breeding ground for future leaders." Publ Wkly

Singer, P. W.
Wired for war; the robotics revolution and conflict in the twenty-first century. Penguin Press 2009 499p il $29.95 **355**
1. Robots 2. Military weapons 3. Military art and science
ISBN 978-1-59420-198-1; 1-59420-198-6
This is "a vivid picture of the current controversies and dazzling possibilities of war in the digital age." Kirkus
Includes bibliographical references

Sites, Kevin
The **things** they cannot say; stories soldiers won't tell you about what they've seen, done or failed to do in war. Kevin Sites. HarperCollins 2013 336 p. $15.99 **355**
1. Soldiers -- Psychology 2. Afghan War, 2001- -- Personal narratives 3. Iraq War, 2003-2011 -- Personal narratives
ISBN 0061990523; 9780061990526
In this book author Kevin Sites asks soldiers, "many of whom Sites first met while in Afghanistan and Iraq, . . . difficult questions. . . . One struggles to recover from a head injury he believes has stolen his ability to love; another attempts to make amends for the killing of an innocent man; yet another finds respect for the enemy fighter who tried to kill him. Sites also shares the unsettling narrative of his own failures during war--including his complicity in a murder." (Publisher' note)

Sunzi bing fa
★ The **illustrated** art of war; [by] Sun Tzu; the definitive English translation by Samuel B. Griffith. Oxford University Press 2005 272p il map $29.95 **355**
1. Military art and science
ISBN 0-19-518999-X; 978-0-19-518999-5
LC 2005-10651
An illustrated version of The art of war, a military treatise written in China during the 6th century BC discussing different military tactics and strategies.
Includes bibliographical references

Sutherland, Jonathan

★ **African** Americans at war; an encyclopedia. [by] Jonathan D. Sutherland. ABC-CLIO 2004 2v set $185 **355**

1. Reference books 2. African American soldiers 3. United States -- Armed forces -- Encyclopedias 4. African Americans -- Biography -- Encyclopedias

ISBN 1-57607-746-2

LC 2003-21501

"There are more than 250 [alphabetically arranged] entries conveying biographical, thematic, and conceptual information. Well-known leaders (Colin Powell), groups (Buffalo Soldiers), specific units [and battles] . . . have their own entries. . . . This is a superb resource for any . . . library looking to enrich its history, military or African American studies collections." Booklist

★ **Voices** of war; stories of service from the home front and the front lines. edited by Tom Wiener. National Geographic Society 2004 336p il $30; pa $6.95 **355**

1. Veterans 2. United States -- Military history 3. United States -- Armed forces -- Military life

ISBN 0-7922-7838-0; 0-7922-4204-1 pa

LC 2004-49986

This book showcases "the oral histories collected by the Veteran's History Project, the Library of Congress's nationwide effort to collect and preserve the stories not only of war veterans, but also of those who served in support of the frontline troops. . . . The personal accounts cover the major conflicts of the 20th century, from World War I to the Persian Gulf War, and include letters, diaries, and journals. The chapters are nicely arranged to show the commonalities of military experience, e.g., basic training, daily life, combat, the home front, and returning home." Libr J

★ **War:** from ancient Egypt to Iraq; editorial consultant, Saul David. DK 2009 512p il $50 **355**

1. Reference books 2. War -- Encyclopedias 3. Military history -- Encyclopedias

ISBN 978-0-7566-5572-3

LC 2010-278612

"From the Punic wars to the Crusades to the wars of the league of Cognac and modern conflicts like those in the former Yugoslavia, War is an outstanding catalog of conflict. Each of the seven chapters . . . opens with a time line and is peppered with sidebars of military superlatives such as youngest commanders, famous female warriors, and even landmark war movies. . . . An essential reference title for all libraries." Libr J

355.009 History, geographic treatment, biography

Brands, H. W.

★ The **man** who saved the union; Ulysses Grant in war and peace. H. W. Brands. Doubleday 2012 736 p. $35.00 **355.009**

1. Civil rights 2. Presidents -- United States 3. Generals -- United States -- Biography 4. Presidents

-- United States -- Biography

ISBN 0385532415; 9780385532419

LC 2011043795

This book offers a biography of U.S. President Ulysses S. Grant. Here, "Pulitzer [prize] finalist [H. W.] Brands . . . treats Grant's entire life, showing its full arc. He breaks with earlier interpretations . . . , concluding that Grant did the best he could in trying circumstances, particularly in the area of civil and minority rights." (Library Journal)

Keegan, John

Fields of battle; the wars for North America. Knopf 1996 348p il maps hardcover o.p. pa $15 **355.009**

1. North America -- Military history

ISBN 0-679-42413-X; 0-679-74664-1 pa

LC 96-154385

First published 1995 in the United Kingdom with title: Warpaths: travels of a military historian in North America

The author "demonstrates how North America's geography has influenced its history: how its mountain chains and river systems have determined where people fought, and fought repeatedly. For example, the defenses that Cornwallis built at Yorktown to deter American forces were improved and reused by the Confederates almost a century later. Keegan's tour of the continent skips the Mexican War, and his book is atypically discursive. For Americans, the charm is the familiarity of its sites—Brooklyn, Pittsburgh, Laramie, and other home towns." New Yorker

★ **New** York at war; Steven H. Jaffe. Basic Books 2012 p. cm. **355.009**

1. War 2. New York (N.Y.) -- History, Military

ISBN 9780465029709; 9780465036424

LC 2012000454

In this book "historian Steven H. Jaffe offers a . . . history of New York City" from a local, military perspective. "Beginning with an Indian attack on one of Henry Hudson's crewmen (who in 1609 became the first recorded fatality of an act of war in the region's history), Jaffe describes, in turn, each of the city's encounters with war over the past four centuries. . . . [including] how New York became hugely powerful . . . during the Civil War . . . during the build-up to World War I . . . during World War II, and in the atomic era." The book's scope discusses the impact of military and ethnic conflicts in the city "stretching from the colonial era to 9/11 and beyond." (Publisher's note)

Includes bibliographical references

The **Oxford** companion to American military history; editor in chief, John Whiteclay Chambers II; editors, Fred Anderson [et al.] Oxford Univ. Press 1999 xxxiv, 916p il maps $75 **355.009**

1. Reference books 2. United States -- Military history -- Dictionaries

ISBN 0-19-507198-0

LC 99-21181

This reference work covers "battles and soldiers, ships and weapons, services and doctrines—as well as the social and cultural impact of the U.S. military at home and around the world. . . . There are entries on relevant acts of Congress and on diplomatic policies such as the Monroe Doctrine and the Marshall Plan; on peace and antiwar movements; on war in film, literature, music, and photography; and on war viewed through the disciplinary lenses of anthropology, economics, gender studies, and psychology." Publisher's note

Includes bibliographical references

Reader's guide to military history; edited by Charles Messenger. Fitzroy Dearborn Pubs. 2001 xxxvi, 948p $135   **355.009**
1. Military history
ISBN 1-57958-241-9

LC 2002-275907

Topics covered "include land, sea, and air services; conflicts; types of warfare; military theory; prominent military leaders; and national armed services. . . . {This} is a unique, well-designed reference tool." Booklist

Includes bibliographical references

Ricks, Thomas E.
★ The **generals**; American military command from World War II to today. Thomas E. Ricks. Penguin Press 2012 576 p.   **355.009**
1. Command of troops 2. United States -- Military history 3. Generals -- United States -- History -- 20th century 4. Command of troops -- History -- 20th century -- Case studies 5. United States -- History, Military -- 20th century -- Case studies
ISBN 1594204047; 9781594204043

LC 2012015110

This book, by Thomas E. Ricks, presents an overview of U.S. military leadership since 1945. "History has been kind to the American generals of World War II--Marshall, Eisenhower, Patton, and Bradley--and less kind to the generals of the wars that followed. . . . Thomas E. Ricks sets out to explain why that is. . . . [W]e meet great leaders and suspect ones, generals who rose to the occasion and those who failed themselves and their soldiers." (Publisher's note)

Includes bibliographical references and index

Wheelan, Joseph
★ **Terrible** swift sword; the life of General Philip H. Sheridan. Joseph Wheelan. Da Capo Press 2012 387 p. (hardcover : alk. paper) $26   **355.009**
1. Native Americans -- History 2. United States -- History -- 1861-1865, Civil War -- Campaigns 3. United States. Army -- Biography 4. Generals -- United States -- Biography 5. Indians of North America -- Wars -- 1866-1895 6. United States -- History -- Civil War, 1861-1865 -- Campaigns
ISBN 0306820277; 9780306820274; 9780306821097

LC 2012018587

This book, by Joseph Wheelan, is a biography of the Civil War general Philip H. Sheridan. "Sheridan is the least known of the triumvirate of generals most responsible for winning the Civil War. . . . It was General Sheridan who introduced scorched-earth warfare to the South. . . . After the war, Sheridan ruthlessly suppressed the raiding Plains Indians much as he had the Confederates, . . . but he also defended reservation Indians from corrupt agents and contractors." (Publisher's note)

Includes bibliographical references and index

355.02   War and warfare

Gentile, Gian P.
Wrong turn; America's deadly embrace of counterinsurgency. Colonel Gian Gentile. The New Press 2013 208 p. (hardback) $24.95   **355.02**
1. Counterinsurgency 2. Iraq War, 2003-2011 3. Counterinsurgency -- Case studies 4. Counterinsurgency -- Iraq -- History -- 21st century 5. Counterinsurgency -- Malaya -- History -- 20th century 6. Counterinsurgency -- Government policy -- United States 7. Counterinsurgency -- Vietnam -- History -- 20th century 8. Counterinsurgency -- Afghanistan -- History -- 21st century
ISBN 1595588744; 9781595588746

LC 2012049114

In this book about the U.S. Iraq war, Gian Gentile "argues that the U.S. military's appropriation of COIN [counterinsurgency], a strategy with a long and fraught history, as the author explains, was a dangerously misguided attempt 'to refight the Vietnam War—but this time in Iraq.' COIN, in Gentile's estimation, is little more than 'a recipe for perpetual war.'" (Publishers Weekly)

Includes bibliographical references and index

Hedges, Chris
War is a force that gives us meaning. PublicAffairs 2002 211p $23   **355.02**
1. War
ISBN 1-58648-049-9

LC 2002-68136

"War can only be sustained, Hedges affirms, by imbuing events with meanings they do not have. These 'mythic realities' are essential to suspending the normal rules of human behavior and justifying the mayhem and personal sacrifice war entails. Each side comes to see itself as the embodiment of absolute goodness; each demonizes the other and reduces its enemies to objects. The killing is thus made easy, but communication is impossible." New Leader

"This should be required reading in this post-9/11 world." Libr J

Includes bibliographical references

Scahill, Jeremy
Dirty wars; the world is a battlefield. Jeremy Scahill. Nation Books 2013 680 p. (hbk.) $29.99   **355.02**
1. Military intelligence 2. Terrorism -- Prevention 3. Military art and science 4. United States -- History, Military -- 21st century 5. United States -- Military policy -- History -- 21st century 6. Targeted killing -- United States -- History -- 21st century 7. United States -- Military policy -- Moral and ethical aspects 8. Intelligence service -- United States -- History -- 21st century 9. Special operations (Military science) -- United States -- History -- 21st century 10. Terrorism -- Prevention -- United States -- Government policy -- History -- 21st century
ISBN 156858671X; 9781568586717

LC 2012051769

In this book, author Jeremy Scahill "questions the legality and command methods of the ongoing war against al-Qaida. Focusing on the career of Anwar al Awlaki, an American citizen and reported al-Qaida leader killed by a drone in Yemen, and the evolution of special forces-led global strikes, the author seeks to establish his case that Barack Obama's military policies are best seen as a continuation of the policies of George W. Bush." (Kirkus Reviews)

Includes bibliographical references (pages 531-613) and index

Wilson, Ward

Five myths about nuclear weapons; Ward Wilson. Houghton Mifflin Harcourt 2013 208 p. $22 **355.02**
1. Arms control 2. Nuclear warfare 3. Nuclear weapons 4. Strategy 5. Nuclear weapons -- Psychological aspects
ISBN 054785787X; 9780547857879
LC 2012017322

This book, by Ward Wilson, offers a "rethinking of the power and purpose of nuclear weapons--and a call for radical action. Nuclear weapons have always been a serious but seemingly insoluble problem: while they're obviously dangerous, they are also, apparently, necessary. This . . . study shows why five central arguments promoting nuclear weapons are, in essence, myths." (Publisher's note)

"This slim, persuasively argued, tightly written book provides much food for thought." Booklist

355.1   Military life and customs

Scott, Jeff

Raising children in the military; Cheryl Lawhorne-Scott, Don Philpott, and Jeff Scott. Rowman & Littlefield 2014 224 p. (Military life) (cloth : alk. paper) $36 **355.1**
1. Children of military personnel 2. Child rearing -- United States -- Handbooks, manuals, etc 3. United States -- Armed Forces -- Military life -- Handbooks, manuals, etc 4. Families of military personnel -- United States -- Handbooks, manuals, etc
ISBN 1442227486; 9781442227484
LC 2013046688

This book by Cheryl Lawhorne-Scott, Don Philpott, and Jeff Scott, part of the Military Life series, describes how "[m]ilitary life places unique demands on military families with children including frequent moves, disruptions in schooling, family separation, health care issues, loss of friends. . . . It also covers other critical issues such as wellness, family solidarity, benefits, insurance and problems such as addiction and domestic violence." (Publisher's note)

"This is a helpful guide aimed at the special challenges of military families." Booklist

355.3   Organization and personnel of military forces

Geraghty, Tony

Soldiers of fortune; a history of the mercenary in modern warfare. Pegasus Books 2009 392p il $27.95 **355.3**
1. Mercenary soldiers
ISBN 978-1-60598-048-5; 1-60598-048-X

"Covering the 1960s to the present, with revealing interviews, Geraghty looks at the virtues and failings of the world's second-oldest profession. . . . This serious study should find its way to most readers of military history." Libr J

Includes bibliographical references

Lawhorne-Scott, Cheryl

★ **Military** mental health care; a guide for service members, veterans, families, and community. Cheryl Lawhorne and Don Philpott. Rowman & Littlefield Publishers, Inc. 2012 240 p. (Military life) (cloth : alk. paper) $34.95 **355.3**
1. Mental health services 2. Military personnel -- Health and hygiene 3. Psychology, Military -- Handbooks, manuals, etc 4. Veterans' families -- United States -- Handbooks, manuals, etc 5. Soldiers -- Mental health -- United States -- Handbooks, manuals, etc 6. Veterans -- Mental health -- United States -- Handbooks, manuals, etc
ISBN 1442220937; 9781442220935; 9781442220942
LC 2012034879

This book is a "reference guide on mental health for returning veterans. Chapters cover problems (e.g., PTSD, head injuries), symptoms (e.g., stress, anger, depression), social issues (e.g., suicide, homelessness, family relationships), resilience, and wellness. Self-help sections include bulleted lists, suggested websites, and resources from the Veterans Administration and other service agencies." (Library Journal)

Includes bibliographical references and index

Paglen, Trevor

Blank spots on the map; the dark geography of the Pentagon's secret world. Dutton/Penguin Group 2009 324p il map **355.3**
1. Military bases 2. Intelligence service -- United States
ISBN 9780525951018
LC 2008042862

The author "explores the clandestine activities of the U.S. military and the CIA, giving readers a thorough and provocative tour of places that officially do not exist. Paglen has a brisk reporting style and is an engaging storyteller. His journey into what he calls the 'black world' of classified locations—from research facilities to secret prisons—this time takes him across the country and around the world." Libr J

Includes bibliographical references

355.4 Military operations

Kilcullen, David

The **accidental** guerrilla; fighting small wars in the midst of a big one. Oxford University Press 2009 xxviii, 346p il map $27.95 **355.4**

1. Guerrilla warfare 2. War on terrorism

ISBN 978-0-19-536834-5

LC 2008-54870

This "excellent book has an anthropologist's sense of social dynamics and a reporter's eye for telling detail. . . . [The author's] account of how the Americans use soft and hard power to pacify parts of eastern Afghanistan . . . should be compulsory reading in military academies on both sides of the Atlantic." Economist

Includes bibliographical references

355.5 Military training

Man, John

Ninja; 1,000 years of the shadow warrior. John Man. William Morrow 2013 304 p. (hardcover) $25.99 **355.5**

1. Ninja 2. Ninjutsu 3. Ninja -- History 4. Ninjutsu -- History

ISBN 0062222023; 9780062222022

LC 2012031912

This book, by John Man, offers a popular history "of the Japanese stealth assassins. . . . [The book] is a . . . blend of mythology, anthropology, travelogue, and history of the legendary shadow warriors. Spies, assassins, saboteurs, and secret agents, Ninja have become the subject of countless legends that continue to enthrall us in modern movies, video games, and comics--and their arts are still practiced in our time by dedicated acolytes who study the ancient techniques." (Publisher's note)

Includes bibliographical references and index

355.6 Military administration

Vogel, Steve

The **Pentagon**; a history: the untold story of the wartime race to build the Pentagon--and to restore it sixty years later. Random House 2007 xxv, 626p il map $32.95 **355.6**

1. Public buildings -- United States 2. United States -- Dept. of Defense 3. Pentagon (Arlington, Va.: Building)

ISBN 978-1-4000-6303-1; 1-4000-6303-5

LC 2006-50873

Vogel's "work recounts the construction of one of the world's most iconic buildings—the Pentagon. But more compelling by far, he relates the human stories underlying this huge construction effort. . . . All this would of itself be enough to warrant a book but Vogel plunges on to an appropriate second story: the terrorist assault of 9/11 and the Pentagon's subsequent resurrection. This section of the book, due perhaps to the proximity of the event, is all the more compelling." New York Post

Includes bibliographical references

355.8 Military equipment and supplies (Mat??riel)

Baggott, J. E.

The **first** war of physics; the secret history of the atom bomb, 1939-1949. [by] Jim Baggott. Pegasus Books 2010 576p il $35 **355.8**

1. Atomic bomb

ISBN 978-1-60598-084-3; 1-60598-084-6

First published 2009 in the United Kingdom with title: Atomic

"Baggott contributes a novel perspective to the story, looking at the Anglo-American, German, and Soviet atomic programs, and as such provides a broad thematic history." Libr J

Includes bibliographical references

Light, Michael

100 suns, 1945-1962. Knopf 2003 208p il $49.95 **355.8**

1. Nuclear weapons -- Pictorial works

ISBN 1-4000-4113-9

LC 2003-106275

"The 'suns' Light presents to readers in this . . . photography collection are manmade: aboveground atomic detonations captured on film both in the Nevada desert and at sea, terrifyingly beautiful images that remind readers of the apocalyptic might of nuclear weapons." Booklist

Includes bibliographical references

Pollack, Kenneth M.

Unthinkable; Iran, the Bomb, and American Strategy. Kenneth M. Pollack. Simon & Schuster 2013 560 p. illustration, maps $30 **355.8**

1. Nuclear weapons 2. Iran -- Foreign relations -- United States 3. United States -- Foreign relations -- Iran 4. Nuclear weapons -- Iran 5. Nuclear nonproliferation -- Iran 6. Iran -- Politics and government -- 21st century 7. Nuclear arms control -- Government policy -- United States

ISBN 1476733929; 9781476733920

LC 2013431171

In this book on U.S. relations with Iran, author Kenneth Pollack "clearly states his preference for containment but not before thoroughly exploring the pros and cons of a military attack (including one by Israel) and not without conceding the dangers of the policy he recommends. As the Cold War demonstrated, the path of nuclear deterrence and containment is a difficult slog, but this choice . . . is likely less bad than the alternative." (Kirkus Reviews)

Includes bibliographical references (pages 429-512) and index

Preston, Diana

Before the fallout; from Marie Curie to Hiroshima. Walker 2005 438p il $27 **355.8**

1. Atomic bomb

ISBN 0-8027-1445-5

LC 2004-61953

"Avidly researched and gracefully constructed, Preston's revelatory history is rich in telling moments, powerful personalities, intense confrontations, and indelible images of the devastation delivered by nuclear weapons, our Damoclean sword." Booklist

Includes bibliographical references

356   Specific kinds of military forces and warfare

Carney, John T.

No room for error; the covert operations of America's special tactics units from Iran to Afghanistan. {by} John T. Carney Jr. and Benjamin F. Schemmer. Ballantine Books 2003 334p il map $25.95   **356**
1. Military art and science   2. United States -- Army -- Special Forces
ISBN 0-345-45333-6

LC 2002-28158

The author's "dramatic tales place special operations history in perspective, particularly as the war in Afghanistan has been led by special forces units." Publ Wkly

Includes bibliographical references

Clancy, Tom

Special forces; a guided tour of U.S. Army Special Forces. written with John Gresham. Berkley Bks. 2001 366p il pa $16   **356**
1. United States -- Special Operations Command
ISBN 0-425-17268-6

LC 00-65121

"The book covers recruitment and training of personnel . . . equipment, which includes an exotic mixture of high, low, and no tech components; and the variety of missions special forces execute." Booklist

Includes bibliographical references

Couch, Dick

Sua sponte; the forging of a modern American Ranger. Dick Couch. Berkley Books 2012 364 p.   **356**
1. Commando troops 2. United States. Army 3. Special forces (Military science) -- United States 4. United States. Army. Ranger Regiment, 75th 5. United States. Army -- Commando troops -- Training of 6. United States. Army. Ranger Regiment, 75th -- Recruiting, enlistment, etc
ISBN 0425247589; 9780425247587

LC 2011038693

This book, by Dick Couch, profiles the U.S. Army Rangers. "They stand alone, even among our other Special Operations forces, as the most active brigade-sized force in the current Global War on Terrorism. . . . Granted . . . access to the training of this highly-restricted component of America's Special Operations Forces in a time of war, . . . Couch tells the personal story of the young men who begin this difficult and dangerous journey to become a Ranger." (Publisher's note)

Halevi, Yossi Klein

Like dreamers; the story of the Israeli paratroopers who reunited Jerusalem and divided a nation.

Yossi Klein Halevi. HarperCollins Publishers 2013 608 p. (hardcover : alk. paper) $35   **356**
1. Israel -- History 2. Israel-Arab War, 1967 3. Arab-Israeli conflict -- 1967-1973 4. Arab-Israeli conflict -- 1973-1993 5. Israel -- Parachute troops -- Biography 6. Israel. Tseva haganah le-Yiśra'el -- Parachute troops -- History -- 20th century 7. Israel. Tseva haganah le-Yiśra'el. Hel-ha-tsanhanim -- History -- 20th century
ISBN 0060545763; 9780060545765; 9780060545772; 9780062274823

LC 2013018850

National Jewish Book Awards: Jewish Book of the Year (2013)

In this book, author Yossi Klein Halevi, "interweaves the stories of a group of 1967 paratroopers who reunited Jerusalem, tracing the history of Israel and the divergent ideologies shaping it from the Six-Day War to the present. Following the lives of seven young members from the 55th Paratroopers Reserve Brigade . . . Halevi reveals how this band of brothers played pivotal roles in shaping Israel's destiny long after their historic victory." (Publisher's note)

Includes bibliographical references

Haney, Eric L.

★ Inside Delta Force; the story of America's elite counterterrorist unit. Delacorte Press 2002 324p il hardcover o.p. pa $14   **356**
1. United States -- Army -- Delta Force
ISBN 0-385-33603-9; 0-385-33936-4 pa

LC 2001-58408

The author relates his "experiences during the formation and early operations of 1st Special Forces Operational Detachment-Delta. . . . He served three times in Beirut guarding the American ambassador, participated in the invasion of Grenada, served in several Central American countries and narrowly escaped death during the abortive rescue attempt of the American hostages in Iran. . . . Readers of other special forces memoirs will find this one distinctive for Haney's attention to interservice rivalries . . . that he believes compromised several missions, as well as for Haney's nuanced, often disgusted descriptions of the human cost of war." Publ Wkly

Mazzetti, Mark

The way of the knife; the CIA, a secret army, and a war at the ends of the Earth. Mark Mazzetti. The Penguin Press 2013 400 p. $29.95   **356**
1. Terrorism 2. Military policy -- United States 3. United States. Dept. of Defense 4. Interagency coordination -- United States 5. United States. Central Intelligence Agency 6. United States -- Military policy -- Decision making 7. National security -- United States -- Decision making
ISBN 1594204802; 9781594204807

LC 2013006820

In this book, "Pulitzer Prize-winning New York Times national security correspondent [Mark] Mazzetti demonstrates in . . . detail how the new-style warfare approved by both George W. Bush and Barack Obama has led to controversial assassinations by the U.S. government and blowback yielding new terrorists determined to harm American citizens." (Kirkus Reviews)

Includes bibliographical references and index

357 Mounted forces and warfare

Cotterell, Arthur

Chariot; from chariot to tank, the astounding rise and fall of the world's first war machine. Overlook Press 2005 344p il map $29.95   **357**

1. Military art and science

ISBN 1-58567-667-5

LC 2004-65980

"This work is a welcome addition to a collection specializing in military history or ancient history but will appeal to general readers as well because the writing is accessible despite the plethora of detail." Libr J

Includes bibliographical references

358 Air and other specialized forces and warfare; engineering and related services

Engelberg, Stephen

Germs; America's secret war against biological weapons. Judith Miller, Stephen Engelberg, William Broad. Simon & Schuster 2001 382p $27; pa $14   **358**

1. Biological warfare

ISBN 0-684-87158-0; 0-684-87159-9 pa

LC 2001-42690

Three reporters survey the history of biological weapons and recount incidents of their use by terrorist groups. They explain why advances in biology and the spread of germ weapons poses grave risks as countries such as Iran, Iraq and North Korea continually engage in research

Includes bibliographical references

Guillemin, Jeanne

★ **Biological** weapons; from the invention of state-sponsored programs to contemporary bioterrorism. Columbia University Press 2005 258p $75; pa $22.95   **358**

1. Biological warfare

ISBN 0-231-12942-4; 0-231-12943-2 pa

LC 2004-51911

This is a "history of biological weaponry, beginning with the British, American and Japanese programs that predate WWII. . . . Admirably free of finger-pointing, shrillness and Luddite tendencies, the book ranks high as a historical introduction to the subject and a handbook on contemporary remedies." Publ Wkly

Includes bibliographical references

Lockwood, Jeffrey A.

Six -legged soldiers; using insects as weapons of war. Oxford University Press 2009 xx, 377p il $27.95   **358**

1. Biological warfare 2. Insects as carriers of disease

ISBN 978-0-19-533305-3; 0-19-533305-5

LC 2008-6935

"Both science and military history buffs will learn much from Lockwood." Publ Wkly

Includes bibliographical references (p. 315-322)

Tucker, Jonathan B.

★ **War** of nerves; chemical warfare from World War I to al-Qaeda. Pantheon Books 2006 479p il $30; pa $17.95   **358**

1. Chemical warfare

ISBN 0-375-42229-3; 978-0-375-42229-4; 1-4000-3233-4 pa; 978-1-4000-3233-4 pa

LC 2005-50053

This "book makes a sobering case for a less poisonous world." N Y Times Book Rev

Includes bibliographical references

Weapons of mass destruction; an encyclopedia of worldwide policy, technology, and history. Eric A. Croddy and James J. Wirtz, editors. ABC-CLIO 2004 2v il set $185   **358**

1. Nuclear weapons 2. Chemical warfare 3. Biological warfare

ISBN 1-85109-490-3

LC 2004-24651

"No other reference source covers such a wide array of topics related to WMD. It will dispel many myths but will also draw attention to the lethal consequences of WMD." Booklist

Includes bibliographical references

358.4 Air forces and warfare

Jacobsen, Annie

Area 51; an uncensored history of America's top secret military base. Little, Brown 2011 523p il map $27.99   **358.4**

1. Area 51 (Nev.)

ISBN 978-0-316-13294-7; 0-316-13294-2

"Seventy-five miles north of Las Vegas sits a land parcel in the middle of the desert. Called Area 51, the parcel is just outside of the abandoned Nevada Test and Training Range, where more than 100 atmospheric bomb tests were conducted in the 1950s. Officially, the U.S. government has never acknowledged the existence of Area 51. Unofficially, it has become a place associated with conspiracy theories, alien landings and tiny spaceships. Journalist Annie Jacobsen . . . [reveals] that the site has remained classified for many years — not because of aliens or spaceships, but because the government once used the site for top-secret nuclear testing and weapons development. . . Jacobsen details how several agencies — including the Atomic Energy Commission, the Department of Defense and the CIA — once used the site to conduct controversial and secretive research on aircraft and pilot-related projects." NPR

Includes bibliographical references

Wildsmith, Snow

Joining the United States Air Force; a handbook. Snow Wildsmith. McFarland & Co. 2012 x, 229 p.p (Joining the military) (pbk. : alk. paper) $25 **358.4**

1. Employment 2. United States -- Armed forces 3. Military personnel -- United States 4. United States. Air Force -- Vocational guidance

ISBN 0786447583; 9780786447589

LC 2012010677

Author Snow Wildsmith presents a book on the U.S. Air Force. "This book is for the teenager or young adult who is interested in enlisting in the United States Air Force. It will walk him or her through the enlistment and recruit training process: making the decision to join the military, talking to recruiters, getting qualified, preparing for and learning what to expect at basic recruit training." (Publisher's note)

Includes bibliographical references and index

359   Sea forces and warfare

Berman, Larry

Zumwalt; the life and times of Admiral Elmo Russell "Bud" Zumwalt, Jr. Larry Berman. Harper 2012 528 p. **359**

1. United States. Navy 2. Vietnam War, 1961-1975 -- Naval operations 3. Admirals -- United States -- Biography 4. United States. Navy -- Officers -- Biography 5. Vietnam War, 1961-1975 -- Naval operations, American 6. United States. Office of the Chief of Naval Operations -- History -- 20th century

ISBN 0061691305; 9780061691300

LC 2012032320

This book, by Larry Berman, offers a biography of "Admiral Elmo Russell Zumwalt, Jr. . . . In a career spanning forty years, he rose to the top echelon of the U.S. Navy as a commander of all navy forces in Vietnam and then as CNO from 1970 to 1974. His tenure came at a time of scandal and tumult, from the Soviets' challenge to the U.S. for naval supremacy and a duplicitous endgame in Vietnam to Watergate and an admirals' spy ring." (Publisher's note)

Includes bibliographical references

Bruce, Anthony

An **encyclopedia** of naval history; [by] Anthony Bruce and William Cogar. Fitzroy Dearborn 1998 440p il $100 **359**

1. Reference books 2. Naval history -- Encyclopedias

ISBN 1-579-58109-9

An "encyclopedia of world naval history from the 15th century to the present. Its 1,000 articles cover all manner of detail from sea battles and great commanders to warship evolution, naval technology and tactics, organizations, and naval-oriented details of specific campaigns. Although international in scope, the work clearly emphasizes the US and Britain." Choice

Crowley, Roger

Empires of the sea; the siege of Malta, the battle of Lepanto, and the contest for the center of the world. Random House 2008 336p il map $30; pa $16 **359**

1. Naval battles 2. Christianity and other religions 3. Europe -- Naval history 4. Islam -- Relations -- Christianity

ISBN 978-1-4000-6624-7; 1-4000-6624-7; 978-0-8129-7764-6 pa; 0-8129-7764-5 pa

LC 2007-33794

This book "is well-crafted narrative history in the best sense of the word, lucid, colorful, and beautifully written. . . . Crowley draws on a wealth of sources reflecting a multiplicity of viewpoints and the results are convincing." Journal of Military History

Includes bibliographical references

Grant, R. G.

Battle at sea; 3,000 years of naval warfare. written by R.G. Grant. DK Pub. 2008 360p il map $40 **359**

1. Naval history 2. Naval art and science

ISBN 978-0-7566-3973-0

LC 2008-10019

"This oversized book . . . is perhaps the most comprehensive one-volume history of war at sea, covering engagements large and small, from 1200 B.C.E. to the present day. . . . Highly recommended." Libr J

★ **Naval** warfare; an international encyclopedia. edited by Spencer C. Tucker; associate editors, John Fredriksen {et al.}; introduction by James C. Bradford. ABC-CLIO 2002 3v il maps set $295 **359**

1. Reference books 2. Naval art and science -- Encyclopedias

ISBN 1-57607-219-3

LC 2002-4401

This set "explores the history of combat at sea, from ancient Greek galleys to the sophisticated ships of the U.S. Sixth Fleet. More than 1500 signed entries . . . describe the three key eras: Age of Galley Warfare, Age of Sail, and Age of Steam or Modern Era. . . . Each new development is examined in painstaking detail." Libr J

Includes bibliographical references

Toll, Ian W.

★ **Six** frigates; the epic history of the founding of the U.S. Navy. Norton 2006 560p il map $27.95 **359**

1. United States -- Navy

ISBN 978-0-393-05847-5; 0-393-05847-6

LC 2006-20769

This is "a must-read for fans of naval history and the early American Republic." Publ Wkly

Includes bibliographical references

Taylor, Stephen

Commander; the life and exploits of Britain's greatest frigate captain. Stephen Taylor. W.W. Norton 2012 320 p. **359.009**

1. War 2. Biography 3. Military personnel 4. Great

Britain -- History, Naval -- 18th century 5. Great Britain -- History, Naval -- 19th century 6. Great Britain. Royal Navy. Officers -- Biography 7. Frigates -- Great Britain -- History -- 18th century 8. Frigates -- Great Britain -- History -- 19th century
ISBN 9780393071641

LC 2012027783

This book by Stephen Taylor presents a biography of British naval commander Edward Pellew. He discusses "Pellew's meteoric rise to midshipman within four years and his first command by age 25. Rare in a seaman, he could swim and more than once dove into the sea to save a crewmember, and his physical prowess . . . was the stuff of legend." In addition, Taylor describes "life at sea during wars in America, the English Channel, the Indian Ocean and the Mediterranean." (Kirkus Reviews)

Includes bibliographical references and index

359.9 Specialized combat forces; engineering and related services

Couch, Dick

The **warrior** elite; the forging of Seal Class 228. photographs by Cliff Hollenbeck. Crown 2001 319p il hardcover o.p. pa $14.95   **359.9**
   1. United States -- Navy -- Sea Air Land Team
   ISBN 1-4000-4695-5 pa

LC 2001-28368

This is an account of the Basic Underwater Demolition course, (BUD) training for the U.S. Navy Sea Air Land Team (SEALs)

This book "is unique. Couch, a Vietnam-era SEAL and retired naval reserve captain was given the most complete access possible. . . . On view is much serious thought by serious thinkers on the making of warriors at the dawn of the twenty-first century." Booklist

Parrish, Thomas

★ The **submarine**; a history. Viking 2004 576p il $29.95; pa $16   **359.9**
   1. Submarines
   ISBN 0-670-03313-8; 0-14-303519-3 pa

LC 2003-70515

"This brilliant, dramatic account of submarines and the men who sailed in them is a required acquisition for every military history collection." Choice

Includes bibliographical references

361.2 Social action

Rieff, David

A **bed** for the night; humanitarianism in crisis. Simon & Schuster 2002 367p $26; pa $15   **361.2**
   1. International agencies 2. War relief 3. Humanitarianism 4. International relief
   ISBN 0-684-80977-X; 0-7432-5211-X pa

LC 2002-29432

This book argues that "humanitarian organizations trying to bring relief in an ever more violent and dangerous world are often betrayed and misused, and have increasingly lost sight of their purpose." (Publisher's note) Index.

Readers "will come away from this passionate, eloquent argument with a distinctly clearer understanding of the complex moral issues facing humanitarian aid in a world filled with brutality and suffering." Publ Wkly

Includes bibliographical references

361.7 Private action

Budd, Ken

The **voluntourist**; a six-country tale of love, loss, fatherhood, fate, and singing Bon Jovi in Bethlehem. Ken Budd. 1st ed. William Morrow 2012 451 p. ill. (acid-free paper) $15.99   **361.7**
   1. Social action 2. Volunteer work 3. Self-realization 4. Voluntarism 5. Social service 6. Parents -- Death 7. Adult children -- Psychology
   ISBN 006194646X; 9780061946462

LC 2011032000

"In this . . . memoir, [Ken] Budd . . . records how he changes 'emotionally, physically, spiritually' as he travels to work with 'people with real problems and different perspectives.' Budd begins his journey in New Orleans . . . then moves on to . . . rural Costa Rica. But these two experiences become the genesis of a broader project -- the heart of his memoir -- to make four more trips in nine months, volunteering in Asia, South America, the Middle East, and Africa." (Publishers Weekly)

Zunz, Olivier

Philanthropy in America; a history. Olivier Zunz. Princeton University Press 2012 x, 381 p.p $29.95   **361.7**
   1. Charities 2. Philanthropy -- History 3. Philanthropy -- United States 4. Humanitarianism -- History 5. Charities -- United States -- History 6. Endowments -- United States -- History 7. Nonprofit organizations -- United States -- History
   ISBN 0691128367; 9780691128368 (hardcover : alk. paper)

LC 2011017479

This book "trace[s]the evolution of American philanthropy over the past 150 years and its contribution to democracy and civil society." It "focus[es] . . . on the extent to which foundations and other grantmaking programs have been involved in shaping national affairs and public policy. . . . Zunz explains the transformation of charitable giving from individual acts of financial relief to the formidable efforts of institutions to influence education, health, and welfare policies." (Nation)

Includes bibliographical references and index

362 Specific social problems and services

America's top doctors. Castle Connolly Medical $79.95; pa $29.95   **362**
   1. Reference books 2. Physicians -- Directories
   ISBN 1-883769-38-8; 1-883769-36-1 pa

LC 2003-100260

First published 2001

This guide identifies and provides information about more than 4,000 top specialists for care and treatment of more than 2,000 diseases and medical conditions, provides information about accessing and using clinical trials, and explains services provided at the National Institutes of Health and how to get the most from your specialist's appointment

Critser, Greg

Fat land; how Americans became the fattest people in the world. Houghton Mifflin 2003 232p il $24; pa $13   **362**

1. Obesity

ISBN 0-618-16472-3; 0-618-38060-4 pa

LC 2002-32282

The author "succeeds in letting laypersons grasp agricultural policy, astute marketing ploys, lipid chemistry, human physioloy, and the follies of institutional feeding schemes and weight-loss quackery." Choice

Manguso, Sarah

The **two** kinds of decay. Farrar, Straus and Giroux 2008 184p $22; pa $14   **362**

1. Poets 2. Authors 3. Editors 4. Guillain-Barré syndrome

ISBN 978-0-374-28012-3; 0-374-28012-6; 978-0-312-42844-0 pa; 0-312-42844-8 pa

LC 2008-1766

"What makes this lightning-quick book extraordinary is not just Manguso's deadpan delivery of often unthinkable details, nor her poet's struggle with the damaging metaphors of disease, but the compassion she acquires as she comes to understand her pain in relation to the pain of others." Publ Wkly

362.1   People with illnesses and disabilities

Blumenthal, David

The **heart** of power; health and politics in the Oval Office. [by] David Blumenthal and James A. Morone. University of California Press 2009 484p il $26.95   **362.1**

1. Medical care -- Government policy 2. Presidents -- United States -- Health

ISBN 978-0-520-26030-6; 0-520-26030-9

LC 2008-54361

"More than an excellent primer on American health policy, the book offers a thorough, incisive look at the presidency as an institution and the men who have occupied the office." Publ Wkly

Includes bibliographical references

Chase, Marilyn

The **Barbary** plague; the Black Death in Victorian San Francisco. Random House 2003 276p map $25.95; pa $13.95   **362.1**

1. Plague 2. San Francisco (Calif.)

ISBN 0-375-50496-6; 0-375-75708-2 pa

LC 2002-68102

The author offers a "portrait of the roles played by Chinese merchant societies, the white press, and Sacramento officials that initially enabled the disease to gain a foothold. She then turns most of her attention to detailing the scientific and personal strengths and weaknesses of the national public health officials who worked to determine efficient ways to diagnose, treat, and eventually halt the spread of the disease." SLJ

This is "a pleasure to read, full of people, dramatic situations, individual foibles and collective hard work. I closed the book wishing it had been longer." N Y Times Book Rev

Coste, Joanne Koenig

Learning to speak Alzheimer's; a groundbreaking approach for everyone dealing with the disease. Houghton Mifflin 2003 240p il hardcover o.p. pa $14   **362.1**

1. Caregivers 2. Alzheimer's disease

ISBN 0-618-22125-5; 0-618-48517-1 pa

LC 2003-51141

"Key elements of Coste's approach include simplifying the environment for the patient, capitalizing on his or her remaining skills, and making an effort to understand what life must be like for the memory impaired. Because such Alzheimer's behaviors as agitation and physical aggression are often rooted in frustration, she also offers caregivers techniques to help patients compensate for cognitive and sensory losses. . . . Directions for simple activities, recipes for nutritious 'finger foods,' and tips for hiring home caregivers are included. . . . A fine addition to Alzheimer's and caregiving collections." Libr J

Includes bibliographical references

Crosby, Molly Caldwell

Asleep; the forgotten epidemic that remains one of medicine's greatest mysteries. Berkley Books 2010 291p il $24.95   **362.1**

1. Epidemics 2. Encephalitis

ISBN 978-0-425-22570-7; 0-425-22570-4

LC 2009-34928

"Crosby is a fine storyteller, peppering her case studies with facts about the history of neurology and details about 1910s New York. She also provides fully realized portraits of not only her case studies' patients, but also the brilliant doctors who treated them. . . . A capable, readable account of a medical mystery." Kirkus

Includes bibliographical references

Douglas, Kirk, 1916-

My stroke of luck. Morrow 2002 196p il hardcover o.p. pa $12.95   **362.1**

1. Actors

ISBN 0-06-001404-0 pa

LC 2002-727755

"Entertaining and uplifting, Douglas's story is a lesson in survival, one that will entice readers whether or not they have had similar illnesses. . . . This book is a natural for the 65-plus crowd." Publ Wkly

Encyclopedia of public health; edited by Lester Breslow. Macmillan Ref. USA 2001 4v set $475   **362.1**
1. Reference books 2. Public health -- Encyclopedias
ISBN 0-02-865354-8

LC 2001-31501

"Information on more than 900 programs, services, organizations, health behaviors, and the prevalence, epidemiology, and costs of communicable diseases. Although the work focuses on the United States, there are also references to worldwide problems." Libr J

Garrett, Laurie
Betrayal of trust; the collapse of global public health. Hyperion 2000 754p il $30; pa $16.95 **362.1**
1. Medical care 2. Public health
ISBN 0-7868-6522-9; 0-7868-8440-1 pa

LC 00-33425

This book examines contemporary "health systems in the former Soviet Union, India, central Africa, and the United States." N Y Times Book Rev

Greenspan, Stanley I.
The **child** with special needs; encouraging intellectual and emotional growth. [by] Stanley I. Greenspan, Serena Wieder, with Robin Simons. Addison-Wesley 1998 496p $32   **362.1**
1. Child psychology 2. Children with disabilities 3. Handicapped children
ISBN 0-201-40726-4

LC 97-32101

This offers advice to parents on helping children with such disabilities as cerebral palsy, autism, retardation, ADD, and language problems.
This "is an important work for libraries." Libr J
Includes bibliographical references

Gruber, Jonathan
Health care reform; what it is, why it's necessary, how it works. Jonathan Gruber, with HP Newquist ; illustrated by Nathan Schreiber. Hill and Wang 2011 151 p.   **362.1**
1. Medical care 2. Access to health care 3. Medical care -- Costs 4. Medical policy -- United States 5. Health care reform -- United States 6. Medical care -- United States
ISBN 0809053977; 0809094622; 9780809053971; 9780809094622

LC 2011020495

This book is "[a] cartoon-driven examination of what's wrong with the American way of health care--and why the legislative reform of 2010 was necessary." (Kirkus) "It delivers information . . . through an earnest but informal lecture by a cartoon version of an expert--in this case [Jonathan] Gruber, an MIT economics professor who helped craft Massachusetts's successful health care reform plan as well as the Affordable Care Act, which has been the subject of so much confusion and deliberate misinformation. He begins the presentation by confronting a small group of people with the enormous medical bills they could receive after medical treatment, then moves from the individual to the national

level to show that our present system is unfair and unsustainable." (Publishers Wkly)

Hoffman, Beatrix
Health care for some; rights and rationing in the United States since 1930. Beatrix Hoffman. University of Chicago Press 2012 xxxv, 319 p.p (cloth : alkaline paper) $30   **362.1**
1. Access to health care 2. Medical care -- Costs 3. Health care reform -- United States 4. Right to health -- United States -- History 5. Health care rationing -- United States -- History
ISBN 0226348032; 9780226348032

LC 2012000338

Author Beatrix Rebecca Hoffman looks at "America's long tradition of unequal access to health care. . . . Hoffman argues that two main features have characterized the US health system: a refusal to adopt a right to care and a particularly American type of rationing." The book "shows that the haphazard way the US system allocates medical services--using income, race, region, insurance coverage, and many other factors--is a disorganized, illogical, and powerful form of rationing." (Publisher's note)
Includes bibliographical references and index.

Hurley, Dan
Diabetes rising; how a rare disease became a modern pandemic, and what to do about it. foreword by Zachary T. Bloomgarden. Kaplan Pub. 2010 xxiii, 312p $26.95   **362.1**
1. Diabetes
ISBN 978-1-60714-458-8

LC 2009-29382

The author, "diagnosed at age 18 with type 1 diabetes, recounts the 3500-year history of the disease, its possible causes, and the latest promising treatments and cures with a professional writer's skills and a patient's passion. . . . [This is] a compelling layperson's overview of diabetes research, enlivened by multiple interviews with scientists in the field. Diabetics and those who love them will find this a fascinating and hope-filled read." Libr J
Includes bibliographical references

Kaufman, Sharon R.
--And a time to die; how American hospitals shape the end of life. Scribner 2005 400p $28 **362.1**
1. Death 2. Terminal care -- Ethical aspects
ISBN 0-7432-6476-2

LC 2004-52530

The author "reveals the dilemmas of hospital death in America today: the shift to patients' control of decision making despite the doctors' greater knowledge; the ethics and practical effects of resuscitation versus pain relief; the complexities of assessing 'quality of life' while guessing at the desires of an unconscious patient. . . . This deeply probing study lays bare the cultural and institutional assumptions and rhetoric that frame our search for 'a good death.'" Publ Wkly
Includes bibliographical references

Kessler, Lauren

✓ **Dancing** with Rose; finding life in the land of Alzheimer's. Viking 2007 260p $24.95   **362.1**
   1. Caregivers 2. Alzheimer's disease
   ISBN 0-670-03859-8; 978-0-670-03859-6
                 LC 2006-35699

This is the author's "account of the months she worked as an unskilled resident assistant in an Alzheimer's facility on the West Coast." Publ Wkly

"Invaluable intelligence, especially for anyone considering a residential facility for a loved one." Booklist

✓ **Monette, Paul**

   Borrowed time; an AIDS memoir. Harcourt Brace Jovanovich 1988 342p $22; pa $13   **362.1**
   1. AIDS (Disease)
   ISBN 0-15-113598-3; 0-15-600581-6 pa
                 LC 88-7215

"The memoir transcends the particulars of the AIDS epidemic to stand as an eloquent testimonial to the power of love and the devastation of loss." Publ Wkly

Orbach, Susie

✓ **Bodies**. Picador 2009 216p (Big ideas/small books) pa $14   **362.1**
   1. Body image
   ISBN 978-0-312-42720-7; 0-312-42720-4
                 LC 2008-50352

The author "delves into the touchy subject of commercial exploitation of 'the body' and explores how modern culture is eroding individual appreciation of the unaltered human form. She uses specific case studies from her own practice to show the long-term effects that can result from body dissatisfaction. . . . Orbach's timely analysis is a key addition to the growing discussion of what is becoming a national trend, the favoring of delusion over reality, a troubling tendency that is threatening to steadily encompass all facets of American life." Booklist
   Includes bibliographical references

Price, Reynolds

✓ A **whole** new life. Atheneum Pubs. 1994 213p $23; pa $13   **362.1**
   1. Authors 2. Novelists 3. Essayists 4. College teachers 5. Short story writers 6. Cancer -- Personal narratives
   ISBN 0-684-87255-2; 0-7432-3854-0 pa
                 LC 93-35967

Price gives an "account of his 'mid-life collision with cancer and paralysis.' In 1984, he was found to have a malignant tumor of the spinal cord, and three surgeries and radiation therapy arrested the growth but left him unable to walk. Although he has not written an essay on illness per se, he embraces elements of an essay as he pauses to ponder nature's systemic breakdowns, the importance of friendships in times of stress, or how to handle pain psychologically. His book is primarily a chronological narrative of events in the treatment of his disease and his rehabilitation." Booklist

Reid, T. R.

✓ The **healing** of America; a global quest for better, cheaper, and fairer health care. Penguin Press 2009 277p il $25.95   **362.1**
   1. Medical care -- Government policy
   ISBN 9781594202346
                 LC 2009-9555

The author "explores health-care systems around the world in an effort to understand why the U.S. remains the only first world nation to refuse its citizens universal health care." Publ Wkly

"Reid's concise—and surprisingly humorous—study is recommended to anyone following the ongoing debate over health-care reform." Libr J
   Includes bibliographical references

Shah, Sonia

✓ The **body** hunters; testing new drugs on the world's poorest patients. New Press 2006 242p $24.95   **362.1**
   1. Drug industry 2. Medical ethics 3. Developing countries
   ISBN 1-56584-912-4; 978-1-56584-912-9
                 LC 2005-58394

The author "uncovers a series of recent unethical drug trials conducted on impoverished and sick people in the developing world. . . . Meticulously researched and packed with documentary evidence, Shah's tautly argued study will provoke much needed public debate about this disturbing facet of globalization." Publ Wkly
   Includes bibliographical references

Shilts, Randy

✓ ★ **And** the band played on; politics, people, and the AIDS epidemic. 20th anniversary ed.; St Martin's Griffin 2007 630p pa $17.95   **362.1**
   1. AIDS (Disease)
   ISBN 978-0-312-37463-1
   First published 1987

The author traces the history of the AIDS epidemic in the United States.

"Shilts successfully weaves comprehensive investigative reporting and commercial page-turner pacing, political intrigue and personal tragedy into a landmark work." Publ Wkly
   Includes bibliographical references

Silver, Daniel B.

   Refuge in hell; how Berlin's Jewish hospital outlasted the Nazis. Houghton Mifflin 2003 xxii, 311p $24   **362.1**
   1. Jews -- Germany 2. Holocaust, 1933-1945 3. Jüdisches Krankenhaus (Berlin, Germany)
   ISBN 0-618-25144-8
                 LC 2003-47896

"This enlightening work is essential for public and academic libraries." Libr J
   Includes bibliographical references

Smith, Tom

A **balanced** life; 9 strategies for coping with the mental health problems of a loved one. Hazelden 2008 147p pa $14.95 **362.1**
  1. Mentally ill
  ISBN 978-1-59285-662-6

LC 2008-18794

"Through extensive research and his own experience with his daughter's mental illness and subsequent suicide, . . . [the author] suggests nine strategies for coping, including helping loved ones find and continue to take their medication, urging them to maintain a supportive relationship with a therapist, and recognizing the warning signs. . . . Smith provides empathetic information that has the potential to buoy people up." Libr J

Includes bibliographical references

Sommer, Alfred

Getting what we deserve; health and medical care in America. Johns Hopkins University Press 2009 133p il map $21.95 **362.1**
  1. Social medicine 2. Public health -- United States 3. Medical care -- Government policy
  ISBN 978-0-8018-9387-2; 0-8018-9387-9

LC 2009-6039

"Opposing what we've been led to believe about the health-care situation in the United States, . . . [the author] posits that there's less complexity than meets the eye and that solutions are possible. . . . First illustrating how much improvement there was in life expectancy in the 20th century even before the advent of antibiotics and advanced technology, he proceeds to emphasize the importance of environment—e.g., hygiene, pollution, smoking—in creating public health problems and the relatively simple steps to improvement. . . . Sommer keeps it short and clear, with plenty of understandable graphs and charts. His common-sense points will interest consumers trying to understand the ongoing debate as well as policymakers." Libr J

Includes bibliographical references

Starr, Paul

Remedy and reaction; the peculiar American struggle over health care reform. Yale University Press 2011 324p $28.50 **362.1**
  1. Health insurance 2. Medical care -- Government policy
  ISBN 978-0-300-17109-9

LC 2011019577

The author "recounts the long and largely unsuccessful fight to provide all Americans with health care. . . . Starr shows how the window of opportunity for health-care reform has opened several times in the last 100 years and how each time it has been slammed shut by powerful interests including the American Medical Association, big insurance companies, and the conservative politicians they support. . . . This is a must-read in order to understand why health-care reform has been and continues to be so difficult to achieve in America." Libr J

Includes bibliographical references

Steinberg, Jonny

Sizwe's test; a young man's journey through Africa's AIDS epidemic. Simon & Schuster 2008 349p il $26 **362.1**
  1. AIDS (Disease) 2. South Africa
  ISBN 978-1-4165-5269-7; 1-4165-5269-3

LC 2007-29672

This book "focuses on Lusikisiki, a district in [South Africa's] Eastern Cape Province. . . . Almost one out of three pregnant women in Lusikisiki was H.I.V. positive, but the area also had a first-rate AIDS treatment program. . . . Steinberg presents the district largely through the eyes of one man, whom he calls Sizwe Magadla. Sizwe is 30, healthy and literate." N Y Times Book Rev

The author "becomes intertwined with his subject, but balances critical distance and compassion with gleanings from his own psychological barriers to HIV testing that further deepen the concern and understanding he accords to Sizwe's story." Publ Wkly

Includes bibliographical references

Torrey, E. Fuller (Edwin Fuller), 1937-

The **insanity** offense; how America's failure to treat the seriously mentally ill endangers its citizens. W.W. Norton 2008 265p il **362.1**
  1. Mentally ill -- Institutional care
  ISBN 0-393-06658-4; 978-0-393-06658-6

LC 2008-2697

"Released en masse from institutions beginning in the 1960s, the most severely ill are most likely to become homeless, incarcerated, victimized, and/or violent. Torrey details how civil liberties suits have prevented such people from being involuntarily institutionalized, leaving them a danger both to themselves and to others. . . . Chilling and well documented, this text has many no-nonsense solutions to protect the mentally ill themselves as well as society as a whole." Publ Wkly

Includes bibliographical references

362.106 Management

Friedman, Leonard H.

101 careers in healthcare management; by Leonard H. Friedman, Anthony R. Kovner. Springer Pub. Co. 2013 xix, 332 p.p ill. (paperback) $25.00; (eBook) $25.00 **362.106**
  1. Vocational guidance 2. Medical personnel -- Employment 3. Health Services Administration -- United States
  ISBN 082619334X; 9780826193346; 9780826193353 pdf

LC 2012033692

This book by Leonard H. Friedman and Anthony R. Kovner is a "resource describing the many career opportunities in healthcare management. The book begins with general chapters providing an overview of the field of healthcare management, information on educational requirements, and advice on finding a job in the field. Following chapters outline specific job titles and feature many real-life examples." (Choice)

362.109   History, geographic treatment, biography

Atlas, Scott W.

In excellent health; setting the record straight on America's health care and charting a path for future reform. Scott W. Atlas, MD. Hoover Institution Press, Stanford University 2011 xxiv, 359 p.p (cloth : alk. paper) $24.95   **362.109**
   1. Technological innovations 2. Medical care -- United States 3. Health insurance -- United States 4. Health care reform -- United States
ISBN 0817914447; 9780817914448

                    LC 2011037058

In this book, "[Scott W.] Atlas admits that U.S. health care faces serious challenges . . . , [but] he asserts that we have made remarkable advances in the past 60 years" and that "we lead the world in" developing medical innovations. "He argues for substantive tax reforms, an overhaul of private insurance, and the 'minimization of the role of government as direct insurer' as essential." (Library Journal)
Includes bibliographical references and index.

Brawley, Otis Webb

How we do harm; Otis Webb Brawley with Paul Goldberg. St. Martin's Press 2012 256p.   **362.109**
   1. Medical care 2. Access to health care 3. Medical policy -- United States 4. Medical care -- United States 5. Health care reform -- United States
ISBN 9780312672973

                    LC 2011035843

'In this book, Dr. Otis Webb Brawley, M.D., explores "how medicine is really practiced in America. Brawley tells of doctors who select treatment based on payment they will receive, rather than on demonstrated scientific results; hospitals and pharmaceutical companies that seek out patients to treat even if they are not actually ill (but as long as their insurance will pay); a public primed to swallow the latest pill, no matter the cost; and rising healthcare costs for unnecessary—and often unproven—treatments that we all pay for. Brawley calls for rational healthcare, healthcare drawn from results-based, scientifically justifiable treatments, and not just the peddling of hot new drugs." (Publisher's note)

362.11   Services of specific kinds of institutions

Fink, Sheri

★ Five days at Memorial; life and death in a storm-ravaged hospital. Sheri Fink. Crown Publishers 2013 432 p. $27   **362.11**
   1. Hospitals 2. Disaster relief 3. Hurricane Katrina, 2005 4. Memorial Medical Center (New Orleans, La.) 5. Disaster medicine -- Louisiana -- New Orleans -- Case studies 6. Disaster hospitals -- Louisiana -- New Orleans -- Case studies 7. Forensic pathology -- Louisiana -- New Orleans -- Case studies 8. Health facilities -- Louisiana -- Administration -- Case studies
ISBN 0307718964; 9780307718969

                    LC 2013019693

Andrew Carnegie Medal for Excellence in Nonfiction Shortlist (2014)

Author Sheri Fink's book "unspools the mystery of what happened in" the days after Hurricane Katrina, "bringing the reader into a hospital fighting for its life and into a conversation about the most terrifying form of health care rationing. . . . Fink exposes the hidden dilemmas of end-of-life care and reveals just how ill-prepared we are in America for the impact of large-scale disasters--and how we can do better." (Publisher's note)

"Pulitzer Prize–winning medical journalist/investigator Fink (War Hospital, 2003) submits a sophisticated, detailed recounting of what happened at Memorial Medical Center in New Orleans during and after Hurricane Katrina... Fink draws those few days in the hospital's life with a fine, lively pen, providing stunningly framed vignettes of activities in the hospital and sharp pocket profiles of many of the characters. She gives measured consideration to such explosive issues as class and race discrimination in medicine, end-of-life care, medical rationing and euthanasia, and she presents the injection of some patients with a cocktail of drugs to reduce their breathing in such a manner that readers will be able to fully fashion their own opinions...The obvious villains are the usual suspects: nature, for sending Katrina forth; big business, in the guise of Memorial owner Tenet Healthcare, for its failure to act and subsequent guilty posturing; and government, feds to local, for the bungling incompetence that led to dozens of deaths. The street thugs and looters didn't help much, either." (Kirkus)
Includes bibliographical references and index

Manheimer, Eric

Twelve patients; life and death at Bellevue Hospital. Eric Manheimer. Grand Central Pub. 2012 vii, 355 p.p (regular) $26.99   **362.11**
   1. Patients 2. Hospitals 3. Cancer -- Patients 4. Physicians -- Biography 5. Bellevue Hospital 6. Hospital care -- New York (State) -- New York -- Case studies 7. Hospital patients -- New York (State) -- New York -- Case studies
ISBN 1455503886; 9781455503889

                    LC 2012005513

This book presents "a memoir from the Medical Director of Bellevue Hospital that uses the plights of twelve very different patients -- from dignitaries at the nearby UN . . . to illegal immigrants, and Wall Street tycoons -- to illustrate larger societal issues. . . . As the book unfolds, the narrator is diagnosed with cancer, and he is forced to wrestle with the end of his own life even as he struggles to save the lives of others." (Publisher's note)

362.17   Specific services

Gawande, Atul

★ Being mortal; medicine and what matters in the end. Atul Gawande. Henry Holt & Co. 2014 288 p. illustrations (hardcover) $26   **362.17**
   1. Hospices 2. Terminal care 3. Elderly -- Medical care 4. Prognosis 5. Quality of life 6. Attitude to death 7. Aging -- Physiology
ISBN 0805095152; 9780805095159

                    LC 2014017442

"In 'Being Mortal,' . . . author Atul Gawande . . . addresses his profession's ultimate limitation, arguing that quality of life is the desired goal for patients and families. Gawande offers examples of freer, more socially fulfilling models for assisting the infirm and dependent elderly, and he explores the varieties of hospice care to demonstrate that a person's last weeks or months may be rich and dignified." (Publisher's note)

"A sensitive, intelligent and heartfelt examination of the processes of aging and dying." Kirkus

Includes bibliographical references

362.196 Specific conditions

Baroni, Bill

Fat kid got fit; Bill Baroni with Damon DiMarco; with a foreword by Howard Eisenson. Lyons Press 2012 x, 245p.p **362.196**
1. Weight loss 2. Autobiography 3. Physical fitness 4. Overweight persons -- New Jersey -- Biography
ISBN 9780762770472

LC 2011028047

This book tells the story of "Bill Baroni [who] was just twenty years old, [when] he was convinced he was dying. He thought he was having a heart attack because it felt like he had an elephant sitting on his chest. It turned out to be only indigestion, but more than that, it was the wake up call he needed to save his life. Bill weighed 320 pounds and was hooked on junk food. He set about to change his life forever. . . . He lost his weight using common sense. It took dedication, and even some gumption. But it worked! He lost 120 pounds and, more importantly, he has kept it off! He has maintained a healthy 185 pounds for fifteen years. At 65", he is trim, handsome, and healthy." (Publisher's note)

"[Baroni] traces his own path and, with humor and style, passes the information he learned along to readers. This can work for anyone." (Libr J)

Includes bibliographical references (p. 241-245).

Brzezinski, Mika, 1967-

Obsessed; America's Food Addiction -- And My Own. Perseus Books Group 2013 256 p. $26 **362.196**
1. Eating habits 2. Eating disorders
ISBN 1602861765; 9781602861763

This book by Mika Brzezinski looks at eating habits in the U.S. As a television host for "Morning Joe," she "admonish[es] viewers about the importance of proper diet and exercise. Few would suspect that her vehemence stems from a personal addiction to junk food and binge eating that has plagued her all her life and that her ironclad willpower actually border on an unhealthy obsession to stay thin at any cost." (Booklist)

Cody, Joshua

[Sic] W.W. Norton 2011 266 p. **362.196**
1. Autobiographies 2. Cancer -- Patients
ISBN 9780393081060

LC 2011026035

In this book "Joshua Cody, a . . . young composer, was about to receive his PhD when he was diagnosed with an

aggressive cancer. Facing a bone-marrow transplant and full radiation, he charts his struggle: the fury, the tendency to self-destruction, and the ruthless grasping for life and sensation; the encounter with a strange woman on Canal Street that leads to sex at his apartment; the detailed morphine fantasy complete with a bride called Valentina while, in reality, hospital staff are pinning him to his bed." (Publisher's note)

Includes bibliographical references.

Forrest, Emma

Your voice in my head; a memoir. Other Press 2011 215 p. **362.196**
1. Authors 2. Bulimia 3. Novelists 4. Journalists 5. Self-mutilation 6. Screenwriters 7. Biography, Individual
ISBN 1590514467; 9781590514467; 978-1-59051-446-7; 1-59051-446-7

LC 201030930

This book presents a memoir by writer Emma Forrest which details a period in her life in which, despite "the support of her parents . . . as well as a precocious career in journalism and a first novel . . . already on the way, she became a bulimic and an obsessive cutter, and soon began walking 'hand in hand with the thought of suicide.' She also had a knack for acquiring terrible boyfriends whose bad behavior inspired her to hurt herself more, and who sometimes aided and abetted the abuse." Particular focus is given to "the therapist who ultimately changed her life, a man she refers to as Dr. R. . . . [and his] unexpected death." Also included are "letters from Dr. R.'s other patients . . . [and] a sermon by her rabbi." (N Y Times)

Iweala, Uzodinma

Our kind of people; a continent's burden, a country's hope. by Uzodinma Iweala. 1st ed. HarperCollins 2012 228 p. (hardback) $24.99 **362.196**
1. Health 2. Nigeria 3. Epidemics 4. AIDS (Disease) -- Social aspects -- Nigeria 5. HIV infections -- Social aspects -- Nigeria
ISBN 0061284904; 9780061284908

LC 2011047861

Author Uzodinma "Iweala embarks on a . . . journey through his native Nigeria, meeting individuals and communities that are struggling daily to understand both the impact and meaning of HIV/AIDS. He speaks with people from all walks of life--the ill and the healthy, doctors, nurses, truck drivers, sex workers, shopkeepers, students, parents, and children. Their testimonies are . . . [a] personal exploration of life, love, and connection in the face of disease, and an incisive critique of our existing ideas of health and happiness." (Publisher's note)

Leavitt, Sarah

Tangles; A Story About Alzheimer's, My Mother, and Me. Sarah Leavitt. Skyhorse Pub. 2012 127 p. ill., port. (paperback) $14.95 **362.196**
1. Family life 2. Autobiographies 3. Alzheimer's disease
ISBN 1616086394; 9781616086398

"In this . . . graphic memoir, Sarah Leavitt reveals how Alzheimer's disease transformed her mother Midge -- and her family -- forever. . . . Sarah shares her family's journey . . . managing to find moments of happiness. Midge, a Harvard-educated intellectual, struggles to comprehend the simplest words; Sarah's father Rob slowly adapts to his new role as full-time caretaker . . . Sarah and her sister Hannah argue, laugh, and grieve together." (Publisher's note)

Stratton, Stephen E.

The **encyclopedia** of HIV and AIDS; Stephen E. Stratton, Evelyn J. Fisher ; foreword by Edward A. Morales. 3rd ed. Facts On File 2012 414 p. (hardcover) $75   **362.196**

1. AIDS (Disease) 2. HIV infections 3. Reference books 4. AIDS (Disease) -- Dictionaries
ISBN 0816077231; 9780816077236

LC 2011017597

First published 1998 with title: The AIDS dictionary

This book is the third edition of an encyclopedia of HIV and AIDS. "Coverage includes definitions of AIDS and HIV; information on medications used to treat the conditions--including side effects, dosage, and drug interactions; and related medical conditions. Further research is supported by the inclusion of a bibliography for each essay. The appendixes include frequently used abbreviations, lists of online resources, and U.S. and global HIV and AIDS statistics." (Library Journal)

This volume includes "entries covering the basic biological, medical, financial, legal, political, and social issues and terms associated with HIV and AIDS. Entries explain symptoms and treatments, opportunistic infections, prevention strategies, and much more. Appendixes include HIV/AIDS associations, education centers, clinical trials, hotlines, publications, and additional material." Publisher's note

Includes bibliographical references and index.

Zimmer, Carl

A **planet** of viruses; Carl Zimmer. University of Chicago Press 2011 x, 109p.p col. ill.   **362.196**

1. Viruses
ISBN 9780226983356 pa; 0226983358 pa;
9780226983363; 9780226983332

LC 2010036742

"This . . . book explores the hidden world of viruses. . . . Here Carl Zimmer, popular science writer and author of Discover magazine's award-winning blog The Loom, presents the latest research on how viruses hold sway over our lives and our biosphere, how viruses helped give rise to the first life-forms, how viruses are producing new diseases, how we can harness viruses for our own ends, and how viruses will continue to control our fate for years to come. In this . . . tour of the frontiers of biology, . . . we learn that some treatments for the common cold do more harm than good; that the world's oceans are home to an astonishing number of viruses; and that the evolution of HIV is now in overdrive, spawning more mutated strains than we care to imagine." (Publisher's note)

Includes bibliographical references (p. 97-101) and index.

362.2   People with mental illness and disabilities

Schüll, Natasha Dow

Addiction by design; machine gambling in Las Vegas. Natasha Dow Schüll. Princeton University Press 2012 xi, 442 p.p (hardcover) $35   **362.2**

1. Casinos -- Nevada -- Las Vegas 2. Gambling -- Nevada -- Las Vegas 3. Compulsive gambling -- Nevada -- Las Vegas 4. Gambling -- Equipment and supplies -- Nevada -- Las Vegas
ISBN 0691127557; 9780691127552

LC 2012004339

In this book, Natasha Dow Schüll looks at problem gambling. "She begins by tracing the spectacular growth of machine gambling over the last several decades to where it now stands as the dominant gambling form in the US. Applying an anthropological perspective, the author focuses especially on the Las Vegas gambling industry." (Choice)

Includes bibliographical references (p. 385-423) and index

362.28   Suicide

Ackerman, Diane, 1948-

A **slender** thread. Random House 1997 305p hardcover o.p. pa $14   **362.28**

1. Suicide 2. Crisis centers 3. Hotlines (Telephone counseling)
ISBN 0-679-77133-6 pa

LC 96-8721

This is an account of the author's work as a volunteer counselor at a suicide-prevention and crisis center in a New York college town

"In a narrative that is lush with her signature gift for metaphor and delight in the senses and taut with the drama of her often frightening negotiations with people in the throes of every imaginable form of crisis, Ackerman illuminates the bewildering workings of the resilient human psyche." Booklist

362.29   Substance abuse

Clegg, Bill

Ninety days; a memoir of recovery. Bill Clegg. Little, Brown and Co. 2012 194 p.   **362.29**

1. New York (N.Y.) 2. Drug addicts -- Rehabilitation 3. Literary agents -- Personal narratives 4. Recovering addicts -- Personal narratives 5. Drug addicts -- United States -- Biography 6. Literary agents -- United States -- Biography
ISBN 9780316122528

LC 2011032542

"In this . . . memoir, a follow-up to Portrait of an Addict as a Young Man, literary agent and author [Bill] Clegg describes his struggle to stay clean. Returning to New York City after a stint in rehab, Clegg faces the ruin he's made of his life: his literary agency has closed, his lover has moved on, and he faces mounting debts with no income to speak of. Making matters worse, in spite of the many meetings Clegg attends, he's helplessly drawn to vice. Many organizations dealing with substance abuse emphasize 90 days sober as a real signpost toward recovery. Clegg discovers that reaching that signpost is going to take him a lot longer than three months." (Publishers Weekly)

Courtwright, David T.

Forces of habit; drugs and the making of the modern world. Harvard Univ. Press 2001 277p $24.95; pa $16.95 **362.29**

1. Drug abuse 2. Psychotropic drugs
ISBN 0-674-00458-2; 0-674-01003-5 pa

LC 00-61466

"In charting the mostly covert impact of drugs on modern civilization, Courtwright . . . contends that governmental, religious and economic institutions have a centuries-old love-hate relationship with psychoactive substances ranging from alcohol and caffeine to cocaine and peyote." Publ Wkly

"Reasoned and informative, Courtwright's book is a cogent source of dispassionate information on drugs and their role in society." Booklist

Includes bibliographical references and index

Feiling, Tom

Cocaine nation; how the white trade took over the world. Pegasus Books 2010 350p $27.95 **362.29**

1. Cocaine 2. Drug traffic
ISBN 978-1-60598-101-7; 1-60598-101-X

First published 2009 in the United Kingdom with title: The candy machine

"Studying the cultivation, distribution, and use of cocaine, . . . [the author] probes the drug's meteoric rise in sales and traces traffic from Colombian coca fields to Miami, Kingston, Tijuana, London, and New York. He follows consumers, traders, producers, police officers, doctors, and custom officials. . . . Packed with facts and figures, this is a well-researched survey of the subject." Publ Wkly

Includes bibliographical references

Fletcher, Anne M.

Inside rehab; the surprising truth about addiction treatment : and how to get help that works. Anne M. Fletcher. Penguin Group USA 2013 448 p. $27.95 **362.29**

1. Substance abuse 2. Drug abuse -- Treatment 3. Drug addicts -- Rehabilitation 4. Addicts -- Rehabilitation 5. Substance abuse -- Treatment
ISBN 0670025224; 9780670025220

LC 2012037030

This book is an "overview of modern treatment methods for substance abuse." Anne M. Fletcher "conducted interviews with patients and the administrators and staff of addiction programs, visiting more than a dozen such programs (both residential and outpatient). The author challenges the notion that an addict is powerless to overcome an addiction on his or her own or with minimal professional counseling." (Kirkus)

Includes bibliographical references and index

Hart, Carl

High Price; A Neuroscientist's Journey of Self-discovery That Challenges Everything You Know

About Drugs and Society. Carl Hart. HarperCollins 2013 352 p. $26.99 **362.29**

1. Scientists 2. Drug education
ISBN 0062015885; 9780062015884

In this book, "combining memoir, popular science, and public policy" author Carl Hart "lambasts current drug laws as draconian and repressive, arguing that they're based more on assumptions about race and class than on a real understanding of the physiological and societal effects of drugs. . . . Central to his work is the idea that addiction is actually a combination of physiological and social factors, and the use of drugs does not itself lead to violence and crime." (Publishers Weekly)

"An eye-opening, absorbing, complex story of scientific achievement in the face of overwhelming odds." Kirkus

Proctor, Robert N.

Golden holocaust; origins of the cigarette catastrophe and the case for abolition. Robert N. Proctor. University of California Press 2011 x, 737 p.p ill. (cloth : alk. paper) $49.95 **362.29**

1. Cigarettes 2. Tobacco habit 3. Smoking cessation programs 4. Tobacco use -- Health aspects 5. Smoking -- Psychological aspects 6. History, 20th Century -- United States 7. Smoking -- psychology -- United States 8. Persuasive Communication -- United States 9. Smoking -- adverse effects -- United States 10. Tobacco Industry -- history -- United States 11. Tobacco industry -- United States -- History 12. Tobacco Industry -- economics -- United States 13. Government Regulation -- history -- United States
ISBN 0520270169; 9780520270169

LC 2011003825

Author Robert N. Proctor discusses the cigarette, "the deadliest artifact in the history of human civilization . . . [and] how the cigarette came to be the most widely-used drug on the planet, with six trillion sticks sold per year . . . [He looks at] tobacco manufacturers conspiring to block the recognition of tobacco-cancer hazards, even as they ensnare legions of scientists and politicians in a web of denial." (Publisher's note)

Includes bibliographical references and index

Reding, Nick

Methland; the death and life of an American small town. Bloomsbury 2009 255p $25 **362.29**

1. Methamphetamine 2. Iowa 3. Methamphetamine abuse
ISBN 1-59691-650-8; 978-1-59691-650-0

LC 2008-45398

This is an account of the effect of crystal methamphetamine on "the community of Oelwein, Iowa (pop. 6,159), a once-thriving farming and railroad community." (Publisher's note)

The author traces "rise of meth use across the Midwest, focusing on Oelwein, an Iowa railroad town (pop. 6,772) that by 2005 had been 'destroyed' by the drug. . . . An important report on an extremely dangerous drug and the consequences of addiction." Kirkus

Includes bibliographical references

Ruta, Domenica

With or without you; a memoir. Domenica Ruta. Spiegel & Grau 2013 224 p. $25   **362.29**

1. Substance abuse 2. Children of drug addicts 3. Drug addicts -- Massachusetts -- Biography 4. Children of drug addicts -- Massachusetts -- Biography

ISBN 0812993241; 9780679645023; 9780812993240

LC 2012017991

This book is Domenica Ruta's memoir of her relationship with "her drug-dealer, addict mother. . . . Ruta holds nothing back as she . . . portrays her childhood in Massachusetts, whether she's writing about school events at her Catholic school, her mother's ascent as a millionaire and subsequent loss of money due to drug use, or the sexual abuse at the hands of . . . one of her mother's friends." (Kirkus Reviews)

Streatfeild, Dominic

Cocaine; an unauthorized biography. Thomas Dunne Bks./St. Martin's Press 2002 510p il $27.95; pa $15   **362.29**

1. Cocaine 2. Drug abuse 3. Drug traffic

ISBN 0-312-28624-4; 0-312-42226-1 pa

First published 2001 in the United Kingdom

"Thorough, engrossing, balanced, and entertaining, it is important social history in palatable form." Booklist

Includes bibliographical references

362.292   Alcohol

Dorris, Michael

The **broken** cord; with a foreword by Louise Erdrich. Harper & Row 1989 300p il hardcover o.p. pa $14   **362.292**

1. Alcoholism 2. Native Americans 3. Father-son relationship

ISBN 0-06-016071-3; 0-06-091682-6 pa

LC 88-45893

"The alarming statistics and consequences of fetal alcohol syndrome are skillfully interwoven with the human story of one of its victims in 'The Broken Cord.' Mr. Dorris's prose is clear and affecting." N Y Times Book Rev

Includes bibliographical references

Glaser, Gabrielle

Her best-kept secret; why women drink -- and how they can regain control. Gabrielle Glaser. Simon & Schuster 2013 256 p. $24   **362.292**

1. Alcoholism 2. Women -- Alcohol use 3. Women -- Alcohol use -- United States 4. Women alcoholics -- Rehabilitation -- United States

ISBN 1439184380; 9781439184387

LC 2013001088

This book by Gabrielle Glaser looks at U.S. women's alcohol consumption. She "traces the increasingly besotted history of women's relationship with alcohol (focusing mostly on middle-class women), but . . . argues against the efficacy of Alcoholics Anonymous (AA) for women. Rather than guiding women down a healing path of humility and acceptance, AA and its Twelve Steps, Glaser argues, have failed to protect women from predatory men, thereby consigning many" women to failure. (Publishers Weekly)

Includes bibliographical references

Johnston, Ann Dowsett

Drink; the intimate relationship between women and alcohol. by Ann Dowsett Johnston. HarperWave 2013 320 p. (hardback) $27.99   **362.292**

1. Alcoholism 2. Women -- Alcohol use 3. Women alcoholics

ISBN 0062241796; 9780062241795

LC 2013026103

In this book, author "Anne Dowsett Johnston combines in-depth research with her own personal story of recovery, and delivers a[n] . . . examination of a shocking yet little recognized epidemic threatening society today: the precipitous rise in risky drinking among women and girls." (Publisher's note)

Includes bibliographical references

362.4   People with physical disabilities

Nielsen, Kim E.

A **disability** history of the United States; Kim E. Nielsen. Beacon Press 2012 272 p. (alk. paper) $26.95   **362.4**

1. Autonomy (Psychology) 2. United States -- History 3. People with disabilities -- Legal status, laws, etc. 4. Sociology of disability -- United States -- History 5. People with disabilities -- United States -- History 6. People with disabilities -- Legal status, laws, etc. -- United States -- History

ISBN 0807022020; 9780807022023

LC 2012014236

This book "seeks to define the pivotal role of people with disabilities in [the U.S.'s] past and their contribution to our laws, policy, economics, popular culture, and our collective identity. Disability, with its presumed need for dependency, challenges the American ideal of independence and autonomy. [Kim E.] Nielsen uses various concepts of disability and dependency that go to 'the heart of both human and American experience.'" (Publisher's Weekly)

Includes bibliographical references and index.

Sacks, Oliver W.

Seeing voices; a journey into the world of the deaf. [by] Oliver Sacks. Vintage Books 2000 222p il pa $13.95   **362.4**

1. Deaf 2. Sign language 3. Gallaudet University

ISBN 0-375-70407-8

LC 00-42340

First published 1989 by University of California Press

"With his philosopher's penchant for profound discovery and his neurologist's knowledge of biology and the brain, Sacks offers provocative connections and acute observations about the nature of language and culture." Booklist

Includes bibliographical references

Solomon, Andrew

✓★ **Far** from the tree; parents, children and the search for identity. Andrew Solomon. Scribner 2012 962 p. (hbk. : alk. paper) $37.50   **362.4**

1. Parenting 2. Family life 3. Exceptional children 4. Slow learning children 5. Identity (Psychology) -- United States 6. Parents of exceptional children -- United States 7. Exceptional children -- United States -- Psychology 8. Parents of children with disabilities -- United States 9. Children with disabilities -- United States -- Psychology 10. Parent and child -- United States -- Psychological aspects

ISBN 0743236718; 9780743236713; 9780743236720; 9781439183106; 9781442356108; 9781442357433

LC 2012020878

In this book, Andrew Solomon "writes about families coping with deafness, dwarfism, Down syndrome, autism, schizophrenia, multiple severe disabilities, with children who are prodigies, who are conceived in rape, who become criminals, who are transgender. . . . All parenting turns on a crucial question: to what extent parents should accept their children for who they are, and to what extent they should help them become their best selves." (Publisher's note)

Includes bibliographical references (p. 831-906) and index.

Witter, Bret

Until Tuesday; a wounded warrior and the golden retriever who saved him. [by] Luis Carlos Montalvan with Bret Witter. Hyperion 2011 272p illustrations hardcover $23   **362.4**

1. Veterans 2. Army officers

ISBN 9781401324292

LC 2010051147

"A highly decorated captain in the U.S. Army, Luis Montalvan never backed down from a challenge during his two tours of duty in Iraq. After returning home from combat, however, the pressures of his physical wounds, traumatic brain injury, and crippling post-traumatic stress disorder began to take their toll. . . . Then Luis met Tuesday, a beautiful and sensitive golden retriever trained to assist the disabled. Tuesday had lived amongst prisoners and at a home for troubled boys, blessing many lives; he could turn on lights, open doors, and sense the onset of anxiety and flashbacks. But because of a unique training situation and sensitive nature, he found it difficult to trust in or connect with a human being--until Luis." (Publisher's note)

"Montalvan's mixture of memoir, military history, and pet story results in an urgently important tale." Booklist

362.5   Poor people

Kozol, Jonathan, 1936-

✓ **Rachel** and her children; homeless families in America. Three Rivers Press 2006 303p pa $13.95   **362.5**

1. Homeless persons

ISBN 0-307-34589-0

LC 2007-281899

A reissue of the title first published 1988

"While the individual stories that Kozol tells so affectingly point out the vivid realities of urban poverty, the book also supplies statistics that detail the more abstract-and inhuman-attitudes that contemporary society assumes when attempting to deal with its victims." Booklist

Includes bibliographical references

Vollmann, William T.

✓★ **Poor** people. Ecco 2007 314p il $29.95; pa $16.95   **362.5**

1. Poor 2. Poverty

ISBN 0-06-087882-7; 978-0-06-087882-5; 0-06-087884-3 pa; 978-0-06-087884-9 pa

LC 2006-48547

The author "brings to bear his keen powers of observation on the world around him and, not incidentally, on himself; he is unabashed about allowing his emotional reactions to inform his thoughts about what it means to be poor. This remarkable book is sui generis and should be in all collections." Libr J

362.6   People in late adulthood

Carnot, Edward J.

Is your parent in good hands? protecting your aging parent from financial abuse and neglect. Capital Books 2004 261p pa $18.95   **362.6**

1. Caregivers 2. Aging parents 3. Elderly -- Care

ISBN 1-931868-37-9

LC 2003-12140

The author "offers advice for adult children who may live far from their elderly parents about the importance of planning, how to find reliable caregivers, how to use the legal system when abuse occurs, and how to keep track of a parent's condition from a distance. This cautionary tale belongs in all aging collections." Libr J

Includes bibliographical references

Delehanty, Hugh

Caring for your parents; the complete AARP guide. [by] Hugh Delehanty & Elinor Ginzler; foreword by Mary Pipher. Rev. and expanded ed.; Sterling Pub. 2008 xvii, 238p il pa $12.95   **362.6**

1. Aging parents 2. Elderly -- Care

ISBN 1-4027-5857-X; 978-1-4027-5857-7

LC 2008-277441

First published 2005

The authors "provide information on everything from the first difficult conversations with parents about their changing situation to coping with terminal illness and death. The book has a wealth of data on long-distance caregiving, financial matters, community-based and professional case management, Medicare, and age-related physical changes." Libr J

Includes bibliographical references

Hogan, Paul Ross

✓ **Stages** of senior care; your step-by-step guide to making the best decisions. by Paul Hogan and Lori Hogan. McGraw-Hill 2009 292p il pa $18.95 **362.6**

1. Aging parents 2. Elderly -- Care

ISBN 978-0-07-162109-0

LC 2009-20572

This is "a helpful guide for families choosing among home care-giving and other assisted-living options for aging or ailing parents." Publ Wkly

Includes bibliographical references

362.7   Young people

Caughman, Susan

You can adopt; an Adoptive Families guide. [by] Susan Caughman and Isolde Motley; with the editors and readers of Adoptive Families magazine. Ballantine Books 2009 296p il pa $16   **362.7**

1. Adoption

ISBN 978-0-345-50401-2; 0-345-50401-1

LC 2009-20252

"This thorough and honest resource stands out among other books on the topic in both its comprehensiveness and the authors' candor in discussing potentially controversial adoption-related issues. Domestic or international adoption? An infant or an older child? A sibling group? What about adopting transracially? These questions and many more are addressed here via a straightforward text interspersed with firsthand, sometimes wrenching accounts by adoptive parents, birth parents, and adoptees themselves." Booklist

Includes bibliographical references

Gammage, Jeff

China ghosts; my daughter's journey to America, my passage to fatherhood. William Morrow 2007 255p il $25.95   **362.7**

1. Adoption

ISBN 978-0-06-124029-4; 0-06-124029-X

LC 2007-61204

"A father's account of going to China with his wife to adopt their first and second daughters. . . . Gammage, a staff writer for the Philadelphia Inquirer, had been happily married without children for many years, although he knew his wife really wanted children. By the time they discovered they couldn't have biological children, the best option was adopting from China. While there were tensions over their first daughter's medical problems (an infected scalp injury), both adoptions went reasonably smoothly. Back home, Gammage wrestled with his mixed feelings about the birth parents and his burden of good fortune, that guilty knowledge that his own happiness came from someone else's misfortune. Realizing that his own relationship to China was being shaped by the process of raising two Chinese girls, he ends this upbeat memoir by wondering about the impact of this new wave of immigrants on the future of Sino-American relations." Publ Wkly

Kozol, Jonathan, 1936-

Amazing grace; the lives of children and the conscience of a nation. HarperPerennial 1996 284p pa $14.95   **362.7**

1. Inner cities 2. Children with social disabilities 3. Poor -- New York (N.Y.) 4. Socially handicapped children

ISBN 0-06-097697-7; 978-0-06-097697-2

First published 1995 by Crown

Kozol's "powerfully understated report takes us inside rat-infested homes that are freezing in winter, overcrowded schools, dysfunctional clinics, soup kitchens. . . . While his narrative offers no specific solutions, it forcefully drives home his conviction: a civilized nation cannot allow this situation to continue." Publ Wkly

Includes bibliographical references

Fire in the ashes; twenty-five years among the poorest children in America. Jonathan Kozol. 1st ed. Crown Publishers 2012 x, 368 p.p $27   **362.7**

1. Poor -- United States 2. Poor children -- United States 3. Children -- United States -- Social conditions 4. Child welfare -- United States 5. Poor families -- United States

ISBN 1400052467; 9781400052462

LC 2012005183

In this book, author Jonathan Kozol profiles "a group of inner-city children he has known for many years, . . . as they grow into adulthood. . . . Jonathan tells the stories of young men and women who have come of age in one of the most destitute communities of the United States. Some of them never do recover from the battering they undergo in their early years, but many more battle back with fierce . . . determination to overcome the formidable obstacles they face." (Publisher's note)

Includes bibliographical references and index.

Leach, Penelope

Child care today; getting it right for everyone. Alfred A. Knopf 2009 350p $25.95   **362.7**

1. Child care

ISBN 978-1-4000-4256-2

LC 2008-38373

The author "evaluates the state of child care in the Western world in the context of caring for children (as opposed to rearing children). . . . There's no doubt Child Care Today will become the bible on the subject. Stock up." Booklist

Includes bibliographical references

Tough, Paul

Whatever it takes; Geoffrey Canada's quest to change Harlem and America. Houghton Mifflin Co. 2008 296p il map   **362.7**

1. Poverty 2. Poverty -- Prevention 3. Organization officials 4. Social welfare leaders 5. Poor -- Social conditions 6. Education -- United States 7. African American children -- Education 8. Harlem (New York, N.Y.) -- Economic conditions

ISBN 0-618-56989-8; 978-0-618-56989-2

LC 2008-13303

This is an account of Geoffrey Canada's creation of "the Harlem Children's Zone, a ninety-seven-block . . . [area] in central Harlem where he is testing new . . . ideas about poverty in America." (Publisher's note) Index.

"Tough profiles educational visionary Geoffrey Canada, whose Harlem Children's Zone—currently serving more than 7,000 children and encompassing 97 city blocks—represents an audacious effort to end poverty within underserved communities. . . . This book gives readers a solid look at the problems facing poor communities and their reform-

ers, as well as good cause to be optimistic about the future."
Publ Wkly

Includes bibliographical references

Tucker, Neely

Love in the driest season; a family memoir. Crown Publishers 2004 242p il hardcover o.p. pa $14   **362.7**

1. Adoption 2. Zimbabwe

ISBN 0-609-60976-9; 1-4000-8160-2 pa

LC 2002-154095

This is a "narrative of two Mississippians in Africa—a white reporter and his African-American wife—who struggle against Third World bureaucracy to adopt an abandoned Zimbabwean baby, as the continent is torn by crisis." SLJ

"This story about the adoption of a tiny, critically ill Zimbabwean orphan appeals to the head as much as the heart." Christ Sci Monit

362.73   Institutional and related services

Beam, Cris

★ To the end of June; the intimate life of American foster care. Cris Beam. Houghton Mifflin Harcourt 2013 336 p. $26   **362.73**

1. Foster home care 2. United States -- Social conditions 3. Foster home care -- United States

ISBN 0151014124; 9780151014125

LC 2013001331

This book looks at the foster care system in the U.S. "Following the lives of foster children, meeting their natural and foster parents, and interviewing experts, [Cris] Beam developed a broad overview. Intended to be a temporary arrangement, foster care frequently fails to lead either to resolution of the biological parents' problems and restoration of the birth family or to the children's permanent adoption into a new home." (Kirkus Reviews)

Includes bibliographical references

Bernstein, Nina

The lost children of Wilder; the epic struggle to change foster care. Pantheon Bks. 2001 482p hardcover o.p. pa $15   **362.73**

1. Child welfare 2. Foster home care

ISBN 0-679-75834-8 pa

LC 00-57456

"Bernstein explores the genesis and aftermath of the landmark 1973 legal case filed by young ACLU attorney Marcia Lowry against the New York State foster-care system. Known as Wilder for its 14-year-old African-American plaintiff, Shirley 'Pinky' Wilder, the suit claimed Jewish and Catholic child welfare services had a lock on foster care funding and placements. . . . This viscerally powerful history of institutionalized child abuse and the criminalization of poverty, of civil rights and social change, is compelling and essential reading." Publ Wkly

Includes bibliographical references

362.734   Adoption

Aronson, Jane

Carried in Our Hearts; The Gift of Adoption: Inspiring Stories of Families Created Across Continents. Penguin Group USA 2013 336 p. $25.95   **362.734**

ISBN 0399161058; 9780399161056

"...There is a wealth of information —and hope —here for people looking at possibilities for international adoption, and there is certainly no better advocate on the long journey than the upbeat, passionate Aronson." PubWkly

Joyce, Kathryn

★ The child catchers; rescue, trafficking, and the new gospel of adoption. Kathryn Joyce. PublicAffairs 2013 352 p. (hardback) $26.99   **362.734**

1. Adoption 2. Evangelicalism -- United States 3. Abortion -- Religious aspects -- Christianity 4. Adoption -- Religious aspects -- Christianity

ISBN 1586489429; 9781586489427; 9781586489434

LC 2012044316

This book "examines the rise of adoption as a practice and cause among American evangelical communities . . . . The more than 150 million so-termed orphans and vulnerable children worldwide frequently have living family members . . . capable of raising them, circumstances . . . lost in the mix of aggressive agencies, inadequate regulation, vulnerable families lacking understanding of the concept of adoption as permanent, and adoptive families with emotional and financial resources invested." (Library Journal)

Includes bibliographical references and index

Sweeney, Julia

If it's not one thing, it's your mother; Julia Sweeney. Free Press 2013 256 p. (hardcover) $26   **362.734**

1. Working mothers 2. Adopted children 3. Parenting -- California 4. Motherhood -- California 5. Adopted children -- California

ISBN 145167404X; 9781451674040; 9781451674057

LC 2012049503

This book is comedian Julia Sweeney's "memoir on adopting and raising a family." She writes about "her childhood, finding a suitable nanny during her daughter's childhood, her failed relationships and life as a working mother . . . . Her thoughts swirled around the complexities of educating her daughter about human anatomy and sex." (Kirkus)

362.74   Specific kinds of young people

Phelps, Carissa

Runaway girl; escaping life on the streets, one helping hand at a time. Carissa Phelps with Larkin Warren. Viking 2012 311 p. $19.99   **362.74**

1. Runaway children 2. Juvenile prostitution 3. Prostitution -- California 4. Runaway children -- California -- Biography 5. Sexually abused children -- California -- Biography

ISBN 1561636150; 9780670023721

LC 2011038441

In this memoir, Carissa Phelps discusses "her loveless, troubled childhood." After running away from a state group home at age 12, "she meets crack-addicted Natara, a prostitute, and Icey, a pimp, a pair who promise to take care of her." Eventually, "she lands in the Youth Authority detention center. There, she meets her first mentor, counselor Ron Jenkins. Slowly and with setbacks, Phelps rebuilds her life and graduates from high school thanks to the perseverance of a teacher." (Publishers Weekly)

Includes bibliographical references.

362.82   Families

Dalpiaz, Christina M.

Breaking free, starting over; parenting in the aftermath of family violence. Praeger 2004 232p $39.95   **362.82**
   1. Parenting 2. Domestic violence
   ISBN 0-275-98167-3
                                    LC 2003-62436
This guide provides "techniques for reparenting children who've been exposed to domestic violence. Lacking a safe haven, many of these children exhibit significant behavior, communication, and self-management problems." Libr J
   Includes bibliographical references

Denham, Wes

Arrested; what to do when your loved one's in jail. Chicago Review Press 2010 263p il pa $16.95   **362.82**
   1. Prisoners
   ISBN 978-1-55652-834-7; 1-55652-834-5
                                    LC 2009-42270
This book is an "extended checklist for those coping with the incarceration of a family member or significant friend, from the time the phone rings with news of the arrest onward. Denham shares the jargon, procedures, tricks, and traps in his coverage of jail visits, bail, public defenders, jail medical care, and legal and jail costs, and he outlines a decision-making process that considers the well-being of the entire family. . . . Hard-hitting, blunt, and practical, this book is packed with inside knowledge of the jail experience. It's a necessary purchase for criminal justice collections in public libraries." Libr J
   Includes bibliographical references

Domestic violence sourcebook; edited by Joyce Brennfleck Shannon. 3rd ed.; Omnigraphics 2009 665p il (Health reference series) $84   **362.82**
   1. Reference books 2. Domestic violence
   ISBN 978-0-7808-1038-9; 0-7808-1038-4
                                    LC 2009-4386
First published 2000 under the editorship of Helene Henderson with title: Domestic violence & child abuse sourcebook
   "Provides basic consumer health information about the physical, mental, and social effects of violence against intimate partners, children, teens, parents, and the elderly, along with prevention and intervention strategies." Publisher's note
   Includes bibliographical references

Fessler, Ann

The **girls** who went away; the hidden history of women who surrendered children for adoption in the decades before Roe v. Wade. Penguin Press 2006 354p hardcover o.p. pa $16   **362.82**
   1. Adoption
   ISBN 1-59420-094-7; 0-14-303897-4 pa
                                    LC 2005-58179
This "book is the culmination of interviews with more than 100 women who had been forced to give up their children for adoption between the end of World War II and Roe v. Wade (1973). The book discusses all facets of the complex issue, including the women's discovery that they were pregnant out of wedlock, going away to maternity homes to deliver the babies, and later searching for their adult children." Libr J
   "These knowing oral histories are an emotional boon for birth mothers and adoptees struggling to make sense of troubled pasts." Publ Wkly
   Includes bibliographical references

Forward, Susan

Toxic parents: overcoming their hurtful legacy and reclaiming your life; {by} Susan Forward with Craig Buck. Bantam Bks. 1989 326p hardcover o.p. pa $16   **362.82**
   1. Child abuse
   ISBN 978-0-553-38140-5; 0-553-38140-7
                                    LC 89-6812
The authors identify types of hurtful parents, including alcoholics, verbal and physical abusers, and those who emotionally neglect their children. They also offer advice to adult child abuse victims on how to overcome the harm done
   Includes bibliographical references

Marshall, Samantha

Reunited; an investigative genealogist unlocks some of life's greatest family mysteries. Pamela Slaton ; with Samantha Marshall. St. Martin's Griffin 2012 248 p. (trade pbk.) $14.99   **362.82**
   1. Adoption 2. Genealogy 3. Adoptees -- United States -- Identification -- Case studies 4. Birthparents -- United States -- Identification -- Case studies
   ISBN 0312617321; 9780312617325; 9781250012135
                                    LC 2012004630
This book shares the experience of investigative genealogist Pamela Slaton. An "adopted child herself, the author's sleuthing career began 15 years ago when her husband hired an investigator to locate her birth mother. Although she was raised by a loving adoptive family, Slaton had always wondered about her roots. . . . The author tells about finding her own extended birth family and the touching stories of some of the clients she has helped." (Kirkus Reviews)

Weiss, Elaine

Family & friends' guide to domestic violence; how to listen, talk, and take action, when someone you care about is being abused. Volcano Press 2003 143p pa $17.95 **362.82**

   1. Domestic violence

   ISBN 1-88424-422-X

                         LC 2003-4642

This is a "guide for family and friends, with practical tips for communicating with a likely victim of abuse, including how to broach the subject." Libr J

Includes bibliographical references

Surviving domestic violence; voices of women who broke free. Volcano Press 2004 214p pa $17.95 **362.82**

   1. Domestic violence

   ISBN 1-88424-427-0

                     LC 2003-27829

First published 2000 by Agreka Bks.

The author tells the "stories of 12 survivors, ranging in age and socioeconomic circumstances. She concludes each case study with a reflective commentary that emphasizes the strength and courage of these women." Libr J

Includes bibliographical references

362.83   Women

Kristof, Nicholas D., 1959-

  ★ **Half** the sky; turning oppression to opportunity for women worldwide. [by] Nicholas D. Kristof and Sheryl WuDunn. Alfred A. Knopf 2009 xxii, 294p il $27.95; ebook $15.95; pa $15.95 **362.83**

   1. Women's rights 2. Women -- Developing countries 3. Women's rights -- Developing countries 4. Women -- Crimes against -- Developing countries 5. Women -- Developing countries -- Social conditions

   ISBN 9780307267146; 9780307273154; 9780307387097

                   LC 2009-12270

Kristof and WuDunn address what they consider to be "our era's most pervasive human rights violation: the oppression of women in the developing world. They show that a little help can transform the lives of women and girls abroad and that the key to economic progress lies in unleashing women's potential." (Publisher's note) Index.

This book "is a call to arms, a call for help, a call for contributions, but also a call for volunteers. It asks us to open our eyes to this enormous humanitarian issue. It does so with exquisitely crafted prose and sensationally interesting material." Washington Post Book World

Includes bibliographical references

362.86   Veterans of military service

Finkel, David

  ★ **Thank** You for Your Service; by David Finkel. Farrar, Straus and Giroux 2013 272 p. $27 **362.86**

   1. Veterans -- Employment 2. Veterans -- United States 3. Iraq War, 2003-2011 -- Psychological aspects 4. Post-traumatic stress disorder -- United States 5. Iraq

War, 2003-2011 -- Veterans -- United States

   ISBN 0374180660; 9780374180669

                   LC 2013021990

In this book, author David Finkel "has embedded with some of the men of the 2-16 [Infantry Battalion]--but this time he has done it . . . after their deployments have ended. He is with them in their most intimate, painful, and hopeful moments as they try to recover, and in doing so, he creates a . . . portrait of what life after war is like." (Publisher's note)

"It is impossible not to be moved, outraged, and saddened by these stories, and Finkel's deeply personal brand of narrative journalism is both heartbreaking and gut-wrenching in its unflinching honesty." Booklist

Includes bibliographical references and index

362.88   Victims of war

Crompton, Vicki

  Saving beauty from the beast; how to protect your daughter from an unhealthy relationship. by Vicki Crompton and Ellen Zelda Kessner. Little, Brown 2003 259p il $22.95; pa $13.95 **362.88**

   1. Parenting 2. Abused women

   ISBN 0-316-09058-1; 0-316-73552-3 pa

                   LC 2002-19153

This book "illuminates the problems of dangerous relationships by describing their characteristics, mapping out warning signs of abuse and offering sound advice for parents seeking to empower their daughters. The authors interviewed psychologists, counselors and girls who have had violent boyfriends; the girls' stories, as well as first-person accounts from parents and abusive boyfriends, are woven throughout the text. . . . This book serves as both fervent friend and practical coach to parents whose daughters may be facing abuse." Publ Wkly

Includes bibliographical references

Feinberg, Kenneth R.

  What is life worth? the unprecedented effort to compensate the victims of 9/11. Public Affairs 2005 xxv, 213p $24 **362.88**

   1. September 11 terrorist attacks, 2001

   ISBN 1-58648-323-4

                   LC 2005-47699

"Feinberg's willingness to put himself into the book makes what could have been an alternately dry and self-serving case study crackle with care, frustration, intellectual energy and good writing." Publ Wkly

Surviving sexual violence; a guide to recovery and empowerment. edited by Thema Bryant-Davis. Rowman & Littlefield Publishers 2011 ix, 372 p.p (cloth : alk. paper) $49.95; (electronic) $49.95 **362.88**

   1. Rape 2. Sex crimes 3. Sexual harassment 4. Sexual abuse victims -- Psychology 5. Sexual abuse victims -- Rehabilitation

   ISBN 144220639X; 9781442206397; 9781442206410

                   LC 2011013937

Author Thema Bryant-Davis's "book outlines and describes the impact of particular types of sexual violation .

. . [including] childhood sexual abuse, sexual assault during adulthood, marital rape, sexual harassment, sex trafficking, or sexual violence within the military. . . . [Readers] are introduced to various pathways to surviving sexual violence and moving forward. . . . Survivors can make use of the particular approaches, which include mind-body practices, counseling, group therapies, self-defense training, and others." (Publisher's note)

Includes bibliographical references and index.

362.883   Rape

Ream, Anne K.

Lived through this; listening to the stories of sexual-violence survivors. Anne K. Ream ; with photographs by Patricia Evans. Beacon Press 2014 216 p. illustrations (hardcover : alk. paper) $24.95 **362.883**
1. Sex crimes 2. Rape victims 3. Sex crimes -- Case studies 4. Sexual abuse victims -- Case studies
ISBN 0807033367; 9780807033364

LC 2013045411

This book, by Anne K. Ream, is about "rape and sexual violence survivors. . . . In these pages we are introduced to . . . the women of Atenco, Mexico, victims of rape and political torture who are speaking out about gender-based violence in Latin America; Beth Adubato, a woman who was raped by a popular athlete; . . . and Jenny and Steve Bush, a rape survivor and her father who are working together to share Jenny's testimony of surviving rape at the hands of a veteran." (Publisher's note)

"Ream's prose is approachable, making the book a useful introductory primer for anyone studying sexual violence. The helpful inclusion of statistics at the end, which puts quantitative weight behind these individual stories, enhances the book's educational value." Pub Wkly

Includes bibliographical references

Sebold, Alice

Lucky. Back Bay Books 2002 246p pa $11.95 **362.883**
1. Rape
ISBN 0-316-09619-9
First published 1999 by Scribner

When the author "was a college freshman at Syracuse University, she was attacked and raped on the last night of school. . . . Sebold launches her memoir headlong into the rape itself, laying out its visceral physical as well as mental violence, and from there spins a narrative of her life before and after the incident, weaving memories of parental alcoholism together with her post-rape addiction to heroin. In the midst of each wrenching episode, from the initial attack to the ensuing courtroom drama, Sebold's wit is as powerful as her searing candor." Publ Wkly

363   Other social problems and services

Halpern, Jake

Braving home; dispatches from the Underwater Town, the Lava-Side Inn, and other extreme locales. Houghton Mifflin 2003 240p il $23; pa $13 **363**
1. Home 2. Authors 3. Journalists 4. United States -- Local history 5. United States -- Description and travel
ISBN 0-618-15548-1; 0-618-44662-1 pa

LC 2002-191262

"The book is like a stay-at-home adventure, with all the excitement but none of the hardship. . . . This is the perfect book for armchair travelers interested in virtual visits to 'extreme locations.'" Booklist

Includes bibliographical references

363.1   Public safety programs

Cummins, Ronnie

Genetically engineered food; a self-defense guide for consumers. [by] Ronnie Cummins and Ben Lilliston; foreword by Frances Moore Lappé. [2nd, rev ed]; Marlowe & Co 2004 237p pa $14.95 **363.1**
1. Farm produce 2. Food -- Biotechnology
ISBN 1-569-24469-3

LC 2004-45565

First published 2000

The authors "discuss genetically engineered or modified food focusing on the scientific, political, economic, and health issues. . . . [They] include information on what consumers can do, from smart shopping to grassroots lobbying, to reduce the threat of genetically engineered food." Booklist [review of 2000 edition]

Includes bibliographical references

Genetically modified foods; debating biotechnology. edited by Michael Ruse, David Castle. Prometheus Bks. 2002 355p il (Contemporary issues series) $20 **363.1**
1. Farm produce 2. Food -- Biotechnology
ISBN 1-57392-996-4

LC 2002-70510

In this collection of essays the first section focuses on "the history and the science of genetically modified foods. The next section focuses on the morality of modifying organisms for human use. . . . Succeeding sections include articles discussing religious attitudes toward genetically modified food, legal issues involving patenting and environmental damage, risk assessment, and possible environmental threats and benefits." Publisher's note

Includes bibliographical references

Nestle, Marion

Pet food politics; the Chihuahua in the coal mine. University of California Press 2008 219p il $18.95 **363.1**
1. Product recall 2. Pets -- Food
ISBN 978-0-520-25781-8; 0-520-25781-2

LC 2008-3995

This book "provides a vivid and detailed account of the [contaminated pet food] affair and its aftermath. The book . . . deserves a wider readership." Economist

Includes bibliographical references

Pringle, Peter

★ **Food,** inc; Mendel to Monsanto--the promises and perils of the biotech harvest. Simon & Schuster 2003 239p hardcover o.p. pa $13   **363.1**
  1. Farm produce 2. Food -- Biotechnology
  ISBN 0-7432-2611-9; 0-7432-6763-X pa
                                            LC 2003-42823

The author "believes that there is nothing inherently unsafe about genetically modified (GM) foods and that technology has the potential to relieve hunger and pain for millions of people. However, in this discussion of the aspects of GM foods, he does not hesitate to point out the perils. . . . Especially troubling to the author is the degree to which plant biotechnology gives control to a few international conglomerates that own patents to the products and processes." Libr J

"This is a book to satisfy curiosity and engender concern, and any of its chapters would provide an excellent subject for discussion groups." SLJ

Puleo, Stephen

Dark tide; the great Boston molasses flood of 1919. Beacon Press 2003 263p il $23   **363.1**
  1. Industrial accidents 2. Boston (Mass.) -- History
  ISBN 0-8070-5020-2
                                            LC 2003-10433

"On January 15, 1919, a fifty-foot tall steel tank filled with 2.3 million gallons of molasses collapsed on Boston's waterfront, disgorging its contents as a fifteen-foot high wave of molasses that briefly traveled at thirty-five miles per hour. The Great Boston Molasses Flood claimed the lives of twenty-one people and scores of animals, injured 150, and caused widespread destruction. Tracing the era from the tank's construction in 1915 through the multiyear lawsuit that followed the tragedy, Dark Tide uses the drama of the flood to examine the sweeping changes brought about by World War I, Prohibition, the Anarchist movement, the Red Scare, Immigration, and the role of big business in society." Univ Press Books 2004

Includes bibliographical references

Wilson, Bee

Swindled; the dark history of food fraud, from poisoned candy to counterfeit coffee. Princeton University Press 2008 384p il map $26.95   **363.1**
  1. Food industry 2. Food contamination
  ISBN 978-0-691-13820-6
                                            LC 2008-9688

"In this day and age of tainted milk, pet food and genetically altered food, Bee Wilson has given us an immensely readable history from the 1820's to the 21st century. Timely and purposeful, this book should bring many people to the whole foods world." Univ Press Books for Public and Second Sch Libr, 2009

Includes bibliographical references (351-361)

363.11   Occupational and industrial hazards

Galuszka, Peter A.

Thunder on the Mountain; Death at Massey and the Dirty Secrets Behind Big Coal. Peter A. Galuszka. St. Martin's Press 2012 xvii, 283 p., [8] p. of plates p ill. (hardcover) $25.99   **363.11**
  1. Coal mines and mining 2. Massey Energy (Firm) 3. Coal trade -- Appalachian Region 4. Coal mines and mining -- Appalachian Region
  ISBN 1250000211; 9781250000217
                                            LC 2012028241

This book by journalist Peter A. Galuszka focuses on the U.S. coal industry. He examines a "central dichotomy: the geographical and cultural isolation of the Appalachian people, perpetuated by inaccurate and condescending popular conceptions, has fostered a big-profit environment for Big Coal even as the region remains impoverished." (Publishers Weekly)

Tobar, Héctor

✓ **Deep** down dark; the untold stories of 33 men buried in a Chilean mine, and the miracle that set them free. Hector Tobar. Fararr, Straus & Giroux 2014 320 p. illustrations (cloth : alk. paper) $26   **363.11**
  1. Chile 2. Rescue work 3. Gold mines and mining 4. Copper mines and mining 5. Gold mines and mining -- Accidents 6. Copper mines and mining -- Accidents 7. San José Mine Accident, Chile, 2010
  ISBN 0374280606; 9780374280604
                                            LC 2014008385

This book, by Hector Tobar, focuses on "the San José mine [collapse] outside of Copiapó, Chile, in August 2010, [which] trapped thirty-three miners beneath thousands of feet of rock for a record-breaking sixty-nine days. . . . Even while still buried, they all agreed that if by some miracle any of them escaped alive, they would share their story only collectively." (Publisher's note)

"Rich in local color, this is a sensitive, suspenseful rendering of a legendary story." Pub Wkly

363.12   Transportation hazards

Gonzales, Laurence

Flight 232; A Story of Disaster and Survival. Laurence Gonzales. W.W. Norton & Co Inc. 2014 432 p. illustrations (some color) $27.95   **363.12**
  1. Journalism 2. Aircraft accidents
  ISBN 0393240029; 9780393240023
                                            LC 2014005238

"United Airlines Flight 232 wallowed drunkenly over the bluffs northwest of Sioux City. The plane slammed onto the runway and burst into a vast fireball. . . . Drawing on interviews with hundreds of survivors, crew, and airport and rescue personnel, [author] Laurence Gonzales, a commercial pilot himself, captures, minute by minute, the harrowing journey of pilots flying a plane with no controls and flight attendants keeping their calm in the face of certain death." (Publisher's note)

"Gonzalez presents an absorbing account of the delicate machinery of flight—and the titanic forces it must withstand—and of the investigation that traced the disaster to a tiny flaw therein." Pub Wkly

Includes bibliographical references and index

363.17 Hazardous materials

Brown, Kate

Plutopia; nuclear families, atomic cities, and the great Soviet and American plutonium disasters. Kate Brown. Oxford University Press 2013 416 p. (acid-free paper) $27.95 **363.17**

1. Working class families -- Russia (Federation) -- Ozërsk (Cheliabinskaia oblast) -- History -- 20th century 2. Plutonium industry -- Accidents -- Russia (Federation) -- Ozërsk (Cheliabinskaia oblast) -- History -- 20th century 3. Richland (Wash.) -- History -- 20th century 4. Industrial safety -- Government policy -- Soviet Union -- Case studies 5. Industrial safety -- Government policy -- United States -- Case studies 10. Working class families -- Washington (State) -- Richland -- History -- 20th century 6. Plutonium industry -- Accidents -- Washington (State) -- Richland -- History -- 20th century 7. Ozërsk (Cheliabinskaia oblast, Russia) -- History -- 20th century

ISBN 0199855765; 9780199855766

LC 2012041758

This book, written by Kate Brown, "draws on official records and dozens of interviews to tell the extraordinary stories of Richland, Washington and Ozersk, Russia-the first two cities in the world to produce plutonium. An untold - . piece of Cold War history, Plutopia invites readers to consider the nuclear footprint left by the arms race and the enormous price of paying for it." (Publisher's note)

Includes bibliographical references and index

Iversen, Kristen

★ Full body burden; growing up in the nuclear shadow of Rocky Flats. Kristen Iversen. Crown Publishers 2012 400 p. ill. $25.00 **363.17**

1. Nuclear weapons 2. Women journalists 3. Rocky Flats Plant (U.S.) 4. Rocky Flats Plant (U.S.) -- History 5. Plutonium -- Health aspects -- Colorado 6. Jefferson County (Colorado) -- Biography 7. Rocky Flats Plant (U.S.) -- Health aspects 8. Radioactive waste sites -- Cleanup -- Colorado 9. Rocky Flats Plant (U.S.) -- Environmental aspects 10. Nuclear weapons plants -- Health aspects -- Colorado 11. Radioactive pollution -- Colorado -- Jefferson County

ISBN 030795563X; 9780307955630

LC 2011045902

This book is about "[t]he Rocky Flats nuclear weapons plant near Denver [that] began production in 1953; within four years, the plutonium factory had its first major accident, the first of many. In fact, by the end of its forty-year run, the plant would gain notoriety as 'the most contaminated site in America.' Kristen [Iversen], the author . . . , grew up in the radioactive shadow of this secret facility and she witnessed at close quarters the disastrous effects of its activities." Here, "she combines . . . personal experiences and . . . investigative

reporting to expose [the U.S.] government's betrayal of its responsibility to its citizens." (Barnes & Noble)

Includes bibliographical references and index

Schlosser, Eric, 1959-

★ Command and control; nuclear weapons, the Damascus Accident, and the illusion of safety. Eric Schlosser. The Penguin Press 2013 640 p. $36 **363.17**

1. Nuclear weapons -- United States -- History 2. Nuclear weapons -- Accidents -- United States -- History 3. Titan (Missile) -- History 4. Nuclear weapons -- Accidents -- Arkansas -- History 5. Nuclear weapons -- United States -- Safety measures 6. Nuclear weapons -- Government policy -- United States 7. United States. Air Force. Strategic Air Command. Strategic Missile Wing, 308th

ISBN 1594202273; 9781594202278

LC 2013017151

This book "interweaves the minute-by-minute story of an accident at a nuclear missile silo in rural Arkansas with a historical narrative that spans more than fifty years. It depicts the urgent effort by American scientists, policymakers, and military officers to ensure that nuclear weapons can't be stolen, sabotaged, used without permission, or detonated inadvertently." (Publisher's note)

Includes bibliographical references and index

363.19 Product hazards

Nestle, Marion

Safe food; bacteria, biotechnology, and bioterrorism. University of Calif. Press 2003 350p il (California studies in food and culture) $27.50 **363.19**

1. Terrorism 2. Food adulteration and inspection 3. Food -- Biotechnology

ISBN 0-520-23292-5

LC 2002-27172

The author "argues that ensuring safe food involves more than washing hands or cooking food to higher temperatures. It involves politics. When it comes to food safety, billions of dollars are at stake, and industry, government, and consumers collide over issues of values, economics, and political power—and not always in the public interest." Publisher's note

Includes bibliographical references

363.2 Police services

Bell, Suzanne

Encyclopedia of forensic science; foreword by Barry A.J. Fisher; preface by Robert C. Shaler. rev ed; Facts on File 2008 402p il (Facts on File science library) $85 **363.2**

1. Reference books 2. Forensic sciences -- Encyclopedias

ISBN 978-0-8160-6799-2; 0-8160-6799-6

LC 2008-5862

First published 2003

"In addition to explaining the science of forensics, Bell . . . reviews various disciplines related to forensic science, among them entomology, odontology, and psychology. Other entries cover professional organizations, government agencies, famous names in the field of forensics, evidence, and legal issues. . . . With its clear language and brief entries [this] volume will provide readers with a nuts-and-bolts understanding of the real world of forensic science." Booklist [review of 2003 edition]

Includes bibliographical references

Englert, Rod

Blood secrets; a forensic expert reveals how blood spatter tells the crime scene's story. [by] Rod Englert, with Kathy Passero; foreword by Ann Rule. Thomas Dunne Books 2010 286p il $25.99; ebook $12.99 **363.2**

1. Blood 2. Forensic sciences 3. Criminal investigation
ISBN 978-0-312-56400-1; 0-312-56400-7; 978-1-4299-2921-9 ebook; 1-4299-2921-9 ebook
LC 2009-40294

"This book is aimed at anyone who is interested in the field of forensics or wants to pursue a career in that area. The book also gives a detailed account of the many difficulties involved in crime scene reconstruction. . . . Among the topics covered are blood patterns and their identification." Sci Books Films

"Englert deftly balances real-life examples and detailed scientific analysis, giving readers a richer understanding of this developing avenue of forensic science." Publ Wkly

Includes bibliographical references

Geary, Rick

J. Edgar Hoover; a graphic biography. Hill and Wang 2008 102p il $16.95 **363.2**

1. Graphic novels 2. Biographical graphic novels 3. FBI officials 4. United States -- Federal Bureau of Investigation -- Graphic novels
ISBN 978-0-8090-9503-2; 0-8090-9503-3
LC 2007-25193

Rick Geary has written a biography of J. Edgar Hoover, who served in the federal government for 55 years and under eight presidents, most notably as director of the Federal Bureau of Investigation. He was appointed to that position on May 10, 1924. Geary covers Hoover's sometimes controversial career, including his refusal to involve the FBI directly into investigations of crimes against civil rights workers and the 1963 bombing in Birmingham, Alabama, and the bureau's investigation of Martin Luther King, Jr. He tastefully discusses Hoover's undercover sexual life.

"As solid, thrilling and informative a guide to the life of the America's most powerful authoritarian as one could ask for." Kirkus

Neme, Laurel A.

Animal investigators; how the world's first wildlife forensics lab is solving crimes and saving endangered species. foreword by Richard Leakey. Scribner 2009 230p il $25 **363.2**

1. Poaching 2. Forensic sciences 3. Wild animal trade 4. Endangered species 5. Wildlife conservation 6. U.S.

Fish and Wildlife Service -- Forensics Laboratory
ISBN 978-1-4165-5056-3; 1-4165-5056-9
LC 2008-56004

"Illegal wildlife trafficking is worth an estimated $20 billion a year. That makes it the third most lucrative criminal activity, coming in just behind drug and human trafficking and, incredibly, ahead of arms smuggling. . . . Animal Investigators documents this black market in unflinching and often depressing detail. But the book is more than just a journey into the criminal underworld, a litany of dismal statistics or a roll-call of cowardly, greedy intermediaries. Instead, Laurel A. Neme centres her book on a more inspiring place: the US Fish and Wildlife Service Forensics Lab in Ashland, Oregon, the world's only laboratory dedicated to solving crimes against wildlife." New Sci

Includes bibliographical references

Stillman, Deanne

Desert reckoning; a town sheriff, a Mojave hermit, and the biggest manhunt in modern California history. Deanne Stillman. Nation Books 2012 308 p. (hbk.) $26 **363.2**

1. California -- History 2. Criminal investigation 3. Mojave Desert (Calif.) 4. Criminal investigation -- California -- Mojave Desert -- Case studies
ISBN 1568586086; 1568586914; 9781568586083; 9781568586915
LC 2012004961

This book by author Deanne Stillman features "a brilliant, paranoid, drug-abusing hermit and a former surfer-turned-law enforcement officer, and the subsequent seven-day manhunt . . . Stillman explores . . . the broken families and failed strivings of her two protagonists: hermit Donald Kueck and the murdered sheriff, Steve Sorenson. . . . The details of the manhunt for Kueck are interspersed with Stillman's imaginings about his seven days on the run, with the desert sometimes becoming the main character." (Publishers Weekly)

Includes bibliographical references and index.

Wagner, E. J.

The **science** of Sherlock Holmes; from Baskerville Hall to the Valley of Fear, the real forensics behind the great detective's greatest cases. Wiley 2006 244p il $24.95; pa $16.95 **363.2**

1. Forensic sciences 2. Criminal investigation 3. Holmes, Sherlock (Fictitious character)
ISBN 0-471-64879-5; 978-0-471-64879-6; 0-470-12823-2 pa; 978-0-470-12823-7 pa
LC 2005-22236

The author discusses forensic science in Arthur Conan Doyle's stories of the 'consulting detective' Sherlock Holmes. She compares Holmes's investigative techniques to those used in actual cases such as the killing of Lizzie Borden's parents in 1892, the 1902 murder of Joseph Browne Elwell, and the disappearance of Dr. George Parkman in 1849.

This book "will intrigue readers with incredible stories and amazing tales from the early days of forensic science." Christ Sci Monit

Includes bibliographical references

363.25 Detection of crime (Criminal investigation)

Halber, Deborah

The **skeleton** crew; how amateur sleuths are solving America's coldest cases. Deborah Halber. Simon & Schuster 2014 304 p. (hardcover) $25 **363.25**

1. Private investigators 2. Cold cases (Criminal investigation) 3. Criminal investigation -- United States
ISBN 1451657587; 9781451657586; 9781451657593
LC 2013034949

This book, by Deborah Halber, "provides an entree into the gritty and tumultuous world of Sherlock Holmes-wannabes who race to beat out law enforcement--and one another--at matching missing persons with unidentified remains. In America today, upwards of forty thousand people are dead and unaccounted for. These murder, suicide, and accident victims, separated from their names, are being adopted by the bizarre online world of amateur sleuths." (Publisher's note)

"The author paints a colorful picture of armchair investigators pursuing their first 'solves' amid the conflicting motivations of their peers and of various law enforcement agencies—." LJ

Includes bibliographical references

Lance, Peter

Deal With the Devil; The FBI's Secret Thirty-Year Relationship with a Mafia Killer. by Peter Lance. William Morrow 2013 672 p. (hardcover) $29.99 **363.25**

1. Mafia 2. Criminal investigation -- United States
ISBN 0061455342; 9780061455346

In this book, author Peter Lance draws on three decades of once secret FBI files—and exclusive new interviews—to tell the . . . story of Gregory Scarpa Sr., aka "The Grim Reaper;" a Mafia capo, who "stopped counting" after 50 murders, while secretly betraying the Colombo crime family as a Top Echelon Criminal Informant for the Bureau. Lance draws on thousands of pages of court transcripts, interviews and declassified FBI files, to trace Scarpa's . . . relationship with the Bureau starting in 1960." (Publisher's note)

Weiner, Tim

Enemies; the history of the FBI at war. Tim Weiner. 1st ed. Random House 2011 537 p. (alk. paper) $30 **363.25**

1. National security -- United States 2. Intelligence service -- United States 3. United States -- History -- 20th century 4. Espionage -- United States -- History -- 20th century 5. United States. Federal Bureau of Investigation -- History -- 20th century
ISBN 9780679643890; 9781400067480
LC 2011005353

This book "delivers a . . . history of what has been, in effect, America's secret police. The history of the FBI is easily divided into two periods: the J. Edgar Hoover period and after. In 1924, before he was 30, Hoover took over a tiny, tawdry Bureau and built it into a fearsome empire he ruled as a personal fiefdom until his death in 1972. . . . Weiner focuses on the FBI's activities investigating and attempting to prevent subversion and terrorism." (Kirkus Reviews)

Includes bibliographical references and index

363.28 Services of special kinds of security and law enforcement agencies

Carr, Matthew, 1953-

Fortress Europe; dispatches from a gated continent. Matthew Carr. New Press 2012 xiii, 279 p.p (hbk. : alk. paper) : $27.95 **363.28**

1. Border patrols 2. Illegal aliens 3. Europe -- Immigration and emigration 4. Borderlands -- Europe 5. Border crossing -- Europe 6. Illegal aliens -- Europe -- Social conditions 7. Illegal aliens -- Government policy -- Europe 8. Border security -- Government policy -- Europe 9. Europe -- Emigration and immigration -- Government policy
ISBN 1595586857; 9781595586858
LC 2012012225

This book presents an "exposé of European immigration policy and its devastating effects" focusing on "the 'contradictory character' of the 1985 Schengen Agreement, which opened borders between 25 European states. . . . The grimly ironic result for undocumented immigrants, refugees, and victims of human trafficking has been people 'drowning in the Mediterranean, shot trying to cross border fences, mutilating themselves in detention centers, or reduced to destitution'." (Publishers Weekly)

Includes bibliographical references (p. [255]-266) and index

Mackay, James A.

Allan Pinkerton; the first private eye. {by} James Mackay. Wiley 1997 256p il $35 **363.28**

1. Private investigators 2. Pinkerton's National Detective Agency
ISBN 0-471-19415-8
LC 97-21271

"Though Pinkerton started the first U.S. detective agency after successfully uncovering a counterfeit ring, little was known about him. The author does an excellent job of tracing Pinkerton's early life and his arrival in the United States from Scotland. Then he examines better-known aspects of Pinkerton's career—his part in Lincoln's train ride through Baltimore, investigation of the Confederate spy Rose Greenhow, and association with Gen. George McClellan, his mentor and hero." Libr J

Includes bibliographical references

Miller, Todd

Border patrol nation; dispatches from the front lines of homeland security. Todd Miller. City Lights Publishers 2014 256 p. ill., maps (City lights open media) (pbk.) $16.95 **363.28**

1. Border patrols 2. Immigration law -- United States 3. United States. Immigration Border Patrol -- History 4. Mexican-American Border Region -- Economic conditions
ISBN 0872866319; 9780872866317
LC 2013043754

In this book, author "Todd Miller sounds an alarm as he chronicles the changing landscape. Traveling the country--and beyond--to speak with the people most involved with and impacted by the Border Patrol, he combines these first-hand encounters with careful research to expose a vast and booming industry for high-end technology, weapons, surveillance, and prisons." (Publisher's note)

An "alarming story of U.S. Border Patrol and Homeland Security's ever-widening reach into the lives of American citizens and legal immigrants as well as the undocumented." Pub Wkly

Includes bibliographical references and index. (p. 326-343) and index

363.3   Other aspects of public safety

Maclean, John N.

Fire and ashes; on the front lines of American wildfire. Holt & Co. 2003 238p il map $25; pa $14   **363.3**
1. Wildfires
ISBN 0-8050-7212-8; 0-8050-7591-7 pa
LC 2002-38704

"This work tells of two infernos: a 1999 conflagration in Nevada and a 1953 case of arboreal arson in California that took 15 lives when the fire exhibited unexpected behavior. . . . Careful in analysis, Maclean turns visceral when imparting the sudden terror of life-ending flames, or, as for a survivor of the 1949 Mann Gulch disaster whom he visits, a life-searing whirlwind. A solid choice that will be in demand, particularly during the West's summer fire season." Booklist

363.31   Censorship

1990

Green, Jonathon

The **encyclopedia** of censorship; [by] Jonathon Green, Nicholas J. Karolides. rev ed; Facts on File 2005 xxii, 698p (Facts on File library of world history) $85   **363.31**
1. Reference books 2. Censorship -- Encyclopedias
ISBN 0-8160-4464-3
LC 2004-53211

First published 1990

"The crowded roster of those who have been affected by censorship, as well as the books, films, and other works attacked, are found in these . . . pages. Controversies that have arisen over the years are given historical context; highly valuable national wrap-ups treat the culture, law, and predominant trends of diverse lands." Libr J

Includes bibliographical references

363.32   Social conflict

Allison, Graham T.

Nuclear terrorism; the ultimate preventable catastrophe. [by] Graham Allison. Times Books\Henry Holt 2004 263p il $24   **363.32**
1. Terrorism 2. Nuclear warfare
ISBN 0-8050-7651-4
LC 2004-47427

"Allison's comprehensive but accessible treatment of this vital subject is a major contribution to public understanding." N Y Times Book Rev

Includes bibliographical references

Anderson, Sean

Historical dictionary of terrorism; [by] Sean K. Anderson, with Stephen Sloan. 3rd ed; Scarecrow Press 2009 lxxvi, 800p (Historical dictionaries of war, revolution, and civil unrest) $115   **363.32**
1. Reference books 2. Terrorism -- Dictionaries
ISBN 978-0-8108-5764-3; 0-8108-5764-2
LC 2009-3226

First published 1995

"The dictionary encompasses individuals, groups, events, doctrines, and concepts such as Power law, which is the mathematical relation between the numbers and intensity of events. . . . This is an accurate, objective, and clearly written resource that will be useful in public and academic libraries." Booklist

Includes bibliographical references (p. 713-798)

Aust, Stefan

Baader -Meinhof; the inside story of the R.A.F. translated from the German by Anthea Bell. Rev ed; Oxford University Press 2009 xxi, 457p il $29.95   **363.32**
1. Terrorism 2. Red Army Faction
ISBN 978-0-19-537275-5; 0-19-537275-1
LC 2008-49401

Original German edition, 1985

"The quintessential radical leftist terrorist group, founded in 1970 and eventually known as the Red Army Faction, Baader-Meinhof was responsible for 34 deaths in Germany over a 30-year period. . . . Exhaustively detailing the group's exploits from 1970 until the prison suicides of the leaders in 1977, Aust offers fascinating insights into both the spectacular and the mundane aspects of life in a terrorist cadre." Libr J

Baker, Stewart A.

Skating on stilts; why we aren't stopping tomorrow's terrorism. Hoover Institution Press 2010 370p $19.95   **363.32**
1. Terrorism 2. Right of privacy 3. United States -- Foreign relations 4. United States -- Dept. of Homeland Security
ISBN 978-0-8179-1154-6
LC 2010-20763

"In the years after 9/11, officials scrambled to rethink security at the border and in the air—while privacy groups and foreign governments did their best to stop and then roll back security measures. . . . Baker draws on his experience at Homeland Security to give the reader a ringside seat as the battle unfolds. . . . He describes his agency's post-9/11 strategy to rebuild border security on a foundation of better information about travelers, and the bitter resistance the strategy met from privacy campaigners in the United States and Europe." Publisher's note

Baker "makes a persuasive case against the privacy absolutists." Los Angeles Times

Includes bibliographical references

Bobbitt, Philip

Terror and consent; the wars for the twenty-first century. Alfred A. Knopf 2008 672p il $35 **363.32**
1. Terrorism 2. United States -- Foreign relations
ISBN 1-4000-4243-7; 978-1-4000-4243-2
LC 2007-34194

The author examines "the relationship between the emergent constitutional order and the emergence of modern 'market state terrorism,' which, mirroring the market state and availing itself of the same technological advances, may be lethal enough to pose an existential threat to the very possibility of government by consent of the governed." Booklist

Includes bibliographical references

Dershowitz, Alan M.

Preemption; a knife that cuts both ways. W.W. Norton 2006 348p il (Issues of our time) $24.95 **363.32**
1. Military art and science 2. Violence -- Prevention
ISBN 0-393-06012-8
LC 2005-27728

The author "examines preemptive war, preventative detention, and restrictions on dangerous speech, and claims that in the absence of general legal principles (or even a healthy debate) about preemptive action, society's current trend away from deterrence and toward prevention (as accelerated by the 'war on terrorism') threatens longstanding notions of individual liberty and state sovereignty. . . . This book is an academic and accessible framing of an important debate." Booklist

Includes bibliographical references

Dickey, Christopher

Securing the city; inside America's best counterterror force--the NYPD. Simon & Schuster 2009 321p $26 **363.32**
1. Terrorism 2. Police -- New York (N.Y.) 3. New York (N.Y.) -- Police Dept.
ISBN 978-1-4165-5240-6; 1-4165-5240-5
LC 2008-43085

This is an examination of the "command center of the New York City Police Department's counterterrorism division. . . . Headed by David Cohen, who ran the CIA's operations inside the United States in the 1980s and its global spying in the 1990s, the NYPD's counterterrorism division had up-to-the-minute details of new attacks set in motion to target Manhattan in 2002 and 2003." Publisher's note

"Vivid and thought-provoking. . . . The general reader can enjoy a book that has the pace and drama of a thriller, and for the specialist, . . . there is much to ponder." Economist

Includes bibliographical references

Elshtain, Jean Bethke

Just war against terror; the burden of American power in a violent world. Basic Books 2003 240p $23; pa $14 **363.32**
1. Terrorism 2. War on terrorism
ISBN 0-465-01910-2; 0-465-01911-0 pa
LC 2002-154549

"While this volume is not a radical departure from the abundance of post-September 11 books, it presents well the moral case for U.S. military engagement in the world and gives credence to those who advocate the use of force as a response to terrorism." Publ Wkly

Includes bibliographical references

Encyclopedia of terrorism; Peter Chalk, editor. ABC-CLIO 2013 xviii, 871 p.p ill. (hardcopy) $205; (ebook) $205.00 **363.32**
1. Terrorism -- Encyclopedias
ISBN 0313308950; 9780313308956; 9780313385353
LC 2012016710

This book, edited by Peter Chalk, "provides comprehensive coverage of the events, individuals, groups, incidents, and trends in terrorism in the modern era. [It] . . . presents . . . information on developments since the watershed events of September 11, 2001, providing readers with an invaluable reference tool for understanding major developments that have occurred in domestic and international terrorism." (Publisher's note)

Includes bibliographical references and index

Harris, Shane

The **watchers**; the rise of America's surveillance state. Penguin Press 2010 418p il $27.95; pa $17 **363.32**
1. Terrorism 2. National security -- United States 3. Intelligence service -- United States
ISBN 978-1-59420-245-2; 978-0-14-311890-9 pa
LC 2009-37205

The author examines the development of domestic surveillance programs in the United States intended to prevent terrorist attacks.

"A sharply written, wise analysis of the complex mashup of electronic sleuthing, law, policy and culture." Kirkus

Includes bibliographical references

Herridge, Catherine

The **next** wave; on the hunt for al Qaeda's American recruits. Crown Forum 2011 258p il $25 **363.32**
1. Terrorists 2. Islamic fundamentalism 3. Al Qaeda (Organization) 4. Muslims -- United States 5. Terrorism -- Religious aspects
ISBN 978-0-307-88525-8; 0-307-88525-9
LC 2010-53585

A "report on a new generation of terrorists and the American-born Islamic cleric Anwar al-Awlaki, who has inspired many of them to commit violent acts. Now believed to be in Yemen, al-Awlaki was targeted for killing by the U.S. government in 2010. He is linked to three of the 9/11 hijackers, the massacre at Foot Hood, the attempted Christmas Day 2009 bombing and the cargo printer plot in October 2010. Drawing on documents and interviews, the author shows how the charismatic al-Awlaki has become a leading al-Qaeda propagandist, using the Internet to recruit alienated American youths, many newly arrived in America, to join the terrorist cause. . . . A sobering view of why the 9/11 nightmare continues a decade later. " Kirkus

Includes bibliographical references

Merriman, John M.

The **dynamite** club; how a bombing in fin-de-siecle Paris ignited the age of modern terror. Houghton Mifflin Co. 2009 259p il map $26   **363.32**

1. Bombings 2. Terrorism 3. Anarchism and anarchists 4. Anarchists 5. Paris (France) -- History

ISBN 978-0-618-55598-7; 0-618-55598-6

LC 2008-49470

"Because he neither makes excuses for anyone nor takes simplistic ideological swipes, Merriman is a solid guide through these dark back lanes of European history." Houston Chron

Includes bibliographical references

Pedahzur, Ami

The **Israeli** secret services and the struggle against terrorism. Columbia University Press 2009 215p il $27.50   **363.32**

1. Terrorism 2. Secret service -- Israel 3. Intelligence service -- Israel

ISBN 978-0-231-14042-3; 0-231-14042-8

LC 2008-25949

"Dividing the potential responses to terrorism into four categories (defensive, reconciliatory, criminal justice and war), the author tracks the development of an Israeli war model and demonstrates that rather than sending terrorists running, the approach leads to an escalating cycle of terrorism, citing many examples in which Israels elimination of threats has created the impetus for more violence. . . . While Pedahzurs style leans toward the dryly academic, his insights are so well reasoned and relevant that the pages almost turn themselves." Publ Wkly

Includes bibliographical references

363.325   Terrorism

Bergen, Peter L.

Manhunt; the ten-year search for Bin Laden from 9/11 to Abbottabad. Peter L. Bergen. 1st ed. Crown Publishers 2012 xxi, 359 p.p col. ill., maps $26   **363.325**

1. Terrorists 2. Special forces (Military science) -- United States 3. Qaida (Organization) 4. Terrorists -- Saudi Arabia 5. War on Terrorism, 2001-2009 6. Fugitives from justice -- United States 7. Terrorism -- United States -- Prevention 8. Special operations (Military science) -- United States

ISBN 0307955575; 9780307955579

LC 2012004258

This book provides an "account of the . . . effort to track and kill the al-Qaeda leader. . . . Only in 2010 did the monitoring of a Kuwaiti courier's cellphone use suggest ties to bin Laden, and they followed his car to the compound in the quiet Pakistani town of Abbottabad, where he actually lived with bin Laden's extended family. . . . Bergen . . . delineates the U.S. government decision-making process in pursuing the Special Operations infiltration of the compound, despite the lack of certainty that bin Laden was actually there." (Kirkus Reviews)

Includes bibliographical references and index

Graff, Garrett M.

The **threat** matrix; Garrett M. Graff. 1st ed. Little, Brown and Company 2011 666 p. ill.   **363.325**

1. Terrorism -- Prevention 2. National security -- United States 3. United States. Federal Bureau of Investigation 4. War on Terrorism, 2001-2009 5. Intelligence service -- United States 6. Terrorism -- United States -- Prevention

ISBN 9780316068611

LC 2010053237

In this book, author Garrett M. "Graff shows how . . . [Former FBI Director Louis Freeh's] leadership slowed intelligence operations preceding 9/11 and in what ways the agency still suffers from his tenure. Graff . . . track[s] the ways that the FBI adapted as terrorism changed. He takes seriously even ridiculous threats, such as an absurd letter penned by a Filipino teenager and the realization that the FBI lacked a file on the Japanese cult that released sarin gas in Tokyo even though they were listed in the Manhattan phone book. Some episodes . . . [include a] discussion of the events behind a July 2001 memo's theory that terrorists were in the U.S. training at civil aviation facilities. Graff's focus, though it covers a time span from J. Edgar Hoover's death to the present day, rests particularly on the massive intelligence failures in the 10 years preceding 9/11, and after." (Publishers Weekly)

Includes bibliographical references (p. 638-646) and index

Johnsen, Gregory D.

The **last** refuge; Yemen, al-Qaeda, and America's war in Arabia. Gregory D. Johnsen. W.W. Norton & Co. 2013 p. cm.   **363.325**

1. Yemen 2. Qaida (Organization) 3. War on Terrorism, 2001-2009 4. Terrorism -- Yemen (Republic) 5. United States -- Military policy 6. Terrorism -- Persian Gulf Region -- Prevention

ISBN 9780393082425

LC 2012027875

In this book on Yemen, Gregory D. Johnson presents an "analysis of how a nation that had been a success story in the U.S. effort to defeat al-Qaeda and stabilize the region has been the site for resurgence instead. He examines the historical factors that have contributed to the buildup of al-Qaeda in Yemen as young men were recruited by the government, Yemeni tribes, and mosques in a concerted effort to turn the war in Afghanistan into a broader jihad." (Booklist)

Includes bibliographical references and index

McDermott, Terry

The **hunt** for KSM; inside the pursuit and takedown of the real 9/11 mastermind, Khalid Sheikh Mohammed. Terry McDermott and Josh Meyer. Little, Brown and Co. 2012 350 p.   **363.325**

1. Terrorists 2. September 11 terrorist attacks, 2001

3. Terrorism -- Prevention -- United States 4. Qaida (Organization) 5. Terrorists -- Islamic countries 6. September 11 Terrorist Attacks, 2001 7. Terrorism -- United States -- Prevention
ISBN 9780316186599

LC 2011041533

This book follows "[t]he cat-and-mouse game between American investigators and Khalid Sheikh Mohammed, architect of the 9/11 attacks and other terrorist spectaculars. . . . Journalists [Terry] McDermott . . . and [Josh] Meyer (the L.A. Times's chief terrorism reporter) present a police procedural starring an FBI agent, Frank Pellegrino, Port Authority detective Matt Besheer, and the inter-agency anti-terrorism experts who tracked KSM and his confederates for a decade before his 2003 capture. . . . The authors" . . . profile of Khalid Sheikh Mohammed depicts a resourceful, charismatic man . . . and paints a . . . portrait of the workaday terrorist life of fund-raising, recruitment, bomb-rigging, and general plotting, all carried out while dodging a global manhunt." (Publishers Weekly)
Includes bibliographical references

Molotch, Harvey

Against security; how we go wrong at airports, subways, and other sites of ambiguous danger. Harvey Molotch. Princeton University Press 2012 xv, 260 p.p ill., maps (hardcover) $35.00   **363.325**
1. Fear 2. Security (Psychology) 3. Offenses against public safety 4. National security -- United States 5. Transportation -- Security measures -- United States 6. Terrorism -- Prevention -- Government policy -- United States
ISBN 069115581X; 9780691155814

LC 2012012128

In this book, Harvey Molotch "profiles the workings of our anxieties and fears and how they can be exploited by authorities who have an interest in stoking them. The author is concerned with the complex systems that permit us to feel safe in public places. He traces a path from public toilet facilities through subways and airports to the reconstruction of ground zero before taking on the catastrophic effects of nature in the hurricane damage and flooding of New Orleans in 2005." (Kirkus)
Includes bibliographical references and index

Russell, Jenna

Long mile home; Boston under attack, the city's courageous recovery, and the epic hunt for justice. Scott Helman and Jenna Russell, reporters for the Boston Globe. Penguin Group 2014 352 p. ill. (chiefly col.), col map (hardcover) $27.95   **363.325**
1. Bombings 2. Boston Marathon 3. Terrorism -- United States 4. Boston Marathon Bombing, Boston, Mass., 2013 5. Terrorism -- Massachusetts -- Boston -- Case studies
ISBN 0525954481; 9780525954484

LC 2014000091

This book, by Scott Helman and Jenna Russell, is about "the Boston Marathon bombing and subsequent manhunt for the Tsarnaev brothers. [It tells] the gripping story of the tragic, surreal, and ultimately inspiring week of April 15, 2013: the preparations of the bombers; the glory of the race; the . . .

. emergency response to the explosions; the massive deployment of city, state, and federal law enforcement personnel; and the . . . world's emotional and humanitarian response." (Publisher's note)

"Despite the multitude of sources drawn upon, the writing is seamless and riveting. . . . Sensitive in its treatment and thrilling in its pace and immediacy." LJ
Includes bibliographical references and index

Theoharis, Athan G.

Abuse of power; Athan G. Theoharis. Temple University Press 2011 xvi, 212p (hbk: alk. paper) $29.95   **363.325**
1. Wiretapping 2. Intelligence service 3. Electronic surveillance 4. Cold War 5. September 11 Terrorist Attacks, 2001
ISBN 9781439906644; 9781439906651; 9781439906668

LC 2010042416

In this book, "[Athan G.] Theoharis continues his investigation of U.S. government surveillance and historicizes the 9/11 response. Criticizing the U.S. government's secret activities and policies during periods of 'unprecedented crisis,' he recounts how presidents and FBI officials exploited concerns about foreign-based internal security threats. Drawing on information sequestered until recently in FBI records, Theoharis shows how these secret activities in the World War II and Cold War eras expanded FBI surveillance powers and, in the process, eroded civil liberties without substantially advancing legitimate security interests. . . . [T]his . . . book speaks to the costs and consequences of still-secret post-9/11 surveillance programs and counterintelligence failures [and] . . . makes the case that the abusive surveillance policies of the Cold War years were repeated in the government's responses to the September 11 attacks." (Publisher's note)

Willman, David

The mirage man; David Willman. Bantam Books 2011 xiii, 448p ill.   **363.325**
1. Bioterrorism 2. Iraq War, 2003-2011 3. Governmental investigations -- United States
ISBN 9780553807752; 9780345530219

LC 2011006232

This book "offers . . . [an] account of the . . . FBI investigation into the 'anthrax attacks' as the [George W.] Bush administration strove to use the public panic to strengthen their case to go to war, while the culprit was, in all likelihood, a military microbiologist named Bruce Ivins. . . . [It] traces Ivins's unhappy life, how he endured childhood abuse and privation to become a successful scientist only to find his life unraveling as a result of his . . . obsessions and fixations with women. . . . [David] Willman pivots to focus on the flawed investigation . . . and how . . . Ivins benefited both financially and professionally from the public paranoia about anthrax as his research into an anthrax vaccine became a national priority." (Publishers Weekly)
Includes bibliographical references and index

363.33 Gun control

Guns in American society; an encyclopedia of history, politics, culture, and the law. Gregg Lee Carter, editor. ABC-CLIO 2012 3 v. lxx, 1096 p.p ill. **363.33**
1. Weapons 2. Law -- United States 3. Violence -- Encyclopedias 4. Gun control -- United States -- Encyclopedias 5. Violent crimes -- United States -- Encyclopedias 6. Social movements -- United States -- Encyclopedias 7. Firearms -- Social aspects -- United States -- Encyclopedias 8. Firearms -- Law and legislation -- United States -- Encyclopedias
ISBN 0313386706; 0313386714; 9780313386701; 9780313386718

LC 2011043435

In this book, editor Gregg Lee Carter focuses on the following questions: Is "the high rate of violence in the United States linked to the prevalence of guns--or to a lack of social homogeneity and economic inequality? Should there be support for stricter or more lenient gun control? Should people carry concealed weapons for personal protection? . . . The encyclopedia . . . [offers] the latest thinking and research in the fields of criminology, history, law, medicine, politics, and sociology, [while] providing objective information." (Publisher's note)

Includes bibliographical references and index

363.34 Disasters

De Villiers, Marq

The **end**; natural disasters, manmade catastrophes, and the future of human survival. Thomas Dunne Books/St. Martin's Press 2008 362p il $26.95 **363.34**
1. Human ecology 2. Disaster relief 3. Natural disasters
ISBN 978-0-312-36569-1; 0-312-36569-1

LC 2008-39096

Published in Canada with title: Dangerous world

The author presents an analysis of humanity's role in catastrophic natural disasters to consider whether or not such threats are increasing and how they can be managed.

"This book effectively summarizes the latest scientific thought on disasters, and de Villiers's entrancing prose will hook even the most reluctant reader." Libr J

Includes bibliographical references

Downey, Tom

The **last** men out; life on the edge at Rescue 2 firehouse. H. Holt 2004 300p il $25; pa $15 **363.34**
1. Fire fighters 2. World Trade Center terrorist attack, 2001 3. New York (N.Y.) -- Fire Dept.
ISBN 0-8050-7169-5; 0-8050-7844-4 pa

LC 2003-67770

"Downey's descriptions burn into the pages with searing intensity. Writing with verve and energy in a gritty style, he explores all extremes of the firemen's world, from triumphant moments of heroism to bitter tragedies." Publ Wkly

Ehrlich, Gretel

Facing the wave; a journey in the wake of the tsunami. Gretel Ehrlich. Pantheon Books 2012 240 p. $25 **363.34**
1. Tsunamis 2. Sendai Earthquake, Japan, 2011 3. Fukushima Nuclear Accident, Fukushima, Japan, 2011 4. Tohoku Earthquake and Tsunami, Japan, 2011 5. Tsunami damage -- Japan -- Tōhoku Region 6. Tsunami relief -- Japan -- Tōhoku Region 7. Disaster victims -- Japan -- Tōhoku Region
ISBN 0307907317; 9780307907318

LC 2012020400

In this book, Gretel Ehrlich, winner of PEN New England's Henry David Thoreau Prize, "explains how a fascination with Japanese art and poetry drove her to Japan's devastated Tohoku coast after last year's tsunami." (Library Journal) Ehrlich "made several visits to Japan in the months after the shattering earthquake and tsunami" and tried to make sense of the event by "recording accounts by traumatized survivors and [sharing] her own . . . on-the-ground observations." (Kirkus)

Includes bibliographical references

Halberstam, David

Firehouse. Hyperion 2002 201p $22.95; pa $14 **363.34**
1. Fire fighters 2. World Trade Center terrorist attack, 2001 3. New York (N.Y.) -- Fire Dept.
ISBN 1-4013-0005-7; 0-7868-8851-2 pa

"A journalist's homage to firefighters, their values, their culture and their courage during the martyrdom imposed on the New York Fire Department by the catastrophe of the attack on the World Trade Center." N Y Times Bk Rev

Katz, Jonathan M.

The **big** truck that went by; how the world came to save Haiti and left behind a disaster. Jonathan Katz. Palgrave Macmillan 2013 306 p. $26 **363.34**
1. Humanitarian intervention 2. Haiti Earthquake, Haiti, 2010 3. Disaster response and recovery 4. Disaster relief -- Haiti 5. Earthquake relief -- Haiti 6. Economic assistance, American -- Haiti 7. Humanitarian assistance, American -- Haiti 8. Haiti -- Economic conditions -- 21st century 9. Haiti -- Politics and government -- 21st century
ISBN 023034187X; 9780230341876

LC 2012037217

This book by Jonathan M. Katz is "about the January 2010 earthquake and its aftermath. . . . Katz, a former AP correspondent, was the only full-time American reporter stationed in Haiti when the quake hit; he stayed for more than a year thereafter, reporting on the charitable aftershocks--as small donations were mishandled by NGOs, as big donations never materialized, and as the world gradually lost interest and left Haiti to fend for itself." (Columbia Journalism Review)

Includes bibliographical references (p. [283]-298) and index

Pilkey, Orrin H., 1934-

The **rising** sea; [by] Orrin H. Pilkey and Rob Young. Island Press/Shearwater Books 2009 203p il map $25.95 **363.34**

1. Ocean 2. Coasts 3. Sea level 4. Coast changes 5. Greenhouse effect

ISBN 978-1-59726-191-3; 1-59726-191-2

LC 2009-06152

"This book's title represents the most obvious effect of global warming: the incursion of ocean water onto land due to thermal expansion and, more ominously, the melting of mountain glaciers and polar ice sheets. This phenomenon is often dismissed as inconsequential (or even denied), but as the authors convincingly demonstrate with stories of distress at vulnerable locations (e.g., the Maldives), it is already ravaging coastlines directly and indirectly, helped by human intrusion. . . . This book offers a wealth of opportunities for further reading. Its greatest strength is the cogent, well-organized, layman-friendly narrative that makes up each chapter." Sci Books Films

Includes bibliographical references

Smith, Dennis

Report from ground zero; the story of the rescue efforts at the World Trade Center. Viking 2002 366p il maps $24.95; pa $14 **363.34**

1. Fire fighters 2. World Trade Center terrorist attack, 2001 3. New York (N.Y.) -- Fire Dept.

ISBN 0-670-03116-X; 0-452-28395-7 pa

LC 2002-19840

Based on his personal observations and interviews with other rescue workers, the author describes the efforts of the New York City Fire Department to rescue survivors of the September 11 attack on the World Trade Center

Tougias, Mike

Ten hours until dawn; the true story of heroism and tragedy aboard the Can Do. [by] Michael Tougias. St. Martins Press 2005 322p il map $24.95 **363.34**

1. Blizzards 2. Shipwrecks 3. Rescue work

ISBN 0-312-33435-4

This book is "about the attempt to rescue the original rescuers as well as the rescued when a tanker ran aground off Salem, Massachusetts, in the blizzard of 1978." Booklist

The author "delivers a well-researched, vividly written tale of brave men overwhelmed by the awesome forces of nature." Publ Wkly

Welky, David

The **thousand** -year flood; the Ohio-Mississippi disaster of 1937. University of Chicago Press 2011 355p il $27.50 **363.34**

1. Disaster relief 2. New Deal, 1933-1939 3. Floods -- Mississippi River 4. Floods -- Ohio River valley 5. United States -- Politics and government -- 1933-1945

ISBN 978-0-226-88716-6; 0-226-88716-2; 978-0-226-88718-0 ebook

LC 2011014875

The author "leads the reader though the history of the 1937 Ohio River flood, discussing both the manmade and natural causes for the extreme flood." Publ Wkly

"Vividly written and carefully documented, . . . [this book] masterfully brings a turning point in American history back to life." Wilson Quarterly

Includes bibliographical references

Zebrowski, Ernest

Category 5; the story of Camille, lessons unlearned from America's most violent hurricane. [by] Ernest Zebrowski & Judith A. Howard. University of Michigan Press 2005 276p il map $27.95 **363.34**

1. Hurricanes 2. Gulf Coast (U.S.)

ISBN 0-472-11525-1

LC 2005-28583

"Partly a narrative and partly a pondering of how people and authorities prepare for predictable risk, the work focuses on the areas devastated by the maelstrom: Plaquemines Parish, Louisiana; Mississippi's Gulf Coast; and faraway Nelson County, Virginia. . . . The authors sound a pessimistic note about society's short-term memory in their sobering, able history of Camille." Booklist

Includes bibliographical references

Zeilinga de Boer, Jelle

Earthquakes in human history; the far-reaching effects of seismic disruptions. [by] Jelle Zeilinga de Boer and Donald Theodore Sanders. Princeton University Press 2005 278p il maps $24.95 **363.34**

1. Earthquakes

ISBN 0-691-05070-8

LC 2004-40122

The authors provide "facts and insights on geologic processes and the effects of . . . natural disasters on the course of human history. Narratives on especially impactful earthquakes include events in the Holy Land, Ancient Greece, England, Portugal, Missouri, San Francisco, Japan, Peru and Chile, and Nicaragua. The influence of the earthquakes on religion, politics, economy, wars, and literature is portrayed in fascinating prose, embellished with carefully selected photos, drawings, and maps." Choice

Includes bibliographical references

363.4 Controversies related to public morals and customs

Okrent, Daniel, 1948-

Last call; the rise and fall of Prohibition, 1920-1933. Scribner 2010 468p $30 **363.4**

1. Prohibition 2. Drinking of alcoholic beverages 3. United States -- History -- 20th century 4. Prohibition -- United States -- History -- 20th century 5. Drinking of alcoholic beverages -- United States -- History -- 20th century

ISBN 978-0-7432-7702-0; 0-7432-7702-3

LC 2009-51127

This is a history of "the years 1920-1933, when the U.S. Constitution was amended to restrict . . . drinking alcholic beverages." Publisher's note

"Okrent's style is bracing and wry, his research is vast and impressive and his insight is penetrating. Intoxicating." Kirkus

Includes bibliographical references

Watman, Max

Chasing the white dog; an amateur outlaw's adventures in moonshine. Simon & Schuster 2010 292p $25 **363.4**

1. Liquors 2. Distillation

ISBN 978-1-4165-7178-0; 1-4165-7178-7

LC 2009-24657

"No matter where the chase takes him, from policing a lobster pot full of boiling molasses to getting schnockered at a conference for hobby distillers, Watman is a hands-on, no-holds-barred participant. He gamely learns to race cars to absorb the moonshine/NASCAR culture, and sits through the trial of a group of large-scale bootleggers in a multistate investigation. He profiles local color like Daytona 500 winner Junior Johnson, onetime moonshiner, famous for inventing the 'bootleg turn' to outrun the feds; and 'whitecollar' distillers like George Stranahan in Colorado." PopMatters

363.45 Drug traffic

Ainslie, Ricardo C.

The **fight** to save Juárez; life in the heart of Mexico's drug war. by Ricardo C. Ainslie. 1st ed. University of Texas Press 2013 xii, 282 p.p ill. (paperback) $25 **363.45**

1. Ciudad Juarez (Mexico) 2. Drug traffic -- Mexico 3. Law enforcement -- Mexico 4. Drug control -- Mexico -- Ciudad Juárez 5. Drug traffic -- Mexico -- Ciudad Juárez 6. Violent crime -- Mexico -- Ciudad Juárez

ISBN 9780292738904

LC 2012035822

This book, by Ricardo C. Ainslie, discusses the Mexican drug war. "The city of Juárez is ground zero for the drug war that is raging across Mexico and has claimed close to 60,000 lives since 2007. . . . [The book] takes us into the heart of Mexico's bloodiest city through the lives of four people who experienced the drug war from very different perspectives--Mayor José Reyes Ferriz, a mid-level cartel player's mistress, a human rights activist, and a photojournalist." (Publisher's note)

Includes bibliographical references and index.

Gibler, John

To die in Mexico; dispatches from inside the drug war. City Lights Books 2011 218p (Open media) pa $15.95 **363.45**

1. Drug traffic 2. Crime -- Mexico

ISBN 978-0-87286-517-4; 0-87286-517-7

LC 2011-02970

The author "recounts an endless litany of violence that has exploded during the tenures of Carlos Salinas, Ernesto Zedillo, Vicente Fox and, especially, Felipe Calderon. The various drug cartels—the Gulf cartel, the Zetas, the Sinaloa Cartel, among others—have only grown stronger over the years. . . . Hence, drugs are big business, especially for the banks, who launder the spectacular profits. The corruption of organized crime has infiltrated every segment of Mexican society, as Gibler demonstrates here, visiting prisons and civic groups, who express an utter sense of hopelessness and despair. However, the author has found fighting spirits, such as young murdered men's mothers who show up bravely and demand a police reckoning; and the journalists mourning their murdered fellow colleagues at El Diario de Juarez. Gibler argues passionately to undercut this 'case study in failure.' . . . With legality, both U.S. and Mexican society could address real issues of substance abuse through education and public-health initiatives." Kirkus

Includes bibliographical references

Schou, Nicholas

Orange sunshine; the Brotherhood of Eternal Love and its quest to spread peace, love, and acid to the world. Thomas Dunne Books 2010 306p il $24.99 **363.45**

1. Drug traffic 2. Dissenters 3. Narcotics dealers 4. Brotherhood of Eternal Love

ISBN 978-0-312-55183-4; 0-312-55183-5

LC 2009-40284

"Blue Cheer. Window Pane. Orange Sunshine. Maui Wowie. These were the brand names of the psychedelic counterculture of the 1960s and '70s, a culture led by the Brotherhood of Eternal Love. Chances are, if a brand of acid, pot or hashish was known to stoners, it first made its way into the underground market via the Brotherhood. Originally a marijuana-dealing motorcycle gang of toughs, the Brotherhood had a mass religious experience with LSD in 1965-they believed they'd found a lysergic shortcut to God. They resolved, under the charismatic leadership of John 'the Farmer' Griggs, whom Timothy Leary called 'the holiest man ever to live in this country,' to become apostles of acid with a mission to turn on the entire world. . . . A fascinating read for any audience and essential history for anyone interested in the roots of psychedelia." Kirkus

Includes bibliographical references

363.46 Abortion

Palmer, Louis J.

Encyclopedia of abortion in the United States; [by] Louis J. Palmer, Jr. and Xueyan Z. Palmer. 2nd ed.; McFarland & Co. 2009 624p il $150 **363.46**

1. Reference books 2. Abortion -- Encyclopedias

ISBN 978-0-7864-3838-9; 0-7864-3838-X

LC 2008-31047

First published 2002

"Ranging in length from a single paragraph to several pages, the A-to-Z entries define noteworthy events, significant figures, state and federal legislation, prochoice and prolife organizations, case specifics, abortion methods, and contraceptive devices. . . . This balanced, unblinking, and comprehensive subject reference makes complex legal details accessible to the lay reader." Libr J

Includes bibliographical references

Press, Eyal

Absolute convictions; my father, a city, and the conflict that divided America. Henry Holt and Co. 2006 292p il map hardcover o.p. pa $15 **363.46**

1. Abortion 2. Gynecologists 3. Pro-life movement 4. Abortion providers

ISBN 0-8050-7731-6; 978-0-312-42657-6 pa; 0-312-

42657-7 pa

LC 2005-34064

"In this inside look at a battleground of the abortion debate—Buffalo, N.Y.—the son of an abortion provider examines both sides of the culture clash that envelops his Israeli father's life." Publ Wkly

The author "manages the extraordinary feat of bringing light to a political issue that for far too long has generated nothing but blistering heat." N Y Times Book Rev

Includes bibliographical references

Reagan, Leslie J.

When abortion was a crime; women, medicine, and law in the United States, 1867-1973. University of Calif. Press 1997 387p il hardcover o.p. pa $19.95   **363.46**

1. Abortion 2. Women -- United States
ISBN 0-520-21657-1 pa

LC 96-22568

This is a history of abortion in the United States from its criminalization between 1860 and 1880 to Roe v. Wade in 1973

"Important and original, vigorously written even down to the footnotes, {this book} manages with apparent ease to combine serious scholarship . . . and broad appeal." Atl Mon

Includes bibliographical references

363.5   Housing

Loewen, James W.

Sundown towns; a hidden dimension of American racism. New Press 2005 562p il $29.95 **363.5**

1. Discrimination in housing 2. United States -- Race relations 3. African Americans -- Segregation
ISBN 1-56584-887-X

LC 2005-43855

This is an "account of the towns, suburbs, and neighborhoods throughout the United States that enforced the exclusion of minorities within their borders." Libr J

"This book is sure to become a landmark in several fields and a sure bet among Loewen's many fans." Publ Wkly

Includes bibliographical references

Satter, Beryl

Family properties; race, real estate, and the exploitation of Black urban America. Metropolitan Books 2009 495p il $30   **363.5**

1. Lawyers 2. Discrimination in housing 3. Social activists 4. African Americans -- Chicago (Ill.)
ISBN 978-0-8050-7676-9; 0-8050-7676-X

LC 2008-33005

The book "leaps from the particulars of one man's story to become a panoramic retelling of the Chicago real-estate wars during a period when, after the postwar migration of Southern blacks, that city was the most segregated in the North." N Y Times (Late N Y Ed)

Includes bibliographical references

363.6   Public utilities and related services

Amery, Colin

Vanishing histories; 100 endangered sites from the World Monuments Watch. by Colin Amery, with Brian Curran; foreword by John Berendt; preface by Bonnie Burnham and Marilyn Perry. Abrams 2001 207p il maps $60   **363.6**

1. Monuments 2. Historic sites
ISBN 0-8109-1435-2

LC 2001-22622

"The World Monuments Fund, which has been monitoring the state of precious architectural and artistic sites since 1965, established the World Monuments Watch in 1995 to heighten awareness of endangered cultural sites in the hope of garnering the support necessary for their preservation. Architectural expert Amery and conservator Curran present the histories of 100 such monuments in a volume as notable for the beauty of its photographs as for the urgency of its message." Booklist

Farabee, Charles R.

National park ranger; an American icon. {by} Charles R. "Butch" Farabee Jr. Roberts Rinehart Publishers 2003 180p il pa $18.95   **363.6**

1. United States -- National Park Service 2. National parks and reserves -- United States
ISBN 1-570-98392-5

LC 2003-1022

"In this study of the vocation of park ranger since Maryland's park caretakers in 1696 to the present day, former ranger Farabee not only explores a ranger's role but also touches on the establishment of the National Park Service, the introduction of women rangers, and early resource management. Readers will enjoy the abundance of archival photographs, ranger profiles, and numerous other features." Libr J

Includes bibliographical references

363.7   Environmental problems

Berners-Lee, Mike

How bad are bananas? the carbon footprint of everything. Greystone Books 2011 232p il pa $16.95   **363.7**

1. Carbon 2. Greenhouse effect
ISBN 978-1-55365-831-3 pa; 978-1-55365-832-0 ebook

First published 2010 in the United Kingdom

Discusses the carbon footprint—the carbon emissions used to manufacture and transport—of everyday items, including paper bags and imported produce, and provides information to help build carbon considerations into everyday purchases.

"A book like this risks being preachy or overly serious, but Berners-Lee approaches his topics with humor and curiosity. He rarely advocates radical change. Rather, he gives readers information." Christ Sci Monit

Includes bibliographical references

Bloom, Jonathan

American wasteland; how America throws away nearly half of its food (and what we can do about it) Da Capo Press 2010 360p il $26 **363.7**

1. Salvage 2. Food supply 3. Food industry 4. Waste (Economics)

ISBN 978-0-7382-1364-4

LC 2010-15075

The author "documents some specifics about the nature of wasted food in the twenty-first century and calls into question both the economic efficiency and the morality of such profligacy." Booklist

"An eye-opening account of what used to be considered a sin—the willful waste of perfectly edible food. . . . An urgent, necessary book." Kirkus

Includes bibliographical references

Braasch, Gary

Earth under fire; how global warming is changing the world. Updated ed; University of California Press 2009 xxx, 267p il pa $24.95 **363.7**

1. Greenhouse effect 2. Climate -- Environmental aspects

ISBN 978-0-520-26025-2

First published 2007

"What sets Earth Under Fire apart from other books on the same topic are the inspiring photographs. These images are an effective tool that helps the reader understand what the implications of climate change are—for people, for other organisms, and for entire ecosystems." Sci Books Films

Includes bibliographical references

Busch, Akiko

The incidental steward; reflections on citizen science. Akiko Busch ; illustrations by Debby Cotter Kaspari. Yale University Press 2013 256 p. (hardcover) $25 **363.7**

1. Wildlife conservation 2. Environmental protection 3. Wildlife conservation -- Hudson River Valley (N.Y. and N.J.) 4. Environmental monitoring -- Hudson River Valley (N.Y. and N.J.)

ISBN 0300178794; 9780300178791

LC 2012040301

This book, by Akiko Busch, illustrated by Debby Cotter Kaspari, "highlights factors that distinguish twenty-first-century citizen scientists from traditional amateur naturalists: a greater sense of urgency, helpful new technologies, and the expanded possibilities of crowdsourcing. . . . While not a primer on the prescribed protocols of citizen science, the book combines vivid natural history, a deep sense of place, and reflection about our changing world." (Publisher's note)

Includes bibliographical references and index

Carson, Rachel, 1907-1964

★ Silent spring; introduction by Linda Lear; afterword by Edward O. Wilson. 40th anniversary ed; Houghton Mifflin 2002 378p il **363.7**

1. Pesticides and wildlife 2. Pesticides -- Environmental aspects

ISBN 0-618-24906-0 pa; 0-618-25305-X

First published 1962

In The silent spring, Carson "contended that the indiscriminate use of weed killers and insecticides constituted a hazard to wildlife and to human beings. Her provocative work inspired many subsequent environmental studies." Reader's Ency. 4th edition

Flannery, Tim F.

The weather makers; how man is changing the climate and what it means for life on Earth. [by] Tim Flannery. Atlantic Monthly Press 2006 357p il maps hardcover o.p. pa $15 **363.7**

1. Climate 2. Greenhouse effect

ISBN 0-8711-3935-9; 0-8021-4292-3 pa

LC 2005-52350

This is a "look at the connection between climate change and global warming." Publ Wkly

"This work is distinctive in its marriage of science to an act-now attitude and should energize environmentally minded readers." Booklist

Includes bibliographical references (p. 289-297)

Freudenburg, William R.

Blowout in the Gulf; the BP oil spill disaster and the future of energy in America. [by] William R. Freudenburg and Robert Gramling. MIT Press 2010 254p il $18.95 **363.7**

1. Oil spills 2. Drilling platforms 3. Offshore oil well drilling 4. British Petroleum Co. plc

ISBN 978-0-262-01583-7

LC 2010-937510

The authors "set the deadly BP blowout within a technologically precise history of oil in America, from the first primitively constructed well on land to the development of offshore rigs, explaining that the Deepwater Horizon was actually a technical marvel—if only its operation hadn't been compromised. . . . Science, commerce, and the politics of oil are all newly illuminated here, accompanied by invaluable explanations of the risks of offshore drilling and a pragmatic look at the energy conundrums we now face." Booklist

Includes bibliographical references

Friedman, Thomas L.

Hot, flat, and crowded; why we need a green revolution--and how it can renew America. Farrar, Straus & Giroux 2008 438p il $27.95 **363.7**

1. Energy resources 2. Environmental movement 3. Climate -- Environmental aspects 4. Environmental policy -- United States

ISBN 978-0-374-16685-4; 0-374-16685-4

LC 2008-930589

"Friedman's big, passionate, and solidly specific ecological primer, social manifesto, and realistic plan for a green revolution aimed at restoring America's greatness and securing a sustainable future should serve as a playbook for innovators and civic leaders." Booklist

Gates, Alexander E.

Encyclopedia of pollution; [by] Alexander E. Gates and Robert P. Blauvelt. Facts on File 2011 2v il map (Facts on File science library) set $170 **363.7**

1. Pollution 2. Reference books 3. Pollution --

Encyclopedias
ISBN 978-0-8160-7002-2

LC 2009048190

"Broad topics encompass all aspects of pollutants, including properties, production, uses, environmental release and fate, regulations, and adverse health effects in response to exposure. Summary entries on general subjects, such as water pollution, provide topical overviews. Case studies of pollution events supply instructive background information." Booklist

Includes bibliographical references

George, Rose

The **big** necessity; the unmentionable world of human waste and why it matters. Metropolitan Books 2008 288p il $26 **363.7**

1. Sanitation 2. Sewage disposal

ISBN 978-0-8050-8271-5; 0-8050-8271-9

LC 2008-29999

The author "breaks the embarrassed silence over the economic, political, social and environmental problems of human waste disposal. . . . From the depths of the world's oldest surviving urban sewers in to Japan's robo-toilet revolution, George leads an intrepid, erudite and entertaining journey through the public consequences of this most private behavior." Publ Wkly

Includes bibliographical references

Gore, Al,1948-

★ An **inconvenient** truth; the planetary emergency of global warming and what we can do about it. Rodale 2006 325p il map pa $23.95 **363.7**

1. Human ecology 2. Environmental protection 3. Greenhouse effect 4. Environmental policy -- United States

ISBN 978-1-59486-567-1; 1-59486-567-1

LC 2006-926537

"Gore has put together a coherent account of a complex topic that Americans desperately need to understand. . . . By telling the story of climate change with striking clarity . . . Al Gore may have done for global warming what [Rachel Carson's] Silent Spring [1962] did for pesticides." N Y Rev Books

Our choice; a plan to solve the climate crisis. Rodale 2009 414p il map pa $26.99 **363.7**

1. Human ecology 2. Environmental policy 3. Environmental protection 4. Greenhouse effect

ISBN 978-1-59486-734-7; 1-59486-734-8

LC 2009-38291

The former vice president addresses key environmental issues while profiling and evaluating possible solutions.

This "is an inviting and momentous compendium of environmental discovery . . . that addresses one of the greatest threats our species has encountered with intelligence, knowledge, wisdom, and faith in human empowerment. This is a book that should be displayed and talked about everywhere." Booklist

Grossman, Elizabeth

High tech trash; digital devices, hidden toxins, and human health. Island Press/Shearwater Books 2006 334p hardcover o.p. pa $21.95 **363.7**

1. Refuse and refuse disposal 2. Electronic apparatus and appliances 3. Waste electronic apparatus and appliances 4. Electronic apparatus and appliances -- Environmental aspects

ISBN 1-55963-554-1; 1-59726-190-4 pa; 978-1-55963-554-7; 978-1-59726-190-6 pa

LC 2006-4549

This book "traces the toxic substances (lead, mercury, phosphorus, brominated flame retardants, and others) used in digital devices, along with their health hazards." (Sci Books Films) Index.

The author "traces the toxic substances (lead, mercury, phosphorus, brominated flame retardants, and others) used in digital devices, along with their health hazards. Each of the book's nine chapters has notes and references; there is also an appendix on how to recycle computers. . . . [Grossman] has made a valiant effort to consolidate the information that general, nontechnical readers interested in the subject . . . would find very useful." Sci Books Films

Includes bibliographical references

Hansen, James E.

Storms of my grandchildren; the truth about the coming climate catastrophe and our last chance to save humanity. [by] James Hansen; illustrations by Makiko Sato. Bloomsbury USA 2009 304p il $25 **363.7**

1. Environmental influence on humans 2. Greenhouse effect 3. Climate -- Environmental aspects

ISBN 978-1-60819-200-7

LC 2009-44553

"Rich in invaluable insights into the geopolitics as well as the geophysics of climate change, Hansen's guaranteed-to-be-controversial manifesto is the most comprehensible, realistic, and courageous call to prevent climate change yet. It belongs in every library." Booklist

Includes bibliographical references

Humes, Edward

Eco Barons; the dreamers, schemers and millionaires who are saving our planet. Ecco 2009 367p $25.99 **363.7**

1. Conservationists 2. Environmentalists

ISBN 978-0-06-135029-0; 0-06-135029-X

"The millionaires of the subtitle are Doug Tompkins, who put Esprit clothing profits to work protecting Argentina's Patagonia; Roxanne Quimby, who used Burt's Bees cosmetics earnings to purchase vast wild lands in Maine; and Ted Turner, whose CNN fortune allowed him to become America's single largest landowner, with 15 immense ranches managed for native species. Others featured in the book get the job done through sheer tenacity. . . . Although too fast-paced for much nuance, this book is full of captivating facts and well-told tales of environmentalism's human side." Libr J

Jacobs, Chip

Smogtown; the lung-burning history of pollution in Los Angeles. [by] Chip Jacobs & William J. Kelly. Overlook Press 2008 384p il $26.95   **363.7**

   1. Air pollution 2. Los Angeles (Calif.)

   ISBN 978-1-58567-860-0

"This friendly, accessible history should appeal to any American environmentalist." Publ Wkly

Includes bibliographical references

Jones, Van

The **green** -collar economy; how one solution can fix our two biggest problems. with Ariane Conrad. HarperOne 2008 237p $25.95; pa $14.99 **363.7**

   1. Environmental protection 2. Social policy -- United States 3. Environmental policy -- United States

   ISBN 978-0-06-165075-8; 0-06-165075-7; 978-0-06-165076-5 pa; 0-06-165076-5 pa

The author "argues that developing a sustainable energy industry in America would lessen our dependency on non-renewable and foreign energy sources, as well as provide local and well-paid employment. With a resource list to help individuals become involved." Libr J

Includes bibliographical references

Keizer, Garret

The **unwanted** sound of everything we want; a book about noise. PublicAffairs 2010 385p $27.95   **363.7**

   1. Noise 2. Sound 3. Noise -- Psychological aspects 4. Sound -- Psychological aspects

   ISBN 1586485520; 9781586485528

                  LC 2010-05391

This book presents an "argument about the politics of sound. [Garret] Keizer acknowledges the subjective dimension of noise, which is sometimes defined as unwanted sound. What I deem noise may not be bothersome to someone else, and what bothers me in one context could be acceptable to me in another." Keizer offers an "analysis of power and inequality, noting the disproportionate effect of noise on people on the margins. . . . In response, he argues for a renewed human community of civility and sustainability." (Christian Century)

This "book explores the unforeseen (and sometimes unwanted) side effects of our inventive natures. We usually use the word noise as a pejorative, a term denoting unwanted sound: somebody's loud music, a blaring car alarm, the din from a nearby airport. But, as Keizer points out, noise is often—perhaps even usually—a product of human achievement, invention, or ambition. In broad terms, you can't have civilization without noise. . . . An enlightening look at an issue most of us ignore." Booklist

Includes bibliographical references

Kirby, David

Animal factory; the looming threat of industrial pig, dairy, and poultry farms to humans and the environment. St. Martin's Press 2010 492p $26.99 **363.7**

   1. Livestock industry 2. Agriculture -- Environmental aspects

   ISBN 0-312-38058-5; 978-0-312-38058-8

"Thanks to Kirby's extraordinary journalism, we have the most relatable, irrefutable, and unforgettable testimony yet to the hazards of industrial animal farming." Booklist

Kolbert, Elizabeth

★ **Field** notes from a catastrophe; man, nature, and climate change. Bloomsbury Pub. 2006 210p il map hardcover o.p. pa $14.95 **363.7**

   1. Climate 2. Greenhouse effect

   ISBN 1-59691-125-5; 978-1-59691-125-3; 1-59691-130-1 pa; 978-1-59691-130-7 pa

                  LC 2005-30972

"On the burgeoning shelf of cautionary but occasionally alarmist books warning about the consequences of dramatic climate change, Kolbert's calmly persuasive reporting stands out for its sobering clarity." Publ Wkly

Includes bibliographical references

McKibben, Bill, 1960-

Oil and Honey; The Education of an Unlikely Activist. Bill McKibben. Times Books 2013 272 p. $26   **363.7**

   1. Beekeeping 2. Environmentalists 3. Environmental movement 4. Environmentalism -- United States 5. Beekeepers -- United States -- Biography 6. Climatic changes -- Environmental aspects 7. Environmentalists -- United States -- Biography 8. Petroleum industry and trade -- Environmental aspects 9. Petroleum industry and trade -- Political aspects -- United States

   ISBN 0805092846; 9780805092844

                  LC 2013010995

This book is a memoir by environmental activist Bill McKibben. "McKibben intersperses his accounts of his intense and wide-ranging efforts as an environmental activist with his sometimes-humbling experiences as a novice beekeeper, learning from [farmer Kirk] Webster the art and science of raising bees and making honey." (Kirkus Reviews)

Mooney, Chris

Storm world; hurricanes, politics, and the battle over global warming. Harcourt 2007 392p il map $26   **363.7**

   1. Hurricanes 2. Greenhouse effect

   ISBN 978-0-15-101287-9; 0-15-101287-3

                  LC 2007-09742

"This is certainly one of the most thought-provoking and accessible accounts of climate change to appear since Katrina." Booklist

Includes bibliographical references

Moore, Charles

Plastic ocean; how a sea captain's chance discovery launched a determined quest to save the oceans. [by] Capt. Charles Moore with Cassandra Phillips. Avery 2011 358p il map $26   **363.7**

   1. Plastics 2. Marine pollution

   ISBN 978-1-58333-424-9; 1-58333-424-6

                  LC 2011034559

"The author is an impassioned, fiercely inquisitive writer, detailing the many unorthodox ways he's managed to get these issues into the news and in peer-reviewed science journals. . . . Fast-paced and electrifying, Moore's story is 'gonzo science' at its best." Kirkus

Includes bibliographical references

Pooley, Eric

The **climate** war; true believers, power brokers, and the fight to save the earth. Hyperion 2010 481p $27.99   **363.7**

1. Environmental policy 2. Climate -- Environmental aspects

ISBN 978-1-4013-2326-4

LC 2010-12422

This "is a fascinating, well-researched, behind-the-scenes account of the political twists and turns and efforts of corporate bosses and climate activists. Pooley . . . puts a human face on the topic and writes a gripping account— whether one reads it cover to cover or consults individual chapters in any order." Choice

Includes bibliographical references

Rogers, Heather

Gone tomorrow; the hidden life of garbage. New Press 2005 288p il $23.95   **363.7**

1. Refuse and refuse disposal

ISBN 1-56584-879-9

LC 2005-41562

The author "analyzes the contents of America's garbage and its disposal while also revealing the corporate strategies behind the disposable-goods explosion and assessing the ecological toll of our consumer habits." Booklist

Includes bibliographical references

Royte, Elizabeth

Garbage land; on the secret trail of trash. Little, Brown 2005 311p hardcover o.p. pa $14.99 **363.7**

1. Refuse and refuse disposal

ISBN 0-316-73826-3; 0-316-15461-X pa

LC 2004-24732

The author presents "a cultural tour guided and informed by the things she throws away. Structured around four separate journeys—those of Royte's household trash, compostable matter, recyclables, and sewage—[this] is a literary investigation of the . . . dirty side of consumption." Publisher's note

"There's little waste in Royte's winning words. . . . Seldom has garbage been handled with such care." Christ Sci Monit

Includes bibliographical references

Shulman, Seth

Cooler smarter; practical steps for low-carbon living : expert advice from the Union of Concerned Scientists. Seth Shulman ... [et al.] Island Press 2012 321 p. (pbk.) $21.95   **363.7**

1. Fuel 2. Environmental health 3. Transportation -- Environmental aspects 4. Sustainable living -- United States 5. Environmental protection -- United States -- Citizen participation

ISBN 161091192X; 9781610911924

LC 2012008656

In the book, the Union of Concerned Scientists discusses "proven strategies to cut carbon, with chapters on transpor-

tation, home energy use, diet, personal consumption, as well as how best to influence your workplace, your community, and elected officials. The book explains how to make the biggest impact and when not to sweat the small stuff. It also turns many eco-myths on their head, like the importance of locally produced food or the superiority of all hybrid cars." (Publisher's note)

Stager, Curt

Deep future; Curt Stager. Thomas Dunne Books 2011 284p ill.   **363.7**

1. Global warming 2. Geological time 3. Historical geology 4. Climate -- Research

ISBN 9780312614621; 9780312614638

LC 2010040381

This book, a 'Kirkus Reviews' Best Nonfiction of 2011 title, presents an "exploration of the impact of climate change over geological time. [Curt] Stager takes the long view of global climate change . . . [and] examines both moderate and extreme scenarios. . . . A key point is that humanity has the ability to moderate the release of carbon, shaping the long-range impact on climate. While we are already past the point where significant global warming can be prevented, the author points out that cutting carbon now preserves some for a future era when its release could help prevent another ice age -- a global disaster every bit as threatening to the human race as warming." (Kirkus)

Includes bibliographical references (p. 243-270) and index.

Walker, Gabrielle

The **hot** topic; what we can do about global warming. [by] Gabrielle Walker and Sir David King. Harcourt 2008 276p il map pa $14   **363.7**

1. Greenhouse effect

ISBN 978-0-15-603318-3

LC 2007-45080

The authors "explain how fossil fuels produce carbon dioxide, show how global warming is affecting individual species and changing entire ecosystems, predict how much more climate change we can afford before things become truly catastrophic, and consider economic and political solutions to the problem." Publ Wkly

"This is the best overview of global warming that this reviewer has read. . . . What is most valuable about this book is that the text clearly explains to lay readers a very complex and highly controversial topic." Libr J

Includes bibliographical references

Watts, Jonathan

When a billion Chinese jump; how China will save mankind--or destroy it. Scribner 2010 435p map pa $17; ebook $9.99   **363.7**

1. China -- Economic conditions 2. Environmental policy -- China 3. China -- Politics and government

ISBN 978-1-4165-8076-8 pa; 1-4165-8076-X pa; 978-1-4391-4193-9 ebook; 1-4391-4193-2 ebook

LC 2010-29901

"Watts' comprehensive, revealing study is eye-opening, not only for the way it illuminates how China's population growth and rapid modernization affect the environment, but also for its exposure of the way Western waste contributes to the problem." Booklist

Includes bibliographical references

Winston, Mark L.

Nature wars; people vs. pests. Harvard Univ. Press 1997 210p $27.50; pa $15.95 **363.7**
1. Pest control 2. Human influence on nature 3. Pesticides -- Environmental aspects

ISBN 0-674-60541-1; 0-674-60542-X pa

LC 97-17302

"Winston provides case studies demonstrating alternative methods of pest control, explaining how political, social, economic, and biologic interactions behind pest-management decisions have contributed to our failure to replace toxic chemicals as our first method of choice. . . . Winston has written a convincing and necessary book." Libr J

Includes bibliographical references

363.72 Sanitation

Fagin, Dan

★ Toms River; a small town, a cancer cluster, and the epic quest to expose pollution's hidden consequences. Dan Fagin. Bantam Books 2013 560 p. $28 **363.72**
1. Rivers 2. Pollution 3. Industrial waste 4. Cancer -- Toms River Region 5. Water quality -- New Jersey -- Toms River Watershed 6. Toms River Watershed (N.J.) -- Environmental conditions 7. Groundwater -- Pollution -- Health aspects -- Toms River Region 8. Drinking water -- Contamination -- Health aspects -- Toms River Region

ISBN 055380653X; 9780345538611; 9780553806533

LC 2012017030

Pulitzer Prize: General Nonfiction (2014)

This book by Dan Fagin "recounts the sixty-year saga of rampant pollution and inadequate oversight that made Toms River [New Jersey] a cautionary example for fast-growing industrial towns from South Jersey to South China. He tells the stories of the pioneering scientists and physicians who first identified pollutants as a cause of cancer, and brings to life the everyday heroes in Toms River who struggled for justice." (Publisher's note)

Includes bibliographical references and index

363.73 Pollution

Blackwell, Andrew

★ Visit sunny Chernobyl; and other adventures in the world's most polluted places. Andrew Blackwell. Rodale 2012 xiii, 306 p.p maps (hardcover) $25.99 **363.73**
1. Pollution 2. Ecotourism 3. Environmental degradation 4. Tourism -- Environmental aspects

ISBN 1605294454; 9781605294452

LC 2011053229

"[I]n 'Visit Sunny Chernobyl,' Andrew Blackwell embraces a different kind of travel, taking a jaunt through the most gruesomely polluted places on Earth. . . . From the hidden bars and convenience stores of a radioactive wilderness to the sacred but reeking waters of India, 'Visit Sunny Chernobyl' fuses . . . first-person reporting with satire and analysis, making the case that it's time to start appreciating our planet as it is--not as we wish it would be." (Publisher's note)

Jenkins, McKay

Poison spring; the secret history of pollution and the EPA. by E.G. Vallianatos with McKay Jenkins. Bloomsbury Press 2013 304 p. (alk. paper) $28 **363.73**
1. Political corruption 2. United States. Environmental Protection Agency 3. Corporate power -- United States 4. Pollution -- Research -- United States 5. Environmental responsibility -- United States

ISBN 1608199142; 9781608199143

LC 2013041923

"For twenty-five years [author] E.G. Vallianatos saw the EPA from the inside, with rising dismay over how pressure from politicians and threats from huge corporations were turning it from the public's watchdog into a 'polluter's protection agency.' Based on his own experience . . . and hundreds of documents Vallianatos collected inside the EPA, 'Poison Spring' [co-authored by McKay Jenkins] reveals how the agency has continually reinforced the chemical-industrial complex." (Publisher's note)

"The authors tout healthier living through small, non-toxic family farms while delivering an alarming, comprehensive account of a 'fatally compromised' EPA mission crippled by bad enforcement practices and numerous corrupting influences." Pub Wkly

Includes bibliographical references and index

363.738 Pollutants

Climate change; an encyclopedia of science and history. Brian C. Black, general editor ; David M. Hassenzahl, Jennie C. Stephens, Gary Weisel, and Nancy Gift, associate editors. ABC-CLIO, LLC 2013 xx, 1774 p.p ill. (hardcover) $399 **363.738**
1. Climate change 2. Global warming 3. Climatic changes -- History -- Encyclopedias 4. Climatic changes -- Research -- Encyclopedias

ISBN 1598847619; 9781598847611

LC 2012034673

This book afford a "historical overview of the topic" of climate change. "The volume provides a foundational understanding of climate change for students, policymakers, and the general public. . . . More than 100 subject experts contributed more than 225 articles, typically several pages in length, to the compilation. The articles examine the potential effects of climate change on both human and natural systems; many contain climate change mitigation" strategies. (Booklist)

Includes bibliographical references (pages 1651-1693) and index.

Encyclopedia of global warming & climate change; general editor, S. George Philander. SAGE Pub-

lications, Inc. 2012 3 v.,1641 p. 3v il (cloth)
$375   **363.738**
1. Climate change 2. Encyclopedias and dictionaries 3.
Global warming -- Encyclopedias 4. Climatic changes
-- Encyclopedias
ISBN 1412992613; 9781412992619

LC 2012002545

This encyclopedia has "40 new articles . . . and extensive
revision" and "offers students and . . . 'laymen' close looks
at recent developments. The set also examines broad historical, scientific, national, geographical, political, and thematic
pictures of climate change's mechanisms, effects, and controversies." (School Library Journal)

"The set includes more than 750 articles addressing
major topics related to global warming and climate change
ranging geographically from the North Pole to the South
Pole and thematically from social effects to scientific causes.
Coverage encompasses the science and history of climate
change, the polarizing controversies over climate-change
theories, the role of societies, the industrial and economic
factors, and the sociological aspects of climate change. . . .
This valuable resource provides an excellent historical overview and framework of this topic and serves as a general
resource for geography, oceanography, biology, climatology,
history, and many other subjects." Libr J
Includes bibliographical references and index

The **global** warming reader; A Century of Writing
About Climate Change. Penguin Books 2012
421 p. (paperback) $18.00   **363.738**
1. Climate change 2. Global warming 3. Environmental
sciences 4. Human influence on nature
ISBN 0143121898; 9780143121893

This book, edited by Bill McKibben, "brings together
the essential voices on global warming, from its 19th-
century discovery to the present. . . . [The book] provides
more than thirty-five answers . . . from more than one hundred years of engagement with the topic. Here is Elizabeth
Kolbert's groundbreaking essay 'The Darkening Sea,' . . .
NASA scientist James Hansen's testimony before the U.S.
Congress, and clarion calls for action by Al Gore, Arundhati
Roy, Naomi Klein, and many others." (Publisher's note)

Guzman, Andrew T.
Overheated; The Human Cost of Climate
Change. Andrew T. Guzman. Oxford University
Press 2013 280 p. (hardcover) $29.95   **363.738**
1. Human ecology 2. Climate change 3. Climatic
changes -- Social aspects 4. Climatic changes --
Economic aspects 5. Climatic changes -- Effect of
human beings on
ISBN 0199933871; 9780199933877

LC 2012047000

This book, by Andrew T. Guzman, discusses the political
aspects surrounding climate change. "Guzman takes climate
change out of the realm of scientific abstraction to explore its
real-world consequences. . . . He takes as his starting point
a fairly optimistic outcome in the range predicted by scientists. . . . Even this modest rise would lead to catastrophic . .
. problems. . . . He shows in vivid detail how climate change
is already playing out in the real world." (Publisher's note)
Includes bibliographical references and index

Lerner, Steve
Sacrifice zones; the front lines of toxic chemical
exposure in the United States. Steve Lerner ; foreword by Phil Brown. MIT Press 2010 xiv, 346p
(hardcover : alk. paper) 29.95   **363.738**
1. Pollution 2. United States 3. Chemical spills 4.
Hazardous wastes 5. Hazardous waste sites 6. Pollution
-- United States -- Case studies 7. Hazardous waste
sites -- United States -- Case studies 8. Environmental
toxicology -- United States -- Case studies 9. Chemical
spills -- Health aspects -- United States -- Case studies
10. Hazardous substances -- Health aspects -- United
States -- Case studies
ISBN 0262014408; 9780262014403

LC 2009051289

In this book, author "Steve Lerner tells the stories of
twelve communities, from Brooklyn to Pensacola, that rose
up to fight the industries and military bases causing disproportionately high levels of chemical pollution. He calls these
low-income neighborhoods 'sacrifice zones'—repurposing
a Cold War term coined by U.S. government officials to designate areas contaminated with radioactive pollutants during the manufacture of nuclear weapons. And he argues that
residents of a new generation of sacrifice zones, tainted with
chemical pollutants, need additional regulatory protections."
(Publisher's note)
Includes bibliographical references (p. [315]-337)
and index

Terry, Beth
Plastic -free; how I kicked the plastic habit and
you can too. Beth Terry. Skyhorse Pub. 2012 viii,
344 p.p (alk. paper) $19.95   **363.738**
1. Pollution 2. Recycling 3. Environmental health 4.
Plastic scrap -- Environmental aspects 5. Plastic waste
-- Environmental aspects
ISBN 1616086246; 9781616086244

LC 2012002817

In this book, author Beth "Terry provides personal anecdotes, stats about the environmental and health problems
related to plastic, and personal solutions and tips on how to
limit your plastic footprint. Terry includes . . . lists and charts
for easy reference, ways to get involved in larger community
actions, and profiles of individuals . . . who have gone beyond personal solutions to create a change on a larger scale."
(Publisher's note)
Includes bibliographical references.

363.739   Pollution of specific environments

Woodard, Colin
Ocean's end; travels through endangered
seas. Basic Bks. 2000 300p hardcover o.p. pa
$15   **363.739**
1. Marine pollution 2. Marine resources
ISBN 0-465-01571-9 pa

LC 99-51771

The author contends "that pollution, harmful fishing
practices, ignorance and global warming are destroying the
world's oceans. . . . He uncovers a colorful cast of scientists,
officials, activists, divers and religious missionaries who at-

test to the human and economic costs of ecological decline."
Publ Wkly

Includes bibliographical references

363.8 Food supply

Soussan, Michael

Backstabbing for beginners; my crash course in international diplomacy. Nation Books 2008 332p il $25.95 **363.8**

1. United Nations -- Office of Iraq Programme -- Oil-for-Food Programme

ISBN 978-1-56858-397-6; 1-56858-397-4

LC 2008-31698

The author "recounts his tenure coordinating the Iraq Oil-For-Food program, revealing why bribery and kickbacks were tolerated." Kirkus

"Soussan brings provocative wit, a keen eye for detail and a knack for revealing anecdotes to this important account of the rampant greed, hypocrisy and cynicism festering behind the United Nations' humanitarian credo." Publ Wkly

Includes bibliographical references

Stuart, Tristram

Waste; uncovering the global food scandal. W.W. Norton & Co. 2009 xxii, 451p il $27.95 **363.8**

1. Recycling 2. Food industry 3. Waste minimization

ISBN 978-0-393-06836-8

The author "shows how we could have much more food overnight simply by not tossing away so much of it. This simple concept ingeniously unites many food scandals that often do not get the attention they deserve: the mould that destroys a third or more of Third World harvests; . . . [and] the millions of tonnes of edible food wasted by modern food processing and 'sell-by' dates. . . . Usefully, Stuart offers examples of what we could be doing better, from processing technologies to offal sausages." New Sci

Includes bibliographical references

363.9 Population problems

Bruinius, Harry

Better for all the world; the secret history of forced sterilization and America's quest for racial purity. Knopf 2006 401p il hardcover o.p. pa $16.95; ebook $16.95 **363.9**

1. Eugenics 2. Sterilization (Birth control)

ISBN 0-375-41371-5; 0-375-71305-0 pa; 978-0-307-42496-9 ebook

LC 2005-44150

The author describes how, "in the early years of the 20th century, a fixation on eugenics led several states to approve forced sterilization to keep thousands of Americans from producing 'morally inferior' or 'feeble-minded' offspring." Publ Wkly

"Bruinius' account of one of America's dirty little secrets is . . . a real page-turner." Booklist

Includes bibliographical references

May, Elaine Tyler

America and the pill; a history of promise, peril, and liberation. Basic Books 2010 214p $25.95 **363.9**

1. Birth control 2. Oral contraceptives 3. Women -- Social conditions 4. Oral contraceptives -- Social aspects 5. Birth control -- United States -- History 6. Women -- United States -- Social conditions -- 20th century

ISBN 978-0-465-01152-0

LC 2009-46957

The author describes "the now extravagant-seeming hopes and fears the pill first elicited, how the pill became a symbol of the 1960s sexual revolution without demonstrably affecting it, how feminists used the pill to push for an analogue for men as part of their gender-egalitarian agenda, and how reaction to the pill's ill effects on many women contributed to the late-twentieth-century dissipation of respect for professional and institutional authority. . . . Understanding that the book is fundamentally, nonargumentatively pro-pill, one couldn't ask for a better short history of its subject." Booklist

Includes bibliographical references and index

Tone, Andrea

Devices and desires; a history of contraceptives in America. Hill & Wang 2001 366p hardcover o.p. pa $15 **363.9**

1. Birth control

ISBN 0-8090-3817-X; 0-8090-3816-1 pa

LC 00-50547

"Part 1 examines the 'contraceptive entrepreneurs' who practiced what was for many years an illegal trade, regulated by no one. In part 2, 'From Smut to Science,' Tone considers the development of relatively reliable contraceptive techniques, . . . part 3, 'The Medicalization of Contraceptives,' covers birth control pills, Norplant, and intrauterine devices." Booklist

364 Criminology

Nash, Jay Robert

The **great** pictorial history of world crime. History 2004 2v il set $249 **364**

1. Reference books 2. Crime -- Encyclopedias

ISBN 1-928831-20-6

LC 2004-100992

"Each of these topical sections opens with a general overview and then explores individual crimes in chronological order. As befits the title, there are thousands of black-and-white photographs and illustrations and although their quality varies they are, by and large, helpful and interesting. . . . [This is] the most comprehensive true crime book available." SLJ

Rosen, Fred

The **historical** atlas of American crime. Facts on File 2005 xx, 296p il map (Facts on File crime library) $75; pa $24.95 **364**

1. Crime -- United States

ISBN 0-8160-4841-X; 0-8160-4842-8 pa

LC 2004-11346

The author "brings a fresh point of view to American crime by placing it within the larger context of American history; at the same time he observes multiple disciplines (e.g., history, economics, literature) through the lens of crime." Choice

Includes bibliographical references

Zuckoff, Mitchell

Ponzi's scheme; the true story of a financial legend. Random House 2005 390p il $25.95; pa $14.95   **364**

1. Swindlers

ISBN 1-400-06039-7; 0-8129-6836-0 pa

LC 2004-46770

The author "chronicles Ponzi's mercurial rise and fall as he conjured up one get-rich-quick scheme after another. . . . Zuckoff provides not only a definitive portrait of Ponzi's life but also insights into immigrant life and the social world of early 20th-century Boston." Publ Wkly

Includes bibliographical references

364.1   Criminal offenses

Atwood, Roger

Stealing history; tomb raiders, smugglers, and the looting of the ancient world. St. Martin's Press 2004 337p il map hardcover o.p. pa $15.95 **364.1**

1. Art thefts 2. Antiquities -- Collection and preservation

ISBN 0-312-32406-5; 0-312-32407-3 pa

LC 2004-50862

The author's "ability to bring a story dramatically to life and his keen interest in stemming the illegal antiquities trade makes this an important book for anyone interested in archeology, preservation or the potentially tangled provenance of works they love." Publ Wkly

Includes bibliographical references

Bergreen, Laurence

Capone; the man and the era. Simon & Schuster 1994 701p il hardcover o.p. pa $19   **364.1**

1. Mobsters 2. Bootleggers

ISBN 0-684-82447-7 pa

LC 94-5941

Bergreen "traces Capone's childhood in Brooklyn, his entry into organized crime and his violent rise to the top of the Chicago crime world. He focuses on Capone's battles with law-enforcement agencies that eventually resulted, in 1931, in his conviction on tax evasion charges and imprisonment at Alcatraz." Publ Wkly

"Mr. Bergreen has written a book objective and rigorous enough to meet scholarly standards, yet colorful enough to engross the general reader." N Y Times Book Rev

Includes bibliographical references

Breslin, Jimmy

The good rat; a true story. Ecco 2008 270p $24.95   **364.1**

1. Mafia 2. Organized crime

ISBN 978-0-06-085666-3; 0-06-085666-1

The "main narrative is devoted to the story of Louis Eppolito and Stephen Caracappa, two New York police detectives who were fingered as mob assassins . . . by Burton Kaplan, a drug dealer and friend of the Luchese crime family." N Y Times Book Rev

"Breslin is a delighted tour guide through the underworld. . . . Nobody does it better." Booklist

Bugliosi, Vincent

★ Helter skelter; the true story of the Manson murders. {by} Vincent Bugliosi with Curt Gentry. 25th anniversary ed; Norton 1994 528p il $25; pa $13.95   **364.1**

1. Homicide 2. Prisoners 3. Murderers

ISBN 0-393-08700-X; 0-393-32223-8 pa

LC 94-20957

A reissue of the title published 1974

"This book by the prosecutor at the Tate-LaBianca murder trial tells the inside story of the Manson Family murders, the investigations, and the trial." Libr J

Burns, Sarah

The Central Park Five. Alfred A. Knopf 2011 240p il map $25.95   **364.1**

1. Rape 2. False accusation 3. Victims of crimes 4. Administration of criminal justice 5. Rape victims 6. Investment bankers 7. Crime -- New York (N.Y.) 8. Criminal justice, Administration of -- New York (N.Y.)

ISBN 978-0-307-26614-9; 0-307-26614-1

LC 2010039661

This book recounts "the public frenzy surrounding the April 19, 1989, attack on Trisha Meili in Central Park. The 28-year-old investment banker was out for a run when she was . . . raped, beaten and left for dead. The assault, pinned on a group of black and Hispanic boys aged 13 to 16 who'd been misbehaving in the park that night, incited media diatribes about civic decay. . . . [C]ourt cases found five of the boys guilty in 1990. Then, in 2002, convicted rapist and murderer Matias Reyes confessed to the attack and the five convictions were overturned. [Sarah] Burns's deconstruction of how justice was hijacked is part police procedural, part courtroom drama, part cultural critique . . . Burns . . . reveals how 'winning the case trumped investigating the evidence.'" Particular focus is given to "media and public resistance to Reyes's confession: so entrenched was the 'wilding' narrative that many refused to give it up." (Maclean's)

"An important cultural document, and unquestionably worth reading. . . . Burns's gripping tale may serve as an allegory for some of the most pressing criminal justice issues of our time." N Y Times Book Rev

Includes bibliographical references

Capote, Truman

★ In cold blood; a true account of a multiple murder and its consequences. Random House 2002 343p $22; pa $13   **364.1**

1. Homicide 2. Murderers

ISBN 0-375-50790-6; 0-679-74558-0 pa

LC 2002-282920

A reissue of the title first published 1966

"Truman Capote called his account of the 1959 murder of a Kansas farm family a nonfiction novel. Using information he collected through interviews with townspeople and the killers, Capote created a vivid portrait of the criminals and graphically described the crime, the criminals' escape to Mexico, capture, trial, appeals, and hanging." HarperCollins Reader's Ency of Am Lit. 2nd edition

Carney, Scott

The **red** market; on the trail of the world's organ brokers, bone thieves, blood farmers, and child traffickers. William Morrow 2011 254p il $25.99 **364.1**

1. Procurement of organs, tissues, etc.

ISBN 978-0-06-193646-3; 0-06-193646-4

LC 2010-47807

"The 'red market' of Scott Carney's lucid and alarming book refers to the various medical activities through which the human body can generate a profit: surrogate motherhood, organ transplantation, drug testing, baby selling and blood farming, to mention just a few items on Mr. Carney's disturbing list. The buyers of red-market goods are usually well-to-do Westerners, while the sellers tend to come from developing countries. A surprisingly large number of the sellers are women, and many appear to be forced into the business. Middlemen, beyond taking large profits, encourage the trade by assuring buyers that the transaction is conducted ethically. . . . [This] is not an abstract philosophical meditation or an ethnographic treatise, though it has elements of both. It is a work of investigative journalism, written by an experienced health reporter who lived in India for more than 10 years. Mr. Carney knows how to tell a story and digs deeply." Wall Street J

Includes bibliographical references

Carrere, Emmanuel

The **adversary**; a true story of monstrous deception. translated by Linda Coverdale. Picador USA 2002 191p pa $13 **364.1**

1. Homicide

ISBN 0-312-42060-9; 978-0-312-42060-4

LC 2001-50066

First published 2000 by Metropolitan Books

"In 1933, Jean-Claude Romand, a successful French doctor, seemed devastated when his family was killed in a house fire; then police found evidence of blunt trauma on his wife's skull, and dug bullets out of his children. Soon, the truth began to surface: Romand was not a doctor at all, and he had murdered his family to conceal a web of lies that extended across almost two decades." New Yorker

"In telling Romand's story, [the author] also writes of the process of creating this book. By injecting himself into the narrative, Carrere has managed to make this appalling story both fascinating and highly readable." Libr J

Cullen, Kevin

Whitey Bulger; America's most wanted gangster and the manhunt that brought him to justice. Kevin Cullen and Shelley Murphy. 1st ed. W W Norton & Co Inc 2013 viii, 478 p., 16 unnumbered pages of platesp (hardcover) $26.95 **364.1**

1. Fugitives from justice 2. Organized crime -- United States 3. Gangsters -- Massachusetts -- Boston -- Biography 4. Fugitives from justice -- United States -- Biography 5. Organized crime -- Massachusetts --

Boston -- Case studies

ISBN 0393087727; 9780393087727

LC 2012050752

This book, by Kevin Cullen and Shelley Murphy, "follows the astonishing career and epic manhunt for Whitey Bulger. . . . Raised in a South Boston housing project, James 'Whitey' Bulger became the most wanted fugitive of his generation. . . . Reporters Kevin Cullen and Shelley Murphy follow Whitey's extraordinary criminal career--from teenage thievery to bank robberies to the building of his underworld empire and a string of brutal murders." (Publisher's note)

Includes bibliographical references (pages 431-464) and index.

Dash, Mike

The **first** family; terror, extortion, revenge, murder, and the birth of the American mafia. Random House 2009 375p il map $27 **364.1**

1. Mafia 2. Organized crime 3. Mobsters

ISBN 978-1-4000-6722-0

LC 2009-5681

This account of the early days of the Mafia in the United States focuses on the life of "Giuseppe 'The Clutch Hand' Morello. Arriving in the States in 1892 from Corleone, Sicily, 'The Clutch Hand' is believed to have been the force behind America's first Mafia family." Libr J

"Essential for students of organized crime in America. Murder and mayhem buffs will enjoy it too." Kirkus

Includes bibliographical references (p. 350-357)

Dolnick, Edward

The **rescue** artist; a true story of art, thieves, and the hunt for a missing masterpiece. HarperCollins Publishers 2005 270p il $25.95; pa $14.95 **364.1**

1. Artists 2. Painters 3. Art thefts

ISBN 0-06-053117-7; 978-0-06-053117-1; 0-06-053118-5 pa; 978-0-06053118-8 pa

LC 2004-62060

This is an "account of the 1994 theft of one of the world's most famous paintings, The Scream. . . . This is a tightly woven, fast-paced story." SLJ

Includes bibliographical references

Douglas, John E.

The **cases** that haunt us; from Jack the Ripper to JonBenet Ramsey, the FBI's legendary mindhunter sheds light on the mysteries that won't go away. [by] John Douglas, Mark Olshaker. Pocket Books 2001 487p il pa $7.99 **364.1**

1. Homicide 2. Criminal psychology

ISBN 978-0-671-01706-4; 0-671-01706-3

First published 2000 by Scribner

The authors discuss "eight controversial cases that include the Lindbergh baby kidnapping, the Boston Strangler, the Zodiac Killer, and the JonBenet Ramsey killing." Libr J

Dray, Philip

At the hands of persons unknown; the lynching of Black America. Random House 2002 528p il hardcover o.p. pa $14.95 **364.1**

1. Lynching 2. Southern States -- Race relations 3.

African Americans -- Southern States
ISBN 0-375-75445-8 pa

LC 2001-40366

The author "looks at specific lynchings, the national history of race and politics, and anti-lynching campaigns of black and biracial organizations." Libr J

"Dray balances moral indignation with a sound understanding of history and politics. The result is vital, hard-hitting cultural history." Publ Wkly

Includes bibliographical references

Fisher, Kenneth L.

How to smell a rat; the five signs of financial fraud. [by] Ken Fisher with Lara Hoffmans. Wiley 2009 209p (Fisher investments series) $24.95 **364.1**
1. Fraud 2. Investments 3. Swindlers and swindling
ISBN 978-0-470-52653-8

LC 2009-21631

"With five straightforward rules that would have saved any investor from Bernie Madoff, . . . [Fisher] gives readers a secure plan for fraudproof investing, worthwhile for novices and sophisticated financiers alike. . . . Much more than what to avoid, Fisher's concise guide should be highly illuminating and confidence-building for anyone with a bank account." Publ Wkly

Includes bibliographical references

Geary, Rick

The **Lindbergh** child; America's hero and the crime of the century. written and illustrated by Rick Geary. NBM/ComicsLit 2008 un il map (Treasury of XXth century murder) pa $15.95 **364.1**
1. Generals 2. Air pilots 3. Graphic novels 4. Mystery graphic novels 5. Memoirists 6. Air force officers 7. Homicide -- Graphic novels 8. Kidnapping -- Graphic novels
ISBN 978-1-56163-529-0

Charles Lindbergh was an American hero following his solo crossing of the Atlantic in an airplane. He married into a wealthy family, he and his wife had a baby, they were building their dream home. Then, one night, the baby was abducted from the house. Geary's account retraces all the highly publicized events, ransom notes (false and otherwise), as well as the string of colorful characters who all claimed they could help but instead snookered the Lindberghs. While Bruno Hauptmann was arrested, tried, convicted, and executed, there remain many questions about what really happened. Geary brings them up for readers to consider.

"A good example of the origins of modern forensics, crime-scene investigation, and celebrity hysteria, this work is an excellent choice for most collections." SLJ

Glenny, Misha

McMafia; a journey through the global criminal underworld. Alfred A. Knopf 2008 375p il map $27.95 **364.1**
1. Organized crime
ISBN 978-1-4000-4411-5; 1-4000-4411-1

LC 2007-30522

The author discusses "the ability of organized crime worldwide to find and service markets driven by a seemingly insatiable demand for illegal wares. . . . [He contends

that] organized crime feeds off the poverty of the developing world. . . . Glenny talked to police, victims, politicians, and members of the global underworld in eastern Europe, North and South America, Africa, the Middle East, China, Japan, and India." Publisher's note

"Readers yearning for a deeper understanding of the real-life, international counterparts to The Sopranos need look no further than Glenny's engrossing study." Publ Wkly

Includes bibliographical references

Goldhagen, Daniel Jonah

Worse than war; genocide, eliminationism, and the ongoing assault on humanity. [by] Daniel Jonah Goldhagen. PublicAffairs 2009 658p il **364.1**
1. Racism 2. Genocide 3. Prejudices 4. Mass murder 5. Racism -- Psychological aspects 6. Genocide -- Psychological aspects
ISBN 1-58648-769-8; 978-1-58648-769-0

LC 2009-28035

This is an investigation into the phenomenon of genocide and mass killing—explaining why genocides begin, are sustained, and end; why societies support them and why they happen so frequently; and how the international community should and can successfully stop them.

The author "convincingly disparages bureaucratic 'banality of evil' explanations of genocide and spotlights the ideologies of leaders who exploit ordinary citizens' hate-filled beliefs to instigate mass murder. It's not easy reading, but Goldhagen's vehemence and the sheer weight of horrors that he recounts move one's conscience." Publ Wkly

Includes bibliographical references

Guinn, Jeff

Go down together; the true, untold story of Bonnie and Clyde. Simon & Schuster 2009 467p il $27 **364.1**
1. Criminals 2. Outlaws 3. Murderers
ISBN 978-1-4165-5706-7; 1-4165-5706-7

LC 2008-53342

"As Guinn relates, Bonnie and Clyde didn't commit many of the acts—particularly the murders—they were accused of. Their crime spree only lasted from spring 1932 to May 1934. But in the worst of the Depression, Americans ate up accounts of the Barrow exploits as a form of entertainment. The gang fed the newspapers terrific stuff, including the staged photo of Bonnie holding a gun and smoking a cigar. For folks living hardscrabble lives, the fact that the gang robbed the same bankers who were foreclosing on their farms made the exploits of Bonnie and Clyde even sweeter. Guinn succeeds marvelously in recreating the spirit of the times, the desperation of unemployment and financial ruin." PopMatters

Includes bibliographical references

Ifill, Sherrilyn A.

On the courthouse lawn; confronting the legacy of lynching in the twenty-first century. Beacon Press 2007 xx, 204p il $25.95; pa $16 **364.1**
1. Lynching 2. Reconciliation 3. United States -- Race relations 4. Lynching -- United States -- History
ISBN 978-0-8070-0987-1; 0-8070-0987-3; 978-0-

8070-0988-8 pa; 0-8070-0988-1 pa

LC 2006-16618

The author explores the continued effects of lynching. Ifill contends that "the lynchings implicated average white citizens, some of whom actively participated in the violence while many others witnessed the lynchings but did nothing to stop them. Ifill observes that this history of complicity has become embedded in the social and cultural fabric of local communities, who either supported, condoned, or ignored the violence. She . . . [presents] ideas to help communities heal. . . . Ifill argues that reconciliation and reparation efforts must also be locally based in order to bring both black and white Americans together in an efficacious dialogue." (Publisher's note) Index.

"An intriguing, immodest proposal that itself warrants discussion—and action." Kirkus

Includes bibliographical references

James, Bill, 1949-

Popular crime; reflections on the celebration of violence. Scribner 2011 482p il   **364.1**

1. Crime 2. Homicide 3. Crime -- United States -- History

ISBN 1416552731; 9781416552734

LC 2010-36180

This "book is primarily a history of the murders that have obsessed American newspaper readers since Dec. 22, 1799, when the body of a young Manhattan woman named Elma Sands was found floating in a well at what is now 89 Greene Street. Between . . . accounts of Lizzie Borden, the Boston Strangler and the Zodiac killer, Mr. James offers proposals for penal and judicial reform, theories about the cultural significance of crime stories and brief book reviews." (N Y Times (Late N Y Ed)) Index.

This is a "very entertaining book, and it will instigate arguments even as it scores many important points. . . . James's layman status is a big part of this book's bracing charm. And his real point is more universal. He loves crime books and wants you to love them, too, and not just because they're a good way to pass the time in a motel room or airport. He wants you to take them seriously, as he does, and consider the ways they reflect and reshape the culture, what they say about our justice system and our very concept of justice." Washington Post Book World

Javers, Eamon

Broker, trader, lawyer, spy; inside the secret world of corporate espionage. Harper 2010 306p $26.99; ebook $11.99   **364.1**

1. Espionage 2. Business intelligence

ISBN 978-0-06-169720-3; 978-0-06-196938-6 ebook

LC 2009031010

"Javers traces spying activity, which began in Washington, D.C., in 1790, when the city became the capital, through the Civil War, when Allan Pinkerton was chasing Confederate spies, to Allen Dulles and the CIA developing drugs to enhance interrogations and in 2002 capturing traitor Robert Hanssen. The author also offers a fascinating explanation of the role of spies in today's world economy with hundreds of firms globally in the corporate espionage business using as operatives alumni from the FBI, CIA, Secret Service, British M15 and Russian KGB, and military intelligence officers. . . . This is a must-read, excellent book." Booklist

Includes bibliographical references

Jentz, Terri

Strange piece of paradise. Farrar, Straus & Giroux 2006 542p il $27   **364.1**

1. Criminal investigation 2. Offenses against the person

ISBN 0-374-13498-7; 978-0-374-13498-3

LC 2005-27240

"This book opens 15 years after a horrifyingly brutal assault in which Jentz and a Yale classmate, asleep at an Oregonian campground, were first run over and then attacked by a hatchet-wielding stranger. Jentz first returned to Oregon in 1992 to reclaim the self she lost at 19 and conduct her own investigation into the crime, for which no one was ever prosecuted. Her story is simultaneously riveting and disturbing—not an embellished memoir but a straightforward, chronological account based on notes, crime reports, newspaper accounts, hospital records, lab reports, and the author's own memory of events." Libr J

Jimenez, Stephen

The **Book** of Matt; Hidden Truths About the Murder of Matthew Shepard. Stephen Jimenez. Steerforth Press 2013 viii, 360 p.p $26; $16 **364.1**

1. Homicide 2. Drug traffic 3. Mass media and gays -- United States 4. Gays -- Crimes against -- United States 5. Mass media -- United States -- Influence 6. Hate crimes -- United States -- Public opinion 7. Mass media and public opinion -- United States

ISBN 1586422146; 9781586422141; 9781586422264

LC 2013431178

Author Stephen Jiminez presents his story of "determination to ascertain why Matthew Shepard--a gay University of Wyoming student-- was viciously killed in 1998. Jimenez makes a strong case that the unappreciated lesson of the Shepard murder is one about the dangers of methamphetamine. Shepard and his killer, Aaron McKinney, were not strangers after all. In fact Aaron McKinney was a bisexual, who had had sex with Shepard. And both were dealers of methamphetamine." (Amazon)

"In claiming that Shepard was killed because of drugs, and the 'gay panic' story was offered as a cover and heavily pushed by media and politicians as part of a larger agenda, Jimenez completely changes the meaning and impact of Shepard's death." Pub Wkly

Includes bibliographical references (pages 355-357)

Keefe, Patrick Radden

The **snakehead**; an epic tale of the Chinatown underworld and the American dream. Doubleday 2009 414p map   **364.1**

1. Smuggling 2. Illegal aliens 3. Smugglers 4. Businesspeople 5. Illegal aliens -- United States 6. Human trafficking -- United States 7. China -- Emigration and immigration 8. United States -- Emigration and immigration 9. United States -- Immigration and emigration

ISBN 0-307-27927-8 pa; 0-385-52130-8; 978-0-307-27927-9 pa; 978-0-385-52130-7

LC 2008-50049

This book tells the story of human smuggling and trafficking among Fujianese immigrants to the United States. It focuses on Cheng Chui Ping, a Chinese immigrant who came to New York in the early 1980s. Her path to the American "dream began with an underground bank . . . run out of a noodle shop. . . . She became known as Sister Ping and built a global people-smuggling conglomerate that stretched from China's Fujian province to Africa, Europe, and South America, relying on one of Chinatown's . . . gangs to protect her power and profits. Sister Ping's empire came to light in 1993, when [the Golden Venture], a ship loaded with 300 near-starving immigrants ran aground off Queens. It took . . . nearly ten years to untangle the criminal network and home in on its mastermind." (Publisher's note) Index.

"This is one of the freshest accounts of modern-day migration I've read, one filled with moral ambiguity, one that doesn't pretend to have the answers, one that . . . feels like essential reading." Washington Post Book World

Includes bibliographical references

Lebsock, Suzanne

A **murder** in Virginia; Southern justice on trial. Norton 2003 442p il $26.95; pa $15.95   **364.1**

1. Trials (Homicide) 2. Virginia 3. Southern States -- Race relations

ISBN 0-393-04201-4; 0-393-32606-3 pa

LC 2002-15946

"On a warm afternoon in June 1895, a 56-year-old white woman was brutally murdered in Lunenburg County, VA. Despite the absence of any truly incriminating eyewitness testimony or physical evidence, four blacks—three women and one man—were arrested and tried for the murder. Lebsock . . . recreates the subsequent trials, introducing the defendants, their prosecutors, and the witnesses and placing the proceedings within the context of the black and white communities and deteriorating conditions for African Americans in the post-Reconstruction South. Here historical narrative is every bit as intriguing as fictional mystery but more edifying for the information it gives its readers concerning race relations and criminal justice in the latter part of the 19th century." Libr J

Includes bibliographical references

Lehr, Dick

The **fence**; a police cover-up along Boston's racial divide. Harper 2009 383p il map $25.99; pa $14.99   **364.1**

1. Police brutality 2. Police corruption 3. Boston (Mass.) -- Race relations

ISBN 978-0-06-078098-2; 0-06-078098-3; 978-0-06-078099-9 pa; 0-06-078099-1 pa

The author "details one of the most controversial cases in the annals of the Boston Police Department, involving a brutal assault on a black plainclothes officer by his fellow cops and the resulting 1998 civil rights trial against the police force. Not only does Lehr paint the racial and political turbulence of Boston at the time, but he explores the cultural backgrounds of the black officer, Michael Cox; his attacker and fellow officer, Kenny Conley; and Robert 'Smut' Brown, a drug dealer involved in the killing that started it all. . . . Jolting, nightmarish and potent, this true cop yarn bests

any bogus reality show or overblown tabloid tale with its hardboiled spin." Publ Wkly

Includes bibliographical references

Levitt, Len

NYPD confidential; power and corruption in the country's greatest police force. Thomas Dunne Books 2009 304p $25.99   **364.1**

1. Police corruption 2. Police -- New York (N.Y.) 3. New York (N.Y.) -- Police Dept.

ISBN 978-0-312-38032-8; 0-312-38032-1

LC 2009-7602

"Using the administrations of recent New York City police commissioners Raymond W. Kelly (twice), William J. Bratton, Howard Safir, and Bernard Kerick as a frame, Levitt . . . pries into the inner workings of the NYPD. Levitt spins a fascinating tale of politics, rivalries, infighting, counterterrorism, and corruption inside the police department of America's largest city." Libr J

Includes bibliographical references

Longman, Jere

Among the heroes; United Flight 93 and the passengers and crew who fought back. HarperCollins Pubs. 2002 288p il $24.95; pa $13.95   **364.1**

1. Hijacking of airplanes 2. September 11 terrorist attacks, 2001

ISBN 0-06-009908-9; 0-06-009909-7 pa

LC 2002-68530

This is an account of the United Airlines flight which was hijacked on September 11, 2001 and crashed in Pennsylvania before reaching its intended target

This book "gives us an incredibly detailed and personal tale of that horrific episode." Booklist

Includes bibliographical references

Mallon, Thomas

Mrs. Paine's garage and the murder of John F. Kennedy. Pantheon Bks. 2002 211p $22; pa $13   **364.1**

1. Homemakers 2. Presidents 3. Senators 4. Murderers 5. Members of Congress 6. Spouses of prominent persons

ISBN 0-375-42117-3; 0-15-602755-0 pa

LC 2001-36157

"A journalistic inquiry into Ruth Paine, the woman who welcomed Marina Oswald—and sometimes her husband, Lee—into her suburban Dallas home in 1963; it offers a new theory about the antecedents of the assassination." N Y Times Book Rev

Matthews, Joe

Bringing Adam home; the abduction that changed America. [by] Les Standiford with Detective Sergeant Joe Matthews. Ecco 2011 291p il map   **364.1**

1. Children 2. Homicide 3. Kidnapping 4. Kidnap victims 5. Murder victims

ISBN 0-06-198390-X; 978-0-06-198390-0

LC 2010-43572

"This is the ultimate cold case—tragic, high-profile, and, finally, successfully solved. Six-year-old Adam Walsh was abducted from a crowded Sears store in Hollywood, Florida, in 1981. Later, he was murdered and decapitated. Identifying Adam's killer took 25 years. His parents turned into tireless advocates for missing and abused children; Adam's father, John Walsh, moved from a sales job to being the executive producer and host of America's Most Wanted. This forceful account . . . gives readers the ultimate insider's account of the grueling search for Adam's killer and for the evidence to convict him. While many true-crime books claim to shine a light on society by examining one particular case, this account actually does." Booklist

McGinniss, Joe

★ **Fatal** vision. New American Library 1989 684p il pa $7.99 **364.1**
1. Homicide 2. Surgeons 3. Murderers
ISBN 978-0-451-16566-4; 0-451-16566-7
First published 1983 by Putnam
"The complex story of Jeffrey MacDonald, a Princeton-educated doctor and Green Beret captain who was accused of brutally murdering his wife and their two young daughters on a dreary February night in 1970." Best Sellers
"This is a wisely observant, well-written, and understated book." Harpers
Includes bibliographical references

Murakami, Haruki

Underground; translated from the Japanese by Alfred Birnbaum and Philip Gabriel. Vintage Bks. 2001 366p map pa $14 **364.1**
1. Terrorism 2. Aum Shinrikyo
ISBN 0-375-72580-6
LC 00-69310
"On March 20, 1995, followers of the religious cult Aum Shinrikyo unleashed lethal sarin gas into cars of the Tokyo subway system. Many died, many more were injured. This is {Murakami's} . . . account of this episode." Publ Wkly

Olsen, Jack

I : the creation of a serial killer. St. Martin's Press 2002 365p il $24.95; pa $6.99 **364.1**
1. Homicide 2. Murderers
ISBN 0-312-24198-4; 0-312-98384-0 pa
LC 2001-58892
The author draws "on interviews and his subject's own diaries to . . . reveal the life and inner workings of Keith Hunter Jesperson, currently serving life in prison for the murders of eight women in the 1990s." Publ Wkly
"A truly horrifying account of a serial killer, told with shocking candor." Booklist

Pepper, William F.

An **act** of state; the execution of Martin Luther King. Norton 2003 334p il map $25 **364.1**
1. Clergy 2. Conspiracies 3. Nonfiction writers 4. Civil rights activists 5. Nobel laureates for peace
ISBN 1-85984-695-5
Companion volume to Orders to kill (1995)
This book continues the author's examination of the life and death of Martin Luther King Jr.
"Forget everything you think you know, Pepper insists. James Earl Ray did not pull the trigger. . . . Pepper gradually

introduces the vast cast of characters in a dizzying murder conspiracy that winds from a Memphis bar through the shadows of organized crime to the far reaches of national government. He carefully maps each player's place and role in the tangled web and doggedly tries to stick to a straightforward narrative. . . . Pepper attempts nothing less than a rewrite of history, and a spurring of further investigation." Publ Wkly
Includes bibliographical references

Queen, William

Under and alone; the true story of the undercover agent who infiltrated America's most violent outlaw motorcycle gang. Random House 2005 270p il $24.95 **364.1**
1. Gangs
ISBN 1-400-06084-2
LC 2004-51176
This is an "account of how Queen, a veteran agent within the Bureau of Alcohol, Tobacco and Firearms, posed as a hard-core biker." N Y Times Book Rev
"The strength and white-hot intensity of the writing make this read like a movie, and Hollywood is certain to take note." Publ Wkly

Raab, Selwyn

Five families; the rise, decline, and resurgence of America's most powerful Mafia empires. Thomas Dunne Books 2005 765p il $29.95 **364.1**
1. Mafia 2. Organized crime
ISBN 0-312-30094-8
LC 2005-48416
"With vivid characterizations of a cavalcade of thugs, Raab's account is the most lively and informative Mafia history in years." Booklist
Includes bibliographical references

Reppetto, Thomas A.

American Mafia; a history of its rise to power. {by} Thomas Reppetto. H. Holt 2003 318p il $26; pa $15 **364.1**
1. Mafia
ISBN 0-8050-7210-1; 0-8050-7798-7 pa
LC 2003-56736
"Though this book doesn't answer every question about the Mafia in America, it does present a thought-provoking depiction of the Mob devoid of the sensationalism prevalent in many other portrayals." Publ Wkly
Includes bibliographical references

Rule, Ann

--and never let her go; Thomas Capano, the deadly seducer. Pocket Star Books 2000 680p il pa $7.99 **364.1**
1. Lawyers 2. Homicide 3. Secretaries 4. Missing persons 5. Trials (Homicide) 6. Murderers 7. Murder victims 8. District attorneys 9. State government employees
ISBN 0-671-86871-3; 978-0-671-86871-0
First published 1999 by Simon & Schuster
"In June 1996, Anne Marie Fahey, a 30-year-old secretary to the governor of Delaware, disappeared and was reported missing by her family. In the weeks that followed,

a charming, successful, and well-connected attorney, Tom Capano, was charged with her murder. Rule . . . tells the riveting story of the three-year secret affair between Fahey and Capano and a cruel obsession that led to murder." Booklist

Bitter harvest; a woman's fury, a mother's sacrifice. Simon & Schuster 1998 351p $23   **364.1**
1. Arson 2. Homicide 3. Physicians
ISBN 0-684-81047-6

LC 97-49677

"It is impossible to know what was going on in Dr. Debora Green's mind the night she set fire to her house in Prairie Village, Kan., killing two of her three children. Ann Rule . . . speculates that Green's alcoholism and addiction to prescription drugs, as well as her anger that her estranged husband, Dr. Michael Farrar, was leaving her for another woman, sent Green over the edge." N Y Times Book Rev

"It is Rule's expert attention to detail that makes this Medea-incarnate story so compelling." Publ Wkly

Dead by sunset; perfect husband, perfect killer? Simon & Schuster 1995 429p il hardcover o.p. pa $7.99   **364.1**
1. Trials (Homicide)
ISBN 0-671-00113-2 pa

LC 95-38326

"Eight years after killing his divorced wife in Portland, Oregon, Brad Cunningham was finally convicted of her murder. . . . {Rule} tackles the case of the five-times-married Cunningham, whose loving personality and demeanor changed after each marriage." Booklist

"Rule's writing is crisp and well paced, full of details that give the reader clear insight into circumstances and surroundings, as well as motive." Libr J

Everything she ever wanted; a true story of obsessive love, murder, and betrayal. Simon & Schuster 1992 527p il $23; pa $6.99   **364.1**
1. Homicide
ISBN 0-671-69070-1; 0-671-69071-X pa

LC 92-21541

"Spoiled rotten by her family, Patricia Vann Radcliffe Taylor Allanson, a Georgia beauty whose goal in life was to emulate Scarlett O'Hara, led a life of deadly horror. . . . Her presence was a constant danger to people who stood in her way: her brother a suicide, her new in-laws shot dead, her grandparents-in-law nearly poisoned by arsenic, her employer severely overdosed, her daughter, who finally saw the awful truth about her mother, possibly poisoned. Rule's tautly written study of this diabolical woman constantly fascinates the reader." Libr J

Saviano, Roberto
Gomorrah; translated from the Italian by Virginia Jewiss. Farrar, Straus & Giroux 2007 301p map $25   **364.1**
1. Organized crime 2. Italy
ISBN 978-0-374-16527-7; 0-374-16527-0

LC 2007-31004

Original Italian edition, 2006

This is the "tale of the Camorra, a network of thugs, exploiters and killers who run Naples and the surrounding countryside." Publ Wkly

This "is an eyepopping, hair-raising, stomach-turning book. The mob has never looked so bad—or read so well." Christ Sci Monit

Selby, Scott Andrew
Flawless; inside the largest diamond heist in history. by Scott Andrew Selby and Greg Campbell. Sterling Pub. Co. 2010 319p il map $24.95   **364.1**
1. Theft 2. Diamonds
ISBN 978-1-4027-6651-0

LC 2009-40766

The authors "provide an engrossing nonfiction thriller with a truly improbable story at its center, but they also provide a colorful look at the shadowy world of the diamond trade—how they're graded, sold, secured and stolen." Kirkus

Includes bibliographical references

Sifakis, Carl
The **mafia** encyclopedia; 3rd ed; Facts on File 2005 510p il (Facts on File crime library) $65; pa $21.95   **364.1**
1. Reference books 2. Mafia -- Dictionaries
ISBN 0-8160-5694-3; 0-8160-5695-1 pa

LC 2004-58487

First published 1987

The author provides a "survey of the mob's most influential perpetrators and personalities, including their hangouts and hideaways, their plays for power, their schemes and crimes, and their unique culture and jargon." Publisher's note

"Sifakis provides detailed, informed, and colorful information." Libr J

Smith, Jennie Erin
Stolen world; a tale of reptiles, smugglers and skulduggery. Crown 2011 322p il $25; ebook $25   **364.1**
1. Reptiles 2. Smuggling 3. Rare animals 4. Wild animal trade 5. Rare reptiles 6. Animal dealers 7. Wildlife smuggling 8. Wild animal trade -- Corrupt practices
ISBN 978-0-307-38147-7; 0-307-38147-1; 978-0-307-72026-9 ebook; 0-307-72026-8 ebook

LC 2010-9548

"Smith's affection for these unsavory people gives the book an intriguing moral ambiguity (which might make some environmentalists cringe), but the subculture's brazen shenanigans make for a convoluted, fascinating tale." Publ Wkly

Stewart, James B.
Blind eye; how the medical establishment let a doctor get away with murder. Simon & Schuster 1999 334p il hardcover o.p. pa $14   **364.1**
1. Homicide 2. Physicians 3. Murderers
ISBN 0-684-86563-7 pa

LC 99-37044

Stewart discusses the "case against Dr. Michael Swango, a . . . physician suspected of poisoning between 35 and 60 patients and co-workers." Time

This is "not only a fascinating look at a psychopath masquerading as a healer but also a disturbing exposé of the system that fails to protect the public." Libr J

Welch, Craig

Shell games; rogues, smugglers, and the hunt for nature's bounty. William Morrow 2010 274p il map $25.99   **364.1**

1. Poaching 2. Smuggling 3. Puget Sound region (Wash.)

ISBN 978-0-06-153713-4; 0-06-153713-6

LC 2009-38980

"Welch covers the wildlife crime beat in Puget Sound, where shellfish poachers wreak havoc on the region's once bountiful, now imperiled marine ecosystem. Writing with the sizzle of a mystery novelist, Welch portrays a complex, driven, and irresistible cast of real-life characters, from fish cops Ed Volz and Kevin Harrington to Doug Tobin, a larger-than-life Native American fisherman. . . . Welch's utterly compelling true tale of black-market trade in endangered ocean wildlife is astounding and infuriating." Booklist

Includes bibliographical references

Wittman, Robert

Priceless; how I went undercover to rescue the world's stolen treasures. [by] Robert K. Wittman with John Shiffman. Crown Publishers 2010 324p il $25; ebook $25   **364.1**

1. Art thefts 2. Criminal investigation

ISBN 978-0-307-46147-6; 978-0-307-46149-0 ebook

LC 2009-49083

"During his 20-year career, Wittman recovered more than $225 million worth of artwork and historical artifacts in undercover stings all over the globe. . . . [This is] an account of how he planned and pulled off some of his high-stakes operations, rescuing treasures such as an original copy of the Bill of Rights and paintings by Rembrandt and Renoir." Washington Post

This "book has the excitement of an espionage novel. It's suspenseful, thought provoking, and funny." ARTnews

364.106   Organized crime

Reavill, Gil

Mafia summit; J. Edgar Hoover, the Kennedy Brothers, and the meeting that unmasked the mob. Gil Reavill. Thomas Dunne Books 2012 320 p. (hbk.) $26.99   **364.106**

1. Mafia 2. Mafia -- United States -- History -- 20th century 3. Organized crime -- United States -- Prevention -- History 4. Organized crime -- United States -- History -- 20th century

ISBN 0312657757; 9780312657758; 9781250021106

LC 2012038009

Author Gil Reavill presents a book on the Mafia in the U.S. "For years, FBI director J. Edgar Hoover had adamantly denied the existence of the Mafia, but young Robert Kennedy immediately recognized the shattering importance of the Appalachian summit. As attorney general when his brother JFK became president, Bobby embarked on a campaign to break the spine of the mob, engaging in a furious turf battle with the powerful Hoover." Reavill details "mob killings, the early days of the heroin trade, and the crusade to loosen the hold of organized crime." (Publisher's note)

Includes bibliographical references

364.15   Offenses against the person

Cohan, William D.

★ The **price** of silence; the Duke lacrosse scandal, the power of the elite, and the corruption of our great universities. Willam D. Cohan. Scribner 2014 672 p. (hardcover : alk. paper) $35   **364.15**

1. Rape 2. Lacrosse 3. College sports 4. Duke University 5. Rape -- North Carolina -- Durham 6. Lacrosse players -- North Carolina -- Durham 7. Malicious accusation -- North Carolina -- Durham 8. Prosecution -- Corrupt practices -- North Carolina -- Durham

ISBN 1451681798; 9781451681796; 9781451681802

LC 2013043923

This book, by Willam D. Cohan, presents an account of the "Duke lacrosse team scandal that reveals the pressures faced by America's elite colleges and universities and pulls back the curtain . . . on the larger issues of sexual misconduct, underage drinking, and bad-boy behavior. . . . What transpired at Duke followed upon the university's . . . effort to compete directly with the Ivy League for the best students and with its Division I rivals for supremacy in selected sports." (Publisher's note)

"Cohan explores the usual disconnects that occur in high-profile crime cases between what is reported by the press, chronicled in official records, and perceived as public opinion and what really happened. A gripping account of a sensational case." Booklist

Includes bibliographical references and index.

Foxman, Abraham H., 1940-

Viral hate; containing its spread on the Internet. Abraham H. Foxman and Christopher Wolf. Palgrave Macmillan 2013 256 p. (alk. paper) $27   **364.15**

1. Hate speech 2. Internet -- Social aspects 3. Online hate speech 4. Hate crimes -- Prevention 5. Internet -- Moral and ethical aspects

ISBN 0230342175; 9780230342170

LC 2012047877

Here, the authors explore "the increasingly volatile subject of Internet hate speech and cyberbullying, a 'serious illness' with lethal ramifications. The authors support this statement in chapters . . . defining various types of noxious online rhetoric and the most recognizable extremist groups spreading it through Internet social portals and artistic media." (Kirkus Reviews)

Includes bibliographical references

Garcia Marquez, Gabriel

News of a kidnapping; translated from the Spanish by Edith Grossman. Knopf 1997 291p $25   **364.15**

1. Hostages 2. Kidnapping 3. Drug traffic

ISBN 0-375-40051-6

LC 97-5445

The author discusses kidnappings in Colombia orchestrated by "Pablo Escobar, once head of the Medellín drug cartel. . . . The writer's respondents are mainly the survivors of a group of prominent residents of Bogotá whom the drug lord held hostage during 1990 and 1991." Time

Hatch, Thom

The **Last** Outlaws; The lives and legends of Butch Cassidy and the Sundance Kid. by Thom Hatch. New American Library 2013 xii, 350 p.p ill., maps (The last outlaws) (hardcover) $26.95 **364.15**

1. West (U.S.) -- Biography 2. Outlaws -- West (U.S.) -- Biography

ISBN 0451239199; 9780451239198

LC 2012031697

This book, by Thom Hatch, presents a biography of "Butch Cassidy and the Sundance Kid--as leaders of the Wild Bunch, they planned and executed the most daring bank and train robberies of the day. . . . For several years at the end of the 1890s, the two friends, along with a revolving cast who made up their band of thieves, eluded local law enforcement and bounty hunters, all while stealing from the rich bankers and eastern railroad corporations who exploited western land." (Publisher's note)

King, Joyce

Hate crime: the story of a dragging in Jasper, Texas. Pantheon Bks. 2002 225p $24   **364.15**

1. Homicide 2. Hate crimes 3. Murder victims 4. Southern States -- Race relations 5. African Americans -- Southern States

ISBN 0-375-42132-7

LC 2001-58074

"On a Texas back road in 1998 . . . three young whites wrapped a chain around an African American man and dragged him to his death behind their truck. . . . King covers each of the three trials that followed the atrocity." Libr J

The author "provides both objective reporting and sensitive insight into the players on both sides of America's racial divide." Booklist

Koerner, Brendan I.

The **skies** belong to us; love and terror in the golden age of hijacking. Brendan I. Koerner. Crown Publishers 2013 336 p. illustrations $26   **364.15**

1. Hijacking of airplanes 2. Hijacking of aircraft -- United States -- Case studies

ISBN 0307886107; 9780307886101

LC 2012043203

This book on the history of airplane hijacking "follows the strange and romantic exploits of Willie Roger Holder and Cathy Kerkow, lovers and radicals who became international celebrities when they hijacked Western Airlines Flight 701 in June 1972, demanding a ransom and the release of Angela Davis. Their escape to Algiers and their subsequent adoption by French radicals contributed to the cachet of hijacking." (Library Journal)

"A riveting, highly readable tale of terror in the skies." Kirkus

Includes bibliographical references and index

Larson, Erik

★ The **devil** in the white city; murder, magic, and madness at the fair that changed America. Erik Larson. Crown 2003 xi, 447p ill., maps $25.95 **364.15**

1. Homicide 2. Murderers 3. World's Columbian Exposition (1893: Chicago, Ill.)

ISBN 0609608444; 9780609608449

LC 20020154046

International Horror Guild Awards: Best Nonfiction (2003); Edgar Allan Poe Awards: Best Fact Crime (2004)

This nonfiction "tale of Chicago Worlds' Fair of 1893 focuses primarily on two men: Daniel H. Burnham, the architect who was the driving force behind the fair, and Henry H. Holmes, a sadistic serial killer working under the cover of the busy fair. . . Burnham and his partner, John Root, the leading architects in Chicago, were tapped for the job, and they in turn called on Frederick Law Olmstead, Louis Sullivan, and Richard M. Hunt to help them build the world's greatest fair. . . . Unbeknownst to any of them, Holmes, a charismatic, handsome doctor, had arrived in the city and built a complex with apartments, a drugstore, and a vault, which he used to trap his victims until they suffocated." (Booklist)

This is an account of how "H.H. Holmes (born Herman Webster Mudgett) dispatched somewhere between 27 and 200 people, mostly single young women, in the churning new metropolis of Chicago; many of the murders occurred during (and exploited) the city's finest moment, the World's Fair of 1893. Larson's breathtaking new history is a novelistic yet wholly factual account of the fair and the mass murderer who lurked within it." Publ Wkly

Includes bibliographical references (p. [423]-429) and index.

McConnell, David

American honor killings; desire and rage among men. David McConnell. Akashic Books 2013 256 p. (trade pbk. original) $15.95   **364.15**

1. Homicide 2. Hate crimes 3. Crime -- United States 4. Murder -- United States -- Case studies 5. Murderers -- United States -- Case studies 6. Victims of crimes -- United States -- Case studies

ISBN 1617751324; 9781617751325; 9781617751530

LC 2012939273

Stonewall Book Award: Israel Fishman Non-Fiction Award

Author David McConnell presents a "look at the subculture of violent crime [and] shows how fluid terms like 'gay' and 'straight' can actually be. The author's case studies reflect an intensive investigation into the economic and cultural backgrounds of a wide variety of extremist cultures, research that involved interviews with law enforcement officials, families of victims and the convicted criminals themselves." (Kirkus)

"With no clear answers, but some very intriguing questions, these vignettes of masculine pride and rage will appeal to those interested in gender politics and gay studies as well as true crime fans." LJ

Salamon, Julie

Facing the wind; a true story of tragedy and reconciliation. Random House 2001 302p hardcover o.p. pa $13.95   **364.15**
1. Homicide 2. Brooklyn (New York, N.Y.) -- Social conditions
ISBN 0-375-75940-9 pa

LC 00-42532

"In 1978, Bob Rowe, an out-of-work Brooklyn lawyer, killed his two sons, his daughter and wife by bashing their heads in with a baseball bat. He was found not guilty by reason of insanity, and after several years in a mental institution was released. He later remarried and had another daughter. Although journalist Salamon . . . did not interview Rowe before his death in 1997, this expertly crafted account is informed by diligent research and interviews with his second wife, Colleen, as well as with a women's support group to which Rowe's first wife, Mary, had belonged." Publ Wkly

Schiller, Lawrence

Perfect murder, perfect town. HarperCollins Pubs. 1999 621p hardcover o.p. pa $7.99 **364.15**
1. Children 2. Homicide 3. Homemakers 4. Murder victims 5. Beauty contest winners 6. Computer industry executives 7. Parents of murdered children 8. Boulder (Colo.) -- Police Dept.
ISBN 0-06-109696-2 pa

LC 99-207248

This is an account of the investigation "of the murder of six-year-old child beauty-pageant winner JonBenét Ramsey in Boulder, Colorado, on the night of Christmas 1996." N Y Rev Books

Schiller argues that the "Boulder Police Department bungled the investigation, in large part out of ego and inexperience." N Y Times Book Rev

Sexual violence and abuse; an encyclopedia of prevention, impacts, and recovery. edited by Judy L. Postmus. ABC-CLIO, LLC 2013 2 v. (xxxii, 841 p.)p (hardcover) $189; (ebook) $189.00 **364.15**
1. Sex crimes 2. Sexual harassment 3. Sex crimes -- Prevention
ISBN 1598847554; 9781598847550; 9781598847567 pdf

LC 2012018355

This book, by Judy L. Postmus, provides a "resource on sexual violence and abuse for students, practitioners, and general readers. . . . The two-volume work contains 264 fully cross-referenced entries in alphabetical order, starting with abortion and ending with yoga therapy. The bibliography [also] provides important books, articles, online resources, and videos on a wide range of topics." (Publisher's note)

Includes bibliographical references and index.

Stiles, T. J.

Jesse James; last rebel of the Civil War. Knopf 2002 510p il maps $27.50; pa $16   **364.15**
1. Thieves 2. Outlaws
ISBN 0-375-40583-6; 0-375-70558-9 pa

LC 2002-25493

This is a "revisionist biography of Jesse James, one that takes issue with the traditional image of the Wild West outlaw . . . and with the folk-hero notion of James as a prairie Robin Hood. . . . Mr. Stiles presents James as a Confederate terrorist caught up in the wild political turbulence of his times." N Y Times Book Rev

"This is a well-written and often surprising reinterpretation of the life of a legendary and enigmatic figure." Booklist

Includes bibliographical references

The **Ultimate** Jack the Ripper companion; an illustrated encyclopedia. {compiled by} Stewart P. Evans & Keith Skinner. Carroll & Graf Pubs. 2000 692p il $35; pa $16   **364.15**
1. Homicide 2. Murderers
ISBN 0-7867-0768-2; 0-7867-0926-X pa

LC 00-711560

Published in the United Kingdom with title: Ultimate Jack the Ripper sourcebook

This is a collection of primary and secondary source material pertaining to the Whitechapel murders

"This volume is undoubtedly the single largest resource on this case ever published." Libr J

Includes bibliographical references

Worrall, Simon

The **poet** and the murderer; a true story of literary crime and the art of forgery. Dutton 2002 270p il $23.95; pa $14   **364.15**
1. Forgery 2. Homicide 3. Forgers 4. Murderers
ISBN 0-525-94596-2; 0-452-28402-3 pa

LC 2001-53878

"In 1997, Sotheby's unveiled what experts believed was a newly discovered poem, 'That God Cannot Be Understood,' by Emily Dickinson. A few weeks later, the . . . discovery was revealed a forgery by a man who had already convincingly forged documents by more than 100 literary and historical figures, including Daniel Boone and Betsy Ross. This book examines the psychology of . . . forger and murderer (he killed two people who threatened his unmasking) Mark Hofmann." Booklist

364.152   Homicide

Blum, Howard

American lightning; terror, mystery, moviemaking, and the crime of the century. Crown Publishers 2008 339p il $24.95   **364.152**
1. Bombings 2. Terrorism
ISBN 978-0-307-34694-0

LC 2008-2974

The author "explores the 1910 dynamiting of the Los Angeles Times building." Kirkus

"Blum's prose is tight, his speculations unfailingly sound and his research extensive—all adding up to an absorbing and masterful true crime narrative." Publ Wkly

Includes bibliographical references

Bowden, Charles

Murder city; Ciudad Juarez and the global economy's new killing fields. photographs by Julian Cardona. Nation Books 2010 320p il $27.50 **364.152**
1. Homicide 2. Drug traffic 3. Ciudad Juarez (Mexico)
ISBN 978-1-56858-449-2; 1-56858-449-0

LC 2010-01716

"Bowden uses his tremendous talents to tell a haunting, darkly poetic story of a city's horrifying descent into madness and anarchy. A potent book that readers won't soon forget, and a warning of what can come of an insatiable market that knows no borders." Kirkus

Braude, Joseph

The honored dead; Joseph Braude. 1st ed. Spiegel & Grau 2011 xvi, 318p.p **364.152**
1. Arabs 2. Morocco 3. Homicide 4. Friendship 5. Journalism
ISBN 9780385527033; 0385527039; 9780679604327 ebook

LC 2010046496

This book recounts the author's experiences as a journalist with "'embed-style access' to a police precinct in Casablanca, [Morocco]. . . . The Judiciary Police, an FBI-like agency, were . . . proud of their low crime rate compared to the United States, although bedeviled by a pesky sect of Islamist militants. . . . The particular murder that fascinated the author during this period involved a 41-year-old homeless Berber man, Ibrahim Dey, who was beaten to death in a warehouse where he had been sleeping for five years—ostensibly for theft. Dey was well liked and considered a majdub, or someone who brings fortune to others, and his best friend, Muhammad Bari, whom Braude befriended, swore to vindicate the suspicious murder." (Kirkus)

Brown, Ethan

Shake the devil off; a true story of the murder that rocked New Orleans. Henry Holt and Co. 2009 286p il $25 **364.152**
1. Homicide 2. Soldiers 3. Murderers 4. Bartenders 5. New Orleans (La.)
ISBN 978-0-8050-8893-9; 0-8050-8893-8

LC 2009-06698

"This is an account of a murder and suicide in New Orleans. After military service in Iraq, Zackery Bowen returned to the city to tend bar and deliver groceries. In the weeks before Hurricane Katrina made landfall, he met Addie Hall. . . . In October 2006, Bowen leaped from the rooftop bar of a French Quarter hotel. A note in his pocket directed the police to the body of Addie Hall." Publisher's note

Drawing the parallel between Katrina's aftermath and Bowen's unraveling psyche, Brown creates a riveting portrait of a gruesome crime while detailing the heart of a city in distress. A grim murder-suicide story delivered with skill and verve. Kirkus

Includes bibliographical references

Bryan, Patricia L.

Midnight assassin; a murder in America's heartland. [by] Patricia L. Bryan & Thomas Wolf. Algonquin Books of Chapel Hill 2005 278p $23.95 **364.152**
1. Farmers 2. Homemakers 3. Trials (Homicide)
ISBN 1-565-12306-9

LC 2004-59782

Bryan and Wolf offer "not only an interesting trial drama but also a look into social attitudes of rural America at the beginning of the 20th century, especially toward women." Libr J

Includes bibliographical references

Burke, Timothy M.

The **Paradiso** files; Boston's unknown serial killer. Steerforth Press 2008 346p il $24.95 **364.152**
1. Homicide 2. Murderers 3. Sex offenders
ISBN 978-1-58642-140-3; 1-58642-137-9

LC 2007-42576

"Nearly 24 years after attorney Timothy M. Burke locked up a Revere shellfish huckster for life for killing an East Boston woman, the former prosecutor is making his case that the portly predator is also a Bay State serial killer. . . . Burke alleges Leonard 'The Quahog' Paradiso is linked to the deaths of at least seven young women, including a Havard coed who vanished in 1981." Boston Herald

"Burke tells a compelling story, with chilling accounts of Paradiso's crimes gleaned from victims' accounts and evidence that never made it to court. . . . The story transcends Boston with an insider's view of the criminal justice system." Boston Globe

Buruma, Ian

Murder in Amsterdam; the death of Theo van Gogh and the limits of tolerance. Penguin Press 2006 278p $24.95 **364.152**
1. Ethnic relations 2. Netherlands 3. Television producers 4. Motion picture directors
ISBN 1-59420-108-0; 978-1-59420-108-0

LC 2006-43606

"The Netherlands may be the Western country most affected by radical Muslim violence, with two major assassinations since 9/11, those of politician Pym Fortuyn, who had called for restrictions on Muslim immigration . . . and media celebrity Theo Van Gogh, director of a film lambasting the Qur'an on women. Buruma returned to his homeland after Van Gogh's murder to gain understanding from figures in Dutch and Dutch Muslim politics and society who might provide it." Booklist

This is a "shrewd, subtly argued inquiry into the tensions and resentments underlying two of the most shocking events in the recent history of the Netherlands." N Y Times (Late N Y Ed)

Includes bibliographical references

Collins, Paul

Duel With the Devil; The True Story of How Alexander Hamilton and Aaron Burr Teamed Up to Take on America's First Sensational Murder Mystery. by

Paul Collins. Random House Inc 2013 viii, 289 p.p
map (hardcover) $26.00   **364.152**
   1. Trials (Homicide)
ISBN 0307956458; 9780307956453
                    LC 2013371593

This book, written by Paul Collins, is the "true account
of a . . . turn-of-the-19th century murder and the trial that
ensued — a showdown in which iconic political rivals Alexander Hamilton and Aaron Burr joined forces to make sure
justice was done. Still our nation's longest running 'cold
case,' the mystery of Elma Sands finally comes to a close
with this book, which delivers the first substantial break in
the case in over 200 years." (Publisher's note)

The **murder** of the century; Paul Collins. Crown
2011 viii, 325p ill.   **364.152**
   1. Homicide 2. Journalism 3. Newspapers -- United
States
ISBN 9780307592200; 0307592200
                    LC 2011009390

This book discusses "a sensational 1897 murder case
that fascinated the public as it played out across the front
pages of the New York City's leading newspapers: Joseph
Pulitzer's 'New York World' and William Randolph Hearst's
'New York Journal.' After a group of children discovered
the ghastly severed trunk of William Guldensuppe, a Turkish bath-house attendant, the rival news organs spared no
expense to ferret out the culprits, eventually tracking the
purchase of an oilcloth used to wrap the torso to Mrs. Augusta Nack, a German immigrant midwife and rumored
back-room abortionist. Guldensuppe had been Nack's lover
before being replaced by Martin Thorn, a hotheaded barber.
Things failed to progress smoothly." (Kirkus)

Includes bibliographical references and index.

Cullen, Dave
  Columbine. Twelve 2009 417p $26.99 **364.152**
   1. School shootings 2. Columbine High School
(Littleton, Colo.)
ISBN 978-0-446-54693-5; 0-446-54693-3
                    LC 2008-31441

This is an account of the shootings at Columbine High
School in 1999.

This book "is an excellent work of media criticism,
showing how legends become truths through continual citation; a sensitive guide to the patterns of public grief . . .
and, at the end of the day, a fine example of old-fashioned
journalism." N Y Times Book Rev

Includes bibliographical references

Epstein, Edward Jay
  The **annals** of unsolved crime; by Edward Jay
Epstein. Melville House 2013 347 p. (hardcover)
$26   **364.152**
   1. Cold cases (Criminal investigation) 2. Criminal
investigation 3. Assassination -- History 4.
Assassination -- Investigation
ISBN 1612190480; 9781612190488
                    LC 2012049984

This book by Edward Jay Epstein presents "case studies
of 35 controversial crimes. Several involve conspiracy theories, e.g., JFK's assassination and the Dominique Strauss-

Kahn case. He includes well-known historical cases (e.g.,
Jack the Ripper, the Lindbergh baby kidnapping) . . . and
media-sensation cases such as those of Amanda Knox, O.J.
Simpson, and JonBenet Ramsey. . . . After describing each
case, he outlines theories, and offers his opinion on the most
likely solution." (Library Journal)

Includes bibliographical references (pages [335]-338)
and index.

Flanders, Judith
  ★ The **invention** of murder; how the Victorians
revelled in death and detection and created modern
crime. by Judith Flanders. Thomas Dunne Books
2013 576 p. il (hardcover) $26.99   **364.152**
   1. Homicide 2. Detectives -- Fiction 3. Great Britain
-- History -- Victoria, 1837-1901 4. Murder -- Great
Britain -- History -- 19th century
ISBN 1250024870; 9781250024879
                    LC 2013010535

This book by Judith Flanders is an "exploration of murder in the nineteenth century, [which] examines some of the
most gripping cases that captivated the Victorians and gave
rise to the first detective fiction. Flanders retells the gruesome stories of many different types of murder, both famous
and obscure. Through these stories of murder—from the
brutal to the pathetic—Flanders builds a rich and multi-fac-
eted portrait of Victorian society." (Publisher's note)

Graeber, Charles
  The **good** nurse; America's most prolific serial
killer, the hospitals that allowed him to thrive, and
the detectives who brought him to justice. Charles
Graeber. 1st ed. Twelve 2013 320 p. (hardcover)
$26.99   **364.152**
   1. Serial killers 2. Nurses -- United States -- Biography
3. Serial murderers -- United States -- Biography
ISBN 0446505293; 9780446505291
                    LC 2012041982

This book, by Charles Graeber, profiles the serial murderer and registered nurse "Charlie Cullen. . . . Implicated in
the deaths of as many as 300 patients, he was also perhaps
the most prolific serial killer in American history. . . . Graeber's portrait of Cullen depicts a surprisingly intelligent and
complicated young man whose promising career was overwhelmed by his compulsion to kill, and whose shy demeanor
masked a twisted interior life hidden even to his family and
friends." (Publisher's note)

Includes bibliographical references

Guinn, Jeff
  ★ **Manson**; the life and times of Charles Man-
son. Jeff Guinn. Simon & Schuster 2013 512 p.
$27.50   **364.152**
   1. Criminals -- United States -- Biography 2. Murderers
-- United States -- Biography
ISBN 1451645163; 9781451645163
                    LC 2012050176

This book by Jeff Guinn "reexamines the life of Charles
Manson, interviewing Manson's sister and cousin, who
have not previously spoken out, and gleaning new information from childhood friends, cellmates, and Manson Family
members. Guinn argues that while Manson spouted incoher-

ent race-war rhetoric, the killings were in fact related to his failed ambitions to be a rock star." (Library Journal)

Includes bibliographical references and index

Hakkakiyan, Ru'ya

Assassins of the Turquoise Palace. Grove Press 2011 322p   **364.152**

1. Assassination 2. Trials (Homicide) 3. Political crimes and offenses 4. Iran -- Politics and government

ISBN 0-8021-1911-5; 978-0-8021-1911-7

A "look at the September 17, 1992, terror killing of four Kurdish exiles who were holding a meeting in a small restaurant in Berlin. This crime resulted in a massive German investigation and an equally massive four-year trial that ended with guilty verdicts for the accused and, more importantly, a condemnation of Iran's leaders as the instigators of the murder plot." (Publishers Weekly)

Includes bibliographical references

Hempel, Sandra

The **inheritor's** powder; a tale of arsenic, murder, and the new forensic science. by Sandra Hempel. W W Norton & Co Inc 2013 288 p. (hardcover) $25.95   **364.152**

1. Arsenic 2. Forensic sciences 3. Poisons and poisoning 4. Forensic toxicology 5. Murder -- Great Britain -- History -- 19th century 6. Poisoning -- Great Britain -- History -- 19th century 7. Toxicology -- Great Britain -- History -- 19th century 8. Arsenic -- Toxicology -- Great Britain -- History -- 19th century

ISBN 0393239713; 9780393239713

LC 2013024989

Author Sandra Hempel presents a "look at how the science of poison detection developed. Hempel focuses on a different dilemma for the Victorian medical profession: how to successfully determine when poison is the cause of death. In 1833 the strange death of farmer George Bodle and the investigation of his family members, with whom he lived, frames the history of scientists' struggles to develop foolproof tests for the presence, in the victims' digestive tracts, of arsenic." (Publishers Weekly)

"An unexpected verdict and its aftermath make this a satisfying murder mystery in the grand tradition." Kirkus

Includes bibliographical references and index

Junger, Sebastian

A **death** in Belmont. Norton 2006 266p il $23.95   **364.152**

1. Homicide 2. Homemakers 3. Murderers 4. Murder victims 5. Maintenance workers

ISBN 0-393-05980-4

In 1963, a murder took place in Belmont, Massachusetts, that resembled those committed by the Boston Strangler. A black man, Roy Smith, who had worked in Bessie Goldberg's house that day, was convicted of the crime. "On the day of the murder, Albert DeSalvo—the man who would eventually confess . . . to the Strangler's crimes—was also in Belmont, working as a carpenter at the Jungers' home. . . . Sebastian Junger [here] chronicles three lives that collide." Publisher's note

"In [Albert] DeSalvo's dark world, Junger's clear, beautifully reasonable writing is the literary equivalent of night-vision goggles." Time

Includes bibliographical references

Kirn, Walter

Blood will out; the true story of a murder, a mystery, and a masquerade. Walter Kirn. First edition Liveright Publishing Corporation 2014 272 p. (hardcover) $25.95   **364.152**

1. Murderers -- United States -- Case studies 2. Impostors and imposture -- United States -- Case studies

ISBN 0871404516; 9780871404510

LC 2013046327

This book, by Walter Kirn, is the true story of Clark Rockefeller, an "eccentric son of privilege who ultimately would be unmasked as a brazen serial impostor, child kidnapper, and brutal murderer. . . . As Kirn uncovers the truth about his friend, a psychopath masquerading as a gentleman, he also confronts hard truths about himself. Why, as a writer of fiction, was he susceptible to the deception of a sinister fantasist whose crimes, Kirn learns, were based on books and movies?" (Publisher's note)

"Kirn's reflecting, musing, and personal dealings add a killer punch to this true-crime memoir." Booklist

Kolker, Robert

Lost Girls; An Unsolved American Mystery. by Robert Kolker. HarperCollins 2013 xiv, 399 p.p (hardcover) $25.99   **364.152**

1. Crime 2. Prostitution 3. Young women -- New York (State) -- Long Island 4. Prostitution -- New York (State) -- Long Island 5. Serial murders -- New York (State) -- Long Island 6. Computer crimes -- New York (State) -- Long Island

ISBN 006218363X; 9780062183637

LC 2013021815

This book from Robert Kolker looks at the murder of five prostitutes in Oak Beach, Long Island. He "probes the 21st-century innovations that facilitated these crimes, which launched a media blitz." A major focus of the book is the author's attention to "the girls' back stories and to the efforts of their families and friends to bring the killer to justice." (Kirkus Reviews)

Kraybill, Donald B.

Amish grace; how forgiveness transcended tragedy. [by] Donald B. Kraybill, Steven M. Nolt, [and] David L. Weaver-Zercher. Jossey-Bass 2007 237p $24.95   **364.152**

1. Amish 2. Forgiveness 3. Amish -- Doctrines 4. West Nickel Mines Amish School (Pa.) 5. Amish School Shooting, Nickel Mines, Pa., 2006 6. Forgiveness -- Religious aspects -- Christianity

ISBN 978-0-7879-9761-8; 0-7879-9761-7

This book explains "Amish reaction to the horrific Nickel Mines shootings. . . . This anguished and devastating account of a national tragedy and a hopeful, life-affirming lesson in how to live is itself a marvel of grace." Booklist

Includes bibliographical references

Larson, Erik

Thunderstruck. Crown Publishers 2006 463p il map $25.95   **364.152**

1. Radio 2. Homicide 3. Inventors 4. Murderers 5. Electrical engineers 6. Homeopathic physicians 7. Nobel laureates for physics

ISBN 1-4000-8066-5; 978-1-4000-8066-3

LC 2006-11908

This book "alternates the story of Marconi's quest for the first wireless transatlantic communication amid scientific jealousies and controversies with the tale of [Dr. Hawley Harvey Crippen,] a mild-mannered murderer caught as a result of the invention. . . . A thrilling read." SLJ

Includes bibliographical references

Leake, John

Entering Hades; the double life of a serial killer. Farrar, Straus & Giroux 2007 350p il $25 **364.152**

1. Authors 2. Homicide 3. Criminals 4. Novelists 5. Dramatists 6. Journalists 7. Murderers

ISBN 978-0-374-14845-4; 0-374-14845-7

LC 2007-08644

This is a "study of traveling playwright, poet, and prostitute killer Jack Unterweger. . . . Unterweger started his dual career as criminal and crime reporter in his native Austria, where he was convicted at 18 for murdering a prostitute. While in prison he became something of a cause célèbre for European literati and their associates because of his writings, including a revealing autobiography. Eventually, pronounced rehabilitated, he was released. He decamped for the bloody big time in L.A. when an Austrian magazine engaged him to write about . . . crime. He resumed his other trade in the U.S., using the same method he had used from his first known killing: he strangled his victims with articles of their clothing." Booklist

The author "has written the definitive book—dispassionate, superbly detailed—on Jack Unterweger." N Y Times Book Rev

Includes bibliographical references

Liebman, James S.

The wrong Carlos; anatomy of a wrongful execution. James S. Liebman, Shawn Crowley, Andrew Markquart, Lauren Rosenberg, Lauren Gallo White, and Daniel Zharkovsky. Columbia University Press 2014 464 p. illustrations (pbk. : alk. paper) $27.95   **364.152**

1. Judicial error 2. Trials (Homicide) 3. Capital punishment -- United States 4. Judicial error -- Texas 5. Trials (Murder) -- Texas 6. Capital punishment -- Texas

ISBN 0231167237; 9780231167222; 9780231167239; 9780231536684

LC 2013044147

This book focuses on the history of a wrongful execution. "In 1989, Texas executed Carlos DeLuna, a poor Hispanic man with childlike intelligence, for the murder of Wanda Lopez, a convenience store clerk. His execution passed unnoticed for years until a team of Columbia Law School faculty and students almost accidentally chose to investigate his case and found that DeLuna almost certainly was innocent." (Publisher's note)

"A masterpiece of its type and a disturbing true crime account." LJ

Includes bibliographical references and index

Morris, Errol, 1948-

A wilderness of error; the trials of Jeffrey MacDonald. Errol Morris ; illustrations by Niko Skourti. Penguin Press 2012 xviii, 524 p.p ill. $29.95 **364.152**

1. Administration of criminal justice 2. Murder -- North Carolina -- Case studies 3. Murderers -- United States -- Case studies

ISBN 1594203431; 9781594203435

LC 2012017906

This book by Errol Morris is about the murder trials of Jeffrey MacDonald "that led to the conviction and imprisonment for life of this man for butchering his wife and two young daughters. . . . It shows us that almost everything we have been told about the case is deeply unreliable, and crucial elements of the case against MacDonald simply are not true. . . . Along the way Morris poses bracing questions about the nature of proof, criminal justice, and the media." (Publisher's note)

Includes bibliographical references and index

Parry, Richard Lloyd

People who eat darkness; the true story of a young woman who vanished from the streets of Tokyo and the evil that swallowed her up. Richard Lloyd Parry. Farrar, Straus and Giroux 2012 454 p.   **364.152**

1. Homicide 2. Trials (Homicide) 3. Victims of crimes 4. Murder -- Investigation -- Japan -- Tokyo 5. Young women -- Crimes against -- Japan -- Tokyo

ISBN 9780224079174 Jonathan Cape; 0224079174 Jonathan Cape; 0374230595 Farrar, Straus and Giroux; 9780374230593 Farrar, Straus and Giroux

LC 2011047019

This true crime book by Richard Lloyd Parry tells the story of how "Lucie Blackman--tall, blond, twenty-one years old--stepped out into the vastness of Tokyo in the summer of 2000, and disappeared forever. The following winter, her dismembered remains were found buried in a seaside cave. . . . [The author], an award-winning foreign correspondent, covered Lucie's disappearance and followed the massive search for her, the long investigation, and the even longer trial." (Publisher's note)

Includes bibliographical references.

Rule, Ann

Too late to say goodbye; a true story of murder and betrayal. Free Press 2007 456p il $26 **364.152**

1. Homicide 2. Homemakers 3. Murder victims

ISBN 978-0-7432-3852-6; 0-7432-3852-4

LC 2007-9168

"Rule's meticulous 2½ years of research provides a cinematically satisfying look into how police in two jurisdictions worked together to prove Corbin was a serial murderer of women who tried to leave him." USA Today

Schechter, Harold

Psycho USA; famous american killers you never heard of. Harold Schechter. Ballantine Books 2012 xiii, 396 p.p   **364.152**

1. Homicide 2. Serial Killers -- History 3. Murder -- United States -- Case studies 4. Murderers -- United States -- Biography

ISBN 0345524470; 9780345524478; 9780345524485

LC 2012004990

This book by Harold Schechter focuses on "a bevy of all-but-forgotten homicidal fiends studding the bloody margins of U.S. history. . . . Spurred by profit, passion, paranoia, or perverse pleasure, these killers -- the Witch of Staten Island, the Smutty Nose Butcher, the Bluebeard of Quiet Dell, and many others -- span three centuries and a host of harrowing murder methods." (Publisher's note)

Includes bibliographical references and index

Sides, Hampton

★ Hellhound on his trail; the stalking of Martin Luther King, Jr., and the international hunt for his assassin. Doubleday 2010 459p il $28.95   **364.152**

1. Clergy 2. Murderers 3. Nonfiction writers 4. Civil rights activists 5. Nobel laureates for peace

ISBN 978-0-385-52392-9; 0-385-52392-0

LC 2009-43659

"Sides begins with Ray's escape from a maximum security prison in Missouri the prior April. In short, crisp chapters, Sides then cuts back and forth between Ray's movements during the ensuing year and King's increasing challenges during the same period, as a fraying civil rights movement struggled to transform hard-won legal equality into economic justice. Along the way, we're treated to vignettes featuring J. Edgar Hoover's vicious antiKing smear tactics; George Wallace's race-driven politics of hate during the 1968 presidential campaign; and an embittered Lyndon Johnson's estrangement from King over the ongoing war in Vietnam. None of this is new, but Sides ensures that it's still compulsively readable." Milwaukee Journal Sentinel

Includes bibliographical references

Siegel, Barry

Manifest injustice; the true story of a convicted murderer and the lawyers who want him freed. by Barry Siegel. 1st ed. Henry Holt and Co. 2012 xiv, 384 p.p (hardcover) $28   **364.152**

1. Miscarriage of justice 2. Macumber, William, 1935- -- Trials, litigation, etc. 3. Judicial error 4. Arizona Justice Project 5. Trials (Murder) -- Arizona -- Maricopa County

ISBN 0805094156; 9780805094152

LC 2012028986

In this book, Pulitzer Prize-winning journalist Barry Siegel "describes the efforts of the Arizona Justice Project to free Bill Macumber, who has spent 38 years in prison for a double murder he denies committing. In 1962, a young couple was shot on a lovers lane in Maricopa County, AZ. There were no credible leads at the time, but a decade later Carol Macumber, a clerk in the sherriff's office, claimed that her ex-husband [Bill] was the murderer." (Library Journal)

Includes bibliographical references (p. [365]-371) and index.

Starr, Douglas

The killer of little shepherds; a true crime story and the birth of forensic science. A.A. Knopf 2010 300p il $26.95   **364.152**

1. Homicide 2. Physicians 3. Forensic sciences 4. Trials (Homicide) 5. Murderers 6. Criminologists 7. Law enforcement officials

ISBN 978-0-307-26619-4; 0-307-26619-2

LC 2010-14930

This book is "like an episode of CSI: 19th-Century France. As he prowled the countryside, Joseph Vacher preyed on young shepherds, ultimately slaughtering four times as many people as Jack the Ripper. How the bumbling French authorities finally pieced together the evidence — while learning to study bodies and crime scenes for clues and to compare details about the killings — represents, Starr says, nothing less than the birth of forensic science. In gripping, almost novelistic chapters, he alternates between Vacher and Alexandre Lacassagne, the criminologist who helped crack the case." Entertainment Wkly

Includes bibliographical references

Stashower, Daniel

The beautiful cigar girl; Mary Rogers, Edgar Allan Poe, and the invention of murder. Dutton 2006 326p il $25.95   **364.152**

1. Poets 2. Authors 3. Homicide 4. Essayists 5. Murder victims 6. Short story writers

ISBN 0-525-94981-X; 978-0-525-94981-7

LC 2006-19335

The author "tells the story of New York City cigar store clerk Mary Rogers, whose violent death in 1841 brought on a frenzy of sensational newspaper stories and prompted the interest of Edgar Allan Poe. . . . [He] details how the mystery surrounding Rogers's murder became the inspiration for Poe's story 'The Mystery of Marie Rogêt.' . . . Well researched and accessible, here is a gripping story that is hard to put down." Libr J

Includes bibliographical references

Summerscale, Kate

The suspicions of Mr. Whicher; a shocking murder and the undoing of a great Victorian detective. Walker & Company 2008 360p il map $24.95   **364.152**

1. Homicide 2. Detectives 3. London (England)

ISBN 978-0-8027-1535-7; 0-8027-1535-4

LC 2008-00247

This is the story of Inspector Jonathan Whicher of Scotland Yard, who investigated the 1860 murder of three-year-old Francis Saville Kent in the village of Road, Wiltshire.

The author's "clean writing makes . . . [this book] so dynamic that she can't be accused of 'freezing' the past—instead, she has done a masterly job of reviving it, with all its curiosities and contradictions. But, most strikingly, she has created an enthralling mystery by overlaying the fictional tools of misdirection and suspense onto a nonfiction narrative." Am Scholar

Includes bibliographical references

Swanson, James L.

Manhunt; the 12-day chase for Lincoln's killer. William Morrow 2006 448p il $26.95　**364.152**

1. Actors 2. Lawyers 3. Presidents 4. Murderers 5. State legislators 6. Members of Congress

ISBN 0-06-051849-9

LC 2005-44911

This is an "account of the 12 days following Lincoln's assassination at Ford's Theatre on April 14, 1865." Libr J

While this book "belongs in the history section . . . it's as gripping a page-turner as anything you'll find on the mystery shelf." Entertainment Weekly

Includes bibliographical references

Zacharias, Karen Spears

A **silence** of mockingbirds; the memoir of a murder. by Karen Spears Zacharias. MacAdam/Cage Pub. 2012 322 p. (hardcover) $25.00　**364.152**

1. Homicide 2. Child abuse 3. Autobiographies 4. Murder -- Oregon -- Case studies

ISBN 159692375X; 9781596923751

LC 2012000748

This book is a true crime story by Karen Spears Zacharias. Zacharias "never anticipated that she would become . . . involved in a high-profile murder. But when she reconnects with . . . Sarah, . . . Karen discovers that something unspeakable has happened to Sarah's daughter, Karly. . . . Karen pieces together what happened to Karly through court documents, investigators' interviews, and interviews with friends, family, law enforcement officials, and key witnesses." (Publisher's note)

"Journalist Zacharias presents a searing account of child abuse and murder, bringing to life a tragedy with which she is intimately familiar...A harrowing cautionary tale that will touch fans of Ann Rule's chilling works." LJ

364.16　Offenses against property

Crosby, Molly Caldwell

The **great** pearl heist; London's greatest jewel thief and Scotland Yard's hunt for the world's most valuable necklace. by Molly Caldwell Crosby. Berkely Books 2012 304 p. (alk. paper) $25.95　**364.16**

1. Jewelry theft -- History 2. Great Britain -- History -- 20th century 3. Criminal investigation -- Great Britain -- History 4. Jewelry theft -- England -- London -- Case studies 5. Robbery investigation -- England -- London -- Case studies 6. Burglary investigation -- England -- London -- Case studies 7. Receiving stolen goods -- England -- London -- Case studies

ISBN 0425252809; 9780425252802

LC 2012008261

This book by Molly Caldwell Crosby presents "a World War I-era true-crime tale about the theft of the world's most valuable necklace. . . . The setting is the underworld of London's Hatton Garden jewelry district in the days before the war, and the object of desire is a pink pearl necklace. . . . Criminal mastermind Joseph Grizzard . . . had his eye on the necklace, and he concocted a plan to intercept it as it traveled by mail between two dealers." (Kirkus Reviews)

Includes bibliographical references and index.

Mitnick, Kevin D. (Kevin David), 1963-

Ghost in the wires; my adventures as the world's most wanted hacker. by Kevin Mitnick, with William L. Simon. Little, Brown and Company 2011 xiv, 413 p.p ill. $25.99　**364.16**

1. Thieves 2. Computer hackers 3. Computer crimes -- United States 4. Computer security -- United States 5. Computer hackers -- United States -- Biography 6. Information superhighway -- Security measures -- United States

ISBN 0316037702; 9780316037709

LC 2010043461

In this book, computer hacker Kevin Mitnick "recounts his epic illegal computer hacks of Sun Microsystems, Digital Equipment Corporation, and any number of cellphone makers; his exploits triggered a manhunt that made headlines. He insists he did it not for money but for the transgressive thrill of looking at big, secret computer programs." (Publishers Weekly)

Wambaugh, Joseph

Fire lover; a true story. Morrow 2002 338p $25.95; pa $7.99　**364.16**

1. Arson 2. Arsonists 3. Firefighters

ISBN 0-06-009527-X; 0-06-009528-8 pa

LC 2002-20139

"John Orr was a Glendale, Calif., fire investigator who specialized in arson in more ways than one. . . . Mr. Orr has been linked to four deaths and millions of dollars of property damage. . . . Mr. Wambaugh begins by describing the most lethal fire." N Y Times (Late N Y Ed)

"Wambaugh's painstaking research which included interviews with law-enforcement officers, survivors, and victims' families, is astonishing." Booklist

364.3　Offenders

Paradis, Cheryl

The **measure** of madness; inside the disturbed and disturbing criminal mind. Citadel Press 2010 272p pa $16.95　**364.3**

1. Forensic sciences 2. Criminal psychology

ISBN 978-0-8065-3105-2

LC 2010-924994

The author "has spent more than two decades evaluating mentally ill and violent individuals and giving expert testimony in court. Here she details criminal cases in which the prosecution or defense asked her to establish whether defendants were competent to stand trial, or to vet such psychiatric defenses as insanity and extreme emotional disturbance. The cases, all tried in New York City, are fascinating, unsettling and often horrifying. . . . The author also discusses the psycho-legal issues of cases involving juveniles and abused wives. . . . A welcome inside account." Kirkus

Includes bibliographical references

Rhodes, Richard

Why they kill; the discoveries of a maverick criminologist. Knopf 1999 371p $26.95; pa $14 **364.3**

1. Violence 2. Criminals 3. Criminal psychology 4. College teachers

ISBN 0-375-40249-7; 0-375-70248-2 pa

LC 99-18920

The author discusses the history of violence and the work of social scientist Lonnie H. Athens. "Athens interviewed prisoners in maximum security prisons in Iowa, California and elsewhere, predominantly men. . . . His hope was to bypass inmates' typical narratives and get to what they actually thought and felt when they assaulted or raped or killed." N Y Times Book Rev

Includes bibliographical references and index

364.4   Prevention of crime and delinquency

Stuntz, William J.

The collapse of American criminal justice. Belknap Press of Harvard University Press 2011 413p il $35 **364.4**

1. Crime prevention 2. Administration of criminal justice 3. United States -- Race relations 4. African Americans -- Civil rights

ISBN 978-0-674-05175-1; 0-674-05175-0

LC 2011006905

The author argues that the "rule of law has vanished in America's criminal justice system. Prosecutors decide whom to punish; most accused never face a jury; policing is inconsistent; plea bargaining is rampant; and draconian sentencing fills prisons with mostly minority defendants. . . . [Stuntz] looks to history for the roots of these problems—and solutions." Publisher's note

This is "a fascinating, passionate, compassionate, often brilliant book. Flawless? No. But it's a work that deserves to have a significant influence on American criminal-justice thinkers from across the political spectrum." Natl Rev

Includes bibliographical references

364.66   Capital punishment

Echols, Damien

★ Life after death; Damien Echols. Blue Rider Press 2012 399 p. **364.66**

1. Prisons 2. False imprisonment -- United States 3. Prisoners -- United States -- Biography 4. Death row inmates -- United States -- Biography

ISBN 0399160205; 9780399160202

LC 2012026115

Author Damien Echols, "sentenced to death . . . for the murders of three eight-year-old boys in Arkansas, [and] known worldwide as a symbol of wrongful conviction and imprisonment, . . . shares his story in full -- from abuse by prison guards and wardens, to portraits of fellow inmates and deplorable living conditions, to the incredible reserves of patience, spirituality, and perseverance that kept him alive and sane while incarcerated for nearly two decades." (Publisher's note)

Harrington, Joel F.

The faithful executioner; life and death, honor and shame in the turbulent sixteenth century. Joel F. Harrington. Farrar Straus & Giroux 2013 320 p. (hardcover) $28 **364.66**

1. Executions and executioners 2. Crime -- Germany -- Nuremberg -- History 3. Criminal procedure -- Germany -- Nuremberg -- History 4. Executions and executioners -- Germany -- Nuremberg -- Biography

ISBN 0809049929; 9780809049929

LC 2012029017

This book, by Joel F. Harrington, "takes us deep inside the alien world and thinking of Meister Frantz Schmidt of Nuremberg, who, during forty-five years as a professional executioner, personally put to death 394 individuals and tortured, flogged, or disfigured many hundreds more. But the picture that emerges of Schmidt from his personal papers is not that of a monster. Could a man who routinely practiced such cruelty also be insightful, compassionate--even progressive?" (Publisher's note)

Heard, Alex

The eyes of Willie McGee; a tragedy of race, sex, and secrets in the Jim Crow South. Harper 2010 404p il $26.99 **364.66**

1. Trials 2. Veterans 3. Capital punishment 4. Alleged criminals 5. Mississippi -- Race relations

ISBN 978-0-06-128415-1; 0-06-128415-7

LC 2009-51769

"McGee was mourned in poems, novels and memoirs. But while he clearly did not get a fair trial, was he innocent? Was Willette Hawkins really the guilty party? 'The Eyes of Willie McGee' leaves us wondering, and wondering how many other ghosts remain in Jim Crow's closet." Los Angeles Times

Prejean, Helen

★ The death of innocents; an eyewitness account of wrongful executions. Random House 2005 310p $25.95 **364.66**

1. Capital punishment

ISBN 0-679-44056-9

LC 2004-54154

The author "reexamines the cases of two men she fervently believes were executed for crimes they did not commit. . . . In addition to providing a searing indictment of capital punishment, Prejean also exposes the fundamental inadequacies of the American court system. Expect demand for this extremely thought-provoking book." Booklist

Includes bibliographical references

364.67   Corporal punishment

Spierenburg, Pieter

Violence and punishment; civilizing the body through time. Pieter Spierenburg. Polity 2013 vi, 223 p.p (hbk.) $69.95 **364.67**

1. Human body 2. Punishment 3. Violence -- History 4. Punishment -- History

ISBN 0745653480; 0745653499; 9780745653488;

9780745653495

LC 2012277159

This book is a "study of historical violence, social control, honor codes, and the transformation of punishment. It . . . ranges from homicide trends in Amsterdam to modern notions of the human body, punishment, and even the formation of religions in prehistoric societies. . . . Readers learn that punishments became infused with religious and political ritual in the early modern period as part of the civilizing process. This, in turn, reflected aristocratic notions of the body." (Choice)

Includes bibliographical references (p. [201]-220) and index

365   Penal and related institutions

Abbott, Jack Henry, 1944-2002

In the belly of the beast; letters from prison. with an introduction by Norman Mailer. Random House 1981 166p hardcover o.p. pa $12   365
1. Prisoners 2. Prisons -- United States
ISBN 0-679-73237-3 pa

LC 80-6038

The writer of these letters began them while "chained to the crossbar of his bed in the Butner, North Carolina Federal Correctional Institution. He addressed his letter to Norman Mailer. . . . {In these letters he} wished to convey something about the effect of {prison life on the individual}." Nation

Abbott's "letters belong with the best prison literature, not because of their accounts of atrocity, but for their disturbing picture of daily life behind bars." Time

Applebaum, Anne

★ Gulag; a history. Doubleday 2003 677p il maps $35   365
1. Convict labor 2. Concentration camps 3. Soviet Union -- Politics and government
ISBN 0-7679-0056-1

LC 2002-41344

This "describes how, largely under Stalin's watch, a regulated, centralized system of prison labor—unprecedented in scope—gradually arose out of the chaos of the Russian Revolution. . . . Applebaum details camp life, including strategies for survival; the experiences of women and children in the camps; sexual relationships and marriages between prisoners; and rebellions, strikes and escapes. . . . Applebaum's lucid prose and painstaking consideration of the competing theories about aspects of camp life and policy are always compelling." Publ Wkly

Includes bibliographical references

Bernstein, Nell

Burning down the house; the end of juvenile prison. Nell Bernstein. New Press, The 2014 384 p. (hardback) $26.95   365
1. Juvenile courts 2. Juvenile delinquency 3. Administration of justice -- United States 4. Juvenile justice, Administration of -- United States
ISBN 1595589562; 9781595589569

LC 2013043709

In this book journalist Nell Bernstein "turns her attention to the U.S. juvenile justice system in which more than 66,000 youths are confined. . . . Bernstein introduces adolescents in and out of detention centers, capturing their struggles to overcome traumatic histories. . . . Visiting 'therapeutic' prisons in Minnesota, California, and New York, she concludes that . . . these institutions remain embedded in a larger culture that seems impervious to reform." (Publishers Weekly)

"The combination of muckraking research and absolutism make the book passionate and convincing as advocacy." Kirkus

Includes bibliographical references

Encyclopedia of prisons & correctional facilities; Mary Bosworth, editor. Sage Publications 2005 2v il set $310   365
1. Reference books 2. Prisons -- United States -- Encyclopedias
ISBN 0-7619-2731-X

LC 2004-21802

The entries in this encyclopedia "revolve around 12 themes, among them theories of punishment, prison architecture, prison populations, juvenile justice, prison reform, treatment programs, and race, gender, and class. . . . Those interested in understanding the US's complex system of incarceration will find this encyclopedia a vital reference tool." Choice

Includes bibliographical references

Ferro, Jeffrey

Prisons; Rev. ed; Facts On File, Inc. 2011 312p (Library in a book) $45   365
1. Prisons -- United States
ISBN 978-0-8160-8236-0; 978-1-4381-3398-0 ebook

LC 2010-49855

First published 2006

This book "examines the state of U.S. prisons and related issues. It focuses on the development of prisons in the United States and how the competing goals of punishment and rehabilitation have shaped the evolution of criminal correction. An overview presents statistics on U.S. prisons and explores the issues behind those statistics, including racial disparity among prisoners and the causes of recidivism. The financial costs of running prisons and the mixed record of private prisons are examined, and laws and legislation relating to issues of incarceration are reviewed." Publisher's note

Includes bibliographical references

Figes, Orlando, 1959-

Just send me word; a true story of love and survival in the Gulag. Orlando Figes. Metropolitan Books/Henry Holt and Company 2012 333 p.   365
1. Love stories 2. Political prisoners -- Russia 3. Russia -- History -- 1917-1991, Soviet Union 4. Imprisonment -- Soviet Union 5. Fiancées -- Soviet Union 6. Fiancées -- Soviet Union -- Correspondence 7. Labor camps -- Russia (Federation) -- Pechora (Komi) 8. Political prisoners -- Russia (Federation) -- Pechora (Komi) 9. Political prisoners -- Russia (Federation) -- Pechora (Komi) -- Correspondence
ISBN 0805095225; 9780805095227

LC 2011048355

In this book, "[d]rawing on more than 1,200 letters between Lev and Svetlana 'Sveta' Mishchenko, and interviews with the couple, veteran historian Figes . . . tells their remarkable tale of love and devotion during the worst years of the USSR. Having fallen in love as physics students at Moscow University, they were separated for 13 years: first while Lev seized in WWII, and then after he was sentenced to a Siberian labor camp for the 'crime' of serving as a translator for a German officer while a POW. Lev's letters illustrate the extreme hardships of .the Stalinist camps. . . . Her letters express her extraordinary devotion and determination to visit Lev, which she managed to do four times, despite the long trek, subterfuges, necessary bribes, and dangers involved in the illegal journeys." (Publishers Weekly)

Includes bibliographical references and index

Kizny, Tomasz

Gulag; life and death inside the Soviet concentration camps. Firefly Books 2004 495p il maps $69.95 **365**
1. Convict labor 2. Concentration camps 3. Soviet Union -- Politics and government
ISBN 1-55297-964-4
LC 2005-357207

This book "contains 550 black-and-white photographs of life in the Soviet Gulag. . . . The photos gathered here range from official archival snapshots, showing both inmates and their captors, to scenes of enormous construction projects and snowbound ruins. Kizny has added his own photographs of the abandoned camps or work projects and included a brief history of the camps and personal accounts of survivors. These rare and historically significant photographs can only hint at the appalling horrors committed within the camps, and the importance of the book cannot be overstated." Booklist

Liao Yiwu

For a song and one hundred songs; a poet's journey through a Chinese prison. Liao Yiwu ; translated from the Chinese by Wen Huang. Houghton Mifflin Harcourt 2013 432 p. (hardcover) $26 **365**
1. Political prisoners -- China 2. Tiananmen Square Incident, Beijing (China), 1989 -- Poetry 3. Prisoners -- China -- Biography
ISBN 0547892632; 9780547892634
LC 2012019558

In this book, "exiled Chinese poet Liao [Yiwu] . . . recounts . . . his politicization and imprisonment in the wake of the 1989 government crackdown on the democracy movement centered in Beijing's Tiananmen Square." His poem, "Massacre," about the protest and a subsequent film project resulted in his 1990 arrest. The "bulk of the memoir concerns Liao's four-year imprisonment at a series of facilities in the harrowing Chongqing prison system." (Publishers Weekly)

Oshinsky, David M.

Worse than slavery; Parchman Farm and the ordeal of Jim Crow justice. Free Press 1996 306p il hardcover o.p. pa $14 **365**
1. Prisons -- United States 2. Mississippi State Penitentiary 3. United States -- Race relations
ISBN 0-684-83095-7 pa
LC 95-52880

This book examines Mississippi's "Parchman prison farm in the context of sharecropping, convict leasing, lynching and the legalized segregation that replaced slavery." N Y Times Book Rev

"Oshinsky's beautifully constructed narrative brings to vivid life one of the most shameful chapters in American history." New Yorker

Includes bibliographical references

Solzhenitsyn, Aleksandr, 1918-2008

★ The **Gulag** Archipelago, 1918-1956 v1; an experiment in literary investigation. [by] Aleksandr I. Solzhenitsyn; translated from the Russian by Thomas P. Whitney; foreword by Anne Applebaum. Harper Perennial Modern Classics 2007 xx, 660p pa $21.95 **365**
1. Political prisoners 2. Soviet Union -- Politics and government
ISBN 978-0-06-125371-3; 0-06-125371-5
First published 1974

The first volume of the author's three-volume "'literary investigation' of the network of Soviet prison camps as they existed between 1918 and 1956. . . . A mixture of autobiography, history, and analysis, the relentlessly grim picture of life inside the camps forms the basis for an attack not only on Stalinism and Leninism but also on the whole process of substituting Western rational and secular ideas for Russia's traditional mysticism." Benét's Reader's Ency. 4th edition

★ The **Gulag** Archipelago, 1918-1956 v2; an experiment in literary investigation. [by] Aleksandr I. Solzhenitsyn; translated from the Russian by Thomas P. Whitney; foreword by Anne Applebaum. Harper Perennial Modern Classics 2007 712p il map pa $21.95 **365**
1. Political prisoners 2. Soviet Union -- Politics and government
ISBN 978-0-06-125372-0; 0-06-125372-3
First published 1975

This second volume of a two-volume series describes "the story of Solzhenitsyn's entrance into the Soviet prison camps, where he would remain for nearly a decade." Publisher's note

★ The **Gulag** Archipelago, 1918-1956 v3; an experiment in literary investigation. [by] Aleksandr I. Solzhenitsyn; translated from the Russian by Harry Willetts; foreword by Anne Applebaum. Harper Perennial Modern Classics 2007 558p il map pa $21.95 **365**
1. Political prisoners 2. Soviet Union -- Politics and government
ISBN 978-0-06-125373-7; 0-06-125373-1
First published 1978

The final volume of a three-volume series, this book contains the author's "account of resistance within the Soviet labor camps and his own release after eight years." Publisher's note

366   Secret associations and societies

Ridley, Jasper Godwin

The **Freemasons**; a history of the world's most powerful secret society. [by] Jasper Ridley. Arcade Pub. 2001 357p $25.95; pa $14.95   **366**

1. Freemasons

ISBN 1-55970-601-5; 1-55970-654-6 pa

LC 2001-45745

The author "traces the origins of freemasonry back to the craft guilds in medieval Europe, and then he chronicles their growth and evolution through the modern era. . . . This work of popular history sheds light on a frequently obscure subject." Booklist

Includes bibliographical references

368   Insurance

Boyd, Roddy

Fatal risk; a cautionary tale of AIG's corporate suicide. Wiley 2011 349p   **368**

1. Insurance 2. Financial crises 3. Insurance executives 4. American International Group, Inc.

ISBN 978-0-470-88980-0

LC 2011-01512

An "inside account of how Maurice 'Hank' Greenberg, the storied combat veteran and driven entrepreneur, took a motley collection of insurance companies and built them into the world's most innovative and daring financial conglomerate—only to see it all crash and burn. Made rich and powerful through Greenberg's iron will and vision, AIG was unprepared for his dramatic ouster in 2005. As the company recovered from a bruising regulatory battle, its management did not understand what risks were being taken onto its once mighty balance sheet in the name of a quick buck. . . . Boyd argues that, contrary to conventional wisdom, Goldman Sachs, and the billions in collateral calls it made on AIG's Financial Products unit, was not the sole cause of the company's downfall. Drawing upon a host of sources—from Hank Greenberg to senior Goldman executives; current and former AIG leaders and board members; to legendary short-seller Jim Chanos and Federal Reserve officials—Boyd makes a . . . case that AIG's collapse was an inside job." Publisher's note

"A vivid portrait of the giant insurer at the center of the 2008 financial crisis." Wall Street J

368.4   Government-sponsored insurance

Altman, Nancy J.

The **battle** for Social Security; from FDR's vision to Bush's gamble. Wiley 2005 362p $24.95   **368.4**

1. Social security

ISBN 978-0-471-77172-2; 0-471-77172-4

LC 2005-20700

The author "traces the history of Social Security from its introduction in 1935, and provides a thoughtful, well-researched case against the . . . [Bush] administration's efforts to reduce Social Security protection." Booklist

Includes bibliographical references

Frank, Joshua

The **people's** pension; the struggle to defend social security since Reagan. Eric Laursen, Joshua Frank ; [edited by] 674-A 23rd Street. AK Press 2012 818 p. ill. (alk. paper) $13.99   **368.4**

1. Privitization 2. Social security 3. United States -- Politics and government -- 2001-

ISBN 9781849351010

LC 2012933068

This book looks at the issue of Social Security in terms of the U.S. 2012 presidential election. In "the aftermath of the debt reduction deal between Barack Obama and congressional Republicans, the 2012 election promises to be a kind of referendum on the size and role of government—including economic support programs like Social Security. . . . Eric Laursen suggests that the only solution for Social Security is taking it out of the government's hands altogether." (Barnes and Noble)

Includes bibliographical references (p. [727]-783) and index.

370   Education

Uncle Tom or new Negro; African Americans reflect on Booker T. Washington and Up from slavery one hundred years later. edited by Rebecca Carroll. Broadway Books/Harlem Moon 2006 320p pa $15.95   **370**

1. Slaves 2. Authors 3. Educators 4. African American educators 5. Memoirists 6. Nonfiction writers 7. Tuskegee Institute 8. Civil rights activists 9. African Americans -- Biography

ISBN 0-7679-1955-6; 978-0-7679-1955-5

LC 2005-50161

"This collection of 20 commentaries by contemporary writers offers new perspectives on Booker T. Washington's autobiography and his place in the struggle for racial equality. Among the commentators are Debra Dickerson, Julianne Malveaux, Bill Ethanson, Ronald Walkers, Earl Ofari Hutchinson, and John McWhorter. The book also includes the complete text of Up from Slavery." Booklist

Includes bibliographical references

370.1   Philosophy and theory, education for specific objectives, educational psychology

Dewey, John

Democracy and education; an introduction to the philosophy of education. Free Press 1997 378p pa $17.95   **370.1**

1. Education -- Philosophy

ISBN 0-684-83631-9; 978-0-684-83631-7

First published 1916 by Macmillan

"The author's aim here is to detect and state the ideas implied in a democratic society and to apply those ideas to the problems of education." Boston Transcr

370.15   Educational psychology

Levine, Melvin D.

A **mind** at a time; {by} Mel Levine. Simon &
Schuster 2002 352p $26; pa $14   **370.15**
1. Child development 2. Learning disabilities 3.
Educational psychology
ISBN 0-7432-0222-8; 0-7432-0223-6 pa
LC 2001-57670

The author discusses "eight areas of learning (the memory system, the language system, the spatial ordering system,
the motor system, etc.). He provides chapters describing how
each type of learning works and advises parents and teachers
on how to help kids struggling in these areas. . . . This is a
must-read for parents and educators who want to understand
and improve the school lives of children." Publ Wkly

Includes bibliographical references

370.71   Education

McKeown, Rosalyn

Into the classroom; a practical guide for starting student teaching. Rosalyn McKeown. University of Tennessee Press 2011 xv, 165 p.p (pbk.)
$14.95   **370.71**
1. Teaching 2. Student teaching 3. Student teaching
-- United States
ISBN 1572338164; 9781572338166
LC 2011011282

This book offers suggestions to those "just starting out
in a secondary school classroom. . . . After exploring the
pitfalls of inexperience and providing . . . guidance on maintaining order in the classroom, [Rosalyn] McKeown focuses
on teaching skills. She advises readers on writing objectives
and lesson plans, creating interesting ways to start and end
class, introducing variety into the classroom, lecturing, asking meaningful questions, and using visual aids." (Amazon.
com)

Includes bibliographical references and index.

370.9   Education--History, geographic treatment, biography

Abani, Adesina

Teaching matters; stories from inside city
schools. Beverly Falk and Megan Blumenreich with
Adesina Abani ... [et al.] New Press 2012 xii, 196
p.p ill. (paperback) $19.95   **370.9**
1. Teaching 2. Urban schools 3. Education -- Case
studies 4. Teachers -- United States -- Case studies 5.
Education, Urban -- United States -- Case studies 6.
Children of minorities -- Education -- United States --
Case studies
ISBN 1595584900; 9781595584908
LC 2012004564

This book, by Beverly Falk and Megan Blumenreich,
discusses inner city public schools. "As public schools become increasingly embattled . . . , the burden of these restrictions has drastically changed the way children are expected

to learn. . . . Leading education experts Beverly Falk and
Megan Blumenreich provide an enlightening account of
what our students really need--and how teachers are stepping up to provide what state standards and political posturing cannot." (Publisher's note)

Includes bibliographical references (p. 189-196)

Hirsch, E. D.

The **schools** we need and why we don't have
them; {by} E.D. Hirsch, Jr. Doubleday 1996 317p
hardcover o.p. pa $14.95   **370.9**
1. Education -- United States
ISBN 0-385-49524-2 pa
LC 96-2192

The author argues that "our current educational system
has failed to reduce social inequity or enhance our economic
competitiveness. . . . Hirsch pleads for abandoning Progressivism's 'process' methodology in favor of a curriculum
based on challenging content, common knowledge acquisition, and rigorous standardized testing." Libr J

This "book presents a sophisticated, scholarly and often
compelling argument and it deserves serious consideration,
whatever one's political predilections." N Y Times Book Rev

Includes bibliographical references

Postman, Neil

The **end** of education; redefining the value
of school. Knopf 1995 209p hardcover o.p. pa
$13.95   **370.9**
1. Multiculturalism 2. Technology and civilization 3.
Education -- United States
ISBN 0-679-75031-2 pa
LC 94-46605

"The volume initially investigates American education
in the earlier part of this century. . . . Part 2 shifts focus to
contemporary education, describing the underlying conceptions of today's schools and considering economic utility,
consumership, technology, and separatism. . . . Postman responds creatively to the problems of 'modernity,' holding
out hope for regaining a sense of purpose and respect for
learning." Choice

"Beautifully written, breathtakingly high-minded, this is
Postman's best book on American education." Booklist

Includes bibliographical references

Ripley, Amanda

The **smartest** kids in the world; and how they
got that way. Amanda Ripley. Simon & Schuster
2013 320 p. $28   **370.9**
1. Foreign students 2. Education -- United States
3. Education -- Poland 4. Education -- Finland 5.
Comparative education 6. Education -- Korea (South)
ISBN 1451654421; 9781451654424
LC 2013002021

This book looks at the educational disparities between
the U.S. and other world nations. Journalist Amanda Ripley
"recounts the experiences of three American teens studying
abroad for a year in the education superpowers. Fifteen-
year-old Kim raises $10,000 so she can go to high school
in Finland; Eric, 18, trades a leafy suburb in Minnesota for

a 'city stacked on top of a city' in South Korea; and Tom, 17, leaves Gettysburg, Pa., for Poland." (Publishers Weekly)

Includes bibliographical references and index

371.01   Public schools

Rhee, Michelle A., 1969-

Radical; fighting to put students first. Michelle Rhee. Harper 2013 304 p. (hardcover) $27.99 **371.01**

1. Education -- United States 2. Education -- Aims and objectives 3. Public schools -- United States 4. Educational change -- United States 5. School improvement programs -- United States 6. Education -- Aims and objectives -- United States

ISBN 0062203983; 9780062203984

LC 2012038474

This book, by education reformer Michelle Rhee, "draws on her own life story and delivers her plan for better American schools. . . . Informing her critique are her . . . experiences in education. . . . Rhee draws on dozens of compelling examples from schools she's worked in and studied, from students who've left behind unspeakable home lives and thrived in the classroom to teachers whose groundbreaking methods have produced unprecedented leaps in student achievement." (Publisher's note)

371.1   Schools and their activities

Kozol, Jonathan, 1936-

Letters to a young teacher. Crown Publishers 2007 288p hardcover o.p. pa $14 **371.1**

1. Teaching

ISBN 978-0-307-39371-5; 0-307-39371-2; 978-0-307-39372-2 pa; 0-307-39372-0 pa

LC 2007-2689

"The book will delight and encourage first-year (or for that matter, 40th-year) teachers who need Kozol's reminders of the ways that their beautiful profession can bring joy and beauty, mystery and mischievous delight into the hearts of little people in their years of greatest curiosity." Publ Wkly

Includes bibliographical references

Parini, Jay

The **art** of teaching. Oxford University Press 2005 160p $17.95 **371.1**

1. Teaching 2. Vocational guidance

ISBN 0-19-516969-7

LC 2004-5443

The author offers "musings about teaching's demands and what it takes to not lose one's other, creative self while meeting those demands in this memoir-cum-advice book for novice instructors. . . . This warm guide should inform, entertain, and inspire young teachers as they seek to 'waken a student to his or her potential.'" Publ Wkly

371.102   Teaching

Espinoza, Roberta

Pivotal moments; how educators can put all students on the path to college. Roberta Espinoza. Harvard Education Press 2011 200 p. (pbk.) $26.95 **371.102**

1. Higher education

ISBN 1612501192; 9781612501192; 9781612501208

LC 2011937500

In this book, "sociologist Roberta Espinoza introduces the idea of pivotal moments[:] interventions that point the way toward college, particularly for students from working-class or ethnic minority backgrounds. These pivotal encounters and the relationships that spring from them can help students accumulate procedural knowledge about attending college (cultural capital) and interpersonal support (social capital)." (Amazon.com)

Includes bibliographical references and index.

371.26   Examinations and tests; academic prognosis and placement

Reese, William J.

Testing wars in the public schools; a forgotten history. William J. Reese. Harvard University Press 2013 298 p. $45 **371.26**

1. Public schools -- United States 2. Educational tests and measurements 3. Public schools -- United States -- History -- 19th century 4. Educational tests and measurements -- United States -- History -- 19th century

ISBN 0674073045; 9780674073043

LC 2012033665

Author William J. Reese provides an "examination of the roots of the testing culture in American education and the ramifications for administrators, teachers, and students. Reese organizes the book into six chapters, including those that concentrate upon the origins of large-scale testing, the reform-minded reasons for using such instruments, the procedures by which testing was implemented, the effects of testing, how the content was selected, and how the culture of testing evolved." (Choice)

Includes bibliographical references and index

371.3   Methods of instruction and study

Britton, Lesley

Montessori play & learn; a parents' guide to purposeful play from two to six. with an introduction by Joy Starrey Turner. Crown 1992 144p il pa $19.95 **371.3**

1. Parenting 2. Montessori method of education

ISBN 0-517-59182-0

LC 92-5446

This describes educational activities for two to six year olds according to the Montessori method which parents can introduce at home

Jackson, Rebecca

The **learning** habit; a groundbreaking approach to homework and parenting that helps our children succeed in school and life. Stephanie Donaldson-Pressman, Rebecca Jackson, Robert Pressman. Perigee Trade 2014 320 p. illustrations (paperback) $17   **371.3**

     1. Homework 2. Family life 3. Psychology of learning 4. Families 5. Parenting 6. Study skills

     ISBN 0399167110; 9780399167119

                      LC 2014011124

Written by Stephanie Donaldson-Pressman, Rebecca Jackson, and Robert Pressman, this book "presents new solutions based on the largest study of family routines ever conducted. 'The Learning Habit' offers a blueprint for navigating the maze of homework, media use, and . . . everyday stress . . . ; turning those 'stress times' into opportunities to develop . . . skills including concentration and focus, time management, decision-making, goal-setting, and self-reliance." (Publisher's note)

"The book lists eight essential skill sets that parents should help children cultivate, from time management to fostering self-reliance. An especially useful chapter focuses on ways to help children concentrate." Pub Wkly

Includes bibliographical references and index

Montessori, Maria

     ★ The **Montessori** method; introduction by J. McV. Hunt. Schocken Bks. 1964 xxxix, 376p il hardcover o.p. pa $14   **371.3**

     1. Montessori method of education

     ISBN 0-8052-0922-0 pa

Originally published in Italy; first published 1912 in the United States

This is an introduction to the author's teaching methods. The Montessori system emphasizes the development of individuality in the child and the careful training of the senses. Education is controlled by interpersonal relations between the children rather than between teacher and child

371.33   Teaching aids, equipment, materials

Vander Ark, Tom, 1959-

     Getting smart; how digital learning is changing the world. Tom Vander Ark ; foreword by Bob Wise. 1st ed. Jossey-Bass 2011 xxi, 213 p.p $26.95   **371.33**

     1. Internet in education 2. Computer-assisted instruction 3. Education -- Experimental methods 4. Blended learning -- United States 5. Internet in education -- United States 6. Computer-assisted instruction -- United States

     ISBN 1118007239; 9781118007235

                      LC 2011024028

This book, by Tom Vander Ark, "examines the various facets of educational innovation in the United States and abroad. Vander Ark . . . makes a . . . case for a new model of education that blends online and on-site learning. [He] explains that through the use of technology it is now possible to provide 24/7 access to learning and increase student engagement. . . . By customizing learning . . . each hour of learning can become more effective for all students at all levels." (Publisher's note)

Includes bibliographical references and index

371.4   Student guidance and counseling

Morgan, Genevieve

     Undecided; navigating life and learning after high school. Genevieve Morgan. Zest Books 2014 256 p. $14.99   **371.4**

     1. College choice 2. Vocational guidance 3. Life skills -- Handbooks, manuals, etc.

     ISBN 1936976323; 9781936976324

                      LC 2013951198

Written by Geneieve Morgan, "This comprehensive handbook outlines the different options available to teens after high school and provides suggestions on how to follow each path. . . . It covers everything from SAT preparation and personal statements to trade school pros and cons and advice on how to prepare for life in the military. Full of checklists, anecdotes, brainstorming activities, and journal exercises, 'Undecided' leaves no stone unturned and no option unconsidered." (Publisher's note)

"A helpful guide full of good, sensible advice to teens feeling overwhelmed by the prospect of major life transitions." Kirkus

Includes bibliographical references and index

371.5   School discipline and related activities

Bully; an action plan for teachers and parents to combat the bullying crisis. edited by Lee Hirsch and Cynthia Lowen ; with Dina Santorelli. Perseus Books Group 2012 viii, 295 p.p ill. $15.99   **371.5**

     1. Bullies 2. Bullying 3. Bullying -- Prevention 4. Cyberbullying -- Prevention 5. Bullying in schools -- Prevention

     ISBN 1602861846; 1602861854; 9781602861848; 9781602861855

                      LC 2012289039

"This companion book to the documentary film Bully was edited by filmmaker [Lee]Hirsch and writer/producer [Cynthia] Lowen, with contributing chapters by a number of celebrities, authors, experts, government officials, and educators. Part homage to the film, part resource, the book interweaves the stories of children who have been bullied with practical information and advice for parents and other readers." (Publishers Weekly)

Includes bibliographical references (p. 281-289) and index

371.82 Specific groups of students; schools for specific groups of students

Cahill, Sean

LGBT youth in America's schools; Jason Cianciotto and Sean Cahill. The University of Michigan Press 2012 236 p. (pbk. : alk. paper) $30 **371.82**
1. Bullies 2. Gay youth 3. Discrimination 4. Schools -- Administration 5. Gay students -- United States 6. Sexual minorities -- Education 7. Lesbian students -- United States 8. Bisexual students -- United States 9. Homosexuality and education -- United States 10. Transgender youth -- Education -- United States
ISBN 0472031406; 9780472028320; 9780472031405; 9780472118229

LC 2011045478

In this book, "[Jason] Cianciotto and [Sean] Cahill use statistics and real-life anecdotes to show the pervasiveness of gender- and sexual orientation-based harassment in American schools, and argue for institutional reform and policy changes. . . . [R]esearch shows that . . . more young people are coming out . . . while still technically a minor, and thus subject to the rules of their educational institutions, and increasingly the abuse of their peers, teachers, and school administrators." (Publishers Weekly)

Includes bibliographical references and index.

Mortenson, Greg

Stones into schools; promoting peace with books, not bombs, in Afghanistan and Pakistan. Viking 2009 420p il map $26.95 **371.82**
1. Humanitarian intervention 2. Schools -- Pakistan 3. Schools -- Afghanistan
ISBN 978-0-670-02115-4

LC 2009-30812

In this follow-up to Three cups of tea (2009), the author "continues the story of how the Central Asia Institute (CAI) built schools in northern Afghanistan. Descriptions of the harsh geography and more than one near-death experience impress readers as new faces join Mortenson's loyal 'Dirty Dozen' as they carefully plot a course of school-building through the Badakshan province and Wakhan corridor. . . . To blandly call this book inspiring would be dismissive of all the hard work that has gone into the mission in Afghanistan as well as the efforts to fund it. Mortenson writes of nothing less than saving the future, and his adventure is light years beyond most attempts." Booklist

Three cups of tea; one man's mission to fight terrorism and build nations--one school at a time. [by] Greg Mortenson and David Oliver Relin. Viking 2006 338p il map $25.95; pa $16 **371.82**
1. Humanitarian intervention 2. Schools -- Pakistan 3. Schools -- Afghanistan
ISBN 0-670-03482-7; 978-0-670-03482-6; 0-14-303825-7 pa; 978-0-14-303825-2 pa

LC 2005-43466

This book discusses "Mortenson's one-man mission to counteract extremism by building schools, especially for girls, throughout the breeding ground of the Taliban." Publisher's note

"Laced with drama, danger, romance, and good deeds, Mortenson's story serves as a reminder of the power of a good idea and the strength inherent in one person's passionate determination to persevere against enormous obstacles." Christ Sci Monit

Perez, William

We are Americans; undocumented students pursuing the American dream. foreword by Daniel Solorzano. Stylus 2009 xxxiv, 161p $70; pa $22.50 **371.82**
1. Illegal aliens 2. Discrimination in education 3. United States -- Immigration and emigration
ISBN 978-1-57922-375-5; 978-1-57922-376-2 pa

LC 2009-26206

The author "plumbs the stories of students living with the constant threat of deportation for an answer to the question, 'What does it mean to be an American?' Raised in this country by parents who gained access illegally, the 16 high school, college and postgraduate students profiled here (standing in for 65,000 nationwide) have each embraced our language, culture and collective dream, but are denied pathways to success. . . . No matter what one's position is on legalizing immigrants, this collection of inspiring, heartbreaking stories puts a number of unforgettable faces to the issue, making it impossible to defend any one side in easy terms or generalities." Publ Wkly

Includes bibliographical references

371.9 Special education

Chura, David

I don't wish nobody to have a life like mine; tales of kids in adult lockup. Beacon Press 2010 xxiii, 216p $24.95; pa $14 **371.9**
1. Juvenile delinquency 2. Prisoners -- Education
ISBN 978-0-8070-0064-9; 978-0-8070-0123-3 pa

LC 2009027664

Shares the experiences of teenagers incarcerated in an adult prison in New York, as well as those of the men and women hired to teach and watch over them.

"Chura offers a compelling personal look at the failings of the juvenile justice system." Booklist

Flink, David

Thinking Differently; An Inspiring Guide for Parents of Children With Learning Disabilities. David Flink. HarperCollins 2014 320 p. illustrations $15.99 **371.9**
1. Learning disabilities 2. Students with disabilities
ISBN 0062225936; 9780062225931

This book by David Flink "enlarges our understanding of the learning process and offers powerful, innovative strategies for parenting, teaching, and supporting the 20 percent of students with learning disabilities. . . . Focusing on how to arm students who think and learn differently with essential skills, including meta-cognition and self-advocacy, Flink offers real, hard advice, providing the tools to address specific problems they face." (Publisher's note)

Includes bibliographical references and index

Hayden, Torey L.

Beautiful child; [by] Torey Hayden. HarperCollins Pubs. 2002 326p hardcover o.p. pa $7.99 **371.9**

1. Special education

ISBN 0-380-81339-4; 0-06-050887-6 pa

LC 2001-39928

This is "the story of a scruffy seven-year-old, Venus, who is so unresponsive that Hayden searches for signs of deafness, brain damage or mental retardation. . . . Hayden sets Venus's bittersweet and complex story against the backdrop of other students. . . . In this first-person narrative, Hayden also shares her own thoughts, worries and strained relationship with a mismatched classroom aide, creating a rich tapestry of the dynamics of a group of special needs youngsters and the adults who try to help them." Publ Wkly

Kozol, Jonathan, 1936-

Savage inequalities; children in America's schools. HarperPerennial 1992 261p pa $14.95 **371.9**

1. Public schools 2. Segregation in education 3. Children with social disabilities 4. Socially handicapped children

ISBN 0-06-097499-0; 978-0-06-097499-2

First published 1991 by Crown

"Jonathan Kozol has written an impassioned book, laced with anger and indignation, about how our public education system scorns so many of our children. 'Savage Inequalities' is also an important book, and warrants widespread attention" N Y Times Book Rev

Includes bibliographical references

Salzman, Mark

True notebooks. Alfred A. Knopf 2003 330p hardcover o.p. pa $13.95 **371.9**

1. Creative writing 2. Juvenile delinquency

ISBN 0-375-41308-1; 0-375-72761-2 pa

LC 2002-43435

"While teaching writing to 17-year-olds detained in Los Angeles Central Juvenile Hall, Salzman found himself surprised by the boys' talent. The teens' heartwarming, funny voices are included in his irresistible, provocative memoir." Booklist

Siegel, Bryna

Helping children with autism learn; treatment approaches for parents and professionals. Oxford Univ. Press 2003 498p $30; pa $18.95 **371.9**

1. Autism 2. Special education

ISBN 0-19-513811-2; 0-19-532506-0 pa

LC 2002-151673

"Carefully tailoring her book to multiple audiences, with free use of commentary and introductory notes, Siegel . . . excels at showing what parents and educators need to do to reach autistic children. She includes a valuable section on having successful individualized educational programs (IEPs), the standard for children with special needs." Libr J

Includes bibliographical references

Siegel, Lawrence M.

The **complete** IEP guide; how to advocate for your special ed child. 7th ed.; Nolo 2011 380p pa $34.99 **371.9**

1. Special education 2. Children with disabilities 3. Individualized instruction 4. Individuals with Disabilities Education Act

ISBN 978-1-4133-1313-0 pa; 1-4133-1313-2 pa; 978-1-4133-1336-9 ebook; 1-4133-1336-1 ebook

LC 2010-38386

First published 1999. Frequently revised

This legal guide offer strategies and advice for parents of children who need an individualized special education program. Includes information on special education laws and eligibility rules, how to draw up a blueprint of a child's educational needs, and what to look for in a special education program.

Turkington, Carol

The **encyclopedia** of learning disabilities; [by] Carol Turkington, Joseph R. Harris, American Bookworks. 2nd ed; Facts on File 2006 304p (Facts on File library of health and living) $75; pa $19.95 **371.9**

1. Reference books 2. Learning disabilities -- Encyclopedias

ISBN 0-8160-6399-0; 978-0-8160-6399-4; 0-8160-6400-8 pa; 978-0-8160-6400-7 pa

LC 2005-53045

First published 2002

This book "offers a wealth of information useful to teachers, health-care providers, and parents as they seek to communicate and learn about particular developmental and learning problems." Booklist

Includes bibliographical references

371.91   Students with physical disabilities

Hauser, Peter C.

★ **How** deaf children learn; what parents and teachers need to know. Marc Marschark Peter C. Hauser. Oxford University Press 2012 156 p. $26.50 **371.91**

1. Teaching 2. Deaf children 3. Elementary education 4. Deaf -- Education 5. Deaf -- Means of communication

ISBN 0195389751; 9780195389753

LC 2011012553

This book is "about teaching deaf children. Written primarily for parents and teachers of deaf or hard-of-hearing children, this work covers general information about their education, gives insights into their cognitive development, and provides steps to their school success. The authors also discuss issues such as the value of cochlear implants and the debate over signing vs. speaking." (Library Journal)

Includes bibliographical references.

372 Specific levels of education

Dewey, John

★ The **school** and society, and The child and the curriculum; introduction by Philip W. Jackson. University of Chicago Press 1990 xli, 209p hardcover o.p. pa $11   **372**
   1. Elementary education
   ISBN 0-226-14396-1 pa

                        LC 90-43528

A combined edition of two essays first published separately in 1899 and 1902 respectively

Both of these works stress the functional relationship between classroom learning activities and real life experiences and analyze the social and psychological nature of the learning process. They present and defend the underlying tenets of Dewey's philosophy of education

372.21 Preschool education

Tough, Paul

★ How children succeed; grit, curiosity, and the hidden power of character. Paul Tough. Houghton Mifflin Harcourt 2012 231 p. $27.00   **372.21**
   1. Rich 2. Equality 3. Social classes 4. Poor -- United States 5. Children -- United States 6. Early childhood education -- United States 7. Cognitive styles in children -- United States
   ISBN 0547564651; 9780547564654

                    LC 2012019000

In this book Paul Tough "argues that non-cognitive skills (persistence, self-control, curiosity, conscientiousness, grit and self-confidence) are the most critical to success in school and life. . . . When policymakers favor the belief that disadvantaged kids have insufficient cognitive training, Tough finds that a new generation of researchers are questioning the cognitive hypothesis." (Kirkus Reviews)

"Well-written and bursting with ideas..." Kirkus

Includes bibliographical references and index

372.4 Reading

Fertig, Beth

Why cant U teach me 2 read? three students and a mayor put our schools to the test. Farrar, Straus and Giroux 2009 354p $27   **372.4**
   1. Reading disability 2. Students with disabilities 3. Reading -- Remedial teaching 4. New York (N.Y.) -- Board of Education
   ISBN 978-0-374-29905-7; 0-374-29905-6

                    LC 2009-11520

The author "offers a view of the crisis in education through the lens of three young adults struggling with illiteracy. Yamilka, Alejandro, and Antonio, all products of New York public schools, legally challenged the system when it failed to teach them to read, securing special tutoring arrangements designed to compensate for years of neglect. Fertig intersperses their accounts with the politics of educa-

tion reform in New York during the mayoral administration of Michael Bloomberg." Booklist

This is "an overall excellent, thoroughly grounding survey of the state of literacy and education." Publ Wkly

Includes bibliographical references

Flesch, Rudolf Franz

★ Why Johnny can't read--and what you can do about it. Harper & Row 1955 222p hardcover o.p. pa $13   **372.4**
   1. Reading 2. Phonetics -- Study and teaching
   ISBN 0-06-091340-1 pa

Companion volume to Why Johnny still can't read (1981)

The author advocates the alphabetic-phonetic system of teaching children to read. He includes step-by-step directions and phonetic drills for use by parents

Grover, Sharon

Listening to learn; audiobooks supporting literacy. by Sharon Grover and Lizette D. Hannegan. American Library Association 2011 xi, 188 p.p (alk. paper) $45   **372.4**
   1. Literacy 2. Audiobooks 3. Educational technology 4. Reading -- United States 5. Children -- Books and reading 6. Libraries -- Special collections -- Audiobooks 7. Literacy -- Study and teaching -- United States 8. School librarian participation in curriculum planning
   ISBN 0838911072; 9780838911075

                    LC 2011041814

Authors Sharon Grover and Lizette D. Hannegan "make the case that audiobooks not only present excellent opportunities to engage the attention of young people but also advance literacy. 'Listening to Learn' connects audiobooks with K-12 curricula and demonstrates how the format can support national learning standards and literacy skills." (Publisher's note)

"This informative resource establishes the literacy benefits of audiobooks as an alternate reading delivery method... Discussions of audiobook formats and recommended sources for building an audiobook collection are also included. The authors provide a collaborative resource that would benefit a classroom, library, or home setting." (Library Media Connection)

Includes bibliographical references (p. 175-178) and index

372.5 The arts

Art and social justice education; culture as commons. edited by Therese Quinn, John Ploof, and Lisa Hochtritt. Routledge 2012 xxiii, 201 p.p ill. (some col.)   **372.5**
   1. Culture 2. Educators 3. Education -- Curricula 4. Arts -- Study and teaching 5. Art in education -- Social aspects 6. Social justice -- Study and teaching 7. Teaching -- Social aspects -- United States 8. Education -- Social aspects -- United States
   ISBN 0415879078; 9780203852477; 9780415879064; 9780415879071

                    LC 2011027006

Editor Therese Quinn "offers inspiration and tools for educators to craft critical, meaningful, and transformative arts education curriculum and arts integration projects. The images, descriptive texts, essays, and resources are grounded within a clear social justice framework and linked to ideas about culture . . . Proposing that art can contribute in a wide range of ways to the work of envisioning and making a more just world, this imaginative . . . sourcebook of contemporary artists' works and education resources advances the field of arts education." (Amazon)

Includes bibliographical references and index

372.6   Language arts (Communication skills)

Maguire, James

American bee; the National Spelling Bee and the culture of word nerds: the lives of five top spellers as they compete for glory and fame. Rodale 2006 371p $24.95   **372.6**

1. Spelling bees 2. English language -- Spelling
ISBN 978-1-59486-214-4; 1-59486-214-1

LC 2005-37443

"From the nail-biting denouement of the 2004 Bee, Maguire . . . moves on to brief sketches of some past winners and then takes an informative and wryly humorous look at the English language itself and the evolution of the American spelling bee from Puritan pastime to major media event." Libr J

Includes bibliographical references

Seeger, Pete

Pete Seeger's storytelling book; by Pete Seeger and Paul Du Bois Jacobs. Harcourt 2000 264p $24; pa $14   **372.6**

1. Storytelling
ISBN 0-15-100370-X; 0-15-601311-8 pa

LC 00-29599

"The tales themselves, tape-recorded by Seeger and rewritten by Jacobs . . . are grouped roughly by origin. They range from family stories to versions of Bible tales to stories inspired by songs, history, legends, and Seeger's own imagination. In an introduction to each chapter, Seeger explains the source of the tales and offers suggestions for scouting similar ones. Each story, ready to read aloud or tell, concludes with possible variations, themes, morals, and, sometimes, music." Booklist

373.1   Organization and activities in secondary education

Keizer, Garret

Getting Schooled; The Reeducation of an American Teacher. Garret Keizer. Henry Holt & Co 2014 320 p. $27   **373.1**

1. Teachers 2. Teaching 3. High schools 4. Rural schools 5. Public schools -- Vermont -- Case studies 6. High school teaching -- Vermont -- Case studies 7. High school teachers -- Professional relationships -- Vermont

-- Case studies
ISBN 0805096434; 9780805096439

LC 2013042594

In this book, "teacher and writer Garret Keizer takes us to school--literally--in this arresting account of his return to the same rural Vermont high school where he taught fourteen years ago. Much has changed since then--a former student is his principal, standardized testing is the reigning god, and smoking in the boys' room has been supplanted by texting in the boys' room." (Publisher's note)

"[A]t once a sympathetic portrait of a school, a searing indictment of a culture that uses working-class children as cannon fodder, and, unexpectedly, a page-turner." Pub Wkly

373.22   Private and public secondary schools

Brick, Michael

Saving the school; the true story of a principal, a teacher, a coach, a bunch of kids, and a year in the crosshairs of education reform. Michael Brick. Penguin Press 2012 288 p. (hardback) $25.95   **373.22**

1. High schools 2. Schools -- Administration 3. School superintendents and principals 4. John H. Reagan High School (Austin, Tex.) 5. School improvement programs -- Texas -- Austin
ISBN 159420344X; 9781594203442

LC 2011050569

This book presents an "account of a troubled Austin, Texas, school that endured a year of tough medicine while facing shutdown. . . . When Reagan was given one more chance to bring up test scores or face closure as part of the national get-tough approach to school reform headed by the new president, . . . [Michael] Brick immersed himself in the lives of the teachers and students. . . . He focuses especially on . . . the school's principal, Anabel Garza." (Kirkus Reviews)

374   Adult education

John, Lauren Z.

Running book discussion groups; a how-to-do-it manual. [by] Lauren Zina John. Neal-Schuman Publishers 2006 250p (How-to-do-it manual for librarians) pa $55   **374**

1. Books and reading 2. Discussion groups
ISBN 1-55570-542-1; 978-1-55570-542-8

LC 2006-704

This is a "step-by-step guide to the tasks and responsibilities librarians are likely to encounter as book-group leaders conducting booktalks both on-site and online. . . . This is essential reading for anyone who may be considering taking on the role of a book-discussion-group leader and a refresher for the more experienced among us." Booklist

Includes bibliographical references

Rose, Mike

Back to school; why everyone deserves a second chance at education. Mike Rose. New Press, The 2012 224 p. (hardcover) $21.95 **374**
1. Adult education 2. College students 3. Higher education
ISBN 9781595587862

LC 2012021135

This book by Mike Rose "look[s] at the schools that serve a growing population of . . . [non-traditional students] exploring what higher education . . . can offer our rapidly changing society." (Publisher's note) "Rose explores the need for a reassessment of the post–K-12 educational system, noting that growing sectors of the labor market require a four- or even two-year degree." (Kirkus Reviews)
Includes bibliographical references

378   Higher education (Tertiary education)

Book of Majors 2014. Henry Holt & Co 2013 1368 p. (paperback) $27.99 **378**
1. College majors 2. College students
ISBN 1457300222; 9781457300226

This book is a guide to college majors. "In-depth descriptions of 200 of the most popular majors are followed by complete listings of every major offered at more than 3,800 colleges, including four-year and two-year colleges and technical schools. The 2014 edition covers every college major identified by the U.S. Department of Education—over 1,200 majors are listed in all." (Publisher's note)

College Board Guide To Getting Financial Aid, 2014. Henry Holt & Co 2013 1000 p. (paperback) $22.99 **378**
1. Student aid 2. College costs 3. Education -- Finance
ISBN 1457300192; 9781457300196

This book looks at financial aid for college students. The "FAFSA [Free Application for Federal Student Aid] form is explained with step-by-step instructions, and the College Board's CSS/Financial Aid PROFILE form is explained by the people who administer it. The guide includes information and advice from experts on how to apply for aid, plus easy-to-compare college profiles giving the 'financial aid picture' for more than 3,000 four-year and two-year colleges and technical schools." (Publisher's note)

Dreifus, Claudia

Higher education? how colleges are wasting our money and failing our kids--and what we can do about it. [by] Andrew Hacker and Claudia Dreifus. Times Books 2010 271p il $26 **378**
1. College costs 2. Higher education 3. College teachers -- United States 4. Colleges and universities -- Faculty 5. Education, Higher -- United States -- Finance
ISBN 978-0-8050-8734-5; 0-8050-8734-6

LC 2010-07219

Hacker and Dreifus "draw up a powerful, if rambling, indictment of academic careerism. The authors are not shy about making biting judgments along the way. . . . [They conclude] with capsule summaries of, as they put it, 'Schools

We Like'—that is, schools that offer superior undergraduate educations at relatively low cost." Wall Street J
Includes bibliographical references

Selingo, Jeffrey J.

College (un)bound; the future of higher education and what it means for students. Jeffrey J. Selingo. Houghton Mifflin Harcourt 2013 xviii, 238 p.p (hardcover) $26 **378**
1. Higher education 2. Colleges and universities -- Finance 3. College students -- United States 4. Educational planning -- United States 5. Universities and colleges -- United States 6. Education, Higher -- Aims and objectives -- United States
ISBN 0544027078; 9780544027077

LC 2013001941

This book offers an analysis of "middle-tier American colleges" and highlights "forward-thinking educational models. [Jeffrey J.] Selingo . . . describes a climate in which colleges compete for rankings by improving amenities, falling into an escalating cycle of tuition increases and larger financial aid packages that leave students with crushing debt, and a sense of students as consumers that leads to grade inflation and teaching compromises." (Publishers Weekly)
Includes bibliographical references and index.

Williams, Juan

I'll find a way or make one; a tribute to historically Black colleges and universities. by Juan Williams and Dwayne Ashley. Amistad/HarperCollins 2004 xxiv, 453p il $35 **378**
1. African American universities and colleges 2. African Americans -- Education
ISBN 0-06-009453-2

LC 2004-46450

The authors "explore America's 107 historically black colleges and universities, in existence for 172 years, showing how the schools were created and how black and white abolitionists united to educate newly freed slaves." Libr J
Includes bibliographical references

378.1   Organization and activities in higher education

Albom, Mitch, 1958-

Tuesdays with Morrie; an old man, a young man, and life's greatest lesson. Mitch Albom. Doubleday 1997 192 p. pa $13.99; $20.00 **378.1**
1. Amyotrophic lateral sclerosis 2. Sociologists 3. College teachers 4. Brandeis University -- Faculty -- Biography 5. Death -- Psychological aspects -- Case studies 6. Teacher-student relationships -- United States -- Case studies 7. Amyotrophic lateral sclerosis -- Patients -- United States -- Biography
ISBN 076790592X pa; 0385484518

LC 96052535

This book discusses the author's relationship with his former teacher and mentor, "sociologist Morrie Schwartz. Here [Mitch] Albom recounts how . . . as the old man was dying, he renewed his warm relationship with his revered mentor. This is the . . . record of the teacher's battle with muscle-wasting amyotrophic lateral sclerosis, or Lou Gehrig's disease. The dying man, largely because of his life-affirming attitude toward his death-dealing illness, became a sort of thanatopic guru, and was the subject of three Ted Koppel interviews on Nightline. That was how the author first learned of Morrie's condition. Albom . . . calls his weekly visits to his teacher his last class, and the present book a term paper. The subject: The Meaning of Life . . . Albom does not present a full transcript of the regular Tuesday talks. Rather, he expands a little on the professor's aphorisms." (Kirkus)

"As a student at Brandeis University in the late 1970s, Albom was especially drawn to his sociology professor, Morris Schwartz. On graduation he vowed to keep in touch with him, which he failed to do until 1994, when he saw a segment about Schwartz on the TV program Nightline, and learned that he had just been diagnosed with Lou Gehrig's disease. By then a sports columnist for the Detroit Free Press . . . Albom was idled by the newspaper strike in the Motor City and so had the opportunity to visit Schwartz in Boston every week until the older man died. Their dialogue is the subject of this moving book." Publ Wkly

Bain, Ken

What the best college students do; Ken Bain. The Belknap Press of Harvard University Press 2012 289 p. (alk. paper) $24.95   **378.1**
1. College students 2. College students -- United States 3. Academic achievement -- United States
ISBN 0674066642; 9780674066649
LC 2012015548

In this book, author Ken Bain "identifies the key attitudes that distinguished the best college students from their peers. These individuals started out with the belief that intelligence and ability are expandable, not fixed. This led them to make connections across disciplines, to develop a 'meta-cognitive' understanding of their own ways of thinking, and to find ways to negotiate ill-structured problems rather than simply looking for right answers." (Publisher's note)

"A soundly encouraging guide for college students to think deeply and for as long as it takes." Kirkus

Includes bibliographical references and index

Beyond the asterisk; understanding Native students in higher education. edited by Heather Shotton, Shelly Lowe, and Stephanie J. Waterman. Stylus 2013 xvi, 189 p.p (cloth : alk. paper) $85 **378.1**
1. Foreign students 2. Students -- United States 3. Indian students -- United States 4. Indians of North America -- Education (Higher) -- United States
ISBN 157922623X; 9781579226237; 9781579226244
LC 2012040238

Editor Heather J. Shotton's book discusses Native American students in higher education. "The purpose of this book is to move beyond the asterisk in an effort to better understand Native students, challenge the status quo, and provide an informed base for leaders in student and academic affairs, and administrators concerned with the success of students on their campuses." (Publisher's note)

Includes bibliographical references and index

Crossman, Anne

Getting the best out of college; insider advice for success from a professor, a dean, and a recent grad. Peter Feaver, Sue Wasiolek, Anne Crossman. Rev. and updated, 2nd ed. Ten Speed Press 2012 xiv, 289 p.p (pbk.) $14.99   **378.1**
1. Counseling 2. College students 3. Colleges and universities -- United States 4. College student orientation -- United States
ISBN 160774144X; 9781607741442
LC 2011051246

This book, by authors Peter Feaver, Sue Wasiolek, and Anne Crossman, "reveals insider advice that makes the hefty price tag worth it: how to impress professors, live with a roommate, pick the best courses (and do well in them), design a meaningful transcript, earn remarkable internships, prepare for a successful career after graduation, and much more." (Publisher's note)

Fiske guide to getting into the right college; [by] Edward B. Fiske & Bruce G. Hammond. 4th ed.; Sourcebooks 2010 352p pa $16.99   **378.1**
1. College choice 2. Colleges and universities -- Finance 3. Colleges and universities -- Entrance requirements
ISBN 978-1-4022-4309-7
First published 1997 by Times Bks.

This guide includes advice and information on constructing applications, writing essays, interviews, the application process, using the Internet when applying for college, and finanical aid.

Jager-Hyman, Joie

B + grades, A+ college application; how to present your strongest self, write a stand-out admissions essay, and get into the perfect school for you. by Joie Jager-Hyman, EdD. Random House Inc 2013 ix, 246 p.p (paperback) $14.99   **378.1**
1. Student aid 2. College applications 3. Exposition (Rhetoric) 4. College applications -- United States 5. Universities and colleges -- United States -- Admission
ISBN 1607743418; 9781607743415
LC 2013004970

In this book, college admissions consultant Joie Jager-Hyman "guides students (and their parents) through the college-admissions process, offering a wealth of insider advice. . . . Jager-Hyman covers the usual steps: developing a list of target, reach, and safety schools; writing essays; prepping for the college interview; taking the SATs; and demystifying financial aid." (Publishers Weekly)

"The author emphasizes that even in the highly competitive (and, according to the media, often "gloomy") admissions environment, there is hope for kids who don't have straight A's and perfect SAT scores...Though there is plenty of information on the Internet about the college-application process, this insider perspective is a welcome addition to the toolkit." (Publishers Weekly)

The **Latino** student's guide to college success; Leonard A. Valverde, editor. Greenwood 2012 xiv, 270 p.p (alk. paper) $58   **378.1**
1. Hispanic Americans -- Education (Higher) --

Handbooks, manuals, etc. 2. Universities and colleges -- United States -- Directories 3. Hispanic Americans -- Education (Higher) -- Handbooks, manuals, etc
ISBN 031339797X; 0313397988; 9780313397974; 9780313397981

LC 2012010827

This book, edited by Leonard A. Valverde, provides "advice directed specifically to Latinos contemplating, preparing for, or already in the university or community college setting. This volume contains the 8 Steps to College Success, numerous vignettes of notable Latinos in many fields who give their personal story of how they succeeded in college and their advice for today's students, and a directory of top Latino universities and community colleges." (Publisher's note)

Pekar, Harvey

Students for a Democratic Society; a graphic history. written by Harvey Pekar; art by Gary Dumm; edited by Paul Buhle. Hill & Wang 2008 214p il $22; pa $16   **378.1**
  1. Graphic novels 2. College students -- Political activity -- Graphic novels 3. Students for a Democratic Society -- Graphic novels -- History
ISBN 978-0-8090-9539-1; 978-0-8090-8939-0 pa

LC 2007-40641

Students for a Democratic Society formed as an organization in 1960, but had its roots as a New Left group in the League for Industrial Democracy, founded in 1905 with members such as Jack London and Upton Sinclair. The members in 1960 included Al Haber and Tom Hayden, and one of their most famous documents is the Port Huron Statement of 1962. By the late 1960s, with opposition to the Vietnam War in full swing, a radical subgroup called the Weathermen became more violent. Graphic novelist Pekar is joined by members of the SDS in telling the story of the organization, which dissolved soon after its 1969 convention. The book includes some harsh language and violence.

"The book acts like a sophisticated handbook on an often misunderstood organization. It's good comics and excellent history." Publ Wkly

Rosenfeld, Seth, 1956-

Subversives; the FBI's war on student radicals, and Reagan's rise to power. Seth Rosenfeld. Farrar, Straus and Giroux 2012 752 p. ill., map (alk. paper) $40.00   **378.1**
  1. United States. Federal Bureau of Investigation 2. California -- Politics and government -- 1951- 3. Student movements -- California -- Berkeley -- History 4. University of California, Berkeley -- Students -- History 5. Subversive activities -- California -- Berkeley -- History 6. College students -- Political activity -- California -- Berkeley -- History
ISBN 0374257000; 9780374257002

LC 2011041204

This book "traces the FBI's secret involvement with three iconic figures at Berkeley during the 1960s: the ambitious neophyte politician Ronald Reagan, the fierce but fragile radical Mario Savio, and the liberal university president Clark Kerr. Through these converging narratives, the award-winning investigative reporter Seth Rosenfeld tells .

. . of FBI surveillance, illegal break-ins, infiltration, planted news stories, poison-pen letters, and secret detention lists." (Publisher's note)
Includes bibliographical references

Shachtman, Tom

Airlift to America; how Barack Obama, Sr., John F. Kennedy, Tom Mboya, and 800 East African students changed their world and ours. St. Martin's Press 2009 273p il $24.99   **378.1**
  1. College students 2. African-American Students Federation 3. East Africa -- Foreign relations -- United States 4. United States -- Foreign relations -- East Africa
ISBN 978-0-312-57075-0

LC 2009-13186

"In the late 1950s, before Kenya's independence from Britain, Kenyan leader Tom Mboya and American philanthropist William Scheinman joined to develop a cadre of educated young people to staff the government and schools. Between 1959 and 1963, nearly 800 African students were flown to the U.S. to be educated and to return to become the 'founding brothers and sisters' of their East African nations. Among them were Wangari Maathai, who went on to become an environmentalist and 2004 Nobel Peace Prize winner, and Barack Obama Sr., father of the future president of the U.S. Shachtman provides historical perspective of cold war politics in African nations, countervailing loyalties to European colonial powers, and the appeal of U.S. ideals of independence." Booklist
Includes bibliographical references

Steinberg, Jacques

The gatekeepers; inside the admissions process of a premier college. Viking 2002 xxiii, 292p hardcover o.p. pa $15   **378.1**
  1. College applications 2. Wesleyan University (Middletown, Conn.)
ISBN 0-670-03135-6; 0-14-200308-5 pa

LC 2002-16884

The author follows "the procedures at Wesleyan University for a year . . . [to] see how the admissions process really looks, to the admitters as well as the applicants." N Y Times Book Rev

"This insightful and readable book should be purchased by all academic and large public libraries." Libr J
Includes bibliographical references

378.3   Student aid and related topics

Collinge, Alan

The student loan scam; the most oppressive debt in U.S. history, and how we can fight back. Beacon Press 2008 167p $22.95   **378.3**
  1. Student loan funds
ISBN 978-0-8070-4229-8; 0-8070-4229-3

LC 2008-12230

"Collinge argues that student loans have become the most profitable, uncompetitive, and oppressive type of debt in American history. This has occurred in large part due to federal legislation passed since the mid-1990s that removed standard consumer protections from student loans—and allowed for massive penalties and draconian wealth-extraction mechanisms to collect this inflated debt. Collinge covers the history of student loans, the rise of Sallie Mae, and how universities have profited at the expense of students." Publisher's note

"Comprehensive and stirring, this extraordinary book is whistle-blowing at its finest." Publ Wkly

Includes bibliographical references

378.73   Colleges--United States

Delbanco, Andrew

College; what it was, is, and should be. Andrew Delbanco. Princeton University Press 2012 xiv, 229 p.p (hardcover) $24.95   378.73

1. Higher education 2. Colleges and universities 3. Education, Higher -- Aims and objectives -- United States

ISBN 0691130736; 9780691130736

LC 2011039399

This book presents an "assessment of how American higher education has lost its way. [Andrew Delbanco] starts with the American ideal, dating back to the Puritans, of college as a place that trained the whole person. . . . In modern America, that focus has shifted: Now it's less about the eternal verities than chasing after dollars, more about filling seats than heads and more about science than the humanities." (Kirkus Reviews)

Includes bibliographical references and index

Mettler, Suzanne

Degrees of inequality; how the politics of higher education sabotaged the American dream. Suzanne Mettler. Basic Books, a member of the Perseus Books Group 2014 272 p. illustrations (hardback) $27.99   378.73

1. College costs 2. American dream 3. Higher education 4. Education -- United States 5. Educational change -- United States

ISBN 0465044964; 9780465044962

LC 2013043678

In this book, political scientist Suzanne Mettler "explains why the . . . American Dream is increasingly out of reach for so many. . . . She illuminates how political partisanship has overshadowed America's commitment to equal access to higher education. As politicians capitulate to corporate interests, owners of for-profit colleges benefit, but for far too many students, higher education leaves them with little besides crippling student loan debt." (Publisher's note)

"Though the book orbits the central theme of the for-profits and their outsized political influence, [Mettler] frames this with a history of higher education and its attendant laws, as well as an excellent introduction to political science that explains—in approachable language—the myriad impacts of law and the ways in which the intentions of legislators are often deformed." Pub Wkly

Includes bibliographical references and index

379   Public policy issues in education

Greenawalt, Kent

Does God belong in public schools? Princeton University Press 2005 261p $29.95   379

1. Church and state 2. Religion in the public schools

ISBN 0691121117

LC 2004-45779

The author "considers issues ranging from the teaching of evolution to parents' rights that their children not be exposed to offensive curriculum. He grounds his analyses in a review of the history and purposes of schooling. . . . His legal and philosophical lines of scholarship come together to produce a nonpartisan consideration of the crucial issues facing US courts and the country." Choice

Includes bibliographical references

Kozol, Jonathan

★ The shame of the nation; the restoration of apartheid schooling in America. Crown Publishers 2005 404p $25; pa $14.95   379

1. Segregation in education

ISBN 1-4000-5244-0; 1-4000-5245-9 pa

LC 2005-8626

The author "spent five years interviewing and observing students, teachers, and principals in 60 schools across 11 states, providing further documentation of the growing caste and color segregation in overcrowded and underfunded schools." Choice

"Readers interested in public education will appreciate—and be challenged by—this compelling book." Booklist

Includes bibliographical references

Ravitch, Diane, 1938-

The death and life of the great American school system; how testing and choice are undermining education. Basic Books 2010 283p $26.95   379

1. School choice 2. Educational tests and measurements 3. Public schools -- United States 4. Educational accountability -- United States 5. Educational tests and measurements -- United States

ISBN 978-0-465-01491-0; 0-465-01491-7

LC 2009-50406

Ravitch critiques "ideas for restructuring schools, including privatization, standardized testing, punitive accountability, and the . . . multiplication of charter schools." (Publisher's note) Index.

The author "provides an important and highly readable examination of the educational system, how it fails to prepare students for life after graduation, and how we can put it back on track. . . . Anyone interested in education should definitely read this accessible, riveting book." Libr J

Includes bibliographical references

379.26   Educational equalization (Equal educational opportunity)

Wilder, Craig Steven

★ Ebony and Ivy; Race, Slavery, and the Troubled History of America's Universities. by Craig Wilder. Bloomsbury 2013 448 p. $30   **379.26**
1. Higher education 2. Slavery -- United States -- History 3. Race discrimination -- United States 4. Slavery -- United States 5. United States -- Race relations 6. Racism in education -- United States 7. African Americans -- Education (Higher) History 8. Discrimination in higher education -- United States 9. Universities and colleges -- United States -- History 10. Minorities -- Education (Higher) -- United States -- History
ISBN 1596916818; 9781596916814

LC 2013011971

In this book, author Craig Steven Wilder examines the relationship among "race, slavery, and the American academy. Wilder shows, our leading universities, dependent on human bondage, became breeding grounds for the racist ideas that sustained them . . . revealing a history of oppression behind the institutions usually considered the cradle of liberal politics." (Publisher's note)

Includes bibliographical references and index

381   Commerce (Trade)

Cassidy, John

How markets fail; the logic of economic calamities. Farrar, Straus and Giroux 2009 390p il   **381**
1. Monetary policy 2. Stock exchanges 3. Financial crises 4. Banks and banking
ISBN 0374173206; 9780374173203

LC 2009029529

"Cassidy describes the rising influence of what he calls utopian economics—thinking that is blind to how real people act and that denies the many ways an unregulated free market can produce disastrous unintended consequences." (Publisher's note) Index.

"The author focuses primarily on the rise and fall of free market ideology and the mostly unrealistic ideal of a self-correcting marketplace. An excellent comprehensive history of the economic thought that led to this kind of utopian economics provides a refresher course in Adam Smith, Friedrich August von Hayek, Kenneth Arrow and Hyman Minsky." Publ Wkly

Includes bibliographical references

Dolin, Eric Jay

Fur, fortune, and empire; the epic history of the fur trade in America. W.W. Norton & Co. 2010 442p il map $29.95   **381**
1. Fur trade 2. Europe -- Colonies -- America 3. Fur trade -- North America -- History 4. Fur trade -- Western States -- History 5. Frontier and pioneer life -- North America
ISBN 978-0-393-06710-1

LC 2010016212

This is an "overview of the American fur trade from Colonial times until the beginnings of the conservation movement of the late 19th century. . . . From the Iroquoian 'Beaver Wars' of the mid-1600s to the brutal Russian domination of Alaskan native hunters, Dolin successfully shows how America's natural history is a vital part of our collective national history." Libr J

Includes bibliographical references

Eltis, David

Atlas of the transatlantic slave trade; [by] David Eltis and David Richardson; foreword by David Brion Davis; afterword by David W. Blight. Yale University Press 2010 xxvi, 307p il map (The Lewis Walpole series in eighteenth-century culture and history) $50   **381**
1. Atlases 2. Reference books 3. Slave trade -- Maps
ISBN 978-0-300-12460-6

"For nearly 20 years, the Trans-Atlantic Slave Trade Database project has been diligently tabulating all the slave ship crossings of the Atlantic Ocean, from 1500 to 1900. . . . With 189 informative and handsome maps, Eltis and Richardson relay and interpret the information contained in this rich database, mixing in beautiful historical illustrations and key passages from relevant texts. An accessible narrative, meanwhile, expands on the information in the maps. . . . This marvelous book will change how people think of the slave trade." Foreign Affairs

Mitchell, Stacy

Big -box swindle; the true cost of mega-retailers and the fight for America's independent businesses. Beacon Press 2006 318p $24.95; pa $15   **381**
1. Chain stores 2. Retail trade 3. Small business
ISBN 978-0-8070-3500-9; 0-8070-3500-9; 978-0-8070-3501-6 pa; 0-8070-3501-7 pa

LC 2006-13818

This is an "indictment of Wal-Mart and other 'big box' stores, based on numerous national examples. . . . [The author catalogues the] ways indie-minded consumers can fight back, by campaigning against government subsidies to big-box stores, and advocating for sales tax collection on Internet sales and stronger antitrust enforcement." Publ Wkly

Mitchell's "call to action reveals the hidden costs of those 'low prices' promoted by the big-box bullies and gives hope to local entrepreneurs and concerned citizens alike." Booklist

Includes bibliographical references

Sennett, Frank

Groupon's biggest deal ever; the inside story of how one insane gamble, tons of unbelievable hype, and millions of wild deals made billions for one ballsy joker. Frank Sennett. St. Martin's Press 2012 310 p. (hbk.) $25.99   **381**
1. Groupon (Firm) 2. Internet industry 3. Internet marketing 4. Coupons (Retail trade) 5. Internet advertising
ISBN 125000084X; 1250014948; 9781250000842; 9781250014948

LC 2012009440

This book looks at daily deal website Groupon. The firm's "CEO Andrew Mason takes center stage in this story about the company's founding, development, and explosive assent." Author Frank Sennett starts "from November 2006, when Mason first pitched the idea for Policy Tree (Groupon's precursor) to Eric Lefkofsky, the man who became Groupon's chairman, to early November 2011, when Groupon finally went public on the NASDAQ stock exchange." (Publishers Weekly)

Spector, Robert

The **mom** & pop store; how the unsung heroes of the American economy are surviving and thriving. Walker Pub. Co. 2009 293p $26   **381**

1. Small business 2. Business enterprises

ISBN 978-0-8027-1605-7

    LC 2009-19198

The author "aims to show what life looks like 'from the other side of the counter' in mom-and-pop stores—small, independent businesses—and to help us appreciate the service these types of shops offer our society." Libr J

"Lively lessons about business ethics and practices that Fortune 500 companies, the author suggests, would be wise to follow." Kirkus

Includes bibliographical references

Stanton, Maureen

Killer stuff and tons of money; seeking history and hidden gems in flea-market America. Penguin Press 2011 326p $26.95   **381**

1. Antiques 2. Flea markets

ISBN 978-1-59420-293-3; 1-59420-293-1

    LC 2010-53099

Before Stanton "reconnected with her pseudonymous old college friend, 'Curt Avery,' who had become a professional antiques dealer, she was 'the self-anointed Queen of the Flea-Market Dollar Table.' Like many Americans, she was on the lookout for an appealing bargain and just as happy with an inexpensive reproduction as the real thing. When she and Avery met again in 2000, she agreed to fly across the country to attend an auction where some old bottles that he coveted were on offer. He asked her to be his proxy bidder while he hid at the back and signaled his bids. This was her introduction to a fascinating subculture, which she calls 'the flea realm.' Over the years, she attended many fairs and flea markets with Avery as what she calls a 'participant observer,' getting up before dawn to help him set up displays, grabbing food on the run and camping out next to his truck at night. . . . A treasure-trove of a book, especially for would-be antiquers." Kirkus

Includes bibliographical references

Whitaker, Jan

Service and style; how the American department store fashioned the middle class. St. Martin's Press 2006 342p il $35   **381**

1. Middle class 2. Department stores

ISBN 978-0-312-32635-7; 0-312-32635-1

    LC 2006-40542

"At their peak, department stores were the nation's largest booksellers and many major chains also sold groceries. But it was clothes that made the stores a prime destination for women of all social classes, and Whitaker discusses at significant length the subtle movements through which major chains from one end of the country to the other cultivated their reputations for being up-to-date with the latest Paris fashions, then tapped into additional markets for young adult and children's wear. More than 100 photographs and illustrations are integrated into the text, aptly demonstrating the lengths to which stores went in order to present themselves as elegant yet modern and convenient." Publ Wkly

Includes bibliographical references

Ziegler, Mel

Wild company; the untold story of Banana Republic. Mel and Patricia Ziegler. Simon & Schuster 2012 208 p.   **381**

1. Clothing industry 2. Banana Republic Travel and Safari Company 3. Clothing trade -- United States 4. Fashion merchandising -- United States

ISBN 1451683480; 9781451683486; 9781451683509; 9781451683516

    LC 2012030040

This book, by Mel and Patricia Ziegler, describes how the authors "turned a wild idea into a company that would become the international retail colossus Banana Republic. Re-imagining military surplus as safari and expedition wear, the former journalist and artist created a world that captured the zeitgeist for a generation and spoke to the creativity, adventure, and independence in everyone." (Publisher's note)

382   International commerce (Foreign trade)

Goldstein, Natalie

Globalization and free trade; Natalie Goldstein ; foreword by Joanna G. Moss. 2nd ed. Facts On File 2012 428 p. (ebook) $54.00; (hardcover) $45.00; (paperback) $18.95; (hardcover) $45.00   **382**

1. Free trade 2. Globalization 3. International economic relations 4. Free trade -- Case studies 5. Globalization -- Economic aspects -- Case studies 6. International economic integration -- Case studies

ISBN 9781438109008; 9780816068081; 9780816077397; 0816083657; 9780816083657

    LC 2011004940

This encyclopedia, by Natalie Goldstein, examines international economic issues and "provides an overview of the history of globalization and how it has evolved into its present state." It gives "opinions by proponents and detractors of the issue, and case studies of the United States, East Asia, China, Cochabamba, and Iceland are presented to provide real-world context." (Publisher's note)

Includes bibliographical references and index.

Rose, Sarah

For all the tea in China; how England stole the world's favorite drink and changed history. Viking 2010 261p $25.95   **382**

1. Tea 2. Horticulturists 3. China -- Description and travel

ISBN 0-670-02152-0; 978-0-670-02152-9

    LC 2009-41482

First published 2009 in the United Kingdom

An account of mid-19th-century botanist Robert Fortune's mission to travel to China's remote Wu Yi Shan hills to steal closely guarded secrets of tea horticulture and manufacturing describes his encounters with pirates, threatening weather, and unethical people.

"With her probing inquiry and engaging prose, Sarah Rose paints a fresh and vivid account of life in rural 19th-century China and Fortune's fateful journey into it." Washington Post

Includes bibliographical references

Snyder, Rachel Louise

Fugitive denim; a moving story of people and pants in the borderless world of global trade. W.W. Norton & Company 2008 352p $26.95; pa $16.95 **382**

1. Jeans (Clothing) 2. Clothing industry 3. International trade

ISBN 978-0-393-06180-2; 0-393-06180-9; 978-0-393-33542-2 pa; 0-393-33542-9 pa

LC 2007-24335

This is a "look at how jeans are designed, sewn, and transported as well as how the cotton for denim is grown, regulated, purchased, and processed." Libr J

"Snyder's investigation is an essential read for those curious about fashion or the globe-spanning business that produces their clothes." Publ Wkly

Includes bibliographical references

382.09 International commerce (Foreign trade)--History

Dolin, Eric Jay

When America first met China; an exotic history of tea, drugs, and money in the Age of Sail. Eric Jay Dolin. Liveright Pub. Corp. 2012 394 p. **382.09**

1. China -- History 2. United States -- History 3. China -- Commerce -- United States 4. China -- Foreign economic relations 5. United States -- Foreign economic relations 6. China -- Commerce -- United States -- History -- 18th century 7. China -- Commerce -- United States -- History -- 19th century 8. United States -- Commerce -- China -- History -- 18th century 9. United States -- Commerce -- China -- History -- 19th century

ISBN 0871404338; 9780871404336

LC 2012016598

In this book, Eric Jay Dolin profiles the early history of United States-China trade. The author "traces . . . [America's] fraught relationship with China back to its roots: . . . a brash, rising naval power . . . [and] a battered ancient empire. . . . [T]he furious trade in furs, opium, and beche-de-mer . . . might have catalyzed America's emerging economy, but it also sparked an ecological and human rights catastrophe . . . that . . . can still be felt today." (Publisher's note)

Includes bibliographical references and index

383 Communications and transportation

National five digit zip code and post office directory. U.S. Postal Service 2v maps pa $45 **383**

1. Zip code

ISBN 978-1-59804-282-5; 1-59804-282-3

Annual. Continuation of National zip code and post office directory

"Besides ZIP codes and post offices, this directory includes information on the organization of the Postal Service, addressing, parcel weights and sizes, delivery statistics, and other matters." Recomm Ref Books in Paperback. 2d edition

384 Communications

Gertner, Jon

The **idea** factory; Bell Labs and the great age of American innovation. Jon Gertner. Penguin Press 2012 422 p. ill. $29.95 **384**

1. Bell Telephone Laboratories 2. Telecommunication -- History 3. Technological innovations -- History 4. Inventors -- United States -- History -- 20th century 5. Bell Telephone Laboratories -- History -- 20th century 6. Creative ability -- United States -- History -- 20th century 7. Telecommunication -- United States -- History -- 20th century 8. Technological innovations -- United States -- History -- 20th century

ISBN 1594203288; 9781594203282

LC 2011040207

This book "traces the history of Bell Labs through more than five decades of brilliant thinking and innovation. From the transistor to lasers to satellites and cellular technology, Bell Labs and its scientists invented machines and techniques that . . . ultimately presaged all of modern communications. . . . Bell Labs became a haven for creative and technical minds due to a unique culture of encouraged interdisciplinary research." (Kirkus Reviews)

"The book is a celebration of basic exploratory research. . . . [T]he writing and the longitudinal biographical portraits are engaging." LJ

Includes bibliographical references (p. [409]-412) and index

Knopper, Steve

Appetite for self-destruction; the spectacular crash of the record industry in the digital age. Free Press 2009 301p $26 **384**

1. Music industry

ISBN 978-1-4165-5215-4; 1-4165-5215-4

LC 2008-38739

Knopper "provides a wide-angled, morally complicated view of the current state of the music business. He doesn't let those rippers and burners among us—that is, those who download digital songs without paying for them, and you know who you are—entirely off the hook. But he suggests that with even a little foresight, record companies could have adapted to the Internet's brutish and quizzical new realities and thrived." N Y Times Book Rev

Includes bibliographical references

Lapsley, Phil

Exploding the Phone; The Untold Story of the Teenagers and Outlaws Who Hacked Ma Bell. by Phil Lapsley ; forward by Steve Wozniak. Grove Press 2013 xvi, 431 p.p (hardcover) $26   **384**

1. Bell System 2. Telecommunication -- History

ISBN 080212061X; 9780802120618

In this book, Phil Lapsley "uses more than 100 interviews and 400 Freedom of Information Act requests to present the virtually unknown battle between phone companies and overcurious young tech whizzes determined to explore Ma Bell's networks." He "pieces together a . . . re-creation of 1967, a highly significant period in telecommunications history." (Library Journal)

Wu, Tim

The **master** switch; the rise and fall of information empires. Alfred A. Knopf 2010 366p il $27.95   **384**

1. Telecommunication 2. Information technology 3. Mass media -- History 4. Telecommunication -- History 5. Information technology -- History

ISBN 978-0-307-26993-5; 0-307-26993-0

LC 2010-04137

"Policy quibbles aside, there's a sharp insight and a surprising fact on nearly every page of Wu's masterful survey. Above all, Wu shows that each new communications technology spawns the same old quest for power." Boston Globe

Includes bibliographical references

384.1   Telegraphy

Gordon, John Steele

A **thread** across the ocean; the heroic story of the transatlantic cable. Walker & Co. 2002 240p il $26   **384.1**

1. Telegraph 2. Submarine cables

ISBN 0-8027-1364-5

LC 2002-66385

The author "has written a lively, engaging account of the extraordinary efforts that brought about this remarkable scientific, technological, and business feat." Libr J

Includes bibliographical references

384.3   Computer communication

Blum, Andrew

Tubes; a journey to the center of the Internet. Andrew Blum. Ecco 2012 294 p.   **384.3**

1. Internet 2. Computer networks 3. Information networks 4. Information technology 5. Information highway 6. Internet -- History 7. Telecommunication systems 8. Internet -- Social aspects

ISBN 0061994936; 9780061994937

LC 2012009519

In this book, "journalist Andrew Blum goes inside the Internet's physical infrastructure. . . . From the room in Los Angeles where the Internet first flickered to life . . . [to] a ten-thousand-mile undersea cable just two thumbs wide

[that] connects Europe and Africa, to the wilds of the Pacific Northwest, where Google, Microsoft, and Facebook have built monumental data centers--Blum chronicles the . . . Internet's development, explains how it all works, and takes . . . [a] look inside its hidden monuments." (Publisher's note)

Includes bibliographical references and index.

384.54   Radiobroadcasting

Fisher, Marc

Something in the air; radio, rock, and the revolution that shaped a generation. Random House 2007 374p il $27.95   **384.54**

1. Radio broadcasting

ISBN 978-0-375-50907-0; 0-375-50907-0

LC 2006-47353

"There's not a bit of dead air in this well-written and researched history of radio and its pivotal role in the emergence of American youth culture." Publ Wkly

Includes bibliographical references

Heil, Alan L.

Voice of America; a history. Columbia University Press 2003 538p $75; pa $26.50   **384.54**

1. Radio broadcasting 2. Voice of America

ISBN 0-231-12674-3; 0-231-12675-1 pa

LC 2002-41019

This is a "history of America's largest publicly funded overseas broadcasting network. . . . From the crises in eastern Europe to the student uprising in Tiananmen Square, Mr Heil provides countless examples of people clinging to their shortwave radios to listen to VOA and other international broadcasters, in spite of intense jamming, to know what was really going on in their own countries. . . . Readers fascinated by the technical intricacies of radio and the arcana of Washington's broadcasting policies will no doubt be riveted." Economist

Includes bibliographical references

385   Railroad transportation

Ambrose, Stephen E.

Nothing like it in the world; the men who built the transcontinental railroad, 1863-1869. Simon & Schuster 2000 471p $28; pa $16   **385**

1. West (U.S.) -- History 2. Central Pacific Railroad 3. Railroads -- United States 4. Union Pacific Railroad Company

ISBN 0-684-84609-8; 0-7432-0317-8 pa

LC 00-41005

This is an account of the construction of the transcontinental railroad by the Central Pacific and Union Pacific companies

"Ambrose's scholarship seems impeccable. . . . He writes a brisk, colloquial, straightforward prose that not only is easy to read but also bears the reader on shoulders of wonder and excitement." N Y Times Book Rev

Includes bibliographical references

Bain, David Haward

Empire express; building the first transcontinental railroad. Viking 1999 797p il maps hardcover o.p. pa $30   385

1. West (U.S.) -- History 2. Central Pacific Railroad 3. Railroads -- United States 4. Union Pacific Railroad Company

ISBN 0-670-80889-X; 0-14-008499-1 pa

LC 99-33375

"Bain knits together excellent storytelling and exhaustive research in a rich contextual tale of vision, ambition, and, ultimately, political and personal corruption." Libr J

Includes bibliographical references

Drabelle, Dennis

The **great** American railroad war; how Ambrose Bierce and Frank Norris took on the notorious Central Pacific Railroad. Dennis Drabelle. St. Martin's Press 2012 306 p. $26.99   385

1. Whistle blowing 2. Central Pacific Railroad Company -- History 3. Norris, Frank, 1870-1902 -- Criticism and interpretation 4. Bierce, Ambrose, 1842-1914? -- Criticism and interpretation 5. Railroads -- California -- History -- 19th century 6. Political corruption -- Press coverage -- California

ISBN 0312667590; 9780312667597; 9781250015051

LC 2012010247

Author Dennis Drabelle "examines the role of literature in battling the Central Pacific Railroad monopoly. He recounts the financing of the transcontinental railroad with U.S. government bonds and how the railroad's owners such as Leland Stanford and Collis Huntington enriched themselves in various quasi-legal ways. Though the railroad worked to make itself untouchable by buying influence, Drabelle chronicles how writers Ambrose Bierce and Frank Norris challenged that position." (Library Journal)

Includes bibliographical references

Hayes, Derek

Historical atlas of the North American railroad. University of California Press 2010 224p il map $39.95   385

1. Reference books 2. Historical atlases 3. Railroads -- Canada -- Maps 4. Railroads -- North America -- Maps 5. Railroads -- United States -- Maps 6. North America -- Historical geography 7. Railroads -- North America -- History

ISBN 978-0-520-26616-2

LC 2009-943592

"With 400-plus color maps ranging from 1821 to President Obama's report 'A Vision for High Speed Rail,' this historical atlas reveals the richly variegated visual culture of railroad mapping in the US and Canada. Always utilitarian, railroad maps are differentiated into four types: those required to survey the land for construction and attracting investments, timetable maps for passengers, maps in advertising, and engineering maps. . . . The wealth of visual information, comprehensive coverage, and optimistic stance for the future of railroads on the North American continent make this an important purchase for all reference collections." Choice

Includes bibliographical references

McCommons, James

Waiting on a train; the embattled future of passenger rail service. foreword by James Howard Kunstler. Chelsea Green Pub. Company 2009 285p map pa $17.95   385

1. Transportation 2. Railroads -- United States

ISBN 978-1-60358-064-9; 1-60358-064-6

LC 2009-30142

"McCommons spent almost all of 2008 riding Amtrak trains back and forth across the country, telling folks he met along the way that he was doing research for a book on the future of passenger rail. . . . [The resulting work] is part travel log, chronicling both the horrors and the pleasures of riding Amtrak, and part solid political and business reporting on the rail industry that hardly any other journalist is doing." Washington Monthly

White, Richard

Railroaded; the transcontinentals and the making of modern America. Norton 2011 xxxix, 660p il map $35   385

1. American national characteristics 2. Railroads -- United States 3. Land settlement -- United States 4. National characteristics, American 5. Railroads -- United States -- History -- 19th century

ISBN 978-0-393-06126-0; 0-393-06126-4

LC 2010-54054

In this book, author Richard White "takes on the task of explaining the achievements and failings of the few transcontinental railroads that spanned North America in the latter half of the 19th century. He concentrates on their financial, political, and social impact. . . . He describes the corruption that made the railroad's founders wealthy but hamstrung the companies . . . , the antipathy between management and workers . . . [and] the antimonopoly movements against railroad practices." (Library Journal)

"Focusing on the entrepreneurs who between the 1860s and 1890s built and operated the transcontinental railroads, White judges them and their companies as failures and malignant influences on the settlement of the West." Booklist

Includes bibliographical references

Wolmar, Christian

Blood, iron, & gold; how the railroads transformed the world. PublicAffairs 2009 376p il map $28.95   385

1. Railroads -- History

ISBN 978-1-58648-834-5

LC 2009-38340

First published 2009 in the United Kingdom

The author describes "both how railroads developed worldwide from the 1820s forward and the profound changes they brought." Libr J

This is "a fascinating study not just of a transportation system, but of the Promethean spirit of the modern age." Publ Wkly

Includes bibliographical references

385.09   Railroad transportation--History

Zoellner, Tom

Train; riding the rails that created the modern world : from the Trans-Siberian to the Southwest Chief. Tom Zoellner. Viking Adult 2014 384 p. (hardback) $27.95   **385.09**

  1. Railroads 2. Railroad engineering 3. Railroad travel -- History

  ISBN 0670025283; 9780670025282

LC 2013036816

In this book, Tom Zoellner "examines both the mechanics of the rails and their engines and how they helped societies evolve. Not only do trains transport people and goods in an efficient manner, but they also reduce pollution and dependency upon oil. Zoellner also considers America's culture of ambivalence to mass transit, using the perpetually stalled line between Los Angeles and San Francisco as a case study in bureaucracy and public indifference." (Publisher's note)

"An absorbing and lively reflection on an enduring marvel of modern industrial technology." Booklist

Includes bibliographical references and index

386   Inland waterway and ferry transportation

Bernstein, Peter L.

Wedding of the waters; the Erie Canal and the making of a great nation. W.W. Norton 2005 448p il map $24.95; pa $15.95   **386**

  1. Erie Canal (N.Y.)

  ISBN 0-393-05233-8; 0-393-32795-7 pa

LC 2004-22792

The author discusses the building of the Erie Canal and how, in his opinion, it changed the course of American history.

This "is an important window into a vital and too often neglected period in the American past." Foreign Affairs

Includes bibliographical references

Karabell, Zachary

Parting the desert; the creation of the Suez Canal. Knopf 2003 310p il map $27.50   **386**

  1. Diplomats 2. Suez Canal (Egypt)

  ISBN 0-375-40883-5

LC 2002-34209

Karabell "has written a thorough and entertaining work. . . . The author is quite comfortable discussing any issue, period, or personality in the canal's history, and many of the references in his 150-title bibliography are from primary sources. This is simply an excellent book." Libr J

387.7   Air transportation

Blatner, David

The flying book; everything you've ever wondered about flying on airplanes. Walker & Co. 2003 248p il $22   **387.7**

  1. Airplanes 2. Commercial aeronautics

  ISBN 0-8027-1378-5

"Concentrating on commercial aviation, {the author} offers a compendium of fascinating facts. Chapters zero in on specific aspects of flight: what keeps planes in the air, for example, or how a jet engine functions, or the workings of air-traffic control, or airplane maintenance, or the often-bewildering universe of ticket prices. In addition to technological facts, he also covers the human side of air travel: fear of flying and how to control it, what the pilots are up to in the cockpit, even the horrors of airline food." Booklist

"Engaging, upbeat, and fact-filled, The Flying Book features an open, airy design with lots of charts and sidebars." SLJ

Includes bibliographical references

Fallows, James

China airborne; James Fallows. Pantheon Books 2012 xiii, 268 p.p   **387.7**

  1. China -- History -- 1976- 2. Aerospace industry -- China 3. China -- Economic conditions 4. Commercial aeronautics -- China 5. Aeronautics -- China 6. Aerospace industries -- China 7. Aeronautics, Commercial -- China 8. China -- Economic conditions -- 2000-

  ISBN 0375422110; 9780375422119

LC 2011046805

This book by James Fallows "analyzes the problems and promises of China's economic development through an examination of the efforts to create a world-class aerospace industry. With its unprecedented manufacturing prowess, China has become a world economic power. But how real and sustainable is the development? The test, writes the author, is how well China succeeds in its current effort to build an aerospace industry." (Kirkus Reviews)

Includes bibliographical references (p. [237]-251) and index

Holmes, Richard, 1945-

★ Falling upwards; how we took to the air. Richard Holmes. Pantheon Books 2013 416 p. $35   **387.7**

  1. Flight 2. Balloons 3. Ballooning -- History 4. Balloonists -- History

  ISBN 0307379663; 9780307379665

LC 2013011128

This book by Richard Holmes looks at ballooning. He "mentions Daedalus and Icarus, some balloons in literature, films and popular culture, and then lifts off into another of his . . . histories. He notes that the French were the first to use balloons for military purposes (reconnaissance), then tells us about some of the most notable balloon pioneers, including André-Jacques Garnerin, who also pioneered parachutes." (Kirkus Reviews)

Includes bibliographical references and index

McGee, William J.

Attention all passengers; the airlines' dangerous descent and how to reclaim our skies. William J. McGee. HarperCollins 2012 xii, 354 p.p $26.99 **387.7**

  1. Airlines 2. Air travel 3. Aeronautics -- Safety measures 4. Airlines -- United States

  ISBN 0062088378; 9780062088376

LC 2012026940

Author William J. McGee "derives most of the book from his interviews with, among others, flight attendants, congressmen, [and] an FAA whistleblower. . . . McGee explains how the shortcomings of airlines can and do cost consumers more than a comfortable flight; they result in unsafe conditions. . . . The author exposes the common practice of outsourcing repairs, which can result in crashes because the companies doing the repairs are not as competent or as tightly regulated." (Kirkus Reviews)

Mondor, Colleen Catherine

The **map** of my dead pilots; Colleen Mondor. Lyons Press 2012 256p **387.7**
1. Alaska 2. Air pilots 3. Aircraft accidents
ISBN 9780762773619

LC 2011033005

This book explores the author's experiences "as operations manager for a commercial airline servicing Alaska's remote villages and hamlets. . . . [Colleen] Mondor has had a bird's-eye view of the rigors of flying cargo that often as not included carcasses as well as crates, sleds as well as the dogs that hauled them, and passengers who had no other means of traversing a state whose isolation was both allure and aggravation. The men who flew these missions are—and, all too sadly, were—a lethal combination of danger junkies and hotshots, dreamers and schemers, dedicated professionals and determined daredevils who reveled in the challenges that Alaska's climate and terrain threw their way." (Booklist)

388 Transportation

McPhee, John A.

Uncommon carriers; [by] John McPhee. Farrar, Straus & Giroux 2006 248p $24 **388**
1. Freight 2. Transportation
ISBN 0-374-28039-8; 978-0-374-28039-0

LC 2006-7953

The author "sums up eight years of riding around with people who haul freight in vehicles ranging from 18-wheelers to towboats." Libr J

"McPhee's eye for idiosyncratic detail keeps the stories . . . lively and frequently moves them in interesting directions." Publ Wkly

388.1 Roads

Conover, Ted

The **routes** of man; how roads are changing the world, and the way we live today. Alfred A. Knopf 2010 333p il map $26.95 **388.1**
1. Roads
ISBN 978-1-4000-4244-9; 1-4000-4244-5

LC 2009-24007

"A readable, fact-filled, well-written exploration of how roads work, for good and ill, and what their future likely holds." Kirkus
Includes bibliographical references

388.3 Vehicular transportation

Sperling, Daniel

Two billion cars; driving toward sustainability. [by] Daniel Sperling [and] Deborah Gordon. Oxford University Press 2009 304p il $24.95 **388.3**
1. Automobile industry 2. Alternative fuel vehicles 3. Automobiles -- Fuel consumption
ISBN 978-0-19-537664-7; 0-19-537664-1

LC 2008-21647

"With statistical data, charts, graphs, and erudite analysis, Sperling and Gordon present the most thorough study of the automobile industry general readers could hope to find." Booklist
Includes bibliographical references and index

390 Customs, etiquette, folklore

Jenkins, Jessica Kerwin

All the time in the world; a book of hours. Jessica Kerwin Jenkins. Nan A. Talese 2013 320 p. (hardback) $28.95 **390**
1. Culture 2. Hobbies 3. Manners and customs -- History 4. Manners and customs -- Miscellanea
ISBN 0385535414; 9780385535410

LC 2013000795

In this book, author Jessica Kerwin Jenkins "uses the template of the medieval book of hours, which provided readings and meditations for certain times of the day and seasons, to create an unusual look at 'how we pass the time.'" (Booklist) "Subjects covered include the daylong ceremony of laying a royal Elizabethan tablecloth; the radicalization of sartorial chic in 1890s Paris; [and] Nostradamus's belief in the aphrodisiac power of jam". (Publisher's note)
Includes bibliographical references

391 Customs

Crowe, Lauren Goldstein

The **towering** world of Jimmy Choo; a glamorous story of power, profits and the pursuit of the perfect shoe. [by] Lauren Goldstein Crowe and Sagra Maceira de Rosen. Bloomsbury USA 2009 228p il $26; pa $15 **391**
1. Shoes 2. Fashion design 3. Jimmy Choo (Firm) 4. Clothing industry executives
ISBN 978-1-59691-391-2; 1-59691-391-6; 978-1-60819-040-9 pa; 1-60819-040-4 pa

LC 2008-44378

This book is "about how the worlds of fashion and international business influence each other, with the firm called Jimmy Choo as an illustrative case." Libr J

"A fascinating, well-written chronology that draws a chillingly accurate behind-the-scenes portrait of a contemporary fashion brand." Booklist
Includes bibliographical references

DeJean, Joan E.

The **essence** of style; how the French invented high fashion, fine food, chic cafes, style, sophistication, and glamour. Free Press 2005 303p il $25; pa $15 **391**

1. Kings 2. Fashion -- History 3. France -- Social life and customs

ISBN 0-7432-6413-4; 0-7432-6414-2 pa

LC 2005-40019

A historian of seventeenth-century French culture argues that "the French under Louis XIV set the standards of sophistication, style, and glamour that still rule our lives today." Publisher's note

"An unusual and delightfully educational perspective on snob appeal." Booklist

Includes bibliographical references

Paterek, Josephine

Encyclopedia of American Indian costume. Norton 1996 516p il pa $24.95 **391**

1. Reference books 2. Native American costume -- Encyclopedias

ISBN 0-393-31382-4

First published 1994 by ABC-CLIO

Paterek describes "the clothing used for everyday, war, rites, and ceremonies for men, women, and children in hundreds of tribes in diverse climates stretching over centuries. Well-organized text and 400 drawings and authentic photos plus the cultural essays prefacing the 10 regional groupings and each tribe put the costumes in historical, social, and geographic context. Appendixes cover terminology and the materials used in clothing. The excellent bibliographies in this classic work both document and encourage further reading." Am Libr

Includes bibliographical references

391.009 History, geographic treatment, biography

Stevenson, N. J.

Fashion; a visual history from regency & romance to retro & revolution : a complete illustrated chronology of fashion from the 1800s to the present day. NJ Stevenson. 1st US ed. St. Martin's Griffin 2012 288 p. ill. (chiefly col.) $29.99 **391.009**

1. Hats 2. Painting 3. Women's clothing 4. Clothing and dress 5. Fashion -- History 6. Fashion design -- History 7. Clothing and dress -- History 8. Fashion -- History -- 19th century 9. Fashion -- History -- 20th century 10. Fashion -- History -- 21st century

ISBN 031262445X; 9780312624453

LC 2011278257

Author N. J. Stevenson describes "when distinctive styles that began as extravagances of the very rich permeated through well-dressed society until a cut of cloth or choice of accessory defined fashion. . . . Each spread focuses on a definitive item--be it bowler hat or little black dress, stiletto or caftan--or identifies key shifts in fashion that reflect excess, liberation, austerity, nostalgia, and technology, displaying it in contemporary images ranging from paintings

and illustrated fashion plates to cartoons and photographs." (Publisher's note)

Includes bibliographical references and index

391.6 Personal appearance

Etcoff, Nancy L.

Survival of the prettiest; the science of beauty. {by} Nancy Etcoff. Doubleday 1999 325p il hardcover o.p. pa $14 **391.6**

1. Natural selection 2. Personal appearance 3. Sexual behavior

ISBN 0-385-47942-5 pa

LC 98-41332

The author "presents the evolution of our conception of beauty as a biological adaptation that seeks healthy, fertile mates and makes us instinctively seek partners whose physical characteristics reflect this likelihood." Libr J

"Topics as wide-ranging as penis- or breast-enlargement surgery and the basics of haute couture are treated with wit and insight. Etcoff's arguments are certain to initiate a great deal of discussion." Publ Wkly

Includes bibliographical references

Peiss, Kathy Lee

Hope in a jar; the making of America's beauty culture. {by} Kathy Peiss. Metropolitan Bks. 1998 334p il hardcover o.p. pa $15.95 **391.6**

1. Cosmetics 2. Personal appearance

ISBN 0-8050-5551-7 pa

LC 97-42706

This is a "social history of the origin and development of the U.S. cosmetics industry. . . . An engrossing, highly readable book that should be welcomed by scholars and general readers alike." Libr J

Includes bibliographical references

392 Customs of life cycle and domestic life

Gollaher, David

Circumcision; a history of the world's most controversial surgery. [by] David L. Gollaher. Basic Bks. 2000 253p hardcover o.p. pa $18 **392**

1. Circumcision

ISBN 0-465-02653-2 pa

LC 99-40015

This history of circumcision discusses Jewish, Muslim, and tribal rituals, medical procedures and complications, reasons for the procedure, and its social significance in various cultures and eras

Jellison, Katherine

It's our day; America's love affair with the white wedding, 1945-2005. University Press of Kansas 2008 297p il (CultureAmerica) $29.95 **392**

1. Marriage customs and rites 2. United States -- Social life and customs

ISBN 978-0-7006-1559-9

LC 2007-35444

The author "takes an in-depth look at the history and popularity of the American 'white wedding' and in doing so provides a unique exploration of late 20th- and early 21st-century American culture. She starts right after World War II and progresses through celebrity, royal, and movie weddings to the 'reality weddings' of today and how the ritual of a white wedding has been adapted in many same-sex marriages. . . . An enlightening and fascinating read, her book is sure to be of interest in most libraries." Libr J

Includes bibliographical references

Mead, Rebecca

One perfect day; the selling of the American wedding. Penguin Press 2007 245p $25.95; pa $15 **392**

1. Weddings

ISBN 978-1-59420-088-5; 978-0-14-311384-3 pa

LC 2006-52461

This "critique of the contemporary wedding industry in the US looks at the commercialization of the marriage ceremony from a variety of angles—from the retail side to the ubiquitous wedding planner and in between." Choice

"Part investigative journalism, part social commentary, Mead's wry, insightful work offers an illuminating glimpse at the ugly underbelly of our Bridezilla culture." Publ Wkly

393 Death customs

Jokinen, Tom

Curtains; adventures of an undertaker-in-training. Da Capo Press 2010 279p pa $15.95 **393**

1. Undertakers and undertaking 2. Funeral rites and ceremonies

ISBN 978-0-306-81891-2; 0-306-81891-4

LC 2010-920629

"The narrative pinballs between the many roles Jokinen takes on within the industry—hearse driver, embalming assistant, theatrically solemn host who gestures at coat racks and restrooms. All the while, Jokinen dutifully remains the voice of the curious reader, channeling skepticism, the weirds and awe into laugh-out-loud observations grounded in just enough research to provide context without weighing down the plot." PopMatters

Kammen, Michael G.

Digging up the dead; a history of notable American reburials. [by] Michael Kammen. University of Chicago Press 2010 260p il $25 **393**

1. Burial 2. Exhumation 3. Funeral rites and ceremonies

ISBN 978-0-226-42329-6; 0-226-42329-8

LC 2009-23515

The author relates "stories of exhumation and reburial from throughout American history. Taking us to the contested grave sites of such figures as Sitting Bull, John Paul Jones, Frank Lloyd Wright, Daniel Boone, Jefferson Davis, and even Abraham Lincoln, Kammen explores how complicated interactions of regional pride, shifting reputations, and evolving burial practices led to public, often emotional battles over the final resting places of famous figures." Publisher's note

"Kammen has a good sense of the details that make historical stories memorable. His occasional flashes of humor add a winsome, professionally geeky element to the telling." Dallas Morning News

Includes bibliographical references

Pringle, Heather Anne

The **mummy** congress; science, obsession, and the everlasting dead. {by} Heather Pringle. Hyperion 2001 368p il hardcover o.p. pa $13.95 **393**

1. Mummies 2. Forensic anthropology

ISBN 0-7868-6551-2; 0-7868-8463-0 pa

LC 00-54487

"Besides outstanding members of the scientific association that gathers as the Mummy Congress, Pringle limns the many varieties of mummies, from the world's oldest, preserved by the high-altitude climate of the Andes, to modern Communist dictators, self-mummifying Buddhists, and the subjects of extreme cosmetic surgery. More astounding than all the fright flicks about shambling, gauze-wrapped menaces wound together." Booklist

Includes bibliographical references

394 General customs

Visser, Margaret

The **gift** of thanks; the roots and rituals of gratitude. Houghton Mifflin Harcourt 2009 458p $27 **394**

1. Gratitude

ISBN 978-0-15-101331-9

LC 2009-14018

First published 2008 in Canada

The author "examines the meaning of gratitude, using linguistic, sociological, religious, and other rubrics to consider such matters as why we wrap gifts, what we owe to our parents, and why Japanese speakers say 'I'm sorry' when English speakers would say 'Thank you.'" Libr J

"A book to be thankful for—sympathetic to human foible, deeply learned and a pleasure to read." Kirkus

Includes bibliographical references

394.1 Eating, drinking; using drugs

Anthony, Jason C.

Hoosh; roast penguin, scurvy day, and other stories of Antarctic cuisine. Jason C. Anthony. University of Nebraska Press 2012 286 p. (pbk. : alk. paper) $26.95 **394.1**

1. Food 2. Scientific expeditions 3. Antarctica -- Exploration 4. Food habits -- Antarctica 5. Outdoor cooking -- Antarctica 6. Antarctica -- History -- Anecdotes 7. Antarctica -- Social life and customs

ISBN 0803226667; 9780803226661

LC 2012011994

This book is "[Jason C.] Anthony's debut . . . [and] traces hardships during Antarctic expeditions and the sometimes disconcerting fare borne of isolation. From blubber to penguin meat, and on infamous occasions, sled dogs and horses, supplemented by canned foods as well as pemmican (a concentrated mixture of fat and protein, the 'perfect endurance food used by Native Americans for millennia'), polar cuisine has always had a storied history." (Kirkus)

Includes bibliographical references.

Collingham, E. M. (Elizabeth M.)

Curry; a tale of cooks and conquerors. Oxford University Press 2006 315p il maps $28   **394.1**

1. Eating customs 2. India -- Civilization
ISBN 978-0-19-517241-6; 0-19-517241-8

LC 2005-16641

This is a "history of Indian cuisine, ranging from the imperial kitchen of the Mughal invader Babur to the smoky cookhouse of the British Raj." Publisher's note

The author "with incredibly engrossing detail, unravels the tantalizing mystery of 'curry' in its innumerable forms, which have ravished the taste buds in far-flung kitchens and dining rooms." MultiCult Rev

Includes bibliographical references

Cowen, Tyler

An economist gets lunch; new rules for everyday foodies. Tyler Cowen. Dutton 2012 x, 293 p.p   **394.1**

1. Restaurants 2. Food industry and trade 3. Eating habits -- Economic aspects 4. Food habits -- Economic aspects 5. Food preferences -- Economic aspects
ISBN 0525952667; 9780525952664

LC 2011035174

In this book, economist Tyler Cowen "steers his audience through the contemporary world of eating and drinking. Like many staunch foodies, he respects the local. . . . Cowen finds that, despite what logic may suggest, the most expensive food is not necessarily the best. And he reveals that the same principle holds true in urban America as well as in the Third World. He expands this insight with a survey of barbecue restaurants in the U.S." (Booklist)

Includes bibliographical references and index

Fernandez-Armesto, Felipe

Near a thousand tables; a history of food. Free Press 2002 258p $25; pa $14   **394.1**

1. Food -- History
ISBN 0-7432-2644-5; 0-7432-2740-9 pa

LC 2002-23318

This is a "well-written, thought-provoking overview of food history." Libr J

Includes bibliographical references

Mayle, Peter

French lessons; adventures with knife, fork, and corkscrew. Knopf 2001 227p il $24; pa $12.95   **394.1**

1. Eating customs 2. France -- Social life and customs
ISBN 0-375-40590-9; 0-375-70561-9 pa

Mayle "relives some of his most precious moments reveling in the cuisine of his adopted homeland. . . . {He tells} savory, sensual, positively transporting stories about his encounters with Gallic gustatory delights and about his growing appreciation of the central place food occupies in French life." Booklist

McWilliams, James E.

Just food; where locavores get it wrong and how we can truly eat responsibly. Little, Brown and Company 2009 258p $25.99   **394.1**

1. Food industry 2. Natural foods 3. Eating customs
ISBN 978-0-316-03374-9

LC 2009-15514

The author "argues for moderation and compromise in today's raging food fights. Until recently, the author was a locavore—one who eats locally produced food. Though he still believes that it is a dietary commitment with many virtues, he argues that it's also a feeble, ineffective way to feed the world's hungry billions. . . . McWilliams presents some appealing alternatives to the views of both the agrarian romantics on the left and the agribusiness capitalists on the right. . . . Rich in research, provocative in conception and nettlesome to both the right and the left." Kirkus

Includes bibliographical references

Pollan, Michael

★ The omnivore's dilemma; a natural history of four meals. Penguin Press 2006 450p pa $16; $26.95   **394.1**

1. Eating customs 2. Agriculture -- United States 3. Food supply -- United States 4. Food consumption -- United States
ISBN 0-14-303858-3 pa; 1-59420-082-3

LC 2005-56557

"Pollan has divided The Omnivore's Dilemma into three parts, one for each of the food chains that sustain us: industrialized food, alternative or 'organic' food, and food people obtain by dint of their own hunting, gathering, or gardening. Pollan follows each food chain . . . from the ground up to the table, emphasizing our dynamic co-evolutionary relationship with the species we depend on. He concludes each section by sitting down to a meal—at McDonald's, at home with his family sharing a dinner from Whole Foods, and in a revolutionary 'beyond organic' farm in Virginia. For each meal he traces the provenance of everything consumed, [aiming to] and explain how our taste for particular foods reflects our environmental and biological inheritance." (Publisher's note)

The author "defines the Omnivore's Dilemma as the confusing maze of choices facing Americans trying to eat healthfully in a society that he calls 'notably unhealthy.' He seeks answers to this dilemma by taking readers through the industrial, organic, and hunter-gatherer stages of the food chain. . . . This folksy narrative provides a wealth of information about agriculture, the natural world, and human desires." Libr J

Includes bibliographical references

Schlosser, Eric

★ Fast food nation; the dark side of the all-American meal. Houghton Mifflin 2001 356p il $25   **394.1**

1. Restaurants 2. Food industry 3. Convenience foods
ISBN 0-395-97789-4

LC 00-53886

"Schlosser documents the effects of fast food on America's economy, its youth culture, and allied industries. . . . Starting with a young woman who makes minimum wage working at a Colorado fast-food restaurant, Schlosser relates the oft-told story of Ray Kroc's founding of McDonald's. The author also tells about the development of the franchise method of business ownership and the health and nutrition implications of fast-food consumption." Booklist

Includes bibliographical references

Standage, Tom

An **edible** history of humanity. Walker & Company 2009 269p il map $26 **394.1**

1. Food 2. Agriculture 3. Eating customs
ISBN 0-8027-1588-5; 978-0-8027-1588-3

LC 2009-5610

"Humanity's most basic need, along with water, is food. Earliest civilizations appeared on earth when farmers banded together and exploited their excess crops as a means of trade and currency. This allowed some people to abandon agriculture [leading to] organized communities and cities. Standage traces this ever-evolving story through Europe, Asia, and the Americas and casts human progress as an elaboration and refinement of this foundation. . . . Standage also uncovers the aspects of food distribution that underlay such historic events as the Napoleonic Wars and the fall of the Soviet empire." Booklist

"This meaty little volume [is] cogent, informative and insightful." Kirkus

Includes bibliographical references

A **history** of the world in 6 glasses. Walker & Co. 2005 311p il $25 **394.1**

1. Beverages 2. World history 3. Tea -- History 4. Coffee -- History 5. Beverages -- History 6. Drinking of alcoholic beverages -- History
ISBN 0-8027-1447-1

LC 2004-61209

Mr. Standage's "book divides world history into beer, wine, spirits, coffee, tea and Coca-Cola ages. . . . He begins with humanity's shift from hunting and gathering to agriculture. This transition led to the cultivation of grain, which led to storage and fermentation and, eventually, beer." (N Y Times (Late N Y Ed)) Index.

Standage "has the ability to connect the smallest detail to the big picture and a knack for summarizing vast concepts in a few sentences." Publ Wkly

Includes bibliographical references

United States. Works Progress Administration

The **food** of a younger land; a portrait of American food: before the national highway system, before chain restaurants, and before frozen food, when the nation's food was seasonal, regional, and traditional: from the lost WPA fil. edited and illustrated by Mark Kurlansky. Riverhead Books 2009 397p il $27.95 **394.1**

1. Cooking 2. Eating customs
ISBN 978-1-59448-865-8

LC 2009-8100

"In the late 1930s the WPA farmed out a writing project with the ambition of other New Deal programs: an encyclopedia of American food and food traditions from coast-to-coast similar to the federal travel guides. After Pearl Harbor, the war effort halted the project for good; the book was

never published, and the files were archived in the Library of Congress. . . . [The editor] brought the unassembled materials to light and created this version of the guide that never was. . . . This extraordinary collection—at once history, anthropology, cookbook, almanac and family album—provides a vivid and revitalizing sense of the rural and regional characteristics and distinctions that we've lost and can find again here." Publ Wkly

Includes bibliographical references

394.26   Holidays

Baker, James W.

Thanksgiving; the biography of an American holiday. foreword by Peter J. Gomes. University of New Hampshire Press 2009 273p il (Revisiting New England) pa $26.95 **394.26**

1. Thanksgiving Day
ISBN 978-1-58465-801-6

LC 2009-12348

The author shows "how Thanksgiving is seen through each generation's reality, having morphed from a holiday for pilgrim hats and turkeys to a cause for Native American protests to a holy day to several ancient holidays combined and a full-scale orgy of food and football. . . . [This is] an enjoyable, fascinating read both for students and for anyone looking for a good story." Libr J

Includes bibliographical references

Forbes, Bruce David

Christmas; a candid history. University of California Press 2007 179p il $19.95; pa $12.95 **394.26**

1. Christmas
ISBN 978-0-520-25104-5; 978-0-520-25802-0 pa

LC 2007-00366

The author "presents a brief social history of Christmas from pre-Christian winter celebrations to the commercialization of the holiday in American popular culture. The growth of the holiday to include Christmas cards, music and movies are included in this easy to read overview." Univ Press Books for Public and Second Sch Libr, 2008

Includes bibliographical references

Hillstrom, Laurie

The **Thanksgiving** book; [by] Laurie C. Hillstrom. Omnigraphics 2008 328p il $65 **394.26**

1. Thanksgiving Day
ISBN 978-0-7808-0403-6

LC 2007-25708

"This book is definitely a wonderful tribute to the holiday of Thanksgiving." Am Ref Books Annu, 2008

Includes bibliographical references

Holiday symbols and customs; 4th ed.; Omnigraphics 2009 1321p $94 **394.26**

1. Holidays 2. Festivals
ISBN 978-0-7808-0990-1

LC 2008-28403

First published 1998 with title: Holiday symbols

"Describes the origins of 323 holidays around the world. Explains where, when, and how each event is celebrated, with detailed information on the symbols and customs associated with the holiday. Includes contact information and web sites for related organizations." Publisher's note

Includes bibliographical references

Holidays, festivals, and celebrations of the world dictionary; detailing more than 3,000 observances from all 50 states and more than 100 nations: a compendious reference guide to popular, ethnic, religious, national, and ancient holidays. . . edited by Cherie D. Abbey. 4th ed.; Omnigraphics 2010 1323p $144   **394.26**
1. Reference books 2. Holidays -- Dictionaries 3. Festivals -- Dictionaries
ISBN 978-0-7808-0994-9

                 LC 2009-41138
First edition published 1994 compiled by Sue Ellen Thompson and Barbara W. Carlson

"A comprehensive dictionary that describes more than 3,000 holidays and festivals celebrated around the world. Features both secular and religious events from many different cultures, countries, and ethnic groups. Includes contact information for events; multiple appendices with background information on world holidays; extensive bibliography; multiple indexes." Publisher's note

Rajtar, Steve
United States holidays and observances; by date, jurisdiction, and subject, fully indexed. McFarland & Co. 2003 165p $45   **394.26**
1. Holidays 2. Festivals
ISBN 0-7864-1446-4

                LC 2002-154293
This "concentrates on observances and holidays established by statute in the U.S. and American Samoa, District of Columbia, Guam, the Northern Mariana Islands, Puerto Rico, and the U.S. Virgin Islands. In addition, UN-designated holidays are included. . . . The text is arranged by month, and chapters for each month are divided into 'Observances with Variable Dates' and 'Observances with Fixed Dates.' Each entry identifies the observance as federal or specific to a state and offers a description that ranges in length from three or four lines to a quarter page. . . . [This] would be a good addition to ready-reference desks in public libraries and information centers in schools." Booklist

394.264   Halloween

Morton, Lisa
Trick or Treat; A History of Halloween. Lisa Morton. University of Chicago Press 2012 229 p. (hardcover) $29   **394.264**
1. Halloween
ISBN 1780230478; 9781780230474

This book, by Lisa Morton, offers a history of Halloween. "The popularity of Halloween has spread around the globe to places as diverse as Russia, China, and Japan, but its association with death and the supernatural and its inevitable commercialization has made it one of our most misunderstood holidays. How did it become what it is today?

. . . Lisa Morton provides a thorough history of this spooky day." (Publisher's note)

395   Etiquette (Manners)

Baldrige, Letitia
Letitia Baldrige's new manners for new times; a complete guide to etiquette. illustrations by Denise Cavalieri Fike. Scribner 2003 xxvi, 709p il $35 **395**
1. Etiquette
ISBN 0-7432-1062-X

                 LC 2003-65666
First published 1990 with title: Letitia Baldrige's complete guide to the new manners for the 90's

"Combining correctness, consideration, and common sense in equal measure, Baldrige advises readers on proper ways to approach intricate situations. She addresses same-sex unions, pregnant brides, blended and extended families, and sexual harassment with aplomb." Libr J

Blyth, Catherine
The **art** of conversation; a guided tour of a neglected pleasure. Gotham Books 2009 289p $22.50   **395**
1. Conversation
ISBN 978-1-592-40419-3; 1-592-40419-7

                 LC 2008-24276
"Adopting a chatty, conversational manner to write about conversation, Blyth mixes personal anecdotes into a salmagundi of selected quotes from anthropology, history, literature, philosophy and pop culture to analyze and give advice on the dynamics of good conversation, not to mention the perfect riposte for every situation. She examines everything from small talk to pillow talk, from riotous raconteurs to crashing bores, from flattery to false smiles. . . . Witty, eloquent and insightful, Blyth's book is a delightful encouragement to rediscover conversation as the best communication technology." Publ Wkly

Dresser, Norine
Multicultural manners; essential rules of etiquette for the 21st century. Rev ed; John Wiley & Sons 2005 285p map pa $16.95   **395**
1. Etiquette 2. Manners and customs
ISBN 978-0-471-68428-2; 0-471-68428-7

                 LC 2004-27079
First published 1996

"From body language and table manners to classroom behavior and gift giving, this guide to etiquette provides fascinating information about relations in our multicultural society." Booklist

Includes bibliographical references

Forni, Pier Massimo
The **civility** solution; what to do when people are rude. [by] P.M. Forni. St. Martin's Press 2008 xxi, 166p $19.95   **395**
1. Courtesy 2. Etiquette
ISBN 978-0-312-36849-4; 0-312-36849-6

                 LC 2008-9448

"In Part 1 . . . [the author] describes some of the causes of rudeness (e.g., anger, fear, inflated self-worth) and the negative consequences of rude behavior in daily life. . . . In Part 2, Forni provides over 70 examples of situations in which rudeness arises and solutions for dealing with them. Readers who have been criticized in public or annoyed by a loud cell phone conversation get realistic help." Libr J

Includes bibliographical references

Martin, Judith, 1938-

Miss Manners' guide to excruciatingly correct behavior; illustrated by Gloria Kamen. freshly updated; Norton 2005 858p il $35   **395**
1. Etiquette
ISBN 0-393-05874-3
          LC 2005-00264
First published 1982 by Atheneum Pubs.
This book "covers such modern dilemmas as dealing with intrusive cell phones, handling guests who can't commit, and determining when e-mail is socially correct." Libr J
"Miss Manners is always as entertaining as she is civilized." Booklist

Morrison, Terri

★ **Kiss,** bow, or shake hands; the bestselling guide to doing business in more than 60 countries. [by] Terri Morrison and Wayne A. Conaway. 2nd ed.; Adams Media 2006 593p il pa $24.95   **395**
1. Negotiation 2. Business etiquette 3. Business communication
ISBN 1-59337-368-6
          LC 2006-13587
First published 1994
"Brief information regarding the history of the country, the type of government, languages, religions, and demographics are included. The authors then provide what they call a cultural orientation for each country, identifying 'cognitive styles, negotiation strategies, and value systems.' A summary of business practices (appointment scheduling, negotiating do's and don'ts, business entertaining, and time zone information) follows. Finally, 'protocol' considerations, such as greetings, titles and forms of address, gestures, gift giving, and appropriate dress, are offered." Booklist
"The definitive reference for doing business around the world." Libr J

Oliver, Vicky

301 smart answers to tough business etiquette questions. Skyhorse Pub. 2010 370p pa $12.95 **395**
1. Business etiquette
ISBN 978-1-61608-141-6; 1-61608-141-4
          LC 2010021474
This guide to business etiquette covers "making a good first impression (and how to fix a bad one!); how to behave in elevators, airplanes, and supply closets; surviving cabs, commutes, and coffee shops; why time is not necessarily money everywhere on the planet; pre-approved conversational topics from A to Z; dining rules and regulations for the twenty-first century; what to do when you are suddenly unemployed; [and] electronic communication." Publisher's note
Includes bibliographical references

Outcalt, Todd

Your beautiful wedding on any budget. Sourcebooks 2009 227p pa $12.99   **395**
1. Weddings
ISBN 978-1-4022-1788-3
          LC 2008-46864
"A terrific resource for couples trying to start their marriage on a financially sound footing. The Methodist pastor offers suggestions for building a wedding fund and creative cost-cutting measures based on his debt-free wedding seminars and blog." Libr J

Post, Peggy

Emily Post's Etiquette; 17th ed.; HarperCollins Publishers 2004 876p $39.95   **395**
1. Etiquette
ISBN 0-06-620957-9
          LC 2004-40508
First published 1922 under the authorship of Emily Post. Periodically revised and updated. Title varies. 11th-15th editions revised by Elizabeth Post; 16th-17th editions revised by Peggy Post
"The classic reference for which fork to use has been expanded to include such modern situations as dating, living together, second marriages, and co-ed business traveling." N Y Public Libr Book of How & Where to Look It Up

Emily Post's wedding etiquette; 5th ed.; HarperCollins 2006 xxiv, 405p il $27.95   **395**
1. Weddings 2. Etiquette 3. Marriage customs and rites
ISBN 978-0-06-074503-5; 0-06-074503-7
          LC 2005-40387
First published 1982 under the authorship of Emily Post with title: Emily Post's complete book of wedding etiquette
This guide to wedding planning covers such topics as multicultural and interfaith marriages, second marriages, engagements, prewedding events, postwedding duties, financial matters, working with consultants, and responsibilities of participants, and includes flow charts and ckecklists.

Vivaldo, Denise

Do it for le$$! weddings; how-to create your dream wedding without breaking the bank. Sellers Pub., Inc. 2008 272p il pa $19.95   **395**
1. Weddings
ISBN 978-1-4162-0519-7
          LC 2008-923779
The author "focuses on receptions—venues, logistics, and menus (including numerous recipes). Detailed information and instructive illustrations make this a solid choice for those catering their own affairs." Libr J
Includes bibliographical references

Weiss, Mindy

The **wedding** book; the big book for your big day. by Mindy Weiss with Lisbeth Levine. Workman Pub. Company, Inc. 2007 485p il $35; pa $19.95   **395**
1. Weddings
ISBN 978-0-7611-5094-7; 978-0-7611-3960-7 pa
          LC 2008-15510

This book offers wedding planning advice on topics such as announcing the wedding, setting up a budget, planning the ceremony, wedding parties, and designing the dress and tuxedo.

This "comprehensive, well-organized guide offers good details on contracts and setting priorities." Libr J

398 Folklore

Bane, Theresa

Encyclopedia of vampire mythology. McFarland & Company, Inc., Publishers 2010 199p $75 **398**
1. Reference books 2. Vampires -- Encyclopedias
ISBN 978-0-7864-4452-6

LC 2010-15576

The "introduction presents a survey of the vampire myth's historical roots and continued evolution. Subsequent entries, organized alphabetically by vampire name, include phonetic pronunciations and define the many tangible and intangible vampiric forms that hail from every continent around the globe. . . . A thorough resource for dark mythologists and vampire enthusiasts." Libr J

Includes bibliographical references

Encyclopedia of American folklife; Simon J. Bronner, editor. M.E. Sharpe 2006 4v il set $399 **398**
1. Reference books 2. Folklore -- United States -- Encyclopedias 3. United States -- Social life and customs -- Encyclopedias
ISBN 0-7656-8052-1; 978-0-7656-8052-5

LC 2005-32119

This encyclopedia "provides a survey of the cultural patterns and experiences of diverse communities throughout the United States and the territories of Guam, Samoa, and Puerto Rico as well as other countries and ethnic groups that have influenced American social practices. . . . The encyclopedia covers crafts, foods, architecture, remedies, customs, holidays, narratives, speech, and stereotypes, with an emphasis on contemporary practices." Libr J

Includes bibliographical references

Guiley, Rosemary Ellen

The encyclopedia of vampires & werewolves; foreword by Jeanne Keyes Youngson. 2nd ed; Facts On File 2011 430p il $85; pa $24.95 **398**
1. Reference books 2. Monsters -- Encyclopedias 3. Vampires -- Encyclopedias 4. Werewolves -- Encyclopedias
ISBN 978-0-8160-8179-0; 0-8160-8179-4; 978-0-8160-8180-6 pa; 0-8160-8180-8 pa; 978-1-4381-3632-5 ebook; 1-4381-3632-3 ebook

LC 2010034839

First published 2004 with title: The encyclopedia of vampires, werewolves, and other monsters

"Entries describe supposed true historical accounts, how vampires and werewolves come into existence, beliefs about vampires and werewolves, and real-life creatures and cases that may have inspired their legends. . . . Fictional vampires from a range of media are discussed, along with the people who helped create them." Publisher's note

Includes bibliographical references

Hurston, Zora Neale

Folklore, memoirs, and other writings. Library of Am. 1995 1001p il $35 **398**
ISBN 0-940450-84-4

LC 94-21384

Companion volume to Novels and stories (1995)

"This is the first time the unexpurgated version of Hurston's 1942 autobiography, Dust Tracks on the Road, is being published; sections deemed too provocative (dealing with politics, race, and sex) have been restored. Mules and Men (1935) is a collection of African American folklore she gleaned on travels in the South, while Tell My Horse (1938) tenders her personal findings on African-based religion in Jamaica and Haiti. Additionally, 22 magazine and book articles with anthropological themes . . . that have never been gathered into book form are corralled here." Booklist

Melton, J. Gordon

The vampire book; the encyclopedia of the undead. Completely revamped, fully rev. and expanded, 3rd ed.; Visible Ink Press 2010 909p il pa $29.95 **398**
1. Reference books 2. Vampires -- Encyclopedias
ISBN 978-1-57859-281-4

LC 2010-24263

First published 1994

"This vampire lore tome covers legends from around the world, both classical and current, presenting an overview of the historical, literary, mythological, biographical, and popular aspects of vampires. . . . This book is an excellent and comprehensive addition to any collection serving readers interested in learning more about the vampire in time, place, and society. Aficionados of vampires in popular culture will enjoy it." Libr J

Includes bibliographical references

Prahlad, Anand

The Greenwood encyclopedia of African American folklore; edited by Anand Prahlad. Greenwood Press 2005 xl, 1557p 3v il set $299.95 **398**
1. Reference books 2. African Americans -- Folklore -- Encyclopedias 3. African Americans -- Social life and customs -- Encyclopedias
ISBN 0-313-33035-2

LC 2005-19214

For a fuller review, see: Booklist, Feb. 1, 2006

"The three volume set gives special attention to music, art, folktales, spiritual beliefs, foodways, proverbs, and other topics central to African American folklore, and discusses the Caribbean and African roots of traditional African American culture." Libr Media Connect

Includes bibliographical references

World folklore for storytellers; tales of wonder, wisdom, fools, and heroes. Josepha Sherman, editor. Sharpe Reference 2010 368p il $95 **398**
1. Folklore 2. Storytelling
ISBN 978-0-7656-8174-4

LC 2009-10525

This is "a wonderfully wide-ranging collection of nearly 200 ethnically diverse folktales. Particularly vital is that the stories are organized thematically rather than geographically, allowing for broader symbolic and anthropological comparisons. Each narrative runs several pages, includes a brief explanatory introduction, and consistently concludes with at least two bibliographic references. Pockets of multipage color plates offer images from native folktale anthologies and other relevant artistic renderings." Libr J

Includes bibliographical references

398.2 Folk literature

Ackroyd, Peter

The **death** of King Arthur; Thomas Malory's Le morte d'Arthur. Sir Thomas Malory; a retelling by Peter Ackroyd. Viking 2011 316p $26.95   **398.2**
  1. Authors 2. Kings 3. Britons -- Fiction. 4. Great Britain -- Kings and rulers -- Fiction. 5. Knights and knighthood -- Great Britain -- Fiction.
  ISBN 978-0-670-02307-3; 0-670-02307-8
               LC 2011-21800

First published 2010 in the United Kingdom

"Ackroyd takes the daunting Middle English verse and retells the ancient legends in modern English prose. He also omits most of Malory's medieval tales as perhaps too creaky for modern minds, or maybe simply to make his retelling a niftier little book. All the essential stories are here, among them: Arthur lifting the great sword Excalibur from the stone to become king; the adulterous quarter-century-long love affair of Queen Guinevere and Arthur's most powerful and trusted knight, Lancelot du Lake; the love of Tristram and Isolte; Sir Galahad and the search for the Holy Grail; the awesome power of the wizard Merlin, the exquisite evil of Morgan le Fay, Arthur's half-sister, and finally the doom of Camelot and the death of Arthur at the hand of Sir Mordred, his own son born from an incestuous union of Arthur and Morgan le Fay. . . . Ackroyd tells these stories in such simple, vivid language that they seem as new as they must have when first heard around the peat fires of cold and gloomy England perhaps 1,000 years ago. And they're still a lot of fun." Dallas Morning News

Armstrong, Karen, 1944-

★ A **short** history of myth. Canongate 2005 159p hardcover o.p. pa $14   **398.2**
  1. Mythology
  ISBN 1-84195-716-X; 1-84195-800-X pa

This is an "overview of the ever-evolving partnership between myth and man from Paleolithic times to the present. Succinct and cleanly written, it is hugely readable and, in its journey across the epochs of human experience, often moving. . . . Armstrong's exposition is streamlined and uncluttered without being simplistic." N Y Times Book Rev

Includes bibliographical references

Asma, Stephen T.

On monsters; an unnatural history of our worst fears. Oxford University Press 2009 351p il $27.95   **398.2**
  1. Monsters
  ISBN 978-0-19-533616-0
              LC 2009-7219

The author "is insightful and entertaining in his discussion of monsters of the deep, supernatural doppelgangers, zombies, and vampires, and intense in his discussion of Freud and the science of monstrous feelings. . . . Asma's far-reaching book of monsterology is original, captivating, and profoundly elucidating." Booklist

Includes bibliographical references

Brunvand, Jan Harold

The **vanishing** hitchhiker; American urban legends and their meaning. Norton 1981 208p hardcover o.p. pa $13.95   **398.2**
  1. Legends -- United States 2. Folklore -- United States
  ISBN 0-393-95169-3 pa
              LC 81-4744

A collection of modern urban folktales with an ironic or supernatural twist. The author reports on how such tales are disseminated and discusses their inherent messages for contemporary society

Includes bibliographical references

Bulfinch, Thomas

★ **Bulfinch's** mythology; foreword by Alberto Manguel. Modern Library pbk. ed.; Modern Library 2004 862p pa $17.95   **398.2**
  1. Chivalry 2. Emperors 3. Mythology 4. Mabinogion 5. Folklore -- Europe
  ISBN 0-375-75147-5
             LC 2005-271850

First combined edition published 1913 by Crowell. Originally published in three separate volumes 1855, 1858 and 1862 respectively

"The classic work on mythology, Bulfinch's gives brief summations of Greek, Roman, Norse, Arthurian, and other miscellaneous myths and includes notes on the 'Iliad,' the 'Odyssey,' and the 'Aeneid.'" N Y Public Libr Book of How & Where to Look It Up

Includes bibliographical references

Favorite folktales from around the world; edited by Jane Yolen. Pantheon Bks. 1986 498p hardcover o.p. pa $18   **398.2**
  1. Folklore 2. Fairy tales
  ISBN 0-394-75188-4 pa
              LC 86-42644

"Selections include tales from the American Indians, the brothers Grimm, Italo Calvino's Italian folk-tales, as well as stories from Iceland, Afghanistan, Scotland, and many other countries. Yolen provides each section with a relevant introduction, often including historical and literary factors, thus alerting readers as to what to look for." SLJ

The **Greenwood** encyclopedia of folktales and fairy tales; edited by Donald Haase. Greenwood Press 2008 3v il set $299.95   **398.2**
  1. Reference books 2. Folklore -- Encyclopedias 3. Fairy tales -- Encyclopedias
  ISBN 978-0-313-33441-2
              LC 2007-31698

"Meticulously documented and firmly grounded in scholarly research, most articles feature straightforward language and sufficient background material to be accessible to lay readers and novice researchers." Booklist

Includes bibliographical references

Lavers, Chris

The **natural** history of unicorns. William Morrow 2009 258p il $26.99 **398.2**

1. Unicorns

ISBN 978-0-06-087414-8; 0-06-087414-7

First published 2008 in the United Kingdom

This "is an erudite, scholarly book which uses the unicorn to illuminate millennia of social and geographical change. Unicorns appear in many guises in many cultures. . . . Lavers's achievement is to show how each of these is a chimera based on startlingly accurate reports of real animals, carried over trade routes. . . . Lavers's book offers revelations not only about mythical creatures, but about the extent and effects of globalisation in ancient times. It's eminently readable, too." New Sci

Includes bibliographical references p. 245-248)

Malory, Thomas Sir, 15th cent

Le morte Darthur, or, The hoole book of Kyng Arthur and of his noble knyghtes of the Rounde Table; authoritative text, sources and backgrounds, criticism. [by] Sir Thomas Malory; edited by Stephen H.A. Shepherd. Norton 2004 lii, 954p (A Norton critical edition) pa $16.95 **398.2**

1. Kings

ISBN 0-393-97464-2

LC 2002-26534

Originally published 1485

"The work is a skillful selection and blending of materials taken from the mass of Arthurian legends. The central story consists of two main elements: the reign of King Arthur ending in catastrophe and the dissolution of the Round Table; and the quest of the Holy Grail." Oxford Companion to Engl Lit

Includes bibliographical references

Orenstein, Catherine

Little Red Riding Hood uncloaked; sex, morality, and the evolution of a fairy tale. Basic Bks. 2002 289p il hardcover o.p. pa $14.95 **398.2**

1. Little Red Riding Hood

ISBN 0-465-04126-4 pa; 0-465-04125-6

LC 2002-4240

"Once upon a time, Red Riding Hood was a good little girl. When she foolishly strayed from the path in the forest and spoke to strangers, she fell prey to the wicked wolf, but fortunately, the heroic woodcutter rescued her just in time. . . . With wit and insight, Orenstein makes us look again at the old childhood story, how it has changed and what that says about us. From Perrault and the Brothers Grimm to Bruno Bettelheim and Andrea Dworkin, the lively informal narrative surveys the stories and the scholarship in terms of folklore, psychology, feminism, and pornography." Booklist

Includes bibliographical references

Sir Gawain and the Green Knight; a new verse translation. [translated by] Simon Armitage. W.

W. Norton & Company 2007 198p $25.95; pa $14.95 **398.2**

1. Arthurian romances 2. Poetry -- By individual authors

ISBN 978-0-393-06048-5; 0-393-06048-9; 978-0-393-33415-9 pa; 0-393-33415-5 pa

LC 2007-28520

Armitage "clearly feels a special kinship with the Gawain poet. He captures his dialect and his landscape and takes great pains to render the tale's alliterative texture and drive. . . . His vernacular translation isn't literal—sometimes he alliterates different letters, sometimes he foreshortens the number of alliterations in a line, sometimes he changes lines altogether and so forth—but his imitation is rich and various and recreates the gnarled verbal texture of the Middle English original, which is presented in a parallel text." N Y Times Book Rev

398.208 Folk literature--Groups of people

Encyclopedia of Jewish folklore and traditions; Raphael Patai, founding editor ; Haya Bar-Itzhak, editor. M.E. Sharpe 2012 44 p. (hardcover : alk. paper) $299 **398.208**

1. Jewish folk literature 2. Judaism -- Encyclopedias 3. Folklore -- Encyclopedias 4. Jews -- Folklore -- Encyclopedias 5. Jews -- Social life and customs -- Encyclopedias

ISBN 0765620251; 9780765620255

LC 2012042203

"This encyclopedia covers the long and multifarious history of Jewish folklore and customs from the Bible to bagels. . . . The eclectic content covers holidays (Purim), material artifacts (illuminated manuscripts), and mythical beliefs (Dybbuk) and offers country studies (Afghanistan, Iran) and biographies of notable Jewish ethnographers." (Library Journal)

Includes bibliographical references and index

398.209 Folk literature--History, geographic treatment, biography

Wroe, Ann

Orpheus; the song of life. Ann Wroe. Overlook 2012 262 p. Hardcover $26.95 **398.209**

1. Greek mythology 2. Cross-cultural studies 3. Literature -- History and criticism 4. Orpheus (Greek mythology) 5. Orpheus (Greek mythology) in literature

ISBN 0224091360; 1590207785; 9780224091367; 9781590207789

LC 2011508687

This book by Ann Wroe "traces the obscure origins and tangled relationships of the Orpheus myth from ancient times through today." (Library Journal). After tracing "his adventures with Jason and the Argonauts, his eternal love of Eurydice and interminable mourning for her and descent into Hades . . . the author recounts the influence of Orpheus on a veritable pantheon of writers and musicians, including Ovid, Virgil, Milton, Shelley, Keats, Cocteau and a host of others." (Kirkus Reviews)

Zipes, Jack

The **irresistible** fairy tale; the cultural and social history of a genre. Jack Zipes. Princeton University Press 2012 xvii, 235 p.p (hardcover : alk. paper) $29.95 **398.209**

1. Fairy tales 2. Fairy tales -- Social aspects 3. Fairy tales -- History and criticism

ISBN 0691153388; 9780691153384

LC 2011040188

This book, by Jack Zipes, presents "a provocative new theory about why fairy tales were created and retold--and why they became such an indelible and infinitely adaptable part of cultures around the world. . . . Zipes presents a nuanced argument about how fairy tales originated in ancient oral cultures, how they evolved through the rise of literary culture and print, and how, in our own time, they continue to change through their adaptation in an ever-growing variety of media." (Publisher's note)

Includes bibliographical references and index.

398.8   Rhymes and rhyming games

The **Oxford** dictionary of nursery rhymes; edited by Iona and Peter Opie. 2nd ed; Oxford Univ. Press 1997 xxix, 559p il $55 **398.8**

1. Reference books 2. Nursery rhymes -- Dictionaries

ISBN 0-19-860088-7

LC 98-140995

First published 1951

An anthology of "over 500 rhymes, songs, nonsense jingles, and lullabies. . . . Complementing the rhymes are nearly a hundred illustrations, including reproductions of early art found in ballad sheets and music books, which highlight the development of children's illustrations over the last two centuries. . . . [The editors note] the earliest known publications of the rhyme, describing how it originated, illustrating changes in wording over time, and indicating variations and parallels in other languages." Publisher's note

"The novice as well as the professional will find it an enjoyable read, as well as a learning experience." Am Ref Books Annu, 1999

398.9   Proverbs

Manser, Martin H.

The **Facts** on File dictionary of proverbs; associate editors, Rosalind Fergusson, David Pickering. 2nd ed.; Facts On File 2006 499p (Facts on File library of language and literature) $55; pa $19.95 **398.9**

1. Proverbs

ISBN 0-8160-6673-6; 978-0-8160-6673-5; 0-8160-6674-4 pa; 978-0-8160-6674-2 pa

LC 2006-24535

Original edition published 1983 compiled by Rosalind Fergusson

This dictionary "includes more than 1,700 English-language proverbs . . . that are widely recognized today. Arranged alphabetically, entries provide the meaning of each proverb, the date it was first recorded, variant forms of the proverb, other proverbs that are similar and opposite to it in meaning, and examples of the proverb's use." Publisher's note

Includes bibliographical references

400   LANGUAGE

400   Language

Crystal, David

★ The **Cambridge** encyclopedia of language; 3rd ed; Cambridge University Press 2010 516p il map $99; pa $45 **400**

1. Reference books 2. Language and languages -- Encyclopedias

ISBN 978-0-521-51698-3; 978-0-521-73650-3 pa

LC 2010-502889

First published 1987

"A valuable and concise . . . handbook for linguistic beginners, linguistic researchers looking for a quick overview and, most of all, the general reader interested in language." Linguist List

Includes bibliographical references

Everett, Daniel L.

Language; the cultural tool. Daniel L. Everett. Pantheon Books 2012 351 p. ill. $27.95 **400**

1. Intellect 2. Communication 3. Sociolinguistics 4. Language and culture

ISBN 0307378535; 9780307378538

LC 2011034829

This book looks at whether language is "a genetically programmed instinct or something we pick up from the culture around us . . . . Challenging Noam Chomsky, Steven Pinker, and other partisans of 'nativism,' which holds that certain kinds of knowledge are hard-wired into us . . . , linguist [Daniel L. Everett . . . argues that language is a practical tool for communicating and social bonding . . . that children learn through general intelligence." (Publishers Weekly)

"Everett unfolds a compelling analysis of how language informs all the activities we recognize as distinctively human. A linguistic study certain to attract many general readers." Booklist

Includes bibliographical references (p. [334]-337) and index

Kenneally, Christine

The **first** word; the search for the origins of language. Viking 2007 357p $26.95 **400**

1. Evolution 2. Language and languages

ISBN 978-0-670-03490-1; 0-670-03490-8

LC 2007-3182

The author "explains difficult ideas concisely and clearly, and she maintains a firm grip on the steering wheel, moving the overall argument along in a straight line. Above all, she is scrupulously fair-minded." N Y Times (Late N Y Ed)

Includes bibliographical references

Pinker, Steven

The **language** instinct; how the mind creates language. Harper Perennial 2007 526p il pa $15.95   **400**

1. Language and languages
ISBN 978-0-06-133646-1; 0-06-133646-7
First published 1994 by Morrow

The author "argues that an 'innate grammatical machinery of the brain' exists, which allows children to 'reinvent' language on their own. Basing his ideas on Noam Chomsky's Universal Grammar theory, Pinker describes language as a 'discrete combinatorial system' that might easily have evolved via natural selection. Pinker steps on a few toes . . . but his work, while controversial, is well argued, challenging, often humorous, and always fascinating." Libr J

Includes bibliographical references

401   Philosophy and theory

Crystal, David

★ **How** language works; how babies babble, words change meaning, and languages live or die. Overlook Press 2006 500p $32.50   **401**

1. Linguistics 2. Language and languages
ISBN 1-58567-848-1

Crystal "offers an impeccably organized guide to language and communication that brings clarity to a scholarly subject, and is sure to become a standard reference." Publ Wkly

Includes bibliographical references

Pinker, Steven

The **stuff** of thought; language as a window into human nature. Viking 2007 499p il $29.95   **401**

1. Thought and thinking 2. Language and languages
ISBN 978-0-670-06327-7; 0-670-06327-4

LC 2007-26601

Pinker argues that "the reason language works is that it reflects the world as we jointly experience it. That doesn't mean we always use language to convey reality. Language is a social medium with social purposes. Sometimes, we use it not to communicate facts about the world but to filter them." N Y Times Book Rev

The author's "vivid prose and down-to-earth attitude will once again attract an enthusiastic audience outside academia." Publ Wkly

Includes bibliographical references

Words and rules; the ingredients of language. Perennial 2000 349p il pa $15   **401**

1. Grammar 2. Language and languages
ISBN 978-0-06-095840-4; 0-06-095840-5
First published 1999 by Basic Books

Pinker "studies how the mind works by examining the nature of language. In 'Words and Rules,' he examines irregularities, especially irregular verbs and plurals, from the points of view of biology, child development, psychology, philology, and linguistics." Christ Sci Monit

This book "with its crisp prose and neat analogies, makes required reading for anyone interested in cognition and language." Publ Wkly

Includes bibliographical references

Yang, Charles

★ The **infinite** gift; how children learn and unlearn the languages of the world. Scribner 2006 275p il $25   **401**

1. Language and languages
ISBN 978-0-7432-3756-7; 0-7432-3756-0

The author explains the "process by which children acquire language. He discusses everything from the sounds they hear in the womb to how they distinguish between different languages at three months to their mastery of their language by age five. Throughout this learning process, posits Yang, a child has tested the grammar and sounds that exist in many other languages (and would presumably have no trouble acquiring them) but ultimately settles on the relevant one, and soon after, can no longer distinguish between or articulate nonrelevant sounds. . . . Anyone with the slightest interest in the English language should read his book." Libr J

410   Linguistics

Crystal, David

★ A **dictionary** of language; 2nd ed; University of Chicago Press 2001 390p il pa $17.50   **410**

1. Reference books 2. Language and languages -- Dictionaries
ISBN 0-226-12203-4

LC 00-69076

First published 1992 with title: An encyclopedic dictionary of language and languages; present edition first published in the United Kingdom with title: The Penguin dictionary of language

This dictionary "offers explanations of the most frequently used linguistic terms, particularly those that can occur in texts read by beginners and by interested laypersons. . . . There are also entries concerned with graphology, shorthand writing, and similar peripheral, but interesting, topics. The impression that this dictionary has been written mainly for the general public is enhanced by the humorous jocose caricatures interspersed throughout the text, but the information is still solid. The author has succeeded in creating a handy dictionary that will serve students and laypeople equally well, for both browsing and study." Am Ref Book Annu, 2002

★ **Language** and the internet; 2nd ed.; Cambridge University Press 2006 304p $29.99   **410**

1. Internet 2. Language and languages
ISBN 978-0-521-86859-4; 0-521-86859-9

LC 2006-12916

First published 2001

"Covering a range of Internet genres, including e-mail, chat, and the Web, this is . . . [an] account of how the Internet is radically changing the way we use language." Publisher's note

Includes bibliographical references

Deutscher, Guy
Through the language glass; why the world looks different in other languages. Metropolitan Books / Henry Holt and Co. 2010 304p il $28; ebook $14.99 **410**
1. Linguistics 2. Language and languages
ISBN 978-0-8050-8195-4; 978-1-4299-7011-2 ebook
LC 2010-1042
Deutscher "combines erudition, wry humor, and serious interpretation in this elegant and charmingly accessible study of the relation among language, culture, and thought and of how we have engaged in and reflected upon language over the years." Libr J
Includes bibliographical references

411 Writing systems of standard forms of languages

Houston, Keith
Shady characters; the secret life of punctuation, symbols, & other typographical marks. Keith Houston. W W Norton & Co Inc 2013 352 p. $25.95 **411**
1. Typography 2. Punctuation 3. Writing -- History 4. Punctuation -- History 5. Signs and symbols -- History 6. Type and type-founding -- History
ISBN 0393064425; 9780393064421
LC 2013017324
This book is a "bestiary of lesser-known punctuation marks. . . . Nearly every punctuation symbol in this book gained its start from the annotation marks of monks, scribes, or scholars. (The chapter on daggers and asterisks, of course, uses those symbols to mark the asides.) Some game-changers, like the sudden confines of the typing press or the yet-more-restrictive typewriter, extend their influence across numerous chapters." (Publishers Weekly)
Includes bibliographical references and index

418 Standard usage (Prescriptive linguistics)

Dehaene, Stanislas
Reading in the brain; the science and evolution of a cultural invention. Viking 2009 388p il $27.95 **418**
1. Reading
ISBN 978-0-670-02110-9; 0-670-02110-5
LC 2009-09389
The author "explains what scientists now know about how the human brain performs the feat of reading, and what made this astonishing cultural invention biologically possible." Washington Post Book World
"Dense with ideas and experiments, but richly rewarding for readers willing to put in the effort." Kirkus
Includes bibliographical references

Grossman, Edith
Why translation matters. Yale University Press 2010 135p (Why X matters) **418**
1. Translating and interpreting 2. Literature --

Translations
ISBN 0-300-12656-5; 978-0-300-12656-3
LC 2009-26510
Grossman "argues for the cultural importance of translation and a more encompassing and nuanced appreciation of the translator's role." (Publisher's note) Index.
"In the end, Grossman warmly (after all) and gratefully rehearses the twofold answer to the question of her title: translation matters because it is an expression and an extension of our humanity, the secret metaphor of all literary communication; and because the creation of any literary translation is (or at least must be) an original writing, not a pathetic shadow or tracing of the inaccessible 'original' but the creation, indeed, of a second — and as we have seen, a third and a ninth — but always a new work, in another language." N Y Times Book Rev
Includes bibliographical references

419 Sign languages

Chambers, Diane P.
Communicating in sign; creative ways to learn American Sign Language (ASL) written by Diane P. Chambers, with Lee Ann Chearney; edited by D. Keith Robertson; illustrations by Paul M. Setzer; with an introduction by Bernard Bragg. Fireside 1998 165p il (Flying hands book) pa $12 **419**
1. Sign language
ISBN 0-684-83520-7
LC 97-51145
"By combining vocabulary, grammar, syntax, expression, and movement with commentary on etiquette and other cultural issues, Chambers . . . has created a general resource intended for the lay public." Libr J
Includes bibliographical references

Costello, Elaine
Random House Webster's American Sign Language dictionary: unabridged. Random House Reference 2008 xxxii, 1200p $55 **419**
1. Reference books 2. Sign language -- Dictionaries
ISBN 978-0-375-42616-2; 0-375-42616-7
First published 1994 with title: Random House American Sign Language dictionary
This dictionary includes "over 5,600 signs for the novice and experienced user alike. It includes complete descriptions of each sign, plus full-torso illustrations. There is also a subject index for easy reference as well as alternate signs for the same meaning." Publisher's note

Gallaudet University
★ The Gallaudet dictionary of American Sign Language; Clayton Valli, editor in chief; illustrated by Peggy Swartzel Lott, Daniel Renner, and Rob Hills. Gallaudet University Press 2005 xli, 558p il $49.95 **419**
1. Reference books 2. Sign language -- Dictionaries
ISBN 1-56368-282-6; 978-1-56368-282-7
LC 2005-51129

"This is a very valuable language resource for parents, students, and teachers learning ASL as a first language and as a second language." Choice

Includes bibliographical references

Grayson, Gabriel

Talking with your hands, listening with your eyes; a complete photographic guide to American Sign Language. Square One Pubs. 2002 373p il pa $26.95 **419**

1. Sign language

ISBN 0-7570-0007-X

LC 2002-1125

"The book covers more than 900 signs that represent nearly 1,800 words and phrases, with signs grouped by topic. . . . Grayson provides instructions for each word, explaining the hand shape, the position in front of the body where the sign is made and the type of movement involved in expressing the word." Publ Wkly

"An outstanding, user-friendly resource for those interested in learning ASL." SLJ

Sternberg, Martin L. A.

American Sign Language; a comprehensive dictionary. illustrated by Herbert Rogoff. Unabridged; HarperCollins Pubs. 1998 xxi, 983p il $60; pa $24 **419**

1. Reference books 2. Sign language -- Dictionaries

ISBN 0-06-271608-5; 0-06-273634-5 pa

LC 98-26649

First published 1981

Arranged alphabetically, this dictionary features 7,000 sign entries, with cross-references and more than 12,000 illustrations

Includes bibliographical references

Tennant, Richard A.

The **American** Sign Language handshape dictionary; {by} Richard A. Tennant, Marianne Gluszak Brown; illustrated by Valerie Nelson-Metlay. Gallaudet Univ. Press 1998 407p il $39.95 **419**

1. Sign language

ISBN 1-56368-043-2

LC 97-48389

This work organizes "signs by handshape rather than alphabetically by English word order. In so doing, it acts best as a recognition tool for the ASL learner, leading the user quickly to specific signs without having first to refer to an English-equivalent word." Libr J

420   Specific languages

Bragg, Melvyn

The **adventure** of English; the biography of a language. Arcade Pub. 2004 322p il $27.95 **420**

1. English language -- History

ISBN 1-55970-710-0

LC 2003-19583

First published 2003 in the United Kingdom

The author offers a "biography of the English language, highlighting key individuals, places, and literature that advanced it, as well as the political and social trends that influenced it. . . . Bragg discusses its evolution in the English colonies, devoting four chapters to the United States and one each to India, the West Indies, and Australia. . . . Well researched yet more accessible to a wide audience than scholarly treatments by linguists or historians." Libr J

Bryson, Bill

Made in America; an informal history of the English language in the United States. Avon Books 1996 417p pa $14.95 **420**

1. Americanisms 2. English language -- History

ISBN 978-0-380-71381-3; 0-380-71381-0

First published 1994 by Morrow

"For Bryson's wonderfully sane and reasoned discussion of the issues surrounding 'politically correct' language alone, this book is a worthwhile read." Libr J

Includes bibliographical references

Crystal, David

★ The **Cambridge** encyclopedia of the English language; 2nd ed; Cambridge Univ. Press 2003 499p il hardcover o.p. pa $35 **420**

1. English language

ISBN 0-521-82348-X; 0-521-53033-4 pa

LC 2003-272259

First published 1995

This "volume is divided into six broad topics that cover the English language's history, vocabulary, grammar, writing and speech systems, usage, and acquisition. Within these major topics, the book is divided into logical subtopics and finally into the basic unit of the text—the two-page spread. . . . The clear and spirited text is stunning, enhanced with over 500 illustrations, making this a particularly rich reference work and a browser's dream." Libr J {review of 1995 edition}

★ **English** as a global language; 2nd ed; Cambridge Univ. Press 2003 212p il maps $45; pa $15 **420**

1. English language -- Social aspects

ISBN 0-521-82347-1; 0-521-53032-6 pa

LC 2003-282119

First published 1997

Crystal's "account of the rise of English as a global language explores the history, current status and potential of English as the international language of communication. {Includes} sections on the future of English as a world language, English on the Internet, and the possibility of an English 'family' of languages." Publisher's note

"This is a fascinating and useful book. . . . a fine introduction for a wide variety of potential users." Choice

Includes bibliographical references

Hitchings, Henry

The **language** wars; a history of proper English. Farrar, Straus and Giroux 2011 408p $28 **420**

1. English language -- Usage 2. English language --

History
ISBN 978-0-374-18329-5; 0-374-18329-5

LC 2011-10701

"As the author points out, there is probably not a person alive who does not have some bee in his bonnet about the way other people speak and write. Maybe it is the errant apostrophe, the splitting of the poor old infinitive, or the use of 'like' as a comma. Or perhaps it is the exclamation mark, once known as the 'shriek mark'. Mr Hitchings's book is a corrective to some of these linguistic prejudices. It is bracing to learn, for example, that the prohibition on splitting the infinitive is fairly recent. Pre-Victorians did not object. Chaucer was a splitter, and even Shakespeare had a go. Same story with the apostrophe: in the 18th-century authors were sprinkling apostrophes over everything. . . . Mr Hitchings reviews such matters with cool erudition. He is resolutely relaxed about usage, understanding that correctitude and intelligibility are not the same." Economist

Includes bibliographical references

McCrum, Robert
★ The **story** of English; [by] Robert McCrum, Willam Cran [and] Robert MacNeil. 3rd rev ed; Penguin Bks. 2003 xxi, 468p pa $16 **420**
1. English language -- History
ISBN 0-14-200231-3

LC 2002-29818

First published 1986 by Viking
A "companion to the PBS television series of the same name. . . . The text covers the history of our language from its roots in Latin through its transplanting to other shores and its infusions from other cultures and languages. . . . Good for browsing, this book is a must for word and history buffs." SLJ [review of 1986 edition]

Includes bibliographical references

Metcalf, Allan A.
Predicting new words; the secrets of their success. {by} Allan Metcalf. Houghton Mifflin 2002 206p il $22 **420**
1. New words 2. English language -- Terms and phrases
ISBN 0-618-13006-3

LC 2002-68593

This book traces the origins of an "array of words and phrases: Marlboro Man, Frankenfood, blurb, skycap, quark, scofflaw. It also introduces us to a fascinating array of would-be words, coinages that never quite caught on. . . . The book is jam-packed with treats for word lovers." Booklist

421 Writing system, phonology, phonetics of standard English

★ **Acronyms**, initialisms, & abbreviations dictionary; 40th ed; Gale Res. 2008 4v set $1,190 **421**
1. Reference books 2. Acronyms -- Dictionaries
ISBN 978-1-4144-1902-2; 1-4144-1902-3

First published 1960 in one volume with title: Acronyms dictionary. Frequently revised

A guide to acronyms, initialisms, abbreviations, contractions, alphabetic symbols, and similar condensed apellations

Stahl, Dean
★ **Abbreviations** dictionary; {by} Dean Stahl, Karen Kerchelich; originated by Ralph De Sola. 10th ed; CRC Press 2001 1529p $79.95 **421**
1. Reference books 2. Signs and symbols 3. Abbreviations -- Dictionaries
ISBN 0-8493-9003-6

LC 00-58549

First published 1958 under the authorship of Ralph De Sola
"The classic status of this title endures: abbreviations are again joined by a dazzling array of acronyms, contractions, initials, nicknames, short forms, signs, and symbols. Its 15,000 new terms swell the dictionary to nearly 300,000 entries. Domestic and international terms are harvested from diverse fields, criminology to music. Computing, technology, and government draw special attention due to active abbreviating. Entries are alphabetically and numerically ordered." Choice

Truss, Lynne
Eats, shoots & leaves; the zero tolerance approach to punctuation. Gotham Books 2004 xxvii, 209p $19.95; pa $12 **421**
1. Punctuation
ISBN 1-59240-087-6; 1-59240-203-8 pa

LC 2004-40646

First published 2003 in the United Kingdom
The author "dissects common errors that grammar mavens have long deplored (often, as she readily points out, in isolation) and makes . . . arguments for increased attention to punctuation correctness. . . . Truss serves up delightful, unabashedly strict and sometimes snobby little book, with cheery Britishisms ('Lawks-a-mussy!') dotting pages that express a more international righteous indignation." Publ Wkly

Includes bibliographical references

421.52 Spelling (Orthography) and pronunciation

Crystal, David
Spell It Out; The Curious, Enthralling and Extraordinary Story of English Spelling. David Crystal. St. Martin's Press 2013 336 p. $22.99 **421.52**
1. English language -- Spelling 2. English language -- Orthography and spelling 3. English language -- Orthography and spelling -- History
ISBN 1250003474; 9781250003478

LC 2013010521

In this book author David Crystal "takes readers on a history of English spelling, starting with the Roman missionaries' sixth century introduction of the Roman alphabet and ending with where the language might be going. He looks individually at each letter in the alphabet and its origins. He considers the question of vowels and how people developed a way to tell whether or not it was long or short. He looks at influences from other cultures." (Publisher's note)

422   Etymology of standard English

Adonis to Zorro; Oxford dictionary of reference and allusion. edited by Andrew Delahunty and Sheila Dignen. 3rd ed.; Oxford University Press 2010 406p $34.95   **422**
1. Allusions 2. Reference books
ISBN 978-0-19-956745-4; 0-19-956745-X
LC 2010-549367
First published 2001 with title: The Oxford dictionary of allusions

"This guide to allusions and common references is a moderately priced volume well worth adding to a public, school, community college, or college shelf. Neat and user-friendly, the 1,900 entries, their provenance, definitions, models, and starred cross-references identify a range of familiar terms, from 'Terminator' to 'hobbit,' and from 'My Lai' to the 'sword of Damocles' and 'thirty pieces of silver.' The text makes clever use of fonts, dingbats, and point count to identify authors, sources, and dates." Choice

Barnhart, Robert K.

★ The **Barnhart** dictionary of etymology; Robert K. Barnhart, editor; Sol Steinmetz, managing editor. Wilson, H.W. 1988 xxvii, 1284p $115   **422**
1. Reference books 2. English language -- Etymology
ISBN 0-8242-0745-9
LC 87-27994
This etymological dictionary of current American English "contains some 30,000 entries. Each entry includes spelling variations, pronunciation, . . . part of speech, a short definition, date of first recorded use in English (with original spelling), and information on the language(s) from which the word evolved. . . . The Dictionary includes scientific and technical terms (echovirus, mutagen), regional vocabulary (lagniappe, hoosier), product names (nylon, Xerox), slang (nerd, jeepers creepers), as well as words of recent origin (yuppie, Medicare). Words that originated in the U.S. or are now commonly used only in the U.S. are labeled as American English. The Dictionary also includes a short history of the English language, a glossary of language names and linguistic terms, and a glossary of pre-1600 literary works cited in entries." (Booklist) Bibliography.

This dictionary "focuses on words used in contemporary American English and words of American origin and incorporates current American scholarship. Entries give spelling variations, pronunciation for difficult words, part of speech, definition, and information on word origins. Written for a wide audience, this is a very attractive, readable work suited for most library users." Ref Sources for Small & Medium-sized Libr. 6th edition

Crystal, David

The **story** of English in 100 words; David Crystal. St. Martin's Press 2012 260 p.   **422**
1. Vocabulary 2. English language -- History 3. English language -- Etymology 4. English language -- Foreign words and phrases 5. English language -- Foreign elements
ISBN 9781250003461; 9781466805088
LC 2012003038

This book presents "information about how English grows, changes, adopts and plays. . . . The author . . . teach[es] 100 lessons about English by picking out 100 words from our history, telling us their origin story and showing us how they've changed and spawned. Roughly chronological-beginning in the fifth century, ending in the 21st-[David] Crystal's text begins with what may be the first written word in our language, raihan, the word for roe-deer, and ends with something awfully recent, twittersphere. In between are not just the stories of individual words but the stories of how words become words. Why do we sometimes spell yogurt with an -h? Has there always been a difference between disinterested and uninterested? Why do only poets use certain words like swain?" (Kirkus)

Forsyth, Mark

The **etymologicon**; a circular stroll through the hidden connections of the English language. Mark Forsyth. Berkley Books 2012 XVIII, 252 p.p $16   **422**
1. English language -- Etymology
ISBN 0425260798; 9780425260791; 9781848313071
LC 2011535421
This book by Mark Forsyth presents a "guide to the strange underpinnings of the English language. It explains: how you get from 'gruntled' to 'disgruntled'; why you are absolutely right to believe that your meager salary barely covers 'money for salt'; how the biggest chain of coffee shops in the world (hint: Seattle) connects to whaling in Nantucket; and what precisely the Rolling Stones have to do with gardening." (Publisher's note)

★ **From** bonbon to cha-cha; Oxford dictionary of foreign words and phrases. edited by Andrew Delahunty. 2nd ed; Oxford University Press 2008 411p $24.95; pa $18.99   **422**
1. Reference books 2. English language -- Foreign words and phrases -- Dictionaries
ISBN 978-0-19-954369-4; 0-19-954369-0; 978-0-19-954368-7 pa; 0-19-954368-2 pa
LC 2008-482026
First published 1997 with title: The Oxford dictionary of foreign words and phrases. Paperback has title: Oxford dictionary of foreign words and phrases

This reference "offers coverage of more than 6,000 foreign words and phrases that are in regular use in English today." Publisher's note

Hendrickson, Robert

★ The **Facts** on File encyclopedia of word and phrase origins; 4th ed., [Updated and expanded ed.]; Facts On File 2008 948p (Facts on File library of language and literature) $95; pa $27.95   **422**
1. Reference books 2. English language -- Terms and phrases 3. English language -- Etymology -- Dictionaries
ISBN 978-0-8160-6966-8; 978-0-8160-6967-5 pa
LC 2007-48223
First published 1987
"This encyclopedia features anecdotes and information on the development of a wide range of words, including slang, proverbs, animal and plant names, place names, nick-

names, historical expressions, foreign language expressions, and phrases from literature." Publisher's note

"Because the entries have both scholarly value and the capacity to entertain, the book is ideal for both linguists and lay readers." Libr J

Hitchings, Henry

The **secret** life of words; how English became English. Farrar, Straus and Giroux 2008 440p $27 **422**

1. English language -- Etymology
ISBN 978-0-374-25410-0; 0-374-25410-9

LC 2008-26055

"Hitchings here provides a colorful, thematic history of the English language. Treating borrowings and coinages as psychological windows to history, the author takes the reader on a tour of the lexicon from Anglo-Saxon to the present day and shows how new words answer linguistic needs. . . . Hitchings treats the reader to some 3,000 word histories. . . . With 90-plus pages of notes, sources, and useful indexes, this is a fine choice for libraries and a 'smorgasbord' for language aficionados." Choice

Includes bibliographical references

Korach, Myron

Common phrases and where they come from; [by] Myron Korach in collaboration with John B. Mordock. Lyons Press 2001 200p hardcover o.p. pa $9.95 **422**

1. English language -- Etymology 2. English language -- Terms and phrases
ISBN 1-58574-682-7 pa

LC 00-69016

Korach and Mordock "show how much our culture relies on idiomatic speech to enliven discourse, a point further demonstrated by the more than 150 well-known phrases whose interesting histories they have provided. The arrangement of phrases is loosely thematic, with one to several paragraphs devoted to each." Libr J

Manser, Martin H.

The **Facts** on File dictionary of allusions; David H. Pickering, associate editor. Facts on File 2008 532p (Facts on File library of language and literature) $75; pa $18.95 **422**

1. Allusions 2. Reference books 3. Literature -- Dictionaries
ISBN 978-0-8160-7105-0; 0-8160-7105-5; 978-0-8160-7907-0 pa; 0-8160-7907-2 pa

LC 2007-51375

"In approximately 4,000 entries, this . . . resource explores well-known events, places, people, and phenomena whose names have acquired linguistic significance, conveying a particular message beyond a mere reference to the objects referred to. Entries are drawn from a . . . range of sources, including Shakespeare and the Bible; Greek, Roman, and Norse mythology; texts from literature through the ages; historical events; popular culture; and film and television. Individual entries contain pronunciation guides, defini-

tions, examples, information on derived forms, and more." Publisher's note

Includes bibliographical references

★ The **Facts** on File dictionary of foreign words and phrases; [by] Martin H. Manser; associate editors: Alice Grandison and David H. Pickering. 2nd ed., [New ed.]; Facts on File 2008 469p (Facts on File library of language and literature) $55; pa $19.95 **422**

1. Reference books 2. English language -- Foreign words and phrases -- Dictionaries
ISBN 978-0-8160-7035-0; 978-0-8160-7036-7 pa

LC 2007-29711

First published 2002

This dictionary includes more than 4,500 entries for terms that have entered the English lexicon from foreign languages in the fields of language and literature, religion, law, politics, economics, music, entertainment and cuisine. Examples or quotations are provided to illustrate usage.

"This is a captivating title to browse." SLJ

Includes bibliographical references

More word histories and mysteries; from aardvark to zombie. from the editors of the American Heritage dictionaries. Houghton Mifflin 2006 288p il pa $12.95 **422**

1. Reference books 2. English language -- Etymology
ISBN 978-0-618-71681-4; 0-618-71681-5

LC 2006020835

This "emphasizes the huge number of source languages from which English draws its vast vocabulary—from Sanskrit to French and beyond. The introductory pages give the reader a brief overview of the methods and aims of etymology and a potted history of the origins of English. . . . The editors then present an alphabetical listing of words and their etymology. Each of the 300-plus entries is about half a page to a page long and briefly outlines the origins of the word, its use, and the evolution of its meaning. . . . The book's informative yet informal writing style would appeal to the amateur enthusiast, and accessibility is further enhanced by a useful glossary of linguistic terms." Libr J

Morris, William

Morris dictionary of word and phrase origins; [by] William and Mary Morris; foreword by Isaac Asimov. 2nd ed; Harper & Row 1988 669p $38 **422**

1. English language -- Etymology 2. English language -- Terms and phrases
ISBN 0-06-015862-X

LC 87-45651

Original three volume edition published 1962-1971; one volume edition first published 1977

"Traces the origins of several thousand words and phrases commonly used in the English language, including slang terms and clichés not usually found in more formal works. Entries are listed alphabetically by the first word in the phrase, with an index at the end." Ref Sources for Small & Medium-sized Libr. 6th edition

Quinion, Michael

★ **Ballyhoo,** buckeroo, and spuds; ingenious tales of words and their origins. Smithsonian Books 2004 288p $19.95 **422**

1. English language -- Etymology 2. English language -- Terms and phrases

ISBN 1-588-34219-0

LC 2004-52235

A look at common English "words and phrases most readers will probably have wondered about. We're all familiar with the phrase 'happy as a clam.' but why a clam? We know what a 10-gallon hat is, but how did it get its name? And what the heck is a ballyhoo, anyway? The book is simply organized—alphabetically, of course—and endlessly illuminating. Quinion's research and documentation are impeccable, and when he needs to make a leap of imagination, he does so gracefully. For word lovers, this book is indispensable." Booklist

Includes bibliographical references

Rosten, Leo

The **new** joys of Yiddish; revisions and commentary by Lawrence Bush; illustrations by R. O. Blechman. Rev ed; Crown 2001 xxxii, 458p il $35; pa $18 **422**

1. Yiddish language 2. English language -- Foreign words and phrases

ISBN 0-609-60785-5; 0-609-80692-0 pa

LC 2001-28366

First published 1968 with title: The joys of Yiddish

This "work explores the nuances and complexities of language, clarifying the interrelationship between Yiddish and English (Yinglish, according to Rosten). The lengthy alphabetical listing not only presents multiple spellings, pronunciation guides, definitions, and cross references but also illustrates usage with background information, anecdotes, and jokes, as well as breezy erudition in the form of tidbits of cultural history, Talmudic and biblical references, tips on pronunciation, and thoughtful commentary. . . . The revision incorporates additional material on modern Yiddish literature and culture and updates on changes in American Jewish life and faith. Also included as an appendix is an English-Yiddish dictionary." Libr J

Includes bibliographical references

Word histories and mysteries; from abracadabra to Zeus. from the editors of the American Heritage dictionaries. Houghton Mifflin Co. 2004 xvi, 348p il pa $12.95 **422**

1. Reference books 2. English language -- Etymology

ISBN 978-0-618-45450-1; 0-618-45450-0

LC 2004014798

"The 400 alphabetically arranged entries here illustrate the diversity from which the English language draws its vocabulary, particularly from the prehistoric base that linguists call Proto-Indo-European. As a result, the editors aim to demonstrate links between the ancient base and modern English. . . . An overall quality resource." Libr J

423 Dictionaries of standard English

Adelson-Goldstein, Jayme

The **Oxford** picture dictionary; [by] Jayme Adelson-Goldstein and Norma Shapiro. 2nd ed.; Oxford University Press 2008 285p il pa $16.95 **423**

1. Reference books 2. Picture dictionaries 3. English language -- Dictionaries

ISBN 978-0-19-436976-3; 0-19-436976-5

LC 2007-41017

First published 1998

This picture dictionary features "4,000 words and phrases illustrated with . . . artwork." Publisher's note

The **American** Heritage dictionary of the English language; 5th ed.; Houghton Mifflin Harcourt 2011 xxvii, 2084p il map **423**

1. Reference books 2. Encyclopedias and dictionaries 3. English language -- Usage -- Dictionaries 4. English language -- Dictionaries

ISBN 9780547041018

LC 2011004777

First published 1969

This book, "the fifth edition of "The American Heritage Dictionary of the English Language" (AHD)" includes 10,000 new words, with "color photos in the margin to illustrate the definitions. Countries all have a small map with their location and major cities. . . . [U]sage notes . . . . have been updated . . . AHD also includes example sentences, and many of these have been lengthened with the addition of quotations from writers . . . Synonyms for words have been added . . . The purchase of this print edition contains a passkey for a free app version, and there is a free online version at www.ahdictionary.com." (Booklist)

Ammer, Christine

The **American** Heritage dictionary of idioms. Houghton Mifflin 1997 729p $32; pa $14.95 **423**

1. Americanisms 2. Reference books 3. English language -- Idioms 4. Americanisms -- Dictionaries 5. English language -- Terms and phrases 6. English language -- Idioms -- Dictionaries

ISBN 0-395-72774-X; 0-618-24953-2 pa

LC 97-12390

"This book surveys 10,000 American English expressions. Idioms predominate, but common figures of speech (e.g., blind as a bat), interjections, proverbs, colloquialisms (out in left field), emphatic redundancies whose word order cannot be reversed (far and wide), and slang phrases are also included. Entries and their variants are listed alphabetically in boldface. Where a phrase has more than one meaning, definitions are numbered and ordered by frequency of use. Keywords to phrases are listed alphabetically among the entries and note all the entries that contain that keyword. Entries are labeled to indicate the degree of formality or offensiveness: colloquial, slang, and vulgar slang." (Booklist)

"In addition to idioms, the dictionary includes common figures of speech, formula phrases such as 'take care,' emphatic redundancies whose word order cannot be reversed such as 'cease and desist,' common proverbs, colloquialisms, and slang phrases. Each expression is defined briefly and then illustrated by a short, simple sentence showing how it is used in context." SLJ

Includes bibliographical references

★ **Concise** Oxford American thesaurus. Oxford University Press 2006 996p $19.95   **423**
1. Reference books 2. English language -- Synonyms and antonyms
ISBN 0-19-530485-3; 978-0-19-530485-5

           LC 2005-35868
First published 1997 in the United Kingdom with title: The concise Oxford thesaurus; Original American edition published 1999 with title: The Oxford American thesaurus of current English

This "thesaurus contains over 15,000 entries with more than 350,000 synonyms and is . . . arranged with the typical synonyms listed first. . . . This simple arrangement makes this thesaurus particularly user-friendly." Libr J

Davidson, Mark
★ **Right,** wrong, and risky; a dictionary of today's American English usage. Norton 2006 570p $29.95   **423**
1. Americanisms 2. Reference books 3. English language -- Usage 4. English language -- Dictionaries
ISBN 0-393-06119-1

           LC 2005-17628
The author "offers a dictionary that 'views the real world of today's American English, identifying usage questions that are debatable, citing conflicting answers, and offering risk-free solutions for each conflict.' . . . Browsers will enjoy the colorful, interesting backstories on the origins of terms such as ground zero, on the sudden warming to the phrase girl talk, and on the widely misunderstood use of the word Neanderthal." Booklist

Includes bibliographical references

★ **Dictionary** of confusable words; {edited by} Adrian Room. Fitzroy Dearborn Pubs. 2000 251p $35   **423**
1. English language -- Usage 2. English language -- Synonyms and antonyms
ISBN 1-57958-271-0

A "guide to potentially confusing words. . . . The brief entries give definitions of each of the terms. Each word is then used in at least one sample sentence, clarifying the differences between like terms. The definitions and examples are in simple language and are easy to understand." Libr J

Espy, Willard R.
Words to rhyme with; a rhyming dictionary. 3rd ed.; Facts On File 2006 683p (Facts on File library of language and literature) $75; pa $19.95   **423**
1. English language -- Rhyme
ISBN 0-8160-6303-6; 978-0-8160-6303-1; 0-8160-6304-4 pa; 978-0-8160-6304-8 pa

           LC 2005-51122
First published 1986

"Including a primer of prosody, a list of more than 80,000 words that rhyme, a glossary defining 9,000 of the more eccentric rhyming words, and a variety of exemplary verses, one of which does not rhyme at all." Title page

Garner, Bryan A.
★ **Garner's** modern American usage; 3rd ed; Oxford University Press 2009 lx, 942p $45   **423**
1. Reference books 2. Americanisms -- Dictionaries 3. English language -- Usage -- Dictionaries
ISBN 978-0-19-538275-4

           LC 2009-9539
First published 1998 with title: A dictionary of modern American usage

"One would be tempted to say that this is clearly one of the best works on the topic, but doing so would be using one of Garner's weasel words (intensives such as clearly that 'actually have the effect of weakening a statement'). Suffice it to say that it is highly recommended for most libraries." Booklist

Includes bibliographical references (p. 925-938)

Historical thesaurus of the Oxford English dictionary; with additional material from A Thesaurus of Old English. [edited by] Christian Kay [et al.] Oxford University Press 2009 3952p 2v set $395   **423**
1. Reference books 2. English language -- Synonyms and antonyms
ISBN 978-0-19-920899-9

           LC 2009-935029
This "historical thesaurus claims to be the first to include 'almost the entire vocabulary of English, from Old English to the present day,' covering more than 920,000 words and meanings and documenting, through data from the Oxford English Dictionary, how words with similar meaning have developed over time." Libr J

"The knowledge compiled in this 40-year project is stunning, and promises to revolutionize the study of the language by making wholly new kinds of questions possible." Choice

Includes bibliographical references

Houghton Mifflin Co.
★ The **American** Heritage guide to contemporary usage and style. Houghton Mifflin 2005 512p $19.95   **423**
1. English language -- Usage
ISBN 978-0-618-60499-9; 0-618-60499-5

           LC 2005-16513
"Drawing on the authoritative knowledge of its lexicographers and the considered collective judgment of a panel of noted writers, the book offers guidance on the simple (the pronunciations of bouquet); the perplexingly redundant (free gift); the often imprecisely used (impeach); the no longer distinct (healthful/healthy); the needless but persistent (irregardless); the easily confused (stationary/stationery); the unfortunately conflated (lay/lie); and many more pitfalls. Articles embodying the precision and lucidity of dictionary definitions explain the history of a word's or expression's usage issue, how and why the issue exists, and the preferred usage." Booklist

Little, Brown & Co. Inc.
★ **Bartlett's** Roget's thesaurus. Little, Brown 1996 xxxii, 1415p $21.95; pa $16.95   **423**
1. Americanisms 2. Reference books 3. English

language -- Synonyms and antonyms
ISBN 0-316-10138-9; 0-316-73587-6 pa

LC 96-18343

This thesaurus "reflects the current state of American English, including terminology from the worlds of composers and television, with such sub-categories as 'Living Things,' 'The Arts,' 'Feelings.' But what really makes the book a joy to use is the tremendously useful lists—everything from phobias to styles and periods of furniture." Am Libr

Merriam-Webster Inc.

★ **Merriam** -Webster's collegiate dictionary; Eleventh ed; Merriam-Webster 2003 1623p il $23.95 **423**
1. Reference books 2. English language -- Dictionaries
ISBN 0-87779-808-7

LC 2003-3674

First published 1898

This edition includes over 165,000 entries, 10,000 new words and meanings, 38,000 etymologies, a handbook of style, an essay on the English language, a special section on signs and symbols, and a free one-year subscription to the Collegiate Web site.

★ **Merriam** -Webster's collegiate thesaurus; 2nd ed.; Merriam-Webster 2010 16a, 1162p $21.95 **423**
1. Reference books 2. English language -- Synonyms and antonyms
ISBN 978-0-8777-9269-7; 0-8777-9269-0

LC 2009-42161

First published 1976 with title: Webster's collegiate thesaurus

"Employs a conventional dictionary arrangement, and gives synonyms, related terms, idiomatic equivalents, antonyms, and contrasted words as applicable. Cross-references in small capitals." Guide to Ref Books. 11th edition

★ **Merriam**-Webster's visual dictionary. Merriam-Webster, Inc. 2012 1112 p. (hbk.) $39.95 **423**
1. English language -- Dictionaries
ISBN 0877791511; 9780877791515

This visual dictionary, edited by Jean-Claude Corbeil, has "more than 8,000 highly detailed, full-color illustrations, organized by subject in specialized fields from all aspects of life, . . . [and] nearly 25,000 . . . technical and everyday terms with clear, concise definitions. . . . Themes include a wide variety of fields: astronomy, the earth, human beings, the animal kingdom, plants and gardening, . . . food, arts and architecture, . . . sports and games" and more. (Publisher's note)

Mugglestone, Lynda

Lost for words; the hidden history of the Oxford English Dictionary. Yale University Press 2005 xxi, 273p il $30 **423**
1. Oxford English dictionary
ISBN 0-300-10699-8

LC 2004-29344

This is a "history of the making of the OED." Am Sch

"Serious word lovers will appreciate . . . [this book's] fascinating revelations." Booklist

Includes bibliographical references

★ **New** Oxford American dictionary; 3rd ed.; Oxford University Press 2010 xxvi, 2018p il map $60 **423**
1. Reference books 2. Americanisms -- Dictionaries 3. English language -- Dictionaries
ISBN 978-0-19-539288-3

LC 2010-20033

First published 1980 with title: The Oxford American dictionary. Editors vary

"This dictionary arranges definitions by most current usage and provides additional guidance in usage notes. Although U.S. English is the focus here, regionalisms from other English-speaking areas are also included. More than 1000 illustrations (e.g., photos, drawings, diagrams) clarify definitions. . . . A labor of love and an unparalleled gift to writers and readers worldwide, the New Oxford American Dictionary should be on the reference shelves of every library." Libr J

★ **Oxford** American writer's thesaurus; compiled by Christine A. Lindberg. 2nd ed.; Oxford University Press 2008 xxvi, 1052p $40 **423**
1. Reference books 2. English language -- Synonyms and antonyms
ISBN 978-0-19-534284-0; 0-19-534284-4

LC 2008-31259

First published 2004

"This expansive reference . . . is a functional treasure." Libr J

★ **Oxford** dictionary of English idioms; 3rd ed., Oxford pbk ed.; Oxford University Press 2010 408p (Oxford paperback reference) pa $16.95 **423**
1. Reference books 2. English language -- Idioms
ISBN 978-0-19-954378-6

LC 2010-935315

First published 1999 with title: The Oxford dictionary of idioms

This book "contains entries for over 6,000 idioms. . . . These include a range of idioms such as 'the elephant in the corner,' 'go figure,' 'step up to the plate,' 'a walk in the park,' and 'win ugly.'" Publisher's note

The **Oxford** English dictionary; 2nd ed; Oxford Univ. Press 1989 20v apply to publisher for price **423**
1. Reference books 2. English language -- Dictionaries
ISBN 0-19-861186-2

LC 88-5330

First published 1888 with title: New English dictionary on historical principles

"This is an etymological or word-source dictionary. In addition to definitions, this work gives the history of 290,500 words, both current and archaic, in the English language. Slang entries are very limited. Word histories include early forms, variant forms and roots, and first or exemplary usages in English from ancient to modern times. Short explanatory notes are provided for more common words." N Y Public Libr Book of How & Where to Look It Up

Princeton Language Institute

✓ ★ **Roget's** 21st century thesaurus in dictionary form; the essential reference for home, school, or office. edited by the Princeton Language Institute; Barbara Ann Kipfer, head lexicographer. 3rd ed; Bantam Dell 2005 962p $15; pa $5.99 **423**

1. Reference books 2. English language -- Synonyms and antonyms

ISBN 0-385-33895-3; 0-440-24269-X pa

First published 1992

This thesaurus, cross referencing each word with the same concept, provides 500,000 synonyms and antonyms in a dictionary format and includes recently coined and common slang terms and commonly used foreign terms.

★ **Random** House Webster's unabridged dictionary; 2nd ed.; Random House 2005 xxvi, 2230p il map $59.95 **423**

1. Reference books 2. English language -- Dictionaries

ISBN 0-375-42599-3

First published 1966 with title: The Random House dictionary of the English language

This dictionary contains over 315,000 entries. A new-words section and an essay on the growth of English are included. 2,400 spot maps and illustrations complement the text

★ **Roget's** international thesaurus; 6th ed; HarperResource 2001 xxv, 1248p $20.95; pa $16.95 **423**

1. Reference books 2. English language -- Synonyms and antonyms

ISBN 0-06-273693-0; 0-06-093544-8 pa

LC 2002-276277

First copyright edition published 1911 with title: The standard thesaurus of English words and phrases classified and arranged so as to facilitate the expression of ideas and assist in literary composition

This edition includes 330,000 words and phrases organized into 1,075 categories and a pinpoint reference system that directs the user from a comprehensive index to the numbered category of the right word. Cross-references throughout lead to other categories. Also included are supplemental word lists that supply the names of things which have no synonyms (measurements, wines, state mottoes) as well as quotations that amplify the meanings of selected words

★ **Shorter** Oxford English dictionary on historical principles; [editor-in-chief, Lesley Brown] 6th ed.; Oxford University Press 2007 2v il map set $175 **423**

1. Reference books 2. English language -- Dictionaries

ISBN 978-0-19-923324-3; 0-19-923324-1

LC 2007-37226

First published 1933

This dictionary "has more than half a million definitions drawn from the Oxford English Corpus database of more than 1.5 billion words. . . . It includes 'all words in current English from 1700 to the present day, plus the vocabulary of Shakespeare, the Authorized Version of the Bible and other major works from before 1700.'" Booklist

Includes bibliographical references

Upton, Clive

★ **Oxford** rhyming dictionary; {by} Clive Upton, Eben Upton. Oxford University Press 2004 659p $37.95 **423**

1. English language -- Rhyme

ISBN 0-19-280115-5

LC 2004-53133

In this dictionary "an index of words leads to numbered sections of phonic groupings of end, double, and triple syllable rhymes, with proximate groupings of near rhymes. But the index (95,000 words) . . . provides many word variations." Choice

Winchester, Simon

✓ The **professor** and the madman; a tale of murder, insanity, and the making of the Oxford English dictionary. HarperCollins Pubs. 1998 242p il $22; pa $13 **423**

1. Surgeons 2. Mentally ill 3. Editors 4. Murderers 5. Lexicographers 6. Oxford English dictionary 7. New English dictionary on historical principles 8. English language -- Lexicography -- History -- 19th century 9. United States -- History -- Civil War, 1861-1865 -- Veterans -- Biography

ISBN 0-06-017596-6; 0-06-099486-X pa

LC 98-10204

Winchester examines the relationship between James Murray, editor of the Oxford English Dictionary, and "William C. Minor (1834-1920), . . . a Civil War surgeon whose war experience caused his personality to change. He became paranoid and was eventually diagnosed as schizophrenic. After three years in an asylum, he went to Europe in 1871. . . . {In London} he killed George Merritt. An English court found him not guilty on the ground of insanity, and Minor was sent to Broadmoor. Coming across a leaflet for volunteers to help compile a history of the English language, Minor offered his services. . . . After 17 years of correspondence, the editor of the Oxford English Dictionary came to meet Minor, who had submitted 10,000 definitions to the project." (Libr J)

The author relates the "story of the Oxford English Dictionary's first editor and the expatriate American murderer who contributed more than 10,000 quotations as examples. Best of all, among the entertaining tangents one learns a great deal about the making of that grandest of all reference works." Libr J

Includes bibliographical references

425 Grammar of standard English

Huddleston, Rodney D.

✓ ★ The **Cambridge** grammar of the English language; {by} Rodney Huddleston, Geoffrey K. Pullum in collaboration with Laurie Bauer {et al.} Cambridge Univ. Press 2002 1842p il $160 **425**

1. English language -- Grammar

ISBN 0-521-43146-8

LC 2001-25630

"Each chapter comprises core definitions, detailed analyses, notes explaining alternative interpretations of difficult or controversial points, and brief notes on usage and history." Publisher's note

This "comprehensive and detailed look at the principles of the English language . . . {is} an authoritative addition to the fields of both English grammar and linguistics." Libr J

Includes bibliographical references

427 Historical and geographic variations, modern nongeographic variations of English

Axelrod, Alan

Whiskey tango foxtrot; the real language of the modern American military. Alan Axelrod. Skyhorse Publishing 2013 240 p. (pbk. : alk. paper) $12.95 **427**

1. English language -- Slang 2. United States -- Armed forces 3. Sailors -- United States -- Language -- Dictionaries 4. Soldiers -- United States -- Language -- Dictionaries 5. Military art and science -- United States -- Dictionaries 6. English language -- United States -- Slang -- Dictionaries

ISBN 1620876477; 9781620876473

LC 2013011431

In this book, Alan Axelrod "tours modern military slang via six topical chapters, including 'Cake Eaters and Chicken Guts.' As the author acknowledges, the sources for some of his entries are from 'official' authorities such as the Department of Defense Dictionary of Military Terms . . . , but Axelrod's main focus is 'unofficial' terms, such as soldiers' rework of the 'What the . . .' curse as expressed in this book's title." (Library Journal)

Ayto, John

The **Oxford** dictionary of slang. Oxford University Press 2003 (Oxford paperback reference) pa $16.95 **427**

ISBN 0-19-860763-6

LC 427

A reissue of the title first published 1998

"The 10,000 slang terms defined here originated mainly in the United States, Britain, Australia, or New Zealand and include both old and new coinages. The dictionary's arrangement is topical in thesaurus fashion." Libr J

Bailey, Richard W.

Speaking American; a history of English in the United States. Richard W. Bailey. Oxford University Press 2012 xvi, 207 p.p (alk. paper) $27.95 **427**

1. Americanisms 2. English language -- History 3. English language -- Lexicography -- United States 4. English language -- United States -- Usage 5. English language -- United States -- Grammar 6. English language -- United States -- History 7. English language -- Variation -- United States

ISBN 019517934X; 9780195179347

LC 2011011042

In this book, Richard W. Bailey "identifies eight major centers of influence on American English and describes how each has helped shape the tongue of today. . . . In his introduction, he" refutes "the idea that language can somehow be perfected and standardized and celebrates the ability of

English to change, adapt, adopt, steal and transform. Then he offers a series of . . . chapters, each focusing on a certain region whose influence on the language has been profound." (Kirkus Reviews)

Includes bibliographical references and index.

Crystal, David

By hook or by crook; a journey in search of English. Overlook Press 2008 314p il map $27.95 **427**

1. English language -- Dialects

ISBN 978-1-59020-061-2; 1-59020-061-6

First published 2007 in the United Kingdom

Combines personal reflections, historical allusions, and traveler's observations about the author's encounters with language and its users throughout the English-speaking world.

"In a conversational style that includes plenty of quirky facts, Crystal captures the exploratory, seductive, teasing, quirky, tantalizing nature of language study, and in doing so illuminates the fascinating world of words in which we live." Publ Wkly

Includes bibliographical references

The **stories** of English. Overlook Press 2004 584p il map $35 **427**

1. English language -- History

ISBN 1-585-67601-2

LC 2004-54727

The author "traces the diverse and unpredictable influences that have shaped English into an unruly family of dialects, creoles, and patois. . . . Crystal acknowledges the emergence during the fourteenth and fifteenth centuries of a prestigious standard version of English. Yet he shows in instance after instance that the tempests of linguistic change have often overwhelmed the custodians of the King's English, compelling them to accommodate forces they could not control. And though he never loses his focus on language, Crystal allows some of its more colorful users—including Chaucer, Shakespeare, Samuel Johnson, and Thomas Jefferson—to bring their personalities and voices into the chronicle." Booklist

Includes bibliographical references

Dickson, Paul

★ **Slang!** the topical dictionary of Americanisms. Walker & Co. 2006 418p $24.95 **427**

1. Reference books 2. Americanisms -- Dictionaries 3. English language -- Slang -- Dictionaries

ISBN 0-8027-1531-1; 978-0-8027-1531-9

First published 1990 by Pocket Bks.

"Informative, reliable, entertaining, and modern, this topical slang dictionary complements the more staid slang lexicons and more scholarly general dictionaries." Booklist

Includes bibliographical references

Dictionary of American slang; Barbara Ann Kipfer, editor; Robert L. Chapman, founding editor. 4th ed., fully rev. and updated; Collins 2007 592p $45 **427**

1. Americanisms 2. Reference books 3. English language -- Slang -- Dictionaries

ISBN 978-0-06-117646-3; 0-06-117646-X

First published 1960 by Crowell. Variant title: New dictionary of American slang

This dictionary of American slang terms "features pronunciation guides, word origins, examples of appropriate usage as well as a . . . highlighting system that lets you know which terms should be used with caution, and never in polite company." Publisher's note

Do you speak American ?(Television program)

★ **Do** you speak American? [by] Robert MacNeil and William Cran. 1st Harvest ed.; Harcourt 2005 228p map pa $13   **427**

1. Americanisms 2. English language -- Dialects
ISBN 978-0-15-603288-9; 0-15-603288-0

LC 2005-23093

Sequel to The story of English (1986)
First published 2005 by Nan A. Talese/Doubleday
"Whether talking to crab fishermen in Maryland or country-and-western singers in Tennessee, the authors discover that regional dialects are thriving despite the uniformity of our national tastes in clothing, fast-food chains, and movies. . . . The authors show how mobility, immigration, and racial and ethnic mixing are rapidly and profoundly changing the language. . . . This is colorful, witty, and insightful commentary on American speech patterns." Booklist

Includes bibliographical references

Holder, R. W.

★ **How** not to say what you mean; a dictionary of euphemisms. 4th ed.; Oxford University Press 2007 410p pa $18.95   **427**

1. Reference books 2. Euphemism -- Dictionaries
ISBN 978-0-19-920839-5; 0-19-920839-5

LC 2007-37558

First published 1987 by Bath University Press with title: A dictionary of American and British euphemisms

"Here are almost five thousand euphemistic expressions listed in alphabetical order, ranging from well-known favorites such as 'push up the daisies,' 'fly-by-night,' 'red light district,' 'take to the cleaners,' 'get lucky,' and 'five-fingered discount,' to less amusing expressions from the bureaucratic and military world such as 'restructuring,' 'collateral damage,' and 'extrajudicial killing.' For each word or expression, Holder includes examples from . . . authors, along with . . . explanations of the words' origins and meaning." Publisher's note

Includes bibliographical references

McMahon, Sean

★ **Brewer's** dictionary of Irish phrase & fable; [by] Sean McMahon and Jo O'Donoghue. Brewer's 2009 867p $34.95   **427**

1. Allusions 2. Reference books 3. Folklore -- Ireland
4. Irish literature -- Dictionaries
ISBN 978-0-550-10565-3

First published 2004 by Weidenfeld & Nicholson
"Entries explore the island's history, literature, language, folklore and mythology . . . [with a] mix of people, places, historical events, facts and phrases. . . . 6,000 entries focus on the phrase and fable of Ireland, from ancient myth to modern politics." Publisher's note

★ The **new** Partridge dictionary of slang and unconventional English; Tom Dalzell (senior editor) and Terry Victor (editor) Routledge 2006 2v set $220   **427**

1. Reference books 2. English language -- Slang -- Dictionaries
ISBN 0-415-21258-8; 978-0-415-21258-8

First published 1937
"Entries list the term, identify its part of speech, explain its meaning, identify the country of origin, and cite sources or provide quotations showing how the term is used. . . . This dictionary informs, but it also entertains." Booklist

Includes bibliographical references

Nunberg, Geoffrey

The **ascent** of the A-word; assholism, the first sixty years. Geoffrey Nunberg. PublicAffairs 2012 251 p. (hardcover) $25.99   **427**

1. Popular culture 2. English language -- Slang 3. English language -- History 4. Words, Obscene 5. English language -- Obscene words
ISBN 1610391756; 9781610391757; 9781610391764

LC 2012017027

Author Geoffrey "Nunberg's study of the word 'asshole' . . . breaks down the important place the word 'asshole' occupies in our language and culture. Nunberg begins by charting the rise of 'asshole' from its origins as WWII barracks slang, to its popularization in post-war literature . . . to its eventual adoption as part of Standard English in the 1970s." (Publishers Weekly)

Spears, Richard A.

★ **McGraw** -Hill's dictionary of American slang and colloquial expressions; 4th ed.; McGraw-Hill 2006 xxix, 546p pa $19.95   **427**

1. Americanisms 2. Reference books 3. English language -- Slang -- Dictionaries
ISBN 0-07-146107-8; 978-0-07-146107-8

LC 2005-52220

First published 1989 with title: NTC's dictionary of American slang and colloquial expressions

This book offers "definitions of more than 12,000 slang and informal expressions from various sources, ranging from golden oldies such as . . . golden oldie, to recent coinages like shizzle (gangsta), jonx (Wall Street), and ping (the Internet). Each entry is followed by examples illustrating how an expression is used in everyday conversation and, where necessary, International Phonetic Alphabet pronunciations are given, as well as cautionary notes for crude, inflammatory, or taboo expressions." Publisher's note

Includes bibliographical references

428   Standard English usage (Prescriptive linguistics)

Adolescent literacy in the academic disciplines; general principles and practical strategies. edited by Tamara L. Jetton, Cynthia Shanahan. The Guilford Press 2012 xiv, 274 p.p ill. (paper) $30 **428**

1. Reading 2. Literacy 3. Teaching 4. Secondary

education 5. Language arts (Secondary) 6. Language arts -- Correlation with content subjects

ISBN 1462502806; 9781462502806; 9781462502837

LC 2011035689

This book, edited by Tamara L. Jetton and Cynthia Shanahan, "addresses the particular challenges of literacy learning in each of the major academic disciplines. Chapters focus on how to help students successfully engage with texts and ideas in English/literature, science, math, history, and arts classrooms. The book shows that . . . students also need to learn processing strategies that are quite specific to each subject and its typical tasks or problems." (Publisher's note)

Includes bibliographical references and index

Dunn, Patricia A.

Grammar rants. Heinemann/Boynton/Cook Publishers 2011 xvi, 134 p   **428**

1. Grammar 2. Textbooks 3. English language -- Grammar

ISBN 0867096055; 9780867096057

LC 2011005689

This book presents an analysis of debates and complaints concerning the moral and social implications of grammar. "Each chapter includes actual rants along with . . . editorial commentary, instructional activities and classroom lessons" intended to facilitate student discussion on the social aspects of grammar and the assumptions people make when they encounter incorrect usage. According to the publisher, these "lessons will promote savvy writing by empowering students and teachers to see for themselves how best to raise the quality of their written and spoken language without resorting to ranting." (Publisher's note)

Includes bibliographical references and index.

Florey, Kitty Burns

Sister Bernadette's barking dog; the quirky history and lost art of diagramming sentences. Melville House 2006 154p $19.95   **428**

1. English language -- Grammar

ISBN 978-1-933633-10-7; 1-933633-10-7

LC 2006-24703

The author "writes with verve about the nuns who taught her to render the English language as a mess of slanted lines, explains how diagrams work, and traces the bizarre history of the men who invented this odd pedagogical tool. And unlike so many of today's microhistorians, who seek to demonstrate how zippers, azaleas, or hopscotch explain the world, Florey is refreshingly content to recount her tale without any suggestion that the diagramming of sentences somehow illuminates the American character. It's a great read." Slate

Fowler, H. W.

★ **Fowler's** modern English usage; first edition by H.W. Fowler. Rev. 3rd ed.; Oxford University Press 2004 xxi, 873p $35   **428**

1. Reference books 2. English language -- Usage 3. English language -- Idioms 4. English language -- Etymology

ISBN 0-19-861021-1; 978-0-19-861021-2

LC 2005-271630

First published 1926 with title: A dictionary of modern English usage; 2000 edition published with title: The new Fowler's modern English usage

This alphabetically arranged guide gives "advice on grammar, syntax, style, and choice of words." Publisher's note

Fuhrken, Charles

What every middle school teacher needs to know about reading tests (from someone who has written them) Charles Fuhrken. Stenhouse Publishers 2012 vii, 237 p.p ill. (pbk. : alk. paper) $24   **428**

1. Achievement tests 2. Examinations -- Study guides 3. Educational tests and measurements 4. Reading (Middle school) -- Ability testing

ISBN 1571108858; 1571109455; 9781571108852; 9781571109453

LC 2011037287

This book's author, "Charles Fuhrken, has spent years working with several major testing companies and contributing to the reading assessments of various testing programs." He "offers . . . strategies to help students perform well on test day." Particular focus is given to "information about reading tests, including . . . preparation materials, samples of the most frequently assessed reading standards, and . . . core-reading activities." (Publisher's note)

Includes bibliographical references and index.

O'Conner, Patricia T.

★ **Woe** is I; the grammarphobe's guide to better English in plain English. Riverhead Bks. 2003 240p $19.95; pa $14   **428**

1. English language -- Usage 2. English language -- Grammar

ISBN 1-57322-252-6; 1-59448-006-0 pa

LC 2003-41416

First published 1996

This guide to good English offers advice on punctuation, usage, style and grammar as well as e-mail.

"The author doesn't take herself or the subject matter too seriously, offering a delightful romp through the intricacies of our language. . . . She knows her subject, can convey her message with wit and ease, and does it all in a compact, easy-to-read format. In short, this is an entertaining and useful grammar reference." Libr J

Includes bibliographical references

Peters, Pam

★ The **Cambridge** guide to English usage. Cambridge University Press 2004 608p il $35   **428**

1. Reference books 2. English language -- Usage

ISBN 0-521-62181-X

LC 2004-301888

"Covering over 3000 points of word meaning, spelling, punctuation, grammar, and style, the alphabetically arranged entries often include references to resources where the information was found." Libr J

"Considering the abundance of peculiarities and challenges in English usage, Cambridge will strengthen even a library well stocked with other guides. It is a serious book for those serious about language." Booklist

Strumpf, Michael

The **grammar** bible; everything you always wanted to know about grammar but didn't know whom to ask. [by] Michael Strumpf and Auriel Douglas. Holt 2004 489p pa $18   **428**

  1. English language -- Grammar
ISBN 0-8050-7560-7

                 LC 2003-57129

The authors move "from the parts of speech to the parts of the sentence and then to spelling, vocabulary, and punctuation, even encompassing thorny issues (e.g., sexist language, split infinitives) and complex grammatical terms (e.g., objective complements, gerund phrases). The authors also include a useful list of collocations and intersperse informative and often amusing 'Hot Line' queries throughout. . . This book is thorough, combining practical information not easily found in trade books, and is lively without trying to be too witty, cute, or humorous." Libr J

Includes bibliographical references

433   Dictionaries of standard German

★ **Random** House Webster's German-English, English-German dictionary; Rev. ed; Random House Reference 2006 547p $12.95   **433**

  1. Reference books 2. German language -- Dictionaries
ISBN 0-375-72194-0; 978-0-375-72194-6

First published 1997 with title: Random House German-English English-German dictionary

In addition to more than 60,000 entries this dictionary also includes notes on pronunciation, lists of abbreviations, tables of irregular verbs and lists of geographical names.

439.1   Yiddish

Comprehensive Yiddish-English Dictionary; Hayem Bokhner, Sholem Beynfeld, shef-redaktorn ; Berish Goldshteyn, Yankl Salant, asotsyirte redaktorn = Solon Beinfeld, Harry Bochner, editors-in-chief ; Barry Goldstein, Yankl Salant, associate editors. Indiana University Press 2013 xxxix, 704 p.p (hardcover) $45   **439.1**

  1. Encyclopedias and dictionaries 2. Yiddish language -- Dictionaries
ISBN 0253009839; 9780253009838

                 LC 2012491596

This book is a Yiddish-English dictionary. It contains "more than 37,000 words and a treasure horde of idiomatic phrases." It provides "readers with the most contemporary grammatical and semantic nuances. . . . Included is a . . . user's guide, an introduction and road map through the difficulties inherent in working with two distinct alphabets and language systems." (Choice)

440   French and related Romance languages

Nadeau, Jean-Benoit

★ The **story** of French; [by] Jean-Benoît Nadeau [and] Julie Barlow. St. Martin's Press 2006 483p map $25.95   **440**

  1. French language
ISBN 9780312341831; 0312341830

                 LC 2006-49348

This book explores the origins and evolution of the French language.

This is "a well-told, highly accessible history of the French language that leads to a spirited discussion of the prospects for French in an increasingly English-dominated world." N Y Times (Late N Y Ed)

Includes bibliographical references

443   Dictionaries of standard French

Correard, Marie-Helene

★ The **Oxford** -Hachette French dictionary; French-English, English-French. edited by Marie-Hélène Corréard, Valerie Grundy. 4th ed.; Oxford University Press/Hachette Livre 2007 xxxviii, 1945p $55   **443**

  1. Reference books 2. French language -- Dictionaries
ISBN 978-0-19-861422-7; 0-19-861422-5

                 LC 2007-14213

First published 1994

This work provides coverage of French and English vocabulary in general as well as scientific and technical areas with over 350,000 words and phrases and over 530,000 translations. Supplementary material includes information on French society and culture, including famous places, people and much practical information for those planning to reside in France.

460.9   Spanish--History

Barlow, Julie

The **story** of Spanish; Jean-Benoit Nadeau and Julie Barlow. St. Martin's Press 2013 496 p. (hardcover) $27.99   **460.9**

  1. Linguistics 2. Spanish language -- History
ISBN 0312656025; 9780312656027

                 LC 2013002633

This book, by Jean-Benoit Nadeau and Julie Barlow, asks "just how did a dialect spoken by a handful of shepherds in Northern Spain become the world's second most spoken language, the official language of twenty-one countries on two continents, and the unofficial second language of the United States? . . . [The authors] look at the roots and spread of modern Spanish." (Publisher's note)

Includes bibliographical references and index.

463   Dictionaries of standard Spanish

Houghton Mifflin Co.
The **Concise** American Heritage Spanish diction-
ary; 2nd ed; Houghton Mifflin 2001 xxiv, 616p
$14   463
1. Reference books 2. Spanish language -- Dictionaries
ISBN 0-618-11769-5
LC 00-66461
"This bilingual dictionary includes more than 70,000
words and phrases. The emphasis on American English and
Latin American Spanish as well as the informative guides
and tables will assist students of either language." Booklist

470   Latin and related Italic languages

Ostler, Nicholas
Ad infinitum; a biography of Latin. Walker &
Company 2007 382p il map $27.95   470
1. Latin language
ISBN 978-0-8027-1515-9; 0-8027-1515-X
"In four parts, Ostler covers the origins and development of Latin in the Roman world, Latin's "taking over
the church," its medieval continuation and fracturing into
vernaculars, and a nuanced rebirth in the Renaissance and
its legacy in the contemporary world. Incredibly well documented, with examples from antiquity to the modern era."
Libr J

473   Dictionaries of classical Latin

★ **Oxford** Latin dictionary; edited by P. G. W. Glare.
Oxford Univ. Press 1982 xxiii, 2126p   473
1. Reference books 2. Latin language -- Dictionaries
ISBN 0198642245
LC 8208162
This dictionary looks at the meaning and development of
more than 40,000 classical Latin words and phrases
"Authorized in 1931 and begun two years later, {this dic-
tionary} appeared in eight fascicles published between 1968
and 1982. These have been combined in a single volume."
Wilson Libr Bull

Stone, Jon R.
★ **Latin** for the illiterati; a modern phrase book
for an ancient language. 2nd ed.; Routledge 2009
xxii, 338p pa $24.95   473
1. Reference books 2. Latin language -- Dictionaries
ISBN 978-0-415-77767-4; 0-415-77767-4
First published 1996
"Organized alphabetically within the categories of verba
(common words and expressions), dicta (common phrases
and familiar sayings), and abbreviations, this . . . [is a]
compendium of more than 7,000 Latin words, expressions,
phrases, and sayings taken from the world of art, music, law,
philosophy, theology, medicine and the theatre, as well as .
. . [remarks and] advice from ancient writers such as Virgil,
Ovid, Cicero, and more." Publisher's note
Includes bibliographical references

487   Preclassical and postclassical Greek

Fox, Margalit
★ The **Riddle** of the Labyrinth. HarperCollins
2013 384 p. $27.99   487
1. Ciphers 2. Greece -- Antiquities
ISBN 0062228838; 9780062228833
This book looks at the deciphering of Linear B, a "script
first found on clay tablets excavated on the island of Crete
and later at Pylos on the Greek mainland and dating to the
Mycenaean period, circa 1400 BCE." It was deciphered
by Michael Ventris. This book focuses on the "work of
American classical scholar Alice Kober (1906-50) whose
syllabic grids made Ventris's breakthrough possible."
(Library Journal)

492.4   Hebrew

Zilkha, Avraham
★ **Modern** English-Hebrew dictionary. Yale
Univ. Press 2002 457p (Yale language series) $55;
pa $30   492.4
1. Reference books 2. Hebrew language -- Dictionaries
ISBN 0-300-09004-8; 0-300-09005-6 pa
LC 2001-26830
This dictionary includes 30,000 entries, with listings
for translating words with multiple meanings, newly coined
and slang words, common idioms, vocalization of Hebrew
words, acronyms, and gender identification and plural forms
of irregular nouns

493   Non-Semitic Afro-Asiatic languages

Robinson, Andrew, 1957-
Cracking the Egyptian code; the revolutionary
life of Jean-François Champollion. Andrew Robinson. Oxford University Press 2012 272 p. (tele-
work) $29.95   493
1. Hieroglyphics 2. Rosetta stone 3. Egyptologists
-- France -- Biography 4. Egyptian language -- Writing,
Hieroglyphic
ISBN 0199914990; 9780199914999
LC 2011046769
This book, by Andrew Robinson, "is the first biography
in English of [Jean-François] Champollion, widely regarded
as the founder of Egyptology. . . . Robinson . . . reconstructs
how Champollion cracked the code of the hieroglyphic
script, describing how Champollion . . . sailed the Nile for
a year, studied the tombs in the Valley of the Kings . . . and
carefully compared the three scripts on the Rosetta Stone
to penetrate the mystery of the hieroglyphic text." (Publisher's note)
Includes bibliographical references and index.

495.1   Chinese

Cheng & Tsui English-Chinese lexicon of business
terms with pinyin; compiled by Andrew C. Chang

= [Jianqiao Ying Han shang yong ci hui pin ying ci dian / Zhang Jiezhou bian] Cheng & Tsui Co. 2001 442p (C & T Asian dictionary series) $36.95 **495.1**
1. Reference books 2. Business -- Dictionaries 3. Chinese language -- Dictionaries
ISBN 978-0-88727-394-0; 0-88727-394-7

LC 2001-94244

"A book to hand to your patrons who need to know the Chinese expressions for terms such as Chief Executive Officer, market penetration, and stockholder. More than 9,000 English-language words and phrases are listed with their Chinese simplified characters, with pinyin transliteration equivalents." Booklist

495.7 Korean

Berlitz Korean compact dictionary. Berlitz Publishing 2006 672p pa $12.95 **495.7**
1. Reference books 2. Korean language -- Dictionaries
ISBN 978-981-246-949-6; 981-246-949-4

This book has "45,000 entries that aim to capture the core words of the language. This dictionary features bold, blue headwords [for navigation]." Publisher's note

499 Non-Austronesian languages of Oceania, Austronesian languages, miscellaneous languages

Okrent, Arika
In the land of invented languages; Esperanto rock stars, Klingon poets, Loglan lovers, and the mad dreamers who tried to build a perfect language. Spiegel & Grau 2009 342p il $26 **499**
1. Artificial languages
ISBN 978-0-385-52788-0; 0-385-52788-8

LC 2008-38732

The author "explores some of the themes and shortcomings of 900 years worth of artificial languages. . . . [Her] prose is a model of clarity and grace; through it, she conveys fascinating insights into why natural language, with its corruptions, ambiguities and arbitrary conventions, trips so fluently off our tongues." Publ Wkly

Includes bibliographical references

Pukui, Mary Kawena
Hawaiian dictionary; Hawaiian-English, English-Hawaiian. [by] Mary Kawena Pukui, Samuel H. Elbert. rev & enl ed; University of Hawaii Press 1986 xxvi, 572p $32.95 **499**
1. Reference books 2. Hawaiian language -- Dictionaries
ISBN 0-8248-0703-0

LC 85-24583

Originally published in two separate parts in 1957 and 1964. First combined edition published 1971

"The Hawaiian-English part now comprises 29,000 entries. It is the most comprehensive and up-to-date dictionary for the language." Guide to Ref Books. 11th edition

Includes bibliographical references

500 SCIENCE

500 Natural sciences and mathematics

Aczel, Amir D.
The **artist** and the mathematician; the story of Nicolas Bourbaki, the genius mathematician who never existed. Thunder's Mouth Press 2006 239p il $23.95 **500**
1. Mathematicians
ISBN 978-1-56025-931-2; 1-56025-931-0

"In 1934, a small group of mostly French mathematicians met to reinvent a new math based on a pedagogy of rigorous proofs, clarity, and logical thinking. The group invented a fictitious persona, 'Nicolas Bourbaki,' as a pseudonym under which to author their collective work. Presenting the fascinating story behind the publication of over 40 tomes . . . , Aczel describes the group's cultural context, eccentricities, informal rules, and practices of engagement and offers biographical sketches of such influential members as Andr Weil and Alexandre Grothendieck. Writing in an accessible, conversational style that excludes mathematical proofs, Aczel paints a clear picture of the Bourbaki movement and how it has influenced the way mathematics should be discussed and learned." Libr J

Bais, Sander
In praise of science; curiosity, understanding, and progress. MIT Press 2010 192p il $24.95 **500**
1. Science
ISBN 978-0-262-01435-9; 0-262-01435-1

LC 2009-35675

"Over the course of four short chapters, Sander Bais illustrates in entertaining and often poetic ways not only how all of the sciences are connected to each other, but how they comprise a vital (if not the most vital) endeavor humans has ever undertaken. . . . Among others, the stories in In Praise of Science include the origin of Santa Claus, the history of quantum theory, the invention of the lightning rod, and religious attacks that distorted the theory of evolution and facts surrounding HIV and AIDS. The polemical nature of Bais' arguments might spark debate for some readers, but he never comes across as ranting. He employs many (at times lengthy) quotes from a variety of sources, and near the end of the book there's a tendency to let the quotes make the case for him. But for the vast majority of the book, Bais seems like the quirky professor everyone loves and/or wishes they had, one who inspires lifelong interests." PopMatters

Includes bibliographical references

Bejan, Adrian
Design in nature; Adrian Bejan, J. Peder Zane. Doubleday 2012 vii, 296 p.p (hbk.) $27.95 **500**
1. Evolution 2. Constructal theory 3. Physics -- Philosophy 4. Pattern formation (Physical sciences)
ISBN 0385534612; 9780385534611

LC 2011015398

This book, aimed at a general audience, discusses the "the concept of constructal law, a theory of organization that studies the thermodynamics, shape, structure, and patterns of flow systems." (Libr J) According to the author, "systems change over time to maximize the rate of flow through the system. And this high level of efficiency is achieved in similar ways in any dynamic system, whether water flowing through an ecosystem or blood through a body's circulatory system. [Adrian] Bejan makes the controversial claim that the constructal law explains everything in the world, from the evolution of life to the development of human culture, and can predict how things will evolve--toward the ability to move more freely on Earth." (Publishers Weekly)

Includes bibliographical references and index

Bloom, Howard

The **God** problem; how a godless cosmos creates. by Howard Bloom. Prometheus Books 2012 708 p. (hardcover) $28.00   **500**
  1. Religion and science 2. Cosmology -- Miscellanea
  3. Science -- Social aspects
  ISBN 161614551X; 9781616145514
                                    LC 2012013460

This book, by Howard Bloom, asks "how does an inanimate universe generate stunning new forms and unbelievable new powers without a creator? . . . [The book explains] . . . Howard Bloom's provocative new theory of the . . . universe--the Bloom toroidal model, also known as the big bagel theory--which explains two of the biggest mysteries in physics: dark energy and why, if antimatter and matter are created in equal amounts, there is so little antimatter in this universe." (Publisher's note)

Includes bibliographical references and index

Bronowski, Jacob

Science and human values; revised edition with a new dialogue, The abacus and the rose. Harper & Row 1965 119p il hardcover o.p. pa $12   **500**
  1. Science
  ISBN 0-06-097281-5 pa
  First published 1958 by Messner
Contains the following three essays, which were first given as lectures at the Massachusetts Institute of Technology in 1953: The creative mind; The habit of truth; The sense of human dignity. The abacus and the rose was originally broadcast by the BBC Third Programme in 1962

The dialogue "discusses the theme that 'science is as integral a part of the culture of our age as the arts are.'" Sci Am

Brooks, Michael

13 things that don't make sense; the most baffling scientific mysteries of our time. [by] Michael Brooks. Doubleday 2008 240p $23.95   **500**
  1. Science
  ISBN 0-385-52068-9; 978-0-385-52068-3
                                    LC 2008-12443

This book is based on a 2005 article on scientific anomalies that Brooks wrote for the New Scientist. "13 Things opens at the twenty-third Solvay physics conference, where the scientists present are ready to throw up their hands over an anomaly: is it possible that the universe, rather than slowly drifting apart as the physics of the big bang had once predicted, is actually expanding at an ever-faster speed? . . . [Brooks also examines the questions]: Is a 1977 signal from outer space a transmission from an alien civilization? Might giant viruses explain how life began? Why are some NASA

satellites speeding up as they get farther from the sun—and what does that mean for the laws of physics?" (Publisher's note) Index.

This "book examines such mysteries as dark matter and dark energy, the prospect of life on Mars, sex and death, free will and the placebo effect, among other head-scratchers. . . . This elegantly written, meticulously researched and thought-provoking book provides window into how science actually works, and is sure to spur intense debate." New Sci

Includes bibliographical references

Bryson, Bill

★ A **short** history of nearly everything. Broadway Bks. 2003 544p $27.50; pa $15.95   **500**
  1. Science
  ISBN 0-7679-0817-1; 0-7679-0818-X pa
                                    LC 2003-46006

"Neither oversimplified nor overstuffed, this exceptionally skillful tour of the physical world covers the basic principles and still has room for profiles of some of the more engaging scientists." N Y Times Book Rev

Includes bibliographical references

Cole, K. C.

Mind over matter; conversations with the cosmos. Harcourt 2003 319p $25; pa $14   **500**
  1. Science
  ISBN 0-15-100816-7; 0-15-602956-1 pa
                                    LC 2003-982

The author "gathers 92 short essays that first appeared primarily in her Los Angeles Times science column. The book's four sections are loosely ordered around the subjectivity of inquiry, the physical world, science in practice and the politics of science. Cole's technique is to set her stage with a scientific factoid or news blip and then ruminate on the unexpected insights, inversions or ironies she finds there." Publ Wkly

"These three-page tidbits may not tax your scientific thought processes, but they'll certainly make you think." Libr J

Dawkins, Richard, 1941--

A **devil's** chaplain; reflections on hope, lies, science, and love. Houghton Mifflin 2003 263p il $24; pa $14   **500**
  1. Evolution 2. Religion and science 3. Science -- Philosophy
  ISBN 0-618-33540-4; 0-618-48539-2 pa
                                    LC 2003-50859

This is "a collection of essays that span 25 years of writing on evolution, education and science versus nonsense. . . . Dawkins is creative, articulate and, above all, emotional." N Y Times Book Rev

Includes bibliographical references

Dyson, Freeman J.

The **scientist** as rebel; [by] Freeman Dyson. New York Review Books 2006 360p $27.95   **500**
  1. Science
  ISBN 978-1-59017-216-2; 1-59017-216-7
                                    LC 2006-22081

This is a "collection of 33 previously published and frequently updated essays and reviews. Organized into sections on contemporary issues in science, war and peace, history of science and scientists, and personal and philosophical ruminations, these works demonstrate Dyson's far-ranging interests and skill in writing for educated and curious generalists, qualities that ensure this volume's wide appeal." Booklist

Includes bibliographical references

Eiseley, Loren C.

The **unexpected** universe. 1969 239p hardcover o.p. pa $14 **500**

1. Science 2. Natural history

ISBN 0-15-692850-7 pa

This volume contains personal interpretative meditations on mankind's relationship to nature.

Includes bibliographical references

Feynman, Richard Phillips, 1918-1988

★ The **meaning** of it all; thoughts of a citizen scientist. Basic Books 2005 133p pa $13.95 **500**

1. Science 2. Religion

ISBN 0-465-02394-0

First published 1998 by Addison-Wesley

"Originally delivered as a three-part lecture series at the University of Washington in 1963, this collection touches on such far-ranging topics as the existence or nonexistence of God; the Constitution; and UFOs. . . . These memorable lectures confirm that Feynman's gift of insight extended from the subatomic world to the cosmic, and to the very human as well." Publ Wkly

The **pleasure** of finding things out; the best short works of Richard P. Feynman. by Richard P. Feynman; edited by Jeffrey Robbins; foreword by Freeman Dyson. Perseus Bks. 1999 270p hardcover o.p. pa $15.95 **500**

1. Science

ISBN 0-7382-0349-1 pa

LC 99-64775

These lectures and interviews are "expositions about [Feynman's] life, about technical topics in computing and physics, and about science's general place in society." Booklist

Gardner, Martin

★ **Did** Adam and Eve have navels? discourses on reflexology, numerology, urine therapy and other dubious subjects. Norton 2000 333p il hardcover o.p. pa $15.95 **500**

1. Science

ISBN 0-393-32238-6 pa

LC 00-34870

This is a collection of the author's pieces culled from the Skeptical Inquirer. Gardner "gives succinct and amusing critiques of a number of the fallacies that abound in alternative medicine (including the very peculiar urine-therapy treatment) and many other 'dubious subjects.'" Libr J

Includes bibliographical references

Goldacre, Ben

Bad science; quacks, hacks, and big pharma flacks. Faber and Faber 2010 288p il pa $15 **500**

1. Errors 2. Medical misconceptions

ISBN 978-0-86547-918-0

LC 2010-14401

First published 2008 in the United Kingdom

The author "has written a very funny and biting book critiquing what he calls 'Bad Science.' Under this heading he includes homeopathy, cosmetics manufacturers whose claims about their products defy plausibility, proponents of miracle vitamins, and drug companies and physicians who design faulty studies and manipulate the results. . . . While it is a very entertaining book, it also provides important insight into the horrifying outcomes that can result when willful anti-intellectualism is allowed equal footing with scientific methodology." Boston Globe

Includes bibliographical references

Gould, Stephen Jay, 1941-2002

The **flamingo's** smile; reflections in natural history. Norton 1985 476p il hardcover o.p. pa $15.95 **500**

1. Natural history

ISBN 0-393-30375-6 pa

LC 85-4916

In this collection "the theme is history, both natural and human. . . . The essays are marked by Gould's usual careful scholarship and erudition and clear and nontechnical language." Sci Books Films

Includes bibliographical references

Gribbin, John R.

Almost everyone's guide to science; the universe, life and everything. [by] John Gribbin with Mary Gribbin. Yale Univ. Press 1999 232p $30; pa $11.95 **500**

1. Science

ISBN 0-300-08101-4; 0-300-08460-9 pa

LC 99-26755

First published 1998 in the United Kingdom

In this "general guide to science for the layperson . . . Gribbin combines biographies and history, on the one hand, with the major theories in science, on the other. . . . The text is clear, is based on solid research, and clearly reflects a lifetime love for science." Sci Books Films

Includes bibliographical references

The **handy** science answer book; compiled by the Carnegie Library of Pittsburgh; [edited by] Naomi E. Balaban and James E. Bobick. 4th ed.; Visible Ink Press 2011 679p il pa $21.95 **500**

1. Science 2. Technology

ISBN 978-1-57859-321-7

LC 2011-429

First published 1994

"The text is divided into various subject areas including physics and chemistry, space, earth, climate and weather, minerals and other materials, energy, technology, and environment, gathering answers to reference questions. . . . A comprehensive index . . . makes the material accessible and easy to find. Pages are full of fascinating tidbits, comple-

mented by illustrations, photos, charts, graphs, and maps."
Voice Youth Advocates

Includes bibliographical references

Henderson, Mark

100 most important science ideas; key concepts in genetics, physics and mathematics. [by] Mark Henderson, Joanne Baker, Tony Crilly. Firefly Books 2009 431p il $19.95   **500**

1. Physics 2. Genetics 3. Mathematics

ISBN 978-1-55407-527-0

This book aims to encourage the reader to explore "the 100 most important, groundbreaking ideas that have emerged from the scientific disciplines of genetics, physics, and mathematics. Divided into three sections, each written by one of the authors . . . this work presents complex scientific topics in a simple, understandable way. . . . Text boxes, entertaining quotations, frequent diagrams, and everyday examples hold the reader's attention and make this work engaging to anyone interested in the world of science." Libr J

History of modern science and mathematics; Brian S. Baigrie, editor. Scribner 2002 4v il set $605   **500**

1. Science -- History 2. Mathematics -- History

ISBN 0-684-80636-3

LC 2002-4042

This "set attempts to synthesize the history of scientific developments in anthropology, astronomy, biology, chemistry, mathematics, physics, psychology, and the earth sciences. . . . This work ranges from the 17th century to the present without trying to include the most recent developments." Libr J

Includes bibliographical references

Kipfer, Barbara Ann

How it happens; the extraordinary processes of everyday things. Random House Reference 2005 322p il pa $16.95   **500**

1. Science

ISBN 0-375-72082-0

LC 2005-40453

This "trivia miscellany describes hundreds of processes, from popcorn popping to radio signal transmission to tango dancing." Publisher's note

Maddox, John Royden

What remains to be discovered; mapping the secrets of the universe, the origins of life, and the future of the human race. [by] John Maddox. Kessler Bks./Free Press 1998 434p hardcover o.p. pa $22.95 **500**

1. Science

ISBN 0-684-82292-X; 978-0-684-86300-9 pa; 0-684-86300-6 pa

LC 98-29137

The author reflects "on the nature of science, both its successes and its challenges. . . . By focusing on some of the 'big' fields of science—cosmology, quantum mechanics, cell biology, genetics, evolution and neuroscience, for example—he has crafted a primer worthy of study. But this is not an introduction for the uninitiated." Publ Wkly

Includes bibliographical references

★ **Oxford** dictionary of scientific quotations; edited by W.F. Bynum and Roy Porter; assistant editors, Sharon Messenger, Caroline Overy. Oxford University Press 2005 712p $60; pa $18.95   **500**

1. Science 2. Quotations

ISBN 0-19-858409-1; 0-19-861443-8 pa

LC 2005-277260

"The quotations collected here are not only by scientists but by writers, politicians, and others with something to say about science. . . . Each entry includes the name of the person being quoted, his or her dates, a . . . biographical statement, and several quotes, with their sources." Booklist

"This hefty volume is a great reference but it is also a great read—open it up to any page and expand the mind with a sampling of scientific ideas and philosophy." Choice

Park, Robert L.

Voodoo science; the road from foolishness to fraud. Oxford Univ. Press 2000 230p hardcover o.p. pa $17.95   **500**

1. Fraud 2. Science

ISBN 0-19-513515-6; 978-0-19-514710-0 pa; 0-19-514710-3 pa

LC 99-40911

The author "aims to expose various beliefs and schemes put forth in the popular press and other places as scientifically real and factual. . . . {He} turns a critical eye on cold fusion, magnet therapy, homeopathy, perpetual motion, and other recent examples of fringe science. . . . Park's book should be required reading for all science writers, journalists, and politicians." Libr J

Pohl, Frederik

Chasing science; science as a spectator sport. TOR Bks. 2000 251p $23.95; pa $14.95   **500**

1. Science

ISBN 0-312-86711-5; 0-7653-0829-0 pa

LC 00-57768

In order to witness science in action, Pohl traveled to a variety of sites, museums, laboratories, and observatories around the world. This is an account of his experiences and impressions.

Randall, Lisa

Knocking on heaven's door; how physics and scientific thinking illuminate the universe and the modern world. Ecco 2011 xxi, 442p il $29.99; ebook $14.99   **500**

1. Physics 2. Science

ISBN 978-0-06-172372-8; 978-0-06-209689-0 ebook

LC 2011010521

"To explain how science works, Randall analyzes the way two researchers at Bell Labs turned the annoying static coming through their radio telescope into a cosmic breakthrough. For in this piquant episode—and others that Randall examines—science advances by testing theoretical ingenuity against technologically acquired data. . . . Randall offers an insider's perspective into this cutting-edge science. Yet she illuminates that science with lucid language, laced with references to popular culture, political controversy, and even comic-strip art. The general reader's indispensable passport to the frontiers of science." Booklist

Includes bibliographical references

Ray, C. Claiborne

The **New** York Times second book of science questions and answers; 225 new, intriguing, and just plain bizarre inquiries into everyday scientific mysteries. drawings by Victoria Roberts; edited by Henry Fountain. Anchor Bks. (NY) 2003 228p il pa $13 **500**

1. Science

ISBN 0-385-72258-3

LC 2002-26192

"This eclectic volume of 228 questions with 200-word answers entices readers' interest in science. . . . There is no index and not much structure in this volume, but its charm and interest make up for its informality." Sci Books Films

Includes bibliographical references

Rees, Martin J., 1942-

From here to infinity; a vision for the future of science. Martin Rees. W.W. Norton 2012 144 p (hardcover) $23.95 **500**

1. Overpopulation 2. Nuclear warfare 3. Science and civilization 4. Science -- Philosophy

ISBN 0393063070; 9780393063073

LC 2012003421

This book on science by Martin Rees offers "four of the distinguished Reith lectures, delivered annually over BBC radio by renowned thinkers. . . . He reviews our planet's looming problems, from climate change to overpopulation to nuclear war, emphasizing that there are no solutions outside of science. . . . He also warns about the 'tendency for long-term strategies, however important, to be trumped by more immediate issues that can be resolved within an electoral cycle.'" (Kirkus Reviews)

Sagan, Carl, 1934-1996

Billions and billions; thoughts on life and death at the brink of the millennium. Random House 1997 241p hardcover o.p. pa $14.95 **500**

1. Science

ISBN 0-345-37918-7 pa

LC 96-52730

This collection of essays covers such topics as: "the invention of chess, life on Mars, global warming, abortion, international affairs, the nature of government, and the meaning of morality. Writing with clarity and an understanding of human nature, Sagan offers hope for humanity's future." Libr J

Includes bibliographical references

Broca's brain; reflections on the romance of science. Random House 1979 347p hardcover o.p. pa $7.99 **500**

1. God 2. Science 3. Religion 4. Astronomy 5. Machinery 6. Philosophy 7. Physicians 8. Physicists 9. Psychologists 10. Writers on science 11. Nobel

laureates for physics

ISBN 0-345-33689-5 pa

LC 78-21810

In this volume Sagan considers the following: "the quest for extraterrestrial life, popular science, and religious questions, as well as numerous concerns more immediate to his own specialty, astronomy." Libr J

The author "is a lucid, logical writer with a gift for explaining science to the layman and infecting the reader with his own boundless enthusiasm and curiosity." Natl Rev

Includes bibliographical references

Scientific American's ask the experts; answers to the most puzzling and mindblowing science questions. by the editors of Scientific American. HarperCollins Pubs. 2003 267p il pa $14.95 **500**

1. Science

ISBN 0-06-052336-0

LC 2004-555579

This "is a book that answers questions big, little, and in between. . . . The book uses the familiar question-and-answer format, with a table of contents allowing the reader to flip to a specific question. The questions are answered by a variety of experts. . . . This is one of those books you put on your reference shelf, and pull out whenever the subject turns to matters of scientific interest. Great for trivia buffs, too." Booklist

This explains everything; deep, beautiful, and elegant theories of how the world works. edited by John Brockman. 1st ed. Harper Perennial 2013 xx, 411 p.p (paperback) $15.99 **500**

1. Physics 2. American essays 3. Pattern perception 4. Explanation 5. Science -- Miscellanea

ISBN 0062230174; 9780062230171

LC 2012032107

This book is a "collection of brief essays [that] started with a question posed to the readers of Edge.org, founded by [editor John] Brockman . . . : What is your favorite deep, elegant, or beautiful explanation? The result is 150 brief essays that present . . . explanations of the world around us. The authors include Richard Dawkins, Eric Kandel, Alan Alda, and Brian Eno." (Library Journal)

Wiggins, Arthur W.

The **five** biggest ideas in science; [by] Charles M. Wynn [and] Arthur W. Wiggins; with cartoon commentary by Sidney Harris. Wiley 1997 200p il maps pa $15.95 **500**

1. Science

ISBN 0-471-13812-6

LC 96-27469

Presents five basic scientific hypotheses: the atomic model, the periodic law, the big bang theory, plate tectonics, and evolution

"Each 'Big Idea' is thoroughly described. . . . In explaining the thinking that led to each 'Big Idea,' the authors clear-

ly outline the scientific method and demystify the process."
Libr J

Includes bibliographical references

★ The **five** biggest unsolved problems in science; [by] Arthur W. Wiggins [and] Charles M. Wynn; with cartoon commentary by Sidney Harris. J. Wiley & Sons 2003 234p il pa $14.95   **500**
1. Science
ISBN 0-471-26808-9

LC 2003-284262

"The problems discussed in this volume are the dueling concepts of mass and masslessness (physics), the passage from chemicals to living matter (chemistry), the complete structure of the proteome (biology), long-range weather forecasting (geology), and the expansion of the universe (astronomy)." Sci Books Films

Includes bibliographical references

500.2   Physical sciences

Ball, Philip, 1962-
Nature's patterns; a tapestry in three parts. Oxford University Press 2009 308p il $29.95   **500.2**
1. Shape 2. Chaos (Science) 3. Patterns (Mathematics)
ISBN 978-0-19-923796-8; 0-19-923796-4

LC 2009-280579

"From the curl of a ram's horn to patterns of spider webs and the development of an embryo, Mr Ball examines the possible causes of the shapes and forms we observe. His book contains a lot of fascinating detail about the different physical, chemical and evolutionary processes at work." Economist

Includes bibliographical references

500.5   Space sciences

Launius, Roger D.
Smithsonian atlas of space exploration; [by] Roger D. Launius & Andrew K. Johnston. Collins 2009 230p il map $34.99   **500.5**
1. Outer space -- Exploration -- Pictorial works
ISBN 978-0-06-156526-7

LC 2009-649

This book "relates the story of space exploration in text, photographs, illustrations, and maps from the earliest times to the present. Written at a level geared to the general reader, this topically arranged work is divided into seven parts. . . . Each part contains a number of two or four-page subsections covering topics ranging from the earliest observatories of the ancient world to the possibilities for space flight in the future. . . . Distinguished by outstanding color illustrations and photographs, the very reasonably priced atlas should appeal to a broad audience." Booklist

Includes bibliographical references

Zimmerman, Robert
The **chronological** encyclopedia of discoveries in space. Oryx Press 2000 410p il maps $95 **500.5**
1. Astronautics 2. Outer space -- Exploration
ISBN 1-57356-196-7

"Over 1,000 entries record the date of launch, name of the spacecraft(s), summary of the mission, names of the crew members, experiments, problems, and discoveries in a clear and concise fashion. Seemingly every single space mission is included, encompassing spaceflight with and without human crews, military and civilian ventures, public and commercial ventures, planetary probes, and communications satellites. . . . An excellent, cross-referencing system within the text, as well as extensive subject indices by satellite, mission, and nation or consortia, helps the reader follow particular interests in detail. . . . There is no comparable source to this volume for its comprehensiveness and conciseness." Sci Books Films

Includes bibliographical references

501   Philosophy and theory

Arbesman, Samuel
★ The **half** -life of facts; why everything we know has an expiration date. Samuel Arbesman. Current 2012 viii, 242 p.p ill. (hardback) $25.95 **501**
1. Science 2. Probabilities 3. Theory of knowledge 4. Evolution 5. Science -- Philosophy
ISBN 159184472X; 9781591844723

LC 2012019142

This book by Samuel Arbesman presents a "treatise on the nature of facts: what they are, how and why they change and how they sometimes don't (despite being wrong). . . . [Arbesman argues that] what we know 'changes in understandable and systematic ways.' . . . He introduces 'scientometrics,' the science of science. With scientometrics, we can measure the exponential growth of facts, how long it will take, exponentially, for knowledge in any field to be disproved." (Kirkus Reviews)

Includes bibliographical references (pages 215-234) and index

Costa, Rebecca D.
The **watchman's** rattle; thinking our way out of extinction. with a foreword by E.O. Wilson. Vanguard Press 2010 347p $26.95   **501**
1. Civilization 2. Problem solving 3. Complexity (Philosophy)
ISBN 978-1-59315-605-3; 1-59315-605-7

LC 2010-927900

Explains why the human brain has such difficulty dealing with complex global problems and provides a method for surmounting these limitations in order to end the blights of worldwide recession, global warming, fast-spreading viruses, famine, and poverty.

This book "will give concerned readers new hope in human capability." Libr J

Includes bibliographical references

Dawkins, Richard

Unweaving the rainbow; science, delusion, and the appetite for wonder. Houghton Mifflin 1998 336p $26; pa $14 **501**
1. Science -- Philosophy
ISBN 0-395-88382-2; 0-618-05673-4 pa
LC 98-40879

Dawkins is a "witty popularizer, whether he is offering a crash course in DNA fingerprinting, explaining the origins of 'mad cow disease' in weird proteins that spread like self-replicating viruses or discussing male birdsong as an auditory aphrodisiac for female birds." Publ Wkly

Includes bibliographical references

Dawkins, Richard, 1941-

The **magic** of reality; how we know what's really true. illustrated by Dave McKean. 1st Free Press hardcover ed; Free Press 2011 271p il map **501**
1. Nature 2. Reality 3. Science -- Philosophy
ISBN 1439192812; 1451628927 ebook;
9781439192818; 9781451628920 ebook
LC 2011025607

"In this outstanding 'graphic science book,' evolutionary biologist Dawkins . . . teams up with illustrator Dave McKean . . . to examine questions in everyday science, such as: why seasons occur; what things are made of; and whether there's life on other planets. They explain the answers from mythological and cultural points of view before diving into the chemistry, biology, and physics—all in language that advanced middle school, or most high school, students can absorb." Publ Wkly

Deutsch, David

The **beginning** of infinity; explanations that transform the world. Viking Adult 2011 487p il $30 **501**
1. Infinite 2. Science -- Philosophy
ISBN 978-0-670-02275-5; 0-670-02275-6
LC 2011004120

The book discusses the interaction between humans and the universe they inhabit, challenging concepts such as "the Earth is a maternally inclined spacefaring vessel . . . [and] the utter insignificance of human beings in the cosmic scheme of things. . . . Our cosmic importance derives from our capacity to acquire knowledge, and use it to transform our lives and surroundings. . . . In the short term, this means that we should seek to understand and control the Earth's entire ecosystem. . . . In the medium term we should colonize the Moon, followed by the other planets in our solar system. In the longer term we should aim for the stars - and even beyond: Deutsch argues in some detail that extremely empty intergalactic space is easily capable of sustaining a high population of technologically advanced space-dwellers." (TLS)

"Anyone who loves to grapple with profound ideas should love reading this very ambitious and challenging look at the history and (possibly unlimited) future of human understanding." Sci Books Films

Includes bibliographical references

Firestein, Stuart

Ignorance; how it drives science. Stuart Firestein. Oxford University Press 2012 viii, 195 p.p **501**
1. Ignorance 2. Discoveries in science 3. Science -- Methodology 4. Science -- Philosophy 5. Ignorance (Theory of knowledge)
ISBN 0199828075; 9780199828074
LC 2011051395

This book argues that "[t]he fundamental attribute of successful scientists . . . is a form of ignorance characterised by knowing what you don't know, and being able to ask the right questions. . . . To demonstrate the crucial role of this type of informed ignorance, [Stuart] Firestein highlights two well-known examples. The first, Heisenberg's uncertainty principle, asserts that we cannot know the position and momentum of a particle simultaneously. . . . His second example is Godel's incompleteness theorems. . . . Firestein also includes more modern examples of productive ignorance." (New Scientist)

Includes bibliographical references and index

Henry, John

A **short** history of scientific thought; John Henry. Palgrave Macmillan 2012 xvii, 306 p.p ill. (hbk.) $90 **501**
1. Science -- History 2. Science -- Philosophy 3. Science and civilization 4. Natural history -- History 5. Civilization, Western -- History 6. Science -- Philosophy -- History 7. Science and civilization -- History
ISBN 0230019420; 0230019439; 9780230019423; 9780230019430
LC 2011049038

This book by John Henry offers a "historical survey of the major developments in scientific thought and the impact of science on Western culture, this book takes the reader from ancient times through to the twentieth century. Organized chronologically, the book explores the history of studies of the natural world, and man's role within that world, in a single volume." (Publisher's note)

Includes bibliographical references and index

Mitchell, Melanie

Complexity; a guided tour. Oxford University Press 2009 349p il map $29.95 **501**
1. Complexity (Philosophy) 2. Science -- Philosophy
ISBN 978-0-19-512441-5; 0-19-512441-3
LC 2008023794

The sciences of complexity "seek to explain how large-scale complex, organized, and adaptive behavior can emerge from simple interactions among myriad individuals. . . . Based on her work at the Santa Fe Institute and drawing on its interdisciplinary strategies, Mitchell [attempts to] bring clarity to the workings of complexity across a . . . range of biological, technological, and social phenomena, seeking out the general principles or laws that apply to all of them. She explores as well the relationship between complexity and evolution, artificial intelligence, computation, genetics, information processing, and [other fields]." (Publisher's note) Bibliography. Index.

The author offers a "snapshot of the growing field of complex-systems science. . . . Mitchell explores the historical roots of this area in the work of visionaries such as Henri

Poincaré and Edward Lorenz in dynamical-systems theory, and of John von Neumann, Alan Turing and others in computation. . . . The book hits its stride in its latter half, with an insightful survey of recent developments in complex-network theory and scaling in biology." Nature

Includes bibliographical references (p. 326-336)

Olson, Randy

★ **Don't** be such a scientist; talking substance in an age of style. Island Press 2009 206p il pa $19.95   **501**
1. Science 2. Communication 3. College teachers 4. Marine biologists 5. Communication in science 6. Motion picture directors 7. Science in motion pictures 8. Science -- Study and teaching
ISBN 1-59726-563-2; 978-1-59726-563-8

LC 2009-7081

Olson discusses his evolution "from science professor to Hollywood filmmaker. In Don't Be Such a Scientist, he . . [discusses] talking substance in an age of style. The key, he argues, is to stay true to the facts while tapping into something more primordial, more irrational, and ultimately more human." (Publisher's note) Filmography of movies by Randy Olson. Index.

The author argues "that 'scientists need artists.' He delves into the principle of 'arouse and fulfill,' suggesting that while scientists are great with the fulfillment part, the power of art can help arouse the interest of the broader audience." Publisher's note

Includes bibliographical references

Poe, Mya

Learning to communicate in science and engineering; case studies from MIT. [by] Mya Poe, Neal Lerner, and Jennifer Craig; foreword by James Paradis. MIT Press 2010 256p il $35   **501**
1. Writing 2. Communication 3. Science -- Study and teaching 4. Engineering -- Study and teaching
ISBN 978-0-262-16247-0

LC 2009-24788

"Case studies and pedagogical strategies to help science and engineering students improve their writing and speaking skills while developing professional identities." Barnes and Noble

Includes bibliographical references

Stannard, Russell

The **end** of discovery. Oxford University Press 2010 228p il $24.95   **501**
1. Physics 2. Theory of knowledge 3. Science -- Philosophy
ISBN 978-0-19-958524-3; 0-19-958524-5

LC 2010-930293

The author "believes that science will eventually come to an end, and that we are living in a 'transient age of human development' in which scientific discoveries can be made. But science won't end because we know everything; it will end because we know everything we can know. . . . [This is] a book worth reading. Lucid and provocative, it is a very polite corrective to both the superstitions of the layman . . . and the triumphalism of the experts." New Statesman

This will change everything; ideas that will shape the future. edited by John Brockman; [introduction by Daniel C. Dennett] HarperCollins 2010 xxiii, 390p pa $14.99   **501**
1. Science 2. Forecasting
ISBN 978-0-06-189967-6

"Author and editor Brockman presents 136 answers to the question, 'What game-changing scientific ideas and developments do you expect to live to see?'" Publ Wkly

"With contributions from Ian McEwan, Steven Pinker, Lee Smolin, Craig Venter, Richard Dawkins and 130 others of their ilk, the book is like an intellectual lucky dip." New Sci

502   Miscellany

Lamothe, Matt

The **where,** the why, and the how; 75 artists illustrate wondrous mysteries of science. Matt Lamothe ; Julia Rothman ; Jenny Volvovski. Chronicle Books 2012 160 p. ill. (chiefly col.) (hardcover) $24.95   **502**
1. Physics 2. Life sciences 3. Earth sciences
ISBN 1452108226; 9781452108223

LC 2012289775

In this book by Matt Lamothe, Julia Rothman, and Jenny Volvovski, "some of the biggest (and smallest) mysteries of the natural world are explained in essays by real working scientists, which are then illustrated by artists given free rein to be as literal or as imaginative as they like. The result is a celebration of the wonder that inspires every new discovery." (Publisher's note)

502.8   Auxiliary techniques and procedures; apparatus, equipment, materials

Instruments of science; an historical encyclopedia. editors, Robert Bud, Deborah Jean Warner; associate editor, Stephen Johnston; managing editor, Betsy Bahr Peterson; picture editor, Simon Chaplin. Garland 1998 xxv, 709p il (Garland encyclopedias in the history of science) $175   **502.8**
1. Reference books 2. Scientific apparatus and instruments -- Encyclopedias
ISBN 0-8153-1561-9

LC 97-15296

This "encyclopedia presents 325 historically significant scientific instruments from antiquity to the present. Instruments used for testing and monitoring in addition to those used for research are studied, including laboratory organisms such as E coli. Each of the signed entries explains how the instrument works and how it is used, as well as tracing its invention, development, and distribution. . . . Beautiful illustrations accompany many of the entries." Am Libr

Includes bibliographical references

503 Dictionaries, encyclopedias, concordances

The **Encyclopedia** of science and technology; James S. Trefil, general editor; contributing editors, Harold Morowitz, Paul Ceruzzi. Routledge 2001 554p il maps $50   **503**
1. Reference books 2. Science -- Encyclopedias 3. Technology -- Encyclopedias
ISBN 0-415-93724-8

LC 2001-19983

This reference includes "1000 entries, arranged alphabetically and color-coded to indicate whether the topic is related to life science, physical science, or technology. Accessible to the general reader, the articles range widely. . . . The excellent cross references direct the reader to related articles that cover either more fundamental or more advanced information. . . . A true pleasure to browse and read; highly recommended." Libr J
Includes bibliographical references and index

Encyclopedia of science, technology, and ethics; edited by Carl Mitcham. Macmillan Reference USA 2005 4v il map set $450   **503**
1. Reference books 2. Technology -- Encyclopedias 3. Science -- Ethical aspects -- Encyclopedias
ISBN 0-02-865831-0

LC 2005-6968

This "multivolume work on ethics provides a superb introduction to the issues presented." Booklist
Includes bibliographical references

McGraw-Hill dictionary of scientific and technical terms; 6th ed; McGraw-Hill 2003 2380p il $150   **503**
1. Reference books 2. Science -- Dictionaries 3. Technology -- Dictionaries
ISBN 0-07-042313-X

LC 2002-26436

First published 1974

This dictionary provides "over 100,000 succinct definitions ranging through 102 fields of science, from acoustics to zoology. Many of the definitions contain clear-cut illustrations with labels in the margins of the pages. Phonetics for pronunciation appear at the end of the definition." Sci Books Films

"This continues to be the most comprehensive science and technology dictionary for the student, researcher, and layperson." Booklist

McGraw-Hill Publishing Company

McGraw -Hill concise encyclopedia of science & technology; 6th ed.; McGraw-Hill 2009 2v il map set $295   **503**
1. Reference books 2. Science -- Encyclopedias 3. Technology -- Encyclopedias
ISBN 978-0-07-161366-8

LC 2008-50987

First published 1984

This encyclopedia features over 7100 articles on branches of technology and science ranging from acoustics to zoology.
Includes bibliographical references

★ **Van** Nostrand's scientific encyclopedia; 10th ed.; Wiley 2008 3v il map set $450   **503**
1. Reference books 2. Science -- Encyclopedias
ISBN 978-0-471-74338-5

LC 2007-46658

First published 1938

This encyclopedia contains articles contains over 10,000 entries on topics such as biology, chemistry, earth science, mathematics and engineering, anatomy and physiology, physics, botany, and space science.
Includes bibliographical references

506 Organizations and management

Seeing further; the story of science, discovery, and the genius of the Royal Society. edited & introduced by Bill Bryson; contributing editor, Jon Turney. William Morrow 2010 506p il $35; ebook $21.99   **506**
1. Science 2. Royal Society (Great Britain)
ISBN 978-0-06-199976-5; 978-0-06-203622-3 ebook

Bryson "presents a remarkable collection of essays celebrating the 350th anniversary of the founding of the Royal Society of London and its many contributions to science. Society members have included such illustrious names as Darwin, Newton, Leibniz, and Francis Bacon, to name a few. The volume's 23 contributors are both uniformly excellent and remarkable for their diversity." Publ Wkly
Includes bibliographical references (p. 486-489)

507.8 Use of apparatus and equipment in study and teaching

Experiment central; understanding scientific principles through projects. John T. Tanacredi & John Loret, general editors. U.X.L 2000 6v il set $347   **507.8**
1. Science -- Experiments
ISBN 1-4144-0522-7

LC 99-54142

Demonstrates scientific concepts by means of experiments, including step-by-step instructions, lists of materials, troubleshooter's guide, and interpretation and explanation of the results.

Johnson, George

The **ten** most beautiful experiments. Alfred A. Knopf 2008 192p il $22.95   **507.8**
1. Science -- Experiments
ISBN 978-1-4000-4101-5; 1-4000-4101-5

LC 2007-27839

"Writing up Luigi Galvani's study of frog's legs, James Joule's of heat, Albert Michelson's of light's speed, and Robert Millikan's of the electron's charge, Johnson exerts classic appeal to science readers: presenting the lone genius making a great discovery. Good to go in any library." Booklist
Includes bibliographical references

Sheldrake, Rupert

   Seven experiments that could change the world; a do-it-yourself guide to revolutionary science. {2nd ed}; Park St. Press 2002 303p pa $16.95   **507.8**

   1. Science -- Experiments

   ISBN 0-89281-989-8

                        LC 2002-728157

   First published 1995 by Riverhead Bks.

   "Sheldrake questions many tenets of the mechanistic-materialistic orthodoxy governing most science today and proposes certain practical experiments to raise further doubts about it. He presents experiments by which we can determine how some pets know when their owners are coming home, how homing pigeons find their way, how insect colonies operate, how people know that they are being stared at from behind and how phantom limbs sometimes seem to amputees to be still attached. . . . Finally, he offers details of experiments by which even those who are not trained scientists can measure some of these possibly paranormal phenomena. A well-reasoned, accessible and provocative book." Publ Wkly

   Includes bibliographical references (p. 284-296) and index

508   Natural history

Ackerman, Diane, 1948-

   Cultivating delight; a natural history of my garden. HarperCollins Pubs. 2001 261p hardcover o.p. pa $13.95   **508**

   1. Gardens 2. Natural history 3. Large print books

   ISBN 0-06-050536-2 pa

                        LC 2001-16607

   This book is divided "into 52 passages of meditation, observation and storytelling, following the {author's} garden from spring through winter." (N Y Times Book Rev)

   Although Ackerman's "book is presented as a gardening journal, with sections on the four seasons, her musings know no bounds and verge on stream-of-consciousness. One typical chapter ranges over topics that include landscape architecture, lawns, fences, autumn colors, childhood memories, the difference between labyrinths and mazes, the history and definition of gardens, and compost, all peppered with quotations from a dozen authors." Libr J

Asma, Stephen T.

   Stuffed animals & pickled heads; the culture and evolution of natural history museums. Oxford Univ. Press 2001 302p il hardcover o.p. pa $16.95 **508**

   1. Museums 2. Natural history

   ISBN 0-19-513050-2; 0-19-516336-2 pa

                        LC 00-40674

   The author discusses the development of natural history museums, beginning with the "'cabinets of curiosities', put together in the 17th century. . . . The cabinets changed when Darwin's theory of evolution became widely accepted in the late 19th century, with less emphasis on the exceptional, more on showing how each species fitted into the supposed scheme of things." Economist

   Includes bibliographical references

Carroll, Sean B.

   Remarkable creatures; epic adventures in the search for the origins of species. Houghton Mifflin Harcourt 2009 331p il map $26; pa $14.95   **508**

   1. Evolution 2. Naturalists

   ISBN 978-0-15-101485-9; 0-15-101485-X; 978-0-547-24778-6 pa; 0-547-24778-8 pa

                        LC 2008-25438

   "Examines the contributions of pioneering scientists to the modern understanding of how Earth and the planet's life evolved, recounting such important events as Darwin's trip around the world, Charles Walcott's discovery of pre-Cambrian life, and the Leakeys' probe into humankind's remote past." Publisher's note

   "A stirring introduction to the wonder of evolutionary biology." Kirkus

   Includes bibliographical references

Darwin, Charles

   ★ The **voyage** of the Beagle; journal of researches into the natural history and geology of the countries visited during the voyage of H.M.S. Beagle round the world. introduction by Steve Jones. Modern Lib. 2001 468p il pa $12.95   **508**

   1. Natural history 2. Beagle Expedition (1831-1836) 3. South America -- Description and travel

   ISBN 0-375-75680-9

                        LC 00-46294

   This journal records the author's five year voyage around the world as a naturalist aboard H.M.S. Beagle. The trip was influential in the formulation of Darwin's theories of evolution. During the journey he collected data on wildlife, geological formations, weather, and local customs.

De Villiers, Marq

   Sahara : a natural history; {by} Marq de Villiers and Sheila Hirtle. Walker & Co. 2002 326p il maps $28; pa $13   **508**

   1. Sahara Desert 2. Natural history -- Africa

   ISBN 0-8027-1372-6; 0-8027-7678-7 pa

                        LC 2002-71391

   "Insightful and intelligent, this fascinating book will appeal to anyone with a curiosity about the world's largest desert and the people who inhabit it." Booklist

   Includes bibliographical references

Dunne, Pete, 1951-

   Bayshore summer; finding Eden in a most unlikely place. photographs by Linda Dunne. Houghton Mifflin Harcourt 2010 262p il $24   **508**

   1. Outdoor life 2. Natural history -- New Jersey

   ISBN 978-0-547-19563-6; 0-547-19563-X

                        LC 2009-27928

   "This delightful book, written in the first person, introduces readers to the places that Pete Dunne loves in South Jersey along Delaware Bay. Each chapter relates a particular excursion of his and manages to include an ample amount of natural history, along with regional human history, environmental controversies, and appreciation of the local culture. . . . The book is written with an easygoing style and humor, presenting scientific information in an accessible form, along with local history and culture, with a dose of environmentalism and regret for the loss of the old ways of life for the local population thrown in." Sci Books Films

Includes bibliographical references

Flannery, Tim F.

The **eternal** frontier; an ecological history of North America and its peoples. {by} Tim Flannery. Atlantic Monthly Press 2001 404p il maps $27.50; pa $16 **508**

1. Natural history -- North America

ISBN 0-87113-789-5; 0-8021-3888-8 pa

LC 2001-18841

This "book explores approximately 65 million years of the ecology of the entire North American continent." Libr J

"This book weaves ecological, cultural, and social history together in a marvelous way." Sci Books Films

Fothergill, Alastair

Planet Earth; as you've never seen it before. [by] Alastair Fothergill [et al.]; foreword by David Attenborough. University of California Press 2007 309p il map $39.95 **508**

1. Habitat (Ecology) 2. Earth

ISBN 978-0-520-25054-3; 0-520-25054-0

LC 2006-50073

In this collection of over 400 photographs of natural landscapes and wildlife, the author "takes readers on a kaleidoscopic tour of the flora, fauna and natural history of the Earth's poles, forests, plains, deserts, mountains and oceans." Publ Wkly

Gould, Stephen Jay, 1941-2002

Bully for brontosaurus; reflections in natural history. Norton 1991 540p il hardcover o.p. pa $15.95 **508**

1. Evolution 2. Natural history

ISBN 0-393-30857-X pa

LC 91-6916

A collection of essays from the author's monthly columns in Natural History magazine

"These pithy essays focus on evolution and the workings of science. Gould's fans . . . will find these works fascinating, literate, and often challenging—vintage Gould." Libr J

Leonardo's mountain of clams and the Diet of Worms; essays on natural history. Harmony Bks. 1998 422p il hardcover o.p. pa $15 **508**

1. Evolution 2. Natural history

ISBN 0-609-80475-8 pa

LC 98-11500

"Gould's incomparable style, by turns colloquial, humorous, ironic and insightful, allows readers to revel in his unabashed and contagious enthusiasm." N Y Times Book Rev

Includes bibliographical references

The **lying** stones of Marrakesh; penultimate reflections to natural history. Harmony Bks. 2000 372p il hardcover o.p. pa $15 **508**

1. Evolution 2. Natural history

ISBN 0-609-80755-2 pa

LC 99-36148

In this collection of essays Gould "chronicles the history of paleontology through a biographical lens, then trains his scientific acumen and keen humor on such subjects as Mozart's Requiem and the tragic 1911 Triangle Shirt Factory fire." Booklist

★ The **richness** of life; the essential Stephen Jay Gould. edited by Paul McGarr and Steven Rose; with an introduction by Steven Rose and a foreword by Oliver Sacks. Norton 2007 654p il $35 **508**

1. Evolution 2. Natural history

ISBN 978-0-393-06498-8; 0-393-06498-0

LC 2006-29208

Frist published 2006 in the United Kingdom

"For collections that have room for only one volume of his writing, this is the essential one." SLJ

Includes bibliographical references

Keynes, R. D.

Fossils, finches, and Fuegians; Darwin's adventures and discoveries on the Beagle. by Richard Keynes. Oxford Univ. Press 2003 428p il maps $35 **508**

1. Naturalists 2. Natural history 3. Travel writers 4. Writers on science 5. Beagle Expedition (1831-1836)

ISBN 0-19-516649-3

LC 2002-154176

First published 2002 in the United Kingdom

"Keynes shows readers how his great-grandfather's belief in the immutability of species slowly began to change during his travels. Handsomely illustrated with sketches and paintings made by Darwin and others associated with the Beagle, this is an excellent introduction to the events that led 20 years later to On the Origin of Species." Publ Wkly

Includes bibliographical references

Kress, W. John

The **weeping** goldsmith; discoveries in the secret land of Myanmar. foreword by Wade Davis. Abbeville Press 2009 272p il map $45 **508**

1. Natural history -- Myanmar 2. Myanmar -- Description and travel

ISBN 978-0-7892-1032-6

LC 2008-55031

"A visually stunning and involving chronicle of . . . Kress' daunting and revelatory explorations and discoveries in Myanmar, a land of beauty and tyranny, imperiled biodiversity and resilience." Booklist

Includes bibliographical references

Leach, Amy

Things that are; Amy Leach ; illustrations by Nate Christopherson. Milkweed Editions 2012 xiii, 185 p.p (acid-free paper) $18.00 **508**

1. Essays 2. Natural history 3. Natural history literature

ISBN 1571313346; 9781571313348

LC 2011040887

This book of essays by Amy Leach, winner of a Whiting Writers' Award and a Rona Jaffe Foundation Writers' Award, "explores fantastical and curious subjects pertaining to natural phenomena." It is "divided into two sections -- 'Things of Earth' and 'Things of Heaven' -- containing essays with names such as 'Goats, and Bygone Goats,' 'When Trees Dream of Being Trees' and 'Sail On, My Little Honeybee.' Each of the essays range from three to seven pages, and they are accompanied by . . . pen-and-ink drawings by [Nate] Christopherson." (Kirkus Reviews)

Leopold, Aldo, 1886-1948

A **Sand** County almanac & other writings on ecology & conservation; a sand county almanac & other writings on ecology and conservation. Aldo Leopold ; [edited by] Curt Meine. Literary Classics of the United States, Inc. 2013 832 p. illustrations, maps (Library of America)   **508**
    1. Nature conservation 2. Environmental protection
ISBN 9781598532067

                   LC 2012948207

A reissue of the title first published 1949

By Aldo Leopold and edited by Curt Meine, "the collection opens with Leopold's classic A Sand County Almanac," which "is joined here by over fifty uncollected articles, essays, speeches, and other writings that chart the evolution of Leopold's ideas over the course of three decades. . . . The volume also presents a freshly prepared version of Leopold's extraordinary field journals." (Publisher's note)

"The volume also includes a chronology of Leopold's life; extensive notes; an index to plants/animals, with a mixture of common and scientific nomenclature; and a general index." Choice

Includes bibliographical references and indexes

Lincoln, Roger J.

★ The **Cambridge** illustrated dictionary of natural history; {by} R. J. Lincoln and G. A. Boxshall; illustrations by Roberta Smith. Cambridge Univ. Press 1987 413p il hardcover o.p. pa $29   **508**
    1. Reference books 2. Natural history -- Dictionaries
ISBN 0-521-39941-6 pa

                   LC 87-8018

This "is principally a dictionary of taxonomic groups down to the level of family, with common names cross-referenced to Latin ones, and frequent illustrations. Technical terms are few, and paleontology is given less attention than current classes of plants, animals, and microorganisms." Recomm Ref Books in Paperback. 2d edition

Matthiessen, Peter

End of the earth; voyaging to Antarctica. National Geographic Soc. 2003 242p il maps $26 **508**
    1. Animals -- Antarctica 2. Antarctica -- Exploration
ISBN 0-7922-5059-1

                   LC 2003-51254

This account of the author's voyage describes the wildlife he encountered in the region

"Vivid and empathic accounts of the high drama and petty rivalries of Antarctic exploration alternate with Matthiessen's own adventures as he shares his indelible impressions of this cold, white wonderland in the hope that they will inspire readers to appreciate the beauty and bounty of the earth's 'shimmering web of biodiversity' enough to defend and preserve it." Booklist

Includes bibliographical references

Muir, John

Nature writings; the story of my boyhood and youth, my first summer in the Sierra, the mountains of California, Stickeen, selected essays. Library of Am. 1997 888p il $35   **508**
    1. Authors 2. Naturalists 3. Writers on nature
ISBN 1-88301-124-8

                   LC 96-9664

Muir "is at his best . . . when he is looking intently at something, walking around it, sniffing the air, looking again. As a writer he is a kind of visionary sensualist, a seer who reveals what lies in plain sight." Commentary

Natural history; the ultimate visual guide to everything on Earth. [senior project editor, Kathryn Hennessy] DK 2010 648p il map $50   **508**
    1. Natural history 2. Reference books
ISBN 978-0-7566-6752-8; 0-7566-6752-6

                  LC 2010-283659

"This is an international encyclopedia of life-forms—e.g., fossils, fungi, plants, animals, mammals—that includes vital facts and two to three sentences about each as well as more than 5000 color illustrations in all. Each grouping is introduced by an essay that puts it in biological and evolutionary perspective." Libr J

Nature writing; the tradition in English. edited by Robert Finch and John Elder. Norton 2002 1152p $39.95   **508**
    1. Natural history
ISBN 0-393-04966-3

                  LC 2001-55825

First published 1990 with title: The Norton book of nature writing

This anthology of nature writings from 1789 to 1987 includes such authors as Henry David Thoreau, John Muir, Annie Dillard, and Barry Lopez

Includes bibliographical references

Nicholls, Steve

Paradise found; nature in America at the time of discovery. University of Chicago Press 2009 524p $30   **508**
    1. Human influence on nature 2. America -- Exploration 3. Natural history -- North America
ISBN 978-0-226-58340-2; 0-226-58340-6

                  LC 2008-36076

The author "turns to the writings of forgotten early naturalists to gain understanding both of the natural abundance of the New World when the first Europeans arrived and of how so much of this living bounty was destroyed so quickly. . . . Not only does Nicholls present arresting material, he also offers fresh interpretations and connections in this grandly spanning and affecting look to the past for guidance in facing a future of further diminishment." Booklist

Includes bibliographical references and index

Quammen, David

The **boilerplate** rhino; nature in the eye of the beholder. Scribner 2000 287p hardcover o.p. pa $13 **508**

1. Nature 2. Natural history
ISBN 0-7432-0032-2 pa

LC 99-56894

In this "collection of David Quammen's columns for Outside magazine, the focus is on man's interaction with nature. Sometimes Quammen interacts with the nature he's writing about; at other times he just thinks about it, reads up and summarizes what he's read." N Y Times Book Rev

Includes bibliographical references

Safina, Carl

The **view** from Lazy Point; a natural year in an unnatural world. with drawings by Trudy Nicholson; maps by Jon Luoma. Henry Holt and Co. 2011 401p il map $32; ebook $16.99 **508**

1. Human ecology 2. Marine ecology 3. Coastal ecology 4. Environmental degradation
ISBN 978-0-8050-9040-6; 0-8050-9040-1; 978-1-4299-5035-0 ebook; 1-4299-5035-8 ebook

LC 2009-40108

A conservationist explores various global regions to investigate examples of environmental degradation and renewal while identifying a link between environmental dangers and human rights issues.

"A superb work of environmental reportage and reflection." Kirkus

Includes bibliographical references

Shetterly, Susan Hand

Settled in the wild; notes from the edge of town. Algonquin Books of Chapel Hill 2010 240p $21.95 **508**

1. Wildlife 2. Natural history -- Maine
ISBN 1565126181; 9781565126183

LC 2009-30802

Shetterly "notes the interplay of humanity and wilderness through fishing, forestry, conservation, preservation, hunting, trapping, development and wildlife rehabilitation, but also in quiet, personal appreciation. Shetterly is a less verbose Thoreau, allowing nature's wisdom to seep through her simple yet thorough observations." Kirkus

Stroud, Patricia Tyson

A **glorious** enterprise; the Academy of Natural Sciences of Philadelphia and the making of American science. Robert McCracken Peck and Patricia Tyson Stroud ; photographs by Rosamond Purcell. University of Pennsylvania Press 2012 xvii, 437 p.p (alk. paper) $75 **508**

1. Natural history 2. Science -- History 3. Academy of Natural Sciences of Philadelphia -- History 4. Natural history -- Research -- Pennsylvania -- Philadelphia
ISBN 0812243803; 9780812243802

LC 2011034991

This book by Robert McCracken Peck and Patricia Tyson Stroud focuses on the history of the Academy of Natural Sciences of Philadelphia, which "stands today as the oldest

natural history museum in the Western hemisphere.... What began as a small gathering of devoted amateurs has grown into a vibrant international center for scientific education and research." (Publisher's note)

Includes bibliographical references and index.

Wallace, Joseph

A **gathering** of wonders; behind the scenes at the American Museum of Natural History. St. Martin's Press 2000 288p il $24.95; pa $14.95 **508**

1. Natural history 2. American Museum of Natural History
ISBN 0-312-25221-8; 0-312-28039-4 pa

LC 00-25481

This describes the American Museum of Natural History "through its most famous, colorful or important scientists and administrators, from the 1880s to the 1970s." Publ Wkly

508.2 Seasons

Ackerman, Diane, 1948-

Dawn light; dancing with cranes and other ways to start the day. W.W. Norton 2009 240p il $24.95 **508.2**

1. Nature 2. Seasons 3. Environmental influence on humans
ISBN 978-0-393-06173-4

LC 2009-23459

"This collection of essays is arranged seasonally from spring to winter and ranges geographically between Palm Beach, FL, and Ithaca, NY. Essays cover everything from the behavior of doves in Florida at dawn and Monet's use of light in his art to a discussion of festivals that take place at dawn and teaching young whooping cranes to migrate... . These pieces are accessible and lyrically written, and they flow well, one after another, making reading the book a true pleasure." Libr J

508.747 Natural history--New York

Steinberg, Ted

★ **Gotham** unbound; an ecological history of greater New York, from Henry Hudson to Hurricane Sandy. Ted Steinberg. Simon & Schuster 2014 544 p. illustrations, maps (hardcover : alk. paper) $32 **508.747**

1. Natural history -- New York (State) -- New York
ISBN 1476741247; 9781476741246; 9781476741284; 9781476741307

LC 2013036197

This book, by Ted Steinberg, "is a powerful account of the relentless development that New Yorkers wrought as they plunged headfirst into the floodplain and transformed untold amounts of salt marsh and shellfish beds into a land jam-packed with people, asphalt and steel, and the reeds and gulls that thrive among them." (Publisher's note)

A "fascinating and cautionary unnatural history, a staggering epic of human will, might, and folly that affirms a crucial truth, 'the control of nature is an illusion.'" Booklist

Includes bibliographical references and index

509   History, geographic treatment, biography

Al-Khalili, Jim

The **house** of wisdom; how Arabic science saved ancient knowledge and gave us the Renaissance. Penguin Press 2011 xxix, 302p il map $29.95   **509**
1. Medieval civilization 2. Science -- Philosophy 3. Science -- Arab countries 4. Arab countries -- Intellectual life
ISBN 1-59420-279-6; 978-1-59420-279-7

LC 2010-53136

This is a history of early "Islamic astronomy, mathematics, medicine and philosophy." (N Y Times Book Rev) Glossary. Chronology. Index.

"There is a commonly held view that during the Middle Ages, Arabic scientists focused mainly on translating into Arabic the scientific knowledge of ancient civilizations while contributing little to scientific advancement. Physicist al-Khalili . . . challenges this theory by documenting the remarkable contributions of Arabic astronomers, mathematicians, physicians, physicists, chemists, and philosophers, who were scholars at a scientific academy in Baghdad known as the House of Wisdom. . . . Al-Khalili brings to life a vibrant intellectual period of Islamic history when there was not only tolerance for other religions and cultures but a synergy between science and Islam. Anyone interested in the early history of science or the development of the scientific method before Galileo will find this an engaging study." Libr J

Includes bibliographical references

Concise history of science & invention; an illustrated time line. edited by Jolyon Goddard. National Geographic 2010 352 p. ill., maps (some col.) $40.00   **509**
1. Reference books 2. Science -- History 3. Inventions -- History 4. Science -- History -- Chronology 5. Inventions -- History -- Chronology
ISBN 1426205449; 9781426205446

LC 2009018460

This book presents "a panoramic perspective on humankind's restless quest for the laws, theories, and tools by which we can grasp and master our universe. . . . All human scientific endeavors and achievement are divided into four general fields of inquiry and arrayed into four basic geocultural regions . . . highlighted by 350 photographs, maps, illustrations, and diagrams that add graphic emphasis to key information." (Publisher's note)

Includes glossary and bibliographical references

Crease, Robert P.

The **great** equations; breakthroughs in science from Pythagoras to Heisenberg. W.W. Norton & Co. 2009 315p il $25.95   **509**
1. Equations 2. Science -- History 3. Science --

Philosophy
ISBN 978-0-393-06204-5; 0-393-06204-X

LC 2008-42494

The author "explores 10 rather beautiful equations. He begins with the beguiling simplicity of the equation that bears Pythagoras' name . . . and moves on to Newton's second law of motion and law of universal gravitation, the second law of thermodynamics, Maxwell's celebrated equations, discoveries by Einstein and Schrödinger and, finally, Heisenberg's famous uncertainty principle. . . . Any reader who aspires to be scientifically literate will find this a good starting place." Publ Wkly

Includes bibliographical references

The **prism** and the pendulum; the ten most beautiful experiments in science. Random House 2003 xxii, 244p il hardcover o.p. pa $14.95   **509**
1. Science -- History 2. Science -- Experiments
ISBN 1-400-06131-8; 0-8129-7062-4 pa

LC 2003-54765

Each scientific experiment discussed here "is followed by an 'interlude,' or commentary, on how the experiment qualifies as most beautiful and how art and science both give meaning to the term 'beauty.'" Sci Books Films

Dolnick, Edward

The **clockwork** universe; Isaac Newton, the Royal Society, and the birth of the modern world. HarperCollins 2011 378p il $27.99; ebook $23.99   **509**
1. Science 2. Physicists 3. Mathematicians 4. Writers on science 5. Royal Society of London 6. Royal Society (Great Britain) 7. Scientists -- Great Britain -- History
ISBN 9780061719516; 9780062042262

LC 2010-24321

The subject is "how the scientific attempt to describe the underlying order of the cosmos played out in the life of Isaac Newton." (N Y Times Book Rev) Bibliography. Index.

"Colorful, entertainingly written and nicely paced— a fine introductory text on Newton and the scientific revolution." Kirkus

Includes bibliographical references

Encyclopedia of the scientific revolution; from Copernicus to Newton. editor Wilbur Applebaum. Garland 2000 xxxv, 758p il (Garland reference library of the humanities) $160   **509**
1. Reference books 2. Science -- History -- Encyclopedias
ISBN 0-8153-1503-1

LC 00-25149

A "collection of articles on the progress of scientific discovery in the 16th and 17th centuries. . . . The 437 entries vary in length from just half a page to five pages, and each has a short bibliography directing the reader to recent articles and monographs as well as primary sources." Libr J

Includes bibliographical references

Fara, Patricia

★ **Science**; a four thousand year history. Oxford University Press 2009 408p il map pa $18.95; $34.95 **509**

1. Science and civilization 2. Science -- History
ISBN 019922689X; 0199580278 pa; 9780199226894; 9780199580279 pa; 978-0-19-922689-4; 978-0-19-958027-9 pa; 0-19-958027-8 pa; 0-19-922689-X
LC 2008-50975

This "book explores how science has become so powerful by describing the financial interests and imperial ambitions behind its success. . . . [Fara challenges] notions of European superiority by emphasising the importance of scientific projects based around the world. . . . [This] volume challenges scientific supremacy itself, arguing that science is successful not because it is always indubitably right, but because people have said that it is right. Science dominates modern life, but perhaps the globe will be better off by limiting science's powers and undoing some of its effects." (Publisher's note) Index.

"This survey of 4,000 years of scientific discovery from Babylon to the present confirms that historians of science often have quite different perspectives from those of the actual practitioners. . . . Readers learn about the contributions of famous scientists as though they were almost puppets responding to religious, social, and practical influences in both their choices of research topics and their methods of investigation—in contrast to their possessing an inherent desire to better understand the behavior of nature. In this highly readable book that tells a magnificent story, Fara . . . weaves together the bits and pieces in a unique way." Choice

Includes bibliographical references

Flowers, Charles

★ **Instability** rules; the ten most amazing ideas of modern science. Wiley 2002 228p $24.95 **509**

1. Science -- History
ISBN 0-471-38042-3
LC 2001-6729

A "look at ten milestone discoveries and their discoverers. . . . The stories include Edwin Hubble and the expanding universe, Alfred Wegener and continental drift, Neils Bohr and quantum mechanics, Alan Turing and artificial intelligence, and James Watson and Francis Crick and DNA." (Publisher's note)

Freely, John

The **flame** of Miletus; the birth of science in ancient Greece (and how it changed the world) John Freely. I.B. Tauris 2012 238 p. (hbk.) $29.95 **509**

1. Ancient philosophy 2. Greece -- Civilization 3. Science, Ancient 4. Science -- Greece -- History 5. Greece -- Intellectual life -- To 146 B.C
ISBN 1780760515; 9781780760513
LC 2012472537

This book looks at Ancient Greece and "the great scientific thinkers of that distant age. [John Freely] narrates . . . the story of how the ancient flame lit by Thales and others survived the centuries after the fall of Hellas and Rome, resurfaced in the Islamic world, and was transmitted to western Europe. There it rekindled the spirit of scientific inquiry that led to the germination of modern science." (Choice)

Includes bibliographical references (p. 226-235) and index

Green, Bill

Boltzmann's tomb; travels in search of science. Bellevue Literary Press 2011 208p il **509**

1. Scientists 2. Voyages and travels 3. Discoveries in science 4. College deans 5. College teachers 6. Religious scholars
ISBN 1-934137-35-9; 978-1-934137-35-2

This book discusses Green's visits to "the workplaces and graves of . . . famous scientists whose lives and research were affected in some way by unpredicted events." (Sci Books Films) Index.

"This book is very readable and should be especially appealing to young people contemplating a life in science." Sci Books Films

Gribbin, John R.

The **fellowship**; Gilbert, Bacon, Harvey, Wren, Newton, and the story of a scientific revolution. [by] John Gribbin. Overlook Press 2007 335p il $29.95 **509**

1. Scientists 2. Royal Society (Great Britain)
ISBN 1-58567-831-7; 978-1-58567-831-0
LC 2008-530551

This is a "chronicle of modern science's beginnings. The author devotes a chapter each to the lives of the five titular scientists—William Gilbert, Francis Bacon, William Harvey, Christopher Wren, and Isaac Newton—plus several others who lived between the 1500s and the early 1700s." Libr J

"Gribbin is an ideal and entertaining narrator for this lively story of intellectual discovery and brotherhood." Publ Wkly

Includes bibliographical references

The **scientists**; a history of science told through the lives of its greatest inventors. [by] John Gribbin. Random House 2003 xxii, 646p il hardcover o.p. pa $16.95 **509**

1. Scientists 2. Science -- History
ISBN 1-4000-6013-3; 0-8129-6788-7 pa
LC 2003-46607

First published 2002 in the United Kingdom with title: Science: a history, 1543-2001

"Replete with scientific clarity, Gribbin's work is the epitome of what a general-interest history of science should be." Booklist

Includes bibliographical references

Hofstadter, Dan

The **Earth** moves; Galileo and the Roman Inquisition. W.W. Norton 2009 240p il **509**

1. Popes 2. Astronomy 3. Astronomers 4. Inquisition 5. Writers on science 6. Inquisition -- Italy 7. Science, Renaissance 8. Catholic Church -- Italy -- History 9. Astronomy -- Religious aspects -- Christianity 10. Catholic Church -- Doctrines -- History -- 17th century
ISBN 0-393-06650-9; 978-0-393-06650-0
LC 2009-4325

This book examines the Inquisition in relation to Galileo's arrest, trial, conviction, and the legal processes involved. Bibliography. Index.

This book "allows a clear understanding of one of the major events in the history of science." Sci Books Films

Includes bibliographical references

Holmes, Richard, 1945-

★ The **age** of wonder; how the romantic generation discovered the beauty and terror of science. Pantheon Books 2009 xxi, 552p il $40; pa $17.95 **509**

1. Science -- Great Britain -- History

ISBN 978-0-375-42222-5; 978-1-4000-3187-0 pa

LC 2008-49587

The author focuses on "the science of the Romantic Age, and demonstrates the extent to which the era's scientific and literary endeavors enriched each other and were animated by common ideals." New Yorker

"In this big two-hearted river of a book, the twin energies of scientific curiosity and poetic invention pulsate on every page." N Y Times Book Rev

Includes bibliographical references

Horvitz, Leslie Alan

Eureka! : scientific breakthroughs that changed the world. Wiley 2002 246p il $24.95 **509**

1. Inventors 2. Discoveries in science 3. Inventions

ISBN 0-471-40276-1

LC 2001-46890

This examines twelve scientific discoveries and their discoverers, including Joseph Priestley and oxygen, Friedrich Kekulé and the structure of carbon compounds, Dmitri Mendeleev and the periodic table, Isaac Newton and gravity, Einstein and the theory of relativity, Philo Farnsworth and television, Alexander Fleming and penicillin, Charles Townes and the laser, Alfred Wegener and continental drift, Darwin and the origin of species, Watson and Crick and the double helix, and Benoit Mandelbrot and fractal geometry.

Includes bibliographical references

Jardine, Lisa

Ingenious pursuits; building the scientific revolution. Talese 1999 444p il hardcover o.p. pa $16 **509**

1. Science -- History

ISBN 0-385-72001-7 pa

LC 99-41985

In this history of science in the 17th and early 18th centuries the author "chronicles improvements in the tools of observation (telescopes, microscopes) and measurement (clocks) that were used by a pungent cast of characters who collaborated and squabbled with one another as they sorted out comets and discovered microbes." New Yorker

Includes bibliographical references

Lightman, Alan P.

★ The **discoveries**; great breakthroughs in 20th century science. [by] Alan Lightman. Pantheon Books 2005 553p il $32.50; pa $16.95 **509**

1. Science -- History

ISBN 0-375-42168-8; 0-375-71345-X pa

LC 2005-40854

This book "chronicles 25 landmark findings in astronomy, physics, chemistry, and biology in the 20th century. Beginning with Max Planck's quantum theory and ending with Paul Berg's recombinant DNA, these breakthroughs are academically and playfully explored via the nature of the unknown, the circumstances and influences of discovery, and, most originally, the actual words of the scientists." Libr J

Includes bibliographical references

McCray, W. Patrick

The **visioneers**; how a group of elite scientists pursued space colonies, nanotechnologies, and a limitless future. W. Patrick McCray. Princeton University Press 2012 351 p. (hardback : acid-free paper) $29.95 **509**

1. Nanotechnology 2. Space colonies 3. Visionaries 4. Science -- History

ISBN 0691139830; 9780691139838

LC 2012017061

This book looks at visioneers, a term coined by author W. Patrick McCray "to describe an individual with an an inquiring mind that is not merely scientific or technical but posed imaginatively toward the future. . . . The two primary visioneers examined by McCray are Gerard O'Neil, a prominent Princeton physicist who saw space colonization as an answer to Earth's growing population, and Eric Drexler, who was fascinated by the new field of nanotechnology." (Library Journal)

Includes bibliographical references and index

Notable black American scientists; Kristine M. Krapp, editor. Gale Res. 1999 xxvi, 349p il $125 **509**

1. Reference books 2. Scientists -- Dictionaries 3. African Americans -- Biography -- Dictionaries

ISBN 0-7876-2789-5

LC 98-36338

The "contributors to this compilation of 254 bibliographic profiles emphasize the achievements of black scientists and physicians, men and women, from Colonial times to the present, in the territory that is now the US. . . . Each entry begins with basic information about each subject—name, year of birth and death (if deceased), and specialty. A biographical essay follows." Choice

Includes bibliographical references

★ The **Oxford** companion to the history of modern science; editor in chief, J.L. Heilbron; editors, James Bartholomew {et al.} Oxford Univ. Press 2003 xxviii, 941p il $110 **509**

1. Science -- History

ISBN 0-19-511229-6

LC 2002-153783

This reference on the history of science from the Renaissance through the 20th century includes some 600 articles covering "a broad spectrum of topics in all scientific disciplines (e.g., biotechnology, geology) as well as disciplines that influenced science, such as religion and politics. Also included are the biographies of 100 leading figures (e.g., Isaac Newton, Marie Curie) and coverage of scientific instruments (e.g., microscopes, Geiger counters). Organized alphabetically, the well-written articles include plenty of cross references. Over 100 black-and-white illustrations appear within their appropriate articles, but the eight pages of color illustrations in the middle of the volume are not associated with any article." Libr J

Includes bibliographical references

Piel, Gerard

The **age** of science; what scientists learned in the 20th century. with illustrations by Peter Bradford. Basic Bks. 2001 xx, 460p il maps $40   **509**

1. Science -- History

ISBN 0-465-05755-1

LC 2001-43178

This "survey explores quantum mechanics, subatomic particles, astrophysics, genetics, cell biology, planetary geology, and evolution. . . . While it generally succeeds in making science intelligible to the lay reader, this book is still challenging if rewarding." Libr J

Includes bibliographical references

Reader's guide to the history of science; edited by Arne Hessenbruch. Fitzroy Dearborn Pubs. 2000 xxix, 934p $135   **509**

1. Reference books   2. Science -- History -- Encyclopedias

ISBN 1-884964-29-X

LC 2001-270888

"This volume contains about 600 entries on various aspects of the history of science, including individuals (e.g., Galileo), disciplines (e.g., astronomy), and broad topics (e.g., religion)." Libr J

Includes bibliographical references

Reynolds, Moira Davison

American women scientists; 23 inspiring biographies, 1900-2000. McFarland & Co. 1999 149p il hardcover o.p. pa $24.95   **509**

1. Women scientists

ISBN 0-7864-0649-6; 0-7864-2161-4 pa

LC 99-14603

"Four-to-six page profiles of 23 of the century's premier women scientists, representing a wide variety of disciplines. The entries are arranged chronologically beginning with Cornelia Clapp (1849-1934) and ending with Mary Good (1931-). . . . Each entry includes a black-and-white portrait." SLJ

Includes bibliographical references

Science and its times; understanding the social significance of scientific discovery. Neil Schlager, editor; Josh Lauer, associate editor. Gale Group 2000 8v set $625   **509**

1. Science -- History

ISBN 0-7876-3932-X

LC 00-37542

This set addresses "a wide variety of scientific developments with explanations of underlying factors and their effects on politics, economics, culture and daily life. [It includes] more than 20 topical essays, 25 full biographies and 85 sketches of notable people in each volume." Publisher's note

Snyder, Laura J.

The **philosophical** breakfast club; four remarkable friends who transformed science and changed the world. Broadway Books 2011 439p il map $27; ebook $27   **509**

1. Clergy 2. Economists 3. Scientists 4. Astronomers 5. Philosophers 6. Photographers 7. Mathematicians 8. Writers on science 9. Science -- Philosophy 10. Great Britain -- Intellectual life 11. Scientists -- Great Britain -- History

ISBN 978-0-7679-3048-2; 978-0-7679-3048-2 ebook

LC 2010-25790

The author "shows how four British 'natural philosophers' helped launch modern science. Lifelong friends since 1813, when they were students at Cambridge University, the scientists—William Whewell, Charles Babbage, John Herschel and Richard Jones—shared a belief in the importance of precise measurement and calculations as the basis for the scientific method and advocated public support for science. The author makes a . . . case that not only did each of these men make important individual contributions . . . but together they played a vital role in transforming science." Kirkus

This book "gives a unique view of the background and times in which these men lived, and a peek at the implications that their work and philosophy had on today's modern science." Sci Books Films

Includes bibliographical references

Teresi, Dick

Lost discoveries; the ancient roots of modern science, from the Babylonians to the Maya. Simon & Schuster 2002 453p il $27; pa $15   **509**

1. Ancient civilization 2. Science -- History

ISBN 0-684-83718-8; 0-7432-4379-X pa

LC 2002-75457

"This is a compendium of premodern knowledge of the natural world. Teresi structures his exploration into the science of Sumerian, Babylonian, Mayan, Chinese, and other non-European, premodern cultures around the thesis that classical Greece is not the sole fount of Western science." Booklist

"Teresi offers a great deal of fascinating material largely ignored by many histories of science." Publ Wkly

Includes bibliographical references

Walker, Mark

Nazi science; myth, truth, and the German atomic bomb. Perseus 2001 325p il pa $22.50   **509**

1. Atomic bomb 2. National socialism 3. Science -- Germany

ISBN 0-7382-0585-0; 978-0-7382-0585-4

First published 1995 by Plenum Press

"Walker examines the effect of the Nazi years on German science. Focusing primarily on physics and such . . . individuals as Einstein, Heisenberg, Gerlach, von Weizsacher, Stark, von Laue, and Planck, the author devotes the first seven of 11 chapters to an . . . analysis of how the German physics community evolved during the growth of the Third Reich. In chapters 8-10, the German work on nuclear fission is discussed." Choice

"Although scholarly, this will be accessible to general readers." Libr J

Includes bibliographical references

Whitfield, Peter

Landmarks in western science; from prehistory to the atomic age. Routledge 1999 256p il $65 **509**

1. Science -- History

ISBN 0-415-92533-9

LC 99-24976

This survey "highlights significant discoveries and turning points in mathematics, astronomy, physics, medicine, geology, and many other fields." Publisher's note

Includes bibliographical references

510   Mathematics

Adam, John A.

★ A **mathematical** nature walk. Princeton University Press 2009 248p il $27.95 **510**

1. Mathematics 2. Mathematical analysis

ISBN 978-0-691-12895-5; 0-691-12895-2

LC 2008-44828

"The general reader will find here a remarkably lucid explanation of how mathematicians create a formulaic model that mimics the key features of some natural phenomenon. . . . Ordinary math becomes adventure." Booklist

Includes bibliographical references

Barrow, John D.

100 essential things you didn't know you didn't know; math explains your world. W.W. Norton & Co. 2009 284p il $25.95; pa $15.95 **510**

1. Mathematics

ISBN 978-0-393-07007-1; 978-0-393-33867-6 pa

LC 2008-55910

First published 2008 in the United Kingdom

"For those who find something mysterious and intriguing in solving an equation, this collection is a fascinating look into the mind of a professional mathematician and the way in which math can be not simply a row of numbers but a way of looking at the world." SLJ

Includes bibliographical references

Blastland, Michael

★ The **numbers** game; the commonsense guide to understanding numbers in the news, in politics, and in life. [by] Michael Blastland and Andrew Dilnot. Gotham Books 2009 210p il $22 **510**

1. Statistics 2. Mathematics 3. Number concept

ISBN 978-1-59240-423-0; 1-59240-423-5

LC 2008-30130

First published 2007 in the United Kingdom with title: The tiger that isn't

The authors "embark on a monumental task of interpreting numerical data and showing how its misinterpretation often leads to misinformation. . . . The authors take a close look at statistics that are accepted at face value—many stemming from scientific or medical discoveries." Publ Wkly

Includes bibliographical references

Boyer, Carl B.

A **history** of mathematics; [by] Carl B. Boyer and Uta Merzbach. 3rd ed.; Wiley 2010 xx, 668p il pa $39.95 **510**

1. Mathematics -- History

ISBN 978-0-470-52548-7

LC 2010-3424

First published 1969

This book explores the "history of humankind's relationship with numbers, shapes, and patterns. This revised edition features up-to-date coverage of topics such as Fermat's Last Theorem and the Poincaré Conjecture, in addition to recent advances in areas such as finite group theory and computer-aided proofs." (Publisher's note)

"This good general history of mathematics is understandable to the student as well as authoritative for the mathematician." Malinowsky. Best Sci & Technol Ref Books for Young People

Includes bibliographical references

★ **CRC** Standard Mathematical Tables and Formulae; [editor-in-chief,] Daniel Zwillinger. 32nd edition CRC Press 2011 819 p. ill (hc) $75.95 **510**

ISBN 9781439835487

LC 91659327

First published 1929 with title: Math tables from the Handbook of Chemistry and Physics. Periodically revised

"This standard mathematical handbook contains both textual and tabular material. The contents include constants and conversion factors; algebra; combinatorial analysis; geometry; trigonometry; logarithmic, exponential, and hyperbolic functions; analytical geometry; calculus; differential equations; special functions; numerical methods; probability and statistics; and financial tables." Malinowsky. Best Sci & Technol Ref Books for Young People

Cusick, Thomas W.

Mathematics made simple; 6th ed; Broadway Books 2003 281p il pa $12.95 **510**

1. Mathematics

ISBN 978-0-7679-1538-0; 0-7679-1538-0

LC 2003-41923

First published 1943 by Kenmore Pub. Co.

"This book serves as a review of arithmetic, and an introduction to algebra, geometry, and trigonometry. Combinations and permutations are covered . . . in the Probability chapter. The exercises and answers in this book provide readers with opportunities to test their mastery of each step in these common branches of mathematics." Introduction

Darling, David J.

The **universal** book of mathematics; from Abracadabra to Zeno's paradoxes. [by] David Darling. Wiley 2004 383p il $40 **510**

1. Reference books 2. Mathematics -- Encyclopedias

ISBN 0-471-27047-4

LC 2003-24670

"The book's entries include numerous mathematical terms, brief biographies of mathematicians from ancient times to the present, and famous mathematical problems (both solved and unsolved), as well as problems and puzzles of a more recreational nature. It is a spirit of whimsy, the fanciful, and the outrageous that makes this book much more than a dry encyclopedia of mathematical terms, however. Darling's writing style and choice of entries make this an easy book to pick up and page through." Choice

Includes bibliographical references

Devlin, Keith J.

The **math** gene; how mathematical thinking evolved and why numbers are like gossip. {by} Keith Devlin. Basic Bks. 2000 328p il hardcover o.p. pa $17   **510**
1. Mathematics 2. Number concept
ISBN 0-465-01619-7 pa

LC 2001-520984

"Is the human brain hardwired for mathematical thinking? Just as we have an instinct for language acquisition, Devlin argues that we also possess an innate ability for logical and algorithmic reasoning. This book is an eye-opener for all math phobics." Libr J

Includes bibliographical references

Dewdney, A. K.

200 [percent] of nothing; an eye-opening tour through the twists and turns of math abuse and innumeracy. Wiley 1993 182p il hardcover o.p. pa $15.95   **510**
1. Mathematics
ISBN 0-471-57776-6; 0-471-14574-2 pa

LC 92-42173

The author discusses the media abuse of numbers "as well as 'percentage pumping,' 'irrational ratios,' 'compound blindness,' 'filtering,' and 'dimensional dementia.'" Libr J

Includes bibliographical references

A **mathematical** mystery tour; discovering the truth and beauty of the cosmos. Wiley 1999 218p il $22.95; pa $15.95   **510**
1. Mathematics
ISBN 0-471-23847-3; 0-471-40734-8 pa

LC 98-36470

Dewdney "addresses two closely related, long-pondered questions. Why is mathematics so uncannily effective in describing the physical universe? Is 'new' mathematics invented, or is it a preexisting something that is discovered?. . . He explores these fundamental questions via discussions of the mathematical work of Pythagoras, the medieval Arab mathematicians, modern theoretical physicists, and modern mathematicians." Libr J

★ A **Dictionary** of quotations in mathematics; compiled and edited by Robert A. Nowlan. McFarland & Co. 2002 314p pa $45   **510**
1. Mathematics -- Quotations
ISBN 0-7864-1284-4

LC 2002-5268

"This work contains almost 3,000 quotations in mathematics. It is divided into thirty-eight chapters and 389 sections that present quotations over a spectrum from God and religion to the nature of infinity. . . . Areas covered [include] historical origins, linguistics, the arts, mathematicians themselves, logic, real and idealized space, number theory,

algebra, computers, probability theory, and statistics." Publisher's note

"For anyone writing a term paper, professional paper, or giving a presentation, whether in mathematics, science, or a related discipline, this reference will be a useful resource. For the rest of us, this book is a delightful read all by itself." Am Ref Books Annu, 2003

Includes bibliographical references

Dunham, William

The **mathematical** universe; an alphabetical journey through the great proofs, problems, and personalities. Wiley 1994 314p il hardcover o.p. pa $19.95   **510**
1. Mathematics 2. Mathematicians
ISBN 0-471-17661-3 pa

LC 93-46702

In this history of mathematics, "Dunham sheds light not only on the personalities—eccentric, vain, brilliant—of major mathematicians, but also on contemporary social issues, such as multiculturalism and gender equity. Readers who want to understand the cultural significance of mathematics would do well to begin with this book." Booklist

Includes bibliographical references

Ellenberg, Jordan

★ **How** not to be wrong; the power of mathematical thinking. Jordan Ellenberg. The Penguin Press 2014 480 p. illustrations (hardback) $27.95   **510**
1. Life skills 2. Mathematics 3. Mathematical analysis
ISBN 1594205221; 9781594205224

LC 2014005394

"The math we learn in school can seem like a dull set of rules, laid down by the ancients and not to be questioned. In 'How Not to Be Wrong,' Jordan Ellenberg shows us how terribly limiting this view is: Math isn't confined to abstract incidents that never occur in real life, but rather touches everything we do--the whole world is shot through with it. . . . Ellenberg chases mathematical threads through a vast range of time and space, from the everyday to the cosmic." (Publisher's note)

"Ellenberg finds the common-sense math at work in the everyday world, and his vivid examples and clear descriptions show how 'math is woven into the way we reason.'" Pub Wkly

Includes bibliographical references and index

Glazer, Evan

★ **Real** -life math; everyday use of mathematical concepts. [by] Evan M. Glazer and John W. McConnell. Greenwood Press 2002 165p il $49.95   **510**
1. Mathematics
ISBN 0-313-31998-7

LC 2001-58635

The authors "have written this book as a reply to students' complaints that they'll never use the mathematical concepts they're being taught. They look at dozens of mathematical concepts and . . . show how these math ideas relate to the world in which students live. . . . The book is thorough and accurate." Libr Media Connect

Includes bibliographical references

God created the integers; the mathematical break-throughs that changed history. edited and with commentary by Stephen Hawking. Running Pr. 2005 1160p il $29.95; pa $21.95 **510**
1. Mathematicians
ISBN 0-7624-1922-9; 978-0-7624-1922-7; 0-7624-3004-4 pa; 978-0-7624-3004-8 pa
LC 2005-924493
Follow-up to On the shoulders of giants
This book "features biographies of 17 great figures in the world of mathematics and 31 excerpts of their landmark literature." Libr J
This "is a wonderful resource providing insight into both the mathematics and the personalities involved." Sci Books Films
Includes bibliographical references

Huber, Michael R.
Mythematics; solving the twelve labors of Hercules. Princeton University Press 2009 183p il $24.95 **510**
1. Problem solving 2. Hercules (Legendary character)
ISBN 978-0-691-13575-5
LC 2009-8535
The author takes the ancient Greeks' "early interest in puzzles and the descriptions of Hercules' various labors and reinterpreted each of those labors in terms of several 'tasks,' after which he gives a 'solution' to the mathematical problem(s) implicit in each of the tasks. . . . Given that we tend to think of early Greek mathematics in terms of geometry or, possibly, number theory, the breadth of mathematics required for the various tasks may be surprising." Sci Books Films
Includes bibliographical references

Kanigel, Robert
The **man** who knew infinity; a life of the genius Ramanujan. Washington Sq. Press 1992 438p map il pa $15 **510**
1. Mathematicians
ISBN 0-671-75061-5; 978-0-671-75061-9
LC 91-37763
First published 1991 by Charles Scribner's Sons
This biography traces the life of the Indian mathematician. "Working alone in relative obscurity and lacking the usual academic credentials [Ramanujan] could easily have passed unnoticed. However, with the help of a handful of friends and the ultimate support of renowned English mathematician G.H. Hardy, his work was brought to the attention of the world." Libr J
"Kanigel deserves high praise for a work of arduous research and rare insight." Booklist
Includes bibliographical references

Livio, Mario
Is God a mathematician? Simon & Schuster 2009 308p il $26 **510**
1. Symbolic logic 2. Mathematics -- Philosophy 3. Mathematicians -- Psychology 4. Logic, Symbolic and mathematical
ISBN 978-0-7432-9405-8; 0-7432-9405-X
LC 2008-45850

The author "is concerned with the contentious question: is mathematics a human invention? Or is it the intricate design of the universe that we are slowly discovering?" Publ Wkly
Livio "provides apt quotations and helpful explanations within an enjoyable narrative. This is a good popularization of some decidedly nontrivial questions." Libr J
Includes bibliographical references

Mahajan, Sanjoy
Street -fighting mathematics; the art of educated guessing and opportunistic problem solving. MIT Press 2010 134p il pa $25 **510**
1. Problem solving 2. Approximate computation
ISBN 0-262-51429-X; 978-0-262-51429-3
LC 2009-28867
The author argues that the key to solving complex arithmetic questions "lies in having informal tools on hand that let us attack the problem. Though the result may not be perfectly precise, he believes, intuitive mathematical reasoning is often sufficient for our needs. . . . [The book] is not organized around traditional math topics, such as differential equations, but ways of thinking: reasoning by analogy, visualizing geometric problems, and more. Readers can then answer all manner of questions: Guessing the number of babies in the United States, calculating the bond angles in methane, or determining the drag that air exerts on a 747." Dr. Dobb's
Includes bibliographical references

The **New** York Times book of mathematics; edited by Gina Kolata ; forward by Paul Hoffman. Sterling 2013 xvi, 480 p.p (hardcover) $24.95 **510**
1. Mathematics
ISBN 1402793227; 9781402793226
LC 2012045019
This book about mathematics is "divided into thematic sections and is only occasionally chronological. Among topics covered are the National Security Agency's (NSA's) threats to mathematicians writing papers with code-breaking applications; the celebrated story of Andrew Wiles's proof of Fermat's Last Theorem; Grigori Perelman's confirmation of the Poincaré conjecture and his subsequent, Bobby Fischer-like, disappearance." (Library Journal)

Pasles, Paul C.
Benjamin Franklin's numbers; an unsung mathematical odyssey. Princeton University Press 2008 254p il $26.95 **510**
1. Authors 2. Diplomats 3. Inventors 4. Statesmen 5. Scientists 6. Mathematics 7. Writers on science 8. Members of Congress
ISBN 978-0-691-12956-3; 0-691-12956-8
LC 2006-102508
The author "documents the famous scientist-statesman's lively interest in numerical enigmas, most particularly those known as Magic Squares. . . . An unexpected but welcome perspective on the genial genius of Philadelphia." Booklist
Includes bibliographical references

Paulos, John Allen

Beyond numeracy; ruminations of a numbers man. Knopf 1991 285p il hardcover o.p. pa $14 **510**
1. Mathematics
ISBN 0-679-73807-X pa

LC 90-44999

These seventy short essays "range from summaries of whole disciplines (calculus, trigonometry, topology) to biographical and historical asides (Gödel, Pythagoras, non-Euclidean geometry) to bits of mathematical or quasi-mathematical folklore (infinite sets, Platonic solids, QED)." Introduction

"This well-written and easy-to-follow book gently guides readers through many interesting mathematical topics." SLJ

Includes bibliographical references

A **mathematician** reads the newspaper. Anchor Books 1996 212p il pa $13.95 **510**
1. Mathematics
ISBN 0-385-48254-X

LC 95-46049

First published 1995 by Basic Books

The author uses newspaper features "as vehicles for explaining mathematical concepts and how they figure in the business of being a well-informed citizen. For instance, he uses stories on the economy to illustrate prediction, regression analysis, statistics, and game theory and how those tools are used to both illuminate and obfuscate underlying truth." Booklist

Includes bibliographical references

Pickover, Clifford A.

The **math** book; from Pythagoras to the 57th dimension, 250 milestones in the history of mathematics. Sterling Pub. 2009 527p $29.95 **510**
1. Mathematics -- History
ISBN 978-1-4027-5796-9

LC 2008-43214

"Beginning millions of years ago with ancient 'ant odometers' and moving through time to our modern-day quest for new dimensions, . . . [this book] covers 250 milestones in mathematical history." Publisher's note

"Pickover's love of mathematics shines through the text and images, and it is likely that the reader will catch at least some of his enthusiasm." Choice

Includes bibliographical references

Posamentier, Alfred S.

Magnificent mistakes in mathematics; by Alfred S. Posamentier and Ingmar Lehmann. Prometheus Books 2013 300 p. (hardback) $24 **510**
1. Errors 2. Mathematics 3. Errors, Scientific 4. Discoveries in science 5. Mathematics -- Miscellanea
ISBN 1616147474; 9781616147471

LC 2013012126

Authors Alfred S. Posamentier and Ingmar Lehmann "demonstrate how some mistakes had profound consequences for our understanding of mathematics' key concepts. The authors show that when we "prove" that every triangle is isosceles, we are violating a concept not even

known to Euclid [and how] even using correct procedures can sometimes lead to absurd - but enlightening - results." (Publisher's note)

Includes bibliographical references and index

Rudman, Peter Strom

The **Babylonian** theorem; the mathematical journey to Pythagoras and Euclid. [by] Peter S. Rudman. Prometheus Books 2010 248p il $26 **510**
1. Philosophers 2. Mathematicians 3. Writers on science 4. Mathematics -- History
ISBN 978-1-59102-773-7; 1-59102-773-X

LC 2009-39196

Sequel to How mathematics happened (2007)

"Topics covered include Pythagorean triplets, . . . similar triangles, square-root calculations, and calculations of the volume of a pyramid. . . . This is a well-researched volume on what forms of mathematics existed when similar ideas developed again and again in different cultures. The book's numerous mathematical equations would delight any math student." Sci Books Films

Includes bibliographical references

Seife, Charles

★ **Proofiness**; the dark arts of mathematical deception. Viking 2010 295p il map $25.95 **510**
1. Mathematics
ISBN 978-0-670-02216-8

LC 2010-12127

The author "examines the many ways that people fudge with numbers, sometimes just to sell more moisturizer but also to ruin our economy, rig our elections, convict the innocent and undercount the needy. . . . [This book] reveals the truly corrosive effects on a society awash in numerical mendacity. This is more than a math book; it's an eye-opening civics lesson." N Y Times Book Rev

Includes bibliographical references

Sherlock Holmes in Babylon; and other tales of mathematical history. edited by Marlow Anderson, Victor Katz, Robin Wilson. Mathematical Association of America 2004 387p il maps (Spectrum series) $51.95 **510**
1. Mathematics -- History
ISBN 0-88385-546-1

LC 2003-113541

This "is a compilation of journal articles written by various mathematical historians and published by the Mathematical Association of America over the past 100 years. The stories deal with many important and fundamental topics from ancient up through 18th-century mathematics. The papers are all self-contained, so the reader with some degree of mathematical maturity can jump around in the book." Sci Books Films

Includes bibliographical references

Singh, Simon

The **Simpsons** and their mathematical secrets; Simon Singh. Bloomsbury USA 2013 272 p. (hardback) $26 **510**
1. Mathematics 2. Television programs 3. Simpsons

(Television program)
ISBN 1620402777; 9781620402771

LC 2013020884

Author Simon Singh discusses the television series "The Simpsons," examining how "embedded in many plots are subtle references to mathematics, ranging from well-known equations to cutting-edge theorems and conjectures. That they exist, Simon Singh reveals, underscores the brilliance of the shows' writers, many of whom have advanced degrees in mathematics in addition to their unparalleled sense of humor." (Publisher's note)

"Perhaps Simpsons nerds have known this all along, but for the rest of us who think of the TV show as primarily a sharp piece of comic writing, it may come as a surprise to learn that it is riddled with sophisticated mathematics. . ." Kirkus

Includes bibliographical references and index

Stewart, Ian

The **magical** maze; seeing the world through mathematical eyes. Wiley 1998 268p il $24.95; pa $16.95 **510**
1. Mathematics 2. Mathematical recreations
ISBN 0-471-19297-X; 0-471-35065-6 pa

LC 98-13185

Stewart presents various mathematical puzzles and problems through the metaphorical structure of a maze.

Chapters "contain good discussions of such topics as modular arithmetic, Marilyn vos Savant's Monty-Hall problem, depth-first and other search strategies, static and dynamic symmetry, Turing machines, optimization, fractals, and chaos. This is an excellent mix of topics and the material is very much up-to-date." Choice

Visions of Infinity; The Great Mathematical Problems. Perseus Books Group 2013 352 p. $26.99 **510**
1. Mathematics
ISBN 0465022405; 9780465022403

This looks at mathematical problems. Mathematician Ian Stewart argues that "mathematics is as creative as physics." He discusses Goldbach's Conjecture "that every even number can be written as the sum of two prime numbers," Squaring the Circle, or "constructing a square with an area identical to a given circle," pi, and Newton's laws of motion. (Kirkus)

Strogatz, Steven

★ The **joy** of X; a guided tour of math, from one to infinity. Steven Strogatz. Houghton Mifflin Harcourt 2012 336 p. (hardback) $27.00 **510**
1. Mathematics
ISBN 0547517653; 9780547517650

LC 2012017320

In this book on mathematics, author Steven Strogatz "begins with arithmetic, by way of Sesame Street, then explores algebra, geometry, and, finally, the wonders of calculus. . . . From addition and subtraction, with a glimpse into negative numbers and 'the black art of borrowing,' it's a quick step into the hardcore detective work of algebra's search for the unknown x, with algorithms like the quadratic equation." (Publishers Weekly)

Szpiro, George G.

Numbers rule; the vexing mathematics of democracy from Plato to the present. Princeton University Press 2010 226p **510**
1. Mathematics 2. Voting 3. Democracy -- History
ISBN 978-0-691-13994-4

LC 2009-28615

Szpiro "traces the quest of philosophers, statesmen and mathematicians throughout history to create a more perfect democracy and adapt to the ever-changing demands of each new generation by analyzing the mathematical anomalies in voting results." (Publisher's note) Index,

The author "presents a refreshingly different presentation of the mathematics of voting and apportionment. Topics are organized chronologically, and historical contexts are presented in an engaging way. Unlike mathematics textbooks, the book reads like a collection of stories describing the origin of many mathematical ideas. The mathematical content is not trivial, and it is well written, very clear, and should be accessible to readers with an understanding of arithmetic and a willingness to play with numbers." Choice

Includes bibliographical references

Poincare's prize; the hundred-year quest to solve one of math's greatest puzzles. Dutton 2007 309p $24.95 **510**
1. Mathematics 2. Mathematicians
ISBN 978-0-525-95024-0; 0-525-95024-9

LC 2007-12792

The author "recounts the story of how a geometrical puzzle worthy of the most voracious sphinx finally yielded to an eccentric Russian genius who has since refused the honors and million-dollar prize proffered by an astonished world. The mathematical puzzle, readers learn, originated with the French polymath Henri Poincaré, whose revolutionary topology generated a tantalizing conjecture about how multidimensional bodies might all be transformed into spheres. . . . Never has mathematics provided more fascinating human drama!" Booklist

Includes bibliographical references

Tammet, Daniel

★ **Thinking** in numbers; on life, love, meaning, and math. Daniel Tammet. Little, Brown and Co. 2013 288 p. $26 **510**
1. Numbers 2. Statistics 3. Mathematics
ISBN 0316187372; 9780316187374

LC 2013935728

This is a book of essays by Daniel Tammet. "His topics include the concept of zero, the calendar, prime numbers, chess, time and statistics. . . . Several of his pieces have an autobiographical component. His essay on infinity shows him as a young boy discovering the infinity of fractions between two points on his walk home from school, and readers learn of his amazing memory in his account of reciting aloud the decimals of pi to 22,514 places at the University of Oxford's Pi Day." (Kirkus Reviews)

Tanton, James S.

★ **Encyclopedia** of mathematics; [by] James Tanton. Facts on File 2005 568p il (Facts on File science library) $75 **510**

1. Reference books 2. Mathematics -- Encyclopedias
ISBN 0-8160-5124-0

LC 2004-16785

This encyclopedia "offers more than 800 entries from abacus and compound interest to Bertrand Russell and vector along with essays on the history and evolution of equations and algebra, calculus, functions, geometry, probability and statistics, and trigonometry." SLJ

Includes bibliographical references

Tobias, Sheila

Overcoming math anxiety; rev and expanded; Norton 1993 260p il $23; pa $14.95 **510**

1. Mathematics
ISBN 0-393-03577-8; 0-393-31307-7 pa

LC 93-3648

First published 1978

The author explains common misconceptions about mathematical concepts, analyzes what makes math seem difficult, discusses alleged sex differences in brain function in relation to math, and describes math programs aimed at women

Includes bibliographical references

511　General principles of mathematics

Berlinski, David

The **advent** of the algorithm; the idea that rules the world. Harcourt 2000 345p $28; pa $14 **511**

1. Algorithms
ISBN 0-15-100338-6; 0-15-601391-6 pa

LC 98-43755

Berlinski "chronicles the discovery of algorithms, the codes that control computers, vividly profiling the key thinkers involved. He also identifies the hidden sources of the algorithm's power as a calculating tool, and exposes its defects as a scientific metaphor for explaining the human intellect." Booklist

Includes bibliographical references

Kaplan, Robert

The **nothing** that is; a natural history of zero. illustrations by Ellen Kaplan. Oxford Univ. Press 2000 225p $40; pa $11.95 **511**

1. Zero (The number)
ISBN 0-19-512842-7; 0-19-514237-3 pa

LC 99-29000

"Kaplan presents cultural, philosophical, historical, and mathematical developments that either encouraged or discouraged the recognition of the role of zero in counting and computation." Sci Books Films

Michael, T. S.

How to guard an art gallery and other discrete mathematical adventures. Johns Hopkins University Press 2009 257p il $60; pa $25 **511**

1. Algorithms 2. Computer science 3. Mathematical analysis
ISBN 978-0-8018-9298-1; 0-8018-9298-8; 978-0-8018-9299-8 pa; 0-8018-9299-6 pa

LC 2009-00435

"The time-honored story problem, central to mathematics and an expression of its fascination or frustration (depending on the student's success), is the protagonist of this delightful work on discrete mathematics. Written for . . . [readers with a knowledge of] algebra and geometry, the text contains 7 chapters, each one devoted to a different story problem and its variations. Pick's formula, art gallery problems, quadratic residues of primes and squares, and stamps and coins and Sylvester's formula are some of the problems presented, with each chapter consisting of a group of problems of increasing difficulty." Sci Tech Book News

Includes bibliographical references

Seife, Charles

Zero; the biography of a dangerous idea. Viking 2000 248p il hardcover o.p. pa $15 **511**

1. Zero (The number)
ISBN 0-670-88457-X; 0-14-029647-6 pa

LC 99-36693

"The zero emerges as a daunting intellectual riddle in this . . . chronicle of a once controversial concept as Seife deftly traces the gradual acceptance of the zero and its role as catalyst for the evolution of everything from business to physics to moral thought." Booklist

Includes bibliographical references

511.3　Mathematical logic (Symbolic logic)

Fortnow, Lance

The **golden** ticket; P, NP, and the search for the impossible. Lance Fortnow. Princeton University Press 2013 188 p. (hardback) $26.95 **511.3**

1. Computer algorithms 2. NP-complete problems
ISBN 0691156492; 9780691156491

LC 2012039523

This book by Lance Fortnow "tackles one of the biggest open problems in mathematics. P vs. NP can be succinctly phrased as the issue of whether some of the hardest and most important questions in mathematics have easily computable solutions. The questions themselves can range from how best to match up organ donors and recipients to how one can use the smallest number of different colors when creating a map." (Library Journal)

Includes bibliographical references and index

Stillwell, John

Roads to infinity; the mathematics of truth and proof. A K Peters 2010 203p il $39 **511.3**

1. Infinite 2. Set theory 3. Symbolic logic 4. Logic,

Symbolic and mathematical
ISBN 978-1-56881-466-7; 1-56881-466-6

LC 2010-14077

"This book offers an introduction to modern ideas about infinity and their implications for mathematics. It unifies ideas from set theory and mathematical logic, and traces their effects on mainstream mathematical topics of today, such as number theory and combinatorics." Publisher's note

Includes bibliographical references

512   Algebra

Havil, Julian

The **irrationals**; a story of the numbers you can't count on. Julian Havil. Princeton University Press 2012 298 p. (alk. paper) $29.95   **512**
1. Mathematicians   2. Irrational numbers   3. Mathematics -- History
ISBN 0691143420; 9780691143422

LC 2012931844

This book "tells the story of irrational numbers and the mathematicians who have tackled their challenges, from antiquity to the twenty-first century. Along the way, [author Julian Havil] explains why irrational numbers are surprisingly difficult to define -- and why so many questions still surround them." (Publisher's note)

Livio, Mario

The **equation** that couldn't be solved; how mathematical genius discovered the language of symmetry. Simon & Schuster 2005 353p il $26.95   **512**
1. Symmetry   2. Mathematicians
ISBN 0-7432-5820-7

LC 2005-44123

This "summary of the origins of group theory and symmetry . . . [covers] biographical information on Niels Henrik Abel and Evariste Galois, introductory concepts and problems in group theory, and applications of group theory to broader disciplines." Libr J

"Even the mathematically fainthearted can learn a great deal about symmetry from this book." Sci Books Films

Includes bibliographical references

Singh, Simon

Fermat's enigma; the epic quest to solve the world's greatest mathematical problem. foreword by John Lynch. Anchor Books 1998 315p il pa $13.95   **512**
1. Number theory   2. Mathematicians   3. College teachers
ISBN 0-385-49362-2

First published 1997 in the United Kingdom with title: Fermat's last theorem

"This vivid account is fascinating reading for anyone interested in mathematics, its history, and the passionate quest for solutions to unsolved riddles." SLJ

Includes bibliographical references

512.7   Number theory

Conway, John Horton

The **book** of numbers; [by] John Horton Conway, Richard K. Guy. Copernicus 1996 310p il $35   **512.7**
1. Number theory
ISBN 0-387-97993-X

LC 95-32588

"For 350 years, mathematicians staked whole careers—even lives—on solving Fermat's Last Theorem. The story of this immensely difficult problem involves failure, despair, obsession, and, ultimately triumph." Libr J

"The authors take such joy in the order and patterns of numbers that you can't help being fascinated by what is actually a fairly difficult subject." Libr J

Includes bibliographical references

Derbyshire, John

Prime obsession; Bernhard Riemann and the greatest unsolved problem in mathematics. Plume 2004 422p il pa $16   **512.7**
1. Number theory   2. Mathematicians
ISBN 978-0-452-28525-5; 0-452-28525-9
First published 2003 by Joseph Henry Press

The author "first takes readers through . . . mathematical fundamentals in order to give them a good understanding of Riemann's discovery and its consequences. Interspersed with the hardcore math, other chapters profile Riemann the man and trace the history of mathematics in relation to his still-unproven hypothesis. Derbyshire shows how after 150 years, the world's greatest minds still haven't found a solution." Libr J

Reid, Constance

From zero to infinity; what makes numbers interesting. 5th ed, 50th anniversary ed; A K Peters 2006 188p il pa $19.95   **512.7**
1. Number theory
ISBN 978-1-568812-73-1; 1-568812-73-6

LC 2005-27860

First published 1955 by Crowell

"This book covers selected topics in number theory. Partly expository, it nonetheless challenges the reader's mind in clever and nonthreatening ways." Sci Books Films

Sabbagh, Karl

★ The **Riemann** hypothesis; the greatest unsolved problem in mathematics. Farrar, Straus & Giroux 2002 340p il $25; pa $14   **512.7**
1. Number theory   2. Mathematicians
ISBN 0-374-25007-3; 0-374-52935-3 pa

LC 2003-101178

First published 2002 in the United Kingdom with title: Dr. Riemann's zeroes

"Sabbagh introduces contemporary mathematicians who are working on the problem, one of whom claims, to professional skepticism, to be on the verge of vindicating the hypothesis. Another is working away in search of a single counterexample that would refute it. Such pursuits, which often consume mathematicians' entire lives, may seem incomprehensible or even pointless to the innumerate—but that's a prejudice brilliantly dispelled through Sabbagh's interviews, which are interwoven with his not overly numerical tour of the hypothesis. The drive and competitiveness of mathematicians clearly emerge from Sabbagh's narrative." Booklist

512.9   Foundations of algebra

Mackenzie, Dana

The **universe** in zero words; the story of mathematics as told through equations. Dana Mackenzie. Princeton University Press 2012 224 p. ill. (some col.) (hardcover) $27.95   **512.9**
1. Equations 2. Mathematics -- History
ISBN 0691152829; 9780691152820
LC 2011936364

This book "tells the history of twenty-four . . . equations that have shaped mathematics, science, and society -- from the elementary . . . to the sophisticated . . . and from the famous . . . to the arcane. . . . [Dana] Mackenzie . . . explains what each equation means, who discovered it (and how), and how it has affected our lives." (Publisher's note)

Includes bibliographical references (p. 219-221) and index.

513   Arithmetic

Bellos, Alex

Here's looking at Euclid; a surprising excursion through the astonishing world of math. Free Press hardcover ed.; Free Press 2010 319p il $25; ebook $11.99   **513**
1. Number concept
ISBN 978-1-4165-8825-2; 978-1-4165-9634-9 ebook
LC 2009-36815

The author "offers a lively romp through many different fields of mathematics as he incorporates ancient discoveries and modern developments alike. Topics include geometry, number theory, the development of sudoku, numerous aspects of pi and its calculation, statistics, probability and its application to gambling, and many other historical tidbits." Libr J

Includes bibliographical references

Kogelman, Stanley

The **only** math book you'll ever need; [by] Stanley Kogelman and Barbara R. Heller. rev ed.; HarperPerennial 1995 xx, 268p il pa $15   **513**
1. Mathematics
ISBN 978-0-06-272507-3; 0-06-272507-6
First published 1986 by Facts on File

Step-by-step operations are reviewed in problems encountered on a daily basis such as comparing credit cards, evaluating investments, estimating interest rates, and converting area measurements.

515   Analysis

Ash, Avner

Elliptic tales; curves, counting, and number theory. Avner Ash, Robert Gross. Princeton University Press 2012 253 p. (hardcover) $29.95   **515**
1. Number theory 2. Cubic equations 3. Elliptic curves 4. Curves, Elliptic 5. Elliptic functions
ISBN 0691151199; 9780691151199
LC 2011044712

This book explains a major unsolved problem "in contemporary mathematics—the Birch and Swinnerton-Dyer Conjecture. . . . The key to the conjecture lies in elliptic curves, which are cubic equations in two variables. These equations may appear simple, yet they arise from some very deep—and often very mystifying—mathematical ideas. Using only basic algebra and calculus while presenting numerous eye-opening examples, Ash and Gross make these ideas accessible to general readers." (Barnes and Noble)

Includes bibliographical references and index.

Ouellette, Jennifer

The **calculus** diaries; how math can help you lose weight, win in Vegas, and survive a zombie apocalypse. [illustrations by Jason Torchinsky] Penguin Books 2010 318p il pa $15   **515**
1. Calculus
ISBN 978-0-14-311737-7; 0-14-311737-8
LC 2010-25843

The author "shows how she learned to apply calculus to everything from gas mileage to dieting, from the rides at Disneyland to shooting craps in Vegas." Publisher's note

Includes bibliographical references

516   Geometry

Apostol, Tom M.

New Horizons in Geometry; Tom M. Apostol and Mamikon A. Mnatsakanian. Cambridge University Press 2012 520 p. $75   **516**
1. Calculus 2. Geometry
ISBN 088385354X; 9780883853542

In this book, Tom Apostol and Mamikon A. Mnatsakanian introduce "Mamikon's sweeping-tangent theorem," which "relies on a continuous transformation of a unit tangent to a curve, and then explore its consequences. The authors use this powerful method, which does not fit into the canon of either Euclidean geometry or calculus, to unfold much of classical geometry and to . . . solve problems usually requiring calculus." (Choice)

Gorini, Catherine A.

The **Facts** on File geometry handbook; Rev ed; Facts on File 2009 342p il (Facts on File science library) $40   **516**
1. Geometry
ISBN 978-0-8160-7389-4
LC 2009-5775

First published 2003

This includes a glossary of over 3,000 entries with labeled diagrams, biographies of over 300 scientists and mathematicians from ancient times to the present, a chronology of geometry history, charts, tables, recommended reading and websites.

Includes glossary and bibliographical references

Lehmann, Ingmar

The **secrets** of triangles; a mathematical journey. by Alfred S. Posamentier and Ingmar Lehmann. Prometheus Books 2012 387 p. ill. (hardcover) $26 **516**

1. Geometry 2. Triangle 3. Trigonometry
ISBN 1616145870; 9781616145873

LC 2012013635

This book offers "mathematical insights, intriguing relationships, and surprising results focused on the triangle." Topics include "noteworthy points, special lines, and concentric circles as related to triangles. Ultimately the book is a . . . compendium of results that" may surprise the reader with their simultaneous simplicity and complexity. (Choice)

Includes bibliographical references (p. 367-368) and index.

Mlodinow, Leonard

Euclid's window; the story of geometry from parallel lines to hyperspace. Free Press 2001 306p il hardcover o.p. pa $15 **516**

1. Authors 2. Geometry 3. Physicists 4. Astronomers 5. Philosophers 6. Mathematicians 7. College teachers 8. Writers on science 9. Nobel laureates for physics
ISBN 0-684-86524-6 pa

LC 00-54351

"This engaging history does an excellent job of explaining the importance of the study of geometry without making the reader learn any geometry." Libr J

Includes bibliographical references

O'Rourke, Joseph

How to fold it; the mathematics of linkages, origami, and polyhedra. Cambridge University Press 2011 177p il $80; pa $27.99 **516**

1. Origami 2. Mathematics
ISBN 978-0-521-76735-4; 0-521-76735-0; 978-0-521-14547-3 pa; 0-521-14547-3 pa

LC 2011001236

The author explains "folding problems starting from high school algebra and geometry and introducing more advanced concepts in tangible contexts as they arise. He shows how variations on these basic problems lead directly to the frontiers of current mathematical research and offers ten . . . unsolved problems for the enterprising reader." Publisher's note

516.2   Euclidean geometry

Berlinski, David

★ The **king** of infinite space; Euclid and his Elements. David Berlinski. Basic Books 2013 172 p. illustrations (hardcover : alk. paper) $24 **516.2**

1. Geometry 2. Mathematics, Greek 3. Geometry

-- History
ISBN 046501481X; 9780465014811

LC 2012042492

This book by David Berlinski looks at the ancient mathematician Euclid "and the world of axioms and theorems he created--a geometric world that became the basis for much of modern math, from analytic geometry to the idea of curved space-time. To Berlinski, Euclid's fourth-century B.C., 13-volume 'Elements' is a manifestation of his 'intense demand for an idealized world.'" (Publishers Weekly)

Kaplan, Ellen

Hidden harmonies; the lives and times of the Pythagorean theorem. [by] Robert Kaplan and Ellen Kaplan. Bloomsbury Press 2011 290p il $25 **516.2**

1. Pythagorean theorem 2. Mathematics -- History
ISBN 978-1-59691-522-0; 1-59691-522-6

LC 2010-19959

The authors discuss "the famous theorem that relates the sides of a right triangle. Going through many of the apparently hundreds of proofs of it, the Kaplans sinuously weave personalities into the history of proving Pythagoras correct. . . . Showing the theorem's endless versatility, the Kaplans and their logic- and symbol-permeated text will engage those who delight in doing the math." Booklist

Includes bibliographical references

Livio, Mario

The **golden** ratio; the story of phi, the world's most astonishing number. Broadway Bks. 2002 294p hardcover o.p. pa $14.95 **516.2**

1. Geometry
ISBN 0-7679-0815-5; 0-7679-0816-3 pa

LC 2002-23084

The author examines the history and myths of phi, the "golden ratio" of 1.6180339887 that has been related to phenomena as diverse as the arrangements of petals on roses and the breeding patterns of rabbits.

"Overall, an enjoyable work, amply supported by index, extensive references, and ten appendixes presenting mathematical elaborations of text material." Choice

Includes bibliographical references

Maor, Eli

The **Pythagorean** theorem; a 4,000-year history. Princeton University Press 2007 259p il map $24.95 **516.2**

1. Mathematics -- History
ISBN 978-0-691-12526-8; 0-691-12526-0

LC 2006-50969

The author "presents an account of the Pythagorean Theorem and its approximate 400 proofs, up to its importance in the Theory of Relativity." Univ Press Books for Public and Second Sch Libr, 2008

"This [is an] interesting and well-written book. . . . I recommend the book highly to students, teachers, and the intelligent general reader interested in a very old, beautiful, and useful result." Sci Books Films

Includes bibliographical references

516.22   Plane geometry

Blatner, David

The **joy** of pi. Walker & Co. 1997 129p il
hardcover o.p. pa $12   **516.22**
1. Pi
ISBN 0-8027-1332-7; 0-8027-7562-4 pa
LC 97-23705

The author discusses the history of the number π, as
well as the process of "calculating the ratio of a circle's
circumference to its diameter, which has advanced from
measuring lengths of string and the 'brute force' of measuring polygons to feeding supercomputers sophisticated
algorithms. Sidebars . . . abound, containing a factoid,
joke, or doggerel inspired by π." Booklist

Includes bibliographical references

519.2   Probabilities

Aczel, Amir D.

Chance : a guide to gambling, love, the stock
market & just about everything else.   Thunder's
Mouth Press 2004 161p il $23   **519.2**
1. Chance 2. Probabilities
ISBN 1-56858-316-8
LC 2004-304723

The author "explains the elements of probability theory for lay readers. . . . [He] points out that some of the
results of probabilistic calculations can seem contrary to
common sense and can even surprise experienced mathematicians and scientists such as himself; nevertheless, the
results are mathematically sound and must be accepted. .
. . . It is not often that one can recommend a mathematics
book as good-quality 'light' reading, but this work fits the
bill." Libr J

Includes bibliographical references

Devlin, Keith J.

The **unfinished** game; Pascal, Fermat, and
the seventeenth-century letter that made the world
modern. [by] Keith Devlin. Basic Books 2008
191p il (Basic ideas) $24.95   **519.2**
1. Theologians 2. Probabilities 3. Mathematicians
4. Writers on religion
ISBN 978-0-465-00910-7; 0-465-00910-7
LC 2008-12222

This book "analyzes the correspondence between
17th-century mathematicians Blaise Pascal and Pierre de
Fermat concerning methods of calculating probabilities—
in particular, methods of predicting the outcomes of unfinished gambling games." Sci Books Films

"This informative book is a lively, quick read for anyone who wonders about the science of predicting what's
next and how deeply it affects our lives." Publ Wkly

Includes bibliographical references

Mlodinow, Leonard

The **Drunkard's** walk; how randomness rules our
lives. Pantheon Books 2008 252p il $24.95 **519.2**
1. Chance 2. Probabilities
ISBN 978-0-375-42404-5; 0-375-42404-0
LC 2007-42507

This book "attempts to present the core concepts of
probability theory and statistics in a format that is accessible
to any motivated reader." Choice

"Mlodinow will help readers sort out Mark Twain's
'damn lies' from meaningful statistics and the choices we
face every day." Publ Wkly

Includes bibliographical references

Rosenthal, Jeffrey

Struck by lightning; the curious world of prob-
abilities. [by] Jeffrey S. Rosenthal. HarperCollins
Canada 2005 263p il pa $19.95   **519.2**
1. Chance 2. Probabilities
ISBN 0-309-09734-7; 978-0-309-09734-5
LC 2005-37021

Rosenthal discusses ways in which probability theory affects such areas of everyday life as crime, travel, gambling,
politics, and disease.

"The lighthearted presentation ensures that readers will
not feel burdened by all the knowledge they are gaining and
the concluding summary—disguised as a final exam—is
sure to deliver an A to everyone, which is what Rosenthal
deserves for this clever book." Publ Wkly

Santos, Aaron

How many licks? or, How to estimate damn
near anything. Running Press 2009 175p il pa
$14.95   **519.2**
1. Probabilities
ISBN 978-0-7624-3560-9; 0-7624-3560-7

"How many licks to the center of a Tootsie Pop? How
many people are having sex at this moment? How long
would it take a monkey on a typewriter to produce the
plays of Shakespeare? . . . . Using Enrico Fermi's theory
of approximation, Santos brings the world of numbers into
perspective. For puzzle junkies and trivia fanatics, these 70
word puzzles will show the reader how to take a bit of information, add what they already know, and extrapolate an
answer." Publisher's note

"No matter how you feel about math, Santos' puzzle-
solving prowess shows you just how much you can do when
you put on your thinking cap." Am Profile

519.3   Game theory

Highfield, Roger

★ **Supercooperators**; altruism, evolution, and
why we need each other to succeed. [by] Martin A.
Nowak, with Roger Highfield. Free Press 2011 330p
$27   **519.3**
1. Evolution 2. Game theory 3. Cooperative societies
ISBN 978-1-4391-0018-9; 1-4391-0018-7
LC 2010-35517

"Nowak aims to tackle the mysteries of nature with paper, pencil and computer. By looking at phenomena as diverse as H.I.V. infection and English irregular verbs, he has formally defined five distinct mechanisms that have helped give rise to cooperative behavior, from the first molecules that joined to self-replicate, to the first cells that formed multicellular organisms, all the way to human societies, which exhibit a degree of cooperation unmatched in all creation. In Nowak's view, figuring out how cooperation comes about and breaks down, as well as actively pursuing the 'snuggle for existence,' is the key to our survival as a species." N Y Times Book Rev

Includes bibliographical references

519.5   Statistical mathematics

Cohen, I. Bernard

The **triumph** of numbers; how counting shaped modern life. W. W. Norton 2005 209p il $24.95; pa $14.95   **519.5**
1. Statistics
ISBN 0-393-05769-0; 978-0-393-05769-0; 0-393-32870-8 pa; 978-0-393-32870-7 pa
LC 2004-27322

"This book presents a persuasive narrative on how numbers have maintained a prominent role not only in science and government throughout time, but in the daily operations of life." Sci Books Films

Includes bibliographical references

Everitt, Brian

★ The **Cambridge** dictionary of statistics; [by] B.S. Everitt, A. Skrondal. 4th ed.; Cambridge University Press 2010 468p il $59   **519.5**
1. Reference books 2. Statistics -- Dictionaries
ISBN 978-0-521-76699-9
LC 2010-502891

First published 1998

"This field-specific dictionary explains nearly 4000 terms, concepts, and models relevant to fields employing theoretical, applied, scientific, and survey-related probability methods." Libr J

Silver, Nate

The **signal** and the noise; why so many predictions fail--but some don't. Nate Silver. Penguin Press 2012 534 p. $27.95   **519.5**
1. Statistics 2. Theory of knowledge 3. Knowledge, Theory of 4. Forecasting -- History 5. Forecasting -- Methodology 6. Bayesian statistical decision theory
ISBN 159420411X; 9781594204111
LC 2012027308

This book, by political forecaster Nate Silver, "examines the world of prediction, investigating how we can distinguish a true signal from a universe of noisy data. Most predictions fail, . . . because most of us have a poor understanding of probability and uncertainty. . . . Silver visits the most successful forecasters in a range of areas. . . . He explains and evaluates how these forecasters think and what bonds they share." (Publisher's note)

Includes bibliographical references (p. 459-514)

and index

Wheelan, Charles

Naked statistics; stripping the dread from the data. Charles Wheelan. W W Norton & Co Inc 2013 304 p. (hardcover) $26.95   **519.5**
1. Statistics
ISBN 0393071952; 9780393071955
LC 2012034411

Wheelan "has provided an intuitive presentation of statistical concepts without getting bogged down by extensive data lists or computation. The author begins by generally introducing each idea with an idealized situation to illustrate that statistical setting and its impact on effective interpretation, and then moves on to current real-world settings to legitimize his discussion. He also clearly discusses subtleties that can be encountered, showing how data users must be careful to avoid oversimplifying the implications of a given result. The presentation is nonthreatening, yet readers will find it a suitably thoughtful consideration of statistical ideas." Choice

Includes bibliographical references and index

520   Astronomy and allied sciences

Bakich, Michael E.

The **Cambridge** encyclopedia of amateur astronomy. Cambridge Univ. Press 2003 342p il $69 **520**
1. Reference books 2. Astronomy -- Encyclopedias
ISBN 0-521-81298-4
LC 2002-31551

"The book is arranged in two parts. Part one presents planetary data, such as atmospheric pressure, composition, and future conjunctions and transits. Part two contains a summary on each planet, including its moons. These summaries cover cloud and atmospheric conditions, surface features, historical early ideas about each planet, and recent discoveries from the Hubble Space Telescope and other data collected in the 'late 1990s.'" Booklist

"Any amateur astronomer, or anyone with an interest in seeing what nonprofessionals can do if they are dedicated, would enjoy this book." Sci Books Films

Includes bibliographical references

Bartusiak, Marcia

The **day** we found the universe. Pantheon Books 2009 337p il $27.95   **520**
1. Astronomy -- History
ISBN 978-0-375-42429-8; 0-375-42429-6
LC 2008-34377

"This is a superb book that interweaves the fascinating story of a major scientific quest with a cast of characters, situations, painstaking observations, and imaginative thinking that reminds us all of the human side of scientific endeavors and the ways in which the universe itself continuously surprises us." Sci Books Films

Includes bibliographical references

Couper, Heather

The **history** of astronomy; [by] Heather Couper & Nigel Henbest; foreword by Arthur C. Clarke. Firefly Books 2007 285p il $59.95; pa $29.95 **520**

1. Astronomy -- History
ISBN 978-1-55407-325-2; 1-55407-325-1; 978-1-55407-537-9 pa; 1-55407-537-8 pa

LC 2008-272095

This "history is pieced together through astronomer interviews and visits to historically important astronomy sites around the world. . . . This is a copiously illustrated, straightforwardly written volume that will appeal to readers with and without an astronomy background. In addition to covering astronomy through the ages, the authors do an admirable job explaining current astronomical discoveries and personalities." Choice

Darling, David J.

The **universal** book of astronomy from the Andromeda Galaxy to the zone of avoidance; [by] David Darling. Wiley 2003 570p il $40 **520**

1. Reference books 2. Astronomy -- Dictionaries
ISBN 0-471-26569-1

LC 2003-13941

"Designed for nonspecialists, Darling's volume fills a niche in astronomy ready reference. . . . The volume is . . . highly readable and provides bonuses in 22 star charts outlining all 88 constellations in both north and south celestial hemispheres, instructional aids throughout the text, and charts that accompany entries for many stars, galaxies, and clusters and show size, position, etc." Choice

Includes bibliographical references

Davidson, Keay

Carl Sagan; a life. Wiley 1999 xx, 540p hardcover o.p. pa $24.95 **520**

1. Authors 2. Novelists 3. Astronomers 4. Essayists 5. Astrophysicists 6. Writers on science 7. Science fiction writers
ISBN 0-471-39536-6 pa

LC 99-36206

The author profiles the life and scientific career of the influential American astronomer

"Sagan is presented in such a way that readers can decide whether to view him admirably or with a dose of skepticism." Booklist

Includes bibliographical references

Ferris, Timothy

Seeing in the dark; how backyard stargazers are probing deep space and guarding earth from interplanetary peril. Simon & Schuster 2002 379p il hardcover o.p. pa $14 **520**

1. Astronomy 2. Astronomers
ISBN 0-684-86579-3; 0-684-86580-7 pa

LC 2002-20693

Ferris examines "the 20th-century in spectroscopic analysis of very distant light from celestial bodies through the personal experiences of . . . astronomers, mostly amateurs." Christ Sci Monit

"This book should turn many novices on to astronomy and captivate those already fascinated by the heavens." Publ Wkly

Finkbeiner, Ann

A **grand** and bold thing; the extraordinary new map of the universe ushering in a new era of discovery. [by] Ann Finkbeiner. Free Press 2010 223p $27; ebook $12.99 **520**

1. Astronomical instruments 2. Astrophysicists 3. College teachers
ISBN 978-1-416-55216-1; 978-1-4391-9647-2 ebook

LC 2010-8533

"Finkbeiner reveals the story behind today's most exciting astronomical research program: the Sloan Digital Sky Survey, a massive technological undertaking whose results have allowed everyone, from astronomers to high school students, to create and work with 'the most complete map of the universe ever.' The SDSS began with astronomer Jim Gunn. . . . This delightful book reveals just how much SDSS has changed how astronomers work, and how they—and we—see the universe." Publ Wkly

Includes bibliographical references

Garfinkle, David

Three steps to the universe; from the sun to black holes to the mystery of dark matter. [by] David Garfinkle & Richard Garfinkle. The University of Chicago Press 2008 265p il $25 **520**

1. Black holes (Astronomy) 2. Dark matter (Astronomy) 3. Sun
ISBN 978-0-226-28346-3; 0-226-28346-1

LC 2008-8659

The authors "explore some of the knottiest problems facing modern cosmologists in this tough but informative primer to modern cosmology. . . . Arguing that 'it is necessary to jump the barrier of user-friendliness and discover the fascinating world beyond that layer of comfort,' the Garfinkles aren't afraid to get technical, but this smart, rewarding read is helped by a welcome voice, a feel for narrative and a useful glossary." Publ Wkly

Includes bibliographical references

Kanipe, Jeff

The **cosmic** connection; how astronomical events impact life on Earth. Prometheus Books 2009 296p il $27.95 **520**

1. Astronomy
ISBN 978-1-59102-667-9; 1-59102-667-9

LC 2008-31877

Kanipe sets out to trace "the whole natural history of how events in the near and far universe have influenced life on Earth today, and how they might influence life in the future." Publisher's note

"This extremely well written book would be an engaging read for any person with even the slightest interest in astronomy." Sci Books Films

Includes bibliographical references

Miller, Arthur I.

Empire of the stars; obsession, friendship, and betrayal in the quest for black holes. Houghton Mifflin 2005 364p il $26 **520**
1. Astronomers 2. Mathematicians 3. Black holes (Astronomy) 4. Astrophysicists 5. Writers on science 6. Nobel laureates for physics
ISBN 0-618-34151-X

LC 2004-60909

This history of the discovery of black holes focuses on the bitter rivalry between Indian astrophysicist Subrahmanyan Chandrasekhar and Cambridge astrophysicist Sir Arthur Eddington.

"Astronomy buffs and readers fascinated by the history of science will find this a compelling read." Publ Wkly
Includes bibliographical references

Patrick Moore's data book of astronomy; edited by Patrick Moore and Robin Rees. Cambridge University Press 2011 576p il map $55 **520**
1. Astronomy 2. Reference books
ISBN 978-0-521-89935-2

LC 2010031372

First published 2000 by Institute of Physics Pub. with title: The data book of astronomy

"Readers with no prior interest in amateur astronomy will find a lot to captivate here. It also contains clearly written, up-to-date sections explaining what all these various celestial objects are, and how we've come to know them. . . . This work offers so much more than a handbook for backyard telescopes; it is an atlas for the Universe around us that will surprise every time you dip in." Times Higher Ed

Plait, Philip C.

Death from the skies! these are the ways the world will end . . . [by] Philip Plait. Viking 2008 326p il $25.95 **520**
1. End of the world
ISBN 978-0-670-01997-7; 0-670-01997-6

LC 2008-22943

"The book is extremely informative: Plait explains not only what can destroy the planet but also how it would happen. It's a crash course in astronomy as well as a cautionary tale about the (possibly brief) future of our world." Booklist

Raymo, Chet

An **intimate** look at the night sky. Walker & Co. 2001 242p il $25; pa $16 **520**
1. Astronomy
ISBN 0-8027-1369-6; 0-8027-7670-1 pa

Raymo discusses astronomy and cosmology. "The narrative follows earth's path through the four seasons {around the sun}." Christ Sci Monit

"A delightful, inspiring introduction to astronomy." Booklist
Includes bibliographical references

Ridpath, Ian

★ **Stars** and planets; the most complete guide to the stars, planets, galaxies, and the solar system. illustrated by Wil Tirion. Fully rev. and expanded ed.;

Princeton University Press 2007 400p il (Princeton field guides) pa $19.95 **520**
1. Stars 2. Planets 3. Astronomy
ISBN 978-0-691-13556-4; 0-691-13556-8
First published 1998 by DK Pub.

This book features "charts covering all 88 constellations in the Northern and Southern hemispheres; data and notes on all bright stars and other objects of interest; . . . Moon maps and descriptions of the main lunar features; [and] tips on choosing and using binoculars and telescopes." Publisher's note

Sagan, Carl, 1934-1996

Conversations with Carl Sagan; edited by Tom Head. University Press of Mississippi 2006 xxv, 167p (Literary conversations series) $50; pa $20 **520**
1. Authors 2. Novelists 3. Astronomers 4. Essayists 5. Astrophysicists 6. Writers on science 7. Science fiction writers
ISBN 1-57806-735-9; 1-57806-736-7 pa

LC 2005-48747

The editor "has selected 16 engaging conversations from such popular venues as Rolling Stone, Psychology Today, The Charlie Rose Show, and NPR, and it's a boon to connect with Sagan's knowledge, wisdom, and generosity . . . after his early death at 62." Booklist
Includes bibliographical references

Cosmos. Random House 2002 365p $35 **520**
1. Astronomy
ISBN 0-375-50832-5

LC 2002-69744

A reissue of the title first published 1980

Based on the author's television series of the same name, this volume covers "the 10- to 20-billion-year history of the universe, from the big bang and subsequent evolution of molecular material through the evolution of human culture." Libr J {review of 1980 edition}
Includes bibliographical references

Pale blue dot; a vision of the human future in space. Ballantine Books 1997 360p pa $14.95 **520**
1. Outer space -- Exploration
ISBN 978-0-345-37659-6; 0-345-37659-5
First published 1994 by Random House

"In a tour of our solar system, galaxy and beyond . . . Sagan meshes a history of astronomical discovery, a cogent brief for space exploration and an overview of life. . . . His exploration of our place in the universe is illustrated with photographs, relief maps and paintings, including high-resolution images made by Voyager 1 and 2, as well as photos taken by the Galileo spacecraft, the Hubble Space Telescope and satellites orbiting Earth." Publ Wkly
Includes bibliographical references

Schaaf, Fred

The **50** best sights in astronomy and how to see them; observing eclipses, bright comets, meteor

showers, and other celestial wonders. John Wiley 2007 280p il pa $19.95 **520**
1. Astronomy
ISBN 978-0-471-69657-5; 0-471-69657-9
LC 2006-36221

The author "begins with some basic information and terminology (altazimuth system, for example, or right ascension) and then plunges right in with the most easily accessible astronomical sight, the starry sky above our heads. For each sight, he not only explains what it is and the best conditions under which to observe it, he also tells us about its historical, mythological, or scientific importance and explores how these far-off wonders can have a very real effect on our humble home world. This could so easily have been a dry-as-dust tome, but Schaaf's enthusiasm overflows every page." Booklist
Includes bibliographical references

Sobel, Dava
A **more** perfect heaven; how Copernicus revolutionized the cosmos. Walker Pub. 2011 273p il map $25 **520**
1. Astronomy 2. Astronomers 3. Solar system
ISBN 978-0-8027-1793-1
LC 2011024772

"Dava Sobel excels in telling the story of Nicholas Copernicus and his almost-shelved masterpiece, On the Revolutions. Along the way, she brings the social and political milieu of the times into sharp relief providing context for the sheer audacity of his insights into planetary motion and his reticence in pursuing their dissemination." Sci Books Films
Includes bibliographical references

Trefil, James
Space atlas; mapping the universe and beyond. James Trefil ; foreword by Buzz Aldrin. National Geographic 2012 335 p. col. ill. (hardback) $50 **520**
1. Galaxies 2. Astronomy 3. Solar system 4. Stars -- Atlases 5. Galaxies -- Atlases 6. Solar system -- Atlases 7. Astronomy -- Charts, diagrams, etc
ISBN 1426209711; 9781426209710; 9781426210914
LC 2012020000

Author James Trefil presents a "guide to the planets, stars and outer reaches of the universe." The book "explains the nature of planets, stars, galaxies and exotic objects such as black holes alongside photos and art . . . In addition to the latest imagery coming from space telescopes and diagrams explaining key astronomical concepts, this atlas also includes more than 90 pages of detailed maps." (Publisher's note)
Includes bibliographical references

Universe; general editor, Martin Rees. DK 2008 512p il pa $27.95 **520**
1. Cosmology
ISBN 978-0-7566-3670-8; 0-7566-3670-1
LC 2008-299650

First published 2005

This is "a visually stunning reference that makes browsing irresistible. Every page of this oversized volume is full color, with an eye-pleasing balance of text and graphics." Libr J

521 Astronomy

Goodstein, David L.
Feynman's lost lecture; the motion of planets around the sun. {by} David L. Goodstein and Judith R. Goodstein. Norton 1996 191p il $35; pa $19.95 **521**
1. Authors 2. Universe 3. Physicists 4. Astrophysics 5. Solar system 6. Writers on science 7. Nobel laureates for physics
ISBN 0-393-03918-8; 0-393-31995-4 pa
LC 95-38719

This "book consists of four chapters. The first and largest is a brief history of the establishment of the Copernican cosmology, which Feynman gave as a lecture to the freshman class at Caltech. Feynman then revisits the work of Isaac Newton and the watershed proof of the Scientific Revolution that separated the ancient world from the modern. There is also a chapter with some wonderful reminiscences of Feynman." Libr J
Includes bibliographical references

522 Techniques, procedures, apparatus, equipment, materials

Dickinson, Terence
The **backyard** astronomer's guide; [by] Terence Dickinson & Alan Dyer. 3rd ed; Firefly Books 2008 368p il $49.95 **522**
1. Astronomy
ISBN 978-1-55407-344-3; 1-55407-344-8
First published 1991 by Camden House

The authors provide guidance "on the right types of telescopes and other equipment; photographing the stars through a telescope; and star charts, software and other references. They cover daytime and twilight observing, planetary and deep-sky observing, and . . . more." Publisher's note
Includes bibliographical references

Kerrod, Robin
Hubble; the mirror on the universe. [by] Robin Kerrod & Carole Stott. 3rd ed. updated, rev. and expanded.; Firefly Books 2011 224p il pa $29.95 **522**
1. Hubble Space Telescope 2. Outer space -- Exploration
ISBN 978-1-55407-972-8; 1-55407-972-1
LC 2011292195

First published 2003

"Kerrod provides an excellent overview of Hubble's accomplishments (along with a history of the evolution of the telescope), thoughtfully organizing the spellbinding images from space, and clearly and avidly explaining exactly which phenomena they depict." Booklist

523   Specific celestial bodies and phenomena

Gribbin, John R.

Stardust; supernovae and life: the cosmic connection. {by} John Gribbin with Mary Gribbin. Yale Univ. Press 2000 238p $35; pa $13.95 **523**

1. Universe 2. Supernovas 3. Life (Biology)

ISBN 0-300-08419-6; 0-300-09097-8 pa

LC 00-35944

"All the carbon, hydrogen, oxygen and nitrogen (CHON) in our DNA was once floating around in a planetary nebula, to which it had been expelled violently from a red giant star. So how did it get here? Most likely via comets, says Gribbin. . . . The author also argues that we shouldn't necessarily look for life on other planets, but rather on the large moons revolving around the giant planets that orbit distant stars. . . . In a short appendix . . . Gribbin discusses current theories about the evolution of multiple universes." Publ Wkly

"A fine summary of the origin of our elemental constitution." Booklist

Includes bibliographical references

523.1   The universe, galaxies, quasars

Aczel, Amir D.

God's equation; Einstein, relativity, and the expanding universe. Delta Trade Paperbacks 2000 236p il pa $12 **523.1**

1. Cosmology 2. Physicists 3. Relativity (Physics) 4. Nobel laureates for physics

ISBN 978-0-385-33485-3; 0-385-33485-0

First published 1999 by Four Walls Eight Windows

"Though Aczel's analysis of Einstein's work requires familiarity with advanced mathematics, that analysis makes up only a minor portion of his book, and most readers will appreciate the author's inclusion of the great physicist's letters to astronomer Erwin Freundlich." Publ Wkly

Includes bibliographical references

Bojowald, Martin

Once before time; a whole story of the universe. Alfred A. Knopf 2010 309p il $27.95; ebook $27.95 **523.1**

1. Cosmology 2. Physicists 3. Space and time 4. Beginning 5. Quantum gravity

ISBN 978-0-307-27285-0; 978-0-307-59425-9 ebook

LC 2010-15937

Original German edition, 2009

The author "explores loop quantum theory, an idea he developed as a postdoctoral student in 2000, to fill in the gaps left by 20th-century physics." Publ Wkly

"Cutting-edge physics made accessible for readers who pay close attention." Kirkus

Includes bibliographical references

Cox, Brian, 1968-

Wonders of the universe; [by] Brian Cox and Andrew Cohen. Harper Design 2011 256p il $29.99; ebook $14.99 **523.1**

1. Cosmology

ISBN 978-0-06-211054-1; 978-0-06-211561-4 ebook

The author "uses the evidence found in the natural world on Earth to . . . explain the truth of the cosmos. . . . [He shows] how the vast and unfathomable phenomena of deep space can be explained, and even experienced, by re-examining the familiar here on Earth." Publisher's note

Dauber, Philip M.

The **three** big bangs; comet crashes, exploding stars, and the creation of the universe. [by] Philip M. Dauber, Richard A. Muller. Perseus Books 1997 207p il pa $15 **523.1**

1. Cosmology 2. Supernovas 3. Catastrophes (Geology)

ISBN 978-0-201-15495-5; 0-201-15495-1

First published 1996 by Addison-Wesley

The authors discuss the origins of the universe and of life on Earth.

"Dauber and Muller have not only chosen three 'hot topics' in . . . astronomy but also have masterfully woven the underlying scientific strands together. They paint a colorful picture of the theories and techniques of modern astronomy." Choice

Includes bibliographical references

Ferguson, Kitty

Measuring the universe; our historic quest to chart the horizons of space and time. Walker & Co. 1999 342p il $27; pa $16.95 **523.1**

1. Cosmology 2. Measurement

ISBN 0-8027-1351-3; 0-8027-7592-6 pa

LC 99-19476

"Starting with Eratosthenes and his calculation of the earth's circumference using the shadows cast in a well, and moving through Stephen Hawking's work on black holes, Ferguson tells the tale of our search for our place in the universe. This book is nicely illustrated with photos, tables, and diagrams." Libr J

Includes bibliographical references and index

Frank, Adam

About time; cosmology and culture at the twilight of the Big Bang. Free Press 2011 xxi, 406p il $26 **523.1**

1. Cosmology 2. Space and time 3. Big bang theory 4. Life -- Origin

ISBN 978-1-4391-6959-9; 1-4391-6959-4; 978-1-4391-6961-2 ebook

LC 2011011345

The author "delves into the complex relationship between time and culture and concludes that culture and cosmology—even the Big Bang—are linked inextricably together." Kirkus

"Frank offers a unique and fascinating look at complex concepts with an accessible style that is both matter-of-fact and thoroughly entertaining." Publ Wkly

Includes bibliographical references

Gates, Evalyn

Einstein's telescope; the hunt for dark matter and dark energy in the universe. W.W. Norton 2009 305p il $25.95; pa $16.95 **523.1**

1. Dark energy (Astronomy) 2. Dark matter (Astronomy)

ISBN 978-0-393-06238-0; 978-0-393-33801-0 pa

LC 2008-44455

The author "explores the science of . . . [dark matter and dark energy] and the questions they raise about the universe's origins, its present and its future." Publ Wkly

"Gates writes with a freshness and clarity that make complex ideas such as relativity, lensing, black holes, and the cosmic web understandable." Libr J

Includes bibliographical references

Gleiser, Marcelo

The prophet and the astronomer; a scientific journey to the end of time. Norton 2002 256p il $26.95; pa $15.95 **523.1**

1. Cosmology 2. End of the world 3. Religion and science

ISBN 0-393-04987-6; 0-393-32431-1 pa

LC 2002-538

"Gleiser ponders the dark parallels between the apocalyptic visions of ancient seers and the cosmic predictions of modern scientists. . . . Gleiser's musings . . . occasionally will baffle the nonspecialist, but most readers will consider a few moments of perplexity a small price to pay for the opportunity to probe humanity's oldest nightmares and newest aspirations." Booklist

Includes bibliographical references and index

Greene, Brian R.

The fabric of the cosmos; space, time, and the texture of reality. Knopf 2004 569p il $28.95; pa $15.95 **523.1**

1. Cosmology

ISBN 0-375-41288-3; 0-375-72720-5 pa

LC 2003-58918

"Frogs in bowls, falling eggs, loaves of bread, pennies on balloons, ping pong balls in molasses, and babushka dolls are just some of the analogies used to explain complex concepts cleverly. After reading this book, you will never look at a starry night sky the same way again." Libr J

Includes bibliographical references

Gribbin, John R.

The origins of the future; ten questions for the next ten years. [by] John Gribbin. Yale University Press 2006 292p $27.50 **523.1**

1. Cosmology 2. Evolution 3. Life -- Origin

ISBN 978-0-300-11998-5; 0-300-11998-4

LC 2006-11062

"In each of this book's 10 chapters, . . . [the author] describes different eras in the evolution of our universe. Each chapter opens with a question setting forth that chapter's theme. . . . Gribbin lays out the history of the universe and takes care to show its intricate workings for us to admire." Sci Books Films

Includes bibliographical references

Halpern, Paul

Edge of the universe; a voyage to the cosmic horizon and beyond. by Paul Halpern. John Wiley & Sons 2012 236 p. (cloth) $27.95 **523.1**

1. Universe 2. Big bang theory 3. Dark energy (Astronomy) 4. Cosmology -- Popular works

ISBN 0470636246; 9780470636244

LC 2012002028

This book offers a "look at the mysteries that lurk at the edge of the known universe and beyond." Author Paul Halpern "explains what we know about the Big Bang, the accelerating universe, dark energy, dark flow, and dark matter to examine some of the theories about the content of the universe and why its edge is getting farther away from us faster." (Publisher's note)

Includes bibliographical references and index

Hawking, Stephen, 1942-

Black holes and baby universes and other essays; [by] Stephen Hawking. Bantam Bks. 1993 182p hardcover o.p. pa $18 **523.1**

1. Cosmology 2. Science -- Philosophy

ISBN 0-553-37411-7 pa

LC 93-8269

A collection of essays and speeches ranging from autobiographical sketches to theoretical discussions of black holes, relativity and quantum mechanics.

The author "sprinkles his explanations with a wry sense of humor and a keen awareness that the sciences today delve not only into the far reaches of the cosmos, but into the inner philosophical world as well." N Y Times Book Rev

★ A briefer history of time; [by] Stephen Hawking and Leonard Mlodinow. Bantam Dell 2005 162p il $25 **523.1**

1. Cosmology

ISBN 0-553-80436-7

LC 2005-42949

First published 1988 with title: A brief history of time

The authors describe concepts about space and time, black holes, the origin and nature of the universe, the uncertainty principle, and the unification of physics. It also discusses string theory, dark matter, and dark energy.

"Hawking and Mlodinow provide one of the most lucid discussions of this complex topic ever written for a general audience. Readers will come away with an excellent understanding of the apparent contradictions and conundrums at the forefront of contemporary physics." Publ Wkly

Includes bibliographical references

Hooper, Dan

Dark cosmos; in search of our universe's missing mass and energy. HarperCollins Publishers 2006 240p il pa $14.95; $24.95 **523.1**

1. Dark energy (Astronomy) 2. Dark matter (Astronomy)

ISBN 978-0-06-113033-5 pa; 0-06-113033-8 pa; 978-0-06-113032-8; 0-06-113032-X

LC 2006-44333

This book discusses "dark matter" and "dark energy," invisible substances which scientists speculate may make up over 95% of the universe.

"Hooper's clear presentation in very simple, jargon-free prose should appeal especially to young people just starting to get excited about the mysteries that still await them in science." Publ Wkly

Impey, Chris

How it began; a time- traveler's guide to the universe. Chris Impey. W.W. Norton 2012 434 p.   **523.1**
1. Universe 2. Astronomy 3. Cosmology 4. Space and time 5. Cosmology -- Popular works 6. Space and time -- Popular works
ISBN 9780393080025

LC 2011052855

This book about the universe "follow[s] atoms through generation after generation of stellar cores from the Big Bang onward. [Author Chris] Impey's time travelers are astronomers doing cosmic archeology in which the farther out in the universe one goes, the farther back in time one can see. Impey begins close to home, and closest in time, with the formation of our solar system. . . . Moving outward in the universe (and back in time toward the Big Bang), Impey discusses how to measure stellar distances and detect planets orbiting other stars. Stretching farther back, Impey explores galactic evolution, relativity, the large-scale structure of the universe, and the Big Bang. Fictional vignettes narrated by a space/time traveler . . . bookend each chapter to personalize the material." (Publishers Wkly)

Includes bibliographical references and index

How it ends; from you to the universe. W.W. Norton 2010 352p il $26.95   **523.1**
1. Death 2. Universe 3. End of the world
ISBN 978-0-393-06985-3; 0-393-06985-0

LC 2009-47265

"Although dealing with a gruesome subject, Impey's book is a lighthearted romp through all the ways that life and everything else in the universe may end. Along the way, the author not only educates the reader in biology and astronomy, but also provides some tantalizing glimpses into possible future scenarios that avoid such gruesome endings." Sci Books Films

Includes bibliographical references

Kaku, Michio

Parallel worlds; a journey through creation, higher dimensions, and the future of the cosmos. Doubleday 2005 428p il hardcover o.p. pa $15.95 **523.1**
1. Cosmology 2. String theory 3. Big bang theory
ISBN 0-385-50986-3; 1-4000-3372-1 pa

LC 2004-56039

"This is a riveting popular treatment of the string revolution in physics written by a pioneering theorist in the field. Kaku expounds comprehensibly on why astrophysicists love strings and branes and the way they resolve various vexatious cosmological paradoxes." Booklist

Kanipe, Jeff

Chasing Hubble's shadows; the search for galaxies at the edge of time. Hill and Wang 2006 205p il $24; pa $15   **523.1**
1. Hubble Space Telescope 2. Outer space -- Exploration
ISBN 0-8090-3406-9; 0-8090-3407-7 pa

LC 2005-9652

This "is an account of the continuing efforts of astronomers to probe the outermost limits of the observable universe." Publisher's note

The author's "breathless writing conveys his own excitement over the revelations that new advances in astronomy can tell us about our planet and our place in the universe." Publ Wkly

Mitton, Simon

Heart of darkness; unraveling the mysteries of the invisible universe. Jeremiah P. Ostriker, Simon Mitton. Princeton University Press 2013 299 p. (Science essentials) (alk. paper) $27.95 **523.1**
1. Cosmology 2. Dark matter (Astronomy) 3. Cosmology -- Popular works 4. Dark energy (Astronomy)
ISBN 0691134308; 9780691134307

LC 2012950892

This book by Jeremiah P. Ostriker and Mitton explores the history of cosmology. "From humankind's early attempts to comprehend Earth's place in the solar system, to astronomers' exploration of the Milky Way galaxy . . . to the detection of the primordial fluctuations of energy from which all subsequent structure developed, this book explains the physics and the history of how the current model of our universe arose and has passed every test hurled at it by the skeptics." (Publisher's note)

Includes bibliographical references (p. 291-293) and index

Panek, Richard

★ The **4** percent universe; dark matter, dark energy, and the race to discover the rest of reality. Houghton Mifflin Harcourt 2011 297 p. $26.00 **523.1**
1. Physics 2. Cosmology 3. Astrophysics 4. Dark energy (Astronomy) 5. Dark matter (Astronomy)
ISBN 0618982442; 9780618982448

LC 2010-25838

This is an account of the scientific inquiry into the substance of the unseen dark matter and energy that makes up 96% of the universe. Index.

"This is a story about not just science, but also scientists, with enough dueling personalities, epic failures, inspirational triumphs, and out-and-out rivalries to carry a Hollywood blockbuster—should Hollywood ever turn its attention to the world of cosmology." Ad Astra

Includes bibliographical references

Potter, Christopher

You are here; a portable history of the universe. HarperCollins 2009 294p $26.99 **523.1**
1. Cosmology 2. Science -- History 3. Science -- Philosophy
ISBN 978-0-06-113786-0; 0-06-113786-3

An exploration of the universe and our relationship to it.

"A well-executed, consistently readable layperson's exposition of the state of scientific knowledge. . . . One of the best short surveys of science and its history in recent years." Kirkus

Includes bibliographical references (p. 275-279)

Rees, Martin J.

Just six numbers; the deep forces that shape the universe. {by} Martin Rees. Basic Bks. 2000 173p il hardcover o.p. pa $14.95   **523.1**

1. Cosmology 2. Big bang theory
ISBN 0-465-03673-2 pa

          LC 00-268248

First published 1999 in the United Kingdom

"Rees summarizes the history of the universe, pointing out that six numbers related to basic physical constants (for example, the relative strengths of the gravitational and electromagnetic attraction) determine how the universe developed." Libr J

"A brief, readable, and profoundly instructive account of where cosmological knowledge stands at this moment." New Yorker

Includes bibliographical references

Our cosmic habitat; [by] Martin Rees. Princeton Univ. Press 2001 205p il $35; pa $14.95   **523.1**

1. Cosmology
ISBN 0-691-08926-4; 0-691-11477-3 pa

          LC 2001-27835

"In the crowded field of popular writing about the universe, Rees is genuinely in the forefront—an accomplished scientist with the superior writing skills that enable him to connect with nonspecialists." Booklist

Includes bibliographical references

Singh, Simon

Big bang: the origins of the universe. Fourth Estate 2005 532p il $27.95   **523.1**

1. Cosmology 2. Big bang theory
ISBN 0-00716-220-0

The author "presents a brief history of the origins of the universe. . . . He begins with a historical overview of how scientific thought changed from mythology to cosmology, then moves to the debate between the steady state model of an eternal universe and the Big Bang theory, which saw the universe as beginning at a unique moment that was followed by rapid extension. . . . This readable book provides an accessible overview of this complex scientific theory." Libr J

Smoot, George

Wrinkles in time; witness to the birth of the universe. [by] George Smoot and Keay Davidson; with a new preface. Harper Perennial 2007 331p il pa $14.95   **523.1**

1. Cosmology
ISBN 978-0-06-134444-2; 0-06-134444-3

          LC 2008-530705

First published 1993 by William Morrow

"Smoot and Davidson present a historical review of cosmology that takes the reader from the work of Galileo to the recent . . . work on 'COBE' (the Cosmic Background Explorer satellite). An excellent nontechnical study of re-

search into what makes the universe the way it is, the book provides a detailed discussion of the search for and the eventual discovery of what are called the 'wrinkles in time' from the viewpoint of the authors' own experiences in the field." Choice [review of 1993 edition]

Includes bibliographical references

Steinhardt, P. J.

Endless universe; beyond the Big Bang. [by] Paul J. Steinhardt and Neil Turok. Doubleday 2007 284p il $24.95   **523.1**

1. Cosmology
ISBN 0-385-50964-2; 978-0-385-50964-0

          LC 2006-25256

"This volume is not light reading, but the authors lighten the load with stories of how they met and collaborated on an M-theory (a string theory derivative) based cyclical model of the universe. . . . The illustrations, which play a key role in the book, introduce the reader to difficult material through simplified analogies." Sci Books Films

Includes bibliographical references

Tyson, Neil deGrasse

Origins : fourteen billion years of cosmic evolution; {by} Neil deGrasse Tyson, Donald Goldsmith. W.W. Norton 2004 345p il $27.95   **523.1**

1. Cosmology 2. Evolution 3. Life -- Origin
ISBN 0-393-05992-8

          LC 2004-12201

The authors investigate "the connections between subatomic physics and the structure of the universe. With that as background, the authors then flit between the epoch of infinite density and temperature and the contemporary eon of galaxies, and they sign off with ruminations on extraterrestrial life." Booklist

"Amateur astronomers—in fact, any reader who enjoys popular science—will find fascinating information presented in clear but never patronizing language." Libr J

Includes bibliographical references

Universe down to Earth. Columbia Univ. Press 1994 277p il $60; pa $19   **523.1**

1. Cosmology
ISBN 0-231-07560-X; 0-231-07561-8 pa

          LC 93-32259

The author "guides readers through the methods, history, and jargon of cosmology." Booklist

"This book is a genuine joy to read. . . . It is at once witty and profound in its treatment of some of the most 'far-out' concepts of the universe." Sci Books Films

Includes bibliographical references

Vilenkin, Alexander

Many worlds in one; the search for other universes. [by] Alex Vilenkin. Hill and Wang 2006 235p il $24   **523.1**

1. Cosmology
ISBN 978-0-8090-9523-0; 0-8090-9523-8

          LC 2005-27057

The author discusses the "creation of the universe, its likely demise and the growing belief among cosmologists that there are an infinite number of universes. Vilenkin does an impressive job of presenting the background information necessary for lay readers to understand the ideas behind the big bang and related phenomena. . . . Drawing on the work of Stephen Hawking and recent advances in string theory, Vilenkin gives us a great deal to ponder." Publ Wkly

Includes bibliographical references

Weintraub, David A.

How old is the universe? Princeton University Press 2011 370p il $29.95   **523.1**

1. Universe 2. Cosmology 3. Solar system 4. Earth -- Age

ISBN 978-0-691-14731-4

LC 2010-9117

"It's all very well for astronomers to say that the universe is 13.7 billion years old, but you have to wonder just how they figured that out. . . . [The author] starts with how scientists first determined the age of the solar system—about 4.5 billion years—by isotope dating the oldest known rocks: lunar rocks brought back by astronauts, and meteorites that have collided with Earth. He then shows how stellar life cycles indicate an age of about 13 billion years." Publ Wkly

"This is no-nonsense science writing that will be enjoyed for years: David Weintraub is an expert guide, laying out the evidence in just the right amount of detail." New Sci

523.2   Planetary systems

Baker, David

The 50 most extreme places in our solar system; [by] David Baker and Todd Ratcliff. Belknap Press 2010 290p il $27.95   **523.2**

1. Solar system 2. Extreme environments

ISBN 0-674-04998-5; 978-0-674-04998-7

LC 2010-06126

"Descriptions of physical phenomena are given around themes such as 'Surface and Interior' and 'Extreme Climates.'" (Sci Books Films) Glossary. Bibliography. Index.

The authors "discuss phenomena like the potential for diamond rain on Uranus and Neptune and the hardiness of extremophile life forms. As planetary scientists, they write clearly about the most extreme physical aspects of solar system bodies such as planets, moons, and comets, but deftly mix in more familiar comparisons from planet Earth as well." Choice

Includes bibliographical references

Daniels, Patricia

The new solar system; ice worlds, moons, and planets redefined. foreword by Robert Burnham. National Geographic Society 2009 223p il map $35   **523.2**

1. Solar system

ISBN 978-1-4262-0462-3; 1-4262-046-20

LC 2009-10117

This is "a sumptuously illustrated book describing the history, composition, and exploration of the solar system. Aimed at a general audience, the text is highly readable and contains numerous side notes providing fasci-

nating anecdotes and facts about the planets, the sun, and astronomers." Choice

Includes bibliographical references

Jayawardhana, Ray

Strange new worlds; the search for alien planets and life beyond our solar system. Princeton University Press 2011 255p il $24.95   **523.2**

1. Solar system 2. Extrasolar planets 3. Life on other planets 4. Astronomy -- History

ISBN 978-0-691-14254-8; 0-691-14254-8

LC 2010940350

An astronomer discusses the search for extrasolar planets and extraterrestrial life. Bibliography. Index.

"Everything you need to know about alien planet discovery is insightfully described in this engaging book, which will appeal to astronomers, general science buffs, and armchair UFOlogists." Libr J

Includes glossary and bibliographical references

Lang, Kenneth R.

The Cambridge guide to the solar system; Kenneth R. Lang. Cambridge University Press 2003 452p il $60   **523.2**

1. Solar system

ISBN 0-521-81306-9

LC 2002-31562

"The photographs are stunning, the numerous charts and graphs are exemplary, and the narrative is bulging with all the important information about the solar system that is available to date. The author has done a wonderful job of making many of the complicated scientific concepts accessible to the layperson." Booklist

Includes bibliographical references

Lemonick, Michael D.

Mirror Earth; the search for our planet's twin. Michael D. Lemonick. Walker 2012 294 p. (hardback) $26   **523.2**

1. Earth 2. Extrasolar planets 3. Planetology

ISBN 080277900X; 9780802779007

LC 2012009787

AAAS Subaru SB & F Young Adult Science Book Finalist (2013)

This book by Michael Lemonick "offers readers . . . [a] view into the work of 'exoplaneteers': astronomers dedicated to searching out not just planets orbiting distant worlds, but 'Mirror Earths,' Earth-like planets that might harbor life. . . . Lemonick introduces planet-hunting pioneers like mild-mannered Bill Borucki, indefatigable Geoff Marcy . . . and nurse-turned-astrophysicist Debra Fischer, revealing personalities as well as research frustrations and successes." (Publishers Weekly)

"A solid overview of the cutting edge of astronomy and of the new breed of astronomers who are exploring it." Kirkus

Includes bibliographical references and index

Lorenz, Ralph

Titan unveiled; Saturn's mysterious moon explored. [by] Ralph Lorenz and Jacqueline Mitton. Princeton University Press 2008 243p il map $29.95; pa $19.95 **523.2**

    1. Saturn (Planet) 2. Titan (Satellite) -- Exploration

    ISBN 978-0-691-12587-9; 0-691-12587-2; 978-0-691-14633-1 pa; 0-619-14633-0 pa

                            LC 2007-938922

This book "provides the general reader with a lively narrative that combines a reliable, nontechnical account of the Cassini-Huygens mission with personal and often intimate insights into these efforts to explore a fascinating planetary analogue to the Earth." Am Sci

    Includes bibliographical references

523.3 Specific parts of solar system

Mackenzie, Dana

    The **big** splat; or, How our moon came to be. Wiley 2003 232p il $24.95 **523.3**

    1. Moon

    ISBN 0-471-15057-6

                            LC 2003-535402

"Mackenzie's account of humanity's long relationship with Earth's only natural satellite, from a probable lunar calendar found in the Lascaux caves to the new 'giant impact' theory of the moon's origin, is magnetically readable, preternaturally clear, and amazingly concise." Booklist

    Includes bibliographical references

523.4 Planets, asteroids, trans-Neptunian objects of solar system

Boyle, Alan

    The **case** for Pluto; how a little planet made a big difference. Wiley 2010 258p il $22.95; ebook $14.99 **523.4**

    1. Solar system 2. Pluto (Planet)

    ISBN 978-0-470-50544-1; 0-470-50544-3; 978-0-470-54188-3 ebook

                            LC 2009-15961

This volume examines the history of the discovery of planets. Boyle "chronicles the decision by the International Astronomical Union in 2006 to redefine the definition of a planet. . . . [Boyle argues] that Pluto has unjustly been cast out of the 'Planet Family' and recast as a 'dwarf planet.'" Sci Books Films

    Includes bibliographical references

Jones, Barrie William

    Pluto; sentinel of the outer solar system. [by] Barrie W. Jones. Cambridge University Press 2010 231p il $35.99 **523.4**

    1. Solar system 2. Pluto (Planet)

    ISBN 978-0-521-19436-5; 0-521-19436-9

                            LC 2010-15480

This is "a detailed, matter-of-fact, and thoroughly accessible look at Pluto's origins, its history, and what it can tell us about our solar system—especially its outer reaches. . . . The author writes in a clear, matter-of-fact style, including sidebars on related subjects from Kepler's laws of planetary

motion to calculating a planet's surface temperature using nothing more complex than high school algebra." Publ Wkly

    Includes glossary and bibliographical references

Kessler, Andrew

    Martian summer; robot arms, cowboy spacemen, and my 90 days with the Phoenix Mars Mission. Pegasus 2011 340p il $27.95 **523.4**

    1. Space flight to Mars 2. Phoenix Mars Mission (U.S.) 3. Mars (Planet) -- Exploration

    ISBN 978-1-60598-176-5; 1-60598-176-1

The author chronicles the three months he spent in Mission Control for NASA's Phoenix Mars Mission, a project that lead to the discovery of liquid water on Mars, as well as a giant frozen ocean trapped beneath the planet's north pole

    "The author provides some fascinating glimpses of the real work of a space mission: planning activities for the lander, dealing with peremptory orders from NASA and JPL, interpreting the sometimes ambiguous data and occasionally letting one's hair down for a party." Kirkus

Tyson, Neil De Grasse

    The **Pluto** files; the rise and fall of America's favorite planet. W.W. Norton 2009 194p il $23.95; pa $15.95 **523.4**

    1. Pluto (Dwarf planet) 2. Pluto (Planet)

    ISBN 978-0-393-06520-6; 0-393-06520-0; 978-0-393-33732-7 pa; 0-393-33732-4 pa

                            LC 2008-40436

The author, who is the director of the Hayden Planetarium and the Rose Center for Earth and Space at the American Museum of Natural History in New York City, discusses the "history of Pluto and the debate over its planethood. . . [Tyson cites Pluto's] entrenchment in America's cultural and patriotic view of the cosmos to explain its considerable popularity and the reasons why so many people campaigned for the preservation of its status." (Publisher's note)

    The author "uses an engaging mix of facts, photographs, cartoons, illustrations, songs, e-mails, and humor to explain what's up (and down) with Pluto." Christ Sci Monit

    Includes bibliographical references

Weintraub, David A.

    Is Pluto a planet? a historical journey through the solar system. Princeton University Press 2007 254p il $27.95 **523.4**

    1. Planets 2. Solar system 3. Pluto (Planet)

    ISBN 0-691-12348-9; 978-0-691-12348-6

                            LC 2006-929630

The author "places the Pluto controversy in context in his . . . account of the development of our solar system and the evolution of the meaning of the word planet, from Aristotle's theories to recent decrees by the International Astronomical Union." Publ Wkly

    Weintraub "provides a very interesting and thought-provoking history concerning the whole idea of planets, and I recommend the book highly to anyone interested in the solar system." Sci Books Films

    Includes bibliographical references

523.43 Mars

Hubbard, Scott

Exploring Mars; chronicles from a decade of discovery. Scott Hubbard ; foreword by Bill Nye. University of Arizona Press 2011 xix, 194 p.p (hardcover) $45.00 **523.43**

1. Space flight to Mars 2. Mars (Planet) -- Exploration 3. United States. National Aeronautics and Space Administration 4. Space flight to Mars -- History
ISBN 0816521115; 0816528969; 9780816521111; 9780816528967

LC 2011036184

This book presents author Scott Hubbard's "perspective on the logistical issues -- technical, scientific, and political -- that . . . [he] faced as NASA's 'Mars Czar' during a reorganization of its Mars Exploration Program. Covering the period between . . . 1999 and the launch of the Mars Odyssey spacecraft in April 2001, Hubbard details the . . . process of simultaneous planning and approval seeking for multiple missions as far as a decade in advance." (Library Journal)

Morton, Oliver

Mapping Mars; science, imagination, and the birth of a world. Picador 2002 357p il maps $30; pa $16 **523.43**

1. Mars (Planet)
ISBN 0-312-24551-3; 0-312-42261-X pa

The author "traces scientists' efforts to map and understand the surface of Mars. . . . Morton writes eloquently and displays a breadth of knowledge not often found in science writing." Publ Wkly

Includes bibliographical references

523.48 Neptune

Brown, Mike

How I killed Pluto and why it had it coming; Mike Brown. Spiegel & Grau 2010 xiii, 267p 1 ill. (pbk.) $15.00; (alk. paper) o.p.; (alk. paper) o.p.; (ebook) $12.99 **523.48**

1. Planets 2. Astronomers 3. Solar system 4. Pluto (Dwarf planet) 5. Discoveries in science 6. Pluto (Planet) 7. College teachers 8. Eris (Dwarf planet) 9. Discoveries in science -- Anecdotes
ISBN 9780385531108; 0385531087; 9780385531085; 9780385531092

LC 2010015074

This book relates the story of astronomist Mike Brown's research that led to the demotion of Pluto as a planet. "The solar system most of us grew up with included nine planets, with Mercury closest to the sun and Pluto at the outer edge. Then, in 2005, astronomer Mike Brown made the discovery of a lifetime: a tenth planet, Eris, slightly bigger than Pluto. But instead of adding one more planet to our solar system, Brown's find ignited a firestorm of controversy that culminated in the demotion of Pluto from real planet to the newly coined category of 'dwarf' planet. Suddenly Brown was receiving hate mail from schoolchildren and being bombarded by TV reporters—all because of the discovery he had spent

years searching for and a lifetime dreaming about." (Publisher's note)

"Deftly pulling readers along on his journey of discovery and destruction, Brown sets the record straight and strongly defends his science with a conversational, rational, and calm voice that may change the public's opinion of scientists as poor communicators." Publ Wkly

523.5 Meteors, solar wind, zodiacal light

Bevan, A. W. R.

Meteorites : a journey through space and time; [by] Alex Bevan and John de Laeter. Smithsonian Institution Press 2002 215p il maps $35.95 **523.5**

1. Meteorites
ISBN 1-58834-021-X

LC 2001-49551

"The authors trace the formation and breakup of the planets, asteroids, and comets where meteorites originated, their long journey through space, their fall to Earth, their recovery, and what scientists are learning from them. The book contains a great deal of material about the '84001 Martian meteorite, which has raised provocative new questions about life on the red planet." Publisher's note

"Informative and visually appealing, this title meets any library's need for a basic source on meteorites." Booklist

Includes bibliographical references

Cokinos, Christopher

The **fallen** sky; an intimate history of shooting stars. Jeremy P. Tarcher/Penguin 2009 518p $27.95 **523.5**

1. Meteorites
ISBN 978-1-58542-720-8; 1-58542-720-9

LC 2009-17493

"In 1894, fifteen years before his storied expedition to the North Pole, Robert Peary crossed a treacherous expanse of ice in Greenland in search of another prize: a massive meteorite laden with rare metals from outer space. In this hefty, industrious book, Cokinos retraces Peary's steps, and those of other meteor 'obsessives,' in an idiosyncratic hunt of his own." New Yorker

Includes bibliographical references

523.6 Comets

Sagan, Carl, 1934-1996

Comet; [by] Carl Sagan and Ann Druyan. Random House 1985 398p il hardcover o.p. pa $23 **523.6**

1. Comets 2. Halley's comet
ISBN 0-345-41222-2

LC 85-8308

"The authors explore the myth and science of comets in a lavishly illustrated, slightly oversize volume that is both fascinating and authoritative." Booklist

Includes bibliographical references

523.7 Sun

Berman, Bob

The **sun's** heartbeat; and other stories from the life of the star that powers our planet. Little, Brown and Co. 2011 290p il $25.99; ebook $12.99 **523.7**
1. Sun
ISBN 0316091014; 9780316091015; 9780316175395
LC 2010044207

The author "provides facts about the star at the center of our solar system and describes the life of the sun, from its birth and life as a self-sustaining ultra-H-Bomb fusion explosion, to its spectacular and anticipated future death." (Publisher's note) Bibliography. Index.

"An engaging consciousness-raiser that entertains as it informs about our neighborhood nuclear furnace." Booklist
Includes bibliographical references

Clark, Stuart

The **sun** kings; the unexpected tragedy of Richard Carrington and the tale of how modern astronomy began. Princeton Univ. Press 2007 211p il $24.95 **523.7**
1. Astronomers 2. Photographers 3. Sun 4. Writers on science 5. Astronomy -- History
ISBN 978-0-691-12660-9; 0-691-12660-7
LC 2006-940123

"Clark's parade of historical characters dramatize the narrative nicely, and Clark conveys the significance of their scientific observations with plenty of context and thorough references, making this a fascinating work for both casual stargazers and serious astronomy buffs." Publ Wkly
Includes bibliographical references

Cohen, Richard

Chasing the sun; the epic story of the star that gives us life. Random House 2010 xxxi, 574p il $35; ebook $17.99 **523.7**
1. Science and civilization 2. Sun 3. Astronomy -- History
ISBN 978-1-4000-6875-3; 1-4000-6875-4; 978-1-58836-934-5 ebook
LC 2010-05885

"A remarkably comprehensive and engrossing synthesis of the sun's influence on science, art, religion, literature, mythology and politics. . . . Ever enthusiastic, Cohen provides illuminating personal anecdotes, but he includes just the right amount of detail, never allowing the material to sprawl untethered." Kirkus
Includes bibliographical references

Golub, Leon

Nearest star; the surprising science of our sun. {by} Leon Golub & Jay M. Pasachoff. Harvard Univ. Press 2001 267p il $29.95; pa $16.95 **523.7**
1. Sun
ISBN 0-674-00467-1; 0-674-01006-X pa
LC 00-63213

The authors "describe for a nonspecialist audience what is currently known of the structure of the sun, the source of its enormous energy, its history and future, its various effects on Earth and its atmosphere." Libr J

This is "a brilliant, richly illustrated survey." Booklist
Includes bibliographical references

523.8 Stars

Kaler, James B.

Extreme stars; at the edge of creation. Cambridge Univ. Press 2001 236p il maps $40 **523.8**
1. Stars
ISBN 0-521-40262-X
LC 00-58522

"Each chapter covers extreme stars of a different kind, including the faintest, the coolest, the brightest, the largest, the smallest, the youngest, the oldest, and the strangest. . . . {Kaler} piques the curiosity of the novice, while encouraging knowledgeable readers to think about stars from a different perspective. There is a wealth of information, much of it not available elsewhere at this semipopular level." Choice

Ridpath, Ian

The **monthly** sky guide; Ian Ridpath ; illustrated by Wil Tirion. 9th ed. Cambridge University Press 2012 71 p. col. ill. (paperback) $17.99 **523.8**
1. Astronomy 2. Stars -- Atlases 3. Stars -- Identification 4. Stars -- Observers' manuals
ISBN 1107683157; 9781107683150
LC 2012033599

This book, the ninth edition of Ian Ridpath and Wil Tirion's guide to the night sky, "is updated with planet positions and forthcoming eclipses to the end of the year 2017. It contains twelve chapters describing the main sights visible in each month of the year, providing" information for anyone "wanting to identify prominent stars, constellations, star clusters, nebulae and galaxies; to watch out for meteor showers . . . ; or to follow the movements of the four brightest planets." (Publisher's note)
Includes bibliographical references and index.

Scagell, Robin

Stargazing with binoculars; [by] Robin Scagell, David Frydman. 2nd ed., updated and rev.; Firefly Books 2011 208p il pa $19.95 **523.8**
1. Stars 2. Astronomy 3. Binoculars
ISBN 978-1-55407-821-9; 1-55407-821-0
LC 2011-288021

First published 2008

This is a "guide to using binoculars to view the night sky for newcomers to astronomy. The book includes reviews of the wide range of binoculars on the market and provides advice on features to consider before making a purchase. The authors guide the beginner through the first steps of using binoculars to observe the night sky, describe what will be visible and show how to find specific objects." Publisher's note

Scharf, Caleb

Gravity's engines; how bubble-blowing black holes rule galaxies, stars, and life in the cosmos. Ca-

leb Scharf. Scientific American/ Farrar, Straus and Giroux 2012 ix, 252 p.p (hardback) $26   **523.8**
1. Gravity 2. Cosmology 3. Black holes (Astronomy)
ISBN 0374114129; 9780374114121

LC 2011047089

Author Caleb Scharf presents a "journey through the endlessly colorful place we call our galaxy and reminds us that the Milky Way sits in a special place in the cosmic zoo--a 'sweet spot' of properties. Is it coincidental that we find ourselves here at this place and time? Could there be a deeper connection between the nature of black holes and their role in the universe and the phenomenon of life?" (Publisher's note)

Includes bibliographical references and index.

Tyson, Neil deGrasse
Death by black hole; and other cosmic quandaries. Norton 2007 384p $24.95; pa $15.95 **523.8**
1. Cosmology 2. Space biology 3. Religion and science 4. Black holes (Astronomy) 5. Solar system
ISBN 978-0-393-06224-3; 0-393-06224-4; 978-0-393-33016-8 pa; 0-393-33016-8 pa

LC 2006-22058

In this collection of essays that were originally published in Natural History magazine, the author takes readers on a "journey from Earth's hot springs, where extremophiles flourish in hellish conditions, to the frozen, desolate stretches of the Oort Cloud and the universe's farthest reaches, in both space and time. Tyson doesn't restrict his musings to astrophysics, but wanders into related fields like relativity and particle physics. . . . He tackles popular myths (is the sun yellow?) and takes movie directors—most notably James Cameron—to task for spectacular goofs. In the last section the author gives his take on the hot subject of intelligent design." Publ Wkly

"A wonderfully informed viewpoint on the slowly expanding boundaries of human knowledge." Boston Globe

Includes bibliographical references

523.9   Satellites and rings; eclipses, transits, occultations

Sheehan, William
The **transits** of Venus; by William Sheehan, John Westfall. Prometheus Books 2004 407p il $28   **523.9**
1. Venus (Planet)
ISBN 1-59102-175-8

LC 2003-22420

Sheehan and Westfall "chronicle the explorations of scientists and adventurers who studied the transits of Venus in the quest for scientific understanding." Publisher's note

"This volume is a tour de force not only of the history of observing Venus, but of much of astronomy itself." Sci Books Films

Includes bibliographical references

Wulf, Andrea
Chasing Venus; the race to measure the heavens. Andrea Wulf. Alfred A. Knopf 2012 xxvi, 304 p.p (hardback) $26.95   **523.9**
1. Astronomy 2. Scientists 3. Venus (Planet) 4. Venus (Planet) -- Transit 5. Astronomy -- History -- 18th century 6. Geodetic astronomy -- History -- 18th century
ISBN 0307700178; 0307958612; 9780307700179; 9780307958617

LC 2011049136

This book "is concerned with Venus's 1761 and 1769 transits, when the international science community dispatched a remarkable set of expeditions to remote parts of the world to observe and measure the planet's passages across the sun. Their primary objective was to use newly acquired observational data to improve knowledge of the distance between Earth and the Sun and the solar system's dimensions. Many of the traveling scientists underwent great travails, and several died." (Library Journal)

525   Earth (Astronomical geography)

Gribbin, John
Alone in the universe; why our planet is unique. John Gribbin. Wiley 2011 xv, 219 p.p (cloth) $25.95   **525**
1. Earth 2. Astrophysics 3. Life -- Origin 4. Life on other planets 5. Sun 6. Solar system 7. Earth -- Origin 8. Collisions (Astrophysics)
ISBN 1118147979; 9781118147979; 9781118175392; 9781118175408; 9781118175415

LC 2011034995

This book by John Gribbin discusses extraterrestrial life on other planets starting with the question of whether we are "alone in the universe. . . . Gribbin argues that the very existence of intelligent life anywhere in the cosmos is, from an astrophysicist's point of view, a miracle. So why is there life on Earth and (seemingly) nowhere else? . . . Taking us back some 600 million years, Gribbin [shows] the series of unique cosmic events that were responsible for our unique form of life within the Milky Way Galaxy." (Publisher's note)

"Gribbin is a veteran author of popular science books; this new volume should be of great interest for all readers curious about the possibility of life beyond our own planet. Strongly recommended.—" LJ

Includes bibliographical references and index

Our changing planet; the view from space. edited by Michael D. King . . . [et al.] Cambridge University Press 2007 390p il map $47   **525**
1. Remote sensing 2. Environmental sciences 3. Human influence on nature 4. Earth
ISBN 978-0-521-82870-3; 0-521-82870-8

LC 2008-295497

Examines what orbital imagery tells us about the atmosphere, land, ocean, and polar ice caps of our planet and the ways that it changes naturally, and in response to human activity.

"This is a very fine compilation of System Earth through the eyes and experience of remote sensing experts—beautifully made and a pleasure to read." Environmental Geology

526 Mathematical geography

100 maps; the science, art and politics of cartography throughout history. edited by John O. E. Clark; introduction by Jeremy Black. Sterling 2006 256p il map $24.95 **526**
1. Maps
ISBN 1-4027-2885-9
"This atlas contains 100 attractively presented maps, each with a story appended explaining its qualities: scientific, imaginative, propagandistic, etc. . . . The maps range across history from an ancient clay tablet map drawn more than 4,000 years ago in a country now known as Iraq to maps of the tsunami of 2004. . . . This well-wrought production will appeal to both advanced readers and neophytes." Choice
Includes bibliographical references

Alder, Ken
The **measure** of all things; the seven-year odyssey and hidden error that transformed the world. Free Press 2002 422p $27; pa $15 **526**
1. Geography 2. Astronomers 3. Metric system
ISBN 0-7432-1675-X; 0-7432-1676-8 pa
LC 2002-70267
"In 1792, two astronomers set out from Paris in opposite directions to measure the meridian and thereby define the length of the meter. Alder's marvelous account of their quest is a dramatic tale of revolution, science, and human error." Libr J
Includes bibliographical references

Danson, Edwin
Weighing the world; the quest to measure the Earth. Oxford University Press 2005 289p il $29.95 **526**
1. Surveying 2. Earth 3. Science -- History
ISBN 978-0-19-518169-2; 0-19-518169-7
LC 2004-66284
The author "enlivens data about geodetic surveying, transforming them into greatly interesting dramas of science." Booklist
Includes bibliographical references

Felt, Hali
Soundings; the remarkable woman who mapped the ocean floor. Hali Felt. Henry Holt and Co. 2012 340 p. (hardback) $30.00 **526**
1. Women cartographers 2. Oceanography -- History 3. Submarine topography 4. Cartographers -- United States -- Biography 5. Geomorphologists -- United States -- Biography 6. Women cartographers -- United States -- Biography
ISBN 0805092153; 9780805092158
LC 2011044178
This book presents a "biography of a groundbreaking geologist who discovered 'a rift valley running down the center of the Atlantic,' essentially transforming 20th-century geophysics despite . . . gender bias and scientific rivalries. . . . From the 1950s through the '70s, Marie Tharp (1920-2006) mapped the entire ocean floor, an accomplishment honored by the Library of Congress in 1997, when she was named 'one of the four greatest cartographers' of the 20th century." (Kirkus Reviews)

Ferreiro, Larrie D.
Measure of the Earth; the enlightenment expedition that reshaped our world. Basic Books 2011 353p il map $28 **526**
1. Geodesy 2. Scientific expeditions 3. Geodesy -- Europe -- History 4. Scientific expeditions -- Europe -- History -- 18th century
ISBN 978-0-465-01723-2; 0-465-01723-1; 978-0-465-02345-5 ebook; 0-465-02345-2 ebook
LC 2011007173
This book "reads like a script from an Indiana Jones adventure film. . . . [It is] very well written and will interest any reader as it gives insight into the 18th Century and introduces some fascinating and unforgettable characters." Sci Books Films
Includes bibliographical references

Nicastro, Nicholas
Circumference; Eratosthenes and the ancient quest to measure the globe. St. Martin's Press 2008 223p il map $23.95 **526**
1. Astronomers 2. Measurement 3. Weights and measures 4. Geographers 5. Writers on science
ISBN 978-0-312-37247-7; 0-312-37247-7
LC 2008-25773
"Nicastro delivers the deeply human story of a multitalented genius whose tenure as the head of Alexandria's famed library occasioned remarkable achievements in literature, history, linguistics, and philosophy despite the political turmoil that periodically rocked the Ptolemaic world." Booklist
Includes bibliographical references

Raymo, Chet
Walking zero; discovering cosmic space and time along the Prime Meridian. Walker & Co. 2006 194p il maps $22.95 **526**
1. Longitude 2. Great Britain -- Description and travel
ISBN 0-8027-1494-3; 978-0-8027-1494-7
LC 2006-282372
This is the author's "expression of his personal exploration of space, time, and scientific history, inspired partly by his walking the footpaths of southeast England in close proximity to the 0 degrees longitude line. . . . This work is a thought-provoking, highly enlightening discussion of some of the most fascinating concepts in physics, astronomy, and geology, among other subjects." Sci Books Films
Includes bibliographical references

Reinhartz, Dennis
The **Art** of the Map; An Illustrated History of Map Elements and Embellishments. by Dennis Re-

inhartz. Sterling Pub Co Inc 2012 240 p. ill. (hardcover) $40   **526**
1. Maps 2. Map drawing
ISBN 1402765924; 9781402765926

This book, by Dennis Reinhartz, offers an "illustrated history of the golden age of cartography, from the sixteenth through the nineteenth centuries, explor[ing] not only the embellishments on maps but also what they reveal about the world in which they were created. Here there be monsters . . . ; ships actual and archetypical; newly discovered flora such as corn and tobacco; fauna ranging from buffalo to unicorns; [and] godlike beings and fantasy-like depictions of native peoples." (Publisher's note)

Sobel, Dava

★ **Longitude**; the true story of a lone genius who solved the greatest scientific problem of his time. with a new foreword by Neil Armstrong. Hardcover anniversary ed., [10th anniversary ed., 2005 anniversary ed.]; Walker & Co. 2005 184p il $19   **526**
1. Longitude 2. Mechanical engineers 3. Clock and watch makers
ISBN 0-8027-1462-5; 978-0-8027-1462-6
First published 1995

"In 1714, Britain's Parliament offered the modern equivalent of $12 to anybody who could develop a means of determining longitude at sea. While the likes of Isaac Newton and Edmund Halley sought to calculate longitude by celestial measurement, John Harrison, an uneducated clockmaker, solved the problem with his invention of the chronometer. Science writer Sobel tells this story in a way that enables readers 'to see the globe anew.'" Libr J
Includes bibliographical references

Winchester, Simon

The **map** that changed the world; William Smith and the birth of modern geology. illustrations by Soun Vannithone. HarperCollins Pubs. 2001 329p il map $26; pa $13.95   **526**
1. Geologists 2. Stratigraphic geology 3. Civil engineers 4. Writers on science
ISBN 0-06-019361-1; 0-06-093180-9 pa
LC 2001-16603

"In the early years of the nineteenth century, William Smith created the first geological map of Great Britain, a time-consuming, solitary project that helped establish geology as one of the 'fundamental fields of study.' . . . Winchester tells Smith's story, including the dramatic ups and downs of his personal life. . . . This is just the kind of creative nonfiction that elevates a seemingly arcane topic into popular fare." Booklist

529   Chronology

Falk, Dan

In search of time; the science of a curious dimension. Thomas Dunne Books, St. Martin's Press 2008 329p il $25.95; pa $15.99   **529**
1. Time 2. Science and civilization
ISBN 978-0-312-37478-5; 0-312-37478-X; 978-0-
312-60351-9 pa; 0-312-60351-7 pa
LC 2008-24875

The author "explores the origins of calendar time, from primitive astronomical observatories to the precision clocks of today." Publ Wkly

"The book's scope is audaciously broad. Relying on reportage and humour to offset writing that is occasionally prolix, Falk deftly weaves together elements of religion, anthropology, philosophy, and physics into an engaging narrative." Quill Quire
Includes bibliographical references

Galison, Peter Louis

Einstein's clocks and Poincare's maps; empires of time. by Peter Galison. Norton 2003 389p il $23.95   **529**
1. Time 2. Physicists 3. Mathematicians 4. Relativity (Physics) 5. Nobel laureates for physics
ISBN 0-393-02001-0
LC 2002-155114

"Gallison shows how Einstein's work was influenced by French cartographer Henri Poincaré and by the physicist's own experience working in a Bern patent office, where the numerous patent requests for devices designed to coordinate distant clocks may have prompted further inquiry into the problem of simultaneity, which lies at the heart of relativity. Few books have ever made Einstein's theories more accessible—or more engrossing—for general readers." Booklist
Includes bibliographical references

Sims, Michael

Apollo's fire; a day on Earth in nature and imagination. Viking 2007 xxiv, 296p $24.95   **529**
1. Days 2. Time 3. Astronomy
ISBN 978-0-670-06328-4; 0-670-06328-2
LC 2007-6024

The author "takes a single day and guides readers through the history of what we know, and what we've imagined, about sunrises, clouds and other natural phenomena. . . . His delightful tour of day and night skies will inspire many readers to look up with a marveling new perspective." Publ Wkly
Includes bibliographical references

530   Physics

Ananthaswamy, Anil

The **edge** of physics; a journey to Earth's extremes to unlock the secrets of the universe. Houghton Mifflin Harcourt 2010 322p il $25   **530**
1. Physics 2. Cosmology
ISBN 978-0-618-88468-1; 0-618-88468-8
LC 2009-20225

"Despite 20th-century physics' revelations, from relativity and quantum mechanics to the physics of the atom's nucleus and the life cycles of stars, ninety-odd percent of the universe is a complete mystery, says a scientist quoted by Ananthaswamy. . . Dark matter, dark energy, quantum gravity: these are the topics that keep physicists awake at night, requiring bigger, more massive, more extreme experiments to test theories and uncover clues. The author takes readers behind the scenes of these experiments in some of the most inhospitable places in the world." Publ Wkly

"A meticulous, accessible update of the latest ideas and instruments that contribute to the clarification of an increasingly puzzling universe." Kirkus

Includes bibliographical references

Balibar, Sebastien

The **atom** and the apple; twelve tales from contemporary physics. translated by Nathanael Stein. Princeton University Press 2008 190p il $24.95 **530**

1. Physics

ISBN 978-0-691-13108-5

LC 2008-18027

This "is a delightful ramble through many areas of science as well as through the experiences, opinions, passions and frustrations of a leading research physicist. . . . It is a very refreshing read that will do much to bring an understanding of scientific culture to the reader." Times Higher Ed

Includes bibliographical references

Buchanan, Mark

Nexus : small worlds and the groundbreaking science of networks. Norton 2002 235p $25.95; pa $14.95 **530**

1. System analysis 2. Patterns (Mathematics)

ISBN 0-393-04153-0; 0-393-32442-7 pa

LC 2002-518

The author "introduces readers to the dynamics of networks and shows how these networks affect behaviors in both the natural and the social world. . . . {Buchanan} finds the same patterns taking shape in food chains, in the neuronal networks of insects, in the architecture of the Internet and in the cultural backgrounds of elite CEOs. . . . Buchanan's ability as an affable, easygoing storyteller makes up for myriad digressions, and the narrative is, at times, spellbinding." Publ Wkly

Includes bibliographical references

The **Cambridge** companion to Newton; edited by I. Bernard Cohen and George E. Smith. Cambridge Univ. Press 2002 500p il $65; pa $23 **530**

1. Physicists 2. Mathematicians 3. Writers on science

ISBN 0-521-65177-8; 0-521-65696-6 pa

LC 2001-37836

This is "the best available brief overview of Newton's contributions to mechanics, cosmology, optics, mathematics, alchemy, and theology. The contributors have produced 16 well-written and admirably focused chapters. Some will be challenging for nonspecialist readers, but even those that discuss mechanics in detail are so well organized and clearly written that they amply repay close attention." Choice

Includes bibliographical references

Close, F. E.

Nothing; a very short introduction. [by] Frank Close. Oxford University Press 2009 157p (Very short introductions) pa $11.95 **530**

1. Physics -- Philosophy

ISBN 978-0-19-922586-6; 0-19-922586-9

LC 2009-281157

First published 2007 in the United Kingdom with title: The void

This history of "nothing" covers the "history of the vacuum: how the efforts to make a better vacuum led to the discovery of the electron; the ideas of Newton, Mach, and Einstein on the nature of space and time; the mysterious aether and how Einstein did away with it; and the . . . [idea] that the vacuum is filled with the Higgs field." Publisher's note

Includes bibliographical references

Cole, K. C.

First you build a cloud; and other reflections on physics as a way of life. Harcourt Brace & Co. 1999 231p il pa $14 **530**

1. Physics

ISBN 0-15-600646-4

LC 98-47050

First published 1985 by Morrow with title: Sympathetic vibrations

"Cole offers reflections on the place of physics in modern life. . . . Especially compelling are the essays on the aesthetic force behind scientific endeavors—the beauties of theory. For readers without scientific background, Cole gracefully introduces relativity, quantum theory, optics, astrophysics, and other significant disciplines, never getting bogged down in unnecessary explanation." Booklist

Includes bibliographical references

Conant, Jennet

Tuxedo Park; a Wall Street tycoon and the secret palace of science that changed the course of World War II. Simon & Schuster 2002 330p il $26; pa $14 **530**

1. Physicists 2. Atomic bomb 3. Investment bankers 4. Foundation officials

ISBN 0-684-87287-0; 0-684-87288-9 pa

LC 2002-21001

In 1928 Alfred Loomis, a wealthy financier and amateur physicist, "established a premier research facility in Tuxedo Park, N.Y., that attracted such brilliant minds as Einstein, Bohr and Fermi and became instrumental in the Allies' WWII victory. Conant . . . draws on studies, family papers and interviews with Loomis's friends, family and colleagues . . . to trace the story of the tycoon's professional and social life." Publ Wkly

"Conant displays a real feel for the personal lives and sensibilities of the era's leading scientists and industrialists in a fascinating, never-before-told bit of American history." Booklist

Includes bibliographical references

Darling, David J.

Gravity's arc; the story of gravity, from Aristotle to Einstein and beyond. [by] David Darling. J. Wiley 2006 278p $24.95 **530**

1. Gravity

ISBN 0-471-71989-7; 978-0-471-71989-2

LC 2005-30772

This is a "historical review of the human understanding of gravity from the ancient Greeks to the 21st century. Included are examinations of Greek philosophers and their debates, medieval and Arabic developments, Galileo, Tycho,

Kepler, Newton, Eotvos, [and] Einstein. . . . The writing style is clear and reader friendly. . . . Read this book to learn about gravity and experience a model scientific exposition for the scientist and general reader alike." Sci Books Films

Includes bibliographical references

Deutsch, David

The **fabric** of reality; the science of parallel universes--and its implications. Allen Lane/The Penguin Press 1997 390p il hardcover o.p. pa $16   **530**

1. Life 2. Reality 3. Cosmology 4. Physics --Philosophy
ISBN 0-14-027541-X

LC 97-6171

"Deutsch describes a reality where parallel universes are 'stacked like a pack of playing cards' to comprise a 'multiverse,' with computers communicating between them, where the mechanics and likelihood of time travel exist and where the universe comes to an end. . . . An intellectually stimulating read for the science-literate and motivated lay person." Publ Wkly

"A thoroughly mesmerizing scientific/philosophical view of reality." Libr J

Includes bibliographical references

Einstein, Albert, 1879-1955

★ The **evolution** of physics; the growth of ideas from early concepts to relativity and quanta. by Albert Einstein and Leopold Infeld. Simon & Schuster 1938 320p il hardcover o.p. pa $13 **530**

1. Quantum theory 2. Relativity (Physics) 3. Physics -- History
ISBN 0-671-20156-5 pa

An "exposition for the layman of the growth of ideas in physical science." Publ Wkly

Ideas and opinions; with an introduction by Alan Lightman; based on Mein weltbild, edited by Carl Seelig, and other sources; new translations and revisions by Sonja Bargmann. Modern Lib. 1994 418p $16.95; pa $13   **530**

1. Physics 2. Science--Philosophy
ISBN 0-679-60105-8; 0-517-88440-2 pa

LC 94-2115

A reissue of the title first published 1954 by Crown

This is a collection of the scientist's general writings on such subjects as freedom, education, religion, politics and government, the Jewish people, and Germany

The **ultimate** quotable Einstein; collected and edited by Alice Calaprice; with a foreword by Freeman Dyson. Princeton University Press 2011 xxviii, 578p il $24.95; ebook $24.95   **530**

1. Quotations
ISBN 978-0-691-13817-6; 0-691-13817-6; 978-1-4008-3596-6 ebook

LC 2010002855

This collection of Einstein's quotes includes "sections titled 'On and to Children' and 'On Race and Prejudice,'

and a brief selection of Einstein's wry verses. The comments are few on the matters of physics and mathematics, concentrating more on personal, social, political, philosophical, and educational subjects." Choice

Includes bibliographical references

Feynman, Richard Phillips, 1918-1988

★ **Six** easy pieces; essentials of physics explained by its most brilliant teacher. [by] Richard P. Feynman; originally prepared for publication by Robert B. Leighton and Matthew Sands; introduction by Paul Davies. Basic Books 2005 xxix, 144p il pa $13.95   **530**

1. Atoms 2. Physics 3. Gravitation 4. Quantum theory 5. Energy conservation
ISBN 978-0-465-02392-9

First published 1995 by Helix Bks.

This book reprints six chapters from Feynman's Lectures on Physics. "In these six chapters, Feynman introduces the general reader to the following: atoms, basic physics, the relationship of physics to other topics, energy, gravitation, and quantum force." Publisher's note

Goldberg, Dave

A **user's** guide to the universe; surviving the perils of black holes, time paradoxes, and quantum uncertainty. [by] Dave Goldberg and Jeff Blomquist. Wiley 2010 296p il $24.95   **530**

1. Physics
ISBN 978-0-470-49651-0; 0-470-49651-7

Surveys the major discoveries of modern physics, from relativity to the Large Hadron Collider. The authors discuss subjects such as special relativity, quantum mechanics, randomness, time travel, and the expanding universe. Illustrated with cartoons

"With a large measure of humor and a minimum of math (one equation), physics professor Goldberg and engineer Blomquist delve into the fascinating physics topics that rarely make it into introductory classes. . . . This nearly-painless guide is . . . involved and scientific, aimed at science hobbyists rather than science-phobes." Publ Wkly

Includes bibliographical references

Kaku, Michio

Physics of the impossible; a scientific exploration into the world of phasers, force fields, teleportation, and time travel. Doubleday 2008 xxi, 329p $26.95   **530**

1. Physics
ISBN 978-0-385-52069-0; 0-385-52069-7

LC 2007-30290

"There is a surprising amount of heavyweight, cutting-edge science woven into the fabric of the book. String theory, dark energy, metamaterials and quantum theory are just a few topics—Physics of the Impossible is, in fact, an easy-to-read physics primer in disguise." New Sci

Includes bibliographical references

Kragh, Helge

Quantum generations; a history of physics in the twentieth century. Princeton Univ. Press 1999 494p $65; pa $22.95 **530**

1. Physics -- History

ISBN 0-691-01206-7; 0-691-09552-3 pa

LC 99-17903

The author "details the explosive course physics has taken from the introduction of X rays in the mid-1890's to superstring theory in the present day. . . . {He} explains not only how the groundbreaking ideas of physics progressed but also how they are actively applied." Publisher's note

Includes bibliographical references and index

Krauss, Lawrence Maxwell

★ **Fear** of physics; a guide for the perplexed. [by] Lawrence M. Krauss. Rev ed; Basic Books 2007 257p il pa $29.95 **530**

1. Physics

ISBN 978-0-465-00218-4; 0-465-00218-8

LC 2007-04700

First published 1993

This overview describes what physics is and the work of physicists.

"The writing style genuinely keeps the reader interested. . . . This book is a great resource if you want insight into what physics really is and what physicists do." Sci Books Films

Includes bibliographical references

Levi, Mark

Why cats land on their feet; and 76 other physical paradoxes and puzzles. Mark Levi. Princeton University Press 2012 x, 190 p.p ill. (pbk. : alk. paper) $19.95 **530**

1. Puzzles 2. Science -- Miscellanea

ISBN 0691148546; 9780691148540

LC 2011045728

This book by Mark Levi presents "a compendium of paradoxes and puzzles that readers can solve using their own physical intuition. . . . Levi introduces each physical problem, sometimes gives a hint or two, and then fully explains the solution. Here readers can test their critical-thinking skills against a whole assortment of puzzles and paradoxes. . . . This . . . collection also features an appendix that explains all physical concepts used in the book." (Publisher's note)

Includes bibliographical references and index

Ohanian, Hans C.

Einstein's mistakes; the human failings of genius. W.W. Norton & Company 2008 394p il $24.95 **530**

1. Physics 2. Physicists 3. Nobel laureates for physics

ISBN 978-0-393-06293-9; 0-393-06293-7

LC 2008-13155

This book examines Einstein's "mistakes and the role they played in the discovery of his theories." Publisher's note

This "clearly written, fascinating, and exciting book is a gem." Sci Books Films

Includes bibliographical references

Simonyi, Károly, 1916-2011

A **cultural** history of physics; Károly Simonyi ; translated by David Kramer. CRC Press 2012 622 p. (alk. paper) $59.00 **530**

1. Physics 2. Science -- History 3. Science and the humanities 4. Physics -- History

ISBN 1568813295; 9781568813295

LC 2010009407

In this book, "Hungarian scientist and educator Károly Simonyi" describes "the experimental methods and theoretical interpretations that created scientific knowledge, from ancient times to the present day, within the cultural environment in which it was formed." He "explores the interplay of science and the humanities to convey the wonder and excitement of scientific development throughout the ages." (Barnes and Noble)

Includes bibliographical references and index.

Suplee, Curt

Physics in the 20th century; edited by Judith R. Franz and John S. Rigden. Abrams 1999 223p il $49.50; pa $19.95 **530**

1. Physics

ISBN 0-8109-4364-6; 0-8109-9084-9 pa

LC 98-41306

In this overview of physics Suplee "leads us through the structure and function of atoms, the astonishing intimacy of light and matter, the often amusing improbabilities of quantum mechanics, the architecture of exotic materials, the elusive lives of subatomic particles that are the stuff of all creation, and chaos and order in nature—until we arrive at a vision of the entire universe. He does it without equations or misleading analogies, and often with humor." N Y Times Book Rev

530.01   Philosophy and theory

Cole, K. C.

The **hole** in the universe; how scientists peered over the edge of emptiness and found everything. Harcourt 2001 274p il hardcover o.p. pa $14 **530.01**

1. Physics

ISBN 0-15-601317-7 pa

LC 00-44947

Cole discusses the history of nothing, "combining the history of zero (a mathematical nothing) with that of the vacuum (a physical nothing). . . . Until Einstein showed that light needed no tangible medium through which to travel, theorists filled the vacuum with 'ether'—the 'enfant terrible' of substances, as Einstein put it. It was subsequently banished." Atl Mon

Includes bibliographical references

530.092   Physicists

Kaiser, David

How the hippies saved physics; science, counterculture, and the quantum revival. David Kaiser. 1st

ed. W.W. Norton 2011 xxvi, 372 p.p ill. (hardcover)
$26.95   **530.092**
　　1. Quantum theory 2. Counter culture 3. Physicists
-- Biography 4. Counterculture -- United States 5.
Fundamental Fysiks Group (Berkeley, Calif.)
ISBN 0393076369; 9780393076363
　　　　　　　　　　　　　　　LC 2010053415
　　This book by David Kaiser looks at "a coterie of physicists who, during the 1970s, embraced New Age fads and
sometimes went on to make dramatic discoveries. . . . They
explored complex, hitherto ignored areas such as Bell's
theorem and quantum entanglement while annoying the establishment by exploring their links to the paranormal. The
end result was a transformation in cutting-edge physics and
major discoveries in quantum information science, now a
thriving industry." (Kirkus Reviews)
　　"This entertaining, worthwhile read is as much about the
nature of society at the dawn of the New Age as it is about
quantum physics." Choice
　　Includes bibliographical references

530.1　Theories and mathematical physics

Baggott, J. E
　　The **quantum** story; [by] Jim Baggott. Oxford
University Press 2011 469p il $29.95   **530.1**
　　1. Quantum theory 2. Quantum theory -- History
　　ISBN 978-0-19-956684-6; 0-19-956684-4
　　In this history of quantum theory, Baggott examines
"how, over the space of three decades, Einstein, Bohr,
Heisenberg, and others formulated and refined the theory. .
. . To take us from the story's beginning to the present day,
Baggott organizes his narrative around forty turning-point
moments of discovery." (Publisher's note)
　　"Quantum theory—challenging, disconcerting, and
heavy on math—is not going to be pinned down and dissected for lay readers without a lot of kicking and screaming.
Baggott succeeds, however, imbuing the narrative with important context, his own communicable enthusiasm and the
instances of dense theoretical exposition mediated by historical and biographical storytelling. His survey runs roughly chronologically, starting with Max Planck's contention
that energy is composed of a definite number of equal finite
packages, through Einstein, Bohr, Heisenberg, Dirac, Feynman, Hawking et al. the author then looks at the Standard
Model and the more amorphous superstring theory." Kirkus
　　Includes bibliographical references

Bodanis, David
　　E; a biography of the world's most famous equation. Walker & Company 2005 337p il $25 **530.1**
　　1. Physicists 2. Space and time 3. Force and energy 4.
Nobel laureates for physics
　　ISBN 0-8027-1463-3
　　First published 2000
　　The author relates the story of "Einstein's formulation of
the equation in 1905 and its association ever after with relativity and nuclear energy. Parallel with the science, Bodanis
populates his tale with dramatic lives." Booklist [review of
2000 edition]

Bolles, Edmund Blair
　　Einstein defiant; genius versus genius in the
quantum revolution. Joseph Henry Press 2004 348p
il $27.95   **530.1**
　　1. Physicists 2. Quantum theory 3. Nobel laureates
for physics
　　ISBN 0-309-08998-0
　　　　　　　　　　　　　　　LC 2003-23735
　　"This carefully researched book achieves a nice balance
between science and history. The author provides enough
scientific information to illuminate the unfolding drama for
nonscientists and constructs a marvelously choreographed
tale of how just about every physicist of note in the last century contributed to the debate." Sci Books Films
　　Includes bibliographical references

Carroll, Sean M.
　　★ **From** eternity to here; the quest for the ultimate theory of time. [by] Sean Carroll. Dutton 2009
438p il $25   **530.1**
　　1. Space and time
　　ISBN 978-0-525-95133-9; 0-525-95133-4
　　　　　　　　　　　　　　　LC 2009-23828
　　"Understanding time requires an acquaintance with entropy, relativity, cosmology, thermodynamics and statistical
mechanics, which Carroll enthusiastically delivers at great
length. Not for the scientifically disinclined, but determined
readers will come away with a rewarding grasp of a complex
subject." Kirkus
　　Includes bibliographical references

Close, F. E.
　　The **infinity** puzzle; quantum field theory and the
hunt for an orderly universe. [by] Frank Close. Basic
Books 2011 435p il $28.99   **530.1**
　　1. Infinite 2. Quantum theory
　　ISBN 978-0-465-02144-4; 978-0-465-02803-0 ebook
　　　　　　　　　　　　　　　LC 2011022966
　　Close "offers a compelling history and sociology of
modern particle theory. We discover the motivations and
achievements of a rich cast of brilliant individuals, and get
enough of the science to grasp what they were trying to do.
Where Close really shines is in exposing the fraught process
of recognition in science, focusing on key players such as
Pakistani theoretical physicist Abdus Salam and the man af-
ter whom the famous boson is named, British physicist Peter
Higgs." Nature
　　Includes bibliographical references

Einstein, Albert, 1879-1955
　　The **meaning** of relativity; 5th ed; Princeton
University Press 2005 xxiv, 166p il pa $16.95 **530.1**
　　1. Relativity (Physics)
　　ISBN 0-691-12027-7
　　　　　　　　　　　　　　　LC 2004-111082
　　First published 1922. Translated by Edwin Plimpton Ad-
ams, Ernst G. Straus and Bruria Kaufman
　　"Though few can understand it, most readers in phys-
ics and librarians in charge of science collections know this
book as one of the landmarks of modern knowledge. . . .
The book is not intended for general reading. Instead it is
addressed to . . . those whose training enables them to under-

stand the mathematical expressions of relativity." N Y Public Libr. New Tech Books

★ A **stubbornly** persistent illusion; the essential scientific works of Albert Einstein. [edited, with commentary, by Stephen Hawking] Running Press 2007 468p il $29.95 **530.1**
1. Relativity (Physics) 2. Physics -- Philosophy
ISBN 978-0-7624-3003-1; 0-7624-3003-6
LC 2007-935658
The editor presents with introductions writings by Albert Einstein on relativity, the history of physics and philosophy.
"Hawking adds a brief but effective introduction to each section, making this gem of a collection really shine." Publ Wkly
Includes bibliographical references

Ford, Kenneth W.
101 quantum questions; what you need to know about the world you can't see. [by] Kenneth W. Ford. Harvard University Press 2011 291p il **530.1**
1. Quantum theory
ISBN 9780674050990
LC 2010-34791
"Ford explains the essential concepts of quantum reality, our small-fast world, full of uncertainty and probability, where all matter can exist in more than one state simultaneously. Ford brings interesting and entertaining anecdotal and historical material into his answers, organizing and shaping his book around 15 subjects. By using humor and straight talk to answer questions that often bedevil the nonscientist who attempts to grasp this knotty subject, Ford has created an entertaining read and an excellent companion piece to more detailed popular treatments of modern physics." Publ Wkly
Includes bibliographical references

Gell-Mann, Murray
The **quark** and the jaguar; adventures in the simple and the complex. Holt & Co. 1995 392p il pa $17 **530.1**
1. Particles (Nuclear physics) 2. Science -- Philosophy
ISBN 0-8050-7253-5
First published 1994 by W.H. Freeman
The author "ponders the universe's mix of simplicity and complexity, regularity and randomness, as he ranges from quarks (the fundamental subatomic particles which he discovered) to complex adaptive systems like bacteria developing resistance to antibiotics, mobile robots, jaguars, and people interacting with and learning from their environment." Publ Wkly
"While the topics are technical in nature, Gell-Mann's presentation is clear and will be readily understood by scholars and informed lay readers." Libr J

Gilder, Louisa
The **age** of entanglement; when quantum physics was reborn. Alfred A. Knopf 2008 443p il $27.50 **530.1**
1. Quantum theory
ISBN 978-1-4000-4417-7; 1-4000-4417-0
LC 2008-11796

This is "the story of quantum mechanics and its lively cast of supporters. . . . Gilder's history is rife with curious characters and dramatizes how difficult it was for even these brilliant scientists to grasp the paradigm-changing concepts of quantum science." Publ Wkly
Includes bibliographical references

Greene, B. (Brian), 1963-
★ The **hidden** reality; parallel universes and the deep laws of the cosmos. [by] Brian Greene. Alfred A. Knopf 2011 370p il $29.95 **530.1**
1. Cosmology 2. Quantum theory 3. Relativity (Physics) 4. Physics -- Philosophy
ISBN 0-307-26563-3; 978-0-307-26563-0
LC 2010-42710
The Hidden Reality aims to show how major developments in different branches of fundamental theoretical physics—relativistic, quantum, cosmological, unified, computational—have all led us to consider one or another variety of parallel universe. Index.
The author "explores the possibility that there is not one big uncharted universe, but many. Those universes take the form of Swiss cheese, suds in a bubble bath, passageways right out of 'Star Trek,' and realms right next to us. The danger of writing a mind-blower like 'The Hidden Reality' is that, if the author isn't careful, it can become mind-numbing to read. A caution here upfront: There are points where Greene walks perilously close to that precipice. Black holes, parallel universes, the idea that we and our world may have doppelgängers in different dimensions are heady concepts. For some, such conjecture is religious heresy; for others, it aims to answer the ultimate questions as to how and why we are here, with science, not faith, forming a necessary and—so far—inadequate, bridge to explore the mystery. What Greene . . . does exceedingly well is to lay out the prevailing theories, advanced by the brightest human minds, as to how the whole of everything may be ordered." Christ Sci Monit
Includes bibliographical references

Gribbin, John R.
In search of Schrodinger's cat; quantum physics and reality. Bantam Bks. 1984 302p il pa $15.95 **530.1**
1. Reality 2. Quantum theory
ISBN 0-553-34253-3
LC 84-2975
This history of quantum mechanics discusses the work of Huygens, Einstein, Schrödinger, Bohr, Planck and Everett
This book "contains many vignettes from the history of science and many insights into the researchers and the work that has led to our current understanding of the quantum theory. Excellent analogies and graphic illustrations are used to present difficult ideas." Sci Books Films
Includes bibliographical references

Schrodinger's kittens and the search for reality; solving the quantum mysteries. {by} John Gribbin. Little, Brown 1995 261p il hardcover o.p. pa $14.95 **530.1**
1. Light 2. Reality 3. Physicists 4. Quantum theory

5. Nobel laureates for physics
ISBN 0-316-32819-7 pa

LC 95-75652

In this sequel to In search of Schrödinger's cat, Gribbin attempts to "explain recent experimental and theoretical findings about the . . . nature of the submicroscopic world of the atom. The 'Copenhagen interpretation' of quantum mechanics offered by Niels Bohr and his colleagues has prevailed for almost 70 years, but there {are} now . . . competing interpretations. Gribbin reviews this . . . {field and} indicates his personal preference for one of the new theoretical models." Libr J
Includes bibliographical references

Guillen, Michael
Five equations that changed the world; the power and poetry of mathematics. Hyperion 1995 277p hardcover o.p. pa $14.95 **530.1**
1. Physics 2. Chemists 3. Physicists 4. Mathematics 5. Mathematicians 6. College teachers 7. Writers on science 8. Nobel laureates for physics
ISBN 0-7868-6103-7; 0-7868-8187-9 pa

LC 95-15199

"A seamless blend of dramatic biography and mathematical documentary that links the personal with the scientific." Publ Wkly

Hawking, Stephen, 1942-
★ The **grand** design; [by] Stephen Hawking and Leonard Mlodinow. Bantam Books 2010 198p il $28; ebook $28 **530.1**
1. Universe 2. Cosmology 3. String theory 4. Quantum theory 5. Life -- Origin 6. Science -- Philosophy
ISBN 978-0-553-80537-6; 0-553-80537-1; 978-0-553-90707-0 ebook; 0-553-90707-7 ebook

"The three central questions of philosophy and science: Why is there something rather than nothing? Why do we exist? Why this particular set of laws and not some other? . . . Along with Caltech physicist Mlodinow . . . Hawking deftly mixes cutting-edge physics to answer those key questions. . . . This is an amazingly concise, clear, and intriguing overview of where we stand when it comes to divining the secrets of the universe." Publ Wkly
Includes bibliographical references

Hawking, Stephen, 1942-
The **nature** of space and time; [by] Stephen Hawking and Roger Penrose. [New ed.]; Princeton University Press 2010 145p il (Isaac Newton Institute series of lectures) pa $14.95; ebook $14.95 **530.1**
1. Astrophysics 2. Quantum theory 3. Space and time
ISBN 978-0-691-14570-9 pa; 978-1-4008-3474-7 ebook
First published 1996
This volume "takes the form of a debate between Hawking and Penrose at Cambridge in 1994. At the center of the discussion is a pair of powerful theories: the quantum theory of fields and the general theory of relativity. The issue is how—if at all—one can merge the two into a quantum

theory of gravity. . . . A substantial background in theoretical physics is needed for full comprehension." Libr J
Includes bibliographical references

★ The **universe** in a nutshell; [by] Stephen Hawking. Bantam Bks. 2001 216p il $35 **530.1**
1. Quantum theory
ISBN 0-553-80202-X

LC 2001-35757

Hawking "explains the basic laws of physics that govern the universe, beginning with a brief history of the concept of relativity, and then he is off and running to explore time, space, the future, and the possibility of time travel, among other fundamental rules of the universe's road. Admirers of Hawking's previous book will continue to appreciate his ability not only to air fresh, provocative ideas but also to say what he means clearly and without watering down his material or condescending to his audience—he even injects humor into his narrative. The profuse, beautifully rendered illustrations contribute greatly to the reader's understanding of his points." Booklist

Kakalios, James
The **amazing** story of quantum mechanics; a math-free exploration of the science that made our world. Gotham Books 2010 318p il $26 **530.1**
1. Quantum theory
ISBN 978-1-59240-479-7; 1-59240-479-0

LC 2010-29568

"Though the book does not quite live up to the subtitle's promise of a 'math-free' text, readers need no more than basic algebra to accompany comic-book heroes into well-illustrated explanations of quantum packets of light energy, of the wave functions of particles, and even of the angular spin inherent in both energy and matter. These basic principles illuminate the solid-state physics of semiconductors, the atomic magnetism of MRIs, and the nanotechnology of high-capacity storage batteries. And all of this conceptual heavy lifting comes with entertaining episodes from DC Comics and H. G. Wells' fiction. Physics has never been more fun!" Booklist
Includes bibliographical references

Kaku, Michio
Hyperspace; a scientific odyssey through parallel universes, time warps, and the tenth dimension. illustrations by Robert O'Keefe. Oxford Univ. Press 1994 359p il $35 **530.1**
1. Space and time 2. Relativity (Physics)
ISBN 0-19-508514-0

LC 93-7910

This is an "overview of the major scientists, discoveries, and ideas involved in an ongoing quest for synthesizing quantum mechanics and relativity physics into a superstring theory of our entire universe." Libr J
Includes bibliographical references

Kumar, Manjit

★ **Quantum**; Einstein, Bohr and the great debate about the nature of reality. W.W. Norton 2010 448p il $27.95 **530.1**
1. Quantum theory
ISBN 978-0-393-07829-9; 0-393-07829-9
LC 2009-51249

"A staggering account of the scientific revolution that still challenges our notions of reality. . . . Kumar evokes the passion and excitement of the period and writes with sparkling clarity and wit. Expertly delineates complex scientific issues in nontechnical language, using telling detail to weave together personal, political and scientific elements." Kirkus
Includes bibliographical references

Lloyd, Seth

★ **Programming** the universe; a quantum computer scientist takes on the cosmos. Knopf 2006 221p il $25.95 **530.1**
1. Quantum theory 2. Microcomputers
ISBN 1-4000-4092-2; 978-1-4000-4092-6
LC 2005-50408

The author argues that "the universe is a computer that feeds on information and generates complexity." N Y Times Book Rev

"Exploring big questions in accessible, comprehensive fashion, Lloyd's work is of vital importance to the general-science audience." Booklist
Includes bibliographical references

Nadis, Steve

The **shape** of inner space; string theory and the geometry of the universe's hidden dimensions. Shing-tung Yau and Steve Nadis; illustrations by Xianfeng (David) Gu and Xiaotian (Tim) Yin. Basic Books 2010 xix, 377 p.p $30 **530.1**
1. Geometry 2. String theory 3. Fourth dimension 4. Hyperspace 5. String models
ISBN 978-0-465-02023-2; 0-465-02023-2; 9780465020232; 0465020232
LC 2010009956

"It is a testimony to [Yau's] careful prose (and no doubt to the skills of co-author Steve Nadis) that this book so compellingly captures the essence of what pushes string theorists forward in the face of formidable obstacles. It gives us a rare glimpse into a world as alien as the moons of Jupiter, and just as fascinating. . . . Yau and Nadis have produced a strangely mesmerizing account of geometry's role in the universe." New Scientist
Includes bibliographical references (p. 331-343) and index

Parker, Barry R.

Albert Einstein's vision; remarkable discoveries that shaped modern science. [by] Barry Parker. Prometheus Books 2004 286p il $28 **530.1**
1. Physicists 2. Quantum theory 3. Relativity (Physics) 4. Nobel laureates for physics
ISBN 1-59102-186-3
LC 2004-3990

"The book takes the ideas generated by Einstein, before his death in 1955, and follows the work of other scientists as they continued to build modern physics and cosmology." Sci Books Films
Includes bibliographical references

Rigden, John S.

★ **Einstein** 1905; the standard of greatness. Harvard University Press 2005 173p il $21.95; pa $14.95 **530.1**
1. Physicists 2. Quantum theory 3. Nobel laureates for physics
ISBN 0-674-01544-4; 0-674-02104-5 pa
LC 2004-54049

The author "chronicles the . . . theories that Einstein put forth beginning in March 1905: his particle theory of light, rejected for decades but now a staple of physics; his overlooked dissertation on molecular dimensions; his theory of Brownian motion; his theory of special relativity; and the work in which his famous equation, . . . [energy equals mass times the speed of light squared] , first appeared." Publisher's note

"The book is a delight to read, with a lot of interesting, useful information." Choice
Includes bibliographical references

Smolin, Lee

The **trouble** with physics; the rise of string theory, the fall of a science, and what comes next. Houghton Mifflin Co. 2006 392p il $26 **530.1**
1. String theory 2. Science -- Methodology
ISBN 978-0-618-55105-7; 0-618-55105-0
LC 2006-07235

"This is a well-written, critical profile of the theoretical physics community, free of equations, from the perspective of a member." Libr J
Includes bibliographical references

Susskind, Leonard

The **black** hole war; my battle with Stephen Hawking to make the world safe for quantum mechanics. Little, Brown 2008 470p il $27.99; pa $15.99 **530.1**
1. Physicists 2. Quantum theory 3. Space and time 4. Relativity (Physics) 5. Black holes (Astronomy) 6. People with disabilities 7. College teachers 8. Writers on science
ISBN 978-0-316-01640-7; 0-316-01640-3; 978-0-316-01641-4 pa; 0-316-01641-1 pa
LC 2007-48355

The author "delves into the related and disturbingly dangerous subject of black holes. Here, he describes disagreements that he and his Dutch friend, Gerard d'Hooft, had with the famous British mathematician/physicist Stephen Hawking on his predictions regarding the interaction of objects with black holes. This book provides an anecdotal, highly readable discussion of the background to black holes and the consequences of their existence." Choice
Includes glossary

Thorne, Kip S.

Black holes and time warps; Einstein's outrageous legacy. Norton 1994 619p il hardcover o.p. pa $18.95   **530.1**

    1. Physics 2. Astrophysics 3. Relativity (Physics) 4. Black holes (Astronomy)

    ISBN 0-393-31276-3 pa

                           LC 93-2014

This book is "about black holes, white holes, wormholes, parallel universes, time travel, 10-dimensional space-time, the origin and fate of the universe and a lot of other subjects dear to science fiction fans." N Y Times Book Rev

Includes bibliographical references

Toomey, David M.

The new time travelers; a journey to the frontiers of physics. [by] David Toomey. W. W. Norton 2007 391p il $28   **530.1**

    1. Space and time

    ISBN 978-0-393-06013-3; 0-393-06013-6

                           LC 2007-11307

This book on the physics of time travel "illustrates dimension-bending concepts with space-time diagrams, M. C. Escher drawings, and the plot of H.G. Wells' Time Machine. Toomey gets a grip on bending the fourth dimension by historically chronicling physicists who have theorized about time travel . . . . If you dream of getting outside your personal light cone, Toomey shows how it might be imagined." Booklist

Includes bibliographical references

Wertheim, Margaret

Physics on the fringe; Smoke rings, circlons, and alternative theories of everything. Margaret Wertheim. Walker & Company 2011 336 p. il   **530.1**

    1. Physics

    ISBN 0802715133; 9780802715135

This book "describes work done by amateur . . . [scientists], people rejected by the academic establishment and rejecting orthodox academic beliefs. . . . Margaret Wertheim's . . . leading character is Jim Carter. . . . Carter's . . . belief in a theory of the universe [is] based on endless hierarchies of circlons. Circlons are mechanical objects of circular shape. . . . He verified the behavior of circlons by doing experiments with smoke rings at his home." (New York Review of Books)

The author "offers a look into the hearts and minds of the 'outsider' physicists: solitary figures who, usually with little or no formal training, strive to explain our world. Wertheim builds the book around the affable Jim Carter, explorer, self-taught physicist, trailer park owner, and proponent of circlon synchronicity, with atoms shaped like tiny circles of coiled spring. . . . This sympathetic portrayal of one outsider's work offers an entry point into a fascinating corner of pseudoscience." Publ Wkly

Includes bibliographical references

Wolfson, Richard

Simply Einstein; relativity demystified. Norton 2003 261p il $24.95   **530.1**

    1. Relativity (Physics)

    ISBN 0-393-05154-4

                           LC 2002-2984

"Wolfson's economical and vivid tutorial should open doors for lay readers encountering Einstein's principles for the first time. His popular style, with a minimum of math, should make this a must-have book for Einstein buffs as well." Publ Wkly

Includes bibliographical references

530.11   Relativity theory

Gott, J. Richard

Time travel in Einstein's universe; the physical possibilities of travel through time. {by} J. Richard Gott, III. Houghton Mifflin 2001 291p il hardcover o.p. pa $14   **530.11**

    1. Space and time 2. Fourth dimension

    ISBN 0-395-95563-7; 0-618-25735-7 pa

                           LC 00-54243

"Gott tackles the complexities of attempting to turn the fantasy of time travel into a theoretical possibility in a lively and lucid discussion." Booklist

Includes bibliographical references

Magueijo, Joao

Faster than the speed of light; the story of a scientific speculation. Perseus Bks. 2003 279p il $26   **530.11**

    1. Light 2. Physics

    ISBN 0-7382-0525-7

                         LC 2002-112394

In this study theoretical physicist Magueijo presents the idea that light traveled faster in the early universe than it does today. He also documents the reactions other scientists are having to this theory, which contradicts Einstein's theory of relativity.

"Breaking the old speed limit posted by . . . Albert Einstein in his 20s, this book deploys a racy and provocative text to convey its popularized content of a new cosmology. Jocular, ironic, witty, self-centered, even indignant, Magueijo is all too ready to castigate his adversaries." Sci Am

530.12   Quantum mechanics (Quantum theory)

Cox, Brian

The quantum universe; (and why anything that can happen, does) [by] Brian Cox [and] Jeff Forshaw. Da Capo Press 2012 256p   **530.12**

    1. Physics 2. Quantum theory 3. Science -- Methodology

    ISBN 9780306819643; 9780306820601; 0306819643

                           LC 2011942393

In this book, "Brian Cox and Jeff Forshaw approach the world of quantum mechanics . . . and make fundamental scientific principles accessible . . . to everyone. The subatomic realm has a reputation for weirdness, spawning any number of profound misunderstandings." This book "asks what observations of the natural world made it necessary, how it was constructed, and why we are confident that, for all its apparent strangeness, it is a good theory." (Publisher's note)

Parker, Barry R.

Quantum legacy; the discovery that changed our universe. {by} Barry Parker. Prometheus Bks. 2002 282p il $29   **530.12**
1. Quantum theory
ISBN 1-57392-993-X

LC 2002-67966

The author describes the theory of quantum mechanics, its practical applications, and the work of such scientists as Max Planck, Albert Einstein, Niels Bohr, Werner Heisenberg, Erwin Schrodinger, and Richard Feynman

Includes bibliographical references (p. 269-273) and index

530.4   States of matter

Frankel, Felice

On the surface of things; images of the extraordinary in science. [by] Felice Frankel and George M. Whitesides. Harvard University Press 2007 160p il pa $26.50   **530.4**
1. Optical images 2. Surfaces (Physics)
ISBN 978-0-674-02688-9

First published 1997 by Chronicle Bks.

Text and photographs explore the way light interacts with various surfaces.

"Materials science bears an unfortunate reputation for dullness, dealing as it does with the stuff of everyday life. A ramble through the pages of this poetic volume, however, exposes the field's underlying luster." Sci Am [review of 1997 ed.]

Includes bibliographical references

530.8   Measurement

Barrow, John D.

The **constants** of nature; from Alpha to Omega--the numbers that encode the deepest secrets of the universe. Pantheon Books 2002 352p il $26; pa $15   **530.8**
1. Measurement
ISBN 0-375-42221-8; 1-4000-3225-3 pa

LC 2002-75975

"Barrow traces scientists' evolving understanding of natural constants, like the speed of light, in this erudite and enthralling work of popular science." Publ Wkly

Includes bibliographical references

Robinson, Andrew

The **story** of measurement. Thames & Hudson 2007 224p il map $34.95   **530.8**
1. Measurement
ISBN 978-0-500-51367-5; 0-500-51367-8

LC 2007-921450

"Robinson has the knack to explain any number of complex concepts lucidly and with simplicity, without being condescending. . . . He has produced a highly readable book." Times Lit Suppl

Includes bibliographical references

535   Light and related radiation

Park, David

The **fire** within the eye; a historical essay on the nature and meaning of light. Princeton Univ. Press 1997 377p il hardcover o.p. pa $19.95   **535**
1. Light 2. Optics
ISBN 0-691-05051-1 pa

LC 96-45573

A history of the concept and science of light from classical times to the present. Cultural, philosophical, intellectual and theological perspectives are explored and works by Aristotle, Grosseteste, Plotinus and Bohr are among those discussed

"Whether it is Fermat and Huygens on optics or Faraday and Maxwell on electromagnetism, the writing is lively and informed. . . . The very readable style and helpful glossary, along with an excellent bibliography and references, make this work suitable for . . . general readers." Choice

Pendergrast, Mark

Mirror mirror; a history of the human love affair with reflection. Basic Books 2003 404p il $27.50; pa $17   **535**
1. Mirrors
ISBN 0-465-05470-6; 0-465-05471-4 pa

LC 2003-2544

"Those with a historical and scientific bent may profitably read this book for insight into the manufacture of mirrors—along with descendents the telescope and microscope—down through the ages. . . . Whether for pleasure or profit, this well-written, entertaining book, packed with historical information, should be read!" Choice

Includes bibliographical references

535.6   Color

Eckstut, Arielle

The **Secret** Language of Color; Science, Nature, History, Culture, Beauty and Joy of Red, Orange, Yellow, Green, Blue, and Violet. Joann Eckstut and Arielle Eckstut. Black Dog & Leventhal Pub 2013 240 p. color illustrations $29.95   **535.6**
1. Color 2. Vision 3. Physics
ISBN 1579129498; 9781579129491

LC 2014397031

This book, by Joann Eckstut and Arielle Eckstut, is "organized into chapters that begin with . . . [an] explanation of the physics and chemistry of color. . . . In these chapters we learn about how and why we see color, the nature of rainbows, animals with color vision far superior and far inferior to our own, how our language influences the colors we see, and much more." (Publisher's note)

"The book's dynamic design and short entries make it easy to skim, but it's likely that those intending just a casual perusal will find themselves engrossed by this terrifically entertaining and informative volume." Pub Wkly

Includes bibliographical references (p. [234]-235) and index.

536   Heat

Shachtman, Tom

Absolute zero and the conquest of cold. Houghton Mifflin 1999 261p hardcover o.p. pa $14   **536**
1. Thermodynamics 2. Low temperatures -- Research
ISBN 0-395-93888-0; 0-618-08239-5 pa

LC 99-33305

The author "analyzes the social impact of the chill factor, explains the science of cold and tells the curious tales behind inventions like the thermometer, the fridge and the thermos flask." N Y Times Book Rev

Includes bibliographical references

537   Electricity and electronics

Bodanis, David

Electric universe; the shocking true story of electricity. Crown Publishers 2004 308p hardcover o.p. pa $31   **537**
1. Electricity 2. Force and energy
ISBN 1-4000-4550-9; 0-307-33598-4 pa

LC 2004-11275

The author "examines electricity's theoretical development and how 19th- and 20th-century entrepreneurs harnessed it to transform everyday existence. Going from 'Wires' to 'Waves' to computers and even the human body, Bodanis pairs electrical innovations with minibiographies of their developers, among them Thomas Edison, Alexander Graham Bell, Guglielmo Marconi, Heinrich Herz and Alan Turing." Publ Wkly

"As a storyteller, author David Bodanis is wonderful. . . . This book is directed at a general audience, but it should be required reading for all scientific professionals." Sci Books Films

Includes bibliographical references

539.2   Radiation (Radiant energy)

Biddle, Wayne

A **field** guide to radiation; Wayne Biddle. Penguin Books 2012 258 p.   **539.2**
1. Cosmic rays 2. Radioactivity 3. Radiation -- Physiological effect 4. Radiation 5. Radioisotopes 6. Radioactive substances
ISBN 0143121278; 9780143121275

LC 2012009025

In this book, Wayne Biddle offers a "guide to understanding how radiation affects our everyday lives. Nuclear energy, X-rays, radon, cell phones . . . radiation is part of the way we live on a daily basis, and yet the sources and reper-

cussions of our exposure to it remain mysterious." Biddle provides "the history, meaning, and health implications of . . . radiation poisoning, alpha particles [and] cosmic rays." (Publisher's note)

Includes bibliographical references and index

Blatner, David

Spectrums; our mindboggling universe from infinitesimal to infinity. David Blatner. Walker & Co. 2012 183 p. (hardback) $25   **539.2**
1. Size 2. Science 3. Measurement 4. Spectrum analysis
ISBN 0802717705; 9780802717702

LC 2012010727

This book, by David Blatner, asks "how can we understand the world of the atom or the size of our galaxy? How do we grasp a billionth of a second or a billion years? . . . Blatner re-introduces us to six fundamental spectrums in the world around us: numbers, size, light, sound, heat, and time. Offering fascinating glimpses of hidden realities, full of comparisons, facts, and anecdotes." (Publisher's note)

539.7   Atomic and nuclear physics

Aczel, Amir D.

Present at the creation; the story of CERN and the Large Hadron Collider. [by] Amir Aczel. Harmony Books 2010 271p il $25.99; ebook $12.99   **539.7**
1. Large Hadron Collider (France and Switzerland) 2. CERN
ISBN 978-0-307-59167-8; 978-0-307-59168-5 ebook

LC 2010-14835

Aczel "has produced an excellent review of past, current, and possible future theories of particle physics and how they relate to the field of cosmology. He uses the Large Hadron Collider (LHC), the most energetic particle accelerator ever built, as a focal point for a discussion of these theories." Choice

Includes bibliographical references

Carroll, Sean

The **particle** at the end of the Universe; how the hunt for the Higgs boson leads us to the edge of a new world. Sean Carroll. Penguin Group USA 2012 352 p. $27.95   **539.7**
1. Higgs bosons 2. Dark matter (Astronomy)
ISBN 0525953590; 9780525953593

In this book "Sean Carroll takes readers behind the scenes of the Large Hadron Collider at CERN to meet the scientists and explain . . . the Higgs boson [particle], the key to understanding why mass exists. . . . The fact is, while we have now essentially solved the mass puzzle, there are things we didn't predict and possibilities we haven't yet dreamed. A doorway is opening into the mind boggling, somewhat frightening world of dark matter." (Publisher's note)

Includes bibliographical references and index.

Feynman, Richard Phillips, 1918-1988

QED; the strange theory of light and matter. [by] Richard Feynman. Princeton Univ. Press 1985

158p (Alix G. Mautner memorial lectures) $55; pa $15.95   **539.7**
  1. Light 2. Electrons 3. Quantum theory
  ISBN 0-691-08388-6; 0-691-02417-0 pa
                                                LC 85-42685
The author attempts to describe the interaction between light and electrons

"Feynman describes with accuracy, insight, self-deprecating humor, and clarity the centerpiece of modern elementary particle theory—quantum electrodynamics. . . . 'QED' will challenge the mind." Christ Sci Monit

Goldberg, Dave

The **Universe** in the Rearview Mirror; How Hidden Symmetries Shape Reality. Dave Goldberg. Dutton 2013 336 p. illustrations $27.95   **539.7**
  1. Physics 2. Universe 3. Reality 4. Symmetry 5. Cosmology
  ISBN 0525953663; 9780525953661
                                                LC 2013016178
Author Dave Goldberg examines "space, time and everything in between showing that our elegant universe--from the Higgs boson to antimatter to the most massive group of galaxies--is shaped by hidden symmetries that have driven all our recent discoveries about the universe and all the ones to come." (Publisher's note)

An "informative, math-free, and completely entertaining look at the concept of symmetry in physics." Pub Wkly

Includes bibliographical references and index

Greene, Brian R.

★ The **elegant** universe; superstrings, hidden dimensions, and the quest for the ultimate theory. [by] Brian Greene. Vintage Books 2000 448p il pa $15.95   **539.7**
  1. Cosmology 2. String theory
  ISBN 0-375-70811-1; 978-0-375-70811-4
                                                LC 99-42018
First published 1999 by Norton

The author "makes the terribly complex theory of strings accessible to all. He possesses a remarkable gift for using the everyday to illustrate what may be going on in dimensions beyond our feeble human perception." Publ Wkly

Includes bibliographical references

Hall, Christopher

Beyond the god particle; Leon M. Lederman, Christopher T. Hill. Prometheus Books 2013 340 p. ill hc $24.95   **539.7**
  1. Matter 2. Particles (Nuclear physics) 3. Higgs bosons
  ISBN 9781616148010
                                                LC 2013022346
The coauthors "discuss the 2012 discovery of the Higgs boson particle . . . and what's next for subatomic particle physics research. This is essentially a sequel to The God Particle, in which the titular term for Higgs boson was coined. Both descriptive and prescriptive, this new book presents enjoyable overviews of discoveries of the physical world, from molecules to atoms and subatomic particles, including a clear description of the need for huge machines to provide energy to accelerate tiny particles. . . . The authors aim to offer "coulds and shoulds," and do, including a directive thoroughly to study strong interactions in particle physics." Booklist

Includes bibliographical references and index

Malley, Marjorie Caroline

Radioactivity; a history of a mysterious science. [by] Marjorie C. Malley. Oxford University Press 2011 xxi, 267p il map $21.95   **539.7**
  1. Radioactivity
  ISBN 978-0-19-976641-3
                                                LC 2010038979
"Malley presents a timely tale about the discovery of radioactivity, the development of our knowledge of the physical universe, and the way radioactivity has changed our world. . . . [She] manages to make the periodic table and the giants involved in its creation interesting. . . . Malley does a wonderful job of demonstrating how scientific discovery functions, as opposed to the usual approach in which facts and figures are given as tidbits along a chronology." Libr J

Includes bibliographical references

Nelson, Craig

The **age** of radiance; the epic rise and dramatic fall of the atomic era. Craig Nelson. Scribner 2014 416 p. illustrations (hardcover) $29.99   **539.7**
  1. Radiation 2. Radioactivity 3. Nuclear energy 4. Nuclear physics 5. Nuclear weapons
  ISBN 145166043X; 9781451660432; 9781451660449
                                                LC 2013042192
This book, by Craig Nelson, is a "history of the Atomic Age. . . . From the discovery of X-rays in the 1890s, through the birth of nuclear power in an abandoned Chicago football stadium, to the bomb builders of Los Alamos, . . . Nelson illuminates a pageant of fascinating historical figures: Marie and Pierre Curie, Albert Einstein, Niels Bohr, Franklin Roosevelt, J. Robert Oppenheimer, Harry Truman, Curtis LeMay, John F. Kennedy, Robert McNamara, Ronald Reagan, and Mikhail Gorbachev." (Publisher's note)

"An engaging history that raises provocative questions about the future of nuclear science." Kirkus

Includes bibliographical references and index

Seife, Charles

Sun in a bottle; the strange history of fusion and the science of wishful thinking. Viking 2008 294p il map $25.95   **539.7**
  1. Nuclear fusion
  ISBN 978-0-670-02033-1; 0-670-02033-8
                                                LC 2008-13135
"Ever since the first hydrogen bomb tests in the 1950s, scientists have hoped to reproduce the sun's magic in a controlled fashion, unlocking an unlimited source of energy. But the dream has been elusive. With great explanatory skill, Seife . . . explains how fusion works and why it is so hard to get power out of it. Seife reviews the parade of hubristic and sometimes comic or outright dishonest claims that fusion scientists have made over the decades." Sci News

Includes bibliographical references

Stewart, Ian

Why beauty is truth; a history of symmetry. Basic Books 2007 290p il $26.95   **539.7**
1. Symmetry
ISBN 978-0-465-08236-0; 0-465-08236-X
LC 2006-38274

"Beginning with the early struggles of the Babylonians to solve quadratics, Stewart guides his readers through the often-tangled history of symmetry, illuminating for non-specialists how a concept easily recognized in geometry acquired new meanings in algebra. . . . An exciting foray for any armchair physicist!" Booklist

Includes bibliographical references

540   Chemistry and allied sciences

Cobb, Cathy

Creations of fire; chemistry's lively history from alchemy to the atomic age. [by] Cathy Cobb and Harold Goldwhite. Perseus Pub. 2001 475p il pa $20.95   **540**
1. Chemistry -- History
ISBN 0-7382-0594-X; 978-0-7382-0594-6
LC 2001-99001

First published 1995 by Plenum Press

This history "begins with chemistry in the Stone Age and ends with current areas of interest such as superheavy elements and the polymerase chain reaction. Along the way, the coverage includes alchemy, cold fusion, and . . . topics like the contributions of Lise Meitner and Marie Lavoisiere. . . . This book's light and often humorous style makes it especially appealing to the general reader." Libr J

Includes bibliographical references

The joy of chemistry; the amazing science of familiar things. [by] Cathy Cobb & Monty L. Fetterolf. Prometheus Books 2005 393p il hardcover o.p. pa $19   **540**
1. Chemistry
ISBN 1-591-02231-2; 1-591-02771-3 pa
LC 2004-20144

The authors cover "the material of a general chemistry course along with organic, inorganic and analytical chemistry and biochemistry; there's even a chapter on forensic chemistry. . . . They explain everything from flatulence (the chemical composition of intestinal gas) to pizza cheese (why mozzarella rather than, say, parmesan?)." Publ Wkly

Includes bibliographical references

Coffey, Patrick

Cathedrals of science; the personalities and rivalries that made modern chemistry. Oxford University Press 2008 379p il $29.95   **540**
1. Chemists 2. College teachers 3. Chemistry -- History 4. Science -- Ethical aspects 5. Nobel laureates for chemistry
ISBN 978-0-19-532134-0; 0-19-532134-0
LC 2007-48304

The author writes about the careers of such chemists as Gilbert Lewis, Irving Langmuir, Fritz Haber, Glenn Seaborg, Harold Urey, Linus Pauling, and Dorothy Wrinch.

This is "is an engaging, well-written, balanced account of 13 chemists who built modern chemistry." Choice

Includes bibliographical references

CRC Handbook of Chemistry and Physics; W. M. Haynes, editor-in-chief. 95th edition CRC Press 2014 various pagings $169.95   **540**
1. Reference books 2. Physics -- Tables 3. Chemistry -- Tables
ISBN 1482208679; 9781482208672

First published 1913. Periodically revised

A "reference book containing much-used information on mathematics, chemistry, and physics, including tables, physical constants of chemical elements and compounds, definitions, formulae, etc." AAAS Sci Book List for Young Adults

Includes bibliographical references

A dictionary of chemistry; edited by John Daintith. 6th ed.; Oxford University Press 2008 584p il (Oxford paperback reference) pa $17.95   **540**
1. Reference books 2. Chemistry -- Dictionaries
ISBN 978-0-19-920463-2; 0-19-920463-2
LC 2008-274475

This book covers "biochemistry, chemoinformatics, forensic chemistry, metallurgy, and geology. The dictionary includes chronologies, biographies, illustrations, tables, chemical structures, feature articles, and eight appendixes." Choice

Greenberg, Arthur

The art of chemistry; myths, medicines, and materials. Wiley 2003 357p $59.95   **540**
1. Alchemy 2. Medicine -- History 3. Chemistry -- History
ISBN 0-471-07180-3
LC 2002-9950

This book "tracks chemistry's incremental progress from myth to modern science, featuring the figures and diagrams that early chemists used to explain their craft." Publisher's note

"A very interesting mix of information. Although it is not something that a reader would sit down and read through in one sitting, each of the eight sections was interesting by itself." Sci Books Films

Includes bibliographical references

From alchemy to chemistry in picture and story. Wiley-Interscience 2007 xxiii, 637p il $69.95 **540**
1. Chemistry -- History
ISBN 978-0-471-75154-0; 0-471-75154-5
LC 2006-33564

According to the author, this "is a combination of his two previous books, A Chemical History Tour and The Art of Chemistry, with some additions and revisions. . . . One could open the book at almost any page to learn something about the remarkable history of the chemical sciences." Sci Books Films

Includes bibliographical references

Lange's handbook of chemistry; 16th ed.; Mc-Graw-Hill 2005 various paging il $150 **540**
1. Chemistry -- Tables
ISBN 0-07-143220-5; 978-0-07-143220-7
First published 1934. Periodically revised
"A standard reference source for both students and professional chemists. Sections for: organic compounds; general information, conversion tables, and mathematics; inorganic chemistry; properties of atoms, radicals, and bonds; physical properties; thermodynamic properties; spectroscopy; electrolytes, electromotive force, and chemical equilibrium; physiochemical relationships; polymers, rubbers, fats, oils, and waxes; and practical laboratory information." Guide to Ref Books. 11th edition

Le Couteur, Penny
Napoleon's buttons; how 17 molecules changed history. [by] Penny Le Couteur, Jay Burreson. Jeremy P. Tarcher/Penguin Books 2003 375p il hardcover o.p. pa $14.95 **540**
1. Chemistry
ISBN 1-58542-220-7; 1-58542-331-9 pa
LC 2002-032247
"Napoleon's Buttons is a fascinating attempt at recognizing the role of chemistry in the wider world. With its many structural diagrams, the book can resemble a course in organic chemistry, but the chemist-authors are good guides. . . . The best chapter is the one on dyes." Quill & Quire
Includes bibliographical references

541 Chemistry

Atkins, Peter William, 1940-
Reactions; the private life of atoms. by Peter Atkins. Oxford University Press 2011 191 p. **541**
1. Chemical reactions
ISBN 9780199695126; 0199695121
LC 2011275047
The author "provides detailed descriptions of the reactions that occur in everyday life, using language that, while elevated, will be accessible for the armchair scientist. Each chapter focuses on a particular type of reaction, including: precipitation, neutralization, combustion, reduction, oxidation separately and in combination, catalysis, and more." Publ Wkly

546 Inorganic chemistry

Aldersey-Williams, Hugh, 1959-
Periodic tales; a cultural history of the elements, from arsenic to zinc. Ecco 2011 428p il $29.99 **546**
1. Periodic law 2. Chemical elements
ISBN 978-0-06-182472-2; 0-06-182472-0
"Because Aldersey-Williams's ultimate subject is human civilization rather than simply the elements, he gives himself room to expound on just about everything, treating the components of the table as though they were 'sorted by an anthropologist.' So his book is organized (loosely) into five sections: power (elements hoarded as riches or used to exert control); fire (elements that can best be understood by what happens when they are burned); craft (elements used to create and the cultural meaning we ascribe to them); beauty (elements used to 'colour our world'); and earth (elements that have marked the place where they were discovered in a notable way). It's an ambitious project. . . . [The book] is swollen with names, places, and long-forgotten (or simply unknown to most of us) figures, with zigzagging detours into almost every subject imaginable. It is almost more of a question of what the book does not touch upon than what it does." Boston Globe
Includes bibliographical references

Bernstein, Jeremy
Plutonium; a history of the world's most dangerous element. National Academies Press 2007 194p il map $27.95 **546**
1. Plutonium
ISBN 978-0-309-10296-4; 0-309-10296-0
LC 2006-38466
This book "relates the 'life story' of the chemical element plutonium." Sci Books Film
"Bernstein's book should play a useful role by helping to demystify plutonium and by encouraging interested members of the public and Congress to start constructing a more rational policy to deal with the dangers posed by this manmade element." Am Sci
Includes bibliographical references

Gray, Theodore
★ The **elements**; a visual exploration of every known atom in the universe. photographs by Theodore Gray and Nick Mann. Black Dog & Leventhal Publishers 2009 240p il $29.95 **546**
1. Periodic law 2. Chemical elements
ISBN 1579128149; 9781579128142
LC 2009-34931
This is a collection of "photographic representations of the 118 elements in the periodic table. . . . [The book also contains] facts, figures, and stories of the elements as well as data on the properties of each, including atomic weight, density, melting and boiling point, valence, electronegativity, and the year and location in which it was discovered." (Publisher's note) Index.
This is a collection of "photographic representations of the 118 elements in the periodic table. . . . Organized in order of appearance on the periodic table, each element is represented by a spread that includes a . . . full-page, full-color photograph that most closely represents it in its purest form. . . . [Also included are] facts, figures, and stories of the elements as well as data on the properties of each, including atomic weight, density, melting and boiling point, valence, electronegativity, and the year and location in which it was discovered." Publisher's note
Includes bibliographical references

Kean, Sam
★ The **disappearing** spoon; and other true tales of madness, love, and the history of the world from

the periodic table of the elements. Little, Brown and Co. 2010 391p $24.99   **546**
1. Chemical elements
ISBN 978-0-316-05164-4; 0-316-05164-0
LC 2009-40754

"Kean's traipse among the elements leads him through a warren of subjects, as he examines how these basic building blocks have factored prominently in astronomy, biology, literature, history, politics, and even cryptozoology. With the anecdotal flourishes of Oliver Sacks and the populist accessibility of Malcolm Gladwell, but without the latter's occasional facileness, he makes even the most abstract concepts graspable for armchair scientists. His keen sense of humor is a particular pleasure." Entertainment Wkly

Includes bibliographical references

Rigden, John S.

Hydrogen; the essential element. Harvard Univ. Press 2002 280p il $28; pa $15.95   **546**
1. Hydrogen 2. Science -- History
ISBN 0-674-00738-7; 0-674-01252-6 pa
LC 2001-51708

The author chronicles "how one enduring conundrum—that of explaining the element hydrogen—has challenged two centuries of brilliant scientists. . . . In the process, he clarifies for general readers the nature of the scientific enterprise, in which elegant theories must meet the test of empirical verification." Booklist

Includes bibliographical references

Zoellner, Tom

Uranium; war, energy, and the rock that shaped the world. Viking 2009 337p $26.95; pa $16 **546**
1. Uranium
ISBN 978-0-670-02064-5; 0-670-02064-8; 978-0-14-311672-1 pa; 0-14-311672-X pa
LC 2008-29023

This is an overview of the radioactive mineral.

"Zoellner vividly conveys both the potential benefits and the harm that uranium holds for human civilization. . . . Policymakers and citizens alike need to read 'Uranium.'" Washington Post Book World

Includes bibliographical references

547 Organic chemistry

Gorman, Hugh S.

The **story** of N; a social history of the nitrogen cycle and the challenge of sustainability. by Hugh S. Gorman. Rutgers University Press 2012 xiii, 241 p.p (Studies in modern science, technology, and the environment) (hardcover : alk. paper) $49.95   **547**
1. Nitrogen 2. Climate change 3. Sustainability 4. Nitrogen cycle 5. Sustainable development
ISBN 0813554381; 9780813554389; 9780813554396
LC 2012009901

In this book, author Hugh S. "Gorman analyzes the notion of sustainability from a fresh perspective--the integration of human activities with the biogeochemical cycling of nitrogen--and provides a supportive alternative to studying

sustainability through the lens of climate change and the cycling of carbon." (Publisher's note)

Includes bibliographical references (p. 209-233) and index

548 Crystallography

Holden, Alan

Crystals and crystal growing; {by} Alan Holden and Phylis Morrison; introduction by Philip Morrison. MIT Press 1982 318p il pa $19.95   **548**
1. Crystals
ISBN 0-262-58050-0
LC 81-23639

First published 1960 by Anchor Bks.

This book "sets for itself three major goals: 1. Describing the atomistic character of crystallinity; 2. Describing some techniques for preparing large single crystals; and 3. Describing some experiments that display the unexpected properties which flow from crystallinity." Preface

"An excellent introduction to crystallography (and, incidentally, to much basic physics) written in plain language." Libr J

549 Mineralogy

Chaline, Eric

Fifty minerals that changed the course of history; Eric Chaline. Firefly Books 2012 223 p. ill. (chiefly col.), ports. $29.95   **549**
1. Minerals 2. Mines and mineral resources
ISBN 1554079845; 9781554079841

This book by Eric Chaline is a "guide to the minerals that have had the greatest impact on human civilization. These are the materials used from the Stone Age to the First and Second Industrial Revolutions to the Nuclear Age and include metals, ores, alloys, salts, rocks, sodium, mercury, steel and uranium. The book also includes minerals used as currency, as jewelry and as lay and religious ornamentation when combined with gem minerals like diamonds, amber, coral, and jade." (Publisher's note)

Includes bibliographical references and index.

Chesterman, Charles W.

★ The **Audubon** Society field guide to North American rocks and minerals; scientific consultant, Kurt E. Lowe. Knopf 1979 850p il $19.95   **549**
1. Rocks 2. Minerals
ISBN 0-394-50269-8
LC 78-54893

"Pocket guide providing color photos and descriptions of some 232 mineral species and forty types of rocks. Includes guide to mineral environments, glossary, bibliography, and indexes by name and locality." Ref Sources for Small & Medium-sized Libr. 5th edition

Johnsen, Ole

Minerals of the world. Princeton Univ. Press 2002 439p il (Princeton field guides) pa $24.95 **549**
1. Crystals 2. Minerals
ISBN 0-691-09537-X

LC 2001-97695

Originally published in hardcover with title: Photographic guide to minerals of the world

The author "provides descriptive information for the identification of more than 500 minerals. . . . This book follows the standard mineralogy textbook approach in which the mineral sections are arranged according to mineral composition and structure. . . . The book's suitability as a field guide is completed by the addition of hundreds of excellent color photographs and drawings. . . . The content material is solid, and superb illustrations on high-quality paper make for an attractive volume." Choice

Klein, Cornelis

Manual of mineral science; [by] Cornelis Klein, Barbara Dutrow. 23rd ed; Wiley 2007 xxi, 675p il $150.95 **549**
1. Minerals
ISBN 978-0-471-72157-4; 0-471-72157-3

LC 2007-273750

First published 1848 under the authorship of James D. Dana. Periodically revised. Variant title: Manual of mineralogy

This is a standard introductory reference book for the use of students and collectors. It covers physical, chemical, determinative, and descriptive mineralogy, discusses mineral occurrence, association, and use, and includes both a subject and mineral index

Includes bibliographical references

Pough, Frederick H.

★ A **field** guide to rocks and minerals; photographs by Jeff Scovil. 5th ed; Houghton Mifflin 1996 396p il hardcover o.p. pa $20 **549**
1. Rocks 2. Minerals
ISBN 0-395-72778-2; 0-395-91096-X pa

LC 94-49005

First published 1953

This illustrated guide utilizes traditional identification methods and includes discussions of crystallography, mineralogy and home laboratory techniques.

Includes bibliographical references

Rocks and minerals; 1st American ed. DK Publishing 2012 352 p. col. ill. (DK Smithsonian nature guide) $14.95 **549**
1. Rocks 2. Minerals
ISBN 0756690420 ; 9780756690427

LC 2012470083

"[P]acked full of stunning images that reveal intricate details and unique characteristics of each rock and mineral. . . . Us[es] close-up photographs of every specimen and profiles containing examples from all over the world [and] brings revealing key facets and details perfect for quick identification." (Publisher's note)

550 Earth sciences

Childs, Craig

Apocalyptic planet; field guide to the everending Earth. Craig Childs. Pantheon Books 2012 xvii, 343 p.p $27.95 **550**
1. Earth 2. End of the world 3. Earth -- History -- Popular works
ISBN 0307379094; 9780307379092

LC 2012006012

In this book "[Craig] Childs makes clear that ours is not a stable planet, that it is prone to sudden, violent natural disasters and extremes of climate. Alternate futures, many not so pretty, are constantly waiting in the wings. Childs refutes the idea of an apocalyptic end to the earth and finds clues to its more inevitable end in some of the most physically challenging places on the globe." (Publisher's note)

Includes bibliographical references (p. 331-343)

★ **Earth;** the definitive visual guide. editors-in-chief, James F. Luhr and Jeffrey E. Post. Revised and updated ed. DK Publishing 2013 528 p. ill. (chiefly col.) (hc) $50 **550**
1. Earth
ISBN 9781465414373; 1465414371

LC 2013444093

First published 2003

Presents an overview of the Earth, discussing its internal structure, the major features of its lands, mountains, and oceans, its climate, weather, and place in the universe.

"Specially commissioned new 3-D digital artwork provides a striking, informative guide to the features of our planet, explains the scientific processes that govern our world, and looks at the complex relationship between humans and the natural environment." Publisher's note

Hazen, Robert M.

★ The **story** of Earth; the first 4.5 billion years, from stardust to living planet. Robert M. Hazen. Viking 2012 306 p. **550**
1. Evolution 2. Earth -- Age 3. Earth sciences 4. Earth -- Internal structure 5. Earth
ISBN 0670023558; 9780670023554

LC 2011043713

This book on the history of Earth, by Robert M. Hazen, argues that "'Earth's living and nonliving spheres' have coevolved over the past four billion years. . . . Describing the 'discoveries of organisms in places long considered inhospitable [to life] -- in superheated volcanic vents, acidic pools, Arctic ice and stratospheric dust,' he argues for the dating of the origin of life more than a billion years earlier than estimates based on Nobel Prize winner Harold Urey's groundbreaking experiments." (Kirkus Reviews)

Shubin, Neil H., 1960-

The **universe** within; discovering the common history of rocks, planets, and people. Neil Shubin. Pantheon Books 2012 240 p. $25.95 **550**
1. Geology 2. Universe 3. Human body 4. Petrology 5. Earth -- Origin
ISBN 0307378438; 9780307378439

LC 2012007541

This book by Neil Shubin addresses "how . . . the events that formed our solar system billions of years ago [are] embedded inside each of us. . . . Starting . . . with fossils, [Shubin] turns his gaze skyward, showing us how the entirety of the universe's fourteen-billion-year history can be seen in our bodies. As he moves from our very molecular composition . . . to the workings of our eyes, Shubin makes clear how the evolution of the cosmos has profoundly marked our own bodies." (Publisher's note)

Includes bibliographical references and index.

Williams, David B.

Stories in stone; travels through urban geology. Walker 2009 260p il   **550**

1. Urban geology

ISBN 978-0-8027-1622-4

LC 2009-5609

The author "describes the mineralogy and history of some of the world's most common building materials. . . . Each chapter showcases a different stone. By describing how the stones formed and how they are used, this book reveals that natural and cultural history may lie no farther than the building next door." Sci News

Includes bibliographical references

551   Geology, hydrology, meteorology

Flannery, Tim, 1956-

Here on Earth; a natural history of the planet. [by] Tim Flannery. Atlantic Monthly Press 2011 316p il   **551**

1. Evolution 2. Earth sciences 3. Earth 4. Earth -- Origin 5. Evolution -- History 6. Earth sciences -- History

ISBN 080211976X; 9780802119766

The author "expands on the proposition that humans inherently exhaust their resources, triggering all manner of ecological and societal trauma. To evaluate the idea, he ranges over the entirety of human existence, remarking within each subtopic he raises--for example, the Aborigines' relation to Australian ecosystems--the ramifications of human use of available natural resources." Booklist

Includes bibliographical references

Lamb, Simon

Devil in the mountain; a search for the origin of the Andes. Princeton University Press 2004 335p il $29.95   **551**

1. Andes

ISBN 0-691-11596-6

LC 2003-64124

The author gives "a clear, solid lecture on geological theory and practice with a few personal snapshots of the unseen hazards of fieldwork and occasional local color. . . . Those interested in geology will find it informative and its conclusion satisfying." Publ Wkly

Includes bibliographical references

Lambert, David

The field guide to geology; [by] David Lambert and the Diagram Group. New ed.; Checkmark Books 2006 304p il map $39.95; pa $16.95   **551**

1. Geology

ISBN 0-8160-6509-8; 978-0-8160-6509-7; 0-8160-6510-1 pa; 978-0-8160-6510-3 pa

LC 2006-48533

First published 1988

This is an "overview of the processes that forged the planet and the technologies that have revolutionized the way that scientists investigate Earth's systems." Publisher's note

Includes bibliographical references

551.2   Volcanoes, earthquakes, thermal waters and gases

Calderazzo, John

Rising fire: volcanoes and our inner lives. Lyons Press 2004 268p $22.95   **551.2**

1. Volcanoes

ISBN 1-59228-389-6

"Calderazzo climbs volcanoes, presents dramatic accounts of major eruptions, portrays people who live within a volcano's reach, and muses on the impact volcanoes have had on humankind's sense of the sacred." Booklist

Feldman, Jay

★ When the Mississippi ran backwards; empire, intrigue, murder, and the new Madrid earthquakes. Free Press 2005 307p il maps $27   **551.2**

1. Mississippi River valley 2. Earthquakes -- United States

ISBN 0-7432-4278-5

LC 2004-57537

"Through four historical figures, Feldman recreates the frontier world of 1811-12, when the New Madrid earthquakes devastated the lower Ohio and mid-Mississippi valleys. . . . Synthesizing lives and times, Feldman composes a fluent, coherent narrative that culminates in the War of 1812." Booklist

Includes bibliographical references

Gates, Alexander E.

★ Encyclopedia of earthquakes and volcanoes; [by] Alexander E. Gates, PH.D and David Ritchie. 3rd ed.; Facts on File 2007 346p il map (Facts on File science library) pa $21.95; $75   **551.2**

1. Reference books 2. Volcanoes -- Encyclopedias 3. Earthquakes -- Encyclopedias

ISBN 9780816071203; 0-8160-6302-8

LC 2005-46619

First published 1994

"The book's entries cover information on key environmental issues, economic dilemmas, ethical concerns, advances in research and technology, organizations, and individuals who have left their mark on the fields of volcanology and seismology." Publisher's note

Includes bibliographical references

Oppenheimer, Clive

Eruptions that shook the world. Cambridge University Press 2011 392p il map $30 **551.2**
1. Volcanoes
ISBN 978-0-521-64112-8

LC 2011004246

The author "pieces together our volcanic past by connecting major historic and prehistoric eruptions to the course of human civilization. . . . A fascinating work that will engage not just volcano experts but also those with an interest in history, climatology, archaeology, and geochronology." Libr J

Includes bibliographical references

Scarth, Alwyn

Vesuvius : a biography. Princeton University Press 2009 342p il map $29.95 **551.2**
1. Volcanoes 2. Vesuvius (Italy)
ISBN 978-0-691-14390-3; 0-691-14390-0

LC 2009-925151

"Vesuvius has been central to Western civilization's unfolding understanding of volcanoes. While the detailed descriptions of historic eruptions here are valuable, if repetitious, the real strength of the book lies in the quotations from primary sources. These range from Pliny the Younger's description of the C.E. 79 eruption that destroyed Pompeii and Herculaneum, to medieval and Counter-Reformation reactions invoking the supernatural (after a brief naturalistic approach in the Renaissance), to the beginnings of a modern scientific understanding of volcanoes in the late 18th century with the work of Sir William Hamilton, the British envoy in Naples. The chronology concludes with current concerns about the safety of the increasing population around Vesuvius." Libr J

Includes bibliographical references

Winchester, Simon

Krakatoa : the day the world exploded, August 27, 1883. HarperCollins Pubs. 2003 416p il maps $25.95; pa $13.95 **551.2**
1. Volcanoes
ISBN 0-06-621285-5; 0-06-083859-0 pa

"This book chronicles the underlying causes, utter devastation and lasting effects of the cataclysmic 1883 eruption of the volcano island Krakatoa in what is now Indonesia. . . . [The author] demonstrates a keen knack for balancing rich and often rigorous historical detail with dramatic tension and storytelling." Publ Wkly

"As a rich blend of science and history, this book is highly recommended for most public and academic libraries." Libr J

551.21 Volcanoes

Thompson, Dick

Volcano cowboys; the rocky evolution of a dangerous science. St. Martin's Press 2000 326p il map $26.95; pa $14.95 **551.21**
1. Volcanoes 2. Mount Saint Helens (Wash.)
ISBN 0-312-20881-2; 0-312-28668-6 pa

LC 00-26158

This describes the work of U.S. Geological Survey scientists in predicting volcanic eruptions, focusing on the eruptions of Mount St. Helens in 1980 and Mount Pinatubo in 1991

"An informative book about science's communication with the lay public." Booklist

Includes bibliographical references

551.22 Earthquakes

Dvorak, John

Earthquake Storms; The Fascinating History and Volatile Future of the San Andreas Fault. by John Dvorak. W W Norton & Co Inc 2014 352 p. illustrations $27.95 **551.22**
1. Faults (Geology) 2. California -- History 3. Earthquakes -- California
ISBN 1605984957; 9781605984957

LC 2014395154

Author John Dvorak "treats Californians and other tectonics enthusiasts to an enjoyable history of the Golden State's earthquakes alongside a bracing look at potential future ones. Dates, locations, magnitudes, and damage figures are all embedded in these stories of quakes and in the stories of those who studied them, like Andrew Lawson, the University of California geology professor who named the San Andreas Fault in 1895, and Charles Richter, developer of the eponymous magnitude scale." (Publishers Weekly)

"Although almost entirely focused on California, this is a fine popular primer on the subject, lucidly written and no more technical than necessary." Kirkus

551.3 Surface and exogenous processes and their agents

Fredston, Jill A.

Snowstruck; in the grip of avalanches. [by] Jill Fredston. Harcourt 2005 342p il $24; pa $14 **551.3**
1. Avalanches 2. Survival skills
ISBN 978-0-15-101249-7; 0-15-101249-0; 978-0-15-603254-4 pa; 0-15-603254-6 pa

LC 2005-20454

"As avalanche experts, . . . [the author and her husband] are often called upon to forecast, trigger, and teach about avalanches as well as rescue survivors—or, sadly, more often to recover remains. Fredston's decades of experience distilled into this instructive and personal narrative will leave readers with a newfound appreciation for the force, the fury, and the cold sorrow of avalanches." Libr J

Gosnell, Mariana

Ice; the nature, the history, and the uses of an astonishing substance. Knopf 2005 560p il $30 **551.3**
1. Ice
ISBN 0-679-42608-6

LC 2005-45126

The author "opens with a description of the sound and sight of a small lake freezing, expanding from there to discuss the seasonal advance and retreat of ice, as on the Great Lakes or Lake Baikal. Taking the next natural step, the persistence of ice through the summer, brings Gosnell to the 1800s origin of glaciology in Louis Agassiz's study of Mont Blanc's Mer de Glace, and subsequently into the contemporary specialty of ice cores in ice-age research. En route through the science, which Gosnell condenses from the technical literature, the author imparts eclectic information through excerpts from poems, adventure and disaster stories, and discussions of ice sports and diversions." Booklist

Pollack, H. N.

A **world** without ice; [by] Henry Pollack. Avery 2009 287p il map $26; pa $16   **551.3**

1. Ice 2. Glaciers 3. Greenhouse effect

ISBN 978-1-58333-357-0; 978-1-58333-407-2 pa

LC 2009-30326

"Seldom has a scientist written so well and so clearly for the lay reader. Pollack's explanations of how researchers can tell that the climate is warming faster than normal are free of the usual scientific jargon and understandable. All readers concerned about global warming and students writing papers on the topic will want this excellent and important volume." Libr J

Includes bibliographical references

551.41   Geomorphology

Streever, Bill

Heat; adventures in the world's fiery places. Bill Streever. Little, Brown, and Co. 2013 368 p. (hardback) $26.99   **551.41**

1. Fire 2. Heat 3. Arid regions -- Description and travel

ISBN 0316105333; 9780316105330

LC 2012020861

In this book, Bill Streever "explores any place hot or anything that creates heat, like Death Valley, forest fires, coal, oil, nuclear bombs, cooking, and volcanoes. . . . In this . . . companion to 'Cold,' Streever is able to mix the pop science, personal experiences, and historic asides into a . . . commentary on a subject that few people think about." (Publishers Weekly)

551.46   Oceanography and submarine geology

Ballard, Robert D.

The **eternal** darkness; a personal history of deepsea exploration. {by} Robert D. Ballard with Will Hively. Princeton Univ. Press 2000 388p il maps $55; pa $18.95   **551.46**

1. Underwater exploration

ISBN 0-691-02740-4; 0-691-09554-X pa

LC 99-43072

Ballard "blends his personal experiences exploring hydrothermal vents and shipwrecks with stories of earlier deep-sea pioneers, focusing especially on the technology. . . . Ballard's volume is easy to read and will be an excellent addition to collections at all levels on oceanography, history of science, and exploration." Libr J

Includes bibliographical references (p. 315-374) and index

Broad, William

The **universe** below; discovering the secrets of the deep sea. {by} William J. Broad; illustrations by Dimitry Schidlovsky. Simon & Schuster 1997 432p il maps hardcover o.p. pa $15   **551.46**

1. Oceanography 2. Underwater exploration

ISBN 0-684-83852-4 pa

LC 96-50337

This work focuses "on the ships, subs, divers, underwater vehicles both manned and robotic, and satellites used in a variety of applications, from discovering the Titanic to observing unusual or new marine species." Libr J

"Intensively researched and crisply told, this is an illuminating, stimulating portrait of one of Earth's last frontiers." Publ Wkly

Includes bibliographical references

Carson, Rachel, 1907-1964

The **sea** around us. Oxford Univ. Press 2003 274p il maps $45   **551.46**

1. Ocean 2. Oceanography

ISBN 0-19-514701-4

LC 2002-29299

This is a reissue of the title first published 1951

This is a new edition of a "work originally published in 1951 and revised in 1961." (Sci Books Films)

Casey, Susan

The **wave**; in pursuit of the rogues, freaks and giants of the ocean. Doubleday 2010 326p il map $27.95   **551.46**

1. Surfing 2. Ocean waves

ISBN 978-0-7679-2884-7; 0-7679-2884-9

LC 2010-10193

Casey "estimates that freak waves might have a hand in sinking about two dozen large ships every year. She embarked on a five-year odyssey to meet the people who know these monsters best—from salvagers working a graveyard of ships off the South African coast to a convention of wave scientists, from researchers and mariners who have battled these beasts to surfers who roam the world in search of the ultimate thrill. Reading the 'The Wave' is almost like riding one, paddling in the expositional surf of vivid imagery and colorful description, thrown at you in ever-escalating surges." Cleveland Plain Dealer

Includes bibliographical references

Day, Trevor

Oceans; illustrations by Richard Garratt. rev ed; Facts on File 2008 318p il map (Ecosystem) $70   **551.46**

1. Ocean 2. Oceanography

ISBN 0-8160-5932-2; 978-0-8160-5932-4

LC 2006-100769

First published 1999

This volume describes the oceans of the world with regard to their geography, geology, history, chemistry, biology, ecology, exploration, relationship to the atmosphere, economic resources, and management.

Includes glossary and bibliographical references

Earle, Sylvia A.

The **world** is blue; how our fate and the ocean's are one. National Geographic 2009 303p il map $26 **551.46**
1. Oceanography 2. Marine biology 3. Marine ecology 4. Marine pollution 5. Human influence on nature
ISBN 978-1-4262-0541-5; 1-4262-0541-4

LC 2009-23972

The author "illustrates, in ways both humorous and discomforting, how our cavalier attitude toward the ocean and its inhabitants is causing our slow but certain destruction. Even more importantly, Earle offers solutions and discusses ongoing actions that have been taken to reverse this frightening cycle of obliteration. Even those who do not consider themselves environmentalists will find themselves easily caught up in Earle's heroic fight to save our 'blue world.'" Choice

Includes bibliographical references (p. 286-303)

Ebbesmeyer, Curtis

Flotsametrics and the floating world; how one man's obsession with runaway sneakers and rubber ducks revolutionized ocean science. [by] Curtis Ebbesmeyer and Eric Scigliano. Smithsonian Books 2009 286p il $26.99 **551.46**
1. Ocean currents
ISBN 978-0-06-155841-2; 0-06-155841-9

LC 2008-38805

Ebbesmeyer's "primary interest is ocean currents, especially gyres—great circular, interlocking currents that sweep the Earth's waters with clockwork regularity—and the flotsam they carry around the planet. Everything from athletic shoes and bathtub toys to messages in bottles and corpses have provided data to help Ebbesmeyer trace currents. He recounts how flotsam guided colonization and exploration, from Norse explorers to Christopher Columbus (the first to master the North Atlantic Subtropical Gyre). Today, Ebbesmeyer says, the human propensity for creating garbage has also made flotsam an environmental concern." Publ Wkly

Includes bibliographical references

Hohn, Donovan

★ **Moby** -Duck; The True Story of 28,800 Bath Toys Lost at Sea. Donovan Hohn. Viking 2011 402p. map (pbk) $16 **551.46**
1. Journalism 2. Oceanography
ISBN 0-670-02219-5; 978-0-670-02219-9; 9780143120506

LC 2010-33608

This book presents the author's investigations into "28,800 bath toys lost at sea over a period of nearly 20 years. . . . Found by beachcombers in the most unlikely locations, the toys provided rich data for those studying the notoriously difficult subject.

Nichols, C. Reid

Encyclopedia of marine science; [by] C. Reid Nichols and Robert G. Williams. Facts on File 2009 626p il map (Facts on File science library) $85 **551.46**
1. Reference books 2. Marine sciences -- Encyclopedias
ISBN 978-0-8160-5022-2; 0-8160-5022-8

LC 2007-45166

This "book consists of (a) some 600 encyclopedic definitions of applied science, technology, and engineering terms, (b) twenty 'Feature Essays' distributed among the encyclopedic definitions, and (c) a set of appendices." Sci Books Films

"The expert contributors have packed these pages with top-notch information that will be invaluable to students and reference librarians." SLJ

Includes bibliographical references

Prager, Ellen J.

Chasing science at sea; racing hurricanes, stalking sharks, and living undersea with ocean experts. [by] Ellen Prager. University of Chicago Press 2008 162p il $22.50; pa $13 **551.46**
1. Oceanography
ISBN 978-0-226-67870-2; 0-226-67870-9; 978-0-226-67874-0 pa; 0-226-67874-1 pa

LC 2007-49486

This book "assembles anecdotes from colleagues such as marine biologists, geologists and engineers. Their tales range from divers chasing parrotfish poo with plastic bags to oceanographers seeing an actual step in the surface of the sea at the edge of the Gulf Stream. In bringing these briny tales together, Prager explores some of their common themes to convey why many of us study the ocean—and why it matters." Times Higher Ed

Includes bibliographical references

Roberts, Callum

The **ocean** of life; the fate of man and the sea. Callum Roberts. Viking 2012 405 p. paperback $17; hardcover o.p. **551.46**
1. Ocean mining 2. Human ecology 3. Climate change 4. Marine ecology 5. Ocean -- History 6. Ocean and civilization
ISBN 9780143123484; 9780670023547; 067002354X

LC 2012000252

This book by Callum Roberts addresses how the ocean "has been used as a dumping ground while being indiscriminately overharvested." It also looks at "noise pollution, invasive species, plastic pollution, and the effects of climate change on reefs and sea levels as well as ocean acidification. . . . Roberts . . . provides . . . arguments against some of the technological 'fixes' some scientists have proposed." (Choice: Current Reviews for Academic Libraries)

Includes bibliographical references and index.

Stow, Dorrik A. V.

★ **Oceans** : an illustrated reference; [by] Dorrik Stow. University of Chicago Press 2006 256p il map $55 **551.46**
1. Ocean 2. Oceanography 3. Marine biology
ISBN 0-226-77664-6

LC 2004-55333

This "reference work presents a thorough overview of the physical, geological, chemical, and biological properties of the world's oceans. . . . [The author's] up-to-date and well-organized volume would make a valuable introduction to a huge field of knowledge." Libr J

Includes bibliographical references

Ulanski, Stan L.

The **Gulf** Stream; tiny plankton, giant bluefin, and the amazing story of the powerful river in the Atlantic. [by] Stan Ulanski. University of North Carolina Press 2008 212p il map $28; pa $22   **551.46**

    1. Gulf Stream

    ISBN 978-0-8078-3217-2; 0-8078-3217-0; 978-0-8078-8709-7 pa; 0-8078-8709-9 pa

                 LC 2008-4746

This "book provides the layperson a synopsis of the physical origin, general biology, and rich exploration history of the Gulf Stream. Ulanski . . . offers a concise, engaging blend of science and history for anyone interested in learning about the general flow dynamics, the intricate food webs, and the human use and exploitation of this vital western-boundary current of the North Atlantic Ocean." Choice

    Includes bibliographical references

Winchester, Simon

Atlantic; great sea battles, heroic discoveries, titanic storms, and a vast ocean of a million stories. Harper 2010 495p il map $27.99   **551.46**

    1. Atlantic Ocean

    ISBN 978-0-06-170258-7; 0-06-170258-7

                 LC 2010-15229

"Writing the history of the Atlantic Ocean — from tectonic labor pains to its lead role in modern European and American history — might be one of the more difficult tasks Simon Winchester has set for himself. . . . Luckily, the author comes armed with a knowledge almost as vast and deep as his subject, as well as a clever yet functional organizational scheme that divides his oceanic biography Atlantic into the seven ages of a man's life as proposed by Shakespeare. A formidable writer and storyteller, Winchester still gets distracted by the occasional unworthy anecdote or superfluous specificity, but for all the densely packed information in this work, the one thing it never becomes, quite appropriately, is dry." Entertainment Wkly

551.48   Hydrology

Montgomery, David R.

★ The **rocks** don't lie; a geologist investigates Noah's flood. David R. Montgomery. W.W. Norton 2012 320 p. (hardcover) $26.95   **551.48**

    1. Geology 2. Noah's ark 3. Creationism 4. Paleohydrology 5. Paleolimnology

    ISBN 0393082393; 9780393082395

                 LC 2012015146

In this book, geologist David R. Montgomery "offers a . . . critique of creationist worldviews (including Noah's flood) . . . , reflecting on both ancient and modern debates . . . . He admits that geologists have often stifled dissent and stubbornly rejected the idea that massive floods could have ever occurred, discounting such ideas as myths though there have, in fact, been many throughout human history." (Library Journal)

    Includes bibliographical references and index

Pielou, E. C.

Fresh water. University of Chicago Press 1998 275p il maps $24; pa $14   **551.48**

    1. Water

    ISBN 0-226-66815-0; 0-226-66816-9 pa

                 LC 97-51562

This "is a wonderful natural history of one of life's necessities, a refreshing break from grand theory and special pleading of many a science book. . . . Sometimes Pielou gets political. . . . But the mind-boggling details always hold the attention best." New Scientist

    Includes bibliographical references (p. {247}-267) and index

551.5   Meteorology

Buckley, Bruce

★ **Weather** : a visual guide; [by] Bruce Buckley, Edward J. Hopkins [and] Richard Whitaker. Firefly Books 2004 303p il maps $29.95; pa $27.95 **551.5**

    1. Weather 2. Meteorology

    ISBN 1-55297-957-1; 978-1-55297-957-0; 1-55407-430-4 pa; 978-1-55407-430-3 pa

                 LC 2004-303909

This is "a comprehensive academic resource with information and glorious color photographs on virtually every aspect of weather." SLJ

Logan, William Bryant

Air; the restless shaper of the world. William Bryant Logan. W.W. Norton & Co. 2012 416 p. (hardcover) $26.95   **551.5**

    1. Air 2. Atmosphere 3. Air pollution 4. Environmental protection 5. Air -- Social aspects

    ISBN 039306798X; 9780393067989

                 LC 2012013823

This environmental book by William Bryant Logan discusses air. "Air sustains the living. Every creature breathes to live, exchanging and changing the atmosphere. . . . Ignorance of the air is costly. The artist Eva Hesse died of inhaling her fiberglass medium. Thousands were sickened after 9/11 by supposedly 'safe' air." The author describes the scope of the atmospheric ecosystem and the importance of its preservation. (Publisher's note)

    "For everyone who has wondered just how a 747 manages to get off the ground, luxuriated in the intoxicating aroma of a bed of roses, or marveled at a tropical sunset, Logan's meticulously researched and engagingly presented treatise is a breath of, well, fresh air." Booklist

    Includes bibliographical references and index

McGuire, Bill

Waking the giant; how a changing climate triggers earthquakes, tsunamis, and volcanoes. Bill McGuire. Oxford University Press 2012 xiv, 303 p.p (acid-free paper) $29.95   **551.5**

    1. Climate change 2. Natural disasters 3. Tsunamis 4. Earthquakes 5. Volcanic eruptions 6. Climatic changes

-- Environmental aspects
ISBN 0199592268; 9780199592265

LC 2011278933

This book by Bill McGuire describes how "an astonishing transformation over the last 20,000 years has seen . . . not only a huge temperature hike but also the Earth's crust bouncing and bending in response to the melting of the great ice sheets and the filling of the ocean basins. . . . McGuire argues that now that human activities are driving climate change as rapidly as anything seen in post-glacial times, the sleeping giant beneath our feet is stirring once again." (Publisher's note)

Includes bibliographical references (p. 271-282) and index

Walker, Gabrielle

An **ocean** of air; why the wind blows and other mysteries of the atmosphere. Harcourt 2007 272p il map $25   **551.5**
1. Atmosphere
ISBN 978-0-15-101124-7; 0-15-101124-9

LC 2006-32359

The author "brings a new perspective to centuries-old stories of wonder and discovery and sheds light on the personalities of the 19th and 20th centuries who have also contributed to the world's body of knowledge. Witty and full of fascinating information, this is a captivating book." Libr J

Includes bibliographical references

Williams, Jack

★ The **AMS** weather book; the ultimate guide to America's weather. University of Chicago Press 2009 316p il map $35   **551.5**
1. Climate 2. Weather 3. Meteorology
ISBN 0-226-89898-9; 978-0-226-89898-8

LC 2008-35916

This book "provides a clearly written, profusely illustrated narrative guide to weather that affects the US. . . . Topics in this 12-chapter volume range from how rainbows are formed and what makes the wind blow, to climate change and how weather satellites work. In addition, Williams highlights profiles of meteorologists and other scientists influential in weather prediction and research, including many women and minorities. This work, with its attractive, easy-to-understand graphics, offers a useful, engaging basic introduction to a wide variety of weather-related topics." Choice

Includes glossary

551.51   Composition, regions, dynamics of atmosphere

Bowen, Mark

Thin ice; unlocking the secrets of climate in the world's highest mountains. Henry Holt 2005 463p il $30; pa $17   **551.51**
1. Upper atmosphere 2. Climate -- Research
ISBN 0-8050-6443-5; 0-8050-8135-6 pa

LC 2005-40426

The author "documents the specialized techniques that Thompson used to extract and preserve ice cores from the highest mountains around the world's equator while also examining Thompson's research, which is based on the provocative premise that equatorial mountain glaciers, rather than polar ice, provide the clues to understanding global warming." Libr J

"This book will appeal to mountaineering and climatology buffs, but should be read by everyone concerned about the future of our planet." Publ Wkly

551.55   Atmospheric disturbances and formations

Emanuel, Kerry A.

★ **Divine** wind; the history and science of hurricanes. [by] Kerry Emanuel. Oxford Univ. Press 2005 285p il $45   **551.55**
1. Hurricanes
ISBN 0-19-514941-6

LC 2004-13078

This is a study of hurricanes.
"A gripping popular treatment of peril, that will have great resonance in light of recent disasters." Booklist
Includes bibliographical references

Sandlin, Lee

★ **Storm** kings; the untold history of America's first tornado chasers. Lee Sandlin. Pantheon Books 2013 xxv, 266 p., [16] p. of platesp ill., maps (hardcover) $26.95   **551.55**
1. Tornadoes 2. Storm chasers
ISBN 0307378527; 9780307378521

LC 2012027314

This book, by Lee Sandlin, "explores America's fascination with and unique relationship to tornadoes. . . . Drawing on memoirs, letters, eyewitness testimonies, and archives, Sandlin brings to life the forgotten characters and scientists who changed a nation--including James Espy, America's first meteorologist, and Colonel John Park Finley, who helped place a network of weather 'spotters' across the country." (Publisher's note)

551.56   Atmospheric electricity and optics

Bogard, Paul

The **end** of night; searching for natural darkness in an age of artificial light. Paul Bogard. Little, Brown and Co. 2013 336 p. $27   **551.56**
1. Sky 2. Light 3. Night 4. Light pollution 5. Lighting -- Social aspects 6. Night -- Psychological aspects 7. Lighting -- Physiological aspects
ISBN 0316182907; 9780316182904

LC 2012027287

Author Paul Bogard presents a "blend of environmental and cultural history . . . about light pollution. As he travels the world looking for dark spaces that best reveal the night skies, Bogard considers our affinity for artificial light, the false sense of security it provides, and its implications. He studies the skies of Las Vegas and Paris, Walden Pond and Mantua, Italy. He walks with lighting designers, naturalists, and astronomers while pondering the best way to embrace the night." (Booklist)

"In this artful blend of environmental and cultural history, Bogard manages to make a book about light pollution pure reading pleasure." Booklist

Includes bibliographical references

551.57   Hydrometeorology

Hamblyn, Richard

The **invention** of clouds; how an amateur meteorologist forged the language of the skies. Picador 2002 292p il pa $15   **551.57**
1. Clouds 2. Chemists 3. Meteorology 4. Meteorologists
ISBN 0-312-42001-3; 978-0-312-42001-7
LC 2002-25152

First published 2001 by Farrar, Straus and Giroux

This is a study of Luke Howard, an unknown amateur scientist who in 1802 "gave a lecture in which he named and defined the different types of clouds-cirrus, cumulus, stratus and their various hybrid forms. . . . [His taxonomy] gave scientists a standardised way to record and compare observations and begin to form theories." Economist

"A remarkable, remarkably pleasing story." Booklist

Includes bibliographical references

551.6   Climatology and weather

DeBuys, William Eno

A **great** aridness; climate change and the future of the American southwest. [by] William deBuys. Oxford University Press 2011 369p il map   **551.6**
1. Droughts 2. Water supply 3. Southwestern States 4. Climate -- Environmental aspects
ISBN 978-0-19-977892-8
LC 2011033298

The author discusses "the untenable water situation in the Southwest. . . . While he focuses on the environmental science of heat and aridity, he also acknowledges the uncertain nature of climate variability itself. . . . With wide-eyed wonder and the clearest of prose, deBuys explains why we should care about these places, the people he portrays, and the conundrums over land and water he illuminates." Booklist

Includes bibliographical references

Dow, Kirstin, 1963-

The **atlas** of climate change; mapping the world's greatest challenge. Kirstin Dow and Thomas E. Downing. 3rd edition University of California Press 2011 128 p. col. ill., col. maps pbk $24.95   **551.6**
1. Atlases 2. Climate 3. Reference books
ISBN 9780520268234
LC 2011922284

First published 2006

"This atlas examines the causes of climate change and considers its possible impact on subsistence, water resources, ecosystems, biodiversity, health, coastal megacities, and cultural treasures. It reviews historical contributions

to greenhouse gas levels, progress in meeting international commitments, and local efforts to meet the challenge of climate change." Publisher's note

Includes bibliographical references

Dumanoski, Dianne

★ The **end** of the long summer; why we must remake our civilization to survive on a volatile Earth. Crown Publishers 2009 311p $25   **551.6**
1. Climate -- Environmental aspects
ISBN 978-0-307-39607-5; 0-307-39607-X
LC 2009-281272

An environmental journalist discusses the possible ecological consequences beyond global warming resulting from modern human activity and describes the possibility of massive instability and climate swings, including a possible return to ice ages of the past.

"A passionate, precise account of climate change and a persuasive strategy for dealing with 'Nature's return to center stage as a critical player in human history.'" Kirkus

Includes bibliographical references

Fagan, Brian M.

The **long** summer: how climate changed civilization. Basic Books 2003 284p il hardcover o.p. pa $16   **551.6**
1. Climate 2. Civilization -- History
ISBN 0-465-02281-2; 0-465-02282-0 pa
LC 2003-13917

Fagan discusses global climate change and its relation to human society. He "argues that as humans have organized themselves in increasingly complex ways, their susceptibility to large-scale devastation wrought by climate change has also risen. Ice Age hunter-gatherers were vulnerable to the vagaries of their harsh world, but they had a 'flexibility, mobility, and opportunism' that allowed them to move on if their immediate environment became too difficult. As people formed villages, cities, and empires, they became rooted to environments that inevitably changed." Archaeology

"This book is highly recommended for general audiences considering the implications and the challenges posed by human-induced global climate change." Sci Books Films

Includes bibliographical references

Fleming, James Rodger

Fixing the sky; the checkered history of weather and climate control. [by] James Rodger Fleming. Columbia University Press 2010 325p il (Columbia studies in international and global history) $27.95   **551.6**
1. Global warming 2. Weather control 3. Human influence on nature 4. Climatic changes
ISBN 978-0-231-14412-4
LC 2010-15482

This is a "look at the history of weather modification and similar efforts." N Y Times (Late N Y Ed)

This book "should be read by all who want a better understanding of global climate change and the debate over geoengineering our environment." Sci Books Films

Includes bibliographical references

Fry, Juliane L.

The **encyclopedia** of weather and climate change; a complete visual guide. [authors, Juliane L. Fry ... [et al.] University of California Press 2010 512 p. col. ill., col. maps **551.6**

1. Reference books 2. Weather -- Encyclopedias 3. Climatology -- Encyclopedias 4. Meteorology -- Encyclopedias 5. Climatic changes -- Encyclopedias

ISBN 0520261011; 9780520261013

LC 2009943908

"Major sections fall under the following headings: Engine, Action, Extremes, Watching, Climate, and Change. Chapters within the sections begin with a broad overview of a particular topic, then move on to greater detail. The regional climate guide, focusing on 43 specific locations around the world, is particularly noteworthy. . . . The profuse illustrations carry the information; this title could be just the thing for visual learners." Libr J

Includes index.

Goodell, Jeff

How to cool the planet; geoengineering and the audacious quest to fix Earth's climate. Houghton Mifflin Harcourt 2010 262p $26 **551.6**

1. Greenhouse effect 2. Climate -- Environmental aspects

ISBN 978-0-618-99061-0; 0-618-99061-5

LC 2009-46565

"There is no trace of climate alarmism or political advocacy here. Goodell takes a detailed look at the range of hard choices humanity faces and explores how complicated moral and ethical considerations will dictate our response. Goodell is also a skilled writer. He splices complicated ideas into pithy turns of phrase." Business Week

Includes bibliographical references

Linden, Eugene

The **winds** of change; climate, weather, and the destruction of civilizations. Simon & Schuster 2006 302p il map $26 **551.6**

1. Climate 2. Weather 3. Social change

ISBN 0-684-86352-9; 978-0-684-86352-8

LC 2005-54434

The author argues that there is "a recurring pattern in which civilizations become prosperous and complacent during good weather, only to collapse when climate changes— either through its direct effects, such as floods or drought, or indirect consequences, such as disease, blight, and civil disorder." Publisher's note

"Relatively restrained in tone, and consequently more persuasive by its sobriety, Linden's presentation of scientists' theories on historical climate change will provoke readers concerned about the implications of global warming for modern civilization." Booklist

Ludlum, David M.

The **Audubon** Society field guide to North American weather. Knopf 1991 656p il maps $19.95 **551.6**

1. Weather forecasting

ISBN 0-679-40851-7

LC 91-52707

"The opening essays provide in-depth information on topics such as clouds, snowstorms, floods, etc. About half of the book is comprised of labelled, high-quality photographs. The third section gives description, environment, season, range, and significance of each type of weather. Clear diagrams, simple definitions, and a readable text make this an excellent selection." SLJ

Lynas, Mark

★ **Six** degrees; our future on a hotter planet. National Geographic 2008 335p $26 **551.6**

1. Environmental influence on humans 2. Greenhouse effect 3. Climate -- Environmental aspects

ISBN 978-1-4262-0213-1

LC 2007-30864

First published 2007 in the United Kingdom

"In 2001, the Intergovernmental Panel on Climate Change released a landmark report projecting average global surface temperatures to rise between 1.4 degrees and 5.8 degrees Celsius (roughly 2 to 10 degrees Fahrenheit) by the end of this century. Based on this forecast, author Mark Lynas outlines what to expect from a warming world, degree by degree." Publisher's note

Includes bibliographical references

Pearce, Fred

With speed and violence; why scientists fear tipping points in climate change. Beacon Press 2007 xxvi, 278p $24.95; pa $15 **551.6**

1. Greenhouse effect 2. Climate -- Environmental aspects

ISBN 978-0-8070-8576-9; 0-8070-8576-6; 978-0-8070-8577-6 pa; 0-8070-8577-4 pa

LC 2006-19901

The author "covers many ways in which the climate could change dramatically within years or decades." Choice

"Important reading for policymakers, climate-change skeptics and anyone planning a future beyond the next decade." Kirkus

Includes bibliographical references

Weart, Spencer R.

★ The **discovery** of global warming; Spencer R. Weart. Rev. and expanded ed. Harvard University Press 2008 x, 230 p.p il pbk $21 **551.6**

ISBN 9780674031890

LC 2008013675

The author "reports the history of global warming theory, including the internal conflicts plaguing the research community and the role government has had in promoting climate studies. . . . Without resorting to fear-mongering, Weart gives an informed history and offers his readers solutions to consider." Publ Wkly

551.63 Weather forecasting and forecasts, reporting and reports

Cullen, Heidi

The **weather** of the future; heat waves, extreme storms, and other scenes from a climate-changed

planet. HarperCollins 2010 329p il map $25.99;
pa $15.99   **551.63**
  1. Forecasting 2. Climate -- Environmental aspects
  ISBN 978-0-06-172688-0; 0-06-172688-5; 978-0-06-
  172694-1 pa; 0-06-172694-X pa
  "A lively and troubling but not entirely doomsday scenario of our warmer future, which will hopefully persuade
readers to pay greater attention." Kirkus
  Includes bibliographical references

Monmonier, Mark S.
  Air apparent; how meteorologists learned to
map, predict, and dramatize weather. {by} Mark
Monmonier. University of Chicago Press 1999 309p
il $27.50; pa $17   **551.63**
  1. Meteorology 2. Weather forecasting
  ISBN 0-226-53422-7; 0-226-53423-5 pa
                                    LC 98-25797
  The author presents a "history of more than 200 years
of weather maps, an account that embraces technological
advances from the telegraph and mercury barometer to the
satellite and Doppler radar." Booklist
  Includes index

551.69   Geographic treatment of climate

Tape, Ken D.
  The **changing** arctic landscape; Ken D. Tape.
University of Alaska Press 2010 viii, 56p ill. (some
col.), col. maps (cloth : alk. paper) $35.00   **551.69**
  1. Alaska 2. Arctic regions 3. Climate change 4.
Alaska -- Climate 5. Alaska -- Environmental conditions
-- Pictorial works 6. Climatic changes -- Environmental
aspects -- Alaska -- Pictorial works
  ISBN 9781602230804; 1602230803
                                    LC 2009035478
  It was the author's intent to demonstrate "how the work
of several generations of earth scientists can be integrated
into a picture of arctic Alaska landscapes that are responding
to both natural and human influences. Decades-old photos
from pioneering studies of the geology, vegetation, glaciers,
and landforms of Brooks Range and North Slope were used
to select specific environments for change detection. . . .
The author concludes that the changes are consisted with a
warming climate, but the argument for warming is not as
solid as the argument for the changes themselves." (Environment)
  Includes bibliographical references and index.

551.7   Historical geology

Alvarez, Walter
  T. rex and the Crater of Doom. Princeton Univ.
Press 1997 185p il $35   **551.7**
  1. Dinosaurs 2. Catastrophes (Geology)
  ISBN 0-691-01630-5
                                    LC 96-49208
  The author relates the story of how he "along with four
other Berkeley scientists, found the geologic evidence that

implicated a cosmic collision in the extinction of the dinosaurs. . . . {Their research involved} the evaluation of a thin
iridium-rich layer of clay found in Italy and the search for an
impact crater." Booklist
  This book "gets the facts across in a lighthearted, almost
playful manner. But it's also solid science, a clear and efficient exposition." N Y Times Book Rev
  Includes bibliographical references

Bjornerud, Marcia
  Reading the rocks; the autobiography of the
earth. Basic Books 2005 237p $26   **551.7**
  1. Geology
  ISBN 0-8133-4249-X
                                    LC 2004-22738
  In this "volume of pop-geology, . . . Bjornerud chronicles the watersheds in Earth's history from the primordial
supernova that seeded the nascent solar nebula to the man-
made cataclysms of global warming and habitat destruction." Publ Wkly
  "This wonderful book should be examined by anyone
with a curiosity about the natural history of our planet and
how one science in particular has done such an impressive
job of deciphering key mysteries of its origin and evolution."
Sci Books Films
  Includes bibliographical references

Fortey, Richard A.
  ★ **Earth**; an intimate history. by Richard Fortey.
Knopf 2004 429p il hardcover o.p. pa $19   **551.7**
  1. Stratigraphic geology
  ISBN 0-375-40626-3; 0-375-70620-8 pa
                                    LC 2004-46470
  The author "relates his walks in places that visually reveal the deep earth (Vesuvius, Hawaii, the Grand Canyon) as
well as sites, which, if not so spectacular, contain puzzling
elements that provoked great interpretive controversies. . . .
The Alps, the Scottish Highlands, Newfoundland, the Dec-
can Traps of India—these are among Fortey's destinations
as he explains the theory of plate tectonics, showing how
the theory came to be, as well as the continents and oceans
whose skein of connections it explains. This is a marvelously inviting presentation." Booklist
  Includes bibliographical references

Hancock, Graham
  Underworld : the mysterious origins of civilization; photographs by Santha Faiia. Crown 2002
769p il maps $27.50; pa $16.95   **551.7**
  1. Prehistoric peoples 2. Ancient civilization 3.
Stratigraphic geology
  ISBN 1-4000-4612-2; 1-4000-4951-2 pa
  The author presents theories on how "civilization rose
about 17,000 years ago (rather than about 6,000) and vanished beneath a rising sea level, leaving its traces in flood
myths in Sumerian and Vedic texts, in early maps of the Age
of Discovery, and more plausibly, in submerged ruins. Hancock throws up a fantastic amount of data on these points in
this work, ranging from his personal textual interpretations
to his dives at coastal sites in Malta, India, Japan, and the
Bahamas." Booklist
  Includes bibliographical references

Macdougall, J. D.

 Frozen earth; the once and future story of ice ages. [by] Doug Macdougall. University of California Press 2004 256p il $24.95; pa $15.95   **551.7**
   1. Ice Age
   ISBN 0-520-23922-9; 0-520-24824-4 pa
                             LC 2004-8502
   The author "presents the scientific history behind ice ages, emphasizing the roles of four great scientists in the field: Louis Agassiz, James Croll, Milutin Milankovitch, and Harlan Bretz. . . . Macdougall's account promotes a welcome reasoning attitude toward ice-age research and its relevance to global warming." Booklist
   Includes bibliographical references

 Nature's clocks; how scientists measure the age of almost everything. University of California Press 2008 271p il $40; pa $17.95   **551.7**
   1. Geochronometry 2. Geological time 3. Radiocarbon dating 4. Radioisotopes in geology
   ISBN 978-0-520-24975-2; 978-0-520-26161-7 pa
                           LC 2007-46955
   The author "looks at fixed dating via decay rates of radioactive isotopes of carbon, uranium, and potassium. He examines relational dating via dendrochronology, ice cores, and stratigraphy. And he tells the stories of the scientists who teased out these techniques with excruciating patience." Libr J
   "Rich in historical titbits, this book is a delightful study of how scientists figured out analytical techniques that revealed the history of the Earth." New Sci
   Includes bibliographical references

 A **short** history of planet earth; mountains, mammals, fire, and ice. Wiley 1996 266p il maps (Wiley popular science) hardcover o.p. pa $16.95   **551.7**
   1. Stratigraphic geology 2. Life -- Origin
   ISBN 0-471-19703-3 pa
                            LC 95-46399
   In "this survey of four-and-a-half billion years of Earth's past . . . MacDougall traces the rise of continents and the origins of life in each era. He discusses tectonic plates, the major extinctions and their probable causes, climate and the Ice Ages, and he speculates on the future of our planet. To compress Earth's history into a single, lucidly written volume is a major achievement." Publ Wkly
   Includes bibliographical references

Richet, Pascal

 A **natural** history of time; translated by John Venerella. University of Chicago Press 2007 471p il $29   **551.7**
   1. Geological time 2. Earth -- Age
   ISBN 978-0-226-71287-1; 0-226-71287-7
                           LC 2006-33992
   Original French edition, 1999
   "How old is the Earth? Mr. Richet sets out to explore humanity's attempts to answer this most perplexing of questions, which acted as a spur and a baffle to human ingenuity for 2,500 years. . . . The book is translated from the French—capably, considering how much scientific terminology it contains, but not gracefully—and . . . can be rough going.

Still, 'A Natural History of Time' more that repays the effort it requires. Not only does it shed light on key advances in the history of science, from the ancient Greeks to the X-ray, it reminds us of the real heroism and nobility of the scientific enterprise." N Y Sun

Seeley, Thomas D.

 Honeybee democracy. Princeton University Press 2010 273p $29.95   **551.7**
   1. Bees 2. Democracy 3. Honeybee -- Behavior
   ISBN 978-0-691-14721-5
                           LC 2010-10265
   "In the late spring and early summer, as a bee colony becomes overcrowded, a third of the hive stays behind and rears a new queen, while a swarm of thousands departs with the old queen to produce a daughter colony. Seeley describes how these bees evaluate potential nest sites, advertise their discoveries to one another, engage in open deliberation, choose a final site, and navigate together—as a swirling cloud of bees—to their new home. Seeley investigates how evolution has honed the decision-making methods of honeybees over millions of years, and he considers similarities between the ways that bee swarms and primate brains process information." Publisher's note
   Seeley's "enthusiasm and admiration for honeybees is infectious. His accumulated research seems truly masterly, doing for bees what E. O. Wilson did for ants." N Y Times Book Rev
   Includes bibliographical references

552   Petrology

Coenraads, Robert Raymond

 Rocks and fossils; a visual guide. [by] Robert R. Coenraads. Firefly Books 2005 304p il $29.95 **552**
   1. Rocks 2. Fossils 3. Minerals
   ISBN 1-55407-068-6
   In this "introduction to geology and paleontology . . . [the author presents the] facts of how fossils are formed, how rocks are formed, and how plate tectonics work. . . . A science work perfectly suited for general use." Booklist

553.6   Other economic materials

Kurlansky, Mark

 ★ **Salt** : a world history. Penguin Books 2003 484p il map pa $16   **553.6**
   1. Salt
   ISBN 0-14-200161-9
                           LC 2004-270006
   First published 2002 by Walker & Co.
   "Throughout his engaging, well-researched history, Kurlansky sprinkles witty asides and amusing anecdotes. A piquant blend of the historic, political, commercial, scientific and culinary, the book is sure to entertain as well as educate." Publ Wkly
   Includes bibliographical references

Welland, Michael

Sand; the never-ending story. University of California Press 2009 343p il map $24.95   **553.6**
1. Sand
ISBN 978-0-520-25437-4

LC 2008-9084

The author "discusses the science, geology, and cultural significance of sand as a critical ingredient in so many aspects of our lives. Learn about arenophiles, sand forensics, extraterrestrial sand, Udden-Wentworth scale, Bagnold formula, and how sand shapes our environment. . . . Anyone who has walked on a beach, run up a sand dune, or built a sand castle will be fascinated by this excellent book." Libr J

Includes bibliographical references

553.7   Water

Fagan, Brian

Elixir; a history of water and humankind. Brian Fagan. 1st U.S. ed. Bloomsbury Press 2011 384 p. ill., maps $28   **553.7**
1. Water supply 2. Drinking water 3. Water -- History 4. Water and civilization -- History 5. Water -- Social aspects -- History
ISBN 160819003X (alk. paper); 9781608190034 (alk. paper)

LC 2010032082

Author Brian Fagan presents "anecdotes and historical episodes showing how pre-industrial people . . . properly appreciated water, from the San hunters of the Kalahari, who see the whole world as a sometimes grudging source of the substance, to John Wesley Powell's efforts to create political divisions in the American West not based on surveyors' straight lines but on natural watersheds." (Kirkus ReviewS)

"Supplying intriguing historical background, Fagan well informs those pondering freshwater's role in contemporary environmental problems." Booklist

Includes bibliographical references and index.

Kandel, Robert S.

★ Water from heaven; the story of water from the big bang to the rise of civilization, and beyond. [by] Robert Kandel. Columbia Univ. Press 2003 311p il maps $29.95; pa $24   **553.7**
1. Water
ISBN 0-231-12244-6; 0-231-12245-4 pa

LC 2002-31229

Original French edition, 1998

The author "explains the earth's elaborate and essential-to-life water cycle . . . beginning cosmologically with the birth of the solar system and an analysis of various theories as to where the earth's water . . . originated." Booklist

"While dense with facts and figures, Kandel's aquatic history is riveting, an exhaustive and complex examination of our most precious chemical compound." Publ Wkly

Includes bibliographical references

Solomon, Steven

Water; the epic struggle for wealth, power, and civilization. Harper 2010 596p il map   **553.7**
1. Water 2. World history 3. Water and civilization 4. Water-supply -- Government policy
ISBN 0060548304; 9780060548308

LC 2009-27500

This is "a narrative account of how water has shaped human society from the ancient past to the present." (Publisher's note) Bibliography. Index.

"Solomon's unprecedented inquiry into the history, science, and politics of water use provides fascinating and ample testimony to the need to place a higher value on water and its preservation." Booklist

Includes bibliographical references

553.8   Gems

Hart, Matthew

Diamond : a journey to the heart of an obsession. Walker & Co. 2001 276p il maps $26 **553.8**
1. Diamonds
ISBN 0-8027-1368-8

LC 2001-26348

Hart's "account of the glittering business of mining and marketing diamonds is also a story of avarice, theft, aesthetics, monopoly, and war. A thoroughly entrancing book." Booklist

Includes bibliographical references

Oldershaw, Cally

★ Firefly guide to gems. Firefly Bks. 2004 224p il map $14.95   **553.8**
1. Gems 2. Precious stones
ISBN 1-55297-814-1

This book "opens with extensive introductory material including history, various properties, and lore. Then, each gem is presented with text and charts of specific chemical properties. While most gems are discussed on a single page, some that are well known have longer articles." SLJ

Zoellner, Tom

The heartless stone; a journey through the world of diamonds, deceit, and desire. St. Martins Press 2006 293p map hardcover o.p. pa $16 **553.8**
1. Diamonds
ISBN 0-312-33969-0; 978-0-312-33969-2; 0-312-33970-4 pa; 978-0-312-33970-8 pa

LC 2005-33037

The author "probes how 'blood diamonds' are used to fund vicious civil wars in Africa; how De Beers, seeing new markets to exploit, linked diamonds to the ancient yuino ceremony in Japan and played on caste obsession in India; and how India is pushing Belgium and Israel out of the gem trade. . . . This is a superior piece of reportage." Publ Wkly

Includes bibliographical references

557 Earth sciences of North America

McPhee, John A.

    Annals of the former world; [by] John McPhee. Farrar, Straus & Giroux 1998 695p maps $35; pa $20   **557**

  1. Geology -- United States

  ISBN 0-374-10520-0; 0-374-51873-4 pa

                    LC 97-39660

  This volume combines edited and revised sections from Basin and range (1981), In suspect terrain (1983), Rising from the plains (1986), and Assembling California (1993), with two new essays

  "As in any McPhee work, there are gemlike sentences, richly rhythmic paragraphs, nicely burnished synecdoches, metaphors as pungent as wasabi and, behind those felicities, vast amounts of painstaking research." N Y Times Book Rev

559.9 Earth sciences of extraterrestrial worlds

Sykes, Bryan

    DNA USA; a genetic portrait of America. Bryan Sykes. Liveright Pub. Corp. 2012 369 p.   **559.9**

  1. Genetics 2. Genealogy 3. Chromosomes 4. DNA fingerprinting 5. United States -- Population 6. Human genetics -- Popular works 7. Human population genetics -- United States -- Popular works

  ISBN 0871404125; 9780871404121

                  LC 2011053182

  In this book, "America's gorgeous mosaic emerges from its DNA in this . . . treatise on genetics and genealogy. Oxford geneticist [Bryan] Sykes . . . traveled across the United States collecting DNA samples, recording family histories. . . . The resulting 'chromosomal portraits,' painted by analyzing markers that correlate with African, European, or Asian-Native American populations, reveal DNA tell-tales of unsuspected centuries-old migrations and mixings: Mexican-American Catholics descended from Spanish Jews; white Southerners with substantial African-American ancestry; possible journeys from Europe to North America 10,000 years ago, Sykes gives . . . explanations of new genetic techniques and their startling success at tracing familial ties across continents and millennia." (Publishers Weekly)

  Includes bibliographical references and index

560 Paleontology

Fortey, Richard A.

    ★ **Fossils**; the key to the past. [by] Richard Fortey. 3rd ed; Smithsonian Institution Press 2002 232p il maps $55; pa $27.50   **560**

  1. Fossils

  ISBN 1-58834-023-6; 1-58834-048-1 pa

                  LC 2001-49439

  First published 1982 by Van Nostrand Reinhold

  In this volume, fossils "from earliest Precambrian forms onward are discussed, emphasizing evolutionary trends and extinctions, and relationships with habitat environments and geologic processes, such as volcanism and meteorite impacts, are evaluated. . . . Aspects of preservation, discovery,

collection, and identification are discussed." Choice {review of 1991 edition}

  Includes bibliographical references

    Trilobite! eyewitness to evolution. by Richard Fortey. Knopf 2000 284p il $26; pa $14   **560**

  1. Fossils 2. Evolution

  ISBN 0-375-40625-5; 0-375-70621-6 pa

                  LC 00-34908

  The author's "unabashed trilobite-centric view of the evolution of life on Earth is full of personal anecdotes and asides, but it's also full of excellent science." Libr J

  Includes bibliographical references

Poinar, George O.

    The **quest** for life in amber; {by} George and Roberta Poinar. Addison-Wesley 1994 219p il hardcover o.p. pa $18   **560**

  1. Amber 2. Fossils

  ISBN 0-201-48928-7

                  LC 94-3043

  This is an account of the authors' search for and work with amber, a fossilized resin. The Poinars also include details of their scientific analyses of the insects trapped within this host material

  This is "one of those books that educates the general reader about a scientific topic without requiring very much scientific background. Although educational, it is also highly entertaining and should be read for pleasure as much as for knowledge." Choice

  Includes bibliographical references

Rea, Tom

    Bone wars; the excavation and celebrity of Andrew Carnegie's dinosaur. University of Pittsburgh Press 2001 276p il hc o.p.; pa $16   **560**

  1. Fossils 2. Dinosaurs 3. Philanthropists 4. Metal industry executives

  ISBN 0-8229-4173-2; 9780822958468

                  LC 2001-3336

  This describes the history of the excavation of the dinosaur fossil Diplodocus carnegii in 1899 which was financed by Andrew Carnegie

  "Rea pieces together countless bits of information to construct an overall picture of this period of scientific discovery." Booklist

  Includes bibliographical references and index

Thompson, Ida

    ★ The **Audubon** Society field guide to North American fossils; with photographs by Townsend P. Dickinson; visual key by Carol Nehring. Knopf 1982 846p il maps flexible bdg $19.95   **560**

  1. Fossils

  ISBN 0-394-52412-8

                  LC 81-84772

  "This softbound field guide to fossils is divided into a section of color photographs followed by a section of detailed descriptions. It covers 420 fossils of marine and freshwater invertebrates, insects, plants, and vertebrates that are likely to be found by the amateur." Malinowsky. Best Sci & Technol Ref Books for Young People

Travels with the fossil hunters;   edited by Peter Whybrow. Cambridge Univ. Press 2000 211p il $40   **560**
1. Fossils 2. Scientists
ISBN 0-521-66301-6

LC 99-30134

A collection of essays by paleontologists from London's Natural History Museum describing their work in such places as China, India, the Sahara, Latvia, and Antarctica

"The essayists give enough details of their quests to explain their presence in these places and keep science buffs entertained. . . . Heightening the impact of the stories is an abundance of beautiful, colorful photos of the places, the people, and the fossils." SLJ

Wallace, David Rains
The **bonehunters'** revenge; dinosaurs, greed, and the greatest scientific feud of the gilded age. Houghton Mifflin 1999 366p il $25; pa $14   **560**
1. Fossils 2. Zoologists 3. Paleontologists
ISBN 0-395-85089-4; 0-618-08240-9 pa

LC 99-31904

This is an account of the rivalry between 19th century paleontologists Edward Drinker Cope and Othniel Charles Marsh.

"This curious century-old feud comes alive with momentum and understanding in Wallace's skillful hands." Booklist
Includes bibliographical references

567.9   Reptiles

★ **Dinosaurs**; edited by John J. Meier. H.W. Wilson Co. 2011 221p il (Reference shelf) pa $55   **567.9**
1. Dinosaurs
ISBN 978-0-8242-1107-3

LC 2011007540

A collection of articles discussing dinosaurs "from their origins and evolution to their much-debated extinction. . . . Coverage includes . . . background information distilled from the fossil record as well as more speculative and theoretical material." Publisher's note
Includes bibliographical references

Fiffer, Steve
Tyrannosaurus Sue; the extraordinary saga of the largest, most fought over T. rex ever found. foreword by Robert T. Bakker. Freeman, W.H. 2000 248p hardcover o.p. pa $14.95   **567.9**
1. Dinosaurs 2. Paleontologists
ISBN 0-7167-9462-4 pa

LC 00-21596

In 1990 "South Dakota fossil-hunters Sue Hendrickson and Peter Larson dug up an exceptional T. rex—only the 12th tyrannosaur ever found, and the biggest and best-preserved to date. . . . The ensuing legal, political and scientific imbroglio set Native Americans against the federal government, the government against itself, the feds against established scientists and the world's great research universities against independent operators like Larson. Fiffer's thorough

account should prove irresistible to readers with even a marginal interest in the legendary lizards." Publ Wkly

Horner, John R.
How to build a dinosaur; extinction doesn't have to be forever. [by] Jack Horner and James Gorman. Dutton 2009 246p il $25.95   **567.9**
1. Dinosaurs 2. Evolution
ISBN 978-0-525-95104-9; 0-525-95104-0

LC 2008-48042

"Dinosaurs could walk the earth again within five years, says paleontologist Jack Horner. It won't happen the way it did in Jurassic Park, the novel and movie inspired in part by Horner's work. No active DNA from history's big lizards is likely ever to be found, he says. But birds carry dinosaur DNA. As embryos, they sprout the beginnings of teeth, claws, and a lizard tail before certain genes cancel and redirect that growth. Horner's dream these days is to bring out a chicken's inner dinosaur by turning off those controlling secondary genes. . . . The great value of How to Build a Dinosaur is that it illuminates how the work of paleontologists has changed in the past few decades." Week
Includes bibliographical references

Larson, Peter L.
Rex appeal; the amazing story of Sue, the dinosaur that changed science, the law, and my life. {by} Peter Larson, Kristin Donnan. Invisible Cities Press 2002 404p il $26.95   **567.9**
1. Fossils 2. Dinosaurs
ISBN 1-931229-07-4

LC 2002-24207

Larson's "team discovered the largest and most complete Tyrannosaurus rex skeleton that the world had seen. Almost immediately, however, the team . . . became embroiled in a dispute with the U.S. government about who owns the fossil, during which the skeleton was seized by the National Guard. . . . The book recounts the heated legal battles but focuses primarily on Larson's adventures in South Dakota, where his group eventually found six more T. rex fossils." Publ Wkly
Includes bibliographical references

Nothdurft, William E.
The **lost** dinosaurs of Egypt; {by} William Nothdurft with Josh Smith {et al.} Random House 2002 242p il maps $24.95; pa $13.95   **567.9**
1. Fossils 2. Dinosaurs
ISBN 0-375-50795-7; 0-375-75979-4 pa

LC 2002-75172

"Between 1910 and 1914, Ernst Stromer . . . unearthed a wealth of dinosaur fossils in Egypt's Bahariya Oasis. Thirty years later, Stromer's discoveries were destroyed in a WWII Allied bombing raid, and the oasis lay neglected for decades until Josh Smith, a Penn State doctoral candidate in paleontology, decided to retrace Stromer's footsteps in 1999. . . . {This} account highlights Stromer's discoveries . . . and chronicles recent findings by Smith and his colleagues. . . . An engaging mix of history and desert drama, this . . . is first-rate popular science." Publ Wkly

Paul, Gregory S.

The **Princeton** field guide to dinosaurs. Princeton University Press 2010 320p il map (Princeton field guides) $35 **567.9**

1. Dinosaurs

ISBN 978-0-691-13720-9; 0-691-13720-X

LC 2010-14916

"Though not a field guide to stuff in your backpack, this exciting addition to dinosaur reference is essential for high school through university libraries and is highly recommended for all students of dinosaurs." Libr J

Includes bibliographical references

Sampson, Scott D.

Dinosaur odyssey; fossil threads in the web of life. University of California Press 2009 332p il map $29.95 **567.9**

1. Fossils 2. Dinosaurs

ISBN 978-0-520-24163-3; 0-520-24163-0

LC 2009-6150

"Sampson reconstructs the odyssey of the dinosaurs from their humble origins on the supercontinent Pangaea, to their reign as the largest animals the planet has ever known, and finally to their abrupt demise." Publisher's note

"This book draws scientifically accurate pictures in a style that is accessible to researchers and general readers alike." Libr J

Includes bibliographical references

569 Fossil mammals

Lister, Adrian

★ **Mammoths**; giants of the ice age. [by] Adrian Lister and Paul Bahn; foreword by Jean M. Auel. Rev ed; University of California Press 2007 192p il $29.95 **569**

1. Mammoths

ISBN 978-0-520-25319-3; 0-520-25319-1

LC 2007-26369

First published 1994 by Macmillan

This book integrates "research to piece together the story of mammoths, mastodons, and their relatives, icons of the Ice Age." Publisher's note

Includes glossary and bibliographical references

569.9 Humans and related genera

Johanson, Donald C.

Lucy's legacy; the quest for human origins. [by] Donald Johanson and Kate Wong. Harmony Books 2009 309p il map $25 **569.9**

1. Human origins

ISBN 978-0-307-39639-6; 0-307-39639-8

LC 2008-39907

"In 1974 paleontologist Donald C. Johanson found a female skeleton 3.2 million years old that exhibited both ape and human characteristics. Johanson and Kate Wong . . . recount the stunning discovery of Lucy, and then they venture far beyond that to bring readers up-to-date on what has been

unearthed since and the implications of these new finds for what it means to be human. . . . Conversational, knowledgeable, flowing logically from one topic to the next, the book is packed with information of the kind that will be especially intriguing to general readers." Sci Am

Includes bibliographical references

Sarmiento, Esteban

★ The **last** human; a guide to twenty-two species of extinct humans. created by G.J. Sawyer and Viktor Deak; text by Esteban Sarmiento, G.J. Sawyer, Richard Milner; with contributions by Donald C. Johanson, Meave Leakey, and Ian Tattersall. Yale University Press 2006 256p il map $45 **569.9**

1. Evolution 2. Human beings 3. Fossil hominids

ISBN 978-0-300-10047-1; 0-300-10047-7

This book "covers 22 species of extinct humans, concluding with the only surviving one, Homo sapiens. . . . Provided for each is information on its emergence, chronology, geographic range, classification, physiology, environment, habitat, cultural achievements, coexisting species, and possible reasons for extinction. Summaries of fossil discoveries for each species are also provided, along with historical notes mentioning publications and controversies." Libr J

"This is fascinating stuff, not least because it drives home just how much of our knowledge about the past is based on inference." New Sci

Includes bibliographical references

Walter, Chip

Last ape standing; the seven-million year story of how and why we survived. Chip Walter. Walker & Co. 2013 240 p. $17; $26 **569.9**

1. Evolution 2. Human origins 3. Fossil hominids 4. Human evolution 5. Primates -- Evolution

ISBN 9781620405215; 080271756X; 9780802717566

LC 2012037484

In this book, Chip Walter considers human evolution. He "argues that neotony, 'the retention of juvenile features in the adult animal,' is most responsible for differences between humans and other hominids. . . . In the end, Walter posits that the next evolutionary step might be Cyber sapiens: immortal superhuman hybrids of humans and machines." (Publishers Weekly)

"An exceptionally well-written overview of man's evolutionary history as well as an accessible guide to the underappreciated field of paleoanthropology." Booklist

Includes bibliographical references and index

570 Biology

Gould, Stephen Jay, 1941-2002

An **urchin** in the storm; essays about books and ideas. Norton 1987 255p il hardcover o.p. pa $11.95 **570**

1. Biology

ISBN 0-393-30537-6 pa

LC 87-21718

This collection of Gould's book reviews is arranged in broad subject areas: evolutionary theory, biological determinism, time and geology.

Wilson, Edward O., 1929-

★ **Letters** to a Young Scientist; by Edward O. Wilson. Liveright 2013 256 p. $21.95   **570**

1. Science -- Vocational guidance 2. Observation (Scientific method) 3. Biologists -- United States -- Correspondence 4. Naturalists -- United States -- Correspondence
ISBN 0871403773; 9780871403773

LC 2012051412

In this book, author Edward O. Wilson "draws on the experiences of a long career to offer encouraging advice to those considering a life in science. . . . After a prologue in which the author assures would-be scientists of their importance in our technoscientific world, he groups 20 letters into five sections. . . . In Part II, 'The Creative Process,' Wilson discusses the nature of science, the scientific method, how scientists think creatively and what it takes to succeed." (Kirkus Reviews)

"In five thematic sections, he presents 20 "letters" (five-to ten-plus pages each) examining the scientist's role in the 21st century, the foundations and credos that remain in place, and the manner in which the field has changed...Although the title and small format may suggest the book as a gift for graduates, it ought to be on the shelves of all high school and public libraries, as well as some undergraduate collections." (Library Journal)

570.1   Philosophy and theory

Bulletproof feathers; how science uses nature's secrets to design cutting-edge technology. edited by Robert Allen. University of Chicago Press 2010 192p il $35   **570.1**

1. Robots 2. Bionics
ISBN 978-0-226-01470-8

LC 2009037097

This book "is a fascinating introduction to the field of biomimetics, or bionics. Biomimetics refers to efforts to understand the design and complexity of natural, biological systems and the application of this knowledge to achieve useful new technologies. . . . This book, beautifully illustrated with many real-world examples and explanatory diagrams, will be a joy to read for any fan of science and technology." Choice

Includes bibliographical references

Capra, Fritjof

The **web** of life; a new scientific understanding of living systems. Anchor Bks. (NY) 1996 347p il hardcover o.p. pa $14.95   **570.1**

1. System theory 2. Life (Biology)
ISBN 0-385-47676-0 pa

LC 96-12576

This discourse on the life sciences incorporates "elements from such contemporary schools of thought as the Gaia hypothesis, deep ecology, complexity theory, systems theory, and . . . eco-feminism." Libr J

This is "a rewarding synthesis that will challenge serious readers." Publ Wkly
Includes bibliographical references

Lovelock, James

The **ages** of Gaia; a biography of our living earth. Norton 1988 xx, 252p il hardcover o.p. pa $13.95   **570.1**

1. Biosphere 2. Life (Biology) 3. Gaia hypothesis 4. Biology -- Philosophy
ISBN 0-393-31239-9 pa

LC 87-36567

"Gaia is the Greek goddess of the earth. For James Lovelock she is the embodiment of a hypothesis: the earth is not merely the abode of life but is a single living organism. He proposes that all living species are components of that organism, as cells are components of the human body." N Y Times Book Rev
Includes bibliographical references

Margulis, Lynn

What is life? foreword by Niles Eldredge. University of California Press 2000 288p il pa $24.95   **570.1**

1. Life (Biology) 2. Life -- Origin 3. Biological diversity 4. Biology -- Philosophy
ISBN 0-520-22021-8

LC 00-25833

First published 1995 by Simon & Schuster

"Continuing Margulis's contention that organelles within cells, such as mitochondria, were originally free-living organisms that fused with others to form complex cells and bodies, the authors extend this concept to the Earth as a superorganism. Although following traditional evolutionary pathways, the authors argue that life has played a role in its own evolution." Choice
Includes bibliographical references

Thomas, Lewis

The **lives** of a cell; notes of a biology watcher. Viking 1974 153p hardcover o.p. pa $13   **570.1**

1. Biology -- Philosophy
ISBN 0-14-004743-3 pa

In this collection of twenty-nine short essays "the author does not confine his scientist's eye to a microscope. He takes a much wider view of the world, looking at insect behavior and the possibility of intelligent life in outer space or bird songs and the evolution of language. He also offers a modest proposal for saving ourselves from nuclear self-destruction." Time
Includes bibliographical references

Yoon, Carol Kaesuk

Naming nature; the clash between instinct and science. W.W. Norton 2009 344p il $27.95   **570.1**

1. Names 2. Biology -- Classification
ISBN 978-0-393-06197-0; 0-393-06197-3

LC 2009-14332

This is "a wondrous history of taxonomy—the science of ordering and naming living things—and how it has disconnected us from the natural world. . . . Yoon is an outstanding science writer who takes a seemingly dull topic and rivets unsuspecting readers to the page. Superb." Kirkus

Includes bibliographical references

571 Internal biological processes and structures

Roach, Mary, 1959-

★ **Packing** for Mars; the curious science of life in the void. W.W. Norton 2010 334p il **571**

1. Space biology

ISBN 0-393-06847-1; 978-0-393-06847-4

LC 2010-17113

This book examines space travel and life without gravity. (Publisher's note)

The author "explores the organic aspects of the space program, such as the dangerous bane of space motion sickness and the challenges of space hygiene. . . . She devotes one chapter to space food and another to zero-gravity elimination, which is a serious matter, even with a term like 'fecal popcorning.' An impish and adventurous writer with a gleefully inquisitive mind and a standup comic's timing, Roach celebrates human ingenuity (the odder the better), and calls for us to marshal our resources, unchain our imaginations, and start packing for Mars." Booklist

Includes bibliographical references

Toomey, David

Weird Life; The Search for Life That Is Very, Very Different from Our Own. David Toomey. 1st ed. W W Norton & Co Inc 2013 288 p. ill pbk $15.95; (hardcover) $25.95 **571**

1. Life 2. Ecology 3. Organisms 4. Life (Biology) 5. Adaptation (Biology) 6. Extreme environments 7. Life on other planets 8. Curiosities and wonders

ISBN 9780393348262; 0393071588; 9780393071580

LC 2012042391

This book looks at living organisms. The "author begins by describing 'extremophiles,' which thrive in wildly harsh conditions: chemical hot springs, inside sea ice, . . . or at the ocean's bottom. Having dealt with creatures that, however weird, exist, he proceeds to even stranger life that may exist on Earth, the planets, elsewhere throughout the universe, and in the minds of writers and philosophers. Along the way, he addresses surprisingly difficult questions, such as how to define life." (Kirkus)

"Toomey manages to make this panoply of life forms at once strange and familiar, and in doing so will entrance his readers." LJ

Includes bibliographical references and index.

571.7 Biological control and secretions

Foster, Russell G.

Rhythms of life; the biological clocks that control the daily lives of every living thing. Yale University Press 2004 276p il $30; pa $18 **571.7**

1. Biological rhythms

ISBN 0-300-10574-6; 978-0-300-10574-2; 0-300-10969-5 pa; 978-0-300-10969-6 pa

LC 2004-105609

The authors "survey the biological clocks that dictate circadian rhythms, the daily cycles that affect creatures from cockroaches to humans. . . . Biology buffs will marvel at the fascinating material." Publ Wkly

Includes bibliographical references

571.8 Reproduction, development, growth

Carroll, Sean B.

Endless forms most beautiful; the new science of evo devo and the making of the animal kingdom. with illustrations by Jamie W. Carroll, Josh P. Klaiss, Leanne M. Olds. W.W. Norton & Co. 2005 350p il $25.95 **571.8**

1. Evolution

ISBN 0-393-06016-0

LC 2004-29388

The author's "highly detailed and well-illustrated technical discussions are enriched by his appreciation for the philosophical, aesthetic, and ethical implications of the biological wonders he decodes, adding up to a vital and enjoyable introduction to a field with profound implications." Booklist

Includes bibliographical references

Haycock, David Boyd

Mortal coil; a short history of living longer. Yale University Press 2008 308p il **571.8**

1. Aging 2. Longevity 3. Death 4. Medicine -- Philosophy 5. Immortality (Philosophy)

ISBN 0-300-11778-7; 9780300117783

LC 2007-35341

This book "explores the medical, scientific, and philosophical theories behind the quest for the prolongation of human life. [According to Haycock], it was a conundrum that intrigued Sir Francis Bacon and underpinned the scientific revolution; ideas of ultimate perfectibility, indefinite progress, and worldly rather than heavenly immortality fed directly into the spirit of the Enlightenment and even further into the nineteenth and twentieth centuries. In today's world of genetic research, cryonics, and nanotechnology, we still seek the same elusive philosopher's stone." (Publisher's note) Index.

This book is "fully successful in managing to drum up excitement for the future of human development while steering clear of propaganda." PopMatters

Includes bibliographical references

572 Biochemistry

Finkel, Elizabeth

The **Genome** Generation; by Elizabeth Finkel. Melbourne University Publishing 2012 256 p. $32.95 **572**

1. Genomes 2. Evolution 3. Medical technology

ISBN 0522856470; 9780522856477

This book, by Elizabeth Finkel, covers revolutionary genetic developments in areas as diverse as medicine, agriculture, and evolution. From Botswana to Boston and from Australia to Mexico, the contributors to this work reveal what it means to be part of the genome generation. [It answers questions] such as What have we learned about evolution? How has it changed the way we practice medicine, grow crops, and breed livestock? and Is the genomic revolution an overhyped flop?" (Publisher's note)

Morton, Oliver

★ **Eating** the sun; how plants power the planet. HarperCollins 2008 457p il $28.95   **572**
    1. Photosynthesis
    ISBN 978-0-00-716364-9; 0-00-716364-9
               LC 2008-23433

First published 2007 in the United Kingdom

The author discusses "how biologists discovered photosynthesis and through it found a new understanding of the history of our planet and how life is inconceivable without it." Publisher's note

This book "is a work of flowing prose that makes vivid why our leafy nub of cosmic dust, swirling around an average star, is an extraordinarily beautiful and rare place to reside in the universe." Christ Sci Monit

Includes bibliographical references

572.8   Biochemical genetics

Carroll, Sean B.

★ The **making** of the fittest; DNA and the ultimate forensic record of evolution. with illustrations by Jamie W. Carroll and Leanne M. Olds. W.W. Norton & Co. 2006 301p il map $25.95   **572.8**
    1. DNA 2. Evolution
    ISBN 978-0-393-06163-5; 0-393-06163-9
               LC 2006-17197

The author presents "discoveries gathered from DNA evidence that confirm Charles Darwin's theory of evolution 'beyond any reasonable doubt.' . . . Readers will gain insight into the evolutionary process and expand their knowledge of how the 'fittest' species were made, from fish that live in subfreezing water to birds that communicate via ultraviolet colors." Libr J

Includes bibliographical references

Cook-Deegan, Robert M.

The **gene** wars; science, politics, and the human genome. Norton 1994 416p il $25; pa $14.95 **572.8**
    1. Gene mapping 2. Human Genome Project
    ISBN 0-393-03572-7; 0-393-31399-9 pa
               LC 93-10762

This "account of the Human Genome Project is as much about the politics, economics, and personalities as it is about the science of this . . . project to map the 100,000 chromosome sequences of the human genome." Libr J

Includes bibliographical references

Francis, Richard C.

Epigenetics; the ultimate mystery of inheritance. W.W. Norton 2011 234p il $25.95   **572.8**
    1. Genetics 2. Adaptation (Biology)
    ISBN 978-0-393-07005-7; 0-393-07005-0
               LC 2011-00696

The author "sets out to dethrone the notion that genes are the 'directors' of the 'plays' that are our lives, orchestrating our development and determining our risk for disease and sundry physical and behavioral traits. Yes, genes are important, writes the author, but they are subject to regulation by forces that can turn them on or off, sometimes for a lifetime, sometimes across generations. These forces can come via the cell housing of the genes, other parts of the body or the environment, in each instance initiating the actions of chemicals that bind (or unbind) one or more parts of a gene, preventing (or activating) its transcription. This is an 'epigenetic' process—epigenetics is the science that studies the ways in which DNA can undergo long-term regulatory changes that do not involve mutations of the genes themselves. To illustrate, Francis provides a dizzying array of examples." Kirkus

Includes bibliographical references

Kean, Sam

The **violinist's** thumb; and other lost tales of love, war, and genius, as written by our genetic code. Sam Kean. Little, Brown and Co. 2012 ix, 401 p.p (hardback) $25.99   **572.8**
    1. DNA 2. Genetics 3. Human genome 4. Behavior genetics 5. Human genetics -- Miscellanea
    ISBN 0316182311; 9780316182317
               LC 2012007029

In this book, author Sam Kean "attempts to take the mystery out of DNA by explaining its structure, its historical impact, and how the science of genetics continues to influence our lives. A good portion of the book examines how modern genetic breakthroughs have helped to explain our evolutionary and historical past. . . . The latter part of the book concentrates on what the future may hold as computer technology and our base of genetic knowledge expands." (Library Journal)

Includes bibliographical references and index.

Lewontin, Richard C.

The **triple** helix; gene, organism, and environment. [by] Richard Lewontin. Harvard Univ. Press 2000 136p il $25; pa $15   **572.8**
    1. Ecology 2. Evolution 3. Genetic code 4. Molecular biology
    ISBN 0-674-00159-1; 0-674-00677-1 pa
               LC 99-53879

In this book the author "demonstrates how all organisms, including humans, are the product of intricate interactions between their genes and the environment in which they live. . . . Although the issues Lewontin addresses are huge, he writes about them in a manner fully accessible to the nonspecialist." Publ Wkly

Includes bibliographical references

Segrè, Gino

Ordinary geniuses; Max Delbruck, George Gamow, and the origins of genomics and big bang cosmology. Gino Segrè. Viking 2011 xxi, 330 p.p $27.95   **572.8**
    1. Physicists -- United States -- Biography 2. Molecular

biologists -- United States -- Biography
ISBN 9780670022762; 0670022764

LC 2011009309

The author "explores the extraordinary lives and scientific accomplishments of two far-from-ordinary men, Max Delbrück and George Gamow. . . . An exuberant dual biography that integrates developments in quantum physics, cosmology and genetics since the 1920s with the lives of these two scientists." Kirkus

Includes bibliographical references (p. 309-318) and index

Sulston, John

The **common** thread; a story of science, politics, ethics, and the human genome. [by] John Sulston, Georgina Ferry. Joseph Henry Press 2002 310p il $24.95 **572.8**

1. Human Genome Project
ISBN 0-309-08409-1

LC 2002-14007

The author gives an "account of the excitement, hard work, vision, and daring needed to move from worm biology to recommending sequencing of the human genome, while senior and influential colleagues argued vigorously against it. He speaks forcefully of the necessity of keeping the sequence public and freely available. . . . {This title is} recommended for almost any library, particularly those with readers willing to go beyond sound bites and media hype." Libr J

Includes bibliographical references

Watson, James D., 1928-

★ The **annotated** and illustrated double helix; James D. Watson ; edited by Alexander Gann & Jan Witkowski. Simon & Schuster 2012 345 p. (hardcover) $30 **572.8**

1. DNA 2. Genetic Code 3. Molecular Biology
ISBN 1476715491; 9781476715490;
9781476715506; 9781476715513

LC 2012037483

This book, by James D. Watson, Alexander Gann and Jan Witkowski, was "published to mark the 50th anniversary of the Nobel Prize for Watson and Crick's discovery of the structure of DNA, an annotated and illustrated edition of . . . his 1968 memoir, 'The Double Helix,' the brash young scientist James Watson chronicled the drama of the race to identify the structure of DNA, a discovery that would usher in the era of modern molecular biology." (Publisher's note)

"Numerous appendices include a chapter about his Nobel Prize experiences, the first letters about the double helix, a previously unpublished chapter, and reviews of the original edition. Watson strikes a balance between science for the layman and science for the scientist, resulting in a memoir that will hold the interest of a broad, scientifically-minded audience." Pub Wkly

Includes bibliographical references and index

573.6   Reproductive system

Friedman, David M.

A **mind** of its own; a cultural history of the penis. Penguin Books 2003 358p il pa $16 **573.6**

1. Penis
ISBN 978-0-14-200259-9; 0-14-200259-3
First published 2001 by Free Press

This is a social and medical history of the male organ. Topics discussed include religious teachings about sex, efforts to overcome male impotence throughout history, attitudes toward masturbation, and racial stereotypes relating to phallus size.

"This valuable analysis of the origins of male sexuality and how the conception of maleness has shaped understanding of female sexuality isn't just educational . . . it's entertaining." Booklist

Includes bibliographical references

573.7   Musculoskeletal system

Winchester, Simon

Skulls; An Exploration of Alan Dudley's Curious Collection. Black Dog & Leventhal Pub 2012 240 p. $29.95 **573.7**

1. Skull
ISBN 1579129129; 9781579129125

This book by Simon Winchester focuses on the "story of skulls, both human and animal, from every perspective imaginable: historical, biographical, cultural, and iconographic. . . . At the center of 'Skulls' is a . . . never-before-seen-in-any-capacity visual array of the skulls of more than 300 animals. . . . The skulls are from the collection of Alan Dudley, a British collector and owner of what is probably the largest and most complete private collection of skulls in the world." (Publisher's note)

573.8   Nervous and sensory systems

Hughes, Howard C.

Sensory exotica; a world beyond human experience. MIT Press 1999 345p $40; pa $18.95 **573.8**

1. Senses and sensation 2. Comparative physiology
ISBN 0-262-08279-9; 0-262-58204-X pa

LC 98-51875

This is a compendium of stories and information regarding the vast array of sensory systems that are utilized by different species, ranging from insects to aquatic mammals to humans. . . . Hughes does an excellent job of presenting the facts and the science behind the vast array of sensory systems." Sci Books Films

Includes bibliographical references and index

Iacoboni, Marco

Mirroring people; the new science of how we connect with others. Farrar, Straus and Giroux 2008 308p il $25   **573.8**
1. Nervous system
ISBN 978-0-374-21017-5; 0-374-21017-9
LC 2007-47322

The author introduces "readers to the world of mirror neurons and what they imply about human empathy, which, the author says, underlies morality. . . . Iacoboni's expansive style and clear descriptions make for a solid introduction to cutting-edge neurobiology." Publ Wkly
Includes bibliographical references

575   Specific parts of and physiological systems in plants

Dawkins, Richard, 1941-

River out of Eden; a Darwinian view of life. illustrations by Lalla Ward. Basic Bks. 1995 172p il (Science masters series) hardcover o.p. pa $14 **575**
1. Genetics 2. Evolution
ISBN 0-465-06990-8 pa
LC 94-37146

The author "explores the evolution of humans from a single ancestor; evolutions of specific organs (e.g., eyes) and coadaptation of species (e.g., wasps and orchids); nature's physical and behavioral mechanisms to maximize survival of DNA; and, finally, the ultimate results when our DNA reaches out in space. His arguments and examples are clear, compelling, and often amusing." Libr J
Includes bibliographical references

575.5   Roots and leaves

Vogel, Steven

The **life** of a leaf; Steven Vogel. The University of Chicago Press 2012 xi, 303 p.p (hardcover : alkaline paper) $35   **575.5**
1. Leaves 2. Leaves -- Growth 3. Leaves -- Physiology
ISBN 0226859398; 9780226859392
LC 2011037295

In this book, Steven Vogel "demonstrates how a scientist can unite micro and macro perspectives in looking at the natural world. Using the leaf of a plant as his model system of life, he explores aspects of structure, function, and physiology while embedding specific questions in a broader evolutionary context. Thus, as we learn how a leaf . . . uses various strategies to maintain appropriate water balance, we also learn why these strategies are important." (Publishers Weekly)
Includes bibliographical references (pages 287-293) and index

576   General and external biological phenomena

Dawkins, Richard

★ The **selfish** gene; 30th anniversary ed; Oxford University Press 2006 xxiii, 360p il pa $15.95 **576**
1. Genetics 2. Evolution
ISBN 978-0-19-929115-1; 0-19-929115-2 pa
LC 2007-271478
First published 1976

The author examines evolution and contends that genes that benefit individual members of a species will be passed on to future generations, rather than those which may benefit the entire group
Includes bibliographical references

576.5   Genetics

Beckwith, Jonathan R.

Making genes, making waves; a social activist in science. Harvard Univ. Press 2002 242p il $27.95   **576.5**
1. Genetics 2. Ethicists 3. Microbiologists 4. College teachers
ISBN 0-674-00928-2
LC 2002-22747

"The text traces Beckwith's development as both a scientist and an activist, essentially in a chronological narrative form, with a few chapters providing expanded coverage of specific examples of the interaction between scientific research and societal effects. Those working in scientific fields or students who plan to pursue such a career would enjoy this book." Sci Books Films
Includes bibliographical references

Endersby, Jim

A **guinea** pig's history of biology. Harvard University Press 2007 499p il $27.95; pa $18.95 **576.5**
1. Genetics 2. Heredity 3. Biology -- History
ISBN 978-0-674-02713-8; 0-674-02713-2; 978-0-674-03227-9 pa; 0-674-03227-6 pa
LC 2007-20824

Endersby chronicles "the history of heredity and genetics, tracing the slow, uncertain path . . . that led us from the ancient world's understanding of inheritance to modern genetics." Publisher's note

"This book would be of interest to anyone fascinated or intrigued by genetics or biological research, as well as any professional or lay student of history and science." Sci Books Films
Includes bibliographical references

Henig, Robin Marantz

The **monk** in the garden: how Gregor Mendel and his pea plants solved the mystery of inheritance. Houghton Mifflin 2000 292p il $24; pa $14 **576.5**
1. Geneticists
ISBN 0-395-97765-7; 0-618-12741-0 pa
LC 00-24341

The author explores "Mendel's personality and experiments. The latter lasted but a few years in the 1850s and 1860s, ending when Mendel became the abbot of his monastery in what is now Brno in the Czech Republic. Henig crisply conveys how the laws of inheritance that Mendel derived from his statistical analysis remained unnoticed until several botanists who discovered them independently in 1900 also learned that Mendel found them first. This biography itself rediscovers a scientist often mentioned but insufficently known." Booklist

Keller, Evelyn Fox

The **century** of the gene. Harvard Univ. Press 2000 186p il $25; pa $15.95   **576.5**

1. Genetics

ISBN 0-674-00372-1; 0-674-99825-1 pa

LC 00-38319

The author "traces the evolution of genetic science over the course of the twentieth century, during which Gregor Mendel's theories of inheritance were rediscovered, the structure of DNA revealed, and the human genome mapped." Booklist

"In this tight, clearly written survey, Keller does a wonderful job of explaining and demonstrating how our knowledge of genetics has accumulated to the extent that we can fathom what we don't understand." Publ Wkly

Includes bibliographical references

Knight, Jeffrey A.

★ **Genetics** & inherited conditions; editor, Jeffrey A. Knight. Salem Press 2010 3v il (Salem health) set $395   **576.5**

1. Reference books 2. Genetics -- Encyclopedias 3. Medical genetics -- Encyclopedias

ISBN 978-1-587-65650-7; 1-587-65650-7

LC 2010-5289

First published 1999 with title: Encyclopedia of genetics

"The subjects covered include all aspects of genetics, such as diseases, biology, genetic engineering, social issues, and more. . . . Articles covering diseases and syndromes include such information as definition, risk factors, etiology and genetics, symptoms, screening and diagnosis, treatment and therapy, and prevention and outcomes. For other types of articles, essays are preceded by a brief summary of the significance of the topic and definitions of key terms." Booklist

Includes bibliographical references

576.8   Evolution

Ayala, Francisco J.

Darwin's gift to science and religion. Joseph Henry Press 2007 237p il map $24.95   **576.8**

1. Evolution 2. Creationism 3. Naturalists 4. Natural selection 5. Travel writers 6. Writers on science

ISBN 978-0-309-10231-5; 0-309-10231-6

LC 2007-05821

"This elegant book provides the single best introduction to Darwin and the development of evolutionary biology now available." Publ Wkly

Includes bibliographical references

Billings, Lee

Five billion years of solitude; the search for life among the stars. by Lee Billings. Current 2013 304 p. $27.95   **576.8**

1. Universe 2. Life -- Origin 3. Extrasolar planets 4. Life on other planets

ISBN 1617230065; 9781617230066

LC 2013017672

This book presents an "overview of the still-evolving field of 'exoplanetary' research (discovery and characterization of planets orbiting other stars). Early dreams that we would locate and visit intelligent, technologically sophisticated beings elsewhere in space have been tempered as declining governmental funding has restricted our planet hunting." (Library Journal)

"A great outline of the subject, bringing what's often treated as science fiction down to Earth, where it can be understood." Kirkus

Includes bibliographical references and index

Browne, Janet

★ **Darwin's** Origin of species; a biography. Atlantic Monthly Press 2007 174p (Books that changed the world) hardcover o.p. pa $14   **576.8**

1. Naturalists 2. Travel writers 3. Writers on science

ISBN 0-87113-953-7; 978-0-87113-953-5; 0-8021-4346-6 pa; 978-0-8021-4346-4 pa

LC 2007-275116

In this "biography" of Darwin's book, the author "describes the long genesis of Darwin's theories, from his early readings as a university student and his five-year voyage on the Beagle, to his debates with contemporaries and experiments in his garden." Publisher's note

"This excellent introduction is highly recommended for all readers who want to better understand the heated debates that this book still causes today." Publ Wkly

Includes bibliographical references

Byrne, Eugene

Darwin; a graphic biography. by Eugene Byrne ; illustrated by Simon Gurr. Smithsonian Books 2013 96 p. ill. (paperback) $9.95   **576.8**

1. Evolution 2. Graphic novels 3. Natural selection -- Comic books, strips, etc 4. Evolution (Biology) -- Comic books, strips, etc

ISBN 1588343529; 9781588343529

LC 2012951786

This work of graphic nonfiction by Eugene Byrne and Simon Gurr presents a "summary of [Charles] Darwin's life and achievement. . . . Darwin was an indifferent student . . .until he received an invitation to take a voyage that 'would change the course of history.'. . .The animals he encountered seemed so different . . . that he theorized that if it weren't a matter of different conditions that resulted in such 'transmutation,' they might well have had a different creator." (Kirkus Reviews)

Includes bibliographical references.

Catling, David C.

Astrobiology; a very short introduction. David C. Catling. Oxford University Press 2013 xiv, 142

p.p illustrations (Very short introductions) (pbk.)
$11.95   **576.8**
    1. Life on other planets 2. Exobiology
    ISBN 9780199586455; 0199586454
                 LC 2013940856

A "very good treatment of astrobiology. In eight chapters and just about 130 pages, it covers the full gamut of the discipline, which really only came about in the 1990s. Importantly, in spite of the necessary requirement of brevity, Catling . . . does not neglect key historical elements in his topical discussions." Choice

Includes bibliographical references and index

Challenger, Melanie

On extinction; how we became estranged from nature. Melanie Challenger. Granta 2011 330 p. $28   **576.8**
    1. Polar regions 2. Extinct animals 3. Environmental protection 4. Human influence on nature 5. Extinction (Biology) 6. Environmental responsibility 7. Polar regions -- Description and travel
    ISBN 1619020181; 1847081878; 9781619020184; 9781847081872
                 LC 2012358414

In this book, "realizing the link between her own estrangement from nature and the cultural shifts that led to a dramatic rise in extinctions, . . . writer Melanie Challenger travels in search of the stories behind these losses. From an exploration of an abandoned mine in England to an Antarctic sea voyage to South Georgia's old whaling stations, . . . to a stay among an Inuit community in Canada, she uncovers species, cultures, and industries touched by extinction." (Publisher's note)

Includes bibliographical references (p. [314]-325)

Coyne, Jerry A.

★ **Why** evolution is true. Viking 2009 xx, 282p il map $27.95   **576.8**
    1. Evolution
    ISBN 978-0-670-02053-9
                 LC 2008-33973

Presents the threads of modern work in genetics, paleontology, geology, molecular biology, and anatomy that demonstrate the stamp of the evolutionary processes first proposed by Darwin.

"Readers looking to understand the case for evolution and searching for a response to many of the most common creationist claims should find everything they need in this powerful book, which is clearer and more comprehensive than the many others on the subject." Publ Wkly

Includes bibliographical references

Darwin, Charles, 1809-1882

The **Beagle** letters; edited by Frederick Burkhardt; with an introduction by Janet Browne. Cambridge University Press 2008 xxx, 470p il map $32   **576.8**
    1. Evolution 2. Beagle Expedition (1831-1836)
    ISBN 978-0-521-89838-6; 0-521-89838-2
                 LC 2009-417801

"The complete correspondence both to and from Charles Darwin during his five years circumnavigating the globe on the HMS Beagle, beginning in 1831, documents his growth as a naturalist and offers a picture of life in the England he left behind. . . . It is fascinating to watch Darwin attempt to come to grips with the huge amount of data he collected and make sense of the patterns he observed. We get an intimate look at an adventurous young Darwin, so unlike his more familiar, sedentary older self who would write On the Origin of Species." Publ Wkly

Includes bibliographical references

The **Darwin** reader; edited by Mark Ridley. 2nd ed; Norton 1996 315p il pa $21.30   **576.8**
    1. Evolution 2. Natural selection
    ISBN 0-393-96967-3
                 LC 95-50297

First published in the United Kingdom with title: The essential Darwin; first Norton edition published 1987

This collection presents excerpts from Darwin's most important works including Origin of the species, The descent of man and Coral reef. Illustrations are taken from the original editions

Includes bibliographical references

On the origin of species; David Quammen, general editor. Illustrated ed.; Sterling Pub. 2008 544p il $35   **576.8**
    1. Heredity 2. Evolution 3. Human origins 4. Natural selection
    ISBN 978-1-4027-5639-9
                 LC 2008-6902

Illustrated edition of the book first published 1859 with title: The origin of species by means of natural selection

"As a milestone not only in the history of science but also in cultural history, On the Origin of Species belongs in every library, high school and above. . . . [Quammen] offers a gloriously illustrated and richly annotated volume, which testifies to the book's enduring legacy. Throughout the text, relevant sidebars from other of Darwin's writings, including his Autobiography, field notes from the HMS Beagle, and his myriad letters, are presented for their insight. Illustrations include historical images, such as sketches, woodcuts, and portraits of people and places, but also included are contemporary photographs of the flora and fauna that Darwin described." Libr J

Includes bibliographical references

★ The **origin** of species by means of natural selection, or, The preservation of favored races in the struggle for life. Modern Library 1993 689p $21.95   **576.8**
    1. Heredity 2. Evolution 3. Human origins 4. Natural selection
    ISBN 0-679-60070-1
                 LC 93-3598

First published 1859. Variant title: The origin of species by means of natural selection

The classic exposition of the "theory of evolution by natural selection. Darwin argues that every species develops or evolves from a previous one and that all life is a continuing pattern. His objects of study were the variations from generation to generation in domestic plants and animals. . . . While subsequent investigation has superseded some of Darwin's arguments, Origin of Species remains one of the most influential books ever published." Reader's Ency. 4th edition

Davies, P. C. W.

The **eerie** silence; renewing our search for alien intelligence. [by] Paul Davies. Houghton Mifflin Harcourt 2010 241p il $27   **576.8**

1. Life on other planets 2. Extraterrestrial beings 3. Unidentified flying objects

ISBN 978-0-547-13324-9; 0-547-13324-3

LC 2010-3088

"After 50 years of scanning the skies for signs of extraterrestrial intelligence, astronomers have only silence to report — an eerie silence, Davies argues. Part history of the search, part road map for its future and (large) part mind-stretching exercise, the book provides Davies' perspective on profound questions that have implications far beyond alien hunting." Sci News

Includes bibliographical references

Dawkins, Richard

★ The **ancestor's** tale; a pilgrimage to the dawn of evolution. with additional research by Yan Wong. Houghton Mifflin 2004 673p il $28; pa $16.95   **576.8**

1. Evolution

ISBN 0-618-00583-8; 0-618-61916-X pa

LC 2004-59864

The author "sets out on a pilgrimage tracing the history of the human species back to the very origins of life, marking along the way 39 rendezvous points where the human genealogical path crosses that of other terrestrial species. . . . Lively and daring, a book certain to draw even casual readers deep into the adventure—and controversy—of science." Booklist

Includes bibliographical references

The **greatest** show on Earth; the evidence for evolution. Free Press 2009 470p il map $30 **576.8**

1. Evolution

ISBN 978-1-4165-9478-9; 1-4165-9478-7

LC 2009-25330

The author offers "not a discussion of the magnificence of the evolutionary view of life but several basic proofs of its validity. He argues that this is necessary because of recent assaults from creationists upon the very concept of evolution by natural selection." Libr J

"A pleasure in the face of so much scientific ignorance—biology rendered accessible and relevant to the utmost degree." Kirkus

Includes bibliographical references

Eiseley, Loren C.

★ The **immense** journey; [by] Loren Eisley. Random House 1957 210p hardcover o.p. pa $10   **576.8**

1. Evolution 2. Human origins

ISBN 0-394-70157-7 pa

"Essays on biology and paleontology by an anthropologist speculating on the origin of man and the theory of evolution." Publ Wkly

Dr Eiseley's "style is beautiful, compelling in impact and poetic in its imagery. His subject is one of the epics of natural science—the 'immense journey' of life as known on this planet." Christ Sci Monit

★ **Evolution**; the first four billion years. edited by Michael Ruse [and] Joseph Travis; with a foreword by Edward O. Wilson. Belknap Press of Harvard University Press 2009 979p il map $39.95   **576.8**

1. Evolution

ISBN 9780674031753

LC 2008-30270

This book is in two parts. "The first part contains 16 substantive, semischolarly essays on overarching topics, such as 'The Origin of Life,' 'Paleontology and the History of Life,' 'Evolution and Society,' and 'Evolution and Religion.' The book's second part contains . . . an alphabetical encyclopedia of evolution, containing shorter essays on more focused subjects." Libr J

"If ever there were an education in a book, there's one in this massive volume." Booklist

Includes bibliographical references

Fortey, Richard A.

★ **Life**; a natural history of the first four billion years of life on earth. [by] Richard Fortey. Knopf 1998 346p il $32.59; pa $15   **576.8**

1. Evolution 2. Life -- Origin

ISBN 0-375-40119-9; 0-375-70261-X pa

LC 97-49466

First published 1997 in the United Kingdom with subtitle: an unauthorized biography

This work is "written for readers with no science. It will help them understand the specialized and often technical books on evolution that make headlines but leave most people wondering why." N Y Times Book Rev

Includes bibliographical references

Gould, Stephen Jay, 1941-2002

★ **Hen's** teeth and horse's toes. Norton 1983 413p il hardcover o.p. pa $15.95   **576.8**

1. Evolution

ISBN 0-393-31103-1 pa

LC 82-22259

The theme of this collection is "biological evolution. {The author} has grouped the 30 essays into seven categories: Sensible Oddities, Personalities, Adaptation and Development, Teilhard and Piltdown, Science and Politics, Extinction and a Zebra Trilogy." America

Includes bibliographical references

The **panda's** thumb; more reflections in natural history. Stephen Jay Gould. Norton 1980 343p il hardcover o.p. pa $15.95   **576.8**

1. Evolution 2. Natural selection

ISBN 0-393-30819-7 pa

LC 80-15952

In these essays "a variety of creatures, including humans, dinosaurs, pandas, turtles, and microscopic organisms, are considered in light of their reflection of Darwin's theory. One intriguing theme which runs throughout the selections is how imperfectly designed anatomy or haphazardly applied anatomical evolution best supports Darwinism." Booklist

Includes bibliographical references

The **structure** of evolutionary theory. Belknap Press 2002 xxii, 1433p il $39.95   **576.8**
1. Evolution 2. Evolution (Biology) 3. Punctuated equilibrium (Evolution)
ISBN 0-674-00613-5

LC 2001-43556

This is a summation of the author's "life work, building on Darwinism to provide a . . . synthesis of how {in Gould's view} evolution has shaped the living world. . . . Gould says of his book that it 'cycles through the three central themes of Darwinian logic at three scales—by brief mention of a framework in (the introduction), by full exegesis of Darwin's presentation in Chapter 2, and by lengthy analysis of the major differences and effects in historical (part 1) and modern critiques (part 2) of these three themes in the rest of the volume.'" (N Y Rev Books) Index.

This is a "history and analysis of classical and twentieth-century evolutionary theory." Booklist

Includes bibliographical references

Johnson, Paul, 1928-
Darwin; portrait of a genius. Paul Johnson. Viking 2012 176 p. $25.95   **576.8**
1. Biography 2. Evolution 3. Social Darwinism 4. Naturalists -- England -- Biography
ISBN 0670025712; 9780670025718

LC 2012003433

In this book, Paul Johnson presents a biography of Charles Darwin. He "summarizes the key events of Darwin's formative days, then devotes the meat of the book to his development of the theory and the publication of 'The Origin of Species.' . . . Johnson also points to what he considers two central flaws in Darwin's work: a too-literal acceptance of Malthus' theories and insufficient understanding of anthropology." He also discusses social Darwinism. (Kirkus Reviews)

Jones, Steve
Darwin's ghost; the origin of species updated. Random House 2000 xxix, 377p il hardcover o.p. pa $15.95   **576.8**
1. Evolution 2. Natural selection
ISBN 0-345-42277-5 pa

LC 99-53246

First published 1999 in the United Kingdom with title: Almost like a whale

Jones "has updated Charles Darwin's On the origin of species (1859) so that the fact of organic evolution is both understandable and relevant to today's general reader. . . . Very informative and cogently argued, this book is an important addition to the natural history literature." Libr J

Includes bibliographical references

Kaufman, Marc
First contact; scientific breakthroughs in the hunt for life beyond Earth. Simon & Schuster 2011 213p il $26; ebook $12.99   **576.8**
1. Life on other planets
ISBN 978-1-4391-0900-7; 978-1-4391-3030-8 ebook

LC 2010-44630

Kaufman "takes us from beneath the surface of our planet, where scientists hunt for and study 'extremophile' microbes that alter our views of what is necessary for life to exist, to observatories and labs searching deep space for extraterrestrial signals or exoplanets, planets outside the solar system. Not only does the book suggest the breadth of the effort, it reveals how each aspect reveals ideas and science never before suspected. . . . [The author] does what excellent science reporters do—he translates at times difficult concepts into language those of us who barely passed 'Bonehead Chemistry' can understand." Seattle Post-Intelligencer

Includes bibliographical references

Keller, Michael
Charles Darwin's On the Origin of Species; a graphic adaptation. [by] Michael Keller; art by Nicolle Rager Fuller. Rodale 2009 192p il $19.99; pa $14.99   **576.8**
1. Naturalists 2. Graphic novels 3. Travel writers 4. Writers on science 5. Heredity -- Graphic novels 6. Evolution -- Graphic novels 7. Human origins -- Graphic novels 8. Natural selection -- Graphic novels
ISBN 978-1-60529-697-5; 1-60529-697-X; 978-1-60529-948-8 pa; 1-60529-948-0 pa

LC 2009-11387

"The graphic novel follows Origin's original chapters, combining snippets of Darwin's text with quotes from letters, illustrative examples from his time and from the present, and occasional invented dialog. Fuller's images of people seem clumsy, but her full-color plants, animals, charts, maps, and scientific accoutrements are attractive and effective. . . . [This] version well conveys both the science and the wonder of Origin." Libr J

Kolbert, Elizabeth
★ The **sixth** extinction; an unnatural history. Elizabeth Kolbert. First edition. Henry Holt and Co 2014 336 p. illustrations, map (hardback) $28 **576.8**
1. Extinction (Biology) 2. Environmental degradation 3. Human influence on nature 4. Mass extinctions 5. Environmental disasters
ISBN 0805092994; 9780805092998

LC 2013028683

"In 'The Sixth Extinction,' [author] Elizabeth Kolbert draws on the work of scores of researchers in half a dozen disciplines, accompanying many of them into the field: geologists who study deep ocean cores, botanists who follow the tree line as it climbs up the Andes, marine biologists who dive off the Great Barrier Reef. She introduces us to a dozen species, some already gone, others facing extinction." (Publisher's note)

"Kolbert . . . weaves a relatable element into the at-times heavily scientific discussion, bringing the sites of past and present extinctions vividly to life with fascinating information that will linger with readers long after they close the book. A highly significant eye-opener rich in facts and enjoyment." Kirkus

Includes bibliographical references and index

Larson, Edward J.

Evolution : the remarkable history of a scientific theory. Modern Library 2004 337p il (Modern Library chronicles) $21.95; pa $14.95   **576.8**
1. Evolution
ISBN 0-679-64288-9; 0-8129-6849-2 pa

LC 2003-64888

This is an "overview of evolutionary thought from ancient speculations to the emergence of a neo-Darwinian synthesis. It focuses on those essential facts, events, and ideas that have contributed to the successes of scientific evolutionism. . . . Larson is to be commended for stressing the value of both scientific inquiry and the evolutionary framework. This outstanding book is highly recommended for all academic and public libraries." Libr J

Includes bibliographical references

Margulis, Lynn

Symbiotic planet; a new look at evolution. Basic Bks. 1998 147p il (Science masters series) hardcover o.p. pa $14   **576.8**
1. Evolution 2. Symbiosis 3. Gaia hypothesis
ISBN 0-465-07272-0 pa

LC 98-38921

"From the origin of life to the classification and phylogeny of living organisms, from a discussion of Gaia—the belief that Earth operates like a living being—to a discussion of the underlying reasons for sex, iconoclastic biologist Margulis . . . takes on many of the big questions in biology. . . . In a book that is part autobiography and part biological primer, Margulis . . . advances the idea that a large part of organic evolution can be explained by symbiosis." Publ Wkly

Includes bibliographical references

Mayr, Ernst

What evolution is. Basic Bks. 2001 318p il maps hardcover o.p. pa $16   **576.8**
1. Evolution
ISBN 0-465-04426-3 pa

LC 2001-36562

This introduction to the theory of evolution offers "insights into taxonomy, adaptation, common descent, biodiversity, and those mechanisms of organic evolution that result in the process of speciation." Libr J

"A wise and illuminating examination, by an illustrious evolutionary biologist, that sorts out the complexities of evolution." N Y Times Book Rev

Includes bibliographical references

McCalman, Iain, 1947-

Darwin's armada; four voyages and the battle for the theory of evolution. W.W. Norton & Co. 2009 422p il map   **576.8**
1. Botanists 2. Evolution 3. Biologists 4. Naturalists 5. Essayists 6. Travel writers 7. Writers on science
ISBN 0-393-06814-5; 978-0-393-06814-6

LC 2009-16055

"This geographically expansive account of the rise of evolutionary theory traces the lives and travels of four titans of nineteenth-century biology: Darwin, the botanist Joseph Hooker, the physiologist Thomas Huxley, and Alfred Russel Wallace, a fearless globetrotter whose dangerous and often unpleasant journeys in the Amazon and the Malay Archipelago were the source of biological epiphanies and tens of thousands of specimens. Though these stories have been told before, McCalman's central conceit—that the four naturalists, who all travelled at length in the Southern Hemisphere, share a 'special bond of the salt'—supplies a fresh, antipodean perspective." New Yorker

Includes bibliographical references

Newitz, Annalee

Scatter, adapt, and remember; how humans will survive a mass extinction. Annalee Newitz. Doubleday 2013 320 p. illustrations, maps (hardcover : alk. paper) $26.95   **576.8**
1. Human beings 2. Survival skills 3. Extinction (Biology) 4. Survival
ISBN 0385535910; 9780385535915

LC 2012042409

LA Times Book Prize Finalist: Science & Technology (2013)

In this book, author Annalee Newitz "explains that although global disaster is all but inevitable, our chances of long-term species survival are better than ever. [She] focuses on humanity's long history of dodging the bullet, as well as on new threats that we may face in years to come. Most important, it explores how scientific breakthroughs today will help us avoid disasters tomorrow." (Publisher's note)

"Humans may be experts at destroying the planet, but we are no slouches at preserving it, either, and Newitz's shrewd speculations are heartening." Kirkus

Includes bibliographical references and index

Novacek, Michael J.

Terra; our 100-million-year-old ecosystem--and the threats that now put it at risk. [by] Michael Novacek. Farrar, Straus and Giroux 2007 xxiv, 451p il map $27   **576.8**
1. Ecology 2. Evolution 3. Environmental degradation 4. Human influence on nature
ISBN 978-0-374-27325-5; 0-374-27325-1

LC 2007-9126

The author takes a "look at what humans have done over time and in more recent years. Combining paleontology, evolutionary biology, and environmental science, he shows how these three perspectives can bring us to a better understanding of the 'mass extinction event' that threatens this planet if changes aren't implemented now." Libr J

Includes bibliographical references

Palumbi, Stephen R.

The evolution explosion; how humans cause rapid evolutionary change. Norton 2001 277p il $24.95; pa $14.95   **576.8**
1. Evolution 2. Pesticides 3. Antibiotics 4. Human influence on nature
ISBN 0-393-02011-8; 0-393-32338-2 pa

LC 00-67004

This describes human causes of rapid evolutionary change, focusing on bacteria which have evolved strains resistant to antibiotics and insects resistant to pesticides

"Palumbi's writing is lively and lucid, and his analogies are felicitous." Booklist

Includes bibliographical references and index (p.)

Rutherford, Adam

Creation; how science is reinventing life itself. Adam Rutherford. Current 2013 288 p. (hardback) $27.95   **576.8**

1. Life -- Origin 2. Genetic engineering 3. Biogenesis -- Popular Works
ISBN 1617230057; 9781617230059

LC 2013013441

Author Adam Rutherford's book brings "genomics and synthetic biology to life in this accessible overview of the past and future of the fields. In the first half," Rutherford "describes what we know about cellular biology, while the second portion explores where and how we might apply our growing knowledge base in the future. He argues that the theory of evolution does not aim to explain the origin of life, but he also insists that in order to know where we're going, we have to know where we're from, and one of the best ways to do that is to trace evolution at the cellular level." (Publisher's note)

Includes bibliographical references and index

Sasselov, Dimitar

The **life** of super-Earths; Dimitar Sasselov. Basic Books 2012 xvi, 202 p.p ill.   **576.8**

1. Exobiology 2. Extrasolar planets 3. Life on other planets 4. Life -- Origin 5. Synthetic biology
ISBN 9780465021932; 9780465023400

LC 2011036888

This book discusses the research supporting the claim for extra-terrestrial life beyond Earth. Author Dimitar "Sasselov (Astronomy/Harvard Univ.) reviews the hard evidence in favor . . . before proceeding to explain discoveries and simulations that suggest we are not alone. No telescope has directly observed an extra-solar planet, but the author delivers a[n] . . . explanation of how instruments and, since 2009, a satellite are detecting subtle changes in a star's light or movement that reveal not only the presence of planets (600 so far) but their size, orbits and a hint of their composition. Sasselov maintains that the minority of 'super-earths' possess conditions favorable to life: proper temperature, protective atmosphere, volcanism and tectonic movements." (Kirkus)

Includes bibliographical references and index

Schopf, J. William

Cradle of life; the discovery of earth's earliest fossils. Princeton Univ. Press 1999 367p il $55; pa $20.95   **576.8**

1. Fossils 2. Life -- Origin
ISBN 0-691-00230-4; 0-691-08864-0 pa

LC 98-42443

An "exploration of how Precambrian fossils came to light and what they've taught us. The author covers the history of evolutionary thought and the exploits of field pa-

leontologists, as well as the trajectory of his own career." Publ Wkly

"Schopf's chapter on the evolution of biochemical pathways is a fascinating and wonderfully clear exposition of a difficult topic." Libr J

Includes bibliographical references

Stott, Rebecca

★ **Darwin's** ghosts; the secret history of evolution. Rebecca Stott. Spiegel & Grau 2012 xviii, 396 p.p   **576.8**

1. Evolution 2. Naturalists 3. Biology -- History 4. Scientists -- Biography 5. Naturalists -- Biography
ISBN 1400069378; 9781400069378

LC 2011041951

This book "draws for readers stories of the people who came before [Charles] Darwin and who presented ideas that were precursors to the theory of evolution. . . . Many of the thinkers and ideas presented in this book . . . Darwin was not aware of until after the publication of 'On the Origin of Species.' After receiving a critical letter, he compiled a list of his scientific predecessors to be included in the foreword of later editions . . . including Aristotle, Al-Jahiz, Leonardo da Vinci, and Denis Diderot." (Library Journal)

Includes bibliographical references (p. [357]-376) and index

Switek, Brian

Written in stone; evolution, the fossil record and our place in nature. Brian Switek. 1st ed. Bellevue Literary Press 2010 320p il pa $17.95   **576.8**

1. Fossils 2. Evolution 3. Fossil hominids 4. Human evolution
ISBN 1-934137-29-4 pa; 978-1-934137-29-1 pa

This is a "history of evolutionary discovery." (Publisher's note) Index.

The author "presents a popular account of fossil discoveries, historical debates related to evolution, and how the unearthing of these missing links is filling in the gaps in evolutionary history. . . . Armchair scientists and general readers interested in evolution will enjoy this informative book." Libr J

Ward, Peter Douglas

Life as we do not know it; the NASA search for (and synthesis of) alien life. Peter D. Ward. Viking 2005 xxvii, 292p ill. hardcover o.p. (pbk.) $15.00; o.p.   **576.8**

1. Science 2. Solar system 3. Life (Biology) 4. Life on other planets 5. Life -- Origin
ISBN 9780143038498; 0670034584

LC 2005056299

This book "sets a research agenda aimed at unraveling science's most profound questions: What is life, and where does it exist? To that query, he adds this philosophical discussion: What is humanity's role in life's unfolding on Earth and in the rest of the Solar System? . . . [Author Peter] Ward begins with a generally agreed-upon set of criteria — life metabolizes, has complexity and organization, reproduces, develops, evolves, and is autonomous — but then proposes the controversial hypothesis that this definition should include viruses. . . . Ward leaves no solar-system world unvisited. He quickly dismisses Mercury but spends a number of pages discussing the possibility of life floating high in the sulfuric-acid-laced clouds of Venus. . . . Mars gets the most attention outside of Earth." (National Space Society)

The author "believes researchers might be taking the wrong approach by looking only for earthly DNA-based life forms. Truly alien life, he argues, might have completely different origins. . . . The science is neatly laid out, and readers willing to follow his daring, scientifically based speculations will find their imaginations spurred." Publ Wkly

Includes bibliographical references (p. [257]-278) and index

Wilson, David Sloan

★ **Evolution** for everyone; how Darwin's theory can change the way we think about our lives. Delacorte Press 2007 390p $24 **576.8**

1. Evolution

ISBN 978-0-385-34021-2; 0-385-34021-4

LC 2006-23685

"Rather than catalog its successes, denounce its detractors or in any way present evolutionary theory as the province of expert tacticians like himself, Wilson invites readers inside and shows them how Darwinism is done, and at lesson's end urges us to go ahead, feel free to try it at home. The result is a sprightly, absorbing and charmingly earnest book that manages a minor miracle, the near-complete emulsifying of science and the 'real world,' ingredients too often kept stubbornly, senselessly apart." N Y Times Book Rev

Includes bibliographical references

Young, Christian C.

★ **Evolution** and creationism; a documentary and reference guide. [by] Christian C. Young and Mark A. Largent. Greenwood Press 2007 298p il $85 **576.8**

1. Evolution 2. Creationism

ISBN 978-0-313-33953-0; 0-313-33953-8

LC 2007-10682

"This reference work provides over 40 of the most important documents to help readers understand the [evolution versus creationism] debate in the eyes of the people of the time. Each document is from a major participant in the debates from the predecessors of Darwin to the judges of the influential court cases of the present day." Publisher's note

Includes bibliographical references

577 Ecology

Burdick, Alan

★ **Out** of Eden; an odyssey of ecological invasion. Farrar, Straus & Giroux 2005 324p il $25; pa $14 **577**

1. Ecology 2. Biological invasions

ISBN 0-374-21973-7; 0-374-53043-2 pa

LC 2005-922517

This book argues that "exotic animals and plants are crossing the globe, borne on the . . . tide of human traffic to places where nature never intended them to be. . . . [These species] increasingly crowd native and endangered species out of existence." Publisher's note

"A sober report, Burdick's work still sounds an alarm for readers concerned with the way humans alter nature." Booklist

Roston, Eric

The **carbon** age; how life's core element has become civilization's greatest threat. Distributed to the trade by Macmillan 2008 309p il $25.99 **577**

1. Carbon 2. Atmosphere

ISBN 978-0-8027-1557-9; 0-8027-1557-5

LC 2008-2754

"The first half traces carbon's history from the beginning of the universe, the Big Bang, and the nucleosynthesis (the formation of the elements) through the life cycle of stars, and then covers the development of life and dynamics of the 'natural' carbon cycle of Earth. The second section spans the last 150 years and delves into the impact of humans on the climate in creating what Roston calls the 'industrial carbon cycle.' Without using a great deal of scientific jargon, Roston leads us patiently and clearly through this complex issue." Libr J

Includes bibliographical references

Stolzenberg, William

Where the wild things were; life, death, and ecological wreckage in a land of vanishing predators. Bloomsbury 2008 291p $24.99; $24.99 **577**

1. Ecology 2. Predatory animals 3. Endangered species

ISBN 9781596912991; 978-1-59691-299-1; 1-59691-299-5

LC 2008-2392

A look at how the disappearance of the world's great predators has upset the delicate balance of the environment, and what their disappearance portends for the future.

This "is one of those rare books that provide not just an enriching story, but a new, clarifying lens through which to understand the world around us." Christ Sci Monit

Includes bibliographical references

Wills, Christopher

Green Equilibrium; The Vital Balance of Humans and Nature. Christopher Wills. Oxford University Press 2013 320 p. $34.95 **577**

1. Ecology 2. Evolution 3. Ecosystem health 4. Biotic communities 5. Ecosystem management 6. Nature -- Effect of human beings on 7. Human beings -- Effect of environment on

ISBN 0199645701; 9780199645701

LC 2012277418

In this book, Christopher Wills "recounts visits to diverse wildlife reserves around the world, illustrated with his photographs, while discussing many aspects of evolution. The author describes a green equilibrium as balance among organisms that maintains a local ecosystem. No paradise, it includes predation, disease, and starvation." Humans' effects, both positive and negative, on ecosystems are considered. (Library Journal)

Includes bibliographical references (p. 247-267) and index

577.2 Specific factors affecting ecology

Global weirdness; severe storms, deadly heat waves, relentless drought, rising seas, and the weather of the future. produced by Climate Central. Pantheon Books 2012 214 p. ill. $22.95 **577.2**
1. Climate change 2. Global warming 3. Weather forecasting 4. Global environmental change 5. Greenhouse gases -- Environmental aspects
ISBN 0307907309; 9780307907301

LC 2011047699

This book, "[p]roduced by Climate Central, . . . summarizes . . . everything we know about the science of climate change; explains what is likely to happen to the climate in the future; and lays out in practical terms what we can and cannot do to avoid further shifts. Sixty . . . entries tackle such questions as: Is climate ever 'normal'? . . . [and w]hat risks does climate change pose for human health?" (Publisher's note)
Includes bibliographical references (p. 201-214).

Montaigne, Fen
Fraser's penguins; a journey to the future in Antarctica. Henry Holt and Co. 2010 288p il map $26 **577.2**
1. Penguins 2. Human influence on nature 3. Ecologists 4. Climate -- Environmental aspects 5. Antarctica -- Description and travel
ISBN 978-0-8050-7942-5; 0-8050-7942-4

LC 2010-07151

The author "spent five months tracking penguins through the breeding season on the northwestern Antarctica peninsula with the scientist Bill Fraser, and his book is a bittersweet account of the stark beauty of the continent and the climate change that threatens its delicate ecosystem. . . . Montaigne poetically portrays the daunting Antarctic landscape and gives readers an intimate perspective on its rugged, audacious, and charming penguin and human inhabitants." Publ Wkly
Includes bibliographical references

577.3 Ecology of specific environments

Haskell, David George
The forest unseen; a year's watch in nature. David George Haskell. Viking 2012 268 p **577.3**
1. Philosophy of nature 2. Natural history -- Tennessee 3. Forests and forestry -- Tennessee 4. Seasons -- Tennessee 5. Nature observation -- Tennessee 6. Old growth forests -- Tennessee 7. Old growth forest ecology -- Tennessee
ISBN 9780670023370

LC 2011037552

In this book, "biologist David Haskell uses a one-square-meter patch of old-growth Tennessee forest as a window onto the entire natural world. Visiting it almost daily for one year to trace nature's path through the seasons, he brings the forest and its inhabitants to . . . life. Each of this book's short chapters begins with a simple observation: a salamander scuttling across the leaf litter; the first blossom of spring wildflowers. From these, Haskell spins a . . . web of biol-

ogy and ecology, explaining the science that binds together the tiniest microbes and the largest mammals and describing the ecosystems that have cycled for thousands- sometimes millions-of years." (Publisher's note)
Includes bibliographical references and index

Preston, Richard
The wild trees; a story of passion and daring. Random House 2007 294p il map $25.95; pa $16 **577.3**
1. Redwood 2. Botanists 3. College teachers
ISBN 978-1-4000-6489-2; 1-4000-6489-9; 978-0-8129-7559-8 pa; 0-8129-7559-6 pa

LC 2006-48646

The author tells the story of Steve Sillett, Marie Antoine and other naturalists and researchers who climb and explore giant redwoods in northern California
"There is something so elementally boyish in searching out the biggest and tallest, poring over maps and measurements, dubbing these trees with names lifted from J.R.R. Tolkien's Middle Earth. . . . Preston knows how to fold the science into the seams of his narrative, and his dry humor crops up, pleasurably, at the edges of his observations." Cleveland Plain Dealer

577.34 Rain forest ecology

Lowman, Margaret
Life in the treetops; adventures of a woman in field biology. [by] Margaret D. Lowman. Yale Univ. Press 1999 219p il maps hardcover o.p. pa $13.95 **577.34**
1. Botanists 2. Women scientists
ISBN 0-300-07818-8; 978-0-300-07818-3; 0-300-08464-1 pa; 978-0-300-08464-1 pa

LC 98-48691

Lowman "gives a funny, unassuming and deeply idiosyncratic chronicle of her trials and triumphs as a field biologist of tree canopies and other ecosystems in Australia, New England, Belize, Panama and elsewhere." N Y Times Book Rev
Includes bibliographical references
Followed by It's a jungle up there! (2006)

Royte, Elizabeth
The Tapir's morning bath; mysteries of the tropical rain forest and the scientists who are trying to solve them. Houghton Mifflin 2001 328p maps $25; pa $14 **577.34**
1. Rain forest ecology 2. Panama -- Description
ISBN 0-395-97997-8; 0-618-25758-6 pa

LC 2001-24989

Royte discusses time spent with scientists studying the ecology of Barro Colorado, an island in the Panama Canal.
This is "a superb introduction to tropical ecology and theoretical biology, as well as original and thoroughly engaging travel writing." Publ Wkly
Includes bibliographical references

577.4   Grassland ecology

Manning, Richard

Grassland; the history, biology, politics, and promise of the American prairie. Viking 1995 306p hardcover o.p. pa $15   **577.4**
   1. Grassland ecology 2. Human influence on nature
   ISBN 0-14-023388-1 pa

                     LC 95-10073

"Our culture's disrespect for grasslands has produced an environmental catastrophe, charges the author. By allowing overgrazing on public lands, our government is wiping out an ecosystem as vital as the Brazilian rain forests. In this sweeping exploration of the prairie, Manning . . . makes an eloquent plea to restore it." Publ Wkly

   Includes bibliographical references

577.5   Ecology of miscellaneous environments

Barilla, James

★ My Backyard Jungle; The Adventures of an Urban Wildlife Lover Who Turned His Yard into Habitat and Learned to Live With It. James Barilla. Yale University Press 2013 376 p. $28   **577.5**
   1. Wildlife conservation 2. Human-animal relationship 3. Habitat (Ecology) 4. Urban ecology (Biology) 5. Animals and civilization
   ISBN 0300184018; 9780300184013

               LC 2012040298

In this book, James Barilla "takes readers on his personal journey to explore human and animal relationships in shared habitats around the world. To begin with, he had his own property in Columbia, SC, certified by the National Wildlife Federation as a wildlife habitat. . . . Going between his backyard and distant locations, his chapters cover topics from idealized children's toys . . . to the illegal wildlife trade." (Library Journal)

   Includes bibliographical references (pages 349-353) and index

577.6   Aquatic ecology

Douglas, Marjory Stoneman

The Everglades; river of grass. illustrated by Robert Fink; [update by Michael Grunwald] 60th anniversary ed; Pineapple Press 2007 447p $19.95   **577.6**
   1. Everglades (Fla.)
   ISBN 978-1-56164-394-3

             LC 2007-28384

First published 1947 by Rinehart

A natural history of South Florida focusing on the unique ecosystem of the Everglades. Discusses environmental changes, scientific research, and political responses to conservation efforts.

   Includes bibliographical references

577.7   Marine ecology

Carson, Rachel, 1907-1964

The **edge** of the sea; with illustrations by Bob Hines. Houghton Mifflin 1955 276p il hardcover o.p. pa $14   **577.7**
   1. Seashore 2. Marine biology
   ISBN 0-395-92496-0 pa

"The seashores of the world may be divided into three basic types: the rugged shores of rock, the sand beaches, and the coral reefs and all their associated features. Each has its typical community of plants and animals. The Atlantic coast of the United States [provides] clear examples of each of these types. I have chosen it as the setting for my pictures of shore life." Preface

Ellis, Richard

★ The **empty** ocean; plundering the world's marine life. written and illustrated by Richard Ellis. Island Press 2003 367p il hardcover o.p. pa $25; pa $37.50   **577.7**
   1. Marine ecology 2. Endangered species
   ISBN 1-55963-974-1; 1-55963-637-8 pa; 9781559636377

"Rather than writing the 'Silent Spring' of the oceans, [Ellis] has produced a book that is likely to provide the inspiration and source materials for such a badly needed work . . . It is also a splendid example of history illuminating ecology, with well-chosen facts that enable us to picture a largely invisible catastrophe." N Y Times Book Rev

   Includes bibliographical references

578   Natural history of organisms and related subjects

Weidensaul, Scott

★ **Return** to wild America; a yearlong journey in search of the continent's natural soul. North Point Press 2005 xx, 394p il map $26; pa $15   **578**
   1. Artists 2. Illustrators 3. Ornithologists 4. Writers on nature 5. Natural history -- North America
   ISBN 0-8654-7688-8; 0-8654-7731-0 pa

             LC 2005-47720

Fifty years after the publishing of Roger Tory Peterson's and James Fisher's Wild America, the author retraces Peterson and Fisher's steps "from Newfoundland's craggy coastline, down the East Coast, into Mexico and up the West Coast to Alaska. . . . This engrossing state-of-nature memoir, making a vibrant case for preserving America's wild past for future Americans, promises to become a classic in its own right." Publ Wkly

   Includes bibliographical references

578.4   Adaptation

Barrington, Rupert

Life; extraordinary animals, extreme behaviour. [by] Martha Holmes and Mike Gunton; [with] Rupert

Barrington ... [et al.] University of California Press 2010 311p il map   **578.4**

    1. Animal behavior 2. Adaptation (Biology)
    ISBN 0-520-26537-8; 978-0-520-26537-0

                     LC 2009-31158

    First published 2009 in the United Kingdom

    "In 2009, to commemorate the 200th anniversary of Charles Darwin's birth, the BBC premiered the ten-episode television documentary Life to great acclaim. . . . Written by the documentary's producers, this impressive companion volume showcases species of fish, amphibians, reptiles, insects, birds, mammals, and plants that have developed unique or unusual strategies for solving 'the eternal problems of life': finding food, escaping predators, attracting mates, and raising young. . . . Even the most casual reader will be awed by the beauty, complexity, and ingenuity of nature as celebrated here." Libr J

Forbes, Peter

    Dazzled and deceived; mimicry and camouflage. Yale University Press 2009 283p il map $27.50   **578.4**

    1. Camouflage (Biology)
    ISBN 978-0-300-12539-9; 0-300-12539-9

                     LC 2009-23577

    "Forbes has produced a colorful look at camouflage in nature and battle, with a focus on the two world wars. . . . [The book] straddles the worlds of evolutionary biology, art, and military strategy with a world-class cast of characters, among them Charles Darwin, Pablo Picasso, Vladimir Nabokov, Theodore Roosevelt, and Winston Churchill. A pivotal character is Abbott Handerson Thayer, the eccentric New England painter who studied the animals near his summer home in Dublin, N.H., and is one of the few artists to have a scientific law (Thayer's Law of Concealing Coloration) named after him." Boston Globe

    Includes bibliographical references

578.6   Miscellaneous nontaxonomic kinds of organisms

Hamilton, Garry

    Super species; the creatures that will dominate the planet. Firefly Books 2010 271p il $35   **578.6**

    1. Nonindigenous pests 2. Biological invasions
    ISBN 978-1-55407-630-7; 1-55407-630-7

                     LC 2011286604

    "This book details a number of invasive species that have expanded into new regions or are in the process of expanding their range. These are the species, as the author explains, that will be dominating the earth of the future as they continue to invade new areas and become more dominant." Sci Books Films

    "Well researched and written, with an abundance of excellent photos, this work provides an outstanding, balanced look at this group of species." Choice

    Includes bibliographical references

578.68   Rare and endangered species

Ackerman, Diane, 1948-

    The **rarest** of the rare; vanishing animals, timeless worlds. Random House 1995 xxi, 184p hardcover o.p. pa $12   **578.68**

    1. Rare animals 2. Endangered species
    ISBN 0-679-77623-0 pa

                     LC 95-8499

    In these essays the author "tells of her adventures in several relatively isolated habitats of several endangered animal species: monk seals in Hawaii, golden lion tamarins in the Brazilian rain forest, short-tailed albatrosses on a Japanese volcanic island, and monarch butterflies in southern California. For each of the habitats Ackerman has recruited the company of one or more biologically sophisticated guides." Choice

    "Every species that is endangered or becomes extinct deserves so poetic a chronicler as Ackerman." Libr J

578.7   Organisms characteristic of specific kinds of environments

Burt, William

    Marshes; the disappearing Edens. Yale University Press 2007 179p il $35   **578.7**

    1. Marshes
    ISBN 978-0-300-12229-9; 0-300-12229-2

                     LC 2006-26961

    This book combines photographs of marsh life with information about wetland habitat in North America.

    "This well-structured, readable book will be valuable for students, teachers, researchers, and sundry readers interested in a unique kind of wetland. Reading this book is an excellent way to understand marshes as wild places." Choice

    Includes bibliographical references

Carson, Rachel, 1907-1964

    Under the sea wind; introduction by Linda Lear; illustrations by Howard Frech. Penguin Books 2007 xx, 184p il (Penguin classics) pa $15   **578.7**

    1. Marine biology
    ISBN 978-0-14-310496-4

                     LC 2006-50707

    First published 1941 by Simon & Schuster

    A series of narratives describe the birds and sea creatures that inhabit the Eastern coasts of North America.

    Includes bibliographical references

Cramer, Deborah

    Smithsonian ocean; our water, our world. Smithsonian Books 2008 295p il map $39.95 **578.7**

    1. Marine biology 2. Marine ecology
    ISBN 978-0-06-134383-4; 0-06-134383-8

                     LC 2008-15633

    In this study, Cramer contends that "the vital partnership between earth and the life it nourishes has recently been disrupted." Publisher's note

    "With its hundreds of beautiful photographs, the volume is visually enchanting. It is also a vividly, accurately, and clearly written survey of the state of our understanding . . . of the history and current condition of the ocean." Sci Books Films

Includes bibliographical references

Crist, Darlene Trew

World ocean census; a global survey of marine life. [by] Darlene Trew Crist, Gail Scowcroft, James M. Harding, Jr. Firefly Books 2009 256p il map $40   **578.7**

1. Marine animals 2. Marine biology 3. Science -- Methodology 4. Census of Marine Life (Project)

ISBN 978-1-55407-434-1; 1-55407-434-7

"The Census of Marine Life is a global network of scientists in more than 80 nations involved in a ten-year project to assess and explain the diversity of life in the oceans. . . . [The authors] describe the various aspects of the Census for the educated layperson. Illustrated with examples of creatures found in all parts of the oceans, including many newly discovered and never-before-described species, chapters cover the different project groups, how they are gathering and publishing data, and why this is important." Libr J

The authors "have produced a highly readable text with stunning photos that should fully engage the public imagination." Publ Wkly

Includes bibliographical references

DeStefano, Stephen

Coyote at the kitchen door; living with wildlife in suburbia. Harvard University Press 2010 196p il $24.95   **578.7**

1. Coyotes 2. Urbanization 3. Suburban life 4. Wildlife conservation

ISBN 978-0-674-03556-0; 0-674-03556-9

The author "examines the expanding field of 'urban ecology' in this pithy volume. Urban ecologists study changes in human-animal interactions caused by factors like sprawl, traffic, and noise pollution, in an attempt to understand why some species (the mountain lion, say) are badly disrupted by human developments, while others, such as the coyote, appear to be thriving—turning up in more and more Eastern back yards. DeStefano cites some alarming facts . . . but, having experienced the benefits of a suburban childhood, he refuses to reduce his thinking to a view in which wilderness preservation is the only solution." New Yorker

Includes bibliographical references

Kirby, Richard R.

Ocean drifters; a secret world beneath the waves. Firefly Books 2011 192p il $29.95   **578.7**

1. Marine plankton

ISBN 978-1-55407-982-7; 1-55407-982-9

LC 2011284690

"Kirby (Marine Inst. Research Fellow, Plymouth Univ., UK), who has published widely in scientific journals, combines in this book his area of expertise-plankton-with magnificent color photography of each species. He details the importance of the ocean's plankton layer to the health of the globe and its effects on sea and human life in the photos' descriptions...Recommended for readers interested in the smaller denizens of the natural world, the ocean, or microphotography." (Library Journal)

Koslow, J. Anthony

★ The silent deep; the discovery, ecology, and conservation of the deep sea. [by] Tony Koslow. University of Chicago Press 2007 270p il map $35   **578.7**

1. Marine ecology 2. Marine resources 3. Conservation of natural resources

ISBN 978-0-226-45125-1; 0-226-45125-9

LC 2006-22282

"The Census of Marine Life is a global network of scientists in more than 80 nations involved in a ten-year project to assess and explain the diversity of life in the oceans. . . . [The authors] describe the various aspects of the Census for the educated layperson. Illustrated with examples of creatures found in all parts of the oceans, including many newly discovered and never-before-described species, chapters cover the different project groups, how they are gathering and publishing data, and why this is important." Libr J

"This important book should be read by everyone who cares about Earth's future." Choice

Includes bibliographical references

Rice, Stanley A.

Encyclopedia of biodiversity; author, Stanley A Rice. Facts On File 2012 598 p. $95   **578.7**

1. Biology -- Encyclopedias 2. Evolution -- Encyclopedias 3. Biodiversity -- Encyclopedias

ISBN 0816077266; 9780816077267

LC 2010050557

This biology and evolutionary science encyclopedia, by Stanley A. Rice, provides "information about groups of organisms (from bacteria to mammals) and about ecological concepts and processes (such as biogeography and ecological succession). . . . Tables at the end of each entry . . . allow . . . readers to see how environmental conditions and biodiversity have changed through evolutionary time." (Publisher's note)

"The text is suitable for high school students but advanced enough for adult readers, too. Although there are many encyclopedias on ecology, resources, and science, this one presents important biodiversity topics in one volume, providing a handy overview for term papers and class presentations." LJ

Includes bibliographical references and index

Wolfe, David W.

Tales from the underground; a natural history of subterranean life. Perseus Bks. 2001 221p il hardcover o.p. pa $18   **578.7**

1. Soil microbiology

ISBN 0-7382-0679-2 pa

The author discusses the ecology of life in the soil and the earth's rocky crust, including Darwin's experiments with earthworms, Lewis and Clark's first encounter with prairie dogs, the use of genetic tools, and the possible role of primitive underground microbes in evolution.

Wolfe "explains in a straightforward, readable style that there is probably as much biodiversity and even as much biomass below ground as above." New Sci

Includes bibliographical references

579   Natural history of microorganisms, fungi, algae

Ben-Barak, Idan

The **invisible** kingdom; from the tips of our fingers to the tops of our trash, inside the curious world of microbes. Basic Books 2009 204p $24   **579**
1. Microbiology
ISBN 978-0-465-01887-1; 0-465-01887-4

LC 2009-19655

The author "gives an enthusiastic tour of single-celled life. . . . He touches on myriad microbes in a range of environments, from the abyss of the sea to the inside of humans, explaining how they defend themselves, eat, move, and reproduce." Booklist

Includes bibliographical references

Dunn, Rob

The **wild** life of our bodies; predators, parasites, and partners that shape our evolution. Harper 2011 290p $26.99   **579**
1. Evolution 2. Parasites 3. Human ecology 4. Microorganisms
ISBN 978-0-06-180648-3; 0-06-180648-X

LC 2010-43564

The author "shares the view of modern human life as a paradise lost, but the loss he laments is not merely of a vague sense of being one with nature. What we have sacrificed, he argues, is a physical connection with the species that shaped our bodies from our physique to the immune system. As humans became urban and industrial, we also separated ourselves from other species. Pets aside, we have laboured to rid our houses and cities of creatures — not just visible predators and pests but also the microbes on our countertops and hands. Some of these steps were sensible acts of self-preservation, but others were driven by an ideology of humans as separate from nature. Dunn . . . catalogues the dangers of that ideology." New Scientist

Includes bibliographical references

Sankaran, Neeraja

★ **Microbes** and people: an A-Z of microorganisms in our lives. Oryx Press 2000 297p il $62.95   **579**
1. Reference books 2. Microbiology -- Dictionaries
ISBN 1-57356-217-3

LC 00-10117

"Entries cover environmental, industrial, and food microbiology, in addition to the microbiology of health and disease. Scientific techniques used for studying microorganisms are discussed, and biographies of key individuals are provided. A chronology of infections and disease epidemics from 430 BC to the present is included as an appendix." Publisher's note

"Because it provides very readable coverage of topics so much in the news lately, this dictionary will be much used in high school, undergraduate, and public libraries." Booklist

Includes bibliographical references

579.3   Prokaryotes (Bacteria)

Zimmer, Carl

Microcosm; E. coli and the new science of life. Pantheon Books 2008 243p il $25.95   **579.3**
1. Bacteria
ISBN 978-0-375-42430-4; 0-375-42430-X

LC 2007-37155

This is a study of the E. coli bacteria. Zimmer shows "how scientists used it to discover how genes work and then to launch the . . . biotechnology industry." Publisher's note

The author "renders an absorbing picture of what E. coli says about the history and future of life." Booklist

Includes bibliographical references

579.5   Fungi

Hudler, George W.

Magical mushrooms, mischievous molds. Princeton Univ. Press 1998 248p il hardcover o.p. pa $18.95   **579.5**
1. Fungi
ISBN 0-691-07016-4 pa

LC 98-10163

The author shows how fungi "have dramatically influenced the course of human history. With chapters on yeasts used to make bread and to brew alcoholic beverages, on the medicinal uses of fungi from penicillin to possible treatments for AIDS, on edible mushrooms like the common button mushroom and the more exotic truffle, and on hallucinogenic mushrooms, Hudler takes readers on an enthralling and informative tour of this much maligned kingdom." Publ Wkly

Includes bibliographical references

579.6   Mushrooms

McKnight, Kent H.

A **field** guide to mushrooms, North America; [by] Kent H. McKnight and Vera B. McKnight; illustrations by Vera B. McKnight. Houghton Mifflin 1987 429p il hardcover o.p. pa $21   **579.6**
1. Mushrooms
ISBN 0-395-91090-0 pa

LC 86-27799

"More than 500 species [of mushrooms] are described and depicted. . . . Edibility of each species is noted and signified by marginal pictograms both in the text and on the colorplates. . . . Appended: a genial chapter of recipes by Anne Dow, glossary, selected references, and index." Booklist

Smith, Alexander Hanchett

The **mushroom** hunter's field guide; {by} Alexander H. Smith and Nancy Smith Weber. all color & enlarged; University of Mich. Press 1980 316p il $24.95   **579.6**
1. Mushrooms
ISBN 0-472-85610-3

LC 80-10514

First published 1958

This is a "field guide for both novices and experts alike. The introductory chapter explains basic terminology and what to look for when identifying fungi. More than 280 mushrooms are described, including identifying marks, edibility, habitat, native range, and type of spore. A color photograph . . . of each mushroom is most valuable for accurate information." Booklist

Includes bibliographical references

580   Natural history of plants and animals

Goodall, Jane, 1934-
Seeds of Hope; Wisdom and Wonder from the World of Plants. Jane Goodall with Gail Hudson. 1st ed. Grand Central Pub. 2013 384 p. (hardcover) $26.99   **580**
   1. Plants 2. Trees 3. Human-plant relationships
   ISBN 1455513229; 9781455513222
                              LC 2012045482
This book, by Jane Goodall with Gail Hudson, "examines the critical role that trees and plants play in our world. . . She introduces us to botanists around the world, as well as places where hope for plants can be found, such as The Millennium Seed Bank, where one billion seeds are preserved. She shows us the secret world of plants with all their mysteries and potential for healing our bodies as well as Planet Earth." (Publisher's note)

Kassinger, Ruth, 1954-
   ★ A **Garden** of Marvels; How We Discovered That Flowers Have Sex, Leaves Eat Air, and Other Secrets of Plants. Ruth Kassinger. HarperCollins Publishers 2014 416 p. illustrations $25.99   **580**
   1. Gardening 2. Botanists -- United States -- Anecdotes
   3. Women gardeners -- United States -- Anecdotes
   ISBN 0062048996; 9780062048998
                              LC 2014002824
In this book, author Ruth Kassinger "sets out to understand the basics of botany in order to become a better gardener. She retraces the progress of the first botanists who banished myths and misunderstandings and discovered that flowers have sex, leaves eat air, roots choose their food, and hormones make morning glories climb fence posts. She also visits modern gardens, farms, and labs to discover the science behind extraordinary plants." (Publisher's note)

"[A]n informal, entertaining account of how early researchers discovered how plants work and what scientists are still learning about plants today." Kirkus

Includes bibliographical references and index

   ★ **Magill's** encyclopedia of science; plant life. editor, Bryan D. Ness. Salem Press 2002 4v il map set $457   **580**
   1. Reference books 2. Botany -- Encyclopedias
   ISBN 1-58765-084-3
                              LC 2002-13319
This encyclopedia provides "information for any study related to plants, archaea, bacteria, algae, or fungi, from molecular-level processes to planet-wide economic or environmental issues. The 379 signed articles, about half of

which are published with revisions and updated bibliographies from several of the publisher's earlier reference books, are arranged into a single alphabet." SLJ

Includes bibliographical references

581.6   Miscellaneous nontaxonomic kinds of plants

Angier, Bradford
   Field guide to edible wild plants; revisions by David K. Foster; illustrations by Arthur J. Anderson; additional illustrations by Jacqueline Mahannah, Michelle L. Meneghini, and Kristen E. Workman. 2nd ed.; Stackpole Books 2008 282p il pa $21.95 **581.6**
   1. Edible plants
   ISBN 978-0-81173-447-9; 0-81173-447-1
                              LC 2007-40125
First published 1974

"Plants are arranged alphabetically by one of their common names. Each entry includes genus, family affiliation, other common names, a lengthy plant description (including many interesting facts about the plant), notes on distribution, and a statement concerning edibility and preparation of the plant parts." Libr J

Davis, Wade
   One river; explorations and discoveries in the Amazon rain forest. Simon & Schuster 1996 537p il hardcover o.p. pa $16   **581.6**
   1. Botanists 2. Ethnobotany 3. Hallucinogens 4. Medical botany 5. Ethnobiologists 6. College teachers 7. Writers on nature 8. Writers on science 9. Amazon River valley
   ISBN 0-684-83496-0 pa
                              LC 96-21516
"This is the story of Timothy Plowman, a young ethnobotanist who died while looking for medicinal plants in the South American rain forests. . . . Plowman was the brilliant protégé of Richard Evans Schultes, one of the world's leading authorities on hallucinogenic plants and the Amazon rain forest. The author mixes the backgrounds and travels of the two men with sociology of South American tribes and their sacred plants." Libr J

Davis "writes magnificently, with verve when describing his many adventurous field trips, accurately and efficiently when telling science or history, and with vivid fantasy when portraying hallucinogenic trances." N Y Times Book Rev

Includes bibliographical references

Foster, Steven
   ★ **Peterson** field guide to medicinal plants and herbs of eastern and central North America; Steven Foster and James A. Duke ; photographs by Steven Foster. Houghton Mifflin Harcourt 2014 456 p. col. ill. (Peterson field guides) $21   **581.6**
   1. Medical botany 2. Plants -- Identification
   ISBN 0547943989; 9780547943985
In this book, authors "Steven Foster and James A. Duke have used recent advances in the study of medicinal plants and their combined experience of over 100 years to

completely update the 'Peterson Field Guide to Medicinal Plants.' The clear and concise text identifies the key traits, habitats, uses, and warnings for more than 530 of the most significant medicinal plants in the eastern and central United States and Canada including both native and alien species." (Publisher's note)

"A hefty handbook to haul over marsh and meadow, but invaluable to searchers and researchers alike.—" LJ

Includes bibliographical references (p. 422-425) and indexes

Gibbons, Euell

Stalking the wild asparagus; with illustrations by Margaret F. Schroeder; including a remembrance of the author by John McPhee. 25th anniversary ed; Hood, A.C. 1987 303p il hardcover o.p. pa $17.50 **581.6**

1. Cooking 2. Edible plants
ISBN 0-911469-036 pa

LC 87-16933

A reprint of the title first published 1962 by McKay

In this series of brief anecdotal essays the naturalist discourses on the identification and preparation of roots, flowers and plants, old Indian legends, and wilderness survival.

Stewart, Amy

★ The **drunken** botanist; the plants that create the world's great drinks. Amy Stewart. Algonquin Books of Chapel Hill 2013 400 p. $19.95 **581.6**

1. Edible plants 2. Alcoholic beverages 3. Cocktails 4. Plants, Edible 5. Plants, Useful
ISBN 1616200464; 9781616200466

LC 2012041725

This book by Amy Stewart "explores the botanical beginnings of our favorite drinks. . . . Each plant description includes history, propagation, and usage details. Stewart includes sidebars with recipes, field guides, planting instructions, a description of the role of bugs in getting from seed to plant to table, and in-depth historical details. She includes archaeological finds such as the presence of barley beer on clay pot fragments dated to 3400 B.C.E." (Library Journal)

Sumner, Judith

The **natural** history of medicinal plants; foreword by Mark Plotkin. Timber Press 2000 235p il hardcover o.p. pa $24.95 **581.6**

1. Medical botany
ISBN 0-88192-483-0; 978-0-88192-957-7 pa; 0-88192-957-3 pa

LC 99-76555

In this "introduction to the botanical compounds used medicinally, Dr. Sumner describes their biological and ecological importance as toxins and deterrents in protecting plants." Publisher's note

Sumner presents an "accessible introduction to the world of medicinal plants. . . . Some of her most interesting revelations are about the relationships that animals have with plants." Booklist

Includes bibliographical references

Turner, Nancy J.

★ The **North** American guide to common poisonous plants and mushrooms; [by] Nancy J. Turner and Patrick von Aderkas. Timber Press 2009 375p il $29.95 **581.6**

1. Mushrooms 2. Poisonous plants
ISBN 0-88192-929-8; 978-0-88192-929-4

LC 2008-35095

First published 1991 with title: Common poisonous plants and mushrooms of North America

"The book is split into four main categories: mushrooms, wild plants, ornamental and crop plants, and houseplants. Each plant entry includes a . . . photograph to aid the task of identification, a description of the plant, notes on where they commonly occur, and a description of their toxic properties." Publisher's note

Includes bibliographical references

Van Wyk, Ben-Erik

★ **Food** plants of the world; an illustrated guide. Timber Press 2005 480p il $39.95 **581.6**

1. Edible plants
ISBN 0-88192-743-0; 978-0-88192-743-6

LC 2005-44048

This is an "illustrated guide to more than 350 commercially important plants that are sources of cereals, nuts, fruits, vegetables, drinks, herbs, and spices." Choice

Includes bibliographical references

582.1 Herbaceous and woody plants, plants noted for their flowers

Symonds, George W. D.

The **shrub** identification book; the visual method for the practical identification of shrubs, including woody vines and ground covers. photos by A. W. Merwin. William Morrow & Company 1963 379p il pa $22 **582.1**

1. Shrubs
ISBN 978-0-688-05040-5; 0-688-05040-9

First published 1963 by Barrow

"Part I gives pictorial keys for thorns, leaves, flowers, fruit, twigs and bark of broad-leaved upright shrubs. Part II contains 200 master pages arranged under four categories, with data on habitat, blooming period, etc., accompanying the photographs." Wilson Libr Bull

Includes bibliographical references

582.13 Plants noted for their flowers

Heywood, V. H.

Flowering plant families of the world; [by] V.H. Heywood . . . [et al.] Updated & rev.; Firefly Books 2007 424p il map $59.95 **582.13**

1. Flowers
ISBN 978-1-55407-206-4; 1-55407-206-9

LC 2007-272849

First published 1978 in the United Kingdom with title: Flowering plants of the world

"At the core of the book are . . . entries on 504 flowering plant families. Each entry describes distribution, anatomy, habitat, classification and commercial uses." Publisher's note

Includes bibliographical references

Spellenberg, Richard

National Audubon Society field guide to North American wildflowers, western region; 2nd ed rev; Knopf 2001 862p il map $19.95   **582.13**
   1. Wild flowers
   ISBN 0-375-40233-0
                      LC 2001-269242
   First published 1979
   "More than 940 . . . full-color images show the wildflowers of western North America close-up and in their natural habitats. . . . Images are grouped by flower color and shape and keyed to . . . descriptions that reflect current taxonomy." Publisher's note

Thieret, John W.

National Audubon Society field guide to North American wildflowers: eastern region; revising author, John W. Thieret; original authors, William A. Niering and Nancy C. Olmstead. Knopf 2001 879p il map (National Audubon Society field guide series) $19.95   **582.13**
   1. Wild flowers
   ISBN 0-375-40232-2
                      LC 2001-269241
   First published 1979 under the authorship of William A. Niering and Nancy C. Olmstead
   "Covers the area east of the Rockies and east of the Big Bend area of Texas to the Atlantic. Color photographs together with family and species descriptions make this a most useful field guide." Sci News {review of 1979 edition}

Wells, Diana

100 flowers and how they got their names; illustrated by Ippy Patterson. Algonquin Bks. 1997 257p il $17.95   **582.13**
   1. Flowers 2. Popular plant names
   ISBN 1-56512-138-4
                      LC 96-22296
   The author "describes the mythology and history behind 100 favorite garden plants, emphasizing the exploits of botanists and plant explorers who brought them out of their native habitats." Libr J

Includes bibliographical references

582.16   Trees

Hugo, Nancy Ross

   ★ **Seeing** trees; Nancy Ross Hugo ; photography by Robert J. Llewellyn. 1st ed; Timber Press 2011 242p. col. ill.   **582.16**
   1. Trees
   ISBN 9781604692198
                      LC 2010052455

National Outdoor Book Awards: Nature and the Environment (2011)

This book, "[f]ocusing on widely grown trees, . . . describes the rewards of careful and regular tree viewing, outlines strategies for improving your observations, and describes some of the most visually interesting tree structures, including leaves, flowers, buds, leaf scars, twigs, and bark. . . . [P]rofiles of ten familiar species -- including such beloved trees as white oak, southern magnolia, white pine, and tulip poplar -- show you how to recognize and understand many of their most compelling (but usually overlooked) physical features." (Publisher's note)

Includes bibliographical references and index.

Johnson, Hugh

The **world** of trees; consultant editor, John Grimshaw; preface by Thomas Pakenham. University of California Press 2010 400p il map $34.95   **582.16**
   1. Trees
   ISBN 978-0-520-24756-7
   First published 1973 with title: The international book of trees
   "The first section of the book provides general information on how trees grow, the life cycle of trees, their classification, and morphological characteristics. Next comes a compendium of more than 600 taxa of trees, divided into conifers and broadleaves. Beautiful color photographs, including portraits and landscape scenes, grace every page. The last section includes a guide to choosing trees for the landscape and a chart comparing the ornamental traits of trees throughout the seasons." Am Gardener

Little, Elbert Luther

   ★ The **Audubon** Society field guide to North American trees; [by] Elbert L. Little; photographs by Sonja Bullaty and Angelo Lomeo [et. al.]; visual key by Susan Rayfield and Olivia Buehl. Knopf 1980 2v il v1 $19.95; v2 $19.95   **582.16**
   1. Trees -- North America
   ISBN 0-394-50760-6 v1; 0-394-50761-4 v2
                      LC 79-3474
   These "guides are unusual in that they contain many color photographs of parts of a living tree. The identification keys are easy to use, being based on an arrangement by leaf shapes, flowers, fruit, and fall leaves, and giving drawings of winter silhouettes. The eastern guide covers 364 species, the western guide describes 314 species; they divide the country at central Texas and the Rockies." Libr J

Nadkarni, Nalini

Between earth and sky; our intimate connections to trees. [by] Nalini M. Nadkarni. University of California Press 2008 322p il $45; pa $17.95   **582.16**
   1. Trees
   ISBN 978-0-520-24856-4; 978-0-520-26165-5 pa
                      LC 2008-2162
   "This book presents a multifaceted, multidisciplined approach to the appreciation of trees that combines science, art, literature, poetry, and spirituality, including a discussion of the practical use of trees throughout history. . . . Beginning with a very enlightening chapter defining just what a tree is and describing the attributes of trees, the book thor-

oughly explores the human affinities to trees, explaining that trees fulfill human needs at every level of our existence. The chapters cover physical needs, security, health, recreation, time and history, symbols and language, and finally spirituality and mindfulness." Choice

Includes bibliographical references

Pakenham, Thomas

Remarkable trees of the world; text and photographs by Thomas Pakenham. Norton 2002 191p il $49.95; pa $27.95   **582.16**

1. Trees

ISBN 0-393-04911-6; 0-393-32529-6 pa

LC 2002-21934

The author presents descriptions and photographs of sixty exceptional trees from around the world

"This beautiful and unique book is sure to be appreciated by nature lovers. And though it is a highly personal work and not a scientific text, it demonstrates keen and accurate observation; it could also serve as an excellent supplement to studies in science, history, and geography." SLJ

Includes bibliographical references

Sibley, David

The **Sibley** guide to trees; written and illustrated by David Allen Sibley. Alfred A. Knopf 2009 xxxviii, 426p il map $39.95   **582.16**

1. Trees -- North America

ISBN 978-0-375-41519-7

LC 2009-927625

"With more than 4,100 . . . paintings, the Guide highlights the . . . similarities and distinctions between more than 600 tree species—native trees as well as many introduced species." Publisher's note

This "is an outstanding book that should be available in all public libraries, schools, colleges, universities, and homes. The text is comprehensive and the illustrations are pertinent, accurate, and clear." Sci Books Films

Wells, Diana

Lives of the trees; an uncommon history. illustrated by Heather Lovett. Algonquin Books of Chapel Hill 2010 369p il $19.95   **582.16**

1. Trees

ISBN 978-1-56512-491-2; 1-56512-491-X

LC 2009-31669

"A compendium, from acacia to yew, of uncommon tree tales—enough esoterica and darn-good yarns to chew on for quite some time. You'll learn all sorts of delectable lore and legend, history and science." Seattle Times

"Wells explores people's relationship with about 100 trees and the stories behind their names." NPR

Includes bibliographical references

583   Dicotyledons

Anderson, Edward F.

★ The **cactus** family; with a foreword by Wilhelm Barthlott; and a chapter on cactus cultivation by

Roger Brown. Timber Press 2001 776p il maps $99.95   **583**

1. Cactus

ISBN 0-88192-498-9; 978-0-88192-498-5

LC 00-60700

This reference work on cactaceae covers 125 genera and 1810 species

"While more than 1,000 photographs overall illustrate the extraordinary diversity and beautiful flowers of cacti, the main section—an alphabetically arranged reference—will arguably rank as the definitive work readers will use to examine and identify cactus genera, species, and subspecies." Booklist

Includes bibliographical references

Pappalardo, Joe

Sunflowers; the secret history; the unauthorized biography of the world's most beloved weed. Overlook Press 2008 256p il $22.95   **583**

1. Sunflowers

ISBN 978-1-58567-991-1; 1-58567-991-7

A "look at a flower so ubiquitous that its critical role in cultural development since the dawn of time often goes overlooked. A glib, upbeat writer and fiercely determined researcher, Pappalardo intrepidly investigates everything from the sunflower's genetic history and recent bioengineering discoveries to its influence on global economies from the U.S. to Uganda." Booklist

590   Animals

Lavers, Chris

Why elephants have big ears; understanding patterns of life on Earth. St. Martin's Press 2001 269p il $24.95; pa $13.95   **590**

1. Animals 2. Evolution

ISBN 0-312-26902-1; 0-312-30333-5 pa

LC 00-45997

"Lavers analyzes why animals look the way they do, why they live where they live, and why their physiology is either warm or cold-blooded. . . . He then examines the evolution of animal life and the corollary evolution of warmbloodedness." Booklist

Includes bibliographical references

590.73   Collections and exhibits of living mammals

Anthony, Lawrence

Babylon's ark; the incredible wartime rescue of the Baghdad Zoo. [by] Lawrence Anthony with Graham Spence. Thomas Dunne Books 2007 248p il hardcover o.p. pa $14.95   **590.73**

1. Zoos 2. Iraq War, 2003-2011 3. Wildlife conservation 4. Iraq War, 2003- 5. Baghdad Zoo (Iraq)

ISBN 978-0-312-35832-7; 0-312-35832-6; 978-0-312-38215-5 pa; 0-312-38215-4 pa

LC 2006-50573

"This remarkable story recounts the recent wartime rescue of the once-world-renowned Baghdad Zoo through the experiences of a South African conservationist and heroic Iraqi zookeepers." Booklist

Baratay, Eric
★ **Zoo** : a history of zoological gardens in the West; [by] Eric Baratay, Elisabeth Hardouin-Fugier. Reaktion Bks. 2002 400p il $40   **590.73**
1. Zoos
ISBN 1-86189-111-3
In this history of zoos the authors "take a social history focus, examining how people view wild animals and how that has changed over time. . . . One can read the text or spend hours simply enjoying the images. Libraries that have other titles on zoos will still want to purchase this." Libr J
Includes bibliographical references

French, Thomas
Zoo story; life in the garden of captives. Hyperion 2010 288p $24.99   **590.73**
1. Zoos 2. Lowry Park Zoo
ISBN 978-1-4013-2346-2
The author "chronicles the rise of Lowry Park from one of the worst zoos in the country to one of the best. . . . This behind-the-scenes look will both entertain and enlighten animal lovers. It is a story that needs to be told, and French does it superbly." Libr J
Includes bibliographical references

Hanson, Elizabeth
Animal attractions; nature on display in American zoos. Princeton Univ. Press 2002 243p il $29.95   **590.73**
1. Zoos
ISBN 0-691-05992-6
LC 2001-55198
This book "examines the meaning of nature in the city by looking at the ways zoos have assembled and displayed their animal collections." Publisher's note
"If ever a book lived up to its title and subtitle, this one, an interesting and readable history of zoos and influences on their development in the US, certainly does." Choice
Includes bibliographical references

Robinson, Phillip T.
★ **Life** at the zoo: behind the scenes with the animal doctors. Columbia University Press 2004 293p il $27.95; pa $17.95   **590.73**
1. Zoos
ISBN 0-231-13248-4; 0-231-13249-2 pa
LC 2004-43893
"It would be difficult to cover even one aspect, such as animal health, that might affect the overall management of a zoo, but Dr. Philip Robinson manages to provide an excellent coverage of just about everything that might be involved in the operation of a zoo." Sci Books Films
Includes bibliographical references

590.75 Museum activities and services

Milgrom, Melissa
Still life; adventures in taxidermy. Houghton Mifflin Harcourt 2010 285p $25   **590.75**
1. Taxidermy
ISBN 978-0-618-40547-3
LC 2009-13511
"An animated initiation to the realm of taxidermy—its cultural significance, its hybrid status between art, craft and science, and the obsessive, idiosyncratic personalities who practice it. . . . Brimming with respect and immersive vitality." Kirkus

591.3 Genetics, evolution, age characteristics

Nielsen, Claus
Animal evolution; interrelationships of the living phyla. Claus Nielsen. Oxford University Press 2012 x, 402 p.p (hbk) $69.99   **591.3**
1. Evolution 2. Developmental biology 3. Unicellular organisms 4. Phylogeny 5. Evolution (Biology)
ISBN 0199606021; 019960603X; 9780199606023; 9780199606030
LC 2011941928
In this book, Claus Nielsen "examines the unity of the animal kingdom by tracing the evolution of all the 31 living phyla from their unicellar ancestor. The second edition incorporates new morphological data and new topic areas from the past decade, including histological/ultrastructural and embriological data, numerical cladistic analyses, DNA sequencing and developmental biology." (Booknews)
Includes bibliographical references and index.

591.5 Behavior

American Museum of Natural History
Animal life; Charlotte Uhlenbroek, [editor in chief] DK Pub. 2008 512p il map $50   **591.5**
1. Animal behavior 2. Animals -- Pictorial works
ISBN 978-0-7566-3986-0; 0-7566-3986-7
LC 2008-300010
This book "provides an excellent overview of the animal world written at a level accessible to students and the general public. Introductory sections cover basics of animal life such as evolution, animal history, classification, and anatomy. Animal behavior receives the most extensive treatment, encompassing living space, hunting and feeding, defense mechanisms, sex and reproduction, birth and development, society, communication, and intelligence." Booklist

Balcombe, Jonathan
The **exultant** ark; a pictorial tour of animal pleasure. University of California Press 2011 214p il $34.95   **591.5**
1. Pleasure 2. Animal behavior
ISBN 978-0-520-26024-5; 0-520-26024-4
LC 2010-43747

"As animal behaviourist Jonathan Balcombe sees it, too often the animal kingdom is portrayed solely as a realm of dire and perpetual struggle for survival. He argues that observations of playfulness or expressions of pleasure by non-human creatures of all stripes, feathers and fins are depicted as nothing more than evolutionary adaptation. The Exultant Ark, his pictorial exploration of pleasure among creatures from primate to porpoise, challenges this idea. It intersperses glorious images of animals preening, grooming and gallivanting with snippets of studies suggesting such behaviours belie an overly utilitarian interpretation." New Sci

Includes bibliographical references

Pleasurable kingdom; animals and the nature of feeling good. Macmillan 2006 274p il $24.95; pa $14.95   **591.5**
1. Pleasure 2. Animal behavior
ISBN 1-4039-8601-0; 978-1-4039-8601-6; 1-4039-8602-9 pa; 978-1-4039-8602-3 pa

LC 2006-41734

This is an "examination of positive feelings in animals. . . . [The author] first defines what is meant by pleasure and why it is worthy of study, then looks at several potentially pleasure-causing activities: play, eating, sex, touching, and love. Full of examples both anecdotal and from refereed journals . . . this book not only makes a case for animal pleasure but calls for more research on the science of pleasure in animals, allowing humans to view them in a new way." Booklist

Includes bibliographical references

Second nature; the inner lives of animals. foreword by J.M. Coetzee. Palgrave Macmillan 2010 242p il $27.00; $27.00   **591.5**
1. Animal behavior 2. Animal intelligence 3. Animal psychology 4. Social behavior in animals
ISBN 0230613624; 9780230613621

LC 2009-30770

The author of Pleasurable Kingdom (2006) argues that animals are "sentient beings capable of feelings and pain and emotions." (Publisher's note) Index.

The author "draws on the latest research, observational studies and personal anecdotes to reveal the full gamut of animal experience—from emotions, to problem solving, to moral judgment. Balcombe challenges the widely held idea that nature is red in tooth and claw, highlighting animal traits we have disregarded until now: their nuanced understanding of social dynamics, their consideration for others, and their strong tendency to avoid violent conflict." Publisher's note

Includes bibliographical references

Bekoff, Marc
Wild justice; the moral lives of animals. [by] Marc Bekoff and Jessica Pierce. University of Chicago Press 2009 188p il $26; pa $17   **591.5**
1. Animal behavior 2. Animal intelligence 3. Animal psychology 4. Motivation in animals 5. Social behavior in animals
ISBN 0-226-04161-1; 0-226-04163-8 pa; 978-0-226-04161-2; 978-0-226-04163-6 pa

LC 2008-40173

Bekoff and Pierce argue "that animals exhibit a broad repertoire of moral behaviors, including fairness, empathy, trust, and reciprocity. Underlying these behaviors is a complex and nuanced range of emotions, backed by a high degree of intelligence and surprising behavioral flexibility. . . . [The authors draw the] conclusion that there is no moral gap between humans and other species: morality is an evolved trait that we unquestionably share with other social mammals." (Publisher's note) Index.

The authors "discuss recent scientific studies documenting that great apes, monkeys, wolves, coyotes, hyenas, dolphins, whales, elephants, rats, and mice are capable of a wide range of moral behavior. They strongly urge the scientific and philosophical communities to recognize that these animals can act as moral agents within the context of their own social groups. This provocative and well-argued view of animal morality may surprise some readers as it challenges outdated assumptions about animals." Libr J

Includes bibliographical references and index

Berger, Joel
The **better** to eat you with; fear in the animal world. University of Chicago Press 2008 305p il map $29   **591.5**
1. Fear 2. Animal behavior
ISBN 978-0-226-04363-0; 0-226-04363-0

LC 2008-00418

The author "ostensibly attempts to answer whether the fear of predation in animals is innate or learned. In reality, his book is a memoir of a research career spent in some of the most inhospitable places on Earth, including Alaska, Greenland, Siberia, and Mongolia. . . . [He] recounts his research as a series of adventure stories that portray the rewards and pitfalls of conducting biological field investigations." Choice

This is "an engaging book about how an understanding of predator-prey dynamics can inform conservation biology." Times Higher Ed

Includes bibliographical references (p. 287-292)

Boysen, Sarah Till
The **smartest** animals on the planet; with a contribution from Deborah Custance. Firefly Books 2009 192p il map $35   **591.5**
1. Animal behavior 2. Animal intelligence
ISBN 978-1-5540-7456-3; 1-5540-7456-8

In this study on animal intelligence, "each animal is placed into one of seven categories—tool making and use, communication, learned social behaviors, individual self-awareness, numerical ability, language learning and group cooperation/mutual protection . . . showing how animals place on different axes of intelligence." Publ Wkly

"Succinctly written and sumptuously illustrated with photographs and diagrams, this appealing book is sure to fascinate the general reader and inspire the science student considering a career in animal behavior or cognition." Libr J

Braitman, Laurel
Animal madness; how anxious dogs, compulsive parrots, and elephants in recovery help us understand

ourselves. Laurel Braitman. Simon & Schuster 2014 384 p. (hardback) $28   **591.5**
   1. Mental illness 2. Animal behavior 3. Comparative psychology 4. Animal psychology
ISBN 1451627009; 9781451627008

LC 2014000791

This book by Laurel Braitman "draws evidence from across the world to show how humans and other animals are astonishingly similar when it comes to their feelings and the ways in which they lose their minds. . . . Nonhuman animals can lose their minds. And when they do, it often looks a lot like human mental illness." (Publisher's note)

"Braitman's gradual accretion of reasons to believe in animal emotional states that we can relate to, including the loopy ones, gives pause and sparks curiosity." Kirkus

★ **Encyclopedia** of animal behavior; edited by Marc Bekoff; foreword by Jane Goodall. Greenwood Press 2004 3v il set $349.95   **591.5**
   1. Animal behavior
ISBN 0-313-32745-9

LC 2004-56073

This encyclopedia describes "what makes animals tick using techniques that range from molecular approaches to analysis of species. The 300 entries, some stretching to 7000 words, discuss topics as diverse as concept learning in pigeons and stress in dolphins." Libr J
Includes bibliographical references

Grandin, Temple, 1947-
   ★ **Animals** in translation; using the mysteries of autism to decode animal behavior. [by] Temple Grandin and Catherine Johnson. Scribner 2010 356p $28; ebook $18.99   **591.5**
   1. Autism 2. Animal behavior
ISBN 978-1-4391-8710-4; 978-1-4391-3084-1 ebook
First published 2005
"This fascinating book will teach readers to see as animals see, to be a little more visual and a little less verbal, and, as a unique analysis of animal behavior, it belongs in all libraries." Booklist
Includes bibliographical references

Griffin, Donald Redfield
   Animal minds; beyond cognition to consciousness. {by} Donald R. Griffin. {Rev and expanded}; University of Chicago Press 2001 355p $27.50 **591.5**
   1. Animal behavior
ISBN 0-226-30865-0

LC 00-10006

First published 1992
The author "moves beyond considerations of animal cognition to argue that scientists can and should investigate questions of animal consciousness. Using examples from studies of species ranging from chimpanzees and dolphins to birds and honeybees, he demonstrates how communication among animals can serve as a 'window' into what animals think and feel, just as human speech and nonverbal communication tell us most of what we know about the thoughts and feelings of other people." Publisher's note

"Griffin's book will enlighten, delight and even ruffle some feathers." Publ Wkly
Includes bibliographical references (p.) and index

Linden, Eugene
   The **octopus** and the orangutan; more true tales of animal intrigue, intelligence, and ingenuity. Dutton 2002 242p $23.95; pa $14   **591.5**
   1. Animal behavior 2. Animal intelligence
ISBN 0-525-94661-6; 0-452-28411-2 pa

LC 2002-67434

The author "presents anecdotes that illustrate the workings of the minds of both domestic and wild creatures—how they use tools, play games and adapt to change." Publ Wkly
"Linden's chatty writing style, along with the science behind the stories that he occasionally slips in, makes for entertaining and enlightening reading." Booklist
Includes bibliographical references (p.)

Masson, J. Moussaieff
   The **pig** who sang to the moon; the emotional world of farm animals. {by} Jeffrey Moussaieff Masson. Ballantine Books 2003 277p il $25.95; pa $13.95   **591.5**
   1. Domestic animals 2. Animal intelligence
ISBN 0-345-45281-X; 0-345-45282-8 pa

LC 2003-61773

The author "makes the case that the animals humans eat on a regular basis—pigs, chickens, sheep, cows and ducks—feel, think and suffer. Each animal gets a chapter, in which Masson interweaves folklore, science and literature (he quotes Darwin, Gandhi and the Bible) with his observations of the animals' behaviors." Publ Wkly
"Masson is passionate in his beliefs, and a strong thread of animal rights runs through his entire narrative. Readers not convinced by his philosophy will learn quite a bit about the animals we mostly take for granted." Booklist
Includes bibliographical references

   When elephants weep; the emotional lives of animals. {by} Jeffrey Moussaieff Masson and Susan McCarthy. Delacorte Press 1995 xxiii, 291p il hardcover o.p. pa $15.95   **591.5**
   1. Animal behavior 2. Animal intelligence
ISBN 0-385-31428-0 pa

LC 94-23819

The authors gather "the evidence to date for the existence of emotions and, hence, something approaching human consciousness in animals. . . . Masson and McCarthy do a commendable job of synthesizing the material they tackle . . . making it efficiently readable." Booklist
Includes bibliographical references

McCarthy, Susan
   ★ **Becoming** a tiger; how baby animals learn to live in the wild. HarperCollins 2004 418p hardcover o.p. pa $13.95   **591.5**
   1. Animal intelligence
ISBN 0-06-620924-2; 0-06-093484-0 pa

LC 2003-67553

The author examines "the ways that animals figure out how to function in their worlds. . . . One of the basic things a baby animal must learn is how to get from one place to another in a manner appropriate to its species. Other basics involve learning to recognize your own species, to communicate, to find food, and not to become some other species' food. McCarthy discusses species as various as horses, bonobos, zebra finches, and fruit-fly maggots to illustrate the learning process." Booklist

"McCarthy writes clearly and her penchant for humor . . . makes the book an easy read, both for students of learning and those who can't get enough of television's Animal Planet." Publ Wkly

Includes bibliographical references

Morell, Virginia

Animal wise; the thoughts and emotions of our fellow creatures. Virginia Morell. Random House Inc 2013 304 p. $26   **591.5**
   1. Animal behavior 2. Thought and thinking 3. Cognition in animals 4. Human-animal communication
   ISBN 0307461440; 9780307461445
                                                        LC 2012031503
This book, by Virginia Morell, "explores the frontiers of research on animal cognition and emotion. . . . [The book] takes us . . . into the inner world of animals, from ants to elephants to wolves, and from sharp-shooting archerfish to pods of dolphins that rumble like rival street gangs. . . . She probes the moral and ethical dilemmas of recognizing that even 'lesser animals' have cognitive abilities such as memory, feelings, personality, and self-awareness." (Publisher's note)

Smoller, Jordan

The other side of normal; how biology is providing the clues to unlock the secrets of normal and abnormal behavior. Jordan Smoller. HarperCollins 2012 390 p.   **591.5**
   1. Psychology 2. Human behavior 3. Mental illness 4. Behavior genetics 5. Abnormal psychology 6. Psychobiology 7. Norm (Philosophy) 8. Biological psychiatry
   ISBN 0061492191; 9780061492198; 9780061492204
                                                        LC 2011040827
In this book, "[t]he author uses the 2010 announcement by the American Psychiatric Association of provisional plans to revise the Diagnostic and Statistical Manual of Mental Disorders as an opportunity to revisit the hot-button issue of what constitutes mental disease. In his opinion, one of the shortcomings of the DSM is its creation of 'categories from constellations of symptoms' without understanding how they connect to the 'functional organization of the mind and brain.'" (Kirkus)

Includes bibliographical references

Weiner, Jonathan

Time, love, memory; a great biologist and his quest for the origins of behavior. Knopf 1999 300p il $27.50; pa $14   **591.5**
   1. Behavior genetics 2. Biophysicists 3. Neuroscientists 4. College teachers
   ISBN 0-679-44435-1; 0-679-76390-2 pa
                                                        LC 98-43128

An exploration of the work of "one of the unsung pioneers of molecular biology: brash, eccentric physicist-turned-biologist Seymour Benzer. By studying tiny genetic mutations in the fruit fly, Benzer seeks to shed light on the question of whether genes determine behavior. Weiner . . . presents an elegant scientific detective story." Publ Wkly

Includes bibliographical references

Wynne, Clive D. L.

Do animals think? Princeton University Press 2004 268p il $26.95   **591.5**
   1. Animal intelligence
   ISBN 0-691-11311-4
                                                        LC 2003-60019
The author "shows how bats, bees, pigeons, and dolphins perceive their worlds quite differently from the way humans do. . . . Readers will delight in this insightful, well-referenced book." Choice

Includes bibliographical references

591.56   Behavior relating to life cycle

Bagemihl, Bruce

Biological exuberance; animal homosexuality and natural diversity. illustrated by John Megahan. St. Martin's Press 1999 751p il map $40; pa $21.95   **591.56**
   1. Homosexuality 2. Animal behavior
   ISBN 0-312-19239-8; 0-312-25377-X pa
                                                        LC 98-28528
The author "challenges the belief that homosexuality is an aberration in nature by revealing the documented homosexual or transgendered behavior of 450 animal species. Contesting the idea that scarcity and functionality are the primary agents of biological change, biologist Bagemihl persuasively argues that abundance and extravagance are just as crucial to the mosaic of life." Publ Wkly

Includes bibliographical references

Wilcove, David S.

No way home; the decline of the world's great animal migrations. with illustrations by Louise Zemaitis. Island Press/Shearwater Books 2008 253p il map $24.95   **591.56**
   1. Environmental degradation 2. Animals -- Migration
   ISBN 978-1-55963-985-9; 1-55963-985-7
                                                        LC 2007-26205
The author presents a "report on the status of the world's great migratory species: songbirds, butterflies, locusts, bison, wildebeest, whales, sea turtles, and salmon. Citing both anecdotal and scientific evidence, he describes what these spectacular migrations were like at their peak, what they have dwindled to today, and what they are likely to become in the future." Libr J

"Absorbing and thought provoking, [this work] deserves to be widely read and used to promote conservation action." Science

Includes bibliographical references

Zuk, M.

Sexual selections; what we can and can't learn about sex from animals. {by} Marlene Zuk. University of Calif. Press 2002 239p il $40; pa $16.95 **591.56**

1. Sexual behavior in animals

ISBN 0-520-21974-0; 0-520-24075-8 pa

LC 2001-5771

This book "exposes the anthropomorphism and gender politics that have colored our understanding of the natural world and shows how feminism can help move us away from our ideological biases." Publisher's note

"Fascinating and persuasive. Zuk is not an idealogue, just an unusually clear-eyed scholar." N Y Times Book Rev

Includes bibliographical references and index

591.59   Communication

Friend, Tim

Animal talk; breaking the codes of animal language. Free Press 2004 274p il $25; pa $15 **591.59**

1. Animal communication

ISBN 0-7432-0157-4; 0-7432-0158-2 pa

LC 2003-63107

"The author describes the methods of, and reasons behind, animal communication and demonstrates that human and animal communication are not so widely disparate as once believed. Friend also gives background details on the basics of communication theory, genetics, evolution, and the progression of scientific thought regarding animal communication. . . . His humorous and engaging prose style makes this a captivating read." Libr J

Includes bibliographical references

591.6   Miscellaneous nontaxonomic kinds of animals

Grice, Gordon

Deadly kingdom; the book of dangerous animals. Dial Press 2010 xxv, 324p il $27; ebook $27 **591.6**

1. Dangerous animals

ISBN 978-0-385-33562-1; 978-0-385-33562-1 ebook

LC 2009-33933

Describes the author's lifelong obsession with dangerous animals that prompted his amateur studies with virtually all dangerous creatures, from sharks and bears to alligators and spiders.

"This darkly fascinating book might add a few words to your vocabulary: anthropophagy (the eating of humans), or the verb to flense (to strip off skin). . . . Grice was clearly the sort of kid who left the house at dawn with a packed lunch and a bag full of bug jars. He peppers Deadly Kingdom with his own stories, and defends animals as only behaving as they are meant to." Maclean's

Includes bibliographical references

Quammen, David

★ **Monster** of God; the man-eating predator in the jungles of history and the mind. Norton 2003 513p maps $26.95; pa $15.95 **591.6**

1. Dangerous animals 2. Predatory animals 3. Endangered species

ISBN 0-393-05140-4; 0-393-32609-8 pa

LC 2003-7812

This is an "account of efforts to preserve large top-of-the-food-chain carnivores like tigers and crocodiles, and a meditation on what life would be like without them." N Y Times Book Rev

"Rich with personal stories that clarify humanity's true place in the universe, this book will leave the reader eager for more. . . . This has all the makings of a science book of the year. Highly recommended." Libr J

Includes bibliographical references

591.68   Rare and endangered animals

Weidensaul, Scott

The **ghost** with trembling wings; science, wishful thinking, and the search for lost species. North Point Press 2002 341p il maps $26; pa $15 **591.68**

1. Rare animals 2. Extinct animals

ISBN 0-374-24664-5; 0-86547-668-3 pa

LC 2001-54605

"Weidensaul's narrative concerns those rare occurrences when a supposedly extinct animal makes a surprise reappearance, and the much more frequent occasions when scientists or civilians only think they've sighted a vanished creature." Publ Wkly

"Weidensaul is a graceful writer who works an amazing amount of scientific theory into his narrative." Booklist

Includes bibliographical references

591.7   Animal ecology, animals characteristic of specific environments

Heinrich, Bernd

Life everlasting; the animal way of death. Bernd Heinrich. Houghton Mifflin Harcourt 2012 xiv, 236 p.p **591.7**

1. Death 2. Zoology 3. Animal behavior 4. Animal communication 5. Life cycles (Biology) 6. Animal ecology 7. Animal life cycles 8. Animals -- Psychological aspects

ISBN 0547752660; 9780547752662

LC 2012010583

This book "explores the taboos and relevance of scavengers, the 'life-giving links that keep nature's systems humming along smoothly.' After a friend asked if he could be buried on the author's woodland property in Maine, he reexamined his curiosity with the natural world . . . [Bernd] Heinrich presents five major sections outlining how bodies and plants are recycled and broken down: small to large . . . north to south . . . plant undertakers . . . watery deaths . . . and changes (metamorphosis and death rituals). Above all, temperature affects how and what breaks down carrion as the flies and insects of summer are replaced by various birds in the winter. The author also tracks how trees decompose, a process that often begins before they die". (Kirkus Reviews)

Summer world; a season of bounty. Ecco 2009 253p il $26.95 **591.7**

1. Summer 2. Animals

ISBN 978-0-06-074217-1; 0-06-074217-8

A discussion of animal survival in the hot season explores the ways in which animals make the most of the summer's short span by efficiently compacting most of their procreative and survival activities.

"Heinrich presents natural science at its engaging best." Kirkus

Includes bibliographical references

Naskrecki, Piotr

The **smaller** majority; the hidden world of the animals that dominate the tropics. Belknap Press of Harvard University Press 2005 278p il $35 **591.7**

1. Invertebrates 2. Tropics 3. Animals -- Pictorial works

ISBN 0-674-01915-6; 978-0-674-01915-7

LC 2005-46060

In this book the author "includes over 400 . . . full-color photographs of animals that are generally smaller than the human finger. The author . . . [has] collected images of animals from Costa Rica, Guinea, the Dominical Republic, the Solomon Islands, Australia, South Africa, Botswana, and Namibia." Choice

"Naskrecki's exuberant, expert knowledge of this microscopic world has been distilled down to the most arresting details. Crisp, enjoyable prose, clearly explains complex biological processes." Publ Wkly

Includes bibliographical references

Zimmer, Carl

★ **Parasite** rex; inside the bizarre world of nature's most dangerous creatures. Free Press 2000 xxii, 298p il hardcover o.p. pa $14 **591.7**

1. Parasites

ISBN 0-7432-0011-X pa

LC 00-37593

This is a chronicle of the effects of parasites on plants and animals

"The importance of Zimmer's book lies not only in its accessible presentation of the new science of evolutionary parasitology but in its thoughtful treatment of the global strategies and policies that scientists, health workers and governments will have to consider in order to manage parasites in the future." N Y Times Book Rev

Includes bibliographical references

591.9 Animals by specific continents, countries, localities

Bambaradeniya, Channa N. B.

The **illustrated** atlas of wildlife; [by] Channa Bambaradeniya [et al.] University of California Press 2009 288p il map $39.95 **591.9**

1. Atlases 2. Biogeography 3. Reference books

ISBN 978-0-520-25785-6; 0-520-25785-5

LC 2008-40625

"This gorgeous book, featuring detailed, customized maps and more than 800 photographs . . . and original artworks, presents a spectacular visual survey of wild animals across the globe and describes in detail their habitats, physical characteristics, diet, and behavior. . . . [It also includes] conservation and preservation data, information about human impact upon the world's complex ecosystems, and chronicles of the evolution and adaptation of animals over the ages." Education Digest

Includes glossary and bibliographical references

592 Specific taxonomic groups of animals

Attenborough, David

Life in the undergrowth. Princeton University Press 2006 288p il $29.95 **592**

1. Invertebrates

ISBN 0-691-12703-4

LC 2005-934727

The author "explores the lives of the planet's land-based invertebrates. Concentrating mainly on insects and spiders, the author investigates all aspects of the animals' life cycles." Booklist

"This wonderful exploration of invertebrates exceeds the requirements for a great nature book through the strength of its photographs and the quality of its prose." Publ Wkly

Hubbell, Sue

Waiting for Aphrodite; journeys into the time before bones. with illustrations by Liddy Hubbell. Houghton Mifflin 1999 242p il $24; pa $13 **592**

1. Invertebrates

ISBN 0-395-83703-0; 0-618-05684-X pa

LC 98-49811

"These essays on natural history discuss everything from the orange-humped crickets that are unique to Missouri and the iridescent butterflies of Costa Rica to the furry sea mice that live in the coastal waters near the writer's new house, in Maine. Hubbell is both a delighted home scientist and a glinting memoirist, and her observations are interspersed with accounts of her fresh life in the East." New Yorker

Includes bibliographical references

Stewart, Amy

The **earth** moved; on the remarkable achievements of earthworms. Algonquin Bks. 2004 223p $23.95; pa $12.95 **592**

1. Worms 2. Earthworms

ISBN 1-56512-337-9; 1-56512-468-5 pa

LC 2003-52379

Stewart discusses earthworms. "This peaceful, delicate creature, Stewart writes, has posed a large task for scientists, who have taken more than 100 years to piece together a portrait of the earthworm's dark life. But the subterrestrials still have more to teach us, even as creatures like the giant Oregon earthworm are being pushed to the brink of extinction." (Christ Sci Monit)

The author explores "the impact worms have on humans and on our planet. . . . {She} educates on the vital roles these creatures play in growing crops, how they can neutralize the effects of nuclear waste on soil, and their ability to regenerate new body parts. . . . A book that's as enlightening as it is entertaining." SLJ

Includes bibliographical references

594 Mollusks and molluscoids

Harasewych, M. G.

The **book** of shells; a life-size guide to identifying and classifying six hundred seashells. [by] M.G. Harasewych & Fabio Moretzsohn. University of Chicago Press 2010 655p il map $55   **594**

1. Shells 2. Mollusks 3. Reference books
ISBN 978-0-226-31577-5; 0-226-31577-0

LC 2009-34321

This book "provides an excellent introduction to the major classes of sea-living mollusks worldwide. Students and the lay enthusiast will find the 600 entries accessible and engaging. . . . A table lists the family, shell-size range, distribution, abundance, depth, habitat, feeding habit, and the presence or absence of an operculum. A color range map, genus and species and common name, a paragraph-long description of the species, a listing of related species, a color life-size illustration, and, for small shells, a larger, more detailed image complete the information." Booklist

Includes bibliographical references

Williams, Wendy

Kraken; the curious, exciting, and slightly disturbing science of squid. Abrams Image 2011 223p il $21.95   **594**

1. Squids
ISBN 978-0-8109-8465-3

LC 2010032489

This book "traces sightings of the giant squid throughout the centuries. . . . Discussion of the anatomy, physiology, reproduction, evolution, and taxonomy of Architeuthis is provided, along with accounts of the author's visits to various scientific laboratories and descriptions of research studies being conducted on the animal. . . . This serves as a good introduction to the subject for general readers and an inspiration to young people interested in marine biology." Libr J

Includes filmography and bibliographical references

595 Arthropods

Fortey, Richard

Horseshoe crabs and velvet worms; the story of the animals and plants that time has left behind. by

Richard Fortey. Alfred A. Knopf 2012 320 p. ill. (some col.) $28.95   **595**

1. Botany 2. Zoology 3. Paleontology 4. Worms 5. Plant conservation 6. Arthropoda -- Conservation 7. Invertebrates -- Conservation 8. Limulus polyphemus -- Conservation
ISBN 9780307263612

LC 2011039941

This book by Richard Fortey introduces "the reader to organisms that seemingly have undergone little change since their ancient origins. . . . Evolution has never stopped, and Fortey discusses changes that occur at the molecular level in response to predation pressure and other changing environmental conditions. He starts his journey by witnessing the spectacular spawning of horseshoe crabs, the closest living relatives of his specialty, the trilobites." (Choice: Current Reviews for Academic Libraries)

"Informative, engrossing and delightful." Kirkus

595.4 Chelicerates

Beccaloni, Jan

Arachnids. University of California Press 2009 320p il $39.95   **595.4**

1. Mites 2. Ticks 3. Spiders
ISBN 978-0-520-26140-2; 0-520-26140-2

LC 2009-18657

"This book is overflowing with scientific data and crystal-clear images of strange insects that are certain to make your skin crawl. Free of myths and misconceptions, this book delivers the real facts on the diverse arachnid family which includes a wide variety of scorpions, ticks, mites, and over 38,000 species of spiders. They vary from bizarre to beautiful and a few are even deadly but all are interesting and sure to spark your imagination." Shutterbug

Includes bibliographical references

595.7 Insects

Alcock, John

In a desert garden; love and death among the insects. with illustrations by Turid Forsyth. Norton 1997 186p il $27.50   **595.7**

1. Insects 2. Desert ecology
ISBN 0-393-04118-2

LC 97-589

The focus of this "work is the author's own front yard in Tempe, Arizona, and its insect inhabitants. . . . Readers will gain insights into how science is practiced as the author's lively, often humorous observations of assorted beetles, bugs, wasps, bees, caterpillars, and butterflies are related to broad concepts of animal behavior, ecology, and survival." Libr J

Includes bibliographical references

Brock, James P.

★ **Kaufman** field guide to butterflies of North America; [by] Jim P. Brock and Kenn Kaufman; with the collaboration of Rick and Nora Bowers and Lynn

Hassler. Houghton Mifflin 2006 391p il map pa
$19.95   **595.7**

1. Butterflies

ISBN 0-618-76826-2; 978-0-618-76826-4

LC 2006-287515

First published 2003 with title: Butterflies of
North America

"Each species is listed by common name and scientific
name and receives a several-sentence description, including
flight time and larval food plants. All except very local or accidental species also are shown on range maps. The illustrations are opposite the written description, with most species
pictured in multiple images. . . . The illustrations are created
by digital enhancement of photographs. . . . An essential
purchase for all libraries." Booklist [review of 2003 edition]

Capinera, John L.

Field guide to grasshoppers, crickets, and katydids of the United States; [by] John L. Capinera,
Ralph D. Scott, and Thomas J. Walker. Cornell University Press 2004 249p il maps hardcover o.p. pa
$29.95   **595.7**

1. Crickets 2. Grasshoppers

ISBN 0-8014-4260-5; 0-8014-8948-2 pa

LC 2004-10727

This "field guide to U.S. and Canadian orthoptera introduces 206 of the most common species. . . . It explains classification, morphology (illustrated), biology, sound production, and collection and preservation, and presents pictorial
keys to families and subfamilies." Libr J

"The highlight is certainly the 50 pages of Scott's color
illustrations. . . . For those who want to know what's plaguing them when locusts descend, this is the book." Publ Wkly

Includes bibliographical references

Carde, Ring T.

Encyclopedia of insects; editors, Vincent H.
Resh, Ring T. Cardé. 2nd ed; Elsevier/Academic
Press 2009 xxxiii, 1132p il map $120   **595.7**

1. Reference books 2. Insects -- Encyclopedias

ISBN 978-0-12-374144-8

First published 2003

This book covers "all aspects of insect anatomy, physiology, evolution, behavior, reproduction, ecology, and disease,
as well as issues of exploitation, conservation, and management." Publisher's note

Includes bibliographical references

Eisner, Thomas

For love of insects. Belknap Press of Harvard
University Press 2003 448p il $35; pa $19.95 **595.7**

1. Insects

ISBN 0-674-01181-3; 0-674-01827-3 pa

LC 2003-44399

"Ranging from a caterpillar who feeds on flowers while
disguising as one by affixing petals to his back, to a beetle
who can resist a pull 200 times his own weight, the book
is full of little known information about how insects feed,

fight, and reproduce." Univ Press Books for Public and Second Sch Libr, 2006

Includes bibliographical references

★ **Secret** weapons; defenses of insects, spiders,
scorpions, and other many-legged creatures. [by]
Thomas Eisner, Maria Eisner, Melody V.S. Siegler.
Belknap Press of Harvard University Press 2005
372p il $29.95; pa $18.95   **595.7**

1. Insects 2. Spiders 3. Animal defenses

ISBN 0-674-01882-6; 0-674-02403-6 pa

LC 2005-41042

"This volume presents 69 case studies of organisms from
4 orders of spiders, 2 of centipedes, 5 of millipedes, and 10
of insects. Most of the studies address defensive chemistry
and identify the chemical(s) involved, how each is acquired,
stored, and deployed." Sci Books Films

"This very readable and well-illustrated book will appeal
to all those interested in disciplines like biology, entomology, and ecology." Choice

Includes bibliographical references

Ellis, Hattie

Sweetness & light; the mysterious history of the
honeybee. Harmony Books 2004 243p il hardcover
o.p. pa $13.95   **595.7**

1. Bees 2. Beekeeping

ISBN 1-4000-5405-2; 1-4000-5406-0 pa

LC 2004-4116

"What a delightful volume on the honeybee this is: Not
only is the reader treated to a wealth of information on the biology, ecology, and economic importance of that insect, but
the interrelationship of the honeybee and humanity throughout history is very nicely presented." Sci Books Films

Includes bibliographical references

Evans, Arthur V.

An inordinate fondness for beetles; [by] Arthur V. Evans, Charles L. Bellamy; photography by
Lisa Charles Watson; illustrations by Patricia Wynne. University of California Press 2000 208p il pa
$31.95   **595.7**

1. Beetles

ISBN 0-520-22323-3; 978-0-520-22323-3

LC 99-46118

First published 1996 by Henry Holt and Company

"The six chapters cover beetle numbers and diversity,
their body plan and functions, their life histories, habits, and
defenses, their evolution, their interactions with humans,
and their aesthetic importance and conservation." Libr J

"The incredible full-color photographs bring readers up
close without a magnifying lens at hand, and the seemingly
infinite variations within the species due to size, structure,
and color are easily seen. . . . While the text is scientific, it is
very readable." SLJ

Includes bibliographical references

Himmelman, John

Cricket radio; tuning in the night-singing insects. Belknap Press of Harvard University Press 2011 254p il $22.95 **595.7**

1. Crickets 2. Katydids

ISBN 978-0-674-04690-0

LC 2010-35203

The author explores "what moves crickets and katydids to sing, how they produce their distinctive sounds, how they hear the songs of others, and how they vary cadence, volume, and pitch to attract potential mates, warn off competitors, and evade predators." Publisher's note

Includes bibliographical references

Hölldobler, Bert

The leafcutter ants; civilization by instinct. [by] Bert Hölldobler and Edward O. Wilson. Norton 2010 160p il pa $19.95 **595.7**

1. Ants

ISBN 978-0-393-33868-3

LC 2010-16202

The authors "introduce the general reader to earth's most evolved animal society. With the colony's queen as its reproductive organ; the various ages and types of workers as the brain, heart, and other organs; and the communication among the ants similar to the communication of nerves and ganglia, a leafcutter ant colony can be truly considered as a superorganism." Booklist

Includes bibliographical references

The superorganism; the beauty, elegance, and strangeness of insect societies. [by] Bert Hölldobler and Edward O. Wilson; line drawings by Margaret C. Nelson. W.W. Norton & Company 2009 xxi, 522p il $55 **595.7**

1. Insects

ISBN 978-0-393-06704-0; 0-393-06704-1

LC 2008-38547

"This study covers mathematical analysis as well as field data, but in a straightforward manner that guides readers from one remarkable fact or concept to the next, inspiring wonder at the origin of our own societies." Publ Wkly

Includes bibliographical references

Keller, Laurent

The lives of ants; by Laurent Keller and Élisabeth Gordon; translated by James Grieve. Oxford University Press 2009 252p il $27.95; pa $15.95 **595.7**

1. Ants

ISBN 978-0-19-954186-7; 0-19-954186-8; 978-0-19-954187-4 pa; 0-19-954187-6 pa

LC 2008-943416

The authors "provide a lucid . . . overview of any evolution, ecology, biology, behavior, and genetics that easily communicates complex research in these areas to a wide audience." Sci Books Films

Includes bibliographical references

Laufer, Peter

The dangerous world of butterflies; the startling subculture of criminals, collectors, and conservationists. Lyons Press 2009 271p $24.95 **595.7**

1. Butterflies

ISBN 978-1-59921-555-6; 1-59921-555-1

LC 2009-03115

"Laufer wants you to do more than just love them; he wants you to have some notion of the extraordinary circumstances which butterflies live through every day, whether it is as part of a hotly contested captive breeding program, or a participant in a thousand-mile, five year Monarch migration, or death at the hands of the sinister traders in endangered insect species. . . . So consider yourself warned: The Dangerous World of Butterflies might change the way you notice the world. For a book such as this, that's the highest praise of all." PopMatters

Includes bibliographical references

Milne, Lorus Johnson

The Audubon Society field guide to North American insects and spiders; [by] Lorus and Margery Milne; visual key by Susan Rayfield. Knopf 1980 989p il $19.95 **595.7**

1. Insects 2. Spiders

ISBN 0-394-50763-0

LC 80-7620

The authors "have based their field guide on 702 excellent color photographs (75 of which are of spiders and other arachnids). In addition to some general information, the text (two thirds of the book) is made up of brief comments on each kind of arthropod pictured." Choice

Includes glossary

Moffett, Mark W.

Adventures among ants; a global safari with a cast of trillions. University of California Press 2010 280p il $29.95 **595.7**

1. Ants 2. Ants -- Ecology 3. Ants -- Behavior

ISBN 978-0-520-26199-0; 0-520-26199-2

LC 2009-40610

"This superb book by a first-class writer with an unsurpassed feel for ants begins at the ground level as we come face to face with the creatures, move into their minds, and begin to understand what makes them tick. Moffett organizes his text around six ant lifestyles, each represented by an insect that dominates its habitat: Indian Marauder ants, African army ants, African Weaver ants, Amazon slavemaking ants, Neotropical leaf cutter ants, and the Argentine ant, a global invader. . . . This marvelous volume illustrated with the author's closeup photographs will delight biologists, naturalists, and general readers with a natural history bent." Libr J

Includes bibliographical references

The monarch butterfly; biology & conservation. edited by Karen S. Oberhauser & Michelle J. Solensky. Cornell University Press 2004 248p il maps (A Comstock book) $39.95 **595.7**

1. Monarch butterflies 2. Wildlife conservation

ISBN 0-8014-4188-9

LC 2004-884

"Covered is every facet of monarch breeding, migration, and overwintering, as well as population modeling and management. . . . The text is clearly written, and the mathematical formulas included in certain chapters are not essential to understanding the main ideas. The most up-to-date and comprehensive publication on monarch butterfly biology, this will be an important reference tool." Libr J

Includes bibliographical references

Pyle, Robert Michael

★ The **Audubon** Society field guide to North American butterflies; visual key by Carol Nehring and Jane Opper. Knopf 1981 916p il $19.95 **595.7**
1. Butterflies
ISBN 0-394-51914-0

LC 80-84240

This guide "introduces more than 600 species of North American butterfly, including those native to the Hawaiian Islands. A section of brilliant color plates (more than 1,000 of them) featuring butterflies in their natural habitats, follows a general introduction and notes on text organization and use." Booklist

Mariposa road; the first butterfly big year. Houghton Mifflin Harcourt 2010 558p il map $27 **595.7**
1. Butterflies
ISBN 978-0-618-94539-9

LC 2010-5763

The author "goes in search of as many butterfly species as he can find north of the Mexican border during 2008." Kirkus

"This is engaging writing—always compelling, always approachable; it should inspire all of us to set out on our own long quests on the road." Sci Books Films

Raffles, Hugh

Insectopedia. Pantheon Books 2010 465p il **595.7**
1. Insects 2. Human-animal relationships
ISBN 0375423869; 9780375423864

LC 2009-24302

"For as long as humans have existed, insects have existed, too. Wherever we've traveled, they've traveled, too. Yet we hardly know them. . . . Organizing his book alphabetically with one entry for each letter, weaving together brief vignettes, meditations, and extended essays, Raffles embarks on an . . . exploration of history and science, anthropology and travel, economics, philosophy, and popular culture to show us how insects have triggered our obsessions, stirred our passions, and beguiled our imaginations." (Publisher's note) Index.

"In addition to the fine writing, Raffles includes many intriguing drawings and illustrations, as well as a fascinating Notes section. Because of his manner of organization, there is little reason to read the book in order; you can simply open it anywhere and discover a new way to reflect on not only insects but people." Seattle Times

Includes bibliographical references

Schappert, Phil

The **last** Monarch butterfly; conserving the Monarch butterfly in a brave new world. Firefly Books 2004 113p il pa $19.95 **595.7**
1. Monarch butterflies 2. Wildlife conservation
ISBN 1-55297-969-5

LC 2005-357220

Overview of both eastern and western monarch butterflies, including their life cycle and migratory patterns. The impact of natural disasters and increasing residential and industrial development on monarch butterfly populations is also discussed.

"The narrative is enhanced by beautiful photographs and backed up by some 180 references to the scientific literature. . . . Let's hear it for the monarch, an amazing insect; if the reader has any doubts about that, this book will put them to rest." Sci Books Films

Stokes, Donald W.

The **butterfly** book; an easy guide to butterfly gardening, identification, and behavior. {by} Donald and Lillian Stokes and Ernest Williams. Little, Brown 1991 95p il maps pa $12.95 **595.7**
1. Butterflies
ISBN 0-316-81780-5

LC 91-15323

This book discusses plants which will attract butterflies, explains butterfly life cycles and behavior, and provides information for identification of over 140 species

Waldbauer, Gilbert

Insects through the seasons. Harvard Univ. Press 1996 289p il $27.50; pa $14.95 **595.7**
1. Moths 2. Insects
ISBN 0-674-45488-X; 0-674-45489-8 pa

LC 95-35171

"Waldbauer uses the yearly cycle of the cecropia moth as a base to which he periodically returns while presenting an impressive array of the tactics the moth's fellow insects and arthropod relatives use to live and thrive." Booklist

"The scientific information is excellent and the writing is fascinating." Sci Books Films

Includes bibliographical references

Millions of monarchs, bunches of beetles; how bugs find strength in numbers. Harvard Univ. Press 2000 264p il $27.50; pa $16.95 **595.7**
1. Insects
ISBN 0-674-00090-0; 0-674-00686-0 pa

LC 99-42453

The author "examines many of the reasons that insects form groups. . . . Insects come together for a host of reasons, Waldbauer explains: to find mates, to avoid predators, to enhance their food-gathering abilities, to manipulate their environment and to subdue prey. In each case, Waldbauer provides evocative descriptions of particular species' behaviors while discussing the underlying evolutionary reasons for that behavior." Publ Wkly

Includes bibliographical references

✓ ★ **What** good are bugs? insects in the web of life. Harvard University Press 2003 384p il hardcover o.p. pa $17.50 **595.7**
    1. Insects
    ISBN 0-674-01027-2; 0-674-01632-7 pa
                                LC 2002-27335
This "is an excellent work about the beneficial insects, that vast majority of insect species of which we are generally unaware. . . . The author is an excellent writer and provides many interesting examples." Choice

Includes bibliographical references

Zuk, Marlene
✓ **Sex** on six legs; lessons on life, love, and language from the insect world. [by] Marlene Zuk. Houghton Mifflin Harcourt 2011 262p $25 **595.7**
    1. Insects 2. Sexual behavior in animals
    ISBN 978-0-15-101373-9
                                LC 2010025829
"Despite the title, . . . the book gives clear accounts of a wide range of research beyond sex: insect personalities, wasp facial recognition, fruit flies artificially bred for intelligence, slave-making ants, hitchhiking blister beetles and much more." Sci News

Includes bibliographical references

595.77   Flies (Diptera) and fleas

Spielman, A.
Mosquito; a natural history of man's most persistent and deadly foe. {by} Andrew Spielman and Michael D'Antonio. Hyperion 2001 247p il maps hardcover o.p. pa $12 **595.77**
    1. Mosquitoes
    ISBN 0-7868-8667-6 pa
                                LC 2001-16815
The authors tell us about the mosquito's "life cycle, its natural enemies and predators, and, of course, its monumental impact on human history. . . . This is truly an unexpected delight, an informative, entertaining, and sometimes skin-crawly book that should appeal to anyone with a taste for popular science." Booklist

595.78   Moths and butterflies

Leach, William
Butterfly people; an American encounter with the beauty of the world. William R. Leach. Pantheon Books 2012 416 p. $32.50 **595.78**
    1. Entomologists -- United States 2. Butterflies -- United States -- History -- 19th century 3. Entomologists -- United States -- History -- 19th century 4. Industrial revolution -- United States -- History -- 19th century
    ISBN 0375422935; 9780375422935
                                LC 2012000389

This book, by William R. Leach, "is [a] . . . chronicle of nineteenth-century America's infatuation with butterflies, and the story of the naturalists who unveiled the mysteries of their existence. . . . Leach focuses on the correspondence and scientific writings of half a dozen pioneering lepidopterists who traveled across the country and throughout the world, collecting and studying unknown and exotic species." (Publisher's note)

Includes bibliographical references and index

595.79   Hymenoptera

Hölldobler, Bert
✓ The **ants**; [by] Bert Hölldobler and Edward O. Wilson. Belknap Press 1990 732p il $95 **595.79**
    1. Ants
    ISBN 0-674-04075-9
                                LC 89-30653
This volume includes coverage of ant "evolution, taxonomy, life history, chemical ecology, kin recognition, community organization, {and} symbiosis. . . . Army ants, fungus growers, harvesting ants and weaver ants . . . are each given a chapter of their own. . . . The book's last chapter tells the reader how to collect, culture and observe live ants." Sci Am

"Science is rarely good literature. 'The Ants' is an exalting exception." N Y Times Book Rev

Includes bibliographical references

✓ **Journey** to the ants; a story of scientific exploration. {by} Bert Hölldobler and Edward O. Wilson. Belknap Press 1994 228p il $27.50; pa $16.95 **595.79**
    1. Ants
    ISBN 0-674-48525-4; 0-674-48526-2 pa
                                LC 94-13386
"Based on their field studies ranging from the Arctic Circle and Finland to rain forests in Brazil, the authors relate various aspects of ant natural history including foraging behavior, colony structure and organization, and chemical communication." Choice

"A skillful blend of natural lore, autobiography, and history." Libr J

596   Chordates

Dinerstein, Eric
ϙ The **kingdom** of rarities; Eric Dinerstein. Island Press 2013 312 p. (cloth : alk. paper) $29.95 **596**
    1. Ecology 2. Rare animals 3. Rare vertebrates
    ISBN 1610911954; 1610911962; 9781610911955; 9781610911962
                                LC 2012025535
In this book, Eric Dinerstein "demonstrates that while rarity is a phenomenon of nature, few scientists have sought to study the more 'uncommon' species in a given ecosystem, and therefore may be missing key issues to better understand the natural world. He has cumulated over 40 years of his studies and experiences to highlight how rare species have developed intricate and complex webs, and how their exis-

tence has profound impacts on the ecosystem(s) in which they live." (Choice)

Includes bibliographical references and index

597 Cold-blooded vertebrates

Behnke, Robert J.

★ **Trout** and salmon of North America; illustrated by Joseph R. Tomelleri; foreword by Thomas McGuane; introduction by Donald S. Proebstel; edited by George Scott. Free Press 2002 359p il maps $40 **597**

1. Trout 2. Salmon

ISBN 0-7432-2220-2

LC 2002-69256

This is a "guide to the more than 70 types of trout and salmon of North America." Libr J

"Along with full and clearly written scientific explanations, statistics and analysis, the author provides anecdotal and historical details that make this not just a field guide, but a fascinating read for those interested in the natural world." Publ Wkly

Includes bibliographical references

Compagno, Leonard J. V.

Sharks of the world; [by] Leonard Compagno, Marc Dando, Sarah Fowler. Princeton University Press 2005 368p il map (Princeton field guides) hardcover o.p. pa $29.95 **597**

1. Sharks

ISBN 0-691-12071-4; 0-691-12072-2 pa

LC 2004-111901

First published in the United Kingdom with title: Field guide to the sharks of the world

The authors cover "over 450 species, including many as-yet-unnamed species and some that are only known from a single specimen. Each is illustrated with both a line drawing and a beautifully rendered color painting; in most cases a ventral view of the head and illustrations of the teeth are included. . . . Packed with information, this is an invaluable guide for anyone interested in this fascinating group." Choice

Includes bibliographical references

Eilperin, Juliet

Demon fish; travels through the hidden world of sharks. Pantheon Books 2011 xxi, 295p il $26.95 **597**

1. Sharks

ISBN 978-0-375-42512-7

LC 2010-30264

Eilperin "describes her travels throughout Asia, South Africa, and the United States in search of shark information and folklore. . . . The author provides a well-written overview of current and past attitudes toward sharks and discusses shark species, physiology, genetics, reproduction, evolution, navigation, and attacks on swimmers." Libr J

Includes bibliographical references

Gilbert, Carter Rowell

★ **National** Audubon Society field guide to fishes, North America; [by] Carter R. Gilbert, James D. Williams. rev ed, 2nd ed, fully rev; Alfred A. Knopf 2002 607p il maps pa $19.95 **597**

1. Fishes -- North America

ISBN 0-375-41224-7

LC 2002-20773

First published 1983 with title: The Audubon Society field guide to North American fishes, whales, and dolphins

This guide covers over 600 freshwater and saltwater species in detail, with notes on 771 more species.

McPhee, John A.

The **founding** fish; {by} John McPhee. Farrar, Straus & Giroux 2002 358p $25; pa $14 **597**

1. Shad

ISBN 0-374-10444-1; 0-374-52883-7 pa

LC 2002-25012

The author considers the shad's "role in nature and American history." Libr J

"McPhee is in great form here, as informative as always but also funny, unusually self-revealing, and quite passionate." Booklist

Page, Lawrence M.

★ **Peterson** field guide to freshwater fishes of North America north of Mexico; [by] Lawrence M. Page, Brooks M. Burr; illustrations by Eugene C. Beckham III . . . [et al.]; maps by Griffin E. Sheehy. 2nd ed.; Houghton Mifflin Harcourt 2011 663p il map pa $21 **597**

1. Fishes -- North America

ISBN 978-0-547-24206-4; 0-547-24206-9

LC 2010-49219

First published 1991 with title: A field guide to freshwater fishes: North America north of Mexico

This guide to identifying different species of freshwater fish in North America includes "maps and information showing where to locate each species of fish—whether that species can be found in miles-long stretches of river or small pools that cover only dozens of square feet." Publisher's note

Includes glossary and bibliographical references

Pepperell, Julian G.

Fishes of the open ocean; a natural history & illustrated guide. illustrated by Guy Harvey. University of Chicago Press 2010 266p il map $35 **597**

1. Fishes

ISBN 978-0-226-65539-0; 0-226-65539-3

LC 2009032290

This book "details the biology and brief ecology of various open-ocean fishes. The first half of the book details the importance of pelagic fish in the oceans, the food web of oceanic life, and the relationship between form (fish shape) and function, along with a historical perspective of interactions between fish and humans. The second half of the book illustrates the distribution range, migratory patterns and behavior, reproductive patterns, and trophic information of various fishes. . . . the book is not exhaustive in detail, it provides a very useful overall description of various fishes and their life in the oceans." Choice

Includes bibliographical references

Prosek, James

Eels; an exploration, from New Zealand to the Sargasso, of the world's most amazing and mysterious fish. Harper 2010 287p il map   **597**

1. Eels 2. Religion and sociology 3. Maori (New Zealand people)

ISBN 0-06-05661-6; 978-0-06-056611-1

LC 2010-06803

This is an account of the "life history and cultural associations of the freshwater eel." (Publisher's note)

This is "much more than a fish book. It is an impassioned defense of nature itself, rescued from the tired rhetoric of 1970s-style environmentalism by good, honest shoe-leather reporting. And yet it contains the untainted germ of Age-of-Aquarius eco-consciousness by centering on an essential question: Does a tidy scientific analysis of a creature really tell us all we need to know, or are there numinous qualities to every life-form that require a different kind of meditation?" N Y Times Book Rev

Includes bibliographical references

Rigney, Matt

In pursuit of giants; one man's global search for the last of the great fish. Matt Rigney. Viking 2012 336 p. ill., map $26.95   **597**

1. Fishes 2. Overfishing 3. Corporations -- Environmental aspects 4. Fishing -- History 5. Fisheries -- History 6. Wildlife conservation 7. Marine fishes -- Ecology 8. Rare fishes -- Conservation 9. Fish populations -- Research 10. Marine fishes -- Conservation 11. Endangered species -- Research

ISBN 0670023353; 9780670023356

LC 2012003442

Author Matt Rigney "debuts with this personal investigation into the decline of big-game fish like marlin, swordfish and bluefin tuna. His travels took him to the Mediterranean, Japan, Cabo San Lucas, Mexico, Georges Bank off Nova Scotia, the Great Barrier Reef, and New Zealand. . . . Everywhere he traveled he discovered a similar story: Corporations entered an area, manipulated or ignored government regulations, and, using long lines and huge nets, laid waste to massive populations of sea creatures." (Kirkus Reviews)

Includes bibliographical references and index

Schultz, Ken

Ken Schultz's field guide to saltwater fish. Wiley 2004 274p il pa $17.95   **597**

1. Fishes

ISBN 0-471-44995-4

LC 2003-15773

"Arranged alphabetically by species, each entry covers the identification, size/age, distribution, habitat, life history/behavior, and feeding habits of each fish." Publisher's note

Schweid, Richard

Consider the eel. University of North Carolina Press 2002 181p il map pbk $27.95   **597**

1. Eels

ISBN 9781469615134; 0-8078-2693-6

LC 2001-48067

The author "tries to fill in the gaps in the eel's astonishing natural history and tie that to sketches of fishery traditions, folklore, literary excerpts and reportage. . . . Anyone with a curiosity about the sea will find Schweid's taste of the eel strangely appealing." Publ Wkly

Includes bibliographical references

Smith, C. Lavett

National Audubon Society field guide to tropical marine fishes of the Caribbean, the Gulf of Mexico, Florida, the Bahamas, and Bermuda. Knopf 1997 720p il maps $19.95   **597**

1. Tropical fish

ISBN 0-679-44601-X

LC 97-7690

This illustrated guide to tropical fishes describes nearly 1,200 species and includes color photographs, classification and identification information.

597.3 Selachii, Holocephali, fleshy-finned fishes

Weinberg, Samantha

A fish caught in time; the search for the coelacanth. HarperCollins Pubs. 2000 xx, 220p il map hardcover o.p. pa $13   **597.3**

1. Coelacanth

ISBN 0-06-093285-6 pa

LC 99-44800

First published 1999 in the United Kingdom

"In 1938, a fish believed to be extinct for 70 million years was caught off the South African coast, triggering the 'greatest scientific find of the century.' The search for the coelacanth . . . is a fascinating story, and Weinberg . . . tells it well." Libr J

Includes bibliographical references

597.8 Amphibians

Souder, William E.

A plague of frogs; unraveling an environmental mystery. [by] William Souder. University of Minnesota Press 2002 309p pa $18.95   **597.8**

1. Frogs

ISBN 0-8166-4178-1

First published 2000 by Hyperion

The author examines "the disturbing increase in deformed frogs found in Minnesota in 1995. . . . So far, the biologists have not reached a consensus, but Souder's deep-drilling reportage of their work informs readers how these sentinels of science track 'indicator' species such as frogs." Booklist

Includes bibliographical references

597.9   Reptiles

Attenborough, David
    Life in cold blood. Princeton University Press
2008 288p il $29.95   **597.9**
    1. Reptiles 2. Amphibians
    ISBN 978-0-691-13718-6; 0-691-13718-8
                                            LC 2007-938089
    This discussion of amphibians and reptiles was first pub-
lished as a companion volume to the BBC television series
of the same name. "Basic life history including diet, locomotion, reproductive habits, and geographic distribution are
presented." Choice
    "The writing is crisp and lively, the examples are up to
date, and the photography is beautiful. . . . This is a very interesting book, which provides many examples of organisms
some of us often overlook." Am Biology Teacher

Conant, Roger
    A **field** guide to reptiles & amphibians; eastern
and central North America. [by] Roger Conant and
Joseph T. Collins; illustrated by Isabelle Hunt Conant
and Tom R. Johnson. 3rd ed, expanded; Houghton
Mifflin 1998 616p il map (Peterson field guide series) pbk $21   **597.9**
    1. Reptiles 2. Amphibians
    ISBN 9780395904527
                                              LC 98-13622
    First published 1958 with title: A field guide to reptiles
and amphibians of the United States and Canada east of the
100th meridian
    This guide describes 595 species and subspecies, fea-
turing color photos, black and white drawings, and color
distribution maps of reptiles and amphibians of the region.
Also includes information on transporting live reptiles
and amphibians
    Includes glossary and bibliographical references

Ernst, Carl H.
    Venomous reptiles of the United States, Canada,
and northern Mexico; Carl H. Ernst and Evelyn M.
Ernst. Johns Hopkins University Press 2011 424 p.
ill. (some col.), maps (v. 2 : alk. paper) $75   **597.9**
    1. Reptiles 2. Poisonous animals 3. Animals -- North
America 4. Heloderma -- North America 5. Poisonous
snakes -- North America
    ISBN 0801898757; 0801898765; 9780801898754;
9780801898761
                                           LC 2010036966
    This book presents a reference guide to the venomous
reptiles of North America. "The first volume contains species accounts of the venomous lizards and elapid and viperid
snakes found north of Mexico's twenty-fifth parallel. Volume 2 of this definitive work covers the twenty-one species
of the genus Crotalus found in the United States, Canada,
and . . . northern Mexico." (Publisher's note)
    "A current, vital addition to herpetology collections." LJ
    Includes bibliographical references and index

Stebbins, Robert C.
    A **field** guide to Western reptiles and amphibians;
text and illustrations by Robert C. Stebbins. 3rd ed
newly rev; Houghton Mifflin 2003 533p il map
(Peterson field guide series) pa $22   **597.9**
    1. Reptiles 2. Amphibians
    ISBN 0-395-98272-3
                                            LC 2002-27561
    First published 1966
    This "covers all the species of reptiles and amphibians
found in western North America. More than 650 full-color
paintings and photographs show key details for making accurate identifications. . . . Color range maps give species'
distributions. . . . [Includes] information on conservation efforts and survival status." Publisher's note
    Includes bibliographical references

Tyning, Thomas F.
    A **guide** to amphibians and reptiles; edited by
Donald W. Stokes and Lillian Q. Stokes; illustrations
by Andrew Finch Magee; range maps by Thomas F.
Tyning and Timothy J. Flanagan. Little, Brown 1990
400p il hardcover o.p. pa $14.95   **597.9**
    1. Reptiles 2. Amphibians
    ISBN 0-316-81713-9 pa
                                             LC 89-28444
    This guide covers common frogs, salamanders, alliga-
tors, snakes, turtles, and lizards
    Includes bibliographical references

597.92   Turtles

Safina, Carl
    Voyage of the turtle; in pursuit of the Earth's
last dinosaur. Holt 2006 383p il map $27.50; pa
$17   **597.92**
    1. Turtles
    ISBN 978-0-8050-7891-6; 0-8050-7891-6; 978-0-
8050-8318-7 pa; 0-8050-8318-9 pa
                                            LC 2005-55023
    The author's "main subject is the leatherback, Dermo-
chelys coriacea, largest of all living turtles, which grows to
800 pounds as an average adult." N Y Times Book Rev
    "This is a well-written natural history/conservation nar-
rative. General readers will enjoy the book and hopefully
will become excited to learn more about critical environmental issues." Sci Books Films
    Includes bibliographical references

Spotila, James R.
    Sea turtles; a complete guide to their biology, be-
havior, and conservation. Johns Hopkins University
Press 2004 227p il $24.95   **597.92**
    1. Sea turtles
    ISBN 0-8018-8007-6
                                             LC 2004-8935
    "The volume covers various aspects of sea turtle biology,
such as their life history, diving physiology, sense organs,
and magnetic orientation. Following the general chapters,

individual chapters are devoted to each of the seven species of extant sea turtles." Sci Books Films

"The author is eloquent in his appeal for the conservation of sea turtles. The best single book on the subject." Booklist

Includes bibliographical references

597.96 Snakes

Campbell, Jonathan

The **venomous** reptiles of the Western Hemisphere; by Jonathan A. Campbell and William W. Lamar, with contributions by Edmund D. Brodie III [et al.] Comstock Pub. Associates 2004 2v il maps (Comstock books in herpetology) set $149.95 **597.96**
1. Reptiles 2. Poisonous animals
ISBN 0-8014-4141-2

LC 2003-7834
The authors "describe two species of lizards (the Gila monster and the beaded lizard) and 190 species of dangerously venomous snakes of North, Central and South America. Provided are . . . accounts of each species—from the smallest to the largest—complete with descriptions, habitats, and geographic distribution." Libr J

Includes bibliographical references

Ernst, Carl H.

Snakes of the United States and Canada; [by] Carl H. Ernst, Evelyn M. Ernst. Smithsonian Books 2003 668p il map $70 **597.96**
1. Snakes
ISBN 1-58834-019-8

LC 2002-26924
"This current and comprehensive volume contains all the information currently available on the 131 species of snakes living in North America." Libr J

Includes bibliographical references

Greene, Harry W.

Snakes; the evolution of mystery in nature. with photographs by Michael and Patricia Fodgen. University of Calif. Press 1997 351p il $55; pa $29.95 **597.96**
1. Snakes
ISBN 0-520-20014-4; 0-520-22487-6 pa

LC 96-21928
The author examines the "biology and ecology of snakes. Throughout, facts on the form, function, habitat, and evolution of these reptiles are mixed with the author's experiences, and the over 200 natural-setting color photographs that complement the text are commendable in their own right." Libr J

Includes bibliographical references

Mattison, Christopher

The **new** encyclopedia of snakes. Princeton University Press 2007 272p il map $35 **597.96**
1. Reference books 2. Snakes -- Encyclopedias
ISBN 0-691-13295-X; 978-0-691-13295-2

LC 2007-922951
First published 1995 by Facts on File with title: The encyclopedia of snakes

This encyclopedia "covers all aspects of snake biology and habitat. This is not a field guide aimed at snake identification. . . . But the work contains a wealth of information about our scaled friends, including patterns of distribution and matters relating to evolution and morphology, feeding, reproduction, and defensive strategies. . . . This captivating work will appeal to students and snake lovers everywhere." Libr J

Includes bibliographical references

★ **Snakes** of the world; [by] Chris Mattison. Facts on File 2003 190p il map $35 **597.96**
1. Snakes
ISBN 0-8160-5213-1

LC 2002-34737
A reissue of the title first published 1986
Snake morphology, reproduction, diet, self-defense, ecology and behavior are discussed

"Mattison provides an enjoyable introduction to snake biology and snake diversity for the interested general reader. . . . Many of the numerous color photographs are spectacular." Choice [review of 1986 edition]

Includes bibliographical references

Murphy, John C.

Tales of giant snakes; a historical natural history of anacondas and pythons. [by] John C. Murphy and Robert W. Henderson. Krieger 1997 221p il map $32.50 **597.96**
1. Pythons 2. Anacondas
ISBN 0-89464-995-7

LC 96-54033
Accounts of encounters between large snakes and humans include newspaper articles, adventure writings, and reports of explorers

Includes bibliographical references

O'Shea, Mark

Venomous snakes of the world. Princeton University Press 2005 160p il map $29.95 **597.96**
1. Snakes 2. Poisonous animals
ISBN 0-691-12436-1

LC 2005-920576
The author "has produced a compendium of more than 170 venomous snakes, along with their markings, geographical distribution, maximum length, venom, prey, and similar species. But instead of opting for the traditional taxonomic arrangement, he lists these snakes geographically by continent (a final chapter on sea snakes is also included)." Libr J

"Fascinating photographs and descriptions will make this title a favorite." Univ Press Books for Public and Second Sch Libr, 2006

Includes bibliographical references

Perez, Larry

Snake in the grass; an Everglades invasion. Larry Perez. Pineapple Press 2012 xvii, 220 p.p col. ill., col. maps (paperback) $16.95 **597.96**
1. Pythons 2. Everglades (Fla.) 3. Biological invasions 4. Snakes -- Florida -- Everglades National Park
ISBN 1561645133; 9781561645138

LC 2011043280

This book, by Larry Perez, explores the ecological disruption of the Florida Everglades due to the introduction of Burmese pythons. "Over the past decade, thousands of pythons have made themselves at home across the landscape. And . . . methods of control remain elusive. Many questions remain in the wake of this troubling discovery. . . . The story unfolding in the Florida Everglades provides new opportunities to revisit our understanding of wilderness and man's place within it." (Publisher's note)

Includes bibliographical references and index

Rubio, Manny

Rattlesnake; portrait of a predator. Smithsonian Institution Press 1998 xxvii, 239p il $49.95   **597.96**

1. Rattlesnakes

ISBN 1-56098-808-8

LC 98-22935

This book contains "more than 120 color photographs of various North American rattlesnakes. . . . The text discusses many aspects of rattlesnake evolution, anatomy and physiology, and ecology, including several chapters on interactions between snakes and people." Sci Books Films

Includes bibliographical references

598   Birds

Alderfer, Jonathan

★ National Geographic birding essentials; all the tools, techniques, and tips you need to begin and become a better birder. [by] Jonathan Alderfer and Jon L. Dunn. National Geographic 2007 224p il pa $15.95   **598**

1. Bird watching

ISBN 978-1-4262-0135-6; 1-4262-0135-4

LC 2007-30960

This "book offers data on how to begin and how to improve your bird-watching skills. Chapters deal with the pleasures of birding, getting started, where and when birds are found, how common or rare they are at different seasons, parts of a bird, how to identify them, and variations in birds. . . . With a helpful glossary, this is an essential volume for all birdwatchers." Booklist

Includes bibliographical references

Arctic wings; birds of the Arctic National Wildlife Refuge. edited by Stephen Brown; foreword by Jimmy Carter; introduction by David Allen Sibley. Mountaineers Books 2006 192p il map $39.95; pa $27.95   **598**

1. Birds

ISBN 0-89886-975-7; 978-0-89886-975-0; 0-89886-976-5 pa; 978-0-8988-6976-7 pa

LC 2006-865

"The unique aspect of this book is the vivid photographs of bird behavior and the birds in their habitats, showing the importance of the habitats to the birds' continued existence. A great addition is a CD with 60 bird calls recorded on the refuge." Sci Books Films

Includes bibliographical references

★ The atlas of bird migration; tracing the great journeys of the world's birds. general editor Jonathan Elphick; foreword by Thomas E. Lovejoy. Firefly Books 2007 176p il map hardcover o.p. pa $24.95   **598**

1. Birds -- Migration

ISBN 978-1-55407-248-4; 1-55407-248-4; 978-1-55407-971-1 pa; 1-55407-971-3 pa

First published 1995 by Random House

"The first section is a primer on bird migration and habitat usage patterns, consisting of short, illustrated essays on topics like the evolution of migration, the mechanics of flight, birds' navigational methods and how human development affects migration patterns. Succeeding sections examine different families of migrating birds according to geographical distribution, and each has carefully designed maps that show birds' seasonal ranges and migratory routes. The use of color to describe, clarify, distinguish and compare migration patterns is exceptional, and clear explanations of complicated topics (e.g., how birds fly) make it an excellent text for middle and high school students as well as adults." Publ Wkly

Attenborough, David

The life of birds. Princeton Univ. Press 1998 320p il $29.95   **598**

1. Birds

ISBN 0-691-01633-X

LC 98-30705

This survey of bird behavior describes "eating habits, flight, communication, mating, parenthood and environmental adaptability." Publ Wkly

"Well illustrated with color photographs, Attenborough's latest goes a long way to converting all readers into bird lovers." Booklist

Includes bibliographical references

Birkhead, Tim

Bird sense; what it's like to be a bird. by Tim Birkhead. Walker & Company 2012 265 p. $25   **598**

1. Nightingales 2. Birds -- Behavior 3. Senses and sensation in animals 4. Birds -- Physiology 5. Birds -- Psychology

ISBN 0802779662; 9780802779663

LC 2011043684

This book attempts to answer the question "what would an avian existence be like?" Zoologist Tim Birkhead examines "a bird's basic senses. . . . Birkhead describes, for example, ducks that keep half of their brain awake during sleep so they can still spot predators. Then there are the great grey owls that pinpoint their rodent prey using asymmetric ears." (New Scientist)

Includes bibliographical references and index

Bull, John L.

★ The National Audubon Society field guide to North American birds, Eastern region; [by] John Bull and John Farrand, Jr.; revised by John Farrand, Jr.; visual key by Amanda Wilson and Lori Hogan. rev ed; Knopf 1994 797p il maps pa $19.95   **598**

1. Birds -- North America

ISBN 0-679-42852-6

LC 94-7768

Companion volume to National Audubon Society field guide to North American birds, Western region, by Miklos D. F. Udvardy

First published 1977

This pictorial guide to 508 eastern species arranges birds by color and shape to simplify identification. It also includes information on bird-watching and conservation status

Includes bibliographical references

Clark, William S.

★ A **field** guide to hawks of North America; {by} William S. Clark and Brian K. Wheeler; illustrations by Brian K. Wheeler. 2nd ed; Houghton Mifflin 2001 316p il maps $30; pa $22 **598**

1. Hawks

ISBN 0-395-67068-3; 0-395-67067-5 pa

LC 2001-2477

First published 1987

"Accounts are presented for all 39 of North America's diurnal raptors, including eagles, falcons, and vultures. Each species account reviews details of plumages and molts, useful identification features, patterns of flight, and general behavior. . . . The guide also provides size data (weight, length, and wingspread) for all species, as well as the etymology of common and scientific names. Basically, the reference is essential for any student of raptors and useful for serious birders in general." Am Ref Books Annu, 2002

Includes bibliographical references

Cocker, Mark

Birders; tales of a tribe. Atlantic Monthly Press 2002 229p $24; pa $13 **598**

1. Bird watching

ISBN 0-87113-844-1; 0-8021-3996-5 pa

LC 2001-56490

First published 2001 in the United Kingdom

In a "memoir cum essay collection, the author brings the reader into the sometimes obsessive world of bird-watching. . . . Stories of the author and friends going to great lengths and distances to see rare birds, of birding in exotic locales, or of unmasking a fellow birder's claims to finding a rare species are both thought-provoking and amusing." Booklist

Includes bibliographical references

Dunne, Pete, 1951-

Pete Dunne on bird watching; the how-to, where-to, and when-to of birding. Houghton Mifflin 2003 334p il pa $12 **598**

1. Bird watching

ISBN 0-395-90686-5

LC 2002-27558

This "book is a superlative introduction to bird watching." Libr J

Includes bibliographical references

Pete Dunne's essential field guide companion. Houghton Mifflin Co. 2006 710p $29.95 **598**

1. Birds -- North America

ISBN 0-618-23648-1; 978-0-618-23648-0

LC 2005-21110

Dunne presents "information on status, distribution, habitat, cohabitants, movement and migration, behavior, flight, and vocalizations for all species of North American birds." (Sci Books Films)

This "title should appeal . . . to the serious birder striving to become more accomplished. No serious bird collection should be without it." Libr J

Floyd, Ted

Smithsonian field guide to the birds of North America; [by] Ted Floyd; edited by Paul Hess and George Scott; designed by Charles Nix; maps by Paul Lehman; photographs by Brian E. Small . . . [et al.] HarperCollins Publishers 2008 512p il map pa $24.95 **598**

1. Birds -- North America

ISBN 978-0-06-112040-4; 0-06-112040-5

LC 2008-1395

This "guide to American birds . . . has 2000 color photographs, hundreds of range maps, and many other . . . features, including a DVD disc of five and a half hours of downloadable songs, totaling 587 from 138 species." Libr J

"Ideal for beginners, but also has formidable resources for experienced birders. . . . Perfect for field use. Birders of any experience level will be happy with this volume on their bookshelf." Publ Wkly

Includes bibliographical references

Gehrman, Elizabeth

Rare birds; the extraordinary tale of the Bermuda petrel and the man who brought it back from extinction. Elizabeth Gehrman. Beacon Press 2012 256 p. **598**

1. Rare birds 2. Bermuda petrel

ISBN 0807010766; 9780807010761

LC 2012014237

This book by Elizabeth Gehrman is the "story of David Wingate . . . who brought . . . the cahow, or Bermuda petrel . . . back from presumed extinction. . . . In 1951, two scientists invited fifteen-year-old Wingate along on a bare-bones expedition to find the bird. The team . . . locat[ed] seven nesting pairs, and Wingate knew his life had changed forever. He would spend the next fifty years battling natural and man-made disasters, bureaucracy, and personal tragedy." (Publisher's note)

Includes bibliographical references and index

Hanson, Thor

Feathers; the evolution of a natural miracle. Basic Books 2011 336p il **598**

1. Birds 2. Feathers

ISBN 0-465-02013-5; 978-0-465-02013-3

LC 2011003272

Hanson "presents the natural history of feathers, applying the findings of paleontologists, ornithologists, biologists, engineers and art historians to answer questions about the origin of feathers, their evolution and their uses throughout the ages." (Publisher's note) Index.

"Divided into sections that cover such categories as evolution, insulation, flight and adornment, 'Feathers' stretches from the ancient mists of the late Jurassic to the laboratories of today's Smithsonian Museum, where 'snarge'—science slang for what's produced when a bird meets a plane—is analyzed for data. In between, you learn that a falcon thrown out of an airplane can dive at a speed of 242 miles per hour, that the word pen is itself derived from the Latin word for feather and that the most valuable cargo on the Titanic wasn't gold or jewels but more than 40 cases of plumes intended for women's hats, a fashion craze that nearly caused the extinction of several species and led to the formation of the Audubon Society, as well as America's first National Wildlife Refuge, Florida's Pelican Island. Mr. Hanson may be a scientist but he writes like a man who believes in the value of story. . . . [He] offers more than a fanciful, associative style. He is a very good explainer of serious biology." Wall Street J

Includes bibliographical references

Heinrich, Bernd

   Mind of the raven; investigations and adventures with wolf-birds. HarperCollins 1999 380p il pa $14.99   **598**

   1. Ravens

   ISBN 9780061136054

                LC 99-18129

   Heinrich "describes his field experiments in the feeding habits, play, intelligence, social structure, territoriality, and hunting methods of ravens as well as an array of topics from their skill as mimics to their suspected emotional natures. He brings alive the romance of field research, where the discipline of science is often harder to achieve than in the lab but is at least as rewarding. A splendid book." Libr J

   Includes bibliographical references

Kaufman, Kenn

   Kaufman field guide to birds of North America; with the collaboration of Rick and Nora Bowers and Lynn Hassler Kaufman. Houghton Mifflin 2005 392p il map pa $18.95   **598**

   1. Birds -- North America

   ISBN 0-618-57423-9; 978-0-618-57423-0

   First published 2000 with title: Birds of North America

   For this identification guide "Kaufman selected over 2000 digitally edited photographs, enhanced to improve contrast, color, and the like. The excellent result will appeal to beginning birders perhaps intimidated by illustrations. . . . Kaufman's text is simple and uncluttered, a plus for novices." Libr J

Kiser, Joy M.

   America's other Audubon; Joy M. Kiser. Princeton Architectural Press 2012 191 p. (hardcover : alk. paper) $45.00   **598**

   1. Birds in art 2. Birds -- North America -- Pictorial works 3. Ornithological illustration -- North America 4. Ornithologists -- United States -- Biography

   ISBN 1616890592; 9781616890599

                LC 2011039605

   This book is a reprinted collection of "almost unknown late 19th-century color paintings of birds' nests and eggs by an obscure Ohio family. Begun by Genevieve Jones, who died young, it was eventually completed by her brother Howard, mother Virginia, and friend Eliza Schulze. . . . The

accompanying detailed notes and paintings of the eggs are more in the nature of a scientific contribution at a time when there were no guides to such." (Library Journal)

Kroodsma, Donald E.

   The **singing** life of birds; the art and science of listening to birdsong. drawings by Nancy Haver. Houghton Mifflin 2005 482p il $28   **598**

   1. Birdsongs

   ISBN 0-618-40568-2

                LC 2004-65130

   "Kroodsma is a warm, encouraging guide to the world of birdsong, and his enthusiasm is contagious." Publ Wkly

   Includes bibliographical references

Leahy, Christopher W.

   The **birdwatcher's** companion to North American birdlife; illustrations by Gordon Morrison. Princeton University Press 2004 1039p il hardcover o.p. pa $19.95   **598**

   1. Birds -- North America

   ISBN 0-691-09297-4; 0-691-11388-2 pa

                LC 2003-66383

   First published 1982 by Hill & Wang

   "This alphabetical compendium of ornithology offers entries ranging from single-line definitions of avian terminology ('Erne') to 12-page essay-style articles ('Systemics') that concentrate primarily on the US and Canada. Entries include a substantial number of biographies and black-and-white drawings. . . . Comprehensive entries on conservation, evolution of birdlife, optical equipment, and human threats to birdlife provide welcome up-to-date information. . . . Leahy's style is by turns serious and scholarly or personal and whimsical, appropriate to a comprehensive reference for both novice and expert birders. There is no recent comparable work." Choice

   Includes bibliographical references

Lynch, Wayne

   Penguins of the world; text and photographs by Wayne Lynch. 2nd ed.; Firefly Books 2007 175p il map $34.95; pa $24.95   **598**

   1. Penguins

   ISBN 978-1-55407-334-4; 1-55407-334-0; 978-1-55407-274-3 pa; 1-55407-274-3 pa

                LC 2007-299218

   First published 1997

   This is a "look at Lynch's discoveries about these flightless seabirds in the field and in scientific journals, during day-to-day as well as birth-to-death observations, and from the smallest to the largest type. While Lynch presents detailed descriptions of everything from mating rituals to eating habits, the best parts of his book are the photographs. Lynch's gorgeous and gorgeously printed images . . . display such a refined visual sensibility that even without accompanying text, the images would still achieve Lynch's goal of presenting the scientific and aesthetic appeal of this unique family of birds." Publ Wkly

   Includes bibliographical references

Montgomery, Sy

Birdology; lessons learned from a pack of hens, a peck of pigeons, cantankerous crows, fierce falcons, hip hop parrots, baby hummingbirds, and one murderously big cassowary. Free Press 2010 260p il $25 **598**

1. Birds

ISBN 978-1-4165-6984-8; 1-4165-6984-7

LC 2009-31303

"Montgomery assists a hummingbird rehabilitator in the delicate raising of two tiny orphans, and meets the 'most dangerous bird on earth,' the enormous, razor-clawed cassowary in Australia, one bird whose dinosaur ancestry is blazingly apparent. She also writes from unexpected perspectives about falcons, crows, pigeons, chickens, and parrots. . . . Inspired equally by all that we share with birds—similarities in intelligence, emotion, language, and music—and all that is mysterious (birds 'remain fundamentally wild'), Montgomery expresses profound appreciation for the living web of life in a book that both bird lovers and readers new to bird lore will find evocative, enlightening, and uplifting." Booklist

Includes bibliographical references

National Audubon Society

Bird; the definitive visual guide. Audubon; [senior editor, Peter Frances; contributors, BirdLife International, David Burnie] DK Pub. 2007 512p il map $50 **598**

1. Birds

ISBN 978-0-7566-3153-6; 0-7566-3153-X

LC 2007-282186

"From flyleaf to fore edge, the visuals are astounding. . . . An enclosed CD with bird calls and songs adds yet another dimension to a glorious work." Libr J

Nigge, Klaus

Whooping crane; images from the wild. introduction by Krista Schlyer. Texas A&M University Press 2010 217p il map $45 **598**

1. Cranes (Birds)

ISBN 978-1-60344-209-1; 1-60344-209-X

LC 2009048496

"On the flock's wintering grounds at Aransas National Wildlife Refuge in Texas, photographer Klaus Nigge has captured the daily activity of a single family over several weeks in two separate years, documenting their life in the salt marshes of the central Texas coast and, in one year, the happy arrival from the north of twin adolescents. . . . Then, with the backing of National Geographic magazine, he received unprecedented permission from the Canadian government to photograph the cranes' summer nesting sites in remote areas of Wood Buffalo National Park. . . . [This collection of his photos is divided into] three galleries, each containing portfolios of images of these magnificent birds in their natural habitat." Publisher's note

Includes bibliographical references

Peterson, Roger Tory, 1908-1996

Peterson field guide to birds of Eastern and Central North America; [by] Roger Tory Peterson, with contributions from Michael DiGiorgio [et al.] 6th ed; Houghton Mifflin Harcourt 2010 445p il map (Peterson field guide series) $19.95 **598**

1. Birds -- North America

ISBN 978-0-547-15246-2; 0-547-15246-9

LC 2009-37681

First published 1934 with title: A field guide to the birds

This guide to birds found east of the Rocky Mountains contains colored illustrations painted by the author, with a description of each species on the facing page. Views of young birds and seasonal variations in plumage are included.

★ **Peterson** field guide to birds of North America; with contributions from Michael DiGiorgio . . . [et al.] Houghton Mifflin Co. 2008 527p il map (Peterson field guide series) $26 **598**

1. Birds -- North America

ISBN 0-618-96614-5; 978-0-618-96614-1

LC 2007-39803

First published 1934 with title: A field guide to the birds. Previously published in two separate parts as A field guide to western birds (1990) and A field guide to the birds of eastern and central North America (2002)

This guide to birds found in North America contains colored illustrations painted by the author, with a description of each species on the facing page. Views of young birds and seasonal variations in plumage are included. The book also includes a URL to video podcasts.

"This field guide is of high quality and should be in millions of birders' and other nature lovers' backpacks." Sci Books Films

Peterson field guide to birds of Western North America; with contributions from Michael DiGiorgio [et al.] 4th ed; Houghton Mifflin Harcourt 2010 493p il map (Peterson field guide series) pa $19.95 **598**

1. Birds -- North America

ISBN 978-0-547-15270-7; 0-547-15270-1

LC 2009-39158

First published 1941 with title: A field guide to western birds

This guide illustrates over 600 species of birds on 176 color plates. In addition, over 588 range maps are included.

★ The **Princeton** encyclopedia of birds; edited by Christopher Perrins. Princeton University Press 2009 656p il map pa $35 **598**

1. Reference books 2. Birds -- Encyclopedias

ISBN 978-0-691-14070-4; 0-691-14070-7

First published 1985 by Facts on File with title: The encyclopedia of birds. Previous edition published 2003 by Firefly Bks. with title: Firefly encyclopedia of birds

The editor "combines the work of 150 contributors and more than 1000 great color photographs, maps, and other illustrations to produce a stunning book that informs both amateurs and experts. Coverage includes form and function, distribution, diet, breeding biology, and conservation and environment." Libr J

Includes bibliographical references

Sibley, David

The **Sibley** field guide to birds of Eastern North America; written and illustrated by David Allen Sibley. Knopf 2003 431p il pa $19.95 **598**
1. Birds -- North America
ISBN 0-679-45120-X

LC 2002-114931

"All the qualities to be expected in a field guide are here. . . . Image reproduction is crisp, colors are distinct, shading shows well, and despite the very small size, range map colors are clear. . . . Sibley has accomplished the difficult task of condensing . . . [The Sibley guide to birds] to practical field size." Libr J

★ The **Sibley** field guide to birds of Western North America; written and illustrated by David Allen Sibley. Knopf 2003 473p il pa $19.95 **598**
1. Birds -- North America
ISBN 0-679-45121-8

LC 2002-114930

"All the qualities to be expected in a field guide are here. . . . Image reproduction is crisp, colors are distinct, shading shows well, and despite the very small size, range map colors are clear. . . . Sibley has accomplished the difficult task of condensing . . . [The Sibley guide to birds] to practical field size." Libr J

★ The **Sibley** guide to bird life & behavior; illustrated by David Allen Sibley; edited by Chris Elphick, John B. Dunning, Jr., David Allen Sibley. Knopf 2001 588p il maps hardcover o.p. pa $39.95 **598**
1. Birds -- North America
ISBN 0-679-45123-4; 1-4000-4386-7 pa

LC 2001-33903

This companion volume to The Sibley guide to birds provides "information about birds' lives and behavior. . . . Part 1 ('The World of Birds') discusses basic avian biology, including form, distribution, population, and conservation, in about 100 pages. Part 2 ('Bird Families of North America'), to which over 40 ornithologists contributed, uses a standard format to describe taxonomy, foraging, breeding, range, nests, eggs, longevity, conservation, and more." Libr J

The **Sibley** guide to birds; written and illustrated by David Sibley. Knopf 2000 544p il maps pa $35 **598**
1. Birds -- North America
ISBN 0-679-45122-6

LC 00-41239

"The treatments of each of the 810 species have detailed paintings to show the natural variations in plumage (e.g., juveniles, male/female adults, seasonal and geographic changes). In all, there are more than 6,600 full-color illustrations. . . . The text for each species has a short summary of identification key points, description of vocalizations, and an up-to-date range map." Choice

Sibley's birding basics; written and illustrated by David Allen Sibley. Knopf 2002 154p il pa $15.95 **598**
1. Bird watching
ISBN 0-375-70966-5

LC 2002-20768

Sibley "explores general aspects of birding such as getting started, misidentification, voice, understanding feathers, age variation, ethics and conservation, taxonomy, and finding birds. If being a field naturalist is a craft, then this book is essential in helping to develop and understand the required skills." Libr J

Stiteler, Sharon

1001 secrets every birder should know; tips and trivia for the backyard and beyond. by Sharon "Birdchick" Stiteler ; foreword by Bill Oddie. Running Press 2013 296 p. col. photos. (paperback) $20.00 **598**
1. Bird watching 2. Birds -- Handbooks, manuals, etc.
ISBN 0762447346; 9780762447343

LC 2012954930

Here, author Sharton Stiteler's "purpose is to spark general birding-inclined readers' interest; her method involves getting beyond mere identification by encouraging a deeper understanding of avian biology and behavior. The text flits from topic to topic easily and includes feeding, nesting, adaptations, migration, and mating. The tools of the birder's trade are also discussed, and many vacation ideas (bird-related) are provided." (Library Journal)

Stokes, Donald W.

The **bird** feeder book; an easy guide to attracting, identifying, and understanding your feeder birds. {by} Donald and Lillian Stokes; illustrations of feeders by Gordon Morrison; range maps by Leslie Cowperthwaite. Little, Brown 1987 90p il maps pa $12.95 **598**
1. Bird watching
ISBN 0-316-81733-3

LC 87-3016

"This guide for beginners features 72 dramatic color photographs of the most common backyard birds. The text offers chapters on attracting and identifying birds (which types of feeders to use, etc.), dealing with squirrels and other yard pests, and planting shrubbery layouts that offer food and nest sites. A nicely illustrated, logically organized handbook." Booklist
Includes bibliographical references

The **new** Stokes field guide to birds; western region. Donald Stokes, Lillian Stokes. Little, Brown and Co. 2013 574 p. $19.99 **598**
1. Birds -- North America 2. Birds -- Handbooks, manuals, etc.
ISBN 0316213926; 9780316213929

LC 2012945368

This guide offers information about North American birds in two volumes, one devoted to the eastern region and one to the western region. "Much of the data is directly taken from the earlier 1996 editions," but there are "many new photos and inclusions. . . . The tiny range maps include not only the year-round, summer, and winter ranges, but migration routes as well." (Library Journal)

Swash, Andy

The **world's** rarest birds; Erik Hirschfeld, Andy Swash & Robert Still; with contributions by Nick Langley ... [et al.] ; and illustrations by Tomasz Cofta. Princeton University Press 2013 360 p. ill. (chiefly col.), col. maps (WILDGuides) $45   **598**
    1. Birds 2. Extinct birds 3. Birds -- Conservation 4. Rare birds -- Geographical distribution
    ISBN 0691155968; 9780691155968

LC 2012945960

This book, by Erik Hirschfeld, Andy Swash & Robert Still, "depicts the most endangered birds in the world and provides the latest information on the threats each species faces and the measures being taken to save them. Today, 571 bird species are classified as critically endangered or endangered, and a further four now exist only in captivity. . . . [It] has introductory chapters that explain the threats to birds, the ways threat categories are applied, and the distinction between threat and rarity." (Publisher's note)

"The scope, depth and organization is exemplary. The links to regularly updated information through the QR codes means the book's value will continue." LJ

Tudge, Colin

The **bird**; a natural history of who birds are, where they came from, and how they live. Crown Publishers 2009 462p il $30   **598**
    1. Birds
    ISBN 978-0-307-34204-1
    First published 2008 in the United Kingdom with title: Consider the birds

"The author writes with clarity and cheerful wit about the physics and mechanics of flight, evolution and the archaeological record [of birds] . . . [Tudge] covers the avian landscape like a tarp, from amusing anecdotes about bird behavior, to a critique of behavioralism, to the abuse of Darwin's theories, to the complex structure of avian taxonomy. . . . Entertaining, charming and knowledgeable." Kirkus

Includes bibliographical references

Udvardy, Miklos D. F.

★ **National** Audubon Society field guide to North American birds, Western region; revised by John Farrand, Jr.; visual key by Amanda Wilson and Lori Hogan. rev ed; Knopf 1994 822p il maps pa $19.95   **598**
    1. Birds -- North America
    ISBN 0-679-42851-8

LC 94-7415

Companion volume to National Audubon Society field guide to North American birds, Eastern region by John L. Bull

First published 1977

In this guide, "virtually every bird found in North America is brought to life in a full-color photograph and with textual information on the bird's voice, nesting habits, habitat, range, and interesting behaviors. Accompanying range maps; overhead flight silhouettes; sections on birdwatching, accidental species, and endangered birds" are also included. (Publisher's note)

Includes bibliographical references

Unwin, Mike

The **atlas** of birds; diversity, behavior, and conservation. Princeton University Press 2011 144p il map pa $22.95   **598**
    1. Birds 2. Atlases 3. Reference books
    ISBN 978-0-691-14949-3

LC 2011920367

This "is neither a textbook nor an encyclopedia but rather a compendium of interesting factoids and bird trivia, with each two-page layout addressing one aspect of bird biology. This is a book for general readers who enjoy studying birds." Choice

Includes bibliographical references

Weidensaul, Scott

Living on the wind; across the hemisphere with migratory birds. North Point Press 1999 420p il hardcover o.p. pa $15   **598**
    1. Birds -- Migration
    ISBN 0-86547-591-1 pa

LC 99-11693

"Starting at a wildlife refuge in Alaska, the author follows birds on their southward migration; watches them on their wintering grounds in Central America, Jamaica, Argentina, and the U.S. . . . and then follows them north again. Along the way he discovers how birds navigate on their journeys, using the sun during the day, the stars to orient by night, or even the Earth's magnetic field as a compass." Booklist

"The book will be of interest to biologists and amateur naturalists; birders will particularly appreciate the discussion of key 'fallout' areas." Libr J

Includes bibliographical references

Of a feather; a brief history of American birding. Harcourt, Inc. 2007 358p il $25; pa $15   **598**
    1. Bird watching
    ISBN 0-15-101247-4; 0-15-603355-0 pa; 978-0-15-101247-3; 978-0-15-603355-8 pa

LC 2007-07364

This narrative history of birding in America "begins in colonial America, where new arrivals from Europe 'made awed note of the continent's teeming skies and waterways.'" (N Y Times Book Rev) Index.

The author's "vivid descriptions of his own experiences should send many a reader out of doors to look for the small, contained miracle that is a bird." Publ Wkly

Includes bibliographical references

Williamson, Sheri L.

A **field** guide to hummingbirds of North America;
{by} Sheri L. Williamson. Houghton Mifflin 2001
263p il maps $30; pa $22   **598**
    1. Hummingbirds
    ISBN 0-618-02495-6; 0-618-02496-4 pa
                        LC 2001-24473

"The habits, habitats, migratory patterns, physical traits,
diet, mating practices, where to find them in short, all the
information that a good wildlife guide offers are the stuff
of Williamson's book. Clear, engaging prose and 180 full
color photographs make this a natural for birdwatchers everywhere." Publ Wkly

Zickefoose, Julie

The **bluebird** effect; uncommon bonds with
common birds. Julie Zickefoose. Houghton Mifflin
Harcourt Co. 2012 355 p.   **598**
    1. Naturalists 2. Bird watching 3. Birds -- Behavior 4.
    Wildlife rehabilitation 5. Human-animal relationship 6.
    Birds -- United States
    ISBN 9780547003092
                        LC 2011036692

This book by bird rehabilitator Julie Zickefoose presents
an "account of her rescues of cardinals, robins and more
than 20 other bird species. . . . The birds are a disparate lot:
the starlings with their imitations of car alarms and barking
dogs; the potentially home-wrecking chickadees; the lean
and sinewy ospreys; the barn sparrows that haunt the eaves
of large home-improvement stores." (Kirkus Reviews)

Includes bibliographical references and index

598.09   Ornithology

Birkhead, Tim

★ **Ten** thousand birds; ornithology since Darwin. Tim Birkhead, Jo Wimpenny, Bob Montgom-
erie. Princeton University Press 2014 544 p. ill
(some color), color maps   **598.09**
    1. Birds 2. Evolution 3. Ornithologists 4. Ornithology
    -- History -- 19th century 5. Ornithology -- History --
    20th century 6. Ornithology -- History -- 21st century
    ISBN 9780691151977; 0691151970
                        LC 2013939390

This book, by Tim Birkhead, "provides a . . . history of
modern ornithology, tracing how the study of birds has been
shaped by a succession of visionary and often-controversial
personalities, and by the unique social and scientific contexts
in which these . . . individuals worked. . . . It describes how in
the early 1900s pioneering individuals such as Erwin Strese-
mann, Ernst Mayr, and Julian Huxley recognized the importance of studying live birds in the field." (Publisher's note)

An "engaging, readable history of ornithology, replete
with dozens of color and black-and-white illustrations and
vivid, frequently humorous descriptions of the people who
advanced ornithology because of, and often in spite of, their
personalities. The charming and witty work fills the needs
of academic scientists and researchers as well as serious
birders." Choice

Includes bibliographical references (pages 467-496)
and index

598.4   Miscellaneous orders of water birds

Safina, Carl

Eye of the albatross; visions of hope and survival. Holt & Co. 2002 377p il maps hardcover o.p.
pa $16   **598.4**
    1. Albatrosses
    ISBN 0-8050-6229-7 pa
                        LC 2001-51644

The author "recounts his travels to remote portions of the
northwest Hawaiian Islands to witness albatross breeding
season, during which parent birds fly across entire oceans—
as much as 25,000 miles—to hunt sufficient food to nourish
their single chicks. . . . Safina's encyclopedic knowledge and
spirited prose provide a stunningly intimate portrait of an
environment." Publ Wkly

Includes bibliographical references

598.7   Miscellaneous orders of land birds

Gallagher, Tim

★ **Imperial** Dreams; Tracking the Imperial
Woodpecker Through the Wild Sierra Madre. Tim
Gallagher. Pocket Books 2013 304 p. $26   **598.7**
    1. Imperial woodpecker 2. Natural history -- Mexico 3.
    Sierra Madre Occidental Region (Mexico) -- Description
    and travel
    ISBN 1439191522; 9781439191521
                        LC 2013005233

In this book by explorer and naturalist Tim Gallagher, he
journeys "deep into Mexico's . . . Sierra Madre Occidental,
home to rich wildlife, as well as to Mexican drug cartels,
in a perilous quest to locate the most elusive bird in the
world--the imperial woodpecker. Gallagher's . . . quest takes
a harrowing turn as he encounters armed drug traffickers,
burning houses, and fleeing villagers. His mission becomes
a life-and-death drama that . . . as he chases truth in the most
dangerous of habitats." (Publisher's note)

Includes bibliographical references and index

598.8   Perching birds (Passeriformes)

Young, Jon

What the robin knows; how birds reveal the secrets of the natural world. Jon Young ; with science
and audio editing by Dan Gardoqui. Houghton Mifflin Harcourt 2012 xxviii, 241 p.p   **598.8**
    1. Birdsongs 2. Bird watching 3. Philosophy of nature
    4. Nature observation 5. Songbirds -- Behavior 6.
    Natural history -- New Jersey
    ISBN 0547451253; 9780547451251
                        LC 2012002403

In this book naturalist Jon Young teaches "three basic
premises: the robin, junco, and other songbirds know everything important about their environment, be it backyard or
forest; by tuning in to their vocalizations and behavior, we
can acquire much of this wisdom for our own pleasure and
benefit; and the birds' companion calls and warning alarms
are just as important as their songs. Birds are the sentries—

and our key to understanding the world beyond our front door. Unwitting humans create a zone of disturbance that scatters the wildlife. Respectful humans who heed the birds acquire an awareness that radically changes the dynamic. We are welcome in their habitat." (Publisher's note)

Includes bibliographical references and index.

598.9 Falconiformes, Caprimulgiformes, owls

Gessner, David, 1961-

Return of the osprey; a season of flight and wonder. Algonquin Bks. 2001 286p map pa $14.95 **598.9**

1. Ospreys

ISBN 9780345450166; 1-56512-254-2

LC 00-68230

"Over 90 percent of the osprey population in New England was wiped out between 1950 and 1975, and then DDT was banned. Gessner writes of the return of nesting ospreys to Cape Cod. . . . This beautifully written story of a season with birds of prey makes for engrossing reading as we learn about osprey life from a master essayist." Booklist

Includes bibliographical references

Mikkola, Heimo

Owls of the world; a photographic guide. Heimo Mikkola. Firefly Books 2012 512 p. $49.95 **598.9**

1. Owls

ISBN 1770851364; 9781770851368

LC 2012288505

This book is "a complete guide to identifying the world's owls. Photographers spend hours waiting to capture them and birders seek them out with determination, but owls have been tough to identify--until now. . . .Owls are shown as adults from a perspective that clearly shows markings which assist in identification. Photographs of similar-looking species are included where identification is particularly difficult." (Publisher's note)

Includes bibliographical references (p. 504) and index

Taylor, Marianne

Owls; [text by Marianne Taylor ; photos by Markus Varesvuo ... et al.] Cornell University Press 2012 224 p. col. ill. (hardcover) $35 **598.9**

1. Owls

ISBN 0801451817; 9780801451812

LC 2012023191

This book, by Marianne Taylor, presents an introduction to various species of owls. "From tiny Elf and Pygmy Owls through the familiar Tawny and Barn Owls to the giant Eagle and Fish Owls, these fierce hunters of dawn, dusk and night have long held a fascination for people around the world. This . . . book, covering all owl species found in the northern hemisphere, looks closely at how owls live their lives, and how best to recognize them." (Publisher's note)

Includes bibliographical references (p. 220) and index.

599 Mammals

Elbroch, Mark

Mammal tracks & sign; a guide to North American species. Stackpole Bks. 2003 779p il maps $44.95 **599**

1. Mammals 2. Animal tracks

ISBN 0-8117-2626-6

LC 2002-10549

The author "brings an ideal combination of practical experience and careful research to this work. . . . A definitive treatment, Elbroch's book will set the standard for years to come and is essential to anyone interested in tracking this continent's mammals." Libr J

Includes bibliographical references

★ The **Peterson** field guide to animal tracks; [by] Mark Elbroch and Olaus J. Murie. 3rd ed.; Houghton Mifflin Company 2005 (The Peterson field guide series) hardcover o.p. pa $19.95 **599**

1. Animal tracks

ISBN 978-0-618-51742-8; 978-0-618-51743-5 pa

LC 2005-13108

First published 1954

"Murie's handbook is recognized as the classic work on the subject. . . . The illustrated guide describes the tracks, droppings, and marks left on bones and leaves by an army of wild animals-bats, bears, rabbits, reptiles, moles, weasels, and others. A fascinating collection of miscellaneous information about the habits of these creatures is part of the descriptive text." Wynar. Ref Books in Paperback. 2d edition

Mares, Michael A.

A **desert** calling; life in a forbidding landscape. Harvard Univ. Press 2002 318p il maps $29.95 **599**

1. Mammals 2. Desert animals

ISBN 0-674-00747-6

LC 2001-51786

The author describes his studies of "small mammals in the deserts of North America, South America, Egypt, and Iran. . . . The wonder of field research and of the discoveries that result shines through his matter-of-fact tone." Booklist

Includes bibliographical references

Nowak, Ronald M.

Walker's mammals of the world; 6th ed; Johns Hopkins Univ. Press 1999 2v il set $135 **599**

1. Mammals 2. Reference books

ISBN 0-8018-5789-9

LC 98-23686

First published 1964

"A goal of the work . . . [is] to provide a quality photograph of a living representative of every genus of mammal. . . . Each genus entry contains information on the number of species known, key literature references, physical description, comparison of characteristics of representative species, description of habitat, general behavior, breeding and care of young, and information on the species' endangered status." Am Ref Books Annu, 2000

Includes bibliographical references

Owens, Mark

Secrets of the savanna; twenty-three years in the African wilderness unraveling the mysteries of elephants and people. [by] Mark and Delia Owens. Houghton Mifflin 2006 230p il map $26; pa $14.95   **599**

1. Elephants 2. Wildlife conservation

ISBN 978-0-395-89310-4; 0-395-89310-0; 978-0-618-87250-3 pa; 0-618-87250-7 pa

LC 2005-23842

Sequel to The eye of the elephant

The authors "describe traveling to the 'remote and ruggedly beautiful' Luangwa Valley, in northeastern Zambia, to help save the North Luangwa National Park, where the elephant population had been decimated by poachers." Publ Wkly

"This book, full of adventure and a few hair-raising moments, deserves a wide readership." Libr J

Includes bibliographical references

The **Princeton** encyclopedia of mammals; edited by David W. Macdonald. Princeton University Press 2009 936p il map pa $45   **599**

1. Reference books 2. Mammals -- Encyclopedias

ISBN 978-0-691-14069-8; 0-691-14069-3

This encyclopedia features a "general introduction to mammals followed by . . . accounts of species and groups that . . . describe form, distribution, behavior, status, conservation, and more." Publisher's note

Includes bibliographical references

Whitaker, John O.

★ **National** Audubon Society field guide to North American mammals; rev ed; Knopf 1996 937p il maps pa $19.95   **599**

1. Mammals

ISBN 0-679-44631-1

LC 95-81456

First published 1980

This field guide describes 390 species of mammals of North America and includes keys for identification, range maps, information on tracks and anatomy, and 375 color photos

599.2   Marsupials and monotremes

Flannery, Tim F.

Chasing kangaroos; a continent, a scientist, and a search for the world's most extraordinary creature. Grove Press 2007 258p il map hardcover o.p. pa $14   **599.2**

1. Kangaroos 2. Australia -- Description and travel

ISBN 978-0-8021-1852-3; 0-8021-1852-6; 978-0-8021-4371-6 pa; 0-8021-4371-7 pa

LC 2006-52628

First published 2004 in Australia with title: Country

"In a time where pride in one's country is a rarity, Flannery has written a love letter to his. . . . Just as much as Chasing Kangaroos is about the evolution of a creature, it's also Flannery's acknowledgement of Australia's inherent unique-

ness, a uniqueness he begs is not casually lost in the growing conformity of the global landscape." Paste

599.5   Cetaceans and sea cows

Bortolotti, Dan

Wild blue; a natural history of the world's largest animal. Thomas Dunne Books 2008 315p il map $24.95   **599.5**

1. Whales

ISBN 978-0-312-38387-9; 0-312-38387-8

LC 2008-24933

The author "provides the most comprehensive title yet on blue whales for the general reader. Encapsulating everything from statistical analysis of geographic populations to the reports of whalers from centuries past, Wild Blue is an effective twenty-first-century fusion of marine biology and international politics." Booklist

Includes bibliographical references

Folkens, Pieter A.

National Audubon Society guide to marine mammals of the world; illustrated by Pieter A. Folkens; written by Randall R. Reeves [et al.] Knopf 2002 527p il maps $26.95   **599.5**

1. Marine mammals

ISBN 0-375-41141-0

LC 2001-38103

"Just about everything one could hope for in a guide can be found in this info-packed yet extremely user-friendly tome. . . . A liberal dose of superb, high-quality action color photographs shows the creatures in their natural surroundings." SLJ

Includes bibliographical references

Herzing, Denise L.

Dolphin diaries; my 25 years with spotted dolphins in the Bahamas. St. Martin's Press 2011 xxi, 314p $26.99; ebook $12.99   **599.5**

1. Dolphins

ISBN 978-0-312-60896-5; 978-1-4299-8744-8 ebook

LC 2011005995

"Tales of diving with wild dolphins, recalcitrant equipment, living on boats, and hurricanes really bring both the excitement and the drudgery of field research to life." Booklist

Includes bibliographical references

Hoare, Philip

The **whale**; in search of the giants of the sea. Ecco 2010 453p il map $27.99   **599.5**

1. Whales 2. Whaling

ISBN 978-0-06-197621-6; 0-06-197621-0

First published 2009 in the United Kingdom with title: Leviathan; or, The whale

A "chronicle of the tragic interaction between humans and whales. Using Herman Melville's life and 'Moby-Dick' as touchstones, Hoare traces the whaling industry from its origins in 18th century New England to the present." Los Angeles Times

Includes bibliographical references

Kelsey, Elin

Watching giants; the secret lives of whales. with photographs by Doc White; additional photographs by François Gohier. University of California Press 2009 201p il $24.95   **599.5**

1. Whales

ISBN 978-0-520-24976-9; 0-520-24976-3

LC 2008-7782

"An appealing, agitating foray into the world of whales that ignites both protective instincts and a hungry curiosity to know more." Kirkus

Includes bibliographical references

Rothenberg, David

Thousand mile song; whale music in a sea of sound. Basic Books 2008 287p il $27.50   **599.5**

1. Whales

ISBN 978-0-465-07128-9; 0-465-07128-7

LC 2007-48161

"Biologists know that whale songs, which may carry for hundreds of miles, change over time and are passed on from one generation to the next, but they don't fully understand what these complex sounds are for. . . . [The author] proposes that music played by humans can help us find answers. He tested this theory by playing his clarinet into an underwater speaker and recording the whales' responses on an underwater hydrophone. His intriguing book includes sonograms and a CD demonstrating that the orcas, belugas and humpbacks he played for seemed to interact with his music. . . . His paean to the beautiful music these great mammals make should lend further support to attempts to save the whales at a time when they are increasingly threatened." Publ Wkly

Includes bibliographical references

599.53   Dolphins and porpoises

Kirby, David

Death at SeaWorld; Shamu and the dark side of killer whales in captivity. David Kirby. St. Martin's Press 2012 469 p. (hardcover) $26.99   **599.53**

1. Amusement parks 2. Captive marine mammals 3. Marine mammals -- Behavior 4. Sea World 5. Killer whale 6. Animal attacks 7. Marine biologists 8. Aquatic animal welfare

ISBN 1250002028; 9781250002020; 9781250008312

LC 2012009433

In this book, investigative journalist David Kirby examines the marine mammal theme park SeaWorld. "SeaWorld trainer Dawn Brancheau's death in 2010 after being attacked by a killer whale made headlines, but the story goes deeper. Marine biologist and animal advocate Naomi Rose had already spent two decades challenging SeaWorld's captivity of killer whales as dangerous to both whales and humans." (Library Journal)

Montgomery, Sy

Journey of the pink dolphins; an Amazon quest. Simon & Schuster 2000 317p il maps hardcover o.p. pa $16   **599.53**

1. Dolphins 2. Amazon River valley

ISBN 0-7432-0026-8 pa

LC 99-45840

The author "recounts her Amazonian adventures in search of the botos, the famously elusive freshwater pink dolphins, a quest that yields not only invaluable scientific observations but profound insights into the significance of myth." Booklist

Includes bibliographical references

599.638   Giraffe and okapi

Peterson, Dale

★ **Giraffe** reflections; text by Dale Peterson ; photographs by Karl Ammann. University of California Press 2013 221 p. (cloth : alk. paper) $39.95   **599.638**

1. Animals -- Pictorial works 2. Giraffe

ISBN 0520266854; 9780520266858

LC 2012038611

Author Dale Peterson's book features a book on endangered giraffes. The book presents "a natural and cultural history of the world's tallest and second-biggest land animals, describing in detail their biology and behavior. He offers a new perspective on the giraffes' place in our world, and argues for the stronger protection of these imposing yet endangered creatures and their elusive forest relatives, the okapis." (Publisher's note)

Includes bibliographical references and index

599.64   Bovids

Rinella, Steven

American buffalo; in search of a lost icon. Spiegel & Grau 2008 277p il map $24.95   **599.64**

1. Bison

ISBN 978-0-385-52168-0; 0-385-52168-5

LC 2008-13624

"In 2005, [Rinella] won an Alaska state lottery permit making him one of 24 hunters allowed to kill one wild buffalo each to thin out the Copper River herd in the Wrangell-Saint Elias National Park. The book's core is Rinella's entertaining and often harrowing account of that hunting trip into Alaska's frozen south-central wilderness, where he bagged his first buffalo. But entwined throughout that story line is an engaging back story — a stampede of facts and factoids, legends and lore, hard-core science and staggering history of North America's largest land animal. Everything you ever wanted to know about the buffalo — or didn't — going back to Pleistocene days." USA Today

Includes bibliographical references

599.67   Elephants

Ammann, Karl

Elephant reflections; photographs by Karl Ammann; text by Dale Peterson. University of California Press 2009 272p il $39.95   **599.67**
1. Elephants
ISBN 978-0-520-25377-3; 0-520-25377-9

LC 2008-42391

"Ammann's photographs capture an astonishing range of elephant behavior, but Peterson's text—with its scope, synthesis of history and observation, précis of the ivory trade and conservation—is what distinguishes this book. He spins the history of elephant research into mini-mysteries of how scientists struggled to understand elephants' secretive behaviors. . . . The photographs and text complement each other beautifully in their respective odes to the 'improbable' physicality of the elephant's body." Publ Wkly

Includes bibliographical references

Anthony, Lawrence, 1950-2012

The **elephant** whisperer; my life with the herd in the African wild. [by] Lawrence Anthony with Graham Spence. Thomas Dunne Books/St. Martin's Press 2009 368p il $24.99   **599.67**
1. Elephants 2. Wildlife refuges
ISBN 978-0-312-56578-7

LC 2009-23815

This is the author's "robust portrait of Thula Thula, the game land he owns, in cooperation with a number of Zulu tribes, in Zululand—5,000 acres of raw landscape that is thought to have been part of the exclusive hunting grounds of the Zulu king. No longer, since Anthony now runs it as a conservationist lodge, but it continues to produce colorful tales of wild discovery. Most prominent are the many fascinating stories that surround his adoption of the elephants, an unruly bunch he endeavors to make at home on the reserve. With a combination of intuition and experience, the author intelligently discusses many aspects of elephant behavior." Kirkus

599.7   Carnivores

Nicholls, Henry

The **way** of the panda; the curious history of China's political animal. Pegasus Books 2011 319p il map $25   **599.7**
1. Giant panda 2. Wildlife conservation 3. China -- Foreign relations
ISBN 978-1-60598-188-8; 1-60598-188-5
First published 2010 in the United Kingdom

"When the Chinese government brings Giant Pandas to the negotiating table, the stakes change. Whole populations and their leaders clamor for access to these animals, as if they were toddlers reaching for toys. Washington, London and Moscow have all succumbed to this awesome (a chorus of 'Awwwwwww!' accompanies every panda appearance) force. That is only one reason that Henry Nicholls refers to the Giant Panda as a political animal in his charmingly written 'The Way of the Panda.' At times everything concerning the creatures seems to have a political angle: not only

their value as state gifts (with heavy strings attached) but also their precise scientific classification; their mating habits and offspring; and the efforts to ensure their preservation. The author compares the history of the panda in the modern world to that of China itself, complete with a 'great leap forward' in the 1960s, when the captive breeding of pandas first became possible." Wall Street J

Includes bibliographical references

599.74   Land carnivores

Thomas, Elizabeth Marshall

The **tribe** of tiger; cats and their culture. illustrated by Jared Taylor Williams. Simon & Schuster 1994 240p il hardcover o.p. pa $13.95   **599.74**
1. Cats 2. Lions 3. Tigers
ISBN 0-7434-2689-4 pa

LC 94-20195

The author offers a "look into the lives of various members of the cat family—small and large, domestic and wild, Old World and New. She begins with the evolution and spread of different feline species, explaining the physiology and behavior of cats, including house cats, as meat eaters, that is, in the light of their hunting instincts. She then examines the changes over a period of more than 30 years in the culture . . . of different lion communities in several parts of Africa. In conclusion, she discusses the need for tiger conservation." Booklist

Includes bibliographical references

599.75   Cat family

Adamson, Joy

Born free; a lioness of two worlds. Pantheon Bks. 1987 220p il hardcover o.p. pa $14.95 **599.75**
1. Lions 2. Kenya -- Description and travel
ISBN 0-375-71438-3 pa

LC 86-42972

A reissue of the title first published 1960

This is the "story of a lioness who bridged the gulf between two worlds, that of the jungle and of man. The author and her husband, a Kenya game warden, reared a cub to kill and fend for herself when she was returned to the jungle. At the same time they were able to preserve the bond of confidence and affection established with her as a pet." Cincinnati Public Libr

Vaillant, John

The **tiger**; a true story of vengeance and survival. Alfred A. Knopf 2010 329p il map $26.95; pa $15   **599.75**
1. Tigers 2. Tiger hunting 3. Tigers -- Behavior 4. Human-animal relationships 5. Siberia (Russia) -- Description and travel 6. Russian Far East (Russia) -- Description and travel
ISBN 978-0-307-26893-8; 0-307-26893-4; 978-0-307-38904-6 pa; 0-307-38904-9 pa; 978-0-307-59379-5 ebook; 0-307-59379-7 ebook

LC 2010-04068

"What makes 'The Tiger' a grand addition to the animal-pursuit subgenre is the sensitive way in which Vaillant . . . evokes his cat. Few writers have taken such pains to understand their monsters, and few depict them in such arresting prose." N Y Times Book Rev

Includes bibliographical references

599.756 Tiger

Matthiessen, Peter

Tigers in the snow; introduction and photographs by Maurice Hornocker. Farrar, Straus & Giroux 1999 169p il hardcover o.p. pa $15 **599.756**
1. Tigers 2. Endangered species
ISBN 0-86547-596-2 pa

LC 99-44866

"Mixing information about the lives of all the races of wild tigers with firsthand tales of his visits to Russia, the author brings an immediacy to his narrative that stirs the reader to awe of these great cats. . . . [An] evocative look at one of our rarest animals." Booklist

Includes bibliographical references

599.77 Dog family

Busch, Robert

The **wolf** almanac; a celebration of wolves and their world. by Robert H. Busch. New & rev ed; Lyons Press 2007 274p il map pa $19.95 **599.77**
1. Wolves
ISBN 978-1-59921-069-8; 1-59921-069-X
First published 1995

This offers information about "the evolution and history of wolves; their biology and physiology; their behavior and sociology; and their influence in ancient cultures and mythology. . . . The author also discusses the conservation politics of all wolf species." Publisher's note

Includes bibliographical references

Lopez, Barry Holstun

★ **Of** wolves and men; with photographs by John Bauguess; including a new afterword by the author and expanded bibliography. 1st Scribner Classics ed.; Scribner Classics 2004 323p il $45 **599.77**
1. Wolves
ISBN 0-7432-4936-4

LC 2004-45429

First published 1978

The author "infuses his natural history of the long relationship between wolves and humankind with both myth and science, then revisits the controversial subject of wolf reintroduction." Booklist

Includes bibliographical references

McAllister, Ian

The **last** wild wolves; ghosts of the rain forest. with contributions by Chris Darimont; introduction

by Paul C. Paquet. University of California Press 2007 191p il map $39.95 **599.77**
1. Wolves
ISBN 978-0-520-25473-2; 0-520-25473-2

LC 2007-10887

This is an account of the author's experiences following two packs of wolves on the north coast of British Columbia. In text and photographs, the wolves are depicted "as they fish for salmon in the fall, target seals [are] hauled out on rocks in winter, and [the wolves] give birth to their young." Publisher's note

"The text is particularly well written and engaging. . . . However, it is the dozens of unique photos sprinkled liberally throughout the book that provide the greatest appeal." Sci Books Films

Mowat, Farley

Never cry wolf. Back Bay Books 2001 246p pa $12.99 **599.77**
1. Wolves
ISBN 978-0-316-88179-1; 0-316-88179-1
First published 1963 by Little, Brown

"A biologist for the Canadian government describes his experiences in the Arctic watching and tracking the activities of a wolf family." Publ Wkly

Smith, Douglas W.

★ **Decade** of the wolf; returning the wild to Yellowstone. [by] Douglas W. Smith & Gary Ferguson. Lyons Press 2005 212p il maps $23.95; pa $16.95 **599.77**
1. Wolves 2. Endangered species 3. Yellowstone National Park
ISBN 1-59228-700-X; 1-59228-886-3 pa

LC 2005-40767

"Well illustrated with black-and-white and color photographs, this intimate history of the return of the top predator to Yellowstone will find an eager audience." Booklist

Includes bibliographical references

599.78 Bears

Croke, Vicki

★ The **lady** and the panda; the true adventures of the first American explorer to bring back China's most exotic animal. [by] Vicki Constantine Croke. Random House 2005 372p il $25.95; pa $14.95 **599.78**
1. Explorers 2. Giant panda
ISBN 0-375-50783-3; 0-375-75970-0 pa

LC 2004-51356

The author tells the "story of Ruth Harkness, the Manhattan bohemian socialite who, against all but impossible odds, trekked to Tibet in 1936 to capture the most mysterious animal of the day: a bear that had for countless centuries lived in secret in the labyrinth of lonely cold mountains." Publisher's note

"This well-written, exhaustively researched and documented book should be on every library's shelves." Libr J

Includes bibliographical references

Ellis, Richard

✓ On thin ice; the changing world of the polar bear. Alfred A. Knopf 2009 400p il $28.95   **599.78**

1. Polar bear 2. Greenhouse effect

ISBN 978-0-307-27059-7; 0-307-27059-9

LC 2009-20017

This profile of the habitat and life cycle of the polar bear covers the species' venerated position in Inuit culture, its reproductive habits, and the environmental factors that are compromising its ability to survive.

"The real strength of the book is its focus on the polar bear as the poster child of global warming, of how tied the bears are to the arctic ice and what will happen if the ice melts, and of the national and international wrangling over the politics of climate change and the listing of the bear as an endangered species. The polar bear could not ask for a better champion than Ellis in this highly recommended work." Booklist

Includes bibliographical references

599.79   Marine carnivores

Williams, Terrie M.

The **odyssey** of KP2; an orphan seal, a marine biologist, and the fight to save a species from extinction. Terrie M. Williams. Penguin Press 2012 xvi, 283 p.p ill. (hardcover) $27.95   **599.79**

1. Animal rescue 2. Seals (Animals) 3. Wildlife rehabilitation 4. Endangered species -- Hawaii 5. Wildlife conservation -- Hawaii 6. Wildlife rehabilitation -- Hawaii 7. Hawaiian monk seal -- Conservation

ISBN 1594203393; 9781594203398

LC 2011050415

AAAS/Subaru SB&F Prize for Excellence in Science Books: Young Adult Science Book (2013)

This book "chronicles . . . an orphaned Hawaiian monk seal's . . . rescue and first years of life. . . . [Terrie M.] Williams and her team of researchers began an intense study of the young male, and they collected important data on KP2's growth rates, feeding habits and sociability, with the 'survival of [the] entire species' resting on his shoulders." (Kirkus Reviews)

599.8   Primates

Among African apes; stories and photos from the field. edited by Martha M. Robbins and Christophe Boesch. University of California Press 2011 182p il map pa $29.95; ebook $29.95   **599.8**

1. Apes

ISBN 978-0-520-26710-7 pa; 978-0-520-94883-9 ebook

LC 2010033131

This book on apes contains some violent content. "The authors want to raise awareness about the plight of African apes. To do so, they draw upon research careers that go back at least 30 years. Included in the text are day-to-day accounts of what it takes to organize and find a research site in Africa, what it's like to track a gorilla, what it's like to experience a chimp or bonobo community, and what hap-

pens to these communities as a result of their encounters with various human communities. . . . Rarely does a book so perfectly illustrate the scientific process. The interaction between researcher and subject comes alive in these pages." Sci Books Films

Includes bibliographical references

Bearzi, Maddalena

Beautiful minds; the parallel lives of great apes and dolphins. [by] Maddalena Bearzi & Craig B. Stanford. Harvard University Press 2008 351p $24.95; pa $14.95   **599.8**

1. Apes 2. Dolphins 3. Comparative psychology

ISBN 978-0-674-02781-7; 0-674-02781-7; 978-0-674-04627-6 pa; 0-674-04627-7 pa

LC 2007-46199

"Endowed through evolution with large brains, the great apes (chimpanzees, bonobos gorillas and orangutans) and the cetaceans (dolphins and whales) are second only to humans in intelligence. In this delightful and intriguing book, . . . [the authors] discuss the similarities between these groups." Publ Wkly

Includes bibliographical references

Goodall, Jane, 1934-

★ In the shadow of man; photographs by Hugo van Lawick; [with a new preface; foreword by Richard Wrangham] Mariner Books 2009 xxx, 302p il map pa $15.95   **599.8**

1. Chimpanzees

ISBN 978-0-547-33416-5

LC 2009044848

First published 1971

The author describes the chimpanzee group she studied during ten years of field observation in the Gombe Stream Chimpanzee Reserve in Tanzania.

Includes bibliographical references

✓ **Through** a window; my thirty years with the chimpanzees of Gombe. [with a new preface and a new afterword] Houghton Mifflin Harcourt 2010 xx, 337p il map pa $15.95   **599.8**

1. Chimpanzees

ISBN 978-0-547-33695-4; 0-547-33695-0

LC 2009045230

First published 1990

This continuation of In the shadow of man "tells two stories: first of how the chimps of Gombe in Tanzania have grown, changed and died, and second, how Goodall and her dedicated group of Tanzanian observers have survived the rigours of the past thirty years. It is beautifully written, and evokes both sympathy and understanding of these animals." Times Lit Suppl

Includes bibliographical references

Morris, Desmond

Planet ape; [by] Desmond Morris with Steve Parker. Firefly Books 2009 288p il $49.95   **599.8**

1. Apes

ISBN 978-1-55407-566-9

Detail of the great apes, including: where they live, how they live and the challenges they face. Illustrations compare apes with human beings, including their anatomy, social life, physical and mental development, diet and communication.

"Published in a large format (approximately 10 by 11 inches) with hundreds of full-color glossy photographs and illustrations, this beautiful volume is a cross between a coffee-table book and a thorough compendium of ape behavior, anatomy, taxonomy, and lore. . . . The book reads well, is packed full of exciting information, and is just plain fun to browse for hours." Sci Books Films

Redmond, Ian

The **primate** family tree; the amazing diversity of our closest relatives. foreword by Jane Goodall. Firefly Books 2008 176p il map $35; pbk $24.95 **599.8**
1. Primates
ISBN 978-1-55407-378-8; 1-55407-378-2; 9781554079643
The Primate Family Tree "is beautifully designed, and the contents are well organized and will be interesting to all. . . . This is a very attractive, interesting, and informative publication." Sci Books Films
Includes bibliographical references

Sapolsky, Robert M.

A **primate's** memoir. Scribner 2001 304p pa $14; $25 **599.8**
1. Baboons 2. Baboons -- Behavior -- Africa, East -- Anecdotes
ISBN 0-7432-0241-4 pa; 0-7432-0247-3
LC 00-63522
This is an account of the author's experiences observing baboons in Kenya
"One closes Sapolsky's book a lot more knowledgeable about plenty of baboon-related matters. But mostly one has already begun to miss the company of this sometimes cranky but always impassioned, learned and winningly irreverent man." N Y Times Book Rev

★ **World** atlas of great apes and their conservation; edited by Julian Caldecott and Lera Miles; foreword by Kofi A. Annan. University of California Press, in association with UNEP-WCMC 2005 456p il map $45 **599.8**
1. Apes 2. Atlases 3. Biogeography 4. Reference books 5. Wildlife conservation
ISBN 0-520-24633-0; 978-0-520-24633-1
LC 2006-272653
"Each great ape specie is given a separate chapter that contains information on behavior and ecology, communication and tool use, threats and conservation, and exceptionally detailed distribution maps. What sets this book apart is the section that details each country in which apes are found and exactly what conservation efforts are underway." Univ Press Books for Public and Second Sch Libr, 2006
Includes bibliographical references

599.88   Great apes and gibbons

Fossey, Dian

★ **Gorillas** in the mist. Houghton Mifflin 1983 326p il hardcover o.p. pa $14 **599.88**
1. Gorillas
ISBN 0-618-08360-X pa
LC 82-23332
This book "recounts some of the events of the thirteen years that I have spent with the mountain gorillas in their natural habitat and includes data from the fifteen years of continuing field study." Preface
Includes bibliographical references

Stanford, Craig B.

Planet without apes; Craig B. Stanford. Belknap Press of Harvard University Press 2012 262 p. ill. (hardcover) $25.95 **599.88**
1. Apes 2. Endangered species 3. Extinct animals
ISBN 0674067045; 9780674067042
LC 2012023985
This book, by Craig B. Stanford, "warns that extinction of the great apes--chimpanzees, bonobos, gorillas, and orangutans--threatens to become a reality within just a few human generations. We are on the verge of losing the last links to our evolutionary past, and to all the biological knowledge about ourselves that would die along with them. The crisis we face is tantamount to standing aside while our last extended family members vanish from the planet." (Publisher's note)
"Stanford has brilliantly distilled scientific research, African and Asian economic issues, and ethical concerns surrounding the exploitation of these intelligent, highly social creatures into a powerful plea for primate protection." LJ
Includes bibliographical references and index

Waal, Frans de

Bonobo; the forgotten ape. photographs, Frans Lanting. University of Calif. Press 1997 210p il maps $50; pa $29.95 **599.88**
· 1. Apes
ISBN 0-520-20535-9; 0-520-21651-2 pa
LC 96-41095
The subject of this monograph is the bonobo, a species of ape. "In six chapters, de Waal describes the history of the discovery of bonobos as a separate species; he compares them with common chimps; he describes their natural habitat and their . . . use of sex as social currency, particularly in moderating aggression; he examines bonobo social structure in relation to that of common chimps and humans; and he finishes with an exploration of bonobos' highly developed sense of empathy." New Sci
. Includes bibliographical references

599.885   Chimpanzees

Halloran, Andrew R.

The **song** of the ape; Andrew R. Halloran. 1st ed. St. Martin's Press 2012 x, 276p.p **599.885**
1. Chimpanzees 2. Animal sounds 3. Animal

communication 4. Zoo keepers 5. Primatologists
ISBN 9780312563110; 9781429933278

LC 2011041344

The premise for this book began when, "working as a zookeeper at a drive-through animal park in south Florida, [author and primatologist Andrew R.] Halloran witnessed the escape of a group of chimpanzees who capitalized on an unsecured boat to flee from their island habitat and an upstart group of rival chimps. To react so quickly and uniformly, the group, Halloran surmises, must have been communicating in a complex manner that allowed them to plan and orchestrate such an escape. To examine this idea further, Halloran . . . embarks on a . . . study of five of the chimps involved, delving into their histories, their calls, and the meaning of their calls. The result is an . . . account of communication development among these intelligent animals . . . showing how they communicate with each other on their own terms and how numerous factors cause dialects to emerge." (Publishers Weekly)

Includes bibliographical references and index

599.9   Humans

Fabian, Ann

The **skull** collectors; Ann Fabian. The University of Chicago Press 2010 xi, 270 p.p ill.   **599.9**
   1. Anthropometry 2. Race relations 3. Craniology
-- History
   ISBN 978-0-226-23348-2; 0-226-23348-0

LC 2009047712

This book tells the "story of [naturalist Samuel] Morton, his contemporaries, and their search for a scientific foundation for racial difference. From cranial measurements and museum shelves to heads on stakes, bloody battlefields, and the 'rascally pleasure' of grave robbing, [author Ann] Fabian paints a . . . picture of scientific inquiry in service of an agenda of racial superiority, and of a society coming to grips with both the deadly implications of manifest destiny and the mass slaughter of the Civil War. . . . Fabian also . . . traces the continuing implications of this history, from lingering traces of scientific racism to debates over the return of the remains of Native Americans that are held by museums to this day." (Publisher's note)

Includes bibliographical references and index

Olson, Steve

Mapping human history; discovering the past through our genes. Houghton Mifflin 2002 292p il $25; pa $14   **599.9**
   1. Human beings 2. Physical anthropology
   ISBN 0-618-09157-2; 0-618-35210-4 pa

LC 2001-51880

The author "traces the history of human civilization in five regions of the world—Africa, the Middle East, Asia, Australia, and Europe and the Americas, plus a final chapter on Hawaii—to explain how physical differences originated and to provide evidence of our essential sameness." Publ Wkly

Includes bibliographical references and index

599.93   Genetics, sex and age characteristics, evolution

Diamond, Jared

The **third** chimpanzee; the evolution and future of the human animal. {by} Jared Diamond. Harper-Collins Pubs. 1992 407p il maps hardcover o.p. pa $14.95   **599.93**
   1. Evolution 2. Human origins 3. Anthropology 4. Social change 5. Human influence on nature
   ISBN 0-06-018307-1; 0-06-084550-3 pa; 978-0-06-084550-6 pa

LC 91-50455

First published 1991 in the United Kingdom with title: The rise and fall of the third chimpanzee

The author "argues that the human being is just a third species of chimpanzee but nevertheless a unique animal essentially due to its capacity for innovation, which caused a great leap forward in hominoid evolution. After stressing the significance of spoken language, along with art and technology, Diamond focuses on the . . . propensities of our species to kill each other (genocide and drug abuse) and to destroy the environment (mass extinctions). He also discusses human sexuality, geographic variability, and ramifications of agriculture (metallurgy, cultivated plants, and domesticated animals)." (Libr J) Bibliography. Index.

The author "argues that the human being is just a third species of chimpanzee but nevertheless a unique animal essentially due to its capacity for innovation, which caused a great leap forward in hominoid evolution. After stressing the significance of spoken language, along with art and technology, Diamond focuses on the self-destructive propensities of our species." Libr J

Includes bibliographical references

Johanson, Donald C.

★ **From** Lucy to language; [by] Donald Johanson & Blake Edgar; principal photography, David L. Brill. Rev., updated, and expanded; Simon and Schuster 2006 288p il map $65   **599.93**
   1. Human origins 2. Fossil hominids
   ISBN 0-7432-8064-4; 978-0-7432-8064-8

LC 2007-270098

First published 1996

This is a "photographic showcase of the essential physical evidence of human origins. . . . Permitting a face-to-face encounter with human ancestors, this work furnishes essential information, [and] an incomparable visual experience." Booklist

Includes bibliographical references

Lucy: the beginnings of humankind; [by] Donald C. Johanson and Maitland A. Edey. Simon & Schuster 1981 409p il hardcover o.p. pa $16   **599.93**
   1. Human origins 2. Fossil mammals 3. Fossil hominids
   ISBN 0-671-72499-1 pa

LC 80-21759

In November 1974 at a place called Hadar in Ethiopia Donald Johanson "discovered the partial skeleton of an extremely primitive female, erect-walking primate or hominid. . . . The skeleton received the name 'Lucy.' Much later, Lucy received the scientific name, Australopithecus afarensis, and it was determined she was some 3.5 million years old. . . . This book is Johanson's own story of the events leading up to and subsequent to Lucy's discovery." Best Sellers

Includes bibliographical references

Jolly, Alison

Lucy's legacy; sex and intelligence in human evolution. Harvard Univ. Press 1999 518p il hardcover o.p. pa $18.95 **599.93**

1. Evolution 2. Intellect

ISBN 0-674-00069-2; 0-674-00540-6 pa

LC 99-32252

"Lucy is the name given to the fossil skeleton of an Australopithecine, a human ancestor, discovered in Ethiopia. The name may be a misnomer, since there's no way yet of telling whether Lucy was female. No matter. Primatologist Jolly's interest is not so much in Lucy as in the crucial role that females in general have played in human evolution. . . . In clear and clever prose, Jolly shows us how we got so smart, what sex had to do with it, and how our brains have become the central force in evolution." Booklist

Includes bibliographical references

Leakey, Richard E.

The **origin** of humankind; [by] Richard Leakey. Basic Bks. 1994 171p il maps (Science masters series) hardcover o.p. pa $14.95 **599.93**

1. Human origins

ISBN 0-465-05313-0 pa

LC 94-3617

"Leakey summarizes the evolution of theories, from Darwin's to his own, in the process demonstrating the scientific method in action. . . . Covering the taxonomy of skeletons and craniums, shapes of tools, and the first sprouts of art and culture, Leakey knowledgeably points the enthralled neophyte to the wide avenues of future discoveries." Booklist

This "is a worthwhile addition to many kinds of libraries—public, general, science, biological, and psychological." Sci Books Films

Includes bibliographical references

Origins reconsidered; in search of what makes us human. [by] Richard Leakey and Roger Lewin. Doubleday 1992 375p il hardcover o.p. pa $16.95 **599.93**

1. Human origins

ISBN 0-385-46792-3 pa

LC 92-6661

"Leakey and Lewin discuss how conceptions of human anatomical and behavioral development have been radically altered within the last 12 years by new discoveries and research in other fields. They review the developments and assert Leakey's own hypotheses based on these discoveries. . . . This is an engrossing book written for the layperson, fully explaining anthropological terms and theories when necessary. It's a solid introduction to current theory concerning human development." SLJ

Marks, Jonathan

★ **What** it means to be 98[percent] chimpanzee; apes, people, and their genes. University of Calif. Press 2002 312p $27.50 **599.93**

1. Genetics 2. Evolution 3. Human beings

ISBN 0-520-22615-1

LC 2001-7085

"With plenty of entertaining sarcasm as well as scientific argument and moral indignation, Marks blasts the pretensions of grandiose geneticists pretty thoroughly out of the water. This may be the science book to read this year." Booklist

Includes bibliographical references

Ridley, Matt

Genome; the autobiography of a species in 23 chapters. HarperCollins Pubs. 2000 344p hardcover o.p. pa $14.95 **599.93**

1. Genomes 2. Genetics

ISBN 0-06-019497-9; 978-0-06-089408-5 pa; 0-06-089408-3 pa

LC 99-40933

Ridley presents a "summation of our ever increasing understanding of the roles that genes play in disease, behavior, sexual differences, and even intelligence. More important, though, he addresses not only the ethical quandaries faced by contemporary scientists but the reductionist danger in equating inheritability with inevitability." New Yorker

Includes bibliographical references

Swisher, Carl C.

Java Man; how two geologists changed our understanding of human evolution. [by] Carl C. Swisher III, Garniss H. Curtis, Roger Lewin. University of Chicago Press 2001 256p il $16 **599.93**

1. Human origins 2. Fossil hominids

ISBN 978-0-226-78734-3; 0-226-78734-6

LC 2001-37337

First published 2000 by Scribner

The authors "offer a lively writeup of the technicalities of geochronology, bio-sketches of the discoverers of the erectus fossils, travelogues of their travel in Java, and their side of a spat with paleoanthropology celebrity Don Johansen. An engrossing contribution to the general-interest literature about human origins." Booklist

Includes bibliographical references

Sykes, Bryan

Adam's curse; a future without men. Norton 2004 318p il $25.95; pa $15.95 **599.93**

1. Genetics 2. Chromosomes 3. Sex

ISBN 0-393-05896-4; 0-393-32680-2 pa

LC 2004-3628

First published 2003 in the United Kingdom

The author argues that "all human existence . . . stems from the battle between the X and Y chromosomes to further their own reproduction at the expense of the other." Publ Wkly

"This book incorporates many genres—scientific protocol, biography, harlequin romance, and historical fiction—all expertly executed by Sykes." Sci Books Films

The **seven** daughters of Eve. Norton 2001 306p il map hardcover o.p. pa $15.95　　**599.93**
1. Genetics 2. Human origins
ISBN 0-393-32314-5 pa

The author "contends that most Europeans can trace their roots back to seven women—seven daughters of Eve. One of them lived about 10,000 years ago, around the time farmers first cultivated European soil; the six others go back much farther, to Europe's early hunter-gatherers." N Y Times Book Rev

Tattersall, Ian

The **fossil** trail; how we know what we think we know about human evolution. 2nd ed.; Oxford University Press 2009 xxiii, 327p il map pa $24.95　　**599.93**
1. Fossils 2. Evolution 3. Human origins
ISBN 978-0-19-536766-9
LC 2008-13654

First published 1995

"The task of organising such complex material into a narrative account would have defeated most writers, but Tattersall has mastered it with remarkable skill." New Sci [review of 1995 edition]

Includes bibliographical references

Masters of the planet; Ian Tattersall. Palgrave Macmillan 2012 272p.　　**599.93**
1. Biology 2. Evolution 3. Human origins
ISBN 9780230108752
LC 2011034415

'This book examines the evolution of humans. "When homo sapiens made their entrance 100,000 years ago they were confronted by a wide range of other early humans - homo erectus, who walked better and used fire; homo habilis who used tools; and of course the Neanderthals, who were brawny and strong. . . . [Author Ian Tattersall] explores how the physical traits and cognitive ability of homo sapiens distanced them from the rest of nature. Even more importantly, 'Masters of the Planet' looks at how our early ancestors acquired these superior abilities; it shows that their strange and unprecedented mental facility is not, as most of us were taught, simply a basic competence that was refined over unimaginable eons by natural selection. Instead, it is an emergent capacity that was acquired quite recently and changed the world definitively." (Publisher's note)

Includes bibliographical references and index.

The **monkey** in the mirror; essays on science and what makes us human. Harcourt 2002 203p hardcover o.p. pa $13　　**599.93**
1. Evolution 2. Human origins
ISBN 0-15-602706-2 pa
LC 2001-24122

The author "explores the current understanding of organic evolution in terms of science and reason." Libr J

"A perceptive and persuasive introduction to human origins." Booklist

Taylor, Timothy

The **artificial** ape; how technology changed the course of human evolution. Palgrave Macmillan 2010 256p il $27　　**599.93**
1. Evolution 2. Human origins
ISBN 9780230617636
LC 2010-7924

The author "proposes that it was our early adoption of tools, objects, and, now, technology that changed us [from apes], demonstrating how: baby slings made out of animal fur freed up our arms up to use tools; clothes kept us warm, reducing our need for body hair; [and] shelter protected us from the elements and led our bodies to become slighter and physically weaker. . . . Taylor shows how humans made choices that assumed greater control over their own evolution." Publisher's note

Includes bibliographical references

Wade, Nicholas

Before the dawn; recovering the lost history of our ancestors. Penguin Press 2006 312p il map $24.95　　**599.93**
1. Evolution 2. Social change
ISBN 1-59420-079-3; 978-1-59420-079-3
LC 2005-55293

This is a "survey of human evolution for lay readers which considers the emergence of man in his entirety: physical, psychological, and social. . . . Wade's book concentrates on the recent evolutionary past: our last 50,000 years. . . . [It] emphasizes genetic over paleontological evidence." N Y Rev Books

"This is highly recommended for readers interested in how DNA analysis is rewriting the history of mankind." Publ Wkly

Includes bibliographical references

Walker, Alan

The **wisdom** of the bones; in search of human origins. [by] Alan Walker and Pat Shipman. Knopf 1996 338p il maps hardcover o.p. pa $14　　**599.93**
1. Evolution 2. Human origins 3. Fossil hominids
ISBN 0-679-74783-4 pa
LC 95-37525

"In 1984 Walker, along with colleague Richard Leakey and their 'hominidgang' of experienced Kenyan excavators, discovered a near-intact fossil of Homo erectus. The find was a veritable trove of theory-busting information, which the authors take up after recounting the scientists who preceded Walker in investigating the species. . . . A fluidly presented portrait of the people and process of paleoanthropology." Booklist

Includes bibliographical references

Wilson, Edward O., 1929-

★ The **social** conquest of earth; Edward O. Wilson. W. W. Norton & Co 2012 viii, 330 p.p　　**599.93**
1. Evolution 2. Human origins 3. Human behavior 4. Natural selection 5. Human evolution -- Philosophy 6. Social evolution -- Philosophy 7. Evolution (Biology) -- Philosophy
ISBN 0871404133; 9780871404138
LC 2011052680

This book by Edward O. Wilson provides an "explanation of why humans rule the Earth. After a respectful nod to the old favorites (big brains, tools, language, fire), the author maintains that these merely provide the background to our overpowering 'eusociality'; we are the world's most intensely social creatures, living in complex societies of mutually dependent individuals. . . . Group selection--as opposed to kin selection . . . --is the author's big idea." (Kirkus Reviews)

Includes bibliographical references and index.

600 TECHNOLOGY

600 Technology (Applied sciences)

Arthur, W. Brian

The **nature** of technology; what it is and how it evolves. Free Press 2009 246p $27   **600**
1. Technology -- Philosophy
ISBN 978-1-4165-4405-0; 1-4165-4405-4

LC 2009-7015

"What is technology in its nature, in its deepest essence? Where does it come from? How does it evolve? . . . [The author] tries to answer these and other questions. . . . Arthur's arguments will likely alter the reader's way of thinking about technology and its relationship to humanity." Publ Wkly

Includes bibliographical references

Edgerton, David

The **shock** of the old; technology and global history since 1900. Oxford University Press 2007 270p il $26   **600**
1. Technology -- History
ISBN 978-0-19-532283-5; 0-19-532283-5

LC 2006-26435

Edgerton "challenges us to view the history of technology in terms of what everyday people have actually used—and continue to use around the world—rather than just what was invented." Publisher's note

This book "is a necessary reminder of just how important things are in our lives, and how important we are in the life of things." New Yorker

Includes bibliographical references (240-247)

Harman, Jay

The **shark's** paintbrush; biomimicry and how nature is inspiring innovation. Jay Harman. White Cloud Press 2013 326 p. ill $26.95   **600**
1. Biomimicry 2. Sustainable development
ISBN 1935952846; 9781935952848

LC 2012015185

This book, by Jay Harman, describes how, "in a world of depleted natural resources, entrepreneurs and scientists are turning to nature to inspire future products that are more energy- and cost-efficient. Biomimicry, the science of employing nature to advance sustainable technology, is arguably one of the hottest new business concepts." Harman "shows business leaders and aspiring entrepreneurs how we can reconcile creating more powerful, lucrative technologies with maximizing sustainability." (Publisher's note)

"A useful update on recent developments in biomimicry and an intriguing case for innovative green technology that goes beyond sustainability." Kirkus

Macaulay, David

The **new** way things work; [by] David Macaulay with Neil Ardley. Houghton Mifflin 1998 400p il $35   **600**
1. Machinery 2. Inventions 3. Technology
ISBN 0-395-93847-3

LC 98-14224

First published 1988 with title: The way things work

Arranged in five sections this volume provides information on "the workings of hundreds of machines and devices—holograms, helicopters, airplanes, mobile phones, compact disks, hard disks, bits and bytes, cash machines. . . . Explanations [are also given] of the scientific principles behind each machine—how gears make work easier, why jumbo jets are able to fly, how computers actually compute." Publisher's note

609 History, geographic treatment, biography

Denny, Mark

Ingenium; five machines that changed the world. Johns Hopkins University Press 2007 176p il $27   **609**
1. Machinery 2. Inventions -- History
ISBN 978-0-8018-8586-0; 0-8018-8586-8

LC 2006-26085

Denny analyzes "the bow and arrow, waterwheels and windmills, counterpoise siege engines, the pendulum clock anchor escapement mechanism, and the centrifugal governor." Sci Books Films

The author "has authored a well-written, illustrated, and informative book that is readable to all but the mentally lazy." Choice

Includes bibliographical references

Macdonald, Anne L.

Feminine ingenuity; women and invention in America. {by} Anne Macdonald. Ballantine Bks. 1992 xxiv, 514p il hardcover o.p. pa $25   **609**
1. Inventions 2. Women inventors
ISBN 0-345-38314-1 pa

LC 91-55502

This is a "study of American women's contribution to science, engineering, and technology as represented in the issuance of U.S. patents. From the first patent issued to a woman in 1809, Macdonald traces the uphill struggle women have faced in their efforts to obtain equal rights—in the area of patent awards as well as in the broader educational, economic, and social arenas." Libr J

Includes bibliographical references

Petroski, Henry

The **evolution** of useful things. Knopf 1992 288p il hardcover o.p. pa $13.95   **609**
1. Patents 2. Inventions
ISBN 0-679-74039-2 pa

LC 91-39524

The author "provides an intricate look, in lay reader's terms, at the technology and basic rationale behind a number of items we often take for granted. The list is comprehensive: kitchen utensils, zippers, tools, paper clips, fast-food packaging, and more. The text is far from a recital of mere facts. Petroski's anecdotes and stories about individual designers and inventors are told with warm regard. He also provides illuminating thoughts on the theoretical, historical, and cultural frameworks that influenced these creations." Libr J

Includes bibliographical references

Popular mechanics magazine.

The **wonderful** future that never was; flying cars, mail delivery by parachute, and other predictions from the past. Gregory Benford and the editors of Popular mechanics. Hearst Communications 2010 207p il $24.95   **609**
1. Forecasting 2. Technological innovations 3. Inventions -- History
ISBN 978-1-58816-822-1
LC 2010-3998

"Profusely illustrated (there's something on nearly every page), the book is endlessly fascinating, a collage of snapshots of the present the way people saw it when it was still the distant future." Booklist

Tobin, James

Great projects; the epic story of the building of America: from the taming of the Mississippi to the invention of the Internet. Free Press 2001 322p il maps hardcover o.p. pa $31.95   **609**
1. Engineering -- History
ISBN 0-7432-1064-6; 1-4516-1301-6 pa
LC 2001-33016

This describes eight construction projects and innovations including "the flood-control works of the lower Mississippi, Hoover Dam, Edison's lighting system, the spread of electricity across the nation, the great Croton Aqueduct, the bridges of New York City, Boston's revamped street system, known as the Big Dig, and the [Internet]." Publisher's note

"The clearly written, nontechnical narratives are lively and comprehensive." Libr J

Includes bibliographical references

Van Dulken, Stephen

Inventing the 19th century; 100 inventions that shaped the Victorian Age from aspirin to the Zeppelin. New York Univ. Press 2001 218p il $30   **609**
1. Inventions
ISBN 0-8147-8810-6
LC 2001-30831

This briefly describes the inventions of the 19th century with text and diagrams from the patent applications

Includes bibliographical references

Inventing the 20th century; 100 inventions that shaped the world: from the airplane to the zipper. {by} Stephen Van Dulken; with an introduction by

Andrew Phillips. New York Univ. Press 2000 246p il hardcover o.p. pa $17.95   **609**
1. Inventions
ISBN 0-8147-8808-4; 0-8147-8812-2 pa
LC 00-41141

This briefly describes inventions of the 20th century, arranged by decade, with text and diagrams from the patent applications

"A fascinating compendium for trivia seekers." Publ Wkly

Includes bibliographical references

609.2   Biography

Kendall, Joshua

★ **America's** obsessives; the compulsive energy that built a nation. Joshua Kendall. GCP 2013 304 p. (hardcover) $27   **609.2**
1. Success 2. Compulsive behavior 3. United States -- Biography 4. Scholars -- United States -- Biography 5. Inventors -- United States -- Biography 6. Successful people -- United States -- Biography 7. Motivation (Psychology) -- United States -- Case studies
ISBN 1455502383; 9781455502387; 9781611138320
LC 2012051196

Author Joshua Kendall "profiles a 'ticker-tape parade of American icons' in an effort to understand how their 'obsessions and compulsions. . . fueled their stratospheric success.' Across a range of disciplines, from sexuality to sports, these seven legendary figures revolutionized their fields, and they all likely had obsessive-compulsive personality disorder (OCPD)." Subjects include Thomas Jefferson, Henry Heinz, Melvil Dewey, Alfred Kinsey, Charles Lindbergh, and Ted Williams. (Publishers Weekly)

Includes bibliographical references and index

Vare, Ethlie Ann

Patently female; from AZT to TV dinners: stories of women inventors and their breakthrough ideas. [by] Ethlie Ann Vare, Greg Ptacek. Wiley 2002 220p il $27.95   **609.2**
1. Women inventors
ISBN 0-471-02334-5
LC 2001-26950

Sequel to: Mothers of invention (1988)

The authors "detail how women's ideas like the cotton gin, automatic sewing machine and even the Brooklyn Bridge have often been attributed to men and how history books and museums like the Smithsonian and the National Inventors Hall of Fame have ignored women's achievements." Publ Wkly

Includes bibliographical references

610   Medicine and health

Adler, Robert E.
Medical firsts; from Hippocrates to the human genome. Wiley 2004 232p il $24.95   **610**
1. Medicine -- History
ISBN 0-471-40175-7

LC 2003-14212

"The contributors to the annals of medical knowledge [the author] cites include the most famous names—Hippocrates, Pasteur, Freud, Alexander Fleming—and some not so commonly known, such as pioneering gynecologist Soranus (first century C.E.); Ibn al-Nafis (ca. 1210-88), credited as the first to understand and describe pulmonary circulation; and John Snow, an important figure in the war on cholera. . . . Adler discusses each figure's personal, social, and political history as it affected his or her contribution." Booklist

"Adler ably combines good storytelling, clear and cogent scientific explanations [and] a respect for science over superstition." Publ Wkly

Includes bibliographical references

Ball, Philip, 1962-
The **devil's** doctor; Paracelsus and the world of Renaissance magic and science. Farrar, Straus and Giroux 2006 430p il map $27   **610**
1. Physicians 2. Alchemists 3. Writers on science
ISBN 0-374-22979-1

LC 2005-19848

This biography "illuminates the life of alchemist, physician, theologian, and astrologer Paracelsus (1493-1541), placing him . . . in the context of the Reformation. . . . Ball captures and explains all of Paracelsus's idiosyncrasies and contradictions in writing that is clear and enjoyable." Libr J

Includes bibliographical references

Bortolotti, Dan
Hope in hell; inside the world of Doctors Without Borders. Firefly Bks. 2004 303p il $29.95; pa $19.95   **610**
1. Médecins Sans Frontières (Organization)
ISBN 1-55297-865-6; 1-55407-142-9 pa

LC 2005-357206

This "portrait of Doctors Without Borders/Médecins Sans Frontières (aka MSF), the nonprofit that won the Nobel Peace Prize in 1999, emphasizes the inner workings of the organization and is animated by interviews with mid-level staffers and by site visits to MSF projects in Angola, Afghanistan and Pakistan. In between, . . . Bortolotti traces the history of the world's largest independent medical humanitarian organization, whose genesis was the Biafran horrors of the late '60s." Publ Wkly

"Much of what Bortolotti reports is noticeably absent from the daily headlines, so this eye-opening account is all the more chilling, and MSF's efforts achingly more compelling." Booklist

Includes bibliographical references

The **Cambridge** illustrated history of medicine; edited by Roy Porter. Cambridge Univ. Press 1996 400p il maps hardcover o.p. pa $35   **610**
1. Medicine -- History
ISBN 0-521-44211-7; 0-521-00252-4 pa

LC 95-38000

This is a history of medicine from antiquity to the present. In ten "chapters, Roy Porter and his collaborators examine the changing form of medicine and . . . {the} technical successes that it has achieved." Sci Am

Includes bibliographical references

Cassedy, James H.
Medicine in America: a short history. Johns Hopkins Univ. Press 1991 187p (American moment) hardcover o.p. pa $18.95   **610**
1. Medicine -- United States -- History
ISBN 0-8018-4208-5 pa

LC 91-7058

This history of American medicine traces medical and health-related matters from colonial times to the present

This book "is scholarly, well written, very useful, and fills a void." Choice

Includes bibliographical references

★ **Dorland's** illustrated medical dictionary; 32nd ed; Elsevier/Saunders 2011 xxvii, 2147p il $51.95   **610**
1. Reference books 2. Medicine -- Dictionaries
ISBN 978-1-4160-6257-8

LC 2011-9789

First published 1900. Periodically revised

This standard reference includes terms used in medicine, surgery, dentistry, pharmacy, chemistry, nursing, veterinary science, biology, and medical biology. Pronunciation, derivation, and definitions are given.

"This is considered one of the most comprehensive medical dictionaries in print." N Y Public Libr Book of How & Where to Look It Up

Includes bibliographical references

Finger, Stanley
Doctor Franklin's medicine. University of Pennsylvania Press 2006 379p il $39.95   **610**
1. Authors 2. Diplomats 3. Inventors 4. Statesmen 5. Scientists 6. Writers on science 7. Medicine -- History 8. Members of Congress
ISBN 978-0-8122-3913-3; 0-8122-3913-X

LC 2005-45659

The author presents the "story of Benjamin Franklin's contributions to modern medicine and hygiene. The book is an important tribute to America's quintessential Enlightenment scholar and statesman." Choice

Includes bibliographical references

Groopman, Jerome E.
★ **How** doctors think; [by] Jerome Groopman. Houghton Mifflin Co. 2007 307p il $26   **610**
1. Medicine 2. Diagnosis 3. Physicians
ISBN 978-0-618-61003-7; 0-618-61003-0

LC 2006-35718

This book is comprised of a series of "essays that explore the rational and irrational factors that influence medical decision-making. By turns inspired and dismaying, it explains how even the best doctor can draw the wrong conclusion, and why that same doctor might also come up with a brilliant diagnosis that has eluded his peers. Uncertainty hovers over the practice of medicine, which Dr. Groopman, a clear writer and a humane thinker, presents as an art as well as a science, despite the spectacular advances in medical technology." N Y Times (Late N Y Ed)

Includes bibliographical references

Second opinions; stories of intuition and choice in a changing world of medicine. {by} Jerome Groopman. Viking 2000 243p hardcover o.p. pa $14   **610**
    1. Medicine 2. Diagnosis
    ISBN 0-14-029862-2 pa

                      LC 99-36692

"Through vivid accounts of the dilemmas he has faced—not only as a doctor but as a patient, a parent, a grandson and a friend—the author illuminates the art, and the perils, of interpreting other people's symptoms." Newsweek

Your medical mind; how to decide what is right for you. [by] Jerome Groopman and Pamela Hartzband. Penguin Press 2011 308p $27.95   **610**
    1. Medicine 2. Decision making 3. Physician-patient relationship
    ISBN 978-1-59420-311-4

                      LC 2011019808

The authors "present readers with a fascinating look into medical decision making. Through detailed portraits of socially and ethnically diverse real-life individuals who must make medical choices, the authors show how patients' family history, culture, profession, and attitudes toward medicine and technology can shape their decisions about treatment. . . . This engaging, insightful, and illuminating book should be read by general audiences as well as medical and healthcare professionals, who are often baffled by the choices their patients make." Libr J

Includes bibliographical references

Magill's medical guide; medical editors: Bryan C. Auday, Ph.D., Gordon College, Michael A. Buratovich, Ph.D., Spring Arbor University, Geraldine F. Marrocco, Ed.D., APRN, CNS, ANP-BC, Yale University School of Nursing, Paul Moglia, Ph.D., South Nassau Communities Hospital. 6th ed.; Salem Press 2014 2537 p. 6v il (Salem health) $425   **610**
    1. Reference books 2. Medicine -- Encyclopedias
    ISBN 1619252147; 9781619252141

                      LC 2010-31862

First published 1995

Covers diseases, disorders, treatments, procedures, specialties, anatomy, biology, and issues in an A-Z format, with sidebars addressing recent developments in medicine and concise information boxes for all diseases and disorders.

Includes bibliographical references and index.

★ The **Merck** manual of diagnosis and therapy; Robert S. Porter, editor-in-chief; Justin L. Kaplan, senior assistant editor. 19th ed.; Merck Sharp & Dohme Corp. 2011 xxxii, 3754p il $79.95 **610**
    1. Reference books 2. Medicine -- Handbooks, manuals, etc.
    ISBN 978-0-911910-19-3
    First published 1899

"A one-volume reference that attempts to cover all but the most obscure diseases. Sections are organized by type of disease or medical specialty." N Y Public Libr Book of How & Where to Look It Up

Meyers, Morton A.

Happy accidents; serendipity in modern medical breakthroughs. [by] Morton Meyers. Arcade Pub. 2007 390p il $29.95; pa $16.99   **610**
    1. Medicine -- Research
    ISBN 978-1-55970-819-7; 978-1-55970-845-6 pa

                    LC 2006-100551

The author "details dozens of medicines currently saving millions of lives that are the results of serendipity, which he defines as 'chance plus judgment'—medicines discovered while researchers were looking in quite another, often the opposite, direction. . . . Meyers' accounts of such happy accidents as the discoveries of the lifesaving anticoagulant Coumadin, the manic-depression therapeutic lithium, and others is a significant brief on creativity's critical role in medical research." Booklist

Includes bibliographical references

Mosby's medical dictionary; [editor, Marie T. O'Toole] 9th ed Elsevier/Mosby 2013 xiv, A1-A43, 1921 p.p ill. (chiefly col.) (hardcover : alk. paper) $43.95   **610**
    1. Reference books 2. Medicine -- Dictionaries
    ISBN 0323085415; 9780323085410

                    LC 2012028208

First published 1983 with title: Mosby's medical & nursing dictionary; published 2002 with title: Mosby's medical, nursing, and allied health dictionary. Periodically revised

"Many definitions are discursive. Emphasizes allied health professions, with . . . categories of entries in physical therapy, occupational therapy, and respiratory care." Guide to Ref Books. 11th edition

Orbinski, James

An **imperfect** offering; humanitarian action in the twenty-first century. Walker & Co. 2008 431p il $27   **610**
    1. War relief 2. Medical assistance 3. Médecins Sans Frontières (Organization)
    ISBN 978-0-8027-1709-2; 0-8027-1709-8

"Orbinski was president of Doctors Without Borders when it received the Nobel Peace Prize in 1999, and this book echoes and expands on his acceptance speech. He argues that humanitarian action must be free of political influence, must not become a tool of war and must not be silent in the face of human-rights violations. . . . An important, consciousness-raising work." Kirkus

Includes bibliographical references

Pollack, Robert

The **missing** moment; how the unconscious shapes modern science. Houghton Mifflin 1999 240p $25 **610**

1. Psychology 2. Medicine -- Philosophy
ISBN 0-395-70985-7

LC 99-26241

"The collective myth of science and of biomedicine, in Pollack's diagnosis, involves misplaced beliefs in the omnipotence of rational thought, absolute control over nature and triumph over death. With eloquence and wit, he contends that biomedicine's heroic goals of beating infectious microbes into total submission, of eradicating cancer and of dramatically extended life expectancy should give way to emphasis on disease prevention and methods to slow the aging process." Publ Wkly

Includes bibliographical references

Porter, Roy

The **greatest** benefit to mankind; a medical history of humanity. Norton 1998 831p il $35; pa $18.95 **610**

1. Medicine -- History 2. Social medicine -- History
ISBN 0-393-04634-6; 0-393-31980-6 pa

LC 98-10219

First published 1997 in the United Kingdom

Porter's "study traces Western medical thought and practices from their origins in classical Greece to today's biomedical developments. Although scholarly, the text is elegantly written, accessible to the general reader, and filled with fascinating details." Libr J

Includes bibliographical references

Teresi, Dick

★ The **undead**; organ harvesting, the ice-water test, beating heart cadavers : how medicine is blurring the line between life and death. Dick Teresi. Pantheon Books 2012 256 p. **610**

1. Death 2. Brain death 3. Medical ethics 4. Physicians -- Attitudes 5. Transplantation of organs, tissues, etc. -- Ethical aspects 6. Death -- Autobiography 7. Persistent Vegetative State 8. Tissue and Organ Harvesting
ISBN 9780375423710

LC 2011032025

"In this . . . look at how doctors determine the moment of death, skeptical science writer . . . [Dick] Teresi . . . relishes ripping into the 1968 Harvard team that formulated new criteria for determining death: 'loss of personhood,' or brain death. Doctors, Teresi says, can now 'declare a person dead in less time than it takes to get a decent eye exam' by testing reflexes: 'a flashlight in the eyes, ice water in the ears, and then an attempt to gasp for air' when the respirator is disconnected. Teresi interviews scientists who question the finality of brain death when the heart is still beating, and even the concept that personhood is located solely in the brain. . . . Teresi charges that the brain-death revolution is driven by the $20 billion-a-year organ transplant business." (Publishers Weekly)

Includes bibliographical references and index

Western medicine: an illustrated history; edited by Irvine Loudon. Oxford Univ. Press 1997 347p il $65; pa $27.50 **610**

1. Medicine -- History
ISBN 0-19-820509-0; 0-19-924813-3 pa

LC 97-218848

This history "extends from ancient Greece to the present. . . . The book consists of chapters by 20 historians from England, Germany, and the United States. An introductory chapter describes the long historical relationship between medicine and the visual arts. Seven subsequent chapters offer a chronological history of medicine, including a discussion of the influence of Islamic medicine on medieval and Renaissance physicians. The 11 final chapters deal with medicine in its social context, such as histories of childbirth, nursing, and mental illness." Libr J

Includes bibliographical references

610.1 Medicine -- philosophy

Szczeklik, Andrzej

★ **Kore**; on sickness, the sick, and the search for the soul of medicine. Andrzej Szczeklik ; translated by Antonia Lloyd-Jones ; with an introduction by Adam Zagajewski. Counterpoint 2012 320 p. (hardback : alk. paper) $26 **610.1**

1. Sick 2. Soul 3. Medicine 4. Humanities 5. History of Medicine 6. Philosophy, Medical 7. Physician-patient relations
ISBN 161902019X; 9781619020191; 9781619021389

LC 2012042867

In this book, translated by Antonia Lloyd-Jones, author Andrzej Szczeklik "insists that only with a curiosity thoroughly at home in both [science and the humanities] . . . can one expect to discover what we should mean about sickness and about the soul. . . . Anecdotes drawn from a personal immersion in art, music, and literature are woven with reports on experimental medicine and daily clinical experience." (Publisher's note)

Includes bibliographical references and index

610.22 Medical illustration

Anderson, Julie, 1965-

The **art** of medicine; over 2,000 years of images and imagination. Julie Anderson, Emm Barnes, and Emma Shackleton; foreword by Antony Gormley. Ilex Press 2011 256p il **610.22**

1. Medical illustration; 2. Medicine -- History; 3. Medicine in art
ISBN 9780226749365; 0226749363

LC 2011019933

This book on visual representations of medicine "offers a . . . gallery of rarely seen paintings, artifacts, drawings, prints, and extracts from manuscripts and manuals to provide . . . visual insight into our knowledge of the human body and mind, and how both have been treated with medicine. Julie Anderson, Emm Barnes, and Emma Shackleton take readers on a . . . journey through the history of medical practice, exploring contemporary biomedical images, popular art, and caricature." (Publisher's note)

610.28   Auxiliary techniques and procedures; apparatus, equipment, materials

Friedman, David M.

The **immortalists**; Charles Lindbergh, Dr. Alexis Carrel, and their daring quest to live forever. HarperCollins Ecco 2007 337p il $26.95   **610.28**
1. Generals 2. Surgeons 3. Longevity 4. Air pilots 5. Biologists 6. Physicians 7. Immortality 8. Preservation of organs, tissues, etc. 9. Memoirists 10. Air force officers 11. Writers on medicine 12. Nobel laureates for physiology or medicine
ISBN 978-0-06-052815-7; 0-06-052815-X

LC 2007-299304

This book discusses "the relationship between famed aviator Charles Lindbergh and the Noble Prizewinning French surgeon Alexis Carrel. Driven by a desire to cure his ailing sister-in-law, Elizabeth Morrow, Lindbergh contacted Carrel in 1930 for the purpose of developing an artificial heart." Libr J

The author "makes complex science accessible and serves as an absorbing cautionary tale on how two heroic reputations were marred by fascism and anti-Semitism." Publ Wkly

Gawande, Atul

★ The **checklist** manifesto; how to get things right. Metropolitan Books 2010 209p $24.50 **610.28**
1. Lists 2. Medical care -- Quality control
ISBN 9780805091748

LC 2009-46888

"We live in a world of great and increasing complexity, where even the most expert professionals struggle to master the tasks they face. Longer training, ever more advanced technologies—neither seems to prevent grievous errors. But in [this book], . . . Gawande finds a remedy in the . . . simplest of techniques: the checklist. First introduced decades ago by the U.S. Air Force, checklists have enabled pilots to fly aircraft of mind-boggling sophistication. Now innovative checklists are being adopted in hospitals around the world. . . . Gawande takes us from Austria, where an emergency checklist saved a drowning victim who had spent half an hour underwater, to Michigan, where a cleanliness checklist in intensive care units virtually eliminated a type of deadly hospital infection. He explains how checklists actually work to prompt striking and immediate improvements." (Publisher's note) Index.

"Few medical writers working today can transmit the gore-drenched terror of an operation that suddenly goes wrong—a terror that has a special resonance when it is Dr. Gawande himself who makes the initial horrifying mistake. And few can make it as clear as he can what exactly is at stake in the effort to minimize calamities." N Y Times (Late N Y Ed)

Includes bibliographical references

Topol, Eric

The **creative** destruction of medicine; Eric Topol. Basic Books 2012 xi, 303p.p   **610.28**
1. Medical technology 2. Access to health care 3. Technological innovations 4. Internet 5. Health Communication 6. Biomedical Technology 7. Diffusion of Innovation 8. Medical Informatics Applications 9. Delivery of Health Care -- trends
ISBN 9780465025503; 9780465029341

LC 2011041162

This book offers information about "how academic healthcare organizations . . . can collaborate with for-profit companies to accelerate technological progress in medicine. . . . The author says that no single innovation will have a more profound effect than the conversion of biological data. . . . Dr. [Eric] Topol focuses much of his attention on the development of 'theranostics,' or the integrated use of treatments and diagnostics . . . to better guide therapy." (Wall Street Journal)

Includes bibliographical references and index.

610.3   Medicine -- dictionaries

Taber's cyclopedic medical dictionary; editor, Donald Venes ... [et. al.] 22nd ed F.A. Davis 2013 2846 p. col. ill. (indexed : alk. paper) $42.95   **610.3**
1. Medicine -- Dictionaries
ISBN 080362977X; 9780803629776; 9780803629783; 9780803629790

LC 2012034064

First published 1940. Periodically revised

This work gives "definitions of medical terms and words. Pronunciation is given for all but very common terms and the etymology of most words is included. Appendixes include such information as emergency treatment, dietetic charts, Latin and Greek nomenclature, and normal reference laboratory values." Guide to Ref Books

Includes bibliographical references and index

610.69   Medical personnel and relationships

Newman, David H.

Hippocrates' shadow; secrets from the house of medicine. Scribner 2008 236p il $26   **610.69**
1. Physician-patient relationship
ISBN 1-4165-5153-0; 978-1-4165-5153-9

LC 2008-12485

"Newman shares information about the practice of medicine not generally known or discussed but which could have a significant impact on health care costs, access, and outcomes. With this book he makes a valuable contribution to the dialogue on reform of the US health care system." Choice

Includes bibliographical references

Ofri, Danielle

What doctors feel; how emotions affect the practice of medicine. Danielle Ofri. Beacon Press 2013 232 p. (alk. paper) $24.95   **610.69**
   1. Physicians 2. Physician-patient relationship 3. Empathy -- Personal Narratives 4. Physicians -- Psychology -- Personal Narratives
   ISBN 0807073326; 9780807073322

LC 2012049349

Here, Dr. Danielle Ofri offers a "take on the inner life of medical professionals, describing not only her own bumpy path from med student to M.D., but also the difficulty of maintaining empathy for patients over the years. 'Emotional layers' in medicine are more subtle and pervasive than anyone wants to believe, and they often become the 'dominant players in medical decision-making,' she argues." (Publishers Weekly)

Includes bibliographical references

610.73 Nursing and services of allied health personnel

Lake, Nell

The **caregivers**; a support group's stories of slow loss, courage, and love. Nell Lake. Scribner 2014 320 p. (hardback : alk. paper) $26   **610.73**
   1. Caregivers 2. Medical care 3. Self-help groups 4. Long-Term Care -- Methods -- Personal Narratives
   ISBN 1451674147; 9781451674149

LC 2013037357

This book, by Nell Lake, "chronicles the experiences of a group of long-term caregivers and illuminates critical issues of old age, end-of-life care, medical reform, and social policy. . . . Her work considers important . . . social issues. . . . How can we care for the aging, ill, and dying with skill and compassion, even as the costs and labors of care increase? How might the medical profession take into account the needs of caregivers as well as patients?" (Publisher's note)

"This profound study on the effects of tending to ill loved ones offers powerful testimony to friendship and mutual support." Pub Wkly

Includes bibliographical references and index

610.730 Organizations and management

Makary, Marty

Unaccountable; what hospitals won't tell you and how transparency can revolutionize health care. by Marty Makary. Bloomsbury Press 2012 246 p. ill. (hardback) $26   **610.730**
   1. Medical records 2. Health care reform -- United States 3. Medical errors 4. Patient education 5. Medical personnel and patient 6. Medical care -- Quality control 7. Health facilities -- Public relations
   ISBN 1608198367; 9781608198368

LC 2012007740

In this book, surgeon Marty Makary "suggests that providing patients with more access to their own medical information, as well as to the volume and safety records of facili-

ties and doctors, would improve the overall quality of health care and save money. . . . He takes on what he believes is the health-care profession's inept self-regulation, poor communication caused by fear of speaking up, obfuscation of available statistics, and nonprofit hospital CEO compensation." (Library Journal)

Includes bibliographical references and index

610.9 Medicine--history

Mattern, Susan P.

Prince of medicine; Galen in the Roman world. Susan P. Mattern. Oxford University Press 2013 368 p. $29.95   **610.9**
   1. Medicine -- History 2. Physicians -- Biography
   ISBN 019976767X; 9780199767670

LC 2012035656

Susan P. Mattern presents a "biography of Galen of Pergamum (circa 130-212 C.E.), a Greek who practiced medicine and philosophy in the Roman-dominated Mediterranean, first rising to fame at home in Asia Minor before becoming preeminent in Rome during the reign of Marcus Aurelius." (Library Journal)

Includes bibliographical references and index

610.92 Biography

Chopra, Deepak

Brotherhood; dharma, destiny, and the American dream. by Deepak Chopra and Sanjiv Chopra. New Harvest/Houghton Mifflin Harcourt 2013 384 p. (hardcover) $28.00   **610.92**
   1. Immigrants -- United States -- Biography 2. Siblings -- India 3. Siblings -- United States 4. Delivery of Health Care -- India 5. Emigrants and Immigrants -- India 6. Cross-Cultural Comparison -- India 7. Physicians -- India -- Autobiography 8. Delivery of Health Care -- United States 9. Emigrants and Immigrants -- United States 10. Cross-Cultural Comparison -- United States 11. Physicians -- United States -- Autobiography
   ISBN 0544032101; 9780544032101

LC 2013001928

"This 'double memoir' tracks the lives of two prominent physicians and brothers. Deepak and Sanjiv Chopra were born and raised in India, then came to America for postgraduate medical training. They became U.S. citizens, distinguished doctors, and influential figures. . . . Both men reflect on their Indian heritage, karma, dharma, and pursuit of the American dream." (Booklist)

Sweet, Victoria

God's hotel; a doctor, a hospital, and a pilgrimage to the heart of medicine. Victoria Sweet. Riverhead Books 2012 384 p. ill. (hardback) $27.95 **610.92**
   1. Medicine 2. Hospitals 3. Physicians 4. Laguna Honda Hospital (San Francisco, Calif.) -- History 5. Hospital care -- California -- San Francisco -- Anecdotes
   ISBN 1594488436; 9781594488436

LC 2011049340

This book offers a "portrait of a . . . physician on a quest to understand the heart, as well as the art, of medicine. Laguna Honda Hospital, the last remaining almshouse in the United States--a therapeutic community that houses and cares for the chronically ill or impoverished--offers . . . [author and physician Victoria] Sweet . . . a[n] . . . education in ministering to the body, heart, and soul." (Library Journal)

Includes bibliographical references

611   Human anatomy, cytology, histology

Balaban, Naomi E.

The **handy** anatomy answer book; [by] Naomi E. Balaban and James E. Bobick. Visible Ink Press 2008 362p il pa $21.95   **611**

1. Physiology 2. Human anatomy
ISBN 978-1-57859-190-9

"This book can provide an excellent way to read and self-test for health and human biology classes. Adults wanting to know more about the subjects covered will also find a wealth of useful and accessible information." Voice Youth Advocates

Gray's anatomy; the anatomical basis of clinical practice. 40th ed.; Churchill Livingstone 2008 xxiv, 1551p il $209   **611**

1. Human anatomy 2. Reference books
ISBN 978-0-443-06684-9

First published 1858. Periodically revised. Publisher varies

A comprehensive standard reference work with illustrations, descriptions and definitions.

"Holds its place as a major and authoritative text on systematic anatomy. Recommended." Annals of Internal Medicine

Includes bibliographical references

McElheny, Victor K.

Drawing the map of life; inside the Human Genome Project. Victor K. McElheny. Basic Books 2010 xiii, 361 p.p   **611**

1. Genomics 2. Human Genome Project -- History
ISBN 046504333X (alk. paper); 40018025006; 9780465043330 (alk. paper)

LC 2010003339

Drawing the Map of Life is the "story of the Human Genome Project from its origins, through the race to order the 3 billion subunits of DNA, to the surprises emerging as scientists seek to exploit the molecule of heredity." (Publisher's note) Index.

McElheny's "description of the politics that led to the human genome project becoming the first megascale biology research program . . . is clear and illuminating. Similarly, McElheny does an impressive job at explaining the current and future benefits likely to arise from the genetics data flooding into scientists' laboratories." Publ Wkly

Includes bibliographical references and index

Roach, Mary, 1959-

★ **Stiff**; the curious lives of human cadavers. Norton 2003 303p il $23.95; pa $13.95   **611**

1. Dead 2. Dissection 3. Human experimentation in medicine
ISBN 0-393-05093-9; 0-393-32482-6 pa

LC 2002-152908

The author "explains how surgeons and doctors use cadavers donated for research purposes to help the living, and also examines potential new variations on how we bury the dead." Libr J

"For those who are interested in the fields of medicine or forensics and are aware of some of the procedures, this book makes excellent reading." SLJ

Includes bibliographical references

Shubin, Neil

Your inner fish; a journey into the 3.5-billion-year history of the human body. Pantheon Books 2008 229p il map $24   **611**

1. Evolution 2. Human anatomy
ISBN 978-0-375-42447-2; 0-375-42447-4

LC 2007-24699

This is a "look at how the human body evolved into its present state. . . . Shubin excels at explaining the science, making each discovery an adventure, whether it's a Pennsylvania roadcut or a stony outcrop beset by polar bears and howling Arctic winds." Publ Wkly

Includes bibliographical references

612   Human physiology

Aldersey-Williams, Hugh, 1959-

Anatomies; A Cultural History of the Human Body. by Hugh Aldersey-Williams. 1st American ed. W W Norton & Co Inc 2013 xxv, 294 p.p ill. (hardcover) $26.95   **612**

1. Human body 2. Human anatomy 3. Human body -- Popular works 4. Human anatomy -- Popular works 5. Human physiology -- Popular works
ISBN 0393239888; 9780393239881

LC 2013002982

This book by Hugh Aldersey-Williams offers a cultural history of the human body. "Although he divides the corpus into part-specific chapters, Aldersey-Williams avoids a reductionist view of the subject, reflecting instead on how our components come together to make us fully human. Along the way he relates myriad" stories on topics ranging from autocannibalism, ballet, facial recognition, and shrunken heads. (Publishers Weekly)

Includes bibliographical references and index.

Ashcroft, Frances

The **spark** of life; electricity in the human body. Frances Ashcroft ; illustrations by Ronan Mahon. Norton 2012 339 p. ill.   **612**

1. Biology 2. Electrophysiology 3. Human physiology
ISBN 0393078035; 9780393078039

LC 2012021264

This book, by Frances Ashcroft, presents an "exploration of the surprising role that electricity plays in our bodies. What happens during a heart attack? Can someone really die of fright? What is death, anyway? How does electroshock treatment affect the brain? What is consciousness? The answers to these questions lie in the electrical signals constantly traveling through our bodies, driving our thoughts, our movements, and even the beating of our hearts." (Publisher's note)

Includes bibliographical references and index

Brenkus, John

The **perfection** point. HarperCollins 2010 242p $26.99; ebook $9.99   **612**
1. Sports records
ISBN 978-0-06-184545-1; 978-0-06-200884-8 ebook

This is an "exploration of the limits of human athletic ability. . . . The book is full of startling facts: the current U.S. record for holding one's breath, for example, is a breathtaking 7 minutes and 21 seconds. But here's the book's most arresting element: using a variety of disciplines, including physics and physiology, Brenkus extrapolates into the future, showing us when we will reach our absolute limit of performance. . . . Sure to spark debate in sporting and scientific circles, the book is engagingly written, well argued, and—even when the conclusions seem almost science fictiony—entirely plausible." Booklist

The **Human** body; an illustrated guide to its structure, function, and disorders.   editor-in-chief, Charles Clayman.   Dorling Kindersley 1995 240p il $30   **612**
1. Physiology 2. Human anatomy
ISBN 1-56458-992-7

LC 94-37165

"This body atlas uses current medical illustration techniques to provide unique views of human anatomical features. Color-enhanced microscope photographs and computer-generated images accompany detailed drawings to illustrate various organs, demonstrate body functions, and depict problems or complications. The introduction explains various types of medical illustration such as computerized tomography, ultrasound, and magnetic resonance imaging." Booklist

"This absolutely stunning book succeeds immeasurably as a guide to the human body." Sci Books Films

Lieberman, Daniel, 1964-

The **story** of the human body; evolution, health, and disease. Daniel Lieberman.   Pantheon Books 2013 464 p. illustrations $27.95   **612**
1. Evolution 2. Human body 3. Adaptation (Biology)
ISBN 0307379418; 9780307379412

LC 2013011811

This book, by Daniel E. Lieberman, presents the "story of human evolution consisting of five biological transformations (walking upright, eating a variety of different foods, accumulating physical traits aligned to hunting and gathering, gaining bigger brains with larger bodies, and developing unique capacities for cooperation and language) and two cultural ones (farming and reliance on machines)." (Booklist)

"Lieberman's discussion of type 2 diabetes, heart disease, and breast cancer are as clear as any yet published, and he offers a well-articulated case for why an evolutionary perspective can greatly enrich the practice of medicine." Pub Wkly

Includes bibliographical references and index

McCredie, Scott

Balance: in search of the lost sense. Little, Brown and Company 2007 296p il $24.99   **612**
1. Balance
ISBN 978-0-316-01135-8; 0-316-01135-5

LC 2006-38089

"After the shock of seeing his fit father fall for no apparent reason, . . . McCredie became curious about the physiology of equilibrium. His extensive and creative research has led him to conclude that balance is the overlooked sixth sense and crucial to our survival. . . . McCredie offers practical advice for maintaining one's equilibrium and acuity and rekindles deep appreciation for life's incredible exactitude and grace." Booklist

Includes bibliographical references (p. 283-287)

McMillan, Beverly

Human body; a visual guide. Firefly Books 2006 304p il $29.95   **612**
1. Physiology 2. Human anatomy
ISBN 978-1-55407-188-3; 1-55407-188-7

This book provides "scientific information on the human body, using microphotography, advanced medical imaging and annotated illustrations. The book reveals all the intricacy and beauty of the human body and shows the structure and functions of all the systems that make up a human being." Publisher's note

Includes bibliographical references

612.1   Specific functions, systems, organs

Amidon, Stephen

The **sublime** engine; a biography of the human heart. [by] Stephen Amidon and Thomas Amidon. Rodale 2011 242p $24.99   **612.1**
1. Heart
ISBN 978-1-60529-584-8

LC 2010-30227

This book "presents a multifaceted picture of the heart's influences on mythology, science, and popular culture through the ages. In six lyrically written chapters, they trace humanity's perennial fascination with the heart through the eyes of history's greatest artists and medical explorers, beginning with the Greeks and fancifully ending with a peek into the future of cardiological innovation." Booklist

Includes bibliographical references

612.3   Digestive system

Roach, Mary, 1959-

  ★ **Gulp**; adventures on the alimentary canal. Mary Roach. W W Norton 2013 336 p.   **612.3**

  1. Alimentary canal -- Popular works 2. Digestive organs -- Popular works 3. Gastrointestinal system -- Popular works

  ISBN 9780393081572

                  LC 2012050391

In this book, science writer Mary Roach explores "the alimentary canal. Roach asks the questions that some readers may have always wondered: Does saliva have curative properties? Do pets taste food differently than their owners do? Could Jonah have survived three days in a whale's stomach? . . . As she investigates these questions, Roach encounters many an eccentric scientist who has worked tirelessly to unlock the mysteries of saliva, gastrointestinal gases, and mastication." (Library Journal)

  "Roach's approach is grounded in science, but the virtuosic author rarely resists a pun, and it's clear she revels in giving readers a thrill... Adventurous kids and doctors alike will appreciate this fascinating and sometimes ghastly tour of the gastrointestinal system." Pub Wkly

  Includes bibliographical references

612.4   Hematopoietic, lymphatic, glandular, urinary systems

Arikha, Noga

  Passions and tempers; a history of the humours. Ecco 2007 xxi, 376p il $27.95   **612.4**

  1. Body fluids 2. Medicine -- History

  ISBN 978-0-06-073116-8; 0-06-073116-8

  This is "an erudite book, drawing on historical and scientific sources in several languages, but a gracefully written one. There are many superb illustrations [and] informative notes. . . . One of the best things about Ms. Arikha's study, in addition to its wealth of intriguing detail, is that it is thoughtful." N Y Sun

612.6   Reproduction, development, maturation

Angier, Natalie

  Woman; an intimate geography. Houghton Mifflin 1999 398p $25   **612.6**

  1. Physiology 2. Gender role 3. Sex role 4. Women -- Psychology

  ISBN 0-395-69130-3

                  LC 98-47634

  "Angier proves a knowledgeable, witty guide on our illustrative journey through hordes of cultures and species." Ms

  Includes bibliographical references

Doubilet, Peter M.

  Your developing baby, conception to birth; [by] Peter M. Doubilet, Carol B. Benson, [and] Roanne Weisman. McGraw-Hill 2008 194p il pa $18.95   **612.6**

  1. Pregnancy 2. Embryology

  ISBN 978-0-07-148871-6; 0-07-148871-5

                  LC 2007-35278

  "Using 250 diagnostic ultrasound images, . . . [the authors] present a marvelous book charting the growth of babies in the womb. Readers are taken through the entire reproductive process, from ovulation through the third trimester. . . . This virtual tour of a life in the making will attract future parents in droves." Libr J

Eliot, Lise

  Pink brain, blue brain; how small differences grow into troublesome gaps--and what we can do about it. Houghton Mifflin Harcourt 2009 420p il $25   **612.6**

  1. Child development 2. Sex differences (Psychology)

  ISBN 978-0-618-39311-4

                  LC 2009-14746

  The author "argues that infant brains are so malleable that small differences at birth become amplified over time, as parents and teachers—and the culture at large—unwittingly reinforce gender stereotypes." Publisher's note

  "This is an important book and highly recommended for parents, teachers, and anyone who works with children." Libr J

  Includes bibliographical references

Kim, Susan

  Flow; the cultural story of menstruation. [by] Elissa Stein and Susan Kim. St. Martin's Griffin 2009 270p $27.99   **612.6**

  1. Menstruation

  ISBN 978-0-312-37996-4

                  LC 2009-17046

  "There is probably no better book for moms who want their daughters to respect themselves in every aspect, and for female preteens and teens who would never say a word about their moms reading a book about menses but surely would like several sneak peeks into its pages." Booklist

  Includes bibliographical references

Lachs, Mark

  Treat me, not my age; a doctor's guide to getting the best care as you or a loved one gets older. Viking 2010 386p il $27.95   **612.6**

  1. Aging 2. Elderly -- Health and hygiene

  ISBN 978-0-670-02210-6

                  LC 2010-17487

  The author "discusses for seniors and their caregivers the aging process, ageism in society, choosing and communicating with a physician, financial issues, medications, complementary and alternative medicine, and end-of-life planning. Writing in a witty, conversational style, Lachs provides a great deal of useful information." Libr J

  Includes bibliographical references

Martin, Robert

How we do it; the evolution and future of human reproduction. Robert Martin. Basic Books 2013 xii, 304 p.p (hardcover) $27.99 **612.6**

1. Evolution 2. Reproduction 3. Human fertility 4. Human evolution 5. Human reproduction

ISBN 0465030157; 0465037844; 9780465030156; 9780465037841

LC 2012278031

In this book, "primatologist Robert Martin draws on forty years of research to locate the roots of everything from our sex cells to the way we care for newborns. He examines the procreative history of humans as well as that of our primate kin to reveal what's really natural when it comes to making and raising babies, and distinguish which behaviors we ought to continue--and which we should not." (Publisher's note)

"The author explains potentially complicated topics in a marvelously clear manner; although the focus is clearly evolutionary, he does not shy from considering practical implications." Choice

Includes bibliographical references and index

Nilsson, Lennart

A child is born; [photography], Lennart Nilsson; text, Lars Hamberger; translated from the Swedish by Linda Schenck. 4th ed, completely rev and updated; Delacorte Press 2003 239p il $35; pa $21 **612.6**

1. Pregnancy 2. Childbirth 3. Embryology

ISBN 0-385-33754-X; 0-385-33755-8 pa

LC 2003-43854

Original Swedish edition, 1965; first United States edition, 1966

An illustrated look at male and female reproductive anatomy and physiology, the processes of ovulation and fertilization, fetal development, and labor and delivery.

Roach, Mary, 1959-

Bonk; the curious coupling of science and sex. Norton 2008 319 p. il **612.6**

1. Sex (Biology)

ISBN 0393064646; 9780393064643

LC 2007-51990

This is an overview of the research on sexual physiology. "Tucked between the jokes and anecdotes, you will find lessons on impotence, orgasm, unusual and unusually brave scientists, and the sexual behaviour of other species, including a hilarious description of porcupine sex." New Sci

Includes bibliographical references (p. 307-319)

Stipp, David

The **youth** pill; scientists at the brink of an anti-aging revolution. Current 2010 308p $26.95 **612.6**

1. Longevity 2. Drug industry

ISBN 978-1-61723-000-4; 1-61723-000-6

LC 2010-7114

The author possesses "a singular style, crafting complex explanations of scientific discoveries (and failures) into eminently enjoyable reading. Whether or not the notion of living energetically to the age of 150 appeals, Stipp makes the research compelling." Booklist

Includes bibliographical references

Weil, Andrew

Healthy aging; a lifelong guide to your physical and spiritual well-being. Alfred A. Knopf 2005 293p $27.95 **612.6**

1. Aging

ISBN 0-375-40755-3

LC 2005-45183

The author "explores common Western beliefs and attitudes about aging and urges readers to develop healthier perspectives. The 60-year-old author assesses the growing and lucrative field of anti-aging medicine, takes the position that aging is not reversible, and offers many ways for readers to prevent conditions and illnesses that limit mortality and ensure well-being into the later years. . . . The real value is Weil's courageous stand, one likely to meet resistance in a culture devoted to external indicators of eternal youth." Publ Wkly

Includes bibliographical references

Weiner, Jonathan

Long for this world; the strange science of immortality. Ecco/HarperCollins Publishers 2010 310p $27.99 **612.6**

1. Longevity 2. Immortality

ISBN 978-0-06-076536-1; 0-06-076536-4

This is "a brilliant and improbably funny look inside the mind-bending science of immortality. . . . [The author's] ability to write simply and swiftly about complex evolutionary processes makes him an ideal guide through the burgeoning field of gerontology." Village Voice

Includes bibliographical references

Williams, Florence

Breasts; a natural and unnatural history. Florence Williams. W.W. Norton & Co. 2012 338 p. ill. (hardcover) $25.95 **612.6**

1. Breast 2. Breast cancer 3. Human ecology 4. Cancer -- Environmental aspects 5. Breast -- History 6. Breast -- Psychological aspects

ISBN 0393063186; 9780393063189

LC 2011053153

This book is a "comprehensive 'environmental history' of the only human body part without its own medical specialty, [in which] . . . [Florence] Williams . . . the reader along a journey extending from the evolution of human breasts from sweat glands, through cosmetic breast enhancements, the science and politics of breastfeeding, and possible links between pollutants and breast cancer in both women and men." (Publishers Weekly)

Includes bibliographical references

612.7 Musculoskeletal system, integument

Dickey, Colin

Cranioklepty; grave robbing and the search for genius. Unbridled Books 2009 308p il $25.95 **612.7**

1. Skull 2. Phrenology 3. Grave robbing

ISBN 978-1-932961-86-7

LC 2009-18527

The author relates the story of "the plucky grave robbers who stole the craniums of famed composers Haydn and Beethoven, Swedish mystic Emanuel Swedenborg, artist Francisco Goya, the English doctor and philosopher Sir Thomas Browne and others to sell, study or put on public display. The skull obsession was triggered by the infamous Gall system, created in the late 18th century by Franz Joseph Gall, who theorized that the bumps and dents of the skull could provide a measure of intelligence. . . . Blending science with historical drama, Dickey's book illuminates the mystery and controversy of a bizarre tradition throughout the ages." Publ Wkly

Includes bibliographical references

612.8   Nervous system

Aamodt, Sandra

Welcome to your brain; why you lose your car keys but never forget how to drive and other puzzles of everyday life. [by] Sandra Aamodt and Sam Wang. Bloomsbury USA 2008 220p il $24.95   **612.8**
    1. Brain
    ISBN 978-1-59691-283-0; 1-59691-283-9
                                LC 2007-26739
    This is a "'user's guide' to our brains. . . . The text is divided into six main parts, covering the brain's basic structure and function, the senses, the brain's development, emotions, rational processes, and altered states. . . . Rather than didactically lecturing, the authors very effectively engage the reader in a comfortable, interesting, and informative dialog." Sci Books Films

Alexander, Brian

The **chemistry** between us; love, sex, and the science of attraction. Larry Young and Brian Alexander. Current 2012 310 p. $26.95   **612.8**
    1. Sex -- Physiological aspects 3. Sex -- Psychological aspects 4. Love -- Psychological aspects 5. Sexual attraction 6. Love -- Physiological aspects
    ISBN 1591845130; 9781591845133
                                LC 2012019129
    This book by Larry Young and Brian Alexander presents an "analysis of the complex brain chemicals behind lust and love. . . . In interviews with scientists of all stripes (psychiatrists, neuroscientists, researchers), Young and Alexander examine their ideas and how they pertain to us, often illuminating their explanations with funny, and sometimes raunchy, anecdotes." (Kirkus Reviews). Topics include "love, sex, gender, sexual orientation, and family life." (Publisher's note)
    Includes bibliographical references (p. 267-299) and index

Biever, John A.

The **wandering** mind; understanding disassociation, from daydreams to disorders. John A. Biever and Maryann Karinch. Rowman & Littlefield Publishers 2012 xv, 167 p.p (hardcover) $35; (ebook) $34.99   **612.8**
    1. Mental illness 2. Dissociation (Psychology) 3. Consciousness 4. Mental health
    ISBN 1442216158; 1442216174; 9781442216150;

9781442216174 pdf
                                LC 2012013303
    In this book by John A. Biever and Maryann Karinch, Biever "describes daydreaming, fantasy-prone personalities, and charismatic leaders. He differentiates dissociate identity disorder (DID) from dissociative fugue, dissociative amnesia, depersonalization disorders, and false memories, using examples from the literature as well as his own case studies." (Choice)
    Includes bibliographical references   (p. 155-156) and index.

Bor, Daniel

The **ravenous** brain; how the new science of consciousness explains our insatiable search for meaning. Daniel Bor. Basic Books 2012 xviii, 326 p.p ill. (some col.) (hardcover) $27.99   **612.8**
    1. Brain 2. Consciousness 3. Mind and body 4. Consciousness -- Physiological aspects
    ISBN 046502047X; 9780465020478; 9780465032969
                                LC 2012016971
    This book, by Daniel Bor, "propose[s] a new model for how consciousness works. . . . This model explains our brains' ravenous appetite for information--and in particular, its constant search for patterns. . . . Such behavior . . . led our ancestors to discover fire and farming, pushed modern society to forge ahead in science and technology, and guides each one of us to understand and control the world around us." (Publisher's note)
    Includes bibliographical references and index

Buonomano, Dean

Brain bugs; how the brain's flaws shape our lives. W. W. Norton & Co. 2011 310p $25.95 **612.8**
    1. Brain 2. Memory
    ISBN 978-0-393-07602-8
                                LC 2011014934
    The author explains "that as the human brain has evolved over the past 100,000 years, it has added layer upon layer of networked neural connections to cope with a rapidly changing world. But, he writes, the brain's most detrimental malfunctions are often traceable to its most ancient structures—those that compose the limbic system. . . . Drawing on real-world examples and current research in neuroscience, Buonomano guides the reader through the unexpected ways in which our lives are influenced by the messiness of our busiest, most intricate, and often most error-prone organ." The Scientist
    Includes bibliographical references

Carr, Nicholas G., 1959-

The **shallows**; what the Internet is doing to our brains. W.W. Norton 2010 276p $26.95   **612.8**
    1. Neuropsychology 2. Neurophysiology 3. Internet -- Psychological aspects
    ISBN 978-0-393-07222-8; 0-393-07222-3
                                LC 2010-07639
    "Drawing from neuroscience, history and social-science research, Carr reviews evidence that learning how to solve a problem, how to play a piece of music or how to speak a language physically changes the brain. It's a mistake, he argues, to think of the brain as a hard drive that stores information;

it's far more than that and changes dynamically as it processes information, altering itself as it confronts challenges — for better or worse. Reading a book, he notes, is vastly different from reading hyperlinked Internet text. Reading a book is solitary, requiring deep thought, analysis of the text and sustaining a narrative thread for the duration. By contrast, Internet reading invites shallow skimming for relevant passages, incessant clicking to hyperlinked articles and reliance on Google's search algorithms to determine relevance. . . . Carr argues that the result is an emerging nation of shallow and impatient readers." Seattle Times

Includes bibliographical references

Carter, Rita

The **human** brain book; [by] Rita Carter; Susan Aldridge, Martyn Page, Steve Parker; consultants, Chris Frith, Uta Frith, and Melanie Shulman. Dk Pub. 2014 264 p. il $40   **612.8**
   1. Brain 2. Reference books
   ISBN 1465416021; 9781465416025

"This outstanding reference is filled with interesting, detailed information about every possible aspect of the human brain. Three-dimension images and other unique computer-generated visuals complement the massive volume, which also includes more than 50 brain-related diseases and disorders." National Science Teachers Association

Includes glossary

Chorost, Michael

World wide mind; the coming integration of humanity, machines and the Internet. Free Press 2011 242p il $26; ebook $12.99   **612.8**
   1. Brain 2. Internet 3. Telepathy 4. Communication 5. Thought and thinking 6. Brain mapping 7. Computational neuroscience 8. Interpersonal communication
   ISBN 978-1-4391-1914-3; 1-4391-1914-7; 978-1-4391-4120-5 ebook; 1-4391-4120-7 ebook
                      LC 2010-11875

This "is a thought-provoking story about how technology will connect with the brain ever more intimately, merging humanity and the internet, providing technologically shared experiences and emotions. It forces the reader to think again—not just about neuro-technology but also about communication, about how important eye-to-eye and body-to-body contact is." New Sci

Includes bibliographical references

Churchland, Patricia S.

Braintrust; what neuroscience tells us about morality. [by] Patricia S. Churchland. Princeton University Press 2011 273 p. (hardcover) $24.95   **612.8**
   1. Ethics 2. Philosophy 3. Neuropsychology 4. Neurobiology 5. Neurosciences
   ISBN 069113703X; 9780691137032
                      LC 2010043584

In this book, "[Patricia S.] Churchland argues that morality originates in the biology of the brain. She describes the 'neurobiological platform of bonding' that, modified by evolutionary pressures and cultural values, has led to human styles of moral behavior. . . . Moral values, Churchland ar-

gues, are rooted in a behavior common to all mammals -- the caring for offspring." (Publisher's note)

Includes bibliographical references and index

DeSalle, Rob

★ The **brain**; big bangs, behaviors, and beliefs. Rob DeSalle and Ian Tattersall ; illustrated by Patricia J. Wynne. Yale University Press 2012 xiv, 354 p.p ill. (clothbound : alk. paper) $29.95   **612.8**
   1. Brain 2. Evolution 3. Nervous system 4. Cognition 5. Neurophysiology 6. Brain -- Evolution
   ISBN 0300175221; 9780300175226
                      LC 2011044329

This book by Rob DeSalle and Ian Tattersall presents a "step-by-step account of the evolution of the brain and nervous system." The authors "explain how the cognitive gulf that separates us from all other living creatures could have occurred. They discuss the development and uniqueness of human consciousness, how human and nonhuman brains work, the roles of different nerve cells, the importance of memory and language in brain functions, and much more." (Publisher's note)

Includes bibliographical references (p. 327-336) and index

Doidge, Norman

The **brain** that changes itself; stories of personal triumph from the frontiers of brain science. Viking 2007 427p $24.95   **612.8**
   1. Brain 2. Neuroplasticity
   ISBN 978-0-670-03830-5; 0-670-03830-X
                      LC 2006-49224

"A woman who perpetually feels like she's falling, a man addicted to hard-core pornography, an amputee with excruciating pain in his phantom elbow: all cured thanks to neuroplasticity, the brain's ability to rewire itself. Doidge provides a history of the research in this growing field, highlighting scientists at the edge of groundbreaking discoveries and telling fascinating stories of people who have benefited. An engaging read for anyone interested in the science behind how our surprisingly moldable brains are changed by our experiences." Psychology Today

Dowling, John E.

Creating mind; how the brain works. Norton 1998 212p il hardcover o.p. pa $17.50   **612.8**
   1. Brain
   ISBN 0-393-97446-4 pa
                      LC 98-9365

"In this guide to the 'nuts and bolts' of the human brain, neurobiologist Dowling explains how basic brain functions work and are interconnected. He then explores in clear, concise prose the brain's major functions: vision, language, memory, emotion, perception, and consciousness. A good jumping off point for learning about neuroscience and its fascinating discoveries." Libr J

Includes bibliographical references

Eliot, Lise

What's going on in there? how the brain and mind develop in the first five years of life. Bantam Bks. 1999 533p hardcover o.p. pa $18   **612.8**
1. Brain 2. Developmental psychology
ISBN 0-553-37825-2 pa

LC 99-35423

"This book is both theoretical and practical, combining scientific reportage with 'how-to' advice for new parents... . With clear, mostly simple language, {Eliot} guides readers through a fascinating array of new research—on infant balance, the development of language and memory, and the relationship between the birthing process and the brain." Libr J

Gazzaniga, Michael S.

Human; the science behind what makes us unique. Ecco 2008 447p $27.50   **612.8**
1. Brain 2. Human beings 3. Consciousness
ISBN 978-0-06-089288-3; 0-06-089288-9

LC 2008-297703

The author's "main premise is that human brains are not only proportionately larger than those of other primates but have a number of distinct structures, which he explores along with evolutionary explanations for their existence... . Throughout, Gazzaniga addresses the nature of consciousness." Publ Wkly

"A savvy, witty guide to neuroscience today." Kirkus
Includes bibliographical references

Johnson, Steven

Mind wide open; your brain and the neuroscience of everyday life. Scribner 2004 274p il $25; pa $15   **612.8**
1. Brain
ISBN 0-7432-4165-7; 0-7432-4166-5 pa

LC 2003-63308

"Johnson fills this book with important, big-picture ideas, including enough description of the details to give the reader a sense of the science without becoming overwhelmed. His knowledgeable and thoughtful approach makes neuroscience accessible to all." Choice

Includes bibliographical references

Kaku, Michio

The future of the mind; the scientific quest to understand, enhance, and empower the mind. Dr. Michio Kaku, professor of Theoretical Physics, City University of New York. Doubleday 2014 400 p. illustrations $28.95   **612.8**
1. Mind and body 2. Neurosciences 3. Neuropsychology 4. Brain-computer interfaces 5. Cognitive neuroscience 6. Brain -- Mathematical models
ISBN 038553082X; 9780385530828

LC 2013017338

In this book, "theoretical physicist [Michio] Kaku . . . explores fantastical realms of science fiction that may soon become our reality. His futurist framework merges physics with neuroscience to model how our brains construct the future, and is loosely applied to demonstrations that 'show proof-of-principle' in accomplishing what was previously fictional: that minds can be read, memories can be digitally stored, and intelligences can be improved to great extents." (Publishers Weekly)

Kaku "delivers ingenious predictions extrapolated from good research already in progress." Kirkus
Includes bibliographical references

Kurzweil, Ray, 1948-

How to create a mind; the secret of human thought revealed. Ray Kurzweil. Viking 2012 336 p. $27.95   **612.8**
1. Brain 2. Consciousness 3. Artificial intelligence 4. Self-consciousness (Awareness) 5. Brain -- Localization of functions
ISBN 0670025291; 9780670025299

LC 2012027185

In this book, "[Ray] Kurzweil . . . provides insight into how the human brain functions, while speculating on the possibilities and philosophical implications of creating a nonbiological mind. Underlying this analysis is the Pattern Recognition Theory of Mind, a process in the neocortex, the seat of higher brain functions such as perception, memory, and language and, by extension, consciousness." (Publishers Weekly)

Includes bibliographical references and index.

Lilienfeld, Scott O.

Brainwashed; The Seductive Appeal of Mindless Neuroscience. Sally Satel and Scott O. Lilienfeld. Perseus Books Group 2013 256 p. $26.99   **612.8**
1. Mind and body 2. Neurosciences
ISBN 0465018777; 9780465018772

In this book, "a psychiatrist and a clinical psychologist... argue against the use of brain scans as the basis for marketing efforts, addiction treatment, lie detection, and decisions in criminal trials. . . . The authors explain how particular mental states cannot be pinned directly onto active brain regions. They assert that a comprehensive understanding of behavior requires consideration of not only brain activity but also psychological, social, and cultural influences." (Library Journal)

Linden, David J.

The compass of pleasure; how our brains make fatty foods, orgasm, exercise, marijuana, generosity, vodka, learning, and gambling feel so good. Viking 2011 230p il $26.95   **612.8**
1. Pleasure 2. Neuropsychology
ISBN 978-0-670-02258-8

LC 2010-35380

The author "addresses provocative questions about the relationship between pleasure and addiction while exploring many of the broader implications of the nexus of the two... . Linden's conversational style, his abundant use of anecdotes, and his successful coupling of wit with insight makes the book a joy to read. Even the footnotes are sprinkled with hidden gems." Publ Wkly

Includes bibliographical references

McDermott, Terry

101 theory drive; a neuroscientist's quest for memory. Pantheon Books 2010 271p il $25.95 **612.8**
1. Brain 2. Memory 3. Biologists 4. Neurologists 5.

College teachers 6. Medicine -- Research 7. University of California, Irvine
ISBN 978-0-375-42538-7; 0-375-42538-1

LC 2009-34251

The author "profiles UC-Irvine psychobiologist Gary Lynch and his decades-long effort to understand the biochemical processes and structural changes in neurons that underlie memory. . . . In McDermott's portrayal, Lynch comes off as a hippie-ish, hard-drinking, foul-mouthed visionary at odds with the neuroscientific establishment, who both inspires and exploits the students and post-docs under his sway. . . . This is an engrossing story of science and the brilliant, flawed people who make it." Publ Wkly

Includes bibliographical references

Palca, Joe

Annoying; the science of what bugs us. [by] Joe Palca and Flora Lichtman. Wiley 2011 272p $25.95 **612.8**

1. Physiology 2. Neuropsychology
ISBN 978-0-470-63869-9

LC 2010-54046

Palca and Lichtman "skitter all over the map in pursuit of their subject, and at first their progress seems peculiarly random, like one of those robotic vacuums. But in the end they do indeed cover every part of the terrain: from physics and psychology to aesthetics, genetics and even treatment for the miserably, terminally annoyed." N Y Times (Late N Y Ed)

Includes bibliographical references

Randall, David K.

Dreamland; adventures in the strange science of sleep. David K. Randall. W.W. Norton 2012 304 p. $25.95; (hardcover) $25.95 **612.8**

1. Sleep 2. Dreams 3. Sleepwalking
ISBN 039308020X; 9780393080209

LC 2012014932

This book offers an "examination of the science behind the little-known world of sleep. . . . [David K.] Randall explores the research that is investigating those dark hours that make up nearly a third of our lives. Taking readers from military battlefields to children's bedrooms, [the book] shows that sleep isn't as simple as it seems. Why did the results of one sleep study change the bookmakers' odds for certain Monday Night Football games? Do women sleep differently than men? And if you happen to kill someone while you are sleepwalking, does that count as murder?" (Publisher's note)

Includes bibliographical references

Tammet, Daniel

Embracing the wide sky; a tour across the horizons of the mind. Free Press 2009 292p il $25 **612.8**

1. Brain 2. Memory 3. Intellect 4. Savants (Savant syndrome)
ISBN 978-1-4165-6969-5; 1-4165-6969-3

LC 2008-30551

"In chapters on intelligence, memory, language, the perception of numbers as instinctual, and ways in which the brain works, Tammet relates savant capabilities to normal functions, theorizes from sound research about what enables savant capabilities, cashiers the notion of computers ever becoming genuinely intelligent, and offers tips on how to calculate and learn languages better." Booklist

Includes bibliographical references

Zimmer, Carl

Soul made flesh; the discovery of the brain--and how it changed the world. Free Press 2004 367p il $26 **612.8**

1. Brain
ISBN 0-7432-3038-8

LC 2003-63144

Zimmer tells "the story of the 'discovery' of the human brain by physician Thomas Willis. Exploring the effects of this breakthrough on 17th-century Oxford, the author traces and investigates the subsequent discoveries and theories in neurology and medicine that flowed from Willis and others (e.g., Harvey, Hobbes, Descartes, Boyle, and Locke) in Oxford and on the continent. . . . Zimmer's elegant writing combines these multiple perspectives to produce a fascinating tour-de-force of a man, a time, and a place that readers will greatly enjoy." Libr J

Includes bibliographical references

613 Personal health and safety

Boston Women's Health Book Collective

★ Our bodies, ourselves; [by] Boston Women's Health Book Collective. 40th anniversary ed.; Touchstone 2011 928p il pa $26; ebook $12.99 **613**

1. Women -- Psychology 2. Women -- Health and hygiene
ISBN 978-1-4391-9066-1 pa; 1-4391-9066-6 pa; 978-1-4391-9665-6 ebook; 1-4391-9665-6 ebook

LC 2011022749

First published 1971

This encyclopedia of women's health covers such topics as body image, food, alcohol and drugs, holistic healing, psychotherapy, occupational health, violence, relationships and sexuality, sexual health and controlling fertility, childbearing, aging and politics of women and health.

This is "the bible for women's health; an outstanding resource that belongs in all health collections." Libr J

Columbia University/Health Service

The Go ask Alice book of answers; a guide to good physical, sexual, and emotional health. [by] Columbia University's Health Education Program. Holt & Co. 1998 345p pa $15.95 **613**

1. Adolescence 2. Sex education 3. Youth -- Health and hygiene
ISBN 0-8050-5570-3

LC 98-3318

"The title within the title refers to a Web site maintained by Columbia University Health Services. Set up to answer questions about relationships, sex, physical and mental health, nutrition, and related matters, the site eventually was opened to the general public as a quick-reference forum. The book's seven chapters round up queries the site has received and responses to them from Columbia-associated health educators." Booklist

Includes bibliographical references

Delgado, Jane L.

The **Latina** guide to health; consejos and caring answers. foreword by Antonia Novello. Newmarket Press 2010 239p pa $15.95   **613**

1. Hispanic American women -- Health and hygiene
ISBN 978-1-55704-854-7; 1-55704-854-1

LC 2009-36591

This book "contains useful information about psychosocial and environmental issues, access to health care, common diseases and conditions, and medical decision-making. An excellent addition to all consumer health collections and home libraries." Libr J

Includes bibliographical references

Guiliano, Mireille

French women don't get facelifts; the secret of aging with style and attitude. Mireille Guiliano. Grand Central Life & Style 2013 272 p. (hardcover) $25   **613**

1. Women -- France 2. Women -- Health and hygiene 3. Aging -- Psychological aspects 4. Older women -- France -- Attitudes 5. Older women -- Health and hygiene -- France
ISBN 1455524115; 9781455524112

LC 2013017824

Author Mireille Guiliano's book "presents an insightful guide to the French way of aging with style, grace, and attitude. She encourages midlife women to adopt French-inspired remedies for aging woes, such as antiaging foods, regular exercise, sufficient sunlight, proper skin care, and plenty of water . . . The author provides a list of superfoods paired with easy-to-follow recipes, a straightforward skin-care routine, product recommendations, and ways to stay physically active." (Library Journal)

Health and social relationships; the good, the bad, and the complicated. edited by Matthew L. Newman and Nicole A. Roberts. American Psychological Association 2013 ix, 262 p.p $69.95 **613**

1. Health 2. Social networking 3. Interpersonal relations 4. Health -- Social aspects 5. Social networks -- Health aspects 6. Social interaction -- Health aspects 7. Interpersonal relations -- Health aspects
ISBN 1433812223; 9781433812224

LC 2012019789

Editor Matthew L. Newman's book examines "the psychological and physiological linkages between relationships and health, but also offer[s] clinical implications -- such as how to foster good social relationships in our personal lives and in our communities at large. . . . Most of our relationships -- relatives, coworkers, caregivers, and romantic partners among them -- are complicated, providing varying degrees of both support and stress." (Publisher's note)

Includes bibliographical references and index

Healthy women, healthy lives; a guide to preventing disease from the landmark Nurses' Health Study. senior editors, Susan E. Hankinson {et al.} Si-

mon & Schuster 2001 xxviii, 546p il $26; pa $16   **613**

1. Women -- Diseases 2. Women -- Health and hygiene
ISBN 0-684-85519-4; 0-7432-1774-8 pa

LC 2001-34154

"In 'Lowering the Risk of Disease', the risks of coronary heart disease, breast cancer, lung cancer, stroke, diabetes, colon cancer, osteoporosis, endometrial cancer, ovarian cancer, and skin cancer are discussed. Another chapter covers asthma, arthritis, age-related eye disease, and Alzheimer's disease. . . . The final chapters look at changing behaviors and making decisions that can affect women's health." Libr J

Includes bibliographical references

Kaye, Lenard W.

A **man's** guide to healthy aging; stay smart, strong, and active. Edward H. Thompson, Jr. and Lenard W. Kaye. The Johns Hopkins University Press 2013 584 p. illustrations (A Johns Hopkins Press health book) (pbk. : alk. paper) $30.95   **613**

1. Longevity 2. Elderly men 3. Men -- Health and hygiene 4. Older men -- Health and hygiene
ISBN 1421410559; 1421410567; 9781421410555; 9781421410562

LC 2012047831

This book, by Edward H. Thompson Jr. and Lenard W. Kaye, is a "guide that covers major health problems, preventative care, and social and spiritual concerns that contribute to [men's] good health. . . . Chapters devoted to health management, [emphasize] the importance of staying active, eating healthy food, and maintaining social connections. . . . Alongside . . . subjects like cancer and heart disease, the authors discuss sexuality, holistic medicine, retirement, and caregiving." (Publishers Weekly)

Includes bibliographical references and index

Levkoff, Logan

Got teens? the doctor moms' guide to sexuality, social media and other adolescent realities. Logan Levkoff, Ph.D. and Jennifer Wider, M.D. Seal Press 2014 296 p. (pbk.) $16   **613**

1. Parenting 2. Teenagers 3. Mothers and sons 4. Parent and teenager 5. Adolescent psychology 6. Health behavior in adolescence
ISBN 1580055060; 9781580055062

LC 2013040092

"In 'Got Teens?,' [authors Logan Levkoff and Jennifer Wider] combine their medical and psychological knowledge with their own personal experiences to address the most cringeworthy and difficult questions that kids often ask their parents. . . . Topics include body development, emotional changes, bullying, social media, substance abuse, and more--giving parents the confidence to tackle these subjects with authority and compassion." (Publisher's note)

"This work zeroes in on the peskiest questions that teens ask and gives sound, friendly advice for challenging topics." LJ

Includes bibliographical references (pages 263-267) and index

Pollan, Michael

In defense of food; an eater's manifesto. Penguin Press 2008 244p $21.95; pa $16 **613**

1. Nutrition 2. Eating customs

ISBN 978-1-59420-145-5; 1-59420-145-5; 978-0-14-311496-3 pa; 0-14-311496-4 pa

LC 2007037552

The author "proposes a . . . way to think about the question of what to eat that is informed by ecology and tradition rather than by the prevailing nutrient-by-nutrient approach." Publisher's note

"Pollan will succeed in making you think twice about what you are piling up in your grocery cart or on your plate." Christ Sci Monit

Includes bibliographical references

Smith, Rick

Toxin toxout; getting harmful chemicals out of our bodies and our world. Bruce Lourie, Rick Smith. St. Martin's Press 2014 304 p. (hardcover) $25.99 **613**

1. Pesticides 2. Environmental health 3. Detoxification (Health) 4. Environmentally induced diseases -- Nutritional aspects

ISBN 1250051339; 9781250051332

LC 2013049688

This book presents a "guide to the toxins in our everyday environment and how best to avoid them or get them out of our bodies. . . . The authors . . . focus on providing practical advice on how to avoid toxins (the short answer is to buy organic and natural products) and eliminate those that have accumulated from our bodies. . . . Toward the end of their book, [Bruce] Lourie and [Rick] Smith discuss some of the broader implications of their findings." (CCPA Monitor)

"In a collegial, straightforward style, Lourie and Smith quiz doctors and researchers, converse with wellness activists, visit organic stores and companies and, most interestingly, engage in a variety of experiments to track how the more than 80,000 synthetic chemicals in use today got into our bodies and what it will take to get them out." Booklist

Includes bibliographical references and index

Weil, Andrew

Eight weeks to optimum health; a proven program for taking full advantage of your body's natural healing power. Knopf 1997 276p $25; pa $13.95 **613**

1. Health self-care 2. Alternative medicine

ISBN 0-679-44715-6; 0-449-00026-5 pa

LC 96-51918

The book's "strength lies in its design, which uses small easy steps to achieve big changes. . . . As a physician, Weil is careful to substantiate every claim, and he debunks some of today's more extreme alternative health theories." Libr J

Includes bibliographical references

613.2 Dietetics

Bittman, Mark

Food matters; a guide to conscious eating with more than 75 recipes. Simon & Schuster 2009 326p il $24 **613.2**

1. Nutrition 2. Agriculture 3. Weight loss 4. Food industry 5. Eating customs

ISBN 978-1-4165-7564-1; 1-4165-7564-2

LC 2008-39593

The "Minimalist" columnist and author of How to Cook Everything outlines an eating plan that is comprised of environmentally responsible choices, in a guide that shares insight into the risks associated with livestock production.

Burke, Louise

The complete guide to food for sports performance; a guide to peak nutrition for your sport. [by] Louise Burke, Greg Cox. 3rd ed., Updated and expanded; Allen & Unwin 2010 xxii, 522p il pa $24.95 **613.2**

1. Physical fitness 2. Athletes -- Nutrition

ISBN 978-1-7411-4390-4; 1-7411-4390-X

LC 2010-537626

First published 1992

"This book presents nutrition as an integrated part of an athlete's total performance-enhancing package. General nutrition and exercise physiology information are converted into a plan for day-to-day practice for training and competition preparation. It outlines important differences in nutritional needs for different sports, including the timing of food and liquid intake, and the best foods to achieve maximum energy output." Publisher's note

Duyff, Roberta Larson

American Dietetic Association complete food and nutrition guide; Roberta Larson Duyff. 4th ed. rev. and updated John Wiley & Sons Inc 2012 708 p. ill. $24.95 **613.2**

1. Diabetes 2. Nutrition

ISBN 0470912073; 9780470912072

"The author's goal is 'to answer the whats, hows, and whys about food and nutrition' for wellness. This new edition . . . is divided into six sections covering food choices for wellness; the basics of nutrition; food selection and safety; special needs for various life stages; food choices for some selected health problems; and a selected list of resources." Choice

Includes bibliographical references and index

Friedman, Howard S.

The longevity project; surprising discoveries for health and long life from the eight-decade study. [by] Howard S. Friedman and Leslie R. Martin. Hudson Street Press 2010 248p $25.95 **613.2**

1. Longevity

ISBN 978-1-594630-75-0; 1-594630-75-5

LC 2010-22833

"Analyzing the data from the Terman study and following up on the 1500 participants, . . . [the authors] investigate why some people live until old age while others die or become ill prematurely. Unlike most studies, this work looks at key psychological factors, habits, and patterns that affect health and longevity over time. Some of the authors' conclusions about achieving longevity are surprising. Factors such as the study participants' sociability, conscientiousness, happiness, and religious involvement were analyzed to show which patterns lead over time to an increased life span. The authors have provided a well-written and easy-to-follow analysis of this interesting study." Libr J

Includes bibliographical references

Heller, Marla

The **everyday** DASH diet cookbook; over 150 fresh and delicious recipes to speed weight loss, lower blood pressure, and prevent diabetes. by Marla Heller, MS, RD ; with Rick Rodgers. Grand Central Life & Style 2013 214 p. (hardback) $26   **613.2**
1. Cookbooks 2. Hypertension -- Prevention 3. Reducing diets -- Recipes 4. Salt-free diet -- Recipes 5. Diabetes -- Diet therapy 6. Hypertension -- Diet therapy
ISBN 1455528064; 9781455528066
LC 2012045485

This cookbook looks at the "research-based DASH (dietary approaches to stop hypertension) diet," which "emphasizes 'real foods' and minimizes processed sugars, salt, cholesterol, and fats. Writing with veteran cookbook author [Rick] Rodgers . . . , leading DASH expert [Marla] Heller . . . offers easy recipes (e.g., crunchy broccoli slaw, rosemary pork chops with balsamic glaze) for readers living a healthy lifestyle." (Library Journal)

Includes bibliographical references and index

Jones, Heather K.

Good housekeeping drop 5 lbs; the small changes, big results diet. edited [and foreword] by Rosemary Ellis. Hearst Books 2010 270p il pa $19.95 **613.2**
1. Metabolism 2. Weight loss
ISBN 978-1-58816-786-6
LC 2010-18434

The author "highlights five eating misbehaviors, including skipping meals and mindless munching. Throughout, there are specific tips to help eliminate bad habits. . . . An effective, attractive, and informative ready reference diet manual. Readers will love the achievable results, and it is refreshing to have a book that does not expect great sacrifice and total lifestyle change." Libr J

Kolata, Gina

Rethinking thin; the new science of weight loss--and the myths and realities of dieting. Farrar, Straus, and Giroux 2007 257p $24   **613.2**
1. Weight loss
ISBN 978-0-374-10398-9; 0-374-10398-4
LC 2006-33816

The author "traces the history of dieting fads back to the 19th century; discusses our changing ideas about the ideal body (thinner and thinner); and, most importantly, explains how genetic and biochemical understanding has (at least among researchers) replaced the view of obesity as a lack of self-control. . . . This book will change your thinking about weight, whether you struggle with it or not." Publ Wkly

Includes bibliographical references

Moss, Michael

★ **Salt,** sugar, fat; how the food giants hooked us. Michael Moss. Random House Inc 2013 480 p. (hardcover) $28   **613.2**
1. Obesity 2. Junk food -- Marketing 3. Food industry -- United States 4. Food industry and trade -- United States 5. Nutrition -- Economic aspects -- United States 6. Food habits -- Economic aspects -- United States
ISBN 1400069807; 9780679604778; 9781400069804
LC 2012033034

Pulitzer prize winner Michael Moss offers an exposé of the U.S. food industry. He "explains the two-faced science of salt, sugar, and fat, which impart tantalizing tastes and luscious mouth-feel that light up the same neural circuits that narcotics do . . . while causing epidemic obesity, cardiovascular disease, and diabetes. But he also crafts an . . . insiders' view of the food industry, where these ingredients are the main weapons in a brutally competitive war for stomach-share." (Publishers Weekly)

Nesheim, Malden

Why calories count; from science to politics. Marion Nestle and Malden Nesheim. University of California Press 2012 288 p. (California studies in food and culture) (hardback : alk. paper) $29.95   **613.2**
1. Diet 2. Nutrition 3. Weight loss 4. Eating customs 5. Food -- Caloric content 6. Politics 7. Marketing 8. Food Industry 9. Obesity -- prevention & control
ISBN 9780520262881
LC 2011044785

This book "assists readers in evaluating diet claims, formulating strategies to lose, gain, or maintain weight, and learning how to make healthy food choices. [Marion] Nestle . . . and [Malden] Nesheim . . . focus on the history of the calorie and its relationship to body weight, the science behind metabolism, how to estimate calories in a given portion, and . . . the role of big business in creating calorie-laden food." (Library Journal)

Includes bibliographical references and index.

Nestle, Marion

What to eat. North Point Press 2006 611p $30   **613.2**
1. Diet 2. Health 3. Nutrition
ISBN 0-8654-7704-3; 978-0-8654-7704-9
LC 2006-07886

This book presents "a guided tour of the supermarket, . . . section by section: produce, dairy, meat, fish, packaged foods, breads, juices, bottled waters, and more. . . . [The author] tells us how to make sensible choices based on freshness, taste, nutrition, health, effects on the environment, and . . . price." (N Y Times Book Rev). Index.

The author's "intelligent and reassuring approach will likely make readers venture more confidently through the jungle of today's super-sized stores." Publ Wkly

Includes bibliographical references

Sears, William

The **family** nutrition book; everything you need to know about feeding your children from birth through adolescence. Little, Brown 1999 416p il hardcover o.p. pa $19 **613.2**

1. Infants -- Nutrition 2. Children -- Nutrition

ISBN 0-316-77715-3 pa

LC 98-51879

"The book progresses from an overview of nutrients (water and fiber among them) to an extensive evaluation of food groups, including discussions of vegetarianism, organic foods and decoding packaging labels. Additional sections address weight control and the specific roles various foods play in disease prevention, stamina building, etc. Reference tables and an updated food pyramid will prove indispensable to the reader." Publ Wkly

Includes bibliographical references

Willett, Walter

Eat, drink and be healthy; the Harvard Medical School guide to healthy eating. {by} Walter C. Willett with P. J. Skerrett; contributions by Edward L. Giovannucci; recipes by Maureen Callahan. Simon & Schuster 2001 299p il $25; pa $13 **613.2**

1. Nutrition

ISBN 0-684-86337-5; 0-7432-2322-5 pa

LC 2001-20565

The author contends that the USDA Food Pyramid, which recommends 6 to 11 servings of carbohydrate-rich foods per day, is wrong and dangerous, and he offers an alternate nutritional plan emphasizing fruits, vegetables, fish, chicken, legumes, and whole grains

Includes bibliographical references

613.6   Personal safety and special topics of health

Bailey, Elizabeth

Safe kids, smart parents; what parents need to know to keep their children safe. Rebecca Bailey, Ph.D. with Elizabeth Bailey ; introduction by Terry Probyn. Simon & Schuster 2013 224 p. (trade paper : alk. paper) $15 **613.6**

1. Children 2. Safety education 3. Parenting 4. Children -- Protection 5. Critical thinking in children 6. Children -- Crimes against -- Prevention

ISBN 1476700443; 9781476700441

LC 2012047452

This book is a guide to children's safety. It is "divided into two sections, one intended for parents and guardians, the other written especially for children. The message in both is the same: the need for parents and children (whether toddlers or teens) to be aware of their environment and vigilant. The authors emphasize the difficult reality that, these days, children must be taught to be wary of all strangers, even those who appear to be in trouble and are requesting help." (Kirkus Reviews)

Drago, Dorothy A.

From crib to kindergarten; the essential child safety guide. Johns Hopkins University Press 2007 195p il $45; pa $15 **613.6**

1. Parenting 2. Accidents -- Prevention

ISBN 978-0-8018-8569-3; 0-8018-8569-8; 978-0-8018-8570-9 pa; 0-8018-8570-1 pa

LC 2006-20809

"In an effort to help readers 'recognize and reduce hazards so . . . children can be as safe from injury as possible,' Drago offers hundreds of tips on how to provide a safe environment for daily activities, concentrating on small children in the home setting. . . . This book is packed with indispensable advice and is an essential resource and reference guide for parents and caregivers." Libr J

Includes bibliographical references

Gervasi, Lori Hartman

Fight like a girl-- and win; defense decisions for women. St. Martin's Griffin 2007 285p pa $14.99 **613.6**

1. Safety education 2. Self-defense for women

ISBN 978-0-312-35772-6; 0-312-35772-9

LC 2007-17216

"Although the author has a black belt in karate, she maintains that 90 percent of self-defense is awareness and common sense. She helps readers set up absolute rules and boundaries, sharpen their observation skills, and trust in their intuition. Physical fitness is stressed, and resources are provided for further training." Libr J

Includes bibliographical references

Stilwell, Alexander

The **encyclopedia** of survival techniques. Lyons Press 2007 192p il map pa $19.95 **613.6**

1. Survival skills 2. Wilderness survival

ISBN 978-1-59921-314-9

First published 2000

This guide covers preparation, basic skills, equipment, various terrains, natural disasters, and first aid.

Wiseman, John

SAS survival handbook; for any climate, in any situation. [by] John ¿Lofty¿ Wiseman. Rev. ed.; Collins 2009 576p il pa $19.99 **613.6**

1. Survival skills 2. Wilderness survival 3. Survival after airplane accidents, shipwrecks, etc.

ISBN 978-0-06-173319-2; 0-06-173319-9

LC 2009-502549

First published 1986 in the United Kingdom

This book "is the Special Air Service's complete course in being prepared for any type of emergency. John Wiseman presents real strategies for surviving in any type of situation, from accidents and escape procedures, including chemical and nuclear to successfully adapting to various climates (polar, tropical, desert), to identifying edible plants and creating fire." Publisher's note

613.7 Physical fitness

American College of Sports Medicine

★ **Complete** guide to fitness & health; Barbara Bushman, editor. Human Kinetics 2011 396p il pa $21.95 **613.7**

1. Health 2. Exercise 3. Physical fitness
ISBN 978-0-7360-9337-8; 0-7360-9337-0

LC 2011-6563

"Contributions from a range of academics (many affiliated with the ACSM) distill the current thinking on nutrition and exercise for all ages and for adults with chronic conditions such as arthritis and diabetes. They discuss how to determine your current levels of fitness, create a graduated fitness plan and coordinate it with proper eating habits, and measure your progress and maintain your optimum level. Chapters include recommendations for those with special health and medical conditions, such as diabetes, high cholesterol, high blood pressure, and arthritis. . . . Anyone who is serious about getting in shape will want this guide." Libr J

Includes bibliographical references

Basic weight training for men and women; Thomas D. Fahey. 8th ed McGraw-Hill 2013 251 p. ill. (alk. paper) $73.15 **613.7**

1. Weight training
ISBN 0078022622; 9780078022623

LC 2011053194

"Each chapter presents the most important and up-to-date weight training exercises with free weights and on the most popular exercise machines found in schools and health clubs in the United States. Nutrition information, workout schedules, proper techniques, and research articles debunking fitness myths" are also included. "The text also includes a discussion of functional training exercises and stresses the concept that the key to building strength and power is to train movements rather than specific muscles." Publisher's note

Includes bibliographical references and index

Bonifonte, Philip

T'ai chi for seniors; how to gain flexibility, strength, and inner peace. New Page Bks. 2004 213p il pa $16.99 **613.7**

1. Tai chi
ISBN 1-564-14697-9

LC 2003-60207

The author describes the ancient Chinese exercise that focuses "on easy, gentle movements that increase aerobic capacity, decrease blood pressure and stress, and improve balance and joint function. Along with a short history of various tai chi styles philosophies, the text features breathing techniques, warm-up exercises, movement forms, and meditation exercises with modifications for those with limited mobility." Libr J

Broad, William J.

The **science** of yoga; William J. Broad. Simon & Schuster 2012 xxxi, 298p ill. **613.7**

1. Exercise 2. Hatha yoga 3. Yoga -- History
ISBN 9781451641424; 9781451641431;
9781451641448

LC 2011020408

This book, "[f]ive years in the making, . . . draws on more than a century of . . . research to present the first impartial evaluation of a practice thousands of years old. It celebrates what's real and shows what's illusory, describes what's uplifting and beneficial and what's flaky and dangerous--and why. Broad illuminates how yoga can lift moods and inspire creativity. He exposes moves that can cripple and kill. . . . [The book] presents a . . . body of evidence that raises questions about whether humans have latent capabilities for entering states of suspended animation and unremitting sexual bliss. 'The Science of Yoga' takes us on a . . . tour of unknown yoga that goes from old archives in Calcutta to the world capitals of medical research, from storied ashrams to spotless laboratories, from sweaty yoga studios with master teachers to the cozy offices of yoga healers." (Publisher's note)

Callahan, Lisa

The **fitness** factor; every woman's key to a lifetime of health and wellbeing. Lyons Press 2002 xxi, 314p il $24.95 **613.7**

1. Exercise 2. Physical fitness 3. Women -- Health and hygiene
ISBN 1-58574-501-4

LC 2001-50729

In this guide the author stresses the importance of exercise in "preventing heart disease; beating osteoporosis; lowering cholesterol; decreasing cancer risk; losing weight; increasing energy; reducing stress; having better sex and much more." Publisher's note

Includes bibliographical references

Cohen, Jennifer

Strong is the new skinny; how to eat, live, and move to maximize your power. Jennifer Cohen and Stacey Colino ; foreword by David Kirchhoff. Harmony Books 2014 240 p. illustrations (paperback) $18 **613.7**

1. Exercise 2. Physical fitness
ISBN 0804140510; 9780804140515

LC 2014021072

This book by Jennifer Cohen and Stacey Colino says that "it's time for a new conversation--and a new plan for treating, feeding, and moving your body in ways that build on your strengths inside and out. . . . 'Strong Is the New Skinny' offers a reality-based diet, lifestyle, and fitness program (the 'SINS' plan, for short)." (Publisher's note)

"Cohen and Colino's guide is encouraging, empowering, and accessible." Pub Wkly

Devi, Gayatri

A **calm** brain; unlocking your natural relaxation system. Gayatri Devi. Dutton 2012 ix, 275 p.p $25.95 **613.7**

1. Stress management 2. Biofeedback training 3. Self-help techniques 4. Relaxation 5. Cognitive-analytic therapy
ISBN 0525952691; 9780525952695

LC 2011046555

This medical self-help book by Dr. Gayatri Devi "shows . . . how you can cultivate [a] . . . state of focused peaceful awareness by tapping into your body's hard-wired natural relaxation system. . . . Our bodies have been trained to react to the beeps and alarms of all our different technologies. . . . The result is chronic stress and a learned inability to relax, . . . but our bodies have strong wiring that makes true enduring calm possible . . . through the vagus nerve." (Publisher's note)

Includes bibliographical references and index

Epstein, David

The **sports** gene; inside the science of extraordinary athletic performance. David Epstein. Current 2013 352 p. $26.95   **613.7**
1. Athletes 2. Genetics 3. Human genetics 4. Sports -- Physiological aspects
ISBN 1591845114; 9781591845119

LC 2013013443

In this book, David Epstein investigates the connection between genetics and athletic ability. "Drawing on interviews with athletes and scientists, he points out that 'a nation succeeds in a sport not only by having many people who practice prodigiously at sport-specific skills, but also by getting the best all-around athletes into the right sports in the first place.'" (Publishers Weekly)

"[T]his book is essential reading for sports fans interested in the science of sports, and for readers (not scholars) interested in the science of human differences." LJ

Includes bibliographical references and index

Fitness and exercise sourcebook; edited by Amy L. Sutton. 3rd ed; Omnigraphics 2007 663p il (Health reference series) $87   **613.7**
1. Exercise 2. Physical fitness
ISBN 978-0-7808-0946-8; 0-7808-0946-7

LC 2006-36852

First published 1996
Includes bibliographical references

Hesson, James L.

Weight training for life; 9th ed.; Wadsworth/Cengage Learning 2010 178p il $59.95   **613.7**
1. Weight lifting
ISBN 978-0-495-55909-2; 0-495-55909-1

LC 2010291364

First published 1985 by Morton

"The text contains hundreds of full-color photos demonstrating exercises and proper techniques. It also contains forms for writing goals, planning a personal weight-training program, and recording circumference, strength, and muscle endurance measurements." Publisher's note

Includes bibliographical references

Hines, Emmett W.

Fitness swimming; [by] Emmett Hines. 2nd ed.; Human Kinetics 2008 224p il pa $18.95   **613.7**
1. Swimming 2. Physical fitness
ISBN 978-0-7360-7457-5; 0-7360-7457-0

LC 2008-13353

First published 1999

The author "has created 60 . . . workouts and 16 sample programs, each arranged into suggested training zones to correspond to your fitness level and performance goals. . . . The text covers stretching, warm-up and cool-down meth-

ods, heart rate zone targets, expanded instruction for stroke efficacy, progressive drills, conditioning tips, and fitness assessments." Publisher's note

Includes bibliographical references

Idzikowski, Chris

Sound Asleep; The Expert Guide to Sleeping Well. Sterling Pub Co Inc 2013 224 p. $17.95 **613.7**
1. Brain 2. Sleep 3. Dreams
ISBN 1780281188; 9781780281186

In this book, sleep expert Chris Idzikowski "covers everything from the nature of dozing and dreaming to the disorders and poor habits that can infringe on getting a good night's rest. Scientific topics covered include the different kinds of brainwaves and how they relate to the 90-minute sleep cycle and REM sleep, as well as more speculative subjects like lucid dreaming and the causes of nightmares." (Publishers Weekly)

Kolata, Gina

Ultimate fitness; the quest for truth about exercise and health. Farrar, Straus & Giroux 2003 292p il $24; pa $14   **613.7**
1. Exercise 2. Physical fitness
ISBN 0-374-20477-2; 0-312-42322-5 pa

LC 2002-192523

The author " investigates 30 years of the American physical fitness craze, looking at issues like athlete's heart, maximum heart rates, fat-burning zones, training, runner's high, weightlifting, walking, food, water, {and} the fitness business. . . . Fascinating historical information about fitness, understandable facts and figures, and a conversational writing style make this an enormously readable book." Libr J

Includes bibliographical references

Lorr, Benjamin

Hell -bent; obsession, pain, and the search for something like transcendence in competitive yoga. Benjamin Lorr. St. Martin's Press 2012 viii, 312 p.p (hardcover) $25.99   **613.7**
1. Yoga 2. Physical fitness 3. Stretching exercises 4. Yoga -- Philosophy
ISBN 031267290X; 9780312672904; 9781250017529

LC 2012034514

This book by Benjamin Lorr is an "examination of hot, competitive yoga, its cultlike following and the author's immersion into the practice. Named for its founder, Bikram Choudhury, Bikram Yoga is a strict series of 26 postures performed in a heated room set to at least 105 degrees with 40 percent humidity." (Kirkus)

Includes bibliographical references

Pagano, Joan

Strength training for women; tone up, burn calories, stay strong. Dorling Kindersley 2005 160p il pa $15   **613.7**
1. Weight lifting 2. Physical fitness 3. Women -- Health and hygiene
ISBN 0-7566-0595-4; 978-0-7566-0595-7

LC 2005-295208

The author "begins with a three-part fitness test and questionnaire to assess whether the reader should consult a doctor before beginning her program. For true beginners, she provides an anatomy chart that depicts the major muscle groups and the exercises that are best suited to them. She dispels fitness myths like 'lifting weights will bulk you up' and 'you can spot reduce,' and talks about the risk factors, exercise guidelines and restrictions of osteoporosis. . . . This book may be one of the best substitutes for pricey gym memberships and personal trainers." Publ Wkly

Pilates; Rael Isacowitz. 2nd ed Human Kinetics 2014 373 p. illustrations $22.95   **613.7**
1. Pilates method
ISBN 1450434169; 9781450434164
LC 2013019507

This guide to Pilates exercises includes information on mat work, breathing, and equipment.

Includes bibliographical references and index

Reynolds, Gretchen
The **first** 20 minutes; surprising science reveals how we can exercise better, train smarter, live longer. Gretchen Reynolds. Hudson Street Press 2012 xvii, 266 p.p   **613.7**
1. Health 2. Exercise 3. Physical fitness 4. Exercise -- Popular Works 5. Exercise -- Physiological aspects 6. Physical Fitness -- Popular Works 7. Exercise -- physiology -- Popular Works 8. Physical education and training -- Physiological aspects
ISBN 1594630933; 9781594630934
LC 2012000321

This book by Gretchen Reynolds offers "findings about the mental and physical benefits of exercise, personal stories from scientists and laypeople alike, as well as researched-based prescriptions for readers, . . . show[ing] what kind of exercise—and how much—is necessary to stay healthy, get fit, and attain a smaller jeans size. Inspired by Reynolds's . . . 'Phys Ed' column for 'The New York Times,' this book explains how exercise affects the body in distinct ways and provides the tools readers need to achieve their fitness goals, whether that's a faster 5K or staying trim." (Publisher's note)

Sivananda Yoga Vedanta Center (London, England)
★ **Yoga;** your home practice companion. DK 2010 256p il $25   **613.7**
1. Yoga 2. Physical fitness
ISBN 978-0-7566-5729-1; 0-7566-5729-6
LC 2010-291655

This is "one of the best yoga guides for all levels of experience. . . . The yogic principles of proper exercise, breathing, diet, and meditation are covered. . . . Color photo spreads of models depict easy-to-follow classic poses as well as corrective poses for physical ailments. Accompanying anatomical drawings demonstrate how yoga affects and benefits the musculoskeletal and nervous systems. . . . Readers are given all of the necessary information to start and maintain a home yoga practice. Best of all, the information is comprehensive without being overwhelming." Libr J

Taubes, Gary
Why we get fat and what to do about it. Alfred A. Knopf 2011 257p $24.95   **613.7**
1. Obesity 2. Weight loss 3. Low-carbohydrate diet
ISBN 978-0-307-27270-6; 0-307-27270-2
LC 2010-34248

The author "assures readers that overweight and obesity are not character flaws but a disorder of fat accumulation; most of the book deals with this issue in detail. This brave, paradigm-shifting man uses logic and the primary literature to unhinge the nutritional mantra of the last 80 years that an imbalance of 'calories in versus calories out' leads to weight change." Choice

Includes bibliographical references

613.9   Birth control, reproductive technology, sex hygiene, sexual techniques

Comfort, Alex, 1920-2000
The **joy** of sex; The Ultimate Revised Edition. Alex Comfort, Susan Quilliam. Rev. ed. Crown Publishers 2008 288 p. ill. (some col.) (hc) $29.95 **613.9**
1. Sex 2. Sex education 3. Sex -- Psychological aspects
ISBN 9780307452030
LC 2008017531

"An international bestseller since it was first published in 1972, Dr. Alex Comfort's classic work dared to celebrate the joy of human physical intimacy with such authority and candor that a whole generation felt empowered to enjoy sex. . . . Substantial revisions from sex expert and relationship psychologist Susan Quilliam include new information on [k]ey scientific discoveries in the fields of psychology, physiology, and sexology." (Publisher's note)

Includes bibliographical references and index

Vernacchio, Al
For goodness sex; changing the way we talk to teens about sexuality, values, and health. Al Vernacchio, with Brooke Lea Foster. HarperWave 2014 272 p. (hardback) $25.99   **613.9**
1. Sex education 2. Teenagers -- Sexual behavior 3. Sexual ethics 4. Parent and teenager 5. Sex instruction for teenagers
ISBN 0062269518; 9780062269515
LC 2014019134

This book by Al Vernacchio offers a "progressive, effective, and responsible approach to sex education for parents and teens that challenges traditional teaching models and instead embraces 21st century realities by promoting healthy sexuality, values, and body image in young people." The book contains "examples from the classroom, exercises and quizzes, and a wealth of sample discussions and crucial information." (Publisher's note)

613.907   Education

Roffman, Deborah
Talk to me first; everything you need to know to become your kids' "go-to" person about sex, by

Deborah Roffman. 1st ed. Da Capo Lifelong 2012 xii, 281 p.p (pbk. : alk. paper) $14.99 **613.907**

1. Parenting 2. Conversation 3. Sex education 4. Parent and child 5. Parent and teenager 6. Sexual ethics for teenagers 7. Sex instruction for children 8. Sex instruction for teenagers

ISBN 0738215082; 9780738215082; 9780738215877

LC 2012006068

This book presents a "guide for parents contemplating how to talk to their children about [sex]. . . . [Deborah] Roffman discusses a laundry list of commonly used statements about sex and doesn't shy away from more sensitive material such as abstinence, gay and transgendered kids, sexually transmitted infections and rape. Throughout, she emphasizes the importance of positive, direct interaction with children." (Kirkus Reviews)

Includes bibliographical references (p. 245-251) and index.

614 Forensic medicine; incidence of injuries, wounds, disease; public preventive medicine

Bass, William M.

Death's acre; inside the legendary forensic lab the Body Farm where the dead do tell tales. [by] Bill Bass and Jon Jefferson; foreword by Patricia Cornwell. Putnam 2003 304p il $24.95; pa $15 **614**

1. Forensic anthropology

ISBN 0-399-15134-6; 0-425-19832-4 pa

LC 2003-46908

"The author explains the process of decomposition and how bones give clues to identify: approximate age, sex, height, and race, all of which are needed to bring the forensic scientist one step closer to putting a name to a corpse. He describes some of the cases he has been involved with and laughs at himself when he shares stories of mistakes and assumptions. Young adults will gain insight into the forensic process and appreciate Bass's dedication to the truth and his work." SLJ

Blum, Deborah

The **poisoner's** handbook; murder and the birth of forensic medicine in Jazz Age New York. Penguin Press 2010 319p $25.95; pa $16 **614**

1. Toxicology 2. Forensic sciences 3. Poisons and poisoning

ISBN 978-1-59420-243-8; 1-59420-243-5; 978-0-14-311882-4 pa; 0-14-311882-X pa

LC 2009-26461

Chronicles the story of New York City's first forensic scientists to describe Jazz Age poisoning cases, including a family's inexplicable balding, Barnum and Bailey's Blue Man, and the crumbling bones of factory workers.

"Blum effectively balances the fast-moving detective story with a clear view of the scientific advances that her protagonists brought to the field. Caviar for true-crime fans and science buffs alike." Kirkus

Includes bibliographical references

Maples, William R.

Dead men do tell tales; [by] William R. Maples and Michael Browning. Doubleday 1994 292p il hardcover o.p. pa $15.95 **614**

1. Forensic anthropology

ISBN 0-385-47968-9 pa

LC 94-12290

Maples, a forensic anthropologist, "describes the remains (or, when burnt, cremains) presented to him, describes what he looks for, and guides us through his thinking and the search for additional clues and information. His most difficult, fascinating, and perplexing case dealt with a 1985 apparent double murder and burning, while among historic bodies, Maples dealt with those of Francisco Pizarro, Zachary Taylor, Czar Nicholas II, and Joseph Merrick, 'the Elephant Man.'" Booklist

614.4 Incidence of and public measures to prevent disease

Alcabes, Philip

Dread; how fear and fantasy have fueled epidemics from the Black Death to avian flu. PublicAffairs 2009 313p $26.95 **614.4**

1. Fear 2. Anxiety 3. Epidemics 4. Communicable diseases

ISBN 978-1-58648-618-1; 1-58648-618-7

LC 2009-00248

"Alcabes examines epidemics through history to show how they reflect the particular social and cultural anxieties of their times. From Typhoid Mary to bioterrorism, as new outbreaks are unleashed or imagined, new fears surface, new enemies are born, and new behaviors emerge." Publisher's note

"Showing how even epidemics hinge on societal attitudes and expectations, Alcabes presents an engrossing, revealing account of the relationship between progress and plague." Publ Wkly

Includes bibliographical references

Allen, Arthur

Vaccine; the controversial story of medicine's greatest lifesaver. Norton 2007 523p il $27.95 **614.4**

1. Vaccination

ISBN 0-393-05911-1; 978-0-393-05911-3

LC 2006-19480

The author "records the miracles, controversies, and tragedies that have accompanied the development of vaccines since Edward Jenner first combated smallpox in the 18th century. . . . This compelling narrative of the vaccine's undoubted triumphs and troubling challenges is highly recommended to serious readers interested in medicine and public health." Libr J

Includes bibliographical references

Encyclopedia of pestilence, pandemics, and plagues; edited by Joseph P. Byrne; foreword by Anthony S. Fauci. Greenwood Press 2008 2v il map set $199.95 **614.4**

1. Reference books 2. Epidemics -- Encyclopedias 3.

Communicable diseases -- Encyclopedias
ISBN 978-0-313-34101-4

LC 2008-19487

"A useful resource, especially for those trying to learn about the cultural issues like news reporting on epidemic disease or societal reactions to leprosy, this well-written work would be a good starting point for research." Libr J

Includes bibliographical references

Encyclopedia of plague and pestilence; from ancient times to the present. George Childs Kohn, editor. 3rd ed; Facts On File 2008 529p il map (Facts on File library of world history) $85   **614.4**
1. Reference books 2. Epidemics -- Encyclopedias
ISBN 978-0-8160-6935-4; 0-8160-6935-2

LC 2006-41296

First published 1995

This encyclopedia provides "descriptions of more than 700 epidemics, listed alphabetically by location of the outbreak. Each . . . entry includes when and where a particular epidemic began, how and why it happened, whom it affected, how it spread and ran its course, and its outcome and significance." Publisher's note

Includes bibliographical references

Garrett, Laurie
The **coming** plague; newly emerging diseases in a world out of balance. Penguin 1995 750p maps pa $20   **614.4**
1. Viruses 2. Epidemics 3. Ebola virus 4. AIDS (Disease) 5. Communicable diseases
ISBN 0-14-025091-3; 978-0-14-025091-6

First published 1994 by Farrar, Straus & Giroux

"The author demonstrates that the emerging global village means not only superior communication and trade among nations but also the deadly swap of microbes. Analyzing the spread of both familiar diseases like cholera and new viruses like Ebola, this is 'a meticulously researched, genuinely disturbing' account." N Y Times Book Rev

Includes bibliographical references

Offit, Paul A.
★ **Deadly** choices; how the anti-vaccine movement threatens us all. Basic Books 2010 270p il $27.50   **614.4**
1. Vaccination
ISBN 978-0-465-02149-9; 0-465-02149-2

LC 2010-22446

This "is a thorough dismantling of antivaccine notions and a sober warning about the resurgence of deadly childhood infections stemming from declining vaccination rates. Worried parents, especially, will find this a lucid, compelling riposte to antivaccine fear-mongering." Publ Wkly

Includes bibliographical references

Oldstone, Michael B. A.
Viruses, plagues, and history; past, present, and future. by Michael B.A. Oldstone. Rev and updat-

ed ed; Oxford University Press 2010 383p il map $17.95   **614.4**
1. Viruses 2. Epidemics 3. Communicable diseases
ISBN 978-0-19-532731-1; 0-19-532731-4

LC 2009-03550

First published 1998

Oldstone "focuses his tale on a few of the most famous viruses humanity has battled, beginning with some we have effectively defeated, such as smallpox, polio, and measles. . . . [He] then describes the fascinating viruses that have captured headlines in more recent years: Ebola and other hemorrhagic fevers, which literally turn their victims' organs to a bloody pulp; the Hantavirus outbreaks in the southwestern United States and elsewhere; mad cow disease, a frightening illness made worse by government mishandling and secrecy; and, of course, AIDS." Publisher's note

Includes bibliographical references (p. 343-369) and index. (BLCM)

Quammen, David, 1948-
★ **Spillover**; animal infections and the next human pandemic. David Quammen. W.W. Norton & Co. 2012 587 p. (hardcover) $28.95   **614.4**
1. Epidemics 2. Animals -- Diseases 3. Animals as carriers of disease
ISBN 0393066800; 9780393066807

LC 2012029300

This book by David Quammen "sums up . . . what we know about some of the world's scariest scourges: Ebola, AIDS, pandemic influenza--and what we can do to thwart the 'NBO,' the Next Big One. The author discusses zoonoses, infectious diseases that originate in animals and spread to humans. . . . They persist because they are endemic in a reservoir population through a process of mutual adaptation." (Kirkus Reviews)

Includes bibliographical references and index

The vaccine book; making the right decision for your child. Robert W. Sears. 2nd ed. Little, Brown & Co. 2011 335 p. (Sears parenting library) pbk $16   **614.4**
1. Vaccination of children 2. Immunization of children
ISBN 9780316180528; 0316180521

LC 2011293797

"The first 12 chapters discuss each vaccination in the childhood series, providing explanation of the relative disease, how the vaccine is made and points to assess a child's at-risk level when considering if the vaccine is necessary. Sears does offer guidance for those who are indecisive, offering his opinion based on clinical experience and 13 years of research taken from product inserts, pediatric reference books, articles and databases. Additional chapters illuminate more controversial aspects of the debate, such as how vaccine safety is researched and what the findings are, side effects and how to minimize them, common myths and questions." Publisher's note

Includes bibliographical references and index

Wills, Christopher

✓ **Yellow** fever, black goddess; the coevolution of people and plagues. Addison-Wesley 1996 324p il hardcover o.p. pa $16.50 **614.4**
1. Epidemics 2. Communicable diseases
ISBN 0-201-32818-6 pa

LC 96-23934

Published in the United Kingdom with title: Plagues: their origins, history, and future

The author manages "to provide a good read while weaving seamlessly between historical accounts, scientific detective stories, and personal (or family) anecdotes." New Sci

Includes bibliographical references

614.5 Incidence of and public measures to prevent specific diseases and kinds of diseases

Allen, Arthur

★ The **fantastic** laboratory of Dr. Weigl; how two brave scientists battled typhus and sabotaged the Nazis. Arthur Allen. W.W. Norton & Co. Inc 2014 400 p. illustrations, maps (hardcover) $26.95 **614.5**
1. Typhus 2. Zoologists 3. World War, 1939-1945 -- Poland 4. Scientists -- Poland -- Biography 5. Typhus fever -- Poland -- History 6. World War, 1939-1945 -- Underground movements -- Poland
ISBN 039308101X; 9780393081015

LC 2014003246

This book by Arthur Allen describes how "In the 1920s, [zoologist Rudolf] Weigl had created the first typhus vaccine . . . . giving him cover during the Nazi's violent occupation of Lviv. His lab soon flourished as a hotbed of resistance. Weigl hired otherwise doomed mathematicians, writers, doctors, and other thinkers, protecting them from atrocity. Among the scientists saved by Weigl, who was a Christian, was a gifted Jewish immunologist named Ludwik Fleck." (Publisher's note)

"Allen is unflinching in his retelling of this monstrous era, but he manages to avoid writing a depressing narrative. Instead, Weigl, Fleck and their vaccines illuminate the inherent social complexities of science and truth and reinforce the overriding good of man." Kirkus

Includes bibliographical references and index

Barry, John M.

✓ The **great** influenza; the epic story of the deadliest plague in history. Viking 2004 546p il $29.95; pa $16 **614.5**
1. Influenza
ISBN 0-670-89473-7; 0-14-303649-1 pa

LC 2003-57646

In this account of the 1918 influenza pandemic, the author "explores how the deadly confluence of biology (a swiftly mutating flu virus that can pass between animals and humans) and politics (President Wilson's all-out war effort in WWI) created conditions in which the virus thrived, killing more than 50 million worldwide and perhaps as many as 100 million in just a year." Publ Wkly

Includes bibliographical references

Cantor, Norman F.

✓ **In** the wake of the plague; the Black death and the world it made. 1st Perennial ed.; Perennial/HarperCollins 2002 245p il map pa $13.95 **614.5**
1. Plague
ISBN 0-06-001434-2

LC 2001-51819

First published 2001 by Free Press

"By animating history and demonstrating our times' connections to even as remote an event as the Black Death, Cantor's erudite excursion proves most engrossing." Booklist

Includes bibliographical references

Crosby, Molly Caldwell

✓ The **American** plague; the untold story of yellow fever, the epidemic that shaped our history. Berkley Books 2006 308p il $24.95 **614.5**
1. Yellow fever 2. Yellow fever -- History
ISBN 0-425-21202-5; 978-0-425-21202-8

LC 2006050497

This is an "account of the 1878 yellow fever epidemic." (N Y Times Book Rev) Index.

The author "offers a forceful narrative of a disease's ravages and the quest to find its cause and cure." Publ Wkly

Includes bibliographical references

Fenn, Elizabeth A.

✓ **Pox** Americana; the great smallpox epidemic of 1775-82. Hill & Wang 2001 370p $25; pa $15 **614.5**
1. Smallpox 2. United States -- History -- 1775-1783, Revolution
ISBN 0-8090-7820-1; 0-8090-7821-X pa

LC 2001-16886

The author describes the effects of smallpox during the American Revolution, including the disease's toll on Native Americans, the greater vulnerability of Americans as compared to the British, and the conditions which transmitted the disease.

"Noteworthy as scholarship, Fenn's insightful, readable narrative is a welcome addition to literature about the revolutionary period." Booklist

Includes bibliographical references

Foege, William F.

House on fire; the fight to eradicate smallpox. University of California Press/Milbank Memorial Fund 2011 218p il map (California/Milbank books on health and the public) $29.95 **614.5**
1. Smallpox
ISBN 978-0-520-26836-4

LC 2010-41703

"Foege's emphasis on the personal does enliven the myriad statistics he presents. But he seems a reluctant memoirist, uncomfortable with the spotlight, and as a consequence, the story gets bogged down, at times, by Foege's need to mention (and compliment) every colleague with whom he ever collaborated. Still, though Foege is anything but self-congratulatory, it is impossible to read 'House on Fire' without admiring him and feeling grateful for the gift he gave to mankind." Boston Globe

Includes bibliographical references

Halperin, Daniel

Tinderbox; How the West Sparked the AIDS Epidemic and How the World Can Finally Overcome It. Craig Timberg and Daniel Halperin. Penguin Press HC 2012 421 p. ill. (hardback) $29.95 **614.5**

1. AIDS (Disease) 2. Communicable diseases -- History 3. Epidemiology -- Africa -- History 4. Pakistan -- History 5. HIV Infections -- etiology -- Africa 6. HIV Infections -- epidemiology -- Africa

ISBN 159420327X; 9781594203275

LC 2011040206

It was the authors' intent to "trace the history, growth and spread of HIV and present what will in the minds of many be a controversial approach to addressing the disease. . . . The key factor in the spread of the disease was the expansion of European colonialism in Africa. . . . [Craig] Timberg and [Daniel] Halperin examine how to confront it." (Kirkus Reviews)

Includes bibliographical references and index.

Holt, Nathalia

Cured; how the Berlin patients defeated HIV and forever changed medical science. Nathalia Holt. Dutton, published by the Penguin Group 2014 336 p. $27.95 **614.5**

1. Gene therapy 2. HIV infections 3. Gene therapy -- Germany -- Berlin -- History 4. HIV infections -- Treatment -- Germany -- Berlin

ISBN 0525953922; 9780525953920

LC 2013037181

In this book, HIV researcher Nathalia Holt "offers increasing hope for a cure by spotlighting the two male 'Berlin Patients' . . . who chemically bombarded and expunged the HIV virus from their bodies. The author tracks the enduring histories of these men--German-born Christian Hahn and Timothy Brown, an American. . . . Holt also profiles HIV specialists Heiko Jessen, Bruce Walker and David Ho." (Kirkus Reviews)

"[I]n this accessible and fascinating account, Holt . . . juggles genetic mysteries, research perils, the agonies of these two reserved and sensitive men diagnosed with what was considered a death sentence, and the dogged doctors who successfully treated them during the later stages of AIDS epidemic." Pub Wkly

Includes bibliographical references

Johnson, Steven

The ghost map; the story of London's most terrifying epidemic--and how it changed science, cities, and the modern world. Riverhead 2006 299p il map $26.95 **614.5**

1. Cholera 2. Physicians 3. Writers on medicine

ISBN 1-59448-925-4; 978-1-59448-925-9

LC 2006-23114

"From Snow's discovery of patient zero to Johnson's compelling argument for and celebration of cities, this makes for an illuminating and satisfying read." Publ Wkly

Includes bibliographical references

Kelly, John

The **great** mortality; an intimate history of the Black Death, the most devastating plague of all time. HarperCollins Publishers 2005 364p hardcover o.p. pa $14.95 **614.5**

1. Plague

ISBN 0-06-000692-7; 0-06-000693-5 pa

LC 2004-54213

"Western Europe is the primary focus of Kelly's compact history, which is 'intimate' in that it highlights many particular persons' passages through the crucible years, 1348-49. . . . Kelly proceeds chronologically, beginning with the plague's prehistory in north central Asia and its spread through China before empire-building Mongols brought it west. . . . This sweeping, viscerally exciting book contributes to a literature of perpetual fascination: the chronicles of pestilence." Booklist

Includes bibliographical references

Kolata, Gina

★ **Flu**; the story of the great influenza pandemic of 1918 and the search for the virus that caused it. Simon & Schuster 2001 330p il pa $15 **614.5**

1. Influenza 2. Epidemiology 3. Influenza -- History -- 20th century

ISBN 0-7432-0398-4; 978-0-7432-0398-2

LC 00-64861

First published 1999 by Farrar, Straus & Giroux

"Clearly explaining both the science and the social toll of the pandemic, Kolata writes an admirable history and soberly spells out how the U.S. government is prepared—or unprepared—for a similar public health threat today." Publ Wkly

Includes bibliographical references

Murphy, Monica, 1970-

Rabid; a cultural history of the world's most diabolical virus. Bill Wasik and Monica Murphy. Viking 2012 240 p. $25.95 **614.5**

1. Rabies 2. Diseases in literature 3. Communicable diseases -- History 4. Rabies -- Treatment -- History 5. Rabies -- Epidemiology -- History

ISBN 0670023736; 9780670023738

LC 2011043903

This book "chart[s] four thousand years in the history, science, and cultural mythology of rabies. . . . A disease that spreads avidly from animals to humans, rabies has served throughout history as a symbol of savage madness, of inhuman possession. And today, its history can help shed light on the wave of emerging diseases, from AIDS to SARS to avian flu, that we now know to originate in animal populations." (Publisher's note)

Oshinsky, David M.

★ **Polio**; an American story. Oxford University Press 2005 342p il $30; pa $16.95 **614.5**

1. Poliomyelitis vaccine

ISBN 0-19-515294-8; 0-19-530714-3 pa

LC 2004-25249

This book "is a rich and illuminating analysis that convincingly grounds the ways and means of modern American research in the response to polio." N Y Times Book Rev
Includes bibliographical references

Pisani, Elizabeth
The **wisdom** of whores; bureaucrats, brothels, and the business of AIDS. W. W. Norton & Co. 2008 372p $25.95   **614.5**
1. Sexual behavior 2. AIDS (Disease) -- Prevention
ISBN 978-0-393-06662-3; 0-393-06662-2
LC 2007-51396
The author discusses various aspects of international AIDS prevention.
This is "an eye-opening look at who gets AIDS how, when and where. . . . Delivers a strong, well-told and believable message." Kirkus
Includes bibliographical references

Preston, Richard
The **hot** zone. Random House 1994 300p hardcover o.p. pa $14   **614.5**
1. Ebola virus 2. Animal experimentation
ISBN 0-385-49522-6 pa
LC 94-13415
"Ebola, a lethal virus that slumbers in an unknown host somewhere in the rain forest, sneaked into the United States in 1989 in a shipment of primates that ended up in a monkey house in Reston, Virginia. This virus jumps between species easily, and takes only weeks to kill its victim, with gory hemorrhaging from various orifices. Preston tells the suspenseful tale of its detection, and gives vivid life to the members of the SWAT team that, for eighteen bio-hazardous days, combatted the strain now known as Ebola Reston." New Yorker

Rhodes, Richard
Deadly feasts; tracking the secrets of a terrifying new plague. Simon & Schuster 1997 259p il hardcover o.p. pa $13   **614.5**
1. Prion diseases
ISBN 0-684-84425-7 pa
LC 97-320
"Rhodes offers the first popular documentation of a disaster with profound implications." Booklist

Shah, Sonia
The **fever**; how malaria has ruled humankind for 500,000 years. Sarah Crichton Books/Farrar, Straus, and Giroux 2010 307p $26   **614.5**
1. Malaria 2. Malaria -- History
ISBN 0-374-23001-3; 978-0-374-23001-2
LC 2010-2374
This is a chronicle of the illness and its influence on human lives. (Publisher's note) Index.
"This fascinating, mordant pop-sci account tells us why malaria is one of the world's greatest scourges, killing a million people every year and debilitating another 300 million, and why we have remained complacent about it. . . . [This] is an absorbing account of human ingenuity and progress, and of their heartbreaking limitations." Publ Wkly
Includes bibliographical references

Spurlock, Morgan
Don't eat this book; fast food and the supersizing of America. G. P. Putnam's Sons 2005 308p hardcover o.p. pa $14   **614.5**
1. Restaurants 2. Food industry 3. Convenience foods
ISBN 0-399-15260-1; 0-425-21023-5 pa
LC 2005-43196
The author "describes America's obesity epidemic, its relation to the fast food industry, the industry's cozy relations to U.S. government agencies and how the problem is spreading worldwide. . . . His book is a powerful tool in his rip-roaring campaign to turn around America's love-hate relationship with fast food." Publ Wkly
Includes bibliographical references

Tayman, John
★ The **Colony**; John Tayman. Scribner 2006 421p il maps $27.50   **614.5**
1. Leprosy 2. Hawaii -- History
ISBN 0-7432-3300-X
LC 2005-47767
This is a "history of the leper colony at the Hawaiian island Molokai. . . . Tayman's crisp, flowing writing and inclusion of personal stories and details make this an utterly engrossing look at a heartbreaking chapter in Hawaiian history." Booklist

615   Pharmacology and therapeutics

Dasgupta, Amitava
The **science** of drinking; how alcohol affects your body and mind. Rowman & Littlefield Publishers 2011 265p il $34.95; ebook $34.95   **615**
1. Drinking of alcoholic beverages 2. Alcohol -- Physiological effect
ISBN 978-1-4422-0409-6; 978-1-4422-0411-9 ebook
LC 2010-51613
The author "outlines what constitutes healthy drinking and its attendant health benefits, offers advice on how to drink responsibly, and provides insight into just how alcohol works on the brain and the body." Publisher's note
Includes bibliographical references

Hager, Thomas
The **demon** under the microscope; from battlefield hospitals to Nazi labs, one doctor's heroic search for the world's first miracle drug. Harmony Books 2006 340p $24.95   **615**
1. Sulfonamides 2. Microbiologists 3. Writers on science 4. Nobel laureates for physiology or medicine
ISBN 1-4000-8213-7; 978-1-4000-8213-1
LC 2006-4510
The author "narrates the story of the race [by doctors such as Gerhard Domagk] to find the 'magic bullet' to eliminate diseases such as pneumonia, childbed fever, and gonorrhea. . . . Hager connects early innovations in medicine to the fortuitous and intuitive leaps that allowed early 20th-century researchers to create sulfa, the first antibiotic. . . . One is left

with a sense of gratitude for the relative safety of modern medical practices." Libr J

Includes bibliographical references

The **Merck** index; an encyclopedia of chemicals, drugs, and biologicals. Maryadele J. O'Neil, editor; Patricia E. Heckelman, senior associate editor; Cherie B. Koch, associate editor; Kristin J. Roman, assistant editor; Catherine M. Kenny, editorial assistant; Maryann R. D'Arecca, administrative assistant. 14th ed.; Merck 2006 various paging il $125 **615**
1. Reference books 2. Drugs -- Dictionaries 3. Materia medica -- Dictionaries
ISBN 0-911910-00-X; 978-0-911910-00-1
First published 1889. Periodically revised
"Technical descriptions of the preparation, properties, uses, commercial names, and toxicity of drugs and medicines." N Y Public Libr Book of How & Where to Look It Up

Physicians' Desk Reference 2015; 69th ed Physicians Desk Reference Inc 2014 2500 p. il $97.95 **615**
1. Drugs -- Dictionaries
ISBN 1563638312; 9781563638312
Annual. First published 1947. Title varies
"Latest available information intended for physicians on over 2,000 products. Covers dosage, contraindications, precautions, side effects, and undesirable interactions. The information is furnished by the manufacturers of the various products. Product identification in color." N Y Public Libr Book of How & Where to Look It Up

Tucker, Holly
Blood work; a tale of medicine and murder in the scientific revolution. W.W. Norton 2011 xxix, 304p il $25.95 **615**
1. Homicide 2. Physicians 3. Human experimentation in medicine 4. Science -- History 5. Blood -- Transfusion
ISBN 978-0-393-07055-2; 0-393-07055-7
LC 2010-46340
This is "more than a simple medical history; it's a true crime picaresque, with Denis as a roguish, ethically-challenged antihero beset on all sides by intrigue and villainy. It's also a provocative exploration of the often strained relationship between science and the morality of the society it seeks to enlighten." PopMatters
Includes bibliographical references

615.107 Research

Goldacre, Ben
Bad Pharma; How Drug Companies Mislead Doctors and Harm Patients. Ben Goldacre. Faber & Faber 2013 448 p. $28 **615.107**
1. Drug industry 2. Drugs -- Testing 3. Drugs --Testing 4. Drugs --Quality control 5. Clinical trials --Moral and ethical aspects 6. Drugs --Testing --Moral and ethical

aspects 7. Pharmaceutical industry --Moral and ethical aspects
ISBN 0865478007; 9780865478008
LC 2012038902
In this book, physician Ben Goldacre "reveals how pharmaceutical companies mislead doctors and hurt patients. They 'sponsor' trials, which tend to yield favorable results, while negative results often remain unreported. He also reports that drug companies spend twice as much on marketing and advertising as on researching and developing new drugs." (Booklist)
Includes bibliographical references and index.

615.5 Therapeutics

Bausell, R. Barker
Snake oil science; the truth about complementary and alternative medicine. Oxford University Press 2007 324p il $24.95 **615.5**
1. Alternative medicine
ISBN 978-0-19-531368-0; 0-19-531368-2
LC 2007-10217
The author builds a "case against CAM, beginning with a look at the history of CAMs and placebos, then the 'poorly trained scientists' and flawed studies (among more than 300 analyzed for this book) that have historically supported CAM's efficacy. . . . Entertaining and informative, with plenty of diverting anecdotal examples, Bausell offers non-professionals and pros a thorough look at the science on CAM, along with a complementary lesson in the methods of good medical research." Publ Wkly
Includes bibliographical references

Bruce, Debra Fulghum
Miracle touch; a complete guide to hands-on therapies that have the amazing ability to heal. {by} Debra Fulghum Bruce; foreword by Dolores Krieger. Three Rivers Press 2003 xxi, 216p pa $12.95 **615.5**
1. Touch 2. Alternative medicine
ISBN 0-609-80734-X
LC 2002-7443
The author covers "the various types of TT {Therapeutic Touch}, including acupuncture and acupressure, massage, reflexology, and Reiki. For each therapy, they include how it originated, how it works, what it can treat, how therapists are trained and/or certified, and research or case studies. . . . This practical, well-written guide is recommended for most alternative health and consumer health collections." Libr J
Includes bibliographical references

The **encyclopedia** of natural medicine; Michael T. Murray, Joseph E. Pizzorno. 3rd ed Atria Books 2012 x, 1219 p.p ill. (trade paper : alk. paper) $29.99 **615.5**
1. Naturopathy -- Encyclopedias
ISBN 1451663005; 9781451663006; 9781451663013; 9781451687347
LC 2012023268
First published 1991
The authors "present an evidence-based approach to wellness, based on firm scientific findings. They aim to dis-

pel the notion that natural medicine isn't 'real medicine,' offering examples and studies that show the efficacy of a holistic approach to patient care."

Includes bibliographical references and index

The **Gale** encyclopedia of alternative medicine; Laurie J. Fundukian, editor. 4th ed Gale / Cengage Learning 2014 2848 p. 4v (set : hbk. : alk. paper) $714   **615.5**
1. Reference books 2. Internal Medicine -- Encyclopedias 3. Complementary Therapies -- Encyclopedias -- English
ISBN 1573027308; 9781573027304

LC 2013045439

"The four volumes contain more than 800 entries, approximately 400 color images, and many informative illustrations and charts pertaining to herbs and flowers, therapies and procedures, nutrition, and diseases and conditions. More than 50 new entries were added" for the fourth edition. (Publisher's note)

Includes bibliographical references and index

Speid, Lorna
Clinical trials; what patients and healthy volunteers need to know. Oxford University Press 2010 186p il pa $19.95   **615.5**
1. Drugs -- Testing
ISBN 978-0-19-973416-0

LC 2010-9154

"If informed consent is the gold standard for clinical-trial participants, this book raises the bar to become the platinum standard. A must-have for anyone—healthy or sick—who is considering volunteering." Booklist

Includes bibliographical references

615.7 Pharmacokinetics

Blaser, Martin J.
★ **Missing** microbes; how the overuse of antibiotics is fueling our modern plagues. Dr. Martin Blaser. Henry Holt & Co. 2014 288 p. illustrations (hardback) $28   **615.7**
1. Bacteria 2. Antibiotics 3. Drug resistance in microorganisms
ISBN 0805098100; 9780805098105; 9780805098112

LC 2013042578

"In 'Missing Microbes,' Dr. Martin Blaser invites us into the wilds of the human microbiome where for hundreds of thousands of years bacterial and human cells have existed in a peaceful symbiosis that is responsible for the health and equilibrium of our body. . . . Taking us into both the lab and deep into the fields where these troubling effects can be witnessed firsthand, Blaser . . . provides cutting edge evidence for the adverse effects of antibiotics." (Publisher's note)

A "masterful work of preventive health and superb science writing." Booklist

Includes bibliographical references (pages 221-256) and index

Buzzed; The Straight Facts About the Most Used and Abused Drugs From Alcohol to Ecstasy. by

Cynthia Kuhn, Scott Swartzwelder, Wilkie Wilson with Leigh Heather Wilson and Jeremy Foster. 4th edition W W Norton & Co Inc 2014 385 p. pbk $19.95   **615.7**
1. Drugs 2. Drug abuse
ISBN 0393344517; 9780393344516

"[S]urveys the most used and abused drugs from caffeine to heroin to methamphetamine. In both quick-reference summaries and in-depth analysis, it reports on how these drugs enter the body, how they manipulate the brain, their short-term and long-term effects, the different highs they produce, and the circumstances in which they can be deadly." Publisher's note

Includes bibliographical references and index

Newton, David E.
Marijuana; a reference handbook. David E. Newton. ABC-CLIO 2013 330 p. (Contemporary world issues) (alk. paper) $58   **615.7**
1. Marijuana 2. Drug legalization 3. Cannabis 4. Government Regulation 5. Cannabinoids -- Therapeutic use 6. Marijuana Smoking -- Legislation & jurisprudence
ISBN 1610691490; 9781610691499; 9781610691505

LC 2012036276

This book, part of the Contemporary World Issues series, "examines the production, consumption, and regulation of the Cannabis plant; the plant's commercial, recreational, medicinal, and religious applications; and the various attempts to regulate the production and consumption of marijuana in the United States and other parts of the world. Additionally, it provides . . . the arguments for and against its legalization or decriminalization." (Publisher's note)

Includes bibliographical references and index

615.8 Specific therapies and kinds of therapies

Quest, Penelope
Reiki for life; the complete guide to reiki practice for levels 1, 2 & 3. Jeremy P. Tarcher/Penguin 2010 310p il pa $16.95   **615.8**
1. Reiki (Healing system)
ISBN 978-1-58542-790-1

LC 2009-51213

This book covers "basic routines, details about the power and potential of each level, special techniques for enhancing Reiki practice, and . . . direction on the use of Reiki toward spiritual growth. Penelope Quest also compares the origins and development of Reiki in the West and the East, revealing methods specific to the original Japanese Reiki tradition." Publisher's note

Includes bibliographical references

615.9 Toxicology

Booth, Michael
Eating dangerously; why the government can't keep your food safe-- and how you can. Michael Booth and Jennifer Brown. Rowman & Littlefield

Publishers, Inc. 2013 200 p. (cloth : alk. paper) $24.95 **615.9**

1. Food supply 2. Food industry 3. Food poisoning 4. Food -- Safety measures 5. Food adulteration and inspection -- Government policy -- United States
ISBN 1442222662; 9781442222663

LC 2013037125

This book, by Michael Booth and Jennifer Brown, "explains to the American consumer how their food system works--and more importantly how it doesn't work. It also dishes up course after course of useful, friendly advice gleaned from the cutting-edge laboratories, kitchens and courtrooms where the national food system is taking new shape. Anyone interested in knowing more about how their food makes it from field and farm to store and table will want the inside scoop." (Publisher's note)

An "eye-opening exposé of foods, grocery shopping, and government oversight in America." Booklist

Includes bibliographical references and index

Fagin, Dan

Toxic deception; how the chemical industry manipulates science, bends the law, and endangers your health. [by] Dan Fagin, Marianne Lavelle, and the Center for Public Integrity. Common Courage Press 1999 xxv, 271p pa $17.95 **615.9**

1. Chemicals 2. Chemical industry
ISBN 1-56751-162-7

LC 99-13742

First published 1996 by Carol Pub. Group

This work examines "the regulatory foundations of four suspect chemicals—atrazine, alachor, formaldehyde, and perchloroethylene—and the chemical industry's role in the design and calculation of risk assessments. . . . This well-researched expose is recommended." Libr J

Includes bibliographical references

Smith, Rick

Slow death by rubber duck; the secret danger of everyday things. [by] Rick Smith, Bruce Lourie; with Sarah Dopp. Counterpoint 2009 328p il $25 **615.9**

1. Pollution 2. Toxicology 3. Environmental health
ISBN 978-1-58243-567-1

"The authors manage to stay this side of apocalyptic without sounding flippant. Not only is the book scary, it's hard to put down." Quill Quire

Includes bibliographical references

616 Diseases

Bacci, Ingrid

Effortless pain relief; a guide to self-healing from chronic pain. Free Press 2005 255p $24 **616**

1. Chronic pain
ISBN 0-7432-6075-9

LC 2005-295415

This book presents an "explanation of how stress creates chronic pain, along with . . . self-help techniques for reducing and even eliminating pain." Publisher's note

Biddle, Wayne

A **field** guide to germs; 2nd Anchor Books ed; Anchor Bks. (NY) 2002 209p il pa $13.95 **616**

1. Microbiology 2. Germ theory of disease
ISBN 1-400-03051-X

LC 2002-511927

First published 1995 by Holt & Co.

"Relaying essential information about the 100 most prevalent, powerful, or literarily famous microbiological malefactors in dictionary-encyclopedia style, Biddle injects social and political history into the exposition to provide fuller understanding of germs, their roles in society, their histories, and their current statuses. . . . Eminently entertaining, the book yet has the serious purpose of showing how concerns other than science and the relief of human suffering have affected the course of medical history." Booklist {review of 1995 edition}

Includes bibliographical references

Collins, Francis S.

The **language** of life; DNA and the revolution in personalized medicine. Harper 2010 332p il $26.99 **616**

1. Medical genetics 2. Genetic screening
ISBN 978-0-06-173317-8; 0-06-173317-2

LC 2009-25832

"This readable book . . . can help anyone understand more about how genetics and our DNA contribute to our health." Libr J

Includes bibliographical references

Crawford, Dorothy H.

Virus Hunt; The Search for the Origin of HIV/AIDS. by Dorothy H. Crawford. Oxford University Press 2013 224 p. (hardcover) $27.95 **616**

1. Epidemiology 2. AIDS (Disease)
ISBN 0199641145; 9780199641147

In this book, "virologist Dorothy H. Crawford takes us inside . . . the search for the origin of AIDS. . . . Crawford follows the trail of the virus back to its roots deep in Africa. We track wild monkeys and apes through the jungle . . . to discover from which primates HIV first jumped to our species. . . . We then time travel back to colonial Africa around the turn of the 20th century, when the virus first spread to humans." (Publisher's note)

Current Medical Diagnosis & Treatment 2015; [edited by] Stephen J. McPhee, Maxine A. Papadakis; associate editor Michael W. Rabow. McGraw-Hill 2014 1887 p. ill. $85 **616**

1. Medicine -- Handbooks, manuals, etc.
ISBN 0071824863; 9780071824866

Annual. First published 1974 as a successor to Current diagnosis & treatment

"Provides concise information on the diagnosis and treatment of diseases and disorders for medical practitioners. Uses common medical terminology, but is generally understandable to the layperson." N Y Public Libr Book of How & Where to Look It Up

Gawande, Atul

Better; a surgeon's notes on performance. Metropolitan 2007 273p $24 **616**

1. Medicine 2. Medical ethics

ISBN 978-0-8050-8211-1; 0-8050-8211-5

LC 2006-46962

"Mostly, and repeatedly, the question Gawande pose at the heart of each of his essays is deceptively straightforward and can-do: How do we get it right, or barring that, just an ioat better? . . . Gawande is unassuming in every way, and yet his prose is infused with steadfast determination and hope." Boston Globe

Groopman, Jerome E.

The **anatomy** of hope; how people prevail in the face of illness. [by] Jerome Groopman. Random House 2004 248p hardcover o.p. pa $14.95 **616**

1. Hope 2. Physician-patient relationship

ISBN 0-375-50638-1; 0-375-75775-9 pa

LC 2003-46692

The author "discovered that hope could actually cause physiological change, blocking pain and improving respiratory, circulatory, and motor function. He shares personal experiences from his own life and his patients' case histories that illustrate the power and importance of hope. . . . An excellent narrative for public libraries." Libr J

Includes bibliographical references

Harrington, Anne

The **cure** within; a history of mind-body medicine. W.W. Norton 2008 336p il $25.95 **616**

1. Mind and body 2. Mental healing 3. Psychosomatic medicine

ISBN 978-0-393-06563-3; 0-393-06563-4

LC 2007-30906

This is a history of alternative and complementary medicine.

The author "has produced a book that desperately needed to be written." N Y Times Book Rev

Includes bibliographical references (p. 299-321)

Moalem, Sharon

Survival of the sickest; a medical maverick discovers why we need disease. [by] Sharon Moalem, with Jonathan Prince. William Morrow 2007 267p $25.95 **616**

1. Diseases 2. Genetics 3. Evolution 4. Natural selection

ISBN 978-0-06-088965-4; 0-06-088965-9

LC 2006-50128

The author "uses numerous examples to show how analyzing history might help explain why a certain genetic trait that seems useless—even harmful—to us now made perfect sense in our ancestors' environment. He also introduces such recent research topics as host manipulation, noncoding DNA, and epigenetics. The particularly coherent writing style makes complex ideas accessible to people without a science background. With the book's emphasis on evolution's goals of survival and reproduction, readers will gain insights into why evolution may have selected for certain traits and why having that insight may better our lives." Libr J

Parks, Tim

Teach us to sit still; a skeptic's search for health and healing. Rodale Books 2011 322p il **616**

1. Chronic pain 2. Mind and body

ISBN 1609611586; 9781609611583

LC 2011-08512

First published 2010 in the United Kingdom

"In a hallmark of conversion narratives, the original mania reproduces itself as a mirror image: in the old days, hyperbolically anxious; in the new, hyperbolically anxious to enumerate the old anxiety. To his credit, Parks doesn't pretend otherwise. Moreover, his personal account, never preachy, engages some serious matters about contemporary life, notably what it's like to be a patient, as nearly all of us, sooner or later, are or will be." N Y Times Book Rev

Spector, Tim

Identically Different. Weidenfeld & Nicolson 2012 338 p. $26.95 **616**

1. Twins 2. Epigenetics

ISBN 0297866311; 146830660X; 9780297866312; 9781468306606

This book by genetic epidemiologist Tim Spector looks at genes and epigenetics. Specifically, it considers "the concept of 'acquired inheritance,' whereby environmental, hormonal, or other external stimuli modify one's genetic makeup. Perhaps the most interesting consequence of this is that such an altered blueprint can then be passed on to future generations. But drastic changes can occur even within one's own lifetime." (Publishers Weekly)

Twelve breaths a minute; end-of-life essays. edited by Lee Gutkind; foreword by Karen Wolk Feinstein; introduction by Francine Prose. Southern Methodist University Press 2011 267p (Medical humanities) $23.95 **616**

1. Death 2. Caregivers 3. Terminal care 4. Terminally ill

ISBN 978-0-87074-571-3; 0-87074-571-9

LC 2010-45874

"A collection of creative nonfiction essays about end-of-life issues. How depressing, a friend said. I thought the same thing until I read one and then another and then another. Sad, yes. But depressing? No. 'Twelve Breaths a Minute,' a book commissioned by the Jewish Healthcare Foundation as part of its ongoing end-of-life initiative, is uplifting. The 23 essays, chosen from among more than 400 submissions, also are beautifully written. The writers are the sons, daughters and parents who have had to deal with the deaths of family, as well as members of the medical profession who have had to balance the oath to save lives with the desires of a patient to die without extraordinary medical measures. Sometimes they are both." Pittsburgh Post-Gazette

Van Tilburg, Christopher

Mountain rescue doctor; wilderness medicine in the extremes of nature. St. Martin's Press 2007 293p il hardcover o.p. pa $14.95 **616**

1. Rescue work 2. Mountaineering

ISBN 978-0-312-35887-7; 0-312-35887-3; 978-0-312-35888-4 pa; 0-312-35888-1 pa

LC 2007-28304

The author "is a member of the Hood River Crag Rats, the oldest search-and-rescue (S&R) team in the United States. Both adults and teens will relish his vivid recountings of efforts to rescue sports enthusiasts who got lost or injured in the mountains." Libr J

616.02   Special topics of diseases

Anthes, Emily

Frankenstein's cat; cuddling up to biotech's brave new beasts. Emily Anthes. 1st ed. Scientific American / Farrar, Straus and Giroux 2013 256 p. (hardcover) $26   **616.02**
>   1. Biotechnology 2. Transgenic animals
>   ISBN 0374158592; 9780374158590
>   LC 2012029045

This book, by Emily Anthes, "takes us from petri dish to pet store as she explores how biotechnology is shaping the future of our furry and feathered friends. . . . [Visiting] a 'frozen zoo' where scientists are storing DNA from the planet's most exotic creatures, she discovers how we can use cloning to protect endangered species, craft prosthetics to save injured animals, and employ genetic engineering to supply farms with disease-resistant livestock." (Publisher's note)

"[A] quick, often surprising review of current advances, giving accessible treatment to a weighty subject and employing clear descriptions of complex science." Booklist

Includes bibliographical references and index.

Brody, Jane E.

Jane Brody's guide to the great beyond; a practical primer to help you and your loved ones prepare medically, legally, and emotionally for the end of life. [by] Jane Brody. Random House 2009 xxiv, 287p il $26   **616.02**
>   1. Death 2. Terminal care 3. Terminally ill
>   ISBN 978-1-4000-6654-4
>   LC 2008-16583

"With bulleted lists itemizing what needs to be done and how to do it, short portraits and anecdotes throughout, Brody covers the importance of preparation; the necessity of an advance directive and why a living will is not enough; funeral plans; living with a bad prognosis and dealing with uncertainty; caregiving; hospice; communicating with doctors; assisted dying; organ donation and autopsy; and legacies. An instructive, inspiring and reassuring work full of compassion and humor (along with several cartoons from various New Yorker illustrators), this volume belongs on every family's bookshelf." Publ Wkly

Butler, Katy

Knocking on Heaven's Door; the path to a better way of death. Katy Butler. Simon & Schuster 2013 336 p. illustrations $25   **616.02**
>   1. Death 2. Right to die 3. Terminal care -- Decision making 4. Euthanasia -- Moral and ethical aspects 5. Adult children of aging parents -- Family relationships
>   ISBN 1451641974; 9781451641974
>   LC 2013017659

In this book, "when doctors refused to disable the pacemaker that caused her eighty-four-year-old father's heart to outlive his brain, Katy Butler . . . embarked on a quest to understand why modern medicine was depriving him of a humane, timely death. After his lingering death, Katy's mother, nearly broken by years of nonstop caregiving, defied her doctors, refused open-heart surgery, and insisted on facing death the old-fashioned way: bravely, lucidly, and head on." (Publisher's note)

"With candidness and reverence, Butler examines one of the most challenging questions a child may face: how to let a parent die with dignity and integrity when the body has stopped functioning." Kirkus

Includes bibliographical references

Gibney, Mike

Something to chew on; challenging controversies in food and health. Mike Gibney. University College Dublin Press 2012 xiv, 177 p.p (paperback) $38.95   **616.02**
>   1. Food 2. Nutrition 3. Food supply 4. Public health 5. Genetic engineering
>   ISBN 1906359679; 9781906359676
>   LC 2012405919

This book, by Mike Gibney, discusses the scientific perspective on many of "the worldwide controversies dominating the popular press in relation to the modern food chain. It deals with the topics of organic food, GM foods, obesity, growing old, the integrity of food research, global warming, global malnutrition, consumer perception of food-borne risk, our gut bacteria, and how nutrition during pregnancy primes us for health in later life." (Publisher's note)

Norton, Trevor

Smoking ears and screaming teeth; a celebration of scientific eccentricity and self-experimentation. Pegasus Books 2011 404p il $24.95   **616.02**
>   1. Eccentrics and eccentricities 2. Human experimentation in medicine 3. Medicine -- Research
>   ISBN 978-1-60598-254-0

"Though some chapters (e.g., 'A Diet of Worms') shouldn't be read over breakfast, Norton conveys more than just a carnival of the grotesque; he also introduces forgotten and under-appreciated scientists whose curious curiosity saved lives." Kirkus

Includes bibliographical references

Preston, Richard

Panic in level 4; cannibals, killer viruses, and other journeys to the edge of science. Random House 2008 xli, 188p il $26; pa $15   **616.02**
>   1. Science 2. Medicine
>   ISBN 978-1-4000-6490-8; 1-4000-6490-2; 978-0-8129-7560-4 pa; 0-8129-7560-X pa
>   LC 2007-41770

A collection of the author's science essays, all first published in the New Yorker.

"Whether hanging out with genetics entrepreneur J. Craig Venter, the restorers of the Cloisters' famous unicorn tapestries, or the sufferers of Lesch-Nyhan syndrome, Preston personifies perceptiveness and empathy in journalism." Booklist

616.07   Pathology

Biss, Eula

★ **On** immunity; an inoculation. Eula Biss. Graywolf Press 2014 216 p. (alk. paper) $24 **616.07**
1. Immunity 2. Immunization
ISBN 1555976891; 9781555976897

LC 2014935701

In this book, author Eula Biss "addresses a chronic condition of fear--fear of the government, the medical establishment, and what is in your child's air, food, mattress, medicine, and vaccines. She finds that you cannot immunize your child, or yourself, from the world. . . . Biss investigates the metaphors and myths surrounding our conception of immunity and its implications for the individual and the social body." (Publisher's note)

Includes bibliographical references

Bracken, Michael B.

Risk, chance, and causation; investigating the origins and treatment of disease. Michael B. Bracken. Yale University Press 2013 xiii, 330 p.p illustrations (cloth : alk. paper) $60 **616.07**
1. Diseases 2. Therapeutics 3. Risk Factors 4. Disease -- Etiology
ISBN 0300188846; 9780300188844

LC 2012045173

In this book, epidemiologist Michael B. Bracken "explains the scientific techniques used to discover if a drug is efficacious or if a mysterious cluster of illnesses can be explained in terms of an apparently obvious environmental phenomenon. Understanding cause and effect can be extremely complex for the scientifically trained." (Choice)

"This is a very successful book, elucidating technical information for concerned citizens." Choice

Includes bibliographical references (p. 303-304) and index

Mosby's diagnostic and laboratory test reference; Kathleen Deska Pagana, Timothy J. Pagana. 12th edition Elsevier/Mosby 2014 1088 p. il pbk $54.95 **616.07**
1. Nursing 2. Diagnosis 3. Reference books 4. Diagnosis, Laboratory -- Handbooks, manuals, etc
ISBN 9780323225762
First published 1992. Frequently revised

"Concise test entries are arranged alphabetically and reflect the latest in research and diagnostic testing. Each test entry includes vital information such as type of test, alternate or abbreviated test names, test explanation, normal and abnormal findings, possible critical values, contraindications, potential complications, interfering factors, and patient care. To simplify lookup, related tests are cross-referenced." Publisher's note

Includes bibliographical references and index

Nuland, Sherwin B.

How we die; reflections on life's final chapter. Knopf 1994 278p hardcover o.p. pa $14 **616.07**
1. Death
ISBN 0-679-74244-1 pa

LC 93-24590

"Nuland is one of those rare physicians who know a great deal about a great deal, not only medicine but also its history and, beyond that, literature and the humanities." Commentary

Sanders, Lisa

Every patient tells a story; medical mysteries and the art of diagnosis. Broadway 2009 xxvii, 276p $25 **616.07**
1. Diagnosis
ISBN 978-0-7679-2246-3; 0-7679-2246-8

LC 2008-41478

The author "discusses how doctors deal with diagnostic dilemmas. . . . Sanders not only collects difficult cases, she reflects on what each means for both patient and struggling physician. . . . Readers who enjoy dramatic stories of doctors fighting disease will get their fill, and they will also encounter thoughtful essays on how doctors think and go about their work, and how they might do it better." Publ Wkly

Includes bibliographical references

Zuk, M.

Riddled with life; friendly worms, ladybug sex, and the parasites that make us who we are. Harcourt 2007 328p il $25 **616.07**
1. Diseases 2. Parasites 3. Pathology 4. Human ecology 5. Adaptation (Biology)
ISBN 978-0-15-101225-1; 0-15-101225-3

LC 2006-28642

"Zuk has an amazing gift for turning experiments and facts into stories. . . . She is urging the public to take a new look at disease, though it's one that's well supported by the research. There are moments where she's speculating ahead of the science a bit, but those moments are clearly marked. Riddled with Life will change the way you look at public and private health." PopMatters

Includes bibliographical references

616.2   Diseases of respiratory system

Ackerman, Jennifer

Ah -choo! the uncommon life of your common cold. Twelve 2010 245p $22.99 **616.2**
1. Cold (Disease)
ISBN 978-0-446-54115-2; 978-0-446-57401-3 ebook

LC 2010-4794

The author "parses the variety and durability of the cold, its wellknown miseries, paradoxes (a highly active immune system may actually make you sicker with a cold), and myriad mysteries (why do poorer people get more colds? what roles do stress and sleep play? is our clean obsession making us more susceptible to sickness?) with the thoroughness of a scientist, the doggedness of a journalist, and the verve of a thriller writer. . . . There's a nifty collection of comforting recipes as well, including a nonalcoholic hot toddy (and a delicious sounding boozy one, too), banana pudding, and yes, chicken soup." Publ Wkly

Includes bibliographical references

616.3   Diseases of digestive system

Lavie, Carl J.

The **obesity** paradox; when thinner means sicker and heavier means healthier. Carl J. Lavie, M.D. ; with Kristin Loberg. Hudson Street Press 2014 288 p. (hardback) $25.95   **616.3**
1. Obesity 2. Body weight 3. Weight loss 4. Human body -- Composition 5. Overweight persons -- Health and hygiene
ISBN 1594632448; 9781594632440

LC 2013045483

This book, by Carl J. Lavie, "reveals the science behind the obesity paradox and shows us how to achieve maximum health rather than minimum weight. Lavie not only explains how extra fat provides additional fuel to help fight illness, he also argues that we've gotten so used to framing health issues in terms of obesity that we overlook other potential causes of disease." (Publisher's note)

"Comprehensible, practical advice that shuns yo-yo dieting and exhaustive exercise regimens for a more lenient lifestyle in which having some body fat is actually good for you." Kirkus
Includes bibliographical references and index

616.4   Diseases of endocrine, hematopoietic, lymphatic, glandular systems; diseases of male breast

American Diabetes Association

American Diabetes Association complete guide to diabetes; 5th ed.; American Diabetes Association 2011 499p il pa $22.95   **616.4**
1. Diabetes
ISBN 978-1-58040-330-6

LC 2010-41272

First published 1996
This book describes types of insulin and the best ways to use them, insulin pumps and injection-free insulin techniques in research, new oral diabetes medications and therapies, the use of carbohydrate counting techniques as a meal planning tool as well as information on diabetes in the workplace, school, and day care.
Includes bibliographical references

Crowe, Lynn

The **diabetes** manifesto; take charge of your life. [by] Lynn Crowe, Julie Stachowiak. Demos Medical Publisher 2011 266p pa $18.95   **616.4**
1. Diabetes
ISBN 978-1-932603-94-1

LC 2010-38543

The authors "strive to provide information that enables diabetics to gain a healthy perspective in managing daily tasks and accepting the inevitable setbacks that occur in the course of the disease. . . . Their well-written, tangible, and achievable advice is outstanding. An essential title for diabetes patients, their families, and health-care workers." Libr J
Includes bibliographical references

Hoffman, Brian B.

Adrenaline; Brian B. Hoffman. Harvard University Press 2013 304 p. (hardcover) $24.95   **616.4**
1. Adrenaline 2. Medicine -- History 3. History, 19th Century 4. History, 20th Century 5. History, 21st Century 6. Epinephrine -- history
ISBN 0674050886; 9780674050884

LC 2012035120

This book by professor Brian B. Hoffman looks at the medical history of adrenaline. He reveals "the blend of genius, guts, and luck that transformed a hunch into a breakthrough—from 19th-century physician Thomas Addison's insights into the function of the adrenal glands to the beginnings of endocrinology," the "Nobel Prize snub of a canny Japanese scientist and biotechnology pioneer, and the myriad other drugs developed after the discovery of adrenaline." (Publishers Weekly)
Includes bibliographical references and index.

Mayo Clinic, the essential diabetes book; medical editor, M. Regina Castro, M.D. 2nd ed Time Home Entertainment, Inc. 2014 vii, 223 p.p color illustrations (pbk.) $19.95   **616.4**
1. Diabetes
ISBN 0848743393; 9780848743390

LC 2014933598

"This title covers: the pre-diabetes stage - taking charge to prevent diabetes; types of diabetes; symptoms and risk factors; treatments and strategies for managing your blood sugar; avoiding serious complications; advances in insulin delivery and new medications; and recipes." Publisher's note

616.8   Diseases of nervous system and mental disorders

★ The 36-Hour Day; A Family Guide to Caring for People Who Have Alzheimer Disease, Related Dementias and Memory Loss. [by] Nancy L. Mace, Peter V. Rabins. 5th ed Johns Hopkins University Press 2011 353 p. hc $45   **616.8**
1. Senile dementia 2. Alzheimer's disease
ISBN 1421402793; 9781421402796

"This best-selling book features thoroughly revised chapters on the causes of dementia, managing the early stages of dementia, the prevention of dementia, and finding appropriate living arrangements for the person who has dementia when home care is no longer an option." Publisher's note

Ali, Naheed

Understanding Alzheimer's; an introduction for patients and caregivers. Naheed Ali. Rowman & Littlefield Publishers 2012 367 p. (cloth : alk. paper) $35   **616.8**
1. Alzheimer's disease 2. Alzheimer Disease
ISBN 1442217537; 9781442217539

LC 2012013305

This book by Naheed Ali "illustrate[s] how Alzheimer's works, how we can prevent it, and how we can address it once symptoms begin to appear. Covering diet and lifestyle, medical interventions and the stages of Alzheimer's, . . . [Ali] draws readers into a fuller understanding of the disease." (Publisher's note)

Includes bibliographical references and index.

Alzheimer's Early Stages; First Steps for Family, Friends and Caregivers. Daniel Kuhn. 3rd ed Hunter House 2013 296 p. $17.95 **616.8**
1. Caregivers 2. Alzheimer's disease
ISBN 0897936671; 9780897936675
Includes bibliographical references and index

"The third edition . . . offers new research findings, treatment approaches, and information on the three key areas of Alzheimer's disease: medical aspects, day-to-day care, and care for the caregiver." Publisher's note

B., David

★ **Epileptic**. Pantheon Books 2005 361p il $25; pa $18.95 **616.8**
1. Graphic novels 2. Autobiographical graphic novels 3. Epilepsy -- Graphic novels
ISBN 0-375-42318-4; 0-375-71468-5 pa
LC 2004-53419

Original French edition, 2002

The author's "artwork is magnificent—gorgeously bold, impressionistic representations of the world not as it is but as he's taught himself to perceive it. . . . B.'s illustrations constantly underscore his writing's wrenching psychological depth; readers can literally see how the chaos of his childhood shaped his vision and mind." Publ Wkly

Burton, Robert A.

A **skeptic's** guide to the mind; what neuroscience can and cannot tell us about ourselves. Robert A. Burton, M.D. St. Martin's Press 2013 272 p. (hardback) $24.99 **616.8**
1. Neurosciences 2. Human behavior 3. Brain -- Physiology 4. Mind and body
ISBN 1250001854; 9781250001856
LC 2012041265

In this book, "neurologist [Robert A.] Burton . . . focuses on new, key aspects of human behavior, specifically the control and lack of control humans have over their minds, treading a fine line of conscious and unconscious actions, thoughts, and decisions." (Library Journal) The book "provid[es] a critical overview of recent advances . . . in neuroscience" and "examines the inherent difficulties and flaws of the field." (Publishers Weekly)

Includes bibliographical references (pages 235-253) and index

Gillies, Andrea

Keeper; one house, three generations, and a journey into Alzheimer's. Broadway Books 2010 323p $25; ebook $25 **616.8**
1. Caregivers 2. Journalists 3. Alzheimer's disease 4. Memoirists
ISBN 978-0-307-71911-9; 978-0-307-71913-3 ebook
LC 2010-6659

First published 2009 in the United Kingdom

In this "chronicle of her troubled two years taking care of her mother-inlaw in the throes of dementia, . . . Gillies reveals the 'dehumanizing' toll of the disease on the whole family. Gillies, her husband, and three children moved to a rambling Victorian house in the wilds of a Scottish peninsula and took in Chris's parents, Edinburgh residents who had been showing signs of needing increasing care: irascible Morris had 'bad legs,' while his strong-willed wife, Nancy, at 79, was spiraling deeper into Alzheimer's. As Nancy's memory deteriorated the entire family unit began to collapse under the strain of constant caretaking. . . . [This] memoir is an invaluable resource on the stages of Alzheimer's, history, drugs, brain function, care-giving options, even literary works." Publ Wkly

Includes bibliographical references

Horstman, Judith

The **Scientific** American day in the life of your brain. Jossey-Bass 2009 236p il $25.95 **616.8**
1. Brain 2. Mind and body 3. Human behavior
ISBN 978-0-470-37623-2
LC 2009-13923

The author "reviews a full day of brainwork by accounting for the mental processes of everyday activities, arranged by hour. . . . Information-packed and fully referenced, this Scientific American publication is perfect for anyone with interest in mind/body interaction, mental health or aging." Publ Wkly

Includes bibliographical references

Kuhn, Daniel

Alzheimer's early stages; first steps for families, friends and caregivers. 2nd ed; Hunter House 2003 306p hardcover o.p. pa $15.95 **616.8**
1. Alzheimer's disease
ISBN 0-89793-398-2; 0-89793-397-4 pa
LC 2002-151932

First published 1999

This book covers "the importance of getting a diagnosis, risk factors (including the role of depression), early symptoms, treatment and prevention, and information on physical health, safety concerns, caring for the caregiver, and financial and end-of-life planning—all illustrated with brief, first-person narratives. Of special interest are chapters on relationships, including telling others about the diagnosis, and the . . . section on current available treatments. . . . Intelligently written with numerous references to professional and consumer literature, this book is an excellent choice for Alzheimer's and consumer health collections." Libr J

Includes bibliographical references

Lang, Anthony E.

★ **Parkinson's** disease; a complete guide for patients and families. [by] William J. Weiner, Lisa M. Shulman, Anthony E. Lang. 2nd ed.; Johns Hopkins University Press 2007 278p il $55; pa $17.95 **616.8**
1. Parkinson's disease
ISBN 0-8018-8545-0; 978-0-8018-8545-7; 0-8018-8546-9 pa; 978-0-8018-8546-4 pa
LC 2006-18814

First published 2001

This book contains "information for managing this complex condition, including details on the use of medications, diet, exercise, complementary therapies, and surgery." Publisher's note

Max, D. T.

The **family** that couldn't sleep; a medical mystery. Random House 2006 xxxi, 299p hardcover o.p. pa $15.95 **616.8**

1. Insomnia 2. Prion diseases 3. Sleep disorders
ISBN 1-4000-6245-4; 978-1-4000-6245-4; 978-0-8129-7252-8 pa; 0-8129-7252-X pa

LC 2006-43885

This book discusses fatal familial insomnia and the history of one family in the Veneto region of Italy that has suffered from this disease for more than two centuries.

This is a "gracefully written medical detective story." N Y Times (Late N Y Ed)

Includes bibliographical references

Moore, Lisa

Encyclopedia of Alzheimer's disease; with directories of research, treatment and care facilities. Elaine A. Moore with Lisa Moore ; illustrated by Marvin G. Miller ; foreword by David Perlmutter. 2nd edition McFarland 2012 viii, 447 p.p ill. (softcover : alk. paper) $95 **616.8**

1. Alzheimer's disease 2. Alzheimer's disease -- Directories 3. Alzheimer's disease -- Encyclopedias
ISBN 0786464585; 9780786464586

LC 2011046545

This reference volume discusses Alzheimer's disease. "For this second edition . . . medical writer [Elaine A.] Moore has updated her alphabetical entries. This volume notes discontinued trials and reflects the current emphasis on lifestyle changes to reduce the risk of Alzheimer's disease, relevant environmental factors, and the search for better diagnostic techniques. Black-and-white diagrams aid the entries' explanations. Three revised sections are featured." (Choice)

Includes bibliographical references and index

Ramachandran, V. S.

The **tell** -tale brain; a neuroscientist's quest for what makes us human. W. W. Norton 2011 xxvi, 357p il $26.95 **616.8**

1. Brain 2. Nervous system
ISBN 978-0-393-07782-7

LC 2010-44913

"Ramachandran produces an exhilarating and at times funny text that invites discussion and experimentation." Kirkus

Includes bibliographical references

Ropper, Allan H.

★ **Reaching** down the rabbit hole; a renowned neurologist explains the mystery and drama of brain disease. Dr. Allan H. Ropper and Brian David Burrell. St. Martin's Press 2014 272 p. (hardback) $25.99 **616.8**

1. Neurosciences 2. Nervous system 3. Brain -- Diseases 4. Neurology -- Anecdotes 5. Brain -- Diseases -- Anecdotes 6. Neurologists -- Massachusetts

-- Boston -- Biography
ISBN 1250034981; 9781250034984

LC 2014017011

In this book, authors Dr. Allan H. Ropper and Brian David Burrell "take the reader behind the scenes at Harvard Medical School's neurology unit to show how a seasoned diagnostician faces down bizarre, life-altering afflictions." (Publisher's note)

Sacks, Oliver W.

An **anthropologist** on Mars; seven paradoxical tales. [by] Oliver Sacks. Knopf 1995 327p il hardcover o.p. pa $14 **616.8**

1. Nervous system -- Diseases
ISBN 0-679-75697-3 pa

LC 94-26733

In this "collection of previously published essays, the noted neurologist describes his meetings with seven people whose 'abnormalities' in brain function generate new perspectives on the workings of that organ, the nature of experience and concepts of personality and consciousness. . . . Writing with eloquent particularity and compassionate respect, Sacks enlarges our view of the nature of human experience." Publ Wkly

Includes bibliographical references

★ The **man** who mistook his wife for a hat and other clinical tales; [by] Oliver Sacks. Simon & Schuster 1998 243p il pa $14 **616.8**

1. Nervous system -- Diseases
ISBN 0-684-85394-9

LC 98-4723

First published 1985 by Summit Bks.

"Sacks introduces the reader to real people who suffer from a variety of neurological syndromes which includes symptoms such as amnesia, uncontrolled movements, and musical hallucinations. Sacks recounts their stories in a riveting, compassionate, and thoughtful manner." Libr J

Includes bibliographical references

Uncle Tungsten; memories of a chemical boyhood. [by] Oliver Sacks. Knopf 2001 337p il hardcover o.p. pa $14 **616.8**

1. Physicians 2. Neurologists 3. Writers on science 4. Writers on medicine
ISBN 0-375-40448-1; 0-375-70404-3 pa

LC 2001-33738

"Sacks' first scientific love was chemistry, and he presents an avid history of the field within a memoir that pays tribute to his uncle, who welcomed Sacks into his lab, thus encouraging his passion for chemistry and learning." Booklist

Sharpe, Katherine, 1979-

Coming of age on Zoloft; how antidepressants cheered us up, let us down, and changed who we are. Katherine Sharpe. Harper Perennial 2012 314 p. $14.99 **616.8**

1. Teenagers 2. Antidepressants 3. Adolescent psychiatry 4. Depression (Psychology)
ISBN 0062059734; 9780062059734

LC 2012374063

This book, by Katherine Sharpe, describes "what it is like to grow up on psychiatric medications. . . . The author questions the effect of such medication on adolescents. . . . Besides her personal story and those of her interviewees, Sharpe provides a history of antidepressants, a . . . look at the politics behind the evolution of the Diagnostic and Statistical Manual of Mental Disorders and . . . the rise of the biomedical model of mental illness." (Kirkus Reviews)

Includes bibliographical references.

Shenk, David

The **forgetting** : Alzheimer's, portrait of an epidemic. Doubleday 2001 290p $24.95; pa $13.95 **616.8**

1. Alzheimer's disease
ISBN 0-385-49837-3; 0-385-49838-1 pa
LC 2001-28012

The author "traces the development of knowledge about Alzheimer's in the work of individuals and such groups as the National Institute of Aging; describes various tests that help in identifying possible sufferers; and discusses the early, middle, and end stages of the malady. . . . Lucid and well organized, this is one of the best books on this increasingly prevalent illness." Booklist

Includes bibliographical references

616.85   Miscellaneous diseases of nervous system and mental disorders

Bass, Ellen

The **courage** to heal; a guide for women survivors of child sexual abuse. by Ellen Bass and Laura Davis. 20th anniversary edition; 4th revised edition; Collins Living 2008 xxxiv, 606p pa $22.95 **616.85**

1. Child sexual abuse 2. Adult child sexual abuse victims 3. Women -- Psychology
ISBN 978-0-06-128433-5; 0-06-128433-5
LC 2008-11616

First published 1988

"This book offers help and encouragement to women who were sexually abused in childhood. Through moving firstperson narratives, it illustrates how to come to terms with the past and work constructively towards the future. Along the way it describes the effects of sexual abuse, maps the stages survivors pass through, and offers practical guidance on dealing with self-defeating behaviors and building self-esteem. . . . Compassionate and supportive." Libr J

Includes bibliographical references

Bulik, Cynthia M.

Midlife eating disorders; your journey to recovery. Cynthia M. Bulik, Ph. D. Walker & Company 2013 352 p. $17 **616.85**

1. Eating disorders 2. Middle aged persons 3. Middle-aged persons 4. Middle age -- Psychological aspects
ISBN 080271269X; 9780802712691
LC 2012037481

In this book, clinical psychologist and director of the University of North Carolina Eating Disorders Program Cynthia M. Bulik "reviews the causes, features, and age-appropriate treatments of midlife eating disorders from an-

orexia nervosa to binge eating, bulimia nervosa, and purging. She explores some of the challenges facing adults with eating problems, including parenting, intimacy, pregnancy, and breastfeeding." (Booklist)

"[Bulik] discusses treatment options, finding compassionate care, and the importance of support from health professionals as well as family and friends. The book has extensive notes as well as a resource list of American and British organizations." LJ

Includes bibliographical references and index

Driven to Distraction; Recognizing & Coping With Attention Deficit Disorder From Childhood to Adulthood. by Edward M. Hallowell and John Ratey. Rev. and updated ed. Anchor Books 2011 382 p. $15.95 **616.85**

1. Attention deficit disorder
ISBN 0307743152; 9780307743152
LC 9329536

"Through vivid stories and case histories of patients--both adults and children--Hallowell and Ratey explore the varied forms ADHD takes, from hyperactivity to daydreaming. They dispel common myths, offer helpful coping tools, and give a thorough accounting of all treatment options as well as tips for dealing with a diagnosed child, partner, or family member." Publisher's note

Includes bibliographical references and index

Frost, Randy O.

Stuff. Houghton Mifflin Harcourt 2010 290p $27 **616.85**

1. Compulsive hoarding 2. Collectors and collecting 3. Obsessive-compulsive disorder
ISBN 978-0-15-101423-1; 0-15-101423-X
LC 2009-28273

"Writing with authority and compassion, the authors tell the stories of diverse men and women who acquire and accumulate possessions to the point where their apartments or homes are dangerously cluttered with mounds of newspapers, clothing and other objects. . . . An absorbing, gripping, important report." Kirkus

Includes bibliographical references

Grandin, Temple, 1947-

★ The **autistic** brain; thinking across the spectrum. Temple Grandin and Richard Panek. Houghton Mifflin Harcourt 2013 256 p. (hardcover) $28 **616.85**

1. Autism 2. Neurosciences 3. Autism -- Research 4. Psychology, Pathological 5. Autism spectrum disorders 6. Autistic people -- Mental health
ISBN 0547636458; 9780547636450
LC 2013000662

This book, by Temple Grandin and Richard Panek, presents an "account of the latest science of autism. . . . Autism studies have moved from the realm of psychology to neurology and genetics, and there is far more hope today than ever before thanks to groundbreaking new research into causes and treatments. Now Temple Grandin reports from the forefront of autism science, bringing her singular perspective to a thrilling journey into the heart of the autism revolution." (Publisher's note)

Greenberg, Gary

Manufacturing depression; the secret history of a modern disease. Simon and Schuster 2010 432p $27   **616.85**

1. Antidepressants 2. Depression (Psychology) 3. Depression, Mental 4. Psychotherapy -- United States -- History

ISBN 1-4165-6979-0; 9781416569794

LC 2009-24310

"Greenberg draws on sources ranging from the Old Testament to current medical journals and scholarship to his twenty-five years as a psychotherapist and his own experience as a depression patient to show how the idea that depression is a widespread chronic disease has been packaged by . . . scientists, doctors, and marketing experts—and why it is has become wildly successful in the marketplace of ideas. Rather than asking whether or not depression is a disease, or whether or not we should take drugs to ease our pain, Greenberg asks what we gain and lose by taking this approach, and who benefits when we do." (Publisher's note) Index.

The author "ponders depression and its treatment through the ages. . . . [He] focuses heavily on the human element lurking behind the symptoms of depression and their context and meaning. During this tour of depression, the author engages in extended, illuminating discussions of a host of therapeutic techniques, the confounding power of the placebo effect, the evolution of psychopharmacology and the ways in which expectations shape response. A humanistic, witty exploration of the human response to depression." Kirkus

Includes bibliographical references

Grinker, Roy Richard, 1961-

Unstrange minds; remapping the world of autism. Basic Books 2006 340p hardcover o.p.   **616.85**

1. Autism

ISBN 0465027636; 0465027644; 9780465027637; 9780465027644

LC 2006-23003

Part 1 of this work examines "the history of the classification of psychiatric disorders. . . . The second part of the book explores the cultural issues related to autism in . . . India, South Korea, and South Africa and how the place of the autistic child is changing in those countries." (Sci Books Films) Index.

"The first part of the book is an expanded essay on the history of the classification of psychiatric disorders and how these definitions continue to evolve. . . . The second part of the book explores the cultural issues related to autism in societies as diverse as those of India, South Korea, and South Africa and how the place of the autistic child is changing in those countries. Grinker's experiences as a father of an autistic child are woven throughout the volume. . . . The text is scholarly, but easily read, and is useful not only for providing an understanding of autism, but also for understanding the issues associated with changing diagnoses of psychiatric disorders." Sci Books Films

Includes bibliographical references

Hornbacher, Marya

Wasted : a memoir of anorexia and bulimia. HarperCollins Pubs. 1998 268p hardcover o.p. pa $13.95   **616.85**

1. Bulimia 2. Anorexia nervosa

ISBN 0-06-018739-5; 978-0-06-085879-7 pa; 0-06-085879-6 pa

LC 97-21375

This "is a gritty, unflinching look at eating disorders. . . . Hornbacher is at her best when she zeroes in on the specifics of eating disorders and their origins." N Y Times Book Rev

Includes bibliographical references

Kluger, Jeffrey

The **Narcissist** Next Door; Understanding the Monster in Your Family, in Your Office, in Your Bed- -in Your World. Jeffrey Kluger. Riverhead Books 2014 288 p. $27.95   **616.85**

1. Narcissism

ISBN 1594486360; 9781594486364

LC 2014006297

This book, by Jeffrey Kluger, is an "exploration of narcissism, how to recognize it, and how to handle it. . . . Kluger frames the surprising new research on narcissism and explains the complex, exasperating personality disorder. He reveals how narcissism and narcissists affect our lives at work and at home, on the road, and in the halls of government; what to do when we encounter narcissism; and how to neutralize its effects before it's too late." (Publisher's note)

"In addition to being informative and engaging, Kluger's account provides some effective tools for dealing with potential narcissists." Pub Wkly

Kramer, Peter D.

Listening to Prozac; a psychiatrist explores mood-altering drugs and the new meaning of the self. Viking 1993 409p hardcover o.p. pa $15 **616.85**

1. Psychiatry 2. Psychotherapy 3. Psychotropic drugs 4. Personality disorders

ISBN 0-14-026671-2 pa

LC 92-50733

"Kramer's thesis is that Prozac, in addition to its antidepressant effects, can also act upon aspects of the personality that were previously conceptualized as enduring individual traits (i.e., sensitivity to rejection, social inhibition, and reactivity to stressors). Medication with Prozac appears to have beneficial effects on self-esteem, the ability to experience pleasure, and mental acuity. Kramer is favorable to Prozac, although he documents its side effects, unknown long-term affects, and controversial publicity." Choice

Machoian, Lisa

The **disappearing** girl; learning the language of teenage depression. Dutton 2005 xxiv, 244p $24.95; pa $15   **616.85**

1. Teenagers 2. Depression (Psychology)

ISBN 0-525-94866-X; 0-452-28710-3 pa

LC 2004-25777

The author "sets out to determine why so many young women seem to emotionally withdraw and to explain how parents and others can help them." Publ Wkly

Includes bibliographical references

McBride, Karyl

Will I ever be good enough? healing the daughters of narcissistic mothers. Free Press 2008 243p il $24 **616.85**

1. Narcissism 2. Self-acceptance 3. Mother-daughter relationship

ISBN 978-1-4165-5132-4; 1-4165-5132-8

LC 2008-14676

In this book aimed at women whose mothers have narcissistic personality disorder, "McBride presents specific steps toward recovery that daughters of any age can use as they grieve for the love and support they didn't receive, set healthy boundaries with their mothers and access an 'internal mother' as a source of self-comforting. The author provides parenting tips as well as advice on maintaining healthy love relationships and friendships—all of which tend to be weak points of the daughters of narcissistic mothers." Publ Wkly

Includes bibliographical references

Nathan, Debbie

Sybil exposed; the extraordinary story behind the famous multiple personality case. Free Press 2011 xxi, 297p il $26; ebook $12.99 **616.85**

1. Artists 2. Painters 3. Mentally ill 4. Multiple personality

ISBN 978-1-4391-6827-1; 978-1-4391-6829-5 ebook

LC 2011009164

The author "claims that the subject of the 1973 international bestseller, Sybil by Flora Schreiber, and the blockbuster film that followed, was a deliberate fabrication that not only fooled a mass popular audience but shaped the practice of psychiatry, opening the door to mass hysteria and misdiagnosis. . . . A nuanced, not-entirely-unsympathetic account of the women who perpetrated a sensational literary fraud." Kirkus

Includes bibliographical references

Raine, Adrian

The anatomy of violence; the biological roots of crime. Adrian Raine. 1st ed. Pantheon Books 2013 xv, 478 p.p ill. (some col.) (hardcover) $35 **616.85**

1. Genetics 2. Violence 3. Mind and body 4. Violence -- Physiological aspects 5. Violence -- Psychological aspects

ISBN 0307378845; 9780307378842

LC 2012036952

This book, by Adrian Raine, researches "the biological roots of violence. . . . Raine documents from genetic research that the seeds of sin are sown early in life, giving rise to abnormal physiological functioning that cultivates crime. Drawing on classical case studies of well-known killers in history . . . Raine illustrates how impairments to brain areas controlling our ability to experience fear, make good decisions, and feel guilt predispose us to violence." (Publisher's note)

Includes bibliographical references (pages 375-453) and index.

Ronson, Jon

The psychopath test; Jon Ronson. Riverhead Books 2011 275 p. **616.85**

1. Research 2. Abnormal psychology 3. Mentally ill

-- Institutional care 4. Psychopaths

ISBN 978-1-59448-801-6; 1-59448-801-0

LC 201103133

This book provides an "exploration of psychiatry's attempts to understand and treat psychopathy, [in which] British journalist Ronson . . . reveals that psychopaths are more common than we'd like to think. Visiting Broadmoor Psychiatric Hospital, where some of Britain's worst criminal offenders are sent, Ronson discovers the difficulties of diagnosing the complex disorder when he meets one inmate who says he feigned psychopathy to get a lighter sentence, and instead has spent 12 years in Broadmoor. The psychiatric community's criteria for diagnosing psychopathy . . . is a checklist developed by the Canadian prison psychologist Robert Hare. Using Hare's rubric, which includes 'glibness,' 'grandiose sense of self-worth,' and 'lack of remorse,' Ronson sets off to interview possible psychopaths, many of them in positions of power, from a former Haitian militia leader to a power-hungry CEO." (Publishers Weekly)

Includes bibliographical references (p. [273]-275).

Sacks, Oliver, 1933-

The mind's eye. Alfred A. Knopf 2010 263p il $26.95 **616.85**

1. Perception 2. Nervous system 3. Vision disorders 4. Communicative disorders 5. Neurology 6. Face perception 7. Cognition disorders

ISBN 978-0-307-27208-9; 0-307-27208-7

LC 2010-12791

Sacks "offers case histories of six individuals adjusting to major changes in their vision. A renowned pianist has lost the ability to read music scores and must cope with the fear of an ever-shrinking life as her vision worsens. A prolific writer develops 'word blindness' and is unable to read even what he himself writes, forcing him to develop memory books in his mind, adaptations that he later incorporates into his fiction writing. Sacks recalls his own struggle to cope with a tumor in his eye that left him unable to perceive depth. He includes diary entries and drawings of his harrowing experience. . . . [A] riveting exploration of how we use our vision to perceive and understand the world and our place in it and how our brains teach us to 'see' those things we need to lead a complete, fulfilled life." Booklist

Includes bibliographical references

Schreiber, Flora Rheta

Sybil. Warner Books 1995 460p il pa $7.99 **616.85**

1. Multiple personality

ISBN 978-0-446-35940-5; 0-446-35940-8

First published 1973 by Regnery Pub.

This is the "true story of Sybil I. Dorsett, a battered child possessed by 16 different personalities. . . . The author skillfully evokes Sybil's patient work during 11 years of psychoanalysis and her eventual success in integrating these selves into a unified personality." Libr J

Slone, Laurie B.

★ After the war zone; a practical guide for returning troops and their families. [by] Laurie B.

Slone and Matthew J. Friedman. Da Capo Lifelong
2008 279p pa $14.95   **616.85**
> 1. Veterans 2. Mental health 3. Post-traumatic stress
> disorder
> ISBN 978-1-60094-054-5; 1-60094-054-4
> > LC 2008-5555

"Far more than a practical guide, this is an informative,
insightful, and riveting text that should be required reading
for everyone because no one is left untouched by war. Essential for all libraries." Libr J
> Includes bibliographical references

Smith, Daniel

Monkey mind; a memoir of anxiety. Daniel B.
Smith. 1st Simon & Schuster hardcover Simon &
Schuster 2012 viii, 212 p.p (hardcover) $25 **616.85**
> 1. Anxiety 2. Journalists 3. Interpersonal relations
> 4. Anxiety disorders 5. Mentally ill -- United States
> -- Biography
> ISBN 1439177309; 9781439177303; 9781439177327
> > LC 2011025971

In this memoir, "afflicted journalist and editor [Daniel]
Smith uses humor . . . as he explains the excess of thought
and emotion also known as 'Monkey Mind' in Buddhism."
After college "graduation, he embarks on his first romance
and lands a fact-checking job at the Atlantic. . . . Reading
the harsh comments posted online about his article and
tracking his thoughts and behavior for triggers helps him
reroute his psychological circuitry and win his ex back."
(Publishers Weekly)

Solomon, Andrew

The **noonday** demon; an atlas of depression.
Scribner 2001 569p $28; pa $16   **616.85**
> 1. Depression (Psychology)
> ISBN 0-684-85466-X; 0-684-85467-8 pa
> > LC 2001-18884

"The author draws on his own life story and other
sources for a deeply moving and provocative exploration of
depression." Booklist
> Includes bibliographical references

Stossel, Scott

My age of anxiety; fear, hope, dread, and the
search for peace of mind. Scott Stossel. Alfred A.
Knopf 2014 416 p. (hardcover) $27.95   **616.85**
> 1. Anxiety 2. Anxiety -- Chemotherapy 3. Tranquilizing
> drugs -- Social aspects
> ISBN 0307269876; 9780307269874; 9780307390608
> > LC 2013006336

This book, by Scott Stossel, presents an "account of the
author's struggles with anxiety, and of the history of efforts
by scientists, philosophers, and writers to understand the
condition. . . . He ranges from the earliest medical reports of
Galen and Hippocrates, through later observations by Robert
Burton and Soren Kierkegaard, to the investigations by great
nineteenth-century scientists, such as Charles Darwin, William James, and Sigmund Freud." (Publisher's note)

"[T]he author's beautiful prose and careful research
combine to make this book informative, thoughtful and fun
to read. Powerful, eye-opening and funny." Kirkus
> Includes bibliographical references

Styron, William

Darkness visible; a memoir of madness. Random House 1990 84p hardcover o.p. pa $11 **616.85**
> 1. Depression (Psychology)
> ISBN 0-679-73639-5 pa
> > LC 90-53141

This is an account of the author's experience of suicidal
depression and his recovery

"The book's virtues—considerable—are twofold. First,
it is a pitiless and chastened record of a nearly fatal human
trial far commoner than assumed—and then a literary discourse on the ways and means of our cultural discontents."
Publ Wkly

Wansink, Brian

Mindless eating; why we eat more than we think.
Bantam Books 2006 276p il hardcover o.p. pa
$14   **616.85**
> 1. Eating habits
> ISBN 978-0-553-80434-8; 0-553-80434-0; 978-0-553-
> 38448-2 pa; 0-553-38448-1 pa
> > LC 2006-47532

The author "explores some of the psychological aspects
of overeating to explain why we in fact consume more than
we believe we do. . . . Wansink's dual approach emphasizing
food knowledge and self-knowledge offers a sensible route
to permanent weight loss." Booklist
> Includes bibliographical references

616.86   Substance abuse (Drug abuse)

Beattie, Melody

Beyond codependency; and getting better all
the time. Hazelden Foundation 1989 252p pa
$15.95   **616.86**
> 1. Drug abuse 2. Applied psychology
> ISBN 0-89486-583-8

The author discusses "the process of recovering from the
self-defeating behaviors adopted as survival tactics by adult
children of families rendered dysfunctional by parental alcoholism or similar traumas." Publ Wkly
> Includes bibliographical references

★ Codependent no more; how to stop controlling others and start caring for yourself. 2nd ed.; Hazelden 1992 250p pa $15.95   **616.86**
> 1. Drug abuse 2. Codependency 3. Health self-care
> ISBN 0-89486-402-5
> > LC 2004-351623

First published 1987
This guide offers advice on how to overcome codependency, aimed at the spouses and other caretakers of people
who abuse drugs or alcohol.
> Includes bibliographical references

Goldfarb, Toni L.

American Lung Association 7 steps to a smoke-free life; [by] Edwin B. Fisher, Jr. with Toni L. Goldfarb. Wiley 1998 226p pa $14.95   **616.86**
1. Tobacco habit 2. Smoking cessation programs
ISBN 0-471-24700-6

LC 97-38826

"Based on the American Lung Association's smoking cessation program, this book coaches smokers through discovering their own personal motivations and obstacles to quitting, planning effective strategies to meet and conquer the temptation to pick up a cigarette, and tailoring a cessation program to individual lifestyles." Libr J

616.89   Mental disorders

Adamec, Christine

When your adult child breaks your heart; coping with mental illness, substance abuse, and the problems that tear families apart. Joel L. Young, MD., Christine Adamec. Lyons Press, an imprint of Globe Pequot Press 2013 251 p. (pbk.) $19.95   **616.89**
1. Mental illness 2. Substance abuse 3. Self-care, Health 4. Parent and adult child 5. Parents of mentally ill children -- Psychology
ISBN 0762792973; 9780762792979

LC 2013023047

"Behind nearly every adult who is accused of a crime, . . . addicted to drugs or alcohol, or . . . severely mentally ill . . . , there is . . . one extremely stressed-out parent." This book by Joel L. Young, with Christine Adamec, "presents families with quotations and scenarios from real suffering parents . . . , practical advice, and tested strategies for coping. It also discusses the fact that parents of adult children may themselves need therapy and medications." (Publisher's note)

"The book offers practical advice, stories, and resources—and, perhaps most importantly, comfort for any parent facing one of the biggest parenting challenges." Pub Wkly

Includes bibliographical references and index

Burns, Tom

★ Our Necessary Shadow; The Nature and Meaning of Psychiatry. Tom Burns. W.W. Norton & Co Inc. 2014 384 p. $27.95   **616.89**
1. Psychiatry 2. Medicine -- History
ISBN 1605985708; 9781605985701

Introduction: What is psychiatry and what is it for? -- What to expect if you are referred to a psychiatrist -- Part one. How modern psychiatry developed. The origins of institutional psychiatry -- The discovery of the unconscious -- The rise and fall of psychoanalysis -- The first medical model (between the wars) -- The impact of war -- Out of the asylum - the origins of community care -- Part two. The questions psychiatry asks about us and the questions we ask of it. Is mental illness real? Psychiatry's legitimacy -- Is psychiatry trustworthy? Psychiatry's sins and abuses -- Is bad behavior any of our business? Psychiatry and the law -- A diagnosis for everything and the medicalization of everyday life -- New treatments but old dilemmas -- The rise of neuroscience and the future of psychiatry -- Epilogue

"This is the first attempt in a generation to explain the whole subject of psychiatry. . . . Tom Burns reviews the historical development of psychiatry, throughout alert to where psychiatry helps, and where it is imperfect. What is clear is that mental illnesses are intimately tied to what makes us human in the first place and the drive to relieve the suffering they cause is even more human." (Publisher's note)

"There are fine chapters on neuroscience and pharmaceuticals . . ., and Burns covers antipsychiatry movements, the insanity defense, and the impact of war." LJ

Includes bibliographical references (p. 306-309) and index

Engel, Jonathan

American therapy; the rise of psychotherapy in the United States. Gotham Books 2008 351p $27.50   **616.89**
1. Psychotherapy
ISBN 978-1-59240-380-6; 1-59240-380-8

LC 2008-23517

Engel "does a thorough job of synopsizing the history of psychology in general, and studiously relates how psychoanalysis—a European-born oddity—took the United States by storm a century ago." Baltimore City Paper

Includes bibliographical references

Frances, Allen

★ Saving Normal; An Insider's Revolt Against Out-of-control Psychiatric Diagnosis, Dsm-5, Big Pharma, and the Medicalization of Ordinary Life. Allen Frances. HarperCollins 2013 xx, 314 p.p (hardcover) $27.99   **616.89**
1. Psychiatry 2. Mental health 3. Mental illness
ISBN 0062229257; 9780062229250

This book, by Allen Frances, "warns that mislabeling everyday problems as mental illness has shocking implications for individuals and society. . . . We also shift responsibility for our mental well-being away from our own naturally resilient and self-healing brains . . . into the hands of 'Big Pharma,' who are reaping multi-billion-dollar profits." (Publisher's note)

Porter, Roy

Madness; a brief history. Oxford Univ. Press 2002 241p il hardcover o.p. pa $12.95   **616.89**
1. Psychiatry 2. Mental illness
ISBN 0-19-280267-4 pa

LC 2001-52329

This is a study on the many ways madness has been perceived and misperceived from antiquity to modern times. The author "also discusses topical issues, including the relationship between lunacy and creativity, the drive to institutionalize, which peaked in the mid-20th century; the rise and demise of psychoanalysis; and the development of the antipsychiatry movement. This book combines the appeal of history as narrative with the intellectual stimulation derived from cogent analysis." Libr J

Includes bibliographical references

Sederer, Lloyd I.

The family guide to mental health care; Lloyd I Sederer, MD ; foreword by Glenn Close. W.W.

Norton & Co Inc. 2013 xxii, 312 p.p (hardcover)
$25.95   **616.89**
1. Mental health services 2. Families of terminally
ill 3. Mental illness -- United States 4. Mental health
services -- United States 5. Families of the mentally ill
-- Counseling of
ISBN 0393707946; 9780393707946
LC 2013007244

This book, by Lloyd I. Sederer, offers advice for families
navigating the U.S. mental health care system. "More than
fifty million people a year are diagnosed with some form
of mental illness. . . . Family members and friends are often the first to realize when someone has a problem. . . .
From understanding depression, bipolar illness and anxiety
to eating and traumatic disorders, schizophrenia, and much
more, readers will learn what to do and how to help." (Publisher's note)

Includes bibliographical references and index.

Shorter, Edward
A **history** of psychiatry; from the era of the asylum to the age of Prozac. Wiley 1997 436p il hardcover o.p. pa $30   **616.89**
1. Psychiatry
ISBN 0-471-24531-3 pa
LC 96-15292

This "social history of 200 years of psychiatry in the
U.S., Great Britain, France, and Germany is informative and at times lively. . . . Dealing ably with the major
trends, Shorter does not fail to also illuminate such engaging and horrifying byways as the 'fever cure' and ice pick
lobotomy." Booklist

Includes bibliographical references

Slater, Lauren
Prozac diary. Penguin Bks. 1999 203p pa
$15   **616.89**
1. Mental illness 2. Psychotropic drugs
ISBN 0-14-026394-2; 978-0-14-026394-7
LC 97-35727

First published 1998 by Random House

The author "was among the first patients to be given Prozac, and she has now been on it, almost without interruption,
for ten years. She credits the drug with enabling her, after an
incapacitating adolescence, not only to taste and see but to
complete a doctorate; marry; and, as director of a clinic, be
useful. But she also ponders what it means to one's sense of
self to be more or less permanently under the influence of a
personality (and libido) altering drug." New Yorker

Whitaker, Robert
Anatomy of an epidemic; magic bullets, psychiatric drugs, and the astonishing rise of mental illness in America. Crown Publishers 2010 404p il
$26   **616.89**
1. Psychiatry 2. Mental illness 3. Psychotropic drugs
ISBN 978-0-307-45241-2; 0-307-45241-7
LC 2009-49467

This is the "first book to investigate the long-term outcomes of patients treated with psychiatric drugs, and Whitaker finds that, overall, the drugs may be doing more harm
than good. Adhering to studies published in prominent

medical journals, he argues that, over time, patients with
schizophrenia do better off medication than on it. Children
who take stimulants for ADHD, he writes, are more likely
to suffer from mania and bipolar disorder than those who
go unmedicated. Intended to challenge the conventional wisdom about psychiatric drugs, 'Anatomy' is sure to provoke
a hot-tempered response, especially from those inside the
psychiatric community." Salon

Includes bibliographical references

616.9   Other diseases

Horowitz, Richard I.
Why can't I get better? solving the mystery
of lyme and chronic disease. Richard Horowitz,
M.D. St. Martin's Press 2013 544 p. (hardback)
$29.99   **616.9**
1. Diagnosis 2. Lyme disease 3. Chronic diseases 4.
Symptoms
ISBN 1250019400; 9781250019400
LC 2013013336

This book, by doctor Richard Horowitz, is "about diagnosing, treating and healing Lyme, and peeling away the
layers that lead to chronic disease. . . . [He] covers in detail
Lyme's leading symptoms and co-infections, including immune dysfunction, sleep disorders, chronic pain and neuro-
degenerative disorders–providing a . . . health care model . .
. for physicians and health care providers to effectively treat
Lyme and other chronic illnesses." (Publisher's note)

"Less self-help and more educational, this work is recommended for health sciences professionals and medically
literate audiences, not necessarily for introductory or casual
readers." LJ

Includes bibliographical references) and index

McKenna, Maryn
Superbug; the fatal menace of MRSA. Free
Press 2010 271p $26   **616.9**
1. Methicillin-Resistant Staphylococcus aureus
ISBN 978-1-4165-5727-2; 1-4165-5727-X
LC 2009-37793

"McKenna suggests that vaccines might be the answer,
but it seems a distant hope — and too late for the patients
whose heartbreaking stories she tells. A meticulously researched, frightening report on a deadly pathogen." Kirkus

Includes bibliographical references

Piot, Peter, 1949-
No time to lose; a life in pursuit of deadly viruses.
Peter Piot with Ruth Marshall. W.W. Norton & Co.
2012 387 p.   **616.9**
1. Ebola virus 2. Public health 3. AIDS (Disease) 4.
Autobiographies 5. History, 20th Century -- Belgium
6. History, 20th Century -- England 7. History,
21st Century -- Belgium 8. History, 21st Century --
England 9. Virology -- Belgium -- Autobiography 10.
Virology -- England -- Autobiography 11. Joint United
Nations Programme on HIV--AIDS 12. Hemorrhagic
Fever, Ebola -- history -- Belgium 13. Hemorrhagic
Fever, Ebola -- history -- England 14. International
Cooperation -- Belgium -- Autobiography 15.

International Cooperation -- England -- Autobiography
ISBN 039306316X; 9780393063165

LC 2012011911

In this book, Peter Piot describes his "career, from identifying the Ebola virus to pioneering AIDS research and policy. . . . Piot was sent to Central Africa as part of a team tasked with identifying a grisly new virus. Crossing into the quarantine zone on the most dangerous missions, he studied local customs to determine how this disease--the Ebola virus--was spreading. Later, Piot found himself in the field again when another mysterious epidemic broke out: AIDS." (Publisher's note)

Preston, Richard

The **demon** in the freezer; a true story. Random House 2002 240p hardcover o.p. pa $7.99   **616.9**

1. Smallpox 2. Biological warfare
ISBN 0-375-50856-2; 0-345-46663-2 pa

The author explains "the chemical properties of the smallpox virus; how a single infected person . . . can set off an epidemic; and what this horrendous disease can be like. . . . We learn how the disease was eliminated by an international vaccination campaign in the 1970's; why there are reasons to believe that the Soviet Union grew staggering quantities of the virus, allegedly in part to arm intercontinental missiles; and how the virus might now be used by others as a 'strategic weapon.'" N Y Times Book Rev

Weintraub, Pamela

Cure Unknown; Inside the Lyme Epidemic. Pamela Weintraub. Revised ed. St Martins Pr 2013 456 p. ill $17.99   **616.9**

1. Lyme disease
ISBN 1250044561; 9781250044563

"When Pamela Weintraub, a science journalist, learned that her oldest son tested positive for Lyme disease, she thought she had found an answer to the symptoms that had been plaguing her family for years. . . . Almost everything about Lyme disease turned out to be deeply controversial, from the microbe causing the infection, to the length and type of treatment and the kind of practitioner needed." Publisher's note

Includes bibliographical references and index

Wolfe, Nathan

The **viral** storm; the dawn of a new pandemic age. Times Books 2011 304p il map $26; ebook $12.99   **616.9**

1. Viruses 2. Diseases 3. Evolution
ISBN 978-0-8050-9194-6; 978-1-4299-7359-5 ebook

LC 2011011321

In this book, author Nathan Wolfe attempts to answer the questions "'How do pandemics start? Why are we now plagued with so many pandemics? What can we do to prevent pandemics in the future?' . . . Wolfe delivers the message that pandemics are imminent threats, a product of our evolutionary history and today's globalized world. . . . According to Wolfe, our best hope for preventing pandemics is . . . to hunt down deadly pathogens before they have a chance to become front-page news." (Science)

The author presents "an eloquent argument for why we need better ways to predict and thus prevent major disease outbreaks. . . . Wolfe makes clear that most bugs are harmless; some are even helpful. But his wide experience confronting killer diseases in Africa and Asia makes for important, graphic reading and underscores his passion for prevention." Kirkus

616.97   Diseases of immune system

Sicherer, Scott H.

Food allergies; a complete guide for eating when your life depends on it. Scott H. Sicherer ; foreword by Maria Laura Acebal ; introduction by Hugh A. Sampson. Johns Hopkins University Press 2013 279 p. ill. (hdbk. : alk. paper) $45   **616.97**

1. Food allergy 2. Food allergy -- Diet therapy
ISBN 1421408449; 1421408457; 1421408988; 9781421408446; 9781421408453; 9781421408989

LC 2012025274

In this book, Scott H. Sicherer "addresses the full spectrum of food allergies, from mild to life threatening, from single foods to food families, clearing up misconceptions along the way. He explains how exposure to foods can bring about an allergic response, describes the symptoms of food allergy, and illuminates how food allergies develop. He also recommends tests for diagnosing both food allergies and chronic health problems caused by food allergies." (Publisher's note)

"This book is practical and informative without being overwhelming." LJ

Includes bibliographical references and index

Velasquez-Manoff, Moises

An **Epidemic** of Absence; A New Way of Understanding Allergies and Autoimmune Diseases. by Moises Velasquez-Manoff. Simon & Schuster 2012 vii, 385 p.p ill.   **616.97**

1. Health 2. Immune system 3. Parasitic diseases
ISBN 1439199388; 9781439199381

LC 2012289041

Author Moises Velasquez-Manoff looks at "worm theory"--deliberate infection with parasitic worms--in development to treat autoimmune disease. It explains why farmers' children so rarely get hay fever, why allergy is less prevalent in former Eastern Bloc countries, and how one cancer-causing bacterium may be good for us. It probes the link between autism and a dysfunctional immune system. It investigates the newly apparent fetal origins of allergic disease--that a mother's inflammatory response imprints on her unborn child, tipping the scales toward allergy." (Publisher's note)

Includes bibliographical references (p. 313-356) and index.

Walsh, William E.

★ **Food** allergies; the complete guide to understanding and relieving your food allergies. Wiley 2000 286p pa $16.95   **616.97**

1. Allergy
ISBN 0-471-38268-X

LC 00-24608

"While providing an overview of the physiology and types of food allergies, Walsh concentrates on what he terms 'MALS' (monosodium glutamate, acidic foods, low-calorie sweeteners, and refined sugar), the most common allergens identified in his patients. He lists MALS foods, provides a sample elimination diet, and includes information on common fast-food restaurant choices." Libr J

Includes bibliographical references

616.99   Tumors and miscellaneous communicable diseases

Gubar, Susan
Memoir of a debulked woman; enduring ovarian cancer. Susan Gubar. W.W. Norton & Co. 2012 288 p.   **616.99**
1. Ovaries -- Cancer -- Patients 2. Ovaries -- Cancer -- Treatment 3. Women -- United States -- Biography 4. Cancer -- Psychological aspects 5. Ovaries -- Cancer -- Patients -- United States -- Biography
ISBN 9780393073256
LC 2011053073
This book presents an "account of the author's ovarian cancer treatment and a staunch protest against the state of contemporary approaches to the disease. In telling her personal story, feminist scholar Gubar . . . remains the academic, looking for understanding not just in the medical literature but also in Frida Kahlo's art . . . and other women's writings." (Kirkus Reviews)

Includes bibliographical references

Jacobs, Hollye
The **Silver** Lining; A Supportive and Insightful Guide to Breast Cancer. text by Hollye Jacobs, RN, MS, MSW; photography by Elizabeth Messina. Pocket Books 2014 288 p. ill. (some col.) $35   **616.99**
1. Breast cancer 2. Cancer -- Patients 3. Cancer -- Patients -- Attitudes
ISBN 147676350X; 9781476763507
LC 2013019103
Author Hollye Jacobs "offers an unabashedly candid account of her experience with breast cancer. Each chapter . . . focuses on a particular point in the breast cancer journey and discusses how to handle challenges . . . including: diagnosis; relaying the news; . . . surgery; chemotherapy; the isolating nature of the disease; radiation; nutritional and other therapies to ease treatment; discovering the new normal; and redefining your life post-treatment." (Publishers Weekly)

"With her humorous and approachable style, Jacobs has written an essential title for patients facing a cancer diagnosis." LJ

Johnson, George
The **cancer** chronicles; unlocking medicine's deepest mystery. by George Johnson. Alfred A. Knopf 2013 304 p. $27.95   **616.99**
1. Cancer 2. Medicine -- History 3. Cancer -- Etiology

-- Popular works
ISBN 0307595145; 9780307595140
LC 2012048474
In this book, author George Johnson "tackles cancer on a technical and personal level. Johnson's discussion of the science of cancer is entwined with two tales of loss. Despite aggressive treatment, his youngest brother dies from cancer of the head and neck. His wife is diagnosed with uterine cancer and recovers, but their 17-year marriage ends." (Publisher's note)

"A thorough and nuanced presentation of the state of the science of cancer research, refreshing in its honest appraisal that the war is far from over." Kirkus

Includes bibliographical references and index

Leaf, Clifton
The **truth** in small doses; why we're losing the war on cancer-and how to win it. Clifton Leaf. 1st S&S hardcover ed Simon & Schuster 2013 512 p. illustrations (hbk. : alk. paper) $27   **616.99**
1. Cancer 2. Medicine -- Research 3. Drug Discovery -- History
ISBN 1476739986; 9781476739984; 9781476739991; 9781476740003
LC 2013005817
This book, by Clifton Leaf, offers a "history of the war on cancer. . . . [The author] began to investigate why we had made such limited progress fighting this terrifying disease. The result is a gripping narrative that reveals why the public's immense investment in research has been badly misspent." (Publisher's note)

"Leaf believes that the system must be revamped now, arguing that free exchange of information and a major upgrade in preventative medicine are the keys to improvement. An important evaluative study meriting serious public discussion." Kirkus

Includes bibliographical references and index

Lung cancer; a guide to diagnosis and treatment. Walter J. Scott. 2nd ed. Addicus Books 2012 vii, 110 p.p ill. (pbk.) $19.95   **616.99**
1. Cancer 2. Lung cancer
ISBN 1886039097; 9781886039094
LC 2011042503
"The completely revised second edition has been updated to include a discussion of the movement towards customized chemotherapy; treatment options for early-stage lung cancer including minimally invasive surgery; and the most promising treatments, among them multimodality therapy--a combination of surgery, chemotherapy, and radiation." Publisher's note

Includes bibliographical references and index

Mukherjee, Siddhartha
★ The **emperor** of all maladies. Scribner 2010 571p il $30; ebook $14.99   **616.99**
1. Cancer
ISBN 978-1-4391-0795-9; 1-4391-0795-5; 978-1-4391-8171-3 ebook; 1-4391-8171-3 ebook
LC 2010-24114
The author explores how cancer has been perceived throughout history.

"Mukherjee's formidable intelligence and compassion produce a stunning account of the effort to disrobe the 'emperor of maladies.'" Publ Wkly

Includes bibliographical references

Prijatel, Patricia

Surviving triple negative breast cancer; hope, treatment, and recovery. Patricia Prijatel. Oxford University Press 2013 256 p. (hardback : alk. paper) $7.95 **616.99**

1. Breast cancer 2. Cancer -- Patients 3. Breast cancer -- Treatment

ISBN 1616518898; 9780195387629

LC 2012012425

This book, by health journalist Patricia Prijatel, "delivers . . . information on . . . [triple-negative breast cancer]; the role of genetics, family history, and race; how to navigate treatment options; understanding a pathology report; and a plethora of strategies to reduce the risk of recurrence. . . . Woven throughout the book are stories of women who have faced TNBC, . . . who went through a variety of medical treatments and then got on with life." (Publisher's note)

Includes bibliographical references and index.

Schwalbe, Will

★ The **end** of your life book club; Will Schwalbe. 1st ed. Alfred A. Knopf 2012 viii, 336 p.p (hardcover) $25.00; (paperback) $15.00; (ebook) $25.00 **616.99**

1. Terminally ill 2. Books and reading 3. Mother-son relationship 4. Families of terminally ill 5. Cancer -- Patients -- United States -- Biography 6. Cancer -- Patients -- Family relationships -- United States

ISBN 0307594033; 9780307594037; 9780307739780; 9780307961112

LC 2012018989

In this book by Will Schwalbe, after his mother is "diagnosed with a form of advanced pancreatic cancer" the pair "start a 'book club' that brings them together as her life comes to a close. . . . Their list jumps from classic to popular, from poetry to mysteries, from fantastic to spiritual. The issues they discuss include questions of faith and courage as well as everyday topics such as expressing gratitude and learning to listen." (Publisher's note)

Schwartz, Anna

Cancer fitness; exercise programs for cancer patients and survivors. {by} Anna L. Schwartz. Simon & Schuster 2004 283p il pa $13 **616.99**

1. Cancer 2. Exercise

ISBN 0-7432-3801-X

LC 2004-45340

This guide "details the physical and mental benefits of exercise before, during, and after cancer. Following a review of the science behind her book (including selected references), . . . {the author} explains how and when to start exercising and presents examples of safe and effective aerobic and strength-building exercises designed for both men and women, young and old. . . . This unique guide is highly recommended for all public, consumer health, and nursing collections." Libr J

Sikka, Madhulika

A **breast** cancer alphabet; Madhulika Sikka. Crown Publishers 2014 224 p. $19 **616.99**

1. Breast cancer 2. Cancer -- Patients

ISBN 0385348517; 9780385348515

LC 2013003652

In this book, Madhulika Sikka "has gathered together her reflections and discoveries of being in 'Cancerland' in an A-to-Z guidebook to the entire process of cancer diagnosis, treatment and life afterward. The author examines the process of coping with the waves of feelings one will experience (anxiety, guilt, indignity and others), the need for pampering and the odds of a diagnosis--one in eight women in the United States will get breast cancer." (Kirkus Reviews)

"Whether discussing turbans and other headwear, omnipresent anxiety, or the relief that pillows can provide from post-surgery pain, Sikka's voice is calm and earnest, poetic and descriptive, and occasionally even uplifting." Pub Wkly

Includes bibliographical references

Silver, Marc

Breast cancer husband; how to help your wife (and yourself) through diagnosis, treatment, and beyond. foreword by Frederick P. Smith. Rodale 2004 319p pa $14.95 **616.99**

1. Caregivers 2. Breast cancer

ISBN 1-579-54833-4

LC 2004-7914

"Silver's prose is funny, tender, and filled with rock-solid advice." Libr J

Smith, Claire Bidwell, 1978-

The **rules** of inheritance; a memoir. Claire Bidwell Smith. Hudson Street Press 2012 298 p. **616.99**

1. Bereavement 2. Autobiographies 3. Self-realization 4. Women -- United States -- Biography 5. Daughters -- United States -- Biography 6. Psychotherapists -- United States -- Biography 7. Women psychotherapists -- United States -- Biography 8. Children of cancer patients -- United States -- Biography

ISBN 1594630887; 9781594630880

LC 2011025136

This memoir by Claire Bidwell Smith describes "a young woman who loses her family but finds herself in the process. . . . Smith is just fourteen years old when both of her charismatic parents are diagnosed with cancer. With an impatience typical of youth, Claire throws herself at anything she thinks might help her cope with the weight of this harsh reality: boys, alcohol, traveling, and the anonymity of cities like New York and Los Angeles. By the time she is twenty-five years old they are both gone and Claire is very much alone in the world." (Publisher's note)

Straight Talk about Breast Cancer; from diagnosis to recovery. Suzanne W. Braddock [et al] 5th ed Addicus Books 2014 180 p $19.95 **616.99**

1. Breast cancer

ISBN 9781940495705 ; 1940495709

"Twenty years and five editions later, dermatologist and cancer survivor Braddock continues along with her physician colleagues to offer information for those going through the breast cancer process. This update expands the treatment picture and includes new photos of reconstructions and additional resources." LJ

Includes bibliographical references

Wapner, Jessica

The **Philadelphia** chromosome; a mutant gene and the quest to cure cancer at the genetic level. Jessica Wapner ; foreword by Robert A. Weinberg, PhD. The Experiment, LLC 2013 320 p. ill. (some col.) (pbk.) $25.95   **616.99**
1. Chromosomes 2. Gene therapy 3. Philadelphia Chromosome -- United States
ISBN 1615190678; 9781615190676; 9781615191659
LC 2012047686

This book by Jessica Wapner "describes the path from the first description of a chromosomal abnormality in cancer cells to the successful deployment of a gene-targeted medicine against what had previously been a lethal leukemia. Along the way, she pays homage to various scientific underdogs. . . . In the last chapter, Wapner surveys the current landscape of cancer research, noting hurdles to continued progress such as difficulties in sequencing tumors." (Science)

"Wapner weaves together the basic and applied science with the stories of the dedicated researchers, the broader supporting superstructure of modern medicine and the process of bringing pharmaceuticals to market. An absorbing, complex medical detective story." Kirkus

Includes bibliographical references and index

Wheelwright, Jeff

The **wandering** gene and the Indian princess; Jeff Wheelwright. W.W. Norton & Co. 2012 304p.   **616.99**
1. Race 2. Genetics 3. Religion 4. Breast cancer 5. Genes, BRCA1 6. History of Medicine 7. Breast Neoplasms -- genetics 8. Genetic Predisposition to Disease
ISBN 9780393081916
LC 2011030178

This book tells the story of a "vibrant young Hispano woman, Shonnie Medina, [who] inherits a breast-cancer mutation known as BRCA1.185delAG. It is a genetic variant characteristic of Jews. The Medinas knew they were descended from Native Americans and Spanish Catholics, but they did not know that they had Jewish ancestry as well. The mutation most likely sprang from Sephardic Jews hounded by the Spanish Inquisition. The discovery of the gene leads to a fascinating investigation of cultural history and modern genetics by Dr. Harry Ostrer and other experts on the DNA of Jewish populations. Set in the isolated San Luis Valley of Colorado, this . . . book tells of the Medina family's five-hundred-year passage from medieval Spain to the American Southwest and of their surprising conversion from Catholicism to the Jehovah's Witnesses in the 1980s." (Publisher's note)

Includes bibliographical references and index

617   Surgery, regional medicine, dentistry, ophthalmology, otology, audiology

Current surgical diagnosis & treatment; edited by Gerard M. Doherty, Lawrence W. Way. 12th ed; Lange Medical Books/McGraw-Hill 2006 1453p il pa $66.95   **617**
1. Surgery
ISBN 978-0-07-142315-1; 0-07-142315-X
LC 2006-278501

First published 1977. Periodically revised

This book "covers over 1,000 diseases and disorders managed by surgeons . . . {and} emphasizes quick recall of major diagnostic features and succinct descriptions of disease processes, followed by procedures for definitive diagnosis and treatment, epidemiology, pathophysiology, and pathology." Publisher's note

Includes bibliographical references

Dr. Mütter's Marvels; A True Tale of Intrigue and Innovation at the Dawn of Modern Medicine. by Cristin O'Keefe Aptowicz. Gotham Books 2014 384 p. ill (hardcover) $27.50   **617**
1. Surgery -- History 2. Physicians -- Biography 3. Mutter Museum 4. Museums -- History -- Pennsylvania 5. Pathology -- History -- Pennsylvania 6. History, 19th Century -- Pennsylvania 7. Physicians -- Pennsylvania -- Biography 8. General Surgery -- History -- Pennsylvania 9. General Surgery -- Pennsylvania -- Biography
ISBN 1592408702; 9781592408702
LC 2014014747

This book, by Cristin O'Keefe Aptowicz, is a biography of surgeon Thomas Dent Mütter. "Mütter was . . . [a] medical innovator who pioneered the use of ether as anesthesia, the sterilization of surgical tools, and a compassion-based vision for helping the severely deformed, which clashed spectacularly with the sentiments of his time. . . . He . . . amassed an immense collection of medical oddities that would later form the basis of Philadelphia's Mütter Museum." (Publisher's note)

Includes bibliographical references and index

Gawande, Atul

Complications : a young surgeon's notes on an imperfect science. Metropolitan Bks. 2002 269p $24   **617**
1. Surgery
ISBN 0-8050-6319-6
LC 2001-55884

The author describes the work of a trainee surgeon. The pieces "range from edgy accounts of medical traumas to sobering analyses of doctors' anxieties and burnout. . . . These exquisitely crafted essays, in which medical subjects segue into explorations of much larger themes, place Gawande among the best in the field." Publ Wkly

Includes bibliographical references

Tilney, Nicholas L.

Invasion of the body; revolutions in surgery. Harvard University Press 2011 358p il **617**

1. Surgery -- History

ISBN 978-0-674-06228-3

LC 2011013287

"Touching on everything from sanitation-free barber surgeons to robotics, he discusses the evolving science of surgery, the growth of the profession, the individuals responsible for incremental developments and breakthroughs, the technologies now available, and the directions in which the field might be headed. . . . A broad subject is nicely condensed into a very readable book that should prove fascinating to both lay readers and professionals."

"Touching on everything from sanitation-free barber surgeons to robotics, he discusses the evolving science of surgery, the growth of the profession, the individuals responsible for incremental developments and breakthroughs, the technologies now available, and the directions in which the field might be headed. . . . A broad subject is nicely condensed into a very readable book that should prove fascinating to both lay readers and professionals." Libr J

Includes bibliographical references

617.1   Injuries and wounds

Fainaru, Steve

League of Denial; The NFL, Concussions and the Battle for Truth. Mark Fainaru-Wada and Steve Fainaru. Random House Inc 2013 416 p. illustrations (chiefly color) $27 **617.1**

1. Brain -- Concussion 2. National Football League

ISBN 0770437540; 9780770437541

LC 2012276088

"Both ESPN investigative reporters, the authors reveal how the NFL, over a period of nearly two decades, sought to cover up and deny mounting evidence of the connection between football and brain damage. This narrative moves between the NFL trenches, America's research labs and the boardrooms where the NFL went to war against science; it examines how the league used its power and resources to attack independent scientists and elevate its own flawed research." Publisher's note

"The narrative is fast-paced and almost cinematic in the way it describes the culture of the gridiron, and in the picture it provides of the NFL research labs where scientists drew their conclusions, and the NFL boardrooms where football executives decided to go to war." Pub Wkly

617.4   Surgery by systems and regions

Krug, Louise

Louise; amended. Louise Krug. Black Balloon Pub. 2012 192 p. (trade paper : alk. paper) $14 **617.4**

1. Brain -- Wounds and injuries

ISBN 1936787016; 9781936787012

LC 2011938591

This memoir by Louise Krug describes "A beautiful young woman from Kansas [who] is about to embark on the life of her dreams--California! Glossy journalism! French boyfriend!--only to suffer a brain bleed that collapses the right side of her body, leaving her with double vision, facial paralysis, and a dragging foot. . . . The memoir presents not only Louise's perspective, but also the reaction of her loved ones. . . in fictional interludes." (Publisher's note)

Mukand, Jon

The man with the bionic brain; and other victories over paralysis. Jon Mukand. Chicago Review Press 2012 xiv, 353 p.p (hardback) $26.95 **617.4**

1. Bionics 2. Brain-computer interfaces 3. Paralytics -- Rehabilitation 4. Neurosciences 5. Implants, Artificial 6. Quadriplegia -- Treatment -- Technological innovations

ISBN 1613740557; 9781613740552

LC 2012008154

In this book, "[Jon] Mukand, a physician and rehabilitation medicine specialist, recounts the stories of people who are paralyzed from strokes or spinal-cord injuries. Most of the narrative reports on the life of . . . Matthew Nagle. . . . His spinal cord fully severed, Matt . . . volunteers . . . in a clinical trial of the BrainGate Neural Interface System. . . . The apparatus records signals of individual neurons in his brain and allows his thoughts to direct the cursor of a computer." (Booklist)

Includes bibliographical references and index.

Snyder, Rich, d. 1993

What you must know about dialysis; the secrets to surviving and thriving on dialysis. Rich Snyder. Square One Publishers 2013 197 p. (pbk.) $17.95 **617.4**

1. Chronic disease 2. Kidneys -- Diseases 3. Hemodialysis -- Patients 4. Hemodialysis -- Popular works

ISBN 0757003494; 9780757003493

LC 2012028692

In this book, "osteopathic physician and nephrologist [Rich] Snyder . . . arms patients with . . . information to aid in coping with chronic kidney conditions that require dialysis or a kidney transplant. . . . Focusing primarily on controlling fluid intake and blood pressure, Snyder discusses a dietary regimen, diet supplements, and caring for emotional and spiritual as well as physical well-being." (Publishers Weekly)

Includes bibliographical references and index

Stoler, Diane Roberts

Coping with concussion and mild traumatic brain injury; a guide to living with the challenges associated with post concussion syndrome and brain trauma. Diane Roberts Stoler, Ed.D., and Barbara Albers Hill. Avery 2013 400 p. illustrations (alk. paper) $18 **617.4**

1. Brain -- Concussion 2. Brain -- Wounds and injuries 3. Brain damage 4. Brain damage -- Psychological aspects

ISBN 1583334769; 9781583334768

LC 2013016860

This book, by Diane Roberts Stoler and Barbara Albers Hill, is a "guide for improving memory, focus, and quality of life in the aftermath of a concussion. Often presenting itself after a head trauma, concussion-- or mild traumatic brain injury (mTBI)-- can cause chronic migraines, depression, memory, and sleep problems that can last for years, referred to as post concussion syndrome (PCS)." (Publisher's note)

"Filled with practical advice on understanding and living with concussion and TBI, this well-written and well-organized volume is an excellent resource for patients who have suffered from this condition and for their family members." LJ

Includes bibliographical references and index

617.6   Dentistry

Wynbrandt, James

The **excruciating** history of dentistry; toothsome tales & oral oddities from Babylon to braces. St. Martin's Press 1998 248p il hardcover o.p. pa $14.95   **617.6**
    1. Dentistry -- History
    ISBN 0-312-26319-8 pa
                     LC 98-9794

The author "discusses the development of dentistry as a profession, the use of different anesthetics, and the evolution of dentures and dental prosthetics, among other topics. Much of the book is devoted to anecdotes illustrating discontinued dental practices." Libr J

Includes bibliographical references

617.7   Ophthalmology

Sacks, Oliver W.

The **island** of the colorblind; and, Cycad island. {by} Oliver Sacks. Knopf 1997 298p il maps hardcover o.p. pa $13   **617.7**
    1. Color blindness 2. Parkinson's disease 3. Islands of the Pacific
    ISBN 0-375-70073-0 pa
                    LC 96-34252

First published 1996 in the United Kingdom

"As a travel writer, Sacks ranks with Paul Theroux and Bruce Chatwin. As an investigator of the mind's mysteries, he is in a class by himself." Publ Wkly

Includes bibliographical references

617.8   Otology and audiology

Bouton, Katherine

★ **Shouting** won't help; why I - and 50 million other Americans - can't hear you. Katherine Bouton. Sarah Crichton Books/Farrar, Straus, and Giroux 2013 288 p. (hardcover : alk. paper) $26   **617.8**
    1. Deaf 2. Hearing impaired 3. Deafness 4. Deaf women -- New York (State) -- New York -- Biography
    ISBN 0374263043; 9780374263041
               LC 2012029096

This book, by Katherine Bouton, describes the author's personal experiences struggling with hearing loss. "For twenty-two years, Katherine Bouton had a secret that grew harder to keep every day. . . . She had gone profoundly deaf in her left ear; her right was getting worse. . . . Using her experience as a guide, Bouton examines the problem [of hearing loss] personally, psychologically, and physiologically." (Publisher's note)

Includes bibliographical references and index

617.9   Operative surgery and special fields of surgery

Cheney, Annie

Body brokers; inside America's underground trade in human remains. Broadway Books 2006 205p $23.95; pa $14   **617.9**
    1. Procurement of organs, tissues, etc.
    ISBN 0-7679-1733-2; 978-0-7679-1733-9; 0-7679-1734-0 pa; 978-0-7679-1734-6 pa
               LC 2005-54278

This book "speeds along like a circular saw through a thigh joint. It's a zippy, entertaining read, and more formal, scholarly works on the topic are not." N Y Times Book Rev

Includes bibliographical references

618.1   Gynecology and obstetrics

Eig, Jonathan

★ The **birth** of the pill; how four crusaders reinvented sex and launched a revolution. Jonathan Eig. W W Norton & Co Inc 2014 416 p. (hardcover) $27.95   **618.1**
    1. Oral contraceptives
    ISBN 0393073726; 9780393073720
               LC 2014019355

This book on this history of birth control, by Jonathan Eig, "revolves around four principal characters: . . . feminist Margaret Sanger, who was a champion of birth control, . . . Katharine McCormick, who owed her fortune to her wealthy husband, . . . scientist Gregory Pincus, who was dismissed by Harvard in the 1930s as a result of his experimentation with in vitro fertilization, . . . and the telegenic John Rock, a Catholic doctor from Boston." (Publisher's note)

Includes bibliographical references and index

Greer, Germaine

The **change**; women, aging and the menopause. Ballantine 1993 422p pa $23   **618.1**
    1. Aging 2. Menopause 3. Self-realization 4. Women -- Psychology
    ISBN 0-449-90853-4; 978-0-449-90853-2

First published 1991 in the United Kingdom

This is a discussion of menopause in Western society. Greer looks at medical, psychological and social aspects of the cessation of menstruation and the aging process. She views the climateric as an important turning-point in a woman's life.

"In a wise, witty and inspiring book, Greer rebukes doctors, psychiatrists—and women themselves—who blame the aging female for her menopausal distress. . . . Greer dispels all manner of myths and misconceptions about menopause." Publ Wkly

Includes bibliographical references

Love, Susan M.

Dr. Susan Love's breast book; [by] Susan M. Love, with Karen Lindsey. 5th ed., 1st Da Capo Press ed.; Da Capo Press 2010 736p il pa $22   **618.1**
1. Breast
ISBN 978-0-7382-1359-0

LC 2010-21598

First published 1990 by Addison-Wesley

This book covers breast development, plastic surgery, common problems, and breast cancer diagnosis, treatment, and screening.

Includes bibliographical references

Napoletano, Erika

The **insider's** guide to egg donation; a compassionate and comprehensive guide for all parents-to-be. by Wendie Wilson-Miller and Erika Napoletano. Demos Health 2012 xix, 204 p.p (pbk.) $16.95 **618.1**
1. Infertility 2. Reproductive technology 3. Infertility -- Popular works 4. Human reproductive technology -- Popular works
ISBN 1617051047; 1936303302; 9781617051043; 9781936303304

LC 2012005052

This book by Wendie Wilson-Miller and Erika Napoletano "helps families of all types navigate the less talked about but widely practiced egg donor landscape. . . . In their search for alternative means for building a family, those who face infertility turn to the nearly 500 reproductive specialty clinics across the United States. While egg donors enter into the picture for a variety of reasons, every reason has the same desired result: a family to call one's own." (Publisher's note)

Includes bibliographical references and index

Sheehy, Gail

The **silent** passage: menopause; Rev and updated with four brand-new chapters; Pocket Bks. 1998 xxvi, 293p pa $7.50   **618.1**
1. Menopause
ISBN 0-671-56777-2

LC 98-65873

First published 1992

The author examines the medical, psychological, and social aspects of menopause and includes interviews with women in various stages of menopause and with experts. Discussions of herbal remedies, exercise and diet, menopause in the workplace, estrogen and brainpower, and new frontiers in treatment are included

618.2   Obstetrics

Boston Women's Health Book Collective

Our bodies, ourselves: pregnancy and birth; [by] the Boston Women's Health Book Collective. Simon & Schuster 2008 370p il pa $15   **618.2**
1. Pregnancy 2. Childbirth
ISBN 978-0-7432-7486-9; 0-7432-7486-5

LC 2007-49498

This book includes "information on making health-care decisions (e.g., choosing a provider and a birth setting), nutrition, labor and delivery, Cesarean birth, recovery, feeding an infant, and life as a new mother. It also addresses special situations such as prenatal testing and pregnancy loss. . . . This is an excellent book for public and consumer health library collections; highly recommended." Libr J

Includes bibliographical references

Epstein, Randi Hutter

Get me out; a history of childbirth from the Garden of Eden to the sperm bank. W.W. Norton 2010 302p il $24.95   **618.2**
1. Childbirth
ISBN 978-0-393-06458-2

LC 2009-34751

The author "provides a sharp, sassy history of childbirth. The book is as much a study in sociology as historical snapshot of human birthing practices and gynecological advances, with particular emphasis on developments in the late 19th- and 20th-century United States. . . . The author's engaging sarcasm . . . lends this chronicle a welcome punch and vitality often absent from medical histories." Kirkus

Includes bibliographical references

Greene, Alan R.

Raising baby green; the earth-friendly guide to pregnancy, childbirth, and baby care. [by] Alan Greene; with Jeanette Pavini and Theresa Foy DiGeronimo; illustrations by Val Lawton. Jossey-Bass 2007 306p il pa $16.95   **618.2**
1. Pregnancy 2. Environmental protection 3. Infants -- Care
ISBN 978-0-7879-9622-2; 0-7879-9622-X

LC 2007-23342

This "informative guide for raising children in the most environmentally friendly way possible makes for some fascinating (and surprising) reading. . . . An excellent choice for those who don't know where to begin when it comes to environmental parenting." Booklist

Includes bibliographical references

The **mommy** docs' ultimate guide to pregnancy and birth; [by] Yvonne Bohn, Allison Hill, Alane Park with Melissa Jo Peltier. Da Capo Lifelong 2011 526p il pa $15.95   **618.2**
1. Pregnancy 2. Childbirth 3. Infants -- Care
ISBN 978-0-7382-1460-3

"Chapters are arranged from preparing for pregnancy to first, second, and third trimesters; birth; and early days at home. Additional chapters handle complications of early pregnancy, high-risk pregnancies, and 'frequently asked questions . . . and frequently repeated myths.' They offer reassurance for a healthy pregnancy even for those with health conditions such as hypertension or diabetes. Throughout, the authors deliver practical tips and emotional support for coping with both complicated and uncomplicated pregnancies as well as the things that can go wrong, such as miscarriages or infertility. . . . A great resource for anyone seeking information on pregnancy, childbirth, and the first weeks after birth." Libr J

Includes bibliographical references

Murkoff, Heidi Eisenberg

What to expect before you're expecting; by Heidi Murkoff and Sharon Mazel; foreword by Charles J. Lockwood. Workman Pub. 2009 275p il $23.95; pa $12.95   **618.2**
1. Pregnancy 2. Childbirth 3. Prenatal care
ISBN 978-0-7611-5552-2; 978-0-7611-5276-7 pa
LC 2009-7466

The authors "present a preconception program that includes tips on what to eat (and not eat), how to maintain a healthy weight and advice about preconception medical care, such as having a physical and dental checkup. . . . Couples who are trying to conceive will find plenty of useful ideas to consider and implement in the months preceding their baby's debut." Publ Wkly

What to expect when you're expecting; by Heidi Murkoff and Sharon Mazel; foreword by Charles J. Lockwood. 4th ed.; Workman 2008 xxiii, 614p il pa $14.95   **618.2**
1. Pregnancy 2. Childbirth
ISBN 978-0-7611-4857-9; 0-7611-4857-4

First published 1984 under the authorship of Arlene Eisenberg, Heidi E. Murkoff, and Sandee E. Hathaway

"The book is arranged by month, from pregnancy test through labor and delivery. Each section offers answers to frequently asked questions, along with features such as 'What You May Be Feeling' . . . This book remains an indispensable guide for pregnant women and their partners." Publ Wkly [review of 2002 edition]

Vincent, Peggy

Baby catcher; chronicles of a modern midwife. Scribner 2002 336p $26; pa $13   **618.2**
1. Midwives
ISBN 0-7432-1933-3; 0-7432-1934-1 pa
LC 2001-54988

This is an account of a midwife specializing in home births who "over the course of 40 years, brought some 2,000 babies into the world. . . . A solid writer, Vincent doesn't preach the virtues of unmedicated birthing; she just lays consistent stories of women doing it—Christian Science moms, Muslim moms, spiritualist moms, lesbian moms, teen moms and just plain ordinary moms." Publ Wkly

Your pregnancy week by week; Glade B. Curtis, Judith Schuler. Da Capo Lifelong 2011 673 p. 7th ed ill. (paperback) $15.95   **618.2**
1. Pregnancy 2. Fetus -- Growth
ISBN 0738214639; 0738214647; 9780738214634;

9780738214641
LC 2011037019

First published 1989 by Fisher Books

"[T]his guide provides everything expectant parents need for a healthy, happy pregnancy, including descriptions of the fetus's development each week, up-to-date information about medical tests and procedures, safe weekly exercises to help expectant moms stay in shape, and helpful hints for the father-to-be." Publisher's note

618.3   Diseases, disorders, management of pregnancy, childbirth, puerperium

Kohn, Ingrid

A **silent** sorrow; pregnancy loss: guidance and support for you and your family. [by] Ingrid Kohn and Perry-Lynn Moffitt, with Isabelle A. Wilkins. 2nd ed; Routledge 2000 xx, 299p pa $16.95 **618.3**
1. Bereavement 2. Miscarriage
ISBN 0-415-92481-2
LC 99-25720

First published 1993 by Delacorte Press

The authors provide "suggestions to validate parents' grief; cope with the unique concerns of early loss, crisis pregnancies, stillbirth, and newborn death; find medical, religious, and family support; and manage their lives afterwards. The writing is insightful and the tone respectful and supportive." Libr J [review of 1993 edition]

Includes bibliographical references

Lerner, Henry M.

Miscarriage : a doctor's guide to the facts; why it happens and how best to reduce your risks. with contributions by Alice Domar; introduction by Robert Barbieri. Perseus Bks. 2003 291p pa $16.95 **618.3**
1. Miscarriage
ISBN 0-7382-0634-2
LC 2002-114586

This book provides "explanations to questions concerning the etiology, diagnosis, prevention, and treatment of miscarriage. His medical and scientific discussion, while exceedingly thorough, is easy to understand. . . . Especially helpful are the concluding chapters, which focus on dealing with the emotional trauma of miscarriage." Libr J

Paul, Annie Murphy

Origins; how the nine months before birth shape the rest of our lives. Free Press 2010 306p $26; ebook $12.99   **618.3**
1. Fetus 2. Pregnancy 3. Prenatal diagnosis 4. Fetus -- Development 5. Pregnancy -- Psychological aspects
ISBN 0-7432-9662-1; 1-4391-7184-X ebook; 978-0-7432-9662-5; 978-1-4391-7184-4 ebook
LC 2010-15249

Paul writes that "'fetal origins research suggests that the lifestyle that influences the development of disease is often not only the one we follow as adults, but the one our mothers practiced when they were pregnant with us as well.'" (N Y Times Book Rev) Index.

"Just what effect do the things that women inhale, consume and experience have on a fetus? In 'Origins,' Annie Murphy Paul sets out to discover the answer. Along the way she explodes myths, reviews scientific evidence and explores the new frontier of fetal-origins research, the study of how we are shaped in utero by a combination of genes and environment." Wall Street J

Includes bibliographical references

Rope, Kate

The **Complete** Guide to Medications During Pregnancy and Breastfeeding; Carl P. Weiner and Kate Rope. St. Martin's Press 2013 viii, 1062 p.p (paperback) $9.99　　　　　　　　　　　**618.3**

1. Pregnancy 2. Pharmacology 3. Breast feeding
ISBN 1250028388; 9781250028389

This book, by Carl P. Weiner and Kate Rope, offers a "comprehensive pharmaceutical guide . . . to help . . . make informed decisions while pregnant and nursing. Sometimes even physicians disagree or appear confused about what medications are appropriate choices for pregnant and breastfeeding women. . . . This . . . guide combines authority and empathy with an A-to-Z directory of more than six hundred drugs to help you make the best possible decisions for you and your baby." (Publisher's note)

618.4　Childbirth

Birth without violence; Frédérick Leboyer ; new translation by Yvonne Fitzgerald and the author. 3rd ed Healing Arts Press 2009 xiii, 130 p.p ill. (pbk.) $14.95　　　　　　　　　　　**618.4**

1. Natural childbirth 2. Childbirth
ISBN 1594772975; 9781594772979

LC 2009001028

Original French edition, 1974; first English translation published 1975 by Knopf

A new edition of the book that "revolutionized the way we perceive the process of birth, urging us to consider birth from the infant's point of view." It shows how to "ease the transition from womb to world without trauma or fear." (Publisher's note)

Gaskin, Ina May

Ina May's guide to childbirth. Bantam Books 2003 348p il pa $14.95　　　　　　　　　　**618.4**

1. Natural childbirth
ISBN 0-553-38115-6

LC 2002-29901

Gaskin "explains that the female body is well designed for normal birth and provides techniques for dealing with the discomforts of labor. A whole chapter devoted to women's birthing experiences supports her stance. More than a childbirth guide, this comprehensive book provides insight into the sociological and historical aspects of the natural childbirth movement." Libr J

Includes bibliographical references

618.92　Pediatrics

Asperger Syndrome; The Oasis Guide: Advice, Inspiration, Insight, and Hope, from Early Intervention to Adulthood. Patricia Romanowski Bashe. 3rd ed Random House Inc 2014 592 p. $17　　　　　　　　　　　　　　　**618.92**

1. Autism 2. Asperger's syndrome
ISBN 0385344651; 9780385344654
First published 2001

"This edition includes new developments made in AS research over the past four years, new thinking on diagnosis and evaluation, the latest approaches to medication and social skills development, and tips on navigating the maze of interventions, therapies, and special education." Publisher's note

Includes bibliographical references

Brown, Ian, 1954-

The **boy** in the moon; Ian Brown. St. Martin's Press 2011 293p.　　　　　　　　　　**618.92**

1. Journalists 2. Children -- Diseases 3. Father-son relationship 4. Parents of children with disabilities
ISBN 0312671830; 9780312671839

LC 2011378371

This book, based on "a series of pieces [the author wrote] about his son Walker [for 'The Globe and Mail'],"
presents an "account of raising, loving, and trying to connect with and gain insight into his severely disabled son. . . Walker was born with cardiofaciocutaneous (CFC) syndrome, an extremely rare genetic disorder. . . . The author writes of the struggle to raise a self-destructive child who could not speak and suffered numerous physical deformities and medical problems. . . . He seeks out and profiles other families with CFC children, interviews a genetic researcher who found mutations in three genes related to the disorder, looks for clues to CFC through an MRI of Walker's brain and travels to France to visit L'Arche, a faith-based organization that operates communities for the developmentally disabled." (Kirkus)

Chicoine, Brian

The **guide** to good health for teens & adults with Down syndrome; [by] Brian Chicoine & Dennis McGuire. Woodbine House 2010 391p il pa $29.95　　　　　　　　　　　　　　　**618.92**

1. Down syndrome
ISBN 978-1-890627-89-8

LC 2010-18783

"This excellent book provides a wealth of information for DS caregivers. . . . The authors describe diagnosis, treatment, and prevention of common health conditions impacting DS people and cover mental and emotional issues that can affect physical health. Sexuality and birth control are discussed, as is abuse prevention. The book also includes information on residential options as well as coverage of end of life issues." Libr J

Includes bibliographical references

Cohen, Scott W.

Eat, sleep, poop; a common sense guide to your baby's first year--essential information from an

award-winning pediatrician and new dad. Scribner
2010 291p il pa $16 **618.92**
 1. Infants -- Care
 ISBN 978-1-4391-1706-4; 1-4391-1706-3
           LC 2009-37966
 "Cohen is great at identifying parental concerns, and he
responds with reassuring answers, providing just enough
information to assuage worries. Of the multitude of baby
guides out there, this is, hands down, one of the best in
years." Libr J
 Includes bibliographical references

Edwards, Laurie

 Life disrupted; getting real about chronic illness
in your twenties and thirties. Walker & Company
2008 272p pa $14.99 **618.92**
 1. Chronic diseases
 ISBN 978-0-8027-1649-1; 0-8027-1649-0
           LC 2008-245
 The author, who "manages bronchiectasis, thyroid disease, and celiac disease, among other conditions, ably describes the realities of people living longer with chronic
(often rare) illnesses. . . . Using her own life story, Edwards
shares practical advice about going to college, looking for a
job, finding a partner, and deciding whether to have children,
all the while juggling demanding health issues." Libr J
 Includes bibliographical references

Foss, Ben

 The **dyslexia** empowerment plan; a blueprint for
renewing your child's confidence and love of learning. by Ben Foss. Ballantine Books 2013 336 p.
(hardback) $27 **618.92**
 1. Parents 2. Dyslexia 3. Child psychology 4. Dyslexic
children -- Rehabilitation 5. Parents of children with
disabilities
 ISBN 0345541235; 9780345541239
           LC 2013023931
 In this book, author Ben Foss "describes dyslexia as a
characteristic and a disability that should be accommodated
in the same way as blindness or mobility issues. Foss reframes the use of film, audiobooks, and material read aloud
as ear-reading, in contrast to the eye-reading that is the educational standard. He hopes that parents can learn to explain
their child's needs in a way that will win them essential support, and that they can help their child build self-esteem."
(Publishers Weekly)
 Includes bibliographical references and index

Frith, Uta

 Autism : explaining the enigma; 2nd ed; Blackwell 2003 249p il $59.95; pa $26.95 **618.92**
 1. Autism
 ISBN 0-631-22900-0; 0-631-22901-9 pa
           LC 2002-12932
 First published 1989
 This "book is valuable for educated parents interested
in learning about autism in a larger historical context. Frith
writes a great deal on the problem that autistic people have
with 'mind blindness,' the inability to look at and see other
people." Libr J
 Includes bibliographical references

Hayden, Torey L.

 Twilight children; three voices no one heard until a therapist listened. [by] Torey Hayden. William
Morrow 2005 331p $24.95 **618.92**
 1. Child abuse 2. Psychotherapy
 ISBN 0-06-056088-6
           LC 2004-47376
 "The author documents the particulars of her approach to
treating a volatile, manipulative nine-year-old abuse victim;
a mute but sociable and atypically charismatic four-year-old;
and, in a change of pace, an 82-year-old stroke victim. The
dysfunctional family dynamics impacting each patient are
explored, as are impediments to the therapist's interfacing
with relatives." SLJ

Hilden, Joanne M.

 Shelter from the storm; caring for a child with
a life-threatening condition. {by} Joanne M. Hilden
and Daniel R. Tobin, with Karen Lindsey. Perseus
2003 224p pa $15.95 **618.92**
 1. Terminally ill children
 ISBN 0-7382-0534-6
 This guide "empowers parents to ask the right questions
so that they can get necessary information and make the
best decisions about their child's care. It also supports them
through death and the grieving process if treatment fails. Using a combination of medical advice and quotes from parents who have been there, the authors have created a sensitive and useful resource." Libr J
 Includes bibliographical references

Ives, Martine

 Caring for a child with autism; a practical guide
for parents. {by} Martine Ives and Nell Munro; illustrations by Fiona Bleach. Kingsley, J. 2002 304p
il pa $18.95 **618.92**
 1. Autism
 ISBN 1-85302-996-3
           LC 2001-38436
 This "guide answers the questions commonly asked by
parents and carers following a diagnosis of autism, and discusses the challenges that can arise in home life, education
and socializing." Publisher's note
 Includes bibliographical references and index

Jackson, Luke

 Freaks, geeks and asperger syndrome; a user
guide to adolescence. foreword by Tony Attwood.
Kingsley, J. 2002 217p il pa $17.95 **618.92**
 1. Autism 2. Asperger's syndrome 3. Adolescent
psychology
 ISBN 1-8431-0098-3
           LC 2002-70930
 "In this terrific book that is sure to inspire other adolescents with the same condition, 13-year-old Jackson offers a teenager's perspective on what it's like to live with
Asperger's. He also writes about his younger brother, who
has a more severe condition on the ASD spectrum." Libr J
 Includes bibliographical references

Jassey, Jonathan

The **newborn** sleep book; a simple, proven method for training your new baby to sleep through the night. Dr. Lewis Jassey and Dr. Jonathan Jassey. Perigee Trade 2014 224 p. (paperback) $15 **618.92**
1. Sleep 2. Infants -- Health and hygiene 3. Infants -- Sleep
ISBN 0399167986; 9780399167980

LC 2014011339

This book by Lewis Jassey and Jonathan Jassey provides advice on getting newborn babies to sleep through the night by strictly regulating feeding times despite an infant's hunger. "The Jassey Way uses a feeding schedule that allows newborns (and their parents) a full night's sleep at a younger age than other sleep training techniques." (Publisher's note)

"Parent testimonials and numerous checklists are appended to this manageable plan." Pub Wkly

Includes bibliographical references

Martin, Katherine L.

Does my child have a speech problem? Chicago Review Press 1997 160p il pa $16.95   **618.92**
1. Speech disorders 2. Children -- Health and hygiene
ISBN 1-55652-315-7

LC 96-35302

The author addresses stuttering, fluency and articulation issues. Listening and auditory processing skills are discussed

"Martin's writing style is clear and engaging, making this slim volume a quick, easy read." Libr J

Includes bibliographical references

Preemies; the essential guide for parents of premature babies. Dana Wechsler Linden, Emma Trenti Paroli, and Mia Wechsler Doron. 2nd ed Gallery Books 2010 xxii, 633 p.p ill. $26.99   **618.92**
1. Premature infants 2. Premature infants -- Care 3. Pregnancy -- Complications 4. Birth weight, Low -- Complications
ISBN 1416572325; 9781416572329

LC 2011289347

This guide "covers risk factors, the first day, the first week, surgery, taking the baby home and many other topics. Each section contains personal observations from parents of preemies, insightful comments from 'the doctor's perspective' and information on procedures, equipment, common problems and other issues." Publ Wkly

Rapp, Emily

The **still** point of the turning world; Emily Rapp. The Penguin Press 2013 272 p. (hardcover) $25.95   **618.92**
1. Tay-Sachs disease 2. Parents of children with disabilities
ISBN 1594205124; 9781594205125

LC 2012039516

This book, by Emily Rapp, is a memoir of a mother struggling to parent her terminally ill child. "Ronan was diagnosed at nine months old with Tay-Sachs disease, a rare and always-fatal degenerative disorder. . . . Rapp and her husband were forced to re-evaluate everything they thought they knew about parenting. They would have to learn to live with their child in the moment; to find happiness in the midst of sorrow; to parent without a future." (Publisher's note)

Richman, Shira

Raising a child with autism; a guide to applied behavior analysis for parents. Kingsley, J. 2000 173p pa $19.95   **618.92**
1. Autism 2. Parent-child relationship
ISBN 1-85302-910-6

LC 00-47818

"Behavior therapy consultant Richman clearly outlines the applied behavior analysis (ABA) activities that parents can use with ASD children. Included is helpful guidance for toilet training, daily living, and increasing communication and sibling interaction. Since ABA consultants may be out of the financial or geographic reach of many parents, having a strong resource like this is invaluable." Libr J

Includes bibliographical references and index

Saul, Richard

ADHD does not exist; the truth about attention deficit and hyperactivity disorder. Richard Saul. HarperWave 2013 336 p. (hardback) $25.99 **618.92**
1. Psychology 2. Hyperactivity 3. Mental health 4. Attention deficit disorder
ISBN 006226673X; 9780062266736

LC 2013030794

In this book, "behavioral neurologist Dr. Richard Saul draws on five decades of experience treating thousands of patients labeled with Attention Deficit and Hyperactivity Disorder--one of the fastest growing and widely diagnosed conditions today--to argue that ADHD is actually a cluster of symptoms stemming from over 20 other conditions and disorders." (Publisher's note)

Includes bibliographical references and index

Sicherer, Scott H.

Understanding and managing your child's food allergies. Johns Hopkins University Press 2006 312p il $45; pa $18.95   **618.92**
1. Parenting 2. Food allergy
ISBN 0-8018-8491-8; 978-0-8018-8491-7; 0-8018-8492-6 pa; 978-0-8018-8492-4 pa

LC 2006-5261

This "book provides parents with practical advice for managing a child's environment at home, at school, or out in the world at large. In Part 2, 'Diagnosing a Food Allergy,' the practice of taking a detailed medical history is espoused and case studies serve to bring the issue home. An action plan for anaphylaxis, a life-threatening type of allergic reaction, as well as a chapter on food allergy resources are included." Libr J

Includes bibliographical references

★ **Sleep;** what every parent needs to know. American Academy of Pediatrics ; [edited by] Rachel Moon, MD, FAAP. American Academy of Pediatrics 2013 250 p. ill. $16.95   **618.92**
1. Sleep 2. Parenting 3. Sleep therapy
ISBN 1581107811; 9781581107814

LC 2012953639

This book, edited by Rachel Moon, "incorporates the expertise of more than 20 pediatricians and covers numerous issues regarding how to create and maintain healthy sleep habits in children. . . . The book is divided into two sections: Ages, Stages and Phases and Childhood Sleep Challenges. Part one guides readers from the first year of life through adolescence, with chapters along the way about toddlers, preschoolers, and school-age kids." (Publisher's note)

Suskind, Ron

Life, animated; a story of sidekicks, heroes, and autism. by Ron Suskind. Kingswell 2014 358 p. illustrations, some color (hardback) $26.99 **618.92**
1. Autism 2. Communication 3. Animated films 4. Parents of autistic children 5. Autistic children
ISBN 1423180364; 9781423180364

LC 2014006760

"This is the real-life story of Owen Suskind, the son of the Pulitzer Prize-winning journalist Ron Suskind and his wife, Cornelia. An autistic boy who couldn't speak for years, Owen memorized dozens of Disney movies, turned them into a language to express love and loss, kinship, brotherhood.The family was forced to become animated characters, communicating with him in Disney dialogue and song; until they all emerge, together, revealing how, in darkness, we all literally need stories to survive." (Publisher's note)

"The Disney effect may be distinctive to this experience, but the family dynamic should resonate with a much wider readership." Kirkus

Taking Charge of ADHD; The Complete, Authoritative Guide for Parents. Russell A. Barkley, PHD. 3rd ed The Guilford Press 2013 363 p. pbk $19.95; hc $55 **618.92**
1. Attention deficit disorder 2. Child rearing 3. Attention-deficit hyperactivity disorder
ISBN 1462508510; 1462507891; 9781462507894; 9781462508518
First published 1995

Presents "science-based information . . . about attention-deficit/hyperactivity disorder (ADHD) and its treatment. It also presents a proven eight-step behavior management plan specifically designed for 6- to 18-year-olds with ADHD. Updated throughout with current research and resources, the third edition includes the latest facts about medications and about what causes (and doesn't cause) ADHD." Publisher's note

Includes bibliographical references and index

Terr, Lenore

Magical moments of change; how psychotherapy turns kids around. W. W. Norton 2008 304p $27.95 **618.92**
1. Psychotherapy 2. Child psychiatry
ISBN 978-0-393-70530-0; 0-393-70530-7

LC 2007-16745

The author "has compiled 48 vignettes offered by 33 psychiatrists dealing with myriad cases, from mild development problems to juvenile delinquency to schizophrenia, recounting the almost magical moments of breakthrough." Booklist

Includes bibliographical references

618.97 Geriatrics

Mace, Nancy L.

★ The **36** -hour day; a family guide to caring for people with Alzheimer disease, other dementias, and memory loss in later life. [by] Nancy L. Mace, Peter V. Rabins. 4th ed.; Johns Hopkins University Press 2006 xxii, 324p (Johns Hopkins Press health book) $45; pa $16.95 **618.97**
1. Alzheimer's disease
ISBN 978-0-8018-8510-5; 0-8018-8510-8; 978-0-8018-8509-9 pa; 0-8018-8509-4 pa

LC 2006-9627

First published 1981

A guide designed for families of Alzheimer's sufferers. Current research on the brain, behavior and personality is included.

620 Engineering and allied operations

Molotch, Harvey Luskin

Where stuff comes from; how toasters, toilets, cars, computers, and many other things come to be as they are. [by] Harvey Molotch. Routledge 2003 324p il $35; pa $29.95 **620**
1. Engineering
ISBN 0-415-94400-7; 0-415-95042-2 pa

LC 2003-1191

The author examines "the complicated, dynamic relationships between inventor, society, corporation, regulator, shopkeeper, community, family and customer. . . . Myriad links, he argues, ultimately produce and constantly change what we want, buy, keep and throw away; thus, neither consumers nor producers are to be blamed for our numerous possessions. . . . Molotch's description of systemic person-product complexes could work to end blame-the-consumer guilt-mongering in the popular discourse." Publ Wkly

Includes bibliographical references

Petroski, Henry

The **essential** engineer; why science alone will not solve our global problems. Alfred A. Knopf 2010 274p il $26.95 **620**
1. Engineering 2. Technological innovations 3. Technology and civilization
ISBN 978-0-307-27245-4; 0-307-27245-1

LC 2009-21216

"Petroski presents a book-length argument for the place of engineering in humanity's future, especially when it comes to ensuring that future in the face of climate change, natural disasters, dwindling oil supplies and other global problems. . . . Scientists get the credit for everything from the moon landing to the construction of the Large Hadron Collider, he complains, when in reality those and myriad other projects large and small couldn't have been achieved without the creative, intelligent and rigorous input of engineers." Washington Post Book World

Includes bibliographical references

Invention by design; how engineers get from thought to thing. Harvard Univ. Press 1996 242p il map hardcover o.p. pa $14.95 **620**

1. Inventions 2. Engineering
ISBN 0-674-46368-4 pa

LC 96-19227

"Every case study includes well-chosen pictures and schematic drawings to clarify how inventors resolve technical difficulties, and the carefully research text explains how they make their new creations economically feasible and socially acceptable." Booklist

Includes bibliographical references

Remaking the world; adventures in engineering. Knopf 1997 239p il hardcover o.p. pa $13 **620**

1. Engineering
ISBN 0-375-70024-2 pa

LC 97-29328

A collection of the author's essays originally written for American Scientist. "Several pieces are about particular engineers . . . or engineering projects (the Channel Tunnel, the Ferris Wheel); others are provocative (the flaws of engineering software, the creep of technology)." Libr J

Includes bibliographical references

Success through failure; the paradox of design. Princeton University Press 2006 235p il hardcover o.p. pa $21.95 **620**

1. Design 2. Engineering
ISBN 978-0-691-12225-0; 0-691-12225-3; 978-0-691-13642-4 pa; 0-691-13642-4 pa

LC 2005-34126

An "engaging and readable book. . . . Petroski uses countless interesting case histories to show how failure motivates technological advancement." IEEE Spectrum

Includes bibliographical references

Petroski, Henry, 1942-

★ **To** forgive design; understanding failure. Henry Petroski. Belknap Press of Harvard University Press 2012 xii, 410 p.p ill. **620**

1. Design 2. Engineering 3. Structural failures 4. System failures (Engineering)
ISBN 0674065840; 9780674065840

LC 2011044194

This book, by Henry Petroski, "looks not only at how people contribute to the failure of engineering designs but also at how analyzing those failures can improve subsequent models. He considers many different types of failures, from several infamous bridge collapses to carefully designed intentional failures, which are engineered specifically to prevent greater failures." (Library Journal)

"Even the layman will find Petroski's study to be accessible, informative, and interesting." Pub Wkly

Includes bibliographical references and index.

Sale, Kirkpatrick

The **fire** of his genius: Robert Fulton and the American dream. Free Press 2001 242p il $24; pa $13 **620**

1. Engineers 2. Inventors
ISBN 0-684-86715-X; 0-7432-2321-7 pa

LC 2001-23064

Sale examines the life of the American inventor, "explaining how his North River steamboat opened up the North American continent to settlement and how it became the key factor that influenced the beginnings of the American industrial revolution. . . . This is an informative, moving story that personalizes the relatively obscure life of a self-taught tinkerer who had a genius for self-promotion and exploiting the discoveries of others." Libr J

Includes bibliographical references

620.1 Engineering mechanics and materials

Freinkel, Susan

Plastic; a toxic love story. Houghton Mifflin Harcourt 2011 324p $27 **620.1**

1. Plastics
ISBN 978-0-547-15240-0

LC 2010-43019

"At first a godsend, [plastic] reduced dependence on shrinking natural resources, such as the shell of the hawksbill turtle (combs) or elephants' ivory (billiard balls and piano keys.) Ultimately it democratized materialism, making everything available to everybody, cheaply. Now, the partner we've found in plastic 'can rightly inspire both our deepest admiration and our strongest disgust.' To describe its history, wonders and dangers, journalist Freinkel reviews eight products: the comb, the chair, the Frisbee, the IV bag, the disposable lighter, the grocery bag, the soda bottle and the credit card. You will not look casually at any of them again." Cleveland Plain Dealer

Includes bibliographical references

621 Applied physics

Alley, Richard B.

Earth; the operators' manual. W.W. Norton 2011 479p il $27.95 **621**

1. Energy development 2. Renewable energy resources 3. Greenhouse effect
ISBN 978-0-393-08109-1

LC 2010-54016

The author "presents a primer on combatting global warming. The book begins with a history of how fuel—from trees, whale oil, and petroleum—has been instrumental to civilization and how we tend to exhaust our sources. He goes on to explain how scientists study climate change and why the evidence is convincing, and ends with a call to action and an overview of possible solutions. . . . This optimistic book ought to convince even the most obstinate climate-change denier." Publ Wkly

Includes bibliographical references

Marks' standard handbook for mechanical engineers; [edited by] Eugene A. Avallone, Theodore Baumeister, Ali Sadegh. 11th ed; McGraw-Hill 2006 1800p il $199.95   **621**
1. Mechanical engineering -- Handbooks, manuals, etc.
ISBN 978-0-07-142867-5; 0-07-142867-4
First published 1916 under the editorship of Lionel S. Marks with title: Mechanical engineers' handbook. Periodically revised. Editors vary
This volume presents concisely the basic scientific and technical data of mechanical engineering, covering theory, basic mechanism, standard practice, often-needed mathematical formulae and technical data
Includes bibliographical references

621.3   Electrical, magnetic, optical, communications, computer engineering; electronics, lighting

American electricians' handbook; Terrell Croft, Frederic P. Hartwell, Wilford I. Summers [editors] 16th ed McGraw-Hill 2013 1712 p. ill. $90   **621.3**
1. Electric engineering -- Handbooks, manuals, etc
ISBN 0071798803; 9780071798808
"The Sixteenth Edition is revised to complywith the 2011 National Electrical Code and the 2012 National Electrical Safety Code, and covers current energy-efficient technologies, such as photovoltaics and induction lighting. Detailed photos, diagrams, charts, tables, and calculations are included throughout." Publisher's note

Kaplan, Steven M.
    Wiley electrical and electronics engineering dictionary. John Wiley & Sons 2004 885p pa $73.50   **621.3**
1. Reference books 2. Electronics -- Dictionaries 3. Electrical engineering -- Dictionaries
ISBN 0-471-40224-9
                                LC 2003-66068
This "will be an asset to any university library that supports an electrical and electronics engineering curriculum, or to any professional engineering library. . . . A superb resource." Choice
Includes bibliographical references

McGraw-Hill's national electrical code handbook 2014; Frederic P. Hartwell, Joseph F. McPartland, Brian J. McPartland. 28th ed McGraw-Hill 2014 1678 p. $99   **621.3**
1. Electrical engineering -- Handbooks, manuals, etc.
ISBN 0071834788; 9780071834780
First published 1932 with title: National Electrical Code handbook. Periodically revised to reflect changes in the code. Title varies
    28th ed
This handbook presents analysis and commentary on the National Electrical Code, as it pertains to wiring of appliances, buildings, emergency systems, and other types of electrical construction.

National electrical code handbook 2014; [edited by] Mark W. Earley, P.E., Christopher D. Coache, Mark Cloutier, Gil Moniz. National Fire Protection Association 2013 1259 p. $165.50   **621.3**
1. Electrical engineering -- Handbooks, manuals, etc.
ISBN 1455905445; 9781455905447
                                LC 2013941415
First published 1978. Periodically revised
This "is a nationally accepted guide to the safe installation of electrical conductors and equipment, and is, in fact, the basis for all electrical codes used in the United States." Ref Sources for Small & Medium-sized Libr. 5th edition

Shulman, Seth
    ★ The **telephone** gambit; chasing Alexander Graham Bell's secret. W. W. Norton & Co. 2008 256p il $24.95   **621.3**
1. Inventors 2. Telephone 3. Teachers of the deaf 4. Telecommunications executives
ISBN 978-0-393-06206-9; 0-393-06206-6
                                LC 2007-30904
The author argues that Alexander Graham Bell is not the true inventor of the telephone.
This book "does a neat job of painting, in rapid brush strokes, a portrait of the thrilling era of innovation in which Bell lived and also of the interesting circumstances of his life. . . . [He] also manages to lace his work with just enough technology to tell his story without losing the interest of any low-tech readers." Christ Sci Monit
Includes bibliographical references

Standard Handbook for Electrical Engineers; H. Wayne Beaty, Donald G. Fink. 16th ed McGraw-Hill 2012 2144 p. ill $150   **621.3**
1. Electrical engineering -- Handbooks, manuals, etc.
ISBN 0071762329; 9780071762328
First published 1908. Periodically revised
    16th ed
Edited by H. Wayne Beaty and Donald G. Fink, "Completely revised throughout to address the latest codes and standards, the 16th Edition of this renowned reference offers new coverage of green technologies such as smart grids, smart meters, renewable energy, and cogeneration plants. Modern computer applications and methods for securing computer network infrastructures that control power grids are also discussed." (Publisher's note)
Contains data on all branches of electrical engineering including material in the field of nuclear physics, plastics and resins, transistors and television.

621.31   Generation, modification, storage, transmission of electric power

Fletcher, Seth
    Bottled lightning; superbatteries, electric cars, and the new lithium economy. Hill and Wang 2011 260p $26   **621.31**
1. Lithium 2. Electronics 3. Electric batteries
ISBN 978-0-8090-3053-8; 0-8090-3053-5
                                LC 2010-47695

"Provides an entertaining, surprisingly eventful history of human efforts to harness energy in the form of battery power . . . . A fine, readable work of popular science." Kirkus

Includes bibliographical references

Schlesinger, Henry R.

The **battery**; how portable power sparked a technological revolution. [by] Henry Schlesinger. Smithsonian Books 2010 308p il $25.99 **621.31**

1. Storage batteries 2. Electric batteries

ISBN 978-0-06-144293-3

LC 2009-34303

"From its witty subtitle ('sparked,' get it?), to its lively writing style, to its sheer abundance of fascinating and frequently surprising stories, this is a delightful book." Booklist

Includes bibliographical references

621.319 Transmission

The **complete** guide to wiring; current with 2014-2017 electrical codes. 6th ed Cool Springs Press 2014 335 p. color illustrations (paperback) $24.99 **621.319**

1. Electric wiring 2. Electric wiring, Interior -- Amateurs' manuals 3. Dwellings -- Electric equipment -- Amateurs' manuals 4. Dwellings -- Maintenance and repair -- Amateurs' manuals

ISBN 159186612X; 9781591866121

LC 2014000449

First published 1998 by Cowles Creative Pub.

Includes "an overview of electricity and wiring safety; wire, cable, and conduits; boxes and panels; switches; and receptacles. . . [and] foolproof circuit maps for 30 common wiring set-ups and step-by-step walkthroughs of every essential home wiring and electrical repair project." Publisher's note

Includes bibliographical references and index

621.32 Lighting

Brox, Jane

Brilliant; the evolution of artificial light. Houghton Mifflin Harcourt 2010 360p $25 **621.32**

1. Lighting

ISBN 978-0-547-05527-5; 0-547-05527-7

LC 2009-35441

The author "examines our relationship with light, our attempts to harness it to brighten places we cannot see, and its impact on American psychology and culture. . . . This well-written, well-researched, and thought-provoking book has much to offer. The general reader with an interest in the (social) history of technology will find it . . . a source of inspiration for considering technology's impact on our lives." Libr J

Includes bibliographical references

621.381 Electronics

Schultz, Mitchel E.

Grob's basic electronics; 11th ed.; McGraw-Hill 2011 xxvi, 1206p il $155.31 **621.381**

1. Electricity 2. Electronics

ISBN 978-0-07-351085-9; 0-07-351085-8

LC 2010-8273

First published 1959 under the authorship of Bernard Grob. Periodically revised

An introductory text on the fundamentals of electricity and electronics for technicians in radio, television, and industrial electronics.

Includes glossary

621.383 Specific communications systems

Silverman, Kenneth

Lightning man; the accursed life of Samuel F.B. Morse. Knopf 2003 503p il $35 **621.383**

1. Artists 2. Painters 3. Inventors 4. Telegraph 5. Cipher and telegraph codes

ISBN 0-375-40128-8

LC 2002-43613

This is a "biography of Samuel F.B. Morse, the inventor of the Morse code and the disputed inventor of the electromagnetic telegraph. . . . Silverman shows how Morse's never-ending battle with negative self-image, a result of his strict Calvinist upbringing, was the common thread that tied together the disparate events of his life. And Silverman's well-paced, character-driven storytelling brings Morse's raw, emotional persona to life. Strongly recommend for public libraries and for academic library collections at all levels." Libr J

621.388 Television

Abramson, Albert

The **history** of television, 1942 to 2000; foreword by Christopher H. Sterling. McFarland & Co. 2003 309p il hardcover o.p. pa $75 **621.388**

1. Television -- History

ISBN 0-7864-1220-8; 978-0-7864-3243-1 pa; 0-7864-3243-8 pa

LC 2002-326

"No reference work available in print right now matches the attention to detail that is obvious here. A significant work on how the machinery of television has evolved, this . . . should stand as the authority for years to come." Libr J

Includes bibliographical references

621.43 Internal-combustion engines

★ **Small** engines and outdoor power equipment; a care & repair guide for lawn mowers, snowblowers & small gas-powered implements. edited by

Peter Hunn. Cool Springs Press 2014 144 p. color illustrations (pbk) $19.99   **621.43**
1. Household equipment and supplies -- Maintenance and repair 2. Small gasoline engines -- Maintenance and repair 3. Gardening -- Equipment and supplies -- Maintenance and repair
ISBN 1591865875; 9781591865872

LC 2013028515

"Small engine repair and maintenance is well covered here, starting with an introduction to common engine types, with interior systems and components clearly illustrated. Tools needed and safety considerations are carefully detailed, followed by a lengthy troubleshooting chart. A section on annual maintenance is accompanied by large photos and step-by-step instructions; it's followed by basic repairs, which focus on common issues. The book finishes with more difficult repairs that involve interior systems, such as rebuilding or replacing parts." LJ

621.48   Nuclear engineering

Smith, Gar
  Nuclear roulette; the truth about the most dangerous energy source on earth. Gar Smith ; foreword by Jerry Mander and Ernest Callenbach. Chelsea Green Pub. 2012 xxx, 279 p.p (hardcover) $29.95 **621.48**
1. Nuclear energy 2. Nuclear power plants 3. Nuclear power plants -- Accidents
ISBN 1603584773; 9781603584340; 9781603584357; 9781603584777

LC 2012027407

Author Gar Smith argues that "nuclear power is not clean, cheap, or safe. . . . While some critiques are familiar-nuclear power is too costly, too dangerous, and too unstable-others are surprising: Nuclear Roulette exposes historic links to nuclear weapons, impacts on Indigenous lands and lives, and the ways in which the Nuclear Regulatory Commission too often takes its lead from industry, rewriting rules to keep failing plants in compliance." (Publisher's note)
  Includes bibliographical references (p. [233]-267) and index

621.8   Machine engineering

Gurstelle, William
  Adventures from the technology underground; catapults, pulsejets, rail guns, flamethrowers, tesla coils, air cannons, and the garage warriors who love them. Clarkson Potter 2006 224p $25; pa $13.95   **621.8**
1. Machine design
ISBN 1-4000-5082-0; 0-307-35125-4 pa

LC 2005-20412

The author takes "readers into the hidden communities of people involved in developing hurling machines (catapults and trebuchets), pulse jet engines, flamethrowers, tesla coil-powered electric current theater, air cannons, robots, high-powered rockets, and magnetic linear accelerator guns. . . . Gurstelle balances scientific explanations of the technol-

ogies with profiles of the people who built them and descriptions of the events at which they were showcased." Libr J
  Includes bibliographical references

622   Mining and related operations

Prud'homme, Alex
  Hydrofracking; Alex Prud'homme. Oxford University Press 2013 184 p. (What everyone needs to know) (pbk. : alk. paper) $16.95   **622**
1. Hydraulic fracturing 2. Environmental protection 3. Hydraulic fracturing -- Popular works 4. Shale gas reservoirs -- Popular works 5. Gas wells -- Hydraulic fracturing -- Popular works 6. Oil wells -- Hydraulic fracturing -- Popular works
ISBN 0199311250; 9780199311255; 9780199311262

LC 2013028962

"A timely addition to Oxford's What Everyone Needs to Know series, 'Hydrofracking' tackles this contentious topic, exploring both sides of the debate and providing a clear guide to the science underlying the technique. In . . . question-and-answer format, Alex Prud'homme . . . [covers] key points, from the economic and political benefits of fracking to the health dangers and negative effects on the environment." (Publisher's note)
  "Most useful are the point/counterpoint discussions on the pros and cons of fracking." Choice
  Includes bibliographical references and index

Reece, Erik
  Lost mountain; a year in the vanishing wilderness: radical strip mining, and the devastation of Appalachia. foreword by Wendell Berry; photographs by John J. Cox. Riverhead Books 2006 250p il $24.95; pa $14   **622**
1. Coal mines and mining 2. Human influence on nature 3. Appalachian region
ISBN 1-59448-908-4; 1-59448-236-5 pa

LC 2005-52921

The author explores the effects of strip mining on the landscape of Eastern Kentucky.
  Reece "has written an impassioned account of a business rife with industrial greed, devious corporate ownership and unenforced environmental laws. It's also a heartrending account of the rural residents whose lives are being ruined by strip-mining's relentless, almost unfettered, encroachment." Publ Wkly
  Includes bibliographical references

622.4   Mine environment

Carter, Bill
  Boom, Bust, Boom; A Story About Copper, the Metal That Runs the World. Bill Carter. Simon & Schuster 2012 288 p. $26   **622.4**
1. Copper 2. Copper mines and mining
ISBN 1439136440; 9781439136447

This book by Bill Carter is "a sweeping account of civilization's complete dependence on copper and what it means for people, nature, and our global economy. Copper is a miraculous and contradictory metal, essential to nearly every human enterprise. . . . Yet . . . copper mining causes irrevocable damage to the Earth . . . . and the mines themselves have significant effects on the economies and wellbeing of the communities where they are located." (Publisher's note)

Includes bibliographical references and index.

623.4 Ordnance

Chivers, C. J.

The **gun**; the AK-47 and the evolution of war. Simon & Schuster 2010 481p il $28 **623.4**
1. Rifles 2. Firearms 3. Military history 4. AK-47 rifle 5. Machine guns 6. War -- History
ISBN 978-0-7432-7076-2; 0-7432-7076-2

LC 2010-20459

The author "chronicles the evolution and employment of fully automatic firearms, the development of the Kalashnikov and how the rifle redefined modern warfare from its use in Hungary in 1956 to Afghanistan today." Washington Post

This "is gripping and original interpretive history, highly recommended." Libr J

Includes bibliographical references

Conant, Jennet

109 East Palace; Robert Oppenheimer and the secret city of Los Alamos. Simon & Schuster 2005 425p map hardcover o.p. pa $14 **623.4**
1. Physicists 2. Atomic bomb 3. Office workers 4. College teachers 5. Manhattan Project 6. Government employees 7. Government officials 8. Los Alamos Scientific Laboratory
ISBN 0-7432-5007-9; 0-7432-5008-7 pa

LC 2005-42497

In this history of the creation of the atomic bomb, the author focuses "on daily life in Los Alamos. She tells the story largely through the eyes of Dorothy McKibben, who was in charge of the project's Santa Fe office, at 109 East Palace Street. This unassuming storefront was the portal to Los Alamos for all the physicists and military personnel who arrived in New Mexico." Booklist

"Anyone interested in the history of atomic weapons will find this book totally engrossing." Sci Books Films

Includes bibliographical references

Hodge, Nathan

A **nuclear** family vacation; travels in the world of atomic weaponry. [by] Nathan Hodge and Sharon Weinberger. Bloomsbury 2008 324p $24.99 **623.4**
1. Arms control 2. Nuclear weapons 3. Nuclear engineering
ISBN 978-1-59691-378-3; 1-59691-378-9

LC 2008-2013

This "is a book that is both entertaining and informative. Hodge and Weinberger are shrewd and observant nuclear tour guides who are knowledgeable about their subject without being didactic." Am Sci

Includes bibliographical references

Rhodes, Richard

Dark sun; the making of the hydrogen bomb. Simon & Schuster 1995 731p il hardcover o.p. pa $18 **623.4**
1. Spies 2. Cold war 3. Generals 4. Arms race 5. Physicists 6. Hydrogen bomb 7. College teachers 8. Air force officers 9. Writers on science 10. Government officials
ISBN 0-684-82414-0

LC 95-11070

This is a "chronicle of the rivalry between the U.S. and the U.S.S.R. to invent, build, test and stockpile hydrogen bombs. . . . Rhodes places the story of the bomb's development in the context of politics, science, technical hurdles and espionage. . . . He also brings in the case of convicted atomic spies Julius and Ethel Rosenberg." Publ Wkly

"This meticulously documented treatise presents a gripping story." Libr J

The **making** of the atomic bomb. Simon & Schuster 1986 886p il hardcover o.p. pa $20 **623.4**
1. Atomic bomb
ISBN 0-684-81378-5 pa

LC 86-15445

"The book provides portraits of the many players from Szilard and Einstein to Oppenheimer. . . . The book is heavily documented and includes a 13-page bibliography. This is a definitive work, well written, with a gripping story. It is not an easy book to read, but is well worth the effort." Libr J

Sheinkin, Steve

Bomb; the race to build and steal the world's most dangerous weapon. Steve Sheinkin. Roaring Brook Press 2012 266 p. ill. (hc) $19.99 **623.4**
1. Nuclear warfare 2. Nuclear weapons 3. Atomic bomb -- History 4. Operation Freshman, 1942 5. Atomic bomb -- Germany -- History 6. World War, 1939-1945 -- Secret service -- Soviet Union 7. World War, 1939-1945 -- Secret service -- Great Britain 8. World War, 1939-1945 -- Commando operations -- Norway -- Vemork
ISBN 1596434872; 9781596434875

LC 2011044096

Robert F. Sibert Informational Book Medal (2013)
YALSA Award for Excellence in Nonfiction for Young Adults (2013)
John Newbery Honor Book (2013)

Author Steve Sheinkin's "story unfolds in three parts, covering American attempts to build the [atomic] bomb, how the Soviets tried to steal American designs and how the Americans tried to keep the Germans from building a bomb. It was the eve of World War II, and the fate of the world was at stake . . . all along the way spies in the United States were feeding sensitive information to the KGB." (Kirkus Reviews)

Includes bibliographical references (p. [243]-259) and index

Weapons & warfare; editor, John Powell. 2nd ed.; Salem Press 2010 3v il map set $395 **623.4**
1. Reference books 2. Military weapons 3. Military

art and science
ISBN 978-1-58765-594-4

LC 2009-50491

First published 2001

"Volume 1, Ancient & Medieval, . . . covers warfare from prehistoric times to approximately 1500; Volume 2, Modern, covers 1500 to the present. The organization is chronological by geographic region, and both volumes open with essays discussing weapons and forces used in that era of history, how and why those tools of warfare have evolved or been discontinued, and the military achievement of the forces, weapons, uniforms and armor, military organizations, and doctrine strategy and tactics. In the third volume, Culture and Concepts, essays cover social aspects of war, technological achievements used in warfare, and morality of behavior during war. . . . This useful overview of warfare's evolution will be appreciated by students as well as general readers." Libr J

623.7 Communications, vehicles, sanitation, related topics

Macy, Edward

Apache : inside the cockpit of the world's most deadly fighting machine. Atlantic Monthly Press 2008 xxvi, 374p il map $25   **623.7**
1. Afghan War, 2001- 2. Military airplanes 3. Great Britain -- Army -- Air Corps
ISBN 978-0-8021-1894-3; 0-8021-1894-1

"Macy, now retired from the British army, spent an active tour in Afghanistan's Helmand Province flying Apache helicopter combat sorties in support of the NATO ground mission there. He loved the work, which was demanding, violent, and incredibly expensive. An absorbing, exciting chronicle of a 21st-century soldier fighting on the high-tech side of asymmetric warfare." Libr J

623.8 Nautical engineering and seamanship

Ujifusa, Steven

A **man** and his ship; America's greatest naval architect and his quest to build the S.S. United States. Steven Ujifusa. Simon & Schuster 2012 x, 437 p., [32] p. of platesp ill. (hc : alk. paper) $29.99 **623.8**
1. Ocean liners 2. United States -- Military history 3. World War, 1939-1945 -- Naval operations 4. United States (Steamship) 5. Gibbs & Cox -- History -- 20th century 6. Naval architects -- United States -- Biography 7. Ocean liners -- United States -- History -- 20th century
ISBN 9781451645071; 9781451645088

LC 2011049883

Author Steven Ujifusa tells the story of William Francis Gibbs, who, in 1915, "completed plans for the world's largest and fastest superliner . . . Setting up his own company in 1922, Gibbs made his name building modest liners for American companies . . . As World War II loomed, Gibbs became the leading designer for the U.S. Navy and Merchant Marine. It took the Cold War and energetic lobbying to achieve Gibbs' dream . . . Launched in 1952 to national

acclaim, the SS United States was a technological triumph; rival liners never matched her speed, reliability or safety." (Kirkus)

Includes bibliographical references and index

623.88 Seamanship

Pawson, Des

The **handbook** of knots; Expanded ed.; DK 2004 176p il pa $17   **623.88**
1. Rope 2. Knots and splices
ISBN 0-7566-0374-9; 978-0-7566-0374-8

LC 2004-274491

First published 1998

"This is a step-by-step guide to tying and using more than 100 knots. . . . There's a chapter on rope construction, rope materials, and properties of ropes and their main uses. It's very informative and put together concisely." BAYA Book Rev [review of 1998 edition]

623.89 Navigation

Cutler, Thomas J.

Dutton's nautical navigation; [by] Thomas J. Cutler; with the U.S. Naval Institute Navigation Board. 15th ed; Naval Inst. Press 2004 447p il map $55   **623.89**
1. Navigation
ISBN 1-557502-48-X

LC 2003-11183

First published 1926 under the authorship of Benjamin Dutton with title: Navigation and nautical astronomy. Variant title: Dutton's navigation & piloting

This guide for the coastal and seagoing mariner focuses on piloting, celestial navigation, radio navigation and dead reckoning

624.2 Bridges

Blockley, D. I.

Bridges; the science and art of the world's most inspiring structures. Oxford University Press 2010 312p il $29.95   **624.2**
1. Bridges
ISBN 978-0-19-954359-5

"In this fascinating exploration for lay readers, Blockley lucidly explains both the basic forces at work on every bridge—tension, compression, and shear—and the structural elements combating those forces: beams, arches, trusses, and suspension cables. . . . Bold, insightful statements help make this a remarkable work." Publ Wkly

Includes bibliographical references

Petroski, Henry

Engineers of dreams; great bridge builders and the spanning of America. Knopf 1995 479p il hardcover o.p. pa $16   **624.2**
1. Bridges 2. Civil engineering 3. Civil engineers 4.

Bridge engineers
ISBN 0-679-76021-0 pa

LC 94-48893

"An exhilarating saga of ingenuity and sheer determination." Publ Wkly
Includes bibliographical references

625.2 Railroad rolling stock

Jensen, Joel

Steam : an enduring legacy; the railroad photographs of Joel Jensen. introduction by Scott Lothes; essay by John Gruber; afterword by Jeff Brouws. W. W. Norton & Company 2011 160p il $50 **625.2**
1. Steam engines 2. Railroads -- Pictorial works
ISBN 978-0-393-08248-7; 0-393-08248-2

"Jensen has been photographing trains and rail stations west of the Mississippi River for some 25 years, and this long-overdue collection of his work features black-and-white shots that capture the bygone majesty and sense of history inspired by these steam-powered machines, preserved and operated in the latter-day era by dedicated rail-fans. Besides the 150 photos, there are essays by John Gruber and Scott Lothes—both of the Center for Railroad Photography and Art—examining the economics and cultural importance of trains in America." BookPage

627 Hydraulic engineering

Earth ponds; the country pond maker's guide to building, maintenance, and restoration. Tim Matson. 3rd ed Countryman Press 2012 150 p. ill. $21.95 **627**
1. Ponds 2. Water supply engineering
ISBN 9781581571479

A "complete overview of the country pond.Illustrations guide the pond builder through every step of the process; chapters carefully describe the issues and decisions." (Publisher's note)
Includes bibliographical references

Finch, Phillip

Diving into darkness; a true story of death and survival. St. Martin's Press 2008 310p il $25.95 **627**
1. Diving 2. Divers
ISBN 978-0-312-38394-7; 0-312-38394-0

LC 2008-24271

"In January 2005, extreme diver David Shaw entered Bushman's Hole, a watery crater in the Kalahari Desert. Easing himself through a narrow fissure, he aimed himself at the bottom of the crater, roughly 900 feet below him. Soon after, his diving partner, Don Shirley, followed Shaw down. In less than an hour, one of the men was dead, and the other faced a harrowing 10-hour decompression, during which he scrambled for every breath. This is a dramatic and emotional story. . . . A solid addition to the sport-diving genre." Booklist

Hiltzik, Michael A.

✓ **Colossus**; Hoover Dam and the making of the American century. Free Press 2010 496p il map $30 **627**
1. Hoover Dam (Ariz. and Nev.) 2. Civil engineers
ISBN 978-1-4165-3216-3; 1-4165-3216-1

LC 2009-33833

In this account of the Hoover Dam story, Hiltzik "explains the technological and physical difficulties posed by the dam project, but he also fixes the endeavor in its time and captures the personalities of the people involved. . . . The author is at his best in a masterly portrayal of Frank Crowe, the central figure in the dam's construction. A born engineer who demanded much from his workmen, Crowe had to solve a myriad of problems on the fly as he confronted the unexpected difficulties of an unprecedented project in an unprecedented location. . . . One of the nice things about nonfiction such as 'Colossus' is that the stories don't need to be believable; they just need to be true." Wall Street J
Includes bibliographical references and index

628.4 Waste technology, public toilets, street cleaning

Humes, Edward

✓ **Garbology**; our dirty love affair with trash. Edward Humes. Avery 2012 277 p. **628.4**
1. Pollution 2. Consumption (Economics) 3. United States -- Social life and customs 4. Refuse and refuse disposal -- United States 5. Salvage (Waste, etc.) -- China 6. Environmental engineering -- United States
ISBN 1583334343; 9781583334348

LC 2012001701

In this book, "Edward Humes . . . [makes the case] that the United States—the world's largest generator of trash—will soon confront a new crisis of garbage. . . . Humes spotlights a turning point in the history of American garbage: the postwar rise of consumer culture, birthed by a new generation of advertisers who saw their mission in life as persuading Americans to throw away perfectly good things in order to buy bigger, better replacements. . . . Humes argues that an economy whose health depends on how much disposable stuff people buy is driving us toward a precipice. Making and trashing all those things will generate economic activity and jobs, to be sure, but the waste-driven model of mass consumption also eats up tremendous amounts of increasingly scarce resources." (Bookforum)
Includes bibliographical references and index

628.9 Other branches of sanitary and municipal engineering

National Fire Protection Association

Fire protection handbook; Arthur E. Cote, editor-in-chief; Casey C. Grant, John R. Hall, Jr., Robert E. Solomon, asoociate editors; Pamela A. Powell, managing editor. 20th ed; National Fire Protection Assn. 2008 2v il $233.75   **628.9**

1. Fire prevention
ISBN 978-0-87765-758-3; 0-87765-758-0

LC 2007-928644

First published 1896. Periodically revised. Title varies

"A handbook of approved practice in the fields of fire prevention and fire protection. Will be useful to owners and superintendents of buildings, and to architects and engineers interested in designing safe buildings and planning for their protection against fire." Carnegie Libr of Pittsburgh

Walliser, Jessica

Attracting beneficial bugs to your garden; a natural approach to pest control. Jessica Walliser. Timber Press 2014 240 p. col. ill. $24.95   **628.9**

1. Gardening 2. Beneficial insects 3. Garden pests -- Biological control
ISBN 1604693886; 9781604693881

LC 2013015303

Written by Jessica Walliser, "'Attracting Beneficial Bugs to Your Garden' is a book about bugs and plants, and how to create a garden that benefits from both. In addition to information on companion planting and commercial options for purchasing bugs, there are 19 detailed bug profiles and 39 plant profiles." (Publisher's note)

"While the subject matter and close-up photographs of insects eating insects may make some readers squirm, dedicated gardeners will discover enough solid information and genuine motivation to finally put down their bug spray." Booklist

Includes bibliographical references and index

629   Other branches of engineering

Bizony, Piers

The **man** who ran the moon; James E. Webb and the secret history of Project Apollo. Thunder's Mouth 2006 242p il $24.95   **629**

1. Lawyers 2. Diplomats 3. Apollo project 4. NASA officials 5. Government officials 6. United States -- National Aeronautics and Space Administration
ISBN 1-56025-751-2; 9781560257512

LC 2006-298038

"Emerging from the bureaucratic thickets with an ultimately praiseworthy portrait of Webb, this should circulate with the space program set." Booklist

Includes bibliographical references

Mullane, R. Mike

Riding rockets; the outrageous tales of a space shuttle astronaut. [by] Mike Mullane. Scribner 2006 368p il hardcover o.p. pa $15   **629**

1. Astronauts 2. Air force officers
ISBN 978-0-7432-7682-5; 978-0-7432-7683-2 pa; 0-7432-7683-3 pa

LC 2005-56123

This is a memoir by the American astronaut.

"A strong addition to science and space collections of any size." Booklist

629.1   Aerospace engineering

Branson, Richard

Reach for the skies; ballooning, birdmen, and blasting into space. Current 2011 343p il $26.95   **629.1**

1. Aeronautics -- History
ISBN 978-1-61723-003-5

LC 2010-52340

"The Virgin Atlantic Airlines founder and billionaire adventurer celebrates the exploits of airborne daredevils— his own prominently among them—in this lively history of aviation pioneers. Branson ranges from the Montgolfier brothers' 1783 invention of the hot-air balloon to today's nascent space tourism industry . . . highlighting men and women who risked their money and lives to advance aerial technology or just put on a good show. It's a colorful assemblage of engineers, test pilots, barnstormers, and fighter aces. . . . Branson's enthusiasm for avant-garde flight and his firsthand understanding of its rigors make this a rousing— sometimes even elevating—read." Publ Wkly

Includes bibliographical references

Hickam, Homer H.

★ **Rocket** boys; a memoir. [by] Homer H. Hickam, Jr. Delacorte Press 1998 368p $25.95; pa $14   **629.1**

1. Authors 2. Novelists 3. Aerospace engineers 4. Memoirists 5. West Virginia 6. Authors, American 7. Writers on science
ISBN 0-385-33320-X; 0-385-33321-8 pa

LC 98-19304

"Even if Hickam stretched the strict truth to metamorphose his memories into Stand By Me-like material for Hollywood . . . the embellishing only converts what is a good story into an absorbing, rapidly readable one that is unsentimental but artful about adolescence, high school, and family life." Booklist

629.13   Aeronautics

Alexander, David E.

Why don't jumbo jets flap their wings? flying animals, flying machines, and how they are different. Rutgers University Press 2009 278p il $26.95   **629.13**

1. Aeronautics 2. Animal flight
ISBN 978-0-8135-4479-3; 0-8135-4479-3

LC 2008-35425

Alexander discusses the mechanics and physics of how animals and aircraft fly.

"Anyone interested in the flight of birds or insects or the flight of various types of aircraft will find this volume fascinating. . . . [This book] is very well written and approaches complex topics in a manner that readers at any level of expertise will find understandable and interesting." Sci Books Films

Includes glossary and bibliographical references

Berg, A. Scott

★ **Lindbergh**. Putnam 1998 628p il $30; pa
$16   **629.13**
1. Generals 2. Air pilots 3. Memoirists 4. Air force
officers
ISBN 0-399-14449-8; 0-425-17041-1 pa
LC 98-18548

"The first biographer to be granted unfettered access to
Lindbergh's private papers, Berg provides enough fresh detail to trace the roots of Lindbergh's personality, its strengths
as well as its maddening flaws, all the way back to his turbulent boyhood." N Y Times Book Rev

Includes bibliographical references (p. {569}-612)
and index

Butler, Susan

East to the dawn; the life of Amelia Earhart. Da
Capo Press 1999 489p il map pa $15.95   **629.13**
1. Air pilots 2. Missing persons 3. Women air pilots
4. Memoirists
ISBN 978-0-306-81837-0
First published 1997 by Addison-Wesley

In this biography of the pilot and women's rights advocate "Butler shows a mastery of aviation history, and considerable sophistication about the technology of flight and
navigation . . . The mountain of new material it marshals
guarantees 'East to the Dawn' a permanent place on the shelf
of Amelia Earhart references." N Y Times Book Rev

Includes bibliographical references

Chaikin, Andrew

Air and space; the National Air and Space Museum's story of flight. Little, Brown 1997 317p il
$50; pa $29.95   **629.13**
1. National Air and Space Museum (U.S.)
ISBN 0-8212-2082-9; 0-8212-2670-3 pa
LC 96-31929

This illustrated work connects artifacts on display at the
Smithsonian's aeronautics museum with a brief history of
air and space flight

"A few photos, as of the DC-3, show the vehicle in
its exhibit hall, but most pictures depict planes or rockets
in action, right up through the latest images of the space
age—Mars as viewed from Pathfinder. An enthusiast's
delight." Booklist

Goldstone, Lawrence

★ **Birdmen**; The Wright Brothers, Glenn Curtiss, and the Battle to Control the Skies. Lawrence
Goldstone. Random House Inc 2014 448 p. illustrations $28   **629.13**
1. Aeronautics -- History
ISBN 034553803X; 9780345538031
LC 2014001424

This book, by Lawrence Goldstone, tells the "story of
the . . . feud between . . . great air pioneers, the Wright brothers and Glenn Curtiss. . . . On one side, a pair of tenacious
siblings who together had solved the centuries-old riddle of
powered, heavier-than-air flight. On the other, an audacious
motorcycle racer whose innovative aircraft became synony-
mous in the public mind with death-defying stunts. For more

than a decade, they battled each other in court, at air shows,
and in the newspapers." (Publisher's note)

"A superbly crafted retelling of a story familiar to aviation buffs, here greatly strengthened by fresh perspectives,
rigorous analyses, comprehensible science, and a driving
narrative." LJ

Includes bibliographical references (pages 401-404)
and index

Grant, R. G.

Flight : 100 years of aviation. DK Pub. 2002
440p il hardcover o.p. pa $24.95   **629.13**
1. Aeronautics -- History
ISBN 0-7894-8910-4; 0-7566-1902-5 pa
LC 2002-73935

"The impressive illustrations include over 300 gorgeous,
full-color profiles of the world's major military and civilian
aircraft and space vehicles." Libr J

Gubert, Betty Kaplan

Distinguished African Americans in aviation and
space science; {by} Betty Kaplan Gubert, Miriam
Sawyer, and Caroline M. Fannin. Oryx Press 2002
319p il (Distinguished African Americans series)
$64.95   **629.13**
1. Astronauts 2. African American pilots
ISBN 1-57356-246-7
LC 2001-34821

This profiles 80 men and 20 women in aviation and
space science covering 80 years of the 20th century

"Libraries should not hesitate to add this title to their
collections." Booklist

Includes bibliographical references

Haynsworth, Leslie

Amelia Earhart's daughters; the wild and glorious story of American women aviators from World
War II to the dawn of the space age. {by} Leslie
Haynsworth and David Toomey. Morrow 1998 322p
il hardcover o.p. pa $14   **629.13**
1. Air pilots 2. Women air pilots 3. Women astronauts
4. Cosmetics industry executives
ISBN 0-380-72984-9 pa
LC 98-8727

This "study of American women aviators concentrates
almost exclusively on the WASPs of World War II and the
would-be female astronauts of the early 1960s." Booklist

Includes bibliographical references

Lindbergh, Charles

The **spirit** of St. Louis; [by] Charles A. Lind-
bergh. Scribner 1998 562p il hardcover o.p. pa
$20   **629.13**
1. Spirit of St. Louis (Airplane) 2. Aeronautics --
Flights
ISBN 0-684-85277-2; 0-7432-3705-6 pa
LC 98-33556

First published 1953

This is an account of the first solo transatlantic flight
from New York to Paris, as well as a detailed description of

the preparation for the flight which in turn mirrors aviation of the 1920's.

Lovell, Mary S.

The **sound** of wings: the life of Amelia Earhart. St. Martin's Press 1989 xxv, 420p il hardcover o.p. pa $17.99   **629.13**
1. Air pilots 2. Missing persons 3. Women air pilots 4. Memoirists
ISBN 978-0-312-58733-8 pa

LC 89-34935

This biography concentrates on Earhart's "personality and character and the relationships with family and friends as they contributed to her accomplishments. . . . The book also contains excerpts from Last Flight, Earhart's reworked logbook and notes on the fateful 1937 flight." Libr J
Includes bibliographical references

Straight on till morning: the biography of Beryl Markham. St. Martin's Press 1987 xxiv, 408p il hardcover o.p.   **629.13**
1. Air pilots 2. Memoirists 3. Horse trainers 4. Air pilots -- Great Britain -- Biography

LC 87-16329

Lovell does not "record only the high points of Beryl's life, nor does she eulogize her; rather, she gives the whole picture of a woman. . . . Her biography provides an enthralling study, not simply of a remarkable personality, but of a place, a period, and a culture." Wilson Libr Bull
Includes bibliography

Mortimer, Gavin

Chasing Icarus; the seventeen days in 1910 that forever changed American aviation. Walker & Co 2009 305p il $26   **629.13**
1. Aeronautics -- History
ISBN 978-0-8027-1711-5

The author "argues that three aeronautic events in 1910 vouchsafed the primacy of U.S. aviation and the triumph of heavier-than-air flight. Interweaving the events—Walter Wellman's failed attempt to cross the Atlantic in his dirigible, America; the International Balloon Cup Race, which embarked from St. Louis; and the country's first international aircraft contest, held above the Belmont Park racetrack in New York—Mortimer effectively places the reader at the vital center of all three. . . . A singular contribution to early aviation history." Libr J
Includes bibliographical references

Rich, Doris L.

Amelia Earhart; a biography. Smithsonian Institution Press 1989 321p il hardcover o.p. pa $16.95   **629.13**
1. Air pilots 2. Missing persons 3. Women air pilots 4. Memoirists
ISBN 1-56098-725-1 pa

LC 89-32181

A "fast-paced, richly detailed biography." Publ Wkly
Includes bibliographical references

Smithsonian atlas of world aviation; charting the history of flight from the first balloons to today's

most advanced aircraft. [compiled by] Dana Bell. HarperCollins 2008 230p il map $39.95 **629.13**
1. Reference books 2. Historical atlases 3. Aeronautics -- History
ISBN 978-0-06-125144-3; 0-06-125144-5

LC 2007-47574

"Bell's writing . . . adds immeasurably to the value of this atlas: it is articulate, clear, informative, and, above all, accurate." SLJ
Includes bibliographical references

Tobin, James

To conquer the air; the Wright Brothers and the great race for flight. Free Press 2003 433p il hardcover o.p. pa $16   **629.13**
1. Inventors 2. Aeronautics -- History 3. Aircraft industry executives
ISBN 0-684-85688-3; 0-7432-5536-4 pa

LC 2002-44778

"This book represents the most forceful argument to date for the brothers' monumental legacy to the history of flight. . . . This lucidly written and exhaustively researched study is recommended for all aviation collections and all libraries." Libr J
Includes bibliographical references

Trzebinski, Errol

The **lives** of Beryl Markham; Out of Africa's hidden free spirit and Denys Finch Hatton's last great love. Norton 1993 396p il maps hardcover o.p. pa $12   **629.13**
1. Air pilots 2. Memoirists 3. Horse trainers
ISBN 0-393-31252-6 pa

LC 93-9919

The author offers "confirmation of the rumor that Beryl's third husband actually wrote her best-selling memoir, West with the Night." Booklist
Includes bibliographical references

629.130   Biography of flight

Jackson, Joe

Atlantic fever; Lindbergh, his competitors, and the race to cross the Atlantic. Joe Jackson. Farrar, Straus and Giroux 2012 x, 525 p.p   **629.130**
1. Aeronautics -- History 2. Air pilots -- Biography 3. Aeronautics -- Competitions 4. Transatlantic flights -- History -- 20th century 5. Aeronautics -- Competitions -- History -- 20th century
ISBN 0374106754; 9780374106751

LC 2011046068

In this book, Joe Jackson "places Lindbergh's historic flight of May 20-21, 1927, in the dramatic framework of the 'Great Atlantic Air Race,' which began eight years earlier when Franco-American hotelier Ramond Orteig sponsored a $25,000 prize to the first aviator to cross the Atlantic. . . . Jackson traces the futile attempts to win the Orteig Prize until the spring of 1927, when a bevy of pilots stepped forth to compete for the honor no matter the cost. Jackson's compelling portraits of these contenders . . . place Lindbergh's successful bid in perspective. The reader is reminded that 'Lindy' was the last contestant to arrive in New York but the first to depart, owing to the simplicity of his effort compared with the technical, funding, and personnel complexities of his rivals' preparations." (Libr J)

Includes bibliographical references and index

629.132   Mechanics of flight; flying and related topics

Tennekes, H.

The **simple** science of flight; from insects to jumbo jets. [by] Henk Tennekes. Rev and expanded ed; MIT Press 2009 201p il pa $21.95   **629.132**
1. Flight 2. Aerodynamics
ISBN 978-0-262-51313-5; 0-262-51313-7

LC 2009-12431

Original German edition 1992; first English language edition 1996

The author "explains to lay readers the aerodynamic principles that underlie the flight of everything, including paper airplanes, kites, gliders, and human powered aircraft. He also explains such concepts as lift, drag, wing loading, and cruising speed; and the impact of fuel efficiency, headwind, tailwind, and other factors." Booknews

Includes bibliographical references

629.133   Aircraft types

Botting, Douglas

Dr. Eckener's dream machine; the great Zeppelin and the dawn of air travel. Holt & Co. 2001 331p il maps $27.50; pa $16   **629.133**
1. Airships 2. Aeronautics -- Flights 3. Graf Zeppelin (Airship) 4. Aircraft industry executives
ISBN 0-8050-6458-3; 0-8050-6459-1 pa

LC 2001-24770

Botting discusses the history of the Zeppelin, a rigid airship designed by a Prussian army officer, Ferdinand Count von Zeppelin, and the career of Hugo Eckener, who promoted and flew the dirigible

"A truly exciting book, filled with colorful characters and plenty of derring-do and laced with just the right amount of sadness and tragedy." Booklist

Includes bibliographical references

Chiles, James R.

The **god** machine; from boomerangs to black hawks, the story of the helicopter. Bantam Dell 2007 354p il hardcover o.p. pa $16   **629.133**
1. Helicopters
ISBN 978-0-553-80447-8; 978-0-553-38352-2 pa

LC 2007-28575

This "is an engaging blend of pop science and pop culture." Publ Wkly

Includes bibliographical references

Spenser, Jay P.

The **airplane**; how ideas gave us wings. [by] Jay Spenser. HarperCollins 2008 340p il $25.95 **629.133**
1. Aeronautics -- History 2. Airplanes -- Design and construction
ISBN 978-0-06-125919-7; 0-06-125919-5

LC 2008-23423

This "is a very well written book that is organized in a way to make it both readable and informative. The writing makes it obvious that the author knows his subject and is fascinated by it." Sci Books Films

Includes bibliographical references

629.222   Gasoline-powered, oil-powered, manpowered vehicles

Adler, Dennis

The **art** of the sports car; the greatest designs of the 20th century. written and with photographs by Dennis Adler. HarperCollins Pubs. 2002 236p il $44.95   **629.222**
1. Sports cars
ISBN 0-06-018885-5

LC 2001-51810

In this illustrated history of the sports car the author provides an "account of the evolution of small cars with big engines, recounting the travails of famous auto designers, the engineering and styling innovations they pioneered and the races and road rallies at which cars proved (and advertised) themselves. His narrative dwells mostly on European makes such as Jaguar, Porsche and Ferrari, but also discusses the American Corvette and muscle cars like the Ford Thunderbird and the Dodge Challenger. . . . Hard-core aficionados will derive much gratification from the detailed descriptions of mechanical design and performance. . . . But just about anyone will be entranced at the pictures of classic cars meticulously restored, polished to a sheen and photographed on opulent country estates." Publ Wkly

The Beaulieu encyclopedia of the automobile; editor in chief, Nick Georgano; foreword by Lord Montagu of Beaulieu. Fitzroy Dearborn Pubs. 2000 2v il set $325   **629.222**
1. Reference books 2. Automobiles -- Encyclopedias
ISBN 1-57958-293-1

LC 2001-316285

"The most comprehensive automobile encyclopedia available today." Am Libr

Ingrassia, Paul

Engines of change; a history of the American dream in fifteen cars. Paul Ingrassia. 1st Simon & Schuster hc ed. Simon & Schuster 2012 xx, 395 p., [32] p. of platesp ill. (some col.) (hardcover) $30.00; (paperbook) $18.00   **629.222**
1. Popular culture -- United States 2. Automobiles -- United States -- History 3. Automobiles -- Social aspects -- United States -- History
ISBN 1451640633; 9781451640632; 9781451640649;

9781451640656

LC 2012002303

This book, by Paul Ingrassia, offers a cultural history of automobiles in the United States. "From the assembly lines of Henry Ford to the open roads of Route 66, from the lore of Jack Kerouac to the sex appeal of the Hot Rod, America's history is a vehicular history. . . . Ingrassia offers a[n] . . . epic in fifteen automobiles, . . . as well as the personalities and tales behind them." (Publisher's note)

Includes bibliographical references (p. 373-375) and index.

Parissien, Steven

The **life** of the automobile; a history of the motor car. Steven Parissien. Thomas Dunne Books 2014 448 p. (hardback) $27.99   **629.222**
    1. Automobiles -- History
    ISBN 1250040639; 9781250040633

LC 2013045750

This book, by Steven Parissien, "is the first comprehensive world history of the car. . . . The author examines the advances of the interwar era, the Golden Age of the 1950s, and the iconic years of the 1960s to the decades of doubt and uncertainty following the oil crisis of 1973, the global mergers of the 1990s, the bailouts of the early twenty-first century, and the emergence of the electric car." (Publisher's note)

"This elegant and authoritative work demonstrates the historical links among people, machines, and cultures on a global scale." LJ

Includes bibliographical references and index

Swift, Earl

Auto Biography; A Classic Car, an Outlaw Motorhead, and 57 Years of the American Dream. by Earl Swift. HarperCollins 2014 368 p. illustrations (some color) $26.99   **629.222**
    1. American dream 2. Criminals -- Fiction 3. Automobiles -- Fiction
    ISBN 0062282662; 9780062282668

This book, by Earl Swift, "follows an outlaw auto dealer as he struggles to save a rusted '57 Chevy--a car that has already passed through twelve pairs of hands before his--while financial ruin, government bureaucrats and the FBI close in on him. . . . [H]assled by a growing assortment of challengers, the Chevy's thirteenth owner--an orphan, grade-school dropout and rounder, a felon arrested seventy-odd times, and a man who's been written off as a ruin himself--embarks on a mission to save the car." (Publisher's note)

"A big, weird, heartfelt book about a badass who could give a damn whether you root for him or not." Kirkus

Includes bibliographical references

Vuic, Jason

The **Yugo**; the rise and fall of the worst car in history. Hill & Wang 2010 262p il $26   **629.222**
    1. Foreign automobiles 2. Yugo America Inc.
    ISBN 978-0-8090-9891-0; 0-8090-9891-1

LC 2009-25612

A "meticulous and wide-ranging social history of a troubled car." Minneapolis Star Tribune

Includes bibliographical references

629.223   Light trucks

Perry, Michael

Truck : a love story. HarperCollins Publishers 2006 281p $24.95   **629.223**
    1. Trucks
    ISBN 978-0-06-057117-7; 0-06-057117-9

LC 2006-43394

Perry "propels the story forward as if he were writing a novel, helped by a cast of characters who range from the lightly offbeat to the totally bizarre." Booklist

629.227   Cycles

Herlihy, David

Bicycle : the history; [by] David V. Herlihy. Yale University Press 2004 470p il $40   **629.227**
    1. Bicycles
    ISBN 0-300-10418-9

LC 2004-12992

Herlihy "takes us from the mathematician Jacques Ozanam's 1696 challenge to develop a 'human-powered carriage' to the creation of the draisine and the velocipede and eventually to the development of the bicycle. . . . The author demonstrates how the development and success of the bicycle were contingent on engineering, marketing, patents, the culture of various regions, and changing views of recreation and health; therefore, this book will also appeal to anyone interested in the history of those fields." Libr J

Includes bibliographical references

629.28   Tests, driving, maintenance, repair

Ramsey, Dan

Teach yourself visually car care & maintenance; by Dan Ramsey and Judy Ramsey. Visual / Wiley 2009 210p il (Visual read less, learn more) pa $24.95   **629.28**
    1. Automobiles -- Maintenance and repair
    ISBN 978-0-470-37727-7

LC 2009-920042

This book covers "how to change oil and other fluids; rotate tires; replace fuel pumps, air filters, and batteries; and . . . more." Publisher's note

Includes glossary

Vanderbilt, Tom

Traffic; why we drive the way we do (and what it says about us) Alfred A. Knopf 2008 402p $24.95   **629.28**
    1. City traffic 2. Automobile drivers
    ISBN 978-0-307-26478-7

LC 2008-11507

"This may be the most insightful and comprehensive study ever done of driving behavior and how it reveals truths about the types of people we are." Booklist

Includes bibliographical references

629.4 Astronautics

Brzezinski, Matthew

Red moon rising; Sputnik and the hidden rivalries that ignited the Space Age. Times Books 2007 322p il $26 **629.4**

1. Cold war 2. Artificial satellites 3. Outer space -- Exploration 4. Astronautics -- Soviet Union 5. Astronautics -- United States

ISBN 978-0-8050-8147-3; 0-8050-8147-X

LC 2007-08227

"Matthew Brzezinski's history of 1957 is not a potted retelling of the space race highlights we have perhaps encountered once too often in television documentaries and Sunday supplements, but a vivid and anecdotal account of the nerve-wracking delays, tormented decisions and agonizing uncertainties that unquestionably lent a human, and even heroic, aspect to his subject." Times Lit Suppl

Includes bibliographical references

Burrows, William E.

This new ocean; the story of the first space age. Random House 1998 723p il hardcover o.p. pa $18.95 **629.4**

1. Astronautics 2. Outer space -- Exploration

ISBN 0-375-75485-7 pa

LC 98-3252

"'This New Ocean' is most distinguished by the successful integration of three different story lines: manned space flight, the militarization of space and space science." N Y Times Book Rev

Includes bibliographical references

Cadbury, Deborah

Space race; the epic battle between America and the Soviet Union for dominion of space. HarperCollins 2006 370p il hardcover o.p. pa $15.95 **629.4**

1. Cold war 2. Outer space -- Exploration 3. Astronautics -- Soviet Union 4. Astronautics -- United States

ISBN 0-06-084553-8; 0-06-117628-1 pa

LC 2005-52693

First published 2005 in the United Kingdom

"From the opening account of Washington and Moscow's race to grab the models, machines, drawings, and personnel from Hitler's V-2 missile program at the end of World War II to Sputnik and then to Neil Armstrong's moonwalk, this is an utterly engrossing book—largely because of the two characters around whom the story unfolds, and because Cadbury has the material to tell it from the inside." Foreign Affairs

Includes bibliographical references

Hardesty, Von

Epic rivalry; the inside story of the Soviet and American space race. [by] Von Hardesty and Gene Eisman; foreword by Sergei Khrushchev. National Geographic Society 2007 275p il map $28; pa $16.95 **629.4**

1. Cold war 2. Outer space -- Exploration 3. Astronautics -- Soviet Union 4. Astronautics -- United

States

ISBN 978-1-4262-0119-6; 978-1-4262-0321-3 pa

LC 2007-17393

"This is a true saga, full of daring, danger, death, ego conflicts, and triumphs. . . . All readers should love this fabulous and profusely illustrated combined story." Sci Books Films

Includes bibliographical references

National Geographic Society (U.S.)

National Geographic encyclopedia of space; [compiled by] Linda K. Glover; with Andrew Chaikin . . . [et al.]; foreword by Buzz Aldrin. National Geographic Society 2004 400p il map $40 **629.4**

1. Astronautics 2. Reference books 3. Astronomy -- Encyclopedias 4. Outer space -- Exploration

ISBN 0-7922-7319-2

LC 2004-55229

The essays in this encyclopedia "discuss deep space, our solar system and space travel. There are also sections on using space to study Earth and on the military and intelligence uses of space. The essays in general are readable and show the implications of astronomy for life on Earth, such as the impact of solar flares on the weather. . . . This volume will suit astronomy enthusiasts better than total novices. Everyone, however, can enjoy the gorgeous photos." Publ Wkly

Tyson, Neil deGrasse, 1958-

Space chronicles; facing the ultimate frontier. Neil deGrasse Tyson ; edited by Avis Lang. W.W. Norton 2012 364 p. ill. $26.95 **629.4**

1. Space flight -- Forecasting 2. Astronautics -- United States 3. Astronautics and state -- United States 4. United States. National Aeronautics and Space Administration 5. Astronautics 6. Space flight 7. Outer space -- Exploration 8. United States -- National Aeronautics and Space Administration

ISBN 0393082105; 9780393082104

LC 2011032481

In this book, Neil DeGrasse Tyson "delivers . . . [an] argument for space exploration even in the face of a disastrous economy. In this collection of articles and talks, the author investigates what space travel means to us as a species and, more specifically, what NASA means to America. . . . 'When science does advance, when discovery does unfold . . . ,' he writes, 'they happen as an auxiliary benefit and not as a primary goal of NASA's geopolitical mission statement.'" (Kirkus Reviews)

"Tyson is an articulate popularizer of astrophysics. . . . His writing style, while necessarily a bit technical, is as engaging as his screen presence." LJ

629.43 Unmanned space flight

Zimmerman, Robert

The universe in a mirror; the saga of the Hubble Telescope and the visionaries who built it. Princeton University Press 2008 287p il $29.95 **629.43**

1. Hubble Space Telescope

ISBN 978-0-691-13297-6; 0-691-13297-6

LC 2007-943159

"Must reading for armchair astrophysicists." Booklist
Includes bibliographical references

629.44   Auxiliary spacecraft

Aldrin, Buzz, 1930-

Mission to mars; my vision for space exploration. by Buzz Aldrin and Leonard David. National
Geographic 2013 272 p. $26   **629.44**
   1. Outer space -- Exploration   2. Mars (Planet) --
Exploration
   ISBN 1426210175; 9781426210174

                 LC 2012953599

In this book, by Buzz Aldrin and Leonard David, Aldrin
"speaks out as a vital advocate for the continuing quest to
push the boundaries of the universe as we know it. As a pioneering astronaut who first set foot on the moon during mankind's first landing of Apollo 11--and as an aerospace engineer who designed an orbital rendezvous technique critical
to future planetary landings--Aldrin has a vision, and in this
book he plots out the path he proposes, taking humans to
Mars by 2035." (Publisher's note)

"Aldrin makes a daring proposal for further space exploration in this exciting glimpse of the new new frontier."
Pub Wkly

629.45   Manned space flight

Chaikin, Andrew

A **man** on the moon; the voyages of the Apollo
astronauts. Viking 1994 670p il hardcover o.p. pa
$18   **629.45**
   1. Apollo project   2. Space flight to the moon
   ISBN 0-670-81446-6; 978-0-14-311235-8 pa; 0-14-
311235-X pa

                 LC 93-48680

In this chronicle of NASA's Apollo program "diary-like
reports mix with first- and third-person accounts as Chaikin
. . . delivers a chronological view of the missions and those
who planned and flew them. Focusing closely on the Apollo
astronauts, including Buzz Aldrin, Pete Conrad and Neil
Armstrong, Chaikin gives his topic a sense of immediacy."
Publ Wkly

Includes bibliographical references

French, Francis

In the shadow of the moon; a challenging journey
to Tranquility, 1965-1969. [by] Francis French and
Colin Burgess; with a foreword by Walter Cunningham. University of Nebraska Press 2007 425p il
(Outward odyssey) $29.95   **629.45**
   1. Apollo project   2. Space flight to the moon   3.
Astronautics -- Soviet Union   4. Astronautics -- United
States
   ISBN 978-0-8032-1128-5; 0-8032-1128-7

                 LC 2006-103047

"This book will have an important place in the recorded
history of space exploration." Sci Books Films
Includes bibliographical references

Koppel, Lily

The **Astronaut** Wives Club; A True Story. Lily
Koppel. Grand Central Pub. 2013 384 p. (hardcover) $28   **629.45**
   1. United States -- History   2. Astronauts' spouses --
Biography   3. Astronautics -- United States -- History
   4. Astronauts' spouses -- Texas -- Houston -- Biography
   5. Women -- Texas -- Houston -- Social life and customs
-- 20th century
   ISBN 1455503258; 9781455503254

                 LC 2012045976

This book, by Lily Koppel, profiles the lives of U.S. astronauts' wives during the 1960s and onward. "As America's
Mercury Seven astronauts were launched on death-defying
missions, television cameras focused on the brave smiles
of their young wives. Overnight, these women were transformed from military spouses into American royalty. . . .
They formed the Astronaut Wives Club, meeting regularly
to provide support and friendship." (Publisher's note)

Kranz, Eugene F.

Failure is not an option; mission control from
Mercury to Apollo 13 and beyond. {by} Gene Kranz.
Simon & Schuster 2000 415p il $26   **629.45**
   1. Space flight   2. Astronautics -- United States   3.
United States -- National Aeronautics and Space
Administration
   ISBN 0-7432-0079-9

                 LC 00-27720

"A welcome contribution to the history of space flight.
More than any previous book, it gives the view of that history as lived by the brotherhood of Mission Control. The writing, like Kranz himself, is brisk, unadorned and informative,
but warmed from time to time by characteristic expressions
of irony and humor." N Y Times Book Rev

Nelson, Craig

Rocket men; the triumph and tragedy of the
first Americans on the moon. Viking 2009 404p il
$27.95   **629.45**
   1. Apollo project   2. Space flight to the moon   3.
Astronautics -- United States
   ISBN 978-0-670-02103-1

                 LC 2008-51175

"A thorough recounting—as full in human terms as in
scientific and technical detail—of NASA's first manned
Moon landing. . . . The definitive account of a watershed in
American history." Kirkus
Includes bibliographical references

Piantadosi, Claude A.

Mankind beyond Earth; the history, science, and
future of human space exploration. Claude A. Piantadosi. Columbia University Press 2012 336 p. (cloth
: alk. paper) $35   **629.45**
   1. Interplanetary voyages   2. Outer space -- Exploration
   3. Outer space -- Exploration -- Popular works   4.
Manned space flight -- History -- Popular works   5.
Astronautics -- United States -- Forecasting -- Popular
works
   ISBN 0231162421; 9780231162425; 9780231531030

                 LC 2012017631

In this book, Claude A. Piantadosi "offers a brief history of human space exploration; a discussion of various strategies for extending human excursions to asteroids, the Moon (again), Mars, the outer planets of the Sun, and even targets beyond the solar system; and a rigorous examination of the very special and expensive conditions needed for human survival on such trips." (Library Journal)

Includes bibliographical references and index

Pyle, Rod

Destination moon; the Apollo missions in the astronauts' own words. HarperCollins Publishers 2005 192p il $24.95; pa $14.95   **629.45**

1. Space flight to the moon 2. Project Apollo
ISBN 0-06-087349-3; 0-06-087350-7 pa

LC 2005-51350

This "survey of the Apollo moon program includes a brief summary of each flight and attempted flight of the great effort, from the fatal fire on Pad 34 in 1967 to the landing of a scientist on the moon in Apollo 17 in 1972. . . . Space collections of all sizes should welcome Pyle's book, and smaller ones will find it invaluable." Booklist

Schefter, James L.

The **race**; the uncensored story of how America beat Russia to the moon. by James Schefter. Doubleday 1999 303p il hardcover o.p. pa $14   **629.45**

1. Astronautics 2. Apollo project 3. Space flight to the moon
ISBN 0-385-49254-5 pa

LC 98-54430

Schefter chronicles the early days of space flight competition describing "the subtle infighting among the astronauts, the complex nature of lesser-known people like manned-flight champion Bob Gilruth, and the American leaders struggling with military, scientific and public relations concerns." Publ Wkly

Wolfe, Tom

★ The **right** stuff. Picador 2008 352p pa $16   **629.45**

1. Astronauts 2. Astronautics -- United States
ISBN 0-312-42756-5; 978-0-312-42756-6
First published 1979 by Farrar, Straus & Giroux

This volume chronicles "the handful of adrenaline-junkie military test pilots who became the Mercury astronauts. Their story is juxtaposed against that of Chuck Yeager, the ace of aces pilot who broke the sound barrier but couldn't apply to the space program because he lacked a college degree. . . . A terrific read from beginning to end." Libr J

Zimmerman, Robert

Genesis : the story of Apollo 8; the first manned flight to another world. Dell 1999 350p il pa $7.99   **629.45**

1. Apollo project 2. Space flight to the moon
ISBN 978-0-440-23556-9; 0-440-23556-1
First published 1998 by Four Walls Eight Windows

The author tells the story of "Apollo 8 from the time it blasted into space on December 21, 1968, until it splashed down in the Pacific nearly a week later. He focuses on three brave men—Frank Borman, Jim Lovell, and Bill Anders—

who volunteered to ride an inadequately tested space vehicle equipped with a primitive computer on a journey of some quarter-million miles to orbit the Moon and return. He also focuses on the astronauts' wives." Choice

Includes bibliographical references

629.46   Engineering of unmanned spacecraft

Dickson, Paul

Sputnik : the shock of the century. Walker & Co. 2001 310p il $28   **629.46**

1. Astronautics 2. Artificial satellites 3. United States -- Politics and government -- 20th century
ISBN 0-8027-1365-3

LC 2001-26156

"Paul Dickson skillfully puts the story of Sputnik and its aftermath into . . . perspective in his informative and readable book." Christ Sci Monit

Includes bibliographical references

629.47   Astronautical engineering

Dyson, George

Project Orion; the true story of the atomic spaceship. Holt & Co. 2002 345p il $26; pa $16 **629.47**

1. Astronautics 2. Nuclear rockets
ISBN 0-8050-5985-7; 0-8050-7284-5 pa

LC 2001-46500

The author "charts the history of the failed Project Orion, which called for a massive rocket to be built atop a nuclear-powered piston. . . . Dyson's explanations of the nuclear science behind the system are lucid. A great strength of Dyson's project is the interviews he conducted with surviving Orion team members." Publ Wkly

Includes bibliographical references

629.8   Automatic control engineering

Bascomb, Neal

The **new** cool; a visionary teacher, his FIRST robotics team, and the ultimate battle of smarts. Crown Publishers 2010 337p il $25; ebook $12.99 **629.8**

1. Robots 2. FIRST (Organization)
ISBN 978-0-307-58889-0; 978-0-307-58891-3 ebook

LC 2010-21646

The author "charts the marathon play-by-play teamwork of a group of fourth-year Southern California students from Dos Pueblos High School Engineering Academy as they competed in a robot-building contest. Since 2002, physics teacher and mentor Amir Abo-Shaeer has administered an experimental science curriculum culminating in a team entry in 'FIRST' (For Inspiration and Recognition of Science and Technology), a worldwide robotics competition created by Dean Kamen. . . . Aside from a mind-numbing plethora of physics terminology, Bascomb skillfully translates the exhilarating challenge to the page via intricately descriptive, expertly paced sketches of the group and their combined handiwork. A nail-biting thrill ride for techies and armchair engineers." Kirkus

Includes bibliographical references

Dufty, David F.

How to build an android; the true story of Philip K. Dick's robotic resurrection. David F. Dufty. 1st US ed. H. Holt 2012 272 p. ill. (hbk.) $26.00 **629.8**

1. Robots 2. Artificial intelligence 3. Roboticists -- Biography 4. Androids -- Popular works 5. Robotics -- Popular works 6. Artificial intelligence -- Popular works

ISBN 0805095519; 9780805095517

LC 2011043674

This book by David F. Dufty tells "the story of the roboticists who created a fully functioning android replica of renowned writer Philip K. Dick." (Kirkus Reviews) "Dufty focuses on two main developers . . . David Hanson . . . who created Phil's head only to later lose it on an airplane, and Andrew Olney, a computer programmer who was obsessed with science fiction books as a youngster. Dufty examines how their differing outlooks influenced the project." (Publishers Weekly)

Long, John

Darwin's devices; what evolving robots can teach us about the history of life and the future of technology. John Long. Basic Books 2012 273 p. **629.8**

1. Biology -- Simulation methods 2. Evolution -- Study and teaching 3. Robots -- Design and construction 4. Technological innovations -- Forecasting 5. Evolutionary robotics 6. Technological forecasting

ISBN 0465021417; 9780465021413; 9780465029280

LC 2011051804

The author "traces his path from a doctoral student studying the evolution of fish vertebrae to his present position as director of Vassar's Interdisciplinary Robotics Laboratory. . . . [John] Long explains how a blunder in an early version of his doctoral thesis led to his later work with robots. . . . Long's first self-propelled robot had a fairly simple design--an embedded minicomputer, one light sensor and a backbone built to mimic varying structural aspects of a marlin vertebrae. . . . More complex robots allowed him to model predator/prey relationships and target acquisition more realistically, and he was able to consider broader issues such as the relationship between goal-directed behavior and animal intelligence." (Kirkus)

Includes bibliographical references and index

Robot building for beginners; David Cook. 2nd ed Apress 2009 xxxiv, 453 p.p ill. (pbk.) $34.99 **629.8**

1. Robots -- Design and construction

ISBN 1430227486; 9781430227489

LC 2010282774

This book contains instructions on how to build a robot. "General sources for tools and parts are provided in a consolidated list, and specific parts are recommended throughout the book. . . . {The book also features information on} basic safety precautions and essential numbering and measuring systems." Publisher's note

630   Agriculture and related technologies

Berry, Wendell

Bringing it to the table; on farming and food. introduction by Michael Pollan. Counterpoint 2009 234p pa $14.95 **630**

1. Family farms 2. Sustainable agriculture 3. Agriculture -- United States

ISBN 978-1-58243-543-5

LC 2009-24437

"The essays [included] address such concerns as: How does organic measure up against locally grown? What are the differences between small and large farms, and how does that affect what you put on your dinner table? What can you do to support sustainable agriculture?" Publisher's note

Includes bibliographical references

Carpenter, Novella

Farm city; the education of an urban farmer. Penguin Press 2009 276p $25.95 **630**

1. Farmers 2. Journalists 3. Urban agriculture

ISBN 978-1-59420-221-6; 1-59420-221-4

LC 2008-54666

This is "easily the funniest, weirdest, most perversely provocative gardening book I've ever read. . . . Though always entertaining, . . . [Carpenter] occasionally lapses into the grating lingo of the blogger, but toward the end, as she contemplates the place of her garden in the greater scheme of life, she shows what she's capable of and the writing soars." N Y Times Book Rev

Hanson, David

Breaking through concrete; building an urban farm revival. David Hanson and Edwin Marty ; photographs by Michael Hanson ; foreword by Mark Winne. University of California Press 2012 xv, 181 p.p (cloth : alk. paper) $29.95 **630**

1. Gardening 2. Teenage mothers 3. Homeless persons 4. Community gardens 5. Urban agriculture 6. Community gardens -- United States 7. Urban agriculture -- United States

ISBN 0520270541; 9780520270541

LC 2011024485

For this book, "[b]rothers David (a freelance journalist) and Michael (a freelance photographer) Hanson, together with Marty, founder of the nonprofit Jones Valley Farm in downtown Birmingham, AL, traveled cross-country to 12 urban gardens, starting in Seattle and ending in Illinois. Featured projects include a Santa Cruz garden tended by the homeless, a New Orleans congregational garden run by Vietnamese immigrants, and a Detroit teaching farm for teenage mothers." (Library Journal)

Includes bibliographical references.

631.5 Cultivation and harvesting

Cummings, Claire Hope

★ **Uncertain** peril; Genetic engineering and the future of seeds. Beacon Press 2008 232p $24.95 **631.5**

1. Seeds 2. Biotechnology

ISBN 978-0-8070-8580-6

LC 2007-26298

This "authoritative portrait of another way in which our planet is at peril provides stark food for thought." Publ Wkly

Includes bibliographical references

631.6 Clearing, drainage, revegetation

Fukuoka, Masanobu

Sowing seeds in the desert; natural farming, global restoration, and ultimate food security. Masanobu Fukuoka ; edited by Larry Korn. Chelsea Green Pub. 2012 168 p. (hardback) $22.50 **631.6**

1. Sustainable agriculture 2. Agricultural innovations 3. Agriculture -- Environmental aspects 4. Revegetation 5. Desert reclamation 6. Desertification -- Control

ISBN 9781603584180; 1603584188; 9781603584197

LC 2012007330

This book "calls on modern-day farmers to reconsider their methods and heed the needs of the land. . . . [Masanobu Fukuoka] illuminates regional disparities in environmental and agricultural thought and practice. . . . In clarifying popular misconceptions about organic and natural farming, he advises that we must not focus on cash crops. . . . Only by the co-existence of myriad micro-organisms and vegetation will we be able to preserve and maintain our land." (Publishers Weekly)

Includes bibliographical references.

631.8 Fertilizers, soil conditioners, growth regulators

Pleasant, Barbara

★ The **complete** compost gardening guide; banner batches, grow heaps, comforter compost, and other amazing techniques for saving time and money, and producing the most flavorful, nutritious vegetables ever. [by] Barbara Pleasant & Deborah L. Martin. Storey Pub. 2008 319p il map $29.95; pa $19.95 **631.8**

1. Compost 2. Gardening

ISBN 978-1-58017-703-0; 978-1-58017-702-3 pa

LC 2007-49729

The authors "provide both a reference guide and an introduction to composting. The first section . . . includes a number of interesting facts, definitions, and even recipes (e.g., for Miracle Leaf Mold). The second section, on compost gardening techniques, examines easy methods of composting with piles, bins, and cans as well as more elaborate approaches involving pits and trenches. It also discusses the use of earthworms in composting. Finally, the third section treats in detail the kinds of plants that will do well in a composter's garden. . . . Essential reading for any gardener interested in composting, this should find its way into many public libraries with active gardening communities and academic and special libraries with an interest in horticulture and gardening." Libr J

632 Plant injuries, diseases, pests

Lockwood, Jeffrey A.

Locust; the devastating rise and mysterious disappearance of the insect that shaped the American frontier. Jeffrey A. Lockwood. 1st ed; Basic Books 2004 xxiii, 294p il $25; pa $14.95 **632**

1. Locusts 2. West (U.S.) -- History

ISBN 0-7382-0894-9; 0-465-04167-1 pa

LC 2003-25538

The author "tells the fascinating story of how the Rocky Mountain locust invasions shaped American life in the 1870s. . . . This book is great for natural-history lovers, American history lovers, mystery lovers, and all who love a well-told real-life tale." Sci Books Films

Mabey, Richard

Weeds; in defense of nature's most unloved plants. HarperCollins 2011 324p il $25.99; ebook $12.99 **632**

1. Weeds

ISBN 978-0-06-206545-2; 978-0-06-206547-6 ebook

LC 2011010483

First published 2010 in the United Kingdom

"This lively, erudite work invites readers to take a new look at the lowly and unloved weed. Mabey explains how weeds have cunningly evolved to survive natural disasters, human devastation, climate change, and almost every attempt to eradicate them. He weaves together a complex, fascinating tale of history and botany that travels from the first farm fields of Mesopotamia to the bomb craters of the London Blitz and the lowly industrial outfields of our modern cities." Publ Wkly

Includes bibliographical references

Stewart, Amy

Wicked bugs; the louse that conquered Napoleon's army & other diabolical insects. etchings and drawings by Briony Morrow-Cribbs. Algonquin Books of Chapel Hill 2011 271p il $18.95 **632**

1. Mites 2. Ticks 3. Spiders 4. Insect pests

ISBN 978-1-56512-960-3

LC 2011-3629

"Ranging from verdant South American jungles to Manhattan's cold concrete canyons, Stewart amusingly but analytically profiles the baddest bugs around in quick but attention-grabbing snapshots of little creatures that pack a lot of punch. Bed bugs and bookworms, rat fleas and filth flies all come under Stewart's curious gaze as she exposes their evil habits and lethal charms. No alarmist setting out to stoke preexisting phobias, Stewart shares her natural fascination with the insect world to help readers recognize both the threats and the wonders that could be lurking in corner crevices or come wafting in on the next gentle breeze." Booklist

Includes bibliographical references

633.5   Fiber crops

Fine, Doug

Hemp bound; dispatches from the front lines of the next agricultural revolution. Doug Fine. Chelsea Green Publishing Company 2014 192 p. (pbk.) $14.95   **633.5**

1. Hemp 2. Agriculture -- United States 3. Hemp industry

ISBN 1603585435; 9781603585439; 9781603585446

         LC 2013048926

"In 'Hemp Bound: Dispatches from the Front Lines of the Next Agricultural Revolution,' . . . author Doug Fine embarks on a . . . journey to meet the men and women who are testing, researching, and pioneering hemp's applications for the twenty-first century. . . . Fine learns how . . . possible it is for this misunderstood plant to help us end dependence on fossil fuels, heal farm soils damaged [by] growing monocultures, and bring . . . taxable revenue into the economy." (Publisher's note)

"A short, sweet, logical and funny argument for the potential of one of the world's most dynamic cash crops." Kirkus

Includes bibliographical references and index

634   Orchards, fruits, forestry

Deardorff, David

What's wrong with my fruit garden? 100% organic solutions for berries, trees, nuts, vines, and tropicals. David Deardorff and Kathryn Wadsworth. Timber Press 2014 312 p. color illustrations $24.95   **634**

1. Gardening 2. Fruit culture 3. Fruit-culture 4. Organic gardening 5. Fruit -- Diseases and pests -- Control 6. Fruit trees -- Wounds and injuries -- Diagnosis

ISBN 1604693584; 9781604693584; 9781604694888

         LC 2013009257

Written by David Deardorff and Kathryn Wadsworth, "'What's Wrong With My Fruit Garden?' offers a path toward a healthy garden packed with fresh fruit. In addition to learning how to diagnose a plant problem through clear visual keys, you will also learn the most effective organic solutions for every problem. Detailed plant portraits include information on growth; seasonality; temperature, light, and soil requirements; and planting techniques." (Publisher's note)

"Deardorff and Wadsworth arm the gardener with needed strategies that lessen the risk of failure and encourage robust growth." Pub Wkly

Includes bibliographical references and index

634.9   Forestry

Brown, Daniel

Under a flaming sky; the great Hinckley firestorm of 1894. [by] Daniel James Brown. Lyons Press 2006 256p il map $22.95   **634.9**

1. Forest fires 2. Minnesota

ISBN 1-59228-863-4; 978-1-59228-863-2

"On September 1, 1894, a firestorm consumed timber-boomtown Hinckley, Minnesota, and three nearby hamlets. Brown, grandson of an 11-year-old survivor, makes riveting, affecting, white-knuckle reading of that horrifying, internationally reported day's lethal passage." Booklist

Includes bibliographical references

Connors, Philip

Fire season; field notes from a wilderness lookout. Ecco 2011 246 p. (trade) $24.99   **634.9**

1. Authors 2. Solitude 3. New Mexico 4. Forest fires 5. Essayists 6. Fire lookouts 7. Newspaper editors 8. Writers on nature 9. Fire lookout stations 10. Gila National Forest (N.M.)

ISBN 0061859362; 9780061859366

The content of this book is based on author "Philip Connors[' time] . . . spent . . . in a seven-by-seven foot fire-lookout tower, ten thousand feet above the ground in one of the remotest territories of New Mexico. One of the least developed parts of the country, the first region designated as an official wilderness area in the world, the section he tends is also one of the most fire-prone, suffering more than thirty thousand lightning strikes each year. . . . Connors' time up on the peak is filled with drama—there are fires large and small; spectacular midnight lightning storms and silent mornings awakening above the clouds; surprise encounters with long-distance hikers, smokejumpers, bobcats, black bears, and an abandoned, dying fawn." (Blackstone Audio)

"For almost a decade, former Wall Street Journal reporter Connors has spent half a year keeping vigil over 20,000 square miles of desert, forest, and mountain chains from atop a tower 10,000 feet above sea level. One of a handful of seasoned, seasonal fire-watchers in New Mexico's Gila National Forest, Connors introduces us to his wilderness in this ruminative, lyrical, occasionally suspenseful account." Publ Wkly

Maclean, John N.

The Thirtymile fire; a chronicle of bravery and betrayal. Henry Holt 2007 241p il map $25 **634.9**

1. Wildfires 2. Fire fighters 3. Cascade Range region

ISBN 978-0-8050-7578-6; 0-8050-7578-X

         LC 2006-45846

Maclean "interviewed families, survivors, investigators and fire experts, and the result is an evenhanded, lucid recreation of catastrophe and its aftermath. The author gives a human face to national headlines, capturing the dignity and sense of mission of the lost firefighters." Publ Wkly

635   Garden crops (Horticulture)

Adam, Judith

Landscape planning; practical techniques for the home gardener. 2nd ed., rev. and expanded; Firefly 2008 247p il $39.95; pa $29.95   **635**

1. Landscape gardening

ISBN 978-1-55407-381-8; 1-55407-381-2; 978-1-55407-258-3 pa; 1-55407-258-1 pa

First published 2002

"Adam's language is both practical and reflective of a love of gardening. A sound resource for any size collection." Libr J [review of 2002 edition]

American Horticultural Society

The **American** Horticultural Society gardening manual. Dorling Kindersley 2000 420p il map $40   635

1. Gardening
ISBN 0-7894-5952-3

LC 00-22644

"The book is divided into four parts, the first of which covers garden planning, illustrating various garden styles, hardscape choices, and advice on designing the space. . . Part 2, which is arranged by plant type . . . covers the care and maintenance of the plants. . . . Part 3 offers thumbnail descriptions, including hardiness zones and the mature size of reliable, recommended plants arranged by the season they are at their best. The final part summarizes the routine but essential tasks the gardener should do each month." Libr J

★ **New** encyclopedia of gardening techniques; American Horticultural Society editors, David J. Ellis . . . [et al.]; additional contributors, Simon Akeroyd . . . [et al.] Mitchell Beazley 2009 480p il map $45   635

1. Reference books 2. Gardening -- Encyclopedias
ISBN 978-1-84533-484-0

"Expert gardeners and garden writers have been assembled to execute this tour de force, which every serious gardener will want to repeatedly consult. Abundantly illustrated with thousands of illustrations and photographs, each clearly and sensibly written section of this volume offers helpful advice, step-by-step techniques, tips for identifying and correcting common problems, suggested plants for various situations, and lots of ideas." Booklist

Balick, Michael J.

Rodale's 21st-century herbal; a practical guide for healthy living using nature's most powerful plants. Michael J. Balick ; foreword by Andrew Weil. Rodale 2013 498 p. color illustrations (hardcover) $35   635

1. Herbs -- Therapeutic use 2. Encyclopedias and dictionaries 3. Herbs 4. Herbals 5. Herb gardening 6. Organic gardening
ISBN 1609618041; 9781609618049

LC 2013022312

Written by Michael J. Balick, "'Rodale's 21st-Century Herbal' first explores the historical relationship between people and herbal plants and how it has evolved over time. In the second part, readers will delve into an A-to-Z encyclopedia of 180 of the most useful herbs from around the globe. . . . The final section highlights how herbs create a 'fuller' life and features herbal cooking techniques, ways to use herbs for beauty and the bath, ideas for daily herbal use." (Publisher's note)

Barrett, Judy

What can I do with my herbs? how to grow, use, and enjoy these versatile plants. art by Vic-

tor Z. Martin. Texas A&M University Press 2009 134p il (W.L. Moody, Jr., natural history series) pa $19.95   635

1. Herbs 2. Herb gardening
ISBN 978-1-60344-092-9; 1-60344-092-5

LC 2008-31016

A "look at forty common herbs and the creative and useful things people do with them. Each herb description includes the plant's history and a list of popular uses. . . . [Barrett conveys] information about how to successfully grow herbs (start a ginger plant with a root from the grocery store), how to enjoy herbs in the garden (watch the swallowtail butterflies and caterpillars that love fennel), and how to use them in the kitchen (substitute the yellow flowers of calendula for saffron). Along the way, she even shares some of her favorite recipes." Publisher's note

Bartholomew, Mel

All new square foot gardening; the revolutionary way to grow more in less space. Mel Bartholomew. 2nd ed. Cool Springs Press 2013 272 p. col. ill. (softcover) $24.99   635

1. Vegetable gardening 2. Vertical gardening 3. Square foot gardening 4. Gardening for children
ISBN 1591865484; 9781591865483

LC 2012042837

In this book, author and gardener Mel Bartholomew "furthers his discussion on one of the most popular gardening trends today: vertical gardening. He also explains how you can make gardening fun for kids by teaching them the square foot method. Finally, an expanded section on pest control helps you protect your precious produce." (Publisher's note)

Cohen, Whitney

The **book** of gardening projects for kids; 101 ways to get kids outside, dirty, and having fun. Whitney Cohen and John Fisher. 1st ed. Timber Press 2012 264 p. col. ill. $29.95   635

1. Gardening 2. Gardens -- Guidebooks 3. Gardens -- Activity projects 4. Gardening for children
ISBN 1604693738; 9781604692457

LC 2011036778

In this book, "Whitney Cohen and John Fisher draw on years of experience in the Life Lab Garden Classroom and gardening with their own children to teach parents how to integrate the garden into their family life, no matter its scope or scale. The book features . . . gardening advice, including how to design a play-friendly garden, ideas for fun-filled theme gardens, and how to cook and preserve the garden's bounty. 101 . . . garden activities are also featured." (Publisher's note)

Coleman, Eliot

Winter harvest handbook; year-round vegetable production using deep-organic techniques and unheated greenhouses. Chelsea Green Pub. Co. 2009 247p il map pa $29.95   635

1. Greenhouses 2. Organic farming 3. Vegetable

gardening
ISBN 978-1-60358-081-6

LC 2008-53184

"Coleman's opus is as much a call to action for town planners to embrace local farms as it is a bible for small farmers. This book is for people who know what they're doing." N Y Times Book Rev

Includes bibliographical references

Coombes, Allen J.

The **A** to Z of plant names; a quick reference guide to 4000 garden plants. Allen J. Coombes. 1st ed. Timber Press 2012 312 p. $19.95   **635**

1. Popular plant names 2. Botany -- Nomenclature 3. Botany -- Great Britain -- Dictionaries 4. Botany -- North America -- Dictionaries 5. Plants -- Great Britain -- Nomenclature -- Dictionaries 6. Plants -- North America -- Nomenclature -- Dictionaries
ISBN 1604691964; 9781604691962

LC 2011029271

This guide to plant names "features the botanic names of the plants that gardeners really grow. Additional information includes suggested pronunciation, the common name, the derivation of the scientific name, the number of species currently accepted, the type of plant and the distribution." (Publisher's note)

Includes bibliographical references (p. 311-312).

Damrosch, Barbara

The **garden** primer; illustrations by Linda Heppes Funk, Ray Maher, and Carol Bolt. 2nd ed.; Workman Pub. 2008 820p il map $28.95; pa $18.95 **635**

1. Gardening
ISBN 978-0-7611-4856-2; 978-0-7611-2275-3 pa

LC 2007-51425

First published 1988

This is a "book for the new gardener that clearly explains the basics of garden planning, plant care, and equipment. Detailed chapters on the different categories of plants—annuals, perennials, vegetables, fruits, lawns, shrubs, roses, vines, trees, wildflowers, and even house plants—give general advice on how to use and care for these varieties. A valuable book for public libraries." Libr J

Includes bibligoraphical references

Deardorff, David C.

What's wrong with my plant (and how do I fix it?) a visual guide to easy diagnosis and organic remedies. [by] David Deardorff and Kathryn Wadsworth. Timber Press 2009 451p il pa $24.95   **635**

1. Plant diseases 2. Ornamental plants 3. Natural pesticides
ISBN 978-0-88192-961-4; 0-88192-961-1

LC 2009-19447

"The book allows readers to select a suitable starting point that describes a plant's symptom—for example, wilting leaves or holes in the stems—and answer simple questions that eventually lead to a solution to the problem. . . . The book is divided into three parts. The first features clear keys that help identify the cause. . . . Once the problem is identified, the reader just goes to the suggested page in the second section, which contains a hierarchy of remedies. The

third section, also referenced by individual page numbers in the previous two, contains excellent pictures of symptoms to help confirm the diagnosis of the problem and offer remedies. . . . [This book] is an important reference that will help gardeners successfully diagnose their own plant problems and make educated decisions about how to solve them." Am Gardener

Includes bibliographical references

DiSabato-Aust, Tracy

The **well**-designed mixed garden; building beds and borders with trees, shrubs, perennials, annuals, and bulbs. Timber Press 2003 460p il map $39.95   **635**

1. Landscape gardening
ISBN 0-88192-559-4

LC 2002-23191

The author focuses on "the mixed border, which incorporates permanent woody plants as well as perennials, annuals, and other plants that die back to the ground every year. . . . Particularly impressive are the author's designs for using the mixed-garden approach in small properties, such as townhouse gardens and around foundations. . . . The motivated gardener will find a wealth of information and ideas in this book." Libr J

Includes bibliographical references

Eck, Joe

Our life in gardens; [by] Joe Eck and Wayne Winterrowd. Farrar, Straus and Giroux 2009 322p il $30   **635**

1. Gardening
ISBN 978-0-374-16031-9; 0-374-16031-7

LC 2008-45349

"In nearly 50 erudite and entertaining essays stretching alphabetically from Agapanthus to Xanthorrhoea quadrangulate, Eck and Winterrowd share the history of their Vermont garden, writing about the plants they have lived with, nurtured and nourished." Publ Wkly

Hatch, Peter J.

A rich spot of earth; Thomas Jefferson's revolutionary garden at Monticello. Peter J. Hatch ; foreword by Alice Waters. Yale University Press 2012 263 p. (clothbound : alk. paper) $35.00   **635**

1. Gardens 2. Presidents -- United States 3. Vegetable gardening -- United States 4. Monticello (Va.) 5. Vegetable gardening -- Virginia
ISBN 9780300171143

LC 2011038043

This book presents an account of U.S. President Thomas Jefferson's garden at his estate, Monticello. "Beginning with an extensive examination of Jefferson's structural plans and implementation strategies for Monticello's complex system of vegetable gardens, [Peter J.] Hatch then chronicles his own lengthy effort at the helm of a vast restoration project that owes much of its success to the meticulous records Jefferson left behind. Along with providing plant profiles of the myriad vegetables cultivated there over the centuries, he also offers . . . insights into the arduous physical tasks involved in eighteenth-century gardening as well as Jefferson's prudent establishment of seed-saving techniques that continue to affect the marketplace." (Booklist)

Includes bibliographical references and index.

Hill, Fionna

Microgreens; how to grow nature's own superfood. Firefly Books 2010 107p il pa $17.95 **635**
1. Salad greens
ISBN 978-1-55407-769-4

"Hill explains how to plant, raise, and harvest crops of delicious and highly nutritious microgreens. The book is informative and accessible, delivering in a buoyant voice all you need to know about the ultimate in local eating—making a meal of houseplants. It is nicely illustrated as well, with tantalizing photographs of microgreens at every stage, from seed to planting to plate. And there are more than a dozen recipes included here along with the chapters on plant care, individual crops of microgreens from amaranth to mustard to rocket, and involving children in the operation." Libr J

Includes bibliographical references

Homegrown harvest; a season-by-season guide to a sustainable kitchen garden. Rita Pelczar, editor in chief. Rev. American ed.; American Horticultural Society 2011 304p il $32.50 **635**
1. Vegetable gardening
ISBN 978-1-84533-560-1

"The American Horticultural Society shows temperate-climate gardeners how to make their ways through the gardening year. The book is arranged by season, from early spring to late winter, with how-to advice on growing vegetables and fruits, subdivided into tasks for the different vegetable families and fruit trees, bushes, and vines in each subseason, individualized for mild-winter, medium-temperature, and cold-winter regions. . . . The book's sumptuous tone, instructive photographs, and detailed directions should give beginning gardeners the enthusiasm and confidence to get started and organizationally challenged old-timers a sigh of relief that they won't have to figure out what to do next." Publ Wkly

Hutchinson, Carolyn

Time -saving gardener; tips and essential tasks, season by season. Firefly Books 2008 144p il pa $19.95 **635**
1. Gardening
ISBN 978-1-55407-372-6; 1-55407-372-3

First published 1999 in the United Kingdom with title: The once-a-week gardener

"For gardeners too busy to plan, this eminently practical book takes care of the distracting work of planning, organizing and prioritizing." Publ Wkly

Jabbour, Niki

Groundbreaking food gardens; 73 plans that will change the way you grow your garden. by Niki Jabbour. Storey Pub. 2014 272 p. col. ill. (pbk. : alk. paper) $19.95 **635**
1. Fruit 2. Vegetables 3. Edible plants 4. Vegetable gardening 5. Food crops 6. Edible landscaping
ISBN 161212061X; 9781603428446; 9781612120614
LC 2013030517

In this book, author Niki Jabbour "has collected 73 plans for novel and inspiring food gardens from her favorite superstar gardeners, including Amy Stewart, Amanda Thomsen, Barbara Pleasant, Dave DeWitt, and Jessi Bloom. You'll find a garden that provides salad greens 52 weeks a year, another that supplies your favorite cocktail ingredients, one that you plant on a balcony, one that encourages pollinators, one that grows 24 kinds of chile peppers, and dozens more." (Publisher's note)

"Every plan is accompanied by full-color illustrations, growing tips, and tweakable lists of crop possibilities. The abundance of creative advice here will help perk up the gardens of both novice and professional growers." Booklist

Seventy-three plans that will change the way you grow your garden

Land, Leslie

The **New** York times 1000 gardening questions & answers; based on the column Gardeners Q & A. with additional material by Leslie Land; botanical illustrations by Bobbi Angell; how-to illustrations by Elayne Sears. Workman 2003 852p il $34.95; pa $19.95 **635**
1. Gardening
ISBN 0-7611-2886-7; 0-7611-1997-3 pa
LC 2002-34206

"The text uses a Q&A format to address a gamut of gardening topics. The result is a substantial reference work useful to novice and experienced gardeners alike, with the Q&As organized into five sections: 'Flowering Plants,' 'Landscaping,' 'Edible Plants,' 'Container Gardening,' and 'Maintenance.' The subtopics within each section are many and diverse, including historically appropriate plantings, houseplants, over-wintering, and organic vegetable growing, as well as standard topics such as deer damage, roses, pruning, soil types and amendment, and recommended plant lists for specific situations." Libr J

Learn to garden; [contributors, Guy Barter ... [et al.]] 1st American ed.; DK Pub. 2008 352p il pa $22.95 **635**
1. Gardening
ISBN 978-0-7566-3443-8; 0-7566-3443-1
LC 2008-297619

This book covers how to "plant perennials, annuals and bulbs; prune trees and shrubs; make a new lawn or a gravel garden; select and grow roses, grasses, and ferns; grow vegetables and herbs in containers; [and] keep pests and diseases under control." Publisher's note

Markham, Brett L.

Mini farming; self sufficiency on a 1/4 acre. rev. and expanded; Skyhorse Pub. 2010 227p il pa $16.95 **635**
1. Farms 2. Agriculture 3. Self-reliance
ISBN 978-1-60239-984-6
LC 2009041561

"An excellent guide for gardeners wanting to eliminate most of their grocery bills. Markham's approach combines his own experience with the best practices from several raised-bed methods. Advice includes how to select vegetables that are calorie-dense and budget friendly, how to raise poultry, how to build both a plucker and a thresher, and how to preserve food." Libr J

Includes bibliographical references

Pleasant, Barbara

Starter vegetable gardens. Storey Pub. 2010 179p il pa $19.95　　　**635**

1. Vegetable gardening

ISBN 978-1-60342-529-2

LC 2009-49114

"From simple bag gardens to bountiful food cornucopias, each garden plan is . . . laid out with precise lists of materials and plants based on detailed landscape plans suitable for small city gardens as well as larger suburban backyards. Along with year-by-year overviews that allow gardeners to anticipate growth and adapt to changes, Pleasant provides essential cultivation and maintenance techniques." Booklist

Rodale's ultimate encyclopedia of organic gardening; the indispensible green resource for every gardener. edited by Fern Marshall Bradley, Barbara W. Ellis, and Ellen Phillips. Newly rev. and updated; Rodale 2009 707p il map pa $24.99　　**635**

1. Reference books 2. Organic gardening -- Encyclopedias

ISBN 978-1-59486-917-4; 1-59486-917-0

LC 2008-35329

First published 1959 with title: Rodale's encyclopedia of organic gardening; this is a revision of the 1992 edition published with title: Rodale's all-new encyclopedia of organic gardening

This volume presents alphabetically arranged entries about topics relating to organic gardening.

"The book marches through its business, Acer to Zucchini. The chart of common organic fertilizers is nifty, especially for those of us who can ferret out that blood meal we've lost in the pantry. Scarification, permaculture, crop rotation and cover crops are clarified. Diagrams are used judiciously." N Y Times Book Rev

Includes bibliographical references

Sayre, April Pulley

Touch a butterfly; wildlife gardening with kids. April Pulley Sayre. 1st ed. Roost Books 2013 xiv, 207 p.p (paperback) $19.95　　　**635**

1. Wildlife attracting 2. Gardening -- Juvenile literature 3. Garden animals 4. Gardening to attract wildlife

ISBN 1590309170; 9781590309179

LC 2012021579

This book, by April Pulley Sayre, offers instructions on how to "turn your garden into a hummingbird hotspot, a haven for butterflies, and a thriving ecosystem that will delight and inspire the young and young-at-heart. . . . Begin to see your yard from an animal's perspective; discover plants that attract colorful birds and bugs; embrace sensory experiences that native plants and creatures bring; and understand how your yard fits into the surrounding landscape." (Publisher's note)

Smith, Charles W. G.

The **beginner's** guide to edible herbs; 26 herbs everyone should grow & enjoy. introduction by Edward C. Smith; photography by Saxon Holt. Storey Pub. 2010 145p il pa $12.95　　　**635**

1. Herbs 2. Herb gardening 3. Cooking -- Herbs

ISBN 978-1-60342-528-5

LC 2010-845

"While Smith's beginner's guide may be a gem of simplicity, it's also chock-full of supplemental information including sumptuous recipes and inventive tips for household applications. Each herb's profile covers the many ways it can be harvested and used, and Smith includes helpful at-a-glance charts summarizing pertinent cultural information such as soil and light requirements, mature height, and planting distances. Perfect for novice gardeners, Smith's compact guide can also be appreciated by experienced hands who want to get back to the basics." Booklist

Smith, Edward C.

★ The **vegetable** gardener's bible; discover Ed's high-yield W-O-R-D system for all North American gardening regions. 2nd ed., [Fully updated 10th anniversary ed.]; Storey Pub. 2009 351p il map $34.95; pa $24.95　　　**635**

1. Organic gardening 2. Vegetable gardening

ISBN 978-1-60342-476-9; 978-1-60342-475-2 pa

LC 2009-23862

First published 2000

The author "explains everything novice and experienced gardeners need to know to grow vegetables and herbs using his system of wide, deep, raised beds. He gives detailed instructions on siting, preparing, and planning a vegetable garden, then goes on to cover choosing plant varieties, starting seed, and growing plants. Smith discusses compost creation, companion planting, crop rotation, succession planting, and ecologically friendly methods of dealing with plant diseases and pests." Libr J

Includes bibliographical references

The **vegetable** gardener's container bible. Storey Pub. 2011 263p il map $29.95; pa $19.95　**635**

1. Container gardening 2. Vegetable gardening

ISBN 978-1-60342-976-4; 978-1-60342-975-7 pa

LC 2010-51167

First published 2006 with title: Incredible vegetables from self-watering containers

The author discusses "how to choose the right plants, select containers and tools, care for plants throughout the growing season, control pests without chemicals, and . . . more." Publisher's note

Smith, Jeremy N.

Growing a garden city; how farmers, first graders, counselors, troubled teens, foodies, a homeless shelter chef, single mothers, and more are transforming themselves and their neighborhoods through the intersection of local. [by] Jeremy N. Smith; foreword by Bill McKibben; photographs by Chad Harder and Sepp Jannotta. Skyhorse Pub. 2010 225p il $24.95　　　**635**

1. Community gardens

ISBN 978-1-61608-108-9

LC 2010-12369

This book offers "photographs and personal narratives of community garden members, graduate students and first graders, a low-income senior and troubled teen, a foodie, a food bank officer, and . . . more. They describe their setbacks and successes involved with community gardening and show how to build on and emulate their achievements anywhere across the country and around the world." Publisher's note

"Bright, vibrant, and buoyantly accessible, this effervescent celebration of the local food movement thrums with regional, national, and international implications." Booklist

Speichert, C. Greg

Encyclopedia of water garden plants; [by] Greg Speichert & Sue Speichert; foreword by Ann Lovejoy. Timber Press 2004 386p il $49.95 **635**
1. Freshwater plants 2. Landscape gardening
ISBN 0-88192-625-6

LC 2003-16619

"The authors devote separate chapters to hardy waterlilies, tropicals, lotus, marginal plants, irises, waterlily-like plants (such as water snowflakes), floaters, and submerged plants. . . . This is the most comprehensive guide to all types of water plants and would make an excellent addition to gardening collections." Libr J

Springer, Lauren

Passionate gardening; good advice for challenging climates. essays and photography by Lauren Springer & Rob Proctor. Fulcrum 2000 336p il $34.95 **635**
1. Gardening
ISBN 1-55591-348-2

LC 99-49511

The "authors dispense practical advice to gardeners facing difficult growing conditions, such as poor soil, dry shade, etc. . . . {They also} discuss what plants to select—whether working with bulbs or ornamental grasses—and how to use them in conjunction with other plants." Libr J

Includes bibliographical references (p.   )

Tucker, Arthur O.

The **encyclopedia** of herbs; a comprehensive reference to herbs of flavor and fragrance. [by] Arthur O. Tucker and Thomas DeBaggio; edited by Francesco DeBaggio. [2nd ed.]; Timber Press 2009 604p il $39.95 **635**
1. Reference books 2. Herbs -- Encyclopedias
ISBN 978-0-88192-994-2

LC 2009-16700

First published 2000 by Interweave Press with title: The big book of herbs

The authors "describe more than 500 herbs that are most common in home gardens, catalogs, restaurants, and markets used for flavor or fragrance, from the acorus (sweet flag) used in the Oil of Holy Ointment to Zingiber mioga (mioga ginger) used for soups and stir fry." Libr J

Includes bibliographical references

Wulf, Andrea

The **brother** gardeners; botany, empire, and the birth of an obsession. Alfred A. Knopf 2008 354p il map $35 **635**
1. Gardening 2. Horticulture
ISBN 978-0-307-27023-8; 0-307-27023-8

LC 2008-55080

First published 2008 in the United Kingdom

"A garden will never look quite the same after you've read this book. . . . Wulf's book will be of interest to anyone with a garden, even if it's on a windowsill." Libr J

Includes bibliographical references

Wyman, Donald

Wyman's gardening encyclopedia; new expanded 2nd ed; Macmillan 1986 xxvi, 1221p il $65 **635**
1. Reference books 2. Gardening -- Encyclopedias 3. Ornamental plants -- Encyclopedias
ISBN 0-02-632070-3

LC 86-12509

First published 1961

Contains information on major horticultural practices, including use of pesticides and herbicides, and on ornamental and agricultural plant species. Includes scientific names according to Hortus third, with cross-references for common names

Zachos, Ellen

Down & dirty; 43 fun & funky first-time projects & activities to get you gardening. Storey Pub. 2007 248p il map $30; pa $19.95 **635**
1. Gardening
ISBN 978-1-58017-642-2; 978-1-58017-641-5 pa

LC 2006-23059

This book "describes more than 40 'fun and funky' projects and activities designed for novice gardeners, including children. . . . The book also includes . . . activities such as some garden photography basics, and instructions for building a containerized water garden and using cold frames." Am Gardener

Includes bibliographical references

635.092   Gardeners

Obama, Michelle, 1964-

American grown; the story of the White House kitchen garden and gardens across America. Michelle Obama. Crown Publishers 2012 271 p. $30.00 **635.092**
1. United States. White House Office 2. Vegetable gardening -- United States 3. Gardening -- United States 4. Food habits -- United States 5. Kitchen gardens -- Washington (D.C.) 6. White House Gardens (Washington, D.C.)
ISBN 0307956024; 9780307956026; 9780307956033

LC 2012015935

In this book U.S. "First Lady [Michelle] Obama presents the . . . tale of the White House Kitchen Garden." In 2009, "the first food-producing garden since Eleanor Roosevelt's WWII-era 'victory garden'" was planted. Here, Obama details the evolution of the current 1,100 square foot patch, and expands her story to touch on community gardens, farmers' markets, the importance of the availability of fresh foods, and her 'Let's Move!' initiative to fight childhood obesity." (Publishers Weekly)

Includes bibliographical references and index.

635.9   Flowers and ornamental plants

The **American** Horticultural Society A-Z encyclopedia of garden plants; Christopher Brickell, H. Marc Cathey, editors-in-chief. Rev. US ed.; DK Pub. 2004 1099p il map $80   **635.9**
1. Reference books 2. Ornamental plants -- Encyclopedias
ISBN 0-7566-0616-0

LC 2004-559196

First published 1997

"Equal parts gem and tool, this book is like a diamond. Clear, concise, and thoroughly useful, it fits the needs of all gardeners." Am Ref Books Annu, 2005

American Horticultural Society encyclopedia of plants & flowers; editor-in-chief, Christopher Brickell. Rev ed DK Publishing 2011 744 p. col. ill., maps $60   **635.9**
1. Ornamental plants
ISBN 0756668573; 9780756668570

LC 2011290703

First published 1989 in the United Kingdom with title: The Royal Horticultural Society gardeners' encyclopedia of plants and flowers

"This fully revised and updated edition features a brighter, clearer design and improved navigation--cataloging plants by color, season, and size--that makes the book more intuitive for the reader." Publisher's note

Armitage, Allan M.
Armitage's native plants for North American gardens. Timber Press 2006 451p il $49.95   **635.9**
1. Ornamental plants
ISBN 0-88192-760-0; 978-0-88192-760-3

LC 2005-22495

This book provides "information on more than 630 native species and cultivars of perennials, biennials, and annuals that are readily available to mainstream gardeners... . With more than 400 color photos, this is an essential reference book for nursery people and horticulturalists, home gardeners, and all libraries." Libr J

Includes bibliographical references

Armitage's vines and climbers. Timber Press 2010 212p il $29.95   **635.9**
1. Climbing plants 2. Ornamental plants
ISBN 978-1-60469-039-2

LC 2009-32437

This book is "written with authority, in simple language, with humor. Anyone trying to build a gardening library should think about adding this one." Philadelphia Inquirer

Includes bibliographical references

Bryant, Geoff
Annuals and perennials; a gardener's encyclopedia. [by] Geoff Bryant and Tony Rodd. Firefly Books 2011 304p il pa $19.95   **635.9**
1. Reference books 2. Perennials -- Encyclopedias 3. Annuals (Plants) -- Encyclopedias
ISBN 978-1-55407-837-0; 1-55407-837-7

LC 2011499056

This guide provides a selection table with characteristics, growth habits, and needs of each plant, as well as information on subspecies, hybrids, and cultivars.

"This well-designed and practical book deserves a green thumbs-up for public libraries and most gardeners." Libr J

Cullina, William
Understanding perennials; a new look at an old favorite. Houghton Mifflin Harcourt 2009 247p il $40   **635.9**
1. Perennials
ISBN 978-0-618-88346-2; 0-618-88346-0

LC 2008-36760

This book provides "a chance to learn what soil is composed of, why it's acid or alkaline and why you should care. Cullina will straighten out your understanding of roots, bulbs, rhizomes, stolons, corms and tubers; he clarifies osmosis, photosynthesis, secretory structures, nitrogen fixes and plant hormones. . . . [He] is an engaging, clear and congenial writer." N Y Times Book Rev

Includes bibliographical references

Darke, Rick
The **American** woodland garden; capturing the spirit of the deciduous forest. text and photography by Rick Darke. Timber Press 2002 377p il $49.95   **635.9**
1. Gardening 2. Forest plants
ISBN 0-88192-545-4

LC 2002-20474

This "is both a pictorial and narrative account of a wooded locale in Pennsylvania that the author spent years studying, as well as a design and planting guide. . . . He explains the different elements of a woodland garden and thoroughly describes the plants (features, zones, and growth ranges) that will perform well. The author's photographs illustrate both the overall effect and the beauty of individual plants." Libr J

Includes bibliographical references

Dash, Mike
Tulipomania; the story of the world's most coveted flower and the extraordinary passions it aroused. Crown 2000 273p hardcover o.p. pa $13.95 **635.9**
1. Tulips 2. Netherlands -- History
ISBN 0-609-80765-X pa

LC 99-39186

"The centerpiece of this story is a stunning two months, December 1636 and January 1637, when fortunes were made and lost in the Netherlands—in tulip bulb futures trading. Stripped to its basics, this would be a dry case study in an economics textbook. But Dash adds depth to the tale by including relevant bits of botany, sociology and history, as well as glimpses of the personalities involved in the creation of the tulip market." Publ Wkly

Includes bibliographical references

Dirr, Michael

Dirr's Hardy trees and shrubs; an illustrated encyclopedia. by Michael A. Dirr. Timber Press 1997 493p il $69.95 **635.9**

1. Trees 2. Shrubs 3. Landscape gardening
ISBN 0-88192-404-0

LC 96-54032

"Depicting both character and traits (fruit, flower, bark, or autumn color), the volume covers over 500 species and some additional varieties and cultivars. Each entry enumerates scientific name, common name, detailed plant description, environmental conditions, place in the landscape, i.e., woodlawn tree or lawn tree, and hardiness zones." Libr J

Dirr's trees and shrubs for warm climates; an illustrated encyclopedia. by Michael A. Dirr. Timber Press 2002 446p il map $69.95 **635.9**

1. Trees 2. Shrubs 3. Ornamental plants 4. Landscape gardening
ISBN 0-88192-525-X

LC 2001-35810

"This volume, in conjunction with Dirr's Hardy Trees and Shrubs, completes [the author's] coverage of the woody ornamentals cultivated in North America. In a witty and informative style, Dirr presents botanic, cultural, and landscaping details on over 400 species. Entries are accompanied by magnificent color photos." Libr J

Dirr, Michael A.

Dirr's encyclopedia of trees and shrubs; Michael A. Dirr. Timber Press 2011 951 p. col. ill. $79.95 **635.9**

1. Trees 2. Shrubs 3. Ornamental plants 4. Ornamental trees -- Encyclopedias 5. Ornamental shrubs -- Encyclopedias
ISBN 0881929018; 9780881929010

LC 2011007951

This reference book, by Michael A. Dirr, focuses on trees and shrubs. "From majestic evergreens to delicate vines and flowering shrubs, Dirr features thousands of plants and all the essential details for identification, planting, and care, plus full-color photographs showing a tree's habit in winter, distinctive bark patterns, fall color, and more." (Publisher's note)

"With beautiful, artistic photographs and succinct text, this volume is nearly as attractive as one of the gorgeous blossoming shrubs discussed within. . . . The chatty descriptions incorporate information often limited to tables—disease resistance, size, shape, and zone hardiness as well as some history and taxonomy. These descriptions are accompanied by high-quality photographs." Booklist

Includes bibliographical references and index

DiSabato-Aust, Tracy

The **well** -tended perennial garden; planting & pruning techniques. Expanded ed; Timber Press 2006 383p il map $34.95 **635.9**

1. Perennials
ISBN 978-0-88192-803-7; 0-88192-803-8

LC 2006-10388

First published 1998

In addition to details on pruning and maintenance this work contains an A-Z encyclopedia of perennials

Includes bibliographical references

Duffield, Mary Rose

Plants for dry climates; how to select, grow, and enjoy. {by} Mary Rose Duffield and Warren D. Jones. rev ed; Perseus Pub. 2001 216p il pa $27.50 **635.9**

1. Gardening 2. Desert plants
ISBN 1-55561-251-2

LC 2001-280011

First published 1981

The authors "explore strategies for gardening in dry or arid climates. . . . They cover climate conditions and predesign concerns such as possible planting restrictions by neighborhood covenants, the use of professional landscaping services, costs, and maintenance. A detailed plant guide identifies more than 300 species best suited to arid gardens, explaining conditions in which they thrive or are compromised." Libr J

Includes bibliographical references

Ellis, Barbara W.

Covering ground; unexpected ideas for landscaping with colorful, low-maintenance ground covers. Storey Pub. 2007 224p il map $29.95; pa $19.95 **635.9**

1. Grasses 2. Climbing plants 3. Ornamental plants
ISBN 1-58017-664-X; 978-1-58017-664-4; 1-58017-665-8 pa; 978-1-58017-664-4 pa

LC 2007-335

"Divided into three main sections, the book addresses why one should consider using ground covers, types of plants for different areas, and planting, growing, and propagating. . . . Suitable for all gardening collections, this easy and fun read is essential for the home gardener looking for low-maintenance or problem-area ground covers." Libr J

Taylor's guide to annuals; how to select and grow more than 400 annuals, biennials, and tender perennials. Houghton Mifflin 1999 441p il (Taylor's guides to gardening) pa $23 **635.9**

1. Annuals (Plants) 2. Flower gardening
ISBN 0-395-94352-3

LC 99-33188

First published 1986

This guide features information on over five hundred popular plants and cultivars for landscaping and gardening

Taylor's guide to perennials; more than 600 flowering and foliage plants, including ferns and or-

namental grasses. Houghton Mifflin 2001 490p il map (Taylor's guide to gardening) pa $23 **635.9**
1. Perennials 2. Flower gardening
ISBN 0-395-98363-0

LC 00-33436

First published 1986

Text and numerous illustrations cover popular perennials, their cultivars, ornamental grasses, and ferns

Fell, Derek

Encyclopedia of hardy plants; annuals, bulbs, herbs, perennials, shrubs, trees, vegetables, fruits & nuts. Derek Fell. Firefly Books 2007 224p il map $29.95 **635.9**
1. Reference books 2. Plants -- Encyclopedias
ISBN 978-1-55407-240-8; 1-55407-240-9

LC 2007-296324

This reference features descriptions of more than 700 hardy plants, each with color photos and hardiness zone ranges. Also contains indexes of both common plant names and botanical names.

Fisher, Kathleen

Taylor's guide to shrubs; how to select and grow more than 500 ornamental and useful shrubs for privacy, ground covers, and specimen plantings. Houghton Mifflin 2001 441p il map (Taylor's guides to gardening) pa $23 **635.9**
1. Shrubs
ISBN 0-618-00437-8

LC 00-36941

First published 1987

This guide covers information on popular shrubs and their cultivars and includes growing instructions

Flora: a gardener's encyclopedia; over 20,000 plants. chief consultant, Sean Hogan. Timber Press 2003 2v il map set $99.95 **635.9**
1. Flowers 2. Reference books 3. Ornamental plants -- Encyclopedias
ISBN 0-88192-538-1

LC 2003-59663

"Although gardening books abound, none matches this work's range of detail." Libr J

Garden perennials

Armitage's garden perennials; 2nd ed., fully rev. and updated; Timber Press 2011 347p il $49.95 **635.9**
1. Reference books 2. Perennials -- Encyclopedias
ISBN 978-1-60469-038-5

LC 2011293867

First published 2000

This is an "illustrated compilation of 136 genera of garden-worthy perennials. Alphabetical entries feature illuminating descriptions of plant habits and forms, along with essential cultural advice. Armitage recommends countless varieties that can be depended on to perform well or are particularly lovely specimens. Appropriate U.S.D.A. zones and regions where the plants will thrive are noted, too. With its accessible writing style, abundant color photographs, and

final section listing plants suggested for specific conditions or purposes, Armitage's latest work should be considered an essential addition to gardening collections." Booklist

Gardiner, Jim

The **Timber** Press encyclopedia of flowering shrubs; Jim Gardiner. Timber Press 2011 p. cm. **635.9**
1. Shrubs 2. Gardening 3. Garden design 4. Flowering shrubs -- Encyclopedias 5. Flowering shrubs -- Pictorial works
ISBN 9780881928235

LC 2011020264

This book, by Jim Gardiner, is a reference work for gardening with flowering shrubs. "Rich attributes . . . make flowering shrubs the most rewarding of garden plants, but this vast group with its scores of tempting plants . . . requires careful navigation. Leading expert on woody plants Jim Gardiner has distilled several decades of knowledge and experience into . . . [a] pictorial reference of hardy shrubs that excel in temperate-zone gardens." (Publisher's note)

Includes bibliographical references and index

Greenlee, John

The **American** meadow garden; creating a natural alternative to the traditional lawn. photography by Saxon Holt. Timber Press 2009 278p il $34.95 **635.9**
1. Grasses 2. Landscape gardening
ISBN 978-0-88192-871-6; 0-88192-871-2

LC 2009-19438

"Meadow gardening is an exciting, fresh approach to horticulture. By taking advantage of native plant life and soil conditions, gardeners can create an ecologically friendly yard that requires less water and mowing. Greenlee . . . focuses on the conditions of regional types of American grasslands, emphasizing throughout that gardeners must first understand local ecology (using professional help where necessary) to be successful. With Holt's photographs, this is a large and colorful showcase of Greenlee's extensive knowledge and great passion for gardening." Libr J

Includes bibliographical references

Hansen, Eric

Orchid fever; a horticultural tale of love, lust, and lunacy. Pantheon Bks. 2000 288p hardcover o.p. pa $13 **635.9**
1. Orchids
ISBN 0-679-77183-2 pa

LC 99-44582

"Most of Hansen's sketches are fundamentally vehicles for illustrating his serious and provocative argument against CITES (the Convention on International Trade in Endangered Species of Wild Fauna and Flora). According to the author, CITES thwarts orchid conservation and perversely legitimizes plant smuggling by botanical institutions." Libr J

Heffernan, Cecelia

Flowers A to Z; buying, growing, cutting, arranging. photography T.K. Hill. Abrams 2001 160p $49.50; pa $17.95 **635.9**
1. Flowers 2. Flower gardening 3. Flower arrangement
ISBN 0-8109-3348-9; 0-8109-2122-7 pa
LC 00-64282
"Recommendations for the best tools and containers are followed by in-depth profiles of 55 of the most popular garden and hothouse flowers, in which Heffernan shares such trade secrets as the flower's vase life and its cost at different seasons. . . .Straightforward directions are supported by close-up photographs." Booklist

Hewitt, Terry

The **complete** book of cacti & succulents. Dorling Kindersley 1993 176p il hardcover o.p. pa $20 **635.9**
1. Cactus 2. Succulent plants
ISBN 1-56458-337-6; 0-7894-1657-3 pa
LC 93-22107
An illustrated look at the history and cultivation of more than 300 plants. Ideas for containers and display are included.

The **Hillier** gardener's guide to trees & shrubs; editor, John Kelly; consultant editor, John Hillier. Reader's Digest Assn. 1997 640p il maps $50 **635.9**
1. Trees 2. Shrubs
ISBN 0-89577-973-0
LC 97-4282
First published 1995 in the United Kingdom
"Alphabetically arranged plant directory covering more than 4000 plants with over 400 genres represented. . . . {It discusses} basic biology, theory and practice, selection and purchase, care and maintenance, pest and diseases, plant propagation, plant names, and plant selection." Libr J

Hillier, Malcolm

Container gardening through the year; photography by Matthew Ward. Dorling Kindersley 1995 160p il hardcover o.p. pa $13.95 **635.9**
1. Container gardening
ISBN 0-7894-3296-X pa
LC 94-26717
"Hillier advises on how to match surprising plant combinations with an array of containers. Various themes (shape and proportion, texture, and harmonizing or contrasting colors) are represented in lovely color plates that provide a pleasing supplement to Hillier's reassuring guidance." Booklist

Hodgson, Larry

Perennials for every purpose; choose the plants you need for your conditions, your garden, and your taste. Rodale 2000 502p il $29.95; pa $19.95 **635.9**
1. Perennials
ISBN 0-87596-823-6; 0-87596-893-7 pa
LC 99-6968

"Preliminary chapters cover the basics such as getting started, creating a design, and keeping plants healthy. The highlight, however, is the 14 chapters that profile perennials that can be used in unique situations (e.g., dry, wet, sunny, shade, easy-care). Each plant profile includes a photograph, a sidebar listing plant characteristics, and informative paragraphs detailing good companion plants, problems and solutions, and the top performers and recommended varieties for each plant." Libr J
Includes bibliographical references

Kelaidis, Gwen Moore

Hardy succulents; tough plants for every climate. photography by Saxon Holt. Storey Pub. 2008 159p il map $29.95; pa $19.95 **635.9**
1. Succulent plants
ISBN 978-1-58017-701-6; 978-1-58017-700-9 pa
LC 2007-39890
The author "offers practical tips on siting, planting, soil requirements, and care of succulents for every hardiness zone in a clear and confident voice. Advice on pairing succulents with perennials, using them as focal points in the garden, and protecting them from the cold of winter is dispensed in lively prose. . . . This delightful book will be practical and inspiring for both novice and experienced gardeners." Libr J

Martin, Tovah

The **new** terrarium; creating beautiful displays for plants and nature. [by] Tovah Martin and Kindra Clineff. Clarkson Potter/Publishers 2009 176p il $25 **635.9**
1. Terrariums
ISBN 978-0-307-40731-3; 0-307-40731-4
LC 2008-27713
"With beguiling photographs by Kindra Clineff, this attractive volume contains everything you need to know about growing plants under glass." N Y Times Book Rev

The **unexpected** houseplant; 220 extraordinary choices for every room in your home. Tovah Martin ; photography by Kindra Clineff. 1st ed. Timber Press 2012 328 p. col. ill. (paperback) $22.95; (ebook) $22.95 **635.9**
1. House plants 2. Indoor gardening 3. Container gardening
ISBN 160469243X; 9781604692433; 1604694262; 9781604694260
LC 2011045164
It was author Tovah Martin's intent to demonstrate "how correctly chosen plants placed in creative containers can enhance indoor living space. Martin shows how imagination and use of fundamental ground rules for growing and proper placement should result in an indoor horticultural paradise year round. Martin covers over 220 plants, ranging from exotic to conventional. . . .Growth requirements, propagation advice, problems, and attributes of plants are outlined." (Library Journal)
Includes bibliographical references and index.

McGowan, Alice

Bulbs in the basement, geraniums on the window-sill; how to grow and overwinter 165 tender plants. [by] Alice McGowan, Brian McGowan. Storey Pub. 2008 208p il pa $17.95   **635.9**
1. Perennials 2. Greenhouses 3. Ornamental plants
ISBN 978-1-60342-042-6; 1-60342-042-8
LC 2008-22440

"After offering readers a brief history of gardening with 165 plants, the McGowans give advice on choosing a container, on container combinations, and on the best type of soil to use. They stress the importance of the correct temperature and give instructions on setting up a site. There's a color photograph of each plant, along with information on its shape, color, and foliage, what the genus comprises, and design ideas. There also are instructions on how to use the guide, as well as suggested reading." Booklist

Includes bibliographical references

Michener, David

Taylor's guide to ground covers; more than 400 flowering and foliage ground covers for every garden situation. {by} David Michener and Nan Sinton. completely rev and updated; Houghton Mifflin 2001 375p il maps (Taylor's guides to gardening) pa $23   **635.9**
1. Grasses 2. Climbing plants 3. Ornamental plants
ISBN 0-618-03010-7
LC 2001-39566

First published 1987 with title: Taylor's guide to ground covers, vines & grasses

"In this guide luscious photographs of 400 ground covers are paired with information about gardening zones and sun tolerance. . . . The splendor of the photography aside, the no-nonsense approaches are recommended." Am Ref Books Annu, 2003

O'Sullivan, Penelope

The **homeowner's** complete tree & shrub handbook; the essential guide to choosing, planting and maintaining perfect landscape plants. photography by Karen Bussolini. Storey Pub. 2007 408p il map $39.95; pa $29.95   **635.9**
1. Trees 2. Shrubs 3. Ornamental plants
ISBN 978-1-58017-571-5; 978-1-58017-570-8 pa
LC 2007-10718

This guide to planting trees and shrubs discusses planning the landscape and buying, planting and caring for trees and shrubs. Includes descriptions of 348 trees and shrubs.

"The real jewel of this volume is the extensive AZ directory of nearly 350 trees and shrubs, many offering more than one season of interest. There is even a handy pronounciation guide for every plant name." Libr J

Includes webliography and bibliographical references

Ondra, Nancy J.

Taylor's guide to roses; how to select, grow, and enjoy more than 380 roses. Houghton Mifflin 2001 474p il maps (Taylor's guides to gardening) pa $23   **635.9**
1. Roses
ISBN 0-618-06888-0
LC 00-68248

First published 1986

Text and numerous full color illustrations describe classes of roses including floribundas, grandifloras, miniatures, and climbers. Suggestions are provided for carefree border and ground cover roses. Entries are given for each plant, noting its uses and limitations

Pavord, Anna

Bulb. Mitchell Beazley 2009 544p il map $39.99   **635.9**
1. Bulbs
ISBN 978-1-84533-532-8

This book features "advice on the purchase and care of bulbs. The approximately 600 entries include detailed descriptions of the blooms, some comparisons with related cultivars, plant size, hardiness, native areas, and bloom season. . . The entries are accompanied by photographs of individual blossoms. These are interspersed with lush two-page-spread images of gardens, masses of blooms, and single spectacular blooms. Pavord's writing style is delightfully conversational while providing important technical information for the gardener." Booklist

Includes bibliographical references

★ The plant finder; the right plants for every garden. senior consultants, Tony Rodd and Geoff Bryant. Firefly Books 2007 992p il map $49.95   **635.9**
1. Gardening 2. Ornamental plants 3. Landscape gardening
ISBN 978-1-55407-265-1; 1-55407-265-4
LC 2007-298960

This book "gives basic descriptions and growing conditions for more than 5,000 plants, with a focus on the temperate zones. . . . Beginning gardeners as well as plant fanatics may find this comprehensive volume an indispensable midwinter reference for yearly garden planning, as well as a useful outdoor planting companion come spring." Publ Wkly

Pleasant, Barbara

The **complete** houseplant survival manual; essential know-how for keeping (not killing) more than 160 indoor plants. photography by Rosemary Kautzky. Storey Pub. 2005 365p il pa $24.95   **635.9**
1. House plants
ISBN 1-58017-569-4
LC 2005-14205

"Following an enlightening introduction that discusses the history, uses, and benefits that houseplants bestow, the manual is divided into three main sections. The first two are plant directories offering in-depth plant profiles of first flowering, then foliage, houseplants. The third is an extensive compilation of houseplant-care topics, from acclimatization to watering. With vivid color photographs, precise illustrations, appendixes listing helpful resources, definitions, and a cross-reference chart of botanical and common names, this is a must-have manual for anyone who shares home or office space with potted plants." Booklist

Taylor's encyclopedia of garden plants; edited by Frances Tenenbaum. Houghton Mifflin 2003 464p il map (Taylor's guides to gardening) $45 **635.9**
1. Reference books 2. Ornamental plants -- Encyclopedias
ISBN 0-618-22644-3

LC 2002-27630

"This beautifully illustrated encyclopedia offers North American gardeners a definitive resource for all their questions, from flowers to trees to shrubs." Publ Wkly

Taylor's master guide to gardening; editor-in-chief: Frances Tenenbaum; editors: Rita Buchanan, Roger Holmes; designer: Deborah Fillion; illustrator: Steve Buchanan; copy editor: Nancy J. Stabile. Houghton Mifflin 1994 612p il $60 **635.9**
1. Gardening 2. Landscape gardening
ISBN 0-618-15907-X

LC 93-48865

The first part of this book consists of a discussion of "30 topics (annuals, perennials, trees, design, color, containers, shade, water, etc.) . . . Next, a 200-page 'Gallery' of recommended plants is arranged alphabetically by Latin name, with photographs and climate zone numbers. The third section, a 300-page encyclopedia, list 3000 unillustrated species and cultivars with a short paragraph about each." Libr J
Includes bibliographical references

636   Animal husbandry

Belozerskaya, Marina
The **Medici** giraffe; and other tales of exotic animals and power. Little, Brown and Co. 2006 414p il $24.99 **636**
1. Exotic animals
ISBN 0-316-52565-0; 978-0-316-52565-7

LC 2006-09659

"This is a sumptuous read—smart, funny and utterly compelling." Publ Wkly
Includes bibliographical references

Grandin, Temple
★ **Animals** make us human; creating the best life for animals. [by] Temple Grandin and Catherine Johnson. Houghton Mifflin Harcourt 2009 342p $26 **636**
1. Animal behavior
ISBN 978-0-15-101489-7; 0-15-101489-2

LC 2008-34892

The authors "investigate four basic driving forces behind behaviors in dogs, cats, horses, cows, pigs, poultry, wildlife, and zoo animals. They discuss how humans must understand these drives in order to provide a 'good mental life' for their animals." Libr J
"Packed with fascinating insights, unexpected observations and a wealth of how-to tips, Grandin's peppy work ably challenges assumptions about what makes animals happy." Publ Wkly

Halligan, Karen
Doc Halligan's What every pet owner should know; prescriptions for happy, healthy cats and dogs. illustrations by Liz Wells. HarperCollins Publishers 2007 324p il $24.95; pa $15.95 **636**
1. Cats 2. Dogs 3. Pets -- Health and hygiene
ISBN 978-0-06-089859-5; 0-06-089859-3; 978-0-06-089860-1 pa; 0-06-089860-7 pa

LC 2007-60869

"Emphasizing canine (and feline) wellness, . . . [the author] gives clear advice about preventing illness and injuries through sensible nutrition, regular grooming, dental care, and partnering with your veterinarian." Libr J

Katz, Jon
Dog days; dispatches from Bedlam Farm. Villard Books 2007 273p il $23.95 **636**
1. Domestic animals 2. Farm life -- New York (State)
ISBN 978-1-4000-6404-5; 1-4000-6404-X

LC 2006-52804

This is a "collection of stories from upstate New York's Bedlam Farm. . . . Bedlam Farm, a cross between a working and a hobby farm, is the home of the animals that are . . . [the author's] inspiration. . . . A must-read for all animal lovers." Booklist

Wells, Jeff
All my patients have tales; favorite stories from a vet's practice. St. Martin's Press 2009 226p il $24.95; pa $13.99 **636**
1. Veterinary medicine
ISBN 978-0-312-53739-5; 0-312-53739-5; 978-0-312-60639-8 pa; 0-312-60639-7 pa

LC 2008-35868

"Newly minted veterinarian Wells is on one of his first calls—a cow trying to deliver a dead calf—when after two hours of unceasing labor, he decides to try another approach, and one of the on-looking farmers says, 'That's what you should have done to begin with!' So begins the education of a young vet, the on-the-job training that no amount of schooling can provide. . . . A move to Colorado didn't immediately improve his finances but did improve his buffalo-wrangling skills and his ability to remove porcupine quills from overzealous dogs and donkeys. Another winning veterinary memoir deserving of space next to the immortal James Herriot and his heirs." Booklist

636.088   Animals for specific purposes

Sutherland, Amy
Kicked, bitten, and scratched; life and lessons at the world's premier school for exotic animal trainers. Viking 2006 320p hardcover o.p. pa $15 **636.088**
1. Animals -- Training 2. Moorpark College -- Exotic Animal Training and Management Program
ISBN 0-670-03768-0; 978-0-670-03768-1; 0-14-311194-9 pa; 978-0-14-311194-8 pa

LC 2005-57474

"Readers will acquire new and enhanced respect for a little-studied profession." Booklist

636.089   Veterinary medicine

Black's veterinary dictionary;   edited by Edward
Boden and Anthony Andrews. 22nd ed A. & C.
Black 2015 790 p. il $52   **636.089**
1. Reference books   2. Veterinary medicine --
Dictionaries
ISBN 0713663626; 140817572X; 9781408175729
First published 1928 by Macmillan with title: Black's
veterinary cyclopedia
  "There is greatly expanded coverage of topics relating to
popular breeds of dog and cat, and the inheritable conditions
that might affect their health.
  Advances in medicine, surgery and diagnostic tech-
niques; descriptions of newly identified diseases such as
Schmallenberg virus; the resurgence of old scourges such as
TB in cattle, and ongoing enzootic infections such as bird flu
are included in this new edition." Publisher's note

Bowers, Kathryn
  Zoobiquity; What Animals Can Teach Us About
Health and the Science of Healing. Barbara Natter-
son-Horowitz and Kathryn Bowers. Alfred A. Knopf
2012 308 p.   **636.089**
1. Medicine 2. Pathology 3. Veterinary medicine 4.
Comparative psychology 5. Pathology, Veterinary 6.
Disease Models, Animal 7. Physiology, Comparative
8. Psychology, Comparative
ISBN 0307593487; 9780307593481
                                        LC 2012005051
  "In this . . . book, cardiologist and psychiatrist [Barbara]
Natterson-Horowitz, along with science journalist [Kathryn]
Bowers, explore some of humanity's most pressing health
problems (cancer, obesity) through the eyes of the animal
kingdom. The authors argue in favor of the 'One Health'
worldview, which brings doctors and veterinarians into close
collaboration to discuss causation and treatment of diseases." (Publishers Weekly)
  "Clearly, we have much to learn from animals and from
this profoundly illuminating new fusion of veterinary, human, and evolutionary medicine." Booklist
  Includes bibliographical references and index

Goldstein, Martin
  The **nature** of animal healing; the path to your
pet's health, happiness, and longevity. Knopf 1999
357p hardcover o.p. pa $16   **636.089**
1. Pets 2. Veterinary medicine
ISBN 0-345-43919-8 pa
                                          LC 98-38193
  "Goldstein outlines an approach to healing that revolves
around strengthening the immune system through diet and
such holistic healing techniques as acupuncture and homeopathy, so that an animal can heal itself. . . . This is a life-affirming book that should interest any pet owner." Publ Wkly

Herriot, James
  Every living thing. St. Martin's Press 1992 342p
$22.95   **636.089**
1. Authors 2. Veterinarians 3. Large print books 4.

Memoirists
ISBN 0-312-08188-X
                                          LC 92-18526
  Sequel to The Lord God made them all, entered in
main catalog
  "Herriot regales us with additional tales of his veterinary
practice in Yorkshire. He picks up his story after World War
II, when medicines and treatment have improved, his chil-
dren are growing up and the family moves to a new house.
. . . There are no surprises here, just the expected mix of
gentle humor and compassion for animals and people alike.
Herriot's many fans will not be disappointed." Publ Wkly

  James Herriot's animal stories; with an introduction by Jim Wright; illustrations by Lesley Holmes.
St. Martin's Press 1997 142p il   **636.089**
1. Domestic animals 2. Large print books 3. Veterinary
medicine
                                          LC 97-13863
  This is a compilation of ten previously published stories
from the author's autobiographical accounts of the practice
of veterinary medicine in 1930's Yorkshire England

Kahn, Cynthia M.
  The **Merck** veterinary manual; [edited by Cynthia M. Kahn and Scott Line] 10th ed. Merck 2010
2945 p. $60   **636.089**
1. Veterinary medicine
ISBN 091191093X; 9780911910933
                                          LC 2010923995
  This book, edited by Cynthia M. Kahn and Scott Line,
"is the most comprehensive, reliable reference for veterinary professionals. . . . [It has] been updated to reflect the
latest advances in veterinary medicine. . . . The section on
behavior has been thoroughly revised, and includes the most
current information on diagnosing and treating behavioral
disorders in dogs, cats, and other domestic animals." (Publisher's note)

  The **Merck** /Merial manual for pet health; Cynthia M. Kahn, editor. Home ed.; Merck & Co. 2007
xxvii, 1345p il $29.95; pa $22.95   **636.089**
1. Pets -- Health and hygiene 2. Veterinary medicine
-- Handbooks, manuals, etc.
ISBN 978-0-911910-22-3; 0-911910-22-0; 978-0-
911910-99-5 pa; 0-911910-99-9 pa
                                          LC 2007-933381
  Covers basic care and diseases of dogs, cats, horses, and
exotic pets.
  "An in-depth, thoroughly indexed reference featuring
high-quality information." Libr J

  Petspeak; you're closer than you think to a great
relationship with your dog or cat! by the editors
of Pets, part of the family books. Rodale 2000
485p il $29.95; pa $16.95   **636.089**
1. Cats 2. Dogs
ISBN 1-57954-077-5; 1-57954-337-5 pa
                                            LC 00-9290
  This volume "attempts to explain pet behavior to improve pet-owner relationships. Addressing the habits of both

cats and dogs, this book helps make sense out of pet peculiarities and offers practical solutions and advice." Booklist

Pinney, Chris C.

The **complete** home veterinary guide. McGraw-Hill 2004 736p il $29.95   **636.089**

1. Veterinary medicine 2. Pets -- Diseases
ISBN 0-07-141272-7

LC 2003-52668

First published 1992 by Tab Bks. with title: The illustrated veterinary guide for dogs, cats, birds & exotic pets

This guide covers "preventive health care, diet, grooming, training, diseases, traveling with pets, selection, first aid, anatomy, {and} holistic pet care." Publisher's note

Schoen, Allen M.

Kindred spirits; how the remarkable bond between humans and animals can change the way we live. Broadway Bks. 2001 280p hardcover o.p. pa $14   **636.089**

1. Pets 2. Veterinary medicine
ISBN 0-7679-0431-1 pa

LC 00-57891

This book "covers the benefits of the human-animal bond; seven ways to foster a spiritual bond with your animal; wellness approaches, such as diet therapy and preventing and treating cancer the natural way; finding veterinary support; and how to let go when there is nothing further that can be done." Libr J

Includes bibliographical references

636.1   Horses

Faurie, Bernadette

The **horse** riding & care handbook. Lyons Press 2000 160p il hardcover o.p. pa $19.95   **636.1**

1. Horses 2. Horsemanship
ISBN 1-58574-058-6; 1-58574-517-0 pa

"Each section contains pictures or diagrams to clarify the explanations, from horse evolution and history with humans to markings, colors, and breeds. Topics such as tack, how to mount, a first riding lesson, and techniques of western riding are all simply described with wonderful graphics." Libr J

Richards, Susan

Chosen by a horse; a memoir. Soho Press 2006 248p $20   **636.1**

1. Horses
ISBN 1-56947-419-2

LC 2005-52337

"Richards adopts an emaciated mare and her foal, overriding the small voice telling her that she already has three horses to care for and a herniated disk. Her experience with her new charges proves profoundly instructive in terms of how love can foster growth of the human spirit and help in overcoming pain and loss. The abused mare, Lay Me Down, proves to be one of those rare creatures that remain gentle despite years of mistreatment, responding profoundly to the kind treatment that is part of everyday life for Richards' animals. Fascinated by the affection this animal accords a stranger, Richards notes the mare's courage and slowly be-

gins to emulate it in her own life, opening up to a love affair and its aftermath." Booklist

Storey's horse-lover's encyclopedia; an English and Western A-to-Z guide. edited by Deborah Burns. Storey Bks. 2001 471p il $37.50; pa $24.95   **636.1**

1. Horses
ISBN 1-58017-336-5; 1-58017-317-9 pa

LC 00-46329

"The alphabetically arranged entries vary in length from a few sentences to a few pages, with the most thorough coverage going to extensive topics like breeding, foot care, and feeding. Most entries consist of one or two paragraphs and provide a good definition of the term at hand." Libr J

636.2   Cattle and related animals

Kardashian, Kirk

Milk money; cash, cows, and the death of the American dairy farm. Kirk Kardashian ; foreword by Senator Bernie Sanders. University of New Hampshire Press 2012 xv, 253 p., [6] p.p (cloth : alk. paper) $27.95   **636.2**

1. Dairying -- Economic aspects -- United States 2. Dairy farmers -- United States 3. Dairy farming -- Economic aspects -- United States
ISBN 1611680271; 9781611680270; 9781611683400

LC 2012012528

This book by Kirk Kardashian "uncovers the hidden forces behind dairy farm consolidation, and explains why milk--a staple commodity subject to both government oversight and industry collusion--has proven so tricky to stabilize. Meanwhile, every year we continue to lose scores of small dairy farms. . . . Kardashian asks whether it is right that family farmers in America should toil so hard, produce a food so wholesome and so popular, and still lose money." (Publisher's note)

Includes bibliographical references and index

636.4   Swine

Montgomery, Sy

The **good** good pig; the extraordinary life of Christopher Hogwood. Ballantine Books 2006 228p il $21.95; pa $13.95   **636.4**

1. Pigs
ISBN 0-345-48137-2; 978-0-345-48137-5; 0-345-49609-4 pa; 978-0-345-49609-6 pa

LC 2005-57094

This is a "description of the 14-year life of a 750-pound pet pig who was named after the conductor [Christopher Hogwood]. Anyone who has ever loved a pet can enjoy reading about the relationship between Montgomery and her Christopher." Sci Books Films

636.7 Dogs

American Kennel Club

★ The **complete** dog book; American Kennel Club. 20th ed.; Ballantine Books 2006 xxi, 858p il $35 **636.7**

1. Dogs

ISBN 0-345-47626-3; 978-0-345-47626-5

LC 2005-48263

First published 1935. Periodically revised

"The official guide to 124 AKC registered breeds and their history, appearance, selection, training, care and feeding, and first aid. Some color plates." N Y Public Libr. Ref Books for Child Collect. 2d edition

Arden, Andrea

★ **Dog** -friendly dog training; illustrations by Tracy Dockray. 2nd ed.; Wiley Pub. 2007 232p il $18.99 **636.7**

1. Dogs -- Training

ISBN 978-0-470-11514-5; 0-470-11514-9

LC 2007-7079

First published 2000 by Howell Book House

"This straightforward, color-illustrated book by a charter member of the APDT [Association of Pet Dog Trainers] focuses on a dog-friendly, positive approach [to training]. The essential title for libraries with tight budgets." Libr J

Bradshaw, John

★ **Dog** sense; how the new science of dog behavior can make you a better friend to your pet. John Bradshaw. Basic Books 2011 xxiv, 324 p.p il $25.99 **636.7**

1. Dogs -- Behavior 2. Dogs -- Psychology 3. Human-animal relationship 4. Animal intelligence 5. Human-animal relationships

ISBN 0465019447; 9780465019441

LC 2010054337

The author discusses "how humans can live in harmony with their canine friends, explaining why positive reinforcement is a more effective way to control behavior and how to weigh a dog's unique personality against the stereotypes of its breed." (Publisher's note) Bibliography. Index.

"Pet owners and those interested in the animal mind will learn from this balanced, well-referenced guide to the science of canine behavior.—" LJ

Includes bibliographical references and index

Burch, Mary R.

Citizen canine; ten essential skills every well-mannered dog should know. Kennel Club Books 2010 256p il pa $14.95 **636.7**

1. Dogs -- Training

ISBN 978-1-593786-44-1

LC 2009-28847

"Often a component of therapy dog assessment, the Canine Good Citizen (CGC) test has become a popular way to document a dog's manners. . . . [The author] outlines the ten test items and demonstrates how to teach your dog these skills. . . . This well-indexed guide is essential reading for dog owners, whether the goal is obedience training, therapy dog work, or simply polite pets." Libr J

Charleson, Susannah

Scent of the missing; love and partnership with a search-and-rescue dog. Houghton Mifflin Harcourt 2010 288p il $26 **636.7**

1. Rescue dogs

ISBN 978-0-547-15244-8; 0-547-15244-2

LC 2009-33783

"Humans have long used dogs, with their remarkable scenting abilities, to find lost, injured, or dead people. However, recent tragedies and disasters—9/11, Hurricane Katrina—have brought search-and-rescue recovery to the forefront. Charleson introduces us to this world as she trains her dog Puzzle to work with Dallas's elite Metro Area Rescue K9 unit. Interspersed with stories of such routine activities as housebreaking and walking on a leash are the hold-your-breath moments when the author describes actual rescue/recovery missions such as the shuttle Columbia explosion." Libr J

Coile, D. Caroline

Encyclopedia of dog breeds. Barron's Educational Series 2005 352p il $29.95 **636.7**

1. Reference books 2. Dogs -- Encyclopedias

ISBN 0-7641-5700-0

LC 2004-52977

First published 1998

"More than 150 breed descriptions are grouped along American Kennel Club divisions: the sporting group, the hound group, the working group, and so on. . . . Breed descriptions are organized into subsections entitled 'History,' 'Temperament,' 'Upkeep,' 'Health,' and 'Form and Function.'" Booklist

Coppinger, Raymond

Dogs; a new understanding of canine origin, behavior, and evolution. [by] Raymond Coppinger and Lorna Coppinger. University of Chicago Press 2002 352p il pa $18 **636.7**

1. Dogs

ISBN 0-226-11563-1

LC 2002-20404

First published 2001 by Scribner

"This important book belongs in all libraries." Booklist

Includes bibliographical references

Coren, Stanley

Why we love the dogs we do; how to find the dog that matches your personality. Free Press 1998 308p il hardcover o.p. pa $13 **636.7**

1. Dogs

ISBN 0-684-85502-X pa

LC 97-50333

"Coren offers insight into dog-and-owner personality conflicts and shows prospective owners how to choose the dog that is right for them. His book shows why some breeds of dogs turn out to be disasters for certain people, provides personality tests for readers to determine their own distinctive personality types, and includes amusing 'famous pet' anecdotes. Humanitarian, witty, and full of common sense, this is a perfect primer for novice dog owners." Booklist

Includes bibliographical references

De Vito, Dominique

★ **World** atlas of dog breeds; [by] Dominique De Vito with Heather Russell-Revesz and Stephanie Fornino. 6th ed.; T.F.H. Publications 2009 959p il $99.95   **636.7**

1. Dogs 2. Reference books
ISBN 978-0-7938-0656-0

      LC 2008-55261

First published 1989 with title: Atlas of dog breeds of the world. Periodically revised

"Covering more than 420 breeds, the guide is easy to use, alphabetically arranged with ratings for a number of important breed characteristics such as compatibility with children, with other pets, grooming, and energy level. Beautiful photographs portray each breed, accompanied by origin and history, recognized by the seven foremost breed clubs and registries." Publ Wkly

Includes bibliographical references

★ **Decoding** Your Dog; The Ultimate Experts Explain Common Dog Behaviors and Reveal How to Prevent or Change Unwanted Ones. by American College of Veterinary Behaviorists ; edited by Debra Horwitz, John Ciribassi, and Steve Dale. Houghton Mifflin Harcourt 2014 384 p. illustrations $27   **636.7**

1. Dogs -- Behavior 2. Dogs -- Training
ISBN 0547738919; 9780547738918

      LC 2014395601

This book, edited by Debra Horwitz, John Ciribassi, and Steve Dale, is a "dog behavior guide. . . . Experts analyze problem behaviors, decipher the latest studies, and correct common misconceptions and outmoded theories. The book includes: effective, veterinary-approved positive training methods [and] expert advice on socialization, housetraining, diet, and exercise." (Publisher's note)

"A fascinating and detailed exploration of the reasons behind common dog behaviors and of how to interpret dogs' communication signals in order to train them to be happy, healthy, obedient companions." LJ

Dogs: the ultimate care guide; good health, loving care, maximum longevity. edited by Matthew Hoffman; medical advisor, Lowell Ackerman. Rodale Press 1998 450p il hardcover o.p. pa $19.95   **636.7**

1. Dogs
ISBN 1-57954-244-1 pa

      LC 97-46600

Subjects covered range "from bringing up puppy, basic training, and emergency first aid, to easing common complaints." Booklist

Eldredge, Debra

Dog owner's home veterinary handbook; [by] Debra M. Eldredge . . . [et al.] 4th ed; Wiley Pub. 2007 xxviii, 628p il $34.99   **636.7**

1. Dogs -- Diseases
ISBN 978-0-4700-6785-7; 0-4700-6785-3

      LC 2007-16275

First published 1980

"The authors discuss all of the major organ systems with descriptions of normal functions and infectious and parasitic diseases. Writing in easy-to-understand terms, they identify emergency situations and explain first-aid care. . . . It contains information on Lyme disease and other recently recognized problems." Libr J [review of 1992 edition]

Fogle, Bruce

Dog owner's manual. DK Pub. 2003 288p il pa $25   **636.7**

1. Dogs
ISBN 0-7894-9321-7

      LC 2002-41146

"Fogle's succinct writing style packs a tremendous amount of information into each sentence. Heavily illustrated with beautiful photographs." Booklist

★ **Dog** : the definitive guide for dog owners. Firefly Books 2010 384p il $39.95; pa $29.95   **636.7**

1. Dogs
ISBN 978-1-55407-779-3; 978-1-55407-700-7 pa

This is a "one-volume compendium on everything canine. He begins with an explanation of the dog's evolution, genetics, and classification. Then he delves into the human-dog relationship, giving . . . information and advice about selecting and training a new puppy, surviving its adolescence, enjoying its adulthood, coping with its declining years, and, finally, coming to grips with its demise. . . . [This is] an easy-to-read, attractive, indispensable guide for the novice and veteran dog owner alike." Libr J

Includes bibliographical references

New dog; choosing wisely and ensuring a happily ever after. with Patricia Holden White. Firefly Books 2008 192p il $29.95; pa $19.95   **636.7**

1. Dogs -- Training
ISBN 978-1-55407-356-6; 1-55407-356-1; 978-1-55407-357-3 pa; 1-55407-357-X pa

      LC 2008-299624

"In advising how to choose and welcome a new dog, . . . [the author's] attractive and sensible guide addresses training, behavior issues, and health care." Libr J

The **new** encyclopedia of the dog; photography by Tracy Morgan. 2nd American ed; Dorling Kindersley 2000 416p il $40   **636.7**

1. Reference books 2. Dogs -- Encyclopedias
ISBN 0-7894-6130-7

      LC 00-22642

First published 1995 with title: The encyclopedia of the dog

This describes over 420 breeds and varieties of dogs, including their histories, temperments, and physical features.

√ **Franklin, Jon**

★ The **wolf** in the parlor; the eternal connection between humans and dogs. Henry Holt 2009 283p $25   **636.7**

1. Dogs
ISBN 978-0-8050-9077-2; 0-8050-9077-0

      LC 2009-2227

Building on evolutionary science, archaeology, behavioral science, and the firsthand experience of watching his own dog evolve from puppy to family member, Franklin posits that man and dog are more than just inseparable; they are part and parcel of the same creature.

"Among a plethora of books on breeding, disciplining, loving and lamenting the loss of man's best friend, this thoughtful discourse is a best of breed." Publ Wkly

Healy, Thomas

I have heard you calling in the night. Harcourt 2006 204p $22   **636.7**
1. Dogs 2. Alcoholism
ISBN 978-0-15-10125-6; 0-15-101259-8
LC 2006-6363

"Novelist Healy was a raging, brawling drunk until, on a whim, he adopted a Doberman pinscher puppy he named Martin. He nursed Martin through illness and wounds; Martin in turn stood guard over him while he lay passed out in fields. Their bond, and the slight but persistent duty of caring for Martin enabled Healy to very fitfully begin to recover from his alcoholism and propensity to violence and gently nudged him toward an understanding of himself and God. Healy embeds the story in a memoir of his life in the slums of Glasgow, his relationship with his parents, his conflicted attitude toward the church and his many loves. . . . In Healy's heartfelt prose, this eccentric friendship becomes the core of a moving meditation on the mysterious nature of redemption." Publ Wkly

Herriot, James

James Herriot's dog stories. St. Martin's Press 1986 xxxiii, 426p il $23.95; pa $7.99   **636.7**
1. Dogs
ISBN 0-312-43968-7; 0-312-92558-1 pa
LC 86-6637

Herriot "has gathered 50 recollections of canines, some of them sentimental, a few tragic and at least one—the story of a terrier male who abruptly becomes attractive to other males—as odd as anything in the Decameron. Herriot recalls that in his student days domestic animals were customarily listed in descending order of importance: horse, ox, sheep, pig, dog. In the latest work, he has brought his favorites to the front and given them a new leash on life." Time

James Herriot's favorite dog stories; illustrations by Lesley Holmes. St. Martin's Press 1996 169p il $17.95   **636.7**
1. Dogs 2. Large print books
ISBN 0-312-14841-0
LC 96-18796

This is a collection of 10 previously published dog "stories written in Herriot's heartwarming style. Each tale is accompanied by new attractive watercolor illustrations. A dog-lover's delight." SLJ

Horowitz, Alexandra

Inside of a dog; what dogs see, smell, and know. Scribner 2009 353p $27   **636.7**
1. Dogs -- Psychology
ISBN 978-1-4165-8340-0; 1-4165-8340-8
LC 2008-45842

Includes bibliographical references

Katz, Jon

★ **Katz** on dogs; a commonsense guide to training and living with dogs. Villard 2005 xxviii, 240p il $24.95   **636.7**
1. Dogs -- Training
ISBN 1-4000-6403-1
LC 2005-46209

Katz's "commonsense approach and skill as a storyteller make this an appealing, informative book." Libr J
Includes bibliographical references

The **new** work of dogs; tending to life, love, and family. Villard Bks. 2003 xxiii, 225p $19.95; pa $13.95   **636.7**
1. Dogs
ISBN 0-375-50814-7; 0-375-76055-5 pa
LC 2002-44915

The author "explores the bond between dogs and their owners. Focusing on 12 people-dog relationships in Montclair, N.J., and drawing on current research into attachment theory, interviews with animal workers and psychiatrists, as well as conversations with dog owners, Katz offers nuanced portraits of what happens when humans depend on dogs to satisfy their emotional needs. . . . In this well-written and thoughtful account, Katz makes a convincing case that dog owners must be more self-aware and responsible when they use their pets as human substitutes." Publ Wkly

Kerasote, Ted

Merle's door; lessons from a freethinking dog. Harcourt, Inc. 2007 398p $25   **636.7**
1. Dogs
ISBN 978-0-15-101270-1
LC 2006-38041

"In telling Merle's story, Kerasote also explores the science behind canine behavior and evolution, weaving in research on the human-canine bond and musing on the way dogs see the world. Merle is a true character, yet Merle is also Everydog. An absolute treasure of a book." Booklist
Includes bibliographical references

Pukka's Promise; The Quest for Longer-lived Dogs. Ted Kerasote. Houghton Mifflin Harcourt 2013 464 p. $28   **636.7**
1. Dogs 2. Animals -- Longevity 3. Dog owners -- Anecdotes
ISBN 0547236263; 9780547236261
LC 2012289472

This book, by Ted Kerasote, discusses dogs as pets and their health and longevity, "questioning our conventional wisdom and emerging with vital new information that will surprise even the most knowledgeable dog lovers. . . . Interviewing breeders, veterinarians, and leaders of the animal-welfare movement, Kerasote pulls together the latest research to help us rethink the everyday choices we make for our companions." (Publisher's note)

Kihn, Martin

Bad dog; a love story. Pantheon Books 2011 213p **636.7**

1. Dogs

ISBN 978-0-307-37915-3; 978-0-307-37987-0 ebook

LC 2010035355

"Meet Hola, a gorgeous purebred Bernese mountain dog so badly managed by her human that walks were 'a haphazard dance of death' and greetings 'full-body slam[s] . . . just this side of actionable.' Now meet the human: Kihn, a Yale grad with an M.B.A., a deep neurotic streak, and a serious drinking problem. When his wife leaves, Kihn realizes he must get his life under control, and that includes Hola. Soon man and dog are enrolled in various training programs so that Hola can earn her Canine Good Citizen certificate from the American Kennel Club. . . . This sharply written, darkly funny memoir-cum-dog story-cum-recovery tale is a quick, absorbing read that will serve a wide audience well." Libr J

Kotler, Steven

A small furry prayer; dog rescue and the meaning of life. Bloomsbury 2010 307p il $24 **636.7**

1. Dogs

ISBN 978-1-608-19002-7; 1-608-19002-1

LC 2010-12019

The author "became involved with dog rescue when he became involved with novelist Joy Nicholson, a committed rescuer; in a matter of weeks, they were compelled to move their dogs . . . from California to Chimayo, NM, a rough neighborhood but the only place they could afford that offered enough room. As he recounts their life in Chimayo (the pack at times approaches 50, all entertainingly delineated), Kotler seamlessly blends a history of Chimayo, a well-articulated understanding of how humans and dogs coevolved, and background on animal welfare efforts in this country with his witty, sharp-edged, and rewarding reflections on life." Libr J

Includes bibliographical references

Lufkin, Elise

To the rescue; found dogs with a mission. photographs by Diana Walker; foreword by Bonnie Hunt. Skyhorse Pub. 2009 150p il $19.95 **636.7**

1. Dogs 2. Animals and people with disabilities

ISBN 978-1-60239-772-9

LC 2009-12164

"This feel-good book should please animal and dog-lovers, especially those who live with a working dog." Publ Wkly

Includes bibliographical references

McConnell, Patricia

For the love of a dog; understanding emotion in you and your best friend. Ballantine Books 2006 332p il hardcover o.p. pa $15.95 **636.7**

1. Dogs

ISBN 0-345-47714-6; 978-0-345-47714-9; 0-345-47715-4 pa; 978-0-345-47715-6 pa

LC 2006-45200

"This is not a book on how to train dogs, but McConnell's examination of cases from her veterinary practice, backed up by her scientific study of animal behavior, will help readers better understand their closest companions." Booklist

Monks of New Skete

How to be your dog's best friend; the classic training manual for dog owners. {by} the Monks of New Skete. completely rev and updated, 2nd ed; Little, Brown 2002 336p il $25.95 **636.7**

1. Dogs -- Training

ISBN 0-316-61000-3

LC 2002-102894

First published 1978

This guide to dog training focuses on important aspects of the canine-human relationship, including discipline and choosing a breed that fits the owner's personality and lifestyle

This book's "unique value lies in the monks' insights and thoughts about the human-canine bond. . . . Without devolving into New Age psychobabble, the monks make philosophical and spiritual observations that no dog lover could resist." Publ Wkly

Includes bibliographical references

Orlean, Susan

★ Rin Tin Tin. Simon & Schuster 2011 324p il $26.99; ebook $12.99 **636.7**

1. Working dogs 2. Rin-Tin-Tin (Dog)

ISBN 978-1-4391-9013-5; 978-1-4391-9015-9 ebook

LC 2011024476

This book discusses the "story of Lee Duncan (1893-1960), a young American soldier and dog-lover who found the German shepherd puppy that became Rin Tin Tin (Rinty) in France, got the dog home and spent the rest of his life training and promoting Rinty, breeding other German shepherds. . . . [The author] also provides the biography of Duncan, as well as Bert Leonard, writer and producer, and she includes interviews with Duncan's daughter, the current keeper of the latest Rinty and scores of others. The author tells the story of silent films (where Rinty began his career), the transition to talkies and to color, the rise of television, the popularity of dog ownership in America (especially of German shepherds and collies--because of Lassie) and the evolving tastes of American youth." (Kirkus)

"A terrific dog's tale that will make readers sit up and beg for more." Kirkus

Includes bibliographical references

Rosenfelt, David

Dogtripping; 25 rescues, 11 volunteers, and 3 RVs on our canine cross-country adventure. David Rosenfelt. St. Martin's Press 2013 288 p. color illustrations (hardcover) $25.99 **636.7**

1. Dogs 2. Moving 3. Human-animal relationship 4. Dog adoption 5. Dogs -- Biography 6. Human-animal relationships 7. Authors, American -- 21st century -- Biography

ISBN 1250014697; 9781250014696

LC 2013009168

This book, by David Rosenfelt, is an "account of a cross-country move from California to Maine, and the beginnings of a dog rescue foundation. When . . . Rosenfelt and his family moved from Southern California to Maine, he thought he had prepared for everything. . . . But traveling with twenty-five dogs turned out to be a bigger ordeal than he anticipated, despite the RVs, the extra kibble, volunteers, and camping equipment." (Publisher's note)

"Spirited and absolutely absorbing reading for fans of canine capers." Booklist

Rutherford, Clarice

How to raise a puppy you can live with; [by] Clarice Rutherford, David H. Neil. 4th ed., rev. & updated; Alpine Blue Ribbon Books 2005 153p il pa $11.95   **636.7**

1. Dogs -- Training
ISBN 1-57779-076-6

LC 2005-41038

First published 1981

This book features "practical advice on puppy selection, development, training, and problem-solving." Libr J

Includes bibliographical references

Thomas, Elizabeth Marshall

The **social** lives of dogs; the grace of canine company. illustrated by Jared Taylor Williams. Simon & Schuster 2000 253p hardcover o.p. pa $13.95   **636.7**

1. Dogs
ISBN 0-7434-2236-8 pa

LC 99-87357

Thomas discusses how dogs interact with various members of the household, including other dogs and pets of other species

The author "draws upon her extensive knowledge of the behavior and treatment of feral dogs in East Africa to explain the domestication of the dog. Appendixes containing advice on controlling dogs' behavior and on keeping parrots as pets conclude this entertaining and informative book." Libr J

Warren, Cat

What the dog knows; the science and wonder of working dogs. Cat Warren. Simon & Schuster 2013 352 p. $26.99   **636.7**

1. Working dogs 2. Search dogs -- Anecdotes
ISBN 1451667310; 9781451667318

LC 2013012006

This book, by Cat Warren, focuses on working dogs. She "interviews cognitive psychologists, historians, medical examiners, epidemiologists, and forensic anthropologists, as well as the breeders, trainers, and handlers who work with and rely on these . . . animals daily. Along the way, she discovers story after story that proves the . . . capabilities—as well as the . . . limits—of working dogs and their human partners." (Publisher's note)

"Warren writes with verve and provides rare insight into our working partnership with canines." Kirkus

Woestendiek, John

Dog, Inc. the uncanny inside story of cloning man's best friend. Avery 2010 310p il $26   **636.7**

1. Dogs 2. Cloning
ISBN 978-1-58333-391-4; 1-58333-391-6

LC 2010-23697

"A valuable contribution illuminating the hubris and futility of trying to replicate dead pets (or people) that will appeal to dog lovers and those interested in cloning and science." Libr J

636.8   Cats

Bradshaw, John, 1950-

★ **Cat** sense; how the new feline science can make you a better friend to your pet. John Bradshaw. Basic Books 2013 336 p. (hardcover) $27.99 **636.8**

1. Cats 2. Pets 3. Animal intelligence 4. Cat owners 5. Cats -- Behavior 6. Cats -- Psychology 7. Human-animal relationships
ISBN 0465031013; 9780465031016

LC 2013020749

In this book, author John Bradshaw takes readers "further into the mind of the domestic cat . . . using cutting-edge scientific research to dispel the myths and explain the true nature of our feline friends. Tracing the cat's evolution from lone predator to domesticated companion, Bradshaw shows that although cats and humans have been living together for at least eight thousand years, cats remain independent, predatory, and wary of contact with their own kind." (Publisher's note)

"Bradshaw teases out a better understanding of what our cats want (and need) from their owners. . . . This fascinating book will be a bible for cat owners." Booklist

Includes bibliographical references and index

Cooper, Gwen

Homer's odyssey; a fearless feline tale, or how I learned about love and life with a blind wonder cat. Delacorte Press 2009 287p il $20   **636.8**

1. Cats
ISBN 978-0-385-34385-5; 0-385-34385-X

LC 2009-17602

A pet rescue volunteer and literacy outreach coordinator describes her relationship with a three-pound blind cat whose daredevil character and affectionate personality saw the author through six moves, a burglary, and the healing of her broken heart.

"This tender and affecting book reveals Homer's lessons about love and acceptance—and how he transformed Cooper into the woman she had always wanted to be." Publ Wkly

Herriot, James

James Herriot's cat stories; with illustrations by Lesley Holmes. St. Martin's Press 1994 161p $17.95   **636.8**

1. Cats
ISBN 0-312-11342-0

LC 94-20131

A "collection of favorite cat tales from Herriot's veterinary practice. Retired after over 50 years in practice,

Herriot continues to entertain young and old alike with his storytelling ability. His current collection includes 'Alfred, the Sweet-Shop Cat,' 'Boris and Mrs. Bond's Cat Establishment,' 'Moses Found Among the Rushes,' and others." Libr J

Myron, Vicki

Dewey; a small-town library cat who touched the world. Grand Central Publisher 2008 277p il $19.99   **636.8**

1. Cats

ISBN 978-0-446-40741-0; 0-446-40741-0

LC 2008-4498

The story of Dewey Readmore Books, the beloved library cat of Spencer, Iowa.

"Myron's beguiling, poignant, and tender tale of survival, loyalty, and love is an unforgettable study in the mysterious and wondrous ways animals, and libraries, enrich humanity." Booklist

636.9   Other mammals

Westoll, Andrew

The **chimps** of Fauna Sanctuary; a true story of resilience and recovery. Houghton Mifflin Harcourt 2011 268p il $25   **636.9**

1. Chimpanzees 2. Wildlife refuges 3. Animal rescue 4. Fauna Foundation 5. Chimpanzees -- Behavior 6. Animal experimentation -- Moral and ethical aspects

ISBN 978-0-547-32780-8; 0-547-32780-3

LC 2010049783

"This is both an inspiring and a disturbing book. It is inspiring because of the devotion of caregivers to welfare of the chimps; it is disturbing because of the callous treatment to which chimps in research are subjected." Sci Books Films

Includes bibliographical references

637   Processing dairy and related products

English, Ashley

Home dairy with Ashley English; all you need to know to make cheese, yogurt, butter & more. Lark Crafts 2011 135p il (Homemade living) $19.95 **637**

1. Dairy products

ISBN 978-1-60059-627-8

LC 2010020669

"English is no slouch at demystifying the intricacies of home dairy; from the simplicities of churning out your own delectable butter to pressing your very first gouda, the author covers it all in clean, unpretentious, step-by-step instruction. Excellent for those looking to take a slight step off the grid." Kirkus

Includes bibliographical references

Lucero, Claudia

One -hour cheese; ricotta, mozzarella, chèvre, paneer--even burrata, fresh and simple cheeses you can make in an hour or less! by Claudia Lucero, founder of Urban Cheesecraft and Creator of DIY

Cheese Kit. Workman Pub. Company, Inc. 2014 260 p. color illustrations (alk. paper) $14.95   **637**

1. Cheesemaking

ISBN 0761177485; 9780761177487

LC 2014001166

In this cookbook Claudia Lucero "shows step by step— with every step photographed—exactly how to make sixteen fresh cheeses at home, using easily available ingredients and tools, in an hour or less. The approach is basic and based on thousands of years of cheesemaking wisdom: Heat milk, add coagulant, drain, salt, and press. Simple variations produce delicious results across three categories—Creamy and Spreadable, Firm and Chewy, and Melty and Gooey." (Publisher's note)

"A fantastic introduction for novices who want simple, delicious, DIY cheese." LJ

Includes bibliographical references and index

638   Insect culture

Hubbell, Sue

A **book** of bees; and how to keep them. drawings by Sam Potthoff. Houghton Mifflin 1998 193p il pa $13   **638**

1. Bees

ISBN 0-395-88324-5

LC 98-10191

First published 1988 by Random House

"Following the seasons of the beekeeper's year the author imparts practical hints along with literary, mythological, entomological, and anecdotal commentary." Booklist

Jacobsen, Rowan

Fruitless fall; the collapse of the honey bee and the coming agricultural crisis. Bloomsbury USA 2008 279p il $25   **638**

1. Bees

ISBN 978-1-59691-537-4; 1-59691-537-4

LC 2008-26126

The author "celebrates the marvels of the honeybee, reveals the many ways we've endangered this essential pollinator, and calls for action to prevent a 'fruitless fall'." Booklist

Includes bibliographical references

Nordhaus, Hannah

The **beekeeper's** lament; how one man and half a billion honey bees help feed America. Harper Perennial 2011 269p il pa $14.99   **638**

1. Bees 2. Beekeeping 3. Beekeepers

ISBN 978-0-06-187325-6; 0-06-187325-X

"Nordhaus centers her account on John Miller, a migratory beekeeper who hauls truckloads of bees from crop to crop to help farmers who don't have natural pollinators. Honey bees are crucial to American agriculture, pollinating crops of 90 different fruits and vegetables. We would lose our almond crops almost entirely without bees, for example. Nordhaus meticulously details this process, demonstrating how modern apiculture affects everyone from keeper to bee to farmer to consumer. . . . [She] provides an almost overwhelming amount of information in a relatively short amount of space, but it's a fascinating read from cover to cover, and Miller makes a genuinely likable American hero." Stamford Advocate

639   Hunting, fishing, conservation, related technologies

Greenlaw, Linda

The **lobster** chronicles; life on a very small island. Hyperion 2002 238p $22.95; pa $13.95 **639**

1. Lobster fisheries 2. Isle au Haut (Maine)
ISBN 0-7868-6677-2; 0-7868-8591-2 pa

In this companion to The hungry ocean, the author gives "up swordfishing to return to her parents' home on Isle Au Haut off the coast of Maine and fish for lobster. . . . She intersperses her narrative with plenty of eccentrics who live on her tiny island. . . . Self-speculation and uncertainties . . . nicely balance her delightfully cocky essays of island life." Publ Wkly

Landers, Jackson

Eating aliens; one man's adventures hunting invasive animal species. by Jackson Landers. Storey Pub. 2012 xii, 226 p.p ill. $14.95 **639**

1. Pest control 2. Biological invasions 3. Hunting stories 4. Hunting -- Anecdotes
ISBN 161212027X; 9781612120270

LC 2012017449

This book "chronicles the 16 months [Jackson] Landers spent traveling around the United States hunting and eating invasive species, often in the company of colorful characters." He argues the way to combat invasive species like Asian carp and green iguanas is to "create a demand for them as food, then eat them until they're under control." (Library Journal)

639.2   Commercial fishing, whaling, sealing

Dolin, Eric Jay

Leviathan; the history of whaling in America. W.W. Norton & Company 2007 479p il $27.95 **639.2**

1. Whaling -- History
ISBN 978-0-393-06057-7; 0-393-06057-8

LC 2007-06113

The author "chronicles the long history of whaling in North America, from the voyages of Capt. John Smith, who, like many after him, 'found this Whale-fishing a costly conclusion,' to the last voyage of the Wanderer, a whaler that set sail from the once-teeming port of New Bedford, Mass., in 1924 and promptly wrecked in the shallows before a crowd of curious onlookers. . . . Anyone whose knowledge of whaling begins and ends with 'MobyDick' will get a solid education from Mr. Dolin, who fills in the historical record and sets the stage for the glory years when men like Melville set out from Nantucket, New Bedford, Sag Harbor and dozens of other ports on voyages lasting as long as four years." N Y Times (Late N Y Ed)

Includes bibliographical references

Fagan, Brian M.

Fish on Friday; feasting, fasting, and the discovery of the New World. [by] Brian Fagan. Basic Books 2006 338p il maps hardcover o.p. pa $16.95 **639.2**

1. Fish as food 2. Commercial fishing
ISBN 0-465-02284-7; 0-465-02285-5 pa

LC 2005-21322

The author "traces the rise of the European fishing industry. He posits the root of popular demand for fish in the early church's cycle of fasts and feasts. . . . Fagan intersperses his account with delightfully rendered, updated versions of ancient and modern fish-based recipes from Roman, British, and Jamaican traditions." Booklist

Greenlaw, Linda

The **hungry** ocean; a swordboat captain's journey. Hyperion 1999 265p map $22.95; pa $14 **639.2**

1. Fishing
ISBN 0-7868-6451-6; 0-7868-8541-6 pa

LC 98-51985

The author "details a 30-day swordfishing trip from Gloucester to the Grand Banks. Greenlaw describes her boat, equipment, and various electronic gear, including the 'temperature bird' that is lowered to measure the temperature at the fishing depth, as well as her technique for finding just the right area to fish. . . . An exciting and detailed look inside the commercial fishing industry." Libr J

Kurlansky, Mark

★ The **last** fish tale; the fate of the Atlantic and survival in Gloucester, America's oldest fishing port and most original town. Riverhead Books 2009 xxix, 269p il map pa $16 **639.2**

1. Commercial fishing 2. Gloucester (Mass.)
ISBN 978-1-59448-374-5

First published 2008 by Ballantine Books

The author "provides a delightful, intimate history and contemporary portrait of the quintessential northeastern coastal fishing town: Gloucester, Mass., on Cape Anne. Illustrated with his own beautifully executed drawings, Kurlansky's book vividly depicts the contemporary tension between the traditional fishing trade and modern commerce, which in Gloucester means beach-going tourists." Publ Wkly

Includes bibliographical references

639.3   Culture of cold-blooded vertebrates

Halverson, Anders

An **entirely** synthetic fish; how rainbow trout beguiled America and overran the world. Anders Halverson. Yale University Press 2010 xxi, 257 p.p **639.3**

1. Rainbow trout 2. Fisheries -- United States 3. Introduced fishes -- United States 4. Rainbow trout industry -- United States -- History
ISBN 0300140878; 9780300140873

LC 2009036200

Halverson provides an "account of the rainbow trout and why it has become the most commonly stocked and controversial freshwater fish in the United States. Discovered in the remote waters of northern California, rainbow trout have been artificially propagated and distributed for more than 130 years by government officials eager to present Americans with an opportunity to get back to nature by going fishing. . . . Dubbed 'an entirely synthetic fish' by fisheries managers, the rainbow trout has been introduced into every state and province in the United States and Canada and to every continent except Antarctica, often with devastating effects on the native fauna, [according to the author]." (Publisher's note) Bibliography. Index.

this is not one of those whiny, hand-wringing catalogs of environmental gloom and doom. With prose as engaging as it is thoughtful, Halverson has crafted an absorbing cautionary tale of ecological trial and error, documenting our tardy but increasing understanding of biological interdependence and its immeasurable value. Washington Post

Includes bibliographical references (p. 211-244) and index

639.34   Fish culture in aquariums

Alderton, David

Encyclopedia of aquarium & pond fish. Dorling Kindersley 2005 400p il hardcover o.p. pa $24.95   **639.34**

1. Reference books 2. Fishes -- Encyclopedias
ISBN 0-7566-0941-0; 0-7566-3678-7 pa
The author "has created the definitive work on the subject, with photos to match." Libr J

Mills, Dick

Aquarium fish. DK 2004 72p il (101 essential tips) pa $5   **639.34**

1. Fishes 2. Aquariums
ISBN 0-7566-0611-X; 978-0-7566-0611-4

LC 2004-303366

Reprint of paperback printed by DK Pub. in 1996
This book offers advice on choosing fish for aquariums, aquarium equipment, decoration, feeding, and health care, and describes various species of tropical, coldwater, freshwater, and marine fishes.

"Accurate, clear, and concise writing is enhanced with wonderful color photographs on each page." Voice Youth Advocates [review of 1996 edition]

639.9   Conservation of biological resources

Apfelbaum, Steven I.

Nature's second chance; restoring the ecology of Stone Prairie Farm. Beacon Press 2009 242p $25.95   **639.9**

1. Prairie ecology
ISBN 978-0-8070-8582-0

LC 2008-13071

"Ecologist Apfelbaum wanted to put into practice what he learned about restoring damaged ecosystems on land of his own. He purchased a 150-year-old farmhouse and eventually, thanks to the success of his visionary consulting business, Applied Ecological Services, acquired 80 acres of southern Wisconsin farmland. By dint of ardent research and relentless hard work, Apfelbaum and his partner, Susan Marie Lehnhardt, transformed land long depleted by corn crops, pesticides, and invasive species into a thriving prairie resplendent with wildflowers and resurgent birds, butterflies, and wildlife. . . . [The] book is as rich in farming adventure, environmental ideas, and profound insights as a restored prairie is rich in life and beauty." Booklist

DeNapoli, Dyan

The **great** penguin rescue; 40,000 penguins, a devastating oil spill, and the inspiring story of the world's largest animal rescue. Free Press 2010 307p il map $26   **639.9**

1. Penguins 2. Oil spills
ISBN 978-1-4391-4817-4; 1-4391-4817-1

LC 2010-17156

This "firsthand account of the rescue of the oiled penguins (all of whom fought against their rescuers), repeated washing of each bird, force-feeding, and guano cleanup plunges the reader into the maelstrom of animal rescue and rehabilitation on such a large scale." Booklist
Includes bibliographical references

Jacobsen, Rowan

The **living** shore; rediscovering a lost world. illustrated by Mary Elder Jacobsen. Bloomsbury 2009 167p il map $20   **639.9**

1. Oysters 2. Commercial fishing 3. Puget Sound region (Wash.)
ISBN 978-1-59691-684-5; 1-59691-684-2

LC 2009-8903

A marine scientist, together with Rowan and a conservancy group interested in habitat restoration, suggests a possible blueprint for cleaning up our oceans by observing an isolated pocket of oysters living on the western side of Vancouver Island.

"Lovely science writing, and a smart look into where the work of ecological restoration is headed." Kirkus
Includes bibliographical references

Varty, Boyd

Cathedral of the wild; an African journey home. Boyd Varty. Random House Inc 2014 304 p. illustrations (acid-free paper) $27   **639.9**

1. Game reserves 2. Africa -- Social conditions 3. Londolozi Game Reserve (South Africa) -- History 4. Wildlife conservation -- South Africa -- Londolozi Game Reserve -- History
ISBN 1400069858; 9781400069859

LC 2013022706

Author Boyd Varty presents a "memoir of his life in [Londolozi Game Reserve in South Africa]. At Londolozi, Varty gained the confidence that emerges from living in Africa. It was there that young Boyd and his equally adventurous sister learned to track animals, raised leopard and lion cubs, followed their larger-than-life uncle on his many adventures filming wildlife, and became one with the land. An intense spiritual quest takes him across the globe and back again." (Publisher's note)

An "intense, insightful memoir that brings together several wise observations about the relationship between nature and humanity." Pub Wkly

Includes bibliographical references and index

640   Home and family management

Bried, Erin

How to sew a button; and other nifty things your grandmother knew. Ballantine Books 2009 xxii, 278p il pa $15   **640**
    1. Handicraft 2. Life skills 3. Home economics
    ISBN 978-0-345-51875-0; 0-345-51875-6
                  LC 2009036046

"These anecdotes and tutorials gleaned from subject experts and grandmothers who were children during the Great Depression cover a broad swath of homemaking skills. Instead of systematic how-tos, Bried presents these lessons as a means to improve the quality of the reader's life. Excellent information, but definitely written to a female audience." Libr J

Mendelson, Cheryl

Home comforts; the art and science of keeping house. illustrations by Harry Bates. Scribner 1999 884p il hardcover o.p. pa $21   **640**
    1. Home economics
    ISBN 0-684-81465-X; 0-7432-7286-2 pa
                  LC 99-37555

Mendelson includes "sections on food, clothing, cleanliness, daily life, and safety, with information on negligence, domestic employment laws, insurance, and even the impact of clothing label laws on our laundry. Preferred methods are explained in detail, and some alternatives are offered for those who need to compromise. This is a valuable tool." Libr J

Includes bibliographical references

Nakone, Lanna

Organizing for your brain type; finding your own solution to managing time, paper, and stuff. St. Martin's Griffin 2005 xlvii, 222p pa $13.95   **640**
    1. Home economics 2. Time management
    ISBN 0-312-33977-1
                  LC 2004-60159

"A quiz at the beginning assigns readers to the maintaining, harmonizing, innovating, or prioritizing style. Nakone then describes the strengths and weaknesses of each type and matches a prescription for how that type can best manage time. . . . This book should do well in most libraries." Libr J

Includes bibliographical references

Walsh, Peter

How to organize just about everything; more than 500 step-by-step instructions for everything from organizing your closets to planning a wedding to creat-

ing a flawless filing system. Free Press 2005 501p $25   **640**
    1. Home economics
    ISBN 0-7432-5494-5
                  LC 2004-56277

"Inside the 16 sections are 501 activities, both the usual and out-of-the-ordinary tasks, from getting organized and planning a remodeling project to joining the Peace Corps or becoming an astronaut. Each features the step-by-step procedures, tips, a warning (if necessary), and 'who knew?'—additional advice designed to make the activity a success. . . . A great humane reference anytime, anywhere, for any occasion." Booklist

640.73   Evaluation and purchasing guides

Coyne, Kelly

Making it; radical home ec for a post-consumer world. [by] Kelly Coyne and Erik Knutzen. Rodale 2010 310p il pa $19.99   **640.73**
    1. Simplicity 2. Home economics 3. Consumer education
    ISBN 978-1-60529-462-9; 1-60529-462-4
                  LC 2010023680

"Motivated to reduce household consumption, Coyne and Knutzen offer 70 projects that reintroduce production-based homemaking skills. Ranging in difficulty from making cleaning products to building a chicken coop, the projects are parsed into segments of time, giving readers an idea of how often a project should be repeated during the year." Libr J

Includes bibliographical references

Levine, Judith

Not buying it; my year without shopping. Simon & Schuster 2006 274p $25   **640.73**
    1. Shopping 2. Consumer education
    ISBN 0-7432-6935-7
                  LC 2005-55517

The author discusses her experiences when she decided not to buy any nonessential items for a year.

"This honest and humorous tale of a nonspending year is well worth putting aside a few hours to read." Christ Sci Monit

641   Food and drink

101 classic cookbooks; 501 classic recipes. Marvin J. Taylor, Clark Wolf, The Fales Library, New York University. Rizzoli 2012 688 p. $50   **641**
    1. Cookbooks 2. American cooking
    ISBN 0847837939; 9780847837939
                  LC 2012940384

This "collection, edited by [Marvin J.] Taylor . . . and food consultant [Clark] Wolf, offers signature recipes from 20th-century classics such as Fannie Farmer's 'The Boston Cooking-School Cook Book,' James Beard's 'American Cookery,' and Mark Bittman's 'How To Cook Everything.' Books are organized chronologically in entries that explain each title's historical significance and include bibliographic information, images of the first edition, and a list of notable recipes." (Library Journal)

The **backyard** homestead; edited by Carleen Madigan. Storey Pub. 2009 367p il pa $18.95 **641**
1. Vegetable gardening 2. Food -- Preservation
ISBN 978-1-60342-138-6

LC 2009-01338

"Madigan presents the information in clear chapters, starting with vegetables, herbs, and fruit and nut trees; moving on through growing grains and grinding them into flour; and then tackling keeping chickens, cows, pigs, and more. The last chapter, 'Food from the Wild,' delves into beekeeping, foraging for berries and mushrooms, and making your own maple syrup. None of the information is particularly in-depth—if you decide to pursue something, you'll likely want to get another book on that one subject. But as an inspiration and an introduction to the various possibilities, it's perfect." Epicurious

Includes bibliographical references

Bourdain, Anthony

A **cook's** tour; global adventures in extreme cuisines. Ecco 2002 274p il pa $14.99 **641**
1. Food 2. Cooking
ISBN 0-06-001278-1

LC 2002-23507

First published 2001 by Bloomsbury Press

This is an "account of the author's global search for the 'perfect mix of food and context' that takes the reader to the culinary corners of the earth: from Vietnam (a live cobra heart) and Japan (poisonous blowfish) to England (roasted bone marrow) and Scotland (deep-fried Mars bar)." N Y Times Book Rev

David, Elizabeth

An **omelette** and a glass of wine. Lyons Press 2010 xxiii, 368p (The cook's classic library) pa $16.95 **641**
1. Cooking
ISBN 978-1-59921-860-1

LC 2010-6369

First published 1984 in the United Kingdom

A collection of book reviews, restaurant reviews, articles and recipes that originally appeared in The Spectator, Gourmet magazine, Vogue, and The (London) Sunday Times, among others.

Fisher, M. F. K. (Mary Frances Kennedy), 1908-1992

The **art** of eating; M.F.K. Fisher ; with an introduction by Clifton Fadiman ; an appreciation by James A. Beard ; and a retrospective essay by Joan Reardon. Wiley Pub. 2004 xxxiv, 749 p.p $24.95 **641**
1. Cooking 2. Eating habits 3. Gastronomy
ISBN 0764542613; 9780764542619

LC 2003026124

James Beard Cookbook Hall of Fame (1990)

IACP Culinary Classics Book Award (2012)

This book, by Mary Frances Kennedy Fisher, is a "50th anniversary paperback reprint . . . [of the author's collected best writings on food and cooking. M. F. K.] Fisher (1908-

1992) was one of this country's earliest food writers. . . . The 784-page collection brings together five works originally published under separate titles. . . . There are also recipes scattered throughout." (Publisher's note)

A **stew** or a story; an assortment of short works by M.F.K. Fisher. gathered and introduced by Joan Reardon. Shoemaker & Hoard 2006 364p $28; pa $15.95 **641**
1. Food 2. Cooking
ISBN 978-1-59376-115-8; 1-59376-115-5; 978-1-59376-165-3 pa; 1-59376-165-1 pa

LC 2006-08708

"Fisher's food writing was ahead of its time; a frequent contributor to Gourmet, Bon App tit, and other publications, Fisher had lived in both France and the California wine country and offered cooking tips that predate the American culinary 'revolution' of the 1960s. As these enjoyable pieces show, she was also a witty writer who offered astute observations along with the occasional recipe. The topics chosen for this collection include coffee making, borscht, olives, picnics, holidays, and places." Libr J

Includes bibliographical references

Jacobsen, Rowan

American terroir; savoring the flavors of our woods, waters, and fields. Bloomsbury 2010 272p il $25 **641**
1. Food 2. Cooking
ISBN 978-1-59691-648-7

LC 2010-6125

"Jacobsen eases readers into discussions of chemistry, history, geography, and gastronomy with cavalier charm and worldly wit, but his knack for cutting to the core restores exoticism to our backyard. Inspirational and highly engaging." Libr J

Kamp, David

The **United** States of Arugula; how we became a gourmet nation. Broadway Books 2006 392p il $26 **641**
1. Dining
ISBN 0-7679-1579-8

LC 2006-42599

The author "details the development of fine dining in the U.S. and proves healthy, even exotic food movements are having an effect on our diet. . . . This cultural history makes for an engrossing read, documenting the dramas and rivalries of the food industry." Publ Wkly

Includes bibliographical references

Kingsolver, Barbara, 1955-

★ **Animal,** vegetable, miracle; a year of food life. [by] Barbara Kingsolver, with Steven L. Hopp and Camille Kingsolver; original drawings by Richard A. Houser. HarperCollins Publishers 2007 370p il $26.95; pa $15.99 **641**
1. Farm life 2. Eating customs 3. Appalachian region 4. Agriculture and energy
ISBN 978-0-06-085255-9; 0-06-085255-0; 978-0-06-

085256-6 pa; 0-06-085256-9 pa

LC 2006-53516

"This is a serious book about important problems. Its concerns are real and urgent. It is clear, thoughtful, often amusing, passionate and appealing. It may give you a serious case of supermarket guilt, thinking of the energy footprint left by each out-of-season tomato, but you'll also find unexpected knowledge and gain the ability to make informed choices about what—and how—you're willing to eat." Washington Post Book World

Includes bibliographical references

Lappé, Anna, 1973-

Diet for a hot planet; the climate crisis at the end of your fork and what you can do about it. with a forward by Bill McKibben. Bloomsbury 2010 xxi, 313p il　　　　**641**

1. Food supply 2. Food industry 3. Eating customs 4. Greenhouse effect

ISBN 1-59691-659-1; 978-1-59691-659-3

LC 2010-17363

The author "argues that food is 'the integrating lens' for the innumerable responses to climate change. At three meals or more per day, Lappe writes, we are faced with either supporting or resisting industrial food production. So-called conventional food production and distribution—ecologically and economically fragile—contributes to nearly one-third of total human-caused global warming and paradoxically creates hunger out of plenty. Organic, local, plant-based foods, on the other hand, have the potential to not only mitigate but ultimately repair this damage. Lappe bolsters her support for a local, organic diet with a substantial bibliography of peer-reviewed science, studies, policies and interviews." Kirkus

Includes bibliographical references

New Yorker (Periodical)

Secret ingredients; the New Yorker book of food and drink. edited by David Remnick. Random House 2007 xv, 582p il $29.95　　　　**641**

1. Food 2. Cooking 3. Eating customs

ISBN 978-1-4000-6547-9

LC 2007-14490

"A wide range of authors are represented, from the familiar A.J. Liebling and M.F.K. Fisher to the piquant Anthony Bourdain and the delightful Calvin Trillin. Those seeking an introduction to fiction and nonfiction food writing would do well to graze this work; seasoned readers will enjoy the nostalgic places and tastes depicted, and the quintessential New Yorker cartoons are a delightful addition." Libr J

Oliver, Jamie, 1975-

Jamie's dinners; with photographs by David Loftus and Chris Terry and illustrations by Marion Deuchars. Hyperion 2004　　　　**641**

1. Cooking

ISBN 1-4013-0194-0

The **Oxford** companion to food; Alan Davidson ; edited by Tom Jaine ; illustrations by Soun Van-

nithone. 3rd ed Oxford University Press 2014 xxx, 921p illustrations $65　　　　**641**

1. Food 2. Reference books

ISBN 9780199677337

LC 2013957569

First published 1999

"There is new coverage of attitudes to food consumption, production and perception, such as food and genetics, food and sociology, and obesity. New entries include terms such as convenience foods, drugs and food, Ethiopia, leftovers, medicine and food, pasta, and many more. There are also new entries on important personalities who are of special significance within the world of food." Publisher's note

Includes bibliographical references and index

641.2　Beverages (Drinks)

Acitelli, Tom

The **audacity** of hops; the history of America's craft beer revolution. Tom Acitelli. Chicago Review Press 2013 416 p. (pbk.) $19.95　　　　**641.2**

1. Beer 2. Brewing 3. Microbreweries 4. Beer -- United States

ISBN 1613743882; 9781613743881

LC 2013002264

This book by Tom Acitelli is a "look at craft beer from the 1960s onward, from its birth out of the home brewing movement to ultimately revitalize an industry—and the drinking habits of millions. The author traces craft brewing's passage from an unorthodox business decision to a potentially logical investment. His book provides the histories of dozens of breweries, from familiar names to more obscure, long-shuttered institutions, and takes in numerous industry-wide controversies." (Library Journal)

Includes bibliographical references and index

Beaumont, Stephen

The **world** atlas of beer; The Essential Guide to the Beers of the World. Sterling Epicure 2012 256 p. (hardcover) $30　　　　**641.2**

1. Beer 2. Brewing

ISBN 1402789610; 9781402789618

This book presents the "global history of beer. . . . Color photographs accompany the text, which offers information on buying and drinking beer, as well as a geographic survey of beers around the world. Other topics covered include the various types of beer, brewing methods and technologies, trends, brands, and more." (Booklist)

Exploring wine; Steven Kolpan, Brian H. Smith, Michael A. Weiss. 3rd ed Wiley 2010 792 p. col. ill., col. maps (cloth) $70　　　　**641.2**

1. Wine and wine making

ISBN 0471770639; 9780471770633

LC 2009014016

"This new edition of the critically acclaimed guide features more comprehensive coverage of the wine regions of the world, grape varietals, winemaking, purchasing, tasting, service, and pairing." Publisher's note

Includes bibliographical references and index

Larousse encyclopedia of wine; general editor, Christopher Foulkes. Ed fully updated in 2001 by Larousse; Larousse 2001 624p il maps $45   **641.2**

1. Reference books 2. Wine and wine making

ISBN 2-03-585013-4

LC 2003-269288

First published 1994

This book is a "reference to the world's vineyards and to the enjoyment of wine. . . . Full-color photographs, maps and drawings illustrate the country-by-country, vineyard-by-vineyard descriptions of all the world's wine regions from the United States and Europe to New Zealand and the Orient. . . . The book also details the intricacies of pairing wine with food, wine selection and etiquette, as well as historical and technical information about how wine is made." Publisher's note

★ The **Oxford** companion to wine; edited by Jancis Robinson. 3rd ed; Oxford University Press 2006 840p il map $65   **641.2**

1. Reference books 2. Wine and wine making

ISBN 0-19-860990-6; 978-0-19-860990-2

LC 2006-50303

First published 1994

The contributors "write with zesty enthusiasm about everything from the different varieties of grapes to the world's greatest wineries and geographic areas of production." Libr J

Peynaud, Emile

The **taste** of wine; the art and science of wine appreciation. {by} Emile Peynaud; with the assistance of Jacques Blouin; translated from the French by Michael Schuster; with a foreword by Michael Broadbent. 2nd ed; Wiley 1996 xxi, 346p il $95 **641.2**

1. Wine and wine making

ISBN 0-471-11376-X

LC 96-24181

Original French edition 1980; first English translation published 1987 in the United Kingdom

"Long considered the definitive tome on winetasting." Libr J

Includes bibliographical references

Risen, Clay

American Whiskey, Bourbon & Rye; A Guide to the Nation's Favorite Spirit. by Clay Risen. Sterling Pub Co Inc 2013 304 p. color illustrations $24.95   **641.2**

1. Whiskey 2. Alcoholic beverages

ISBN 1402798407; 9781402798405

This book, by Clay Risen, is a "guide devoted solely to US-made whiskey, rye, and bourbon. Arranged alphabetically by distillery and/or brand, it offers histories, ratings, and tasting notes for over 200 whiskeys. Each main account includes the name and address of the maker, including website URL and contact information, along with its various products." (Publisher's note)

"Risen . . . deftly combines history and assessment in this informative volume that covers more than 200 of the titular spirits." LJ

Includes bibliographical references (pages 281-284) and index

Wallace, Benjamin

The **billionaire's** vinegar; the mystery of the world's most expensive bottle of wine. Crown Publishers 2008 319p $24.95; pa $14.95   **641.2**

1. Wine and wine making

ISBN 978-0-307-33877-8; 0-307-33877-0; 978-0-307-33878-5 pa; 0-307-33878-9 pa

LC 2007-31645

"This is a gripping story, expertly handled by Benjamin Wallace who writes with wit and verve, drawing the reader into a subculture strewn with eccentrics and monomaniacs. . . . Full of detail that will delight wine lovers. It will also appeal to anyone who merely savours a great tale, well told." Economist

Includes bibliographical references

Wondrich, David

Punch; the delights (and dangers) of the flowing bowl. Perigee 2010 296p $23.95   **641.2**

1. Punches (Beverages)

ISBN 978-0-399-53616-8; 0-399-53616-7

Wondrich "argues that British sailors, making the best of the ingredients available to them far from home, first improvised Punch using an exotic eastern distillate called arrack, local limes or lemons, sugar, spice and water. In Mr. Wondrich's account, it often seems the main activity at the English East India Company's trading posts in South Asia—aside from welcoming or sending off the occasional ship—was the making and downing of Punch. The humble quaff soon came to be the drink of the British Empire, beloved not only in India, but in the Caribbean, the American colonies, and of course England herself. As the concept spread, it was adapted to the ingredients at hand. . . . Mr. Wondrich's noble effort to restore Punch's good name offers sound advice on the basics of Punch-making along with a variety of vintage recipes." Wall Street J

Zraly, Kevin

Windows on the World Complete Wine Course; Kevin Zraly. 30th anniv ed Sterling Pub Co Inc 2014 368 p. il $27.95   **641.2**

1. Wine and wine making

ISBN 1454913649; 9781454913641

Annual. First published 1985

"Zraly deftly takes the mystery out of choosing wine, explains the basics, and suggests hundreds of new wines to try. . . . [T]his thoroughly redesigned edition also presents a beautiful tribute to Windows on the World, the renowned restaurant where Zraly's course began. User-friendly smartphone tags and audio guides are featured throughout." Publisher's note

641.3   Food

Barber, Dan

The **third** plate; field notes on a new cuisine. by
Dan Barber. The Penguin Press 2014 496 p. illustra-
tions (hardback) $29.95   **641.3**
1. Agriculture 2. Natural foods 3. Eating customs 4.
Seasonal cooking -- United States
ISBN 1594204071; 9781594204074
LC 2013039966

This book, by Dan Barber, advocates for "an integrated
system of vegetable, grain, and livestock production that
is fully supported--in fact, dictated--by what we choose
to cook for dinner. The third plate is where good farming
and good food intersect. While the third plate is a novelty
in America, Barber demonstrates that this way of eating is
rooted in worldwide tradition." (Publisher's note)

"In this bold and impassioned analysis, Barber insists
that chefs have the power to transform American cuisine to
achieve a sustainable and nutritious future." Kirkus
Includes bibliographical references and index

Bittman, Mark

The **food** matters cookbook; 500 revolutionary
recipes for better living. Simon & Schuster 2010
645p $35; ebook $16.99   **641.3**
1. Food 2. Health 3. Cooking 4. Nutrition
ISBN 978-1-4391-2023-1; 978-1-4391-4123-6 ebook
LC 2010-28623

The author "provides a rational approach to eating that
not only improves health but also helps the environment.
Extolling the benefits of a plant-heavy diet, Bittman offers
more than 500 healthful recipes that feature unprocessed
fruits, vegetables, legumes, nuts, and whole grains and reduce all types of meat to backup players. In addition, he
shares five basic principles for sane eating that are easy to
implement and understand as well as an unusually helpful
pantry section and handy charts for substituting produce and
seafood by season. . . . Practical and balanced, this collection will shape the way we cook at home for years to come."
Publ Wkly

Colquhoun, Kate

Taste : the story of Britain through its cooking.
Bloomsbury 2007 460p il $34.95   **641.3**
1. Eating customs 2. British cooking
ISBN 978-1-59691-410-0; 1-59691-410-6
The author offers a culinary history of Great Britain.
"Colquhoun's enthusiasm for her subject leaps from ev-
ery page." Economist
Includes bibliographical references

Crosby, Guy

The **science** of good cooking; master 50 simple
concepts to enjoy a lifetime of success in the kitch-
en. the editors at America's Test Kitchen and Guy
Crosby ; illustrations by Michael Newhouse and John

Burgoyne. America's Test Kitchen 2012 486 p.
$40   **641.3**
1. Food 2. Cooking 3. Cookbooks
ISBN 1933615982; 9781933615981
LC 2012012807

This book by the editors of America's Test Kitchen and
Guy Crosby, part of the Cook's Illustrated Cookbooks series,
"brings science to the stove. . . . In addition to explaining
how food science works (and why you should care), 'The
Science of Good Cooking' shows you the science. This book
brings you into the test kitchen with 50 . . . experiments engineered to illustrate (and illuminate) the science at work."
(Publisher's note)

Darlington, Tenaya

Dibruno Bros. House of Cheese; by Tenaya Darlington ; photographs by Jason Verney. 1st ed. Running Press 2013 256 p. (hardcover) $25.00   **641.3**
1. Cheese
ISBN 0762446048; 9780762446049
LC 2012942524

In this book, Tenaya Darlington "draws on the offerings
at long-established Philadelphia cheese monger Di Bruno
Bros. and the expertise of its staff to highlight a range of
cheeses according to such personalities as 'mountain men,'
'vixens,' 'quiet types,' and 'pierced punks.' . . . The description of each cheese briefly captures its history and its flavor,
complemented with suggestions for beverage pairings and
accompaniments." (Library Journal)

Foer, Jonathan Safran

Eating animals. Little, Brown and Company
2009 341p $25.99; pa $14.99   **641.3**
1. Vegetarianism
ISBN 978-0-316-06990-8; 978-0-316-06988-5 pa
LC 2009-34434

The novelist presents a critique of the food industry
and explores arguments in favor of humane agriculture
and vegetarianism.

"A blend of solid—and discomforting—reportage
with fierce advocacy that will make committed carnivores
squeal." Kirkus
Includes bibliographical references

Katzinger, Jennifer

Gluten -free & vegan pie; more than 50 sweet
and savory pies to make at home. Jennifer Katzinger ;
photographs by Charity Burggraaf. Sasquatch Books
2013 xvii, 140 p.p color illustrations (alk. paper)
$23.95   **641.3**
1. Pies 2. Veganism 3. Cookbooks 4. Gluten-free diet
5. Vegetarian cooking 6. Gluten-free diet -- Recipes
ISBN 1570618682; 9781570618680
LC 2012050141

This book, by Jennifer Katzinger with photographs by
Charity Burggraaf, offers "more than 55 gluten-free and
vegan pie recipes. . . . Baking your favorite pies without
dairy, eggs, gluten, or animal products calls for a different
approach to both fillings and dough. Here you'll find techniques and tips for mixing and working with dough that
doesn't contain butter or lard, and for luscious fillings that
contain neither cream nor egg." (Publisher's note)

"Katzinger presents a breadth of pastry doughs, press-in crusts, and sweet and savory fillings that can be used to make pies, turnovers, cobblers, crisps, galettes, tarts, and more." LJ

Gluten-free and vegan pie

★ **Larousse** gastronomique; the world's greatest culinary encyclopedia. with the assistance of the Gastronomic Committee, president Joël Robuchon. Clarkson Potter Publishers 2009 1206p il map $90   **641.3**
1. French cooking 2. Reference books 3. Food -- Encyclopedias 4. Cooking -- Encyclopedias
ISBN 978-0-307-46491-0

Original French edition published 1938 under the authorship of Prosper Montagné; first United States edition 1961

"The alphabetical entries range in length from a few sentences to several pages. They cover types of food (Apples, Locusts); cooking techniques (Braising, Grilling); famous chefs (Auguste Escoffier, Alice Waters); culinary jobs (Maître d'hôtel, Sommelier); countries (China, Greece); and tools of the trade (Knife, Saucepan). . . . This is an essential resource for most library reference collections as well as a wonderful book to browse." Booklist

Masson, J. Moussaieff
The **face** on your plate; the truth about food. W.W. Norton & Co. 2009 288p $24.95   **641.3**
1. Food of animal origin
ISBN 978-0-393-06595-4; 0-393-06595-2

LC 2008-52733

The author presents "arguments for not eating animal products: the link to global warming, the horrors of factory farming, and the negative influence aquaculture is having on wild fish populations. He concludes that we are in a state of denial about the origins of our food and demonstrates that veganism is not as difficult as it may sound by presenting a day in his life as a vegan. Well footnoted with ample suggestions for further reading." Libr J

McLagan, Jennifer
Odd bits; how to cook the rest of the animal. photography by Leigh Beisch. Ten Speed Press 2011 248p il $35   **641.3**
1. Cooking -- Meat
ISBN 978-1-58008-334-8

LC 2011-11575

A "unique, informative, and readable cookbook. The ingredients used for the 100 recipes include lungs, necks, spleens, tongues, cheeks, testicles, and feet, as well as a few more common cuts (ribs, brisket, and shanks). In her introduction, McLagan traces the history of eating meat and why in earlier times the odd bits were considered the prime parts. In the last 75 to 100 years, most of these parts have been discarded or used for cat and dog food in the United States. McLagan encourages readers with a detailed and clear discussion of how to choose, prepare, and cook them. She draws the line at eyeballs and notes that lungs are not sold in the United States." Libr J

Norman, Jill
Herbs & spices; photography, Dave King. DK Pub. 2002 336p il $30   **641.3**
1. Herbs 2. Spices
ISBN 0-7894-8939-2

LC 2003-544667

First published in the United Kingdom with title: Herb & spice

"Ranging from one to four pages each, the entries for 60 different herbs and 60 different spices include an overview, tasting notes, the parts of the herb or spice used in cooking, buying and storage information, culinary uses, and some details on cultivation. Separate chapters on preparation, recipes for blending herbs and spices (as in sauces and pastes), recipes that draw on cuisines around the world, and purchasing sources are also included . . . Norman's volume excels at giving the practical details and clear illustrations cooks need when it comes to using these ingredients in the kitchen." Libr J

Includes bibliographical references

Ornelas, Kriemhild Conee
The **Cambridge** world history of food; editors, Kenneth F. Kiple, Kriemhild Coneè Ornelas. Cambridge Univ. Press 2000 2v set $190   **641.3**
1. Diseases 2. Nutrition 3. Edible plants 4. Food -- History
ISBN 0-521-40216-6

LC 00-57181

"The two volumes are arranged in eight parts covering the diet of early man, staple foods, dietary liquids, nutrients and food-related disorders, food and drink around the world, nutrition and health, current food-related issues and concluding with a dictionary of plant foods. . . . The Cambridge World History of Food is a thorough study of a topic that is eternally popular. It should become a standard source in reference collections." Booklist

Includes bibliographical references

The **Oxford** encyclopedia of food and drink in America; Andrew F. Smith, editor in chief. Oxford University Press 2004 2v il set $250   **641.3**
1. Beverages 2. Reference books 3. Food 4. Cookery, American 5. Food -- Encyclopedias
ISBN 0-19-515437-1; 978-0-19-515437-5

LC 2003-24873

In some 800 articles, this work "covers the significant events, inventions, and social movements in American history that have affected the way Americans view, prepare, and consume food and drink. In an A-Z format, this two-volume set details the regions, people, ingredients, foods, drinks, publications, advertising, companies, historical periods, and political and economic aspects pertinent to American cuisine."

"Whether readers make a living studying culinary traditions or just enjoy eating, they'll find this book a marvel. . . . For food lovers of all stripes, this work inspires, enlightens and entertains." Publ Wkly

Parsons, Russ

How to pick a peach; the search for flavor from farm to table. Houghton Mifflin 2007 412p $27   **641.3**
1. Cooking -- Fruit 2. Cooking -- Vegetables
ISBN 978-0-618-46348-0; 0-618-46348-8
LC 2006-35462

"Equal parts cookbook, agricultural history, chemistry lesson and produce buying guide. . . . [Parsons begins with a] tale of agribusiness trumping our taste buds en route to supplying year-round on-demand produce, and how farmer's markets are bringing back both appreciation of, and access to, local and seasonal foods. He then takes readers on a delectable season-by-season produce tour, from springtime Artichokes Stuffed with Ham and Pine Nuts to midwinter Candied Citrus Peel, and provides readers with the lowdown on where each fruit or vegetable is grown and how to choose, store and prepare it." Publ Wkly

Pierson, Stephanie

The **brisket** book; a love story with recipes. photographs by Roger Sherman. Andrews McMeel Publishing 2011 208p il $29.99   **641.3**
1. Cooking -- Meat
ISBN 978-1-4494-0697-4
LC 2011-921500

"The book is both humorous and serious: from a section called Found in Translation—how to order brisket in sixteen languages—to The Last Brisket, a joke by David Minkoff. Pierson shares cooking tips, chef interviews, information on beef cuts, different cooking techniques and more than 30 brisket recipes. It took Stephanie a year to select and test the recipes that are included in the book. They come from notable chefs, cookbook authors, cowboys, pit masters and home cooks." KosherEye

Reese, Jennifer

Make the bread, buy the butter; what you should and shouldn't cook from scratch--over 120 recipes for the best homemade foods. Jennifer Reese. 1st Free Press hardcover ed; Free Press 2011 295 p. il $24   **641.3**
1. Cookbooks 2. Natural foods 3. Agricultural processing 4. Processed foods -- Costs 5. Natural foods -- Processing
ISBN 1451605870; 9781451605877; 9781451605891 ebook
LC 2011009088

This book, by Jennifer Reese, "gives 120 recipes with . . . practical yet . . . fun 'Make or buy' recommendations. Reese . . . relates her food and animal husbandry adventures. . . . Her tales include living with a backyard full of . . . chickens, . . . ducks, and . . . baby goats. . . . Here's . . . what is involved in a truly homemade life--with the good news that you shouldn't try to make everything yourself--and how to get the most out of your time in the kitchen." (Publisher's note)

Rosenblum, Mort

Chocolate : a bittersweet saga of dark and light. North Point Press 2005 290p il $24; pa $14 **641.3**
1. Chocolate
ISBN 0-86547-635-7; 0-86547-730-2 pa
LC 2004-54734

The author "unveils chocolate's history and its various incarnations, including in his fresh and insightful discussions the origins of mole; the differences between, say, Hershey's kisses and Valrhona's products; the invention of Nutella; and the small boutique chocolate artisans found nearly everywhere. . . . A compelling and tasty read." Booklist

World cheese book; editor-in-chief, Juliet Harbutt; contributors, Martin Aspinwall . . . [et al.] DK 2009 352p il map $25   **641.3**
1. Cheese
ISBN 978-0-7566-5442-9

"Harbutt has compiled a comprehensive illustrated guide to more than 750 artisanally and industrially produced cheeses from around the globe. . . . Organized by country, cheeses are listed alphabetically and each has a uniform data table, making information easy to find. Key cheeses such as Parmigiano Reggiano, Stilton, Roquefort, Halloumi, and the like have much longer entries detailing production methods." Booklist

Includes bibliographical references

Wrangham, Richard W.

Catching fire; how cooking made us human. [by] Richard Wrangham. Basic Books 2009 309p $26.95   **641.3**
1. Fire 2. Cooking 3. Eating customs 4. Prehistoric peoples
ISBN 978-0-465-01362-3
LC 2009-1742

This "is a plainspoken and thoroughly gripping scientific essay that presents nothing less than a new theory of human evolution. . . . [This book] contains serious science yet is related in direct, no-nonsense prose. It is toothsome, skillfully prepared brain food." N Y Times (Late N Y Ed)

Includes bibliographical references

641.4   Food preservation and storage

Costenbader, Carol W.

The **big** book of preserving the harvest; {foreword by Joanne Lamb Hayes} rev ed; Storey Bks. 2002 347p il pa $18.95   **641.4**
1. Canning and preserving
ISBN 1-58017-458-2
LC 2002-21172

First published 1997

In addition to recipes this book provides instructions for food preservation techniques, including canning, drying, freezing, the preparation of jams and jellies, pickles, relishes and chutneys, vinegars and seasonings, and cold storage. Includes a section on gift giving, directions on building a food dehydrator, a table of equivalents, and a conversion chart to metric measures

Includes bibliographical references

Field, Rick

The **Art** of preserving; authors, Lisa Atwood, Rebecca Courchesne, Rick Field ; photographer, France Ruffenach. Weldon Owen 2010 239 p. col. ill. (pbk) $19.95 **641.4**

1. Food -- Preservation 2. Canning and preserving
ISBN 9781740899789; 9781616283834; 1616283831

This book, by Lisa Atwood, Rick Field, and Rebecca Courchesne, "[p]acked with . . . recipes for preserves, from Apricot Jam to Pickled Fennel with Orange Zest to Preserved Lemons, . . . provides a wealth of ideas for making the most of the harvest. Additional recipes showcase the many ways that preserved foods can be used in finished dishes, from savory starters to flavorful main courses to sweet desserts." (Publisher's note)

The **Good** Housekeeping step-by-step cookbook; edited by Susan Westmoreland with the assistance of Susan Deborah Goldsmith and Elizabeth Brainerd Burge. Hearst Books 2008 576p il $29.95 **641.4**

1. Cooking
ISBN 978-1-58816-760-6; 1-58816-760-7
First published 1997

This offers over 1,000 basic recipes illustrated by 1,800 color photographs divided into sections such as appetizers, soups, eggs and cheese, shellfish, poultry, meat, vegetables, pasta, grains and beans, breads, and desserts.

Mackenzie, Jennifer

The **complete** book of pickling; 250 recipes from pickles & relishes to chutneys & salsas. Robert Rose 2009 335p il pa $24.95 **641.4**

1. Canning and preserving
ISBN 978-0-77880216-7; 0-7788-0216-7

This is a "terrific collection of 250 pickles, sauces, chutneys and relishes. . . . Even readers without an appreciation for the tang of a good pickle will appreciate MacKenzie's 50 chutneys, including variations such as Sangria Citrus, classic cranberry and peach, pineapple ginger and spiced tomato; six chili sauces; 18 salsas; and homemade ketchup." Publ Wkly

West, Kevin

Saving the season; the essential guide to home canning, pickling, and preserving. by Kevin West. Alfred A. Knopf 2013 544 p. (hardback) $35 **641.4**

1. Fruit -- Preservation 2. Canning and preserving
ISBN 0307599485; 9780307599483

LC 2012037844

In this book, Kevin West "explores the various preserves available through the four seasons. Each base recipe includes variations to please any palate; the recipe for Black Mission Fig Jam offers directions to flavor it with Syrah, Madeira, or Smoky Black Tea. . . . Appendixes of peak seasons by region and tables of fruit varieties provide extensive information for cooks in any region. More than just recipes, the book also contains stories of the author's travels." (Library Journal)

Includes bibliographical references and index

Ziedrich, Linda

The **joy** of pickling; 250 flavor-packed recipes for vegetables and more from garden or market. foreward by Chuck Williams. Rev. ed.; Harvard Common Press 2009 418p $29.95; pa $18.95 **641.4**

1. Canning and preserving
ISBN 978-1-55832-374-2; 978-1-55832-375-9 pa

LC 2008-36446

First published 1998

"There are chapters on fresh, sweet, quick, and freezer pickles, as well as cabbage pickles, miso and soy pickles, pickle relishes, and even pickled meat, seafood, and eggs. . . . [It also includes information on] pickling techniques, procedures, safety, and equipment, as well as . . . recipes." Publisher's note

Includes bibliographical references

641.5   Cooking

The **150** best American recipes; edited by Fran McCullough and Molly Stevens; foreword by Rick Bayless; photography by Ben Fink; [selected by the editors of The best American recipes] Houghton Mifflin 2006 352p il $30 **641.5**

1. Cooking
ISBN 978-0-618-71865-8; 0-618-71865-6

LC 2006-5604

The editors "have selected the 'best of the best' recipes from . . . [The Best American Recipes series], choosing from more than 1000 contenders. The recipes come from a variety of sources, from cookbooks to web sites to cooking schools, and the result is a mouthwatering array: Charred Tomatillo Guacamole; Tuscan Pork Roast with Herbed Salt; Mussels with Smoky Bacon, Lime, and Cilantro; and Mocha Fudge Pudding." Libr J

Adrià, Ferran, 1962-

The **family** meal; home cooking with Ferran Adria. Phaidon Press 2011 383p il $29.95 **641.5**
ISBN 978-0-7148-6253-8; 0-7148-6253-3

"Even if you're more comfortable navigating cobblestone streets in platforms than wielding a microplane in the kitchen, this book will show even the most harried and clueless of cooks how to prepare a simple dinner at home. And, as an unexpected bonys, it will also be a meal that will forever impress guests." Vogue

Ahern, Shauna James

Gluten -free girl every day; Shauna James Ahern, with Daniel Ahern ; photography by Penny De Los Santos. John Wiley & Sons, Inc. 2013 319 p. col. ill. (cloth) $29.99 **641.5**

1. Cookbooks 2. Gluten-free diet 3. Gluten-free diet -- Recipes
ISBN 111811521X; 9781118115213

LC 2012030520

James Beard Award (2014)

This cookbook, by Shauna James Ahern, was the winner of a James Beard Foundation cookbook award. "Vegetables in season are the key to these healthy, relatively simple recipes, along with whole grains, beans, and a few key spices and homemade sauces. . . . [The book] also includes practical tips on how to stock a gluten-free pantry, as well as helpful insights into how to bake gluten-free." (Publisher's note)

Alford, Jeffrey

     Beyond the Great Wall; recipes and travels in the other China. [by] Jeffrey Alford and Naomi Duguid; studio photography by Richard Jung; location photographs by Jeffrey Alford and Naomi Duguid. Artisan 2008 376p il map $40   **641.5**
     1. Chinese cooking 2. Tibet (China) -- Description and travel
     ISBN 978-1-57965-301-9

                           LC 2007-28556
     The authors "explore the food and peoples of the outlaying regions of present-day China, historically home to those not ethnically Chinese. Part travel guide and part cookbook, this collection looks at the cultural survival and preservation of food in smaller societies including that of the Tibetan, Mongol, Tuvan and Kirghiz peoples, among others. . . . A handsome and engaging collection suitable for travelers and cooks alike, this book will delight anyone with an interest in this part of the world." Publ Wkly
     Includes bibliographical references

     The **America's** Test Kitchen healthy family cookbook; a new, healthier way to cook everything from America's most trusted test kitchen. the editors at America's test kitchen ; photography, Daniel J. Van Ackere, Carl Tremblay. America's Test Kitchen 2010 viii, 520 p.p ill. (chiefly col.) (looseleaf) $34.95   **641.5**
     1. Cookbooks 2. American cooking 3. Cooking, American 4. Families -- Health and hygiene
     ISBN 1933615567; 9781933615561

                           LC 2011278441
     This cookbook, produced by the editors at America's Test Kitchen, "[p]resents advice on cooking techniques, equipment, food preparation, and selection of ingredients, along with more than 750 recipes for healthy dishes, including appetizers, soups, meats, fish, vegetables, sauces, breads, and desserts." (Publisher's note)
     "[A] well-tested collection of more than 750 recipes that employ vetted techniques and abundant flavor to create dishes that are as healthy as they can be, given what they are, without sacrificing a pleasurable eating experience." Pub Wkly

     The **America's** Test Kitchen new family cookbook; all-new edition of the best-selling classic with 1,100 new recipes. the editors at America's Test Kitchen. America's Test Kitchen 2014 928 p. col. ill. $40   **641.5**
     1. Cooking, American
     ISBN 1936493853; 9781936493852

                           LC 2014009517

American food writing; an anthology with classic recipes. edited by Molly O'Neill. Library of America 2007 753p il $40   **641.5**
     1. Cooking
     ISBN 978-1-59853-005-6; 1-59853-005-4
     This "collection of essays, anecdotes, and recipes spans three centuries of American food writing, from Meriwether Lewis's account of killing 'two bucks and two buffaloe' during his famous trek across the continent, to Michael Pollan's up-to-the-minute account of the politics of organic food. . . . With so many wonderful ingredients, this rich, delectable treat is a must-have for American foodies." Publ Wkly
     Includes bibliographical references

American Institute for Cancer Research

     The **new** American plate cookbook; recipes for a healthy weight and a healthy life. American Institute for Cancer Research. University of California Press 2005 306p il $24.95   **641.5**
     1. Cooking
     ISBN 0-520-24234-3

                           LC 2004-17993
     The recipes in this book are "built around vegetables and whole grains, with an emphasis on brown rice, wheat pasta, and other healthful foods, rather than protein. . . . Recipes are appealing and easy to make and cover every course of a meal. Well-known dishes are reworked, e.g., New England Clam Chowder, to help with the transition to healthier eating." Libr J

Anderson, Jean

     The **food** of Portugal; color photography by the author. Morrow 1986 304p il map hardcover o.p. pa $19.95   **641.5**
     1. Portuguese cooking
     ISBN 0-688-13415-7 pa

                           LC 86-2510
     The author "first covers Portugal's geography and touches on distinctive regional cooking styles. The following glossary delineates Portuguese food, drink, and dining terminology. . . . Part 2, . . . is a guide to the country's best food." Booklist
     Includes bibliographical references

Anderson, Pam

     How to cook without a book; recipes and techniques every cook should know by heart. Broadway Bks. 2000 290p $25   **641.5**
     1. Cooking
     ISBN 0-7679-0279-3

                           LC 99-43776
     "In chapters organized mostly by course or by technique, Anderson provides basic templates for tossed salads, pasta

dishes with vegetables, simple stir-fries, and so forth, with easy suggestions for variations on the theme." Libr J

Perfect recipes for having people over; photographs by Rita Maas. Houghton Mifflin 2005 304p il $35 **641.5**
1. Cooking 2. Entertaining
ISBN 0-618-32972-2
LC 2005-46370
Anderson "offers 200 recipes from entrées to desserts. Most are easy to make; some require guest participation, such as shish kebabs, with a variety of ingredients for all tastes. The book begins with main courses since they will dictate the accompaniments. Each recipe has a question section–e.g., 'Any Shortcuts?' 'What Should I Serve with It?' 'How Far Ahead Can I Make It?' There are many familiar dishes like macaroni and cheese and deviled eggs, but readers will also encounter innovative recipes." Libr J

Andrews, Colman
Country cooking of Ireland; photographs by Christopher Hirsheimer; foreword by Darina Allen. Chronicle 2009 383p il map $50 **641.5**
1. Irish cooking
ISBN 978-0-8118-6670-5
The author "provides new perspectives on the often maligned Irish cuisine. The breathtakingly beautiful photographs are alone enough to convince, but Andrews, calling Irish cuisine one of the most exciting food stories in the world today, lets the dishes make his case. Robust soups such as butternut and apple and roast pork belly start the mouth juices flowing. Andrews offers a culinary feast with everything from nested eggs and steak-and-kidney pie to Arlington chicken liver pâté and battered sausages. . . . Andrews has done the near impossible in elevating a cuisine thought to be humble and drab into tantalizing fare that will have worldwide appeal." Publ Wkly
Includes bibliographical references

Anthony, Michael
The **Gramercy** Tavern cookbook; Michael Anthony ; with a history by Danny Meyer ; produced by Dorothy Kalins ; photographs by Maura McEvoy. Clarkson Potter Publishers 2013 352 p. color illustrations (hardback) $50 **641.5**
1. Cookbooks 2. Restaurants 3. American cooking 4. Gramercy Tavern 5. Seasonal cooking 6. Cooking, American
ISBN 0307888339; 9780307888334
LC 2012047367
This cookbook, by Michael Anthony, focuses on the New York City restaurant Gramercy Tavern. "Opened in 1994, Gramercy Tavern . . . has become a New York institution earning dozens of accolades, including six James Beard awards. . . . The restaurant has its own magic--a sense of community and generosity--that's captured in these pages for everyone to bring home and savor through 125 recipes." (Publisher's note)
"[T]he authors encourage cooks to approach their restaurant recipes as inspirational points of departure to produce dishes that 'look great by virtue of the beauty of the ingredients.' Signature tavern cocktails are followed by recipes

organized by season, from appetizers through main dishes to desserts." Pub Wkly

Antine, Stacey, 1968-
Appetite for life; the thumbs up, no yucks guide to getting your kid to be a great eater-including over 100 kid-approved recipes. Stacey Antine. HarperCollins 2012 272 p. ill. $26.99 **641.5**
1. Cooking 2. Cookbooks 3. Children -- Nutrition
ISBN 0062103709; 9780062103703
LC 2012002471
This book, by Stacey Antine, founder of HealthBarn USA, offers advice for encouraging healthy, nutritious eating in children and families along with multiple cooking recipes. The book "encourages giving children a voice: with her 'no yucks allowed' method, kids use a thumbs-up/thumbs-down rating system for each new food they try, but they always have to try at least one bite." (Publisher's note)
"Frustrated parents will find plenty of encouraging and practical ideas as well as more than 100 recipes for breakfast, lunch, dinner, and snack time." Pub Wkly
Includes bibliographical references and index

Bastianich, Lidia
Lidia cooks from the heart of Italy; by Lidia Matticchio Bastianich and Tanya Bastianich Manuali, with David Nussbaum; full-page photographs by Christopher Hirsheimer; other photographs by Lidia Matticchio Bastianich. Alfred A. Knopf 2009 411p il $35 **641.5**
1. Italian cooking
ISBN 978-0-307-26751-1; 0-307-26751-2
LC 2009-22021
"Bastianich and daughter Tanya take readers on a culinary tour of Italy's 12 regions. Grouped by those areas, the recipes are simple enough for novice cooks. Included are appetizers, soups, salads and side dishes, condiments, pastas and risottos/rice, vegetarian main courses (aside from pasta), fish and seafood, meat and poultry, and desserts. In addition, there are stories about the history of the dishes." Libr J

Bastianich, Lidia Matticchio
★ **Lidia's** family table; Lidia Matticchio Bastianich, with David Nussbaum ; photographs by Christopher Hirsheimer. Random House Inc 2004 419 p. col. ill. $35 **641.5**
1. Cookbooks 2. Italian cooking
ISBN 1400040353; 9781400040353
LC 2004022411
In this cookbook, author and television chef "Lidia Bastianich, . . . gives us her most generous, instructive, and creative cookbook. The emphasis here is on cooking for the family, and her book is filled with unusually delicious basic recipes for everyday eating Italian-style, as well as imaginative ideas for variations and improvisations." (Publisher's note)
"Step-by-step photographs illustrate kitchen techniques, and charming photos of the author's grandchildren and other family scenes add to the appeal of this engaging, immensely practical book." LJ

Batali, Mario

Italian grill; [by] Mario Batali with Judith Sutton; photography by Beatriz da Costa; art direction by Lisa Eaton and Douglas Riccardi. Ecco 2008 246p il $29.95   **641.5**

  1. Italian cooking 2. Barbecue cooking

  ISBN 978-0-06-145097-6; 0-06-145097-9

A collection of eighty recipes for grilled Italian food is divided into categories for antipasti, pizza, meat, fish, and vegetables, and includes information on grilling basics, different heat-source options, and differences in grilling equipment.

"This is an essential collection for any serious backyard cook." Publ Wkly

Bayless, Rick

Fiesta at Rick's; fabulous food for great times with friends. [by] Rick Bayless with Deann Groen Bayless; photographs by Paul Elledge. W. W. Norton 2010 348p il $35   **641.5**

  1. Menus 2. Entertaining 3. Mexican cooking

  ISBN 978-0-393-05899-4

                       LC 2010-13128

"The book loosely packages recipes around fiestas, from a luxury guacamole and cocktail party for 12 to classic mole for 24, complete with game-plan checklists. . . . The hardest thing about using this book isn't finding the ingredients (today, practically every small town has a great Mexican grocery), it's keeping yourself from eating everything before the guests arrive." N Y Times Book Rev

Beard, James

The **armchair** James Beard; edited by John Ferrone; foreword by Barbara Kafka. Lyons Press 1999 346p $24.95   **641.5**

  1. Cooking

  ISBN 1-55821-737-1

                       LC 98-29728

This collection assembles "essays on everything from main courses to condiments; dining in restaurants, hospitals, and al fresco; libations and desserts; and broader philosophical concerns on gastronomy. Each chapter has captured Beard's feeling for food, his wicked sense of humor, his consummate excellence as a writer, and even his love of controversy. . . . The 150 recipes cover the globe and honor the palate." Libr J

The **fireside** cook book; a complete guide to fine cooking for beginner and expert. [by] James A. Beard; illustrated by Alice Provensen and Martin Provensen; foreword by Mark Bittman. Simon & Schuster 2008 336p il $30   **641.5**

  1. Cooking

  ISBN 978-1-4165-8967-9; 1-4165-8967-8

                       LC 2008-25094

First published 1949

This volume "includes more than 12,000 recipes and variations, with chapters on every course of a meal, as well as 'Outdoor Cookery,' 'Frozen Foods and PickUp Meals,' and more. This 60th-anniversary edition includes the original watercolor illustrations and a brief new foreword by cookbook author Mark Bittman. While some of the information

and language is dated, of course, it's amazing how ahead of his time Beard often was. . . . The amount of information the book provides is equally impressive, and Beard's straightforward, opinionated prose remains a delight to read." Libr J

★ **James** Beard's American cookery. Little, Brown 1972 877p hardcover o.p. pa $24.95 **641.5**

  1. Cooking

  ISBN 0-316-08566-9 pa

"Comprehensive in scope the cookbook gives eighteenth-and nineteenth-century recipes as well as modern directions for preparation of a full range of U.S. cookery. . . . The format is attractive and the historical data add to the value of an authoritative guide." Booklist

Includes bibliographical references

Berley, Peter

The **modern** vegetarian kitchen; [by] Peter Berley with Melissa Clark. ReganBooks 2000 450p il hardcover o.p. pa $21.99   **641.5**

  1. Vegetarian cooking

  ISBN 0-06-039295-9; 0-06-098911-4 pa

                       LC 00-42524

The author "organizes his recipes first by type (e.g., soups, salads, pasta, and beans) and then by season. . . . He also provides lots of background information and recommendations on ingredients, necessary utensils and appliances, and techniques." Libr J

Includes bibliographical references

Besh, John

Cooking from the heart; my favorite lessons learned along the way. John Besh. Andrews McMeel Pub., LLC 2013 320 p. $40   **641.5**

  1. Cooking 2. Cookbooks

  ISBN 1449430562; 9781449430566

                       LC 2013936654

In this book "James Beard Award-winning chef John Besh shares the lessons he learned from his mentors through 140 accessible recipes and cooking lessons. . . . From Germany's Black Forest to the mountains of Provence, each chapter highlights . . . memories and . . . recipes--the framework for his love of food." (Publisher's note)

The **best** American recipes 2005-2006; the year's top picks from books, magazines, newspapers, and the Internet. Fran McCullough and Molly Stevens, series editors; with a foreword by Mario Batali. Houghton Mifflin 2004 303p il (The Best American series)   **641.5**

  1. Cooking

  ISBN 978-0-0618-57478-0; 0-618-57478-6

Annual. First published 1999

This is a compilation of popular recipes taken from cookbooks, newspapers, magazines, and other sources

Better homes and gardens

Better homes and gardens new cook book; 15th ed.; J. Wiley 2010 660p il $29.95   **641.5**
1. Cooking
ISBN 978-0-470-55686-3

LC 2010-25417

First published 1930 with title: My Better Homes and Gardens cook book. Periodically revised

"A standard cookbook . . . with staple recipes and types of cooking." N Y Public Libr. Book of How & Where to Look It Up

★ Betty Crocker cookbook; everything you need to know to cook today. 10th ed.; Wiley 2005 575p il $29.95; pa $17.95   **641.5**
1. Cooking
ISBN 0-7645-6877-9; 978-0-7645-6877-0; 0-7645-8374-3 pa; 978-0-7645-8374-2 pa

LC 2006-281166

First published with this title 1969 by Golden Press. Periodically revised. Publisher varies. Variant title: Betty Crocker's new cookbook

"This book gives easily readable and understandable recipes. Also has a glossary of cooking terms in back, as well as nutritional guidelines and 'special helps.'" N Y Public Libr. Book of How & Where to Look It Up

Betty Crocker's cooking basics; learning to cook with confidence. Macmillan 1998 280p il $19.95   **641.5**
1. Cooking
ISBN 0-02-862451-3

LC 98-20522

In addition to recipes, this illustrated volume contains tips on food selection, grocery shopping, thawing, and nutrition. Cooking equipment is discussed

Bittman, Mark

★ **How** to cook everything; 2,000 simple recipes for great food. illustrations by Alan Witschonke. 2nd ed.; J. Wiley 2008 1044p il $35   **641.5**
1. Cooking
ISBN 978-0-76-457865-6; 0-76-457865-0

LC 2008-18984

First published 1998 by Macmilllan

The author presents "more than 1000 basic recipes and simple and inventive variations. The enormous breadth of recipes along with Bittman's engaging, straightforward prose will appeal to cooks looking for reliable help with kitchen fundamentals." Publ Wkly

Includes bibliographical references

★ **How** to cook everything vegetarian; simple meatless recipes for great food. illustrations by Alan Witschonke. Wiley 2007 996p il $35   **641.5**
1. Vegetarian cooking
ISBN 978-0-7645-2483-7; 0-7645-2483-6

LC 2006-36937

This vegetarian cookbook "presents more than 2000 recipes and variations. Most of the recipes are quick and easy; prep times are given for each one, and icons indicate those that are especially fast, can be made ahead, and/or are vegan. . . . An essential purchase for all cookery collections." Libr J

Mark Bittman's Kitchen express; 404 inspired seasonal dishes you can make in 20 minutes or less. Simon & Schuster 2009 233p $26   **641.5**
1. Quick and easy cooking
ISBN 978-1-4165-7566-5

LC 2008-54823

"Bittman here offers a sampling of 404 inspiring recipes. . . . The no-sweat recipes are divided into four sections: summer, fall, winter and spring, capitalizing on the freshest ingredients of each season while whittling down the prep time of ordinarily elaborate dishes like coq au vin and ricotta cheesecake to 10 minutes or less. The book includes a drill-down of how best to stock your kitchen, and given the impromptu nature of the book, the substitution grid proves indispensable." Publ Wkly

Bittman, Mark, 1950-

The **VB6** cookbook; 320 all-new recipes that help you eat healthy vegan meals all day and delicious flexitarian dinners at night. Mark Bittman ; photographs by Quentin Bacon. Clarkson Potter 2014 272 p. color illustrations $29.95   **641.5**
1. Veganism 2. Cookbooks 3. Vegetarian cooking 4. Vegan cooking 5. Reducing diets -- Recipes
ISBN 0385344821; 9780385344821

LC 2013050637

"When [author Mark] Bittman committed to a vegan before 6:00 pm diet, he quickly realized that everything about it became easier if he cooked his own meals at home. In The VB6 Cookbook he makes this proposition more convenient than you could imagine. Drawing on a varied and enticing pantry of vegan staples strategically punctuated with 'treat' foods . . . , he has created a versatile repertoire of recipes that makes following his plan simple, satisfying, and sustainable." (Publisher's note)

"Rather than overload readers with prescriptive rules, unfamiliar ingredients, and complicated preparations, Bittman gives them a memorable charge (eat more plants, less meat and processed foods) and tools to help them follow it." LJ

Bracken, Peg

The **I** hate to cook book; with a new foreword by Jo Bracken; drawings by Hilary Knight. 50th anniversary ed.; Grand Central Pub. 2010 207p $22.99; ebook $10.99   **641.5**
1. Cooking 2. Quick and easy cooking
ISBN 978-0-446-54592-1; 978-0-446-56894-4 ebook

LC 2009-1249

First published 1960 by Harcourt, Brace

"This book's strident title belies both its usefulness and its popularity. Peg Bracken faced the burden of being a full-time writer, a full-time mother and a full-time housewife. To buy herself a bit more time for other pursuits, she and her friends collected a host of easy, stress-free recipes. What's truly wonderful is Bracken's droll delivery and the more than 200 recipes that run the gamut from appetizers to desserts." Washington Post

Brennan, Kathy

Keepers; two home cooks share their tried-and-true weeknight recipes and the secrets to happiness in the kitchen. Kathy Brennan and Caroline Campion ; photographs by Christopher Testani. Rodale Books 2013 256 p. color illustrations (hardcover) $26.99   **641.5**

    1. Menus 2. Cookbooks 3. American cooking 4. Quick and easy cooking 5. Cooking, American 6. Low budget cooking 7. Cooking -- Philosophy 8. Kitchens -- Management

    ISBN 1609613546; 9781609613549

                      LC 2013005481

    IACP Cookbook Award (2014)

    In this cookbook, chefs Kathy Brennan and Caroline Campion "offer 120 appealing, satisfying recipes ideal for weeknight meals. There's an array of master recipes for classic dishes with options for substitutions, updated old favorites, one-pot meals, 'international' dishes, super-fast ones, and others that reheat well or can be cooked in individual portions." (Publisher's note)

Bryant, George

    The **paleo** kitchen; finding primal joy in modern cooking. George Bryant and Juli Bauer. Victory Belt Publishing Inc 2014 327 p. color illustrations $34.95   **641.5**

    1. Cookbooks 2. Paleo cooking

    ISBN 1628600101; 9781628600100

    This cookbook, by George Bryant and Juli Bauer, "bring[s] a myriad of bold and delectable gluten & grain-free Paleo recipes straight from their kitchens to yours in their new cookbook. . . . [It] boasts over 100 brand new recipes consisting of appetizers, entrées, side dishes, and decadent desserts that are sure to invigorate and please the fearless caveman palate." (Publisher's note)

    Includes bibliographical references (page 314) and index

Buford, Bill

    Heat; an amateur's adventures as kitchen slave, line cook, pasta-maker, and apprentice to a Dante-quoting butcher in Tuscany. Knopf 2006 318p $25.95   **641.5**

    1. Cooks 2. Italian cooking 3. Television personalities 4. Restaurateurs 5. Cookbook writers

    ISBN 1-4000-4120-1; 978-1-4000-4120-6

                      LC 2005-57868

    "Mr Buford also has a biographer's gift of bringing characters to life. . . . [He] fills his book with people as pungent and spicy as the food." Economist

Burke, David

    David Burke's new American classics; [by] David Burke and Judith Choate. Knopf 2006 300p il $35   **641.5**

    1. Cooking

    ISBN 0-375-41231-X

                      LC 2005-44960

    "Burke presents each dish in three separate and distinctive guises: classic, contemporary, and second day (leftovers). This tripartite approach allows him to address cooks possessing different levels of expertise and sophistication. . . . A large number of these recipes require advanced kitchen techniques so that only the most experienced cooks will have the skills to reproduce Burke's results. Color photographs help guide when the instructions alone fail to communicate the chef's intent." Booklist

Chang, David

    Momofuku; [by] David Chang and Peter Meehan; photographs by Gabriele Stabile. Clarkson Potter 2009 303p il $40   **641.5**

    1. Asian cooking

    ISBN 978-0-307-45195-8

    "Chang's Virginia upbringing, upscale restaurant experience and love of certain Korean and Japanese flavors result in the kind of dishes that will jam your eyeballs into the back of your head, like brussels sprouts with bacon and kimchi puree. This fawningly produced book . . . is fueled by Chang's hard-core attitude and punctuated with a 'Hell's Kitchen' season's worth of unprintable words. The dude's intense, and he wants you to know it. The food is intense, too, especially as the recipes increase in difficulty as the chapters move up the Momofuku restaurant scale, from Noodle Bar to Ssam Bar to Ko." N Y Times Book Rev

Child, Julia

    From Julia Child's kitchen; photographs and drawings by Paul Child; additional technical photographs by Albie Walton. Knopf 1975 687, xxvip il $13.99   **641.5**

    1. French cooking

    ISBN 0-517-20712-5

    The author "has taken many of the recipes she demonstrated in her 72 'French Chef' TV shows; grouped them by subject {soups, appetizers, egg dishes, fish, poultry, meat, vegetables, salads, bread} added variations and additional recipes; and introduced each section and most recipes with commentaries." Libr J

    Includes bibliographical references

    ★ **Mastering** the art of French cooking; by Julia Child, Louisette Bertholle, Simone Beck. updated ed; Knopf 1983 2v il v1 $40; v1 pa $30; v2 $60; v2 pa $30   **641.5**

    1. French cooking

    ISBN 0-375-41340-5 v1; 0-394-72178-0 v1 pa; 0-394-40152-2 v2; 0-394-72177-2 v2 pa

                      LC 83-48113

    Volume 1 first published 1961 with Beck's name first; volume 2 by Julia Child and Simone Beck

    Volume one includes, in addition to usual categories, a chapter dealing with entrees and luncheon dishes, including quiches, pâtés, and crepes, and other cold buffet items. Volume two emphasizes French bread and pastries, with chapters also devoted to soups, meats, chickens, vegetables, and desserts. Appendices discuss stuffings and kitchen equipment.

★ The **way** to cook; photographs by Brian Leatart and Jim Scherer; food designer, Rosemary Manell. Knopf 1989 511p il $65; pa $39.95 **641.5**
1. Cooking
ISBN 0-394-53264-3; 0-679-74765-6 pa

LC 88-45838

"With her sensible-as-always approach to food, Child has produced a comprehensive cooking bible, filled with stunning photographs and practical illustrations, that will aid the novice {and} inspire the gourmet. . . . A masterwork from a master chef." Libr J

Clark, Melissa

Cook this now; 120 easy and delectable dishes you can't wait to make. Hyperion 2011 396p il $29.99 **641.5**
1. Cooking
ISBN 978-1-4013-2398-1

LC 2011010420

"Clark presents readers with 120 recipes organized by season and month. With a candid opening essay on weekly trips to her local NYC farmers' market in the dead of winter—think frosty fingers, and ice-topped milk—Clark sets the course for this down-to-earth, realistic guide to cooking throughout the year, finding and highlighting seasonal gems in mains, side dishes, and desserts. . . . Even with a multitude of cooking-by-season titles in the marketplace, the author's inspiring use of fresh ingredients and flexible attitude toward cooking make this a solid addition to any kitchen cookbook shelf." Publ Wkly

In the kitchen with a good appetite. Hyperion 2010 444p il $27.50 **641.5**
1. Cooking
ISBN 978-1-4013-2376-9

LC 2010-5760

Includes bibliographical references

Colwin, Laurie

Home cooking; a writer in the kitchen. Laurie Colwin ; illustrated by Anna Shapiro. Vintage Books 2010 x, 193 p.p ill. $15.95 **641.5**
1. Cooking 2. Cookbooks
ISBN 0307474410; 9780307474414

LC 2010455796

James Beard Cookbook Hall of Fame (2012)

This autobiographical cookbook, "is [author] Laurie Colwin's manifesto on the joys of sharing food and entertaining. From the humble hotplate of her one-room apartment to the crowded kitchens of bustling parties, Colwin regales us with tales of meals gone both magnificently well and disastrously wrong." (Publisher's note)

Cook's illustrated (Periodical)

The **best** International recipe; a home cook's guide to the best recipes in the world. by the editors of Cook's Illustrated. America's Test Kitchen 2007 579p il $35 **641.5**
1. Cooking
ISBN 978-1-933615-17-2; 1-933615-17-6

This volume contains more than 300 recipes from around the world. Each has been tested to ensure success. Includes explanations of ingredients and what to look for, and in some cases, what you can substitute without compromising flavor. Specialty equipment is also discussed. Core techniques are highlighted throughout the book.

The **new** best recipe; by the editors of Cook's illustrated; photography, Carl Tremblay, Daniel J. Van Ackere; illustrations, John Burgoyne. 2nd ed.; America's Test Kitchen 2004 1028p il $35 **641.5**
1. Cooking
ISBN 978-0-936184-74-6; 0-936184-74-4

First published 1999 by Boston Common Press

A compendium of more than 1,000 recipes. "Twenty-two chapters cover appetizers to desserts. Even the simplest tasks, such as blanching vegetables or peeling an egg, are explained and illustrated in detail. More involved techniques include brining poultry and roasting a turkey. . . . Well organized and extremely clear." Publ Wkly

Crumpacker, Bunny

How to slice an onion; cooking basics and beyond--hundreds of tips, techniques, recipes, food facts, and folklore. Thomas Dunne Books 2009 303p il $25.99 **641.5**
1. Cooking
ISBN 978-0-312-53718-0

LC 2009-16741

"Beginning with the properly sliced onion, Crumpacker explains the hows of cooking as well as the whys: readers will learn why roasting a chicken upside-down is preferable (it keeps the white meat moist), how you can salvage overcooked scrambled eggs (a little butter or sour cream), and the best way to crush tomatoes for homemade marinara sauce (by hand). These and other tips won't bowl over veteran cooks, but Crumpacker's simple advice will rapidly build cookery confidence in those used to dining on canned or premade products. . . . Though bolstered with recipes, Crumpacker's crisp prose makes this volume a winner—the next best thing to having a chef at your side as you prepare to tackle a new dish." Publ Wkly

Includes bibliographical references

Cunningham, Marion

The **Fannie** Farmer cookbook; illustrated by Lauren Jarrett. 13th ed; Knopf 1996 874p il $30 **641.5**
1. Cooking
ISBN 0-679-45081-5

LC 97-162330

First published 1896 under the authorship of Fannie Merritt Farmer. Periodically revised

This standard cookbook focuses on the selection, preparation, and serving of a wide variety of foods

David, Elizabeth

A **book** of Mediterranean food; decorated by John Minton. 2nd rev. ed.; New York Review Books 2002 203p il (New York Review Books classics) pa $14.95 **641.5**

1. Mediterranean cooking
ISBN 978-1-59017-003-8; 1-59017-003-2

LC 2002-749

First published 1950 in the United Kingdom

This is a "mixture of recipes, culinary lore, and frank talk. In bleak postwar Great Britain, when basics were rationed and fresh food a fantasy, David set about to cheer herself—and her audience—up with dishes from the south of France, Italy, Spain, Portugal, Greece, and the Middle East." Publisher's note

French provincial cooking. Grub Street 2008 519p il $34.95 **641.5**

1. French cooking
ISBN 978-1-904943-71-6; 1-904943-71-3

LC 2008-411778

First published 1960 in the United Kingdom

This book "should be approached and read as a series of short stories, as well as written and evocative as the best literature. The voice is highly personal and opinionated, sometimes sharp but always true and always entertaining. This book is a long essay on French cuisine, offering background stories and sketches of recipes very different from the prescriptive type of recipes that most modern readers might be used to today." Living France

Is there a nutmeg in the house? compiled by Jill Norman. Viking 2001 318p il hardcover o.p. pa $15 **641.5**

1. Food 2. Cooking
ISBN 0-14-200166-X pa

LC 2001-26185

Companion volume to An omelette and a glass of wine (1985)

An "evocative and entertaining exploration of cooking and the time, place and personalities that shaped it.'" Publ Wkly

Includes bibliographical references

Italian food; rev ed; Penguin Books 1999 xxxiii, 376p pa $16 **641.5**

1. Italian cooking
ISBN 978-0-14-118155-4; 0-14-118155-9

LC 99-200031

First published 1958 in the United Kingdom

"David studies and analyzes cooking the way a scholar analyzes literature, and, as a result, her titles are far more than just cookbooks. Along with the recipes, of which there are many, she explains at length the histories of the dishes and offers splendid advice on serving wine with the meals." Libr J

Includes bibliographical references

Summer cooking; illustrated by Adrian Daintrey. New York Review Books 2002 234p il (New York Review Books classics) pa $12.95 **641.5**

1. British cooking
ISBN 978-1-59017-004-5; 1-59017-004-0

LC 2002-744

First published 1955 in the United Kingdom

"Don't let the unsophisticated subject fool you into expecting only cheese sandwiches and potato salads. For all its simplicity, 'Summer Cooking' is a wonderfully subversive volume — every bit as unexpected and enchanting to read today as it must have been 50 years ago, when England was just stirring from its wartime fast and garlic was an ingredient still capable of provoking controversy. . . . David earned her place in gastronomic history by being one of the first writers to suggest that thoughtful food and cooking itself could be a means of escape. Now, 15 years after her death, that voice remains a singular note in the chorus of her contemporaries and acolytes, neither frankly amiable like Julia Child, nor seductively literate like M.F.K. Fisher, nor playfully mod like Nigella Lawson. No matter how trivial the point, David speaks her mind." Salon.com

Davies, Katie Quinn

What Katie Ate; Recipes and Other Bits and Pieces. photography by Katie Quinn Davies. Penguin Group USA 2012 304 p. col. ill. $40 **641.5**

1. Cookbooks 2. Cooking
ISBN 0670026182; 9780670026180

LC 2012289524

James Beard Foundation Award: Photography (2013)

In this book, food photographer Katie Quinn Davies "shares her favorite simple dishes with a . . . collection of recipes and . . . images. . . . Showcasing her extraordinary eye, this debut cookbook is a unique combination of food diary and how-to, with tips and tricks, photographs, recipes, and stories. . . . Featured dishes range from Wild Mushrooms on Toast with Parmesan and Herbs to Roasted Pork Tenderloin with Apple, Prune & Pine Nut Stuffing and Cider Cream Gravy." (Publisher's note)

"Davies built her fan base with a blog that chronicles her meals and work, and her debut book gives readers a tangible record—part recipe collection, part scrapbook, laden with sumptuous color and extravagant, full-page layouts." Pub Wkly

DiSpirito, Rocco

Now eat this! 150 of America's favorite comfort foods, all under 350 calories. Ballantine Books 2010 xxiii, 246p il pa $22; ebook $22 **641.5**

1. Cooking 2. Low-calorie diet
ISBN 978-0-345-52090-6 pa; 0-345-52090-4 pa; 978-0-307-76753-0 ebook; 0-307-76753-1 ebook

LC 2009-52470

"Lower-calorie brownies, gravy, spaghetti and meatballs, and beef stroganoff will delight readers who have been avoiding favorite foods." Libr J

Dojny, Brooke

The **New** England cookbook; 350 recipes from town and country, land and sea, hearth and home. illustrations by John MacDonald. Harvard Common Press 1999 652p il $29.95; pa $21.95 **641.5**

1. Cooking

ISBN 1-55832-138-1; 1-55832-139-X pa

LC 99-14393

This volume includes traditional dishes as well as "dozens of ethnic specialties from the various immigrant groups who have helped populate New England: Oregano-Scented Greek Lamb Shanks, Portuguese Tuna Escabeche, and Garlicky Mussels, Italian-style, to name a few." Libr J

Includes bibliographical references and index

Dusoulier, Clotilde

The **French** market cookbook; vegetarian recipes from my Parisian kitchen. by Clotilde Dusoulier. Clarkson Potter Publishers 2013 224 p. (pbk.) $22.50 **641.5**

1. French cooking 2. Vegetarian cooking 3. Cooking, French

ISBN 0307984826; 9780307984821

LC 2012554926

In this book author Clotilde Dusoulier "takes [readers] through the seasons in 82 recipes--and explores the love story between French cuisine and vegetables. [Recipes include] carrots are lightly spiced with star anise and vanilla in a soup made with almond milk; tomatoes are jazzed up by mustard in a gorgeous tart; winter squash stars in golden Corsican turnovers; and luscious peaches bake in a cardamom-scented custard." (Publisher's note)

"Organized by season and peppered with tips on how to select and store vegetables, this cookbook will excite readers looking for substantial vegetarian meals they can feel good about eating." LJ

Easy, delicious home cooking; 250 recipes for every season and occasion. edited by Allie Lewis Clapp, Lygeia Grace, and Candy Gianetti. Real Simple Books 2012 368 p. col. ill. $24.95 **641.5**

1. Cooking 2. Cookbooks

ISBN 1603209239; 9781603209236

Includes index

The editors of this cookbook, Allie Lewis Clapp, Lygeia Grace, and Candy Gianetti, offer "recipes [that] can be prepared in 30 minutes or less, and include tips along the way point to additional time-savers and other tricks of the trade. The recipes are arranged by season, to help you take advantage of what's fresh at the market, and are accompanied by photos so you know exactly what you're getting." (Publisher's note)

The **essential** New York times grilling cookbook; more than 100 years of sizzling food writing and recipes. edited by Peter Kaminsky ; foreword by Mark Bittman ; other contributors include Craig Claiborne, Pierre Franey, Florence Fabricant, Steven Raichlen, Molly O'Neill, Julia Moskin, and many more. Sterling Epicure 2014 400 p. illustrations (some color) $24.95 **641.5**

1. Cookbooks 2. Barbecue cooking 3. Barbecuing

ISBN 1402793243; 9781402793240

LC 2013026602

Edited by Peter Kaminsky, this book shows how "Over the past 100 years, the 'New York Times' has published thousands of articles on barbecuing and grilling, along with mouthwatering recipes--and this unique collection gathers the very best. These essential pieces are worth savoring not only for their time-tested advice and instruction, but also for the quality of the storytelling: even non-cooks will find them a delight to read." (Publisher's note)

"A fascinating look at how various innovators, personalities, and cultural trends have shaped the evolution of grilling and barbecue." LJ

Includes bibliographical references and index

Estrine, Darryl

Harvest to heat; cooking with America's best chefs, farmers, and artisans. [by] Darryl Estrine and Kelly Kochendorfer; foreword by Alice Waters. Taunton Press 2010 295p il $40 **641.5**

1. Cooking

ISBN 978-1-60085-254-1

LC 2010-11943

"The authors match farmers and artisans with chefs and restaurants across the country to present 100 original recipes from, e.g., Eric Ripert (Le Bernardin, New York), Paul Kahan (Blackbird, Chicago), and Vitaly Paley (Paley's Place, Portland, OR), for the home cook, for starters and salads, main courses, sides, and desserts. . . . Each recipe is accompanied by a description of the farmer or artisan who provided the main ingredients. Sustainable food is in, and this book will encourage home cooks to follow the tenets of the movement." Libr J

Fairchild, Barbara

The **Bon** appetit cookbook. Wiley 2006 xxiv, 792p il $34.95 **641.5**

1. Cooking

ISBN 0-7645-9686-1; 978-0-7645-9686-5

LC 2005-5181

"Mirroring the magazine on which it is based, this collection of 1,200 recipes is accessible, applicable to most home cooks' lives and a pleasure to cook from." Publ Wkly

The **Bon** appetit fast easy fresh cookbook. J. Wiley 2008 xxix, 770p il $34.95 **641.5**

1. Cooking

ISBN 978-0-470-22630-8

LC 2007-44562

This cookbook "presents hundreds of quick and simple recipes from the magazine's popular 'Fast Easy Fresh' feature. An introductory 'Shopping Guide' covers buying and storing produce, meat, and fish, and dozens of sidebars and boxes provide more information on ingredients and techniques. . . . Sure to appeal to any busy cook as well as the magazine's numerous fans, this is highly recommended." Libr J

Farris, Efisio

Sweet myrtle & bitter honey; the Mediterranean flavors of Sardinia. [by] Efisio Farris with Jim Eber; food photography by Laurie Smith; location photography by Rohan Van Twest. Rizzoli 2007 272p il map **641.5**

    1. Italian cooking

    ISBN 9780847829927; 0847829928

                    LC 2007-925274

Fearnley-Whittingstall, Hugh

The **River** Cottage cookbook; photography by Simon Wheeler. Ten Speed Press 2008 447p il $35 **641.5**

    1. English cooking 2. Cooking -- Natural foods

    ISBN 978-1-58008-909-8; 1-58008-909-7

                    LC 2007-43795

First published 2001 in the United Kingdom

"The author writes with passion and humor, and his unusual book will be useful as both a reference and a cookbook." Libr J

Includes bibliographical references

River Cottage every day; photography by Simon Wheeler. Ten Speed Press 2011 415p il $32.50 **641.5**

    1. British cooking 2. Cooking -- Natural foods

    ISBN 978-1-60774-098-8

                    LC 2010-46949

First published 2009 in the United Kingdom

"An advocate of a back-to-basics approach to cooking and sustainable agriculture, . . . [the author] delivers thoughtful insight and colorful narratives that celebrate the joy of good family food, which will inspire and compel readers into the kitchen, book in hand. Simple ingredients become brilliant when combined in fresh and easy recipes like Baked Breakfast Cheesecake, Curried Fish Pie, breads, boxed lunches, and frittatas." Libr J

River Cottage Veg; 200 Inspired Vegetable Recipes. Hugh Fearnley-Whittingstall. Random House Inc. 2013 416 p. (hardcover) $35 **641.5**

    1. Cookbooks 2. Vegetarian cooking

    ISBN 1607744724; 9781607744726

This book, by Hugh Fearnley-Whittingstall, offers "a comprehensive collection of 200+ recipes that embrace vegetarian cuisine as the centerpiece of a meal. . . . In this . . . illustrated cookbook, you'll find handy weeknight one-pot meals, pure and simple raw dishes, and hearty salads as well as a chapter of meze and tapas dishes to mix and match." (Publisher's note)

Fertig, Judith

The **back** in the swing cookbook; recipes for eating and living well every day after breast cancer. Barbara C. Unell and Judith Fertig ; foreword by Rachel S. Beller ; photography by Sara Remington.

Andrews McMeel Pub., LLC 2012 261 p. col. ill. $29.99 **641.5**

    1. Cookbooks 2. Breast cancer

    ISBN 1449418325; 9781449418328

                    LC 2011944354

IACP Cookbook Award (2013)

This cookbook, by Barbara C. Unell and Judith Fertig, "is . . . full of 150 feel-good recipes that are easy to prepare, with fresh ingredients specifically designed to help breast cancer survivors get back in the swing of joyful, healthy living. . . . In addition to . . . food and drinks, . . . [it] include[s] . . . friendly nuggets on topics ranging from genetics, lifestyle choices, and the environment to the influence of all three on living a full and happy life." (Publisher's note)

Flinn, Kathleen

The **kitchen** counter cooking school; how a few simple lessons transformed nine culinary novices into fearless home cooks. Viking Adult 2011 285p il $26.95 **641.5**

    1. Cooking -- Study and teaching

    ISBN 978-0-670-02300-4

                    LC 2011016222

"A successful, ambitious graduate of Paris' Le Cordon Bleu culinary academy, Flinn scrutinized average American supermarket shoppers and concluded that far too many rely on prepackaged, processed foods. Pressing them about their food choices, she learned that these timid souls simply believed that they lacked the time and certainly the ability to regularly prepare meals for their families from fresh, seasonal ingredients. Flinn eventually recruited nine motivated volunteers who spent time with her to learn how to plan meals confidently, shop effectively, cook thoughtfully, and serve attractively. She taught them such basic techniques as braising as well as simple but important recipes such as roasted chicken. . . . Flinn winningly offers inspiration to anyone who cares about cooking but lacks basic tools and skills." Booklist

Includes bibliographical references

Foose, Martha Hall

★ **Screen** doors and sweet tea; recipes and tales from a Southern cook. Clarkson Potter/Publishers 2008 248p il $32.50 **641.5**

    1. Southern cooking

    ISBN 978-0-307-35140-1; 0-307-35140-8

                    LC 2007031646

Foung, Jessica Goldman

Sodium girls limitless low-salt cookbook; Jessica Goldman ; photography by Matt Armendariz. Wiley 2012 256 p. (pbk.) $24.99 **641.5**

    1. Cookbooks 2. Food -- Sodium content 3. Salt-free diet -- Recipes

    ISBN 1118123778; 9781118123775

                    LC 2011040042

This is a cookbook by blogger Jessica Goldman Foung, who documents her experiences with living a low-sodium lifestyle on her blog Sodium Girl. Here, "she shares . . . recipes (some new, some from her blog, and some from celebrity chefs) and useful advice, such as how to cut salt from your favorite recipes, including buffalo wings and Bloody Marys.

Also provided is information on handling diet-challenging situations and environments (e.g., restaurant outings, trips abroad, college dining halls)." (Library Journal)

Friedman, Andrew

Knives at dawn; the American quest for culinary glory at the legendary Bocuse d'Or competition. Free Press 2009 304p $26   **641.5**
   1. Cooking -- Competitions
   ISBN 978-1-4391-5307-9

            LC 2009-35271

"A vibrant portrait of the world's most significant cooking competition, the Bocuse d'Or, in Lyon, France. . . . [The author] dynamically illustrates the colorful personalities, ego-battering conflicts, career-defining aspirations, politicking, precision planning, naked missteps and the final judges' decisions regarding the 2009 U.S. team's shot for the culinary gold medal. . . . The book is infused with the muscular, meticulous gusto of a sportswriter covering the Olympics. Edge-of-your-seat food writing of the highest caliber." Kirkus

   Includes bibliographical references

Fuentes, Laura

The **best** homemade kids' lunches on the planet; make lunches your kids will love with over 200 deliciously nutritious lunchbox ideas. Laura Fuentes. Fair Winds Press 2014 240 p. color illustrations $24.99   **641.5**
   1. Cookbooks 2. School children -- Food 3. Lunchbox cooking
   ISBN 1592336086; 9781592336081

            LC 2013049151

This cookbook dedicated to school child lunches, written by Laura Fuentes, "[f]ull of recipes to suit every age and stage, . . . shows you how simple and easy it is to prepare food that'll be the envy of the lunch table. . . . There are even entire lunchbox meals that are gluten-, soy-, and/or nut-free." (Publisher's note)

Gand, Gale

Gale Gand's brunch! Clarkson Potter/Publishers 2009 208p il $27.50   **641.5**
   1. Cooking
   ISBN 978-0-307-40698-9

            LC 2008-36988

Gand "starts with an enticing assortment of drinks (e.g., white hot chocolate and a three-alarm Bloody Mary), then a chapter on brunch's eggy foundations—omelets, stratas, frittatas, quiches and crêpes, each with appetizing variations—that will please any brunch crowd. In subsequent chapters, Gand hits the sweet and savory high points, from pancakes and doughnuts to onion tarts and cheddar grits. . . . Accessible instructions, basic preparation tips and make-ahead hints ensure that both beginners and those who think cooking brunch is too bothersome will find this volume to be inspiring." Publ Wkly

Garten, Ina

Barefoot Contessa at home; everyday recipes you'll make over and over again. photographs by Quentin Bacon. Clarkson Potter 2006 p. cm. **641.5**
   1. Menus. 2. Cooking
   ISBN 1400054346

            LC 2006014257

Barefoot Contessa family style; easy ideas and recipes that make everyone feel like family. photographs by Maura McEvoy; food styling by Rori Trovato. Potter 2002 240p il $35   **641.5**
   1. Cooking
   ISBN 0-609-61066-X

            LC 2002-74979

This is "simple, elegant home cooking with good ingredients and a minimum of fuss. It takes a certain amount of chutzpah to include ordinary chicken noodle soup and mashed potatoes and gravy in a cookbook, but Garten pulls it off with heart and style." Publ Wkly

Barefoot Contessa, how easy is that? Ina Garten. 1st ed.; Clarkson Potter 2010 p. cm. $35   **641.5**
   1. Cooking 2. Barefoot Contessa (East Hampton, N.Y.: Store)
   ISBN 978-0-307-23876-4

            LC 2010-2025

Barefoot in Paris; easy French food you really can make at home \ Ina Garden ; photographs by Quentin Bacon ; Food Stuyleing by Rori Trovato ; Prop Styling by Miguel Flores-Vianna. Clarkson Potter\Publishers 2004 p. cm   **641.5**
   1. Cooking
   ISBN 1-400-04935-0 (hardcover)

Gentry, Ann

The **Real** Food Daily cookbook; really fresh, really good, really vegetarian. [by] Ann Gentry with Anthony Head. Ten Speed Press 2005 232p $24.95   **641.5**
   1. Vegetarian cooking
   ISBN 1-58008-618-7

            LC 2005-16245

The author presents "what she has learned about seasonal, organic, macrobiotic and vegan cooking. Gentry doesn't break new ground—sandwiches made with tempeh instead of meat, and nut cheeses like cashew cheddar will be familiar to most vegans—but she provides clear and comprehensive directions on how to make them more interesting and flavorful. . . . Gentry explains the basics without preaching or condescending to readers, and discusses nutritional benefits without unnecessary jargon." Publ Wkly

Gerson, Fany

My sweet Mexico; recipes for authentic breads, pastries, candies, beverages, and frozen treats. Ten Speed Press 2010 215p il $30   **641.5**
   1. Desserts 2. Mexican cooking
   ISBN 978-1-58008-994-4

            LC 2010-14469

The author "has dutifully catalogued the confections of her native Mexico. . . . American readers who have only encountered the occasional tres leches cake in a Mexican restaurant will be stunned by the breadth and depth of recipes here, ranging from coffee-flavored corn cookies to guava caramel pecan rolls and hibiscus ice pops, all culled from Gerson's family, friends, and generous strangers. . . . Gerson's vivid descriptions, exacting instruction, and obvious passion for her subject matter make this volume a substantial read about the most tempting indulgences." Publ Wkly

Includes bibliographical references

Goin, Suzanne

The **A.O.C.** cookbook; by Suzanne Goin. Alfred A. Knopf 2013 448 p. (alkaline paper) $35   **641.5**
1. American cooking 2. Wine and wine making 3. Appetizers 4. Cooking, American 5. A.O.C. (Restaurant) 6. Food and wine pairing
ISBN 030795823X; 9780307958235

LC 2013005068

In this book, author Suzanne Goin "brings readers recipes from A.O.C., her restaurant known for its relaxed atmosphere and small dishes, meant to be shared. Goin shares personal anecdotes and explains how she chooses ingredients. The book opens with sections on cheese and charcuterie. Chapters on salads, fish, meat, vegetables, and desserts are organized by season." (Publisher's note)

Includes bibliographical references and index

★ **Sunday** suppers at Lucques; [by] Suzanne Goin with Teri Gelber; photographs by Shimon and Tammar. Knopf 2005 398p il $35   **641.5**
1. French cooking
ISBN 1-4000-4215-1

LC 2004-58604

The author "writes with passion and humor, and while her recipes are sophisticated and sometimes complicated, they are written with the home cook in mind." Libr J

Good housekeeping (Periodical)

★ The **Good** Housekeeping cookbook; 1,275 recipes from America's favorite test kitchen. edited by Susan Westmoreland. 125th anniversary ed.; Hearst Books 2010 752p il $35   **641.5**
1. Cooking
ISBN 978-1-58816-813-9

LC 2010-18437

Provides over 1,200 traditional and contemporary American recipes and offers information on cooking techniques, tools, ingredients, food handling, nutrition, canning, freezing, and holiday celebrations.

"Quick recipes and simple dessert preparations, like Fire-Roasted Nectarines and Coffee Granita, will please anyone pressed for time, but the encyclopedic inclusion of recipes for everything from Egg Salad, Lobster Bisque, and Chocolate Souffle to Pad Thai, Salmon with Mustard-Dill Sauce, and Muffuletta is its true benefit, making it a cookbook readers will grow with." Publ Wkly

Goodall, Tiffany

The **ultimate** student cookbook; from chicken to chili. photography by Claire Peters. Firefly Books 2010 160p il pa $14.95   **641.5**
1. Cooking 2. Quick and easy cooking
ISBN 978-1-55407-602-4

The author "outlines basic kitchen equipment, pantry ingredients, and food hygiene. Writing for the student with no cooking experience, she offers step-by-step photos that will make cooking a breeze. Goodall discusses basics like how to cook noodles, rice, and potatoes and presents dishes like wraps, salads, soups, chili, pizza, kebabs, and cakes. Two alcoholic drinks are included. Highly recommended for the numerous photographs and the variety of recipes." Libr J

The gourmet cookbook; more than 1000 recipes. edited by Ruth Reichl. Houghton Mifflin 2004 1040p $40   **641.5**
1. Cooking
ISBN 0-618-37408-6

LC 2004-47873

Recipes culled from issues of Gourmet magazine include "concoctions like Coq au Vin, Beef Wellington, Coulibiac, Chop Suey, Bananas Foster, and Black Forest Cake. . . . Every chapter begins with an overview of its subject; each recipe has an introduction; and many dishes feature helpful 'cook's notes,' which give tips for food preparation, technique and storage." Publ Wkly

Gourmet today; more than 1000 all-new recipes for the contemporary kitchen. edited by Ruth Reichl. Houghton Mifflin Harcourt 2009 1008p il $40   **641.5**
1. Cooking
ISBN 978-0-618-61018-1

LC 2009-19781

The editor "offers a diverse range of recipes that reflect the ever-changing American palate and the many cultures that have influenced it. Alongside Stilton cheese puff are recipes for babaghanouj, bangers and mash, Armenian lamb pizza, arepas with black beans and feta, and Vietnamese fried spring rolls. Informative sidebars provide details on a huge array of topics, from what salt to use when to preserving fish. . . . Comprehensive, appetizing and thoroughly tested, this mammoth collection is the book no kitchen should be without." Publ Wkly

Greenspan, Dorie

Around my French table; more than 300 recipes from my home to yours. photographs by Alan Richardson. Houghton Mifflin Harcourt 2010 530p il $40   **641.5**
1. French cooking
ISBN 978-0-618-87553-5; 0-618-87553-0

LC 2010-14232

"A part-time Paris resident for more than a decade, Greenspan focuses on what French people really eat at home: easy-to-prepare yet flavorful dishes that are suitable for just about any time of day. From Bacon and Eggs and Asparagus Salad to Chicken in a Pot to Veal Chops with Rosemary Butter, her offerings are hardy, mostly uncomplicated, and superbly appetizing. She also provides sidebars on a wide range of topics, including whether or not to wash raw chicken, several ways of cooking beets, mussels, and more." Publ Wkly

The **grilling** book; the definitive guide from Bon Appetit. edited by Adam Rapoport ; photography by Peden + Munk. Andrews McMeel Pub., LLC 2013 432 p. color illustrations $45   **641.5**
1. Cookbooks 2. Barbecue cooking
ISBN 1449427529; 9781449427528
LC 2012952341
This cookbook, edited by Adam Rapoport, focuses on grilling. "Offering more than 350 foolproof recipes, dozens of luscious full-color photographs, crystal clear illustrations, and plenty of plainspoken, here's-how-to-do-it guidelines, [it] welcomes you to everything that is sensational (and sensationally simple) about grilling." (Publisher's note)

Gur, Janna
The **book** of New Israeli food; a culinary journey. photography, Eilon Paz; contributing writers Rami Hann . . . [et al.] Schocken Books 2008 303p il $35   **641.5**
1. Israeli cooking
ISBN 978-0-8052-1224-2; 0-8052-1224-8
First published 2007 in Israel
"Beautiful and comprehensive, this book will become an immediate favorite with anyone with even a passing interest in Israeli cuisine." Publ Wkly

Hair, Jaden
The **steamy** kitchen cookbook; 101 Asian recipes simple enough for tonight's dinner. photography by Jaden Hair. Tuttle Pub. 2009 160p il $27.95 **641.5**
1. Asian cooking
ISBN 978-0-8048-4028-6
LC 2009-17461
The author, a food blogger, "shares recipes drawn from her mother's kitchen, other food bloggers, and her own delightful archives. Her focus is mostly simple Asian dishes (from China, Vietnam, Japan, and Thailand), with several more complicated ones thrown into the mix. . . . For home cooks of all levels of experience seeking to expand their repertoire of Asian recipes, Hair has written an extremely accessible cookbook that blends great recipes with mouthwatering photographs she took." Libr J

Hazan, Marcella
Marcella says . . . Italian cooking wisdom from the legendary teacher's master classes, with more than 120 of her irresistible new recipes. HarperCollins Publishers 2004 390p il $29.95   **641.5**
1. Italian cooking
ISBN 0-06-620967-6
LC 2004-42892
The author shares lessons in Italian cooking, discussing techniques, ingredients and planning and preparing Italian dishes

Henry, Diana
A **Change** of Appetite; where healthy meets delicious. Diana Henry. Octopus Pub Group 2014 336 p. color illustrations $34.99   **641.5**
1. Cookbooks 2. Asian cooking 3. Middle Eastern cooking
ISBN 1845338928; 9781845338923
LC 2014412876
"What happened when one of today's best-loved food writers had a change of appetite? Here are the dishes that Diana Henry created when she started to crave a different kind of diet--less meat and heavy food, more vegetable-, fish-, and grain-based dishes--often inspired by the food of the Middle East and Far East, but also drawing on cuisines from Georgia to Scandinavia." (Publisher's note)
"Broken down by season, the book offers a nice mix of food from around the world that will not take a toll on the digestive system." Pub Wkly
Includes bibliographical references (page 328-329) and index

Pure simple cooking; effortless meals everyday. photography by Jonathan Lovekin. Ten Speed Press 2009 192p il pa $21.95   **641.5**
1. Quick and easy cooking
ISBN 978-1-58008-948-7; 1-58008-948-8
LC 2008-35099
First published 2007 in the United Kingdom
This "collection of 150 recipes focuses on simple weeknight dishes, most of which can be prepared in under an hour and with only a handful of ingredients. Strong emphasis is placed on seasonal produce, with vegetable and fruit chapters broken down into 'spring and summer' or 'autumn and winter' categories. . . . Endless variations for savory sauces, poultry stuffing, roasted potatoes and even whipped cream pepper the text, and many of the recipes contain footnotes offering simple substitutions. . . . One hundred sumptuous, full-color photographs serve as both illustration and inspiration." Publ Wkly

Roast figs, sugar snow; food to warm the soul. photographs by Jason Lowe. Mitchell Beazley 2009 191p il pa $19.99   **641.5**
1. Cooking
ISBN 978-1-84533-524-3
First published 2005 in the United Kingdom
This "is an appealing collection of winter dishes from the Northern Hemisphere (including northern Italy, France, Russia, Switzerland, and Vermont), certain to make cooks yearn for a long winter." Libr J

Hesser, Amanda
The **essential** New York Times cook book; classic recipes for a new century. W.W. Norton 2010 932p il $40   **641.5**
1. Cooking
ISBN 978-0-393-06103-1; 0-393-06103-5
LC 2010-33311
The author "spent six years combing the Times's vast recipe archive, cooking her way through more than 1000 recipes to assemble this indispensible tome culled from 150 years of the paper's food columns. This daunting compen-

dium features both noteworthy classics (Osso Buco) and modern recipes (Smoked Mashed Potatoes) that have been tested and, in some cases, updated for the contemporary cook. Chapters begin with a time line and are arranged by type of food (e.g., soups, vegetables, cakes) then chronologically within the chapter, making for a fascinating historic overview of the interests of American cooks." Libr J

Includes bibliographical references

Hirsheimer, Christopher

Canal house cooks every day; Melissa Hamilton, Christopher Hirsheimer. Andrews McMeel Pub., LLC 2012 359 p. col. ill. $45   **641.5**
1. Cooking 2. Cookbooks
ISBN 1449421474; 9781449421472

LC 2012936742

James Beard Foundation Award: General Cooking (2013)

This book, by Melissa Hamilton and Christopher Hirsheimer, was the 2013 James Beard Foundation Award winner for General Cooking. "The delicious, easy-to-prepare recipes celebrate the everyday practice of simple cooking and the enjoyment of eating. . . . In addition to the recipes, this wonderful cookbook includes menus for all the great holidays throughout the year, plus twelve intimate essays . . . that introduce each month and capture the feeling and vibe of that special time of the year." (Publisher's note)

Hyman, Gwen

Urban Italian; simple recipes and true stories from a life in food. [by] Andrew Carmellini, and Gwen Hyman; photographs by Quentin Bacon. Bloomsbury 2008 311p il $35   **641.5**
1. Italian cooking
ISBN 978-1-59691-470-4

The author "presents spectacular recipes while opening a window onto his life with food, from his Italian-American boyhood and cooking school to revelations while traveling in Italy and being a top New York chef. . . . The recipes, which come from all over Italy and mix regional Italian and American influences, are arranged classically, from antipasti to dolci." Publ Wkly

Iyer, Raghavan

660 curries; the gateway to the world of Indian cooking. by Raghavan Iyer. Workman Pub. 2008 809p il $32.50; pa $22.95   **641.5**
1. Cooking -- Curry
ISBN 978-0-7611-4855-5; 0-7611-4855-8; 978-0-7611-3787-0 pa; 0-7611-3787-4 pa

LC 2008-1288

"A wide-ranging guide to the curries of the Indian subcontinent, including Pakistan, Nepal, and Sri Lanka. Iyer explains that Indian curries are not based on a can of curry powder and that the term 'curry' refers to any dish simmered in or covered with a fragrant, spicy (though not necessarily hot) sauce or gravy. The hundreds of recipes include appetizer curries such as Skewered Chicken with Creamy Fenugreek Sauce, main-course curries like Yogurt-Marinated Lamb with Ginger and Garlic, and 'contemporary curries' such as Wild Salmon with Chiles, Scallions, and Tomato;

there are also recipes for 'curry cohorts'—rice, bread, and other accompaniments." Libr J

Jaffrey, Madhur

At home with Madhur Jaffrey; simple, delectable dishes from India, Pakistan, Bangladesh, and Sri Lanka. Alfred A. Knopf 2010 301p il $35; ebook $35   **641.5**
1. Asian cooking
ISBN 978-0-307-26824-2; 978-0-307-59440-2 ebook

LC 2010-19678

This is a "cookbook of easily prepared, thoughtful, and unusual dishes from India, Pakistan, Bangladesh, and Sri Lanka. Anyone looking to explore Indian cooking for the first time will find this volume uniquely helpful." Booklist

Madhur Jaffrey's world vegetarian. Potter 1999 760p $40; pa $24.95   **641.5**
1. Vegetarian cooking
ISBN 0-517-59632-6; 0-609-80923-7 pa

LC 98-30318

A compendium of vegetarian "recipes from all over the world. Grouped mostly into broad categories by main ingredient (beans, grain, vegetables, etc.), they are as likely to come from a Palestinian restaurant in Toronto, the nuns at the Ormylia Monastery in Macedonia, or a home cook in Mexico as from Jaffrey's own Indian background or her experience as a cooking teacher." Libr J

Jamison, Cheryl Alters

The big book of outdoor cooking and entertaining; spirited recipes and expert tips for barbecuing, charcoal and gas grilling, rotisserie roasting, smoking, deep-frying, and making merry. [by] Cheryl and Bill Jamison. Morrow 2006 548p $24.95   **641.5**
1. Entertaining 2. Barbecue cooking
ISBN 0-06-073784-0; 978-0-06-073784-9

LC 2006-41918

This book features "more than 850 recipes and information on every aspect of backyard cooking. There are dozens of 'Party-Time Tips' and other helpful hints, menu suggestions, and sidebars and boxes on techniques, ingredients, and more. . . . New grilling books appear as the season approaches every year, but this one is an essential purchase." Libr J

Jenkins, Nancy Harmon

The new Mediterranean diet cookbook; a delicious alternative for lifelong health. with a foreword by Marion Nestle. Bantam Books 2009 496p $26.95   **641.5**
1. Low-fat diet 2. Mediterranean cooking
ISBN 978-0-553-38509-0; 0-553-38509-7

LC 2008-40982

First published 1994 with title: The Mediterranean diet cookbook

Jenkins' "knowledge of these cuisines is both personal and informed. . . . An essential purchase." Libr J

Includes bibliographical references

Jones, Judith

The **pleasures** of cooking for one. Alfred A. Knopf 2009 273p il $27.95 **641.5**

1. Cooking

ISBN 978-0-307-27072-6

LC 2009-12307

Counsels readers on how to enjoy a solitary culinary life by preparing meals in accordance with one's own preferences, outlining a range of basic through sophisticated recipes that work in weekly menus and make use of leftovers.

This is a "civilized, unfussy guide to cooking—and cooking well—for solitary diners. . . . [The author] doesn't skip desserts, entertaining or self-indulgence, and best of all, her whole book benefits from the diverse and cumulative gleanings of work with many of the great cooks and cookbook writers (including Julia Child, of course) of the latter half of the 20th century." Publ Wkly

Includes bibliographical references

Joulwan, Melissa

Well fed; Paleo recipes for people who love to eat. by Melissa Joulwan ; foreword by Melissa and Dallas Hartwig ; photos by David Humphreys ; design by Kathleen Shannon. Greenleaf Book Group Llc 2012 160 p. ill. (chiefly col.) $29.95 **641.5**

1. Cookbooks 2. Paleo cooking 3. Reducing diets 4. High-protein diet -- Recipes 5. Prehistoric peoples -- Nutrition

ISBN 061557226X; 9780615572260

This paleo-diet cookbook, by Melissa Joulwan, "explains how to get in the habit of a Weekly Cookup so that you have ready-to-go food for snacks and meals every day. It will also show you how to make Hot Plates, a mix-and-match approach to combining basic ingredients with spices and seasonings. . . . The recipes are as simple as possible, without compromising taste." (Publisher's note)

Kamozawa, Aki

Ideas in food; great recipes and why they work. [by] Aki Kamozawa and H. Alexander Talbot. Clarkson Potter 2010 320p il $25 **641.5**

1. Cooking 2. Chemistry

ISBN 978-0-307-71740-5; 978-0-307-71974-4 ebook

LC 2010-17633

"The authors break down the science behind correctly and deliciously preparing everything from bread, pasta, and eggs (including soft scrambled eggs; hardboiled eggs, and brown butter hollandaise sauce) to homemade butter and yogurt. Most recipes fall into the 'Ideas for Everyone' category, which composes about the first three-quarters of the book; the final section is 'Ideas for Professionals,' which explores trendy molecular gastronomy topics like liquid nitrogen-used to make popcorn gelato-and carbon dioxide, a necessary tool for making coffee onion rings. Straightforward prose and anecdotes with personality keep this from being a dry food science tome. And accessible recipes for such dishes as a simple roast chicken, green beans almondine, and root beer-braised short ribs mean it never gets too lofty." Publ Wkly

Includes bibliographical references

Katz, Rebecca

The **cancer** -fighting kitchen; nourishing big-flavor recipes for cancer treatment and recovery. [by] Rebecca Katz with Mat Edelson. Celestial Arts 2009 222p il $32.50 **641.5**

1. Cooking for the sick 2. Cancer -- Diet therapy

ISBN 978-1-58761-344-9

LC 2009-14359

"Katz's experience with cancer patients and their long, often frustrating recovery lends authority to her wise, common-sense approach, suitable for cooks of all skill levels." Publ Wkly

Includes bibliographical references

Katzen, Mollie

Get cooking; 150 simple recipes to get you started in the kitchen. [by] Mollie Katzen, with photographs by the author. HarperStudio 2009 xx, 268p il pa $24.99 **641.5**

1. Cooking

ISBN 978-0-06-173243-0

LC 2009-32815

This book "offers an invaluable list of equipment and advice (you can never have too many cutting boards), plus an illustrated vegetable-chopping guide. The 150 recipes for such common dishes as chicken noodle soup, potato salad, and spaghetti and meatballs are a good starting place for beginners. The recipes note variations, complementary dishes, and vegan dishes. Highly recommended for new cooks." Libr J

The **heart** of the plate; vegetarian recipes for a new generation. Mollie Katzen ; photographs and illustrations by Mollie Katzen. Houghton Mifflin Harcourt 2013 464 p. $34.99 **641.5**

1. Cookbooks 2. Vegetarian cooking 3. International cooking 4. Cooking (Natural foods)

ISBN 0547571593; 9780547571591

LC 2013010180

This cookbook by Mollie Katzen promotes vegetables, focusing "on their natural flavors rather than rich accompaniments such as butter, cream, and cheese." The recipes "combine everyday vegetables in appetizing ways." Chapters on soups, salads, grains, burgers, pasta, and desserts are included. (Publishers Weekly)

Keller, Thomas

★ **Ad** Hoc at home. Artisan Books 2009 359p il $50 **641.5**

1. Cooking

ISBN 978-1-57965-377-4

LC 2009-13258

For this cookbook, the author focuses on "family-style meals for the home cook in this accessible and dazzlingly beautiful book based on the fare served at his Ad Hoc restaurant, in Napa, Calif. . . . [He provides] a thorough primer on the foundations of cooking, offering clear and easy-to-follow instructions on techniques such as butchering and trussing chickens and tying a pork loin. . . . Dishes such as braised beef short ribs, buttermilk fried chicken, and fig-stuffed roast pork loin highlight a vast array of offerings that range from crab cakes to shortbread cookies." Publ Wkly

Kennedy, Diana

From my Mexican kitchen; techniques and ingredients. photographs by Michael Calderwood; and styled by the author. Clarkson Potter 2003 320p il $40   **641.5**

1. Mexican cooking
ISBN 0-609-60700-6

LC 2002-70405

The author "explains how to produce authentic enchiladas, tacos, tamales, sopes, panuchos, and other Mexican classics. Kennedy also provides a guide to wild greens, items rarely seen outside provincial markets. Her advice on freezing excess quantities of cuitlacoche (corn fungus) will reward fans of that uncommon mushroom. This is an indispensable addition to any library cookbook collection." Booklist

Kiros, Tessa

Food from many Greek kitchens. Andrews McMeel Pub. 2011 333p il $35   **641.5**

1. Greek cooking
ISBN 978-1-4494-0652-3

LC 2010943021

First published 2010 in Australia

"For each recipe, [the author] gives the title in English and Greek and offers an introduction to the dish and thorough instruction. From Baklava to Keftedes Fried Meatballs to Pita Bread, the accessible dishes are accompanied by beautiful photography. Greek cookbooks written for the beginner are rare, so this book is a gem. It provides a good foundation and is sure to be a gateway to more advanced Greek cooking." Lirb J

Ko, Genevieve

Home cooking with Jean-Georges; [by] Jean-Georges Vongerichten with Genevieve Ko. Clarkson Potter/Publishers 2011 256p il $40   **641.5**

1. Cooking
ISBN 978-0-307-71795-5; 0-307-71795-X

LC 2010-53808

"After working 18-hour days six days a week, Vongerichten buys a weekend country home and rediscovers the joys of unfussy cooking. He shares recipes for the meals he and his family enjoy in this pleasingly accessible volume. Chicken liver and pancetta crostini, swiss chard braised in shiitake butter, shortbread are among the recipes that cover salads, fish and seafood, meat, desserts, and brunch. All focus on flavor yet rely on a minimal number of ingredients that don't take a lot of time and effort to prepare. . . . Dotted with culinary reminiscences both personal and professional, this book shows Vongerichten at his simple best and offers his many fans the opportunity to cook and enjoy his favorite meals without being chained to the kitchen for hours." Publ Wkly

Lagasse, Emeril

From Emeril's kitchens; favorite recipes from Emeril's restaurants. William Morrow/HarperCollins 2003 342p il $27.50   **641.5**

1. Cooking
ISBN 978-0-06-018535-0; 0-06-01853-5

LC 2002-27568

"Spreading his philosophy and history in the introduction, [Emeril] entreats the user not to be put off by the complexity of many of the recipes, but to use the components and mix and match the dishes. The first chapter, 'Basics,' contains the building blocks of many of the dishes, ranging from the customary stocks to Hard Boiled Eggs and Roast Duck. Subsequent chapters are structured in the usual manner ranging from appetizers and first courses through desserts. Each dish is attributed to its restaurant or chef and results in a range of styles and inspirations." Publ Wkly

Lang, Adam Perry

Serious barbecue; smoke, char, baste, and brush your way to great outdoor cooking. [by] Adam Perry Lang, with J.J. Goode and Amy Vogler. Hyperion Books 2009 390p il $35   **641.5**

1. Barbecue cooking
ISBN 978-1-4013-2306-6

LC 2009-1765

The author's "definition of barbecue includes grilling as well as 'low and slow cooking,' and he presents a wide variety of tasty recipes here, along with a detailed introduction to barbecue basics and many useful sidebars on techniques and other tips. Highly recommended for all collections." Libr J

Lawson, Nigella

Nigella express; good food, fast. photographs by Lis Parsons. Hyperion 2007 390p il $35   **641.5**

1. Cooking
ISBN 978-1-4013-2243-4; 1-4013-2243-3

"Recipes in this book run the gamut from retro crepe suzettes to modern favorites like quesadillas and smoothies; and from orange French toast for breakfast to cocktail nibbles for a party. In the interest of speed Lawson uses prepared ingredients, but they're the ones many of us use already, like mayonnaise from a jar or frozen puff pastry. And if her tastes are sometimes nostalgically British (Eton mess, roly poly pudding) she also has a whole chapter on quick Tex-Mex food." WeightWatchers.com

Lee, Cecilia Hae-Jin

Quick and easy Korean cooking; more than 70 everyday recipes. photographs by Julie Toy and Cecilia Hae-Jin Lee. Chronicle Books 2009 168p il pa $22.95   **641.5**

1. Korean cooking
ISBN 978-0-8118-6146-5

LC 2008-33629

"Quality, accessible, authentic Korean cookbooks are hard to come by. Ably filling that gap is [this book]. . . . It's filled with more than 70 recipes, most of which only call for about six ingredients. If you're skeptical that such simple recipes can produce the flavor bombs that are Korean dishes, know that three recipes were tested, and all worked perfectly as written. Each one was lively with the flavors of garlic, chiles, soy sauce, and sesame." Village Voice

Lee, Matthew

★ The **Lee** Bros. southern cookbook; stories and recipes for southerners and would-be southerners. [by] Matt Lee and Ted Lee; color photography by Gentl & Hyers. W.W. Norton 2006 589p il $35 **641.5**

1. Southern cooking

ISBN 978-0-393-05781-2; 0-393-05781-X

LC 2006-22745

This "cookbook begins with a collection of drink recipes, from sweet tea to potent planters' punch. To accompany these beverages, the Lee brothers array a long series of snack and party foods. A section on preserves and pickles documents some rarely seen regional treats, such as Jerusalem artichoke relish. Meats, seafood, sweets, and breads round out the book. Every recipe has a story attached, and the large format makes for easy reading." Booklist

Leite, David

The **new** Portuguese table; exciting flavors from Europe's western coast. photographs by Nuno Correia. Clarkson Potter 2009 256p il $32.50 **641.5**

1. Portuguese cooking

ISBN 978-0-307-39441-5; 0-307-39441-7

LC 2008-51283

The author "begins by outlining Portugal's diverse regional cuisines and then describes traditional ingredients. From there it is a straightforward listing of appetizers, soups, fish, meat, poultry, vegetable/egg/rice dishes, breads, sweets, liqueurs, and condiments, with approximately 150 recipes overall. . . . Full of delicious-sounding recipes, this title is sure to appeal to adventurous cooks wanting to try a new ethnic cuisine and will also be popular with Portuguese American communities." Libr J

Lewis, Edna

★ The **taste** of country cooking; [with a foreword by Alice Waters] 30th anniversary ed.; Knopf 2006 xxi, 268p il $22.95 **641.5**

1. Southern cooking

ISBN 0-307-26560-9; 978-0-307-26560-9

First published 1976

"Recipes are categorized by the four seasons and are ones . . . [the author] grew up with in a small Virginia farming community (personal reminiscences about her family life appear throughout the text)." Booklist

Liddon, Angela

The **oh** she glows cookbook; over 100 vegan recipes to glow from the inside out. Angela Liddon. Avery 2014 313 p. color illustrations (pbk.) $25 **641.5**

1. Veganism 2. Cookbooks 3. Vegetarian cooking 4. Vegan cooking

ISBN 1583335277; 9781583335277

LC 2013037135

This cookbook, by Angela Liddon, presents collected recipes taken from the author's "blog, ohsheglows.com, to spread the word about her journey to health and the powerful transformation that food can make. . . . [This book] is packed with more than 100 delicious recipes such as go-to breakfasts, protein-packed snacks, hearty entrées, and decadent desserts." (Publisher's note)

"Liddon's authentic voice and candidly shared successes will motivate nonvegans to try healthy recipes." LJ

Lim, Allen

The **feed** zone cookbook; fast and flavorful food for athletes. Biju Thomas & Allen Lim. Velo Press 2011 xi, 315 p.p col. ill. (hardcover : alk. paper) $24.95 **641.5**

1. Cookbooks 2. Athletes -- Nutrition 3. Snack foods

ISBN 1934030767; 9781934030769

LC 2011028918

In this athlete-centered cookbook, by Biju Thomas and Allen Lim, "provides 150 delicious recipes that even the busiest athletes can prepare in less time than it takes to warm up for a workout. . . . [The book] strikes the perfect balance between science and practice so that athletes will change the way they think about food, replacing highly processed food substitutes with real, nourishing foods that will satisfy every athlete's cravings." (Publisher's note)

Feed zone portables; a cookbook of on-the-go food for athletes. Biju Thomas & Allen Lim. VeloPress 2013 xv, 271 p.p color illustrations (hardback) $24.95 **641.5**

1. Cookbooks 2. Athletes -- Nutrition 3. Snack foods

ISBN 1937715000; 9781937715007

LC 2013003073

In this cookbook, author "[Allen] Lim joined professional chef Biju Thomas to make eating delicious and practical. . . . Their groundbreaking 'Feed Zone Cookbook' brought the favorite recipes of the pros to everyday athletes. In [this,] their new cookbook . . . , Chef Biju and Dr. Lim offer 75 all-new portable food recipes for cyclists, runners, triathletes, mountain bikers, climbers, hikers, and backpackers." (Publisher's note)

Link, Donald

Real Cajun; rustic home cooking from Donald Link's Louisiana. [by] Donald Link with Paula Disbrowe; photographs by Chris Granger. Clarkson Potter Publishers 2009 255p il $35 **641.5**

1. Cooking -- Louisiana

ISBN 978-0-307-39581-8; 0-307-39581-2

LC 2008-36989

"Link shares the fare he ate growing up on the bayou, as well as what he cooks for family, friends and funerals. Some recipes are aspirationally insane—fried chicken and andouille gumbo, or 'game day' choucroute with sausage, tasso and duck confit—while others I simply aspire to make, like a fried oyster and bacon sandwich (bacon recipe included), and Link's outstanding boudin, which he also uses as a heart-stopping beignet filling. The tone is easygoing, the explanations clear." N Y Times Book Rev

Lukins, Sheila

The **Silver** Palate cookbook; Julee Rosso & Sheila Lukins with Michael McLaughlin ; photographs by Patrick Tregenza and Susan Goldman ; illustrations by Sheila Lukins. Workman Pub Co 2007 xi, 452 p.p col. ill. (pbk) $22.95 **641.5**

1. Cookbooks 2. American cooking 3. Cooking

ISBN 9780761145981; 9780761145974; 0761145974

LC 2007276244

James Beard Cookbook Hall of Fame (1992)

IACP Culinary Classics Book Award (2014)

This cookbook, by Julee Rosso & Sheila Lukins, is a 25th anniversary edition that "brings a new passion for food and entertaining into American homes. Its 350 . . . dishes make every occasion special, and its recipes, featuring vibrant, pure ingredients, are a pleasure to cook. Brimming with kitchen wisdom, cooking tips, information about domestic and imported ingredients, menus, quotes, and lore, this . . . book feels as fresh and exciting as the day it was first published." (Publisher's note)

Madison, Deborah

The **new** vegetarian cooking for everyone; Deborah Madison. Ten Speed Press 2014 665 p. $40 **641.5**

1. Cookbooks 2. Vegetarian cooking
ISBN 1607745534; 9781607745532

LC 2013046540

Originally published: New York : Broadway Books, 1997

This cookbook, by Deborah Madison, "originally published in 1997, . . . has endured as one of the world's most popular vegetarian cookbooks, winning both a James Beard Foundation award and the IACP Julia Child Cookbook of the Year Award. Now, . . . [this edition] picks up where that culinary legacy left off, . . . including a new introduction, more than 200 new recipes, and comprehensive, updated information on vegetarian and vegan ingredients." (Publisher's note)

★ **Vegetarian** cooking for everyone; 10th anniversary ed; Broadway Books 2007 742p il $40 **641.5**

1. Vegetarian cooking
ISBN 978-0-7679-2747-5; 0-7679-2747-8

LC 2007-10075

First published 1997

Following information on ingredients and techniques, the recipes focus "mainly on vegetables and grains, aiming at flavor and variety, both often arrived at via assorted ethnic approaches." Publ Wkly

Vegetarian suppers from Deborah Madison's kitchen; Deborah Madison. Broadway Books 2005 228 p. ill. (pbk) $19.99 **641.5**

1. Cookbooks 2. Vegetarian cooking 3. Suppers
ISBN 076792472X; 9780767916271; 9780767924726

LC 2004045899

This vegetarian cookbook, by Deborah Madison, "solves the perennial question of what to cook for dinner in her first collection of suppertime solutions, with more than 100 inspiring recipes to enjoy every night of the week. . . . For vegetarians and health-conscious nonvegetarians, the quest for recipes that don't call for meat often can seem daunting." (Publisher's note)

"[O]ffers everything from quickie suppers to subtle, sophisticated dinner-party dishes while encouraging local, seasonal eating and unfussy kitchen artisanship. . . . Madison's recipes do call for good kitchen gear (Dutch ovens, double-boilers, numerous gratin pans and casseroles) and some hard-to-find ingredients (fromage blanc, blanched nettles, Thai basil), but they're flexible enough to allow for substitutions." Pub Wkly

Mallmann, Francis

Seven fires; grilling the Argentine way. [by] Francis Mallmann, with Peter Kaminsky. Artisan 2009 278p il $35 **641.5**

1. Outdoor cooking 2. Barbecue cooking 3. Argentine cooking
ISBN 978-1-57965-354-5

LC 2008-37367

"Mallmann cooks with the elegant purity achieved only after attaining a mastery of complicated food. . . . He also reconnects us to the primal simplicity and visceral pleasure of cooking over a fire—though his recipes can be made over charcoal or in a grill pan, too." N Y Times Book Rev

Marks, Gil

The **world** of Jewish cooking; more than 500 traditional recipes from Alsace to Yemen. Simon & Schuster 1996 406p il hardcover o.p. pa $17 **641.5**

1. Jewish cooking
ISBN 0-684-83559-2 pa

LC 96-2848

This cookbook is "loosely arranged by food category, with chapters on appetizers, soups, and main dishes, as well as side items, breads, and desserts. . . . You'll find recipes from India, Africa, even China, here, alongside many dishes that originated in one of the two major Jewish cultural communities, Ashkenazic and Sephardic." Booklist

Massaad, Barbara Abdeni

Man'oushé; inside the Lebanese street corner bakery. Barbara Abdeni Massaad ; photography by Barbara Abdeni Massaad and Raymond Yazbeck. Interlink Books, An imprint of Interlink Publishing Group, Inc. 2014 200 p. color illustrations $30 **641.5**

1. Cookbooks 2. Lebanese cooking 3. Cooking, Lebanese
ISBN 1566569281; 9781566569286

LC 2013032109

This cookbook, by Barbara Abdeni Massaad, "is dedicated entirely to the art of creating the perfect man'oushé. With over 70 simple recipes, it offers you a way to enjoy these typical [Lebanese] pies traditionally baked in street corner bakeries in the comfort of your own home." (Publisher's note)

"A reasonably adept home baker will find Massaad's recipes easy to follow. . . . The book's full-color photographs bring into focus not just the foods but also the lively characters who constitute a remarkably diverse nation." Booklist

McGee, Harold

Keys to good cooking; a guide to making the best of foods and recipes. Harold McGee. Penguin Books 2012 552 p. $20 **641.5**

1. Cooking 2. Food -- Composition
ISBN 0143122312; 9780143122319

LC 2010017303

This reference book, by Harold McGee, "is a concise and authoritative guide designed to help home cooks navigate the ever-expanding universe of ingredients, recipes, food safety, and appliances, and arrive at the promised land of a satisfying dish. . . . [The book] distills the modern scientific understanding of cooking and translates it into immediately useful information." (Publisher's note)

Includes bibliographical references and index

Moosewood Restaurant cooks at home; fast and easy recipes for any day. the Moosewood Collective. Simon & Schuster 1994 416 p. ill. $25 **641.5**
1. Cookbooks 2. Vegetarian cooking 3. Cooking -- Natural foods 4. Moosewood Restaurant 5. Cooking (Natural foods)
ISBN 0671679929; 0671879545; 9780671679927
LC 93039126
James Beard Award (1995)
Written by the Moosewood Collective, this book features "over 150 carefully honed and tested recipes calling for the best ingredients, accompanied by time-saving tips and planning suggestions, add up to a delicious whole-foods cuisine that is versatile and healthful and can be prepared with a minimum of effort." (Publisher's note)

Moosewood restaurant favorites; the 250 most-requested, naturally delicious recipes from one of America's best-loved restaurants. The Moosewood Collective. St. Martin's Press 2013 416 p. ill. (chiefly col.) (hardback) $29.99 **641.5**
1. Veganism 2. Vegetarian cooking 3. Cooking -- Vegetables 4. Cooking -- Natural foods 5. Moosewood Restaurant
ISBN 1250006252; 9781250006257
LC 2013013841
This book focuses on "Moosewood Restaurant, founded in 1973. . . . [It] contains 250 of their most requested recipes completely updated and revised to reflect the way they're cooked now--increasingly vegan and gluten-free, benefitting from fresh herbs, new varieties of vegetables, and the wholesome goodness of newly-rediscovered grains." (Publisher's note)
"This collection of some of Moosewood's cooks' and customers' most admired recipes has something for just about everyone." Booklist

Morris, Julie
Superfood Kitchen; Cooking with Nature's Most Amazing Foods. Sterling Pub Co Inc 2012 256 p. **641.5**
1. Cookbooks 2. Nutrition 3. Cooking -- Natural foods
ISBN 145490352X; 9781454903529
This cookbook, by Julie Morris, presents "dishes . . . entirely composed of plant-based, nutrient-dense, and whole foods that energize, nourish, and taste delicious. Each recipe . . . combines natural ingredients that deliver . . . antioxidants, essential fatty acids (like omega-3), minerals, vitamins, and more. The . . . superfood meals--from Goldenberry Pancakes to Quinoa Spaghetti with Cashew Cream Sauce and Chard-- will make you feel as good as they taste." (Publisher's note)

Moskowitz, Isa Chandra
Vegan pie in the sky; 75 out-of-this-world recipes for pies, tarts, cobblers & more. [by] Isa Chandra

Moskowitz & Terry Hope Romero. Da Capo Lifelong 2011 223p il pa $17 **641.5**
1. Pies 2. Vegetarian cooking
ISBN 978-0-7382-1274-6
The authors focus on "dessert in this collection of 75 egg, dairy and animal-free pies, cheesecakes, cobblers and tarts. . . . The duo deserves plaudits for their user-friendly approach as well as their ability to keep scarcer ingredients to a minimum. Bakers who fear they won't be able to recreate these will be happy to discover that once they've mastered a crust or two they'll be able to whip together a Strawberry Field Hand Pie, Chocolate Mousse Tart, or even a Coconut Cream with confidence." Publ Wkly

Nathan, Joan
Jewish cooking in America; expanded ed; Knopf 1998 518p il $35 **641.5**
1. Jewish cooking
ISBN 0-375-40276-4
LC 98-27952
First published 1994
This companion volume to the PBS television series contains nearly 300 recipes. It "is also a history of the Jewish people through their food. Nathan introduces both people and food in a preface that discusses dietary laws, Jewish holidays, Jewish immigration to the U.S., and the impact of Jews—and their food—on American culture. With every recipe comes an original story or a reprint of an article or a personal vignette that intrigues and/or edifies." Booklist
Includes bibliographical references

Quiches, kugels, and couscous; my search for Jewish cooking in France. Alfred A. Knopf 2010 387p il $39.95; ebook $40 **641.5**
1. French cooking 2. Jewish cooking 3. Jews -- France
ISBN 978-0-307-26759-7; 978-0-307-59450-1 ebook
LC 2010-20280
"Nathan's multi-layered, narrative approach makes this treasury of tempting flavors an entertaining and compelling read." Publ Wkly
Includes bibliographical references

Natkin, Michael
Herbivoracious; a flavor revolution with 150 vibrant and original vegetarian recipes. Michael Natkin. Harvard Common Press 2012 367 p. **641.5**
1. Cookbooks 2. Nutrition 3. Vegetarian cooking
ISBN 1558327452; 9781558327450
LC 2011030819
This vegetarian cookbook "offers up 150 . . . recipes. . . . A third of the book is taken up with hearty main courses, ranging from a robust Caribbean Lentil-Stuffed Flatbread across the Atlantic to a comforting Sicilian Spaghetti with Pan-Roasted Cauliflower and around the Cape of Good Hope to a delectable Sichuan Dry-Fried Green Beans and Tofu. An abundance of soups, salads, sauces and condiments, sides, appetizers and small plates, desserts, and breakfasts round out the recipes. [Michael] Natkin . . . provides lots of advice on how to craft vegetarian meals that amply deliver protein and other nutrients, and the . . . menus he presents deliver balanced and complementary flavors. . . . The many dozens

of vegan and gluten-free recipes are clearly noted." (Publisher's note)

Neely, Pat

Down home with the Neelys; a Southern family cookbook. [by] Patrick Neely and Gina Neely; with Paula Disbrowe. Alfred A. Knopf 2009 278p il $27.95   **641.5**

1. Barbecue cooking 2. Southern cooking
ISBN 978-0-307-26994-2; 0-307-26994-9
LC 2008-54393

This cookbook written by "husband-and-wife television personalities with their own Tennessee chain of barbecue joints . . . [is] full of 120 recipes that pull back the curtain on their award-winning seasonings, sauce, and fixings. Emphasizing their personal story and family recipes, this cookbook is brimming with down-home personality . . . and dishes that are 'simple, stylish, and not too fussy.'" Publ Wkly

New American Heart Association cookbook

The new American Heart Association cookbook; 8th ed.; Clarkson Potter 2010 xxi, 696p il $35 **641.5**

1. Cooking 2. Low-cholesterol diet 3. Heart diseases
-- Diet therapy
ISBN 978-0-307-40757-3
LC 2009-44692

First published 1973 with title: American Heart Association cookbook

"Each recipe comes with a breakdown of calories, protein content, carbohydrates, cholesterol, fats (broken down by saturated, polyunsaturated and monounsaturated) and sodium content, along with a table of dietary exchange. . . . This book remains a basic in many heart-conscious kitchens." Publ Wkly

The New York Times Jewish cookbook; more than 825 traditional and contemporary recipes from around the world. edited by Linda Amster; introduction by Mimi Sheraton. St. Martin's Press 2003 xxvi, 614p $35   **641.5**

1. Jewish cooking
ISBN 978-0-312-29093-1; 0-312-29093-4
LC 2002-68358

"Included here are hundreds of recipes from Jewish communities all over the world, reflecting Mimi Sheraton's introductory comment that Jewish food is 'the world's oldest fusion cuisine.' Recipes range from Persian Chicken Soup with Chickpea Dumplings to Alain Ducasse's Rib-Eye Steaks with Peppered Cranberry Marmalade to Fresh Corn and Red Pepper Blini. All the classics are here, too, and there's a separate chapter on 'Trimmings,' including an array of condiments and garnishes. . . . This is an essential purchase." Libr J

The New York Times Passover cookbook; more than 200 holiday recipes from top chefs and writers. edited by Linda Amster. Morrow 1999 xxii, 328p il $25   **641.5**

1. Passover 2. Jewish cooking
ISBN 0-688-15590-1
LC 98-41282

This book's recipes "range from the traditional to the innovative and are drawn from European, Mediterranean and Middle Eastern traditions. . . . Amster has produced what may be the definitive word in Passover cookbooks, from recipes to the feelings evoked by sitting at a beautifully set, bountifully laden table." Publ Wkly

Includes bibliographical references (p. 314-315) and index

Newgent, Jackie

The all -natural diabetes cookbook; the whole food approach to great taste and healthy eating. American Diabetes Association 2007 337p il pa $18.95   **641.5**

1. Cooking -- Natural foods 2. Diabetes -- Diet therapy
ISBN 978-1-58040-275-0
LC 2007-11961

The author presents a "cookbook designed to provide diabetes-friendly recipes that emphasize fresh and organically grown produce. . . . A wide variety of food styles are presented, ranging from Southern Black-Eyed Pea Salad to Vietnamese-Style Beef and Soba Noodle Soup. Even desserts are here, with such enticing options as Fudgy Brownies and New Fashioned Oatmeal Cookies. Highly recommended for all cooking collections." Libr J

O'Neill, Molly

One big table; a portrait of American cooking 600 recipes from the nation's best home cooks, farmers, fishermen, pit-masters, and chefs. Simon & Schuster 2010 864p il $50; ebook $37.99   **641.5**

1. Cooking
ISBN 978-0-7432-3270-8; 978-1-4516-0977-6 ebook
LC 2010-28841

"This collection celebrates the nation's culinary diversity, both ethnically and agriculturally, and offers a uniquely intimate look at what home cooking in America is truly like today. O'Neill crossed the country, interviewing home cooks and spending time in the kitchens of recent immigrants. The results are enticing recipes that intertwine family stories, personal histories, and food. From stuffed Danish pancakes in Utah to tamales in Santa Fe and Vietnamese shrimp pancakes in Mississippi, this eclectic collection showcases the best this country has to offer." Publ Wkly

Oliver, Jamie, 1975-

Cook with Jamie; my guide to making you a better cook. photography: David Loftus and Chris Terry. Hyperion 2007 447p il $37.50   **641.5**

1. Cooking
ISBN 978-1-4013-2233-5; 1-4013-2233-6

"Aiming to educate readers on cooking basics, Oliver offers more than 175 recipes, which emphasize flavor and freshness over labor-intensive preparation. With a conversational style that favors general guidelines over strict instructions—recipes often call for a 'knob of butter,' a 'handful of shelled peas' or 'a big handful of freshly grated Parmesan'—Oliver's friendly and enthusiastic approach handily deflates new-cook anxiety. Loaded with photos that cover common skills like cleaning and preparing fresh lobster, discerning degrees of doneness in meat and crafting homemade pasta, Oliver's patient explanations leave little room for confusion.

His dishes, many of which are updated versions of classics, are impressive and accessible." Publ Wkly

Ortega, Simone

1080 recipes; [by] Simone and Ines Ortega; illustrations, Javier Mariscal. Phaidon 2007 975p il $39.95   **641.5**

1. Spanish cooking

ISBN 978-0-7148-4836-5; 0-7148-4836-0

First published 1977 in Spain

"Something like the Joy of Cooking for the Spanish home cook, . . . [this book] includes recipes for both traditional regional fare and dishes inspired by a variety of other cuisines. . . . An essential purchase." Libr J

Ottolenghi, Yotam

★ **Jerusalem**; a cookbook. Yotam Ottolenghi, Sami Tamimi. Ten Speed Press 2012 318 p. (hardcover) $35.00   **641.5**

1. Cookbooks 2. Jewish cooking 3. Israeli cooking 4. Cooking, Middle Eastern 5. Jerusalem -- Description and travel

ISBN 1607743949; 9781607743958; 9781607743941

LC 2012017560

James Beard Foundation Award: International (2013).

This is a cookbook of recipes from Jerusalem. "London chefs and business partners [Yotam] Ottolenghi and [Sami] Tamimi both grew up in Jerusalem (the former in the Jewish west, the latter in the Arab east). Drawing on their childhood experiences for inspiration, they've updated traditional recipes (e.g., Falafel, Tabbouleh, Lamb Shawarma) to suit the lifestyles and preferences of modern home cooks." (Library Journal)

Ottolenghi; the cookbook. Yotam Ottolenghi and Sami Tamimi. Ebury 2008 288 p. col. ill. (hardcover) $35   **641.5**

1. Cookbooks 2. Mediterranean cooking 3. Cooking 4. Ottolenghi (Restaurant)

ISBN 9781607744184; 160774418X

LC 2014397522

This cookbook, by Yotam Ottolenghi and Sami Tamimi, "features 140 recipes culled from the popular Ottolenghi restaurants and inspired by the diverse culinary traditions of the Mediterranean. . . . The recipes reflect the authors' upbringings in Jerusalem yet also incorporate culinary traditions from California, Italy, and North Africa, among others." (Publisher's note)

"This vibrant and bold collection lives up to the authors promise that 'cooking can be enjoyable, simple, and fulfilling, yet look and taste amazing.'" Pub WKly

Page, Karen

The **flavor** bible; the essential guide to culinary creativity, based on the wisdom of America's most imaginative chefs. [by] Karen Page and Andrew Dornenburg; photographs by Barry Salzman. Little, Brown and Company 2008 380p il $35   **641.5**

1. Cooking

ISBN 978-0-316-11840-8; 0-316-11840-0

LC 2007-33064

"The authors first discuss the four basic tastes and the roles played by weather, the season of the year, and other environmental factors in cooking. The rest of the book is an extensive alphabetic guide to different culinary ingredients. . . . . Rather than just another collection of recipes, this is a unique resource that both beginning cooks and serious chefs will find wonderfully inspiring and immensely useful." Libr J

Pascal, Cybele

The **whole** foods allergy cookbook; two hundred gourmet & homestyle recipes for the food allergic family. Vital Health Pub. 2006 213p pa $18.95   **641.5**

1. Cooking 2. Diet therapy 3. Food allergy

ISBN 1-890612-45-6; 978-1-890612-45-0

LC 2005-931263

"Each and every dish offered is free of dairy, eggs, wheat, soy, peanuts, tree nuts, fish, and shellfish. . . . [The book includes] recipes for breakfast pancakes, breads, and cereals; lunch soups, salads, spreads, and sandwiches; dinner entrées and side dishes; dessert puddings, cupcakes, cookies, cakes, and pies; and even after-school snacks ranging from trail mix to pizza and pretzels. Included is a resource guide to organizations that can supply information and support, as well as a shopping guide for hard-to-find items." Publisher's note

Includes bibliographical references

Pepin, Jacques

The **apprentice** : my life in the kitchen. Houghton Mifflin 2003 318p il $26   **641.5**

1. Cooks 2. Cooking 3. Television personalities 4. Cookbook writers

ISBN 0-618-19737-0

LC 2002-192158

"Pépin relates how his interest in food and culinary techniques developed into passions for cooking and teaching. He does this deftly, neatly capturing personalities and events with clear, concise writing." Libr J

Essential Pepin; more than 700 all-time favorites from my life in food. Houghton Mifflin Harcourt 2011 685p il $40   **641.5**

1. French cooking

ISBN 978-0-547-23279-9

LC 2011-16057

Pepin "offers more than 700 of his best French and French-accented dishes from decades of cooking and teaching. They're simple without being dumbed down; approachable yet still adventurous. Whether he's explaining how to make Escoffier quenelles with mushroom sauce; black sea bass gravlax; chicken livers sautéed with vinegar; duck cassoulet; artichoke hearts with tarragon and mushrooms; or tarte tatin, he makes it seem doable and shares tidbits of wisdom to boost confidence and kitchen knowledge. His head notes are brief but informative, warm but not cloying. Pepin's own line drawings accompany the recipes, and they are, appropriately, at once homey and sophisticated. A DVD teaching a variety of cooking techniques accompanies the book, promising to make even the more challenging recipes less intimidating. For serious cooks and beginners alike, this is an instant classic." Publ Wkly

Jacques Pepin celebrates; by Jacques Pépin with Claudine Pépin; photographs by Christopher Hirsheimer; illustrations by Jacques Pépin. Knopf 2001 458p il $40   **641.5**
1. Cooking 2. Entertaining
ISBN 0-375-41209-3
LC 2001-29929

"In this companion to a new PBS series, Pépin builds on a broad definition of celebrations—encompassing holidays, special occasions, and simply nice weather—to present a collection of typically solid French recipes and numerous useful tips and techniques. . . . More valuable than the recipes . . . are the many notes on chopping, garnishing, carving and so forth." Publ Wkly

Perelman, Deb
★ The **smitten** kitchen cookbook; Deb Perelman. Alfred A. Knopf 2012 p. cm.   **641.5**
1. Cooking 2. Kitchens 3. Cookbooks
ISBN 9780307595652
LC 2012007711

This book is a cookbook by "Deb Perelman of Smitten Kitchen--home cook, photographer, and celebrated food blogger." The book is "all about approachable, uncompromised home cooking. Here you'll find better uses for your favorite vegetables: asparagus blanketing a pizza; ratatouille dressing up a sandwich; cauliflower masquerading as pesto. . . . Deb tells you her favorite summer cocktail; how to lose your fear of cooking for a crowd; and the essential items you need for your own kitchen." (Publisher's note)

Peterson, James
Cooking. Ten Speed Press 2007 534p il $40   **641.5**
1. Cooking
ISBN 978-1-580-08789-6; 1-580-08789-2
LC 2007-21065

This book "opens with a fairly brief description of ten basic cooking techniques and then moves on to Recipes To Learn By, organized by course or main ingredient. Many of the recipes are traditional French standbys, from Celeriac Rémoulade to Beef à la Mode, although there are dishes inspired by Thai, Mexican, and other cuisines as well. . . . Essentially an intensive course for home cooks in the classic techniques that underlie good cooking, this is recommended for all cookery collections." Libr J

Glorious French food; a fresh approach to the classics. Wiley 2002 xxv, 742p il map $45 **641.5**
1. French cooking
ISBN 0-471-44276-3
LC 2001-46972

The author presents "50 classic recipes as the starting point for his wide-ranging exploration of French food and techniques; each recipe serves both to demonstrate a variety of techniques and as the inspiration for a diverse collection of other recipes related to it in one way or another. . . . Each chapter includes boxes and charts on improvising with different ingredients and flavors. The suggested variations for individual recipes, often mini-essays in themselves, open up dozens of other possibilities. Peterson is both passionate and knowledgeable about his subject, and his . . . book is an essential purchase." Libr J

Includes bibliographical references

Kitchen simple; essential recipes for everyday cooking. Ten Speed Press 2011 244p il $30 **641.5**
1. Cooking
ISBN 978-1-58008-318-8
LC 2011-04435

"With a solid background in culinary instruction, Peterson easily articulates the basics of cooking and baking the selected recipes for even the most adventurous cook. This diverse assortment of 200 recipes strikes a perfect balance between fundamental and more advanced dishes, making it a useful source for cooks at every level of expertise. The straightforward language and full-color photographs, taken by Peterson himself, combine to create an accessible, well-organized guide to cooking for any occasion." Shelf Awareness

Pollan, Michael
★ **Cooked**; a natural history of transformation. Michael Pollan. Penguin Press 2013 480 p. **641.5**
1. Food industry -- United States 2. Cooks 3. Cooking
ISBN 9781594204210
LC 2012039705

It was author Michael Pollan's intent to demonstrate that "taking back control of cooking may be the single most important step anyone can take to help make the American food system healthier and more sustainable. Reclaiming cooking as an act of enjoyment and self-reliance, learning to perform the magic of these everyday transformations, opens the door to a more nourishing life." (Publisher's note)

Includes bibliographical references

Poses, Steven
The **Frog** Commissary cookbook; by Steven Poses, Anne Clark, and Becky Roller ; illustrated by Becky Roller. Camino Books 2002 272p pa $19.95   **641.5**
1. Cooking
ISBN 978-0-940159-73-0; 0-940159-73-2
LC 2001-43691

"Lighthearted, full of ideas. . . . Could inject new life into your dining and entertaining style." Bon Appetit

The **professional** chef; the Culinary Institute of America. 8th ed; Wiley 2006 1215p il map $70   **641.5**
1. Cooking 2. Restaurants
ISBN 978-0-7645-5734-7; 0-7645-5734-3
LC 2004-27110

First published 1962

"The nation's most prestigious training school for food careerists concentrates the essence of its course work within a comprehensive volume that competent students must master. Every aspect of the restaurant business is addressed, from nutrition and portion sizing to fiscal and human resource management. Sections on equipment, from major appliances to handheld tools, show the bond between chef and technology. Chapters on world cooking identify the most typical cooking processes and give examples of commonly appearing ingredients in each style. Recipes record classic preparations that form the foundation for myriad elaborations and personalization to move cooking from mere technique to high art. Although beyond the need of most home cooks, this massive tome is a necessary reference-collection purchase for any library whose community includes food-service-training programs." Booklist

Psilakis, Michael

How to roast a lamb; new Greek classic cooking. [by] Michael Psilakis with Brigit Binns & Ellen Shapiro; foreword by Barbara Kafka; photography, Christopher Hirsheimer & Melissa Hamilton. Little, Brown and Company 2009 288p il $35 **641.5**
1. Greek cooking 2. Mediterranean cooking
ISBN 978-0-316-04121-8
LC 2008-54932
This "cookbook is an emotional autobiography in narrative and recipe form. It's also an introduction to the marvels of Hellenic cuisine. Psilakis, beginning with childhood favorites, moves from simple home cooking to complex restaurant fare. The bulk of the dishes—precise and lavishly illustrated—are easy enough to replicate (although some of his Anthos creations require dozens of ingredients and could take all day to make)." Time Out N Y

Puck, Wolfgang

Live, love, eat! the best of Wolfgang Puck. Gramercy Books 2006 243p il $14.99 **641.5**
1. Cooking
ISBN 978-0-517-22868-5; 0-517-22868-8
LC 2006-41232
First published 2002 by Random House
This volume contains more than 125 recipes for appetizers, a variety of seasonal soups and salads, and, along with pasta and risotto recipes, the California-style pizzas that first made Puck and his original Spago Hollywood a favorite of international celebrities. Puck also serves up all manner of main courses, including seafood recipes, poultry dishes, and meat recipes. To round out the collection, he offers a variety of vegetable and other side-dish recipes, plus desserts. A section covering basics, sauces, and techniques provides guidance for beginning and experienced cooks alike. Illustrated throughout with more than 150 color images of finished dishes and closeup how-to shots demonstrating key techniques and tips.

Quessenberry, Sara

The good neighbor cookbook; 125 easy and delicious recipes to surprise and satisfy the new moms, new neighbors, recuperating friends, community-meeting members, book club cohorts, and block party pals in your life! [by] Sara Quessenberry and Suzanne Schlosberg. Andrews McMeel 2011 195p il pa $16.99 **641.5**
1. Cooking
ISBN 978-0-7407-9355-4
Provides 125 recipes for appetizers, soups, salads, entrées, and snacks suitable for a variety of gatherings, including block parties, potluck dinners, book clubs, and recuperating friends.

"This distinctive approach that highlights the communality of cooking is highly recommended." Libr J

Raichlen, Steven

★ The barbecue! bible; photography by Ben Fink. 10th anniversary edition; Workman Pub. 2008 556p il **641.5**
1. Barbecue cooking
ISBN 978-0-7611-4944-6; 978-0-7611-4943-9
First published 1998

Ramineni, Shubhra

Entice with spice; easy Indian recipes for busy people. photography by Masano Kawana; styling by Christina Ong and Magdalene Ong. Tuttle Pub. 2010 160p il map $27.95 **641.5**
1. Indic cooking
ISBN 978-0-8048-4029-3
LC 2009-49092
This is a "cookbook full of traditional Indian recipes adapted for busy American kitchens. Beginning with thorough explanations, from terminology to spice mixtures, she provides time-saving suggestions and tips for preparing ingredients. . . . This may be the Indian cookbook that American foodies have been waiting for." Publ Wkly

Ramsay, Gordon, 1966-

Gordon Ramsay's fast food; more than 100 delicious, super-fast, and easy recipes. by Gordon Ramsay. Sterling 2012 208 p. col. ill. $24.95 **641.5**
1. Cookbooks
ISBN 1402797877; 9781402797873
In this cookbook, celebrity chef Gordon Ramsay "serves up a feast of doable ideas: more than 100 recipes and 15 great menus for putting food on the table each and every day. Many of the dishes take only 15 minutes to prepare and cook; none takes longer than half an hour--and you can put together an entire meal in only 30-45 minutes. Ramsay also offers time-saving shortcuts, plus info on how to stock your pantry." (Publisher's note)

Recipes from an Italian summer; [translation by Mary Consoni; photographs by Joel Meyerowitz, Andy Sewell; illustrations by Jeffrey Fisher] Phaidon Press Limited 2010 431p il $39.95 **641.5**
1. Italian cooking
ISBN 978-0-714857732
This collection, "from the editors behind The Silver Spoon cookbook, is comprised of a glorious 400+ pages of recipes for picnics, barbecues, light suppers and summer entertaining (with the chapters thus organized, along with chapters on salads, desserts and ice cream/beverages). It's a compilation of dishes from popular Italian vacation regions. . . . The dishes are simple yet glorious in that Italian way (meaning without good ingredients first press olive oil, farmers market greens, real Parmigiano-Reggiano, there's little point in making many of the recipes)." L A Wkly

Ridge, Brent

The **Beekman** 1802 heirloom dessert cookbook; 100 delicious heritage recipes from the farm and garden. by Brent Ridge, Josh Kilmer-Purcell, and Sandy Gluck. Rodale Books 2013 272 p. (hardback) $32.50   **641.5**
1. Farm produce 2. American cooking 3. Farm life -- United States 4. Desserts 5. Cooking, American 6. Farm life -- New York (State) -- Upstate New York 7. Farm produce -- New York (State) -- Upstate New York
ISBN 1609615735; 9781609615734
LC 2013010502
This book, by Josh Kilmer-Purcell, Brent Ridge, and Sandy Gluck, " will show off the delicious and decadent recipes that the Beekman Boys have collected from across the generations of their family, from Brent's grandmother's Fourth of July Fruitcake to Josh's mother's Hot Chocolate Dumplings. Each recipe will be accompanied by a personal memory from the authors or a story about how that recipe came to be." (Publisher's note)

Robertson, Robin

Vegan planet; 400 irresistible recipes with fantastic flavors from home and around the world. Harvard Common Press 2003 576p hardcover o.p. pa $21.95   **641.5**
1. Vegetarian cooking
ISBN 1-55832-210-8; 1-55832-211-6 pa
LC 2002-7435
The author "offers dozens of imaginative vegan recipes inspired by a wide range of cuisines, from Five-Spiced Portobello Satays and Lebanese Fattoush (bread salad) to Cajun-Style Collards and Moroccan Fava Bean Stew." Libr J

Roden, Claudia

Arabesque : a taste of Morocco, Turkey, and Lebanon. Knopf 2006 341p il $35   **641.5**
1. Turkish cooking 2. Lebanese cooking 3. Moroccan cooking
ISBN 0-307-26498-X; 978-0-307-26498-5
LC 2006-45258
First published 2005 in the United Kingdom
The author "has chosen more than 150 recipes from Morocco, Turkey, and Lebanon, some newly discovered, some variations on more familiar dishes, and a selection of favorite classic dishes. Each section opens with a fascinating insider's guide, providing both cultural and culinary history as well as information on specific ingredients and techniques. . . . An essential purchase." Libr J

The **book** of Jewish food; an odyssey from Samarkand to New York. Claudia Roden. Knopf 1996 668 p. il $45   **641.5**
1. Cookbooks 2. Jewish cooking 3. Jewish civilization
ISBN 0394532589; 9780394532585
LC 96028758
James Beard Award (1997)
This cookbook, written by Claudia Roden, "traces the development of both Ashkenazic and Sephardic Jewish communities and their cuisine over the centuries. The 800 . . . recipes, many never before documented, represent treasures garnered by Roden through nearly 15 years of traveling around the world." (Publisher's note)
Includes bibliographical references and index

The **food** of Spain. Ecco Press 2011 $39.99 **641.5**
1. Spanish cooking
ISBN 978-0-06-196962-1

Rombauer, Irma von Starkloff

★ **Joy** of cooking; [by] Irma S. Rombauer, Marion Rombauer Becker, Ethan Becker; illustrated by John Norton. 75th anniversary ed.; Scribner 2006 1132p il $30   **641.5**
1. Cooking
ISBN 978-0-7432-4626-2; 0-7432-4626-8
LC 2006-51231
First published 1931
This is the "backbone for any library's cookery reference collection, its nearly 4,000 recipes defining essential American home cooking." Booklist

Rosenthal, Mitchell

Cooking my way back home; recipes from San Francisco's Town Hall, Anchor & Hope, and Salt House. Mitchell Rosenthal with Jon Pult, foreword by wolfgang Puck ; photography by Paige Green. Ten Speed Press 2011 vii, 263 p.p col. ill. (hbk.) $35   **641.5**
1. Cookbooks 2. American cooking 3. Southern cooking 4. Salt House (Restaurant) 5. Anchor & Hope (Restaurant) 6. Cooking, American -- Southern style 7. Cooking, American -- California style 8. Town Hall (Restaurant : San Francisco, Calif.)
ISBN 158008592X; 9781580085922
LC 2011011631
This cookbook, by Mitchell Rosenthal with Jon Pult, "blends Southern-inspired comfort food with urban sophistication and innovation, for exciting results. Reflecting on the classics (Shrimp Étouffée), updating regional specialties (Poutine), elevating family favorites (Chopped Liver), and reveling in no-holds-barred, all-out indulgences (Butterscotch Chocolate Pot de Crème) are what's on order in this collection of 100 . . . recipes." (Publisher's note)
Includes bibliographical references

Ruggiero, Tina

The **truly** healthy family cookbook; mega-nutritious meals that are inspired, delicious and fad free. by Tina Ruggiero. Page Street Publishing 2013 224 p. (pbk.) $22.99   **641.5**
1. Cookbooks 2. Nutrition
ISBN 1624140084; 1624140092; 9781624140082; 9781624140099
LC 2013933895
This book, by Tina Ruggiero, contains "recipes based on modern nutrition science. It takes a flexitarian approach that includes the best parts of the current health movements. Ruggiero offers up her best 120 mega-nutritious recipes . . . that focus on . . . tasty, fresh, real food ingredients, simple preparation and proven nutrition." (Publisher's note)

Ruhlman, Michael

Ratio; the simple codes behind the craft of everyday cooking. Scribner 2009 xxv, 224p il $27 **641.5**
1. Cooking
ISBN 978-1-416-56611-3; 1-416-56611-2

LC 2008-32679

"While Ruhlman was attending the Culinary Institute of America for a book project, a chef showed him a copy of the golden rules, which boiled down the elements of (French) cooking into ratios. . . . [In this volume] Ruhlman guides readers through the ratios for a variety of doughs, batters, stocks, sauces, custards and sausages, explaining their chemical and culinary basis in clear, earnest prose and providing tasteful recipes that lay out the technique for each formula." N Y Times Book Rev

Ruhlman's twenty; the ideas and techniques that will make you a better cook. Michael Ruhlman ; photographs by Donna Turner Ruhlman. Chronicle Books 2011 367 p. col. ill. (alk. paper) $40 **641.5**
1. Cooking 2. Cookbooks
ISBN 9780811876438

LC 2011036735

IACP Award (2012)
James Beard Award (2012)

This cookbook "distills [author Michael] Ruhlman's decades of cooking, writing, and working with the world's greatest chefs into twenty essential ideas from ingredients to processes to attitude that are guaranteed to make every cook more accomplished. Whether cooking a multi-course meal, the juiciest roast chicken, or just some really good scrambled eggs, Ruhlman reveals how a cook s success boils down to the same twenty concepts." (Publisher's note)

"Thorough, clearly explained, and stunningly beautiful, this collection will appeal to cooks of all levels." Pub Wkly

Includes bibliographical references and index

Saltsman, Amelia

The **Santa** Monica Farmers' Market Cookbook; seasonal foods, simple recipes, and stories from the market and farm. Amelia Saltsman ; foreword by Deborah Madison. Blenheim 2007 216 p. col. ill. $22.95 **641.5**
1. Markets 2. Cookbooks 3. Farm produce 4. Santa Monica (Calif.) 5. Cooking 6. Santa Monica Farmers' Market (Santa Monica, Calif.)
ISBN 0979042909; 9780979042904

LC 2007901323

This cookbook, by Amelia Saltsman, is "a celebration of the [Santa Monica Farmers' Market]. . . . What s the difference between white and green zucchini? What are amaranth, sapote, and ramps? With Amelia as your guide, you'll learn the answers to these questions and more. You'll also find advice on how to select and store produce, stories about farmers and their crops, chef and farmer cooking tips, and more than 100 of Amelia's simple, tempting recipes." (Publisher's note)

Includes bibliographical references (p. 205-206) and index

Samuelsson, Marcus

The **soul** of a new cuisine; a discovery of the foods and flavors of Africa. foreword by Desmond Tutu. Wiley 2006 xxii, 344p il map $40 **641.5**
1. African cooking
ISBN 0-7645-6911-2

For this African cookbook, the author "traveled to Africa and even took cooking lessons in Ethiopia, the country of his birth. Samuelsson emphasizes that this is not the definitive cookbook of an area with over 800 languages and dialects, but an overview of what he saw and ate in his travels. . . . This is a unique cookbook about a little-known cuisine, including travel essays and enhanced by beautiful color photographs that depict the food and the people of Africa. A necessary acquisition for international cookery collections." Libr J

Includes bibliographical references

Sanfilippo, Diane

Practical paleo; a customized approach to health and a whole-foods lifestyle. Diane Sanfillipo, with photography by Bill Staley. Victory Belt Pub. 2012 416 p. col. ill. $39.95 **641.5**
1. Cookbooks 2. Paleo cooking
ISBN 1936608758; 9781936608751

This Paleo cookbook, by Diane Sanfilippo, illustrated by Bill Staley, "explains why avoiding both processed foods and foods marketed as 'healthy'--like grains, legumes, and pasteurized dairy--will improve how you look and feel and lead to lasting weight loss. . . . [This book] is jam-packed with over 120 easy recipes, all with special notes about common food allergens including nightshades and FODMAPs. Meal plans are also included." (Publisher's note)

Shulman, Martha Rose

The **simple** art of vegetarian cooking; templates and lessons for making delicious meatless meals every day. Martha Rose Shulman. Rodale Books 2014 270 p. color illustrations (hardback) $32.50 **641.5**
1. Cookbooks 2. Vegetarian cooking 3. Quick and easy cooking
ISBN 162336129X; 9781623361297

LC 2013049184

"In 'The Simple Art of Vegetarian Cooking,' . . . Martha Rose Shulman offers a . . . method for creating delicious plant-based meals every day. . . . It teaches the reader how to cook basic dishes via templates--master recipes with simple guidelines for creating an essential dish, such as a frittata or an omelet, a stir-fry, a rice bowl, a pasta dish, a soup--and then how to swap in and out key ingredients as desired based on seasonality and freshness." (Publisher's note)

The **very** best of recipes for health; 250 recipes and more from the popular feature on NYTimes.com. Martha Rose Shulman. Rodale 2010 xvi, 352 p.p col. ill. (hardcover) $37.50 **641.5**
1. Cookbooks 2. Cooking -- Natural foods 3. Health 4. Nutrition 5. Cooking (Natural foods)
ISBN 9781605295732; 1605295736

LC 2010021608

This cookbook, by Martha Rose Shulman, "shows how to fill your refrigerator, freezer, and cabinets with healthy staples such as beans, grains, extra virgin olive oil, tuna, eggs, yogurt, and tomato sauce, so that you are prepared to cook delicious dishes like Asparagus and Herb Frittata, Quinoa Salad with Lime Ginger Dressing and Shrimp, or Pizza Marinara with Tuna and Capers in minutes." (Publisher's note)

Shulman, Martha Rose.

Mediterranean harvest; vegetarian recipes from the world's healthiest cuisine. Martha Rose Shulman. Rodale 2007 p. cm.   **641.5**
   1. Vegetarian cookery. 2. Cookery, Mediterranean.
ISBN 9781594862342 (hardcover); 1594862346 (hardcover)

                    LC 2007031561
Includes bibliographical references and index..

The silver spoon. Phaidon Press 2005 1263p il $39.95   **641.5**
   1. Italian cooking
ISBN 978-0-7148-4531-9; 0-7148-4531-0
Original Italian edition, 1950
"The book contains recipes for everything from basic sauces and marinades to salads, game, fish and baked goods, with each section color-coded for easy browsing. Recipes emphasize fresh ingredients and are to-the-point, typically summed up in a paragraph sans photo illustrations. Those who know their way around a kitchen will appreciate the brevity. . . . Almost all of the ingredients called for can be found in a typical supermarket. . . . Globe-trotting gourmands will appreciate the menu and 'signature dish' contributions by famous Italian chefs that round out the book. The most exhaustive Italian cookbook in recent memory, this volume offers something for every cook, regardless of their skill level, and deserves to be a fixture in American kitchens." Publ Wkly

Simonds, Nina

  ★ **Spices** of life; simple and delicious recipes for great health. Nina Simonds ; photographs by Tina Rupp. 1st ed.; Random House Inc 2005 383 p. col. ill. $24.95   **641.5**
   1. Cookbooks 2. Cooking -- Herbs 3. Quick and easy cooking 4. Spices
ISBN 0375411607; 9780375411601
                    LC 2004021089
James Beard Award (2006)
IACP Cookbook Award (2006)
In this cookbook, author and chef "Nina Simonds offers us more than 175 . . . recipes, along with practical tips for a sensible lifestyle, that demonstrate that health-giving foods not only provide pleasure but can make a huge difference in our lives. With her emphasis on the tonic properties of a wide variety of foods, herbs, and spices, this book also brings us up to date on the latest scientific research" (Publisher's note)
Simonds' book is "full of straightforward but practical recipes, and peppered with loads of health information." Pub Wkly
Includes bibliographical references (p. 362-364)

and index

Spieler, Marlena

Paris; authentic recipes celebrating the foods of the world. recipes and text Marlena Spieler; photographs Jean-Blaise Hall; general editor Chuck Williams. Oxmoor House 2004 191p il map (Williams-Sonoma foods of the world) $24.95   **641.5**
   1. French cooking
ISBN 978-0-8487-2854-8
Illustrated with full-color photographs. "Dozens of stories reveal the secrets of making long-cherished foods and profile people, places, and influences that have shaped the Parisian food scene. More than 45 recipes allow you to sample traditional dishes, such as Boeuf en Daube, Steak withe Shallot Sauce, or Raspberry Charlotte, as well as such innovations as Duck Breasts with Port and Figs or Strawberry Soup." Publisher's note

Splendid table (Radio program)

The **Splendid** table's how to eat supper; recipes, stories, and opinions from public radio's award-winning food show. [by] Lynne Rossetto Kasper and Sally Swift. Clarkson Potter/Publishers 2008 338p il $35   **641.5**
   1. Dining 2. Cooking
ISBN 978-0-307-34671-1
                    LC 2007-24749
"This superb book should grace the shelves of even the most infrequent of cooks." Publ Wkly

Spungen, Susan

Recipes; a collection for the modern cook. Susan Spungen ; foreword by Martha Stewart ; photographs by Maria Robledo. William Morrow 2005 272 p. col. ill. $34.95   **641.5**
   1. Cooking 2. Cookbooks
ISBN 0060731249; 9780060731243
                    LC 2005045710
IACP Cookbook Award Winner (2006)
In this cookbook, by Susan Spungen, the "founding food editor and editorial director for food at 'Martha Stewart Living Omnimedia' for twelve years presents her own easy, unfettered ideas for cooking simple food rich with freshness and flavors to share with family and friends." This cookbook is organized primarily by technique. (Publisher's note)

Stewart, Martha

Martha Stewart's cooking school; lessons and recipes for the home cook. by Martha Stewart with Sarah Carey; photographs by Marcus Nilsson; portraits by Ditte Isager. Clarkson Potter 2008 504p il $45   **641.5**
   1. Cooking 2. Entertaining
ISBN 978-0-307-39644-0; 0-307-39644-4
                    LC 2008-531117
This "cookbook is the result of what Stewart refers to as her 'mission to teach the methods of home cooking.' Chapters are organized by technique, from 'How To Make White Stock' to 'How To Make Pâte à Choux.' Master recipes are followed by others that build on them, and there are hun-

dreds of color photographs, including many step by steps for essential techniques. The illustrated 'Basics' section that opens the book covers equipment, knife skills, herbs and spices, 'the onion family,' and citrus fruits. Charts, buying guides, and sidebars are featured throughout, along with dozens of tips on ingredients, special techniques, and more." Libr J

Streiff, Fritz

The **art** of simple food; notes, lessons, and recipes from a delicious revolution. [by] Alice Waters, with Patricia Curtan, Kelsie Kerr & Fritz Streiff ; illustrations by Patricia Curtan. Clarkson Potter 2007 405p il $35   **641.5**
   1. Quick and easy cooking
   ISBN 978-0-307-33679-8; 0-307-33679-4
                       LC 2007-300393
"After a useful discussion of ingredients and equipment come chapters on techniques, such as making broth and soup. Each of these includes three or four recipes that rely on the technique described. . . . The final third of the book divides many more recipes traditionally into salads, pasta and so forth. Waters taps an almost endless supply of ideas for appealing and fresh yet low-stress dishes." Publ Wkly

Swanson, Heidi

Super natural every day; well-loved recipes from my natural foods kitchen. Heidi Swanson. Ten Speed Press 2011 p. cm. pa $23   **641.5**
   1. Cooking -- Natural foods
   ISBN 978-1-58008-277-8
                       LC 2010-43749
'A collection of 100 vegetarian recipes for nutritious, weekday-friendly dishes from the blogger behind 101 Cookbooks'--

Tanis, David

Heart of the artichoke and other kitchen journeys. Artisan 2010 344p il $35   **641.5**
   1. Menus 2. Cooking 3. Entertaining
   ISBN 978-1-57965-407-8
                       LC 2010-4538
The author "begins with 14 'Kitchen Rituals' (ordinary pleasures perfect for one or two people) such as Jalapeño Pancakes and raw artichokes for lunch. Menus are arranged by season and feature, e.g., Fork-Mashed Potatoes and Spring Lamb with Rosemary. There are also menus for a long table (for a large crowd) such as A Perfect Suckling Pig. Simple recipes, eloquent writing, and Tanis's great reputation make this an essential purchase." Libr J

A **platter** of figs and other recipes; foreword by Alice Waters; photographs by Christopher Hirsheimer. Artisan 2008 294p il $35   **641.5**
   1. Menus 2. Cooking 3. Entertaining
   ISBN 978-1-57965-346-0; 1-57965-346-4
                       LC 2007-49384
This volums is "both a meditation on the powerful rites of cooking and serving a meal and a gentle but serious education in doing both. . . . With 24 menus distributed over the course of a year, Tanis emphasizes seasonality with ingredients (blueberry-blackberry crumble in summer; celery root mashed potatoes in winter) and with the types of dishes provided for each menu (as with a divine, warming lobster risotto as part of a menu for a cold spring day). Anecdotes from his peripatetic life of enjoying good food around the world, from Venice to Morocco to New Mexico, add another intimate dimension and help the book appear written just for the reader by a kind, patient friend." Publ Wkly
   Includes bibliographical references

Tausend, Marilyn

Cocina de la familia; more than 200 authentic recipes from Mexican-American home kitchens. {by} Marilyn Tausend with Miguel Ravago. Simon & Schuster 1997 415p hardcover o.p. pa $20 **641.5**
   1. Mexican American cooking
   ISBN 0-684-85259-4 pa
                       LC 97-26979
This cookbook includes recipes for "Green Enchiladas with Spinach and Tofu, Chicken with Spicy Prune Sauce made with Coca-Cola, and Mexican Beef Chow Mein, {as well as} more traditional Mexican fare like Guacamole and Braised Chicken with Rice and Vegetables." Publ Wkly
   Includes bibliographical references

Terry, Bryant

Vegan Soul kitchen; fresh, healthy, and creative African American cuisine. Da Capo Press 2009 223p il pa $18.95   **641.5**
   1. Southern cooking 2. African American cooking
   ISBN 978-0-7382-1228-9; 0-7382-1228-8
                       LC 2008-46945
   Includes bibliographical references

Theroux, Jessica

Cooking with Italian grandmothers; recipes and stories from Tuscany to Sicily. introduction by Alice Waters. Welcome Books 2010 296p $25.99 **641.5**
   1. Italian cooking
   ISBN 978-1-59962-089-3
                       LC 2010-21657

Thomas, Anna

Love soup; 160 all-new vegetarian recipes from the author of The Vegetarian Epicure. illustrations by Annika Huett. W. W. Norton & Company 2009 528p il $35; pa $22.95   **641.5**
   1. Soups 2. Vegetarian cooking
   ISBN 978-0-393-06479-7; 978-0-393-33257-5 pa
                       LC 2009-19632
The author presents 160 "enticing recipes that may just charm even a die-hard carnivore. Soups are organized by season and range from hearty selections like rustic leek and potato, and minestrone for a crowd, to lighter summer options including tomato and fennel soup with blood orange and sweet corn. . . . Recipes for breads, dips and spreads, salads and a collection of desserts, as well as sample menus at the start of each chapter, make it easy to plan a full meal." Publ Wkly

Thompson, David

Thai food; with photography by Earl Carter. Ten Speed Press 2002 673p $40 **641.5**

1. Thai cooking

ISBN 978-1-580-08462-8; 1-580-08462-1

LC 2002-18117

"The first section of the book provides detailed cultural and social history and a guide to the regions and regional cuisines of Thailand. Then a detailed glossary of ingredients and a guide to techniques introduce the hundreds of recipes. These are grouped into chapters on relishes, soups, curries, salads, and sides, followed by one of menus with recipes. . . . [This] culinary history/cookbook is unique and will be an important purchase for any Asian cookery collection." Libr J

Includes bibliographical references

Tourles, Stephanie L.

Raw energy; 124 raw food recipes for energy bars, smoothies, and other snacks to supercharge your body. [by] Stephanie Tourles. Storey Pub. 2009 271p il pa $16.95 **641.5**

1. Snack foods 2. Vegetarian cooking 3. Cooking -- Natural foods

ISBN 978-1-60342-467-7

LC 2009-28675

"This delightful addition is easily accessible even to readers looking to make small changes in their diets. . . . [The author] shares a list of ingredients with pictures of each item. A list of kitchen equipment is also provided to accompany these recipes for shakes, bars, and soups, some of which require the use of a juicer or dehydrator. For libraries that don't have any books on the topic, this is an excellent introduction." Libr J

Includes bibliographical references

Trang, Corinne

Essentials of Asian cuisine; fundamentals and favorite recipes. black-and-white photographs by Corinne Trang; color photographs by Christopher Hirscheimer. Simon & Schuster 2003 592p il hardcover o.p. pa $34.99 **641.5**

1. Asian cooking

ISBN 0-7432-0312-7; 1-4391-9108-5 pa

LC 2002-30490

"Authoritative and thoroughly researched, this will be invaluable as both a reference and a cookbook." Libr J

Includes bibliographical references

Tsai, Ming

Blue Ginger; East-meets-West cooking with Ming Tsai. by Ming Tsai and Arthur Boehm. Potter 1999 275p $32.50 **641.5**

1. Cooking 2. Asian cooking

ISBN 0-609-60530-5

LC 99-36393

"Chapters divide the 125-plus recipes into soups, dim sum, rice and noodles, poultry, meat, seafood, elaborate side dishes and desserts, with mail-order sources. . . . Instructions are clearly written and often include tips for wine and food pairings and advice on ingredient substitutions and techniques." Publ Wkly

Ultimate curry bible

Madhur Jaffrey's ultimate curry bible; India, Singapore, Malaysia, Indonesia, Thailand, South Africa, Kenya, Great Britain, Trinidad, Guyana, Japan, USA. Ebury 2003 352p il $51.65 **641.5**

1. Cooking -- Curry

ISBN 978-0-09-187415-5; 0-09-187415-7

With over 150 recipes, "Madhur starts with the best curry recipes in India today, moves on to Asian curries, and even includes European curry ideas such as French curry sauces. Some recipes have never before appeared in print, such as fish seasoned with tamarind and coconut and lamb braised with oranges. Also included are Madhur's tips for the best accompanying foods — she gives us ideas for rice, bread, chutneys, relishes and sweets — the perfect complement for any curry." Publisher's note

Vetri, Marc

Il viaggio di Vetri; a culinary journey. [by] Marc Vetri with David Joachim; wine notes by Jeff Benjamin; photography by Douglas Takeshi Wolfe. Ten Speed Press 2008 289p il $40 **641.5**

1. Italian cooking

ISBN 978-1-58008-888-6; 1-58008-888-0

LC 2008-21667

"More than a cookbook, this . . . is a guide through the particular Italian cuisine and culture on which . . . [the author] has based his career. . . . Amateur chefs may have only dreamed of having a culinary journey like Vetri's, but with this book he has given them a reliable key to turning dream into reality." Publ Wkly

Waters, Alice

In the green kitchen; techniques to learn by heart. photographs by Hirsheimer & Hamilton. Clarkson Potter/Publishers 2010 151p il $28 **641.5**

1. Slow food movement 2. Vegetarian cooking 3. Cooking -- Natural foods

ISBN 978-0-307-33680-4; 0-307-33680-8

LC 2010-278664

The author "showcases basic cooking techniques every cook can and should master along with recipes using each method in this slim and attractive book. Derived from a Slow Food Nation event she helped organize, where notable chefs and foodies provided demonstrations on foundational procedures, Waters highlights a set of techniques that are universal to all cuisines. She covers the most basic of the basics, from stocking the pantry and washing lettuce to boiling pasta and wilting greens. . . . Ideal for the cooking novice, this gem of a book captures the expertise of world-class chefs in an accessible, straightforward manner." Publ Wkly

Weight Watchers 50th anniversary cookbook; 280 delicious recipes for every meal. St. Martin's Griffin 2013 335 p. $29.99 **641.5**

1. Cookbooks 2. Weight loss

ISBN 1250036402; 9781250036407

This cookbook of updated recipes "supplements the new Weight Watchers 360 program. Emphasizing retro comfort foods like chicken cordon bleu, cheddar corn pudding, and Boston cream pie, the book aims to dispel notions that diet food can't be crave-worthy. Each recipe includes nutritional analysis and a 'PointsPlus' value based on the amount of protein, carbohydrates, fat, and fiber per serving. Using the secondary index, readers can easily choose recipes by points value." (Library Journal)

Weil, Andrew

The **healthy** kitchen; recipes for a better body, life, and spirit. {by} Andrew Weil and Rosie Daley; photographs by Sang An, Amy Haskell, and Eric Studer. Knopf 2002 xxxvii, 325p il $24.95; pa $16.95   **641.5**
1. Cooking 2. Natural foods
ISBN 0-375-41306-5; 0-375-71031-0 pa
LC 2001-50391

This volume features "healthful recipes and information on topics ranging from growing herbs to wine to the Mediterranean diet. Recipes contain nutrition information, but this is not 'diet food': recipes include Smoked Fish with Horseradish Sauce, Roasted Cornish Hens with Roasted Garlic, and Thai Shrimp and Papaya Salad." Libr J

This is "a stimulating invitation to healthy, pleasurable eating." Publ Wkly

Weinstein, Bruce

Cooking know-how; be a better cook with hundreds of easy techniques, step-by-step photos, and ideas for over 500 great meals. [by] Bruce Weinstein & Mark Scarbrough; photography by Lucy Schaeffer. John Wiley 2009 406p il $34.95   **641.5**
1. Cooking
ISBN 978-0-470-18080-8
LC 2008-44375

"The recipes are structured without being fussy and the majority are relatively easy. This is a welcome rarity, imparting a useful, innovative framework as well as the confidence to depart from it." Publ Wkly

Wells, Patricia

Patricia Wells' trattoria; simple and robust fare inspired by the small family restaurants of Italy. William Morrow 2003 338p il pa $18.95   **641.5**
1. Italian cooking
ISBN 978-0-06-093652-5
First published 1993

This "collection of informal, robust recipes, gathered from Italy's small family-run restaurants, should appeal to anyone who appreciates the unmasked flavors of high-quality fresh ingredients, simply but lovingly prepared. Wells's often lengthy headnotes are full of personal reminiscences but also paint a colorful picture of the country's relaxed, generous lifestyle. Wine suggestions follow each recipe, and there are sensible cooking tips throughout." Libr J

The **Provence** cookbook; 175 recipes and a select guide to the markets, shops, & restaurants of France's sunny south. HarperCollins 2004 338p il $29.95   **641.5**
1. French cooking
ISBN 978-0-06-050782-4; 0-06-050782-9
LC 2003-56977

Wells offers "her own recipes, along with some from her butcher, fishmonger, other merchants, neighborhood restaurants, and other sources slightly farther afield. Most of the dishes are simple, allowing the flavors of Provence's wonderfully fresh produce and other ingredients to come through. . . . Wine suggestions are included throughout— sometimes for Wells's own label, since her vineyard is now productive—and she provides addresses and other relevant details about her favorite restaurants and purveyors." Libr J

Wolfert, Paula

The **slow** Mediterranean kitchen; recipes for the passionate cook. Wiley 2003 350p il $34.95 **641.5**
1. Mediterranean cooking
ISBN 0-471-26288-9
LC 2002-153265

The author offers "dishes from all the countries of the region: brodetto Pasquale (Italian Easter Lamb Soup), Expatriate Roast Chicken with Lemon and Olives from Morocco, and Catalonian Fall-Apart Lamb Shanks. Although many recipes call for braising, stewing, and other techniques of long cooking, others are not limited to those techniques, for Wolfert's definition of slow cooking also encompasses marinating and similar techniques." Libr J

Workman, Katie

The **mom** 100 cookbook; 100 recipes every mom needs in her back pocket. Katie Workman ; photographs by Todd Coleman. Workman Pub Co 2012 xxix, 366 p.p col. ill. (alk. paper) $16.95 **641.5**
1. Cooking 2. Cookbooks 3. Parenting
ISBN 0761166033; 9780761166030
LC 2012001330

This cookbook, by Katie Workman, "offers recipes, tips, techniques, attitude, and wisdom for staying happy in the kitchen while proudly keeping it homemade--because homemade not only tastes best, but is also better (and most economical) for you. . . . [It presents] 20 dilemmas every mom faces, with 5 solutions for each: including terrific recipes for the vegetable-averse, the salad-rejector, for the fish-o-phobe, or the overnight vegetarian convert." (Publisher's note)

Worrall-Thompson, Antony

The **essential** diabetes cookbook; good healthy eating from around the world. [by] Anthony Worrall Thompson, with Louise Blair. Kyle: Kyle Cathie 2010 287p il $35   **641.5**
1. Cooking 2. Diabetes -- Diet therapy
ISBN 978-1-906868-15-4
LC 2010-932221

200 recipes for diabetics that take their inspiration from cuisines around the world, including nutritional information for each recipe.

"From fish (Grilled Sea Bass with Spiced Cabbage) to crepes (Asian Surf and Turf Crêpes) to pork (Tofu, Pork, and Shellfish Hot Pot), these dishes bring life back into diabetic cooking. . . . Adventurous cooks will cheer for this diabetes cookbook." Libr J

641.509 History, geographic treatment, biography

Cherniavsky, Mark

The **cookbook** library; four centuries of the cooks, writers, and recipes that made the modern cookbook. Anne Willan ; with Mark Cherniavsky and Kyri Claflin. University of California Press 2012 xii, 328 p.p (cloth : alk. paper) $50   **641.509**
1. Cooking -- History
ISBN 0520244001; 9780520244009
LC 2011024489
Includes bibliographical references (p. 296-306) and indexes

Spitz, Bob

★ **Dearie**; the remarkable life of Julia Child. Bob Spitz. A.A. Knopf 2012 viii, 557 p.p ill.   **641.509**
1. French cooking 2. Cooks -- Biography 3. Cooks -- France -- Biography 4. Cooks -- United States -- Biography
ISBN 0307272222; 9780307272225
LC 2012019632
This book, by Bob Spitz, offers a biography of the television cooking personality Julia Child. "At its heart, [the book] is a story about a woman's search for her own unique expression. . . . Julia Child was a directionless . . . woman who ran off halfway around the world to join a spy agency during World War II. She eventually settled in Paris, where she learned to cook and collaborated on . . . a book that changed the food culture of America." (Publisher's note)
"An engrossing biography of a woman worthy of iconic status." Kirkus
Includes index.

641.59 Cooking characteristic of specific geographic environments, ethnic cooking

Acheson, Hugh

A **New** Turn in the South; Southern Flavors Reinvented for Your Kitchen. Hugh Acheson. Clarkson Potter 2011 299 p. color illustrations $35   **641.59**
1. Cookbooks 2. American cooking 3. Southern cooking
ISBN 0307719553; 9780307719553
LC 2010052632
James Beard Award (2012)
In this cookbook, by Hugh Acheson, "you'll find libations, seasonal vegetables that take a prominent role, salads and soups, his prized sides, and fish and meats--all of which turn Southern food on its head every step of the way. Hugh's recipes include: Oysters on the Half Shell with Cane Vinegar and Chopped Mint Sauce; . . . Chanterelles on Toast with Mushrooms; . . . Braised and Crisped Pork Belly with Citrus Salad; . . . and Lemon Chess Pies with Blackberry Compote." (Publisher's note)

Alford, Jeffrey

★ **Hot,** sour, salty, sweet; a culinary journey through Southeast Asia. Jeffrey Alford and Naomi Duguid ; studio photographs by Richard Jung ; location photographs by Jeffrey Alford and Naomi Duguid. Artisan 2000 346 p. col. ill. $45   **641.59**
1. Cookbooks 2. Southeast Asian cooking
ISBN 1579651143; 9781579651145
LC 00022092
In this cookbook, written by Jeffrey Alford and Naomi Duguid, "more than 175 recipes for spicy salsas, welcoming soups, grilled meat salads, and exotic desserts are accompanied by evocative stories about places and people. The recipes and stories are . . . illustrated throughout with more than 150 full-color food and travel photographs." (Publisher's note)
"Part travel essay and part culinary exploration, this is a perfect choice for both adventurous cooks and armchair travelers." LJ
Includes bibliographical references (p. 325-327) and index

Algar, Ayla Esen

Classical Turkish cooking; traditional Turkish food for the American kitchen. {by} Ayla Algar. HarperCollins Pubs. 1991 306p $35; pa $17 **641.59**
1. Turkish cooking
ISBN 0-06-016317-8; 0-06-093163-9 pa
LC 91-55096
"A cuisine that melds the fragrances and flavors of the Far East, Central Asia, Iran, Anatolia, and the Mediterranean is enriched by Algar as she goes well beyond the standard recipes (160 of them) to explain Turkey's historical, cultural, and culinary traditions—and, along the way, to include a glimpse of her personal family heritage." Booklist
Includes bibliographical references

Alger, Kajsa

Susan Feniger's street food; Susan Feniger, Kajsa Alger, and Liz Lachman. Random House Inc. 2012 224 p. $27.50   **641.59**
1. Salads 2. Cooking 3. Asian cooking 4. Street food 5. International cooking
ISBN 0307952584; 9780307952585
LC 2011041175
Author Susan Feniger "shares 83 of her favorite recipes with home cooks, giving them a taste of these . . . dishes. On her globe-trotting adventures, with cooking and eating as the only shared language, Susan has forged friendships with rice farmers in Vietnam, women baking flatbread in Turkey, and nomadic cheesemakers in Mongolia. . . . [Recipes are featured, such as] Saigon Chicken Salad, . . . Thai Drunken Shrimp with Rice Noodles, or sweet-savory Korean Glazed Short Ribs with Sesame and Asian Pear." (Publisher's note)

Barr, Luke

Provence, 1970; M.F.K. Fisher, Julia Child, James Beard, and the Reinvention of American Taste. Luke Barr. Clarkson Potter 2013 320 p. (alkaline paper) $26   **641.59**
1. Cooks 2. French cooking 3. Provence (France) -- Biography 4. Cooking, American -- Philosophy 5. Cooking, American -- History -- 20th century 6. Provence (France) -- Social life and customs -- 20th

718

century
ISBN 0307718344; 9780307718341

LC 2013007782

This book discusses winter 1970, when "culinary icons M.F.K. Fisher, Julia Child, James Beard, Simone Beck, and Richard Olney all found themselves in Provence, France. This period was a turning point both for these figures and for the culture of food. . . . [Luke] Barr, Fisher's great-nephew, pieces together the events of that winter from diaries and letters, chronicling the dinner parties that took place and the food that was eaten." (Library Journal)

Includes bibliographical references and index

Barrenechea, Teresa

The **Basque** table; passionate home cooking from one of Europe's great regional cuisines. {by} Teresa Barrenechea, with Mary Goodbody. Harvard Common Press 1998 232p il hardcover o.p. pa $16.95   **641.59**
1. Basque cooking
ISBN 1-55832-140-3; 978-1-55832-327-8 pa; 1-55832-327-9 pa

LC 98-29295

The author's "Basque dishes are characterized by fresh, lively flavors; garlic, hot chilis, and roasted sweet peppers, fish of all types, and beef and lamb are favorite ingredients. While home-style dishes are her emphasis here, there are some entries from nueva cocina as well. A chapter on pinchos, the Basque version of tapas, is a highlight, and there are sidebars on Basque ingredients and traditions throughout." Libr J

Bastianich, Lidia

Lidia's Italian-American kitchen; by Lidia Matticchio Bastianich; photographs by Christopher Hirsheimer. Knopf 2001 xxvi, 432p il $35 **641.59**
1. Italian cooking
ISBN 0-375-41150-X

LC 2001-45009

"Bastianich has a warm, engaging style, and she's a teacher as well as a chef: throughout, she provides thoughtful head-notes and sidebars along with useful boxes on cooking with wine, 'resting' soup, and other such practicalities." Libr J

Baxter, John, 1939-

The **perfect** meal; in search of the lost tastes of France. John Baxter. Harper Perennial 2013 382 p. ill. (pbk.) $14.99   **641.59**
1. French cooking 2. France -- Description and travel 3. Cooking (Game)
ISBN 0062088068; 9780062088062

LC 2012019240

IACP Cookbook Award (2014)

This book, by John Baxter is "part grand tour of France, part history of French cuisine, taking readers on a journey to discover and savor some of the world's great cultural achievements before they disappear completely. Some of the most revered and complex elements of French cuisine are in danger of disappearing as old ways of agriculture, butchering, and cooking fade and are forgotten." (Publisher's note)

"Baxter skillfully blends what could be considered merely entertaining food trivia into a satisfying full-course meal." Pub Wkly

Bayless, Rick

Rick Bayless's Mexican kitchen; capturing the vibrant flavors of a world-class cuisine. [by] Rick Bayless with Deann Groen Bayless and JeanMarie Brownson; photographs by Maria Robledo; illustrations by John Sandford. Scribner 1996 448p il $35   **641.59**
1. Mexican cooking
ISBN 0-684-80006-3

LC 96-218444

This cookbook "includes more than 200 tantalizing recipes and is packed with information on Mexican ingredients and cooking techniques, regional cuisine, and history. . . . A serious guide to an often underestimated cuisine, this is important as both a reference and a cookbook." Libr J

Includes bibliographical references

Besh, John

My family table; a passionate plea for home cooking. John Besh. Andrews McMeel Pub., LLC 2011 264 p. col. ill. $35   **641.59**
1. Family 2. Kitchens 3. American cooking 4. Cooking, American
ISBN 1449407870; 9781449407872

LC 2011923008

IACP Cookbook Award (2012)

In this book, "[r]enowned chef and James Beard award-winner John Besh invites us into his home and shows us how we can put good, fresh, healthy food on the table for our families every day. . . . From organizing your kitchen and stocking your pantry to demystifying fish cookery, [he] shares his favorite recipes he cooks with his family every day." (Publisher's note)

"Recipes like Risotto of Almost Anything and Whole Roasted Sole with Brown Butter reinforce Besh's Jamie Oliver-like argument that practical home cooking does not require reliance on processed products. Includes some excellent holiday recipes." LJ

My New Orleans; the cookbook : 200 of my favorite recipes & stories from my hometown. by John Besh. Andrews McMeel Universal 2009 374 p. ill. (chiefly col.) $45   **641.59**
1. Cookbooks 2. Cooking -- Louisiana 3. New Orleans (La.) -- Social life and customs 4. Cooking, Cajun 5. Cooking, Creole 6. Cooking -- Louisiana -- New Orleans 7. Cooking, American -- Louisiana style
ISBN 0740784137; 9780740784132

LC 2009920846

IACP Cookbook Award (2010)

In this cookbook, by John Besh, "archival, four-color, location photography along with ingredient information make the Big Easy easy to tackle in home kitchens. Cooks will salivate over the 200 recipes that honor and celebrate everything New Orleans. . . . From Mardi Gras, to the shrimp season, to the urban garden, to gumbo weather, boucherie (the season of the pig), and everything tasty in between, Besh gives a sampling of New Orleans." (Publisher's note)

Bishara, Rawia

Olives, lemons & za'atar; the best middle eastern home cooking. Rawia Bishara. Kyle Books 2014 224 p. (hardcover) $29.95   **641.59**
  1. Cookbooks 2. Middle Eastern cooking
  ISBN 1906868840; 9781906868840

LC 2013952643

This cookbook by Rawia Bishara is "Organized by Breakfasts, Mezze, Salads, Soups and Stews, Main Courses (including vegetarian, fish, chicken, lamb and beef), Sides, Pickles and Sauces, and Desserts. . . . A dish like Egyptian Rice with Lamb and Pine Nuts shows this cookbook goes beyond Nazareth, and is more of a bible of Middle Eastern food." (Publisher's note)

"Themes of food, family, and personal growth flow throughout this gorgeous cookbook, which balances both simple and challenging recipes." LJ

Caggiano, Biba

Biba's Italy; favorite recipes from the splendid cities. Biba Caggiano. Artisan 2006 xv, 320 p.p ill. $29.95   **641.59**
  1. Italian cooking 2. Italy -- Description and travel
  ISBN 1579653170; 9781579653170

LC 2006045951

This cookbook, by Biba Caggiano, presents "the very best food from our very favorite cities--the glorious dining destinations Rome, Florence, Bologna, Milan, and Venice. . . . The 100 delicious, simple recipes range from time-honored home-cooking traditions to restaurant classics and even startling innovations by Italy's star chefs, and are accompanied by invaluable cooking tips and rich, evocative atmosphere. And each chapter offers travel tips galore." (Publisher's note)

Child, Julia

Julia and Jacques cooking at home; by Julia Child and Jacques Pepin, with David Nussbaum. Knopf 1999 430p il $40   **641.59**
  1. French cooking
  ISBN 0-375-40431-7

LC 98-32418

A companion volume to the PBS series. "For each show, the two chefs started out with ideas and ingredients but no set recipes, so they improvised as they went along, cooking a lot of their favorite traditional dishes and coming up with new ones as well. . . . Dozens of boxes throughout the text provide information on a wide variety of topics." Libr J

Currence, John

Pickles, pigs & whiskey; recipes from my three favorite food groups and then some. John Currence. Andrews McMeel Pub., LLC 2013 259 p. col. ill. $40   **641.59**
  1. Cookbooks 2. American cooking 3. Southern cooking
  ISBN 1449428800; 9781449428808

LC 2013940033

This cookbook, by John Currence, presents "130 recipes organized by 10 different techniques, . . . [including] Pickled Sweet Potatoes, Whole Grain Guinness Mustard, Deep South 'Ramen' with a Fried Poached Egg, Rabbit Cacciato-re, Smoked Endive, Fire-Roasted Cauliflower, and Kitchen Sink Cookie Ice Cream Sandwiches. Each recipe has a song pairing with it." (Publisher's note)

"Recipes for mint julep redux, deep South "ramen" with fried poached eggs, hill country cioppino, and bourbon-pecan pie with tonka bean ice cream, showcase some of the most exciting trends in Southern food and drink." LJ

Duguid, Naomi

★ **Burma**; rivers of flavor. Naomi Duguid. Artisan 2012 372 p. col. ill. $35   **641.59**
  1. Myanmar 2. Cookbooks 3. Asian cooking 4. Food -- Burma 5. Cooking (Spices) 6. Cooking, Burmese 7. Burma -- Social life and customs
  ISBN 1579654134; 9781579654139

LC 2011052121

IACP Cookbook Award (2013)

"Located at the crossroads between China, India, and the nations of Southeast Asia, Burma has long been a land that absorbed outside influences into its everyday life. . . . Interspersed throughout the 125 recipes are intriguing tales from the author's many trips to this fascinating but little-known land." (Publisher's note)

"A colorful immersion into the daily market and table of the Burmese people, this volume is an invitation to celebrate the Burmese people and their transformation." Pub Wkly

Includes bibliographical references and index

Dunlop, Fuchsia

Every grain of rice; simple Chinese home cooking. Fuchsia Dunlop ; photography by Chris Terry. W W Norton & Co Inc 2013 351 p. illustrations (hardcover) $35   **641.59**
  1. Cookbooks 2. Chinese cooking
  ISBN 0393089045; 9780393089042

LC 2012004741

James Beard Award (2014)

In this book, author "Fuchsia Dunlop trained as a chef in China's leading Sichuan cooking school and possesses the rare ability to write recipes for authentic Chinese food that you can make at home. Following her two seminal volumes on Sichuan and Hunan cooking, . . . [this cookbook] is inspired by the vibrant everyday cooking of southern China, in which vegetables play the starring role, with small portions of meat and fish." (Publisher's note)

Dupree, Nathalie

Mastering the art of Southern cooking; Nathalie Dupree & Cynthia Graubart ; photographs by Rick McKee ; with a foreword by Pat Conroy. Gibbs Smith 2012 720 p. col. ill. $45   **641.59**
  1. Cookbooks 2. American cooking 3. Southern cooking
  ISBN 1423602757; 9781423602750

LC 2012017365

James Beard Foundation Award: American Cooking (2013)

"Through more than 600 recipes and hundreds of step-by-step photographs, Dupree and Graubart make it easy to learn the techniques for creating the South's fabulous cuisine. . . . Traditional Southern recipes and ingredients are also given modern twists to make them relevant for today's healthy lifestyle." (Publisher's note)

Includes bibliographical references and index

Foose, Martha Hall

A **southerly** course; recipes & stories from close to home. Martha Hall Foose. Clarkson Potter 2011 256 p. col. ill. $32.50   **641.59**

1. Cookbooks 2. American cooking 3. Southern cooking

ISBN 0307464288; 9780307464286

LC 2010022969

This cookbook, by Martha Hall Foose, "delves deep into Mississippi Delta flavors and foodways. . . . In her signature style, she pairs each recipe with an anecdote or words of advice. . . . Martha's beloved Southern cuisine is a fresh take on homey favorites fiercely protected by the locals, including Skillet Fried Corn, Sweet Pickle Braised Pork Shoulder, and Blackberry Jelly Roll." (Publisher's note)

"Offering meditations on subjects like congealed salads and family china, Foose has all the savvy of a local tour guide, leading the way through her native state with poetry and wit." Pub Wkly

Friedman, Andrew, 1967-

Classico e moderno; Michael White and Andrew Friedman. Ballantine Books 2013 448 p. (hardcover : alk. paper) $50   **641.59**

1. Italian cooking 2. Cooking, Italian

ISBN 0345530527; 9780345530523

LC 2013009625

In this book by Michael White and Andrew Friedman, "White brings his passion for authentic Italian cuisine to the home kitchen, with recipes--nearly 250--that cover both the traditional and contemporary dishes of the region. White shares such iconic dishes as Meatballs Braised in Tomato Sauce; Pasta and Bean Soup; Cavatelli with Lamb Ragù and Bell Peppers; and Roasted Pork Leg with Rosemary and Black Pepper." (Publisher's note)

Includes bibliographical references and index

Hazan, Marcella

★ **Essentials** of classic Italian cooking; illustrated by Karin Kretschmann. Knopf 1992 688p il $30   **641.59**

1. Italian cooking

ISBN 0-394-58404-X

LC 92-52954

Revised and updated edition of the author's The classic Italian cookbook (1973) and More classic Italian cooking (1978)

A guide to the products, techniques and dishes of classic Italian cooking. Regional specialities are dealt with at length

This "could readily assume the mantle of the definitive resource for Italian cuisine." Booklist

Marcella cucina; photography by Alison Harris, design by Joel Avirom. HarperCollins Pubs. 1997 471p il $35   **641.59**

1. Italian cooking

ISBN 0-06-017103-0

LC 97-1253

This book includes both the author's "old favorites and recent creations, along with her versions of regional dishes from chefs and home cooks throughout Italy. . . . She offers an intimate, at times nostalgic glimpse at her life with cooking." Libr J

Helou, Anissa

Mediterranean street food; stories, soups, snacks, sandwiches, barbecues, sweets, and more, from Europe, North Africa, and the Middle East. Anissa Helou. William Morrow 2006 277 p. ill. $19.99   **641.59**

1. Cookbooks 2. Mediterranean cooking

ISBN 0060891513; 9780060891510

LC 2001051451

In this cookbook by Anissa Helou, readers will "join her on a fascinating adventure around the Mediterranean, where eating on the street is a way of life. . . . With . . . black-and-white photographs from Anissa's travels and more than eighty-five fast, flexible, flavorful recipes, . . . [this book] offers home cooks the chance to experience the tastes of distant lands without leaving the kitchen." (Publisher's note)

Includes bibliographical references and index

Hiroko Shimbo

Hiroko's American kitchen; cooking with Japanese flavors. Hiroko Shimbo ; photography by Frances Janisch. Andrews McMeel Pub., LLC 2012 215 p. col. ill. $24.99   **641.59**

1. Cookbooks 2. Japanese cooking 3. Cooking, Japanese

ISBN 1449409784; 9781449409784

LC 2012936725

IACP Cookbook Award (2013)

This cookbook, by Hiroko Shimbo, presents "125 . . . recipes that highlight the best of Japanese cuisine. . . . The recipes are organized in chapters, each using one of two stocks or four sauces. By preparing and storing these easily made items, with a minimum of time and fuss you can enjoy a wide variety of delicious dishes every day. These are recipes . . . are prepared and served in dishes that are familiar to American tastes and dining habits." (Publisher's note)

Hoyer, Daniel

Mayan cuisine; recipes from the Yucatan region. Daniel Hoyer ; photographs by Marty Snortum. Gibbs Smith 2008 224 p. ill. (chiefly col.) $34.95 **641.59**

1. Cookbooks 2. Mayan cooking 3. Maya cooking 4. Cooking -- Mexico -- Yucatán (State)

ISBN 1423601319; 9781423601319

LC 2007033541

In this cookbook, author "Daniel Hoyer brings us the authentic recipes of the . . . [Maya of the Yucatan Region,] along with his personal experiences that make the historical and cultural background of this people accessible and enjoyable." Recipes include "Sweet Corn and Cilantro Cream Soups, Yucatan BBQ Shrimp, Smoked Pork Loin, Jicama-Orange Salad, and Chicken in Red Chile and Pumpkinseed Sauce." (Publisher's note)

"Hoyer is encouraging and enthusiastic, offering salient tips for key techniques like working with tamale wrappers and charring tomatoes, as well as sources for hard-to-locate ingredients." Pub Wkly

Humm, Daniel

I love New York; ingredients and recipes : a moment in New York cuisine. Daniel Humm and Will Guidara. Ten Speed Press 2013 512 p. col. ill. $50   **641.59**

1. Local foods 2. American cooking 3. New York (State) 4. Cooking, American 5. Cooking -- New York (State) -- New York

ISBN 1607744406; 9781607744405

LC 2012026491

IACP Cookbook Award (2014)

Chef Daniel Humm and restaurant manager Will Guidara present a "cookbook showcasing the foods, ingredients, and culinary history of New York. . . . [They take] an in-depth look at the region's centuries-old farming traditions along with nearly 150 recipes that highlight its outstanding ingredients. . . . Included among these dishes designed explicitly for the home cook are reinterpretations of New York classics." (Publisher's note)

Iyer, Raghavan

Indian cooking unfolded; a master class in Indian cooking, with 100 easy recipes using 10 ingredients or less. by Raghavan Iyer ; photography by TK. Workman Publishing 2013 340 p. color illustrations (alk. paper) $19.95   **641.59**

1. Cookbooks 2. Indian cooking

ISBN 0761165215; 9780761165217

LC 2013004247

This cookbook, by Raghavan Iyer, focuses on Indian cooking. "The book's 100 authentic recipes use only ingredients readily available at the local supermarket. Taking into account time restraints, each dish can be quickly assembled and will give home cooks the confidence to create knockout Tandoori Chicken, Coconut Squash with Chiles, Turmeric Hash Browns, Saffron-Pistachio Ice Cream Bars, and Mango Bread Pudding with Chai Spices." (Publisher's note)

Includes bibliographical references and index

Jaffrey, Madhur

An **invitation** to Indian cooking; Madhur Jaffrey ; with a new preface by the author. Ecco Press/Alfred A. Knopf 1999 285, 15 p.p ill hardcover o.p.; paperback $16.95   **641.59**

1. Cookbooks 2. Indian cooking

ISBN 0880016647; 9780375712111; 0375712119

LC 98030321

First published 1973

James Beard Cookbook Hall of Fame (2006)

IACP Culinary Classics Book Award (2014)

This cookbook, by Madhur Jaffrey, "originally published in 1973, introduced the richly fascinating cuisine of India to America--and changed the face of American cooking. Now, as Indian food enjoys an upsurge of popularity in the United States, a whole new generation of readers and cooks will find all they need to know about Indian cooking in Madhur Jaffrey's . . . book." (Publisher's note)

Jamison, Bill

The **border** cookbook; authentic home cooking of the American Southwest and Northern Mexico. {by} Cheryl Alters Jamison and Bill Jamison. Harvard Common Press 1995 500 p. ill. pbk $21.95; hardcover o.p.   **641.59**

1. Cookbooks 2. American cooking 3. Cooking 4. Mexican cooking 5. Cooking -- Southwestern style

ISBN 9781558321038; 9781558321021; 1558321039

LC 95010799

James Beard Award (1996)

In this "James Beard Book Award-winning cookbook, authors Cheryl Alters Jamison and Bill Jamison combine the best of Mexican and Southwest cooking, bringing together this large region's Native American, Spanish, Mexican, and Anglo culinary roots into one big, exuberant book. . . . In over 300 recipes they explore the common elements and regional differences of border cooking." (Publisher's note)

Joachim, David

Rustic Italian food; Marc Vetri with David Joachim ; beverage notes by Jeff Benjamin ; photography by Kelly Campbell ; foreword by Mario Batali. Ten Speed Press 2011 291 p. col. ill. $35   **641.59**

1. Sauces 2. Cookbooks 3. Italian cooking 4. Cooking -- Pasta products 5. Cooking, Italian

ISBN 158008589X; 9781580085892

LC 2011015301

In this cookbook, "Philadelphia chef Marc Vetri celebrates the handcrafted cuisine of Italy, advocating a hands-on, back-to-the-basics approach to cooking. . . . [It presents] an education in kitchen fundamentals, with detailed, step-by-step instructions for making terrines, dry-cured salami, and cooked sausage; a thorough guide to bread and pasta making; and a primer on classic Italian preserves and sauces." (Publisher's note)

"Advanced cooks looking to master bread and pasta will value Vetri's patient, masterful explanation of underlying techniques." LJ

Jones, Catherine Cheremeteff

A **year** of Russian feasts; Catherine Cheremeteff Jones ; illustrations by Barbara Stott McCoy. Jelly-roll Press 2002 192 p. ill. $16.95   **641.59**

1. Russian cooking 2. Religious holidays 3. Russian Orthodox Church 4. Food habits -- Russia (Federation) 5. Russia (Federation) -- Social life and customs

ISBN 0971601305; 9780971601307

LC 2001129493

This cookbook, by Catherine Cheremeteff Jones, illustrated by Barbara Stott McCoy, "explains to Western readers the regularly recurring Russian Orthodox feasts, those traditional dishes associated with them, and the holidays' significance in the life of the church and the people. In Orthodoxy, prior to feasting comes fasting, so Jones' first recipes exemplify ascetic vegetarian dishes. Then it's on to the celebrations . . . : beet soups, meat-stuffed dumplings, sweetly spiced and aromatic Easter bread, and many variations on potatoes." (Booklist)

Kennedy, Diana

The **essential** cuisines of Mexico. Potter 2000 526p $35 **641.59**
1. Mexican cooking
ISBN 0-609-60355-8

LC 00-23156

The author has gathered "the recipes from her first cookbook, the groundbreaking Cuisines of Mexico (1972), as well its two successors, The Tortilla Book (1975) and Mexican Regional Cooking (1978) . . . in this new collection. She's revised the recipes and simplified some, and there are also 30 or so new recipes. Kennedy's books became classics long ago; this compilation of her early works is an essential purchase." Libr J

Includes bibliographical references

Kijac, Maria Baez

The **South** American table; the flavor and soul of authentic home cooking from Patagonia to Rio de Janeiro, with 450 recipes. Maria Baez Kijac ; foreword by Charlie Trotter. Houghton Mifflin Harcourt 2003 478 p. ill., 1 map (alk. paper) $29.95 **641.59**
1. Cookbooks 2. Latin American cooking 3. South America -- Social life and customs
ISBN 9781558322486; 1558322485

LC 2003011100

This South American-themed cookbook, by Maria Baez Kijac, "reflects a true mix of history and cultures, melding the bounty of the New World (tomatoes, potatoes, corn, beans, hot peppers) and the cooking traditions of its indigenous peoples with the influences and culinary heritage of the Conquistadors, African slaves, and immigrants from Italy, Germany, China, and elsewhere." (Publisher's note)

Author Kijac "offers a thorough volume that is part reference book and part cookbook. Long chapters about the geography of South America and its pre-Columbian civilizations, as well as a history of cooking in South America precede the hundreds of recipes. A glossary of South American ingredients as well as a dictionary of ingredients are included as well. The recipes are wonderful, if overwhelming in number." Pub Wkly

Kochilas, Diane

The **glorious** foods of Greece. Morrow 2000 496p map $40 **641.59**
1. Greek cooking
ISBN 0-688-15457-3

LC 00-28158

This cookbook includes over 400 recipes from various "regions, starting with the Peloponnesus and the Ionian Islands, moving on to Macedonia, the islands of the Aegean, and Crete, and finishing up in the city of Athens. . . . Kochilas also provides extensive historical background, cultural as well as culinary, along with detailed descriptions and explanations of ingredients." Libr J

Includes bibliographical references

Koehler, Jeff

Spain; Recipes and Traditions from the Verdant Hills of the Basque Country to the Coastal Waters of Andalucía. by Jeff Koehler ; location photographs by Jeff Koehler , plated food photographs by Kevin

Miyazaki. Chronicle Books 2013 352 p. color illustrations (hardback) $40 **641.59**
1. Spanish cooking 2. Cooking, Spanish
ISBN 0811875016; 9780811875011

LC 2013026594

This book of Spanish recipes, by food writer Jeff Koehler, is "organized by food type rather than local. . . . A tasty section on tapas covers classics like dates wrapped in bacon, as well as more intense options, such as Galician octopus with paprika on potatoes. . . . In addition to the food itself, Koehler explores a variety of the country's food-related traditions." (Publishers Weekly)

Lebovitz, David

My Paris kitchen; recipes and stories. David Lebovitz. Ten Speed Press 2014 345 p. ill. (chiefly col.) (hardback) $35 **641.59**
1. French cooking 2. Paris (France) -- Civilization 3. Paris (France) -- Description and travel 4. Cooking -- France -- Paris 5. Food habits -- France -- Paris -- Anecdotes 6. Paris (France) -- Social life and customs -- Anecdotes
ISBN 1607742675; 9781607742678

LC 2013032561

"In 'My Paris Kitchen,' [author] David [Lebovitz] remasters the classics, introduces lesser-known fare, and presents 100 sweet and savory recipes that reflect the way modern Parisians eat today. You'll find Soupe à l'oignon, Cassoulet, Coq au vin, and Croque-monsieur, as well as Smoky barbecue-style pork, Lamb shank tagine, Dukkah-roasted cauliflower, Salt cod fritters with tartar sauce, and Wheat berry salad with radicchio, root vegetables, and pomegranate." (Publisher's note)

"French food personalized and demystified for the home cook in the best way." Pub Wkly

Includes bibliographical references and index

Lee, Edward

Smoke and pickles; recipes and stories from a new southern kitchen. Edward Lee. Workman Pub Co 2013 304 p. illustrations $29.95 **641.59**
1. Cookbooks 2. American cooking 3. Southern cooking 4. Cooking, American -- Southern style
ISBN 1579654924; 9781579654924

LC 2012039653

This cookbook, by Edward Lee, presents a "collection of contemporary, complex Southern favorites features strong Asian influences: darkly braised lamb shoulder simmers in a mix of bourbon, sorghum, black bean paste, and chocolate, for example, and chicken-fried pork steak gets breaded in crushed ramen noodles. Distinctive pickles, cocktails, sides, snacks, and desserts round out this meaty cookbook." (Library Journal)

An "irresistible collection for any adventurous home cook." Pub Wkly

Lee, Matt

The **Lee** Bros. Charleston kitchen; Matt Lee and Ted Lee. Clarkson Potter 2012 240 p. col. ill., col. maps $35 **641.59**
1. Cookbooks 2. American cooking 3. Southern cooking 4. Cooking, American -- Southern style 5.

Cooking -- South Carolina -- Charleston
ISBN 0307889734; 9780307889737

LC 2012013331

IACP Cookbook Award (2014)

This cookbook, by Matt Lee and Ted Lee, features recipes for Southern U.S. cuisine. "The 100 offerings represent a mix of the classic and the newfangled. There's peach leather, a Charleston chew dating back to the 19th century, which requires two days of sun-drying. And then there's a totally nontraditional tomato and watermelon gazpacho with shrimp." Chapters "cover drinks, snacks, soups, vegetables, fish, meat, and desserts." (Publishers Weekly)

"The brothers also provide two excellent addendums: a comprehensive bibliography of Charleston cookbooks dating back to 1756 and directions for a walking or driving tour featuring eateries from which many of their recipes were derived." Pub Wkly

Includes bibliographical references (p. 232-[235]) and index

Lewis, Edna

The **gift** of Southern cooking; recipes and revelations from two great Southern cooks. by Edna Lewis and Scott Peacock. Knopf 2003 352p il $29.95   **641.59**
1. Southern cooking
ISBN 0-375-40035-4

LC 2002-73153

"If you care—and I mean really care—about coleslaw, pan-fried chicken, trout, . . . greens simmered in pork stock and Southern-style ketchups, relishes and vinegars, this is a book you shouldn't be without." N Y Times Book Rev

Lo, Eileen Yin-Fei

Mastering the art of Chinese cooking; Eileen Yin-Fei Lo ; photographs by Susie Cushner ; brush calligraphy by San Yan Wong. Chronicle Books 2009 384 p. col. ill. $50   **641.59**
1. Cookbooks 2. Chinese cooking
ISBN 0811859339; 9780811859332

LC 2010027670

IACP Cookbook Award (2010)

This cookbook, by Eileen Yin-Fei Lo, offers "a series of lessons [to] build skill, knowledge, and confidence as Lo guides the home cook step by step through the techniques, ingredients, and equipment that define Chinese cuisine. With more than 100 classic recipes and technique illustrations throughout, ... [It] makes . . . this ancient cuisine utterly accessible." (Publisher's note)

"[V]isually stunning—with brush calligraphy, decorative borders, and full-page color photographs—as well as a comprehensive and educational guide that fulfills the promise of how to master Chinese cooking." Pub Wkly

Miller, Adrian

Soul food; the surprising story of an American cuisine, one plate at a time. by Adrian Miller. University of North Carolina Press 2013 344 p. (cloth : alk. paper) $30   **641.59**
1. American cooking 2. African American cooking 3. African American cooking -- History 4. Cooking,

American -- Southern style
ISBN 146960762X; 9781469607627

LC 2013002823

In this book author Adrian Miller "delves into the influences, ingredients, and innovations that make up the soul food tradition. Focusing each chapter on the culinary and social history of one dish--such as fried chicken, chitlins, yams, greens, and 'red drinks'--Miller uncovers how it got on the soul food plate and what it means for African American culture and identity." (Publisher's note)

"An engaging, tradition-rich look at an often overlooked American cuisine--certainly to be of interest to foodies from all walks of life." Kirkus

Includes bibliographical references and index

Nguyen, Andrea

Asian dumplings; mastering gyoza, spring rolls, samosas, and more. Andrea Quynhgiao Nguyen ; photography by Penny De Los Santos. Ten Speed Press 2009 234 p. col. ill. (hardcover) $30 **641.59**
1. Dumplings 2. Asian cooking 3. Cooking, Asian
ISBN 1580089755; 9781580089753

LC 2010286323

This cookbook, by Andrea Quynhgiao Nguyen, focuses on preparing Asian style dumplings. "Plump pot stickers, spicy samosas, and tender bāo (stuffed buns) are enjoyed by the million every day in dim sum restaurants, streetside stands, and private homes worldwide. Wrapped, rolled, or filled; steamed, fried, or baked--Asian dumplings are also surprisingly easy to prepare, as [the author] . . . demonstrates." (Publisher's note)

Includes bibliographical references (p. 227-228) and index

Nguyen, Luke

The **food** of Vietnam; Luke Nguyen. Hardie Grant Books 2013 367 p. $50   **641.59**
1. Cookbooks 2. Vietnamese cooking 3. Vietnam -- Description and travel
ISBN 1742706207; 9781742706207

A journey to discover food & heritage -- Saigon & south -- From coast to countryside -- Salt water people -- Princes & paupers -- The dragon & the turtle -- Mountain people -- Basic recipes -- Glossary -- Index

This cookbook and travel memoir, by Luke Nguyen, "follows his trip from northern Vietnam down to the south, through marketplaces and kitchens of strangers and family alike to find the best recipes Vietnam has to offer. Luke records his experiences with the people he meets and the places he visits along the way, breathing life into the classic recipes of Vietnam, from pho to banh mi and everything in between." (Publisher's note)

Oliver, Jamie, 1975-

Jamie's Italy; Jamie Oliver ; photographs by David Loftus and Chris Terry. Hyperion 2006 319 p. il $34.95   **641.59**
1. Cookbooks 2. Italian cooking
ISBN 1401301959; 9781401301958

LC 2006445348

This cookbook by Jamie Oliver focuses on Italian cuisine. "Italy and its wonderful flavors have always had a major influence on Jamie Oliver's food and cooking. . . . [Here] he travels this famously gastronomic country paying homage to the classic dishes of each region and searching for new ideas to bring home. The result is a . . . collection of Italian recipes, old and new." (Publisher's note)

Olney, Richard

Lulu's Provencal table; the food and wine from Domaine Tempier Vineyard. by Richard Olney; foreword by Alice Waters; photographs by Gail Skoff. Grub Street 2013 364 p. il (hc) $29.95 **641.59**
1. Cookbooks 2. Vineyards 3. French cooking 4. Domaine Tempier 5. Domaine Tempier Vineyard 6. Cookery, French -- Provencal style
ISBN 9781909166189; 1909166189
First published 1994
This book, by Richard Olney, describes how the author "moved to Provence[, France] in 1961 and had the good fortune to befriend Lulu and Lucien Peyraud, the owners of the noted Domaine Tempier vineyard in Provence, not far from Marseilles. . . . [The book provides] Olney's descriptions of the regional food served as the vineyard meals at the domaine. Then he lovingly transcribes Lulu's recipes." (Publisher's note)

Simple French food; Richard Olney ; new foreword by Mark Bittman ; foreword by James Beard ; introduction by Patricia Wells ; drawings by Richard Olney. Houghton Mifflin Harcourt 2014 455 p. ill. (hbk.) $24.99 **641.59**
1. Cookbooks 2. French cooking 3. Cooking, French -- Provencal style
ISBN 0544242203; 9780544242203
LC 2014012324
IACP Culinary Classics Book Award (2013)
"This new edition of [Richard Olney's] classic cookbook includes a fresh cover, new interior design, and a foreword by Mark Bittman. . . . Olney's 175 recipes are so straightforward that cooks will be inspired to go right into the kitchen: herb omelets, fish with zucchini, lamb shanks with garlic, and many more. He also shares techniques (several featuring his own illustrations), such as fermenting vinegar, in line with the back-to-basics trend in cooking." (Publisher's note)

Phan, Charles

Vietnamese home cooking; Charles Phan with Jessica Battilana ; photography by Eric Wolfinger. Ten Speed Press 2012 xxix, 222 p.p col. ill. $35 **641.59**
1. Cookbooks 2. Vietnamese cooking 3. Cooking, Vietnamese
ISBN 1607740532; 9781607740537; 9781607743859
LC 2012014119
IACP Cookbook Award (2013)
In this cookbook, chef Charles Phan "introduces traditional Vietnamese cooking to home cooks by focusing on fundamental techniques and ingredients. . . . With solid instruction and encouraging guidance, perfectly crispy imperial rolls, tender steamed dumplings, delicately flavored whole fish, and meaty lemongrass beef stew are all deliciously close at hand." (Publisher's note)

Phillips, Michael

The **Chelsea** Market cookbook; 100 recipes from New York's premier indoor food market. by Michael Phillips with Rick Rodgers. Stewart, Tabori & Chang 2013 223 p. color illustrations $29.95 **641.59**
1. Cookbooks 2. American cooking 3. Cooking, American 4. International cooking 5. Chelsea Market (New York, N.Y.)
ISBN 1617690376; 9781617690372
LC 2013009924
IACP Cookbook Award (2014)
This book, by Michael Phillips and Rick Rodgers, "collects the most interesting and famous recipes from the [Chelsea New York City] market's eclectic vendors and celebrity food personalities. Archival images, gorgeous food photography, and cooking and entertaining tips and anecdotes accompany the 100 recipes, ranging from Buddakan's Hoisin Glazed Pork Belly, to Sarabeth's Velvety Cream of Tomato Soup, to Ruthy's Rugelach." (Publisher's note)

Plum, Camilla

The **Scandinavian** Kitchen; Camilla Plum ; photography by Anne-Li Engstrom. Natl Book Network 2011 272 p. col. ill. hardcover o.p. $35 **641.59**
1. Cookbooks 2. Scandinavian cooking 3. Cooking, Scandinavian
ISBN 1906868476; 9781906868475
This cookbook, by Camilla Plum, "shares Scandinavian tastes, broken down by group of ingredient, easy to recreate in your own kitchen. Scandinavian cooking achieves a delicate balance between extravagance and the humble, producing a wealth of seasonal daily food, and more luxurious festive food." (Publisher's note)
"Plum, a leading Danish food writer, broadcaster, and cookbook author, extols the virtues of Scandinavian cuisine in this beautiful and fascinating collection. More of a guide to Scandinavian agriculture and its bounty than a full-fledged cookbook, this work showcases the diverse ingredients that make up the Scandinavian diet, including the wide array of both fresh and preserved fish, meat, and vegetables. Recipes are numerous but feel almost secondary." Pub Wkly

Presilla, Maricel E.

★ **Gran** cocina latina; the food of Latin America. Maricel E. Presilla ; photography by Gentl & Hyers/Edge ; illustrations by Julio Figueroa. Norton & Company 2012 vii, 901 p., [32] p. of platesp ill. (some col.) (hardcover) $45 **641.59**
1. Cookbooks 2. Latin American cooking 3. Cooking, Mexican 4. Cooking, Caribbean
ISBN 0393050696; 9780393050691
LC 2012017701
James Beard Foundation Award: Cookbook of the Year (2013)
Author Maricel E. Presilla, "who runs a restaurant in Hoboken, N.J., and holds a doctorate in medieval Spanish history, offers this bible of Latin American food." It "covers dishes from Mexico, Argentina, and the Hispanic Caribbean. . . . Presilla includes more than 500 recipes for everything from tropical roots to empanadas and meat dishes of every kind." (Publishers Weekly)

Richardson, Alan

The **breath** of a wok; unlocking the spirit of Chinese wok cooking through recipes and lore. Grace Young and Alan Richardson ; with text and recipes by Grace Young. Simon & Schuster 2004 240 p. ill. (some col.) $37.50   **641.59**
1. Cookbooks 2. Wok cooking 3. Cooking, Chinese 4. Food habits -- China
ISBN 0743238273; 9780743238274

LC 2003070403

IACP Cookbook Award (2005)

This cookbook, written by Grace Young and Alan Richardson, "brings the techniques and flavors of old-world wok cooking into today's kitchen, enabling anyone to stir-fry with wok hay. . . . The 125 recipes are a testament to the versatility of the wok, with stir-fried, smoked, pan-fried, braised, boiled, poached, steamed, and deep-fried dishes." (Publisher's note)

Includes bibliographical references and index

Roden, Claudia

The **new** book of Middle Eastern food; rev ed; Knopf 2000 513p il $35   **641.59**
1. Middle Eastern cooking
ISBN 0-375-40506-2

LC 00-708864

Originally published 1968 in the United Kingdom; first United States edition published 1972 with title: A book of Middle Eastern food

This volume "includes 800 recipes and variations, as well as historical background, an introduction to essential ingredients and regional dietary practices, folktales, and a vast amount of other information." Libr J

Includes bibliographical references

Rouxel, Sebastien

★ **Bouchon** Bakery; Thomas Keller, with Sebastien Rouxel and Matt McDonald ; along with Susie Heller, Michael Ruhlman, and Amy Vogler ; photographs by Deborah Jones. Artisan 2012 399 p. col. ill. $50   **641.59**
1. Baking 2. Pastry 3. Cookbooks 4. Bouchon Bakery
ISBN 1579654355; 9781579654351

LC 2012000695

IACP Cookbook Award (2013)

This cookbook, by Thomas Keller, was the winner of the 2013 IACP Cookbook Award for Food Photography & Styling. "[I]n this . . . amalgam of American and French baked goods, you'll find recipes for the beloved TKOs and Oh Ohs (Keller's takes on Oreos and Hostess's Ho Hos) and all the French classics he fell in love with as a young chef apprenticing in Paris: the baguettes, the macarons, the millefeuilles, the tartes aux fruits." (Publisher's note)

"[T]his lovely volume is a must-have for cooks who want to take baking to the next level." Pub Wkly

Includes index

Santibañez, Roberto

Truly Mexican; Essential Recipes and Techniques for Authentic Mexican Cooking. [by] Roberto Santibanez, with J.J. Goode and Shelley Wise-

man. John Wiley & Sons, Inc. 2011 264 p. col. ill. $35   **641.59**
1. Cookbooks 2. Mexican cooking 3. Sauces
ISBN 0470499559; 9780470499559

LC 2010013151

This cookbook, by Roberto Santibanez, is "[a]n introduction to Mexican cooking. [It] covers the main ingredients as well as how they're best prepared--from toasting tortillas to roasting tomatoes--and offers a few simple kitchen commandments that make great results a given. Recipes cover main dishes, sides, salsas, guacamoles, moles, adobos, and more." (Publisher's note)

"[T]he author's expertise is conveyed in a straightforward and inspiring tone that will instill confidence in cooks eager to prepare Mexican meals at home, regardless of previous experience or skill level." Pub Wkly

Speck, Maria

Ancient grains for modern meals; Mediterranean whole grain recipes for barley, farro, kamut, polenta, wheat berries & more. Maria Speck ; photogaphy by Sara Remington. Ten Speed Press 2011 ix, 210 p.p col. ill. (hardback) $29.99   **641.59**
1. Cookbooks 2. Cooking -- Grains 3. Alternative grains 4. Grain 5. Cooking (Cereals) 6. Cooking, Mediterranean
ISBN 1580083544; 9781580083546

LC 2010045867

IACP Cookbook Award (2012)

This cookbook, by Maria Speck, presents recipes for alternative, traditional grains including "farro, barley, polenta, and wheat berries." It contains "rustic but elegant dishes--Creamy Farro with Honey-Roasted Grapes, Barley Salad with Figs and Tarragon-Lemon Dressing, Lamb Stew with Wheat Berries in Red Wine Sauce, and Purple Rice Pudding with Rose Water Dates." (Publisher's note)

Includes bibliographical references and index

Sterling, David

Yucatán; recipes from a culinary expedition. by David Sterling. University of Texas Press 2014 576 p. ill. (chiefly col.), col. map (hardbound : alk. paper) $60   **641.59**
1. Maya cooking 2. Yucatan (Mexico) 3. Cooking -- Yucatan Peninsula 4. Mayas -- Social life and customs 5. Yucatán Peninsula -- Description and travel 6. Yucatán Peninsula -- Social life and customs
ISBN 0292735812; 9780292735811

LC 2013021911

This book, by David Sterling, "takes you on a gastronomic tour of the [Yucatan] peninsula in this unique cookbook. . . . Throughout the journey, Sterling serves up over 275 authentic, thoroughly tested recipes. . . . He also discusses pantry staples and basic cooking techniques and offers substitutions for local ingredients that may be hard to find elsewhere." (Publisher's note)

Includes bibliographical references and index

Terry, Bryant

Afro -vegan; farm-fresh African, Caribbean & Southern flavors remixed. Bryant Terry ; photogra-

phy by Paige Green. Ten Speed Press 2014 215 p. ill. (chiefly col.), col. map (hardback) $27.50 **641.59**
1. Veganism 2. Caribbean cooking 3. African American cooking 4. Vegan cooking 5. Cooking, African 6. Cooking, American -- Southern style
ISBN 1607745313; 9781607745310

LC 2013048560

"With more than 100 modern and delicious dishes that draw on [author Bryant] Terry's personal memories as well as the history of food that has traveled from the African continent, Afro-Vegan takes you on an international food journey. Accompanying the recipes are Terry's insights about building community around food, along with suggested music tracks from around the world and book recommendations." (Publisher's note)
Includes bibliographical references and index

Thielen, Amy
The **New** Midwestern table; 200 heartland recipes. Amy Thielen. Clarkson Potter/Publishers 2013 399 p. color illustrations (hardback) $35 **641.59**
1. Cookbooks 2. Midwestern cooking 3. Cooking, American -- Midwestern style
ISBN 0307954870; 9780307954879

LC 2012047058

James Beard Award (2014)
This cookbook, by Amy Thielen, "reveals all that she's come to love--and learn--about the foods of her native Midwest, through updated classic recipes and numerous encounters with spirited home cooks. . . . [The book also contains] 150 color photographs capturing these fresh-from-the-land dishes and the striking beauty of the terrain." (Publisher's note)

Van Aken, Norman
New World kitchen; Latin American and Caribbean cuisine. Norman Van Aken, with Janet Van Aken ; photographs by Tim Turner. Ecco 2003 xiv, 322 p.p ill. (some col.) $34.95 **641.59**
1. Cookbooks 2. Caribbean cooking 3. Latin American cooking 4. Cooking, Caribbean 5. Cooking, Latin American
ISBN 0060185058; 9780060185053

LC 2002027158

This cookbook, by Norman Van Aken with Janet Van Aken, "explores the rich influence of Latin American cuisine on the American palate. From the African-influenced Creole cuisines of Cuba, Puerto Rico, and Jamaica to South American flavors from Brazil, Peru, and Argentina to the distinct tastes of Mexico, Van Aken works his particular magic on this luscious cornucopia and emerges with a wealth of brilliant recipes." (Publisher's note)
"Combined with Van Aken's many thoughtful sidebars and notations, the sophistication of these recipes make this a treat for serious home cooks." Pub Wkly
Includes bibliographical references and index

Von Bremzen, Anya
Mastering the art of Soviet cooking; a memoir of love and longing. by Anya von Bremzen. Crown Publishers 2013 352 p. $26 **641.59**
1. Russian cooking 2. Russia -- History -- 1917-

1991, Soviet Union 3. Food habits -- Soviet Union 4. Moscow (Russia) -- Biography 5. Russian Americans -- Biography 6. Soviet Union -- Social life and customs 7. Women cooks -- Soviet Union -- Biography 8. Food writers -- United States -- Biography 9. Cooking, Russian -- History -- 20th century 10. Russia (Federation) -- Social conditions -- 1991-
ISBN 0307886816; 9780307886811

LC 2013007787

This book by Anya von Bramzen presents "a memoir of life in Soviet Russia. The book is subdivided by decade, and von Bremzen . . . weaves her own memories together with stories from her grandmother and mother, beginning in 1910. The common denominator--and recurring touchstone--is food. . . . Von Bremzen concludes with nine recipes." (Library Journal)
"With anecdotes, history and recipes, the author delivers a lively, precisely detailed cultural chronicle." Kirkus
Includes bibliographical references

Wells, Patricia
Patricia Wells at home in Provence; recipes inspired by her farmhouse in France. Patricia Wells ; photographs by Robert Freson. Fireside 1999 355 p. col il (paperback) $24 **641.59**
1. Cookbooks 2. Provence (France) -- Description 3. French cooking -- Provencal style
ISBN 9780684815695; 9780684863283; 0684863286

LC 00266924

James Beard Award (1997)
In this French cookbook, Patricia Wells, "the award-winning journalist and author invites readers to share the passion, the joy, and, best of all, the cooking of her adopted home. Provence is uniquely blessed with natural beauty as well as some of the world's most appealing foods and liveliest wines. . . . Here are 175 recipes from Patricia's farmhouse kitchen." (Publisher's note)

Willan, Anne
The **country** cooking of France; by Anne Willan ; photographs by France Ruffenach. Chronicle Books 2007 390 p. ill. (chiefly col.), col. map $50 **641.59**
1. Cookbooks 2. French cooking
ISBN 0811846466; 9780811846462

LC 2007004773

James Beard Award (2008)
This cookbook, by Anne Willan, "combines years of hands-on experience with extensive research to create a brand new classic. More than 250 recipes range from the time-honored La Truffade, with its crispy potatoes and melted cheese, to the Languedoc specialty Cassoulet de Toulouse, a bean casserole of duck confit, sausage, and lamb." (Publisher's note)

Wolfert, Paula
Couscous and other good food from Morocco; Introd. by Gael Green. Color photos. by Bill Bayer. Drawings by Sidonie Coryn. Harper & Row 1973 xv, 351 p.p illus. (part col.) $19.99 **641.59**
1. Cookbooks 2. Moroccan cooking
ISBN 0060147210; 0060913967; 9780060913960

LC 72009165

IACP Culinary Classics Book Award (2013)

James Beard Cookbook Hall of Fame (2008)

"Since it was first published in 1973, 'Couscous and Other Good Food from Morocco' has established itself as the classic work on one of the world's great cuisines, and in 2008 it was inducted into the James Beard Cookbook Hall of Fame. From the magnificent bisteeyas . . . to endless varieties of couscous, [author] Paula Wolfert reveals not only the riches of the Moroccan kitchen but also the variety and flavor of the country itself." (Publisher's note)

Bibliography: p. 342

The **food** of Morocco; Paula Wolfert ; photographs by Quentin Bacon ; drawings by Mark Marthaler. Ecco 2011 518 p. ill. (chiefly col.), col. maps $45   **641.59**

1. Cookbooks 2. Moroccan cooking 3. Cooking, Moroccan

ISBN 0061957550; 9780061957550

LC 2011278431

James Beard Award (2012)

This cookbook, by Paula Wolfert, "provides food lovers with the definitive guide to the food of Morocco. Lavishly photographed and packed with tantalizing recipes to please the modern palate, . . . [the book] provides helpful preparation techniques for chefs, home cooks, and any serious student of the culinary arts and culture." (Publisher's note)

Deftly balancing authenticity with ease of preparation, . . . Wolfert is an eager and encouraging host, walking readers through the various regions and their signature dishes as well as the handful of ingredients that make the cuisine so distinctive." Pub Wkly

Includes bibliographical references and index

Mediterranean clay pot cooking; traditional and modern recipes to savor and share. Paula Wolfert. John Wiley & Sons 2009 xviii, 334 p.p ill. (chiefly col.) (cloth) $34.95   **641.59**

1. Cookbooks 2. Clay pot cooking 3. Mediterranean cooking 4. Cooking, Mediterranean

ISBN 076457633X; 9780764576331

LC 2008055912

In this cookbook, author Paula Wolfert, "shares her inimitable passion for detail and insatiable curiosity about cultural traditions and innovations. . . . Here, the self-confessed clay pot 'junkie'--having collected in her travels ceramic pots of all sorts . . . shares recipes as vibrant as the Mediterranean itself along with the delightful stories behind the earthy pots, irresistible dishes, and outstanding cooks she has met along the way." (Publisher's note)

"Wolfert is a true cook's author, and . . . this book is not for the casual home cook. But for those willing to tackle them, Wolfert's clay pot dishes do indeed merit the hype." Pub Wkly

Includes bibliographical references and index

Zanger, Mark H.

The **American** history cookbook. Greenwood Press 2003 xxiii, 459p il (Cookbooks for students) pa $29.95   **641.59**

1. Cooking

ISBN 1-57356-376-5

LC 2002-69608

"This book uses historical commentary and recipes to trace the history of American cooking from the first European contact with Native Americans to the 1970s. Each of 50 chronologically arranged topical chapters contain 500-1,000 words of general commentary followed by descriptions and . . . step-by-step instructions for 3-4 recipes. The recipes are drawn from a wide variety of historical cookbooks and other historical sources." Publisher's note

Includes bibliographical references

641.594

Clark, Melissa

Franny's; simple seasonal Italian. by Andrew Feinberg, Francine Stephens, Melissa Clark. Artisan 2013 ix, 366 p.p ill. (some col.) (hardcover) $35.00   **641.594**

1. Cooking 2. Cookbooks 3. Cooking, Italian 4. Cooking -- New York (State) -- Brooklyn

ISBN 1579654649; 9781579654641

LC 2012028954

In this book, Andrew Feinberg and Francine Stephens, owners of the Brooklyn, New York restaurant Franny's, offer recipes "for everything from soups, salads, and fritti to fish, vegetables, and cocktails." For more complicated recipes, "the authors provide straightforward step-by-step instructions accompanied by photos that demonstrate the proper technique." (Publishers Weekly)

Includes index.

641.5973   Cooking -- United States

The **America's** test kitchen do-it-yourself cookbook; 100+ foolproof kitchen projects for the adventurous home cook. by the editors at America's test kitchen ; photography by Anthony Tieuli. America's Test Kitchen 2012 viii, 360 p.p $26.95   **641.5973**

1. Cookbooks 2. American cooking

ISBN 193649308X; 9781936493081

LC 2012022144

In this book, the editors of the television cooking show America's Test Kitchen "walk home cooks step-by-step through more than 100 of their favorite D.I.Y. kitchen projects. . . . This book delivers a wide variety of projects, from jams and pickles like Grandma used to make to artisanal cheeses and cured meats that you usually have to pay top dollar for at a specialty shop." (Publisher's note)

641.6 Cooking specific materials

Aidells, Bruce

The **complete** meat cookbook; a juicy and authorative guide to selecting, seasoning, and cooking today's beef, pork, lamb, and veal. {by} Bruce Aidelle and Denis Kelly; photographs by Beatriz Da Costa; illustrations by Mary De Palma. Houghton Mifflin 1998 604p il $35   **641.6**
   1. Cooking -- Meat
   ISBN 0-618-13512-X

                      LC 98-28216

"More than 230 recipes, many with several variations, are presented along with charts and illustrations to help the reader understand different types of meat." Libr J

Byres, Tim

Smoke; new firewood cooking : how to build flavor with fire, on the grill and in the kitchen. Tim Byres. Rizzoli International Publications 2013 255 p. ill. (chiefly col.) $40   **641.6**
   1. Cookbooks 2. Barbecue cooking
   ISBN 0847839796; 9780847839797

              LC 2012950104

James Beard Award (2014)

This cookbook, by Tim Byres, was the winner of the 2014 James Beard Award in the General Cooking Category. "Byres . . . gives innovative ideas for easy ways to use smoke in your everyday kitchen arsenal of flavors--such as smoking safely on the stovetop with woodchips, putting together relishes and salsas made with smoked peppers and other vegetables, grilling with wood planks, and using smoke-cured meats to add layers of flavor to a dish." (Publisher's note)

Cameron, Angus

The **L.L.** Bean game and fish cookbook; by Angus Cameron and Judith Jones; illustrations by Bill Elliott. Random House 1983 475p il $25.95 **641.6**
   1. Cooking -- Fish 2. Cooking -- Game
   ISBN 0-394-51191-3

              LC 82-15089

"With handsome wildlife and botanical drawings by Bill Elliott, the book was written by two experts and is complete and comprehensive." Christ Sci Monit

Cole, Tyson

Uchi : the cookbook; by Tyson Cole and Jessica Dupuy; foreword by Lance Armstrong. Umaso Publishing 2011 268p $39.95   **641.6**
   1. Sushi 2. Japanese cooking 3. Cooking -- Seafood 4. Uchi (Austin, Tex.: Restaurant)
   ISBN 978-0-292-77129-1; 0-292-77129-0

"Every now and then a cookbook comes along that is such a great read and has such dazzling photography that I can't put it down. Uchi, the Cookbook is one of those." Texas Monthly

Cook's illustrated (Periodical)

The **best** chicken recipes; by the editors of Cook's illustrated; photography, Keller + Keller, Carl Tremblay, and Daniel J. Van Ackere; illustrations,

John Burgoyne. America's Test Kitchen 2008 422p il $35   **641.6**
   1. Cooking -- Poultry
   ISBN 978-1-933615-23-3; 1-933615-23-0

This volume "offers more than 300 recipes for chicken, along with a primer called 'Chicken 101,' information on techniques (including step-by-step illustrations), and ratings of equipment and ingredients." Libr J

Culinary Institute of America

Vegetables; recipes and techniques from the world's premier culinary college. the Culinary Institute of America; photography by Ben Fink. Lebhar-Friedman Books 2007 293p il $40   **641.6**
   1. Cooking -- Vegetables
   ISBN 978-0-86730-918-8; 0-8673-0918-0

            LC 2007-298057

Includes "over 150 recipes for soups, appetizers, salads, entrees, side dishes, and a chapter devoted to sauces and relishes made from vegetables or perfect to serve with vegetables. Accompanied by 75 full-color photos." Publisher's note

Fraioli, James O.

Culinary birds; the ultimate poultry cookbook. Chef John Ash, James O. Fraioli. Running Press 2013 319 p. color illustrations (hardcover) $30 **641.6**
   1. Cookbooks 2. Cooking -- Poultry
   ISBN 0762444843; 9780762444847

            LC 2013938633

James Beard Award (2014)

This cookbook, by John Ash and James O. Fraioli, "offers more than 170 savory ways to enjoy poultry. . . . Because it is important to know where your bird comes from, [the book also] . . . provides a brief history of poultry, the rise of factory farms, and the progression of the sustainability movement." (Publisher's note)
   Includes index

Grescoe, Taras

Bottomfeeder; how to eat ethically in a world of vanishing seafood. Bloomsbury USA 2008 327p $24.99; pa $16   **641.6**
   1. Seafood 2. Marine resources 3. Conservation of natural resources 4. Cooking -- Seafood
   ISBN 978-1-59691-225-0; 1-59691-225-1; 978-1-59691-625-8 pa; 1-59691-625-7 pa

            LC 2007-49843

The author, a food and travel writer, presents an account of his experiences eating fish and seafood around the world and looks at the ecological ramifications of our diet. He argues that we need to redesign our relationship with seafood.

This is "a comprehensive, lively and illuminating guide." Nation
   Includes bibliographical references

Grigson, Jane

Charcuterie and French pork cookery; Jane Grigson. Grub Street 2001 347 p. ill. $34.95 **641.6**
   1. French cooking 2. Cooking -- Pork 3. Cooking,

French
ISBN 1902304888; 9781902304885

LC 2008426563

IACP Culinary Classics Book Award (2013)

This book, by Jane Grigson, "first published in 1969 but unavailable for many years, . . . is a guidebook and a recipe book. She describes every type of charcuterie available for purchase and how to make them yourself. She describes how to braise, roast, pot-roast and stew all the cuts of pork, how to make terrines, how to cure your own ham and make your own sausages." (Publisher's note)

Guggiana, Marissa

Primal cuts; cooking with America's best butchers. Marissa Guggiana ; foreword by Dario Cecchini ; introduction by Andrew Zimmern. Welcome Books 2012 287 p. col. ill. (hardcover) $40   **641.6**
1. Cookbooks 2. Cooking -- Meat 3. Carving (Meat, etc.) 4. Cooking (Meat) 5. Meatcutting -- United States
ISBN 1599621150; 9781599621159

LC 2012018389

This cookbook describes how "Marissa Guggiana, food activist, writer, and fourth generation meat purveyor traveled the country to discover 50 of our most gifted butchers and share their favorite dishes, personal stories, and cooking techniques. From the Michelin star chef to the small farmer who raises free-range animals--butchers are the guide for this unique visual cookbook, packed with tons of their most prized recipes and good old-fashioned know-how." (Publisher's note)

Jacoby, Kate

Vedge; 100 plates, large and small, that place vegetables in the spotlight. Rich Landau and Kate Jacoby. The Experiment 2013 256 p. (cloth) $24.95 **641.6**
1. Veganism 2. Cooking -- Fruit 3. Cooking -- Vegetables 4. Vegan cooking 5. Vedge (Restaurant : Philadelphia, Pa.)
ISBN 1615190856; 9781615190850

LC 2013012098

In this cookbook, chefs Rich Landau and Kate Jacoby "share their passion for ingenious vegetable cooking. The more than 100 recipes here--such as Fingerling Potatoes with Creamy Worcestershire Sauce, Pho with Roasted Butternut Squash, Seared French Beans with Caper Bagna Cauda, and Eggplant Braciole--explode with flavor but are surprisingly straightforward to prepare." (Publisher's note)

Kafka, Barbara

★ **Vegetable** love; a book for cooks. [by] Barbara Kafka with Christopher Styler; photographs by Christina Cornish. Artisan 2005 708p il $35 **641.6**
1. Vegetables 2. Cooking -- Vegetables
ISBN 1-57965-168-2

LC 2005-47818

The author "has triumphed with an outstanding, indispensable cookbook that not only summons the reader to get into the kitchen and cook but also constitutes a valuable and comprehensive reference tool." Booklist

Includes bibliographical references

La Place, Viana

Verdura; vegetables, Italian style. Viana La Place. Grub Street 2010 320 p. il (pbk) $24.95 **641.6**
1. Cookbooks 2. Cooking -- Vegetables 3. Italian cooking
ISBN 1906502781; 9781906502782

LC 2010537034

Originally published: New York: Morrow, 1991. London: Macmillan, 1994

This cookbook, by Viana La Place, offers "300 irresistible recipes [that] represent the best of the Italian approach to vegetable preparation, an earthy yet spirited technique that celebrates fresh ingredients simply treated. . . . Contending that eating well-prepared vegetables helps us to appreciate life's natural cycles, [the volume] . . . presents recipes for antipastos, salads, soups, sandwiches, pasta, risottos, pizzas, and much more." (Publisher's note)

Includes bibliographical references (p. 307) and index

Lobel, Stanley

The **meat** bible; all you need to know about meat and poultry from America's master butchers. by Stanley Lobel ... [et al.]; with Mary Goodbody and David Whiteman; photographs by Lucy Schaeffer. Chronicle Books 2009 319p il $40   **641.6**
1. Cooking -- Meat 2. Cooking -- Poultry
ISBN 978-0-8118-5826-7; 0-8118-5826-X

LC 2008-33441

"Recipes number 135, well photographed and indexed." Publ Wkly

Madison, Deborah

Vegetable literacy; exploring the affinities and history of the vegetable families, with 300 recipes. Deborah Madison. 1st ed. Ten Speed Press 2013 416 p. col. ill. (hardcover) $40.00   **641.6**
1. Cooking -- Vegetables 2. Food crops -- Identification
ISBN 9781607741916; 1607741911

LC 2012030968

Includes bibliographical references (page 395) and index.

Mast, Rick

Mast Brothers Chocolate; a family cookbook. Rick Mast & Michael Mast ; foreword by Thomas Keller ; photography by Tuukka Koski. Little Brown & Co 2013 276 p. illustrations, some color (hbk.) $40   **641.6**
1. Desserts 2. Cookbooks 3. Cooking -- Chocolate 4. Mast Brothers Chocolate
ISBN 0316234842; 9780316234849

LC 2013938865

IACP Cookbook Award (2014)

In this cookbook, authors Rick Mast and Michael Mast "share their unique story and recipes for classic American desserts like chocolate cookies and cakes, brownies, bars, milkshakes, and even home-made whoopie pie. There are mouthwatering savory dishes as well, like Pan-seared Scallops with Cocoa Nibs and Cocoa Coq au Vin." (Publisher's note)

Moonen, Rick

Fish without a doubt; the cook's essential companion. [by] Rick Moonen and Roy Finamore; photographs by Ben Fink. Houghton Mifflin Co. 2008 496p il $35 **641.6**

1. Cooking -- Fish 2. Cooking -- Seafood
ISBN 978-0-618-53119-6; 0-618-53119-X

LC 2007-52084

In this cookbook that covers the preparing of sustainable fish, the authors "show how to clean, bone, and portion both finfish and shellfish. Recipes are organized by cooking method—broiling, poaching, roasting, grilling, steaming, [and] frying. . . . Succeeding chapters cover such fish basics as chowders, fish cakes, and salads. . . . Both the book's organization and its comprehensive coverage make this a necessary addition to any cookbook collections." Booklist

Ottolenghi, Yotam

Plenty more; vibrant vegetable cooking from London's Ottolenghi. Yotam Ottolenghi. Ten Speed Press 2014 352 p. color illustrations (hardcover) $35 **641.6**

1. Cookbooks 2. Vegetarian cooking 3. Cooking (Vegetables) 4. Ottolenghi (Restaurant)
ISBN 1607746212; 9781607746218

LC 2014017924

In this vegetarian cookbook, author Yotam Ottolenghi "continues to explore the diverse realm of vegetarian food with a wholly original approach. Organized by cooking method, more than 150 dazzling recipes emphasize spices, seasonality, and bold flavors." It also includes "120 vegetarian dishes organized by cooking method." (Publisher's note)

While the recipes "require time and finesse . . . they are often revelatory, introducing textures and flavor combinations that readers won't find elsewhere." LJ

Peterson, James

Meat; a kitchen education. Ten Speed Press 2010 326p il $35 **641.6**

1. Cooking -- Meat
ISBN 978-1-58008-992-0; 1-58008-992-5

LC 2010-21759

"Though his introduction addresses vegans, admonishing all to 'follow your conscience' about the consumption of animals, the rest of [Peterson's] text advocates only the use of the best lamb, rabbit, beef, and chicken available. Thoroughly review the first two chapters; in them Peterson sets forth the proper ways to sauté, grill, braise, and poach (among other methods), illustrates such fundamental preparation methods as julienning a leek and sectioning a turnip, and identifies the flavors associated with different international cuisines. Next, the fun: 175 recipes and, more important, instructions and sidebars to ensure that expensive roasts and whole birds emerge with great taste." Booklist

Seaver, Barton

For cod and country. Sterling Epicure 2011 294p il $30 **641.6**

1. Cooking -- Seafood
ISBN 978-1-4027-7775-2

A "a user's manual for any seafood lover who wants to eat sustainably—and very well. Seaver's book vibrates with personality, practical advice, photographs (both evocative and how-to), and stovetop wisdom: never be shy about adding butter, but go easy on the black pepper. With the help of step-by-step photographs, he demonstrates seafood-savvy techniques, everything from how to fillet a bass to how to open an oyster without severing one of your arteries. He also provides a list of substitutions for overexploited species: Use Pacific cod in place of Atlantic cod; sablefish instead of Chilean sea bass; squid instead of octopus." Atlantic

Slater, Nigel

Ripe; a cook in the orchard. Nigel Slater ; photography by Jonathan Lovekin. Ten Speed Press 2012 591 p. col. ill. (hardback) $40 **641.6**

1. Cookbooks 2. Gardening 3. Cooking -- Fruit 4. Cooking (Fruit)
ISBN 1607743329; 9781607743323

LC 2011043551

James Beard Foundation Award: Single Subject (2013)

This cookbook, by food writer Nigel Slater, "focuses on sweet and savory applications for fruits grown in his London garden. Organized alphabetically, the fruit-focused chapters offer historical and varietal information, gardening tips, and suggested flavor pairings, followed by simple recipes like Baked Peaches with Maple Syrup and Vanilla, Slow-Cooked Quinces with Cassis, and Roast Leg of Pork with Spiced Rhubarb." (Library Journal)

Stein, Rick

Rick Stein's complete seafood; a step-by-step reference with over 150 recipes and 550 photographs. Rick Stein [photography by James Murphy] Ten Speed Press 2004 264 p. col. ill. $27.99 **641.6**

1. Cookbooks 2. Cooking -- Fish 3. Cooking -- Seafood
ISBN 1580085687; 1580089143; 9781580089142

LC 2006298920

James Bead Award (2005)

This cookbook, by Rich Stein, "offers an almost limitless repertoire [of seafood recipes], with detailed instructions and extensive charts. Hundreds of photographs and illustrations show how to scale and gut fish for the grill, bake whole fish in a salt or pastry casing, hot-smoke fish, prepare live crabs, and clean and stuff squid, along with other essential techniques." (Publisher's note)

Vegetables from an Italian garden; season-by-season recipes. Phaidon 2011 431p il $39.95 **641.6**

1. Vegetable gardening 2. Cooking -- Vegetables
ISBN 978-0-7148-6117-3; 0-7148-6117-0

This book, assembled by the editors at Phaidon Press, "is divided into four chapters, following the four seasons. Each chapter has its own colored ribbon, which makes it easy to go to the season you want to cook from. . . . Each season starts with an explanation of the vegetables available that season. There is a short history of the vegetable, then an explanation of how to select and buy them, along with stunning photos by Andy Sewell. Following this is a description of how and when to plant these vegetables in your own garden. The scrumptious recipes are taken from all parts of Italy. Well written and clear, they let you jump in and start cooking." Super Chef

Vinton, Sherri Brooks

Put 'em up! a comprehensive home preserving guide for the creative cook, from drying and freezing to canning and pickling. Storey Pub. 2010 303p il pa $19.95   **641.6**

1. Cooking -- Fruit 2. Cooking -- Vegetables 3. Fruit -- Preservation 4. Vegetables -- Preservation
ISBN 978-1-60342-546-9

LC 2010009609

"Vinton provides an excellent introduction to multiple food preservation methods. Organized first by technique, then by fruit or vegetable, this volume contains many easy-to-follow options for prepared and preserved foods." Libr J

Includes bibliographical references

Wells, Patricia

Vegetable harvest; vegetables at the center of the plate. William Morrow 2007 324p il $34.95 **641.6**

1. Cooking -- Vegetables
ISBN 978-0-06-075244-6; 0-06-075244-0

LC 2006-43723

"After surveying the bounty of her backyard garden, Wells became inspired to build meals around vegetables rather than starting with meat, fish or poultry. She tripled the number she served at each meal and tried different cooking methods, looking for the best-tasting, most wholesome ways of cooking each type. She includes nutritional information and an equipment list for each recipe, and selectively offers wine suggestions, translations of French food idioms, and nuggets of folklore connected to the dish or main ingredient. . . . This collection is highly recommended for cooks and gardeners alike." Publ Wkly

641.65   Cooking with vegetables

Wilkinson, Matt

Mr. Wilkinson's vegetables; a cookbook to celebrate the garden. Matt Wilkinson. Black Dog & Leventhal Pub. 2013 287 p. $27.95   **641.65**

1. Cooking -- Vegetables
ISBN 157912934X; 9781579129347

In this cookbook, "Melbourne, Australia-based chef [Matt] Wilkinson takes a 'veg-first approach' to cooking, building dishes around fresh, seasonal produce. In 25 chapters named for vegetables, he shares inspiring and beautifully photographed recipes that range from rustic (braised eggplant, tomato and meatballs) to playful ('Shepherd's Pie' croquettes) to unconventional (frozen vanilla syrup-coated fennel)." (Library Journal)

641.675   Dairy products -- cooking

Ruhlman, Michael

Egg; a culinary exploration of the world's most versatile ingredient. Michael Ruhlman ; photography

by Donna Turner Ruhlman. Little Brown & Co 2014 xix, 235 p.p col. ill. $40   **641.675**

1. Cooking -- Eggs
ISBN 0316254061; 9780316254069

LC 2013948058

In this cookbook Michael Ruhlman "explains why the egg is the key to the craft of cooking. . . . He starts with perfect poached and scrambled eggs and builds up to brioche and Italian meringue. Along the way readers learn to make their own mayonnaise, pasta, custards, quiches, cakes, and other preparations that rely fundamentally on the hidden powers of the egg." (Publisher's note)

"Ruhlman's regard for this simple ingredient is evident as he describes the multiple functions it serves and then offers up recipes for a wide array of appetizing dishes." Pub Wkly

641.7   Specific cooking processes and techniques

Child, Julia

Baking with Julia; based on the PBS series hosted by Julia Child. written by Dorie Greenspan; photographs by Gentl & Hyers. Morrow 1996 480p il $40   **641.7**

1. Baking
ISBN 0-688-14657-0

LC 96-23061

"The 200 recipes are organized as a course in baking, with an early, energetic section on the basic batters and doughs for cakes and pastries. The book moves on to recipes of varying degrees of complexity. . . . But the book's success is due to more than organization: the text never misses a chance to explain, expand and entertain." N Y Times Book Rev

Includes bibliographical references

Cook's illustrated (Periodical)

Best skillet recipes; a best recipe classic. by the editors of Cook's illustrated; photography, Keller + Keller, Carl Tremblay, and Daniel J. Van Ackere; illustrations, John Burgoyne. America's Test Kitchen 2009 335p il $35   **641.7**

1. Cooking
ISBN 978-1-933615-41-7; 1-933615-41-9

This cookbook celebrates the "versatility of that ordinary workhorse, the 12-inch skillet. An indispensable tool for eggs, pan-seared meats and sautéed vegetables, the skillet can also be used for stovetop-to-oven dishes such as All-American Mini Meatloaves; layered dishes such as tamale pie and Tuscan bean casserole; and even desserts such as hot fudge pudding cake. . . . Whether or not you properly appreciate your skillet, this book will at least teach you to wield it gracefully." Publ Wkly

Farmer, Fannie Merritt

The **Fannie** Farmer baking book; illustrated by Lauren Jarrett. Knopf 1984 624p il hardcover o.p. pa $12.99   **641.7**
  1. Baking
  ISBN 0-517-14829-3

LC 84-47862

"Separate chapters cover pies and tarts, cookies, cakes, yeast breads, quick breads, and crackers in encyclopedic detail with brisk but reassuring professionalism. Many of the 800 recipes are standard favorites." Libr J

Kaminsky, Peter

Charred & scruffed; Bold New Techniques for Explosive Flavor On and Off the Grill. Adam Perry Lang with Peter Kaminsky. Artisan 2012 xiv, 266 p.p col. ill.   **641.7**
  1. Barbecue cooking 2. Barbecuing
  ISBN 9781579654658

LC 2011031786

In this book, chef Adam Perry Land "employs his extensive culinary background to refine and concentrate the flavors and textures of barbecue and reimagine its possibilities. Adam's new techniques, from roughing up meat and vegetables ('scruffing') to cooking directly on hot coals ('clinching') to constantly turning and moving the meat while cooking ('hot potato'), produce crust formation and layers of flavor." (Publisher's note)
  Includes index

Stevens, Molly

★ **All** about braising; the art of uncomplicated cooking. Molly Stevens ; color photographs by Gentl & HyersEdge ; black-and-white illustrations by Yevgeniy Solovyev ; wine notes and selections by Tim Gaiser. 1st ed; W W Norton & Co Inc 2004 481 p. ill. (some col.) $35   **641.7**
  1. Cookbooks 2. Braising (Cooking)
  ISBN 0393052303; 9780393052305

LC 2004017907

IACP Award (2005)
James Beard Foundation Award (2005)
This book, by Molly Stevens, offers a cookbook dedicated to braising. "Written to instruct a cook at any level . . . , [it includes] 125 . . . recipes for meat, poultry, seafood, and vegetables, ranging from quick-braised weeknight dishes to slow-cooked weekend braises." It also includes "a thorough explanation of the principles of good braising with helpful advice on the best cuts of meat, the right choice of fish and vegetables, and the right pots." (Publisher's note)

"[T]he book contains interesting tasting notes and cultural information, and Stevens's lengthy instructions will be particularly valuable to beginners." Pub Wkly
  Includes bibliographical references and index

All about roasting; a new approach to a classic art. photographs by Quentin Bacon; wine pairings by Tim Gaiser. W. W. Norton 2011 573p il $35 **641.7**
  1. Roasting (Cooking)
  ISBN 978-0-393-06526-8

LC 2011022692

The author "begins with a 45-page introduction to the art and science of roasting that should be required reading for anyone in possession of a chunk of meat and an oven. Topics covered include the differences in employing high versus low heat, the reasons to rest meat before carving, the joys of convection ovens, and why fat is always a critical component. Next come 150 recipes divided into chapters on beef, pork, poultry, fish, and vegetables. . . . [This] is a compelling collection that drives home the difference between a chef merely showing off some recipes and a teacher exploring her craft." Publ Wkly
  Includes bibliographical references

641.8 Cooking specific kinds of dishes and preparing beverages

Alexander, William

52 loaves; one man's relentless pursuit of truth, meaning, and a perfect crust. Algonquin Books of Chapel Hill 2010 339p il $23.95   **641.8**
  1. Bread
  ISBN 978-1-56512-583-4

LC 2009-49656

Charts the author's attempts to bake the perfect loaf of bread, including growing, harvesting, and milling his own wheat.

"Bakers will delight in his often humorous mission as he relates leaving out salt, growing his own wheat, discovering parchment paper, and splashing water into the oven in an effort to create steam. . . . This humorous memoir is recommended for anyone who has ever tried to bake a loaf." Libr J
  Includes bibliographical references

Alford, Jeffrey

Flatbreads and flavors; a baker's atlas. Jeffrey Alford and Naomi Duguid. Morrow 1995 xvi, 441 p.p ill. (some col.) $21.99   **641.8**
  1. Bread 2. Cookbooks 3. International cooking
  ISBN 0061673269; 0688114113; 9780061673269

LC 94030892

James Beard Award (1996)
In this cookbook, "Jeffrey Alford and Naomi Duguid have found an internationally shared and nourishing element of culture and cuisine: flatbreads, humankind's simplest, oldest, and most remarkably varied form of bread. . . . In addition, they provide 150 recipes for traditional accompaniments to the flatbreads, from chutneys and curries, salsas and stews." (Publisher's note)
  Includes bibliographical references (p. 421-425) and index

The **America's** test kitchen family baking book; [by] the editors at America's Test Kitchen; photography, Daniel J. Van Ackere, Carl Tremblay, Keller + Keller. America's Test Kitchen 2008 544p il $34.95   **641.8**
  1. Baking 2. America's test kitchen (Television program)
  ISBN 978-1-933615-22-6; 1-933615-22-2

"Expert bakers and novices scared of baking's requisite exactitude can all learn something from this hefty, all-purpose home baking volume." Publ Wkly

Anderson, Pam

Perfect one-dish dinners; all you need for easy get-togethers. photographs by Judd Pilossof. Houghton Mifflin Harcourt 2010 266p il $32   **641.8**

1. Entertaining 2. One-dish cooking

ISBN 978-0-547-19595-7

LC 2010-21447

This is an "accessible, engaging collection of meals based around a singular dish. Grouped into four sections—summer salads and grilled platters; casseroles; the roasting pan; and stews—Anderson smartly mixes classics like Osso Bucco, Paella, and Lasagna with riffs on standards like Coq Au Vin (here with white wine and spring vegetables) and a Spanish beef stew (with bell peppers, chickpeas, saffron, paprika, and orange). . . . Whether readers are new to cooking or simply looking for new ideas for meals, Anderson's winning collection is sure to encourage and inspire." Publ Wkly

Andres, Jose

Tapas; a taste of Spain in America. [by] José Andrés with Richard Wolffe. Clarkson Potter 2005 256p il $35   **641.8**

1. Appetizers 2. Spanish cooking

ISBN 1-4000-5359-5

LC 2004-27466

The author presents some of the small-plate dishes "he serves at his tapas restaurants, including traditional favorites recreated with American ingredients. . . . Recipes are organized by ingredient, from olives and olive oil to citrus to fish, shellfish, and meat, and they are mouth-watering: Oven-Roasted Potatoes and Oyster Mushrooms, for example, or Lobster with Pimentón and Olive Oil." Libr J

Includes bibliographical references

Baking illustrated; a best recipe classic. by the editors of Cook's illustrated; illustrations, John Burgoyne; photography, Carl Tremblay, Keller + Keller, Daniel Van Ackere. America's Test Kitchen 2004 515p il $35   **641.8**

1. Baking

ISBN 0-936184-75-2

"Test kitchen cooks analyzed brand-name baking ingredients and equipment and . . . make 'best buy' recommendations. . . . The test summaries preceding each recipe include both successes and failures; the resulting recipes (more than 350) cover everything from the simplest quick breads to more complex yeast breads and cookies and pastries. . . . This is the best instructional book on baking this reviewer has seen." Libr J

Bauer, Jeni Britton

Jeni's splendid ice creams at home. Artisan 2011 217p il $23.95   **641.8**

1. Ice cream, ices, etc.

ISBN 978-1-57965-436-8; 1-57965-436-3

LC 2010-39453

"This inspiring collection of seasonal ice cream recipes from Ohio-based ice cream whiz Bauer stands apart for its

creative, unconventional flavors like Sweet Basil & Honeyed Pine Nut and Sweet Potato with Torched Marshmallows." Libr J

Beard, James

Beard on bread; drawings by Karl Stuecklen. Knopf 1973 230p il hardcover o.p. pa $15   **641.8**

1. Bread

ISBN 0-679-75504-7 pa

"An inclusive guide to the preparation of a variety of breads with recipes for coffee cakes, rolls, flat breads, fried cakes. . . . The recipes included are those Beard considers the best from around the world which can be made in a U.S. kitchen." Booklist

Beranbaum, Rose Levy

The **cake** bible; edited by Maria D. Guarnaschelli; photographs by Vincent Lee; foreword by Maida Heatter. Morrow 1988 555p il   **641.8**

1. Cake

ISBN 0-688-04402-6; 978-0-688-04402-2

LC 8801369

This collection of cake recipes includes "discussions on ingredients and equipment and concludes with a . . . section on the chemistry of cake baking and on making . . . professional wedding cakes." (Libr J) Bibliography. Index.

Includes bibliographical references

The **best** one-dish suppers; a best recipe classic. by the editors of Cook's Illustrated; photography, Keller + Keller, Carl Tremblay, and Daniel J. Van Ackere; illustrations, John Burgoyne. America's Test Kitchen 2011 342p il $35   **641.8**

1. One-dish cooking 2. Quick and easy cooking

ISBN 978-1-933615-81-3

"This volume presents recipes (180 of them, further clarified by 169 illustrations) for supremely simple meals (including many versions of tempting classics) prepared in one cooking vessel. There are dinners that can be made in just a sheet pan, a single pot, a dutch oven, or a slow cooker, plus stews and chilis, casseroles, and stir-frys. . . . This book could easily become a go-to resource for busy home cooks." Publ Wkly

Blakeslee, Robert L.

Your time to bake; a first cookbook for the novice baker. by Robert L. Blakeslee. Square One Publishers 2012 384 p. (hardback) $29.95   **641.8**

1. Baking 2. Desserts 3. Cookbooks 4. Cake decorating

ISBN 9780757003554

LC 2011014622

In this cookbook, "[Robert L.] Blakeslee includes 'step by step photo instructions, with a finished shot of each recipe.' . . . He provides recipes for every simple sweet treat imaginable. . . . Explaining that baking is 'more about chemistry,' Blakeslee . . . discusses 'important baking variables and how to control them,' with helpful tips: measuring ingredients exactly and making sure ingredients such as eggs and butter are the correct temperature. Also . . . [included] are sections on essential items needed for baking--such as different flours, sugars, spices and cheeses--important equipment, and baking terms from A to Z. . . . [T]here are more than 150 recipes . . . and a final chapter on decorating cookies, tarts, and cupcakes and making fondant." (Publishers Weekly)

Boyle, Tish

The **cake** book; the definitive guide to making great cakes with nearly 200 recipes. Tish Boyle ; photography by John Uher. Houghton Mifflin Harcourt 2006 376 p. ill. (some col.) $39.95   **641.8**
  1. Cake 2. Cookbooks 3. Cake decorating
  ISBN 0471469335; 9780471469339
                                         LC 2005021384
This cake cookbook, written by Tish Boyle, "includes recipes ranging from pound cakes and coffee cakes to meringue, mousse, and ice cream cakes to fillings, frostings, and more. Throughout, color and black-and-white photographs and drawings show you important techniques and spectacular end results. A difficulty rating with each recipe helps you decide which to make, depending on how much time--or ambition--you have." (Publisher's note)

"Well written, easy to read, and beautifully photographed." LJ

Colicchio, Tom

'**wichcraft**; craft a sandwich into a meal--and a meal into a sandwich. [by] Tom Colicchio with Sisha Ortúzar; text by Rhona Silverbush; photographs by Bill Bettencourt. Clarkson Potter/Publishers 2009 208p il $27.50   **641.8**
  1. Sandwiches
  ISBN 978-0-609-61051-0
                                         LC 2008-27803
The authors offer "an entire cookbook featuring the sandwiches served at . . . [their] New York restaurant, 'wichcraft. . . . This book's table of contents alone will have grab-and-go eaters and sophisticated gastronomes alike salivating." Booklist

The **Complete** book of pasta and noodles; by the editors of Cook's illustrated; preface by Christopher Kimball; illustrations by Judy Love; photographs by Daniel J. van Ackere. Potter 2000 483p il hardcover o.p. pa $19.95   **641.8**
  1. Cooking -- Pasta products
  ISBN 0-609-80930-X pa
                                         LC 99-40076
This work brings "together information and recipes covering pasta's worldwide range from North America's beloved macaroni and cheese through Italy's sophisticated sauces, across China's exotic rice noodles, and up to Japan's modest Zen noodles in broth. . . . Content and organization combine to make this a superior cooking reference book for libraries." Booklist

Corriher, Shirley

BakeWise; the hows and whys of successful baking with over 200 magnificent recipes. [by] Shirley O. Corriher. Scribner 2008 532p $40   **641.8**
  1. Baking
  ISBN 978-1-4165-6078-4; 1-4165-6078-5
                                         LC 2008-32681

This "collection of more than 200 recipes offers amateur and expert bakers alike clear, numbered steps and a plethora of information on ingredients, equipment and method. Invaluable troubleshooting sections solve pesky problems on everything from pale and crumbly cookies to fallen soufflés. . . . Astute references to a variety of chefs, cookbook authors and restaurants add a knowing punch to this solid collection that's sure to please bakers of all skill levels." Publ Wkly

Crocker, Betty

★ **Betty** Crocker cookie book; rev ed; Wiley 2003 xxix, 322p il $22.95   **641.8**
  1. Cookies
  ISBN 0-7645-3940-X
                                         LC 2003-270127
First published 1963 by Golden Press with title: Cooky book
This book features "over 240 cookie favorites, from heirloom showstoppers to contemporary treats . . . [including] everything from chocolate chip cookies to brownies, oatmeal cookies to date bars and more." Publisher's note

Daley, Regan

In the sweet kitchen; the definitive baker's companion. Artisan 2001 692p il hardcover o.p. pa $24.95   **641.8**
  1. Baking
  ISBN 1-57965-208-5; 1-57965-427-4 pa
                                         LC 2001-41289
"While other books include some details on baking ingredients and tools as part of their introduction to the craft, . . . [this] is the definitive guide to all the equipment, techniques, and ingredients a baker uses." Libr J
Includes bibliographical references

DeMasco, Karen

The **craft** of baking; cakes, cookies, & other sweets with ideas for inventing your own. [by] Karen DeMasco & Mindy Fox; photographs by Ellen Silverman. Clarkson Potter Publishers 2009 256p il $35   **641.8**
  1. Cake 2. Candy 3. Baking 4. Cookies 5. Desserts
  ISBN 978-0-307-40810-5; 0-307-40810-8
"In the first sections, [DeMarco] covers ingredients and techniques accessible even to novice bakers. Then come her 'new modern-day treats,' created with 'traditional recipes and familiar home baking techniques,' e.g., Lemon Olive Cake (an interesting variation on the traditional lemon cake using butter and extra virgin olive oil). Sources are listed for hard-to-find items. Owing to DeMasco's well-respected culinary pedigree, home bakers will want this." Libr J

Desaulniers, Marcel

Death by chocolate cakes; an astonishing array of chocolate enchantment. recipes with Brett Bailey and Kelly Bailey; photography by Duane Winfield. Morrow 2000 216p il $35   **641.8**
  1. Cake 2. Cooking -- Chocolate
  ISBN 0-688-16297-5
                                         LC 00-56247

This "cookbook features indulgent showstoppers, from Happy All the Time Cakes to Excessively Expressive Espresso Ecstasy, each one shown in a full-page color photograph. Although many of the recipes are complicated, instructions are detailed and clear; there are no headnotes per se to introduce these creations, but 'The Chef's Touch' section at the end of each recipe provides tips and some background." Libr J

Includes bibliographical references

Fine cooking appetizers; 200 recipes for small bites with big flavor. from the editors and contributors of Fine cooking. Taunton Press 2010 252 p. col. ill. $19.95   **641.8**
1. Cookbooks 2. Appetizers
ISBN 1600853307; 9781600853302

LC 2010028598

"In [this collection] the editors of Fine Cooking have gathered a tempting--and satisfying--range of recipes on favorite topics. . . . As always, clear instructions, full-color photos, plus tips and techniques help you get delicious results." This cookbook features 200 recipes for appetizers. (Publisher's note)

The **Gourmet** cookie book; the single best recipe from each year 1941-2009. Houghton Mifflin Harcourt 2010 161p il $18   **641.8**
1. Cookies
ISBN 978-0-547-32816-4

LC 2010-18882

This cookbook "features one recipe for every year Gourmet magazine was in business. . . . The recipes are grouped by decade, from the ration-era pluck of the 1940s (honey refrigerator cookies and Scotch oat crunchies), when the magazine was published out of a penthouse in the Plaza Hotel, to the twisted classics of the oughts (cranberry turtle bars and glittering lemon sandwich cookies). The wistful headnotes offer historical insight into our past tastes and aspirations." N Y Times Book Rev

Haedrich, Ken
    ★ **Pie** : 300 tried-and-true recipes for delicious homemade pie. The Harvard Common Press 2004 639p il $37.95; pa $24.95   **641.8**
1. Baking
ISBN 1-558-32253-1; 1-558-32254-X pa

LC 2004-3635

Haedrich's "zeal and solid expertise make this book a worthy addition to the baker's bookshelf." Publ Wkly

Heatter, Maida
    Maida Heatter's book of great desserts; drawings by Toni Evins. Andrew McMeel 1999 xxxii, 528p il $26.95   **641.8**
1. Desserts
ISBN 0-8362-7861-5

LC 98-45993

First published 1974 by Knopf

This cookbook features nearly 300 dessert recipes for both light and rich desserts including Queen Mother's Cake, Mushroom Meringues, and East 62nd Street Lemon Cake

    Maida Heatter's brand-new book of great cookies; illustrations by the author. Random House 1995 244p il hardcover o.p. pa $19   **641.8**
1. Cookies
ISBN 0-8129-9175-3 pa

LC 95-5250

First published 1977 with title: Book of great cookies

"The instructions here are true to a long line of Heatter recipes: foolproof. Ms. Heatter's instructions are famously meticulous. They are also lengthy and chatty, full of learned asides." N Y Times Book Rev

Hellmich, Mittie, 1960-
    Ultimate bar book; the comprehensive guide to over 1,000 cocktails. by Mittie Hellmich ; illustrations by Arthur Mount. Chronicle Books 2006 474 p. ill. (jacket) $19.95   **641.8**
1. Cocktails 2. Bartending
ISBN 0811843513; 9780811843515

LC 2005030720

This alcoholic mixed-drinks guidebook, by Mittie Hellmich, features "essential-to-know topics such as barware, tools, and mixing tips. . . . Illustrations show precisely what type of glass should be used for each drink. With dozens of recipes for garnishes, rims, infusions, and syrups; punches, gelatin shooters, hot drinks, and non-alcoholic beverages." (Publisher's note)

Includes bibliographical references and indexes

Hensperger, Beth
    The **best** quick breads; 150 recipes for muffins, scones, shortcakes, gingerbreads, cornbreads, coffeecakes, and more. Beth Hensperger. Harvard Common Press 2000 256p pa $22.95   **641.8**
1. Bread
ISBN 1-55832-171-3

LC 00-36962

First published 1994 by Chronicle Books with title: The art of quick breads

This book includes about 150 recipes. "In addition to quick loaves, both sweet and savory, there are waffles, dumplings, biscuits, popovers, and a variety of other easy baked goods, along with some tasty accompaniments, such as the Fruit Salsa for her Hopi Blue Corn Hotcakes." Libr J

Hirigoyen, Gerald
    Pintxos; small plates in the Basque tradition. [by] Gerald Hirigoyen with Lisa Weiss; photography by Maren Caruso. Ten Speed Press 2009 201p il $24.95   **641.8**
1. Cooking 2. Basque cooking
ISBN 978-1-58008-922-7; 1-58008-922-4

LC 2008-43518

Lebovitz, David
    The **perfect** scoop; ice creams, sorbets, granitas, and sweet accompaniments. David Lebovitz ; pho-

tography by Lara Hata. Ten Speed Press 2007 256 p. il (pbk) $18.99; (hbk) $24.99 **641.8**
1. Desserts 2. Cookbooks 3. Ice cream, ices, etc.
ISBN 9781580082198; 9781580088084; 158008219X
LC 2006037610

This cookbook, by David Lebovitz, offers a "guide to the pleasures of homemade ice creams, sorbets, granitas, and more. With an emphasis on intense and sophisticated flavors and a bountiful helping of the author's expert techniques, this collection of frozen treats ranges from classic . . . to comforting . . ., contemporary . . . to cutting edge." (Publisher's note)

"The author's 25 years of experience as a frozen-dessert maker are put to excellent use in this wittily written, detailed volume. Step-by-step photos and advice on selecting an ice cream machine will reassure ice cream amateurs." Pub Wkly

Matheson, Christie

Flour; spectacular recipes from Boston's Flour Bakery + Cafe. by Joanne Chang, with Christie Matheson ; photographs by Keller + Keller. Chronicle Books 2010 319 p. col. ill. (hbk.) $35 **641.8**
1. Flour 2. Baking 3. Cookbooks 4. Baked products 5. Flour Bakery + Cafe 6. Baking -- Massachusetts -- Boston 7. Cooking -- Massachusetts -- Boston
ISBN 081186944X; 9780811869447
LC 2011377998

This baking cookbook, by Joanne Chang with Christie Matheson, features Boston, Massachusetts-based "Flour Bakery-owner Joanne Chang's repertoire of baked goods. . . . Almost 150 Flour recipes such as Milky Way Tart and Dried Fruit Focaccia are included, plus Joanne's essential baking tips." (Publisher's note)

Medrich, Alice

Chewy gooey crispy crunchy melt-in-your-mouth cookies. Artisan Books 2010 384p il $25.95 **641.8**
1. Cookies
ISBN 978-1-57965-397-2
LC 2010-19491

"Medrich presents a compendium of exciting and enticing cookie recipes that reflects every aspect of our widening culinary landscape. . . . The recipes are organized by texture, hence the title, but there's also a section grouping cookies into categories like those containing whole grains, those that keep at least two weeks, ridiculously quick and easy cookies, and cookies to make with kids. This book has redesigned and reframed the often-overlooked cookie and is a boon to the modern, conscious baker." Publ Wkly

Mix shake stir; cocktails for the home bar: recipes from Danny Meyer's acclaimed New York City restaurants. foreward by Danny Meyer. Little, Brown 2009 223p il $29.99 **641.8**
1. Cocktails
ISBN 978-0-316-04512-4; 0-316-04512-8
LC 2008-934947

Restauranteur Meyers "delivers a terrific collection of 140 tempting recipes for cocktails created by bartenders in his award-winning dining establishments. Included are old favorites like the Ritz as well as new classics like the Winter Mojito, and the book's clear instructions and luscious pho-

tographs will inspire even nondrinkers to pick up a cocktail shaker. As a bonus, basic tips on mixing drinks, recipes for simple syrups and garnishes, and a concise collection of recipes for bar snacks are offered." Libr J

Mushet, Cindy

The **art** and soul of baking; [by] Sur La Table with Cindy Mushet; foreword by Alice Medrich; photography by Maren Caruso. Andrews McMeel Pub. 2008 454p il $40 **641.8**
1. Baking
ISBN 978-0-7407-7334-1; 0-7407-7334-8
LC 2008-8232

This guide to baking "covers both sweet and savory baking. . . . Two lengthy introductory chapters cover techniques, equipment, and ingredients, and dozens of sidebars on 'Tips for Success' and 'What the Pros Know' offer further helpful insider advice. . . . Mushet's style is engaging and never intimidating. Essential." Libr J

Ojakangas, Beatrice

The **Best** Casserole cookbook ever; by Beatrice Ojakangas; photographs by Susie Cushner. Chronicle Books 2008 640 p. col. ill. (alk. paper) $24.95 **641.8**
1. Baking 2. Cookbooks 3. Casserole cooking
ISBN 0811856240; 9780811856249
LC 2007042019

This cookbook, by Beatrice Ojakangas, with photography by Susie Cushner, is dedicated to baking casseroles. "From a breakfast of Eggs Florentine to a dinner of Pork Chops with Apple Stuffing, soon even the most casserole-wary cook will be dishing about these delights. Yummy treats like Parmesan and Sun-Dried Tomato Quiche and Strawberry Rhubarb Crisp are just right for parties. Even appetizers are reinvented in casserole form!" (Publisher's note)

Parsons, Brad Thomas

Bitters; a spirited history of a classic cure-all, with cocktails, recipes, and formulas. Brad Thomas Parsons ; photographs by Ed Anderson. Ten Speed Press 2011 231 p. col. ill. $24.99 **641.8**
1. Cocktails 2. Alcohol -- History 3. Alcoholic beverages 4. Bitters
ISBN 1580083595; 9781580083591
LC 2011017774

A brief history of bitters -- A bitters boom -- Making your own bitters -- Setting up your bar -- Bitters hall of fame -- Old-guard cocktails -- New-look cocktails -- Bitters in the kitchen
IACP Award (2012)
James Beard Award (2012)

This book, by Brad Thomas Parsons with photography by Ed Anderson, "traces the history of the world's most storied elixir, [bitters,] from its earliest 'snake oil' days to its near evaporation after Prohibition to its ascension as a beloved (and at times obsessed-over) ingredient on the contemporary bar scene." (Publisher's note)
Includes bibliographical references and index

Pasta, atlante dei prodotti tipici/English

Encyclopedia of pasta; translated by Maureen B. Fant; with a foreword by Carol Field. University of

California Press 2009 xxi, 374p il map (California studies in food and culture) $29.95   **641.8**
1. Reference books 2. Cooking -- Pasta products 3. Pasta products -- Encyclopedias
ISBN 978-0-520-25522-7

LC 2009-10522

This book provides "a complete history of pasta in Italy, showcasing more than 300 types of pasta—from bucatini and gnocchetti to tortellini and ziti. . . . Each entry is nicely displayed in a box and includes an overview of each pasta type: the primary ingredients, preparation techniques, the different names for each kind of pasta, how it is served, the region where it is found, and the author's remarks. . . . This wonderful resource is destined to become the definitive book on pasta. It succeeds both as a scholarly achievement and as an entertaining and authentic overview of Italian history and geography." Libr J

Includes bibliographical references

Patent, Greg

Baking in America; traditional and contemporary favorites from the past 200 years. Houghton Mifflin 2002 552p il $35   **641.8**
1. Baking
ISBN 0-618-04831-6

"Patent's cookbook will be irresistible to anyone interested in the rich traditions and history of American baking." Libr J

Peterson, James

Baking. Ten Speed Press 2009 378p il $40 **641.8**
1. Baking
ISBN 978-1-58008-991-3

"This workhorse of a guidebook . . . is a worthy baking school between covers. . . . The work features over 300 recipes, mostly classics based in the French tradition. The five chapters—Cakes; Pies, Tarts and Pastries; Cookies; Breads, Quick Breads, and Bread-based Desserts; and Custards, Soufflés, Fruit Curds and Mousses—include a comprehensive overview, sidebars on techniques and recipes designed to teach techniques that can be used in more than the recipe listed." Publ Wkly

Pillsbury Co.

Pillsbury best cookies cookbook; favorite recipes from America's most-trusted kitchens. [by] the Pillsbury Company. Wiley Pub 2003 255p il $22.95   **641.8**
1. Cookies
ISBN 0-7645-8854-0; 978-0-7645-8854-9
First published 1997 by Potter

This "cookbook includes more than 175 recipes for cookies, brownies, and other bars, from old favorites like Chocolate Chips to new ones like Cherry Poppy Seed Twinks. . . . There are also lots of tips and hints, suggestions to 'Make It Special,' and variations, as well as 'real-time' prep times and nutrition analyses for each recipe." Libr J [review of 1997 edition]

Robertson, Chad

Tartine; by Elisabeth M. Prueitt and Chad Robertson ; foreword by Alice Waters ; photographs by

France Ruffenach. Chronicle Books 2006 223 p. ill. (chiefly col.) $35   **641.8**
1. Pastry 2. Desserts 3. Cookbooks 4. Tartine (Bakery)
ISBN 0811851508; 9780811851503

LC 2006004651

In this cookbook, "pastry chef Elisabeth Prueitt and . . . baker Chad Robertson share not only their fabulous recipes, but also the secrets and expertise that transform a delicious homemade treat into a great one." Recipes featured include "moist Brioche Bread Pudding; luscious Banana Cream Pie; [and] the sweet-tart perfection of Apple Crisp. . . . Practical advice comes in the form of handy Kitchen Notes. These "hows" and "whys" convey the authors' know-how." (Publisher's note)

Tartine bread; photographs by Eric Wolfinger. Chronicle Books 2010 304p il $40   **641.8**
1. Bread
ISBN 978-0-8118-7041-2

"This 'baker's guidebook' is divided into four parts: Basic Country Bread; Semolina and Whole-Wheat Breads; Baguettes and Enriched Breads; and Day-Old Bread. Robertson's basic recipe is explained in depth with numbered steps, and consists of making a natural leaven and baking in a cast-iron cooker. The author's passionate tone and tales of baking apprenticeships, along with top-notch step-by-step photos, elevate the title from mere manual to enjoyable read." Publ Wkly

Sax, Richard

★ **Classic** home desserts; a treasury of heirloom and contemporary recipes from around the world. Richard Sax ; photography by Alan Richardson. Houghton Mifflin Harcourt 2010 648 p. col il $35   **641.8**
1. Desserts 2. Cookbooks 3. International cooking
ISBN 0618057080; 9780618057085

LC 2010025552

James Bead Award (1995)
IACP Cookbook Award (1995)

This dessert cookbook, by Richard Sax with photography by Alan Richardson, winner of the James Beard Award and the Julia Child Award, offers "350 of the best and most beloved home desserts. Everything the cook longs for is here: cobblers and crisps, cakes and cookies, puddings and soufflés, pies and pastries, ice creams and sauces." (Publisher's note)

Includes bibliographical references and index

Schreiber, Cory

Rustic fruit desserts; crumbles, buckles, cobblers, pandowdies, and more. [by] Cory Schreiber and Julie Richardson; photography by Sara Remington. Ten Speed Press 2009 164p il $22   **641.8**
1. Desserts 2. Cooking -- Fruit
ISBN 978-1-58008-976-0; 1-58008-976-3

LC 2008-49349

"A seasonal mini-bible that goes beyond basics." N Y Times Book Rev

Tosi, Christina

Momofuku Milk Bar; Christina Tosi. 1st ed.; Clarkson Potter 2011 p. cm. $35 **641.8**
1. Baking 2. Desserts 3. Momofuku Milk Bar
ISBN 978-0-307-72049-8
LC 2011007720

Walter, Carole

Great cookies; secrets to sensational sweets. Carole Walter ; photographs by Duane Winfield. 1st ed; Clarkson Potter 2003 418 p. col. ill. $35 **641.8**
1. Cookbooks 2. Cookies
ISBN 0609609696; 9780609609699
LC 2003007633
IACP Cookbook Award Winner (2004)
This cookbook, by Carole Walter with photography by Duane Winfield, is "packed with more than 200 . . . recipes and more than 150 . . . photographs [of cookies,] . . . from traditional favorites like Snickerdoodles, Oatmeal Raisin, and Favorite Lemon Squares to future stars of the cookie jar like the trail mix-inspired Teton Trailers and chewy, chocolaty Midnight Macaroons." (Publisher's note)
Includes bibliographical references (p. 404) and index

Zabar, Tracey

One sweet cookie; celebrated chefs share favorite recipes. photography by Ellen Silverman. Rizzoli 2011 191p il $30 **641.8**
1. Cookies
ISBN 978-0-8478-3666-6
LC 2011927545
"When cookie-obsessed baker Zabar couldn't convince friends to participate in a cookie swap, she orchestrated a virtual exchange, the result of which is this outstanding collection of recipes from more than 50 well-known New York City chefs. . . . [It features] contributions from Dorie Greenspan, Michael Laiskonis, Maury Rubin, Laurent Tourondel, and others." Libr J
Includes bibliographical references

641.81   Side dishes, sauces, garnishes

Beranbaum, Rose Levy

★ The **baking** Bible; Rose Levy Beranbaum. Houghton Mifflin Harcourt 2014 576 p. (hardback) $40 **641.81**
1. Baking 2. Cookbooks
ISBN 1118338618; 9781118338612
LC 2014016319
"With all-new recipes for the best cakes, pies, tarts, cookies, candies, pastries, breads, and more, this magnum opus draws from [author] Rose [Levy Beranbaum's] passion and expertise in every category of baking. As is to be expected from the woman who's been called 'the most meticulous cook who ever lived,' each sumptuous recipe is truly foolproof--with detail-oriented instructions that eliminate guesswork, 'plan-aheads,' ingenious tips, and highlights for success." (Publisher's note)
"Berenbaum successfully bridges the gap between popular home baking collections and professional texts." LJ

Forkish, Ken

Flour water salt yeast; the fundamentals of artisan bread and pizza. Ken Forkish ; photographs by alan Weiner. Ten Speed Press 2012 265 p. col. ill. (hardback) $35 **641.81**
1. Bread 2. Pizza 3. Baking 4. Cookbooks
ISBN 160774273X; 9781607742739; 9781607742746
LC 2012012080
James Beard Foundation Award: Baking and Dessert (2013)
IACP Cookbook Award (2013)
This book, by Ken Forkish, is "[d]ivided into four sections ('The Principles of Artisan Bread,' 'Basic Bread Recipes,' 'Levain Bread Recipes,' and 'Pizza Recipes'), with recipes broken down by breads made with store-bought yeast, breads made with long-fermented simple doughs, and doughs made with pre-ferments. . . . [The] book presents recipes accessible to novices, while providing a different approach for making dough to experienced bakers." (Publishers Weekly)

Peterson, James

★ **Sauces**; classical and contemporary sauce making. James Peterson. 3rd ed.; J. Wiley 2008 612 p. ill. (chiefly col.) $49.95 **641.81**
1. Sauces 2. Cookbooks
ISBN 0470194960; 9780470194966
LC 2007046546
James Bead Award (1992)
This cookbook, the third edition by James Peterson, is the "former winner of the prestigious James Beard Cookbook-of-the-Year award and the ultimate reference for saucemaking. . . . With more 325 recipes in all, [it] includes all-new chapters on Asian sauces and pasta sauces, plus new recipes that cater to lighter, contemporary tastes. Includes a 32-page color insert with more than 100 color photos of sauce-making techniques." (Publisher's note)
"In the third edition, the sections have been organized so the entries are easier to use as a reference. Peterson has also added 60 recipes that showcase the sauces with a variety of foods." LJ
Includes bibliographical references and index

Robertson, Chad

Tartine Book No. 3; modern, ancient, classic, whole. Chad Robertson. Chronicle Books 2013 336 p. color illustrations $40 **641.81**
1. Baking 2. Cookbooks 3. Alternative grains 4. Pastry 5. Cooking (Bread) 6. Tartine (Bakery)
ISBN 1452114307; 9781452114309
LC 2012276745
This book, by Chad Robertson, the third cookbook published "from Tartine Bakery & Cafe. . . . is a revolutionary, and altogether timely, exploration of baking with whole grains. The narrative of Chad Robertson's search for ancient flavors in heirloom grains is interwoven with 85 recipes for whole-grain versions of Tartine favorites." (Publisher's note)
"Acclaimed baker and Tartine Bakery cofounder Robertson's third cookbook is as visually impressive as its predecessors. . . . Its recipes, however, are far more challenging, providing spare instructions and assuming considerable technical knowledge. Robertson breaks up chapters

of intriguing and innovative breads, crispbreads, and pastries (e.g., sprouted quinoa kamut bread, lemon-poppy-kefir pound cake) with accounts of baking-related travels in Denmark, Sweden, Germany, Austria, France, and Mexico." LJ

641.82 Main dishes

Green, Aliza

Making artisan pasta; how to make a world of handmade noodles, stuffed pasta, dumplings, and more. [Aliza Green ; with photography by Steve Legato] Quarry Books 2012 176 p. col. ill. (pbk.) $24.99 **641.82**

1. Cookbooks 2. Cooking -- Pasta products 3. Noodles 4. Cooking (Pasta)
ISBN 1592537324; 9781592537327

LC 2011031326

This cookbook offers "chef Aliza Green's pasta expertise and encyclopedic knowledge of all things culinary, plus hundreds of . . . photos by acclaimed food photographer Steve Legato, [so that readers can] learn how to use the best ingredients and simple, classic techniques to make fresh, homemade pasta in . . . [their] own kitchen." (Publisher's note)

"The book contains many useful extras such as nutrition information, resources, and a glossary, but those who want to serve a homemade sauce along with their pasta fresca may need to consult another resource." LJ

Includes bibliographical references (p. 168-169) and index

Marchetti, Domenica

The **glorious** pasta of Italy; by Domenica Marchetti. Chronicle Books 2011 280 p. col. ill. (alk. paper) $30 **641.82**

1. Cookbooks 2. Italian cooking 3. Cooking -- Pasta products 4. Cooking, Italian
ISBN 0811872599; 9780811872591

LC 2011030010

This pasta-centered Italian cookbook, by Domenica Marchetti, "draws from her Italian heritage to share 100 classic and modern recipes. Step-by-step instructions for making fresh pasta offer plenty of variations on the classic egg pasta, while a glossary of pasta shapes, a source list for unusual ingredients, and a handy guide for stocking the pantry with pasta essentials encourage the home cook to look beyond simple spaghetti." (Publisher's note)

Includes index

Parachini, Chris

Roberta's; Carlo Mirarchi, Brandon Hoy, Chris Parachini and Katherine Wheelock, art direction by Ryan Rice. Clarkson Potter 2013 287 p. color illustrations $35 **641.82**

1. Pizza 2. Cookbooks 3. Restaurants 4. Roberta's (Restaurant)
ISBN 0770433715; 9780770433710

LC 2013004300

The authors of this cookbook, Carlo Mirarchi, Brandon Hoy, Chris Parachini and Katherine Wheelock, "share recipes, photographs, and stories meant to capture the ex-

perience of [the Brooklyn-based pizza restaurant] Roberta's for those who haven't been, and to immortalize it for those who've been there since the beginning." (Publisher's note)

Segan, Francine

Pasta modern; new & inspired recipes from Italy. Francine Segan. Stewart, Tabori & Chang 2013 208 p. $35 **641.82**

1. Italian cooking 2. Cooking -- Pasta products
ISBN 1617690627; 9781617690624

LC 2013935989

In this book, author Francine Segan "challenges the notion that pasta must be traditional or old-world. . . . Segan details . . . unusual pasta dishes from Italy's food bloggers, home cooks, artisan pasta makers, and vanguard chefs. . . . Tips and anecdotes culled from Segan's Italian travels enhance the easy-to-follow directions, and a glossary of more than 50 . . . dried pastas showcases shapes to revive any pasta lover's repertoire." (Publisher's note)

"Meticulously researched, thoughtfully curated, and artfully designed, this unique collection will inspire readers to try new preparations and flavors." LJ

Tanis, David

One good dish; by David Tanis. Artisan 2013 256 p. $25.95 **641.82**

1. Cookbooks 2. One-dish meals
ISBN 1579654673; 9781579654672

LC 2013006289

Author David Tanis "turns his focus to an eclectic array of simple, casual meals that satisfy and are appropriate to be eaten at any time of day. Tanis's whimsy runs from bread, snacks, and condiments to vegetables, griddled foods, desserts, and more. Waffle-iron grilled cheese, gorgonzola and walnut crostini; and ham and gruyere bread pudding are highlights among the rustic offering of bread entries." (Publishers Weekly)

641.83 Salads

Romero, Terry Hope

Salad samurai; 100 cutting-edge, ultra-hearty, easy-to-make salads you don't have to be vegan to love. Terry Hope Romero. Da Capo Lifelong 2014 180 p. col. ill. (pbk.) $19.99 **641.83**

1. Salads 2. Veganism 3. Cookbooks 4. Vegan cooking
ISBN 0738214876; 9780738214870

LC 2014002618

This vegan cookbook, by Terry Hope Romero, offers a "guide to real salad bushido: a hearty base, a zesty dressing, and loads of seriously tasty toppings. . . . Based on whole food ingredients and seasonal produce, these versatile meatless, dairy-free dishes are organized by season for a full year of memorable meals." (Publisher's note)

641.86   Desserts

Greenspan, Dorie

★ **Baking** chez moi; recipes from my paris home to your home anywhere. Dorie Greenspan ; photographs by Alan Richardson. Houghton Mifflin Harcourt 2014 496 p. ill. (chiefly col.) (hardback) $40   **641.86**

1. Baking 2. Desserts 3. French cooking 4. Cooking, French

ISBN 0547724241; 9780547724249

LC 2014016312

In this cookbook, author Dorie Greenspan "explores the fascinating world of French desserts, bringing together a charmingly uncomplicated mix of contemporary recipes, including original creations based on traditional and regional specialties, and drawing on seasonal ingredients, market visits, and her travels throughout the country." (Publisher's note)

Kave, Allison

First prize pies; Shoo-fly, candy apple & other deliciously inventive pies for every week of the year (and more) Allison Kave. Stewart, Tabori & Chang 2014 224 p. color illustrations $29.95   **641.86**

1. Pies 2. Cookbooks

ISBN 161769102X; 9781617691027

LC 2013945638

In this cookbook, author "Allison Kave made pies as a hobby, until one day her boyfriend convinced her to enter a Brooklyn pie-making contest. . . . [Now] people can't get enough of her Bourbon Ginger Pecan pie, her whimsical Root Beer Float Pie, her addictive Chocolate Peanut Butter Pretzel Pie. . . . Organized by month, the book includes pies for every sweet tooth, from inventive pies like Chocolate Lavender Teatime to old-school comfort pies like Candy Apple." (Publisher's note)

Includes bibliographical references and index

Richardson, Julie

Vintage cakes; timeless cupcakes, flips, rolls, layer, angel, snack, chiffon, and icebox cakes for today's sweet tooth. Julie Richardson ; photography by Erin Kunke. Ten Speed Press 2012 166 p. col. ill. (hbk.) $24   **641.86**

1. Cake 2. Cookbooks

ISBN 1607741024; 9781607741022

LC 2011041262

This cookbook by Julie Richardson focuses on cakes. She "consulted classic cookbooks, submissions from family and friends, and vintage recipes dating back to the 1920s. . . . Richardson includes familiar (e.g., Wacky, Texas Sheet, Red Velvet, Caramel, and Watergate cakes) and lesser-known classics and a few originals, all updated to suit modern palates." (Library Journal)

Includes bibliographical references (p. 157) and index

Robicelli, Allison

Robicelli's; A Love Story, With Cupcakes: With 50 Decidedly Grown-up Recipes. by Allison Robi-

celli and Matt Robicelli. Penguin Group USA 2013 320 p. $35   **641.86**

1. Baking 2. Family 3. Cupcakes

ISBN 0670785873; 9780670785872

Authors Allison Robicelli and Matt Robicelli present a "guide to gourmet cupcakes, featuring grown-up flavors (figs! whiskey! fried chicken!) and the delicious story of a family saved by a love of sweets. Nixing cutesy, pastel-colored dollops of fluff for real ingredients and rich French buttercreams, the husband and wife team have reinvented the cupcake craze for a more sophisticated palate." (Publisher's note)

"Photos are lick-the-page enticing and proof that home bakers are going to enjoy the best bleeping cupcakes their side of the Brooklyn Bridge." Pub Wkly

Shulman, Martha Rose

★ The **art** of French pastry; Jacquy Pfeiffer ; with Martha Rose Shulman ; photographs by Paul Strabbing. Alfred A. Knopf 2013 432 p. (hardback) $85   **641.86**

1. Baking 2. Pastry 3. French cooking 4. Cooking, French

ISBN 0307959368; 9780307959355

LC 2013017643

In this cookbook, pastry chef Jacquy Pfeiffer provides "an intimate knowledge of the fundamentals of pastry. . . . By teaching you how to make everything from pâte à choux to pastry cream, Pfeiffer builds on the basics until you have an understanding of the science behind the ingredients used, how they interact with one another, and what your hands have to do to transform them into pastry." (Publisher's note)

"Anyone studying to be a professional baker will profit from Pfeiffer's guidance, and the amateur cook can vastly improve family desserts." Booklist

641.87   Preparing beverages

Conigliaro, Tony, 1971-

The **cocktail** lab; unraveling the mysteries of flavor and aroma in drink, with recipes. Tony Conigliaro. Ten Speed Press 2013 224 p. color illustrations (hardback) $29.99   **641.87**

1. Bartending 2. Alcoholic beverages 3. Cocktails

ISBN 1607745674; 9781607745679

LC 2013004969

James Beard Award (2014)

In this book, bartender Tony Conigliaro presents a "collection of 60 revolutionary cocktails, all grounded in the classics but utilizing technologies and techniques from the molecular gastronomy movement. . . . Tony presents his best and boldest creations: drinks like the Vintage Manhattan, Dirty Martini by the Sea, and Cosmo Popcorn." (Publisher's note)

Includes bibliographical references (pages 217-218) and index

Fauchald, Nick

★ **Death** & Co; modern classic cocktails. David Kaplan, Nick Fauchald, Alex Day ; photographs by

William Hereford ; illustrations by Tim Tomkinson. Ten Speed Press 2014 320 p. ill. (some col.) (hardcover) $40   **641.87**

1. Bars 2. Cocktails 3. Bartending 4. Death & Co. (Bar : New York, N.Y.)

ISBN 1607745259; 9781607745259

LC 2014004245

This book, by David Kaplan, Nick Fauchald, and Alex Day, is a "guide to the contemporary craft cocktail movement. . . . [M]ore than just a collection of recipes, [it] is also a complete cocktail education, with information on the theory and philosophy of drink making, a complete guide to buying and using spirits, and step-by-step instructions for mastering key bartending techniques." (Publisher's note)

Includes bibliographical references and index

Morgenthaler, Jeffrey

Bar Book; Elements of Cocktail Technique. Jeffrey Morgenthaler with Martha Holmberg ; photographs by Alanna Hale. Chronicle Books Llc 2014 288 p. color illustrations (hc) $30   **641.87**

1. Cocktails 2. Bartending 3. Alcoholic beverages

ISBN 9781452113845; 145211384X

"Written by renowned bartender and cocktail blogger Jeffrey Morgenthaler, 'The Bar Book' is the only technique-driven cocktail handbook out there. . . . More than 60 recipes illustrate the concepts explored in the text, ranging from juicing, garnishing, carbonating, stirring, and shaking to choosing the correct ice for proper chilling and dilution of a drink." (Publisher's note)

642   Meals and table service

Colwin, Laurie

More home cooking; a writer returns to the kitchen. Laurie Colwin. HarperPerennial 2000 224 p. $12.99   **642**

1. Cookbooks 2. Food 3. Cookery 4. Cooking 5. Entertaining

ISBN 0060955317; 9780060955311

James Beard Cookbook Hall of Fame (2012)

This book, "like its predecessor, 'Home Cooking,' is an expression of [author] Laurie Colwin's lifelong passion for cuisine. In this . . . mix of recipes, advice, and anecdotes, she writes about often overlooked food items such as beets, pears, black beans, and chutney. . . . Colwin also discusses the many pleasures and problems of cooking at home in essays such as 'Desserts That Quiver,' 'Turkey Angst,' and 'Catering on One Dollar a Head.'" (Publisher's note)

643   Housing and household equipment

Becker, Norman

The **complete** book of home inspection; 3rd ed; McGraw-Hill 2002 289p il pa $19.95   **643**

1. Houses -- Inspection

ISBN 0-07-139125-8

LC 2002-27892

First published 1980

The author "provides the novice homebuilder and buyer with inspection information for roofs, exterior landscaping, plumbing, and electrical, as well as tips on searching for insects and rotting materials. Helpful checklists guide readers in inspecting all parts of a home from the exterior walkway to the interior basement." Libr J

Black & Decker Corp.

The **complete** guide to finishing basements; step-by-step projects for adding living space without adding on. Creative Pub. International 2009 255p il pa $24.99   **643**

1. Basements 2. Houses -- Remodeling

ISBN 978-1-58923-454-3; 1-58923-454-5

LC 2008-45813

"Thorough and filled from beginning to end with handy reference information, this tome more than adequately demostrates how to evaluate, upgrade, and remodel the . . . basement." Booklist

The **complete** photo guide to home improvement; [created by the editors of Creative Publishing International, Inc., in cooperation with Black & Decker] Creative Pub. International 2009 560p il $35   **643**

1. Houses -- Remodeling 2. Houses -- Maintenance and repair

ISBN 978-1-58923-452-9; 1-58923-452-9

LC 2008-45755

First published 2001

This home improvement guide covers such topics as flooring, ceilings and walls, windows and doors, and remodeling different rooms including kitchens, bathrooms, and basements.

This "guide is basic, easy to follow, and completely illustrated. The organization is sensible and information easy to find." Libr J

The **complete** photo guide to home repair. Creative Pub. International 2008 559p il $35   **643**

1. Houses -- Maintenance and repair

ISBN 978-1-58923-417-8; 1-58923-417-0

LC 2008-16520

First published 1999

"Features more than 200 . . . home repair projects, including common wiring, plumbing, interior and exterior repairs." Publisher's note

Bray, Ilona M.

Nolo's essential guide to buying your first home; [by] Ilona Bray, Alayna Schroeder & Marcia Stewart. 3rd ed.; Nolo 2010 426p il pa $24.99   **643**

1. Houses -- Buying and selling

ISBN 978-1-4133-1322-2 pa; 1-4133-1322-1 pa; 978-1-4133-1348-2 ebook; 1-4133-1348-5 ebook

LC 2010-31334

First published 2007. Frequently revised

Provides information on selecting the right house, the right mortgage, the right agent, the right inspections and more. CD-ROM contains a "Homebuyer's Toolkit" with forms and other resources.

Includes bibliographical references

Bryson, Bill

At home; a short history of private life. Doubleday 2010 497p il $28.95 **643**

1. Rooms 2. Houses

ISBN 978-0-7679-1938-8; 0-7679-1938-6

LC 2010-04008

The author takes readers on a tour of his house, a rural English parsonage, showing how each room has figured in the evolution of private life.

"It takes a very particular kind of thoughtfulness, as well as a bold temperament, to stuff all this research into a mattress that's supportive enough to loll about on while pondering the real subject of this book—the development of the modern world. . . . Bryson is fascinated by everything, and his curiosity is infectious." N Y Times Book Rev

Includes bibliographical references

Corbett, Michael

Before you buy! the homebuyer's handbook for today's market. Plume 2011 xxiii, 277p il pa $15 **643**

1. Real estate investment 2. Houses -- Buying and selling

ISBN 978-0-452-29680-0

LC 2010050910

A real estate developer offers advice on buying a home during the economic crisis, covering common mistakes made by buyers and offering advice on how to handle foreclosure, mortgages, inspections, and other issues.

Crook, David

The **Wall** Street Journal complete home owner's guidebook; make the most of your biggest asset in any market. Three Rivers Press 2008 260p il pa $14.95 **643**

1. Real estate investment 2. Houses -- Buying and selling

ISBN 978-0-307-40592-0; 0-307-40592-3

LC 2008-25355

This is a "look at the pros and cons of owning a home—rather than renting one from a bank via a mortgage—along with its ultimate costs. . . . For those aspiring to own a home and those trying to manage the affordability of their biggest asset, this is a must read." Publ Wkly

Includes bibliographical references

Do it yourself kitchens; stunning spaces on a shoestring budget. Wiley 2011 192p **643**

1. Kitchens

ISBN 9781118031629

"Ranked by budget, from $1000 up to $10,000, sample kitchen makeovers showcased here illustrate a range of possibilities. With spending breakdowns, stunning before-and-after shots, and lots of tips that make big differences, this book has wide appeal. For each makeover there are detailed instructions for selected projects, such as installing fixtures, resurfacing, and tiling. This is not in-depth how-to, but ideas and inspiration. Each sample kitchen is brimming with creativity and innovation."

"Ranked by budget, from $1000 up to $10,000, sample kitchen makeovers showcased here illustrate a range of possibilities. With spending breakdowns, stunning before-and-after shots, and lots of tips that make big differences, this book has wide appeal. For each makeover there are detailed instructions for selected projects, such as installing fixtures, resurfacing, and tiling. This is not in-depth how-to, but ideas and inspiration. Each sample kitchen is brimming with creativity and innovation." Libr J

Family Handyman

Refresh your home; simple projects and tips to save money, update, and renovate. editors of the Family handyman. Reader's Digest 2011 287p il pa $16.95 **643**

1. Houses -- Remodeling

ISBN 978-1-60652-201-1

LC 2010029903

First published 2010 with title: Family handyman home improvement 2010

"The coverage of a wealth of home fixes with a dose of humor makes this DIY guide a delight. . . . There are tips and insights on every page. New gadgets, considerations for appliance purchases, and fun little projects populate this book. The section on power tool safety is important, and 'dos and don'ts' suggestions are peppered throughout. Even common goofs are shared with chuckles. A charming and friendly collection of tips and projects." Libr J

German, Roger

Remodeling a basement; Rev. ed.; Taunton Press 2010 170p il (Taunton's build like a pro) pa $19.95 **643**

1. Basements 2. Houses -- Remodeling

ISBN 978-1-60085-292-3

LC 2009-33545

First published 2004

"Beginning with solving moisture problems, then renovating space, this book walks the reader through a logical process for repair and remodeling, with easy-to-follow instruction and illustrations. Design ideas and the latest building code data are also included." Libr J

Home Depot, Inc.

Home improvement 1-2-3; 3rd ed., Newly expanded and rev.; Home Depot Books 2008 607p il $34.95 **643**

1. Interior design 2. Houses -- Remodeling 3. Houses -- Maintenance and repair

ISBN 978-0-696-23850-5

LC 2008-924090

First published 1995

This book offers illustrated instructions for home remodeling, decorating, and repair.

Jackson, Albert

Popular mechanics complete home how-to; [by] Albert Jackson and David Day. Hearst Books 2004 514p il $24.95 **643**

1. Houses -- Maintenance and repair

ISBN 1-58816-302-4

LC 2003-56853

"Interior and exterior repairs are included, from simple tasks like replacing an electrical switch to difficult ones like constructing a wall or building a pond, as well as common upgrades. Everything is explained in detail, with a wealth of clear photos and illustrations. A section on skills and tools shows the use of woodworking, building, decorating, plumbing, and electrical equipment, and a reference section describes hardware/materials and defines commonly used terminology. A great general guide to home repairs of all types, this book will see heavy use in most collections." Libr J

Litchfield, Michael W.

Renovation; [by] Michael Litchfield; Chip Harley, technical editor. 3rd ed, completely rev and updated; Taunton Press 2005 534p il $39.95   **643**

1. Houses -- Remodeling
ISBN 978-1-5615-8588-5; 1-5615-8588-2

LC 2005-110

First published 1982 by Wiley

This "guide covers all aspects of home renovation, including how to assess a house's structure, tools, materials, wiring, plumbing, painting, flooring, etc. Instructions are to the point—there is less hand-holding here than in other titles because some remodeling experience is assumed. A classic." Libr J

Papolos, Janice

The **virgin** homeowner; the essential guide to owning, maintaining, and surviving your first home. Norton 1997 444p il pa $24.95   **643**

1. Houses
ISBN 0-393-04035-6; 978-0-393-33496-8 pa; 0-393-33496-1 pa

LC 96-31304

"Beginning with how to get the most out of the initial home inspection, Papolos takes the reader through a house, describing each system, its quirks, and its potential problems. Later, she covers pest control, security, and safety. This highly readable book will prove useful to both new homeowners and those just thinking of making a purchase, and veteran homeowners will undoubtedly learn something, too." Libr J

Includes bibliographical references

Reader's Digest Association, Inc.

Complete do-it-yourself manual; with the editors of Family handyman. rev and updated; Reader's Digest 2005 528p il $35   **643**

1. Houses -- Maintenance and repair
ISBN 0-7621-0579-8

LC 2004-50945

First published 1973 with title: Reader's Digest complete do-it-yourself manual

This manual for homeowners covers topics such as power tools, plumbing, landscaping, and storage projects with photos, diagrams and illustrations

"Intriguing sidebars on wood refinishers (the fastest drying versus the safest), the financial benefits of renting specialty tools for a large drywall project and other subjects round out this must-have guide." Publ Wkly

Solakian, Susan E.

The **homeowner's** guide to managing a renovation; tough-as-nails tactics for getting the most from your money. Sterling 2008 288p il pa $19.95 **643**

1. Houses -- Remodeling
ISBN 978-1-4027-2754-2

LC 2008-03797

"While dollar figures used will quickly be outdated, the principles presented are constant. This is really an underrepresented topic in how-to collections, and Solakian's book is an especially good offering." Libr J

Soles, Clyde

The **fire** smart home handbook; preparing for and surviving the threat of wildfire. Clyde Soles ; foreword by Molly Mowery. Lyons Press 2014 288 p. illustrations (some color) (pbk.) $19.95   **643**

1. Wildfires 2. Houses -- Safety measures 3. Wildfires -- United States -- Prevention and control 4. Dwellings -- Fires and fire prevention -- United States
ISBN 0762796901; 9780762796908

LC 2013050242

Written by Clyde Soles, "this highly detailed and practical guide will help you live safely in the wildfire zone and save you time and money along the way, providing various methods of risk mitigation along with the financial level of each action. . . . This book will help you create a survivable space that will not only enhance the scenery but may increase the value of your home." (Publisher's note)

"While not everyone has to worry about wildfire, some of this advice applies to fire preparedness in most any home." Pub Wkly

Sussman, Julie

Dare to repair; a do-it-herself guide to fixing (almost) anything in the home. {by} Julie Sussman and Stephanie Glakas-Tenet; illustrations by Yeorgos Lampathakis. HarperCollins Pubs. 2002 253p il pa $14.95   **643**

1. Houses -- Maintenance and repair
ISBN 0-06-095984-3

LC 2002-27625

The authors "show women how to perform a number of the most common repairs, including unclogging drains and toilets, replacing electrical switches and outlets, leveling appliances, lighting pilot lights, unsticking windows, and installing a door peephole. . . . This is a wonderful book that should be purchased by every public library." Libr J

Ultimate guide: home repair and improvement; 3rd ed.; Creative Homeowner 2011 607p il $29.95   **643**

1. Houses -- Remodeling 2. Houses -- Maintenance and repair
ISBN 978-1-58011-528-5

First published 2000 with title: Home book

This guide "completely covers the repairs most home owners need. . . . This strong manual is highly recommended." Libr J

Wilson, Bee

Consider the fork; a history of how we cook and eat. Bee Wilson ; with illustrations by Annabel Lee. Basic Books 2012 xxiii, 327 p.p (hardback) $26.99 **643**

1. Food writing 2. Eating habits 3. Eating customs 4. Cooking -- History 5. Kitchen utensils -- History 6. Dinners and dining -- History

ISBN 0547773943; 9780465021765; 9780465033324

LC 2012016283

Author Bee Wilson presents an "evolution of cooking around the world, revealing the hidden history of everyday objects we often take for granted. Knives . . . predate the discovery of fire, whereas the fork endured centuries of ridicule before gaining widespread acceptance . . . Blending history, science, and anthropology, Wilson reveals how our culinary tools and tricks came to be, and how their influence has shaped modern food culture." (Publisher's note)

Includes bibliographical references and index.

Wing, Charlie

How your house works; a visual guide to understanding & maintaining your home. RSMeans 2007 152p il pa $21.95 **643**

1. Houses -- Maintenance and repair

ISBN 978-0-87629-015-6; 0-87629-015-2

This book "teaches the basics of home systems and appliances. Providing clean and detailed diagrams, Wing describes the purpose and function of that system or fixture. Also accompanying each is a list of tips to use before you call in a professional. This book is more a 'how' than a 'how-to' and fills its role quite nicely." Libr J

645 Household furnishings

Montano, Mark

The big -ass book of home decor; photographs by Auxy Espinoza. Stewart, Tabori & Chang 2010 271p il pa $22.50 **645**

1. Interior design

ISBN 978-1-58479-825-5

LC 2009-36376

The author "presents over 100 projects for decorating, creating, and repurposing furniture and decorative accessories. He offers clearly written instructions illustrated with color photographs of the steps. The wealth of inspiring projects that require only basic skills—e.g., decoupage, spray paint, glue gun—will make this a popular choice for both experienced and inexperienced crafters." Libr J

646 Sewing, clothing, management of personal and family life

Moebes, Deborah

Stitch Savvy; 25 Skill-Building Projects to Take Your Sewing Technique to the Next Level: Home Decor, Patchwork & Quilting, Bags, Sewing for Children, Clothing. F & W Media Inc 2012 224 p. (hardcover) $27.99 **646**

1. Sewing -- Technique

ISBN 1440229473; 9781440229473

This book by Deborah Moebes "focuses on sewists who are ready to move past basic beginner projects. The title is organized into five 'tracks' (home decor, patchwork and quilting, bags, sewing for children, and clothing), each with five progressively more difficult projects. The author's goal is to further refine basic sewing skills and bring beginners to the next level. . . . [E]ach project includes a sidebar that serves as a guide to possible 'next steps'." (Library Journal)

646.2 Sewing and related operations

Bednar, Nancy

The encyclopedia of sewing machine techniques; [by] Nancy Bednar, JoAnn Pugh-Gannon. Sterling Pub. 2007 336p il pa $24.95 **646.2**

1. Sewing

ISBN 1-4027-4293-2; 978-1-4027-4293-4

First published 1999

Among the techniques covered in this illustrated step-by-step guide are beading, fringing, pintucks, and puffing.

Cheetham, Kathleen

Singer perfect plus; sew a mix-and-match wardrobe in plus and petite-plus sizes. Quayside Pub. Group 2009 144p il $25 **646.2**

1. Sewing 2. Tailoring 3. Women's clothing

ISBN 978-1-58923-394-2; 1-58923-394-8

LC 2008-30415

"Cheetham's projects for casual and workplace fashions are accessible for beginning sewers. The mix-and-match tips are reminiscent of fashion magazine features, providing hints for assembling creative outfits. It's refreshing to see the clothes modeled on an actual plus-sized woman (the author herself)." Libr J

Colgrove, Debbie

Teach yourself visually sewing. Wiley 2006 283p il (Visual read less, learn more) pa $24.99 **646.2**

1. Sewing

ISBN 0-471-74991-5; 978-0-471-74991-2

LC 2005-939196

This visual guide explains the "basics of hand sewing and sewing with a machine. . . . [It includes] information about tools and fabrics." Publisher's note

Creative Publishing International

The complete photo guide to window treatments; [edited by Linda Neubauer] 2nd ed; Creative Publisher International 2011 320p il pa $24.99 **646.2**

1. Draperies

ISBN 978-1-58923-607-3

LC 2010046925

First published 2007

"Fabric recommendations and materials lists introduce each style of window treatment, with clear, step-by-step instructions. Organization is consistent and well thought out, making this an easy manual to follow." Libr J

Includes bibliographical references

Creative Publishing International, Inc.

★ The **complete** photo guide to sewing; 1200 full-color how-to photos. [created by the editors of Creative Publishing International] Rev. + expanded ed.; Creative Pub. International 2009 352p il pa $24.99   **646.2**

1. Sewing

ISBN 978-1-58923-434-5; 1-58923-434-0

LC 2008-31264

First published 1999

"Sections include choosing the right tools and notions, using conventional machines and sergers, fashion sewing, tailoring, and home décor projects. Included are step-by-step instructions for basic projects like pillows, tablecloths, and window treatments." Publisher's note

Gardiner, Wendy

The **sewing** machine accessory bible; get the most out of your machine from using basic feet to mastering specialty feet. [by] Wendy Gardiner & Lorna Knight. Griffin: St. Martin's 2011 128p il pa $22.99   **646.2**

1. Sewing machines

ISBN 978-0-312-67658-2

This book focuses "on sewing machine accessories—feet, needles, and other attachments. . . . [The authors] briefly cover the basics of sewing machines, but they focus on the specialized feet that come with the machine. A photo of a sewing machine foot is included at the top left corner of each spread, allowing for quick and easy identification. There's also information about how to use each foot—what it's for and how to sew with it. Beginners will find this book especially handy." Libr J

James, Chris

The **complete** serger handbook. Sterling 1997 159p il hardcover o.p. pa $17.95   **646.2**

1. Sewing 2. Sewing machines

ISBN 0-8069-9807-5 pa

LC 96-39316

This "is a concise guide to the serger and serger techniques. Major sections of the book include identifying the parts of a serger (with photos of each part), serger accessories, types of threads, threading and testing the threading, learning to regulate tension, and techniques." Libr J

Lee, Linda

Sewing edges and corners. Taunton Press 2000 134p il pa $19.95   **646.2**

1. Sewing

ISBN 1-56158-418-5

LC 00-29919

The author offers about 40 corner and edge techniques for garments and home decorating projects

"Readers appreciate the clarity of Lee's instructions, since each step is numbered, photographs and other illustra-

tions ease difficult tasks, and sidebars ensure the comfortableness of the sewing." Booklist

The **new** sewing essentials; Updated and rev. ed.; Creative Publishing International 2008 144p il pa $16.99   **646.2**

1. Sewing

ISBN 978-1-58923-432-1; 1-58923-432-4

First published 1984 by Random House with title: Sewing essentials

This guide to sewing clothes and other items includes information on equipment, patterns, fabrics, and techniques.

Reader's Digest Association, Inc.

New complete guide to sewing; step-by-step techniques for making clothes and home accessories. from the editors at Reader's digest. Reader's Digest Assn. 2002 384p il $35   **646.2**

1. Sewing

ISBN 0-7621-0420-1

LC 2002-69944

First published 1976 with title: Complete guide to sewing

This illustrated guide begins with an overview of basic equipment and techniques. A discussion of patterns and fabrics is included. The bulk of the book provides step-by-step instructions for making clothes and home furnishings.

Yaker, Rebecca

Little one-yard wonders; by Rebecca Yaker and Patricia Hoskins. Storey Publishing 2014 360 p. color illustrations (One-yard wonders series) (paper w/concealed wire-o and patterns : alk. paper) $29.95   **646.2**

1. Handicraft 2. Children's clothing 3. Machine sewing 4. Children's paraphernalia

ISBN 1612121241; 9781612121246

LC 2013045043

Written by Rebecca Yaker and Patricia Hoskins, "[t]his newest addition to the best-selling One-Yard Wonders series features 101 . . . projects for babies and kids, each using just one yard of fabric and many requiring just a few hours to complete. Step-by-step illustrated instructions, . . . close-up photographs, and pattern pieces included in a bound-in envelope make it easy and fun to create all kinds of adorable items." (Publisher's note)

"This title is a treasure trove of handmade kid's stuff, and sewists of all skill levels will find ideas and inspiration in this lighthearted collection." LJ

646.4   Clothing and accessories construction

Abousteit, Nora

BurdaStyle sewing vintage modern; mastering iconic looks from the 1920s to 1980s. Nora Abousteit with Jamie Lau and David Leon Morgan. 1st ed. Potter Craft 2012 216 p. illustrations (chiefly color) (hardcover) $29.99; (ebook) $85.00   **646.4**

1. Sewing 2. Dressmaking -- Patterns 3. Dressmaking

ISBN 0307586758; 9780307586759; 9780770434397

LC 2012010976

This book is a collection of sewing patterns. "Five adaptable master patterns for tops, dresses, and pants are transformed into nineteen unique projects for both women and men that draw inspiration from key fashion moments. These influential looks—from the Roaring Twenties to the Awesome Eighties—are all modernized and reinterpreted for today's sewing enthusiasts." (Publisher's note)

Armstrong, Helen Joseph

Patternmaking for fashion design; technical illustrator, Vincent James Maruzzi; fashion illustrator, Kathryn Hagen. 4th ed; Pearson Prentice Hall 2006 xxi, 805p il $104.40 **646.4**

1. Dressmaking -- Patterns

ISBN 978-0-13-194893-9; 0-13-194893-8

LC 2005-283500

First published 1987 by Harper & Row

"Covers the three steps in the development of design patterns—dart manipulation, added fullness, and contouring—with a central theme that all designs are based on one, or more of these three major patternmaking and design principles." Publisher's note

Includes bibliographical references

Betzina, Sandra

Power sewing step-by-step. Taunton Press 2000 231p il $34.95; pa $24.95 **646.4**

1. Sewing 2. Dressmaking

ISBN 1-56158-363-4; 1-56158-572-6 pa

LC 00-23431

"Vests, pants, shirts, dresses, and jackets for women are the focus of this book, with Betzina guiding the reader step by step through her thinking process in planning, constructing, fitting, customizing, and finishing each type of garments. More than 500 color photos illustrate many tricks of the trade, shortcuts, and tips. This will be a core title in any sewing collection." Libr J

Doh, Jenny

Signature styles; 20 stitchers craft their look. Lark Crafts 2011 144p il pa $19.95 **646.4**

1. Sewing 2. Dressmaking 3. Dress accessories

ISBN 978-1-60059-791-6; 1-60059-791-2

LC 2010040531

Reveals how 20 women authors, bloggers, entrepreneurs and more developed their own distinctive looks. Each crafter shares her studio, style, a key technique, and an exclusive project.

This is "a surprisingly varied collection, ranging from costumey retroquirk to urban couture to modern country." Libr J

White, Betz

Sewing green; projects and ideas for stitching with organic, repurposed, and recycled fabrics: plus tips and resources for earth-friendly stitching. Stewart, Tabori & Chang 2009 143p il pa $24.95 **646.4**

1. Recycling 2. Clothing and dress

ISBN 978-1-58479-758-6; 1-58479-758-4

LC 2008023649

"White's collection of green sewing projects features garments and accessories made from thrift-store clothing, scrap fabric, and recycled goods. The looks are contemporary—you won't find any 1970s-era hippie patchwork dresses—and the designer profiles and tips are inspirational. Nicely cutting edge." Libr J

646.7 Management of personal and family life

Atik, Chiara

Modern Dating; A Field Guide. Chiara Atik ; foreword by Brian Schechter & Aaron Schildkrout. Harlequin Books 2013 224 p. illustrations $19.95 **646.7**

1. Online dating 2. Dating (Social customs) 3. Interpersonal relations

ISBN 0373892772; 9780373892778

LC 2013478066

This book, by Chiara Atik, is a "guide for navigating the modern dating world. . . . Rather than listing a set of 'rules,' [it] offers advice on modern challenges, like how to send a relatively unembarrassing sext, how to create a failproof first date idea, and how to make sure you're getting into a relationship for the right reasons." (Publisher's note)

"Atik's smart, youthful appraisal of today's social landscape makes her seem like an expert that's just one step ahead of you. Informed by research and delivered with style, this is big-sister advice at its best." Pub Wkly

Begoun, Paula

Don't go to the cosmetics counter without me; [by] Paula Begoun with Bryan Barron. 8th ed.; Beginning Press; distributed to the U.S. book trade by Publishers Group West 2010 1191p pa $29.95 **646.7**

1. Cosmetics 2. Consumer education 3. Skin -- Care

ISBN 978-1-877988-34-9

First published 1992

"From drugstores and home shopping to department stores and catalogs, Begoun reviews all of the major cosmetic and skin care lines product by product—more than 30,000 in all. . . . Begoun covers product websites, efficacy, and whether claims such as youth extension are accurate. Individual chapters are devoted to best products, a cosmetic ingredients dictionary, and animal testing." Publisher's note

Berg, Rona

Beauty : the new basics; illustrations by Anja Kroencke; photography by Deborah Jaffe. Workman 2001 404p il pa $19.95 **646.7**

1. Personal appearance

ISBN 0-7611-0186-1

LC 00-43631

The author discusses "hair and skin care, bath and body, aging, skin cancer, makeup, home spa treatments, aromatherapy, and cosmetic surgery. She includes a directory of day and destination spas and recommended salons. Amusing time lines give thumbnail histories of style and popular products. Essential for small collections in particular." Libr J

Brandon, Ruth

Ugly beauty; Helena Rubinstein, L'Oreal, and the blemished history of looking good. Harper 2011 290p il $26.99; ebook $21.99   **646.7**

1. Chemists 2. Personal appearance 3. L'Oreal SA 4. Cosmeticians 5. Art collectors 6. Cosmetics industry executives

ISBN 978-0-06-174040-4; 0-06-174040-3; 978-0-06-204156-2 ebook; 0-06-204156-8 ebook

LC 2010-24435

"A clearheaded discussion of current beauty standards, vanity, and the gender politics of the modern cosmetic industry rounds out this lively history of the founding of the beauty business as we know it." Publ Wkly

Includes bibliographical references

Cullinane, Jan

The **new** retirement; the ultimate guide to the rest of your life. [by] Jan Cullinane and Cathy Fitzgerald. Rev. and updated ed.; Rodale 2007 484p pa $19.95   **646.7**

1. Retirement

ISBN 978-1-59486-479-7; 1-59486-479-9

LC 2007-15947

First published 2004

This guide provides "information about particular locales, financial planning and tax considerations, lifelong learning opportunities, leisure and volunteer activities, and working after retirement." Publisher's note

Includes bibliographical references

DuPriest, Laura

Natural beauty; pamper yourself with salon secrets at home. Prima Pub. 2002 230p il pa $10.95   **646.7**

1. Cosmetics 2. Personal appearance 3. Skin -- Care

ISBN 0-7615-2099-6

LC 2002-72554

The author's "obvious knowledge about everything from waxing to massaging to not being taken in at the cosmetics counter, as well as her inventive concoctions . . . make this a solid beauty resource." Publ Wkly

Essence total makeover; body, beauty, spirit. [by the editors of Essence]; Patricia Mignon Hinds, editor; introduction by Susan L. Taylor. Crown 2000 216p il hardcover o.p. pa $18   **646.7**

1. Personal appearance 2. African American women -- Health and hygiene

ISBN 0-609-80527-4 pa

LC 99-14442

"Hinds provides practical tips on caring for skin, hair, body, and spirit. Glossy and attractive, this comprehensive volume is aimed at African American women." Libr J

Includes bibliographical references

Hinden, Stan

How to retire happy; the 12 most important decisions you must make before you retire. [foreword by John C. Bogle] 3rd ed., fully rev. and updated; McGraw-Hill 2010 233p pa $18.95; ebook $18.95   **646.7**

1. Retirement

ISBN 978-0-07-170247-8 pa; 978-0-07-171298-9 ebook

First published 2001

This retirement planning guide covers such topics as Social Security, pension plans, investments after retirement, health insurance, preparing for serious illness, and where to live after retirement.

Includes bibliographical references

Kashuk, Sonia

Real beauty; concept by Sonia Kashuk; written with Amie Valentine. Potter 2003 137p il + 1 DVD ROM $27.50   **646.7**

1. Personal appearance 2. Women -- Health and hygiene

ISBN 1-4000-4774-2

LC 2003-535298

The author "showcases women of all ages and ethnic types, covering nutrition and fitness in addition to the usual hair and skin care. The accompanying DVD shows the suggested makeup techniques being performed." Libr J

Kirsch, Melissa

The **girl's** guide to absolutely everything. Workman Pub. 2006 477p il $26.95; pa $15.95   **646.7**

1. Young women 2. Conduct of life

ISBN 978-0-7611-4213-3; 0-7611-4213-4; 978-0-7611-3579-1 pa; 0-7611-3579-0 pa

LC 2006-41840

The author provides "advice for women in their twenties and thirties on everything from body image and friendship to first jobs and money. . . . Her well-designed book is pleasurable to read and encourages healthy, responsible behavior." Libr J

Includes bibliographical references

Lofas, Jeannette

Stepparenting; Rev. and updated.; Citadel Press 2004 241p pa $12.95   **646.7**

1. Parenting 2. Stepparents 3. Stepchildren

ISBN 0-8065-2652-1; 978-0-8065-2652-2

LC 2004-556219

First published 1985 by Zebra Books

"Acknowledging the difficulty of a stepparent's role, this standout title guides readers through carefully forming a stepfamily, with straightforward coverage of the usual issues (e.g., etiquette, praising positive behavior)." Libr J

Massey, Lorraine

Curly girl; more than just hair--it's an attitude: a celebration of curls: how to cut them, care for them, love them & set them free. Workman 2001 148p il pa $9.95   **646.7**

1. Hair

ISBN 0-7611-2300-8

LC 2001-26842

This book features "tips on shampoo . . . conditioners . . . drying, combing . . . styling, getting the right cut, and how to Heal Thy Hair after years of strong detergents and damaging blow-dryers. There are before-and-after photographs . .

. self-help tests, confessions from curly girls {and} advice."
Publisher's note

Romanowski, Perry

Can you get hooked on lip balm? top cosmetic scientists answer your questions about the lotions, potions, and other beauty products you use every day. [by] Perry Romanowski and the creators of TheBeautyBrains.Com. Harlequin 2011 194p pa $16.95 **646.7**
  1. Cosmetics
  ISBN 978-0-373-89234-1

               LC 2010-44199
"Women who subscribe to such magazines as InStyle and Self will devour this question-and-answer guide to cosmetics, shampoos, and nail polishes." Booklist
Includes bibliographical references

646.700 Management of personal and family life with respect to people in specific stages of adulthood

Blake, Jenny

Life after college; the complete guide to getting what you want. Jenny Blake. Running Press 2011 293 p. (pbk.) $17 **646.700**
  1. Personal finance 2. College graduates 3. Life skills -- Handbooks, manuals, etc. 4. Professional developmen -- Handbooks, manuals, etc. 5. College graduates -- Employment 6. Young men -- Life skills guides 7. Young women -- Life skills guides 8. Young adults -- Life skills guides 9. College graduates -- Life skills guides
  ISBN 0762441275; 9780762441273

               LC 2010940614
The book is "full of . . . advice to encourage young adults who are on the precipice of a new life, a life that can be tenuous and daunting. It covers money, relationships (both romantic and familial), friends, health, fun and relaxation, life planning, and personal and professional growth." (Library Journal)

647 Management of public households (Institutional housekeeping)

Ripert, Eric

On the line; [by] Eric Ripert, Christine Muhlke. Artisan 2008 239p il $35 **647**
  1. Restaurants 2. Le Bernardin (New York, N.Y.: Restaurant)
  ISBN 978-1-57965-369-9; 1-57965-369-3

               LC 2008-05930
"A behind-the-scenes look at the famed New York restaurant Le Bernardin. . . . Chef Ripert and New York Times writer Muhlke recount the restaurant's history, from its founding in 1986 by Gilbert and Maguy Le Coze, through Ripert's joining the team in 1991, to the present day. This thorough guide to how the restaurant operates teaches about various kitchen stations, tools of the trade, key personnel

and their duties, how new dishes are born and what it's like to spend a night 'on the line.' . . . [Some recipes are included.] A huge treat for industry insiders, fans of Le Bernardin and foodies everywhere." Publ Wkly

647.9 Specific kinds of public households and institutions

Ottolenghi, Yotam

  ★ **Plenty**; vibrant vegetable recipes from London's Ottolenghi. by Yotam Ottolenghi. Chronicle Books 2011 287p il $35 **647.9**
  1. Cooking -- Vegetables 2. Ottolenghi (Restaurant)
  ISBN 978-1-4521-0124-8

               LC 2011036741
Includes bibliographical references

Schultz, Howard

  Onward; how Starbucks fought for its life without losing its soul. [by] Howard Schultz with Joanne Gordon. Rodale 2011 350p il $25.99 **647.9**
  1. Leadership 2. Coffee industry 3. Starbucks Coffee International (Firm)
  ISBN 978-1-60529-288-5

               LC 2011003239
"Throughout this book, readers get a very intimate look at the conviction that drives leaders, the resiliency of employees, the passion that customers feel about a brand, and the global community that one brand can inspire. Whether or not you are a coffee lover or have a fondness for the Starbucks experience, Onward details tremendous leadership lessons from which everyone can learn." T + D

647.95 Eating and drinking places

McMillan, David

  The **art** of living according to Joe Beef; a cookbook of sorts. Frederic Morin, David McMillan, and Meredith Erickson ; photographs by Jennifer May. Ten Speed Press 2011 291 p. ill. (chiefly col.) $40 **647.95**
  1. Cookbooks 2. Restaurants 3. Montreal (Quebec) 4. Joe Beef (Restaurant) -- History
  ISBN 1607740141; 9781607740148

               LC 2011020857
"Located in a working-class neighborhood of Montreal, Joe Beef is at the center of Montreal's growing reputation as a culinary destination." In this book, "co-owners/chefs Frédéric Morin and David McMillan, along with writer and former Joe Beef staff member Meredith Erickson, present 135 unforgettable recipes showcasing Joe Beef's unconventional approach to French market cuisine." (Publisher's note)
The authors "combine forces to create a savvy page-turner full of meats, oysters, attitude and irreverence." Pub Wkly

Wizenberg, Molly

Delancey; a man, a woman, a restaurant, a marriage. Molly Wizenberg. Simon & Schuster 2014 256 p. illustrations   **647.95**
1. Marriage 2. Restaurants 3. Married people 4. Delancey (Pizzaria : Seattle, Wash.) 5. Food writers -- United States -- Biography 6. Pizzerias -- Washington (State) -- Seattle 7. Restaurateurs -- United States -- Biography
ISBN 9781451655094; 9781451655117; 9781451655124

LC 2013034429

In this memoir, author Molly Wizenberg "recounts how opening a restaurant sparked the first crisis of her young marriage. . . . [W]hen Brandon decided to open a pizza restaurant, Molly was supportive. . . . The restaurant, Delancey . . . became a success, and Molly tried to convince herself that she was happy in their new life until--in the heat and pressure of the restaurant kitchen--she realized that she hadn't been honest with herself or Brandon." (Publisher's note)

"Wizenberg candidly describes her fears and doubts, as well as her struggles with trying to be a supportive wife." LJ

647.954   Bars (drinking establishments) -- London

Brown, Pete, 1968-

Shakespeare's Pub; A Barstool History of London As Seen Through the Windows of Its Oldest Pub - the George Inn. Pete Brown. St. Martin's Press 2013 368 p. (hardcover) $26.99   **647.954**
1. Bars 2. George Inn (Enfield, London, England) -- History 3. Great Britain -- History 4. HISTORY -- Europe -- Great Britain 5. Enfield (London, England) -- History 6. London (England) -- Buildings, structures, etc. -- History 7. Bars (Drinking establishments) -- England -- London -- History
ISBN 1250033888; 9781250033888

LC 2013010139

This book, by Pete Brown, offers a history of London through focusing on the "George Inn near London Bridge; a cosy, wood-paneled, galleried coaching house a few minutes' walk from the Thames. . . . Chaucer and his fellow pilgrims almost certainly drank in the George on their way out of London to Canterbury. It's fair to say that Shakespeare popped in from the nearby Globe for a pint, and we know that Dickens certainly did." (Publisher's note)

648   Housekeeping

Friedman, Virginia M.

Field guide to stains; how to identify and remove virtually every stain known to man. by Virginia M. Friedman, Melissa Wagner, and Nancy Armstrong. Quirk Bks. 2003 280p il pa $14.95   **648**
1. Cleaning
ISBN 1-931686-07-6

LC 2002-104065

This guide to identifying and removing over 100 stains features sections on sauces, fruits and vegetables, office products, and yard and garage stains. It also includes information on when and where certain stains are most likely to occur

Platt, Stacey

What's a disorganized person to do? Artisan 2010 277p il pa $16.95   **648**
1. House cleaning 2. Storage in the home
ISBN 978-1-57965-372-9

LC 2009-13493

The author "offers quick tips (e.g., storing sterling silver with chalk to prevent tarnish), instructions (e.g., folding silk scarves correctly), and one-hour projects (e.g., taking back the junk drawer) that anyone can immediately put into practice. Guidelines for organizing office space are designed for those who like to file and those who prefer to pile, and detailed steps for vacation packing and cross-country moving are also included. The employment of one idea alone is worth the price of the book." Libr J

Includes bibliographical references

649   Child rearing; home care of people with disabilities and illnesses

Agnew, Connie L.

Twins! pregnancy, birth, and the first year of life. [by] Connie L. Agnew, Alan H. Klein, and Jill Alison Ganon; illustrations by Victor Robert. 2nd ed.; Collins 2005 360p il pa $18.95   **649**
1. Twins
ISBN 0-06-074219-4; 978-0-06-074219-5

LC 2005-45585

First published 1997

An overview of the physical, medical, emotional, and psychological issues involved in having twins. Fetal and embryonic development, nutrition, and exercise are among the topics covered. Includes interviews with parents of twins.

Includes bibliographical references

American Academy of Pediatrics

Caring for your school-age child; ages 5 to 12. editor-in-chief, Edward L. Schor. rev trade pa. ed; Bantam Bks. 1999 xxviii, 624p il pa $19.95   **649**
1. Child care 2. Child rearing
ISBN 0-553-37992-5

LC 99-12639

First published 1995

This book "offers comprehensive information about the growth, development, and behavior of children from five to 12 years of age. . . . Bicycle safety, latchkey children, dealing with violence and crime, guns in the home, prejudice, gender identity and sexual orientation, and physical and sexual abuse appear along with the usual information about immunization, diet, school problems, illness, and first aid. The text also offers sound, practical advice about how parents in traditional and nontraditional families can handle a wide variety of situations, stating clearly when they should seek professional help. . . . This book belongs in all parenting and consumer health collections." Libr J {review of 1995 edition}

Ames, Louise Bates

Your eight-year-old; lively and outgoing. by Louise Bates Ames and Carol Chase Haber; illustrated with photographs by Betty David. Delacorte Press 1989 147p il hardcover o.p. pa $12.95   **649**
> 1. Child rearing
> ISBN 0-440-50681-6 pa
>> LC 88-31150
> A discussion of the basic personality and typical physical and mental development of the eight-year-old
> Includes bibliographical references

Your five-year-old; sunny and serene. by Louise Bates Ames and Frances L. Ilg, Gesell Institute of Child Development; illustrated with photographs by Betty David. Delacorte Press 1979 123p il hardcover o.p. pa $12.95   **649**
> 1. Child rearing
> ISBN 0-440-50673-5 pa
>> LC 78-11622
> Beginning with a description of the general characteristics of the five-year-old, the authors go on to discuss how the child relates to parents and others
> Includes bibliographical references

Your four-year-old; wild and wonderful. by Louise Bates Ames and Frances L. Ilg, Gesell Institute of Child Development. Delacorte Press 1976 152p il hardcover o.p. pa $12.95   **649**
> 1. Child rearing
> ISBN 0-440-50675-1 pa
> A discussion of the basic personality and typical physical and mental development of the four-year-old
> Includes bibliographical references

Your one-year-old; the fun-loving, fussy 12-to-24-month-old. by Louise Bates Ames, Frances L. Ilg, and Carol Chase Haber (Gesell Institute of Child Development); illustrated with photographs by Betty David. Delacorte Press 1982 178p il hardcover o.p. pa $12.95   **649**
> 1. Child rearing
> ISBN 0-440-50672-7 pa
>> LC 81-17275
> A discussion of the basic personality and typical physical and mental development of the one-year-old
> Includes bibliographical references

Your seven-year-old; life in a minor key. by Louise Bates Ames and Carol Chase Haber; illustrated with photographs by Betty David. Delacorte Press 1985 165p il hardcover o.p. pa $12.95   **649**
> 1. Child rearing
> ISBN 0-440-50650-6 pa
>> LC 84-15627

A discussion of the basic personality and typical physical and mental development of the seven-year-old
Includes bibliographical references

Your six-year-old; defiant but loving. by Louise Bates Ames and Frances L. Ilg, Gesell Institute of Child Development. Delacorte Press 1976 132p il hardcover o.p. pa $12.95   **649**
> 1. Child rearing
> ISBN 0-440-50674-3 pa
> A discussion of the basic personality and typical physical and mental development of the six-year-old
> Includes bibliographical references

Your two-year-old; terrible or tender. by Louise Bates Ames, and Frances L. Ilg, Gesell Institute of Child Development. Delacorte Press 1976 149p il hardcover o.p. pa $12.94   **649**
> 1. Child rearing
> ISBN 0-440-50638-7 pa
> A discussion of the basic personality and typical physical and mental development of the two-year-old
> Includes bibliographical references

The **baby** book; everything you need to know about your baby from birth to age two. William Sears, MD, Martha Sears, RN, Robert Sears, MD, and James Sears, MD. 3rd ed Little, Brown & Co. 2013 xiv, 770 p.p ill., charts (pbk.) $21.99 **649**
> 1. Infants -- Care 2. Infants -- Development 3. Newborn infants -- Care
> ISBN 0316198269; 9780316198264
>> LC 2012953605
> "The authors teach new parents how to bond with their babies through seven fundamental behaviors, including breastfeeding, 'babywearing' and setting proper boundaries. . . . From tips for a healthy birth, getting your baby to sleep and feeding him the 'right fats,' to information about early health concerns, the major steps in infant development and troublesome but typical toddler behavior, the authors of this comprehensive volume . . . are assured and reassuring experts." Publ Wkly
> Includes bibliographical references and index

Brain rules for baby; how to raise a smart and happy child from zero to five. John Medina. 2nd ed; updated Pear Press 2014 323 p. ill pbk $15.95 **649**
> 1. Parenting 2. Child rearing 3. Child development
> ISBN 0983263388; 9780983263388
> Medina "presents the best of the refereed literature to examine how infants process information at the molecular, cellular, and behavioral levels. . . . Covering such topics as pregnancy, relationships, and 'moral' babies, the book will educate even the most learned parents. Medina's humorous, conversational style makes this an absolute pleasure to read." LJ

Brazelton, T. Berry

Touchpoints birth to 3; your child's emotional and behavioral development. revised with Joshua

Sparrow. 2nd ed.; Da Capo Lifelong Books 2006 xxvi, 500p il pa $17.95 **649**

1. Child rearing 2. Child psychology 3. Child development

ISBN 978-0-7382-1049-0; 0-7382-1049-8

LC 2008-274711

First published 1992 by Addison-Wesley with title: Touchpoints

The author "defines 'touchpoints' as the periods of development and regression which every child experiences while growing up. He describes the first six years of life and the touchpoints of that period. . . . Worried new parents will be put at ease after reading this book. Brazelton is knowledgeable, warm, and kind, and his book is a pleasure to read." Libr J

Includes bibliographical references

Brooks, Robert B.

Raising resilient children; fostering strength, hope, and optimism in your child. {by} Robert Brooks, Sam Goldstein. Contemporary Bks. 2001 317p hardcover o.p. pa $14.95 **649**

1. Child rearing 2. Parent-child relationship

ISBN 0-8092-9765-5 pa

LC 00-60316

The authors "synthesize research on children's coping skills; define and describe resilience (the capacity to cope and feel competent); and offer specific strategies for nurturing resilience in children." Booklist

Includes bibliographical references

Brott, Armin A.

The **expectant** father; facts, tips, and advice for dads-to-be. [by] Armin A. Brott and Jennifer Ash. 3rd ed.; Abbeville Press 2010 373p il $18.95; pa $12.95 **649**

1. Fathers 2. Pregnancy

ISBN 978-0-7892-1079-1; 978-0-7892-1077-7 pa

LC 2010-15973

First published 1995

This book "gives dads-to-be a month-by-month breakdown of what to expect as they prepare to welcome a baby into their family. For each month, Brott and Ash give a rundown of what mothers, babies, and fathers are experiencing physically and emotionally, from moodiness and food cravings (which fathers aren't exempt from) to balancing fatherhood with work. . . . Brott and Ash's measured, experienced tone offers assurance and guidance for those new to the stresses and worries of impending fatherhood, making this a must-have for anyone expecting." Publ Wkly

Includes bibliographical references

Brown, Christia Spears

Parenting beyond pink and blue; how to raise your kids free of gender stereotypes. Christia Spears Brown, PhD. Ten Speed Press 2014 240 p. illustrations (pbk) $14.99 **649**

1. Parenting 2. Gender role 3. Sex differences (Psychology) 4. Stereotype (Social psychology)

ISBN 160774502X; 9781607745020

LC 2014001259

This book, by developmental psychologist Christia Spears Brown, is "a guide that helps parents focus on their children's unique strengths and inclinations rather than on gendered stereotypes to more effectively bring out the best in their individual children, for parents of infants to middle schoolers. . . . [It] addresses all the issues that contemporary parents should consider--from gender-segregated birthday parties and schools to sports, sexualization, and emotional intelligence." (Publisher's note)

Brown "argues that children are 'free to flourish' when gender is deemphasized and covers both the neuroscience and cultural influences of sex in language that is accessible and at times even humorous." LJ

Includes bibliographical references and index

Bullard, Sara

Teaching tolerance; raising open-minded empathetic children. Doubleday 1996 235p hardcover o.p. pa $19 **649**

1. Children 2. Parenting 3. Prejudices 4. Toleration

ISBN 0-385-47265-X pa

LC 95-36045

Bullard "states the principles of tolerance adults need to impart to children and provides guidelines for modeling the behavior we want to encourage." Libr J

Cohen, Lawrence J.

Playful parenting; a bold new way to use play in raising your children. Ballantine Bks. 2001 307p $23.95; pa $14 **649**

1. Play 2. Games 3. Parenting

ISBN 0-345-43897-3; 0-345-44286-5 pa

LC 00-66809

"According to Cohen, children of all ages have an ongoing need for connectedness, security and attachment; playful interaction with parents is an important way to develop such bonds. Through play, parents can help their kids develop greater confidence, express bottled up or difficult feelings, recover from daily emotional upheavals, negotiate agreements, express love and—not least—have fun." Publ Wkly

Deak, JoAnn

Girls will be girls; a parent's guide to cultivating confident, competent and connected daughters. by JoAnn Deak with Teresa Barker. Hyperion 2002 287p $23.95; pa $14.95 **649**

1. Girls 2. Teenagers 3. Child rearing

ISBN 0-7868-6768-X; 0-7868-8657-9 pa

LC 2001-39247

"Deak discusses the differences between fathers and daughters and mothers and daughters and also some of the more common problems faced by teens, such as body image and peer pressure." Publ Wkly

Edgerton, Clyde

Papadaddy's book for new fathers; advice to dads of all ages. Clyde Edgerton ; drawings by Daniel Wallace. Little, Brown and Co. 2013 192 p. $25 **649**

1. Fatherhood 2. Child rearing 3. Father-child

relationship
ISBN 0316056928; 9780316056922

LC 2012033851

Author Clyde Edgerton "is a 68-year-old father with four children between the ages of 6 and 30. Here, he offers the fruits of the many ruminations and experiences that informed them, coming at his subject with a wisdom that is still being surprised, daily. Enjoy the good stuff, he writes, and make sure your children are the best of the good stuff." (Kirkus Reviews)

Egan, Amy

Is it a big problem or a little problem? when to worry, when not to worry, and what to do. [by] Amy Egan . . . [et al.] St. Martin's Press 2007 335p il pa $15.95 **649**
1. Child psychology 2. Child development
ISBN 978-0-312-35412-1

LC 2007-17218

The authors "divide the book into three sections, 'The Basics,' 'Understanding Development,' and 'Where Children Struggle.' Within these, they illustrate specific concerns (e.g., 'She can hear, why doesn't she understand?'), explore the range of normal, and examine signals that indicate a need for professional intervention. . . . Never using an alarmist tone, the authors strike a perfect balance between advocating for early intervention and appreciating the ups and downs of typical childhood behavior." Libr J
Includes bibliographical references

Elman, Natalie Madorsky

The **unwritten** rules of friendship; simple strategies to help your child make friends. by Natalie Madorsky Elman and Eileen Kennedy-Moore. Little, Brown 2003 340p il pa $14.95 **649**
1. Friendship 2. Child rearing 3. Socialization
ISBN 0-316-91730-3

LC 2002-40611

The authors "formulate nine prototypes of children with friendship problems. These range from passive (e.g., 'sensitive soul') to more aggressive (e.g., 'intimidating' children, 'short-fused' children, and born leaders) personalities. Chapters provide checklists for evaluation, social rules such children need to know, learning activities, and case studies. . . . Colorfully written and practical, Unwritten Rules offers many tips for anxious parents." Libr J
Includes bibliographical references

Faber, Adele

★ **How** to talk so kids will listen & listen so kids will talk; [by] Adele Faber and Elaine Mazlish; illustrations by Kimberly Ann Coe. 1st Avon Books rev (20th anniversary) print., 20th anniversary ed updated; Avon Books 1999 286p il pa $13.95 **649**
1. Parenting 2. Communication
ISBN 0-380-81196-0

LC 99-94868

First published 1980 by Rawson, Wade Publishers
This book designed to facilitate communication between parents and their children discuss how to cope with an unhappy child, resolving family conflicts, and how to set boundaries for a child without damaging goodwill.
Includes bibliographical references

Furedi, Frank

Paranoid parenting; why ignoring the experts may be best for your child. Chicago Review Press 2002 233p pa $14.95 **649**
1. Parenting 2. Child rearing 3. Parent-child relationship
ISBN 1-55652-464-1

LC 2002-4121

"This book is provocative, well argued, and clearly written, though the rhetoric can be stinging." Libr J
Includes bibliographical references and index

Huggins, Kathleen

★ The **nursing** mother's companion; foreword by Ruth A. Lawrence. 5th ed.; Harvard Common Press 2005 308p il hardcover o.p. pa $14.95 **649**
1. Breast feeding
ISBN 1-55832-303-1; 1-55832-304-X pa

LC 2004-21182

First published 1986
This offers advice on preventing and solving breast feeding problems and includes sections on premature babies, babies at risk for underfeeding, and breast pumps, as well as an appendix on drug safety.
Includes bibliographical references

Ilg, Frances Lillian

Your three-year-old; friend or enemy. by Louise Bates Ames, and Frances L. Ilg, Gesell Institute of Child Development. Delacorte Press 1976 168p il hardcover o.p. pa $12.95 **649**
1. Child rearing
ISBN 0-440-50649-2 pa
A discussion of the basic personality and typical physical and mental development of the three-year-old
Includes bibliographical references

Karp, Harvey

The **happiest** baby on the block; the new way to calm crying and help your baby sleep longer. Bantam Bks. 2002 267p il $21.95; pa $13.95 **649**
1. Child rearing 2. Parent-child relationship 3. Infants -- Care
ISBN 0-553-80255-0; 0-553-38146-6 pa

LC 2001-56734

To calm a crying baby the author "recommends a series of five steps designed to imitate the uterus. These steps include swaddling, side/stomach position, shhh sounds, swinging and sucking. The book includes detailed advice on the proper way to swaddle a child, the difference between a gentle rocking versus shaking and more." Publ Wkly

Kazdin, Alan E.

The **Everyday** Parenting Toolkit; The Kazdin Method for Easy, Step-by-step, Lasting Change for

You and Your Child. Alan E. Kazdin. Houghton Mifflin Harcourt 2013 208 p. $25 **649**

1. Child rearing 2. Parent-child relationship 3. Parenting

ISBN 0547985541; 9780547985541

LC 2012537349

Here, Alan E. Kazdin "offers practical strategies to help parents manage everyday behavioral problems. His science-based method may surprise some readers, particularly those who favor a more authoritarian approach. The core of the book focuses on the 'ABC's': antecedents, behavior, and consequences. According to Kazdin, parents can effect desired behavior in their children by offering choices and speaking in pleasant tones." (Publishers Weekly)

Includes bibliographical references (p. [178]-181) and index

Kennedy-Moore, Eileen

Smart parenting for smart kids; nurturing your child's true potential. Eileen Kennedy-Moore, Mark S. Lowenthal. John Wiley & Sons inc. 2011 xii, 306 p.p (pbk.) $16.95 **649**

1. Child rearing 2. Academic achievement 3. Parent-child relationship 4. Gifted children 5. Parents of gifted children

ISBN 0470640057; 9780470640050

LC 2010043005

Author Eileen Kennedy-Moore discusses child-rearing and offers "a perceptive guide to help smart children succeed academically and socially." The author offers suggestions for parents on how they can "help lead their children to new intellectual and emotional growth. Near the end of each chapter are suggestions for how parents can model healthy behaviors for their kids. . . . This . . . look at raising smart children will help parents teach their kids that there's more to life than academic achievement." (Kirkus Reviews)

Includes bibliographical references and index.

La Leche League International

The **Womanly** art of breastfeeding; 7th rev ed; Plume 2004 463p il pa $18 **649**

1. Breast feeding

ISBN 978-0-452-28580-4; 0-452-28580-1

LC 2004-557599

First published 1956. Periodically revised

This guide explains the benefits of breastfeeding and offers advice on avoiding problems, breastfeeding and working mothers, family life, and weaning.

Includes bibliographical references

Leach, Penelope

The **essential** first year. DK Publishing 2010 288p il pa $17.95 **649**

1. Child rearing 2. Infants -- Care

ISBN 978-0-7566-5799-4

"Leach empowers parents without overwhelming or guilting them, ultimately making the world a better place for families and children everywhere. Warning: this will make you want to have babies." Libr J

Includes bibliographical references

Your baby & child; from birth to age five. photographs by Jenny Matthews. 3rd ed completely rev; Knopf 1997 559p il $35; pa $20 **649**

1. Child care 2. Child development 3. Infants -- Care

ISBN 0-375-40007-9; 0-375-70000-5 pa

LC 97-29325

First published 1977 in the United Kingdom with title: Baby and child; first United States edition 1978

The author explores the psychosocial needs of children along with their physical growth and progress. Parental concerns are addressed

"Public and academic libraries would do well to stock . . . this primer on children and their development for circulation as well as for the reference shelf." Libr J

Lev, Arlene Istar

The **complete** lesbian & gay parenting guide; Berkeley trade pbk. ed.; Berkley Books 2004 379p pa $17 **649**

1. Parenting 2. Gay parents

ISBN 0-425-19197-4; 978-0-425-19197-2

LC 2004-57080

"This book addresses the concerns of transgendered parents, as well as those of lesbian and gay parents. . . . [The author] knows how to tackle relevant issues, e.g., dealing with the homophobia that children of GLBT parents will inevitably encounter. Humorous and replete with valuable narratives." Libr J

Includes bibliographical references

Lippincott, Jenifer Marshall

7 things your teenager won't tell you; and how to talk about them anyway. [by] Jenifer Marshall Lippincott and Robin M. Deutsch. Ballantine Books 2005 223p pa $14.95 **649**

1. Parenting 2. Teenagers 3. Adolescent psychology 4. Parent-child relationship

ISBN 0-8129-6959-6

LC 2005-297256

"The first section of the book reviews psychological and physiological research on brain development in adolescents. The authors then identify seven important facts to keep in mind, among them: truth is a malleable concept for teens, they suffer from distorted self-images, and they are attracted to risks. . . . Parents of teens will recognize the us-and-them dialogues and will find encouragement and guidance." Booklist

Includes bibliographical references

Margulis, Jennifer

The **business** of baby; what doctors don't tell you, what corporations try to sell you, and how to put your pregnancy, childbirth, and baby before their bottom line. Jennifer Margulis. Scribner 2013 368 p. (hardcover) $27 **649**

1. Pregnancy -- Economic aspects 2. Parenthood --

Economic aspects
ISBN 1451636083; 1451636091; 9781451636086; 9781451636093

LC 2012031245

This book, by Jennifer Margulis, "exposes how our current cultural practices during pregnancy, childbirth, and the first year of a baby's life are not based on the best evidence or the most modern science, . . . [but are] being undermined by corporate interests. . . . [Combining] research and in-depth interviews . . . , Margulis's . . . critique . . . arms parents with the information they need to make informed decisions about their own health and the health of their infants." (Publisher's note)

Includes bibliographical references and index.

Mayes, Linda C.

The **Yale** Child Study Center guide to understanding your child; healthy development from birth to adolescence. {by} Linda C. Mayes and Donald J. Cohen with John E. Schowalter and Richard H. Granger; J. L. Bell, editorial consultant; W. Rodney Torbert, illustrator. Little, Brown 2002 548p $40; pa $21.95 **649**

1. Child rearing 2. Child development 3. Parent-child relationship
ISBN 0-316-95432-2; 0-316-79432-5 pa

LC 00-39116

"The book offers three perspectives: the scientific, with basic information about meeting a growing child's needs; the emotional, with attention to understanding a child's feelings; and the parental, with emphasis on the feelings and expectations the parent brings to the relationship. . . . The objective is to help parents balance the three perspectives. . . . This approach lends the guide a broad and deep perspective on parenting even as it covers typical issues such as imaginary friends and sibling rivalry." Booklist

Murkoff, Heidi Eisenberg

What to expect the first year; [by] Heidi Murkoff, Arlene Eisenberg & Sandee Hathaway. 2nd ed, rev and updated; Workman 2003 704p $25.95; pa $15.95 **649**

1. Child rearing 2. Infants -- Care
ISBN 0-7611-3184-1; 0-7611-2958-8 pa

LC 2003-57578

First published 1996 with Eisenberg's name appearing first

This guide to "taking care of a newborn through the milestone of his or her first birthday . . . [covers] issues such as newborn screening, home births and the resulting at-home newborn care, vitamins and vaccines, milk allergies, causes of colic, sleep problems, SIDS, returning to work, dealing with siblings, weaning, sippy cups, . . . [and] the expanded role of the father." Publisher's note

★ **What** to expect the second year; from 12 to 24 months. [by] Heidi Murkoff and Sharon Mazel; foreword by Mark D. Widome. Workman Pub Co 2011 512p il $24; pa $15.95 **649**

1. Toddlers 2. Child rearing
ISBN 978-0-7611-6364-0; 978-0-7611-5277-4 pa

This is a "look at the toddler from 12 to 24 months. In 15 chapters the authors cover feeding, sleeping, learning, playing, health and safety, injuries and developmental disorders, discipline, and other issues with a meaty center section on behavior. . . . Murkoff offers sound advice and reassurance that will help parent and toddler stay grounded during this whirlwind period of growth and change." Publ Wkly

Neifert, Marianne R.

Great expectations; the essential guide to breastfeeding. [by] Marianne Neifert. Sterling 2009 312p il pa $14.95 **649**

1. Breast feeding
ISBN 978-1-4027-5817-1

LC 2009-5248

"The author combines detailed, readable medical explanations with practical tips for success and addresses potential challenges honestly rather than glossing over them with bland reassurances. Each chapter seems designed to stand alone, making it easy for time-pressed mothers to find the information they need without reading the entire book." Libr J

Pitman, Teresa

Sweet sleep; nighttime and naptime strategies for the breastfeeding family. Diane Wiessinger and [three others] Ballantine Books 2014 512 p. illustrations (paperback : acid-free paper) $20 **649**

1. Parenting 2. Breast feeding 3. Sleeping customs 4. Sleep 5. Breastfeeding 6. Breastfeeding -- Safety measures
ISBN 0345518470; 9780345518477

LC 2014019411

Written by Diane Wiessinger, Diana West, Linda J. Smith, and Teresa Pitman, "'Sweet Sleep' includes extensive information on creating a safe sleep space, helping children learn to sleep on their own and defusing criticism of your family's choices. . . . This book is nothing but supportive of whatever your choices are about nursing and sleeping." (BookPage)

"The core of the book offers detailed, practical advice on bed sharing and breast-feeding, with basic guidelines for safe bed sharing outlined in seven steps." Pub Wkly

Includes bibliographical references and index

Sears, William

Parenting the fussy baby and high-need child; everything you need to know--from birth to age five. {by} William Sears and Martha Sears. Little, Brown 1996 237p il hardcover o.p. pa $12.95 **649**

1. Parenting 2. Child psychology
ISBN 0-316-77916-4 pa

LC 95-48381

To cope with a high-need child the authors "recommend the approach they label attachment parenting; it includes such techniques as on-demand feeding and weaning; nighttime parenting; sharing sleep; soothing through motion, sound, visual distraction, and physical contact; and learning via close study how to anticipate the baby's needs." Booklist

Includes bibliographical references

Siegel, Daniel J.

No -drama discipline; the whole-brain way to calm the chaos and nurture your child's developing mind. Daniel J. Siegel, M.D., Tina Payne Bryson, Ph.D. Bantam Books 2014 288 p. illustrations (hardback) $26   **649**
1. Parenting 2. Child rearing 3. Child development
ISBN 0345548043; 9780345548047

LC 2014008270

Written by Daniel J. Siegel and Tina Payne Bryson, "'No-Drama Discipline' provides an effective, compassionate road map for dealing with tantrums, tensions, and tears--without causing a scene." It includes "strategies that help parents identify their own discipline philosophy--and master the best methods to communicate the lessons they are trying to impart." (Publisher's note)

"With lucid, engaging prose accompanied by cartoon illustrations, Siegel and Bryson help parents teach and communicate more effectively." Pub Wkly

Small, Meredith F.

Our babies, ourselves; how biology and culture shape the way we parent. Anchor Bks. (NY) 1998 xxii, 292p il hardcover o.p. pa $14.95   **649**
1. Parent-child relationship 2. Infants -- Care 3. Infants -- Development
ISBN 0-385-48362-7 pa

LC 97-44348

The author "explores ethnopediatrics, an interdisciplinary science that combines anthropology, pediatrics, and child development research in order to examine how child-rearing styles across cultures affect the health and survival of infants. Small describes the different parenting styles of several cultures, including . . . the nomadic Ache tribe of Paraguay, the agrarian !Kung San society of the Kalahari Desert in Africa, and the American industrialized society." Libr J

Includes bibliographical references

Spock, Benjamin

Dr. Spock on parenting; sensible advice from America's most trusted child care expert. Simon & Schuster 1988 318p hardcover o.p. pa $16.95 **649**
1. Parenting
ISBN 0-7434-2683-5 pa

LC 88-15792

"The author presents a personal critique on parenting, often bordering on the autobiographical. . . . He discusses in depth and with great conviction contemporary and traditional parent concerns, such as divorce, discipline, sex education, and the father's role." Libr J

Dr. Spock's the first two years; the emotional and physical needs of children from birth to age two. edited by Martin T. Stein. Pocket Bks. 2001 153p pa $13.95   **649**
1. Child care 2. Child rearing 3. Child development
ISBN 0-7434-1122-6

In these articles culled from Redbook and Parenting Spock's advice to parents is that they should "trust themselves" and "expands on this idea in his reply to the ques-

tion, 'What has eroded so many parents' self-asssurance in asking for reasonably good behavior?'" Libr J

Dr. Spock's the school years; the emotional and social development of children. edited by Martin T. Stein. Pocket Bks. 2001 283p pa $15.95   **649**
1. Child care 2. Child rearing 3. Child development
ISBN 0-7434-1123-4

This volume collects Spock's essays published in Redbook and Parenting. They address "our contemporary culture's tendency to overschedule children." Libr J

Wiseman, Rosalind

Masterminds and wingmen; helping our boys cope with schoolyard power, locker-room tests, girlfriends, and the new rules of Boy World. Rosalind Wiseman. Harmony Books 2013 384 p. illustrations $25   **649**
1. Masculinity 2. Boys -- Psychology 3. Adolescent psychology 4. Parent and teenager 5. Teenage boys -- Psychology
ISBN 0307986659; 9780307986658

LC 2013372427

This book offers information "for every parent--or anyone who cares about boys--to know. Collaborating with a large team of middle- and high-school-age editors, Rosalind Wiseman has created an unprecedented guide to the life your boy is actually experiencing--his on-the-ground reality. Not only does Wiseman challenge you to examine your assumptions, she offers innovative coping strategies aimed at helping your boy develop a positive, authentic, and strong sense of self." (Publisher's note)

"Wiseman's sound and steady assistance provides a calm response to every twist and turn on the multifaceted road of parenthood. . . . A wealth of sensible information for parents of boys." Kirkus

Includes bibliographical references (pages 365-366) and index

649.1   Child rearing

Swanson, Wendy Sue

Mama doc medicine; finding calm and confidence in parenting, child health, and work-life balance. Wendy Sue Swanson, MD, MBE, FAAP. American Academy of Pediatrics 2014 389 p. illustrations $16.95   **649.1**
1. Parenting 2. Mother-child relationship 3. Parent-child relationship
ISBN 1581108370; 9781581108378

LC 2013943971

Pediatrician Wendy Sue Swanson "helps decipher today's conflicting medical opinions, offers helpful online resources, and shares what she's learned over many years from her patients, friends and family in this . . . guide to parenting." (Publisher's note)

"Arranged in four sections ("Prevention," "Social-Emotional Support," "Immunizations," and "Work-Life Balance/

Mothering"), [Swanson's] guide is practical as well as personal."

Includes bibliographical references and index.

649.8 Home care of people with disabilities and illnesses

Carter, Rosalynn
Helping yourself help others; a book for caregivers. {by} Rosalynn Carter with Susan K. Golant. Times Bks. 1994 278p hardcover o.p. pa $14 **649.8**
1. Caregivers 2. Home care services
ISBN 0-8129-2591-2 pa

LC 94-11924

The authors "describe the stages the caregiver progresses through, from first facing the illness or declining health of a loved one to the 'long-term, hard-work phase of caregiving.' Questions regarding in-home professional care and nursing homes are addressed, and the authors provide information on strategies, support groups, program recommendations, helpful organizations, and books." Booklist

McFarlane, Rodger
The complete bedside companion; no-nonsense advice on caring for the seriously ill. {by} Rodger McFarlane, Philip Bashe. Simon & Schuster 1998 544p hardcover o.p. pa $25.95 **649.8**
1. Caregivers 2. Home nursing 3. Terminal care
ISBN 0-684-84319-6 pa

LC 97-43746

"This primer provides information on general illness and specific diseases, questions to ask the physician, basic nursing skills, making hospital visits, dealing with insurance companies, sources of additional information, and support groups. The authors . . . supplement this material with case studies and personal experiences." Libr J

Includes bibliographical references

650 Management and auxiliary services

The business book; senior editor, Sam Atkinson. Dk Pub 2014 352 p. illustrations (chiefly color) (Big Ideas Simply Explained) $25 **650**
1. Business 2. Encyclopedias and dictionaries
ISBN 1465415858; 9781465415851

LC 2013478653

A "comprehensive coverage of business, addressing such topics as money management, leadership and human resources, starting and growing a business, marketing, production, and operations. Discussed is not only what has worked for successful businesses but also what has not worked, and why being the first with an idea is not always the best." VOYA

Kaufman, Josh
The personal MBA; a world-class business education in a single volume. Portfolio Penguin 2010 402p $27.95 **650**
1. Business 2. Commerce 3. Management
ISBN 978-1-59184-352-8

LC 2010-27919

The author "argues that those interested in business would be better served by skipping the M.B.A. and focusing on the critically important concepts that really make or break a business. According to the author, much of what is taught in business schools is outdated; you're better off saving the expense and finding other ways to learn about these core principles—which Kaufman synthesizes—in such areas as value creation, marketing, sales, and finance. . . . While Kaufman's rallying call will not eradicate the need or desire for M.B.A. degrees, he does provide a surprisingly solid alternative full of information that even those already in the workplace will respond to." Publ Wkly

650.1 Personal success in business

Godin, Seth
Linchpin; are you indispensible? illustrations by Jessica Hagy and Hugh MacLeod. Portfolio 2010 244p il $26.95 **650.1**
1. Employees 2. Creative thinking 3. Motivation (Psychology)
ISBN 978-1-59184-316-0

LC 2009036957

The author explains why some people make a difference in their professional fields and others do not, and shows readers how to make more meaningful contributions at work.

Includes bibliographical references

Goulston, Mark
Just listen; discover the secret to getting through to absolutely anyone. foreword by Keith Ferrazzi. American Management Association 2009 234p il $24.95 **650.1**
1. Business communication 2. Interpersonal relations
ISBN 978-0-8144-1403-3

LC 2009-14386

This is "a primer on dealing with hard-to-reach people in virtually every scenario—defiant executives, angry employees, families in turmoil, warring couples—through use of well-honed psychological techniques. . . . Chapter summaries feature action steps preparing readers to encounter similar scenarios, yielding a guide that is as entertaining as it is useful." Publ Wkly

Hill, Napoleon
Think and grow rich; the landmark bestseller-now revised and updated for the 21st century. rev. and expanded by Arthur R. Pell. 1st Jeremy P. Tarcher/Penguin ed.; Jeremy P. Tarcher/Penguin 2005 302p pa $10 **650.1**
1. Success 2. Entrepreneurship
ISBN 1-585-42433-1

LC 2005-44133

First published 1937 by The Ralston Society

A motivational guide to achieving wealth and success, drawing upon stories of successful millionaires as examples.

Kotter, John P., 1947-

Buy -in; saving your good idea from being shot down. [by] John P. Kotter and Lorne A. Whitehead. Harvard Business Review Press 2010 192p   **650.1**

    1. Creative ability   2. Public relations

    ISBN 978-1-4221-5729-9

                        LC 2010016497

"This book explains how to protect a good idea and win support for it. The authors welcome naysayers, nitpickers, and handwringers into the room during the discussion, because they show you in this book how to respond to the unfair attacks to find success. Readers learn about the four attack strategies—death by delay, confusion, fear mongering, and character assassination—and how to show respect for all and use simple, clear, and common-sense responses. . . . This book helps you gain the upper hand by giving you practical responses to more than 24 generic attacks that people often use to shoot down good ideas." T + D

McCormack, Mark H.

What they don't teach you at Harvard Business School. Bantam Bks. 1984 256p hardcover o.p. pa $16.95   **650.1**

    1. Success   2. Management

    ISBN 0-553-34583-4 pa

                        LC 84-45172

McCormack's firm, the International Management Group, merchandises professional sports figures and markets the international television rights to sporting events. In this book, McCormack offers advice on business management.

Shell, G. Richard

Springboard; launching your personal search for success. G. Richard Shell. Portfolio/Penguin 2013 320 p. $26.95   **650.1**

    1. Success   2. Vocational guidance   3. Satisfaction   4. Job satisfaction   5. Self-realization

    ISBN 1591845475; 9781591845478

                        LC 2013017451

Author G. Richard Shell "offers a guide to a more fruitful life. . . . The reader learns about developing his or her own definition of success. . . . Citing research on happiness and wealth, as well as anecdotes and spiritual wisdom, Shell concludes that meaningful work--i.e., work that uses your talents, 'ignites you emotionally,' and is financially rewarding, in addition to building health and strong relationships--is the true measure of success." (Publishers Weekly)

    Includes bibliographical references and index

Spaulding, Tommy

It's not just who you know; transform your life (and your organization) by turning colleagues and contacts into lasting, genuine relationships. Broadway Books 2010 307p $23; ebook $12.99   **650.1**

    1. Success   2. Interpersonal relations

    ISBN 978-0-307-58913-2; 0-307-58913-7; 978-0-307-58915-6 ebook

                        LC 2010012355

In this "guide to reaching out to others, Spaulding . . . [discusses] how to create lasting relationships that go well beyond mere superficial contacts and 'second floor' relationships." Publisher's note

    Includes bibliographical references

Swanepoel, Stefan

Surviving your Serengeti; 7 skills to master business and life: a fable of self-discovery. Wiley 2011 176p il $21.95; ebook $14.99   **650.1**

    1. Success   2. Life skills   3. Industrial efficiency

    ISBN 978-0-470-94780-7; 0-470-94780-2; 978-1-1180-0859-1 ebook

                        LC 2010039905

"In this business fable, Swanepoel offers a . . . tale of life in the Serengeti and what lessons it holds for today's beleaguered workforce. The book follows the story of corporate executive Sean Spencer as he embarks on a three day visit to Africa. Without cell phone coverage or any other form of technology to keep him wired in, Sean is forced to disconnect from the worries of his troubled business thousands of miles away, and instead, he becomes engrossed in the animals that rule this untamed land and the wisdom the Serengeti has to offer." Publisher's note

Syed, Mathew

Bounce; Mozart, Federer, Picasso, Tiger, and the science of success. Harper 2010 312p il $25.99   **650.1**

    1. Ability   2. Success

    ISBN 978-0-06-172375-9; 0-06-172375-4

                        LC 2009-48135

"At the age of 24, Syed became the #1 British table tennis player, an achievement he initially attributed to his superior speed and agility. But in retrospect, he realizes that a combination of advantages—a mentor, good facilities nearby, and lots of time to hone his skills—set him up perfectly to become a star performer. . . . He takes on the myth of the child prodigy, emphasizing that Mozart, the Williams sisters, Tiger Woods, and Susan Polgar, the first female grandmaster, all had live-in coaches in the form of supportive parents who put them through a ton of early practice. Cogent discussions of the neuroscience of competition, including the placebo effect of irrational optimism, self-doubt, and superstitions, all lend credence to a compelling narrative." Publ Wkly

    Includes bibliographical references

Williams, Joan, 1952-

What works for women at work; four patterns working women need to know. Joan C. Williams, Rachel Dempsey ; [foreword by] Anne-Marie Slaughter. NYU Press 2014 384 p. (hardback) $24.95   **650.1**

    1. Gender role   2. Work environment   3. Women -- Employment   4. Women -- Psychology   5. Sex role in the work environment

    ISBN 1479835455; 9781479835454

                        LC 2013029819

This book, by Joan C. Williams and Rachel Dempsey, "is a comprehensive and insightful guide for mastering office politics as a woman. . . . Distilling over 35 years of research, Williams and Dempsey offer four crisp patterns that affect working women: Prove-It-Again!, the Tightrope, the Maternal Wall, and the Tug of War. Each represents different challenges and requires different strategies—which is why women need to be savvier than men to survive and thrive in high-powered careers." (Publisher's note)

"[F]illed with street-smart advice and plain old savvy about the way life works in corporate America." Booklist

Includes bibliographical references and index

650.1082   Success in business -- women

White, Kate

I shouldn't be telling you this; success secrets every gutsy girl should know. by Kate White. HarperBusiness 2012 345 p.   **650.1082**
1. Time management 2. Vocational guidance 3. Women -- Employment 4. Women in the workplace 5. Career development 6. Success in business 7. Businesswomen -- Psychology
ISBN 0062122126; 9780062122124

LC 2012027067

In this book, "former 'Cosmopolitan' editor-in-chief [Kate] White . . . offers straight-shooting career advice to women at all stages of their professional lives." White "discusses how to gain a foothold in the workplace, . . . what to do after a career begins to gather momentum, . . . [and] how to enjoy being at the top. . . . She offers tips for time management, including ways to handle maternity leave." (Kirkus Reviews)

650.14   Success in obtaining jobs and promotions

Asher, Donald

Cracking the hidden job market; how to find opportunity in any economy. Ten Speed Press 2011 198p pa $14.99; ebook $11.99   **650.14**
1. Success 2. Job hunting 3. Vocational guidance
ISBN 978-1-58008-494-9 pa; 978-1-58008-639-4 ebook

LC 2010010857

The author "invites job seekers to develop strategies for finding jobs—before they've been posted. He provides specific rules for figuring out what job is the best fit, and offers templates for structuring informational interviews, e-mail, conversations, and other forms of contact that can be adapted for use according to individual job seeker's needs. . . . Valuable assistance from a leading authority." Publ Wkly

Berger, Lauren

All work, no pay; finding an internship, building your resume, making connections, and gaining job experience. Lauren Berger. Ten Speed Press 2012 xii, 194 p.p $12.99   **650.14**
1. Job hunting 2. Internship programs 3. Employees -- Training 4. Vocational guidance
ISBN 1607741687; 9781607741688

LC 2011034540

This book is a "guide [that] reveals insider secrets to scoring the perfect internship, building invaluable connections, boosting transferable skills, and ultimately moving toward your dream career." Topics include "internship opportunities," writing "effective resumes and cover letters," and "network[ing] like a pro." (Publisher's note)

Includes bibliographical references and index.

Boldt, Laurence G.

Zen and the art of making a living; a practical guide to creative career design. 2010 ed., 3rd rev. ed.; Penguin Books 2009 xxxiii, 569p il pa $22 **650.14**
1. Vocational guidance
ISBN 978-0-14-311459-8

LC 2009-19516

First published 1992 by Lightning Press with title: Zen and the art of making a living in the post-modern world

This "career development guide helps the reader identify 'work purpose,' key talents, and objectives. . . . Boldt moves beyond the basics to address unusual practical and psychological issues such as starting a business, freelancing, founding a nonprofit corporation, maintaining a healthy self-esteem, and building marketing strategy." Libr J

Includes bibliographical references

Cohen, Carol Fishman

Back on the career track; a guide for stay-at-home moms who want to return to work. [by] Carol Fishman Cohen and Vivian Steir Rabin. Warner Books 2007 297p il $24.99   **650.14**
1. Vocational guidance 2. Women -- Employment
ISBN 978-0-446-57820-2; 0-446-57820-7

LC 2006-20986

The authors present a "step-by-step relaunch guide for stay-at-home moms. Both Harvard MBA relaunchers themselves, they explore the role career plays in the quality of life for professional women. . . . A listing of resources, recommended reading, and sample résumés are provided. One of only a few books for the millions of professional women/mothers who are not working for pay; highly recommended for public libraries." Libr J

Includes bibliographical references

Enelow, Wendy S.

Cover letter magic; trade secrets of professional resume writers. Wendy S. Enelow and Louise M. Kursmark. JIST Works 2010 xviii, 443 p.p (alk. paper) $18.95   **650.14**
1. Business letters 2. Resumes (Employment) 3. Cover letters
ISBN 1593577354; 9781593577353

LC 2009036718

In this book, by Wendy S. Enelow and Louise M. Kursmark, "professional resume and cover letter writers reveal their inside secrets for creating phenomenal cover letters that get attention and land interviews." Contents include more than 100 sample cover letters for various types of positions and advice on making changes to existing documents to improve them. (Publisher's note)

Includes bibliographical references and index

Ghilani, Mary E.

Working in your major; how to find a job when you graduate. Mary E. Ghilani. Praeger 2012 xi, 234 p.p (hardcover) $48; (paperback) $24.00 **650.14**
   1. Job hunting 2. College graduates -- Vocational guidance 3. Career education 4. School-to-work transition 5. Résumés (Employment)
ISBN 1440803110; 9781440803116; 9781440803123; 9781440828775

LC 2012014873

This book is meant to assist recent college graduates with their job searches. "Thirteen chapters clearly lay out the steps point the process of landing a job and positioning oneself for sustained employability; chapters include guidance on writing a resumé, using social media and networking, interviewing for a job, surviving a first year on the job, and acquiring skills for marketability in the future." (Choice)

Includes bibliographical references and index

Kay, Andrea

This is how to get your next job; an inside look at what employers really want. Andrea Kay ; foreword by Richard Nelson Bolles. American Management Association 2013 245 p. (pbk.) $16   **650.14**
   1. Job hunting 2. Vocational guidance 3. Career development 4. Employment interviewing
ISBN 0814432212; 9780814432211

LC 2012051814

In this book, Andrea Kay "offers practical advice for the job seeker based on her expertise as a career consultant. The first chapter, 'You Are What You Seem,' lists 17 characteristics employers look for, such as consistent, stable behavior; clear, critical thinking; and initiative. Her approach highlights multiple ways to reassess strengths and weaknesses and offers readers the opportunity to glean the employer's perspective." (Library Journal)

Lore, Nicholas

The **pathfinder**; how to choose or change your career for a lifetime of satisfaction and success. by Nicholas Lore. Touchstone Book 2012 x, 430 p.p ill. $16.99   **650.14**
   1. Occupations 2. Vocational guidance 3. Career changes 4. Job satisfaction
ISBN 1451608322; 9781451608328; 9781451626032

LC 2011043709

Author Nicholas Lore's book serves as a "guide . . . to more engaging, fulfilling work . . . whether you are a seasoned professional in search of a career change or just starting out. . . . Based on . . . techniques . . . [the book] offers more than fifty self-tests, diagnostic tools, and the acclaimed Rockport Career Design Method to help you choose an entirely new career, an entrepreneurial path, or the ideal job in your present field." (Publisher's note)

Mackay, Harvey

Use your head to get your foot in the door; job search secrets no one else will tell you. Portfolio 2010 329p il $25.95; pa $16   **650.14**
   1. Job hunting
ISBN 978-1-59184-321-4; 1-59184-321-9; 978-1-

59184-343-6 pa; 1-59184-343-X pa

LC 2009039791

"This collection of job search tips by Mackay . . . [comes] complete with humorous examples and 'Quickie' one-page stories that illustrate his main points. Don't let the cover or any worry about his sense of humor dissuade you: this is a very useful book. The short chapters with descriptive titles make it easy to navigate, and Mackay offers tips—from changing your attitude to getting hired—both for those currently employed but wishing to position themselves better in their current companies and for those who are out of work." Libr J

Includes bibliographical references

Martini, Kitty

Thank you for firing me! how to catch the next wave of success after you lose your job. [by] Kitty Martini and Candice Reed. Sterling Publishing Company 2010 232p pa $14.95   **650.14**
   1. Job hunting 2. Career changes 3. Vocational guidance
ISBN 978-1-4027-6956-6

LC 2009-34298

"For readers who have lost their jobs, are thinking about venturing forth as freelancers or consultants, or are searching for a new career, this is an invigorating and very helpful book. . . . [The authors'] book is clear, enthusiastic, and, most importantly, loaded with direct, uncluttered advice with tons of specifics. A resource guide in the back lists almost 30 pages' worth of web sites and some print materials, corresponding to the chapter topics, which range from how to develop a support network and how to tune into Gen Y job networking to specifics on global, artistic, and green industries, among others. A great choice for most job hunters." Libr J

Includes bibliographical reference

652   Processes of written communication

The book of codes; understanding the world of hidden messages: an illustrated guide to signs, symbols, ciphers, and secret languages. Paul Lunde, general editor. University of California Press 2009 279p il map $29.95   **652**
   1. Ciphers
ISBN 978-0-520-26013-9

"Whether or not you're fascinated by the world of Dan Brown's 'The Last Symbol,' there is probably something of interest in this densely researched, beautifully illustrated book. 'The Book of Codes' is so complete — with chapters that include information about everything from religions to body language to digital communication — reading this book won't peg you as a secret-society nut." St. Louis Post-Dispatch

Florey, Kitty Burns

Script and scribble; the rise and fall of handwriting. Melville House 2009 190p $22.95   **652**
   1. Handwriting
ISBN 978-1-933633-67-1; 1-933633-67-0

LC 2008-26964

A "pithy account of the history of handwriting . . . Florey makes a solid case for handwriting as a social indicator, and her affection for its art is thoughtful and aesthetically informed." Bookforum

657   Accounting

Siegel, Joel G.

Accounting handbook; [by] Joel G. Siegel, Jae K. Shim. 4th ed; Barron's 2006 993p il $35   **657**
1. Accounting
ISBN 0-7641-5776-0

LC 2005-45279

First published 1990

This reference includes sections on financial accounting, tax preparation, auditing, personal financial planning, and governmental and nonprofit accounting and includes a dictionary of accounting terms

658   General management

Ahmed, Mumtaz

The **three** rules; how exceptional companies think. Michael E. Raynor and Mumtaz Ahmed. Portfolio 2013 384 p. $29.95   **658**
1. Corporations 2. Business planning 3. Success in business 4. Organizational effectiveness
ISBN 1591846145; 9781591846147

LC 2013007590

In this book about rules for exceptional companies, authors Michael E. Raynor and Mumtaz Ahmed "base their proposed rules on an extensive financial data-mining project involving 25,000 companies from 1966 to 2010. From this, they identified companies that had exceptional return on assets over the 44-year span. In addition, they identified runner-up companies in each of the nine major industries covered, as well as companies that exemplified average financial performance." (Library Journal)

Includes bibliographical references and index

Collins, James C.

Good to great; why some companies make the leap, and others don't. {by} Jim Collins. HarperBusiness 2001 300p il $27.50   **658**
1. Leadership 2. Management
ISBN 0-06-662099-6

LC 2001-24818

"Starting with every company that ever appeared in the Fortune 500, Collins identifies 11 great ones and looks for similarities among them, and what he finds will both surprise and fascinate anyone involved in management." Booklist

Includes bibliographical references

Connors, Richard J.

Warren Buffett on business; principles from the sage of Omaha. John Wiley & Sons 2010 259p il $24.95; ebook $16.99   **658**
1. Management
ISBN 978-0-470-50230-3; 978-0-470-57071-5 ebook

LC 2009024946

Material drawn from Berkshire Hathaway shareholders' letters from 1977–2008, in Warren Buffett's own words.

Includes bibliographical references

Drucker, Peter F.

The **Drucker** lectures; essential lessons on management, society, and economy. edited and with an introduction by Rick Wartzman. McGraw-Hill 2010 266p $29.95; ebook $29.95   **658**
1. Management
ISBN 978-0-07-170045-0; 0-07-170045-5; 978-0-07-175950-2 ebook; 0-07-175950-6 ebook

LC 2010484567

This book presents thirty-three of Peter F. Drucker's speeches and talks delivered at professional gatherings and in the classroom.

"From his concern with continuous and full employment in the 1950s to globalization, nonprofit management, and the future of the corporation in the early 2000s, these lectures reflect a Drucker that many scholars and practitioners knew, but they also reveal new insights into the currency . . . of his thinking." Choice

Includes bibliographical references

Fenn, Donna

Alpha dogs; how your small business can become a leader of the pack. Collins 2005 224p il $24.95; pa $14.95   **658**
1. Success 2. Businesspeople 3. Small business 4. Entrepreneurship
ISBN 0-06-075867-8; 978-0-06-075867-7; 0-06-075868-6 pa; 978-0-06-075868-4 pa

LC 2006-275386

The author "takes us inside the reality of small businesses by showcasing eight successful entrepreneurs who share their stories and strategies. . . . This book offers valuable insight for current and aspiring entrepreneurs." Booklist

Includes bibliographical references

Gerber, Michael E.

The **most** successful small business in the world; the ten principles. John Wiley & Sons 2010 xxv, 162p il $24.95; ebook $16.99   **658**
1. Small business
ISBN 978-0-470-50362-1; 0-470-50362-9; 978-0-470-59432-2 ebook

LC 2009038789

The author presents ten principles toward building and maintaining a successful small business.

Includes bibliographical references

Jacobs, Charles S.

Management rewired; why feedback doesn't work and other surprising lessons from the latest brain science. Portfolio 2009 216p $25.95; pa $16 **658**

1. Applied psychology 2. Personnel management 3. Interpersonal relations

ISBN 978-1-59184-262-0; 978-1-59184-337-5 pa

LC 2009-1724

"Well argued and substantiated, this book turns prevalent management theory on its head and will have lasting impact on how it is taught in business schools and implemented in organizations." Publ Wkly

Includes bibliographical references

Kelley, Robert Earl

How to be a star at work; nine breakthrough strategies you need to succeed. Times Business 1998 xxi, 312p il hardcover o.p. pa $13 **658**

1. Success 2. Office workers

ISBN 0-8129-3169-6 pa

LC 97-28117

Kelley's "program is commonsense advice to workers: take initiatives, network for useful information, self-manage, know whom you're trying to please, be a biddable follower when necessary, be a reliable leader when that's called for, work effectively in teams, know your organization and how to present your ideas." Publ Wkly

Includes bibliographical references

Michelli, Joseph A.

The **Starbucks** experience; 5 principles for turning ordinary into extraordinary. McGraw-Hill 2006 208p $21.95 **658**

1. Success 2. Management 3. Starbucks Corporation

ISBN 978-0-07-147784-0; 0-07-147784-5

LC 2006-16788

The author "takes an in-depth look at Starbucks's proven and practical strategies for building a successful, multinational corporation. His chapters illustrate the company's five basic success principles: make it your own, everything matters, surprise and delight, embrace resistance, and leave your mark. Readers will discover a rich mix of ideas and techniques that will help them apply the Starbucks vision, creativity, and leadership to their own careers, workplaces, and companies." Libr J

Includes bibliographical references

Mintzberg, Henry

Managing. Berrett-Koehler Publishers 2009 306p il $26.95 **658**

1. Management

ISBN 978-1-57675-340-8

"This is a great read: a work of rich description and insight rather than a theory of managing, and it will stand the test of time." Management Today

Includes bibliographical references

O'Reilly, Charles A.

Hidden value; how great companies achieve extraordinary results with ordinary people. {by}

Charles A. O'Reilly III, Jeffrey Pfeffer. Harvard Business School Press 2000 286p il $29.95 **658**

1. Management 2. Human capital

ISBN 0-87584-898-2

LC 00-25016

"Through eight case studies, Hidden Value shows how a firm can use existing talent rather than how firms can attract talent. Smart organizations make it possible for ordinary people to perform as stars by engaging their emotional and intellectual resources." Libr J

Includes bibliographical references

Shipley, David

Send; the essential guide to email for office and home. [by] David Shipley and Will Schwalbe. Alfred A. Knopf 2007 247p hardcover o.p. pa $14.95 **658**

1. E-mail 2. Business communication 3. Electronic mail systems

ISBN 978-0-307-26364-3; 978-0-307-27599-8 pa

LC 2006-35235

A "humorous, pithy, and much-needed guide to the art and science of e-mail. . . . These tutorials are peppered with true tales of e-mail misuse that are both illustrative and amusing. For the more technically inclined, sidebars spell out e-mail's history, . . . briefly explain how it works, and define great moments in e-mail history." Christ Sci Monit

Stephenson, James

Ultimate homebased business handbook; how to start, run and grow your own profitable business. [by] James Stephenson with Rich Mintzer. 2nd ed.; Entrepreneur Press 2008 xxxi, 516p $29.95 **658**

1. Small business 2. Home-based business 3. Business enterprises

ISBN 978-1-59918-185-1

LC 2008-4944

First published 2004 with title: Entrepreneur's ultimate homebased business handbook

"Stephenson's comprehensive publication covers all topics of concern for the would-be side business owner. It is distinguished by comprehensive coverage of marketing, advertising, and PR and a list of business ideas and franchise opportunities." Libr J

Includes bibliographical references

Strauss, Steven D.

The **small** business bible; everything you need to know to succeed in your small business. 2nd ed.; Wiley 2008 526p il pa $19.95 **658**

1. Small business 2. Business enterprises

ISBN 978-0-470-26124-8; 0-470-26124-2

LC 2008-12277

First published 2005

"Chapters cover green businesses, online advertising and marketing, emerging technologies, and cutting-edge business building strategies." Libr J

Thompson, Mark

Now, build a great business! 7 ways to maximize your profits in any market. [by] Mark Thompson and Brian Tracy; foreword by Frances Hesselbein.

American Management Association 2011 xxii, 228p
$24.95 **658**
1. Marketing 2. Leadership
ISBN 978-0-8144-1697-6; 0-8144-1697-7

LC 2010030612

The authors "offer easy, tried-and-true ways to think about and plan organizational growth, especially in tough economic times. In seven steps (with a chapter devoted to each), the authors identify sustainable strategies for attracting customers and recruiting better leaders. They share seven simple questions that leaders ask themselves and provide helpful checklist exercises on a variety of key topics including creating a great business plan, designing an effective marketing plan, and creating a good customer experience." Publ Wkly

Wall Street journal

√ The **Wall** Street Journal essential guide to management; lasting lessons from the best leadership minds of our time. Harper Business 2010 xxvii, 207p pa $16.99 **658**
1. Management
ISBN 978-0-06-184033-3

LC 2010-2879

The author "lays out in helpful order and understandable prose what he considers the best practices for a good manager to follow; especially instructive are his discussions of 'six different styles that leaders use to motivate others.' . . . For serious consideration for any library business collection." Booklist
Includes bibliographical references

Wooldridge, Adrian

√**Masters** of management; how the business gurus and their ideas have changed the world--for better and for worse. HarperBusiness 2011 446p $29.99 **658**
1. Management
ISBN 978-0-06-177113-2; 9780061771132

LC 2011015690

First published 1996 by Times Bks. with title: The witch doctors

"The core of the book is a solid examination of the effects of entrepreneurship, globalization, and the free-agency economy on corporate governance. Wooldridge offers a balanced look at how business schools have spawned a guru industry that offers a gamut of theories on learning, innovation, and strategy. Peter Drucker, Tom Peters, and the 'Journo-Gurus' (Thomas Friedman, Malcolm Gladwell, and Chris Anderson) receive focused attention as the main influences in contemporary theory. . . . This is one of the best overviews of management theory in the 20th century. It is written in a clear and accessible style that will appeal to both MBA students and the general reader." Libr J

658.02   Management of enterprises of specific sizes and scope

Sarillo, Nick, 1963-

A **slice** of the pie; how to build a big little business. Nick Sarillo. Portfolio 2012 272 p. $26.95 **658.02**
1. Small business 2. Entrepreneurship 3. Business planning 4. Success in business 5. Industrial management 6. Employees -- Training of 7. New business enterprises
ISBN 1591844584; 9781591844587

LC 2012019321

In this book, Nick Sarillo, "founder and CEO of Nick's Pizza & Pub, offers a personal account of being a small business owner, sharing his perspectives, challenges he's faced and overcome, and the way he's transformed his company into a thriving success. More than a mere autobiography, it's also the story of his company and the people he works with. Sarillo expounds on the paths that he has chosen and why, what those choices have produced, and where the results have led." (Publishers Weekly)

658.1   Organization and financial management

Duffy, Scott

Launch! the critical ninety days from idea to market. Scott Duffy. Portfolio Hardcover 2013 240 p. (hardback) $26.95 **658.1**
1. New products 2. Entrepreneurship 3. New business enterprises
ISBN 1591846064; 9781591846062

LC 2013039077

In this book, entrepreneur Scott Duffy "has developed a practical approach for turning your big idea into a thriving venture by focusing on the crucial period of 90 days immediately before, during, and after starting your business. Based on his own experiences, . . . Duffy . . . emphasizes the personal side of entrepreneurship, including balancing finances, relationships, and your health." (Publisher's note)

"A breezy handbook for entrepreneurs on how to launch a new business, product or service. . . . Solid advice for novice risk-takers." Kirkus
Includes bibliographical references and index

Johnson, Victoria M.

Grant writing 101; everything you need to start raising funds today. McGraw-Hill 2011 269p pa $20; ebook $20 **658.1**
1. Fund raising 2. Grants-in-aid
ISBN 978-0-07-175018-9 pa; 978-0-07-175018-9 ebook

LC 2010039599

This guide to grant writing offers "ten tactics for writing a compelling proposal; tips for finding the best grantor for your needs; important components of various types of grants; [and] next steps for when you're approved." Publisher's note

Kidder, David S.

The **Startup** playbook; secrets of the fastest-growing startups from their founding entrepreneurs / David S. Kidder. David S. Kidder. Chronicle Books 2013 292 p. $29.99   **658.1**

1. Entrepreneurs 2. Entrepreneurship 3. New business enterprises 4. New business enterprises -- Management
ISBN 1452105049; 9781452105048

LC 2012019684

This book by David S. Kidder "shares the hard-hitting experiences of some of the world's most influential entrepreneurs and CEOs, revealing their most closely held advice. Face-to-face interviews with 40 founders give readers key insights into what it took to build PayPal, LinkedIn, AOL, TED, Flickr, and many others into household names. Special sections include topics ranging from how to select the right idea to pursue to finding funding and overcoming inevitable obstacles." (Publisher's note)

McGuckin, Frances

Business for beginners; from research and business plans to money, marketing and the law. Sourcebooks, Inc. 2005 318p il pa $16.95   **658.1**

1. Management 2. Small business 3. Entrepreneurship
ISBN 1-4022-0392-6

LC 2005-3351

First published 1997 in Canada

This "is the ultimate of primers, starting with a good self-assessment—do you have the skills for success?—and concluding with real-life tales of seven entrepreneurs." Booklist

McKeever, Mike P.

How to write a business plan; by Mike McKeever. 10th ed.; Nolo 2010 273p pa $34.99; ebook $34.99   **658.1**

1. Small business 2. Business planning 3. Business enterprises
ISBN 978-1-4133-1280-5 pa; 1-4133-1280-2 pa; 978-1-4133-1297-3 ebook; 1-4133-1297-7 ebook

LC 2010-21162

First published 1984 with title: Startup money. Frequently revised

"This is an outstanding step-by-step guide to writing a professional and sound business plan. Using examples and worksheets, McKeever helps the reader evaluate the profitability of a business idea, estimate expenses, prepare a cash-flow statement, create profit and loss forecasts, and more." Libr J

Root, Hal

The **small** business start-up guide; a surefire blueprint to successfully launch your own business. [by] Hal Root and Steve Koenig. 4th ed.; Sourcebooks, Inc. 2005 246p il pa $16.95   **658.1**

1. Small business
ISBN 1-4022-0602-X; 978-1-4022-0602-3

LC 2006-279673

First published 1996 by Information Int.

This guide covers such topics as finding investors and capital, bank loans, becoming incorporated, and business plans.

Slim, Pamela

Escape from cubicle nation; from corporate prisoner to thriving entrepreneur. Portfolio 2009 340p $25.95; pa $15   **658.1**

1. Success 2. Entrepreneurship 3. Business enterprises
ISBN 978-1-59184-257-6; 1-59184-257-3; 978-0-425-23284-2 pa; 0-425-23284-0 pa

LC 2008-50022

"Slim shows readers how to navigate the terrifying yet gratifying transition from corporate drone to entrepreneur. . . . What's here is: the nitty-gritty of getting a business off the ground, legal considerations, making the best use of social networking sites, the components of a business model, organized creative brainstorming, financial advice, shopping for self-paid insurance and benefits, and helpful anecdotes of real-life entrepreneurship. With her humorous insights into corporate life and an appealing no-nonsense yet empathic tone, Slim deals swiftly and incisively with anxiety, fear and hesitation. . . . This is a standout in the start-your-own business genre." Publ Wkly

Includes bibliographical references

Wasserman, Noam

The **founder's** dilemmas; anticipating and avoiding the pitfalls that can sink a startup. Noam Wasserman. Princeton University Press 2012 p. cm.   **658.1**

1. Management 2. Entrepreneurship 3. New business enterprises 4. New business enterprises -- Management
ISBN 9780691149134

LC 2011037954

This book, by Noam Wasserman, is part of the Kauffman Foundation Series on Innovation and Entrepreneurship. "Often downplayed in the . . . starting up a new business venture is . . . [the question] should they go it alone, or bring in co-founders, hires, and investors to help build the business? . . . Bad decisions at the inception of a promising venture lay the foundations for its eventual ruin. . . . Wasserman reveals the common pitfalls founders face and how to avoid them." (Publisher's note)

Includes bibliographical references and index

658.11   Initiation of business enterprises

Barringer, Bruce

Launching a Business; The First 100 Days. Bruce Barringer. Business Expert Pr 2013 254 p. illustrations (Entrepreneurship and small business management collection) $43.95   **658.11**

1. Management 2. Entrepreneurship 3. New business enterprises
ISBN 1606493973; 9781606493977

This book by Bruce R. Barringer "focuses on the tasks that a new business owner must complete in the first 100 days of launching a business. . . . Examples include securing the proper business licenses and permits, setting up a bookkeeping system, negotiating a lease, buying insurance, entering into contracts with vendors, recruiting and hiring employees, making the first sale, and so on." (Publisher's note)

"[Offers] tactical advice on things important during early launch of a business that an experienced founder should know but a novice likely will not." Choice

658.3 Personnel management (Human resource management)

Elton, Chester

All in; how the best managers create a culture of belief and drive big results. Adrian Gostick and Chester Elton. Free Press 2012 viii, 243 p.p (hbk.) $25   **658.3**
1. Leadership 2. Executive ability 3. Personnel management 4. Corporate culture 5. Employee motivation 6. Organizational behavior
ISBN 1451659822; 9781451659825

LC 2011045590

Author Adrian Gostick answers today's leadership questions, such as why are managers "able to get their employees to commit wholeheartedly to their culture and give that extra push that leads to outstanding results? . . . [The author presents] a simple seven-step road map for creating a culture of belief: define a burning platform; create a customer focus; develop agility; share everything; partner with your talent; root for each other; and establish clear accountability." (Publisher's note)

Includes bibliographical references and index.

Hallowell, Edward M.

Shine; using brain science to get the best from your people. Harvard Business Review Press 2011 197p il $26.95   **658.3**
1. Management 2. Job satisfaction 3. Interpersonal relations 4. Motivation (Psychology)
ISBN 978-1-59139-923-0; 1-59139-923-8

LC 2010024950

"Edward Hallowell draws on brain science, performance research, and his own experience helping people maximize their potential to present a . . . process for getting the best from your people." Publisher's note

Includes bibliographical references

Kelly, Matthew

The **dream** manager. Hyperion 2007 158p $19.95   **658.3**
1. Employee morale 2. Personnel management 3. Motivation (Psychology)
ISBN 978-1-4013-0370-9; 1-4013-0370-6

LC 2007-13597

This "business fable extols the virtues of helping those working for and with you to achieve their dreams. In this way . . . managers can boost morale and control turnover. . . . This one's sure to appeal to business readers." Libr J

Tracy, Brian

Full engagement! inspire, motivate, and bring out the best in your people. American Management Association 2011 226p $22   **658.3**
1. Employee morale 2. Personnel management 3.

Motivation (Psychology)
ISBN 978-0-8144-1689-1; 0-8144-1689-6

LC 2010048293

The author "shows managers how they can supercharge their employees' efforts." Publisher's note

658.4 Executive management

Bones, Christopher

The **cult** of the leader; a manifesto for more authentic business. Christopher Bones. Wiley 2011 296 p. $29.95   **658.4**
1. Business 2. Leadership 3. Management 4. Executive ability
ISBN 0470666048; 9780470666043

LC 2011410609

Chartered Management Trust Book of the Year 2011/12

This book, by Christopher Bones, offers "[a] critical look at the way that business leadership has gone so badly wrong. Modern business is obsessed with leaders. We talk about leadership all the time, but its real meaning is becoming more and more obscure. Recent corporate crises have shown that all too often, our leaders are missing in action when we need them most. In this . . . new book, Chris Bones shows how we need to . . . [change.]" (Publisher's note)

Includes bibliographical references.

Bossidy, Larry

Execution : the discipline of getting things done; {by} Larry Bossidy & Ram Charan; with Charles Burck. Crown Business 2002 278p $27.50   **658.4**
1. Management 2. Executive ability
ISBN 0-609-61057-0

LC 2002-18743

"This is a terrific book that will make smart managers rethink how business gets done within every level of their organization or department." Publ Wkly

Bryant, Adam

The **corner** office; indispensable and unexpected lessons from CEOs on how to lead and succeed. Times Books 2011 249p $25; ebook $11.99 **658.4**
1. Leadership 2. Management 3. Executive ability
ISBN 978-0-8050-9306-3; 0-8050-9306-0; 978-1-4299-5916-2 ebook; 1-4299-5916-9 ebook

LC 2010042970

The author "offers compelling advice for the aspiring executive. With interviews with more than 75 CEOs and other top executives at companies of all sizes, he compiles insights on such questions as what does it take to lead an organization? what are the keys to achieving the highest levels of success? . . . The conversational format makes these valuable lessons easy to comprehend and digest, and readers are left with a new understanding of leadership—why it's important, how these experts have worked to attain it, and how they can do the same." Publ Wkly

Camp, Jim

Start with no; the negotiating tools that the pros don't want you to know. Crown Business 2002 271p $22.95   **658.4**

  1. Business 2. Management 3. Negotiation
  ISBN 0-609-60800-2

                    LC 2001-47742

"Camp has developed a system of negotiating that reflects the common concept of 'win-win,' and the result is an excellent book with valuable insights." Booklist

Chan, Ronald W.

Behind the Berkshire Hathaway curtain; lessons from Warren Buffett's top business leaders. John Wiley & Sons 2010 178p il $24.95; ebook $16.99   **658.4**

  1. Success 2. Business 3. Management 4. Executive ability 5. Financiers 6. Berkshire Hathaway Inc.
  ISBN 978-0-470-56062-4; 0-470-56062-2; 978-0-470-64297-9 ebook

                    LC 2010281776

"Chan shares some of the business philosophies, strategies, and mindsets learned from exclusive interviews with leaders of Buffett's Berkshire Hathaway, including David Sokol of MidAmerican Energy, Cathy Baron Tamraz of Business Wire, Brad Kinstler of See's Candies, and Maria Gottschalk of Pampered Chef. The detailed stories of these executives' early career decisions bring to life practical lessons for personal and professional success." T + D

Conant, Douglas R.

Touchpoints; creating powerful leadership connections in the smallest of moments. [by] Douglas R. Conant, Mette Norgaard. Jossey-Bass 2011 xxxi, 173p (Warren Bennis signature series) $26.95; ebook $12.99   **658.4**

  1. Leadership
  ISBN 978-1-1180-0435-7; 978-1-1180-7554-8 ebook
                    LC 2011008907

"In an engaging personal style, Doug Conant, the CEO of Campbell Soup Company, discusses a leadership philosophy that he and leadership development expert Mette Norgaard refer to as 'TouchPoints'—those daily encounters with staff, co-workers, or colleagues that leaders can use to 'touch' others in meaningful ways, such as influencing, inspiring, or providing clarity. The book highlights ways to develop that ability and ways to practice leadership in the moment." T + D

Connors, Roger

Change the culture, change the game; the breakthrough strategy for energizing your organization and creating accountability for results. [by] Roger Connors and Tom Smith. Portfolio Penguin 2011 222p il $25.95   **658.4**

  1. Management 2. Responsibility 3. Corporate culture -- United States
  ISBN 978-1-59184-361-0; 1-59184-361-8
                    LC 2010032892

"If you don't like the results the company is producing, take a look at the culture, say [the authors.] . . . The book describes a 'Results Pyramid,' which presents three critical components of organizational culture that work together to produce results—experiences, beliefs, and actions. Part one of the book covers how to use each of the elements to help implement the change, and part two provides specific tools and best practices to use throughout the process." T + D

Convis, Gary L.

The Toyota way to lean leadership; achieving and sustaining excellence through leadership development. Jeffrey Liker, Gary L. Convis. McGraw-Hill 2011 280 p. il (hardback) $30   **658.4**

  1. Leadership 2. Personnel management 3. Leadership -- Japan 4. Lean manufacturing -- Japan 5. Toyota Jidōsha Kabushiki Kaisha -- Management 6. Automobile industry and trade -- Japan -- Management
  ISBN 0071780785; 9780071780780

                    LC 2011032234

In this book on Lean production methods, "Jeffrey Liker and Gary L. Convis, a former executive V.P. and managing officer of Toyota, help executives and senior managers get employees to refocus their efforts -- from simply performing their singular function to continuously improving in collaboration across the organization. Case studies from Toyota . . . illustrate the methods that create powerful, effective Lean leadership." (Publisher's note)

Cortada, James W.

Information and the modern corporation; James W. Cortada. MIT Press 2011 xiv, 159 p.p $11.95   **658.4**

  1. Corporations 2. Knowledge management 3. Information technology 4. Information resources management 5. Information technology -- Management
  ISBN 0262516411; 9780262516419

                    LC 2011005885

Author James W. Cortada's "book offers a guide to the role of information in modern business, mapping the use of information within work processes and tracing flows of information across supply-chain management, product development, customer relations, and sales. The emphasis is on information itself, not on information technology. Information, overshadowed for a while by the glamour and novelty of IT, is the fundamental component of the modern corporation." (Publisher's note)

Includes bibliographical references and index

Covey, Sean

The 4 disciplines of execution; achieving your wildly important goals. Chris McChesney, Sean Covey, Jim Huling. 1st Free Press hardcover ed. Free Press 2012 xxvi, 326 p.p ill. (hbk.) $28   **658.4**

  1. Leadership 2. Responsibility 3. Executive ability 4. Organization 5. Goal -- Psychology 6. Goal setting in personnel management
  ISBN 145162705X; 9781451627053

                    LC 2012001672

Authors Chris McChesney and Sean Covey provide "a simple repeatable, and proven formula for executing on your most important strategic priorities in the midst of the whirlwind. . . . Leaders can produce breakthrough results, even when executing the strategy requires a significant change in behavior from their teams [through] focusing on the wildly important, acting on lead measures, keeping a compelling scoreboard, [and] creating a cadence of accountability." (Publisher's note)

Includes bibliographical references and index

Gallo, Carmine

Talk like TED; the 9 public speaking secrets of the world's top minds. Carmine Gallo. St. Martin's Press 2014 288 p. illustrations (hardcover : alk. paper) $24.99   **658.4**
1. Public speaking 2. Business presentations
ISBN 1250041120; 9781250041128

LC 2013031049

In this book about public speaking, author Carmine Gallo "identifies the common elements that make TED Talks so successful. He offers nine secrets, including mastering the art of storytelling, being passionate about the subject matter, speaking conversationally, using humor, . . . and keeping presentations to 18 minutes. Gallo divides the lessons into three parts, focusing on the emotional, novel, and memorable." (Booklist)

"The author . . . includes successful outlines and guides to using both audio-visual aides and effective body language. Dramatic composition and vigorous presentation make this a powerful tool to improve mastery of speaking skills." Kirkus

Includes bibliographical references and index

Giuliani, Rudolph W.

Leadership; by Rudolph W. Giuliani with Ken Kurson. Miramax Bks. 2002 407p $25.95   **658.4**
1. Management
ISBN 0-7868-6841-4

This is a "book of guidelines about exemplary management skills {by} New York City's former mayor. . . . {He includes} opening and closing segments about the destruction of the World Trade Center." N Y Times (Late N Y Ed)

Goleman, Daniel

Primal leadership; realizing the power of emotional intelligence. {by} Daniel Goleman, Richard Boyatzis, Annie McKee. Harvard Business School Press 2002 306p $26.95   **658.4**
1. Leadership 2. Management 3. Executive ability
ISBN 1-57851-486-X

LC 2001-41207

This "book is well written, intelligent, approachable, and stimulating." Booklist

Includes bibliographical references

Guber, Peter

Tell to win; connect, persuade, and triumph with the hidden power of story. Crown Business 2011 255p $26; ebook $13.99   **658.4**
1. Success 2. Storytelling 3. Creative ability 4. Entrepreneurship
ISBN 978-0-307-58795-4; 0-307-58795-9; 978-0-307-58797-8 ebook

LC 2010019828

The author "offers insight on how to craft and deliver a story that will bring an idea to life. Guber liberally draws on the wealth of stories from his years of experience as a Hollywood studio executive and includes anecdotes from former President Bill Clinton, Michael Jackson, Deepak Chopra, Alice Walker, Gene Simmons, Wolfgang Puck, and dozens of others on how they have used personal stories to motivate." Libr J

Klubeck, Martin

Why organizations struggle so hard to improve so little; overcoming organizational immaturity. Martin Klubeck, Michael Langthorne, and Donald Padgett. Praeger Pub 2010 xvi, 222 p.p ill. (hardcover : alk. paper) $34.95; (ebook) $49.00   **658.4**
1. Organizational change 2. Organizational behavior
ISBN 0313380228; 0313380236; 9780313380228; 9780313380235

LC 2009046410

This book by Martin Klubeck, Michael Langthorne, and Donald Padgett "explains the difficulties and dangers of organizational immaturity, then provides proven, effective tools and ideas for achieving change within the limitations of an immature organization. With this guide, leaders and other stakeholders will be able to determine the maturity level of an organization, get beyond prevailing myths about how change gets derailed, and identify potential areas for improvement." (Publisher's note)

Includes bibliographical references and index.

Kouzes, James M.

The truth about leadership; the no-fads, heart-of-the-matter facts you need to know. [by] James M. Kouzes, Barry Z. Posner. Jossey-Bass 2010 xxv, 197p $24.95; ebook $16.99   **658.4**
1. Leadership 2. Executive ability
ISBN 978-0-470-63354-0; 978-0-470-87243-7 ebook

LC 2010018715

"It's hard to think of a better introduction for a new manager—or back-to-basics review for a veteran." Conference Board Rev

Includes bibliographical references

Penenberg, Adam L.

Play at work; how games inspire breakthrough thinking. Adam L. Penenberg. Portfolio Hardcover 2013 256 p. (hardback) $26.95   **658.4**
1. Play 2. Problem solving 3. Work environment 4. Creative thinking 5. Management games
ISBN 1591844797; 9781591844792

LC 2013024878

In this book, author Adam L. Penenberg "explores how, by understanding the way successful games are designed, we can apply them to become more efficient, come up with new ideas, and achieve even the most daunting goals. He shows how game mechanics are being applied to make employees happier and more motivated, improve worker safety, create better products, and improve customer service." (Publisher's note)

"The book's highlights include sections explaining the social satisfaction of gaming . . . as well as an exploration of how even the simplest point systems can provide necessary motivation." Pub Wkly

Includes bibliographical references and index

Peshawaria, Rajeev

Too many bosses, too few leaders; the art of being a true leader. Free Press 2011 xxii, 222p $26; ebook $12.99   **658.4**

1. Leadership

ISBN 978-1-4391-9774-5; 978-1-4391-9776-9 ebook

"Peshawaria's book ought to become required reading for all business people—from students to executives." Publ Wkly

Includes bibliographical references

Peters, Thomas J.

The **little** big things; 163 ways to pursue excellence. [by] Tom Peters. HarperStudio 2010 xxix, 538p $24.99; ebook $11.99   **658.4**

1. Management

ISBN 978-0-06-189408-4; 978-0-06-196350-6 ebook

LC 2009051160

The author "combines observations he has gleaned from his travels, current news items, conversations, and followers of his blog in a compact guide that aims to help readers realize effective projects, customer contentment, employee engagement, and business profitability. No doubt, Peters is on target as he advises readers to appreciate the angry customer, work on their last impressions, make sure that the restroom is clean, and 160 other ways to guarantee success. Each suggestion contains a rationale, example, and method of implementation, all in two pages apiece." Libr J

Pinson, Linda

Anatomy of a business plan; the step-by-step guide to building your business and securing your company's future. 7th ed.; Out of Your Mind...and Into the Marketplace 2008 356p il pa $22.95 **658.4**

1. Business planning 2. Business enterprises

ISBN 978-0-944205-37-2; 0-944205-37-2

LC 2008-277443

This book "features chapters on financing resources and business planning for nonprofits, as well as a sample restaurant business plan. Blank forms and worksheets help readers write a thoughtful, thorough, and professional business plan." Libr J

Ramsey, Dave

Entreleadership; 20 years of practical business wisdom from the trenches. Howard Books 2011 305p   **658.4**

1. Success 2. Leadership 3. Christian life 4. Entrepreneurship 5. Executive ability

ISBN 978-1-4516-1785-6; 978-1-4516-4601-6 ebook

LC 2011016820

"The author 'paid his stupid tax' in his 20s when his successful real-estate investment business failed due to massive debt. Broke and humbled, Ramsey embraced Christian principles in every facet of his life, including his work. This framework would lead to his new venture, a financial consulting firm, which, more than 20 years later, has earned the author tens of millions of dollars in revenues and helped countless others find success as well. Ramsey's faith may serve as his foundation, but any entrepreneur will find inspiration in his nuts-and-bolts advice. He touches on everything from time management and organization to the three things successful businesses never skip: contracts, vendors and collections."

"The author 'paid his stupid tax' in his 20s when his successful real-estate investment business failed due to massive debt. Broke and humbled, Ramsey embraced Christian principles in every facet of his life, including his work. This framework would lead to his new venture, a financial consulting firm, which, more than 20 years later, has earned the author tens of millions of dollars in revenues and helped countless others find success as well. Ramsey's faith may serve as his foundation, but any entrepreneur will find inspiration in his nuts-and-bolts advice. He touches on everything from time management and organization to the three things successful businesses never skip: contracts, vendors and collections." Kirkus

Rubinfeld, Arthur

Built for growth; expanding your business around the corner or across the globe. [by] Arthur Rubinfeld, Collins Hemingway. Wharton School Pub. 2005 xxiv, 343p il map $25.95   **658.4**

1. Management 2. Retail trade

ISBN 0-13-146574-0

LC 20040114697

"The authors intend the book to be 'a valuable primer on all aspects of retail: brand, location, people, finance, property management, expansion strategy and long-term thinking.' . . . An informative read for both beginners and seasoned retailers, this outstanding book abounds with insightful case studies and expert advice that should enhance the success of any retail brand." Libr J

Sandberg, Sheryl, 1969-

Lean in; women, work, and the will to lead. Sheryl Sandberg. Alfred A. Knopf 2013 240 p. (hardcover) $24.95   **658.4**

1. Leadership 2. Women in the workplace 3. Women executives 4. Leadership in women

ISBN 0385349947; 9780385349949

LC 2012043371

This book, by Sheryl Sandberg, "examines why women's progress in achieving leadership roles has stalled, explains the root causes, and offers compelling, commonsense solutions that can empower women to achieve their full potential. . . . Sandberg digs . . . into these issues, combining personal anecdotes, hard data, and compelling research to cut through the layers of ambiguity and bias surrounding the lives and choices of working women." (Publisher's note)

Sutton, Robert I.

Good boss, bad boss; how to be the best--and learn from the worst. Business Plus 2010 308p $23.99; ebook $10.99   **658.4**

1. Personnel management

ISBN 978-0-446-55608-8; 978-0-446-55847-1 ebook

LC 2009-53414

"With examples from such diverse workplaces as Pixar and Anchor Steam brewery, Sutton reveals how the best bosses take diverse and intertwined steps to create effective and humane workplaces, and offers tips on taking control, getting and giving credit appropriately, taking responsibility, staying in tune with employees, and squelching your potential inner jerk. . . . This entertaining, satisfying guide is a wakeup call for bosses everywhere—and a survival guide for those who work for them." Publ Wkly

Includes bibliographical references

Tarr-Whelan, Linda

Women lead the way; your guide to stepping up to leadership and changing the world. Berrett-Koehler Publishers 2009 213p $24.95   **658.4**

1. Leadership 2. Women executives

ISBN 978-1-60509-135-8; 1-60509-135-9

LC 2009-21826

"Conversational and eye-opening, with many narrative illustrations and concrete advice, Tarr-Whelan's text could prove an important volume for working women looking to advance and enrich their careers." Publ Wkly

Includes bibliographical references

Taylor, William

Practically radical; not-so-crazy ways to transform your company, shake up your industry, and challenge yourself. [by] William C. Taylor. William Morrow 2011 xxi, 293p $27.99; pa $14.99 **658.4**

1. Leadership 2. Business enterprises

ISBN 978-0-06-173461-8; 0-06-173461-6; 978-0-06-203522-6 pa; 0-06-203522-3 pa

LC 2010028021

The author "takes us on an inside look at 25 companies that have grown ever more adaptive to not merely survive but thrive in today's challenging environment. . . . An engaging and briskly written read, this will captivate and benefit business people interested in change and innovation." Publ Wkly

Includes bibliographical references

Walsh, Bill

The score takes care of itself; my philosophy of leadership. [by] Bill Walsh with Steve Jamison and Craig Walsh. Portfolio 2009 251p $25.95   **658.4**

1. Leadership 2. Management 3. Football -- Coaching

ISBN 978-1-59184-266-8

LC 2009-10651

"This posthumous leadership guide by the acclaimed head coach of the San Francisco 49ers is a fascinating compendium of Walsh's philosophy, as compiled by his son and Jamison. . . . Walsh reveals a simple and strict philosophy that prizes people above all and focuses on core values, principles and ideals. . . . Enlightening, informative and engaging, this powerful book is a must-read for executives and managers at every level." Publ Wkly

Welch, John F.

Winning; [by] Jack Welch with Suzy Welch. HarperBusiness 2005 384p $27.95   **658.4**

1. Success 2. Business

ISBN 0-06-075394-3

LC 2005-40337

The author offers business advice "from practices he employed at GE (e.g., the much-debated differentiation, which includes winnowing 10% of the workforce at regular intervals), to the personal qualities that lead to success (to Welch, candor is essential), to advice on job hunting and how to

work with a bad boss, to ways to maximize the budget process. . . . It's difficult to think of anyone in business who wouldn't benefit from reading this savvy, engaging cubicle-to-boardroom guide to success." Publ Wkly

Wheeler, Michael

The art of negotiation; how to improvise agreement in a chaotic world. by Michael Wheeler. Simon & Schuster 2013 320 p. (hardcover : alk. paper) $26   **658.4**

1. Negotiation 2. Business planning 3. Negotiation in business

ISBN 1451690428; 9781451690422; 9781451690439

LC 2013005793

This book, by Michael Wheeler, "hows how master negotiators thrive in the face of chaos and uncertainty. Wheeler illuminates the improvisational nature of negotiation, drawing on his own research and his work with Program on Negotiation colleagues. He explains how the best practices of diplomats such as George J. Mitchell, dealmaker Bruce Wasserstein, and Hollywood producer Jerry Weintraub apply to everyday transactions." (Publisher's note)

658.452   Oral communication

McGowan, Bill

Pitch Perfect; How to Say It Right the First Time, Every Time. by Bill McGowan. HarperCollins 2014 288 p. illustrations $27.99   **658.452**

1. Communication

ISBN 0062273221; 9780062273222

In this book, Bill McGowan "teaches you how to get your message across and get what you want with pitch perfect communication. . . . Saying the right thing the right way can make the difference between sealing the deal or losing the account, getting a promotion, or getting a pink slip. It's essential to be pitch perfect--to get the right message across to the right person at the right time." (Publisher's note)

"In this engaging, enlightening, and full-of-practical-advice text, McGowan calls out poor public speaking doctrine and replaces it with examples of better ways to persuade and communicate." LJ

658.5   Management of production

Greene, Jay

Design is how it works; how the smartest companies turn products into icons. Portfolio 2010 231p il $25.95   **658.5**

1. Marketing 2. Industrial design

ISBN 978-1-59184-322-1

LC 2010004030

"Greene introduces us to eight companies (Porsche; Nike; LEGO; OXO, design-centric kitchenware; REI, outdoor outfitter; energy-food company Clif Bar; Ace Hotels; and Virgin Atlantic) of different sizes, in different industries and locations, new and old, publicly traded and privately held to show that design is something in which any company can succeed. Greene provides valuable information and insight for companies in all businesses as he explains the importance of design thinking." Booklist

Includes bibliographical references

658.8 Management of marketing

Anderson, Christopher

The **long** tail; why the future of business is selling less of more. [by] Chris Anderson. Hyperion 2006 238p il $24.95 **658.8**

1. Internet marketing

ISBN 1-4013-0237-8; 978-1-4013-0237-5

LC 2006-43378

This "book does an excellent job of spotting trends and fitting them into an easily accessible theoretical framework that helps explain the changing culture around us." N Y Times (Late N Y Ed)

Includes bibliographical references

Burcher, Nick

Paid, owned, earned; maximizing marketing returns in a socially connected world. Nick Burcher. Kogan Page 2012 xiv, 279 p.p **658.8**

1. Mass media 2. Social media 3. Digital media 4. Internet marketing 5. Online social networks 6. Marketing -- Management

ISBN 074946562X; 9780749465629; 9780749465636

LC 2011038487

This book by Nick Burcher "defines the constituents of each area of 'paid,' 'owned' and 'earned' media and shows how they are linked together. The complexity of media that now sees multiple channels accessed through multiple devices has created major challenges for today's marketing and advertising professionals. [Burcher] proposes a blueprint for how to think and navigate across this space." (Publisher's note)

Includes bibliographical references and index

Cook, Sarah

Customer care excellence; how to create an effective customer focus. 6th ed.; Kogan Page 2011 278p il pa $39.95; ebook $39.95 **658.8**

1. Quality control 2. Customer services 3. Customer relations

ISBN 978-0-7494-5705-1 pa; 0-7494-5705-8 pa; 978-0-7494-6257-4 ebook

LC 2010023892

First published 1992 with title: Customer care

"This book explains how to develop and sustain a customer-service focus within a company. Emphasizing both strategic and practical aspects of customer service, the author explains how gaining customer commitment and motivating employees to deliver excellent service can ensure successful results and satisfied customers." Publisher's note

Includes bibliographical references

Fox, Scott

Click millionaires; work less, live more with an internet business you love. Scott C. Fox. American Management Association 2012 278 p. **658.8**

1. Small business 2. Personal finance 3. Electronic commerce 4. Small business -- Management

ISBN 0814431917; 9780814431917

LC 2012004882

This book "offers a guide to escaping the daily grind. . . . [It offers a] program [that] leads readers through every step of the transition from cubicle to home office. . . . [The author] urges readers to create a lifestyle business, in which they prioritize a flexible schedule and independent work over profits and stress, using Web sites, e-commerce, digital publishing, and social media to build businesses that work on their own schedules--first part-time and then developing a niche business online that generates recurring revenues automatically. His comprehensive, pragmatic approach covers online presence, social networking, production and operations, and online advertising, and includes interviews from those who've succeeded." (Publishers Weekly)

Includes bibliographical references and index

Goldman, Aaron

Everything I know about marketing I learned from Google. McGraw-Hill 2011 341p il $26.95; ebook $26.95 **658.8**

1. Marketing 2. Google (Web site) 3. Internet marketing

ISBN 978-0-07-174289-4; 978-0-07-174621-2 ebook

LC 2010025355

The author "outlines 20 lessons that laypeople can use to market their products and services successfully online. Lessons include how to get near the top of search results, keeping marketing simple, and testing and tracking everything you do. . . . Written with humor and frankness, this book is as appealing as a manual for marketing as it is for armchair reading. Anyone interested in the pop culture of Google will appreciate it." Libr J

Handley, Ann

Content rules; how to create killer blogs, podcasts, videos, ebooks, webinars (and more) that engage customers and ignite your business. [by] Ann Handley & C.C. Chapman. Wiley 2011 xxii, 282p il (New rules of social media series) $24.95; ebook $9.99 **658.8**

1. Internet marketing 2. Digital media 3. Web sites -- Design

ISBN 978-0-470-64828-5; 0-470-64828-7; 978-0-470-94872-9 ebook

LC 2011280622

A one-stop source on the art and science of developing marketing content that people care about. This coverage is interwoven with case studies of companies successfully spreading their ideas online—and using them to establish credibility and build a loyal customer base.

Includes bibliographical references

Jantsch, John

The **referral** engine; teaching your business how to market itself. Portfolio 2010 243p $25.95 **658.8**
1. Marketing 2. Advertising
ISBN 978-1-59184-311-5

LC 2009-49521

The author "argues that typical methods of advertising and marketing are not as effective as fostering good word of mouth and referral buzz for your business. To that end, he suggests numerous ways to encourage referrals, including using social media and hiring, training, and treating employees as courteously as you expect them to treat your customers." Libr J

"This practical, smart, and original guide is essential reading for any company looking to grow without a fat marketing budget." EContent

Kaputa, Catherine

Breakthrough branding; how smart entrepreneurs and intrapreneurs transform a small idea into a big brand. Catherine Kaputa. Nicholas Brealey Pub. 2012 272 p. (pbk.) $19.95 **658.8**
1. Business planning 2. Success in business 3. Branding (Marketing)
ISBN 1857885813; 9781857885811

LC 2011044338

The author Catherine Kaputa "instructs readers on how to develop ideas into successful brands. She presents numerous case studies to illustrate success stories: . . . Reed Hasting and Netflix, Jack Dorsey and Twitter, and Mark Zuckerberg and Facebook. Readers are grounded in such . . . topics as selecting a brand name, creating the company or product's logo, seeking celebrity endorsements, marketing the brand, creating a company culture, and using social media to promote the brand." (Library Journal)

Includes bibliographical references and index.

Kawasaki, Guy

Enchantment; the art of changing hearts, minds, and actions. Portfolio/Penguin 2011 xxiii, 211p il **658.8**
1. Marketing 2. Persuasion (Psychology)
ISBN 978-1-59184-379-5

LC 2010046009

The author discusses "the tricky art of influence and persuasion. Kawasaki . . . transforms the otherwise exhausted and overwrought tropes of how to win friends and influence people with a complete makeover here, whether he's talking about wardrobe choice or tips for effective swearing. . . . Informative, concise guide from one of America's most influential and, yes, enchanting entrepreneurs." Kirkus

Includes bibliographical references

Mainwaring, Simon

We first; how brands and consumers use social media to build a better world. Palgrave Macmillan 2011 250p $26; ebook $12.99 **658.8**
1. Capitalism 2. Social change 3. Social networking 4. Internet marketing 5. Digital media
ISBN 978-0-230-11026-7; 978-0-230-12053-2 ebook

LC 2010048454

"A must-read for those who want to understand and engage the power and potential of social media to promote a healthier, more equitable world." Kirkus

Includes bibliographical references

Massengill, Rebekah Peeples

Wal -Mart wars; moral populism in the twenty-first century. Rebekah Peeples Massengill. New York University Press 2013 256 p. (hbk. : alk. paper) $75 **658.8**
1. Capitalism 2. Corporations 3. Wal-Mart Stores, Inc. 4. Retail trade 5. Wal-Mart (Firm) 6. Marketing -- Political aspects 7. Marketing -- Moral and ethical aspects
ISBN 0814763332; 9780814763339; 9780814763346

LC 2012040760

This book, by Rebekah Peeples Massengill, focuses on the retail store Wal-Mart. "It is . . . a central symbol in America's increasingly polarized political discourse over consumption, capitalism and government regulations. In many ways the battle over Wal-Mart is the battle between 'Main Street' and 'Wall Street' as the fate of workers under globalization and the ability of the private market to effectively distribute precious goods like health care take center stage." (Publisher's note)

"This is first-rate sociology, deftly packaged to offer insight for both academic and popular audiences." LJ

Includes bibliographical references and index

Moffitt, Sean

Wikibrands; reinventing your company in a customer-driven marketplace. [by] Sean Moffitt and Mike Dover. McGraw-Hill 2011 318p il $28; ebook $28 **658.8**
1. Marketing 2. Internet marketing 3. Wikis (Computer science)
ISBN 978-0-07-174927-5; 0-07-174927-6; 978-0-07-175235-0 ebook; 0-07-175235-8 ebook

LC 2010029785

"There is a wealth of important information in this broad-based report on the new customer-controlled marketplace; it is an excellent wakeup call, a strategic guide, and an execution road map for business leaders." Booklist

Includes bibliographical references

Resnick, Lynda

Rubies in the orchard; how to uncover the hidden gems in your business. with Francis Wilkinson. Doubleday 2009 xx, 204p il $24.95 **658.8**
1. Business 2. Marketing 3. Advertising
ISBN 978-0-385-52578-7; 0-385-52578-8

LC 2008-23167

"Real-life tales of marketing strategies that rocketed Resnick and her husband to astounding success with companies like Fiji Water, Teleflora, the Franklin Mint and Pom Wonderful, the wildly successful pomegranate juice. The author charms with her winning wit and a self-deprecating tone as she distills the secrets of her extraordinary career into a series of philosophies illustrated through behind-the-scenes looks at various marketing campaigns. . . . A must-read for anyone who aspires to Resnick's level of promotional genius, success or commitment to environmental sustainability." Publ Wkly

Schaefer, Mark W.

Return on influence; the revolutionary power of Klout, social scoring, and influence marketing. Mark Schaefer. McGraw-Hill 2012 xviii, 215 p.p (alk. paper) $25   **658.8**

    1. Social influence 2. Internet marketing 3. Online social networks 4. Social media -- Marketing
    ISBN 0071791094; 9780071791090

                       LC 2011052315

    This book, by Mark Schaefer, "is the first book to explore how brands are identifying and leveraging the world's most powerful bloggers, tweeters, and YouTube celebrities to build product awareness, brand buzz, and new sales. . . . [In it] marketing consultant and college educator Mark W. Schaefer shows you how to use the latest breakthroughs in social networking and influence marketing to achieve your goals." (Publisher's note)

    Includes bibliographical references and index.

Siegel, David

    Pull; the power of the Semantic Web to transform your business. Portfolio 2009 270p il $27.95 **658.8**

    1. Internet marketing 2. Electronic commerce 3. Information technology
    ISBN 978-1-59184-277-4

                       LC 2009-35779

    "Siegel envisions the future of 'smart computing' which will unfold over the next 10 years, where your data 'follows you around' and is accessible from anywhere through the Web, predicting that hardware and operating systems will become obsolete as the Web itself becomes the computer." Booklist

    "This thought-provoking read is sure to spark ideas about what it will take to succeed in tomorrow's marketplace." Publ Wkly

    Includes bibliographical references

Underhill, Paco

    ★ **Why** we buy; the science of shopping. Updated and rev.; Simon & Schuster Pbks. 2009 306p pa $16; ebook $12.99   **658.8**

    1. Shopping 2. Consumers 3. Marketing
    ISBN 978-1-4165-9524-3 pa; 1-4165-9524-4 pa; 978-1-4165-6174-3 ebook; 1-4165-6174-9 ebook

                       LC 2010-483248

    First published 1999

    "Each chapter delves into a particular aspect of a store environment and its interface with customers: the importance of signage and why less is more, how men shop, . . . and clues about waiting time. Throughout, insights are peppered with one or several examples." Booklist [review of 1999 edition]

Walker, Rob

    Buying in; the secret dialogue between what we buy and who we are. Random House 2008 xxi, 291p $25   **658.8**

    1. Marketing 2. Brand name products
    ISBN 978-1-4000-6391-8; 1-4000-6391-4

                       LC 2007-39973

    This "is a thoughtful and unhurried investigation into consumerism that pushes the analysis to the maximum and builds a thesis that refutes the myth of the brand-proof consumer." Publ Wkly

    Includes bibliographical references

Yellin, Emily

    Your call is (not that) important to us; customer service and what it reveals about our world and our lives. Free Press 2009 291p $26   **658.8**

    1. Customer services 2. Customer relations
    ISBN 978-1-4165-4689-4; 1-4165-4689-8

                       LC 2009-2468

    The author "dives into the often dysfunctional world of customer service, exploring the multimillion-dollar industry from various points of view, interviewing exasperated consumers, displeased CEOs and infuriated customer service reps themselves. . . . While Yellin's study offers more industry anecdotes than concrete solutions, readers will likely look at the industry differently and with more empathy for those who participate in it." Publ Wkly

    Includes bibliographical references

658.85   Personal selling

The **art** of the sale; learning from the masters about the business of life. Philip Delves Broughton. Penguin Press 2012 291 p.   **658.85**

    1. Selling 2. Sales management 3. Business -- Psychological aspects
    ISBN 1594203326; 9781594203329

                       LC 2011040209

    This book examines "the keys to success in sales." "Broughton has met with top sellers around the world, traveling to Japan, Morocco and the United Kingdom . . . . In addition to his interview research, he examines academic studies, history, self-help literature, academic research on the psychology of selling and the character attributes of sales people. He explores the differences in theory and practice, and he draws from the history of the field, by way of P.T. Barnum and Joseph Duveen, who brought fine-art sales to the U.S." (Kirkus)

    Includes bibliographical references (p. [277]-281) and index

659.1   Advertising

Doucett, Elisabeth

Creating your library brand; communicating your relevance and value to your patrons. American Library Association 2008 124p il pa $50   **659.1**
    1. Marketing 2. Libraries -- Public relations
    ISBN 978-0-8389-0962-1; 0-8389-0962-0

LC 2008-983

The author "defines marketing and branding and then offers practical advice on the different aspects, from creating a logo to using templates, working with outside help, and creating and evaluating the branding plan. She emphasizes including staff, patrons, and board members in the process and offers helpful examples with which one can follow up online. . . . This type of guide can serve as a useful ready reference, but be forewarned—marking helpful pages will require a book full of tabs." Voice Youth Advocates

Tungate, Mark

Adland; a global history of advertising. Mark Tungate. Kogan Page 2013 259 p. il $24.95 **659.1**
    1. Advertising industry 2. Advertising -- History
    ISBN 0749464313; 9780749464318

LC 200716432

This book, by Mark Tungate, offers an "examination of modern advertising, from its early origins, to the evolution of the current advertising landscape. . . . Exploring the roots of the advertising industry in New York and London, and going on to cover the emerging markets of Eastern Europe, Asia and Latin America, . . . [the book] offers a comprehensive examination of a global industry and suggests ways in which it is likely to develop in the future." (Publisher's note)

"As a definitive record of what happened and why, there is none finer. Whether you're a novice in the industry or . . . a veteran of 25 years, there is much to learn." Management Today

Includes bibliographical references

Turow, Joseph

The **daily** you; how the new advertising industry is defining your identity and your world. Joseph Turow. Yale University Press 2011 xi, 234 p.p (hardback) $28.00 **659.1**
    1. Advertising 2. Internet marketing 3. Consumer profiling 4. Marketing -- Technological innovations 5. Customer services -- Technological innovations
    ISBN 0300165013; 9780300165012

LC 2011028202

This book presents "a warning about the impact of the 'Web 3.0' revolution . . . on individual freedom and privacy. . . . It is via this avalanche of personal data, available through networks like Facebook . . . [Joseph] Turow warns, 'the new advertising industry is defining your identity and your world.' . . . The root of the problem, Turow explains, is the disappearance of boundaries between advertising and content that shaped 20th-century media." (New Scientist)

Includes bibliographical references and index.

659.2   Public relations

Fertik, Michael

Wild west 2.0; how to protect and restore your online reputation on the untamed social frontier. [by] Michael Fertik and David Thompson. American Management Association 2010 264p il $24.95 **659.2**
    1. Web 2.0 2. Public relations 3. Social networking 4. Internet -- Social aspects
    ISBN 978-0-8144-1509-2

LC 2009-42255

"Full of invaluable information that readers will be very grateful to have when they need it, this book explains the rules and provides the tools for overcoming online attacks and regaining a positive reputation." Publ Wkly

Includes bibliographical references

660.6   Biotechnology

Hubbell, Sue

Shrinking the cat; genetic engineering before we knew about genes. with illustrations by Liddy Hubbell. Houghton Mifflin 2001 175p il $25; pa $13 **660.6**
    1. Cats 2. Corn 3. Silk 4. Apples 5. Breeding 6. Genetic engineering
    ISBN 0-618-04027-7; 0-618-25748-9 pa

LC 2001-24547

This is a "history of how genetic engineering began, how it has been used, and how humankind has benefited from a combination of natural selection and scientific manipulation of genes. Hubbell . . . shows that genetic engineering has always been with us, illustrating by way of silkworm breeding from its origins in China to the New World, where it spawned an industry that depends on genetics to thrive; the domestication of corn from its wild state to the product we eat today; {and} how we turned wildcats into house cats by selective breeding that changed size, color, and demeanor." Libr J

"An engaging synthesis of material that will appeal to Hubbell's well-established audience." Booklist

Includes bibliographical references and index

Kurpinski, Kyle

How to defeat your own clone; and other tips for surviving the biotech revolution. [by] Kyle Kurpinski and Terry D. Johnson. Bantam Books Trade Paperbacks 2010 180p il pa $14 **660.6**
    1. Cloning 2. Biotechnology
    ISBN 978-0-553-38578-6; 0-553-38578-X

LC 2009-45899

"Kurpinski and Johnson have written a science book that is irreverent, timely, accessible, and, best of all, compulsively readable." Publ Wkly

664   Food technology

Adamchak, Raoul W.

✓ **Tomorrow's** table; organic farming, genetics, and the future of food. [by] Pamela C. Ronald [and] Raoul W. Adamchak. Oxford University Press 2008 208p il map $29.95   **664**

1. Organic farming 2. Genetic engineering 3. Genetically modified foods 4. Food -- Biotechnology
ISBN 9780195301755

LC 2007-7071

"The format is easy to follow and effective at highlighting . . . [the authors'] seemingly adverse positions on the subject. By the book's conclusion, their argument is elegantly presented in a logical fashion." Choice

Includes bibliographical references (p. 179-197)

Katz, Sandor Ellix

The **art** of fermentation; an in-depth exploration of essential concepts and processes from around the world. Sandor Ellix Katz ; foreword by Michael Pollan. Chelsea Green Pub. 2012 498 p. ill. (some col.) (hardback) $39.95   **664**

1. Fermentation 2. Canning and preserving 3. Fermented foods
ISBN 160358286X; 9781603582865; 9781603583640

LC 2011052014

James Beard Foundation Award: Reference and Scholarship (2013)

This book, by Sandor Ellix Katz, was the winner of the 2013 James Beard Foundation Book Award for Reference and Scholarship. "Readers will find detailed information on fermenting vegetables; sugars into alcohol; . . . sour tonic beverages; milk; grains and starchy tubers; beers (and other grain-based alcoholic beverages); beans; seeds; nuts; fish; meat; and eggs, as well as growing mold cultures, using fermentation in agriculture, art, and energy production, and considerations for commercial enterprises." (Publisher's note)

"Katz takes fermentation down to the molecular level while keeping it conversational and accessible to the generalist." LJ

Includes bibliographical refererences and index

Robinson, Jancis

Wine grapes; a complete guide to 1,380 vine varieties, including their origins and flavors. by Jancis Robinson, Julia Harding, and Jose Vouillamoz. Ecco/HarperCollins 2012 1242 p. (hardback) $175 **664**

1. Grapes 2. Wine and wine making 3. Viticulture 4. Grapes -- Varieties
ISBN 0062206362; 9780062206367

LC 2012019224

James Beard Foundation Award: Beverage (2013)

This book by Jancis Robinson, Julia Harding, and Jose Vouillamoz provides information "about the . . . fruit that care, love, skill, and time transform into [wine]. [It] is the first complete compendium in more than a century to all grape varieties relevant to the wine lover. 'Wine Grapes' charts the relationships of the grapes . . . , discusses . . . where and how they are grown, and, most importantly, what the wines made from them will ultimately taste like." (Publisher's note)

Winter, Ruth

A **consumer's** dictionary of food additives; 7th ed.; Three Rivers Press 2009 595p pa $17.95; ebook $17.95   **664**

1. Reference books 2. Food additives -- Dictionaries
ISBN 978-0-307-40892-1 pa; 978-0-307-45259-7 ebook

LC 2008-40601

First published 1972. Periodically revised

This guide provides "facts about the safety and side effects of more than 12,000 ingredients—such as preservatives, food-tainting pesticides, and animal drugs—that end up in food as a result of processing and curing." Publisher's note

Includes bibliographical references

664.362   Olive oil

Mueller, Tom

✓ **Extra** virginity; Tom Mueller. 1st ed. W. W. Norton 2011 238 p.   **664.362**

1. Fraud 2. Olive oil 3. Food adulteration and inspection 4. Olive -- History 5. Olive -- Folklore 6. Olive oil -- History 7. Olive oil industry -- Moral and ethical aspects
ISBN 9780393070217

LC 2011041459

In this book, author "Tom Mueller . . . [an] expert on olive oil and olive oil fraud . . . [tells] a story of globalization, deception, and crime in the food industry from ancient times to the present, and a[n] . . . indictment of today's lax protections against fake and even toxic food products in the United States. . . . [The book] is also an . . . account of the artisanal producers, chemical analysts, chefs, and food activists who are defending the extraordinary oils that truly deserve the name 'extra-virgin.'" (Publisher's note)

666   Ceramic and allied technologies

Garfield, Simon

✓ **Mauve**; how one man invented a color that changed the world. Norton 2001 222p il hardcover o.p. pa $13.95   **666**

1. Chemists 2. Dyes and dyeing
ISBN 0-393-32313-7 pa

LC 00-69533

This volume discusses how a British student, William Henry Perkin, while trying to synthesize quinine from coal tar, developed mauve, "the first mass-produced artificial dye. . . . By the turn of the 20th century, because of Perkin's novel idea, dye makers had 2,000 synthesized colors at their disposal." N Y Times Book Rev

"The text is understandable by the average layman and is enjoyable reading for the scientist and non-scientist alike." Sci Books Films

Includes bibliographical references

Macfarlane, Alan

Glass : a world history; {by} Alan Macfarlane and Gerry Martin. University of Chicago Press 2002 255p il $27.50 **666**

1. Glass
ISBN 0-226-50028-4

LC 2002-20493

The authors "make the case for the centrality of glass in the artistic renaissance and scientific revolution that took place in Western Europe from the 14th to 17th centuries. They discuss the origins of glass making and trace its development and usage across centuries and multiple cultures (Europe, the Middle East, China, India, and Japan). Their discussion combines cultural, artistic, and aesthetic viewpoints of glass within these cultures with history and developments in science. The result is a thoroughly readable, carefully argued work, filled with delightful surprises. . . . An excellent example of microhistory . . . this is required for history of science collections and recommended for large public and academic collections." Libr J

Includes bibliographical references

667 Cleaning, color, coating, related technologies

Greenfield, Amy Butler

A **perfect** red; empire, espionage, and the quest for the color of desire. Amy Butler Greenfield. 1st ed; HarperCollins 2005 338p il $26.95 **667**

1. Dyes and dyeing
ISBN 0-06-052275-5

LC 2004-42376

The author "combines the investigative prowess of a detective with the intellectual reasoning of an academician to create an eminently entertaining and educational read." Booklist

Includes bibliographical references

668 Technology of other organic products

Turin, Luca

The **secret** of scent; adventures in perfume and the science of smell. Ecco 2006 207p il $23.95; pa $13.95 **668**

1. Perfumes
ISBN 0-06-113383-3; 978-0-06-113383-1; 0-06-113384-1 pa; 978-0-06-113384-8 pa

LC 2006-46273

The author "investigates the reason things smell they way they do." N Y Times Book Rev

Includes bibliographical references

674 Lumber processing, wood products, cork

The Encyclopedia of wood; a tree-by-tree guide to the world's most versatile resource. general edi-

tor, Aidan Walker. Facts on File 2005 192p il map $35 **674**

1. Reference books 2. Wood -- Encyclopedias
ISBN 0-8160-6181-5

LC 2004-60849

First published 1989

"A nice addition to libraries with strong interior design or DIY collections." Libr J

Includes bibliographical references

Petroski, Henry

The **pencil**; a history of design and circumstance. Knopf 1990 434p il hardcover o.p. pa $20 **674**

1. Pencils
ISBN 0-394-57422-2; 0-679-73415-5 pa

LC 89-45362

The author discusses the manufacture, design, history, and sociological significance of the pencil.

"An incredibly rich and complex history of this entirely unremarkable instrument of communication." SLJ

Includes bibliographical references

676 Pulp and paper technology

Grummer, Arnold E.

Trash -to-treasure papermaking. Storey Publishing 2011 207p il pa $16.95 **676**

1. Paper 2. Papermaking
ISBN 978-1-60342-547-6

LC 2010-43056

"Grummer begins with basic papermaking, then progresses to more advanced skills. Ample tips on everything from proper technique to troubleshooting problems with finished paper are included. A gallery of clever projects with directions rounds out this friendly, accessible guide to papermaking." Libr J

Includes bibliographical references

Hiebert, Helen, 1965-

The **papermaker's** companion; the ultimate guide to making and using handmade paper. Helen Hiebert. Storey Books 2000 219 p. $18.95 **676**

1. Papermaking 2. Paper, Handmade
ISBN 1580172008; 9781580172004

LC 99087351

This book by Helen Hiebert "covers absolutely everything you need to know about papermaking, from the basics to advanced techniques such as shaped sheets, embossing, laminating, and watermarking. . . . [The book] also includes thorough step-by-step instructions for processing pulp, building papermaking equipment, and making paper-based projects." (Publisher's note)

Includes bibliographical references and index.

676.092   Pulp and paper technology

Basbanes, Nicholas A.

★ **On** paper; the everything of its two-thousand-year history. Nicholas A. Basbanes. Alfred A. Knopf 2013 448 p. $35   **676.092**

1. Paper 2. Paper industry 3. Paper -- History 4. Papermaking -- History 5. Paper industry -- History
ISBN 0307266427; 9780307266422

LC 2012050267

Andrew Carnegie Medal for Excellence in Nonfiction Shortlist (2014)

This book, by Nicholas A. Basbanes, presents "a consideration of all things paper: its invention that revolutionized human civilization; its thousand-fold uses (and misuses), proliferation, and sweeping influence on society; its makers, shapers, collectors, and pulpers. Basbanes writes about the ways in which paper has been used to record history, make laws, conduct business, and establish identities." (Publisher's note)

Includes bibliographical references

677   Textiles

Schoeser, Mary

World textiles: a concise history. Thames & Hudson 2003 224p il (World of art) pa $14.95 **677**

1. Fabrics 2. Textile industry
ISBN 0-500-20369-5

LC 2002-110919

"Arranged roughly into chronological periods, the book . . . details technique, materials, and designs and puts them in historical and cultural context. This is truly a fantastic history of textile arts. . . . The text itself is a delight to read and more comprehensive than in other comparable works." Libr J

Includes bibliographical references

678   Elastomers and elastomer products

Korman, Richard

The **Goodyear** story; an inventor's obsession and the struggle for a rubber monopoly. Encounter Bks. 2002 230p il $25.95; pa $16.95   **678**

1. Rubber 2. Inventors 3. Manufacturing executives 4. Goodyear Tire & Rubber Company
ISBN 1-89355-437-6; 1-89355-482-1 pa

LC 2001-55635

"Charles Goodyear began his obsessive quest to find the recipe for making rubber in the 1830s and ended up becoming an American industrial legend. Besides tracing the life of this inspiring entrepreneur, Korman's social history of factory life and debtors prison in the early to mid-1800s is exceedingly well drawn." Booklist

Includes bibliographical references

Slack, Charles

Noble obsession; Charles Goodyear, Thomas Hancock, and the race to unlock the greatest indus-

trial secret of the nineteenth century. Hyperion 2002 274p il $24.95; pa $14.95   **678**

1. Rubber 2. Inventors 3. Manufacturing executives 4. Goodyear Tire & Rubber Company
ISBN 0-7868-6789-2; 0-7868-8856-3 pa

LC 2002-68932

This is the story of how Charles Goodyear discovered the process of vulcanization of rubber, making possible the manufacture of rubber tires carried out by Thomas Hancock and the company which bears Goodyear's name

"Slack brings Charles Goodyear back to life and redeems the man who gave up everything to give his gift to the world." Booklist

Includes bibliographical references

681   Precision instruments and other devices

Angel, Solly

The **tale** of the scale; an odyssey of invention. Oxford University Press 2003 304p il $28   **681**

1. Inventions 2. Industrial design
ISBN 0-19-515868-7

LC 2003-48699

This is the "story of one man's attempt to design a novel personal (bathroom) scale. . . . The book is more than simply a narrative of the author's successes and failures; it also contains his musings on topics that should be of interest to scientists and engineers: the . . . scientific method, the relationship between form and function, design theory, and creativity, among others. . . . I highly recommend this very interesting, very entertaining account of how one person went through the product design and development process." Sci Books Films

Includes bibliographical references

681.1   Instruments for measuring time, counting and calculating machines and instruments

Marchant, Jo

Decoding the heavens; a 2,000-year-old computer--and the century-long search to discover its secrets. Da Capo Press 2009 328p il $25   **681.1**

1. Clocks and watches 2. Greece -- Antiquities
ISBN 978-0-306-81742-7; 0-306-81742-X

LC 2008-939733

First published 2008 in the United Kingdom

The author "relates the century-long struggle of competing amateurs and scientists to understand the secrets of a 2000-year-old clock-like mechanism found in 1901 by Greek divers off the coast of Antikythera, a small island near Tunisia. . . . This globe-trotting, era-spanning mystery should absorb armchair scientists of all kinds." Publ Wkly

Includes bibliographical references

682   Small forge work (Blacksmithing)

Parkinson, Peter

The **artist** blacksmith; design and techniques.
Crowood Press 2002 160p il $40   **682**
1. Blacksmithing
ISBN 1-86126-428-3
"Parkinson explains the tools, materials, and equipment
needed by blacksmiths as well as the most commonly used
techniques. Numerous illustrations of beautiful creations
(such as gates, sculptures, household items, and furniture)
appear throughout this fascinating title." Libr J

683.4   Small firearms

Gun Digest 2014; edited by Jerry Lee. F & W Media
Inc 2013 568 p. ill. (paperback) $34.99 **683.4**
1. Firearms 2. Ammunition
ISBN 1440235422; 9781440235429
This book is the 68th edition of Gun Digest, which looks
at firearms. It contains "articles about about the world's
most fascinating guns, testfire reports on the latest models, insights about fine collectibles and one of a kind custom creations, plus roundups of what's new and trending in
firearms, ammo, reloading and optics from today's leading
manufacturers." (Publisher's note)

683.400973   Firearms owners – United States

Baum, Dan

Gun guys; a road trip. Dan Baum. 1st ed. Knopf
2013 352 p. (hardcover) $26.95   **683.400973**
1. Firearms industry 2. United States -- Social
conditions 3. Firearms ownership -- United States 4.
Firearms owners -- United States 6. Firearms -- Social
aspects -- United States
ISBN 0307595412; 9780307595416
LC 2012028767
This book, by Dan Baum, discusses gun culture in the
United States. "Many Americans love guns--which horrifies
and fascinates many other Americans, and much of the rest
of the world. . . . [The author] grabs his licensed concealed
handgun and hits the road to meet some of the 40 percent
of Americans who own guns." Baum interviews gun owners and enthusiasts along with victims of gun crime. (Publisher's note)
Includes bibliographical references (pages [321]-323)
and index

684   Furnishings and home workshops

Abram, Norm

Measure twice, cut once; lessons from a master
carpenter. Little, Brown 1996 196p il $18.95 **684**
1. Woodwork 2. Carpentry
ISBN 0-316-00494-4
LC 96-7584

In this book about woodwork and carpentry the author
"deals mainly with hand tools. Abram covers items such as
levels, chalk lines, and plumb-bobs, detailing his experiences with them and his preferences. . . . Even experienced
woodworkers will pick up a tip or two from this book."
Libr J

Bird, Lonnie

The **complete** illustrated guide to shaping wood.
Taunton Press 2001 294p il $39.95   **684**
1. Woodwork
ISBN 1-56158-400-2
LC 2001-27430
This guide shows "the many ways of shaping wood (cutting, edge treatments, decorative techniques, turning, and
carving). Techniques of all types and complexity are covered, usually including several means to accomplish each
task, such as using hand or power tools. Profusely illustrated
with drawings and photos, this book offers something for
every woodworker." Libr J
Includes bibliographical references

Taunton's complete illustrated guide to woodworking; [by] Lonnie Bird . . . [et al.]. Taunton Press
2005 311p il $29.95   **684**
1. Woodwork
ISBN 1-56158-769-9
LC 2004-28678
This "guide covers a wide array of woodworking topics. . . . The arrangement is consistent and well thought out,
with illustrated referencing at the beginning of each chapter." Libr J

Davy, Phil

Ultimate woodwork bible; a complete reference
with step-by-step techniques. [by] Phil Davy and Ben
Plewes. Sterling Pub. Co. 2011 288p il (C & B
crafts) $29.95   **684**
1. Woodwork
ISBN 978-1-84340-574-0; 1-84340-574-1
"A nicely organized manual on a wide range of woodworking basics, from types of tools to techniques. A British book, this guide includes terminology and tool names
that may be unfamiliar to U.S. readers. In the large section
on tool selection, there are a few items detailed that are not
available on this side of the Atlantic. Instructions come with
minimal drawings and concise text." Libr J

Hoadley, R. Bruce

Understanding wood; a craftsman's guide to
wood technology. 2nd ed; Taunton Press 2000 280p
il $39.95   **684**
1. Wood 2. Woodwork
ISBN 1-56158-358-8
LC 00-44322
First published 1980
This guide "covers the nature of wood and its properties,
the basics of wood technology, and the woodworker's raw
materials." Publisher's note
Includes bibliographical references and index

Kelsey, John

Woodworking; Techniques & Projects for the First Time Woodworker. John Kelsey. Fox Chapel Publishing 2013 111 p. ill. (chiefly col.) $14.99 **684**

    1. Woodwork 2. Woodwork -- Handbooks, manuals, etc 3. Carpentry -- Handbooks, manuals, etc

    ISBN 156523801X; 9781565238015

                            LC 2013017981

This book, by John Kelsey, is a guidebook for woodworking. "Each of the woodworking projects in this book can be completed in just a few hours. Designed to teach basic woodworking skills, they require only ordinary lumber and simple hand and power tools that you may already own. Each new project builds on what you learned before, allowing you to become more self-confident as your skills increase." (Publisher's note)

"Aimed at nine-year-olds through adults, this beautifully arranged title starts logically with wood selection and tool overviews and contains simple skill-building tasks that will develop DIYers' confidence and help them to learn technique. The quality of instruction is high, with large color photos showing each step." LJ

Peters, Rick

Woodworker's guide to wood; softwoods, hardwoods, plywoods, composites, veneers. Sterling 2000 192p il pa $24.95 **684**

    1. Wood 2. Lumber and lumbering

    ISBN 0-8069-3687-8

                            LC 99-86641

Peters' book is "geared toward hobbyist woodworkers. He covers the process of making lumber from start to finish, including how trees grow, their structure, common ways of milling and drying lumber, grading, and possible defects found in wood. One section shows wood samples (both finished and plain) and describes their basic working characteristics." Libr J

Popular woodworking

The **weekend** woodworker's project collection; 40 projects for the time-challenged craftsman. from the editors of Popular woodworking. Popular Woodworking Books 2010 255p il pa $22.99 **684**

    1. Woodwork

    ISBN 978-1-4403-0888-8

                         LC 2010-15396

"These quick projects for intermediate and advanced woodworkers are quite stylish. From frames and clocks to shelving and boxes, they exhibit enough variety for every taste. Project plans come with exploded views offering dimensions and technique tips. Tool familiarity and woodworking skills are assumed. The photos are attractive and the pieces appealing. . . . [This is] a great addition to any collection." Libr J

Warner, Pat

The **router** book. Taunton Press 2001 185p pa $19.95 **684**

    1. Woodwork 2. Power tools

    ISBN 1-56158-423-1

                        LC 2001-27149

"Warner shows readers how to get the most from their router, covering tools, accessories, and its use. Fixed-base, plunge routers, and laminate trimmers are introduced with excellent evaluations of specific models of each type." Libr J

Woodwork; a step-by-step photographic guide to successful woodworking. [writers, Alan Bridgewater . . . [et al]; illustrator, Simon Rodway] DK Pub. 2010 400p il $40 **684**

    1. Woodwork

    ISBN 978-0-7566-4306-5

                         LC 2010-279214

Thsi book "offers instruction in basic woodworking techniques and pairs profiles of common and exotic woods with great photos. The 25 projects, including furnishings and household products, start from simple and build to complex. While the projects are not particularly distinctive, the supporting materials make this a key purchase for any woodworking collection. Highly recommended." Libr J

684.1   Furniture

Cone, Steve

Singer upholstery basics plus; complete step-by-step photo guide. Creative Pub. International 2007 155p il pa $19.95 **684.1**

    1. Upholstery

    ISBN 978-1-58923-329-4; 1-58923-329-8

                        LC 2007-7252

First published 1997 with title: Upholstery basics

"If there ever was an upholstery bible, this is it." Libr J

Dobson, Cherry

The **complete** guide to upholstery; stuffed with step-by-step techniques for professional results. St. Martin's Griffin 2009 143p il pa $24.95 **684.1**

    1. Upholstery 2. Furniture -- Repairing

    ISBN 978-0-312-38327-5; 0-312-38327-4

"Want to recycle your old furniture with reupholstery? This lovely manual . . . contains fine step-by-step photos and tips on technique. Master upholsterer Dobson easily walks the confident beginner through the basics." Libr J

Hingley, Brian D.

Furniture repair & restoration. Creative Homeowner 2010 175p il pa $14.95 **684.1**

    1. Furniture finishing 2. Furniture -- Repairing

    ISBN 978-1-58011-478-3

First published 1998 with title: Furniture repair & refinishing

"With special sections on evaluation and repair of structural issues, this volume features an array of valuable information on furniture repair and refinishing. . . . Geared toward beginners in wood restoration, the book highlights the author's professional experience, which shows through in the advice and thorough directions." Libr J

Storage & shelving solutions; over 70 projects and ideas that fit your budget, space, and lifestyle. with

the editors of The Family Handyman. Reader's Digest Association 2006 255p il $26.95 **684.1**
1. Cabinetwork 2. Storage in the home
ISBN 978-0-7621-0636-3; 0-7621-0636-0

LC 2005-50772

"These home storage projects are neatly packaged, each accompanied by a box listing skill level, tools needed, and approximate cost (a nice feature) as well as a box with a shopping and cutting list. . . . This polished book on a great topic is recommended for public libraries." Libr J

686 Printing and related activities

Lee, Marshall

Bookmaking : editing, design, production; technical consultant Joseph Gannon. 3rd ed; Norton 2004 494p il $49.95 **686**
1. Books 2. Book industry
ISBN 0-393-73018-2

LC 2003-59672

First published 1965 by Bowker

This book describes "the business and art of transmitting an author's manuscript to readers by means of a book. The process includes editing, physical and visual design, costing, production planning, scheduling, procurement, and distribution. . . . This timeless classic should be acquired while it is still available." Choice

Includes bibliographical references

686.2 Printing

Garfield, Simon

Just my type; a book about fonts. Gotham Books 2011 356p il $27.50 **686.2**
1. Printing 2. Fonts 3. Type and type-founding -- History
ISBN 978-1-59240-652-4

LC 2011379019

First published 2010 in the United Kingdom

"Conveying the richness and the personality of typefaces with love and passion, this is an accessible and entertaining introduction to the world of lettering." Blueprint

Includes biblliographical references

Spiekermann, Erik

★ **Stop** Stealing Sheep and Find out How Type Works; Erik Spiekerman. 2nd ed; Pearson P T R 2013 213 p. il (some col) $39.99 **686.2**
1. Typography 2. Graphic design 3. Type and type-founding
ISBN 0321934288; 9780321934284

LC 2014378096

"In this third edition, acclaimed type designer Erik Spiekermann brings his type classic fully up to date on mobile and web typography. . . . If you use type--and these days, almost everyone does--Spiekermann's engaging, commonsense style will help you understand how to look at type, work with type, choose the best typeface for your message,

and express yourself more effectively through design." (Publisher's note)

"This updated edition uses an easygoing style to get readers from a variety of backgrounds up to speed on good use of type and general typography. The examples, images, and guidance not only are helpful to illustrate concepts, but also are up-to-date with current web and mobile trends and technologies." Choice

Includes bibliographical references and indexes

686.3 Bookbinding

Cambras, Josep

Bookbinding; techniques and projects. [translation from the Spanish, Michael Brunelle and Beatriz Cortabarria] Barron's 2007 143p il (Decorative techniques) pa $26.99 **686.3**
1. Bookbinding
ISBN 978-0-7641-6084-4; 0-7641-6084-2

LC 2007-924989

"Beginning with a historical overview, continuing to an explanation of tools and materials, Cambras showcases his expertise in chapters devoted to half a dozen techniques and the same quantity of paper-painting methods." Booklist

Diehn, Gwen

Real life journals: designing & using handmade books. Lark Books 2010 180p il (Live & learn) $24.95 **686.3**
1. Diaries 2. Bookbinding
ISBN 978-1-60059-492-2

LC 2009-32647

"Chapters on tools, covers, paper choices, and bindings are detailed and fully illustrated, but Diehn . . . goes well beyond that, making a point to include information on creating a purposeful design, enriching textual content, and binding the words to the visual elements to reflect a bookmaker's interests and personality. . . [This is] a lovely, helpful volume that will inspire and attract journalers and scrapbookers alike." Booklist

Golden, Alisa

Making handmade books; 100+ bindings, structures & forms. Lark Crafts 2010 256p il pa $19.95 **686.3**
1. Books 2. Bookbinding
ISBN 978-1-60059-587-5

LC 2010-1546

"This volume updates and combines Golden's previous Creating Handmade Books and Unique Handmade Books to provide an introduction to the fascinating world of artists' books. The specimens highlighted are far from your traditional book—they are works of art that will challenge readers' ideas of what books can be. Though there are plenty of inspiring photographs, there is also ample direction to guide readers interested in creating their own books. Golden also intersperses tidbits of bookmaking history and lore throughout, making this guide not only pleasurable and inspiring to look at but fun to read. " Libr J

Includes bibliographical references

690   Construction of buildings

The **Art** of natural building; design, construction, resources. editors: Joseph F. Kennedy, Michael Smith, Catherine Wanek; illustrated by Joseph F. Kennedy. New Soc. Pubs. 2002 291p il pa $26.95   **690**
1. Building 2. Building materials 3. House construction
ISBN 0-86571-433-9
"The authors, who are practitioners in the natural building movement, introduce a variety of nontraditional construction options, including underground building and building with alternative materials such as adobe, recycled agricultural materials, rammed earth, and straw bale. They also address energy efficiency, design, and the desire to create a healthy environment. The final chapters include case studies." Libr J
Includes bibliographical references

Black & Decker Corp.
The **complete** guide to flooring; updated with new products & techniques. 3rd ed.; Creative Pub. International 2010 271p il $24.99   **690**
1. Floors
ISBN 978-1-58923-521-2

LC 2010-4486
First published 2003
This book covers methods of installing different types of flooring, including "information on renewable flooring materials, such as bamboo, reclaimed floorboards, and natural stone. It also includes . . . techniques for polished and etched concrete flooring. The DVD add-on product includes 50 minutes of real-time demonstration of . . . layout and installation techniques, as well as the entire print edition in electronic form." Publisher's note

The **complete** guide to patios & walkways; money-saving do-it-yourself projects for improving outdoor living space. Creative Pub. International 2010 255p il pa $24.99   **690**
1. Patios
ISBN 978-1-58923-481-9
This is a guide to plan, build, repair, and maintain patios and walkways. It "stands out for its detailed photos and step-by-step, logically arranged instructions. . . . There is an original section on drainage options with projects." Libr J

Bollinger, Don
Hardwood floors; laying, sanding and finishing. Taunton Press 1990 137p il pa $19.95   **690**
1. Floors
ISBN 0-942391-62-4

LC 90-11065
The author "addresses the three types of flooring: strip, plank, and parquet—covering such topics as estimating costs; selecting wood types and grades; preparing the underlayment; planning the layout; sanding; and applying various finishes." Libr J
Includes bibliographical references

The **complete** outdoor builder; from arbors to walkways : 150 DIY projects. Creative Pub. International 2009 528 p. (pbk.) $19.99   **690**
1. Masonry 2. Garden structures 3. Masonry -- Amateurs' manuals 4. Woodwork -- Amateurs' manuals 5. Building, Wooden -- Amateurs' manuals 6. Do-it-yourself work -- Amateurs' manuals 7. Outbuildings -- Design and construction -- Amateurs' manuals 8. Garden structures -- Design and construction -- Amateurs' manuals
ISBN 1589234839; 9781589234833

LC 2009028983
This book, edited by Mark Johnson, Tracy Stanley, and Jennifer Gehlhar, provides advice on adding "patios and walkways to the yard. . . . From low-cost, curb-appeal walkways to expensive, estate-quality decorative concrete patios . . . this book presents each project with step-by-step instructions and full-color photographs as well as . . . tips, tricks, and inspiration. Each project uses the most current materials, tools, common practices, codes, and construction techniques." (Publisher's note)
Includes bibliographical references and index.

Cory, Steve
Ultimate guide: porches; building techniques for adding a new porch to your home. Creative Homeowner 2011 191p il pa $16.95   **690**
1. Porches
ISBN 978-1-58011-491-2

LC 2009941175
In this manual, the author "shares numerous, clear illustrations and detailed construction information and techniques. His confident, expert instruction . . . is apparent in the projects presented here. . . . A solid addition to any home improvement collection." Libr J

Kidder, Tracy
House. Houghton Mifflin 1985 341p il hardcover o.p. pa $14   **690**
1. House construction
ISBN 0-618-00191-3 pa

LC 85-7630
"The saga of a couple who supervised the building of their house in Massachusetts, this report interweaves the personal lives of those involved in the project with New England history, the sociology of building, popular lore and practical tips for would-be homebuilders." Publ Wkly
Includes bibliographical references

Levy, Matthys
Why buildings fall down; how structures fail. {by} Matthys Levy and Mario Salvadori; illustrations by Kevin Woest. Norton 1992 334p il hardcover o.p. pa $14.95   **690**
1. Building failures 2. Structural failures
ISBN 0-3933-1152-X pa

LC 91-34954
"Two structural engineers examine puzzling structural failures and collapses and the destruction of ancient and modern buildings, bridges, dams, and other constructions. Plenty of illustrations accent the lively text." Booklist

Nash, George

Do -it-yourself housebuilding; the complete handbook. illustrations by Roland Dahlquist. Sterling 1995 704p il pa $24.95   **690**

1. House construction 2. House construction -- Amateurs' manuals
ISBN 0-8069-0424-0

LC 94-2371

This "book covers every step of house construction from site selection to finishing touches. The authors discuss both rough and finish carpentry and show how to install plumbing, and electrical, heating, and air-conditioning systems. The text is supplemented by numerous excellent photographs and illustrations." Libr J

Includes bibliographical references

Peters, Rick

Popular mechanics garage makeovers; adding space without adding on. Hearst Books 2006 192p il pa $17.95   **690**

1. Garages
ISBN 978-1-58816-513-8; 1-58816-513-2

LC 2006-7912

"The book is divided into three main parts: planning, which covers basic construction methods and styles; real-life examples of different projects (including budget estimates); and plans for implementing any or all of the features shown. . . . Peters covers everything from basic construction techniques such as drywalling a ceiling and building walls to installing garage door openers and wall-mounted storage systems. . . . Those considering tackling a garage renovation will find the book's common-sense approach and practical advice invaluable." Publ Wkly

Schoenherr, Matthew

House transformed; getting the home you want--with the house you have. [by] Matthew Schoenherr with Linda Hunter and Wendy Jordan. Taunton Press 2005 186p il $32   **690**

1. Houses -- Remodeling
ISBN 1-56158-711-7

LC 2004-26818

This book outlining projects for home renovation describes "seven keys to a successful remodel, whether you are redoing a kitchen, building an addition, or making over the whole house." Publisher's note

Stiles, David

Backyard Building; Treehouses, Sheds, Arbors, Gates and Other Garden Projects. Jeanie Stiles and David Stiles. W.W. Norton & Co. Inc 2014 256 p. col. ill. $19.95   **690**

1. Building 2. Garden structures 3. Life skills -- Handbooks, manuals, etc.
ISBN 1581572387; 9781581572384

This book by Jeanie Stiles and David Stiles, part of the Countryman Know How series, covers "backyard accessories, the fundamentals of tools and materials, and useful tips based on real-life questions from the couple's popular website." It features "hand-drawn illustrations to guide the reader through the building process in a user-friendly way." (Publisher's note)

690.837   Houses -- construction

Johnston, Amy

What your contractor can't tell you; the essential guide to building and renovating. Amy Johnston. Shube Pub. 2008 208 p. $24.95   **690.837**

1. House construction 2. Houses -- Remodeling
ISBN 0979983800; 9780979983801

This book by Amy Johnston "is a comprehensive guide to getting the best results while building or renovating a home. . . . Chapters give detailed coverage of critical topics: design; selecting and supervising the architect and contractor; cost estimates; budget; plan specifications; contracts; dealing with town officials; and keeping track of everything along the way. For each stage of the project, there is detailed information on common pitfalls and how to avoid them." (Publisher's note)

Includes bibliographical references and index.

695   Roof covering

Black & Decker Corp.

The complete guide to roofing, siding & trim; created by: the editors of Creative Publishing International, Inc., in cooperation with Black & Decker. Updated 2nd ed.; Creative Pub. International 2008 271p il pa $24.99   **695**

1. Roofs 2. Siding (Building materials)
ISBN 978-1-58923-418-5

LC 2008-26823

First published 2004 with title: The complete guide to roofing & siding

This guide to installing and maintaining roofing and siding includes a "section on trim work as well as a section on ecofriendly roofs. . . . The photo gallery is quite attractive and fresh, reflecting current and popular house styles. The evaluation of materials—relating to home style, maintenance, duration, and drawbacks—is particularly nice. Text is matter-of-fact and clear, with no topic overdone. A useful and usable guidebook, this is recommended for all public libraries." Libr J

696   Utilities

Black & Decker Corp.

The complete guide to plumbing; modern materials and current codes all new guide to working with gas pipe. Expanded 4th ed.; Creative Pub. International 2008 334p il pa $24.99   **696**

1. Plumbing
ISBN 978-1-58923-378-2; 1-58923-378-6

LC 2008-8636

First published 1998

This guide to plumbing covers fixtures, installations, repairs, materials, tools, and skills.

"The sequential directions for many common household repairs are the real asset here. Excellent photos with simple instruction for each project are also valuable. Includes a DVD with demonstrations of many of the jobs described in the book." Libr J

Ferington, Esther

You can build: plumbing; by Esther Ferington and the editors of Sunset Books. Sunset 2010 239p il pa $24.95   696

1. Plumbing

ISBN 978-0-376-01468-9

"Concise and informative, this title offers valuable assistance to homeowners with plumbing problems and no plumbing expertise. Although not extensive, it focuses on proper fixes to common problems and is an excellent money-saving guide. Guidance for minor renovation is also included." Libr J

Henkenius, Merle

Plumbing : complete projects for the home; New expanded ed.; Creative Homeowner 2006 287p il pa $19.95   696

1. Plumbing

ISBN 1-58011-311-7; 978-1-58011-311-3

LC 2006-924699

First published 2002 with title: Plumbing: basic, intermediate & advanced projects

The author "shows homeowners how to tackle expensive plumbing repairs (e.g., replacing a washer in a leaky faucet). . . . The skill level of each project is rated, and photos walk users step by step through the instructions. . . . Strongly recommended for all collections." Libr J

697   Heating, ventilating, air-conditioning engineering

Ewing, Rex A.

Got sun? go solar; harness nature's free energy to heat and power your grid-tied home. [by] Rex A. Ewing and Doug Pratt. Expanded 2nd ed.; PixyJack Press 2009 191p il map pa $20   697

1. Wind power 2. Solar energy 3. Photovoltaic power generation

ISBN 978-0-9773724-6-1

LC 2009-19053

First published 2005

"This is an excellent primer on home application of solar energy. Written in a chatty and amusing style, the book is more informational than mechanical." Libr J

Includes bibliographical references

698   Detail finishing

Garskof, Josh

Tiling; by Josh Garskof and the editors of Sunset Books. Sunset Books 2009 240p il pa $21.95 698

1. Tiles

ISBN 978-0-376-01680-5

This book introduces "materials and techniques for tiling various surfaces, both inside and outside the home. Garskof offers great step-by-step instructions for some required basics. A wonderful addition to public library collections." Libr J

Santos, Brian

Painting and wallpapering secrets from Brian Santos, the Wall Wizard. Wiley 2011 240p il pa $21.99   698

1. Paperhanging 2. House painting

ISBN 978-0-470-59360-8; 0-470-59360-1

LC 2010-28548

"This guide contains useful information for wall treatments. The practical and reassuring advice includes important directions on what not to do. This is nitty-gritty do-it-yourself, with outstanding prep instruction, tool selection, well-thought-out tips and tricks, and technique photos. While inspirational wall-treatment photo books abound, . . . this is the guide you'll need to achieve those looks." Libr J

700   ARTS

700   The arts

★ **Arts** and humanities through the eras. Gale 2004 5v il set $450   700

1. Arts -- History 2. Civilization -- History

ISBN 0-7876-5695-X

LC 2004-10243

"Each volume consists of nine chapters covering the major branches of the humanities: architecture and design, dance, fashion, literature, music, philosophy, religion, theater, and visual arts. . . . This outstanding series offers a wealth of information; the chapters on architecture, dance, and theater alone are worth the price of each volume." Libr J

Includes bibliographical references

Davenport, Guy

The **Hunter** Gracchus, and other papers on literature and art. Counterpoint 1996 339p il hardcover o.p. pa $19.95   700

ISBN 978-1-887178-55-6; 1-887178-55-4

LC 96-43090

The author "announces blithely that this collection of essays and comments 'has for a semblance of unity only their being written on the same typewriter'. . . . Davenport is what the ancient Greek poet Antolochus would call a fox, or one who knows many things, rather than a hedgehog, who has a single central vision. These writings on Kafka, Darwin, Picasso, Shakers, and snake handlers have more in common than their means of production, however, because each is in its own way brilliant, the stylish work of a master stylist." Libr J

Impelluso, Lucia

Gods and heroes in art; edited by Stefano Zuffi; translated by Thomas Michael Hartmann. Getty Mus. 2003 383p il pa $19.95 **700**
1. Reference books 2. Art and mythology -- Dictionaries 3. Classical mythology -- Dictionaries
ISBN 0-89236-702-4

LC 2002-13422

The characters of ancient Greek and Roman mythology "are each described in entries summarizing their distinctive stories, their special attributes, and the ways in which artists have depicted them. Each entry is . . . illustrated with reproductions of works of art in which the god or hero is pictured. . . . The book concludes with . . . indexes, including a list of iconographic symbols associated with the subjects, and a bibliography." Publisher's note

Includes bibliographical references

The **muses** go to school; inspiring stories about the importance of arts in education. edited by Herbert Kohl and Tom Oppenheim. New Press 2012 xxvii, 200 p.p **700**
1. Celebrities 2. Arts -- Study and teaching 3. Education -- Aims and objectives
ISBN 1595585397; 9781595585394

LC 2011042803

In this book, edited by Herbert Kohl and Tom Oppenheim, "autobiographical pieces with well-known artists and performers are paired with . . . essays by . . . educators to produce a . . . case for positioning the arts at the center of primary and secondary school curriculums. Spanning a range of genres from acting and music to literary and visual arts, these . . . voices make surprising connections between the arts and the development of intellect, imagination, spirit, emotional intelligence, self-esteem, and self-discipline of young people." (Publisher's note)

Nelson, Maggie

The **art** of cruelty; Maggie Nelson. W.W. Norton & Co. 2011 288p. **700**
1. Cruelty 2. Violence in art 3. Cultural critique 4. Cruelty in art 5. Art -- Moral and ethical aspects
ISBN 978-0-393-07215-0; 0-393-07215-0

LC 2011001828

This book of "art and cultural criticism takes on . . . representations of violence in art. . . . The pervasiveness of images of torture, horror, and war has all but demolished the twentieth-century hope that such imagery might shock us into a less alienated state, or aid in the creation of a just social order. . . . [A]uthor Maggie Nelson . . . navigates this contemporary predicament, with an eye to the question of whether or not focusing on representations of cruelty makes us cruel. In a journey through high and low culture (Kafka to reality TV), the visual to the verbal (Paul McCarthy to Brian Evenson), and the apolitical to the political (Francis Bacon to Kara Walker), Nelson offers a model of how one might balance strong ethical convictions with an equally strong appreciation for work that tests the limits of taste, taboo, and permissibility." (Publisher's note)

Includes bibliographical references and index.

Oakes, Kaya

Slanted and enchanted; the evolution of Indie culture. Henry Holt and Company 2009 256p pa $14 **700**
1. Arts -- United States
ISBN 978-0-8050-8852-6; 0-8050-8852-0

LC 2008-45286

"Although the term indie is most associated with rock music, Oakes explores a variety of artists and DIY art forms that operate with some degree of independence from the mainstream. She traces this phenomenon back to the 1950s — to the New York School poets, particularly Frank O'Hara, and the Beats — and from there, she explores a myriad of indie angles: riot-grrrl culture, the crafting world, the growth of underground comics and the music of bands such as Operation Ivy, the Minutemen and Pavement. Oakes is no dry outsider. She believes in what she describes, she contributes to it and she speaks its language. . . . Oakes also shines when she examines an irony of indie life: It often thrives on collaboration and community." Cleveland Plain Dealer

Includes bibliographical references

Updike, John, 1932-2009

Always looking; essays on art. by John Updike ; edited by Christopher Carduff. Alfred A. Knopf 2012 xiii, 204 p.p ill. $45 **700**
1. Art criticism 2. Art -- Psychology
ISBN 0307957306; 9780307957306

LC 2012005986

This book presents "the previously uncollected art writings of the prolific and award-winning novelist and critic [John] Updike, who died in 2009. . . . The essays explore works by artists including [Claude] Monet . . . [Edgar] Degas . . . [and Rene] Magritte; the major movements of Impressionism, Surrealism, Pop art, and Minimalism; and the habits and tastes of the collectors who shape our understanding of fine art's place in American culture." (Publishers Weekly)

700.1 Philosophy and theory of the arts

Larson, Kay

Where the heart beats; John Cage, Zen Buddhism, and the inner life of artists. Kay Larson. Penguin Press 2012 474 p. (hardcover) $29.95 **700.1**
1. Zen Buddhism 2. Postmodernism 3. Zen Buddhism -- Influence
ISBN 1594203407; 9781594203404

LC 2011044714

This book, by Kay Larsen, "part biography, part cultural history," presents "reflections on [John] Cage's encounters with and absorption of Zen Buddhism. . . . Weaving threads of the teachings of Zen Buddhist writer D.T. Suzuki and Alan Watts, along with Cage's own reflections and writings on art, music, dance, and life, [Kay] Larson . . . covers Cage's growing understanding of the nature of noise and silence and the roles that each plays in music." (Publishers Weekly)

Includes bibliographical references and index

700.9 History, geographic treatment, biography of the arts

Fitzgerald, Kenneth

Volume; writings on graphic design, music, art, and culture. written by Kenneth FitzGerald ; liner notes by Rudy VanderLans. Princeton Architectural Press 2010 254 p. (alk. paper) $24.95   **700.9**

1. Graphic design 2. American essays 3. Cultural critique 4. Arts, Modern -- 20th century 5. Arts, Modern -- 21st century 6. Graphic arts -- United States -- History -- 20th century 7. Graphic arts -- United States -- History -- 21st century

ISBN 1568989644; 9781568989648

LC 2009045011

This book is a "collection of both new and classic writings by . . . educator Kenneth FitzGerald that survey the discipline of graphic design in context with the parallel creative fields of contemporary music and art. The topics of the writings are diverse: the roles of class in design, design education, Lester Bangs and 'Creem' magazine, pornography, album cover art, independent record labels, anonymity and imaginary creative identities, and design as cultural chaosmaker." (Publisher's note)

700.92 Biography

Currey, Mason

Daily rituals; how artists work. by Mason Currey. 1st ed. Alfred A. Knopf 2013 xviii, 278 p.p ill. (hardcover) $24.95   **700.92**

1. Artists -- Psychology

ISBN 0307273601; 9780307273604

LC 2012036279

"How artists work, how they ritualize their days with the comforting (mundane) details of their lives: their daily routines, fears, dreams, naps, eating habits, and other prescribed, finely calibrated "subtle maneuvers" ... From Beethoven and Kafka to George Sand, Picasso, Woody Allen and Agatha Christie; from Leo Tolstoy and Henry James to Charles Dickens and John Updike, here are writers, composers, painters, choreographers, playwrights, philosophers, caricaturists, comedians, poets, sculptors, and scientists on how they create (and avoid creating) their creations." (Publisher's note)

Kaplan, Carla

Miss Anne in Harlem; The White Women of the Black Renaissance. by Carla Kaplan. Harper 2013 512 p. $28.99   **700.92**

1. Whites 2. Harlem Renaissance 3. Women -- United States

ISBN 0060882387; 9780060882389

In this book, author Carla Kaplan "focuses on white women, collectively called 'Miss Anne,' who became Harlem Renaissance insiders. [She] focuses on six of the unconventional, free-thinking women, some from Manhattan high society, many Jewish, who crossed race lines and defied social conventions to become a part of the culture and heartbeat of Harlem." (Publisher's note)

Ross, Clifford

The world of Edward Gorey; by Clifford Ross and Karen Wilkin. Abrams 1996 190p il hardcover o.p. pa $19.95   **700.92**

1. Artists 2. Authors 3. Novelists 4. Illustrators 5. Set designers 6. Children's authors

ISBN 0-8109-9083-0 pa

LC 95-47900

This book includes an "interview with Mr. Ross, {in which} Edward Gorey speaks of his likes and dislikes and aspects of his career. . . . Ms. Wilkin discusses Gorey's work as illustrator, author, stage designer, and miscellaneous creator." Atl Mon

Includes bibliographical references

701 Philosophy and theory of fine and decorative arts

Dutton, Denis

The art instinct; beauty, pleasure, and human evolution. Bloomsbury Press 2009 278p $25   **701**

1. Art 2. Instinct 3. Evolution 4. Aesthetics 5. Art -- Philosophy 6. Evolution (Biology)

ISBN 978-1-59691-401-8; 1-59691-401-7

LC 2008-28304

"Marshaling intriguing examples and analogies in a cogent, animated argument destined to provoke debate, Dutton formulates the best answer yet to the question, 'What's art good for?'" Booklist

Includes bibliographical references (p. 259-268)

Higgins, Hannah B.

The grid book; [by] Hannah B. Higgins. MIT Press 2009 300p il map pa $24.95   **701**

1. Design 2. Grids (Crisscross patterns)

ISBN 978-0-262-51240-4; 0-262-51240-8

LC 2008-29430

"Higgins traces the grid from its origins in agriculture and urbanism of 9000 BCE to the developing architectures of digital computers. Indeed, a complete list of the grids she uncovers would mean nothing less than offering a full index of her book, which would include everything from the Code of Hammurabi to meditations on mail-order catalogs and fractal geometry. . . . [The work's] ambition is breathtaking but deftly handled, as Higgins metaphorically detaches the grid off a brick wall, throws it down on city streets, plucks it up into a stave, stretches it into a screen, a net, and finally the web. Though it sounds as if this project would be endless, in fact the book comprises ten intimate and compelling essays, written with a light and playful touch." PopMatters

Includes bibliographical references

Rothenberg, David

Survival of the beautiful; art, science, and evolution. Bloomsbury Press 2011 311p il $30   **701**

1. Aesthetics 2. Art and science

ISBN 978-1-60819-216-8

LC 2011014964

It was the author's intent "to understand why beauty exists in the first place, and what that means to our existence. Evolution and mutation determine what features are passed on in each species, but nature also offers 'case after case of wild, untrammeled craziness," patterns, colors, and behavior that are clearly not needed for survival.' [David] Rothenberg notes with amusement how Darwin thought ornamentation--colorful feathers, brilliant songs, mating dances--existed to 'delight the mind of potential mates, throwing evolutionary control into female hands, an idea that didn't sit well with Victorians.' Rothenberg goes on to discuss how animal patterns (animal art) have influenced human creativity in cubist and abstract art as well as military camouflage." (Publishers Weekly)

The author "presents a leaps-and-bounds inquiry into the role beauty plays in evolution. . . . Rothenberg argues that to understand nature's 'frills and flourish,' including the wildly impractical peacock's tail, we must look beyond the rigid pragmatism at the core of current evolutionary theory and accept that beauty is not utilitarian. . . . With verve, multidisciplinary fluency, and an encompassing vision, Rothenberg accomplishes his mission to change the way we perceive and understand the intertwining of natural evolution and human cultural evolution, beauty and life, art and science." Booklist

Includes bibliographical references

701.15 Psychological principles

Bennett, Cat

Making Art a Practice; 30 Ways to Paint a Pipe (How to Be the Artist You Are) Cat Bennett. Findhorn Press 2013 128 p. $16.95 **701.15**
1. Creative ability 2. Art -- Guidebooks 3. Creation (Literary, artistic, etc.)
ISBN 1844096076; 9781844096077

"This guide walks the artist through exercises designed to develop the personal qualities critical to being an artist in the world, such as courage, the ability to look and see, and connection to the true creative self. This is a hands-on, experiential action book designed to get the reader creating art and exploring a variety of possibilities for being an artist." (Publisher's note)

702 Miscellany of fine and decorative arts

★ **American** art directory 2009; 63rd ed; National Register Publishing 2008 1035p $297 **702**
1. Reference books 2. Art -- Directories 3. American art -- Directories 4. Canadian art -- Directories
ISBN 978-0-87217-755-0; 0-87217-755-6
Biennial. First published 1898 by Bowker with title: American art annual

This book identifies "key characteristics for thousands of art institutions in the U.S. and Canada. This . . . resource provides . . . information on museums, art organizations, art schools, libraries, art editors and critics, scholarships, fellowships, exhibitions and state art councils." Publisher's note

Michels, Caroll

★ **How** to survive and prosper as an artist; selling yourself without selling your soul. 6th ed.; Henry Holt and Co. 2009 381p pa $20 **702**
1. Art -- Marketing 2. Art -- Vocational guidance
ISBN 978-0-8050-8848-9; 0-8050-8848-2
LC 2008-39615
First published 1983

This is a "guide to taking control of your career and making a good living in the art world . . . [that includes] information on getting into a gallery, being your own PR agent, and negotiating prices, as well as innovative marketing, exhibition, and sales opportunities for various artistic disciplines." Publisher's note

Includes bibliographical references

702.8 Auxiliary techniques and procedures; apparatus, equipment, materials

The **Grove** encyclopedia of materials and techniques in art; edited by Gerald W.R. Ward. Oxford University Press 2008 828p il lib bdg $150 **702.8**
1. Reference books 2. Art -- Technique -- Encyclopedias 3. Artists' materials -- Encyclopedias
ISBN 978-0-19-531391-8; 0-19-531391-7
LC 2008-2486
Ward "has revised and updated approximately 1440 entries and full-length articles . . . from the venerable 34-volume Grove Dictionary of Art and added some new entries on topics of 'emerging importance' to produce a comprehensive one-volume resource on all aspects of materials and techniques of the fine arts and crafts, from acrylic painting, alabaster, and aquatint to upholstery, varnish, wood-engraving, and zinc. . . . An essential work for artists, historians, and art students and for the libraries that serve them." Libr J

Includes bibliographical references

Hoving, Thomas

False impressions; the hunt for big-time art fakes. Simon & Schuster 1996 366p il hardcover o.p. pa $22 **702.8**
1. Art -- Forgeries
ISBN 0-684-83148-1 pa
LC 95-53800
Hoving "is a magnetic storyteller, achieving just the right blend of humor and mettle." Booklist
Includes bibliographical references

Shay, Bee

Collage lab; experiments, investigations, and exploratory projects. Quarry Books 2010 144p il pa $22.99 **702.8**
1. Collage
ISBN 978-1-59253-565-1; 1-59253-565-8
LC 2009-22988
"This is a sophisticated and accessible lab manual for all but the complete novice. Shay . . . offers 52 labs that reinforce the basics of art and set the artist on a path to experimental collage with brilliant textures, colors, and images." Libr J

Smith, Ray

★ The **artist's** handbook; [equipment, materials, procedures, techniques] 3rd. ed.; DK Pub. 2009 384p il pa $21.95 **702.8**

1. Artists' materials 2. Art -- Technique
ISBN 978-0-7566-5722-2; 0-7566-5722-9

LC 2010-502586

First published 1987 by Knopf

An illustrated handbook offers step-by-step projects, reproductions of works by master artists, and instruction in creative techniques, covering everything from drawing and painting to printmaking and digital media.

702.81 Mixed-media and composites

Plowman, Randel

The **collage** workbook; how to get started & stay inspired. Randel Plowman. Lark Crafts, An Imprint of Sterling Pub. Co. 2012 132 p. ill. (mostly col.) (pb-trade pbk. : alk. paper) $17.95 **702.81**

1. Collage 2. Art -- Technique 3. Collage -- Technique
ISBN 9781454701996

LC 2011030969

This book offers advice on making collages from artist Randel Plowman, who "has been making at least one small collage per day for many years and has chronicled his work since 2006 on the blog acollageaday.com. Plowman covers design basics, tools, and techniques before inviting readers to make their own mixed-media found-object artworks using 50 short exercises. Hundreds of examples of . . . collages are included." (Library Journal)

Includes bibliographical references (p. 130) and index

703 Dictionaries, encyclopedias, concordances of fine and decorative arts

The **Concise** Oxford dictionary of art and artists; edited by Ian Chilvers. 3rd ed; Oxford University Press 2003 653p pa $14.95 **703**

1. Reference books 2. Art -- Dictionaries 3. Artists -- Dictionaries
ISBN 0-19-860477-7

LC 2003-278290

First published 1990

This "is an abbreviated lexicon based on 'The Oxford Dictionary of Art'.... It includes western art from the fifth century B.C.E., but has been expanded to include more recent artists born prior to 1965 instead of 1945. Entries include biographies of artists, sculptors, writers, leading collectors and dealers, materials and techniques, and galleries and museums." Am Ref Books Annu, 2004

Frazier, Nancy

The **Penguin** concise dictionary of art history. Penguin Ref. 1999 774p hardcover o.p. pa $20 **703**

1. Reference books 2. Art -- Dictionaries
ISBN 0-14-051420-1 pa

LC 98-56089

"This volume seeks to present an interdisciplinary approach to art history. It uses information from a number of fields, such as literature, psychology, history, geography, and economics, to give a cultural context to the changes in art. There are more than 1,500 alphabetically arranged entries. . . . Each biographical entry includes birth and death dates when known, nationality, medium used, and style of work or school of art." Booklist

"An easy-to-read, scholarly yet not lofty, fascinating, and very well-organized book." Libr J

Includes bibliographical references (p. {731}-736) and index

Langmuir, Erika

✓ **Yale** dictionary of art and artists; {by} Erika Langmuir and Norbert Lynton. Yale Univ. Press 2000 753p $30; pa $12.95 **703**

1. Reference books 2. Art -- Dictionaries 3. Artists -- Dictionaries
ISBN 0-300-08702-0; 0-300-06458-6 pa

LC 00-25800

"Varying in length from a few lines to several pages for artists such as Leonardo da Vinci, Pablo Picasso, or John Constable, the 3000 entries cover Western art from 1300 until the present. The work covers painters, sculptors, graphic artists, patrons, technical processes, movements, and terminology." Libr J

Lucie-Smith, Edward

✓ ★ The **Thames** & Hudson dictionary of art terms; 2nd ed; Thames & Hudson 2004 240p il (World of art) pa $16.95 **703**

1. Reference books 2. Art -- Dictionaries
ISBN 0-500-20365-2

LC 2003100802

First published 1984; this edition first published 2003 in the United Kingdom

"More than 2,000 entries define and explain terms used to describe painting, sculpture, architecture, graphic arts, decorative and applied arts, and photography, including the terminology of non-Western art. Several entries contain cross-references, and the book's 400 illustrations and diagrams, although reproduced in black and white, help explain the concepts defined. The thorough and clear entries make this volume appropriate for any beginning art history student." Choice

704 Special topics in fine and decorative arts

The **female** gaze; women artists making their world. edited by Robert Cozzolino with contributions by Glenn Adamson, Linda Lee Alter, Diane Burko, Anna C. Chave, Robert Cozzolino, Anna Havemann, Joanna Gardner-Huggett, Melanie Anne Herzog, Janine Mileaf, Mey-Yen Moriuchi, Jodi Throckmorton, Michele Wallace. Pennsylvania Academy of the Fine Arts 2012 335 p. (alk. paper) $60 **704**

1. Women artists 2. Art -- Exhibitions 3. Women artists -- Exhibitions 4. Art, Modern -- 20th century --

Exhibitions 5. Art, Modern -- 21st century -- Exhibitions 6. Art -- Pennsylvania -- Philadelphia -- Exhibitions 7. Pennsylvania Academy of the Fine Arts -- Exhibitions
ISBN 1555953891; 9781555953898

LC 2012036714

This "catalog was created in conjunction with an exhibition of the same title at the Pennsylvania Academy of the Fine Arts, where [art collector Linda Lee] Alter eventually donated her collection" of women-made art. The book features "essays by an internationally diverse group of scholars and curators who focus on Alter's collection." (Library Journal)

Includes bibliographical references (pages 323-330)

Holladay, Wilhelmina Cole

A **museum** of their own; National Museum of Women in the Arts. text contributions by Philip Kopper. Abbeville Press 2008 240p il $50   **704**
1. Women artists 2. National Museum of Women in the Arts (U.S.)
ISBN 978-0-7892-1003-6; 0-7892-1003-7

LC 2008-21646

"The National Museum of Women in the Arts . . . opened in 1987. It changed the status of women artists and the life of its founder, who now tells the museum's fascinating success story in an entertainingly anecdotal, inspiring, and beautifully illustrated [book]. . . . This invaluable work of art history is enlivened by Holladay's encounters with artists . . . and gorgeous reproductions, many of works that will be new to even the most art-expert readers." Booklist

In harmony; the Norma Jean Calderwood collection of Islamic art. edited by Mary McWilliams ; with essays by Jessica Chloros and Katherine Eremin, Walter B. Denny, Penley Knipe, Oya Pancaroğlu, David J. Roxburgh, Sunil Sharma, Anthony B. Sigel, Marianna Shreve Simpson. Harvard Art Museum Distributed by Yale University Press 2013 303 p. (Yale University Press) $75   **704**
1. Islamic art 2. Art collections 3. Islamic art -- Exhibitions 4. Art, Iranian -- Exhibitions 5. Arthur M. Sackler Museum -- Exhibitions 6. Art -- Private collections -- Massachusetts -- Cambridge -- Exhibitions
ISBN 9781891771620; 9780300176414; 0300176414

LC 2012030304

Editor Mary McWilliams' book features the Norma Jean Calderwood collection of Islamic art. The book features nine essays that "explore issues of conservation as well as the cultural and historical significance of various objects in this largely unpublished collection. Topics include the influence of calligraphic line and physical gesture on Safavid drawings; figurative imagery on Iranian ceramics; and what cobalt pigment reveals about an object's origins." (Publisher's note)

Includes bibliographical references (pages 274-290) and index

Kort, Carol

A to Z of American women in the visual arts; {by} Carol Kort and Liz Sonneborn. Facts on File 2002 258p il (Facts on File library of American history) $44   **704**
1. Reference books 2. American art -- Dictionaries 3. Women artists -- Dictionaries
ISBN 0-8160-4397-3

LC 2001-40231

A "handy, well-written volume. . . . The biographical entries are filled with interesting personal and career details that make for absorbing reading." Voice Youth Advocates

Includes bibliographical references and index

704.03   Ethnic and national groups

The **James** T. Bialac Native American Art Collection; Selected Works. Mark Andrew White, General Editor. University of Oklahoma Press 2012 xi, 223 p.p ill. (hardcover) $49.95; (paperback) $29.95   **704.03**
1. Art collections 2. Native American art 3. Indian art -- Catalogs 4. Fred Jones Jr. Museum of Art -- Catalogs 5. Art -- Private collections -- Oklahoma -- Norman -- Catalogs
ISBN 0806143045; 9780806142999; 9780806143040

LC 2012003005

This book, published by the Fred Jones Museum of Art, presents a catalogue of the James T. Bialac Native American Art Collection of "easel paintings and three-dimensional works. . . . The collection comprises nearly four thousand items, including drawings, sculptures, prints, kachinas, jewelry, ceramics, rattles, baskets, and textiles. . . . The Bialac Collection represents indigenous cultures across North America." (Publisher's note)

Includes bibliographical references (pages 205-209) and index

Patton, Sharon F.

African -American art. Oxford Univ. Press 1998 319p il maps (Oxford history of art) hardcover o.p. pa $18.95   **704.03**
1. African American art
ISBN 0-19-284213-7 pa

LC 98-190459

"Comprehensively and with sharp, scholarly accuracy, Patton has closed gaps between the chronological and thematic directions of Black American art and complexities of Euro-American art history." Choice

704.039   Indian art -- North America

Russell, Karen Kramer

Shapeshifting; transformations in native american art. Karen Kramer Russell. Yale University Press 2012 248 p. $65   **704.039**
1. Indian art 2. Native American art 3. Native Americans -- North America
ISBN 0300177321; 9780300177329

LC 2011928735

Author Karen Kramer Russell "aims to dispel the notion that Native American art is 'predictable.' . . . This confluence of past and present is enacted in many of the pieces featured in this . . . volume, such as Brian Jungen's Cetology . . . [and] Dwayne Wilcox's After Two or Three Hundred Years You Will Not Notice. . . . Russell and her colleagues . . . achieve their goal of asserting the . . . relevancy of Native American art." (Publishers Weekly)

704.9   Iconography

Bussagli, Marco

Angels. Abrams 2007 780p il $19.95   **704.9**
1. Angels 2. Art and religion
ISBN 978-0-8109-9436-2; 0-8109-9436-4
LC 2007-010749

"Art historian Marco Bussagli has organized the book by significant Biblical events. . . . Each work of art is accompanied by the Biblical passage it illustrates, along with a commentary exploring its form and meaning." Publisher's note
Includes bibliographical references

Fliegel, Stephen N.

A **higher** contemplation; sacred meaning in the Christian art of the Middle Ages. Stephen N. Fliegel. Kent State University Press 2012 xi, 115 p.p (hardcover : alk. paper) $42.00   **704.9**
1. Byzantine art 2. Christian art 3. Christian art and symbolism -- Medieval, 500-1500
ISBN 1606350935; 9781606350935
LC 2011000686

This is a "guidebook to the content and symbolism of medieval Christian visual art," in which curator "[Stephen N.] Fliegel . . . explains the early Christian and Byzantine perception of images and then explores in detail pictures of saints and angels, images of the cross and crucifixion, and the many visual varieties of the cult of Mary in the later Middle Ages. The book also briefly describes Byzantine and western European societies as well as their evolution between 300 and 1600 C.E." (Library Journal)
Includes bibliographical references and index.

Levine, Lee I.

Visual Judaism in late antiquity; historical contexts of Jewish art. Lee I. Levine. Yale University Press 2012 x, 582 p.p (cloth : alk. paper) $75 **704.9**
1. Antiquities 2. Jewish art and symbolism 3. Middle East -- Civilization -- To 622
ISBN 0300100892; 9780300100891
LC 2012003770

Here, Lee I. Levine "focuses on the art of the Jewish people inside and outside the synagogue, from c. 1200 BCE to seventh century CE, using 'the immediate social, cultural, and religious contexts as the main points of reference in interpreting Jewish art of Late Antiquity.' . . . Levine argues: 'the picture that emerges from the archaeological remains of Late Antiquity is far more diverse, heterogeneous, and locally oriented than that derived from literary sources.'" (Library Journal)
Includes bibliographical references (pages 483-557) and index

★ The **Renaissance** portrait; from Donatello to Bellini. edited by Keith Christiansen and Stefan Weppelmann ; essays by Patricia Rubin ... [et al.] Metropolitan Museum of Art -- Distributed by Yale University Press 2011 xii, 420 p.p (hc: Yale University Press) $65   **704.9**
1. Renaissance portrait painting -- Italy 2. Art, Italian -- Exhibitions 3. Portraits, Renaissance -- Italy -- Exhibitions
ISBN 0300175914; 1588394255; 1588394263; 9780300175912; 9781588394255; 9781588394262
LC 2011027471

This book, edited by Keith Christiansen and Stefan Weppelmann, "provides new research and insight into the early history of portraiture in Italy, examining in detail how its major art centers--Florence, the princely courts, and Venice--saw the rapid development of portraiture as closely linked to Renaissance society and politics, ideas of the individual, and concepts of beauty." (Publisher's note)
Includes bibliographical references and index.

706   Organizations and management of fine and decorative arts

Artist's & graphic designer's market 2014; by Mary Burzlaff Bostic. North Light Books 2013 671 p. ill. $34.99   **706**
1. Graphic arts 2. Art -- Marketing 3. Art -- Vocational guidance
ISBN 9781440329432

This book presents a "reference guide for any artist who wants to establish or expand a career in fine art, illustration or graphic design." It includes "contact information for more than 1,700 art market resources, including galleries, magazines, book publishers, greeting card companies, ad agencies, syndicates, art fairs and more" as well as "information on grants, residencies, organizations, publications and websites that offer support and direction for visual artists." (Publisher's note)

708   Galleries, museums, private collections of fine and decorative arts

Meier, Richard

Building the Getty. University of California Press 1999 204p il pa $25.95   **708**
1. Getty Center (Los Angeles, Calif.)
ISBN 0-520-21730-6; 978-0-520-21730-0
LC 99-20219

First published 1997 by Knopf

"Charting his involvement in the Getty's construction, Meier recounts in an intriguingly candid, eminently personal style the formidable bureaucratic process entailed upon undertaking to realize this grandiose endeavor. Beginning with the competition itself, Meier's detailed reminiscences offer fascinating insights into the design process and the extraordinarily intricate procedures and systems, as well as endless setbacks, associated with executing a modern-day megalithic structure." Booklist

National Gallery of Art (U.S.)

★ **National** Gallery of Art; [foreword by Earl A. Powell III] 2nd ed.; Thames and Hudson 2006 332p il (World of art) pa $18.95 **708**

1. National Gallery of Art (U.S.)

ISBN 0-500-20390-3; 978-0-500-20390-3

LC 2005-904459

First published 2004 by National Gallery of Art; Based on John Walker's National Gallery of Art, published 1984

"The collection of the National Gallery of Art in Washington includes works by the greatest masters of Western art from the twelfth century to the present. . . . [In this] look at the National Gallery's masterpieces . . . the works are illustrated in full color, and the curators have written the texts." Publisher's note

708.1 Geographic treatment

Walsh, John

The **J.** Paul Getty Museum and its collections; a museum for the new century. {by} John Walsh, Deborah Gribbon. Getty Mus. 1997 288p hardcover o.p. pa $40 **708.1**

1. Philanthropists 2. Art collectors 3. J. Paul Getty Museum 4. Energy industry executives

ISBN 0-89236-476-9 pa

LC 97-12170

This volume is a history of the J. Paul Getty Museum and a guide to its collections

This is "a lavish visual compendium of J. Paul Getty's amazing art collection; in addition, the text reveals important background details surrounding Getty's life and his passion for art. Walsh and Gribbon communicate just how the magnate's fortunes were put to the test as planned acquisitions of artwork flourished." Booklist

708.13 United States

Loebl, Suzanne

America's art museums; a traveler's guide to great collections large and small. Norton 2002 426p il pa $18.95 **708.13**

1. Art museums

ISBN 0-393-32006-5

LC 2001-44208

This is a "guide to some of America's finest art museums. Not only does it focus on the major and more familiar art museums, it also supplies some much-needed information and marketing for some of the small and little-known, yet important, art galleries in the United States. The book is alphabetically arranged by state and then by city, and provides information on times open, strengths of the museum's collection, activities for children, the museum's history, and Websites." Am Ref Books Annu, 2003

Includes bibliographical references and index

709 History, geographic treatment, biography

The **Art** Book; Phaidon Press. Phaidon Press 2012 592 p. (hardcover) $59.95 **709**

1. Art 2. Artists

ISBN 0714864676; 9780714864679

This book by Phaidon Press is an "A - Z guide to artists from medieval times to the present day . . . including paintings, photographs, sculptures, video, installations and performance art. Each artist is represented on a full page with a definitive work and explanatory . . . information." The book features "examples of all periods, schools, visions and techniques." (Publisher's note)

★ **Atlas** of world art; edited by John Onians. Oxford University Press 2004 352p il maps $150 **709**

1. Art -- History -- Maps

ISBN 0-19-521583-4

LC 2003-55029

This atlas offers a "framework for coverage of art activity around the world from prehistoric times to 2000. . . . Each of the book's seven parts (each covers a period in art history) includes a brief illustrated introduction followed by a standardized sequence of sections on World, American, European, African, Asian and Pacific Art." Choice

Includes bibliographical references

Barnitz, Jacqueline

Twentieth -century art of Latin America. University of Tex. Press 2001 400p il $70; pa $34.95 **709**

1. Latin American art 2. Art -- 20th century

ISBN 0-292-70857-2; 0-292-70858-0 pa

LC 99-50871

A survey of 20th century Latin American art which includes coverage of regional movements, and discussion of historical, political, and cultural influences

"Latin American art, the fruit of violent collisions among diverse indigenous, European, and African cultures, is revealed as provocative and vibrant in Barnitz's well-illustrated and groundbreaking overview of its dazzling twentieth-century flowering." Booklist

Includes bibliographical references

Beckett, Wendy

Sister Wendy's American collection; {by} Sister Wendy Beckett. HarperCollins Pubs. 2000 288p il $40 **709**

1. Art appreciation 2. Art -- History

ISBN 0-06-019556-8

LC 00-40953

The author provides a "discussion of works in six of America's renowned art museums. . . . {She} includes a variety of media-- paintings, sculpture, decorative arts, armor, and other art objects-- and the individual works originate from a dizzying array of time periods and several countries." Libr J

Bramly, Serge

Leonardo; the artist and the man. translated by Sian Reynolds. Penguin Bks. 1994 493p il pa $25 **709**

1. Artists 2. Painters 3. Scientists 4. Artists, Italian

5. Writers on science

ISBN 0-14-023175-7; 978-0-14-023175-5

Original French edition, 1988

In this account Bramly "sheds light on the more personal aspects of Leonardo. . . . As he follows da Vinci's often frustrating career and ever-widening sphere of inquiries, inventions, and discoveries, he also patches together overlooked clues about his private life, causing us to marvel anew at Leonardo's fertile and versatile mind while acquiring a sharper image of Leonardo the man. A richly detailed, expansive, and thoroughly enjoyable portrait." Booklist

Includes bibliographical references

Contemporary artists; editors, Sara Pendergast and Tom Pendergast; advisers, Jean-Christophe Ammann [et al.] 5th ed; St. James Press 2001 2v il set $265   **709**

1. Reference books 2. Artists -- Dictionaries

ISBN 1-55862-407-4

LC 2001-48443

First one volume edition published 1977

In this reference "nearly 850 prominent artists (those who have exhibited works in major galleries or museums) are listed. . . . Alphabetic entries provide biographical information (e.g., nationality, education, address), individual and select group exhibitions, collections in which the artist's work is contained, publications by or about the individual, a critical essay or essays, and occasionally a statement by the artist. The essays highlight the artist's achievements and offer insight into their work. . . . As a reference tool, this publication remains a classic, indispensable part of every art library's collection and is highly recommended." Am Ref Books Annu, 2003

Craven, Wayne

    American art; history and culture. McGraw-Hill 2003 687p il pa $69   **709**

1. American art

ISBN 978-0-07-282329-5; 0-07-282329-1

LC 2002-035777

First published 1994

The author "establishes seven main stylistic periods—colonial, Federal, romantic, the American Renaissance, early modern, postwar modern, and postmodern—and then goes into great detail within each section, profiling individual artists and discussing the effects of various social, political, and technological changes on aesthetics and the role of art in daily life. . . . Coverage of American photography and twentieth-century art are particularly dynamic, but his examples and emphases prove to be insightful and creative throughout." Booklist

Includes bibliographical references

Cuba: art and history, from 1868 to today; [edited by Nathalie Bondil; translation, Timothy Bernard et al.] Montreal Museum of Fine Arts 2008 424p il map $85   **709**

1. Cuban art

ISBN 3-7913-4019-0; 978-3-7913-4019-7

LC 2008-396997

"This momentous, dazzling volume interweaves history, biography, and artistic expression to explicate Cuba's distinctive vibrancy and glorious creativity." Booklist

Includes bibliographical references

Dippie, Brian W.

    The **Frederic** Remington Art Museum collection. Abrams 2000 264p il $49.50   **709**

1. Artists 2. Painters 3. Sculptors 4. West (U.S.) in art 5. Drafters

ISBN 0-8109-6711-1

LC 00-49339

This biography examines the artist's life and work and follows his evolution from illustrator to artist

"Photographs and comparative images enhance the author's discussions of Remington himself and of the individual paintings, drawings, and sculptures." Libr J

Includes bibliographical references

Encyclopedia of artists; [consulting editor, William Vaughan; contributors, Christopher Ackroyd, et al.] Oxford Univ. Press 2000 6v il set $195 **709**

1. Reference books 2. Art -- Dictionaries 3. Artists -- Dictionaries

ISBN 0-19-521572-9

LC 00-27167

"The first five volumes of this set alphabetically profile more than two hundred artists, covering western art from the Middle Ages to the present. Each artist is accorded a two-page spread consisting of three parts. The main introductory section details the artist's life and work. . . . Each entry then provides a data file that lists the major facts about each artist: nationality, style, dates, key works with dates, things to look for in the art, comparable artists, and related glossary terms. . . . Volume six consists of articles on art movements and styles mentioned in the other volumes." Voice Youth Advocates

"This set is beautifully written and illustrated. It will not only provide reliable information for researchers but will also entertain the interested browser." Am Ref Books Annu, 2001

Encyclopedia of Latin American & Caribbean art; edited by Jane Turner. Oxford University Press 2006 803p il (Grove library of world art) $250   **709**

1. Reference books 2. Caribbean art -- Encyclopedias 3. Latin American art -- Encyclopedias

ISBN 978-0-19-531075-7; 0-19-531075-6

First published 1999 by Grove's Dictionaries

"This work covers the art of every country in Central and South America and the Caribbean, from the colonial period to the present. The entries, expanded and updated from the publisher's mammoth Dictionary of Art, cover countries, artists, and artistic styles, with cross-referencing where appropriate." Libr J [review of 1999 edition]

Includes bibliographical references

Farrington, Lisa E.

★ **Creating** their own image; the history of African-American women artists. Oxford University Press 2005 354p il $55 **709**

1. Women artists 2. African American women 3. African American artists

ISBN 0-19-516721-X

LC 2003-66171

"A richly detailed yet fluent work of trailblazing research, fresh interpretations, and cogent argument, Farrington's treatise discusses vital aesthetic as well as social and cultural issues and creates a vibrant context for such seminal artists as Augusta Savage, Faith Ringgold, Barbara Chase-Riboud, Kara Walker, and many more." Booklist

Fenton, James

Leonardo's nephew; essays on art and artists. University of Chicago Press 2000 283p il pa $15 **709**

1. Art -- History

ISBN 0-226-24147-5; 978-0-226-24147-0

LC 99-55666

First published 1998 by Farrar, Straus, and Giroux

Fenton presents a collection of fifteen essays on various aspects of art history. Subjects "include Freud's collection of antique statuettes, Egyptian funerary portraits and Joseph Cornell. These essays educate, enlighten, surprise and thrill, unfailingly." N Y Time Book Rev

Includes bibliographical references

FitzGerald, Michael C.

★ **Picasso** and American art; [by] Michael FitzGerald; with a chronology by Julia May Boddewyn. Whitney Museum of American Art; in association with Yale University Press 2006 400p il $65 **709**

1. Artists 2. Painters 3. American art

ISBN 9780300114522; 0-300-11452-4

LC 2006-1402

A "study of Picasso's influence on some of the most significant American artists of the 20th century. Fitzgerald moves chronologically, from the earliest Americans who engaged cubism in the teens (Max Weber, Mardsen Hartley, Man Ray, Stuart Davis), through the modernist investigations of Arshile Gorky, Willem De Kooning and Jackson Pollack, and winds up with Roy Lichtenstien's pop-art and Jasper Johns' postmodern responses to Picasso. Fitzgerald takes great pains to triangulate exhibition specifics with the work and words of each artist to document the precise nature and extent of the influence in each case. . . . There is a generous supply of images presented with the text, and they are as successful as Fitzgerald's prose in illuminating the complexities of Picasso's influence on these artists." Publ Wkly

Includes bibliographical references

Gardner, Helen

★ **Gardner's** art through the ages; a global history. [revised by] Fred S. Kleiner. Enhanced 13th ed.; Wadsworth, Cengage Learning 2010 1088p il map $165.99 **709**

1. Art -- History

ISBN 978-0-495-79986-3; 0-495-79986-6

LC 2009-932089

First published 1926 by Harcourt Brace & Co.

This book surveys world art from prehistoric times to the present day. Painting, sculpture, architecture and some decorative arts are considered. Although the focus is on European art, there are also chapters on ancient Near Eastern, Asian, pre-Columbian, American Indian, African and Oceanic art.

Includes bibliographical references

Gombrich, E. H.

★ The **story** of art; 16th ed rev and expanded; Phaidon Press 1995 688p il $49.95; pa $29.95 **709**

1. Art -- History

ISBN 0-7148-3355-X; 0-7148-3247-2 pa

LC 96-140698

First published 1950

This survey of art examines artistic achievements in historical context to consider how prevailing social, political, and economic factors may have influenced the succession and popularity of certain artistic styles.

Includes bibliographical references

Gompertz, Will

What Are You Looking at? the Surprising, Shocking & Sometimes Strange Story of 150 Years of Modern Art. Will Gompertz. Dutton 2012 432 p. (hardcover) $28.95 **709**

1. Art -- 20th century 2. Art -- 21st century

ISBN 0525952675; 9780525952671

LC 2012027995

It was author Will "Gompertz's aim . . . to demystify modern art, to provide a basic history of each of its 'isms,' and show how these movements are interconnected." He "begins with [Marcel] Duchamp's omnipresent influence on the history of modern art and then chronicles movements that led up to and followed Duchamp's Fountain (1917), from pre-Impressionist artists Manet and Courbet to contemporary artists Banksy and Ai Weiwei." (Publishers Weekly)

The **Grove** encyclopedia of American art; editor in chief, Joan Marter. Oxford University Press 2011 5 v. ill. (some col.), map **709**

1. American art -- Encyclopedias

ISBN 9780195335798; 0199739269; 9780199739264; 0195335791

LC 2010030274

This reference book "contains entries . . . that comprise a . . . survey . . . art history. It covers American painting, architecture, sculpture, and photography from the Pre-Columbian sources to the colonial period to the twenty-first century devoting coverage to many previously underrepresented areas of inquiry, including African American artists, Asian American artists, and Native American art, both historical and contemporary. Artists, major movements, institutions, critics, and the architecture found in major cities of the United States are covered, as are new media and methodologies, including digital art, performance art, and installation art. In addition to American artists such as John Singer Sargent,

Robert Rauschenberg, Maya Lin, and Kiki Smith, attention is also paid to individuals who have had a significant impact on American art and art history through their activity in the United States, including Marcel Duchamp, Erwin Panofsky, Renzo Piano, and Max Beckmann." (Publisher's note)

Includes bibliographical references and index.

Hamilton, George Heard

The **art** and architecture of Russia. Yale University Press 1983 482p il map (Pelican history of art) pa $32   **709**

1. Russian art 2. Christian art 3. Church architecture

ISBN 978-0-300-05327-2; 0-300-05327-4

First published 1954 by Penguin Bks.

Hamilton traces the development of Russian art from the height of the Byzantine Empire, through its flowering under Peter the Great, to contemporary work and the influence of Western European culture.

Includes bibliographical references

Harclerode, Peter

The **lost** masters; World War II and the looting of Europe's treasurehouses. [by] Peter Harclerode & Brendan Pittaway. Welcome Rain 2000 402p il hardcover o.p. pa $18.95   **709**

1. Art thefts 2. World War, 1939-1945 -- Destruction and pillage

ISBN 1-56649-165-7; 1-56649-253-X pa

LC 00-42867

The authors "trace the elusive web of collaborators, opportunists and dealers who exploited the Third Reich's lust for prestigious trophies. Gripping vignettes and revelatory anecdotes illuminate the fates of specific works of art, including the outstanding story of four paratroopers who contrived to rescue the largest cache of stolen art sequestered by the Nazis." Publ Wkly

Includes bibliographical references

Harvey, Eleanor Jones

The **Civil** War and American art; Eleanor Jones Harvey. Smithsonian American Art Museum 2012 xvii, 316 p.p ill. (hardcover) $65   **709**

1. American art 2. Art collections 3. United States -- History -- 1861-1865, Civil War -- Pictorial works 4. Art, American -- 19th century -- Themes, motives -- Exhibitions 5. Art and society -- United States -- History -- 19th century -- Exhibitions 6. United States -- History -- Civil War, 1861-1865 -- Art and the war -- Exhibitions

ISBN 0300187335; 9780300187335; 9780937311981

LC 2012029342

This book, by Eleanor Jones Harvey and released by the Smithsonian American Art Museum, "looks at the range of artwork created before, during, and following the [U.S. Civil War], in the years between 1852 and 1877. [The] author . . . surveys paintings made by some of America's finest artists, including Frederic Church, Sanford Gifford, Winslow Homer, and Eastman Johnson, and photographs taken by George Barnard, Alexander Gardner, and Timothy H. O'Sullivan." (Publisher's note)

Includes bibliographical references (pages 274-293) and index.

Haskell, Barbara

The **American** century; art and culture. Norton 2000 2v il boxed set $120   **709**

1. American art 2. Arts -- United States

ISBN 978-0-393-04859-9; 0-393-04859-4

A reissue of the title first published 1999

Based on exhibitions at the Whitney Museum, these illustrated volumes cover 20th century American painting, sculpture, printmaking, and photography through political, historical, social, economic, and culture contexts

Hearn, Maxwell K.

Splendors of Imperial China; treasures from the National Palace Museum, Taipei. Metropolitan Mus. of Art 1996 144p il hardcover o.p. pa $29.95 **709**

1. Chinese art 2. National Palace Museum (Taipei, Taiwan)

ISBN 0-87099-766-1 pa

LC 95-46590

Hearn "selected more than 100 works to present here, drawn from an extensive traveling exhibition featuring Neolithic and Bronze Age works, as well as Sung, Ming, and other dynasty masterpieces. This beautifully produced book contains fine quality reproductions that illuminate a splendid collection of rare artwork. . . . The text describes in accessible terms important background information, including cultural climate, historical events, and artistic elements." Booklist

Herrera, Hayden

Frida : a biography of Frida Kahlo. Harper & Row 1983 507p il hardcover o.p. pa $24.95   **709**

1. Artists 2. Painters 3. Artists, Mexican

ISBN 0-06-008589-4 pa

LC 80-8688

This biography of the Mexican painter and wife of Diego Rivera "is a mesmerizing story of radical art, romantic politics, bizarre loves and physical suffering. . . . Herrera resolves Kahlo the public figure and Kahlo the artist in a perceptive portrait of a woman who rose above a circumscribed content with a grand style." Time

Includes bibliographical references

Hoving, Thomas

Art for dummies; foreword by Andrew Wyeth. IDG Books Worldwide, Inc 1999 382p il (--For dummies) $24.99   **709**

1. Art appreciation 2. Art -- History

ISBN 978-0-7645-5104-8; 0-7645-5104-3

LC 99-65838

"In this delightful book, Hoving . . . leads readers gently through thousands of years of art history. . . . His breathless enthusiasm is avuncular, scholarly, and quite infectious—an attitude that happily precludes condescension. . . . A terrific book for students, travelers, tyros, and old hands alike." Libr J

Includes bibliographical references

Hughes, Robert

American visions; the epic history of art in America. Knopf 1997 635p il $65; pa $39.95 **709**

1. American art

ISBN 0-679-42627-2; 0-375-70365-9 pa

LC 96-45111

"Hughes has orchestrated a spectacular integration of facts, observations, and insights in this ambitious, lively, and gloriously illustrated volume." Booklist

Includes bibliographical references

Janson, H. W.

★ Janson's history of art; the western tradition. Penelope J.E. Davies ... [et. al] 8th ed.; Prentice Hall 2011 xxxi, 1152p il map $170.40 **709**

1. Art -- History

ISBN 978-0-205-68517-2; 0-205-68517-X

LC 2009-22617

First published 1962 by Abrams with title: History of art

A history of art from prehistoric cave paintings to video art. While the focus is primarily on Western art, brief discussions of Oriental, Near Eastern, Islamic, African and Latin American arts are included.

Includes bibliographical references

Johnson, Paul

★ Art : a new history. HarperCollins Pubs. 2003 777p il $39.95 **709**

1. Art -- History

ISBN 0-06-053075-8

"While {Johnson's} narrative is for the most part a conventional journey through the canon, his headlong pace, quirky views and pungent prose make it anything but dull." Publ Wkly

Khalili, Nasser D.

Islamic art and culture; a visual history. Overlook Press 2006 186p il $60 **709**

1. Islamic art 2. Islamic civilization

ISBN 1-58567-839-2; 978-1-58567-839-6

This "visual history of Islamic art introduces readers to the diverse peoples, cultures, and styles making up Islam today. Spanning 12 centuries and covering everything from miniature painting to architecture, it shows, e.g., various Qur'ans, coins, armor, and scientific instruments. . . . This is an excellent introduction to the subject that combines aptly chosen and beautifully reproduced photographs with a concise and informative text." Libr J

Includes bibliographical references

King, Ross

Art : over 2,500 works from cave to contemporary; foreword by Ross King. DK Pub. 2008 612p il $50 **709**

1. Reference books 2. Art appreciation 3. Art -- History

ISBN 978-0-7566-3972-3; 0-7566-3972-7

LC 2008-301471

Within each time period, provides examples of significant works in painting, sculpture, drawing and other media. Highlights themes that were important at various times such as nudes, landscape, still life, and love. Includes brief biographies of some artists and a "closer look" in depth for the most significant works.

"Easy to read and use, . . . both newcomers to art and art connoisseurs will enjoy this picturesque work." Libr J

Includes glossary

Kirwin, Liza

Lists; to-dos, illustrated inventories, collected thoughts, and other artists' enumerations from the Smithsonian's Archives of American Art. with a foreword by John W. Smith. Princeton Architectural Press 2010 205p il pa $24.95 **709**

1. Lists 2. Archives of American Art 3. Artists -- United States

ISBN 978-1-56898-888-7; 1-56898-888-5

LC 2009-25316

"Collecting work from close to 70 list-makers, including Joseph Cornell, Elaine and Willem de Kooning, Lee Krasner, H.L. Mencken, Pablo Picasso and N.C. Wyeth, Kirwin's beautiful book uses an unusual medium to glimpse into the minds of artists. . . . As an 'entry point', the book seems to presuppose a level of familiarity with the various artists. Fortunately for the unfamiliar (like me), each entry includes a brief bit of text from Kirwin that provides biographical information and analysis of each list. However, with its full-colour reproductions, the book seems more appealing as an unusual, mesmerizing, and intimate collection of outsider-like art." PopMatters

Klein, Stefan

Leonardo's legacy; how Da Vinci reimagined the world. translated by Shelley Frisch. Da Capo Press 2010 291p il $26 **709**

1. Artists 2. Painters 3. Inventors 4. Scientists 5. Artists, Italian 6. Writers on science

ISBN 978-0-306-81825-7; 0-306-81825-6

LC 2010-00130

Original German edition, 2008

The author "makes a compelling case that DaVinci's ability to trigger an empathetic physical response in the viewer lay in his scientific acumen: the asymmetry of the Mona Lisa's smile, for instance, deliberately reflects the asymmetry of the human brain. While Leonardo is remembered primarily as an artist, his accomplishments as a scientist were at least as important. . . . Including a detailed chronology of the artist's life, this makes an illuminating new look at Leonardo's unique genius." Publ Wkly

Includes bibliographical references

Langdon, Helen

Caravaggio; a life. Westview Press 2000 436p il map pa $22 **709**

1. Artists 2. Painters 3. Artists, Italian

ISBN 0-8133-3794-1; 978-0-8133-3794-4

First published 1998 in the United Kingdom

In this study of the Renaissance painter, "Langdon's masterly achievement is to integrate Caravaggio's art and life in a convincing and vividly delineated recreation of his world." Libr J

Includes bibliographical references

Little, Stephen

. . . isms: understanding art. Universe 2004 159p il pa $16.95 **709**

1. Art -- History

ISBN 0-7893-1209-3

LC 2004-94996

The author "identifies four types of isms: trends specific to the visual arts (perspectivism), broad cultural trends (romanticism), artist-defined movements (cubism), and retrospectively named movements (mannerism). He then moves forward chronologically, deftly defining more than 50 isms, naming key artists, and showcasing splendid examples." Booklist

Lottman, Herbert R.

Man Ray's Montparnasse. Abrams 2001 261p il $29.95 **709**

1. Artists 2. Painters 3. Photographers 4. Paris (France) -- Intellectual life

ISBN 0-8109-4333-6

LC 2001-633

Lottman presents a "snapshot of Man Ray between the two world wars, emphasizing the 1920s, with the developing Montparnasse section of Paris as the backdrop. Here are the cutting-edge dadaists and surrealists flanking Man Ray and his unerring camera eye, along with poets and artists, collectors, lovers, and other assorted characters. . . . Lottman's vivid exploration of 20th-century art events will serve the art historian and student of Paris very well in documenting an essential epoch and place." Libr J

Includes bibliographical references and index

Marin, Cheech

Chicano visions; American painters on the verge. essays by Max Benavidez, Constance Cortez, Tere Tomo. Little, Brown 2002 160p il $35; pa $19.95 **709**

1. American painting 2. Mexican Americans

ISBN 0-8212-2805-6; 0-8212-2806-4 pa

LC 2002-104645

"Marin's extraordinary collection forms the foundation for this exciting and invaluable showcase . . . {which includes works by} John Valadez, Gronk, Diane Gamboa, Patssi Valdez, Adan Hernandez, and Carlos Almaraz." Booklist

Includes bibliographical references

Martin, Barnaby

Hanging man; the arrest of Ai Weiwei. Barnaby Martin. Faber and Faber, Inc. 2013 256 p. (hardback) $27 **709**

1. Political activists 2. China -- Social conditions -- 2000- 3. China -- Politics and government -- 2002- 4. Dissenters, Artistic -- China -- Social conditions -- 21st century

ISBN 0374167753; 9780374167752

LC 2013015010

This book focuses on the arrest of Chinese artist and activist Ai Weiwei. Journalist Barnaby Martin interviewed "the artist about his experience, to inform the larger world of his treatment, to learn why he was arrested and ultimately released, and, finally, to shed light on the current state of the Chinese government itself. . . . Martin covers . . . the political trajectory of China through the 20th century, contemporary art movements in the post-Mao era, and Ai Weiwei's own life." (Library Journal)

"A book that offers great clarity on an important subject without succumbing to oversimplification." Kirkus

McPhee, John A.

The **ransom** of Russian art; {by} John McPhee. Farrar, Straus & Giroux 1994 181p il $20; pa $12 **709**

1. Economists 2. Russian art 3. Art collectors 4. College teachers

ISBN 0-374-24682-3; 0-374-52450-5 pa

LC 94-14723

"McPhee's engaging narrative sheds light on this suppressed creative milieu." Publ Wkly

Muller, Melissa

Lost lives, lost art; Jewish collectors, Nazi art theft, and the quest for justice. [by] Melissa Muller [and] Monika Tatzkow; with contributions from Thomas Blubacher and Gunnar Schnabel; foreword by Ronald S. Lauder. Vendome Press 2010 248p il $40 **709**

1. Art thefts 2. Jews -- Europe 3. Art -- Collectors and collecting 4. World War, 1939-1945 -- Destruction and pillage

ISBN 978-0-8656-5263-7; 0-8656-5263-7

LC 2010-15337

Original German edition, Verlorene Bilder, Verlorene Leben, 2009.

The authors "cover 15 Jewish/possibly Jewish families with vast art collections looted by the Nazis. Jewish collectors either had to sell their treasures for a pittance or had them seized. The Bloch-Bauer family's story is famous, but the unknown histories of other prominent families are compellingly told here, and there is a final historical-legal commentary by expert Gunnar Schnabel on Nazi-looted art and the German laws that perpetuated these crimes. . . . Richly illustrated with excellent art reproductions and family photographs." Libr J

North American women artists of the twentieth century; a biographical dictionary. edited by Jules Heller and Nancy G. Heller. Garland 1995 xxii, 612p il (Garland reference library of the humanities) hardcover o.p. pa $41.95 **709**

1. Reference books 2. Women artists -- Dictionaries

ISBN 0-8153-2584-3 pa

LC 94-49710

This is a "guide to more than 1500 Canadian, Mexican, and United States women artists born between 1850 and 1960. Artists are listed alphabetically, and each artist . . . is briefly treated in several paragraphs that end with bibliographical citations, often to important journal articles. More than 100 illustrations provide a small sampling of their work. . . . An essential acquisition for all art reference libraries." Libr J

Nuland, Sherwin B.

Leonardo da Vinci. Viking 2000 170p il (Penguin lives series) pa $13 **709**

1. Artists 2. Painters 3. Scientists 4. Artists, Italian 5. Writers on science
ISBN 0-670-89391-9; 978-0-14-303510-7 pa; 0-14-303510-X pa

LC 00-32061

"Nuland . . . elegantly sketches Leonardo's life of constant employment by noblemen eager to enjoy the prestige he reflected on them and of even more constant curiosity, which drove him to become the greatest anatomist before Vasari. . . . A scintillating addition." Booklist

Paglia, Camille, 1947-

Glittering images; a journey through art from Egypt to Star Wars. Camille Paglia. Pantheon 2012 xviii, 202 p.p col. ill. **709**

1. Painting 2. Sculpture 3. Digital photography 4. Art -- History 5. Art and society -- History -- 21st century
ISBN 9780375424601

LC 2012005220

In this book, author Camille Paglia offers a history of the "themes of Western art." The book shows "more than two dozen seminal images, some famous and some obscure or unknown--paintings, sculptures, architectural styles, performance pieces, and digital art that have defined and transformed our visual world." Paglia presents information on Jackson Pollock, Renée Cox, and George Lucas. (Publisher's note)

Penrose, Roland

★ **Picasso** : his life and work; 3rd ed; University of Calif. Press 1981 517p il hardcover o.p. pa $21.95 **709**

1. Artists 2. Painters
ISBN 0-520-04207-7 pa

LC 80-54015

First published 1958 by Harper

The author "has produced a painstaking, comprehensive biography . . . and, what is more, a popular biography, assuming neither knowledge of nor sympathy with twentieth-century art on the part of the reader." Times Lit Suppl {review of 1958 edition}
Includes bibliographical references

Petropoulos, Jonathan

The **Faustian** bargain; the art world in Nazi Germany. Oxford Univ. Press 2000 395p il $42.50 **709**

1. Art thefts 2. National socialism 3. World War, 1939-1945 -- Destruction and pillage
ISBN 0-19-512964-4

LC 99-33372

"Spotlighting five groups--art museum directors, art dealers, art journalists, art historians, and artists--Petropoulos . . . details how each of these groups either directly or indirectly facilitated the theft of countless works of art and legitimized the Nazi regime." Libr J
Includes bibliographical references

Robinson, Roxana

★ **Georgia** O'Keeffe: a life. University Press of New England 1999 639p il pa $22.95 **709**

1. Artists 2. Painters
ISBN 0-87451-906-3

LC 98-30944

A reissue of the title first published 1989 by Harper & Row

"This biography, the first to draw on sources unavailable during O'Keeffe's lifetime—and the first to be granted her family's cooperation—offers a persuasive feminist analysis of the life and work of an iconic figure in American art. . . . [The author's] detailed, sensitive critique of O'Keeffe's work . . . alternates with an absorbing, intimate narrative of O'Keeffe's personal life." Publ Wkly
Includes bibliographical references

Schama, Simon

The **power** of art. Ecco 2006 448p il $50 **709**

1. Art -- History
ISBN 0-06-117610-9; 978-0-06-117610-4

LC 2007-270937

The author "presents eight remarkable artists who created their masterworks against a backdrop of personal and professional distress. From politically charged commentaries (David, Picasso, Turner and Rembrandt) to intensely personal visions of the world (van Gogh and Rothko) and the reinvention of the divine (Bernini and Caravaggio), Schama takes these masters' hallowed works off the museum wall and drags them through the mud and muck that went into their creation." Publ Wkly
Includes bibliographical references

Scott, John F.

Latin American art; ancient to modern. University Press of Fla. 1999 xxiv, 240p il $49.95; pa $29.95 **709**

1. Latin American art
ISBN 0-8130-1645-2; 0-8130-1826-9 pa

LC 98-46535

A study "of Latin American art from pre-Columbian times to the present, encompassing media ranging from sculpture, pottery, and painting to architecture. Scott . . . addresses the major styles and artists that define each period." Libr J
Includes bibliographical references

Tomkins, Calvin

Duchamp; a biography. Holt & Co. 1996 550p il map hardcover o.p. pa $20 **709**

1. Artists 2. Painters 3. Artists, French
ISBN 0-8050-5789-7

LC 96-3080

"Tomkins organizes the facts of Duchamp's life and work into a sober, coherent whole, and for this alone his book makes valuable reading for anyone seeking to understand how art's cutting edge was honed." New Repub
Includes bibliographical references

Tregear, Mary

Chinese art; rev ed; Thames & Hudson 1997 216p il maps (World of art) pa $14.95   **709**

1. Chinese art

ISBN 0-500-20299-0

First published 1980 by Oxford Univ. Press

An introduction to major decorative, ceremonial, figurative and narrative aspects of Chinese art. Coverage ranges from works of Neolithic groups and the bronzes of the Shang dynasty to Buddhist sculpture, ceramics, garden design and architecture. Emphasis is also placed on the interaction of poetry, painting and calligraphy.

Includes bibliographical references

Visona, Monica Blackmun

A **history** of art in Africa; [by] Monica Blackmun Visona, Robin Poynor, Herbert M. Cole; with contributions by Suzanne Preston Blier (introduction), Rowland Abiodun (preface) and Michael D. Harris (chapter 16) 2nd ed; Pearson/Prentice Hall 2007 560p il pa $111   **709**

1. African art

ISBN 978-0-13-612872-4; 0-13-612872-6

LC 2007-15831

First published 2000

"Treating the subject from an art historical rather than an anthropological perspective, this groundbreaking book is organized geographically to cover the entire continent. Each of the five regional sections focuses on selected major art traditions. . . . Accompanying the text are over 700 photos and scores of maps, plans, drawings, etc." Libr J [review of 2000 edition]

Includes bibliographical references (p. 544-551)

Wittkower, Rudolf

Art and architecture in Italy, 1600-1750; revised by Joseph Connors and Jennifer Montagu. 6th ed; Yale Univ. Press 1999 3v il maps (Pelican history of art) set $160; pa set $80   **709**

1. Baroque art 2. Italian art

ISBN 0-300-07890-0; 0-300-07889-7 pa

LC 98-49066

First published 1958 by Penguin Bks.

The author examines works produced during the Early, High, and Late Baroque periods of Italian art, covering such artists as Caravaggio, Bernini, Borromini and Cortona.

Includes bibliographical references

709.01   Periods of development, and arts of nonliterate peoples

Berlo, Janet Catherine

Native North American art; by Janet Catherine Berlo and Ruth B. Phillips. Oxford Univ. Press 1999 291p il map (Oxford history of art) hardcover o.p. pa $24.95   **709.01**

1. Native American art

ISBN 0-19-284218-8 pa

LC 99-177938

This survey covers the "artistic output of most Native American tribes across the northern hemisphere over a period of more than eight centuries. . . . In an introduction that stresses the commonality of themes—cosmology, vision quests, love of ornament, reverence of materials—[the authors] emphasize the importance of today's Native art as a natural extension. Five regional chapters then incorporate history, outstanding crafts and arts, some prominent figures, and social, religious, and cultural aspects." Libr J

709.02   6th-15th centuries, 500-1499

Adams, Laurie

Italian Renaissance art. Westview Press 2001 420p il map $75; pa $65   **709.02**

1. Italian art 2. Art -- 15th and 16th centuries

ISBN 978-0-8133-3690-9; 0-8133-3690-2; 978-0-8133-3691-6 pa; 0-8133-3691-0 pa

LC 2001-269582

"Adams has produced a near-perfect introduction to the people, places, and events of the Italian Renaissance. . . . The text follows Italian art as it transforms from a highly religious activity into a very human one, and culminates with a focus on the multitalented genius of da Vinci, Raphael, and Michelangelo. . . .The side boxes are helpful and provide further information about the religious figures, ideas, and historical events that directly influenced the era, such as Dante and the black death. . . . This, along with numerous superb photographs, adds incalculable value to the understanding of the Italian Renaissance." Booklist

Includes bibliographical references

Lowden, John

Early Christian & Byzantine art. Chronicle Bks. 1997 447p il (Art & ideas) pa $24.95   **709.02**

1. Medieval art 2. Byzantine art 3. Christian art

ISBN 0-7148-3168-9

In this illustrated history of the origins and growth of Christian art Lowden works "deftly through fascinatingly complex and epoch-defining artistic and theological debates, including the so-called Iconoclast Controversy." Booklist

Includes bibliographical references

Snyder, James

★ **Art** of the Middle Ages; [by] James Snyder, Henry Luttikhuizen, Dorothy Verkerk. 2nd ed.; Prentice Hall 2006 530p il map hardcover o.p. pa $134.40   **709.02**

1. Medieval art 2. Christian art 3. Medieval architecture

ISBN 0-13-193825-8; 0-13-192970-4 pa

LC 2004-60135

First published 1989 with title Medieval art

"Church architecture and decoration receive the bulk of Snyder's attention, with manuscript illumination and sumptuary and secular arts presented rather briefly. The volume is well illustrated, though chiefly in black-and-white photographs." Libr J [review of 1989 edition]

Includes bibliographical references

709.03 Modern period, 1500-

Craske, Matthew

Art in Europe, 1700-1830; a history of the visual arts in an era of unprecedented urban economic growth. Oxford Univ. Press 1997 320p il (Oxford history of art) hardcover o.p. pa $21.50 **709.03**
1. Art -- 19th century 2. World history -- 18th century
ISBN 0-19-284206-4 pa

LC 96-37917

This study analyzes "the fundamental historical causes of change that took place from the early 1700s to 1839. . . . Craske . . . provides a series of four stimulating chapters devoted respectively to the function of the artist, art worlds, the appreciation of the visual arts, and evolving ideas of history and civilization. The text is enhanced by 129 high-quality illustrations." Choice

Escritt, Stephen

Art Nouveau. Phaidon 2000 447p il map (Art & ideas) $24.95 **709.03**
1. Art nouveau
ISBN 0-7148-3822-5; 978-0-7148-3822-9

LC 00-344423

In this book "Stephen Escritt defines Art Nouveau broadly, analyzing the work of such diverse designers as Victor Horta in Belgium, Emile Galle in France, Charles Rennie Mackintosh in Glasgow and Antoni Gaudi in Barcelona." Publisher's note

Includes bibliographical references

709.04 20th century, 1900-1999

Arnason, H. Harvard

★ History of modern art; painting, sculpture, architecture, photography. [by] H.H. Arnason, Elizabeth C. Mansfield. 6th ed.; Pearson Prentice Hall 2009 830p il $130.67; pa $122.67 **709.04**
1. Modern art
ISBN 0-205-67367-8; 978-0-205-67367-4; 0-13-606206-7 pa; 978-0-13-606206-6 pa

LC 2009-15436

First published 1969

This covers artists and movements in art from the 19th century to the present, discussing such schools as cubism, surrealism, and abstract impressionism. Video, installation and performance art, sculpture, architecture, and photography are also surveyed.

"An ideal primer on modern art." Libr J

Includes glossary and bibliographical references

★ Art deco 1910-1939; edited by Charlotte Benton, Tim Benton, and Ghislaine Wood. Bulfinch Press 2003 464p il $65 **709.04**
1. Art deco
ISBN 0-8212-2834-X

LC 2002-113762

This exhibition catalog includes 40 essays about the Art Deco movement and its sources and expression throughout the world in such fields as architecture, ceramics, fashion, jewelry, graphic design, metalwork, glasswork, and film

Includes bibliographical references

Balken, Debra Bricker

Abstract expressionism. Distributed in North America by Harry N. Abrams 2005 80p il (Movements in modern art) $16.50 **709.04**
1. American art 2. Abstract expressionism
ISBN 1-85437-306-4; 978-1-85437-306-9

LC 2004-111326

This book has "60 color illustrations of works created by the artists of the movement . . . [and] examines the critical response to Abstract Expressionism from the time of its heyday up until the present day." Publisher's note

Includes bibliographical references

Brandon, Ruth

Surreal lives; the surrealists, 1917-1945. Grove Press 1999 527p il hardcover o.p. pa $16 **709.04**
1. Surrealism
ISBN 0-8021-3727-X pa

LC 99-25492

This study of surrealism "gives an account of the school's major practitioners, from Apollinaire to Dali; their flamboyant eccentricities and unconventional sexual entanglements prove a lively and absorbing complement to their work." New Yorker

Includes bibliographical references

Castle, James

James Castle; a retrospective. edited by Ann Percy; essays by Ann Percy . . . [et al.]; interview with Terry Winters by Jeffrey Wolf. Philadelphia Museum of Art in association with Yale University Press 2008 251p il $60 **709.04**
1. Outsider art
ISBN 978-0-300-13730-9; 0-300-13730-3

LC 2008-21792

"James Castle (1899-1977), born profoundly deaf, lived within his own silent world, communicating solely through his art. . . . [Percy] has brought together an amazing collection of his art as well as scholarly essays and biographical pieces. Castle used everyday items like soot, swabs, sticks, and food containers to create intricate constructions, surrealistic images, and collages of words and pictures. . . . The book also examines Castle's materials and techniques and his obsession with the ephemera of life around him. A major contribution to the literature of 20th-century art as well as outsider art; the accompanying DVD features an excellent film, Jeffrey Wolf's James Castle: Portrait of an Artist." Libr J

Includes bibliographical references

Dempsey, Amy

Art in the modern era; a guide to styles, schools & movements 1860 to the present. Abrams 2002 304p il $55 **709.04**
1. Reference books 2. Modern art -- Encyclopedias 3. Art -- 20th century -- Encyclopedias
ISBN 0-8109-4172-4

LC 2001-46261

This guide to art from 1860 to the present describes 300 schools and movements and includes a fold-out timeline

"All major and minor movements are mentioned in this very comprehensive guide, which could easily become a standard for modern art survey courses, making it a sensible purchase for most libraries." Libr J

Includes bibliographical references

Dickerman, Leah

★ **Dada**; Zurich, Berlin, Hannover, Cologne, New York, Paris. with essays by Brigid Doherty [et al.] National Gallery of Art in association with Distributed Art Publishers 2005 519p il $65   **709.04**
1. Dadaism
ISBN 1-933045-20-5

LC 2005-17984

"Seven scholars and curators contribute essays that examine each of the various Dada centers in turn. . . . Each essay examines key locations (e.g., the Cabaret Voltaire), individuals, publications (including Merz magazine), and inventions (such as ready-mades and photomontage.) . . . Its comprehensive scholarship and color illustrations of many rarely seen works make this book essential for all art collections." Choice

Includes bibliographical references

Fineberg, Jonathan David

Art since 1940; strategies of being. {by} Jonathan Fineberg. 2nd ed; Abrams 2000 528p il $65   **709.04**
1. Modern art 2. Art -- 20th century
ISBN 0-18-094209-7

LC 99-51584

First published 1995

This surveys American and European art from 1940 to 2000 through a series of biographical profiles of individual artists linked by discussions of the cultural influences on their work

"Fineberg surveys the visual arts in Europe, England, and North America from 1940 to the present, focusing on the avant-garde artist in the major Western capitals. . . . The text is arranged in 15 chapters in chronological order. Within each chapter the individual artist is discussed, as are the ideas and events relevant to understanding how cultural and social situations influenced the artist." Choice {review of 1995 edition}

Includes bibliographical references

Hunter, Sam

Modern art; painting, sculpture, architecture, photography. [by] Sam Hunter, John Jacobus, Daniel Wheeler. 3rd ed, rev and expanded; Prentice Hall 2005 472p il hardcover o.p. pa $126.20   **709.04**
1. Modern art
ISBN 978-0-13-150519-3; 0-13-150519-X; 978-0-13-189565-2 pa; 0-13-189565-6 pa

LC 2004-46659

First published 1985

This book explains "how European and American vanguard culture created modernist art by heeding the call 'to make it new.'. . . Coverage ranges across a broad spectrum of visual arts, from painting, sculpture, and photography to conceptual forms, installation and video art, and architecture." Publisher's note

Includes bibliographical references

Livingstone, Marco

Pop art; a continuing history. 2nd ed. Thames & Hudson 2000 272p il $29.95   **709.04**
1. Pop art
ISBN 978-0-500-28240-3; 0-500-28240-4

LC 00-100788

First published 1991 in the United Kingdom

With 300 color plates this volume chronicles the work of 130 artists of the Pop Art movement, including Jasper Johns, Robert Rauschenberg, Andy Warhol, and Roy Lichtenstein.

"Recommended as the best single historical survey on Pop Art." Libr J

Lucie-Smith, Edward

Art today. Phaidon Press 1995 511p il hardcover o.p. pa $45   **709.04**
1. Art -- 20th century
ISBN 0-7148-3888-8 pa

This "survey attempts to essay the scope and aims of the art of the world over the past 30 years. . . . As well as such . . . ground as Pop Art, Lucie-Smith covers Conceptual Art, Installation Art, and Neo-Expressionism. He also covers . . . artists and works from the former Soviet Union, Africa, the Far East, and Latin America. Chapters are also included on 'Racial Minorities' and 'Feminist and Gay' art. . . . The book offers brief biographies of all artists mentioned, a chronology, and bibliography." Libr J

Marquis, Alice Goldfarb

The **pop!** revolution; how an unlikely concatenation of artists, aficionados, businessmen, collectors, critics, curators, dealers, and hangers-on radically transformed the art world. MFA Publications 2010 221p il $29.95   **709.04**
1. Pop art 2. American art
ISBN 978-0-87846-744-0

This volume "will delight both the friends of Pop and its foes, for the book confirms the prejudices of each group. Pop's friends will read it as an account of an aesthetic revolution that displaced the humorless and posturing European-derived formalism of the postwar years. . . and substituted a content-rich art that was deeply engaged with American life and subject matter. . . . Pop's foes, by contrast, will read 'The Pop Revolution' as the saga of a crass commercial enterprise in which a mindless populist fad cut short the career of Abstract Expressionism, America's only meaningful contribution to the world art. . . . Ms. Marquis's principal contribution is that she tells the story of Pop not by profiling the artists themselves, as is usually done, but by tracing the interlocking network of galleries and collectors that sustained them. The result is a Pop social history." Wall Street J

Surrealism; edited by Mary Ann Caws. Phaidon 2004 304p il (Themes and movements) $75   **709.04**
1. Surrealism
ISBN 978-0-7148-4259-2; 0-7148-4259-1

"In this well-organized and nicely illustrated survey of Surrealism, Caws . . . discusses many of the basic ideas and tenets of the movement, emphasizing chance and freedom as the central surrealist concepts." Libr J

Includes bibliographical references

Theories and documents of contemporary art; a sourcebook of artists' writings. [edited] by Kristine Stiles. University of California Press 2012 xxii, 1141 p.p ill. (California studies in the history of art) (hardcover) $75.00; (paperback) $34.95 **709.04**

1. Art -- 20th century 2. Art -- 21st century
ISBN 0520257189; 9780520253742; 9780520257184
LC 2011038212

This book, edited by Kristine Stiles and Peter Selz, offers writings by "a diverse roster of artists, including many who have emerged since the 1980s, such as Julie Mehretu, Carrie Mae Weems, Damien Hirst, Shirin Neshat, Cai Guo-Qian, Olafur Eliasson, Matthew Barney, and Takashi Murakami. The writings, which . . . take the form of artists' statements, interviews, and essays, make vivid each artist's aesthetic approach and capture the flavor and intent of his or her work." (Publisher's note)

Includes bibliographical references (p. 1071-1088) and index

709.05 21st century, 2000-2099

Thornton, Sarah
Seven days in the art world. W.W. Norton 2008 274p il $24.95 **709.05**
1. Art -- Marketing 2. Art -- Exhibitions
ISBN 978-0-393-06722-4; 0-393-06722-X
LC 2008-35056

"The book is cleverly divided into seven day-in-the-life chapters, each focusing on a different facet of the contemporary art world: an auction (at Christie's New York), an art school 'crit' (at the California Institute of the Arts in Valencia), an art fair (Art Basel), an artist's studio (that of the Japanese star Takashi Murakami), a prize (Britain's prestigious Turner Prize), a magazine (Artforum) and a biennale (Venice). Thornton is a smart and savvy guide with a keen understanding of the subtle power dynamics that animate each of these interconnected milieus." N Y Times Book Rev

Includes bibliographical references

709.1 Areas, regions, places in general

Bloom, Jonathan
The **Grove** encyclopedia of Islamic art and architecture; edited by Jonathan M. Bloom and Sheila S. Blair. Oxford University Press 2009 3v il map set $395 **709.1**
1. Reference books 2. Islamic art -- Encyclopedias 3. Islamic architecture -- Encyclopedias
ISBN 978-0-19-530991-1
LC 2008-28208

This "encyclopedia expands and updates the Islamic art entries from the . . . Grove Dictionary of Art. Rewritten, reedited, and reorganized, these entries amount here to over 1600 A-to-Z articles and over 450 illustrations, drawings, and maps detailing 'the art made by artists and artisans whose religion was Islam, for patrons who lived in predominantly Muslim lands, or for purposes that are restricted or peculiar to a Muslim population or in a Muslim setting.' . . . This volume is everything that one has come to expect from a Grove title: literate, comprehensive, and authoritative." Libr J

Includes bibliographical references

O'Kane, Bernard
★ **Treasures** of Islam; artistic glories of the Muslim world. Duncan Baird; Distributed in the USA by Sterling Pub. 2007 224p il map $35 **709.1**
1. Islamic art 2. Islamic civilization
ISBN 978-1-84483-483-9; 1-84483-483-2

The author "combines an overview of Islamic art and architecture with a cursory history of Islam's empires and dynasties. Beginning with a brief discussion of the earliest mosque from the seventh century, and showing how Islamic architects created a distinctive artistic tradition, O'Kane . . . follows architectural and artistic ideas to the 19th century. . . . The wealth of glorious full-color illustrations make this beautifully designed book an excellent introduction to the art of Islam." Publ Wkly

Includes bibliographical references

709.2 Biography

Dictionary of women artists; editor, Delia Gaze; picture editors, Maja Mihajlovic, Leanda Shrimpton. Fitzroy Dearborn Pubs. 1997 2v il set $310 **709.2**
1. Reference books 2. Women artists -- Dictionaries
ISBN 1-88496-421-4
LC 97-206872

"The chronological coverage extends from 975 A.D. to artists born in 1945. Each of the alphabetically arranged entries includes a brief biography, information about the genre of art produced, and an example of the artist's work. These volumes also present 20 introductory surveys on such topics as 'Court Artists' and 'Training and Professionalism,' and include an overview of women's art in the 19th and 20th centuries by country. Together with their chronological list of artists, the volumes include a range of information not ordinarily found in a resource of this type." Am Libr

Hirst, Michael
★ **Michelangelo**; v1 Michael Hirst. Yale University Press 2011 x, 438 p.p v1 ill. (some col.) $40.00 **709.2**
1. Poets 2. Italian art 3. Mural painting and decoration 4. Artists 5. Painters 6. Sculptors 7. Architects 8. Biography, Individual
ISBN 0300118619; 9780300118612
LC 2011042294

In this book, author Michael Hirst presents a biography of Michelangelo, following "the artist from his apprenticeship in Ghirlandaio's workshop to his final move to Rome in 1534, when, at the age of 59, he left behind his native Florence, never to return. During these years he created such outstanding works as the marble 'Pietà,' the giant marble 'David,' commissioned for the cathedral in Florence, the Sistine Ceiling frescoes, and the new sacristy and library for the Medici family at San Lorenzo." (Publisher's note)

Includes bibliographical references (p. [378]-415) and index

Kosinski, Dorothy

Angels, demons and savages; Pollock, Ossorio, Dubuffet. Klaus Ottmann, Dorothy Kosinski ; introduction by Dorothy Kosinski and Terrie Sultan with an essay by Alicia G. Longwell, a text by Jean Dubuffet, and contributions by Elizabeth Steele, Sylvia Albro, Scott Homolka, and Chantal Bernicky. Yale University Press 2013 ix, 145 p.p ill. (hardcover) $45   **709.2**

  1. Modernism in art
  ISBN 0300186487; 9780300186482

                      LC 2012021496

This book looks at the "artistic relationships among Jackson Pollock (1912-1956), Alfonso Ossorio (1916-1990), and Jean Dubuffet (1901-1985)" and their influence on the development of postwar art. The book "reveals previously unrecognized technical and thematic affinities in the artists' work, from Dubuffet's 'raw,' unconventional style to Ossorio's use of Christian iconography and grotesque elements to Pollock's emphasis on medium and gestural force." (Publisher's note)

Includes bibliographical references and index.

709.3   Specific continents, countries, localities

Boardman, John

Greek art; 4th ed, rev and expanded; Thames & Hudson 1996 304p il map (World of art) pa $16.95   **709.3**

  1. Greek art
  ISBN 0-500-20292-3

                      LC 96-60184

First published 1964 by Praeger Pubs.

Partial contents: The beginnings and geometric Greece; Greece and the arts of the East and Egypt; Archaic Greek art; Classical sculpture and architecture; Hellenistic art; Selected bibliography

"This is a classic in the field made even more readable and useful than before. Highly recommended for all collections." Libr J

Frankfort, Henri

The **art** and architecture of the ancient Orient; 5th ed; Yale Univ. Press 1996 483p il maps (Pelican history of art) pa $35   **709.3**

  1. Ancient art 2. Middle East -- Antiquities
  ISBN 0-300-06470-5

                      LC 97-224901

First published 1954 in the United Kingdom, 1955 in the United States

This traces the development of art in the Near East from 3500 B.C. to 539 B.C., covering the Sumerians, Assyrians, Babylonians, Hittites, Aramaeans, Levants, and Phoenicians

Includes bibliographical references

Robins, Gay

The **art** of ancient Egypt; Rev ed; Harvard University Press 2008 271p il map pa $27.95   **709.3**

  1. Egyptian art 2. Egypt -- Antiquities
  ISBN 978-0-674-03065-7; 0-674-03065-6

                      LC 2008-4264

First published 1997

"The first chapter orients the reader in the cultural, technical, and iconographic contexts needed to explore the evolution of the Egyptian artistic tradition in subsequent chapters. Beginning with the predynastic origins (5000 BCE) and concluding in the Ptolemaic Period (304-30 BCE), Robins traces the development of sculpture, painting, funerary and religious art, and architecture with over 300 illustrations, many in color." Libr J [review of 1997 edition]

Includes bibliographical references (p. 256-266)

Smith, William Stevenson

The **art** and architecture of ancient Egypt; [by] W. Stevenson Smith. rev with additions; Yale Univ. Press 1998 296p il map (Pelican history of art) hardcover o.p. pa $35   **709.3**

  1. Egyptian art 2. Egypt -- Antiquities
  ISBN 0-300-07715-7; 0-300-07747-5 pa

                      LC 98-24893

First published 1958 by Penguin Bks.

"This book shows the tombs at Thebes, including the treasure-filled burial place of Tutankhamen, the temples of Luxor and Karnak, and the palaces of Akhenaten at Tell el Amarna and of Amenhotep III at Thebes. It also presents many revealing portraits depicting a range of subjects from the kings and queens who built the pyramids at Giza and Saqqara to their own civil servants." Publisher's note

Includes bibliographical references

709.5   Oriental arts

Brougher, Kerry

Ai weiwei; according to what? Kerry Brougher, Mami Kataoka, Charles Merewether ; edited by Kerry Brougher, Mami Kataoka, Charles Merewether. Del Monico Books 2012 176 p. ill. (some col.) (hardcover) $39.95   **709.5**

  1. Artists, Chinese 2. Installations (Art) -- Exhibitions
  ISBN 3791352407; 9783791352404

                      LC 2012949559

This book features dissident Chinese artist Ai Weiwei's work, ranging from furniture, videos, and photographs to sculpture and ceramics, [and] is published in conjunction with an exhibition . . . . Curator Mami Kataoka (Mori) summarizes the artist's life . . . and influences on his work. Two short chapters follow: Charles Merewether . . . elaborates on Ai's social concerns; Kerry Brougher . . . presents an interview with the artist." (Choice)

Includes bibliographical references (p. 142-144)

711 Area planning (Civic art)

McGregor, James H.
★ **Rome** from the ground up; [by] James H.S. McGregor. Belknap Press of Harvard University Press 2005 344p il map $29.95; pa $18.95 **711**
1. Rome -- History 2. City planning -- Rome
ISBN 0-674-01911-3; 0-674-02263-7 pa
LC 2005-48213
The author "chronologically traces the successive periods of intense architecture and planning that helped Rome achieve strategic greatness, from the Etruscan management of the Tiber Island ford 3,000 years ago, to the city's unparalleled artistic stamp by Bramante and Michelangelo during the Renaissance, to Mussolini's monumental Fascist vision, to the precarious repairs heralding the Jubilee Year of 2000. . . . Here is a walking tour in stately, inviting prose that renders wonderfully manageable a massive history lesson for the intellectually curious and adept." Publ Wkly
Includes bibliographical references

711.4 Local community planning (City planning)

Shane, David Grahame
Urban design since 1945; a global perspective. David Grahame Shane. Wiley 2011 360 p. (paperback) $45.00 **711.4**
1. City planning -- History 2. Urban renewal -- History 3. Urban renewal 4. Architecture, Modern -- 20th century 5. Architecture, Modern -- 21st century 6. City planning -- History -- 21st century
ISBN 0470515260; 9780470515259; 9780470515266
LC 2011283507
This book by David Grahame Shane "reviews the emergence of urban design as a global phenomenon. The book opens with the urgent need to rebuild cities and re-house the millions of refugees living in camps and shantytowns at the end of the Second World War. Against this background, the book traces the collapse of the modernist, comprehensive state-planning schemes on both sides of the Iron Curtain as global corporations emerged, concentrating on networks and enclaves." (Publisher's note)
Includes bibliographical references and index

712 Landscape architecture (Landscape design)

Buchanan, Rita
Taylor's master guide to landscaping. Houghton Mifflin 2000 384p il $40 **712**
1. Landscape gardening
ISBN 0-618-05590-8
LC 99-54110
Companion volume to Taylor's master guide to gardening
"Buchanan offers a comprehensive treatment of landscape design, emphasizing designing with plants and including extensive information about choosing and caring for plants, trees, shrubs, vines, and ground covers. . . . A landmark work destined to become a classic." Libr J

Clausen, Ruth Rogers
Dreamscaping; 25 easy designs for home gardens. Hearst Bks. 2002 127p il $30 **712**
1. Garden design
ISBN 1-58816-067-X
LC 2001-16928
The author provides "plans, plant lists, and well-illustrated planting directions for all sorts of situations in sun or shade, outdoors and in the home. Tips and reminders are used to address design issues and maintenance, and to point out poisonous species. . . . The book's pretty layout and colorful photographs should entice novices to try something new in the garden." Booklist

Goodwin, Nancy
Montrose; life in a garden. with illustrations by Ippy Patterson; foreword by Maureen Quilligan. Duke University Press 2005 292p il $34.95 **712**
1. Gardening
ISBN 0-8223-3604-9
LC 2005-11387
"Goodwin and her husband, Craufurd, searched for 10 years for a larger piece of property before buying Montrose, a nineteenth-century estate in historic Hillsborough, North Carolina. . . . Godwin taught piano and ran a mail-order nursery before she settled into the full-time gardening . . . that has shaped the rhythm of her life since 1994. This lovely little book, exquisitely illustrated with a friend's penciled and watercolored botanical drawings, chronicles a year in her garden. It's a story of the seasons, the weather, hard work, triumphs, and disappointments. Goodwin's voice, precise and detailed when discussing the differences between various hellebores and snowdrops, remains fondly appreciative of the treasures she grows so lovingly and well." Horticulture

Graham, Wade
American Eden; from Monticello to Central Park to our backyards: what our gardens tell us about who we are. Harper 2011 459p il $35; ebook $27.99 **712**
1. Gardens 2. Landscape architecture
ISBN 978-0-06-158342-1; 978-0-06-207886-5 ebook
LC 2010-24940
"Graham unveils the aesthetic, political, psychological, and ethical dimensions of the American garden. . . . Graham is able to gently mock the fashions of history while astutely observing that we are still as vulnerable to gardening fads today. After more than 250 years, the American gardening tradition has bequeathed to us treasured public parks, suburban sprawl, Kentucky bluegrass lawns in the desert, and kitchen gardens at the White House. Graham's history is a fascinating and illuminating tour of this American landscape." Publ Wkly
Includes bibliographical references

Griswold, Mac K.
The **golden** age of American gardens; proud owners, private estates, 1890-1940. {by} Mac Griswold, Eleanor Weller; with research assistance by

Helen E. Rollins. Abrams 1991 408p il $75; pa $34.95 **712**

1. Gardens

ISBN 0-8109-3358-6; 0-8109-2737-3 pa

LC 91-8283

A "history of owners, designers, and the ultimate country retreats resulting from their collaborations. . . . Weller's compilation of rare, hand-colored lantern slides and hundreds of black-and-white historical photographs of the era are particularly noteworthy." Booklist

Includes bibliographical references

Hayward, Gordon

Stone in the garden; inspiring designs and practical projects. Norton 2001 224p il $39.95 **712**

1. Landscape gardening

ISBN 0-393-04779-2

LC 00-69945

"The book's first half focuses on the philosophical and design considerations of stone forms as varied as walls, paths, terraces, and even benches. The second half is more practical, covering topics such as estimating the amount of stone needed for a wall, the methods of cutting and laying stone, and building pools and fountains." Libr J

Includes bibliographical references

Messervy, Julie Moir

Home outside; creating the landscape you love. Taunton Press 2009 249p il $30 **712**

1. Outdoor living spaces 2. Landscape architecture

ISBN 978-1-60085-008-0; 1-60085-008-1

LC 2008-32956

"This book helps home lovers make their outdoor spaces as comfortable and beautiful as their interiors. I like the 'before' and 'after' photos (which I always find more trustworthy in garden design books than drawings.)" Boston Globe

Includes bibliographical references

Miller, Lynden

Parks, plants, and people; beautifying the urban landscape. Norton 2009 206p il $49.95 **712**

1. Parks 2. City planning 3. Landscape gardening

ISBN 978-0-393-73203-0; 0-393-73203-7

LC 2009-04536

This "authoritative book should be required reading for any study of urban planning, but it's equally relevant to the home gardener. It's full of useful design and planting advice, clearly and unpretentiously presented." N Y Times Book Rev

Includes bibliographical references

Nagel, Vanessa Gardner

Understanding garden design; the complete handbook for aspiring designers. Timber Press 2010 235p il $34.95 **712**

1. Garden design

ISBN 978-0-88192-943-0

LC 2009-53692

"With novice gardeners and aspiring designers in mind, garden designer Nagel offers an overview of the whole enterprise, explaining why design is important, factors to consider, and how to get started. Accessing the site, gathering desired components, incorporating basic design principles, and implementing a design are detailed with photos, diagrams, and construction schedules." Libr J

"Thorough and thoroughly accessible, Nagel's reasoned yet personable approach to an often intimidating subject will benefit both homeowners and design professionals." Booklist

Includes bibliographical references

Newbury, Tim

The **ultimate** garden designer; New ed.; Hamlyn 2009 256p il pa $22.50 **712**

1. Garden design 2. Landscape gardening

ISBN 978-0-600-61987-1

First published 1995 by Cassell. Alternate title: 20 best garden designs

This primer to garden design features design plans for different types of gardens (including family gardens, water gardens, Japanese-style gardens, and roof gardens), information on different types of garden highlights (such as pools, gazebos, fences, and trellises), and a plant directory.

Rybczynski, Witold

A **clearing** in the distance: Frederick Law Olmsted and America in the nineteenth century. Scribner 1999 480p il $28; pa $15.95 **712**

1. Travel writers 2. Urban planners 3. Landscape architects

ISBN 0-684-82463-9; 0-684-86575-0 pa

LC 99-18094

"Rybczynski, celebrated for his sparkling prose as well as for his deep knowledge of architectural history, adeptly chronicles the life of the man who 'was a landscape architect before that profession was founded.'" Booklist

Includes bibliographical references

Van Sweden, James A.

★ **Architecture** in the garden; {by} James van Sweden with Thomas Christopher; foreword by Penelope Hobhouse. Random House 2002 264p il $39.95 **712**

1. Garden design 2. Landscape architecture

ISBN 0-375-50154-1

LC 2002-69702

The author attempts "to show that architectural elements are essential in developing a successful garden design. Van Sweden focuses on such components as paths, edgings, fences, walls, water, and artwork, explaining that a garden is not a garden without a sound structural organization that uses these elements. . . . A well-illustrated glossary is included. Recommended for most gardening and landscape architecture collections." Libr J

Includes bibliographical references

Wulf, Andrea

Founding gardeners; the revolutionary generation, nature, and the shaping of the American nation. Knopf 2011 349p il map $30; ebook $14.99 **712**

1. Gardens 2. Gardening 3. American national characteristics 4. Statesmen -- United States

ISBN 978-0-307-26990-4; 0-307-26990-6; 978-0-307-59554-6 ebook

LC 2010-52920

The book discusses how the "leaders of the American Revolution and the early republic were engaged plantation owners keenly interested in scientific agriculture. Andrea Wulf argues that this interest, shared by other Founding Fathers, was no mere sideline activity, but rather something central to their identities as leaders and political thinkers." The author examines "the political role of horticulture/agriculture in the Constitutional Convention and the landmark battle over the Hamilton Bank Bill in 1791 that brought party political differences into the open." (Journal of American History)

The author demonstrates "that the garden, the natural world and the shape of a new nation were, for the men who launched the United States, parts of a whole. The image of the farmer-statesman is an ideal of republican government dating back to Romans. It's no accident that the men who led the Revolution and wrote the Constitution owned plantations and farms. . . . [Wulf is a] writer of considerable grace and breadth of vision, and 'Founding Gardeners' is an excellent portrait of the early years of the federal republic. It will delight the general reader, not just the garden buff. But for the garden enthusiast, this is a book of special interest, reminding us that a garden has a purpose, a character, a soul—that it's an expression of our relationship not just to the soil, but to a vision of the world." Cleveland Plain Dealer

720   Architecture

Altman, Adelaide
  Elderhouse : planning your best home ever. Chelsea Green 2002 232p il pa $19.95   **720**
  1. Elderly -- Housing 2. Domestic architecture -- Designs and plans
  ISBN 1-931498-11-3
                                         LC 2002-31481
  "The first section is full of ideas for creating a safe and comfortable home for wheelchair access or for a time in our lives when we are less nimble. The second section addresses the psychology of moving to a new smaller space in the later years of life." Libr J
  Includes bibliographical references

Curl, James Stevens
  ★ A **dictionary** of architecture and landscape architecture; with line-drawings by the author. 2nd ed.; Oxford University Press 2006 xxv, 880p il $45 **720**
  1. Reference books 2. Architecture -- Dictionaries 3. Landscape architecture -- Dictionaries
  ISBN 978-0-19-280630-7; 0-19-280630-0
                                         LC 2006-40248
  First published 1999 with title: Oxford dictionary of architecture
  For a fuller review, see: Booklist, Nov. 15, 2006
  This is a dictionary of the "many stylistic and technical terms used in architecture today. The work covers all periods of Western architectural history in more than 5000 articles." Libr J
  Includes bibliographical references

Davies, Colin
  Thinking about architecture; an introduction to architectural theory. Colin Davies. Chronicle Books Llc. 2011 160 p. ill. (paperback) $29.95; (ebook) $29.95   **720**
  1. Architecture -- Philosophy
  ISBN 185669755X; 9781856697552; 9781780670911
  It was author Colin Davies' intent "to provide designers, teachers, students, and interested laypersons with a set of ideas that will enrich their conversation, their writing, and above all their thinking about architecture." The book introduces "basic concepts such as representation, form, and space." (Publisher's note)

  ★ **Dictionary** of architecture & construction; edited by Cyril M. Harris. 4th ed.; McGraw-Hill 2005 1089p il $74.95   **720**
  1. Reference books 2. Building -- Dictionaries 3. Architecture -- Dictionaries
  ISBN 0-07-145237-0
                                         LC 2005-42340
  First published 1975
  "The handy one-volume format, the reasonable cost, the clarity and accuracy of entries, the legible type and drawings, and the inclusive approach to current developments in the design, building, and scholarly professions related to architecture make this publication a crucial tool." Choice

O'Gorman, James F.
  ✓ **ABC** of architecture; drawings by Dennis E. McGrath. University of Pa. Press 1997 127p il pa $13.45; $35   **720**
  1. Architecture
  ISBN 0-8122-1631-8 pa; 0-8122-3423-5
                                         LC 97-22616
  The author discusses the history of architecture, types of buildings, advances in technology, and architectural analysis. Glossary. Index.
  This book, "a model of brevity and clarity, may be the best-written work on the subject in English for lay people." N Y Times Book Rev
  Includes bibliographical references

Palladio, Andrea
  ✓ The **four** books on architecture; translated by Robert Tavernor and Richard Schofield. MIT Press 1997 xxxv, 436p il $69.95; pa $24.95   **720**
  1. Architecture
  ISBN 0-262-16162-1; 0-262-66133-0 pa
                                         LC 96-36406
  "Drawing on the monuments of ancient Rome as well as the author's own villas and public works, this philosophical treatise and practical guide served as the pattern book for countless Palladian buildings by other architects around the world. Elegantly translated (in the first new English translation since 1738) and illustrated with the lyrical, rarely seen woodcuts of Palladio's original." N Y Times Book Rev
  Includes bibliographical references

Watkin, David, 1925-2008

A **history** of Western architecture; David Watkin. Watson-Guptill Publications 2005 720 p. (paperback) $40.00   **720**

1. Architecture -- History 2. Classicism in architecture
ISBN 0823022773; 1856697908; 9781856697903
LC 2005921992

This book by David Watkin "traces the history of western architecture from the earliest times in Mesopotamia and Egypt to the eclectic styles of the twenty-first century. The author emphasizes the ongoing vitality of the Classical language of architecture, underlining the continuity between, say, the work of Ictinus in fifth-century BC Athens and that of McKim, Mead and White in twentieth-century New York." (Publisher's note)

Includes bibliographical references (p. 704-708) and index

720.9   History, geographic treatment, biography

Boucher, Bruce

Andrea Palladio; the architect in his time. principal photography by Paolo Marton. 2nd ed; Abbeville Press 2007 324p il pa $39.95   **720.9**

1. Architects
ISBN 978-0-7892-0940-5; 0-7892-0940-3
First published 1994

"In this careful, comprehensive, stunningly illustrated survey, Boucher . . . capably illuminates Palladio's stylistic evolution. . . . Among the 300 plates are more than 100 newly commissioned photographs of building interiors and exteriors, which superbly capture Palladio's distincitve blend of simplicity and grandeur." Publ Wkly

Includes bibliographical references (p. 301-312)

Ching, Frank

A **global** history of architecture; [by] Francis D.K. Ching, Mark Jarzombek, Vikramaditya Prakash. J. Wiley & Sons 2006 800p il map $75   **720.9**

1. Architecture -- History
ISBN 978-0-471-26892-5; 0-471-26892-5
LC 2005-34527

"Ching and colleagues comprehensively look at the history of architecture worldwide from 3500 BCE to CE 1950. . . . The book includes most of the major monuments found in other architectural surveys, plus many more, especially from the non Western world. . . . The book's most informative and attractive feature is its illustrations, hundreds of drawings by Ching, a noted author and architectural illustrator. . . . Includes a portfolio of color photographs, companion Web site, and list of coordinates for Google Earth to provide satellite images of the major monuments." Choice

Includes bibliographical references

Glancey, Jonathan

The **story** of architecture. Dorling Kindersley 2000 240p il hardcover o.p. pa $25   **720.9**

1. Architecture -- History
ISBN 0-7894-5965-5; 0-7894-9334-9 pa
LC 00-30434

"Devoting nearly half the text to the modern period, Glancey condenses history's panorama into a series of colorful vignettes, each described as having some contemporary relevance. Driven by a contagious enthusiasm, the narrative is enlivened by chatty, sometimes offbeat commentary." Libr J

Hollis, Edward

The **secret** lives of buildings; from the ruins of the Parthenon to the Vegas Strip in thirteen stories. Metropolitan Books 2009 338p il $28   **720.9**

1. Buildings 2. Architecture
ISBN 978-0-8050-8785-7; 0-8050-8785-0
LC 2009-18715

This book is "built around thirteen chapters, each telling the story of a building that changed dramatically over time, either in physical terms (the Parthenon, Gloucester Cathedral) or conceptual ones (the Venetian hotel and casino in Las Vegas, which seeks to capture the image of the Most Serene Republic if not, exactly, the spirit). Hollis's stories are engrossing—his history of the Hulme housing estates in Manchester, and their role as incubator for British post-punk rock, was completely new to me—and his writing is engaging." Bookforum

Includes bibliographical references (p. 315-322)

Mathewson, Casey C. M.

Frank O. Gehry: selected works; 1969 to today. Firefly Books 2007 599p il $69.95   **720.9**

1. Architects
ISBN 978-1-55407-276-7; 1-55407-276-X
LC 2008-271852

First published 2006 in Germany

"Mathewson reviews Gehry's windows, furniture, and his use of natural light, as well as highlights specific buildings and includes hundreds of artfully composed color photographs of Gehry's interior and exterior projects." Libr J

Ruan Xing

New China architecture; by Xing Ruan; photography by Patrick Bingham-Hall. Periplus Editions 2006 239p il $49.95   **720.9**

1. Asian architecture
ISBN 978-0-7946-0389-2; 0-7946-0389-0

"China's remarkable economic boom is generating prodigious architectural and building activity. Ruan . . . offers a sampling by presenting 43 recent and projected buildings or complexes. . . . A diverse parade of designs is featured throughout, including airports, offices, stores, theaters, libraries, museums, villas, and sport showcases for the 2008 Olympic Games. Each rates a brief description and several excellent photographs or artist renderings. Floor plans or sections are often included." Libr J

Rybczynski, Witold

The **perfect** house: a journey with the Renaissance architect Andrea Palladio. Scribner 2002 266p il $25; pa $15   **720.9**

1. Architects 2. Architecture -- 15th and 16th centuries
ISBN 0-7432-0586-3; 0-7432-0587-1 pa
LC 2002-66838

The author offers a historical and architectural analysis of ten villas attributed to 16th century Italian architect Andrea Palladio

"With its intriguing biographical detail, precise descriptions of design elements, and engaging insights into daily life in the 16th century, Rybczynski's book is a small but lasting gift to the reader." Libr J

Includes bibliographical references

The **Seventy** wonders of the modern world; 1500 years of extraordinary feats of engineering and construction. edited by Neil Parkyn. Thames & Hudson 2002 304p il $40   **720.9**
1. Architecture 2. Curiosities and wonders
ISBN 0-500-51047-4

LC 2002-100549

Published in the United Kingdom with title: The seventy architectural wonders of our world

"Most of the featured 'wonders' date from the second half of the 20th century. The selections are divided into seven categories: churches, palaces, public buildings, towers and skyscrapers, bridges and railways, canals and dams, and statues. Each entry includes basic information on history, structural and engineering details, innovations, aesthetics, and a sidebar 'fact-file.'" Libr J

Includes bibliographical references

Storrer, William Allin

The **Frank** Lloyd Wright companion; Rev ed; University of Chicago Press 2006 492p il $99 **720.9**
1. Architects 2. Nonfiction writers
ISBN 0-226-77621-2

LC 2006-44502

First published 1993

This "volume covers more than 450 buildings designed by master architect Wright between 1886 and 1959. Storrer documents each structure with plans, drawings, photographs, and commentary. Each presentation is both complete and concise, following each stage of Wright's aesthetic development, each leap of his imagination, and each instance of technical innovation." Booklist

Wiseman, Carter

Shaping a nation; twentieth-century American architecture and its makers. Norton 1998 412p il $45   **720.9**
1. Architects 2. Architecture -- 20th century 3. Architecture -- United States
ISBN 0-393-04564-1

LC 97-9896

In this survey the author is "concerned to trace the ways in which buildings express an American identity. Though his subject is twentieth-century architecture, his search for roots extends back to the colonial vernacular and Thomas Jefferson. ... Wiseman has written a solid mainstream history in which the look of buildings is seen as important. More significantly, he argues the case for social relevance alongside beauty." Archit J

Includes index

Wolfe, Tom

From Bauhaus to our house. Bantam Books 1999 111p il pa $15   **720.9**
1. Bauhaus -- Influence 2. Architecture -- 20th century 3. Architecture -- United States
ISBN 978-0-553-38063-7; 0-553-38063-X
First published 1981 by Farrar, Straus & Giroux

A humorous history of American architecture in the 20th century.

721   Architectural materials

Maliszewski-Pickart, Margaret

Architecture and ornament; an illustrated dictionary. McFarland & Co. 1998 198p il $35   **721**
1. Architecture -- Details
ISBN 0-7864-0383-7

LC 97-33112

This source pairs a traditional dictionary of architectural elements with a series of illustrations of the same elements. The names located in the numbered illustrations may be found alphabetically in the dictionary; and cross-references in the dictionary refer to specific illustrations. The illustrations are grouped by category: windows and doors; walls; roofs; columns; stairs; ornament and moldings; arches, vaults, and domes

Rybczynski, Witold

The **look** of architecture. Oxford Univ. Press 2001 130p il hardcover o.p. pa $9.95   **721**
1. Design 2. Architecture
ISBN 0-19-513443-5; 0-19-515633-1 pa

LC 00-53077

"The author's deeply informed enthusiasm is infectious, and his removal of architectural writing from an airily theoretical discourse to the realm of practical experience is empowering for the lay reader." Publ Wkly

Includes bibliographical references

724   Architecture from 1400

Curtis, William J. R.

Modern architecture since 1900; 3rd ed [rev, expanded, and redesigned]; Phaidon 1996 736p il $59.95; pa $39.95   **724**
1. Architecture -- 20th century
ISBN 978-0-7148-3524-2; 0-7148-3524-2; 978-0-7148-3356-9 pa; 0-7148-3356-8 pa

LC 97-112837

First published 1982

"The volume's well-detailed text is buttressed with 650 color and black-and-white illustrations. This should be a standard volume in all architecture collections." Lib J

Includes bibliographical references

Gossel, Peter

Case study houses; 1945-1966 : the Californian impetus. Elizabeth A.T. Smith. Taschen 2006 96 p. ill. (some col.), maps (some c (pbk.) $14.99　　**724**

1. Domestic architecture -- History 2. Architecture -- United States -- History -- 20th century 3. Architecture, Domestic -- California -- Los Angeles 4. Dwellings -- California -- Los Angeles -- Design and construction
ISBN 3836513013; 9783822846179; 9783836513012

LC 2008386132

This book by Elizabeth Smith and Peter Gossel explores "The Case Study House program (1945-1966) which concentrated on the Los Angeles area and oversaw the design of 36 prototype homes, [seeking] to make available plans for modern residences that could be easily and cheaply constructed during the postwar building boom. Highly experimental, the program generated houses that were designed to redefine the modern home." (Publisher's note)

Includes bibliographical references (p. 96) and index

Gropius, Walter

The **new** architecture and the Bauhaus; translated from the German by P. Morton Shand; with an introduction by Frank Pick. MIT Press 1965 112p il pa $14.95　　**724**

1. Bauhaus 2. Architecture -- 20th century
ISBN 0-262-57006-8

LC 65-10279

Original German edition, 1925; this is a reissue of the translation first published 1935 in the United Kingdom

The founder of the Dessau Bauhaus describes the work of that institution, and his own architectural theories

Huxtable, Ada Louise

On architecture; collected reflections on a century of change. Walker 2008 478p il $35　　**724**

1. Architecture -- 20th century
ISBN 978-0-8027-1707-8; 0-8027-1707-7

The author "presents her penetrating and tough-minded criticism spanning half a century. . . . Centering largely on modernism, its masters and its discontents, the volume opens with an overview of the past four decades, including startlingly powerful pieces on the late '60s urban decay and the '90s reinvention of architecture." Publ Wkly

726　Buildings for religious and related purposes

Adams, Henry

Mont -Saint-Michel and Chartres; with an introduction by Ralph Adams Cram. Princeton Univ. Press 1981 401p il hardcover o.p. pa $40　　**726**

1. Middle Ages 2. Mont-Saint-Michel (France) -- Abbey 3. Notre-Dame (Cathedral: Chartres, France)
ISBN 0-691-00335-1 pa

LC 81-47279

"This classic study of medieval civilization is written as the commentary of Henry Adams to an imaginary niece as they tour the Abbey Church at Mont-Saint-Michel and the Chartres Cathedral." Benet's Reader's Ency of Am Lit

King, Ross

Brunelleschi's dome; how a Renaissance genius reinvented architecture. Penguin Books 2001 194p il pa $14　　**726**

1. Artists 2. Sculptors 3. Architects 4. Church buildings 5. Santa Maria del Fiore (Cathedral: Florence, Italy)
ISBN 0-14-200015-9

LC 2001-280068

First published 2000 by Walker & Co.

"King illuminates the mysterious sources of inspiration and the secretive methods of architectural genius Filippo Brunelleschi in a fascinating chronicle of the building of his masterwork, the dome of Santa Maria del Fiore in Florence. A remarkable saga of how one incandescent mind performed the one matchless feat that would forever transform architecture from a mechanical craft into a creative art." Booklist

Includes bibliographical references

727　Buildings for educational and research purposes

Holway, Tatiana

The **flower** of empire; the Amazon's largest water lily, the quest to make it bloom, and the world it helped create. Tatiana Holway. Oxford University Press 2013 328 p. $29.95　　**727**

1. Botany -- History 2. Victorian architecture 3. Victoria amazonica 4. Botanical gardens -- England -- History -- 19th century
ISBN 0195373898; 9780195373899

LC 2012034518

The "central narrative of [Tatiana] Holway's book pivots around an 1837 British discovery in Guiana of an immense water lily, and the mission to make one bloom in England. Along with the story of a quest for germination is the author's . . . description of the botany-obsessed Victorian England where the building of glass greenhouses influenced the design of the Crystal Palace in Hyde Park for the Great Exposition of 1851." (Library Journal)

728　Residential and related buildings

Cox, Reuben

The **work** of Joe Webb; Appalachian master of rustic architecture. photographs and essay by Reuben Cox. The Jargon Society 2009 116p il $64.95　**728**

1. Log cabins
ISBN 0-912330-85-6

"During the 1920s and 1930s, builder Joe Webb constructed nearly three dozen log homes in the tiny Appalachian town of Highlands, North Carolina. The cabins were built without the aid of power tools—or architectural plans. . . . Using a large-format field camera, Cox has documented all of Webb's extant cabins. . . . [Cox] also includes an essay that places the work within a regional and historical context." Publisher's note

Eck, Jeremiah

★ The **distinctive** home; a vision of timeless design. Taunton Press 2003 234p il $40 **728**
1. Building 2. Domestic architecture -- Designs and plans
ISBN 1-561-58528-9

LC 2002-151820

"Eck firmly believes it is possible to build creative houses without a large budget. He discusses a home's site placement, examines the flow of activity within a modern home, and encourages the reader to think of rooms beyond their traditional uses. Eck's book encourages creativity and provides a series of color photographs for developing sound ideas." Libr J

★ The **elements** of style; an encyclopedia of domestic architectural detail. general editor, Stephen Calloway ; consultant editor, Elizabeth Cromley. Firefly Books 2005 592 p. ill. (some col.) $85 **728**
1. Domestic architecture 2. Architecture -- Great Britain 3. Architecture -- United States 4. Interior architecture 5. Architecture -- Details 6. Architecture, Domestic -- Great Britain 7. Architecture, Domestic -- United States
ISBN 1554070791; 9781770850866

LC 2006276161

This book, edited by Stephen Calloway, Alan Powers, and Elizabeth Cromley, presents a "visual survey, period by period, feature by feature, of the key styles in American and British domestic architecture from the Tudor period to present day. . . . The book is designed for owners of period houses, restorers, architects, interior designers and all those interested in our architectural heritage." (Publisher's note)

Includes bibliographical references (p. 581-583) and index

Friedman, Avi

The **adaptable** house; designing homes for change. McGraw-Hill 2002 271p il $45 **728**
1. Prefabricated houses 2. Domestic architecture -- Designs and plans
ISBN 0-07-137746-8

LC 2002-141433

"Friedman urges the reader to reimagine the traditional static home as dynamic space that changes as the needs of the occupants change. A single house, according to the author, should be able to accommodate an individual and/or family throughout their lives. Friedman examines how space functions within a house and the ways a house can be expanded and contracted based on the needs of its owners." Libr J

Includes bibliographical references and index

The **Greenwood** encyclopedia of homes through American history; Thomas W. Paradis, general editor. Greenwood Press 2008 4v il set $399.95 **728**
1. Reference books 2. Decorative arts -- Encyclopedias 3. Domestic architecture -- Encyclopedias
ISBN 978-0-313-33496-2; 0-313-33496-X

LC 2008-2946

"The set covers ten historical eras beginning with the Colonial era and ending with the period 1986 to present. Each era is introduced by a time line and short historical essay. Other essays synthesize research under topics such as building materials, house plans, interior design, and landscaping. . . .The value of the set lies behind the pretty facade of the American home, in the contributors' exploration of the interaction of physical house and family life." Choice

Includes bibliographical references

Jordan, Wendy Adler

Universal design for the home; great looking, great living design for all ages, abilities, and circumstances. Quarry Books 2008 207p il pa $24.99 **728**
1. Domestic architecture -- Designs and plans
ISBN 978-1-59253-381-7; 1-59253-381-7

LC 2007-32663

This book "shows how a home that is accommodating to all can also have a stylish decor. . . . Color photographs and some before-and-after floor plans show how accessibility standards have been incorporated. A list of resources is provided." Libr J

Lind, Carla

The **Wright** style. Simon & Schuster 1992 224p il $50 **728**
1. Architects 2. Domestic architecture 3. Nonfiction writers
ISBN 0-671-74959-5

LC 91-44553

This book "takes us inside dozens of Frank Lloyd Wright's 'organic' houses, including his home and studio in Oak Park, Illinois, and the two Taliesins. . . . Carla Lind's text traces the development and components of Wright's unique, revolutionary aesthetic while 250 color photographs allow readers to appreciate the harmony of Wright's light-filled, graciously rectilinear rooms." Booklist

Includes bibliographical references

McAlester, Virginia Savage

A **field** guide to American houses; the definitive guide to identifying and understanding America's domestic architecture. Virginia Savage McAlester ; with drawings by Suzanne Patton Matty and photographs by Steve Clicque. Random House Inc 2013 848 p. ill. $50 **728**
1. Architecture -- United States 2. Domestic architecture -- Guidebooks 3. United States -- Guidebooks 4. Architecture, Domestic -- United States -- Guidebooks
ISBN 140004359X; 9781400043590

LC 2013018432

This book "covers more than 50 styles of American residential architecture, from early settlement homes of the seventeenth century to the modern 'Millennium Mansions' of the present day. Expanded and completely revised from the 1984 edition, this edition includes American house design from the last three decades and adds more than 600 new photographs and illustrations." (Booklist)

Includes bibliographical references and index

Meisel, Paul

Bird -friendly nest boxes and feeders; Paul Meisel. Fox Chapel Pub. 2012 111 p. (pbk.) $14.95   **728**

1. Birdhouses 2. Handicraft 3. Bird watching 4. Birdhouses -- Design and construction 5. Bird feeders -- Design and construction

ISBN 1565236920; 9781565236929

LC 2011039673

This book, by Paul Meisel, "offers ten simple and classic designs for building traditional birdhouses and feeders, plus valuable insights on creating the perfect backyard bird environment. More than just a set of plans, it covers how to attract the right kinds of birds and ensure that they will keep coming back.

This book includes complete plans for making basic, practical bird-welcoming structures, accompanied by patterns, illustrations and full color photographs." (Publisher's note)

Petroski, Henry, 1942-

The **house** with sixteen handmade doors; a tale of architectural choice and craftsmanship. Henry Petroski ; with photographs by Catherine Petroski. W.W. Norton & Co. Inc. 2014 384 p. illustrations, maps (hardcover) $27.95   **728**

1. Maine 2. Domestic architecture 3. Architecture, Domestic -- Maine 4. Arrowsic (Me.) -- Buildings, structures, etc

ISBN 0393242048; 9780393242041

LC 2014006423

"When Henry Petroski and his wife Catherine bought a . . . six-decades-old island retreat in coastal Maine, Petroski couldn't help but admire its unusual construction. An . . . expert on engineering, history, and design, he began wondering about the place's origins and evolution. . . . Sleuthing around dimly lit closets, knotty-pine wall panels, and even a secret passage . . . Petroski zooms in on the details but also steps back to examine the structure in the context of its time and place." (Publisher's note)

"Though this fascinating history of a house includes painstaking attention to woodcrafting techniques that may excite professional and amateur architects and carpenters a bit more than general readers, the book is replete with Petroski's usual fascinating details and elegant prose." Booklist

Includes bibliographical references and index

Susanka, Sarah

Creating the not so big house; insights and ideas for the new American home. photographs by Grey Crawford. Taunton Press 2000 258p il $34.95; pa $24.95   **728**

1. Interior design 2. Domestic architecture

ISBN 1-56158-377-4; 1-56158-605-6 pa

LC 00-44323

Susanka provides photographs and plans of houses that are designed to look bigger than their actual size

"Architect Susanka has big ideas about small design. . . . {This book promotes} well-designed, efficient, interesting modest-size homes. . . . {She} includes 25 delightful examples of houses designed by architects from around the country." Booklist

Not so big solutions for your home. Taunton Press 2002 155p il pa $22.95   **728**

1. Interior design 2. Domestic architecture -- Designs and plans

ISBN 1-56158-613-7

LC 2002-7101

The author presents a compilation of 31 essays from her "Drawing Board" column in Fine Homebuilding magazine "that offer a number of solutions to household design problems both big and small. . . . Susanka offers an eclectic mix: tips on site selection, mud room design, planning to fit specific furniture, creating a family room that works, personalizing with tile, and planning window seats, pantries, TV placement, and floor plan changes." Libr J

728.8   Large and elaborate private dwellings

Wiencek, Henry

National Geographic guide to America's great houses; more than 150 outstanding mansions open to the public. by Henry Wiencek and Donna M. Lucey. National Geographic Soc. 1999 320p il pa $25   **728.8**

1. Domestic architecture 2. American architecture 3. Architecture -- United States

ISBN 0-7922-7424-5

LC 98-53013

Arranged by state, this guide includes information on past owners, furnishings, renovations, room descriptions, and excursion plans for other nearby houses of note. The text is accompanied by 170 full-color photos

730.9   History, geographic treatment, biography of sculpture and related arts together, of sculpture alone

Manca, Joseph

1000 sculptures of genius; [by] Joseph Manca, Patrick Bade and Sarah Costello. English version; Sirrocco 2007 543p il $24.95   **730.9**

1. Sculpture

ISBN 978-1-84484-215-5; 1-84484-215-0

"This sculpture collection offers a vision of western art. . . . It also includes references, comments on masterworks and biographies." Publisher's note

730.92   Biography

McPhee, Sarah

Bernini's beloved; a portrait of Costanza Piccolomini. Sarah McPhee. Yale University Press 2012 260p.   **730.92**

1. Sculptors 2. Artists' models 3. Mistresses -- Italy -- Biography 4. Art -- Collectors and collecting --

Biography 5. Marble sculpture, Italian -- Italy -- Rome -- 17th century 6. Art -- Collectors and collecting -- Italy -- Rome -- History -- 17th century
ISBN 9780300175271

LC 2011038171

This book is a biography of Costanza Piccolomini, whose "marble portrait" was "[c]arved by sculptor Gianlorenzo Bernini in1636-37." For "centuries Costanza was identified only as Bernini's mistress, who later incited his rage by betraying him for her brother. Author Sarah McPhee corrects and expands this story . . . [which] sets the bust and Costanza's own life . . . against the backdrop of Baroque Rome." (Publisher's note)

Includes bibliographical references and index

731.4 Techniques and procedures

Belcher, Judy
Polymer clay creative traditions; techniques and projects inspired by the fine and decorative arts. principal photography by Steve Payne. Watson-Guptill 2006 144p il $21.95 **731.4**
1. Clay 2. Modeling
ISBN 0-8230-4065-8; 978-0-8230-4065-0

LC 2005-927912

"Addressing novices to the medium of polymer clay as well as more advanced crafters in the field, Belcher prepares an attractive handbook on making clay items." Booklist

Butz, Richard
How to carve wood; a book of projects and techniques. Taunton Press 1984 215p il pa $19.95 **731.4**
1. Wood carving
ISBN 0-918804-20-5

LC 83-50680

The author introduces "the most common types of carving, whittling, chip carving, relief carving, lettering, and architectural carving. The information on tools and their care is very helpful. This is the best book available on the subject." Libr J

Includes bibliographical references

Hessenberg, Karin
Sculpting basics; everything you need to know to create fantastic three-dimensional artwork. Barron's 2005 128p il $23.99 **731.4**
1. Sculpture -- Technique
ISBN 978-0-7641-5843-8; 0-7641-5843-0

The author "presents a fine overview for beginning sculptors. . . . [The book] touches on a wide range of sculptural forms and styles, including the traditional figure, symbolic compositions, and abstract reliefs. . . .For such a slight book, [it] bundles a surprising amount of information." Libr J

Includes bibliographical references

Plowman, John
The **encyclopedia** of sculpting techniques; a comprehensive visual guide to traditional and con-

temporary techniques. Sterling 2003 176p il pa $16.95 **731.4**
1. Sculpture -- Technique
ISBN 978-1-4027-0394-2; 1-4027-0394-5
First published 1995 in the United Kingdom

This book on sculpting covers "more than 30 techniques . . . [including] clay, plaster, wood, stone, and papier mâché, as well as . . . aerated concrete block, rubber, and found objects." Publisher's note

736 Other plastic arts

Engel, Peter
10 -fold origami; fabulous paperfolds you can make in just 10 steps! Tuttle 2009 96p il $19.95 **736**
1. Origami
ISBN 978-4-8053-1069-4

LC 2009-920075

This craft book features 26 origami models, all of which can be completed with ten major folds. All models are rated in difficulty from Easy to Advanced.

The author's "art subjects range from the wonderfully whimsical to the eminently practical. . . . Who could resist a plateful of sunny-side up eggs and bacon or the stolidly silent black-and-white penguin? Or not be tempted to use a brightly patterned picture frame or decorative party pinwheels?" Booklist

Hayakawa, Hiroshi
Kirigami menagerie; 38 paper animals to copy, cut & fold. Sterling Pub. 2009 128p il pa $17.95 **736**
1. Paper crafts 2. Animals in art
ISBN 978-1-60059-318-5

LC 2008-50622

The author shows how to cut and fold paper shapes to make 38 different types of animals, including sheep, pandas, and dragons.

Van Sicklen, Margaret
The **joy** of origami. Workman 2005 152p il pa $16.95 **736**
1. Origami
ISBN 0-7611-3988-5; 978-0-7611-3988-1

LC 2005-43687

"The 57 [origami] models [included] range in difficulty from a simple Elephant in Pajamas to a more challenging Tyrannosaurus Rex." Publisher's note

737.4 Coins

Cuhaj, George S.
★ **2012** standard catalog of world coins, 1901-2000; George S. Cuhaj, editor; special contributors: Mahdi Bseiso, Ivan Rakitin, Joeseph Zaffern. 39th ed; Krause Pub. 2011 2345p il map pa $65 **737.4**
1. Coins
ISBN 978-1-4402-1572-8
Annual. First published 1972

This illustrated volume covers coins from throughout the world minted 1901-2000. Prices are provided for each coin in up to four grades of preservation. Includes commemorative issues.

Yeoman, R. S.

★ A **guide** book of United States coins; [by] R.S. Yeoman; editor, Kenneth Bressett; research editor, Q. David Bowers; valuations editor, Jeff Garrett. 64th ed; Whitman Pub. 2010 429p il (Official red book series) $16.95   **737.4**

1. Coins 2. Reference books

ISBN 978-0-7948-3148-6

Annual. First published 1946 by Whitman

This guide "known as the 'Red Book' is an outstanding reference on U.S. coins designed for use in identifying and grading coins. All issues from 1616 to the present are covered. The guide provides historical data, statistics, values, and detailed photographs for each coin. Additional sections deal with specialties such as Civil War and Hard Times tokens, misstruck coins, and uncirculated and proof sets." Nichols. Guide to Ref Books for Sch Media Cent. 4th edition

★ **Handbook** of United States coins 2009; by R. S. Yeoman; edited by Kenneth Bressett. 66th ed; Whitman Publishing 2008 256p il $12.95; pa $9.95   **737.4**

1. Coins

ISBN 978-0-7948-2539-3; 0-7948-2539-7; 978-0-7948-2540-9 pa; 0-7948-2540-0 pa

Annual. First published 1942

This companion volume to A Guide book of United States coins gives the wholesale values of U.S. coins from colonial times to the present

737.4973   Coins--United States

Nolte, Steve

Coins 2009; Steve Nolte. Frederick Fell Publishers 2008 272 p. (pbk. : alk. paper) $18.95 **737.4973**

1. Numismatics 2. Money -- United States 3. Coins -- Collectors and collecting 4. Coins, American -- Collectors and collecting -- Handbooks, manuals, etc

ISBN 0883911671; 9780883911679

LC 2008035759

This book on coins and coin collecting by Steve Nolte is part of the Numismatic Library Series. It includes "updated pricing of all United States coins . . . new minted coins . . . a detailed 50 State quarter program chart . . . over 500 photographs. . . [and a] pricing system . . . [which] includes 7 grades." (Publisher's note)

738   Ceramic arts

Kovel, Ralph M.

Kovels' dictionary of marks: pottery and porcelain; by Ralph M. and Terry H. Kovel. 2nd ed; Crown 1995 278p il $17   **738**

1. Pottery -- Marks 2. Porcelain -- Marks

ISBN 0-517-70137-5

LC 95-3361

First published 1953 with title: Dictionary of marks¿pottery and porcelain

This is a guide to identification of American, English, and European pottery and porcelain including an "index of 5,000 marks, listed by prominent features and with a complete cross-reference {showing} at a glance (a) geographical location of mark, (b) factory or family name of manufacturer, (c) type of ware, (d) method of producing the mark on the object, (e) color of the mark, and (f) date when the mark was used. The authors have included a foreword, bibliography, index of manufacturers and a . . . guide to the often misunderstood marks of Delft, Sevres, and England 1842-1883." Publisher's note

Kovels' new dictionary of marks; {by} Ralph and Terry Kovel. Crown 1986 290p il $19   **738**

1. Pottery -- Marks 2. Porcelain -- Marks

ISBN 0-517-55914-5

LC 85-15146

Covering pottery and porcelain from 1850 to the present this volume is regarded as a complimentary volume to the one covering 1650 to 1850

738.1   Techniques, procedures, apparatus, equipment, materials

Burleson, Mark

The **ceramic** glaze handbook; materials, techniques, formulas. Lark Bks. 2001 144p il hardcover o.p. pa $24.95   **738.1**

1. Glazes 2. Pottery

ISBN 1-57990-439-4 pa

LC 00-63486

"Burleson covers glaze chemistry, application techniques, firing, and problem solving. Color photographs comparing fired samples are particularly good. A collection of formulas by other artists is categorized by type of clay body and firing temperature. Useful for studio potters and hobbyists." Libr J

Hamer, Frank

The **potter's** dictionary of materials and techniques; Frank and Janet Hamer. 5th ed; University of Pa. Press 2004 L 45.00 : CIP entry (Jun.)   **738.1**

1. Reference books 2. Pottery -- Dictionaries 3. Ceramics -- Dictionaries

ISBN 0-8122-3810-9

First published 1975 by Watson-Guptill

Articles in this "potter's reference include soda firing, paper clay, computer glaze calculations, and fuming. . . . Alphabetically arranged entries range in length from a brief paragraph or half-page . . . to longer essays on subjects such as formulas, health hazards, and cones. Subject matter ranges widely, covering all the processes and materials involved in pottery formation, decoration, and firing." Am Ref Books Annu, 1998 {entry for 4th edition}

Muller, Kristin

The **potter's** studio handbook; a start-to-finish guide to hand-built and wheel-thrown ceramics. Quarry Books 2007 192p il (Back yard series) pa $24.99 **738.1**

1. Pottery

ISBN 978-1-59253-373-2; 1-59253-373-6

LC 2007-16693

The author "guides beginners through advanced students in equipping a ceramic studio, handling the design, preparing the clay, constructing slab projects, throwing on a wheel, glazing, and firing. The 16 clay projects featured here include teapots, vases, and dinner plates. Readers can draw inspiration from the creative painting and underglazing examples, as well as the unusual firing techniques for color and texture." Libr J

Nelson, Glenn C.

★ **Ceramics** : a potter's handbook; [by] Glenn C. Nelson, Richard Burkett. 6th ed; Wadsworth/Thomson Learning 2002 439p il pa $90.95 **738.1**

1. Pottery 2. Ceramics

ISBN 0-03-028937-8

LC 2001-96329

First published 1960. Periodically revised

This manual for beginner to advanced potters presents forming and decorating techniques, body and glaze recipes, and sources for raw materials and equipment.

Includes bibliographical references

Otterbein, Kim

Polymer clay 101; [by] Angela Mabray and Kim Otterbein. Creative Pub. International 2011 192p il pa $18.95 **738.1**

1. Clay 2. Modeling

ISBN 978-1-58923-470-3

LC 2010-16772

"With the guidance of polymer clay artists Mabray and Otterbein, crafters can get a handle on all of the basics of working with this distinctive medium. The projects are the highlight here—the authors expect readers to learn by doing, and a variety of techniques, including Skinner blends, canes, snakes, mold making, and stamping, are outlined. The DVD features further step-by-step directions for many techniques." Libr J

Pavelka, Lisa

The **complete** book of polymer clay; step-by-step instructions, original projects, inspirational gallery. Taunton Press 2010 221p il pa $24.95 **738.1**

1. Clay 2. Modeling

ISBN 978-1-60085-128-5

LC 2009-42430

This book presents projects with complete instructions showing readers how to make pendants, curio boxes, a necklace and a bracelet.

Includes bibliographical references

738.4 Specific products and techniques of making them

Darty, Linda

The **art** of enameling; techniques, projects, inspiration. Lark Books 2004 176p il $24.95 **738.4**

1. Enamel and enameling

ISBN 1-579-90507-2

LC 2004-5540

This is an "introduction to enameling fundamentals with practice exercises for techniques such as cloisonné and champlevé. There are also a dozen jewelry projects by other artists. This is an excellent and beautifully illustrated summary of a difficult craft." Libr J

Includes bibliographical references

739.2 Work in precious metals

Faber, Toby

Faberge's eggs; the extraordinary story of the masterpieces that outlived an empire. Random House 2008 302p il $30 **739.2**

1. Artists 2. Emperors 3. Empresses 4. Artisans 5. Jewelers 6. Metalworkers

ISBN 978-1-4000-6550-9; 1-4000-6550-X

LC 2007-49635

"Faber moves beyond mere description and illustration as he traces the fascinating history and sociology of these turn-of-the-century status symbols." Booklist

Includes bibliographical references

739.27 Jewelry

Codina, Carles

The **complete** book of jewelry making. Lark Bks. 2000 160p il hardcover o.p. pa $19.95 **739.27**

1. Jewelry

ISBN 1-57990-188-3; 1-57990-304-5 pa

LC 00-42809

This book covers "the basics, from the ABCs of metallurgy to such complicated techniques as enameling and lacquering. . . . Most of the examples are contemporary, taken from European designers, and all blessed with great color photographs." Booklist

DeCoster, Marcia

★ **Marcia** DeCoster's beaded opulence; elegant jewelry projects with right angle weave. Lark Books 2009 128p il (Beadweaving master class) $24.95 **739.27**

1. Jewelry 2. Beadwork

ISBN 978-1-60059-292-8

LC 2008-50857

This book features jewelry projects using beading stitches with right-angle weave designs.

Gollberg, Joanna

★ The **art** & craft of making jewelry; a complete guide to essential techniques. Lark Books 2006 176p il (A Lark jewelry book) $27.95   **739.27**

1. Jewelry

ISBN 978-1-57990-570-5; 1-57990-570-6

LC 2005-34040

"This is an overview of contemporary jewelry-making techniques for studio artists. Individual chapters cover various aspects of metalworking, color addition, and the use of findings, with project instructions and color photographs of finished works by multiple artists supplementing the technical information and practice exercises. This beautifully illustrated book should find a place in public library collections needing additional material on jewelry making." Libr J

Haab, Sherri

The **art** of metal clay; techniques for creating jewelry and decorative objects. Rev. and expanded ed.; Watson-Guptill Publications 2010 160p il pa $24.99   **739.27**

1. Jewelry 2. Metalwork 3. Precious metal clay

ISBN 978-0-82309-932-0

LC 2009-43781

First published 2003

"An essential project book for anyone interested in learning to work with metal clay. . . . [The projects included involve] bronze and copper metal clays, etching, and enameling. An included DVD has additional projects." Libr J

Miller, Judith

Miller's costume jewelry. Miller's 2010 256p il $34.99   **739.27**

1. Jewelry

ISBN 978-1-84533-563-2

"The highly informative and entertaining introduction highlights the rise and continued use of costume jewelry from ancient times to the present and features many of the influences that make vintage costume jewelry so popular. The book's remainder is divided into four sections focusing on major designers, classic designers, galleries (special collections), and designers to watch. . . . This delightful book will captivate costume jewelry enthusiasts." Libr J

Young, Anastasia

The **workbench** guide to jewelry techniques. Interweave Press LLC 2009 320p il $34.95   **739.27**

1. Jewelry

ISBN 978-1-59668-169-9

LC 2009-41385

This is a "reference guide for all jewelers, amateur or professional. Includes extensive photographic illustrations of virtually all techniques needed to create quality jewelry. Also has an excellent chapter on design, and additional sections on photographing, exhibiting, marketing, and selling work." Libr J

Includes bibliographical references

740   Graphic arts

Eskilson, Stephen J.

Graphic design; a new history. [by] Stephen J. Eskilson. Yale University Press 2011 464 p. il (cloth : alk. paper) $65.00   **740**

1. Graphic arts -- History 2. Commerical art -- History 3. Commercial art -- History

ISBN 0300172605; 9780300172607

LC 2011025963

This book on "the history of graphic design explores its evolution from the 19th century to the present day. Author Stephen J. Eskilson demonstrates how a new era began for design arts under the influence of Victorian reformers, tracing the emergence of modernist design styles in the early 20th century, and examining the wartime politicization of regional styles." (Publisher's note)

The author focuses "on the evolution of graphic design since the 19th century as well as on what recent developments in the field of information technology mean for today's designers. . . . The result is an effective description of the political effects of design (e.g., strategies used by illustrators of war posters) and countercultural influences (e.g., drugs and graffiti) supported beautifully by 400-plus large color reproductions." Libr J

Includes bibliographical references and index

741   Drawing and drawings

Barnet, Will

Will Barnet; a sketchbook 1932-1934. with an essay by Robert C. Morgan. George Braziller 2008 90p il $49.95   **741**

1. Figure drawing

ISBN 978-0-807-61597-3; 0-807-61598-6

LC 2008-22376

"Eight decades of American artist Barnet's work have reflected trends from social realism to abstract formalism in prints, drawing, and paintings. Published here is a recently uncovered collection of sketches figurative in their style. Vibrant yet precise, these were executed en plein air in the early 1930s while Barnet was a student at the Art Students League in Manhattan. The drawings evoke the life and vitality of city dwellers in summertime, enjoying New York's Central Park as a communal backyard. The 36 pen-and-ink drawings portray young lovers, sailors and their girlfriends, and mothers with children." Libr J

Includes bibliographical references.

Beever, Julian

Pavement chalk artist; the three-dimensional drawings of Julian Beever. Firefly Books 2010 110p il $29.95   **741**

1. Street art

ISBN 978-1-55407-661-1

"With these 58 chalk drawings, street artist Beever takes us around the world—to Brussels, Istanbul, London, Tokyo—to the public squares and piazzas where he creates breathtaking colored chalk anamorphic drawings—pictures rendered in perspective and appearing three-dimensional when viewed from a particular angle. The photographs of his immense paintings leap off the page, creating a whimsical wonderland of giant insects and animals, superheroes, gaping chasms, and subterranean waterways that ape and then distort reality. . . . Beever's mastery and unbridled humor are on full display in these dazzling drawings, each accompanied by a description that details artistic techniques, discusses challenges the artist faced, and offers an inside look into his process." Publ Wkly

Johnston, Daniel

Daniel Johnston; with contributions by Jad Fair, Phillippe Vergne, Harvey Pekar; and an interview with Daniel Johnston. Rizzoli 2009 147p il $45 **741**

ISBN 978-0-8478-3230-9; 0-8478-3230-0

LC 2008-933726

This book features "more than 80 of [Johnston's] pieces, all saturated in color and trippy in content. There are chiseled superheroes, flying ducks, multi-eyed monsters, and a variety of demons floating across the pages. The only thing that punctuates the book are occasional pull-quotes from Johnston, as well as short essays from art curator Philippe Vergne, musician Jad Fair, and comic book writer Harvey Pekar. And unlike some other musicians who pursue success in the visual arts, Johnston's already got the respect of the art world establishment; his work was featured in the 2006 Whitney Biennial. No doubt that with this book, he'll win over the respect of his music fans." Nylon

Salisbury, Martin

Children's Picturebooks; The Art of Visual Storytelling. by Martin Salisbury. Chronicle Books Llc 2012 **741**

1. Illustration of books 2. Picture books for children
ISBN 185669738X; 9781856697385

Author Martin Salisbury's "book covers the key stages of conceiving a narrative, creating a visual language, and developing storyboards and design of a picturebook. There are interviews with leading children's picturebook illustrators, as well as case studies of their work. The picturebooks and artists featured hail from Australia, Belgium, Cuba, France, Germany, Hungary, Ireland, Italy, Japan, Norway, Poland, Portugal, Russia, Singapore, South Korea, Spain, Taiwan, the UK, and the USA." (Publisher's note)

Satrapi, Marjane

Embroideries. Pantheon Books 2005 134p il $16.95 **741**

1. Graphic novels 2. Iran -- Graphic novels 3. Women -- Iran -- Graphic novels
ISBN 0-375-42305-2

LC 2004-58660

"Discussions of sex are frank and explicit and laced with high humor. . . . Satrapi's simple black-and-white cartooning style is tremendously effective, expertly portraying emotional nuances with just a few lines." Libr J

741.092   Biography

Bair, Deirdre

Saul Steinberg; a biography. Deirdre Bair. Nan A.Talese/Doubleday 2012 732 p. illustrations (some color) (alk. paper) $40 **741.092**

1. Artists -- United States -- Biography
ISBN 038552448X; 9780385524483

LC 2011050601

This book by Deirdre Bair is a "biography of Saul Steinberg, one of The New Yorker's most iconic artists. . . . Born in Romania, Steinberg was educated in Milan and was already famous for his satirical drawings when World War II forced him to immigrate to the United States. . . . His wife was the artist Hedda Sterne, . . . but his truly great love was the United States, where he traveled extensively by bus, train, and car, drawing, observing, and writing." (Publisher's note)

Includes bibliographical references and index

Lester, Toby

Da Vinci's ghost; genius, obsession, and how Leonardo created the world in his own image. Toby Lester. 1st ed.; Free Press 2012 275 p. **741.092**

1. Art criticism 2. Art -- History 3. Figure drawing
ISBN 1439189234; 9781439189238; 9781439189252 (ebook)

LC 2011027966

This book tells "the story of Vitruvian Man: Leonardo da Vinci's famous drawing of a man in a circle and a square. Deployed today to celebrate subjects as various as the nature of genius, the beauty of the human form, and the universality of the human spirit . . . it has become the world's most famous cultural icon, yet almost nobody knows anything about it. . . . Toby Lester weaves together a century-spanning saga of people and ideas. Assembled here is an eclectic cast of . . . characters . . . and, of course, in the starring role, Leonardo himself—whose ghost Lester resurrects in the . . . unfamiliar context of his own times." (Publisher's note)

Includes bibliographical references.

Genius, obsession, and how Leonardo created the world in his own image

741.2   Techniques, procedures, apparatus, equipment, materials

Birch, Helen (Artist)

Freehand; sketching tips and tricks drawn from art. by Helen Birch. Chronicle Books 2013 224 p. color illustrations (pbk.) $18.95 **741.2**

1. Composition (Art) 2. Drawing -- Technique 3. Creation (Literary, artistic, etc.)
ISBN 1452119775; 9781452119779

LC 2013036430

This book, written and illustrated by Helen Birch, "breaks down basic drawing techniques . . . and reveals their practical application in dazzling examples by today's coolest artists. Over 200 innovative works of art demonstrate all the fundamentals--line, tone, composition, texture, and more--and are presented alongside friendly text explaining the simple techniques used to achieve each stylish effect." (Publisher's note)

"Employing the formula of examples + explanations = inspiration, journalist and artist Birch presents the work of dozens of practicing contemporary artists, highlighting prominent techniques so that the reader can emulate and build upon them. Illustrations can be found on nearly every page, including many close-up views that break down for the reader what is happening in the more elaborate drawings." LJ

Includes bibliographical references and index

Box, Richard

Drawing step-by-step; [by] Richard Box . . . [et al.] Search Press 2009 144p il (Step-by-step series) pa $19.95   **741.2**

1. Drawing -- Technique

ISBN 978-1-84448-439-3

Based on the following books: Basic drawing techniques by Richard Box (2000); Water soluble pencils by Csrole Massey (2001); Drawing landscapes by Ronald Swanwick (2001); Drawing trees by Denis John-Naylor (2004); Drawing pets by Sally Michel (2005)

"This series title is gathered from five previous Search Press books. It features a wide variety of realistic styles and a number of media, including graphite, colored pencils, charcoal, chalks, pastels, water-soluble pencils, and pens." Libr J

Edwards, Betty

Drawing on the Right Side of the Brain; A Course in Enhancing Creativity & Artistic Confidence. Betty Edwards. 4th ed. Tarcher/Penguin 2012 xxxiii, 284 p.p ill. (hbk.) $32.95; (pbk.) $19.95; (deluxe) $29.95; (hbk.) $32.95; (pbk.) $19.95; (deluxe) $29.95   **741.2**

1. Laterality 2. Drawing -- Technique 3. Visual perception 4. Cerebral dominance

ISBN 1585429198; 1585429201; 158542921X; 9781585429196; 9781585429202; 9781585429219

LC 2012001232

"This new edition of the hugely popular and influential drawing manual first published over 30 years ago incorporates new findings from neuroscience, like the discovery of brain plasticity, together with the tried-and-true exercises included in past editions." LJ

Includes bibliographical references (p. 270-274) and index

Kaupelis, Robert

Experimental drawing; 30th anniversary ed.; Watson-Guptill 2010 192p il pa $22.99   **741.2**

1. Drawing -- Technique

ISBN 978-0-8230-1622-8; 0-8230-1622-6

LC 2009-931354

First published 1980

The author "shares the tutorials that he used with his students, offering illustrations of drawings and paintings from old masters to contemporary artists (and even some outstanding works from his students) to explain techniques. . . . [It covers topics ranging] from creating form through contour drawings to drawing with new technology." Publisher's note

"This classic work is a perfect next step for artists who have mastered the basics." Libr J

Includes bibliographical references

Lawlor, Veronica

One drawing a day; a 6-week course exploring creativity with illustration and mixed media. Quarry Books 2011 128p il pa $22.99   **741.2**

1. Drawing -- Technique

ISBN 978-1-59253-724-2; 1-59253-724-3

"Each spread in the book features a . . . drawing by one of 8 professional illustrators, with a description and comments by the illustrator as well as a companion exercise. Each exercise includes suggestions for various mediums or mixed-media solutions, advice on how to approach and execute the drawing, as well as professional tips. The book also includes exercises designed to spark new ideas and increase creativity." Publisher's note

Micklewright, Keith

★ **Drawing** : mastering the language of visual expression. Harry N. Abrams 2005 168p il (Abrams studio) pa $29.95   **741.2**

1. Drawing -- Technique

ISBN 0-8109-9238-8

LC 2005-5862

"Using examples of master artists such as Ingres and Michelangelo as well as more contemporary work of Cezanne, Hockney, and others, different aspects of drawing are examined. Each chapter ends with 'Ideas to Explore,' in which the reader is given suggestions for practice. . . . This book is valuable for those learning the theory behind the elements of drawing and for those looking for practical instruction." Voice Youth Advocates

Includes bibliographical references

Price, Maggie

Painting with pastels; easy techniques to master the medium. North Light Books 2007 128p il pa $24.99   **741.2**

1. Pastel drawing

ISBN 978-1-58180-819-3; 1-58180-819-4

LC 2006-029048

"This book shows the reader . . . [how] to paint with pastels, from materials and techniques to painting from photographs. . . . Hand-in photos show how to hold and apply the pastel, and the twenty-two step-by-step demonstrations cover . . . preparing your surface, underpainting, figure drawing and more." Publisher's note

741.5   Cartoons, graphic novels, caricatures, comics

101 top tips from professional manga artists; Sonia Leong, Hayden Scott Baron. Barrons Educational Series, Inc. 2013 176 p. $22.99   **741.5**

1. Japanese art 2. Drawing -- Technique 3. Manga -- Study and teaching

ISBN 1438002068; 9781438002064

LC 2012948428

This book, by Sonia Leong and Hayden Scott Baron, focuses on the Japanese drawing known as manga. "With additional insights from a select group of fellow professionals, this illustration-packed book covers all aspects of manga art, presenting advice and instruction on . . . everything an illustrator needs to know in order to create successful manga art for a variety of media." (Publisher's note)

"Freelance comic artist and illustrator Leong and several contributing artists provide over 100 tips grouped and organized around basic topics, highlighting key aspects of manga such as character design, backgrounds, props, software and media, and even practices of successful professionals." LJ

Abel, Jessica

Drawing words & writing pictures; making comics: from manga, graphic novels, and beyond. [by] Jessica Abel & Matt Madden. First Second Books 2008 xxi, 282 p.p il $34.99   **741.5**
1. Drawing -- Technique 2. Cartooning -- Technique 3. Graphic novels -- Authorship 4. Comic books, strips, etc. -- Authorship
ISBN 1596431318; 9781596431317
LC 2007044125
Authors Jessica Abel and Matt Madden present "a course on comic creation -- for college classes or for independent study -- that centers on storytelling and concludes with making a finished comic. With chapters on lettering, story structure, and panel layout, the fifteen lessons offered -- each complete with homework, extra credit activities and supplementary reading suggestions -- provide a solid introduction for people interested in making their own comics." (Publisher's note)

This "book offers step-by-step entry into a complicated series of skills in a nonscary and approachable way." Libr J

Includes bibliographical references (p. 261-265) and index

Mastering comics; drawing words & writing pictures continued. by Jessica Abel and Matt Madden. 1st ed. First Second 2012 xvii, 318 p.p chiefly ill. (some col.) (hardcover) $34.99   **741.5**
1. Drawing 2. Cartoonists 3. Cartooning -- Technique 4. Comic books, strips, etc. -- Technique
ISBN 1596436174; 9781596436176
LC 2011037023
Jessica Abel's book "Mastering Comics," written with her husband Matt Madden, is a "course of study for the budding cartoonist. Covering advanced topics such as story composition, coloring, and file formatting, [the book] is a vital companion to the introductory content of the first volume" entitled "Drawing Words & Writing Pictures." (Publisher's note)

An **anthology** of graphic fiction, cartoons & true stories, vol. 2; edited by Ivan Brunetti. Yale University Press 2008 400p il $28   **741.5**
1. American wit and humor 2. Comic books, strips, etc.
ISBN 978-0-300-12671-6; 0-300-12671-9
"Brunetti's second collection of his favorite cartoonists' work is even better than the first—more far-ranging, more personal and eccentric. Clearly a tour of one person's singular tastes, it's arranged in a stream-of-consciousness 'oh,

and you have to see this one' sort of way: work by 80-odd cartoonists, mostly from the past few decades, but also incorporating some early-1900s comic strips, a 1940s-vintage Fletcher Hanks story and several circa 1950 Harvey Kurtzman pieces as well as a smattering of previously unpublished gems." Publ Wkly

An **Anthology** of graphic fiction, cartoons, and true stories; edited by Ivan Brunetti. Yale University Press 2006 400p il $28   **741.5**
1. American wit and humor 2. Comic books, strips, etc.
ISBN 978-0-300-11170-5; 0-300-11170-3
LC 2006-14095
Brunetti presents "an overview of the art-comics movement, complete with a handful of the classic newspaper strips that informed today's creators. He finds room for such established veterans as R. Crumb, Lynda Barry, Gilbert and Jaime Hernandez, Daniel Clowes, Gary Panter, and Chester Brown as well as many less-familiar creators. . . . Brunetti admits that his selection criteria are highly personal, but as a cartoonist himself, whose work combines a socially transgressive spirit and impressive formal capability, his idiosyncratic approach is based in professional expertise. If his choices are sometimes arguable, his iconoclasm makes the book livelier and less predictable than such anthologies are wont to be." Booklist

Barry, Lynda

What it is. Drawn & Quarterly 2008 209p il $24.95   **741.5**
1. Authorship -- Graphic novels 2. Creative writing -- Graphic novels
ISBN 978-1-897299-35-7; 1-897299-35-4
LC c2007-9047319
Independent cartoonist Lynda Barry presents an unconventional book that encourages its readers to write by using her colorful art and asking questions such as "How are monsters different? And how are they the same?" "Can/Do images exist without thinking?" "What is the difference between lying and pretending?" Each question appears with illustrated writing prompts and Barry's own ruminations on the topics. It's a workbook of sorts, but it also exists as a book to be read for itself.

"Every so often a book comes along that surpasses expectations, taking readers on an inspirational voyage that they don't want to leave. This is one such book." SLJ

Batman unauthorized; vigilantes, jokers, and heroes in Gotham City. edited by Dennis O'Neil. Benbella Books, Inc. 2008 219p il (Smart pop series) $17.95   **741.5**
1. Graphic novels 2. Batman (Fictional character) 3. Comic books, strips, etc. -- History and criticism
ISBN 978-1-93377130-4; 1-933771-30-5
LC 2007-46504
Former Batman comics editor and comic book writer O'Neil edits this collection of essays about Batman and his world, written by comics writers, magazine editors, and others. Topics include the cost of being Batman, calculated to the last dollar; why Batman is the most American of superheroes; whether Bruce Wayne might be mentally ill; why Batman needs Robin more than Robin needs Batman; why

Arkham Asylum is doing more harm than good for Gotham City; why Batman works better when his world remains closer to reality; and more.

Includes bibliographical references

Beatty, Scott

★ The **DC** Comics encyclopedia; the definitive guide to the characters of the DC universe. text by Scott Beatty . . . [et al.]; updated text by Dan Wallace. Updated and expanded; DK Pub. 2008 399p il $40   **741.5**

  1. Reference books 2. DC Comics Group 3. Comic books, strips, etc. -- Encyclopedias

ISBN 978-0-7566-4119-1; 0-7566-4119-5

LC 2008-300609

First published 2004

The authors "meticulously profile 1000 DC heroes and villains created since DC's 1935 founding. The entries are organized alphabetically, by character name, while introductory insets consistently detail first appearance, hero/villain status, physical statistics, and special powers. A genuinely essential DC character reference." Libr J

Bechdel, Alison

★ **Are** you my mother? a comic drama. Alison Bechdel. Houghton Mifflin Harcourt 2012 286 p.   **741.5**

  1. Cartoonists -- Biography 2. Autobiographical graphic novels 3. Mother-daughter relationship -- Graphic novels 4. Cartoonists -- United States -- Comic books, strips, etc

ISBN 0618982507; 9780618982509

LC 2012010582

In this book, "[Alison] Bechdel not only searches for keys to [her relationship with her mother] but perhaps even for surrogate mothers, through therapy, girlfriends and the writing of Virginia Woolf, Adrienne Rich, Alice Miller and others. Yet the primary inspiration in this literary memoir is psychoanalyst Donald Winnicott, whose life and work Bechdel explores along with her own." (Kirkus Reviews)

Fun home; a family tragicomic. Houghton Mifflin 2006 232p il $19.95   **741.5**

  1. Artists 2. Authors 3. Novelists 4. Cartoonists 5. Graphic novels 6. Autobiographical graphic novels 7. Essayists 8. Comic book writers 9. Biography, Individual

ISBN 0-618-47794-2; 978-0-618-47794-4

LC 2005-30304

Time Magazine Book of the Year for 2006

This is a memoir in graphic novel format about the author's "childhood, her father's death and their shared homosexuality. . . . The death was deemed an accident—a truck hit [Mr. Bechdel] as he crossed a road with an armful of garden brush—but Ms. Bechdel suspects suicide." (N Y Times (Late N Y Ed))

This "is one of the very best graphic novels ever." Booklist

Beland, Tom

True story swear to God archives, vol. 1. Image Comics 2008 528p il pa $19.99   **741.5**

  1. Cartoonists 2. Graphic novels 3. Romance graphic novels 4. Autobiographical graphic novels

ISBN 978-1-58240-881-1

They met at a bus stop at Disneyworld, by chance: he was a cartoonist from Napa, California, and she was a radio personality from Puerto Rico. Their chance meeting blossomed into a romance that survived a long-distance separation, a Category 5 hurricane, his leaving home to move to a new world. Tom Beland writes candidly about the ups and downs of his relationship with Lily, with his family, and all the slings and arrows of life one has to deal with daily. He originally self-published these comics, and they were collected in several trade paperbacks from AiT/PlanetLar. The book includes occasional harsh language (including s-bombs and f-bombs), sexual situations, and frank talk about sex.

Brunetti, Ivan

Cartooning; philosophy and practice. Yale University Press 2011 77p il pa $13   **741.5**

  1. Cartooning -- Technique

ISBN 978-0-300-17099-3; 0-300-17099-8

LC 2010-940419

"The first half of the book is devoted to the basic terminology and materials of the medium, while the second half is devoted to an intensive and full 15-week comics course. The course should make the non-draftsperson comfortable with drawing and progressively able to translate the panels of the story from head to page. It also breaks down the drawing process so that anyone can draw a couple characters without having to fret about making realistic, Marvel-style, detailed renderings or obsessive crosshatch shading. Cartooning is set to become the next de-facto book for breaking into the comics medium." Molossus

Includes bibliographical references

Chast, Roz

★ **Can't** We Talk About Something More Pleasant? A Memoir. Roz Chast. St. Martin's Press 2014 240 p. color illustrations $28   **741.5**

  1. Aging parents

ISBN 1608198065; 9781608198061

In this memoir, author Roz Chast "brings her signature wit to the topic of aging parents. Spanning the last several years of their lives and told through four-color cartoons, family photos, and documents, and a narrative as rife with laughs as it is with tears, Chast's memoir is both comfort and comic relief for anyone experiencing the life-altering loss of elderly parents." (Publisher's note)

Chast "brings her parents and herself to life in the form of her characteristic scratchy-lined, emotionally expressive characters, making the story both more personal and universal." Pub Wkly

★ The **complete** cartoons of the New Yorker; edited by Robert Mankoff; foreword by David Remnick. Black Dog & Leventhal 2004 655p il $60 **741.5**

  1. Cartoons and caricatures 2. New Yorker (Periodical) 3. New Yorker Magazine, Inc.

ISBN 1-579-12322-8

LC 2004-46371

"Issued as part of the New Yorker's eightieth anniversary celebration, this . . . volume collects, in two formats, the cartoons that have appeared in the pages of that magazine over the course of its distinguished publishing history. . . . The book itself gathers 2,500 of the most representative cartoons for display, but two accompanying CDs contain all the cartoons (68,647, to be exact) ever published in the magazine. Arrangement is by chapter, with each covering a decade of the New Yorker's existence. . . . A testament—a tribute—to the great magazine but also an absolutely special way to spend quality time." Booklist

Critical survey of graphic novels; heroes & superheroes. editors, Bart H. Beaty, Stephen Weiner. Salem Press 2012 2 v. xvi, 818 p.p (set) $295 **741.5**
1. Superheroes -- Psychology 2. Heroes and heroines in literature 3. Graphic novels -- History and criticism 4. American literature -- History and criticism 5. Graphic novels 6. Heroes in literature 7. Comic books, strips, etc 8. Superheroes in literature
ISBN 1587658658; 9781587658655; 9781587658662; 9781587658679
LC 2011046278
This reference book, edited by Bart H. Beaty and Stephen Weiner, offers "insight into over 130 of the most popular and studied graphic novels. . . . Essays look beyond the 'pop culture' aspects of the medium to show the wide range of literary themes and artistic styles used to convey beliefs and conflicts, some harking back to ancient times." (Publisher's note)
Includes bibliographical references and index.

Daniels, Les
Marvel; five fabulous decades of the world's greatest comics. introduction by Stan Lee. Abrams 1991 287p il hardcover o.p. pa $26.95 **741.5**
1. Comic books, strips, etc. 2. Marvel comics (New York, N.Y.)
ISBN 0-8109-2566-4
LC 91-8783
"Daniels' behind-the-scenes look at the development of Marvel, his profiles of the line's foremost heroes and villains, and biographies of leading writers and artists will entice . . . young fans. . . . But the book's strongest appeal lies in the generous samplings of artwork spread throughout." Booklist

De Haven, Tom
Our hero; Superman on Earth. Yale University Press 2010 224p il $24 **741.5**
1. Superman (Fictitious character)
ISBN 978-0-300-11817-9; 0-300-11817-1
LC 2009-18206
De Haven "offers an extended meditation on the role the flying Krypton orphan has played in comic books, cartoons, movies, and TV. Our Hero: Superman on Earth is part history — a summary of the ways Superman creators Jerry Siegel and Joe Shuster were ripped off will break your heart — and part philosophy. De Haven contends that since his creation in 1938, Superman has seen many reinventions, but he always represents a uniquely American desire: to have 'the freedom to act in ways that are satisfying to him. It makes him feel good, dammit.' This book will make you feel the same." Entertainment Wkly
Includes bibliographical references

Delisle, Guy
★ **Pyongyang** : a journey in North Korea; translated by Helge Dascher. Drawn & Quarterly 2005 176p il map hardcover o.p. pa $14.95 **741.5**
1. Graphic novels 2. Korea (North) -- Graphic novels
ISBN 1-896597-89-0; 1-897299-21-4 pa
This book "documents the two months French animator Delisle spent overseeing cartoon production in North Korea. . . . He records everything from the omnipresent statues and portraits of dictators Kim Il-Sung and Kim Jong-Il to the brainwashed obedience of the citizens." Booklist
"Pyongyang will appeal to multiple audiences: current events buffs, Persepolis fans and those who just love a good yarn." Publ Wkly

Eisner, Will, 1917-2005
★ **Comics** and sequential art; principles and practices from the legendary cartoonist. W.W. Norton 2008 175p il (The Will Eisner library) pa $22.95 **741.5**
1. Drawing -- Technique 2. Graphic novels -- Authorship 3. Comic books, strips, etc. -- Authorship
ISBN 978-0-393-33126-4; 0-393-33126-1
LC 2008-20042
First published 1985 by Poorhouse Press
This book offers the author's ideas, theories, and advice about graphic storytelling and the uses to which the comic book art form can be applied.

Glidden, Sarah
How to understand Israel in 60 days or less. Vertigo/DC Comics 2010 206p il map $24.99 **741.5**
1. Graphic novels 2. Israel-Arab conflicts -- Graphic novels 3. Israel -- Description and travel -- Graphic novels
ISBN 978-1-4012-2233-8
The author, "a progressive American Jew who is sharply critical of Israeli policies vis-à-vis the Occupied Territories, went on an all-expense-paid 'birthright' trip to Israel in an attempt to discover some grand truths at the heart of the Arab-Israeli conflict. This graphic memoir tells the . . . story of her utter failure to do so." Publ Wkly
"Glidden's soft, watercolor palette and realistic art complement without overshadowing this thoughtful exploration of the role that cultural heritage plays in the search for personal identity." SLJ

Goldstein, Nancy
Jackie Ormes; the first African American woman cartoonist. University of Michigan Press 2008 225p il $35 **741.5**
1. Cartoonists 2. African American women -- Biography
ISBN 978-0-472-11624-9; 0-472-11624-X
LC 2007-35395
This book covers the life and career of Jackie Ormes, who was the first African American woman cartoonist. She wrote and drew comic strips that ran in Black newspapers such as the Pittsburgh Courier and the Chicago Defender. She was part of the Black elite in Chicago and knew other luminaries such as singer Eartha Kitt and musician/composer/conductor Duke Ellington. She was also investigated by the FBI because of her Leftist political ideas and activi-

ties. While she did such things as create Torchy paper dolls, based on her beautiful and sexy cartoon character, and cute Patty-Jo dolls, Ormes also used her comic strips to put forth her political views. This book reproduces some of her cartoons and comic strips, in both black and white and in color.

Includes bibliographical references

Guibert, Emmanuel

Alan's war. First Second 2008 304p il pa $24   **741.5**

1. Soldiers 2. Veterans 3. Graphic novels 4. Biographical graphic novels 5. Soldiers -- Graphic novels 6. World War, 1939-1945 -- Graphic novels

ISBN 978-1-59643-096-9; 1-59643-096-6

LC 2007-46190

French cartoonist Guibert met and became friends with Alan Cope and interviewed him at length to create this book. It recreates Cope's memories of being an eighteen-year-old G.I. during World War II. Unlike the war movies that focus on battles, this book focuses on more everyday, mundane memories of the day-to-day life of a soldier. Cope frankly describes a bout with crabs (genital lice), matter-of-factly tells of casual man-to-man sexual encounters among the soldiers, and gives the reader a feel for what happened back then. He also talks about postwar relationships and travels.

This is a "poignant and frank graphic memoir of young soldier who was told to serve his country in WWII and how it changed him forever. . . . Cope and Guibert forge a story that resonates with humanity." Publ Wkly

★ The **photographer**; [by] Emmanuel Guibert, Didier Lefèvre and Frédéric Lemercier; translated by Alexis Siegel. First Second 2009 267p il map pa $29.95   **741.5**

1. Graphic novels 2. Photojournalism -- Graphic novels 3. Médecins Sans Frontières (Organization) -- Graphic novels 4. Afghanistan -- History -- Soviet occupation, 1979-1989 -- Graphic novels

ISBN 978-1-59643-375-5; 1-59643-375-2

"Originally published as three volumes in France from 2003 to 2006, this graphic novel follows photojournalist Didier Lefèvre during his three months in Pakistan and Afghanistan in 1986 as he documented the medical missions of Doctors without Borders. . . . The graphic novel combines traditional comic art with some of the four thousand photographs Lefevre shot while in Afghanistan. . . . Many images will stay with readers as both horrifying and glorious. The Afghan children being treated for burns, bullet wounds, and shrapnel are page by page next to the beauty of the Afghan mountainous landscapes. . . . [This book] has a powerful message and images of a part of the world that should be discussed more often." Voice Youth Advocates

Hajdu, David

The **ten** -cent plague; the great comic-book scare and how it changed America. Farrar, Straus and Giroux 2008 434p $26   **741.5**

1. Comic books, strips, etc.

ISBN 978-0-374-18767-5; 0-374-18767-3

LC 2007-25024

"Hajdu offers captivating insights into America's early bluestocking-versus-blue-collar culture wars, and the later

tensions between wary parents and the first generation of kids with the buying power to mold mass entertainment." Village Voice

Includes bibliographical references

Hart, Christopher

Cartooning for the beginner. Watson-Guptill 2000 144p il pa $19.95   **741.5**

1. Cartooning -- Technique

ISBN 0-8230-0586-0

LC 00-101905

This guide to cartooning techniques "covers the world of cartoon animals, animation, and 'edgy 'toons.'" Libr J

Hirschfeld, Al

Hirschfeld on line. Applause Theatre Bk. Pubs. 1998 343p $59.95   **741.5**

1. Entertainers 2. Cartoons and caricatures

ISBN 1-55783-356-7

Hirschfeld "is the irreplaceable M.V.P. of the New York theatre world, and this compendium of his drawings amounts to a historic work of droll, generous-minded theatre criticism. The artist himself has annotated the drawings, which cover a range of the performing arts . . . and his comments are as swooping and witty as his lines." New Yorker

Holtz, Allan

American newspaper comics; an encyclopedic reference guide. Allan Holtz. The University of Michigan Press 2011 624 p. (cloth : alk. paper) $150   **741.5**

1. Cartooning 2. Cartoons and caricatures 3. Newspapers -- Sections, columns, etc. -- Comics 4. Comic books, strips, etc. -- United States -- History and criticism

ISBN 0472117564; 9780472117567

LC 2010033752

The author Allan Holtz focuses on the history of the newspaper comic strip, discussing "the evolution of newspaper cartoon features and . . . [correcting] misinformation that has circulated for years in other references. . . . [The book includes] start and end dates of features, their format, frequency, creators, and distribution companies. . . . [It also] includes a CD with samples of more than 2,000 cartoon features." (Publisher's note)

The **Horror!** The horror! comic books the government didn't want you to read! selected, edited, and with commentary by Jim Trombetta; introduction by R. L. Stine. Abrams ComicArts 2010 304p il $29.95   **741.5**

1. Comic books, strips, etc. 2. Censorship -- United States 3. Horror comic books, strips, etc.

ISBN 0810955954; 9780810955950

LC 2008-54346

The Horror! The Horror! examines "the pre-Code horror comics of the 1950s." (Publisher's note). Index.

"Bonus DVD--Confidential File, a rare 25-minute TV show that first aired on October 9, 1955, about the 'evils 'of comic books and their effect on juvenile delinquency is included with the book." Publisher's note

Includes bibliographical references (p. 302) and index.

Howe, Sean

Marvel Comics; the untold story. by Sean Howe. Harper 2012 485 p. (hardback) $26.99   **741.5**
1. Superhero comic books, strips, etc. 2. Comic books, strips, etc. -- History 3. United States -- History -- 20th century 4. Marvel Comics Group 5. COMICS & GRAPHIC NOVELS -- Superheroes 6. HISTORY -- United States -- 20th Century 7. Comic books, strips, etc. -- United States -- History and criticism
ISBN 0061992100; 9780061992100

LC 2012015058

Author Sean Howe presents a book on the history of Marvel Comics. Howe "reveals the outsized personalities behind the scenes, including Martin Goodman, the self-made publisher who forayed into comics after a get-rich-quick tip in 1939 . . . and Jack Kirby, the World War II veteran who'd co-created Captain America in 1940 and, twenty years later, developed with Lee the bulk of the company's marquee characters in a three-year frenzy of creativity that would be the grounds for future legal battles and endless debates." (Publisher's note)

Includes bibliographical references and index

Howlett, Mike

The **weird** world of Eerie Publications; comic gore that warped millions of young minds. introduction by Stephen R. Bissett. Feral House 2010 xxv, 310p il $32.95   **741.5**
1. Comic books, strips, etc. 2. Eerie Publications (Firm)
ISBN 978-1-932595-87-1; 1-932595-87-2

"Mike Howlett resurrects both Eerie Publications, publisher of many of the post-pulp newsstand magazines, and the grotesque stories and images that filled adolescent minds a decade after the crackdown in 1954, when the Comics Code placed strict puritanical limits on the amount of gore, crime and sex in comic books. Former comic-book publishers took refuge in the unregulated realm of magazines. . . . This colorful book follows the evolution and devolution of these and other horror and novelty magazines and their artists. Even if you're not a fan of this genre, it is a curiously wonderful, weird and eerie tale of magazine history." N Y Times Book Rev

Humbug; [editor, Harvey Kurtzman; art, Jack Davis . . . [et al.]] Fantagraphics 2009 2v il set $60   **741.5**
1. American wit and humor 2. Comic books, strips, etc.
ISBN 978-1-56097-933-3; 1-56097-933-X

"MAD's early years have been justly lauded for their japing assault on postwar American culture, but this . . . two-volume boxed set reflects the history of comedy in the period after staff stars like Kurtzman jumped ship in 1956. . . . [Humbug's] 11 monthly issues published in 1957 and 1958 are all collected here." Publ Wkly

Isabella, Tony

1,000 comic books you must read. Krause Publications 2009 271p il $29.99   **741.5**
1. Best books 2. Comic books, strips, etc. -- Bibliography
ISBN 978-0-89689-921-6; 0-89689-921-7

Isabella "has the great fortune of not having to decide the thousand finest but rather the thousand that he finds compelling. This lends his hardcover a kaleidoscopic approach to deconstructing the evolution of the American comic rather than focusing on the creme de la creme alone. With its chapters predominantly broken up by decade ('The Fighting Forties,' 'The Fearful Fifties,' etc.), 1000 Comic Books provides short summaries (under 75 words) for each title as well as clear cover scans and creator/ publishing information. A plethora of obscure information is sprinkled through the book. . . . There is no discrimination of subject matter, and even the most ardent comic book reader is bound to learn something new." Cincinnati City Beat

Jacobson, Sidney

The **9** /11 report; a graphic adaptation. by Sid Jacobson and Ernie Colón; [with a foreword by Thomas H. Kean and Lee H. Hamilton] Hill and Wang 2006 133p il $30; pa $16.95   **741.5**
1. Graphic novels 2. September 11 terrorist attacks, 2001 -- Graphic novels
ISBN 0-8090-5738-7; 978-0-8090-5738-2; 0-8090-5739-5 pa; 978-0-8090-5739-9 pa

"The book aims to make . . . [The 9/11 Commission Report] more accessable to all readers and draw in young adults. . . . This graphic adaptation is an important and necessary part of any collection." Libr J

After 9/11: America's war on terror (2001-) Hill and Wang 2008 149p il map pa $16.95   **741.5**
1. Graphic novels 2. Terrorism -- Graphic novels 3. Iraq War, 2003- -- Graphic novels 4. United States -- Foreign relations -- Graphic novels 5. United States -- Politics and government -- Graphic novels
ISBN 978-0-8090-2370-7

LC 2008-13298

In 2006, longtime comic book veterans Jacobson and Colon adapted the 9/11 Commission's report into a graphic format that made it a readable, comprehensible work for teens and adults. Now they have used the comic book treatment to cover America's War on Terror since 2001, including the wars in Iraq and in Afghanistan, summarizing events and showing the major players throughout the years. Some images can be disturbing, such as the depiction of prisoner mistreatment at Abu Ghraib and other facilities, as well as depictions of the victims of sectarian violence.

Jones, Gerard

Men of tomorrow; geeks, gangsters and the birth of the comic book. Basic Books 2004 320p il $26; pa $15   **741.5**
1. Cartoonists 2. Comic books, strips, etc.
ISBN 0-465-03656-2; 0-465-03657-0 pa

LC 2004-9031

This book tells "the surprising story of the young Jewish misfits, hustlers and nerds who invented the superhero and the comic book industry. . . . Springing unheralded out of working-class Jewish immigrant neighborhoods in the depths of the Depression, these young men transformed an odd mix of geekdom, science fiction, and outsider yearnings into blue-eyed chisel-nosed crime-fighters and adventurers who quickly captured the mainstream imagination. . . . He chronicles how the comics sparked a frightened counterattack that nearly destroyed the industry in the 1950's and how later they surged back at an underground level, to inspire a new generation to transmute those long-ago fantasies into art, literature, blockbuster movies and graphic novels." Publisher's note

Kanfer, Stefan

Serious business; the art and commerce of animation in America from Betty Boop to Toy story. Da Capo Press 2000 256p il pa $17.50   741.5
1. Animated films
ISBN 0-306-80918-4; 978-0-306-80918-7
LC 98-50687

First published 1997 by Scribner
"As an art form, animation is magically irresistible; as a reflection of broader American popular culture, it is amazingly on target. . . . Kanfer here shows how the people, politics, prejudices, trends, and technologies of various eras have been so aptly reflected in each set of frames. . . . While Kanfer's humbly stated intention is to augment previous writings on the subject, his work should certainly join the ranks of important literature in the field." Libr J

Karp, Jesse

Graphic novels in your school library; Jesse Karp ; illustrated by Rush Kress. American Library Association 2012 xi, 146 p.p ill. (alk. paper) $50 741.5
1. School libraries 2. Graphic novels -- Bibliography 3. Libraries -- Collection development 4. Graphic novels 5. Graphic novels in education -- United States 6. Libraries -- Special collections -- Graphic novels 7. School libraries -- Collection development -- United States
ISBN 0838910890; 9780838910894
LC 2011026353

This book, by Jesse Karp, "takes a look at the term graphic novel, how the format has become entwined in our culture, and the ways in which graphic novels can be used in the library and in the classroom. . . . Karp . . . [i]ntroduces the history . . . and the conventions of the form, . . . [p]rovides annotated lists of core titles, [and] . . . [o]ffers lesson plans that use graphic novels . . . from life skills and dating to history." (Publisher's note)
Includes bibliographical references (p. 131-132) and index

Kitchen, Denis

The art of Harvey Kurtzman; the mad genius of comics. by Denis Kitchen and Paul Buhle; introduction by Art Spiegelman; designed by Kitchen, Lind & Associates. Abrams Comicarts 2009 241p il $40   741.5
1. Cartoonists 2. Cartoons and caricatures
ISBN 978-0-8109-7296-4; 0-8109-7296-4
LC 2008-04809

"Retrace the strands that led to a lot of current American satire — including The Simpsons, Saturday Night Live and The Daily Show — and sooner or later you end up at Harvey Kurtzman. A comic mastermind who created Mad Magazine and Playboy's 'Little Annie Fanny,' Kurtzman also happened to discover Robert Crumb and gave Gloria

Steinem her first job. . . . [This volume] explores the life and art of the famous satirist, weaving together the story of Kurtzman's career with a collection of the artist's images and illustrations." NPR

Kleist, Reinhard

★ Johnny Cash; I see a darkness: a graphic novel. [translated from the German edition by Michael Waaler] Abrams ComicArts 2009 221p il pa $17.95   741.5
1. Singers 2. Graphic novels 3. Country musicians 4. Biographical graphic novels 5. Songwriters 6. Country musicians -- Graphic novels
ISBN 978-0-8109-8463-9
LC 2010-279149

Original German edition, 2006
The author "presents a biography (with seemingly invented dialog that stays true to the facts) focusing on Cash's turning points: from his poor family's 1935 relocation to a New Deal-created cotton farming community, through his troubled first marriage, endless touring, the amphetamine abuse of his early musical career, and climaxing with a famous, highly charged 1968 concert at California's Folsom Prison. Kleist also dramatizes several of Cash's songs and relates the tragic story of Glen Sherley, a Folsom inmate who sent Cash a song he had written hoping Cash would play it in the show. The ruggedness of Kleist's black-and-white illustrations suits their subject, as the stark portrayal of Cash's withdrawal from drugs is inventive and harrowing. . . . This thoughtful and compelling portrait of a towering talent with a tortured soul is recommended for all teen and adult music fans." Libr J
Includes bibliographical references

Lee, Stan, 1922-

★ Stan Lee's How to draw comics; from the legendary co-creator of Spider-Man, the Incredible Hulk, Fantastic Four, X-Men, and Iron Man. Watson-Guptill Publication 2010 224p il pa $24.99 741.5
1. Drawing -- Technique 2. Comic books, strips, etc. -- Authorship
ISBN 978-0-8230-0083-8
LC 2010-5781

The author "includes chapters on creating comics with computer programs and online resources and how to get work in the 21st century. The book begins with a brief history of comics, then focuses on action-adventure style, romance, humor, horror, and Japanese manga. This is the one book anyone interested in drawing comics should own." Libr J
Includes bibliographical references

Lewis, John R., 1940-

★ March; Book One. John Lewis ; [co-written by] Andrew Aydin ; [art by] Nate Powell. Top Shelf Productions 2013 121 p.   741.5
1. African Americans -- Civil rights -- Graphic novels 2. Civil rights movements -- United States -- Comic books, strips, etc
ISBN 9781603093002
LC 2013218903

King Author Honor Book (2014)

This graphic novel, by U.S. congressman John Lewis, "in collaboration with co-writer Andrew Aydin and New York Times best-selling artist Nate Powell . . . spans John Lewis' youth in rural Alabama, his life-changing meeting with Martin Luther King, Jr., the birth of the Nashville Student Movement, and their battle to tear down segregation through nonviolent lunch counter sit-ins, building to a . . . climax on the steps of City Hall." (Publisher's note)

"This is superb visual storytelling that establishes a convincing, definitive record of a key eyewitness to significant social change." SLJ

★ **Masters** of American comics; essay by John Carlin; with contributions by Stanley Crouch . . . [et al.]; edited by John Carlin, Paul Karasik, and Brian Walker. Yale University Press 2005 316p il $45   741.5
    1. Cartoonists 2. Comic books, strips, etc.
    ISBN 0-300-11317-X
                      LC 2005-19449
This book focuses "on the 15 'Masters' of American comics, including George Herriman, Jack Kirby and R. Crumb. . . . Jules Feiffer, Pete Hamill and Matt Groening, among others, contribute essays on each of the artists." Publ Wkly

"Hundreds of color reproductions allow the ingenuity of the artists' work to speak for itself." New Yorker
    Includes bibliographical references

McCloud, Scott

★ **Making** comics; storytelling secrets of comics, manga, and graphic novels. HarperCollins 2006 264p il pa $22.95   741.5
    1. Graphic novels -- Drawing 2. Comic books, strips, etc. -- Authorship
    ISBN 0-06-078094-0; 978-0-06-078094-4
The author "explores practical matters, including comics devices such as panels, word balloons, and sound effects; facial expressions and body language; the creation of convincing and evocative settings; and the different tools artists can use for the job, from pencils to computers. He also delves into the framing of images in panels, the flow of panels on a page, and the relationships between words and pictures in comics. . . . This is thoughtful, fascinating, stimulating, potentially controversial, and inspiring." Libr J
    Includes bibliographical references

Reinventing comics; how imagination and technology are revolutionizing an art form. Paradox Press 2000 237p il pa $22.95   741.5
    1. Cartoons and caricatures 2. Comic books, strips, etc.
    ISBN 0-06-095350-0
                      LC 00-710457
The author maps out "'12 revolutions', which, he believes, need to take place for comics to survive and finally be recognized as a legitimate art form. The topics progress from the oldest of comic-related arguments (seeking respect) to the use of computer technology to renew and expand its audience. These brilliantly presented discussions concern comics as literature, comics as art, creators' rights, industry innovation, and public perception, among other topics." Libr J

Morrison, Grant

Supergods; what masked vigilantes, miraculous mutants, and a sun god from Smallville can teach us about being human. Spiegel & Grau 2011 444p il   741.5
    1. Superheroes 2. Comic books, strips, etc. 3. Heroes 4. Comic books, strips, etc. -- United States
    ISBN 1-4000-6912-2; 978-1-4000-6912-5
                      LC 2010053712
A graphic novelist presents a history of the superhero in American comic books and movies. Index.

Morrison chronicles the "rise, fall, rise, fall and rise again of comic-book superheroes, from Superman's auspicious beginning as a Depression-era symbol of the power of the individual to Wolverine's rise to prominence in a more morally ambiguous era." Kirkus
    Includes bibliographical references

My friend Dahmer; written & illustrated by Derf Backderf. Abrams ComicArts 2012 221 p.   741.5
    1. Comic books, strips, etc. 2. Friendship -- Graphic novels 3. High school -- Graphic novels 4. Autobiographical graphic novels
    ISBN 9781419702167
                      LC 2011285306
    Alex Award (2013)
This book is an "exploration of notorious serial killer Jeffrey Dahmer by his high-school classmate. . . . In this graphic novel, [Derf] Backderf interweaves his memories of Dahmer with additional information gleaned from news reports, public interviews, and the memories of other classmates and community members. The book traces Dahmer's progression from experimenting with roadkill to . . . his first human victim just post-high school." (Bulletin of the Center for Children's Books)

Nadel, Dan

Art in time; unknown comic book adventures 1940-1980. Abrams ComicArts 2010 301p il $40   741.5
    1. Comic books, strips, etc.
    ISBN 978-0-8109-8824-8; 0-8109-8824-0
                      LC 2009-31672
Nadel "rescues from oblivion an array of fascinatingly offbeat comics in a variety of genres (superhero, thriller, Western). In Art in Time, these meticulously reprinted full-length comic-book stories range from a terrifically sexy noir comic by Harry Lucey, 'The Cutie Killer Caper,' to Matt Fox's 'I Was a Vampire,' whose weirdly wooden art can be downright terrifying. Throughout, Nadel offers plenty of biographical details and brisk art criticism that make these riotous pages even more thrilling to rediscover." Entertainment Wkly
    Includes bibliographical references

Neufeld, Josh

A.D. New Orleans after the deluge. Pantheon Books 2009 193p il $24.95   741.5
    1. Graphic novels 2. New Orleans (La.) -- Graphic novels 3. Hurricane Katrina, 2005 -- Graphic novels
    ISBN 978-0-307-37814-9; 0-307-37814-4
                      LC 2008-55687

"Graphic artist Neufeld paints an emotive portrait of New Orleans during and after Hurricane Katrina, as seen through the eyes of seven of the city's citizens. The opening panels coalesce into a long cinematic pan, a thrumming set-up for the disaster. The half-page and quarter-page panels—satellite views of weather patterns and close inspections of neighborhoods—are crisp, and the two-page spreads are softly focused. . . . Neufeld's words and images are commensurable and rhythmic, and the vernacular is sharp. Bristling with attitude and pungent with social awareness." Kirkus

Newave! the underground mini comix of the 1980s. edited by Michael Dowers. Fantagraphics Books 2010 888p il $24.99   **741.5**
   1. Cartoonists 2. Comic books, strips, etc.
   ISBN 978-1-60699-313-2; 1-60699-313-5

"In his introduction to this fascinating treasure trove of an anthology, Dower describes drawing, folding, and stapling his first minicomic back in 1982. Many others were doing the same and their combined efforts added up to a do-it-yourself scene in which 'obsessed nutballs' drew like crazy and made trips to the copy shops to get their work out there before the Web. In addition to work by greats like Artie Romero, Rick Geary, and Mary Fleener, and 50 or so others, the book serves as the history of a movement. The Newave Manifesto, written by Clay Geerdes in 1983 starts things off, and introductions and interviews preceding each creator's work puts it in context, while the list of artist Web sites at the end gives readers much more to discover." Publ Wkly

O'Neil, Dennis
   The **DC** comics guide to writing comics; introduction by Stan Lee. Watson-Guptill 2001 128p il $19.95   **741.5**
   1. Comic books, strips, etc. -- Authorship
   ISBN 0-8230-1027-9
                                         LC 2001-26101
   The author "discusses story structure, characterization, script preparation, and other general writing topics. He also covers those more specific to comics writing such as miniseries, maxiseries, and continuity. O'Neil addresses the visual component of the art, the importance of page layout, and the relationship between the writer and the artist." SLJ
   "O'Neil addresses the universals of writing in a way that makes the book useful to all aspiring scripters, regardless of their knowledge of comics." Booklist

The **psychology** of superheroes; an unauthorized exploration. edited by Robin S. Rosenberg with Jennifer Canzoneri. BenBella Books, Inc. 2008 259p bibl f il (BenBella Books psychology of popular culture series) pa $17.95   **741.5**
   1. Conduct of life 2. Superheroes (Fictional characters) -- Psychology
   ISBN 1-933771-31-3; 978-1-933771-31-1
                                         LC 2007-41418
   This book collects essays about superheroes from several psychological viewpoints, ranging from the positive moral aspects of superheroes to gender stereotypes, prejudice, anti-heroes, the place of Arkham Asylum (the notorious place where DC super villains get locked up), the role of rage in The Incredible Hulk, and more. Editor Rosenberg

is a clinical psychologist, and many of the contributors hold degrees in psychology and have faculty positions at various universities.
   Includes bibliographical references

Rhoades, Shirrel
   A **complete** history of American comic books; afterword by Steve Geppi. Peter Lang Publishing Inc. 2008 353p il $119.95; pa $39.95   **741.5**
   1. Graphic novels -- History and criticism 2. Comic books, strips, etc. -- History and criticism
   ISBN 978-1-4331-0110-6; 1-4331-0110-6; 978-1-4331-0107-6 pa; 1-4331-0107-6 pa
                                         LC 2007-43460
   Rhoades, former publisher of Marvel Comics (after Stan Lee stepped down to move to Hollywood and focus on Marvel Comics in the movies), dates the beginning of the American comic book to the 1930s, when the format was first used. He covers the history of comics from that time to the present, covering all the big names (Will Eisner, Jack Kirby, Stan Lee, etc.). The book is peppered with fun sidebars with such labels as "flashback," "comics trivia," "looking back," "true facts," and so one. These help to make the book fun to read. Rhoades doesn't employ a straight narrative, but includes interviews, the side bars, comics milestones, a list of fanboys who have and had careers in comics, and a comic book quiz.
   Includes bibliographical references

Rosenkranz, Patrick
   Rebel visions: the underground comix revolution, 1963-1975. Fantagraphics Books 2008 292p il pa $34.99   **741.5**
   1. Cartoonists 2. Graphic novels 3. Comic books, strips, etc. -- History and criticism
   ISBN 978-1-56097-706-3
   "The most lasting artistic legacy of the 1960s hippie movement, other than its music, is its eye-poppingly transgressive underground comics—black-and-white pamphlets that spread the counterculture message of sex, drugs, and rebellion to freak and straight alike. Rosencranz thoroughly documents the phenomenon, providing a year-by-year account of the underground scene, from 1968's Zap #1, which artist R. Crumb sold from a baby carriage on the streets of Haight Ashbury, to its crash in 1973 in the wake of obscenity rulings and a crackdown on head shops. . . . Rosencranz's writing may lack flair, but with personalities this colorful (the artists themselves provide fly-on-the-wall reminiscences) and art this outrageous (reprinted on nearly every page) to write about, who needs it?" Booklist

Salkowitz, Rob
   Comic -con and the business of pop culture; strategies for success in the digital transmedia era. by Rob Salkowitz. McGraw-Hill 2012 304 p. (alk. paper) $27   **741.5**
   1. Marketing 2. Trade shows 3. Comic books, strips, etc. 4. Popular culture -- Conferences 5. Webcomics 6. Popular culture -- Economic aspects 7. Comic books, strips, etc. -- Marketing 8. Comic books, strips, etc. -- Authorship -- Marketing 9. Comic books, strips, etc.

-- Technological innovations
ISBN 0071797025; 9780071797023

LC 2012009412

In this book, "author Rob Salkowitz, . . . explores how the humble art form of comics ended up at the center of the 21st-century media universe. From Comic-Con's massive exhibit hall and panels to its exclusive parties and business suites, Salkowitz peels back the layers to show how comics culture is influencing communications, entertainment, digital technology, marketing, education, and storytelling." (Publisher's note)

Includes bibliographical references and index.

Satrapi, Marjane, 1969-

★ The **complete** Persepolis. Pantheon Books 2007 341p il pa $24.95   **741.5**
   1. Artists 2. Authors 3. Novelists 4. Cartoonists 5. Graphic novels 6. Autobiographical graphic novels 7. Memoirists 8. Iran -- Graphic novels
ISBN 978-0-375-71483-2

LC 2007-60106

Originally published in two separate volumes 2003-2004

This "is the story of Satrapi's . . . childhood and coming of age within a large and loving family in Tehran during the Islamic Revolution; of the contradictions between private life and public life in a country plagued by political upheaval; of her high school years in Vienna facing the trials of adolescence far from her family; of her homecoming—both sweet and terrible; and, finally, of her self-imposed exile from her beloved homeland." Publisher's note

Small, David, 1945-

★ **Stitches**; a memoir. W.W. Norton 2009 329p il $23.95   **741.5**
   1. Artists 2. Authors 3. Illustrators 4. Graphic novels 5. Comic books, strips, etc. 6. Autobiographical graphic novels 7. Art teachers 8. Children's authors 9. Cancer -- Graphic novels 10. Family life -- Graphic novels
ISBN 978-0-393-06857-3; 0-393-06857-9

LC 2009-22526

David Small grew up in a dysfunctional family, with a radiologist father who was distant, an angry mother who expressed her anger in eloquent silences, and an older brother who played drums a lot to express his frustrations. When he was eleven, he had a lump, a growth, on the side of his neck. Nothing was done until he was fourteen. He thought he was going in for a minor surgery to remove the cyst from his neck; instead, there were two surgeries, and when he woke up, he had no voice—a vocal cord was removed. He later learned he had cancer, something his parents refused to discuss. After he finds his mother in bed with another woman and his father confesses that he exposed him to x-rays when he was very young, Small leaves home at age sixteen, with little except his dreams that his art could be his life. In one early scene, Small shows the indignities wrought upon his body by his father, including an enema. In another scene, young Small and his older brother look at their father's medical books and see a woman's breast and a man's penis; towards the end of the book, Small draws his grandmother stripping all her clothes off and dancing wildly after setting her house on fire. Other than these few images, Small's depictions of his horrible childhood and teen years are quiet and low-key.

"Emotionally raw, artistically compelling and psychologically devastating graphic memoir of childhood trauma." Kirkus

Spiegelman, Art, 1948-

★ **Co** -Mix; A Retrospective of Comics, Graphics, and Scraps. by Art Spiegelman. Farrar Straus & Giroux 2013 120 p. $39.95   **741.5**
   1. Comic books, strips, etc.
ISBN 1770461140; 9781770461147

This book, "a companion piece to a retrospective exhibition . . . collects some of [Art] Spiegelman's best work spanning nearly six decades along with biographical information and critical essays. The editors trace his career from commercial work for Playboy to his underground, experimental work, including the Raw anthology where he first serialized 'Maus'. . . . The book also features many of Spiegelman's controversial 1990's New Yorker covers and autobiographical comics." (Publishers Weekly)

"Maus did much to 'legitimize' comics to the wider world, but this thoughtfully curated, elegantly presented volume is an even more convincing testament to the potential of the medium." Booklist

★ **MetaMaus**. Pantheon Books 2011 299p il $35   **741.5**
   1. Authors 2. Cartoonists 3. Graphic novels 4. Autobiographical graphic novels 5. Nonfiction writers 6. Cartoonists -- Graphic novels 7. Holocaust survivors -- Graphic novels 8. Holocaust, 1933-1945 -- Graphic novels
ISBN 978-0-375-42394-9

LC 2010052045

The New York cartoonist traces the creative process that went into drawing his Pulitzer Prizewinning classic, revealing the sources of his inspiration and describing his parents' emotional struggles as Holocaust survivors after the end of World War II.

"Informative about everything you may or may not have thought to ask about Maus and the Spiegelmans, this exhaustive purgative has been well organized and packaged and succeeds in being grimly entertaining, indeed almost addictive." Libr J

Steinberg, Saul

Steinberg at the New Yorker; introduction by Ian Frazier. H.N. Abrams 2005 239p il $50   **741.5**
   1. Artists 2. Cartoonists 3. Illustrators 4. Cartoons and caricatures 5. New Yorker Magazine, Inc.
ISBN 0-8109-5901-1

LC 2004-19498

The author "surveys six decades of Steinberg's pieces, including all 89 New Yorker covers (in full color), cartoons, wartime sketches from overseas, evocative (but never literal-minded) illustrations for articles, and unpublished items from the artist's portfolio. The material is arranged thematically, examining such recurring motifs as cats, pedestals and rubber-stamped figures and documenting the turn to visual metaphor in Steinberg's later work. . . . Steinberg's cartoons usually made readers think before they laughed, and so will this splendid memorial to a 20th-century artistic landmark." Publ Wkly

Includes bibliographical references

Studio space; the world's greatest comic illustrators at work. Image Comics 2008 318p il $49.99; pa $29.99   **741.5**

1. Cartoonists 2. Graphic novels 3. Comic books, strips, etc.

ISBN 978-1-58240-909-2; 978-1-58240-908-5 pa

Twenty modern comics artists talk about their careers, their work, and their working methods. Each of them is photographed in his studio, and samples of their artwork are included. The artists are: Brian Bolland, Tim Bradstreet, Howard Chaykin, Steve Dillon, Tommy Lee Edwards, Duncan Fegredo, Dave Gibbons, Adam Hughes, Joe Kubert, Jim Lee, Mike Mignola, Frank Miller, Sean Phillips, George Pratt, Alex Ross, Tim Sale, Walt Simonson, Bryan Talbot, Dave Taylor, and Sergio Toppi.

Torres, Alissa

American widow; illustrated by Sungyoon Choi. Villard Books 2008 209p il $22   **741.5**

1. Educators 2. Graphic novels 3. Autobiographical graphic novels 4. Memoirists 5. Widows -- Graphic novels 6. September 11 terrorist attacks, 2001 -- Graphic novels

ISBN 978-0-345-50069-4

LC 2008-08396

Alissa Torres' husband Luis had just started his new job in the World Trade Center on September 10, 2001. The next day, he died in the terrorist attacks that destroyed the twin towers. Alissa was more than seven months pregnant. In this book, she recounts the personal struggles she suffered as a pregnant "terror widow," first heaped upon with sympathy, then publicly scorned. She describes the tragedies suffered by all the families who lost loved ones on September 11, 2001 and the frustrations they experienced dealing with bureaucrats as they tried to get even the smallest physical trace of their loved ones.

The author's "tragedy of errors inspires anger on her behalf, although the story is calmly and beautifully told. Choi's simple and attractive line art is set off by turquoise wash, yielding to a full-color photo at the end when Alissa embraces her life anew." Libr J

Tran, G. B.

Vietnamerica; a family's journey. written and illustrated by GB Tran. Villard Books 2010 279 p. chiefly col. ill. $30   **741.5**

1. Artists 2. Illustrators 3. Graphic novels 4. Vietnamese Americans -- Biography 5. Cartoonists 6. Vietnamese refugees -- Graphic novels 7. Vietnamese Americans -- Graphic novels 8. Vietnam War, 1961-1975 -- Graphic novels

ISBN 0345508726; 9780345508720

LC 2011283144

In "this personal memoir," drawn in the style of a graphic novel, the author "tries to make sense of a shattered family history. [G. B.] Tran was born in America shortly after his family fled Vietnam during the fall of Saigon. However, he sees how deeply his parents still feel connected to their homeland, even as they can't fully admit their dismay at being cut off from it. . . . By visiting Vietnam and exploring memories, Tran learns how his grandfather, a lifelong Vietminh supporter, was horrified at the brutal results of the Communist victory and how his father became a glum autocrat after his career as an artist was destroyed. He watches how his parents interact uneasily with the swarm of relatives and friends they left behind." (Publishers Weekly)

"Engaging, challenging, and disturbing, Tran's family memoir belongs in all public and academic libraries; older teens and up for occasionally strong language and violence. The swirly, jagged color art fits the story perfectly." Libr J

Watterson, Bill

The **complete** Calvin and Hobbes. Andrews McMeel Pub. 2005 3v il set $150   **741.5**

1. Comic books, strips, etc.

ISBN 0-7407-4847-5; 978-0-7407-4847-9

LC 2004-62709

This is a collection of the entire run of the comic strip Calvin and Hobbes, which ran from 1985 to 1995.

"This is one of the all-time great comic strips, absolutely essential for every library." Libr J

Wednesday comics. DC Comics 2010 200p il $49.99   **741.5**

1. Superhero graphic novels 2. Comic books, strips, etc.

ISBN 978-1-401227470; 1-401227473

LC 2010-282211

"A must-have book for DC comics fans, fans of any comic art, or even those who used to read comics but haven't done so for years. These classic characters still captivate our imaginations – as they have for decades." Christ Sci Monit

741.6   Graphic design, illustration, commercial art

Aldridge, Alan

The **man** with kaleidoscope eyes. Harry N. Abrams 2009 239p il $35   **741.6**

1. Posters 2. Graphic arts 3. Commercial art

ISBN 978-0-8109-0596-2; 0-8109-0596-5

LC 2008-939189

"This book lives up to its title, capturing the lyrical and visual pop of Aldridge's signature psychedelic poster art, which made him a favorite artist among the Beatles, the Who, Cream, Elton John, and Incubus. Readers also get a good sense of the 1960s generation that best defines Aldridge, who is still producing art today. An 'illustrated autobiography,' this work excels at presenting the amusing anecdote and scrapbook aesthetic rather than a historical or critical approach, particularly in terms of other artists working in a similar vein." Libr J

Bowring, Joanna

The **art** of romance; Harlequin Mills & Boon cover designs. [by] Joanna Bowring and Margaret O'Brien. Prestel 2008 253p il pa $25   **741.6**

1. Book covers 2. Mills and Boon (Firm) 3. Harlequin

Enterprises Ltd.

ISBN 978-3-791341-22-4; 3-791341-22-7

The authors "trace a century of lovelorn fiction through its covers. Predictably, the formula of a beautiful woman looking longingly at a handsome man has not changed all that much (except now there's more photography). Mills & Boon, Britain's leading publisher of romantic fiction, is 101 years old; Harlequin, which owns the company, is 60. Throughout these years loyal romance readers have been treated to some enduring fantasies—for example, the sheik as hero. . . . Although sheiks have changed, the covers continue to tell the story of undying male and female stereotypes." N Y Times Book Rev

Brower, Steven

Breathless homicidal slime mutants; the art of the paperback. foreword by Steven Heller. Universe 2010 304p il pa $24.95 **741.6**

1. Book covers 2. Paperback books

ISBN 978-0-7893-1804-6; 0-7893-1804-0

"Packed with worthy representatives from numerous genres, Breathless Homicidal Slime Mutants is a visual and visceral feast that provides a compelling introduction to the history of pop art in the 20th century." PopMatters

Crumb, R.

R. Crumb: the complete record cover collection. W. W. Norton & Co. 2011 un il $27.95 **741.6**

1. Popular music 2. Sound recordings -- Album covers

ISBN 978-0-393-08278-4

This volume is "filled with the artist's designs for such ephemera as 'Unknown Detroit Bluesmen' or Cliff Edwards's 'I'm a Bear in a Ladies' Boudoir.' Starting in the 1970s, Mr. Crumb produced covers for reissues from labels like Yazoo, Blue Goose and Barrelhouse Records, and his love for the music is evident—a stippled Robert Johnson stares out in stark black and white, Bessie Smith sings 'Put a Little Sugar in My Bowl' and Charlie Patton gets his own mini-graphic novel. . . . (The biggest act here is Big Brother and the Holding Company, with Janis Joplin done over to fit Crumb's zaftig ideal.) In this journeyman work, however, the discipline of playing second fiddle to his favorite musicians keeps the artist's self-loathing in check without taming the ribald humor that is also a hallmark of the blues. Few Crumb projects seem like so much fun—to read about, to look at or to listen along to." Wall Street J

Donahue, Daniel

Ultraviolet; 69 backlight posters from the Aquarian age and beyond. [by] Dan Donahue. Abrams Image 2009 un il pa $22.50 **741.6**

1. Posters

ISBN 978-0-8109-7999-4; 0-8109-7999-3

The book features posters, "all produced between 1967 and 1972 (apparently—a few don't have years attributed to them), and covering a wide range of subjects. . . . Every page evokes nostalgia, perhaps a flashback, and conveys a strong sense of the wild power and energy of the times. Counterculture historian Dan Donahue compiled the book, and contributed a lucid and thorough essay that covers the development of the oddball art form associated most often with the late '60s." PopMatters

Fernandes, Teresa

Becoming a graphic designer; a guide to careers in design. Steven Heller & Teresa Fernandes. John Wiley & Sons 2010 368 p. (paperback) $39.95 **741.6**

1. Artists 2. Graphic arts -- Marketing 3. Graphic arts -- Vocational guidance 4. Commercial art -- Vocational guidance

ISBN 0470575565; 9780470575567

LC 2010004729

This book by Steven Heller and Teresa Fernandes "provides a . . . survey of the graphic design market, including . . . coverage of print and electronic media and . . . digital design disciplines. . . . Featuring 65 interviews with today's leading designers, this visual guide has more than 600 illustrations and covers everything from education and training, design specialties, and work settings to preparing an effective portfolio and finding a job." (Publisher's note)

Hayes, Clay

Gig posters volume 1; rock show art of the 21st century. Quirk Books 2009 208p il $40 **741.6**

1. Posters 2. Rock music

ISBN 978-1-59474-326-9; 1-59474-326-6

LC 2008-938830

"There is no single style for gig posters — they are punk, grunge, new wave, neo-modern, comic, retro, parodic and satirical. Some are beautiful, others ugly; some derivative, others novel. Most are eye-catching, and some are memorable. Those that are wheat-pasted on hoardings or taped to lampposts are usually removed within days, so GigPosters has been a terrific archive of the good, the bad and the ugly. But digital versions just don't compare with the printed posters, which is why . . . [this book, compiled by the] founder of GigPosters, is such a useful resource. The book contains posters by leaders of the art form (including Emek, Eleanor Grosch, Lil Tuffy and Luke Drozd), who offer brief commentaries about their work." N Y Times Book Rev

I heart design; remarkable graphic design selected by designers, illustrators, and critics. [edited by] Steven Heller. Rockport Publishers 2011 214p il $45 **741.6**

1. Design 2. Graphic arts

ISBN 978-1-59253-682-5; 1-59253-682-4

LC 2010-41709

Heller "asked 80 experts in the field — including designers, typographers and academics — to each pick an influential example of graphic design that resonates beyond the context in which it was made and place it within the historical framework of the discipline. Heller also asked each to explain why that particular piece moves their souls. . . . Selections run the gamut — magazines, logos, posters, maps, illustrations, architecture, album covers, sculptures, film title sequences, everyday objects and other ephemera. . . . Some of the short essays get bogged down by their academic tone, but in general, readers will enjoy clear discussions of the ability of the best designs to inform, distill and clarify information and, ultimately, to cut through the visual cacophony that litters our lives." Los Angeles Times

Includes bibliographical references

Neuburger, Emily K.

Show me a story; 40 craft projects and activities to spark children's storytelling. by Emily K. Neuburger. Storey Pub. 2012 144 p. ill. (pbk. : alk. paper) $16.95; (hardcover) $26.95 **741.6**

1. Storytelling 2. Handicraft for children 3. Illustrators -- Interviews 4. Illustrated children's books

ISBN 1612121489; 9781603429887; 9781612121482

LC 2012004610

This book presents "40 creative projects and activities [designed to] encourage [children] to free their storytelling instincts." Activities for "[y]ounger children" include "making story stones and a storytelling jar . . . while older kids will enjoy word grab bags, story walks, and journaling exercises." The book is intended "[f]or everyone ages 5 to 12". (Publisher's note)

Includes bibliographical references and index.

The **poster;** 1,000 posters from Toulouse-Lautrec to Sagmeister. edited by Cees V. de Jong, Alston W. Purvis, Martijn F. Le Coultre; text by Alston W. Ourvis; intorduction by Cees W. de Jong. Abrams 2010 567p il pa $35 **741.6**

1. Posters

ISBN 978-0-8109-9588-8; 0-8109-9588-3

LC 2010-14458

"In the history of art, the poster occupies a strange no-man's-land, a middle ground at the intersection of design and commerce. However masterful they might be in terms of composition and execution, the fact remains that posters are used to sell something else—a product, an idea, a critical bit of wartime propaganda. Whether it's cookies or patriotism that is on the block, the purpose of a poster seems to rest uneasily alongside the artistic spirit that impels it. The Poster is a book that aims not to apologize for this duality, but to acknowledge it and then move on. In purely artistic terms, posters can be marvelous works of skill and imagination—powerfully designed and skillfully executed. . . . Overall, the collection succeeds admirably." PopMatters

Includes bibliographical references

Powell, Aubrey

For the love of vinyl; the album art of Hipgnosis. compiled and written by Aubrey Powell and Storm Thorgerson; designed by Peter Curzon and Storm Thorgerson. PictureBox 2008 232p il $45 **741.6**

1. Hipgnosis (Firm) 2. Sound recordings -- Album covers

ISBN 978-0-98156221-6; 0-98156221-3

"Soon, physical album covers will be as extinct as eight-track tapes. Passionate collectors are hoarding classic record sleeves, some of the most memorable of which were created by a British design firm called Hipgnosis. Founded by Aubrey Powell and Storm Thorgerson in 1968, the firm was known for eerie and erotic staged photography that wed magic realism to Surrealism. Hipgnosis employed comedy, mystery and sexuality (sometimes all at once) in its elaborately composed tableaus. Among the bands branded by its images were Led Zeppelin, Pink Floyd, Black Sabbath, Genesis and Wishbone Ash. Covers for these groups and many more are reproduced in [this volume,] . . . which comes with additional commentary on specific albums by various artists and designers, including Peter Blake and Paula Scher." N Y Times Book Rev

Reaves, Wendy Wick

Ballyhoo! posters as portraiture. National Portrait Gallery, Smithsonian; distributed by the University of Washington Press 2008 159p il pa $19.95 **741.6**

1. Posters 2. Celebrities

ISBN 978-0-295-98862-7; 0-295-98862-2

LC 2008-925960

"The book is a compact historical survey of the medium from its earliest days as a proto-Wanted poster to the massive ad campaigns of today's blockbuster films—from John Wilkes Booth to Johnny Depp, literally. Though the book's subtitle stresses the portraiture aspect, many of the posters reproduced are as much about events as people, with wartime propaganda and social statement mixed in with entertainment. Overall, this is a condensed overview of the cultural landscape, with the 70 or so images serving as telling visible index." PopMatters

Includes bibliographical references

Rees, Darrell

How to Be an Illustrator; by Darrel Rees. Chronicle Books LLC 2014 167 p. ill (some col) $24.95 **741.6**

1. Illustrators 2. Vocational guidance

ISBN 1780673280; 9781780673288

This book, by Darrel Rees, "offers practical help and guidance to aspiring illustrators. . . . International illustrators are interviewed, discussing how they got their break in the industry, their experiences with clients, their methods of promoting work, and more. In addition, leading art directors describe their approach to commissioning illustration, how they spot new talent, their thoughts on promotional material, and their advice to up-and-coming illustrators." (Publisher's note)

'This guide . . . shares the author's insights on everything except the artistic aspects of the occupation, i.e., business concerns such as education, job hunting, project management, billing, and promoting yourself." LJ

Includes bibliographical references

Salisbury, Martin

Illustrating children's books; creating pictures for publication. Barron's Educational Series 2004 144p il pa $22.95 **741.6**

1. Illustrators 2. Illustration of books 3. Picture books for children

ISBN 0-76412-717-9

The author "surveys the genre's distinguished history with examples from Caldecott, Greenaway, N. C. Wyeth, Maxfield Parrish, and Howard Pyle. . . . Through sketches and annotations, Salisbury explains how to create fantasy, fairy tale, realism, and nature drawing. Written for advanced students, the book covers storyboards and layouts, contracts, copyrights, and how to present one's work professionally. Highly recommended for all collections." Libr J

Includes bibliographical references

Schiller, Justin

Maurice Sendak; a celebration of the artist and his work. by Justin Schiller and illustrated by Maurice Sendak. Harry N. Abrams 2013 223 p. (alk. paper) $45 **741.6**
1. Artists -- Biography
ISBN 1419708260; 9781419708268

LC 2013007227

In this book, by Justin Schiller, "the preeminent children's book artist of the twentieth century, Maurice Sendak and his sixty-year career are celebrated in this full-color catalog of more than two hundred images being exhibited at the Society of Illustrators in New York City. [Images are] accompanied by twelve essays by such noted scholars and historians as Leonard S. Marcus, Iona Opie, Steven Heller, and Paul O. Zelinsky." (Publisher's note)

Includes bibliographical references and index

741.9 Collections of drawings

Berger, John, 1926-

Bento's sketchbook; 1st American ed. Pantheon Books 2011 167p ill. (mostly col.) **741.9**
1. Art appreciation 2. Drawing -- Technique 3. Drawing -- Psychological aspects
ISBN 9780307379955

LC 2011010841

This is "a meditation, in words and images, on the practice of drawing, by the author of Ways of Seeing (1972)." (Publisher's note)

743 Drawing and drawings by subject

Robins, Clem

The art of figure drawing. North Light Bks. 2003 143p il pa $22.99 **743**
1. Figure drawing
ISBN 1-58180-204-8

LC 2002-69598

"Robins' guide considers the elements—line, light and shade, mass, texture, foreshortening, and more—using basic geometric shapes to achieve accurate renderings of the nude human figure. His explanation of equilibrium and center of gravity as applied to figure drawing is particularly helpful to the novice exploring this essential foundational skill, and the index makes for user-friendliness." Booklist

Watson, Lucy

Life drawing class. Watson-Guptill Publications 2003 125p il pa $24.95 **743**
1. Figure drawing
ISBN 0-8230-2767-8

LC 2003-102105

"Watson presents each chapter as a class in which she introduces basic concepts such as measuring angles, plotting positions, perspective light and tone, and so on. Also included in each section are suggestions for pose lengths, lists of materials, and clearly explained, illustrated step-by-step instructions. Throughout Watson includes examples of

her and other professionals' work in a wide range of styles and media." Booklist

743.4 Drawing human figures

Hart, Christopher

Human anatomy made amazingly easy. Watson-Guptill 2000 114p il pa $19.95 **743.4**
1. Figure drawing 2. Artistic anatomy
ISBN 0-8230-2497-0

LC 00-43514

In this work for the beginning artist "Hart simplifies the process in an accessible manual that concentrates on line and forgoes the complexity of color." Libr J

745 Decorative arts

American Folk Art Museum

★ Encyclopedia of American folk art; Gerard C. Wertkin, editor; Lee Kogan, associate editor; in association with the American Folk Art Museum. Routledge 2004 xxxiii, 612p il $125 **745**
1. American folk art
ISBN 0-415-92986-5

LC 2003-18051

This volume "covers more than three centuries of folk artists and provides information about museum collections, institutions that collect and sponsor folk art, and subjects related to the various forms of folk art. Entries tend to be detailed, and in some cases, extensive. . . . The work is heavily and usefully cross-referenced. Most entries end with brief bibliographies. Although not heavily illustrated, the work offers a number of interesting color and black-and-white illustrations keyed to specific entries." Choice

Includes bibliographical references

Lauria, Jo

Craft in America; celebrating two centuries of artists and objects. [by] Jo Lauria and Stephen Fenton; prologue by Jimmy Carter. Clarkson Potter 2007 320p il $60 **745**
1. Decorative arts -- United States
ISBN 978-0-307-34647-6; 0-307-34647-1

LC 2006-34839

This collection of photographs and "prose pays homage to two centuries' worth of baskets, textiles, furniture, pottery, and jewelry from U.S. artisans. . . . Famous artisans, from Revolutionary War silversmith Paul Revere to modern-day jewelers Denise and Sam Wallace, and their works are featured, as are the numerous schools and workshops inspiring those creations and today's student crafts movement. . . . A wondrous companion to read over and over and over again." Booklist

Includes bibliographical references

Tracy, Lisa

Objects of our affection. Bantam Books 2010 233p il $25 **745**
1. Auctions 2. Personal belongings 3. Souvenirs

(Keepsakes)

ISBN 978-0-553-80726-4; 0-553-80726-9

LC 2009-47841

"Following their mother's death, Tracy and her sister were faced with the daunting task of sifting through her belongings. A military family whose history dated back to the American Revolution, the Tracys had acres of heirlooms, from an elegant, satin-bottomed chair that might have once been occupied by George Washington to a pair of dueling pistols purportedly owned by Aaron Burr. But while these items made for tantalizing stories to be told by the fire, what was their worth if one couldn't establish provenance? When the sisters decide to put selected pieces up for auction, they are both sobered—and occasionally surprised—by the prices they fetch. What they didn't account for was the remorse they would feel after the auction was completed. . . . This will definitely attract the Antiques Roadshow crowd." Booklist

745.1 Antiques

Miller's antiques encyclopedia; general editor, Judith Miller. new ed.; Distributed in the United States and Canada by Sterling Publ. 2008 592p il $50 **745.1**

1. Reference books 2. Antiques -- Encyclopedias

ISBN 978-1-84533-470-3; 1-84533-470-1

First published 1998

"Richly illustrated with high-quality photos, this volume packs significant amounts of information on what is considered antique or collectible, how various items are manufactured, how to evaluate them, what their current value is, and how to care for them. . . . If you aren't already an antiques fiend, this work is likely to make you one!" Libr J

Includes bibliographical references

★ **Miller's** antiques handbook & price guide; [edited by] Judith Miller. Octopus Books 2011 648p il $45 **745.1**

1. Antiques

ISBN 978-1-84533-638-7

Annual. First published 1979. Variant title: Miller's international antiques price guide

This guide includes photographs, prices and brief descriptions of museum-quality antiques sold at auction or by dealers during the past year.

"Although this is a best-of resource, not covering attic knickknacks, it is an alluring look book with inherent educational value." Libr J

745.2 Industrial art and design

Norman, Don

The **design** of everyday things; Don Norman. Basic Books 2013 xviii, 347 p.p illustrations (pbk.) $17.99 **745.2**

1. Human engineering 2. Industrial design -- Psychological aspects

ISBN 0465050654; 9780465050659

LC 2013024417

"The Design of Everyday Things shows that good, usable design is possible. The rules are simple: make things visible, exploit natural relationships that couple function and control, and make intelligent use of constraints." Author "Don Norman hails excellence of design as the most important key to regaining the competitive edge in influencing consumer behavior." (Publisher's note)

"The revised edition updates examples; the original work preceded the Web and mobile devices. It also expands and refines the treatment of psychology, analyzing how affordances are signified to people, how emotion impacts everything people do and experience, and how culture can modulate what is 'natural' in design. Most notably, the revised edition articulates a broader view of design's goals and constraints." Choice

Includes bibliographical references (pages 321-330) and index

745.4 Pure and applied design and decoration

Albrecht, Donald

The **Work** of Charles and Ray Eames; a legacy of invention. essays by Donald Albrecht . . . {et al.} Abrams 1997 205p il hardcover o.p. pa $24.95 **745.4**

1. Design 2. Architects 3. Exhibit designers 4. Interior designers 5. Furniture designers 6. Industrial designers 7. Motion picture producers

ISBN 0-8109-1799-8; 978-0-8109-9232-0 pa; 0-8109-9232-9 pa

LC 97-4086

This overview of the work of two prominent American postwar designers features "pictures of famous furniture, toys, exhibitions, promotional material, informal snapshots, stills from films, comics, advertisements, exhibitions for the federal government, and much more. The work features six major essays, each with extensive notes, by scholars, designers, academics, and architecture/design writers." Choice

Includes bibliographical references

745.5 Handicrafts

Chapin, Kari

★ **Grow** your handmade business; how to envision, develop, and sustain a successful creative business. Kari Chapin ; illustrations by Jennifer Judd-McGee. Storey Pub. 2012 271 p. (pbk. : alk. paper) $16.95 **745.5**

1. Handicraft 2. Small business 3. Entrepreneurship 4. Selling -- Handicraft 5. Handicraft -- Marketing 6. Handicraft industries -- Management

ISBN 1603429891; 9781603429894

LC 2012004612

This book is about business planning, focusing on handicraft businesses. "There are two main sections: 'Mapping Your Dream' and 'Planning for Success.' The first section . . . covers identifying the best type of business to create, discovering skills and strengths, setting goals and benchmarks, and getting help from a mentor. The second section focuses more on the nuts and bolts of running a business and covers business models, time and money management, marketing, legal aspects, etc." (Library Journal)

The **complete** book of home crafts; projects for adventurous beginners. edited by Carine Tracanelli. Skyhorse 2011 352p il $24.95   **745.5**
1. Handicraft 2. Decoration and ornament
ISBN 978-1-61608-322-9
First published 2000 in the United Kingdom
"This extensive collection of projects focuses mainly on home decor, with a brief foray into decorative beadwork. The projects are beginner friendly, and individual steps are illustrated with color photographs, making it easy to follow along. Each section contains a brief introduction, familiarizing crafters with the tools and techniques involved in each type of project. The broad coverage includes picture framing, decorative painting on a variety of different surfaces, decoupage, and tile work." Libr J

Kilby, Janice Eaton
By hand; 25 beautiful objects to make in the American folk art tradition. [by] Janice Eaton Kilby with the assistance of Veronika Alice Gunter. Lark Bks. 2001 144p il hardcover o.p. pa $17.95 **745.5**
1. Handicraft
ISBN 1-57990-376-2 pa
LC 00-54974
This is a "survey collection of two dozen projects for familiar items, such as samplers, decoys, and copper weathervanes, that have been designed by professional artists. Each type of craft has a historic introduction and is illustrated by photographs of museum and gallery pieces. . . . A handy all-in-one source for public libraries." Libr J
Includes bibliographical references

Martha Stewart living
★ **Martha** Stewart's encyclopedia of crafts; an A-to-Z guide with detailed instructions and endless inspiration. [by the editors of Martha Stewart living] Potter Craft 2009 416p il $35   **745.5**
1. Handicraft
ISBN 978-0-307-45057-9
LC 2008-33415
"In alphabetical order, from albums to wreaths, with intermediate stops at beading, jewelry making, mosaics, quilling, soap making, and more, Stewart presents easily absorbed directions for 200 projects; in each project profile, sumptuous illustrations are partnered with rich, full, stimulating discussion of materials, techniques, and tips. . . . Of primary importance to all crafts collections." Booklist

Pretty little pincushions; [Susan Brill, ed.] Lark Books 2007 128p il $17.95   **745.5**
1. Pincushions
ISBN 978-1-6005-9144-0; 1-6005-9144-2
LC 2007-18423
"Several crafters submitted designs [for pincushions], which range from a felt beehive complete with miniscule straight-pin bees to tiny cushions to wear on a finger as the needle flies. . . . Front matter provides information on materials, techniques, and project embellishments, including diagrams of several embroidery stitches. . . . Functional, fun,

and oh-so-easy, these clever pin holders put the ubiquitous red strawberry in the sewing basket to shame." Booklist

Tapper, Joan
Craft activism; people, ideas, and projects from the new community of handmade and how you can join in. photography by Gale Zucker; foreword by Faythe Levine. Potter Craft 2011 159p il pa $22.99   **745.5**
1. Handicraft 2. Social movements
ISBN 978-0-307-58662-9; 0-307-58662-6
LC 2011003675
The author, "inspired by a yarn graffiti installation in Washington state, explores the motivations of creative people who use their skills to make public statements about everything from the environment to the role of traditional 'women's work' in contemporary society. . . . The profiles and the projects that follow them are diverse, and readers are bound to find inspiration in this nicely curated volume." Libr J
Includes bibliographical references

Taylor, Terry
Altered art; techniques for creating altered books, boxes, cards & more. Lark Books 2004 144p il $19.95   **745.5**
1. Handicraft
ISBN 1-57990-550-1
LC 2004-5313
Taylor "begins with a brief history of altered art (Joseph Cornell was an early practitioner), discusses copyright issues with regard to borrowed images, then moves straight into techniques, tools, and a . . . gallery of a variety of artists' works. The author includes a few projects with step-by-step instructions. . . . [This book] is without a doubt one of the finest craft books available." SLJ

Wasinger, Susan
Eco -craft; recycle, recraft, restyle. Lark Books 2009 128p il $24.95   **745.5**
1. Salvage 2. Handicraft 3. Interior design
ISBN 978-1-60059-343-7
LC 2008-31192
The author, a graphic designer, "promotes her own brand of sustainability, starting with the materials (recycled paper with agri-based ink) used to fashion her 30-item craft collection. Everything here is fresh in terms of style, dynamic, and fairly easy to complete, thanks to the step-by-step photographs, well-labeled directions, and notes to ensure a quality finished product." Booklist

745.54   Papers

Helfand, Jessica
Scrapbooks : an American history; A Winterhouse edition; Yale University Press 2008 244p il $45   **745.54**
1. Scrapbooks 2. Paper crafts
ISBN 978-0-300-12635-8; 0-300-12635-2

The author "offers both an overview of the history of the creation of scrapbooks and a visual feast for readers via the integration of texts, images, and memorabilia of all types. . . . Helfand has made a brilliant selection of unusual examples by visiting numerous archives, and she weaves a narrative based on examples that she found. . . .The book is sumptuous, a superb marriage in fine design, paper, and print." Choice

Melichson, Henya

The **art** of paper cutting. Quarry Books 2009 128p il pa $19.99   **745.54**

1. Paper crafts
ISBN 978-1-59253-525-5

"Decorative paper cutting using a single sheet of paper produces lacy silhouettes. Melichson's very elaborate designs draw on religious and ethnic motifs from Mediterranean countries and take some practice to draw out and execute. Templates that may be photocopied and traced are provided for less-intricate projects." Libr J

Reeder, Dan

Papier -mache monsters; turn trinkets and trash into magnificent monstrosities. photographs by Julie, Jeff and Dan Reeder. Gibbs Smith 2009 144p il pa $16.99   **745.54**

1. Paper crafts 2. Monsters in art
ISBN 978-1-4236-0555-3; 1-4236-0555-1

LC 2009-3827

"For lovers of the truly grotesque, Reeder . . . provides detailed photo instructions for large figures constructed of clothes hangers, newspaper, and glue. Cloth skin, teeth, and slathered-on paint finish them off. The toothy dragons are particularly effective." Libr J

745.55   Shells

Marshall, Marlene Hurley

Shell chic; the ultimate guide to decorating your home with seashells. photographs by Sabine Vollmer von Falken. Storey Bks. 2002 152p il $35 **745.55**

1. Shells 2. Handicraft
ISBN 1-58017-440-X

LC 2002-1140

This "contains step-by-step projects for traditional items of shell art such as flower arrangements and shell-encrusted boxes, all interspersed with a colorful running narrative describing decorative uses of shells by contemporary designers." Libr J

745.58   Beads, found and other objects

Benson, Ann

Beading for the first time. Sterling 2000 112p il $19.95   **745.58**

1. Beadwork
ISBN 0-8069-6098-1

LC 00-48265

"Step-by-step instructions for jewelry and accessories are accompanied by large color photographs and line drawings. There are sections on materials and equipment with a gallery of the work of several bead artists." Libr J

Fitzgerald, Diane

Diane Fitzgerald's shaped beadwork; dimensional jewelry with peyote stitch. Sterling Pub. Co. 2009 120p il $24.95   **745.58**

1. Beads 2. Beadwork
ISBN 978-1-60059-277-5

LC 2008-25703

"Although the majority of the book is devoted to the actual fashioning of . . . [different types of] bead shapes, Fitzgerald adds her personal inspiration by way of a dozen-plus items to make, including a Celtic trefoil, Berber earrings, and a trillium necklace. A true breakthrough in the art of beadwork." Booklist

Includes bibliographical references

Wells, Carol Wilcox

The **art** & elegance of beadweaving; new jewelry designs with classic stitches. Lark Bks. 2002 160p il hardcover o.p. pa $14.95   **745.58**

1. Jewelry 2. Beadwork
ISBN 1-57990-200-6; 1-57990-533-1 pa

LC 2001-38958

Includes instructions for craft projects using beads and five types of weaving stitches.

What the author "conjures up in more than 30 bracelets, earrings, and necklaces is nothing short of breathtaking." Booklist

745.59   Making specific objects

Heynen, Jennifer

Ceramic bead jewelry; 30 fired & inspired projects. Lark Books 2008 128p il $24.95   **745.59**

1. Jewelry 2. Beadwork 3. Ceramics
ISBN 978-1-60059-142-6

LC 2007-46536

"About half of . . . [this] book demonstrates the fundamentals: tools and materials and the making, decorating, and firing (bisque as well as glaze) of beads, along with techniques, like raku, metal clay, and luster, among others. Then on to the 30 projects, ranging from a boyfriend black-and-white bead on a cord necklace to an elaborate autumn-bounty (with acorns and leaves) necklace, with rings, brooches, and bracelets well represented in the projects. Each design includes the requisite list, color photographs, and instructions." Booklist

Michaels, Chris Franchetti

Teach yourself visually jewelry making & beading. Wiley Publishing 2007 290p il (Visual read less, learn more) pa $24.99   **745.59**

1. Beads 2. Jewelry 3. Beadwork
ISBN 978-0-470-10150-6; 0-470-10150-4

This book explains how "to craft designs that are chic but inexpensive. With hundreds of detailed photos, this book covers tools and supplies, bead stringing and weaving, wire wrapping, and more." Publisher's note

Oppenheimer, Betty
   Candlemaker's companion; a complete guide to rolling, pouring, dipping, and decorating your own candles. Completely rev and updated; Storey Bks. 2001 199p il pa $18.95 **745.59**
   1. Candles
   ISBN 1-58017-366-7

LC 00-53802
   First published 1997
   This offers a brief history of candles followed by information about wicks, waxes and additives, color and scent, and equipment. Step-by-step instructions on candlemaking techniques and decoration, and a list of suppliers
   Includes bibliographical references

Pickering Rothamel, Susan
   Encyclopedia of greeting card tools and techniques. Lark Books 2008 304p il $24.95 **745.59**
   1. Handicraft 2. Greeting cards
   ISBN 978-1-6005-9029-0; 1-6005-9029-2

LC 2007-50641
   Rothamel offers "a one-stop annotated and illustrated dictionary of greeting card information, whether the subject is mechanics (accordion fold, wrinkling); how-to's (past paper, thermal embossing); arcane bytes (deltiology is the art of collecting postcards); or relevant tips (the use and safety of craft knives). . . . The author provides a good overview of the craft along with profiles of 14 practitioners, a historical time line, and advice for the wannabe professional (such as card submission and composition guidelines)." Booklist

Wire, CeCe
   Creative metal clay jewelry; techniques, projects, inspiration. Lark Bks. 2003 144p il hardcover o.p. pa $14.95 **745.59**
   1. Jewelry 2. Precious metal clay
   ISBN 1-57990-301-0; 1-60059-182-5 pa

LC 2002-34398
   Metal clay "consists of precious metal particles combined with an organic binder and water to make a substance that looks and feels like potters clay. It is worked, dried, and fired like clay. Firing burns off the organic material leaving a fused piece of pure gold or silver. The piece can then be finished like any other metal. Wire . . . gives detailed instructions for using it as a jewelry medium, with step-by-step projects for earrings, bracelets, and other pieces. Contemporary in style, these items tend to resemble cast pieces. This book on an interesting new craft belongs in every crafts collection." Libr J

745.592   Toys, models, miniatures, related objects

Hrachovec, Anna
   Super -scary mochimochi; 20+ cute & creepy creatures to knit. Anna Hrachovec ; photography by

Brandi Simons. Potter Craft 2012 144 p. (pbk. : alk. paper) $19.99 **745.592**
   1. Knitting 2. Soft toy making 3. Needlework -- Patterns 4. Amigurumi -- Patterns
   ISBN 0307965767; 9780307965769

LC 2011046773
   This book, by Anna Hrachovec, offers patterns for knitting stuffed Amigurumi monsters. "What creatures lurk in the darkest shadows of Mochimochi Land? Only the most adorable assortment of knitted monsters, such as tiny vampire brats, a teenage werewolf, and a miniature gang of killer bees. . . . After all, nothing is scarier than a clever knitter armed with yarn, needles, and a wild imagination." (Publisher's note)

745.593   Useful objects

Ure, Susan
   Scrapbooking your vacations; 200 page designs. Sterling Pub 2004 127p il $24.95 **745.593**
   1. Scrapbooks 2. Photograph albums
   ISBN 1-402-70819-X

LC 2003-23619
   This is a "collection of more than 200 page plans, which brings together designs inspired by choice vacation spots across the globe. Crafters will find great-looking, full-color pages motivated by trips to Asia, Africa, Europe, and more to copy or adapt as they choose. For each sample scrapbook page, Ure provides a list of the materials used to create it and commentary about the design itself, often including hints that can be applied to other scrapbook projects." Booklist

745.594   Decorative objects

Beaman, Sarah
   Ultimate cardmaking; a collection of over 100 techniques and 50 inspirational projects. Collins & Brown; Distributed in the U.S. by Sterling Pub. 2008 192p il $24.95 **745.594**
   1. Paper crafts 2. Greeting cards
   ISBN 978-1-84340-438-5; 1-84340-438-9
   "What distinguishes this from other books on making cards? A clean contemporary-design perspective, with an emphasis on the 'less is more' philosophy; great attention to crafter needs; and quite a few 'fast cards' for those with limited time. Truly timeless and creative ways to invite, thank, and celebrate." Booklist

Deeb, Margie
   The **beader's** color palette; 20 creative projects, 220 inspired combinations for beaded and gemstone jewelry. Watson-Guptill 2008 192p il pa $24.95 **745.594**
   1. Color 2. Jewelry 3. Beadwork
   ISBN 978-0-8230-0474-4; 0-8230-0474-0

LC 2007-936519
   The author "provides meticulously worked-out color palettes to capture the essence of period artworks or natural objects. Each palette indicates the proportion of dominant

and secondary hues so that the finished piece will reflect the colors of the original period artwork or natural object." Libr J

Includes bibliographical references

Geary, Theresa Flores

The **illustrated** bead bible; terms, tips & techniques. photographs by Debra Whalen. Sterling Pub. 2008 406p il $29.95   **745.594**

1. Beads 2. Beadwork

ISBN 978-1-4027-2353-7; 1-4027-2353-9

LC 2007-026120

"This may be the ultimate bead reference book. The majority of the text is made up of an illustrated alphabetical encyclopedia of beads, broadly defined, and beading terms. Additional chapters include tips and techniques, charts illustrating bead characteristics, and stitch diagrams." Libr J

Includes glossary and bibliographical references

Mann, Elise

★ The **bead** directory; the complete guide to choosing and using more than 600 beautiful beads. Interweave Press 2006 256p il $24.95   **745.594**

1. Beads 2. Beadwork

ISBN 1-59668-002-4; 978-1-59668-002-9

LC 2005-24503

This is a "handbook of currently available beads made of metal, wood, and plastic as well as of the more usual glass, stone, and clay. Entries for each bead include name, description, suggested use, relative cost, and country of origin and are accompanied by color photos. . . . This resource will prove crucial for public library patrons." Libr J

745.6   Calligraphy, heraldic design, illumination

Gauthier, Jeaneen

Calligraphy 101; a workshop in a book. Creative Pub. International 2010 240p il (101 series) $24.99   **745.6**

1. Calligraphy

ISBN 978-1-58923-503-8; 1-58923-503-7

LC 2010-16769

"After introducing a few simple tools and supplies, . . . [the author] teaches the basic strokes and alphabets. Then she presents a full array of tools, methods, and styles with which to create professional-looking cards, invitations, and artists' books. . . . This is a solid manual for beginners." Libr J

Godfrey-Nicholls, Gaye

Mastering calligraphy; the complete guide to hand lettering. by Gaye Godfrey-Nicholls. Chronicle Books 2013 288 p. color illustrations $40   **745.6**

1. Calligraphy

ISBN 1452101124; 9781452101125

This book, by Gaye Godfrey-Nicholls, offers a "comprehensive and up-to-date volume on this traditional craft [of caligraphy] and its contemporary practice. . . . Inside are step-by-step instructions accompanied by examples of current work, plus historical information, artist profiles,

troubleshooting tips, and an extensive resource section." (Publisher's note)

"Godfrey-Nicholls, an Australia-based artist, elucidates the art of hand-lettering in this comprehensive work. The majority of the book is devoted to calligraphic hands, or different styles of writing. Each hand includes a brief history, exercises for practicing the basic shapes and strokes, foundational groups of letters arranged by type, and variations on the alphabet. Appropriate supplies are suggested for each hand." LJ

Includes bibliographical references (pages 278-281) and index

Kespersaks, Veiko

Calligraphy in 24 hours. Barron's 2011 160p il pa $21.99   **745.6**

1. Calligraphy

ISBN 978-0-7641-4506-3

This book "starts with basic instruction and progresses through sessions that challenge readers with projects of increasing difficulty. An opening lesson introduces students to the standard calligraphy tools—pens, inks, and papers. Tutorials that follow go on to teach the basic strokes for constructing 15 different alphabets, letter-by-letter. Timed exercises are presented to help learners build speed and confidence. . . . They will learn how to create professionally designed greeting cards, wall hangings, place settings, wedding invitations, and more." Publisher's note

Shepherd, Margaret

Learn calligraphy; the complete book of lettering and design. Broadway Bks. 2001 167p il pa $16.95   **745.6**

1. Calligraphy

ISBN 0-7679-0732-9

LC 00-53016

This guide presents historical background, and advice on materials, technique, and workspace organization. Also included are recommended usages for the various alphabets. Step-by-step illustrations are provided

745.7   Decorative coloring

Fresh & fabulous painted furniture. Sterling 2000 128p il hardcover o.p. pa $14.95   **745.7**

1. Furniture 2. Stencil work

ISBN 0-8069-7797-3 pa

LC 99-55370

This describes 25 projects for painting furniture employing techniques such as stenciling, stamping, block-printing, and découpaging.

745.92   Floral arts

Hillier, Malcolm

Flowers. Dorling Kindersley 2000 516p il $40   **745.92**

1. Flower arrangement

ISBN 0-7894-5954-X

LC 00-29485

This book "features 150 floral display ideas using fresh and dried flowers. . . . {The author explains} elements of design (color, shape, and texture) and how to create displays for use in the home, for Thanksgiving and Christmas, at weddings, and in churches." Booklist

Packer, Jane

Jane Packer at home with flowers; beautifully simple arrangements for every room in the house. photography by Catherine Gratwicke. Ryland Peters & Small 2011 144p il $29.95 **745.92**

   1. Interior design 2. Flower arrangement

   ISBN 978-1-84975-119-3; 1-84975-119-6

LC 2010-51126

Packer "shares her flower design philosophy with photos of floral arrangements throughout the home. The over 100 color photographs are accompanied by Packer's recommendations on color, container, arrangement, and flowers, in contrast to her other recent book, Color , which shows fanciful arrangements grouped by color. A list of resources is given for both UK and U.S. firms as well as instructions on the proper care of cut flowers. Recommended to those looking for contemporary ideas for decorating with flowers, which add natural, seasonal touches to interiors." Libr J

746 Textile arts

Searle, Teresa

Felt jewelry; 25 pieces to make using a variety of simple felting techniques. St. Martin's Griffin 2008 128p il pa $21.95 **746**

   1. Fabrics 2. Jewelry 3. Handicraft

   ISBN 978-0-312-38356-5; 0-312-38356-8

LC 2008-40066

"The book is filled with detailed, eye-catching color photographs that will aid beginners and inspire the more accomplished felters." SLJ

Wasinger, Susan

The feisty stitcher; sewing projects with attitude. Lark Books 2009 128p il pa $19.95 **746**

   1. Sewing 2. Fabrics

   ISBN 978-1-60059-465-6

LC 2009-15553

"In the first chapter, . . . [the author] covers how to finish up with sturdy French seams; the use of grommets, snaps, and closures; how to sew with fat thread and reinforce with X's; and sewing machines that work (that is, those that can sew straight, zigzag, and overcast stitches). Every one of her 30 projects follows a similar offbeat tone—and design. With every item, she features a guide to 'ease level,' time, cost, and unexpected materials—as well as a snappy description for at least one . . . with an immediate segue into a step-by-step narrative and color photographs. Pick among oilcloth bike bags; an eco-version of Uggs' boots; a see-through punctured lampshade; and a one-day planner fashioned from an inner tube." Booklist

White, Christine

Uniquely felt; dozens of techniques from fulling and shaping to nuno and cobweb: includes 46 creative projects. Storey Pub. 2007 311p il pa $24.95 **746**

   1. Fabrics 2. Handicraft

   ISBN 978-1-58017-673-6; 1-58017-673-9

LC 2007-23531

The author covers "basic feltmaking techniques as well as needle, nuno, cobweb, 3-D, and carved techniques and featuring 46 projects. . . . What makes this a title of lasting value for libraries is the depth of solid information it offers on the craft and its history, on various artists, and on related topics like setting up a feltmaking studio, teaching felt making, and leading community feltmaking projects." Libr J

Includes bibliographical references

746.1 Products and processes

Dixon, Anne

The handweaver's pattern directory; over 600 weaves for 4-shaft looms. Interweave Press 2007 254p il $34.95 **746.1**

   1. Weaving

   ISBN 978-1-59668-040-1

LC 2007-26351

This "guide to more than 600 different weaving patterns for four-shaft looms divides weaves into basic groups by structure (e.g., basic threadings, block drafts). Each weave is accompanied by warp threading and weaving drafts (the latter, explained in a handy extended flap), a tieup grid, closeup photos of the weave, and color photos of the actual woven fabric. Beginning weavers will appreciate the sections on weaving basics and finishing techniques as well as the glossary of common weaving terms." Libr J

Murphy, Marilyn

Woven to wear; 17 thoughtful designs with simple shapes. Marilyn Murphy. Interweave Press 2013 143 p. color illustrations (pbk.) $26.95 **746.1**

   1. Weaving 2. Clothing and dress 3. Hand weaving

   ISBN 1596686510; 9781596686519

LC 2012048056

This garment-weaver's handbook, by Marilyn Murphy, "offers guidance for weaving scarves, wraps, and more. She also provides advice for designing garments, cutting and sewing fabric, adding edgings and closures, and combining woven fabrics with other techniques. In addition, nine contributing designers share their working philosophies." (Publisher's note)

"Beginners (or experienced weavers who could use a refresher) will appreciate the thorough introduction to weaving tools and technique." LJ

Patrick, Jane

The weaver's idea book; creative cloth on a rigid-heddle loom. Interweave Press 2010 239p il $29.95 **746.1**

   1. Weaving

   ISBN 978-1-59668-175-0

LC 2009-39518

"Patrick's collection of patterns and projects explores the possibilities of weaving on a rigid heddle loom. From basic plain weaves to finger-controlled and pick-up techniques, Patrick guides weavers of all skill levels. . . . This is an excellent addition to any weaving collection." Libr J

Includes bibliographical references

746.2 Laces and related fabrics

Carey, Jacqui

Japanese braiding; the art of Kumihimo. Search Press 2009 96p il pa $21.95   **746.2**

1. Weaving
ISBN 978-1-84448-426-3

First published 1997 in the United Kingdom with title: Beginner's guide to braiding

"Kumihimo braiding is a traditional craft worked with threads on bobbins strung over a marudai, a donut-shaped disk on four legs. Threads are laid in sequence to form the braid pattern. . . . [This guide is] filled with photos and diagrams showing the sequences for each project." Libr J

746.3 Pictures, hangings, tapestries

Brosens, Koenraad

European tapestries in the Art Institute of Chicago; [by] Koenraad Brosens; with contributions by Pascal-Fran¿cois Bertrand [et al.]; Christa C. Mayer Thurman, general editor. Yale University Press 2008 407p il $75   **746.3**

1. Tapestry
ISBN 978-0-300-11960-2; 0-300-11960-7
LC 2008-930401

Brosens, "along with a distinguished group of art historians and curators, argues for the historical and artistic importance of tapestry as an art form. Designed to accompany the Art Institute of Chicago's exhibition The Divine Art: Four Centuries of European Tapestries, this is a genuinely unique text. Its pioneering scholarship is both precise in its claims and accessibly written for a wide audience. After introductory essays, the tapestries are arranged by region and then subdivided by chronology. These works range from medieval through baroque art styles. The color illustrations and the essays that analyze each tapestry are exquisite." Libr J

Includes bibliographical references

746.4 Needlework and handwork

Daniel, Nancy Brenan

The **art** of the handmade quilt. Sterling 2008 176p il $24.95   **746.4**

1. Quilting
ISBN 978-1-40273-351-2; 1-40273-351-8
LC 2008-299642

Daniel "focuses on hand quilting in this book of vintage and vintage-inspired quilt patterns. Ranging from a classic nine-patch to a whimsical windblown daisy design, there are plenty of options for beginning and advanced quilters.

Daniel includes a difficulty rating for each pattern, as well as directions to guide novice quilters through every step of their project. Colorful piecing diagrams, combined with step-by-step instructions, make construction foolproof, and templates are provided for all pieces and quilting patterns." Libr J

Gordon, Maggi McCormick

The **needlecraft** book; [by] Maggi Gordon, Sally Harding, Ellie Vance. DK 2010 400p il $40 **746.4**

1. Quilting 2. Crocheting 3. Needlework
ISBN 978-0-7566-6170-0

This "compilation of five needlework specialties—knitting, crocheting, embroidery, needlepoint, and quilting/appliqué/patchwork—surveys tools and materials, basic skills, patterns (and how to read/use them), and specifics for each specialty. All projects are brilliantly photographed in color, with good explanations given in just a few choice words, especially when picturing yarns and equipment." Booklist

Includes bibliographical references

746.43 Knitting, crocheting, tatting

Bernard, Wendy

Up, down, all-around stitch dictionary; a collection of stitch patterns to knit top down, bottom up, back and forth, and in the round. Wendy Bernard ; photography by Thayer Allyson Gowdy. Stewart Tabori & Chang 2014 288 p. ill. (some col.) $29.95   **746.43**

1. Knitting 2. Handicraft 3. Life skills -- Handbooks, manuals, etc.
ISBN 1617690996; 9781617690990
LC 2013945660

"In the 'Up, Down, All-Around Stitch Dictionary,' designer Wendy Bernard . . . presents instructions for working 150 popular stitch patterns four different ways: top down, bottom up, back and forth, and in the round. This hefty collection, ranging from lace and cables to colorwork and fancy edgings, is loaded with . . . swatches of each pattern, plus charted and text instructions." (Publisher's note)

"As with any solid stitch dictionary, the swatches show multiple repeats of the pattern, and the color photos are clear and large enough to display detail. Charts are present as needed." LJ

Bestor, Leslie Ann

Cast on, bind off; 54 step-by-step methods. by Leslie Ann Bestor. Storey Pub. 2012 215 p. color illustrations (paper w/partially concealed wire-o : alk. paper) $16.95   **746.43**

1. Knitting -- Technique
ISBN 1603427244; 9781603427241
LC 2012002769

This book on knitting by Leslie Ann Bestor "presents more than 50 ways to cast on and bind off, creating edges that are tighter, looser, stretchier, lacier, longer-lasting, prettier. . . . Detailed instructions for each technique are combined with step-by-step photography. . . . At-a-glance charts identify the best cast on or bind off for various types of knitting, as well as cast on/bind off pairs that work well together." (Publisher's note)

Includes bibliographical references (page 209) and indexes

Budd, Ann

★ The **knitter's** handy book of patterns; basic designs in multiple sizes and gauges. Interweave Press 2002 112p pa $24.95   **746.43**
  1. Knitting
  ISBN 1-931499-04-7

                        LC 2001-59208

The patterns in this book "allow the knitter to create garments in any size from toddler to extra-large adult in any weight of yarn, from fingering to bulky. The knitter has only to knit a generous swatch with yarn and needles of her/his choice and plug the resulting gauge information into the charted instructions and schematics provided. Highly recommended for all knitting collections." Libr J

Crochet edgings & trims; 150 stitches. edited by Kate Haxell. Interweave 2009 143p il (The harmony guides) pa $19.95   **746.43**
  1. Crocheting
  ISBN 978-1-59668-172-9

This "is a collection of 150 crochet edgings, all geared to turn a plain Jane garment or blanket into a designer-worthy item or gift. The basics are admirably covered, with special attention paid to black-and-white illustrations of stitch how-to's. The stitches follow, each with a close-up color photograph of the finished products along with prose direction and stitch diagrams. . . . A welcome, detail-laden supplement to long-treasured references." Booklist

Crowfoot, Jane

Ultimate crochet bible; a complete reference with step-by-step techniques. Collins & Brown; Distributed in the U.S. and Canada by Sterling Pub. 2010 304p il (C & B crafts) $29.95   **746.43**
  1. Crocheting
  ISBN 978-1-84340-563-4

This guide begins "with an overview of the craft's origins and its requirements and necessities (for instance, hooks, needles, and knowledge of how to read a chart). Each chapter truly exposes the how-to details, not only in words but also, most important, in oversize illustrations. Included are a well-explained section of basics (for instance, how to differentiate between front and reverse sides and how to work crochet for left-handed crafters) and specific stitch categories: texture and lace, thread, Tunisian entrelac, color, beads and sequins, edgings, and professional finishing techniques." Booklist

Eaton, Jan

The **new** encyclopedia of crochet techniques; a comprehensive visual guide to traditional and contemporary techniques. Jan Eaton. Running Press 2012 160 p. (pbk.) $19.95   **746.43**
  1. Crocheting
  ISBN 0762447494; 9780762447497

                        LC 2012938528

his book by Jan Eaton discusses "all the essential tools and techniques for crochet in more than 400 diagrams and photographs. . . . Readers will discover new twists on the basics, and learn how to create complex-looking stitches, openwork and lace, multi-colored patterns, shaped motifs, Afghan squares, and much more. A 16-page gallery in the back of the book features a wide range of crochet items from designers around the world." (Publisher's note)

Eckman, Edie

The **crochet** answer book. Storey Pub. 2005 320p il pa $12.95   **746.43**
  1. Crocheting
  ISBN 1-58017-598-8

                        LC 2005-16484

This book features "chapters on topics ranging from equipment needs to resources for more information. . . . Appended are standard crochet abbreviations, common crochet terms and phrases, standard body measurements and sizing, suggested sizes for accessories and household items, and yarn care symbols." Booklist

Includes bibliographical references

Epstein, Nicky

Crocheting on the edge; ribs & bobbles, ruffles, flora, fringes, points & scallops: the essential collection of more than 200 decorative borders. Nicky Epstein Books 2008 199p il (Knitting over the edge) $29.95   **746.43**
  1. Crocheting
  ISBN 978-1-9330-2735-7; 1-9330-2735-5

                        LC 2007-937748

"Starting out with crocheted edges on knitting, Epstein quickly moves on to decorative edgings for crocheted pieces. . . . The edgings are grouped by stitch family . . . The book concludes with a variety of patterns utilizing the decorative edgings presented in the book. An essential addition to any library's collection." Libr J

Haxell, Kate

The **knitted** alphabet; how to knit letters from A to Z. Kate Haxell, Sarah Hazell. Barrons Educational Series, Inc. 2013 256 p. ill. (some col.) $21.99   **746.43**
  1. Knitting
  ISBN 1438002955; 9781438002958

                        LC 2013941173

"This book shows readers how to hand knit every letter of the alphabet, plus numbers and punctuation marks, in 26 different fonts--from simple classic lettering to more ornate calligraphy and contemporary handwritten styles." It includes "patterns for 26 different alphabets, including numbers, punctuation, emoticons and dingbats" and patterns for ten projects. (Publisher's note)

Includes index

Hubert, Margaret

The **complete** photo guide to crochet. Creative Pub. International 2010 272p il pa $24.99 **746.43**
  1. Crocheting
  ISBN 978-1-58923-472-7

                        LC 2009-31798

"Reference for crocheters; includes instructions and diagrams for 200 stitch patterns, basic information about how to crochet, plus 20 patterns." Publisher's note

Keim, Cecily

Teach yourself visually crochet; [by] Cecily Keim and Kim P. Werker. 2nd ed.; Wiley Publishing, Inc. 2011 333p il (Visual read less, learn more) pa $24.99 **746.43**
1. Crocheting
ISBN 978-0-470-87997-9

LC 2010-941213

First published 2006 with authors' names in reverse order

This guide to crocheting contains techniques, color photos, step-by-step instructions and tips for additional guidance.

Kimmelstiel, Laurie

Exquisite little knits; hand-knitting with luxurious specialty yarns. [by] Laurie Kimmelstiel, Iris Schreier. 1st ed; Lark Books 2004 144p il $19.95 **746.43**
1. Knitting
ISBN 1-579-90536-6

LC 2004-5314

"The book is divided by both project and type of yarn. Much information is given about each yarn and how it knits up, and several projects are offered for each. There is nothing very complicated among the projects: lots of scarves, shawls, and caps. But by using yarns as varied as lattice, mohair, eyelash, and fur, everything ends up looking great." Booklist

Knight, Erika

Men's knits; 20 new classics. Potter Craft 2009 144p il pa $21.99 **746.43**
1. Knitting 2. Men's clothing
ISBN 978-0-307-46049-3

First published 2008 in the United Kingdom

"The first chapter delves into more know-how than how-to's; its contents cover types of yarn and garment care, not casting on and off or the stitches of knitting and purling. The rest of . . . [this] book showcases 25 men and a dog (Rufus) wearing 20 sharp, well-designed knits that will look good no matter the man's age or size. In fact, all patterns—in addition to materials, gauge, and directions—feature full-color finished photographs of the garment worn by different male models. . . . [The garments covered include] an ombre-striped full zip cardigan; a bulked-up collegiate cable sweater; and vests in plain style, argyle, or checkered patterns. Recommended yarns listed." Booklist

KnitLit: sweaters and their stories and other writing about knitting; Linda Roghaar & Molly Wolf, editors. Three Rivers Press (NY) 2002 270p pa $13 **746.43**
1. Knitting
ISBN 0-609-80824-9

LC 2002-5962

This book "is really about what it means to create something. Sometimes, as many knitters know, there is only the dream of what could be, as unused yarn gathers dust. But that's what's so nice about this book of knitters' personal remembrances. . . . People who love to knit will love this book." Booklist

Includes bibliographical references

Merrick, Kathy

Crochet in color; techniques and designs for playing with color. Interweave Press 2009 127p il pa $22.95 **746.43**
1. Color 2. Crocheting
ISBN 978-1-59668-112-5

LC 2009-8961

The author "has created a book that veterans and novice stitchers will keep at their immediate beck and call, boasting exquisite patterns, subtle colors, precise directions (in symbols and in words), color photographs that encourage trial and experimentation and tips, and techniques that result in professional garments." Booklist

Includes bibliographical references

Parkes, Clara

The knitter's book of socks; the yarn lover's ultimate guide to creating socks that fit well, feel great, and last a lifetime. Potter Craft 2011 207p il $30 **746.43**
1. Knitting 2. Socks
ISBN 978-0-307-58680-3

LC 2011002682

"Parkes educates knitters on the ins and outs of fiber and makes minutiae interesting. Here, she describes the qualities that make yarn suitable for sock knitting, explores the different types of fibers that can be used in sock yarn, and analyzes stitches and stitch patterns commonly used in sock knitting. There's also a beautifully curated selection of sock patterns, including new designs by some of the biggest names in the field. Though the instructions are clear, the majority of the patterns are best suited for those with sock-knitting experience. An essential addition." Libr J

Radcliffe, Margaret

The knowledgeable knitter; understand the inner workings of knitting and make every project a success. by Margaret Radcliffe. Storey Publishing 2014 296 p. ill. (chiefly col.) (hardcover : alk. paper) $34.95 **746.43**
1. Knitting 2. Needlework -- Patterns 3. Knitting -- Patterns
ISBN 1612124143; 9781612120409; 9781612124148

LC 2014016057

This book by Margaret Radcliffe is a "reference for any knitter seeking better results, whether the challenge is reading a pattern chart, substituting yarn, modifying a pattern, fixing a mistake, shaping a collar, or adjusting an armhole." It "covers everything from how to identify a well-written pattern to evaluating schematics, revising a pattern so it fits perfectly, and making adjustments throughout a project." (Publisher's note)

Includes bibliographical references and index

Righetti, Maggie

   Crocheting in plain English; 2nd ed.; Thomas Dunne Books 2008 268p il pa $16.95   **746.43**
   1. Crocheting
   ISBN 978-0-312-35354-4; 0-312-35354-5
                                            LC 2008-43913
   First published 1988
   This is "one of the most comprehensive and accessible guides to crochet available. This isn't a quick-start guide: Righetti provides an overview of the necessary supplies, a brief history of crochet, and information about gauge before guiding beginners through their first stitch, an ideal approach for readers who wish to understand crochet in-depth." Libr J
   Includes bibliographical references

Silverman, Sharon Hernes

   ★ **Basic** crocheting; all the skills and tools you need to get started. Annie Modesitt, consultant; photographs by Alan Wycheck; illustrations by Marjorie Leggitt. Stackpole Books 2006 112p il pa $19.95   **746.43**
   1. Crocheting
   ISBN 978-0-8117-3316-8; 0-8117-3316-5
                                            LC 2005-37862
   This book begins with a look at the yarn, hooks, and other tools one needs to get started, and then moves on to cover the fundamental techniques and stitches. Instuctions are provided for creating a wide variety of home accessories and wearables. Skill workshops accompany each project. Instructions for every step of each project are supplemented with photographs and illustrations.

Square, Vicki

   ★ The **knitter's** companion; Expanded and updated, deluxe ed.; Interweave 2010 138p il $24.95   **746.43**
   1. Knitting
   ISBN 978-1-59668-314-3
   First published 1996
   This is "an excellent ready reference for a variety of knitting techniques, including cast-ons, bind-offs, finishing, and other basics. . . . The demonstrations on the DVDs show knitters exactly what they should be doing. Every knitting collection needs a reference; this one is affordable and accessible." Libr J

Stafford, Jennifer

   Domiknitrix; whip your knitting into shape. North Light Books 2007 256p il pa $19.99 **746.43**
   1. Knitting
   ISBN 978-1-58180-853-7
                                            LC 2006-20117
   "Mastering knitting skills requires discipline, attitude, and wit to transform a ho-hum stitcher into a badass knitter—a domiknitrix. Stafford uses the dominatrix language well and with humor in this entertaining, beautifully designed, and instructive book." Booklist
   Includes bibliographical references

Stoller, Debbie

   ★ **Stitch** 'n bitch; the knitter's handbook. illustrations by Adrienne Yan; fashion photography by John Dolan. Workman 2003 248p il hardcover o.p. pa $13.95   **746.43**
   1. Knitting
   ISBN 0-7611-3258-9; 0-7611-2818-2 pa
                                            LC 2003-53543
   "An introduction chronicles the history of knitting from the female perspective, while subsequent chapters cover topics such as yarn type, instruments, stitches, and patterns. Perhaps the most exciting bit is Stoller's 'knit as you learn' technique: with every new stitch, she presents a new pattern, thereby allowing knitters to build on their knowledge. . . . Essential for all crafts collections and perfect for a display." Libr J

Tracy, Gloria

   Crochet your way; a learn to crochet afghan, over 40 projects for home and family, easy-to-understand text and symbols, special instructions for left-handers. [by] Gloria Tracy and Susan Levin. Taunton Press 2000 218p il pa $22.95   **746.43**
   1. Crocheting
   ISBN 1-56158-310-3
                                            LC 99-58398
   An explanation of basics "including simple and complex stitches, alternative chain techniques, color tips, and felting instructions." Booklist

Turner, Pauline

   ★ **How** to crochet; the definitive crochet course, complete with step-by-step techniques, stitch libraries, and projects for your home and family. Collins & Brown 2001 160p il $29.95   **746.43**
   1. Crocheting
   ISBN 1-85585-827-4
   "This is a complete crochet course presented as a series of workshops that cover not only standard crochet but also those varieties of crochet that do not employ a standard crochet hook, such as Tunisian, broomstick, and hairpin crochet. Each workshop features an illustrative project, full-color illustrations of techniques, and step-by-step instructions. . . . Public libraries will want to add this title to their short list of essential crochet books." Libr J

Turner, Sharon

   Teach yourself visually knitting; 2nd ed.; Wiley Pub. 2010 339p il (Visual read less, learn more) pa $22.99   **746.43**
   1. Knitting
   ISBN 978-0-470-52832-7; 0-470-52832-X
                                            LC 2009-941352
   First published 2006
   This guide to knitting contains techniques, color photos, step-by-step instructions and tips for additional guidance.

Vogue knitting stitchionary: cables; the ultimate stitch dictionary. from the editors of Vogue knit-

ting magazine. Sixth & Spring Books 2006 200p
il $29.95 **746.43**
1. Knitting
ISBN 978-1-931543-89-7; 1-931543-89-5

This book presents a "collection of cable stitches. . . .
The options range from simple to expert level . . . and all the
stitches . . . are organized thematically and shown in large,
closeup images." Publisher's note

746.44 Embroidery

★ The **encyclopedia** of stitches; with 245 stitches
illustrated and 24 exquisite projects. edited by
Karen Hemingway. New Holland 2005 176p il
pa $19.95 **746.44**
1. Embroidery
ISBN 1-84537-203-4; 978-1-84537-203-3

"Each technique is prefaced with history, fabrics,
threads, needles, and uses and then segues into the practice.
Plus, each is accompanied by, for the most part, a sampler
of stitches with occasional real-life items—like a shisha bag
and a Hardanger table mat—to try." Booklist

Kendrick, Helen Winthrope
Stitch -opedia; the only embroidery reference
you'll ever need. St. Martin's Griffin 2010 224p il
$24.99 **746.44**
1. Embroidery
ISBN 978-0-312-61159-0; 0-312-61159-5

"Following a comprehensive introduction to the basics
of embellishing with needle and thread, Kendrick devotes
one section to each individual technique, including crewel,
Hardanger, stump work, and canvas work. Thirty projects,
both practical and decorative, provide practice in each technique, and a full-color stitch dictionary allows novices to
compare their work with the examples." Libr J

Prain, Leanne
Hoopla; the art of unexpected embroidery. photography by Jeff Christenson. Arsenal Pulp Press
2011 400p il pa $29.95 **746.44**
1. Embroidery
ISBN 978-1-55152-406-1

"In this combination overview of embroidery and exploration of its current trends, Prain takes a traditional approach, beginning with a cursory look at the craft's history
and highlighting practicalities, such as tools and equipment,
finishing techniques, and stitching resources. But it is between these lines that the author's true innovation and fun
starts: specifically, with interviews with 28 working embroi-
derers and the same number of unusual projects to complete.
. . . Projects don't disappoint, with directions as clear as
the designs are funky: handkerchiefs emblazoned with microbes, a modern cuckoo clock stitched on Aida cloth, and
knuckle-tattoo church gloves." Booklist
Includes bibliographical references

Reader's Digest Association
The **big** book of cross-stitch designs; over 900
simple-to-stitch decorative motifs. Reader's Digest
Association 2007 320p il $29.95 **746.44**
1. Cross-stitch 2. Needlework -- Patterns
ISBN 0-7621-0673-5; 978-0-7621-0673-8
LC 2006-044634

"When editors at Reader's Digest identify a subject to
publish, they explore its history, plumb the most popular
techniques, then apply those learnings pragmatically. Here,
cross-stitching takes on a more artistic bent, starting with the
book's layout-big type fonts, step-by-step illustrations with
full-color photographs of the projects—and ending with
more than 900 designs." Booklist

Rowan, Margaret
Handsewn; The Essential Techniques for Tailoring and Embellishment. Perseus Distribution Services 2013 256 p. (hardcover) $29.95 **746.44**
1. Handicraft 2. Sewing -- Technique
ISBN 1596687568; 9781596687561

In this book, sewing instructor Margaret Rowan offers
a "collection of handsewing stitches and techniques. The
stitches are divided into functional and decorative, with
functional stitches including such useful ones as hem stitches, buttonhole stitches, basting, and tailor's tacks. Decorative techniques include basic hand embroidery stitches such
as stem stitch and cross-stitch . . . . Each entry includes a full-
color spread with step-by-step directions," (Library Journal)

Van Niekerk, Di
Embroidered alphabets; with ribbon embroidery. Search 2009 128p il pa $25.95 **746.44**
1. Alphabet 2. Embroidery
ISBN 978-1-84448-446-1

Offering 26 "monograms in ribbon embroidery and the
instructions for applying them to quilts, toys, journals, cards,
and home decor pieces, each step-by-step demonstration in
this manual instructs crafters on basic techniques." Publisher's note

746.46 Patchwork and quilting

Beyer, Jinny
★ The **quilter's** album of patchwork patterns;
more than 4050 pieced blocks for quilters. Breckling
Press 2009 488p il $49.95 **746.46**
1. Quilting
ISBN 978-1-933308-08-1
LC 2009-21009

The author "pored through newspapers, catalogs, patterns, and magazines of the 1800s and 1900s to prepare illustrations—along with grids, dates, and multiple names—of
more than 4,000 quilting blocks, the foundation of this genre
of stitching. Yet providing that resource wasn't enough;
Beyer enhances her encyclopedic reference by featuring
mini catalogs of like-minded design styles, like bow ties,
airplanes, the Red Cross, and kaleidoscope blocks. She also
details her sources with commentary and explains how she

categorized the blocks. Worthy of any quilting (and quilter's) library." Booklist

Includes bibliographical references

Brackman, Barbara

Facts & fabrications: unraveling the history of quilts and slavery; 8 projects - 20 blocks - first-person accounts. C & T Pub. 2006 110p il $27.95 **746.46**

1. Quilting 2. Slavery -- United States

ISBN 978-1-57120-364-9; 1-57120-364-8

LC 2006-13689

"Enslaved peoples in the American South preserved their memories with quilts. . . . Quilt historian and artist Barbara Brackman guides readers through the stories they told—and lets crafters create quilts and samplers that capture their own memories." Publisher's note

Includes bibliographical references

Causee, Linda

★ **Quilts** A to Z; 26 techniques every quilter should know. Sterling 2006 192p il $24.95 **746.46**

1. Quilting

ISBN 978-1-4027-2318-6; 1-4027-2318-0

LC 2006-42345

"Deciding to arrange techniques and patterns according to the 26 letters of the alphabet, . . . Causee treats readers to some unusual information in her presentation. . . . In addition to the incorporated instructions for 14 techniques, Causee also delights with examples of new-fashioned quilting-stained glass, or a pictorial representation outlined by mini black fabric strips; and watercolor, in which print fabrics are treated as color gradations. For new and experienced stitchers." Booklist

Cox, Meg

★ The **quilter's** catalog; a comprehensive resource guide. Workman Pub. Co. 2007 598p il pa $18.95 **746.46**

1. Quilts 2. Quilting

ISBN 978-0-7611-3881-5; 0-7611-3881-1

LC 2007-36314

This is a "sourcebook on all aspects of quilts and quilting in the United States and Canada. . . . It is a descriptive manual including specialty shops and mail-order sources for quilting fabrics, batting, and tools; suppliers of kits, patterns, and printed designs; dealers in antique and contemporary quilts; specialists in the finishing, restoring, and/or appraising of quilts; quilting shows, workshops, and teachers; quilting organizations; and museums displaying quilts." Libr J

"This book is an essential resource for hobbyists and professionals alike, and is sure to be a classic for years to come." Publ Wkly

Includes bibliographical references

Ford, Joan

Scraptherapy cut the scraps! 7 steps to quilting your way through your stash. Taunton Press 2011 202p il pa $24.95 **746.46**

1. Quilts

ISBN 978-1-60085-333-3

LC 2010047873

The author presents "her system for organizing and using scrap fabric—oddly sized pieces too large for a thrifty quilter to throw away but too small to use in most quilts. After a thorough overview of the system, which involves cutting scrap fabric into squares of three specific sizes, Ford offers a variety of patterns that use the scraps. The directions are thorough enough for beginning quilters, and there's intelligent advice throughout. Whether your stash fits in a shoe box or threatens to take over your home, you'll find this book useful." Libr J

Includes bibliographical references

Gaudynski, Diane

Guide to machine quilting. American Quilter's Soc. 2002 143p il pa $24.95 **746.46**

1. Quilting

ISBN 1-57432-796-8

LC 2002-9502

The author "covers every aspect of quilting with a sewing machine, from choosing equipment and supplies to marking and quilting the design and finishing the quilt. Of special note are the sections on free-motion quilting and dealing with the bulk of a quilt in the machine. The text is rounded out by three machine-quilting projects designed to illustrate techniques taught in the book." Libr J

Includes bibliographical references

Hargrave, Harriet

Heirloom machine quilting; comprehensive guide to hand-quilting effects using your sewing machine. 4th ed; C&T Pub 2004 176p il spiral bdg $29.95 **746.46**

1. Quilting

ISBN 1-571-20236-6

LC 2004-781

First published 1987 by Burdett Publications

The author "addresses everything from choosing a chair to selecting thread and batting to marking, basting, and sewing. Exquisite examples of finished quilts will inspire." Libr J

Includes bibliographical references and index

Kavaya, Karol

Community quilts; how to organize, design, and make a group quilt. by Karol Kavaya and Vicki Skemp. Lark Bks. 2001 136p il $27.95; pa $17.95 **746.46**

1. Quilts 2. Quilting

ISBN 1-57990-181-6; 1-57990-377-0 pa

LC 00-46378

This work presents three beginners projects and "a gallery of community quilts that includes background information, full-color photos, and working notes as well as a practical, step by-step method for planning, organizing, and making a group quilt." Libr J

Includes bibliographical references

Michler, J. Marsha

Crazy quilting; the complete guide. Krause Publications 2008 255p il $29.99   **746.46**

1. Quilting 2. Needlework -- Patterns

ISBN 978-0-89689-520-1; 0-89689-520-3

LC 2007-940515

This book contains "methods of patching a crazy quilt, more than 100 embroidery stitches, step-by-step illustrations and how-to directions for finishing a crazy quilt." Publisher's note

The **magic** of crazy quilting; a complete resource for embellished quilting. 2nd ed; Krause Publs. 2004 160p il pa $24.99   **746.46**

1. Quilting 2. Needlework

ISBN 0-87349-724-4

First published 1998

"Michler takes the reader step by step through the creation of a crazy quilt and in the process teaches four different piecing methods, 15 embellishments, and more than 1000 embroidery stitch variations. Stitches are divided into broad groups and include stitch diagrams, color photos, and suggestions for use." Libr J

Includes bibliographical references

Pink, Tula

Tula Pink's city sampler; 100 modern quilt blocks. Tula Pink. David & Charles 2013 255 p. ill. (chiefly col.) $27.99   **746.46**

1. Quilts 2. Quilting

ISBN 1440232148; 9781440232145

In this book, author "Tula Pink gives you an inspiring quilt block collection. . . . Make a beautiful, modern quilt of your own design with the 100 original quilt blocks or try one of the 5 city-themed sampler quilts designed by Tula." (Publisher's note)

746.6   Printing, painting, dyeing

Callahan, Gail

Hand dyeing yarn and fleece; dip-dyeing, hand-painting, tie-dyeing, and other creative techniques. photography by John Polak. Storey Pub. 2010 168p il $18.95   **746.6**

1. Wool 2. Yarn 3. Dyes and dyeing

ISBN 1-60342-468-7; 978-1-60342-468-4

LC 2009-28676

This guide to dyeing yarn and fleece "includes instructions for designing self-striping and multicolored yarns with dip-dyeing, tie-dyeing, hand-painting, and other [techniques, as well as] . . . advice on color theory and types of dyes, including food colors and other 'grocery store' dyes." Publisher's note

Includes bibliographical references

Swearington, Jen

Printing on fabric; techniques with screens, stencils, inks, & dyes. Jen Swearington. 1st ed. Lark Crafts 2013 160 p. (paperback) $21.95   **746.6**

1. Textile design 2. Textile printing

ISBN 1454703946; 9781454703945

LC 2012006729

This book, by Jen Swearington, offers "an essential and accessible guide to printing by hand on fabric. She starts by explaining how to translate design ideas into prints, from single motifs to repeating patterns. Jen then goes on to cover various methods of transfer: stencils, photo emulsion, dye baths, bleach resists, and more." (Publisher's note)

746.9   Other textile products

Faerm, Steven

Fashion : design course. Barron's 2010 144p il pa $23.99   **746.9**

1. Fashion design

ISBN 978-0-7641-4423-3

LC 2009-940543

The author "takes readers through a thorough exploration of the fashion industry, from history to inspiration to the design process to landing a job. There are also 14 practical assignments to help budding designers learn more about the industry. Teens exploring careers in fashion will enjoy the practical advice from industry insiders, and fashion-mad readers of all ages will appreciate the information about how fashion design works." Libr J

Webber, Carmen

Chic sweats; 22 ways to transform and restyle your sweatshirts. [by] Carmen Webber and Carmia Marshall. St. Martin's 2009 152p il pa $21.95 **746.9**

1. Sweatshirts

ISBN 978-0-312-37861-5; 0-312-37861-0

LC 2008-37596

Provides step-by-step instructions for transforming sweatshirts and sweatpants into fashionable pieces of clothing and accessories.

"The aesthetic is edgy, hip, and fashion-forward, and readers will be surprised at the imaginative garments that can be made out of humble sweatshirts. Especially outstanding is the introductory material on dressing for your shape." Libr J

747   Interior decoration

Bradbury, Dominic

The **iconic** interior; private spaces of leading artists, architects, and designers. Dominic Bradbury ; with photographs by Richard Powers. Abrams Books 2012 351 p. (alk. paper) $65   **747**

1. Interior design 2. Domestic architecture 3. Interior decoration -- History -- 20th century -- Themes, motives 4. Interior decoration -- History -- 21st century --

Themes, motives
ISBN 1617690058; 9781617690051

LC 2012007221

In this book, author Dominic Bradbury "visits homes whose interiors 'sum up a design movement or define a particular style' of 20th-century interior design. Descriptions of the homes, located primarily in the United States and Europe, include text, color photographs . . . , and a brief biography of the resident or designer. The inhabitants, including Alvar Aalto, Billy Baldwin, Donna Karan, Todd Oldham, and Russel Wright, represent the epitome of 20th-century design and style." (Library Journal)

Includes bibliographical references and index

Brown, Amanda

★ **Spruce**; a step-by-step guide to upholstery and design. by Amanda Brown. Storey Publishing 2013 400 p. ill. (chiefly col.) (hardcover : alkaline paper) $35 **747**

1. Upholstery
ISBN 1612121373; 9781612121376

LC 2013012590

This book, by Amanda Brown, "is the only book you'll need to learn the craft and art of upholstery from start to finish. With clear instructions illustrated by more than 900 step-by-step photographs, the five projects included here are designed to teach all of the techniques and skills you need to reupholster any piece of furniture to suit your own taste and style." (Publisher's note)

"[P]erfectly matches complete, precisely written directions with correspondingly crisp, helpful photographs." Booklist

Includes bibliographical references and index

Cregan, Lisa

House Beautiful Color; the perfect shade for every room. Lisa Cregan ; edited by David Cobb Craig. Sterling Pub Co Inc 2013 336 p. color illustrations $40 **747**

1. Color 2. Interior design 3. Interior decoration 4. Color in interior decoration
ISBN 1588169790; 9781588169792

This book, by Lisa Cregan and edited by David Cobb Craig, offers a "vibrant . . . guide to using color in the home, filled with photos, swatches, and . . . commentary from designers explaining exactly how and why they make their choices. Going shade by shade, it shows how to select the perfect hue for any room, create modern twists on traditional colors, make a subtle statement or a bold one, [and] experiment with colors you might never have considered." (Publisher's note)

Features "more than 400 color photographs of professionally designed interiors and gardens. Cregan includes comparisons of how a particular color is used in contemporary vs. traditional styles and its use for walls and as an accent in various rooms of the home. There is also a section in which designers describe how they employed a specific hue as they decorated a room, along with examples of various color schemes." LJ

Crochet, Treena

Bungalow style; creating classic interiors in your arts and crafts home. Taunton Press 2005 186p il $29.95 **747**

1. Interior design 2. Domestic architecture 3. Houses -- Remodeling
ISBN 978-1-56158-623-3; 1-56158-623-4

LC 2004-9748

This book pictures a "variety of interior details and describes how to add or restore elements that suggest a historic flair while keeping the home comfortable and functional. Common problems such as integrating modern conveniences or gaining needed space are also addressed." Publisher's note

Gillingham-Ryan, Maxwell

Apartment Therapy presents real homes, real people, hundreds of real design solutions; [by] Maxwell Gillingham-Ryan with Jill Slater and Janel Laban. Chronicle Books 2008 264p il $27.50 **747**

1. Interior design 2. Apartment houses
ISBN 978-0-8118-5982-0; 0-8118-5982-7

LC 2007-17179

This "book features 40 homes decorated by real people. Over 400 photos show details of . . . abodes from a tiny rental in Brooklyn to a condo in San Diego to a ranch-style in Miami. Each home profile includes floor plans, . . . resource lists, and 'how I did it' explanations from the renters and owners." Publisher's note

House beautiful colors for your home; 300 designer favorites. Hearst Books 2008 288p il pa $14.95 **747**

1. Color 2. Interior design
ISBN 1-58816-739-9; 9781588167392

LC 2008001533

Jordan, Wendy Adler

New kidspace idea book; [by] Wendy A. Jordan. Taunton Press 2005 153p il pa $19.95 **747**

1. Interior design
ISBN 1-56158-694-3

LC 2004-19929

First published 2001 with title: The kidspace idea book

"Jordan believes that functional space should be designed for children and adults throughout the house. Large and colorful photographs illustrate details described in the text. Ideas include creating fun yet safe bathrooms, dynamic and playful bedrooms, and built-in storage space." Libr J [review of 2001 edition]

New decorating book. John Wiley & Sons 2011 312 p. (paperback) $24.99 **747**

1. Interior design
ISBN 0470887141; 9780470887141

This book on interior design "mix[es] styles for personal expression with an awareness of budget. Organized in two parts, the first section is filled with room-by-room decorating guides and home tours to cover broad sweeps of decorating topics. The second section is organized by integral design topic: color, furniture arrangement, flooring, lighting, etc." (Publisher's note)

Novogratz, Cortney

Downtown chic; designing your dream home : from wreck to ravishing. Robert and Courtney Novogratz, with Elizabeth Novogratz. Rizzoli 2009 175 p. (hbk.) $45   **747**
1. Interior design 2. Houses -- Remodeling 3. Decoration and ornament 4. Interior decoration
ISBN 0847831736; 9780847831739
     LC 2008944143

This book by Cortney, Robert, and Elizabeth Novogratz "offer[s] . . . advice on how to create original, warm interiors with ease. One part practical guide, one part inspirational volume on creating a look for the home, the book pairs . . . anecdotes about the pitfalls and pleasures of renovation with a treasure trove of decorating tips. . . . In each of the ten projects featured . . . before and after shots document the agony and ecstasy of any renovation project." (Publisher's note)

Includes bibliographical references.

Sheridan, Judy

How to work with an interior designer. Gibbs Smith, Publisher 2008 134p il pa $24.95   **747**
1. Interior design
ISBN 978-1-4236-0195-1; 1-4236-0195-5
     LC 2007-48220

The author "discusses how to find and work with a decorator, including developing a budget and what to do if things go wrong." Libr J

Smith, P. Allen

P. Allen Smith's bringing the garden indoors; containers, crafts, and bouquets for every room. photographs by Jane Colclasure and Kelly Quinn. Clarkson Potter/Publishers 2009 224p il $32.50   **747**
1. Indoor gardening
ISBN 978-0-307-35109-8; 0-307-35109-2
     LC 2008-14868

The author "takes readers on a detailed tour of his home to show the various ways he utilizes cut and live plants inside and around the house. A reference guide provides recommended tools and plants for specific interior and seasonal use." Libr J

"A fun-filled how-to retort to those who claim they suffer from black-thumb syndrome." Booklist

Includes bibliographical references

748.2   Blown, cast, decorated, fashioned, molded, pressed glass

Chihuly; edited by Diane Charbonneau. Montreal Museum of Fine Arts ; DelMonico Books, an imprint of Prestel 2013 230 p. illustrations (chiefly color) (Del Monico Books/Prestel) $65   **748.2**
1. Glass sculpture 2. Glass art -- 20th century -- Exhibitions 3. Glass art -- 21st century -- Exhibitions
ISBN 2891923685; 3791353241; 9782891923682; 9783791353241
     LC 2012277913

In this book on artist Dale Chihuly, the authors "examine Chihuly's personal and artistic development, working environment and collections, and collaborative working methods, in addition to recognizing Chihuly's important achievements and contributions to craft and art history." Particular focus is given to his studio glass artwork. "Also included are Chihuly's energetic acrylic paintings and innovative burned drawings." (Choice)

The book "covers a rich set of vibrant work inspired predominantly by natural forms and makes the most of its large format. The documentation is superb, the scope is expansive, and the text is expertly presented." LJ

Includes bibliographical references

748.5   Stained, painted, leaded, mosaic glass

Howell, Karen

Painting on glass & ceramic; [by] Karen Embry. Sterling Pub. 2008 128p il $24.95   **748.5**
1. Ceramics 2. Glass painting and staining 3. Painting -- Technique
ISBN 978-1-4027-5264-3; 1-4027-5264-4
     LC 2007-31742

The author "presents not just a helpful rundown of . . . paints and glazes but also descriptions of brushes and other tools and their uses. She provides instructions for how to get started tracing your design onto your piece, as well as details on techniques as varied as sponging, reverse painting, stamping, stenciling, and more, and useful tips about what works well with different surfaces. . . . A truly useful crafting resource." Booklist

Zaccaria, Donatella

Stained glass crafting. Sterling 1998 159p il hardcover o.p. pa $19.95   **748.5**
1. Glass painting and staining
ISBN 0-8069-4329-7 pa
     LC 98-3575

The author "gears her explanations to both beginners and experienced crafters through step-by-step projects illustrated with photographs. Five patterns . . . become the basis for learning two stained-glass techniques: copper foil with lead and 'straight' lead soldering. Each technique includes excellent closeup photographs of the cutting, trimming, welding, and sealing processes, with enough text to guide unsteady hands." Booklist

749   Furniture and accessories

Kistler, Vivian Carli

The **complete** photo guide to framing & displaying artwork; 500 full-color how-to photos. Creative Pub. International 2009 192p il pa $24.99   **749**
1. Picture frames and framing
ISBN 978-1-58923-422-2; 1-58923-422-7
     LC 2008-46612

In this guide, the author "teaches the do-it-yourselfer to frame like a pro. Hundreds of photos illustrate conservation matting, working with premade elements or frame-building from scratch, glazing, and hanging." Libr J

Miller, Judith

Furniture; [world styles from classical to contemporary] [foreword by David Linley] DK Publishing 2005 560p il $60   **749**
1. Furniture
ISBN 0-7566-1340-X

LC 2005-296398

The author "presents a lavish four-color and highly educational book, and the result will never lose its library-patron appeal." Booklist

Includes bibliographical references

751   Techniques, procedures, apparatus, equipment, materials, forms

Ganz, Nicholas

★ **Graffiti** world; street art from five continents. edited by Tristan Manco. Updated ed.; Abrams 2009 391p il $35   **751**
1. Graffiti 2. Street art 3. Mural painting and decoration
ISBN 978-0-8109-8049-5

LC 2009-922509

First published 2004

Ganz's survey of graffiti art includes "upward of 2,000 full-color photographs. . . . An ephemeral, often despised, yet irrefutably powerful mode of expression, graffiti has always been political, and although many of the street artists Ganz succinctly profiles have moved away from illegal spray painting, they have not compromised the inherent subversiveness of their work. . . . Ganz's global array captures the power and synergy of this vibrant alternative art world in which artists form crews and collectiveness to ensure that their art is seen." Booklist [review of 2004 edition]

Includes bibliographical references

Jennings, Simon

The **complete** artist's manual; the definitive guide to painting and drawing. Simon Jennings. Chronicle Books 2014 399 p. ill. (chiefly col.) (pbk.) $29.95   **751**
1. Artists' materials 2. Drawing -- Technique 3. Painting -- Technique
ISBN 1452127166; 9781452127163

LC 2013040718

This painting and drawing handbook, by Simon Jennings, "is packed with easy to follow instructions, including comprehensive information about all varieties of materials and tools, along with hundreds of critical techniques for mastering composition, color, line, tone, and more. Copiously illustrated in 1,300 color photos and examples from working artists, this new edition is the definitive guide for artists of every skill level looking to begin, develop, and perfect their skills." (Publisher's note)

"This newly updated manual will have broad appeal to beginning and intermediate artists, and can even help experienced professionals hone their craft." LJ

Sanmiguel, David

Complete guide to materials and techniques for drawing and painting; [text, David Sanmiguel; trans-

lation, Michael Brunelle and Beatriz Cortabarria] English language ed.; Barrons Educational Series 2008 239p il $26.99   **751**
1. Artists' materials 2. Drawing -- Technique 3. Painting -- Technique
ISBN 978-0-7641-6111-7; 0-7641-6111-3

LC 2007-931258

Original Spanish edition, 2007

"From applicators like pencils and spatulas to auxiliary materials such as fillers and cleaners . . . [this book] covers a variety of artistic media including paint, paper, canvas, and cardboard. . . . The second half of the book describes drawing and painting techniques. . . . Basic enough for a beginning art student and complete enough to hold the interest of practicing artists, this book is a good choice for any collection." Voice Youth Advocates

751.4   Techniques and procedures

★ **All** about techniques in acrylics; an indispensable manual for artists. {author, Parramón's Editorial Team} Barron's 2004 143p il (All about techniques) $26.95   **751.4**
1. Acrylic painting -- Technique
ISBN 0-7641-5710-8

LC 2003-68843

Originally published in Spain

"A brief history of the use of acrylics by people such as Jackson Pollack is followed by sections on the varieties of acrylics available, tools for their use, and techniques for skies, vegetation, landscapes, still lifes, interiors, animals, and the nude. The demonstrations of color mixing, sgraffito, texturing, transparent impastos, and layering with glazes are especially well done." Libr J

"The book is a delight for anyone interested in acrylics." Voice Youth Advocates

Weber, Mark Christopher

Brushwork essentials; how to render expressive form and texture with every stroke. North Light Bks. 2002 143p il $28.99   **751.4**
1. Painting -- Technique
ISBN 1-58180-168-8

LC 2001-52162

This "book deals exclusively with oil brushwork. Painters learn how to render expressive form and texture using the myriad shapes and types of brushes available. Mixing and loading paint, cleaning and shaping brushes for maximum control, and picking the right paint for specific types of strokes are all covered." Libr J

"Weber writes with humor and confidence, keeping things lighthearted whether he is teaching the mechanics of holding a brush or a wet-into-wet application of paint on canvas." Booklist

751.42   Use of water-soluble mediums

Bellamy, David

  David Bellamy's complete guide to watercolour painting. Search 2009 128p il $29.95; pa $19.95   **751.42**

    1. Watercolor painting -- Technique

    ISBN 978-1-84448-338-9; 978-1-84448-734-9 pa

  "In this short general guide to watercolor painting, Bellamy . . . covers the basics of materials, technique, color, and composition. Advice and suggestions about subject matter are also provided. Bellamy includes numerous sketches, simple step-by-step projects, and diagrammed finished paintings to fully explain the process. Readers will discover the many creative possibilities of this medium, albeit within a traditional figurative framework." Libr J

O'Connor, Birgit

  Watercolor essentials; hands-on techniques for exploring watercolor in motion. North Light Books 2009 127p il $29.99   **751.42**

    1. Watercolor painting -- Technique

    ISBN 978-1-60061-094-3

                  LC 2008-36576

  This guide to watercolor painting covers topics such as types of watercolor paint, painting tools and materials, using color, values, and painting techniques.

  "This is an exciting, comprehensive package for the beginning watercolor artist. O'Connor . . . keys her lessons to a 70-minute DVD. Her wet and loose technique and the personal touch of the DVD make this a great choice at a good price." Libr J

751.45   Oil painting

Sanmiguel, David

  Oil; text, David Sanmiguel; translated from the Spanish by Michael Brunelle. Sterling Publishing Co. 2008 159p il (Painting class) pa $17.95 **751.45**

    1. Painting -- Technique

    ISBN 978-1-4027-4913-1

  "This unusually good introduction to oil painting is at once practical, approachable, and inspiring. Instructions tell how to mix oil colors, work with solvents and dryers, use brushes and spatulas to shape paint, and execute more advanced techniques like chiaroscuro. Exercises cover the characteristics of warm, cool, and neutral colors and illustrate how to approach figure drawing, still lifes, and landscapes." Libr J

Willenbrink, Mark

  Oil painting for the absolute beginner; a clear & easy guide to successful oil painting. by Mark and Mary Willenbrink. North Light Books 2010 127p il pa $24.99   **751.45**

    1. Painting -- Technique

    ISBN 978-1-60061-784-3

                  LC 2010-5056

  "Unlike less successful art books for beginners, this one starts simply and takes the rank amateur to a satisfying level of accomplishment. . . . The accompanying DVD offers useful demonstrations of two complete paintings." Libr J

751.7   Specific forms

Felisbret, Eric

  Graffiti New York; Eric Felisbret DEAL CIA ; contributions by Luke Felisbret SPAR ONE ; foreword by James Prigoff. Abrams 2009 339 p. ill. (chiefly col.)   **751.7**

    1. Street art 2. Artists -- United States 3. Mural painting and decoration 4. Graffiti -- New York (N.Y.) -- History 5. Graffiti -- New York (State) -- New York 6. Street art -- New York (State) -- New York 7. Mural painting and decoration, American -- New York (State) -- New York

    ISBN 0810951460; 9780810951464

                  LC 2009011736

  This book explores the history and influence of New York City as a "mecca of graffiti culture. . . . This is the city where it all began, yet few know the back story. 'Graffiti New York' fills that gap, detailing the concepts, aesthetics, ideals, and social structures that have served as a cultural blueprint for graffiti movements across the world. The book features approximately 1,000 images, complemented by texts by the authors and relevant players in the movement, as well as descriptive graphics and sidebars. [The book describes] . . . the birth of simple signature tags to today's vibrant murals, and covering the ups and downs of the movement, the culture's value system, its social framework, the various forms of graffiti, and significant artists and crews." (Publisher's Note)

752   Color

Edwards, Betty

  Color; a course in mastering the art of mixing colors. Jeremy P. Tarcher/Penguin 2004 206p il $27.95; pa $17.95   **752**

    1. Color in art

    ISBN 978-1-58542-199-2; 1-58542-199-5; 978-1-58542-219-7 pa; 1-58542-219-3 pa

                  LC 2003-67215

  "This new guide distills the . . . existing knowledge about color theory into a practical method of working with color to produce harmonious combinations. . . . Using techniques tested and honed in her five-day intensive color workshops, Edwards provides a basic understanding of how to see color, how to use it, and—for those involved in art, painting, or design—how to mix and combine hues." Publisher's note

  Includes bibliographical references

759 History, geographic treatment, biography

Bailey, Anthony

Velazquez : surrendering at Breda. Holt 2011 264p il $32; ebook $16.99 **759**

1. Artists 2. Painters 3. Artists, Spanish

ISBN 978-0-8050-8835-9; 978-1-4299-7377-9 ebook

LC 2010049809

The author "uses Velázquez's painting of the 1625 surrender of the Dutch town of Breda to Spanish forces as an entry point into a richly detailed portrait of the court of King Philip IV as Spain's Hapsburg empire crumbled around him." Kirkus

Includes bibliographical references

Baillio, Joseph

Claude Monet, 1840-1926; Paris, Galeries nationales, Grand Palais, September 22, 2010-January 24, 2011. [authors of the catalogue, Joseph Baillio . . . [et al.]] Abrams 2010 384p il $65 **759**

1. Artists 2. Painters 3. Impressionism (Art)

ISBN 978-0-8109-9709-7

"In this splendid retrospective catalog for a show at the Galéries Nationales, Grand Palais in Paris through January 2011, Monet's paintings are presented in philosophical, psychological, physical, and personal context in a series of concise, thoughtful, informative, and well-translated essays by noted art historians. . . . This book is what a retrospective catalog should be—expansive and precise, looking over a beloved artist's life and work with many color reproductions." Libr J

Includes bibliographical references

Beckett, Wendy

✓ ★ The story of painting; contributing consultant, Patricia Wright. 2nd American ed, enhanced & expanded ed; Dorling Kindersley 2000 736p il $40 **759**

1. Painting

ISBN 0-7894-6805-0

LC 2001-266885

First published 1994

This history of painting over the past 800 years chronicles movements such as Romanticism, Impressionism, Post-Impressionism and Modernism, focusing on 450 masterpieces and including timelines.

Brainard, Joe

The Nancy book; essays by Ann Lauterbach [and] Ron Padgett; collaborations with Bill Berkson . . . [et al.] Siglio Press 2008 144p il **759**

1. Cartoonists 2. Nancy (Fictitious character) 3. Poets 4. Artists 5. Authors 6. Set designers

ISBN 097995620X; 9780979956201

From 1963 to 1978 Joe Brainard created some 100 Nancy comic strips. "The Nancy Book includes 78 full page reproductions . . . and features collaborations with poets Bill Berkson, Ted Berrigan, Robert Creeley, Frank Lima, Frank O'Hara, Ron Padgett, and James Schuyler." (Publisher's note)

"The guileless heroine of Ernie Bushmiller's long-running comic strip 'Nancy' is an unlikely icon in contemporary art, recurring in work by postmodern cartoonists like Bill Griffith and Scott McCloud, in an Andy Warhol painting, and in rock posters by Frank Kozik. But no one put her to better use than Joe Brainard, in whose irreverent, effervescent paintings, drawings, and collages (occasionally produced in collaboration with poet friends like Ron Padgett and Frank O'Hara) Nancy appears as an ashtray; a medical illustration; the subject of pieces by de Kooning, Picasso, and Leonardo; and part of Mt. Rushmore. Updating the old 'Tijuana Bibles,' Brainard also gleefully depicts Nancy in flagrante delicto and tripping on hallucinogens. Brash but never bratty, fanciful without descending into preciousness." New Yorker

Brewer, John

The American Leonardo; a tale of obsession, art and money. Oxford University Press 2009 310p il $24.95 **759**

1. Artists 2. Painters 3. Scientists 4. Art collections 5. Art dealers 6. Art collectors 7. Art -- Expertising 8. Writers on science 9. Patrons of the arts 10. Art -- 15th and 16th centuries 11. Art -- Collectors and collecting 12. Painting, Renaissance -- Expertising

ISBN 978-0-19-539690-4; 0-19-539690-1

LC 2009008681

"In 1919, a Midwestern auto salesman named Harry Hahn and his French war bride, Andrée, got in touch with Joseph Duveen, the famous New York art dealer, with an offer to sell what they claimed was an original painting by Leonardo da Vinci. Duveen publicly dismissed the work as a fake, and the Hahns, taking him to court for slander, began a decades-long struggle for authentication that scrutinized not only the art world's élitism but the validity of connoisseurship itself. Brewer skillfully outlines the conditions that made America ripe for such an incident and explores how Old Master art became the currency with which the country's new millionaires established their cultural credibility." New Yorker

Includes bibliographical references and index

Brown, David Alan

Leonardo da Vinci; origins of a genius. Yale Univ. Press 1998 240p il $65 **759**

1. Artists 2. Painters 3. Scientists 4. Writers on science

ISBN 0-300-07246-5

LC 98-15164

The author traces the "early influences and the emergence of da Vinci's intense curiosity about nature and ability to re-create it in drawing and painting. The chapter on 'Ginevra de'Benci' is a splendid example of how art history and contemporary scientific techniques can be combined in the examination and attribution of a painting. The excellent full page reproductions and small detail examples are carefully placed within the text for ease of reference." Libr J

Includes bibliographical references

Dali; curated by Dawn Ades and Michael R. Taylor with the assistance of Montse Aguer. Rizzoli 2004 607p il $75 **759**

1. Artists 2. Painters

ISBN 978-0-8478-2673-5; 0-8478-2673-2

Original Italian edition, 2004

This "retrospective of the artist's work from his early years. . . . [includes] comparative illustrations and photographs." Publisher's note

Includes bibliographic references

De Vecchi, Pierluigi

Raphael. Abbeville Press 2002 380p il $125 **759**

1. Artists 2. Painters 3. Architects

ISBN 0-7892-0770-2

LC 2002-23206

This is a survey of the life and work of the Italian Renaissance painter including some 300 illustrations

Includes bibliographical references and index

Dolnick, Edward

★ The **forger's** spell; a true story of Vermeer, Nazis, and the greatest art hoax of the twentieth century. HarperCollins 2008 349p il $26.95 **759**

1. Artists 2. Painters 3. Art forgers 4. Art -- Forgeries 5. World War, 1939-1945 -- Art and the war

ISBN 978-0-06-082541-6; 0-06-082541-3

LC 2007-36578

This is an account of the Vermeer forgeries done by the Dutch painter Han van Meegeren during the late 1930s and early 1940s.

"Dolnick's zesty, incisive, and entertaining inquiry illuminates the hidden dimensions and explicates the far-reaching implications of this fascinating and provocative collision of art and ambition, deception and war." Booklist

Includes bibliographical references

Hensbergen, Gijs van

Guernica : the biography of a twentieth-century icon. Bloomsbury 2004 373p il $35; pa $16.95 **759**

1. Artists 2. Painters

ISBN 1-582-34124-9; 1-582-34606-2 pa

LC 2004-55054

This is a "study of Picasso's antiwar masterpiece, which folds the disciplines of art criticism, political history and biography into a passionate, detailed and well-argued narrative." Publ Wkly

Includes bibliographical references

Kelder, Diane

The **great** book of French impressionism; 2nd Abbeville ed; Abbeville Press 2001 400p il $85 **759**

1. French painting 2. Impressionism (Art)

ISBN 978-0-7892-0688-6; 0-7892-0688-9

LC 2001-266313

First published 1980

This book "traces the development of Impressionism from its roots in landscape and Realist painting through its focus on modern urban life. . . . The works of the major Impressionists and Post Impressionists, Manet, Monet, Renoir, Degas, Toulouse-Lautrec, Seurat, and Cezanne, are featured." Publisher's note

Includes bibliographical references

King, Ross

The **judgment** of Paris; the revolutionary decade that gave the world impressionism. Walker 2006 448p il $28 **759**

1. Artists 2. Painters 3. Sculptors 4. French art 5. Illustrators 6. Impressionism (Art)

ISBN 0-8027-1466-8

LC 2005-31089

"The book serves as an entertaining if broad account of a revolutionary transformation in vision—not least of all through art." Libr J

Includes bibliographical references

★ **Leonardo** and the Last supper; Ross King. Walker & Company 2012 352 p. $28.00 **759**

1. Religious art 2. Art -- History 3. Last Supper in art 4. Italy -- Politics and government -- 1268-1559

ISBN 0802717055; 9780802717054

LC 2012005358

This book presents an account "of the political situation in 15th-century Italy and how it informs our understanding of [Leonardo da Vinci's] 'The Last Supper' . . . interspersed with analysis of history's many interpretations of the painting. . . . The book addresses such topics as the groupings of the apostles and their hand placement; readings of the painting as glorifying faith; and whether the figure next to Jesus depicts the apostle John or Mary Magdalene." (Publishers Weekly)

Michelangelo & the Pope's ceiling. Walker & Co. 2002 371p il hardcover o.p. pa $15 **759**

1. Artists 2. Painters 3. Sculptors 4. Architects 5. Mural painting and decoration 6. Italy -- History -- 0-1559 7. Vatican -- Cappella Sistina

ISBN 0-8027-1395-5; 0-14-200369-7 pa

LC 2002-38074

"This engaging narrative sets the record straight on a few points and is highly recommended for most public library collections." Libr J

Includes bibliographical references

Leal, Brigitte

The **ultimate** Picasso; {by} Brigitte Léal, Christine Piot, Marie-Laure Bernadac; preface by Jean Leymarie. Abrams 2000 535p il hardcover o.p. pa $ **759**

1. Artists 2. Painters

ISBN 0-8109-9114-4 pa

These "essays detail events in Picasso's life and the circumstances surrounding the creation of his art, his influences, and world events. This lavish, handsome book contains more than 1200 reproductions, nearly 800 in full color." SLJ

Includes bibliographical references

Museum of Modern Art (New York, N.Y.)

Joan Miro; painting and anti-painting, 1927-1937. edited by Anne Umland. Museum of Modern Art 2008 242p il $50 **759**

1. Artists 2. Painters

ISBN 978-0-87070-734-6; 0-87070-734-5

LC 2008-932020

"Miro's work is presented with concise attention to detail from the artist's passion for painting. Stripped to its essence, this work captures Miro's artistic roughness, while covering most of his best work. His passion for detail in the mediums he chose to present his art is reflected in the Dutch painters as well as those of Salvador Dali and Pablo Picasso. Entirely represented in color, the book's plates aptly represent paintings on all kinds of mediums from unprimed canvas to still life on mesonite backdrops. The book is printed and bound on museum-quality paper, with a multiplicity of color plates representing the artist's work. A must-have for any library collection." Univ Press Books for Public and Second Sch Libr, 2009

Includes bibliographical references

National Gallery of Art (U.S.)
Edouard Vuillard; [by] Guy Cogeval with Kimberly Jones [et al.] National Gallery of Art, in association with Yale University Press 2003 501p il $70 **759**
1. Artists 2. Painters
ISBN 0-300-09737-9
LC 2002-151120
"A superb display of the surprising colors, forceful textures, and mysterious atmosphere of Vuillard's paintings, accompanied by commentaries in which aesthetics, art history, and biography are perfectly balanced." Booklist

Includes bibliographical references

Renoir, Jean
Renoir : my father; introduction by Robert Herbert; translated by Randolph and Dorothy Weaver. New York Review of Bks. 2001 437p il pa $17.95 **759**
1. Artists 2. Painters
ISBN 0-940322-77-3
LC 2001-2539
First published 1962 by Little, Brown
The author "tells the life story of his father, Pierre Auguste Renoir, the great Impressionist painter. Recounting Pierre-Auguste's extraordinary career, beginning as a painter of fans and porcelain, recording the rules of thumb by which he worked, and capturing his unpretentious and wonderfully engaging talk and personality. . . . {This volume} includes 12 pages of color plates and 18 pages of black and white images." Publisher's note

Robb, Peter
M : the man who became Caravaggio. Holt & Co. 2000 570p il pa $20 **759**
1. Artists 2. Painters 3. Artists, Italian
ISBN 0-8050-6356-0; 978-0-312-27474-0 pa; 0-312-27474-2 pa
LC 99-43576
First published 1998 in Australia
The author examines the life and work of the Italian painter
Robb's "mettlesome assertions regarding M's ruthlessness, 'hairtriggered touchiness,' resiliency, and homosexuality, as well as his confident theories regarding his crimes

and punishments, make for great narrative vitality and drama." Booklist

Includes bibliographical references

Roe, Sue
The **private** lives of the impressionists. HarperCollins Publishers 2006 356p il map $29.95 **759**
1. Artists, French 2. Impressionism (Art)
ISBN 0-06-054558-5; 978-0-06-054558-1
LC 2006-43621
This is a "group portrait of the revolutionary artists dubbed the impressionists for their atmospheric landscapes and forthright depictions of everyday life. Here, masterfully set against a panoramic rendering of their turbulent times, are Manet, Pissarro, Degas, Monet, Renoir, Cezanne, Sisley, Morisot, and Cassatt, each incisively defined as an individual and in terms of their complex interactions as they devoted themselves to paintings that met only with derision." Booklist

Includes bibliographical references

Sassoon, Donald
Becoming Mona Lisa; the making of a global icon. Harcourt 2001 337p il $30; pa $16 **759**
1. Artists 2. Painters 3. Scientists 4. Writers on science
ISBN 0-15-100828-0; 0-15-602711-9 pa
LC 2001-24956
This is a history of Leonardo's most famous portrait and its meanings and popularization in the centuries since it was painted
"Sassoon's knowledge of the minutiae of history and his respect for the image drive the narrative. . . . {This work is} thoroughly researched and highly readable." Libr J

Includes bibliographical references

Scotti, R. A.
Vanished smile; the mysterious theft of Mona Lisa. Knopf 2009 241p il map $24.95 **759**
1. Artists 2. Painters 3. Art thefts 4. Scientists 5. Writers on science
ISBN 978-0-307-26580-7; 0-307-26580-3
LC 2008-47851
The author reports on the "1911 theft of Mona Lisa. The lovely woman with the enigmatic smile was simply lifted off the wall and spirited away. The scandal was immense, the investigation feverish, the headlines screaming, and Scotti revels in every turn. Her lively, expert coverage encompasses the fascinating, many-chaptered story of Mona Lisa and ironic revelations about the frenzy among America's robber barons for old masters and the corresponding renaissance in art fraud. . . . Scotti's avid, exciting true-life mystery yields intriguing disclosures and reaffirms Mona Lisa's unique powers." Booklist

Silverman, Debora
Van Gogh and Gauguin; the search for sacred art. Farrar, Straus & Giroux 2000 494p il $60; pa $25 **759**
1. Artists 2. Painters 3. Art and religion
ISBN 0-374-28243-9; 0-374-52932-9 pa
LC 00-37146

"Silverman's scholarship and lucid writing makes this one of the most refreshing and insightful texts on these two artists in years." Libr J

Includes bibliographical references

Thomson, Belinda

Gauguin. Thames & Hudson 1987 215p il (World of art) pa $14.95　　　**759**

1. Artists 2. Painters

ISBN 0-500-20220-6

LC 87-50203

This "covers the artist's private life and professional development in great detail and captures the dramatic appeal inherent in both these areas. Some of the controversies of Gauguin's life are also clarified." Booklist

Includes bibliographical references

Wach, Kenneth

Salvador Dali; masterpieces from the collection of the Salvador Dali Museum. Harry N. Abrams, Publishers in association with the Salvador Dali Museum, St. Petersburg, Fla 1996 128p il $35　　**759**

1. Artists 2. Painters

ISBN 978-0-8109-3235-7; 0-8109-3235-0

LC 96-3544

"In this slim volume, 40 of the museum's paintings are exquisitely reproduced in full color and accompanied by brief commentaries. . . . A number of Dalí's drawings are included in the introduction, and there is an extensive chronology of the artist's life and a bibliography." Publ Wkly

Includes bibliographical references

759.05　1800-1899

Art Institute of Chicago

Impressionism and post-impressionism in the Art Institute of Chicago; selected by James N. Wood. The Institute 2000 168p il $50　　　**759.05**

1. Impressionism (Art)

ISBN 978-0-86559-176-9; 0-86559-176-8

LC 99-067929

"The 147 paintings, drawings, prints, and sculptures are presented chronologically and in full color. Brief descriptions by art historians, accompanying each illustration, point out details that may not be obvious to a casual viewer and also concentrate on the influences of other artists as well as interactions among artists. . . . This volume is international in scope, especially with its inclusion of American impressionists, and does provide a good overview." Libr J

759.06　1900-1999

Godfrey, Tony

Painting today. Phaidon Press 2009 448p il $75　　　**759.06**

1. Painting -- 20th century 2. Painting -- 21st century

ISBN 978-0-7148-4631-6

"Weighing in at over ten pounds, the book is overflowing with gorgeous full-page reproductions of paintings sprinkled with Godfrey's smartly organized commentary. . . . The most exciting part of the book is how the image placement creates a rowdy dialogue between paintings. If this book could talk, it would roar like a raging party in an echoing art museum." KQED

759.13　United States

Biel, Steven

American Gothic; a life of America's most famous painting. W.W. Norton & Co. 2005 215p il $21.95; pa $13.95　　　**759.13**

1. Artists 2. Painters

ISBN 0-393-05912-X; 0-393-32855-4 pa

LC 2005-4726

"In this ingenious gem of a book, Stephen Biel . . . weaves together a rich cultural history of this unforgettable picture and asks why it has become, for better or for worse, America's most popular painting." Economist

Includes bibliographical references

Breslin, James E. B.

Mark Rothko; a biography. University of Chicago Press 1993 700p il $45; pa $27.50　**759.13**

1. Artists 2. Painters

ISBN 0-226-07405-6; 0-226-07406-4 pa

LC 93-14966

This book "is painstakingly researched, fluently written and unfailingly intelligent in tracing the tragic course of its subject's tormented character." N Y Times Book Rev

Includes bibliographical references

Carter, Alice A.

The Red Rose girls; an uncommon story of art and love. Abrams 2000 216p il hardcover o.p. pa $19.95　　　**759.13**

1. Artists 2. Painters 3. Illustrators

ISBN 0-8109-9068-7 pa

LC 99-39866

"Three of the first American women artists to achieve fame and fortune in the Victorian era—Jessie Willcox Smith, Elizabeth Shippen Green and Violet Oakley—lived unconventional lives marked by a remarkable degree of collaboration. In this . . . study, Carter explores the trio's internecine artistic and romantic relations." Publ Wkly

Includes bibliographical references

Cikovsky, Nicolai

Winslow Homer; {by} Nicolai Cikovsky, Jr., Franklin Kelly; with contributions by Judith Walsh and Charles Brock. National Gallery of Art 1995 420p il $80　　　**759.13**

1. Artists 2. Painters

ISBN 0-300-06555-8 Yale Univ. Press

LC 95-19025

In this catalog of the American artist's retrospective exhibition, the contributors "present a contextually rich and vibrant analysis of Homer's life and groundbreaking work." Booklist

Includes bibliographical references

Claridge, Laura P.
  Norman Rockwell; a life. {by} Laura Claridge. Random House 2001 546p il hardcover o.p. pa $16.95 **759.13**
    1. Artists 2. Painters 3. Illustrators
    ISBN 0-8129-6723-2 pa
                                          LC 2001-19784
  The author "isn't overwhelmed by the complexities and contradictions of Rockwell's temperament, relationship, and oeuvre but rather is invigorated by them, and her insightful portrait matches Rockwell's paintings in its judicious detail, layers of perception, delight in discovery, and reflections on 'the slippery nature of truth in art' and life." Booklist
    Includes bibliographical references

Cohen-Solal, Annie
  ★ **Painting** American; the rise of American artists, Paris 1867-New York 1948. translated from the French with Laurie Hurwitz-Attias. Knopf 2001 436p il $30 **759.13**
    1. American painting
    ISBN 0-679-45093-9
                                          LC 2001-32669
  Original French edition, 2000
  "When writing about the founders, trustees, directors and staffs of museums, {the author} is consistently rewarding. . . . Ms Cohen-Solal is at her best when mining the private history of the art trade." Economist
    Includes bibliographical references

Elderfield, John
  De Kooning: a retrospective; [by] John Elderfield; with Lauren Mahoney [et al.]; edited by David Frankel. Museum of Modern Art 2011 504p il $75 **759.13**
    1. Artists 2. Painters
    ISBN 978-0-87070-797-1
  "A superlative exhibition. (Its catalogue is equally fantastic.)." ARTINFO
    Includes bibliographical references

Gerdts, William H.
  American impressionism; William H. Gerdts. 2nd ed; Abbeville Press 2001 368p il $85 **759.13**
    1. American art 2. Impressionism (Art)
    ISBN 978-0-7892-0737-1; 0-7892-0737-0
                                          LC 2001-22419
  First published 1984
  "The best general source available on American Impressionism. . . . [The] book covers the major artists in the movement, including expatriates working in Europe and regional schools throughout the United States during the late 19th and early 20th centuries. . . . The well-chosen illustrations include many full-page color reproductions as well as photographs of many of the artists." Libr J
    Includes bibliographical references

Hennessey, Maureen Hart
  Norman Rockwell; pictures for the American people. [by] Maureen Hart Hennessey and Ann Knutson. Abrams 1999 199p il $35 **759.13**
    1. Artists 2. Painters 3. Illustrators
    ISBN 0-8109-6392-2
                                          LC 99-73071
  A catalogue of a traveling exhibition of Rockwell's work. "Colorplates reproduce Rockwell's paintings in . . . detail, and the essays set them in fresh contexts, discussing such themes as Rockwell's urban scenes; the reaction by both black and white Southerners to Rockwell's historic civil rights painting The Problem We All Live With; and Rockwell's role in the development of American illustration." Publisher's note
    Includes bibliographical references

Hirshler, Erica E.
  Sargent's daughters; the biography of a painting. MFA Publications 2009 262p il $29.95 **759.13**
    1. Artists 2. Painters
    ISBN 978-0-87846-742-6; 0-87846-742-4
                                          LC 2009-927634
  "This 'life' of Sargent's stirring 'Daughters of Edward Darley Boit' wields a novel's power." N Y Times Book Rev
    Includes bibliographical references

Indiana, Gary
  Andy Warhol and the can that sold the world. Basic Books 2010 175p $22 **759.13**
    1. Artists 2. Pop art 3. Avant-garde (Aesthetics) 4. Motion picture directors
    ISBN 9780465002337; 0-465-00233-1
  A "look at how Warhol's iconic Soup Cans paintings sparked the Pop Art movement, bringing American artists—Warhol especially—to the forefront of artistic and sociological discourse." Kirkus
    Includes bibliographical references

Livingston, Jane
  The **paintings** of Joan Mitchell; with essays by Linda Nochlin, Yvette Lee. University of Calif. Press 2002 237p il $65; pa $35 **759.13**
    1. Artists 2. Painters
    ISBN 0-520-23568-1; 0-520-23570-3 pa
                                          LC 2001-58514
  This is a "vivid portrait of the artist. . . . Mitchell's compositions {are} gorgeously reproduced here in vibrant color." Booklist
    Includes bibliographical references

Mathews, Nancy Mowll
  Mary Cassatt; a life. Yale Univ. Press 1998 383p il pa $21 **759.13**
    1. Artists 2. Painters 3. Artists -- United States
    ISBN 0-300-07754-8
                                          LC 98-8028
  First published 1994 by Villard Bks.
  This "is an evenly written, well-documented, and sympathetic—but not patronizing—biography that should be acquired by most libraries." Libr J
    Includes bibliographical references

Philadelphia Museum of Art

Thomas Eakins; organized by Darrel Sewell with essays by Kathleen A. Foster {et al.}; chronology by Kathleen Brown. Yale Univ. Press 2001 xli, 446p il $75 **759.13**

1. Artists 2. Painters 3. Sculptors 4. Art teachers
ISBN 0-300-09111-7

LC 2001-53142

"This enormous volume accompanies the largest retrospective of {Eakins' work}. . . . {It} includes some 120 photographs as well as examples of his work in watercolor, drawing, and sculpture. . . . Several lengthy and interesting biocritical essays, themselves making up 175 pages of text, separate four sections of color plates. This is clearly the definitive monograph on one of the most significant artists America has produced." Libr J

Includes bibliographical references

Vaill, Amanda

Everybody was so young; Gerald and Sara Murphy, a lost generation love story. Broadway Bks. 1999 470p il pa $16.95 **759.13**

1. Artists 2. Painters 3. Patrons of the arts 4. Artists -- United States 5. Spouses of prominent persons
ISBN 0-7679-0370-6; 978-0-7679-0370-7

LC 99-10416

First published 1998 by Houghton Mifflin

"Often considered minor Lost Generation celebrities, the Murphys were in fact much more than legendary party givers. Vaill's compelling biography unveils their role in the European avant-garde movement of the 1920s." Libr J

Includes bibliographical references

Wilton, Andrew

American sublime; landscape painting in the United States, 1820-1880. {by} Andrew Wilton & Tim Barringer. Princeton Univ. Press 2002 284p il $49.95; pa $35 **759.13**

1. American painting 2. Landscape painting
ISBN 0-691-09670-8; 0-691-11556-7 pa

"Wilton, of the Tate Gallery, considers the influence of Edmund Burke's theory of sublimity and the surge in scientific development on American painters, while Barringer . . . discusses the profound effect on the painters' imaginations of a pristine land free of Western religious, literary, and historical associations. . . . Wilton and Barringer's commentary is stimulating and important, and the exceptional plates are bliss unadulterated." Booklist

Includes bibliographical references

759.2 European painting

Asleson, Robyn

Albert Moore. Phaidon Press 2000 240p il hardcover o.p. pa $29.95 **759.2**

1. Artists 2. Painters
ISBN 0-7148-3846-2; 978-0-7148-4392-6 pa; 0-7148-4392-X pa

LC 00-421386

"This book focuses on the artist's interaction with the Victorian art world as well as his formal pictorial concerns. . . . In addition, the author looks at the politics of Victorian art institutions. This is an excellent book filled with gorgeous color reproductions. Recommended for general collections as well as libraries that support art programs." Libr J

Includes bibliographical references

759.36 Austrian painting

O'Connor, Anne-Marie

The **lady** in gold; the extraordinary tale of Gustav Klimt's masterpiece, Portrait of Adele Bloch-Bauer. by Anne-Marie O'Connor. Knopf 2012 349 p. **759.36**

1. Jews -- Austria 2. Portrait painting 3. Vienna (Austria) -- History
ISBN 9780307265647

LC 2011033578

This book explores "one of Gustav Klimt's most celebrated paintings. . . . [Anne-Marie] O'Connor traces the multifaceted history of Portrait of Adele Bloch-Bauer (1907). . . . The [book] . . . evokes the intellectually precocious and ambitious Adele's rich cultural and social milieu in Vienna, and how she became entwined with the charismatic, sexually charged, and irreverent Klimt, who may have been Adele's lover before and also during her marriage. During WWII, Adele's portrait was renamed by the Nazis as the Dame in Gold to erase her Jewish identity. O'Connor's final arguments about the tragic yet redemptive symbolism of Adele's portrait . . . while it represents the failure of the dream of Jews like Adele to assimilate, through the painting she achieves "her dream of immortality."" (Publishers Weekly)

Includes bibliographical references and index.

759.4 French painting

Bocquet, José-Louis

Kiki de Montparnasse; Catel & Bocquet ; [translated from the Belgian edition by Nora Mahony] SelfMadeHero 2011 416 p. chiefly ill. (pbk.) $24.95 **759.4**

1. Painters 2. Artists' models 3. Women -- France -- History 4. Artists' models -- France -- Biography -- Comic books, strips, etc
ISBN 9781906838256

LC 2011431146

This book offers a graphic biography of artist model and actress Alice Prin, better known as Kiki de Montparnasse. In "bohemian Montparnasse [in Paris, France] of the 1920s, Kiki escaped poverty to become one of the most charismatic figures of the avant-garde years between the wars. Partner to [artist] Man Ray, and one of the first emancipated women of the 20th century, Kiki made her mark with her freedom of style, word, and thought that could be learned from only one school—the school of life." (Amazon.com)

Includes bibliographical references (p. 413-415)

Danchev, Alex

Cézanne; a life. Alex Danchev. Pantheon Books 2012 xx, 488 p.p (hardback) $40 **759.4**

1. French painting 2. Artists -- Biography 3. Painters -- France -- Biography

ISBN 0307377075; 9780307377074

LC 2012007182

Author Alex Danchev presents a biography on Paul Cézanne. "One of the most influential painters of his time and beyond, Cézanne was the exemplary artist-creator of the modern age who changed the way we see the world. . . . Danchev tells the story of an artist who was originally considered a madman, a barbarian, and a sociopath. . . . [He] shows us how the beliefs Cézanne held and the life he led became the obsession and inspiration of artists, writers, poets, and philosophers from Henri Matisse and Pablo Picasso to Samuel Beckett and Allen Ginsberg." (Publisher's note)

Includes bibliographical references and index.

759.5 Italian painting

Ebert-Schifferer, Sybille

Caravaggio; the artist and his work. Sybille Ebert-Schifferer. J. Paul Getty Museum 2012 319 p. (hardback) $59.95 **759.5**

1. Painters 2. Art -- History

ISBN 1606060953; 9781606060957

LC 2011045619

This book is a biography of painter Michelangelo Merisi da Caravaggio. "Rather than accept the stories of the artist as merely an uneducated troublemaker (albeit a wildly talented one), . . . [Sybille] Ebert-Schifferer instead strictly focuses her attention on historical documents and technical research. Beholden to incontrovertible evidence, and taking advantage of X-ray examinations of the paintings, the author finds her way to frequent insight." (Publishers Weekly)

Includes bibliographical references and index.

Graham-Dixon, Andrew

Caravaggio; a life sacred and profane. Andrew Graham-Dixon. Allen Lane 2010 544p **759.5**

1. Artists 2. Painters 3. Painting, Italian 4. Biography, Individual

ISBN 0713996749; 9780713996746

LC 2010497954

This book presents a biography of "Michelangelo Merisi, known as Caravaggio (1571-1610), . . . contextualizing the artist's early life in the town of Caravaggio and in Milan. . . . The author then chronicles Caravaggio's artistic success in Rome. . . . He created many masterpieces there, but the rejection of The Death of the Virgin by its ecclesiastical commissioners, the author argues, may have prompted Caravaggio to commit murder." (Publishers Weekly)

Hale, Sheila

Titian; His Life. Sheila Hale. HarperCollins 2012 **759.5**

1. Painters -- Biography 2. Venice (Italy) -- History

ISBN 006059876X; 9780060598761

This book by Sheila Hale presents a "biography of [painter] Tiziano Vecellio (c.1480-1576), better known as

Titian. . . . Hale examines Titian's life and career within the cultural, economic, political, and social contexts of 16th-century Venice and Italy. As she details his ambitious rise through Venetian society, she also tells the broader story of the artist's stylistic evolution and the world he lived in." (Library Journal)

759.9 Other geographic areas

Bosch, Hieronymus

Hieronymus Bosch; the complete paintings and drawings. {by} Jos Koldeweij, Paul Vandenbroeck, Bernard Vermet. Nai Pubs. 2001 207p il $60 **759.9**

ISBN 0-8109-6735-9

LC 2001-092544

"As keen as the book's historical and technical sections are, its most enthralling passages contain the authors' insights into Bosch's original and satiric worldview and cosmic iconography." Booklist

Includes bibliographical references

Hamill, Pete

Diego Rivera. Abrams 1999 207p il $49.50; pa $24.95 **759.9**

1. Artists 2. Painters 3. Artists, Mexican

ISBN 0-8109-3234-2; 0-8109-9082-2 pa

LC 99-28100

The author examines "Rivera's work and diverse styles. He also describes the pivotal role Rivera's art played in Mexico's development." N Y Times Book Rev

Includes bibliographical references

Liedtke, Walter A.

Vermeer and the Delft school; by Walter Liedtke in collaboration with Michiel C. Plomp and Axel Rüger; with contributions by Reinier Baarsen {et al.} Metropolitan Mus. of Art 2001 626p il $85 **759.9**

1. Artists 2. Painters 3. Dutch painting

ISBN 0-300-08848-5

LC 00-49550

"This is the catalog of an exhibition held at the Metropolitan Museum of Art, New York, N.Y., Mar. 8-May 27, 2001 and at the National Gallery, London, June 20-Sept. 16, 2001. It includes fifteen works by Vermeer and paintings, tapestries and drawings by other Delft artists, including Gerard Houckgeest, Emanuel de Witte, Carel Fabritius, Paulus Potter, Leonaert Bramer, Jan de Bisschop and Pieter de Hooch. . . . Liedtke believes that Vermeer was nurtured and goaded exclusively by Dutch art of his time and by the traditions of his hometown." N Y Rev Books

Includes bibliographical references

Lozano, Luis-Martin

Frida Kahlo. Bulfinch Press 2001 245p il $85 **759.9**

1. Artists 2. Painters

ISBN 0-8212-2766-1

LC 2001-89093

Original Mexican edition, 2000

In this "illustrated survey of Frida Kahlo's work Lozano . . . explores her life and paintings in a series of essays that range from a poetic study by noted Mexican cultural critic Carlos Monsiváis to a short, prosaic piece written in 1943 by her husband, Diego Rivera, to an academic essay by Lozano himself. . . . Lozano uses Kahlo's own stunning images, offering high-quality reproductions of some of Kahlo's most famous works as well as some of her lesser-known pieces. Previously unseen photos of Kahlo at work in her studio are also included. The detail and clarity of the images is incredible." Libr J

Magritte, Rene

The **portable** Magritte; with an essay by Robert Hughes. Universe 2002 438p il $29.95   759.9
ISBN 978-0-7893-0665-4; 0-7893-0665-4
LC 2001-095170

"A glossy, compact collection of 400 works spanning the career of the phlegmatic Belgian painter. . . . [This book is] supplemented by lesser known experiments in cubism, impressionism and expressionism." Publ Wkly

Includes bibliographical references

Naifeh, Steven

Van Gogh; [by] Steven Naifeh and Gregory White Smith. Random House 2011 xiii, 953 p.p some colored ill, maps   759.9
1. Painters 2. Mental illness 3. Biography, Individual
ISBN 9781588360472; 9780375507489; 0375507485
LC 2010053005

This book offers a biography of Vincent van Gogh. The book explores "his early struggles to find his place in the world; his intense relationship with his brother Theo; his impetus for turning to brush and canvas; and his move to Provence, where in a brief burst of . . . productivity he painted some of the best-loved works in Western art. The authors also shed . . . light on . . . Van Gogh's inner world: his deep immersion in literature and art; his erratic and tumultuous romantic life; and his bouts of depression and mental illness." (vangoghbiography.com)

Includes bibliographical references and index.

Saltzman, Cynthia

Old masters, new world; America's raid on Europe's great pictures, 1880-World War I. Viking 2008 336p il $27.95   759.9
1. European painting 2. Art -- Collectors and collecting
ISBN 978-0-670-01831-4; 0-670-01831-7
LC 2008-22141

"The frenzied acquisition of Old Masters by Gilded Age industrialists determined to prove that raw, booming, mercantile America had culture was a blood sport, involving cutthroat competition and calculated deceit. Saltzman . . . draws on both her art history and business backgrounds in this vivacious, anecdotal, and perceptive chronicle of the 'great migration of art' across the Atlantic. Saltzman's close scrutiny of overlooked financial documents led to the resurrection of forgotten players and the exposure of all kinds of shenanigans as tycoons haggled over paintings by such giants as Titian and Rembrandt." Booklist

Includes bibliographical references

Portrait of Dr. Gachet; the story of a van Gogh masterpiece, modernism, money, politics, collectors,

dealers, taste, greed, and loss. Viking 1998 xxii, 406p il hardcover o.p. pa $14.95   759.9
1. Artists 2. Painters 3. Physicians
ISBN 0-14-025487-0 pa
LC 97-37006

"In van Gogh's portrait of his physician, the painter sought to convey the 'heartbroken expression' of his time; Saltzman has taken up where he left off, charting the portrait's progress through our century. From the Nazis who confiscated it as an example of 'degenerate art,' to the Japanese tycoon who bought it for over eighty million dollars, only to keep it hidden in a Tokyo warehouse, the list of the painting's owners is a who's who of modernity, and touches upon the rise and fall of empires and individuals alike." New Yorker

Includes bibliographical references

Thomson, Belinda

Van Gogh paintings; the materpieces. Thames & Hudson 2007 190p il $45   759.9
1. Artists 2. Painters
ISBN 978-0-500-23838-7; 0-500-23838-3

This book "offers a general survey of Van Gogh's paintings. . . . [and] discusses Van Gogh's paintings in terms of a chronological and biographical progression . . . . Filled with beautifully written descriptive passages of the works and careful analysis of the artist's style. . . . This book is a solid introduction to Van Gogh's paintings." Choice

Includes bibliographical references

760   Printmaking and prints

Caplin, Steve

The **complete** guide to digital illustration; [by] Steve Caplin and Adam Banks; Nigel Holmes, consultant editor. Watson-Guptill 2003 192p il pa $35   760
1. Computer art 2. Computer graphics
ISBN 0-8230-0784-7
LC 2002-33190

"This picture-rich resource boasts a glossary, bibliography, and listing of further readings, ensuring that digital designers who are manipulating photos, doing 3D modeling, and exploring the complexities of stacking and layers in illustration will have a wealth of useful instruction and information at hand." Booklist

Includes bibliographical references

Hughes, Robert

★ **Goya**. Knopf 2003 429p il $40   760
1. Artists 2. Etchers 3. Painters 4. Printmakers
ISBN 0-394-58028-1
LC 2002-43281

This is "a remarkably vital, delectably discursive, and deeply affecting study." Booklist

Includes bibliographical references

Riley, Charles A.

The **art** of Peter Max; by Charles Riley II. Abrams 2002 240p il $49.95 **760**
1. Artists
ISBN 0-8109-3270-9

LC 2002-18229

"Peter Max's gorgeous, technically innovative 1960s rock-music posters and album covers made him an instant success and celebrity. Amid a gallery of brilliant reproductions, Riley charts his life before and after as well as during his star turn." Booklist

760.9 History, geographic treatment, biography

Hammond, Wayne G.

J.R.R. Tolkien, artist & illustrator; {by} Wayne G. Hammond, Christina Scull. Houghton Mifflin 1995 207p il hardcover o.p. pa $25 **760.9**
1. Authors 2. Novelists 3. Linguists 4. Philologists 5. Fantasy writers 6. Children's authors
ISBN 0-618-08361-8 pa

LC 96-105237

Along with biographical material and text describing his artwork, this book reproduces more than 200 drawings, sketches and paintings Tolkien made throughout his life. Included are the "Father Christmas" letters to his children and images created in connection with The Hobbit and The Lord of the Rings

"The open and inviting format and the reproductions of his art make this a Tolkien lover's dream, and the insightful text will quickly capture attention as well." Booklist

Includes bibliographical references

770 Photography, computer art, cinematography, videography

Adams, Ansel

Ansel Adams, an autobiography; {by} Ansel Adams with Mary Street Alinder. Little, Brown 1985 400p il $65; pa $14.95 **770**
1. Photographers
ISBN 0-8212-1596-5; 0-8212-2241-4 pa

LC 85-8135

"Consisting of an almost perfect mix of interacting text and images, including some unexpected candid snapshots of Adams himself, this work is an outstanding document of 20th-century American photography." Choice

Includes bibliographical references

Alinder, Mary Street

Ansel Adams; a biography. Holt & Co. 1996 xx, 489p il hardcover o.p. pa $17.95 **770**
1. Photographers
ISBN 0-8050-5835-4 pa

LC 95-44741

"As Alinder traces the straightforward course of Adams' dazzling career . . . she emphasizes the connection between his stunning landscape photography and his zealous work with the Sierra Club. Alinder is as lucid on the topic of Ad-

ams' technical mastery as on his environmentalism and aesthetics, and she also tackles the muddle of his contentious private life with aplomb and candor." Booklist

Includes bibliographical references

Magnum Photos, Inc.

New York September 11; by Magnum photographers; introduction by David Halberstam. PowerHouse Bks. 2001 140p il $29.95 **770**
1. Documentary photography 2. World Trade Center terrorist attack, 2001
ISBN 1-57687-130-4

LC 2001-52330

This collection of photographs documents the attack on the World Trade Center on September 11, 2001. The book is organized essentially as a series of picture essays by individual photographers

Matter, Jordan

Dancers among us; a celebration of joy in the everyday. Jordan Matter. Workman Publishing 2012 229 p. color illustrations (alk. paper) $17.95 **770**
1. Dance in art 2. Dance -- Pictorial works 3. Dancers -- Portraits 4. Portrait photography
ISBN 0761171703; 9780761171706

LC 2012033655

This book by Jordan Matter presents photographs of "dancers leaping, laughing, reclining, and soaring in some of the most unconventional spots: in offices, crossing a busy street, high up in a leafy tree limb, and even in the shower!" The "images [are] around themes like work, play, love, exploration, and dreaming." Also included are "Matter's personal anecdotes about life, learning, and family". (Dance Magazine)

Photos that changed the world; the 20th century. edited by Peter Stepan; with contributions by Claus Biegerd [et al.] Prestel-Verlag 2000 183p il hardcover o.p. pa $19.95 **770**
1. Photojournalism
ISBN 3-7913-2395-4; 3-7913-3628-2 pa

Stepan provides "105 images that had the lasting visual power to capture a moment that could be the image of an era held in the instant of a shutter's click for distribution to a generation. . . . The photos are well reproduced and gain from the explanations of time, place, and context included in the excellent short essays that accompany each." Libr J

Plowden, David

David Plowden: vanishing point; fifty years of photography. foreword by Richard Snow; introduction by Steve Edwards. W.W. Norton 2007 340p il $100 **770**
1. Photography
ISBN 978-0-393-06254-0; 0-393-06254-6

LC 2007-5992

This "book chronicles the American photographer's finest work over a 50-year career that has included some 20 books and numerous exhibits. . . . The breadth, depth, and sheer abundance of Plowden's work over the years are just amazing. Destined to be a classic, this is one of the finest photography books to come along in quite a while." Libr J

Stieglitz, Alfred

★ **Alfred** Stieglitz: the key set; the Alfred Stieglitz collection of photographs. [text by] Sarah Greenough. Abrams 2002 2v il set $150   **770**
ISBN 0-8109-3533-3

LC 2002-5066

This is a "captioned catalog of 1,642 Stieglitz photographs. . . . It contains 'the finest print of every mounted photograph in Stieglitz's possession at the time of his death.' . . . Greenough's essay examines 'what is and is not in the key set in order to clarify the evolution of Stieglitz's understanding of modernist photography. . . .' The set contains very useful, dense chronologies of Stieglitz's process and techniques (1882-1944) and of exhibitions (1888-1944), a bibliography (1875-2001), and an essay on Stieglitz's concern with reproduction printing and publishing." Choice

Includes bibliographical references

770.2   Miscellany

Drager, Kerry

Scenic photography 101; a crash course in shooting better pictures outdoors. AMPHOTO 1999 144p il $24.95   **770.2**
1. Outdoor photography
ISBN 0-8174-5819-0

LC 99-29592

This guide discusses equipment, light and color, composition, and how to capture specific details.

McDarrah, Gloria S.

The **photography** encyclopedia; [by] Gloria S. McDarrah, Fred W. McDarrah, and Timothy S. McDarrah. Schirmer Bks. 1999 689p il $125 **770.2**
1. Reference books 2. Photography -- Encyclopedias
ISBN 0-02-865025-5

LC 98-46084

This work "covers all angles of photographers and the tools of their craft. . . . It is filled with carefully selected photographs portraying the irony and beauty of life seen through the camera lens. As a reference work, the photographs are the glue between biographies and terminology. Additional sections list book reviews, films about photographers, and a time line of photography. Additional appendixes include lists of US museums, galleries, manufacturers, booksellers, etc." Choice

770.9   History, geographical treatment, biography

★ **Encyclopedia** of nineteenth-century photography; John Hannavy, editor. Taylor & Francis Group 2007 2v il set $545   **770.9**
1. Reference books 2. Artistic photography -- Encyclopedias
ISBN 0-415-97235-3; 978-0-415-97235-2

LC 2007-18144

"These two volumes will no doubt remain the standard reference work for 19th-century photography for many years." Choice

Includes bibliographical references

Morris, Errol, 1948-

Believing is seeing; observations on the mysteries of photography. Penguin Press 2011 xxv, 310p il map $40   **770.9**
1. Documentary photography
ISBN 978-1-59420-301-5; 1-59420-301-6

LC 2011013101

The book "takes the reader on a walking tour of photojournalistic hot spots, from 1855 to 2006 to 2003 to 1936 to 2006 to 1863 , in that order . . . Mostly, Morris tries to clear up unsolved mysteries in the crevices of the history of photography—things like whether Walker Evans moved some knickknacks in a sharecropper's house he photographed; which of two photographs by Roger Fenton, from the Crimean War, was taken first; and how much guilt can be inferred from a digital photo of an American soldier grinning over a dead Iraqi at Abu Ghraib." (Nation)

"Morris' assiduous and profound inquiry into the relationship between reality and photography is eye-opening, mind-expanding, and essential in this age of ubiquitous digital images." Booklist

Includes bibliographical references

Newman, Cathy

Women photographers at National Geographic. National Geographic Soc. 2000 271p il $40; pa $25   **770.9**
1. Women photographers
ISBN 0-7922-7689-2; 0-7922-6934-9 pa

LC 00-41575

This look at the life and careers of the photographers "describes their conflicted lives as they balance assignments that took them away from families, homes, and communities for long periods of time. . . . But it is the 144 photographs that attest to the place these women deserve in the history of photography." Libr J

Includes bibliographical references

Photography past forward: Aperture at 50; with a history by R. H. Cravens; and excerpts from Aperture issues 1952-2002; {Melissa Harris, editor} Farrar, Straus & Giroux 2002 239p il $50 **770.9**
1. Artistic photography 2. Aperture (Periodical) 3. Photography -- History
ISBN 0-89381-996-4

LC 2002-107716

"Aperture celebrates 50 years as the premier venue for art photography in the United States with a book worthy of its founders' ideals. An anecdotal history lovingly details its transformation from a bright idea for a magazine—conceived by the likes of Minor White and Ansel Adams—to the publisher of hundreds of books, sampled in the accompanying photos, themselves a dizzying display of artistic variety." Libr J

770.92   Biography

Burrows, Larry

Vietnam; introduction by David Halberstam.
Knopf 2002 243p il $50   **770.92**
    1. Vietnam War, 1961-1975 -- Pictorial works
    ISBN 0-375-41102-X

                                        LC 2002-19100
    This "confirms that {Burrows} was an artist as well as a
journalist, capable of arousing the great tragic emotions, pity
and terror." Booklist
    Includes bibliographical references

Egan, Timothy

★   **Short** nights of the Shadow Catcher; the
epic life and immortal photographs of Edward Curtis. Timothy Egan. Houghton Mifflin Harcourt 2012
384 p. ill. (hardback) $28.00   **770.92**
    1. Photographers 2. Native Americans -- History 3.
HISTORY -- Native American 4. HISTORY -- United
States -- General 5. Indians of North America -- Pictorial
works 6. Photographers -- United States -- Biography
    ISBN 0618969020; 9780618969029

                                        LC 2012022390
    This book by "National Book Award winner Timothy
Egan" is a biography of photographer Edward Curtis that
"recaptures the story of a man both entrapped by his time
and ahead of it." In 1900, Curtis "made a decision that
changed his life . . . . He largely abandoned his lucrative
portrait studio work and began a thirty-year project to record
images of Native Americans who, he believed, were doomed
to extinction, [which] destroyed his marriage and left him
destitute." (Barnes and Noble)

Huffman, Alan

    Here I Am; The Story of Tim Hetherington, War
Photographer. Alan Huffman. Grove Press 2013
256 p. (hardcover) $25   **770.92**
    1. War photography
    ISBN 0802120903; 9780802120908
    This book, by Alan Huffman, offers a biography of "Tim
Hetherington (1970-2011) . . . , one of the world's most distinguished and dedicated photojournalists, whose career was
tragically cut short when he died in a mortar blast while covering the Libyan Civil War. . . . Huffman recounts Hetherington's life from his first interests in photography, through his
critical role in reporting the Liberian Civil War, to his tragic
death in Libya." (Publisher's note)

Panzer, Mary

    Mathew Brady and the image of history; with
an essay by Jeana K. Foley. Smithsonian Institution Press 1997 xxiii, 232p il hardcover o.p. pa
$19.95   **770.92**
    1. Photographers 2. United States -- History -- 1861-
1865, Civil War -- Pictorial works
    ISBN 1-56098-793-6; 978-1-58834-143-3 pa;
1-58834-143-7 pa

                                          LC 97-9493
    In this reassessment of the life and work of the iconic
19th-century photographer, the author "points out that Brady
seldom stood behind the camera, preferring the role of studio

chief executive officer and entrepreneur to that of a mere
'operator.' . . . Moreover, Brady was an incompetent businessman, often leaving his creditors in the lurch, and ended
his career in bankruptcy. This is enough to make us think
twice about Brady, but Panzer's most audacious assertion
is that we also need to think twice about the meaning of the
pictures attributed to him." N Y Times Book Rev
    Includes bibliographical references

Willis, Deborah

    Reflections in Black; a history of Black photog-
raphers, 1840-1999. Norton 2000 348p il $50; pa
$35   **770.92**
    1. African Americans in art 2. African American
photographers 3. Photography -- History
    ISBN 0-393-04880-2; 0-393-32280-7 pa

                                        LC 99-55185
    Companion volume to A Smithsonian traveling exhibition
    "Willis sketches important figures and traces both de-
velopments in photographic techniques and the practice of
photography by African Americans. . . . A beautiful and informative album." Booklist
    Includes bibliographical references and index

Wilson, Robert

    Mathew Brady; Portraits of a Nation. Robert
Wilson. St. Martin's Press 2013 320 p. $28 **770.92**
    1. United States -- History -- 1861-1865, Civil War
-- Photography 2. Photographers -- United States --
Biography 4. United States -- History -- Civil War,
1861-1865 -- Photography
    ISBN 1620402033; 9781620402030

                                        LC 2013016928
    In this biography of photographer Mathew Brady, author
Robert Wilson "examines surviving business registers, articles, advertisements, and documents of Brady's associates
and prestigious clients. . . . Wilson shows how Brady's artistic genius . . . his awareness of the commercial value and
historical impact of his art; his congenial personality; and his
relentless and savvy promotion of himself, his business, and
his craft made him the preeminent 19th-century photographer." (Library Journal)
    Includes bibliographical references and index

775   Digital photography

Ang, Tom

    ★ **Digital** photographer's handbook; Fully up-
dated 4th ed.; Dorling Kindersley 2008 408p il pa
$24.95   **775**
    1. Digital cameras 2. Digital photography
    ISBN 978-0-7566-4310-2

                                        LC 2009-419082
    First published 2002

This guide covers topics such as different types of cameras and lenses, scanners, photography techniques, computers, software, digital manipulation, and printing photos.

Includes bibliographical references

Digital photography masterclass. DK 2008 360p il $30   **775**

1. Digital photography 2. Photography -- Processing

ISBN 978-0-7566-3672-2; 0-7566-3672-8

LC 2008-299944

The author "teaches how to look at the world with a photographer's eye and offers tutorials, photographic assignments, and step-by-step image-manipulation exercises. Combining technical and artistic aspects of photography, Ang completes the volume with sections on travel, documentary, portrait, nature, sports, and architecture photography. . . . A fine selection for all libraries." Libr J

Freeman, Michael

The **photographer's** mind; creative thinking for better digital photos. Focal Press 2011 192p il pa $29.95   **775**

1. Digital photography

ISBN 978-0-240-81517-6

The author "shares experience he has gained as a professional photographer to improve the quality of the digital pictures nearly everyone is now creating. The content is streamlined into three chapters, on intent, style, and process, that tackle both the practical and the intangible aspects of photography more thoughtfully than many similar books. Freeman is as adept at explaining composition as he is at discussing the problem of cliché or the philosophy of the sublime." Libr J

Includes bibliographical references

Johnson, Dave

★ **How** to do everything: digital camera; 5th ed.; McGraw-Hill 2008 xx, 428p il pa $24.99   **775**

1. Digital cameras 2. Digital photography

ISBN 978-0-07-149580-6

LC 2008-4602

First published 2001

This book teaches "the fundamentals of photography, composition, lighting, and exposure, and . . . techniques for different subjects and situations. The book also explains how to use a variety of photo-editing tools and offers . . . tips for storing, sharing, and printing your photographs." Publisher's note

Ritchin, Fred

After photography. W.W. Norton 2008 199p il $29.95   **775**

1. Digital photography

ISBN 978-0-393-05024-0; 0-393-05024-6

LC 2008-19178

The author "offers a supple, politically astute and fascinating account of the dizzying impact of the digital revolution on the trajectory of the photographic image that, like all new media, changes the world in the very act of observing it. The myth of photographic objectivity has concealed fakery as old as the medium itself, he notes, but in the digital era,

concealment and manipulation come to shape the very experience of the image as sui generis." Publ Wkly

Zuckerman, Jim

Pro secrets to dramatic digital photos. Lark Books 2010 176p il pa $19.95   **775**

1. Composition (Art) 2. Digital photography

ISBN 978-1-60059-638-4

LC 2010-8098

The author "compiles 15 critical steps to achieving great pictures. He covers methods for choosing subjects, the use of color for impact, capturing motion, one-of-a-kind perspectives, and thinking as the lens sees. The book is filled with stunning landscapes, portraits, and abstract images." Libr J

776   Computer art (Digital art)

Ligon, Scott

Digital art revolution; creating fine art with Photoshop. Watson-Guptill 2010 256p il pa $29.99 **776**

1. Digital art 2. Computer art 3. Adobe Photoshop (Computer program)

ISBN 978-0-8230-9536-0

LC 2009-22670

The author "begins with the basics of the Photoshop environment and adds increasingly complex digital techniques, illustrated by 40 noted digital artists. . . . Ligon's book is among the best for beginning and intermediate artists." Libr J

Includes bibliographical references

777   Cinematography and videography

Ball, Edward, 1959-

The **inventor** and the tycoon; a Gilded Age murder and the birth of moving pictures. Edward Ball. Doubleday 2013 464 p. (hardcover : alk. paper) $29.95   **777**

1. Businesspeople -- California -- Biography 2. Cinematography -- United States -- History 3. Cinematographers -- California -- Biography 4. Motion pictures -- United States -- History 5. Trials (Murder) -- California -- San Francisco

ISBN 0385525753; 9780385525756; 9780385535496; 9780767929400

LC 2012019977

This book by Edward Ball "interweaves [Eadweard] Muybridge's quest to unlock the secrets of motion through photography, an obsessive murder plot, and the peculiar partnership of an eccentric inventor and a driven entrepreneur. . . . The artist and inventor Muybridge was also a murderer who killed coolly and meticulously, and his trial is one of the early instances of a media sensation. His patron was railroad tycoon (and former California governor) Leland Stanford." (Publisher's note)

Includes bibliographical references

778 Specific fields and special kinds of photography

Yeros, Dimitris

Shades of love; photographs inspired by the poems of C.P. Cavafy. Insight Editions 2011 168 p. **778**

1. Love poetry 2. Greek poetry 3. Artists -- Portraits 4. Gay men -- Portraits 5. Homosexuality -- Poetry
ISBN 1608870138; 9781608870134

This photography book "give[s] visual form to the poems of C.P. Cavafy, the preeminent craftsman of modern Greek verse . . . and one of the twentieth century's earliest lyricists of openly same-sex desire. . . . Mixing genres and sitters, celebrity and anonymity, [Dimitris] Yeros's volume brings to Cavafy's writing a visual range. . . . Cavafy's poem 'The Souls of Old Men' is paired with a group portrait of elderly gentleman from a small Greek town. . . . Other juxtapositions are redolent of less specific erotics, setting verse on love and longing next to anonymous nudes. . . . A number of openly gay literati and artworld luminaries sat for Yeros . . . from Gore Vidal and Edmund White, to Edward Lucie-Smith and Edward Albee. . . . But unexpected figures crop up as well, including Chuck Close, Jeff Koons, Naguib Mahfouz, and Gabriel Garcia Marquez." (Afterimage)

778.3 Special kinds of photography

Benson, Michael

Far out; a space-time chronicle. Abrams 2009 328p il **778.3**

1. Space photography
ISBN 0810949482; 9780810949485

LC 2009-929096

This is a "collection of astronomical images from observatories around the world and in space." (Publisher's note) Index.

"Here are stars packed like golden sand, gas combed in delicate blue threads, piled into burgundy thunderheads and carved into sinuous rilles and ribbons, and galaxies clotted with star clusters dancing like spiders on the ceiling. . . . You can sit and look through this book for hours and never be bored, . . . or you can actually read the accompanying learned essays. Mr. Benson's prose is up to its visual surroundings, no mean feat." N Y Times (Late N Y Ed)

Includes bibliographical references

Dillard, Ted

Black & white pipeline; converting digital color into striking grayscale images. Lark Books 2009 240p il pa $29.95 **778.3**

1. Digital photography
ISBN 978-1-60059-400-7; 1-60059-400-X

LC 2009-14894

"Shooting in full color and converting to black and white . . . [the author] produces a vast range of luminous grays. A must for serious photographers." Libr J

Includes bibliographical references

778.5 Cinematography and videography

Harryhausen, Ray

The **art** of Ray Harryhausen; [by] Ray Harryhausen & Tony Dalton; with a foreword by Peter Jackson. Billboard Books 2006 230p il $50 **778.5**

1. Animated films 2. Cinematography
ISBN 0-8230-8400-0

LC 2005-930364

First published 2005 in the United Kingdom

"The text is fun and informative, but the main feast here is the art, and the reproductions of the concept drawings and photos of the models are superb." Libr J

Netzley, Patricia D.

The **encyclopedia** of movie special effects. Oryx Press 2000 291p il $73.95 **778.5**

1. Cinematography
ISBN 1-57356-167-3

LC 99-47733

"This volume provides 366 entries on visual, mechanical, and makeup effects and techniques used in film and includes discussions of every movie to win an Oscar for special effects." Libr J

Includes bibliographical references

Weishar, Peter

Blue Sky; the art of computer animation: featuring Ice Age and Bunny. Abrams 2002 86p il pa $24.95 **778.5**

1. Computer animation
ISBN 0-8109-9069-5

LC 2001-58988

This goes behind the scenes at "Blue Sky Studios and uses their . . . film Ice Age to illustrate computer modeling, rigging, texture mapping, and special effects. Weishar entertainingly details the technological wizardry used to create 3-D animation of everything from storms and smoke to fully realized film sets and woolly mammoths." Libr J

778.9 Photography of specific subjects

National Audubon Society

National Audubon Society guide to nature photography; Digital ed; Firefly Books 2008 207p il $24.95 **778.9**

1. Nature photography
ISBN 978-1-5540-7392-4; 1-5540-7392-8

LC 2009-285060

First published 1990 by Little, Brown with title: Audubon Society guide to nature photography

"The author provides practical advice for both the craft and art of nature photography, beginning with choosing the right equipment and learning essential skills before moving on to the specifics of photographing wildlife, landscapes, and closeup subjects. The final section deals with digital processing and adjustment of images via such programs as Photoshop. Although the text assumes that the user has basic knowledge of photographic principles, it will be useful for just about anyone who wants to move beyond a simple point-and-shoot camera." Booklist

Includes bibliographical references

Watkins, Carleton Emmons

Carleton Watkins: the complete mammoth photographs; Weston Naef and Christine Hult-Lewis; with contributions by Michael Hargraves, Jack von Euw, and Jennifer A. Watts. J. Paul Getty Museum 2011 xxv, 572p il map $195 **778.9**

1. Photography 2. California -- Pictorial works
ISBN 978-1-60606-005-6; 1-60606-005-8

LC 2011-05241

" A monumental achievement in the pictorial historiography of 19th-century America, loaded with new images and data, this will be an indispensable resource for students of photography and U.S. history." Libr J

Includes bibliographical references

779 Photographic images

Adams, Robert

Summer nights, walking; along the Colorado front range, 1976-1982. Aperture; Yale University Art Gallery 2009 un il $50 **779**

1. Artistic photography
ISBN 978-1-59711-117-1

LC 2009-928119

Expanded and revised edition of: Summer nights, first published 1985 by Aperture

"The book exalts the aftershocks of twilight in images Adams began making in the 1970s around his hometown of Longmont, Colorado. Snapping away into the night, Adams, the quintessential Western American photographer, produced a body of work in which the illuminative sources—often floodlights and moon glow—become the primary subject matter. In his images, the tactile beauty of a warm summer evening becomes anachronistically more evident when placed against the sad sprawl of ever-looming industry." V

Barnes, Richard

Animal logic; with contributions by Susan Yelavich, Jonathan Rosen, Mark Strand. Princeton Architectural Press 2009 un il $65 **779**

1. Artistic photography 2. Animals -- Pictorial works
ISBN 978-1-56898-861-0; 1-56898-861-3

LC 2009-06086

"The first monograph for acclaimed photographer Richard Barnes. Focusing on his work of the past decade, and his 2004 solo exhibition of the same name, the book presents over 100 photographs that explore the collecting and display of animals in natural history museums. His measured, pensive images illustrate the process involved in creating the artificial dioramas and displays." i before e

Includes bibliographical references

Brandow, Todd

Edward Steichen; lives in photography. [by] Todd Brandow and William A. Ewing. W. W. Norton & Company 2008 355p il $100 **779**

1. Photographers 2. Artistic photography
ISBN 978-0-393-06626-5

LC 2007-20128

"One of the finest photography books published in many years; highly recommended for all libraries." Libr J

Includes bibliographical references (p. 309-316)

Burtynsky, Ed

Burtynsky : oil; photographs, Edward Burtynsky; essays, Michael Mitchell, William E. Rees, Paul Roth; [editor, Marcus Schubert] Steidl 2009 215p il $128 **779**

1. Artistic photography 2. Petroleum industry -- Pictorial works
ISBN 978-3-86521-943-5; 3-86521-9438

"The extraction, distribution, consumption, and declining availability of petroleum are all explored through [Burtynsky's] large-format photographs. The opening section examines extraction and refinement. The immense size, geometric order and rectilinear shapes of production fields and refineries make for images of striking formal beauty despite the subject matter, all rendered in fine-grained detail. . . . Next is 'Motor Culture,' images of the world oil has made. Aerial shots of geometric highway interchanges, the immensity of exurban sprawl, endless rows of new cars awaiting shipment—even Bike Week in Sturgis, South Dakota, gets the same monumental treatment. Last, and darkest, is 'The End of Oil.' In this section Burtynsky shows us the final result of the process: rusted out, oozing abandoned oil fields, endless ranks of junked cars and airplanes." Online Photographer

Carter, Graydon

Vanity Fair, the portraits; a century of iconic images. by Graydon Carter and the editors of Vanity Fair; foreword by Graydon Carter; essays by Christopher Hitchens, David Friend, and Terence Pepper. Abrams 2008 383p il $65 **779**

1. Celebrities 2. Portrait photography
ISBN 978-0-8109-7298-8; 0-8109-7298-0

LC 2008-05033

"Culled from the pages of Vanity Fair magazine by its editor, Graydon Carter, and his staff, and shot by many of the greatest photographers in the history of the medium, these pictures are engrossing less because of the people they portray than because of the breathtaking ingenuity with which each subject is captured. . . . Whether taken by Baron de Meyer, Edward Steichen or Man Ray, or by latter-day geniuses like [Annie] Leibovitz, Helmut Newton or Herb Ritts, these pictures stand as some of the finest examples of photographic craft ever to appear in the mainstream press." N Y Times Book Rev

Coles, Robert

★ When they were young; a photographic retrospective of childhood from the Library of Congress.

preface by James H. Billington. Kales Press 2002 160p il $39.95 **779**
1. Library of Congress 2. Artistic photography 3. Children -- Pictorial works
ISBN 0-9670076-5-8
LC 2002-7177
This is an "illustrated portrayal of early life and the legacies that live on from coming of age. . . . Spanning the history of photography from the daguerreotype to the documentary, each tritone image in this volume is illustrated on a full page. Works by internationally renowned photographers such as Edward Curtis and Dorothea Lange are included." Publisher's note

Eggleston, William
William Eggleston; democratic camera, photographs, and video, 1961-2008. [introduced and edited by] Elisabeth Sussman and Thomas Weski; with contributions by Donna De Salvo, Tina Kukielski, and Stanley Booth. Whitney Museum of American Art 2008 304p il $65 **779**
1. Videotapes 2. Artistic photography
ISBN 978-0-300-12621-1; 0-300-12621-2
LC 2008-32248
"Eggleston saturates his extraordinary photographs with light and color, and this makes the banal seem exalted and infused with heightened significance. . . . [He] is a deservedly venerated master, and a full tribute such as this is as compelling as it is overdue." Libr J
Includes bibliographical references

Elkins, Ken
Picture taker. Univ. of Alabama 2005 120p il $35 **779**
1. Photojournalism
ISBN 0-8173-1478-4
LC 2004-25921
A collection of 100 black-and-white photographs taken by the chief photographer of the Anniston Star.
"Elkins is very good at the perfect image caught on the fly. See the picture of a man in a boat who has just paddled it one stroke forward . . . ; a curled ribbon of water is caught leaping from the misted, glassy surface. See the baby crawling on pavement in the driving rain . . . . See the dogs wading in floodwater while fog swallows the whole scene. . . . Perhaps even more than the many exquisitely casual portraits of housedress- and overalls-clad farmers, such visions become engraved in one's memory instantaneously, ineradicably." Booklist

Epstein, Mitch
American power. Steidl 2009 un il $70 **779**
1. Photojournalism 2. Electric power plants -- Pictorial works
ISBN 978-3-86521-924-4; 3-86521-924-1
"In his ravishing new book, American Power, acclaimed art photographer Mitch Epstein succeeds at both enthralling and horrifying with his 63 images of our widely polluted land. After witnessing the evacuation of an Ohio town in the wake of environmental contamination, he decided to explore the ramifications of American production and consumption of energy. For five years he traveled the country photograph-

ing energy production sites, mines, factories, rigs, and deserted gas pumps, as well as the power-related devastation caused by Hurricane Katrina." Artinfo

Haas, Robert B.
Through the eyes of the Vikings; an aerial vision of Arctic lands. Robert B. Haas. Ragged Bears [distributor] 2010 219p il map $50 **779**
1. Aerial photography 2. Arctic regions -- Pictorial works
ISBN 978-1-4262-0638-2; 1-4262-0638-0
LC 2010549763

Jackson, Bruce
Pictures from a drawer; early 20th century portraits from a Southern prison. Temple University Press 2009 204p il $85; pa $34.95 **779**
1. Prisoners 2. Portrait photography
ISBN 978-1-59213-948-4; 978-1-59213-949-1 pa
LC 2008-24250
"The book comprises entry and exit photos of prisoners at Cummins in the first half of the 20th century—mugshots that Jackson found, as the title states plainly, in a drawer. These remarkable photos, preserved by Jackson and resurrected through judicious use of Photoshop, are bracketed by an essay on photography and its uses, neatly balanced by Jackson's reflections on the two decades he spent working in prisons, and a convict's first-person account of what Cummins was like in the decades before Jackson first came there in 1971." Artvoice
Includes bibliographical references

Keep Your Eye on the Wall; Palestinian Landscapes. Edited by Mitchell Albert and Olivia Snaije. Saqi Books 2014 192 p. chiefly col. ill. $69.95 **779**
1. Palestine 2. Photography 3. Israel-Arab conflicts
ISBN 0863567592; 9780863567599
"In art and literature, walls are frequently used as powerful symbols of division. For the people of Palestine, however, the wall that cuts deeply into their land and society is all too real, snaking through over seven hundred kilometres of the West Bank." Edited by Mitchell Albert and Olivia Snaije, "'Keep Your Eye on the Wall' brings together seven . . . artist-photographers and four essayists, all responding to the Wall in images or words." (Publisher's note)
The contributors "searingly present the wall in pictures and text, in a beautiful accordion bound book, that like the wall, extends in a long line from beginning to end." Pub Wkly
Includes bibliographical references

Lee, Russell
Russell Lee photographs; images from the Russell Lee photograph collection at the Center for American History. foreword by John Szarkowski; introduction by J. B. Colson; photographs selected and arranged by Linda Peterson. University of Texas

Press 2007 236p il (Focus on American history series) $50   **779**
1. Documentary photography
ISBN 978-0-292-71499-1; 0-292-71499-8
LC 2006-15020
"Lee's quietly passionate images are masterful works. They set a high standard for a kind of reflective journalism that reminds us that a fine artist may tell you most about himself when first he focuses on others." Texas Observer

Leibovitz, Annie
Annie Leibovitz at work; [Sharon DeLano, editor] Random House 2008 237p il $40   **779**
1. Portrait photography
ISBN 978-0-375-50510-2; 0-375-50510-5
LC 2008-933724
Leibovitz "discusses her personal approaches, trials, and discoveries as a professional photographer, pairing detailed memories and technical discussions with images of her most iconic celebrity portraits (including the Rolling Stones, Demi Moore, John Lennon, and Queen Elizabeth). The book adheres to a chronological format—from Leibowitz's earliest black-and-white photos of the Rolling Stones and John Lennon to her conceptual color portraits from the 1980s. . . . Also included are personal and family photographs as well as her most recent photo shoots for Vanity Fair, including the Obama and Clinton campaigns." Libr J

A **photographer's** life, 1990-2005. Random House 2006 un il $75   **779**
1. Portrait photography
ISBN 978-0-375-50509-6; 0-375-50509-1
LC 2006-45765
This is a collection of Leibovitz's "work from 1990-2005. . . . [Portraits of] Johnny Cash, Nicole Kidman, Mikhail Baryshnikov, Keith Richards, Michael Jordan, Joan Didion, R2-D2, Patti Smith, Nelson Mandela, Jack Nicholson, William Burroughs, [and] George W. Bush with members of his Cabinet appear alongside pictures of Leibovitz's family and friends, reportage from the siege of Sarajevo in the early Nineties, and landscapes." Publisher's note

Women; {photographs by} Annie Leibovitz; {essay by} Susan Sontag. Random House 1999 239p il $75; pa $49.95   **779**
1. Women -- Portraits
ISBN 0-375-50020-0; 0-375-75646-9 pa
LC 99-24968
"Leibovitz greatly increases our lexicon of womanhood with her brilliant photographs of musicians, doctors, teachers, trapeze artists, gangbangers, nude women, a woman in chador, women soldiers, and girls with their Barbies, all commanding attention and respect." Booklist

Life: World War 2; history's greatest conflict in pictures. edited by Richard B. Stolley. Little, Brown 2001 351p il hardcover o.p. pa $29.95   **779**
1. World War, 1939-1945 -- Pictorial works 2. World history -- 20th century -- Pictorial works
ISBN 0-8212-2771-8; 0-8212-5713-7 pa
LC 2001-93633

This "album of 665 photographs taken from the archives of Life magazine and other collections begins with the years 1919 to 1939, the two decades leading up to World War II. Editor Stolley then proceeds to chronicle the war, year by year through 1945, and ends with what he calls 'the war's aftermath,' 1946 to 2001. . . . For World War II buffs, the book is a natural treasure." Booklist

Lyon, Danny
Memories of myself; essays. Phaidon 2009 207p il $90   **779**
1. Documentary photography
ISBN 978-0-7148-4851-8; 0-7148-4851-4
"What happens when you hang out in brothels, derby pits, and dark alleys for forty years? For starters, you take some damn memorable photos. That's been the path of American photographer Danny Lyon, who, like a Method actor, immersed himself in the subcultures he documented. His iconic work from the '60s (pre–Easy Rider photos of bikers on the road) led to exhibitions in MoMA and the Whitney and two Guggenheim fellowships, and he's credited with pioneering the New Journalism movement in photography. In Memories of Myself . . . he shares 134 mostly unpublished pictures—of Colombian prostitutes in hair curlers, chain-smoking greasers, and Brooklyn teens playing Wiffle Ball—that are so intimate they could have come from the photo albums of the subjects themselves. This is the genius of Lyon's work: He inhabits, rather than invades, the personal space of his subjects." GQ

Maisel, David
Library of dust; essays by Geoff Manaugh, Michael S. Roth, and Terry Toedtemeier. Chronicle Books 2008 un $80   **779**
1. Artistic photography
ISBN 978-0-8118-6333-9; 0-8118-6333-6
LC 2008-18899
In 2005 Maisel "was immediately intrigued when he read a small news item describing the efforts of the Oregon State Hospital to move the cremated remains of thousands of psychiatric patients who had died between 1913 and 1971. The article hardly suggested an art treasure — except to Maisel, who noticed that the remains were stored in copper canisters, which he guessed had probably turned to dazzling colors over the decades. . . . [In this book] he shows dozens of the canisters in larger-than-life size, their turquoise, pink and gold colors so sumptuous they look more like oil paintings than photographs. . . . The abstract beauty of the canisters is a jolting contrast to their grim origins." Time

McCartney, Linda
Life in photographs; texts by Paul McCartney, Linda McCartney, Annie Leibovitz, Mary McCartney, Martin Harrison, Stella McCartney; edited by Alison Castle. Taschen 2011 un $69.99   **779**
1. Portrait photography
ISBN 978-3-8365-2728-6
This volume "offers a portrait of Beatledom from a singularly intimate point of view: that of Paul's wife of nearly three decades, the late Linda McCartney. While the couple's famous friends — Mick Jagger, Steve McQueen, Willem de Kooning — are well represented, the fly-on-the-wall shots

of the McCartneys' idyllic intercontinental life . . . are just as enthralling. But the real highlights are the images of Paul with John Lennon, capturing the electric chemistry and childlike joy that informed the Beatles' greatest work." Entertainment Wkly

Mermelstein, Jeff

Twirl /run; text by Robin Hemley. Powerhouse Books 2010 41p $40 **779**
1. Artistic photography
ISBN 978-1-57687-518-6; 1-57687-518-0

"Mermelstein sees New York not from the comfort of an office or as a city of interiors, but rather as an organism of millions, all the parts of which intersect in a classic Rube Goldbergian contraption. The pictures shown illustrate two generic, ubiquitous, nearly involuntary gestures: mostly young women mindlessly twirling their hair as well as the citizens of this hyperactive city – mostly men – running in the street. Mermelstein, a quintessential New Yorker, photographs his hometown and its quirky inhabitants with the eye of a dedicated uncle or an insightful sociologist, schooled in the universities of Garry Winogrand, André Kértész, Robert Frank and Joel Meyerowitz. . . . The power of these pictures, like a good film, is that once entrenched in them, it is impossible not to identify with the characters or see the world in any other way." Art Knowledge News

National Geographic Society (U.S.)
★ **In** focus; National Geographic greatest portraits. National Geographic Society 2004 504p il $30 **779**
1. Portrait photography
ISBN 0-7922-7363-X
LC 2004-44953

"Comprising 280 portraits by 150 of National Geographic's celebrated photographers . . . the book spans over 100 years and covers the entire globe. Organized chronologically as well as thematically and enriched with essays on the development of photographic styles through decades, it is a tasteful celebration of the medium but even more so of human diversity." Libr J

Through the lens; National Geographic greatest photographs. National Geographic Soc. 2003 504p il $30 **779**
1. Documentary photography
ISBN 0-7922-6164-X
LC 2003-52757

This is a "collection of 250 photos, mostly in color and drawn from the National Geographic Society's archive. . . . The society's signature blend of dramatic, rigorously composed natural shots and 'family of nations'-style culture peeps are backed by broad captions and text. . . . The six sections ('Europe'; 'Asia'; 'Africa & the Middle East'; 'The Americas'; 'Oceans and Isles'; 'The Universe') include the first color underwater photographs, as well as collaborative work with NASA, and prominently credit the 84 photographers whose work is featured." Publ Wkly

Penn, Irving

Irving Penn: small trades; [text by] Virginia A. Heckert and Anne Lacoste. J. Paul Getty Museum 2009 269p il $64.95 **779**
1. Artistic photography
ISBN 978-0-89236-996-6; 0-89236-996-5
LC 2009-930114

"The book is a work of art in its own right; both an object of beauty, and a Noah's ark for vanishing trades. Penn may have had an entomologist's eye, but this is no catalogue of specimens; it is an encyclopaedia of humanity." Jewish Chron
Includes bibliographical references

San Francisco Museum of Modern Art.

Brought to light; photography and the invisible, 1840-1900. edited by Corey Keller; with essays by Jennifer Tucker, Tom Gunning, Maren Groning. San Francisco Museum of Modern Art in association with Yale University Press 2008 215p il $50 **779**
1. Photography -- Scientific applications
ISBN 978-0-300-14210-5; 0-300-14210-2
LC 2008-24251

A "collection of scientific photographs taken between 1840 and 1900. From the ornate structure of a tiny mite to the violent splash of stars on an astronomical plate, these pictures document the emergence of the camera as an important scientific tool. Elegant design and thoughtful explanatory text enhance the wonderful, even poignant, power of these images." Entertainment Wkly
Includes bibliographical references

The **Scurlock** Studio and Black Washington; picturing the promise. edited by Paul Gardulo . . . [et al.] National Museum of African American History and Culture: In collaboration with the National Museum o 2009 224p il $35 **779**
1. Scurlock Studio (Firm) 2. African Americans -- Pictorial works 3. Washington (D.C.) -- Social life and customs
ISBN 978-1-58834-262-1; 1-58834-262-X
LC 2008-32847

"In 1911 Addison Scurlock opened a photography studio in Washington, D.C., and went on to chronicle the aspirations and ambitions of the black community into the 1990s. . . . Photographs include the famous (Marian Anderson, Duke Ellington, Ralph Bunche, W. E. B. DuBois, and Muhammad Ali) as well as the influential but perhaps less well known (business owners, churchgoers, civic leaders, members of high society). With more than 100 images, this book is a proud celebration of a vibrant community from the early to the late twentieth century." Booklist
Includes bibliographical references

Shaughnessy, Jim

The **call** of trains; railroad photographs of Jim Shaughnessy. text by Jeff Brouws. W.W. Norton 2008 224p il $65 **779**
1. Railroads -- Pictorial works
ISBN 978-0-393-06592-3; 0-393-06592-8
LC 2008-1295

"Shaughnessy began shooting trains in downtown Troy, New York (his hometown), in the middle 1940s. He eventually took lengthy trips, first in New England and Canada, later across the Midwest to the Southwest, to photograph trains. He initially focused on the big engines but quickly extended his purview to include railway workers, railway buildings, and the countrysides through which the trains rolled. A civil engineer rather than a professional photographer, he became as skilled as any pro. . . . Appearing on full pages of this oversize volume, his pictures are engrossing, stunning masterpieces of photodocumentation." Booklist

Includes bibliographical references

Smith, Joel

Edward Steichen: the early years. Princeton Univ. Press 1999 167p il $65 **779**
1. Photographers 2. Artistic photography
ISBN 0-691-04873-8

LC 99-26617

Smith examines the photography of Edward Steichen. Alfred Stieglitz was a patron of Steichen's, and Smith discusses "the interrelationship between Steichen's work and Stieglitz's shifting aesthetic interests, as well as the influence of Paris on Steichen's development." N Y Times Book Rev

Includes bibliographical references

Smith, W. Eugene

The **jazz** loft project; photographs and tapes of W. Eugene Smith from 821 Sixth Avenue, 1957-1965. [compiled] by Sam Stephenson. Knopf 2009 268p il $40 **779**
1. Jazz music 2. Musicians -- Portraits 3. New York (N.Y.) -- Pictorial works
ISBN 978-0-307-26709-2; 0-307-26709-1

LC 2009-20875

"After having a breakdown in the midst of working on a photo-essay on Pittsburgh in 1957, legendary photographer W. Eugene Smith holed up in a loft in New York's Chelsea, in the Tin Pan Alley area. There, over the next several years, he became deeply embroiled in the New York City jazz scene, opening his home as a practice and performance space for some of the great artists of mid-century jazz, including Thelonious Monk, Zoot Sims and many others. Of course, he took pictures—both of musicians and of a window-size view of mid-century New York—and also wired the place for recording, logging hours and hours of tape, capturing the music and the talk around it. These photos and tapes had been thought lost—the stuff of rumor, buried in Smith's archive—until Stephenson dug them out and culled the best, along with transcriptions of material from the tapes, for this landmark book. . . . This will be an essential book for jazz fans, photography lovers and those interested in the history of New York." Publ Wkly

Sommer, Frederick

★ The **art** of Frederick Sommer; photography, drawing, collage. [essay by Keith F. Davis; interview by Michael Torosian; chronology by April M. Watson] Yale University Press 2005 251p il $65 **779**
1. Artistic photography
ISBN 0-300-10783-8

LC 2004-118000

"The book's sequencing of images wholly succeeds in creating a powerful contemplative experience, and the enticing arguments Davis offers in his introductory remarks incite a hunger for fresh, detailed scholarship about each of Sommer's works." Publ Wkly

Stamolis, Tony

Frezno. Process Media 2008 un $29.95 **779**
1. Fresno (Calif.) -- Pictorial works
ISBN 978-1-934170-04-5; 1-934170-04-6

This book "examines life in California's sixth largest city with vivid, stark and honest imagery. Stamolis captures his hometown, once a beacon of booming surburbia, with a seedy, fluorescent pallor. . . . The downtrodden Fresno that Stamolis depicts is an affectionately upclose look at pure Americana frozen in the frame." Cool Hunting

Stein, Sally

John Gutmann; the photographer at work. foreword by Douglas R. Nickel; with a contribution by Amy Rule. In association with Yale University Press 2009 180p il $50 **779**
1. Artists 2. Painters 3. Photographers 4. Photojournalism 5. Art teachers
ISBN 978-0-300-12331-9; 0-300-12331-0

LC 2009-921441

"Gutmann's camera eye moves with the times themselves in the dynamic America in which he inserted himself, trying to understand but happy to just go. A secondary theme Stein advances concerns the peculiarity of popular English, as on billboards, to a man for whom it is a language acquired as an adult. The photos themselves are exceptionally varied in angle of regard, subject, and place, though all do tend to look caught-on-the-fly and kinetic even when their subjects are stationary. They're so captivating one can't help wishing there were many more than 108 plates in the book." Booklist

Includes bibliographical references

Steinmetz, Mark

Greater Atlanta. Nazraeli Press 2009 85p il $100 **779**
1. Artistic photography 2. Atlanta (Ga.) -- Pictorial works
ISBN 978-1-59005-259-4; 1-59005-259-5

LC 2009-504431

"Mark Steinmetz's Greater Atlanta continues this photographer's sexy chronicling of the American South. His photos of junkyards and deserted gas stations exude an Ed Ruscha-like iconicism, yet his strongest pieces remain his photographs of young couples in the awkward blush of adolescence. In these tender, uniquely Southern portraits, you can feel the muggy Georgia air, you can smell the scent of magnolia and mosquito repellent wafting between the girl and boy, the nervous tension and the elixir of estrogen and testosterone searching one another out." Willamette Week

Testino, Mario

Let me in! [photographs by] Mario Testino ; [foreword by Nicole Kidman ; essays by Michael Roberts, Mario Testino and Patrick Kinmoth ; Ger-

man translation, Clara Drechsler ; French translation, Philippe Safavi] Taschen 2007 il $39.99 **779**
1. Portrait photography
ISBN 978-3-8228-4418-2; 3-8228-4418-7

"It's tough to tell where fashion photography ends and celebrity photography begins but both are getting some respect from the world of high art these days, and nothing proclaims that fact more eloquently than this . . . book of Mario Testino's behind-the-scenes photographs of celebrities in fashionable garb." Miami Herald

Thompson, Michael
Michael Thompson: Portraits; edited by Vince Aletti. Damiani 2011 216p il $65 **779**
1. Artistic photography
ISBN 978-8-86208-156-6; 8-86208-156-1

"There aren't very many successful commercial photographers whose work is considered to be fine art and exhibited in galleries. . . . It's a fine line that one walks to gain that respect, especially for a photographer who specializes in fashion and celebrity. . . . Michael Thompson is one such photographer who has blurred the line and broken the boundary. The memorable portraits in this book of celebrity tell a story of our culture as much as about the person being photographed." Full Frontal Fashion

Towell, Larry
The **world** from my front porch. Chris Boot; Archive of Modern Conflict 2008 224p il $75 **779**
1. Photojournalism
ISBN 978-1-905712-09-0

"Unlike most contemporary photojournalists, who shoot with high-end digital cameras and print their work with ink and paper, Towell only uses traditional black and white film, whether he is in Gaza, Lebanon, or South Africa, or on his own back porch. . . . That Towell is concerned with the poetics of photography should come as no surprise. His meticulously realized compositions are saturated with the history of photography and the history of painting. . . . Towell's work is astounding in its coherence. He treats people facing poverty, dispossession, and violent conflict in the same spirit as his own family." Walrus

Veasey, Nick
X -ray. Viking Studio 2008 224p il $40 **779**
1. Artistic photography
ISBN 978-0-670-02040-9; 0-670-02040-0

Veasey's "works are beautifully simple, often containing a purpose–to reveal a side never seen before, to evoke emotional response. . . . The images are divided into several categories including humans/animals, objects, nature, abstract, and fashion." Revealed

Wolf, Michael
The **transparent** city. Aperture 2008 111p il $60 **779**
1. Artistic photography 2. Chicago (Ill.) -- Pictorial works
ISBN 978-1-59711-076-1; 1-59711-076-0

"The ground is nowhere in sight in Wolf's dramatically geometric, nearly abstract photographs of Chicago's Loop towers. Shot from strategically selected rooftops and per-

fectly printed in an aptly large, vertical book, Wolf's subtly modulated color photographs are monumental studies in grays, whites, blacks, golds, and occasional splashes of green and blue. . . . With intimations of surveillance and vulnerability, these intensely beautiful cityscapes seem austere and inhuman until one lands on a magnified picture of a man giving the distant photographer the finger." Booklist

780 Music

Allman, Gregg, 1947-
My cross to bear; Gregg Allman with Alan Light. Morrow 2012 390 p. ill. (some col.) $27.99 **780**
1. Drugs 2. Rock musicians 3. Rock musicians -- United States -- Biography
ISBN 0062112031; 9780062112033
LC 2012563465

In "his memoir, . . . Gregg Allman lays bare his soul, carrying us back to his childhood with his older brother, Duane, their days at military school, the first time he picked up a guitar and started making music, the first songs he wrote, his love for Duane, his voracious appetite for drugs and sex, and his countless sexual conquests, his broken relationships and his addictions, and his deep love for music." (Publishers Weekly)

The **complete** classical music guide; general editor, John Burrows with Charles Wiffen and contributions from Robert Ainsley ... [et al.] DK Pub. 2012 352 p. ill. (hc) $25 **780**
1. Music 2. Musical instruments 3. Music appreciation
ISBN 0756692563; 9780756692568
LC 2012562384

This "illustrated guide is arranged by period—'early' (ie 1000-1600), baroque, classical, romantic (with additional chapters on romantic opera and national schools) and modern. Each period is introduced by an overview, and the book opens with a general guide to classical music—its elements, instruments and performance." (Classical Music)

Curtis, Susan
Dancing to a black man's tune: a life of Scott Joplin. University of Mo. Press 1994 xx, 265p il (Missouri biography series) $29.95 **780**
1. Pianists 2. Composers 3. Jazz musicians
ISBN 0-8262-0949-1
LC 93-46116

A "study of the life and world of ragtime creator Scott Joplin (1868-1917). Lapsing only occasionally into academic jargon, the author ably places Joplin in the context of an emerging biracial society and culture as a man who was denied rights because of his color yet applauded as a musician." Publ Wkly
Includes bibliographical references

Forney, Kristine
★ The **enjoyment** of music; an introduction to perceptive listening. Kristine Forney, Joseph Mach-

lis. W. W. Norton 2011 xxxiii, 595 p.p ill. (chiefly col.), col. maps (hardcover) $116.45   **780**
   1. Music appreciation 2. Music -- Social aspects 3. Music -- History and criticism
ISBN 0393935205; 9780393935202

                                LC 2010026215

This book by Kristine Forney and Joseph Machlis "reflects how today's students learn, listen to, and live with music. . . . It emphasizes context to show how music fits in the everyday lives of people throughout history, and connects culture, performance, and technology to the lives of students today. The new edition features . . . cultural and historical context, and in-text features that encourage and develop critical thinking skills." (Publisher's note)

   Includes bibliographical references and index

Glover, Jane

   Mozart's women; the man, the music, and the loves of his life. HarperCollins 2006 406p il $27.95; pa $15.95   **780**
   1. Composers
ISBN 0-06-056350-8; 978-0-06-056350-9; 0-06-056351-6 pa; 978-0-06-056351-6 pa

                                  LC 2005-52699

The author "writes perceptively and knowledgeably about the theatrical genius of Mozart's operas, . . . and her expertise contributes significantly to the pleasures afforded by this volume." Christ Sci Monit

   Includes bibliographical references

Gutman, Robert W.

   Mozart; a cultural biography. Harcourt Brace & Co. 1999 839p hardcover o.p. pa $25   **780**
   1. Composers
ISBN 978-0-15-601171-6 pa; 0-15-601171-9 pa

                                  LC 99-31953

The author interweaves "the chronology of Mozart's life and musical compositions with essays on the social, political, and religious fabrics of the 18th century, offering extended discourses on the Enlightenment, Sturm und Drang, Freemasonry, and other movements that influenced the composer both personally and in his works." Libr J

   Includes bibliographical references

The **Harvard** biographical dictionary of music; edited by Don Michael Randel. Belknap Press 1996 1013p il $39.95   **780**
   1. Reference books 2. Music -- Bio-bibliography
ISBN 0-674-37299-9

                                  LC 96-16456

"International in scope and covering all eras of music from the ancient to the present, this important new reference source has information concerning 5,500 individuals. Most are associated with classical concert music, although prominent jazz, rock , folk, and popular personalities are also represented: Madonna, Mozart, Zoot Sims, Mick Jagger, and Dolly Parton are included. Musicologists, educators, teachers, and reviewers, no matter how influential, are excluded. Entries consist of brief to long paragraphs that may include a bibliography or a list of compositions. . . . This is an authoritative and significant new reference work which all libraries must purchase." Choice

The **Harvard** concise dictionary of music and musicians; edited by Don Michael Randel. Belknap Press 1999 757p il hardcover o.p. pa $18.95 **780**
   1. Reference books 2. Music -- Dictionaries 3. Music -- Bio-bibliography
ISBN 0-674-00084-6; 0-674-00978-9 pa

                                  LC 99-40644

"Entries are arranged alphabetically and encompass terms, musical forms and styles, individual works, and instruments, as well as composers, performers, and theorists." Booklist

   The Harvard dictionary of music; edited by Don Michael Randel. 4th ed; Belknap Press 2003 978p il (Harvard University Press reference library) $39.95   **780**
   1. Reference books 2. Music -- Dictionaries
ISBN 0-674-01163-5

                                  LC 2003-58262

First published 1944 under the authorship of Willi Apel

This reference "includes entries on all the styles and forms in Western music; . . . articles on the music of Africa, Asia, Latin America, and the Near East; descriptions of instruments . . . {with} historical background, and articles that reflect today's best, including popular music, jazz, and rock." Publisher's note

Hoffman, Miles

   The **NPR** classical music companion; an essential guide for enlightened listening. Houghton Mifflin 2005 306p pa $15   **780**
   1. Reference books 2. Music -- Dictionaries
ISBN 978-0-618-61945-0; 0-618-61945-3

                                  LC 2006-273343

First published 1997 with title: The NPR classical music companion: terms and concepts from A to Z

This musical guide includes This musical guide includes "entries that are at least a good-size paragraph in length and liable to include, besides technical information, historical and listener's advisory material." Booklist

Holoman, D. Kern

   Berlioz. Harvard Univ. Press 1989 687p il $36   **780**
   1. Composers
ISBN 0-674-06778-9

                                  LC 88-35788

This is a biography of the nineteenth-century composer, conductor, and music critic

"There may be aspects of Berlioz's life which Holoman has not fathomed, but he paints as full a picture as has yet been attempted." New Statesman (1913)

   Includes bibliographical references

Hyland, William G.

   George Gershwin; a new biography. Praeger Pubs. 2003 312p il $39.95   **780**
   1. Composers
ISBN 0-275-98111-8

                                  LC 2003-46303

"This fresh and well-researched biography of one of America's great composers is highly recommended for all libraries." Libr J

Includes bibliographical references

Joseph, Charles M.

Stravinsky inside out. Yale Univ. Press 2001 xx, 320p il $29.95 **780**

1. Composers

ISBN 0-300-07537-5

LC 2001-913

This study "reveals a . . . flawed and fragile human being, who craved approval, dealt ungenerously with colleagues, loved James Bond movies, and tried hard to further his son's musical career. Although the aged Stravinsky's eagerness to play the role of celebrity composer for the golden age of television . . . was an embarrassment, most of these episodes testify to the protean survival skills of an artist whose sense of identity was always in flux and whose cunning was commensurate with his talent." New Yorker

Includes bibliographical references

Morrison, Simon

Lina and Serge; the love and wars of Lina Prokofiev. Simon Morrison. Houghton Mifflin Harcourt 2013 336 p. (hardcover) $26 **780**

1. Composers' spouses -- Biography 2. Sopranos (Singers) -- Biography

ISBN 0547391315; 9780547391311

LC 2012042185

This book, by Simon Morrison, profiles the life of the 20th-century Russian composer Serge Prokofiev and his wife Lina. "The contrast between Lina and Serge is one of strength and perseverance versus utter self-absorption, a remarkable human drama that draws on the forces of art, sacrifice, and the struggle against oppression." (Publisher's note)

Mozart, Wolfgang Amadeus

Mozart's letters, Mozart's life; selected letters. edited and newly translated by Robert Spaethling. Norton 2000 479p il $35; pa $19.95 **780**

1. Composers

ISBN 978-0-393-04719-6; 978-0-393-32830-1 pa

LC 00-25530

This is a "wonderful collection that gives Mozart a voice as a son, husband, brother and friend. Mozart's main subjects were his composing and performing, but he usually digresses into love for his parents, his sister and his wife, Constanze. And there was a bawdy side, too, to the composer of such elegant music." N Y Times Book Rev

Includes bibliographical references

★ The **New** Grove dictionary of music and musicians; edited by Stanley Sadie; executive editor, John Tyrrell. 2nd ed; Oxford University Press 2004 29v set $1, 500 **780**

1. Reference books 2. Music -- Dictionaries

ISBN 978-0-19-517067-2

First published 1980 in twenty volumes to supersede Grove's dictionary of music and musicians; this edition first published 2000

"Grove is not fat, it is limitless. Whether Grove is on the reference shelf or online, teachers, students, researchers, and the common reader will find it an abiding source of satisfaction." Commonweal

Includes bibliographical references

✓ The **Oxford** companion to music; edited by Alison Latham. Oxford Univ. Press 2002 1434p il $65 **780**

1. Reference books 2. Music -- Dictionaries 3. Musicians -- Dictionaries

ISBN 0-19-866212-2

LC 2002-537302

"Among the 8000 entries are articles on composers, theorists, and some performers; instruments, forms, and terms; subjects like electronic music, individual countries, and politics and music; and some pieces (and even some famous arias). Each entry is presented in a dictionary format, with a select index of names appended and sometimes with bibliographic references. . . . The bias is still English, but the book provides cross references to American terms and includes plenty of American composers and musical subjects. A solid reference with a grand pedigree, usefully improved for home and general library use, this is highly recommended for all public libraries." Libr J

Includes bibliographical references

Ross, Alex

Listen to this. Farrar, Straus and Giroux 2010 364p il $27; ebook $12.99 **780**

1. Musical criticism 2. Music -- History and criticism

ISBN 978-0-374-18774-3; 0-374-18774-6; 978-1-4299-7761-6 ebook; 1-4299-7761-2 ebook

LC 2010-10283

"Though the bulk of the book examines classical work both historical and contemporary, Ross veers effortlessly from Mozart to Radiohead, from Kurt Cobain to Brahms, bringing a pop fan's enthusiasm to the composers and treating the rock stars seriously as musicians. . . . The triumph of 'Listen to This' is that Ross dusts off music that's centuries old to reveal the passion and brilliance that's too often hidden from a contemporary audience. It's a joy for a pop fan or a classical aficionado." N Y Times Book Rev

Includes bibliographical references

Schonberg, Harold C.

✓ ★ The **lives** of the great composers; 3rd ed; Norton 1997 653p il $35 **780**

1. Composers

ISBN 0-393-03857-2

LC 96-13308

First published 1970

This book traces the lives of important musical figures from Monteverdi to Ives and includes information on the serialists, minimalist composers and the new tonalists of the 1990s

"Schonberg writes for the lay reader. His intention is to humanize the composers and the writing, always highly readable, emphasizes biographical information rather than musical analysis." Libr J

Includes bibliographical references

Simmons, Sylvie

★ **I'm** your man; the life of Leonard Cohen.
Sylvie Simmons. Ecco 2012 570 p.   **780**
ISBN 0061994987; 9780061994982

Author Sylvie Simmons' biography of Leonard Cohen,
"[t]he legend behind such songs as 'Suzanne,' 'Bird on the
Wire' and 'Hallelujah' and the poet and novelist behind such
groundbreaking literary works as 'Beautiful Losers' and
'Book of Mercy,' . . . traces the arc of his prodigious achievements to his remarkable retreat in the mid-nineties -- when
. . . he entered a monastery on a rocky mountaintop above
Los Angeles -- and finally to his reemergence for a sold-out
world tour." (Publisher's note)

Swafford, Jan

Charles Ives; a life with music. Norton 1996
525p il hardcover o.p. $18.95   **780**
1. Composers
ISBN 978-0-393-31719-0; 0-393-31719-6

LC 95-22549

"Ives was a professional organist, a successful insurance
executive, a political idealist, and an immensely prolific
composer. The author believes that Ives's transcendentalism
was central to his identity, ceaselessly inspiring him while
also spurring him on to an inevitable physical collapse.
Swafford—a composer himself—intersperses his biography
with valuable 'entr'actes' of approachable musical analysis,
and ends with a ringing endorsement of Ives as an ideal composer for a democratic society." New Yorker

Includes bibliographical references

Johannes Brahms; a biography. Knopf 1997
xxii, 699p il hardcover o.p. $20   **780**
1. Composers
ISBN 978-0-679-74582-2; 0-679-74582-3

LC 97-29308

"Swafford's study, clearly a labor of profound affection,
is a model biography: eloquent, clear-sighted and often moving." Publ Wkly

Includes bibliographical references

Walker-Hill, Helen

From spirituals to symphonies; African-Ameri-
can women composers and their music. Greenwood
Press 2002 401p il $94.95   **780**
1. Poets 2. Singers 3. Teachers 4. Composers 5.
Violinists 6. African American women
ISBN 0-313-29947-1

LC 2001-40600

This profiles the lives and works of Undine Smith
Moore, Julia Perry, Margaret Bonds, Irene Britton Smith,
Dorothy Rudd Moore, Valerie Capers, Mary Watkins, and
Regina Harris Baiocchi

This is "an accessible, thoughtful, and humanist study. .
. . Detailed works lists and an appendix enumerating other
black women composers add reference value." Libr J

Includes bibliographical references

Wolff, Christoph

Johann Sebastian Bach; the learned musician.
Norton 2000 599p il hardcover o.p. $21.95   **780**
1. Composers
ISBN 9780393322569; 0393322564

LC 99-54364

This work "is likely to be the standard one-volume Bach
biography for some time to come. It is a solid, richly informative treatment, presenting the copious details of Bach's
life in a coherent, readable narrative." N Y Rev Books

Includes bibliographical references

780.2   Miscellany; texts; treatises on music scores and recordings

Calamar, Gary

Record store days; from vinyl to digital and back
again. [by] Gary Calamar and Phil Gallo. Sterling
2010 238p il $19.95   **780.2**
1. Record stores 2. Music industry
ISBN 978-1-4027-7232-0

"Packed with quotes from musicians, shop owners, and
fans, this volume is a treat for readers, with its inside look at
the importance of vinyl in people's lives throughout the 20th
century. Major vinyl shops such as Tower Records, Rhino
Records, and Bleecker Bob's are profiled. Nearly every page
is graced with vintage photographs and interesting sidebars
filled with facts, from the format history of recorded music
over the century to vinyl oddities. The authors stress the importance of record stores as community meeting places and
discuss the demise of the record industry, the rise of digital
music, and the comeback of vinyl thanks to bands releasing
limited-edition vinyl singles." Libr J

Cutler, David

The **savvy** musician; building a career, earning
a living & making a difference. Helius Press 2009
350p il pa $19.99   **780.2**
1. Music industry -- Vocational guidance
ISBN 978-0-9823075-0-2

This book "is a guide to the aspiring musician who wants
to make their living doing what they love. A . . . blend of music and marketing book, David Cutler encourages musicians
to learn how to sell themselves and adapt technology to their
approaches, to get themselves out there with a recognizable
brand. An honest book about making it in the music industry,
'The Savvy Musician' is a read that can't be missed by music
lovers." Midwest Book Rev

Includes bibliographical references

Kot, Greg

★ **Ripped**; how the wired generation revolutionized music. Scribner 2009 262p $25; pa $14 **780.2**
1. Music industry 2. Music -- Internet resources
ISBN 978-1-4165-4727-3; 1-4165-4727-4; 978-1-
4165-4731-0 pa; 1-4165-4731-2 pa

LC 2008-40839

The author's "breezy, entertaining, journalistic style and
sympathetic tone consistently draw in the reader. Essential
for all those interested in the intersection of music and technology." Libr J

780.26 Texts; treatises on music scores and recordings

Day, Timothy

★ A **century** of recorded music; listening to musical history. Yale Univ. Press 2000 306p il $40; pa $19   **780.26**

1. Sound recordings -- History 2. Music -- History and criticism 3. Sound -- Recording and Reproducing -- History

ISBN 0-300-08442-0; 0-300-09401-9 pa

LC 00-43490

This work provides a "narrative of the evolution of recording from cylinders (1887), shellac discs, and acoustic rerecording through the reproducing piano, electrical amplifications (1925), and magnetic tape to the long-playing record (1948) and compact disc of the 1980s. Day also discusses studio practices and the emergence of influential record producers, the role of radio and recordings in creating a mass audience, the expansion of recorded repertoire, and new ways to experience music. Recommended for all music collections." Choice

Includes bibliographical references

780.3

Bourne, Joyce

The **Oxford** Dictionary of Music; Tim Rutherford-Johnson ; Michael Kennedy ; Joyce Bourne. Oxford Univ Pr 2012 976 p. $49.95   **780.3**

1. Music 2. Music -- Dictionaries

ISBN 0199578109; 9780199578108

This book by Tim Rutherford-Johnson, Michael Kennedy, and Joyce Bourne, "offers broad coverage of a wide range of musical categories spanning many eras, including composers, librettists, singers, orchestras, important ballets and operas, and musical instruments and their history. Over 250 new entries have been added to this [sixth] edition to expand coverage of popular music, ethnomusicology, modern and contemporary composers, music analysis, and recording technology." (Publisher's note)

780.7 Education, research, related topics; performances

Tunstall, Tricia

Changing lives; Tricia Tunstall. Norton 2012 320 p.   **780.7**

1. Conductors (Music) 2. Music -- Study and teaching 3. Music -- Instruction and study -- Venezuela 4. Music -- Instruction and study -- United States 5. Fundación del Estado para el Sistema Nacional de las Orquestas Juveniles e Infantiles de Venezuela -- History

ISBN 9780393078961

LC 2011026504

This book tells the "story of conductor . . . Gustavo Dudamel, and the music education program, El Sistema, . . . the music education program that nurtured his musical talent, first as a young violinist and then as a budding conductor

under the mentorship of its founder, José Antonio Abreu. . . . No matter the location, the overarching goal of El Sistema is unwavering: to rescue children from the depredations of poverty through music." (Publisher's note)

780.89 Ethnic and national groups

Murray, Albert

The **blue** devils of Nada; a contemporary American approach to aesthetic statement. Pantheon Bks. 1996 238p $23; pa $12   **780.89**

1. Poets 2. Artists 3. Authors 4. Singers 5. Pianists 6. Composers 7. Novelists 8. Blues music 9. Jazz musicians 10. African American arts 11. Band leaders 12. Trumpet players 13. Short story writers 14. Nobel laureates for literature

ISBN 0-679-44213-8; 0-679-75859-3 pa

LC 95-23331

In these essays Murray "presents Louis Armstrong, Count Basie, Duke Ellington, painter Romare Bearden and Ernest Hemingway as embodying, in their work and their lives, a peculiarly American strain of existential improvisation and epic storytelling. His theme, variously elaborated, is the effort of the engaged artist to document and give shape to the rootlessness and chaos underlying contemporary life in general—and African American life, in particular—in a way that transcends 'agitprop journalism.'" Publ Wkly

780.9 History, geographic treatment, biography

Blanning, T. C. W.

The **triumph** of music; the rise of composers, musicians and their art. [by] Tim Blanning. Belknap Press of Harvard University Press 2008 416p il $29.95   **780.9**

1. Musicians 2. Music -- Social aspects

ISBN 978-0-674-03104-3; 0-674-03104-0

LC 2008-26753

"This is not intended to be a history of music; it is a brilliantly written history of the steady growth of the power of music and its performers." Libr J

Includes bibliographical references (p. 343-352)

Crawford, Richard

America's musical life; a history. Norton 2000 976p il hardcover o.p. pa $23.95   **780.9**

1. American music -- History and criticism

ISBN 0-393-04810-1; 978-0-393-32726-7 pa; 0-393-32726-4 pa

LC 99-47565

This survey of music in America covers "blues, jazz, swing, pop, rock, hip hop . . . with economics and history as cultural backdrops. Well researched and sensitively constructed, this is highly recommended." Libr J

Includes bibliographical references

Mithen, Steven J.

The **singing** neanderthals; the origins of music, language, mind, and body. [by] Steven Mithen. Harvard University Press 2006 374p il map $25.95; pa $16.95   **780.9**

1. Music 2. Evolution
ISBN 0-674-02192-4; 978-0-674-02192-1; 978-0-674-02559-2 pa; 0-674-02559-8 pa

LC 2005-30187

First published 2005 in the United Kingdom

The author argues "that as a species, humans most likely made musical noises that led to language, not the other way around. . . . This book is a rich resource." Choice

Includes bibliographical references

Moody, Rick

On celestial music; and other adventures in listening. Rick Moody. Little, Brown and Company 2012 439 p.   **780.9**

1. American essays 2. Music appreciation 3. Popular music -- History and criticism 4. Music -- History and criticism
ISBN 9780316105217

LC 2011030556

This book offers a collection of essays on music. ""On Celestial Music," which was included in "Best American Essays," 2008, begins with a lament for the loss in recent music of the vulnerability expressed by Otis Redding's masterpiece, "Try a Little Tenderness;" moves on to [Rick] Moody's infatuation with the . . . music of the Velvet Underground; and ends with an appreciation of Arvo Part and Purcell. . . . Contemporary groups covered include Magnetic Fields (their love songs), Wilco (the band's and Jeff Tweedy's evolution), Danielson Famile (an evangelical rock band), The Pogues (Shane McGowan's problems with addiction), The Lounge Lizards (John Lurie's brilliance), and Meredith Monk." (Publisher's note)

Includes bibliographical references and index

Norton Anthology of Western Music; edited by J. Peter Burkholder and Claude V. Palisca. 7th ed. W.W. Norton & Co. Inc. 2014 883 p. pa $48.30   **780.9**

1. Music appreciation 2. Music -- History and criticism 3. Musical analysis 4. Music collections
ISBN 9780393921618

LC 2009543431

"Offers an historical selection of Gregorian chant, opera, chamber, orchestral, and choral music by composers from ancient and medieval times to Vivaldi, Bach, Handel, Beethoven, Haydn, Mozart, Debussy, Stravinsky, Copeland, and Britten." (Publisher's Note)

Rosen, Charles

The **classical** style; Haydn, Mozart, Beethoven. expanded ed; Norton 1997 xxx, 533p il $35; pa $19.95   **780.9**

1. Composers 2. Music -- History and criticism
ISBN 0-393-04020-8; 0-393-31712-9 pa

LC 96-27335

First published 1971 by Viking

"This remains simply the most important book on the classical style in music." Choice

Includes bibliographical references

The **romantic** generation. Harvard Univ. Press 1995 723p il hardcover o.p. pa $18.95   **780.9**

1. Music -- History and criticism
ISBN 0-674-77934-7 pa

LC 94-46239

The author "explains and describes the first half of the 19th century in conjunction with literature, art, and social changes. . . . Rosen also examines the lives of the composers and pursues some detailed analysis of numerous compositions to make his points. The result is a fresh, challenging, and stimulating view of the society in which Chopin, Liszt, Berlioz, and Schumann flourished." Libr J

Terkel, Studs, 1912-2008

And they all sang; adventures of an eclectic disc jockey. New Press 2005 xxii, 301p $25.95; pa $16.95   **780.9**

1. Musicians
ISBN 978-1-59558-003-0; 1-59558-003-4; 978-1-59558-118-1 pa; 1-59558-118-9 pa

LC 2005-43866

In this "collection of 40 interviews, . . . Terkel recalls his venerable radio program, The Wax Museum, which premiered shortly after the end of WWII in 1945, profiling composers, entertainers and impresarios of nearly every type of music. . . . Insightful and daring, Terkel always asks the right questions, whether culturally or musically." Publ Wkly

780.92   Biography

Geck, Martin

Robert Schumann; the life and work of a romantic composer. Martin Geck ; translated by Stewart Spencer. The University of Chicago Press 2012 320 p. (cloth : alkaline paper) $35   **780.92**

1. Composers -- Germany -- Biography
ISBN 0226284697; 9780226284699

LC 2012007981

This book by Martin Geck is a biography of Robert Schumann, "one of the most important and representative composers of the Romantic era. . . . Geck shows Schumann to be not only a major composer and music critic . . . but also a political activist, the father of eight children, and an addict of mind-altering drugs. . . . Schumann was able to control his demons and channel the tensions that seethed within him into music that mixes the popular and esoteric." (Publisher's note)

Includes bibliographical references and index

Gilbert, Steven E.

The **music** of Gershwin. Yale Univ. Press 1995 255p music (Composers of the twentieth century) $47   **780.92**

1. Composers
ISBN 0-300-06233-8

LC 95-12086

This book analyzes major musical works of George Gershwin including Rhapsody in Blue, Concerto in F, An American in Paris, Porgy and Bess, and some of his popular songs and lesser known works

"With this book, Gershwin's music finally gets the attention it deserves. . . . Gilbert's book is not for the casual reader, since it requires an understanding of music theory and notation." Libr J

Includes bibliographical references

Lockwood, Lewis
Beethoven : the music and the life. Norton 2002 604p il music $39.95   **780.92**
1. Composers
ISBN 0-393-05081-5
                                                     LC 2002-75397
The author "concentrates primarily on his subject's music and development as a composer before dedicating separate chapters to biography and the historical, political, and cultural milieus. . . . All of Lockwood's narrative, including the discussion of specific compositions, will be accessible to serious music lovers with only a modest technical background. This results partly from an interesting innovation . . . 100 additional musical examples are available on a companion web site. . . . Lockwood's study offers a new and authoritative interpretation of a prodigiously gifted and complex man and artist." Libr J

Includes bibliographical references

The **Norton**/Grove dictionary of women composers; edited by Julie Anne Sadie & Rhian Samuel. Norton 1995 xliii, 548p il $45   **780.92**
1. Reference books 2. Women composers -- Dictionaries
ISBN 0-393-03487-9
First published 1994 in the United Kingdom with title: The New Grove dictionary of women composers
"This important volume does not merely recycle material from the 1980 New Grove but collects 900 newly written articles, the longer ones signed." Libr J

Porter, Cecelia Hopkins
Five lives in music; women performers, composers, and impresarios from the baroque to the present. Cecelia Hopkins Porter. University of Illinois Press 2012 xiv, 244 p.p ill. (cloth : alk. paper) $45 **780.92**
1. Women composers -- Biography 2. Women musicians -- Biography 3. Composers -- Biography 4. Musicians -- Biography
ISBN 0252037014; 9780252037016
                                                     LC 2011051102
This book, by Cecelia Hopkins Porter, profiles women musicians through history. It "brings to light the private and performance lives of five remarkable women musicians and composers. . . . Porter probes each musician's social and economic status, her education and musical training, the cultural expectations within the traditions and restrictions of each woman's society, and other factors." (Publisher's note)

Includes bibliographical references (p. [229]-237) and index

Smith, Richard D.
Can't you hear me callin': the life of Bill Monroe, father of bluegrass. Little, Brown 2000 365p il $25.95   **780.92**
1. Singers 2. Mandolin players 3. Bluegrass musicians
ISBN 0-316-80381-2
                                                     LC 99-54372
The author traces Monroe's "life from a music-rich but isolated childhood in the pastoral backroads of Kentucky to his early years as a struggling professional musician to his well-deserved status as an acclaimed elder statesman and musical ambassador. . . . A sensitive, tasteful, well-balanced portrait of a complicated man." Booklist

Includes   discography,   videography   and bibliographical references

Troupe, Quincy
Miles and me: biography of Miles Davis. University of Calif. Press 2000 189p il $25; pa $12.95   **780.92**
1. Jazz musicians 2. African American musicians 3. Band leaders 4. Flugelhornists 5. Trumpet players
ISBN 0-520-21624-5; 0-520-23471-5 pa
                                                     LC 99-54370
"In the late 1970s, Troupe met Davis in New York, became friends with him, and eventually collaborated with him on Miles' autobiography. This slim memoir tells the intimate story of their unlikely friendship. . . . This is both a revealing look at a musical genius and a tender, surprisingly sweet remembrance of a good but demanding friend." Booklist

781   Principles, forms, ensembles, voices, instruments

Kennedy, Dan
Rock on. Algonquin Books 2008 224p pa $14.95   **781**
1. Authors 2. Music industry 3. Memoirists
ISBN 978-1-565-12509-4; 1-565-12509-6
                                                     LC 2007-17025
This is a memoir of the author's experiences in the music industry.

"Kennedy's style—hilarious, paranoid and vulnerable—captures wonderfully the absurdity of the corporate music industry." Publ Wkly

Mannes, Elena
The power of music; pioneering discoveries in the new science of song. foreword by Dr. Aniruddh Patel. Walker & Company 2011 263p il $26   **781**
1. Music and science 2. Music -- Psychological aspects
ISBN 978-0-8027-1996-6; 0-8027-1996-1
                                                     LC 2010-48255
An "investigation of how music affects people and other animals. Detailing a variety of scientific experiments, [the author] shows the effects of sound frequencies and vibrations on body organs and brain waves; her study culminates in documentation supporting music therapy. Mannes's intercontinental explorations range from songbird studies to infants' melodic preferences to the origins of the universe

(one topic on which her discussions seem rather far-fetched if fascinating). Interviews with influential musicians such as Bobby McFerrin help lighten an otherwise rather dense text." Libr J

Includes bibliographical references.

781.1   Basic principles of music

Byrne, David, 1952-
★ **How** Music Works; David Byrne. Pgw 2012   **781.1**
ISBN 1936365537; 9781936365531

In this book, David Byrne "explores how profoundly music is shaped by its time and place, and he explains how the advent of recording technology in the twentieth century forever changed our relationship to playing, performing, and listening to music. Acting as historian and anthropologist, raconteur and social scientist, he searches for patterns." (Publisher's note)

Includes bibliographical references.

Toop, David
Sinister resonance; the mediumship of the listener. Continuum 2010 256p $24.95   **781.1**
1. Sound perception 2. Music -- Psychological aspects
ISBN 1-4411-4972-4; 978-1-4411-4972-5
LC 2009-47734

"An exploration of sound in novels, poems, and paintings from before the era of sound reproduction. . . . Toop doesn't translate mute works into sound by color or verbal line; rather, he uses the aural environments the works themselves depict as jumping-off points to examine both the objects under study and the nature of humanity's relationship to sound itself. . . . Toop's clear sense of mission gives him and his book a firm grip on this slipperiest subject." AV Club

Includes bibliographical references

781.2   Elements of music

Piston, Walter
Counterpoint. Norton 1947 235p music $41.75   **781.2**
1. Counterpoint
ISBN 978-0-393-09728-3; 0-393-09728-5
This work covers the principles and techniques of counterpoint as represented in the works of 18th and 19th century composers

Harmony; 5th ed; Norton 1987 575p $59.95   **781.2**
1. Harmony
ISBN 0-393-95480-3
LC 86-23901
First published 1941
A presentation of the harmonic structures utilized by composers of the 18th and 19th centuries. Includes examples and exercises

781.49   Recording of music

Milner, Greg
Perfecting sound forever; an aural history of recorded music. Faber and Faber 2009 416p il $35   **781.49**
1. Sound recordings 2. Sound -- Recording and reproducing
ISBN 0-571-21165-8; 978-0-571-21165-4
LC 2008-55444

"The author begins in the late 19th century, tracing the evolution from Edison's invention of the phonograph to the contemporary use of digital music files. Broad in scope and steeped in detail, the book strikes a mostly well-maintained balance between the history of the technological development of recordings and the more approachable accounts of the people and events surrounding it." Kirkus

781.6   Traditions of music

Horowitz, Joseph
★ **Classical** music in America; a history of its rise and fall. W. W. Norton & Company 2005 606p il $39.95; pa. $19.95   **781.6**
1. Music -- United States
ISBN 0-393-05717-8; 9780393330557
LC 2004-27754

"As a comprehensive, convincing analysis of the contemporary dilemma, and a riveting portrait of the century and a half of events and personalities which brought it about, Mr Horowitz's account would be hard to beat." Economist

Includes bibliographical references

Plotkin, Fred
Classical music 101; a complete guide to learning and loving classical music. Hyperion 2002 673p pa $18.95   **781.6**
1. Music appreciation
ISBN 0-7868-8627-7
LC 2002-69075

This introduction to classical music "revolves almost entirely around the orchestra's instruments and the listening experience. {The author} presents material as coursework, and his strictures about really listening (as opposed to mere 'hearing') are well taken and certainly apply to all kinds of music. A valuable feature are the interviews with classical musicians interspersed throughout. . . . Recommended for libraries desiring an up-to-date and informative general introduction to classical music." Libr J

Discography: p; Includes bibliographical references and index

781.62   Folk music

American ballads and folk songs; [compiled by] John A. Lomax and Alan Lomax; with a foreword

by George Lyman Kittredge. Dover Publications 1994 xxxix, 625p pa $21.95 **781.62**
1. Ballads 2. Folk music -- United States
ISBN 0-486-28276-7; 978-0-486-28276-3
First published 1934 by MacMillan

Treasury of authentic songs, many recorded on location by noted father-and-son folklorists. Music and lyrics for over 200 ballads about the railroads, mountain songs, chain gang songs, creole songs, songs about cocaine and whisky, reels, minstrel songs, songs of childhood and much more. Includes such time-honored favorites as John Henry, Goin Home, Frankie and Albert, Down in the Valley, Little Brown Jug, Alabama-Bound, Shortenin Bread, Skip to My Lou, Frog Went a-Courtin and a host of others. Notes about the origin of each melody, a bibliography and an index are included.

★ Our singing country; folk songs and ballads. collected and compiled by John A. Lomax and Alan Lomax; music editor, Ruth Crawford Seeger; introduction to the Dover edition by Judith Tick; includes bibliography by Harold W. Thompson. Dover 2000 pa $16.95 **781.62**
1. Ballads 2. Folk music -- United States
ISBN 978-0-486-41089-0 pa; 0-486-41089-7 pa
First published 1941 by MacMillan

This includes melodies and words for tunes from all parts of the United States. Songs include spirituals, hollers, game songs, lullabies, courting songs, chain-gang work songs, Cajun airs, breakdowns, and many more. Includes over 200 authentic folk songs and ballads.

Sandburg, Carl
The **American** songbag; [compiled by] Carl Sandburg; introduction by Garrison Keillor. Harcourt Brace Jovanovich 1990 xxix, 495p pa $35 **781.62**
1. Folk music -- United States
ISBN 978-0-15-605650-2 pa; 0-15-605650-X pa

A reissue of the title first published 1927

"Sandburg was not only a poet but also a noted collector and performer of American folk music. This anthology contains words and music to 290 songs that people have sung in the making of Americana." Publisher's note

Strom, Yale
The **book** of Klezmer; the history, the music, the folklore. A Cappella Bks. 2002 381p il music $28 **781.62**
1. Klezmer music
ISBN 1-55652-445-5

LC 2002-2701

This history of Klezmer music is divided into "four chapters: 'From King David to Duvid the Klezmer,' 'From the Enlightenment to the Holocaust,' 'Klezmer in the New World, 1880-1960,' and 'From Zev to Zorn: The Masters of the Culture.' The first appendix, 'Klezmer Memories in the Memorial Books,' is one of the most moving sections, featuring a collection of commentaries on klezmer music and musicians from hundreds of memorial books written by Holocaust survivors." Libr J

Includes discography and bibliographical references

Wade, Stephen
The **beautiful** music all around us; field recordings and the American experience. Stephen Wade. University of Illinois Press 2012 xvii, 477 p.p ill., music (Music in American life) (hardcover) $24.95 **781.62**
1. Sound recordings 2. Folk music -- United States 3. Archive of Folk Culture (U.S.) 4. Field recordings -- United States -- History 5. Folk music -- United States -- History and criticism
ISBN 0252036883; 9780252036880

LC 2011044092

This book, by Stephen Wade, is part of the "Music in American Life" series. It describes the "backstories of thirteen performances captured on Library of Congress field recordings between 1934 and 1942 in locations reaching from Southern Appalachia to the Mississippi Delta and the Great Plains. . . . Alongside loving and expert profiles of these performers and their locales and communities, Wade also untangles the histories of these iconic songs and tunes." (Publisher's note)

Includes bibliographical references (p. [423]-445) and index.

Ware, Charles Pickard
Slave songs of the United States; the complete 1867 collection of slave songs. [collected and compiled] by William Francis Allen, Charles Pickard Ware, and Lucy McKim Garrison ; piano accompaniments by Irving Schlein; Peter Schlein, editor. Hal Leonard 2007 183p pa $15.95 **781.62**
1. Spirituals (Songs) 2. African American music 3. Folk music -- United States 4. Slavery -- United States -- Songs
ISBN 978-1-42342-262-4 pa; 1-42342-262-7 pa

"One of the first documentary collections of Negro folk songs was compiled in 1867 by William Francis Allen, Charles Pickard Ware and Lucy McKim Garrison. . . . This collection of 136 authentic folk songs of the Negro people revolutionized America's understanding of this music. The book, which contains spirituals, work songs, field hollers, soldier songs of Civil War days, and freedom songs, has become a classic of its kind. . . . In 1965, composer Irving Schlein created . . . piano settings for every song from the original edition. Chords for guitar have also been added to the musical notation." Publisher's note

Young, Rob
Electric Eden; unearthing Britain's visionary music. Faber and Faber 2011 664p il pa $25 **781.62**
1. Folk music -- Great Britain
ISBN 978-0-86547-856-5; 0-86547-856-2

LC 2011-01987

First published 2010 in the United Kingdom

"It is a commonplace that rock and R&B came out of the folk and blues revivals of the early 1960s, and Young shows, through enchanting storytelling and brilliant commentary, that a similar revival in England inspired the Beatles and Pink Floyd, Led Zeppelin and Traffic, Kate Bush and Talk Talk. Folklorists notated old songs and dances. Marxists put folk music forward as the true voice of the people. Composers like Benjamin Britten and Ralph Vaughan Williams devised rich neo-traditional pageantry. Today, the pioneers of the "acid folk" movement see this music as a model for their own." (Publisher's Note)

"Young's narrative slips fluidly forward, backward, and through the cracks of canonical music history. And he doesn't just stick to music; like Greil Marcus with a thirst for ancient paganism and postmodern urban theory, Young weaves a poetic, philosophical tapestry as rich and heady as the songs he champions." AV Club

Includes bibliographical references and discography

781.64   Western popular music

Bradley, Andy

House of hits; the story of Houston's Gold Star/SugarHill Recording Studios. by Andy Bradley and Roger Wood. University of Texas Press 2010 334p il (Brad and Michele Moore roots music series) $34.95   **781.64**
1. Popular music 2. Music industry 3. SugarHill Recording Studios (Firm)
ISBN 978-0-292-71919-4

LC 2009-44441

"A complete and well-annotated history of Gold Star/SugarHill, the oldest continuously operating recording studio in the U.S., the book is a trove of interesting stories and first-person narratives from many of the major players who made the records that are now an indelible part of the lexicon of American music." Houston Press

Includes bibliographical references

Broven, John

Record makers and breakers; voices of the independent rock 'n' roll pioneers. University of Illinois Press 2008 584p il $50   **781.64**
1. Popular music 2. Music industry
ISBN 978-0-252-03290-5; 0-252-03290-X

LC 2008-27204

"This volume is an engaging and exceptional history of the independent rock 'n' roll record industry from its raw regional beginnings in the 1940s with R & B and hillbilly music through its peak in the 1950s and decline in the 1960s. John Broven combines narrative history with extensive oral history material from numerous recording pioneers including Joe Bihari of Modern Records; Marshall Chess of Chess Records; Jerry Wexler, Ahmet Ertegun, and Miriam Bienstock of Atlantic Records; Sam Phillips of Sun Records; Art Rupe of Specialty Records; and many more." (Publisher's Note)

"The depth of factual detail is incredible, but it's presented in the style of a rich oral history. . . . It's a chronicle of the entrepreneurial American spirit, liberally punctuated by the creation of some of the most exciting and innovative music of all time." Record Collector

Includes bibliographical references (p. 545-556)

Chang, Jeff

Can't stop, won't stop; a history of the hip-hop generation. introduction by D.J. Kool Herc. St.

Martin's Press 2005 546p il hardcover o.p. pa $16   **781.64**
1. Rap music
ISBN 0-312-30143-X; 0-312-42579-1 pa

LC 2004-56656

"A fascinating, far-reaching must for pop-music and pop-culture collections." Booklist

Includes bibliographical references, discography, and filmography

Charnas, Dan

The **big** payback; the history of the business of hip-hop. New American Library 2010 660p il $24.95   **781.64**
1. Hip-hop 2. Rap music 3. Music industry
ISBN 978-0-451-22929-8; 0-451-22929-0

LC 2010-16062

On this four-decade-long journey from the studios where the first rap records were made to the boardrooms where the big deals were inked, "The Big Payback" tallies the list of who lost and who won along the 40-year road to hip-hop's dominance.

This "history of the rap industry is a classic of music-business dirt-digging as well as a kind of pulp epic. . . . Tomorrow's Diddys should sleep with this book under their pillow." Rolling Stone

The **Encyclopedia** of Country Music; the ultimate guide to the music. compiled by the staff of the Country Music Hall of Fame and Museum ; edited by Paul Kingsbury, Michael McCall, and John W. Rumble with the assistance of Michael Gray and Jay Orr. 2nd ed. Oxford University Press 2012 xi, 626 p.p $65.00   **781.64**
1. Music industry 2. Country musicians 3. Folk music -- United States 4. Country music -- Encyclopedias
ISBN 0195395638; 9780195395631

LC 2010045104

This country music encyclopedia, edited by Michael McCall, John Rumble, and Paul Kingsbury, is a revised edition of the previous 1998 publication. "This . . . edition includes more than 1,200 A-Z entries covering nine decades of history and artistry. . . . Compiled by . . . experts at the Country Music Hall of Fame and Museum, the encyclopedia has been brought completely up-to-date, with new entries on the artists who have profoundly influenced country music in recent years." (Publisher's note)

Fletcher, Tony

All hopped up and ready to go; music from the streets of New York, 1927-77. W. W. Norton 2009 476p il pa $18.95   **781.64**
1. Popular music -- History and criticism 2. New York (N.Y.) -- Social life and customs
ISBN 978-0-393-33483-8; 0-393-33483-X

LC 2009-20630

"Anyone interested in popular music and the rich cultural heritage of New York—indeed, all of the U.S.—should read this book." Booklist

Includes bibliographical references

Govenar, Alan B.

Texas blues; the rise of a contemporary sound. [by] Alan Govenar. Texas A&M University Press 2008 599p il (John and Robin Diskson series in Texas music) $40   **781.64**
1. Blues music 2. Rhythm and blues music 3. Texas
ISBN 978-1-58544-605-6; 1-58544-605-X
LC 2007-39152

As this "study shows, the importance of Texas Blues is demonstrated by the number of musicians who have practiced or are practicing this art. The coverage is expansive, with introductory essays, interviews conducted by Govenar and others, and a wealth of photographs. Govenar . . . manages to profile an amazing number of guitarists, pianists, singers, and others, both well known and obscure, who show how much pioneering blues musicians like T-Bone Walker and Lightnin' Hopkins influenced their own development. The discussion of the role played by tiny establishments, radio stations, country music, and several key record labels is particularly enlightening." Libr J

Includes discography and bibliographical references

Hermes, Will

Love goes to buildings on fire; five years in New York that changed music forever. Faber and Faber 2011 368p il $30   **781.64**
1. Popular music 2. Music -- New York (N.Y.)
ISBN 978-0-86547-980-7
LC 2011-08445

"New York City might have been dead broke, crime-ridden and garbage-infested in the 1970s, but the music sure was great. Bob Marley opened a club date for Bruce Springsteen, Bronx DJs stole power from streetlights to fiddle with turntables in new ways, Philip Glass drove classical purists nuts with his sweeping, hypnotic compositions, and The Fania All Stars remade salsa. Down at CBGB's, the Talking Heads were double-billed with the Ramones. New York City has been pumping out great music from Gershwin to Gaga, but veteran music writer Will Hermes shows in his episodic and idiosyncratic book, 'Love Goes to Buildings on Fire,' how 1973 through 1977 stood out as a time for innovation. Not only did the grimy time plant the seeds of hip-hop, it also fostered the highly influential scenes in jazz, Latino music, punk, disco, new wave and classical." Huffington Post

Includes bibliographical references

Houghton, Mick

Becoming Elektra; the true story of Jac Holzman's visionary record label. Jawbone 2010 304p il pa $29.95   **781.64**
1. Popular music 2. Music industry 3. Elektra Records (Firm) 4. Recording industry executives
ISBN 978-1-906002-29-9

Includes "full-color reproductions of virtually every title in Elektra's catalog, themselves a revealing portrait of changing tastes and evolving consumer sophistication. Houghton's research is meticulous but he avoids the minutia that clogs many music books." Seattle Post-Intelligencer

Lauterbach, Preston

The chitlin' circuit; and the road to rock 'n' roll. W. W. Norton & Company 2011 338p il $26.95   **781.64**
1. African American musicians 2. Jazz music -- History and criticism 3. Rock music -- History and criticism
ISBN 9780393076523
LC 2011007209

"The 'chitlin' circuit,' a thriving African American subculture that few outsiders know much about, formed the brash underbelly of the rock 'n' roll story. In this terrific popular history, . . . Lauterbach uncovers a secret world that involves not only music but also racketeering and bribery, bootlegging, and various scandals. Lauterbach focuses on how the chitlin' circuit developed from the late 1930s to the early 1940s, with a particular emphasis on how it nurtured early rock 'n' roll. . . . A major achievement and an important contribution to American musical history." Booklist

Includes bibliographical references

Meltzer, Marisa

Girl power; the nineties revolution in music. Faber and Faber 2010 162p pa $14   **781.64**
1. Riot grrrl movement 2. Women rock musicians
ISBN 978-0-86547-979-1; 0-86547-979-8
LC 2009-25435

"Drawn early to the riot grrrl movement, [Meltzer] subsequently attended Evergreen State College in Olympia, WA, where it flourished and spread. Riot grrrls formed bands, composed and performed their singular brand of punk rock, dressed in girlish outfits and combat boots, spoke openly about politics and gender, and bonded through grass-roots fanzines. They defined their own style of music and feminism." Libr J

Includes bibliographical references and filmography

The Oxford American book of great music writing; edited by Marc Smirnoff; foreword by Van Dyke Parks. University of Arkansas Press 2008 xxii, 421p il $34.95   **781.64**
1. Popular music -- History and criticism
ISBN 978-1-557-28887-5; 1-557-28887-9
LC 2008-26298

A collection of fifty-five essays taken from Oxford American magazine's Southern Music Issues from 1996 to 2007.

"With contributions from Nick Tosches, Robert Palmer, Robert Gordon, and Peter Guralnick, some of the top music writers, Smirnoff reminds us what good music writing is. This compilation is full of little gems, including Susan Straight's tender reminiscence of the music of Al Green, Tom Piazza's harrowing account of his encounter with bluegrass legend Jimmy Martin, and John Fergus Ryan's report of his time backstage with Jerry Lee Lewis in 1970. Also included are Jerry Wexler on Dusty Springfield, Roy Blount Jr. on Ray Charles, and John Jeremiah Sullivan on Chris Bell (of Big Star)." Booklist

Includes bibliographical references

Reynolds, Simon

✓ **Retromania**; pop culture's addiction to its own past. Faber & Faber 2011 458p   **781.64**

1. Rock music 2. Popular culture 3. Popular culture -- History 4. Popular music -- Social aspects 5. Popular music -- History and criticism
ISBN 978-0-571-23208-6 pa; 0-571-23208-6 pa
LC 2011-930771

In this book, "Simon Reynolds, . . . a prominent journalist of popular music, . . . explores one of the most important facets of contemporary popular culture: the ongoing 'uses and abuses of the pop past.' . . . Reynolds touches on this trend as manifested in various cultural forms--fashion, television, movies, theater--but the spotlight is squarely on music. . . . The various issues explored include those of musical style, . . . recreations, . . . collections, . . . and digital technology." (Notes)

"Noting that 'there has never been a society in human history so obsessed with the cultural artifacts of its own immediate past,' Reynolds . . . offers cogent examples of the 'lame and shameful' retromania in pop music, including revivals, reissues, reunions, tribute albums, golden oldie shows, boxed sets and music documentaries. Part of a broader societal obsession with nostalgia—e.g., remakes of blockbuster movies, iconic TV shows and vintage fashions—this constant use and abuse of the past prevents the making of groundbreaking music. New styles like hip hop and rave culture can no longer emerge; instead, pop musicians of the 2000s tweak established musical genres and raid archives. Much of Reynolds's absorbing, brightly written and rambling book focuses on the evolution of pop nostalgia. . . . Important—and alarming—reading for pop-music aficionados." Kirkus

Includes bibliographical references

✓ The **riot** grrrl collection; edited, with an introduction by Lisa Darms. Feminist Press 2013 362 p. illustrations (chiefly color) $34.95   **781.64**

1. Fanzines 2. Punk culture 3. Women's movement 4. Zines 5. Punk rock music -- Periodicals 6. Riot grrrl movement -- Periodicals
ISBN 1558618228; 9781558618220
LC 2013014331

Publishers Weekly Best Books: Nonfiction (2013)

"Against the backdrop of the culture wars and before the rise of the Internet or desktop publishing, the zine and music culture of the Riot Grrrl movement empowered young women across the country to speak out against sexism and oppression." This book, edited by Lisa Darms, "reproduces a sampling of the original zines, posters, and printed matter for the first time since their initial distribution in the 1980s and '90s, and includes an original essay by Johanna Fateman." (Publisher's note)

"The writers' desperation, anger, and desire translate vividly into the 21st century and will resonate strongly with today's feminists, misfits, and punks." Pub Wkly

Includes bibliographical references

Roden, Steve

. . . i listen to the wind that obliterates my traces; music in vernacular photographs, 1880-1955. Dust-to-Digital 2011 un $50   **781.64**

1. Folk music 2. Popular music 3. Artistic photography 4. Musical instruments -- Pictorial works
ISBN 978-09817342-4-8

This volume is "compiled from the personal collection of interdisciplinary sound and visual artist Steve Roden. It contains a book of photographs of musicians mostly unknown and others related to the hearing of music. This beautifully hardbound book also contains two CDs containing 51 songs recorded between approximately 1914-1955, taken from 78s and acetates. The music ranges from the well known Bradley Kincaid's 1928 recording of 'Froggie Went A-Courtin' and Ukulele Ike's '(I'm Cryin' 'Cause I Know I'm) Losing You' to virtually unknown sides taken from home recordings. This is all annotated by a lengthy poetic essay by Roden that attempts to create a social and poetic context from the ephemeral, and is underscored by epigraphs from writers from James Agee, Joseph Roth, and William Wordsworth to Pär Lagerqvist and Gerhart Hauptmann." Allmusic.com

Thompson, Gordon

✓ **Please** please me; change and sixties British pop. Oxford University Press 2008 340p il $99; pa $24.95   **781.64**

1. Rock music 2. Popular music 3. Music industry
ISBN 978-0-19-533318-3; 978-0-19-533325-1 pa
LC 2007-47545

"As history books go, this one is more engaging than most. The selected discography is a nice addition, and a song index (in addition to a general book index) makes it easy to find passages related to your favorite tunes." Goldmine

Includes discography and bibliographical references (p. 307-314)

Wald, Elijah

✓ **How** the Beatles destroyed rock 'n' roll; an alternative history of American popular music. Oxford University Press 2009 323p il $24.95   **781.64**

1. Popular music -- History and criticism
ISBN 978-0-19-534154-6
LC 2008-42265

"A bracing, inclusive look at the dramatic transformation in the way music was produced and listened to during the 20th century." Kirkus

Includes bibliographical references (p. 281-289)

Watkins, S. Craig

★ **Hip** hop matters; politics, pop culture, and the struggle for the soul of a movement. Beacon Press 2005 295p $24.95; pa $16   **781.64**

1. Rap music
ISBN 0-8070-0982-2; 0-8070-0986-5 pa
LC 2004-24187

The author "presents a concise, clear history of the hip-hop movement in the US and uses it as a springboard for discussion of contemporary issues of politics, pop culture, and struggle." Choice

Includes bibliographical references

Westhoff, Ben

Dirty South; Outkast, Lil Wayne, Soulja Boy, and the Southern rappers who reinvented hip-hop. Chicago Review Press 2011 298p il pa $14.95 **781.64**
1. Rap music
ISBN 978-1-56976-606-4; 1-56976-606-1

LC 2010-53907

An "exploration of the musical and personal terrain of what has come to be known as the Southern sound of rap by such artists as Lil Wayne, Young Jeezy, and Ludacris. Westhoff convincingly details how Southern rap music— 'party music, full of hypnotic hooks and sing-along choruses'—took over from dominant East Coast and West Coast rap styles by replacing 'normal rap structures and metaphor-heavy rhymes. . . in favor of chants, grunts and shouts.' In fact, the beauty of Westhoff's descriptions of the genre as a whole and various songs in particular will make old fans as well as newbies want to search out and play classic CDs such as OutKast's 'Aquemini' and 'Kings of Crunk' by Lil Jon. And Westhoff's personal trips to the home bases of each artist he presents show how the personalities of the artists reinforce their music." Publ Wkly

Includes bibliographical references

781.642   Country music

Escott, Colin

The **Grand** ole opry; the making of an American icon. Brenda Colladay, photo editor. Center Street 2006 250p il $24.99   **781.642**
1. Country music 2. Grand ole opry (Radio program)
ISBN 978-1-931722-86-5; 1-931722-86-2

LC 2006-7796

"Escott's overview of the long-running Saturday-night performance showcase takes the form of oral history. The preponderance of the text consists of statements by Grand Ole Opry producers, sponsors, and stars, with the older comments drawn from old books and newspaper stories and the newer from Escott's interviews. . . . With decade-by-decade lists of the Opry's members and scads of performance photos, it's a honey of a book for every American library." Booklist

Jennings, Dana Andrew

Sing me back home; love, death, and country music. [by] Dana Jennings. Faber and Faber 2008 257p $24   **781.642**
1. Country music -- History and criticism
ISBN 978-0-86547-960-9; 0-86547-960-7

LC 2007-47955

This "quirky, endearing combination memoir, family history, music criticism, and love-of-place offering, made up of short, punchy chapters and sharp observations about country's appeal and how country has expressed the inchoate emotions of its largely rural following, essentiallypresents the music as the portrayal of a way of life and a way of being." Booklist

Includes discography and bibliographical references

Kagarise, Leon

Pure country; the Leon Kagarise archives 1961-1971. foreword by Robert Gordon; introduction and text by Eddie Dean. Process Media 2008 191p il $35   **781.642**
1. Country music -- Pictorial works
ISBN 978-1-93417-003-8

"Kagarise was an obsessive fan of 'real' country and bluegrass musics, and he amassed a giant collection of records, live tapes and ephemera, mostly during the 1960s. This volume collects many of the color slides he shot at a couple of outdoor venues in Maryland and Pennsylvania, and the views of this lost scene they provide is unparalleled. Well-known figures like Johnny Cash, George Jones and Skeeter Davis mix with more legendary unknowns (at least to proles), like the Stoneman family, with whom Kagarise had a special connection, and who he rates far above the Carter family in terms of sheer talent. The main text . . . provides a very boss thumbnail history of country music in the pre-modern era." Arthur

Russell, Tony

Country music originals; the legends & the lost. Oxford University Press 2007 258p il $29.95   **781.642**
1. Country music 2. Country musicians
ISBN 978-0-19-532509-6

LC 2007-8471

"Russell has accomplished a spectacular feat in that he has written a thorough reference book that is as pleasing to read as the best of narrative nonfiction." Publ Wkly

Includes bibliographical references

Zwonitzer, Mark

Will you miss me when I'm gone? the Carter Family and their legacy in American music. [by] Mark Zwonitzer with Charles Hirshberg. Simon & Schuster 2002 417p il hardcover o.p. pa $15   **781.642**
1. Carter family (Musical group)
ISBN 0-684-85763-4; 0-7432-4382-X pa

LC 2002-22395

The author "follows the Carter family's history from the 1891 birth of A.P. Carter, the musical founder, up through the late 1970s, offering background on the social, economic and technological developments that spawned American folk, country and rock music. . . . Zwonitzer writes with flair, weaving anecdotes into a compelling study that will intrigue historians and music lovers alike." Publ Wkly

781.643   Blues

Ferris, William

Give my poor heart ease; voices of the Mississippi blues. [interviews by] William Ferris. University of North Carolina Press 2009 302p il $35 **781.643**
1. Blues music 2. African Americans -- Mississippi
ISBN 0-8078-3325-8; 978-0-8078-3325-4

LC 2009-16647

Ferris "presents transcriptions of stories he captured via films and recording devices from the 1960s and 1970s of

Mississippi blues practitioners, preachers, and Parchman Prison inmates. The enclosed CD and DVD bring the package together with stories, blues songs, and gospel recordings. B.B. King and Willie Dixon are the most famous artists included, but the stories of desperately poor sharecroppers and ex-inmates are just as engrossing. The comprehensive bibliography is a great resource." Libr J

Includes bibliographical references

Gioia, Ted

✓ **Delta** blues; the life and times of the Mississippi Masters who revolutionized American music. artwork by Neil Harpe. W. W. Norton 2008 449p il $27.95; pa $16.95   **781.643**

1. Blues music
ISBN 978-0-393-06258-8; 0-393-06258-9; 978-0-393-33750-1 pa; 0-393-33750-2 pa

LC 2008-09412

Gioia describes the "beginnings of the Delta sound with Charley Patton and former Parchman inmates Son House and Bukka White. He relates the stories of such obscure Delta artists as Tommy Johnson and Big Joe Williams before delivering the bulk of the book, which describes the lives and influences of Delta blues icons Robert Johnson, Muddy Waters, Howlin' Wolf, B.B. King, and John Lee Hooker. Gioia ends with a chapter about the rediscovery of Delta legends by rabid blues collectors during the 1960s and then oddly leaps to 1990s performers such as Chris Thomas King and Junior Kimbrough in the last few pages. . . . Though presenting little new information and not geared for the blues fanatic, this is an excellent introduction to Delta blues for the novice and the general reader." Libr J

Includes bibliographical references

King, B. B.

✓ ★ **Blues** all around me; the autobiography of B.B. King. [by] B.B. King with David Ritz. Avon Bks. 1996 336p il hardcover o.p. pa $15.99 **781.643**

1. Singers 2. Guitarists 3. Blues music 4. Blues musicians 5. African American musicians
ISBN 0-380-97318-9; 0-06-206103-8 pa

LC 96-27773

King recounts his humble beginnings and his career as a prominent blues guitarist.

"This is one of the best recent pop-music bios. King speaks straight from the soul, it seems, just like he plays the guitar." Booklist

Lomax, Alan

✓ ★ The **land** where the blues began. New Press 2002 539p il pa $21.95   **781.643**

1. Blues music 2. African American music 3. African Americans -- Mississippi
ISBN 1-56584-739-3; 978-1-56584-739-2

LC 2004-268632

First published 1993 by Pantheon

This is an account of the folklorist and musicologist's travels in the Mississippi Delta in the 1940s as he recorded the work of African American blues musicians.

"If it were a novel, Alan Lomax's long-awaited account of his adventures in the Mississippi Delta would be called

'sprawling' and a 'must read.' . . . It is as delightful and hard to put down as any fictional epic." Booklist

Includes bibliographical references, discography and filmography

✓ **Nothing** but the blues; the music and the musicians. {edited by} Lawrence Cohn. Abbeville Press 1993 432p il hardcover o.p. pa $39.95 **781.643**

1. Blues music
ISBN 0-7892-0607-2 pa

LC 93-2791

The essays in this volume aim to :trace the metamorphosis of the blues from its African roots and the 'hollers,' work songs, and party music of the rural south to the . . . rhythms of urban blues and on to R & B and blues rock. . . . Blues styles associated with specific regions are described. . . . Other topics include the impact of radio and recording technology on the popularity of the blues, the link between gospel and blues, and the blues revival of the 1960s." (Booklist)

This "illustrated compilation of articles by 10 notable writers examines the origins of blues and the music's various styles and artists, including women." Booklist

Includes discography and bibliographical references

781.644   Soul

Danielsen, Anne

✓ **Presence** and pleasure; the funk grooves of James Brown and Parliament. Wesleyan University Press 2006 262p il (Music/culture) $65; pa $24.95   **781.644**

1. Singers 2. Funk (Music) 3. Soul musicians 4. Parliament (Musical group)
ISBN 978-0-8195-6822-9; 0-8195-6822-8; 978-0-8195-6823-6 pa; 0-8195-6823-6 pa

LC 2006-10987

The author "brings a unique perspective to this book. . . . Her discussion of funk comes from the dual angles of musicologist and longtime performer." Choice

Includes bibliographical references

781.646   Reggae

Bradley, Lloyd

✓ **This** is reggae music; the story of Jamaica's music. Grove Press 2001 572p il pa $17   **781.646**

1. Reggae music
ISBN 0-8021-3828-4

LC 2001-33462

First published 2000 in the United Kingdom with title: Brass culture: when reggae was king

Presented "in a witty and engaging manner. . . . For enthusiasts, this book is fabulous." Libr J

Includes bibliographical references and indexes

781.65 Jazz

Armstrong, Louis

Louis Armstrong, in his own words; selected writings. edited and with an introduction by Thomas Brothers; annotated index by Charles Kinzer. Oxford Univ. Press 1999 xxvii, 255p il hardcover o.p. pa $14.95 **781.65**
  1. Singers 2. Jazz musicians 3. Band leaders 4. Trumpet players
  ISBN 0-19-514046-X

  LC 99-17040

In this collection Armstrong "recounts episodes from his childhood in New Orleans, pays tribute to other musicians, and extolls the virtues of marijuana, laxatives, and rice and beans while speaking candidly about race relations, the music business, and his extramarital affairs. The joy he took in expressing himself on paper is abundantly evident." New Yorker

Includes bibliographical references

Cook, Richard

The **Penguin** guide to jazz recordings; [by] Richard Cook and Brian Morton. 9th ed.; Penguin 2008 pa $37.50 **781.65**
  1. Jazz music -- Discography 2. Sound recordings -- Reviews
  ISBN 978-0-14-102327-4; 0-14-102327-9
  Biannual. First published 1992

"Entries include very brief descriptions of the artists and a list of their recordings, with reviews and ratings by the authors. The lengths of the CD entries vary from very short (label, catalog number, issue date, and performers) to extensive, multiparagraph descriptions of the album's history, reception, and individual songs. The authors are clearly devout jazz historians, and the character of the entries is as much admiring as it is strictly factual. Their detailed descriptions of albums, songs, and even artists' tone colors and interpretations within specific songs are testament to their expertise." Booklist

Cooke, Mervyn

The **chronicle** of jazz; Mervyn Cooke. Oxford University Press 2013 272 p. illustrations (hardback : alk. paper) $39.95 **781.65**
  1. Jazz ensembles 2. Jazz musicians 3. Jazz music -- History and criticism 4. Jazz -- Chronology 5. Jazz -- History and criticism
  ISBN 0199341001; 9780199341009

  LC 2013019617

This book, by Mervyn Cooke, "charts the evolution of jazz from its roots in Africa and the southern United States to the myriad urban styles heard around the world today. . . . Featuring hundreds of rare images, from record-cover artwork to pictures of live performances, each chronologically arranged section contains special box features on such topics as the unique tonal qualities of the bass clarinet, jazz clubs in Paris, personality sketches, and seminal gigs and albums." (Publisher's note)

"This handsome and attractive volume by music professor and writer Cooke covers the entire history of the jazz medium in one accessible and colorful resource." Booklist

Includes discography (pages 264-265), bibliographical references (page 266), and indexes

Crouch, Stanley

★ **Considering** genius; writings on jazz. Basic Civitas Books 2006 359p $27.50 **781.65**
  1. Jazz music -- History and criticism
  ISBN 0-465-01517-4

  LC 2006-2225

"This collection brings together a healthy sampling of [Crouch's] jazz writings dating from 1977 to the present. A long and spirited prologue, 'Jazz Me Blues,' lays out Crouch's jazz aesthetic, but he really shows his stuff in the essays on particular musicians, combining trenchant analysis of the artist with fascinating biographical material and feeling free to speculate at will about the psychology and inner lives of such jazz greats as Miles Davis, Thelonious Monk, and John Coltrane. . . . Essential reading for jazz fans." Booklist

Feather, Leonard

The **biographical** encyclopedia of jazz; [by] Leonard Feather and Ira Gitler, with the assistance of Swing journal, Tokyo. Oxford Univ. Press 1999 xx, 718p hardcover o.p. pa $29.95 **781.65**
  1. Jazz musicians
  ISBN 0-19-507418-1; 978-0-19-532000-8 pa; 0-19-532000-X pa

  LC 98-15485

This book is based in part on Leonard Feather's Encyclopedia of jazz, The new encyclopedia of jazz, The encyclopedia of jazz in the sixties, and on a subsequent work by Mr. Feather and Ira Gitler, The encyclopedia of jazz in the seventies

This reference source "is made up of more than 3,000 biographies, listed in alphabetical order. Musicians, singers, songwriters, and producers are included. Each entry begins with birth and death information, instruments played, and music-education information. This is followed by a listing of groups each individual played with for significant periods of time. Concluding each entry are lists of recordings, broadcast appearances, and record labels. . . . An indispensable reference source for its comprehensiveness and quality of scholarship." Booklist

Includes discographies

Friedwald, Will

Jazz singing; America's great voices from Bessie Smith to bebop and beyond. Da Capo Press 1996 505p il pa $18.50 **781.65**
  1. Singers 2. Jazz music 3. Jazz vocals -- History and criticism
  ISBN 0-306-80712-2

  LC 96-23837

First published 1990 by Scribner, this edition has a new discography

"This is an absolutely essential book for anybody who cares in the slightest about adult popular music." Booklist

Includes discography

Gennari, John

Blowin' hot and cool; jazz and its critics. University of Chicago Press 2006 480p $35   **781.65**
1. Jazz music -- History and criticism
ISBN 0-226-28922-2

LC 2005-30539

"Gennari's book does for jazz critics what most of them were unable to do for themselves, but with a postmodern twist: The scholar demystifies and historicizes the journalists. The first sustained scholarly book exclusively about jazz criticism—and, not least, about the passions that have driven and surrounded it—Blowin' Hot and Cool is thorough, absorbing and original, an obsessive study of professional obsessives that will circumvent the need for any other." Nation
Includes bibliographical references

Giddins, Gary

Jazz; [by] Gary Giddins & Scott DeVeaux. W. W. Norton 2009 704p il $39.95   **781.65**
1. Jazz music -- History and criticism
ISBN 978-0-393-06861-0; 0-393-068617

LC 2009-24880

The authors "split duties: DeVeaux provides blow-by-blow, laymen-friendly listening guides to musical examples (there's an accompanying four-CD set, though you have to buy that separately) and Giddins writes the historical narrative. . . . Jazz history for Giddins and DeVeaux isn't a matter of exposition so much as argument, and those arguments — never strident or agenda-driven, but arguments nonetheless — are what provide the 'plot' of this story and carry it through the music's many disparate, colorful characters, styles, and transformations." Boston Phoenix
Includes bibliographical references

Visions of jazz; the first century. Oxford Univ. Press 1998 690p hardcover o.p. pa $18.95 **781.65**
1. Jazz musicians 2. Jazz music -- History and criticism
ISBN 0-19-513241-6 pa

LC 98-12199

"Alongside his virtuoso considerations of Ellington, Monk, Mingus, and the predictable greats, Giddins illuminates the contributions to be found in the likes of Al Jolson's minstrel posing and Stan Kenton's florid kitsch. His writing, like the music he loves, is joyously polyphonic, with history, legend, musicology, biography, and performance all rising out of the mix." New Yorker

Weather bird; jazz at the dawn of its second century. Gary Giddins. Oxford University Press 2004 xxiv, 632p $35   **781.65**
1. Jazz music -- History and criticism
ISBN 0-19-515607-2

LC 2004-654

"This book collects more than 140 essays, articles, and reviews that Giddins wrote from 1990 to November 2003. . . . The breadth and depth of his knowledge is extremely impressive, his ear is astounding, and his masterly style routinely achieves the near impossible in writing engagingly about something that inherently eludes description." Libr J

Gioia, Ted

The history of jazz; 2nd ed.; Oxford University Press 2011 444p il pa $19.95   **781.65**
1. Jazz music -- History and criticism
ISBN 978-0-19-539970-7; 0-19-539970-6

LC 2010-23182

First published 1997

The author "relates the story of African American music from its roots in Africa to the international respect it enjoys today. . . . This well-researched, extensively annotated volume covers the major trends and personalities that have shaped jazz. The excellent bibliography and list of recommended listening make this a valuable purchase for libraries building a jazz collection." Libr J
Includes discography and bibliographical references

Grosse Jazzbuch./English

The jazz book; from ragtime to the 21st century. [by] Joachim-Ernst Berendt and Gunther Huesmann; translated by H. and B. Bredigkeit ... [et al.]. 7th ed., rev. and expanded.; Lawrence Hill Books 2009 754p il $49.95; pa $29.95   **781.65**
1. Jazz music -- History and criticism
ISBN 978-1-55652-820-0; 1-55652-820-5; 978-1-55652-823-1 pa; 1-55652-823-X pa

LC 2008-53770

First published 1953 in Germany; first English translation 1975; periodically revised.

"Should this be your first book about jazz? Yes, but you must start with small portions and use the Internet to sample freely as you proceed. The sheer amount of information on offer here makes this most decidedly a Jazz Tome, but one that can be dipped into freely, any time, for any reason." Open Letters
Includes discography

Kahn, Ashley

The house that Trane built; the story of Impulse Records. Norton 2006 338p il $29.95   **781.65**
1. Jazz music 2. Jazz musicians 3. Saxophonists 4. Impulse Records (Firm)
ISBN 0-393-05879-4

LC 2005-037218

The author "offers a fascinating insider's view of the sessions that produced not only Coltrane's classics but also top-grade albums by both fiery radicals and such timeless stars as Duke Ellington, Coleman Hawkins and Benny Carter." Economist

Lees, Gene

You can't steal a gift; Dizzy, Clark, Milt, and Nat. foreword by Nat Hentoff. Yale Univ. Press 2001 269p il $27.95   **781.65**
1. Singers 2. Pianists 3. Photographers 4. Jazz musicians 5. Bassists 6. Band leaders 7. Flugelhornists 8. Trumpet players 9. United States -- Race relations
ISBN 0-300-08965-1

LC 2001-3444

Lees discusses the lives and careers of four jazz musicians: Dizzy Gillespie, Terry Clark, Milt Hinton, and Nat King Cole. A theme of the book is how these artists were affected by race relations in the United States

The author "has a natural ease with words and a graceful prose style that captures the reader's attention." Booklist

Marsalis, Wynton

Moving to higher ground; how jazz can change your life. [by] Wynton Marsalis with Geoffrey C. Ward. Random House 2008 181p il **781.65**

1. Jazz music -- History and criticism

ISBN 1400060788; 9781400060788

LC 2008-16560

The author "explains in lay readers' terms how jazz works as a diverse musical genre and, more important, how an understanding and appreciation of jazz can enrich one's life. . . . This work is highly recommended." Libr J

Morgenstern, Dan

Living with jazz; a reader. edited by Sheldon Meyer. Pantheon Books 2004 712p $35 **781.65**

1. Jazz music -- History and criticism

ISBN 0-375-42072-X

LC 2004-43432

This is a compilation of "nearly half a century of Morgenstern's profiles, liner notes, record and show reviews and other musings. . . . Morgenstern reminisces about his introduction to jazz in a brief opening memoir, then segues into lengthy sections on his greatest heroes, Louis Armstrong and Duke Ellington. . . . His exuberant characterizations make this monumental volume a stimulating guide to jazz in the second half of the 20th century." Publ Wkly

Myers, Marc

Why jazz happened; Marc Myers. University of California Press 2013 267 p. (hardcover) $34.95 **781.65**

1. Jazz music -- History and criticism 2. Jazz -- History and criticism

ISBN 0520268784; 9780520268784

LC 2012022218

This book, by Marc Myers, offers a "social history of jazz. It provides a . . . look at the many forces that shaped this most American of art forms and the many influences that gave rise to jazz's post-war styles. . . . This book views jazz's evolution through the prism of technological advances, social transformations, changes in the law, economic trends, and much more." (Publisher's note)

Includes bibliographical references and index

Paulo, Joaquim

Jazz covers; ed. Julius Wiedemann; interviews with Bob Ciano . . . [et al.] by Joaquim Paulo; top-10 favorite records lists by jazz DJs Amir Abdullah . . . [et al.] Taschen 2008 494p il pa $39.99 **781.65**

1. Jazz music 2. Sound recordings -- Album covers

ISBN 978-3-8228-2366-8; 3-8228-2366-X

This volume "manages to sum up the genre with the thoroughness of a scholarly essay. Vivid photographs are accompanied by pithy back-story writeups of the jazz artists and album designers." Time Out Hong Kong

Ratliff, Ben (2009)

The **jazz** ear; conversations over music. Times Books 2008 256p il $25 **781.65**

1. Jazz music -- History and criticism

ISBN 978-0-8050-8146-6; 0-8050-8146-1

LC 2008-10122

"Originally published as a series in the New York Times, the 15 conversations presented here consist of Ratliff sitting down with such diverse and talented luminaries as Sonny Rollins, Pat Metheny, Paul Motian, and Dianne Reeves. The treasure of these conversations is not just their fluid and intimate manner but their focus on the recordings that had the greatest influence on the artists and their musical paths. . . . An added bonus is the recommended-listening section, in which Ratliff shares his list of his subjects' seminal recordings. Highly recommended." Libr J

Includes bibliographical references

Sandke, Randall

Where the dark and the light folks meet; race and the mythology, politics, and business of jazz. Scarecrow Press 2010 277p (Studies in jazz) $40; ebook $40 **781.65**

1. Jazz music -- History and criticism

ISBN 0-8108-6652-8; 0-8108-6990-X ebook; 978-0-8108-6652-2; 978-0-8108-6990-5 ebook

LC 2009-37977

The author "tackles a controversial question: Is jazz the product of an insulated African-American environment, shut off from the rest of society by strictures of segregation and discrimination, or is it more properly understood as the juncture of a wide variety of influences under the broader umbrella of American culture?" Publisher's note

Includes bibliographical references

Santoro, Gene

Myself when I am real: the life and music of Charles Mingus. Oxford Univ. Press 2000 452p hardcover o.p. pa $17.95 **781.65**

1. Composers 2. Jazz musicians 3. Bassists

ISBN 0-19-509733-5; 0-19-514711-1 pa

LC 99-46734

The author "has attempted not only to capture the complex, contradictory character of jazz bassist and composer Mingus, but also to assert his music's towering significance in American culture as a whole." Publ Wkly

Includes discography and bibliographical references

Ward, Geoffrey C.

Jazz; a history of America's music. based on a documentary film by Ken Burns written by Geoffrey C. Ward; with a preface by Ken Burns. Knopf 2000 489p il $65; pa $29.95 **781.65**

1. Jazz music

ISBN 0-679-44551-X; 0-679-76539-5 pa

LC 00-22604

The authors "have assembled a comprehensive history with a focus on the musicians and the sociology of jazz. . . . The short articles by Wynton Marsalis, Dan Morgenstern, Gerald Early, Stanley Crouch, and Gary Giddins, which are woven into the text, provide a . . . specific focus on a number of jazz's aspects." Libr J

Includes bibliographical references

Williams, Richard

The **blue** moment; Miles Davis's Kind of blue and the remaking of modern music. W. W. Norton & Company 2010 309p **781.65**

1. Jazz musicians 2. Band leaders 3. Flugelhornists 4. Trumpet players 5. Jazz music -- History and criticism
ISBN 978-0-393-07663-9

LC 2009053270

First published 2009 in the United Kingdom

"'Kind of Blue,' the book jacket notes, is the only jazz album many people own. And while that might turn off jazz fans, even purists bow down to the 1959 Miles Davis release. Williams, a writer for The Guardian in Britain, details the recording sessions (it took only nine hours and was recorded in a Manhattan church); the band, which included John Coltrane, Cannonball Adderly and Gil Evans; and the tenor of the times, which helps explain why it's so extraordinary." N Y Post

Includes bibliographical references

781.66 Rock (Rock 'n' roll)

Almond, Steve

Rock and roll will save your life; a book by and for the fanatics among us (with bitchin' soundtrack) Random House 2010 216p $23 **781.66**

1. Rock music -- History and criticism 2. Popular music -- History and criticism
ISBN 978-1-4000-6620-9; 1-4000-6620-4

"As a young writer plagued by self-doubt, Almond reveled in the emotional escape of music; the joy of his fanaticism is conveyed poignantly—and so completely—that we're infected with his touted salvation too. With well-placed 'interludes' or 'reluctant exegeses,' Almond peppers his pages with biting insights and funny vignettes; dismissing, for instance, Toto's 'Africa' as '. . . the lovechild of Muzak and Imperialism.' Though the language feels a bit highbrow, Almond ultimately crafts a playful and intelligent read." Paste

Aronowitz, Nona Willis

★ **Out** of the vinyl deeps; Ellen Willis on rock music. edited by Nona Willis Aronowitz; foreword by Sasha Frere-Jones; afterword by Daphne Carr and Evie Nagy. University of Minnesota Press 2011 232p il $69; pa $22.95 **781.66**

1. Rock music 2. Rock music -- History and criticism
ISBN 978-0-8166-7282-0; 978-0-8166-7283-7 pa

LC 2010-50856

"Willis's work is crystalline enough that reading each essay takes the reader on a trip back to the era when it originally appeared, but it's a testimony to her intellect and talent that those journeys look completely unlike any hagiography you might stumble across." Village Voice

Includes bibliographical references

Bangs, Lester (2602?)

Mainlines, blood feasts and bad taste; a Lester Bangs reader. edited by John Morthland. Anchor Books 2003 409p pa $15.95 **781.66**

1. Rock music -- History and criticism
ISBN 978-0-375-71367-5; 0-375-71367-0

LC 2003-40392

Mothland includes includes Bangs's "riffs on jazz, heretofore not seen by many eyes. Readers will be reminded of what Bangs . . . should really be famous for: his lust for life and 'soul' music, any tune that hits a nerve and the heart at the same time. Truly, this is a time capsule of when pop music still crackled and people held the stuff to an emotional standard." Libr J

Psychotic reactions and carburetor dung; edited by Greil Marcus. Knopf 1987 386p hardcover o.p. pa $16 **781.66**

1. Rock music -- History and criticism
ISBN 0-394-53896-X; 0-679-72045-6 pa

LC 87-45122

"For rockers whose tastes demand more than Madonna and who remember back before Bruce, this is a gem." Libr J

Blecha, Peter

Sonic boom; the history of Northwest rock, from Louie Louie to Smells like Teen Spirit. Backbeat Books 2009 304p il pa $19.99 **781.66**

1. Rock music
ISBN 978-0-87930-946-6

LC 2008-51529

This book "lends substantial weight to the big fish—long established legends like Jimi Hendrix and Kurt Cobain, as well as newer names like Death Cab for Cutie and Fleet Foxes—but it also pays respect to the lesser known little guys who contributed to 60-plus years of local rock, and as such, . . does a commendable service to the musical history and the sonic identity of the area and its artists." PopMatters

Includes discography

Browne, David

Fire and rain; the Beatles, Simon & Garfunkel, James Taylor, CSNY, and the lost story of 1970. Da Capo Press 2011 369p il $26 **781.66**

1. Singers 2. Rock music 3. Beatles 4. Songwriters 5. Simon and Garfunkel 6. Rock music -- History and criticism 7. Crosby, Stills and Nash (Musical group)
ISBN 9780306818509; 0-306-81850-7

"Browne skillfully interleaves the stories of these musicians during this tumultuous year, making room for substantial walk-ons by other significant industry figures like Bill Graham, Peter Yarrow, Phil Spector, Rita Coolidge, Carole King and Joni Mitchell. Intimately familiar with the music, fully comprehending the cross-pollination among the artists, thoroughly awake to the dynamics of the decade's last gasp, the author expertly captures a volatile and hugely interesting moment in rock history." Kirkus

Includes bibliographical references

Buckland, Gail

Who shot rock & roll; a photographic history, 1955 to the present. Alfred A. Knopf 2009 319p il $40 **781.66**

1. Rock music -- Pictorial works
ISBN 978-0-307-27016-0; 0-307-27016-5

LC 2009-19122

"Here are nearly 300 iconic photographs by those photographers who understood the power of the image in the formation and sustenance of rock-and-roll culture from 1955 onward. The care with which Buckland selects representative photographers and their most significant images is matched by her interpretive prowess. . . . [She] carefully but deliberately argues that the art of rock photography has been sacrificed to the paparazzi and corporate art departments. In light of this inclusive, heady and visceral collection of the genre's best, it would be hard to argue otherwise." Publ Wkly

Includes bibliographical references

Bukszpan, Daniel

The encyclopedia of new wave; by Daniel Bukszpan ; foreword by Gerald Casale. Sterling 2012 304 p. (pbk.) $24.95 **781.66**

1. New wave music 2. Popular music -- Encyclopedias
3. Popular music -- History and criticism
ISBN 1402784724; 9781402784729

LC 2012564140

This book by Daniel Bukszpan "look[s] at the New Wave era in pop music (roughly, late 1970s through the end of the 1980s and defined within as 'a straightforward songwriting approach relying heavily on synthesizers and other electronic equipment')" and "covers more than 150 artists and bands. . . . Best-selling acts such as Duran Duran . . . are included alongside one-hit wonders like the Flying Lizards. . . . Influential music-related personalities of the era . . . are also featured." (Publisher's note)

Includes bibliographical references and index.

Christgau, Robert

Grown up all wrong; 75 great rock and pop artists from vaudeville to techno. Harvard Univ. Press 1998 495p $32.50; pa $18.95 **781.66**

1. Rock music -- History and criticism
ISBN 978-0-674-44318-1; 0-674-44318-7; 978-0-674-00382-8 pa; 0-674-00382-9 pa

LC 98-25779

Christgau's subjects "include Elvis Presley, the punk girl band Sleater-Kinney, the rap artist KRS-One, the country singer Geroge Jones and the minstrel singer Emmett Miller, among many, many others. He writes on each with equal erudition, examining the artists and their music as both cultural products and influences." N Y Times Book Rev

Cutler, Sam

You can't always get what you want; my life with the Rolling Stones, the Grateful Dead and other wonderful retrobates. ECW Press 2010 326p il pa $17.95 **781.66**

1. Rock music 2. Rolling Stones 3. Grateful Dead (Musical group)
ISBN 978-1-55022-932-5

First published 2008 in Australia

"Effortlessly readable, packed with entertaining, sleazy, behind-the-scenes tales. " Portland Mercury

DeRogatis, Jim

The Beatles vs. the Rolling Stones; sound opinions on the great rock 'n' roll rivalry. [by] Jim DeRogatis and Greg Kot. Voyageur Press 2010 191p il $35 **781.66**

1. Rock music 2. Beatles 3. Rolling Stones
ISBN 978-0-7603-3813-1; 0-7603-3813-2

LC 2010-03192

"The authors' discussion draws from other works in the large canon of Beatles and Rolling Stones literature, debunking some myths and validating others. Some sections are bound to raise a few eyebrows. . . . No doubt most readers will approach 'The Beatles vs. the Rolling Stones' with their own opinions, but even the most steadfast loyalists will appreciate the authors' eloquent and insightful arguments in favor of each act." Boston Globe

Includes bibliographical references

Ellis, Iain

Rebels wit attitude; subversive rock humorists. Soft Skull Press 2008 341p pa $15.95 **781.66**

1. Rock music
ISBN 978-1-59376-206-3; 1-59376-206-2

LC 2008-27013

Ellis "traces the history of humorous rebellion in American rock from the 1950s (Chuck Berry, Little Richard, Screamin' Jay Hawkins) to the 1990s (Eminem, Nirvana, Marilyn Manson), in sections on 'Bawdy Women' (e.g., Big Mama Thornton, Wanda Jackson), rap, and sundry other designations. The anecdotes and insights are rich and plentiful. . . . Madonna, Dylan, the Ramones, and bubblegum as a precursor to punk are among Ellis' other specific subjects. Despite the occasional dreary academic expostulation, good enough for general-interest rock lit collections, excellent for episodic reading." Booklist

Epting, Chris

Led Zeppelin crashed here; the rock and roll landmarks of North America. Santa Monica Press 2007 327p il map pa $16.95 **781.66**

1. Rock music 2. United States -- Description and travel
ISBN 978-1-59580-018-3; 1-59580-018-2

LC 2007-6246

"Discover where Bob Dylan's motorcycle crashed, where Elvis Presley first performed, where Ozzy Osbourne bit the head off a bat and the real location of Bruce Springsteen's E Street. The book includes nearly 600 landmarks along with historical information, trivia, photos and backstage lore. Chapters cover topics such as sex and drugs, live performance locations, recording sites, blues and jazz shrines, places where homicides and suicides occurred, and rock and roll museums. There's also a list of 100 classic road trip songs, 100 road trip albums and 30 great North American music stores. An appendix lists rock and roll landmarks by state." Salt Lake Tribune

German, Bill

Under their thumb; how a nice boy from Brooklyn got mixed up with the Rolling Stones (and lived to tell about it) Villard Books 2009 354p il $25 **781.66**

1. Rolling Stones

ISBN 978-1-4000-6622-3; 1-4000-6622-0

LC 2008-45533

"The epic tale of an obsessive teenager who launched a Rolling Stones fanzine and spent the next two decades capturing the band's whirlwind metamorphosis from behind the scenes. . . . First-rate, firsthand account of the world's greatest rock 'n' roll band, and a disenchanted chronicle of its increasingly crass commercialization." Kirkus

Gruen, Bob

New York Dolls; the photographs of Bob Gruen. introduction by Lenny Kaye; featuring commentary by David Johansen and Sylvain Sylvain and quotes collected by Legs McNeil; afterword by Morrissey. Abrams Image 2008 158p il $24.95   **781.66**

1. Rock musicians 2. New York Dolls (Musical group)

ISBN 978-0-8109-7271-1; 0-8109-7271-9

LC 2008-13074

"Gruen met singer David Johansen, guitarists Johnny Thunders and Sylvain Sylvain, drummer Jerry Nolan and bassist Arthur 'Killer' Kane at the beginning of 1973, months after the untimely death of original drummer Billy Murcia. The book chronicles the glam-rock band's career over 230 photographs, only 30 of which have previously been seen by the public. The last picture in the book is of their 2004 reunion in London. Lenny Kaye wrote the book's foreword and interviewed the group's surviving members, Johansen and Sylvain Sylvain." Rolling Stone

Klosterman, Chuck

Killing yourself to live; 85[percent] of a true story. Scribner 2005 245p hardcover o.p. pa $14   **781.66**

1. Death 2. Rock musicians

ISBN 0-7432-6445-2; 978-0-7432-6445-7; 0-7432-6446-0 pa; 978-0-7432-6446-4 pa

LC 2005-42498

"Klosterman's keen eye for American pop-cultural themes and undercurrents facilitates thoughtful observation, and his prose brings those themes and undercurrents together in strange, fresh ways. A treat for the adventurous." Booklist

Lang, Michael

The road to Woodstock; with Holly George-Warren. Ecco 2009 304p il $29.99   **781.66**

1. Woodstock Festival, 1969

ISBN 978-0-06-157655-3; 0-06-157655-7

"The author is a generous raconteur with a good memory for specifics, but what elevates this book above the level of most rock memoirs is the inclusion of voices other than Lang's—including scenesters and key Woodstock players like Jimi Hendrix, Roger Daltrey, Pete Townshend, Jerry Garcia, Abbie Hoffman, John Sebastian, Greil Marcus and Wavy Gravy. . . . Well-written, informative and tons of fun, Lang's book will be appreciated by rockers and musicologists of all ages." Kirkus

Includes bibliographical references

Marcus, Greil

The Doors; a lifetime of listening to five mean years. PublicAffairs 2011 210p $21.99   **781.66**

1. Doors (Musical group)

ISBN 978-1-58648-945-8

LC 2011-27931

"Some of the best passages in The Doors: A Lifetime of Listening to Five Mean Years are the extended descriptions of what Marcus calls 'the drama of a band at war with its audience,' in which lead singer Jim Morrison and listeners exchange taunts that would be unthinkable today at a concert by Usher or Taylor Swift. . . . Like Morrison and the Doors, Marcus likes to set the reader up and then go his own way, and when I say he's a writer's writer, I mean that he has a knack for saying whatever he wants but in a way only he can pull off. Thus in mid-book he riffs on lesser-known bands (Moby Grape) and movies ('Pump Up the Volume') and completely obscure novels (Wayne Wilson's 'Loose Jam'). . . . The thing is, it works. A three-minute song is comforting, and so is a tight prose argument; both distract us briefly, console us, and return us to our everyday lives. Both are escapist, whereas Marcus and his subjects want us to look at life, not avert our glance." Christ Sci Monit

Marcus, Sara

Girls to the front; the true story of the Riot grrrl revolution. HarperPerennial 2010 367p il pa $14.99   **781.66**

1. Feminism 2. Riot grrrl movement

ISBN 978-0-06-180636-0; 0-06-180636-6

This book is "a brash, gutsy chronicle of the empowering music and feminist movement of the early 1990s." Publ Wkly

Margotin, Philippe

All the Songs; The Story Behind Every Beatles Release. Jean-Michel Guesdon & Philippe Margotin ; preface by Patti Smith ; Scott Freiman, consulting editor. Black Dog & Leventhal Pub 2013 672 p. ill, portraits (chiefly color) $50   **781.66**

1. Beatles

ISBN 1579129528; 9781579129521

In this book, by Philippe Margotin and Jean-Michel Guesdon, "every album and every song ever released by the Beatles—from 'Please Please Me' to 'The Long and Winding Road'—is dissected, discussed, and analyzed. . . . Here, we learn that one of John Lennon's favorite guitars was a 1958 Rickenbacker 325 Capri. . . . We also learn that 'Love Me Do,' recorded in Abbey Road Studios in September 1962, took 18 takes to get right, even though it was one of the first songs John and Paul ever wrote together." (Publisher's note)

"Arranged chronologically by album, the book includes for each song basic information (songwriter, track length, number of takes, etc.), a brief discussion of how it was written and recorded, and an overall assessment. . . . [N] umerous anecdotes and quotations from the group keep the book entertaining and accessible even to more casual music fans." LJ

Includes bibliographical references, discography, and indexes

Marshall, Jim

Trust; photographs of Jim Marshall. Omnibus Press 2009 165p il $39.95 **781.66**

1. Rock music -- Pictorial works

ISBN 978-1-84772-110-5; 1-84772-110-9

Jim Marshall "devoted himself to photographing musicians. But more than just taking pictures, Marshall had a knack for capturing moments, snapshots of when the music and the individual collided, which, in turn, revealed something special or private about the artist. His pictures were often windows into the souls of those who were so revered but not always understood. . . . Dr. John sits backstage in full concert regalia, beside him a shrunken human head. Bob Dylan and Johnny Cash casually chat on the set of The Johnny Cash Show. John Coltrane looks contemplative in the backyard of his Queens, NY home. The vast majority of pictures in Trust are split among jazz, blues, and '60s rock and roll. . . . The photographs are paired with short anecdotes about the artists or stories about the images, and in doing this, Marshall lends just enough of his own story to the pictures he presents. But largely, it is Marshall's body of work that does the talking, and, in that, these photographs are revelatory." Under the Radar

McDermott, John

Ultimate Hendrix; an illustrated encyclopedia of live concerts and sessions. [by] John McDermott with Eddie Kramer and Billy Cox. Backbeat Books 2009 256p il $34.95 **781.66**

1. Singers 2. Guitarists 3. Rock music 4. Rock musicians

ISBN 978-0-87930-938-1; 0-87930-938-5

LC 2008-40226

This survey "begins in 1963, when the guitarist began playing backup for such acts as the Isley Brothers, Curtis Squire, and Little Richard. It wasn't until the summer of 1966, when Hendrix met Animals bassist and future manager Chas Chandler, that things really took off, and at this point the book's broad seasonal headings, such as 'Summer 1965' or 'Fall 65', change to the more consecutive 'Thursday, 13 October 1966 . . . Friday, 14 October 1966 . . . Saturday, 15 October 1966', with rarely a date unfilled. The book's day-to-day entries oscillate between high productivity and very low frustration, with peaks and valleys dictated by Hendrix's fortunes and later his moods. . . . Ultimate Hendrix describes songs being built from the bottom up, listing the many takes and practical procedures behind some of the most familiar, impractical sounds." PopMatters

McMurray, Jacob ✓

Taking punk to the masses; from nowhere to Nevermind; a visual history from the permanent collection of Experience Music Project. Fantagraphics Books 2011 253p il pa $29.99 **781.66**

1. Punk rock music

ISBN 978-1-60699-433-7

This volume "visually documents the explosion of Grunge, the Seattle Sound, within the context of the underground punk subculture that was developing throughout the U.S. in the late 1970s and 1980s. This musical journey is represented entirely through the collection of Experience Music Project, Seattle's museum of music and popular culture . .

. . Featuring over 100 key artifacts from EMP's collection, Taking Punk to the Masses illustrates the evolution of punk rock from underground subculture to mainstream embrace." Publisher's note

Moore, Thurston

No wave; post-punk, underground, New York, 1976-1980. by Thurston Moore and Byron Coley; introduction by Lydia Lunch. Abrams Image 2008 143p il $24.95 **781.66**

1. Punk rock music 2. Experimental music

ISBN 978-0-8109-9543-7; 0-8109-9543-3

LC 2007-34093

"A treasure trove of rare photographs and oral history of a fleeting moment of New York underground that continues to reverberate 30 years later." Booklist

Robb, John

Punk rock; an oral history. John Robb ; edited by Oliver Craske ; introduction by Henry Rollins. PM 2012 xv, 562 p.p illustrations $19.95 **781.66**

1. Punk culture 2. Punk rock music 3. Rock musicians -- Anecdotes 4. Punk rock musicians -- Anecdotes 5. Punk rock music -- History and criticism

ISBN 1604860057; 9781604860054

LC 2011939680

Author John Robb presents a history of punk rock music. "John Robb talks to many of those who cultivated the movement, such as John Lydon, Lemmy, Siouxsie Sioux, Mick Jones, Chrissie Hynde, Malcolm McLaren, Henry Rollins, and Glen Matlock, weaving together their accounts to create a . . . history of UK punk. . . . Over 150 interviews" are presented from groups like The Clash, the Stranglers, and The Sex Pistols on the period's "roots in the late 1960s to its enduring influence on the bands, fashion, and culture of today" are presented. (Publisher's note)

Russell, Ethan A.

Let it bleed; the Rolling Stones, Altamont, and the end of the sixties. Ethan A. Russell, with Gerard Van der Leun. Springboard Press 2009 239p il $35 **781.66**

1. Rolling Stones 2. Altamont Festival

ISBN 978-0-446-53904-3

LC 2008-53229

"In 1969, Russell was one of 16 people and the only photographer to join the Rolling Stones on their tour of America. . . . Russell's 200-plus photos, most in stark and clear black and white, range from the band rehearsing and relaxing in a bucolic setting before the tour to Mick Jagger in front of a mirror applying makeup to a closeup of Keith Richards intensely tuning up. Wide onstage shots illustrate the band's relationship with their adoring public. Including interviews and comments from many of the members of the touring group and a haunting narrative of the desolation at Altamont, Russell, with Van Der Leun . . . presents a definitive and authoritative picture of the Stones." Libr J

✓**Sounes, Howard**

27; a history of the 27 club through the lives of Brian Jones, Jimi Hendrix, Janis Joplin, Jim Morrison, Kurt Kobain, and Amy Winehouse. Howard Sounes. Da Capo Press 2013 384 p. illustrations (hardcover) $26.99 **781.66**

1. Music industry 2. Musicians -- United States
ISBN 0306821680; 9780306821684
LC 2013948939

In this book, Howard Sounes "conducts . . . [an] investigation into the lives and deaths of . . . six . . . iconic members of the [27] Club, plus another forty-four music industry figures who died at 27, to discover what, apart from coincidence, this phenomenon signifies. . . . The fantasies, half-truths, and mythologies that have become associated with Jones, Hendrix, Joplin, Morrison, Cobain, and Winehouse are debunked." (Publisher's note)

"A compelling examination of the effects of sudden fame on mentally fragile artists." Kirkus

Includes bibliographical references and index

Thompson, Dave

I hate new music; the classic rock manifesto. Backbeat Books 2008 225p $24.95 **781.66**

1. Rock music
ISBN 978-0-87930-935-0
LC 2008-39492

"In classic pundit style, [Thompson] tauntingly waves the red flag at the contemporary music scene and counter-intuitively stabs some of rock's greatest icons in the back, before delivering an exquisitely executed coup de grace to the music industry as a whole. . . . The book's subtitle is telling, for this is not a history of classic rock, although it partially works as a potted one, nor a critical analysis of the movement, even though there's a great deal of analysis and criticism found within. Instead, Thompson provides a critique of all that made a specific period of rock classic, explains its eventual destruction, and explores the reasons why rock is unlikely to reach such heady heights again. What makes the book impossible to put down, however, is the author's gonzo approach to the subject — laugh-out-loud funny, peppered with jokes and awash in wry amusement, irony and a touch of biting sarcasm." Goldmine

London's burning; true adventures on the frontlines of punk, 1976-1977. Chicago Review Press 2009 327p il pa $18.95 **781.66**

1. Punk rock music
ISBN 978-1-55652-769-2; 1-55652-769-1
LC 2008-40527

"Thompson, 16 when punk exploded on the London scene in 1976, chronicles that pivotal year month-by-month, starting with American Patti Smith's appearance on BBC-TV's Old Grey Whistle Test. . . . Soon Thompson and friends were wading through a cornucopia of the Ramones, Television, and the rest of the New York punks and New Wavers as well as English acts like the Sex Pistols and the Clash. Reggae surfaced, and the punk and Rasta communities came together after years of violent racial and class strife. It was a heady, creative time, reminiscent of the 'Swingin' London' of Beatlemania days. Excellent anecdotal pop-music history." Booklist

Turman, Katherine

Louder Than Hell; The Definitive Oral History of Metal. By Jon Wiederhorn and Katherine Turman. HarperCollins 2013 736 p. $32.50 **781.66**

1. Rock musicians 2. Heavy metal (Music)
ISBN 006195828X; 9780061958281

Written by Jon Wiederhorn and Katherine Turman, this book is an "oral history of heavy metal," which "includes hundreds of interviews with the giants of the movement, conducted over the past 25 years." It "features more than 250 interviews with some of the biggest bands in metal, including Black Sabbath, Metallica, Megadeth, Anthrax, Slayer, Iron Maiden, Judas Priest, Spinal Tap, Pantera, White Zombie, Slipknot, and Twisted Sister." (Publisher's note)

Victor, Adam

The **Elvis** encyclopedia. Overlook Duckworth 2008 598p il $65 **781.66**

1. Actors 2. Singers 3. Rock musicians
ISBN 978-1-58567-598-2; 1-58567-598-9

An alphabetical compendium of topics related to Elvis Presley. Includes personal and place names, movie and song titles, events, and general subjects.

"This obsessively detailed and completely entertaining chronicle . . . of every possible aspect of Elvis Preley's life is mesmerizing and deserves a wide audience." Publ Wkly

Waksman, Steve

This ain't the summer of love; conflict and crossover in heavy metal and punk. University of California Press 2009 408p **781.66**

1. Punk rock music 2. Heavy metal (Music)
ISBN 0520253108; 0520257170; 9780520253100; 9780520257177
LC 2008025957

This survey of heavy metal and punk music "begins on the cusp of the '70s with the colossal arena performances of Grand Funk Railroad, setting up the relationship between performer and (in this case, enormous) audience, which is an ongoing point of reference. From here, Waksman uses subsequent artists to deconstruct the rock concert, moving through the performative stage antics of Alice Cooper and Iggy Pop, to the metal and hardcore bands of the early '80s. . . . The number of fanzines and interviews cited is evidence that this is a comprehensively and enthusiastically researched book. As a critical study it provides an original critique of both the genres involved, and of genre itself; the only flipside is that this ends up playing second fiddle to a damn good story." PopMatters

Includes discography and bibliographical references

Yarm, Mark

Everybody loves our town; an oral history of Grunge. Crown Archetype 2011 567p il $25; ebook $12.99 **781.66**

1. Rock music -- History and criticism
ISBN 978-0-307-46443-9; 978-0-307-46445-3 ebook
LC 2011009192

A tribute to the Pacific Northwest's grunge genre draws on the observations of individuals at the forefront of the movement from Soundgarden and the Melvins to Nirvana and Pearl Jam, citing such influences as the rise of Seattle's Sub Pop record label and the death of Kurt Cobain.

"Yarm's affectionate, gossipy, detailed look at the highs and lows of the contemporary Seattle music scene is one of the most essential rock books of recent years." Kirkus

782   Vocal music

The **Cambridge** companion to singing; edited by John Potter. Cambridge Univ. Press 2000 286p il (Cambridge companions to music) hardcover o.p. pa $24   **782**
1. Singing 2. Vocal music
ISBN 0-521-62225-5; 0-521-62709-5 pa

LC 99-32948

"Articles on popular traditions, including world music, rock, rap, and jazz, describe the major singers and songwriters in each. Then come histories of theatrical singing encompassing twentieth-century stage and screen artists, the beginnings of opera, and grand opera. The growth of choral music and art songs is traced next. . . . The last and largest section concerns performance practices in choral and ensemble singing, medieval singing techniques, singing in the pre-romantic and contemporary periods, teaching singing, children's singing, and vocal production. . . . The guide covers its wide range of topics accessibly as well as thoroughly for a one-volume work." Booklist
Includes bibliographical references

Robeson, Paul

The **undiscovered** Paul Robeson; the early years (1898-1939) Wiley 2001 383p il $30   **782**
1. Actors 2. Singers 3. Football players 4. Civil rights activists 5. African Americans -- Biography
ISBN 0-471-24265-9

LC 2001-17656

This is the first volume of a biography of the African American actor, singer and political activist by his son. It covers the years from Robeson's birth in Princeton, N.J., through the 1930s

"Extensively illustrated with personal photographs, this is a unique account of a brilliant but troubled man." Libr J
Includes bibliographical references

Sudhalter, Richard

Stardust melody: the life and music of Hoagy Carmichael; [by] Richard M. Sudhalter. Oxford Univ. Press 2002 432p il hardcover o.p. pa $18.95 **782**
1. Actors 2. Singers 3. Pianists 4. Jazz musicians 5. Songwriters
ISBN 0-19-513120-7; 0-19-516898-4 pa

LC 2001-34612

"Among the legends of American popular music, Carmichael, composer of such standards as 'Star Dust' and 'Skylark,' is not getting his due, argues the author, who intends to rectify this injustice. The result is a thorough and engaging profile of the great American composer and performer." Booklist
Includes bibliographical references

782.1   Vocal forms

Berger, William

Verdi with a vengeance; an energetic guide to the life and complete works of the king of opera. Vintage Bks. 2000 497p il pa $15   **782.1**
1. Composers
ISBN 0-375-70518-X

LC 00-42261

The author "provides a brief overview of the composer's life and times and examines the connections between contemporary politics and Verdi's creative output. . . . A glossary and recommended recordings, films, and soundtracks are included. Informative and eminently readable for the novice and scholar alike." Libr J
Includes bibliographical references

Bordman, Gerald

American musical theatre; a chronicle. Gerald Bordman, Richard Norton. Oxford University Press 2011 xiv, 1017 p.p $160   **782.1**
1. Musicals 2. Theater -- United States -- History 3. Musicals -- United States -- History and criticism
ISBN 0199729700; 9780199729708

LC 2010033708

This book by Gerald Bordman and Richard Norton "covers more than 250 years of musical theatre in the United States, from a 1735 South Carolina production of Flora, or Hob in the Well to The Addams Family in 2010. Authors Gerald Bordman and Richard Norton . . . blend history, critical analysis, and . . . description to illustrate the transformation of American musical theatre through such incarnations as the ballad opera, revue, Golden Age musical, [and] rock musical." (Publisher's note)

Fiedler, Johanna

Molto agitato; the mayhem behind the music at the Metropolitan Opera. Doubleday 2001 393p il $30; pa $15.95   **782.1**
1. Metropolitan Opera (New York, N.Y.)
ISBN 0-385-48187-X; 1-4000-3231-8 pa

LC 2001-27158

This book is about "the business of New York City's Metropolitan Opera and the personalities who have shaped it from its beginnings in the late 19th century to the present day. . . . {The author} spins a fascinating account of strong egos, clashing personalities, power plays, and frequent major disasters. There are enough heroes, villains, and side plots to fill a dozen adventure novels. . . . For those interested in the dirt behind the golden curtain, this will be a feast." Libr J

Gage, Nicholas

Greek fire; the story of Maria Callas and Aristotle Onassis. Knopf 2000 xxi, 422p il $26.95; pa $7.99   **782.1**
1. Opera singers 2. Shipping executives
ISBN 0-375-40244-6; 0-446-61076-3 pa

LC 00-40553

The author traces "Onassis's and Callas's pasts, their relationship, and the Jackie Kennedy years." Libr J

This "biography is perhaps the most understanding of La Callas yet to be published, and its appeal will extend beyond opera lovers to anyone with an interest in the lives of the rich and famous." Booklist

Includes bibliographical references

Marmorstein, Gary

A **ship** without a sail; the life of Lorenz Hart. Gary Marmorstein. Simon & Schuster 2012 531p. $30.00 **782.1**

1. Lyricists 2. Musicians 3. Lyricists -- United States -- Biography

ISBN 1416594256; 9781416594253

LC 2011040654

This book by Gary Marmorstein offers a "biography of Lorenz Hart (1895-1943), the talented, troubled lyricist of film and Broadway fame. . . . Here, the author details Hart's short life, explores his most productive professional partnership with composer Richard Rodgers, chronicles his descent into the alcoholism that killed him, speculates about his sexuality (his colleagues knew he was gay; the public did not), and provides numerous examples of Hart's witty, sometimes risqué lyrics." (Kirkus Reviews)

Includes bibliographical references, discography, and index.

McBrien, William

Cole Porter; a biography. Knopf 1998 459p il hardcover o.p. $16 **782.1**

1. Composers 2. Lyricists

ISBN 978-0-679-72792-7; 0-679-72792-2

LC 97-46116

In this biography of the American songwriter, the author "weaves a complex and groundbreaking portrait of Porter, interspersed with lyrics and 72 illustrations, recounting his affluent upbringing in Peru, Ind., and his emergence in the 1930s as the musical theater's reigning sophisticate. . . . This astute biography will help to create a standard-setting portrait of Porter as a homosexual artist in a heterosexual world." Publ Wkly

Includes bibliographical references

Mordden, Ethan

Anything goes; a history of American musical theatre. Ethan Mordden. Oxford University Press 2013 360 p. illustrations (alk. paper) $29.95 **782.1**

1. Musicals 2. Theater -- United States -- History 3. Musicals -- United States -- History and criticism

ISBN 0199892830; 9780199892839

LC 2013000208

This book by Ethan Mordden examines "the musical from the 1920s through the 1970s. . . . He also explores the changing structure of musical comedy and operetta, and the evolution of the role of the star. " (Publisher's note)

"Mordden brightly differentiates those forms, citing hundreds and analyzing dozens of examples of them in a sweeping narrative that, with plenty of sass and tang, wit and even a little snark, not to mention scholarly precision, is obviously the best-ever history of the musical and likely to remain so for a very long time." Booklist

Includes bibliographical references, discography and index

The **Richard** Rodgers reader; edited by Geoffrey Block. Oxford Univ. Press 2002 356p il music (Readers on American musicians) $55; pa $38 **782.1**

1. Composers 2. Composers -- United States

ISBN 0-19-513954-2; 0-19-531343-7 pa

LC 2001-37505

"A fine combination of anecdote, music criticism, and biography, this is recommended for all libraries interested in American popular culture and American musical theater." Libr J

Includes bibliographical references

Rose, Michael

The **birth** of an opera; fifteen masterpieces from Poppea to Wozzeck. Michael Rose. W.W. Norton & Company 2013 480 p. (hardcover) $35 **782.1**

1. Opera 2. Composers 3. Librettists 4. Operas -- Analysis, appreciation

ISBN 0393060438; 9780393060430

LC 2012039470

This book by Michael Rose discusses "how operas are written and the personalities . . . and musical circumstances that have shaped their composition. . . . From Monteverdi and Mozart to Puccini and Berg, each chapter focuses on a well-known opera and tells the story that lies behind its creation." Rose describes "Verdi deep in Shakespearian discussion with Boito as they remodel . . . 'Otello;' and Debussy coming almost literally to blows with Maeterlinck over . . . 'Pelléas et Mélisande.'" (Publisher's note)

Includes bibliographical references and index

Schebera, Jurgen

Kurt Weill; an illustrated life. translated by Caroline Murphy. Yale Univ. Press 1995 381p il $55; pa $38 **782.1**

1. Composers

ISBN 0-300-06055-6; 0-300-07284-8 pa

LC 94-41444

Original German edition, 1990

"Schebera makes wonderful use of archival illustrations: concert programs, advertisements, photos, even a few record labels from the Twenties and Thirties. This is a scholarly work, but the appealing subject, complete with the drama of Nazi persecution and flight from prewar Germany, makes it a good choice for most music collections." Libr J

Includes discography and bibliographical references

Sondheim, Stephen, 1930-

Look, I made a hat; collected lyrics (1981-2011) with attendant comments, amplifications, dogmas, harangues, wafflings, diversions and anecdotes. by Stephen Sondheim. 1st ed; Alfred A. Knopf 2011 480p hardcover $45 **782.1**

1. Musicals 2. Lyricists 3. Popular song lyrics 4. Composers -- United States 5. Songs--Texts. 6. Musicals--Excerpts--Librettos.

ISBN 978-0307593412

LC 2011014604

"Picking up where he left off in Finishing the Hat, Sondheim gives us all the lyrics, along with excluded songs and early drafts, of the Pulitzer Prize winning Sunday in the Park with George, Into the Woods, Assassins and Passion. Here, too, is an in-depth look at the evolution of Wise Guys, which subsequently was transformed into Bounce and eventually became Road Show. Sondheim takes us through his contributions to both television and film, some of which may surprise you, and covers plenty of never-before-seen material from unproduced projects as well." (Publisher's Note)

"With this chronological continuation of Finishing the Hat, musical theater lyricist and composer Sondheim has produced another delightful book that melds lyrics, anecdotes, opinions, and whimsy...As in the previous volume, Sondheim includes descriptions about each show, as well as running commentary. Sondheim's general essays (the "harangues" and "dogmas" of the subtitle) show him at his opinionated and literate best....certainly all libraries owning the first volume will want the second." (Library Journal)

Includes bibliographical references and index.

782.27 Hymns

Christ-Janer, Albert

American hymns old and new; {compiled by} Albert Christ-Janer, Charles W. Hughes, Charles Sprague Smith. Columbia Univ. Press 1980 838p music $130   **782.27**

1. Hymns
ISBN 9780231034586

This is an interdenominational compilation of 625 hymns sung in America since 1615

782.42 Songs

Foster, Stephen Collins

Stephen Foster & Co. lyrics of America's first great popular songs. edited by Ken Emerson. Library of America 2010 xxii, 182p il (American poets project) $20   **782.42**

1. Popular music 2. American songs
ISBN 978-1-59853-070-4

LC 2009-973459

The editor "introduces and annotates the lyrics to more than thirty of Foster's best and best-known songs. . . . Alongside are fifty other 19th-century American popular songs that influenced Foster or that he in turn influenced, from 'Home! Sweet Home!' in the 1820s to 'Western Home' (the original 'Home on the Range') in the 1870s." Publisher's note

Includes bibliographical references

Gioia, Ted

Work songs; [by] Theodore Gioia. Duke University Press 2006 352p $27.95   **782.42**

1. Folk music 2. Labor -- Songs
ISBN 0-8223-3726-6; 978-0-8223-3726-3

LC 2005026241

Gioia "poignantly tells the story of work songs sung by everyone from prehistoric hunters to today's consumers. His task involved drawing on multilayered and diverse resources that include travel literature, slave narratives, his-

torical accounts and personal journals, myths and legends, biographies, and labor union writings; the focus is on the rhythms, melodies, and lyrics of music that has accompanied such tasks as raising and lowering sails, felling trees, and weaving and sewing garments. . . . This book provides an opportunity to re-experience the history and dignity of our human toils. Highly recommended for public and academic libraries." Libr J

Includes bibliographical references

Gray, Michael

The **Bob** Dylan encyclopedia. Continuum 2006 832p il $40   **782.42**

1. Singers 2. Folk musicians 3. Songwriters
ISBN 0-82646-933-7; 978-0-82646-933-5

LC 2006-12728

This book "covers many of his songs, albums, and film work, as well as just about every personality associated with the folk singer/rock star. . . . Overall, this is an amazingly well-researched and surprisingly readable work." Libr J

Includes bibliographical references

Greenman, Ben

Mo' meta blues; the world according to questlove. Ahmir. Grand Central Pub. 2013 288 p. (hardcover) $26   **782.42**

1. Musicians
ISBN 1455501352; 9781455501359

LC 2013932326

This book is a memoir by "Questlove" Thompson, the cofounder and drummer of the band the Roots. Here, he "tells of his work as a DJ and producer with some of the biggest names in the music business, such as Jay-Z and Common, and Dave Chappelle," His "recollections touch on everything from drumming at age five in his father's professional doo-wop and soul band to roller-skating as an adult with Eddie Murphy at a bizarre party hosted by Prince." (Publishers Weekly)

Guthrie, Woody

The **Woody** Guthrie songbook. Hal Leonard Corporation 2000 61p il pa $10.95   **782.42**

1. Songs 2. Folk music
ISBN 978-0-63402-405-4 pa; 0-63402-405-1 pa

This features 48 of Guthrie's songs along with a bio, introduction, complete lyrics, a discography, photos and sketches. Songs include: Jig Along Home, Roll On, Columbia, Sinking of the Reuben James, This Land Is Your Land, Tom Joad and more.

Hischak, Thomas

The **Tin** Pan Alley song encyclopedia; {by} Thomas S. Hischak. Greenwood Press 2002 530p $74.95   **782.42**

1. Reference books 2. Popular music -- Encyclopedias
ISBN 0-313-31992-8

LC 2002-23250

Companion volume to The American musical film song encyclopedia and The American musical theatre song encyclopedia (1995)

"Tin Pan Alley refers to the American popular music business from the mid-nineteenth through the mid-twentieth centuries, and the songs written for parlor pianos, sing-alongs, dance orchestras, radio broadcasts, etc. This book is an A-Z listing of more than 1,200 popular songs. . . . Each entry includes the year the song was published and highly readable information about its composition and performance history." Booklist

Includes bibliographical references (p.　) and index

Leadbelly

The **Leadbelly** songbook; the ballads, blues, and folksongs of Huddie Ledbetter. Oak Publications 1962 96p il pa $17.95　　　　　　　　　**782.42**
1. Songs 2. African American music 3. Folk music -- United States

ISBN 978-0-82560-042-5 pa; 0-82560-042-1 pa

More than 70 songs by Huddie Ledbetter, with chord names, musical transcriptions, and biographical notes. Includes: Midnite Special, Backwater Blues, John Henry, and House Of The Rising Sun.

Lehman, David

A **fine** romance; Jewish songwriters, American songs. Nextbook/Schocken 2009 249p (Jewish encounters) $23　　　　　　　　　　　　　　**782.42**
1. Composers 2. Lyricists 3. Songwriters and songwriting 4. Jews -- United States 5. Popular music -- History and criticism

ISBN 978-0-8052-4250-8; 0-8052-4250-3

LC 2009-05942

"Lehman investigates the lasting impact of 20th-century Jewish popular songwriters in America, ranging from Irving Berlin's and Jerome Kern's early efforts in the 1910s through George Gershwin, Harold Arlen, Richard Rodgers, Lorenz Hart, and Oscar Hammerstein II to Leonard Bernstein and the early 1960s. In fluid prose and expert foreshadowing and summations, the author conveys the personality of each musician or writer and recommends selected versions of his favorite songs." Libr J

Includes bibliographical references

Lynskey, Dorian

33 revolutions per minute; a history of protest songs, from Billie Holiday to Green Day. Ecco 2011 660p il pa $19.99　　　　　　　　　　　　**782.42**
1. Political ballads and songs 2. Popular music -- 20th century 3. Popular music -- 21st century 4. Popular music -- Political aspects 5. Popular music -- History and criticism 6. Protest songs -- History and criticism

ISBN 0061670154; 9780061670152

LC 2010-24247

The author presents a history of protest music through an examination of thirty-three songs, from Strange Fruit (1939) to American Idiot (2008). Index.

The author "delves into the protest song movement from 1939 to the present. Dividing the time into discrete sections, he focuses on particular examples but also provides information on related songs. The author traces the historical context, using valuable contemporary sources and quotations from the artists. . . . Lynskey's flowing prose and well-turned phrases bring the times to life. He is especially adept at integrating the songs into the wider social milieu, which

extends the appeal to cultural historians as well as music lovers." Libr J

Includes bibliographical references

Marcus, Greil

When that rough god goes riding; listening to Van Morrison. PublicAffairs 2010 195p $22.95 **782.42**
1. Singers 2. Rock musicians 3. Songwriters 4. Rock music -- History and criticism

ISBN 978-1-58648-821-5; 1-58648-821-X

LC 2010-01656

This is a "collection of short 'close listenings'—some as brief as a page or two—concerning performances and recordings from Morrison's 45-year career. The essays are organized by theme rather than chronology, organized as such because Marcus sees Van Morrison's music as 'a story made of fragments', the story of a 'quest', a damned messy epic with ever-changing monsters to slay and enough digressive journeys to rival Don Quixote. This story has no ending, and Marcus' satisfyingly realistic viewpoint is not, despite its organization, grandly and thematically synoptic." PopMatters

Includes bibliographical references

★　**National** anthems of the world; edited by Michael Jamieson Bristow. 11th ed.; Weidenfeld & Nicolson 2006 629p $90　　　　　　**782.42**
1. National songs

ISBN 0-304-36826-1

First published 1943 in the United Kingdom with title: National anthems of the United Nations and France

This volume contains national anthems of about 198 nations, including melody and accompaniment. Words are presented in the native language with transliteration provided where necessary. English translations follow. Brief historical notes on the adoption of each anthem are included

"An essential reference resource for all libraries." Libr J

Porter, Cole

Selected lyrics; Robert Kimball, editor. Library of America 2006 178p (American poets project) $20　　　　　　　　　　　　　　　　**782.42**
1. American songs

ISBN 978-1-93108-294-5; 1-93108-294-4

LC 2006-40809

"For those hankering after a happy medium between American poetry and American Idolatry, Kimball's reading edition affords a golden opportunity to brush up on your Porter—just be sure to listen up, too, if you really want to be wowed." N Y Times Book Rev

Sheed, Wilfrid

The **house** that George built; with a little help from Irving, Cole, and a crew of about fifty. Random House 2007 xxvi, 335 p il $29.95 * **782.42**
1. Composers--United States 2. Lyricists 3. Popular music

ISBN 978-14000-6105-1; 1-4000-6105-9

LC2006-51030

This is a "look at the classic era of American popular song from the 'piano era' of Irving Berlin abd George Gershwin to the post-World War II era." Libr J

This book "is a big rich stew of an homage that makes you want to listen to Gershwin and Berlin and Porter and Arlen all over again. Wilfrid Sheed's jazzy prose is a joy to read." N Y Times Book Review

782.421   Rock (Rock 'n' roll) songs

The **Beatles** anthology. Chronicle Bks. 2000 367p il $60; pa $35   782.421
1. Beatles
ISBN 0-8118-2684-8; 0-8118-3636-3 pa
LC 00-23685
The story of the Beatles as "told through quotes from John, Paul, George, and Ringo, as well as the group's closest aides: George Martin, Neil Aspinall, and Derek Taylor. . . . The density of the text is daunting, but the book's browsability makes it as appealing to casual readers as it is indispensable to Beatlemaniacs." Libr J
Includes bibliographical references

Carlin, Peter Ames
Bruce; Peter Ames Carlin. Simon & Schuster 2012 xi, 494 p.p ill.   782.421
1. Rock musicians -- Biography 2. Rock musicians -- United States -- Biography
ISBN 9781439191828; 9781439191835; 9781439191842
LC 2012020890
"A painstakingly traced chronicle of the remarkable career of powerhouse proletarian rocker Bruce Springsteen... The author presents his subject as a supremely gifted musician and truly heroic figure, albeit one with a lot on his troubled mind... An epic look at the man and his music." Kirkus
Includes bibliographical references and index.

Clarke, Gerald (?ool)
Get happy: the life of Judy Garland. Random House 2000 510p il hardcover o.p. pa $15.95   782.421
1. Actors 2. Singers
ISBN 0-385-33515-6 pa
LC 99-36285
"This exhaustively researched and illuminating biography . . . is as compassionate as it is wrenching." Publ Wkly
Includes bibliographical references

Dunn, Jancee
Cyndi Lauper; a memoir. Cyndi Lauper with Jancee Dunn. Atria Books 2012 338 p. 16 unnumbered pages of plates $26   782.421
1. Women rock musicians 2. Singers -- United States -- Biography
ISBN 143914785X; 9781439147856
LC 2013560375
Author Cyndi Lauper "left her home in Ozone Park, Queens, at age 17 to escape a sexually abusive stepfather and the limitations on life—especially for women—imposed by a hardscrabble working-class neighborhood and male-dominated family culture. . . . Her life changed in 1983, however, with the release of She's So Unusual, which . . .

made Lauper an instant star. . . . Inevitably, her superstar aura faded, but her eclectic musical output did not." (Kirkus)

Dyson, Michael Eric
Holler if you hear me: searching for Tupac Shakur. Basic Bks. 2001 292p il hardcover o.p. pa $15   782.421
1. Poets 2. Actors 3. Hip-hop 4. Rap music 5. African American musicians 6. Rap musicians
ISBN 0-465-01755-X; 0-465-01728-2 pa
LC 2001-36564
"Dyson's discussion goes beyond slogans and poses to the actualities of 'thug life' and the consequences of Shakur's passions and allegiances. Piquant and analytical." Booklist
Includes bibliographical references

Feinstein, Michael, 1956-
The **Gershwins** and me; a personal history in twelve songs. by Michael Feinstein with Ian Jackman. Simon & Schuster 2012 351 p. illustrations (some color) (hc : alk. paper) $45   782.421
1. Popular music -- Writing and publishing -- United States
ISBN 1451645309; 9781451645309; 9781451645316; 9781451645323; 9781451645330
LC 2012006833
Here, author Michael Feinstein "begins with a swift account of how he met Ira Gershwin, the lyricist of the celebrated duo, and how he subsequently went to work for him for six years. . . . Although he tells the Gershwins' stories, childhood to grave, he also . . . discusses the Gershwins' love lives, the significant performers of their work (from Fred Astaire to Ethel Merman), their successes and flops, their experiences in Hollywood and the devastation of George's shocking death at 38 (brain tumor)." (Kirkus)
Includes bibliographical references and index

Fisher, Eddie
Been there, done that; {by} Eddie Fisher, with David Fisher. St. Martin's Press 1999 341p il $24.95; pa $7.99   782.421
1. Singers
ISBN 0-312-20972-X; 0-312-87558-9 pa
LC 99-27236
"What makes this memoir engaging is Fisher's sharp, often self-deprecating wit and his willingness to dish about his cohorts and conquests." N Y Times Book Rev

Friedwald, Will
★ **Sinatra!** the song is you; a singer's art. Da Capo Press 1997 559p il pa $18.50   782.421
1. Actors 2. Singers
ISBN 0-306-80742-4
LC 96-43855
A reprint of the title first published 1995 by Scribner
Friedwald's "commentary is alert and perceptive, and even more valuable is the wealth of pointed reminiscence drawn from interviews he has done with musicians who worked closely with Mr. Sinatra." N Y Times Book Rev
Includes discography and bibliographical references

Gordon, Robert

Can't be satisfied: the life and times of Muddy Waters. Little, Brown 2002 xx, 408p il $25.95; pa $15.95   **782.421**

1. Singers 2. Guitarists 3. Blues musicians
ISBN 0-316-32849-9; 0-316-16494-1 pa

LC 2001-50473

In this biography of the blues musician "Gordon details the gritty life reflected in Muddy's lyrics. . . . He makes Muddy the musician, Muddy the man, Muddy the parent, and Muddy the tool of the (not so) sainted Chess brothers come alive. . . . Packed with facts, copiously referenced, and featuring a foreword by . . . Keith Richards, this book is absolutely essential for any popular music collection worthy of the name." Booklist

Includes bibliographical references

Guralnick, Peter

Last train to Memphis: the rise of Elvis Presley. Little, Brown 1994 560p il $27.95; pa $17.95   **782.421**

1. Actors 2. Singers 3. Rock musicians
ISBN 0-316-33220-8; 0-316-33225-9 pa

LC 94-10763

The author "depicts Elvis as a naive yet extremely talented boy whose dream of stardom came true, leaving him a virtual prisoner of his own success. . . . Taking pains to keep the story fresh and flowing and refraining from foreshadowing and editorializing, Guralnick lets the facts speak for themselves." Booklist

Includes bibliographical references

Hamm, Charles

Irving Berlin; songs from the melting pot: the formative years, 1907-1914. Oxford Univ. Press 1996 292p il $42.50   **782.421**

1. Composers 2. Lyricists 3. Centenarians
ISBN 0-19-507188-3

LC 96-6335

The author "shows an informed sensitivity for the social and historical atmosphere in which these songs were produced, and . . . makes effective use of period recordings . . . in an effort to understand how they were meant to play to their first listeners." N Y Times Book Rev

Includes discography and bibliographical references

Mason, Bobbie Ann

Elvis Presley. Viking 2002 178p (Penguin lives series) hardcover o.p. pa $13   **782.421**

1. Actors 2. Singers 3. Rock musicians
ISBN 0-670-03174-7; 0-14-303889-3 pa

LC 2002-28873

The author "chronicles Elvis' sad story: humble origins, 1954 breakthrough, adoption by 'the Colonel' (manager Tom Parker), early TV appearances, army hitch, the death of his mother, marriage to Priscilla, Hollywood, 1968 'comeback', Las Vegas headliner, prescription drug abuse, meeting with Nixon, and death at 42 in 1977." Booklist

Includes   discography,   filmography   and bibliographical references

McDonough, Jimmy

Shakey : Neil Young's biography. Villard Bks. 2002 786p il $29.95; pa $16.95   **782.421**

1. Singers 2. Guitarists 3. Rock musicians 4. Songwriters 5. Rock musicians -- Canada -- Biography
ISBN 0-679-42772-4; 0-679-75096-7 pa

LC 2001-43528

"When Young talks, the book sparkles and offers a warm, engaging portrait of the man who keeps on rockin' in the free world." Libr J

McNally, Dennis

A long strange trip; the inside history of the Grateful Dead. Broadway Bks. 2002 684p il $30; pa $18.95   **782.421**

1. Grateful Dead (Musical group)
ISBN 0-7679-1185-7; 0-7679-1186-5 pa

LC 2002-25561

A history of the rock music group led by Jerry Garcia which first became popular in the 1960's

"As the Dead's publicist for more than 20 years, McNally packs this . . . full of intimate details otherwise unavailable. . . . The most exhaustively researched book on the band to date." Publ Wkly

Includes bibliographical references

Nicholson, Stuart

Billie Holiday. Northeastern Univ. Press 1995 311p il $42.50; pa $18.95   **782.421**

1. Singers 2. Blues musicians 3. African American singers
ISBN 1-55553-248-9; 1-55553-303-5 pa

LC 95-16155

"Nicholson's fact-filled biography conveys not only the details of African American jazz singer Holiday's stormy life, but also a sense of the musical and social environments that produced her." Booklist

Includes discography and bibliographical references

Riordan, James

Break on through: the life and death of Jim Morrison; [by] James Riordan and Jerry Prochnicky. Morrow 1991 544p il hardcover o.p. pa $15 **782.421**

1. Singers 2. Rock musicians 3. Songwriters 4. Doors (Musical group)
ISBN 0-688-11915-8 pa

LC 90-26580

This look at the life and work of Jim Morrison is "well documented and avoids unfounded speculation and unnecessary tales of debauchery common to many other rock 'n' roll biographies. . . . An excellent biography of a true rock icon." Choice

Includes discography and bibliographical references

Smith, R. J.

The one; the life and music of James Brown. RJ Smith. Gotham Books 2012 455 p. $18   **782.421**

1. Funk (Music) 2. Soul musicians -- United States -- Biography
ISBN 1592406572; 1592407420; 9781592406579; 9781592407422

LC 2011028536

This is R.J. Smith's "look at the life and times of the late, great James Brown, self-proclaimed Soul Brother Number One and Hardest Working Man in Show Business and leading inspiration to a generation of singers like [Mitch] Ryder. . . . Smith considers Brown's life and career story, right down to brushes with the law, including his incarcerations at both and early age and later in life, when age and substance abuse overcame Brown's legendary control of his image and lifestyle." (Booklist)

Includes bibliographical references and index

Sounes, Howard ✓

Down the highway: the life of Bob Dylan. Grove Press 2001 527p il $27.50; pa $16   **782.421**
1. Singers 2. Folk musicians 3. Rock musicians 4. Songwriters
ISBN 0-8021-1686-8; 0-8021-3891-8 pa
LC 00-69463
"Through extensive interviews Sounes aptly captures the contradictory facets of an American folk legend." Publ Wkly
Includes bibliographical references

White, Charles

The **life** and times of Little Richard; the quasar of rock. Updated ed; Da Capo Press 1994 282p il pa $16   **782.421**
1. Singers 2. Rock musicians 3. African American musicians
ISBN 0-306-80552-9; 978-0-306-80552-3
LC 93-48054
First published 1984 by Harmony Bks.
This biography of the American singer discusses "his flamboyant stage antics; his blatant flaunting of racial taboos; his sexual experiences; his bewildering career that careened between show business and the church; and exactly how he created the music that would become a symbol of rebellion for kids all over the world." Publisher's note
Includes discography and filmography

782.5   Vocal executants

Steinberg, Michael ✓

Choral masterworks; a listener's guide. Michael Steinberg. Oxford University Press 2005 321p $30   **782.5**
1. Choral music
ISBN 0-19-512644-0
LC 2004-13619
"Well-written, concise introductions that record collectors, concertgoers, and chorus members alike should enjoy." Booklist

784   Instruments and their music

Piston, Walter

Orchestration. Norton 1955 477p il music $56.75   **784**
1. Musical instruments 2. Instrumentation and orchestration
ISBN 978-0-393-09740-5; 0-393-09740-4
This text on writing for the orchestra begins with a discussion of individual instruments and their playing techniques. The last two sections cover analysis and specific problems of orchestration

784.192   Techniques and procedures for instruments themselves

Pagliaro, Michael

The **musical** instrument desk reference; a guide to how band and orchestral instruments work. Michael J. Pagliaro. Scarecrow Press 2012 189 p. (cloth : alk. paper) $65   **784.192**
1. Musical instruments 2. Wind instruments -- Construction 3. Bowed stringed instruments -- Construction
ISBN 0810882701; 9780810882706; 9780810882713
LC 2012007244
This book "begins with an 'easy-reference quick start' section on woodwinds, followed by more in-depth chapters on the flute, clarinet, saxophone, oboe, and the bassoon. For the brass instruments, there are fingering charts, an expanded in-depth study chapter, and a chapter on functioning. Nonfretted string instruments . . . are also given a chapter on producing sound and an expanded in-depth study chapter. The final chapter consists of an overview of percussion instruments." (Booklist)

784.2   Full orchestra (Symphony orchestra)

Osborne, Richard

Herbert von Karajan; a life in music. Northeastern Univ. Press 2000 851p il $37.50   **784.2**
1. Conductors (Music)
ISBN 1-55553-425-2
LC 99-59108
First published 1998 in the United Kingdom
"Because Karajan's career developed in Nazi Germany, Osborne dwells at length . . . on Karajan's involvement with the regime and his postwar exoneration. Drawing on a vast variety of source materials and quoting some in full, Osborne takes us on the enthralling musical journey that was the life of one of the greatest of conductors." Booklist
Includes bibliographical references

Steinberg, Michael

The **symphony**; a listener's guide. Oxford Univ. Press 1995 678p music $42.50; pa $25   **784.2**
1. Symphony 2. Composers 3. Music appreciation
ISBN 0-19-506177-2; 0-19-512665-3 pa
LC 95-5568
"Steinberg describes 36 composers and, movement by movement, 118 symphonies, including all the standard repertory . . . as well as a few by less well known composers such as Gorecki, Harbison, Martinu, and Sessions. The writing varies from formal and factual to chatty, with candid

asides and stories relevant to the composer, the composition, or an important performance." Libr J

Includes bibliographical references

784.4 Light orchestra

Ritchie, Jean

Singing family of the Cumberlands. University Press of Ky. 1988 258p il $35; pa $20   **784.4**
1. Singers 2. Folk musicians 3. Songwriters 4. Appalachian region 5. Folk music -- United States
ISBN 978-0-8131-1679-2; 0-8131-1679-1; 978-0-8131-0186-6 pa; 0-8131-0186-7 pa

LC 88-17337

First published 1955 by Oxford University Press

The youngest of the Ritchies, a Cumberland mountain family, whose singing was the order of the day, writes about her own life and that of her family. The Ritchies still sing the songs and ballads brought from Virginia in 1768, by Jean's three times great grandfather. Words and music of 42 songs are included.

"Ritchie writes as she sings—naturally and with an instinctive sense for rhythms. Her story of her rearing in the hill-circled town of Viper is simple, vivid, and moving. . . . A beautiful story of American living." NY Herald Tribune

785 Ensembles with only one instrument per part

Sachs, Harvey

The **Ninth**; Beethoven and the world in 1824. Random House 2010 225p il   **785**
1. Composers 2. Romanticism in music 3. Music -- Social aspects 4. Music -- Political aspects 5. Music -- History and criticism 6. Music -- Social aspects -- Europe -- History
ISBN 1-4000-6077-X; 1-58836-981-1 ebook; 978-1-4000-6077-1; 978-1-58836-981-9 ebook

LC 2009-19716

This analysis of Beethoven's seminal Ninth Symphony identifies it as a key cultural event that reflected major social upheavals, including the emergence of a dynamic Western world and changes in philosophical perspectives on individuality.

"This discussion of the cornerstone of Romantic music, whose influence extended deep into the twentieth century, is concise, thorough, and written from the heart of a great biographer, musicologist, and lover of fine music." Booklist

Includes bibliographical references

786.2 Keyboard instruments

De Barros, Paul

Shall we play that one together? the life and art of jazz piano legend Marian McPartland. Paul de Barros. St. Martin's Press 2012 496 p. (hardcover) $35.00   **786.2**
1. Pianists -- United States -- Biography 2. Jazz

musicians -- United States -- Biography
ISBN 0312558031; 9780312558031; 9781250019011

LC 2012028242

This biography of Marian McPartland, by Paul de Barros, is "[t]he story of the distinguished female jazz pianist who devoted herself to her art and won popularity, the respect of her colleagues and just about every honor the profession bestows. . . . De Barros tells us about her albums . . . [and] McPartland's versatility and success with Piano Jazz, her NPR show that began in 1978. . . . The author also charts her fierce devotion to jazz education and, sadly, her physical decline." (Kirkus)

Includes bibliographical references

Isacoff, Stuart

A **natural** history of the piano; the instrument, the music, the musicians--from Mozart to modern jazz, and everything in between. Alfred A. Knopf 2011 361p il   **786.2**
1. Pianos 2. Piano music -- History and criticism
ISBN 9780307266378; 978030770142-8 ebook

LC 2011011557

"Isacoff offers an encyclopedic history of the beloved instrument and profiles such masters as Beethoven, Gershwin, and Oscar Peterson in this big slice of heaven for piano lovers." Booklist

Includes bibliographical references

786.5 Organs

Whitney, Craig R.

All the stops; the glorious pipe organ and its American masters. Public Affairs 2003 xxv, 323p il $30; pa $17.95   **786.5**
1. Organs (Musical instruments)
ISBN 1-586-48173-8; 1-586-48262-9 pa

LC 2002-37025

"Whitney extolls the organ's eclectic heritage at a time when the instrument seems poised for a return to the mainstream, and his glossary of its colorful terminology will help novices tell a windchest from a bombarde." New Yorker

Includes bibliographical references

787.3 Violas

Siblin, Eric

The **cello** suites; J.S. Bach, Pablo Casals, and the search for a Baroque masterpiece. Atlantic Monthly Press 2009 319p $24   **787.3**
1. Composers 2. Music appreciation 3. Cellists
ISBN 978-0-8021-1929-2; 0-8021-1929-8

The author explores the history of Bach's six suites for unaccompanied cello.

"Siblin's curiosity and passion for his subject is evident throughout, and his method of structuring the story according to the arrangement of the music is inspired. . . . Meticulous in his research, as evidenced by copious notes and resources collected over his travels to several European countries, Siblin makes convincing connections and offers possible answers to the questions surrounding the suites. In the process, he sheds considerable light on the lives of Bach and Casals." Quill Quire

Includes bibliographical references

787.4   Cellos (Violoncellos)

Wilson, Elizabeth

Jacqueline du Pre; her life, her music, her legend. Arcade Pub. 1999 466p il $27.95; pa $14.95 **787.4**

1. Cellists 2. Classical musicians
ISBN 1-55970-490-X; 1-55970-519-1 pa

LC 98-49664

This is a biography of "the classical cellist, who flourished briefly as the brightest young star in the firmament in the 1960s and early '70s, only to see her career ended before she was 30 by multiple sclerosis." Publ Wkly

"Wilson, a professional cellist, has given priority to the music. Her method is discreet, methodical, informed and accurate. Above all it is measured in its tone." N Y Times Book Rev

Includes bibliographical references

787.8   Plectral lute family

Seeger, Pete

How to play the 5-string banjo; a manual for beginners. 3rd ed; Oak Publications 2002 72p il pa $16.95   **787.8**

1. Banjos
ISBN 9781597731645 pa; 1597731641 pa
First published 1948 by People's Songs

A basic manual for banjo players, with melody line, lyrics, and banjo accompaniment and solos notated in standard form of tablature. Appendix includes material on where to buy a banjo, books on the banjo, books of songs to sing and phonograph records

787.87   Guitars

Chapman, Richard

The **new** complete guitarist; rev American ed; DK 2003 208p il pa $20   **787.87**

1. Guitars
ISBN 0-7894-9701-8

LC 2004-271630

First published 1993 with title: The complete guitarist

This work ranges "from fundamentals such as tuning, scales, chords, picking, and strumming, to advanced techniques of various styles such as rock, blues, and jazz. . . . [It also] includes discussions on such topics as sound and amplification, choosing a guitar, studio and home recording, plus care and maintenance of the instrument. An appealing book in the style of the 'Eyewitness' series." SLJ [review of 1993 edition]

Includes bibliographical references

Chappell, Jon

Guitar All-in-one for Dummies; by Jon Chappell. 2nd edition Wiley 2014 628 p. pa $34.99   **787.87**

1. Guitars 2. Guitar 3. Guitar -- methods -- self instruction
ISBN 978-0-470-48133-2

"There's no denying that guitar players have cachet. The guitar is an ever-present part of our collective musical heritage, and the sound can be sensual, aggressive, or a million things in between. Whether you're hoping to conquer Free Bird, Bouree, or Bolero Mallorquin, you need to learn to walk before you can run. Even once you can run, you need something to help you clear hurdles along the way.

That's where Guitar All-In-One For Dummies, 2nd Edition, comes in. It's your complete compendium of guitar instruction, written in clear, concise For Dummies style. It covers everything from positioning and basic chords to guitar theory and playing styles, and even includes maintenance advice to keep your instrument sounding great. It's an amazing resource for newbies and veterans alike, and offers you the opportunity to stretch beyond your usual genre." (Publisher's Note)

Murray, Charles Shaar

Crosstown traffic: Jimi Hendrix and the post-war rock'n'roll revolution. St. Martin's Press 1990 247p il hardcover o.p. pa $12   **787.87**

1. Singers 2. Guitarists 3. Rock musicians
ISBN 0-312-06324-5 pa

LC 89-77681

First published 1989 in the United Kingdom with title: Crosstown traffic: Jimi Hendrix and post-war pop

"This informed, textured account will be irresistible to devotees of Hendrix and psychedelic rock as well as fans of blues, funk, jazz and rock 'n' roll." Booklist

Includes discography and bibliographical references

788   Wind instruments (Aerophones)

Gabbard, Krin

Hotter than that; the trumpet, jazz, and American culture. Faber and Faber 2008 251p il $25   **788**

1. Trumpet 2. Jazz musicians
ISBN 9780571211999; 0-571-21199-2

LC 2008-31349

The author "tells the story of how the trumpet came to be the alpha-male instrument of jazz. . . . This engaging and informative book goes well beyond a who's who of jazz trumpet with thought-provoking discussions of jazz trumpet playing as an expression of freedom for African American musicians and as an expression of sexuality." Libr J

Includes bibliographical references

790   Recreational and performing arts

Denmead, Ken

Geek dad; awesomely geeky projects and activities for dads and kids to share. foreword by Chris Anderson. Gotham Books 2010 222p pa $17; ebook $9.99   **790**

1. Amusements 2. Father-son relationship

ISBN 978-1-59240-552-7 pa; 978-1-101-40431-7 ebook

LC 2010-8860

This book contains projects for activities such as creating a customized comic strip, building a lamp with CDs and LEGOs, and launching a video camera with balloons.

Includes bibliographical references

790.1   General kinds of recreational activities

Conner, Bobbi

Unplugged play; no batteries, no plugs, pure fun. illustrations by Amy Patacchiola. Workman Pub. 2007 xxv, 401p il $27.95; pa $16.95   **790.1**

1. Play 2. Games

ISBN 978-0-7611-4114-3; 978-0-7611-4390-1 pa

LC 2007-23999

"Conner has compiled more than 710 games and activities sorted by age level. Good old-fashioned play and fun are the motto here with simple props from around the house or just an imagination. The book is separated into three major parts: 'Toddler Play,' 'Preschool Play,' and 'Grade School Play.' Each has a section on solo play, ideas for parent and child, playing with others, and birthday-party activities. Each chapter and section is loaded with ideas and suggestions for simple crafts. There is such a wealth of information in this book." SLJ

Ferrer, J. J.

The **art** of stone skipping and other fun old-time games; stoopball, jacks, string games, coin flipping, line baseball, jump rope, and more. by J.J. Ferrer ; illustrated by Todd Dakins. Charlesbridge Pub., Inc. 2012 192 p. (paperback) $14.95   **790.1**

1. Games

ISBN 1936140748; 9781936140749

LC 2012015052

This book, by J. J. Ferrer, offers a "collection of timeless games that guarantees kids a good time- by themselves, with a group of friends, or with family. Includes ball games . . . , card games . . . , sack races, and old favorites such as Duck, Duck, Goose and Red Rover. There is also a chapter for car games. Simple instructions explain the rules, how many people can play, the object of the game, and what you need." (Publisher's note)

Includes bibliographical references and index.

Rowell, Victoria

Tag, toss & run; 40 classic lawn games. Paul Tukey & Victoria Rowell. Storey Pub. 2012 207 p. (pbk. : alk. paper) $14.95   **790.1**

1. Games 2. Outdoor recreation 3. Games -- Juvenile literature 4. Outdoor games -- Juvenile literature

ISBN 1603425608; 9781603425605

LC 2011049410

This book on "family lawn games" presents a "guide to 40 time-tested favorites -- from classics like capture the flag,

croquet, badminton, and bocce to the lesser-known Cherokee marbles, cornhole, and Kubb. The authors offer a quick overview of the basic structure of each game, as well as strategies for playing and tips for creating fun variations." (Publisher's note)

Includes bibliographical references and index.

791   Public performances

Austen, Jake

Darkest America; black minstrelsy from slavery to hip-hop. Yuval Taylor and Jake Austen. W. W. Norton 2012 368 p. (hardcover) $26.95   **791**

1. Hip-hop culture 2. African Americans -- History 3. Popular culture -- United States 4. Blackface entertainers -- United States -- History 5. Hip-hop -- United States -- History 6. Minstrel shows -- United States -- History

ISBN 0393070980; 9780393070989

LC 2012007307

This book, by Yuval Taylor and Jake Austen, "investigate[s] the complex history of black minstrelsy, adopted in the mid-nineteenth century by . . . performers who played the grinning blackface fool to entertain . . . audiences. We now consider minstrelsy an embarrassing relic, but once blacks and whites alike saw it as a black art form. . . . And . . . black minstrelsy remains deeply relevant to popular black entertainment, particularly in the work of contemporary artists." (Publisher's note)

"An innovative, marvelous book about comedy, stereotypes and the struggle to steer through the sometimes-fierce internal debates over African-American identity in a society still struggling with its racial past." Kirkus

Includes bibliographical references and index

The **Cinema** of Terry Gilliam; It's a Mad World. edited by Jeff Birkenstein, Anna Froula & Karen Randell. Wallflower Press 2013 256 p. (Directors' Cuts) $75   **791**

1. Motion picture producers and directors

ISBN 023116534X; 9780231165341

LC 2013474654

This book, edited by Jeff Birkenstein, "argues that when [film director Terry] Gilliam makes a movie, he goes to war: against Hollywood caution and convention, against American hyper-consumerism and imperial militarism, against narrative vapidity and spoon-fed mediocrity, and against the brutalizing notion and cruel vision of the 'American Dream.'" (Publisher's note)

"[Gilliam's] mercurial, idiosyncratic approach to filmmaking is a subject ripe for detailed analysis, which this short, sharp, elegantly argued volume brilliantly supplies." Choice

Fine, Marshall (2005)

Accidental genius; how John Cassavetes invented the American independent film. Miramax Books 2006 482p il $27.95   **791**

1. Actors 2. Motion picture directors

ISBN 1-4013-5249-9

The author "argues that mainstream moviegoers ought to care about maverick director Cassavetes (1929-89) as the progenitor of today's American independent film movement." Booklist

Server, Lee

Ava Gardner; love is nothing. St. Martin's Press 2006 551p il $29.95 **791**

1. Actors

ISBN 0-312-31209-1; 978-0-312-31209-1

LC 2005-51697

This is a biography of the actress.

"No matter how objective Server tries to appear in detailing the highs and lows of [Gardner's] 67 years—the three marriages, the numerous affairs, the binges, the nightlong cruising of low-life byways and bordellos, the mainly poor movies she was in—he cannot really hide his essential fondness for her. It is the kind of affection virtually every one of the more than 100 people he interviewed felt and spoke of with enthusiasm, the kind a reader too will find hard to resist." N Y Times Book Rev

Includes filmography and bibliographical references

Terkel, Studs, 1912-2008

The **spectator**. New Press 1999 364p $26.95; pa $16.95 **791**

1. Dramatists 2. Entertainers

ISBN 1-56584-553-6; 1-56584-633-8 pa

LC 99-17129

"Telling portraits of a wide range of artists in conversation with a passionately involved, prodigiously well prepared interlocutor." Booklist

791.3 Circuses

Daly, Michael

Topsy; The Startling Story of the Crooked Tailed Elephant, P.T. Barnum, and the American Wizard, Thomas Edison. by Michael Daly. Pgw 2013 viii, 369 p.p $27 **791.3**

1. Circus 2. Elephants

ISBN 0802119042; 9780802119049

This book, by Michael Daly, examines how "in 1903, on Coney Island, an elephant named Topsy was electrocuted, and over the past century, this bizarre, ghoulish execution has reverberated through popular culture with the whiff of urban legend. But it really happened, and many historical forces conspired to bring Topsy, Thomas Edison, and those 6600 volts of alternating current together that day. Daly weaves together a fascinating popular history, the first book on this astonishing tale." (Publisher's note)

Jensen, Dean

Queen of the air; a true story of love and tragedy at the circus. Dean Jensen. Crown Publishers 2012 336 p. $26 **791.3**

1. Circus 2. Interpersonal relations 3. Aerialists -- United States -- Biography 4. Woman circus performers -- United States -- Biography

ISBN 030798656X; 9780307986566

LC 2012018066

This book by Dean Jensen presents the "true story of renowned trapeze artist and circus performer Leitzel, Queen of the Air, the most famous woman in the world at the turn of the 20th century, and her star-crossed love affair with Alfredo Codona, of the famous Flying Codona Brothers." (Publisher's note)

791.4 Motion pictures, radio, television

San Filippo, Maria

The **B** word; bisexuality in contemporary film and television. Maria San Filippo. Indiana University Press 2013 x, 281 p.p **791.4**

1. Bisexuality 2. Film criticism 3. Television programs 4. Bisexuality on television 5. Bisexuality in motion pictures

ISBN 9780253008794; 9780253008855

LC 2012042177

Lambda Literary Awards - Bisexual Nonfiction Winner (2014)

It was the author's intent 'explore the central role bisexuality plays in contemporary screen culture, establishing its importance in representation, marketing, and spectatorship. By examining a variety of media genres including art cinema, sexploitation cinema and vampire films, 'bromances,' and series television, [Maria] San Filippo discovers 'missed moments' where bisexual readings of these texts reveal a more malleable notion of subjectivity and eroticism." (Publisher's note)

"San Filippo—a multidisciplinary scholar of film, television, sexuality, and gender studies—draws on all of those sources for this comprehensive, no-holds-barred examination of the portrayal and impact of bisexuality in modern entertainment....San Filippo seeks to redefine our perception of bisexuality; in this study, she's off to a good start." (Publishers Weekly)

Includes bibliographical references and index

Schickel, Richard, 1933-

Conversations with Scorsese; Richard Schickel [interviewer] Alfred A. Knopf 2011 423p il **791.4**

1. Motion picture producers and directors 2. Motion picture directors

ISBN 9780307268402; 9780307595461

LC 2010-34250

"Schickel recently sat down with Scorsese for a series of late-night conversations. Stitched together here, they form an illuminating autobiography-cum-film-studies-course from one of the nation's foremost directors. Scorsese speaks candidly about his childhood in Little Italy and his escape into the movies of the 1950s; his pivotal experiences at the NYU film school and his early student efforts; and, of course, his phenomenal filmmaking career, from his 1967 debut, Who's That Knocking at My Door, through . . . Shutter Island. The in-depth treatment provides fascinating insights into Scorsese's films; even his most obsessed fans will discover new revelations, and hearing him discuss his entire body of work in a single lengthy narrative ties such outliers as The Age of Innocence and Kundun to more-characteristic masterworks like Taxi Driver and Raging Bull." Booklist

Includes filmography and bibliographical references

791.43   Motion pictures

Allen, Woody, 1935-

Woody Allen on Woody Allen; in conversation with Stig Björkman. Grove Press 1995 288 p. $22; $15.95   **791.43**
1. Motion picture producers and directors -- United States -- Interviews
ISBN 080211556X; 0802142036; 9780802142030
LC 94026866

This book by Woody Allen is "a unique self-portrait of this uncompromising filmmaker that offers a revealing account of his life and work. In a series of rare, in-depth interviews, Allen brings us onto the sets and behind the scenes of all his films. Since its original publication, 'Woody Allen on Woody Allen' has been the primary source of Allen's own thoughts on his work, childhood, favorite films, and inspirations." (Publisher's note)
Includes filmography.

Auiler, Dan (2000)

Vertigo; the making of a Hitchcock classic. foreword by Martin Scorsese. St. Martin's Press 1998 220p il hardcover o.p. pa $17.95   **791.43**
1. Motion picture directors 2. Vertigo (Motion picture)
ISBN 0-312-26409-7 pa
LC 97-31654

In this account of the film's production Auiler "reconstructs the sometimes uneasy give-and-take between Hitchcock and his players—actors Jimmy Stewart, Kim Novak and Barbara Bel Geddes; screenwriters Samuel Taylor and Alec Coppel; Robert Burks and his second-unit cameraman who created the now-famous Vertigo effect . . . and Bernard Hermann, who composed the mesmerizing score. Interesting factoids abound." Publ Wkly
Includes bibliographical references

Austerlitz, Saul

Another fine mess; a history of American film comedy. Chicago Review Press 2010 512p il pa $24.95   **791.43**
1. Comedy films 2. Motion pictures -- History and criticism
ISBN 978-1-55652-951-1
LC 2010-9010

"An enthusiastic, well-observed, fresh look at old favorites that makes a compelling case for the genius of American film comedy." Kirkus
Includes bibliographical references

Banner, Lois

Marilyn; the passion and the paradox. Lois Banner. 1st US ed. Bloomsbury 2012 528 p. (hardback) $30   **791.43**
1. Actresses 2. Motion picture actors and actresses -- United States -- Biography
ISBN 1608195317; 9781608195312
LC 2012002395

This book offers a biography of actress Marilyn Monroe. Author Lois Banner presents the premise that "Marilyn is steeped in paradoxes so profound that, even under the microscope, they stir and shift without ever settling into a singular picture." She "weav[es] together exclusive interviews, material from previous books and . . . the contents of Monroe's two long-lost personal filing cabinets" in this book. (New York Times Book Review)

Biskind, Peter

Easy riders, raging bulls; how the sex-drugs-and-rock-'n'-roll generation saved Hollywood. Simon & Schuster 1998 506p il hardcover o.p. pa $15   **791.43**
1. Motion pictures 2. Motion picture producers and directors
ISBN 0-684-85708-1 pa
LC 98-2919

"Biskind does relish the tales of outlandish behaviour. . . . But in kicking over the traces of survivors' more or less reliable memories, he shows that libidinal and pharmaceutical urges were intrinsic to the film-makers' ferocious need to outdo each other as auteurs along the lines of the European greats they studied and worshipped." Sight Sound
Includes filmography and bibliographical references

My Lunches With Orson; Conversations Between Henry Jaglom and Orson Welles. edited by Peter Biskind. Henry Holt and Co. 2013 320 p. $28 **791.43**
1. Motion picture producers and directors -- United States 2. Motion picture producers and directors -- United States -- Anecdotes
ISBN 0805097252; 9780805097252
LC 2013000291

Here, film historian Peter Biskind has edited recordings captured when Orson Welles lunched with his friend, film director Henry Jaglom. In the montage offered, "Welles offers a montage of opinion on his career, his disappointments, and acquaintances from Marlene Dietrich and Laurence Olivier to Winston Churchill." (Library Journal)

Bogle, Donald

Bright boulevards, bold dreams; the story of Black Hollywood. One World Ballantine Books 2005 411p il $26.95; pa $15.95   **791.43**
1. African American actors 2. African Americans in motion pictures
ISBN 0345454189; 0345454197 pa
LC 2004-54781

"Starting with Madame Sul-Te-Wan's work in D.W. Griffith's 1915 The Birth of a Nation and ending with the 1960s deaths of Louise Beavers, Nat 'King' Cole and Dorothy Dandridge, Bogle tells the stories of the stars of Black Hollywood: their outfits, their love affairs and their struggles for better roles. . . . Bogle's lively style . . . and his many anecdotes will entertain and inform film students and black history buffs alike." Publ Wkly
Includes bibliographical references

Bosworth, Patricia

Jane Fonda. Houghton Mifflin Harcourt 2011 596 p. [16] p of plates   **791.43**
1. Actresses 2. Women -- United States -- Biography 3. Biography, Individual
ISBN 978-0-547-15257-8; 0-647-15257-4
LC 201109144

'In this book, "[Author Patricia] Bosworth goes behind the image of . . . American . . . [actress] Jane Fonda . . . whose struggles for high achievement, love, and successful motherhood mirror the conflicts of a generation of women. . . . Jane Fonda emerged from a . . . Hollywood family drama to become a '60s onscreen ingénue and then an Oscar-winning actress. At the top of her game she risked all, rising against the Vietnam War and shocking the world with a trip to Hanoi. Later, while becoming one of Hollywood's most committed feminists, she financed her husband Tom Hayden's political career in the '80s with exercise videos that began a fitness craze and brought in millions of dollars. . . . Fonda's next turn, as a Stepford Wife of the Gulfstream set, [was] marrying Ted Turner and seemingly walking away from her ideals and her career." (Publisher's note)

Includes bibliographical references and index

Cavalier, Stephen
The **world** history of animation; Stephen Cavalier. University of California Press 2011 416 p. ill. (some col.) (cloth : alk. paper) $39.95   **791.43**
1. Animated films 2. Animation (Cinematography) 3. Animated television programs 4. Animators 5. Animated films -- History and criticism
ISBN 0520261127; 9780520261129
LC 2010931052
This book on animation by Stephen Cavalier "tells the genre's 100-year-old story around the globe, featuring key players in Europe, North America, and Asia." It is "organized chronologically and covers pioneers, feature films, television programs, digital films, games, independent films, and the web. . . . The book explains the evolution of animation techniques, from rotoscoping to refinements of cel techniques, direct film, claymation, and more." (Publisher's note)
Includes bibliographical references (p. 404-405) and index.

Chadwick, Bruce (2002)
The **reel** Civil War; mythmaking in American film. Knopf 2001 366p il hardcover o.p. pa $15   **791.43**
1. Motion pictures 2. United States -- History -- 1861-1865, Civil War -- Motion pictures and the war
ISBN 0-375-70832-4 pa
LC 2001-91008
"One-third of 'The Reel Civil War' concentrates on {'The Birth of a Nation' and 'Gone With the Wind'}. Given their prominence, that seems a reasonable balance, and Chadwick's dissection of the myths they helped to foster is superb." N Y Times Book Rev
Includes bibliographical references

★ **Conversations** at the American Film Institute with the great moviemakers; the next generation. edited and with an introduction by George Stevens, Jr. Alfred A. Knopf 2012 xxiii, 737 p.p (hbk.) $39.95   **791.43**
1. Motion pictures 2. Motion picture industry 3. Motion picture producers and directors 4. Motion pictures -- Production and direction 5. Motion picture

producers and directors -- United States -- Interviews
ISBN 0307273474; 9780307273475
LC 2011043741
This book presents conversations with "directors, producers, writers, actors, cameramen, composers, editors": "men and women working in pictures, beginning in 1950, when the studio system was collapsing and people could no longer depend on, or were bound by, the structure of studio life to make movies." Others, "who began to work long after the studio days were over," are featured as well. (Barnes and Noble)
Includes bibliographical references and index.

Corliss, Richard
Mom in the movies; the iconic screen mothers you love (and a few you love to hate) by Richard Corliss ; foreword by Debbie Reynolds and Carrie Fisher; [with editorial assistance from Turner Classic Movies] Simon & Schuster 2014 192 p. illustrations $35   **791.43**
1. Mothers 2. Women in motion pictures 3. Mothers in motion pictures
ISBN 1476738262; 9781476738260
LC 2013044850
"Turner Classic Movies and film historian Richard Corliss present 'Mom in the Movies: The Iconic Screen Mothers You Love (and a Few You Love to Hate),' the . . . fully illustrated book that shares the many ways Hollywood has celebrated, vilified and otherwise memorialized dear old Mom. . . . Here, you will meet the Criminal Moms . . . and the eccentric Showbiz Moms. . . . You'll also find Great American Moms, as warm and nourishing as apple pie." (Publisher's note)
A "comprehensive retrospective of mothers as portrayed on film from the earliest "Silent Moms" . . . to the most recent figures." LJ

Decharne, Max
Hardboiled Hollywood; the true crime stories behind the classic noir films. Pegasus Books 2010 240p $27.95; pa $14.95   **791.43**
1. Mystery films 2. Motion pictures
ISBN 978-1-60598-076-8; 1-60598-076-5; 978-1-60598-083-6 pa; 1-60598-083-8 pa
First published 2002 in the United Kingdom
"A lively exploration of the origins of some of Hollywood's most vivid plots – not only the reworked novels and screenplays, but real events. Police reports, Mafiosi and serial killers are never far away. Décharné renders an intriguing picture of the powerful place this art form has come to occupy in society, and why." Financial Times
Includes filmography and bibliographical references

Dixon, Wheeler W., 1950-
A **Short** History of Film; Wheeler Winston Dixon & Gwendolyn Audrey Foster. 2nd edition Rutgers University Press 2013 449 p. illustrations (some color) pa. $29.95   **791.43**
1. Motion picture industry 2. Motion picture industry -- History 3. Motion pictures -- History. 4. Motion

picture industry -- History.
ISBN 9780813560557

LC 2012533144

"A Short History of Film, Second Edition, provides a concise and accurate overview of the history of world cinema, detailing the major movements, directors, studios, and genres from 1896 through 2012. Accompanied by more than 250 rare color and black-and-white stills - including many from recent films - the new edition is unmatched in its panoramic view, conveying a sense of cinema's sweep in the twentieth and early twenty-first centuries as it is practiced in the United States and around the world.

Wheeler Winston Dixon and Gwendolyn Audrey Foster present new and amended coverage of the industry in addition to updating the birth and death dates and final works of notable directors. Their expanded focus on key films brings the book firmly into the digital era and chronicles the death of film as a production medium." (Publisher's Note)
"This excellent introduction stands out in a crowded field with its lively, accessible writing, broad coverage, and particular focus on traditionally marginalized figures in film history...The most striking aspect of the book is the coverage of women, African Americans, and Third World filmmakers, which strongly complements its solid coverage of American and European film. Illustrations abound, and even the best-versed cineaste will find new films to track down after reading the breezy, enthusiastic analysis in this book. Highly recommended for all collections, this text would also make an excellent textbook for introductory film-studies courses.—" (Library Journal)

Drazin, Charles

French cinema. Faber and Faber 2011 448p il pa $22   791.43
1. Motion pictures -- France
ISBN 978-0-571-21173-9
A "history of French film, from the fanciful, whimsical inventions of pioneer Georges Méliès to the formalist daring and intellectual rigor of contemporary artists like Olivier Assayas and Catherine Breillat. . . . Drazin charts the economic and social conditions that nurtured French film, providing fascinating insights into the pragmatic methods of the Pathé studio, the shift to more escapist, 'Hollywood' style films that characterized the Nazi occupation, the rise of film culture supported by magazines like Cahiers du cinéma and the attendant New Wave spearheaded by directors including François Truffaut and Jean-Luc Godard, and the vital but often uneasy relationship between French and American cinema. Drazin's account is endlessly readable, alternating penetrating analysis of classics like Jean Renoir's La Règle du Jeu with serious appraisals of less well-known figures like Julien Duvivier and Agnès Varda." Kirkus
Includes bibliographical references

Dyer, Geoff

Zona; Geoff Dyer. Pantheon Books 2012 228 p.   791.43
1. Film criticism 2. Stalker (motion picture)
ISBN 0307377385; 9780307377388

LC 2011011727

In this book, author "Geoff Dyer attempts to unlock the mysteries of a film that has haunted him ever since he first saw it thirty years ago: Andrei Tarkovsky's 'Stalker', widely regarded as one of the greatest films of all time. . . . As Dyer guides us into the zone of Tarkovsky's imagination, we realize that the film is only the entry point for a radically original investigation of the enduring questions of life, faith, and how to live." (Publisher's note)
Includes bibliographical references

Eagan, Daniel

America's film legacy; the authoritative guide to the landmark movies in the National Film Registry. Continuum 2010 xxvii, 818p il $130; pa $39.95   791.43
1. Reference books 2. Motion pictures -- Catalogs
ISBN 978-0-826-41849-4; 0-826-41849-X; 978-0-826-42977-3 pa; 0-826-42977-7 pa

LC 2009-42778

The author "chronologically catalogues 500 Registry films, from 1893's 30-second Blacksmithing Scene to 1995's Fargo, jumbling Hollywood classics together with obscure art films, cartoon shorts, documentaries, industrial and student films, newsreel footage from the Hindenburg disaster and the Zapruder film. Each entry includes complete cast and credits lists and an engaging one to two-page historical and interpretive essay. . . . [This is] an erudite, perceptive, always entertaining cinematic encyclopedia." Publ Wkly

Eyman, Scott

Print the legend; the life and times of John Ford. Johns Hopkins Univ. Press 2000 656p il pa $23.50   791.43
1. Motion picture directors 2. Motion picture producers and directors -- Biography
ISBN 0-8018-6560-3; 978-0-8018-6560-2

LC 00-33044

First published 1999 by Simon & Schuster
This is a biography chronicling the life and career of the director of "such classics as The grapes of wrath, The searchers and The man who shot Liberty Valance. . . . Eyman has written a quietly magnificent biography of an American original who has shaped our perception of movies as serious art." Publ Wkly
Includes bibliographical references

Farber, Manny

★ Farber on film; the complete film writings of Manny Farber. edited by Robert Polito. Library of America 2009 824p $40   791.43
1. Motion pictures -- History and criticism
ISBN 978-1-59853-050-6

LC 2009-928058

"Manny Farber (1917-2008), critic and painter, wrote movie reviews for publications ranging from the starchy New Republic to the raunchy girlie mag Cavalier. This is your first bit of proof that Farber had an itch to get his opinions in print anywhere he could (one measure of a critic who wants to communicate, not just simmer in theory-juice). He never followed the pack, or became part of any 'school' of criticism, or held back a judgment because he thought he'd be jeered at or not allowed at the cool-kids' table. . . . Farber covered movies from 1942 to 1977, which means that in this book he weighs in vividly on everything from Casablanca . . . to Taxi Driver." Entertainment Wkly

Film noir; the encyclopedia. edited by Alain Silver . . . [et al.]; co-editor: Carl Macek; designed by Bernard Schleifer. [4th ed.]; Overlook Duckworth 2010 511p il   **791.43**
1. Mystery films 2. Motion pictures
ISBN 978-1-590201442
First published 1979

An introductory essay "lays out the history and parameters of noir in a succinct but undogmatic way, offering an intro for the new viewer as well as food for thought for the hardboiled fan. Most of the rest of the book consists of synopses of noir films, providing a brief plot summary followed by a paragraph or two detailing key aspects of each film. Important flicks like Kiss Me Deadly and Double Indemnity get a bit more space and consideration, and the authors, for the most part, avoid subjective reviews and concentrate on chasing down each film's address in the naked city of noir. . . . This new edition of the definitive text on film noir is a perfect companion for a foray into the dreamlike world of some of the most dark and mesmerizing movies ever made." PopMatters

Frankel, Glenn
The **searchers**; the making of an American legend. Glenn Frankel. Bloomsbury USA 2013 416 p. (hardcover) $28   **791.43**
1. Searchers (Motion picture) 2. Native Americans -- Captivities 3. Motion pictures -- History and criticism 4. Indian captivities -- Texas 5. Motion pictures and history 6. Massacres -- Texas -- History -- 19th century 7. Comanche Indians -- Texas -- History -- 19th century 8. Historical films -- United States -- History and criticism
ISBN 1608191052; 9781608191055
LC 2012029453

This book, by Glenn Frankel, explores the popular history of how "in 1836 in East Texas, nine-year-old Cynthia Ann Parker . . . , kidnapped by Comanches . . . , was raised by the tribe and eventually became the wife of a warrior. Twenty-four years after her capture, she was reclaimed by . . . Texas Rangers. . . . The myth . . . would be adapted into one of Hollywood's most legendary films, 'The Searchers.'" (Publisher's note)

Includes bibliographical references and index

Goldman, William
Adventures in the screen trade; a personal view of Hollywood and screenwriting. Warner Bks. 1983 418p $17.50   **791.43**
1. Motion picture industry 2. Motion picture authorship. 3. Hollywood (Los Angeles, Calif.)--History.
ISBN 0-446-51273-7
LC 82-17602

"No one knows the writer's Hollywood more intimately than William Goldman. Two-time Academy Award-winning screenwriter and the bestselling author of Marathon Man, Tinsel, Boys and Girls Together, and other novels, Goldman now takes you into Hollywood's inner sanctums...on and behind the scenes for Butch Cassidy and the Sundance

Kid, All the President's Men, and other films...into the plush offices of Hollywood producers...into the working lives of acting greats such as Redford, Olivier, Newman, and Hoffman...and into his own professional experiences and creative thought processes in the crafting of screenplays. You get a firsthand look at why and how films get made and what elements make a good screenplay." (Publisher's Note)

Goldman devotes several "chapters to separate categories like Stars, Producers, Executives, the basic elements a screenplay requires, then other chapters to specific reminiscences of movies with which he was associated (e.g., 'Harper,' 'The Great Waldo Pepper,' 'Marathon Man,' 'A Bridge Too Far'), and he ends with a sequence of . . . examples of how a short story (he uses one of his own as illustration) could be adapted first into a screenplay and gradually into a movie." (America) Index.

Which lie did I tell? more adventures in the screen trade. William Goldman. Vintage 2001 384p $17.95   **791.43**
1. Screenwriters 2. Motion picture industry
ISBN 0375703195; 9780375703195

This book by William Goldman, "the Oscar-winning screenwriter of 'Butch Cassidy and the Sundance Kid' and 'The Princess Bride' (he also wrote the novel), and the bestselling author of 'Adventures in the Screen Trade' . . . is as much a screenwriting how-to (and how-not-to) manual as it is a feast of insider information. "Which Lie Did I Tell?" is [designed] for anyone even slightly intrigued by the process of how a movie gets made." (Publisher's Note)

"[Goldman] discusses screenwriting perils, explains how successful movies like Charade and The Sound of Music wreaked havoc by siring copycat films, describes how Andre the Giant always paid for lunch, complains that MTV's impact on quick-cutting has helped make 1990s films awful, reveals that only Clint Eastwood and Sean Connery are tall, investigates how great comedy scenes worked in When Harry Met Sally and There's Something About Mary, debunks auteurs, and divulges why no big star would play Superman in 1978...An engaging expos that is not mean-spirited; recommended for public and academic libraries and film collections." (Library Journal)

Gora, Susannah
You couldn't ignore me if you tried; the Brat Pack, John Hughes, and their impact on a generation. Crown Publishers 2010 367p il $26   **791.43**
1. Teenagers in motion pictures 2. Screenwriters 3. Motion picture directors 4. Motion picture producers
ISBN 978-0-307-40843-3; 0-307-40843-4

"Though Gora discusses the work of Hughes's colleagues, she places the sharpest lens on the godfather of the genre himself. . . . Through extensive research and interviews with insiders, she reveals the romantic undertones in the relationship between the late director and his pouty-lipped muse, Molly Ringwald, 18 years his junior. But, the author argues, perhaps it was his ability to relate to adolescents and his respect for their seemingly insignificant plights that allowed Hughes to capture coming-of-age so candidly. While a long and involved read, Gora's book offers an all-access pass to the Brat Pack, the films they starred in, and those behind the cameras of a movie era that is still relevant today." Paste

Includes bibliographical references

Halberstadt, Michele

La petite; a memoir. Michèle Halberstadt ; translated from the French by Linda Coverdale. Other Press 2012 111 p. (trade pbk.) $14.95   **791.43**
1. Women in the motion picture industry 2. Motion picture producers and directors 3. Women motion picture producers and directors -- France -- Biography
ISBN 1590515315; 9781590515310; 9781590515327
LC 2012000401

Author Michéle Halberstadt presents a biography, discussing the "painful events that surrounded the death of her beloved grandfather, which led to a suicide attempt when she was twelve years old. Michéle's mother favored her older sister, her father was emotionally remote, . . . and her peers a foreign species. Her grandfather alone had given her an image of herself that she could embrace. After he died, there seemed to be nothing left for her. One day . . . the pills in the bathroom were within reach and the temptation of falling asleep forever was irresistible." (Publisher's note)

Harris, Mark

★ Five Came Back; A Story of Hollywood and the Second World War. Mark Harris. Penguin Group USA 2014 480 p. illustrations $29.95   **791.43**
1. Motion picture industry 2. World War, 1939-1945 -- Motion pictures and the war 3. Motion picture producers and directors -- United States 4. Motion pictures -- United States -- History 5. Motion picture industry -- California -- Los Angeles -- History
ISBN 1594204306; 9781594204302
LC 2013039983

This book tells "the untold story of how Hollywood changed World War II, and how World War II changed Hollywood, through the prism of five film directors caught up in the war: John Ford, William Wyler, John Huston, Frank Capra, and George Stevens." (Publisher's note) "Some of the five worked together (Capra and Stevens), but others worked separately on feature-length documentaries, short subjects and films for military use only." (Kirkus Reviews)

"Narrative nonfiction that is as gloriously readable as it is unfailingly informative." Booklist

Includes bibliographical references (pages 449-494) and index

★ Pictures at a revolution; five movies and the birth of the new Hollywood. Penguin Press 2008 490p il $27.95   **791.43**
1. Motion pictures
ISBN 978-1-59420-152-3; 1-59420-152-8
LC 2007-32633

The author examines the five films nominated for the Academy Award for Best Picture in 1967: Bonnie and Clyde, The Graduate, Guess Who's Coming To Dinner, In the Heat of the Night, and Dr. Dolittle.

"Harris gives us a juicy, multilayered chronicle of a turning point in American culture. This is page-turning social history; someone reading this book who didn't live

through those days would understand why 'the '60s' had to happen." Newsweek

Includes bibliographical references

Harvey, James

Movie love in the 50's. Da Capo Press 2002 448p il pa $18.95   **791.43**
1. Motion pictures
ISBN 978-0-306-81177-7; 0-306-81177-4
First published 2001 by Knopf

"For every 'sanitized' movie that came out of the Fifties, there were others that shook up old formulas. Critic and essayist Harvey explores—and ultimately eulogizes—Hollywood films of this era, a time of transition when the Production Code was being scrapped and the studio system abandoned. . . . His movie love is inspired and infectious." Libr J

Includes bibliographical references

Haskell, Molly

Frankly, my dear; Gone With the Wind revisited. Yale University Press 2009 244p il   **791.43**
1. Authors 2. Novelists 3. Motion pictures -- History 4. Gone with the wind (Motion picture)
ISBN 978-0-300-11752-3
LC 2008-37296

This book "deals simultaneously with Margaret Mitchell's . . . novel and David Selznick's . . . film version of Gone With the Wind." (Publisher's note) Bibliography. Index.

The author "applies her deep movie knowledge, feminist eye, and Southern roots to Frankly, My Dear, a fiercely smart appreciation of Gone With the Wind. Passionate about the topic since her teens in Richmond, Haskell turns her attention from making-of stories to meaning-of insights, as crisp in her presentation of Hollywood gossip as she is in her scholarly analysis of why the book-turned-movie has such a hold on us." Entertainment Wkly

Includes bibliographical references

Howard, Jean

Jean Howard's Hollywood; a photo memoir. photographs by Jean Howard; text by Jim Watters. Abrams 1989 248p il hardcover o.p. pa $24.95   **791.43**
1. Motion picture industry -- Pictorial works
ISBN 978-0-8109-2679-0; 0-8109-2679-2
LC 89-264

"Miss Howard has recorded the rarefied behind-the-gates lives of some of the most famous personalities in the history of the motion picture business. No outsider was she, hired for the occasion to 'snap' the swells. Miss Howard is very much one of the swells herself; her pictures are shot from the intimate perspective of the insider, either as a guest at the party or, frequently, as the hostess." N Y Times Book Rev

Jones, G. William

Black cinema treasures; lost and found. foreword by Ossie Davis. University of N. Tex. Press 1991 242p il hardcover o.p. pa $17.95   **791.43**
1. Motion pictures 2. African Americans in motion

pictures
ISBN 1-57441-028-8 pa

LC 91-10882

This book "documents black independent filmmaking from the 1920s to the 1950s, spotlighting sixteen films salvaged from a warehouse in Tyler, Texas, by the author. . . . There are also brief biographies of pioneers such as Oscar Micheaux and Spencer Williams. . . . For anyone with an interest in the social history of the movie industry, this book helps bring to light a much-neglected body of work." San Francisco Rev Books

Includes filmography

Kael, Pauline

The **age** of movies; selected writings of Pauline Kael. edited by Sanford Schwartz. Library of America 2011 xxiv, 828p $40   **791.43**
    1. Motion pictures -- Reviews
    ISBN 978-1-59853-109-1; 1-59853-109-3

LC 2011-23053

"Spanning 1965 to 1990, the volume holds many sparkling radio essays [Kael] delivered over the East Bay airwaves and had reprinted in places like Film Quarterly before heading east, and a wealth of reviews from magazines, especially from her residency at The New Yorker, where she opined from 1967 to 1991. The full range of Kael's smarts, vision, wit, prejudices, and downright cruelty are on full, wicked display." Millions

Kashner, Sam

The **bad** & the beautiful; Hollywood in the fifties. {by} Sam Kashner and Jennifer MacNair. Norton 2002 380p il $26.95; pa $15.95   **791.43**
    1. Motion pictures
    ISBN 0-393-04321-5; 0-393-32436-2 pa

LC 2002-317

This "is a series of vignettes capturing a Hollywood in transition, pressured by television, the studio system's decline, and the postwar emerging permissiveness. Topics include the influence of the short-lived but much-feared Confidential; the clout of aging gossip queens Louella Parsons, Hedda Hopper, and Sheila Graham; and the uproar over an interracial romance between Sammy Davis and Kim Novak." Libr J

"These accounts, often dipped in acid, will keep readers flipping pages." Publ Wkly

Includes bibliographical references

Keaton, Eleanor

Buster Keaton remembered; {by} Eleanor Keaton and Jeffrey Vance; afterword by Kevin Brownlow; Manoah Bowman, photographic editor; photographs from the collection of the Academy of Motion Picture Arts and Sciences. Abrams 2001 238p il $45   **791.43**
    1. Actors 2. Motion picture directors
    ISBN 0-8109-4227-5

LC 00-61853

A "photographic tribute . . . comprising formal and behind-the-scenes stills, staged publicity shots, and previously unpublished personal photos, this book is the most comprehensive pictorial retrospective on Keaton to date." Libr J

Filmography: p. 219-233; Includes bibliographical references (p. 217-218) and index

Lane, Anthony

Nobody's perfect; writings from the New Yorker. Knopf 2002 xx, 752p $30; pa $16.95   **791.43**
    1. Motion pictures -- Reviews
    ISBN 0-375-41448-7; 0-375-71434-0 pa

LC 2002-20809

"One of the best aspects of Lane's column, and of this anthology, is that it wanders across cultural and intellectual borders." Libr J

Lanzmann, Claude, 1925-

The **Patagonian** hare; a memoir. Claude Lanzmann ; translated from the French by Frank Wynne. Farrar, Straus & Giroux 2012 x, 528 p.p ill.   **791.43**
    1. Autobiographies 2. Journalists -- Biography 3. Motion picture producers and directors -- Biography 4. Journalists -- France -- Biography 5. Motion picture producers and directors -- France -- Biography
    ISBN 0374230048; 9780374230043

LC 2011048058

This book is the memoir of the "journalist and filmmaker Claude Lanzmann. . . . Raised as a secular Jew in a family with deep communist sympathies . . . the author served in the French Resistance and narrowly missed capture by the Nazis. . . . He became editor of Jean-Paul Sartre's journal 'Le Temps Modernes' . . . and had an intense seven-year affair with Sartre's lover, Simone de Beauvoir, who was happy to take him on as her 'sixth man.' Faithfulness wasn't anyone's game then, and Lanzmann seemed to seduce nearly every woman he ever met. He also became deeply immersed in his own Jewish heritage and documentary filmmaking, ultimately resulting in his nine-hour magnum opus Shoah." (Kirkus)

Lax, Eric

★ **Conversations** with Woody Allen; his films, the movies, and moviemaking. A.A. Knopf 2007 390p il $30   **791.43**
    1. Actors 2. Humorists 3. Motion picture producers and directors 4. Screenwriters 5. Motion picture directors
    ISBN 978-0-375-41533-3; 0-375-41533-5

LC 2007-06350

This book contains interviews with Woody Allen from 1971 to the present.

"A fine, never-disappointing achievement, this book is in competition with no other." Choice

Leider, Emily Wortis

Becoming Mae West. Farrar, Straus & Giroux 1997 431p il hardcover o.p. pa $18.95   **791.43**
    1. Actors 2. Authors 3. Novelists 4. Dramatists 5. Memoirists 6. Screenwriters
    ISBN 978-0-374-10959-2; 978-0-306-80951-4 pa; 0-306-80951-6 pa

LC 96-43803

This exploration of the West persona "focuses on the first four decades of West's career, up to 1938. Yet Leider's biography is also a portrait of an era: she devotes a great deal of the book to rendering the historical context, particularly the moral landscape, of the early 1900's, in order to more clearly define West's place in it and ultimately her mastery of it." N Y Times Book Rev

Dark lover: the life and death of Rudolph Valentino; [by] Emily W. Leider. Farrar, Straus & Giroux 2003 514p il $35; pa $16 **791.43**
1. Actors
ISBN 0-374-28239-0; 0-571-21114-3 pa
LC 2002-29779
"A comprenhensive . . . portrait of the great screen lover." Booklist
Includes bibliographical references

Lumet, Sidney
Making movies. Knopf 1995 220p hardcover o.p. pa $12 **791.43**
1. Motion pictures -- Production and direction
ISBN 0-679-75660-4 pa
LC 94-34449
"A fascinating look at the artist at work." Libr J

Lynn, Kenneth S.
★ **Charlie** Chaplin and his times. Cooper Square Press 2003 604p il pa $19.95 **791.43**
1. Actors 2. Motion picture directors 3. Motion picture producers 4. Motion picture producers and directors -- Biography
ISBN 0-8154-1255-X; 978-0-8154-1255-7
LC 2002-31420
First published 1997 by Simon & Schuster
The author "interweaves Chaplin's life with the events and personalities of his era, including British music hall impresario Fred Karno, silent screen star and pal Douglas Fairbanks, numerous lovers and wives, brother Sydney, and Adolf Hitler. . . . Lynn addresses his subject's leftist views and makes sense of the House Committee on Un-American Activities investigations of 1947 that led to Chaplin's European exile until 1973. All a biography should be, this is enthusiastically recommended." Libr J
Includes bibliographical references

Maltin, Leonard
Leonard Maltin's movie guide; edited by Leonard Maltin; managing editor, Darwyn Carson; associate editor, Luke Sader; contributing editors, Mike Clark ... [et al.]; video editor, Casey St. Charnez; contributors, Jerry Beck, Jessie Maltin. 2015 ed. Plume 2015 1643p pa $25 **791.43**
1. DVDs 2. Videotapes 3. Motion pictures 4. Reference books
ISBN 9780142181768
Annual. First published 1969 with title: TV movies. Title varies
"Maltin offers 17,000 summary movie reviews. . . . Also included are more than 25,000 combined DVD and video listings. . . . Less commercially familiar works, like foreign films, indies, and cult classics, are given equal billing. Rated on a star system, including a category for 'bomb,' paragraph-long reviews contain actor listings and concise nar-

rative synopses, along with incisive critical considerations. A highly useful, quick reference for film studies and general collections." Libr J

Mamet, David
Bambi vs. Godzilla; on the nature, purpose, and practice of the movie business. Pantheon Books 2007 250p $22 **791.43**
1. Authorship 2. Motion pictures
ISBN 978-0-375-42253-9; 0-375-42253-6
LC 2006-20018
Mamet's "essay collection focuses on the movie industry, and his stance is that of someone who has seen Hollywood's facelift scars and whose advice to eager novices just off the bus can be summarized thusly: 'Go back.' . . . . He outlines the Hollywood caste system with a precision that reflects the bitter experience of the person at the bottom— the screenwriter. Scorn, betrayal, and subjugation—this is the lot of the writer, who, according to Mamet, is resented by nearly everyone in the business. Miraculously, though, great drama is occasionally realized on the screen, and Mamet offers writers some guidelines on how to approach it." Booklist
Includes filmography

On directing film. Viking 1991 107p hardcover o.p. pa $14 **791.43**
1. Motion pictures -- Production and direction
ISBN 0-14-012722-4 pa
LC 90-50428
"Noted playwright, screenwriter, and director Mamet offers his views on film directing taken, some in transcript form, from lectures and classes at Columbia. . . . Refreshingly untheoretical, particularly regarding acting technique, this is fitfully interesting stuff." Libr J

Mann, William J.
Behind the screen; how gays and lesbians shaped Hollywood, 1910-1969. Viking 2001 xxiv, 422p il $29.95; pa $16 **791.43**
1. Motion picture industry 2. Homosexuality in motion pictures
ISBN 0-670-03017-1; 0-14-200114-7 pa
LC 2001-17984
In this study "Mann examines how the movie capital of the world was transformed by a host of writers, directors, designers, actors, and producers often at odds with the official codes, and mores of the times. . . . Mann's book is important reading for anyone interested in the history of American film. Essential for all film and gay studies collections." Libr J

McAllister, Marvin
Whiting up; whiteface minstrels & stage Europeans in African American performance. Marvin McAllister. University of North Carolina Press 2011 xiii, 330 p.p ill. (cloth : alk. paper) $39.95 **791.43**
1. Minstrel shows 2. African American actors 3. United States -- Race relations 4. Minstrel shows -- United States -- History 5. African Americans in the

performing arts -- History
ISBN 0807835080; 9780807835081

LC 2011020426

"In this work, [Marvin] McAllister defines and explores whiting up, a . . . tradition in which African American actors, comics, musicians, and even everyday people have assumed white racial identities in a performative context. Whether in . . . minstrel shows . . . in musicals and satires . . . or in one-person shows . . . McAllister argues that this form of cross-racial play creates unexpected intercultural alliances even as it . . . critiques racial stereotypes and cultural norms." (Publisher's note)
Includes bibliographical references and index.

McCann, Graham
   Cary Grant; a class apart. Columbia Univ. Press 1997 346p il hardcover o.p. pa $19.95   **791.43**
   1. Actors
   ISBN 0-231-10885-0 pa

LC 96-38577

First published 1996 in the United Kingdom
"McCann's biography shows how working-class Archie Leach transformed himself into Cary Grant. Unlike many self-made successes, Grant never renounced his humble origins but incorporated them into his persona. As a result, he became, McCann says, a 'democratic gentleman,' at ease in any element, who shone in both serious dramas and screwball comedies and, unlike most male stars, appealed equally to men and women." Booklist
   Includes bibliographical references

McKay, Sinclair
   The **man** with the golden touch; how the Bond films conquered the world. Overlook Press 2010 396p il $25.95   **791.43**
   1. Motion pictures 2. Bond, James (Fictional character)
   ISBN 978-1-59020-298-2

First published 2008 in the United Kingdom
"Not a 'making-of' film book, like so many others, but rather an exploration of the themes and impact of the James Bond movies, this lively volume is sure to appeal to fans of 007. The author, clearly a huge Bond fan himself, writes with a wry tone, but he's brimming with knowledge and insight. He tracks the movies from their origin, as cold-war spy adventures, through their transition to fantastic adventures in supervillainy, to—horror of horrors!—quaint artifacts of a bygone era, and then, inevitably, back around to relevance again. He compares and contrasts the movies to their source material, Ian Fleming's novels and short stories, and he fills the book with delightful Bond arcana." Booklist
   Includes bibliographical references

Muir, John Kenneth
   The **encyclopedia** of superheroes on film and television; 2nd ed.; McFarland & Co. 2008 696p il $75   **791.43**
   1. Reference books 2. Superhero films -- Encyclopedias 3. Superhero television programs -- Encyclopedias
   ISBN 978-0-7864-3755-9; 0-7864-3755-3

LC 2008-19724

First published 2004

"Entries start with description and background of the hero. Live-action films are presented with reviewer comments and cast and crew. TV series also present reviewer comments and a description of the series. Episode guides include title, writer and director credits, and air dates as well as episode descriptions and guest casts. . . . A good addition to the pop-culture collection." Booklist
   Includes bibliographical references

Neupert, Richard
   A **history** of the French new wave cinema; [by] Richard Neupert. University of Wis. Press 2002 368p il (Wisconsin studies in film) $50; pa $24.95 **791.43**
   1. New wave films -- France 2. Motion pictures -- France
   ISBN 0-299-18160-X; 0-299-18164-2 pa

LC 2002-2305

"Refreshingly jargon-free and full of interesting details and anecdotes, this book is a pleasure to read." Libr J
   Includes bibliographical references

O'Brien, Geoffrey
   Stolen glimpses, captive shadows; writing on film, 2002-2012. Geoffrey O'Brien. Counterpoint 2013 288 p. (hardcover) $25   **791.43**
   1. Film criticism 2. Motion pictures
   ISBN 1619021706; 9781619021709

LC 2013002370

This book, by Geoffrey O'Brien, "gathering the best of a decade's worth of writing on film . . . , ranges freely over the past, present, and future of the movies, from the primal visual poetry of the silent era to the dizzying permutations of the merging digital age. Here are 38 searching essays on contemporary blockbusters . . . , recent innovative triumphs . . . , and the intricacies of genre mythmaking from Chinese martial arts films to the horror classics." (Publisher's note)

Obst, Lynda
   Sleepless in Hollywood; From the New Abnormal in the Movie Business. Lynda Obst. Simon & Schuster 2013 272 p. $26   **791.43**
   1. Motion picture industry 2. Motion pictures -- United States 3. Motion picture industry -- United States
   ISBN 1476727740; 9781476727745

LC 2012051638

In this book, Lynda Obst "examines how Hollywood has transitioned from what she calls the Old Abnormal to the New Abnormal." She "shares trivia, personal experiences, and second-hand anecdotes to explain how and why the entire movie-making system has changed. From the death of the DVD market, to the meteoric rise of the marketing department's influence, from the growing involvement of international partnerships to social media, she dissects the business." (Publishers Weekly)

Osborne, Robert A.
   75 years of the Oscar; the official history of the Academy Awards. {by} Robert Osborne. Abbeville Press 2013 416p il $75   **791.43**
   1. Academy Awards (Motion pictures)
   ISBN 9780789211422

First published 1989 with title: 60 years of the Oscar. Published every five years.

This includes a history of the Academy of Motion Picture Arts and Sciences, overviews of Academy Award nominees and winners, award ceremonies, and a complete listing of nominees and winners in every category

Includes bibliographical references

Rabin, Nathan

My year of flops; the A.V. Club presents one man's journey deep into the heart of cinematic failure. Scribner 2010 264p il pa $15   **791.43**
  1. Motion pictures
  ISBN 978-1-4391-5312-3; 1-4391-5312-4
                                LC 2010-18224

"Follow Nathan Rabin on his quest 'to provide a sympathetic reappraisal of some of the most reviled films of all time,' and what do you learn? 'Pennies From Heaven'and 'Freddy Got Fingered' are better than you might think, and 'Ishtar' offers an 'exquisitely jaundiced take' on American foreign policy. Mostly, though, Mr. Rabin sits slack-jawed watching the everlasting dreadfulness of 'Mame,' 'Battlefield Earth' and 'Exit to Eden' ('the mother of all unsexy sex films'). Always glad to snark it up, Mr. Rabin can also be mournful when reflecting on how worthwhile failures like 'Heaven's Gate' diminished Hollywood's ambitions, then and now. The book, which collects columns that first appeared on The Onion's pop-culture Web site, includes more bad movies and interviews with actors caught up in the cinematic wreckage." N Y Times Book Rev

Reilly, Thomas A.

The **big** picture; filmmaking lessons from a life on the set. St. Martin's Press 2009 239p $25.95 **791.43**
  1. Cinematography 2. Motion pictures -- Production and direction
  ISBN 978-0-312-38038-0; 0-312-38038-0
                                LC 2008-44615

The author "has written a valuable guide that film students and novice filmmakers will find illuminating and insightful. In 50 short essays Reilly analyzes the problems that often surface on movie sets, and offers solutions. . . . Reilly opens with film set slang and jargon ('martini' = last shot of the day) and then moves on to cover everything from schedules, blocking actor movements, camera angles and master shots to variables in sunlight and the color palette." Publ Wkly

Rich, B. Ruby

New queer cinema; the director's cut. B. Ruby Rich. Duke University Press 2013 360 p. (cloth : alk. paper) $94.95   **791.43**
  1. Queer theory 2. Film criticism 3. Gays in motion pictures 4. Homosexuality in motion pictures
  ISBN 082235411X; 9780822354116; 9780822354284
                                LC 2012048672

This book by B. Ruby Rich focuses on new queer cinema. "Based almost entirely on edited selections from Rich's previous work, including the 1992 'Village Voice' article in which she coined the NQC term, this book ambitiously seeks to capture both the author's personal experience and the NQC movement's development from the mid-1980s to the present day." (Library Journal)

Includes bibliographical references and index

Richards, Jeffrey

Hollywood's ancient worlds. Continuum 2008 227p il $29.95   **791.43**
  1. Motion pictures
  ISBN 978-1-8472-5007-0; 1-8472-5007-6

The author "examines how the ancient world has been presented in the movies, placing particular emphasis on Hollywood films but also including some European films and television productions. He excludes comedies for reasons of space and authorial preference, but otherwise Hollywood's Ancient Worlds includes consideration of every epic film set in the ancient world which was created between 1916 and 2006. . . . [The book] is packed with information. . . . However, Richards has also produced a jargon-free book which is fun to read and maintains a sense of proportion about the films he discusses." PopMatters

Rough Guides (Firm)

The **Rough** Guide to film; [by] Richard Armstrong . . . [et al.] Distributed by Penguin Putnam 2007 649p il pa $27.99   **791.43**
  1. Reference books 2. Motion picture producers and directors -- Biography -- Dictionaries
  ISBN 978-1-84353-408-2; 1-84353-408-8
                                LC 2007-300132

"This volume looks beyond the Hollywood mainstream to provide assistance to anyone who is browsing rental-store shelves or online DVD catalogs in search of something new. More than 800 directors from around the globe are profiled, and more than 2,000 of their most important films are briefly reviewed. . . . If you're in a hurry, you can turn to the various categorized lists of five great directors, five classic films, and five 'lesser-known gems.'" Booklist

Schickel, Richard

Clint Eastwood; a biography. Knopf 1996 557p il hardcover o.p. pa $15   **791.43**
  1. Actors 2. Mayors 3. Motion picture directors
  ISBN 0-679-74991-8 pa
                                LC 96-32836

Schickel examines the life and career of the actor-director

"No mere celebrity bio, this is a beautifully written, comprehensive and astonishingly insightful study of a man who, seemingly against all odds, has achieved world renown as both a pop culture icon and an accomplished film artist." Publ Wkly

Includes bibliographical references

Scovell, Jane

Oona; living in the shadows: a biography of Oona O'Neill Chaplin. Warner Bks. 1998 354p il hardcover o.p. pa $14.99   **791.43**
  1. Actors 2. Motion picture directors 3. Motion picture producers 4. Spouses of prominent persons
  ISBN 0-446-67541-5 pa
                                LC 98-21592

A "biography of Oona O'Neill Chaplin, daughter of playwright Eugene O'Neill and wife of film legend Charlie Chaplin." Publ Wkly

Includes bibliographical references

Spacek, Sissy

My extraordinary ordinary life; Sissy Spacek with Maryanne Vollers. Hyperion 2012 271 p.   **791.43**
1. Family life 2. Spacek, Sissy, 1949- 3. Motion picture industry -- History 4. Actors -- United States -- Biography 5. Motion picture actors and actresses -- United States -- Biography
ISBN 1401324363; 9781401324360
LC 2011047858

In this memoir, actress "Sissy Spacek writes about her idyllic, barefoot childhood in a small East Texas town. . . . [S]he describes how she arrived in New York City one star-struck summer as a seventeen-year-old carrying a suitcase and two guitars; and how she built a career that has spanned four decades with films such as 'Carrie,' 'Coal Miner's Daughter,' '3 Women,' and 'The Help.' She details working with some of the great directors of our time, including Terrence Malick, Robert Altman, David Lynch, and Brian De Palma. . . . She also reveals why, at the height of her fame, she and her family moved away from Los Angeles to a farm in rural Virginia." (Publisher's note)

Includes bibliographical references.

Spoto, Donald

The **dark** side of genius; the life of Alfred Hitchcock. {with a new introduction by the author} Centennial ed; Da Capo Press 1999 594p il pa $22   **791.43**
1. Motion picture directors
ISBN 0-306-80932-X
LC 99-37941

This is a reissue of the title first published 1983 by Little, Brown

This is a biography of the director of such films as The man who knew too much, The thirty-nine steps, The lady vanishes, Rebecca, Spellbound, Strangers on a train, Rear window, and Psycho

This "is a vivid and perceptive portrait of a man whose character was as strange and shadowed as his films. . . . Hitchcock's final obsession was secretiveness, but he has been well served by a knowledgeable and revealing biography." Time

Includes bibliographical references

Thomson, David, 1941-

★ The **big** screen; the story of the movies. David Thomson. 1st ed. Farrar, Straus and Giroux 2012 viii, 595 p.p (alk. paper) $35.00   **791.43**
1. Motion pictures -- Social aspects 2. Motion pictures -- United States -- History 3. Motion pictures -- Social aspects -- United States
ISBN 9780374191894; 0374191891
LC 2012009140

This book by David Thomson is "is a wide-ranging narrative about the movies and their signal role in modern life. Thomson takes us around the globe, through time, and across many media--moving from Eadweard Muybridge to Steve Jobs, from 'Sunrise' to 'I Love Lucy,' from John Wayne to George Clooney, from television commercials to streaming video--to tell the complex, gripping, paradoxical story of the movies." (Publisher's note)

Includes bibliographical references and index.

The **moment** of Psycho; how Alfred Hitchcock taught America to love murder. Basic Books 2009 192p $22.95   **791.43**
1. Motion picture directors 2. Psycho (Motion picture: 1960)
ISBN 978-0-465-00339-6
LC 2009-30821

"Though readers may not agree with all of Mr. Thomson's arguments here, he makes a powerful—and sometimes surprising—case for the movie's importance in film and cultural history. Building on the work of Francois Truffaut (who first helped establish Hitchcock's reputation as an auteur) and the writings of the critic Robin Wood, Mr. Thomson does a deft job in this volume of reappraising Hitchcock's work, even as he deconstructs Psycho and its complex cinematic legacy." N Y Times (Late N Y Ed)

Includes bibliographical references

★ The **whole** equation; a history of Hollywood. Knopf 2005 402p il hardcover o.p. pa $15 **791.43**
1. Motion picture industry -- History 2. Motion pictures -- History and criticism
ISBN 0-375-40016-8; 0-375-70154-0 pa
LC 2004-48358

"Peeling back the layers, goring sacred cows, correcting misconceptions, and revealing truth rather than reprinting legends, Thomson offers history, yes, but also a philosophical meditation on how the movie industry has inspired and influenced L.A. and America, and vice versa." Booklist

Includes bibliographical references

Tobolowsky, Stephen

The **Dangerous** Animals Club; Stephen Tobolowsky. 1st Simon & Schuster hc ed. Simon & Schuster 2012 viii, 338 p.p ill. (hardcover) $24.00; (paperback) $15.00   **791.43**
1. American wit and humor 2. Actors -- United States 3. Tobolowsky, Stephen, 1951-
ISBN 1451633157; 9781451633153; 9781451633160
LC 2011277873

In this book, "veteran character actor [Stephen] Tobolowsky . . . offers a . . . collection of autobiographical essays detailing his experiences in and out of show business. . . . He has been held hostage at gunpoint by a lunatic, suffered an apocalyptic infestation of fleas, barely eluded a goring by a bull, and auditioned with a broken neck. . . . Tobolowsky recounts his various heartbreaks, struggles as a young artist and status as a bemused member of the human race." (Kirkus Reviews)

Tropiano, Stephen

Obscene, indecent, immoral, and offensive; 100+ years of censored, banned, and controversial films. Limelight Editions 2009 364p il pa $19.95 **791.43**

1. Motion pictures -- Censorship
ISBN 978-0-87910-359-0

LC 2008-52582

"Though the book is grounded in examples from specific films, the main issues are not the instances of offensive material within a given film but the ensuing controversies and attempts to censor it. . . . This book is a quintessential work for any readers interested in studying issues of censorship in film . . . . It is written in such a way that the casual movie-goer is given enough background to understand the issues and in enough detail that even the most seasoned cinephile is likely to find new and interesting information." PopMatters

Urwand, Ben

The collaboration; Hollywood's pact with Hitler. Ben Urwand. The Belknap Press of Harvard University Press 2013 320 p. (hardcover : alk. paper) $26.95 **791.43**

1. National socialism 2. Germany -- History -- 1933-1945 3. Motion picture industry -- History 4. National socialism and motion pictures 5. Germany -- Civilization -- American influences 6. Motion picture industry -- United States -- History -- 20th century
ISBN 0674724747; 9780674724747

LC 2013013576

This book looks at the "alliance Hollywood made with the Nazis, which allowed both to keep packing movie theaters in Germany up until the outbreak of war. Concomitant with Hollywood's golden era of the 1930s was the rise of the Nazi Party, whose chief officials admired American films. . . . The result of this complicated and slippery relationship . . . was the absolute disappearance from film of Nazis and Jews until the end of the decade." (Kirkus Reviews)

Includes bibliographical references and index

Walker, Alexander (2000)

Stanley Kubrick, director; a visual analysis by Sybil Taylor and Ulrich Ruchti. rev and expanded; Norton 1999 376p il $35; pa $25 **791.43**

1. Motion picture directors
ISBN 0-393-04601-X; 0-393-32119-3 pa

LC 98-24086

First published 1998 in the United Kingdom

"Walker describes Kubrick as a guarded, suspicious, obsessive, controlling, paranoid workaholic, and makes us feel that he's bestowing a compliment. Each movie is given a thorough analysis, reinforced by the extensive use of stills in each case." Publ Wkly

Includes bibliographical references

Walker, Brent E.

Mack Sennett's Fun Factory; a history and filmography of his studio and his Keystone and Mack Sennett comedies, with biographies of players and personnel. [by] Brent E. Walker. McFarland Publishing 2009 671 p. il (pbk) $50; (hc) o.p. **791.43**

1. Motion picture producers and directors 2. Motion picture directors 3. Motion picture producers
ISBN 0786477113; 9780786477111; 9780786436101

LC 2009030637

This book, by Brent E. Walker, "is a comprehensive career study and filmography of Mack Sennett, cofounder of Keystone Studios, home of the Keystone Kops and other vehicles that showcased his innovative slapstick comedy. The filmography covers the more than 1,000 films Sennett produced, directed, wrote or appeared in between 1908 and 1955, including casts, credits, synopses, production and release dates." (Publisher's note)

Includes bibliographical references, filmography, and index

Warren, Bill

Keep watching the skies! American science fiction movies of the fifties. research associate, Bill Thomas; foreword by Howard Waldrop. 21st century ed.; McFarland & Co. 2010 1004p il $99 **791.43**

1. Reference books 2. Science fiction films
ISBN 978-0-7864-4230-0; 0-7864-4230-1

LC 2009-20594

First published in two volumes 1982-1986

Covers "nearly 300 films released between 1950 and 1962. . . . Although prominent films like Forbidden Planet, Them! The Time Machine, and The Fly receive more extensive coverage, all of the essays . . . include production, cast, and distribution credits; a plot synopsis; production details and fun background facts; discussion of the direction, acting, effects, and other prominent elements of the film; and information about public and critical reaction. Attractive photos accompany most of the essays, and posters for the best-known films are reproduced in 35 color plates. . . . Although the audience for 1950s science fiction may be dwindling, this is the kind of reference that not only informs but also creates new fans." Booklist

Includes bibliographical references

Wasson, Sam

Fifth Avenue, 5 AM; Audrey Hepburn, Breakfast at Tiffany's, and the dawn of the modern woman. HarperStudio 2010 xx, 231p il map $19.99 **791.43**

1. Actors 2. Breakfast at Tiffany's (Motion picture)
ISBN 978-0-06-177415-7

LC 2009-52439

The author "presents an irresistibly gossipy account of the production of Breakfast at Tiffany's (1961), charting the transformation of actress Audrey Hepburn into an icon of emerging sexual liberation—the good/bad girl, the lovable 'kook,' independent and sexually experienced but sufficiently charming to bring home to mother. Rich in incident and set among the glitterati of America's most glamorous era, the book reads like a novel." Kirkus

White, Rob

Todd Haynes; by Rob White. University of Illinois Press 2013 176 p. **791.43**

1. Motion picture producers and directors
ISBN 9780252037566; 9780252079108; 9780252094811

LC 2012032489

Author Rob White presents a study of film director Todd Hayne's work. Special attention is paid to the fascination with music culture (from the Carpenters to glam rock) and to the rich pattern of allusions to, or affinity with, predecessor filmmakers (Fassbinder, Ophuls, Sirk, and many more). But White's chief concern is the persistence of a queer impulse to explore social coercion." (Publisher's note)

Includes bibliographical references (p. [169]-172) and index

Includes filmography

Young, Clive

Homemade Hollywood; fans behind the camera. Continuum 2008 297p il $85; pa $19.95 **791.43**
1. Fan films
ISBN 978-0-8264-2922-3; 0-8264-2922-X; 978-0-8264-2923-0 pa; 0-8264-2923-8 pa

LC 2008-24007

An "overview of the fan-film experience and the renegades who've made the fan film both a refreshing puncture of the movie industry's inflated self-importance and a way to gauge how particular big-budget productions resonate, or fail to resonate, with the moviegoing public. Author Clive Young brings the rigors of a scholar and the inside-baseball of a fan to this well-researched and written survey of how doing it yourself has both helped drive our enduring love of motion pictures and to articulate the populist roots of that obsession." PopMatters

Includes bibliographical references

Zinoman, Jason

Shock value; how a few eccentric outsiders gave us nightmares, conquered Hollywood, and invented modern horror. Penguin Books 2011 274p il $25.95 **791.43**
1. Horror films 2. Horror films -- History and criticism
ISBN 978-1-59420-302-2; 1-59420-302-4

LC 2010-52279

"Today's filmgoers may think nothing of going to the local multiplex to see the latest incarnation of the Saw franchise, but New York Times theater reporter Zinoman reminds us of a time when such fare was restricted to drive-ins, while 'mainstream' horror consisted of cheesy Vincent Price movies or vampire films from Britain's Hammer studios. The change is attributed to a group of maverick writers and directors including Wes Craven, John Carpenter, Tobe Hooper and George Romero, makers of such films a Night of the Living Dead, The Last House on the Left, The Texas Chainsaw Massacre and Halloween, which created a new type of horror based on reality instead of fantasy. The author investigates the cultural conditions that made the 'New Horror' possible. . . . An engrossing look at an important cultural moment and a valuable addition to the canon of popular film history." Kirkus

Includes bibliographical references

791.44 Radio

Ely, Melvin Patrick

The **adventures** of Amos 'n' Andy; a social history of an American phenomenon. University Press of Va. 2001 xxi, 322p il pa $18.50 **791.44**
1. African Americans on television 2. Amos 'n' Andy (Radio program) 3. Amos 'n' Andy (Television program)
ISBN 0-8139-2092-2

LC 2001-45538

First published 1991 by Free Press

A "historian examines one of America's greatest cultural enigmas—the amazing popularity, among blacks as well as whites, of 'Amos 'n' Andy' on radio for more than 30 years." N Y Times Book Rev

Includes bibliographical references

791.45 Television

Becker, Christine

It's the pictures that got small; Hollywood film stars on 1950s television. Wesleyan University Press 2008 293p il (Wesleyan film) $70; pa $24.95 **791.45**
1. Actors 2. Television programs
ISBN 0819568937; 0819568945; 9780819568939; 9780819568946

LC 2008-29056

"Based on extensive archival research and amply documented, It's the Pictures That Got Small qualifies both as a contribution to the scholarly literature and as a general-interest book which is fun to read and would not be out of place in your beach bag. It includes an extensive bibliography and endnotes and four appendices documenting the appearances of established film stars on television programs." PopMatters

Bianculli, David

Dangerously funny; the uncensored story of The Smothers Brothers Comedy Hour. Simon & Schuster 2009 382p il $24.99 **791.45**
1. Smothers Brothers comedy hour (Television program)
ISBN 978-1-4391-0116-2; 1-4391-0116-7

LC 2009-36843

"By the time the Smothers got fired in 1969 (they bristle at the notion that the show was cancelled), Comedy Hour had become a benchmark for political expression and satire in prime time. . . . Bianculli devotes the bulk of his work to the period when Comedy Hour was conceived, produced and ultimately removed from its Sunday-night slot, leaving only a few chapters on Tom and Dick Smothers' career before and after the show. This feels right—the best stories are the increasingly dramatic week-to-week battles between the idealistic, strong-willed Tom Smothers and CBS censors and brass." Paste

Includes bibliographical references

Brooks, Tim

The **complete** directory to prime time network and cable TV shows, 1946-present; [by] Tim Brooks and Earle Marsh. 9th ed, completely rev and updated; Ballantine Books 2007 xxi, 1832p il pa $29.95 **791.45**

1. Television programs

ISBN 978-0-345-49773-4; 0-345-49773-2

First published 1979. Periodically revised

"Provides coverage of more than 5,000 nighttime series on commerical networks, with information on the type of show, broadcast history, cast, spin-offs, and plot or format. Index to actors and actresses. Appendixes list each season's prime time schedules, Emmy award winners, long-running and highly rated programs, and spin-offs. Coverage of original cable series began with the sixth edition." Ref Sources for Small & Medium-sized Libr. 6th edition

Davis, Michael

Street gang; the complete history of Sesame Street. Viking 2008 379p il $27.95 **791.45**

1. Sesame Street (Television program)

ISBN 978-0-670-01996-0; 0-670-01996-8

LC 2008-35498

This is a history of the children's television series that premiered on November 10, 1969.

"Any grown-up fan will relish this account, gaining an even greater appreciation for the cultural contributions of Kermit, Big Bird, Oscar the Grouch and all their neighbors." Publ Wkly

Includes bibliographical references

Giddins, Gary

Warning shadows; home alone with classic cinema. W. W. Norton & Company 2010 416p pa $18.95 **791.45**

1. Motion pictures -- History and criticism

ISBN 978-0-393-33792-1 pa; 0-393-33792-8 pa

LC 2009-49298

Giddins is as much of a fan as a critic, and since he's not a daily film reviewer, he hasn't been beaten down by constant exposure to insufferable movies. It's a mark of his enthusiasm that Warning Shadows makes me want to watch or re-watch nearly every movie he discusses. That includes Disney's insane-sounding 1945 musical The Three Caballeros featuring Donald Duck, Carmen Miranda's sister Aurora and Doa Luz as a disembodied head. The book begins with a new essay tracing, with regret, cinema's century-long migration from Radio City Music Hall to streaming laptops. The rest of the pieces cover directors, stars, genres and individual films. Giddins is especially good at assessing the totality of an artist's work. . . . [His] observations about actors' strengths and significance are consistently keen and often stingingly funny. Los Angeles Times

Harris, Bob

Prisoner of Trebekistan; a decade in Jeopardy! Crown Publishers 2006 339p $23.95 **791.45**

1. Jeopardy (Television program)

ISBN 0-307-33956-4; 978-0-307-33956-0

LC 2006-06267

"Harris' account is a personal story and manages to cram in enough fun facts to keep any trivia nut happy." Booklist

Includes bibliographical references

Hewitt, Don

Tell me a story; 50 years and 60 minutes in television. PublicAffairs 2001 272p il $26; pa $15 **791.45**

1. Television producers 2. 60 minutes (Television program)

ISBN 1-58648-017-0; 1-58648-141-X pa

LC 2001-16222

"Hewitt has positive things to say about most of the reporters and anchors he discusses, but his comments about the several generations of CBS executives and owners for whom he has worked are less consistently sunny. At 78, Hewitt remains blunt, opinionated, and full of ideas about where TV news has been and where it's going. His life may be one of the more interesting stories the veteran newsman has ever told." Booklist

Kanfer, Stefan

Ball of fire; the tumultuous life and comic art of Lucille Ball. Knopf 2003 361p il $25.95; pa $15 **791.45**

1. Actors

ISBN 0-375-41315-4; 0-375-72771-X pa

LC 2002-43090

This is a biography of the comedian and star of the television shows I Love Lucy, The Lucy Show, and Here's Lucy

"A fine accumulation of research . . . balanced by Kanfer's insight into what Ball's contribution means in the context of entertainment history, this is the first study to examine all aspects of Ball's life, work, and business acumen." Libr J

Includes bibliographical references

Larsen, Darl

Monty Python's flying circus; an utterly complete, thoroughly unillustrated, absolutely unauthorized guide to possibly all the references: from Arthur Two-Sheds Jackson to Zambesi. Scarecrow Press 2008 563p $150 **791.45**

1. Monty Python's flying circus (Television program)

ISBN 978-0-8108-6131-2; 0-8108-6131-3

LC 2007-52082

"American readers will benefit from definitions of uniquely British phenomena (e.g., anything associated with cricket). Along with explication, the essays on occasion look at the series within the cultural context of the late 1960s, touching on such topics as its treatment of homosexuality or women. Larsen . . . is a devoted fan who exhaustively analyzes the series without ever obscuring its unique brand of humor." Libr J

Includes bibliographical references

Martin, Brett

Difficult men; behind the scenes of a creative revolution: from The Sopranos and The Wire to Mad Men and Breaking Bad. by Brett Martin. The Penguin Press 2013 320 p. (hardcover) $27.95 **791.45**

1. Television -- History 2. Characters and characteristics on television 3. Television series -- United States 4. Television program genres -- United States 5. Cable television -- United States -- History 6. Television

broadcasting -- Social aspects -- United States
ISBN 1594204195; 9781594204197

LC 2012047001

Here, Brett Martin "names the period spanning 1999 to 2013 'the third golden age of television,'" and considers what made it possible. He looks at the rise of shows with a "serialized narrative, as opposed to the syndication-friendly stand-alone episodes common in broadcast television. A little later, shows like The Wire, The Sopranos, and Mad Men subverted network formulas to present flawed, even nihilistic antiheros wrestling with inner demons." (Publishers Weekly)

Includes bibliographical references.

Miller, James Andrew

Those guys have all the fun; inside the world of ESPN. [by] James Andrew Miller and Tom Shales. Little, Brown and Company 2011 763p il $27.99 **791.45**

1. ESPN, Inc. 2. Television broadcasting of sports
ISBN 0316043001; 9780316043007

This book "presents the history of sports channel ESPN based on interviews with . . . current and former employees, featuring announcers and analysts as well as sports stars including LeBron James, Peyton Manning, and Jeff Gordon." (Publisher's note) Index.

"Compiled from more than 550 interviews, Those Guys traces ESPN from its birth as an underdog to its current status as a money-printing behemoth. Some of the best sections deal with the early days of cable, when the network invented itself through savvy business decisions and slow-pitch-softball coverage. But it's the big libidos and bigger egos that will get the most attention. The book is packed with entertaining stories of unpleasant people and awful behavior: booze-fueled boorishness, absurdly arrogant execs, and the endlessly fascinating Olbermann. . . . Miller and Shales offer compelling behind-the-scenes tales of many major sports moments, including the Rush Limbaugh–Donovan McNabb flap and ESPN's takeover of Monday Night Football." Entertainment Wkly

Richards, Thomas

The **meaning** of Star Trek. Doubleday 1997 194p hardcover o.p. pa $15 **791.45**

1. Star trek: The next generation (Television program)
ISBN 0-385-48439-9 pa

LC 97-6845

"One of the best recent Star Trek books and also one of the most cogent, exciting recent literary analyses." Booklist

Stelter, Brian

Top of the morning; inside the cutthroat world of morning tv. Brian Stelter. Grand Central Pub. 2013 320 p. (hardcover) $28 **791.45**

1. Television broadcasting of news 2. Today show (Television program) 3. Good morning America (Television program)
ISBN 1455512877; 9781455512874; 9781455545360

LC 2013932327

This book looks at the struggles between the morning news television programs "Today" and "Good Morning America." It "commences with the decision of producer Jim

Bell to remove struggling co-host Ann Curry from Today. As that story unfolds, Stelter periodically returns us to the earliest days of Today (1952: with Dave Garroway and chimp J. Fred Muggs) and to the beginnings of GMA in 1975." (Kirkus Reviews)

791.5   Puppetry and toy theaters

Blumenthal, Eileen

★ **Puppetry**; a world history. Abrams 2005 272p il $65 **791.5**

1. Puppets and puppet plays
ISBN 0-8109-5587-3

LC 2004-29349

This is a "history of the puppet world, from prehistoric times to Tony-winning Broadway hit Avenue Q. . . . This would be a welcome addition to the libraries of performing arts buffs who want to learn more about a lesser known form." Publ Wkly

Includes bibliographical references

791.8   Animal performances

Buffalo Bill, 1846-1917

The **Wild** West in England; William F. Cody ; edited and with an introduction by Frank Christianson. University of Nebraska Press 2012 xii, 207 p.p (The papers of William F. "Buffalo Bill" Cody) (paperback) $17.95; (hardcover) $75.00 **791.8**

1. Rodeos 2. Pioneers -- West (U.S.) -- Biography 3. Wild west shows -- England -- History 4. Entertainers -- United States -- Biography
ISBN 0803240546; 9780803240544; 9780803243880

LC 2012014820

This book, edited by Frank Christianson, offers the papers of the U.S. Western showman William F. "Buffalo Bill" Cody. "Here Cody describes his Wild West exhibition, the show that offered audiences a mythic experience of the American frontier. Focusing on the show's first season of performances in England, Cody includes excerpts of numerous laudatory descriptions of his show from the English press as well as stories of his time spent with British nobility." (Publisher's note)

Includes bibliographical references (p. [203]-204) and index

Hemingway, Ernest

The **dangerous** summer; introduction by James A. Michener. Scribner 1985 228p il hardcover o.p. pa $13 **791.8**

1. Bullfights 2. Spain -- Description
ISBN 0-684-83789-7 pa

LC 84-27578

A look at the "personal and professional rivalry of the two greatest bullfighters since the death of Manolete in 1947: Luis Miguel Dominguín and Antonio Ordóñez. The Dangerous Summer provides an insider's view based on extensive experience, mingles memory and desire, and is essential reading for anyone interested in the subject or the author." Natl Rev

★ **Death** in the afternoon. Scribner 1999 397p il $35   **791.8**
    1. Bullfights
    ISBN 0-684-85922-X

                         LC 99-231717

First published 1932

"A loosely organized book on bullfighting in Spain. . . . Hemingway depicts the bullfight as an emblematic tragedy, a test of courage, with a bloody and not entirely predictable end. Throughout, he digresses to philosophize on life and death in exchanges with a character he calls the Old Lady." HarperCollins Reader's Ency of Am Lit. 2nd edition

Lewine, Edward

    Death and the sun; a matador's season in the heart of Spain. Houghton Mifflin 2005 258p map $24   **791.8**
    1. Bullfights
    ISBN 0-618-26325-X

                         LC 2005-40424

This is an account of a year spent observing the Spanish matador Francisco Rivera Ordonez.

"What Lewine has created may be the most in-depth, incisively written literary guide to bullfighting available in English. Every drunken sophomore riding the rails to Pamplona this summer ought to keep a volume in his backpack." N Y Times Book Rev

Includes bibliographical references

Peter, Josh

    Fried twinkies, buckle bunnies & bull riders; a year inside the professional bull riders tour. Rodale 2005 246p il $24.95   **791.8**
    1. Bull riding 2. Professional Bull Riders, Inc.
    ISBN 1-59486-119-6

                         LC 2005-17297

"The argument can be made that the Professional Bull Riders Tour may be the most dangerous, least financially rewarding of all sporting endeavors. Skull fractures, punctured lungs, and destroyed knees are all relatively routine injuries. At least now there is a million-dollar payout for the overall champion each season, but even that is in deferred dollars. Peter, a sportswriter for the New Orleans Times-Picayune, spent the 2004 season with the PBR tour and offers a penetrating portrait of a sport that stands at that awkward stage between minor league and national acceptance. . . . Fried Twinkies are a genuine but rare concession delicacy, and buckle bunnies are the young ladies who curry the favor of the young macho men who ride the bulls. This is a tough book to walk away from." Booklist

792   Stage presentations

Adler, Stella

    ★ **Stella** Adler: the art of acting; compiled and edited by Howard Kissel. Applause Theatre Bk. Pubs. 2000 271p il $25.95   **792**
    1. Acting
    ISBN 1-55783-373-7

In this collection of Adler's papers Kissel "has taken tapes, transcriptions, notebooks, and other sources to reconstruct an acting course in 22 lessons. . . . The lessons are graduated from very basic matters to quite complex issues of textual analysis and decorum. Though mostly monologs, they include enough exercises and student responses to get the flavor of Adler's work. . . . This is required reading for anyone interested in theater practice." Libr J

Bernhardt, Sarah

    My double life: the memoirs of Sarah Bernhardt; translated by Victoria Tietze Larson. State Univ. of N.Y. Press 1999 345p $26.50; pa $25.95   **792**
    1. Actors
    ISBN 0-7914-4053-2; 0-7914-4054-0 pa

                         LC 98-30036

This is a newly translated abridgment of Bernhardt's autobiography originally published 1907

"The most tempestuous and possibly the most famous actress of her time, Bernhardt . . . is presented as both melodramatic and frustratingly discreet." Publ Wkly

Includes bibliographical references (p. 331-332) and index

Brestoff, Richard

    The **actor's** wheel of connection; how to integrate your skills and refine your performance. Smith and Kraus 2005 160p (Career development series) $16.95   **792**
    1. Acting
    ISBN 1-57525-391-7

                         LC 2005-44120

"Brestoff draws on the teachings of the great acting teachers–such as Strasberg, Adler, Meisner, Grotowski, and Stanislavsky–in shaping and explaining his methods. Although probably not appropriate for beginners, his wheel will appeal to actors grappling with disparate techniques." BackStage

Briggs, Jody

    ★ **Encyclopedia** of stage lighting; foreword by Scott Nolte. McFarland & Co. 2003 334p il $95; pa $49.95   **792**
    1. Reference books 2. Stage lighting -- Encyclopedias
    ISBN 0-7864-1512-6; 0-7864-4043-0 pa

                         LC 2003-7619

"Peppered with some 300 simple line drawings and diagrams to illustrate basic concepts, this work emphasizes the principles and practices of the founding fathers of theatrical lighting, among whom are Stanley McCandless, Ariel Davis, Adolphe Appia, and Gordan Craig. . . . This book often goes beyond most encyclopedias, addressing standard lighting procedures and practices, briefly outlining the historical development of theatrical lighting, and providing strategies for dealing with theater directors and other theatrical personalities." Choice

Includes bibliographical references

Brook, Peter

The **empty** space. Atheneum 1968 141p hardcover o.p. pa $11   **792**
1. Drama 2. Theater
ISBN 0-684-82957-6 pa

LC 68-12531

The author "distinguishes four types of theater: the Deadly Theatre (conventional), the Holy Theatre (ritualistic), the Rough Theatre (combative), and the Immediate Theatre (mutative and organic). An impassioned treatise that is also very accessible and direct." Libr J

Chekhov, Michael

To the actor; {rev and expanded ed. by Mala Powers}; Routledge 2002 lii, 222p il $75; pa $19.95   **792**
1. Acting
ISBN 0-415-25875-8; 0-415-25876-6 pa
First published 1953 by Harper & Row

"Chekhov is among a handful of master acting teachers who have profoundly influenced not only a constellation of famous stars but also shaped an acting style and sensibility. . . . This new edition contains all of Chekhov's brilliant insights, techniques, and exercises, as well as a previously unpublished chapter on the 'Psychological Gesture,' a central precept of his system." Libr J

Includes bibliographical references

Clinton, Catherine

Fanny Kemble's civil wars. Oxford Univ. Press 2001 302p il pa $24   **792**
1. Poets 2. Actors 3. Novelists 4. Abolitionists 5. Memoirists
ISBN 0-19-514815-0

LC 2001-21405

First published 2000 by Simon & Schuster

"This biography is every bit as sharp, evocative and eloquent as Kemble's Journal." Publ Wkly

Includes bibliographical references

Corson, Richard

Stage makeup; [by] Richard Corson, Beverly Gore Norcross, James Glavan. 10th ed.; Ally & Bacon/Pearson 2009 xx, 407p il $141.40   **792**
1. Theatrical makeup
ISBN 978-0-205-64454-4

LC 2008-53845

First published 1942 by Appleton. Periodically revised

The authors discuss the art and technique of theatrical makeup, covering such topics as facial anatomy, various methods for applying greasepaint and other makeup, and the use of beards, wigs, and prosthetic pieces.

Croall, Jonathan

Gielgud; a theatrical life, 1904-2000. Continuum 2001 579p il $35; pa $24.95   **792**
1. Actors 2. Theatrical directors 3. Theatrical producers
ISBN 0-8264-1333-1; 0-8264-1403-6 pa

LC 2001-28019

Croall examines the life and career of the British actor, director, and producer

"Witty and well-written as well as well-researched, Croall's fine and complete portrait of the man and his endearing charm often reads more like a novel than like nonfiction." Booklist

Includes bibliographical references and index

Gillette, J. Michael

Designing With Light: An Introduction to Stage Lighting; an introduction to stage lighting. Michael Gillette, Michael J. McNamara. 6th ed. McGraw-Hill 2013 379 p. ill. (some col.) pa. $143.45 **792**
1. Stage lighting
ISBN 9780073514239

LC 2012034637

"Designing with Light' is a comprehensive survey of the practical and aesthetic aspects of stage lighting design. The authors approach stage lighting design as an art that integrates the vision of director, actor, and playwright, and as a craft that provides practical solutions for the manipulation of stage space. The sixth edition offers a wealth of new information on new trends in lighting design." (Publisher's Note)

The author "divides his standard text for undergraduate lighting design students into the two constituent elements of his craft—technology and design. He clearly and completely presents both technical and aesthetic design aspects." Libr J

Theatrical design and production; An Introduction to Scene Design and Construction, Lighting, Sound, Costume, and Makeup. 7th ed. McGraw-Hill Higher Education 2012 624 p. hardcover $192.45   **792**
1. Theaters -- Stage setting and scenery 2. Stage management. 3. Theater--Production and direction. 4. Theaters--Stage-setting and scenery.
ISBN 9780073382227

LC 2012020022

First published 1987 by Mayfield

"Theatrical Design and Production is a comprehensive and practical survey that examines the technical and design aspects of play production, including scene design and construction, lighting, sound, costume, and makeup. Design is presented as both an art closely integrated with the director's, actor's, and playwright's visions, and a craft that provides practical solutions for the physical manipulation of stage space."

Includes bibliographical references

Hagen, Uta

Respect for acting; by Uta Hagen with Haskel Frankel. Macmillan 1973 227p $19.95   **792**
1. Acting
ISBN 0-02-547390-5

This "classic treatise on the process and craft of acting has significantly benefited actors for three decades. Juxtaposed with Hagen's aesthetic is a wealth of practical information, creative ideas, and her uniquely useful object exercises." Libr J

Lewis, Roger

The **real** life of Laurence Olivier. Applause Theatre Bk. Pubs. 1997 272p il $25.95; pa $18.95 **792**
1. Actors
ISBN 1-55783-298-6; 1-55783-413-X pa

LC 97-31702

First published 1996 in the United Kingdom
This is a life of the English stage and screen actor
"Lewis enjoys exploring the details that make up such a rich life—Olivier seemed to have met everyone, known everyone, and played every major role in existence. The indexing and photographs are quite good." Libr J

Lipton, James

Inside Inside. Dutton 2007 492p il $27.95 **792**
1. Actors Studio 2. Inside the Actors Studio (Television program)
ISBN 978-0-525-95035-6; 0-525-95035-4

LC 2007-12790

This book from the host of the television program Inside The Actors Studio interweaves anecdotal stories from the author's own life with excerpts from interviews with actors given on that program.
"The anecdotes from the fine actors who have appeared on Inside the Actors Studio and the manifold insights into the craftsmanship of acting together justify the purchase of this exemplary book. An unqualified hit among this season's theatrical offerings and a necessary purchase for all performing arts collections." Libr J

Mamet, David

True and false; heresy and common sense for the actor. Pantheon Bks. 1997 127p hardcover o.p. pa $11 **792**
1. Acting
ISBN 0-679-77264-2 pa

LC 97-19336

"Mamet exhorts actors to show up early, have their lines down cold, and have a single objective for each scene. He contends that overthinking and too much emotional interpretation is not the actor's role. Essential reading for theater collections." Libr J

Marasco, Ron

Notes to an actor. Ivan R. Dee 2007 214p $24.95 **792**
1. Acting
ISBN 978-1-56663-757-2; 1-56663-757-0

LC 2007-11653

This is "a compendium of suggestions, inspirations, warnings, and musings about the art of acting. Marasco speaks to actors who already possess at least a basic knowledge of their craft, seeking to heighten their abilities, clarify their artistic choices, eliminate blocks, and make their work more exciting and enriching. . . . This book is truly unique among acting resources. Useful both to those seeking to further their development as actors and to those for whom

acting has long been a profession, this is an insightful, invaluable, and definitive work." Choice
Includes bibliographical references

Moore, Sonia

★ The **Stanislavski** system; the professional training of an actor. digested from the teachings of Konstantin S. Stanislavski. 2nd rev ed; Penguin Bks. 1984 96p pa $12.95 **792**
1. Acting 2. Actors 3. Theatrical directors
ISBN 0-14-046660-6

LC 84-2855

First published 1960 with title: The Stanislavski method
This is a concise, simplified guide to the teachings of the great master of the Moscow Art Theater

★ The **Oxford** companion to theatre and performance; edited by Dennis Kennedy. Oxford University Press 2010 689p $45 (2011) **792**
1. Reference books 2. Theater -- Encyclopedias 3. Performing arts -- Encyclopedias
ISBN 978-0-19-957419-3
"This is a one-volume updated version of the two-volume Oxford Encyclopedia of Theatre & Performance published in 2003. Kennedy . . . has succeeded in pulling together 2400 entries intended to educate, delight, and encourage the reader to pursue more in-depth information." Libr J

Stanislavsky, Konstantin

★ An **actor's** work; a student's diary. [by] Konstantin Stanislavski; translated and edited by Jean Benedetti. Routledge 2008 693p $35 **792**
1. Acting
ISBN 9780415422239; 0-415-42223-X

LC 2007-45357

A combined translation of Stanislavsky's An actor prepares and Building a character, which describe and illustrate the principles of method acting.
This "translation by Benedetti of Stanislavski's famous works . . . will be greeted with excitement by actors everywhere." Libr J
Includes bibliographical references

Creating a role; [by] Constantin Stanislavski; translated by Elizabeth Reynolds Hapgood; edited by Hermine I. Popper; foreword by Robert Lewis. Routledge 2003 271p pa $19.95 **792**
1. Acting
ISBN 0-87830-981-0

LC 91-228412

"Stanislavski unifies his conceptual canon and applies it to detailed preparatory work for the roles of Othello and Gogol's Inspector General." Libr J

Thomas, Mike

The **Second** City unscripted; revolution and revelation at the world-famous comedy theater. Villard 2009 272p il $26 **792**
1. Comedians 2. Second City (Comedy troupe)
ISBN 978-0-345-51422-6; 0-345-51422-X

LC 2009-33132

"For 50 years, Chicago's Second City Theater has been the training ground for legendary comedians. From John Belushi to Stephen Colbert, many of America and Canada's finest comic talents have honed their skills on Second City's stage, and this collection of interviews brings together comedians and behind-the-scenes players to bare the secrets of the comedy laboratory where improv was birthed by lesser-known genius Del Close. . . . Though occasionally meandering, Thomas corrals his subjects' testimony in a historical framework paralleling the larger baby boomer narrative, progressing from fringe revolutionaries to institutional stalwarts." Publ Wkly

bibliography: p. 259-264

Tynan, Kenneth, 1927-1980

The **diaries** of Kenneth Tynan; edited by John Lahr. Bloomsbury Press 2001 439p il $32.95; pa $16.95 **792**

1. Drama critics 2. Authors, English -- 20th century -- Diaries 3. Theater critics -- Great Britain -- Diaries
ISBN 1-58234-160-5; 1-58234-245-8 pa

LC 2001-35274

These are the diaries of the English theater critic who wrote the musical "Oh! Calcutta!"

Tynan "was one of Britain's foremost drama critics; here, he spent two seasons as theater critic for the New Yorker. Along with Laurence Olivier, he helped found London's National Theater, where he functioned as literary manager for 10 years. Not surprisingly, Tynan dissects theatrical foibles and politicking with a keen inside perspective; he can also discourse on the European common market, Spaniards' attitudes toward homosexuality, cricket, French cuisine, Ethel Merman and much more. . . . Celebrated names are not merely dropped (from Katharine Hepburn and Princess Margaret to W.H. Auden and Jerry Lewis), but integral to his revelatory anecdotes." Publ Wkly

792.09 History, geographic treatment, biography

Brockett, Oscar G.

History of the theatre; [by] Oscar G. Brockett, Franklin J. Hildy. 10th ed; Pearson 2008 688p il map $113 **792.09**

1. Theater -- History 2. Drama -- History and criticism
ISBN 978-0-205-51186-0

LC 2009-291794

First published 1968

This work traces the development of the theater from primitive times to the present, with an emphasis on European theater.

Includes bibliographical references

792.5 Opera

Grout, Donald Jay

★ A **short** history of opera; {by} Donald Jay Grout and Hermine Weigel Williams. 4th ed; Columbia University Press 2003 1030p $65 **792.5**

1. Opera
ISBN 0-231-11958-5

LC 2002-41470

First published 1947

"After surveying anticipations of the operatic form in the lyric theater of the Greeks, medieval dramatic music, and other forerunners, the book reveals the genre's beginnings in the seventeenth century and follows its progress to the present day. . . . The section on twentieth-century opera {is organized} around national operatic traditions, including a chapter devoted solely to opera in the United States that incorporates material on the American musical and ties between classical opera and popular musical theater. A separate section on Chinese opera is also included." Publisher's note

Includes bibliographical references

Osborne, Charles

The **complete** operas of Mozart; a critical guide. Da Capo Press 1986 349p il pa $17.95 **792.5**

1. Composers 2. Opera -- Stories, plots, etc.
ISBN 978-0-306-80190-7; 0-306-80190-6

First published 1978 by Atheneum

In this introduction to Mozart's operas, "each opera is treated as a separate chapter. . . . Each chapter begins with a separate page containing the dramatis personae and their voice range . . . the date, place, and cast for the first performance . . . the name of the librettist, and the Kochel number." Choice

The **complete** operas of Puccini; a critical guide. Da Capo Press 1983 279p il pa $9.95 **792.5**

1. Composers 2. Opera -- Stories, plots, etc.
ISBN 0-306-80200-7; 978-0-306-80200-3

LC 83-10142

First published 1982 by Atheneum

The author "provides general background information on all 13 Puccini operas. . . . Unencumbered by technical language, this enjoyably written book is accessible to all admirers of one of the most popular opera composers of all time." Choice

Includes bibliographical references

The **complete** operas of Richard Wagner. Da Capo Press 1993 288p il pa $16.95 **792.5**

1. Composers 2. Opera -- Stories, plots, etc.
ISBN 0-306-80522-7; 978-0-306-80522-6

LC 92-34417

First published 1990 in the United Kingdom

In this book, "biography—often in Wagner's own words—combined with criticism by Wagner's contemporaries, literary background, Wagner's librettos, plot summaries, descriptions of musical elements illustrated with musical examples, and Osborne's own insights form a clear picture of Wagner, his world, and the operas." Libr J

Includes bibliographical references

792.6   Musical plays

Bloom, Ken

Broadway musicals; the 101 greatest shows of all time. [by] Ken Bloom & Frank Vlastnik; new preface by Broadway's leading ladies; foreword by Jerry Orbach. Rev. and updated ed.; Black Dog & Leventhal 2010 344p il $40   **792.6**
1. Musicals
ISBN 978-1-57912-849-4
First published 2004

This is a history of Broadway musicals from the past 100 years. Each entry features commentary, photos and brief features on performers and creators.

Boland, Robert

Musicals! directing school and community theatre. {by} Robert Boland and Paul Argentini. Scarecrow Press 1997 xxv, 202p il pa $35   **792.6**
1. Musicals -- Production and direction
ISBN 0-8108-3323-9

LC 97-11996

This is "a handbook for novice directors of the musical. This illustrated nuts-and-bolts compendium includes 22 chapters divided among three major sections addressing preparation, production, and performance. Through accessible prose and a you-can-do-it tone, the authors provide an overview of preproduction planning, auditioning and casting, blocking, stage composition, rehearsals, and choreography, as well as the more technical layers of set design, costumes, and lights." Libr J
Includes bibliographical references

Hischak, Thomas

The Oxford companion to the American musical; theatre, film, and television. [by] Thomas S. Hischak. Oxford University Press 2008 923p il $39.95 **792.6**
1. Reference books 2. Musicals -- Dictionaries
ISBN 9780195335330

LC 2007-52436

This is an "overview of the American musical theater on the stage, silver screen, and small screen. The 2000-plus entries are brief but detailed accounts of plots; production histories; careers of actors, dancers, musicians, lyricists, composers, choreographers, and directors; organizations; and genres (animated musicals, frontier musicals). . . . This thorough work provides enjoyable reading for anyone interested in American theatrical history in general and musicals in particular." SLJ
Includes discography and bibliographical references (p. 899-902)

Kantor, Michael

★ Broadway : the American musical; [by] Michael Kantor; Laurence Maslon. Bulfinch Press 2004 480p il $60   **792.6**
1. Musicals
ISBN 0-8212-2905-2

LC 2003-69715

This companion volume to a PBS documentary includes interviews and photographs of Broadway musicals from 1893 to 2004
"With its beguiling blend of entertainment and history, this splendid work is a must-have." Publ Wkly
Includes bibliographical references

Stempel, Larry

Showtime; a history of the Broadway musical theater. W. W. Norton & Company 2010 xx, 826p il $39.95   **792.6**
1. Musicals 2. Musicals -- New York (N.Y.)
ISBN 978-0-393-06715-6; 0-393-06715-7

LC 2010-19704

Beginning in the seventeenth-century United States, well before Broadway existed, Stempel presents the multiple theatrical adventures that would lead from various directions to 'West Side Story' (1957) and 'Les Misérables' (1987). He examines not only minstrelsy, vaudeville, and European operetta—the musical's well-known precursors—but also the Astor Place riot of 1849, an event that publicly performed the ever-hardening divisions of class and culture among American audiences. Later, Stempel describes off-Broadway performances . . . beginning with the Works Progress Administration and the Little Theatre movement, progressing to 'Hair' (1968), which eventually transferred to Broadway, and nodding to regional theaters where many shows originated." (Journal of American History)
"Theater buffs will be delighted to find that this scholarly, definitive work is also a hugely entertaining read." Publ Wkly
Includes discography and bibliographical references

792.7   Variety shows and theatrical dancing

Downer, Lesley

Women of the pleasure quarters; the secret history of the geisha. Broadway Bks. 2001 288p il hardcover o.p. pa $14.95   **792.7**
1. Geishas 2. Japan -- Social life and customs
ISBN 0-7679-0490-7 pa

LC 00-49409

The author "skillfully intertwines her profiles of Kyoto personalities and tea-house customs with a fluidly written geisha history that's unabashedly aimed at a Western audience. . . . Written in dynamic, highly readable prose, the book is supported by exhaustive research and a lengthy bibliography." Publ Wkly
Includes bibliographical references and index

Josephson, Barney

Cafe Society; the wrong place for the right people. Barney Josephson; with Terry Trilling-Josephson; foreword by Dan Morgenstern. University of Illinois Press 2009 376p il (Music in American life) $32.95   **792.7**
1. Café Society (New York, N.Y.: Nightclub) 2. Greenwich Village (New York (N.Y.) -- Social life and customs
ISBN 978-0-252-03413-8; 0-252-03413-9

LC 2008-27205

"An epic ode to personal integrity, creative vision and entrepreneurial tenacity, shedding timely light on the germination of the civil-rights movement." Kirkus

Includes bibliographical references

Kohen, Yael

We killed; the rise of women in American comedy. Yael Kohen. Sarah Crichton Books 2012 xxviii, 308 p.p ill.   **792.7**

1. Stand-up comedy -- United States 2. Women comedians -- United States -- Biography 3. Women comedians -- United States -- Interviews

ISBN 9780374287238

LC 2012018565

In this book, Yael Kohen "pieces together the revolution that happened to (and by) women in American comedy, gathering the country's most prominent comediennes and the . . . colleagues who revolved around them. She starts in the 1950s, when comic success meant ridiculing and de-sexualizing yourself; when Joan Rivers and Phyllis Diller emerged as America's favorite frustrated ladies. . . . Kohen brings us into the sixties and seventies, when the appearance of smart, edgy comedians (Elaine May, Lily Tomlin) and the women's movement brought a new wave of radicals." (Publisher's note)

Nachman, Gerald

★ Seriously funny; the rebel comedians of the 1950s and 1960s. Pantheon Bks. 2003 659p il $29.95   **792.7**

1. Comedians 2. Wit and humor

ISBN 0-375-41030-9

LC 2002-30713

Nachman examines American comedians, including "Mort Sahl, Sid Caesar, Tom Lehrer, Steve Allen, Stan Freberg, Ernie Kovacs, Phyllis Diller, Jonathan Winters, Shelley Berman, Nichols and May, Bob & Ray, Bob Newhart, Lenny Bruce, the Smothers Brothers, Mel Brooks, Dick Gregory, Woody Allen, Bill Cosby, [and] Joan Rivers. . . . 'Taken together, [Nachman writes], they made up the faculty of a new school of vigorous, socially aware satire, a dazzling group of voices that reigned roughly from 1953 to 1965.'" N Y Times Book Rev

Includes bibliographical references

Robinson, Ray

American original: a life of Will Rogers. Oxford Univ. Press 1996 288p il $34   **792.7**

1. Actors 2. Humorists 3. Entertainers 4. Columnists

ISBN 0-19-508693-7

LC 95-31578

In this biography of the American humorist, Robinson attempts "to separate fact from legend and build up a composite portrait of the man. As such, the book is so complete and thorough that until, if ever, new material comes to light, it can scarcely be superseded. Robinson's admiration for Rogers is evident on every page, but that does not blind him to Rogers's faults." Libr J

Tray S. D.

No applause, just throw money; or, The book that made vaudeville famous; a high-class, refined entertainment. Faber and Faber 2005 328p il $25 **792.7**

1. Vaudeville

ISBN 0-571-21192-5

LC 20050-9787

This book documents the history and legacy of vaudeville in the United States.

"One of the year's best historical performing arts texts; a wonderful story wonderfully told." Libr J

Includes bibliographical references

Vollmann, William T.

Kissing the mask; beauty, understatement, and femininity in Japanese Noh theater: with some thoughts on muses (especially Helga Testorf), transgender women, kabuki goddesses, porn queens, poets, housewives, makeup arti. Ecco 2010 504p il $29.99   **792.7**

1. Kabuki 2. Geishas 3. Gender role 4. Transgender people 5. Nō 6. Sex role 7. Femininity 8. Nō plays 9. Women -- Psychology 10. Transgendered people 11. Feminine beauty (Aesthetics) 12. Women in the theater -- Japan

ISBN 0-06-122848-6; 978-0-06-122848-3

Vollmann looks "into the Japanese craft of Noh theater, using the medium as a prism to . . . [examine] the conception of beauty itself." (Publisher's note) Glossary. Chronology. Bibliography.

"Characteristically peripatetic, 'Kissing the Mask' rambles across vast territory in an effort to corral — or at least contemplate — the concept of feminine beauty. Throughout, Vollmann focuses an obsessed and adoring lens on the Noh master Umewaka Rokuro, the Kabuki geishas, and a transgender community in Los Angeles while simultaneously traipsing through Indian, American, European and Norse cultures in an effort to identify what it is (presumption? physiology? carriage?) that makes a woman a woman. Along the way, he pays homage yet again to his pet subject — prostitutes — about whom he has notoriously raved and written throughout his career. Courting controversy, flouting convention, 'Kissing the Mask' is classic Vollmann, right down to the dilettante manner in which he inserts himself directly into his subject." Portland Oregonian

Includes bibliographical references

Yagoda, Ben

Will Rogers; a biography. Knopf 1993 409p il pa $24.95   **792.7**

1. Actors 2. Humorists 3. Air pilots 4. Entertainers 5. Columnists 6. Theatrical producers

ISBN 0-8061-3238-8

LC 92-40177

This is a biography of "the rope-twirling vaudeville monologist, salty political commentator, silent film actor and New York Times columnist. . . . [This is] a resonant portrait imbued with Rogers's irreverent spirit, yet attuned to both the strengths and limitations of his commonsense, cracker-barrel world view." Publ Wkly

Includes bibliographical references

792.7092   Variety shows--biography

Faleiro, Sonia

Beautiful thing; inside the secret world of Bombay's dance bars. Sonia Faleiro. Black Cat 2012 216 p.   **792.7092**

1. Dancers 2. Poverty 3. Bombay (India) 4. Women -- India 5. Human trafficking
ISBN 9780670084050

LC 2010347432

In this book, author Sonia Faleiro "mines the gritty underworld of Bombay's dance bars, where dancers perform for male patrons in . . . the hope of escape from poverty. She spent five years shadowing Leela, a teenage dancer. . . . Leela and . . . Priya, her confidante and fellow dancer, consider themselves a cut above women who sell their services on the streets and in brothels. But when a self-seeking politician . . . shut[s] down Bombay's dance bars, the two are left with few options. Faleiro paints a . . . picture of rape, physical abuse, and sexual slavery, often perpetrated on women like Leela by their own families. But Leela's fearlessness keeps her afloat . . . where the cops are as corrupt as the gangsters and HIV an unspoken but constant threat." (Publishers Weekly)

792.8   Ballet and modern dance

Craine, Debra

★ The Oxford dictionary of dance; [by] Debra Craine, Judith Mackrell. 2nd ed.; Oxford University Press 2010 502p il (Oxford paperback reference) pa $18.95   **792.8**

1. Reference books 2. Dance -- Dictionaries
ISBN 978-0-19-956344-9; 0-19-956344-6

LC 2010-930321

Based on The concise Oxford dictionary of ballet by Horst Kroegler. First published 2000

"The work covers all aspects of the diverse dance world from classical ballet to modern, from flamenco to hip-hop, from tap to South Asian dance forms and includes . . . entries on technical terms, steps, styles, works and countries, in addition to many biographies of dancers, choreographers, and companies." Publisher's note

Includes bibliographical references

Goldner, Nancy

Balanchine variations. University Press of Florida 2008 132p il pa $24.95   **792.8**

1. Ballet 2. Dancers 3. Choreographers
ISBN 978-0-8130-3226-9; 0-8130-3226-1

LC 2007-38092

The author discusses twenty-two ballets choreographed by George Balanchine.

"Now at last we can say, 'If you like Balanchine, you must read Nancy Goldner's [book].' Slim enough to fit into a jacket pocket, . . . it's good-humored, enthusiastic and undictatorial; it gives you numerous things to look out for in any performance; and it abounds with insights. . . . 'Balanchine Variations' is in every sense a vade-mecum ('Go with me'): a pocket-size reference book that is also a companion, a guide, a friend." N Y Times (Late N Y Ed)

Includes bibliographical references

Homans, Jennifer

★ Apollo's angels. Random House 2010 643p il $35   **792.8**

1. Ballet 2. Ballet -- History
ISBN 978-1-4000-6060-3; 1-4000-6060-5

LC 201006945

This book "places ballet . . . in the larger context of the times and societies in which it evolved, flourished and flagged, only be revitalized by an infusion of fresh ideas. That revitalization could come from a ballet master like Jean-Georges Noverre, presented by Homans as an important Enlightenment figure whose ideas on reforming ballet were consonant with those of Diderot on reforming theater. Renewal came from the genius of dancers like Marie Taglioni, the incarnation of romanticism . . . But in a closing section . . . [the author]sounds a despairing note: "ballet is dying," she declares. Not only is the creative well running dry and performances dull, but more crucially, Homans sees today's values as inimical to those of ballet." (Publishers Weekly)

"A book of this breadth is going to have its own biorhythms—chapters that engage the author's mind and heart wholly, where everything clicks and the thinking is virtually kinetic, and chapters that don't come as easily. Ms. Homans is at her best when the ideological agenda at hand aspires to discipline, precision and refinement. Her French section is masterful, as are the chapters on the rise of the ballerina, the Danish style, Imperial Russian classicism, and British ballet." Wall Street J

Includes bibliographical references

Reynolds, Nancy

No fixed points; dance in the twentieth century. [by] Nancy Reynolds and Malcolm McCormick. Yale Univ. Press 2003 907p il $50   **792.8**

1. Dance 2. Ballet 3. Modern dance
ISBN 0-300-09366-7

LC 2003-10754

"Although everyone will be using the book for reference, Reynolds and McCormick have produced a work that is completely unlike a standard reference book; you don't just look things up in it—you read it. Here is a coherent, reasoned and entertaining chronicle of dance performance in the West over the hundred years that are unquestionably the fullest and most complicated in the long history of this fragmented and elusive art." N Y Times

Includes bibliographical references

Volynskii, A. L.

Ballet's magic kingdom; selected writings on dance in Russia, 1911-1925. [by] Akim Volynsky; translated and with an introduction and notes by Stanley J. Rabinowitz. Yale University Press 2008 288p il $35   **792.8**

1. Ballet
ISBN 978-0-300-12462-0; 0-300-12462-7

LC 2008-20365

"The Russian critic Akim Volynsky came late to the art of classical dance but brought to his seat on the aisle a formidable background in philosophy, aesthetics, and polemics. . . . In a sense, editor and translator Stanley J. Rabinowitz, a professor of Russian at Amherst College, has kissed to life one of the most important eras in ballet history—the years when Anna Pavlova and Tamara Karsavina were dancing and when the Imperial classicism of choreographer Marius Petipa was pulled into the twentieth century of Michel Fokine, Sergey Diaghilev, and modernism. How exciting to hear a contemporaneous voice commenting on live performances." Bookforum

Includes bibliographical references

792.802 Specific aspects of ballet and modern dance

Duncan, Isadora, 1877-1927

My life; Isadora Duncan ; introduction by Joan Acocella ; with a prefatory essay by Doree Duncan. Liveright paperback ed. Liveright Publishing Corporation, a division of W. W. Norton & Company 2013 368 p. (paperback) $17.95 **792.802**
1. Dance 2. Women dancers -- Biography
ISBN 0871403188; 9780871403186
LC 2012049575

This book, by Isadora Duncan, presents the autobiography of "the choreographer and dancer . . . [who] not only revolutionized dance in the twentieth century but blazed a path for other visionaries who would follow in her wake. . . . From her early enchantment with classical music and poetry to her great successes abroad, to her sensational love affairs and headline-grabbing personal tragedies, Duncan's story is a dramatic one." (Publisher's note)

Riley, Kathleen, 1974-

The **Astaires**; Fred & Adele. Kathleen Riley. Oxford University Press 2012 xxiii, 241 p.p (alk. paper) $27.95 **792.802**
1. Actors -- United States -- Biography 2. Dancers -- United States -- Biography 3. Actresses -- United States -- Biography
ISBN 0199738416; 9780199738410
LC 2011018462

This book, by Kathleen Riley, offers a biography of the sibling-entertainers Fred and Adele Astaire. "Kathleen Riley traces the Astaires' rise to fame from . . . child performers on small-time vaudeville stages . . . to their 1917 debut on Broadway to star billings on both sides of the Atlantic. . . . Ultimately, Fred's dancing expertise surpassed his sister's, and their paths diverged: Adele married into British aristocracy, and Fred headed for Hollywood." (Publisher's note)

Includes bibliographical references and index.

793 Indoor games and amusements

Lithgow, John

A **Lithgow** palooza! 101 ways to entertain and inspire your kids. Simon & Schuster 2004 351p il pa $15 **793**
1. Games 2. Amusements 3. Recreation
ISBN 0-7432-6124-0
LC 2004-42820

"One dictionary defines a lollapalooza as 'something outstanding of its kind,' which adequately describes Lith-

gow's latest book. . . . Essential for all child-rearing collections." Libr J

793.2 Parties and entertainments

Sedaris, Amy

I like you; hospitality under the influence. Warner Books 2006 303p il $27.99 **793.2**
1. Cooking 2. Entertaining
ISBN 978-0-446-57884-4; 0-446-57884-3
LC 2006-07521

"Novice party-planners will actually find some helpful hints along the way as Sedaris offers instructions and real recipes. . . . [This book] is an outrageous and deadpan delight, greatly enhanced by her deliriously kitschy illustrations and photos." Publ Wkly

793.3 Social, folk, national dancing

Soffee, Anne Thomas

Snake hips; belly dancing and how I found true love. Chicago Review Press 2002 xxii, 262p $22.95 **793.3**
1. Belly dancing
ISBN 1-55652-458-7
LC 2002-572

This is the author's story of how she cured a broken heart and changed her life for the better through belly-dancing

"Soffee's witty, flowing prose draws readers into this unlikely but captivating story." Booklist

Includes bibliographical references

793.73 Puzzles and puzzle games

Arnot, Michelle

Four -letter words; and other secrets of a crossword insider. Penguin Group 2008 xxi, 214p pa $13.95 **793.73**
1. Crossword puzzles
ISBN 978-0-399-53435-5; 0-399-53435-0
LC 2008-14260

"The book is full of little-known (to most of us, anyway) nuggets of information: the first crossword puzzle appeared in a New York newspaper on Christmas Day 1913; there are strict rules for composing a puzzle (no more than one-sixth of the spaces can be black, for example); future publishing giant Simon & Schuster's very first book was a collection of crossword puzzles. . . . The book is like a crash course in crossword puzzles and should appeal equally to veteran solvers and novices." Booklist

Includes bibliographical references

Drabble, Margaret, 1939-

The **pattern** in the carpet; a personal history with jigsaws. Houghton Mifflin Harcourt 2009 353p $25; pa $14.95 **793.73**
1. Jigsaw puzzles
ISBN 978-0-547-24144-9; 0-547-24144-5; 978-0-547-

38609-6 pa; 0-547-38609-5 pa

LC 2009-12214

"Part memoir, part rigorously researched historical perspective, Drabble's book is a multi-layered look at jigsaw puzzles and their role through the ages for society, individuals, and herself; it's also a charming homage to Drabble's beloved Auntie Phyl, who passed her lifelong love of jigsaws on to Drabble." Publ Wkly

Includes bibliographical references

★ The **Official** Scrabble players dictionary; 4th ed.; Merriam-Webster 2005 704p $24.95; pa $7.50   **793.73**
1. Reference books 2. Scrabble (Game) -- Dictionaries
ISBN 978-0-87779-420-2; 0-87779-420-0; 978-0-87779-929-0 pa; 0-87779-929-6 pa

LC 2005-5110

First published 1978

This is a dictionary of words which can be used in the game of Scrabble including 100,000 2 to 8 letter words.

Random House Webster's crossword puzzle dictionary; 3rd ed; Random House 1998 854p $27.95; pa $18.95   **793.73**
1. Reference books 2. Crossword puzzles -- Dictionaries
ISBN 0-679-45856-5; 0-375-70624-0 pa

LC 98-67266

First published 1989 with title: The Random House crossword puzzle dictionary

Each entry lists a variety of terms that may be substituted for the entry term. The arrangement within each term listing is alphabetical and by number of letters

"A useful and entertaining companion for both crossword puzzle and trivia buffs." Ref Sources for Small & Medium-sized Libr. 6th edition

793.74   Mathematical games and recreations

Tahan, Malba

The **man** who counted; a collection of mathematical adventures. illustrated by Patricia Reid Baquero & translated by Leslie Clark and Alastair Reid. Norton 1993 244p il hardcover o.p. pa $15.95 **793.74**
1. Mathematical recreations
ISBN 0-393-30934-7 pa

LC 92-18822

"This small book is a joy. . . . These are beautifully expressive tales that find mathematical puzzles and numerical intrigue in human situations and speak not just of solving the problems but of the needs we all have for friendship, love, and beauty." Booklist

793.8   Magic and related activities

Brandon, Ruth (2003)

The **life** and many deaths of Harry Houdini. Random House 1994 355p il hardcover o.p. pa $14.95   **793.8**
1. Magicians 2. Nonfiction writers
ISBN 0-8129-7042-X pa

LC 94-4080

The author provides a psychological "portrait of the great and enigmatic escape artist Harry Houdini. She not only reveals Houdini's impressive technical secrets but also identifies the sources of his unabashed melodramatics and puzzling innocence. . . . Houdini was one of the most compelling 'idols of popular culture' in the early years of this mass-appeal century, and he still works his magic through the medium of Brandon's bold and magnetic interpretation." Booklist

Includes bibliographical references

Gardner, Martin

The **colossal** book of short puzzles and problems; combinatorics, probability, algebra, geometry, topology, chess, logic, cryptarithms, wordplay, physics and other topics of recreational mathematics. edited by Dana Richards. Norton 2006 494p il $35   **793.8**
1. Scientific recreations 2. Mathematical recreations
ISBN 0-393-06114-0; 978-0-393-06114-7

LC 2005-24080

This is a compilation of puzzles from Martin Gardner's "column, 'Mathematical Games,' which appeared for over 25 years in Scientific American. . . . [The topics] include combinatorics, probability, algebra, plane and solid geometry, topology, games, chess, logic, wordplay, and physics, among others. . . . Anyone interested in recreational mathematics should like this book. The puzzles are fascinating and the book is easily browsed. It can also serve as a good reference for (high school and college) teachers seeking interesting problems to complement routine ones in mathematics texts." Sci Books Films

Stone, Alex

Fooling Houdini; magicians, mentalists, math geeks, and the hidden powers of the mind. Alex Stone. Harper 2012 x, 301 p.p ill. (hardback) $26.99   **793.8**
1. Magicians 2. Perception 3. Magic tricks 4. Autobiographies 5. Magic -- Social aspects 6. Magicians -- United States 7. Magic -- Psychological aspects 8. Magicians -- United States -- Biography
ISBN 0061766216; 9780061766213

LC 2011041927

This book by Alex Stone recounts his "quest to join the ranks of master magicians. As he navigates this . . . subculture, Stone pulls back the curtain on a community shrouded in secrecy . . . and organized around a single overriding need: to prove one's worth by deceiving others. . . . In trying to understand how expert magicians manipulate our minds to create their astonishing illusions, Stone uncovers . . . insight into human nature and the nature of perception." (Publisher's note)

794   Indoor games of skill

Botermans, Jack

The **book** of games; strategy, tactics & history. [by] Jack Botermans; [translated from the Spanish by Edgar Loy Fankbonner] Sterling 2008 736p il $29.95   **794**

1. Board games 2. Indoor games
ISBN 978-1-4027-4221-7; 1-4027-4221-5

LC 2007-10173

"Some 65 international games are described and demonstrated in this colorful book. Ranging from dominoes to mancala and shogi to Yut, each entry highlights the game's origins, versions, and playing rules. . . . Color illustrations and diagrams are used liberally to illustrate strategic moves and the variations of game boards and pieces, while photographs show the games being played. . . . Libraries should consider this for their circulating collections." Booklist

794.1   Chess

Capablanca, Jose Raul

Chess fundamentals. McKay Co. 1988 246p il (McKay chess library) pa $14.95   **794.1**

1. Chess
ISBN 978-0-679-14004-7; 0-679-14004-2

First published 1921 by Harcourt Brace & Co.

Explains the general principles of chess through eighteen illustrative games, so that, when grounded in these, the novice may understand the whole elementary science of the game.

Fischer, Bobby

Bobby Fischer teaches chess; by Bobby Fisher, Stuart Margulies, Donn Mosenfelder. Bantam 1972 334p il pa $7.99   **794.1**

1. Chess
ISBN 0-553-26315-3; 978-0-553-26315-2

First published 1966 by Basic Systems, Inc.

In this book the authors give specific advice and hints aimed at both the beginning and advanced player. Each step-by-step lesson is fully illustrated.

Hallman, J. C.

The **chess** artist. Thomas Dunne Bks. 2003 334p il map $25.95; pa $13.95   **794.1**

1. Chess
ISBN 0-312-27293-6; 0-312-33396-X pa

LC 2003-46872

"Educational, fanciful, entertaining, this is a book that will make every reader see the game of chess in an entirely new—if slightly weird—light." Booklist

Includes bibliographical references

United States Chess Federation

★ **U.S.** Chess Federation's official rules of chess; compiled and sanctioned by the U.S. Chess Federation; Tim Just, chief editor; Daniel B. Burg, editor.

5th ed; Random House Puzzles & Games 2003 xxxvii, 370p il (McKay chess library) pa $18.95 **794.1**

1. Chess
ISBN 0-8129-3559-4

LC 2003-278349

First published 1974

This "edition features the latest rules, including guidelines for the popular game of speed chess, an updated quick rating system, and the latest conventions of governing tournaments. It also contains explanations of every legal move, a guide to calculating lifetime rankings, guidelines for sponsoring and running a tournament, and a lesson on how to read and write chess notation." Publisher's note

794.7   Ball games

Byrne, Robert

Byrne's new standard book of pool and billiards. Harcourt Brace & Co. 1998 xxv, 406p il hardcover o.p. pa $20   **794.7**

1. Billiards 2. Pool (Game)
ISBN 0-15-100325-4; 0-15-600554-9 pa

LC 98-14656

First published 1978 with title: Byrne's standard book of pool and billiards

The author explains the rules of pool and billiards and offers advice on strategy with diagrams of various shots.

Includes bibliographical references

McCumber, David

Playing off the rail; a pool hustler's journey. Avon Books 1997 384p pa $14.95   **794.7**

1. Pool (Game) 2. Pool players
ISBN 0-380-72923-7

First published 1996 by Random House

A "look at the game of pool, which is a gambling sport not yet sanitized by what McCumber calls the 'Fellowship of Christian Athletes types.' He plays financial backer to a sharp-tongued player named Tony Annigoni, and takes him on the road across North America in search of highstakes games. . . . This is a terrific book." New Yorker

794.8   Electronic games

Bissell, Tom

Extra lives; why video games matter. Pantheon Books 2010 218p   **794.8**

1. Video games
ISBN 0-307-37870-5; 978-0-307-37870-5

LC 2009-39602

This is a volume of essays about video games. Portions of the work originally appeared in The New Yorker, Tin House, and Kill Screen. Mr Bissell explains: "I wrote this book as a writer who plays a lot of games, and in these pages you will find one man's opinions and thoughts on what playing games feels like, why he plays them, and the questions they make him think about. In the portions of the book where I address game design and game designers, it is . . . to a formally explanatory rather than technically informative end." (Author's note) Index.

The "first truly indispensable work of literary nonfiction about society's most lucrative entertainment medium. Bissell's commentary is marvelously astute and his enthusiasm for games makes even his words on the printed page feel positively backlit. Any breathless adoration for the medium he doles out, however, takes on additional weight because of his willingness to admit when a game falls on its face." Paste

Chatfield, Tom

Fun Inc. why gaming will dominate the twenty-first century. Pegasus Books 2010 258p $27.95 **794.8**

    1. Video games

    ISBN 978-1-60598-143-7; 1-60598-143-5

"A lively, thought-provoking and thoughtful read on an entertainment juggernaut many of us have failed to properly recognize. A good book, too, for parents, who might feel far more comfortably informed about a sector that can come across as—literally—an alien world their kids inhabit." Irish Times

Neiburger, Eli

    ★ Gamers . . . in the library?! the why, what, and how of videogame tournaments for all ages. American Library Association 2007 178p pa $42 **794.8**

    1. Video games 2. Computer games 3. Young adults' libraries

    ISBN 978-0-8389-0944-7; 0-8389-0944-2

                       LC 2007-10512

"With the writing as vibrant as its topic, . . . [this book] is a must-have professional tool." Voice Youth Advocates

    Includes bibliographical references

Wark, McKenzie

Gamer theory. Harvard University Press 2007 un il $19.95 **794.8**

    1. Computer games

    ISBN 978-0-674-02519-6; 0-674-02519-9

                   LC 2006-102852

"For Wark, video games are worth studying because they offer insights into contemporary society and culture. For example, Katamari Damacy exemplifies the way digital technology has altered the experience of space and time; Rez demonstrates how individual identity is now a matter of action not essence, doing not being; Vice City maps out the territory of the new world order of seemingly unending risk and reward. Gamer Theory devotes complete chapters to particular games and the key concepts they clarify. . . . Gamer Theory concerns itself with more than just the interpretation of video games; it's about gaming ambience—that is, gamespace—as the kinetic field within which game players exist." PopMatters

    Includes bibliographical references

795.4   Card games

Bellin, Andy

    Poker nation; a high stakes, low-life adventure into the heart of a gambling country. HarperCollins Pubs. 2001 258p il hardcover o.p. pa $12.95 **795.4**

    1. Card games

    ISBN 0-06-095847-2 pa

                   LC 2001-42409

"Bellin offers the best of both worlds, combining detailed advice on how to play the game with engagingly written, humorous stories about those who play it with passion." Booklist

    Includes bibliographical references

Hoyle, Edmond

    ★ Hoyle's rules of games; descriptions of indoor games of skill and chance, with advice on skillful play: based on the foundations laid down by Edmond Hoyle, 1672-1769. edited by Albert H. Morehead and Geoffrey Mott-Smith. 3rd rev. & updated ed.; Plume 2001 362p il pa $14 **795.4**

    1. Card games

    ISBN 0-452-28313-2

                  LC 2002-278550

This guide "includes rules, strategies, and playing odds for more than 250 games." Publisher's note

    Includes bibliographical references

McManus, James

    Cowboys full; the story of poker. Farrar, Straus, and Giroux 2009 516p il $30 **795.4**

    1. Poker

    ISBN 978-0-374-29924-8; 0-374-29924-2

                  LC 2009-29533

The story of poker, from its roots in China, the Middle East, and Europe to its ascent as a global—but especially an American—phenomenon, braiding history with poker's relevance to our military, diplomatic, business, and personal affairs.

    "The epic story of how poker has grown from disreputable roots to become America's—and the world's—game. . . . A satisfying, useful overview." Kirkus

    Includes bibliographical references (p. 471-474)

    Positively Fifth Street; murderers, cheetahs, and Binion's World Series of Poker. Farrar, Straus & Giroux 2003 422p il $26 **795.4**

    1. Poker

    ISBN 0-374-23648-8

                  LC 2002-33882

"McManus went to Las Vegas in May 2000 on assignment for Harper's to cover the World Series of Poker. . . . He was to throw in coverage of the trial of Sandy Murphy, an ex-stripper, and her boyfriend, Rick Tabish, accused of murdering Ted Binion, the tournament's host. . . . To satisfy his own gambling urge, McManus enter the poker competition and spends 10 days immersed in the culture of Vegas and gambling, rendering a fast-paced, riveting account of his progress through the tournament. . . . A delicious inside look." Booklist

Includes bibliographical references

Scarne, John

Scarne's encyclopedia of card games. Quill 2001 475p il pa $18   **795.4**
1. Card games
ISBN 0-06-273155-6; 978-0-06-273155-5

A reissue of the title first published 1983 by Harper & Row

The material in this book has been excerpted, with alterations and additions, from Scarne's encyclopedia of games (1973)

796   Athletic and outdoor sports and games

Barrow, John D.

Mathletics; a scientist explains 100 amazing things about the world of sports. John D. Barrow. W. W. Norton & Company 2012 xiv, 298 p.p ill. (hardcover) $26.95   **796**
1. Physics 2. Kinesiology 3. Mathematics 4. Force and energy 5. Sports sciences 6. Sports -- Mathematical models
ISBN 0393063410; 9780393063417

LC 2012009794

This math-and-science book is a collection of "100 short essays explaining a variety of sports-related topics, such as various applications of statistics, the physics of wheelchair racing, how different scoring methods affect the outcome of multi-event sports like the decathlon, and how a new rule led to 'the most bizarre soccer match ever played.'" (Publishers Weekly)

Includes bibliographical references

Berkow, Ira

The minority quarterback, and other lives in sports. Dee, I.R. 2002 307p $26; pa $16.95   **796**
1. Sports
ISBN 1-56663-422-9; 1-56663-502-0 pa

LC 2001-47578

"Berkow brings together essays on a theme: athletes overcoming hardships. Whether his subject is minority football players struggling to win recognition as quarterbacks—a position once restricted to whites—or baseball pitcher Jim Abbott working past the handicap of having only one arm, he writes with skill, empathy, and insight." Booklist

The Best American sports writing of the century; edited by David Halberstam. Houghton Mifflin 1999 776p $30; pa $18   **796**
1. Sports
ISBN 0-395-94513-5; 0-395-94514-3 pa

"Although there are pieces about mountain climbing, tennis and chess, fully half of the selections are about two sports: baseball and boxing. The book begins with a Best of the Best section led by Gay Talese's 1966 profile of Joe DiMaggio, 'The Silent Season of a Hero.'. . . The final section is a special six-piece tribute to a man who himself claimed to be the best of the best—Muhammad Ali." Publ Wkly

Clotfelter, Charles T.

Big -time sports in American universities. Cambridge University Press 2011 313p il $29   **796**
1. College sports 2. College sports -- United States
ISBN 1-107-00434-9; 978-1-107-00434-4

LC 2010-50331

This book presents "findings about the size, importance and effects of big-time college sports." (Publisher's note) Glossary. Index.

"Clotfelter sets himself an ambitious goal: using an analytical, data-rich approach to the questions of why many leading American universities embrace big-time, commercial athletics (while failing to fully acknowledge the size of its footprint), and whether the marriage is a good one for institutions and society as a whole. . . . He collects information on how much of The New York Times coverage of various universities focuses on their sports programs (much greater at institutions with big-time sports programs than at their peers without them), for instance, and mines a forthcoming study to show that undergraduates at one group of highly selective universities with commercial sports programs spend less time on academics than do their counterparts at institutions without top-level programs. In true economist's fashion, he asks: Do the benefits outweigh the costs? Clotfelter's answers, he acknowledges, are something less than fully satisfactory, and the book uncovers ample evidence for fanatics and haters of big-time sports alike." Inside Higher Ed

Includes bibliographical references

Dierker, Larry

This ain't brain surgery; how to win the pennant without losing your mind. Simon & Schuster 2003 289p il $25   **796**
1. Baseball players 2. Houston Astros (Baseball team) 3. Sportscasters 4. Baseball managers
ISBN 0-7432-0400-X

LC 2003-52809

"Dierker, a pitcher and then radio commentator for the Houston Astros, stepped out of the announcer's booth to become the Astros' manager in 1997. . . . Baseball and the Houston Astros have been Dierker's professional adult life, but unlike many baseball lifers, he has a healthy perspective about the game and his role in it, as reflected in the title of this literate, humorous, and entertaining memoir." Booklist

Guttmann, Allen

Women's sports; a history. Columbia Univ. Press 1991 339p il hardcover o.p. pa $24   **796**
1. Sports 2. Women athletes
ISBN 0-231-06957-X pa

LC 90-28692

The author explores "the social and cultural contexts of women's athletics in ancient civilizations, the Middle Ages, and the Renaissance. This lays the groundwork for a subsequent discussion of the subject's current state, in which he . . . exposes controversial issues which threaten the development of women's sports." Libr J

Includes bibliographical references

Halberstam, David

The **teammates**. Hyperion 2003 217p il $22.95   **796**

1. Baseball players 2. Sportscasters 3. Baseball managers 4. Baseball -- Biography 5. Boston Red Sox (Baseball team)

ISBN 1-401-30057-X

LC 2003-42334

This is an "account of the lives and friendships of four legendary Boston Red Sox: Ted Williams, Dominic DiMaggio, Johnny Pesky and Bobby Doerr; the story unfolds in a series of flashbacks as DiMiggio and Pesky drive 1,300 miles to Florida to visit the ailing Williams." N Y Times Book Rev

"This account of good people living full lives and appreciating the experience will move readers." Booklist

Haskins, Don

★ **Glory** road; my story of the 1966 NCAA basketball championship and how one team triumphed against the odd and changed America forever. [by] Don Haskins with Daniel Wetzel. Hyperion 2006 254p il pa $14.95   **796**

1. Basketball coaches

ISBN 1-4013-0791-4

LC 2005-50349

This is an "autobiography of Don Haskins, Texas college basketball icon and inadvertent civil rights pioneer." Publ Wkly

"This is one of the best sports autobiographies in many years." Booklist

Hoyland, Graham

Last Hours on Everest; by Graham Hoyland. HarperCollins 2013 320 p. (hardcover) $26.99 **796**

1. Mount Everest Expedition (1924)

ISBN 0007455755; 9780007455751

In this book, Graham Hoyland posits that explorers George Mallory and Sandy Irvine suffered a fall off the peak of Mount Everest. "Hoyland combines personal memoir, Everest history, and scientific investigation as he sets Everest in the context of the history of surveying, exploration, and mountaineering, and of imperial Britons seeking higher and higher peaks to ascend. He includes literary, scientific, and historical anecdotes." (Library Journal)

Kindred, Dave

Sound and fury; two powerful lives, one fateful friendship. Free Press 2006 368p il $27   **796**

1. Lawyers 2. Television personalities 3. Sportscasters 4. Boxers (Persons)

ISBN 0-7432-6211-5; 978-0-7432-6211-8

LC 2005-55217

This is an account of the friendship of Muhammad Ali and Howard Cosell.

"Even if the shelves are sagging with books about Ali, room should be made for this approachable, touching, and altogether fascinating buddy comedy." Booklist

Includes bibliographical references

Krantz, Les

Not till the fat lady sings; the most dramatic sports finishes of all time. foreword by Doug Flutie. Triumph Books 2003 148p il $29.95; pa $19.95 **796**

1. Sports

ISBN 1-57243-558-5; 1-57243-767-7 pa

LC 2003-47331

"This compendium of the 50 most dramatic endings to sports events divides the great plays into first, second and third place rankings, along with honorable mentions. . . . Many of the book's finishes concern football, baseball and basketball, with just a smattering of other sports (such as golf, tennis and hockey) thrown in. Photos accompany each entry. . . . The supplementary DVD, narrated by Jim McKay, adds a dramatic edge to the package, with commentators relating moments with wild excitement and fans roaring." Publ Wkly

This is "an excellent addition to any sports collection." Booklist

Levine, Peter

Ellis Island to Ebbet's Field; sport and the American-Jewish experience. Oxford Univ. Press 1992 328p il (Sports history and society) hardcover o.p. pa $38   **796**

1. Sports 2. Jews -- United States -- History

ISBN 0-19-505128-9; 0-19-508555-8 pa

LC 91-42016

The author "explores the importance of sport in transforming Jewish immigrants into American Jews. Drawing on interviews with celebrities as well as lesser-known neighborhood stars, Levine vividly recounts the stories of Red Auerbach, Hank Greenberg, Moe Berg, and many others who became Jewish heroes and symbols of the difficult struggle for American success." Univ Press Books for Public and Second Sch Libr

Includes bibliographical references

McDermott, Mickey

A **funny** thing happened on the way to Cooperstown; {by} Mickey McDermott with Howard Eisenberg. Triumph 2003 270p il $24.95   **796**

1. Baseball players 2. Baseball -- Biography

ISBN 1-57243-532-1

LC 2002-45573

McDermott "won 18 games for the Boston Red Sox in 1951 and seemed a sure thing, but he finished a lackluster career with 69 wins and 69 losses. . . . After leaving baseball, McDermott struggled at various jobs until, unbelievably, he won $7 million in the Arizona state lottery in 1991. With the help of coauthor Eisenberg, he tells the story of his life and wild times in this thoroughly engaging memoir." Booklist

Miller, Stephen G.

★ **Ancient** Greek athletics. Yale University Press 2004 288p il map $35   **796**

1. Athletics 2. Olympic games 3. Greece -- Civilization

ISBN 0-300-10083-3

LC 2003-16875

"Five chapters discuss the origins and history of the [Olympic] games and their sociopolitical significance, but at the core of the book are the 11 chapters that use archaeological and textual evidence . . . to reconstruct the physical reality of Greek athletics. Particularly valuable are the vivid reconstruction of the ancient Olympic program and the lucid discussion of the evidence for female athletic contests in ancient Greece." Choice

Includes bibliographical references

Overman, Steven J.

Icons of women's sport; Steven J. Overman and Kelly Boyer Sagert. Greenwood 2012 623 p. ill. (hardback) $173.00 **796**

1. Sports for women 2. Celebrities -- Biography 3. Women athletes -- Biography

ISBN 0313385483; 9780313385483; 9780313385490

LC 2011041561

This book, by Kelly Boyer Sagert and Steven J. Overman, "identifies and examines the individuals who have impacted history, challenged the status quo, influenced sport culture, and garnered wide public interest. Including stars from the past and present, ranging from Babe Didrikson Zaharias . . . to . . . Venus and Serena Williams, the featured athletes are iconic not only because of their achievements in the sports arena, but also because of their contributions to society." (Publisher's note)

Includes bibliographical references and index

Rhoden, William C.

$40 million slaves; the rise, fall, and redemption of the Black athlete. Crown Publishers 2006 286p il $23.95 **796**

1. Sports 2. Race discrimination 3. African American athletes

ISBN 0-609-60120-2; 978-0-609-60120-4

LC 2005-34952

"In his provocative, passionate, important and disturbing book—part memoir, part history, part journalism—William Rhoden . . . builds a historic framework that both accounts for the varieties of African-American athletic experience in the past and continues to explain them today." N Y Times Book Rev

Includes bibliographical references

Rivals; legendary matchups that made sports history. edited by David K. Wiggins and R. Pierre Rodgers. University of Arkansas Press 2010 xx, 465p $75; pa $29.95 **796**

1. Athletes 2. Sports -- History

ISBN 978-1-55728-920-9; 978-1-55728-921-6 pa

LC 2009053650

"In putting together this unique, ambitious volume, Wiggins and Rodgers . . . had four goals: to outline the origin of each rivalry; to uncover the societal conditions that gave rise to it; to reveal the ways the rivalry was maintained; and to discover the meaning of the rivalry for its participants and its fans. They divide the book into three parts, each devoted to a particular type of rivalry. Part 1 covers 'one-on-one' rivalries between two elite athletes; part 2, rivalries between two franchises; and part 3, rivalries between the US and other countries." Choice

Includes bibliographical references

Tuchman, Robert

The **100** sporting events you must see live; an insider's guide to creating the sports experience of a lifetime. BenBella Books 2009 337p pa $17.95 **796**

1. Sports 2. Travel

ISBN 978-1-933771-45-8

LC 2008-45905

The author "gives aficionados of most sports, from golf to baseball, basketball, tennis, hockey, cycling, to football, both American and soccer, a virtual bible of information on the top 100 sporting events worldwide that he recommends traveling to for the live experience. Tuchman presents each sport or event (e.g., the Head of the Charles, the World Cup) with a brief history, followed by specific ticketing information, hotel and restaurant guides, and important phone numbers, i.e, the essentials to plan your trip. . . . Tuchman's book is not only a great resource for vacation planning but also for general sports interest." Libr J

★ The unlevel playing field; a documentary history of the African American experience in sport. {edited by} David K. Wiggins and Patrick B. Miller. University of Ill. Press 2003 xxi, 493p il (Sport and society) hardcover o.p. pa $24.95 **796**

1. African American athletes

ISBN 0-252-02820-1; 0-252-07272-3 pa

LC 2002-14269

"This collection contains several of the most significant primary documents tracing the sports experiences of African Americans. Athletes, sports historians, and some of the nation's foremost intellectuals deliver commentaries on a wide range of subjects and athletic events." Libr J

Includes bibliographical references

Winston, Wayne L.

Mathletics; how gamblers, managers, and sports enthusiasts use mathematics in baseball, basketball, and football. [by] Wayne Winston. Princeton University Press 2009 358p il $29.95 **796**

1. Mathematics 2. Sports -- Statistics

ISBN 978-0-691-13913-5; 0-691-13913-X

LC 2008-51678

"Sports fans will learn much from probability theory and statistical models. . . . A rare fusion of sports enthusiasm and numerical acumen." Booklist

Includes bibliographical references (p. 343-352)

796.04   General kinds of sports and games

Figone, Albert J.

Cheating the spread; gamblers, point shavers, and game fixers in college football and basketball. by Albert J. Figone. University of Illinois Press 2012 xv, 196 p.p ill. (paperback) $21.95 **796.04**

1. Gambling 2. College basketball 3. Sports betting -- United States 4. Football -- Betting -- United States 5. Basketball -- Betting -- United States 6. College sports -- Economic aspects -- United States

ISBN 0252078756; 9780252037283; 9780252078750

LC 2012037767

This book is a "history of game fixing in college basketball and football. Basketball, of course, has been the favorite of fixers through the years, likely because there are fewer variables (players) competing and a couple of key basketball players can have a very effective yet subtle influence on a game. Gambling and fixing games became a real issue after WWII and was centered on the East Coast," according to the author. (Booklist)

Includes bibliographical references (pages 171-185) and index.

796.22   Skateboarding

Beal, Becky

Skateboarding; the ultimate guide. Becky Beal. ABC-CLIO, LLC 2013 xx, 150 p.p ill. (Greenwood guides to extreme sports) (hardcover) $37.00; (ebook) $37.00   **796.22**
1. Skateboarding
ISBN 0313381127; 9780313381126; 9780313381133 pdf

LC 2012035631

This book, by Becky Beal, part of the "Greenwood Guides to Extreme Sports," profiles skateboarding. "In the last half century, skateboarding has evolved from a simple, idyllic child's pastime that originated in southern California to becoming a worldwide youth culture phenomenon. This now-mainstream action sport has spawned a multi-billion-dollar commercial market." (Publisher's note)

Includes bibliographical references (p. 125-135) and index.

796.3   Ball games

Chetwynd, Josh

The **secret** history of balls; Josh Chetwynd ; Illustrations by Emily Stackhouse. Perigee Trade 2011 xiv, 221p ill.   **796.3**
1. Ball games 2. Sporting goods 3. Sports -- History
ISBN 9780399536748

LC 2010054221

This book "mines the stories and lore of sports and recreation to offer insight into 60 balls - whether they're hollow, solid, full of air, or stuffed with twine or made of leather, metal, rubber, plastic, or polyurethane - that give us joy on playing fields and in every arena from backyards to stadiums around the globe." (Publishers' note)

Dawidoff, Nicholas

Collision Low Crossers; A Year Inside the Turbulent World of NFL Football. Nicholas Dawidoff. Little Brown & Co 2013 352 p. $87   **796.3**
1. Football 2. National Football League 3. Football -- United States 4. New York Jets (Football team)
ISBN 0316196797; 9780316196796

LC 2013030013

This book by Nicholas Dawidoff follows the football team the New York Jets throughout 2011, "operations, from the February scouting 'combine' of collegiate talent, through the May draft of college players, the torturous preseason of practices and games, and, finally, to the entire 16-game, regular season schedule and subsequent coaches' postmortem. Head coach Rex Ryan and his staff receive the primary focus." (Booklist)

Includes bibliographical references and index

Riley, Glenda

The **life** and legacy of Annie Oakley. University of Okla. Press 1994 252p il (Oklahoma western biographies) hardcover o.p. pa $19.95   **796.3**
1. Marksmen 2. Frontier and pioneer life -- West (U.S.)
ISBN 0-8061-2656-6; 978-0-8061-3506-9 pa

LC 94-10260

"To provide a factual and intimate biography of Annie Oakley, the legendary female sharpshooter and star of Buffalo Bill Cody's Wild West Show, Riley attempts to place her seemingly mythical subject firmly into historical, cultural, and sociological contexts. . . . What emerges is a multidimensional portrait of an entertainer and a businesswoman whose enduring fame and popularity both reflected and defied the conventions of her era." Booklist

Includes bibliographical references

796.323   Basketball

Araton, Harvey

When the Garden was Eden; Clyde, the captain, dollar bill, and the glory days of the New York Knicks. photographs by George Kalinsky. Harper 2011 352p il $26.99; ebook $12.99   **796.323**
1. Basketball 2. New York Knicks (Basketball team)
ISBN 978-0-06-195623-2; 978-0-06-209705-7 ebook

LC 2011018792

"A warm, accessible celebration of the dynamic early-1970s New York Knicks basketball teams. Populated by such colorful personalities as the flashy but cerebral point guard Walt Frazier, silky-smooth combo guard Earl 'The Pearl' Monroe, hard-nosed forward/center Willis Reed and quirky bench anchor Phil Jackson, this version of the Knicks is near-legendary, even though they were far from a dynasty, only managing a pair of championships (1970 and 1973)." Kirkus

Includes bibliographical references

Barkley, Charles

I may be wrong but I doubt it; edited and with an introduction by Michael Wilbon. Random House 2002 245p $22.95; pa $12.95   **796.323**
1. Sportscasters 2. Basketball players
ISBN 0-375-50883-X; 0-8129-6628-7 pa

LC 2002-29169

The retired NBA champion "explores a wide range of interests. Each chapter has a theme, and Barkley has no problem speaking his mind on any topic, whether it is politics . . . or lack of minority control in sports. . . . In between these chapters are other sections that retell some of the great and not-so-great moments in his career. . . . This is a very entertaining look at one of the most intelligent minds in pro sports, and like Barkley's career, it's bound to produce fierce arguments." Publ Wkly

Blais, Madeleine

In these girls, hope is a muscle. Warner Bks. 1996 266p pa $13.95 **796.323**

1. Basketball 2. Cathedral High School (Springfield, Mass.)

ISBN 0-446-67210-6; 978-0-446-67210-8

First published 1995 by Atlantic Monthly Press

"Alternately funny, exciting and moving, the book should be enjoyed not only by girls and women who have played sports but also those who wanted to but let themselves be discouraged." Publ Wkly

Bradley, Bill

Values of the game. Artisan 1998 160p il $30 **796.323**

1. Basketball 2. National Basketball Association

ISBN 1-57965-116-X

LC 98-7280

In this book, the former senator and New York Knick presents a "blend of sports memoir and inspirational advice interspersed with more than 100 dramatic photos of basketball players past and present. . . . While some may dismiss much of his volume as a collection of copybook maxims, the whole is larger than the sum of its parts, not only because it is so personal but because Bradley moves so deftly from the specific to the general." Publ Wkly

Conroy, Pat

My losing season. Talese 2002 402p hardcover o.p. pa $14.95 **796.323**

1. Authors 2. Novelists 3. Authors, American

ISBN 0-385-48912-9; 0-553-38190-3 pa

LC 2002-66212

"A wonderfully rich, informative, and well-researched reminiscence." Libr J

D'Orso, Michael

Eagle blue; a team, a tribe, and a high school basketball season in Arctic Alaska. Bloomsbury Pub. 2006 323p il map $23.95 **796.323**

1. Basketball 2. School sports 3. Fort Yukon (Alaska)

ISBN 978-1-58234-623-6; 1-58234-623-2

LC 2005-25430

The author "follows the Fort Yukon Eagles through their 2005 season to the state championship, shifting between a mesmerizing narrative and the thoughts of the players, their coach and their fans. What emerges is more than a sports story; it's a striking portrait of a community consisting of a traditional culture bombarded with modernity, where alcoholism, domestic violence and school dropout rates run wild." Publ Wkly

Davis, Seth

When March went mad; the game that transformed basketball. Henry Holt 2009 323p il $26 **796.323**

1. Basketball 2. Indiana State University 3. Michigan State University

ISBN 978-0-8050-8810-6; 0-8050-8810-5

LC 2008-47628

The author "chronicles the 1979 NCAA basketball championship game, which featured two future legends: Earvin

'Magic' Johnson and Larry Bird. The game was a pivotal moment in the development of the sport, leading to an explosion in popularity and a change in the way the game was played and promoted. . . . An essential primer for tournament junkies, and ideal reading material for TV timeouts." Kirkus

Includes bibliographical references

Dohrmann, George

Play their hearts out; a coach, his star recruit, and the youth basketball machine. Ballantine Books 2010 422p il $26 **796.323**

1. Basketball 2. Basketball coaches 3. Basketball players

ISBN 978-0-345-50860-7; 0-345-50860-2

LC 2010-15470

The author "follows California phenom Demetrius Walker through the cycle of Amateur Athletic Union (AAU) summer league hoops, from playing for ambitious hustler and coach Joe Keller to the face of grassroots basketball, longtime coach Pat Barrett. In a constant search for the next Lebron, just as before for the next Michael Jordan, AAU coaches, with support and financing from shoe giants Nike and Adidas, woo youngsters to their summer league basketball teams with gear, shoes, and promises of a college scholarship. . . . [Dohrmann's] insights into the seamy side of youth basketball are investigative journalism at its best." Libr J

Feinstein, John

Last dance; behind the scenes at the Final Four. John Feinstein. Little, Brown 2006 369p il $25.95 **796.323**

1. Basketball

ISBN 0-316-16030-X

LC 2005-28478

The author "employs the 2005 [Final Four] weekend as the catalyst to discuss the history of the event, the key people, and, most significantly, the effect that involvement in the Final Four has had on participants' lives. . . . The anecdotes are entertaining, and the insights into the tournament's logistics fascinating, but what will linger most are the remembrances of players, especially those who ended up on the losing side." Booklist

A march to madness; the view from the floor in the Atlantic Coast Conference. Little, Brown 1997 464p il hardcover o.p. pa $14 **796.323**

1. Basketball 2. Atlantic Coast Conference

ISBN 0-316-27740-1; 0-316-27712-6 pa

LC 97-31060

Feinstein "covers one year with all of the teams in the perennially powerful Atlantic Coast Conference. After introducing each of the schools, their teams, their coaches, and their expectations for the 1996/97 basketball season, the book describes their progress week by week, culminating with Dean Smith's run to the NCAA Final Four. Such a detailed accounting of a sports season could seem interminable to readers, but Feinstein has again produced a narrative that is not only interesting but often exciting." Libr J

FreeDarko presents the macrophenomenal pro basketball almanac; styles, stats and stars in to-

day's game. Bloomsbury USA 2008 219p il
$23   **796.323**
1. Basketball 2. National Basketball Association
ISBN 978-1-59691-561-9; 1-59691-561-7

"This is a wonderful basketball book that blends a unique
perspective, arresting presentation, and superior knowledge
of its subject." Booklist

Kent, Richard G.

Inside women's college basketball; anatomy of a
season. {by} Richard Kent. Taylor, W.T. 2000 222p
il hardcover o.p. pa $16.95   **796.323**
1. Basketball
ISBN 0-87833-188-3; 978-0-87833-278-6 pa;
0-87833-278-2 pa
                                    LC 00-42589
"Kent chronicles the 1999-2000 season as experienced
by four top women's programs: Tennessee, Connecticut,
Rutgers, and Sacred Heart. . . . This is a fine overview for
those looking for insights into the women's game." Booklist

McCallum, Jack

★ **Dream** team; how Michael, Magic, Larry,
Charles, and the greatest team of all time conquered
the world and changed the game of basketball forever.
Jack McCallum. Ballantine Books 2012 xxix, 352
p.p col. ill. (hardback) $28   **796.323**
1. Olympic games 2. Basketball -- History 3. Basketball
players -- United States -- Biography 4. Basketball --
United States -- History 5. Basketball teams -- United
States -- History
ISBN 0345520483; 0345520505; 9780345520487;
9780345520500
                                    LC 2012006253
In this book "sports journalist Jack McCallum delivers
the . . . story of . . . the 1992 U.S. Olympic Men's Basketball
Team that captivated the world. . . . He offers a . . . look at
the controversial selection process. . . . [a]nd he narrates . .
. the legendary July 1992 intrasquad scrimmage that pitted
the Dream Teamers against one another in what may have
been the greatest pickup game--and the greatest exhibition
of trash talk--in history." (Publisher's note)

"...[McCallum] effectively evokes the remarkable team
while placing it within the larger historical context. Basketball and Olympics fans will welcome this nostalgic trip
through the recent past." Kirkus

Merlino, Doug (2012)

✓ The **hustle**; one team and ten lives in Black and
White. Bloomsbury USA 2010 309p il $26 **796.323**
1. Basketball 2. School sports 3. Lakeside School
(Seattle, Wash.) 4. Washington (State) -- Race relations
ISBN 978-1-60819-215-1; 1-60819-215-6
                                    LC 2010-23030
"This book, both memoir and social analysis, is an es-
sential read as a recent social history and personal story of
America." Libr J

Rosen, Charles, 1941-

Crazy basketball; a life in and out of bounds.
foreword by Phil Jackson. University of Nebraska
Press 2011 301p $24.95   **796.323**
1. Authors 2. Sportswriters 3. Basketball coaches
4. Basketball -- Biography 5. Continental Basketball
Association
ISBN 978-0-8032-1793-5
                                    LC 2010-26921
The author "recalls his years as a coach in the Continental Basketball Association. . . . The shining star here isn't
Rosen or any of the players, it's the game itself. The last
half-dozen pages will bring a tear to the eye of anyone for
whom the game was or is a passion." Booklist

Simmons, Bill

The **book** of basketball; the NBA according to
the sports guy. Ballantine/ESPN Books 2009 715p
il $30; pa $18   **796.323**
1. Basketball 2. National Basketball Association
ISBN 978-0-345-51176-8; 0-345-51176-X; 978-0-
345-52010-4 pa; 0-345-52010-6 pa
                                    LC 2009-36006
The author "summarizes the history of the league, discusses his personal fandom, includes a great 'what if?' chapter (what if Michael Jordan had been drafted second by Portland instead of third by Chicago?), analyzes Most Valuable
Player choices through the years, and dissects the careers of
the league's all-time best players. The true NBA fan will dive
into this hefty volume and won't resurface for about a week,
emerging from the man cave unshaven, smelling of beer and
pizza, grinning, and armed with NBA history, insight, anecdotes, statistics, and a dozen new examples of Simmons'
Unintentional Comedy Scale. This is just plain fun. Expect
significant demand from hoops junkies." Booklist

Includes bibliographical references

Swidey, Neil

The **assist**; hoops, hope, and the game of their
lives. PublicAffairs 2008 358p il $26   **796.323**
1. Basketball 2. School sports 3. Basketball coaches
4. Charlestown High School (Boston, Mass.)
ISBN 978-1-58648-469-9; 1-58648-469-9
                                    LC 2007-35826
"This is a prodigiously reported, compulsively readable
book that readers (sport fans or not) will savor." Publ Wkly

Wolff, Alexander

✓**Big** game, small world; a basketball adventure. Warner Bks. 2002 xxiv, 424p il $24.95; pa
$15.95   **796.323**
1. Basketball
ISBN 0-446-52601-0; 0-446-67989-5 pa
"Wolff traveled to 16 countries and 10 states to assess
basketball's impact as a global phenomenon. He profiles a
cloistered nun who was once a talented hoopster and investigates the origins of the crossover dribble. Wolff's passion for
the game burns feverishly throughout." Booklist

796.332   American football

Anderson, Lars

Carlisle vs. Army; Jim Thorpe, Dwight Eisenhower, Pop Warner, and the forgotten story of football's greatest battle. Random House 2007 349p il $24.95   **796.332**

1. Football 2. Generals 3. Presidents 4. Decathletes 5. Pentathletes 6. Football coaches 7. Olympic athletes 8. College presidents 9. United States Indian School (Carlisle, Pa.)

ISBN 978-1-4000-6600-1; 1-4000-6600-X

LC 2007-8410

"A forgotten football game in 1912, between Carlisle, led by Jim Thorpe and coached by the legendary Pop Warner, and Army, led by Dwight Eisenhower, becomes the launching point for a fascinating look at multiple levels of American popular culture." Booklist

Includes bibliographical references

Billick, Brian

More than a game; the glorious present and uncertain future of the NFL. [by] Brian Billick with Michael MacCambridge. Scribner 2009 229p $26   **796.332**

1. Football 2. National Football League

ISBN 978-1-4391-0918-2

LC 2009-27874

"With provocative ideas and an engaging style, this is essential reading for all football fans." Libr J

Includes bibliographical references

Bissinger, H. G.

★ Friday night lights; a town, a team, and a dream. Da Capo Press 2000 367p il pa $15.95   **796.332**

1. Football 2. Permian High School (Odessa, Tex.)

ISBN 0-306-80990-7

LC 00-40510

First published 1990 by Addison-Wesley

"It is a tricky balancing act, but Mr. Bissinger carries it off: 'Friday Night Lights' offers a biting indictment of the sports craziness that grips not only Odessa but most of American society, while at the same time providing a moving evocation of its powerful allure." N Y Times Book Rev

Bowden, Mark

The best game ever; Giants vs. Colts, 1958, and the birth of the modern NFL. Atlantic Monthly Press 2008 279p il $35   **796.332**

1. Football 2. Baltimore Colts (Football team) 3. New York Giants (Football team)

ISBN 978-0-87113-988-7; 0-87113-988-X

"Bowden dives into the trenches of the 1958 NFL Championship game, where New York and Baltimore waged an overtime battle that wowed TV audiences and ensured the future of pro football. He astutely contrasts Frank Gifford's glamorous Giants with the blue-collar Colts of Johnny Unitas, who moonlighted at a local steel factory, and Raymond Berry, the training-obsessed wide receiver. The mistake-laden title game was hardly the 'best,' but it ushered in an era of riches: While Unitas earned $17,500 in 1958, rookie Joe Namath signed for $200,000 just five years later." Entertainment Wkly

Cosell, Greg

★ The games that changed the game; the evolution of the NFL in seven Sundays. [by] Ron Jaworski, with Greg Cosell and David Plaut. ESPN Books 2010 312p il $26; ebook $26   **796.332**

1. Football 2. National Football League

ISBN 978-0-345-51795-1; 978-0-345-51797-5 ebook

LC 2010-31008

"Filled with anecdotes, player recollections, and other wonderful details, this should be the most popular football book of the season. Terrific reading." Booklist

Curtis, Brian

Every week a season; a journey inside big-time college football. Ballantine Books 2004 299p il $24.95; pa $14.95   **796.332**

1. Football 2. College sports

ISBN 0-345-47014-1; 0-345-48337-5 pa

LC 2004-303037

Curtis provides "an appreciation for the preparation and emotional investment at the foundation of every college football game. Legions of fans will savor every word." Booklist

Dent, Jim

Courage beyond the game; Jim Dent. Thomas Dunne Books/St. Martin's Press 2011 xi, 333 p.p ill.   **796.332**

1. College football 2. Football players 3. Cancer -- Patients

ISBN 9780312652852; 9781250007001

LC 2011009348

This book, a 2011 "Kirkus Reviews" Best Nonfiction title, tells the story of "Freddie Steinmark [who] was an under-sized but scrappy young man when he arrived in Austin as a freshman at the University of Texas in 1967. Despite the pronouncement by many coaches that he was too small to play football at the college level, Freddie was a tenacious competitor who vowed to start every game as a varsity Longhorn. By the start of the 1969 season, Freddie was making his mark on the college gridiron and national stage as UT's star safety, but he'd also developed a crippling pain in his thigh that worried his high school sweetheart, Linda. Despite the increasingly debilitating pain, Freddie continued to play throughout the season, helping the Longhorns to rip through opponents like pulpwood. His final game was for the national championship at the end of 1969, when the Longhorns rallied to beat Arkansas in a legendary game that has become known as 'the Game of the Century.' Tragically, bone cancer took Freddie off the field when nothing else could." (Publisher's note)

Includes bibliographical references (p. [317]-318)

and index.

The **Junction** boys; how ten days in hell with Bear Bryant forged a champion team. St. Martin's Press 1999 290p il $24.95; pa $13.95   **796.332**
   1. Football 2. Football coaches
   ISBN 0-312-19293-2; 0-312-26755-X pa
                    LC 99-22179
"In February 1954, Paul 'Bear' Bryant took the head football coaching position at Texas A & M. The story of his first Aggie team, vividly recounted here by journalist Dent, is a little-known but memorable chapter in the legendary coach's career." Booklist

Resurrection; the miracle season that saved Notre Dame. Thomas Dunne Books 2009 306p il $25.99   **796.332**
   1. Football 2. Sportscasters 3. Football coaches 4. Notre Dame Fighting Irish (Football team)
   ISBN 978-0-312-56721-7
                 LC 2009-16738
"The ubiquitous Notre Dame fan base will seek this [book] out in every corner of the country." Booklist
Includes bibliographical references

The **undefeated**; the Oklahoma Sooners and the greatest winning streak in college football history. St. Martin's Press 2001 288p il $24.95; pa $14.95   **796.332**
   1. Football 2. Oklahoma Sooners (Football team)
   ISBN 0-312-26656-1; 0-312-30326-2 pa
                 LC 2001-34896
The author recounts how "Oklahoma Sooner football coach Bud Wilkinson won an all-time record 47 straight games over five seasons, which included three undefeated years, from 1954 through 1956. . . . {This} is a fascinating account of an extraordinary athletic achievement that is unlikely to be approached, let alone equaled." Booklist
Includes bibliographical references

Drape, Joe
   Soldiers first; duty, honor, country, and football at West Point. Joe Drape. Times Books 2012 275 p.   **796.332**
   1. United States Military Academy 2. United States Corps of Cadets -- History 3. United States Military Academy -- Football -- History
   ISBN 0805094903; 9780805094909
                 LC 2012013054
This book by Joe Drape "reveals the unique pressures and expectations that make a year of Army football so much more than just a tally of wins and losses. . . . Drape introduces us to this special group of young men and their achievements on and off the field. . . . Together with Coach Ellerson, his staff, and West Point's officers and instructors, they and their teammates embrace the demands made on them and learn crucial lessons that will resonate throughout their lives." (Publisher's note)

Eisenberg, John
   Ten -gallon war; the NFL's Cowboys, the AFL's Texans, and the feud for Dallas's pro football future. John Eisenberg. Houghton Mifflin Harcourt 2012 308 p. $27.00   **796.332**
   1. Football -- History 2. Dallas Texans (Football team) 3. Dallas Cowboys (Football team) 4. Dallas Cowboys (Football team) -- History 5. Houston Texans (Football team) -- History
   ISBN 0547435509; 9780547435503
                 LC 2012016241
This book, by John Eisenberg, "recounts the story of the birth of pro football in Dallas. . . . In the 1960s, . . . professional football began to flourish across the country. . . . [T]wo young oil tycoons started their own professional football franchises in Dallas the very same year: the NFL's Dallas Cowboys and, as part of a new upstart league designed to thwart the NFL's hold on the game, the Dallas Texans of the AFL. Almost overnight, a bitter feud was born." (Publisher's note)

Feinstein, John
   Next man up; a year behind the lines in today's NFL. Little, Brown 2005 502p il $25.95   **796.332**
   1. Football 2. Baltimore Ravens (Football team)
   ISBN 0-316-00964-4
Feinstein's look at the current state of the National Football League (NFL) focuses on the 2004 Baltimore Ravens' season.
"Even those who are not fanatical football fans will find that, beyond the information provided on players and coaches, there are two other engaging topics in the book: Feinstein's ruminations on how reporting and writing about football are different from reporting and writing about other sports, and his portrayal of the business side of the game through conversations with Ravens owner Steve Bisciotti. . . . Professional football fans cannot lose by reading this book. As for the rest of us, [it] provides interesting glimpses into a strange but popular cultural realm." Christ Sci Monit

Lazarus, Adam
   Super Bowl Monday; from the Persian Gulf to the shores of west Florida: the New York Giants, the Buffalo Bills and Super Bowl XXV. Taylor Trade Pub. 2011 325p il $24.95; ebook $11.99 **796.332**
   1. Football 2. Persian Gulf War, 1991 3. Super Bowl Game (Football) 4. Buffalo Bills (Football team) 5. New York Giants (Football team)
   ISBN 978-1-58979-600-3; 978-1-58979-602-7 ebook
                 LC 2011010710
"This is a wonderful account of a great game and also a look at sports as a diversion from the strife-filled real world. An excellent mix of sports reporting and social history." Booklist
Includes bibliographical references

Miller, John J.
   The **big** scrum; how Teddy Roosevelt saved football. HarperCollins 2011 258p il $25.99; ebook $12.99   **796.332**
   1. Football 2. Governors 3. Presidents 4. College

sports 5. Vice-presidents 6. Nobel laureates for peace
ISBN 978-0-06-174450-1; 0-06-174450-6; 978-0-06-207899-5 ebook; 0-06-207899-2 ebook

LC 2010-32233

"A worthy addendum to the story of football's rise, even though the case for Roosevelt as a cornerstone of its development feels overstated. A good yarn." Kirkus

Includes bibliographical references (p. [227]-245) and index.

Piascik, Andy

Gridiron gauntlet; the story of the men who integrated pro football, in their own words. Taylor Trade Pub. 2009 258p $24.95 **796.332**
1. Football 2. African American athletes 3. National Football League
ISBN 978-1-58979-442-9

LC 2009-9660

For this history of the integration of professional football, the author "interviewed a dozen black football players who played in the AAFC, the NFL, or the AFL between 1946 and 1961. The players ranged from Hall of Fame fullback Joe Perry and stars George Taliaferro and Bob Mann to lesser lights like Eddie Macon, Eddie Bell, Charlie Powell, and John Brown. . . . The stories they tell are humorous, disturbing, angry, sad, and uplifting. An involving and essential read for anyone interested in football." Libr J

Rielly, Edward J.

Football; an encyclopedia of popular culture. University of Nebraska Press 2009 439p pa $26.95 **796.332**
1. Reference books 2. Football -- Encyclopedias
ISBN 978-0-8032-9012-9; 0-8032-9012-8

LC 2009-5245

"Rielly's interest is not so much in football per se as in football as a force in American culture. . . . [This volume offers] short essays arranged alphabetically on topics which the author feels are significant both to football and to American history and culture. Some of the selected topics are expected (Bowl Games, Forward Pass, Television Broadcasting) while others are more surprising (Jewelry, September 11 Terrorist Attacks, Wine). Rielly has a relaxed and informal writing style which practically invites you to pull up a chair and make yourself comfortable while he discourses on his chosen topics." PopMatters

Includes bibliographical references

St. John, Warren

Rammer jammer yellow hammer; a journey into the heart of fan mania. Crown Publishers 2004 275p $24 **796.332**
1. Football 2. Alabama Crimson Tide (Football team)
ISBN 0-609-60708-1

LC 2003-24718

"Wearing a thin veneer of journalistic detachment, St. John followed his beloved Alabama Crimson Tide football team during the 1999 season. The result is a sharp, sneaky-funny, but loving portrait of the team and its incredibly loyal fans." Booklist

796.334 Soccer (Association football)

Anderson, Chris

The numbers game; why everything you know about soccer is wrong. Chris Anderson and David Sally. Penguin Books 2013 384 p. $16 **796.334**
1. Soccer 2. Mathematical analysis 3. Soccer -- Mathematical models 4. Soccer -- Statistical methods
ISBN 0143124560; 9780143124566

LC 2013011448

This book from Chris Anderson and David Sally is "about the use of analytics in soccer." Topics include "what percentage of possession determines victory," "whether it is best to focus on scoring goals or not conceding them," "how much coaches matter to a team's success," among others. (Kirkus Reviews)

Includes bibliographical references and index

Dubois, Laurent

Soccer empire; the World cup and the future of France. University of California Press 2010 xx, 329p il ebook $18.95; $45; pa $18.95 **796.334**
1. Soccer 2. World Cup (Soccer) 3. Soccer players 4. France -- History -- 20th century
ISBN 978-0-520-94574-6; 9780520259287; 9780520269781

LC 2009042962

"Laurent Dubois illuminates the connections between empire and sport by tracing the story of World Cup soccer, from the Cup's French origins in the 1930s to Africa and the Caribbean and back again. . . . [He] recounts the lives of two of soccer's most electrifying players, [Zinedine] Zidane and his outspoken teammate, Lilian Thuram." Publisher's note

Includes bibliographical references

Galeano, Eduardo

Soccer in sun and shadow; by Eduardo Galeano ; translated by Mark Fried. Perseus Books Group 2013 320 p. $16.99 **796.334**
1. Soccer
ISBN 1568584946; 9781568584942

LC 986769

This is a "revised and updated version" of Uruguayan author Eduardo Galeano's 1995 book about soccer. "Like so many children born in Latin America, Galeano . . . grew up wanting to play soccer. In his dreams, he was a star. During the day, however, he 'was the worst wooden leg ever to set foot on the little soccer fields of my country.' Nonetheless, his love affair with the sport continued." (Kirkus Reviews)

Hirshey, David

The **ESPN** World Cup companion; everything you need to know about the planet's biggest sporting event. [by] David Hirshey and Roger Bennett; [foreword by Steve Nash] ESPN Books 2010 251p il $30 **796.334**
1. World Cup (Soccer)
ISBN 978-0-345-51792-0

LC 2010-7273

"Arranged chronologically, the guide takes readers through cup competitions of the past 80 years. . . . Unburdened by endless statistics and scores, the guide does include three pages of facts and figures at the end and dozens of photos throughout. An affordable purchase, an enduring value." Libr J

Includes bibliographical references

Kuper, Simon

Soccernomics; why England loses, why Germany and Brazil win, and why the US, Japan, Australia, Turkey--and even Iraq--are destined to become the kings of the world's most popular sport. [by] Simon Kuper and Stefan Szymanski. Nation Books 2009 328p pa $14.95   **796.334**

1. Soccer
ISBN 978-1-56858-425-6

LC 2009-23502

"Whether analyzing the relationship of spending to winning or applying game theory to the penalty kick, the authors' delight in discovery proves both persuasive and contagious. It's a fascinating book with the potential to effect genuine change in the sport." Booklist

Includes bibliographical references

St. John, Warren

Outcasts united; a refugee team, an American town. Spiegel & Grau 2008 307p hardcover o.p. pa $15   **796.334**

1. Soccer 2. Refugees 3. Soccer coaches 4. Maintenance services executives
ISBN 978-0-385-52203-8; 0-385-52203-7; 978-0-385-52204-5 pa; 0-385-52204-5 pa

LC 2008-40697

This is a "book about an unlikely soccer program in the outlying Atlanta burb of Clarkston, Georgia. . . . Clarkston's residents woke up one morning and found that the city's housing projects had become havens of resettlement for refugee families from war-ravaged locales including Liberia, Afghanistan and Bosnia. Soccer is a pastime like sandlot baseball or touch football to the often-traumatized boys on the Fugees, a ramshackle intramural team of nine to 17-year-olds that St. John follows, along with its Jordanian founder Luma Hassan Mufleh, a Smith-educated woman whose role as volunteer coach quickly expands to extended family member and social worker. St. John's aim is to draw a portrait of small-town America in transition, and his eye for detail is compelling from start to finish." Time Out N Y

Includes bibliographical references

Vecsey, George

Eight world cups; my journey through the beauty and dark side of soccer. George Vecsey. Times Books 2014 304 p. illustrations (hardback) $28   **796.334**

1. Soccer 2. World Cup (Soccer)
ISBN 0805098488; 9780805098488

LC 2013042574

In this book, "sports columnist George Vecsey offers a personal perspective on the beautiful game. Blending witty travelogue with action on the field . . . Vecsey offers an . . . account of the last eight World Cups. He immerses himself in the great national leagues, historic clubs, and devoted fans and provides his up-close impressions of charismatic stars like Sócrates, Maradona, Baggio, and Zidane, while also

chronicling the rise of the U.S. men's and women's teams." (Publisher's note)

"Vecsey's insights offer a unique look at the grace of the game as well as the underside of world soccer." LJ

Includes bibliographical references and index

796.342   Tennis (Lawn tennis)

Fisher, Marshall

A **terrible** splendor; three extraordinary men, a world poised for war, and the greatest tennis match ever played. [by] Marshall Jon Fisher. Crown Publishers 2009 336p $25   **796.342**

1. Tennis 2. Davis cup 3. National socialism 4. Tennis players
ISBN 978-0-307-39394-4; 0-307-39394-1

LC 2008-50527

"Richly detailed . . . the story moves from one nail-biting set to the next against a backdrop of improbably high personal and political stakes." Boston Globe

Includes bibliographical references

McEnroe, John

You cannot be serious; {by} John McEnroe with Jams Kaplan. Putnam 2002 342p il $25.95; pa $14   **796.342**

1. Art dealers 2. Tennis players
ISBN 0-399-14858-2; 0-425-19008-0 pa

LC 2002-23875

Tennis star McEnroe's "recollections fall into three categories: accounts of key matches, life as a jet-setting celebrity, and reflections on the emotional roller coaster that has been his personal life." Booklist

Wertheim, L. Jon

Strokes of genius; Federer, Nadal, and the greatest match ever played. Houghton Mifflin Harcourt 2009 211p $24   **796.342**

1. Tennis 2. Wimbledon Championship (Tennis) 3. Tennis players
ISBN 978-0-547-23280-5; 0-547-23280-2

LC 2009-05595

"Wertheim's compelling account of the five-set 2008 Wimbledon final between Roger Federer and Rafael Nadal captures a classic sports rivalry in its prime." Booklist

796.35   Ball driven by club, mallet, bat

Will, George F. (1990)

Men at work; the craft of baseball. HarperPerennial 1991 353p il pa $9.95   **796.35**

1. Baseball 2. Baseball players 3. Sportscasters 4. Baseball managers
ISBN 0-06-097372-2

LC 90-55518

First published 1990 by Macmillan

"The author's own devotion to detail in defining the components of the game is sure to instill in readers a greater appreciation of what is required to master the sport at the major league level, thereby providing a deeper understanding of the foundation of the game. Altogether, this is hard-core baseball presented in fluent style" Libr J

796.352 Golf

Chopra, Deepak

Golf for enlightenment; seven lessons for the game of life. Harmony Bks. 2003 200p $21 **796.352**
1. Golf 2. Spiritual life
ISBN 0-609-60390-6

LC 2002-27636

The author tells a story about "Adam, who, on a day particularly productive of shanks and slices, is accosted by an apparition who adjures the despairing soul to consult golf pro Wendy, likewise an ethereal being. In a seven-part 'fable,' Wendy heightens Adams' awareness of 'now,' relieves him of his control compulsions, and restores his golfing life to balance and harmony. The authorial brand and publicity ensure that Chopra's confection will be highly, if transiently, popular." Booklist

Feinstein, John

A **good** walk spoiled; days and nights on the PGA tour. Little, Brown 1995 xx, 475p il hardcover o.p. pa $14.95 **796.352**
1. Golf 2. PGA Tour Inc.
ISBN 0-316-27737-1 pa

LC 94-49552

Along with "profiles of the game's big names—Norman, Price, Watson—Feinstein's sojourn through the 1994 PGA tour also offers remarkable glimpses of the marginal players who struggle to first qualify for the tour and then maintain their tenuous places on it. . . . Golfers of all ages simply won't be able to put this book down." Booklist

Frost, Mark

The **greatest** game ever played; Harry Vardon, Francis Ouimet, and the birth of modern golf. Hyperion 2002 488p il $30 **796.352**
1. Golf 2. Golfers
ISBN 0-7868-6920-8

LC 2002-68930

"The climax of the narrative . . . is genuinely exciting, a marvelous re-creation of a signature moment in golf history." Booklist

Haney, Hank

The **big** miss; my years coaching Tiger Woods. Hank Haney. 1st ed. Crown Archetype 2012 262 p. $26 **796.352**
1. Haney, Hank 2. Golf -- Coaching 3. Golfers -- United States -- Biography 4. Golf coaches -- United States
ISBN 0307985989; 9780307985989; 9780307985996

LC 2012003092

This memoir details Hank Haney's experiences as "American golfer [Tiger Woods's] former coach. . . . Haney assiduously monitored Woods's moods and frustrations, his silences and sulks. . . . This book is a[n] . . . account of an often-strained partnership as well as a . . . record of what it costs a man not only to dare to be the best of his generation but a champion for all the ages -- until, that was, he suffered the biggest miss of all." (New Statesman)

Nicklaus, Jack

Jack Nicklaus; my story. with Ken Bowden. Simon & Schuster 1997 505p il $30; pa $24.95 **796.352**
1. Golf 2. Golfers
ISBN 0-684-83628-9; 0-684-83870-2 pa

LC 97-3824

"What comes across most forcibly in this fine book is Nicklaus' respect for the complexity of golf and the never-ending challenges it affords players at every level." Booklist

Sampson, Curt

Masters; golf, money, and power in Augusta, Georgia. Villard Bks. 1998 xxxiv, 263p il hardcover o.p. pa $14.95 **796.352**
1. Golf 2. Augusta National Golf Club
ISBN 0-375-75337-0 pa

LC 97-49143

This history of one of the PGA's most prestigious events "traces the tournament's history since 1933, revealing both the dramatic moments and the controversial secrets, most notably racism—certainly a book to raise eyebrows at the Augusta National Golf Club." Libr J

796.357 Baseball

Achorn, Edward

Fifty -nine in '84; old Hoss Radbourn, barehanded baseball, and the greatest season a pitcher ever had. Smithsonian Books/HarperCollins 2010 366p il $25.99 **796.357**
1. Baseball 2. Baseball players
ISBN 978-0-06-182586-6; 0-06-182686-7

LC 2009-34296

"This is not just a recitation of barehanded baseball and old-time brawling, but a story that, with its larger-than-life protagonist, numerous exploits, and a love interest, reads like a novel. Hugely appealing for baseball die-hards." Libr J

Angell, Roger

★ **Game** time: a baseball companion; edited by Steve Kettmann. Harcourt 2003 398p hardcover o.p. pa $15 **796.357**
1. Baseball
ISBN 0-15-100824-8; 0-15-601387-8 pa

LC 2002-152611

"Half of the essays in this compilation of highlights from Angell's 40 years of covering baseball for the New Yorker have not previously appeared in book form, and even those that have are well worth revisiting. Angell . . . remains the dean of baseball writers." Booklist

Once more around the park; a baseball reader. Ivan R. Dee 2001 351p pa $16.95   **796.357**
1. Baseball
ISBN 1-566-63371-0; 978-1-566-63371-0
LC 00-50436

First published 1991 by Ballantine Books

A collection of 21 pieces, some from Angell's earlier books and others previously uncollected.

"Outstanding among the choices . . . are visits with Hall of Famer Bob Gibson and then-91-year-old Smoky Joe Wood." Libr J

Barra, Allen
Clearing the bases; the greatest baseball debates of the last century. foreword by Bob Costas. St. Martin's Press 2002 xxi, 261p $23.95; pa $13.95   **796.357**
1. Baseball
ISBN 0-312-26556-5; 0-312-30253-3 pa
LC 2001-48992

The author "provides considerable insight into many of the most hotly debated topics of baseball's last 100 years." Booklist

Mickey and Willie; Mantle and Mays, the parallel lives of baseball's golden age. Allen Barra. Crown Archetype 2013 xiii, 479 p., [24] p. of platesp ill. (some col.) (hardcover) $27   **796.357**
1. Baseball players -- United States -- Biography
ISBN 0307716481; 9780307716484
LC 2012013345

This book, by Allen Barra, "exposes the uncanny parallels--and lifelong friendship--between two of the greatest baseball players ever to take the field. Culturally, Mickey Mantle and Willie Mays were light-years apart. . . . What their fans also didn't know was that the two men shared a close personal friendship--and that each was the only man who could truly understand the other's experience." (Publisher's note)

Includes bibliographical references and index

Rickwood Field; a century in America's oldest ballpark. W. W. Norton & Company 2010 367p il $27.95   **796.357**
1. Baseball 2. Birmingham (Ala.) 3. Birmingham Barons (Baseball team) 4. Rickwood Field (Birmingham, Ala.) 5. Birmingham Black Barons (Baseball team)
ISBN 978-0-393-06933-4; 0-393-06933-8
LC 2010-10896

"Rickwood Field, a covered-grandstand fossil in Birmingham, Ala., turns 100 this season. Named after iron scion Rick Woodward, the stadium — home to the Birmingham Barons — has outlasted Philadelphia's Shibe Park and Pittsburgh's Forbes Field and every other major and minor league ballpark that stood on Aug. 18, 1910, when Birmingham put 57 extra streetcars into service for Opening Day. Barra . . . takes readers far beyond the who's who of baseball legends who visited Rickwood, including Connie Mack, the stadium's design consultant, and Ty Cobb, Babe Ruth,

Satchel Paige, Hank Aaron and Reggie Jackson. He spins the thorny racial history of Birmingham through the prism of the old ballpark." Minneapolis Star Tribune

Includes bibliographical references

Barry, Dan
★ Bottom of the 33rd; hope and redemption in baseball's longest game. Harper 2011 255p il $26.99   **796.357**
1. Baseball 2. Baseball -- Records 3. Pawtucket Red Sox (Baseball team) 4. Rochester Red Wings (Baseball team) 5. Minor league baseball -- United States -- History
ISBN 978-0-06-201448-1; 0-06-201448-X
LC 2010-51656

"On a frigid evening in April 1981, 1,740 Pawtucket, R.I., Red Sox fans settled into their seats for a game with the Rochester Red Wings of the AAA International League. With the score tied 11 at the end of regulation, the teams played on. And on. On past 12:50 a.m., when the curfew provision, mysteriously missing from that year's edition of the rule book, would have suspended the contest; on past the 21st inning, when each team maddeningly scored a run; on past the 29th and record-tying inning; on past 4:00 a.m., the bottom of the 32nd, when the league president was finally reached and ordered the umpires to suspend the contest." Kirkus

Bissinger, H. G.
Three nights in August; strategy, heartbreak, and joy, inside the mind of a manager. [foreword by Tony La Russa] Houghton Mifflin 2005 xxi, 280p $25; pa $13.95   **796.357**
1. Baseball players 2. Baseball managers 3. St. Louis Cardinals (Baseball team)
ISBN 0-618-40544-5; 0-618-71053-1 pa
LC 2004-65134

For this book, the author "was given complete access to Tony La Russa and his St. Louis Cardinals. . . . La Russa collaborated fully, hid nothing, freely divulged his thoughts, notes, fears. The result is a fascinating look inside the day-to-day, game-by-game, inning by inning managing of a professional baseball team." N Y Times Book Rev

Includes bibliographical references

Boston, Talmage
1939, baseball's tipping point; foreword by John Grisham. Bright Sky Press 2005 288p il $24.95   **796.357**
1. Baseball
ISBN 1-931721-53-X
LC 2004-65046

This is a "terrific collection of stories and profiles of some of the baseball figures that made 1939 one of the most extraordinary years that any sport has ever enjoyed." Newberg Report

Includes bibliographical references

Bradley, Richard

The **greatest** game; the Yankees, the Red Sox, and the playoff of '78. Free Press 2008 286p il hardcover o.p. pa $15   **796.357**

1. Boston Red Sox (Baseball team) 2. New York Yankees (Baseball team)

ISBN 978-1-4165-3438-9; 1-4165-3438-5; 978-1-4165-3439-6 pa; 1-4165-3439-3 pa

LC 2007-45382

"In 1978, the American League East division champion was determined by a one-game playoff, a taut battle between the Yankees and the Red Sox at Fenway Park. Bradley gives a pitch-by-pitch breakdown of the Boston loss (a three-run homer by Bucky Dent in the top of the seventh cemented the Yankees' lead), and an account of the volatile season preceding it. At a time when pro baseball was making the transition from homegrown pastime to big business, emotions ran high and outsized personalities clashed; New York's pugnacious manager, Billy Martin, resigned in tears midseason. Bradley's prosaic style and his penchant for statistics sometimes test the reader's patience, but his portraits of the coaches and players who converged that day in October lend an intimacy and richness to the book." New Yorker

Includes bibliographical references

Bryant, Howard

Shut out; a story of race and baseball in Boston. Routledge 2002 278p il $27.50   **796.357**

1. Baseball 2. Race discrimination 3. Boston Red Sox (Baseball team) 4. Boston (Mass.) -- Race relations

ISBN 0-415-92779-X

LC 2002-69950

"Bryant looks at both sides of the race issue, and backs his conclusions with exhaustive research from a variety of sources." Publ Wkly

Includes bibliographical references

Clavin, Tom

The **DiMaggios**; Three Brothers, Their Passion for Baseball, Their Pursuit of the American Dream. Ecco 2013 320 p. $25.99   **796.357**

ISBN 006218377X; 9780062183774

This book looks at Vincent, Joe and Dominic DiMaggio. "Three brothers of 11 children born to Italian immigrants, the three boys excelled first in the Pacific Coast League for the local San Francisco Seals and then, one-by-one, they rose to play in the major leagues." Their careers during and after baseball and their personal relationships are explored. (Kirkus Reviews)

Colton, Larry

Southern League; a true story of baseball, civil rights, and the deep South's most compelling pennant race. Larry Colton. Grand Central Pub. 2013 336 p. (hardcover) $27.99   **796.357**

1. Birmingham (Ala.) -- Race relations 2. Race discrimination in sports -- History 3. Birmingham Barons (Baseball team) -- History 4. Birmingham Barons (Baseball team) 5. Baseball -- Alabama -- Birmingham -- History 6. Southern League (Baseball league) -- History 7. Minor league baseball -- Alabama -- Birmingham 8. Discrimination in sports -- United States -- History

ISBN 1455511889; 9781455511884

LC 2012051309

This book by Larry Colton presents "an account of the 1964 season of the racially integrated [baseball team the] Birmingham Barons of the Southern League. The author focuses on the fortunes not just of the team, but some key individuals: Barons' owner Albert Belcher, manager Haywood Sullivan, pitchers Paul Lindblad and John Blue Moon Odom, players Hoss Bowlin and Tommie Reynolds. . . . . Colton also keeps track of the explosive racial issues occurring that summer." (Kirkus Reviews)

Costas, Bob

Fair ball; a fan's case for baseball. Broadway Bks. 2000 179p hardcover o.p. pa $12.95 **796.357**

1. Baseball

ISBN 0-7679-0466-4 pa

LC 99-87992

"The root of baseball's ills, the sports broadcaster Bob Costas argues, lies in how teams like the Yankees and Atlanta Braves, by virtue of vastly higher revenues than franchises like the Montreal Expos or Kansas City Royals, threaten the game's legitimacy by having 'a monopoly on sustained success.' Costas's solution is for team owners to start meaningful revenue sharing and force a salary cap on the intransigent players union, even if it takes another strike or lockout to do it." N Y Times Book Rev

Cramer, Richard Ben

Joe DiMaggio; the hero's life. Simon & Schuster 2000 546p $28; pa $16   **796.357**

1. Baseball players

ISBN 0-684-85391-4; 0-684-86547-5 pa

LC 00-49232

In this biography of the baseball player, "Cramer taps every plank in the wall that DiMaggio erected around himself and that protected him from inquiry. In the wall's hollow spots, Cramer locates the girls, finds the Mob guys, and behind the legend of grace and elegance on and off the field discovers a legend who in reality was more often than not graceless and inelegant." New Yorker

Creamer, Robert W.

Stengel; his life and times. University of Neb. Press 1996 349p il pa $18.95   **796.357**

1. Baseball players 2. Baseball managers

ISBN 0-8032-6367-8

LC 95-40143

First published 1984 by Simon & Schuster

"Casey Stengel is remembered as either the shrewd, innovative New York Yankee manager who won 10 pennants and seven World Series from 1949 to 1960 or as the seemingly senile, aged master of malaprop who (mis)-managed the legendarily inept New York Mets in the early 1960s. Creamer . . . dissolves the apparently disparate images and melds them into an inclusive vision of an unexpectedly complex man." Booklist

Dickson, Paul

★ The **Dickson** baseball dictionary; edited and augmented by Skip McAfee. 3rd ed.; Norton 2009 xxiv, 974p il $49.95   **796.357**
1. Reference books 2. Baseball -- Dictionaries
ISBN 978-0-393-06681-4

LC 2008-51238

First published 1989 by Facts on File

This dictionary "includes 10,000 terms and 18,000 individual definitions. . . . The book features baseball terminology, slang, team names, and stadiums—but not individuals. Assorted softball terms appear as well. . . . This volume is a fabulous addition for any library and a must-have for any baseball fan's personal library." Choice

Includes bibliographical references

The **hidden** language of baseball; how signs and sign-stealing have influenced the course of our national pastime. Walker & Co 2003 230p il $22 **796.357**
1. Baseball
ISBN 0-8027-1392-0

LC 2003-41125

"Anyone who has ever played or coached youth baseball or paid close attention to the third-base coach at a big-league game will appreciate the author's guided tour through the history of diamond sign language. Dickson is a fine story-teller, and his latest book is a welcome addition to the rich canon of baseball literature." Booklist

Includes bibliographical references

Feinstein, John

Where nobody knows your name; life in the minor leagues of baseball. John Feinstein. Doubleday 2014 384 p. $26.95   **796.357**
1. Minor league baseball 2. Minor league baseball -- United States -- History
ISBN 0385535937; 9780385535939

LC 2013030645

This book, by John Feinstein, presents a " journey through the world of minor-league baseball. . . . Focusing exclusively on the Triple-A level, one step beneath Major League Baseball, Feinstein introduces readers to nine unique men: three pitchers, three position players, two managers, and an umpire. Through their compelling stories, Feinstein pulls back the veil on a league that is chock-full of gifted baseball players, managers, and umpires." (Publisher's note)

Fleitz, David L.

Shoeless; the life and times of Joe Jackson. McFarland & Co. 2001 314p il pa $29.95   **796.357**
1. Baseball players 2. Chicago White Sox (Baseball team)
ISBN 0-7864-0978-9

LC 2001-18318

"Shoeless Joe Jackson, banned from baseball for his alleged involvement in the 1919 World Series gambling scandal, is viewed by many as an illiterate phenom hustled by city slickers. Fleitz shows it ain't so, Joe, in this provocative biography." Booklist

Includes bibliographical references

Frost, Mark

Game six; Cincinnati, Boston, and the 1975 World Series: the triumph of America's pastime. Hyperion 2009 406p il $26.99; pa $15.99   **796.357**
1. Baseball 2. World Series (Baseball) 3. World series (Baseball) 4. Boston Red Sox (Baseball team) 5. Cincinnati Reds (Baseball team)
ISBN 978-1-4013-2310-3; 1-4013-2310-3; 978-1-4013-1026-4 pa; 1-4013-1026-5 pa

LC 2009-23227

"Game Six of the 1975 World Series between the Boston Red Sox and the Cincinnati Reds has become one of the most storied contests in the history of baseball. . . . [The author] captures all the excitement and tension of the game, and his book reads like a novel, full of suspense and larger-than-life characters." Libr J

Geist, Bill

Little League confidential; one coach's completely unauthorized tale of survival. Dell Pub 1999 217p pa $15   **796.357**
1. Baseball 2. Little League Baseball, Inc.
ISBN 0-440-50877-0

First published 1992 by Macmillan

The author "relates his decade of service as a little-league baseball coach. He admittedly distills his experiences—and those of others—into a season-long 'docudrama' journal. He tells of pompous coaches lecturing their miniplayers on the subtleties of the infield fly rule; he addresses the question of positioning a player with a personal-injury lawyer for a dad. The book is a wonderful effort filled with empathy for kids, impatience for pushy parents, and a good sense of humor." Booklist

Gentile, Derek

★ **Splitters,** squeezes, and steals; the plays, strategies, and rules of baseball. Black Dog & Leventhal 2009 256p il $29.95   **796.357**
1. Baseball
ISBN 978-1-57912-788-6

LC 2009-00639

This examination of the evolution of the plays, moves, rules, equipment, and strategies that make up baseball "is divided into seven parts: Pitching, Batting, Fielding, Baserunning, Umpires and Management, Equipment, and Ballparks. Chapters include 'The Fastball,' 'The Hit and Run,' 'Stealing Bases,' 'The Hidden Ball Trick,' and more—and each play or move is dissected in detail to reveal its history, its execution, and its greatest innovators." Publisher's note

Includes bibliographical references

Golenbock, Peter

Amazin' the miraculous history of New York's most beloved baseball team. St. Martin's Press 2002 654p il $27.95; pa $18.95   **796.357**
1. New York Mets (Baseball team)
ISBN 0-312-27452-1; 0-312-30992-9 pa

LC 2001-48870

This is a history of the New York Mets baseball team

"Golenbock combines his own well-researched commentary with the recollections of eyewitnesses. . . . This is a delightful and painstakingly detailed trip down memory lane that Mets fans will cherish." Publ Wkly

Includes bibliographical references

Goodwin, Doris Kearns

Wait till next year; a memoir. Simon & Schuster 1997 261p il hardcover o.p. pa $14   **796.357**
1. Authors 2. Historians 3. Biographers 4. Nonfiction writers 5. Political commentators 6. Brooklyn Dodgers (Baseball team)
ISBN 0-684-84795-7 pa

LC 97-39766

"For self-esteem-building female role models, for baseball lore and inning-by-inning action and for a lively trip into the recent American past, you could hardly do better." N Y Times Book Rev

Gould, Stephen Jay (2004) ✓

Triumph and tragedy in Mudville; a lifelong passion for baseball. foreword by David Halberstam. Norton 2003 342p il hardcover o.p. pa $14.95   **796.357**
1. Baseball
ISBN 0-393-05755-0; 978-0-393-32557-7 pa; 0-393-32557-1 pa

LC 2002-155523

This is a collection of Gould's "essays about baseball, written over 20 years and published in venues as divergent as the New York Times and Vanity Fair. . . . The essays are uniformly wonderful. . . . Scientific analysis intersects gently with flat-out fandom. Gould could think, he could write, he was funny, and he loved, loved baseball." Booklist

A great and glorious game; baseball writings of A. Bartlett Giamatti. edited by Kenneth S. Robson; foreword by David Halberstam. Algonquin Bks. 1998 121p $15.95   **796.357**
1. Baseball 2. Baseball -- United States 3. Baseball -- Social aspects -- United States 4. National League of Professional Baseball Clubs
ISBN 1-56512-192-9

LC 97-32803

"Giamatti was a professor, a university president, and, briefly, commissioner of baseball. In his spare time he wrote articles on baseball. . . . {This collection} brings together nine such essays, written between 1977 and 1989. Among the pieces . . . are meditations on baseball and the American character, a statement to the press following his lifetime banishment from baseball of superstar Pete Rose for gambling, a tribute to pitcher Tom Seaver, and a . . . reflection on the end of the baseball season." (Christ Sci Monit)

Giamatti's "writings make baseball a metaphor for America and Americans. His imagery, in the nine essays in this . . . book, elevates the game from ordinary to beautiful and sometimes humorous." N Y Times Book Rev

Gruver, Ed

Koufax; by Edward Gruver. Taylor Pub. Co. 2000 264p il $24.95; pa $16.95   **796.357**
1. Baseball players 2. Brooklyn Dodgers (Baseball team)
ISBN 0-87833-157-3; 0-87833-294-4 pa

LC 99-56763

"This is the biography of legendary L.A. Dodgers pitcher Sandy Koufax, who for half a decade mesmerized hitters as few have ever done. . . . Drawing on childhood friends, teammates, opponents, journalists, and Dodger management, Gruver has written a compelling story, complete with appendix of notable statistics." Libr J

Halberstam, David

★ Summer of '49. Morrow 1989 304p il hardcover o.p. pa $14.95   **796.357**
1. Boston Red Sox (Baseball team) 2. New York Yankees (Baseball team)
ISBN 978-0-06-088426-0; 0-06-088426-6

LC 89-2886

"This book is ostensibly about the pennant race between the Yankees and Red Sox {in 1949} and the 'rivalry' between Joe DiMaggio and Ted Williams. . . . It is a study of all the elements and personalities that influenced baseball that year and beyond. Halberstam brings them together in such an enjoyable, interesting, and informative manner that a reader needn't be a baseball fan to appreciate the book." Libr J

Hample, Zack

Watching baseball smarter; a professional fan's guide for beginners, semi-experts, and deeply serious geeks. Vintage 2007 254p il pa $13.95   **796.357**
1. Baseball
ISBN 978-0-307-28032-9; 0-307-28032-2

LC 2007-296737

The author "covers basics such as what to watch for in pitchers, catchers, hitters, fielders and base runners; he also provides answers to such nagging questions as why spectators stretch in the seventh inning and why most ballplayers grab their crotches. . . . Hample hits the equivalent of a reference book home run with his witty and loose style—taking a friendly for-a-fan-by-a-fan approach that doesn't hide his enormous depth of knowledge." Publ Wkly

Hogan, Lawrence D.

★ Shades of glory; the Negro Leagues and the story of African-American baseball. with a foreword by Jules Tygiel. National Geographic 2006 422p il $26   **796.357**
1. Baseball 2. Negro leagues 3. African American athletes
ISBN 0-7922-5306-X; 978-0-7922-5306-8

LC 2006-273216

This book "traces the history of black baseball from the 19th century to the first great teams, such as the Cuban Giants, and on to the era of the vibrant barnstorming teams from the East Coast, Chicago, and Cuba." Publisher's note

Jamieson, Dave

Mint condition; how baseball cards became an American obsession. Atlantic Monthly Press 2010 272p il $25   **796.357**
1. Baseball cards 2. Collectors and collecting
ISBN 978-0-8021-1939-1; 0-8021-1939-5

"For much of his book, Jamieson seems to be saying that greed and grownups have spoiled card collecting forever. But there's comfort in knowing that the cards have always appealed to baseball lovers and bottom-line business types for their own reasons. Even Jamieson holds out hope that they will find their proper place again in American kids' lives even if it's only in their closets." Minneapolis Star Tribune

Includes bibliographical references

Kahn, Roger

Beyond the boys of summer; the very best of Roger Kahn. edited by Rob Miraldi. McGraw-Hill 2005 xxxvi, 364p hardcover o.p. pa $16.95 **796.357**
1. Baseball
ISBN 0-07-144727-X; 0-07-148119-2 pa
LC 2004-24851
"Kahn is a giant among sports journalists, and this is a fine sampling of his most memorable work." Booklist
Includes bibliographical references

The **head** game; baseball seen from the pitcher's mound. Harcourt 2000 xxii, 310p il $25; pa $14   **796.357**
1. Baseball
ISBN 0-15-100441-2; 0-15-601304-5 pa
LC 00-32014
"The title refers to the battle of wits between pitcher and batter, which is the essence of baseball. Kahn sides with pitching, and in a narrative that is both analytical and anecdotal, he rewards the reader with what amounts to a scholarly treatise on the craft. He does so through engrossing portraits of pitching masters, from Candy Cummings, the reputed inventor of the curveball, to Bruce Sutter, the popularizer of the split-finger fastball. Kahn also presents us with Christy Mathewson on the fadeaway, Warren Spahn on the changeup and Don Drysdale on the duster." Sports Illustrated
Includes bibliographical references

October men; Reggie Jackson, George Steinbrenner, Billy Martin, and the Yankees' miraculous finish in 1978. Harcourt 2003 382p il $25 **796.357**
1. Baseball players 2. Baseball managers 3. Baseball executives 4. Shipbuilding executives 5. New York Yankees (Baseball team)
ISBN 0-15-100628-8
LC 2003-536
"When it comes to writing about baseball, especially New York City baseball, Kahn is king of the hill." Publ Wkly

Katz, Harry

Baseball Americana; treasures from the Library of Congress. [by] Harry Katz [et al.] Smithsonian Books 2009 240p il $29.99   **796.357**
1. Baseball -- History
ISBN 978-0-06-162546-6
LC 2009-13148
"A trove of artifacts and photographs that skillfully conveys the evolution of the game and how it has been chronicled and embraced. . . . The book spans nearly two centuries: baseball's genesis in the late 1700s; its expansion in the late 19th century; the 'glory years' of the early 20th century; the period between World War I and the Great Depression; and

from World War II to the 'wonder years' of the '50s and '60s. Each section is anchored by an essay outlining the period in broad strokes, and copious sidebars help round out the details. The pages are busy, but never scattershot." N Y Times Book Rev

Kelly, Jerry

Bushville; life and time in amateur baseball. McFarland & Co. 2001 202p il pa $21   **796.357**
1. Baseball
ISBN 0-7864-0979-7
LC 01-31264
Kelly's "reflections on what the game has meant to him—from fascination with baseball's special geometry to the sensual pleasure he takes in its textures of leather and wood—make the perfect antidote to most fans' disgust with the big money and big egos of today's major leaguers." Booklist
Includes bibliographical references

Kurlansky, Mark

The **Eastern** stars; how baseball changed the Dominican town of San Pedro de Macoris. Riverhead Books 2010 272p $25.95   **796.357**
1. Baseball 2. San Pedro de Macorís (Dominican Republic)
ISBN 978-1-59448-750-7; 1-59448-750-2
LC 2009-41036
"In 1956, Ozzie (Osvaldo) Virgil played his first rookie season with the New York Giants, becoming the first Dominican baseball player to enter the major leagues in America. Over the next half a century, 471 Dominicans played in at least one major league game, and one in six of those players have come from the small sugar mill town of San Pedro de Macorís. . . . Kurlansky weaves a chronicle of the history of San Pedro de Macorís with the stories of young men seeking only to play baseball and escape the drudgery of working the sugarcane fields to produce a colorful social history of sport." Publ Wkly
Includes bibliographical references

Leavy, Jane

Sandy Koufax; a lefty's legacy. HarperCollins Pubs. 2002 xxii, 282p $23.95; pa $13.95 **796.357**
1. Baseball players
ISBN 0-06-019533-9; 0-06-093329-1 pa
LC 2002-68722
The author "delivers an honest and exquisitely detailed examination of a complex man." Publ Wkly

Leifer, Neil

Neil Leifer: Ballet in the dirt; the golden age of baseball. edited by Eric Kroll; introduction by Ron Shelton; captions by Gabriel Schechter. Taschen 2008 293p il $39.99   **796.357**
1. Baseball -- Pictorial works
ISBN 978-3-8228-4550-9; 3-8228-4550-7
"As a photographer for Sports Illustrated in the 1960s and 1970s, Neil Leifer captured many of baseball's defining moments. But it's the routine, workaday shots he took—Mickey Mantle beating a throw to first, Johnny Bench making a play at the plate or Casey Stengel scolding Yogi Berra during a pitching change—that make this collection fasci-

nating. Here, in gorgeous black and white and Kodachrome color, is the game as it looked before the free-agency craze, before Moneyball, when every player pulled his socks to his knees and performance enhancement meant a big wad to chew." ForbesLife

Includes bibliographical references

Lewis, Michael

★ **Moneyball**; the art of winning an unfair game. Norton 2003 288p $23.95; pa $13.95   **796.357**
  1. Baseball 2. Baseball executives
  ISBN 0-393-05765-8; 0-393-32481-8 pa
               LC 2003-5089

"With so many baseball books to choose from, it is difficult to single out a few as must-haves, but this one comes pretty close." Booklist

Light, Jonathan Fraser

★ The **cultural** encyclopedia of baseball; 2nd ed.; McFarland & Co. 2005 1105p il $75 **796.357**
  1. Reference books 2. Baseball -- Encyclopedias
  ISBN 0-7864-2087-1
               LC 2005-1718

First published 1997

This encyclopedia "profiles every Hall of Fame player, as well as every National and American League club (and predecessors). . . . Statistics play a large role in this resource, which includes facts and figures on just about every conceivable event in the game. Cultural references to baseball are noted throughout in numerous quotations. Some of the more fascinating sections include 'Nicknames,' 'Presidents,' and 'Salaries.' Other entries that make for offbeat perusal include 'Freak Accidents,' 'Sex,' and 'Injuries and Illnesses.'" Choice

Includes bibliographical references

Madden, Bill

Pride of October; what it was to be young and a Yankee. Warner Books 2003 453p il $24.95; pa $14.95   **796.357**
  1. Baseball 2. New York Yankees (Baseball team)
  ISBN 0-446-52932-X; 0-446-69269-7 pa
             LC 2002-191063

Madden "has pieced together a loving appreciation of what it means to wear pinstripes. Some of the better profiles are those of lesser lights, like the backup catcher Charlie Silvera and the pitchers Marius Russo and Tommy Byrne." N Y Times Book Rev

Mann, Lucas

Class A; baseball in the middle of everywhere. Lucas Mann. Pantheon Books 2013 336 p. (hardcover) $26.95   **796.357**
  1. Clinton (Iowa) 2. Minor league baseball 3. Clinton (Iowa) -- Social life and customs 4. Minor league baseball -- Iowa -- Clinton -- History
  ISBN 0307907546; 9780307907547
             LC 2012034683

This book by Lucas Mann examines "minor league baseball and some of the major issues of life in small-town America, in this instance, Clinton, IA. . . . Clinton was once home to more millionaires per capita than any other place in America, but is now a dull image of its past; its Class A team in the Seattle Mariners organization is one of around 200 U.S. minor league teams. . . . Mann seeks to humanize not only the players but also the fans." (Library Journal)

Meltzer, Peter E.

So you think you know baseball? a fan's guide to the official rules. Peter E. Meltzer. W W Norton & Co Inc 2013 344 p. (pbk.) $16.95   **796.357**
  1. Baseball 2. Major League Baseball 3. Baseball -- Rules
  ISBN 039334438X; 9780393344387
             LC 2013001520

In this book, "baseball enthusiast Peter E. Meltzer catalogues every noteworthy baseball rule from the Major League rulebook and illustrates its application with actual plays, from the historical to the contemporary." He "analyzes the entire 'Official Baseball Rules' using hundreds of Major League plays involving both plays on the field situations and plays which have involved the official scorer." (Publisher's note)

Includes bibliographical references and index

Murphy, Cait

★ **Crazy** '08; how a cast of cranks, rogues, boneheads, and magnates created the greatest year in baseball history. Smithsonian/Collins 2007 368p il $24.95   **796.357**
  1. Baseball
  ISBN 978-0-06-088937-1; 0-06-088937-3
             LC 2006-50646

This is an account of the 1908 major league baseball season.

"A book that will long claim the attention of serious sports enthusiasts." Booklist

Includes bibliographical references

Pearlman, Jeff

The **bad** guys won; a season of brawling, boozing, bimbo-chasing, and championship baseball with Straw, Doc, Mookie, Nails, the Kid, and the rest of the 1986 Mets, the rowdiest team to put on a New York uniform, and mayb. HarperCollins 2004 287p il $24.95; pa $13.95   **796.357**
  1. Baseball 2. New York Mets (Baseball team)
  ISBN 0-06-050732-2; 0-06-050733-0 pa
             LC 2003-56991

"Baseball aficionados, especially Mets fans, will enjoy this affectionate but critical look at this exciting season." Publ Wkly

Posnanski, Joe

The **soul** of baseball; a road trip through Buck O'Neil's America. Morrow 2007 276p $24.95   **796.357**
  1. Baseball 2. Baseball players 3. Baseball coaches 4. Baseball managers 5. United States -- Description and travel
  ISBN 978-0-06-085403-4; 0-06-085403-0

An account of how the author "spent a year on the road with the iconic Negro Leagues player and manager Buck

O'Neil (1911-2006), recording the magnanimous 94-year-old's encounters with scores of fans and his vast repertoire of entertaining stories." Publ Wkly

Prager, Joshua

★ The **echoing** green; the untold story of Bobby Thomson, Ralph Branca, and the shot heard round the world. Pantheon Books 2006 498p il $26.95   **796.357**

  1. Baseball 2. Baseball players 3. New York Giants (Baseball team)

  ISBN 0-375-42154-8; 978-0-375-42154-9

                  LC 2006-43157

The author exposes "multiple layers of fascinating backstory to the drama within a drama, and his psychobiographies of Thomson and especially Branca are unfailingly compelling." Booklist

  Includes bibliographical references

Ripken, Cal

Play baseball the Ripken way; the complete illustrated guide to the fundamentals. [by] Cal Ripken, Jr. and Bill Ripken with Larry Burke. Random House 2004 236p il hardcover o.p. pa $15.95   **796.357**

  1. Baseball

  ISBN 1-4000-6122-9; 0-8129-7050-0 pa

                  LC 2003-66725

"This book is the next best thing to a personal lesson with the man who broke Lou Gehrig's record of playing in 2,632 consecutive games; it's a comprehensive look at all aspects of how to play baseball that will benefit young players and adult weekend warriors." Publ Wkly

Robinson, Ray

Yankee Stadium; 75 years of drama, glamor, and glory. by Ray Robinson and Christopher Jennison. Penguin Studio 1998 182p il pa $19.95   **796.357**

  1. Yankee Stadium (New York, N.Y.)

  ISBN 0-670-87093-5; 978-0-670-03301-0 pa; 0-670-03301-0 pa

                  LC 97-48496

"This book is about all the great sporting events—including great boxing matches such as Joe Louis's 1938 demolition of Max Schmeling—and some nonsporting events (such as papal visits and religious revivals) that have occurred at Yankee Stadium over its three-quarters of a century. Baseball does predominate, however, in this tale of 'The House That Ruth Built.' . . . Reminiscences by journalist Pete Hamill, broadcaster Bob Costas, and a few Yankee greats add an extra dimension." Libr J

Ruck, Rob

Raceball; how the Major Leagues colonized the Black and Latin game. Beacon Press 2010 273p il $25.95   **796.357**

  1. Baseball 2. Race relations 3. African American athletes 4. Hispanic American athletes 5. Major League Baseball (Organization)

  ISBN 978-0-8070-4805-4; 0-8070-4805-4

                  LC 2010-37079

The book "blends the intertwined histories of African American and Latin baseball, and their usually ill-fated interactions with Major League Baseball (MLB). . . . [It] recasts conventional notions of baseball history by showing how, in the decades before World War I, Havana became the hub of an international baseball culture. . . . Players in the Negro leagues banned from the major leagues commonly played winter ball in the Caribbean . . . until the early 1940s, along with many white big leaguers supplementing their incomes during the off-season. Cuban teams . . . beat the white major leaguers so frequently that MLB banned teams from playing under their own names, to avoid embarrassment." (Journal of American History)

The author "delves deeply into baseball history to explore the inextricable link between the two phenomena, starting with the struggles of black and Latin players in the segregated pre–Jackie Robinson era, continuing through the painful but inspirational period of integration and into the apex of African-American participation in the 1970s (when more than a quarter of players were black), before exploring the current state of a game dominated by Latin Americans. . . . Compellingly weaves together disparate threads of racial and sporting history." Kirkus

  Includes bibliographical references

Shapiro, Michael

Bottom of the ninth; Branch Rickey, Casey Stengel, and the daring scheme to save baseball from itself. Times Books 2009 303p il $26   **796.357**

  1. Baseball 2. Baseball players 3. Baseball managers 4. Baseball executives

  ISBN 978-0-8050-8247-0; 0-8050-8247-6

                  LC 2008-43582

Shapiro "tells a story of backroom ambitions ultimately defeated by the front offices of the MLB. After the 1958 series, William Shea, Branch Rickey, and Casey Stengel announced their plan to build a third major league, the Continental League; it was fated never to field a team. Shapiro ties the arc of his story to the decline of baseball as America's favorite sport. As much a business history as a baseball story; recommended on both counts." Libr J

  bibliography: p. 283-288

The **last** good season; Brooklyn, the Dodgers, and their final pennant race together. Doubleday 2003 356p il $24.95; pa $14.95   **796.357**

  1. Baseball 2. Brooklyn Dodgers (Baseball team)

  ISBN 0-385-50152-8; 0-767-90688-8 pa

                  LC 2002-71410

"Equal parts sports, history, politics and sociology, Shapiro's book is reminiscent of the works of Caro, Halberstam and Kahn, and belongs in every sports fan's library." Publ Wkly

  Includes bibliographical references (p.   ) and index

Smith, Red

★ **Red** Smith on baseball; the game's greatest writer on the game's greatest years. with a foreword

by Ira Berkow. Dee, I.R. 2000 363p il $24.95; pa
$18.95 **796.357**
1. Baseball
ISBN 1-56663-289-7; 1-56663-415-6 pa
LC 99-53675
This volume contains columns written from the 1940s to
the early 1980s. "Smith's essays on Bobby Thomson's 'shot
heard 'round the world,' Mickey Mantle's first game and
Don Larsen's no-hit pitching in the 1956 World Series are
all worthy of memorization, and his trenchant views on the
reserve clause and the night World Series games are strikes
down the middle. As a bonus, the collection offers readers a
fascinating look at how baseball writing has changed over
the years, as have American attitudes." Publ Wkly

Snyder, Brad
Beyond the shadow of the Senators; the untold
story of the Homestead Grays and the integration
of baseball. Contemporary Books 2003 418p il
$24.95; pa $14.95 **796.357**
1. Baseball 2. Homestead Grays (Baseball team) 3.
United States -- Race relations 4. Washington Senators
(Baseball team)
ISBN 0-07-140820-7; 0-07-143197-7 pa
LC 2002-31335
The author "gives a rich panorama of Washington as it
evolved from a Southern provincial town to a large city with
a black majority. . . . Snyder's book is not just the history of
a team but the tale of one city in all its social complexity." N
Y Times Book Rev
Includes bibliographical references

Stout, Glenn
Fenway 1912; the birth of a ballpark, a cham-
pionship season, and Fenway's remarkable first year.
Houghton Mifflin Harcourt 2011 xxii, 392p il
$26 **796.357**
1. Fenway Park (Boston, Mass.) 2. Boston Red Sox
(Baseball team)
ISBN 978-0-547-19562-9
LC 2011016068
"While some sports histories are bone-dry and distant,
Stout imbues his account with a unique vibrancy and a razor-
sharp intelligence. A wonderful sports book." Booklist

Stump, Al
Cobb; a biography. with a foreword by Jimmie
Reese. Algonquin Bks. 1994 436p il hardcover o.p.
pa $15.95 **796.357**
1. Baseball players
ISBN 1-56512-144-9 pa
LC 94-26122
The author, who collaborated with Cobb on his 1961
autobiography (My life in baseball), here presents his own
version of the life and times of the baseball player
"Emphasizing Cobb's bitter final days, Stump's portrait
of the splenetic Hall of Famer is both chilling and oddly
moving." Am Libr
Includes bibliographical references

Thompson, Teri
★ **American** icon; the fall of Roger Clemens
and the rise of steroids in America's pastime. [by]
Teri Thompson, Nathaniel Vinton, Michael O'Keeffe,
and Christian Red. Alfred A. Knopf 2009 454p
$26.95 **796.357**
1. Baseball 2. Steroids 3. Baseball players 4. Athletes
-- Drug use
ISBN 0-307-27180-3; 978-0-307-27180-8
Four sports reporters, who constitute The New York
Daily News Sports Investigative Team, examine corruption
and the steroids era in American baseball. They discuss the
accusations of performance-enhancing drug use that led to
the investigation of Yankees' baseball player Roger Clemens
by the Justice Department in 2007.
This book "does a nimble job of conjuring up the gym-
rat culture in Texas that promoted the use of performance
enhancement and anti-aging drugs, and the must-win culture
in Major League Baseball that made such drugs appealing to
certain players. . . . By focusing on Clemens and the people
around him, the authors have turned the sprawling story of
steroid-use into a sleek narrative that reads like an investigative thriller, peopled by a Dickensian cast of characters." N
Y Times (Late N Y Ed)
Includes bibliographic references

Thorn, John
Baseball in the Garden of Eden; the secret his-
tory of the early game. Simon & Schuster 2011 365p
il $26; ebook $12.99 **796.357**
1. Baseball 2. Baseball -- United States -- History
ISBN 978-0-7432-9403-4; 0-7432-9403-3; 978-1-
4391-7021-2 ebook
LC 2010045155
"Thorn writes with authority, precision and humor."
Minneapolis Star Tribune
Includes bibliographical references

Tofel, Richard J.
A **legend** in the making; the New York Yankees
in 1939. Dee, I.R. 2002 269p $24.95 **796.357**
1. Baseball 2. New York Yankees (Baseball team)
ISBN 1-56663-411-3
LC 2001-40824
This is the "story of the Yankees' 1939 winning season. .
. . The casual racism against Italians and the utter dismissal
of black baseball are not ignored, and Tofel grounds the year
in events outside of baseball: the Wizard of Oz opens, Freud
dies, Germany invades Poland. A fine gift for fans." Booklist
Includes bibliographical references

Turbow, Jason
The **baseball** codes; beanballs, sign stealing, and
bench-clearing brawls: the unwritten rules of Ameri-
ca's pastime. [by] Jason Turbow, with Michael Duca.
Pantheon Books 2010 294p $25 **796.357**
1. Baseball
ISBN 978-0-375-42469-4; 0-375-42469-5
LC 2009-22253
"The premise [of this book] is that ballplayers, manag-
ers, coaches and various other participants in the culture of

baseball are all clued in to a value system, a mode of behavior that defines a gauzy ideal: the right way to play the game. . . . [The authors] have collected dozens of stories from baseball history about situations that are not governed by the rule book but that pertain to the fuzzy notions of rightness and respect and that describe the contours of the so-called baseball codes. . . . The stories the authors have unearthed to illustrate ballpark justice and morality are often delicious." N Y Times Book Rev

Includes bibliographical references

Tygiel, Jules (1983)
Baseball's great experiment; Jackie Robinson and his legacy. [with a new afterword] 25th anniversary ed, expanded ed; Oxford University Press 2008 415p il pa $19.95 **796.357**
1. Baseball 2. Baseball players 3. Army officers 4. United States -- Race relations
ISBN 978-0-19-533928-4; 0-19-533928-2
LC 2008-273059
First published 1983
A history of the segregation and gradual integration of Afro-American athletes into major league baseball. In addition to Jackie Robinson, the author explores the careers of Larry Doby, Luke Easter, Satchel Paige, and others. Tygiel also notes the vast social and demographic changes wrought by WWII that made integration inevitable
Includes bibliographical references

Vecsey, George
Baseball : a history of America's favorite game. Modern Library 2006 252p il (Modern Library chronicles) $21.95 **796.357**
1. Baseball
ISBN 0-679-64338-9; 978-0-679-64338-8
LC 2006-45033
This history of baseball "unfolds much like a highlights tape, with a breezy background narrative of the game from its pre-Civil War roots to its current drug scandals, structured around set pieces spotlighting the outsized deeds of luminaries like Babe Ruth, Jackie Robinson, Branch Rickey and George Steinbrenner. . . . Vivid, affectionate and cleareyed, Vecsey's account makes for an engaging sports history." Publ Wkly
Includes bibliographical references

Ward, Geoffrey C.
Baseball : an illustrated history; narrative by Geoffrey C. Ward; based on a documentary filmscript by Geoffrey C. Ward and Ken Burns; preface by Ken Burns and Lynn Novick; with an introduction by Roger Angell; contributions by John Thorn {et al.} Knopf 1994 xxv, 486p il $65; pa $39.95 **796.357**
1. Baseball
ISBN 0-679-40459-7; 0-679-76541-7 pa
LC 93-39809
"This lavishly produced, gorgeously illustrated history of the game rises far above the often dreary 'companion volume' genre." Booklist

Weber, Bruce
As they see 'em; travels in the land of umpires. Scribner 2009 341p $26 **796.357**
1. Baseball
ISBN 978-0-7432-9411-9; 0-7432-9411-4
LC 2008-41641
"As a 52-year-old student umpire, the author dons the mask and learns the fundamentals, while spending almost three years visiting baseball venues across the country, as well as interviewing former umpires, players and coaches. . . . Baseball fans will love the insightful, richly textured account of Weber trying to master the plate stance, monitoring each pitch and maintaining a proper strike zone in a physically demanding occupation." Publ Wkly
Includes bibliographical references

Weintraub, Robert
The **house** that Ruth built; a new stadium, the first Yankees championship, and the redemption of 1923. Little, Brown and Co. 2011 421p il $26.99; ebook $12.99 **796.357**
1. Baseball 2. Baseball players 3. Yankee Stadium (New York, N.Y.) 4. New York Yankees (Baseball team)
ISBN 978-0-316-08607-3; 978-0-316-17517-3 ebook
LC 2010-48633
The author "examines the 1923 New York Yankees, the team that opened Yankee Stadium and won the first of the Bronx Bombers' record 27 World Series titles. The center of this work is the clash between the Yankees' star, Babe Ruth, with his new 'bashing' style of playing the game, and the classic 'scientific baseball' epitomized by manager John McGraw and his New York Giants." Publ Wkly
Includes bibliographical references

Wendel, Tim
High heat; the secret history of the fastball and the improbable search for the fastest pitcher of all time. Da Capo Press 2010 268p il $25 **796.357**
1. Baseball
ISBN 978-0-306-81848-6; 0-306-81848-5
LC 2009-53843
"A book like this, so breezy, so informative, so vivid, could only have been written by a true fan of the game. . . . Wendel ends his book by identifying, based on his research, the 12 fastest pitchers in baseball. It's a hard list to argue with. But that doesn't mean some won't. Let the fun continue." PopMatters
Includes bibliographical references

Whitaker, Lang
In the time of Bobby Cox; the Atlanta Braves, their manager, my couch, two decades, and me. Scribner 2011 230p $24 **796.357**
1. Baseball 2. Baseball players 3. Baseball managers 4. Atlanta Braves (Baseball team)
ISBN 978-1-4391-4838-9; 1-4391-4838-4
LC 2010-36177
"In his second incarnation as Atlanta Braves manager, from 1990 through 2010, Bobby Cox, now retired, was so predictably successful—14 straight division titles, 14 seasons of 90 wins or more—as to operate almost under the radar of many baseball fans. Whitaker,. . . pays tribute to

Cox and the teams he managed. There's some analysis here—Whitaker's take on future Hall of Fame pitcher Greg Maddux is especially keen—but readers will more likely appreciate the author's undying connection to his team, which includes an apparently complete, annotated list of every player on the Braves during Cox's second tenure and, more important, the life lessons Whitaker drew from Bobby Cox, among them patience, adaptability, resilience, and a dedication to improving the performance of those he managed. Essential reading for Braves' devotees and a fascinating baseball story for fans of all kinds." Booklist

Williams, Ted

Ted Williams; my life in pictures. {by} Ted Williams with David Pietrusza. Total Sports 2001 201p il $45   **796.357**
    1. Baseball players 2. Baseball managers
    ISBN 1-930844-07-7

                           LC 2001-23360
    Featuring over 300 photographs, this pictorial autobiography recounts Williams's life on and off the field, "many from his personal collection and never before published." Publisher's note

796.4   Weight lifting, track and field, gymnastics

Hoffer, Richard

Something in the air; American passion and defiance in the 1968 Mexico City Olympics. Free Press 2009 258p il $26   **796.4**
    1. Olympic games, 1968 (Mexico City, Mex.)
    ISBN 978-1-4165-8894-8; 1-4165-8894-9

                           LC 2009-09045
    "On Oct. 16, [Tommie] Smith won the gold and [John] Carlos the bronze in the 200-meter race. There they stood on the podium, heads hanging almost humbly and gloved fists raised in a defiant black power salute. Something in the Air, Richard Hoffer's skillfully told tale of the Mexico City Olympics, revolves around this arresting image. . . . There were many other dramas played out in Mexico City—involving George Foreman, the long jumper Bob Beamon and the high jumper Dick Fosbury, among others—and Hoffer gracefully brings them all into the same arena. More important, his jaunty but disciplined prose puts the wind at the reader's back and shows us how the leaps, lifts and dashes of 1968 made a significant impact on the civil rights movement and raised the political consciousness of athletes." N Y Times Book Rev
    Includes bibliographical references

796.42   Track and field

Burfoot, Amby

Runner's world complete book of running; everything you need to run for weight loss, fitness, and competition. edited by Amby Burfoot. Rev. & updated ed.; Rodale; Distributed by Macmillan 2009 312p il pa $21.99   **796.42**
    1. Running
    ISBN 978-1-60529-579-4 pa

                           LC 2009-33150
    First published 1997
    Topics covered include: nutrition, injury prevention and treatment, shoe selection, mental readiness, and marathon preparation.

Davis, David

Showdown at Shepherd's Bush; the 1908 Olympic marathon and the three runners who launched a sporting craze. David Davis. St. Martin's Press 2012 308 p. (hardback) $25.99   **796.42**
    1. Olympic games 2. Track athletics 3. Olympic athletes 4. Olympics -- History 5. Long-distance runners 6. Marathon running -- History
    ISBN 0312641001; 9780312641009; 9781250012395

                           LC 2012010297
    Author David "Davis focuses on three runners [in the 1908 Olympic Games]: pre-race favorite Tom Longboat, a Native American running for Canada, the largely unknown Italian pastry cook Dorando Pietri, and the scrappy Irish-American Johnný Hayes. The race became a sensation after a controversial finish, sparking a marathon craze and helping establish the Olympics as the headline-making international gala it is today." (Kirkus Reviews)

Higdon, Hal

Marathon : the ultimate training guide; 3rd ed; Rodale 2005 369p pa $17.95   **796.42**
    1. Marathon running
    ISBN 978-1-59486-199-4; 1-59486-199-4

                           LC 2005-14083
    First published 1993
    This "manual includes training schedules designed for busy runners, nutritional information, motivational tips, and race-day guidance to help runners of all experience levels reach the 26.2-mile mark with speed, safety, and great satisfaction." Publisher's note

Joyner-Kersee, Jackie

  A **kind** of grace; the autobiography of the world's greatest female athlete. {by} Jackie Joyner-Kersee with Sonja Steptoe. Warner Bks. 1997 310p il $28   **796.42**
    1. African American athletes 2. Heptathletes 3. Olympic athletes 4. Child benefactors 5. Basketball players
    ISBN 0-446-52248-1

                           LC 97-14966
    "A competent account of an admirable life." Booklist

McDougall, Christopher

  Born to run; a hidden tribe, superathletes, and the greatest race the world has never seen. Alfred A. Knopf 2009 287p $24.95   **796.42**
    1. Marathon running 2. Tarahumara Indians
    ISBN 978-0-307-26630-9; 0-307-26630-3

                           LC 2009-922861

"Implausibly difficult marathons, hundreds of miles long, and the ultra-elite competitive runners who tackle them for fun. A hidden, almost mythical, tribe in Mexico untouched by modern disease. Shoe manufacturers driven by corporate greed to sustain an industry that has created modern running injuries. An anthropological study of homo sapiens physiology and the course we took to survive while Neanderthals died out. It may seem farfetched, but Born to Run entwines all those strands and even pop-culture references into an engaging and inspirational read." PopMatters

Robbins, Liz

A **race** like no other; 26.2 miles through the streets of New York. Harper 2008 336p il map $24.99   **796.42**

1. Marathon running

ISBN 978-0-06-137313-8; 0-06-137313-3

LC 2009-275043

A narrative account of the 2007 New York City marathon interweaves the stories of professional and amateur participants, from Great Britain's world-record holder Paula Radcliffe and Latvian two-time winner Jelena Prokopcuka to South African former champion Hendrick Ramaala and a young cancer survivor running his first race.

The author "allows readers to experience the event without ever putting on a pair of running shoes." Publ Wkly

Includes bibliographical references

Scott, Dagny

Runner's world complete book of women's running; the best advice to get started, stay motivated, lose weight, run injury-free, be safe, and train for any distance. [by] Dagny Scott Barrios. Rev. and updated ed.; Distributed to the trade by Holtzbrinck Publishers 2007 324p il pa $16.95   **796.42**

1. Running

ISBN 978-1-59486-758-3; 1-59486-758-5

LC 2007-30645

First published 2000

Topics covered include racing, nutrition, running during pregnancy, weight loss, and proper clothing.

796.42092   Track and field--biography

Jones, Bill

The **ghost** runner; The Epic Journey of the Man They Couldn't Stop. Bill Jones. W W Norton & Co Inc 2013 352 p. ill. (hardcover) $26.95 **796.42092**

1. Running 2. Runners (Athletes)

ISBN 1605984132; 9781605984131

This book, by Bill Jones, is a biography of the non-professional runner John Terrant. "The world would know him as 'the ghost runner,' . . . the extraordinary man whom nobody could stop. . . . When he wanted to run, he was banned for life. . . . Now he was fighting back, gate-crashing races all over Britain. No number on his shirt. . . . Soon he would be a record-breaker, one of the greatest long-distance runners the world had ever seen." (Publisher's note)

796.47   Tumbling, trampolining, acrobatics, contortion

Wall, Duncan

The **ordinary** acrobat; a journey into the wondrous world of the circus, past and present. Duncan Wall. Alfred A. Knopf 2013 336 p. (hardcover) $26.95   **796.47**

1. Circus 2. Acrobats and acrobatics 3. Circus -- History 4. Acrobats -- Biography 5. Circus performers -- Biography

ISBN 0307271722; 9780307271723

LC 2012038250

This book, by Duncan Wall, provides the "story of a young man's plunge into the . . . world of the circus--taking readers deep into circus history and its renaissance as a contemporary art form, and behind the (tented) walls of France's most prestigious circus school. When Duncan Wall . . . applied on a whim to the training program at the École Nationale des Arts du Cirque . . . [he] was, to his surprise, accepted." (Publisher's note)

796.48   Olympic games

Guttmann, Allen (1992)

The **Olympics,** a history of the modern games; 2nd ed; University of Ill. Press 2002 214p il (Illinois history of sports) hardcover o.p. pa $16.95 **796.48**

1. Olympic games

ISBN 0-252-02725-6; 0-252-07046-1 pa

LC 2001-41383

First published 1992

"Guttmann discusses the intended and actual meaning of the modern Olympic Games, from 1896 to 2000. Recounting the memorable and significant athletic events of the Olympics in terms of their social and political impact, Guttmann . . . [attempts to demonstrate] that the modern games were revived to propagate a political message and continue to serve political purposes." Publisher's note

Includes bibliographical references

Spivey, Nigel Jonathan

★ The **ancient** Olympics; [by] Nigel Spivey. Oxford University Press 2004 xxi, 273p il $28; pa $14.95   **796.48**

1. Olympic games

ISBN 0-19-280433-2; 0-19-280604-1 pa

LC 2004-46147

This book "lets us imagine both the strangeness and the glory that surrounded sports in its infancy." Christ Sci Monit

Includes bibliographical references

796.51   Walking

Hart, John

★ **Walking** softly in the wilderness; the Sierra Club guide to backpacking. 4th ed, complete rev and

updated; Sierra Club Books 2005 508p il map (Sierra Club outdoor adventure guide) pa $16.95 **796.51**
1. Backpacking 2. Wilderness areas
ISBN 1-57805-123-1

LC 2004-56554

First published 1977

This guide for both the novice and experienced hiker reflects the environmental concerns of the Sierra Club. Among topics covered are: clothing and equipment; making and breaking camp; problem animals and plants; hiking and camping with kids. Listings of conservation and wilderness travel organizations, map and equipment sources, land management agencies, and Internet contacts are appended.

Includes bibliographical references

Kemsley, William
Backpacker and hiker's handbook. Stackpole Books 2008 290p il map pa $24.95 **796.51**
1. Hiking 2. Backpacking
ISBN 978-0-8117-3462-2; 0-8117-3462-5

LC 2007-21147

This book "tells how to plan and prepare for a backpacking trip and discusses equipment, safety, and the essential trail skills of using a compass, purifying water, cooking, and where and how to set up camp." Publisher's note

Includes bibliographical references

Nicholson, Geoff
The **lost** art of walking; the history, science, philosophy, and literature of pedestrianism. Riverhead Books 2008 276p $24.95 **796.51**
1. Walking
ISBN 978-1-59448-998-3; 1-59448-998-X

LC 2008-25182

"Nicholson catalogues every aspect of walking: its origins, its use as a cure for various ills, expert walkers, eccentric walkers, walking songs, spiritual walking, walking on water, walking in prison, and the analysis of perfect and imperfect walks. . . . The book is varied, wide-ranging, and full of a dry and delightful wit. I found myself giggling every few pages. Nicholson's affection for his subjects and his gusto for walking are palpable." Christ Sci Monit

Includes bibliographical references

Solnit, Rebecca
Wanderlust; a history of walking. Viking 2000 326p il hardcover o.p. pa $15 **796.51**
1. Hiking 2. Walking 3. Voyages and travels
ISBN 0-14-028601-2 pa

LC 99-41153

The author presents a "look at how the act of walking . . . has influenced our history, our science, our literature, and the very way that we see ourselves as human beings. Drawing on a multitude of diverse disciplines, Solnit illustrates that walking has led to some of the best, and worst, incidents in all of history." Booklist

Includes bibliographical references

Tilton, Buck
Hiking & backpacking; a complete illustrated guide. photographs by Stephen Gorman. Knack 2009 244p il map (Knack make it easy) pa $19.95 **796.51**
1. Hiking 2. Backpacking
ISBN 978-1-59921-400-9

LC 2008-41371

"Colorful, with a graphically driven and accessible approach that covers the full array of topics from gear to where, when, and how to hike and camp. For varying skill levels." Libr J

Includes bibliographical references

796.52   Walking and exploring by kind of terrain

Hurd, Barbara (2003)
★ **Entering** the stone; on caves and feeling through the dark. Athens 2008 170p pa $16.95 **796.52**
1. Caves
ISBN 978-0-8203-3153-9; 0-8203-3153-8

LC 2007-44844

First published 2003 by Houghton Mifflin

The author "uses the sport of caving Maryland's Devil's Hole cave and Oregon's Siskiyous Mountains . . . as the launching point for observations about the ways we 'use landscape and the people in our lives to orient ourselves.' Hurd often weaves resonant parallels between what she sees in the nature of caves and her own life, such as her moving recollections of her father and of a friend dying of cancer." Publ Wkly

Tabor, James M. (1998)
Blind descent; the quest to discover the deepest place on earth. Random House 2010 304p $26; ebook $26 **796.52**
1. Caves 2. Explorers 3. Spelunkers 4. Structural engineers
ISBN 978-1-4000-6767-1; 978-1-58836-994-9 ebook

LC 2009-33942

"The author examines the two polar opposites at the head of each of two major cave-diving expeditions: the win-at-all-costs, classic alpha-male, American Bill Stone, who led Mexican cave dives in Cheve and Huatula; and mild-mannered organization man, Ukrainian Alexander Klimchouk, who spearheaded the exploration of his country's notorious Krubera cave. Only one of these men came away with the distinction of having descended deeper into the earth's core than anyone else. Tabor expertly fashions a fly-on-the-wall narrative from the firsthand accounts of Stone, Klimchouk and their supporting casts of death-defying followers. . . . A fascinating and informative introduction to the sport of cave diving, as well as a dramatic portrayal of a significant man-vs.-nature conflict." Kirkus

Includes bibliographical references

Taylor, Joseph E.

Pilgrims of the vertical; Yosemite rock climbers and nature at risk. [by] Joseph E Taylor III. Harvard University Press 2010 368p il map $29.95   **796.52**

1. Mountaineering 2. Yosemite National Park (Calif.)

ISBN 978-0-674-05287-1; 0-674-05287-0

LC 2010-21578

Yosemite "has been a climber magnet for decades, and it was here that many of rock climbing's highly ritualized set of norms and mores evolved. . . . [This book] is at once a chronicle of how the sport evolved in Yosemite and a fascinating social history that considers climbing in the larger context of American life. . . . For the general reader, the book makes a fine introduction to the history of climbing and Yosemite's special place in its development. For climbers, 'Pilgrims of the Vertical' offers a somewhat idiosyncratic view of their sport." Wall Street J

Includes bibliographical references

796.522   Mountains, hills, rocks

Blum, Arlene

Breaking trail; a climbing life. Scribner 2005 313p il map $27.50   **796.522**

1. Mountaineering

ISBN 0-7432-5846-0

LC 2005-44053

"In hiker's parlance, the person who 'breaks trail' is one who leads others across difficult terrain, creating a path as they go. This aptly describes Blum's role, not only in her experiences as a climber, but also as a scientist doing innovative, groundbreaking work. Blum . . . covers a cross section of her life as a climber, from her first experience, as a college student in 1964, to 1993, when she semiretired. Through climbing, she experiences a wide range of emotions, from exhilaration at success to grief over the death of friends. Interspersed between the climbing stories are scenes from her childhood that do much to explain the person she became. This is an engaging, well-written adventure that also serves as a social history of women's roles." Booklist

Boukreev, Anatoli

The **climb**; tragic ambitions on Everest. [by] Anatoli Boukreev and G. Weston Dewalt.   St. Martin's Press 1997 255p il hardcover o.p. pa $14.95   **796.522**

1. Mountaineering 2. Mount Everest Expedition (1996)

ISBN 0-312-20637-2 pa

LC 97-23194

"This is a first-person account of the tragic climbing experience in May 1996 on Mount Everest that left eight hikers dead and several others struggling to stay alive. . . . Fast-paced and easy to read, Boukreev's story of adventure and survival will remain in the reader's memory long after the book is finished." Libr J

Coburn, Broughton

Everest : mountain without mercy; introduction by Tim Cahill, afterword by David Breashears. National Geographic Soc. 1997 256p il maps hardcover o.p. pa $24   **796.522**

1. Mountaineering 2. Mount Everest Expedition (1996)

ISBN 0-7922-7014-2; 0-7922-6984-5 pa

LC 97-10765

"Bringing an understated yet powerful Buddhist/Sherpa ethical perspective to the tragedy on Everest chronicled in Jon Krakauer's Into Thin Air, Coburn reports on the IMAX film crew who participated in the rescue effort when the May 1996 expeditions led by guides Rob Hall and Scott Fischer ended in death and crippling injury." Publ Wkly

Jamling Tenzing Norgay

Touching my father's soul; a Sherpa's journey to the top of Everest. [by] Jamling Tenzing Norgay with Broughton Coburn. HarperSanFrancisco 2001 316p il map hardcover o.p. pa $15.95   **796.522**

1. Mountaineering 2. Mountaineers 3. Mount Everest Expedition (1996)

ISBN 0-06-251688-4 pa

LC 00-68723

This "work has considerably more depth than an exposition of the climb. . . . The son's climb is a pilgrimage exploring his relationship to his father, his Sherpa culture, and Buddhism. It is also a fascinating look into the world of climbers and their relationship to the Sherpas who risk their lives to assist them." Booklist

Krakauer, Jon

★ **Into** thin air; a personal account of the Mount Everest disaster. Villard Bks. 1997 xx, 293p il $25.95; pa $14.95   **796.522**

1. Mountaineering 2. Mount Everest Expedition (1996) 3. Mountaineering -- Personal narratives

ISBN 0-679-45752-6; 0-385-49478-5 pa

LC 96-30031

This is an account of the author's May 1996 Mount Everest climbing expedition in which twelve fellow climbers died during a snow storm

"This tense, harrowing story is as mesmerizing and hard to put down as any well-written adventure novel." SLJ

Includes bibliographical references

Lewis-Jones, Huw

Conquest of Everest; George Lowe, Huw Lewis-Jones. Thames & Hudson Inc. 2013 240 p. (hardcover) $39.95   **796.522**

1. Mount Everest (China and Nepal)

ISBN 9780500544235

LC 2012947781

This book about Mount Everest "features a trove of original photographs and other rare materials from the George Lowe collection, many unpublished, complemented by classic images from the final ascent. Stunning landscapes, candid portraits, and action shots describe the day-by-day moments of the historic expedition as never before." (Publisher's note)

Robinson, Victoria

Rock climbing; the ultimate guide. Victoria Robinson. Greenwood 2013 165 p. (Greenwood guides to extreme sports) (hardcover) $37 **796.522**

1. Mountaineering 2. Rock climbing

ISBN 0313378614; 9780313378614; 9780313378621

LC 2012031304

This book, by Victoria Robinson, presents a guide to rock climbing as part of the "Greenwood Guides to Extreme Sports" series. The book "covers the history of rock climbing in the United States from its origins to the present day. . . . The chapters address topics such as the technicalities of the equipment and clothing, training methods, key places and events where the sport takes place, . . . and the evolution of the sport over the years." (Publisher's note)

Includes bibliographical references and index.

Trailside (Television program)

Rock climbing; a trailside guide. illustrations by Ron Hildebrand. Norton 2003 191p il (Trailside series guide) pa $18.95 **796.522**

1. Mountaineering

ISBN 0-393-31653-X

LC 96-52821

"Designed to be carried on the trail, this will ease beginners into the sport of rock climbing, with step-by-step illustrated tutorials, safety and first-aid tips, and more." Libr J

Includes bibliographical references

796.54 Camping

Callan, Kevin

★ The **happy** camper; an essential guide to life outdoors. Boston Mills Press; distributed by Firefly Books 2005 320p il pa $19.95 **796.54**

1. Camping

ISBN 1-55046-450-7; 978-1-55046-450-4

LC 2005-415489

"A great all-around guide by a top camping expert for campers of any skill level. [It includes] lots of color photos and accessible tips (how to pick a camping spot, stake a tent, build a fire, etc.)." Libr J

Includes bibliographical references

★ **Guide** to summer camps and summer schools 2008/2009; an objective, comparative reference source for residential summer programs. 31st ed.; Porter Sargent Pub. 2008 862p il (Porter Sargent Handbook series) $45; pa $27 **796.54**

1. Reference books 2. Camps -- Directories

ISBN 978-0-87558-163-7; 0-87558-163-3; 978-0-87558-164-4 pa; 0-87558-164-1 pa

First published 1936. Periodically revised. Title varies

"This reliable comprehensive source of summer academic and tutorial programs, travel programs, specialized study programs, and recreational camps lists about 1,300 such programs in the U.S. and Canada. An extensive table of contents and an index make it possible to access all of this information." Safford. Guide to Ref Materials For Sch Media Cent. 5th edition

796.6 Cycling and related activities

Armstrong, Lance

Every second counts; [by] Lance Armstrong, with Sally Jenkins. Broadway Books 2003 272p $24.95; pa $14 **796.6**

1. Athletes 2. Cyclists 3. Olympic athletes

ISBN 0-385-50871-9; 0-7679-1448-1 pa

LC 2003-55580

Companion volume to It's not about the bike

"The book is the story of a family man, world-class athlete, and cancer survivor who is determined to get every single drop of enjoyment and excitement out of life. It's a joyous, triumphant book, a celebration of all the things that make life good. It's also, for cyclists, a detailed look at the Tour de France, as seen through the eyes of one of its top competitors. Fascinating and inspiring." Booklist

Bike Snob

The **enlightened** cyclist; commuter angst, dangerous drivers, and other obstacles on the path to two-wheeled transcendence. Bike Snob NYC. Chronicle Books 2012 220 p. ill. (hardback) $16.95 **796.6**

1. Cycling 2. Transportation 3. Bicycle commuting 4. TRANSPORTATION -- General

ISBN 1452105006; 9781452105000

LC 2011041747

This book, by the anonymous urban cyclist "BikeSnobNYC," "takes on the trials and triumphs of bike commuting with snark, . . . asking the question: If we become better commuters, will that make us better people? From the deadly sins of biking to tactics for dealing with cars, pedestrians, and other cyclists, this primer on bike travel is . . . [written for] cyclists new and seasoned alike." (Publisher's note)

Byrne, David

Bicycle diaries. Viking 2009 297p il **796.6**

1. Bicycle touring 2. Singers 3. Songwriters 4. Rock musicians 5. Urban transportation 6. Cycling -- Environmental aspects

ISBN 0670021148; 9780670021147

LC 2009-09390

This book contains accounts of Byrne's travels in New York and other cities, mainly by bicycle.

"In these random musings over many years while cycling through such places as Sydney, Australia; Manila, Philippines; San Francisco; or his home of New York, the former Talking Head, artist and author . . . offers his frank views on urban planning, art and postmodern civilization in general. . . . Candid and self-deprecating, Byrne offers a work that is as engaging as it is cerebral and informative." Publ Wkly

Carmichael, Chris

The **ultimate** ride; get fit, get fast, and start winning with the world's top cycling coach. [by] Chris Carmichael with Jim Rutberg. G.P. Putnam's Sons 2003 325p il hardcover o.p. pa $15 **796.6**

1. Cycling 2. Physical fitness

ISBN 0-399-15071-4; 0-425-19601-1 pa

LC 2003-43214

"This is an excellent guide to obtaining peak performance in cycling competition, but the wealth of training tips and intelligent discussion of nutrition will be almost as valuable to noncompetitive cyclists and even to other athletes serious about conditioning." Booklist

Cossins, Peter

Tour De France 100; The Definitive History of the World's Greatest Race. Octopus Pub Group 2013 288 p. $29.99   **796.6**
1. Cycling -- Competitions 2. Tour de France (Bicycle race)
ISBN 1844037428; 9781844037421

This book looks at the Tour de France. The text "chronicles the year-by-year, stage-by-stage, drama-to-drama evolution of the race and its rules, as well as the riders, the rivalries, and the lengths explored to win (from the assault of riders in the countryside and shortcuts by alternative transport to technological advancements and performance-enhancing drugs) and reveals an event surely deserving of the title 'the people's race.'" (Library Journal)

796.62   Bicycle racing

Hamilton, Tyler

The **Secret** Race; Inside the Hidden World of the Tour de France: Doping, Cover-ups, and Winning at All Costs. Bantam Books 2012 290 p. $28   **796.62**
1. Drug abuse 2. Bicycle racing 3. Sports -- Corrupt practices
ISBN 0345530411; 9780345530417

This book, by Tyler Hamilton and Daniel Coyle, winner of the 2012 William Hill Sports Book of the Year Award, offers a "look at the world of professional cycling--and the doping issue surrounding this sport and its most iconic rider, Lance Armstrong. . . . [The book] . . . takes us . . . inside a shadowy . . . world of unscrupulous doctors, . . . team directors, and athletes so relentlessly driven to succeed that they would do anything . . . to gain the edge they need to win." (Publisher's note)

796.7   Driving motor vehicles

Johnson, Wayne

Live to ride; the rumbling, roaring world of speed, escape, and adventure on two wheels. Atria Books 2010 274p $25; ebook $11.99   **796.7**
1. Motorcycles
ISBN 978-1-4165-5032-7; 978-1-4391-7715-0 ebook
LC 2009-43983

Shares the author's experiences of pursuing ultimate speeds, performing in high-risk motocross jumps, and joining outlaw motorcycle clubs.

"Johnson captures the obsessive excitement of motorcycle culture with enough verve to make nonriders understand, and jealous, although he doesn't undersell its dangers. Enjoyable and informative—one of the best books on the topic in years." Kirkus

796.72   Automobile racing

Baime, A. J.

Go like hell; Ford, Ferrari, and their battle for speed and glory at Le Mans. Houghton Mifflin Harcourt 2009 304p il map $26   **796.72**
1. Sports cars 2. Automobile racing 3. Ferrari SpA 4. Ford Motor Co.
ISBN 978-0-618-82219-5; 0-618-82219-4
LC 2008-52948

"Baime tells an exciting story at a pace that manages to keep up with the drivers." Libr J
Includes bibliographical references

Bechtel, Mark

He crashed me so I crashed him back; the true story of the year the King, Jaws, Earnhardt, and the rest of NASCAR's feudin', fightin', good ol' boys put stock car racing on the map. Little, Brown and Co. 2010 308p il $25.99   **796.72**
1. Automobile racing 2. National Association for Stock Car Auto Racing
ISBN 978-0-316-03402-9; 0-316-03402-9
LC 2009-31952

The story of how Bobby Allison, Donnie Allison, Cale Yarborough, Richard Petty, Dale Earnhardt, Darrell Waltrip, A.J. Foyt, and Kyle Petty came together in an unforgettable season that featured the first nationally televised NASCAR races.

This is "an illuminating, informative, and entertaining read, as the engaging and droll Bechtel is in complete control from start to finish." Publ Wkly
Includes bibliographical references

Hawley, Samuel Jay

Speed duel; the inside story of the land speed record in the sixties. [by] Sam Hawley. Firefly Books 2010 360p il pa $24.95   **796.72**
1. Automobile racing drivers
ISBN 978-1-55407-633-8

"Even readers who don't know a spark plug from a gear shift will be transfixed by Hawley's white-knuckled account of the ever-escalating competition to hold the Land Speed Record in the '60s and early '70s. Drawing from countless articles, profiles, documentaries, and interviews with the men and women who were there, Hawley traces the sport's evolution from its first four-wheeled record of 39mph in 1898, to today's jet-propelled 700mph-plus, recounting the creation, testing, and repair of legendary cars like the humble Green Monster and the charismatic Spirit of America." Publ Wkly
Includes filmography and bibliographical references

Menzer, Joe

The **wildest** ride; a history of NASCAR (or, How a bunch of good ol' boys built a billion-dollar industry out of wrecking cars) Simon & Schuster 2001 311p il hardcover o.p. pa $14   **796.72**
1. Automobile racing 2. National Association for Stock

Car Auto Racing
ISBN 0-7432-0507-3; 0-7432-2625-9 pa
LC 2001-031088

This history focuses on the "legacy of the founding France family, the evolution of the cars from modified stock cars to purpose-built racers, and the fan-base expansion of the 1980s and 1990s. . . . Highly entertaining and full of facts." Libr J

Includes bibliographical references

Waltrip, Michael

In the blink of an eye; Dale, Daytona, and the day that changed everything. by Michael Waltrip and Ellis Henican. Hyperion 2011 223p il $24.99; pa $14.99   **796.72**

1. Automobile racing 2. Automobile racing drivers
ISBN 978-1-4013-2431-5; 978-0-7868-9139-9 pa

An account of the colorful NASCAR driver's career describes his hardscrabble upbringing and strained relationship with brother Darrell, while recounting his historic win at the 2001 Daytona 500 and the death of mentor Dale Earnhardt in the same race.

"This is a genuinely heartfelt memoir that is equal parts autobiography and tribute to Earnhardt. . . . Though sadness and loss are a big part of Waltrip's story, he balances them with humor and joy. A really wonderful read for NASCAR fans." Booklist

Wright, James D.

Fixin' to git; one fan's love affair with NASCAR's Winston Cup. [by] Jim Wright. Duke Univ. Press 2002 305p il $26.95; pa $18.95   **796.72**

1. Automobile racing 2. National Association for Stock Car Auto Racing
ISBN 0-8223-2926-3; 0-8223-3220-5 pa
LC 2002-485

"This is the very best book to surface on auto racing in many years. Informative, entertaining, and eye-opening." Booklist

796.8   Combat sports

At the fights; American writers on boxing. edited by George Kimball & John Schulian; foreword by Colum McCann. Library of America 2011 517p $35   **796.8**

1. Boxing 2. Boxers (Sports)
ISBN 1-59853-092-5; 978-1-59853-092-6

This collection includes "work by the likes of Pete Hamill, Norman Mailer, Joyce Carol Oates, George Plimpton, David Remnick, Budd Schulberg and Gay Talese." (N Y Times Book Rev) Index.

"The book's editors accomplish several things in 'At the Fights.' They sample the work of devotees such as the incomparable A.J. Liebling and Gene Tunney on his defeat of Jack Dempsey, and of comparative outsiders such as James Baldwin and Joyce Carol Oates, whose novelistic fascination with violence, class and gender inevitably led her to ponder the boxing life. The collection plots a zigzag course through a century of boxing milestones, offering a striking range of approaches to the subject. It also throws open controversies racial, moral, legal and medical that have swirled around the sport since it first attained a sort of legitimacy. . . . [This anthology] presupposes an interest in writing as much as in boxing. Many of its contributors, such as Baldwin, Vic Ziegel, Pete Hamill, Bill Barich and Katherine Dunn, pay as much or more attention to stories tributary to fights as to the ring contests themselves. Observations in many different registers form an engrossing counterpoint as the book proceeds." San Francisco Chron

Cohen, Richard

By the sword; a history of gladiators, musketeers, samurai, swashbucklers, and Olympic champions. Random House 2002 xxiv, 519p il $29.95; pa $15.95   **796.8**

1. Fencing
ISBN 0-375-50417-6; 0-8129-6966-9 pa
LC 2002-21309

This is a worldwide history of sword fighting from Ancient Egypt to the present which considers its role in combat and sports, word origins and customs, and the fencing skills of politicians and actors

"A fascinating story told with literary verve and the pride of a longtime practitioner; highly recommended." Libr J

Includes bibliographical references

Hauser, Thomas

Boxing is-- reflections on the sweet science. The University of Arkansas Press 2010 270p pa $22.50   **796.8**

1. Boxing
ISBN 978-1-55728-942-1
LC 2010-15354

"The collection begins with a detailed biographical examination of the career of Sugar Ray Robinson, considered by many to be the greatest pound-for-pound fighter ever. It's a sadly familiar tale of poverty, ascendancy, fame, and decline, related in a respectful, objective style. The rest of the book is focused on the boxing events of 2009, from the high-profile career of Manny Pacquiao to the progress of several relatively unknown young fighters learning the trade in New York's gyms. Hauser also explores the business end of boxing, especially its painful relationship with television, but above all, he is drawn to the people of the sport: the fighters, trainers, promoters, and hangers-on. Virtually every piece is notable for its carefully drawn characters who will linger on the edges of readers' minds long after the book has been shelved." Booklist

Includes bibliographical references

Kelly, Jason

Shelby's folly; Jack Dempsey, Doc Kearns, and the shakedown of a Montana boomtown. University of Nebraska Press 2010 214p il $26.95   **796.8**

1. Boxing 2. Shelby (Mont.) 3. Boxers (Persons)
ISBN 978-0-8032-2655-5; 0-8032-2655-1
LC 2009-40609

"There was a certain nobility in so vast a failure. The men of Shelby had stood fast as the tidal wave of red ink swept over them. Mr. Kelly writes sympathetically, not mockingly, of Shelby, and he has a proper appreciation for the brazen roguery of Doc Kearns, whose greed and manipulativeness made the fight possible—and doomed Shelby's self-promotional hopes." Wall Street J

Includes bibliographical references

Kreidler, Mark

★ **Four** days to glory; wrestling with the soul of the American heartland. HarperCollins Publishers 2007 262p il hardcover o.p. pa $13.99   **796.8**

1. Wrestling 2. School sports

ISBN 978-0-06-082318-4; 0-06-082318-6; 978-0-06-082319-1 pa; 0-06-082319-4 pa

LC 2007-272997

Jay Borschel and Dan LeClere aspire to be four-time high school wrestling champions in Iowa.

The author's "deftness in 'Four Days' is in turning a niche sport into one as accessible as baseball or basketball." N Y Times Book Rev

Levi, Heather

The **world** of lucha libre; secrets, revelations, and Mexican national identity. Duke University Press 2008 xxii, 265p il (American encounters/global interactions) $79.95; pa $22.95   **796.8**

1. Wrestling 2. Wrestling -- Mexico 3. Mexico -- Social life and customs

ISBN 0-8223-4214-6; 0-8223-4232-4 pa; 978-0-8223-4214-4; 978-0-8223-4232-8 pa

LC 2008-23166

"A small but fascinating part of Levi's book is the field-work she did while preparing the text. While living in Mexico, Levi trained as a luchadora with a former professional wrestler.... The experience of training is not the focus of the work, however, but rather a tool the author used to further illuminate her research." PopMatters

Includes bibliographical references

Margolick, David

★ **Beyond** glory; Joe Louis vs. Max Schmeling, and a world on the brink. Knopf 2005 423p il $26.95   **796.8**

1. Boxing 2. Soldiers 3. Boxers (Persons)

ISBN 0-375-41192-5

LC 2005-45141

The author discusses the historical significance of the fights between Joe Louis and German boxer Max Schmeling in 1936 and 1938.

This book "will be the definitive account of Louis versus Schmeling. And it's a hell of a good read besides." Booklist

Includes bibliographical references

Park, Yeon Hwan

Black belt tae kwon do; the ultimate reference guide to the world's most popular martial art. by Y.H. Park & Jon Gerrard. Facts on File 2000 272p il hardcover o.p. pa $16.95   **796.8**

1. Tae kwon do

ISBN 0-8160-4240-3; 0-8160-4241-1 pa

LC 99-57876

Coverage includes practice, warm-up, and advanced techniques and forms, sparring strategies, self-defense, and breaking. Over 700 photographs accompany the text. Ap-

pendixes cover official competition rules, weight classes, governing bodies, and international organizations and associations. Includes two glossaries, English to Korean and Korean to English

Schulberg, Budd

Sparring with Hemingway and other legends of the fight game. Dee, I.R. 1995 256p $25   **796.8**

1. Boxing

ISBN 1-56663-080-0

LC 94-49153

This is a collection of the author's articles about boxing, originally published between 1954 and 1994

"Included are beautifully crafted portraits of legends such as Benny Leonard, Muhammad Ali, and ageless wonder George Foreman. . . . This literate, entertaining collection represents some of the best writing on any sport." Libr J

796.83   Boxing

Anasi, Robert

★ The **gloves**; a boxing chronicle. North Point Press 2002 331p $24; pa $14   **796.83**

1. Boxing

ISBN 0-86547-599-7; 0-86547-652-7 pa

LC 2001-44111

In this "look at the world of amateur boxing, freelance writer Anasi chronicles how jabbing and jump-roping at a grubby gym in San Francisco's Tenderloin district developed into a life-altering quest to compete, in his early 30s, in New York's storied amateur boxing tournament, the Golden Gloves." Publ Wkly

Gildea, William

★ The **longest** fight; in the ring with Joe Gans, boxing's first African American champion. William Gildea. Farrar, Straus and Giroux 2012 245 p. ill. (hbk.) : $26.00   **796.83**

1. Boxing -- Biography 2. Gans, Joe, 1874-1910 3. African American boxers -- Biography 4. Boxers (Sports) -- United States -- Biography

ISBN 0374280975; 9780374280970

LC 2011040170

This book by William Gildea presents a biography of "Joe Gans, who in 1902 became the first African American boxing champion . . . giving special attention to the fighter's . . . championship bout against avowed racist Oscar 'Battling' Nelson. . . . Gildea gives full measure of Gans' remarkable accomplishments as an athlete . . . while also showing Gans' equally remarkable poise in the face of horrific prejudice, officially sanctioned or not, during his entire career." (Booklist)

Includes bibliographical references and index.

Kram, Mark

The **ghosts** of Manila; the fateful, brutal blood feud between Muhammad Ali and Joe Frazier. HarperCollins Pubs. 2001 232p hardcover o.p. pa $12.95 **796.83**

1. Boxing 2. Boxers (Persons)
ISBN 0-06-095480-9 pa

LC 00-53934

This is "a fascinating blend of history and biography." Booklist

Runstedtler, Theresa

Jack Johnson, rebel sojourner; boxing in the shadow of the global color line. Theresa Runstedtler. University of California Press 2012 xxii, 348 p.p (cloth : alk. paper) $34.95 **796.83**

1. Race relations 2. African American athletes 3. Racism in sports 4. Boxing -- United States -- History 5. African American boxers -- Biography 6. United States -- Race relations -- History 7. Boxers (Sports) -- United States -- Biography
ISBN 0520271602; 9780520271609

LC 2011027435

In this book, "[Theresa] Runstedtler . . . makes [boxer Jack] Johnson the centerpiece of what is also a study of global black-white relations during his era." The boxer "was given to living large, embarrassing white opponents, and consorting with white women at a time when Jim Crow flourished at home and the doctrine of the 'white man's burden' was encircling the globe. Therefore, even when he fled the United States after a Mann Act conviction, he couldn't escape racism." (Library Journal)

Includes bibliographical references and index.

Stratton, W. K.

★ **Floyd** Patterson; the fighting life of boxing's invisible champion. W. K. Stratton. Houghton Mifflin Harcourt 2012 xiv, 269 p.p ill. (hardback) $25.00 **796.83**

1. Boxers (Sports) 2. African Americans -- Civil rights 3. African American boxers -- Biography 4. Boxers (Sports) -- United States -- Biography
ISBN 0151014302; 9780151014309

LC 2012017319

This biography "examines one of the most complex fighters ever to wear the heavyweight crown," boxer Floyd Patterson. "Patterson started boxing [in high school] and . . . caught the eye of trainer Cus D'Amato . . . . By focusing on historical context, Stratton clarifies how Patterson could be trumpeted as a hero of the civil rights movement, then labeled an 'Uncle Tom' a few years later." (Publishers Weekly)

Includes bibliographical references and index.

796.9 Ice and snow sports

Bennett, Jeff (2001)

The **complete** snowboarder; {by} Jeff Bennett, Scott Downey and Charles Arnell. 2nd ed; Ragged Mountain Press 2000 148p il pa $14.95 **796.9**

1. Snowboarding
ISBN 0-07-135787-4

LC 00-39059

First published 1994

This offers advice on getting started in snowboarding, equipment, techniques, snowboarding areas and trails, tricks, competitions, safety, and equipment maintenance.

796.962 Ice hockey

Hockey Hall of Fame

Official guide to the players of the Hockey Hall of Fame; Hockey Hall of Fame; compiled by James Duplacey and Eric Zweig. Firefly Books 2010 544p il pa $19.95 **796.962**

1. Hockey 2. National Hockey League
ISBN 978-1-55407-662-8

"Hockey fans throughout North America will enjoy this beautiful and richly illustrated record of the lives and careers of the nearly 400 players, builders, and on-ice officials whose signal contributions to hockey, and not merely the National Hockey League, have led to their enshrinement in the Hall of Fame located in Toronto." Libr J

McKinley, Michael

★ **Hockey** : a people's history. McClelland & Stewart 2006 346p il hardcover o.p. pa $37.50 **796.962**

1. Hockey
ISBN 0-7710-5769-5; 978-0-7710-5769-4; 0-7710-5771-7 pa; 978-0-7710-5771-7 pa

This history "chronicles hockey from its genesis as a winter substitute for lacrosse. A companion to a similarly titled CBC TV series, the lavishly illustrated book combines punchy boxed features celebrating individuals and hockey oddments and a detailed tracing of the game's development. . . . Essential for general sports as well as hockey-intensive collections." Booklist

Includes bibliographical references

796.98 Winter Olympic games

Wallechinsky, David

The **complete** book of the Winter Olympics; [by] David Wallechinsky and Jaime Loucky. 2010 ed.; Aurum 2009 322p il pa $24.95 **796.98**

1. Olympic games
ISBN 978-1-84513-491-4

First published 1984 by Overlook Press

"While the statistics will delight sports geeks, everyone can savor the readable prose accounts that draw out the athletes' character and high points." SLJ

797.1 Aquatic sports

American Canoe Association

★ **Canoeing**; outdoor adventures. editors, Pamela S. Dillon, Jeremy Oyen. Human Kinetics 2008 253p il (Outdoor adventures) pa $22.95 **797.1**

1. Canoes and canoeing
ISBN 978-0-7360-6715-7; 0-7360-6715-9

LC 2008-4392

The authors "discuss fitness basics, food and nutrition needs, and gear and equipment—from the canoe itself to life jackets, paddles, and clothing. They then cover . . . safety and survival guidelines, including weather, river hazards, capsizing, cold-water safety, and rescue protocols. . . [The DVD included contains] an introduction to paddle sports and basic safety and paddling techniques." Publisher's note

Kayaking; editors, Pamela S. Dillon, Jeremy Oyen. Human Kinetics 2009 237p il (Outdoor adventures) pa $22.95   **797.1**
   1. Canoes and canoeing
   ISBN 978-0-7360-6716-4; 0-7360-6716-7
                        LC 2008-32111
"Part I of Kayaking explains the background knowledge, fitness fundamentals, equipment and gear selection, nutritional needs, and safety and survival skills for a successful adventure. Part II helps build basic techniques, strokes, and maneuvers. . . [It includes] tips and instruction for the three most popular types of kayaking: sea, river, and whitewater. This book also includes the Quick-Start Your Kayak DVD to reinforce the paddling strokes and safety information found in the book. It features videos of kayaking maneuvers." Publisher's note
   Includes bibliographical references

Fredston, Jill A.
Rowing to latitude; journeys along the Arctic's edge. [by] Jill Fredston. North Point Press 2001 289p il hardcover o.p. pa $15   **797.1**
   1. Canoes and canoeing 2. Arctic regions -- Description and travel
   ISBN 0-374-28180-7; 0-86547-655-1 pa
                        LC 2001-30049
The author and her husband, Doug Fesler "canoe the Arctic and sub-Arctic coastlines of Alaska, Canada, Greenland, Norway and Sweden for three months out of each year. . . . Fredston ably describes both the big picture—the coastline, encounters with polar bears, the high-stakes game of second-guessing storms and tides—and the details of their travels. . . . A must-read for armchair travelers, as well as a close and loving look at an intimate relationship." Publ Wkly

Stewart, Chris
Three ways to capsize a boat; an optimist afloat. Broadway Books 2010 178p pa $12.99; ebook $12.99   **797.1**
   1. Sailing 2. Boats and boating
   ISBN 978-0-307-59237-8 pa; 978-0-307-59238-5 ebook
                        LC 2009-44105
"This amusing book chronicles . . . [the author's] sailing adventures in the early 1980s, having just turned 30. Despite his lack of experience, a friend recommended him as captain on a sailboat in the Greek islands. He practiced on a boat out of Littlehampton, England, managing to spend hours without moving and then flipping the vessel. His Greek island cruising was punctuated by regular and spectacular engine fires. The final sail he chronicles is a cold and smelly trip from Brighton to Newfoundland (or Vinland), which he spent wearing adventurer Sir Ranulph Fiennes's moleskin trousers. . . . Stewart's eventual love of sailing translates well

to landlubbers, while sailors will be glad to have missed the winter storms and sea ice encountered. A funny, appealing read." Libr J

797.12   Types of vessels

Brown, Daniel James
   ★ The **Boys** in the Boat; Nine Americans and Their Epic Quest for Gold at the 1936 Berlin Olympics. Daniel James Brown. Penguin Group USA 2013 432 p. (hardcover) $28.95   **797.12**
   1. Rowing 2. Olympic games, 1936 (Berlin, Ger.) 3. Rowing -- United States -- History 4. Rowers -- United States -- Biography 5. University of Washington -- Rowing -- History
   ISBN 067002581X; 9780670025817
                        LC 2013001560
This book, by Daniel James Brown, "tells the story of the University of Washington's 1936 eight-oar crew and their . . . quest for an Olympic gold medal, a team that transformed the sport and grabbed the attention of millions of Americans. The sons of loggers, shipyard workers, and farmers, the boys defeated elite rivals first from eastern and British universities and finally the German crew rowing for Adolf Hitler in the Olympic games in Berlin, 1936." (Publisher's note)
   Includes bibliographical references and index.

797.2   Swimming and diving

Beard, Amanda
   In the water they can't see you cry; a memoir. Amanda Beard ; with Rebecca Paley. 1st Touchstone hardcover ed. Simon & Schuster 2012 248 p. ill. (some col.) $24.99   **797.2**
   1. Autobiographies 2. Olympic athletes 3. Depression (Psychology) 4. Swimmers -- United States -- Biography 5. Women swimmers -- United States -- Biography
   ISBN 145164437X; 9781451644371
                        LC 2012006464
This book is a memoir by Olympic swimmer Amanda Beard, with Rebecca Paley. "[S]he competed in three more Olympic games . . . and enjoyed a lucrative modeling career on the side. . . . Unaware that she was suffering from clinical depression, she . . . expressed her emotions through self-destructive behavior. . . . Only when she met her future husband . . . did Amanda realize she needed help." (Publisher's note)

Graver, Dennis
   Scuba diving; [by] Dennis K. Graver. 3rd ed; Human Kinetics 2003 209p il pa $23.95   **797.2**
   1. Scuba diving
   ISBN 0-7360-4539-2
                        LC 2002-152325
First published 1993
"This colorful beginner's guide is used by many diving classes, including the YMCA Scuba Diving program. All

the basics are covered: why dive, equipment, diving science, and what you might see on a dive." Libr J

Includes bibliographical references

Mullen, P. H.

Gold in the water; the true story of ordinary men and their extraordinary dream of Olympic glory. Thomas Dunne Bks. 2001 326p il hardcover o.p. pa $14.95   **797.2**

1. Swimming 2. Olympic games, 2000 (Sydney, Australia)

ISBN 0-312-26595-6; 0-312-31116-8 pa

LC 2001-31955

"Mullen chronicles the U.S. Olympic swimming team on its journey to the 2000 Summer Games in Sydney. The text moves back and forth in time, giving a sense of the athletes as people and showing what motivates someone to structure his or her whole life toward a single goal." Booklist

Nestor, James ✓

Deep; Freediving, Renegade Science, and What the Ocean Tells Us About Ourselves. James Nestor. Houghton Mifflin Harcourt 2014 272 p. illustrations (chiefly color) $27   **797.2**

1. Ocean 2. Skin diving

ISBN 0547985525; 9780547985527

LC 2014002593

"In 'Deep,' [author James] Nestor embeds with a gang of extreme athletes and renegade researchers who are transforming not only our knowledge of the planet and its creatures, but also our understanding of the human body and mind. . . . Most illuminating of all, Nestor unlocks his own freediving skills as he communes with the pioneers who are expanding our definition of what is possible in the natural world, and in ourselves." (Publisher's note)

"[B]rimming with vivid portraits, lucid scientific explanations, gripping (and funny) first-person accounts, and urgent facts about the ocean's endangerment, Nestor's Deep is galvanizing, enlightening, and invaluable." Booklist

Includes bibliographical references and index

797.21   Swimming

Shapton, Leanne ✓

Swimming studies; Leanne Shapton. Blue Rider Press 2012 320 p. (hbk.) $30   **797.21**

1. Swimming 2. Women swimmers -- Canada -- Biography

ISBN 0399158170; 9780399158179

LC 2012011506

This memoir by Leane Shapton "explores the worlds of competitive and recreational swimming. From her training for the Olympic trials as a teenager to enjoying pools and beaches around the world as an adult, . . . Shapton offers a fascinating glimpse into the private, often solitary, realm of swimming. . . . [The book] reveals an intimate narrative of suburban adolescence, spent underwater in a discipline that continues to inspire Shapton's work as an artist and author." (Publisher's note)

797.5   Air sports

Higgins, Matt

Bird dream; adventures at the extremes of human flight. Matt Higgins. The Penguin Press 2014 304 p. color illustrations $27.95   **797.5**

1. Flight 2. Aeronautical sports

ISBN 1594204659; 9781594204654

LC 2014005399

Written by Matt Higgins, "'Bird Dream' shows that recent decades have witnessed an unprecedented revolution in human flight. . . . Wingsuits were not new; they had fascinated men for centuries. Yet a modern design had improved safety and performance, allowing wingsuit pilots to leap from a helicopter or high cliff and soar for miles--using little more than their bodies--before deploying a parachute to reach the ground safely." (Publisher's note)

"A highflying, electrifying story of a treacherous sport in which every triumph is an eye blink away from becoming a disaster." Kirkus

Includes bibliographical references and index

798.4   Horse racing

Clee, Nicholas

Eclipse; Nicholas Clee. Black Swan 2011 352 p.   **798.4**

1. Eclipse (Race horse) 2. Great Britain -- History -- 1714-1837 3. Horse racing -- Great Britain -- History 4. Horse racing -- Great Britain -- History -- 18th century

ISBN 0552774421; 9780552774420

LC 2011293231

This book presents an "account of one of the most famous racehorses in history. Eclipse (1764-89) was a legend in his time and, astonishingly, became the progenitor of all but three of the 50 most recent Kentucky Derby winners. [Nicholas] Clee . . . chronicles both the life of the horse, who started racing at age five, and the Irish gambler Dennis O'Kelly, who purchased him soon thereafter. The author weaves in many other colorful characters who played a part in the story, including Sir Charles Bunbury (founder of the Jockey Club), the Earl of Derby (from whom classic races take their name), and King George IV. . . . For racing fans, Clee also includes histories of famous races, wagers, bloodlines, and the stories of some of Eclipse's most celebrated offspring." (Libr J)

Includes bibliographical references (p. 281-292) and index

Drape, Joe

The **race** for the Triple Crown; horses, high stakes, and eternal hope. Atlantic Monthly Press 2001 261p hardcover o.p. pa $14   **798.4**

1. Horse racing

ISBN 0-8021-3885-3 pa

LC 2001-16044

In this "look at the highest level of horse racing, the author traces the lives of a handful of preeminent horse owners, trainers and jockeys in their preparations for the Kentucky Derby, the Preakness and the Belmont." Publ Wkly

Eisenberg, John

★ The **great** match race; when North met South in America's first sports spectacle. Houghton Mifflin Co. 2006 258p il $25   **798.4**

1. Horse racing

ISBN 978-0-618-55612-0; 0-618-55612-5

LC 2005-31540

The author "succeeds in creating a gripping yarn of sporting contest, portrayal of a historical moment and smart analysis of a country headed eventually for civil war." Publ Wkly

Includes bibliographical references

Hillenbrand, Laura

★ **Seabiscuit**; an American legend. Random House 2001 399p il $25.95; pa $15.95   **798.4**

1. Horse racing 2. Seabiscuit (Race horse)

ISBN 0-375-50291-2; 0-449-00561-5 pa

LC 2001-267852

"This is a remarkable tale well told by a writer who deftly blends history and sport." Economist

Includes bibliographical references

Mitchell, Elizabeth

★ **Three** strides before the wire; the dark and beautiful world of horse racing. Hyperion 2002 403p $24.95; pa $14.95   **798.4**

1. Horse racing

ISBN 0-7868-6723-X; 0-7868-8622-6 pa

LC 2002-68817

The author "tells the story of Charismatic, who exploded out of the proletarian ranks of claiming horses to come within a stone's throw of sweeping the Triple Crown in 1999 before suffering a career-ending injury in the Belmont Stakes. . . . Mitchell's book possesses an appeal that extends well beyond its subject." Booklist

Ours, Dorothy

Man o' War; a legend like lightning. St Martin's Press 2006 342p il $24.95   **798.4**

1. Horse racing 2. Man o' War (Race horse)

ISBN 0-312-34099-0; 978-0-312-34099-5

LC 2006-41631

This is an account of the thoroughbred racehorse Man o' War, also known as Big Red.

This book "is clearly a labor of love, and it certifies Big Red's claim to immortality." N Y Times Book Rev

Includes bibliographical references

Smiley, Jane

A **year** at the races; reflections on horses, humans, love, money, and luck. Knopf 2004 287p $22   **798.4**

1. Horse racing

ISBN 1-4000-4058-2

LC 2003-65655

"The very qualities of mind that make Smiley such a compelling novelist—her keen attentiveness to the sensuous world, her deep sensitivity to psychological states, and her fascination with life's entwinement of chance and inevitability—enable her to write about horses, both their interior and exterior selves, with extraordinary avidity, empathy, wonder, and gratitude." Booklist

Includes bibliographical references

Squires, James D.

Horse of a different color; a tale of breeding geniuses, dominant females, and the fastest Derby winner since Secretariat. {by} Jim Squires. PublicAffairs 2002 300p il $26; pa $14   **798.4**

1. Horse racing 2. Kentucky Derby

ISBN 1-58648-117-7; 1-58648-180-0 pa

LC 2001-59602

This is the story of how the author, a former editor of the Chicago Tribune, became a breeder of thoroughbred race horses, including a horse named Monarchos, the champion of the 2001 Kentucky Derby

This "is fast paced and fun to read. It will appeal not only to horseracing fans but also to people making midlife career changes." Libr J

798.401   Betting

Ainslie, Tom

Ainslie's complete guide to thoroughbred racing; 3rd ed; Simon & Schuster 1986 349p il hardcover o.p. pa $14   **798.401**

1. Gambling 2. Horse racing

ISBN 0-671-65655-4 pa

LC 86-3879

First published 1968

A guide to the fundamentals of handicapping races including such topics as breeding, judging condition of the horses, calculating speed, track ratings and other tips for successful betting

798.8   Dog racing

Paulsen, Gary

Winterdance; the fine madness of running the Iditarod. Harcourt Brace & Co. 1994 256p il $26; pa $15   **798.8**

1. Sled dog racing 2. Iditarod Trail Sled Dog Race, Alaska 3. Authors 4. Sledding 5. Sled dog racers 6. Children's authors 7. Short story writers 8. Young adult authors

ISBN 0-15-126227-6; 0-15-600145-4 pa

LC 93-42096

"The Alaskan Iditarod is an annual 1180-mile dogsled race from Anchorage to Nome that generally takes two to three weeks to complete. Paulsen . . . ran the race in 1983 and 1985 and was again in training when a heart condition forced him to retire. This book is primarily an account of Paulsen's first Iditarod." (Libr J)

"This book is primarily an account of Paulsen's first Iditarod and its frequent life-threatening disasters. . . . However, the book is more than a tabulation of tribulations; it is a meditation on the extraordinary attraction this race holds for some men and women." Libr J

799.1 Fishing

Dorsey, Pat

Fly fishing tailwaters; tactics and patterns for year-round waters. Stackpole Books 2009 198p il $49.95 **799.1**

1. Fly casting

ISBN 978-0-8117-0512-7; 0-8117-0512-9

LC 2008-46861

"The author covers how tailwaters work—how cold waters released from a dam affect the water, the aquatic life, and the fish. This book . . . [covers]: the hatches, the best imitation flies to use in every circumstance, nymphing and dry-fly tactics, all illustrated with drawings by artist Dave Hall and more than 200 color photographs." Publisher's note

"No one brings more knowledge or passion to an examination of tailwater trout fishing than Pat Dorsey." Denver Post

Includes bibliographical references

Frazier, Ian

The **fish's** eye; essays about angling and the outdoors. Farrar, Straus & Giroux 2002 163p pa $12; $20 **799.1**

1. Fishing

ISBN 0-312-42169-9 pa; 0-374-15520-8

LC 2001-54451

A compendium of the author's essays written for The New Yorker over the last two decades

"It's almost impossible to read these heartfelt and lovingly rendered essays without sharing the author's fascination with woods and water and fish." Booklist

Gierach, John

No shortage of good days; illustrations by Glen Wolff. Simon & Schuster 2011 210p il $24; ebook $10.99 **799.1**

1. Fly casting

ISBN 978-0-7432-9175-0; 978-1-4516-1011-6 ebook

LC 2010043739

"The book is a collection of fondly remembered fishing trips and random fishing-related topics, along with miscellaneous other narrative odds and ends thrown in the mix: fishing and firewood, fly-fishing versus bait fishing, fly-fishing's countercultural history, salmon fishing, the experience of fishing with guides and even a random chapter on the perils of combining fishing with the pain-in-the-neck necessity of book tours. The author's strength is his obvious obsessive drive to find the perfect fishing spot and make the perfect cast; his travels take him from his home state of Colorado to Canada, Wisconsin, Washington State and Mexico. . . . Gierach's genial campfire manner and woodsy witticisms should hook more than just the average fishing fanatic." Kirkus

Harrop, Rene

Learning from the water. Stackpole Books 2010 213p il $39.95 **799.1**

1. Fly casting 2. Trout fishing

ISBN 978-0-8117-0579-0; 0-8117-0579-X

LC 2009-50478

"When you see the name Rene Harrop associated with a book on fly fishing you automatically know that you are in for a treat if you are a serious fly fisher." FlyAngles OnLine

Hersey, John

Blues; with drawings by James Baker. Knopf 1987 205p il hardcover o.p. pa $13 **799.1**

1. Fishing

ISBN 0-394-75702-5 pa

LC 86-46008

"People who love and care about nature and their place in it, be they fishermen or not, should thoroughly enjoy 'Blues.'" Wilson Libr Bull

Rosenbauer, Tom

The **Orvis** guide to the essential American flies; how to tie the most successful freshwater and saltwater patterns. Universe 2011 208p il $35 **799.1**

1. Fishing 2. Artificial flies

ISBN 978-0-7893-2269-2

LC 2011-921540

This "resource features twenty quintessential fly patterns, including the Parachute Adams, Clouser Minnow, and Woolly Bugger. [Includes] detailed chapters exploring the history of and variations on each fly, interviews with fly originators, and step-by-step tying 'recipes' and instructions." Publisher's note

Schullery, Paul

★ The **rise;** streamside observations on trout, flies, and fly fishing. photographs by the author; illustrations by Marsha Karle; with additional illustrations from angling literature. Stackpole Books 2006 194p il $26.95 **799.1**

1. Trout fishing 2. Artificial flies

ISBN 978-0-8117-0182-2; 0-8117-0182-4

LC 2005-37913

This work "distills five centuries' worth of angling lore and wisdom about trout feeding behavior and includes a photographic sequence that shows in detail how trout take a fly. . . . [An] examination of flies includes the importance of wings and what they are made of, hooks, soft-hackled flies, and skipping, dapping, and dry-fly techniques." Publisher's note

Includes bibliographical references

Takahashi, Rick

Modern midges; tying & fishing the world's most effective patterns. [by] Rick Takahashi and Jerry Hubka; photos by Brian Yamauchi and Mark Tracy. Headwater Books 2009 282p il $39.95 **799.1**

1. Fly casting

ISBN 978-1-934753-00-2; 1-934753-00-9

"Midges may be small, but in many streams and lakes around the world they are the most important year-round food source for trout. . . . Photos and detailed illustrations show the life cycle of the naturals, fishing and rigging techniques for a wide range of waters, and over 1,000 midge patterns." Publisher's note

Tapply, William G.

Every day was special; a fly fisher's lifelong passion. foreword by Nick Lyons. Skyhorse Publishing 2010 186p $26.95   **799.1**

1. Fly casting

ISBN 978-1-60239-955-6

LC 2009-45558

This volume collects the late author's pieces on fly-fishing

"Tapply clearly knows his stuff. His knowledge of royal wulffs, wooly buggers, and Chernobyl ants will demonstrate this to those who share his wisdom. Those who don't can content themselves with his evocative descriptions of summer streams, elusive fish, and the elements of life that gave the author joy. Recommended for all enthusiasts of outdoor writing, whether or not they are fly fishers." Libr J

799.12   Angling

Gierach, John

All Fishermen Are Liars; by John Gierach. Simon & Schuster 2014 224 p. illustrations $24   **799.12**

1. Fishing 2. Fly fishing -- Anecdotes

ISBN 145161831X; 9781451618310

LC 2013012784

In this book, author John Gierach "travels across North America from the Pacific Northwest to the Canadian Maritimes to seek out quintessential fishing experiences. Whether he's fishing a busy stream or a secluded lake amid snow-capped mountains, Gierach insists that fishing is always the answer--even when it's not clear what the question is." (Publisher's note)

"An engaging autobiographical introduction opens the book, which includes 22 perceptive and witty essays, recalling numerous fishing trips and offering insights on fly rods and fly patterns. . . . These lyrical essays explode with descriptions of beautiful places, big fish, and beautiful fish." Booklist

Includes bibliographical references and index

799.2   Hunting

Jones, Robert F.

The **hunter** in my heart; a sportsman's salmagundi. Lyons Press 2002 268p $24.95   **799.2**

1. Hunting 2. Game and game birds

ISBN 1-58574-465-4

This "is a collection of 30 essays and two short stories. . . . Jones not only tells great outdoor stories but also explores his thoughts on hunting and friendship." Libr J

799.29   History, geographic treatment, biography

Rinella, Steven

Meat eater; a natural history of an American hunter. Steven Rinella. Spiegel & Grau 2012 244 p.   **799.29**

1. Hunting 2. Food of animal origin 3. Hunting stories, American 4. Hunting -- United States -- History 5. Hunters -- United States -- Biography

ISBN 0385529813; 9780385529815; 9780679645283

LC 2012018129

This book by Steven Rinella "chronicles Rinella's life-long relationship with nature and hunting through the lens of ten hunts, beginning when he was an aspiring mountain man at age ten and ending as a thirty-seven-year-old Brooklyn father who hunts in the remotest corners of North America. . . . Rinella grapples with themes such as . . . the disappearance of the hunter himself as Americans lose their connection with the way their food finds its way to their tables." (Publisher's note)

799.3   Shooting other than game

Kasper, Shirl

Annie Oakley. University of Okla. Press 1992 288p il $29.95; pa $19.95   **799.3**

1. Marksmen 2. Frontier and pioneer life -- West (U.S.)

ISBN 0-8061-2418-0; 0-8061-3244-2 pa

LC 91-50864

This biography of the legendary sharpshooter "not only paints a picture of a woman with an unusual occupation for her time; it also colors the whole era of Wild West performers from Buffalo Bill to Will Rogers." Booklist

Includes bibliographical references

800   LITERATURE, RHETORIC & CRITICISM

801   Philosophy and theory

Bloom, Harold, 1930-

The **anatomy** of influence. Yale University Press 2011 357p $32.50   **801**

1. Authors 2. Editors 3. Biographers 4. College teachers 5. Literary critics 6. Authors and readers 7. Literature -- Philosophy 8. Literature -- Appreciation 9. Literature -- History and criticism 10. Influence (Literary, artistic, etc.)

ISBN 978-0-300-16760-3; 0-300-16760-1

LC 2010-42456

It was the author's intention to "reveal . . . how writers struggle with the works of those who came before. He cites Shakespeare as the greatest writer in the English language. Moving forward chronologically from the 16th through the 20th centuries, [Harold] Bloom analyzes the works of such giants as John Milton, Samuel Johnson, Percy Bysshe Shelley, and Alfred, Lord Tennyson, illustrating their connections to Shakespeare. Bloom examines Walt Whitman's poetry in depth then considers James Joyce, D.H. Lawrence, Stephen Crane, and Wallace Stevens, as well as contemporary poets, e.g., A.R. Ammons, John Ashbery, and Mark Strand." (Libr J)

"The subtitle of Bloom's new book, 'Literature as a Way of Life,' is not an overstatement. For him, great authors don't merely imitate life or capture facets of being. They create 'heterocosms,' alternative but accessible worlds, open to us all. He had always been an esoteric populist, like his first subjects, Blake and Shelley." N Y Times Book Rev

Includes bibliographical references

Donoghue, Denis

Speaking of beauty. Yale University Press 2003 209p $24.95; pa $15 **801**
1. Aesthetics 2. English literature -- History and criticism
ISBN 0-300-09893-6; 0-300-10593-2 pa
LC 2002-12243

This book "is an eloquent reflection on the language beauty inspires and a careful critique of its place in literary criticism and cultural theory." N Y Times Book Rev

Includes bibliographical references

The encyclopedia of literary and cultural theory; general editor: Michael Ryan. Wiley-Blackwell 2011 3 v. **801**
1. Semiotics 2. Literature -- History and criticism
ISBN 9781405183123
LC 2010029411

This reference book "is . . . [a] multi-volume encyclopedia of literary and cultural theory. Arranged in three volumes covering Literary Theory from 1900 to 1966, Literary Theory from 1966 to the Present, and Cultural Theory, this encyclopedia provides . . . entries on the important concepts, theorists and trends in post-1900 literary and cultural theory. . . . [It includes] . . . over 300 entries of 1,000-7,000 words, . . . explanations of complex terms, important theoretical concepts, and tools for critical analysis and summaries of the work and ideas of key figures. (Publisher's note)

Includes bibliographical references and index.

Garber, Marjorie

The **use** and abuse of literature. Pantheon Books 2011 320p $28.95 **801**
1. Literature -- Philosophy
ISBN 978-0-375-42434-2; 0-375-42434-2
LC 2010-35417

Garber "examines classic texts like John Donne's 'The Canonization' and Ezra Pound's haiku-like poem 'In a Station of the Metro,' but she is equally happy to devote half a page to listing books with the phrase 'use and abuse' in their titles, and she spends what seems like an inordinate amount of time attacking a 30-year-old book called 'Metaphors We Live By' by George Lakoff and Mark Johnson, for its 'devaluation of the power and nature of words.' This variousness has been a hallmark of Garber's career — she is the author of books on Shakespeare, real estate, bisexuality, and pets — and it enlivens 'The Use and Abuse of Literature' with many incidental insights and pleasures. But the real justification for Garber's method is the way it enacts her

central thesis: that literature is not so much a subject as an activity." Boston Globe

Gardner, John

On moral fiction. Basic Bks. 1978 214p hardcover o.p. pa $18 **801**
1. Literature -- Philosophy
ISBN 0-465-05226-6 pa
LC 77-20409

Gardner "submits that contemporary U.S. art, primarily that of fiction, is generally not of high quality because it is not moral, in that it strives to devalue rather than improve life. Furthermore, Gardner charges that critics have lost track of true, moral art and have failed to denounce that which is false or immoral." Booklist

Kermode, Frank

An **appetite** for poetry. Harvard Univ. Press 1989 242p $32 **801**
1. Blind 2. Poets 3. Authors 4. Lawyers 5. Criticism 6. Dramatists 7. Editors 8. Essayists 9. Literary critics 10. Insurance executives 11. Nobel laureates for literature 12. Poetry -- History and criticism 13. Literature -- History and criticism
ISBN 0-674-04093-7
LC 89-31725

This collection contains critical and textual readings of Milton, T. S. Eliot, Wallace Stevens, William Empson and the Bible

"Kermode is not simply a critic but also an artist. . . . In An Appetite for Poetry we encounter writing of balance and decorum, and reading of unflinching audacity." Commonweal

Includes bibliographical references

Kundera, Milan

★ The **curtain**; an essay in seven parts. translated from the French by Linda Asher. HarperCollins Publishers 2007 168p $22.95 **801**
1. Literature -- Philosophy 2. Fiction -- History and criticism
ISBN 978-0-06-084186-7; 0-06-084186-9
LC 2006-43420

"The immediacy of Kundera's evocative prose and the rich tapestry he weaves compel us to pick up and read, or reread, the bountiful literary treasures of Western literature. This could be a book from which to draw a summer reading list." Libr J

Mendelsohn, Daniel

Waiting for the barbarians; essays from the classics to pop culture. by Daniel Mendelsohn. New York Review Books 2012 423 p. (alk. paper) $24.95 **801**
1. Criticism 2. Classical literature 3. Popular culture -- United States 4. Literature -- History and criticism 5. Canon (Literature) 6. Literature -- Appreciation 7. Popular culture -- 21st century
ISBN 1590176073; 9781590176078
LC 2012012240

This book by Daniel Mendelsohn is a collection of his essays seen in "The New York Review of Books," "The New Yorker," and "The New York Times Book Review." This collection "brings together twenty-four of his recent essays

. . . on a wide range of subjects. . . . Trained as a classicist, Mendelsohn moves easily from . . . considerations of the ways in which the classics continue to make themselves felt in contemporary life . . . to . . . takes on pop spectacles." (Publisher's note)

Weinstein, Arnold

A **scream** goes through the house; what literature teaches us about life. Random House 2003 xxxvii, 423p il $29.95; pa $14.95   **801**

1. Literature -- Philosophy

ISBN 0-375-50624-1; 0-8129-7243-0 pa

LC 2002-31719

"Blending the literary passion of Harold Bloom with the physiological insights of Antonio Damasio, Weinstein offers splendid readings of the creations of James Baldwin, Ingmar Bergman, Edvard Munch, Kafka, Faulkner, William Burroughs, and Toni Morrison." Booklist

Includes bibliographical references

803   Dictionaries, encyclopedias, concordances

Abrams, M. H. (1993)

★ A **glossary** of literary terms; with contributions by Geoffrey Galt Harpham. 8th ed.; Thomson, Wadsworth 2005 370p pa $34.95   **803**

1. Reference books 2. Literature -- Dictionaries

ISBN 1-4130-0218-8; 978-1-4130-0218-8

LC 2004-111345

First published 1957

In a series of essays, the author discusses literary terms and definitions ranging from the traditional to the avant-garde. Subsidiary terms are included under major or generic terms.

Ayto, John

★ **Brewer's** dictionary of modern phrase & fable; by John Ayto & Ian Crofton. 2nd ed.; Chambers Harrap Pub. Ltd. 2010 853p $39.95   **803**

1. Allusions 2. Reference books 3. Literature -- Dictionaries

ISBN 978-0550-105-646

First published 2000 by Cassell

"Focusing on the 20th and 21st centuries, . . . [this book covers a] selection of buzzwords, catchphrases, slang, nicknames, fictional characters and . . . cultural phenomena from pop culture to politics, literature to technology." Publisher's note

★ Benet's reader's encyclopedia; edited by Bruce F. Murphy. 5th ed.; Collins 2008 1210p $60 **803**

1. Reference books 2. Literature -- Dictionaries

ISBN 978-0-06-089016-2

LC 2008-31430

First published 1948 under the editorship of William Rose Benet

This encyclopedia contains over 10,000 entries and covers world literature from early times to the present. Includes entries on authors, literary movements, principal characters, plot synopses, terms, awards, myths and legends, etc.

This is "an edifying staple for any literary library." Libr J

Cuddon, J. A.

The **Penguin** dictionary of literary terms and literary theory; 4th ed; Penguin 1999 1024p (Penguin reference) pa $29   **803**

1. Reference books 2. Literature -- Dictionaries

ISBN 0-14-051363-9; 978-0-14-051363-9

First published 1977 in the United Kingdom with title: A dictionary of literary terms; first United States edition published 1977 by Doubleday; this edition first published 1998 by Blackwell Publishers

"Comprehensive dictionary covering all literatures and time periods with basic definitions as currently used. Categories include technical terms, forms, genres, groups, movements, -isms, character types, phrases, motifs or themes, concepts, objects, and styles. Entries often indicate origin and cite examples. Numerous see and see also references." Guide to Ref Books. 11th edition

Cyclopedia of literary characters; rev ed; Salem Press 1998 5v set $368   **803**

1. Reference books 2. Characters and characteristics in literature 3. Literature -- Dictionaries

ISBN 0-89356-438-9

LC 97-45813

"Entries are arranged alphabetically by the title of the work. . . . {They} begin with the book's title, foreign title if originally published in a language other than English, author's name with birth and death years, date of first publication, genre, locale, time of action, and plot type. Characters are arranged in order of importance; major characters have 100- to 150-word write-ups. Volume 5 contains three indexes: title, author, and character." Booklist

Dictionary of phrase and fable

★ **Brewer's** dictionary of phrase & fable; edited by Camilla Rockwood. 18th ed.; Brewer's 2009 xxv, 1460p il $49.95   **803**

1. Allusions 2. Reference books 3. Mythology -- Dictionaries 4. Literature -- Dictionaries 5. English language -- Terms and phrases

ISBN 978-0-550-10411-3

LC 2009-379960

First published 1870 under the editorship of Ebenezer Cobham Brewer

"Over 15,000 brief entries give the meanings and origins of a broad range of terms, expressions, and names of real, fictitious and mythical characters from world history, science, the arts and literature." N Y Public Libr. Ref Books for Child Collect. 2d edition

★ Oxford dictionary of phrase and fable; edited by Elizabeth Knowles. 2nd ed.; Oxford University Press 2005 805p $40; pa $18.95   **803**

1. Allusions 2. Reference books 3. Literature -- Dictionaries

ISBN 978-0-19-860981-0; 978-0-19-920246-1 pa

First published 2000

This work seeks to define words and phrases of British cultural history.

This "is a highly useful tool to help understand what phrases mean and where they come from and should definitely be added to all reference collections." Booklist

808

★ The **best** American essays 2012; David Brooks (editor) Robert Atwan (editor) Houghton Mifflin Harcourt 2012 310 p. $14.95 **808**
1. American essays
ISBN 0547840098; 9780547840093
"Edited by 'New York Times' columnist and best-selling author David Brooks, this . . . collection of the year's best includes thought-provoking essays from Marcia Angell, Miah Arnold, Mark Doty, Joseph Epstein, Jonathan Franzen, Malcolm Gladwell, Francine Prose, Lauren Slater, Sandra Tsing Loh, Jose Antonio Vargas, and others." (Publisher's note)

★ The **best** American travel writing 2012; William T. Vollman (editor) Jason WIlson (editor) Mariner Books 2012 256 p. $14.95 **808**
1. Travelers' writings, American
ISBN 0547808976; 9780547808970
This book, edited by Jason Wilson and William T. Vollman, is a collection of American travel writing featuring pieces including "including Monte Reel's look at how to explore the world like a Victorian gentleman and Elliott D. Woods' essay on the 'zabaleen,' or garbage pickers, in the Garbage City of Cairo." Other pieces include "Paul Theroux's short piece on the Maine coast and . . . Kimberly Meyer's essay on the elaborate Passion play performed each year in the Holy City of the Wichitas." (Kirkus)

Black nature; four centuries of African American nature poetry. edited by Camille T. Dungy. University of Georgia Press 2009 xxxv, 387p $69.95; pa $24.95 **808**
1. Nature poetry 2. American poetry -- African American authors
ISBN 978-0-8203-3277-2; 0-8203-3277-1; 978-0-8203-3431-8 pa; 0-8203-3431-6 pa
LC 2009-18528
"Since Bryant, Longfellow, Whitman, and Dickinson, the image of 'nature poetry' has stayed traditionally white. This collection helps complete the picture, by including a people who were chained to a foreign land and yet sustained a love for it." Orion
Includes bibliographical references

Brown, Laura
How to write anything; a complete guide. Laura Brown. W W Norton & Co Inc 2014 608 p. illustrations (hardcover) $35 **808**
1. Writing 2. Rhetoric 3. Report writing 4. English language -- Rhetoric
ISBN 0393240142; 9780393240146
LC 2013045078
This book, by Laura Brown, is "a practical guide to everything you'll ever need to write—at work, at school, and in your personal life. With more than two hundred how-to entries and easy-to-use models organized into three comprehensive sections on work, school, and personal life, [it] covers a wide range of topics that make it an essential guide for the whole family." (Publisher's note)
"Comprehensive and accessible, the work guides users through just about any situation where the written word is

necessary: social media for businesses, a plea to a professor for an extension, sympathy notes, wedding toasts, letters to the editor, and more." Booklist
Includes bibliographical references and index

★ The **Chicago** manual of style; 16th ed; The University of Chicago Press 2010 1026p **808**
1. Writing 2. Authorship 3. English language -- Usage 4. Printing -- Style manuals 5. Publishers and publishing 6. Authorship -- Style manuals 7. Authorship -- Handbooks, manuals, etc. 8. Publishers and publishing -- Handbooks, manuals, etc.
ISBN 0226104206; 9780226104201
LC 2009053612
First published 1906 with title: A manual of style
This style manual includes journals and electronic publications, descriptive headings on all numbered paragraphs, and chapters on grammar, usage, and documentation, including guidance on citing electronic sources.
Includes glossary and bibliographical references

Children's writer's & illustrator's market; edited by Alice Pope. Writer's Digest Books il **808**
1. Publishers and publishing 2. Authorship -- Handbooks, manuals, etc.
Annual. First published 1998
This reference includes listings of children's book publishers, magazines, agents, art reps, contests, clubs, conferences, awards, and grants with contact information, along with articles and interviews on a variety of subjects relating to children's writing, illustrating, and publishing
Includes bibliographical references

Conway, Jill K.
When memory speaks; reflections on autobiography. [by] Jill Ker Conway. Knopf 1998 205p hardcover o.p. pa $13 **808**
1. Autobiography 2. Biography as a literary form
ISBN 0-679-76645-6 pa
LC 97-49452
"Conway's small gem is a landmark in eliciting fresh contemplation of the inchoate complexity of memory's manifold voices." Publ Wkly
Includes bibliographical references

Garvey, Mark
Stylized; a slightly obsessive history of Strunk & White's The elements of style. Simon & Schuster 2009 xxv, 208p il **808**
1. Poets 2. Authors 3. Rhetoric 4. Humorists 5. Novelists 6. Essayists 7. Satirists 8. College teachers 9. Children's authors 10. Nonfiction writers 11. English language -- Style 12. Authorship -- Style manuals 13. English language -- Rhetoric 14. Authorship -- Handbooks, manuals, etc.
ISBN 1-4165-9092-7; 978-1-4165-9092-7
LC 2009007166
This is a history of the composition and publication of William Strunk and E.B. White's The Elements of Style, which appeared in 1959.

"A fan's meticulously researched, bighearted tribute to a sturdy, perennial writing guide, this history of Elements of Style is complete and unreservedly affectionate." Publ Wkly

Includes bibliographical references

Glenn, Cheryl (2007)

Hodges' Harbrace handbook; [by] Cheryl Glenn . . . [et al.] 16th ed; Thomson Wadsworth 2007 xxxi, 793p il $81.95 **808**

1. English language -- Grammar 2. English language -- Composition and exercises

ISBN 1-4130-1031-8

LC 2005-937964

First published 1941 under the authorship of John C. Hodges with title: Harbrace handbook of English. Frequently revised

A guide to the fundamentals of grammar, composition, and usage

Gutkind, Lee

You can't make this stuff up; the complete guide to writing creative nonfiction--from memoir to literary journalism and everything in between. Lee Gutkind. Da Capo Press/Lifelong Books 2012 xviii, 270 p.p **808**

1. Authorship 2. Creative writing 3. Creative nonfiction -- Technique 4. Exposition (Rhetoric) 5. Creative nonfiction -- Authorship 6. Reportage literature -- Technique

ISBN 9780738215549; 9780738215860

LC 2012018586

This book, by Lee Gutkind, offers advice for writing creative nonfiction. "From rags-to-riches-to-rags tell-alls to personal health sagas to literary journalism, everyone seems to want to try their hand at creative nonfiction. . . . Gutkind describes and illustrates each and every aspect of the genre, from defining a concept and establishing a writing process to the final product." (Publisher's note)

Includes bibliographical references (p. 255-259) and index

Hooks, Bell

Remembered rapture; the writer at work. Holt & Co. 1999 237p hardcover o.p. pa $13 **808**

1. Authorship 2. American literature -- African American authors

ISBN 0-8050-5910-5 pa

LC 98-7998

"The redoubtable Hooks offers a series of essays on writing, focusing on women, black writers (e.g., why there are so many black women novelists and so few in nonfiction), and what it was like to move to writer-saturated New York." Libr J

Jacob, Dianne

Will write for food; the complete guide to writing cookbooks, blogs, reviews, memoir, and more. 2nd ed.; Da Capo Lifelong 2010 342p pa $15.95 **808**

1. Food writing

ISBN 978-0-7382-1404-7

LC 2010-14224

First published 2005 by Marlowe and Co.

The author "provides detailed, practical advice on such matters as recipe development; how to launch a blog and draw readers, pitch article and book ideas, and refine one's prose style; and where to go to network or study. Also included are writing exercises, extensive suggestions for further reading, lists of publications and websites that accept freelancers, and perspectives drawn from interviews with dozens of well-known food writers such as Mark Bittman, Deborah Madison, and Calvin Trillin. . . . An engaging, informative handbook for hobbyists and aspiring professionals." Libr J

Includes bibliographical references

LaRocque, Paula, 1937-

The **book** on writing; the ultimate guide to writing well. Marion Street Press 2003 240p pa $18.95 **808**

1. Authorship

ISBN 0-9665176-9-5

LC 2003-13308

The author "organizes her book into three sections: mechanical and structural guidelines (i.e. sharpening accuracy and brevity), creative elements of storytelling (e.g., 'Let the Reader Do Some Work'), and style (grammar, usage and punctuation). LaRocque's advice is sane and sound: avoid pretension and over-complication, and stay away from jargon and clichés. . . . Beginning writers should find clear, useful advice here." Publ Wkly

★ **MLA** style manual and guide to scholarly publishing; 3rd ed.; Modern Language Association of America 2008 xxiv, 336p $32.50 **808**

1. Authorship -- Handbooks, manuals, etc.

ISBN 978-0-87352-297-7; 0-87352-297-4

LC 2008-2894

First published 1985 under authorship of Walter S. Achtert and Joseph Gibaldi

This book offers "guidance on writing scholarly texts, documenting research sources, submitting manuscripts to publishers, and dealing with legal issues surrounding publication." Publisher's note

Includes bibliographical references

Modern Language Association of America

★ **MLA** handbook for writers of research papers; 7th ed.; Modern Language Association of America 2009 xxi, 292p il pa $22 **808**

1. Report writing

ISBN 978-1-60329-024-1

LC 2008-47484

First published 1977 with title: MLA handbook for writers of research papers, theses, and dissertations

This manual discusses research strategies, formatting, documenting sources, writing basics and utilizing electronic sources.

Includes bibliographical references

Plotnik, Arthur

Spunk & bite; a writer's guide to punchier, more engaging language & style. Random House 2005 263p hardcover o.p. pa $12.95 **808**
1. Rhetoric
ISBN 0-375-72115-0; 0-375-72227-0 pa
LC 2005-44934

The author "demonstrates how . . . unexpected humor, loquaciousness, and apt description can jolt a writer into engaged authorship. This primer is dotted with illustrative examples that range from Shakespeare and J.K. Rowling to Dave Barry and Maeve Binchy. . . . This is an entertaining and engaging choice for writers." Libr J

Prose, Francine

★ **Reading** like a writer; a guide for people who love books and for those who want to write them. HarperCollins Publishers 2006 273p **808**
1. Rhetoric 2. Creative writing 3. Books and reading 4. English language -- Rhetoric
ISBN 0-06-077704-4; 0-06-077705-2 pa; 978-0-06-077704-3; 978-0-06-077705-0 pa
LC 2005-58457

The author argues that "would-be writers should turn to the classics for inspiration." (N Y Times Book Rev)

This book "should be greatly appreciated in and out of the classroom. Like the great works of fiction, it's a wise and voluble companion." N Y Times Book Rev

Rabiner, Susan

Thinking like your editor; how to write serious nonfiction--and get it published. by Susan Rabiner and Alfred Fortunato. Norton 2002 284p $26.95; pa $14 **808**
1. Authorship
ISBN 0-393-03892-0; 0-393-32461-3 pa
LC 2001-44551

"In part one, on submissions, the authors discuss how to put together a book proposal and, . . . whether to work through an agent or go solo. In part two, they move to the writing process. . . . Part three discusses how authors and editors (both in-house and freelance) can work together well." Publ Wkly

Siegal, Allan

The **New** York times manual of style and usage; [by] Allan M. Siegal and William G. Connolly. rev and expanded ed; Times Bks. 1999 364p hardcover o.p. pa $15 **808**
1. Authorship -- Handbooks, manuals, etc.
ISBN 0-8129-6389-X pa
LC 99-10630

First published 1962 by McGraw-Hill under the editorship of Lewis Jordan with title: Style book for writers and editors

Rules and guidelines observed by The New York Times for consistency of spelling, capitalization, punctuation, abbreviation, and preferred usage

This work "contends with the AP stylebook in authority and usefulness." Columbia J Rev

Stein, Sol

Stein on writing; a master editor of some of the most successful writers of our century shares his craft techniques and strategies. St. Martin's Press 1995 308p $24.95; pa $14.95 **808**
1. Authorship
ISBN 0-312-13608-0; 0-312-25421-0 pa
LC 95-31793

The author discusses the process of writing "fiction and nonfiction in terms of characterization, pacing, revision, evoking emotion, and 'liposuctioning flab.' Stein's own writing demonstrates the 'resonance' and 'particularities' he discusses, and his original checklists, writing exercises, and numerous examples encourage the reader/writer to see and do the same. A chapter of help sources and a glossary of terms provide the finishing touch." Libr J

Strunk, William

★ The **elements** of style; with revisions, an introduction, and a chapter on writing by E.B. White. 4th ed; Allyn & Bacon 1999 105p $14.95; pa $7.95 **808**
1. Rhetoric
ISBN 0-205-31342-6; 0-205-30902-X pa
LC 99-16419

First privately printed in 1918

This work provides guidelines for proper usage and composition. Misused expressions and commonly misspelled words are discussed. Includes examples.

This work is "prescriptive, conservative, and humorous; in sum, it is the best book available on how to write English prose." Nichols. Guide to Ref Books for Sch Media Cent. 4th edition

Turabian, Kate L.

★ A **manual** for writers of research papers, theses, and dissertations; Chicago style for students and researchers. revised by Wayne C. Booth, Gregory G. Colomb, Joseph M. Williams, and University of Chicago Press editorial staff. 7th ed.; University of Chicago Press 2007 466p il (Chicago guides to writing, editing, and publishing) $35; pa $17 **808**
1. Dissertations 2. Report writing
ISBN 978-0-226-82336-2; 0-226-82336-9; 978-0-226-82337-9 pa; 0-226-82337-7 pa
LC 2006-25443

First published 1937 with title: A manual for writers of dissertations

Designed to serve as a guide to suitable style in the presentation of formal papers—term papers, reports, articles, theses, dissertations—both in scientific and in nonscientific fields.

Student's guide to writing college papers; 4th ed; The University of Chicago Press 2010 281p il (Chicago guides to writing, editing, and publishing) $39; pa $15; ebook $15 **808**
1. Dissertations 2. Report writing
ISBN 978-0-226-81630-2; 978-0-226-81631-9 pa; 978-0-226-81633-3 ebook
LC 2009-31583

First published 1963 with title: Student's guide for writing college papers

This guide covers selecting a topic, collecting material, planning and writing the paper, and preparing footnotes and bibliographies.

Includes bibliographical references

United States/Government Printing Office

★ **Style** manual; an official guide to the form and style of Federal Government printing 2008. U.S. Government Printing Office. [30th ed.]; U.S. G.P.O. 2008 453p pa $36   **808**
    1. Printing -- Style manuals 2. Authorship -- Handbooks, manuals, etc. 3. Publishers and publishing -- Handbooks, manuals, etc.
    ISBN 978-0-16-081812-7

                   LC 2009-376600

First published 1908 with title: Manual of style. Frequently revised

"A useful and extensive manual giving the practices of the Government Printing Office on copy preparation, with rules for capitalization, punctuation, abbreviations, etc., and information on foreign languages, including alphabets, with pronunciation, special rules, lists of numbers, etc." Guide to Ref Books. 11th edition

Van Wicklen, Janet

The **tech** writer's survival guide; a comprehensive handbook for aspiring technical writers. Facts on File 2001 269p $35; pa $15.95   **808**
    1. Technical writing
    ISBN 0-8160-4038-9; 0-8160-4039-7 pa

                   LC 00-62231

First published 1992 with title: The tech writing game

"This guide offers some basic principles of document structure and design for both printed and online media and is full of practical advice on how to glean information from product developers and determine the needs of a document's audience. Van Wicklen draws from her own experience as well as giving testimony from colleagues, demonstrating the wide variability of technical writing jobs. It will be a helpful resource for anyone considering or beginning a career in technical writing." Booklist

Includes bibliographical references

Walker, Janice R.

The **Columbia** guide to online style; [by] Janice R. Walker and Todd Taylor. 2nd ed.; Columbia University Press 2006 xxi, 288p il $45; pa $19.50 **808**
    1. Bibliographical citations 2. Authorship -- Data processing -- Handbooks, manuals, etc.
    ISBN 0-231-13210-7; 978-0-231-13210-7; 0-231-13211-5 pa; 978-0-231-13211-4 pa

                   LC 2006-24383

First published 1998

This is a "resource for citing electronic and electronically accessed sources. It is also a . . . style guide for creating documents electronically for submission for print or electronic publication." Publisher's note

Includes bibliographical references

The **Writer's digest** guide to good writing; edited by Thomas Clark {et al.} Writer's Digest Bks. 1994 338p hardcover o.p. pa $14.99   **808**
    1. Authorship -- Handbooks, manuals, etc.
    ISBN 1-58297-138-2 pa

                   LC 93-43554

This collection of articles culled from issues of Writer's Digest magazine contains "essays on how to write with simplicity, plot and pace a story, build suspense, create characters, and tackle certain genres, including mysteries, horror, romance, and various forms of nonfiction. The selections are organized by decades and include essays by Erle Stanley Gardner, Irving Wallace, Louis L'Amour {and} Allen Ginsberg." Booklist

Zinsser, William Knowlton

Writing to learn. Harper & Row 1988 256p hardcover o.p. pa $145   **808**
    1. Rhetoric -- Study and teaching
    ISBN 0-06-272040-6 pa

                   LC 87-45825

"Eschewing theory and philosophical breast-beating, Zinsser uses his own experience to reinforce the fact that clear, eloquent writing can be taught for every subject across the curriculum. A practical manual for teachers and a powerful reminder for everyone that good writing makes possible good thinking." Am Libr

Includes bibliographical referneces

808.02   Authorship techniques, plagiarism, editorial techniques

D'Agata, John

The **lifespan** of a fact; John D'Agata and Jim Fingal. W. W. Norton 2012 160p.   **808.02**
    1. E-mail 2. Journalists 3. Essay -- Authorship 4. Creative nonfiction -- Authorship
    ISBN 9780393340730

                   LC 2011042637

In this book, "an essayist ([John] D'Agata) and his exasperated fact checker ([Jim] Fingal) debate the line between art and reality. . . . The text reproduces D'Agata's article about a teenager who leapt to his death from a Las Vegas Hotel, . . . Fingal's . . . fact-checking commentary, . . . and the authors' barbed e-exchanges on everything from the number of strip clubs in Vegas to the origins of tae kwon do and the existence of D'ata's mother's cat. . . . D'Agata cheerfully admits to embroidering the story with factoids; meanwhile, Fingal's efforts to verify them . . . required seven years and the help of medical journals, academic linguists, satellite photos, and field research." (Publishers Weekly)

Includes bibliographical references.

Kidder, Tracy

Good prose; the art of nonfiction. Tracy Kidder and Richard Todd. Random House 2013 224 p. (acid-free paper) $26   **808.02**
    1. Writing 2. Biography 3. Friendship 4. Authorship 5. Prose literature -- Authorship 6. Creative nonfiction

-- Authorship
ISBN 1400069750; 9780679604723; 9781400069750

LC 2012021165

Author Tracy Kidder "explores three major nonfiction forms: narratives, essays, and memoirs." She looks at "the works of a wide range of writers, novelists as well as nonfiction writers, for models and instruction." Kidder writes "about narrative strategies (and about how to find a story, sometimes in surprising places), about the ethical challenges of nonfiction, and about the realities of making a living as a writer." (Publisher's book)

Includes bibliographical references and index.

Malcolm, Janet

Forty -one false starts; essays on artists and writers. Janet Malcolm. Farrar Straus & Giroux 2013 320 p. (hardcover : alk. paper) $27 **808.02**
1. Artists 2. Authors 3. Authorship
ISBN 0374157693; 9780374157692

LC 2012034570

This book by Janet Malcolm "brings together essays . . . that reflect her preoccupation with artists and their work. Her subjects are painters, photographers, writers, and critics. She explores Bloomsbury's obsessive desire to create things visual and literary; the 'passionate collaborations' behind Edward Weston's nudes; and the character of the German art photographer Thomas Struth, who is 'haunted by the Nazi past,' yet whose photographs have 'a lightness of spirit.'" (Publisher's note)

Includes bibliographical references

MFA vs NYC; the Two Cultures of American Fiction. edited by Chad Harbach. Faber and Faber, Inc. / n+1 Foundation, Inc. 2014 320 p. illustrations (pbk.) $16 **808.02**
1. Authorship 2. Creative writing 3. Vocational guidance 4. Authors and publishers 5. Fiction -- Authorship 6. Authorship -- Vocational guidance 7. Fiction -- Publishing -- United States 8. Authors and publishers -- United States 9. Creative writing (Higher education) -- United States
ISBN 0865478139; 9780865478138

LC 2013048115

This book, edited by Chad Harbach, describes and engages with how "the American literary scene has split into two cultures: New York publishing versus university MFA programs. This book brings together established writers, MFA professors and students, and New York editors, publicists, and agents to talk about these overlapping worlds, and the ways writers make (or fail to make) a living within them." (Publisher's note)

"Essential insights, masterfully assembled, on the precarious state of American publishing." Kirkus

Includes bibliographical references and index

808.06   Rhetoric of specific kinds of writing

Aiken, Joan (1998)

The **way** to write for children. St. Martin's Griffin 1999 97p pa $9.95 **808.06**
1. Authorship 2. Children's literature -- Technique
ISBN 0-312-20048-X

LC 99-166931

First published 1982 in the United Kingdom

"In this crisp, informative and often witty survey of 'the market' Aiken is also giving the customers—teachers, librarians, parents, every one concerned with children's literature of quality-a good general idea of what is available already and of what authors are trying to do." Times Lit Suppl

Kephart, Beth

Handling the truth; on the writing of memoir. Beth Kephart. Gotham Books 2013 224 p. $16 **808.06**
1. Biography 2. Autobiography -- Authorship 3. Biography as a literary form
ISBN 159240815X; 9781592408153

LC 2012043517

In author Beth Kephart's book, "she thinks out loud about the form--on how it gets made, on what it means to make it, on the searing language of truth, on the thin line between remembering and imagining, and, finally, on the rights of memoirists. Drawing on proven writing lessons and classic examples, on the work of her students and on her own memories of weather, landscape, color, and love, Kephart probes the wrenching and essential questions that lie at the heart of memoir." (Publisher's note)

Seuling, Barbara

How to write a children's book and get it published; 3rd ed; Wiley 2005 233p il pa $15.95 **808.06**
1. Authorship 2. Children's literature -- Technique
ISBN 0-471-67619-5

LC 2004-4691

First published 1984

Presents "five essential steps (from researching the current marketplace to submitting your manuscript) to publishing works for children." Libr J

Includes bibliographical references

Shulevitz, Uri

Writing with pictures; how to write and illustrate children's books. Watson-Guptill 1985 271p il hardcover o.p. pa $29.95 **808.06**
1. Picture books for children 2. Children's literature -- Technique
ISBN 0-8230-5935-9 pa

LC 85-15604

"With heavy emphasis on illustration, this detailed book guides aspiring authors/illustrators through telling the story and drawing the pictures to preparing artwork for the printer." Libr J

Includes bibliographical references

Turabian, Kate L.

★ A **manual** for writers of research papers, theses, and dissertations; Chicago Style for students and

researchers. Kate L. Turabian ; revised by Wayne C. Booth, Gregory G. Colomb, Joseph M. Williams, and the University of Chicago Press editorial staff. University of Chicago Press 2013 xv, 448 p.p illustrations (Chicago guides to writing, editing, and publishing) (cloth : alkaline paper) $42.50 **808.06**
1. Dissertations 2. Report writing 3. Academic writing -- Handbooks, manuals, etc 4. Dissertations, Academic -- Handbooks, manuals, etc
ISBN 0226816370; 9780226816371; 9780226816388
LC 2012036981

This book, by Kate L. Turabian, "[begins] with an overview of the steps in the research and writing process . . . [and] provides an overview of citation practices with detailed information on the two main scholarly citation styles. . . . The final section treats all matters of editorial style, with advice on punctuation, capitalization, spelling, abbreviations, table formatting, and the use of quotations." (Publisher's note)

"This edition's new graphic design updates the look and feel of this resource and further develops rules and advice for the use and citation of online sources. In addition to featuring new templates for citing e-books, websites, blogs, social networks, discussion groups, online videos, and podcasts, the eighth edition offers new general advice to help students make good decisions about what information to include for online sources that may not have all the traditional elements useful in citing a print source." Choice

Includes bibliographical references (pages 409-433) and index

808.1   Rhetoric in specific literary forms

★ **2009** poet's market; Nancy Breen, editor. Writer's Digest Bks. 2008 572p pa $27.99 **808.1**
1. Poetry -- Marketing
ISBN 978-1-58297-544-3; 1-58297-544-2
Annual. First published 1989

"Useful for those aspiring to publish their poems in literary journals and magazines. . . . Entries include a brief journal profile, submission requirements, and contact information. Offers advice to beginning poets on getting published, brief articles by working poets/editors, grant information, contests and awards, poetry readings, writing colonies, organizations and publications useful to poets. Indexes for chapbook publishers, publishers by subject, publishers by state, and a general index." Guide to Ref Books. 11th edition

Includes bibliographical references

Abrams, M. H. (Meyer Howard), 1912-
The **fourth** dimension of a poem; and other essays. M.H. Abrams ; foreword by Harold Bloom. W. W. Norton & Company 2012 240 p. (hardcover) $25.95 **808.1**
1. Poetics 2. American essays 3. Poetry -- History and criticism
ISBN 0393058301; 9780393058307
LC 2012020169

This book by M. H. Abrams presents "a collection of nine new and recent essays that challenge the reader to think about poetry in new ways. In these essays . . . Abrams engages . . . with pivotal figures in intellectual and literary history, among them Kant, Keats, and Hazlitt. The centerpiece of the volume is Abrams's . . . essay 'The Fourth Dimension of a Poem' on the pleasure of reading poems aloud." (Publisher's note)

Includes bibliographical references and index.

Addonizio, Kim
The **poet's** companion; a guide to the pleasures of writing poetry. [by] Kim Addonizio and Dorianne Laux. Norton 1997 284p pa $14.95 **808.1**
1. Poetics
ISBN 0-393-31654-8
LC 96-40451

This work contains "three main sections: 'Subjects for Writing' (e.g. death, the erotic), 'The Poet's Craft' (metaphor, rhyme), and 'The Writing Life' (self-doubt, writer's block); four separate appendixes list other writing texts, anthologies, marketing tips, and electronic resources. . . . Both knowledgeable and practical in their approach, the authors offer everything a poet needs, including . . . a gentle yet insistent lesson on grammar." Libr J

Includes bibliographical references

Deutsch, Babette (1969)
Poetry handbook: a dictionary of terms; 4th ed; HarperResource 2002 203p pa $14 **808.1**
1. Reference books 2. Poetry -- Terminology 3. Poetics -- Dictionaries
ISBN 0-06-463548-1
First published 1957 by Funk & Wagnalls

"The craft of verse described in dictionary form. Terms and techniques are defined and illustrated." N Y Public Libr. Ref Books for Child Collect. 2d edition

Higginson, William J. (1548)
The **haiku** handbook; how to write, teach, and appreciate haiku. [by] William J. Higginson and Penny Harter; foreword by Jane Reichhold. 25th anniversary ed.; Kodansha International 2009 331p pa $18 **808.1**
1. Haiku
ISBN 978-4-770-03113-6; 4-770-03113-0
LC 2009-36628

First published 1985 by McGraw-Hill

This book "presents haiku poets writing in English, Spanish, French, German, and five other languages on an equal footing with Japanese poets. Not only are the four great Japanese masters of the haiku represented (Bash'o, Buson, Issa, and Shiki) but also several major Western authors not commonly known to have written haiku. The book presents a . . . history of the Japanese haiku, including the dynamic changes throughout the twentieth century as the haiku has been adapted to suburban and industrial settings. Full chapters are offered on form, the seasons in haiku, and haiku craft, plus background on the Japanese poetic tradition, and the effect of translation on our understanding of haiku." Publisher's note

Includes bibliographical references

Hirsch, Edward

How to read a poem; and fall in love with poetry. Harcourt Brace & Co. 1999 352p $23; pa $15 **808.1**

1. Poetics 2. Poetry -- History and criticism
ISBN 0-15-100419-6; 0-15-600566-2 pa

LC 98-50065

The author "has gathered an eclectic group of poems from many times and places, with selections as varied as postwar Polish poetry, works by Keats and Christopher Smart, and lyrics from African American work songs. A prolific, award-winning poet in his own right, Hirsch suggests helpful strategies for understanding and appreciating each poem. The book is scholarly but very readable and incorporates interesting anecdotes from the lives of the poets." Libr J

Includes bibliographical references

Hirsch, Edward, 1950-

A **Poet's** Glossary; by Edward Hirsch. Houghton Mifflin Harcourt 2014 736 p. $30 **808.1**

1. Poetry -- History and criticism 2. Poetics 3. Poetry -- Glossaries, vocabularies, etc
ISBN 0151011958; 9780151011957

LC 2014011675

In this book, author Edward Hirsch "has delved deeply into the poetic traditions of the world, returning with an inclusive, international compendium. Moving . . . from the bards of ancient Greece to the revolutionaries of Latin America, from small formal elements to large mysteries, he provides thoughtful definitions for the most important poetic vocabulary, imbuing his work with a lifetime of scholarship and the warmth of a man devoted to his art." (Publisher's note)

"Offering definitions, a discussion of poetic techniques, and an unalloyed spiritual quality to his work, Hirsch's . . . alphabetically arranged glossary includes historical explanations, quotes, interpretative material, usage in various languages, and references to additional terms for even more clarification." LJ

Kooser, Ted

★ The **poetry** home repair manual; practical advice for beginning poets. University of Nebraska Press 2005 163p $19.95; pa $13.95 **808.1**

1. Poetics
ISBN 0-8032-2769-8; 0-8032-5978-6 pa

LC 2004-24700

"Among the many books offering advice on writing poetry, . . . [this book] stands out for its usefulness and, at the same time, for its inspiring view of the purposes of poetry." Midwest Quarterly

Includes bibliographical references

Oliver, Mary

A **poetry** handbook. Harcourt Brace & Co. 1994 130p pa $13 **808.1**

1. Poetics
ISBN 0-15-672400-6

LC 93-49676

A "handbook for young poets on the formal aspects and structure of poetry. Oliver excels at explaining the sound and sense of poetry—from scansion to imagery, diction to voice. She stresses the importance of reading poetry, since, in order to write well, 'it is entirely necessary to read widely and deeply.' Sage advice is given in an entire chapter dedicated to revision, wherein Oliver urges poets to consider their first draft 'an unfinished piece of work' that can be polished and improved later. Written in a pleasant and lucid style, this book is a wonderful resource." Libr J

Pinsky, Robert, 1940- (2014)

Singing School; Learning to Write (And Read) Poetry by Studying With the Masters. Robert Pinsky. W W Norton & Co Inc. 2013 160 p. $25.95 **808.1**

1. Poets 2. Poetry 3. Authorship 4. Poetics
ISBN 0393050688; 9780393050684

LC 2013022146

In this book, poet Robert Pinsky "focuses on how poets read poetry in order to learn how to write poetry, taking his instructive title from William Butler Yeats: 'Nor is there singing school but studying / Monuments of its own magnificence.' Pinsky has selected a . . . variety of salient poems and organized them into sections titled 'Freedom,' 'Listening,' 'Form,' and 'Dreaming Things Up.' He introduces each of the 80 selections with an illuminating bit of analysis." (Booklist)

Includes bibliographical references and index

The **Princeton** encyclopedia of poetry and poetics; Roland Greene, editor in chief ; Stephen Cushman, general editor ; Clare Cavanagh, Jahan Ramazani, Paul Rouzer, associate editors ; Harris Feinsod, David Marno, Alexandra Slessarev, assistant editors. Princeton University Press 2012 xxxvi, 1639 p.p **808.1**

1. Poetry -- Dictionaries 2. Poetics -- Dictionaries 3. Poetry -- History and criticism
ISBN 9780691133348; 9780691154916

LC 2012005602

Includes bibliographical references and index

808.2   Rhetoric of drama

Field, Syd

★ **Screenplay**; the foundations of screenwriting. Rev. ed.; Delta Trade Paperbacks 2005 320p il pa $16 **808.2**

1. Motion picture plays -- Technique
ISBN 0-385-33903-8

LC 2005-48491

First published 1979

This book covers the basics of writing a screenplay, including how to build a character, set up a scene, and what to do after the screenplay is written.

Hauge, Michael

Writing screenplays that sell. HarperPerennial 1991 325p pa $12 **808.2**

1. Motion picture plays -- Technique
ISBN 0-06-272500-9; 978-0-06-272500-4

LC 91-55005

First published 1988 by McGraw-Hill

This book provides a "discussion of the craft—characters, story development, etc.—and industry; lays out the all-important details of format; then tells how to market the finished product. Hauge's volume is a detailed manual offering a step-by-step methodology, a scriptual analysis of a hit film, 'The Karate Kid,' and handy chapter summaries." Libr J

Includes bibliographical references

Inside the room; writing TV with the pros at UCLA Extension Writers' Program. edited by Linda Venis, Director, UCLA Extension Department of the Arts and Writers' Program. Gotham Books 2013 272 p.   **808.2**
1. Television authorship 2. Television broadcasting 3. Television authorship -- Vocational guidance
ISBN 9781592408115

LC 2013004221

In this book, edited by Linda Venis, "accomplished writers from the . . . UCLA Extension Writers' Program provide a . . . how-to book for aspiring television writers. . . . Television writers . . . take aspiring writers through the process of writing their first spec script . . . and revising their scripts to meet pro standards. They also learn how to launch and sustain a writing career and get a rare look inside the process of creating, selling, and getting a TV show made." (Publisher's note)

"A practical guide to how TV is made, from bright idea to syndication. A raft of instructors from the UCLA Extension Writers' Program (including director Venis) and a pool of professional TV writers whose credits include such series as Mad Men, Frasier and The Simpsons guide aspiring TV writers through the process of joining the ranks of small-screen scribes, from drafting a first script to thriving in a writers' room to pitching an original series. The advice is clear and specific...An engaging and helpful how-to for hopeful TV writers or anyone interested in the nuts and bolts of this ephemeral art."

Now write! screenwriting; exercises by today's best writers and teachers. [by] Sherry Ellis with Laurie Lamson. Jeremy P. Tarcher/Penguin 2011 343p il pa $14.95   **808.2**
1. Motion picture plays -- Technique
ISBN 978-1-58542-851-9

LC 2010-29424

The editors "compile guidelines from successful screenwriters on all of the details of writing a screenplay, from choosing your story to structure to character development. Readers will be interested to hear the opinions of such estimated screenwriters as Linda Seger and Syd Field and their takes on what motivates them to write screenplays and how they cope with writer's block and revisions. . . . This guide stands out from the crowd by incorporating the techniques of a variety of different screenwriters rather than just one professional's approach. Highly recommended for readers interested in writing, screenwriting, film, and storytelling." Libr J

808.3   Rhetoric of fiction

Bingham, Harry

The **writers'** and artists' yearbook guide to how to write; the essential guide for authors. Bloomsbury 2012 xiv, 364 p.p (paperback) $22.95   **808.3**
1. Fiction -- Technique 2. Authorship -- Handbooks, manuals, etc.
ISBN 1408157179; 9781408157176

This book by Harry Bingham " is all about writing for publication. How to plan, create and edit work that will sell." It features "examples . . . from successful authors" and is designed "for writers of every genre: fiction and narrative non-fiction, literary and commercial, adults and children. The guide tells you how to . . . understand your market . . . deelop strong, empathetic characters [and] structure and maintain a compelling plot." (Publisher's note)

Butler, Robert Olen

From where you dream; the process of writing fiction. edited, with an introduction by Janet Burroway. Grove Press 2005 269p $24; pa $13   **808.3**
1. Authorship 2. Fiction -- Technique
ISBN 0-8021-1795-3; 0-8021-4257-5 pa

LC 2005-40251

This is a collection of lectures the author has given for his creative writing course at Florida State University.

This "is a remarkably candid, clarifying, and profoundly demanding how-to. . . . Incisive and provocative, Butler's tutorials are a must for anyone even thinking about writing fiction, and readers, too, will benefit from his passionate exhortations." Booklist

Eco, Umberto

Confessions of a young novelist. Harvard University Press 2011 231p il (The Richard Ellmann lectures in modern literature) $18.95   **808.3**
1. Authorship
ISBN 9780674058699; 0-674-05869-0

LC 2010-33172

"In the first three essays/lectures here, Eco addresses interesting questions: what is the boundary between fiction and nonfiction? How do novelists put together books? Why do we care about wholly fictional characters like Anna Karenina or Emma Bovary? His answer to the second question—on constructing a novel—is that he builds his novels by scrupulous attention to physical detail. The fourth essay, 'My Lists,' original to this collection, was not a lecture. It seems a throwaway but reflects Eco's pleasure in the detailed, serial listing of names as attempts to exhaust the plenitude of qualities and quiddities potentially attributable to any single object. . . . As always, Eco is diverting to read." Libr J

Includes bibliographical references

Gardner, John

The **art** of fiction; notes on craft for young writers. Knopf 1984 224p hardcover o.p. pa $12.95   **808.3**
1. Fiction -- Technique
ISBN 0-679-73403-1 pa

LC 83-47850

"This essay distills the late Gardner's ripest thoughts about what fiction is and how to go about learning to write it. The initial section deals with 'literary-aesthetic theory,' the second with 'the fictional process.' . . . The book concludes with two sets of exercises, one for class use and one for individual use. Recommended for any young writer or writing class, and for all readers who care about the craft of fiction." Booklist

On becoming a novelist; foreword by Raymond Carver. W.W. Norton 1999 xxv, 150p pa $14.95   **808.3**
1. Authorship 2. Fiction -- Technique
ISBN 0-393-32003-0
First published 1983 by Harper & Row
The author "explores the dynamic chemistry at the heart of the writer's creative process. Gardner's book is a superbly written, thoroughly original, eminently useful volume." Choice

Koch, Stephen
★ The **modern** library writer's workshop; a guide to the craft of fiction. Modern Library 2003 246p pa $12.95   **808.3**
1. Authorship 2. Fiction -- Technique
ISBN 0-375-75558-6
LC 2002-32593
"Koch's tone is both encouraging and forthright, and his accessible, friendly guide will be essential for aspiring writers." Booklist
Includes bibliographical references

Lukeman, Noah
The **plot** thickens; 8 ways to bring fiction to life. St. Martin's Press 2002 221p $19.95; pa $12.95   **808.3**
1. Fiction -- Technique
ISBN 0-312-28467-5; 0-312-30928-7 pa
LC 2001-58564
"Lukeman focuses on the mechanics of storytelling. He introduces budding writers to the techniques of characterization (ask yourself questions about the people you've created), the various ways of generating suspense (danger, a ticking clock), and the importance of conflict." Booklist

Maass, Donald
Writing the breakout novel; winning advice from a top agent and his bestselling client. foreword by Anne Perry. Writer's Digest Bks. 2001 264p hardcover o.p. pa $16.99   **808.3**
1. Fiction -- Technique
ISBN 1-58297-182-X pa
LC 2001-22036
"Using his own clients as case studies, Maass defines the most crucial elements of a breakout novel—a powerful sense of time and place, larger-than-life characters, a high degree of tension, good subplots, and universal themes—and shows the reader how to use these elements efficiently to write a novel that will generate interest and have the potential to hit the best sellers lists. Each section ends with checklists for review." Libr J

Morrell, Jessica Page
Thanks, but this isn't for us; a (sort of) compassionate guide to why your writing is being rejected. Jeremy P. Tarcher-Penguin 2009 357p pa $16.95   **808.3**
1. Authorship
ISBN 978-1-58542-721-5
LC 2009-23252
The author "explores several mistakes new authors make in their manuscripts among them lack of conflict, unbelievable dialogue, and details that lack specific sensory appeal. Each chapter begins with a lively overview of a common problem, then lists what Morrell calls 'deal breakers'—particular habits such as lack of subplots and one-dimensional bad guys—that deter an editor from accepting a manuscript for publication. She concludes each chapter with exercises designed to improve storytelling, and then lists book resources for those wanting to delve more deeply into studies of character, emotion, tension and plot. . . . Emerging and established writers alike will benefit from Morrell's shrewd observations." Writer
Includes bibliographical references

Nabokov, Vladimir Vladimirovich
Lectures on literature; {by} Vladimir Nabokov; edited by Fredson Bowers; introduction by John Updike. Harcourt Brace Jovanovich 1980 xxviii, 385p il hardcover o.p. pa $18   **808.3**
1. Poets 2. Authors 3. Novelists 4. Dramatists 5. Essayists 6. Travel writers 7. Literary critics 8. Short story writers 9. Fiction -- History and criticism
ISBN 978-0-15-602775-5; 0-15-602775-5
LC 79-3690
Companion volume to Lectures on Russian literature
In the early 1950s, before Nabokov became a famous writer, he taught literature at Wellesley and Cornell. The editor, with the help of Nabokov's wife and son, has collected seven lectures on "Mansfield Park," "Bleak House," "Madame Bovary," "The Strange Case of Dr. Jekyll and Mr. Hyde," "The Walk by Swann's Place," "The Metamorphosis" and "Ulysses." There are two additional lectures on other topics related to literature. The volume includes a sample examination for the course and pages of original manuscripts with maps and diagrams which the author used to illustrate his lectures

Piercy, Marge
So you want to write; how to master the craft of writing fiction and memoir. [by] Marge Piercy and Ira Wood. 2nd ed.; Leapfrog Press 2005 324p pa $16.95   **808.3**
1. Biography as a literary form 2. Fiction -- Technique
ISBN 0-9728984-5-X
First published 2001
This book "uses talks, exercises, anecdotes and examples proven in the classroom, to address: How to begin a piece by seducing your reader, How to create characters that embody the infinite contradictions of human behavior, How to master the elements of plotting fiction, How to create a strategy for telling the story of your life, How to learn to read critically, like a professional writer, How to write about painful personal material without coming off as a victim,

[and] How to proceed if your work is continually rejected by publishers." Publisher's note

Includes bibliographical references

Roberts, Gillian

You can write a mystery. Writer's Digest Bks. 1999 124p il pa $12.99   **808.3**

1. Mystery fiction -- Technique

ISBN 0-89879-863-9

LC 99-19316

"Along with analysis of the literary aspects of mystery writing, Roberts also surveys such practical matters as grammar, punctuation, and how to submit the manuscript. If character and setting are what distinguish the best mysteries, failed plot mechanics are invariably what derail the worst. Roberts' basic but too-often-overlooked advice will help keep your story on track." Booklist

Includes bibliographical references

Stein, Sol

How to grow a novel; the most common mistakes writers make and how to overcome them. St. Martin's Press 1999 240p $25.95; pa $14.95   **808.3**

1. Fiction -- Technique

ISBN 0-312-20949-5; 0-312-26749-5 pa

LC 99-36922

"Stein states bluntly right from the beginning that 'liars say they write only for themselves' and that a 'lack of courtesy' toward the reader is one of the chief faults of unsuccessful writing. While this is perhaps a controversial notion, prospective writers will nonetheless be well rewarded by reading this collection of tips, methods, and numerous anecdotes." Libr J

Swain, Dwight V. (20·7)

Creating characters; how to build story people. Writer's Digest Bks. 1990 195p hardcover o.p. pa $14.99   **808.3**

1. Characters and characteristics in literature 2. Fiction -- Technique

ISBN 0-89879-662-8 pa

LC 90-39640

"Swain talks to his readers in a conversational tone, suggesting techniques, giving examples to illuminate his points, and offering activities for sharpening character development skills. This is a book for those already committed to writing fiction and who want to think about the craft of writing." SLJ

Includes bibliographical references

Techniques of the selling writer. University of Okla. Press 1981 330p $24.95   **808.3**

1. Fiction -- Technique

ISBN 0-8061-1191-7

First published 1965 with title: Tricks & techniques of the selling writer

The author offers practical advice for creating and marketing publishable fiction

"Often called 'the bible of fiction writing,' this classic is dated slightly by references to such things as 'carbon copies.' But Swain's tried-and-true scene-and-sequel approach has generated many books and workshops." Libr J

Wheat, Carolyn

How to write killer fiction; the funhouse of mystery & the roller coaster of suspense. Perseverance Press 2003 191p il pa $13.95   **808.3**

1. Mystery fiction -- Technique 2. Suspense fiction -- Technique

ISBN 1-88028-462-6

LC 2002-15588

Wheat begins with a "discussion of the distinction between mystery and suspense . . . and then devotes a section to each genre. She offers up plenty of useful tips, such as how to dispense vital information in subtle ways and how to plant clues without being too obvious about it." Booklist

Includes bibliographical references

Wood, James

★ **How** fiction works. Farrar, Straus and Giroux 2008 265p $24   **808.3**

1. Fiction

ISBN 0-374-17340-0; 978-0-374-17340-1

LC 2008-10290

The author addresses such questions as "What is character, point of view, the value of metaphor and simile, and detail? Is it all artifice or realism, or could it be labeled imaginative truth? His engaging discussion covers narration in all its forms, the impersonal author, the tension that exists between an author's and a character's style, flat vs. round characters, irony, and more. Wood uses excerpts from works by notable authors, from Miguel Cervantes and Jane Austen to Saul Bellow and John Updike, to illustrate his statements with pinpoint precision. Whether he is commenting on a work's weakness or strength, he supports his opinion with reasoned scholarship." Libr J

Includes bibliographical references

808.5   Rhetoric of speech

Detz, Joan

★ **How** to write and give a speech; a practical guide for executives, PR people, the military, fundraisers, politicians, educators, and anyone who has to make every word count. 2nd rev ed; St. Martin's Press 2002 xx, 202p pa $12.95   **808.5**

1. Public speaking

ISBN 0-312-30273-8

LC 2002-67975

First published 1984

Among the various aspects of public speaking discussed are: tips on topic focus, audience assessment, humor, delivery techniques and media coverage.

Flaherty, Francis

The **elements** of story; field notes on nonfiction writing. Harper Collins 2009 xxi, 293p $24.99 **808.5**

1. Rhetoric 2. Storytelling

ISBN 978-0-06-168914-7; 0-06-168914-9

LC 2008-53946

The author offers 50 "tips on the many elements writers can convey in stories. Not a style guide, this is instead a nuts-and-bolts examination of the larger elements of a story.

... This book can be read in one fell swoop to expose your-self to the full spectrum of story elements—such as theme, motion, artfulness, truth and fairness, leads, and titles—or it can be used as a guide during the process of writing nonfiction. An essential read for both freelance writers and students of journalism." Libr J

Includes bibliographical references

Linklater, Kristin

Freeing the natural voice; drawings by Douglas Florian. Drama Bk. Specialists 1976 210p il hardcover o.p. pa $19.95   **808.5**
  1. Voice
ISBN 0-89676-071-5 pa
"Predicated on the basic assumptions that everyone has a voice capable of expressing a full range of emotions within a normal two- to four-octave scale and that daily stress compromises the voice's natural abilities and power {the author} presents a simple and clear narrative, as well as a full set of exercises to cultivate and strengthen the voice." Libr J

Meyers, Peter

As we speak; how to make your point and have it stick. by Peter Meyers and Shann Nix. Atria Books 2011 viii, 275 p.p ill. $25   **808.5**
  1. Public speaking   2. Business communication   3. Communication in management   4. Interpersonal communication
ISBN 1439153051; 9781439153055
                         LC 2011015029
In this book, "Peter Meyers and Shann Nix offer a comprehensive approach for tackling the underlying obstacles that almost all of us experience when faced with speaking in public. In 'As We Speak,' you'll learn to master the three building blocks at the core of their approach: Content . . . Delivery . . . [and] State. . . . . Meyers and Nix also emphasize that effective communication is impossible without first becoming aware of your own true goals and personal beliefs." (Publisher's note)

Includes bibliographical references (p. 273-275)

Pinsky, Robert

The **sounds** of poetry; a brief guide. Farrar, Straus & Giroux 1998 129p hardcover o.p. pa $13   **808.5**
  1. Poetry
ISBN 0-374-52617-6
                         LC 98-18873
"By bringing his passion for the sound of language—so evident in his own poems—to his expert interpretations of the work of others, Pinsky cracks open the glass case that seems to separate poetry from everyday language, allowing the song of each poem to ring bright and clear." Booklist

Includes bibliographical references

808.8   Collections of literary texts from more than two literatures

The **Book** of eulogies; a collection of memorial tributes, poetry, essays, and letters of condolence. ed-ited with commentary by Phyllis Theroux. Scribner 1997 400p $26   **808.8**
  1. Eulogies   2. Bereavement
ISBN 0-684-82251-2
                         LC 97-2197
"Theroux has gathered over 100 eulogies delivered in the form of spoken tributes, editorials, letters of condolence, essays, and poetry. Many of these testimonials are eloquently penned by the well known to commemorate the well known (e.g., Thomas Merton on Flannery O'Connor, Robert F. Kennedy on Martin Luther King). Others are equally compelling memorials to unknown souls by everyday people. There are helpful commentaries by the author." Libr J

Into the garden; a wedding anthology: poetry and prose on love and marriage. edited by Robert Hass and Stephen Mitchell. HarperCollins Pubs. 1993 193p hardcover o.p. pa $13.95   **808.8**
  1. Weddings   2. Poetry -- Collections
ISBN 0-06-092469-1 pa
                         LC 92-53339
This anthology of readings suitable for wedding ceremonies contains "American Indian, aboriginal Australian, ancient Egyptian, Buddhist, Hindu, and Sufi poetry and prose in addition to . . . biblical, classical Greek and Roman, European, and American passages. . . . {Also included are} traditional or tradition-respecting ceremonies." Booklist

Journalistas; 100 years of the best writing and reporting by women journalists. edited by Eleanor Mills with Kira Cochrane. Carroll & Graf 2005 xx, 364p pa $14.95   **808.8**
  1. Women journalists   2. Literature -- Collections
ISBN 0-7867-1667-3
"From Djuna Barnes' 1914 account of being force-fed to end her hunger strike, to Eleanor Roosevelt's 1938 'My Day' column, to Rose George's 2004 article about gang rapes in France, this collection provides a broad and deep look at reporting by women in the past century." Booklist

The **Norton** book of modern war; edited by Paul Fussell. Norton 1991 830p $24.95   **808.8**
  1. War in literature   2. Literature -- Collections
ISBN 0-393-02909-3
                         LC 90-36495
This anthology of 20th century prose and poetry about war covers World War I, the Spanish Civil War, World War II, the Korean War and Vietnam. Authors represented include Heinrich Böll, Marguerite Duras, Ernest Hemingway, Ron Kovic, Norman Mailer, Wilfred Owen and Siegfried Sassoon.

Nothing makes you free; writings by descendants (7603) of Jewish Holocaust survivors. edited by Melvin Jules Bukiet. Norton 2002 394p hardcover o.p. pa $15.95   **808.8**
  1. Holocaust survivors   2. Holocaust, 1939-1945, in literature   3. Literature -- Collections   4. Holocaust, 1933-1945, in literature
ISBN 0-393-05046-7; 0-393-32425-7 pa
                         LC 2001-55863

"Excerpts from the works of 30 writers whose parents survived the Holocaust make up this anthology of fiction and memoirs. . . . In these remarkable pieces issues such as guilt, anger, faith, and accountability are explored. They capture not only the experience of the concentration camps but also its powerful legacy, passed down to a new generation through the bond of love that ties parent and child." Booklist

The **Paris** review book of heartbreak, madness, sex, love, betrayal, outsiders, intoxication, war, whimsy, horrors, God, death, dinner, baseball, travels, the art of writing, and everything else in the world since 1953; by the editors of the Paris review; with an introduction by George Plimpton. Picador 2003 751p $30; pa $19   **808.8**
1. Literature -- Collections
ISBN 0-312-42238-5; 0-312-42239-3 pa
LC 2003-45971
This anthology includes works by "W.H. Auden, Ernest Hemingway, William Faulkner, Jack Kerouac, Elizabeth Bishop, Truman Capote, William Burroughs, Susan Sontag, Joyce Carol Oates, Toni Morrison, Jonathan Franzen, Ian McEwan and Alice Munro." Publ Wkly

Remembrances and celebrations; a book of eulogies, elegies, letters, and epitaphs. edited by Jill Werman Harris. Pantheon Bks. 1999 xxiii, 308p $25; pa $14   **808.8**
1. Eulogies 2. Bereavement
ISBN 0-375-40123-7; 0-375-70125-7 pa
LC 98-32149
"Comprised of eulogies from the 20th century, as well as, poetic elegies, condolence letters and tombstone epitaphs spanning from the 17th century to the present, this eclectic sourcebook offers inspiration for anyone seeking to memorialize a loved one. Since the mourners and the dead in each instance are well-known writers (Lillian Hellman eulogizes Dashiell Hammett) and public figures (Reverend Jesse Jackson lays Jackie Robinson to rest), the collection is a bonanza for the morbidly minded browser as well." Publ Wkly

808.81   Collections in specific forms

★ The **20th** Century in Poetry. W W Norton & Co Inc 2012 860 p. $35.00   **808.81**
1. Poetry -- Collections 2. Poetry -- History and criticism -- 20th century
ISBN 1605983640; 9781605983646
This poetry anthology, edited by Michael Hulse and Simon Rae, "presents in chronological order over four hundred poems written during the twentieth century. The authors, both published poets themselves, give an overview of each period of history, while notes to the poems place each one in its historical context and trace the century's poetic development. Concise biographies for each poet complete the anthology." (Publisher's note)

A **Book** of love poetry; edited and with an introduction by Jon Stallworthy. Oxford Univ. Press 1974 393p hardcover o.p. pa $18.95   **808.81**
1. Love poetry
ISBN 0-19-504232-8
First published 1973 in the United Kingdom with title: The Penguin book of love poetry
A collection of poems written during the past 2000 years arranged thematically from young love to the "long look back" of the aged
Includes indexes of poets, translators, titles and first lines

City lights pocket poets anthology; edited by Lawrence Ferlinghetti. City Lights Bks. 1995 259p $18.95   **808.81**
1. Poetry -- Collections
ISBN 0-87286-311-5
LC 95-31608
"Drawing from the 52 volumes published in the Pocket Poets series since 1956, this selection provides a handy sampler of many of the prominent avant-garde and leftist poets of the post-WW II era. . . . The series' extensive international scope is highlighted in poems culled from German, Russian, Italian, Dutch, Nicaraguan and Spanish poets." Publ Wkly

The **Columbia** Granger's dictionary of poetry quotations; edited by Edith P. Hazen. Columbia Univ. Press 1992 1132p $131   **808.81**
1. Quotations 2. Reference books
ISBN 0-231-07546-4
LC 91-42240
This work contains the "most memorable lines written by the greatest poets of English. Quotations are organized alphabetically by poet, and coded so one can find full text in hundreds of current anthologies. With keyword and subject indexing." Univ Press Books for Public and Second Sch Libr

★ The **Columbia** Granger's Index to poetry in collected and selected works; edited by Keith Newton. 2nd ed, completely rev; Columbia Univ. Press 2004 xxi, 1847p $225   **808.81**
1. Reference books 2. Poetry -- Indexes
ISBN 0-231-12528-3
LC 2003-51469
First published 1996
This "edition includes 315 works, by 266 different poets, locating more than 65,000 poems by title, first line, author, and subject. Included . . . are the works of many of the major American and British poets of the last thirty years, such as Robert Pinsky, Seamus Heaney, and Paul Muldoon; important twentieth-century American poets such as Langston Hughes, Dorothy Parker, and Robert Penn Warren; twentieth-century foreign poets in new translations, such as Eugenio Montale and Paul Celan; and diverse poets from all times and places, collected in new editions, such as Cold Mountain, Jones Very, and Guido Cavalcanti." Publisher's note

Favorite Poem Project (2000)

Americans' favorite poems; the Favorite Poem Project anthology. edited by Robert Pinsky and Maggie Dietz. Norton 1999 327p $27.50 **808.81**
1. Poetry -- Collections
ISBN 0-393-04820-9

LC 99-31979

"People across America, including many teens, share the poetry they love, and talk about what it means in their lives. Their choices—from John Keats to Lucille Clifton—defy stereotypes, and their comments are heartfelt." Booklist

Granger, Edith (1997)

★ The **Columbia** Granger's index to poetry in anthologies; edited by Tessa Kale. 13th ed., completely rev., indexing anthologies published through May 31, 2006; Columbia University Press 2007 xxviii, 2376p $295 **808.81**
1. Reference books 2. Poetry -- Indexes
ISBN 0-231-13988-8; 978-0-231-13988-5

LC 2006-14853

First edition, edited by Edith Granger, published 1904 by A. C. McClurg with title: Index to poetry and recitations. Fifth through eighth editions have title Granger's index to poetry

"The 400 total entries are organized alphabetically into three sections: 'Title, First Line, Last Line,' 'Author,' and 'Subject.' The anthologies referenced appear as abbreviations explained in a 14-page introductory list. An essential purchase for literature and poetry collections." Libr J

Includes bibliographical references

Holocaust poetry; compiled and introduced by Hilda Schiff. St. Martin's Press 1995 xxiv, 234p hardcover o.p. pa $14.95 **808.81**
1. Poetry -- Collections 2. Holocaust, 1933-1945 -- Poetry
ISBN 0-312-13086-4; 0-312-14357-5 pa

LC 95-2708

"In English and in translation from many languages, more than 80 poets—including Wiesel, Fink, Brecht, Yevtushenko, Auden, and Sachs—give voice to what seems unspeakable. Schiff points out that compelling historical accounts document the facts and numbers, but a poem, like a story, makes us imagine how it felt for one person. These poems are stark and deceptively simple." Booklist

Includes bibliographical references

Language for a new century; contemporary poetry from the Middle East, Asia, and beyond. edited by Tina Chang, Nathalie Handal, and Ravi Shankar. W.W. Norton 2008 l, 734p il pa $27.95 **808.81**
1. Poetry -- Collections
ISBN 978-0-393-33238-4; 0-393-33238-1

LC 2007-49424

"Even a diligent reader of contemporary poetry will leave this gathering feeling humbled by ignorance of the immense poetic energy of what used to be called the East." Booklist

Includes bibliographical references

Merwin, W. S. (William Stanley), 1927-

Selected translations 1948-2010; 1948-2011. [compiled by] W.S. Merwin. Copper Canyon Press 2012 407 p. (alk. paper) $40 **808.81**
1. Poetry 2. Translating and interpreting 3. Poetry -- Collections 4. Poetry -- Translations into English
ISBN 1556594097; 9781556594090

LC 2012025545

This poetry collection, translated by W.S. Merwin, "is the lifework from one of America's greatest poets and translators. Dedicated to the art of translation since his undergraduate years at Princeton, Poet Laureate W.S. Merwin achieved an unmatched oeuvre of translated poems from every corner of the earth, from dozens of languages." (Publisher's note)

Milosz, Czeslaw

A **Book** of lumininous things; an international anthology of poetry. edited and with an introduction by Czeslaw Milosz. Harcourt Brace & Co. 1996 xx, 320p hardcover o.p. pa $15 **808.81**
1. Poetry -- Collections
ISBN 0-15-600574-3

LC 95-38060

"Nobel laureate Milosz states in his introduction that the purpose of this personal and eclectic collection is to present poetry that is 'short, clear, readable, and . . . realistic, that is, loyal toward reality and attempting to describe it as concisely as possible.' . . . Most of the selections are from classical Chinese and 20th-century American and European (primarily Eastern European, Scandinavian, and French) poets." Libr J

Music of a distant drum; classical Arabic, Persian, Turkish, and Hebrew poems. translated and introduced by Bernard Lewis. Princeton Univ. Press 2001 222p il hardcover o.p. pa $17.95 **808.81**
1. Arabic poetry -- Collections 2. Hebrew poetry -- Collections 3. Persian poetry -- Collections 4. Turkish poetry -- Collections
ISBN 0-691-15010-9 pa; 0-691-08928-0

LC 2001-19858

"Lewis, one of the foremost scholars of the Middle East, has devoted much of his career to the history of Islam; this volume collects his translations of poems—nearly all appearing in English for the first time—that span eleven centuries and four major Middle Eastern traditions. Many of the most striking works address, in spare, stirring lines, the twin demands of serving the self and serving God." New Yorker

Includes bibliographical references

The **Oxford** book of war poetry; chosen and edit- (1984) ed by Jon Stallworthy. Oxford University Press 2008 xxxi, 358 p.p (paperback) $19.95 **808.81**
1. War poetry 2. Poetry -- Collections 3. War poetry/ Collections
ISBN 0199554536; 9780199554539

LC 8319303

This book is a collection of war poetry, arranged chronologically by conflict. The "250 poems in John Stallworthy's . . . anthology span centuries of human experience of war, from David's 'Lament for Saul and Jonathan,' and Homer's

'Iliad,' to the finest poems of the First and Second World Wars, and beyond." (Publisher's note)

Includes bibliographical references and indexes.

Poems to read; a new favorite poem project anthology. edited by Robert Pinsky and Maggie Dietz. Norton 2002 xxv, 352p $27.95   **808.81**

1. Poetry -- Collections
ISBN 0-393-01074-0

LC 2002-321

"A graceful, sometimes jubilant, sometimes lyrical, sometimes brooding, but always welcoming and stirring collection." Booklist

Includes bibliographical references

The **Poetry** of our world; an international anthology of contemporary poetry. edited by Jeffrey Paine. HarperCollins Pubs. 2000 xxviii, 511p hardcover o.p. pa $18.95   **808.81**

1. Poetry -- Collections
ISBN 0-06-055369-3; 0-06-095193-1 pa

LC 99-34921

In this global anthology "each section is preceded by a thoughtful introduction of several pages by the selector in that area. . . . A stunning and highly readable anthology." Libr J

Till I end my song; a gathering of last poems. edited with commentaries by Harold Bloom. Harper 2010 xxviii, 377p $24.99   **808.81**

1. Poetics 2. Poetry -- History and criticism
ISBN 978-0-06-192305-0; 0-06-192305-2

LC 2010-20773

"These are poems that embrace change, time, life, the self, and death. Poems that have lasted and that will 'reverberate into the coming silence.' A collection of surpassing splendor and resonance." Booklist

University of California (System)

Poems for the millennium; the University of California book of modern and postmodern poetry. edited by Jerome Rothenberg and Pierre Joris. University of Calif. Press 1995 2v il v1 $70; v1 pa $29.95; v2 pa $29.95   **808.81**

1. Poetry -- Collections
ISBN 0-520-07225-1 v1; 0-520-07227-8 v1 pa; 0-520-20864-1 v2 pa

LC 93-49839

The poetry in this anthology is "often self-referential, certainly aware of its own artistry, embedded in political consciousness, and transgressive. It is the work of more than 100 poets, many little known in the U.S. Rothenberg and Joris see twentieth-century poetics as international and have postwar Japanese poet Fujii Sadakazu rubbing shoulders with Amiri Baraka and Andrei Voznesensky, Tomas Tranströmer and Diane di Prima." Booklist {review of v2}

The **Vintage** book of contemporary world poetry; edited and with an introduction by J.D. McClatchy. Vintage Bks. 1996 xxviii, 654p pa $16   **808.81**

1. Poetry -- Collections
ISBN 0-679-74115-1

LC 95-50628

A "varied collection of contemporary poetry from Europe, the Middle East, Africa, Asia, Latin America, and the Caribbean. Here readers will find Nobel laureates and other luminaries, such as Joseph Brodsky, Derek Walcott, Czeslaw Milosz, Octavio Paz, Wole Soyinka, Breyten Breytenbach, and Nguyen Chi Thien, as well as less well known poets. Editor McClatchy has chosen well, selecting poems that illuminate the personal as well as the universal." Booklist

Includes bibliographical references

World poetry; an anthology of verse from antiquity to our time. Katharine Washburn and John S. Major, editors; Clifton Fadiman, general editor. Norton 1998 xxii, 1338p $45   **808.81**

1. Poetry -- Collections
ISBN 0-393-04130-1

LC 97-10879

The anthology's "stated aim—'to surprise and delight the common reader'—may seem rather quaint; yet it is a worthy one, and is, on the whole, impressively fulfilled." Times Lit Suppl

Includes bibliographical references

808.82   Collections of drama

★ **2010:** the best men's stage monologues and scenes; edited and foreword by Lawrence Harbison. Smith & Kraus 2010 176p (Monologue and scene study series) pa $14.95   **808.82**

1. Acting 2. Monologues
ISBN 978-1-57525-773-0

Annual. First published 1991 for the 1990 theater season under the editorship of Jocelyn Beard

This is a "selection of monologues and scenes from plays that were produced and/or published in the 2009-2010 theatrical season. Most are for younger performers (teens through thirties), but there are also some . . . pieces for men in their forties and fifties, and even a few for older performers. Some are comic (laughs), some are dramatic (generally, no laughs)." Publisher's note

★ **2010:** the best women's stage monologues and scenes; edited and with a foreword by Lawrence Harbison. Smith & Kraus Book 2010 193p (Monologue and scene study series) pa $14.95   **808.82**

1. Acting 2. Monologues
ISBN 978-1-57525-774-7

Annual. First published 1991 for the 1990 theater season under the editorship of Jocelyn Beard

This is a "selection of monologues and scenes from plays that were produced and/or published in the 2009-2010 theatrical season." Publisher's note

★ The **best** plays of 2006-2007; edited by Jeffrey Eric Jenkins; illustrated with production photographs. Limelight Eds. 2008 560p il (Best plays theater yearbook) $49.95 **808.82**
1. Drama -- Collections 2. Theater -- United States
ISBN 978-0-8791-0352-1
Annual. First published 1920. Variant titles: The Burns Mantle theater yearbook; The Applause/best plays theater yearbook
Some back volumes published by Dodd, Mead available from Applause Theatre Bk. Pubs.; reprints of older annuals available from Ayer; for full information on availability and price contact publishers.

The **best** stage scenes of 2007; edited by Lawrence Harbison; with a foreword by D.L. Lepidus. Smith & Kraus 2007 202p (Scene study series) pa $14.95 **808.82**
1. Drama 2. Acting
ISBN 978-1-57525-588-0; 1-57525-588-X
Annual. First published 1992 under the editorship of Jocelyn Beard
This title culls "selections from recent plays, divided among scenic groupings for men and women, men, and women. . . . The scenes vary in length and intensity, with each scene providing a setting, description, and the number of needed characters." Libr J

Nine plays of the modern theater; with an introduction by Harold Clurman. Grove Press 1981 896p pa $21 **808.82**
1. Drama -- Collections
ISBN 0-8021-5032-2
LC 79-52121

The **Ultimate** audition book; 222 monologues, 2 minutes & under. edited by Jocelyn A. Beard. Smith & Kraus 1997 2v + v4 (Monologue audition series) ea pa $19.95 **808.82**
1. Acting 2. Monologues
ISBN 1-57525-066-7 v1; 1-57525-270-8 v2; 1-57525-420-4 v4
LC 97-10471
This collection draws "upon lesser-known works from significant writers and those of contemporary favorites and reflects a wide range of tone, age, time period, and voice. Divided among female, male, and unisex categories, all meet the obligatory two minutes or less time limit imposed by most directors and auditions." Libr J [review of volume 2]
Includes bibliographical references

808.84 Collections of essays

The **Norton** book of personal essays; edited by Joseph Epstein. Norton 1997 477p $30 **808.84**
1. Essays
ISBN 0-393-03654-5
LC 96-26975
George Orwell, James Baldwin, Joan Didion, M. F. K. Fisher, Barbara Tuchman and Cynthia Ozick are among the authors chosen by Epstein for inclusion in this collection of "53 personal essays written in English by well-known authors during the past century. They were chosen because he 'found them interesting, touching, pleasing, amusing, delightful—above all, entertaining.' The result is a potpourri of selections that vary widely in subject and style. Topics range from music, racism, and traveling to fathers, children, and childhood." Libr J

Teachers & Writers Collaborative
The **Art** of the personal essay; an anthology from the classical era to the present. selected and with an introduction by Phillip Lopate. Anchor Bks. (NY) 1994 liv, 777p hardcover o.p. pa $17.95 **808.84**
1. Essays
ISBN 0-385-42339-X pa
LC 93-29708
"Not only are the selections a veritable feast, but Lopate's genre-defining introduction is not to be missed." Booklist
Includes bibliographical references

808.85 Collections of speeches

Sutton, Roberta Briggs
Speech index; an index to 259 collections of world famous orations and speeches for various occasions. 4th ed rev & enl; Scarecrow Press 1966 947p $85 **808.85**
1. Reference books 2. Speeches -- Indexes
ISBN 0-8108-0138-8
First published 1935 by the H.W. Wilson Company
"Speeches are indexed by orator, type of speech, and by subject, with a selected list of titles given in the appendix. Particularly useful for amateur speakers in locating examples to use in preparing a speech and models they can adapt to their needs." Ref Sources for Small & Medium-sized Libr. 6th edition

The **World's** great speeches; edited by Lewis Copeland, Lawrence W. Lamm, and Stephen J. McKenna. 4th enl 1999 ed; Dover Publs. 1999 xxii, 920p pa $17.95 **808.85**
1. Speeches
ISBN 0-486-40903-1
LC 99-32880
First published 1942 by Garden City Pub. Co.
An international collection of approximately 300 speeches by over 200 speakers arranged chronologically

808.86 Collections of letters

Mallon, Thomas
Yours ever; people and their letters. Pantheon Books 2009 338p $26.95 **808.86**
1. Letters
ISBN 978-0-679-44426-8; 0-679-44426-2
LC 2009-06315
Companion volume to A book of one's own (1984)

This is "an astute, exhilarating tour of the mailbag. . . . [It] is nuanced, informed, full-blooded, a vigorous literary salute." N Y Times Book Rev

Includes bibliographical references (p. 313-320)

808.88   Collections of miscellaneous writings

Boller, Paul F.

They never said it; a book of fake quotes, misquotes, and misleading attributions. [by] Paul F. Boller, Jr., and John George. Oxford Univ. Press 1989 xxv, 159p hardcover o.p. pa $15.95   **808.88**
1. Errors 2. Quotations 3. Literary forgeries
ISBN 0-19-506469-0 pa

LC 88-22115

In an alphabetical list of attributees' names or titles the authors expose the truth behind more than 200 phony quotations

Lend me your ears; Oxford dictionary of political quotations. edited by Sir Antony Jay. 4th ed; Oxford University Press 2010 xxv, 446p $24.95   **808.88**
1. Reference books 2. Political science -- Quotations
ISBN 978-0-19-957267-0

LC 2010-923325

First published 1996 with title: The Oxford dictionary of political quotations

Entries are organized "by speaker rather than by topic. Don't know the origin of a quotation? Fear not. Turn to the extensive keyword index or the briefer 'selective subject index' in the back of the volume. Helpful also are one-page special category quotes: epitaphs, misquotations, mottoes, slogans, etc. . . . [This is] a great value and an excellent choice for libraries lacking a current work in this area." Libr J

Nowlan, Robert A.

Born this day; a book of birthdays and quotations of prominent people through the centuries. 2nd ed.; McFarland & Co. 2007 511p $55   **808.88**
1. Birthdays 2. Quotations
ISBN 978-0-7864-2935-6; 0-7864-2935-6

LC 2007-3809

First published 1996

"Arranged chronologically by date of the month, the volume offers lists of 12 'significant' people born on each day, with a very brief biography and a representative or telling quotation uttered by the individual. In addition, each date lists the birthdays of a dozen or more lesser-known individuals, noting only name and year. . . . [This is] a fine ready-reference volume offering unique information." Booklist

O'Brien, Geoffrey

Bartlett's familiar quotations; a collection of passages, phrases, and proverbs traced to their sources in ancient and modern literature. by John Bartlett; Geoffrey O'Brien, general editor. 18th ed. Little,

Brown, and Co. 2012 lxi, 1438 p.p (hardcover) $50.00   **808.88**
1. Quotations 2. Quotations, English
ISBN 0316017590; 9780316017596

LC 2012019870

This book, in its 18th edition, presents a collection of quotations "from the times of ancient Egyptians to the present day." (Publisher's note) It "includes 2500 new quotes and more than 800 newcomers, from Julia Child to David Foster Wallace. Quotes have been culled to bring in more foreigners and women and more material from fiction and poetry." (Library Journal)

The **Oxford** book of aphorisms; chosen by John Gross. Oxford University Press 2003 383p pa $19.95   **808.88**
1. Quotations
ISBN 0-19-280456-1

LC 2003-269712

First published 1983

"Contains a well-chosen collection of aphorisms, maxims, quotations, and pensees from ancient times to the present. Entries, arranged under 58 subject sections, are identified with name of aphorist, source, publication date, or approximate date of original statement. Headings include 'nature,' 'good and evil,' 'illusion and reality,' and 'secrets.' An introduction gives definitions of aphorisms and their use throughout history." Wynar. Guide to Ref Books for Sch Media Cent. 3d edition

Includes bibliographical references

The **Oxford** book of death; chosen and edited by D.J. Enright. Oxford University Press 2008 351p pa $19.95   **808.88**
1. Death -- Quotations
ISBN 978-0-19-955652-6

LC 2008-482099

First published 1983

"Much work has gone into this compilation, and the individual introductions to the component sections are, as we would expect, elegant, modest and very wise." Times Lit Suppl

★ **Oxford** dictionary of humorous quotations; edited by Ned Sherrin; with a foreword by Alistair Beaton. 4th ed; Oxford University Press 2008 536p hardcover o.p. pa $24.95   **808.88**
1. Quotations 2. Wit and humor 3. Reference books
ISBN 978-0-19-923716-6; 0-19-923716-6; 978-0-19-957006-5 pa; 0-19-957006-X pa

LC 2008-486673

First published 1995 with title: The Oxford book of humorous quotations

This dictionary "features 5,000 quotations organized into more than 200 subject categories. Quips are arranged by broad themes. . . . Coverage spans the centuries, and you are as likely to find lines by Johnny Depp, Ricky Gervais, and Eddie Izzard are you are those by Noel Coward, William Shakespeare, and George Bernard Shaw. . . . An amusing addition to the reference collection." Booklist

Oxford dictionary of modern quotations; edited by Elizabeth Knowles. 3rd ed.; Oxford University Press 2007 479p $39.95; pa $18.95 **808.88**
1. Quotations 2. Reference books
ISBN 978-0-19-920895-1; 0-19-920895-6; 978-0-19-954746-3 pa; 0-19-954746-7 pa

LC 2007-36871

First published 1991

"Containing more than 5,000 quotations from authors . . . [such] as Bertolt Brecht, George W. Bush, Homer Simpson, Carl Sagan, William Shatner, and Desmond Tutu, the dictionary is organized alphabetically by author, with . . . cross-referencing and keyword and thematic indexes." Publisher's note

★ **Oxford** dictionary of quotations; edited by Elizabeth Knowles. 7th ed.; Oxford University Press 2009 xxvi, 1155p $50 **808.88**
1. Quotations 2. Reference books
ISBN 978-0-19-923717-3; 0-19-923717-4

LC 2009-464901

First published 1941

Collected here are around 20,000 quotations by nearly 3,500 authors from around the world ranging in time from the 8th century BC to the present. Arrangement is alphabetical by the names of authors with sections such as Advertising Slogans, Epitaphs, Film Lines, Prayers, etc. included in the alphabetical order. Indexed by key words.

Includes bibliographical references

Toasts; over 1,500 of the best toasts, sentiments, blessings, and graces. {compiled by} Paul Dickson; illustrated by Rollin McGrail. Crown 1991 256p il $19 **808.88**
1. Toasts 2. Wit and humor
ISBN 0-517-58412-3

LC 91-6967

"Covering traditional occasions such as anniversaries and weddings as well as a variety of other 'toastable' events, this book organizes 1,500 toasts under 75 alphabetically arranged subject headings. Included are ethnic, military, birthday, and holiday toasts. There are also toasts related to sports, aging, food, parents, and even cheese and champagne! The toasts have been gathered from a variety of toast books, many of which date from the late nineteenth and early twentieth centuries. An interesting history of toasting is included." Booklist

Includes bibliographical references

809 History, description, critical appraisal of more than two literatures

Atwood, Margaret, 1939-
In other worlds; SF and the human imagination. Nan A. Talese/Doubleday 2011 255p pa $24.95 **809**
1. Science fiction -- Authorship 2. Science fiction -- History and criticism
ISBN 978-0-385-53396-6

LC 2011013776

"Atwood is well known to sf readers for such novels as The Handmaid's Tale, Oryx and Crake, and The Year of the Flood. In this collection of essays and short fiction, she further explores the genre, beginning with her three previously unpublished Richard Ellman Lectures in Modern Literature, which she delivered at Emory University in 2010. . . . A clever, thoughtful investigation that will appeal to science fiction readers and Atwood's loyal fans." Libr J

Includes bibliographical references

Beacham's encyclopedia of popular fiction; edited by Kirk H. Beetz. Beacham Pub. 1996 19v **809**
1. Reference books 2. Fiction -- Bio-bibliography
ISBN 0-93383-338-5

LC 96-20771

This reference work consists of a three volume set of Biography series and sixteen volumes of Analyses series. Available separately or in sets. Apply to publisher for price

Bentley, Eric
The **life** of the drama. Applause Theatre Bk. Pubs. 1991 371p pa $12.95 **809**
1. Drama -- History and criticism
ISBN 1-55783-110-6

LC 91-28774

First published 1964 by Atheneum

The author discusses plot, character, dialogue, and action in various theatrical genres. Among the dramatists discussed are Aeschylus, Beckett, Brecht, Chekhov, Corneille, Goethe, Ibsen, Ben Jonson, Molière, Pirandello, Racine, Shakespeare, Shaw, and Sophocles

Includes bibliographical references

Black literature criticism; classic and emerging authors since 1950. Jelena O. Krstovic, project editor; forward by Howard Dodson. 2nd ed.; Gale Cengage Learning 2008 3v il set $459 **809**
1. Blacks in literature 2. English literature -- Black authors -- History and criticism 3. American literature -- African American authors -- History and criticism
ISBN 978-1-4144-3170-3; 1-4144-3170-8
First published 1992

"This work includes African American, Caribbean, and African writers who produce works in English. Authors range from relative newcomers . . . to classic authors. . . . [This is] a worthwhile purchase." Booklist

Includes bibliographical references

Bloom, Harold
The **Western** canon; the books and school of the ages. Riverhead Bks. 1995 546p pa $18 **809**
1. Blind 2. Poets 3. Judges 4. Authors 5. Diplomats 6. Novelists 7. Dramatists 8. Essayists 9. Translators 10. Lexicographers 11. Poets laureate 12. Psychoanalysts 13. Literary critics 14. Nonfiction writers 15. Writers on science 16. Short story writers 17. Writers on medicine 18. Writers on religion 19. Nobel laureates for peace 20. Nobel laureates for literature 21. Literature -- History and criticism
ISBN 1-57322-514-2; 978-1-57322-514-4
First published 1994 by Harcourt Brace & Co.

The "book succeeds not as a polemic but as a passionate, erudite and highly idiosyncratic series of essays about the literature dearest to one of America's most influential academics." Publ Wkly

Boyd, Brian

On the origin of stories; evolution, cognition, and fiction. Belknap Press of Harvard University Press 2009 540p il $35   **809**
1. Evolution 2. Authorship 3. Fiction -- Authorship 4. Fiction -- History and criticism
ISBN 978-0-674-03357-3; 0-674-03357-4
LC 2009-07642

The author "has created a compelling, erudite, and thoroughly original work about the nature of humanistic expression in art and literature. Beautifully written and wide-ranging, the book delves into social science, evolutionary biology, art, and literature to create a comprehensive account of the evolutionary origins of art and storytelling." Choice
Includes bibliographical references

Calvino, Italo

Why read the classics? translated from the Italian by Martin McLaughlin. Pantheon Bks. 1999 277p hardcover o.p. pa $13   **809**
1. Literature -- History and criticism
ISBN 0-679-74349-9 pa
LC 99-21535

Original Italian edition, 1991
"Calvino celebrates a wide range of great thinkers in these provocative essays. Here are writers from the ancient world, the Renaissance and recent times, and from the old and new worlds. . . . [These essays] are a reminder to us that 'rereading' the classics can amuse as well as reward." New Sci
Includes bibliographical references

Colby, Vineta

World authors, 1980-1985; editor, Vineta Colby. Wilson, H.W. 1990 938p il (Authors series) $140   **809**
1. Reference books 2. Authors -- Dictionaries 3. Literature -- Bio-bibliography
ISBN 0-8242-0797-1
LC 90-49782

This volume covers 320 contemporary writers

World authors, 1985-1990; a volume in the Wilson authors series. editor, Vineta Colby. Wilson, H.W. 1995 970p il (Authors series) $140   **809**
1. Reference books 2. Authors -- Dictionaries 3. Literature -- Bio-bibliography
ISBN 0-8242-0875-7
LC 95-41656

This volume covers 345 novelists, playwrights, poets, and other authors who have risen to prominence in the late 1980s

★ Critical survey of drama; edited by Carl Rollyson. 2nd rev ed; Salem Press 2003 8v set $499   **809**
1. Reference books 2. Drama -- Dictionaries 3. English drama -- Dictionaries 4. American drama --

Dictionaries
ISBN 1-58765-102-5
LC 2003-2190

This set contains "about 630 essays, of which 570 discuss individual dramatists and 60 cover overview topics. . . . Each essay on a dramatist provides . . . material as birth and death dates, lists of the author's major dramatic works (with dates of first production and publication). Each essay opens with a brief survey of the author's publications in literary forms other than drama, a summary of the writer's professional achievements and awards, an extended biographical sketch that centers on the writer's development as a dramatist, and an extensive critical analysis of the writer's major dramatic works. Following this discussion is a list of major publications in fields other than drama and an annotated bibliography of critical works about the author." Publisher's note
Includes bibliographical references

Critical survey of mystery and detective fiction; editor, Carl Rollyson. Rev ed; Salem Press 2008 5v il set $399   **809**
1. Mystery fiction -- History and criticism
ISBN 978-1-58765-397-1; 1-58765-397-4
LC 2007-40208

First published 1988 in four volumes under the editorship of Frank Northen Magill
This "is the most exhaustive and best-documented account of this genre available." Choice
Includes bibliographical references

★ Cyclopedia of literary places; consulting editor, R. Baird Shuman; editor, R. Kent Rasmussen; introduction by Brian Stableford. Salem Press 2003 3v set $305   **809**
1. Reference books 2. Literary landmarks 3. Literature -- Encyclopedias
ISBN 1-58766-094-0
LC 2002-156159

"This three-volume set completes Salem's trilogy of reference works analyzing stories (Masterplots), characters (Cyclopedia of Literary Characters), and now settings in classic works of literature (mostly novels, though a few plays and poems are included). . . . Literary Places provides details of both real and imaginary geographic places that serve as settings for approximately 1300 titles covered in the previous works. . . . The entries are alphabetized by title, range in length from 300 to 1000 words, and feature author, type of work, type of plot, time of plot, and a brief synopsis. . . . Well written, easy to use, and fun to read, this set . . . is a valuable addition to all libraries." Libr J
Includes bibliographical references

Damrosch, David

The buried book; the loss and rediscovery of the great Epic of Gilgamesh. H. Holt 2007 315p il map hardcover o.p. pa $16.99   **809**
1. Gilgamesh
ISBN 978-0-8050-8029-2; 0-8050-8029-5; 978-0-8050-8725-3 pa; 0-8050-8725-7 pa
LC 2006-49523

"Combining acuity about cultural contexts with wide-ranging knowledge, Damrosch's account is a superb and engrossing popular presentation." Booklist

Includes bibliographical references

Donoghue, Emma ✓

Inseparable; desire between women in literature. Emma Donoghue. Alfred A. Knopf 2010 x, 271p ill. (hc : alk. paper) $27.95 **809**

1. Female friendship 2. Women in literature 3. Lesbianism in literature

ISBN 9780307270948; 0307270947

LC 2009048368

Stonewall Book Awards: Israel Fisherman Non-Fiction Award (2011)

This book "explores the little-known literary tradition of love between women in Western literature, from Chaucer and Shakespeare to Charlotte Brontë, Dickens, Agatha Christie, and many more. . . . [It] examine[s] how desire between women in English literature has been portrayed, from schoolgirls and vampires to runaway wives, from cross-dressing knights to contemporary murder stories. [Author Emma] Donoghue looks at the work of those writers who have addressed the 'unspeakable subject,' examining whether such desire between women is freakish or omnipresent, holy or evil, heartwarming or ridiculous as she excavates a long-obscured tradition of (inseparable) friendship between women, one that is . . . central to our cultural history." (Publisher's note)

Includes bibliographical references (p. [207]-260) and index

Fraser, Kennedy ✓

Ornament and silence; essays on women's lives. Knopf 1996 247p hardcover o.p. pa $13 **809**

1. Poets 2. Artists 3. Authors 4. Painters 5. Botanists 6. Novelists 7. Dramatists 8. Fashion designers 9. Essayists 10. Feminists 11. Biographers 12. Entomologists 13. College teachers 14. Literary critics 15. Magazine editors 16. Nonfiction writers 17. Writers on science 18. Short story writers 19. Writers on politics 20. New Yorker (Periodical)

ISBN 0-375-70112-5 pa

LC 96-11479

A collection of fourteen profiles, personal reminiscences and extended reviews of books.

"A 'daughter of the paternal old New Yorker' in her youth, Fraser . . . has moved on with time, taking for her more mature role models Nina Berberova, Edith Wharton, and Germaine Greer. Fraser's essays are quiet, thorough, and beautifully paced." Libr J

Hollands, Neil ✓

Fellowship in a ring; a guide for science fiction and fantasy book groups. Libraries Unlimited 2010 300p pa $40 **809**

1. Books and reading 2. Book clubs (Discussion groups) 3. Fantasy fiction -- Bibliography 4. Science fiction -- Bibliography 5. Fantasy fiction -- History and criticism 6. Science fiction -- History and criticism

ISBN 978-1-59158-703-3; 1-59158-703-4

LC 2009-46456

This is "is an excellent resource for both novices looking to initiate groups, and veterans seeking to breathe new life into existing factions. The first chapter delineates the practical building blocks necessary to develop a thriving science fiction/fantasy book group, from suggestions of how to ward off potential problems and keep discussions interesting to creative ideas for preventing meetings from becoming stagnant. . . . Included is a list of fifty recommended science fiction and fantasy novels, with helpful information such as author background, plot summaries, a reading guide, and discussion questions. An especially thorough listing of themes for discussion consists of resources, thematic questions, and suggested works." Voice Youth Advocates

Includes bibliographical references

Isherwood, Christopher, 1904-1986

Liberation; Diaries:1970-1983. HarperCollins 2012 928 p. $39.99 **809**

1. Gay men 2. Novelists

ISBN 0062084747; 9780062084743

This book is the "third and final volume of [Christopher] Isherwood's . . . diaries [and] concludes with a 136-page 'glossary' of names . . . . As the 1970's commence, lover Don Bachardy has just had his screenplay for 'Cabaret' . . . rejected. . . . The last diary entry dates to July 4, 1983, exactly two and a half years before Isherwood's death from cancer. In between, he regales readers with accounts of . . . dinners, parties, and foreign travels." (Publishers Weekly)

Iyer, Pico

The **man** within my head; Pico Iyer. Alfred A. Knopf 2012 241 p. **809**

1. Travel 2. Self-realization 3. Fathers and sons 4. Novelists, English -- 20th century -- Biography

ISBN 030726761X; 9780307267610

LC 2011041285

In this book, author Pico "Iyer describes [writer Graham] Greene as constantly in his mind as a kind of imaginative touchstone. . . . In the second half . . . [Iyer] answers the question he poses in the first half. Why Greene? . . . His answer focuses on the ways that Greene's characters-Pyle and Fowler in 'The Quiet American,' for example - have a kind of father-and-son relationship to each other." (Washington Times)

James, Henry

Literary criticism. Library of Am. 1984 2v v1 ea $50 **809**

1. Literature -- History and criticism

ISBN 0-94050-023-2 v1; 0-94050-22-4 v2

LC 84-11241

"Grouped by nationality, alphabetically by author, and chronologically, the essays provide a kind of critical book within a book on such writers as Balzac, George Eliot, and Hawthorne. These groupings enable the reader to see how James approached a writer and to follow the development of his thinking about particular writers over the years." Publisher's note

Includes bibliographical references

Jarrell, Randall

No other book; selected essays. edited and introduced by Brad Leithauser. HarperCollins Pubs. 1999 xx, 376p hardcover o.p. pa $15   **809**

1. Poets 2. Authors 3. Lawyers 4. Novelists 5. Physicians 6. Essayists 7. Memoirists 8. Biographers 9. Translators 10. College teachers 11. Children's authors 12. Short story writers 13. Insurance executives 14. Nobel laureates for literature 15. Literature -- History and criticism 16. American poetry -- History and criticism

ISBN 0-06-095638-0 pa

LC 98-55353

"Jarrell taught his peers to appreciate first the young Robert Lowell and W. H. Auden, then Marianne Moore, William Carlos Williams, Elizabeth Bishop, Walt Whitman and Robert Frost. . . . The later Jarrell divided his prose between appreciations of poets, digressions on idiosyncratic passions, and funny or sad indictments of 1950s-style popular culture. . . . As a convincing, above all personal, guide to modern poets, and as a captivating writer of criticism Jarrell has no obvious 20th century equal." Publ Wkly

Kundera, Milan

Encounter; translated from the French by Linda Asher. Harper 2010 178p $23.99   **809**

1. Art appreciation 2. Music -- History and criticism 3. Literature -- History and criticism

ISBN 978-0-06-189441-1; 0-06-189441-9

LC 2010-04908

Original French edition, 2009

"Of specific interest are chapters comparing Francis Bacon to Samuel Beckett; Kundera's devilish mixing up of Roland Barthes with the dour theologian Karl Barth in a chance conversation; several discussions on the virtues of Rabelais as well as a restoration to prominence of Anatole France, who had been given the French intellectualist bum's rush; a powerful coupling of the bright birth of film with the sad death of Fellini; a scholar's relishing of Bertolt Brecht's body odor; the music of his fellow Czech Leos Janacek. Like the proverbial meal at the Chinese restaurant, the delicious musings of this book are filling at first. Two hours later, one craves more." Publ Wkly

Kurian, George Thomas

★ Timetables of world literature. Facts on File 2003 457p $65   **809**

1. Literature -- Chronology

ISBN 0-8160-4197-0

LC 2002-3891

Chronicles world literature from the Classical Age through the twentieth century, discussing literary developments and the relationship between literature and the political and social climate of each historical period

"This comprehensive reference . . . helps academic researchers place major works of literature from 58 countries in historical and cultural context." Libr J

Includes bibliographical references

Literary movements for students; presenting analysis, context, and criticism on literary movements.

David Galens, project editor. Gale Group 2002 2v il set $185   **809**

1. Literature -- History and criticism

ISBN 0-7876-6517-7

LC 2002-10928

Entries provide "historical background information on each movement as well as modern critical interpretation of each movement's characteristic styles and themes. Approximately 25 movements are covered, including absurdism, Greek drama, modernism, science fiction/fantasy, surrealism and many others." Publisher's note

Includes bibliographical references

Literature and its times; profiles of 300 notable literary works and the historical events that influenced them. Gale Res. 1997 5v set $741   **809**

1. Literature -- History and criticism

ISBN 0-7876-0606-5

LC 97-34339

"The editors chose the selections (fiction, poetry, short stories, plays, biographies, and speeches) with the input of public libraries and secondary-school teachers. . . . Each volume covers a time range subdivided by dates and a general description . . . and begins with a brief overview of the historical events of the era, with a time-line providing a synopsis of each period." Libr J

★ Magill's survey of world literature; edited by Steven G. Kellman. Rev ed; Salem Press 2009 6v il set $499   **809**

1. Reference books 2. Literature -- Bio-bibliography 3. Literature -- History and criticism

ISBN 978-1-58765-431-2

LC 2008-46042

First published 1992 under the editorship of Frank Northen Magill

"A solid choice for anyone in need of an inexpensive, broad biocritical literary reference title on world literature." Libr J

Includes glossary and bibliographical references

Manguel, Alberto

The dictionary of imaginary places; {by} Alberto Manguel & Gianni Guadalupi; illustrated by Graham Greenfield; with additional illustrations by Eric Beddows; maps and charts by James Cook. Newly updated and expanded; Harcourt Brace & Co. 1999 755p il maps $40; pa $24   **809**

1. Reference books 2. Fantasy fiction -- Dictionaries

ISBN 0-15-100541-9; 0-15-600872-6 pa

LC 99-46994

First published 1980 by Macmillan

This resource "contains entries for more than 1,200 imaginary places from literature and folklore. Each entry describes the place, its locale, and history and provides citations to the source work or tale. More than 220 maps and illustrations are included." Booklist

Includes bibliographical references

★ Masterplots II, drama series; editor, Christian H. Moe. rev ed; Salem Press 2003 4v set $404 **809**

1. Drama -- Stories, plots, etc. 2. Drama -- History and

criticism
ISBN 1-58765-116-5

LC 2003-12651

First published 1990

"This newest addition to a reference standard belongs in most public, academic, and secondary libraries." Booklist

Moore, Steven, 1978-

The **novel**; an alternative history: beginnings to 1600. Continuum 2010 698p $39.95   **809**

1. Fiction -- History and criticism

ISBN 9781441177049; 1-4411-7704-3

LC 2010-279268

"Reveling in the most innovative and daring creations, Moore energetically evaluates tales fantastic, chilling, hilarious, erotic, and tragic, comparing centuries-old novels to those of Barth, Gaddis, Pynchon, and Vollmann. Destined for controversy, Moore's erudite, gargantuan, kaleidoscopic, and venturesome alternative history will leave readers feeling as though they've been viewing literature with blinders on." Booklist

Includes bibliographical references

Mystery and suspense writers; the literature of crime, detection, and espionage. Robin W. Winks, editor in chief; Maureen Corrigan, associate editor. Scribner 1998 2v set $250   **809**

1. Reference books 2. Spies in literature 3. Mystery fiction -- Dictionaries

ISBN 0-684-80521-9

LC 98-36812

"Articles on 68 mystery writers ranging from Edgar Allen Poe to Sarah Paretsky run from ten to 20 pages and include information on the life and works as well as solid bibliographies for each author." Libr J

Niebuhr, Gary Warren

Make mine a mystery; a reader's guide to mystery and detective fiction. Libraries Unlimited 2003 605p $65   **809**

1. Reference books 2. Mystery fiction -- Bibliography 3. Mystery fiction -- History and criticism

ISBN 1-56308-784-7

LC 2003-271056

"The book is divided into two parts. In part 1, 'Introduction to Mystery Fiction,' Niebuhr devotes considerable space to background material: discussion of readers'-advisory service in general and the appeal of mystery fiction in particular and how to build and manage a mystery collection, followed by a history of the genre beginning in 1845. Part 2, 'The Literature,' annotates more than 2,500 titles by more than 200 authors. . . . Among guides to mystery fiction, this one stands out as being thorough and current. Essential for public libraries." Booklist

Nissley, Tom

A **reader's** book of days; true tales from the lives and works of writers for every day of the year. Tom Nissley ; with illustrations by Joanna Neborsky. W.W. Norton & Co. Inc. 2014 464 p. (hardcover) $24.95   **809**

1. Authors 2. Anecdotes 3. Authorhip 4. Best books

5. Books and reading 6. Literature -- History and criticism

ISBN 0393239624; 9780393239621

LC 2013031250

This book, by Tom Nissley, "features bite- size accounts of events in the lives of great authors for every day of the year. Fictional events that take place within beloved books are also included. {Authors featured include] Martin Amis, Jane Austen, James Baldwin, . . . [and] F.Scott Fitzgerald." (Publisher's note)

"The book itself is guaranteed to occupy plenty of pleasant hours, but Nissley's recommended reading lists are a bibliophilic bonus." Kirkus

Niven, Penelope, 1939-2014

★ **Thornton** Wilder; A Life. by Penelope Niven ; forward by Edward Albee. HarperCollins 2012 xvi, 832 p.p (hardcover) $39.99; (ebook) $31.99   **809**

1. American authors -- Biography

ISBN 0060831367; 9780060831363; 9780062097774

This book by Penelope Niven presents a biography of "Pulitzer Prize-winning playwright and novelist Thornton Wilder. . . . Niven . . . combed through the author's many published and unpublished personal writings. . . . Through Wilder's own words, the reader is privy to his arrogant thrills and frequent bouts of self-doubt. Chronicling Wilder's successes and failures in various literary forms . . . Niven includes brief criticism and reviews with each of his major works." (Publishers Weekly)

Ozick, Cynthia

★ The **din** in the head; essays. Houghton Mifflin Co. 2006 243p il $24   **809**

1. Literature -- History and criticism

ISBN 978-0-618-47050-1; 0-618-47050-6

LC 2005-16102

The author is "not only one of the finest novelists of our time but an essayist of startling spiritual verve and range." Christ Century

Poe, Edgar Allan

Essays and reviews. Library of Am. 1984 1544p $40   **809**

ISBN 0-940450-19-4

LC 83-19923

This volume is divided into six main divisions: Theory of poetry, Reviews of British and Continental authors; Reviews of American authors and American criticism; Magazines and criticism; The literary and social scene; and Articles and marginalia

Includes bibliographical references

★ Reference guide to world literature; editors, Sara Pendergast, Tom Pendergast. 3rd ed; St. James Press 2003 2v set $350   **809**

1. Reference books 2. Literature -- Bio-bibliography 3. Literature -- History and criticism

ISBN 1-55862-490-2

LC 2002-15410

First published 1984 by St. Martin's Press with title: Great foreign language writers

This work "contains 1,100 entries, about equally divided between entries on authors and on literary works. Each author entry in volume 1 includes a short biography, a signed critical essay, and selected lists of works by and about the author. Each literary work entry in volume 2 includes the author and date of publication (if known), a signed critical essay, and a selected list of critical studies. The scope of coverage is major works in languages other than English from the earliest known manuscripts to present day writers. . . . Because of its comprehensiveness and authority, this sturdily bound set is recommended for ready reference in libraries with large world literature sections and for smaller libraries needing more information in this area." Am Ref Books Annu, 2003

Includes bibliographical references

Roth, Philip

Shop talk; a writer and his colleagues and their work. Houghton Mifflin 2001 160p $23   **809**

1. Authors 2. Literature -- History and criticism
ISBN 0-618-15314-4

LC 2001-24523

"In this collection of encounters with distinguished minds—unguarded interviews with Primo Levi and Aharon Appelfeld, among others; an odd exchange of letters with Mary McCarthy; fondly contentious portraits of Bernard Malamud and the painter Philip Guston—Roth manages to tease from his subjects the convictions that fuel their work and the vulnerabilities that make them human." N Y Times Book Rev

Short story writers; edited by Charles E. May. Rev. ed.; Salem Press 2008 3v il (Magill's choice) set $217   **809**

1. Short stories -- History and criticism
ISBN 978-1-58765-389-6

LC 2007-32789

First published 1997

This set "covers writers from Giovanni Boccaccio and Geoffrey Chaucer to Anton Chekhov and Sandra Cisneros. . . . Readers, whether in need of a brief critical overview or in search of what to read next, will find this set extremely useful. Each entry includes a brief biography, a list of principal works, a note on other literary forms the author explored, and a concise list of achievements as well as brief essays . . . on particular stories." SLJ

Includes bibliographical references

Society for the Study of the Short Story

A Reader's companion to the short story in English; edited by Erin Fallon [et al.]; under the auspices of the Society for the Study of the Short Story. Greenwood Press 2001 xxxiv, 432p $105   **809**

1. Short stories -- History and criticism
ISBN 0-313-29104-7

LC 00-25113

"Although most of the stories covered by Fallon's compilation were written in the later half of the 20th century, the scope is international. . . . Each chapter concisely profiles a writer and contains a biography, a brief review of criticism, a lengthier analysis of specific works, and a bibliography. A

section covers the short story genre. This work is extremely important because of the popularity of the genre." Choice

Includes bibliographical references

The **story** about the story; great writers explore great literature. edited by J. C. Hallman. Tin House Books 2009 420p pa $18.95   **809**

1. Literature -- History and criticism
ISBN 978-0-9802436-9-7

LC 2009-15717

In his introduction, "editor J.C. Hallman writes about what he calls a 'kind of personal literary analysis, criticism that contemplates rather than analyzes'. He goes on to make the case for writers writing about writing from an individual perspective as his ideal approach to critiquing literature and the inspiration behind his compiling these works by notable writers from Virginia Woolf and D.H. Lawrence to Susan Sontag and Milan Kundera. . . . The selections range from well-known essays like Vladimir Nabokov on The Metamorphosis (he tries to figure out exactly what kind of beetle Gregor Samsa had turned into) to quirkier pleasures like Salman Rushdie on The Wizard of Oz." PopMatters

★ **Supernatural** fiction writers; contemporary fantasy and horror. Richard Bleiler, editor. 2nd ed; Scribner 2003 1048p 2v (Scribner writers series) set $250   **809**

1. Fantasy fiction -- History and criticism
ISBN 0-684-31250-6

LC 2002-11128

First published 1985

This edition "is organized alphabetically by writer. Articles range in length from 5 to 12 pages. There is some biographical information but emphasis is on the works, with analysis of important themes, types of work, and, in many cases, individual series and titles. Each article concludes with a selected bibliography of works by the author under discussion, critical and biographical studies, and Web sites if they are available." Booklist

Includes bibliographical references

Symons, Julian

Bloody murder; from the detective story to the crime novel. 3rd rev ed; Mysterious Press 1993 349p pa $30   **809**

1. Mystery fiction -- History and criticism
ISBN 0-89296-496-0

LC 92-54127

First published 1972 in the United Kingdom. Present edition first published 1992 in the United Kingdom

A critical survey of crime fiction, including detective stories, psychological crime stories, thrillers, and espionage, covering authors from Poe to the 1990s

Thompson, Cliff

World authors, 1990-1995; editor, Clifford Thompson. Wilson, H.W. 1999 863p il (Authors series) $155   **809**

1. Reference books 2. Authors -- Dictionaries 3. Literature -- Bio-bibliography
ISBN 0-8242-0956-7

LC 99-48161

This volume offers "articles on more than 300 poets, dramatists, essayists, novelists, and other writers." (Booklist)
Includes bibliographical references

World authors, 1995-2000; editors, Clifford Thompson, Mari Rich [et. al.] Wilson, H.W. 2003 872p il (Authors series) $160 **809**
1. Reference books 2. Authors -- Dictionaries 3. Literature -- Bio-bibliography
ISBN 0-8242-1032-8
LC 2003-45062
This reference includes 320 novelists, poets, dramatists, essayists, social scientists, and biographers who have published significant works from 1995 through 2000. Each profile details the author's life and career, the circumstances under which their works were produced, and their literary significance.
Includes bibliographical references

Yagoda, Ben
Memoir; a history. Riverhead Books 2009 291p $25.95 **809**
1. Autobiography
ISBN 1-59448-886-X; 978-1-59448-886-3
LC 2009-30859
"Yagoda traces the memoir from its birth in early Christian writings and Roman generals' journals . . . [through the] year of 2007." (Publisher's note) Index.
"With its mixture of literary criticism, cultural history and just enough trivia, Yagoda's survey is sure to appeal to scholars and bibliophiles alike." Publ Wkly
Includes bibliographical references

809.1   Literature in specific forms other than miscellaneous writings

Borges, Jorge Luis
This craft of verse; edited by Calin-Andrei Mihailescu. Harvard Univ. Press 2000 154p il (Charles Eliot Norton lectures) $25; pa $14.95 **809.1**
1. Poetry -- History and criticism
ISBN 0-674-00290-3; 0-674-00820-0 pa
LC 00-33541
This volume is based on the Argentine writer's "Charles Eliot Norton lectures [delivered] at Harvard in 1967-68. . . . [Borges] discusses some of his favorite texts, conducting a literary journey that began in his father's library in Buenos Aires." N Y Times Book Rev
Includes bibliographical references

Brodsky, Joseph
Less than one; selected essays. Farrar, Straus & Giroux 1986 501p hardcover o.p. pa $18 **809.1**
1. Poets 2. Authors 3. Essayists 4. College teachers
ISBN 0-374-52055-0 pa
LC 85-15900
The essays in this volume "begin and end with autobiographical pieces; in between there are alternate homages to favorite poets, both Russian and non-Russian, as well as substantial discussions of such topics as geography and

history, political force and ethical choice, and literary tradition." N Y Times Book Rev

Burt, Stephen
Close calls with nonsense; reading new poetry. Graywolf Press 2009 374p bibl f pa $19 **809.1**
1. Poetry -- History and criticism
ISBN 978-1-55597-521-0; 1-55597-521-6
LC 2008-935602
"This collection of 30 essays, many of which began as book reviews, confirms Stephen Burt's reputation as the leading poetry critic of his generation. Informative, matter-of-fact and abounding with an excited spirit more common to film and pop music reviews than to literary criticism, these essays will appeal to the unpracticed reader of contemporary poetry as well as the seasoned reader. . . . Burt comes to the poets he considers—including Rea Armantrout, Juan Felipe Herrera, Paul Muldoon and James Merrill—as both a scholar and a practitioner of the art, but he eschews the specialist's jargon as well as the indulgent lyricality that makes some poets' criticism more dazzling than illuminating." Publ Wkly
Includes bibliographical references

★ **Classic** writings on poetry; edited by William Harmon. Columbia University Press 2003 538p $79; pa $27.50 **809.1**
1. Poetry -- History and criticism
ISBN 0-231-12370-1; 0-231-12371-X pa
LC 2003-40917
This anthology contains "writing on poetry by such philosophical royalty as Plato, Aristotle, Milton, Sir Philip Sidney, Wordsworth, and Emily Dickinson. Readers are given a peek through the hole of history's fence into the lives and worlds of our poetic geniuses and reminded of the poem's matchless role in conveying reverence, remembering wars, recording history, entertaining, expressing deep emotion, and above all, allowing the finite mind, for one moment, to contain infinity." Libr J
Includes bibliographical references

Gioia, Dana (1972)
Can poetry matter? essays on poetry and American culture. Dana Gioia. 10th Anniversary ed; Graywolf Press 2002 231p pa $16 **809.1**
1. Poets 2. Artists 3. Authors 4. Lawyers 5. Painters 6. Criticism 7. Dramatists 8. Editors 9. Translators 10. Poets laureate 11. College teachers 12. Literary critics 13. Magazine editors 14. Writers on nature 15. Short story writers 16. Insurance executives 17. Poetry -- History and criticism
ISBN 1-55597-370-1
LC 2002-102971
First published 1992
In addition to addressing the business of being a poet and the new formalism, the author offers readings of Robinson Jeffers, Weldon Kees, Robert Bly and others.
"Gioia makes his case with erudition and skill, and the best essays bring attention to underappreciated poets like Ted Kooser." Libr J

Hirsch, Edward

Poet's choice; Edward Hirsch. Harcourt 2006
432p $25   **809.1**
1. Poetry -- History and criticism
ISBN 0-15-101356-X; 978-0-15-101356-2
       LC 2005-26890

"Hirsch's aesthetic is unerring, and his interpretations
are profound as he considers our 'collective destiny' and
takes measure of poetry's encompassing vision." Booklist

Iron-Georges, Tracy

Masterplots II, poetry series; rev ed; Salem
Press 2002 8v set $499   **809.1**
1. Poetry -- History and criticism
ISBN 1-58765-037-1
       LC 2001-55059

"This set supersedes the six-volume Masterplots 2: Poetry Series (1992) and the three-volume Masterplots 2: Poetry
Series Supplement (1998). It contains 1,385 signed entries
written by scholars on individual poems, arranged alphabetically by poem title and ranging in length from three to five
pages apiece." Booklist
Includes bibliographical references

Koch, Kenneth

Making your own days; the pleasures of reading
and writing poetry. Simon & Schuster 1999 317p pa
$15   **809.1**
1. Poetry -- Collections 2. Poetry -- History and
criticism
ISBN 0-684-82438-8
       LC 98-115810

First published 1998 by Scribner
"This book is divided into two parts: a series of essays
on subjects such as meter, rhyme, and personification and an
anthology of favorite poems. Most remarkably, non-English
poems often appear with several translations, underscoring
the flexibility of poetic language. Making Your Own Days
will be most useful to writers already familiar with the basics." Libr J

Orr, David

Beautiful & pointless. HarperCollins 2011 200p
$25.99   **809.1**
1. Poetry 2. Poetry -- History and criticism
ISBN 978-0-06-167345-0; 0-06-167345-5
       LC 2011-11599

This book examines "why poetry seems especially
personal and what it means to write 'in form.'" (Publisher's note)
This book presents a guide and cultural critique of the
state of contemporary poetry by David Orr, an attorney, poet,
and poetry reviewer for "The New York Times Book Review." The author looks at themes and influences of various
modern poems, including the poem "Bush's War," by Robert
Haas. He also explores his own history as an appreciator and
writer of poetry. "[David Orr] takes a calisthenic view of
poetry." (Nation)
What makes this book "different from thousands of other
defenses of poetry is that, according to its author, poetry differs from music and stamp collecting in that people's love
for poetry is measurably greater than their love for any other

activity. Poetry fans don't just love poetry a little; they really
love it." N Y Times Book Rev

Paglia, Camille

Break, blow, burn; Camille Paglia. Pantheon
Books 2005 247p $20; pa $12.95   **809.1**
1. English poetry -- History and criticism 2. American
poetry -- History and criticism
ISBN 0-375-42084-3; 0-375-72539-3 pa
       LC 2004-56573

This work "is vintage Paglia: bracing, opinionated, and
deliciously enjoyable." Natl Rev
Includes bibliographical references

Poetry in person; twenty-five years of conversation with America's poets. edited and with an
introduction by Alexander Neubauer; postscript
by Robert Polito. Alfred A. Knopf 2010 343p il
$27.95   **809.1**
1. Poetics 2. Poetry -- Authorship 3. Poetry -- History
and criticism
ISBN 978-0-307-26967-6
       LC 2009-29277

"For almost 30 years, beginning in 1970, Pearl London
taught a course at the New School called Works in Progress,
to which she asked famous poets to come with drafts of new
poems in hand. This book is a series of transcripts of discussions from those classes, taken from a series of previously
unknown recordings found after London's death. . . . Represented in these 23 conversations are such acknowledged
masters of late 20th–century poetry as Robert Hass, Lucille
Clifton, Amy Clampitt, and Charles Simic." Publ Wkly

810   Literatures of specific languages and language families

Acosta-Belen, Edna

The Norton anthology of Latino literature; Ilan
Stavans, general editor; [editors], Edna Acosta-Belen
[et al.] W.W. Norton & Co. 2010 2489p il map
$59.95   **810**
1. American literature -- Hispanic American authors --
Collections
ISBN 978-0-393-08007-0; 0-393-08007-2
       LC 2010-15108

"With a great array of writers celebrated and too little
known, and invaluable supporting materials, this grand and
affecting treasury of culturally rich and aesthetically dynamic poems, fiction, drama, letters, diaries, and essays illuminates every aspect of Latino life." Booklist
Includes bibliographical references

Baseball: a literary anthology; edited by Nicholas
Dawidoff. Library of Am. 2002 721p $35   **810**
1. Baseball 2. American literature -- Collections
ISBN 1-931082-09-X
       LC 2001-38654

"Beginning with Thayer's Casey at the Bat and ending
with Buster Olney, there are more than 700 pages of prose
and poetry, fiction and sportswriting, writers and players.

Scanning the table of contents, it almost seems like everybody wrote about baseball: Damon Runyon, Ring Lardner, James Weldon Johnson, William Carlos Williams, James Thurber. But so did Paul Gallico, Nelson Algren, Tallulah Bankhead, and Jacques Barzun. . . . Ineffable, indispensable, inimitable—just like baseball." Booklist

★ The **Beat** generation; a Gale critical companion. Lynn M. Zott, project editor. Gale 2003 3v (Gale critical companion collection) set $350 **810**
1. Beat generation 2. American literature -- History and criticism
ISBN 0-7876-7569-5

LC 2002-155786
"Volume 1 gathers a variety of sources that place the movement in cultural context. . . . Volumes 2-3 supply entries for 28 Beat authors. . . . Author entries include a brief biography, notes on major works and critical reception, a list of principal works, a selection of primary sources and secondary criticism, and further readings. . . . The selections include contributions by major Beat Generation scholars and provide a well-balanced, representative view of the Beats." Choice
Includes bibliographical references

Black women writers (1950-1980) a critical evaluation. edited by Mari Evans. Anchor Press 1984 xxviii, 543p hardcover o.p. pa $25 **810**
1. Poets 2. Actors 3. Authors 4. Singers 5. Novelists 6. Dramatists 7. Editors 8. Essayists 9. Columnists 10. Memoirists 11. College teachers 12. Literary critics 13. Social activists 14. Children's authors 15. Short story writers 16. Young adult authors 17. Theatrical directors 18. Motion picture directors 19. Nobel laureates for literature 20. American literature -- Women authors 21. American literature -- History and criticism 22. American literature -- African American authors
ISBN 0-385-17125-0 pa

LC 81-43914
Critical essays on Maya Angelou, Alice Childress, Toni Morisson, Lucille Clifton, and 11 other post World War II Afro-American women writers
"This important work, a tribute to the corpus of literature produced by black women, is an indispensable resource for any serious student, scholar or teacher desiring to probe the depths of the Afro-American literary tradition." Freedomways
Includes bibliographical references

The **Cambridge** handbook of American literature; edited by Jack Salzman. Cambridge Univ. Press 1986 286p $60 **810**
1. Reference books 2. American literature -- Dictionaries
ISBN 0-521-30703-1

LC 86-2587
This handbook's "750 entries, two thirds of them about authors, briefly describe the contents and contribution of key works, assess the careers of writers, and explain the tenets and characteristics of literary movements." Wilson Libr Bull

The **Cambridge** history of American literature; general editor, Sacvan Bercovitch; associate editor, Cyrus R.K. Patell. Cambridge Univ. Press 1994 8v set $1,050 **810**
1. American literature -- History and criticism
ISBN 0-521-85760-0

LC 92-42479
Scholars contribute essays assessing major authors, movements and trends in the development of American literature

Cheever, Susan
American Bloomsbury; Louisa May Alcott, Ralph Waldo Emerson, Margaret Fuller, Nathaniel Hawthorne, and Henry David Thoreau: their lives, their loves, their work. Simon & Schuster 2006 223p il $26 **810**
1. Authors, American 2. American literature -- History and criticism
ISBN 0-7432-6461-4; 978-0-7432-6461-7

LC 2006-45015
This book offers a "glimpse into life in Concord, MA, from about 1840 to the mid-1860s, when such luminaries as Louisa May Alcott, Ralph Waldo Emerson, Margaret Fuller, Nathaniel Hawthorne, and Henry David Thoreau lived, worked, and loved. . . . [This] volume examines the dynamic relationships among these remarkable men and women, who constituted what may be considered the first American literary community. . . . Essential reading for anyone with an interest in American letters." Libr J
Includes bibliographical references

★ The **Chronology** of American literature; America's literary achievements from the colonial era to modern times. edited by Daniel S. Burt. Houghton Mifflin 2004 805p il $40 **810**
1. American literature -- Collections
ISBN 0-618-16821-4

LC 2003-51142
"This chronology includes more than 8,400 literary works by more than 5,000 writers. Sections for each year are grouped in five chapters by period, from 1582 to 1999. Within each year, entries are grouped by genre, such as diaries and other personal writings, fiction, essays, literary criticism and scholarship, nonfiction, poetry, and drama. Within each genre, authors are listed alphabetically, generally with birth and death dates and short descriptions of named works for the year. . . . The Chronology of American Literature is easy to browse and, for book lovers, difficult to put down." Booklist
Includes bibliographical references

Columbia literary history of the United States; Emory Elliott, general editor; associate editors, Martha Banta {et al.}; advisory editors, Houston A. Baker {et al.} Columbia Univ. Press 1988 xxviii, 1263p $119 **810**
1. American literature -- History and criticism
ISBN 0-231-05812-8

LC 87-14672

This anthology "expands the traditional subjects of literary history by incorporating current theoretical ideas and newly discovered writers. Includes treatment of recently explored subjects, such as the role of women and minorities in U.S. literature. No separate bibliography other than what is found in the text." N Y Public Libr Book of How & Where to Look it Up

★ The **Continuum** encyclopedia of British literature; Steven R. Serafin and Valerie Grosvenor Myer, editors. Continuum 2003 1184p $175 **810**
1. Reference books 2. English literature -- Encyclopedias
ISBN 0-8264-1456-7

LC 2002-9231

"This reference work provides a fascinating current take on the canon. . . . The historical/literary time line and the lists of prize titles alone will keep researchers happy." SLJ
Includes bibliographical references

Crossing the danger water; three hundred years of African-American writing. edited and with an introduction by Deirdre Mullane. Anchor Bks. (NY) 1993 xxii, 769p pa $20 **810**
1. American literature -- African American authors -- Collections
ISBN 0-385-42243-1

LC 93-17194

This anthology "includes fiction, autobiography, poetry, songs, and letters by such writers as Frederick Douglass, Sojourner Truth, W.E.B. Du Bois, Zora Neale Hurston, and Richard Wright. Many topics are covered, from slavery, education, the Civil War, Reconstruction, and political issues to spirituals, songs of the Civil Rights movement, and rap music." Libr J
Includes bibliographical references

Elie, Paul
The **life** you save may be your own; an American pilgrimage. Farrar, Straus and Giroux 2003 554p il hardcover o.p. pa $16 **810**
1. Monks 2. Poets 3. Authors 4. Novelists 5. Journalists 6. Reference books 7. Essayists 8. Social reformers 9. Newspaper editors 10. Nonfiction writers 11. Short story writers 12. Writers on religion 13. American literature -- Bio-bibliography 14. American literature -- History and criticism
ISBN 0-374-25680-2; 978-0-374-52921-5 pa; 0-374-52921-3 pa

LC 2002-192522

"This thoroughly researched and well-sourced work deserves attention from students of history, literature and religion, but it will be of special significance to Catholic readers interested in the expression of faith in the modern world." Publ Wkly

Encyclopedia of African-American writing; five centuries of contribution: trials & triumphs of writers, poets, publications and organizations. Shari Dorantes Hatch, editor. 2nd ed.; Grey House Pub. 2009 xxii, 863p il $165 **810**
1. Reference books 2. American literature -- African American authors -- Encyclopedias 3. American

literature -- African American authors -- Bio-bibliography
ISBN 978-1-59237-291-1

First published 2000 by ABC-CLIO with title: African-American writers: a dictionary

"This voluminous and inclusive collection consists of 738 entries that cover authors and other topics related to African American writing, such as newspapers, magazines, journals, and publishers and figures such as educators, playwrights, journalists, academics, editors, and librarians from the past 500 years. . . . Although unsigned, the entries are highly accessible, very current, and chock-full of information for a range of audiences." Libr J
Includes bibliographical references

Encyclopedia of American Indian literature; [edited by] Jennifer McClinton-Temple, Alan Velie. Facts on File 2007 466p (Encyclopedia of American ethnic literature) $75 **810**
1. Reference books 2. Native American literature -- Encyclopedias 3. Native Americans in literature -- Encyclopedias
ISBN 0-8160-5656-0; 978-0-8160-5656-9

LC 2006-23762

"This book brings together solid information from scattered sources, facilitating research on an esoteric subject." Libr J
Includes bibliographical references

Facts on File, Inc. (2002)
✓ ★ **Encyclopedia** of American literature; 2nd ed; Facts on File 2008 4v il (Facts on File library of American literature) set $375 **810**
1. Reference books 2. American literature -- Encyclopedias
ISBN 978-0-8160-6476-2

LC 2007-25662

First published 2002

Entries in this encyclopedia cover works, writers, movements and other American literature-related topics from colonial times to the present. Each volume includes a chronology.
Includes bibliographical references

★ The **Greenwood** encyclopedia of African American literature; edited by Hans Ostrom and J. David Macey, Jr. Greenwood Press 2005 5v il set $499.95 **810**
1. Reference books 2. American literature -- African American authors -- Encyclopedias
ISBN 0-313-32972-9

LC 2005-13679

This "set provides coverage of the foundations, development, and proliferation of African American literature, from Colonial times to the present. . . . The depth and breadth of the 1,029 entries make this an invaluable resource." Choice
Includes bibliographical references

★ The **Greenwood** encyclopedia of multiethnic American literature. Greenwood Press 2005 5v il set $499.95 **810**
1. Reference books 2. Minorities -- Encyclopedias 3.

American literature -- Encyclopedias
ISBN 0-313-33059-X

LC 2005-18960

"A comprehensive set unique in its scope, this encyclopedia is an excellent foundational resource that adds much to the growing field of ethnic American literature." Choice
Includes bibliographical references

Hart, James David

★ The **Oxford** companion to American literature; [by] James D. Hart; with revisions and additions by Phillip W. Leininger. 6th ed; Oxford Univ. Press 1995 779p $49.95 **810**
  1. Reference books 2. American literature -- Dictionaries
ISBN 0-19-506548-4

LC 94-45727

First published 1941
In addition to over 2000 entries for individual authors and more than 1,100 for important works this reference includes entries for literary movements, awards, magazines, printers, book collectors and newspapers. A chronological index of literary and social history is appended.

Jewish American literature; a Norton anthology. [compiled and edited by] Jules Chametzky [et al.] Norton 2000 xxiv, 1221p il $39.95 **810**
  1. American literature -- Collections 2. American literature -- Jewish authors
ISBN 0-393-04809-8

LC 00-55393

The editors have attempted "to encompass Jewish literature from 1654 to the present in this collection of poems, cartoons, sermons, diaries, letters, stories, speeches, plays, prayers, novel excerpts, and critical writings either translated from Hebrew or Yiddish or written in English. Major sections group the literature chronologically to help identify large movements. . . . This great anthology is essential for Jewish studies and American literature collections." Libr J
Includes bibliographical references

Kazin, Alfred

An **American** procession. Harvard University Press 1996 408p pa $15.95 **810**
  1. Poets 2. Authors 3. Humorists 4. Novelists 5. Dramatists 6. Historians 7. Naturalists 8. Philosophers 9. Editors 10. Essayists 11. Pacifists 12. Satirists 13. Memoirists 14. Screenwriters 15. Travel writers 16. Literary critics 17. Writers on nature 18. Nonfiction writers 19. Short story writers 20. Nobel laureates for literature 21. American literature -- History and criticism
ISBN 0-674-03143-1

LC 97-220259

First published 1984 by Knopf
"'An American Procession' is a refresher in the best sense: without any fundamental revision of our understanding of our classics, it vivaciously refreshes our awareness of them, and our gratitude for them." New Yorker

★ **Latino** and Latina writers; Alan West-Durán, editor. Charles Scribner's Sons 2004 1072p 2v (Scribner writers series) set $265 **810**
  1. American literature -- Hispanic American authors
ISBN 0-684-31293-X

LC 2003-15728

This set "begins with five essays of social and historical commentary that focus on key elements of Latino culture in this country. What follows is a series of ten to 20-page biocritical essays on nearly 60 authors (e.g., Gary Soto, Pat Mora, Sandra Cisneros, Victor Villase or, Julia Alvarez, Richard Rodriguez, and Lorna Dee Cervantes). . . . One of the most comprehensive anthologies available of Latino writing in the United States." Libr J
Includes bibliographical references

★ **Magill's** survey of American literature; edited by Steven G. Kellman. Rev. ed; Salem Press 2007 6v il set $499 **810**
  1. Reference books 2. Literature -- Bio-bibliography 3. Literature -- History and criticism
ISBN 978-1-58765-285-1; 1-58765-285-4

LC 2006-16503

First published 1992 with two volume supplement published 1996 under the editorship of Frank Northen Magill
"Examining selected works of 339 U.S. and Canadian writers, from Anne Bradstreet and Benjamin Franklin to Edward Bloor and Octavia E. Butler, this clearly written resource provides sturdy support for assignments, and will also be popular with discussion groups and with general readers of literature." SLJ
Includes bibliographical references

Matthiessen, F. O.

★ **American** renaissance; art and expression in the age of Emerson and Whitman. Oxford Univ. Press 1941 xxiv, 678p il hardcover o.p. pa $53 **810**
  1. Poets 2. Artists 3. Authors 4. Novelists 5. Sculptors 6. Naturalists 7. Philosophers 8. Essayists 9. Pacifists 10. Writers on nature 11. Nonfiction writers 12. Short story writers 13. American literature -- History and criticism
ISBN 0-19-500759-X pa
A critical study of works by Emerson, Thoreau, Melville, Hawthorne and Whitman and their impact on American intellectual history.

Modern American memoirs; selected and edited by Annie Dillard and Cort Conley. HarperCollins Pubs. 1995 449p hardcover o.p. pa $16 **810**
  1. Authors, American 2. American literature -- Collections
ISBN 0-06-092763-1 pa

LC 95-30755

The editors "have collected excerpts from the memoirs of 35 20th-century American authors. The selections represent the best in autobiographical writing published between 1917 and 1992. Included are nine women and 26 men, both black and white, some better known than others, all distinguished writers and wonderful storytellers. . . . The editors precede each entry with a biographical and contextual note.

There's an opening essay on the art of the memoirist and an afterword listing additional classics in the genre." Libr J

Morgan, Bill

The **typewriter** is holy; the complete, uncensored history of the beat generation. Free Press 2010 291p il $28   **810**
1. Beat generation 2. American literature -- History and criticism 3. American literature -- 20th century -- History and criticism
ISBN 1-4165-9242-3; 978-1-4165-9242-6
     LC 2009-42224

In this book, Bill Morgan "employs a wide focus to portray the remarkable group of writers and artists that became known as the Beat Generation. He suggests that Jack Kerouac, Lawrence Ferlinghetti, Gary Snyder, Gregory Corso, William Burroughs, and others had such divergent aims and styles that they cannot properly be considered a literary movement. Instead, he sees them as a circle of friends who loved literature and were united by [Allen] Ginsberg." (Library Journal)

"Morgan clearly loves his subjects, but he doesn't gloss over their erratic lifestyle, which involved amazing amounts of drugs and alcohol, and their consummate selfishness. . . . Morgan's own prose is straightforward, even pedestrian, but his ability to draw together so many events and personalities is astonishing." Providence J

Includes bibliographical references

National Story Project (U.S.)

I thought my father was God and other true tales from the National Story Project; edited and introduced by Paul Auster; Nelly Reifler, assistant editor. Holt & Co. 2001 xxi, 383p il hardcover o.p. pa $15   **810**
1. American literature -- Collections
ISBN 0-8050-6714-0; 0-312-42100-1 pa
     LC 00-54397

"These are stop-you-in-your-tracks stories about hair-raising coincidences, miracles, tragedies, redemption, and moments of pure hilarity." Booklist

A **new** literary history of America; edited by Greil Marcus and Werner Sollors. Belknap Press of Harvard University Press 2009 1095p bibl f il (Harvard University Press reference library) $49.95   **810**
1. United States -- Civilization 2. American literature -- History and criticism
ISBN 978-0-674-03594-2; 0-674-03594-1
     LC 2009014255

"This is an adventurous, jazzily choral, and kaleidoscopic book of interpretations, illuminations, and revitalized history." Booklist

Includes bibliographical references and index

★ The **Norton** anthology of African American literature; Henry Louis Gates, Jr., general editor, Nellie Y. McKay, general editor. 2nd ed; Norton 2003 2800p 2 computer laser optical discs pa $70.30   **810**
1. American literature -- African American authors -- Collections
ISBN 0-393-97778-1
     LC 2003-66176

First published 1996

"The anthology is divided into seven sections, each with a separate introduction giving the sociopolitical factors that impacted on the material included therein. Featured are 120 writers, 52 of whom are women, richly representing African American vernacular literature, poetry, drama, short stories, novels, slave narratives, and autobiographies." Libr J [review of 1996 edition]

Includes bibliographical references

The **Oxford** book of the American South; testimony, memory, and fiction. edited by Edward L. Ayers, Bradley C. Mittendorf. Oxford Univ. Press 1997 597p hardcover o.p. pa $22   **810**
1. American literature -- Southern States -- Collections
ISBN 0-19-512493-6 pa
     LC 96-45135

"Not limiting themselves to fiction (short stories and novels, either in full or in extract), the editors also gather memoirs, diaries, and essays. From both genders and races, from opposite poles on the economic scale, from an eighteenth-century naturalist to a former slave, from Thomas Jefferson to Eudora Welty, these writings give ringing voice to the experiences that have engendered a distinctive southern culture." Booklist

The **Oxford** book of women's writing in the United States; edited by Linda Wagner-Martin, Cathy N. Davidson. Oxford Univ. Press 1995 596p hardcover o.p. pa $27.50   **810**
1. American literature -- Women authors -- Collections
ISBN 0-19-513245-9 pa
     LC 95-1499

This anthology provides "samples of the public and private work of 99 women of diverse racial and ethnic backgrounds who write in English and were born in or have lived in the United States over the past four centuries. They include short fiction (almost half of the book), poems, essays, plays, and speeches but have also gone beyond traditional genre categories to include performance pieces, erotica, diaries, letters, and recipes." Libr J

★ The **Oxford** encyclopedia of American literature; Jay Parini, editor-in-chief. Oxford University Press 2004 4v il set $495   **810**
1. Reference books 2. American literature -- Encyclopedias
ISBN 0-19-515653-6
     LC 2002-156325

This set "provides a wealth of reliable information on standard bearers of American literature in an easy-on-the-eyes format for students and general readers." SLJ

Parini, Jay

√ **Promised** land; thirteen books that changed America. Doubleday 2008 385p il $24.95 **810**
1. American national characteristics 2. American literature -- History and criticism
ISBN 978-0-385-52276-2

LC 2008-9990

This is "a mind-expanding book of books guaranteed to provoke discussion and fuel reading groups." Booklist
Includes bibliographical references

Pierpont, Claudia Roth

√ **Passionate** minds; women rewriting the world. Knopf 2000 298p il hardcover o.p. pa $13 **810**
1. Poets 2. Actors 3. Authors 4. Lawyers 5. Novelists 6. Dramatists 7. Philosophers 8. Women authors 9. Diarists 10. Essayists 11. Feminists 12. Memoirists 13. Folklorists 14. Screenwriters 15. College teachers 16. Literary critics 17. Nonfiction writers 18. Short story writers 19. Writers on politics 20. Political scientists 21. Nobel laureates for literature 22. Political and social philosophers 23. English literature -- Women authors -- History and criticism 24. American literature -- Women authors -- History and criticism
ISBN 0-679-43106-3; 0-679-75113-0 pa

LC 99-33349

"A scintillating collection of brief lives of women writers, a book that sparkles with intelligence, wit and human interest. . . . Unfolding with the dramatic élan of a novella, each one is exhaustively researched, sharply focused, convincingly opinionated." N Y Times Book Rev

The **Portable** beat reader; edited by Ann Charters.
√ Viking 1992 xxxvi, 642p hardcover o.p. pa $17 **810**
1. Bohemianism 2. American literature -- Collections
ISBN 0-14-243753-0 pa

LC 91-16155

"Cutting through bohemian posturing and excess, Charters here reprints much of the most vital, readable and relevant material produced by the Beat generation." Publ Wkly
Includes bibliographical references

The **Portable** Harlem Renaissance reader; edited
√ and with an introduction by David Levering Lewis. Viking 1994 xlvii, 766p hardcover o.p. pa $18 **810**
1. Harlem Renaissance 2. American literature -- African American authors -- Collections
ISBN 0-14-017036-7

LC 93-30233

"General categories include essay, memoir, fiction, poetry, and drama; specific writers include such expected names as Langston Hughes, Zora Neale Hurston, and Claude McKay, but lesser-known names are also represented. There is anger in these pages and also frustration, pride, pain, and elation, but above all there is incredible talent. Reading the collection straight through would be a wonderful education, but most readers will dip in here and there, and that is edifying, too." Booklist

The **Portable** sixties reader; edited by Ann Charters.
√ Penguin Bks. 2003 xli, 628p il pa $16 **810**
1. American literature -- Collections 2. United States -- History -- 1961-1974
ISBN 0-14-200194-5

LC 2002-32266

This reader includes "essays, poetry, and fiction under thematic subjects, such as civil rights; women's rights; the sexual revolution; environmental issues; the antiwar, free-speech, and black-arts movements; and the use of drugs in pursuit of enlightenment. . . . [Includes works by] James Baldwin, Thomas Merton, Susan Sontag, Gary Snyder, Allen Ginsburg, Rachel Carson, Kate Millett, Nikki Giovanni, and many more." Booklist
Includes bibliographical references

The **Portable** Western reader; edited and with an introduction by William Kittredge. Penguin Bks. 1997 xxi, 600p pa $14.95 **810**
1. American literature -- West (U.S.) -- Collections
ISBN 0-14-023026-2

LC 96-47243

"Part 1, 'Ancient Stories,' shows the evolution of Native American storytelling from the early legends to contemporary stories and includes writings by Catherine McClellan, John Graves, and Louise Erdrich. Parts 2 and 3 contrast the mythology of the 19th-century 'Western' with the actual experience of living in the West. Most of these authors, from Walt Whitman to Larry McMurtry, will be familiar to readers. Part 4, 'Brilliant Possibilities,' showcases the new generation of Western writers, including Gretel Ehrlich, Jimmy Santiago Baca, and Sherman Alexie." Libr J

★ **Pushcart** Prize XXXVI: best of the small presses 2012; edited by Bill Henderson with the Pushcart Prize editors. Pushcart 2011 569p $35; pa $18.95 **810**
1. American literature -- Collections
ISBN 978-1-88888964-2; 978-1-8888864-5 pa
Annual. First published 1976
Each volume "consists of short stories, poems and essays; includes the work of established and beginning writers, and has a faintly subversive character. Its audience would seem to be primarily the young, yet among its contributors are many of the best writers in America. . . . Like all interesting literary journals, 'The Pushcart Prize' is eclectic and uneven. . . . The number and diversity of journals represented and the sheer length of it are impressive." Books of the Times
Includes bibliographical references

Salem Press Inc.

√ ★ **Notable** Latino writers; from the editors of Salem Press. Salem Press 2005 3v il (Magill's choice) set $207 **810**
1. American literature -- Hispanic American authors -- History and criticism
ISBN 1-58765-243-9; 978-1-58765-243-1

LC 2005-17567

These volumes feature "122 essays about Latino novelists, short-story writers, poets, and playwrights of the Western Hemisphere who write in English, Spanish, or Portuguese. . . . This set may prove to be a useful research tool for students, teachers, and librarians." Libr J

Includes bibliographical references

Samet, Elizabeth D.

★ **Soldier's** heart; reading literature through peace and war at West Point. Farrar, Straus and Giroux 2007 259p $23   **810**

1. United States Military Academy 2. Soldiers -- United States 3. Literature -- Study and teaching

ISBN 978-0-374-18063-8; 0-374-18063-6

LC 2007-9159

"Like the best professors, Samet asks tough questions and offers no easy answers. Her book is filled with lively classroom discussions and poignant e-mails from former students now in Iraq, often writing about the books they're reading there. . . . I know of no other new book that's a better choice for any reading group that loves to debate literature and politics." USA Today

Showalter, Elaine, 1941-

★ A **jury** of her peers; American women writers from Anne Bradstreet to Annie Proulx. Alfred A. Knopf 2009 586p $30   **810**

1. Women in literature 2. Literature -- Women authors 3. American literature -- Women authors 4. Women in literature -- United States 5. Women and literature -- United States -- History 6. American literature -- Women authors -- Bio-bibliography 7. American literature -- Women authors -- History and criticism

ISBN 978-1-4000-4123-7; 1-4000-4123-6

LC 2008-42312

"Showalter's writing is clear, lively, and authoritative; her research is impressive." Libr J

Includes bibliographical references

Taylor, Todd W. (2002)

★ The **Companion** to southern literature; themes, genres, places, people, movements, and motifs. edited by Joseph M. Flora and Lucinda H. MacKethan; associate editor, Todd Taylor. Louisiana State Univ. Press 2001 xxvi, 1054p $69.95   **810**

1. Reference books 2. Southern States -- Intellectual life 3. American literature -- Southern States -- Encyclopedias

ISBN 0-8071-2692-6

LC 2001-29959

"This unique compilation [is] . . . an excellent addition to libraries that support studies of Southern literature." Libr J

Includes bibliographical references

Transcendentalism; a reader. [edited by] Joel Myerson. Oxford Univ. Press 2001 xxxvii, 712p hardcover o.p. pa $32   **810**

1. New England -- Intellectual life 2. Transcendentalism -- Collections

ISBN 0-19-512212-7; 0-19-512213-5 pa

LC 00-21484

This reader "draws together in their entirety the essential writings of the Transcendentalist group during its most active period, 1836-1844. It includes the major publications of the Dial, the writings on democratic and social reform,

the early poetry, nature writings, and all of Emerson's major essays, as well as an . . . introduction and annotations by Myerson." Publisher's note

Includes bibliographical references

Wall, Cheryl A.

Women of the Harlem Renaissance. Indiana Univ. Press 1995 246p il (Women of letters) hardcover o.p. pa $14.95   **810**

1. Nurses 2. Authors 3. Novelists 4. Dramatists 5. Harlem Renaissance 6. Editors 7. Essayists 8. Memoirists 9. Folklorists 10. Literary critics 11. Short story writers 12. American literature -- African American authors

ISBN 0-253-20980-3 pa

LC 95-3132

This study of women writers of the Harlem Renaissance begins with an overview: On being young—a woman—and colored, followed by critical and biographical studies of Jessie Redmond Fauset, Nella Larsen, and Zora Neale Hurston

"Wall offers strong critiques of these women's work, uncovering certain similarities, including, most importantly, the travel motif as not only a reflection of the mass migrations of the day but also a larger dislocation." Publ Wkly

Includes bibliographical references

Wilson, Edmund (1762)

Patriotic gore; studies in the literature of the American Civil War. Norton 1994 816p pa $19.95   **810**

1. Poets 2. Clergy 3. Judges 4. Authors 5. Lawyers 6. Generals 7. Pianists 8. Diplomats 9. Educators 10. Governors 11. Novelists 12. Presidents 13. Journalists 14. Abolitionists 15. Flutists 16. Essayists 17. Memoirists 18. Sociologists 19. Army officers 20. Political leaders 21. State legislators 22. Children's authors 23. Nonfiction writers 24. Secretaries of war 25. White supremacists 26. Members of Congress 27. Novelists, American 28. Short story writers 29. Writers on politics 30. Civil rights activists 31. Supreme Court justices 32. Spouses of prominent persons 33. American literature -- History and criticism 34. United States -- History -- 1861-1865, Civil War 35. United States -- History -- 1861-1865, Civil War -- Poetry 36. United States -- History -- 1861-1865, Civil War -- Biography

ISBN 978-0-393-31256-0; 0-393-31256-9

First published 1962 by Oxford University Press

"A collection of sixteen essays on writing related to the war including the memoirs of Union generals Grant and Sherman and Confederates Mosby and Lee, diaries, political writing, and fiction by writers such as Ambrose Bierce and John De Forest." Benet's Reader's Ency of Am Lit

810.8   American literature (English)--Collections

★ The **best** American science and nature writing 2012; edited by Dan Ariely and Tim Fol-

(1000)

ger. Houghton Mifflin Harcourt 2012 325 p. $14.95 **810.8**
1. Science 2. Natural history
ISBN 0547799535; 9780547799537

This book, edited by Dan Ariely, "presents a smorgasbord of . . . science writing covering everything from the 1,000 species in the human gut to efforts to reverse-evolve a chicken into a dinosaur. The two dozen pieces reflect the conclusion that 'we are extraordinary yet flawed and predictably irrational creatures.' . . . Topics include allergies, marauder ants, lab-grown meat, airborne contaminants, the adolescent brain . . . and the sequencing of the Neanderthal genome." (Kirkus Reviews)

810.9 American literature (English) -- History and criticism

Bram, Christopher
Eminent outlaws; the gay writers who changed America. Christopher Bram. Twelve 2012 372 p. **810.9**
1. Social change 2. American authors 3. Gay men's writings 4. Gay men -- Biography 5. Homosexuality -- United States -- History 6. Gay authors -- United States 7. Authors, American -- 20th century 8. Gays' writings, American -- History and criticism
ISBN 9780446563130

LC 2011029910

"This book is a history, literary critique, and collective biography in one. Novelist [Christopher] Bram . . . discusses gay men . . . from Gore Vidal in the early postwar years up through the 1990s and close to the present. His main thesis, that 'good art can lay the groundwork for social change,' is demonstrated and contextualized in dozens of examples of how literature can be not just a reflection of the times but also a catalyst for change." (Library Journal)

Includes bibliographical references (p. 351-354) and index

A **story** larger than my own; women writers look back on their lives and careers. edited by Janet Burroway. University of Chicago Press 2014 199 p. (cloth : alkaline paper) $55 **810.9**
1. Women poets 2. Women authors 3. Autobiographies 4. Women authors, American -- Literary collections
ISBN 022601407X; 9780226014074; 9780226014104
LC 2013032197

"In this engrossing volume edited by [Janet] Burroway . . ., 19 accomplished female authors reflect on their careers and offer insights on craft and life. The contributors, all of whom are 60 or older, came of professional age during second wave feminism, confronted the prejudice against women writers of the 1950's and 60's, and continue to publish in the digital age. The variety of voices and styles adds up to a mesmerizing tapestry of a generation, made up of both individual experiences and the commonalities between them." Pub Wkly

Writers of the Black Chicago renaissance; edited by Steven C. Tracy. University of Illinois Press 2011 vii, 523 p.p $50 **810.9**
1. African Americans -- Chicago (Ill.) 2. African Americans -- Political activity 3. American literature -- African American authors 4. Chicago (Ill.) -- Intellectual life -- 20th century 5. American literature -- 20th century -- History and criticism 6. American literature -- Illinois -- Chicago -- History and criticism 7. American literature -- African American authors -- History and criticism
ISBN 0252036395; 9780252036392

LC 2011029269

This book, edited by Steven C. Tracy, "explores the contours and content of the Black Chicago Renaissance, a creative movement that emerged from the crucible of rigid segregation in Chicago's 'Black Belt' from the 1930s through the 1960s. . . . The volume covers a vast collection of subjects, including many important writers such as Richard Wright, Gwendolyn Brooks, and Lorraine Hansberry as well as cultural products such as black newspapers, music, and theater." (Publisher's note)

Includes bibliographical references and index

811 American poetry

180 more; extraordinary poems for every day. selected and with an introduction by Billy Collins. Random House 2005 xxiii, 373p pa $14.95 **811**
1. American poetry -- Collections
ISBN 0-8129-7296-1

LC 2005-42798

Sequel to: Poetry 180

This is a second collection of 180 poems for each day of the school year, designed to expose high school students to poetry.

Ackerman, Diane, 1948-
Origami bridges; poems of psychoanalysis and fire. HarperCollins Pubs. 2002 147p $22.95; pa $11.95 **811**
1. Poetry -- By individual authors
ISBN 0-06-019988-1; 0-06-055529-7 pa

LC 2002-24685

"Sometimes addressed to herself and her personal history, at least as often addressed to 'Dr. B—,' Ackerman's passionate free verse (short, fluent and adorned by irregular rhyme) describes with nearly unmixed awe the relationship she created with her analyst, and the personal transformation she achieved." Publ Wkly

Adair, Virginia Hamilton
Ants on the melon; a collection of poems. Random House 1996 158p hardcover o.p. pa $15 **811**
1. Poetry -- By individual authors
ISBN 0-375-75229-3 pa

LC 95-25977

"The appearance of a first collection by a poet now blind and in her 83rd year must be accounted a triumph . . . {Adair} works with equal daring in free verse and more traditional forms; her subjects include social and religious commentary, but her principal theme is ordinary experience and its resistance to facile interpretation." Libr J

Beliefs and blasphemies; a collection of poems. Random House 1998 109p hardcover o.p. pa $15 **811**

1. Poetry -- By individual authors

ISBN 0-8129-9245-8 pa

LC 97-47403

"Adair's searching verses may not always have the ring of the contemporary, and they often stop short here of fully unfurling their insights. But at its best, this collection points the way back to an American tradition of religious poetry understood and cherished by the likes of Elizabeth Bishop and Louise Bogan." Publ Wkly

Adam, Helen

A **Helen** Adam reader; edited, with notes and an introduction by Kristin Prevallet. National Poetry Foundation 2007 492p il $59.95; $29.95 **811**

1. Poetry -- By individual authors

ISBN 978-0-943373-74-4; 0-943373-74-3; 978-0-943373-73-7 pa; 0-943373-73-5 pa

LC 2007-34740

In the Bay Area of the late 1940s Adam "found herself a member—some said godmother, witch or Nurse of Enchantment—of the interlocking Robert Duncan and Jack Spicer poetry circles, which, with the Beats, formed the avant-garde San Francisco Renaissance. . . . Adam combined the narrative economy of ballads—where each line is a discrete unit of information—with the lush sonic tapestry we associate with older Anglo-Saxon and Celtic strains of British verse. . . . On the page, Adam's intricate soundscapes compare with anything by Gerard Manley Hopkins and Dylan Thomas. But to see her sing her ballads—she chants 'Kiltory' on the Reader's accompanying DVD—is to appreciate how the language, trilling and seething by turns, possessed its acolyte." Nation

Includes bibliographical references

African-American poetry of the nineteenth century; an anthology. edited by Joan R. Sherman. University of Ill. Press 1992 506p hardcover o.p. pa $26.95 **811**

1. American poetry -- African American authors -- Collections

ISBN 0-252-06246-9 pa

LC 91-41709

"The introduction surveys the historical and cultural values of African American poetry. The poems themselves have historical as well as lyric value; unfamiliar as well as familiar poets are included. Though the poems are formal, the rhymes are generally unforced. . . . This anthology also includes an extensive bibliography to help researchers find other resources." Libr J

Alexander, Elizabeth, 1962-

Crave radiance; new and selected poems 1990-2010. Graywolf Press 2010 255p **811**

1. Poetry -- By individual authors

ISBN 9781555975685

LC 2010-922921

"This potent retrospective collection offers the best of Alexander's five previous books, including selections from her young-adult title, Miss Crandall's School for Young Girls and Little Misses of Color (2007), which hold their own as poems for adults of all ages here. . . . Alexander brings intellectual power, musicality, sensuousness, and vernacular immediacy to her lyrics, which entwine the personal with the social, the tactile with the imaginary, the past with the present." Booklist

Alexie, Sherman

Face. Hanging Loose Press 2009 159p $28; pa $15 **811**

1. Poetry -- By individual authors

ISBN 978-1-931236-71-3; 1-931236-71-2; 978-1-931236-70-6 pa; 1-931236-70-4 pa

LC 2008-46580

The author "has mastered both the metrical dance and fixed forms. A sequence of sonnets finds the Seven Deadly Sins in marriage, for instance; a villanelle begins with Mount Rushmore but eases into a consideration of America's Presidents, complemented by wry and smart footnotes. . . . There are a lot of serious undercurrents in his poetry, and they are always a pleasure to find." Libr J

Altman, Howard

In this house. Turtle Point Press 2010 81p pa $15.95 **811**

1. Poetry -- By individual authors

ISBN 978-1-933527-33-8

LC 2009-929505

A "collection of poems that look at the world with thought-provoking and elegantly bifurcated awareness: 'Inside every man is another man / He would like to leave behind.' At once sturdy and visionary, Altmann's work has won him a variety of fans that include not just poet John Ashbery but also actor Patricia Clarkson." Time Out N Y

Alvarez, Julia

The woman I kept to myself; poems. Algonquin Books of Chapel Hill 2004 155p hardcover o.p. pa $14.95 **811**

1. Poetry -- By individual authors

ISBN 1-56512-406-5; 1-61620-072-3 pa

LC 2003-70807

This "collection of 75 poems is divided into three sections, and each poem has three stanzas, exactly . . . The poet, who is from the Dominican Republic, writes about being raised with her sisters in New York. The subjects are personal—love, marriage, rejection, divorce, death, religion—but also universal." SLJ

★ **American** poetry, the twentieth century. Library of Am. 2000 2v ea $35 **811**

1. American poetry -- Collections

ISBN 1-88301-177-9 v1; 1-88301-178-7 v2

LC 99-43721

These volumes represent a "remarkable feat of assemblage, with excellent capsule biographies and explanatory notes at the end of each volume—the biographies, especially, are well worth reading." N Y Times Book Rev

Includes bibliographical references

★ **American** poetry: the seventeenth and eighteenth centuries; edited by David Shields. Library of America 2007 xxiii, 952p $40   **811**

1. American poetry -- Collections
ISBN 978-1-931082-90-7; 1-931082-90-1

LC 2007-929763

"Besides hefty helpings of the few figures meagerly represented in general American-lit surveys—Anne Bradstreet, Edward Taylor, John Trumbull, Timothy Dwight, Philip Freneau, Phyllis Wheatley—here are poems short and . . . long by dozens of others, most of them obscure to even thoroughgoing, historically minded poetry lovers. . . . The subject matter isn't all religion and politics. Work, family, leisure, and exceptional events and lives (one man recounts escape from the limited slavery that was indenture) are all written up. And, in regular rhymes and meters, it's all quite readable. Early-American history buffs as much as, if not more than, poetry readers may consider the book a gold mine." Booklist

Includes bibliographical references

American religious poems; an anthology by Harold Bloom. Harold Bloom and Jesse Zuba, editors. Library of America 2006 685p $40   **811**

1. Religious poetry 2. American poetry -- Collections
ISBN 1-931082-74-X

LC 2006-41031

An anthology of "verse on Christian, Jewish, Islamic, Buddhist, Native American spiritual, Transcendentalist and even agnostic themes, from 17th-century European colonists (one poet is Roger Williams, who founded Rhode Island) to up-and-comers in contemporary verse. Pious readers will have no trouble finding high-quality poetry that confirms their beliefs—from the monk Thomas Merton, the Anglican T.S. Eliot, the Jewish liturgical poet Esther Schor and the Louisiana-based Christian poet Martha Serpas. Yet from the 19th century to the present, from the decidedly heterodox Emily Dickinson forwards, the anthology often highlights the ways in which American spirituality has challenged all doctrines about who God is and what God does. . . . More than half of the book is taken up by 20th-century poets, who offer varied takes on what religion has come to mean in America." Publ Wkly

★ **American** war poetry; an anthology. edited by Lorrie Goldensohn. Columbia University Press 2006 413p $27.95   **811**

1. War poetry 2. American poetry -- Collections
ISBN 0-231-13310-3

LC 2005-54762

"Arranged by war, the book begins with the Colonial period and proceeds through Whitman admiring Civil War soldiers crossing a river to end with Brian Turner, who published his first book in 2005, beckoning a bullet in contemporary Iraq. Many voices, by turns elegiac, outraged, rhetorical and ecstatic are represented." Publ Wkly

Includes bibliographical references

American wits; an anthology of light verse. John Hollander, editor. Library of America 2003 xxv, 194p (American poets project) $20   **811**

1. American poetry -- Collections 2. Humorous poetry

-- Collections
ISBN 978-1-931082-49-5; 1-931082-49-9

LC 2003-46636

This anthology "offers some exceptionally clever writing, much of which will be unfamiliar to many readers (and therefore all the more amusing). Hollander sensibly allots the most space to Ogden Nash and Dorothy Parker; the selections from both are solid. But Hollander's good judgment is best demonstrated by the third most represented poet here, the screenwriter Samuel Hoffenstein (1890-1947). . . . The poetry world currently has a surplus of writers who are eager, sometimes even desperate, to be funny, but we're suffering from a shortage of genuine wit." Poetry (Modern Poetry Association)

Angelou, Maya

★ The **complete** collected poems of Maya Angelou. Random House 1994 273p $24.95   **811**

1. Poetry -- By individual authors
ISBN 0-679-42895-X

LC 94-14501

This volume contains all of Angelou's published poems including her inaugural poem On the pulse of morning

I shall not be moved. Random House 1997 48p $15; pa $9.95   **811**

1. Poetry -- By individual authors
ISBN 0-679-45708-9; 0-553-35458-3 pa
First published 1990

"Angelou's themes include loss of love and youth, human oneness in diversity, the strength of blacks in the face of racism and adversity." Publ Wkly

Angles of ascent; a Norton anthology of contemporary African American poetry. edited by Charles Henry Rowell. W.W. Norton & Co. 2012 672 p. (pbk.) $24.95   **811**

1. American poetry -- African American authors 2. American poetry -- 21st century
ISBN 0393339408; 9780393339406

LC 2011042967

This poetry anthology, edited by Charles Henry Rowell, features "more than seventy [African American] poets. . . . These poets bear witness to the interior landscapes of their own individual selves or examine the private or personal worlds of invented personae and, therefore, of human beings living in our modern and postmodern worlds. The anthology focuses on post-1960s poetry and includes such poets as Rita Dove, . . . Natasha Trethewey, . . . and Yusef Komunyakaa." (Publisher's note)

Armantrout, Rae

Versed. Wesleyan University Press 2009 121p (Wesleyan poetry) $22.95   **811**

1. Poetry -- By individual authors
ISBN 978-0-8195-6879-3; 0-8195-6879-1

LC 2008-43809

National Book Award Finalists (2009)
Pulitzer Prize Finalist (2010)
Pulitzer Prize (2010)
National Book Critics Award (2010)

This book "book comprises two sequences — 'Versed' and 'Dark Matter'— of loosely interlinked poems dealing with the prolific poet's usual subjects (the body, contemporary society, violence) as well as more personal explorations of illness and mortality, all relayed in Armantrout's concentrated, crystalline voice, with a predilection for skipping some steps along the way to sense." Publ Wkly

Ashbery, John

Collected poems 1956-1987; [edited by Mark Ford] Library of America 2008 1042p $40 **811**
1. Poetry -- By individual authors
ISBN 978-1-59853-028-5

"This major book, the first collection from Library of America by a living poet, offers a view of Ashbery's artistic development over many decades.... Watching Ashbery's art grow from the slippery romanticism and verbal hijinks of the early poems through the philosophical, if sideways, inquiry of the '70s, to the chattier, colloquial period inaugurated in the early '80s, is arresting. Though Ashbery has confounded and inspired in seemingly equal measure, he is, according to both his admirers and critics, the towering figure in contemporary American poetry." Publ Wkly

Notes from the air; selected later poems. Ecco 2007 364p $34.95 **811**
1. Poetry -- By individual authors
ISBN 978-0-06-136717-5; 0-06-136717-6
LC 2008-270813

This "volume—beginning with poems from April Galleons (1987) and ending with Where Shall I Wander (2005)— presents . . . [a] panoramic view of Ashbery's second phase, in which he explores, celebrates, sends up and revels in the American vernacular. . . . This is an essential book." Publ Wkly

Planisphere; new poems. Ecco 2009 143p $24.99 **811**
1. Poetry -- By individual authors
ISBN 978-0-06-191521-5; 0-06-191521-1

"In his rendering of American speech, slang, cliché, Ashbery has surpassed most of his contemporaries. But his persistent reach into the 'rut' of tradition should not be forgotten. He could say (with the great Nicaraguan poet Rubén Darío) that he is very 18th century and very archaic and very modern, daring and cosmopolitan. When he becomes most serious, it is in the presence of either catastrophe or truth. His onslaughts of tragedy, emotional or physical, are of geological force while not relinquishing the vocabulary of iron." N Y Times Book Rev

Selected poems. Viking 1985 349p hardcover o.p. pa $17.95 **811**
1. Poetry -- By individual authors
ISBN 0-14-058553-2 pa
LC 85-40549

"Ashbery's work is seductive precisely because it alludes to shared traditions and assumptions about poetry. His poems attract us with their gestures of 'meaningful' discourse, the meditative pace of their syntax and the memories and expectations of meaningfulness that it evokes, the care-

ful use of qualifiers, and the precisions and surprises of his diction." Benet's Reader's Ency of Am Lit

★ Where shall I wander; new poems. J. Ecco 2005 81p $22.95 **811**
1. Poetry -- By individual authors
ISBN 0-06-076529-1
LC 2004-53267

This collection of poetry features the poems "Ignorance of the Law Is No Excuse" and "A Visit to the House of Fools."

"Ashbery expresses a sly playfulness, a tender theatricality, a surreal sensibility, and an urbane wit. . . . Mercurial, elegant, funny, and magical, these mind-bending and beautifully haunting poems are the knowing work of a virtuoso." Booklist

★ A worldly country; new poems. Ecco Press 2007 76p $23.95 **811**
1. Poetry -- By individual authors
ISBN 0-06-117383-5; 978-0-06-117383-7
LC 2006-50279

This is a volume of poems by the author of Some Trees (1956); The Tennis Court Oath (1957); Rivers and Mountains (1966); Sunrise in Suburbia (1968); The Double Dream of Spring (1970); Self-portrait in a Convex Mirror (1975); Houseboat Days (1977); As We Know (1979); Shadow Trains (1981); Your Name Here (2000); and Where Shall I Wander (2006).

"Ashbery's syncopated lyrics are sheer pleasure in their music, collaged images, stabbing perceptions. Mysterious and truth-bearing poems that inspire us to 'flame on, flame on.'" Booklist

Auden, W. H.

Collected poems; edited by Edward Mendelson. Vintage Bks. 1991 xxvii, 926p pa $24 **811**
1. Poetry -- By individual authors
ISBN 0-679-73197-0
LC 91-158031

Originally published in hardcover in different form by Random House in 1976

A compilation of all the poems Auden wished to preserve, in his final revisions. Previous collected editions and later shorter poems are included. There is also an absurdist play written 1928: Paid on both sides

Baca, Jimmy Santiago

Spring poems along the Rio Grande. New Directions Pub. 2007 75p pa $12.95 **811**
1. Poetry -- By individual authors
ISBN 978-0-8112-1685-2; 0-8112-1685-3
LC 2006-101678

"The Rio Grande, as both setting and symbol of freedom and life, meanders through the poems, evoking a natural progression of time and the natural ebb and flow of feelings such as love, hope, and connection. The bosque along the river is home to birds both resident and migratory, trees, fish, bushes, insects, and encroaching urban life represented by power lines and interstate traffic noise. Jogging here, Baca evinces a love of his hometown of Albuquerque but, even more, reveals his well of poetic inspiration: Chicano,

Catholic religiosity, Native American symbolism, and universal milestones. . . . With its highly accessible language and thoughtful reflections on the natural world, readers will find Baca's poetry extremely inviting." Booklist

Bang, Mary Jo

The **bride** of E; poems. Graywolf Press 2009 90p $22   **811**

1. Poetry -- By individual authors

ISBN 978-1-55597-539-5; 1-55597-539-9

LC 2009-926850

"The book takes the form of an abecedarian in which E stands for existence, with the engine of the alphabet overriding the entropy of emptiness, in which 'all action is in the mind, a cluster of notions/ in depravity's head independent of the dreadful/ invention of the magnetic temporary where/ a partition is positioned between right and wrong.' Many of these poems refer to the precariousness of human future, with Bang's medical background contributing convincing detail, and her sharp wit buoys the description with bleak meaning." Libr J

Elegy; poems. Graywolf 2007 92p $20   **811**

1. Poetry -- By individual authors

ISBN 978-1-55597-483-1; 1-55597-483-X

LC 2007-924768

The author "captures the complexity and courage of surviving the death of a child, an adult child, an imperfect child. The grief is multilayered, palpable. In this rendition of living in pain, in absence, in an altered reality, the reader never questions the authenticity of the work. . . . This is a book of exceptional grace and strength; it belongs in every library." Libr J

Barnett, Catherine

★ The **game** of boxes; poems. Catherine Barnett. Graywolf Press 2012 88 p. (alk. paper) $15.00   **811**

1. American poetry -- Collections

ISBN 1555976204; 9781555976200

LC 2012936220

This book of poetry by Catherine Barnett "is organized into three . . . sections; the first is called 'endless forms most beautiful.' Scattered amid poems about a mother and her son are pieces written from the first-person plural perspective of an amorphous chorus. . . . Fragmentary poems . . . [about] lust, sex, and sorrow form the book's second section, 'sweet double, talk-talk.' . . . 'The modern period,' the book's last section is . . . the most lucidly personal." (Publishers Weekly)

Beat poets; selected and edited by Carmela Ciuraru. Knopf 2002 250p (Everyman's library pocket poets) $12.50   **811**

1. Beat generation 2. American poetry -- Collections

ISBN 978-0-375-41332-2; 0-375-41332-4

LC 2002-510236

"The defining work of Allen Ginsberg and Jack Kerouac provides the foundation for this collection, which also features statements on Beat poetics, selections from the alternately ardent, incendiary, and earnest correspondence of Beat Generation writers, and the improvisational verse of such Beat legends as Robert Creeley, Diane Di Prima, Greg-

ory Corso, Denise Levertov, Lawrence Ferlinghetti, Philip Whalen, Bob Kaufman, and Peter Orlovsky, along with the work of other women writers and the lesser-known poets of this school." Publisher's note

Berkson, Bill

★ **Portrait** and dream; new and selected poems. Coffee House Press 2009 314p pa $22   **811**

1. Poetry -- By individual authors

ISBN 978-1-56689-229-2; 1-56689-206-6

LC 2008-52607

"There was always something of a mythical aura about Berkson, the collaborator of Frank O'Hara and one of the chiefs of the New York School whose friends included painters as well as poets. . . . Berkson's own poetry is subtle and demonstrably abstract in the manner of, let's say, DeKooning: it has an imagistic hardness and lushness that sweeps aside whatever you might have been thinking before." Exquisite Corpse

Bernstein, Charles, 1950-

All the whiskey in heaven; selected poems. Farrar, Straus and Giroux 2010 300p $26   **811**

1. Poetry -- By individual authors

ISBN 0-374-10344-5; 978-0-374-10344-6

LC 2009-10187

"This gathering of 30 years worth of work by the prominent L=A=N=G=U=A=G=E poet and essayist offers a . . . critique of the art of poetry itself, which means, among other things, a thorough investigation of language and the mind. Varied voices and genres are at play, from a colloquial letter of complaint to the manager of a Manhattan subway station to a fragmentary meditation on the forces that underlie the formation of knowledge." (Publishers Weekly)

"Bernstein takes his place in the mainstream of American poetry, the very 'Official Verse Culture' he's attacked entertainingly for years—a fate awaiting all our best outsiders. . . . Early Bernstein can be opaque, annoying those who see difficulty as elitist and who want poetry to be cuddly and educational. But everyone should love the later Bernstein, a writer who is accessible, enormously witty, often joyful—and even more evilly subversive." N Y Times Book Rev

Berry, Wendell

Collected poems, 1957-1982. North Point Press 1985 268p hardcover o.p. pa $17   **811**

1. Poetry -- By individual authors

ISBN 978-0-86547-197-9

LC 84-62305

"As a nature poet Berry has a grass-roots, homespun quality that reminds one of Frost. He moves easily from witty lyrics and graceful elegies to moving love poems, philosophical odes and confessionals." Publ Wkly

Given; new poems. Shoemaker & Hoard 2005 152p $22   **811**

1. Poetry -- By individual authors

ISBN 1-59376-061-2

LC 2005-3762

"The latter half, 'Sabbaths 1998-2004,' . . . [contains] the meditational poems Berry conceives on Sundays alone in the woods on his farm. The other half's three parts contain, respectively, short poems of observation, hortatory poems varying in length from epigram to six-page public epistle, and a brief verse play. . . . For those who believe that life and the world are gifts, this is an invaluable book." Booklist

A timbered choir; the sabbath poems, 1979-1997. Counterpoint 1998 216p hardcover o.p. pa $14.95   **811**
1. Poetry -- By individual authors
ISBN 978-15823-006-5

LC 98-4925

"Berry has continued periodically to write poems out-of-doors on days of little other work. This book reprints Sabbaths, a collection of that writing, adding to it about one and a half times as much new work. . . . Few other poets have such chaste and precise diction or manage line and stanza with such unaffected serenity." Booklist

Berry, Wendell, 1934-
New collected poems. Counterpoint 2012 391 p. $30.00   **811**
1. Haiku 2. Fathers -- Poetry 3. Poetry -- Collections
ISBN 1582438153; 9781582438153
This book "makes [poet Wendell] Berry's first Collected [volume] since 1987 and draws on volumes up through 'Leavings.'" It includes "a long elegy for Berry's father and a set of haiku-sized poems. Benedictions and prayers coexist with manifestos and georgic, the ancient genre of poems about rural hard work." (Publishers Weekly)

Berryman, John
Collected poems, 1937-1971; edited and introduced by Charles Thornbury. Farrar, Straus & Giroux 1989 347p hardcover o.p. pa $25   **811**
1. Poetry -- By individual authors
ISBN 978-0-374-52281-0; 0-374-52281-2

LC 89-30944

"Berryman's poetry, sometimes mannered, elliptical, and convoluted, is distinguished by precise technical control and continued experiments with style." Reader's Ency. 4th edition

★ The **dream** songs. Farrar, Straus & Giroux 1969 xx, 427p hardcover o.p. pa $18   **811**
1. Poetry -- By individual authors
ISBN 978-0-374-53066-2; 0-374-53066-1
This book contains the author's 385 'dream songs' that originally appeared in various magazines, the Pulitzer Prize winning 77 dream songs (1964) and His toy, his dream, his rest (1968). The poet also provides a brief note about Henry, the poems' central character
"Berryman makes brilliant use of his speaker's indiscriminately retentive perception—the patter of jukeboxes, of cocktail parties, of the gutter and the cathedral—to drop us dizzily into an original world where life is lived naked and unashamed." Va Q Rev

★ **Best** of the Best American Poetry; 25th Anniversary. guest editor, Robert Pinsky ; series editor,

David Lehman. Simon & Schuster 2013 xxviii, 322 p.p (hardcover) $35   **811**
1. American poetry 2. Poetry -- Collections
ISBN 1451658877; 9781451658873
This poetry anthology, edited by David Lehman, "celebrates twenty-five years of the 'Best American Poetry' series. . . . From its inception in 1988, it has been hotly debated, keenly monitored, ardently advocated (or denounced), and obsessively scrutinized. . . . Out of the 1,875 poems that have appeared in 'The Best American Poetry,' here are 100 that Robert Pinsky, the distinguished poet and man of letters, has chosen for this milestone edition." (Publisher's note)

Bidart, Frank
Star dust. Farrar, Straus and Giroux 2005 84p $20   **811**
1. Poetry -- By individual authors
ISBN 0-374-26973-4

LC 2004-56293

This is a collection of poetry by the author of Desire.
"The poems in this collection range from terribly lame confections questioning the appellation of 'poem' itself—to gracefully and powerfully moving lyrics. . . . The more formal Bidart gets, the stronger his work, like a living example of Richard Wilbur's dictum that the genie gains his strength from confinement in the bottle." Am Book Rev

Watching the spring festival. Farrar, Straus & Giroux 2008 61p $25   **811**
1. Poetry -- By individual authors
ISBN 978-0-374-28603-3; 0-374-28603-5

LC 2007-40513

This book is "a collection of masterful, carefully modulated lyrics, glimpses of the millennium's turn and dispatches from an ancient world." Antioch Rev

Bidart, Frank, 1939-
★ **Metaphysical** dog; Frank Bidart. Farrar, Straus and Giroux 2013 128 p. (hardcover) $24 **811**
1. Metaphysics -- Poetry 2. Poetry -- Collections
ISBN 0374173613; 9780374173616

LC 2012048069

National Book Award: Poetry Finalist (2013)
National Book Critics Circle Award (2013)
In this poetry collection by Frank Bidart, the author explores the themes of "words and sex, art and flesh." The book "reflects what the poet sees as fundamental in human feeling, what psychologists and mystics have called the 'hunger for the Absolute'--a hunger as fundamental as any physical hunger. This hunger must confront the elusiveness of the Absolute, our self-deluding, failed glimpses of it." (Publisher's note)
"There is a quiet, stirring grandeur here as Bidart contemplates the spectrum of existence, life's endless transformations, and our 'hunger for the absolute.'" Booklist
Includes bibliographical references and index

Bishop, Elizabeth
Edgar Allan Poe & the juke-box; uncollected poems, drafts, and fragments. edited and annotated by

Alice Quinn. Farrar, Straus, and Giroux 2006 367p
$30 **811**
    1. Poetry -- By individual authors
    ISBN 0-374-14645-4

LC 2005-11511

"The publication of 'Edgar Allan Poe & the Juke-Box,'
which gathers for the first time Bishop's unpublished material, isn't just a significant event in our poetry; it's part of
a continuing alteration in the scale of American life." N Y
Times Book Rev

    Includes bibliographical references

Blackburn, Paul

The **collected** poems of Paul Blackburn; edited,
with an introduction, by Edith Jarolim. Persea Bks.
1985 xxxv, 667p il $55 **811**
    1. Poetry -- By individual authors
    ISBN 978-0-89255-086-9; 0-89255-086-4

LC 85-9309

"Much of Blackburn's poetry is an engaging mix of
sharp, allusive adventuring, humor and wordplay, annotated
fragments of musical speech, and a moderate but distinctive
use of metaphor. Edith Jarolim's introduction provides a
concise view of Blackburn's art and life." Choice

Blues poems; selected and edited by Kevin Young.
Knopf 2003 256p (Everyman's library pocket
poets) $12.50 **811**
    1. Blues music -- Poetry 2. American poetry --
    Collections
    ISBN 978-0-375-41458-9; 0-375-41458-4

LC 2003-53149

A collection of "blues-influenced and blues-inflected
poems from, among others, Gwendolyn Brooks, Allen Ginsberg, June Jordan, Richard Wright, Nikki Giovanni, Charles
Wright, Yusef Komunyakaa, and Cornelius Eady. And here,
too, are classic song lyrics—poems in their own right—from
Bessie Smith, Robert Johnson, Ma Rainey, and Muddy Waters." Publisher's note

Bly, Robert

Eating the honey of words; new and selected poems. HarperFlamingo 1999 270p hardcover o.p. pa
$14.95 **811**
    1. Poetry -- By individual authors
    ISBN 0-06-093069-1 pa

LC 98-51152

"Collecting over 200 poems from 1950 to 1998, this volume is an appealing poetic sampler, although the ten new
poems are unexciting. The poems celebrating discoveries
Bly makes when alone and silent are always striking, and
his imaginative prose poems radiate witty delight." Libr J

The **night** Abraham called to the stars; poems.
HarperCollins Pubs. 2001 95p hardcover o.p. pa
$12.95 **811**
    1. Poetry -- By individual authors
    ISBN 0-06-093444-1 pa

LC 00-66360

"The book's 48 lyrics are written in a single (here ter-
ceted) form, the ghazal, used by such great Islamic poets as
Ghalib, and harness high points of Western art and literature

to draw general, biblically backed conclusions about the human condition out of the mire." Publ Wkly

Bonair-Agard, Roger

Bury my clothes; by Roger Bonair-Agard. Hay-
market Books 2013 160 p. (pbk.) $16 **811**
    1. Art 2. Race 3. Violence 4. POETRY -- American
    -- African American
    ISBN 1608462692; 9781608462698

LC 2013006344

This book, by Roger Bonair-Agard, "is a meditation on
violence, race, and the place in art at which they intersect.
Art—specifically in oppressed communities—is about survival, . . . Bonair-Agard asserts, and establishing personhood
in a world that says you have none. Through poetry, [he attempts to] transform both the world of art and the world itself." (Publisher's note)

Booth, Philip

Selves; new poems. by Philip Booth. Viking
1990 75p hardcover o.p. pa $9.95 **811**
    1. Poetry -- By individual authors
    ISBN 0-14-058646-6 pa

LC 89-40317

This collection "features contemplative poems born of
the observant patience of North country life. The best are
based on concrete observation. . . . Booth's strength is that
he speaks of significant issues like the ultimate privacy of
suffering, the painful hidden destruction of relationships, the
coming of aging and death." Libr J

Bowers, Edgar

Collected poems. Knopf 1997 168p hardcover
o.p. pa $15 **811**
    1. Poetry -- By individual authors
    ISBN 0-679-76607-3 pa

LC 96-38580

"Surety of rhythm, swiftness of thought, and deftness of
phrase animate Bowers' triumphant poems about loss and
the struggle to be whole. He is, above all, a delineator—vital, ironic, capable of panoramic sweep—of his transfiguring
experiences in Germany during and after the Second World
War. His roots are deep in Horace and Pindar, but amid all
the eloquent austerity there are blessed moments of unexpected Mozartian lilt and wit." New Yorker

Brathwaite, Edward Kamau

Elegguas. Wesleyan University Press 2010 123p
il (Wesleyan poetry) $22.50 **811**
    1. Poetry -- By individual authors
    ISBN 978-0-8195-6943-1; 0-8195-6943-7

LC 2009-35923

"This is a handsome, thoughtfully produced volume,
shaped and sized to respect the poems' requirements for special graphic treatments, page formats, and line lengths. . . .
The language varies as much, if not more or more dramatically in many ways, than the graphical treatments, from the
intimate and colloquial diction of the work addressed to Zea
Mexican [the poet's late wife], to the lyrical conventions of
contemporary western poetry, to neologisms and invented
forms, to the grammatical constructs of Caribbean speech.

Brathwaite is equally adept and comfortable in all of these idioms." NewPages

Includes bibliographical references.

Brock-Broido, Lucie

Stay, Illusion; Poems. By Lucie Brock-Broido. Random House Inc 2013 112 p. (Hardcover) $26   **811**
1. Bereavement 2. American poetry 3. Emotions -- Poetry
ISBN 0307962024; 9780307962027

LC 2013023978

Author Lucie Brock-Broido presents a poetry collection designed to "spin, drape, and sculpt its virtuosic figures around the ideas and emotions of mourning. Often Brock-Broido commemorates her father, remembering him on his own, in her family, in conjunction with her own past selves." (Publishers Weekly)

Includes bibliographical references

Bronk, William

Selected poems; selected by Henry Weinfield. New Directions 1995 80p pa $8.95   **811**
1. Poetry -- By individual authors
ISBN 978-0-8112-1314-1; 0-8112-1314-5

LC 95-290

"Bronk's poems are almost entirely abstract and disembodied . . . his language desiccated but also conversationally halting and embedded. There is no flesh, no world, precious little metaphor—as though every human attachment is cheating. If anything seems to work—such as cause and effect—it never adds up to anything. . . . Bronk is thinking and thinking, as purely as possible, about how we want—want not to be alone, want things to matter, want to feel that we are connected to reality. His poems are all about wanting and how there is no end to it." Poetry Foundation

Brooks, Gwendolyn

The **essential** Gwendolyn Brooks; Elizabeth Alexander, editor. Library of America 2005 148p il (American poets project) $20   **811**
1. Poetry -- By individual authors
ISBN 978-1-931082-87-7; 1-931082-87-1

LC 2005-44162

"A book like [this] can't make the statement that needs to be made: Gwendolyn Brooks is as important to twentieth-century American poetry as Robert Lowell. . . . Her best poems offer a curative, not only to the narcissistic gloom that we've inherited from the Confessionals, but to Eliot's over-aestheticized visions of social life. That Brooks's purposes were so different from Eliot's only strengthens the connection. It shows the vitality of true poetic inspiration, how it can cut across time, temperament, race, and even the motives of its own practitioners." Poetry (Modern Poetry Association)

In Montgomery, and other poems. Third World Press 2003 146p $22.95   **811**
1. African Americans -- Poetry 2. Poetry -- By individual authors
ISBN 0-88378-232-4

LC 2003-50749

This is a "posthumous collection consisting primarily of dramatic monologues in a stunning variety of voices, from those of urban children to Winnie Mandela's. Reading the title sequence resembles randomly tuning a radio dial to listen to the diverse voices of Montgomery, Alabama, a city of 'leaning and lostness, glazed paralysis.' . . . Especially moving are the children's monologues. . . . Brooks captures the fierce purity of these children's needs and desires. Her loving witness never sounded more clearly than in these late poems." Booklist

Budbill, David

Happy life. Copper Canyon Press 2011 117p pa $16   **811**
1. Poetry -- By individual authors
ISBN 978-1-55659-374-1

LC 2011

The poems evoke "a recognizable immediacy and honesty, accompanied by an endearing wit. . . . Budbill's economical, brush-stroke approach . . . evinces a hard-won clarity, a pure, human tone." Libr J

Bukowski, Charles

★ The **pleasures** of the damned; poems, 1951-1993. edited by John Martin. Ecco 2007 556p $29.95   **811**
1. Poetry -- By individual authors
ISBN 978-0-06-122843-8; 0-06-122843-5

LC 2007-282394

This book is "an insightful walk through the work of a poet by the man who knew him best, and it reveals Bukowski in the many, often conflicting dimensions that make him such a popular, accessible, and, yes, great artist. . . . This extraordinary collection establishes Bukowski as much more than just another West Coast Beat poet." Washington Post

Burnshaw, Stanley

The **collected** poems and selected prose; foreword by Thomas F Stanley. University of Texas Press 2002 487p il (Harry Ransom Humanities Research Center) $50   **811**
1. Poetry -- By individual authors
ISBN 978-0-292-70909-6; 0-292-70909-9

LC 2001-52226

"Stanley Burnshaw is one of those men of letters who are so variously productive, and for so long, that they can too easily be taken for granted as merely part of the climate. . . . Since any poet considers himself—and deserves to be considered—a poet first of all, it is wonderful news that Burnshaw's work has now been made available for a new generation of readers. The Collected Poems and Selected Prose . . . allows us to see Burnshaw as a genuine and very American heir of the Romantic tradition in poetry, who has pursued the highest themes over his long career." New Republic

Includes bibliographical references

Callow, Philip

From noon to starry night: a life of Walt Whitman. Dee, I.R. 1992 394p il $28.50; pa $14.95 **811**
1. Poets 2. Authors 3. Essayists
ISBN 0-929587-95-2; 1-56663-133-5 pa

LC 92-5311

"Infused with tenderness and respect, this fine biography deciphers the complexity of Whitman's sexuality and passionate creativity while celebrating his abiding compassion and grandeur of spirit." Booklist

Includes bibliographical references

Carr, Julie
100 notes on violence. Ahsahta Press, Boise State University 2010 109p pa $19 **811**
1. Violence -- Poetry 2. Poetry -- By individual authors
ISBN 978-1-934103-11-1; 1-934103-11-X
LC 2009-26057
"In evocative, powerfully disquieting knife thrusts of verse, Carr examines the human propensity to violence, displayed here in 'notes' that range from personal anecdote to news reports to a lullaby shouted down by the voice of a murderer." Libr J

Includes bibliographical references

Carruth, Hayden
★ **Toward** the distant islands; new & selected poems. edited and with an introduction by Sam Hamill. Copper Canyon Press 2006 181p pa $17 **811**
1. Poetry -- By individual authors
ISBN 1-55659-236-1 pa
LC 2005-28705
Carruth's "books encompass Frostian tales of farm life with New England eccentrics, compilations of haiku, long and unguarded poems of erotic devotion, autobiographical laments, and sensitive odes to jazz greats. . . . All sides of Carruth's oeuvre find a place in this welcome volume. . . . The selection here gives just enough of everything Carruth has learned, and he has learned a lot, especially about the ways and landscapes of New England." Publ Wkly

Carson, Anne
Autobiography of red; a novel in verse. Knopf 1998 149p hardcover o.p. pa $12 **811**
1. Poetry -- By individual authors
ISBN 0-375-70129-X pa
LC 97-49472
"Is it poetry? Is it a novel in verse? A fable? A myth? However you define Carson's distinctive and wildly inventive new work, it is riveting reading. . . . Wistful yet whimsical, offhand yet intense, funky yet erudite . . . this is a reading experience like no other." Libr J

The **beauty** of the husband; a fictional essay in 29 tangos. Knopf 2001 147p $24; pa $12 **811**
1. Poetry -- By individual authors
ISBN 0-375-40804-5; 0-375-70757-3 pa
LC 00-62002
This poem is "at once the story of a failed marriage and an exploration of Romantic notions of beauty and truth. But Carson's idiosyncratic voice and her punchy declarative style—'You want a clean life I live a dirty one'—quickly make it clear that hers is a thoroughly modern take on the intimate cruelties of married life. And this is the primary pleasure of her writing: it is both entirely new and strangely familiar, like remembering a private language we thought we'd forgotten." New Yorker

Men in the off hours. Knopf 2000 166p il hardcover o.p. pa $12 **811**
1. Poetry -- By individual authors
ISBN 0-375-70756-5 pa
LC 00-267850
The author "makes bold references to everyone from Oedipus to Akhamatova, but the effect of these astute, gemlike little poems is less a history lesson than a challenging conversation in a sunlit garden." Libr J

Carson, Anne, 1950-
Nox. New Directions 2010 un il $29.95 **811**
1. Poetry -- By individual authors
ISBN 978-0-8112-1870-2; 0-8112-1870-8
LC 2009-01330
This "is an epitaph in the form of a book, a facsimile of a handmade book Carson wrote and created after the death of her brother." (N Y Times Book Rev)
The "book comes in a box the color of a rainy day, with a sliver of a family snapshot on the front. Inside is a Xeroxquality reproduction of a notebook, made after the death of her brother, including text and photographs and letters, pasted-in inkjet printouts, handwriting, paintings and collage. 'Nox' has no page numbers, and it's accordion-folded. It carries a whiff of visual art multiple or gift shop souvenir or 'Griffin & Sabine.' But trust me: it's an Anne Carson book. Maybe her best." N Y Times Book Rev

Red doc>; Anne Carson. 1st ed. Alfred A. Knopf 2013 167 p. (hardcover) $24.95; (ebook) $74.85 **811**
1. Epic poetry 2. Monsters -- Poetry 3. Literature -- Adaptations 4. Epic poetry, Greek -- Adaptations
ISBN 0307960587; 9780307960580; 9780307960597
LC 2012032322
This book, by Anne Carson, is a mixed poetry-prose genre story following the author's character Geryon from her 1988 book "Autobiography of Red." The book "finds a way to push Geryon into new territories of dry, vaudevillian Americana. Whether she's talking war vets, flying cows, Latin etymology or Elvis, Carson once again blurs the lines of prose and poetry, and challenging both genres within a single poem." (American Poet)

Carver, Raymond
All of us; the collected poems. Knopf 1998 xxx, 386p hardcover o.p. pa $15 **811**
1. Poetry -- By individual authors
ISBN 978-0-375-70380-5; 0-375-70380-2
LC 98-15880
"The great short story writer's poems are dark and funny, like the stories, and tell of domestic discord, crazy adven-

tures and sweet intimacies, sometimes with sorrow but more often with thankfulness and affection." Booklist

Includes bibliographical references

A **new** path to the waterfall; poems. introduction by Tess Gallagher. Atlantic Monthly Press 1989 xxxi, 126p hardcover o.p. pa $14 **811**
 1. Poetry -- By individual authors
 ISBN 978-0-87113-374-8 pa; 0-87113-374-1 pa
 LC 88-34989

"In her moving introduction, Carver's widow, writer Tess Gallagher, notes how often a particular poem calls to mind a corresponding story, and the reverse is also true. Indeed, to know Carver by his prose is to know him only partially. Master at illuminating those often mundane moments that starkly dramatize entire lives, Carver was also master at creating mood, and many of those poems have a striking lyrical intensity, especially when Carver unflinchingly faces death while celebrating life. A coda to a remarkable literary career." Libr J

Ciardi, John
 The **collected** poems of John Ciardi; compiled and edited by Edward M. Cifelli. University of Ark. Press 1997 xxxii, 618p hardcover o.p. pa $34.95 **811**
 1. Poetry -- By individual authors
 ISBN 978-1-55728-449-5; 1-55728-449-0
 LC 96-46331

"This volume supersedes the earlier Selected Poems (1984) providing a vastly more comprehensive sampling of Ciardi's work: 450 poems culled from over 20 individual volumes published between 1940 and 1993. In it we find testimony to Ciardi's desire to achieve not 'a voice,' a style formed to forward an author's individuality, but 'voice'— one that is determined by the externals the poet addresses." Libr J

Clark, Tom
 ★ **Light** & shade; new and selected poems. introduction by Amy Gerstler. Coffee House Press 2006 338p pa $20 **811**
 1. Poetry -- By individual authors
 ISBN 1-56689-183-3
 LC 2005-35810

"Disarmingly casual yet saturated with loss, Clark's body of work revels in simplicities: lovers, friends, cities and landscapes (New York, Southern California, the Southwest), baseball, basketball, modern painters, sad weather, brief visions and ethereal promises. All make repeat appearances in a poetry rooted at once in spontaneity and in High Romantic aspiration." Publ Wkly

Clifton, Lucille
 Mercy; poems. 1st ed; BOA Editions 2004 79p (American poets continuum series) $22; pa $14.95 **811**
 1. Poetry -- By individual authors
 ISBN 1-929918-54-2; 1-929918-55-0 pa
 LC 2004-10396

"These are poems where great restraint mingles with disarming primal imagery to convey poems which hold tremendous emotional weight." Va Q Rev

Clifton, Lucille, 1936-2010
 ★ The **collected** poems of Lucille Clifton 1965-2010; edited by Kevin Young and Michael S. Glaser ; foreword by Toni Morrison ; afterword by Kevin Young. BOA Editions 2012 xxxiv, 769 p.p **811**
 1. Women -- Poetry 2. Feminism -- Poetry 3. African Americans -- Poetry
 ISBN 1934414905; 9781934414903
 LC 2012014244

This book, edited by Kevin Young and Michael S. Glaser, "combines all eleven of Lucille Clifton's published collections with more than fifty previously unpublished poems. The unpublished poems feature early poems from 1965-1969 . . . [and] a collection-in-progress titled the book of days (2008). . . . In the last year of her life, she was named the first African American woman to receive the . . . Ruth Lilly Poetry Prize . . . and was posthumously awarded the Robert Frost Medal." (Publisher's note)

Cloud, Abigail
 Sylph; Poems. Abigail Cloud. Pleiades Press 2014 88 p. (pbk. : alk. paper) $17.95 **811**
 1. Poetry -- Collections
 ISBN 0807156930; 9780807156933
 LC 2014931676

In this book of poems, Abigail Cloud "draws inspiration from nineteenth-century European Romantic ballets, which often portrayed scorned females as mystical spirits such as sylphs, shades, and wilis. Some of these creatures seduced men into dancing until they died punishment for inconstancy or lured them into love. For Cloud, the dark gravity that holds these enchanters to the earth is the same as our own and thus these demons are as everyday as air." (Publisher's note)

Cole, Henri
 Middle earth; poems. Farrar, Straus & Giroux 2003 55p $23; pa $11 **811**
 1. Poetry -- By individual authors
 ISBN 0-374-20881-6; 0-374-52928-0 pa
 LC 2002-29776

The author "examines the dichotomies between life and death, animal and human, and the lover and the beloved. Many of the poems, including, 'My Tea Ceremony' and 'Self-Portrait at the Red Princess,' show a marked Japanese influence; others record a grown son's grief over the death of his father. . . . Cole writes with clarity and an emotive resonance. These poems succeed as the best poems do: they transport the reader to other worlds, no less beautiful or complicated than our own. Highly recommended." Libr J

Collins, Billy
 Nine horses; poems. Random House 2002 120p $21.95; pa $12.95 **811**
 1. Poetry -- By individual authors
 ISBN 1-4000-6177-6; 0-375-75520-9 pa
 LC 2002-24868

Collins is "often able to proceed unburdened by many of the tools—assonance, alliteration, wordplay, complex metrics—that hang from the poet's belt; he makes his way in the world by being funny." N Y Times Book Rev

✓★ **Sailing** alone around the room; new and selected poems. Random House 2001 171p $21.95; pa $13.95 **811**
1. Poetry -- By individual authors
ISBN 0-375-50380-3; 0-375-75519-5 pa

LC 99-52861

"Collins will tackle any topic: his subject matter varies from snow days to Aristotle to forgetfulness. The results are accessible but not trite, comical but not laughable, and well crafted but not overly flamboyant. Collins relies heavily on imagery, which becomes the cornerstone of the entire volume." Libr J

✓ The **trouble** with poetry and other poems; Billy Collins. Random House 2005 88p $22.95 **811**
1. Poetry -- By individual authors
ISBN 0-375-50382-X

LC 2005-46562

"Skeptical of love and scornful of pretension, Collins is breathtaking in his appreciation of the earth's beauty and the precious daily routines that define life." Booklist

The **Columbia** history of American poetry; Jay Parini, editor; Brett C. Millier, associate editor. Columbia Univ. Press 1993 xxxi, 894p $86.50 **811**
1. Poetry -- By individual authors 2. American poetry -- History and criticism
ISBN 0-231-07836-6

LC 92-29399

"These 31 essays by various experts in the field interrogate, dismantle, and ultimately reassemble the history of poetry in the United States, from the work of the slave George Moses Horton . . . to the writings of Beat, Black Arts, and Marxist-oriented Language Poets of today. The great figures of the past—Whitman, Poe, Eliot, and so on—still loom, yet each time we are made to see them in some new way. . . . An essential volume that shows how poetry intersects with our lives and vice versa." Libr J
Includes bibliographical references

The **complete** poems; Philip Larkin ; edited by Archie Burnett. Farrar, Straus and Giroux 2012 729 p. **811**
1. English poetry 2. Poetry -- Collections 3. English poetry -- History and criticism
ISBN 0374126968; 9780374126964

LC 2011945978

This collection edited by Archie Burnett "brings together all of Philip Larkin's poems. In addition to those that appear in 'Collected Poems' (1988) and 'Early Poems and Juvenilia' (2005), some unpublished pieces from Larkin's typescripts and workbooks are included, as well as verse . . . that had been tucked away in his letters. . . . Larkin's poems are [also] given a comprehensive commentary. This . . . covers closely relevant historical contexts, persons and places, allusions and echoes, and linguistic usage. Prominence is given to the poet's comments on his own poems, which often out-

line the circumstances that gave rise to a poem or state what he was trying to achieve." (Publisher's note)

Corbett, William
The **Whalen** poem; drawings by Philip Guston. Hanging Loose Press 2011 61p pa $16 **811**
1. Poetry -- By individual authors
ISBN 978-1-934909-13-3

LC 2010-51639

"Corbett composed this book-length poem, he writes in his introduction, over the summer and autumn of 2007 while in Vermont reading an advanced copy of the collected poems of Philip Whalen (1923-2002). The result is truly a poem for summer, as flighty as a hummingbird, now pausing, now darting too fast to follow to the next luminous blooming. The poem's fluidity offers a delightful ride if one is willing to go along with it. Corbett's economy of language gives him the facility to flit between images, allusions and occurrences, be they personal or seasonal, and his wide ken allows him to track events on several planes at once. . . . Whalen seems to be a spiritual adviser for this poem, a teacher who proved that the paths of the mind, traced mindfully, can be poetry. . . . [The poem] displays an open-ended lyricism that resists closure with the awareness — the insistence — that nothing is ever over, life or a work of literature." Prague Post

Cording, Robert
Walking with Ruskin; poems. CavanKerry Press 2010 93p (Notable voices) pa $16 **811**
1. Poetry -- By individual authors
ISBN 978-1-933880-21-1; 1-933880-21-X

LC 2010-13639

These poems combine the "sacred and the mundane in unexpected ways. Even if you don't know much about poetry, Cording's poems tend to be fairly accessible because of their narrative approach, as well as their immersion in the everyday. The poems in this volume take as their subject matter a mother's grief for her child, looking though Czeslaw Milosz's glasses (literally), aging, taking a walk with a dog, and observing woodpeckers, swallows and starlings. . . . Above all, the poems in Walking with Ruskin celebrate the virtue of attentiveness to the created world around us." Christ and Pop Culture

Crane, Hart
★ **Complete** poems and selected letters. Library of America 2006 849p $40 **811**
1. Poetry -- By individual authors
ISBN 1-93108-299-5

LC 2006-40922

This volume "gathers all of the author's poetry and collected prose with a large sampling of his letters, some appearing in print for the first time. The correspondents include top writers William Carlos Williams, Marianne Moore, e.e. cummings, and Katherine Anne Porter. A good one-stop resource for Crane." Libr J

Creeley, Robert

The **collected** poems of Robert Creeley. University of California Press 1982 2v v1 o.p.; v1 pa $27.50; v2 $60; v2 pa $24.95 **811**

1. Poetry -- By individual authors

ISBN 0-520-04243-3 v1; 978-0-520-24158-9 v1 pa; 978-0-520-24159-6 v2; 978-0-520-25620-0 v2 pa

Creeley's style is "notably spare and laconic; his primary subject is love and the infinite incongruities that characterize love relationships. There is a distinct dearth of imagery in his poetry; the themes are rendered in a cerebral rather than sensual manner. For Creeley, the intent of the poem is definition, not description." Reader's Ency. 4th edition

Cronk, Laura

Having been an accomplice; Laura Cronk. 1st ed. Persea Books 2012 68 p. (original trade pbk. : alk. paper) $15 **811**

1. Love poetry 2. Poetry -- Collections 3. American poetry -- Women authors -- Collections

ISBN 0892554134; 9780892554133

LC 2011042830

Lexi Rudnitsky First Prize: Poetry (2011)

This poetry collection, by Laura Cronk, winner of the 2011 Lexi Rudnitsky First Book Prize in Poetry, offers "love poems and interior monologues. . . . Within them, Laura Cronk writes, 'I want to blow up the Law with Language, having run my tongue around my mouth ten thousand times. Instead of not speaking, I want to speak.'" (Publisher's note)

Includes bibliographical references

Cummings, E. E.

★ **Complete** poems, 1904-1962; containing all the published poetry. edited by George J. Firmage. rev corr & expanded ed; Norton 1994 xxxii, 1102p $50 **811**

1. Poetry -- By individual authors

ISBN 978-0-87140-152-6; 0-87140-152-5

LC 91-29158

Expanded version of Complete poems, 1913-1962 (1972)

"This volume has been prepared directly from the poet's original manuscripts, preserving the original typography and format. It includes all the previously published works, from Tulips (1922) to Etcetera (1983), as well as 36 uncollected poems that originally appeared in little magazines or anthologies." Libr J

Dickinson, Emily

★ The **poems** of Emily Dickinson; edited by R.W. Franklin. Reading ed; Belknap Press 1999 692p $34.50; pa $18.50 **811**

1. Poetry -- By individual authors

ISBN 978-0-674-67624-4; 0-674-67624-6; 978-0-674-01824-2 pa; 0-674-01824-9 pa

LC 99-11821

"Within the guidelines Franklin has set himself, his choices of versions and of alternatives within versions are extremely sensible-and they are efficiently recorded at the end of the volume, making this the first time any volume of Dickinson's poems aimed at a general audience has offered information about the derivation of its texts." Raritan

Dickman, Michael

The **end** of the west. Copper Canyon Press 2009 89p pa $15 **811**

1. Poetry -- By individual authors

ISBN 978-1-55659-289-8; 1-556-59289-2

LC 2008-39990

"Some form of light—sunlight, moonlight, starlight, streetlight— appears in every one of the 18 poems in [this book.] . . . Slight and spare, the poems' frequent recurring themes accumulate beneficially, linking all the individual poems into one, more substantial, piece. Nothing grand takes place in these poems, but the quietness of the language and the creeping, sinister subject matter (heroin addiction, abusive fathers) make this . . . book captivating and very readable." Publ Wkly

Donnelly, Timothy

The **cloud** corporation. Wave Books 2010 153p **811**

1. Poetry -- By individual authors

ISBN 9781933517476

LC 2010-13946

This is a book of poems by Timothy Donnelly was the winner of the 2012 Kingsley Tufts Poetry Award. It includes "[p]rocedural poems, such as one that repurposes language from the Patriot Act . . . [and] a pair of . . . long poems [that] introduce a mind agoraphobicly trapped in its vast vocabulary." (Publishers Weekly) Topics include "finance and/ or capitalism . . . the political economy, [and] the environment". (Poetry)

"Timothy Donnelly pushes abstraction to the limits in this book—anything more, and the book would have collapsed. The book consists mostly of free-flowing tercets, lightly stressed, very much like the light feathery movement of clouds or water. The book is almost a manifesto against the utilization of images and making them the backbone of poetry. . . . This is a very existential, Sartrean project, a constant Sysiphian sifting of indispensable abstract thoughts, and a very challenging book to read." Huffington Post

Dorn, Edward

★ **Way** more West; new and selected poems. introduction by Dale Smith; edited by Michael Rothenberg. Penguin Books 2007 321p (Penguin poets) $20 **811**

1. Poetry -- By individual authors

ISBN 978-0-14-303869-6

LC 2006-50727

"Throughout his career, he was the least endearing, domesticated or predictable of poets, always determined to go his own way, no matter what anyone thought. And if he hadn't been that way, American poetry would be a lot less vital and interesting." N Y Times Book Rev

Includes bibliographical references

Doty, Mark

Fire to fire; new and selected poems. Harper 2008 336p $22.95; pa $15.95 **811**

1. Poetry -- By individual authors

ISBN 978-0-06-075247-7; 0-06-075247-5; 978-0-06-075251-4 pa; 0-06-075251-3 pa

LC 2007-44646

The author "combines new poems with the best of his previous volumes. His narrative style is expansive, filled with what has been described as a 'lyric glitter' that creates radiance around the ordinary." Libr J

Includes bibliographical references

Dove, Rita

American smooth; poems. W.W. Norton 2004 143p $22.95; pa $13.95 **811**
1. Poetry -- By individual authors
ISBN 0-393-05987-1; 0-393-32744-2 pa

LC 2004-11793

"In these free-verse poems, Dove speaks from her own perspective—as well as from that of biblical characters, black soldiers from World War I, a ten-year-old girl from Harlem, several musicians, and a pair of dancers. The selections work by lists, line breaks where ideas collide, and a juxtaposition of voices. Then using razor-sharp metaphors, Dove goes for the jugular and usually finds it. Although the book's sense of audience seems inconsistent, with some poems suitable for A Child's Garden of Verses and others for The Kama Sutra, the poems are evocative." Libr J

On the bus with Rosa Parks; poems. Norton 1999 95p hardcover o.p. pa $12.95 **811**
1. Poetry -- By individual authors
ISBN 0-393-32026-X

LC 98-45057

Dove's "poems effortlessly suggest grand narratives and American myths, yet ground themselves tersely in localities, characters, practicalities and particulars. This seventh collection leads off with a Dove specialty, the historical sequence: her 'Cameos' lend broad, social relevance to an intermittently abandoned Depression-era wife and her family." Publ Wkly

Selected poems. Vintage Bks. 1993 xxvi, 210p pa $13 **811**
1. Poetry -- By individual authors
ISBN 0-679-75080-0

LC 93-26112

"This volume places three previous collections under one cover. . . . The selection begins with The Yellow House on the Corner, Dove's first book, most notable for its poems derived from slave narratives. Museum, her second book, offers a potpourri of work that ranges over several continents and many millenia; Dove's tirelessly exact language illuminates the lives of saints, contemporary lifestyles, and Greek myths." Booklist

Downing, Brandon

Lake Antiquity; poems, 1996-2008. Fence Books 2009 184p il pa $40 **811**
1. Poetry -- By individual authors
ISBN 978-1-934200-27-8; 1-934200-27-1

"Drawing on the tradition of fanciful collage practiced by such poets as John Ashbery, David Shapiro, and Joe Brainard, Brandon Downing wields his own scissors to cut a distinctive patch within this New York School specialty. . . . Downing has sequenced his collages with cinematic pacing; you fly through these pages as you might in a dream." Bookforum

Dugan, Alan

★ **Poems** seven; new and complete poetry. Seven Stories Press 2001 422p $35; pa $18.95 **811**
1. Poetry -- By individual authors
ISBN 1-58322-265-0; 1-58322-512-9 pa

LC 2001-41089

This collection documents "Dugan's project of comic, bleak and formally varied commentary on a dirty, terminally frayed and yet attractive America. . . . This carefully constructed, funny and sometimes unvarying volume combines all six of Dugan's previous books with a decade's worth of new verse." Publ Wkly

Duhamel, Denise

Ka -ching! University of Pittsburgh Press 2009 86p il (Pitt poetry series) $14.95 **811**
1. Poetry -- By individual authors
ISBN 978-0-8229-6021-8; 0-8229-6021-4 pa

"What better poetry for the current economic period than Denise Duhamel's hymns to money, ATMs, her IRA accounts, the Treasury, gambling. . .and Sean Penn? . . . Using prose poems, sonnets, sestinas, and other forms in Ka-Ching!, Duhamel is a wily technician, a touching humanist, a poet deserving stardom." Entertainment Wkly

Duncan, Robert Edward

Selected poems; [by] Robert Duncan; edited by Robert J. Bertholf. New Directions 1993 147p hardcover o.p. pa $12.95 **811**
1. Poetry -- By individual authors
ISBN 978-0-8112-1227-4; 0-8112-1227-0

LC 92-35812

Duncan "was one of the true masters of contemporary American poetry. His oeuvre is by turns lyrical, experimental, archaic, visionary and political. . . . In Bertholf's brief, insightful introduction, he makes necessary connections between the often-neglected early work and the later masterpieces." Publ Wkly

Dunn, Stephen

Different hours; poems. Norton 2000 121p $22; pa $12.95 **811**
1. Poetry -- By individual authors
ISBN 0-393-04986-8; 0-393-32232-7 pa

LC 00-30556

"Stephen Dunn's poetry is strangely easy to like: philosophical but not arid, lyrical but rarely glib, his storytelling balanced effortlessly between the casual and the vivid. But don't mistake that ease for lack of staying power." N Y Times Book Rev

Local visitations; poems. Norton 2003 96p $21.95 **811**
1. Poetry -- By individual authors
ISBN 0-393-05200-1

LC 2002-14204

"The opening section of poems recasts Dunn's average American as the mythic Sisyphus, imprisoned by repetitive work ('a repetition/which would never mean more/at the end than at the start') and yet bereft without it ('But more often he finds himself dreaming/of his rock, wishing it back, the better/to defend himself against so many hours'). Nearly half the collection transports 19th-century literary figures to contemporary New Jersey towns ('Mary Shelley in Brigantine,' 'Hawthorne in Tuckerton'), a series of poems more attractive in concept than in practice, where the subjects often fail to transcend the contrivance they inhabit." Libr J

Loosestrife. Norton 1996 96p $19; pa $12 **811**
1. Poetry -- By individual authors
ISBN 0-393-03982-X; 0-393-31683-1 pa
LC 96-1238
"Dunn understands that there is sorrow in beauty and a 'strange loneliness' even in pleasure, and he examines these dichotomies in language and form as clear and chilling as ice. We feel knocked off balance by the end of one line, then steadied by the beginning of the next." Booklist

New & selected poems, 1974-1994. Norton 1994 296p hardcover o.p. pa $16.95 **811**
1. Poetry -- By individual authors
ISBN 978-0-393-31300-0; 0-393-31300-X
LC 93-33212
"Dunn might be called a Neo-Horatian poet. He is level-headed, witty, conversational in his diction, and willing to see in domestic life his means for attaining and imparting wisdom. Yet Dunn's variations on Horatian odes and epodes are rarely the drab reportorial missives from the daily grind which are found in so much contemporary poetry. He knows that his first duty is to keep the quotidian life interesting, and this is no mean feat. . . . This is to say that Dunn's a gifted talker, a kind of querulous raconteur, and even his less successful poems are highly readable." Poetry (Modern Poetry Association)

Eady, Cornelius
Brutal imagination; poems. Putnam 2001 108p $24; pa $13 **811**
1. Poetry -- By individual authors
ISBN 0-399-14718-7; 0-399-14720-9 pa
LC 00-62674
In this "collection of poetry, Eady invokes a chorus of fictional black characters, from Uncle Tom to the invented criminal whom Susan Smith blamed for the kidnapping of her children. A white woman's 'stray thought,' this man haunts the best of these spare, stirring poems. If the poet's premise—the personification of a black figment of the white imagination—is complex, his verse is unsettlingly direct." New Yorker

Edson, Russell
The **rooster's** wife; poems. BOA Editions 2005 91p hardcover o.p. pa $14.95 **811**
1. Poetry -- By individual authors
ISBN 978-1-929918-63-8; 1-929918-63-1
LC 2004-24831
"Edson's prose poems are directly and indirectly concerned with feelings customarily suppressed during wakefulness, whose content is violent, scatological, and, especially, sexual. An Edson prose poem, however amusing and ridiculous—however jokelike—it may be, is disturbing. . . . Laughter never blunts the edges of Edson's elegantly maculate conceptions." Booklist

Eliot, T. S.
★ **Collected** poems, 1909-1962. Harcourt Brace Jovanovich 1963 221p $23 **811**
1. Poetry -- By individual authors
ISBN 0-15-118978-1
This volume contains the complete text of 'Collected poems, 1909-1935,' the 'Four quartets,' and several other poems accompanied by brief prefatory notes

★ The **complete** poems and plays, 1909-1950. Harcourt Brace & Co. 1952 392p $35 **811**
1. Poetry -- By individual authors
ISBN 0-15-121185-X

Ellis, Thomas Sayers, 1963-
Skin, Inc. identity repair poems. Graywolf Press 2010 181p il $23.00 **811**
1. Poetry -- By individual authors
ISBN 1555975674; 9781555975678
LC 2010-922920
This is a collection of poetry by the author of The Maverick Room (2005).
This collection of the author's poems "constitutes an impassioned argument for revitalizing America's calcified literary culture ('Flat, fixed and finished'), whose conventional assumptions about the expression of racial identity severely limit the aesthetic choices available to both writers and readers of color. . . . With honesty, eloquence, and precision, Ellis calls for resistance to the outward imposition of social and personal identity while acknowledging the difficulty of the task. . . . Certain to ignite debate on campuses and blogs, this work is the perfectly realized embodiment of its author's intent, likely to inspire poets of all ethnic backgrounds for some time to come." Libr J

Emerson, Ralph Waldo
★ **Collected** poems & translations. Library of Am. 1994 637p $35 **811**
1. Poetry -- By individual authors
ISBN 0-940450-28-3
LC 93-40245
Contains Emerson's published poetry, plus selections of his unpublished poetry from journals and notebooks, and some of his translations of poetry from other languages, notably Dante's La vita nuova

Encyclopedia of American poetry, the twentieth century; edited by Eric L. Haralson. Fitzroy Dearborn Pubs. 2001 846p $125 **811**
1. Reference books 2. Poets, American -- Dictionaries 3. American poetry -- Bio-bibliography
ISBN 1-57958-240-0
"The volume features more than 400 entries written by academic contributors on individual poets, landmark poems, and major topics. The poet entries are usually 1,000 to 2,000 words long and offer critical treatment of the poet's career and major achievements along with a capsule biography. . . . Approximately one-third of the poet entries include subentries for one or more landmark poems. The 'major topics' entries are longer (around 3,000 words) and include periods or movements (Black Arts movement, Dada), verse traditions (often ethnic, such as Asian American poetry), and styles

and themes (Confessional poetry, War and antiwar poetry)." Booklist

Erdrich, Louise

Original fire; selected and new poems. Harper-Collins Pubs. 2003 158p $23.95; pa $13.95　**811**
　1. Poetry -- By individual authors
　ISBN 0-06-620986-2; 0-06-093534-0 pa

LC 2003-40700

"With this volume, drawn from two previous collections and including 100 pages of new poems, {the author} presents her first collection in over a decade. . . . Poems from the first collection chronicle her Native American childhood and early schooling, while those from the second rework or invent Native American mythology. The new poems are more rooted in Catholicism and life as a middle-class American. . . . Essential reading for fans of Erdrich's fiction, this volume can be expected to draw poetry readers into the fold." Libr J

Estes, Angie

√ Tryst. Oberlin College Press 2009 75p (Field poetry series) pa $15.95　**811**
　1. Poetry -- By individual authors
　ISBN 9780932440358; 0-932440355

LC 2008-54661

"Gleeful and gorgeous, delighted by puns and other wordplay (including words from French, Latin and Italian), Estes's fast-paced free verse, rich with internal rhyme, takes rightful pride in the beauties it flaunts and explains. Her fourth collection finds, for recurrent motifs, saints' lives, medieval manuscripts, gold leaf and the alphabet. . . . Each deft poem weaves together multiple topics—some art-historical, others autobiographical—through chains of homonyms and knotty analogies." N Y Times Book Rev

Everson, Landis

Everything preserved: poems, 1955-2005; edited by Ben Mazer. Graywolf Press 2006 106p pa $15　**811**
　1. Poetry -- By individual authors
　ISBN 978-1-55597-453-4; 1-55597-453-8

LC 2006-924341

"Everson, who makes his book-length debut in his 70's as winner of the Poetry Foundation's Emily Dickinson first book award, swapped poems with a young Jack Spicer and John Ashbery, then stopped writing for 43 years until a recent creative outburst. This volume—divided into two sections, one for nine poems written between 1955 and 1960, and the other comprising the remaining 66, written since 2003—quickly establishes the charms of the playful early work. . . . The recent work is much more uneven—though much of it has been published in major literary magazines—and there are still plenty of pleasures to be found. Everson evokes the ordinary with a continually surprising touch." Publ Wkly

Every shut eye ain't asleep; an anthology of poetry by African Americans since 1945. edited by Michael Harper and Anthony Walton. Little, Brown 1994 327p hardcover o.p. pa $19　**811**
　1. American poetry -- African American authors --

Collections
　ISBN 0-316-34710-8 pa

LC 93-10788

"Using Robert Hayden and Gwendolyn Brooks's poetry as 'emblematic' successes, this anthology selects 35 African American poets (spanning three generations) who were born between 1913 and 1962 and came of age after 1945. Besides the well-known Imamu Baraka, Lucille Clifton, Rita Dove, and Etheridge Knight, the editors feature little-known or younger poets like Elizabeth Alexander, Gerald Barrax, Jayne Cortex, and Dolores Kendrick." Libr J

Fagan, Deirdre

√ Critical companion to Robert Frost; a literary reference to his life and work. Facts on File 2007 454p il $75　**811**
　1. Poets 2. Authors
　ISBN 0-8160-6182-3; 978-0-8160-6182-2

LC 2006-13269

"This encyclopedic guide offers critical entries on each of Frost's published poems, including such classics as 'The Road Not Taken,' 'Stopping By Woods on a Snowy Evening,' and 'The Death of the Hired Man.'" Publisher's note
　Includes bibliographical references

Fay-LeBlanc, Gibson

Death of a ventriloquist; poems. by Gibson Fay-LeBlanc. University of North Texas Press 2012 x, 85 p.p　**811**
　1. Voice -- Poetry 2. Fatherhood -- Poetry 3. Poetry -- Collections 4. Ventriloquism -- Poetry 5. Ventriloquists -- Poetry
　ISBN 157441447X; 9781574414479; 9781574414554

LC 2011042003

2011 Winner, Vassar Miller Prize in Poetry

In this poetry collection, "[Gibson] Fay-LeBlanc's lines . . . lure, guide, and yank us through poems in which 'a redstart in the boneset and spotted knapweed' and 'eel grass winding your ankles' are always waiting to dance upon the tongue. Whether he's overhearing a conversation in a tavern or the music stuck in his head, Fay-LeBlanc uses his ventriloquist to raise important questions about how we perform ourselves through language, creating a voice that locates its source in a 'Prayer of Glass' because it must hide its true source from us. . . . [I]n 'Notes on Colic,' where, in a dream, we suddenly see 'The foreman of the pity factory,/ where they produce the tiniest/ violins known to man// . . .that guy, / who can't stop itching his welts // . . .does a little jig /to make you feel better.'" (Publishers Weekly)
　Includes bibliographical references

Fearing, Kenneth

Selected poems; Robert Polito, editor. Library of America 2004 xxi, 183p (American poets project) $20　**811**
　1. Poetry -- By individual authors
　ISBN 978-1-931082-57-0; 1-932082-57-X

LC 2003-60482

"Kenneth Fearing writes noir poetry, which is no surprise, considering that he also wrote several noir novels. . . . His poems flirt with narrative (but rarely commit), and they're written in a jittery free verse that sounds like the byproduct of a paranoid, slightly strung-out Whitman. . . . There are plenty of people currently writing variations on Fearing (possibly without being aware of it), but it's tough to beat the stylish chill of the original. These poems may be leaves the wind blows from one gutter to another, but sometimes the gutter's the only place to be." Poetry (Modern Poetry Association)

Fenton, James

Selected poems. Farrar, Straus & Giroux 2006 196p pa $14   **811**

1. Poetry -- By individual authors

ISBN 978-0-374-26065-1; 0-374-26065-6

LC 2006-2691

This "collection offers an introduction to the work of a leading British poet and former professor of poetry at Oxford. Love and menace are the principal muses for Fenton's dark wit. Whether describing how an ex is safe because she's no longer loved . . . or narrating war's awful arithmetic . . . the control behind these lines is often terrifying." Publ Wkly

Ferlinghetti, Lawrence

These are my rivers; new & selected poems, 1955-1993. New Directions 1993 308p il hardcover o.p. pa $13.95   **811**

1. Poetry -- By individual authors

ISBN 0-8112-1273-4

LC 93-10383

"Reading this hefty selection from 12 previous volumes, plus 50 pages of new poems, we realize how accurately the poet described himself in 1979: a man who 'thinks he's Dylan Thomas and Bob Dylan rolled together with Charlie Chaplin thrown in.' . . . His style is recognizable throughout—phlegmatic poems running several pages, often lacking stanza breaks, with short lines at the left margin or moving across the page as hand follows eye." Libr J

Ferry, David

Bewilderment; new poems and translations. David Ferry. University of Chicago Press 2012 xii, 113 p.p (paper : alkaline paper) $18   **811**

1. Death -- Poetry 2. Future life -- Poetry 3. Poetry -- Collections

ISBN 0226244881; 0226244903; 9780226244884; 9780226244907

LC 2011050366

National Book Award Finalist: Poetry (2012)

This is a collection of poems from 88-year-old poet David Ferry. The poems here "are concerned with personal memories, death, and life beyond corporeality. The translations that dot the book—of Catullus, Virgil, and Horace; Rilke, Montale, and Cavafy; and the Anglo-Saxon Genesis A ("The Offering of Isaac")—touch those themes, too." (Booklist)

Includes bibliographical references

Finney, Nikky

★ **Head** off & split; poems. TriQuarterly Books/ Northwestern University 2011 97p pa $15.95   **811**

1. Poetry -- By individual authors

ISBN 978-0-8101-5216-8; 0-8101-5216-9

LC 2010-28888

"Finney picks through the past selectively, and with flicks of the blade that are personal, political, poetic and always musical, gives us back the present moment with an intensity that makes a reader feel as if, until reading her volume, we have been unfed." Cleveland Plain Dealer

Flynn, Nick

The **captain** asks for a show of hands; poems. Graywolf Press 2011 94p $22   **811**

1. Poetry -- By individual authors

ISBN 978-1-55597-574-6

LC 2010-937512

In this poetry collection, the author "considers the quandary of soldiers trained never to question authority and the profound betrayal of trust encoded in orders to commit torture. His masterfully concise poems deploy lulling meter, evocative images, and shocking disclosures. . . . Each word is a lit match, a thrown stone, a howling blast, a choking torrent. Flynn has forged daringly intimate and clarion poems of conscience." Booklist

Forche, Carolyn

Blue hour. HarperCollins Pubs. 2003 73p hardcover o.p. pa $13.95   **811**

1. Poetry -- By individual authors

ISBN 0-06-009912-7; 978-0-06-009913-8 pa; 0-06-009013-5 pa

LC 2002-27270

This "gathering of elegiac meditations calls up ghostly memories both personal and universal as the poet mourns the terrible death of her grandmother, gives thanks for the blessing of her son's birth, and alludes with few words and deep feelings to the anguish of war and exile." Booklist

From totems to hip-hop; edited by Ishmael Reed. Thunder's Mouth Press 2003 xxx, 523p $34.95; pa $17.95   **811**

1. American poetry -- Collections

ISBN 1-56025-500-5; 1-56025-458-0 pa

LC 2002-75691

This is "a dynamic and original anthology, an unprecedented amalgam of poets representing many facets of American culture and society." Booklist

Frost, Robert

★ **Collected** poems, prose, & plays. Library of Am. 1995 1036p $35   **811**

1. Poetry -- By individual authors

ISBN 1-883011-06-X

LC 94-43693

This volume contains "all of the plays, a generous selection of prose, all collected poems, and 94 uncollected poems, as well as 17 poems that were previously unpublished." Libr J

Gallagher, Tess

Dear ghosts, poems. Graywolf Press 2006 140p $20   **811**

1. Poetry -- By individual authors

ISBN 1-55597-443-0

LC 2005-938149

"So compelling are Gallagher's graceful poems, they leave the reader feeling 'rearranged from the cells out.'" Booklist

Galvin, Brendan

★ **Habitat**; new and selected poems, 1965-2005. Brendan Galvin. Louisiana State University Press 2005 250p $49.95; pa $26.95 **811**
1. Poetry -- By individual authors
ISBN 0-8071-3046-X; 0-8071-3047-8 pa
LC 2004-22441
"Galvin's work is not only accessible, it turns the commonplace over into something new. A dory, a cormorant, a pack of dogs, a chickadee—all served up with the eye of someone who can take you on a trip of rediscovery into your own backyard." Cape Cod Voice

Gambito, Sarah Verdes

Delivered; poems. [by] Sarah Gambito. Persea Books 2009 64p pa $14 **811**
1. Poetry -- By individual authors
ISBN 978-0-89255-346-4
LC 2008-31269
The poems in this collection "are as much about language as they are about Gambito's Filipina heritage. . . . If disjunction is a way of talking about or recreating immigrant experience, these poems 'deliver'—that is, provide and lead us out of—the incoherences built into cultural transplantation. They are surrealistic, fierce, and playful." Libr J

Gander, Forrest

Core samples from the world; with photographs by Raymond Meeks, Graciela Iburtide and Lucas Foglia. New Directions 2011 95p il **811**
1. Poetry -- By individual authors
ISBN 0-8112-1887-2; 978-0-8112-1887-0
LC 2011-01154
"Gander is an experimental poet in the most literal sense of the word, in that each of his books attempts things that haven't been tried before, either by him or others. In this eighth collection, four sequences of poems respond to pictures by three photographers—Raymond Meeks, Graciela Iturbide, and Lucas Foglia—making of the images metaphors for people and places that are easy to see but difficult to penetrate. The poems don't describe the pictures so much as work in chorus with them. . . . Concluding each section is a piece of jumpy prose, a kind of lyric essay, narrating one of four journeys-to Xinjiang, Mexico, Bosnia-Herzegovina, and Chile. . . . In these pieces, Gander gets as close as one can to the sensations of being an outsider straining toward empathy." Publ Wkly

★ **Eye** against eye; with ten photographs by Sally Mann. New Directions 2005 80p il pa $14.95 **811**
1. Poetry -- By individual authors
ISBN 0-8112-1635-7
LC 2005-14907
The "opener, 'Burning Towers, Standing Wall,' compares the building of a Mayan wall and its destruction–both from political and natural forces–to the collapse of the Twin Towers. In three long poems, linked with pieces that contrast a couple's relationship with a boy's budding adolescence,

the reader is asked to regard the relationships between words and subjects. . . . Owing to the poems' placement and the near absence of punctuation, the reader is propelled through the verse, left with a sense of urgency and awe." Libr J

Torn awake. New Directions 2001 95p pa $13.95 **811**
1. Poetry -- By individual authors
ISBN 0-8112-1486-9
LC 2001-32657
"There is no solid ground in the world Forrest Gander conjures in his new book of poems, yet his tentativeness is one of this book's essential qualities. . . . The voices vary throughout this book's six highly speculative sequences, . . . yet again and again they call from their spectral airiness a single recurring image, an elemental configuration of man, woman and child." N Y Times Book Rev

Getty, Sarah

Bring me her heart; poems. Higganum Hill Books 2006 98p pa $12.95 **811**
1. Poetry -- By individual authors
ISBN 978-0-9741158-8-6; 0-9741158-8-6
LC 2005-23805
The author "makes meter, rhyme, and formal stanzas the vehicles of winning, natural expression." Booklist

Gibbons, Reginald

Creatures of a day; poems. Louisiana State University Press 2008 79p $45; pa $16.95 **811**
1. Poetry -- By individual authors
ISBN 978-0-8071-3317-0; 978-0-8071-3318-7 pa
LC 2007-34185
The author "presents intense encounters with everyday people amidst the historical and social contexts of everyday life. His poems are meditations on memory, obligation, love, death, celebration, and sorrow." Publisher's note
Includes bibliographical references

It's time: poems. Louisiana State Univ. Press 2002 64p $22.95; pa $15.95 **811**
1. Poetry -- By individual authors
ISBN 0-8071-2814-7; 0-8071-2815-5 pa
LC 2002-73076
"If the thoughtful poems in Gibbons' elegant seventh collection were pieces of music, they would be measured piano sonatas, each note, each word, carefully struck, precisely enunciated." Booklist

Gibran, Kahlil

★ The **Prophet**. Knopf 1923 107p il $15 **811**
1. Poetry -- By individual authors
ISBN 0-394-40428-9
A collection of poems by the mystical writer/artist, who was born in Lebanon and died in the United States, in which the prophet Almustafa deals with fundamental aspects of human life such as love, friendship, good and evil, self-knowledge, passion and reason, joy and sorrow, freedom, work, marriage and children, prayer and death

Gilbert, Jack

The **dance** most of all; poems. Alfred A. Knopf
2009 60p $25   **811**

1. Poetry -- By individual authors
ISBN 978-0-307-27076-4; 0-307-27076-9

LC 2008-44670

"These poems are deeply elegiac, looking back over a
long life lived in the various modes one comes to associate
with Gilbert: desire, love, longing and happiness. In short,
Gilbert is as Romantic as ever, but that romance is tinged
with a hard grief, a sense of loss, but ultimately one of acceptance. These are the poems of a man who realizes without reserve that his time is coming to an end. Death lingers
in the background of these lines, reflected in the landscapes
that close readers of Gilbert have come to know: Pittsburgh,
Greece, Italy, Paris, the woods of Massachusetts where he
now resides." Oregonian

★ **Refusing** heaven; poems. Knopf 2005 92p
$25   **811**

1. Poetry -- By individual authors
ISBN 1-4000-4365-4

LC 2004-48844

"Jack Gilbert is a poet of reckless charisma and its aftermaths: a catch-as-catch-can Castiglione, consigned by
the waywardness of his imagination to write his canon of
manners and gestures in lyric poetry. The poems have the
quality of brilliant, searching, addled talk after a wild night
out. There's a sort of strung-out sprezzatura to this poet, as
he bobs and weaves among the memories of old loves in
old, European cities. . . . These poems are the stream-of-consciousness work of a consciousness radically narrowed over
time, practically armored against new experience. At their
best, shuttling associatively between a few old obsessions,
they attain claustrophobic beauty that sounds like nobody
else." Poetry (Modern Poetry Association)

Gilbert, Jack, 1925-2012

Collected poems; by Jack Gilbert. Alfred A.
Knopf 2012 408 p.   **811**

1. Love poetry 2. Grief -- Poetry 3. Marriage -- Poetry
4. Poetry -- Collections
ISBN 9780307269683

LC 2011025743

This book is a collection of "poems about the joys and
complexities of romantic love, about grief and about the
power of experience deeply felt. . . . Here are also many and
many kinds of poems about travel or life in farflung places,
particularly Greece. Plentiful, too, are poems of marriage-
-its difficulties ("Eight years/ and her love for me quieted
away"), its ecstasies, and its ending: divorce is memorably
figured as "looking/ out at the bright moonlight on concrete." Gilbert is perhaps best known, however, for the
grief-stricken poems that chart the dying of and then mourning over his wife, Michiko, of whom he writes, "The arches
of her feet are like voices/ of children calling in the grove
of lemon trees,/ where my heart is as helpless as crushed
birds."" (Publishers Weekly)

Ginsberg, Allen

★ **Collected** poems, 1947-1997. HarperCollins
Publishers 2006 xx, 1189p il hardcover o.p. pa
$25.99   **811**

1. Poetry -- By individual authors
ISBN 978-0-06-113974-1; 0-06-113974-2; 978-0-06-
113975-8 pa; 0-06-113975-0 pa

LC 2006-41191

First published 1984 with title: Collected poems, 1947-
1980

This books "reprints the complete text of 1984's Collected Poems 1947-1980, along with the collections that followed: White Shroud, Cosmopolitan Greetings, and Death
and Fame, including the original book attributes of each
collection. A poet of extremes at times too trusting of his instincts, Ginsberg could be playful, angry, strident, obscene,
graceful, and hilarious in the space of a page, and by now his
readers know they are likely to encounter as many embarrassing poems as enlightening ones. Still, this compendium
provides the most complete edition of Ginsberg available."
Libr J

Spontaneous mind; selected interviews, 1958-
1996. with a preface by Václav Havel; edited by David Carter. HarperCollins Pubs. 2001 601p hardcover o.p. pa $17.95   **811**

1. Poets 2. Authors 3. Beat generation
ISBN 0-06-093082-9 pa

LC 00-40849

"The bulk of the collection [of interviews] dates from
1965-72, Ginsberg's years as countercultural symbol and
spokesman: dialogues at demonstrations and on the road,
transcripts from 'Firing Line' and the Chicago Seven trial."
N Y Times Book Rev

Includes bibliographical references

Gioia, Dana

Disappearing ink; poetry at the end of print culture. Graywolf Press 2004 271p pa $16   **811**

1. Poetry -- By individual authors 2. American poetry
-- History and criticism
ISBN 1-55597-410-4

LC 2004-104190

In this collection of essays, the author discusses the current relevance of poetry and the ways in which it is evolving
with the times.

The author "offers accessible, necessary criticism for lay
and academic readers of serious poetry." Am Book Rev

Giovanni, Nikki

Bicycles; love poems. William Morrow 2009
109p $16.95   **811**

1. Poetry -- By individual authors
ISBN 978-0-06-172645-3

"Disarming, sly, sensual, and knowing, Giovanni's poems scan like the teasing and wise songs favored by Dinah Washington and Etta James." Booklist

Blues; for all the changes: new poems. Morrow 1999 100p $15   **811**
1. Poetry -- By individual authors
ISBN 0-688-15698-3
LC 98-50996

"Giovanni never loses sight of the people in her work. In poems built with broken lines and paragraphs of prose, she spars with the ills that confront us, but every struggle has a human face." Libr J

The **collected** poetry of Nikki Giovanni, 1968-1998; chronology and notes by Virginia C. Fowler. William Morrow 2003 xliii, 452p $24.95   **811**
1. Poetry -- By individual authors
ISBN 0-06-054133-4
LC 2004-302269

"Giovanni observes and embraces the world like few other poets; seize on these poems spanning three decades, and listen to her sing." Booklist

Includes bibliographical references

Quilting the black-eyed pea; poems and not quite poems. William Morrow 2002 110p $16.95   **811**
1. Poetry -- By individual authors
ISBN 978-0-06-009952-7; 0-06-009952-6
LC 2002-66025

Giovanni "entwines the political and the personal and celebrates womanhood and black society and culture. Hers is an embracing, uplifting, and sustaining voice, one given to both anger and humor." Booklist

Giovanni, Nikki, 1943-
Chasing Utopia; Nikki Giovanni. William Morrow 2013 160 p. $19.99   **811**
1. Poetry -- Collections
ISBN 0688156975; 9780688156978
LC 2013008776

This collection of poems, by Nikki Giovanni, focuses on "the everyday where family and lovers gather, friends commune, and those no longer with us are remembered. And at every gathering there is food, food as sustenance, food as aphrodisiac, food as memory. A pot of beans are flavored with her mother's sighs, this sigh part cardamom, that one the essence of clove; a lover requests a banquet as an affirmation of ongoing passion; an homage is paid to the most time-honored appetizer, soup." (Publisher's note)

In Giovanni's "accessible, teasing, and poignant collection, she offers straightforward, plain-speaking, sneakily resonant poems, many in prose form." Booklist

Includes bibliographical references

Gluck, Louise
Averno. Farrar, Straus and Giroux 2006 79p $22   **811**
1. Poetry -- By individual authors
ISBN 0-374-10742-4; 978-0-374-10742-0
LC 2005-42658

"Empathic and unforgiving, the voice that unifies Persephone's despondent homelessness, Demeter's rageful mothering and Hades's smitten jealousy is unique in recent poetry, and reveals the flawed humanity of the divine." Publ Wkly

Glück, Louise
Poems 1962-2012; Louise Glück. Farrar, Straus and Giroux"||"Ecco Press 2012 634 p. (alk. paper) $40   **811**
1. Free verse 2. Poetry -- Collections
ISBN 0374126089; 9780374126087
LC 2011051349

This book, by Louise Gluck, features selections from the American author's poetry published between 1962 and 2012. "With each successive book her drive to leave behind what came before has grown more fierce, . . . she invented a form to accommodate this need, the book-length sequence of poems, like a landscape seen from above, a novel with lacunae opening onto the unspeakable." (Publisher's note)

A village life. Farrar, Straus, and Giroux 2009 72p $23   **811**
1. Poetry -- By individual authors
ISBN 978-0-374-28374-2; 0-374-28374-5
LC 2008-49218

"Glück's achievement in this collection is to show, through the exigencies of the place she has chosen, how interpersonal relationships are formed, shaped and broken by the particular landscape in which they unfurl. Though the poems are intimate and deeply sympathetic, there remains the suggestion of a distance between Glück and the village life she writes about. When she declaims, 'No one really understands/ the savagery of this place,' it feels as though she is speaking less about her chosen subjects than about herself." Publ Wkly

Goldbarth, Albert
★ The **kitchen** sink; new and selected poems, 1972-2007. Graywolf Press 2007 345p $26   **811**
1. Poetry -- By individual authors
ISBN 978-1-55597-462-6; 1-55597-462-7
LC 2006-929502

"Albert Goldbarth just may be the American poet of his generation for the ages. Often humorous but always serious, Goldbarth combines erudite research, pop-culture fanaticism, and personal anecdote in ways that make his writings among the most stylistically recognizable in the literary world." Georgia Rev

Good poems; selected and introduced by Garrison Keillor. Viking 2002 xxvi, 476p $25.95; pa $15   **811**
1. English poetry -- Collections 2. American poetry -- Collections
ISBN 0-670-03126-7; 0-14-200344-1 pa
LC 2002-16881

Keillor "has put together a collection of close to 300 poems he has read during . . . [the] PBS broadcast, The Writer's Almanac. . . . Poems are arranged by 19 general themes, such as 'Snow,' 'Failure,' and 'A Good Life.' Authors range from well-known oldies like Emily Dickinson and Robert Frost to unknowns like C.K. Williams. . . . An outstanding feature of this collection is that the selections are all so accessible—even folks who say they don't like poetry can find something here to enjoy." SLJ

Graber, Kathleen

The **eternal** city; poems. Princeton University Press 2010 78p (Princeton series of contemporary poets) $35; pa $16.95   **811**

1. Poetry -- By individual authors

ISBN 978-0-691-14609-6; 978-0-691-14610-2 pa

LC 2009-49321

"Graber's lengthy, long-lined, poems take in everything from St. Augustine to Pepperidge Farm Goldfish crackers to a rash of deaths in the poet's own family, and that's in just one poem. . . . Perhaps half the poems have an epigraph, from the likes of William Blake, Marcus Aurelius and Walter Benjamin. Those sources, as well as Graber's candid tone, set the poems in the midst of an ongoing conversation with the lessons of history and religion. But what makes Graber's poems so fresh and wild are the associative slips that happen between the distant past and the urgent present." Publ Wkly

Graham, Jorie

The **dream** of the unified field; selected poems, 1974-1994. Ecco Press 1995 199p hardcover o.p. pa $15   **811**

1. Poetry -- By individual authors

ISBN 0-88001-476-8 pa

LC 95-16572

"Combining great vision like Blake's, a Dickinsonian philosophical introspection, and a richly modern sensuality, this selection demonstrates the full range of Graham's poetic gifts." Booklist

Overlord; poems. Ecco 2005 93p $22.95 **811**

1. Poetry -- By individual authors

ISBN 0-06-074565-7

LC 2004-53681

"In a distinctly forthright and empathic collection, Graham has constructed poems of lyrical steeliness and cauterizing beauty." Booklist

Greenbaum, Jessica

The **two** Yvonnes; poems. Jessica Greenbaum. Princeton University Press 2012 57 p. (pbk. : acid-free paper) $12.95   **811**

1. Motherhood -- Poetry 2. Poetry -- Collections

ISBN 0691156638; 9780691156620; 9780691156637

LC 2012020320

This book is Jessica Greenbaum's second poetry collection. "With fluent free verse broken up by sonnets, an abecedary and a pantoun, in allegories, comic anecdotes, and pivotal, confessional memories, Greenbaum lets us travel along with her as she grows from too-patient girl to agitated student, from the mother of a sick young child to all the sensations of being alive' after the child (to judge by the poems) has moved out." (Publishers Weekly)

Gregg, Linda

All of it singing. Graywolf Press 2008 224p $24   **811**

1. Poetry -- By individual authors

ISBN 978-1-55597-507-4; 1-55597-507-0

LC 2008-928247

This retrospective "selects from all of Gregg's published books—from her 1981 debut Too Bright to See to 2006's In the Middle Distance—including a group of new poems that show her ongoing investigations into the inner intensities of everyday brutality and grace. . . . The poems travel the globe, set in New England, California, Mexico, Greece and beyond, though wherever her poems go, Gregg never forgets that 'if paradise is to be here/ it will have to include her.' Gregg offers up poems of love lost and won, and of an average life lived with extraordinary force. . . . The poems always rejoice, however dark their subjects, in a powerful sense of simply being alive." Publ Wkly

Grossman, Allen R.

Descartes' loneliness; [by] Allen Grossman. New Directions 2007 64p il pa $16.95   **811**

1. Poetry -- By individual authors

ISBN 978-0-8112-1711-8; 0-8112-1711-6

LC 2007-26896

"Grossman once claimed poetry to be the historical enemy of human forgetfulness. This interest—or better, faith—in poetry's capacity to perform distinctly human acts of preservation has informed Grossman's writing from the beginning. This most recent book showcases some of Grossman's most affecting and memorable lyrics to date." Publ Wkly

Guest, Barbara

The **collected** poems of Barbara Guest; edited by Hadley Haden Guest. Wesleyan University Press 2008 525p (Wesleyan poetry) $39.95   **811**

1. Poetry -- By individual authors

ISBN 978-0-8195-6860-1; 0-8195-6860-0

LC 2008-20147

"It is impossible for a reader to leave The Collected Poems of Barbara Guest without appreciating the enormous spiritual gift her work has always offered in the form of an aesthetic and philosophical challenge." Boston Rev

Includes index. `Works by Barbara Guest¿: p. xxvii-xxix

H. D.

Collected poems, 1912-1944; edited by Louis L. Martz. New Directions 1983 xxxvi, 629p hardcover o.p. pa $24.95   **811**

1. Poetry -- By individual authors

ISBN 978-0-8112-0971-7; 0-8112-0971-7

LC 83-6380

The editor's textual notes "offer valuable and illuminating scholarly commentary and present the most important of the textual variants. An informative and sensitively written introduction discusses aspects of the interpenetration of H.D.'s biography with her poetic sensibility. This volume is an impressive scholarly work." Choice

Hacker, Marilyn

Selected poems; 1965-1990. Norton 1994 250p $22; pa $13.95 **811**

1. Poetry -- By individual authors

ISBN 0-393-03675-8; 0-393-31349-2 pa

LC 94-27507

"Few poets have been as successful as Hacker in negotiating the boundary of the feminist and lesbian canon while generating a buzz around their early work. Iambic and readable, the pieces in Selected Poems—taken from five previous volumes—use unique inversions to explore self and other through changing situations between friends, lovers, family, and one's surroundings. . . . Often, these are poems of loss, of desire delayed, of pleasure deferred." Libr J

Squares and courtyards. Norton 2000 107p $21; pa $12 **811**

1. Poetry -- By individual authors

ISBN 0-393-04830-6; 0-393-32095-2 pa

LC 99-39110

"With customary fortitude and intelligence, Hacker confronts such sobering subjects as the trauma of her own chemotherapy and the loss of friends, in poems that are at once clear-sighted and emotionally full." New Yorker

Halaby, Laila

My name on his tongue; poems. Laila Halaby. 1st ed. Syracuse University Press 2012 xi, 131 p.p (pbk. : alk. paper) $17.95 **811**

1. Arab Americans 2. Narrative poetry 3. Poetry -- Collections

ISBN 0815632940; 9780815632948

LC 2012006950

In this "poetry collection . . . [Laila] Halaby . . . narrates the need of Arab Americans to navigate new realities while giving voice to old ones. She writes about her personal feelings and daily experiences in a confessional mode. . . . She . . . interweaves insights about peace, war, family, nostalgia, exile, and sociopolitical conflicts, among other subjects, Halaby promotes poetry as both testimony and instrument of change." (Library Journal)

Hall, Donald

The **back** chamber. Houghton Mifflin Harcourt 2011 82p $22 **811**

1. Poetry -- By individual authors

ISBN 978-0-547-64585-8

LC 2011009152

This is "a mix of naughty, funny, sweet, and sad pieces about love, family, death, and the poignancy of things. The old rooms of his grandfather's farmhouse in New Hampshire, where Hall has lived since the 1970s, set the stage for recalled intimacies with his late wife, the poet Jane Kenyon, and recollections of the childhood that first brought him there. . . . Featuring moving, amusing, musical poems about

love, aging, and baseball, this work will have broad appeal and is recommended for all collections." Libr J

White apples and the taste of stone; poems, 1946-2006. Houghton Mifflin Co. 2006 431p $30; pa $16.95 **811**

1. Poetry -- By individual authors

ISBN 978-0-618-53721-1; 0-618-53721-X; 978-0-618-91999-4 pa; 0-618-91999-6 pa

LC 2005-20047

"Given to formal short work in the '50s, to lengthy verse essays and verse memoirs later on, Hall shows consistent topics and moods: adult life among New Hampshire's farms and mountains, childhood in the Connecticut suburbs, equanimity and nostalgia, satire and self-satire, middle age and old age, regret and reserve. Most original in his long poems from the '80s and '90s, Hall achieved popular success in recent years,. . . collecting elegies and laments for his late wife, the poet Jane Kenyon." Publ Wkly

Harjo, Joy

A **map** to the next world; poetry and tales. Norton 2000 138p hardcover o.p. pa $13.95 **811**

1. Poetry -- By individual authors

ISBN 978-0-393-32096-1; 0-393-32096-0

LC 99-41099

"One of the most significant American Indian poets here expands her poetic practice to include what she calls tales but might as easily be considered prose poems. Harjo's verse has lately taken on a flowing, narrative quality; these tales, by contrast, take an imagistic, stream-of-consciousness form. . . . Written with authority and Harjo's trademark exploratory verve, this is fine, mature work." Booklist

Harper's anthology of 20th century Native American poetry; edited by Duane Niatum. Harper & Row 1988 xxxii, 396p hardcover o.p. pa $24.95 **811**

1. American poetry -- Native American authors

ISBN 0-06-250666-8 pa

LC 86-45023

This collection "contains the work of 36 native American poets, with hearty selections from each. Among the 36 are poets near the mainstream (Scott Momaday, James Welch, Louise Erdrich); those in academe (Gerald Vizenor, Linda Hogan, Jim Barnes); those writing in the tribal oral tradition (Barney Bush, Peter Blue Cloud, Wendy Rose); and those working in a modernist voice (Gladys Cardiff, Paula Gunn Allen). This book belongs in every collection that claims to represent the multiple voices of American literature today." Booklist

Includes bibliographical references

Harrington, Janice N.

Even the hollow my body made is gone; poems. foreword by Elizabeth Spires. BOA Editions, Ltd. 2007 85p (A. Poulin Jr. new poets of America series) pa $15.50 **811**

1. Poetry -- By individual authors

ISBN 978-1-929918-89-8; 1-929918-89-5

LC 2006-30823

The author "sets her first poetry collection mainly in Alabama during the civil-rights era. Her rich, colloquial poems, drawing on both folklore and science, are paeans to a weary but tenacious black family and their journey north through 'a night as wide as the River Jordan.' . . . When the poems themselves seem less pioneering than the spirit they evoke, their scope and empathy largely compensate." New Yorker

Harrison, Jim (ᒐᴼᴼᴼ)

In search of small gods. Copper Canyon Press 2009 120p $22 **811**

1. Poetry -- By individual authors
ISBN 978-155659-300-0; 1-55659-300-7

LC 2008-39992

Harrison "writes like a man reconciling the world at large with the natural world he knows well, one that still fascinates and inspires him. Many of his small gods are dogs, and many of them are fish or birds, that is, chickadees and hawks, willow flycatchers and hummingbirds. . . . He looks at them all with awe and ironic amusement. A group of prose poems centers this volume. Whether he imagines an Estonian World War II veteran who is fascinated by light or Vallejo in Paris, collecting empty wine bottles for small change, Harrison is heavily invested in narrative elements that range from the real to the surreal." Libr J

The **shape** of the journey; new & collected poems. Copper Canyon Press 1998 463p $30; pa $20 **811**

1. Poetry -- By individual authors
ISBN 1-55659-095-4; 1-55659-149-7 pa

LC 98-25501

"This large collection, which also includes a new grab bag of nature verse and prose poems called 'Geo-Bestiary,' has a meandering feel, although Harrison's concerns—aging, women, eating and drinking, hunting, the craft of writing and above all the spirit and rhythms of the natural world—are remarkably constant. . . . Harrison's writing is graceful, direct and muscular, even in those occasional places where the poems feel like dashed-off diary entries or, rarer still, when they hit a mawkish note." N Y Times Book Rev

Harrison, Jim, 1937-

Songs of unreason. Copper Canyon Press 2011 143p $22 **811**

1. Poetry -- By individual authors
ISBN 978-1-55659-389-5

LC 2011025560

"It wouldn't be a Harrison collection without the poet, novelist, and food critic's reverence for rivers, dogs, and women, but that's not to say Harrison has grown stale or uninteresting in his late poems. Often, as in 'A Part of My History,' which finds the poet tracking the ghost of García Lorca through Granada, his poems stun us simply, with the richness of the clarity, detail, and the immediacy of Harrison's voice. . . . Pushing his formal boundaries, Harrison closes the collection with the meditative 'Suite of Unreason,' a piece that boils down his sharp, epigrammatic lines into a sequence of fist-pumping short poems. But it also wouldn't be a Harrison poem without the hard melancholy that has come to define his voice." Publ Wkly

Hass, Robert

The **apple** trees at Olema; new and selected poems. Ecco 2010 352p $34.99 **811**

1. Poetry -- By individual authors
ISBN 978-0-06-192382-1; 0-06-192382-6

This "retrospective collection, drawn from five previous books, beginning with Field Guide (1973), opens with a generous selection of new poems redolent of Whitman and the blues. Narrative poems are droll and astringent in their musings over love's paradoxes and history's shifting claims, children's pleasures, poverty, and danger. . . . Hass distills experiences down to their essence as he limns landscapes, portrays friends and loved ones, and imagines the struggles of strangers. The ordinary is cracked open to reveal metaphysical riddles in poems that feel so natural, their formal complexities nearly elude our detection." Booklist

Time and materials; poems, 1997-2005. Ecco 2007 88p $22.95 **811**

1. Poetry -- By individual authors
ISBN 978-0-06-134960-7; 0-06-134960-7

LC 2007-30294

This collection of poetry by the former U.S. poet laureate "show a rare internal variety, even as they reflect his constant concerns. One is human impact on the planet at the century's end. . . . Another concern is biography and memory, not so much Hass's own life as the lives of family and friends. . . . Through it all runs a rare skill with long sentences, a light touch, a wish to make claims not just on our ears but on our hearts, and a willingness to wait—few poets wait longer, it seems—for just the right word." Publ Wkly

Includes bibliographical references

Haxton, Brooks

They lift their wings to cry; poems. Knopf 2008 78p $25 **811**

1. Poetry -- By individual authors
ISBN 978-0-307-26845-7; 0-307-26845-4

LC 2008-05766

"You could place Haxton in the Billy Collins school of poetry. His poems read readily, they are funny, smart, and so much more, as their blithe cleverness and charming humility lightly camouflage a spiritual dimension. But Haxton goes his own way, channels his sages of choice, and keeps it low-key, bemused, and philosophical. His emotional palette is warm. His frame of reference encompasses Heraclitus, Ovid, the Bible, a CAT scan. His fascination with the small creatures that make up the bulk of what we call nature—he writes of crickets, moths, birds, a mouse—has a scientific cast even as it springs from a freeflowing empathy with all of life." Booklist

Hayden, Robert Earl

Collected poems; edited by Frederick Glaysher. Liveright 1985 205p hardcover o.p. pa $15 **811**

1. Poetry -- By individual authors
ISBN 978-0-87140-159-5; 0-87140-159-2

LC 84-28880

"Hayden's poetry is a blend of unrivaled craftsmanship with a sharp, unrestrained vision. His subjects encompass the whole of human experience, from the extremely personal but never obscure ('Approximations') to the historical but never pedantic ('Belsen, Day of Liberation'). His technique is similarly varied. Hayden is as adept with haiku, imitations of Eskimo song-poems, or sonnets as he is with free verse. A particularly important addition to libraries with black literature collections." Booklist

Hayes, Terrance

Lighthead. Penguin Books 2010 95p (Penguin poets) pa $18   **811**
  1. Poetry -- By individual authors
  ISBN 978-0-14-311696-7; 0-14-311696-7
                            LC 2009-53319

This collection is a "celebration and castigation of American culture, one worthy of the term 'Americanist.' The title references the light of inspiration and the fire that pours from the heads of two teenage lynching victims in one of the opening poems. The fact that the title can do both inspiration and elegy is indicative of how meaning is contested terrain in Hayes' work. . . . [He] deftly quilts together different textures of language. Rants move into love poems and biting humor butts up against meditations. . . . Sound is of primary importance to Mr. Hayes. Throughout the book he borrows from hip-hop, jazz, slang, lists, and T-shirt slogans. Content aside, his poems are full of pure pleasure of sound in his startling and sonically dense images." Pittsburgh Post-Gazette

Healey, Steve

10 Mississippi; poems. Coffee House Press 2010 113p pa $16   **811**
  1. Poetry -- By individual authors
  ISBN 978-1-56689-252-0; 1-56689-252-X
                            LC 2010-16259

"Steve Healey is one of our most promising young poets, and this collection is full of circumambulations around the same topics, in a skillful takeoff from Gertrude Stein's poetics. Healey quotes from Elizabeth Bishop 'Everything only connected by 'and' and 'and'' and from Steve Reich 'I discovered that the most interesting music of all was made by simply lining the loops up in unison, and letting them slowly shift out of phase with each other.' This seems to be his operative paradigm as well. The whole book is about the mendacity (and utter veracity) of connection; Healey's circling around the dead corpse of false consolations is extremely hypnotic and enchanting. The '10 Mississippi' sequence is particularly effective as a meditation on finality." Huffington Post

Hecht, Anthony

Collected later poems. Knopf 2003 255p hardcover o.p. pa $16.95   **811**
  1. Poetry -- By individual authors
  ISBN 978-0-375-71030-8; 0-375-71030-2
                            LC 2003-44601
This volume contains: The transparent man (1990), Flight among the tombs (1996), and The darkness and the light (2001)

"From the outset a fastidious craftsman, Hecht developed out of the legacy of modernism a stately, intricate, rigorously formal poetry that slowly expanded in its range of tones and subject matter." Times Lit Suppl

Hillman, Brenda

Cascadia. Wesleyan Univ. Press 2001 77p (Wesleyan poetry) $26; pa $13.95   **811**
  1. Poetry -- By individual authors
  ISBN 0-8195-6491-5; 0-8195-6492-3 pa
                            LC 2001-35504

"Geologists know 'Cascadia' as the name for the landmass that became the American West Coast: Hillman's serial mix of long and short poems links Californian geology, geography, history (a Gold Rush-era diarist named Shirley), continental philosophy, and personal experience. . . . Some poems are content with their lyrical verbal effects; others play with typography for effects that are energetic, familiar to readers of Susan Howe and Jorie Graham." Publ Wkly

Pieces of air in the epic. Wesleyan Univ. Press 2005 87p $22.95; pa $14.95   **811**
  1. Poetry -- By individual authors
  ISBN 978-0-8195-6787-1; 0-8195-6787-6; 978-0-8195-6788-8 pa; 0-8195-6788-4 pa
                            LC 2005-18749

"The second in a tetralogy exploring the four elements, Hillman's expansive new work examines air not just as 'gusts & siroccos, chinooks, hamskin, whooshes' but as voice, song, and spirit. Were it not such a pun, one would be tempted to call this collection literally breathtaking; Hillman has pursued an ambitious program with remarkably fine-tuned language." Libr J

Seasonal works with letters on fire; Brenda Hillman. Wesleyan University Press 2013 144 p. (Wesleyan poetry series) (cloth : alk. paper) $24.95   **811**
  1. Fire 2. Poetry -- Collections
  ISBN 0819574147; 9780819574145
                            LC 2013939069
This collection of poetry by Brenda Hillman focuses on "fire--its physical, symbolic, political, and spiritual forms. . . . Hillman evokes fire as metaphor and as event to chart subtle changes of seasons during financial breakdown, environmental crisis, and street movements for social justice; she gathers factual data, earthly rhythms, chants to the dead, journal entries, and lyric fragments in the service of a radical animism." (Publisher's note)

Hirsch, Edward

Earthly measures; poems. Knopf 1994 93p hardcover o.p. pa $18   **811**
  1. Poetry -- By individual authors
  ISBN 978-0-679-76566-0; 0-679-76566-2
                            LC 93-26410
"Hirsch contemplates manifestations of the divine in this set of ravishing poems infused with a deeply felt sense of place and history, seeking insights into how instances of spiritual revelation occur in the frequently brutal everyday world." Booklist

The **living** fire; new and selected poems, 1975-2010. Alfred A. Knopf 2010 237p $27   **811**
  1. Poetry -- By individual authors
  ISBN 978-0-375-41522-7; 0-375-41522-X
                            LC 2009-24452

In Hirsch's work, things are not always what they seem. Certainly, his poems work to dignify the everyday. But they do more than that. What makes Hirsch so singular in American poetry is the balance he strikes between the quotidian and something completely other an irrational counterforce, the living fire that gives its name to his new selected poems. . . . Literary and allusive, but also domestic and intimate, as it rises toward praise, Hirsch's voice resounds with both force and subtlety. One of the pleasures of reading the new selected poems is the chance to see that voice develop and then range freely and surprisingly. N Y Times Book Rev

On love; poems. Knopf 1998 86p hardcover o.p. pa $15　　**811**
1. Poetry -- By individual authors
ISBN 978-0-375-70260-0; 0-375-70260-1
LC 97-49460
"The affirmation of On Love is its language, and the sense it gives that the language of love is inexhaustible. However conversant with the abyss, however true to the devastating logic of desire, the poems ultimately feel triumphant. They are held aloft by nothing but their own joyous artistry." Yale Rev

Special orders; poems. Alfred A. Knopf 2008 64p $25　　**811**
1. Poetry -- By individual authors
ISBN 978-0-307-26681-1; 0-307-26681-8
LC 2007-40336
This collection "brings its demotic, heartfelt, autobiographical pieces together to form a picture of Hirsch's whole life, with sadness always visible, but joy in the foreground. He begins with his immigrant 'grandfather,/ an old man from the Old World'; remembers 'the second-story warehouse' where the young poet 'filled orders for the factory downstairs'; and moves on to his own life as a struggling, and then a successful, writer, teacher and father. Jewish and Yiddish heritage, in memory and on canvas (Chaim Soutine, Marc Chagall) pervades the first half of the volume. . . . The second half follows Hirsch as an adult, to Houston (where he taught for many years) and back to New York City, where he now heads the Guggenheim Foundation." Publ Wkly

Hirshfield, Jane
After; poems. HarperCollins 2006 97p $23.95　　**811**
1. Poetry -- By individual authors
ISBN 0-06-077916-0
LC 2005-50260
"These poems' topics range from global warming to insomnia, passion, cheese making, and sneezing. . . . [The author] engages historical figures from Rembrandt, Poe, and Tu Fu to Linnaeus, Roget, and Darwin. The beauty of these historically engaging poems, though, is that they remain firmly tied to our contemporary world." Va Q Rev

Hix, H. L.
First fire, then birds; obsessionals 1985-2010. Etruscan Press 2010 291p $27.95　　**811**
1. Poetry -- By individual authors
ISBN 978-0-9819687-4-2; 0-9819687-4-0

"Sometimes achingly beautiful in their accumulated details, sometimes grisly and violent, and sometimes tersely intellectual, Hix's collections have always been hard to forget: since his debut with the sonnets of Perfect Hell (1996), his books have differed greatly one from another, each with its signature long poem or sequence. . . . Formalists cherish Hix's frequent meter and rhyme; devotees of experiment enjoy the bizarre disjunctions and the philosophical demands. This retrospective shuffles individual poems and sequences from his first seven books to good effect, out of chronological order (along with aphorisms from a book of prose). Hix may make new readers' heads spin with his changes of focus, but he also gives them the chance to see his work whole." Publ Wkly

Hoagland, Tony
Unincorporated persons in the late Honda dynasty; poems. Graywolf Press 2010 90p pa $15 **811**
1. Poetry -- By individual authors
ISBN 978-1-55597-549-4; 1-55597-549-6
LC 2009-933818
"There are 15 or 20 better poets in America than Tony Hoagland, but few deliver more pure pleasure. His erudite comic poems are backloaded with heartache and longing, and they function, emotionally, like improvised explosive devices: the pain comes at you from the cruelest angles, on the sunniest of days. . . . On a superficial level Mr. Hoagland's poems — he writes in an alert, caffeinated, lightly accented free verse — resemble those of many writers in what one is tempted to call the Amiable School of American Poets, a group for which Billy Collins serves as both prom king and starting point guard. But Mr. Hoagland's verse is consistently, and crucially, bloodied by a sense of menace and by straight talk." N Y Times (Late N Y Ed)

What narcissism means to me. Graywolf Press 2003 78p pa $14　　**811**
1. Poetry -- By individual authors
ISBN 1-55597-386-8 pa
LC 2003-101172
The author's "speaker devotes considerable energy to unmasking . . . {his} vulnerable self, revealing its ugliness, hatred and social sensitivity. . . . In milder poems, which often revolve around eating dinner, drinking wine and hanging out with friends (typically other creative writing professors), he explores a more social self, slipping into a 'he said, she said' mode, and reporting at great length on friends' witticisms." Publ Wkly

Hodgen, John
Heaven & earth holding company. University of Pittsburgh Press 2010 73p (Pitt poetry series) pa $14.95　　**811**
1. Poetry -- By individual authors
ISBN 978-0-8229-6114-7; 0-8229-6114-8
"Every writer wants to get the strange kaleidoscopic world of ten thousand things into their work; few succeed. But John Hodgen's Heaven and Earth Holding Company delivers that entirety in poem after poem —sun, rain, baseball, Frost and Shakespeare, the birth of a granddaughter, Abraham Lincoln, W.C Fields, saints, dogs, lovers, Viagra, Motel 6, those beeping airport carts. Hodgen's long-lined poems

are propulsive, his sentences hypotactic, muscular, alliterative. . . . If these were just playful, wise-cracking poems they would give us pleasure enough; but Hodgen's poems fast-break from humor to sorrow and the mortal coils of our lives." On the Seawall

Hoffman, Daniel

Beyond silence; selected shorter poems, 1948-2003. Louisiana State Univ. Press 2003 226p $49.95; pa $26.95 **811**

> 1. Poetry -- By individual authors
> ISBN 0-8071-2860-0; 0-8071-2861-9 pa
>> LC 2002-34090

The collection's "organization by theme brings poems from remote parts of his oeuvre into illuminating conversation with one another. And substantial recent poems such as 'Scott Nearing's Ninety-Eighth Year' and 'The Cape Racer' are as strong as anything he's written." NY Times Book Rev

Hollander, John

A **draft** of light; poems. Alfred A. Knopf 2008 109p $26 **811**

> 1. Poetry -- By individual authors
> ISBN 978-0-307-26911-9; 0-307-26911-6
>> LC 2008-4751

"As one would expect of a poet whose work has been set to music, Hollander sees poetry as an oral art even though it is first written on paper. What one might not expect from this 78-year-old poet is the wordplay, lighthearted tone, and general mischievousness that seems to come trippingly from his pen. . . . This volume's title poem, for example, ends with a paraphrase of T.S. Eliot's 'Little Gidding.' Other poems paraphrase Percy Bysshe Shelley, Wallace Stevens, and Joyce Kilmer, to say nothing of William Shakespeare. Like Shakespeare, Hollander fuses a somber tone with comic conventions, resulting in the poetic equivalent of the problem play." Libr J

Includes bibliographical references

Figurehead & other poems. Knopf 1999 89p hardcover o.p. pa $15 **811**

> 1. Poetry -- By individual authors
> ISBN 978-0-375-70433-8; 0-375-70433-7
>> LC 98-14208

Hollander's "justifiably confident in his skills, the solid grace of his constructions, and his ability to make both the light and dark sides of words, thoughts, and even life itself simultaneously visible. It's no wonder that among nimbly philosophic poems about Arachne, Cain, and a painting by Velázquez he disarms, charms, and intrigues his readers with a witty and imaginative tribute to the tabletop sculptures of Saul Steinberg and a bittersweet remembrance of George Moran, an old vaudevillian." Booklist

Hong, Cathy Park

Engine empire; Cathy Park Hong. W.W. Norton & Co. 2012 95 p. **811**

> 1. Art -- Poetry 2. East Asian poetry 3. Computers -- Poetry 4. Poetry -- Collections 5. Frontier and pioneer life -- West (U.S.) -- Poetry
> ISBN 0393082849; 9780393082845
>> LC 2012000596

This book of poetry "renders a triptych of frontiers--the Old West, the new East, and the digital world--where artistic acts are often tantamount to subversion. 'Ballad of Our Jim,' a sequence of cowboy ballads within ballads, follows a crew of outlaws and their kidnapped boy . . . through an unsettled age when 'the whole country is in a duel and we want no part of it.' 'Shangdu, My Artful Boomtown!' . . . grapples with vocation and origin in a globalizing era. . . . 'Adventures in Shangdu,' a sequence of prose poems depict[s] a dystopia whose citizens include a factory worker reproducing Rembrandts. . . . [P]oems in 'The World Cloud' take on digital realms, where 'the search engine is inside us,/ the world is our display.'" (Publishers Weekly)

Howard, Richard

★ **Inner** voices; selected poems, 1963-2003. Farrar, Straus and Giroux 2004 428p $35 **811**

> 1. Poetry -- By individual authors
> ISBN 0-374-25862-7
>> LC 2004-40464

The author "chooses artists and art as the personae and subjects of many of his poems. . . . Besides artists, Howard often chooses writers as personae, including prominent Victorians (Whitman, Ruskin and Browning); correspondents with other writers and artists; and increasingly, himself as traveler, museumgoer, and engaged reader." Booklist

★ The **silent** treatment; new poems. Turtle Point Press 2005 114p pa $16.95 **811**

> 1. Poetry -- By individual authors
> ISBN 1-885586-38-3
>> LC 2004-113837

Hannah Arendt, George Eliot, Cosima Wagner, and a boy in a photograph by Arkansas photographer Mike Disfarmer are among the speakers in this collection.

"In characterizing the poems of Richard Howard's latest collection, one is tempted to bypass 'golden' as a description and head straight on to platinum. Now in his eighth decade, Howard has long been–along with the late James Merrill, who jokingly coined the phrase–one of American poetry's 'Great Fancies.'" Wkly Stand

Without saying; new poems. Turtle Point Press 2008 108p pa $16.95 **811**

> 1. Poetry -- By individual authors
> ISBN 978-1-933527-14-7 pa; 1-933527-14-5 pa
>> LC 2007-907229

"In this 14th collection of his own verse, [the author] returns to the kinds of poems that made him famous: elaborate dramatic monologues, impersonations and dialogues that are intricately alert to literary history and sexual desire. . . . In these thoughtful new poems, Howard offers, and excels in, sophisticated verbal comedy." Publ Wkly

Howe, Susan

Souls of the Labadie tract. New Directions Books 2007 127p pa $16.95 **811**

> 1. Poetry -- By individual authors
> ISBN 978-0-8112-1718-7; 0-8112-1718-3
>> LC 2007-34255

"In her newest book, Howe stands in thrall to a 17th-century history of Deerfield, Mass., and then chases down an obscure reference to 'Labadist' in Wallace Stevens's family tree, which brings her to the story of a short-lived Utopian 'quietest sect,' followers of Jean de Labadie who established a community in Maryland in 1684 that vanished within 40 years. It is in these vast tracts of time made intimate by texts, by language, that Howe operates.... Beginning with a quote from Jonathan Edwards equating the silkworm to 'a type of Christ' and ending with a photograph of a fragment of the silk wedding dress of Edwards's wife, onto which Howe projects a text ('I have already shown that space is God'), this is intense stuff." Publ Wkly

That this. New Directions Pub. 2010 109p il pa $15.95 **811**

1. Poetry -- By individual authors
ISBN 978-0-8112-1918-1 pa; 0-8112-1918-6 pa
LC 2010-41791

"Death is one of the preeminent subjects of poetry, and Howe ... approaches this topic with the gravitas of one who has endured loss.... [This] volume deals chiefly with the death of her husband, Peter Hare. The book juxtaposes Howe's personal recollections with excerpts from an assortment of documents, ranging from 18th-century diaries to an array of half-decayed ephemera, such as bits of Poussin prints and fragments of linguistic sculpture.... An intelligent and unorthodox treatment of grief, this title will appeal to poetry and visual arts enthusiasts." Libr J

Hughes, Langston

Selected poems of Langston Hughes; drawings by E. McKnight Kauffer. Knopf 1959 297p il hardcover o.p. pa $13.95 **811**

1. Poetry -- By individual authors
ISBN 0-679-72818-X; 978-0-679-72818-4

This collection represents Langston Hughes' own decisions as to which of his poems he wanted to preserve and reprint

Hugo, Richard, 1923-1982

Making certain it goes on; the collected poems of Richard Hugo. Norton 1983 xxi, 456p hardcover o.p. pa $19.95 **811**

1. Poetry -- By individual authors
ISBN 0-393-30784-0; 978-0-393-30784-9
LC 83-8016

This book gathers the verse of the American poet.

"Though he would never be a serene poet, his collected poems show Hugo turning toward a calm peace that would mark his best work in 'White Center' (1980) and 'The Right Madness On Skye' (1981), and in the 22 new poems in this volume.... Among the new poems included [here] Hugo was still driving, looking, and naming. If we had not noticed before that his great gift was the elegy, we see it now." N Y Times Book Rev

The **Hungry** Ear; poems of food & drink. edited by Kevin Young. St Martins Pr 2012 336 p. $25 **811**

1. Food -- Poetry 2. Poetry -- Collections
ISBN 1608195511; 9781608195510

This book, edited by Kevin Young, is a collection of poems related to food. "While some of the poems here are explicitly about the food itself: the blackberries, the butter, the barbecue--all are evocative of the experience of eating. Many of the poems are also about the everything else that accompanies food: the memories, the company, even the politics.... Poets include: Elizabeth Alexander, Elizabeth Bishop, Billy Collins, Mark Doty, Robert Frost, [and] Allen Ginsberg." (Publisher's note)

Huntington, Cynthia

Heavenly bodies; Cynthia Huntington. Southern Illinois University Press 2012 vii, 75 p.p (pbk. : alk. paper) $15.95 **811**

1. Nineteen sixties 2. Addiction -- Poetry 3. Sexual liberation -- Poetry
ISBN 0809330636; 0809330644; 9780809330638; 9780809330645
LC 2011022095

In this "collection of lyric poems, Cynthia Huntington gives an intimate view of the sexual revolution and rebellion in a time before the rise of feminism. 'Heavenly Bodies' is a testament to the duality of sex, the twin seductiveness and horror of drug addiction, and the social, political, and personal dramas of America in the 1960s." (Publisher's note)

Includes bibliographical references (p. 74-75)

Ignatow, David

I have a name. University Press of New England 1996 75p (Wesleyan poetry) hardcover o.p. pa $13.95 **811**

1. Poetry -- By individual authors
ISBN 978-0-8195-2240-5; 0-8195-2240-6
LC 96-19350

"Ignatow's words are spare and apparently casual, holding us riveted by the force of what is articulated but not spoken.... The subjects are timeless: loss, age, death, the joy of fleeting moments." Booklist

Shadowing the ground. Wesleyan Univ. Press 1991 68p (Wesleyan poetry) hardcover o.p. pa $13.95 **811**

1. Poetry -- By individual authors
ISBN 978-0-8195-1197-3; 0-8195-1197-8
LC 90-20872

"Here are sixty-five short, spare, untitled poems, their uniformity of appearance (two-thirds of them ten lines or fewer) belying the plural perspectives that David Ignatow brings to his considerations of age and death's imminence. ... Shadowing the Ground celebrates contrary responses to unplanned obsolescence." World Lit Today

Inventions of the March Hare; poems 1909-1917. edited by Christopher Ricks. Harcourt Brace & Co. 1997 xlii, 428p **811**

1. Poetry -- By individual authors
ISBN 0151002746; 0156005875
LC 96-45399

"Though available in manuscript to scholars since 1968, this is the first appearance—for all but five poems—of Eliot's 'lost' notebook of drafts and fragments." (Libr J) Indexes.

"Though available in manuscript to scholars since 1968, this is the first appearance—for all but five poems—of Eliot's 'lost' notebook of drafts and fragments. Eliot never intended this unfinished work to see publication, but in page after page his autumnal sensibility, his signature aura of languid urban malaise—however tentative—surfaces unmistakably. . . . For scholars and devotees, Eliot's rehearsals for immortality will yield a cornucopia of delights." Libr J

Jackson, Major

Holding company. W.W. Norton & Co. 2010 91p $24.95 **811**
1. Poetry -- By individual authors
ISBN 978-0-393-07080-4

LC 2010-17728
"The sonnet sequence has been a staple of love poetry; Major Jackson tries here a sequence of tenline poems, instead of the fourteen of the sonnet, and the form, as always, pressures the poet toward specific meanings. There is greater urgency to get to the point, and it makes the expression of love only more dire, more taut and almost unmanageable. The effect of these poems individually is a certain serenity, a distance toward public turmoil, but cumulatively they amount to a desperate rebellion, a willful declaration of immortality." Huffington Post

Hoops; poems. Norton 2006 125p $23.95 **811**
1. Poetry -- By individual authors
ISBN 0-393-05937-5; 978-0-393-05937-3

LC 2005-33320
The author's "poems are witty, musical, and intelligent; he is equally happy discussing the war on terror . . . or describing early crushes." New Yorker

Jacobsen, Josephine

In the crevice of time; new and collected poems. Johns Hopkins Univ. Press 1995 258p (Johns Hopkins, poetry and fiction) hardcover o.p. pa $25 **811**
1. Poetry -- By individual authors
ISBN 978-0-8018-6339-4; 0-8018-6339-2

LC 95-2798
"In this retrospective spanning nearly six decades of distinguished poetry, the best work comes at the beginning and the end. A contemporary of Robert Penn Warren and Elizabeth Bishop, Jacobsen continues to write stately poems informed by irony, fatalism, and an eloquent appreciation of strength in all its guises, physical and moral. An unabashed formalist, she carefully composes poems that are aggressively metrical . . . and whose surfaces are dense with metaphor, rhyme, assonance, alliteration, and omniscient authority." Libr J

Jarrell, Randall

★ The **complete** poems. Farrar, Straus & Giroux 1969 507p hardcover o.p. pa $22 **811**
1. Poetry -- By individual authors
ISBN 0-374-51305-8 pa

Collected here are the entire contents of three published volumes Selected poems (1955), The woman at the Washington Zoo (1960), and The Lost World (1965) plus poems published from 1934 to 1964 but never collected and some never before published

Jazz poems. Alfred A. Knopf 2006 256p (Everyman's library pocket poets) $12.50 **811**
1. Jazz music -- Poetry 2. American poetry -- Collections
ISBN 978-1-4000-4251-7; 1-4000-4251-8

A collection of poetry inspired by jazz music. Includes poems by Langston Hughes, E. E. Cummings, William Carlos Williams, Frank O'Hara, Gwendolyn Brooks, Yusef Komunyakaa, Charles Simic, Rita Dove, Ntozake Shange, Mark Doty, William Matthews, and C. D. Wright, among others.

Jeffers, Robinson

The **selected** poetry of Robinson Jeffers; edited by Tim Hunt. Stanford Univ. Press 2001 758p pa $34.95 **811**
1. Poetry -- By individual authors
ISBN 978-0-8047-4108-8; 0-8047-4108-5

LC 00-48490
"Hunt's edition strips the punctuation added by contemporary printers (which 'often obscures the rhythm and pacing of what Jeffers actually wrote, and at points even obscures meaning and nuance') and includes a carefully weighed choice of long and short works, as well as unpublished work. . . . This new selection will get readers closer than ever to the poems as Jeffers himself saw them." Publ Wkly

Johnson, James Weldon

Complete poems; edited with an introduction by Sondra Kathryn Wilson. Penguin Bks. 2000 xxxiii, 202p pa $14 **811**
1. Poetry -- By individual authors
ISBN 0-14-118545-7

LC 00-39969
This volume contains Fifty years and other poems (1917), God's trombones (1927), Saint Peter relates an incident of the resurrection day (1935), and a number of previously unpublished poems. The editor's introduction considers Johnson's achievements and influence
Includes bibliographical references

Johnson, Peter

Rants and raves; selected and new prose poems. White Pine Press 2010 107p pa $16 **811**
1. Poetry -- By individual authors
ISBN 978-1-935210-06-1; 1-935210-06-8

"In the course of reading and rereading his poems one may be reminded of a range of writers, ancient and modern, including Theophrastus, Baudelaire, John Berryman, James Thurber (oh yes!). Peter Johnson represents a big constituency; but always concretely. 'American Male, Acting Up' begins: 'They say your whole life flashes before you when you die, but I'm sure I'll witness the lives of others.' These pages swarm with the lives of others, most particularly 'Peter Johnson,' who rants and raves like any free-mouthed cynic of the good old empire. . . . Savage indignation aside, Johnson is a great poet of friendship and family life. His book brims with wild wisdom, aching longing, tenderness, and most importantly, laughter." Providence J

Johnson, Ronald

The **shrubberies**; edited by Peter O'Leary.
Flood Editions 2001 136p pa $14   **811**

1. Poetry -- By individual authors
ISBN 0-9710059-0-7

LC 2002-279220

This "book consists of a loosely linked sequence written
in the last years of the poet's life. With their brevity and almost microscopic wordplay, the poems resemble epigrams.
But where epigrams click into place, these poems leave
implications floating. . . . The pleasure and insight of these
poems come from more than prosodic specifics. Unlike so
many 'experimental poets,' Johnson writes from necessity.
As Peter O'Leary explains in his eloquent afterword, Johnson had a 'sense that these poems completed his work as a
poet.' Several of the poems address mortality with starkness
and force." Poetry (Modern Poetry Association)

Johnston, Devin

★ **Traveler**. Farrar, Straus and Giroux 2011 67p
$23   **811**

1. Poetry -- By individual authors
ISBN 978-0-374-27933-2; 0-374-27933-0

LC 2011-08457

This collection brings Johnston's "careful, graceful, almost neoclassical pen to scenes from all over the world—Japan, Shanghai, 'the Mongol steppes,' the Midwest 'when a
thunderstorm/ trundles down the Wabash,' and the Scottish
holy isle of Iona. . . . Sometimes sublime, more often astringent, Johnston's poems of places and things seen—they
make up most of the volume—should please fans of that
older world traveler, August Kleinzahler. Yet Johnston may
be most original when his subjects turn up close to home:
his cool temperament meets its fruitful complement when he
writes of family and children, most of all his young daughter, who in the brief, fine triptych entitled 'Appetites' 'lies
awake/ talking in confidential tones/ with one she calls/
my friend who eats me.' It would take a hard heart to resist
such humor, such warmth, set amid such control as Johnston
shows." Publ Wkly

Jordan, June

★ **Directed** by desire; the collected poems of
June Jordan. edited by Jan Heller Levi and Sara
Miles. Copper Canyon Press 2005 649p $40   **811**

1. Poetry -- By individual authors
ISBN 1-55659-228-0

LC 2005-11701

Jordan's poems "consistently display a loving devotion
to black English and pride in her femininity, race, and individuality. Directed by Desire is an important addition to
African American or feminist poetry collections." Booklist

Justice, Donald Rodney

★ **Collected** poems. Knopf 2004 288p $25 **811**

1. Poetry -- By individual authors
ISBN 1-4000-4239-9

LC 2003-65735

"Though its primary subject is the past, his work as a
whole is more extraordinarily present—more thrillingly
contemporary—than most of the styles that have advertised

their commitment to 'making it new' over the past half-century." N Y Times Book Rev

Kasischke, Laura

Space, in chains. Copper Canyon Press 2011
113p pa $16   **811**

1. Poetry -- By individual authors
ISBN 978-1-55659-333-8; 1-55659-333-3

LC 2010-40037

"Known for her representations of mothers and teenagers
in her poems and in her many novels, Kasischke now takes
equal interest in illness and old age: rightly celebrated for
her irregular, spiky, and intricately rhyming lines, Kasischke
has now extended her interest (begun with her last book, Lil-
ies Without) in the prose poem, using its fragments for recollection. . . . For all its length and all its lists, the volume ends
up tightly, almost wrenchingly focused on the omnipresence
of suffering, the fact of mortality and the persistence of grief.
Some readers might call it melodramatic; many more ought
to call it symphonic, perceptive, profound." Publ Wkly

Kelly, Robert

Lapis; poems. Godine 2005 221p pa $18.95 **811**

1. Poetry -- By individual authors
ISBN 1-57423-186-3

LC 2004-16724

This collection "offers dream narratives, elegies,
prayers, anecdotes, parables, dialogues, and folktales from
a land that may not exist. . . . Kelly has done something
remarkable. He has given magic back its dignity, finding it
in human warmth." Bookforum

Red actions; selected poems, 1960-1993. Black
Sparrow Press 1995 398p hardcover o.p. pa
$18.95   **811**

1. Poetry -- By individual authors
ISBN 978-0-87685-977-3; 0-87685-977-5

LC 95-35351

"In more than 35 collections of poetry, Kelly has utterly
failed at one thing: to pigeonhole himself into predictability.
This rich selection from more than a quarter-century of work
contains imagistic bits that seem like fragments of poetic
tapestry, long surreal narratives, series poems, and sonorous
chants. Whatever the form, they are marked by Kelly's erudition, which covers Greek archaeology as readily as twentieth-century music, Sumerian gods as well as contemporary
painting. Yet his work is never merely academic, inspired
as it is by a passionate intellect reminiscent of Wallace Stevens. This survey may draw him more of the readers he well
deserves." Booklist

Kendall, Tim

The **art** of Robert Frost; Tim Kendall. Yale University Press 2012 xvi, 392 p.p (cloth : alk. paper)
$35   **811**

ISBN 0300118139; 9780300118131

LC 2011041416

"This book presents a . . . selection of sixty-five poems
from across [Robert] Frost's writing career, beginning in the
1890s and ending with . . . the 1940s. . . . In addition to close
readings of the poems, 'The Art of Robert Frost' traces the
development of Frost's writing career and relevant aspects

of his life. The book also assesses . . . the poet's style, how it changes over time, and how it relates to the works of contemporary poets and movements, including Modernism." (Publisher's note)

Includes bibliographical references (p. 385-388) and index.

Kenner, Hugh

The **Pound** era. University of Calif. Press 1971 606p il hardcover o.p. pa $26.95 **811**

1. Poets 2. Authors 3. Literary critics 4. Poetry -- By individual authors

ISBN 978-0-520-02427-4; 0-520-02427-3

"As a reader of Pound, Kenner is superb. He moves with ease and authority through the most tangled passages of allusion, ideogram and fragments of Greek and Latin." N Y Times Book Rev

Includes bibliographical references

Kenyon, Jane

★ **Collected** poems. Graywolf Press 2005 357p $26 **811**

1. Poetry -- By individual authors

ISBN 1-55597-428-7

"This collected edition reproduces verbatim the four books Kenyon saw through to press; the poems from two posthumous collections, Otherwise and A Hundred White Daffodils; Kenyon's translations of Akhmatova; and four previously uncollected poems. . . . Taken as a whole, Kenyon's poems remain a sustaining record of a life staked out in very difficult terrain." Publ Wkly

Kerouac, Jack

Book of blues. Penguin Bks. 1995 273p (Penguin poets) pa $13.95 **811**

1. Poetry -- By individual authors

ISBN 0-14-058700-4

LC 94-45902

A "set of eight previously unpublished 'blues' poems written between 1954 and 1961. These long poems, series of 'choruses' or sketches, resemble, in form and avidity, Kerouac's amazing verse creation Mexico City Blues (1959). They are strongly tied to place and are, as the allusion to music implies, boldly improvisational." Booklist

★ **Book** of sketches, 1952-53; introduction by George Condo. Penguin Books 2006 413p (Penguin poets) pa $18 **811**

1. Poetry -- By individual authors

ISBN 978-0-14-200215-5; 0-14-200215-1

LC 2005-44535

"Somewhere between diary, verbal sketchbook and play-by-play account of whatever passed before his eyes, this collection of poems transcribed from notebooks Kerouac kept in his pocket between 1952 and 1954 turns out to rank with his most interesting work. . . . Kerouac hits all the notes for which he and his fellow beats are known. While not everything here is golden, the immediacy and unpretentiousness of this off-the-cuff writing makes it an intimate glimpse into

the consciousness of a man who simply couldn't stop observing." Publ Wkly

Pomes all sizes; introduction by Allen Ginsberg. City Lights Bks. 1992 175p pa $13.95 **811**

1. Poetry -- By individual authors

ISBN 0-87286-269-0

LC 92-1204

"This book, which Kerouac prepared for publication before his death in 1969, collects poems written between 1954 and 1965. Most are playful—comments about friends, variations on the sounds of words. Yet a few extremely sensitive longer pieces appear, including 'Caritas,' in which the poet runs after a barefoot beggar boy to give him money for shoes and then begins to doubt the boy's veracity. Other intriguing poems reflect the poet's religious concerns of the moment, running the gamut of Eastern and Western religions." Libr J

Scattered poems. City Lights Bks. 1971 76p pa $7.95 **811**

1. Poetry -- By individual authors

ISBN 0-87286-064-7

This collection "contains poems that either have previously appeared in periodicals or have not appeared in print at all. The poems are delightfully representative of Kerouac: that free and easy style of writing from the music of the imagination, without a score to follow. Those familiar with the San Francisco school of poetry will readily see Kerouac's affinity in style and content with such writers as Rexroth, Everson, Snyder, Ferlinghetti, Ginsberg, et al. . . . Kerouac sings in the American language to an American tune." Libr J

Kinnell, Galway

A **new** selected poems. Houghton Mifflin 2000 173p hardcover o.p. pa $14 **811**

1. Poetry -- By individual authors

ISBN 978-0-618-15445-6; 0-618-15445-0

LC 99-48904

"New England resides in these pages. Kinnell is a native of America's first literary region. Cold snow and clear nights work their way into his poems. The sounds of the woods are everywhere. But these sounds do not echo Emerson. Like any good transcendentalist, Kinnell sees the spiritual in material things." Christ Sci Monit

Strong is your hold. Houghton Mifflin 2006 69p $25; pa $14.95 **811**

1. Poetry -- By individual authors

ISBN 978-0-618-22497-5; 0-618-22497-1; 978-0-547-05366-0 pa; 0-547-05366-5 pa

LC 2006-11292

"To many readers, the most appealing of these poems will be the half dozen in which the aging poet writes about his wife: cuddling with her in sleep, making love with startling ferocity, waking to find they are holding hands, preparing to say goodbye if one dies before the other. Getting old, as we've heard, is not for sissies. The poet who once chased bears may have slowed a step, but here he's still making like Johnny Cash as he walks the line between sex and death, the odd and the normal, domesticity and wildness, this world and the next. . . . 'Strong Is Your Hold' comes with a CD of

Kinnell reading his work in a steady, pleasant voice." N Y Times Book Rev

Kirby, David

Talking about movies with Jesus; poems. Louisiana State University Press 2011 70p (Southern messenger poets) $50; pa $17.95   **811**

1. Poetry -- By individual authors

ISBN 978-0-8071-3771-0; 0-8071-3771-5; 978-0-8071-3772-7 pa; 0-8071-3772-3 pa

LC 2010-24229

"David Kirby's poems will put you and your imagination on a jet plane and fly you both around the world. They'll take you to Italy and France or into conversations with Jesus and Elvis. They'll even force all of you serious critics to crack a smile." Flashpoint

Kizer, Carolyn (7001)

√ **Cool,** calm & collected; poems 1960-2000. Copper Canyon Press 2000 509p $30; pa $20   **811**

1. Poetry -- By individual authors

ISBN 1-55659-146-2; 1-55659-181-0 pa

LC 00-10243

Kizer "covers civil rights, women's rights and almost everything in between, but even when she's writing about more intimate matters, her underlying concern is freedom. . . . Despite her constant railing against the machine, however, Kizer's poetry remains fundamentally optimistic, perhaps because she seems to love existence almost in spite of herself." N Y Times Book Rev

Kleinzahler, August

√ **Sleeping** it off in Rapid City; poems, new and selected. Farrar, Straus and Giroux 2008 234p $26   **811**

1. Poetry -- By individual authors

ISBN 978-0-374-26583-0; 0-374-26583-6

LC 2007-41926

This is a collection of poetry by the author of Earthquake Weather (1989), Red Sauce, Whiskey, and Snow (1996), and Live from the Hong Kong Nile Club (2000).

The author "writes most often in a strongly accented free verse that is among the most articulate and alive sounds American poetry is currently making. He plays effortlessly with forms, voices, registers. And his range of cultural reference—from Catullus to Custer, from Lorca to Eric Dolphy—is wide and artfully deployed. Rarely does high, learned poetic art sound this casual." N Y Times (Late N Y Ed)

Klink, Joanna

Raptus. Penguin Books 2010 60p (Penguin poets) pa $18   **811**

1. Poetry -- By individual authors

ISBN 978-0-14-311772-8; 0-14-311772-6

LC 2010-08246

"What happens when a relationship fails? Klink gets into the nooks and crannies of that question in her third collection. She sinks into every aspect of the life past and present. . . . She has a rhythmic dedication, a sense that every last emotional corner will be examined in its own time and a keen focus aimed as much at herself as at others. As it cycles through need and loss, this book illuminates just how inextricable experiences can be from the people with whom they are shared." Publ Wkly

Includes bibliographical references

Knott, Bill

The **unsubscriber**. Farrar, Straus and Giroux 2004 122p $20; pa $13   **811**

1. Poetry -- By individual authors

ISBN 978-0-374-26415-4; 0-374-26415-5; 978-0-374-53014-3 pa; 0-374-53014-9 pa

LC 2004-41160

"Knott's talent for compression—his awareness of the physicality of language—has remained undiminished since his youth, surfacing in one poem after another. . . . Like a gifted composer also capable of brilliantly playing every instrument in the orchestra, Knott possesses talent beyond the average allotment. In all fairness, you are not likely to find a more imaginative and provocative book of poetry published in the last year than The Unsubscriber, but neither will you find one that can be more at odds with itself." Am Book Rev

Knox, Jennifer L.

The **mystery** of the hidden driveway. Bloof Books 2010 83p pa $15   **811**

1. Poetry -- By individual authors

ISBN 978-0-9826587-1-0

"If Jennifer L. Knox is a lot of 'fun,' she is also one of the bluntest, most cutting poets in the country. And one of the most consistent—The Mystery of the Hidden Driveway is her best book yet, full of ridiculous characters, speedy narratives of scotch-taped sex and drugs, of emotional instabilities that are likeable and addictive. This is a book of odd and unexpected pleasures, a reminder that if nothing is sacred, everything is." Coldfront

Koch, Kenneth

★ The **collected** poems of Kenneth Koch. Knopf 2005 761p $40   **811**

1. Poetry -- By individual authors

ISBN 1-4000-4499-5

LC 2004-63827

"The products of a lifetime of continual inventing are beautifully on display in this awe-inspiring banquet of a book." Publ Wkly

On the edge; collected long poems. Alfred A. Knopf 2007 411p $35   **811**

1. Poetry -- By individual authors

ISBN 978-0-307-26284-4; 0-307-26284-7

LC 2007-24041

"A principal force behind the New York School of poets that flourished at mid-century, Kenneth Koch never quite won the pride of place occupied by the likes of Frank O'Hara and John Ashbery. This volume compiles Koch's long poems, making an eloquent argument for his unique stature." New York

Koertge, Ron

The **ogre's** wife; poems. Ron Koertge. Red Hen Press 2013 80 p. $17.95   **811**

   1. Poetry -- Collections

   ISBN 1597097233; 9781597097239

                                LC 2013004265

In this collection of poems, Ronald Koertge "introduces readers to Little Red Riding Hood all grown up with a fondness for salsa and chips, explores the thorny relationship of Jackie Robinson and Pee Wee Reese, spies a Trojan pony and the children it bamboozles, and offers an alternate reading to the Icarus story. He meets Walt Whitman on the set of an X-rated movie, attends his gardener's funeral, and goes to his beloved race track." (Publisher's note)

Komunyakaa, Yusef

The **chameleon** couch; poems. Farrar, Straus and Giroux 2011 115p il $24   **811**

   1. Poetry -- By individual authors

   ISBN 978-0-374-12038-2; 0-374-12038-2

                                LC 2010-33148

In this collection, the author "shares unusually personal reflections steeped in his intimacy with ancestors, gods, and monsters. These finely formed lyrics are timeless in their shadows and wounds, and startlingly fresh in mood, metaphor, image, and such pairings as gargoyles and power lines, sugar and salt." Booklist

Talking dirty to the gods; poems. Farrar, Straus & Giroux 2000 134p hardcover o.p. pa $13   **811**

   1. Poetry -- By individual authors

   ISBN 0-374-52793-8 pa

                                LC 00-21277

"Komunyakaa's mournful surrealism seems to have found a perfect mathematical embodiment in this . . . collection, which comprises a hundred and thirty-two poems of four four-line stanzas. These are poems about the uncontrollable human and natural mysteries, and they are made sharper and more mysterious by the eternal recurrence of the stanzaic structure." New Yorker

Thieves of paradise. University Press of New England 1998 128p (Wesleyan poetry) $26; pa $14.95   **811**

   1. Poetry -- By individual authors

   ISBN 0-8195-6330-7; 0-8195-6422-2 pa

                                LC 97-40294

"The central subjects of Komunyakaa's poetry—his experiences in the Vietnam War and as an African-American male—have always been made compelling in his hands, and equally compelling has been the moodily energetic, jazz-inspired improvisatory technique that he employs with increasing mastery. But what is most gratifying about Komunyakaa's surrealist riffs, with their almost hallucinatory lushness, is their power to convince us that the individual

imagination is more than equal to the most excruciating historical burden." New Yorker

Warhorses; poems. Farrar, Straus and Giroux 2008 86p $24   **811**

   1. War poetry 2. Poetry -- By individual authors

   ISBN 978-0-3742-8643-9; 0-3742-8643-4

                                LC 2007-51760

"The poems that comprise [this] new collection provide an astonishingly panoramic view of the totality of war. . . . Strongly recommended." Libr J

Kooser, Ted

Delights & shadows; poems. Copper Canyon Press 2004 87p pa $15   **811**

   1. Poetry -- By individual authors

   ISBN 1-55659-201-9

                                LC 2003-18447

These "poems reflect a joy for life through powerful human images and intimate observations of everyday things." Booklist

Flying at night; poems, 1965-1985. University of Pittsburgh Press 2005 142p (Pitt poetry series) $24.95; pa $14.95   **811**

   1. Poetry -- By individual authors

   ISBN 0-8229-4258-5; 0-8229-5877-5 pa

                                LC 2004-28397

"There is a simplicity to these poems, a healthy, peaceful spirit. . . . Kooser is a skilled craftsman, with a sharp eye and fine ear." Libr J

Kumin, Maxine

Connecting the dots; poems. Norton 1996 86p $18.95; pa $11.95   **811**

   1. Poetry -- By individual authors

   ISBN 0-393-03962-5; 0-393-31695-5 pa

                                LC 95-44441

"Kumin's is a poetry of wide sympathy and tact in which the ecumenical flavor is dominant, starting with the author's description of herself as a 'Jewish agnostic' educated at a convent school. Here both the odd and the even are at home: New Hampshire farm country as well as cosmopolitan Boston, Heidegger and Berlioz interwoven among depictions of spring training, Bosnia, and a New Year's Eve party. This collection is full of generational severance and renewal." New Yorker

Jack and other new poems. W.W. Norton & Co 2005 112p hardcover o.p. pa $13.95   **811**

   1. Poetry -- By individual authors

   ISBN 978-0-393-32852-3; 0-393-32852-X

                                LC 2004-21762

This collection of poetry "focuses on three subjects the poet knows well: first, the fauna (wild and domestic) in and around her New Hampshire farm; second, the troubles and lessons of advancing age; third, large-scale political history, 'this century born in blood and bombs' as this Jewish-American poet has known it. . . . Most of her strongest work (the title poem included) concerns elderly or deceased animals, obvious analogues for Kumin's ill, deceased or grieving human beings." Publ Wkly

The **long** marriage; poems. Norton 2001 118p $21; pa $12   **811**

1. Poetry -- By individual authors
ISBN 0-393-04351-7; 0-393-32437-0 pa

LC 2001-34553

"Although several of the poems treat Kumin's 50-plus year marriage, one feels that the book's title may refer to 'marriage' as a kind of covenant between the poet and her environment. . . . Divided into seven sections, this collection also includes poems about sociopolitical situations (capital punishment, extinct wildlife, revolutions), considerations of aging and rehabilitation, and tributes to Hopkins, Wordsworth, Rukeyser, and Rilke." Libr J

Selected poems, 1960-1990. Norton 1997 294p $27.50; pa $17.95   **811**

1. Poetry -- By individual authors
ISBN 0-393-04073-9; 0-393-31836-2 pa

LC 96-42433

"A pastoral poet who was strongly influenced by friend and mentor Anne Sexton, Kumin is quite simply one of the very best poets writing today. The present collection represents a lifetime . . . of Kumin's work and includes selections from all her published volumes." Libr J

Kunitz, Stanley

★ The **collected** poems. Norton 2000 285p $27.95; pa $15.95   **811**

1. Poetry -- By individual authors
ISBN 0-393-05030-0; 0-393-32294-7 pa

LC 00-41130

"What makes this collection of a lifetime's work so valuable is the way it allows us to perceive the interconnectedness of all Kunitz has written. Each poem stands alone, but each also enriches the others." N Y Times Book Rev

Includes bibliographical references

Kyger, Joanne

About now; collected poems. National Poetry Foundation 2007 798p il $49.95; pa $34.95   **811**

1. Poetry -- By individual authors
ISBN 978-0-943373-72-0; 0-943373-72-7; 978-0-943373-71-3 pa; 0-943373-71-9 pa

LC 2006-48192

This volume "begins with poems of the 1950's, written when Kyger first came to San Francisco and joined the circle of poets around Robert Duncan and Jack Spicer, and ends with Night Palace, poems written in 2003 to 2004. . . . What is exciting about Kyger's poetry is the way she highlights moments which might seem mundane, but under her perceptive eye connect the individual with a greater reality, opening readers' awareness in the process. That immersion in the details of everyday life, quail crossing a yard, a phone call from a friend, or a retelling of last night's dream, is plumbed by Kyger to great depth and is epitomized by the collection's title." Jacket

Includes bibliographical references

Laughlin, James

The **collected** poems of James Laughlin; with an introduction by Hayden Carruth. Moyer Bell 1994 xxxi, 574p il $34.95; pa $19.95   **811**

1. Poetry -- By individual authors
ISBN 978-1-559-21067-6; 1-559-21067-2; 978-1-559-21128-4 pa; 1-559-21128-8 pa

LC 91-32232

"These poems are the work of a man of keen intellectual and moral sophistication, who has read, thought, and lived deeply." Libr J

The **secret** room; poems. New Directions 1997 184p $22.95; pa $14.95   **811**

1. Poetry -- By individual authors
ISBN 0-8112-1343-9; 0-8112-1344-7 pa

LC 96-26188

Laughlin "shares his thoughts with humor and tenderness as he wades in the waters of his golden years. The speaker in many of these poems admires young women and thinks, 'I could see I was entirely out of/my depth.' He realizes he is not as strong as he once was, but he can still 'make old, sick words sound new.'" Libr J

Lauterbach, Ann

Or to begin again. Penguin Books 2009 115p (Penguin poets) pa $18   **811**

1. Poetry -- By individual authors
ISBN 978-0-14-311520-5; 0-14-311520-0

LC 2008-38414

"Intelligent but no less deeply feeling, this collection confirms Lauterbach's position as one of the most highly principled and tirelessly innovative poets writing today." Publ Wkly

Lax, Robert

Love had a compass; journals and poetry. edited by James J. Uebbing. Grove Press 1996 253p $22   **811**

1. Poetry -- By individual authors
ISBN 978-0-8021-1587-4; 0-8021-1587-X

LC 96-1255

The author has produced "some of the sparest imagist poetry in English with no thought about publishing where the literary high and mighty would read him. Lax dispenses with metaphor and largely with ego . . . to present what he sees with elemental forcefulness, as if in strong Mediterranean sunlight." Booklist

A **thing** that is; new poems. edited by Paul Spaeth. Overlook Press 1997 77p $25; pa $14.95 **811**

1. Poetry -- By individual authors
ISBN 978-0-87951-699-4; 0-8795-1699-2; 978-0-87951-885-1 pa; 0-87951-885-5 pa

LC 96-29264

"Given to short lines arranged in long columns, Lax's poems link the natural and personal in simple, direct, deadpan narration. The simplicity can be misleading, not in its initially unnoticed depth or metaphor but in its very purity, its almost ascetic singleness of purpose. . . . Lax has been working at the margins for a long time and has found a crisp and comfortable way of ordering and exploring his contemplations. This collection is not for everyone, but it is a essential for that special audience for truly avante-garde work." Libr J

Lazarus, Emma

Emma Lazarus; selected poems. John Hollander, editor. Library of America 2005 151p (American poets project) $20 **811**

1. Poetry -- By individual authors

ISBN 978-1-931082-77-8; 1-931082-77-4

LC 2004-61551

"At the age of eighteen [Lazarus] had written an impressive poem titled 'In the Jewish Synagogue at Newport,' which all readers recognized as a response to Longfellow's dignified and respectful poem about the Jewish cemetery there. . . . Lazarus became perhaps the most accomplished American writer of sonnets between the generations of Longfellow and Robert Frost. . . . [Her] remarkable 'Little Poems in Prose,' the title borrowed from Baudelaire, ranged with visionary power across centuries of Jewish experience." N Y Rev Books

Lee, Li-Young

Behind my eyes. W.W. Norton 2008 106p $24.95 **811**

1. Poetry -- By individual authors

ISBN 978-0-393-06542-8; 0-393-06542-1

"In this fourth collection by [the author], timely immigration issues drive such poems as 'Self-Help for Fellow Refugees,' but Lee swiftly folds them into broader inquiries about inheritance, memory and loss. . . . Lee's ringing clarity and his compelling life story have brought him uncommonly loyal readers: this volume should swell their ranks. A CD of Lee reading many of the poems is included." Publ Wkly

Leiter, Sharon

Critical companion to Emily Dickinson; a literary reference to her life and work. Facts on File 2006 448p il $75 **811**

1. Poets 2. Authors

ISBN 0-8160-5448-7; 978-0-8160-5448-0

LC 2005-28123

This book "opens with a foreword by poet and Dickinson scholar Gregory Orr and includes an introduction; an approximately 20-page biography of Dickinson; explications of 150 of her best-known poems (e.g., 'Because I Could Not Stop for Death'); an A-to-Z dictionary of relevant persons, places, and ideas illustrated with black-and-white photos; a chronology; bibliographies; and a comprehensive index." Libr J

Includes bibliographical references

Lerner, Ben

Angle of yaw. Copper Canyon Press 2006 127p pa $15 **811**

1. Poetry -- By individual authors

ISBN 1-55659-246-9

LC 2006-14260

"Employing the language of aphorism, advertising, parable, personal essay, political tirade, journalism and journal, the collage-like poems of Lerner's . . . collection express the ennui of American life in an era when even war feels like a television event." Publ Wkly

Levertov, Denise

Selected poems; with a preface by Robert Creeley; edited and with an afterword by Paul Lacey. New Directions 2002 220p hardcover o.p. pa $14.95 **811**

1. Poetry -- By individual authors

ISBN 978-0-8112-1554-1; 0-8112-1520-2

LC 2002-11891

This volume "endeavors to do what all 'selecteds' do: give readers a chance to see for themselves the development of a poetic sensibility. Editor Paul A. Lacey has brought together poems from nearly every collection of Levertov's oeuvre, producing a catalogue of the wildly diverse subjects that engaged her throughout her long career. Here are poems about love and war, about religion and art, about sorrow and joy, about political resistance and familial intimacy and, perhaps most significantly for Levertov's legacy, numerous poems about the practice of poetry itself." Harvard Rev

Levine, Philip

Breath; poems. Knopf 2004 82 p. $23 **811**

1. Poetry -- By individual authors

ISBN 1400042917

LC 2004040839

This is a collection of poetry by the author of Ashes, What Work Is, and The Simple Truth.

The author writes "free verse about American manliness, physical labor, simple pleasures and profound grief, often set in working-class Detroit (where Levine grew up) or in central California (where he now resides), sometimes tinged with reference to his Jewish heritage or to the Spanish poets of rapt simplicity (Machado, Lorca) who remain his most visible influence. Levine's 18th book will neither disappoint his devotees nor silence the doubters." Publ Wkly

The mercy; poems. Knopf 1999 81p hardcover o.p. pa $16 **811**

1. Poetry -- By individual authors

ISBN 978-0-375-70135-1; 0-375-70135-4

LC 98-43353

"Levine's poetry has been steadily moving to the front rank of American poetry for three decades. . . . If Walt Whitman's vision contained multitudes, and if Emerson's vision of nature transcended what it saw with its own eyes, Levine's poetic vision, nearly religious, transcends class, transcends natural boundaries, and transcends time." Atl Mon

New selected poems. Knopf 1991 292p hardcover o.p. pa $20 **811**

1. Poetry -- By individual authors

ISBN 978-0-679-74056-8; 0-679-74056-2

LC 90-53422

This selection contains poems Levine chose for his earlier Selected poems (1984), plus 15 new works

"This is a monumental work that somehow remains wonderfully accessible, largely because Levine has chosen pieces carefully, favoring shorter works and poems that address his staple themes of family (like 'Uncle' and 'My Son and I') and childhood ('Coming Home'). Many of the poems are powerfully imagistic." Libr J

News of the world; poems. Alfred A Knopf 2009 65p $25 (2011)   **811**

1. Poetry -- By individual authors
ISBN 978-0-307-27223-2

LC 2009-16517

A volume of prose poems and formal verses includes pieces on breakfasting late-shift Detroit auto workers, a woman who sings with the Spanish dawn, and an Andorran communist black-market supplier.

The author's "flirtations with death in both prose poems and formal verse have a weightiness that remains long after you close the book. . . . These poems exude a certain melancholia, but Levine's ability to examine expertly the beauty in this sadness keeps them from veering toward the unnecessarily depressing. He can paint even the strange with simple, natural language in a way that's subtly moving, and the nostalgic glow he applies to his memories makes this work the perfect addition to the oeuvre that has come to define his life." Libr J

The **simple** truth; poems. Knopf 1994 69p hardcover o.p. pa $16   **811**

1. Poetry -- By individual authors
ISBN 978-0-679-76584-4; 0-679-76584-0

LC 94-14508

This "collection of poetry is largely about the past: friends lost, fates assigned, potatoes eaten, decisions made. . . . Levine's mingling of realism and romanticism, involving many near-meetings between them, produces fascinating, emotionally persuasive shifts and tonal modulations that closely approach a lived truth." Publ Wkly

What work is; poems. Knopf 1991 77p hardcover o.p. pa $15   **811**

1. Poetry -- By individual authors
ISBN 978-0-679-74058-2; 0-679-74058-9

LC 90-53421

"This collection amounts to a hymn of praise for all the workers of America. These proletarian heroes, with names like Lonnie, Loo, Sweet Pea, and Packy, work the furnaces, forges, slag heaps, assembly lines, and loading docks at places with unglamorous names like Brass Craft or Feinberg and Breslin's First-Rate Plumbing and Plating. . . . But Levine's characters are also significant for their inner lives, not merely their jobs." Libr J

Lindsay, Sarah

Twigs & knucklebones. Copper Canyon Press 2008 117p $15   **811**

1. Poetry -- By individual authors
ISBN 9781556591648 pa

LC 2008-19578

This is a book of poems by the author of Primate Behavior (1997) and Mount Clutter (2002).

"Sarah Lindsay uses oddities and 'flukes' as a point of entry to broader questions regarding fate, bygone civilizations, and human nature. Written in finely crafted narrative verse, her poems take place in a diverse set of locales, both ancient and contemporary, and often explore the intersection of the unfamiliar with the everyday. . . . [This] is an enigmatic, evocative, and compelling book." Pedestal

Liu, Xiaobo, 1955-

★ **June** fourth elegies; [Nian nian liu si / Liu Xiaobo] ; translated from the Chinese by Jeffrey Yang ; foreword by Dalai Lama. Liu Xiaobo. Jonathan Cape 2012 xxv, 228 p.p   **811**

1. China -- Poetry 2. Political activists 3. Human rights -- Poetry 4. Chinese poetry -- Collections 5. Tiananmen Square Incident, Beijing (China), 1989 -- Poetry 6. China -- History -- Tiananmen Square Incident, 1989 -- Poetry
ISBN 1555976107; 9780224096812

LC 2012427497

This book is the "first publication of the poetry of 2010 Nobel Peace Prize Winner Liu Xiaobo . . . [who is] the foremost symbol of the struggle for human rights in China. . . . 'June Fourth Elegies' presents Liu's poems written across twenty years in memory of fellow protestors at Tiananmen Square, as well as poems addressed to his wife, Liu Xia. In this bilingual volume, Liu's poetry is . . . published . . . in both English translation and in the Chinese original.' (Publisher's Note) Xiaobo rebukes his nation, 'used to memorializing tombs as palaces,' and his 'city of near perfect/ shamelessness.' He also casts a harsh eye on himself . . . 'Even if I have the courage/ to be jailed again,' Xiaobo writes, 'it isn't courage enough/ to excavate memories of the dead.'" (Publishers Weekly)

Nian nian liu si

Logan, William

Our savage art; poetry and the civil tongue. Columbia University Press 2009 346p bibl $29.50 **811**

1. American poetry -- History and criticism
ISBN 978-0-231-14732-3; 0-231-14732-5

LC 2008-36414

This collection is "the latest installment in William Logan's prolonged and rumbustious assault on the state of American poetry. . . . The most obvious advantage of Logan's Diogenes-like approach to much of the contemporary poetry he writes about is that it transforms the normally rather stultifying genre of the poetry review into something more akin to a blood sport. Logan's hounding and slashing, parodying and chastising, make for what editors call good copy." N Y Times Book Rev

Includes bibliographical references (p. [341]-344) and index

Longfellow, Henry Wadsworth

★ **Poems** and other writings. Library of Am. 2000 854p $35   **811**

1. Poetry -- By individual authors
ISBN 1-88301-185-X

LC 00-26678

This volume includes "Hiawatha, Evangeline, The Courtship of Miles Standish and 'The Midnight Ride of Paul Revere.' Here, too, are some surprisingly powerful lyric and meditative poems—well made, deeply felt, and not much like the schoolhouse favorites." Publ Wkly

Includes bibliographical references

Lorde, Audre

The **collected** poems of Audre Lorde. Norton 1997 489p $35; pa $17.95 **811**

1. Poetry -- By individual authors

ISBN 0-393-04090-9; 0-393-31972-5 pa

LC 97-10878

"Since her death in 1992, Lorde's reputation has continued to grow. In life a tough, eloquent crusader who demanded that we honor the varieties of human experience, she retained her hold on readers despite the unavailability of much of her work. This edition, then, should be welcomed wherever there is interest in women's, minority, and lesbian literature. It includes Lorde's passionately private early work as well as her later, more obviously political work." Booklist

Lowell, Amy

Selected poems; Honor Moore, editor. Library of America 2004 xxxi, 156p (American poets project) $20 **811**

1. Poetry -- By individual authors

ISBN 978-1-93108-270-9; 1-93108-270-7

LC 2004-48505

This volume contains "the 'cadenced verse' of [Lowell's] Imagist . . . works, her experiments in 'polyphonic prose,' her narrative poetry, and her adaptations from the classical Chinese." Publisher's note

Lowell, Robert

★ **Collected** poems; edited by Frank Bidart and David Gewanter, with the editorial assistance of DeSales Harrison. Farrar, Straus & Giroux 2003 1186p il $45 **811**

1. Poetry -- By individual authors

ISBN 0-374-12617-8

This collection includes "Lowell's first book, Land of Unlikeness (1944); and poems from his 11 ensuing collections, including Life Studies (1959) and The Dolphin (1973). . . . Substantial notes, a chronology, glossary, and critical essays make this an essential title. Readers who think they know Lowell's work will discover new facets, and readers just venturing into Lowell's potently rendered and ceaselessly evocative poetic universe will find much to contemplate." Booklist

Includes bibliographical references

Selected poems; rev ed; Farrar, Straus & Giroux 1977 255p hardcover o.p. **811**

1. Poetry -- By individual authors

LC 78-104855

First published 1976

A selection of over 200 poems tracing the development of one of the premier confessional poets of his generation

Lucas, Dave

Weather; poems. University of Georgia Press 2011 68p pa $16.95 **811**

1. Poetry -- By individual authors

ISBN 978-0-8203-3882-8; 0-8203-3882-6

LC 2010-44222

"The first thing one notices in 'Weather,' Dave Lucas' first poetry collection, is the almost shocking formality of the language not in vocabulary so much as in a theatrical phrasing no longer so common in poetry. Lucas frequently writes things like 'I am also seething / in my depths,' which might not be so interesting were it not for the fact that the book's main subject is the contemporary Midwest, most often Cleveland and its surrounding environs, which for Lucas, is a landscape as mythic as Troy. . . . If Lucas' almost oracular tone occasionally spills over into melodrama, he makes up for it by the absolute beauty of so many of his lines and descriptions. . . . This is a lovely, promising and powerful first book, even more so for readers who know its landscape." Cleveland Plain Dealer

Includes bibliographical references.

MacGowan, Christopher J.

Twentieth -century American poetry; [by] Christopher MacGowan. Blackwell Pub 2004 331p (Blackwell guides to literature) $66.95; pa $27.95 **811**

1. Poetry -- By individual authors 2. American poetry -- History and criticism

ISBN 0-631-22025-9; 0-631-22026-7 pa

LC 2003-12196

This guide explores the historical and cultural contexts within which twentieth-century American poetry was created and includes a biographical dictionary of such key writers as Robert Frost, Ezra Pound, T. S. Eliot, Langston Hughes, James Dickey, Adrienne Rich, and Rita Dove

Includes bibliographical references

Mackey, Nathaniel

Splay anthem. New Directions Book 2006 126p pa $15.95 **811**

1. Poetry -- By individual authors

ISBN 0-8112-1652-7

LC 2005-35051

"Often turning adversity to their advantage, the poems sing not of resurrection but repair, and Splay Anthem is the most delicate and delirious installment of Mackey's epic song of salvage. Its poems speak with a torn voice, a rasp punctuated by gasps of anguish and rumbling with the desire for rejuvenation." Nation

MacLeish, Archibald

Collected poems, 1917-1982; with a prefatory note to the newly collected poems by Richard B. McAdoo. Houghton Mifflin 1985 524p hardcover o.p. pa $19 **811**

1. Poetry -- By individual authors

ISBN 0-395-39569-0 pa

LC 85-14392

Collects all the known poetry of the author/public servant. As an expatriate in Paris his early work was heavily influenced by Pound and Eliot. After returning to the States his verse concerned itself more with America's political, social, and cultural heritage

Manning, Maurice

The **common** man. Houghton Mifflin Harcourt 2010 96p $22 **811**

1. Poetry -- By individual authors

ISBN 978-0-547-24961-2; 0-547-24961-6

LC 2009-29080

"The book balances our cynical, back-foot expectations as readers of contemporary poetry with its own unpretentious ambition incredibly well—the natural world becomes strange in Manning's hands, but not unrecognizably so." Sycamore Rev

Mariani, Paul L.

The **broken** tower: a life of Hart Crane; [by] Paul Mariani. Norton 1999 492p il hardcover o.p. pa $15.95   **811**
1. Poets 2. Authors 3. Short story writers
ISBN 0-393-32041-3 pa

LC 98-37726

"Using unpublished letters, manuscripts, and photographs [Mariani] pieces together the life and passions of this brilliant yet tormented man whose creative genius left us 'The Bridge' and whose influence still reverberates among poets today." Libr J
Includes bibliographical references

Lost puritan: a life of Robert Lowell. Norton 1994 527p il hardcover o.p. pa $15   **811**
1. Poets 2. Authors
ISBN 0-393-31374-3 pa

LC 93-48018

"Mariani, for all his moment-by-moment acuteness and lucidity, offers no radically new insights into Lowell's life or art, nor does he provide those powerfully developed thematic and narrative lines that distinguish the greatest literary biographies. Still, this remains an impressive piece of writing and documentation." Choice

Matthews, William

After all; last poems. Houghton Mifflin 1998 55p hardcover o.p. pa $13   **811**
1. Poetry -- By individual authors
ISBN 0-618-05685-8 pa

LC 98-22909

"Since Matthews was one of the few contemporary poets who really knew how to make the vernacular sing, it's sad to think that these are his last poems. Fittingly, some of them are autumnal, but they range widely and brightly from Prague in 1419 to a Caribbean island in 1967 to Martha Mitchell, Finn sheep, and a poetry reading at West Point. A lovely finale." Libr J

Selected poems and translations, 1969-1991. Houghton Mifflin 1992 200p hardcover o.p. pa $22.95   **811**
1. Poetry -- By individual authors
ISBN 978-0-395-66993-8; 0-395-66993-6

LC 91-45716

"Matthews has been widely praised for the solid grounding of his poems, and rightly so. His clear-cut metaphors illuminate the everyday world with the magic of semantic revelation and the grace of othermindedness." Booklist

May, Jamaal

Hum; Jamaal May. Alice James Books 2013 80 p. (pbk.) $15.95   **811**
1. Poetry -- Collections
ISBN 1938584023; 9781938584022

LC 2013022185

In this collection of poems, by Jamaal May, "poems buzz and purr like a well-oiled chassis. Grit, trial, and song thrum through tight syntax and deft prosody. From the resilient pulse of an abandoned machine to the sinuous lament of origami animals, here is the ever-changing hum that vibrates through us all, connecting one mind to the next." (Publisher's note)

"May, a teacher, seems acutely aware of the injustices in our current condition, but he seeks to educate rather than preach; his poems, exquisitely balanced by a sharp intelligence mixed with earnestness, makes his debut a marvel." Pub Wkly

Mayer, Bernadette

Scarlet tanager. New Directions 2005 117p pa $14.95   **811**
1. Poetry -- By individual authors
ISBN 0-8112-1582-2

LC 2005-5539

This collection demonstrates Mayer's "ease in many poetic forms, her attraction to New York City and to the Berkshires (where she now lives), her recovery from a recent stroke and her continued enthusiastic enmeshment with writing itself." Publ Wkly

McClure, Michael

★ **Of** indigo and saffron; new and selected poems. edited and with an introduction by Leslie Scalapino. University of California Press 2011 319p   **811**
1. Poetry -- By individual authors
ISBN 0-520-26287-5; 978-0-520-26287-4

LC 2010-32585

"Scalapino includes those parts of McClure's oeuvre that focus on the questioning of identity, the uncertain position of the self, and the irrelevance of the traditional lyric 'I,' the bete noire of language poets. But Scalapino's selections do give a broad taste of McClure's perennial concerns with the body, alternative forms of consciousness and environmentalism. . . . McClure invented a new form for himself: the poem centered in the middle of the page, with occasional lines in capital letters (he has insisted that these are not meant to be shouted), with the phrase or line equivalent to Olson's notion of whatever encompasses a breath. McClure has been able to accommodate every thematic concern, every mood and temperament, within this form's versatile parameters."

"Scalapino includes those parts of McClure's oeuvre that focus on the questioning of identity, the uncertain position of the self, and the irrelevance of the traditional lyric 'I,' the bete noire of language poets. But Scalapino's selections do give a broad taste of McClure's perennial concerns with the body, alternative forms of consciousness and environmentalism. . . . McClure invented a new form for himself: the poem centered in the middle of the page, with occasional lines in capital letters (he has insisted that these are not meant to be shouted), with the phrase or line equivalent to Olson's notion of whatever encompasses a breath. McClure has been able to accommodate every thematic concern, every mood and temperament, within this form's versatile parameters." San Francisco Chron

McGrath, Thomas
Letter to an imaginary friend. Copper Canyon Press 1997 413p pa $20 **811**
1. Poetry -- By individual authors
ISBN 978-1-55659-078-8; 1-55659-078-4
LC 97-33929
"Although McGrath, who died in 1990 at 74, published the poem's four parts separately, it appears here complete for the first time. . . . A surprisingly accessible long poem in the Pound tradition of personal epics, Letter arrives 'helved, greaved, and garlanded' and compels our intimate attention." Publ Wkly

McHugh, Heather
★ **Upgraded** to serious. Copper Canyon Press 2009 85p $22 **811**
1. Poetry -- By individual authors
ISBN 978-1-55659-306-2
LC 2009-13347
This collection "offers exactly ravishing poetry that digs deeply into big themes: free will, consciousness, ideas of language. . . . Thinking poems are often poems with lots of moving parts, and when reading (and rereading) this book one notes the elegance with which everything – perception, reflection, feeling – is held in play. And 'play' is the operative word: McHugh's method always involves some winning blend of precision and momentum." Globe and Mail

McLane, Maureen N., 1967-
My poets; Maureen N. McLane. Farrar, Straus and Giroux 2012 273 p. (hc : alk. paper) $25.00 **811**
1. Poets 2. Poetry -- History and criticism 3. Poetry -- Influence
ISBN 0374217491; 9780374217495
LC 2011041208
In this book, poet and critic Maureen N. McLane "presents an esoteric tour of her personal pantheon, the poets that have shaped her life." The text is a "mixture of prose criticism, memoir, anecdote, and imitative verse written in tribute." The poets discussed include Geoffrey Chaucer, Elizabeth Bishop, H. D., and Gertrude Stein. (Publishers Weekly)

McMichael, James
Capacity. Farrar, Straus and Giroux 2006 74p $22 **811**
1. Poetry -- By individual authors
ISBN 978-0-374-11890-7; 0-374-11890-6
LC 2005-51628
"Better known for the infrastructural sweep of his work, McMichael is also a poet of the kind of centripetal force and barely contained emotional heat that we more often associate with the short lyric. What makes him unique in American poetry right now is the strength and subtlety with which he blends conceptual ambition with emotional power. It's very common these days to hear poets talking about their 'projects.' But in James McMichael we actually have a poet whose sustained investigation of a small set of obsessions

has produced the most integral and surprising structures." Yale Rev

Melville, Herman
★ The **poems** of Herman Melville; edited by Douglas Robillard. rev ed; Kent State Univ. Press 2000 349p pa $29 **811**
1. Poetry -- By individual authors
ISBN 0-87338-660-4
LC 99-52872
First published 1976 by College and University Press Service
This volume "presents the complete texts of 'Battle-Pieces,' 'John Marr and Other Sailors,' and 'Timoleon,' as well as additional manuscript poems. Also presented are excerpts from the long narrative poem Clarel to give the reader a taste of the style and content of this work. The editor's introduction, as well as his notes at the end of each section, are informative as well as appreciative of Melville's status as a poet." Libr J
Includes bibliographical references

Menashe, Samuel
★ **New** and selected poems; Christopher Ricks, editor. Library of America 2005 191p (American poets project) $20 **811**
1. Poetry -- By individual authors
ISBN 1-931082-85-5
LC 2005-44161
"Menashe is a curious and meticulous writer, whose brief, sparsely punctuated poems depend on difficult rhyme and assonance schemes to relay his observations. A wry but basically optimistic poet, his best writing shows that the stylistic restrictions one selects rapidly cease to be restrictions, even when one identifies them as such." N Y Times Book Rev

Meredith, William
Effort at speech; new and selected poems. Tri-Quarterly Bks. 1997 231p $46; pa $17.95 **811**
1. Poetry -- By individual authors
ISBN 0-8101-5070-0; 0-8101-5071-9 pa
LC 97-9679
Meredith's early poems "are as subtle as aspirin. So easily digestible in their precise meter and perfectly tuned end-rhyme, their power goes virtually unnoticed until the reader lifts his eyes from the page to find himself moved, affected. In work inspired by the poet's service at sea during WWII, devastation comes on the hushed waves of sonnets. . . . The poems in the book's latter half (1970-1987) find formalism surrendering some ground to free verse as Meredith attempts to salve not the sharp pains of war but the blunted ache of aging." Publ Wkly

Merrill, James
The **changing** light at Sandover; with the stage adaptation Voices from Sandover. edited by J.D. McClatchy and Stephen Yenser. 2nd Knopf hardcover ed.; Knopf 2006 627p il $40 **811**
1. Poetry -- By individual authors
ISBN 978-0-307-26321-6; 0-307-26321-5
LC 2006-273431

First published 1982 by Atheneum; 1992 by Knopf, without Voices from Sandover

This "is an arduous poem, steep and lofty, more than a little difficult to climb, explore, and comprehend, its intricate faceting of the serious and unserious, sacred and profane, vexing to many a reader; but it has, I believe, one controlling stratagem, Merrill's persistent use of doubling or 'entwinning.'. . . The trilogy (though it goes on far too long, gets periodically dizzy, has too much felix culpa and not enough mea culpa) is, surely, an astonishing performance." N Y Rev Books

★ The **collected** poems of James Merrill; edited by J.D. McClatchy and Stephen Yenser. Knopf 2001 xx, 885p $40; pa $27.50 **811**
1. Poetry -- By individual authors
ISBN 0-375-41139-9; 0-375-70941-X pa
LC 00-40542

"Excluded are some juvenilia and light verse, as well as Merrill's book-length poem The Changing Light at Sandover, in print as a separate volume. Merrill's sonnets, sapphics, longer sequences and sinuous sentences encompass lyric pathos, ebullient comedy, rapt romance and acrid satire. Their formal sophistication can belie their depth of feeling, which is exactly what some readers love best about Merrill's work." Publ Wkly

Merton, Thomas

In the dark before dawn; new selected poems of Thomas Merton. edited with an introduction and notes by Lynn R. Szabo; preface by Kathleen Norris. New Directions 2005 253p pa $16.95 **811**
1. Poetry -- By individual authors
ISBN 978-0-8112-1613-5; 0-8112-1613-6
LC 2004-30957

"Szabo has drawn widely from the furious poetic writing of Merton's final years. This new spectrum of poems helps us tap into the complexity and mystery of Thomas Merton. Readers of Merton's journals will be aware of his shifting attitude to all sorts of things—being an American, being a monk at Gethsemani, being a writer, in particular a poet. Szabo helps us here by assembling the poems in eight thematic sections, so as to display the multiple Mertons. There was the contemplative, drawn to the silent beauties of Gethsemani Abbey, especially at night. There was the stinging and at times declamatory social critic, the admiring and painstaking translator, the avant garde experimentalist and, toward the end, the lovelorn monk." America

Merwin, W. S.

★ **Migration**; new & selected poems. Copper Canyon Press 2005 545p $40 **811**
1. Poetry -- By individual authors
ISBN 1-55659-218-3
LC 2004-17473

This volume contains poetry from sixteen of Merwin's collections.

"Complex, spiritual, and evocative, Merwin is a major poet, and this is a sublime measure of his achievements." Booklist

Present company. Copper Canyon Press 2005 137p $22 **811**
1. Poetry -- By individual authors
ISBN 1-55659-227-2
LC 2005-08867

"Nearing 80, the Pulitzer Prize winner seems especially mindful of age and mortality, and these poems–like a series of heartfelt thank-you notes–offer homage to the things of this world. In a manner that recalls the cool, spare diction of H.D., Merwin addresses the local and the nondescript . . . as well as the abstract and the universal. . . . The emotional timber rarely rises above muted melancholy, and Merwin's thoughtful, measured pace never quickens, but the poems are suffused with a warmth and clarity achieved over six decades of disciplined dedication to his art." Libr J

The **shadow** of Sirius. Copper Canyon Press 2008 117p $22 **811**
1. Poetry -- By individual authors
ISBN 978-1-55659-284-3; 1-55659-284-1
LC 2008-14578

Merwin "continues to sing of a disappearing world. At one level these are the Zen-guided, misty disappearances of demarcations. . . . This non-dualist philosophy of Merwin's is perfectly expressed in his smooth, unpunctuated poems, calmly voiced and carefully illuminated with spare, vivid images. There is no overexcited narration (it's tonality rather than personality), no linguistic fireworks to awe the reader. Yet Merwin rarely nods. There is an alert simplicity in nearly every poem." Harvard Rev

Merwin, W. S. (William Stanley), 1927-

The **moon** before morning; W.S. Merwin. Copper Canyon Press 2014 xii, 121 p.p $24 **811**
1. Nature poetry 2. American poetry -- Collections
ISBN 1556594534; 9781556594533
LC 2013031662

This poetry collection by "W.S. Merwin examines everything from minute flowers to oceanic destruction, and weaves our complex relationship with the natural world with his own youth, memory, and intense engagement with the passing of days. With considered reverence, subtle might, and generous poetic imagination, Merwin presents a masterful and gorgeous collection." (Publisher's note)

"Merwin's masterfully refined, meditative poems stem from his dwelling mindfully in one beloved place and handling words as though they are seeds, flowers, stones, and water." Booklist

Includes bibliographical references

Middlebrook, Diane Wood

Anne Sexton; a biography. Vintage Bks. 1992 xxiii, 498p il pa $14 **811**
1. Poets 2. Authors 3. Dramatists 4. Poets, American
ISBN 0-679-74182-8
LC 92-50093

First published 1991 by Houghton Mifflin

"Ms. Middlebrook has written a wonderful book: just, balanced, insightful, complex in its sympathies and in its judgment of Sexton both as a person and as a writer." NY Times Book Rev

Includes bibliographical references

Millay, Edna St. Vincent

Collected poems; edited by Norma Millay. Harper & Row 1956 xxi, 738p hardcover o.p. pa $22.95   **811**

1. Poetry -- By individual authors
ISBN 0-06-090889-0 pa

The poems in this collection "are divided into two separate sections of lyrics and sonnets, arranged chronologically and printed in groups under the titles of the original volumes, ranging from 'Renascence' of 1917 to 'Mine the harvest,' published in 1954, four years after the poet's death." Booklist

★ **Selected** poems; J.D. McClatchy, editor. Library of Am. 2003 xxxiii, 231p (American poets project) $20   **811**

1. Poetry -- By individual authors
ISBN 1-931082-35-9

LC 2002-32126

This collection draws from all Millay's "verse books to display her career-long adroitness in her favorite form, the sonnet, and her variety by including even excerpts from an opera libretto. . . . Read occasionally and mixed with her saucy lyrics about erotic love, . . . [her sonnets] reveal their strengths—not of imagery, but of surprising attitudes expressed within strictly observed poetic conventions." Booklist

Mlinko, Ange

Shoulder season; poems. Coffee House Press 2010 81p pa $16   **811**

1. Poetry -- By individual authors
ISBN 978-1-56689-243-8; 1-56689-243-0

LC 2009-51508

This is a book of poems by the author of Matinées (1999) and Starred Wire (2005).

"Pirouetting beyond fields plowed and sown by Frank O'Hara, John Ashbery, James Schuyler, and Alice Notley, Ange Mlinko is creating her own space in the world of poetry and more. To encapsulate her fecund body of work, the word glee keeps coming to mind. And that may be the most American aspect to her work, its joie de vivre. This may be the Shoulder Season, yet no one has to go slumping through it without some ecstasy." Galatea Resurrects

Moore, Marianne

★ The **poems** of Marianne Moore; edited by Grace Schulman. Viking 2003 449p hardcover o.p. pa $18   **811**

1. Poetry -- By individual authors
ISBN 0-14-303908-3 pa

LC 2003-50159

"The great modernist poet finally gets her due with this outstanding compliation." Libr J

Includes bibliographical references

Morrison, Rusty

Beyond the chainlink; Rusty Morrison. Ahsahta Press 2014 76p. (The new series) (pbk. : alk. paper) $18   **811**

1. Poetry -- Collections
ISBN 1934103462; 9781934103463

LC 2013034839

In this collection of poetry, by Rusty Morrison, "her eye is attuned to the ways language both obscures and exposes the seemingly lucid illusions of intimate attraction. How to recognize the past's specters as they beckon and frighten, haunt and call, from just outside the 'chainlink' of one's schoolyard expectations of self and other?" (Publisher's note)

"Vividly serious and adroitly terse, this fifth collection from poet and publisher Morrison . . . steers a sharp course between the free play of figurative language and the demands of insistent memory." Pub Wkly

Muldoon, Paul

★ **Moy** sand and gravel. Farrar, Straus & Giroux 2002 107p $22; pa $12   **811**

1. Poetry -- By individual authors
ISBN 0-374-21480-8; 0-374-52884-5 pa

LC 2002-20129

This collection "shimmers with play, the play of mind, the play of recondite information over ordinary experience, the play of observation and sensuous detail, of motion upon custom, of Irish and English languages and landscapes, of meter and rhyme. Sure enough, everything Muldoon thinks of makes him think of something else, and poem after poem takes the form of linked association." N Y Times Book Rev

Murphy, Russell E.

Critical companion to T.S. Eliot; a literary reference to his life and work. [by] Russell Elliott Murphy. Facts on File 2007 614p il (Facts on File library of American literature) $75   **811**

1. Poets 2. Authors 3. Dramatists 4. Editors 5. Essayists 6. Literary critics 7. Nobel laureates for literature
ISBN 978-0-8160-6183-9; 0-8160-6183-1

LC 2006-34076

"This is an excellent and exhaustive resource and a good buy for most libraries." Booklist

Includes bibliographical references

Nadelberg, Amanda

Bright brave phenomena; poems. Amanda Nadelberg. Coffee House Press 2012 118p.   **811**

1. Emotions -- Poetry 2. Poetry -- Collections 3. Man-woman relationship -- Poetry
ISBN 1566893038; 9781566893039

LC 2011029251

This collection of poetry "focus[es] on the ways life itself changes, depending on emotional shadings: 'I turned into a blanket and went everywhere. With him there was great purpose.' . . . A longer segmented poem chronicles various unhappinesses: 'And when her boyfriend walks to/ her, she looks like death, the/ face of death, big drapes/ in a tall room in France.' The boyfriend in this poem is just as mutable, taking the form of a blue door and a French vampire. Nadelberg's ebullient language captures the giddiness of love and youth. . . . But love can also deflate like 'two people and/ a broken thing/ as a road somewhere.' Her perspective is always staunchly feminine, unfolding like a present, her 'hysteria as a garden, a house/ the colors are beautiful.'" (Publishers Weekly)

Nemerov, Howard

★ The **selected** poems of Howard Nemerov; edited by Daniel Anderson; foreword by Wyatt Prunty. Swallow Press, Ohio University Press 2003 xxi, 154p $24.95; pa $16.95   **811**

1. Poetry -- By individual authors
ISBN 0-8040-1059-5; 0-8040-1060-9 pa
LC 2003-42380

The selections in this volume span Nemerov's entire poetic output

This volume "represents the broad spectrum of Nemerov's virtues as a poet—his intelligence, his wit, his compassion, and his irreverence. It stands as the retrospective collection of the best of what Nemerov left behind." Publisher's note

Niedecker, Lorine

Collected works; edited by Jenny Penberthy. University of Calif. Press 2002 xxiii, 471p $55; pa $25.95   **811**

1. Poetry -- By individual authors
ISBN 978-0-520-22433-9; 0-520-22433-7; 978-0-520-22434-6 pa; 0-520-22434-5 pa
LC 2001-5376

Niedecker "is often likened to Emily Dickinson. She, too, remained in the backwater where she was born. Large-scale interest in her work came only years after her death. Her characteristic poems are, like Dickinson's, short or in short stanzas, short-lined, and elliptical. But she wasn't reclusive; she connected with the Objectivists, New York poets 'led' by Louis Zukofsky. . . . Whereas Dickinson's poetry is metaphysical, Niedecker's mature work is profoundly physical, sparked by wry, class-conscious humor and usually rooted in her Black Lake Island, Wisconsin, neighborhood." Booklist

Includes bibliographical references

Nims, John Frederick

★ The **powers** of heaven and earth; new and selected poems. Louisiana State Univ. Press 2002 247p $36.95; pa $19.95   **811**

1. Poetry -- By individual authors
ISBN 0-8071-2826-0; 0-8071-2827-9 pa
LC 2002-30055

This is a "collection of the work of one of the foremost formalists and classicists among twentieth-century American poets: epigrams, odes, sonnets, shaped verse, and other kinds of poems on life, nature, culture, literature, but first and foremost, on love." Booklist

Norris, Kathleen

Journey : new and selected poems, 1969-1999. University of Pa. 2001 131p hardcover o.p. pa $16.95   **811**

1. Poetry -- By individual authors
ISBN 0-8229-5761-2 pa

A collection of Norris' "poetry spanning 30 years. Here are poems, arranged chronologically in four sections each beginning with a verse from the Song of Solomon, that tenderly describe an event or scene, examine it, and conclude with a flash of seemingly unrelated insight, leaving profound questions in the reader's heart. . . . Carrying her readers along on her deeply Christian journey, Norris avoids spiritual certainty and preachiness, remaining ever the seeker. Her poems are lyrical, accessible, and hauntingly touching to read and to reread." Libr J

North, Charles

★ **What** it is like; new and selected poems. Turtle Point Press/Hanging Loose Press 2011 302p pa $20   **811**

1. Poetry -- By individual authors
ISBN 978-1-933527-48-2

"North is a younger compatriot of O'Hara and Ashbery, and his nonchalance aspiring to greatness finds the same 'risks inside art' that the other New York School poets found in the city. Juggling a satiric self-consciousness with a 'strange mischief,' North pulls death-defying propositions and playful mockeries from thin air." Publ Wkly

Notley, Alice

★ **Grave** of light; new and selected poems, 1970-2005. Wesleyan University Press 2006 364p $29.95   **811**

1. Poetry -- By individual authors
ISBN 0-8195-6772-8
LC 2006-15712

"Experimental in every sense of the word, Alice Notley has produced an extensive body of work over 30 years in print. This new collection unites previously unpublished poems as well as those from both small-press chapbooks and more widely distributed volumes. Arranged in chronological order while maintaining poetic sequences, Notley's poems tell the story of her artistic development and bear witness to the multitude of styles and influences that Notley has explored. . . . Diversity is Notley's most consistent quality, and this makes her not only somewhat of an enigma aesthetically but also appealing to varying poetic tastes." Booklist

In the pines. Penguin Books 2007 131p (Penguin poets) pa $18   **811**

1. Poetry -- By individual authors
ISBN 978-0-14-311254-9; 0-14-311254-6
LC 2007-12076

"Notley takes the title of her 30-somethingth collection from a notorious American folk song: a man tries to get his lover to admit she's been unfaithful, asking her where she's slept, and her ambiguous answer—in the pines—only makes things worse. That menacing rhetorical moment informs the whole of this searing collection, which is part autobiography, part riposte to literary culture, and part lyrical reclamation of feminist territory. . . . This master poet continues to inspire and challenge." Publ Wkly

Nye, Naomi Shihab

You & yours: poems. BOA Editions 2005 87p (American poets continuum series) hardcover o.p. pa $15.50 **811**

1. Poetry -- By individual authors

ISBN 1-929918-68-2; 1-929918-69-0 pa

LC 2005-11360

"Tender yet forceful, funny and commonsensical, reflective and empathic, Nye writes radiant poems of nature and piercing poems of war, always touching base with homey details and radiant portraits of family and neighbors." Booklist

O'Brien, Michael

Sleeping and waking. Flood Editions 2007 63p pa $12.95 **811**

1. Poetry -- By individual authors

ISBN 978-0-9787467-2-8 pa; 0-9787467-2-4

"O'Brien is primarily an observer rather than a debater, and the poems here are heavy on isolated images, dream logic, bits of overheard conversation (typically urban conversation) and memories, with larger themes emerging through juxtapositions and repetitions. . . . While O'Brien's technical skills should be crisp enough to please the iciest avant-gardist, he has one virtue more cerebral poets often lack: he isn't afraid to make a plain statement. In other hands, that virtue can become a self-satisfied vice, but here it lends a necessary sharpness to an otherwise fluid and dreamlike collection." N Y Times Book Rev

O'Hara, Frank

The collected poems of Frank O'Hara; edited by Donald Allen; with an introduction by John Ashbery. University of Calif. Press 1995 xxix, 586p pa $24.95 **811**

1. Poetry -- By individual authors

ISBN 0-520-20166-3

LC 94-24660

A reissue of the title first published 1971 by Knopf

The subjects of this collection "are lunch-time strolls past construction workers and bargains in wrist watches, the lives of artists (whether distant heroes or close friends), the distractions of city life, . . . homosexuality, . . . headlines glimpsed on newstands. . . . Some {are} . . . about friendships, occasional pieces written for a marriage or a departure." Newsweek

Includes bibliographical references

Frank O'Hara: selected poems; edited by Mark Ford. Alfred A. Knopf 2008 288p $30 **811**

1. Poetry -- By individual authors

ISBN 978-0-307-26815-0; 0-307-26815-2

LC 2007-42865

"At his strongest O'Hara profoundly affected the development of American poetry. . . . His acute eye and finely tuned ear combined with his breezy idiolect and thoughtful intelligence to create a style expressive of a generation that returned from a brutal war intent on throwing off old conventions and seeking new sensations. If O'Hara's work lacks the gravitas ultimately achieved by Koch and Ashbery, his clear, youthful voice will nonetheless continue to evoke a heady, hopeful time in our cultural history—before optimism turned to ashes." New Leader

O'Rourke, Meghan

Once; poems. W. W. Norton & Company 2011 89p $24.95 **811**

1. Poetry -- By individual authors

ISBN 978-0-393-08062-9

LC 2011029033

"Capturing a world where the whimsical observations of a child and the agonizing realities of adulthood collide, O'Rourke's poems offer a resonant exploration of relationships with both family and country. Crossing inevitably through the seasons, the collection transitions from summer pools and Popsicles to icy pines and blurred Christmas lights, all the while reverting back to a mother rebelling against a ravenous disease. . . . Bonded by sorrow but never hopeless, the narrator of this powerful collection dives into a gulf of mourning and emerges renewed." Booklist

Olds, Sharon

Blood, tin, straw. Knopf 1999 125p hardcover o.p. pa $16 **811**

1. Poetry -- By individual authors

ISBN 978-0-375-70735-3; 0-375-70735-2

LC 99-15602

"Olds has always been a frank and transcendent poet of the body, and now . . . she expands her profoundly tactile sensibility to embrace the entire cosmos in poems of powerful female eroticism and emotional acuity that celebrate love both earthly and spiritual." Booklist

The unswept room. Knopf 2002 96p $25; pa $15 **811**

1. Poetry -- By individual authors

ISBN 0-375-41489-4; 0-375-70998-3 pa

LC 2002-18444

"Organized like her previous works, this work begins with poems about her early life and then moves on to grade school, her marriage, and up to the present day. Throughout, Olds re-creates her life, building a scrapbook through words. Although many of her subjects (family, love, sex) stay the same, her tone has shifted from an angry questioning of fate to a passionate acceptance of her own mortality and the experiences she has had." Libr J

The wellspring. Knopf 1996 88p hardcover o.p. pa $16 **811**

1. Poetry -- By individual authors

ISBN 978-0-679-76560-8; 0-679-76560-3

LC 95-15835

This collection "takes the form of an intimate family portrait. Olds begins by imagining her parents making love for the first time. This explicitness informs the entire cycle, from poems about her own birth to snapshots of her youth and early sexual experiences, poems remarkable for their integrity, eroticism, tough humor, and unceasing wonder. . . . Olds continues with a series of strikingly original and profoundly moving poems about her children." Booklist

Olds, Sharon, 1942-

★ **Stag's** leap; by Sharon Olds. Alfred A. Knopf 2012 x, 89 p.p **811**

1. Divorced people -- Poetry
ISBN 0307959902; 9780307959904; 9780375712258
LC 2012004426

Pulitzer Prize: Poetry (2013)

This collection of poems by Sharon Olds "tells the story of a divorce, embracing strands of love, sex, sorrow, memory, and new freedom. . . . [Olds] shar[es] the feeling of invisibility that comes when we are no longer standing in love's sight; the surprising physical bond that still exists between a couple during parting; the loss of everything from her husband's smile to the set of his hip." (Publisher's note)

Oliver, Charles M.

Critical companion to Walt Whitman; a literary reference to his life and work. Facts on File 2005 408p il (Facts on File library of American literature) $65 **811**

1. Poets 2. Authors 3. Essayists
ISBN 0-8160-5768-0
LC 2005-4172

The author "begins this work with a biographical essay that includes several illustrations. A large portion of this book addresses Whitman's works, with entries for the individual poems and for the complete volumes. Each entry describes when and where the book was published and includes a brief account of the poem and its context. The third section of the volume covers people, places, publications, and topics related to Whitman's life and work." Choice

Includes bibliographical references

Oliver, Mary

The **leaf** and the cloud; a poem. Da Capo Press 2000 55p hardcover o.p. pa $15 **811**

1. Poetry -- By individual authors
ISBN 0-306-81073-5 pa
LC 00-57008

A "book-length poem by a poet devoted to close scrutiny of the natural world and exact, sensuous, and ecstatic description. Lyrical and philosophical in the American transcendental tradition, Oliver addresses her readers directly to ravishing effect." Booklist

★ **New** and selected poems. Beacon Press 2005 2v v1 $28.50; v1 pa $16; v2 $24.95; v2 pa $16 **811**

1. Poetry -- By individual authors
ISBN 0-8070-6878-0 v1; 0-8070-6877-2 v1 pa; 0-8070-6886-1 v2; 0-8070-6887-X v2 pa

Vol. 1 first published 1992; redesigned ed. to accompany the publication of vol. 2

Volume one contains poems written from 1965 to 1992. Volume two contains poems written from 1994 to 2005.

A **thousand** mornings; poems. Mary Oliver. Penguin Press 2012 82 p. $24.95 **811**

1. Nature poetry 2. Literature -- 21st century 3. American poetry -- Women authors
ISBN 1594204772; 9781594204777
LC 2012027310

In author Mary Oliver's book of poetry, she transports "us to the marshland and coastline of her beloved home, Provincetown, Massachusetts. In these pages, Oliver shares the wonder of dawn, the grace of animals, and the transformative power of attention. Whether studying the leaves of a tree or mourning her adored dog, Percy, she is ever patient in her observations and open to the teachings contained in the smallest of moments." (Publisher's note)

The **Truro** bear and other adventures; poems and essays. Beacon Press 2008 80p $23; pa $14 **811**

1. Animals -- Poetry 2. Poetry -- By individual authors
ISBN 978-0-8070-6884-7; 0-8070-6884-5; 978-0-8070-6885-4 pa; 0-8070-6885-3 pa
LC 2008-15400

"Oliver's poems hearken back to her 19th-century mentors—particularly Emerson, Thoreau and Whitman—in their attentiveness to the natural world and what it teaches us about ourselves; and yet they are compellingly current, given the fragile condition of the earth and its creatures." America

West wind. Houghton Mifflin 1997 63p hardcover o.p. pa $14 **811**

1. Poetry -- By individual authors
ISBN 0-395-85085-1 pa
LC 97-2986

"Although her papers may scatter as the west wind sweeps through her room, Oliver's house is in order. From the chaos of the world, her poems distill what it means to be human and what is worthwhile about life. Echoing the Romantics and Whitman, she affirms the value of aloneness with nature, of watching and listening—not just to get it down as art but simply to live it." Libr J

Winter hours; prose, prose poems, and poems. Houghton Mifflin 1999 109p $22; pa $14 **811**

1. Poetry -- By individual authors
ISBN 0-395-85084-3; 0-395-85087-8 pa
LC 99-19141

"Oliver has set aside the frames of form and the mask of her poetic persona to share memories and meditations in essays made of both poetry and prose. Writing with the knowingness born of many years of devotion to observation and expression, Oliver declares her unceasing love of nature, the source of her art, and her willingness to embrace what most people resent: the shift in tone and meter age brings." Booklist

Olson, Charles

The **Maximus** poems; edited by George F. Butterick. University of Calif. Press 1985 652p hardcover o.p. pa $42 **811**

1. Poetry -- By individual authors
ISBN 978-520-05595-7; 0-520-05595-0
LC 79-65759

This edition contains the entire sequence of poems set in Gloucester, Massachusetts, whose protagonist is the mythical figure, Maximus

"It is impossible to describe in this small space the immensity of Charles Olson's achievement—as poet, theoretician and explorer of the 'human universe.' Just as Ezra Pound's writing energized Western poetry in the first half of this century, Olson in the 1950s redefined its direction and inspired the next generation of writers. . . . 'The Maximus Poems' are a complex far-ranging attempt to grasp the history of human thought." Christ Sci Monit

Olstein, Lisa

Lost alphabet. Copper Canyon Press 2009 92p pa $15   811

1. Poetry -- By individual authors

ISBN 978-1-55659-301-7; 1-55659-301-5

LC 2008-53486

This is a "sequence of prose poems spoken in the voice of a lepidopterist engaged in isolated research on butterflies and moths near a village whose residents reluctantly embrace her presence. Flirting with fiction without quite unfurling a clear narrative, Olstein's speaker finds correlatives for her lonely if exploratory inner life in the insects—living and dead—she is studying." Publ Wkly

Olstein, Lisa, 1972-

Little stranger; Lisa Olstein. Copper Canyon Press 2013 xi, 85 p.p (pbk. : alk. paper) $16   811

1. Fear -- Poetry 2. Poetry -- Collections

ISBN 1556594321; 9781556594328

LC 2012051259

This is Lisa Olstein's third poetry collection. An "uncertain balance between hope and hopelessness, fear and fascination, breaks the calm surface of her poems." The book "is broken into six sections with a breathing space partway through in the form of a poem constructed of letters to 'Sir,' then 'Sire' then 'Siren.'" (Publishers Weekly)

Oppen, George

★ **New** collected poems; edited with an introduction and notes by Michael Davidson; preface by Eliot Weinberger. New Directions 2002 xlv, 433p il $37.95   811

1. Poetry -- By individual authors

ISBN 0-8112-1488-5

LC 2001-44048

Replaces The collected poems of George Oppen (1975)

"Oppen, a Communist and an objectivist poet deeply influenced by Pound and Williams, believed that there were no ideas except in things, but he also believed, fiercely, that our relationship to things was inherently moral. . . . In 1934, he published a book of stunning, elliptical lyrics about 'big-Business' and American capitalism; he then fell silent for the next twenty-five years, during which he struggled to reconcile his fealty to social causes with the demands of aesthetic originality. The culmination of this struggle was his Pulitzer Prize-winning collection 'Of Being Numerous,' published in 1968, which, to a degree unmatched by any book of American poetry since, movingly portrays the individual in a collective world." New Yorker

Includes bibliographical references

Orr, Gregory

The **caged** owl; new and selected poems. Copper Canyon Press 2002 235p pa $16   811

1. Poetry -- By individual authors

ISBN 1-55659-177-2

LC 2001-6504

"The constraints of personal narrative are stretched to their limits in this summation from Orr, . . . as his poems are often based on tragic experiences occurring to those close to him. Orr's archetypal subject in the new poems and selections from six previous collections . . . is fratricide. As a child, Orr accidentally shot and killed his young brother in a hunting accident." Publ Wkly

Ossip, Kathleen

The **cold** war; Kathleen Ossip. 1st ed.; Sarabande Books 2011 77p.   811

1. Poets 2. Poetry -- Collections 3. September 11 terrorist attacks, 2001

ISBN 9781932511956 pa; 1932511954

LC 2010040378

This poetry collection presents a "socio-poetical exploration of post-World War II America, taking as her starting points Karl A. Menninger, who wrote 'The Human Mind'; Vance Packard, author of 'The Status Seekers'; and that scalawag of orgone energy, Wilhelm Reich." (N Y Times) Topics include "confessional writing, social and literary criticism, and history. The book's centerpiece is the traumatized, post-9/11 'Document.'" (Publishers Weekly) "It questions the origins and premises of contemporary American culture." (Publisher's note)

Ostriker, Alicia

No heaven; [by] Alicia Suskin Ostriker. University of Pittsburgh Press 2005 136p (Pitt poetry series) pa $12.95   811

1. Poetry -- By individual authors

ISBN 0-8229-5875-9

In this "collection of clarion poems intimate and worldly, Ostriker writes about her life as a wife, mother, and grandmother with tenderness, but she is also edgy, erotic, funny, and ornery." Booklist

★ The **Oxford** anthology of African-American poetry; edited by Arnold Rampersad; associate editor, Hilary Herbold. Oxford University Press 2006 432p $32.50   811

1. American poetry -- African American authors -- Collections

ISBN 0-19-512563-0; 978-0-19-512563-4

LC 2005-15242

"Predicated on the fact that there is a vast body of poetry written by gifted black poets, this . . . anthology tells the story of African American culture and explicates its crucial role within the larger literary tradition. . . . There is much to admire about the artistry of the poems, and even more to discover about the African American experience." Booklist

★ The **Oxford** book of American poetry; chosen and edited by David Lehman; associate editor, John Brehm. Oxford University Press 2006 lvii, 1132p $35   811

1. American poetry -- Collections

ISBN 0-19-516251-X; 978-0-19-516251-6

LC 2005-36590

First published 1950 with title: The Oxford book of American verse

"The book is not only a sound historical survey, but also gives the reader a powerful taste of poetry's impact upon the wider world." Economist

Includes bibliographical references

Padgett, Ron

How long. Coffee House Press 2011 88p pa $16 **811**
1. Poetry -- By individual authors
ISBN 978-1-56689-256-8

LC 2010-38005

"Padgett's sense of romantic joy is undiminished, as is his thoughtfulness about language and the ways in which time changes meaning, and sense can morph into eloquent absurdity." Entertainment Wkly

How to be perfect. Coffee House Press 2007 114p pa $15 **811**
1. Poetry -- By individual authors
ISBN 978-1-56689-203-2; 1-56689-203-1

LC 2007-17772

"Padgett's plainspoken, wry poems deliver their wisdom through a kind of connoisseurship of absurdity. . . . Yet these observational, reminiscent, and prescriptive verses are also informed by a sense of loss—not just for his late mother and for departed comrades like Kenneth Koch but for the bohemian ideal that drew him to New York to begin with. . . . Even so, Padgett's cockeyed humor is ultimately optimistic." New Yorker

You never know; poems. Coffee House Press 2001 84p pa $14.95 **811**
1. Poetry -- By individual authors
ISBN 978-1-56689-128-8; 1-56689-128-0

LC 2001-52945

"Padgett is the undisputed Zen master of the chicane, maintaining a perfectly readable and casual tone while turning meanings on a dime, or several dimes, on his way to a reliably radiant and melancholy conclusion. . . . These poems make a go at the epistemological concerns of the title, but like his collaborator Ted Berrigan or his predecessors James Schuyler and Kenneth Koch, Padgett shines brightest when he interrupts his crazy word combinations to be serious about love and death." Publ Wkly

Page, P. K.

The **hidden** room; collected poems. {by} Patricia Kathleen Page. Porcupine's Quill 1997 2v ea $18.95 **811**
1. Poetry -- By individual authors
ISBN 0-88984-190-X v1; 0-88984-193-4 v2

LC 98-113870

These two volumes incude the majority of all of the poet's works published in volume form, from Unit of five to Hologram, along with some unpublished poems and poems hitherto published only in magazines

Palmer, Michael

Company of moths. New Directions Books 2005 70p pa $16.95 **811**
1. Poetry -- By individual authors
ISBN 0-8112-1623-3

LC 2005-994

Palmer "combines spare lyricism and nocturnal visions ('This writing inside/ the lids of the eyes') in poems that resemble dream notes or lost translations from the French symbolists. They derive their tropes from an evocative if limited palette (owl, star, stone, book, moth) and create a sense of metaphysical unease through rhetorical questioning . . . , repetition, and paradox. . . . Whether or not one is absorbed by Palmer's deep image aesthetic and metanarrative stance, his enigmatic voice continues to fascinate." Libr J

Pankey, Eric

The **pear** as one example; new & selected poems, 1984-2008. Ausable Press 2008 274p pa $16 **811**
1. Poetry -- By individual authors
ISBN 978-1-931337-39-7; 1-931337-39-X

LC 2007-49674

"Fans of an earlier generation of American poets, such as Elizabeth Bishop, A.R. Ammons, and Robert Bly, will find much to enjoy in this large volume of poetry that showcases an acute poetic prowess, capturing a range of heartfelt emotions and experiences. . . . For Pankey, each new dawn presents a multitude of poetic possibilities, and he incorporates both the ugly and the beautiful, pain and pleasure in his aesthetic vision." NewPages

Pankey, Eric, 1959-

Trace; poems. Eric Pankey. 1st ed. Milkweed Editions 2013 68 p. (paperback) $16 **811**
1. Belief and doubt -- Poetry 2. Depression (Psychology) -- Poetry
ISBN 1571314490; 9781571314499

LC 2012028097

This collection of poems, by Eric Pankey, "locates itself at a threshold between faith and doubt--between the visible and the invisible, the say-able and the ineffable, the physical and the metaphysical. Also a map of the poet's journey into a deep depression, these poems confront one man's struggle to overcome depression's smothering weight and presence." (Publisher's note)

Parini, Jay

Robert Frost; a life. Holt & Co. 1999 514p il $35; pa $16 **811**
1. Poets 2. Authors
ISBN 0-8050-3181-2; 0-8050-6341-2 pa

LC 98-26690

"Rarely has Frost's story been told this dexterously, or with a better understanding of the relation of Frost's personal crises to his accomplishment as a poet." Publ Wkly

Includes bibliographical references

★ The Penguin anthology of twentieth-century American poetry; edited with an introduction by Rita Dove. Penguin Books 2011 lii, 599 p.p **811**
1. American poetry -- Collections 2. American poetry

-- 20th century
ISBN 9780143106432

LC 2011036342

The book provides an anthology of 20th century U.S. poetry. "Selecting from the canon of American poetry throughout the twentieth century, [Rita] Dove has created an anthology that represents the full spectrum of aesthetic sensibilities. . . . Featuring poems both classic and contemporary, this collection reflects both a dynamic and cohesive portrait of modern American poetry and outlines its trajectory over the past century." (Publisher's note)

Perillo, Lucia

On the spectrum of possible deaths; Lucia Perillo. Copper Canyon Press 2012 81 p.   **811**
1. Death -- Poetry 2. American poetry -- Collections 3. American poetry -- Women authors -- Collections 4. POETRY -- American -- General
ISBN 155659397X; 9781556593970

LC 2011050110

This book is a poetry collection written by the 2009 Pulitzer Prize finalist author Lucia Perillo. "Perillo has long lived with, and written about, her struggle with debilitating multiple sclerosis. Her . . . sixth book of poems, published concurrently with her debut story collection, takes a . . . look at mortality." (Booklist) "with subjects ranging from coyotes and Scotch broom to local elections and family history. . . . the mythic and mundane, of media and daily life, as she faces the treachery of illness." (Publisher's note)

Perillo, Lucia Maria

Inseminating the elephant; [by] Lucia Perillo. Copper Canyon Press 2009 93p $22   **811**
1. Poetry -- By individual authors
ISBN 978-1-55659-291-1; 1-55659-291-4

LC 2008-44772

Perillo "writes accessible, often funny poems that border on the profane. The title poem of this collection, her fifth, is about just what it says: zoologists tasked with helping impregnate an elephant (it's not easy). There's also an ode to bad smells, a middle-aged narrator's reluctant acceptance of cell phones and a meditation on a Viagra ad. Perillo has another rare power among versifiers: She is able to make dire, life-or-death concerns go down easy. . . . Physical decline is one of Perillo's major themes, one that she tackles with wry humor." Time Out N Y

Phillips, Carl

Double shadow. Farrar, Straus and Giroux 2011 58p $23   **811**
1. Poetry -- By individual authors
ISBN 978-0-374-14157-8; 0-374-14157-6

LC 2010-33097

"In some ways the perpetually shifting textures and shardlike quality of Phillips' language are reminiscent of John Ashbery, that preeminent poet of modern consciousness. But where Ashbery's universe is a theater of nihilistic yet playful hijinks, Phillips' is a somber, autumnal landscape, one that is illuminated by moments of ephemeral, ethereal beauty. The world of 'Double Shadow' is an old world, a faded, tired and depleted world: it is late in the day, the major events have already happened, the light is fading, and darkness will soon be upon us. . . . [Phillips] work is

quiet, and at times difficult, but its fragile beauty is unique and at times overwhelming." Chicago Tribune

The rest of love. Farrar, Straus and Giroux 2003 70p $20   **811**
1. Poetry -- By individual authors
ISBN 0-374-24953-9

LC 2003-45213

The author presents a "set of poems on love, sex, masculinity and their classical contours. . . . The result will not only please fans, but will send new readers back to recent books, which may be accumulating more quickly than they can be absorbed." Publ Wkly

Rock Harbor. Farrar, Straus & Giroux 2002 110p $20; pa $12   **811**
1. Poetry -- By individual authors
ISBN 0-374-25140-1; 0-374-52885-3 pa

LC 2002-20588

"Phillips reduces lyric poetry to its bare minimum, translating complex states of being into spare and clever syllogisms. His landscapes are stark, singular, and still. The living entities present, be they bird, tree, horse, or man, stand alone in wind and shifting light. Monumental in their carved perfection and deep mystery, they are embodiments of transcendence, objects of desire, instruments of pleasure and pain." Booklist

Speak low. Farrar, Straus & Giroux 2009 68p $23   **811**
1. Poetry -- By individual authors
ISBN 978-0-374-26716-2; 0-374-26716-2

LC 2008-46000

This book "is a quiet yet wounded reflection on Phillips' signature subjects: relationships, distances, identity, and damage. Phillips' remarkable ability to be clear yet illusive, as well as his dizzying syntax, are ever present as the poems coil into places of confusion." Publ Wkly
Includes bibliographical references

Piercy, Marge

Colors passing through us; poems. Knopf 2003 157p $23; pa $15   **811**
1. Poetry -- By individual authors
ISBN 0-375-41537-8; 0-375-71005-1 pa

LC 2002-66145

The author "tempers 1960s politics and 1970s feminism with nostalgia for the world of her childhood. . . . Piercy celebrates daily life on Cape Cod, where she and her husband live, with poems about gardening, cats, cooking, canning, and sex after 60. While all of these poems are eminently readable, the best are angry and funny. . . . Piercy fans, of which there are many, will relish this collection." Libr J

Pinsky, Robert

Democracy, culture, and the voice of poetry. Princeton Univ. Press 2002 96p (University Center for Human Values series) $29.95; pa $12.95   **811**
1. Poetry -- By individual authors 2. American poetry -- History and criticism
ISBN 0-691-09617-1; 0-691-12263-6 pa

LC 2002-25288

This is an "analysis of the way the intimate rhythms of American poetry invoke a social presence. Pinsky, a former poet laureate, passionately argues that American poetry is driven by the anxiety of being forgotten; the solitary poet makes us aware of the presence of others as he yearns for their approval while striving to preserve his uniqueness." N Y Times Book Rev

The **figured** wheel; new and collected poems, 1966-1996. Farrar, Straus & Giroux 1996 303p hardcover o.p. pa $17 **811**

1. Poetry -- By individual authors
ISBN 0-374-52506-4

LC 95-47617

"Brought together here are 16 new poems, the work of Pinsky's four original collections and a sampling of his fine translations, including a canto from his well-received version of the Inferno. Taken as a whole, this is the record of a poet who grows from highly competent to near-transcendent." Publ Wkly

★ **Gulf** music. Farrar, Straus and Giroux 2007 83p $22 **811**

1. Poetry -- By individual authors
ISBN 978-0-374-16749-3; 0-374-16749-4

LC 2007-4325

This collection "presents a carefully tuned yet impassioned vision of a past-haunted present where lessons of history remain unlearned and individuals struggle for comprehension amid atrocities ('In Africa/ The raiders with machetes to cut off hands/ Might make the victim choose, "long sleeve or short"') and contradictions ('Culture the penalty. Culture the escape'). . . . This anthology contains some of Pinsky's most invigorating work." Libr J

Jersey rain. Farrar, Straus & Giroux 2000 52p hardcover o.p. pa $12 **811**

1. Poetry -- By individual authors
ISBN 978-0-374-52772-3; 0-374-52772-5

LC 99-44209

"The discursive mode suits Pinsky because it allows his mind to range, to consider, to try out images and ideas. The pleasure comes less from the poem's perfection as an artifact than from our sense of the poet's sensitive, inquisitive mind at work." N Y Times Book Rev

Plath, Sylvia

★ The **collected** poems; edited by Ted Hughes. Harper & Row 1981 351p hardcover o.p. pa $17.95 **811**

1. Poetry -- By individual authors
ISBN 0-06-155889-3 pa

"Although her best poems deal with suffering and death, others are exhilarating and affectionate, and her tone is frequently witty as well as disturbing." Concise Oxford Companion to Engl Lit

Plath, Sylvia, 1932-1963

Ariel; the restored edition. foreword by Frieda Hughes. HarperCollins Publishers 2004 xxi, 211p $24.95 **811**

1. Poetry -- By individual authors
ISBN 0-06-073259-8

LC 2004-47703

First published 1955 in the United Kingdom

Sylvia Plath's posthumous volume of poetry, Ariel, was first published in the mid-1960s. "This facsimile edition restores, for the first time, the selection and arrangement of the poems as Sylvia Plath left them at the point of her death. In addition to the facsimile pages of Sylvia Plath's manuscript, this edition also includes in facsimile the complete working drafts of the title poem, 'Ariel,' in order to offer a sense of Plath's creative process as well as notes the author made for the BBC about some of the manuscript poems." (Publisher's note)

"Readers can see Plath's actual manuscript in this handsome facsimile, which provides a missing piece in the Plath annals and proves that there's nothing like going to the source." Booklist

Poe, Edgar Allan

Complete poems; edited by Thomas Ollive Mabbott. University of Ill. Press 2000 xxx, 627p il pa $25 **811**

1. Poetry -- By individual authors
ISBN 0-252-06921-8

LC 00-38639

This book contains 101 poems and their variants. In addition to classic poems such as The raven, The bells, and Annabel Lee, this volume contains previously uncollected poems, fragments, verses published in reviews, and poems attributed to Poe

Includes bibliographical references

★ **Poems** and poetics; Richard Wilbur, editor. Library of Am. 2003 xxv, 179p (American poets project) $20 **811**

1. Poetry -- By individual authors
ISBN 1-931082-51-0

LC 2003-46637

"Wilbur wants Poe to be appreciated as a transcendental cosmic theorist and 'the most difficult of the symbolist writers of his century,' and he appends selections from Poe's writings about poetics to help understanding of his cosmology and discusses some of Poe's most intense stories to exemplify his symbolism. The poems, presented chronologically, show again what a young prodigy Poe was, formulating his poetic thought while still in his teens, and what a sonorous Romantic musician he became." Booklist

Includes bibliographical references

Poems from the women's movement; edited by Honor Moore. Library of America 2009 238p (American poets project) $20 **811**

1. Women's movement 2. American poetry -- Women authors -- Collections
ISBN 978-1-59853-042-1

This is an anthology of poetry written by women during the women's movement of the late 1960s and 1970s.

"These direct, vibrant, potent, passionate, wild, strong, free, and freeing poems come less like a breath of fresh air than a strong wind." Booklist

Poems./Selections

Selected poems. Wave Books 2010 154p $24 **811**
1. Poetry -- By individual authors
ISBN 978-1-933517-45-2; 1-933517-45-X
LC 2010-05808
"This first retrospective collection from Ruefle, which selects from her nine previous books of poetry, the earliest of which first appeared in 1982, shows her to be a poet of visionary imagination, abiding sensitivity, and melancholy humor." Publ Wkly

Poems/Selections

★ The **collected** poems of Ted Berrigan; edited by Alice Notley, with Anselm Berrigan and Edmund Berrigan; introduction and notes by Alice Notley. University of California Press 2005 749p $60; pa $24.95 **811**
1. Poetry -- By individual authors
ISBN 978-0-520-23986-9; 0-520-23986-5; 978-0-520-25155-7 pa; 0-520-25155-5 pa
LC 2005-42259
This volume collects the published and unpublished works of a leading figure of the second-generation New York School. Includes the first presentation of the Easter Monday sequence in the order authorized by Berrigan shortly before his death.
"More than 20 years in preparation, this is a major volume of 20th-century American poetry. . . . Berrigan was a notoriously charismatic reader, teacher and participant in the community that developed around the Poetry Project at St. Mark's Church; his persona has been cited as often as his poems. This book closes the gap once and for all." Publ Wkly

Poetry 180; a turning back to poetry. selected and with an introduction by Billy Collins. Random House Trade Paperbacks 2003 xxiv, 323p pa $13.95 **811**
1. American poetry -- Collections
ISBN 0-8129-6887-5
LC 2002-36949
The editor "has collected 180 accessible modern poems: one for each day of the school year and together signifying a 180° turning back to poetry. These are poems, he says, you can 'get' the first time around, and he hopes that high schools will expose students to a poem a day via public address system or assemblies. A fine gathering of contemporary poets." Libr J
Includes bibliographical references

The **Poetry** anthology, 1912-2002; ninety years of America's most distinguished verse magazine. edited by Joseph Parisi & Stephen Young; with an introduction by Joseph Parisi. Ivan R. Dee 2002 lv, 509p $29.95; pa $16.95 **811**
1. American poetry -- Collections
ISBN 1-56663-468-7; 1-56663-604-3 pa
LC 2002-31178
A collection of 600 poems previously published in Poetry magazine, written by such poets as W.H. Auden, Elizabeth Bishop, Sylvia Plath, James Merrill, and Susan Hahn
This is a "comprehensive and thrilling anthology, a veritable history of twentieth-century poetry in English." Booklist

Poetry speaks expanded; hear poets from Tennyson to Plath read their own work. Elise Paschen & Rebekah Presson Mosby, editors; Charles Osgood, narrator. [2nd ed.]; Sourcebooks 2007 384p il $49.95 **811**
1. English poetry -- Collections 2. American poetry -- Collections
ISBN 978-1-4022-1062-4; 1-4022-1062-0
LC 2007-37080
First published 2001 with title: Poetry speaks
"Reluctant poetry readers may find themselves drawn to the printed page by the spoken work, and poetry fans are likely to find much to love here." Publ Wkly

The **poets** laureate anthology; edited and with introductions by Elizabeth Hun Schmidt; foreword by Billy Collins. W.W. Norton & Co. 2010 liii, 762p $39.95 **811**
1. American poetry -- Collections
ISBN 978-0-393-06181-9
LC 2010-21692
Poems by each of the forty-three poets who have been named our nation's Poet Laureate since the post (originally called Consultant in Poetry to the Library of Congress) was established in 1937.
"A hefty and worthy read that everyone will want to savor. Essential for all contemporary poetry collections." Libr J

Poets of the Civil War; J.D. McClatchy, editor. Library of America 2005 211p il (American poets project) $20 **811**
1. American poetry -- Collections 2. United States -- History -- 1861-1865, Civil War -- Poetry
ISBN 978-1-93108-276-1; 1-93208-276-6
LC 2004-61552
"The poems wisely selected represent not only the main kinds of responses to the war but also the radically conflicting sympathies of the poets—with the Union cause or with the Confederacy—and the important postwar theme of reconciliation of North and South. McClatchy's selection has not only breadth of representation but fine choices within forms, causes, and poets." Sewanee Rev

★ **Poets** of World War II; Harvey Shapiro, editor. Library of Am. 2003 xxxii, 262p (American poets project) $20 **811**
1. World War, 1939-1945 -- Poetry
ISBN 1-931082-33-2
LC 2002-32125

The editor's "objective is to show that the American poets of the Second World War were as significant as their English counterparts in the first one, if different in tone. Even at their most biting, Siegfried Sassoon and Wilfred Owen struck a heroic note, penning anthems for 'doomed youth' and the destruction of innocence. . . . But those who survived battles of the second conflict to become important poets avoided the attempt to sound noble, or to celebrate fallen comrades. . . . Shapiro, a B-17 gunner, takes pains to show the spectrum of opinion that actually existed and how it evolved." New Leader

Includes bibliographical references

Ponsot, Marie

Easy; poems. Alfred A. Knopf 2009 82p $26 **811**

1. Poetry -- By individual authors
ISBN 978-0-307-27218-8; 0-307-27218-4

LC 2009-17488

"Poetry and old age are difficult human endeavors, yet in her new, aptly titled book of poems, Marie Ponsot makes both look Easy. And who would know better than she? Well into her ninth decade and still evolving as an artist, Ponsot takes her place among a distinguished company of American poets who wrote—and continue to write—into their 80s and beyond. . . . In a youth-obsessed culture like ours, it is exhilarating to read a collection of poems that celebrates the graces of age, the gift of wisdom and the freedom won through endurance." America

Springing; new and selected poems. Knopf 2002 233p $25; pa $16.95 **811**

1. Poetry -- By individual authors
ISBN 0-375-41389-8; 0-375-70987-8 pa

LC 2001-38432

"Ponsot's poems are built around . . . unflinching observations of intimate interactions and misfires, whether of familial relations ventriloquized through updated Greek dramatis personae, a French woman's accommodation of her mother's married lover or the self's castings about the natural world." Publ Wkly

Porter, Anne

★ **Living** things; collected poems. foreword by David Shapiro. Zoland Books 2006 176p pa $15 **811**

1. Poetry -- By individual authors
ISBN 1-58195-216-3

LC 2005-029944

Porter "deserves to be called a religious poet, for she sees the world, in all its aspects, as whole within a providential design. In her verse there pulsates a probing, praying spiritual intelligence as well as a poet's sensibility and graceful generosity. . . . Living Things offers over 100 of Porter's poems, all 76 that appeared in An Altogether Different Language (1994) . . . and 39 new poems. The new poems come first. Reading this collection from beginning to end lets the newer work enrich and deepen the older, enhancing the reader's appreciation not for Porter's 'development,' but for discerning and valuing this poet's integrity and vision. The cumulative impact is dazzling." America

Postmodern American poetry; a Norton anthology. edited by Paul Hoover. 2nd ed. W W Norton & Co Inc 2013 lvii, 982 p.p (paperback) $39.95 **811**

1. Postmodernism 2. American poetry 3. American poetry -- 20th century 4. American poetry -- 21st century 5. Postmodernism (Literature) -- United States
ISBN 0393341860; 9780393341867

LC 2012039473

This book, edited by Paul Hoover, is a the second edition of an anthology of poems written after 1950, by such authors as "Robert Duncan, Denise Levertov, James Schuyler, Robert Creeley, Allen Ginsberg, Gary Snyder, Ted Berrigan, Clarence Major, Mei-Mei Berssenbrugge, and David Shapiro." (Booklist) It includes "important recent movements such as Newlipo, conceptual poetry, and Flarf." (Publisher's note)

Includes bibliographical references and index.

Pound, Ezra

★ The **cantos** of Ezra Pound. New Directions 1970 802p $42; pa $22.95 **811**

1. Poetry -- By individual authors
ISBN 0-8112-0350-6; 0-8112-1326-9 pa

"The first sections of the 'Cantos' were published in magazine form as early as 1917. Pound's conception of his epic changed several times during different phases of his life. Originally intended as a didactic treatise for 'philistine' Americans, it combined elements from classical myth, ancient Oriental poetry, Provençal ballads, and modern economic theory, to create a vast disjointed panorama of the growth of civilization. A monumental work of poetic enterprise." Reader's Ency. 4th edition

★ **Poems** and translations. Library of America 2003 1363p $45 **811**

1. Poetry -- By individual authors
ISBN 978-1-931082-41-9; 1-931082-41-3

LC 2003-40142

This volume "offers, in addition to the convenience of having Pound's shorter works compacted into a single volume, a useful chronology of his life and some very helpful, if at times overly terse, annotations to the poems' myriad foreign phrases and proper nouns. Richard Sieburth, an award-winning translator and the author of a previous book on Pound, is clearly at home with the material. . . . More important than all of this, however, what emerges from Poems and Translations is a personality, one of the strongest and strangest in modern poetry." Parnassus: Poetry in Review

Powell, D. A.

Chronic. Graywolf Press 2009 79p $20 **811**

1. Poetry -- By individual authors
ISBN 978-1-55597-516-6; 1-55597-516-X

LC 2008-935598

"Richly romantic yet never sentimental, Powell's work in Chronic is often addressed to 'you': a friend, a lover, and you, the reader. It's a lovely, intimate style." Entertainment Wkly

Useless landscape; or, a guide for boys. D. A. Powell. Graywolf Press 2012 80 p. (alk. paper) $22 **811**

1. Youth -- Poetry 2. Gay men -- Poetry 3. Diseases -- Poetry 4. Human body -- Poetry 5. Poetry -- Collections
ISBN 9781555976057

LC 2011942041

In this collection of poetry, D. A. Powell "revisits themes of body and illness, sacred space and seductive desecration. The first section is an examination of beauty divorced from utility; the second a . . . portrait of young people in acts of exploration." (Booklist) The poems vary in tone, . . . some based on life stories and others built on puns . . . the impoverished spaces of [Powell's] youth stand out among his backgrounds and metaphors for ecological disaster, for gay sexual awakening, for sex itself, for illness, and for love." (Publishers Weekly)

Prufer, Kevin

National anthem; poems. Four Way Books 2008 82p pa $15.95 **811**

1. Poetry -- By individual authors
ISBN 978-1-88480-083-2; 1-88480-083-1

LC 2007-37694

This collection "opens with a panoramic vision of the aftermath of apocalypse—'expired' cars, silenced TVs, coffins 'unmoored and happy with the storm'—but ends intimately, with a child's memory of his first encounter with death; the thin wire between political failure and personal grief runs taut throughout. In the eerie centerpiece poem, the suburbs are sealed under an enormous parachute, its nylon shimmering; icicles line the seams and crash into the streets, and the narrator walks for days, never finding the edge." New Yorker

Ramke, Bin

Aerial; Bin Ramke. Omnidawn Pub. 2012 109 p. **811**

1. Imagination 2. Sky -- Poetry 3. Poetry -- Collections
ISBN 1890650609; 9781890650605

LC 2011051410

In this book, author Bin Ramke chooses the sky as the guiding figure for his 11th collection of poems. Ramke's sky is something longed for, wished for, and out of reach . . . also representing the ways loved ones are both near and distant at once. Ramke ("Theory of Mind") also describes the acts of imagination--dreaming, and of course, writing--letting the sky inspire a wish for openness and lucidity. . . . As in previous books, Ramke delves into the anthropology of words ("Art. Article. Articulate. Artifact. Artery. Arthritic") and welcomes the words of other writers, from Weil to Mary Oliver, into his lines. In these poems, Ramke . . . contemplates death, finality, and fear. (Publishers Weekly)

Ras, Barbara

The **last** skin. Penguin Books 2010 63p (Penguin poets) pa $18 **811**

1. Poetry -- By individual authors
ISBN 978-0-14-311697-4 pa; 0-14-311697-5 pa

LC 2009-53320

Nested in this new book of poems by Barbara Ras, we find an ongoing subtext about the loss of her mother (to whom The Last Skin is dedicated). The title poem holds the one piece of her clothing I'd kept/to bed and bury my face/in her flowered blouse to smell her last skin,/but even from the first it was futile. As direct references to her deceased parents and flowering allusions arise, they reveal the poet's primal experience of losing a parent. But what keeps the poetry from being mere confessional self-pity? First, her loss finds context in our shared mortality but without sentimentality. . . . Second, Ras creates several approaches to the unbearable fragility of life beyond personal loss. . . . Third, there are stunning images about natural phenomena (irises, oceans) and also human objects that subtly suggest grief but do not call its name. San Antonio Express-News

Reed, Ishmael

New and collected poems, 1966-2006. Carroll & Graf 2006 xxi, 482p $25.95; pa $17.95 **811**

1. Poetry -- By individual authors
ISBN 978-0-7867-1788-0; 978-1-56858-341-9 pa

LC 2006-299409

"The mixture of humor and anger is . . . a hallmark of Ishmael Reed, whose strength as an editor, essayist, and novelist (and whose reputation as provocateur) has overshadowed his achievement as a poet. That achievement . . . is based in the vernacular, as well as in his use of folk materials, his fearlessness with form, and his 'irrational' tendency toward the spiritual, which stands as an indictment of the impoverished soul of a bottom-line age." Harvard Review

Rekdal, Paisley

Animal eye; Paisley Rekdal. University of Pittsburgh Press 2012 86 p. **811**

1. Love poetry 2. Poetry -- Collections 3. Loss (Psychology) -- Poetry 4. American poetry
ISBN 0822961792; 9780822961796

LC 2011277541

This book is a collection of poetry from Paisley Rekdal. "In poems long and short, Rekdal looks at paintings and wax models . . . , a stuffed fox . . . , a front-yard garden, a bouquet of flowers, all of which become harsh mirrors reflecting the painful lessons of lost love. 'What's the point of pain if it heals,' Rekdal asks, thinking of finding new love after divorce: these poems don't want to be let off easy. Even tango lessons aren't just for fun: 'The point is not to give yourself away but to connect/ as closely as you are able to// your partner's will in the embrace, so that intent/ slides seamlessly through two// sets of veins.' There's a bit of willful masochism in this dance--in any of life's various dances--when the goal is to join 'two separate hearts.'" (Publishers Weekly)

Revell, Donald

The **bitter** withy; new poems. Alice James Books 2009 61p pa $15.95 **811**

1. Poetry -- By individual authors
ISBN 978-1-88229-576-0; 1-88229-576-5

LC 2009-25413

This collection features "poetical lexicon (rainbows, flowers, celestial bodies, trees and birds abound) and hymnlike sentiments. . . . Revell's voice has become ecstatic, but it has also remained clear, so his intensely personal, even visionary accounts and meditations are rendered with lucidity and ease." Publ Wkly

★ **Pennyweight** windows; new & selected poems. Alice James 2005 220p $26.95; pa $18.95 **811**
1. Poetry -- By individual authors
ISBN 1-882295-51-X; 1-882295-52-8 pa
LC 2004-26191

"Using history, mythology, and contemporary events as a backdrop . . . [the author] tries to balance a public, nearly didactic voice with a personal and revealing one. . . . This readable and well-edited collection—mostly culled from eight previous collections, with some new poems added—is a good representation of Revell's work." Libr J

A **thief** of strings. Alice James Books 2007 68p pa $14.95 **811**
1. Poetry -- By individual authors
ISBN 978-1-882295-61-6; 1-882295-61-7
LC 2007-1116

"Revell is a post-Romantic, his natural imagery clear and immediate, his feelings never very far from his sleeve, his tone approaching a prayerful devotion that evinces an unshakable love of the real world despite its—or our—compromised state." Libr J

Rexroth, Kenneth
★ The **complete** poems of Kenneth Rexroth; edited by Sam Hamill & Bradford Morrow. Copper Canyon Press 2003 xxxvi, 764p hardcover o.p. pa $24 **811**
1. Poetry -- By individual authors
ISBN 1-55659-217-5 pa
LC 2002-1706

"If you love looking things up and taking reading sidetrips, Rexroth is one of the most readable and rewarding twentieth-century American poets." Booklist

Reznikoff, Charles
Holocaust. David R. Godine 2007 93p pa $15.95 **811**
1. Poetry -- By individual authors
ISBN 978-1-57423-208-0; 1-57423-208-8
LC 2006-33803

"A book-length poem about the Shoah as recounted by witnesses at the Nuremberg Military Tribunal and the trial of Adolf Eichmann, architect of Hitler's 'Final Solution,' held in Jerusalem. From U.S. government transcripts of these trials, [the author] selected and spliced together witness testimonies. . . . Reznikoff's historicism and objectivism are brought together in an ethical and spiritual climax. By using the language of others he attends to the 'object' of genocide without imaginative or philosophical flourish, and by reciting it again in his own rhythm he becomes a second witness to its truth. Ultimately, the reader responds not to the poet but to the testimony itself. . . . It presents a story already told and a story never to be finished. It is neither novel nor revelatory, only horrific; as a piece of art it does not seduce

us. But this is precisely its moral power as a document." Boston Rev

★ The **poems** of Charles Reznikoff; 1918-1975. edited by Seamus Cooney. David R. Godine 2005 445p $45; pa $21.95 **811**
1. Poetry -- By individual authors
ISBN 1-57423-204-5; 1-57423-203-7 pa
LC 2005-21218

First published 1989 with title: Poems 1918-1975
This collection "of his poems . . . will be welcomed both by old and new readers of his work." Publ Wkly
Includes bibliographical references

Rich, Adrienne
Arts of the possible; essays and conversations. Norton 2001 190p $23.95; pa $13.95 **811**
1. Poetry 2. Feminism
ISBN 0-393-05045-9; 0-393-32312-9 pa
LC 00-51522

This volume "collects Rich's best-known prose from the 1970s and 1980s, with new writing that extends through the 1990s. In letters such as 'Why I Refused the National Medal for the Arts,' and through complaints about feminism as the cult of the personal and a renewed call for a collective global vision, she delights, and is by turns lyrical and polemical." Ms

Collected early poems, 1950-1970. Norton 1993 xxi, 435p hardcover o.p. pa $15 **811**
1. Poetry -- By individual authors
ISBN 0-393-31385-9 pa
LC 92-13150

This collection "contains all of the work included in Rich's first six books, and a few previously uncollected pieces as well. Her poetry of the 1950s stems from a strong, mostly male tradition, obviously and intentionally echoing the work of Frost, Williams, Dickinson and Stevens. . . . The poems written in the 1960s are pervaded by the poet's consciousness of the subversive nature of creativity, especially for women, a gift at risk of being suppressed or curtailed at any moment by the self, family or the male-dominated society. In the last poems of the period, Rich's voice is firm and brave, her language still searingly beautiful and individual. This important volume charts the radical transformation of one of America's most significant poets." Publ Wkly

Fox; poems, 1998-2000. Norton 2001 64p $21; pa $12 **811**
1. Poetry -- By individual authors
ISBN 0-393-04166-2; 0-393-32377-3 pa
LC 2001-31240

"Rich's recent style—developed slowly throughout the 1990s—comes to full fruition here, conveying her familiar attentions to social injustice and intense introspection with and a sometimes harsh, fragmented, versatile line whose sources include George Oppen and Anglo-Saxon accentual verse." Publ Wkly

The **school** among the ruins: poems, 2000-2004. W.W. Norton 2004 113p $22.95 **811**
1. Poetry -- By individual authors
ISBN 0-393-05983-9
LC 2004-8370
"Rich, a clarion poet of conscience, gets the fractured timbre of our times just right in a collection of vigorous lyric poems about cell phones and television, terror and war, commercialization and 'social impotence.'" Booklist

Roberson, Ed
To see the earth before the end of the world. Wesleyan University Press 2010 161p (Wesleyan poetry) $22.95 **811**
1. Poetry -- By individual authors
ISBN 978-0-8195-6950-9; 0-8195-6950-X
LC 2010-27094
"In poems that proceed snakelike across a page or in traditional flush-left frames, Roberson's images and ideas are startling and complex, often difficult in their dreamlike qualities. His lines have been accurately described as syntactically double-jointed and labyrinthine—and, as with any maze, readers must find a hold, an outside wall to guide them through Roberson's sometimes surreal vision of the earth." Libr J

Roeser, Dana
The **theme** of tonight's party has been changed; poems. Dana Roeser. University of Massachusetts Press 2014 88 p. (pbk. : alk. paper) $15.95 **811**
1. Poetry -- Collections
ISBN 1625340974; 9781625340979
LC 2013051027
In this collection, author Dana Roeser "brings a host of characters into her poems--a Catholic priest raging against the commercialism of Mother's Day, the injured tennis player James Blake, a man struck by lightning, drunk partygoers, an ex-marine, Sylvia Plath's son Nicholas Hughes, a neighbor, travelers encountered in airport terminals, various talk therapists--and lets them speak." (Publisher's note)

Roethke, Theodore
The **collected** poems of Theodore Roethke. Doubleday 1966 279p hardcover o.p. pa $14.95 **811**
1. Poetry -- By individual authors
ISBN 0-385-08601-6 pa
Roethke's "refreshingly original rhythms are keenly articulated and often hypnotic. Although his work is uneven and he sometimes gives way to self-indulgence or to surprising naiveté, many of his best poems recreate disconcertingly intense psychic or mystical experience. He also had a flair for the seductively lyrical and the brashly irreverent. He ranks as one of the best poets of the first postmodern generation." Benet's Reader's Ency of Am Lit

Ronk, Martha
Partially Kept; by Martha Ronk. Univ Pr of New England 2012 74 p. (paperback) $15.95 **811**
1. Death -- Poetry 2. Poetry -- Collections
ISBN 1937658015; 9781937658014
This book is Martha Ronk's ninth collection of poems. It is "composed of three sequences of short lyrics that attend to the elusiveness of language and humanity's shifting sense of the past. The poems of the title sequence quote sentences from Sir Thomas Browne, 17th-century essayist and plant lover, weaving his language in with Ronk's to meditate on the fragility of life and the ways ideas." (Publishers Weekly)

Transfer of Qualities; by Martha C. Ronk. University Press of New England 2013 88 p. (pbk.) $17.95 **811**
1. Matter 2. Interpersonal relations
ISBN 9781890650827; 189065082X
National Book Awards: Poetry: Long List (2013)
This book, by Martha C. Ronk, "addresses the uncanny and myriad ways in which people and things, but also people and those around them, exchange qualities with one another, moving in on, unsettling: altering stance, attitude, mood, gesture. Each entry in the book probes the dissolving boundaries between those sharing space with one another; and the various cross-genres in the book--prose poem, creative non-fiction, personal essay--echo the theme of interdependence." (Publisher's note)
"Ronk's collection of "various objects," books, photograms, people and portraits dominate the collection, which moves from prose to lineated poems, to essays, to brief passages of nonfiction, seguing into topics of representation, death, mourning, love, and intimacy with the physical world." Pub Wkly
Includes bibliographical references

Rukeyser, Muriel
Selected poems; Adrienne Rich, editor. Library of America 2004 xxv, 180p (American poets project) $20 **811**
1. Poetry -- By individual authors
ISBN 978-1-931082-58-7; 1-931082-58-8
LC 2003-60484
"Rukeyser was born in 1913, which puts her in the generation of Bishop, Berryman, Lowell, and Jarrell. Her poems range from the sprawling to the epigrammatic; they often have a flat, documentary feel ('The tunnel is part of a huge water power project/begun, latter part of 1929'), and they're formally various (excerpted sections from a single long poem, 'Letter to the Front,' contain both a sonnet and a sestina). . . . At its best, Rukeyser's work can be open, energetic, and well constructed, if a little enamored of its own goody-goodness." Poetry (Modern Poetry Association)

Ryan, Kay
The **best** of it; new and selected poems. Grove Press 2010 288p $24 **811**
1. Poetry -- By individual authors
ISBN 978-0-8021-1914-8; 0-8021-1914-X
Ryan's "poems are as slim as runway models, so tiny you could almost tweet them. Their compact refinement, though, does not suggest ease or chic. Her voice is quizzical and im-

pertinent, funny in uncomfortable ways, scuffed by failure and loss. Her mastery, like Emily Dickinson's, has some awkwardness in it, some essential gawkiness that draws you close. . . . [This] is a generous and nearly career-spanning collection of her verse." N Y Times Book Rev

Elephant rocks. Grove Press 1996 84p $18; pa $14 **811**

1. Poetry -- By individual authors
ISBN 978-0-8021-1586-7; 0-8021-1586-1; 978-0-8021-3525-4 pa; 0-8021-3525-0 pa

LC 95-42668

This volume is comprised of "miniature five-paragraph essays, something like those little books the Brontes wrote for their dolls. They're epigrams or digestifs or, better, aphorisms if we remember the source of such things: Hippocrates making little pills of pithiness, haiku with punch lines, prescriptions not meant for the pharmacist. . . . If John Skelton had been Emily Dickinson's tutor instead of Jane Scrope's, these poems would not surprise us. But they do." Antioch Review

The **Niagara** River; poems. Grove Press 2005 72p (Grove Press poetry series) pa $13 **811**

1. Poetry -- By individual authors
ISBN 0-8021-4222-2

LC 2005-40423

"In two or three shifty sentences per short-lined poem, Ryan brazenly questions the extent to which we are in control of, and thus responsible for, our own and others' suffering. Her work . . . operates in an American tradition stretching from Dickinson through Stevens and Frost to Ammons and Bronk, where fidelity to the natural world works as a scrim for staging such self-exploration. . . . Empathic and wryly unforgiving of the human condition, the poems are equal parts pith and punch. The effect is bracing." Publ Wkly

Say uncle; poems. Grove Press 2000 76p pa $14 **811**

1. Poetry -- By individual authors
ISBN 978-0-8021-3717-3; 0-8021-3717-2

LC 00-26454

"These precise, epigrammatic poems, which come with hook-and-eye rhymes that click sweetly into place, move deftly and economically. . . . Though they dispose of their subjects wittily and ingeniously, they cannot always suppress a smile of self-satisfaction at having mastered their material; and, like macaroons, they should be taken a few at a time. They are cleverly made. . . . Like cat's cradles, they may be taken in or let out, but at their best they alter the fit of the mind." Atl Mon

Sandburg, Carl

★ The **complete** poems of Carl Sandburg; rev and expanded ed; Harcourt Brace Jovanovich 1970 xxxi, 797p $40 **811**

1. Poetry -- By individual authors
ISBN 0-15-100996-1

First published 1950

A collection of seven of the author's books: Chicago poems, 1916; Cornhuskers, 1918; Smoke and steel, 1920;

Slabs of the sunburnt West, 1922; Good morning, America, 1925; The people, yes, 1936; Honey and salt, 1963

"Known for his free verse, written under the influence of Walt Whitman and celebrating industrial and agricultural America, American geography and landscape, figures in American history, and the American common people, {Sandburg} frequently makes use of contemporary American slang and colloquialisms." Herzberg. Reader's Ency of Am Lit

Sanders, Ed

Let's not keep fighting the Trojan War; selected poems, 1986-2008. [by] Edward Sanders; introduction by Joanne Kyger. Coffee House Press 2009 245p il pa $20 **811**

1. Poetry -- By individual authors
ISBN 978-1-56689-234-6 pa; 1-56689-234-1 pa

LC 2009-22843

"Sanders has been an astonishing and fertile presence in our cutlural and political landscape. . . . But it is Sanders's poetry, more than anything else he does, that pulls together all the varied strands of his interests to weave them into the body of one of our century's most coherent poetics." NPR

Thirsting for peace in a raging century; selected poems, 1961-1985. [by] Edward Sanders. New and rev. ed.; Coffee House Press 2009 260p il pa $20 **811**

1. Poetry -- By individual authors
ISBN 978-1-56689-238-4 pa

LC 2009-28061

First published 1987; revised and updated with sixteen additional poems

This collection "restores Edward Sanders to his rightful place at the forefront of the poetry of his time, and reminds us that spending one's days in active pursuit of the betterment of all life on the planet isn't necessarily antithetical to the creation of first-rate writing." San Francisco Chron

Sarton, May

Selected poems of May Sarton; edited and with an introduction by Serena Sue Hilsinger and Lois Brynes. Norton 1978 206p hardcover o.p. pa $25 **811**

1. Poetry -- By individual authors
ISBN 978-0-393-04512-3; 0-393-04512-9

LC 78-14850

"What May Sarton does is to follow the round of a woman's life. Her verse is traditional, warm, ripe with the wisdom of her years as a poet, novelist, autobiographer. She draws on the artifacts of the past for images to live by in the here and now." Christ Sci Monit

Savich, Zach

Annulments. Center for Literary Publishing/Colorado State University 2010 65p pa $16.95 **811**

1. Poetry -- By individual authors
ISBN 978-1-885635-15-0; 1-885635-15-X

LC 2010-20558

This collection "features poems that communicate what is fragmentary at the expense of the concrete. At once meticulous and vertiginous, these poems are grounded by

'The Mountains Overhead,' a long poem of 113 fragments, in which we find 'Dawn stripping you like a cat/ clawing a band of wallpaper' and horses that 'hold themselves like torches so they/ won't burn like themselves.' The result is a collection that is thrilling and inchoate. . . . In keeping with the trope of annulments, the poems often end suddenly, leaving much to be desired in their genesis and construction. One senses that Savich could go on building his fragmentary mountain forever, not unlike a certain well-known biblical tower whose result was the fragmentation of language itself." Publ Wkly

Scalapino, Leslie

It's go in horizontal; selected poems, 1974-2006. University of California Press 2008 241p il (New California poetry) $45; pa $16.95 **811**
    ISBN 978-0-520-25461-9; 0-520-25461-9; 978-0-520-25462-6 pa; 0-520-25462-7 pa
                    LC 2007-50133
    "Most often classified with the language poets, Scalapino is shown in this welcome overview to have developed a distinctive idiom, as fresh and powerful here as when first published in 14 mostly small press editions. Scalapino fuses a richly detached Buddhist mindfulness with an algorithmically precise disjunctive syntax to explore sex, gender and violence—their politics and their moment-to-moment embodiedness. The longish, serial form that she favors works well in the selected format when the poems are presented in full." Publ Wkly

Schulman, Grace

Days of wonder; new and selected poems. Houghton Mifflin 2002 189p $25; pa $14 **811**
    1. Poetry -- By individual authors
    ISBN 0-618-08623-4; 0-618-34082-3 pa
                    LC 2001-39531
    "In a characteristic Schulman poem, large, difficult questions resonate in the small, singular moments of appreciation. . . . There are allusions to canonical painters and canonical poems, and a variety of religious references, which engender equal portions of reverence and lament. Many of the poems' small pleasures are found amid sometimes difficult sometimes serene backdrops." Publ Wkly

Schutt, Will

Westerly; Will Schutt ; foreword by Carl Phillips. Yale University Press 2013 80 p. (Yale series of younger poets) (hardcover) $45.00; (paperback) $18 **811**
    1. History -- Poetry 2. Poetry -- Collections
    ISBN 030018851X; 9780300188509; 9780300188516
                    LC 2012033923
    This poetry collection, by Will Schutt, is the winner of the 2012 "Yale Series of Younger Poets" award. "A young soldier dons Napoleon's hat. An out-of-work man wanders Berlin, dreaming he is Peter the Great. The famous exile Dante finally returns to his native city. . . . Familial and historical apparitions haunt this . . . collection of poems." (Publisher's note)

Schuyler, James

Collected poems. Farrar, Straus & Giroux 1993 429p hardcover o.p. pa $32 **811**
    1. Poetry -- By individual authors
    ISBN 978-0-374-52403-6; 0-374-52403-3
                    LC 92-40977
    "Schuyler's subject is his life, and his poems often read like elegant journal entries. The book presents intimate and conversational accounts of life in the Eastern literary landscape—New York City, New England, Long Island. In urbane free verse, the poet recalls and meditates on music and painting, homosexuality, weekends with friends—John Ashbery and Fairfield Porter among them—deaths, a drive to the Hamptons. . . . Rarely has a poet imparted so much of his experience as honestly and engagingly as Schuyler does here." Publ Wkly

Other flowers; uncollected poems. edited by James Meetze and Simon Pettet. Farrar, Straus and Giroux 2010 220p $28 **811**
    1. Poetry -- By individual authors
    ISBN 978-0-374-53209-3; 0-374-53209-5
                    LC 2009-31891
    "The Velvet Underground, it has been said, did not sell many records, but everyone who bought one went out and started his or her own band. James Schuyler was, perhaps, the Velvet Underground of verse: Almost unknown outside the poetry world, he was massively influential within it. To read Schuyler is, almost inevitably, to be struck with the desire to be a poet. Schuyler's powerful and frequently moving descriptions of nature, of the weather, of domestic engagements — limpid descriptions that lay upon the sensory world like a pellucid dew — have often seemed to constitute the heart of his poetic accomplishment. . . . Such a skill is best showcased by his longer poems, and if the new collection, 'Other Flowers: Uncollected Poems,' feels somewhat slight, it is partly because the recently discovered works gathered here are all short lyrics." Los Angeles Times

Seibles, Tim

Fast Animal; Tim Seibles. Etruscan Press 2012 72 p. $14 **811**
    1. American poetry -- African American authors
    ISBN 0983294429; 9780983294429
    This book is a collection of poems by Tim Seibles written "in concisely unpredictable free verse. Many concern straight boys and young men in love: poems named for childhood friends, for a middle school beauty, for high school girlfriends. . . . Along with them come poems of popular culture, fantasy, and contemporary life." (Publishers Weekly)

Seidel, Frederick

Poems 1959-2009. Farrar, Straus, and Giroux 2009 509p $40 **811**
    1. Poetry -- By individual authors
    ISBN 978-0-374-12655-1; 0-374-12655-0
                    LC 2008-47161
    "Long regarded as a kind of elegant cult figure in poetry circles, Seidel has a reputation that precedes him into every room: decadent, name-dropper, sexual dalliant, Ducati enthusiast, son of privilege. This runs counter to the man himself. He doesn't do poetry readings and has, for the

most part, shunned interviews. There is no doubt that Seidel is one of the best poets alive today, and now, with the release of 'Poems: 1959-2009,' his collected works can be taken at their measure: They are haughty, funny and terrifying, with plenty of delicious contention throughout." Los Angeles Times

Selections.

Selected poems; David Lehman, editor. Library of America 2006 130p (American poets project) $20   **811**

1. Poetry -- By individual authors

ISBN 978-1-931082-93-8; 1-931082-93-6

LC 2006-40807

Ammons "was a difficult figure to pin down. While unassociated with any particular poetic school or group, he picked up threads from Whitman, Williams, Frost and Stevens, weaving them into poetry all his own: equal parts pastoral meditation, philosophical speculation and homespun resignation. In the process, he won nearly every honor a major American poet can. Now, in the first selection to present samplings from the whole of his oeuvre (which ranges from two-line lyrics to book-length sequences), we can survey the extent is his poetic powers." Publ Wkly

Sendak, Maurice, 1928-2012

★ **My** brother's book; Maurice Sendak ; [edited by] Michael di Capua. HarperCollins 2013 32 p. (hardcover bdg.) $18.95   **811**

1. Poetry 2. Poetry -- Collections

ISBN 0062234897; 9780062234896

LC 2012942549

In this book, "with influences from Shakespeare and William Blake, [Maurice] Sendak pays homage to his late brother, Jack, whom he credited for his passion for writing and drawing. Pairing Sendak's . . . poetry with his . . . artwork, . . . Sendak's tribute to his brother is an expression of both grief and love. . . . Pulitzer Prize--winning literary critic and Shakespearean scholar Stephen Greenblatt contributes a[n] . . . introduction." (Publisher's note)

Sexton, Anne

The **complete** poems; with a foreword by Maxine Kumin. Houghton Mifflin 1981 xxiv, 622p hardcover o.p. pa $19   **811**

1. Poetry -- By individual authors

ISBN 0-395-95776-1 pa

LC 81-2482

"Even before her death in 1974, Sexton's work was the subject of critical controversy, often dismissed as mere confessionalism. But, as Maxine Kumin observes in an insightful introductory essay, Sexton 'delineated the problematic position of women—the neurotic reality of the time' and in so doing 'earned her place in the canon.'" Choice

Shapiro, Alan, 1952-

Night of the republic; Alan Shapiro. Houghton Mifflin Harcourt 2012 95 p. $21   **811**

1. Poetry

ISBN 0547329709; 9780547329703

LC 2010049850

This book offers a collection of poems by Alan Shapiro. "Shapiro gathers his poems into four groups. The first focuses on mundane but iconic places, mostly during night-owl hours (these poems bring to mind the paintings of Edward Hopper); the second presents portraits of seemingly ordinary people; the third explores public spaces; and the last appears to approach, though perhaps not quite to be, autobiography. Parts I and III share the same title, which is the title of the book. . . . The majority of the poems in 'Night of the Republic' share a strategy: short lines lead us down the page, forming longer sentences, many with subordinate clauses." (America)

Includes bibliographical references

Shapiro, David

New and selected poems (1965-2006) Overlook Press 2007 267p $21.95   **811**

1. Poetry -- By individual authors

ISBN 978-1-58567-877-8; 1-58567-877-5

LC 2006-52718

"Shapiro is usually thought of as a New York School poet, but from the evidence of this selection it would probably be more accurate to call him a Greater New York School poet. His metropolis radiates outward to comprehend Weequahic Park and the Palisades, and his aleatory, portent-free sophistication seems confident enough to accommodate primitive, endearing, and frankly tender tropes and situations, as when a poet faces an ailing mother or a growing son. A perennial drama in this volume is that of an erudite and restlessly modernizing mind confronting pains and peculiarities that no amount of urbanity can assuage. . . . The effect is of unforeseen intimacy at the heart of abstraction." New Yorker

Shapiro, Karl Jay

★ **Selected** poems; [by] Karl Shapiro; John Updike, editor. Library of Am. 2003 xxxi, 197p il (American poets project) $20   **811**

1. Poetry -- By individual authors

ISBN 1-931082-34-0

LC 2002-32123

"Karl Shapiro, one of the more influential voices of the late 20th century, displayed complex and contrary tendencies in both his life and his poetry. Editor Updike notes that Shapiro's experimentation with voices and forms alienated those who admired the metrical dexterity of his early poems." Libr J

Includes bibliographical references

Shaughnessy, Brenda

Human dark with sugar. Copper Canyon Press 2008 77p pa $15   **811**

1. Poetry -- By individual authors

ISBN 978-1-55659-276-8 pa; 1-55659-276-0 pa

LC 2007-52225

"The book's three sections contain nine, 11 and 10 poems, respectively, and that off-kilter triangulation . . . proves the right three-cornered lens for looking into the darkest corners of human relationships, including their embodiment. .

. . This is a brilliant, beautiful and essential continuation of the metaphysical verse tradition." Publ Wkly

Our Andromeda; Brenda Shaughnessy. Copper Canyon Press 2012 131 p. (alk. paper) $16   **811**
    1. Poetry -- Collections
    ISBN 1556594100; 9781556594106
                      LC 2012021010
This collection of poems by Brenda Shaughnessy "explores dark subjects--trauma, childbirth, loss of faith--and stark questions: What is the use of pain and grief? Is there another dimension in which our suffering might be transformed? Can we change ourselves? Yearning for new gods, new worlds, and new rules, she imagines a parallel existence in the galaxy of Andromeda." (Publisher's note)

Shockley, Evie
  The **new** black; poems. Wesleyan University Press 2011 104p il (Wesleyan poetry)   **811**
    1. Poetry -- By individual authors
    ISBN 978-0-81957-140-3
                      LC 2010046345
In this book, the author "tells the reader not of some oversimplified and inaccurate version of 'the African-American experience' but of the plethora of experiences that inform the consciousness of one black woman in contemporary America. Shockley's work incorporates elements of myth without being patently 'mythical' and is personal without being self-indulgent, sentimental without being saccharine." Libr J

Simic, Charles
  Master of disguises. Houghton Mifflin Harcourt 2010 75p $22   **811**
    1. Poetry -- By individual authors
    ISBN 978-0-547-39709-2; 0-547-39709-7
                      LC 2009-47470
"Simic's edgy, brooding poems are like saxophone solos played under a bridge in the deep, dark hours of the spinning world's bruising insomnia." Booklist

  Selected early poems. Braziller 1999 255p $22; pa $14.95   **811**
    1. Poetry -- By individual authors
    ISBN 0-8076-1456-4; 0-8076-1483-1 pa
                      LC 99-34872
First published 1985 with title: Selected poems, 1963-1983
  "Charles Simic shows that he is among the very few poets for whom surrealism is a genuine vision, a tool of discovery, rather than a collection of abitrary shocks. . . . His skewed vision manages both to capture the alien concreteness of things and to make them reflect his own consciousness. . . . His skill and sure instinct make this book one of the important poetic achievements of our time." N Y Times Book Rev

  That little something; poems. Harcourt 2008 73p $23   **811**
    1. Poetry -- By individual authors
    ISBN 978-0-15-101359-3; 0-15-101359-4
                      LC 2007-32812

"Among contemporary poets, Simic, now 70, is not only one of the most prolific but also one of the most distinctive, accessible and enjoyable—the commonplace critique of contemporary poetry as dull, obscure and lacking in individuality definitely does not apply. . . . Just about the only thing critics complain of is that his style has shown relatively little development over the years. That's true, although in the last decade or so his poems seem to me to have become shorter, simpler, less manic." N Y Times Book Rev

  ★ The **voice** at 3:00 a.m; selected late & new poems. Harcourt 2003 177p $25   **811**
    1. Poetry -- By individual authors
    ISBN 0-15-100842-6
                      LC 2002-38715
"An important purchase for all libraries." Libr J

Simic, Charles, 1938-
  New and selected poems 1962-2012; Charles Simic. Houghton Mifflin Harcourt 2013 384 p. (hardcover) $30   **811**
    1. Poetry -- Collections
    ISBN 0547928289; 9780547928289
                      LC 2012042188
This poetry collection, by Pulitzer-prize winner and U.S poet laureate Charles Simic, "combin[es] for the first time the best of his early poems with his later works—including nearly three dozen revisions—along with seventeen new, never-before-published poems. Simic's body of work draws inspiration from a range of topics, from the inscrutability of ordinary life to American blues, from folktales to marriage and war." (Publisher's note)

Simpson, Louis Aston Marantz
  ★ The **owner** of the house; new collected poems, 1940-2001. [by] Louis Simpson. BOA 2003 407p (American poets continuum series) $30.95; pa $19.95   **811**
    1. Poetry -- By individual authors
    ISBN 1-929918-38-0; 1-929918-39-9 pa
                      LC 2003-45241
The author "opens with 42 new poems and continues with selections from his 11 previous books, ending with There You Are. This work is filled with evocations of places like Jamaica, Manhattan, Paris, and Venice and range over time from tsarist Russia to World War II to the 1960s. Simpson's obsessive theme is the stultifying effect of middle-class suburban life. . . . The result is a collection both timely and accessible. . . . Highly recommended for all poetry collections." Libr J

Smith, Bruce
  Devotions. University of Chicago Press 2011 88p (Phoenix poets) pa $18   **811**
    1. Poetry -- By individual authors
    ISBN 978-0-226-76435-1; 0-226-76435-4
                      LC 2010027119
"Devotion is a worn word, an excess of meaning dulling its essence. Yet Smith titled . . . [this] book Devotions, recalling a religious definition, a form of worship, for private use. Smith's poems interrogate the meaning of form, worship, private, use—every crucial word. Nearly all the poems

are closely observed blocks of free-associative free verse. . . . Smith riffs on film, cooking, physics, Laundromats, baseball, Rimbaud, and more. His devotions are authoritative and capacious. Neither querulous nor slavish, they give pleasure, which is what we ask of them." Booklist

Smith, Patricia

Blood dazzler; poems. Coffee House Press 2008 77p $16 **811**
1. New Orleans (La.) -- Poetry 2. Poetry -- By individual authors 3. Hurricane Katrina, 2005 -- Poetry
ISBN 978-1-56689-218-6 pa
LC 2008-12528

"Simultaneously accessible and daring, these short, fiery verses describe with sorrow and passion the Crescent City just before, during and immediately after Katrina. They describe it from startling points of view—one series of poems takes the vantage point of Luther B, a hardy abandoned dog. Another set speaks for the hurricane itself. . . . [The author's] command of the spoken voice gives her work both speed and pathos. She benefits, too, from her range of forms: rhymed sonnet, sestina, alphabet poem, long and short-lined, and fragmentary free verse. This book will stand out among literary records of Katrina's devastation." Publ Wkly

Shoulda been Jimi Savannah; Patricia Smith. Coffee House Press 2012 115 p. (alk. paper) $16.00 **811**
1. Women poets 2. African American women 3. Chicago (Ill.) -- Poetry
ISBN 1566892996; 9781566892995
LC 2011029282

[Patricia] Smith's mother bestowed on the poet a name fitting for a woman that would 'never idly throat the Lord's name or wear one/ of those thin, sparkled skirts that flirted with her knees./ She'd be a nurse or a third-grade teacher or a postal drone.' . . . But her father, though acquiescing, secretly called her Jimi Savannah, embodying 'the blues-bathed moniker of a ball breaker.' . . . This duality bursts forth in her poems about . . . growing up black and a woman during the 1960s." (Publishers Weekly)

Smith, Tracy K.

Life on Mars. Graywolf Press 2011 75p. pa $15 **811**
1. Poetry -- By individual authors
ISBN 978-1-55597-584-5; 1-55597-584-4
LC 2011920674
Pulitzer Prize: Poetry (2012)

"Smith shows herself to be a poet of extraordinary range and ambition. It's not easy to be so convincing in both the grand gesture and the reverent contemplation of a humble plate of eggs, and the early successes of this collection far outweigh its later missteps. As all the best poetry does, 'Life on Mars' first sends us out into the magnificent chill of the imagination and then returns us to ourselves, both changed and consoled." N Y Times Book Rev

Snodgrass, W. D.

★ **Not** for specialists; new and selected poems. BOA Editions 2006 251p (American poets continuum series) $27.95; pa $21.95 **811**
1. Poetry -- By individual authors
ISBN 1-92991-877-1; 1-92991-876-3 pa
LC 2005-54846

"If you think that writing primarily in rhyme and meter bespeaks equanimity, or sweetness of character, read Snodgrass. Oh, he mellows out in the face of nature, but he's prickly. . . . His many profoundly bemused and persuasive poems of love's tougher moments, his marvelous angry and denunciatory poems, and the chilling Fuehrer Bunker poems in the voices of the major Nazis during the war's last month—all these might have been impossible if Snodgrass was a nice, easygoing guy. He's not that sort, and his best work seems permanent because he isn't." Booklist

Snyder, Gary

Danger on peaks; poems. Shoemaker & Hoard, Distributed by Publishers Group West 2004 112p il $22; pa $14 **811**
1. Poetry -- By individual authors
ISBN 1-59376-041-8; 1-59376-080-9 pa
LC 2004-11649

This is a collection of poetry by the author of Turtle Island (1975), Axe Handles (1984), No Nature (1992), and The Practice of the Wild (1990).

"From the opening prose-and-verse section on several climbs of Mount St. Helens, through short poems of observation and longer ones on daily life, to more prose-and-verse pieces on journeys near and far, Snyder seems more accepting than ever before. His 1960s eco-Marxist scolding is gone, and he's the wiser for it." Booklist

Includes bibliographical references

Mountains and rivers without end. Counterpoint 1996 165p hardcover o.p. pa $14.50 **811**
1. Poetry -- By individual authors
ISBN 1-887178-57-0 pa
LC 96-26064

"Woven of poems written from 1956 to 1996, this vigorous epic, spanning the landscapes of cities and unsullied nature and covering a period that includes the Beats and their survivors, is rooted in both the American geography and an Eastern spiritual orientation." Publ Wkly

No nature; new and selected poems. Pantheon Bks. 1992 390p hardcover o.p. pa $16 **811**
1. Poetry -- By individual authors
ISBN 978-0-679-74252-4
LC 92-54110

"There is an understated majesty about the ease with which Mr. Snyder puts the present into perspective." N Y Times Book Rev

Sobin, Gustaf

The **places** as preludes. Talisman House 2005 76p pa $14.95 **811**
1. Poetry -- By individual authors
ISBN 1-58498-040-0

"One of the most significant poets of his generation, the late Gustaf Sobin's verse was enigmatic, unique, thought-provoking, and memorable." Midwest Book Rev

Spicer, Jack

★ **My** vocabulary did this to me; the collected poetry of Jack Spicer. edited by Peter Gizzi and Kevin Killian. Wesleyan University Press 2008 496p il $35 **811**

    1. Poetry -- By individual authors
    ISBN 978-0-8195-6887-8

                      LC 2008-24997

"Impeccably edited, this collection gathers the remarkable output of a poet whose writing and person were too counter even for the counterculture of the late '50s and '60s. Spicer's work manages to combine heartbreak, hermeticism, and postwar disquiet in a way both completely of its time and still ahead of ours." Village Voice

Stafford, William Edgar

    The **way** it is; new & selected poems. Graywolf Press 1998 xx, 268p $24.95; pa $16 **811**

    1. Poetry -- By individual authors
    ISBN 1-55597-269-1; 1-55597-284-5 pa

                      LC 97-80082

"Including 71 previously unpublished new poems, among them the poem Stafford wrote the day he died, this collection fully reacquaints us with a quiet, generous presence on the American poetic landscape." Publ Wkly

Stern, Gerald

    This time; new and selected poems. Norton 1998 288p hardcover o.p. pa $15.95 **811**

    1. Poetry -- By individual authors
    ISBN 0-393-31909-1 pa

                      LC 97-43670

"At once self-involved and sympathetic, Stern catalogues with wry dexterity a vast range of sensory data and cultural detritus, always united by 'women and men of all sizes and all ages/living together, without satire.' This healthy collection of new poems and selections from his seven previous volumes . . . is remarkable for its generosity of spirit, manifested in a warm surrealism that is often turned with humor toward his own past." Publ Wkly

Stevens, Wallace

    Collected poetry and prose. Library of Am. 1997 xxii, 1032p $35 **811**

    1. Poetry -- By individual authors
    ISBN 1-88301-145-0

                      LC 97-7023

Having all of Stevens' "poems—especially all the late poems—in one volume is a great thing (previously, one had to seek them out in three different books); the 'Adagia' and his replies to questionnaires are marvelous; and even in the somewhat turgid prose pieces, he sometimes expresses himself with exemplary force and concision." N Y Times Book Rev

Stone, Ruth

    In the dark. Copper Canyon Press 2004 113p $22 **811**

    1. Poetry -- By individual authors
    ISBN 1-55659-210-8

                      LC 2004-6039

"Stone appeals to the mind's eye and the physical ear, each word tested for ripeness like fruit, each a perfectly held note. Wry animal parables, spare and intense dramas, gorgeous nature lyrics, and bracing metaphysical musings constitute a clarion collection." Booklist

    In the next galaxy. Copper Canyon Press 2002 99p $20 **811**

    1. Poetry -- By individual authors
    ISBN 1-55659-178-0

                      LC 2001-7424

"Stone writes conversationally, with lyricism, honesty, wit, and plenty of focus on the passage of time. The suicide of her much-loved husband 40 years ago is a frequent theme, as are observations about aging (which she has achieved with great wisdom), the lives of her young students and neighbors, and ecological and political concerns." Libr J

    What love comes to; new & selected poems. foreword by Sharon Olds. Copper Canyon Press 2008 359p $32 **811**

    1. Poetry -- By individual authors
    ISBN 978-1-55659-271-3; 1-55659-271-X

                      LC 2007045832

Pulitzer Prize Finalist (2009)

"In a field in which collections of selected writings are constantly being released, this book stands out because Stone shows that simplicity can be a deceiving doorway into some of the most challenging poems written by an American poet. Stone's poems blend the personal with dimensions of the larger world in a manner reminiscent of the late William Stafford. Few poets have this gift for taking the workings of ordinary life and fusing them with a poetic process that sustains intense emotion, allowing human experience to be felt through the mysteries of language. . . . Ruth Stone belongs to every generation of poets who have taken the responsibility to give back to the world." Bloomsbury Rev

Strand, Mark

    Blizzard of one; poems. Knopf 1998 55p $21; pa $15 **811**

    1. Poetry -- By individual authors
    ISBN 0-375-40139-3; 0-375-70137-0 pa

                      LC 97-49172

"Strand doesn't approach the universal through the particular. He approaches the universal through the universal. In his masterly new collection, 'Blizzard of One,' even the single snowflake that gives the volume its title . . . is a kind of Platonic essence, linked to a continuum of snowflakes out there in the weather and inside, in the reader's consciousness." N Y Times Book Rev

Man and camel; poems. Knopf 2006 51p $24 **811**

1. Poetry -- By individual authors

ISBN 0-307-26296-0; 978-0-307-26296-7

LC 2006-40986

The author "writes spare, melancholy, and haunting poems." Booklist

Swenson, May

Nature; poems old and new. Houghton Mifflin 1994 xxiii, 240p hardcover o.p. pa $15 **811**

1. Poetry -- By individual authors

ISBN 0-618-06408-7 pa

LC 93-45642

This collection of Swenson's poetry "brings together poems from several earlier books, as well as poems published only in magazines, and introduces us to nine splendid poems published here for the first time. This collection . . . is brought together with special attention to poems describing the environment; poems of tides and the sea, of birds and gardens, of moods and seasons, of self and others. . . . This is a collection to be treasured; it belongs in all libraries with even a modest selection of poetry." Libr J

Szybist, Mary

★ **Incarnadine**; Mary Szybist. Graywolf Press 2013 72 p. (paperback) $15 **811**

ISBN 1555976352; 9781555976354

LC 2012953979

This poetry anthology, by the National Book Critics Circle Award finalist Mary Szybist, is her second published collection. "One poem is presented as a diagrammed sentence. Another is an abecedarium made of lines of dialogue spoken by girls overheard while assembling a puzzle. Several poems arrive as a series of Annunciations, while others purport to give an update on Mary, who must finish the dishes before she will open herself to God." (Publisher's note)

Taggart, John

Is music; selected poems. edited by Peter O'Leary; foreword, C.D. Wright. Copper Canyon Press 2010 353p pa $19 **811**

1. Poetry -- By individual authors

ISBN 978-1-55659-304-8 pa; 1-55659-304-X a

LC 2010-04655

"Metaphor, then, is fundamental to Taggart's poetics, particularly a kind of 'serial metaphor,' a process of making metaphor that is always in motion, like Taggart's musical line, always singing into new meanings, approaching it, which cannot be said—which is light, which is silence, which is a poem." Harp & Altar

★ **Pastorelles**. Flood Editions 2004 104p pa $13.95 **811**

1. Poetry -- By individual authors

ISBN 0-974690-21-X

LC 2004-303826

"Among the small number of poets who have followed the difficult path of Zukofsky, George Oppen, Lorraine Nie-

decker, and William Bronk, John Taggart has kept more closely to the Objectivist trail than most, while at the same time developing his own signature style and deepening his explorations into the strata where vision, music, and language converge. Pastorelles may be his most consistent and fully realized collection, one that maintains and enlivens a literary movement that, even after decades, has still not been granted the degree of attention and critical analysis it deserves." Am Book Rev

Tanning, Dorothea, 1910-2012

Coming to that; poems. Graywolf Press 2011 55p **811**

1. Poetry -- By individual authors

ISBN 1555976018 pa; 9781555976019 pa

"Tanning's poems are beautifully created, filled with rich rhythms and imagery. Mostly, they are made of individual tableaux and artistic vistas, sometimes filled with flights of the fantastic. . . . Often ironic and often filled with wisdom and humor, a Tanning poem asks readers to believe in her artistic vision. These are poems of beginnings and choices, of marriage and aging, and of creation—poems still filled with wondering." Libr J

Tarn, Nathaniel

Selected poems; 1950-2000. Wesleyan University Press 2002 335p (Wesleyan poetry) $45; pa $19.95 **811**

1. Poetry -- By individual authors

ISBN 978-0-8195-6541-9; 0-8195-6541-5; 978-0-8195-6542-6 pa; 0-8195-6542-3 pa

LC 2002-1701

"Arranged chronologically, [this volume] has reprints from nineteen of Tarn's thirty-five books. Here the literary reader can find reality hybrids and can experience the camaraderie of whole image systems from the twentieth century. No syllable is lonely or aloof. One is often reminded, by Tarn's references, his subjects, and his dedications, not only of Blake but of Yeats, Vallejo, Charles Olson, and Robert Duncan. Like those writers, his work brings together mythology, Western and Eastern philosophy (including Gnostic thought), political commentary, scientific investigations, naturalist descriptions and very personal love poetry." Jacket

Tate, James

The ghost soldiers; poems. Ecco 2008 217p $22.95 **811**

1. Poetry -- By individual authors

ISBN 978-0-06-143694-9; 0-06-143694-1

LC 2007-29856

"These poems engage everything from war to police-state oppression to romance to small-town family life. Aliens make appearances, as do mythical creatures, talking animals, shadowy government agencies and malevolent corporations. Tate is clearly responding to contemporary issues. . . . By locating humor in tragedy, by highlighting the false connections by which we mortals construct daily life, Tate distills the sad little details of existence into a potent elixir, at once pathetic and noble." PopMatters

Selected poems. Wesleyan Univ. Press 1991 239p hardcover o.p. pa $18.95 **811**
1. Poetry -- By individual authors
ISBN 978-0-8195-1192-8; 0-8195-1192-7

LC 90-50918

Tate has "created a voice and a kind of poem that no one else could have written. His comedy works not only to entertain, which it does marvelously—he has the rare ability to be very, very funny on the page—but partly to cover and partly to reveal underlying disorientation and angst." N Y Times Book Rev

Shroud of the gnome; poems. Ecco Press 1997 72p hardcover o.p. pa $15 **811**
1. Poetry -- By individual authors
ISBN 0-880015-62-4 pa

LC 97-16224

"The master of our idioms takes us on another dizzy, dangerous careen through absurd and disintegrating Americana, with his speakers looking on bemusedly as their folk narratives spin out of control. Tate . . . continues to draw on small-town kitsch, haywire nature documentaries and 'a giantess by the name of Anna Swan' to fuel his often hilarious antistories. The joke has not tired." Publ Wkly

Worshipful Company of Fletchers; poems. Ecco Press 1994 82p hardcover o.p. pa $13 **811**
1. Poetry -- By individual authors
ISBN 0-880014-31-8 pa

LC 94-9821

The author "offers a collection full of confused narrative voices, prosaic images made startlingly fresh, and landscapes that curve at the sides like hallucinations. . . . Tate is at his best when he weaves into his shimmering language such ordinary objects as toy poodles, crayons, Camp Fire Girls, and gum wrappers. In so doing, he solicits the reader with the familiar, then proceeds to act as trail guide to other worlds." Booklist

Trinidad, David
Dear Prudence; new and selected poems. Turtle Point 2011 493p pa $19 **811**
1. Poetry -- By individual authors
ISBN 978-1-933527-47-5

A collection of poetry from gay poet Trinidad.
The author's "lucid, amusing, and sad journal poems, memoir poems, prose poems, couplets, elegies, sonnets, and impressive pantoums may seem to valorize trash, but that trash sustains a flawed yet invaluable soul aching for loving acceptance." Booklist

Troupe, Quincy
★ **Transcircularities**; new and selected poems. Coffee House Press 2002 368p $30; pa $17 **811**
1. Poetry -- By individual authors
ISBN 1-56689-137-X; 1-56689-135-3 pa

LC 2002-71277

Troupe's "verse returns continually to swing, bebop and free-jazz giants, imitating, commemorating or praising Col-

trane, Duke, Bud Powell and others in a series of musicianly poems culminating in the recent 'Back to the Dream Time: Miles Speaks from the Dead.' Troupe's forms, driven by performability, range from ecstatic odes to overtly political expostulations." Publ Wkly

Twentieth-century American poetry; edited by Dana Gioia, David Mason, Meg Schoerke. McGraw Hill 2004 xlvi, 1143p il pa $79.69 **811**
1. American poetry -- Collections
ISBN 0-07-240019-6

LC 2003-61449

"The text is divided into sections like 'Realism and Naturalism' and 'The Harlem Renaissance,' with each section prefaced by a penetrating overview and each poet introduced by a biographical essay. Included are poets as diverse as Sherman Alexie, Ezra Pound, and Lucille Clifton, along with Nuyorican poets, New Formalists, Beats, imagists, and surrealists. Make room for this affordable, remarkable volume." Libr J
Includes bibliographical references

Twichell, Chase
Horses where the answers should have been; new and selected poems. Copper Canyon Press 2010 255p pa $19 **811**
1. Poetry -- By individual authors
ISBN 978-1-55659-318-5; 1-55659-318-X

LC 2009-48885

"To read a well done 'selected poems' is to follow a life, and we find that here as we watch the poet grow from one in love with thought and language to one who quietly yet intensely contemplates the world by leaning toward the essential. Hers is a world of wounded beauty which she confronts and records for us." N Y Journal of Books
Includes bibliographical references

Updike, John
Collected poems, 1953-1993. Knopf 1993 xxiv, 387p il hardcover o.p. pa $25 **811**
1. Poetry -- By individual authors
ISBN 978-0-679-76204-1; 0-679-76204-3

LC 92-28957

"From the outset Updike's poems are crisp and exact. There is a mock humbleness, ready wit, and divine concreteness to his subjects, an unrelenting curiosity behind his descriptions, and a prodding tension between the tactile and the abstract. . . . From the cocky exuberance of 'Midpoint,' a 1968 autobiographical cycle, to the wry, tender mischief of poems about domesticity, marriage, and aging, Updike's thrill over the unending discovery of poetry inspires images and metaphors of time-stopping perfection as well as humor rich in grace and knowingness." Booklist
Includes bibliographical references

Endpoint and other poems. Alfred A. Knopf 2009 97p $25 **811**
1. Poetry -- By individual authors
ISBN 978-0-307-27286-7; 0-307-27286-9

LC 2009-922927

"The heart of 'Endpoint' turns out to be its opening section, which forms a sequence, beginning with poems written on the author's recent birthdays, continuing through his bouts with cancer, and ending a month before his death on the North Shore. The poems, often written in a jauntily varied iambic pentameter, read like lineated journal entries, but a feeling of necessity runs beneath each of them. . . . This blend of urgency and poise shows in the language itself. Line after line, Updike seems driven to get the world, and the word, right. The poems are dignified everywhere by his lucidity of vision and his inventiveness of phrasing." Boston Globe

Valentine, Jean

  Door in the mountain; new and collected poems, 1965-2003. Wesleyan University Press 2004 285p (Wesleyan poetry) $29.95   **811**

  1. Poetry -- By individual authors

  ISBN 0-8195-6712-4

                  LC 2004-16019

"The defiant, angular, yet propulsively emotional recent poems that occupy the first and last parts of the book should please both fans of Valentine's earliest poetry and fans of her strongly feminist middle period." Publ Wkly

  Includes bibliographical references

Van Duyn, Mona

  ★ **Selected** poems. Knopf 2002 218p $27.50; pa $16   **811**

  1. Poetry -- By individual authors

  ISBN 0-375-41369-3; 0-375-70980-0 pa

                  LC 2001-50672

"Characterized by candor and compassion, Van Duyn's poetry depicts the pleasures and drudgeries of middle-class American life, an approach that at its best becomes an exploration of the spiritual and psychological dimensions of that life. . . . The casually formal surfaces of Van Duyn's poems often resemble those of her model, Elizabeth Bishop, and like Bishop she excels at both formal and free verse." N Y Times Book Rev

Vap, Sarah

  Arco iris; Sarah Vap. Saturnalia Books 2012 88 p. $15   **811**

  1. Poetry -- Collections 2. South America -- Poetry 3. Race relations -- Poetry

  ISBN 0983368643; 9780983368649

                  LC 2012945504

In this collection of poetry, "Sarah Vap explores race, tourism, market, history, intimacy, and the vulnerability of lives beneath the stamp of longstanding powers. Whiteness is considered through the action of travel in South America where white bodies disappear, or are invisible, or attempt to become irrelevant, or are impossible to destroy. These . . . poems explore the subtle violence beneath the commonplace in a foreign land, a violence which underscores the naivete of the traveler." (Publisher's note)

The **Vintage** book of African American poetry; edited and with an introduction by Michael S. Harper and Anthony Walton. Vintage Bks. 2000 xxxiii, 403p pa $14.95   **811**

  1. American poetry -- African American authors --

Collections

ISBN 0-375-70300-4

                  LC 99-39428

"Included in chronological order here are over two centuries of poets, from Jupitor Hammon (1720-1800) to Reginald Shepherd (b.1963). . . . The editors' eloquent, outspoken vision provides a springboard for further examination of what constitutes the mainstream of American poetry." Libr J

  Includes bibliographical references

Viscusi, Robert

  Ellis Island; by Robert Viscusi. Bordighera Press 2012 342 p. $28   **811**

  1. American poetry

  ISBN 1599540339; 9781599540337

                  LC 2012906018

This book presents a collection of poetry by American Robert Viscusi. The collection "is a book of changes. This text exists in two very different modes—one that is stable and one that is endlessly changing. Like Ellis Island, it belongs at the same time to the City and the Sea. Belonging to the City, 'Ellis Island' is a poem of 624 sonnets, in a determined and unchangeable order." (Publisher's note)

Wakoski, Diane

  The **diamond** dog. Anhinga Press 2010 110p pa $15   **811**

  1. Poetry -- By individual authors

  ISBN 978-1-934695-15-9; 1-934695-15-7

Wakoski's "work is often associated with the Deep Image school, with its allegiance to the Jungian imagery said to comprise the collective unconscious, as well as the Confessional and Beat movements in poetry. . . . All of these – the Jungian images, the tendency to confess, the wild leaps and unruly rhythms of the Beat poets, the theme of abandonment – figure in 'The Diamond Dog.' By now, though, Wakoski is able to look back over her 22 books and connect these concerns in the essay called 'Creating a Personal Mythology' that begins the book. Here she provides a career perspective that her fans will welcome. Just as important, she describes a way of writing that young poets will be able to make their own. . . . Wakoski's rhythms are jazzy and easygoing; they're accepting of the world in all its crunchy variety, and they invite the reader to accept as well. The best way to describe her poetics is to say that she asks the reader to go for a walk with her." Christ Sci Monit

Walcott, Derek

  Collected poems, 1948-1984. Farrar, Straus & Giroux 1986 515p hardcover o.p. pa $20   **811**

  1. Poetry -- By individual authors

  ISBN 0-374-52025-9 pa

                  LC 85-20688

"It is difficult to think of a poet in our century who—without ever betraying his native sources—has so organically assimilated the evolution of English literature from the Renaissance to the present, who has absorbed the Classical and Judeo-Christian past, and who has mined the history of Western painting as Walcott has. Throughout his entire body of work he has managed to hold in balance his passionate moral concerns with the ideal of art." Poetry

Includes bibliographical references

Omeros. Farrar, Straus & Giroux 1990 325p hardcover o.p. pa $16   **811**

1. Poetry -- By individual authors

ISBN 0-374-52350-9 pa

LC 90-33592

"No poet rivals Mr. Walcott in humor, emotional depth, lavish inventiveness in language or in the ability to express the thoughts of his characters and compel the reader to follow the swift mutations of ideas and images in their minds. This wonderful story moves in a spiral, replicating human thought." N Y Times Book Rev

The prodigal. Farrar, Straus and Giroux 2004 112p $20   **811**

1. Poetry -- By individual authors

ISBN 0-374-23743-3

LC 2004-5147

"The constants in Nobel laureate Walcott's work are the ravishing beauty of his language, his attunement to the sensuous, his feel for the pulse of history in landscape and seascape, and his despair over the contrast between the glory of European art and the prejudice and brutality that stoked the European conquest of the New World." Booklist

Walcott, Derek, 1930-

White egrets; poems. Farrar, Straus and Giroux 2010 86p $24   **811**

1. Poetry -- By individual authors

ISBN 978-0-374-28929-4; 0-374-28929-8

LC 2009-31895

The author draws the poems in this collection from his Caribbean roots, a love of the Western literary tradition, exotic travel, the wonders of nature, and love, both old and new, as well as the passage of time and the complications that attend age. It is the quest for new love, and the recognition of age, celebrated with grace and wisdom in a delightfully lyrical language, that lie at the heart of this collection. Libr J

Waldman, Anne

In the room of never grieve; new and selected poems, 1985-2003. Coffee House Press 2003 494p il $30   **811**

1. Poetry -- By individual authors

ISBN 978-1-566-89145-5; 1-566-89145-0

LC 2003-55096

"If early work found [Waldman] most engaged with the New York School, these later poems integrate her passions for Buddhism and ethnopoetics into a unique style of vocal, unabashedly current-event-laden, collagistic, wide-ranging work. Waldman's quest to find forms appropriate to her shamanistic, didactic content is particularly compelling in Marriage: A Sentence, with its liquefied gender roles and synthesis of influences ranging from Stein to Corso. . . . Waldman's untiring efforts to link language, ritual and political action come through clearly, urgently and often beautifully." Publ Wkly

Includes bibliographical references and indexes

Waldrop, Keith

Transcendental studies; a trilogy. University of California Press 2009 201p (New California poetry) $50; pa $19.95   **811**

1. Poetry -- By individual authors

ISBN 978-0-520-25877-8; 978-0-520-25878-5 pa

LC 2008-25958

"Comprising three sequences—each almost a book in itself—plus an epilogue, it is an extended philosophical meditation on what are, broadly, the major themes of all poetry: perception, the imagination, the body, and how the human inner life interacts with the larger world. In mostly short, jagged free verse pieces, Waldrop goes at these lofty concepts head-on in accessible, if cerebral, language." Publ Wkly

Waldrop, Rosmarie

Driven to abstraction. New Directions 2010 133p pa $16.95   **811**

1. Poetry -- By individual authors

ISBN 978-0-8112-1879-5; 0-8112-1879-1

LC 2010-14992

"Waldrop continues to actualize surprising poems. Language is active and it enacts. In Driven to Abstraction, questions are often answers—'Only God can create out of nothing. But did he use up the void?'— and statements often questions. This specialized form of constructing prose builds many lessons; sidling up against bigger and more layered themes, the book reads like a semester full of engaging seminars." Coldfront

Walker, Alice

Hard times require furious dancing; new poems. foreword and illustrations by Shiloh McCloud. New World Library 2010 165p il $18   **811**

1. Poetry -- By individual authors

ISBN 978-1-57731-930-6

LC 2010-29972

In this poetry collection, the author "writes of loss and disappointment, and the strength that rises from meeting them unflinchingly. . . . These are powerful anthems of womanhood and age, although just as likely to be empowering to men and to the not-yet-old." Booklist

Walsh, Michael

The **dirt** riddles; poems. University of Arkansas Press 2010 74p (University of Arkansas Press poetry series) pa $16   **811**

1. Poetry -- By individual authors

ISBN 9781557289254; 1557289255

LC 2009046590

This poetry "collection depicts childhood on a family farm and a return to the land as an adult. Walsh's love for rural America is palpable in his attention to the senses. . . . Riddles tells an American story—the end of the family farm, a discovery of sexuality in rural America—but also the universal tale of an attempted return to Paradise. Earthy, pared-down, the lyrics comprising Riddles involve little flash, taking instead a tack of honesty and directness." Antioch Rev

Warren, Robert Penn

★ The **collected** poems of Robert Penn Warren; edited by John Burt; with a foreword by Harold

Bloom. Louisiana State Univ. Press 1998 xxvi, 830p
$44.95   **811**

1. Poetry -- By individual authors
ISBN 0-8071-2333-1

LC 98-26104

"This immense volume gathers 15 books of poetry—as
well as uncollected verse from the beginning and end of
his writing life—from a formidable American man of letters and our first poet laureate. . . . Scholars will especially
cherish the careful, copious textual and explanatory notes
provided by Warren's literary executor Burt . . . and fans of
American poetry and literary history alike should welcome
this opportunity to explore the prodigious oeuvre of one of
the New Criticism's most forceful, convincing proponents."
Publ Wkly

Whalen, Philip
    ★ The **collected** poems of Philip Whalen; ed-
ited by Michael Rothenberg. Weseleyan University
Press 2007 871p $49.95   **811**

1. Poetry -- By individual authors
ISBN 978-0-8195-6859-5; 0-8195-6859-7

LC 2007-16905

"Whalen was a Beat writer who read at the famous Six
Gallery event at which Ginsberg debuted 'Howl.' He adored
Jane Austen and Gertrude Stein, had more than a passing
knowledge of several realms of science, read widely in ancient and modern history, and was a thoroughly cultivated
gent, 'a Fat and Silly poet' who rarely took himself seriously.
He committed the last 35 years of his life to Zen Buddhism.
. . . The distinguishing features of Whalen's poetry are its
playful freedom, . . . its whizzing momentum, its offhand
erudition, its quick eye, its radar ear. But what stands out
is his voice. No other American poet sounds like Whalen,
though Ginsberg in his less vatic moments and Kerouac in
his novels come close." Phoenix
    Includes bibliographical references

Wheatley, Phillis
    The **poems** of Phillis Wheatley; edited with an
introduction by Julian D. Mason, Jr. rev & enl ed;
University of N.C. Press 1989 235p hardcover o.p.
pa $22.95   **811**

1. Poetry -- By individual authors
ISBN 0-8078-4245-1 pa

LC 88-23280

First published 1966
    This volume contains all of the poems and letters known
to have been written by Wheatley, America's first significant
black woman writer

Wheeler, Susan, 1955-
    Meme; poems. by Susan Wheeler. University of
Iowa Press 2012 87 p.   **811**

1. Memes 2. Memetics 3. Love -- Social aspects
ISBN 1609381270; 1609381424; 9781609381271;
9781609381424

LC 2012004396

National Book Award Finalist: Poetry (2012)
    In this book of poems Susan Wheeler "turns her atten-
tion to the most intimate of subjects: the absence or loss of
love. . . . A meme is a unit of thought replicated by imitation;

examples of memes, Richard Dawkins wrote, 'are tunes,
ideas, catch-phrases, clothes fashions, ways of making pots
or of building arches.' Occupy Wall Street is a meme, as are
internet ideas and images that go viral. What could be more
potent memes than those passed down by parents to their
children?" (Publisher's note)

Whitman, Walt
    ★ **Complete** poetry and collected prose. Library
of Am. 1982 1380p $35; pa $17.95   **811**

1. Poetry -- By individual authors
ISBN 0-940450-02-X; 1-883011-35-3 pa

LC 81-20768

"Presented here is the great culminating edition of 1891-
92, the last supervised by Whitman himself. Whitman's
prose, no less extraordinary, includes reminiscences of 19th-
century New York City and notes on the Civil War, especially his service in Washington hospitals and glimpses of
President Lincoln." Publisher's Note

    ★ **Leaves** of grass; edited and with a new after-
word by David S. Reynolds. 150th anniversary ed.;
Oxford University Press 2005 167p $23   **811**

1. Poetry -- By individual authors
ISBN 0-19-518342-8

LC 2004-26509

First published 1855
    "The book, radical in form and content, takes its title
from the themes of fertility, universality, and cyclical life. .
. . As he revised and added to the original edition, Whitman
arranged the poems in a significant autobiographical order."
Reader's Ency. 4th edition

    ★ **Selected** poems; Harold Bloom, editor. Li-
brary of Am. 2003 xxxi, 221p (American poets project) $20   **811**

1. Poetry -- By individual authors
ISBN 1-931082-32-4

LC 2002-32124

The editor "is concerned with Whitman's construction
of his all-encompassing persona, and he selects with that in
mind. . . . Bloom connects Whitman's project to the thesis
of his The American Religion (1992) that the tendency of
religion in America is to replace God with man, and with
the fragments, Bloom presents explicit evidence of the
attempt." Booklist
    Includes bibliographical references

Whittier, John Greenleaf
    Selected poems; Brenda Wineapple, editor. Li-
brary of America 2004 xxvii, 187p $20   **811**

1. Poetry -- By individual authors
ISBN 978-1-931082-59-4; 1-931082-59-6

LC 2003-60483

"Touching and effective as [many of] these poems are,
there is a longer one that ensures Whittier's place in our
canon. Of course I have 'SnowBound' in mind. This poem
of over nine hundred lines evokes a rural way of life, already
past when it was written, in its memories of a family isolated
in their farmhouse for a week by a blizzard. . . . This new selection may not restore Whittier to the schoolroom wall, but
surely it will help readers reassess the author of one major

long poem and a score of attractive lyrics and narratives that deserve their place in our poetic tradition." Sewanee Rev

Wilbur, Richard

★ **Collected** poems, 1943-2004. Harcourt 2004 608p il $35   **811**
1. Poetry -- By individual authors
ISBN 0-15-101105-2

LC 2004-9228

A comprehensive collection of works written throughout the course of the poet's more than sixty-year career includes "In Trackless Woods" and several new and previously unpublished pieces

"Technically, Wilbur remains assured and impressive; he is the premier American master of formal verse. His knowledge has expanded with his life, and his wit has grown in humor while mellowing linguistically. . . . He's indispensable." Booklist

Wilbur, Richard, 1921-

Anterooms; new poems and translations. Houghton Mifflin Harcourt 2010 63p $20   **811**
1. Poetry -- By individual authors
ISBN 978-0-547-35811-6; 0-547-35811-3

LC 2010-05772

"The better work in Anterooms, however limited in quantity, is as good as anything Wilbur has ever written, and upholds certain virtues other poets would do well to acknowledge, even if they travel roads different from the relatively straight one Wilbur has followed." N Y Times Book Rev

Williams, C. K.

★ **Collected** poems. Farrar, Straus and Giroux 2006 682p $40   **811**
1. Poetry -- By individual authors
ISBN 978-0-374-12652-0; 0-374-12652-6

LC 2005-51867

"This weighty, even daunting, tome shows new and old readers the long arc of this Pulitzer Prize and National Book Award winner's career, from the morbid sanguinities of his apprentice work to the careful, moving, stanzaic focus evident in 21 new poems." Publ Wkly

On Whitman. Princeton University Press 2010 187p (Writers on writers) $19.95   **811**
1. Poets 2. Authors 3. Essayists
ISBN 978-0-691-14472-6; 0-691-14472-9

Williams "takes us on a tour of Leaves of Grass as if it were an old, beloved neighborhood. His brief but illuminating chapters cover a range of topics including Whitman's vision, his notebooks, his ever-expanding 'I,' his relationship with Ralph Waldo Emerson, his faith in the imagination, his thematic use of nature, sex, and the body, and his spiritual view of death. To readers already acquainted with Leaves of Grass, these are familiar-enough topics. We know this neighborhood well, especially because Whitman himself spent so much time identifying its key landmarks. But while somewhat predictable in its conception, On Whitman

is revelatory when it comes to explaining Whitman's poetic gifts." Philadelphia Inquirer

Wait. Farrar, Straus and Giroux 2010 125p $25; pa $14   **811**
1. Poetry -- By individual authors
ISBN 978-0-374-28591-3; 0-374-28591-8; 978-0-374-53276-5 pa

LC 2009-31893

The author "writes two kinds of poems: proselike pieces that have a narrative drive and tight, short-lined lyrics that seem inspired by haiku. Generally focusing on dramatic situations in which a person—usually an 'I'—muses on his interior life, all of the poems are surprisingly accessible, especially since some of them seem like examinations of conscience. . . . This book belongs on all poetry lovers' shelves." Libr J

Williams, Jonathan

★ **Jubilant** thicket; new & selected poems. Jonathan Williams. Copper Canyon Press 2005 pa $20   **811**
1. Poetry -- By individual authors
ISBN 1-55659-202-7

LC 2004-20436

"Pared down from 1,450 works over 55 years, this selection features jaunty dances through naughty woods . . . , jokes to and about Ezra Pound, selected listings from the Western Carolina Telephone Company phone book, limericks, 'metafours' (poems in which each line has four words), a poem for each Mahler symphony and acrostics using the names of friends like Guy Davenport. . . . By the end of the book, it becomes clear that Williams can make a verse out of whatever's at hand; the result is a kind of commonplace book for a life lived, with wry but inextinguishable enthusiasm, in the company of artists and arts." Publ Wkly

Williams, Miller

Time and the tilting earth; poems. Louisiana State University Press 2008 51p $45; pa $16.95 **811**
1. Poetry -- By individual authors
ISBN 978-0-8071-3352-1; 0-8071-3352-3; 978-0-8071-3353-8 pa; 0-8071-3353-1 pa

LC 2007-47237

This collection "offers many pleasures. Chief among these are Williams's way of entwining the pure earthiness of language as it's spoken with rigorous metrical precision, and, analogously, his affection for the quotidian, with an insistence on confronting unanswerable but unavoidable existential problems. In poem after poem, he mingles the low and the high in both form and content, bringing a sense of cleareyed practicality to life's big questions and a keenly honed poetic technique to the cadences of Arkansas porch talk." N Y Times Book Rev

Williams, Philip Lee

The **flower** seeker; an epic poem of William Bartram. Mercer University Press 2010 454p il $55; pa $25   **811**
1. Poetry -- By individual authors
ISBN 978-0-88146-228-9; 0-88146-228-4; 978-0-

88146-221-0 pa; 0-88146-221-7 pa

LC 2010-20190

"Extracts from Bartram's Travels, reworked by Williams (as Ezra Pound reworked the sources for his Cantos), are the underlying strata of this work, which pays homage to the epic tradition in a distinctively American way. Curiosity and delight, beauty and sadness, loss and yearning, and all the 'fragrant disorder of this world' are mingled here in a narrative that suggests the gratuitous abundance of Creation itself. And the physical book has been crafted with an expansive generosity that catches the spirit of the poem." Books and Culture

Williams, Tennessee

The **collected** poems of Tennessee Williams; edited by David Roessel and Nicholas Moschovakis. New Directions Pub 2002 xxxi, 304p il hardcover o.p. pa $18.95   **811**
1. Poetry -- By individual authors
ISBN 978-0-8112-1691-3; 0-8112-1691-8

LC 2001-55760

"The painful longing and sense of loss that inhabit Williams's plays and stories are no less present in the poems." Oyster Boy Rev

Williams, William Carlos

★ The **collected** poems of William Carlos Williams. New Directions 1986 2v v1 $40; v1 pa $23.95; v2 $38; v2 pa $22.95   **811**
1. Poetry -- By individual authors
ISBN 0-8112-0999-7 v1; 0-8112-1187-8 v1 pa; 0-8112-1063-4 v2; 0-8112-1188-6 v2 pa

"Williams's poetry is firmly rooted in the commonplace detail of everyday American life. He conceived of the poem as an object: a record of direct experience that deals with the local and the particular. He abandoned conventional rhyme and meter in an effort to reduce the barrier between the reader and his consciousness of his immediate surroundings. . . . Williams's original approach to poetry, his insistence on the importance of the ordinary, and his successful attempts at making his verse as 'tactile' as the spoken word had a far-reaching effect on American poetry." Reader's Ency. 4th edition

Paterson; prepared by Christopher MacGowan. rev ed; New Directions 1992 311p hardcover o.p. pa $15.95   **811**
1. Poetry -- By individual authors
ISBN 978-0-8112-1298-4; 0-8112-1298-X

LC 92-22956

First published 1963

"Set in Paterson, N.J., the poem is a statement on contemporary civilization. Williams uses one dominant metaphor throughout: the city is the human mind beside the river of time; the language of contemporary events (the waterfall) gives the only kind of meaning possible in the flux of time. The poem is composed of lyrics, narrative episodes, prose interludes, bits of letters, etc., to comprise an ecstatic statement on human life." Herzberg. Reader's Ency of Am Lit

Wiman, Christian

Every riven thing. Farrar, Straus and Giroux 2010 93p $24   **811**
1. Poetry -- By individual authors
ISBN 978-0-374-15036-5; 0-374-15036-2

LC 2010-12613

"The work here is searingly honest and beautifully crafted, and it establishes Wiman in his most important public role: a gifted poet whose work cannot be ignored. Wiman's talent is apparent from the opening pages, as are his two central struggles – with illness and faith. . . . [His] ability to love the unconventional or unlovely is one of the qualities that makes his work so memorable and, at times, endearing." Christ Sci Monit

Winder, Elizabeth

Pain, Parties, Work; Sylvia Plath in New York, Summer 1953. Elizabeth Winder. HarperCollins 2013 288 p. (hardcover) $25.99   **811**
1. New York (N.Y.)
ISBN 0062085492; 9780062085498

This biography, by Elizabeth Winder, follows "a young Sylvia Plath and the life-changing month that would lay the groundwork for her seminal novel, 'The Bell Jar.' In May of 1953, a twenty-one-year-old Plath arrived in New York City. . . . She was supposed to be having the time of her life. But what would follow was, in Plath's words, twenty-six days of pain, parties, and work, that ultimately changed the course of her life." (Publisher's note)

Winters, Yvor

Selected poems; Thom Gunn, editor. Library of America 2003 xxviii, 171p (American poets project) $20   **811**
1. Poetry -- By individual authors
ISBN 978-1-93108-250-1; 1-93108-250-2

LC 2003-46638

A volume of verse by "one of the most famous critics and teachers of his lifetime, whose poetry was then more respected than discussed. Now it seems to be some of the best from his generation of American poets. His early work . . . exemplifies imagism at its best, and it is based in the American West rather than the classical Greece that predominates in the work of H. D., the best imagist, Winters' later, formally precise poetry is elegant, allusive, profound, and rather dour, demanding careful reading and rereading and always repaying the effort. Adding immense value to this edition is the inclusion of an autobiographical story with an eerie account of self-confrontation in which Gunn sees the pivot between Winters' early and late poetic styles." Booklist

Words for the hour; a new anthology of American Civil War poetry. edited by Faith Barrett and Cristanne Miller. University of Massachusetts Press 2005 xxx, 401p il lib bdg $80; pa $27.95 **811**
1. War poetry 2. American poetry -- Collections 3. United States -- History -- 1861-1865, Civil War -- Poetry
ISBN 1-55849-510-X lib bdg; 1-55849-509-6 pa

LC 2005-18477

For this collection, the editors "limit their selection to work written between 1834 and 1891 by poets who lived through and often actively participated in antebellum, wartime, and aftermath events. . . . An interpretational, literary, and documentary monument." Booklist

Includes bibliographical references

Wright, C. D.

One with others; [a little book of her days] Copper Canyon Press 2010 168p pa $18   **811**

1. Poetry -- By individual authors 2. African Americans -- Civil rights -- Poetry

ISBN 978-1-55659-324-6; 1-55659-324-4

LC 2010-16789

"In August, 1969, a Memphis man known as Sweet Willie Wine led a group of black men on a four-day March Against Fear, from West Memphis to Little Rock, passing through the small towns of the Arkansas delta. . . . [This book] tells the story of the march, and of the only outsider to join it, a small-town white woman, Margaret Kaelin McHugh, whom Wright calls V. . . . [It] represents Wright's most audacious experiment yet in loading up lyric with evidentiary fact. . . . An affecting element of this book is the way its elegiac impulses accord with, even as they chafe against the documentary impulses." New Yorker

★ **Steal** away; selected and new poems. Copper Canyon Press 2002 235p $25; pa $17   **811**

1. Poetry -- By individual authors

ISBN 1-55659-172-1; 1-55659-194-2 pa

LC 2001-7423

Wright's "poems are crazy quilts constructed out of bits of conversation, a to-do list, dreams, a treatment for a harrowing silent film, and a saxophone solo, but Wright also offers sophisticated readings of the routines and cycle of ordinary life, and ponders the amazing persistence of the ever-hungry body and the tricky mind. It's a boon to have such a wealth of her crackling, intelligent, erotic, 'painfully beautiful,' keep-you-on-your-toes poems in one place. New works accompany selections from nine previous, mostly out of print collections, and all are electrifying in their clear-eyed reports on desire, determination, and survival." Booklist

Wright, Charles

Appalachia. Farrar, Straus & Giroux 1998 67p hardcover o.p. pa $12   **811**

1. Poetry -- By individual authors

ISBN 978-0-374-52624-5; 0-374-52624-9

LC 98-16803

Wright's "inquisitive poems reside at the crux of faith and art: the realization that no matter how sincerely one prays, or how devotedly one writes, the universe and the divine force that animates it remain out of reach of language, reason, and imagination. . . . Wright tries to connect with the spiritual by conjuring the ancient beaming of stars, winter's starkness, and the valor of flowers. Finally, in sweet, bemused surrender, he acknowledges both the impossibility of certainty, and our insatiable hunger for it." Booklist

★ **Negative** blue; selected later poems. Farrar, Straus & Giroux 2000 206p $23; pa $15   **811**

1. Poetry -- By individual authors

ISBN 0-374-22020-4; 0-374-52773-3 pa

LC 99-36987

The author "collects a decade's worth of striking description and laid-back meditation in this sample of work from his last three books. . . . Wright's power lies less in whole poems than in lines within them: those linear strenghts owe something to Ezra Pound, and something more to the antiphonal balances of the Psalms. Wright ends the volume with seven new short poems." Publ Wkly

Sestets. Farrar, Straus and Giroux 2009 75p $23   **811**

1. Poetry -- By individual authors

ISBN 978-0-374-26115-3; 0-374-26115-6

LC 2008-33990

"Wright's poems don't bear down toward conclusions, they expand and evanesce as if in a valiant, impossible effort to comprehend and demonstrate Wittgenstein's dictum that 'the world is all that is the case.' Wright's new collection of short poems is less a book unto itself than the next installment in a continuous poem he's been writing for 40-odd years." N Y Times Book Rev

Wright, Charles, 1935-

Caribou; Charles Wright. Farrar Straus & Giroux 2014 96 p. (hardcover) $23   **811**

1. Poetry -- Collections

ISBN 0374119023; 9780374119027

LC 2013034993

This collection of poems by Charles Wright "consider[s] the impermanence of human existence within the relative permanence of the natural world. . . . A generic setting of creeks, clouds, trees, moons, and stars, Wright's strangely depopulated world takes on a haunting yet familiar presence, inspiring both Zen wisdom . . . and dark wit." (Library Journal)

The collection "is rife with nihilism, humor, and beauty." Pub Wkly

Includes bibliographical references

Wright, James Arlington

Above the river; the complete poems. [by] James Wright; with an introduction by Donald Hall. Farrar, Straus & Giroux 1990 xxxvii, 387p hardcover o.p. pa $20   **811**

1. Poetry -- By individual authors

ISBN 978-0-374-52282-7; 0-374-52282-0

LC 89-16538

"The narrowed range of Wright's characteristic subjects and format, the very delicacy of his instincts, confine him. But his best poems, with their grace and intelligence, not only stand as a rebuke to most of the glib work of his time, but remain among the finest examples of the midcentury American lyric." N Y Times Book Rev

Wright, Jay

★ **Transfigurations**; collected poems. Louisiana State Univ. Press 2000 619p $59.95; pa $24.95 **811**

1. Poetry -- By individual authors

ISBN 0-8071-2629-2; 0-8071-2630-6 pa

LC 00-40560

"Lyric poetry is a way of compressing experience into a heightened moment, but what happens when the experience is one of wanting not to be contained? Wright is an African-American poet who has contended with this dilemma for the last thirty years, and the result is a substantial collection of work. His forcefully musical rhythms drive even poems of everyday experience to a pleasingly contradictory transport. And the later, meditative poems are bound to the world by their attention to the sensual within the spiritual." New Yorker

Youmans, Marly

The **throne** of Psyche. Mercer University Press 2011 106p $30; pa $18   **811**

1. Poetry -- By individual authors

ISBN 978-0-88146-246-3; 978-0-88146-232-6

LC 2011-02079

"Youmans is rather the classicist in outlook; some of her poems actually rhyme. The long title piece is a meditation on the myth of Cupid and Psyche, narrated by some of the characters. . . . Youmans is a nature poet, given to the darker forms of wildness. Her poem 'A Fire in Ice' — a 'riposte' to Billy Collins' 'Taking Off Emily Dickinson's Clothes' — concludes 'Here waits the sphinx whose secret power / In riddles found her finest flower.' Well, someone who likes sphinx riddles can be expected to be a little elusive in meaning, and Youmans can be as slippery as A.R. Ammons sometimes. At other times, though, she's quite accessible." Wilmington Star

Young, Kevin

Ardency; a chronicle of the Amistad rebels. compiled from authentic sources by Kevin Lowell Young. Alfred A. Knopf 2011 249p il map $27.95   **811**

1. Slavery -- Poetry 2. Amistad (Schooner) -- Poetry 3. Poetry -- By individual authors

ISBN 0307267644; 9780307267641

LC 2010-30007

"Young gathers here a chorus of voices that tells the story of the Africans who mutinied onboard the slave ship Amistad." (Publisher's note)

This poetry collection "chronicles the slave mutiny aboard the schooner Amistad in 1839. This three-part book focuses on the 53 Africans who rebelled against their would-be slave owners. Young expertly blends cultural and social history as well as religion to dramatize the lives of the rebels. His evocative use of language—punctuated with stunning metaphors—keeps the historical context clear while moving the gripping true story forward." Libr J

Zapruder, Matthew

Come on all you ghosts; Matthew Zapruder. Copper Canyon Press 2010 xi, 111p (alk. paper) $16   **811**

1. American poetry 2. Poetry -- Collections 3. Heroes and heroines -- Poetry 4. Poetry -- By individual authors

ISBN 1556593228; 9781556593222

LC 2010016787

This book of poetry is written by Matthew Zapruder, the winner of the William Carlos Williams Award. "The title poem is an elegy for heroes and mentors—from David Foster Wallace to Zapruder's father—and demonstrates a[n] . . . expansive range for the poet, highlighting as well a larger body of poetry that . . . wrestles with the desires to live rightly, to make art, and to confront the vast events of

the day." (Publisher's note) "Zapruder invokes a variety of second persons: sometimes it's a particular intimate, as in . . . 'Letter to a Lover' or . . . 'Poem for Hannah,' sometimes a recognizable public figure, as in . . . 'Poem for Ferlinghetti.' . . . Greeting and address help the poet to escape the solitary confinement of consciousness." (LA Review of Books)

The poet "speaks 'with a voice that pretends to be shy/ and actually is, always in search of the question/ that might make you ask me one in return.' In his . . . signature, meandering style, he'll often begin with simple, even childlike observations ('Oh this Diet Coke is really good') that set off associative chains in search of subjects that resonate, psychologically or philosophically, with past personal experiences. . . . Seeming to discover themselves as they go, Zapruder's improvisations (or so they appear) enlist the reader as coexplorer, stumbling into candid self-revelations ('I am also/ always balancing/ on the smooth blade of not/ letting other people down') or surreal quips ('I feel like an elk getting a pelvic exam') with wide-eyed grace." Libr J

Zarin, Cynthia, 1959-

An **enlarged** heart; a personal history. by Cynthia Zarin. 1st ed. Alfred A. Knopf 2013 240 p. (ebook) $24.95   **811**

1. Fashion 2. Motherhood 3. American essays 4. Women poets, American -- Biography 5. Poets, American -- New York (State) -- New York -- Biography

ISBN 1400042712; 9780307962195; 9781400042715; 9781400077649

LC 2012036687

This book is a collection of essays by Cynthia Zarin, a poet, children's author, and journalist who was the fashion writer for the "New Yorker" in the 1980s. "Her passion for beautiful fabric and well-tailored attire, especially coats, is the catalyst for many of her . . . descriptive, complexly emotional . . . essays. Even so, marriage and motherhood are the lifeblood of her . . . observations." (Booklist)

Zucker, Rachel

Museum of accidents. Wave Books 2009 78p $14   **811**

1. Poetry -- By individual authors

ISBN 9781933517421 pa

LC 2009-5831

"This is a startling book of poetry about motherhood— not a cooing little picture of mommy love but an effective snapshot of the chaos, emotional and otherwise, that ensues when a child enters your life. . . . Excellent reading for poetry lovers and a good means of persuading others that verse remains engaging and relevant." Libr J

Zukofsky, Louis

Selected poems; Charles Bernstein, editor. Library of America 2006 xxvii, 172p $20   **811**

1. Poetry -- By individual authors

ISBN 978-1-93108-295-2

LC 2006-40808

"Contemporary poet Charles Bernstein uses these pages skillfully to present a compact but diverse selection of Zukofsky's writing, and he supplies a cogent introduction to both the biography and the poetics." Tikkun

811.008

The best American poetry; edited by Mark Doty.
Scribner Poetry 2012 240 p. (paperback)
$16   **811.008**
1. American poetry 2. Poetry -- Collections
ISBN 1439181527; 9781439181522

This is the 25th volume in the Best American Poetry series. This installment "runs the gamut of styles and positions, from the experimentally mixed registers of Rae Armantrout . . . to the unrelenting intensity of Frank Bidart . . . to an extended meditation on art and family by Paisley Rekdal. . . . [Mark] Doty, this year's guest editor . . . believes poetry is available and useful to all who are willing to seek it out, and so he has chosen poems that take the national pulse in the midst of a tensed political moment." (Publishers Weekly)

812   American drama in English

Abbotson, Susan C. W.
Critical companion to Arthur Miller; a literary reference to his life and work. Facts on File 2006 518p il (Facts on File library of American literature) $75   **812**
1. Authors 2. Dramatists 3. Screenwriters
ISBN 0-8160-6194-7; 978-0-8160-6194-5
                                                 LC 2006-22902

This book "covers Miller's entire canon, including plays, screenplays, fiction, short stories, and poetry, as well as many of his important essays and critical pieces. Also included are . . . entries on literary, theatrical, and personal figures important to Miller; key terms and topics connected to his work; and various theatrical companies and places with which he has been associated." Publisher's note

Includes bibliographical references

Adler, Stella
★ Stella Adler on America's master playwrights;
Eugene O'Neill, Thornton Wilder, Clifford Odets, William Saroyan, Tennessee Williams, William Inge, Arthur Miller, Edward Albee. edited and with commentary by Barry Paris. Alfred A. Knopf 2012 xi, 385 p.p ill.   **812**
1. American drama 2. Drama -- Technique 3. American dramatists 4. Drama -- Explication 5. American drama -- 20th century -- History and criticism
ISBN 0679424431; 9780679424437
                                                 LC 2012018983

This book by Stella Adler, edited by Barry Paris "Brings together [Adler's] most important lectures on America's plays and playwrights, the giants of the twentieth century, men she knew, loved, and worked with. Adler considers, among them, Eugene O'Neill, . . . Tennessee Williams, . . . Clifford Odets, . . . [and] Arthur Miller." (Publisher's note)

Albee, Edward
★ Who's afraid of Virginia Woolf? Scribner Classics 2003 243p $24   **812**
ISBN 0-7432-5525-9
                                                 LC 2003-54206

A reissue of the title first published 1962 by Atheneum Pubs.

Characters: 2 men, 2 women. 3 acts. First produced at the Billy Rose Theatre, New York City, October 13, 1962

"The play is a virulent unveiling of the relationship between George, a history professor, and his wife, Martha, the college president's daughter. Another couple, Nick and Honey, get caught in the crossfire of George and Martha's verbal and emotional lacerations, and it becomes clear that each character is engaged in an isolated struggle through a personal hell." Reader's Ency. 4th edition

Auburn, David
Proof; a play. Faber & Faber 2001 83p pa $13   **812**
ISBN 0-571-19997-6
                                                 LC 00-50284

Characters: 2 men, 2 women. 2 acts, 9 scenes. First produced by the Manhattan Theatre Club, New York City, May 23, 2000

"Twenty-five-year-old Catherine, who sacrificed college to care for her mentally ill father (once a brilliant, much-admired mathematician), is left in a kind of limbo after his death. Socially awkward and a bit of a shut-in, she is gruff with Hal, a former student who shows up even before the funeral wanting to root through the countless notebooks her father kept in the years of his decline, hoping to find mathematical gold. On the heels of his arrival comes Claire, Catherine's cosmopolitan, blandly successful, and pushy sister, with plans to sell their father's house and take Catherine . . . with her back to New York." SLJ

Includes bibliographical references and index

Baraka, Imamu Amiri
Dutchman, and The slave; two plays. [by] LeRoi Jones. Morrow 1964 88p hardcover o.p. pa $9.95   **812**
ISBN 978-0-688-21084-7; 0-688-21084-8

In Dutchman Baraka "explores the revolutionary potential of the educated black middle-class intellectual, represented by the protagonist, Clay, a would-be poet. When Clay is exposed as dangerous—that is, as a latent killer—by white society, seductively imaged as a beautiful white woman named Lula, he is summarily executed by that society. The Slave (1964), a fable set in a future of war between the races, continues the theme of black revolutionary militancy." Benet's Reader's Ency of Am Lit

The **Best** American short plays; edited by Howard Stein and Glenn Young. Applause Theatre Bk. Pubs.   **812**
1. One act plays 2. Drama -- Collections

This series of annual collections was begun in 1937 under the editorship of Margaret Mayorga with title: Best one-act plays, and published by Dodd, Mead through 1955 (starting in 1953 title changed to The best short plays). Beacon Press published the volumes from 1956 through 1961 when publication was suspended. Resumed 1968 under the editorship of Stanley Richards. From 1981 through 1989 edited by Ramon Delgado. Changed to current title and editors with 1990/1991 volume. Volumes prior to 1988 o.p. Apply to publisher for availability and price of retrospective annuals

In addition to the plays each annual contains brief biographical and bibliographical data about dramatists represented

Black, Stephen A.

  Eugene O'Neill; beyond mourning and tragedy. Yale Univ. Press 1999 xxiv, 543p $45; pa $17.95   **812**

    1. Authors 2. Dramatists 3. Nobel laureates for literature

    ISBN 0-300-07676-2; 0-300-09399-3 pa

                         LC 99-33897

    When Black "tracks down correspondences between O'Neill's life and art he adds zip to the life but depersonalizes the art. Still, as he brings the life and the art into apposition, new coloring is cast on a number of the plays. His observations will prove enlightening." New Leader

    Includes bibliographical references

Cervantes Saavedra, Miguel de

  Man of La Mancha; a musical play. lyrics by Joe Darion; music by Mitch Leigh. Random House 1966 82p il hardcover o.p. pa $9.95   **812**

    ISBN 0-394-40621-4; 0-394-40619-2 pa

    Winner of the New York Drama Critics Circle award ¿Best Musical 1966¿

    Characters: 14 men, 5 women, extras. First produced at the ANTA Washington Square Theatre, New York City, November 22, 1965

Cruz, Nilo

  Anna in the tropics. Theatre Communications Group 2003 84p pa $12.95   **812**

    ISBN 1-55936-232-4

                         LC 2003-15859

    Characters: 5 men, 3 women. 2 acts, 10 scenes. First produced at the New Theatre, Coral Gables, Florida, October 12, 2002

    "Set in a cigar factory in Tampa, Florida, in 1929, where the Cuban-American employees have just hired a new 'lector' to read novels to them while they work, Anna and the Tropics is written in the lyrical, somewhat formalized parlance of a folktale. The play is both a piece of cultural history and a warm-spirited tribute to the transformative power of art." Time

Dowling, Robert M.

  Critical companion to Eugene O'Neill; a literary reference to his life and work. Facts On File 2009 2v il (Facts on File library of American literature) set $150   **812**

    1. Authors 2. Dramatists 3. Nobel laureates for literature

    ISBN 978-0-8160-6675-9; 0-8160-6675-2

                         LC 2008-24135

    "These volumes are wonderfully organized and very easy to use. . . . Entries are of a length to provide a good background of O'Neill's works and life." Booklist

    Includes bibliographical references

Edson, Margaret

  Wit; a play. Faber & Faber 1999 85p pa $13   **812**

    ISBN 0-571-19877-5

                         LC 99-11921

    Characters: 3 men, 3 women, extras. First produced at Long Wharf Theatre, New Haven, Connecticut, October 31, 1997

Ensler, Eve, 1953-

  In the body of the world; Eve Ensler. Metropolitan Books/Henry Holt and Company 2013 240 p. $25   **812**

    1. Cancer -- Patients 2. Women -- Congo (Republic) 3. Cancer patients' writings, American 4. Women human rights workers -- Biography 5. Authors, American -- 20th century -- Biography 6. Cancer -- Patients -- United States -- Biography 7. Women -- Congo (Democratic Republic) -- Social conditions

    ISBN 0805095187; 9780805095180

                         LC 2012041539

    This book presents author Eve Ensler's "account of how uterine cancer helped her 'find [her] way back to [her] body'. . . . Incest survivor Ensler['s] . . . professional obsessions eventually led her to the Congo, where 'the systematic rape, torture, and destruction of women and girls' . . . was a horrifyingly banal reality . . . only to discover in 2010 that she had uterine cancer. The diagnosis awakened her to the body that until then had only been 'an abstraction.'" (Kirkus Reviews)

Foote, Horton

  Beginnings; a memoir. Scribner 2001 270p il $24; pa $14   **812**

    1. Actors 2. Authors 3. Novelists 4. Dramatists 5. Screenwriters 6. Television scriptwriters

    ISBN 0-7432-1115-4; 0-7432-1116-2 pa

                         LC 2001-47088

    Foote "chronicled his Wharton, TX, childhood in Farewell. . . . Now he continues his story where he left off, leaving Wharton at 17 to study to become an actor. He travels to theater school in Pasadena but eventually makes it to New York by way of Martha's Vineyard, where he soon discovers his talent for writing and hobnobs with the likes of Martha Graham, Tennessee Williams, and Agnes de Mille." Libr J

  Collected plays. v2 Smith & Kraus 1996 216p v2 hardcover o.p. pa $19.95   **812**

    ISBN 978-1-57525-019-9; 1-57525-019-5

    "Foote's ear for naturalistic dialogue never fails him, and even in the midst of telling an exciting story . . . he never lets the potential for melodrama overwhelm things." Booklist

Gardner, Herb

  Herb Gardner: the collected plays and the screenplay Who is Harry Kellerman and why is he saying those terrible things about me? Applause Theatre Bk. Pubs. 2000 489p il $27.95; pa $16.95   **812**

    ISBN 1-55783-394-X; 1-55783-466-0 pa

    These works "have furnished star actors with some of their most memorable roles and star directors with some of their biggest successes. Those favors are returned by the likes of Jason Robards, Judd Hirsch, Elaine May, Charles

Grodin, and Dustin Hoffman, who introduce the plays that brightened their reputations." Booklist

Gibson, William

★ The **miracle** worker. Scribner 2008 112p pa $12.99   812

1. Deaf 2. Blind 3. Authors 4. Memoirists 5. Humanitarians 6. Teachers of the deaf 7. Inspirational writers 8. Teachers of the blind 9. Social welfare leaders

ISBN 978-1-4165-9084-2; 1-4165-9084-6

LC 2008-275273

First published 1957

A text of the television play, intended for reading, of Anne Sullivan Macy's attempts to teach her pupil, Helen Keller, to communicate.

"The present text is meant for reading, and differs from the telecast version in that I have restored some passages that read better than they play and others omitted in performance for simple lack of time." Author's note

Goodrich, Frances

The **diary** of Anne Frank; by Frances Goodrich and Albert Hackett; newly adapted by Wendy Kesselman. Dramatists Play Service 2000 70p il pa $7.50   812

1. World War, 1939-1945 -- Jews -- Drama 2. Netherlands -- History -- 1940-1945, German occupation -- Drama

ISBN 0-8222-1718-X

LC 2006-455205

First published 1956 by Random House

Awarded the Pulitzer Prize and the New York Drama Critics Circle Award for 1956

Characters: 5 men, 5 women. 2 acts. First produced at the Cort Theatre, New York City, October 5, 1955.

Guare, John

Six degrees of separation; a play. Random House 1990 120p hardcover o.p. pa $12.95   812

ISBN 0-679-73481-3 pa

LC 90-53449

Characters: 13 men, 4 women. First produced at the Mitzi Newhouse Theater, New York City, June 1990

Gurney, A. R.

Love letters and two other plays: The golden age and What I did last summer; with an introduction by the playwright. Penguin Bks. 1990 209p pa $14   812

1. American drama -- 20th century

ISBN 978-0-452-26501-1; 0-452-16501-0

LC 90-34177

Love letters dramatizes the 30-year epistolary "exchange between an upper-class man and an upper-upper-class woman. . . . The Golden Age is an updated, romantic-comic variation upon Henry James' Aspern Papers in which a young academic locates an old woman who may possess a missing chapter of The Great Gatsby and schemes to get it from her. What I did Last Summer is about 14-year-old Charlie's bohemian season with Anna, the Pig Woman, who fosters his creativity as she once did his mother's." Booklist

Hansberry, Lorraine

★ A **raisin** in the sun. Modern Lib. 1995 xxvi, 135p $14.95; pa $6.50   812

ISBN 0-679-60172-4; 0-679-75533-0 pa

LC 95-16074

First published 1959

Awarded the New York Drama Critics Circle Award for the 1958-1959 season

Characters: 8 men, 3 women. 6 scenes in 3 acts. First produced at the Ethel Barrymore Theatre, New York City, March 11, 1959

"Hansberry's drama focuses on the Youngers, a 1950s African-American working-class family in Chicago striving to realize their individual dreams of prosperity and education, and their collective dream of a better life. It was the first play by an African-American woman to be produced on Broadway." Reader's Ency. 4th edition

Heintzelman, Greta

Critical companion to Tennessee Williams; [by] Greta Heintzelman, Alycia Smith Howard. Facts on File 2005 436p il (Facts on File library of American literature) $65; pa $19.95   812

1. Authors 2. Novelists 3. Dramatists 4. Short story writers

ISBN 0-8160-4888-6; 0-8160-6429-6 pa

LC 2004-7362

The authors "offer an excellent resource for those studying Williams's life and extensive body of work." Choice

Includes bibliographical references

Hughes, Langston

Five plays; edited with an introduction by Webster Smalley. Indiana Univ. Press 1963 258p hardcover o.p. pa $14.95   812

ISBN 0-253-32230-8; 0-253-20121-7 pa

Inge, William

4 plays. Grove Press 1979 304p pa $16   812

ISBN 0-8021-3209-X

LC 78-73032

First published 1958 by Random House

The author was awarded the Pulitzer Prize, 1953, for Picnic

Kaufman, George S.

★ **Kaufman** & Co. Broadway comedies. [by] George S. Kaufman with Edna Ferber [et al.] Library of America 2004 911p (Library of America) $35   812

ISBN 1-931082-67-7

LC 2004044200

This compilation includes "Animal Crackers . . . a little-known version that was found among Groucho Marx's personal papers and published here for the first time." Libr J

Kushner, Tony

Angels in America; a gay fantasia on national themes. 1st combined pbk. ed.; Theatre Communications Group 2003 289p pa $15.95 **812**

1. Lawyers 2. Government officials

ISBN 1-55936-231-6

LC 2003-17904

Part one awarded the Pulitzer Prize, 1993

Millennium approaches first presented at the Eureka Theatre Company, San Francisco, May 1991. Perestroika first presented at the Mark Taper Forum, Los Angeles, November 1992.

Lawrence, Jerome

Inherit the wind; [by] Jerome Lawrence and Robert E. Lee. Ballantine Books trade pbk. ed.; Ballantine Books 2007 129p pa $9.95 **812**

1. Evolution -- Study and teaching -- Drama

ISBN 978-0-345-50103-5; 0-345-50103-9

LC 2007-281039

Characters: 23 men, 7 women. 3 acts 5 scenes. First produced at the National Theater, New York City, April 21, 1955

Mamet, David

Glengarry Glen Ross; a play. Grove Press 1984 108p pa $14 **812**

ISBN 978-0-8021-3091-4; 0-8021-3091-7

LC 83-49380

Awarded the Pulitzer Prize, 1984

Characters: 7 men. 2 acts, 4 scenes. First produced at The Cottlesoe Theatre, London, England, September 21, 1983

A "comedy is about smalltime, cutthroat real esate salesmen trying to grind out a living by pushing plots of land on reluctant buyers in a never-ending scramble for their fair share of the American dream." Publisher's note

Speed -the-plow. Grove Press 1988 82p (An Evergreen bk) pa $13 **812**

ISBN 978-0-8021-3046-4; 0-8021-3046-1

LC 87-7252

Characters: 2 men 1 woman. 3 acts. First produced on Broadway at the Royale Theater, May 3, 1988

"A brilliant black comedy, a dazzling dissection of Hollywood cupidity and another tone poem by our foremost master of the language of moral epilepsy. . . . On its deepest level it belongs with the darker disclosures of movie-biz pathology like Nathanael West's The Day of the Locust and F. Scott Fitzgerald's The Last Tycoon. In a sense Speed-the-Plow distills all of these to a stark quintessence: there's hardly a line in it that isn't somehow insanely funny or scarily insane." Newsweek

McCullers, Carson

★ The **member** of the wedding; a play. an introduction by Dorothy Allison. New Directions 2006 118p pa $11.95 **812**

ISBN 0-8112-1655-1; 978-0-8112-1655-5

LC 2005-36493

First published 1951

Awarded the New York Drama Critics Circle Award for 1950

Characters: 6 men, 7 women. 3 acts with 3 scenes in the last act. First produced at the Empire Theatre, New York City, January 3, 1950

Based on the author's book of the same title, this is "a study of the loneliness of an overimaginative young Georgian girl." Saturday Rev

Miller, Arthur

★ **Collected** plays, 1944-1961. Library of America 2006 774p $35 **812**

ISBN 978-1-931082-91-4; 1-931082-91-X

LC 2005-49442

Norman, Marsha

Collected plays. v1 Smith & Kraus 1998 412p v1 (Contemporary playwrights series) pa $19.95 **812**

ISBN 1-57525-029-2

LC 97-7665

Norman's "characters, whether they be performers in a struggling two-bit circus, women in an all-night laundromat, or a Western outlaw, are ones we can easily identify with and understand." Libr J

O'Neil, Eugene

Complete plays; edited by Travis Bogard. Literary Classics of the United States 1988 3v (Library of America) v1 $40; v2 $40; v3 $35 **812**

ISBN 978-0-940450-48-6 v1; 978-0-940450-49-3 v2; 978-0-940450-50-9 v3

Parks, Suzan-Lori

Topdog /underdog. Theatre Communications Group 2001 110p pa $12.95 **812**

ISBN 1-55936-201-4

LC 2001-27316

Characters: 2 men. 6 scenes. First produced at The Joseph Papp Public Theater/New York Shakespeare Festival, New York City, July 22, 2001

This is "the story of Lincoln and Booth, two brothers whose names were given to them as a joke foretelling a lifetime of sibling rivalry and resentment. Haunted by the past, the brothers are forced to confront the shattering reality of their future." Publisher's note

The **play** that changed my life; America's foremost playwrights on the plays that influenced them. edited by Ben Hodges. Applause Theatre & Cinema Books 2009 173p il pa $18.99 **812**

1. Authorship 2. Drama -- Technique 3. Dramatists, American

ISBN 978-1-557837-40-0; 1-55783-740-6

LC 2009-32452

"Edited by Hodges, with a foreword by Paula Vogel, the book assembles 19 of the theater's usual suspects, many of them Pulitzer Prize winners, to explain what lured them into their line of work." Arts J

★ **Playwrights** at work; Paris review. edited by George Plimpton. Modern Lib. 2000 411p il pa $14.95 **812**

1. Poets 2. Actors 3. Authors 4. Novelists 5.

Dramatists 6. Essayists 7. Memoirists 8. Screenwriters 9. Short story writers 10. Theatrical directors 11. Motion picture directors 12. Television scriptwriters 13. Nobel laureates for literature
ISBN 0-679-64021-5

LC 99-44064

"This is an excellent gathering of brilliant minds in the theater, and these interviews provide significant insight into the works of the writers." Libr J

Rose, Reginald

Twelve angry men; introduction by David Mamet. Penguin Books 2006 73p (Penguin classics) pa $11 **812**
ISBN 0-14-310440-3; 978-0-14-310440-7

LC 2006-46006

First published 1955 by Dramatic Pub.
Characters: 12 men. 3 acts. Original television broadcast on CBS program Studio One, September 20, 1954.

Shepard, Sam

Fool for love, and other plays; introduction by Ross Wetzsteon. Bantam Bks. 1984 307p pa $15 **812**
ISBN 978-0-553-34590-2; 0-553-34129-4

LC 84-45182

"Sam Shepard fills the role of professional playwright as a good ballet dancer or acrobat fulfills his role in performance. That is, he always delivers, he executes feats of dexterity and technical difficulty that an untrained person could not, and makes them seem easy." Village Voice

Sam Shepard; seven plays; introduction by Richard Gilman. Bantam Bks. 1981 337p pa $16 **812**
ISBN 978-0-553-34611-4; 0-553-34611-3

LC 83-100533

The **unseen** hand and other plays. Vintage Bks. 1996 383p pa $14.95 **812**
ISBN 978-0-679-76789-3; 0-679-76789-4

LC 95-47723

Simon, Neil

Brighton Beach memoirs. Plume 1995 130p pa $12 **812**
ISBN 0-452-27528-8

LC 95-21788

First published 1984 by Random House
Awarded the New York Drama Critics Circle Award for best play, 1983
"Sex and baseball are the primary preoccupations of 15-year-old Eugene Jerome, narrator of a seriocomic slice of lower-middle-class Jewish family life in Depression-era New York City. The several adolescent characters in the extended family add to the teenage appeal of Simon's . . . play." Booklist

★ The **collected** plays of Neil Simon; with an introduction by Neil Simon. Random House 1979

4v hardcover o.p. v1-2 each pa $25, v3 o.p., v4 pa $17 **812**
ISBN 978-0-452-25870-9 v1; 978-0-452-26358-1 v2; 978-0-679-40889-5 v3; 978-0-684-84785-6 v4

Lost in Yonkers. Plume 1993 120p (Plume drama) pa $12 **812**
ISBN 0-452-26883-4

LC 92-29111

First published 1991 by Random House
Awarded the Pulitzer Prize, 1991
Characters: 4 men, 3 women. 2 acts. First presented at the Stevens Center for the Performing Arts, Winston-Salem, December 31, 1990.
This play, "set in 1940s New York, is a sad-funny portrait of a dysfunctional family, headed by a woman who provided for her children but never showed them love." Booklist

The **play** goes on; a memoir. Simon & Schuster 1999 348p il hardcover o.p. pa $14 **812**
1. Authors 2. Dramatists 3. Screenwriters 4. Television scriptwriters
ISBN 0-684-86980-2 pa

LC 99-36449

Sequel to Rewrites
This memoir "recounts the second half of Simon's life, starting with the life-shattering impact of the death of his first wife, Joan, of cancer at 40, and proceeding through the ensuing 30 years, during which Simon had periods of incredible fertility and others in which his creativity dried up and he feared he would never write again." Booklist

Rewrites; a memoir. Simon & Schuster 1996 397p hardcover o.p. pa $14 **812**
1. Authors 2. Dramatists 3. Screenwriters 4. Television scriptwriters
ISBN 0-684-83562-2 pa

LC 96-13691

This first volume of the dramatist's memoirs focuses on his career as it evolved from writing high school skits to TV programs to Broadway
"This is a gentleman's autobiography, and Simon never stoops to dishing the dirt on his show biz cronies." Libr J

Wasserstein, Wendy

An **American** daughter. Harcourt Brace & Co. 1998 105p il hardcover o.p. pa $14 **812**
ISBN 0-15-600645-6 pa

LC 97-36079

Characters: 6 men, 4 women. 2 acts, 8 scenes. First produced by the Lincoln Center Theater, New York City, April 13, 1997

The **Heidi** chronicles and other plays. Vintage Bks. 1991 249p pa $13.95 **812**
ISBN 0-679-73499-6

LC 90-55681

First published 1990 by Harcourt Brace Jovanovich
This collection traces "three decades of changing styles, mores, life objectives, and intellectual challenges. Wasserstein examines her characters and their times with great

good humor, complexity, depth of feeling, and a firm refusal to accept trite and easy images." Libr J

The **sisters** Rosensweig. 1993 109p il hardcover o.p. pa $11   **812**

ISBN 0-15-600013-X pa

LC 93-224

Characters: 4 men, 4 women. 2 acts 7 scenes. First produced at the Mitzi E. Newhouse Theater, New York City, October 22, 1992

This is "a domestic, romantic comedy partly about the three middle-aged sisters of the title and their relations with men and careers and partly about how the eldest sister, international banker Sara, in whose London home the play is set, meets a man who comes to dinner and, through not much effort on her part . . . sweeps him off his feet. Wasserstein's filled the play with the sharp but poignantly revealing developments and dialogue that she writes so well." Booklist

Wilder, Thornton

Collected plays & writings on theater. Library of America 2007 871p $40   **812**

1. Poetry -- By individual authors
ISBN 978-1-59853-003-2; 1-59853-003-8

LC 2006-48620

"Complementing the selection of plays is [a] . . . group of essays that captures Wilder's reflections on his plays and contains a revealing epistolary account of the film adaptation of Our Town, as well as evaluations of dramatists such as Sophocles, George Bernard Shaw, and the Austrian satirist Johann Nestroy (whose farce Einen Jux will er sich machen Wilder . . . transformed into The Matchmaker)." Publisher's note

★ **Our** town; a play in three acts. foreword by Donald Margulies. HarperCollins Pubs. 2003 xx, 181p $19.95; pa $9.95   **812**

ISBN 0-06-053525-3; 0-06-051263-6 pa

A reissue with a new foreword of the title first published 1938 by Coward-McCann

Large mixed cast. First produced at McCarter's Theatre, Princeton, N.J., January 22, 1938.

"Presented without scenery of any kind, utilizing a narrator and loose episodic form, adventurous and imaginative in style, this unique play . . . is one of the most distinguished in the modern repertoire. It deals with the simplest and most touching aspects of life in a small town." HarperCollins Reader's Ency of Am Lit

Williams, Tennessee

★ **Plays,** 1937-1955. Library of America 2000 1054p $40   **812**

ISBN 978-1-883011-86-4; 1-883011-86-4

★ **Plays,** 1957-1980. Library of America 2000 999p $40   **812**

ISBN 978-1-883011-87-1; 1-883011-87-6

★ A **streetcar** named desire; with an introduction by Arthur Miller. New Directions 2004 192p pa $9.95   **812**

ISBN 0-8112-1602-0

LC 2004-11654

First published 1947

Characters: 6 women, 7 men. 11 scenes. First produced at the Barrymore Theatre, New York City, December 3, 1947

"A study of sexual frustration, violence, and aberration, set in New Orleans, in which Blanche Dubois' fantasies of refinement and grandeur are brutally destroyed by her brother-in-law, Stanley Kowalski, whose animal nature fascinates and repels her." Oxford Companion to Engl Lit. 5th edition

Wilson, August

Fences; a play. introduction by Lloyd Richards. New Am. Lib. 1986 101p pa $12   **812**

ISBN 978-0-452-26401-4

LC 86-5264

Awarded the Pulitzer Prize, 1987

Characters: 5 men, 1 woman, 1 girl. 2 acts, 9 scenes. First produced at the Yale Repertory Theatre, New Haven, Connecticut, April 30, 1985

Gem of the ocean. Theatre Communications Group 2006 85p $25; pa $13.95   **812**

1. Pittsburgh (Pa.) -- Drama. 2. African Americans -- Drama. 3. African American neighborhoods -- Drama. 4. Hill District (Pittsburgh, Pa.) -- Drama.
ISBN 978-1-55936-281-8; 1-55936-281-2; 978-1-55936-280-1 pa; 1-55936-280-4 pa

LC 2006-7812

Characters: 5 men, 2 women. First produced at the Eugene O'Neill Theater Center, Waterford, Ct., 2002

"A swelling battle hymn of transporting beauty. Theatergoers who have followed August Wilson's career will find in Gem a touchstone for everything else he has written." N Y Times

Jitney. Overlook Press 2001 96p hardcover o.p. pa $14.95   **812**

ISBN 978-158567-370-4; 1-58567-370-6

LC 2001-33962

Winner of the New York Drama Critics Circle Award, 2000

Characters: 8 men, 1 woman. 2 acts, 8 scenes. This is a revised version of a play written 1979

Joe Turner's come and gone; a play in two acts. New Am. Lib. 1988 94p pa $12   **812**

ISBN 978-0-452-26009-2; 0-452-26009-4

LC 88-1660

Characters: 6 men, 5 women. 2 acts, 10 scenes. 1 setting. First produced at the Yale Repertory Theatre, New Haven, Connecticut, April 29, 1986

King Hedley II. Theatre Communications Group 2005 103p $27.95; pa $13.95   **812**
1. Ex-convicts -- Drama. 2. Pittsburgh (Pa.) -- Drama. 3. African American men -- Drama.
ISBN 978-1-55936-261-0; 1-55936-261-8; 978-1-55936-260-3 pa; 1-55936-260-X pa
      LC 2005-12535
Characters: 4 men, 2 women. First produced at the Seattle Repertory Theatre, Seattle, Wa., 1999
This is a "big play, filled with big emotions and big speeches. These aria-like monologues are rich in humor, heartbreak and the astonishing details that go into creating real people." Associated Press

Ma Rainey's black bottom; a play in two acts. New Am. Lib. 1985 111p pa $12   **812**
ISBN 978-0-452-26113-6; 0-452-26113-9
      LC 84-27156
Characters: 8 men, 2 women. 2 acts. First produced at the Yale Repertory Theatre, New Haven, Connecticut, April 6, 1984

The **piano** lesson. New Am. Lib. 1990 108p hardcover o.p. pa $12   **812**
ISBN 978-0-452-26534-9; 0-452-26534-7
      LC 90-38734
Awarded the Pulitzer Prize and the New York Drama Critics Circle Award, 1990
Characters: 5 men, 3 women. 2 acts, 7 scenes. First presented at the Yale Repertory Theatre, New Haven, November 26, 1987

Radio golf. Theatre Communications Group 2007 81p $25; pa $13.95   **812**
1. African Americans -- Drama. 2. Nineteen nineties -- Drama. 3. Real estate development -- Drama. 4. African American neighborhoods -- Drama. 5. Hill District (Pittsburgh, Pa.) -- Drama.
ISBN 978-1-55936-306-8; 1-55936-306-1; 978-1-55936-308-2 pa; 1-55936-308-8 pa
      LC 2007-32541
Characters: 4 men, 1 woman. First produced at the Cort Theatre, New Haven Connecticut, May 8, 2007
"A play that could well be Mr. Wilson's most provocative." NY Times

Seven guitars. Dutton 1996 107p hardcover o.p. pa $12   **812**
ISBN 978-0-452-27692-5; 0-452-27692-6 pa
      LC 95-50536
Winner of the New York Drama Critics Circle award, 1996
Characters: 4 men, 3 women. 2 acts, 9 scenes. First produced at the Goodman Theater, Chicago, January 21, 1995
"Pittsburgh, summer 1948. Five of his friends gather after the funeral of Floyd Barton, mysteriously murdered at 35, just as his first blues record had become a hit. The sixth play in Wilson's cycle concerned with twentieth-century Af-

rican American lives is mostly a flashback. We learn what happened to Floyd, but before that horrifying climax, Wilson steeps us in the pathos that Floyd glimpsed a way to escape. . . . As powerful as modern drama gets." Booklist

Two trains running; foreword by Laurence Fishburne. Theatre Communications Group 2007 99p $25   **812**
1. Nineteen sixties -- Drama. 2. African Americans -- Drama. 3. African American neighborhoods -- Drama. 4. Hill District (Pittsburgh, Pa.) -- Drama.
ISBN 978-1-55936-303-7
      LC 2007-22095
First published 1992 by Dutton
Characters: 6 men, 1 woman. 2 acts 8 scenes. First produced at the Yale Repertory Theatre, New Haven, Ct., March 27, 1990

Wilson, Lanford
21 short plays. Smith & Kraus 1993 268p pa $19.95   **812**
ISBN 1-880399-31-8
      LC 93-34434
"The plays range in form from finely crafted one-act plays to short 'skits' written for various benefits. They are arranged in chronological order and the collection spans the years from 1963 to 1991. Wilson's dramatic style has been characterized by such phrases as 'lyric realism' and 'poetic realism,' but these short plays represent a far greater range of styles." Voice Youth Advocates

The **Talley** trilogy. Smith & Kraus 1999 272p (Collected works) hardcover o.p.   **812**
"Wilson didn't begin what became, ultimately, a tetralogy with the idea of creating a play cycle. He just wanted to write a play set in the late 1970s that reflected in some way the post-Vietnam, post-Watergate letdown much of young America was feeling. . . . The resultant four-play cycle captures the Talley's foibles and follies as thoroughly—and as entertainingly—as J.D. Salinger's set of stories and short novels did the Glass family." Booklist

Zindel, Paul
The **effect** of gamma rays on man-in-the-moon marigolds; a drama in two acts. drawings by Dong Kingman. Harper & Row 1971 108p il hardcover o.p. pa $6.99   **812**
ISBN 0-06-075738-8 pa
ALA YALSA Margaret A. Edwards Award (2002)
Characters: 5 women. First produced at the Mercer-O'Casey Theatre, New York City, April 7, 1970
"The play, in the naturalistic tradition, deals with a widow and her two daughters, the imagination of one of whom has been captured by the atom and the possibilities it offers of producing mutations." McGraw-Hill Ency of World Drama

813   American fiction in English

Abbott, Alysia

Fairyland; a memoir of my father. by Alysia Abbott. 1st ed. W.W. Norton & Co. Inc. 2013 352 p. (hardcover) $25.95   **813**

1. Gay parents 2. Children of gay parents 3. Gay fathers -- Biography 4. Gay men -- California -- San Francisco -- Biography

ISBN 0393082520; 9780393082524

LC 2013011614

Stonewall Book Awards: Nonfiction Honor Book (2014)
Lambda Literary Awards Finalist (2014)

This book by Alysia Abbot recounts her relationship with her father, Steve Abbot, who "in the early 1970s . . . embraced his homosexuality and moved to San Francisco." The "memoir describes life with her poet-activist father and his openly gay lifestyle.... She watches as friends, and then her father, contract AIDS, and at age 21, she returns home to help care for him and is conflicted over feelings of duty and the desire to begin a life of her own." (Library Journal)

Includes bibliographical references.

Alice Walker; edited and with an introduction by Harold Bloom. New edition; Bloom's Literary Criticism; an imprint of Infobase Publishing 2007 223p (Modern critical views) $45   **813**

1. Poets 2. Authors 3. Novelists 4. Editors 5. Essayists 6. College teachers 7. Short story writers

ISBN 978-0-7910-9611-6

First published 1989

A collection of critical essays discussing the work of The Color Purple author Alice Walker.

Includes bibliographical references

Alice Walker's The color purple; edited and with an introduction by Harold Bloom. New ed.; Bloom's Literary Criticism 2008 191p (Modern critical interpretations) $45   **813**

1. Poets 2. Authors 3. Novelists 4. Editors 5. Essayists 6. College teachers 7. Short story writers

ISBN 978-0-7910-9614-7; 0-7910-9614-9

LC 2008-2775

First published 2000

A collection of ten essays providing international appraisal and interpretation of Walker's novel.

Includes bibliographical references

Atlas, James

Bellow; a biography. Random House 2000 686p il hardcover o.p. pa $29   **813**

1. Authors 2. Novelists 3. Dramatists 4. Authors, American 5. Short story writers 6. Nobel laureates for literature

ISBN 0-375-75958-1 pa

LC 00-42529

"Atlas shares his subject's devotion to literature, intimacy with Chicago (the city Bellow immortalized), and Jewishness, and he succeeds brilliantly in chronicling and interpreting Bellow's very full life, difficult personality, and powerful work." Booklist

Includes bibliographical references

Bailey, Blake

A tragic honesty: the life and work of Richard Yates. Picador 2003 671p $35; pa $18   **813**

1. Authors 2. Novelists 3. Short story writers 4. Authors, American -- 20th century -- Biography

ISBN 0-312-28721-6; 0-312-42375-6 pa

LC 2002-42525

This biography of the novelist discusses his "unhappy Greenwich Village childhood and his struggles to write while teaching and working as a business writer, Hollywood screenwriter, and speechwriter for Robert Kennedy. As Bailey meticulously and perceptively chronicles Yates' arduous translation of experience into art, he exposes the anguish and transcendence of the writing life and the tragedy of mental illness." Booklist

Boyd, Brian

Stalking Nabokov; selected essays. Columbia University Press 2011 452p $35   **813**

1. Poets 2. Authors 3. Novelists 4. Essayists 5. Memoirists 6. Translators 7. College teachers 8. Literary critics 9. Short story writers

ISBN 978-0-231-15856-5; 0-231-15856-4

LC 2011-08348

This "collection of essays, addresses, and introductions written for an assortment of audiences by a noted Nabokov biographer and scholar is a delight. Boyd . ... does more than an able job of exploring Nabokov's varied intellectual interests—beyond what he could convey in his two-volume biography—from examining Nabokov's lepidopterological pursuits to trenchant assessments of Nabokov as a writer. Boyd dissects several major novels and offers comparisons between Nabokov and writers as diverse as Tolstoy and Machado de Assis." Libr J

Includes bibliographical references

Vladimir Nabokov: the American years. Princeton Univ. Press 1991 783p il hardcover o.p. pa $49   **813**

1. Poets 2. Authors 3. Novelists 4. Authors, Russian 5. Essayists 6. Memoirists 7. Translators 8. College teachers 9. Literary critics 10. Short story writers

ISBN 0-691-06797-X; 0-691-02471-5 pa

LC 90-26374

This volume, which completes the biography begun with Vladimir Nabokov: The Russian Years (1990), is an account of the writer's life from 1940, when he arrived in the United States.

Includes bibliographical references

Vladimir Nabokov: the Russian years. Princeton Univ. Press 1990 607p il hardcover o.p. pa $49   **813**

1. Poets 2. Authors 3. Novelists 4. Authors, Russian 5. Essayists 6. Memoirists 7. Translators 8. College teachers 9. Literary critics 10. Short story writers

ISBN 0-691-06794-5; 0-691-02470-7 pa

LC 90-8040

The author aims to "describe the liberal milieu of the aristocratic Nabokovs, their escape from Russia [after the Revolution], Nabokov's education at Cambridge, and the murder of his father in Berlin. Boyd then turns to the years that Nabokov spent, impoverished, in Germany and France, until the coming of Hitler forced him to flee, with wife and son, to the United States." Publisher's note

Includes bibliographical references

Burroughs, Augusten

★ **Running** with scissors; a memoir. St. Martin's Press 2002 304p $23.95; pa $14   **813**

1. Authors 2. Novelists 3. Memoirists
ISBN 0-312-28370-9; 0-312-42227-X pa

LC 2001-58857

In this memoir the author recalls his youth with a mentally ill mother, living with his mother's psychiatrist in a chaotic household, and his early homosexual experiences

"Burroughs tempers the pathos with sharp, riotous humor in stories that are self-deprecating, raunchy, sexually explicit." Booklist

Burroughs, William S., 1914-1997

Rub out the words; the letters of William S. Burroughs 1959-1974. edited and with an introduction by Bill Morgan. Ecco 2012 xxxv, 444 p.p (hardcover) $35   **813**

1. Letters 2. Beat generation -- Correspondence 3. American authors -- Correspondence 4. Authors, American -- 20th century -- Correspondence
ISBN 006171142X; 9780061711428

LC 2012371022

This collection of correspondence by author William S. Burroughs "contains over 300 . . . letters written mostly to friends, family, and business associates between the publication of 'Naked Lunch' and Burroughs's return to New York City to teach at City College. While old friends like Allen Ginsberg are among the recipients, more of the letters are addressed to newer companions whom Burroughs met while living abroad, including Brion Gysin, Paul Bowles, and Alex Trocchi. Many letters evidence Burroughs's obsessions with the cut-up method, Scientology, and the effectiveness of apomorphine as a cure for addiction; others reveal a caring father concerned about his son's well-being and financial security. . . . [Editor Bill] Morgan includes helpful explanatory notes, a chronology, and a list of sources identifying the repositories holding the letters." (Libr J)

Includes bibliographical references and index

Cather, Willa, 1873-1947

The **selected** letters of Willa Cather; edited by Andrew Jewell and Janis Stout. 1st ed. Alfred A. Knopf 2013 752 p. (hardcover) $37.50; (ebook) $85.00   **813**

1. Authors -- Correspondence 2. Novelists, American -- 20th century -- Correspondence
ISBN 0307959309; 9780307959300; 9780307959317

LC 2012036882

This book is a collection of some of author Willa Cather's personal correspondence. "Beginning with a witty missive written in 1888 when she was only 14, the volume continues through her early years as a successful magazine editor for McLure's, into the 1910s and '20s, when she experienced success as a novelist, all the way through to her death in 1947." (Publishers Weekly)

★ The **Columbia** companion to the twentieth-century American short story; Blanche H. Gelfant, editor. Columbia Univ. Press 2000 660p $83.50; pa $24.50   **813**

1. Reference books 2. American fiction -- Bio-bibliography 3. Short stories -- History and criticism 4. American fiction -- History and criticism
ISBN 0-231-11098-7; 0-231-11099-5 pa

LC 00-31610

"The first 100 pages are devoted to thematic essays that focus on the form of the short story, the development of the genre, several distinct subject types (e.g., short stories of the Holocaust or of the working class), and four different ethnic groups (African American, Asian American, Chicano Latino American, and Native American). . . . The remainder of the book is devoted to over 100 individual author essays that focus on reading for pleasure and understanding rather than critical interpretation. Entries discuss the development of each author and the content and meaning of his or her major short stories." Libr J

Includes bibliographical references

Contemporary Jewish-American novelists; a bio-critical sourcebook. edited by Joel Shatzky and Michael Taub; with a foreword by Daniel Walden. Greenwood Press 1997 xxxi, 506p $105   **813**

1. Reference books 2. American fiction -- Jewish authors 3. American fiction -- Bio-bibliography
ISBN 0-313-29462-3

LC 96-37047

This "reference work 'includes alphabetically arranged entries for more than 75 Jewish-American novelists whose major works were largely written after World War II.' While major canonical figures such as Norman Mailer and Saul Bellow are profiled, lesser-known novelists—including Judith Katz, Lev Raphael, and Steve Stern—are covered as well. One of the editors' goals is to show the diversity of Jewish-American literature. . . . Each entry includes a biographical section, a cogent discussion of major works and themes, an overview of each novelist's critical reception, and a bibliography of both primary and secondary sources." Booklist

Crane, Stephen, 1871-1900

Prose and poetry. Library of Am. 1984 1379p $40; pa $15.95   **813**

1. Short stories
ISBN 0-940450-17-8; 1-883011-39-6 pa

LC 83-19908

"This collection also includes both Crane's collections of epigrammatic free verses—'The Black Riders' and 'War is kind'—and selections from his uncollected poems." Publisher's note

Dearborn, Mary V.

Mailer; a biography. Houghton Mifflin 1999 478p il hardcover o.p. pa $15   **813**

1. Authors 2. Novelists 3. Essayists 4. Authors, American
ISBN 0-395-73655-2; 0-618-15460-4 pa

LC 99-32214

"Dearborn supplies a close reading of one of the most controversial American writers of the postwar era. Mailer's body of work, beginning with his career-defining first novel, The Naked and the Dead (1948), is analyzed with remarkable insight. Mailer's notorious personal life is also examined, as Dearborn sorts through the various preoccupations that have obsessed the writer over five decades in the literary spotlight." Booklist

Includes bibliographical references

Doctorow, E. L. (2004)

Reporting the universe. Harvard Univ. Press 2003 125p (The William E. Massey Sr. lectures in the history of American civilization) $22.95; pa $13.95 **813**

1. Authors 2. Novelists
ISBN 0-674-00461-2; 0-674-01628-9 pa
LC 2002-32742

"This potent collection of elegantly distilled essays offers a fresh perspective on our species' capacity for both the sublime and the horrific." Booklist

Facts on File, Inc.

★ The **Facts** on File companion to the American novel; edited by Abby H.P. Werlock; assistant editor, James P. Werlock. Facts on File 2005 3v (Facts on File library of American literature) set $195 **813**

1. Reference books 2. American fiction -- Encyclopedias
3. American fiction -- Bio-bibliography
ISBN 0-8160-4528-3; 978-0-8160-4528-0
LC 2005-12437

"This A-to-Z reference contains 450 biographical overviews of American and foreign-born authors living in the United States and 500 signed analytical essays on their novels. . . . Libraries will value this compact set for including classics as well as hard-to-find contemporary authors." SLJ

Includes bibliographical references

Fargnoli, A. Nicholas

Critical companion to William Faulkner; a literary reference to his life and work. [by] A. Nicholas Fargnoli, Michael Golay, Robert W. Hamblin. Facts On File 2008 562p il (Facts on File library of American literature) $75 **813**

1. Authors 2. Novelists 3. Screenwriters 4. Short story writers 5. Nobel laureates for literature
ISBN 978-0-8160-6432-8
LC 2007-32361

First published 2001 with title: William Faulkner A to Z
"Coverage includes: Faulkner's major works, including novels, short stories, poetry, and nonfiction; descriptions of characters in Faulkner's fiction, such as Benjy and Quentin from The Sound and the Fury; details about Faulkner's family, friends, colleagues, and critics; real and fictional places important to Faulkner's life and literary development, from Yoknapatawpha County, Mississippi to Hollywood; interviews and speeches given by Faulkner; [and] ideas and events that influenced his life and works, including slavery, the Civil War, World War I, and civil rights." Publisher's note
Includes bibliographical references

Farrell, Susan Elizabeth

Critical companion to Kurt Vonnegut; a literary reference to his life and work. [by] Susan Farrell. Facts On File 2008 532p il (Facts on File library of American literature) $75 **813**

1. Authors 2. Novelists 3. Journalists 4. Biographers
5. Short story writers 6. Science fiction writers
ISBN 978-0-8160-6598-1
LC 2007-37900

This "book covers all his works, including his novels, such as the unforgettable Slaughterhouse-Five; his short stories, such as 'Harrison Bergeron'; and his lectures and essays. . . . Entries on his life, related people, places, and topics are also included." Publisher's note
Includes bibliographical references

Critical companion to Tim O'Brien; a literary reference to his life and work. [by] Susan Farrell. Facts on File 2011 480p (Facts on File library of American literature) $75 **813**

1. Authors 2. Novelists 3. Essayists 4. Memoirists 5. Short story writers
ISBN 978-0-8160-7870-7; 978-1-4381-3661-5 ebook
LC 2010038664

This book features a "biography of O'Brien; entries on all O'Brien's works, including his war novels, Going After Cacciato, The Things They Carried, and In the Lake of the Woods; his memoir, If I Die in a Combat Zone, Box Me Up and Ship Me Home; and all his other published novels and short stories, including The Nuclear Age, July, July, and more; [and] entries on related people, places, and topics, such as Green Berets, Ernest Hemingway, metafiction, and Viet Cong." Publisher's note
Includes bibliographical references

Fitzgerald, F. Scott

A **life** in letters; edited by Matthew J. Bruccoli; with the assistance of Judith S. Baughman. Scribner 1994 xxiii, 503p hardcover o.p. pa $18 **813**

1. Authors 2. Novelists 3. Screenwriters 4. Authors, American 5. Short story writers
ISBN 0-684-19570-4; 0-684-80153-1 pa
LC 93-31011

"Essential reading for a full understanding of Fitzgerald as an artist and a man." Libr J

Gillespie, Carmen

Critical companion to Alice Walker; a literary reference to her life and work. Facts on File 2011 452p il (Facts on File library of American literature) $75 **813**

1. Poets 2. Authors 3. Novelists 4. Editors 5. Essayists 6. College teachers 7. Short story writers
ISBN 978-0-8160-7530-0; 978-1-4381-3488-8 ebook
LC 2010-18639

This book contains "entries on all of Walker's major works, including such novels as The Color Purple, Meridian, The Third Life of Grange Copeland, and Possessing the Secret of Joy; essay collections and essays, such as 'Beauty: When the Other Dancer Is the Self'; poetry collections and poems; and short stories. Each entry on a major work of fiction contains subentries on the work's main characters." Publisher's note

Includes bibliographical references

Critical companion to Toni Morrison; a literary reference to her life and work. Facts On File 2008 484p il (Facts on File library of American literature) $75 **813**
1. Authors 2. Novelists 3. Dramatists 4. Essayists 5. College teachers 6. Literary critics 7. Nobel laureates for literature
ISBN 978-0-8160-6276-8

LC 2006-38231

This book "examines Morrison's life and writing, featuring critical analyses of her work and themes, as well as . . . entries on related topics and relevant people, places, and influences." Publisher's note

Includes bibliographical references

Gunn, James E.
Isaac Asimov; the foundations of science fiction. by James Gunn. rev ed; Scarecrow Press 1996 276p hardcover o.p. pa $42 **813**
1. Authors 2. Novelists 3. Biochemists 4. Children's authors 5. Writers on science 6. Short story writers 7. Young adult authors 8. Science fiction writers 9. Science fiction -- History and criticism
ISBN 0-8108-3129-5; 0-8108-5420-1 pa; 978-0-8108-5420-8 pa

LC 96-21068

First published 1982 by Oxford Univ. Press

The author "focuses on Asimov's robots and on the Foundation trilogy, emphasizing throughout Asimov's limited use of background, style, and characterization, and his constantly recurring theme of the rational solution of a problem. The Lucky Starr juveniles get comparatively cursory treatment, but otherwise this is a very fine book indeed—well informed, clearly written, and judicious." Booklist {review of 1982 edition}

Includes bibliographical references

Gura, Philip F., 1950-
Truth's ragged edge; the rise of the American novel. Philip F. Gura. Farrar, Straus and Giroux 2013 352 p. (hardcover) $30 **813**
1. American literature -- History and criticism 2. Religion in literature 3. HISTORY -- United States -- 19th Century 4. American fiction -- History and criticism 5. Religion and literature -- United States -- History
ISBN 0809094452; 9780809094455

LC 2012029936

This book offers a study of pre-Mark Twain U.S. literary tradition. Literature professor Philip F. Gura "shows that this tradition consisted of far more than just Uncle Tom, Captain Ahab, Leatherstocking, and Hester Prynne. The book's main thread is a liberated sense of self that Gura traces back to Jonathan Edwards's passionate sermonizing." (Publishers Weekly)

Haralson, Eric L.
Critical companion to Henry James; a literary reference to his life and work. [by] Eric Haralson and Kendall Johnson. Facts On File 2009 516p il (Facts on File library of American literature) $75 **813**
1. Authors 2. Novelists
ISBN 978-0-8160-6886-9

LC 2008-36451

This book "covers the life and works of Henry James as well as the related people, places, and topics that shaped his writing. Other features in this . . . title include a chronology of James's life, bibliographies of his works and of secondary sources, and black-and-white photographs and illustrations." Publisher's note

Includes bibliographical references

Hardwick, Elizabeth
Herman Melville. Viking 2000 161p (Penguin lives series) $19.95 **813**
1. Authors 2. Novelists 3. Authors, American
ISBN 0-670-89158-4

LC 00-36510

"Interweaving critical readings of his fiction and poetry with events in Melville's life, Hardwick offers glimpses into his tortured writing career, his sometimes difficult family life, and his ambivalent relationship with his friend Nathaniel Hawthorne." Libr J

Includes bibliographical references

Harrison, Jim
Off to the side; a memoir. Atlantic Monthly Press 2002 313p $25; pa $14 **813**
1. Poets 2. Authors 3. Novelists 4. Essayists
ISBN 0-87113-860-3; 0-8021-4030-0 pa

LC 2002-26051

"Harrison reflects on how childhood tragedies and a profound involvement with nature gave rise to . . . [his] passion for writing. . . . A mesmerizing storyteller and down-to-earth philosophizer, Harrison explicates his 'seven obsessions,' which include alcohol, strip clubs, hunting, fishing, and dogs, and offers compelling ruminations on the splendor of nature and the crimes of man, the mysteries of spirit and the revelations of art." Booklist

Harrison, Kathryn, 1961-
The kiss; Kathryn Harrison. Random House 1997 207 p. **813**
1. Authors, American -- Biography 2. Novelists, American -- 20th century -- Biography
ISBN 067944999X; 9780679449997

LC 97153826

In this memoir, Kathryn "Harrison here turns an unflinching eye on the episode in her life that has most influenced those books: a secret, sexual affair with her father that began when she was 20. . . . Abandoned by her father as a child, neglected by an emotionally remote and impetuous mother, Harrison is raised by her grandparents. . . . A minister and amateur cameraman, her father visits Harrison after an absence of 10 years, when she is home from college on spring break. The boundary between flirtation and paternal affection is soon blurred. . . . Gradually consenting to his demands for sex, Harrison drops out of college and moves in with her father's new family, extricating herself from the affair only when her mother is stricken with metastatic breast cancer." (Publishers Weekly)

Herbert, Brian

★ **Dreamer** of Dune; the biography of Frank Herbert. TOR Bks. 2003 576p il $27.95; pa $16.95 **813**
1. Authors 2. Novelists 3. Science fiction writers
ISBN 0-7653-0646-8; 0-7653-0647-6 pa
LC 2002-42951
"This moving, sometimes painfully obsessive biography is an impressive testament of family loyalty and love. A must-read for Herbert fans (both senior and junior), it includes family photos and a bibliography." Publ Wkly

Hickam, Homer H.

The **Coalwood** way; by Homer H. Hickam, Jr. Delacorte Press 2000 318p hardcover o.p. pa $6.99 **813**
1. Authors 2. Novelists 3. Aerospace engineers 4. Memoirists 5. West Virginia 6. Authors, American 7. Writers on science
ISBN 0-440-23716-5
LC 00-35884
This sequel to Rocket boys "continues the author's life story with his senior year in high school, 1959, in the declining West Virginia mining town of Coalwood. The rocket club, featured in the last book, is pushed to the periphery, and the focus shifts to Hickam's teenage problems, which include his parents, girls, and a sadness whose cause he cannot divine." Booklist

Hillerman, Tony

Seldom disappointed; a memoir. HarperCollins Pubs. 2001 341p il hardcover o.p. pa $13.95 **813**
1. Authors 2. Novelists 3. Journalists 4. Mystery writers 5. Authors, American
ISBN 0-06-050586-9 pa
LC 2001-24160
In this memoir Hillerman "relates his childhood in Oklahoma during the Depression, his service in World War II, his university education, his career in journalism and academia, and his eventual turn to writing mysteries. The entire book will appeal to his fans, but the first half is intensely gripping." Libr J
Includes bibliographical references

Hiney, Tom

Raymond Chandler; a biography. Atlantic Monthly Press 1997 310p il hardcover o.p. pa $14 **813**
1. Authors 2. Novelists 3. Screenwriters 4. Mystery writers
ISBN 0-8021-3637-0 pa
LC 97-264
"Hiney traces the writer's nomadic childhood from pre-Mafia Chicago to pre-telephone Nebraska, from Quaker Ireland and Edwardian England to his education south of London at Dulwich College and his 1913 arrival in the 'mean streets' of Los Angeles, the later setting for his crime fiction. . . . Living at over 100 addresses, he sustained no long friend-

ships, and was 'variously rich, poor, drunk, teetotal, sacked, married and suicidal.'. . . No rough edges have been filed off for this revealing, well-written biography." Publ Wkly
Includes bibliographical references

J.D. Salinger; edited with an introduction by Harold Bloom. New ed; Chelsea House 2008 254p (Modern critical views) $45 **813**
1. Authors 2. Novelists 3. Short story writers
ISBN 978-0-7910-9813-4
LC 2007-44662
First published 1987
This collection of nine essays provides a view of Salinger's critical reception. Among the contributors are David Galloway, Anthony Kaufman and Robert Coles.
Includes bibliographical references

John Steinbeck; edited and with an introduction by Harold Bloom. New ed; Bloom's Literary Criticism 2008 176p (Modern critical views) $45 **813**
1. Authors 2. Novelists 3. Screenwriters 4. Nobel laureates for literature
ISBN 978-0-7910-9787-8; 0-7910-9787-0
LC 2007-38676
First published 1987
A selection of criticism, arranged in chronological order of publication, devoted to the fiction of John Steinbeck.
Includes bibliographical references (p. 167-9)

Jones, Sharon L.

Critical companion to Zora Neale Hurston; a literary reference to her life and work. Facts On File 2008 288p il (Facts on File library of American literature) $75 **813**
1. Authors 2. Novelists 3. Dramatists 4. Memoirists 5. Folklorists 6. Short story writers
ISBN 978-0-8160-6885-2; 0-8160-6885-2
LC 2008-10052
This "covers all her writings, including Their Eyes Were Watching God; her landmark works of folklore and anthropology, such as Mules and Men; and shorter works." Publisher's note
Includes bibliographical references

Kerouac, Jack

Door wide open; a beat love affair in letters, 1957-1958. {by} Jack Kerouac and Joyce Johnson; with introduction and commentary by Joyce Johnson. Viking 2000 xxvi, 182p hardcover o.p. pa $13 **813**
1. Authors 2. Novelists 3. Editors 4. Memoirists 5. Short story writers
ISBN 0-14-100187-9 pa
LC 99-53219
"In a hip, literate correspondence marked by high diction and '50s slang, 21-year-old Johnson (born Glassman) and

35-year-old Kerouac chart the flowering of the Beats and their complicated love affair." Publ Wkly

Includes bibliographical references and index

Selected letters, 1957-1969; edited with an introduction and commentary by Ann Charters. Viking 1999 xxvii, 514p hardcover o.p. pa $17   **813**
1. Authors 2. Novelists
ISBN 0-14-029615-8 pa

LC 99-17374

This volume "starts with the publication of On the Road and continues almost to the day Kerouac died. The years 1957-1960, the height of Kerouac's career, occupy more than half the volume. Later letters record his struggle to care for his ailing mother, his efforts to finish his later books and his troubles with money and health. . . . Frequent addressees and subjects include Gary Snyder, Philip Whalen, Lawrence Ferlinghetti, William Burroughs and Allen Ginsberg." Publ Wkly

King, Stephen, 1947-
On writing; a memoir of the craft. Scribner 2000 288p hardcover o.p. pa $14.95   **813**
1. Authors 2. Novelists 3. Authorship 4. Authors, American 5. Short story writers 6. Science fiction writers
ISBN 0-684-85352-3; 0-671-02425-6 pa

LC 00-30105

The author recounts "his life from early childhood through the aftermath of the 1999 accident that nearly killed him. Along the way, King touts the writing philosophies of William Strunk and Ernest Hemingway, advocates a healthy appetite for reading, expounds upon the subject of grammar, critiques a number of popular writers, and offers the reader a chance to try out his theories. . . . Recommended for anyone who wants to write and everyone who loves to read." Libr J

Kirk, Connie Ann
Critical companion to Flannery O'Connor. Facts on File 2008 415p il (Facts on File library of American literature) $75   **813**
1. Authors 2. Novelists 3. Short story writers
ISBN 978-0-8160-6417-5

LC 2007-6512

This book examines O'Connor's "life and works, and includes critical analyses of some of the themes in her writing, as well as entries on related topics and relevant people, places, and influences." Publisher's note

Includes bibliographical references

L'Amour, Louis
The **Sackett** companion; a personal guide to the Sackett novels. Bantam Bks. 1988 341p il maps hardcover o.p. pa $14.95   **813**
ISBN 0-553-37102-9 pa

LC 88-47530

"Each individual profile of the 17 Sackett novels contains a map, a cover painting, brief plot synopsis, and an annotated list of characters. Sackett enthusiasts will also welcome the inclusion of a detailed Sackett genealogy and family tree." Booklist

Lardner, Ring
I'd hate myself in the morning; a memoir. {by} Ring Lardner, Jr. Thunder's Mouth Press 2000 198p il $22.95; pa $14.95   **813**
1. Novelists 2. Screenwriters
ISBN 1-56025-296-0; 1-56025-338-X pa

LC 00-44298

"Of interest to cultural historians as well as general readers, this book belongs in both academic and public libraries." Libr J

McClure, Wendy
The **Wilder** life; my adventures in the lost world of Little house on the prairie. Riverhead Books 2011 336p $25.95   **813**
1. Authors 2. Novelists 3. Frontier and pioneer life in literature 4. Western writers 5. Children's authors 6. Young adult authors
ISBN 978-1-59448-780-4

LC 2010-44960

"Don't worry that McClure's journey . . . is one of those ginned-up-book-proposal-in-hand faux challenges. In Laura World, following Wilder's footsteps turns out to be a surprisingly common rite. McClure is far from alone in her visit to a Laura look-alike contest, or her encounter with pillowy, life-size 'soft sculptures' of the Ingalls family. Her insights and wry honesty elevate the story from gimmickry. Conversational, witty, and questioning, she manages to coexist with her powerful subject." Christ Sci Monit

Includes bibliographical references

Mellow, James R.
Hemingway; a life without consequences. Addison-Wesley 1994 704p il pa $15   **813**
1. Poets 2. Authors 3. Novelists 4. Journalists 5. Authors, American 6. Short story writers 7. Nobel laureates for literature
ISBN 0-201-62620-9; 978-0-201-62620-9

LC 93-24497

First published 1992 by Houghton Mifflin

"In sheer number of pages, Mr. Mellow's version of the life is most heavily weighed toward the years 1921 to 1930, when Hemingway lived in Paris during his first two marriages and published the novels and stories that built his early reputation as one of this country's most important writers. Mr. Mellow seems in a hurry to get through the rest of the story, but he does dutifully summarize Hemingway's childhood, adolescence and the major events of the later years. . . . Mr. Mellow takes careful note of Hemingway's publications in the context of his life and gives sensitive readings, both biographical and critical, to them all." N Y Times Book Rev

Includes bibliographical references

Michaels, J. Ramsey
Passing by the dragon; the Biblical tales of Flannery O'Connor. by J. Ramsey Michaels. Cascade Books 2013 xii, 211 p.p (pbk.) $28   **813**
1. Christian fiction 2. American literature -- History and criticism 3. Christian fiction, American -- Criticism and interpretation
ISBN 1620322234; 9781620322239

LC 2012285239

This book, by J. Ramsey Michaels, "attempts a close reading of the fiction of Flannery O'Connor, story by story, with one eye on her use of the Bible, and her view of the Bible in relation to her own work. After introductory chapters on O'Connor's markings in her own Roman Catholic Bible, her book reviews in diocesan newspapers, and her impatience with her wayward readers, Michaels looks first at her two novels, 'Wise Blood' and 'The Violent Bear It Away,' and then at seventeen of her short stories." (Publisher's note)

Includes bibliographical references (p. 209-211)

Morris, Willie

My dog Skip. Random House 1995 122p il hardcover o.p. pa $10   **813**

1. Dogs 2. Authors 3. Novelists 4. Journalists 5. Essayists 6. Biographers 7. Magazine editors 8. Short story writers

ISBN 0-679-76722-3 pa

LC 94-41637

"Morris remembers back to the boy-and-his-dog days in his small hometown in the Deep South, where Skip was involved in all of his pranks and escapades. Poignancy rather than humor is the pervading tone of this ode to a steadfast presence." Booklist

Murphy, Mary McDonagh

Scout, Atticus, and Boo; a celebration of fifty years of To kill a mockingbird. Harper 2010 217p il $24.99   **813**

1. Authors 2. Novelists 3. Essayists 4. Short story writers

ISBN 978-0-06-192407-1; 0-06-192407-5

LC 2010-06739

The author tells the story of how the quiet, publicity-shy Southerner Harper Lee came to write her classic. She also conducts interviews (which will later be included in a documentary) with famous folks whose childhoods were transformed by the novel, such as Oprah, Tom Brokaw, and Scott Turow. Lee, now 84, didn't talkshe never does, God bless herbut you come away from Murphy's book with a renewed amazement at what Lee was able to achieve with a single perfect novel. Entertaiment Wkly

Nabokov, Vladimir Vladimirovich

Speak, memory; an autobiography revisited. {by} Vladimir Nabokov; with an introduction by Brian Boyd. Knopf 1999 xxxv, 268p il map $17; pa $14   **813**

1. Poets 2. Authors 3. Novelists 4. Authors, Russian 5. Essayists 6. Memoirists 7. Translators 8. College teachers 9. Literary critics 10. Short story writers

ISBN 0-375-40553-4; 0-679-72339-0 pa

LC 98-49237

A revised version of the memoir first published 1951 in the United States with title: Conclusive evidence

These recollections of the author's youthful years give an account of a vanishing world. They offer a picture of the author's family, their flight from Russia, education in England, and émigré life in Paris and Berlin

Includes bibliographical references

Nadel, Ira Bruce

Critical companion to Philip Roth; a literary companion to his life and work. [by] Ira B. Nadel. Facts On File, Inc. 2011 356p il (Facts on File library of American literature) $75   **813**

1. Authors 2. Novelists 3. Short story writers

ISBN 978-0-8160-7795-3; 978-1-4381-3555-7 ebook

LC 2010022769

"Coverage includes: a . . . biography of Roth; entries on all of Roth's works; . . . entries on related people, places, and topics, such as anti-Semitism, Claire Bloom, Newark, satire, and . . . more; [and] appendixes, including a chronology, a bibliography of Roth's works, and a secondary-source bibliography." Publisher's note

Includes bibliographical references

Norman, Howard

I hate to leave this beautiful place; Howard Norman. Houghton Mifflin Harcourt 2013 208 p. $26   **813**

1. Autobiographies 2. American authors

ISBN 0547385420; 9780547385426

LC 2012042186

This memoir by novelist Howard Norman "begins with a portrait . . . of a Midwest boyhood summer working in a bookmobile, in the shadow of a grifter father and under the erotic tutelage of his brother's girlfriend. His life story continues in places as far-flung as the Arctic, where he spends part of a decade as a translator of Inuit tales . . . and in his beloved Point Reyes, California. Norman's story is also stitched together with moments of uncanny solace." (Publisher's note)

Oliver, Charles M.

Critical companion to Ernest Hemingway; a literary reference to his life and work. Facts on File 2006 630p il (Facts on File library of American literature) $75   **813**

1. Poets 2. Authors 3. Novelists 4. Short story writers 5. Nobel laureates for literature

ISBN 0-8160-6418-0; 978-0-8160-6418-2

LC 2006-7970

First published 1999 with title: Ernest Hemingway A to Z

"This volume features entries on all of Hemingway's major and minor works, places and events related to his works, major figures in his life, and more. Appendixes include a complete list of Hemingway's works; a chronology; a genealogy; a . . . map for readers of Islands in the Stream; a list of film, stage, and radio adaptations; and a bibliography of secondary sources." Publisher's note

Includes filmography and bibliographical references

Parker, Hershel

Herman Melville; v1 a biography. Johns Hopkins Univ. Press 1996 942p v1 il maps $50; pa $29.95   **813**

1. Authors 2. Novelists 3. Authors, American 4. Biography, Individual

ISBN 0-8018-5428-8; 0-8018-8185-4 pa

LC 96-18984

This, the first volume of a projected two-volume "biography of Melville, ends in 1851, when the author presented to his . . . friend Nathaniel Hawthorne an inscribed pre-publication copy of Moby-Dick." (Atl Mon) Index.

This, the first volume of a two-volume "biography of Melville, ends in 1851, when the author presented to his . . . friend Nathaniel Hawthorne an inscribed pre-publication copy of Moby-Dick." Atl Mon

Includes bibliographical references

Philbrick, Nathaniel

Why read Moby-Dick? Viking 2011 x, 131 p.p (hbk.) $25 **813**

1. Whaling -- Fiction 2. Shipwrecks -- Fiction 3. American literature -- History and criticism 4. Sea stories -- History and criticism

ISBN 0670022993; 9780670022991

LC 2011019766

This book attempts to offer Herman "Melville's [book 'Moby-Dick' a] . . . broad contemporary audience. . . . [Author] Nathaniel Philbrick . . . unpacked the story of the wreck of the whaleship Essex, the real-life incident that inspired Melville to write 'Moby-Dick.' Now, he sets his sights on the fiction itself, offering a . . . tour of . . . [the] novel. . . . Philbrick . . . navigates Melville's world and illuminates the book's humor and . . . characters-finding the thread that binds Ishmael and Ahab to our own time." (Publisher's note)

"In this cogent and passionate polemic for Melville's masterpiece, Philbrick . . . combines a critical eye and a reader's adoration to make a case for Moby-Dick. The plights of the Pequod, Ishmael and Ahab may seem irrelevant (or worse, quaint) compared to today's troubles, but Philbrick opines that within the pages of this American classic lie timeless archetypes whose relevance stretches across human history. . . . Less lit-crit and more readers' guide, this tome will remind fans why they loved the book in the first place, and whet the appetites of trepid potential readers." Publ Wkly

Includes bibliographical references

Phillips, Julie

James Tiptree, Jr. the double life of Alice B. Sheldon. St. Martin's Press 2006 469p il $27.95 **813**

1. Authors 2. Science fiction writers

ISBN 0-312-20385-3; 978-0-312-20385-6

LC 2006-40095

This is a biography of the American science fiction writer. The author "has achieved a wonder: an evenhanded, scrupulously documented, objective yet sympathetic portrait of a deliberately elusive personality." Publ Wkly

Includes bibliographical references

Plimpton, George

Truman Capote; in which various friends, enemies, acquaintances, and detractors recall his turbulent career. Talese 1997 498p il hardcover o.p. pa $16.95 **813**

1. Authors 2. Novelists 3. Nonfiction writers 4. Short story writers

ISBN 0-385-49173-5 pa

LC 97-14792

"The book is an intoxicating swirl of contradictory stories, serious analysis and rumors, adroitly edited in chapters arranged like those of a picaresque novel." Publ Wkly

Pritchard, William H.

Updike. University of Massachusetts Press 2005 350p pa $24.95 **813**

1. Poets 2. Authors 3. Novelists 4. Short story writers

ISBN 978-1-55849-507-4; 1-55849-507-X

First published 2000 by Steerforth Press

"All in all, Pritchard's book is a gentle and intelligent request for a little more thought and a little less cranky let'smoveon speed in judging the work of one of America's pre-eminent writers." N Y Times Book Rev

Includes bibliographical references

Rand, Ayn

Letters of Ayn Rand; edited by Michael S. Berliner; introduction by Leonard Peikoff. Dutton 1995 xxi, 681p il hardcover o.p. pa $20 **813**

1. Authors 2. Novelists 3. Philosophers 4. Nonfiction writers

ISBN 0-452-27404-4 pa

LC 94-23646

"Imbued with her fiercely held beliefs, the letters most devoted to politics and philosophy fairly blaze off the page. . . . Regardless of one's opinion of her thinking, her letters add greatly to our understanding of a most exceptional woman of letters." Booklist

Rehak, Melanie

Girl sleuth; Nancy Drew and the women who created her. Harcourt 2005 364p il $25; pa $14 **813**

1. Authors 2. Mystery writers 3. Children's authors 4. Young adult authors 5. Drew, Nancy (Fictitious character)

ISBN 0-15-101041-2; 0-15-603056-X pa

LC 2005-9129

"Packed with revealing anecdotes, Rehak's meticulously researched account of the publishing phenomenon that survived the Depression and WWII . . . will delight fans of the beloved gumshoe whose gumption guaranteed that every reprobate got his due." Booklist

Includes bibliographical references

Reynolds, David S., 1948-

Mightier than the sword; Uncle Tom's cabin and the battle for America. W. W. Norton & Co. 2011 351p il $27.95 **813**

1. Authors 2. Novelists 3. Abolitionists 4. Children's authors 5. Nonfiction writers 6. Short story writers

ISBN 978-0-393-08132-9; 0-393-08132-X

LC 2011-00702

"The powerful antislavery message of 'Uncle Tom's Cabin' fueled the flames leading to the Civil War, making it the most influential novel in American history. . . . Stowe claimed the novel came to her in a vision and God was its true author. Accordingly, her book is weighted with religious symbolism, which Reynolds interprets with typical English professor's zeal. He also examines its impacts not just on public attitudes toward slavery, but on women's rights, temperance, capitalism, minstrel shows, sexual customs and other aspects of mid-19th century American life. Reynolds dissects dozens of imitative novels, plays and minstrel shows — some against, others for slavery or segregation — and traces the influence of Stowe's novel into modern times, including film spin-offs. . . .[This is] not easy reading, but it offers virtually everything you ever wanted to know about 'Uncle Tom's Cabin' — and probably a lot more." Seattle Times

Reynolds, Michael S.

Hemingway : the 1930's; [by] Michael Reynolds. Norton 1997 360p il maps hardcover o.p. pa $15.95   **813**

1. Poets 2. Authors 3. Novelists 4. Journalists 5. Authors, American 6. Short story writers 7. Nobel laureates for literature
ISBN 0-393-04093-3; 0-393-31778-1 pa

LC 96-43113

"Filled with fascinating details and anecdotes, this fine biography illuminates our understanding of this crucial decade." Publ Wkly
Includes bibliographical references

Robertson-Lorant, Laurie

Melville; a biography. University of Massachusetts Press 1998 710p il pa $29.95   **813**

1. Authors 2. Novelists 3. Authors, American
ISBN 1-55849-145-7; 978-1-55849-145-8

LC 98-4899

First published 1996 by Potter
"With access to more than 500 recently discovered Melville family letters, which show Melville to have been a functioning member of a problem-torn extended family, Robertson-Lorant corrects our traditional view of the older Melville as isolato. Instead, he appears here to represent the social consciousness of 19th century America. Together with jargon-free, user-friendly commentary on all Melville's major works, Robertson-Lorant offers an array of historical phenomena . . . that provide an invaluable context for Melville's life and art." Libr J
Includes bibliographical references

Roiphe, Anne Richardson

1185 Park Avenue; a memoir. [by] Anne Roiphe. Free Press 1999 257p il hardcover o.p. pa $14.95   **813**

1. Authors 2. Novelists 3. Essayists 4. Authors, American
ISBN 0-684-85731-6; 0-684-85732-4 pa

LC 98-51939

"Roiphe's devastating memoir fully engages the reader in her painful story of hatred and betrayal." Publ Wkly

Rollyson, Carl

Critical companion to Herman Melville; a literary reference to his life and work. [by] Carl Rollyson, Lisa Paddock, and April Gentry. Facts on File 2006 394p il (Facts on File library of world literature) $75   **813**

1. Authors 2. Novelists
ISBN 0-8160-6461-X; 978-0-8160-6461-8

LC 2005-36733

First published 2000 with title: Herman Melville A to Z
Entries in this "volume examine the characters and settings of Melville's novels and short stories, the critics and scholars who commented on his work, and his friends and associates, including such prominent literary figures as Oliver Wendell Holmes and Nathaniel Hawthorne." Publisher's note
Includes bibliographical references

Roth, Philip

The **facts**; a novelist's autobiography. Vintage Bks. 1997 195p pa $14   **813**

1. Authors 2. Novelists 3. Authors, American 4. Short story writers
ISBN 0-679-74905-5; 978-0-679-74905-9

LC 96-28807

First published 1988 by Farrar, Straus & Giroux
"The Facts is a lively and serious version of a novelist's life, but it seems even more interesting as a new way of formulating the questions about the imagination that Roth has been pursuing with increasing complication in the Zuckerman novels." N Y Rev Books

Patrimony; a true story. Vintage Bks. 1996 238p pa $12   **813**

1. Insurance agents 2. Parents of prominent persons
ISBN 0-679-75293-5; 978-0-679-75293-6

LC 95-43453

First published 1991 by Simon & Schuster
This "ordinary, crucial story is well suited to a comic master, and Mr. Roth brings to the tale his gift for attention, his worldly, vernacular heart and the tremendous inventive force that here he keeps largely in check." N Y Times Book Rev

Rowley, Hazel

Richard Wright; the life and times. Holt & Co. 2001 626p il hardcover o.p. pa $18   **813**

1. Authors 2. Novelists 3. Dramatists 4. Essayists 5. Nonfiction writers 6. Short story writers
ISBN 0-8050-7088-5 pa

LC 00-54249

"The strength of {this book} is {the} painstaking research. Rowley . . . has a daunting dedication to primary sources and her documentation is meticulous." N Y Times Book Rev
Includes bibliographical references

Sallis, James

Chester Himes; a life. Walker & Co. 2000 368p il $28; pa $18.95   **813**

1. Authors 2. Novelists 3. Mystery writers 4. Short story writers
ISBN 0-8027-1362-9; 0-8027-7639-6 pa

LC 00-63328

This is a biography of the African-American crime novelist. "Sentenced to 25 years in prison for armed robbery when he was 19, he turned to writing while behind bars and, when released after serving eight years, published two novels. Their poor reception by the white establishment only confirmed Himes's beliefs about racism in America. He eventually moved to Paris, spending most of the rest of his life abroad. . . . The author succeeds splendidly in fleshing Himes out in this riveting biography." Libr J

Includes bibliographical references

Salzman, Mark

Lost in place; growing up absurd in suburbia. Random House 1995 273p hardcover o.p. pa $13 **813**

1. Authors 2. Novelists 3. Memoirists 4. Asian studies specialists

ISBN 0-679-76778-9 pa

LC 95-7847

In this "memoir about his 'existential angst' as a slightly off-center teenager, . . . writer Salzman vividly recalls his unconventional friends, frugal parents, and other memorable characters from his freewheeling, Connecticut youth." Booklist

Savigneau, Josyane

Carson McCullers; a life. translated by Joan E. Howard. Houghton Mifflin 2001 370p il $30 **813**

1. Authors 2. Novelists 3. Dramatists 4. Short story writers

ISBN 0-395-87820-9

LC 00-46547

This is a "heartfelt, honest portrait of one of the great novelists of the American South." Libr J

Includes bibliographical references

Schultz, Jeffrey D.

Critical companion to John Steinbeck; a literary reference to his life and work. [by] Jeffrey Schultz, Luchen Li. Facts on File 2005 406p il (Facts on File library of American literature) $65; pa $19.99 **813**

1. Authors 2. Novelists 3. Screenwriters 4. Nobel laureates for literature

ISBN 0-8160-4300-0; 0-8160-4301-9 pa

LC 2004-26100

"Useful, succinct, and reasonably priced, it packs an abundance of information into one compact resource." Libr J

Includes bibliographical references

Smiley, Jane

Thirteen ways of looking at the novel. Knopf 2005 591p $26.95 **813**

1. Authorship 2. Fiction -- History and criticism

ISBN 1-4000-4059-0

LC 2005-45181

"The book is roughly divided into three sections: the first classifies the novel, beginning with the most simple of definitions (e.g., it's long, in prose, has a protagonist), and adds moral and aesthetic complexity as it moves along. The second section consists of a primer for fledgling novelists. . . . The result is a thorough reflection on the art and craft of the novel from one of its best-known contemporary practitioners." Publ Wkly

Includes bibliographical references

Tate, Mary Jo

Critical companion to F. Scott Fitzgerald; a literary reference to his life and work. foreword by Mat-thew J. Bruccoli. Facts on File 2006 464p il (Facts on File library of American literature) $75 **813**

1. Authors 2. Novelists 3. Screenwriters 4. Short story writers

ISBN 0-8160-6433-4; 978-0-8160-6433-5

LC 2006-11393

First published 1998 with title: F. Scott Fitzgerald A to Z

This book "studies the legacy of this writer, highlighting significant themes and historical references of his various works." Publisher's note

Includes bibliographical references

★ A **Theodore** Dreiser encyclopedia; edited by Keith Newlin. Greenwood Press 2003 xxiii, 431p il $99.95 **813**

1. Authors 2. Novelists

ISBN 0-313-31680-5

LC 2003-40841

This is a "guide to the essential facts surrounding this prolific author's life and works. Dreiser's novels and short stories are covered, as are his plays, which are far less known. Front matter includes a list of entries, a chronology, and a preface that analyzes prior contributions to Dreiser scholarship. Alphabetically arranged essays on his books, short stories, and magazine and newspaper pieces make up the book's core. . . . The book ends with a bibliography arranged by category (books by Dreiser, critical studies, biographies, etc.). Highly recommended." Choice

Includes bibliographical references and index

Turner, Frederick

Renegade; Henry Miller and the making of Tropic of Cancer. Frederick W. Turner. Yale University Press 2011 xi, 244 p.p (hardback) $24.95 **813**

1. United States -- History 2. Popular culture -- United States 3. Literature -- History and criticism 4. Censorship -- United States -- History -- 20th century 5. Authors and publishers -- United States -- History -- 20th century 6. Politics and literature -- United States -- History -- 20th century 7. Publishers and publishing -- United States -- History -- 20th century

ISBN 0300149492; 9780300149494

LC 2011019531

In this book, author Frederick W. Turner "reassesses [writer Henry Miller's book 'Tropic of Cancer']. . . . Turner's story traces Miller's mid-twentieth-century ramble back through the dark passages of US history . . . claiming that Miller (consciously or not) modeled himself and his books on the American-as-outlaw archetype. . . . Turner also argues that Miller's prose is part of a deep strain in American culture that mistrusts highbrow anything, literature especially, but celebrates talk, and loves big talk the best." (Bookforum)

Includes bibliographical references and index.

Vonnegut, Kurt, 1922-2007

Kurt Vonnegut; letters. edited by Dan Wakefield. Delacorte Press 2012 436 p. $35 **813**

1. American letters 2. Authors -- Correspondence

ISBN 0385343752; 9780345535399; 9780385343756

LC 2012001544

Author Kurt Vonnegut and editor Dan Wakefield present Vonnegut's "collection of personal correspondence." It includes "the letter a twenty-two-year-old Vonnegut wrote home immediately upon being freed from a German POW camp" and "wry dispatches from Vonnegut's years as a struggling writer slowly finding an audience and then dealing with sudden international fame in middle age." (Publisher's note)

Walker, Alice

The **same** river twice; honoring the difficult: a meditation on life, spirit, art, and the making of the film The color purple, ten years later. Scribner 1996 302p il hardcover o.p. pa $14   **813**
    1. Poets 2. Authors 3. Novelists 4. Editors 5. Essayists 6. College teachers 7. Short story writers 8. Color purple (Motion picture)
    ISBN 0-671-00377-1 pa
                  LC 95-30056

This "book finds the Pulitzer Prize-winning author still grappling with criticism of the film version of her novel The Color Purple.... Walker's memoir pieces together assorted journal entries, magazine clippings, occasional photographs and even her original screenplay to form an intimate scrapbook of the period." Publ Wkly
    Includes bibliographical references

Walton, Jo, 1947-

What Makes This Book So Great; Re-reading the classics of science fiction and fantasy. Jo Walton. Tor 2014 448 p. (hardback) $26.99   **813**
    1. Books and reading 2. Fantasy fiction -- History and criticism 3. Science fiction -- History and criticism 4. Books and reading -- United States 5. Fantasy fiction, American -- History and criticism 6. Science fiction, American -- History and criticism
    ISBN 0765331934; 9780765331939
                  LC 2013028170

"This collection gathers 130 of [novelist Jo] Walton's blog posts from science fiction site Tor.com about her favorites works of sci-fi and fantasy.... The themes of the essays interweave ... many are meditations on the genre as a whole more than reviews of specific works, and Walton often ties her points back to earlier posts." (Publishers Weekly)

"Walton shares not only her deep love for sf and fantasy in general and these novels in particular but the insights of a truly thoughtful reader." LJ

Weise, Jillian

The **book** of goodbyes; poems. by Jillian Weise. BOA Editions, Ltd. 2013 88 p. (pbk.) $16   **813**
    1. American poetry
    ISBN 1938160142; 9781938160141; 9781938160158
                  LC 2013013139

In this collection of poems, author Jillian Weise "forwards her . . . poetics by chronicling an affair with a man she names 'Big Logos.' These poems throw into question sex, the law, identity, sentiment, and power, shifting between lyric and narrative, hyper-realism and magical realism, fact and fiction." (Publisher's note)

"Throughout, Weise's masterfully balanced voice transforms even unique intricacies of her experience into a way to relate to—not alienate—the reader." Pub Wkly

White, Edmund

★ **My** lives. Ecco 2006 356p il $25.95   **813**
    1. Authors 2. Novelists 3. Memoirists 4. Biographers 5. Short story writers
    ISBN 0-06-621397-5; 978-0-06-621397-2
                  LC 2005-49506

First published 2005 in the United Kingdom

This is an autobiography by "an award-winning author and leader of the gay liberation movement of the 1960s. . . . The stories of his mother's egotism and incessant chatter, struggle to master the French language, obsession with European culture, literary associates, and work as a novelist, teacher, and essayist are largely overshadowed by graphic and explicit tales of the men in his life. . . . White's writing is amusing, descriptive, shocking, and, ultimately, thought-provoking." Libr J

Wideman, John Edgar

Hoop roots. Houghton Mifflin 2001 242p $24; pa $13   **813**
    1. Authors 2. Novelists 3. Memoirists 4. College teachers 5. Nonfiction writers 6. Short story writers
    ISBN 0-395-85731-7; 0-618-25775-6 pa
                  LC 2001-26455

Wideman "examines his lifelong relationship with basketball. He argues that basketball first allowed him to set his own standard in a white world that often imposes definitions of success on black people. A poignant, thought-provoking memoir." Booklist

Wiesel, Elie

All rivers run to the sea; memoirs. Knopf 1995 432p il $35; pa $15   **813**
    1. Authors 2. Novelists 3. Journalists 4. Holocaust survivors 5. Human rights activists 6. Nobel laureates for peace 7. Holocaust, 1933-1945 -- Personal narratives
    ISBN 0-679-43916-1; 0-8052-1028-8 pa
                  LC 95-17607

Original French edition, 1994

"Wiesel's immensely moving, unforgettable memoir has the searing intensity of his novels and autobiographical tales." Publ Wkly

★ **And** the sea is never full; memoirs, 1969-translated from the French by Marion Wiesel. Knopf 1999 429p hardcover o.p. pa $15   **813**
    1. Authors 2. Novelists 3. Journalists 4. Holocaust survivors 5. Human rights activists 6. Nobel laureates for peace 7. Holocaust, 1933-1945 -- Personal narratives
    ISBN 0-8052-1029-6 pa
                  LC 99-15604

Continues the author's memoirs begun in All the rivers run to the sea

Original French edition, 1996

"This concluding volume begins when the author is age 40. He continues his travels . . . and he continues to write, his books including Souls on fire, Four Hasidic Masters, Twilight, and more. . . . Wiesel is the most significant writer to have made the Holocaust the major theme of his work, just as it has been of major importance to his life. The horror of the Holocaust can be felt in this memoir with an intensity beyond words." Booklist

Wild; from lost to found on the Pacific Crest Trail. Cheryl Strayed. Alfred A. Knopf 2012 315 p. **813**

1. Hiking 2. Bereavement 3. Pacific Crest Trail 4. Mountains -- North America 5. Women authors -- Biography 6. Pacific Crest Trail -- Description and travel 7. Authors, American -- 21st century -- Biography ISBN 0307592731; 9780307592736

LC 2011033752

The ten thousand things -- |t Splitting -- |t Hunching in a remotely upright position -- |t The Pacific Crest Trail, volume I : California -- Tracks -- A bull in both directions -- The only girl in the woods -- Corvidology -- Staying found -- Range of light -- The lou out of lou -- This far -- The accumulation of trees -- Wild -- Box of rain -- Mazama -- Into a primal gear -- The queen of the PCT -- The dream of a common language.

The author "recounts her experience hiking the Pacific Crest Trail (PCT) in 1995 after her mother's death and her own subsequent divorce. Designated a National Scenic Trail in 1968 but not completed until 1993, the PCT runs from Mexico to Canada, and [Cheryl] Strayed hiked sections of it two summers after it was officially declared finished. She takes readers with her on the trail, and the transformation she experiences on its course is significant: she goes from feeling out of her element with a too-big backpack and too-small boots to finding a sense of home in the wilderness and with the allies she meets along the way. . . . [She includes] descriptions of the natural wonders near the PCT, particularly Mount Hood, Crater Lake, and the Sierras--what John Muir proclaimed the 'Range of Light.'" (Libr J)

William Faulkner; edited and with an introduction by Harold Bloom. New ed.; Bloom's Literary Criticism 2008 269p (Modern critical views) $45 **813**

1. Authors 2. Novelists 3. Screenwriters 4. Short story writers 5. Nobel laureates for literature ISBN 978-0-7910-9786-1

LC 2007-33754

First published 1986

"This volume of . . . critical essays examines The Sound and the Fury, Light in August, As I Lay Dying, Absalom, Absalom!, and other key works by this preeminent writer of the twentieth century." Publisher's note

Includes bibliographical references

Wright, Sarah Bird

Critical companion to Nathaniel Hawthorne; a literary reference to his life and work. Facts on File 2006 392p il (Facts on File library of American literature) $75 **813**

1. Authors 2. Novelists 3. Short story writers ISBN 0-8160-5583-1; 978-0-8160-5583-8

LC 2005-34648

This book "offers critical entries on Hawthorne's novels, short stories, travel writing, criticism, and other works, as well as portraits of characters, including Hester Prynne and Roger Chillingworth. This . . . reference also provides entries on Hawthorne's family, friends—ranging from Herman Melville to President Franklin Pierce—publishers, and

critics, as well as periodicals that published his work and important places and events in his life." Publisher's note

Includes bibliographical references

Zora Neale Hurston; edited and with an introduction by Harold Bloom. New ed; Chelsea House Publishers 2008 238p (Modern critical views) $45 **813**

1. Authors 2. Novelists 3. Dramatists 4. Memoirists 5. Folklorists 6. Short story writers ISBN 978-0-7910-9610-9

LC 2007-49161

First published 1986

"Featuring supplemental material such as a chronology, a bibliography, and an index, [this book is a] critical look at Hurston's work and its influence on contemporary themes, such as race and gender in American society." Publisher's note

Includes bibliographical references

813.009   American fiction -- History and criticism

Brave new words; the Oxford dictionary of science fiction. edited by Jeffrey Prucher; introduction by Gene Wolfe. Oxford University Press 2007 xxxi, 342p $29.95 **813.009**

1. Reference books 2. Science fiction -- Dictionaries ISBN 978-0-19-530567-8; 0-19-530567-1

LC 2006-37280

This is a "dictionary of the language of science fiction based on historical principles. . . . Entries include part of speech, etymology, definition with cross references to related terms, usage status (e.g., historical, jocular, derogatory, obsolete), variant forms, and . . . dated citations and quotations illustrating the usage of the word over time." Libr J

Includes bibliographical references

814   American essays in English

Aciman, Andre A.

★ **Alibis;** essays on elsewhere. [by] Andre Aciman. Farrar, Straus and Giroux 2011 200p $25 **814**

ISBN 978-0-374-10275-3; 0-374-10275-9

LC 2011-10700

"Many of these essays begin with a city—New York, Barcelona, Rome—before spiraling into images and ideas that connect with other places and times in Aciman's own well-traveled history. Born in Egypt, raised in a French-speaking Jewish family, his complex identity (is he African? French? Jewish?) confronts him with a 'fundamental distortion' that he can make sense of only by the transformative power of art . . . . In a brilliant piece called 'Temporizing,' Aciman examines his own propensity for filtering all experiences through the Egypt in his mind. Writing, even thinking, thus becomes 'an interminable restoration project whose purpose is to prevent all contact with the present.' With his sly self-deprecation and supple, curious mind, Aciman is the perfect guide through the mysteries of time and place." Boston Globe

Als, Hilton, 1960-

★ **White** Girls; Hilton Als. McSweeney's 2013
300 p. $24   **814**

1. Race 2. Culture 3. Gender role

ISBN 1936365812; 9781936365814

Lambda Literary Awards Winner - LGBT Nonfiction
(2014)

This book by Hilton Als presents a collection of essays.
"His eponymous 'white girls' include Louise Brooks, Flannery O'Connor, Truman Capote, Richard Pryor, Malcolm X,
Michael Jackson, Eminem, and others. Using his subjects
as a springboard to analyze literature, photography, films,
music, television, performance, race, gender, sexual orientation, and history, Als offers wry insights throughout."
(Publishers Weekly)

"Whether his subject is his mother, himself, or seminal
artists, Als is a fine, piercing observer and interpreter, a writer of lashing exactitude and veracity." Booklist

Angelou, Maya

Even the stars look lonesome. Random House
1997 145p $18; pa $10   **814**

1. Women authors 2. African American authors

ISBN 0-375-50031-6; 0-553-37972-0 pa

LC 97-17317

Angelou "touches on a number of topics in this brief
collection of essays, including aging, fame, sensuality, art,
and violence. Her opening piece, about the ending of a long
marriage and the beginning of a new life in a new home, is a
winner. Her take on aging is downright amusing; her tribute
to sensuality, enlightening; and her salute to black women,
a treasure." Libr J

Wouldn't take nothing for my journey now. Random House 1993 141p hardcover o.p. pa $6.99 **814**

ISBN 0-679-42743-0; 0-553-56907-4 pa

LC 93-5904

The author "shares her thoughts about humankind: how
to respect others of different cultures, opinions, and values
as taught by universal philosophies. . . . Angelou's prose is
brisk, fluid, and entrancing. This work will provide a taste of
wisdom to all who read it." Libr J

Atwood, Margaret, 1939-

Writing with intent; essays, reviews, personal
prose, 1983-2005. Carroll & Graf Publishers 2005
427p $26   **814**

ISBN 0-7867-1535-9

LC 2005-42086

Some of the essays in this volume were first published
2004 in Canada with title: Moving targets

In these essays, the author "comments on world events,
fellow writers, and her own development. She reviews
books by John Updike, Italo Calvino, Antonia Fraser, and
Dashiell Hammett, as well as the lesser-known Robert Brin-
ghurst, Hilary Mantel, and H. Rider Haggard. . . . This collection will not disappoint Atwood fans as her analyses both
challenge and entertain." Libr J

Includes bibliographical references

Baker, Nicholson, 1957-

The way the world works; essays. Nicholson
Baker. Simon & Schuster 2012 336 p. (hardcover)
$25.00   **814**

1. American essays 2. Electronic books 3. Books and
reading

ISBN 1416572473; 9781416572473

LC 2011052741

This book is a "collection of essays," in which "[Nich-
olson] Baker . . . poses important questions about our era of
digital readership. As he notes in his essay on the Kindle 2,
there is a distinction between a writer's work and its presentation in book form. Many essays staunchly defend the
reading of print books and newspapers. . . . A proud defender
of libraries and newspapers, Baker acknowledges the perception of him as 'a weirdo cultist, a ringleader' for books."
(Publishers Weekly)

Baldwin, James

★ **Collected** essays. Library of Am. 1998 869p
$35   **814**

ISBN 1-883011-52-3

LC 97-23496

The essays in this volume were selected by Toni Morrison. "Morrison has reprinted all of the material contained in
Baldwin's previous collected essays, The Price of the Ticket
(1985). She has added eleven pieces, the earliest of which
dates from 1947—Baldwin's first published review, of a biography of Frederick Douglass, in the Nation—and the latest from 1984." Times Lit Suppl

The beholder's eye; a collection of America's finest
personal journalism. edited and with an introduction by Walt Harrington. Grove Press 2005 xxii,
256p pa $14   **814**

ISBN 0-8021-4224-5

LC 2005-46242

"Each writer takes a unique approach to the subject,
drawing the reader into the experience of pit-bull fighting
or hunting with the Inuit. Among the collection: Harrington,
who is married to a black woman, explores his evolving attitudes on race through the lens of his relationship with his
in-laws, Pete Earley returns to his hometown in search of the
meaning of a sister's death in their youth, Ron Rosenbaum
explores his own outlook on life in a philosophical discourse
with then-New York governor Mario Cuomo, Davis Miller
is unabashedly starstruck in a comfortable and closeup look
at Muhammad Ali at the home of Ali's mother, and Stephen
S. Hall is personally probing in his exploration, via MRI, of
his own brain and its functioning. These stories are amusing, insightful, and touching in a way that only something
personal can be." Booklist

Berry, Wendell

Imagination in place; essays. Counterpoint
2010 196p $24   **814**

ISBN 978-1-58243-562-6; 1-58243-562-6

LC 2009-38104

"For those who've already come to admire Berry's moral
clarity and closely argued critiques of contemporary society,

'Imagination in Place' is a welcome chance to continue the conversation." Christ Sci Monit

Includes bibliographical references

★ The **best** American essays 2010; edited with an introduction by Christopher Hitchens; Robert Atwan, series editor. Houghton Mifflin 2010 xxi, 272p (The best American series) pa $14.95 **814**
ISBN 978-0-547-39451-0
Annual. First published 1986

Editors select essays from general interest magazines that touch on topics political, scientific, historical, religious, and sociological, in addition to the personal and literary.

The **Best** American essays 2013; edited by Cheryl Strayed ; series editor Robert Atwan. Houghton Mifflin Harcourt 2013 336 p. $14.95 **814**
1. American essays
ISBN 0544103882; 9780544103887;

In this book, editor Charyl Strayed presents her choices for the best essays written by American authors in 2013. "Zadie Smith muses at length about her coming to appreciate the artistry of Joni Mitchell, Steven Harvey provides a . . . recollection of his mother and her suicide, Jon Kerstetter writes of the pain of combat triage, and Vanessa Veselka presents a harrowing story of runaway girls who ride with truckers." (Publisher's note)

The "annual reprise of the venerable series takes a decidedly introspective turn. More than two dozen talented authors, selected by Strayed, write about themselves, more or less." Kirkus

★ The **Best** American essays of the century; Joyce Carol Oates, editor; Robert Atwan, coeditor; with an introduction by Joyce Carol Oates. Houghton Mifflin 2000 596p hardcover o.p. pa $18 **814**
ISBN 0-618-04370-5; 0-618-15587-2 pa

This anthology includes essays "that contemplate diverse worlds, from nature to courtrooms, war and family memories. Race is a pervasive theme, explored with candor and insight by many, including James Baldwin, Zora Neale Hurston, and, in a jolting 1912 condemnation of a Coatesville, Pennsylvania, lynching, John Jay Chapman." Booklist

Includes bibliographical references

Bradbury, Ray

Bradbury speaks; too soon from the cave, too far from the stars. William Morrow 2005 243p hardcover o.p. pa $14.95 **814**
ISBN 0-06-058568-4; 0-06-058569-2 pa
LC 2005-41489

In this collection of essays, the author "weighs in on a medley of topics, including the allure of Paris, his enthusiasm for trains, the genesis of his most popular novels, and his reasons for remaining a diehard optimist. . . . By turns whimsical, insightful, and unabashedly metaphoric, his prose is immediately accessible as well as thought-provoking. Fans and nonfans alike should enjoy." Booklist

Burn this book; PEN writers speak out on the power of the word. edited by Toni Morrison. HarperStudio 2009 118p $16.99 **814**
1. Authorship 2. Censorship 3. Freedom of speech
ISBN 978-0-06-177400-3

"Published in conjunction with the PEN American Center, this slim collection of essays has an amazing list of contributors—Toni Morrison, John Updike, David Grossman, Francine Prose, Pico Iyer, Russell Banks, Paul Auster, Orhan Pamuk, Salman Rushdie, Ed Park, and Nadine Gordimer. . . . [They] discuss the importance of writing from various views, political and social. They illustrate the need for freedom of speech and human rights, and they emphasize the target writers become in a tyranny. . . . This is not an easy read, but it is a profound, absorbing, and moving collection of work." Libr J

Includes bibliographical references

Capote, Truman

★ **Portraits** and observations; the essays of Truman Capote. Random House 2007 518p $28.95 **814**
ISBN 978-1-4000-6661-2; 1-4000-6661-1
LC 2007-36624

This is a collection of 42 essays written by Capote from 1946 to 1984.

"The featured works cover the artist's interests in travel, celebrities, the arts—both visual and literary—crimes of passion, and himself. . . . This collection offers the highest quality of writing from a genuine American stylist." Libr J

Chabon, Michael

Maps and legends; reading and writing along the borderlands. McSweeney's 2008 222p $24 **814**
1. Authorship
ISBN 978-1-932416-89-3; 1-932416-89-7

"In 16 essays, Chabon maps his enthusiasms. . . . Although in part a fragmentary memoir—we receive revealing glimpses of Chabon's family, boyhood home of Columbia, Md., and personal history—'Maps and Legends' is also a manifesto, a declaration of literary principles that asserts the value, even necessity, of genre. Especially in the book's first half, Chabon makes this argument through example, by closely examining and celebrating Arthur Conan Doyle's Sherlock Holmes tales, Philip Pullman's 'His Dark Materials' series, M.R. James' ghost stories, and the comics of Howard Chaykin, Ben Katchor and Will Eisner. . . . However disparately engaging you find the ruminations on other writers, the book's concluding quintet of pieces on the inspirations behind Chabon's major work will prove an illuminating delight for those of us who have the same fannish devotion to his work as he does to Conan Doyle's." St. Louis Post-Dispatch

Codrescu, Andrei

New Orleans, mon amour; by Andrei Codrescu. Algonquin Books of Chapel Hill 2006 273p pa $14 **814**
1. New Orleans (La.) -- Social life and customs
ISBN 1-56512-505-3
LC 2005-53599

In this collection of short essays Codrescu sketches "portraits of a fabled city and its equally fabled inhabitants. The author, who has called the Big Easy home for two decades, shows how, like some gigantic bohemian magnet, New Orleans attracts some of the world's most talented, self-indulgent freaks. Codrescu finds himself quite at home there. He expertly weaves pages of New Orleans history through his stories of personal discovery and debauchery. The last few essays, written post-Katrina, radiate simultaneous anger and clarity. Full of pride and defensiveness, Codrescu closes the collection ruminating about rebuilding the city and his longing to return to its rhythms and eccentricities. Despite Codrescu's frustrations, this collection is, in the end, gentle and sweet." Publ Wkly

Connell, Evan S.

★ The **Aztec** treasure house; new and selected essays. Counterpoint 2001 470p hardcover o.p. pa $17.50 **814**

1. Incas 2. Alchemy 3. Vikings 4. Admirals 5. Astronomy 6. Explorers 7. Hieroglyphics 8. Northwest Passage 9. Cliff dwellers and cliff dwellings 10. Kings 11. Alchemists 12. South Pole 13. Government officials 14. America -- Exploration 15. Colonial administrators
ISBN 1-58243-253-8 pa

LC 2001-28899

Connell "writes about polar exploration; linguistic research; astronomy; preposterous, unkillable fantasies like El Dorado and Prester John; inspired travelers like Ibn Batuta and Mary Kingsley; the insane and tragic Children's Crusade—any subject that illustrates the human urge to strain against physical and mental boundaries. Connell is skeptical, clearheaded and a sworn enemy of all dogma." N Y Times Book Rev

Includes bibliographical references

Crosley, Sloane

How did you get this number; essays. Riverhead Books 2010 274p il $25.95 **814**

1. American wit and humor
ISBN 1594487596; 9781594487590

LC 2010-07178

This is a collection of essays by the author of I Was Told There'd Be Cake (2008).

"With wit, humor, and a sophistication that more experienced authors would envy, this compilation focuses on Crosley's late twenties. . . . Reading like the diary entries of a thirtysomething, Crosley's essays are brutally honest about her flaws as well as the flaws of others and, as a result, paint a realistic and hilarious portrait of what it's like to be an adult in today's world." Libr J

Davenport, Guy

The **geography** of the imagination; forty essays. 1st Nonpareil ed; David R. Godine 1997 384p (Nonpareil book) pa $19.95 **814**
ISBN 1-567-92080-2

LC 97-17831

First published 1981 by North Point Press

In addition to essays on modern and classical literature the author also discusses archaeology, biology, lexicography, music and photography. Among his subjects are: Poe,

Agassiz, Pound, Ives, Zukofsky, Meatyard, Tchelitchew and Joyce.

Includes bibliographical references

Didion, Joan

We tell ourselves stories in order to live; collected nonfiction. with an introduction by John Leonard. Knopf 2006 1122p $30 **814**
ISBN 978-0-307-26487-9; 0-307-26487-4

LC 2006-41043

This volume "contains seven books of journalism—all of [Didion's] nonfiction except her 2005 memoir of new widowhood, 'The Year of Magical Thinking.' Didion's writing was from the beginning startlingly individual. . . . Say what you will about her somewhat self-centered style; America needs more courageous thinkers who will write about life as it is lived—not as elites on all sides seek to manufacture it." Nat Rev

Includes bibliographical references

Dirda, Michael

Classics for pleasure. Harcourt 2007 341p $25 **814**

1. Literature -- History and criticism
ISBN 978-0-15-101251-0; 0-15-101251-2

LC 2007-03029

This book is "a pleasure to dip into any time. Like the key that opens up the door to The Secret Garden, it provides easy entry to a colorful array of literary gems." America

Doctorow, E. L.

Creationists : selected essays, 1993-2006. Random House 2006 176p $24.95 **814**

1. Creation (Literary, artistic, etc.) 2. Literature -- History and criticism
ISBN 978-1-4000-6495-3; 1-4000-6495-3

"Doctorow chose his gallery with what may seem a generous dash of whimsy. Many of his writers and other 'creationists' are not exactly habitues of the canon. Standing alongside the likes of Mark Twain, Sinclair Lewis, Scott Fitzgerald and John Dos Passos are Harriet Beecher Stowe; W. G. Sebald; the anonymous translators of Genesis into the King James version; Harpo Marx; Albert Einstein; [and] the makers of the atomic bomb. . . . And yet the writers assembled here efficiently serve the critic's intentions. Each yields in robustly illustrative ways to 'the voice of the book,' a voice more protean than the artist's own; a voice that soars into conjunction with the voice of the region, the nation, the times." N Y Times Book Rev

Du Bois, W. E. B.

★ **Writings**. Library of Am. 1986 1334p $40; pa $15.95 **814**
ISBN 0-940450-33-X; 1-883011-31-0 pa

LC 86-10565

Includes bibliographical references

Ellison, Ralph

The **collected** essays of Ralph Ellison; edited with an introduction by John F. Callahan; preface by

Saul Bellow. Modern Lib. 1995 xxix, 856p hardcover o.p. pa $18 **814**

1. Artists 2. Authors 3. Pianists 4. Educators 5. Novelists 6. Dramatists 7. Economists 8. Journalists 9. Essayists 10. Screenwriters 11. Music teachers 12. Cabinet members 13. Newspaper editors 14. Nonfiction writers 15. Classical musicians 16. Short story writers 17. Civil rights activists 18. Jazz music -- History and criticism 19. International organization officials 20. Nobel laureates for economic sciences
ISBN 978-0-8129-6826-2 pa; 0-8129-6826-3 pa
LC 95-4719

This book "includes posthumously discovered reviews, criticism, and interviews, as well as the essay collections Shadow and Act (1964) . . . and Going to the Territory (1986), an exploration of literature and folklore, jazz and culture, and the nature and quality of lives that black Americans lead." Publisher's note

Emerson, Ralph Waldo

Essays & lectures. Library of Am. 1983 1321p $35 **814**

ISBN 0-940450-15-1
LC 83-5447

Includes bibliographical references
Contents: Nature; Addresses and lectures; Essays, first and second series; Representative men; English traits; The conduct of life; Uncollected prose

Ephron, Nora, 1941-2012

I feel bad about my neck; and other thoughts on being a woman. Knopf 2006 137p $21.95; pa $12.95 **814**

1. Aging 2. Women
ISBN 0307264556; 0307276821; 9780307264558; 9780307276827
LC 2005-57780

In this collection of essays, Ephron looks "at women who are getting older and dealing with the tribulations of maintenance, menopause, empty nests, and life itself." (Publisher's note)

"While very little in the book is meant to be taken seriously, it is clever enough to qualify as more than just an assemblage of one-liners. Whether you agree with her observations or not, Ephron's perspective as an admittedly high-maintenance, New York-dwelling, successful screenwriter will keep you entertained." Christ Sci Monit

The **Most** of Nora Ephron; by Nora Ephron. Alfred A. Knopf 2013 576 p. (hardcover) $35 **814**

1. Anthologies 2. Love stories 3. Women authors
ISBN 038535083X; 9780385350839
LC 2013016426

This posthumously-published book collects writings by Nora Ephron. Ephron and her editor "decided to structure it around the subject matters she explored and the genres she used to explore them. As a result, the text of her novel Heartburn (1983) is included, as is the screenplay for Ephron's most beloved movie, When Harry Met Sally, and her late-in-life play, Lucky Guy. The remainder of the anthology consists of much briefer entries across a . . . diverse set of topics." (Kirkus Reviews)

"Whether Ephron is writing about politics or purses, sexism or soufflé, her appeal is her intelligent, incisive sense of humor." LJ

Epstein, Joseph

In a cardboard belt! essays personal, literary, and savage. Houghton Mifflin 2007 xxii, 410p $26 **814**

ISBN 978-0-618-72193-1; 0-618-72193-2
LC 2007-8515

In this compendium Epstein includes "essays on his father's passing, movies, travel, dining, editing, writer's block, and the strangely gratifying unhappiness of academics; there are moving appreciations of W.H. Auden, Marcel Proust, and John Keats, and fierce depreciations of Edmund Wilson, Mortimer Adler, and poetry prizes. The result is an unusually broad portrait of a thinking man doing his stuff. Epstein is one of the handful of writers in America today whom one can pleasurably read both for substance and style. His writing sparkles with observation and humor." Claremont Rev Books

Epstein, Joseph, 1937-

Essays in biography; Joseph Epstein. Axios Press 2012 xiv, 603 p.p ill. (hardcover) $24 **814**

1. Essay 2. Authors -- Biography 3. Literature -- History and criticism
ISBN 160419068X; 9781604190687
LC 2012010035

This book, by Joseph Epstein, "presents a provocative collection of essays that illustrate the ways a writer can employ biographical detail. Epstein . . . has assembled a motley crew of characters--from Henry Adams to Xenophon, Michael Jordan to Gore Vidal. The author has . . . a wide range of interests, political biases . . . and a vast storehouse of knowledge about literary history--all of which animate and inform his pieces." (Kirkus Reviews)

Includes bibliographical references and index

Essays/Selections

The **selected** essays of Gore Vidal; edited by Jay Parini. Doubleday 2008 458p $27.50 **814**

ISBN 978-0-385-52484-1; 0-385-52484-6
LC 2008-13517

"Regardless of what one thinks of Vidal, what Vidal thinks is never in doubt in these 24 essays, divided here into two groups: literary criticism and historical or cultural commentary. His writing is clear, sharp, and disciplined, and his approbation of William Dean Howells and Italo Calvino are as finely tuned as his excoriation of John Updike and Herman Wouk." Libr J

Includes bibliographical references

Fairlie, Henry

Bite the hand that feeds you; essays and provocations. edited and with an introduction by Jeremy McCarter; foreword by Leon Wieseltier. Yale University Press 2009 355p $30 **814**

1. United States -- Politics and government -- 20th century
ISBN 978-0-300-12383-8; 0-300-12383-3
LC 2008-49888

"A Grub Street transplant, Fairlie brought to America a fluency in history and prose, a jagged wit, a newcomer's affection for the New World, and a set of self-destructive lifestyle habits charming only in hindsight. We could use more of his kind. Fairlie, who had an unmistakable voice—Tory, yet unpredictable—did most of his finest work at The New Republic. This smartly edited collection gets him at his best, a principled conservative with an eye out for the fatuous." New Yorker

Fiedler, Leslie A.

Fiedler on the roof; essays on literature and Jewish identity. by Leslie Fiedler. Godine 1990 184p $19.95; pa $11.95 **814**
1. Jews in literature
ISBN 0-87923-859-3; 0-87923-949-2 pa
LC 90-55282
"Disturbing, provocative, and brilliant." Libr J

Franzen, Jonathan, 1959-

★ **Farther** away; Jonathan Franzen. Farrar, Straus and Giroux 2012 321 p. **814**
1. American essays 2. Literature -- History and criticism 3. Interpersonal relations in literature
ISBN 0374153574; 9780374153571
LC 2011046067
The author presents "a collection of recent essays, speeches, and reviews, in which he lays out a view of literature in which storytelling and character development trump lyrical acrobatics, and unearths a few forgotten classics. . . . [Jonathan Franzen discusses] books that revel in the frustrations, despairs, and near-blisses of human relationships. . . . This intimate read is packed with provocative questions about technology, love, and the state of the contemporary novel." (Publishers Weekly)

The **Fun** of it; stories from The talk of the town, The New Yorker. edited by Lillian Ross; introduction by David Remnick. Modern Lib. 2001 xxi, 478p pa $16.95 **814**
1. New Yorker (Periodical)
ISBN 0-375-75649-3
LC 00-68237
A "selection of stories from 'Talk' in chronologically arranged sections that begin with the 1920s and end in 2000. Many of the early contributions were unsigned, but through archival research Ross ferrets out and reveals the authors of many of those initial pieces. Included in this lively collection are pieces by writers—some of whom became New Yorker regulars—such as Robert Benchley, James Thurber, E. B. White, A. J. Liebling, John Updike, Garrison Keillor, Ann Beattie, Bill McKibben, Roger Angell, Steve Martin, and Susan Orlean." Libr J

Gass, William H.

Finding a form: essays. Cornell University Press 1997 354p pa $21 **814**
1. Poets 2. Authors 3. Novelists 4. Dramatists 5. Philosophers 6. Pulitzer Prizes 7. Biography as a literary form 8. Editors 9. Essayists 10. Logicians 11. Literary critics 12. Short story writers
ISBN 0-8014-8489-8

First published 1996 by Knopf
Gass "is 'as obdurate as nails' when it comes to the best possible use of the written word. Each essay in this wideranging book (be it titled 'Ezra Pound,' 'Nietzche: The Polemical Philosopher,' 'Robert Walser,' 'Nature, Culture, and Cosmos,' 'Pulitzer, The People Prize,' or 'The Music of Prose') offers evidence for such a conclusion. Gass is concerned with how best to use a phrase or word and believes we should be tough-minded when it comes to reading. He reveals a sardonic sense of humor as well, for example, in discussing the winners of the Pulitzer prize, and he dislikes the fact that anyone would enjoy his/her own writing." Libr J

Gay, Roxane

Bad Feminist; essays. Roxane Gay. HarperCollins 2014 336 p. $15.99 **814**
1. Feminism 2. Feminist criticism
ISBN 0062282719; 9780062282712
This book, by Roxane Gay, is a "collection of essays spanning politics, criticism, and feminism. . . . Gay takes us through the journey of her evolution as a woman (Sweet Valley High) of color (The Help) while also taking readers on a ride through culture of the last few years (Girls, Django in Chains) and commenting on the state of feminism today (abortion, Chris Brown)." (Publisher's note)
"Writing about race, politics, gender, feminism, privilege, and popular media, [Gay] highlights how deeply misogyny is embedded in our culture, the careless language used to discuss sexual violence (seen in news reports of sexual assault), Hollywood's tokenistic treatment of race, the trivialization of literature written by women, and the many ways American society fails women and African-Americans." Pub Wkly

Ginsberg, Allen

★ **Deliberate** prose; selected essays, 1952-1995. HarperCollins Pubs. 2000 xxiv, 536p hardcover o.p. pa $17 **814**
ISBN 0-06-093081-0 pa
LC 99-41360
This collection of over 100 prose pieces "organizes the material under several general topics: 'Politics and Prophecies,' 'Drug Culture,' 'Manifestations and Spirituality,' 'Censorship and Sex Laws,' 'Autobiographical Fragments,' 'Literary Techniques and the Beat Generation,' 'Writer,' and 'Further Appreciations,' tributes to artistic collaborators and cultural heroes such as Robert Frank, Philip Glass, Andy Warhol, and the Beatles. . . . Taken together, they provide a rare glimpse into Ginsberg's creative practice, a key to sources and influences, and a good overview of his life and art." Libr J
Includes bibliographical references

Gladwell, Malcolm

What the dog saw and other adventures. Little, Brown and Company 2009 410p $27.99 **814**
ISBN 978-0-316-07584-8; 0-316-07584-1
LC 2009-24010
"An eccentric collection of 19 essays that run the gamut from the trivial (a profile of infomercial maestro Ron Popeil) to the substantial (a less expensive solution for chronic homelessness). What distinguishes each of them is a surpris-

ing, often counterintuitive, insight or two, delivered in a no-frills — even formulaic — writing style that could be a flaw in some other context, but here works beautifully, ensuring that the words don't distract from the ideas. . . . Gladwell excels at making unobvious and intriguing connections, as between football and teaching or Enron and antisubmarine warfare, and readers are swept along." PopMatters

Gottlieb, Robert Adams

★ **Lives** and letters. Farrar, Straus and Giroux 2011 426p $30 **814**
  ISBN 978-0-374-29882-1; 0-374-29882-3
  LC 2010-38530

"Having headed up two formidable cultural institutions, The New Yorker and the Alfred A. Knopf publishing house, Gottlieb is a fairly formidable cultural institution himself. When he passes judgment, we are inclined to listen. Befitting a man of letters, some of the essays meditate on literary figures and questions that attracted Gottlieb's curiosity. In one he examines the unlikely author-editor collaboration between Marjorie Kinnan Rawlings and Maxwell Perkins; in another he ponders how the 'wildly uneven' works of John Steinbeck have all managed to stay in print. The crowd-pleasing portion of the collection is provided by Gottlieb's critical reflections on biographies, many featuring celebrities who soared through life, egos ablaze. Discussing books about prima donnas as diverse as Margot Fonteyn and Judy Garland, Gottlieb is genteelly shocked by salacious revelations he considers an invasion of privacy, though not too shocked to give examples." Boston Globe

Grann, David

The **devil** and Sherlock Holmes; tales of murder, madness, and obsession. Doubleday 2010 304p $26.95 **814**
  ISBN 978-0-385-53316-4; 0-385-53316-0
  LC 2009-42230

"The real strength of Grann's work isn't earthshaking revelations; it's portraiture. He excels at capturing people and showing what makes them tick. His subjects are always interesting and exceptional, if not always sympathetic. Any appreciator of nonfiction, in fact, may find this book heartbreaking. . . . These pieces are evidence of a great nonfiction writer who has come into his own." Miami Herald

Hampton, Howard

★ **Born** in flames; termite dreams, dialectical fairy tales, and pop apocalypses. Harvard University Press 2007 473p $28.95 **814**
  1. Rock music 2. Motion pictures 3. Popular culture
  ISBN 978-0-674-02317-8; 0-674-02317-X
  LC 2006-43680

"The torrent of allusions presupposes an Olympian level of cultural indoctrination, and some sentences are so dense that they require a little thoughtful chewing, but Hampton offers something that grows scarcer as today's media bombardment grows in volume: fresh thinking. Knee-jerk intellectuals may find it easy to lampoon someone who takes pop this seriously, but Hampton is a writer—possibly the only one—who can analyze Buffy the Vampire Slayer in the context of D. H. Lawrence . . . and make it work." Booklist

  Includes bibliographical references

Hemon, Aleksandar, 1964-

The **book** of my lives; Aleksandar Hemon. Farrar, Straus and Giroux 2013 214 p. (hardcover : alk. paper) $25 **814**
  1. Sarajevo (Bosnia and Hercegovina)
  ISBN 0374115737; 9780374115739
  LC 2012034564

This collection of essays by Aleksandar Hemon focuses on "the war in the former Yugoslavia and its transformative effect on the material and metaphysical circumstances of Hemon's life. . . . In 'The Lives of a Flaneur,' in which he meditates on the loss of Sarajevo, he frames the story in geographical terms. . . . In 'Let There Be What Cannot Be,' by contrast, he frames the story of the war in literary terms: as a Serbian epic poem come to life." (The Nation)

Hitchens, Christopher, 1949-2011

Arguably; Essays by Christopher Hitchens. Christopher Hitchens. Twelve 2011 788p $30.00 **814**
  1. American essays 2. Literature -- History and criticism 3. Criticism
  ISBN 085789255X Atlantic Books; 9780857892553 Atlantic Books; 9781455502776; 9781455506781
  LC 2011930917

This collection of essays by Christopher Hitchens "supplies fresh perceptions of such figures as varied as Charles Dickens, Karl Marx, Rebecca West, George Orwell, J.G. Ballard, and Philip Larkin . . . [and] pungent discussions and intrepid observations, gathered from a lifetime of traveling and reporting from such destinations as Iran, China, and Pakistan. . . . [This] volume is an intellectual self-portrait of a writer with . . . [a] vision of the human longing for reason and justice." (Publisher's note)

"Goading, brilliant, funny, and caring, Hitchens is a voice of enlightenment in a wilderness of cant." Booklist

Hoagland, Edward

Tigers & ice; reflections on nature and life. Lyons Press 1999 206p $22; pa $16.95 **814**
  ISBN 1-55821-742-8; 1-58574-182-5 pa
  LC 98-36477

"Edward Hoagland entered his 60's captivated by sight. After three years of legal blindness, a surgeon restored both his vision and his delight for the tableaux of the natural world. . . . In the 11 essays collected in 'Tigers and Ice,' he considers subjects as varied as suicide, friendship, cowardice, man-made ponds, Indian tigers and Antarctic penguins—all colored by his renewed view of the world." N Y Times Book Rev

Hustvedt, Siri

Living, thinking, looking; essays. Siri Hustvedt. Picador 2012 xiii, 384 p.p $18.00 **814**
  1. Authorship 2. American essays 3. Psychologists -- Research 4. Hallucinations and illusions 5. Bunyan, Paul (Legendary character) 6. Human beings
  ISBN 1250009529; 9781250009524
  LC 2011035714

In this essay collection, "[n]ovelist and essayist [Siri] Hustvedt . . . gathers 32 pieces (most previously published), written over the past six years, that she says are linked by

an abiding curiosity about 'what it means to be human.'"
Topics include a premigraine hallucination of Paul Bunyan, researching her novel "The Sorrows of an American," and the artist Louise Bourgeois. (Publishers Weekly)

Includes bibliographical references (p. [355]-380)

The Inevitable; contemporary writers confront death. edited by David Shields and Bradford Morrow; with an introduction by the editors. W. W. Norton & Co. 2011 332p $17.95   **814**

1. Death
ISBN 9780393339369 pa

LC 2010-43479

"Often poetic and at times funny or gruesome while exposing raw grief, the writers . . . tackle the subject of death with honesty and courage." Publ Wkly

Includes bibliographical references

Jamison, Leslie

★ The **empathy** exams; essays. Leslie Jamison. Graywolf Press 2014 256 p. (alk. paper) $15   **814**

1. Pain 2. Essays 3. Empathy
ISBN 1555976719; 9781555976712

LC 2013946927

"Beginning with her experience as a medical actor who was paid to act out symptoms for medical students to diagnose, Leslie Jamison's visceral and revealing essays ask essential questions about our basic understanding of others: How should we care about each other? How can we feel another's pain, especially when pain can be assumed, distorted, or performed? Is empathy a tool by which to test or even grade each other?" (Publisher's note)

"Jamison exhibits at once a journalist's courage to bear witness to acts and conditions that test human limits--incarceration, laboring in a silver mine, ultramarathoning, the loss of a child, devastating heartbreak, suffering from an unacknowledged illness--and a poet's skepticism at her own motives for doing so." Kirkus

Includes bibliographical references

Johnson, Charles Richard

Turning the wheel; essays on Buddhism and writing. [by] Charles Johnson. Scribner 2003 187p hardcover o.p. pa $15.95   **814**

1. Authors 2. Buddhism 3. Novelists 4. African Americans in literature 5. Essayists 6. College teachers 7. Short story writers
ISBN 0-7432-4324-2; 978-1-4165-7243-5; 1-4165-7243-0

LC 2002-44666

"The central leitmotifs of the lucid, fervently reasoned essays collected in 'Turning the Wheel' are 'enlightenment and liberation.'" N Y Times Book Rev

Includes bibliographical references

Jones, Bill T., 1954-

Story /Time; the life of an idea. Bill T. Jones. Princeton University Press 2014 104 p. illustrations (some color) (The Toni Morrison Lecture Series) (hardcover : acid-free paper) $24.95   **814**

1. Choreographers 2. African American dancers 3.

Literature, Experimental
ISBN 0691162700; 9780691162706

LC 2013050410

In this book, "African American dancer, choreographer, and director Bill T. Jones reflects on his art and life as he describes the genesis of Story/Time, a recent dance work produced by his company and inspired by the modernist composer and performer John Cage. . . . The book is filled with telling vignettes--about Jones's childhood as part of a large, poor, Southern family that migrated to upstate New York; about his struggles to find a place for himself in a white-dominated dance world." (Publisher's note)

"Derived from Jones' presentations at Princeton University for the Toni Morrison Lectures in 2012, the text is a hybrid. There is some introductory material explaining what follows. . . . The central--and largest--section is a series of 60 single-page narratives, each designed to consume a minute of dance and reading." Kirkus

Kosinski, Jerzy N.

Passing by; selected essays, 1962-1991. [by] Jerzy Kosinski. Grove Press; Distributed by Publishers Group West 1995 256p pa $12   **814**

ISBN 0-8021-3423-8

LC 95-19519

First published 1992 by Random House

"While the selections would be improved by contextualizing introductions, they portray a man who was impassioned about literature and who saw his role as confronting 'life's threatening encounters.'" Publ Wkly

Includes bibliographical references

Leonard, John, 1939-2008

Reading for my life; writings, 1958-2008. John Leonard ; edited by Sue Leonard ; with an introduction by E.L. Doctorow. Viking 2012 xv, 381 p.p (hbk.) $35   **814**

1. American essays 2. American literature -- History and criticism 3. Criticism 4. Books -- Reviews
ISBN 0670023086; 9780670023080

LC 2011039564

This collection features "a selection of reviews and essays from the celebrated literary critic [John Leonard], followed by a sort of festschrift with contributors ranging from family members to noted authors (Toni Morrison, Mary Gordon and others). . . . Included in the collection are . . . reviews of Maxine Hong Kingston, Robert Stone, Norman Mailer, Don DeLillo, Philip Roth, Amos Oz, Ralph Ellison, Maureen Howard and numerous other luminaries." (Kirkus Reviews)

Lethem, Jonathan

The **ecstasy** of influence; nonfictions, etc. Doubleday 2011 437p $27.95   **814**

ISBN 978-0-385-53495-6; 9780385534956

LC 2011016248

"Mr. Lethem's crowded pantheon, 'The Ecstasy of Influence' makes clear, includes Marvel comic books and misfit writers like Philip K. Dick, J. G. Ballard, Shirley Jackson and Charles Willeford. It includes improvisational filmmakers like John Cassavetes, little-known bands like the Go-Betweens and rumpled, bohemian critics like Manny Farber.

Mr. Lethem is all about the underdogs, and he counts himself snug among their number. 'Most of my heroes,' he declares, 'are partly or entirely out of print.' Mailer gets a hall pass because he is, like Mr. Lethem, from Brooklyn, and because he took a grizzled interest in things like 'graffiti, underground film, marijuana and space travel.' Like almost everything Mr. Lethem has written, 'The Ecstasy of Influence' is a reflection of, and a pixelated homage to, those whose work he fetishizes. If this book has a thesis, it's this: For an artist, influence is everything." N Y Times (Late N Y Ed)

Liebling, A. J.

★ **Just** enough Liebling; classic work by the legendary New Yorker writer. introduction by David Remnick. North Point Press 2004 xxvi, 534p $27.50   **814**

ISBN 0-374-10443-3

LC 2004-50056

"This captivating and appropriately plump . . . collection will bring renewed attention to a master of the man-on-the-street, narrative nonfiction form and celebrate the centenary of Liebling's birth." Booklist

Loewen, Sara

Gaining daylight; life on two islands. Sara Loewen. University of Alaska Press 2013 xii, 140 p.p ill., map (paperback) $15.95   **814**

1. Kodiak (Alaska) 2. Uyak Bay (Alaska) 3. Alaska -- Description and travel 4. Alaska -- Social life and customs

ISBN 1602231982; 9781602231986; 9781602231993

LC 2012033688

This book presents a collection of essays by Sara Loewen, who lives with her family "in Kodiak, Alaska, much of the year, but 'leave[s] every May for the salmon season, moving to . . . Uyak Bay on the west side of the island.' For half the year, she writes, they give up 'fresh produce, telephones, cars, dryer, and dishwasher.' . . . [S]he describes the patient, silent wait for the birth of her second son, [and] reminisces about her childhood friend and their stories of Old Harbor." (Publishers Weekly)

Includes bibliographical references (p. 129-137)

Martin, Steve

Pure drivel. Hyperion 1998 104p $19.95; pa $10.95   **814**

ISBN 0-7868-6467-2; 0-7868-8505-X pa

LC 98-28739

"The short essays, conversations, and proclamations collected here are relayed in a slyly deadpan Valley voice that belies the coiled craziness of their content. Martin also brings his gift for comedic timing to these creations, setting a quirky beat that perfectly sets off their ironic wiles." Booklist

McPhee, John A.

Silk parachute; [by] John McPhee. Farrar, Straus and Giroux 2010 227p $25   **814**

ISBN 978-0-374-26373-7; 0-374-26373-6

LC 2009-31887

"In the age of blogging and tweeting, of writers' near-constant self-promotion, McPhee is an imperative counter-

weight, a paragon of both sense and civility." N Y Times Book Rev

Miller, Arthur, 1915-

Echoes down the corridor; collected essays, 1947-1999. edited by Stephen R. Centola. Viking 2000 332p hardcover o.p. pa $15   **814**

ISBN 0-14-200005-1 pa

LC 00-40427

"The 50 essays collected here range from atmospheric reminiscences of his childhood in Brooklyn and studies at the University of Michigan, to accounts of visits to China, the Soviet Union and Turkey as an advocate for victims of governmental persecution. Deeply influenced by the radical culture of the 1930s and by his youth during the depression, Miller has always been firmly on the political left." Publ Wkly

"This collection is not to be missed." Libr J

Oates, Joyce Carol, 1938-

In rough country; essays and reviews. Ecco 2010 396p pa $14.99   **814**

ISBN 978-0-06-196398-8; 0-06-196398-4

"Oates explains that in choosing the title for this collection of 28 reviews and reflections, she aimed to describe the 'treacherous geographical/psychological terrains' of her subjects (a list that includes Flannery O'Connor, Jim Crace, Margaret Atwood and Edgar Allan Poe) and of herself after her husband's death. The phrase is almost better as a description of her own criticism. . . . Oates seems to take special, even unusual, pains not to bend her subjects into her own narrative. She is, instead, intensely focused on the books at hand, marking highlights, supplying context, guiding the reader through passage after passage. Her attention, even in a critic's mode, is unfailingly generous." N Y Times Book Rev

Includes bibliographical references

Ozick, Cynthia

★ **Quarrel** & quandary; essays. Knopf 2000 247p hardcover o.p. pa $13   **814**

1. Authors 2. Children 3. Novelists 4. Diarists 5. Holocaust victims 6. Short story writers 7. Literature -- History and criticism

ISBN 0-375-72445-9 pa

LC 99-89889

Among the topics discussed in this collection of personal and literary essays are Henry James, Anne Frank, Kafka, poetry, and public intellectuals.

"All the essays collected here began life elsewhere as reviews and higher journalism. This kind of gathering of literary leftovers is usually not worth reprinting. Ozick's work is an exception. Her pieces have genuine durability. They are great essays." N Y Times Book Rev

Packer, George

Interesting times; writings from a turbulent decade. Farrar, Straus and Giroux 2009 409p $28 **814**

ISBN 978-0-3741-7572-6; 0-3741-7572-1

LC 2009-10186

A collection "essays chronicling global political and cultural tumult between 9/11 and the 2008 presidential election.

. . . From Lagos to Myanmar, Tal Afar to Baghdad, the author reports on location and presents on-the-ground particulars that bring robust perspective to issues that are generally broadly reported. . . . In an era marked by the swift decline of well-researched, long-form journalism, these often heart-wrenching essays bring to life social, political and personal elements of far-flung crises in ways that elude more concise mediums." Kirkus

Remnick, David

Reporting; writings from The New Yorker. Knopf 2006 483p $27.95 **814**

1. Poets 2. Authors 3. Emperors 4. Diplomats 5. Empresses 6. Novelists 7. Dramatists 8. Presidents 9. Journalists 10. Mathematicians 11. Prime ministers 12. Vice-presidents 13. Conservationists 14. Computer scientists 15. Political prisoners 16. Hurricane Katrina, 2005 17. Translating and interpreting 18. Hamas 19. Senators 20. Essayists 21. Dissenters 22. Memoirists 23. Cabinet members 24. Sports trainers 25. Boxers (Persons) 26. Political leaders 27. Nonfiction writers 28. Members of Congress 29. Short story writers 30. Writers on politics 31. Newspaper executives 32. Members of Parliament 33. Human rights activists 34. Presidential candidates 35. United Nations officials 36. Nobel laureates for peace 37. Nobel laureates for literature 38. Palestine Liberation Organization

ISBN 0-307-26358-4; 978-0-307-26358-2

LC 2005-44709

The author "is an ideal reporter, combining erudition, curiosity, wit, an eye for the telling anecdote and empathy." Publ Wkly

Rich, Adrienne, 1929-2012

A **human** eye. W.W. Norton & Co. 2009 180p $24.95 **814**

1. Art and society 2. Poetry -- History and criticism

ISBN 978-0-393-07006-4; 0-393-07006-9

LC 2008049972

This book "collects ten years of [writer Adrienne Rich's] forewords, personal statements and reviews." (London Review of Books). "Strong writing, Rich believes, is about 'how we are with each other,' and she finds this encompassing theme in the work of Muriel Rukeyser, whom Rich admires for her 'poetics of historical sensibility'; James Baldwin, who was 'uncanny' in his prescience; and June Jordan, who believed humor and pleasure are essential to social change. Rich deep-reads poetry written in the shadow of AIDS and during tyranny and war in Iraq, and argues that we must all be 'resistant to dogma.'" (Booklist)

This collection includes a "response to the anthology Iraqi Poetry Today, a critique of three classic socialist manifestos, and a rereading of The Dead Lecturer, an early volume of poems by LeRoi Jones. Rich engages the impulse to make art that both impels toward and interacts with social change, a theme she also traces through the letters of poets Robert Duncan and Denise Levertov, gay and lesbian politics and poetry, and influential texts on Zionism and the Jewish diaspora." Publisher's note

Includes bibliographical references

Richardson, Robert D.

Emerson; the mind on fire: a biography. by Robert D. Richardson, Jr.; with a frontispiece by Barry Moser. University of Calif. Press 1995 671p il $50; pa $21.95 **814**

1. Poets 2. Authors 3. Philosophers 4. Essayists

ISBN 0-520-08808-5; 0-520-20689-4 pa

LC 94-36008

"Richardson focuses principally on his subject's inner life, the life of his mind and spirit. But in this subtle portrayal of Emerson the thinker, the reader also sees the clearly limned portrait of Emerson the social activist. . . . A masterful work, this biography will attract the attention of scholars and serious general readers for decades." Booklist

Includes bibliographical references

Robinson, Marilynne, 1943-

When I was a child I read books; Marilynne Robinson. Farrar, Straus & Giroux 2012 xvi, 206 p **814**

1. American essays 2. Political science 3. United States -- Civilization 4. Philosophy, American 5. Theology -- United States 6. Calvinism -- United States 7. Political science -- United States -- Philosophy

ISBN 0374298785; 9780374298784

LC 2011041206

This collection of essays by Marilynne Robinson offers a critique of U.S. culture and politics. "Her enemies are many and varied -- militant atheists, scientists, . . . a political system that sees everything in terms of economic value, a government that commits the arch-crimes of closing libraries and filleting universities. . . . She observes that the idea of a public sector is now condemned by many Americans as 'socialism,' a stance at odds with the civic principles on which the country was founded." (New Statesman)

Includes bibliographical references.

Said, Edward W.

Reflections on exile and other essays. Harvard Univ. Press 2000 xxxv, 617p (Convergences) $36.95; pa $19.95 **814**

1. Authors 2. Criticism 3. Novelists 4. Nationalism 5. Philosophers 6. Psychologists 7. Palestinian Arabs 8. Politics in literature 9. Literary critics 10. Short story writers 11. Egypt -- Civilization 12. Motion picture directors 13. Literature -- History and criticism

ISBN 0-674-00302-0; 0-674-00997-5 pa

LC 00-44996

"Written between 1967 and the present by a literary critic and advocate for the Palestinian cause, these pieces often deal with the self-deceiving fictions of the colonizers about the people they oppress; others deplore some fashionable critical theories as unengaged with real life and history." N Y Times Book Rev

Includes bibliographical references

Sedaris, David

Dress your family in corduroy and denim. Little, Brown 2004 257p $24.95 **814**

ISBN 0-316-14346-4

LC 2003-65673

The author "has a unique ability to supply exactly the right details to bring every funny, awkward, ludicrous, painful, horrible real-life moment into harrowingly crisp focus." Booklist

Me talk pretty one day. Little, Brown 2000 272p $22.95; pa $14.95 **814**
ISBN 0-316-77772-2; 0-316-77696-3 pa
LC 00-25052

"In this collection of 27 fairly short essays, some of which appeared in Esquire and The New Yorker, Sedaris gives the impression of ease and naturalness. Whether he is writing about overcoming a lisp, learning to play the guitar, trying to master French, or taking an IQ test, whether the locales are North Carolina, New York, or France, the author is both amused and amusing." Libr J

When you are engulfed in flames. Little, Brown 2008 323p $25.99 **814**
ISBN 978-0-316-14347-9; 0-316-14347-2
LC 2007-49021

This collection "gets its title from a booklet with tips for 'Disaster Damage Prevention' that Sedaris found in a Hiroshima hotel room when he moved to Japan for three months to quit smoking. . . . [His stay] provides fresh material aplenty for the longest piece, 'The Smoking Section,' which is destined to become a quit-lit (or quitterature) classic. The draw, as always, is Sedaris's utter lack of sanctimony and his use of humor as a portal to deeper feelings. Instead of insufferably touting his new purity, Sedaris recalls all those nasty habits he's overcome—alcohol, marijuana, cigarettes—with wistful fondness. His honesty is refreshing." Christ Sci Monit

Sedaris, David, 1956-
Let's explore diabetes with owls; by David Sedaris. 1st ed. Little, Brown, and Co. 2013 ix, 275 p.p (hardcover) $27.00; (hardcover) $29.00 **814**
1. Swimming 2. Sea turtles 3. American essays
ISBN 0316154695; 9780316154697; 9780316233910 large print
LC 2013930473

This is an essay collection by David Sedaris. He draws on a "well of appalling childhood memories revolving around his mounting fears about being unlike other boys." He shares stories about his swimming competitions where "his irascible father vociferously championed his son's rival," his "courtship of a shy African American girl," and his "inept handling of captured baby sea turtles." (Booklist)

Solnit, Rebecca
The **Faraway** Nearby; Rebecca Solnit. Penguin Group USA 2013 272 p. $25.95 **814**
1. Iceland 2. Dementia 3. American essays 4. Storytelling 5. Autobiography -- Authorship 6. Narration (Rhetoric) -- Psychological aspects
ISBN 0670025968; 9780670025961
LC 2013001563

In this essay collection, National Book Critics Circle Award-winner Rebecca Solnit offers a "study in empathy through these meandering reflections on subjects as diverse as her mother's descent into dementia, Che Guevara, and Solnit's own 'magical rescue' to Iceland for

some months as resident at the Library of Water museum." (Publishers Weekly)

Sontag, Susan, 1933-2004
★ **At** the same time; essays and speeches. edited by Paolo Dilonardo and Anne Jump; with a foreword by David Rieff. Farrar, Straus & Giroux 2007 235p $23 **814**
ISBN 0-374-10072-1; 978-0-374-10072-8
LC 2006-31179

This is a "collection of 16 essays written toward the end of . . . [Sontag's] life. . . . Every public and academic library should crave to own this." Libr J

★ **Styles** of radical will. Picador USA 2002 274p pa $15 **814**
1. Authors 2. Silence 3. Aesthetics 4. Pornography 5. Philosophers 6. Motion pictures 7. Vietnam War, 1961-1975 8. Essayists 9. Nonfiction writers 10. Theatrical directors 11. Motion picture directors 12. United States -- Moral conditions 13. United States -- Social conditions
ISBN 0-312-42021-8
LC 2001-58071

First published 1969 by Farrar, Straus & Giroux

"The book contains essays, some previously published, arranged in groups. The first group of three is aesthetic and philosophical; three deal with film; and the last set is . . . a reply to a Partisan Review questionnaire about America and an . . . essay on a trip to North Vietnam." Libr J

Where the stress falls; essays. Farrar, Straus & Giroux 2001 351p $25; pa $14 **814**
1. Poets 2. Authors 3. Dancers 4. Composers 5. Novelists 6. Dramatists 7. Journalists 8. Choreographers 9. Essayists 10. College teachers 11. Literary critics 12. Nonfiction writers 13. Short story writers 14. Sarajevo (Bosnia and Hercegovina)
ISBN 0-374-28917-4; 0-312-42131-1 pa
LC 2001-33704

The essays in this collection "are organized into three categories. 'Reading' encompasses Sontag's erudite, critical renderings on autobiography and the works and influence of international literary figures such as Machado de Assis, Roland Barthes, Danilo Kîs, Marina Tsvetaeva, and Robert Walser. In the middle section, 'Seeing,' Sontag is more approachable, expressing her perceptive and provocative opinions on cinema, garden history, photography, painting, opera, drama, and dance. Finally, in 'There and Now,' Sontag recounts her experiences in Sarajevo and her feelings regarding travel, activism, writing, and translations." Libr J

Spiegelman, Willard
Seven pleasures; essays on ordinary happiness. Farrar, Straus, and Giroux 2009 197p $23 **814**
1. Pleasure 2. Solitude 3. Happiness
ISBN 978-0-374-23930-5; 0-374-23930-4
LC 2008-45049

This book "explores a range of satisfactions to be enjoyed in the everyday life — or, to put it another way, in the no man's land between religion and pharmacology, what Mr. Spiegelman calls the 'twin pillars of the American happiness

industry.' Individual chapters focus on his own chief pleasures: reading, walking, looking, dancing, listening, swimming and writing. One theme of his 'book of gerunds' is that
ordinariness can yield much more pleasure than is normally
assumed. All the striving for happiness in our culture may
cause us to overlook the riches of the familiar and near to
hand." Wall Street J

Sullivan, John Jeremiah

Pulphead; essays. John Jeremiah Sullivan. Farrar, Straus and Giroux 2011 369p il   **814**
1. American essays
ISBN 9780374532901; 9781429995047
LC 2011024875

This book is a collection essays by John Jeremiah Sullivan. "Several are about music. There are meditations on
Axl Rose, on Christian rock, on Michael Jackson, on Bunny
Wailer and on the blues singer Geeshie Wiley. . . . [the book
also includes] a piece about caves in Tennessee; one about
sharing a house with . . . the last living member of the Southern Agrarian literary movement; one about an eccentric
19th-century naturalist who almost beat Darwin to the idea
of evolution." (New York Times)

"The age-old strangeness of American pop culture gets
dissected with hilarious and revelatory precision in these
scintillating essays. . . . [The author] surveys 10,000 years
of intriguing, inexplicable, and incorrigible socio-aesthetic
phenomena, from the ancient Indian cave paintings of Tennessee (and their hillbilly admirers) to the takeover of his
Wilmington, N.C., house by the teen soap opera One Tree
Hill. Along the way he visits a Christian rock festival brimming with fellowship and frog-devouring savagery; witnesses the collapse of civilization in a post-Katrina gas
line; hangs out in the professional-partying demimonde of
MTV's Real World; marches with exuberant Tea Partiers;
scouts the animal kingdom's gathering war on mankind;
and traces the rise of rocker Axl Rose from his origins as
a weedy adolescent punk in the small-town void of central
Indiana." Publ Wkly

Tan, Amy

The **opposite** of fate; a book of musings. Putnam 2003 398p il $24.95; pa $15   **814**
1. Authors 2. Novelists 3. Essayists 4. Children's
authors 5. Short story writers
ISBN 0-399-15074-9; 0-14-200489-8 pa
LC 2003-47190

This autobiography contains the author's "musings on
topics as varied as rock'n'roll, the film adaptation of The Joy
Luck Club, her reactions to the Cliff Notes' analysis of her
work and life, her recent health problems, and other autobiographical observations. The selections are culled from essays, speeches, interviews, and a commencement address."
Libr J

"No matter how much readers already revere Tan, their
appreciation for her will grow tenfold after experiencing
these provocative and unforgettable revelations." Booklist

Trillin, Calvin

Too soon to tell. Farrar, Straus & Giroux 1995
292p hardcover o.p. pa $22   **814**
ISBN 0-374-27846-6; 978-0-374-52986-4 pa; 0-374-

52986-8 pa
LC 94-24629

"In this collection of nearly 100 syndicated columns,
Calvin Trillin holds forth on everything from the animal
kingdom . . . to the possibility of being labeled a member of
the cultural elite. . . . 'Too Soon to Tell' abounds with Mr.
Trillin's self-deprecating humor and slyly acerbic insights,
not to mention invaluable homespun wisdom." N Y Times
Book Rev

Updike, John

Due considerations; essays and criticism. Alfred
A. Knopf 2007 xxii, 703p il $40   **814**
ISBN 978-0-307-26640-8; 0-307-26640-0
LC 2007-18665

"A lush book to be savored over a long period of
time." Booklist

Vonnegut, Kurt

★ A **man** without a country; edited by Daniel Si-
mon. Seven Stories Press 2005 146p il $23.95 **814**
ISBN 1-58322-713-X
LC 2005-14967

The author discusses politics, human nature, and other
topics "in this collection of articles written over the last five
years, many from the alternative magazine In These Times."
Publ Wkly

Walker, Alice, 1944-

The **cushion** in the road; meditation and wandering as the whole world awakens to being in harm's
way. Alice Walker. The New Press 2013 336 p.
(hardcover) $26.95   **814**
1. Essays 2. Political science
ISBN 1595588728; 9781595588722
LC 2012041852

This book, by Alice Walker, offers a "collection of wide-
ranging meditations. . . . [The book] revisits themes the . .
. [author] has addressed throughout her career: racism, Africa, solidarity with the Palestinian people, the presidential
campaign of Barack Obama, Cuba, healthcare, and the work
of Aung San Suu Kyi. In doing so, Walker explores her conflicting impulses to retreat into inner contemplation and to
remain deeply engaged with the world." (Publisher's note)

Wallace, David Foster, 1962-2008

Both flesh and not; essays. David Foster Wallace. Little, Brown and Co. 2012 328 p. $26.99 **814**
1. Short stories 2. American essays
ISBN 0316182370; 9780316182379; 9780316224116
LC 2012020794

The book is a collection of previously unpublished short
stories and essays by the late author David Foster Wallace.
"'Federer Both Flesh and Not' is a . . . critical study of tennis star Roger Federer at Wimbledon in 2006. . . . 'Fictional
Futures and the Conspicuously Young' is a . . .1988 essay on
the roots of what he felt was largely threadbare minimalist
fiction. 'The Empty Plenum,' an encomium to David Mark-

son's 1988 novel 'Wittgenstein's Mistress,' explores the philosophical machinery behind the book." (Kirkus Reviews)
Includes bibliographical references.

Consider the lobster; and other essays. Little, Brown 2005 343p il $25.95   **814**
ISBN 0-316-15611-6
LC 2005-10886
"Wallace's complex essays are written, and rightfully so, to be read more than once." Booklist
Includes bibliographical references

White, E. B.
Essays of E.B. White. Perennial Classics 1999 364p il pa $14.95   **814**
1. Ornithologists 2. Florida -- Description and travel 3. United States -- Politics and government 4. New York (N.Y.) -- Description and travel
ISBN 0-06-093223-6
LC 98-56019
First published 1977
Most of the essays first appeared in The New Yorker. "They range from a 1934 piece on the St. Nicholas Magazine 'League' and the distinguished writers who were members of it as children, to a 1975 report from Allen Cove, Maine, where White had retreated from the bedlam of the city." Publ Wkly

Williams, Terry Tempest
Finding beauty in a broken world. Pantheon Books 2008 419p $26   **814**
1. Aesthetics
ISBN 978-0-375-42078-8; 0-375-42078-9
LC 2008-7196
The naturalist author of Refuge and An Unspoken Hunger reflects on what it means to be human, the interconnection between the natural and human worlds, and how they combine to produce both tumult and peace, ugliness and beauty.
"Scientific in her exactitude, compassionate in her receptivity, and rhapsodic in expression, Williams has constructed a beautiful mosaic of loss and renewal that affirms, with striking lucidity, the need for reverence for all of life." Booklist
Includes bibliographical references

Williams, William Carlos
In the American grain. New Directions 1956 235p hardcover o.p. pa $13.95   **814**
1. Poets 2. Authors 3. Emperors 4. Diplomats 5. Explorers 6. Inventors 7. Statesmen 8. Scientists 9. Vice-presidents 10. Scouts 11. Pioneers 12. Essayists 13. Missionaries 14. Naval officers 15. Writers on science 16. Members of Congress 17. Short story writers 18. Colonial administrators
ISBN 0-8112-0230-5 pa
LC 56-13360
First published 1925 by A. & C. Boni
Williams portrays "the developing American conscience in sketches of such major figures as Columbus, Cotton Mather, Washington, Franklin, and Poe, and such minor ones as Champlain, Thomas Morton, Père Sebastian Rasles,

and Jacataqua. He sought the grain of American character especially in homely, rather than heroic, incidents of national history." Benet's Reader's Ency of Am Lit

Wilson, Edmund
Literary essays and reviews of the 1920s & 30s. Library of America 2007 958p $40   **814**
1. Modernism (Aesthetics) 2. Literature -- History and criticism
ISBN 978-1-59853-013-1
LC 2007-928898
This volume collects The Shores of Light (1952), a collection of his early reviews and other writings; and Axel's Castle (1931), a book of literary criticism discussing modernism. It also includes several previously uncollected reviews.
"Anyone wishing to revisit the intellectual and literary passions of the period will be well advised to do so in the company of someone who could be a Virgil as well as recommend the reading of him. Edmund Wilson came as close as anybody has to making the labor of criticism into an art." Atl Mon
Includes bibliographical references

Literary essays and reviews of the 1930s & 40s; [Lewis M. Dabney, editor] Library of America 2007 979p $40   **814**
1. Modernism (Aesthetics) 2. Literature -- History and criticism
ISBN 978-1-59853-014-8
LC 2007-928899
This volume gathers together The Triple Thinkers (1938, revised 1948), The Wound and The Bow (1941), Classics and Commercials (1950), along with a selection of uncollected reviews.
"This is a required purchase for all libraries, public and academic—even for those collections already having these texts in separate volumes." Libr J
Includes bibliographical references

Wiman, Christian
My bright abyss; meditation of a modern believer. Christian Wiman. Farrar, Straus and Giroux 2012 192 p. (hardcover) $24   **814**
1. Faith 2. Cancer 3. Religion and poetry 4. Christianity and literature
ISBN 0374216789; 9780374216788
LC 2012021271
This book is a collection of essays that forms award-winning poet Christian Wiman's memoir. It "springboards from a much talked about 2007 essay that laid out his condition, his dark night of the soul, and his reawakening faith. Like Jacob, Wiman wrestles with that which he will not release until he is blessed--and in fact he was, his cancer apparently in remission." (Publishers Weekly)

Wright, Evan
Hella nation; looking for happy meals in Kandahar, rocking the side pipe, wingnut's war against the gap, and other adventures with the totally lost tribes of America. G. P. Putnam's Sons 2009 388p il $25.95   **814**
1. Popular culture -- United States 2. United States --

Social life and customs
ISBN 978-399-15574-1; 0-399-15574-0
LC 2009-02291

"It's refreshing to read first-person journalism by an unorthodox P.T. Barnum who refuses to put himself at the center of a three-ring circus." Washington Post

815   American speeches in English

★ **American** speeches. Library of America 2006 2v ea $35   **815**
1. American speeches
ISBN 1-931082-97-9 v1; 1-931082-98-7 v2
LC 2006-40928

This is a collection of over 120 historical speeches delivered between 1761 and 1997.
Includes bibliographical references

816   American letters in English

Letters of the century; America, 1900-1999. edited by Lisa Grunwald and Stephen J. Adler. Dial Press (NY) 1999 741p il hardcover o.p. pa $18   **816**
1. American letters 2. United States -- Civilization
ISBN 0-385-31590-2; 0-385-31593-7 pa
LC 99-16808

Among the letter writers gathered are "Carl Van Doren, Huey Long, Franklin D. Roosevelt, Lillian Hellman and a Vietnam soldier named Dusty. This is one of the most original literary tributes to the closing century." Publ Wkly
Includes bibliographical references

816.1   American letters in English -- Philosophy and theory

Bernard, Emily
Carl Van Vechten and the Harlem Renaissance; a portrait in black and white. Emily Bernard. Yale University Press 2012 xiii, 358 p.p (cloth : alk. paper) : $30.00   **816.1**
1. Harlem Renaissance 2. African Americans in literature 3. Harlem (New York, N.Y.) -- Intellectual life -- 20th century 4. African Americans -- New York (State) -- New York -- Intellectual life
ISBN 0300121997; 9780300121995
LC 2011034190

This book presents a "biographical treatment of a significant figure in the explosion of black arts that was centered in Harlem in New York City in the 1920s and 1930s . . . As the author posits, Carl Van Vechten was a 'white man with a passion for blackness.' Movie critic, novelist, and photographer Van Vechten possessed enough of his own fame and influence that he could provide struggling black artists not only with emotional sustenance but also lead them to exposure to a wider commercial arena than they might have been able to enter on their own. [Emily] Bernard . . . interprets Van Vechten's life in terms of just how 'messy' was the 'tangle'

of white-black relations within the structure of the Harlem Renaissance." (Booklist)
Includes bibliographical references and index.

817   American humor and satire in English

Allen, Woody
Side effects. Ballantine 1987 213p pa $6.99 **817**
ISBN 978-0-345-34335-2; 0-345-34335-2
First published 1980 by Random House
"The sixteen sketches—which are concerned with themes of love and death, angst and despair, bagels and lox—appeared originally in magazines." Commonweal

Without feathers. Ballantine 1983 221p pa $6.99   **817**
ISBN 0-345-33697-6; 978-0-345-33697-2
First published 1975 by Random House
A collection of sixteen satirical sketches, most of which previously appeared in The New Yorker and other periodicals, and two one-act plays: God, and Death. The sketches include "takeoffs on other writers (Kafka, Bellow, Strindberg), and several 'intellectual' dissertations on such topics as the Irish genius, the origins of slang, the lesser ballets, psychic phenomena, etc." Libr J

Blount, Roy
Alphabet juice; the energies, gists and spirits of letters, words and combinations thereof: their roots, bones, innards, piths, pips and secret parts, tinctures, tonics and essences: with examples of their usage foul. Farrar, Straus and Giroux 2008 364p $25 **817**
1. Vocabulary 2. English language -- Dictionaries
ISBN 978-0-374-10369-9; 0-374-10369-0
LC 2008-08918

"Laid out in A–Z dictionary format, the book ranges from the pointed critique of conjunction dysfunction to the hilarious diatribe under tump, which finds Blount spending weeks looking for his own name in the new edition of American Heritage Dictionary. . . . Although some entries are only tangentially connected to his ostensible subject (see TV, on being on), many others provide Blount with ample opportunity to wax eloquent on the joys of language; his perfect parsing of the allure of the phrase 'wonky exegeses' will elicit smiles from fellow language lovers. A knowledgeable handbook that is also chock-full of funny, colorful opinions on marriage, movies, and Monet." Booklist

Carlin, George
Napalm & silly putty. Hyperion 2001 269p $22.95; pa $12.95   **817**
ISBN 0-7868-6413-3; 0-7868-8758-3 pa
LC 00-54055

The comedian "covers a wide range of issues from rape and religion to the homeless. . . . And any topic is fair game: abortion, airport security, cars, funerals, language, organ donors, sports, technology, TV and war. . . . Over 100 scintillating short pieces are interrupted by loony lists and hundreds of clever one-liners." Publ Wkly

Frazier, Ian

Coyote v. Acme. Picador USA 2002 117p pa $11 **817**

ISBN 0-312-42058-7; 978-0-312-42058-1

LC 2001-50067

First published 1996 by Farrar, Straus & Giroux

"The title essay, with its exposition, in deadly legalese, of one Wile E. Coyote's complaints against a generic purveyor of explosive devices, shows Frazier's great comic range, however trite the subject. Although this book is not Frazier at full-bore, readers of his generation will find an occasional cultural reference long thought lost, and find themselves oddly beholden to a fellow who can resurrect Billy Joe McCallister from beneath the Tallahatchie Bridge." Publ Wkly

Lamentations of the father. Farrar, Straus and Giroux 2008 194p il $22; pa $14 **817**

1. American wit and humor

ISBN 978-0-374-28162-5; 0-374-28162-9; 978-0-312-42835-8 pa; 0-312-42835-9 pa

LC 2008-2137

This is a collection of essays by the American humorist.

"A treat for Frazier fanatics and new readers alike, this compilation from the past 13 years has nary a misstep and begs to be read in one sitting." Publ Wkly

Mirth of a nation; the best contemporary humor. edited by Michael J. Rosen. HarperPerennial 2000 619p pa $15.95 **817**

1. American wit and humor

ISBN 0-06-095321-7

LC 99-44293

An anthology of more than 50 contributors, "most represented by two or three short works. Included are veterans like Dave Barry, Roy Blount Jr., and Fran Lebowitz, and rising stars like David Sedaris, Sandra Tsing Loh, Patricia Marx, and David Rakoff. Though many of the pieces have been published or broadcast previously, some appear in this volume for the first time." Booklist

Nilsen, Alleen Pace

Encyclopedia of 20th century American humor; [by] Alleen Pace Nilsen and Don L. F. Nilsen. Oryx Press 2000 360p il $73.95 **817**

1. Reference books 2. American wit and humor -- Encyclopedias

ISBN 1-57356-218-1

LC 99-47257

This "is a 98-entry reference work. A bibliography that includes scholarly works on humor, biographies, and joke books stretches over 20 pages and rounds out the text. Arranged alphabetically, articles vary in length from one to five pages. A few are illustrated with cartoons and photographs. Some longer articles are broken down into subtopics." Booklist

Includes bibliographical references

Peter, Laurence J.

The **Peter** principle; why things always go wrong. [by] Laurence J. Peter and Raymond Hull.

1st Collins Business ed.; Collins Business 2009 xxvi, 161p il $19.99 **817**

1. Management -- Anecdotes

ISBN 978-0-06-169906-1

LC 2008-44122

First published 1969

"In a delightful spoof of administrative inefficiency in both public and private enterprise, the authors expound their theory known as the Peter Principle—'in a hierarchy every employee tends to rise to his level of incompetence.' From this they develop their science of hierarchiology." Cincinnati Public Libr

Includes bibliographical references

Trillin, Calvin, 1935-

Quite enough of Calvin Trillin; forty years of funny stuff. Calvin Trillin. Random House 2011 340 p. (hardcover) $27.00 **817**

1. American wit and humor 2. Politicians -- Humor 3. Civilization -- Humor 4. Authors, American -- 20th century -- Biography

ISBN 1400069823; 0812982215; 9780812982213; 9781400069828; 9780679604808

LC 2011004050

This is "a collection of author-selected excerpts from [Calvin Trillin's] memoirs, satires, and novels includes entries ranging from descriptions of untraditional holiday celebrations to observations about literary pop culture. . . . He addresses the horrors of witnessing a voodoo economics ceremony and the mystery of how his mother managed for thirty years to feed her family nothing but leftovers. . . . He even skewers deserving political figures in poetry." (Publisher's note)

The author "entertains with this collection of his song lyrics, comic verse, and more than 130 of the brief essays he originally wrote for the New Yorker, the New York Times, the Nation, and his syndicated King Features column. . . . Trillin dances around a subject, examines it from different angles, and often finds fun in the commonplace throughout this huge and hilarious comedic compendium." Publ Wkly

Twain, Mark, 1835-1910

Mark Twain's library of humor; illustrated by E.W. Kemble; Steve Martin, series ed.; introduction by Roy Blount. Modern Library 2000 xl, 560p il pa $17 **817**

1. American wit and humor

ISBN 978-0-679-64036-3

LC 00-25971

"Beginning with the piece that made Mark Twain famous—'The Notorious Jumping Frog of Calaveras County'—and ending with his fanciful 'How I Edited an Agricultural Paper,' this . . . anthology, an abridgment of the 1888 original, collects twenty of Twain's own pieces, in addition to tall tales, fables, and satires by forty-three of Twain's contemporaries, including Washington Irving, Harriet Beecher Stowe, Ambrose Bierce, William Dean Howells, Joel Chandler Harris, Artemus Ward, and Bret Harte." Publisher's note

Weingarten, Gene

The **fiddler** in the subway; the true story of what happened when a world-class violinist played for handouts-- and other virtuoso performances by America's foremost feature writer. Simon & Schuster 2010 363p il **817**

1. American wit and humor

ISBN 978-1-4391-8159-1; 978-1-4391-8160-7 ebook

LC 2009-51668

"A sparkling collection of features by the Pulitzer Prize-winning Washington Post columnist. . . . There are plenty of smiles and laughs scattered throughout the uniformly strong pieces assembled here. But the author is about more than grins and giggles. In even the slightest of the essays—seeing his daughter off to college, honoring the memory of his childhood baseball hero—his storytelling, keen observation and deft reporting startle and amaze." Kirkus

818 American miscellaneous writings in English

Alcott, Louisa May

The **sketches** of Louisa May Alcott; with an introduction by Gregory Eiselein. Ironweed Press 2001 283p (Ironwood American classics) pa $22.95 **818**

ISBN 0-9655309-8-1

LC 00-57259

"Grouped into five categories ('Hospital sketches,' 'Letters from the Mountains,' 'Sketches of Europe,' 'Concord, Massachusetts,' and 'From The Youth's Companion and Merry's Museum),' these by turns frank, witty, ironic, charming and pensive pieces were almost all written when Alcott was between the ages of 28 and 43." Publ Wkly

Includes bibliographical references

Alvarez, Julia

A **wedding** in Haiti; Julia Alvarez. Algonquin Books of Chapel Hill 2012 287 p. **818**

1. Weddings 2. Friendship 3. Dominican Americans 4. Haiti Earthquake, Haiti, 2010 5. Haiti -- Description and travel 6. Haitians -- Dominican Republic -- Biography

ISBN 9781616201302

LC 2012000452

This book by Julia Alvarez presents a memoir "about her pre- and post-earthquake travels around the island of Hispaniola and the Haitian boy who inspired them. The author met Piti, . . . in 2001, on a chance visit to a coffee farm [in] . . . the Dominican Republic. . . . In 2009, she received a surprise call from Piti telling her that she was invited to his wedding. . . . Eventually Piti called . . . to help him care for his extended family in the aftermath of the 2010 earthquake." (Kirkus)

Angelou, Maya

A **song** flung up to heaven. Random House 2002 212p $23.95; pa $13 **818**

1. Poets 2. Actors 3. Singers 4. Dramatists 5. Essayists 6. Memoirists 7. Children's authors

ISBN 0-375-50747-7; 0-553-38203-9 pa

LC 2001-34914

"This sixth installment in Angelou's autobiographical works begins in 1964 as Angelou returned to the U.S. from Ghana. . . . She worked in Watts at the time of the riots, and Malcolm X and Martin Luther King Jr. were both assassi-nated just before she was to begin working with them. . . . She moved to New York, where she rejoined a vibrant group of famous writers, intellectuals, and friends; worried about her young-adult son; and understood the humor and heart-ache of a painful love affair. . . . Spiced with her mother's aphorisms, her often-poetic prose is best at the end, as she muses on the condition of black women and sitting at her mother's table, begins to write I Know Why the Caged Bird Sings." Booklist

Angelou, Maya, 1928-2014

Mom & me & mom; by Maya Angelou. 1st ed. Random House 2012 224 p. (ebook) $66.00; (hardcover) $22.00 **818**

1. Mother-daughter relationship 2. African American authors -- Biography 3. Entertainers -- United States -- Biography 4. Authors, American -- 20th century -- Biography

ISBN 1400066115; 9780679645474; 9781400066117

LC 2012022257

This memoir, by Maya Angelou, "shares . . . her relationship with her mother. . . . Angelou reveals the triumphs and struggles of being the daughter of Vivian Baxter. . . . Vivian famously sent three-year-old Maya and her older brother away from their California home to live with their grandmother in Stamps, Arkansas. The subsequent feelings of abandonment stayed with Angelou for years, but their reunion, a decade later, began a story that has never before been told." (Publisher's note)

Auster, Paul, 1947-

★ **Winter** journal; Paul Auster. Henry Holt and Co. 2012 240 p. **818**

1. Life 2. Death 3. Autobiographies 4. Authors, American -- 20th century -- Biography

ISBN 0805095535; 9780805095531

LC 2011039025

This memoir by Paul Auster presents a "meditation on death and life. . . . The stuff of everyday life--the childhood baseball games, the succession of New York and Paris apartments (21 in total), even the women longed for, two of whom became wives--and the events that shook and shaped him. From the vantage point of the winter preceding his 64th birthday, Auster lets his body and its sensations guide his memories. There is no set chronology; time and place [change] from one year to another, between childhood and adulthood." (Publishers Weekly)

Baraka, Imamu Amiri

The **LeRoi** Jones/Amiri Baraka reader; by Amiri Baraka; edited by William Harris in collaboration with Amiri Baraka. 2nd ed; Thunder's Mouth Press 2000 xxxiii, 586p pa $16.95 **818**

1. Poets 2. Clergy 3. Mayors 4. Authors 5. Dramatists 6. Blues music 7. African American music 8. Television personalities 9. Cuba 10. Essayists 11. Talk show hosts 12. Political leaders 13. Members of Parliament 14. Civil rights activists 15. Presidential candidates

ISBN 1-56025-238-3

LC 99-32364

First published 1991

A collection of Baraka's poems, plays, and other writings. "The selections included are arranged chronologically in four distinct periods: The Beat Period (1957-62), The Transitional Period (1963-65), The Black Nationalist Period (1965-74), and The Third World Marxist Period (1974-present)." Libr J [review of 1991 edition]

Includes bibliographical references

Bishop, Elizabeth

The **collected** prose; edited, with an introduction, by Robert Giroux. Farrar, Straus & Giroux 1984 xxii, 278p hardcover o.p. pa $16   **818**

ISBN 0-374-51855-6 pa

LC 83-16418

A collection of Bishop's autobiographical sketches and short stories

"Whether she is discussing the sensuous joys and dark fears of childhood or diamond mining and the preparation of food in Brazil, Elizabeth Bishop provides warm, unforced revelations on an array of topics. . . . A book to relish as well as to read." Choice

Includes bibliographical references

Poems, prose, and letters; [selected and edited by Robert Giroux and Lloyd Schwartz] Library of America 2008 979p $40   **818**

1. Criticism 2. Poetry -- By individual authors

ISBN 978-1-59853-017-9; 1-59853-017-8

LC 2007-935885

"From the quietly riveting photograph on the dust jacket through the thorough index, the book is an elegant achievement that one imagines even the scrupulous and discriminating Elizabeth Bishop would approve. . . . This generous new collection lets us make connections across boundaries among many genres: poems, some hitherto uncollected and some mighty rough; translations over many years from ancient Greek, French, Spanish, and Portuguese; 'Personal Essays, Reminiscences, and Reporting'; 'Literary Statements and Reviews'; . . . and letters." Yale Rev

Blount, Roy

Alphabetter juice, or, The joy of text; [by] Roy Blount, Jr. Farrar, Straus and Giroux 2011 283p $26; ebook $12.99   **818**

1. Vocabulary 2. American wit and humor 3. English language -- Dictionaries

ISBN 978-0-374-10370-5; 978-1-4299-2278-4 ebook

LC 2010-39937

This book "is almost a subgenre of its own, a reference book from a leading language expert that's also downright funny. . . . Anybody as eclectic as Blount is worth paying attention to; his passion for the sounds and senses of words makes this book infectiously fun reading for word lovers everywhere." Writer

Be sweet; a conditional love story. [by] Roy Blount, Jr. Harcourt Brace & Co. 1999 329p pa $17   **818**

1. Authors 2. Humorists 3. Sportswriters 4. Nonfiction writers

ISBN 0-15-600682-0; 978-0-15-600682-8

LC 99-15146

First published 1998 by Knopf

"Blount figures that at age 57 he has lived long enough to hunt for life-defining moments among sundry episodes, including his stint as coeditor of his college paper with presidential wanna-be Lamar Alexander, his days smokin' dope with '70s slugger Richie Allen when Blount was a Sports Illustrated reporter, and a slew of childhood memories." Booklist

Borich, Barrie Jean

Body geographic; Barrie Jean Borich. University of Nebraska Press 2013 272 p. (American lives) (paperback) $17.95   **818**

1. Minnesota 2. Chicago (Ill.) 3. Mind and body 4. Middle West -- Biography 5. Self-perception in women 6. Maps -- Psychological aspects 7. Lesbian authors -- United States -- Biography 8. Authors, American -- 20th century -- Biography 9. Middle West -- Geography -- Psychological aspects 10. Women -- Sexual behavior -- Psychological aspects

ISBN 0803239858; 9780803239852

LC 2012030607

Lambda Literary Awards Winner - Lesbian Memoir/Biography (2014)

This memoir, by Barrie Jean Borich, "turns personal history into an inspired reflection on the points where place and person intersect, where running away meets running toward, and where dislocation means finding oneself. One coordinate of Borich's story is Chicago . . . and the other is her own port of immigration, Minneapolis, the combined skylines of these two cities tattooed on Borich's own back." (Publisher's note)

Includes bibliographical references

Bryson, Bill

I'm a stranger here myself; notes on returning to America after 20 years away. Broadway Bks. 1999 288p hardcover o.p. pa $14.95   **818**

1. United States -- Description and travel 2. United States -- Social life and customs

ISBN 0-7679-0382-X pa

LC 99-18074

The author collects "columns on America he wrote weekly, while living in New Hampshire in the mid-to-late 1990s, for a British Sunday newspaper. Although he happily describes himself as dazzled by American ease, friendliness and abundance, Bryson has no trouble finding comic targets, among them fast food, computer efficiency and, ironically, American friendliness and putative convenience." Publ Wkly

Capote, Truman

Music for chameleons; new writing. Random House 1980 262p hardcover o.p. pa $13   **818**

ISBN 0-679-74566-1 pa

LC 79-5532

"There are three sections: one of short stories, or something like; one consisting of the 'In cold blood'-like 'short novel, Handcarved coffins;' and one called 'Conversational portraits,' which is precisely that." Choice

Carson, Anne

Decreation; poetry, essays, opera. Knopf 2005
245p $24.95 **818**
ISBN 1-4000-4349-2

LC 2004-63367

"Carson's inquiry into the paradoxical 'decreation' of the
self in the quest for the divine exemplifies her gift for joining
erudition with feeling, insight with wit, and a sense of cosmic continuity with personal liberation." Booklist

Cather, Willa

★ **Stories,** poems, and other writings. Library of
Am. 1992 1039p $35 **818**
ISBN 0-940450-71-2

LC 91-62294

This volume contains the novels Alexander's bridge
(1912) and My mortal enemy (1926); the poetry collection
April twilights, and other poems (1923); the essay collection Not under forty (1936); and the following short story
collections: Youth and the bright Medusa (1920); Obscure
destinies (1932); The old beauty, and others (1948); and uncollected stories from 1892-1929

Dick, Philip K.

The **exegesis** of Philip K. Dick; edited by Pamela
Jackson and Jonathan Lethem; Erik Davis, annota-
tions editor. Houghton Mifflin Harcourt 2011 944p
$40 **818**
1. Technology and civilization 2. Science fiction --
Authorship
ISBN 978-0-547-54925-5; 0-547-54925-3

LC 2011-28561

"'I sure have odd nights,' wrote Philip K. Dick in a July
1974 letter to a young woman writing her thesis on him. It's
a tremendous understatement, and its inclusion in the early
pages of The Exegesis — the long-awaited compendium of
the sci-fi writer's papers — acts as a palate cleanser, a wry
little weigh station wherein Dick pulls back from his own
dense, circuitous investigation of his visions; laughs a little
at himself; and then dives back in, allowing the reader to do
the same.... Dick wrote more than eight thousand pages in
the eight years leading up to his death in 1982, all in his attempts to decipher a series of visionary, multisensory experiences he had in February and March of '74 ('2-3-74') wherein he glimpsed a vast truth of the world." East Bay Express

Dillard, Annie

The **Annie** Dillard reader. HarperCollins Pubs.
1994 455p hardcover o.p. pa $15.95 **818**
ISBN 0-06-092660-0 pa

LC 94-19482

This reader includes Holy the firm; excerpts from Pilgrim at Tinker Creek, An American childhood, and Teaching
a stone to talk; and a reworked version of the 1978 short
story The living

"This selection of writings, chosen by Dillard herself,
provides a perfect sampling of her incisive, versatile, and
impeccable achievements." Booklist

Pilgrim at Tinker Creek. Harper & Row 1974
271p hardcover o.p. pa $14.95 **818**
1. Natural history -- Virginia
ISBN 0-06-123332-3 pa; 978-0-06-123332-6 pa

This work is "in an honored tradition of literature, not
quite environmentalism and not the philosophy of science,
it is rather the refraction of natural philosophy through the
prismatic conscience of art. Highly recommended for the
general reader—any general reader, anywhere—who wishes
to deepen his awareness of his yard of world and to reflect
upon it more profoundly." Choice

Teaching a stone to talk; expeditions and encounters. Harper & Row 1982 177p hardcover o.p.
pa $13 **818**
1. Natural history
ISBN 0-06-091541-2 pa

LC 82-47520

"In the fourteen pensées that make up this book {the au-
thor} bears witness, reflects on her observations of the order
and disorder, the splendor and horror of the natural world."
New Yorker

The **writing** life. Harper & Row 1989 111p
hardcover o.p. pa $11 **818**
1. Poets 2. Authors 3. Essayists 4. Literary critics 5.
Writers on nature
ISBN 0-06-091988-4 pa

LC 89-45034

The author "probes the sorcery that levitates her own
writing, discussing with clear eye and wry wit how, where
and why she writes." Publ Wkly

Eiseley, Loren C.

The **night** country; [by] Loren Eiseley; illustra-
tions by Leonard Everett Fisher; introduction to the
Bison Books edition by Gale E. Christianson. Univer-
sity of Nebraska Press 1997 240p il pa $19.95 **818**
ISBN 0-8032-6735-5; 978-0-8032-6735-0
First published 1971 by Scribner

These poetically expressed reflections "evoke a sense of
wonder and appreciation of nature and man's place in the
universe. The striking black-and-white illustrations preceding each chapter contribute to the mood and tone." Booklist
Includes bibliographical references

The **star** thrower. Harcourt 1979 319p pa
$15 **818**
ISBN 978-0-15-684909-8; 0-15-684909-7
First published 1978 by Times Bks.

A collection of the late scientist's essays and poems.
"The materials are arranged in three categories, 'Nature and
Autobiography,' 'Early Poems,' and 'Science and Human-
ism.'" Christ Sci Monit

"To read this collection is to see the things he points out
to us refracted, transmuted, and clarified through the prism
of his poetic imagination and literate style." Libr J

Ellison, Ralph

★ **Going** to the territory. Random House 1986 338p hardcover o.p. pa $14.95   **818**

1. Artists 2. Authors 3. Composers 4. Novelists 5. Dramatists 6. Jazz musicians 7. Essayists 8. Band leaders 9. Nonfiction writers 10. Short story writers
ISBN 978-0-679-76001-6 pa; 0-679-76001-6 pa

LC 85-28117

"This collection of essays, addresses, and reviews deals with topics in literature, music, and race relations. . . . Ellison tries to view American culture as a cloth of one piece. His analysis of the growth of the culture, and of the dynamic interaction of the diverse elements within it, is perceptive and convincing." Libr J

Franklin, Benjamin

★ **Autobiography,** Poor Richard, and later writings; letters from London, 1757-1775, Paris, 1776-1785, Philadelphia, 1785-1790, Poor Richard's almanack, 1733-1758, The autobiography. Library of America 1997 816p $30   **818**

ISBN 1-883011-53-1

LC 97-21611

"This collection of Franklin's works begins with letters sent from London (1757-1775) describing the events and diplomacy preceding the Revolutionary War. The volume also contains political satires, bagatelles, pamphlets, and letters written in Paris (1776-1785), where he represented the revolutionary United States at the court of Louis XVI, as well as his speeches given in the Constitutional Convention and other works written in Philadelphia (1785-1790), including his last published article, a . . . satire against slavery. Also included are the . . . prefaces to Poor Richard's Almanack (1733-1758). . . . [The] Autobiography, Franklin's last word on his greatest literary creation—his own invented personality—is presented here in a new edition." Publisher's note
Includes bibliographical references

Gibran, Kahlil

The **collected** works; with eighty-four illustrations by the author. Everyman's Library 2007 880p il $27.50   **818**

ISBN 978-0-307-26707-8; 0-307-26707-5

LC 2007-28736

This anthology of writings by the Syrian poet includes The Madman, The Forerunner, The Prophet, Sand and Foam, Jesus the Son of Man, Earth Gods, The Wanderer, The Garden of the Prophet, Prose Poems, Spirits Rebellious, Nymphs of the Valley, and A Tear and a Smile.

Hearn, Lafcadio

★ **American** writings; [edited by Christopher Benfey] Library of America 2009 848p il $40 **818**

ISBN 978-1-59853-039-1

LC 2008-938732

"Some Chinese Ghosts (1887), a stylized retelling of ancient legends, foreshadows Hearn's later fascination with Asian themes. The . . . novels Chita (1889), about the devastation wrought by a Louisiana hurricane, and Youma (1890), about a slave rebellion in Martinique, epitomize his writing at its most luxuriantly romantic. . . [His] travel book Two Years in the French West Indies (1890), presented here with the many illustrations from its first edition, provides a richly impressionistic account of his long stay on Martinique and other Caribbean islands. More than two dozen examples of Hearn's journalism from the 1870s and 1880s are also included here." Publisher's note

Hogan, Linda

The **woman** who watches over the world; a native memoir. Norton 2001 224p $24.95; pa $13.95   **818**

1. Poets 2. Authors 3. Novelists 4. Dramatists 5. Native Americans 6. Essayists 7. Short story writers
ISBN 0-393-05018-1; 0-393-32305-6 pa

LC 00-49005

In this memoir the author chronicles "her difficult childhood, alcoholism, the anguish of her two psychologically damaged adopted children, and struggles with a neuromuscular disease. She also expresses a lacerating yet crucial vision of the tragic legacies of the U.S. government's brutal war on Native Americans." Booklist

Hughes, Langston

★ **I** wonder as I wander; an autobiographical journey. introd. by Arnold Rampersad. 2nd Hill and Wang ed; Hill & Wang 1993 xxii, 405p (American century series) pa $16   **818**

1. Poets 2. Authors 3. Novelists 4. Dramatists 5. African American authors 6. Poets, American 7. Short story writers 8. Young adult authors
ISBN 0-8090-1550-1

LC 92-39307

First published 1956 by Rinehart
Continuing the autobiography begun in The big sea (1940), this volume contains an account of Hughes' journeys through Russia, Spain, China, and Japan, as well as some incidents of his poetry readings in this country

Jefferson, Thomas, 1743-1826

Writings. Library of Am. 1984 1600p $35 **818**

ISBN 0-940450-16-X

LC 83-19917

"Autobiography—A summary view of the rights of British America—Notes on the State of Virginia—Public papers—Addresses, messages, and replies—Miscellany—Letters." Title page
This is "the largest and most skillfully edited single-volume Jefferson ever published." N Y Times Book Rev
Includes bibliographical references

Johnson, James Weldon

The **essential** writings of James Weldon Johnson; edited and with an introduction by Rudolph P. Byrd; foreword by Charles Johnson. Modern Library 2008 xxx, 321p (Modern library classics) pa $15   **818**

ISBN 978-0-8129-7532-1; 0-8129-7532-4

"This collection of poetry, fiction, criticism, autobiography, political writing and two unpublished plays by James Weldon Johnson (1871-1938) spans 60 years of pure triumph over adversity. . . . [Johnson's] nobility, his inspiration shine forth from these pages, setting moral and artistic standards." Los Angeles Times Book Rev

Johnson, Joyce, 1935-

★ The **voice** is all; the lonely victory of Jack Kerouac. Joyce Johnson. Viking 2012 xx, 489 p.p $32.95   **818**

1. American authors -- Biography 2. Beat generation -- Biography 3. Authors, American -- 20th century -- Biography

ISBN 0670025100; 9780670025107

LC 2012000603

In this biography of Jack Kerouac, author Joyce Johnson "peels away layers of the Kerouac legend to show how, caught between two cultures and two languages, he forged a voice to contain his dualities. Looking . . . into how Kerouac's French Canadian background enriched his prose and gave him a unique outsider's vision of America, she tracks his development from boyhood through the phenomenal breakthroughs of 1951." (Publisher's note)

Includes bibliographical references (p 439-471) and index

Kaling, Mindy, 1979-

Is everyone hanging out without me? (and other concerns) Mindy Kaling. Crown Archetype 2011 ix, 222 p.p ill   **818**

1. Actresses 2. American essays 3. American wit and humor

ISBN 9780307886262; 9780307886286

LC 2011033922

'In this book, author "Mindy Kaling . . . [offers thoughts about what she] thinks makes a great best friend (someone who will fill your prescription in the middle of the night), or what makes a great guy (one who is aware of all elderly people in any room at any time and acts accordingly), or what is the perfect amount of fame (so famous you can never get convicted of murder in a court of law), or how to maintain a trim figure (you will not find that information in these pages). . . . Mindy invites readers on a tour of her life and her unscientific observations on romance, friendship, and Hollywood." (Publisher's note)

Kiernan, Frances

Seeing Mary plain: a life of Mary McCarthy. Norton 2000 845p il $35; pa $25   **818**

1. Authors 2. Novelists 3. Essayists 4. Memoirists 5. Literary critics 6. Short story writers

ISBN 0-393-03801-7; 0-393-32307-2 pa

LC 99-41098

Kiernan uses "her interviews with more than 200 sources to provide multiple points of view on McCarthy's life and work. McCarthy knew most of her generation's literary leading lights, from the Partisan Review crowd to anti-Vietnam activists. . . . Each chapter includes commentary by McCarthy, friends, ex-lovers, admirers, and adversaries." Booklist

Includes bibliographical references

Kingston, Maxine Hong

The **fifth** book of peace. Knopf 2003 401p $26; pa $14.95   **818**

1. Peace 2. Vietnam War, 1961-1975

ISBN 0-679-44075-5; 0-679-76063-6 pa

LC 2002-34103

When "Kingston embarked on a sequel to her delightful novel 'Tripmaster Monkey,' she called it 'The Fourth Book of Peace,' echoing a half-remembered Chinese legend about Three Books of Peace. But the manuscript was destroyed in a fire—a suggestive occurrence to Kingston, because the books in the legend were also burned. Here she recreates her lost fictional narrative and sets it alongside an account of her life after the fire. . . . The book is rich in empathy and moral conviction." New Yorker

Liebling, A. J.

The **sweet** science and other writings; [edited by Pete Hamill] Library of America 2009 1057p $40   **818**

ISBN 978-1-59853-040-7

"The Sweet Science (1956) offers a lively and idiosyncratic portrait of boxing in the early 1950s that encompasses boastful managers, veteran trainers, wily cornermen, and the fighters themselves: Joe Louis, Rocky Marciano, Sugar Ray Robinson, and Archie Moore. . . . The Earl of Louisiana (1961) is a vivid account of Governor Earl Long's bid for re-election after his release from a mental asylum in 1959—and an insightful look at Southern politics during the civil rights era. The Jollity Building (1962) collects hilarious stories about Manhattan cigar-store owners, nightclub promoters, and the scheming 'Telephone Booth Indians' of Broadway. . . Between Meals: An Appetite for Paris (1962) is a . . . memoir of Liebling's lifelong love for Paris and French food and wine. The Press (1964) brings together the best of Liebling's influential 'Wayward Press' pieces." Publisher's note

Manguel, Alberto

A **reader** on reading. Yale University Press 2010 308p il $27.50   **818**

1. Books and reading

ISBN 978-0-300-15982-0; 0-300-15982-X

LC 2009-43719

"Lectures, columns, and other occasional writings are gathered here to form a meditation on 'the art of reading.' Thoughtful interrogations of the value of identity labels like 'Jewish fiction' or 'gay fiction' and the relationship between writers and editors mix with ruminations on the 'ideal reader' and the 'ideal library.' Several autobiographical essays detail a restless life that has taken Manguel from Buenos Aires to Tel Aviv, Canada, and, eventually, France, and an equally restless reading life. Predictable touchstones emerge—Dante and Homer, Shakespeare and Cervantes. Above all, there is Manguel's countryman Borges; he recalls reading aloud to the blind master as a young man in Argentina." New Yorker

Includes bibliographical references

Matthiessen, Peter

The **Peter** Matthiessen reader; nonfiction 1959-1991. edited with an introduction by McKay Jenkins. Vintage Bks. 2000 359p pa $14   **818**

ISBN 0-375-70272-5

LC 99-35246

Excerpts and essays highlighting the spiritual, literary, and political aspects of Matthiessen's work from Wildlife in America to Men's lives

McMurtry, Larry

Walter Benjamin at the Dairy Queen; reflections at sixty and beyond. Simon & Schuster 1999 204p il hardcover o.p. pa $12   **818**
1. Authors 2. Novelists 3. Essayists 4. Short story writers
ISBN 0-684-87019-3 pa

LC 99-19346

"When McMurtry recalls reading 'Don Quixote' as a thirteen-year-old on a Texas ranch and imagining himself as a character in the novel, other obsessional readers will immediately feel a kinship with this author. His appealing ruminations about his life and work as a reader, writer, and bookseller explore the differences between 'dense and empty, open and closed, new country and old cities, no society and old society'—the bare land in which he was reared and the crowded universe of literature." New Yorker

Mencken, H. L.

My life as author and editor; edited and with an introduction by Jonathan Yardley. Knopf 1993 xxi, 449p $30; pa $25   **818**
1. Authors 2. Essayists 3. Philologists 4. Social critics 5. Literary critics 6. Newspaper editors
ISBN 0-679-41315-4; 0-679-74102-X pa

LC 92-4496

An "absorbing memoir that anyone who cares about modern American literature will want to read." N Y Times Book Rev

A **second** Mencken chrestomathy; a new selection from the writings of America's legendary editor, critic, and wit. selected, revised, and annotated by the author; edited and with an introduction by Terry Teachout. Johns Hopkins University Press 2006 528p (Maryland paperback bookshelf) pa $35 **818**
ISBN 0-8018-8549-3

LC 2006-11581

First published 1995 by Knopf
"Mencken edited the first Chrestomathy himself in 1948. He called it 'a sort of Mencken Encyclopedia,' but noted that he had 'an excess of copied material about equal in bulk to the matter now in the book.' Mr. Teachout . . . has organized the unused material into discrete sections and provided titles and chapter headings—as well as performing a substantial amount of copy editing." Booklist

Miller, Henry

Henry Miller on writing; selected by Thomas H. Moore from the published and unpublished works of Henry Miller. New Directions 1964 216p pa $11.95   **818**
ISBN 0-8112-0112-0
The author discusses the art and practice of writing with insights on how he set his goals, how he discovered the excitement of using words, how the books he read influenced him, and how he learned to draw on his own experiences

The **moment;** edited by Larry Smith. Harper Perennial 2012 344p.   **818**
1. Autobiographies 2. American authors 3. American literature -- 21st century 4. Authors, American -- 21st century -- Biography
ISBN 9780061719653; 9780062099211

LC 2011033766

This book contains "stories of life-changing events from a cadre of ready, self-aware authors, each done in a page or two. A short selection of the contributors: A.J. Jacobs, Melissa Etheridge, Gregory Maguire, Dave Eggers, Elizabeth Gilbert, Jennifer Egan and Judy Collins. There are many 'wake-up calls,' some smiles and plenty of tears in these first-person explorations of a few eternal truths. Each of the 125 participants . . . tell of coming out and hiding, of seeking the light, the path, the truth, the way and/or the writers' inner selves. Those goals were achieved by aid of a word, sign, teacher, family road trip, some dope, an inner voice or, more than once, a Eurail pass." (Kirkus)

"Each author's ability to concisely describe such big moments pulls the reader in. Book and writing groups will have a lot to talk about after reading this first-rate collection." (Libr J)

★ The **Oxford** companion to Mark Twain; editor, Gregg Camfield. Oxford Univ. Press 2003 xxi, 767p il $75   **818**
1. Authors 2. Humorists 3. Novelists 4. Essayists 5. Satirists 6. Memoirists 7. Travel writers 8. Short story writers
ISBN 0-19-510710-1

LC 2002-151880

This volume "begins with 300 alphabetically arranged entries of varying lengths devoted to all [Twain's] works, places and people related to his life, and analyses of his views on a variety of topics, from animals to spiritualism. Next come a bibliography of his published works collated from other bibliographies, a chronology, and a general index." Choice
Includes bibliographical references

Parker, Dorothy

The **portable** Dorothy Parker; with a new introduction by Brendan Gill. rev and enl ed; Viking 1973 xxvii, 610p hardcover o.p. pa $18   **818**
ISBN 978-0-14-303953-2; 0-14-303953-9
First published 1944 with title: Dorothy Parker
This collection contains: thirty-two short stories; poems; drama reviews; book reviews, including the entire text of Constant reader; and miscellaneous articles
"It is hard to imagine a library that would not want this book." Choice

Percy, Walker (1993)

Lost in the cosmos; the last self-help book. Picador 2000 262p pa $14   **818**
ISBN 0-312-25399-0

LC 99-87846

A reissue of the title first published 1983 by Farrar, Straus & Giroux

"The whole is brought off with that sly humor and intellectual verve that have made the author's novels exceptional." Natl Rev

Signposts in a strange land; edited with an introduction by Patrick Samway. Picador 2000 428p pa $15   **818**

ISBN 0-312-25419-9

LC 99-89573

A reissue of the title first published 1991 by Farrar, Straus & Giroux

This collection's "speeches, interviews, and essays (some published for the first time) investigate various aspects of Percy's lifelong interests: the South; science, language, and literature; and morality and religion." Booklist

Includes bibliographical references

Plath, Sylvia, 1932-1963

The **unabridged** journals of Sylvia Plath, 1950-1962; edited by Karen V. Kukil. Anchor Press 2000 732p il pa $18   **818**

1. Poets 2. Authors 3. Novelists
ISBN 0-385-72025-4

LC 00-42024

First published 2000 in the United Kingdom with title: Journals of Sylvia Plath, 1950-1962

"This is essential for anyone engaged in Plath studies." Libr J

Includes bibliographical references

Poe, Edgar Allan, 1809-1849

★ **Poetry** and tales. Library of Am. 1984 1408p $37.50   **818**

ISBN 0-940450-18-6

LC 83-19931

This volume contains 70 stories and Poe's poetic work in its entirety

Includes bibliographical references

Rampersad, Arnold

★ The **life** of Langston Hughes Volume II: 1941-1967; I dream a world. 2nd ed; Oxford Univ. Press 2002 576p il hardcover o.p. pa $33   **818**

1. Poets 2. Authors 3. Novelists 4. Dramatists 5. African American authors 6. Poets, American 7. Short story writers 8. Young adult authors
ISBN 0-19-515161-5; 0-19-514643-3 pa

LC 2001-58766

First published 1988

This second volume of a two-volume biography of the Harlem Renaissance poet and author "finds Hughes rooting himself in Harlem, receiving stimulation from his rich cultural surroundings. Here he rethought his view of art and radicalism, and cultivated relationships with younger, more militant writers such as Richard Wright, Ralph Ellison, James Baldwin, and Amiri Bakara." Publisher's note

Includes bibliographical references

Rasmussen, R. Kent

Critical companion to Mark Twain; a literary reference to his life and work. with critical commentary

by John H. Davis and Alex Feerst. Rev ed; Facts on File 2007 2v il map (Facts on File library of American literature) set $125   **818**

1. Authors 2. Humorists 3. Novelists 4. Essayists 5. Satirists 6. Memoirists 7. Travel writers 8. Short story writers
ISBN 0-8160-5398-7; 978-0-8160-5398-8

LC 2004-46910

First published 1995 in one volume with title: Mark Twain A to Z

This companion to the life and works of Mark Twain includes a biography, synopses and critical commentaries on each of his works, discussions about major characters and places in his works, and entries on important people, places, and other aspects of his life.

Includes glossary, filmography and bibliographical references

Rollyson, Carl E.

Susan Sontag; the making of an icon. {by} Carl Rollyson and Lisa Paddock. Norton 2000 370p il $29.95   **818**

1. Authors 2. Novelists 3. Essayists 4. Literary critics 5. Short story writers
ISBN 0-393-04928-0

LC 00-20402

The authors "have unearthed a deluge of information on Sontag's personal life—on her early years and family life, her lesbianism. . . her relationship with son David Rieff and her battles with breast cancer. While the authors provide an intelligent, though not strikingly original, analysis of her work, they are best at detailing how Sontag and her publishers have marketed her image as much as her thought." Publ Wkly

Includes bibliographical references

Rothbart, Davy

My heart is an idiot; Davy Rothbart. Farrar, Straus and Giroux 2012 307 p. (alk. paper) $25 **818**

1. Wit and humor 2. American essays 3. American wit and humor
ISBN 0374280843; 9780374280840

LC 2012003821

This book, by Davy Rothbart, is a collection of personal essays. "Davy Rothbart is looking for love in all the wrong places. . . . He's continually coming up with outrageous schemes. . . . But even when things don't work out, Rothbart finds meaning and humor in every moment. Whether it's humiliating a scammer who takes money from aspiring writers or playing harmless . . . goofs on his deaf mother, nothing and no one is off-limits." (Publisher's note)

Silko, Leslie

Storyteller. Arcade Publishing 1989 278p pa $17.95   **818**

ISBN 978-1-55970-005-4; 1-55970-005-X

First published 1981 by Seaver Books

This "consists of short stories, anecdotes, folktales, poems, historical and autobiographical notes, and photographs." N Y Times Book Rev

Sontag, Susan, 1933-2004

As consciousness is harnessed to flesh; journals and notebooks, 1964-1980. Susan Sontag ; edited by David Rieff. Farrar, Straus and Giroux 2012 xii, 523 p.p **818**

1. Politics 2. Art criticism 3. American essays 4. American authors -- Biography 5. Authors, American -- 20th century -- Diaries

ISBN 0374100764; 9780374100766

LC 2011041210

This book, "the second of three volumes of Susan Sontag's journals and notebooks, begins where the first volume left off, in the middle of the 1960s. It traces and documents Sontag's evolution from fledgling participant in the artistic and intellectual world of New York City to world-renowned critic and dominant force in the world of ideas with the publication of the groundbreaking 'Against Interpretation' in 1966. 'As Consciousness is Harnessed to Flesh' follows Sontag through the turbulent years of the 1960s—from her trip to Hanoi at the peak of the Vietnam War to her time making films in Sweden—up to 1981 and the beginning of the Reagan era." (Publisher's note)

Sova, Dawn B.

Critical companion to Edgar Allan Poe; a literary reference to his life and work. Facts on File 2007 458p il (Facts on File library of American literature) $75 **818**

1. Poets 2. Authors 3. Essayists 4. Short story writers

ISBN 0-8160-6408-3; 978-0-8160-6408-3

LC 2006-29466

First published 2001 with title: Edgar Allan Poe, A-Z

"Biographical, historical, and critical material on Poe's life and work is presented in alphabetical order in three sections. The entries on Poe's works each provide a synopsis, a publication history, and character descriptions, while major works such as 'The Cask of Amontillado' and 'The Purloined Letter' have . . . [a] commentary and . . . further-reading suggestions." SLJ

Includes bibliographical references

Stein, Gertrude, 1876-1947

Writings, 1903-1932. Library of Am. 1998 941p $40 **818**

ISBN 978-1-883011-40-6; 1-883011-40-X

LC 97-28915

In Stein's "early works, she sought a new kind of realism exemplified here by Q.E.D. (written 1903, published posthumously), a novel about lesbian entanglements at college, and the modern classic Three Lives (1909), a set of novellas about the lives of three ordinary women, described in the simplest and most direct of prose. In her . . . abstract 'portraits' Stein uses an extraordinary array of verbal techniques to evoke those friends and collaborators—Matisse, Picasso, Apollinaire, Juan Gris, Satie, Mabel Dodge, Carl Van Vechten, Sherwood Anderson, Virgil Thomson—with whom she shared decades of revolutionary ferment in the arts. Her play Four Saints in Three Acts (1927), which became the basis for an opera by Virgil Thomson, is written for a freewheeling theater of the mind where everything becomes possible. In 'Lifting Belly' and other works she joyously celebrates her lifelong relationship with Alice B. Toklas, one of the most famous domestic partnerships of that century. The Autobiography of Alice B. Toklas (1933), Stein's oblique and playful memoir, became an immediate bestseller and sealed Stein's international celebrity." Publisher's note

★ Writings, 1932-1946. Library of Am. 1998 844p $40 **818**

ISBN 1-883011-41-8

LC 97-28916

In addition to theater pieces, fiction, and poetry "memoir, philosophical speculation, literary criticism and theory, all sorts of briefer forms that are hard to account for but easy to marvel at and even to delight in, pack these volumes, and constitute, as the editors surely intended us to discover, the most consistently achieved representation of new ways of responding to life and new possibilities of getting experience into words that American literature has to show." N Y Times Book Rev

Thompson, Hunter S.

The great shark hunt; strange tales from a strange time. Summit Bks. 1979 602p hardcover o.p. pa $16 **818**

ISBN 0-7432-5045-1 pa

LC 79-831

"A retrospective in journalistic theater, this gathers together excerpts from Thompson's 'Fear and Loathing in Las Vegas' and 'Fear and Loathing on the Campaign Trail,' plus his reportage from such diverse journals as 'Rolling Stone,' 'Playboy,' 'The New York Times,' etc., going back to 1962." Publ Wkly

Includes bibliographical references

Thoreau, Henry David, 1817-1862

★ Collected essays and poems. Library of Am. 2001 703p $35 **818**

ISBN 1-883011-95-7

LC 00-46234

Among the 27 essays included are Civil disobedience, Walking, Martyrdom of John Brown, A Yankee in Canada, and Life without principle. Many of the poems were taken from Thoreau's journals and manuscripts

Includes bibliographical references

★ Walden, or, Life in the woods; with an introduction by Verlyn Klinkenborg. Knopf 1992 xxxi, 295p $19 **818**

ISBN 0-679-41896-2

LC 92-54444

First published 1854

"Philosophy of life and observations of nature drawn from the author's solitary sojourn of two years in a cabin on Walden Pond near Concord, Massachusetts." Pratt Alcove

Includes bibliographical references

A week on the Concord and Merrimack rivers; Walden, or, Life in the woods; The Maine woods; Cape Cod. Library of Am. 1985 1114p il $35 **818**

ISBN 0-940450-27-5

LC 85-5175

"Politically the most conscious of the Transcendentalists, an acute observer of natural and social facts, Thoreau was an outstanding prose stylist." Reader's Ency

Includes bibliographical references

Thursby, Jacqueline S.

Critical companion to Maya Angelou; a literary reference to her life and work. Facts On File 2011 430p il (Facts on File of American literature) $75   **818**

1. Poets 2. Actors 3. Singers 4. Dramatists 5. Essayists 6. Memoirists 7. Children's authors

ISBN 978-0-8160-8093-9; 978-1-4381-3610-3 ebook

LC 2010032716

Coverage includes a "biography of Angelou; entries on all of Angelou's major works, including all six of her book-length autobiographies, her major poems and poetry collections, her major essays and essay collections, her children's books, and more; entries on the autobiographical works contain subentries on the main figures in the work; entries on related people, places, and topics, such as Harlem, Michelle Obama, racism, San Francisco, and more; [and] appendixes, including chronologies, a bibliography of Angelou's works, and a secondary source bibliography." Publisher's note

Includes bibliographical references

Trethewey, Natasha D., 1966-

Beyond Katrina; a meditation on the Mississippi Gulf Coast. University of Georgia Press 2010 127p il   **818**

1. Hurricane Katrina, 2005 2. African Americans -- Mississippi

ISBN 0-8203-3381-6; 978-0-8203-3381-6

LC 2010011417

A collection of essays, poems, and letters, chronicling the effects of Hurricane Katrina on the Mississippi Gulf Coast.

"By looking at the vast devastation with sober and poetic eyes, Trethewey has written a hauntingly beautiful book." Publ Wkly

Twain, Mark, 1835-1910

The **wit** and wisdom of Mark Twain; edited by Alex Ayres. Harper & Row 1987 265p hardcover o.p. pa $13.95   **818**

ISBN 978-0-06-075104-3 pa; 0-06-075104-5 pa

LC 87-45020

The editor "provides systematic access to plenty of Twain's bon mots by arranging them in a dictionary of topics from Adam to youth. . . . Where background is needed, Ayres supplies it succinctly and, as an afterword, proffers 'What Mark Twain might say today' on such ponderables as communism, extraterrestrial intelligence, the national debt, terrorism, and the unborn. Much to Ayres' credit, many of these approximations sound markedly Twainian." Booklist

Includes bibliographical references

Updike, John, 1932-2009

Higher gossip; essays and criticism. edited by Christopher Carduff. 1st ed. Alfred A. Knopf

2011 528 p. ill. ebook $21.99; (hbk.) $40; (pbk.) $20   **818**

ISBN 9780307957177; 9780307957153; 9780812983685

LC 2011013586

This book is a "collection of miscellaneous prose [that] opens with a self-portrait of the writer in winter. . . . It concludes with a . . . meditation on a modern world robbed of imagination--a world without religion, without art--and on the difficulties of faith in a disbelieving age. In between are previously uncollected stories and poems, a pageant of scenes from seventeenth-century Massachusetts, five late 'golf dreams,' and several of Updike's commentaries on his own work. At the heart of the book are his . . . reviews--of John Cheever, Ann Patchett, Toni Morrison, William Maxwell, John le Carré, and essays on Aimee Semple McPherson, Max Factor, and Albert Einstein, among others. Also included are two decades of art criticism--on Chardin, El Greco, Blake, Turner, Van Gogh, Max Ernest, and more." (Publisher's note)

This is a compilation of "nearly 100 uncollected pieces by 'the preeminent literary journalist of our times.' Predominantly comprising literary and art criticism from a range of magazines, the volume also embraces poetry, fiction, memoir, and Updike's comments on his own work." Publ Wkly

Von Mehren, Joan

Minerva and the muse: a life of Margaret Fuller. University of Mass. Press 1995 398p il $40; pa $20.95   **818**

1. Feminists 2. Biographers 3. Social reformers

ISBN 0-87023-941-4; 1-55849-015-9 pa

LC 94-18663

"Von Mehren is sympathetic to Fuller's lifelong struggle to achieve fame and public acclamation for her views on Transcendentalism and feminism, but she balances her sympathy with objectivity and distance." Libr J

Includes bibliographical references

Walsh, John Evangelist (1558)

Midnight dreary; the mysterious death of Edgar Allan Poe. St. Martin's Minotaur 2000 199p il pa $14.95   **818**

1. Poets 2. Authors 3. Essayists 4. Short story writers

ISBN 0-312-22732-9; 978-0-312-22732-6

LC 00-25571

First published 1998 by Rutgers Univ. Press

This is an account of the "circumstances leading to Poe's death in Baltimore, in October 1849." Publ Wkly

Walsh "has undertaken a superbly informed speculation on the week proceeding the mysterious death of Edgar Allan Poe 150 years ago." Libr J

Includes bibliographical references

Wayne, Tiffany K.

Critical companion to Ralph Waldo Emerson; a literary reference to his life and work. Facts On File 2010 444p il (Facts on File library of American literature) $75   **818**

1. Poets 2. Authors 3. Philosophers 4. Essayists

ISBN 978-0-8160-7358-0; 978-1-4381-3048-4 ebook

LC 2009-24809

"This reference book examines the life and works of a central thinker in American history. . . . It begins with Emerson's biography for context. Part 2 focuses on 140 significant (in the view of scholars) individual works, including 60 poems (most with one to three pages of synopses, critical commentary, and further reading). Part 3 covers related people, places, and topics. . . . The final appendixes offer a chronology of Emerson's life and times, bibliographies of both his works and relevant secondary sources." Choice

Includes bibliographical references. 'Bibliography of Emerson's works': p. 406-407. (BLCM)

820 English and Old English (Anglo-Saxon) literatures

★ The **Cambridge** guide to literature in English; edited by Dominic Head. 3rd ed; Cambridge University Press 2006 xxiii, 1241p il $50 **820**
1. Reference books 2. English literature -- Dictionaries 3. American literature -- Dictionaries 4. English literature -- Bio-bibliography
ISBN 978-0-521-83179-6; 0-521-83179-2
LC 2006-271458
First published 1988 under the editorship of Ian Ousby
"The scope of material covered . . . extends to the literature of the United Kingdom and well beyond: Africa, Asia, Australia, Canada, the Caribbean, India, New Zealand, and the U.S. are all well represented. . . . Literary terms are explained, literary movements are summarized, and literary magazines are sketched in unsigned entries ranging in length from a few lines to a few paragraphs or more. . . . With its broad coverage, clearly written and accessible text, and relatively modest price, this is a must purchase for most reference collections." Booklist

Coles, Robert
Handing one another along; literature and social reflection. edited by Trevor Hall and Vicki Kennedy. Random House 2010 xxiv, 273p il $27; ebook $27 **820**
1. English literature -- History and criticism 2. American literature -- History and criticism
ISBN 978-1-4000-6203-4; 978-0-679-60403-7 ebook
LC 2009-47337
The author "adapts his undergraduate lectures on literature's contribution to the development of our moral character. . . . While less than comprehensive and eschewing more technical analyses, it delves into a generous handful of writers and artists—perennials like George Orwell, James Agee, Zora Neale Hurston, Tillie Olsen, Ralph Ellison, and Raymond Carver, among others—with uncommon insight and a personal touch, while offering excerpts of poetry and prose that often whet the appetite for more." Publ Wkly
Includes bibliographical references

Greer, Germaine
The **Cambridge** guide to women's writing in English; [edited by] Lorna Sage; advisory editors, Germaine Greer, Elaine Showalter. Cambridge Univ. Press 1999 696p il $80; pa $29 **820**
1. Reference books 2. English literature -- Women

authors -- Dictionaries
ISBN 0-521-49525-3; 0-521-66813-1 pa
LC 98-50778
A "guide to women writers in the English language. The coverage is thorough, crossing historical, national, and generic boundaries as it ranges from Julian of Norwich to Terry Macmillan {sic}, from M.F.K. Fisher to Pauline Kael, from Ghanaian playwright Ama Ata Aidoo to Native American writer Mourning Dove. There are also articles on selected titles and themes. The entries, which range from 160 to 500 words, are informative, critical, and jargon-free." Libr J

Lee, Hermione
Virginia Woolf's nose; essays on biography. Princeton University Press 2005 141p $19.95 **820**
1. Poets 2. Authors 3. Novelists 4. Biography as a literary form 5. Diarists 6. Essayists 7. Military officials 8. Short story writers 9. Government officials 10. Members of Parliament
ISBN 0-691-12032-3
LC 2004-58457
"Lee's immensely enjoyable study will energize debate among thoughtful readers and should become essential reading for aficionados of literary biography." Publ Wkly
Includes bibliographical references

The **Norton** anthology of English literature; Stephen Greenblatt, general editor; M.H. Abrams, founding editor emeritus. 8th ed.; W.W. Norton 2006 2v il map **820**
1. English literature -- Collections
ISBN 0-393-92713-X v1; 0-393-92531-5 v1 pa; 0-393-92715-6 v2; 0-393-92532-3 v2 pa
LC 2005-52313
First published 1962. Periodically revised
Contains representative writings of authors which convey the tone and trends of specific literary movements and periods. Both volumes contain explanatory footnotes, selected bibliographies, notes on literary forms and usage, an author-title index, and marginalia glossaries.
Includes bibliographical references

★ The **Oxford** companion to English literature; edited by Dinah Birch. 7th ed; Oxford University Press 2009 1164p $150 **820**
1. Reference books 2. English literature -- Dictionaries 3. American literature -- Dictionaries 4. English literature -- Bio-bibliography 5. American literature -- Bio-bibliography
ISBN 978-0-19-280687-1
LC 2009-455948
First published 1932 under the editorship of Sir Paul Harvey
"The subjects of the entries include literary works, authors, themes, archetypes, journals, and forms. . . . This companion is a highly authoritative resource, with clear, concise, and approachable entries on literary topics of high interest to students and scholars of English literature. An essential reference for most public, high school, and academic libraries." Libr J

★ The **Oxford** guide to literature in English translation; edited by Peter France. Oxford Univ. Press 2000 xxii, 656p hardcover o.p. pa $29.95 **820**
1. Translating and interpreting 2. Literature -- History and criticism
ISBN 0-19-924784-6 pa

LC 99-28791

This "guide emphasizes 'high-culture' books in translation that have had the most lasting impact on English-speaking culture since the Middle Ages. . . . The first 116 pages cover translation theory and history, while the heart of this guide is the 17 geographic sections that follow, starting with African languages, moving through Latin, and ending with the West Asian languages. There are excellent bibliographies and an author index." Libr J

Includes bibliographical references

Sanders, Andrew

The **short** Oxford history of English literature; 3rd ed; Oxford University Press 2004 756p pa $45 **820**
1. English literature -- History and criticism
ISBN 978-0-19-926338-7; 0-19-926338-8

LC 2004-49555

First published 1994

"The History provides detailed discussion of Old and Middle English literature, the Renaissance, Shakespeare, the seventeenth and eighteenth centuries, the Romantics, Victorian and Edwardian literature, Modernism, and postwar writing. Discussions of key writers and works are combined with analysis of the impact on literature of contemporary political, social, and intellectual developments. The book includes Scottish, Irish, and Welsh writers, and it asks about the future of the canon in the light of the fragmented condition of British writing in the post-imperial period." Publisher's note

Includes bibliographical references

Stewart, Bruce

The **Oxford** companion to Irish literature; edited by Robert Welch, assistant editor, Bruce Stewart. Oxford Univ. Press 1996 xxv, 614p maps $55 **820**
1. Reference books 2. Irish literature -- Dictionaries
ISBN 0-19-866158-4

LC 95-44943

Encompassing "Ireland's literary heritage from the bardic poets and Celtic sagas to twentieth-century authors like Brian Friel, Edna O'Brien, and Nuala Ni Dhomhnaill, the more than 2,000 unsigned entries cover writers, titles of major works, literary genres and motifs, folklore, mythology, periodicals, associations, and historical figures and events." Booklist

Vendler, Helen Hennessy

Coming of age as a poet; Milton, Keats, Eliot, Plath. [by] Helen Vendler. Harvard Univ. Press 2003 174p il $22.95 **820**
1. Blind 2. Poets 3. Authors 4. Novelists 5. Dramatists 6. Editors 7. Essayists 8. Literary critics 9. Writers on medicine 10. Nobel laureates for literature 11. English poetry -- History and criticism 12. American poetry --

History and criticism
ISBN 0-674-01024-8

LC 2002-27287

"Milton's L'Allegro, Keats's On First Looking into Chapman's Homer, Eliot's The Love Song of J. Alfred Prufrock, and Plath's The Colossus are the poems that Helen Vendler considers, exploring each as an accession to poetic confidence, mastery, and maturity." Publisher's note

Vendler "succeeds in revealing the aesthetic power and technical beauty of great poetry." N Y Times Book Rev

Includes bibliographical references

820.9 English literature -- History and criticism

The **history** of British women's writing; edited by Maroula Joannou. Palgrave Macmillan 2010 340 p. (hbk.) $90 **820.9**
1. English authors 2. English literature -- 20th century 3. English literature -- Women authors 4. Women and literature -- Great Britain -- History 5. English literature -- Women authors -- History and criticism
ISBN 0230282792; 9780230282797 (v. 8)

LC 2010026127

This book, edited by Maroula Joannou, examines British women authors who "do not fit into a recognized version of the modernist canon. Their complex and often troubled relationship to modernity – as readers, consumers, and travellers at home and abroad – requires new critical frameworks in which to discuss their writing as well as a revision of the territory that has been staked out as the preserve of Modernism by critical theory and practice." (Publisher's note)

Includes bibliographical references and indexes

821 English poetry

★ **100** essential modern poems; selected and introduced by Joseph Parisi. Ivan R. Dee 2005 305p $24.95 **821**
1. English poetry -- Collections 2. American poetry -- Collections
ISBN 1-56663-612-4

LC 2005-9897

"Preceded by wonderfully conversational and expertly appreciative biocritical essays about each poet, his choices are superb as he lingers over Yeats and Stevens and includes often-overlooked witty and satirical poets, among them Dorothy Parker, Ogden Nash, Kay Ryan, Frank O'Hara, and Billy Collins." Booklist

★ **100** great poems of the twentieth century; [edited by] Mark Strand. Norton 2005 320p $24.95 **821**
1. English poetry -- Collections 2. American poetry -- Collections
ISBN 0-393-05894-8

LC 2005-2150

The editor "has selected works by poets of Europe and North and South America, and because there are so many gifted American poets, he restricted himself to those born before 1927. The result is a marvelously graceful, shimmering cosmos of poems by the likes of Anna Akhmatova, A.

R. Ammons, Amy Clampit, Robert Desnos, Robert Frost, Nazim Hikmet, Kenneth Koch, Edna St. Vincent Millay, Gabriela Mistral, Eugenio Montale, Octavio Paz, and Derek Walcott." Booklist

Adamson, Robert

★ The **goldfinches** of Baghdad. Flood Editions 2006 103p pa $13.95 **821**

1. Poetry -- By individual authors

ISBN 0-9746902-8-7

Adamson "lives on the Hawksbury River in New South Wales. . . . To give an overview of his poetry is difficult, but it is largely concerned with where he is: the river, the natural environment and creatures, his life and history, his neighbours, love and death. It has little of the 'pastoral' feel about it, being obsessively attached to the present condition, and it never gives any sense of a contented settled existence free from urban cares, quite the reverse. There is indication indeed of a quite fraught personal existence, both past and present, without the poetry ever for a moment becoming 'confessional'. It is to objective for that and too poetic." Shearsman

Adcock, Fleur

★ **Poems** 1960-2000. Bloodaxe Books 2000 287p $54.95; pa $24.95 **821**

1. Poetry -- By individual authors

ISBN 1-85224-529-8; 1-85224-530-1 pa

Adcock's "imagination thrives on what threatens her peace of mind, and only when she is unguarded can these threats have their full creative effect. . . . Throughout her writing life, she has made a fine art from holding on to principles of orderliness and good clear sense; but she has made an even finer one from loosening her grip on them." Times Lit Suppl

An **anthology** of modern Irish poetry; edited by Wes Davis. Belknap Press of Harvard University Press 2010 976p $35 **821**

1. Irish poetry -- Collections 2. Irish poetry -- 20th century 3. English poetry -- Irish authors

ISBN 0-674-04951-9; 9780674049512

LC 2009-37231

Collected here is a "representation of Irish poetic achievement in the twentieth and twenty-first centuries, from poets such as Austin Clarke and Samuel Beckett who were writing while Yeats and Joyce were still living; to those who came of age in the turbulent '60s as sectarian violence escalated, including Seamus Heaney and Michael Longley; to a new generation of Irish writers, represented by such . . . voices as David Wheatley (born 1970) and Sinead Morrissey (born 1972). Editor Wes Davis has chosen work by more than fifty leading modern and contemporary Irish poets." (Publisher's note) Index.

This volume, "running to almost a thousand pages, comes from a country with a population roughly equal to that of Tennessee. The book includes upwards of 50 poets—and there's not a dull page in it. Editor Wes Davis's selection is judicious, while his introduction and notes are as informative as they are brief." Wall Street J

Auden, W. H.

★ **Collected** poems; edited by Edward Mendelson. Modern Library 2007 928p $40 **821**

1. Poetry -- By individual authors

ISBN 978-0-679-64350-0; 0-679-64350-8

LC 2006-47163

Originally published in different form by Random House in 1976

A compilation of all the poems Auden wished to preserve, in his final revisions. Previous collected editions and later shorter poems are included. There is also an absurdist play written 1928: Paid on both sides.

Bentley, G. E.

The **stranger** from paradise: a biography of William Blake. Yale Univ. Press 2001 xxvii, 532p il maps $39.95; pa $24.95 **821**

1. Poets 2. Artists 3. Authors 4. Engravers 5. Illustrators

ISBN 0-300-08939-2; 0-300-10030-2 pa

The author "traces Blake from his natal landscape, youth, marriage, and apprenticeship through to his later years as a working engraver, poet, and radical visionary. Bentley is academic and thorough, and this is more of a straight biography than an analysis." Libr J

Includes bibliographical references

★ The **Best** poems of the English language; from Chaucer through Robert Frost. selected and with commentary by Harold Bloom. HarperCollins Publishers 2004 xxviii, 972p $34.95; pa $19.95 **821**

1. English poetry -- Collections 2. American poetry -- Collections

ISBN 0-06-054041-9; 0-06-054042-7 pa

LC 2003-51104

"Arranged chronologically by author, the poems are preceded by commentaries that extol their specific virtues and place them in historical context. Taken together, they provide an overview of Bloom's own theories of writing, such as his notion that the greatest poems manifest an 'inevitability' of phrasing . . . Bloom rarely bores, and at his best he achieves a cogency . . . worthy of the poets he so deeply admires." Libr J

Includes bibliographical references

Blake, William

The **complete** poetry and prose of William Blake; edited by David V. Erdman; with a new foreword and commentary by Harold Bloom. Newly rev. ed., 1st Calif. ed.; University of California Press 2008 xxvi, 990p il $70 **821**

1. Poetry -- By individual authors

ISBN 978-0-520-04473-9

First published 1965 with title: Poetry and prose of William Blake

In addition to all of Blake's poetry, this volume also includes miscellaneous prose, marginalia, and letters

"The crucial preliminary problem [in establishing Blake's text] is simply to make out what Blake wrote. . . . Erdman has used modern aids such as infrared photography and microphotography. . . but his real achievement has been to look at Blake's text more closely and intelligently than any previous editor." N Y Rev Books

Boland, Eavan

New collected poems. W.W. Norton 2008 320p $27.95 **821**

1. Poetry -- By individual authors
ISBN 978-0-393-06579-4; 0-393-06579-0

LC 2007-42554

First published 2005 in the United Kingdom

"Boland's resilient braid of outspoken feminism with Irish identity has given her a following on both sides of the Atlantic. Here is the recent Boland whose rapid verse celebrates women's courage and women's work, both public (several poems acknowledge Mary Robinson, the former president of the Irish Republic) and unsung: the poet remembers herself, when young, asking a statue in Dublin to 'Make me a heroine.' Here is the poet who learned from Adrienne Rich, among others, how to tackle big topics of loyalty, rebellion, descent and dissent." Publ Wkly

British women poets of the Romantic era; an anthology. edited by Paula R. Feldman. Johns Hopkins Univ. Press 1997 xxxvi, 879p hardcover o.p. pa $29.95 **821**

1. English poetry -- Women authors -- Collections
ISBN 0-8018-6640-5 pa

LC 96-47417

An "anthology of works by 62 British women poets writing between 1770 and 1840. . . . The poets are presented in alphabetical order, with each entry including a brief biography with birth and death dates, sample poems, major works, selected works, and the source of the poetry. The result is a singular resource providing information found in no other reference work." Libr J

Includes bibliographical references

Bronte, Emily

The **complete** poems of Emily Jane Bronte; edited from the manuscripts by C. W. Hatfield. Columbia Univ. Press 1941 xxi, 262p $65; pa $20 **821**

1. Poetry -- By individual authors
ISBN 0-231-01222-5; 0-231-10347-6 pa

A re-editing of the complete poems of Emily Brontë, based on all the known manuscripts. About half of the 193 poems are those belonging to the so-called Gondal cycle

Brown, Terence

The **life** of W.B. Yeats; a critical biography. Blackwell 1999 410p il (Blackwell critical biographies) $66.95; pa $29.95 **821**

1. Poets 2. Authors 3. Dramatists 4. Poets, Irish 5. Memoirists 6. Nobel laureates for literature
ISBN 0-631-18298-5; 0-631-22851-9 pa

LC 99-28388

In this biography Brown places "Yeats's work as poet and dramatist in its political and social—as well as personal and erotic—context." N Y Times Book Rev

Includes bibliographical references

Browning, Elizabeth Barrett

★ **Sonnets** from the Portuguese; a celebration of love. St. Martin's Press 1986 [63] il $9.95 **821**

1. Poetry -- By individual authors
ISBN 0-312-74501-X

LC 86-13755

A series of sonnets which "were written during a period of seven years and are considered by some scholars to have been inspired by her love for her husband poet Robert Browning." New Century Handb of Engl Lit

Browning, Robert

Robert Browning; the major works. edited with notes by Adam Roberts; with an introduction by Daniel Karlin. Oxford University Press 2005 xxxii, 828p pa $18.95 **821**

1. Poetry -- By individual authors
ISBN 978-0-19-280626-0; 0-19-280626-2

LC 2006-277696

This "selection includes over eighty of [Browning's] shorter poems, amongst them his most famous and best-loved dramatic monologues, as well as the complete text of many of his longer poems. It contains three books from The Ring and the Book and Browning's critical writing, Essay on Shelley. This edition also selects generously from the love letters between Browning and Elizabeth Barrett." Publisher's note

Includes bibliographical references

★ **Robert** Browning's poetry; authoritative texts, criticism. selected and edited by James F. Loucks and Andrew M. Stauffer. 2nd ed.; W. W. Norton & Co. 2007 689p (A Norton critical edition) pa $14.50 **821**

1. Poetry -- By individual authors
ISBN 978-0-393-92600-2; 0-393-92600-1

LC 2006-47308

First published 1980

This collection of Browning's poetry, which includes Pauline, "reprints the texts of the seventeen-volume 'Fourth and complete edition' (Smith, Elder), of which all but the final volume were approved by Browning before his death. The poems are ordered chronologically according to their first appearance in book form." Publisher's note

Bunting, Basil

Complete poems; associate editor, Richard Caddel. New Directions Books 2003 239p pa $16.95 **821**

1. Poetry -- By individual authors
ISBN 978-0-8112-1563-3; 0-8112-1563-6

LC 2003-15465

This volume "offers adventure, a confident voice, neat takes on history (both recent and archaic), an attractively careworn secular ethics and an even more attractive combination of archaic and vernacular English models. It also offers superb verbal command, chiseling every stanza to the fewest, densest possible words, giving each an aural shape. Those shapes are not always mellifluous—sometimes they are harsh, a mouthful—but each demonstrates Bunting's mastery, proving itself on the page as well as in the ear, where all good poems find their place." Nation

Burns, Robert

Burns; poems. edited and introduced by Gerard Carruthers. Alfred A. Knopf 2007 255p (Everyman's library pocket poets) $12.50 **821**

1. Poetry -- By individual authors

ISBN 978-0-307-26616-3; 0-307-26616-8

LC 2006-47299

"A pioneer of the Romantic movement, Burns wrote in a light Scots dialect with brio, emotional directness, and wit, drawing on classical and English literary traditions as well as Scottish folklore. . . . All of his most famous lyrics and poems are here, from 'A Red, Red Rose,' 'To a Mouse,' and 'To a Louse' to Tam o'Shanter, 'Holy Willie's Prayer,' and 'Auld Lang Syne.'" Publisher's note

Byron, George Gordon Byron

Selected poetry of Lord Byron; edited by Leslie A. Marchand; introduction by Thomas Disch; notes by Jeffrey Vail. Modern Library 2001 745p (The Modern Library classics) pa $16 **821**

1. Poetry -- By individual authors

ISBN 978-0-375-75814-0; 0-375-75814-3

LC 2001-42771

"From 'Manfred,' with its evocation of the figure that came to be called the 'Byronic hero,' to the melancholy 'Childe Harold,' to the satirical masterpiece 'Don Juan' (presented here in judiciously selected form), this . . . [selection seeks to include] the essential Byron." Publisher's note

Chaucer, Geoffrey

★ The **complete** poetry and prose of Geoffrey Chaucer; edited by John H. Fisher. 2nd ed; Harcourt Brace & Co. 1989 1040p il $105.95 **821**

1. Poetry -- By individual authors

ISBN 0-03-028612-3

LC 88-29400

First published 1977

Includes bibliographical references

Christmas poems; selected and edited by John Hollander and J.D. McClatchy. Knopf 1999 254p (Everyman's library pocket poets) $12.50 **821**

1. Christmas -- Poetry 2. English poetry -- Collections 3. American poetry -- Collections

ISBN 0-375-40789-8

LC 99-36265

Contributors to this collection of Christmas poetry include Milton, Tennyson, Rossetti, Thackeray, Eliot, McGinley, Morris, Bishop and Geoffrey Hill

Coleridge, Samuel Taylor

The **complete** poems; edited by William Keach. Penguin 1997 xxx, 626p (Penguin classics) pa $18 **821**

1. Poetry -- By individual authors

ISBN 978-0-14-042353-2

This edition "contains the final texts of all the poems published in the poet's lifetime, together with a substantial selection from the verse still in manuscript on his death. William Keach's notes draw attention to significant variants, and important earlier versions of 'Monody on the Death of Chatterton', 'The Eolian Harp', 'The Rime of the Ancient Mariner' and 'Dejection: An Ode' are included in full. The poems are arranged in chronological order of composition." Publisher's note

The **Columbia** anthology of British poetry; edited by Carl Woodring and James Shapiro. Columbia Univ. Press 1995 xxxi, 891p $41 **821**

1. English poetry -- Collections

ISBN 0-231-10180-5

LC 94-46333

This anthology "contains major British poetry from Beowulf to the present day. Poets receive a short biographical introduction along with their poetry. . . . It includes more female poets than most comparable anthologies, and is conducive to browsing. Major poems such as Coleridge's 'Rime of the Ancient Mariner,' Britain's best-loved poems, and newly rediscovered poems are part of this collection." SLJ

Constantine, David

Collected poems. Bloodaxe Books 2005 384p pa $31.95 **821**

1. Poetry -- By individual authors

ISBN 1-85224-667-7

"From the first line on this book's first page ('As our bloods separate the clock resumes') to the first sentence on its last ('When the kingfisher flitted/ Under the hazels I entered again into boyhood') Constantine declares himself a Romantic, in almost all the loaded, unfashionable and daring senses that once-omnipresent term can bear. In his elaborate lines, intelligence and strong emotion are collaborators, not competitors; he knows how to let them spur each other on." Times Lit Suppl

★ **Contemporary** poets; editor, Thomas Riggs; with a preface by Diane Wakoski. 7th ed; St. James Press 2001 xxiii, 1443p (Contemporary writers series) $230 **821**

1. Reference books 2. Poets, English -- Dictionaries 3. Poets, American -- Dictionaries 4. American poetry -- Bio-bibliography

ISBN 1-55862-349-3

LC 00-45882

First published 1970 with title: Contemporary poets of the English language

"A biographical handbook of contemporary poets, arranged alphabetically. Entries consist of a short biography, full bibliography, comments by many of the poets, and a signed critical essay." Ref Sources for Small & Medium-sized Libr. 6th edition

Includes bibliographical references

Davie, Donald

Collected poems; edited by Neil Powell. Carcanet 2002 xxi, 634p (Poetry pléiade) $49.95; pa $24.95 **821**

1. English poetry -- 20th century 2. Poetry -- By individual authors

ISBN 978-1-85754-579-1; 1-85754-579-6; 978-1-85754-406-0 pa; 1-85754-406-4 pa

"Davie's poetic output, which abundantly stretches from Hardyesque lyrics ('Bride of Reason,' 'A Winter Talent,'

'The Battered Wife') to cognitively powerful long poems ('Six Epistles to Eva Hesse,' 'The Forests of Lithuania'), from translations of Pasternak and Mandelstam to lyrically brutal political commentary ('August, 1968'), evinces a kind of wide sweep and committed imagination that doesn't necessarily close itself off to confrontation and experiential risk, nor resign itself to failure as the phenomenological and lyrical refusal of further inquiry. In this sense, Davie has always seemed to be a poet working in the very high art of his eighteenth-century forebears." Jacket

Davis, Dick

Belonging; poems. Swallow Press 2002 54p $24.95; pa $14.95   **821**
    1. Poetry -- By individual authors
    ISBN 0-8040-1042-0; 0-8040-1043-9 pa
                         LC 2002-17749

Davis' "poems are full of fine emotion, intelligence, wit, and multinational culture. He lithely celebrates the legendary rake Casanova; poignantly conjures 'Kipling's Kim, Thirty Years On'; economically reports a father's aching futility in comforting his child ('A Bit of Paternity'); deftly valorizes the power of art ('Just So'); and often muses on the shortness of life and the limitations of being human, so cogently that a single quatrain can take one's breath away." Booklist

Day Lewis, C.

The complete poems of C. Day Lewis; [edited by] Jill Balcon. Stanford Univ. Press 1992 745p hardcover o.p. pa $32.95   **821**
    1. Poetry -- By individual authors
    ISBN 978-0-8047-2585-9; 0-8047-2585-3
                         LC 91-68076

"The still lively fascination of his verse seems to depend on the variety of tones [Day Lewis] could pick up, change, and discard at will. . . . His modesty was genuine and profound, giving his verse texture its winning versatility, its air that 'tenure is not for me.' . . . Nothing that Day Lewis wrote is lacking its own sort of ephemeral though rediscoverable effectiveness. He was well aware of this, and it was a part of his modesty, as Jill Balcon points out in her thoughtful and sensitive introduction. . . . For anyone who likes poetry there is real interest here in [this] complete record." N Y Rev Books

Donne, John

★ The complete poetry and selected prose of John Donne; edited by Charles M. Coffin; introduction by Denis Donoghue; notes by W. T. Chmielewski. Modern Lib. 2001 xxxii, 697p pa $14.95   **821**
    1. Poetry -- By individual authors
    ISBN 0-375-75734-1
                         LC 2001-30077

A reissue of the Modern Library edition published 1994

This volume contains Donne's love poetry, satires, epigrams, verse letters and holy sonnets. Also includes selected prose and a sampling of private letters.

Poems and prose. A.A. Knopf 1995 256p (Everyman's library pocket poets) $12.50   **821**
    1. Poetry -- By individual authors
    ISBN 978-0-679-44467-1; 0-679-44467-X
                         LC 95-15330

"Contains Songs and Sonnets, Letters to the Countess of Bedford, The First Anniversary, Holy Sonnets, Divine Poems, excerpts from Paradoxes and Problems, Ignatius His Conclave, The Sermons, Essays and Devotions, and an index of first lines." Publisher's note

Dryden, John

John Dryden; the major works. edited with an introduction and notes by Keith Walker. Oxford University Press 2003 xviii, 967p pa $18.95   **821**
    1. Poetry -- By individual authors
    ISBN 978-0-19-284077-6; 0-19-284077-0
                         LC 2003-270051

This "edition brings together a unique combination of Dryden's poetry and prose—all the major poems in full, literary criticism, and translations—to give the essence of his work and thinking. The collection includes the poems, MacFlecknoe and Absalom and Achitophel as well as Dryden's classical translations; his versions of Homer, Horace, and Ovid are reproduced in full. There are also substantial selections from Dryden's Virgil, Juvenal, and other classical writers. Fables, Ancient and Modern, taken from Chaucer, Ovid, Boccaccio, and Homer, his last and possibly greatest work, also appears in full." Publisher's note

Includes bibliographical references

Feinstein, Elaine

Ted Hughes; the life of a poet. Norton 2001 273p il $29.95; pa $15.95   **821**
    1. Poets 2. Authors 3. Poets laureate
    ISBN 0-393-04967-1; 0-393-32362-5 pa
                         LC 2001-44925

This biography of the English poet examines Hughes's relationship with "his first wife, Sylvia Plath, who committed suicide in 1963 during the acrimonious breakup of their marriage, . . . {and with} Assia Wevill, the woman for whom Hughes left Plath, and who later killed herself and their child." Economist

Includes bibliographical references

Fisher, Roy

★ Selected poems; edited by August Kleinzahler. Flood Editions 2011 158p pa $15.95   **821**
    1. Poetry -- By individual authors
    ISBN 978-0-9819520-6-2

"Fisher's texts have never been as well served on the page as they are here. The poems are given real space and the movement of Fisher's breath, rhythm and cadence is as clear as it possibly could be." Manchester Rev

Foster, R. F.

W.B. Yeats: a life. v2 Oxford Univ. Press 2003 xxiv, 798p v2 il $47.50 **821**
1. Poets 2. Authors 3. Dramatists 4. Poets, Irish 5. Memoirists 6. Nobel laureates for literature
ISBN 0-19-818465-4

This second volume of a two-volume biography covers Yeats's final decades, from his 50th year to his death in 1939.
Includes bibliographical references

Foster, R. F. (Robert Fitzroy), 1949-

W.B. Yeats: a life. v1 Oxford Univ. Press 1997 xxxi, 640p v1 il hardcover o.p. pa $29.95 **821**
1. Poets 2. Authors 3. Dramatists 4. Poets, Irish 5. Memoirists 6. Biography, Individual 7. Nobel laureates for literature
ISBN 0-19-211735-1; 0-19-288085-3 pa
LC 96-31671

This is the first installment of a two-volume biography of the Irish poet. Index.

Foulds, Adam

The **broken** word; an epic poem of the British Empire in Kenya, and the Mau Mau uprising against it. Penguin 2011 60p (Penguin poets) pa $16 **821**
1. Kenya -- Poetry 2. Mau Mau -- Poetry
ISBN 978-0-14-311809-1

First published 2008 in the United Kingdom

Offers a lyrical poem about Tom, a young man who gets caught up in the violent 1950s Mau Mau Uprising in Kenya protesting the British colonial control of that country.

"A tour de force of a long narrative poem, rare in contemporary English poetry." Libr J

Geoffrey Chaucer's The Canterbury tales; edited and with an introduction by Harold Bloom. New ed; Chelsea House 2008 286p (Modern critical interpretations) $45 **821**
1. Poets 2. Authors 3. Poetry -- By individual authors
ISBN 978-0-7910-9618-5
LC 2007-49158

First published 1988 in three separate editions focusing on the Prologue, The knight's tale, and The pardoner's tale

A collection of eleven critical essays on Chaucer's well-known work, arranged in chronological order of their original publication.

Includes bibliographical references

Gunn, Thom

Boss Cupid. Farrar, Straus & Giroux 2000 111p hardcover o.p. pa $13 **821**
1. Poetry -- By individual authors
ISBN 0-374-52771-7 pa
LC 99-57739

"Boss Cupid offers a splendid introduction for the uninitiated. Almost all of Gunn's virtues are on display here: his playful, metrical dexterity, his unflinching celebration both of beauty and of transience. . . . Advancing age and the AIDS-related deaths of friends—'my everpresent dead'—

figure prominently in these poems, but so does Gunn's humorous touch." Time

Collected poems. Farrar, Straus & Giroux 1994 495p pa $20 **821**
1. Poetry -- By individual authors
ISBN 978-0-374-52433-3; 0-374-52433-5
LC 93-74183

There is a "a unity of purpose that extends throughout the work, from the watchful early metrics through the syllabics, the reach and skill of the free verse and, in much of the latest work, a return to strong form that might be termed triumphant had it not been called into the service of matter so saddening." Times Lit Suppl

Hardy, Thomas

Thomas Hardy; the complete poems. edited by James Gibson. Palgrave 2001 xxxvi, 1003p il pa $33.95 **821**
1. Poetry -- By individual authors
ISBN 978-0-333-94929-0; 0-333-94929-3
LC 2001-32732

First published 1976

This collection "includes Hardy's more than 900 poems, complemented by detailed notes. Collected here are his eight books of verse, all the uncollected poems, Domicilium, and the songs from The Dynasts. This edition contains an additional poem, The Sound of Her." Publisher's note

Includes bibliographical references

Heaney, Seamus

District and circle. Farrar, Straus and Giroux 2006 78p $20 **821**
1. Poetry -- By individual authors
ISBN 0-374-14092-8; 978-0-374-14092-2
LC 2005-44687

This "collection of robust lyrics celebrates work, memory, and the physicality of existence. Brimming with anvils, hammers, shovels, and pumps, these poems are scored into the page with Heaney's signature accentual and alliterative force." Libr J

Electric light. Farrar, Straus & Giroux 2001 98p hardcover o.p. pa $13 **821**
1. Poetry -- By individual authors
ISBN 0-374-14683-7; 0-374-52841-1 pa
LC 00-67278

Heaney's "book of poems is a compendium of poetic genres set in an array of forms and tuned to many kinds of experience, the work of a mature poet and world citizen, aware of his cultural authority as a public man and of the rights and responsibilities that go with it." N Y Times Book Rev

★ **Finders** keepers; selected prose 1971-2001. Farrar, Straus & Giroux 2002 452p $30; pa $15 **821**
1. Poets 2. Authors 3. Novelists 4. Dramatists 5. Librarians 6. Editors 7. Essayists 8. Memoirists 9. Translators 10. Poets laureate 11. College teachers 12. Literary critics 13. Nobel laureates for literature 14. Poetry -- History and criticism
ISBN 0-374-15496-1; 0-374-52878-0 pa

This collection "gathers Heaney's occasional prose from four decades, much of it meditating upon other poets who have moved him, including familiar members of the canon, such as Eliot and Yeats and Auden, and lesser-known and newer moderns, such as Hugh MacDiarmid, Thomas Kinsella, and Norman MacCaig, whose work draws his interest. Not surprisingly for a poet from a war-wracked land, Heaney comes back again and again to the question of how poetry can matter against human savagery." Booklist

Human chain. Farrar, Straus and Giroux 2010 85p $24 **821**
 1. Poetry -- By individual authors
 ISBN 978-0-374-17351-7

 LC 2010-10274

"Nostalgia and memory, numinous visions and the earthy music of compound adjectives together control the short poems and sequences of the Irish Nobel laureate's 14th collection of verse. . . . Old teachers, schoolmates, farmhands, and even the employees of an 'Eelworks' arrive transfigured through Heaney's command of sound. . . . For all the variety of Heaney's framed glimpses, though, the standout poems grow from occasions neither trivial nor topical: Heaney in 2006 had a minor stroke, and the discreet analogies and glimpsed moments in poems such as 'Chanson d'Aventure' (about a ride in an ambulance) and 'In the Attic' ('As I age and blank on names') bring his characteristic warmth and subtlety to mortality, rehabilitation, recent trauma, and old age." Publ Wkly

Opened ground; selected poems, 1966-1996. Farrar, Straus & Giroux 1998 443p hardcover o.p. pa $16 **821**
 1. Poetry -- By individual authors
 ISBN 0-374-52678-8 pa

 LC 98-4331

"The best of nobel laureate Heaney's poems, gathered from 12 previous collections, create a substantial volume that charts the course of one man's thoroughly examined personal life and reflects a volatile era in the life of his troubled country, Northern Ireland, though the particulars Heaney renders so vibrantly become archetypal and unbounded in their tragedy and bliss." Booklist

Herbert, George
 Herbert : poems. Alfred A. Knopf 2004 253p (Everyman's library pocket poets) $12.50 **821**
 1. Poetry -- By individual authors 2. Christian poetry, English -- Early modern, 1500-1700.
 ISBN 978-1-4000-4329-3; 1-4000-4329-8

 LC 2005-273574

Herbert experimented with a variety of forms, "from hymns and sonnets to 'pattern poems,' the shape of which reveal their subjects. Such technical agility never seems ostentatious, however, for precision of language and expression of genuine feeling were the primary concerns of this poet who admonished his readers to 'dare to be true.' An Anglican priest who took his calling with deep seriousness, he brought to his work a religious reverence richly allied with a playful wit and with literary and musical gifts of the highest order." Publisher's note

Hill, Geoffrey
 ★ The **orchards** of Syon. Counterpoint 2002 72p $24 **821**
 1. Poetry -- By individual authors
 ISBN 1-58243-166-3

 LC 2001-47245

"Cast as a sequence of 72 uniform blank-verse soliloquies compounded out of a dissonant amalgam of demotic jabber and oracular utterance, 'The Orchards of Syon' confirms that Hill, for all his newfound volubility, can be as refractory as ever. . . . But for readers with the patience and stamina to stick with it, Hill's brooding meditations on his ancestral countryside's 'wintry swamp-thickets, brush-heaps of burnt light' or 'the burring air of the fell' carry the haunting force of a last will and testament." N Y Times Book Rev

Selected poems. Yale University Press 2009 276p **821**
 1. Poetry -- By individual authors
 ISBN 978-0-300-12156-8

 LC 2008-930384

First published 2006 in the United Kingdom
"After four decades with just five books, the past 10 years have seen Hill offer six more, including a trio of long works some liken to Dante and Blake. This first selected since 1994 . . . should get instant critical attention (and sustained academic adoption) even though it contains no new work. Here, entire, is Mercian Hymns, with its gorgeously medievalized evocation of a rural English upbringing. Here, complete, are all three recent long poems, with their erudite mix of elegy and jeremiad. . . . Here, too, are the descriptive beauties that sparkle through even Hill's most rebarbative works." Publ Wkly

The **triumph** of love. Houghton Mifflin 1998 82p hardcover o.p. pa $13 **821**
 1. Poetry -- By individual authors
 ISBN 0-618-00183-2 pa

 LC 98-19502

This book-length poem "ends up so much more satisfying than much of Hill's recent work because there is so much more of Hill in it. . . . When we have read [the book] a few times (no one should read it just once) we know, more than we could from his previous work, what vexes and distresses, what heartens and cheers Hill, what gives him his grim satisfactions and how." Yale Rev

Without title. Yale University Press 2007 81p $26; pa $16 **821**
 1. Poetry -- By individual authors
 ISBN 978-0-300-12176-6; 0-300-12176-8; 0-300-12157-1 pa; 978-0-300-12157-5 pa

 LC 2006-926124

First published 2006 in the United Kingdom
"For much of Hill's five-decade career, his forbiddingly allusive and elliptical style, his sometimes peevish tone, his interest in English church history, and his rapt pastoralism have made him an unfashionable figure, but also a highly individual one. His latest collection exhibits typical erudition: who else would name-drop the Jesuit theologian Karl Rahner or describe Jimi Hendrix as an 'exquisite player of neumes' ('neumes' being an archaic form of musical nota-

tion)? Though the method is a magpie one, the impression that emerges is of absolute control and single-mindedness. And while Hill's outlook can seem willfully bleak . . . there is genuine grace in his descriptions of natural beauty." New Yorker

Hopkins, Gerard Manley

Poems and prose. Alfred A. Knopf 1995 256p (Everyman's library pocket poets) $13.50 **821**

1. Poetry -- By individual authors

ISBN 978-0-679-44469-5; 0-679-44469-6

LC 95-15331

This volume "contains a full selection of Hopkins's work, including selected verse, prose, and letters, and an index of first lines." Publisher's note

Housman, A. E.

★ The **collected** poems of A. E. Housman. Holt & Co. 1965 254p pa $16 **821**

1. Poetry -- By individual authors

ISBN 0-8050-0547-1

This anthology "constitutes the authorized canon of A. E. Housman's verse as established in 1939." Note on the text

Hughes, Ted, 1930-1998

Collected poems; edited by Paul Keegan. Farrar, Straus and Giroux 2003 1376p $50; pa $25 **821**

1. Poetry -- By individual authors

ISBN 978-0-374-12538-7; 0-374-12538-4; 978-0-374-52965-9 pa; 0-374-52965-5 pa

LC 2003-59938

"Paul Keegan has taken Hughes's New Selected Poems of 1995 as his model, and intercalated the expected and familiar Faber texts with uncollected or small press works like a Viennese layer cake—in astonishing quantity and quality." Poetry (Modern Poetry Association)

Johnston, Kenneth R.

The **hidden** Wordsworth; poet, lover, rebel, spy. Norton 1998 965 p. ill. $45; pa $24.95 **821**

1. Poets 2. Authors 3. Poets laureate 4. Spies -- Great Britain -- Biography 5. Poets, English -- 19th century -- Biography 6. Revolutionaries -- Great Britain -- Biography

ISBN 0393046230; 0393321592

LC 97-40317

The author seeks "to chronicle Wordsworth's life from 1770 to 1807." (Libr J) Bibliography. Index.

This "volume focuses on the poet's first thirty-six years, the tumultuous decades immortalized in 'The Prelude.' Johnston's spacious, absorbing argument—that Wordsworth's moments of emotion recollected in tranquillity were themselves rather less than tranquil—is amply supported by a thorough documentation of the multifarious life and times of the young poet, at Hawkshead, at Cambridge, in Grasmere, and abroad." New Yorker

Includes bibliographical references

Jonson, Ben

The **complete** poems; edited by George Parfitt. Penguin Books 1988 634p (Penguin classics) pa $17 **821**

1. Poetry -- By individual authors

ISBN 978-0-14-042277-1; 0-14-042277-3

LC 88-196178

"As well as the entire body of Jonson's nondramatic verse, extensively annotated, this edition contains many of the songs from his plays and masques and his translation of 'Horace, of the Art of Poetry'. His 'Conversations with Drummond', which adds much to our sense of the man, appears as an Appendix, as does 'Discoveries'; together they shed valuable light on Jonson's poetic theory and practice." Publisher's note

Keats, John

★ The **complete** poems of John Keats. Modern Lib. 1994 398p $19.95 **821**

1. Poetry -- By individual authors

ISBN 0-679-60108-2

LC 94-4339

The works in this compilation include Lamia, Isabella, The Eve of St. Agnes', Endymion, and La Belle Dame sans Merci

Poems. Knopf 1994 253p (Everyman's library pocket poets) $12.50 **821**

1. Poetry -- By individual authors

ISBN 0-679-43319-8

LC 94-2495

A representative collection by the influential English romantic.

Includes bibliographical references

Kipling, Rudyard, 1865-1936

Complete verse; definitive edition. Doubleday 1989 850p hardcover o.p. pa $20 **821**

1. Poetry -- By individual authors

ISBN 0-385-26089-X pa

LC 88-7364

Replaces Rudyard Kipling's verse: definitive edition, published 1940

This edition includes all of Kipling's published poetry and, in addition, more than 20 poems which have not previously appeared in the inclusive edition of his verse

Langland, William

Piers Plowman; the Donaldson translation, Middle English text, sources and backgrounds, criticism. edited by Elizabeth Robertson and Stephen H.A. Shepherd. Norton 2006 xxviii, 644p pa $15 **821**

1. Poetry -- By individual authors

ISBN 978-0-393-97559-8; 0-393-97559-2

LC 2004-57578

This Middle English poem is "written in 'Alliterative Verse' like Old English poetry and uses a deliberately rustic and archaic dialect. It is an allegorical moral and social satire, written as a 'vision' of the common medieval type." Reader's Ency. 4th edition

Larkin, Philip

★ **Collected** poems; edited and with an introduction by Anthony Thwaite. Farrar, Straus and Giroux 2004 218p pa $15   **821**

1. Poetry -- By individual authors

ISBN 978-0-374-52920-8; 0-374-52920-5

LC 2003-60846

First published 2003 in the United Kingdom

"Thwaite has gathered all the poems Larkin wrote between 1946 and 1985, the year of his death; he also includes a generous selection of work written earlier, before Larkin found his characteristic voice. In all, there are some 240 poems, 83 of them never published before. The unpublished work comes from every period of Larkin's career and increases by half the number of poems in his canon. The poet we now have is considerably more prolific than the one who issued only three small, mature collections in his lifetime. With or without the new poems, Larkin is a major postwar British writer, and this is the best available collection of his poetry." Libr J

Lawrence, D. H.

The **complete** poems; collected and edited with an introduction and notes by Vivian de Sola Pinto and Warren Roberts. Penguin Books 1993 1079p (Penguin twentieth-century classics) pa $24.95   **821**

1. Poetry -- By individual authors

ISBN 978-0-14-018657-4; 0-14-018657-3

First published 1964 by Viking

This "collection of Lawrence's poems, with appendices containing juvenilia, variants, and early drafts, and Lawrence's own critical introductions to his poems, also includes full textual and explanatory notes, glossary, and index." Publisher's note

Lear, Edward

The **complete** verse and other nonsense; compiled and edited with an introduction and notes by Vivien Noakes. Penguin Bks. 2002 566p il pa $18   **821**

1. Nonsense verses 2. Poetry -- By individual authors

ISBN 0-14-200227-5

LC 2002-28998

This volume "presents all of Lear's verse and other nonsense writings, including stories, letters, and illustrated alphabets, as well as previously unpublished material, line drawings, and . . . [an] introduction by scholar Vivien Noakes." Publisher's note

Includes bibliographical references

MacDiarmid, Hugh

Selected poetry; introduction by Eliot Weinberger; edited by Alan Riach & Michael Grieve. New Directions 1993 289p $30.95   **821**

1. Poetry -- By individual authors

ISBN 978-0-8112-1248-9; 0-8112-1248-3

LC 93-5312

"The preface by the poet's son Michael Grieve, 'Recalling Hugh MacDiarmid,' includes major biographical facts which shaped the poet's work. . . . Alan Riach's 'Reading Hugh MacDiarmid' provides a scholarly look at MacDiar-

mid's importance to the Scottish Renaissance and the themes that informed his poetry. . . . In addition to the two introductory essays, the volume also contains a chronology of MacDiarmid's life, illustrating both his private maturation and the public events that influenced him. The real reason to purchase the volume, however, is for the exceptional overview and easy accessibility it provides to a major poetic voice not only in Scotland but in the world." World Lit Today

The **Making** of a poem; a Norton anthology of poetic forms. edited by Mark Strand and Eavan Boland. Norton 2000 xxxi, 366p hardcover o.p. pa $15.95   **821**

1. English poetry -- Collections 2. American poetry -- Collections

ISBN 0-393-32178-9 pa

LC 99-55233

A "collection of villanelles, sestinas, sonnets, elegies, pastorals, ballads, pantoums, odes, and other familiar structures that have shaped English poetry since Beowulf. Each chapter focuses on a single form. . . . Most useful are the selections themselves, which illustrate how particular forms have been employed over time, from canonical classics by Chaucer, Shelley, and Elizabeth Bishop through newer pieces by Hayden Carruth, Michael Palmer, and Thylias Moss." Libr J

Includes bibliographical references

Marvell, Andrew

Poems; [selected by Peter Washington] A. A. Knopf 2004 256p (Everyman's library pocket poets) $12.50   **821**

1. Poetry -- By individual authors

ISBN 978-1-4000-4252-4; 1-4000-4252-6

The "metaphysical poet Andrew Marvell was one of the chief wits and satirists of his time as well as a passionate defender of individual liberty. Today, however, he is known chiefly for his brilliant lyric poems, including 'The Garden,' 'The Definition of Love,' 'Bermudas,' 'To His Coy Mistress,' and the 'Horatian Ode' to Cromwell." Publisher's note

Motion, Andrew

Keats. University of Chicago Press 1999 636p il pa $18   **821**

1. Poets 2. Authors 3. Poets, English 4. Writers on medicine

ISBN 0-226-54240-8; 978-0-226-54240-9

LC 98-41014

First published 1997 in the United Kingdom

"Motion emphasizes that Keats was no otherworldly creature of exquisite sensibilities but a man whose liberal politics and commitment to medicine animated his aesthetics and enlightened his poetry." Booklist

Includes bibliographical references

Muldoon, Paul

★ **Horse** latitudes. Farrar, Straus and Giroux 2006 107p $22   **821**

1. Poetry -- By individual authors

ISBN 978-0-374-17305-0; 0-374-17305-2

LC 2006-306

"Beginning with a sequence of sonnets whose titles start with the letter B, to a series of instant messages formatted as haiku, to an ending that tributes rocker Warren Zevon, readers are in for a lively ride." Libr J

Maggot; poems. Farrar, Straus and Giroux 2010 134p $24   **821**
1. Poetry -- By individual authors
ISBN 978-0-374-20032-9; 0-374-20032-7
LC 2010-05700

"The play on the word maggot, which can also mean a whim or extravagant notion as well as the larva, tells us all we need to know about Paul Muldoon's poetics. So comfortable is he in both worlds, the debased and the ecstatic, that critics often willfully misunderstand him. . . . Everywhere in 'Maggot,' Mr. Muldoon chafes at the bit, belatedly, against duty and responsibility. He is most susceptible to the charge of triviality in his longer poems, and often in 'Maggot,' he does indeed flirt too closely with absurdity. . . . [He] barely squeaks by on the side of seriousness, but just barely! Credit him with continuing to walk that trapeze, with no net underneath him." Pittsburgh Post-Gazette

★ **Poems,** 1968-1998. Farrar, Straus & Giroux 2001 479p $35; pa $19   **821**
1. Poetry -- By individual authors
ISBN 0-374-12543-0; 0-374-52844-6 pa
LC 00-45607

"Language is heightened, experimental, and also utterly mundane, even coarse. His subjects match the language, what with trips on mescaline chockablock with bucolic landscapes. The luck of this collection is that it is long and dense enough to show the poet wrestling not only with craft—his intricate and often hidden rhymes show, right from the start, his obsession with form—but also with the reason for poetry in a technological age." Booklist

Murray, Les A.
The **biplane** houses. Farrar, Straus and Giroux 2007 99p $23   **821**
1. Poetry -- By individual authors
ISBN 978-0-374-11548-7; 0-374-11548-6
LC 2006-31763

First published 2006 in Australia
"Murray's poems, never exactly intimate and often patrolled by details and place-names nearly indecipherable to an outsider, reflect a life lived self-consciously and rather flamboyantly off the beaten track. . . . Pastoral is a sophisticated game pitting poets against earlier poets, like a chess match played across time. No poet writing about the natural world entirely opts out of the game, but Murray's poetry of elk and emus, bougainvillea and turmeric dust, comes close." New Yorker

★ **Conscious** and verbal; [by] Les Murray. Farrar, Straus & Giroux 2001 94p $23; pa $13   **821**
1. Poetry -- By individual authors
ISBN 0-374-12882-0; 0-374-52860-8 pa
LC 2001-40222

"The poet became a minor celebrity when he awoke from a three-week coma and was pronounced 'conscious and verbal,' but this new volume is more concerned with his familiar Australian topography: dead dogs, the 'Internationale,' oysters, soil, the color yellow. Murray sticks to the cheerfully formal lines that distinguish his work while letting his voice shift between chestnuts of local dialect and a brawny but humble standard English." New Yorker

Poems the size of photographs; [by] Les Murray. Farrar, Straus & Giroux 2003 128p $20   **821**
1. Poetry -- By individual authors
ISBN 0-374-23520-1
LC 2002-192520

First published in 2002 in the United Kingdom
"Murray concentrates his muscular style, passion for landscape, and satirical humor into short and pithy poems. Tightly framed, most can be taken in at a glance, and yet, like developing photographs, they fully disclose their finer details and nuances more slowly. Murray begins with a mischievous tribute to the 'new hieroglyphics,' the international symbols of airports and restaurants, pictographs of the forbidden and the required. The contrasts between words and images intrigue Murray and inform his sly, sometimes startling, always colorful and animated lyrics, yarns, and epigrams." Booklist

Murray, Les, 1938-
Taller when prone; poems. [by] Les Murray. Farrar, Straus and Giroux 2011 82p $24   **821**
1. Poetry -- By individual authors
ISBN 978-0-374-27237-1
LC 2010033150

First published 2010 in Australia
This "is Les Murray's first volume of new poems since The Biplane Houses, published five years ago." (Publisher's note)

The title of Murray's collection "plays with the notion of cutting self down to size. He uses humour to restore perspective (although the punchline to the wonderful and ludicrous 'A Frequent Flyer Proposes a Name', in which he suggests a name for a new London airport, does not qualify as a deflationary joke). There are many more serious and ambitious pieces here, too. There are elegies in the tradition of Gerard Manley Hopkins's 'Felix Randal' – 'Rugby Wheels', about a disabled rugby player, and 'Double Diamond', about a gauche octogenarian soldier at his wife's funeral. It is a collection filled with celebrations of ordinary people, extraordinary Australian birds and open endings. Murray has a gentle way with his poems, letting them go, never forcing a conclusion. One of his great gifts is that he is noninterventionist, never blocks a view – art in apparent artlessness." Guardian (UK)

★ The **New** Oxford book of Irish verse; edited, with translations, by Thomas Kinsella. Oxford Univ. Press 2001 xxx, 423p pa $16.95   **821**
1. Irish poetry -- Collections
ISBN 0-19-280192-9
LC 2001-278442

Replaces The Oxford Book of Irish verse, XVIIth century-XXth century, chosen by Donagh MacDonagh and Lennox Robinson (1958); this is a reissue of the 1986 edition

"This selection is divided into three parts. Book I opens with the earliest pre-Christian poetry in Old Irish and ends in the fourteenth century with the first Irish poetry in the

English language. Book II covers the fourteenth to the eighteenth centuries and Book III the nineteenth and twentieth centuries." Publisher's note

★ The **Norton** anthology of modern and contemporary poetry; edited by Jahan Ramazani, Richard Ellmann, Robert O'Clair. 3rd ed; Norton 2003 2v pa set $75   **821**

1. English poetry -- Collections 2. American poetry -- Collections

ISBN 0-393-32429-X

LC 2002-37990

First published 1973 with title: The Norton anthology of modern poetry

This volume includes "1596 poems by 195 poets. . . . The anthology includes the works of such masters as Walt Whitman, Ezra Pound, Dylan Thomas, Langston Hughes, Gertrude Stein, Lucille Clifton, Louise Erdrich, and Allen Ginsberg. . . . Extensive, and beautifully composed introductions provide insight, observations, and historical context for the selections. . . . This ambitious, highly successful work is a veritable tribute to the enduring power of literature and language." SLJ

Includes bibliographical references

O'Driscoll, Dennis

Stepping stones; interviews with Seamus Heaney. Farrar, Straus, and Giroux 2008 xxx, 552p il map $32   **821**

1. Poets 2. Authors 3. Essayists 4. Translators 5. Nobel laureates for literature

ISBN 978-0-374-26983-8; 0-374-26983-1

LC 2008-41252

"The book is a collection of questions and answers, compiled, largely by correspondence, over a period of some seven years. The compiler, Dennis O'Driscolla poet, senior tax inspector and strict questioner—persuades you that there will be no tolerance of arrears for Heaney here. The replies are tantamount to, while not pre-empting, an autobiography, by someone who says he 'inclines to discretion' but is not a 'self-concealing person'. This is a forthright though not a confessional book, inclined both to 'elevated stuff' and to jokes." Times Lit Suppl

Includes bibliographical references

★ The **Oxford** book of comic verse; edited by John Gross. Oxford University Press 2009 xxxiv, 512p pa $19.95   **821**

1. English poetry -- Collections 2. American poetry -- Collections 3. Humorous poetry -- Collections

ISBN 978-0-19-956161-2

LC 2009-291577

First published 1994

The editor "defines comic verse as primarily meant to amuse. From this bland definition he delves his principles of inclusion: funny poems that do not exceed the boundaries of good taste. No bawdy lyrics, no skewering satire here. Within these limits, he surveys the field from Chaucer to Glyn Maxwell (1962)." Publ Wkly

Includes bibliographical references

★ The **Oxford** book of English verse; edited by Christopher Ricks. Oxford Univ. Press 1999 xxxii, 690p $39.95   **821**

1. English poetry -- Collections

ISBN 0-19-214182-1

LC 99-20831

First published 1900 under the editorship of Sir Arthur Quiller-Couch with title: The Oxford book of English verse, 1250-1900. Present edition replaces The New Oxford book of English verse, 1250-1950, edited by Helen Gardner published 1972

This collection "starts with anonymous 13th-century lyric and ends with Seamus Heaney; in between are seven centuries' worth of poems in English from Britain and Ireland. . . . Ricks brings in plenty of dialect verse, excerpts from long poems and verse plays, and a few translations into English. . . . Long after reviewers stop debating how Ricks chose each item, readers will keep returning to these pages to find yet another good poem they've not before seen." Publ Wkly

The **Oxford** book of sonnets; edited by John Fuller. Oxford Univ. Press 2000 xxxiv, 362p $25; pa $15.95   **821**

1. English poetry -- Collections 2. American poetry -- Collections

ISBN 0-19-214267-4; 0-19-280389-1 pa

LC 00-36757

"Indisputable masterpieces appear plentifully, but Fuller's determination to present a large number of distinguished practitioners assures that there are also many superb poems by virtual unknowns. And Fuller's introduction is a sharp-witted miracle of concise comprehensiveness." Booklist

Includes bibliographical references

The **Oxford** companion to Chaucer; edited by Douglas Gray. Oxford University Press 2003 xxiii, 526p il map $95   **821**

1. Poets 2. Authors 3. Poetry -- By individual authors

ISBN 0-19-811765-5

LC 2004-270323

This reference includes "more than 2,000 signed entries on various aspects of Chaucer and his works as well as their larger cultural and literary context." Choice

Includes bibliographical references

Paterson, Don

Rain. Farrar, Straus, and Giroux 2010 61p $24; pa $13   **821**

1. Poetry -- By individual authors

ISBN 978-0-374-24629-7; 978-0-374-53268-0 pa

LC 2009-938696

"There's something of the shadow puppeteer in Don Paterson — reading his poems, you don't know what's real and what's illusion; they play with the reader's perceptions and sense of perspective, so that you aren't quite sure whether what you're looking at are the moving figures themselves or the backlit projection screen. At their best, this gives them a curiously disorienting quality, like looking at a photographic negative, in which the world or its representation has been turned inside out." Guardian (London)

The **Penguin** book of the sonnet; 500 years of a classic tradition in English. edited by Phillis Levin. Penguin Bks. 2001 419p pa $18   **821**
1. English poetry -- Collections 2. American poetry -- Collections
ISBN 0-14-058929-5

LC 00-62350

In an introductory essay, Levin "discusses the sonnet's origins, history, traditions, and possibilities. . . . Interwoven with the history are approaches to interpreting and criticizing this poetic form. The bulk of the text is an anthology of over 600 sonnets composed by more than 230 poets. Over 150 of the poets represented wrote during the 20th century." Libr J

Includes bibliographical references

Pickard, Tom

★ **Hole** in the wall; new & selected poems. Flood Editions 2004 139p pa $15   **821**
1. Poetry -- By individual authors
ISBN 0-9710059-3-1

"In the Objectivist tradition, paring words down to broaden their sound and register meaning, Pickard's work here is of compact, dazzling, Bunting-esque musicality. It also bursts with a fluid sensual appeal reminiscent of D.H. Lawrence." Skanky Possum

Pope, Alexander

Selected poetry; edited with an introduction and notes by Pat Rogers. Oxford University Press 1998 xxiii, 226p (Oxford world's classics) pa $12.95 **821**
1. Verse satire, English. 2. Poetry -- By individual authors
ISBN 978-0-19-283494-2; 0-19-283494-0

LC 98-230887

Pope achieved "success with his first published work at the age of twenty-one. A succession of brilliant poems followed, including An Essay on Criticism (1711), Windsor Forest (1715), and his masterpiece, The Rape of the Lock. A second period of great poetry was begun in 1728 with the appearance of the first Dunciad. All these works . . . are included in this selection of his poetry." Publisher's note

Includes bibliographical references

Presley, Frances

Myne; new & selected poems and prose 1976-2005. Shearsman Books 2006 199p $20   **821**
1. Poetry -- By individual authors
ISBN 0-907562-87-6 pa

"Myne is a survey of Frances Presley's career to date, as well as a new collection of her poems. It begins with two recent cycles: the title sequence inspired by the Somerset landscape, and 'Stone Settings' which retraces the enigmatic patterns of prehistoric stones on Exmoor. Also here are the entire Somerset Letters, and Linocut, both originally published by Oasis Books, plus substantial selections from the author's first two books, The Sex of Art and Hula Hoop." Publisher's note

Raine, Kathleen

The **collected** poems of Kathleen Raine. Counterpoint 2001 368p $30   **821**
1. Imagination -- Poetry 2. Poetry -- By individual authors
ISBN 978-1-58243-135-2; 1-58243-135-3

LC 00-64448

"Here is a signature collection of [Raine's] work that will delight many and introduce her to many others. She deserves a very wide audience, as she has much to teach us. . . . Her personal religious journey was from a strict Protestant upbringing through conversion to Roman Catholicism to Eastern Vedic belief. From first to last, her poetry is unified by a tone of transcendental belief in visions, presence, angels, and oracles rooted in her Scottish mother's experience of nature." World Lit Today

Robinson, Edwin Arlington

Poems; selected and edited by Scott Donaldson. A. A. Knopf 2007 553p (Everyman's library pocket poets) $12.50   **821**
1. Poetry -- By individual authors
ISBN 978-0-307-26576-0; 0-307-26576-5

LC 2006-48269

"Wisely concentrating on poems of short and middling length, Donaldson . . . admits extracts only from Captain Craig and the ending of Lancelot. . . . [He] gives us whole texts of 'Rembrandt to Rembrandt,' 'Isaac and Archibald,' 'Aunt Imogen,' 'John Brown,' and 'Ben Jonson Entertains a Man from Stratford'— major poems all. For texts, he draws entirely from the Collected Poems, save for 'Romance' and four poems given as they appeared in magazines." New Criterion

Ross, David A.

Critical companion to William Butler Yeats; a literary reference to his life and work. Facts On File 2008 652p il (Facts on File library of world literature) $75   **821**
1. Poets 2. Authors 3. Dramatists 4. Memoirists 5. Nobel laureates for literature
ISBN 978-0-8160-5895-2

LC 2008-13642

"Coverage includes: all of Yeats's . . . poems, as well as all his volumes of poetry; all his plays and important drama-related topics, including Dublin's Abbey Theatre, which he helped establish; his critical and other nonfiction writing, including his . . . autobiographies; important themes in his work; [and] friends and literary influences, including Maud Gonne and James Joyce." Publisher's note

Includes bibliographical references

Rossetti, Christina Georgina

Christina Rossetti; the complete poems. text [edited] by R.W. Crump; notes and introduction by Betty S. Flowers. Penguin 2001 lv, 1221p (Penguin Classics) pa $20   **821**
1. Poetry -- By individual authors
ISBN 978-0-14-042366-2; 0-14-042366-4

LC 2002-281810

This "fully annotated collection, based on the definitive texts, brings together fantasy poems such as 'Goblin Market,' terrifyingly vivid verses for children, love lyrics, sonnets, hymns, and ballads, as well as the vast body of her devotional poetry. . . . [This edition] incorporates contextual notes as well as notes on the text and language, an introduction, and a chronology of Rossetti's life and work." Publisher's note

Includes bibliographical references

Rossignol, Rosalyn

√ **Critical** companion to Chaucer; a literary reference to his life and work. Facts on File 2006 648p il $85   **821**

1. Poets 2. Authors
ISBN 0-8160-6193-9; 978-0-8160-6193-8

LC 2006-99

First published 1999 with title: Chaucer A to Z

This book on the works of Chaucer includes a biography of Chaucer, synopses and critical commentary on his works (including the Canterbury Tales), and lists of related people, places and topics.

Includes bibliographical references

Schmidt, Michael

√ ★ **Lives** of the poets. Knopf 1999 975p hardcover o.p. pa $20   **821**

1. Poets, English -- Biography 2. Poetry -- By individual authors 3. English poetry -- History and criticism 4. American poetry -- History and criticism
ISBN 0-375-70604-6 pa

LC 98-51913

First published 1998 in the United Kingdom

In this "survey of poetry in English, Schmidt . . . enthuses about more than 250 poets whose work dates from the 14th century to 1998. More than a critical essay, this friendly and accessible history embodies the life of poetry and conveys its changeable, subjective beauty." Libr J

Includes bibliographical references

Shelley, Percy Bysshe, 1792-1822

Poems. Knopf 1993 250p (Everyman's library pocket poets) $12.50   **821**

1. Poetry -- By individual authors
ISBN 978-0-679-42909-8; 0-679-42909-3

LC 93-78335

"Among the English Romantics, [Shelley] has recovered his position as an undoubted major figure: the poet of volcanic hope for a better world, of fiery inspirations shot upward through bitter gloom." Oxford Companion to Engl Lit. 6th edition rev.

Shelley's poetry and prose; authoritative texts, criticism. selected and edited by Donald H. Reiman and Neil Fraistat. 2nd ed; Norton 2002 xxii, 786p il pa $18.75   **821**

1. Poetry -- By individual authors
ISBN 0-393-97752-8

LC 2001-30903

First published 1977

"This edition includes all of Shelley's greatest poetry and other poems frequently taught or discussed . . . as well as three of his most important prose works." Preface

Includes bibliographical references (p. 775-783)

and index

Sisson, C. H.

Selected poems; foreword by M.L. Rosenthal. New Directions 1996 94p pa $9.95   **821**

1. Poetry -- By individual authors
ISBN 978-0-8112-1327-1; 0-8112-1327-7

LC 95-47599

"C.H. Sisson's Christianity is an austere, rural form that forbids pity for a newborn duckling that will obviously not survive. Yet Sisson, like Frost, sees death and old age as part of a design, not so much insidious as inexorable and thus no occasion for tears. Like Donne, whom he commemorates in 'A Letter to John Donne,' Sisson understands probably better than any contemporary poet the struggle between the call of the flesh and the love of God, and he knows, like Donne, that their reconciliation can only occur in art. . . . The poems [collected here] are sardonic, elegiac, but not despairing." World Lit Today

Smith, Stevie

Collected poems; edited with a preface by James MacGibbon. New Directions 1983 591p il pa $19.95   **821**

1. Poetry -- By individual authors
ISBN 0-8112-0882-6

LC 83-43008

First published 1975 in the United Kingdom

Smith "wrote three novels, but has been more widely recognized for her witty, caustic, and enigmatic verse, much of it illustrated by her own comic drawings." Concise Oxford Companion to Engl Lit

Spark, Muriel

All the poems of Muriel Spark. New Directions 2004 130p pa $13.95   **821**

1. Poetry -- By individual authors
ISBN 978-0-8112-1576-3; 0-8112-1576-8

LC 2004-948

"As one might expect from a novelist who has always made use of the full range of fictional genres and devices, All the Poems does not come in a straightforward, chronological package or arrangement; from the outset, the book, like so much else written by Spark, is amusingly perverse. Beginning with 'A Tour of London' (c1950-51), it then immediately skips, in terms of both time and place, to 'The Dark Music of the Rue du Cherche-Midi' (2000), comes right up to date with 'The Creative Writing Class' (2003), travels back to 'The Victoria Falls' (c1948) and 'Shipton-under-Wychwood' (c1950), before regressing finally to a series of translations from Latin (c1949). The reader is therefore encouraged to search for the persistent themes and obvious connections. There is clearly a concern and interest in certain technical forms; there is a ballad, an ode, a couple of villanelles. There's the sharp intelligence and wry wit demonstrated in poems that function mainly as conundrums, unanswered questions and, possibly, as skipping rhymes. . . . But the most memorable parts of the book are those that give some clue to Spark's lifelong determination and dedication to her craft." Guardian (UK)

Spencer, Bernard, 1909-1963

Complete poetry: translations & selected prose; edited by Peter Robinson. Bloodaxe Books 2011 351p pa $33.95 **821**

1. Poetry -- By individual authors

ISBN 978-1-85224-891-8 pa; 1-85224-891-2 pa

Spencer "was not a natural self-promoter, publishing sparely and modestly; moreover, his semi-expatriate status and the adventurousness of his reading all but excluded him from narrower and more familiar English traditions. . . . This new edition by Peter Robinson, who has worked extensively with the Spencer archive at Reading University, is the first to appear since Roger Bowen's Collected Poems of 1981, and aims to stir new interest in the work. As well as Spencer's two published collections, Aegean Islands and Other Poems (1946) and With Luck Lasting (1963), and the later poems collected by Bowen, Robinson includes previously uncollected and unpublished drafts, prose drawn from interviews, lectures and notes, and Spencer's pioneering translations of George Seferis, Odysseus Elytis and Eugenio Montale. Reading these alongside his own poems, it becomes clearer than ever how much Spencer drew on Greek and Latin traditions, blending them with the green-grass Englishness of Edward Thomas, and the civilised anguish of MacNeice to make what Robinson's excellent introduction calls 'a European poetry in English'." Guardian (UK)

Spenser, Edmund

★ The **faerie** queene; edited by Thomas P. Roche, Jr., with the assistance of C. Patrick O'Donnell, Jr. Penguin Books 1987 1246p (Penguin classics) pa $20 **821**

1. Poetry -- By individual authors

ISBN 978-0-14-043307-8; 0-14-042207-2

"An epic to compare with the great epics of the classical world and of Renaissance Italy, The Faerie Queene is simultaneously a nationalistic paean to the greatness of Elizabeth and her England, an imaginative romance, and a moral allegory of the soul in quest of salvation." Reader's Ency. 4th edition

"The greatest work of Spenser, of which the first three books were entrusted to the printer in Nov. 1589, and the second three were published in 1596." Oxford Companion to Engl Lit

Stevenson, Anne

★ **Poems,** 1955-2005. Bloodaxe Books 2005 413p $64.95; pa $29.95 **821**

1. Poetry -- By individual authors

ISBN 1-85224-721-5; 1-85224-699-5 pa

"While Anne Stevenson is most certainly, and rightly, regarded as one of the major poets of our period, it has never been by virtue of this or that much anthologised poem, but by the work or mind as a whole. It is not so much a matter of the odd lightning-struck tree as of an entire landscape, and that landscape is always humane, intelligent and sane, composed of both natural and rational elements, and amply furnished with patches of wit and fury, which only serve to bring out the humanity." London Magazine

Swift, Daniel

Bomber County; the poetry of a lost pilot's war. Farrar, Straus and Giroux 2010 269p il $26 **821**

1. World War, 1939-1945 -- Poetry 2. Great Britain -- Royal Air Force 3. English poetry -- History and criticism 4. War poetry, English -- History and criticism 5. World War, 1939-1945 -- Literature and the war 6. English poetry -- 20th century -- History and criticism 7. World War, 1939-1945 -- Great Britain -- Literature and the war

ISBN 0374273316; 9780374273316

LC 2010-23402

'Bomber County' narrates the story of Daniel Swift's grandfather, "a pilot with the 83rd Squadron of the Royal Air Force, who on June 12, 1943, climbed aboard a Lancaster bomber, along with six other men for a raid on Münster, Germany. His plane never returned." (N Y Times (Late N Y Ed))

"Swift has found an ingeniously oblique way to throw fresh light on history. His main achievement here is not new facts but what is done with them, in a subtle exercise in traversing genres." Times Lit Suppl

Includes bibliographical references

Tennyson, Alfred Tennyson

Poems. A. A. Knopf 2004 255p (Everyman's library pocket poets) $12.50 **821**

1. Poetry -- By individual authors

ISBN 978-1-4000-4187-9; 1-4000-4187-2

LC 2003-49505

"This collection includes such famous poems as 'The Lady of Shalott' and 'The Charge of the Light Brigade.' There are extracts from all the major masterpieces—Idylls of the King, The Princess, In Memoriam—and several complete long poems, such as 'Ulysses' and 'Demeter and Persephone,' that demonstrate his narrative grace. Finally, there are many of the short lyrical poems, such as 'Come into the Garden, Maud' and 'Break, Break, Break,' for which he is justly celebrated." Publisher's note

Thomas, Dylan, 1914-1953

The **poems** of Dylan Thomas; edited with an introduction and notes by Daniel Jones; with a preface by Dylan Thomas. rev ed; New Directions 2003 xxix, 320p il $34.95 **821**

1. Poetry -- By individual authors

ISBN 978-0-8112-1541-1; 0-8112-1541-5

LC 2002-155790

First published 1971

"To the 90 poems Thomas published in Collected Poems, 1934-1952 Jones has added 102 and placed the total, as far as he could determine, in the chronological order of their composition. Some of the poems were still in manuscript form when Thomas died; others had been published in periodicals and anthologies. In an appendix, Jones offers Thomas' early poems—including one written when the poet was 12." Libr J [review of 1971 edition]

Includes bibliographical references

Tomlinson, Charles

 Selected poems; 1955-1997. New Directions 1997 226p pa $13.95   **821**
   1. Poetry -- By individual authors
   ISBN 978-0-8112-1369-1; 0-8112-1369-2

LC 97-25373

 "These poems are a fine achievement; they are the work of a consciousness mostly at ease with its dwelling in this world, and unabashed by a lack of inclination to dwell unduly on shadows rather than light. The sunniness of disposition, both geographically and psychologically, combined with Tomlinson's canny ability to metrically heighten what still sounds to the ear like the language of common day, give a tone that might be rationally described as Tomlinsonian. This . . . [is] a book essential to any collection of the best poetry of the postwar years." Am Book Rev

 Skywriting and other poems. Ivan R. Dee 2003 96p $18.95   **821**
   1. Poetry -- By individual authors
   ISBN 978-1-566-63541-7; 1-556-63541-1

LC 2003-55504

 "Mr Tomlinson is an eloquent poet of place—in this collection he moves through Mexico, Italy, Japan, and his home county of Gloucestershire—whose work combines visual exactitude with an uncommon gracefulness of expression." Economist

Turnbull, Gael

 ★ **There** are words; collected poems. Shearsman Books 2006 495p pa $30   **821**
   1. Poetry -- By individual authors
   ISBN 0-90756-289-2

 "Restlessly experimental—but never for its own sake—Turnbull was constantly doing what Ezra Pound asked of poets at the beginning of the twentieth century, namely to make it new. His range is very wide. He employed the long line before C.K. Williams or Ciaran Carson; he experimented with prose-poems, found-poems; he wrote ballads, poems meant to be read out loud, poems that deftly rhyme and ones that deftly don't; he shaped poems on the page with varying line-lengths and indentings; he used the spaces between lines and verses functionally; the touch is sometimes light, sometimes profoundly earnest. . . . In the almost 500pp of this superb Collected Poems there isn't one dud piece, one poem that doesn't have genuine poetic power and resonance." Stride (UK)

West, Richard

 Chaucer, 1340-1400; the life and times of the first English poet. Carroll & Graf Pubs. 2000 302p il map hardcover o.p. pa $14   **821**
   1. Poets 2. Authors 3. Great Britain -- History -- 1154-1399, Plantagenets
   ISBN 0-7867-0925-1 pa

LC 00-712752

 West's biography "combines history and literary criticism. He places Chaucer within his historical context and examines his life and writings." Libr J

Wordsworth, William, 1770-1850

 ★ **Selected** poetry of William Wordsworth; edited by Mark Van Doren; introduction by David Bromwich. Modern Lib. 2001 xxii, 687p $24.95; pa $11.95   **821**
   1. Poetry -- By individual authors
   ISBN 0-679-64224-2; 0-375-75941-7 pa

LC 00-66444

 This collection "represents Wordsworth's prolific output, from the poems first published in Lyrical Ballads in 1798 . . . to the late 'Yarrow Revisited.' Wordsworth's poetry is celebrated for its deep feeling, its use of ordinary speech, the love of nature it expresses, and its representation of commonplace things and events." Publisher's note

Yeats, W. B. (William Butler), 1865-1939

 The **collected** poems of W.B. Yeats; edited by Richard J. Finneran. Rev. 2nd ed.; Scribner Paperback Poetry 1996 xxv, 544p pa $20   **821**
   1. Poetry -- By individual authors
   ISBN 978-0-684-80731-7; 0-684-80731-9

LC 96-23314

 First published 1989 by Collier Books
 This volume "includes all of the poems authorized by Yeats for inclusion in his standard canon. . . . Revised and corrected, this edition includes Yeats's own notes on his poetry, complemented by explanatory notes from . . .Yeats scholar Richard J. Finneran." Publisher's note

821.912   English poetry -- 1900-1945

Hollis, Matthew

 Now all roads lead to France; A Life of Edward Thomas. Matthew Hollis. Faber & Faber 2011 416 p. ill., maps   **821.912**
   1. English poets -- Biography 2. World War, 1914-1918 -- Biography 3. Great Britain -- Armed forces -- Recruiting and enlistment -- Biography 4. Poets 5. Authors 6. Essayists 7. Writers on nature 8. Biography, Individual
   ISBN 0571245994; 9780571245994

LC 2011505697

 Costa Biography Award Winner (2011)
 This book presents "a study of [poet Edward] Thomas's life and work from (roughly) the winter of 1913 onwards, with a strong emphasis on his poetic aspirations." (Times Literary Supplement). "[Matthew] Hollis gives a portrait of the artist as a man at work: shaping, revising, making poems. The biography . . . [is] a story of . . . the last four years of his life, during which he developed a close friendship with Robert Frost, decided to enlist in the army and fight in the First World War, and turned himself into a poet." (New Statesman)
 Includes bibliographical references and index.

822   English drama

Bennett, Alan

The **history** boys. Faber and Faber 2006 xxvii, 109p pa $13   **822**

1. England -- Drama. 2. Education -- Drama. 3. Boarding schools -- Drama. 4. Teacher-student relationships -- Drama.

ISBN 978-0-571-22464-7; 0-571-22464-4

LC 2005-936593

First published 2004 in the United Kingdom

Characters: 11 men, 1 woman extras. First produced at the Lyttleton Theatre, London, May 18, 2004

"Nothing could diminish the incendiary achievement of this subtle, deep-wrought and immensely funny play about the value and meaning of education. . . . In short, a superb, life-enhancing play." Guardian

Bolt, Robert

A **man** for all seasons; a play in two acts. Random House 1962 xxv, 163p il hardcover o.p. pa $9.50   **822**

1. Saints 2. Authors 3. Statesmen 4. Writers on law 5. Writers on religion 6. Great Britain -- History -- 1485-1603, Tudors -- Drama

ISBN 0-679-72822-8 pa

Characters: 11 men, 2 women. First produced in the United States at the ANTA Theatre, New York City, November 22, 1961

A play set in sixteenth century England about Sir Thomas More, a devout Catholic, and his conflict with Henry VIII.

Christie, Agatha

The **mousetrap** and other plays. New American Library 2000 742p hardcover o.p. pa $7.99   **822**

1. English drama -- Collections

ISBN 0-451-20118-3; 0-451-20114-0 pa

LC 00-64727

First published 1978 by Dodd, Mead

"The noted mystery writer composed adaptations of seven novels and stories into arresting plays as well as creating one original theater piece ('Verdict'). . . . All are as delightful to read for pleasure as Christie's mystery novels, especially since some that earlier appeared in the latter form have been intriguingly altered." Booklist

Churchill, Caryl

Mad forest; a play from Romania. Theatre Communications Group 1996 87p pa $13.95   **822**

ISBN 1-55936-114-X; 978-1-55936-114-9

LC 96-12875

First published 1991 in the United Kingdom

Large mixed cast. 3 acts. First performed at the New York Theater Workshop, New York, December 4, 1991

This play "explores the reactions of two ordinary families to the confused events of the Romanian revolution: the dreadful damage done to people's lives by years of repression, and the painful difficulties of sudden but lasting change." Publisher's note

Coward, Noel

Three plays; Blithe spirit, Hay fever, Private lives. introduction by Philip Hoare. Vintage Bks. 1999 254p pa $13   **822**

ISBN 0-679-78179-X

LC 98-47414

First published 1965 by Dell

Dryden, John

✓★ **All** for love; edited by David M. Vieth. University of Neb. Press 1972 xxxiv, 146p (Regents Restoration drama series) hardcover o.p. pa $24.95   **822**

1. Queens

ISBN 0-8032-5379-6 pa

An English Restoration tragedy which is an adaptation of Shakespeare's "Antony and Cleopatra" done in blank verse

Everyman, and medieval miracle plays; edited by A. C. Cawley; with a new preface and bibliography by Anne Rooney. Tuttle 1993 256p hardcover o.p. pa $6.95   **822**

1. Mysteries and miracle plays

ISBN 0-460-87280-X pa

First Everyman's library edition published 1909 with title: Everyman, with other interludes including eight miracle plays

In addition to Everyman, this collection includes plays from the Towneley, Coventry, York and Chester cycles.

Includes bibliographical references

Fugard, Athol

Blood knot and other plays. Theatre Communications Group 1991 202p hardcover o.p. pa $15 **822**

ISBN 978-1-55936-019-7; 1-55936-019-4

LC 90-29029

"The brothers of Blood Knot—one dark-skinned, one light—betray their dream of a better future with the impossible wish of passing for white. In Hello and Goodbye, a poor white brother and sister churn through their once-promising past to comprehend their bleak present. Boesman and Lena, black husband and wife, tramp homelessly through a severe and unforgiving landscape, discovering strength and delivering devotion through an encounter with a mysterious old African." Publisher's note

✓★ **Master** Harold-- and the boys. Vintage Books 2009 60p pa $12.95   **822**

1. South Africa -- Race relations -- Drama

ISBN 978-0-307-47520-6; 0-307-47520-4

LC 2010-292381

First published 1982 by Random House

Characters: 3 men. 1 act. First produced at the Yale Repertory theatre, New Haven, Connecticut, 1982.

Drama with racial overtones set in Port Elizabeth tea room focuses on precocious white South African teenager's relationship with two black men who work for his family, both old enough to be his father.

Gay, John

The **beggar's** opera; edited by Edgar V. Roberts; music edited by Edward Smith. University of Neb. Press 1969 xxix, 238p music (Regents Restoration drama series) hardcover o.p. pa $21.95   **822**

ISBN 978-0-8032-5361-2 pa; 0-8032-5361-3 pa

First published 1728

A ballad opera, this is a rogues' comedy satirizing corrupt politics in 18th century England

Heaney, Seamus

The **burial** at Thebes; a version of Sophocles' Antigone. Farrar, Straus and Giroux 2004 79p $18   **822**

ISBN 0-374-11721-7

LC 2004-43986

"There are many translations of Sophocles' Antigone but few with the understated power and spare beauty of . . . Heaney's version. . . . Written in a muscular but lively style, the translation, like Heaney's best poetry, finds music in the language of the streets and reveals the raw, primal power in the most carefully constructed rhetorical tropes." Booklist

Jonson, Ben

Volpone and other plays; edited by Michael Jamieson. Penguin 2004 496p (Penguin classics) pa $12   **822**

ISBN 978-0-14-144118-4; 0-14-144118-6

LC 2004-275516

First published 1966 in the United Kingdom with title: Three comedies

"Ben Jonson created in Volpone and The Alchemist hilarious portraits of cupidity and chicanery, while in Bartholomew Fair he portrays his fellow Londoners at their most festive—and most bawdy." Publisher's note

Osborne, John

Look back in anger. Penguin 1982 96p (Penguin Plays) pa $12   **822**

ISBN 0-14-048-175-3; 978-0-14-048-175-4

LC 82-9144

First published 1957 by Criterion Books

Characters: 3 men, 2 women. First produced at the Royal Court Theatre, London, May 8, 1956

This play "introduced a new strain of realism to British theatre and set the tone for the generation of anti-Establishment writers who became known as the Angry Young Men. Osborne described his own parents as 'impoverished middle class,' but his play deals with the frustrations, crude language, and squalid conditions of working-class life." Reader's Ency. 4th edition

Peters, Sally

Bernard Shaw; the ascent of the superman. Yale Univ. Press 1996 328p il hardcover o.p. pa $22 **822**

1. Authors 2. Novelists 3. Dramatists 4. Dramatists, English 5. Essayists 6. Nonfiction writers 7. Nobel laureates for literature

ISBN 0-300-06097-1; 0-300-07500-6 pa

LC 95-37248

An "exploration of the ambiguities and passions that formed this great playwright and thinker. Shaw's sexuality, always a good topic of speculation, is studied here, but one wishes for more insights and in-depth analysis. Peters does devote a chapter to Shaw's close relationship with the actor and playwright Harley Granville Barker, mainly from Shaw's point of view. One may not agree with Peter's conclusions, but they will prove to be of interest to anyone studying Shaw." Libr J

Includes bibliographical references

Pinter, Harold

Complete works; with an introduction, Writing for the theatre. Grove Weidenfeld 1990 4v v1 pa $14.50; v2 pa $13.50; v3 pa $14; v4 pa $13.50 **822**

ISBN 0-8021-5096-9 v1; 0-8021-3237-5 v2; 0-8021-5049-7 v3; 0-8021-5050-0 v4

LC 90-13933

First Grove Press edition published 1977-1981

Plays

The **complete** plays; edited by Frank Romany and Robert Lindsey. Penguin Books 2003 xliv, 702p (Penguin classics) pa $15   **822**

ISBN 978-0-14-043633-4; 0-14-043633-2

LC 2004-268858

Includes bibliographical references

Shaffer, Peter

★ **Equus**. Scribner 2005 112p pa $12   **822**

ISBN 0-7432-8730-4; 978-0-7432-8730-2

LC 2005-51600

First published 1973 in the United Kingdom

Characters: 5 men, 4 women. 1 act, 35 scenes. First produced by the National Theater, London, July 26, 1973

Drama about "a jolting confrontation between a psychiatrist and a 17-year-old boy who has blinded six horses from the stable where he is employed. As the probe into the boy's attitudes and behavior deepens, this criminal act is revealed to have been a result of his notions of a sexual/religious spirit in horses." Booklist

★ **Peter** Shaffer's Amadeus; with an introduction by the director Sir Peter Hall and a wholly new preface by the author. Perennial Bks. 2001 xxxiv, 124p pa $15   **822**

1. Composers

ISBN 0-06-093549-9

LC 2001-278382

First published 1980 in the United Kingdom

Characters: 9 men, 1 woman, extras. 2 acts. First produced at the National Theater of Great Britain, November 1979

Explores relationship between Autrian court composer Antonio Salieri and the divinely gifted young Wolfgang Amadeus Mozart.

Shaw, Bernard

Arms and the man; a pleasant play. [by] Bernard Shaw; introduction by Rodelle Weintraub; definitive text under the editorial supervision of Dan H. Laurence. Penguin Books 2006 xxvi 73 (Penguin classics) pa $9 **822**

ISBN 978-0-14-303976-1; 0-14-303976-8

LC 2005-56724

First produced 1894. Comedy set in Bulgaria satirizing romantic attitudes about war.

Heartbreak House; a fantasia in the Russian manner on English themes. definitive text under the editorial supervision of Dan H. Laurence; with an introduction by David Hare. Penguin Books 2000 160p il (Penguin Classics) pa $10 **822**

ISBN 978-0-14-043787-4; 0-14-043787-8

LC 2001-266517

Written in 1913, first produced 1920

"A complex allegorical work in which Shaw indicts apathy, confusion, and lack of purpose as the causes of the world's problems. The characters—all larger than life and with symbolic names—are gathered at the home of an eccentric sea captain; they each represent an evil in the modern world. Into their midst comes young Ellie Dunn, whose search for a husband Shaw treats as a new generation searching for a way of life." Benet's Reader's Ency. 4th edition

Includes bibliographical references

Major Barbara; definitive text under the editorial supervision of Dan H. Laurence; with an introduction by Margery Morgan. Penguin Books 2000 156p (Penguin classics) pa $11 **822**

1. Crime 2. Salvation Army 3. Father-daughter relationship

ISBN 978-0-14-043790-4; 0-14-043790-8

LC 2002-275028

In this "comedy, originally staged in 1905, Andrew Undershaft, a millionaire armaments dealer, loves money and despises poverty. His energetic daughter Barbara, however, is a devout major in the Salvation Army. She sees her father as just another soul to be saved. But when the Salvation Army needs funds to keep going, it is Undershaft who saves the day." Publisher's note

Man and Superman; a comedy and a philosophy. definitive text under the editorial supervision of Dan H. Laurence; introduced by Stanley Weintraub. Penguin 2000 264p (Penguin classics) pa $11 **822**

ISBN 978-0-14-043788-1; 0-14-043788-6

"In Man and Superman, Shaw combined seriousness with comedy to create a satirical and buoyant exposé of the eternal struggle between the sexes. . . . This volume includes Shaw's Preface of 1903 and his appendix, 'The Revolutionist's Handbook', the cast list from the first production of Man and Superman and a list of his principal works." Publisher's note

★ **Pygmalion** . . and My fair lady; [Pygmalion] by George Bernard Shaw; and My fair lady/based on Shaw's Pygmalion; adaptation and lyrics by Alan Jay Lerner; music by Frederick Loewe. 50th anniversary ed.; Signet Classic 2006 219p pa $5.95 **822**

ISBN 0-451-53009-8

My fair lady was awarded the New York Drama Critics Circle Award for 1956

This volume includes the complete texts of Shaw's Pygmalion and Lerner's musical adaptation My fair lady.

Saint Joan; a chronicle play in six scenes and an epilogue. definitive text under the editorial supervision of Dan H. Laurence; with `On playing Joan¿ by Imogen Stubbs; and an introduction by Joley Wood. Penguin 2003 xx, 168p (Penguin classics) pa $12 **822**

1. Saints

ISBN 978-0-14-043791-6; 0-14-04379-1

First produced 1923

Chronicle play in "which Joan of Arc, the young girl who led France to victory over the English, emerges as an unlettered country girl gifted with masterful will and innate intelligence." McGraw-Hill Ency World Drama

Sheridan, Richard Brinsley

The **school** for scandal and other plays; edited with an introduction by Eric S. Rump. New ed; Penguin 2004 288p (Penguin classics) pa $12 **822**

1. Great Britain -- Social life and customs

ISBN 978-0-14-043240-4

First published 1988

"In The Rivals, Captain Absolute becomes his own rival for the hand of Lydia Languish wooing her under another name, while her aunt, the verbally inept Mrs Malaprop, wishes her to marry the real Captain. The Critic, featuring the pompous Puff and the arrogant Sneer, is a mocking depiction of the theatre, playwrights and, of course, critics. And The School for Scandal continues the theme of imposture when Sir Oliver Surface tests his nephews by appearing before them in disguise, and learns that reputation and the approval of society are of little value. In his introduction, Eric S. Rump places the plays in their historical and dramatic context and examines their enduring popularity." Publisher's note

Stoppard, Tom

Arcadia. Faber & Faber 1993 97p hardcover o.p. pa $14 **822**

ISBN 0-571-16934-1 pa

LC 94-103754

Characters: 8 men, 3 women. 2 acts, 7 scenes. First produced at the Royal National Theatre, London, 1993. In the U.S., first produced at the Lincoln Center Theater, New York City, March 30, 1995

The **invention** of love. Grove Press 1998 102p pa $12 **822**

1. Poets 2. Authors

ISBN 0-8021-3581-1

LC 98-28331

Characters: 19 men, 1 woman, extras. 2 acts. First performed at the American Conservatory Theater, San Francisco, January 14, 2000

★ **Rosencrantz** and Guildenstern are dead. Grove Press 1967 126p hardcover o.p. pa $12 **822**
1. Poets 2. Authors 3. Dramatists
ISBN 0-8021-3275-8 pa

Characters: 13 men, 2 women, extras. First produced in this form April 11, 1967 in London

This play "took the theatre world on both sides of the Atlantic by storm. The originality of the idea which put Hamlet's two insignificant friends centerstage was matched by the brilliance of the dialogue between these bewildered nonentities." Reader's Ency. 4th edition

Travesties. Grove Press 1975 99p pa $13 **822**
ISBN 0-8021-5089-6

Characters: 5 men, 2 women. Prologue, 2 acts. First produced at the Aldwych Theatre, London, June 10, 1974

Synge, J. M.
The **complete** plays. Vintage Bks. 1960 268p pa $10 **822**
ISBN 0-394-70178-X

Thomas, Dylan, 1914-1953
Under milk wood; a play for voices. New Directions 1954 107p music pa $8.95 **822**
ISBN 0-8112-0209-7

"A radio play for voices. Written in poetic, inventive prose, this play is full of humor, a joyful sense of the goodness of life and love, and a strong Welsh flavor. It is an impression of a spring day in the lives of the people of Llareggub, a Welsh village situated under Milk Wood. It has no plot, but a wealth of characters who dream aloud, converse with one another, and speak in choruses of alternating voices." Reader's Ency. 4th edition

Wilde, Oscar, 1854-1900
★ The **importance** of being earnest and other plays; introduction by Terrence McNally; notes by Michael F. Davis. Modern Library 2003 257p pa $9.95 **822**
ISBN 0-8129-6714-3

LC 2003-44566

The title play, written in 1895, is a drawing room comedy exposing quirks and foibles of Victorian society with plot revolving around amorous pursuits of two men who face social obstacles when they woo young ladies of quality. The book also features Lady Windermere's fan (1893), a four act comedy about a woman who has an affair when she suspects her husband of adultery, and An ideal husband (1895), a comedy about a blackmail scheme involving a lord's investment in the Suez Canal days before the British government's purchase of it, and his wife's reaction to her husband's past misdeeds.

822.3 Drama of Elizabethan period, 1558-1625

Baker, William
The **facts** on file companion to Shakespeare; William Baker and Kenneth Womack. Facts On File 2011 5 v. (acid-free paper) $375.00 **822.3**
1. English drama -- History and criticism
ISBN 0816078203; 9780816078202

LC 2010054012

This book focuses on the author William Shakespeare. "Volume 1 is made up of background essays and more on Shakespeare's times and texts. Poems and sonnets are covered in volume 2, offering for each analysis and a bibliography. In volumes 3, 4, and 5, plays are covered in a 'complete works' fashion designed for use as a textbook. . . . These are followed by an overview essay and excerpts from 'classic criticism.'"(Booklist)

Includes bibliographical references and index

Bate, Jonathan
Soul of the age; a biography of the mind of William Shakespeare. Random House 2009 471p il map $35 **822.3**
1. Poets 2. Authors 3. Dramatists
ISBN 978-1-4000-6206-5

LC 2008-16561

In this biography of Shakespeare, the author uses "the Bard's own 'Seven Ages of Man' speech from As You Like It to envision him as an infant, a school boy, a lover, a soldier, a justice, a pantaloon, and an old man entering 'oblivion.' The result is a fresh new way to look at Shakespeare and a welcome reminder of what literary biography can still do." Libr J

Includes bibliographical references

Bloom, Harold
Hamlet : poem unlimited. Riverhead Bks. 2003 154p hardcover o.p. pa $13 **822.3**
1. Poets 2. Authors 3. Dramatists
ISBN 1-57322-233-X; 1-57322-377-8 pa

LC 2002-31691

"Far superior to existing theories of performance and worth yards of criticism for each well-wrought page." Libr J

Shakespeare : the invention of the human. Riverhead Bks. 1998 xx, 745p hardcover o.p. pa $18 **822.3**
1. Poets 2. Authors 3. Dramatists
ISBN 1-57322-751-X pa

LC 98-21325

In this critical study, Bloom argues "that the plays and poems of Shakespeare are not just 'the center of the Western canon'; they are nothing less than 'secular scripture.'. . . Bloom's book proceeds through genre groupings in rough chronological order." Commentary

"The passion and obsessiveness of Bloom's approach are its greatest recommendation." N Y Rev Books

Boyce, Charles
Critical companion to William Shakespeare; a literary reference to his life and work. Rev. ed; Facts

on File 2005 2v il (Facts on File library of world literature) set $104.50 **822.3**

1. Poets 2. Authors 3. Dramatists
ISBN 0-8160-5373-1

LC 2004-25769

First published 1990 with title: Shakespeare A to Z

"The first two-thirds [of this set] covers the plays. Arranged alphabetically by title, the 3000 entries generally consist of a scene-by-scene summary, a commentary, sources, theatrical history, and character sketches. The last one-third features entries for actors, composers, musicians, places that figured in the plays, and miscellaneous items." Libr J

Includes bibliographical references

Bryson, Bill

Shakespeare; the world as stage. Atlas Books/HarperCollins 2007 199p (Eminent lives) $19.95 **822.3**

1. Poets 2. Authors 3. Dramatists
ISBN 978-0-06-074022-1; 0-06-074022-1

LC 2007-21647

In this biography, the author marshals "the usual little facts that others might overlook—for example, that in Shakespeare's day perhaps 40% of women were pregnant when they got married—to paint a portrait of the world in which the Bard lived and prospered. . . . Bryson is a pleasant and funny guide to a subject at once overexposed and elusive—as Bryson puts it, he is a kind of literary equivalent of an electron—forever there and not there." Publ Wkly

Includes bibliographical references

Butler, Colin

The **practical** Shakespeare; the plays in practice and on the page. Ohio University Press 2005 205p $39.95; pa $19.95 **822.3**

1. Poets 2. Authors 3. Dramatists
ISBN 0-8214-1621-9; 0-8214-1622-7 pa

LC 2004-30580

"Notes on staging, acting behaviors, scenes not shown, entrances, exits, characterizations, prologues, choruses, and staging are each featured in the text. References to specific scenes in the plays are used to illustrate and support the material. Any group preparing a production of one of the plays should find this a useful reference." Univ Press Books for Public and Second Sch Libr, 2006

Includes bibliographical references

Collins, Paul

★ The **book** of William; how Shakespeare's first folio conquered the world. Bloomsbury 2009 246p $25 **822.3**

1. Poets 2. Authors 3. Dramatists 4. Rare books
ISBN 978-1-59691-195-6; 1-59691-195-6

LC 2009-6722

"Witty, detailed, and highly entertaining, . . . [this book] will be appreciated by fans of Shakespeare, history, or human folly." Libr J

Includes bibliographical references

Frye, Northrop

Northrop Frye on Shakespeare; edited by Robert Sandler. Yale Univ. Press 1986 186p hardcover o.p. pa $17 **822.3**

1. Poets 2. Authors 3. Dramatists
ISBN 0-300-04208-6 pa

LC 86-50485

Shakespeare scholar Frye provides in-depth analyses of ten plays.

"Frye's work is completely accessible, its style crisp and engaging. Most of all, it is full of basic 'good sense' about our most abused literary figure." Libr J

Garber, Marjorie

Shakespeare after all. Pantheon Books 2004 989p hardcover o.p. pa $20 **822.3**

1. Poets 2. Authors 3. Dramatists
ISBN 0-375-42190-4; 0-385-72214-1 pa

LC 2004-40063

The author "provides a handbook on Shakespeare's plays. After an introduction supplying standard overviews of the Renaissance theater and Shakespeare's life, she offers a critical essay on each play, complete with bibliographies and filmographies. The strength of this work is that Garber shows how the plays are interrelated by recurring language, characters, and themes, how each era has interpreted Shakespeare for itself, and how Shakespeare continues to shape today's culture." Libr J

Includes bibliographical references

Shakespeare and modern culture. Pantheon Books 2008 326p il $30 **822.3**

1. Poets 2. Authors 3. Dramatists
ISBN 978-0-307-37767-8; 0-307-37767-9

LC 2008-26802

"Writing on ten plays, [Garber] offers examples of their 'uncanny' anticipation of present-day phenomena and our own appropriations of them, as in the now fashionable use of 'Henry V' as a blueprint for success in business. (She quotes one manual that calls Bardolph's hanging the 'ultimate pink slip.') Garber's approach is eclectic, spanning Freud and evolutionary biology; occasionally, she gets caught up in secondary concerns, but she is an inspiring reader." New Yorker

Includes bibliographical references

Greenblatt, Stephen J.

Will in the world; how Shakespeare became Shakespeare. [by] Stephen Greenblatt. Norton 2004 430p il $26.95 **822.3**

1. Poets 2. Authors 3. Dramatists
ISBN 0-393-05057-2

LC 2004-11512

"Greenblatt is at his best when he merges his gifts as a literary critic and scholar with his instincts as a biographer. He writes with real subtlety and skill about the sonnets. . . . He also writes very well about the climate of fear and the use of public punishment and torture in Elizabethan and early Jacobean England, and how this enters into the very spirit of Shakespeare's work." N Y Times Book Rev

Includes bibliographical references

★ The **Greenwood** companion to Shakespeare; a comprehensive guide to students. edited by Joseph Rosenblum. Greenwood Press 2005 4v set $299.95 **822.3**

1. Poets 2. Authors 3. Dramatists
ISBN 0-313-32779-3

LC 2004-28690

"Each of the set's four volumes relates to a specific genre—Overviews and the History Plays (Vol. 1), The Comedies (Vol. 2), The Tragedies (Vol. 3), and The Romances and Poetry (Vol. 4)—and is organized in 'Cliff Notes' fashion, devoting each entry to a single play, long poem, sonnet, or sonnet pair. . . . A great introduction to the Bard." Libr J

Includes bibliographical references

Heylin, Clinton

So long as men can breathe; the untold story of Shakespeare's Sonnets. Da Capo Press 2009 280p $24 **822.3**

1. Poets 2. Authors 3. Dramatists
ISBN 978-0-306-81805-9; 0-306-81805-1

LC 2009-08999

An account of the publication of Shakespeare's Sonnets. The author "introduces us to the 'unholy alliance' involved in this precarious enterprise: Thomas Thorpe, the publisher, a self-described 'well wishing adventurer;' George Eld, the printer, heavily embroiled in large-scale pirating; William Aspley, the prestigious bookseller, who mysteriously ended his association with Thorpe soon after. Leaving the calamitous world of Elizabethan publishing, Heylin goes on to chart the many editions of the Sonnets through the years and the editorial decisions that led to their present configuration." Publisher's note

Includes bibliographical references

Kenji Yoshino

A **thousand** times more fair; what Shakespeare can teach us about justice. Ecco 2011 305p $26.99; ebook $12.99 **822.3**

1. Poets 2. Authors 3. Dramatists 4. Law in literature
ISBN 0-06-176910-X; 0-06-208772-X ebook; 978-0-06-176910-8; 978-0-06-208772-0 ebook

Looks at the roles of justice and law in the lives of modern-day people through the lens of Shakespeare's plays.

"Readers will find Yoshino provocative, often controversial, and Shakespeare, as always, entertaining." Publ Wkly

Includes bibliographical references

Kermode, Frank

Shakespeare's language. Farrar, Straus & Giroux 2000 324p hardcover o.p. pa $15 **822.3**

1. Poets 2. Authors 3. Dramatists
ISBN 0-374-52774-1 pa

LC 99-55846

Kermode "devotes particular attention to the four great tragedies written at the height of Shakespeare's powers: Hamlet, Othello, King Lear and Macbeth. While Kermode's concern is with the Bard's verse, he betrays no simplistic notions about literary language operating in a vacuum. A careful, close analysis of passages in each play is informed by a breathtaking knowledge of Elizabethan history and culture,

as well as by the entire history of Shakespeare criticism from Coleridge to Eliot and the new historicists." Publ Wkly

Includes bibliographical references

Lamb, Charles

Tales from Shakespeare; by Charles & Mary Lamb; with an introduction by Marina Warner. Penguin Books 2007 304p (Penguin classics) pa $12 **822.3**

1. Poets 2. Authors 3. Dramatists
ISBN 978-0-14-144162-7; 0-14-144162-3
First published 1807

A now classic collection of twenty plays by Shakespeare adapted as prose stories—the comedies by Mary Lamb, the tragedies by Charles Lamb

"The Tales were the first version of 'Shakespeare' to be published specifically for children. They are written in a clear, vigorous style, not often encumbered by the attempt to make the language resemble that of the original. A lot is left out. . . . But the literary quality of the Tales makes them outshine almost every other English children's book of this period, and they proved an immediate and lasting success." Oxford Companion to Child Lit

★ **Living** with Shakespeare; essays by writers, actors, and directors. Edited by Susannah Carson ; Foreword by Harold Bloom. Vintage Books, A Division of Random House, Inc. 2013 xxviii, 500 p.p ill. (paperback) $16 **822.3**
ISBN 0307742911; 9780307742919

LC 2012039745

This book, edited by Susanna Carson, presents collected essays reflecting on the works and influence of playwright William Shakespeare. "Carson invites forty actors, directors, scholars, and writers to reflect on why his work is still such a vital part of our culture. We hear from James Earl Jones on reclaiming Othello as a tragic hero, Julie Taymor on turning Prospero into Prospera, Camille Paglia on teaching the plays to actors, . . . [and] Germaine Greer on the playwright's home life." (Publisher's note)

"Editor Carson's eclecticism aims to break down the usual disciplinary borders and reduce the intimidating distance that often yawns between Shakespeare experts and general readers... The essays include much justified reverence, but also some healthy questioning, as well as limited forays into cross-cultural dialogues... [A] consistently stimulating read..." Pub Wkly.

Norwich, John Julius

Shakespeare's kings; the great plays and the history of England in the Middle Ages, 1337-1485. Scribner 2000 401p il hardcover o.p. pa $16 **822.3**

1. Poets 2. Authors 3. Dramatists
ISBN 0-7432-0031-4 pa

LC 99-58271

The author offers "overviews of Edward III; Richard II; Henry IV, parts 1 and 2; Henry V; Henry VI, parts 1, 2, and 3; and Richard III, examining each play through the lens of history. In addition to providing the necessary historical commentary, he also fills in the gaps between the plays, enabling readers to thoroughly comprehend the entire series in the proper historical context." Booklist

Nuttall, A. D.

Shakespeare the thinker. Yale University Press 2007 428p $30   **822.3**

1. England -- Intellectual life -- 16th century 2. England -- Intellectual life -- 17th century

ISBN 978-0-300-11928-2; 0-300-11928-3

LC 2006-35179

The author "traces ideas about motivation, identity, speech, and symbol in Shakespeare's plays. His study is rich in unexpected juxtapositions: Hippolyta, of 'A Midsummer Night's Dream,' finds herself in casual conversation with David Hume, and Titus Andronicus is seen in the context of 'Goodfellas.' The analysis never pulls too far away from the action onstage; indeed, Nuttall painstakingly shows Shakespeare's skill at negotiating abstract ideas through suspense, conflict, and character." New Yorker

Includes bibliographical references

Olsen, Kirstin

All things Shakespeare; an encyclopedia of Shakespeare's world. Greenwood Press 2002 2v il maps set $150   **822.3**

1. Poets 2. Authors 3. Dramatists 4. Reference books

ISBN 0-313-31503-5

LC 2002-69732

This "encyclopedia describes Shakespeare's physical environment, including common objects, daily activities, and popular beliefs and attitudes. Information is grouped into general topic clusters such as 'Behavior,' 'Clothing and Dress,' 'Furniture,' 'Fire,' and 'War and Peace.' . . . Within the 200-plus entries, references are made to the play, act, and scene in which Shakespeare mentions the item or activity being discussed." Libr J

★ The **Oxford** companion to Shakespeare; general editor, Michael Dobson; associate general editor, Stanley Wells. Oxford Univ. Press 2001 xxix, 541p il maps hardcover o.p. pa $39.95   **822.3**

1. Poets 2. Authors 3. Dramatists 4. Reference books

ISBN 0-19-811735-3; 0-19-280614-9 pa

LC 2001-277478

This volume "illuminates not only Shakespeare's life and works but also the many forms that interpretation of Shakespeare has taken in the centuries since his death." Booklist

Includes bibliographical references

Rasmussen, Eric

The **Shakespeare** thefts; in search of the first folios. Palgrave Macmillan 2011 212p il   **822.3**

1. Poets 2. Theft 3. Authors 4. Dramatists 5. Rare books 6. Book collecting

ISBN 9780230109414; 9780230341203 ebook

LC 2011028287

This book discusses "the known surviving copies of the 1623 First Folio, which published 36 of [William] Shakespeare's plays. Of the 232 recorded surviving copies, the majority are in public institutions rather than private hands. [Eric] Rasmussen . . . and his team of researchers were part of the global quest to catalog every extant copy." (Library Journal)

"Part literary history and part detective story, this is an engaging book about the known surviving copies of the 1623 First Folio, which published 36 of Shakespeare's plays. Of the 232 recorded surviving copies, the majority are in public institutions rather than private hands. Rasmussen . . . and his team of researchers were part of the global quest to catalog every extant copy. Rasmussen uses a lively, nonacademic style and engrossing anecdotes to tell us about one of history's most fascinating books." Libr J

Includes bibliographical references

Rosenbaum, Ron

The **Shakespeare** wars; clashing scholars, public fiascoes, palace coups. Random House 2006 601p $35   **822.3**

1. Poets 2. Authors 3. Dramatists

ISBN 0-375-50339-0; 978-0-375-50339-9

LC 2006-42541

The author "conveys the impassioned arguments of leading directors and scholars concerning how Shakespeare should be printed and performed. . . . Balancing academic reportage with his own lively observations, Rosenbaum wrestles with the weightiest issues of Shakespeare studies in a down-to-earth manner that readers will applaud." Publ Wkly

Includes bibliographical references

Shakespeare, William, 1564-1616

★ The **complete** works; general editors, Stanley Wells and Gary Taylor; editors, Stanley Wells . . . [et al.]; with introductions by Stanley Wells. 2nd ed.; Clarendon Press; Oxford University Press 2005 lxxv, 1344p il $40   **822.3**

ISBN 0-19-926717-0

LC 2005-47272

First published 1986

This anthology "features a brief introduction to each work as well as [a] General Introduction. . . . [The volume includes] essay on language, a list of contemporary allusions to Shakespeare, an index of Shakespearean characters, a glossary, a consolidated bibliography, and an index of first lines of the Sonnets." Publisher's note

Shapiro, James

Contested Will; who wrote Shakespeare? James Shapiro. Simon & Schuster 2010 339 p. $26 **822.3**

1. Poets 2. Authors 3. Dramatists

ISBN 978-1-4165-4162-2; 1-4165-4162-4; 1416541624; 9781416541622

LC 2009032710

"A thorough, engaging work whose arguments would prove more persuasive were we not living in an era of such fierce anti-intellectualism and pervasive conspiracy theory." Kirkus

Includes bibliographical references and index

A **year** in the life of William Shakespeare, 1599. HarperCollins Publishers 2005 394p il map $27.95   **822.3**

1. Poets 2. Authors 3. Dramatists

ISBN 0-571-21448-0

LC 2005-43342

The author "offers a critical examination of four plays Shakespeare wrote in the seminal year of 1599—Henry V, Julius Caesar, As You Like It, and Hamlet—and of the

events that influenced the Bard at the time of their writing...
. This work gives the reader a realistic sense of the multilayered and complex political, social, and literary pressures that
influenced Shakespeare as a citizen of England, as a business
partner in the Globe Theatre, and as a writer." Libr J

Includes bibliographical references

Wells, Stanley W.

★ **Shakespeare** : for all time; [by] Stanley Wells.
Oxford Univ. Press 2003 xxi, 442p il $40   **822.3**
1. Poets 2. Authors 3. Dramatists
ISBN 0-19-516093-2

LC 2002-27412

First published 2002 in the United Kingdom

"Chapters on Shakespeare's life in Stratford and in London offer a . . . view of the development of the writer's career
and personality. At the core of the book lies a . . . study of
the writings themselves—how Shakespeare set about writing a play, his relationships with the company of actors with
whom he worked, his developing mastery of the literary
and rhetorical skills that he learned at the Stratford grammar school, the essentially theatrical quality of the structure
and language of his plays. Subsequent chapters trace the
fluctuating fortunes of his reputation and influence." Publisher's note

Includes bibliographical references

Wills, Garry

Verdi's Shakespeare; man of the theater. Viking
2011 220p $25.95   **822.3**
1. Opera 2. Poets 3. Authors 4. Composers 5.
Dramatists 6. Italy -- History -- 19th century
ISBN 978-0-670-02304-2

LC 2011019768

Includes bibliographical references

823   English fiction

Achebe, Chinua, 1930-2013

Home and exile. Anchor Bks. 2001 115p pa
$11   **823**
1. Africa -- Civilization
ISBN 978-0-385-72133-2; 0-385-72133-1

LC 2001-22599

First published 2000 by Oxford University Press

"This slim volume—told in Achebe's subtle, witty and
gracious style—is one of those small gems of literary and
historical analysis that readers will treasure and reread over
the years." Publ Wkly

Includes bibliographical references

There was a country; a personal history of Bi-
afra. Chinua Achebe. Penguin Press 2012 352 p.
$27.95   **823**
1. Autobiographies 2. Authors, Nigerian -- 20th century
-- Biography 3. Nigeria -- History -- Civil War, 1967-
1970 -- Personal narratives
ISBN 1594204829; 9781594204821

LC 2012005603

This memoir recounts author Chinua Achebe's experience of "the Nigerian civil war, also known as the Biafran

War, of 1967-1970. The conflict was infamous for its savage impact on the Biafran people, Chinua Achebe's people,
many of whom were starved to death after the Nigerian government blockaded their borders. . . . [Achebe] took the Biafran side in the conflict and served his government as a roving
cultural ambassador, from which vantage he absorbed the
war's full horror." (Publisher's note)

Includes bibliographical references and index.

Baker, William

Critical companion to Jane Austen; a literary reference to her life and work. Facts on File 2008 644p
il (Facts on File library of world literature) $75 **823**
1. Authors 2. Novelists
ISBN 978-0-8160-6416-8

LC 2006-102848

This book examines Jane Austen's "life and works, and
includes critical analyses of the themes within her writing, as
well as entries on related topics and relevant people, places,
and influences." Publisher's note

Includes bibliographical references

Ballard, J. G., 1930-2009

Miracles of life; Shanghai to Shepperton : an
autobiography. J.G. Ballard. Liveright Pub. Corporation 2013 272 p. il (hardcover) $25.95   **823**
1. Authorship 2. World War, 1939-1945 -- Influence 3.
Novelists, English -- 20th century -- Biography
ISBN 0871404206; 9780871404206

LC 2012033865

This book presents an autobiography by the English novelist and short story writer J. G. Ballard. "the first half of the
book portrays Ballard's experiences in the Lunghua internment camp near Shanghai during World War II and sheds
light on his relationship with his parents. He also describes
the tragic death of his wife, just after he started to establish himself as a writer, and to a lesser degree his unconventional relationship with lifelong partner Claire Walsh."
(Kirkus Reviews)

Barnes, Julian, 1946-

Levels of life; by Julian Barnes. Alfred A. Knopf
2013 144 p. (hardcover) $22.95   **823**
1. Grief 2. Bereavement
ISBN 0385350775; 9780345806581; 9780385350778

LC 2013004601

In this book author Julian Barnes presents his thoughts
on the subject of grief "beginning in the nineteenth century
and leading . . . into an entirely personal account of loss."
(Publisher's note) "It is divided into three . . . parts: a . . .
discussion of ballooning; a . . . short story about the fictional
romance of a real English adventurer named Fred Burnaby
and the celebrated actress Sarah Bernhardt; and a . . .consid-
eration of grief." (New York Review of Books)

Bayley, John

Elegy for Iris. St. Martin's Press 1999 275p il
hardcover o.p. pa $13   **823**
1. Authors 2. Novelists 3. Philosophers 4. Alzheimer's
disease 5. Essayists 6. College teachers 7. Literary

critics
ISBN 0-312-42111-7 pa

LC 98-40895

"This splendid book enlarges our imagination of the range and possibilities of love." N Y Times Book Rev

Bowker, Gordon, 1934-

★ **James** Joyce; a new biography. Gordon Bowker. Farrar, Straus and Giroux 2012 608 p. ill. (hbk. : alk. paper) $35.00   **823**

1. Authors, Irish 2. Authors, Irish -- 20th century -- Biography
ISBN 0374178720; 9780374178727

LC 2011045954

This biography of James Joyce "show[s] the complexities and contradictions of the man. . . . The author charts . . . his struggle to survive in the early days of his adulthood and marriage, the sad madness of his daughter, . . . and his difficulty finding publishers for 'Dubliners' and the more controversial works that followed. . . . We see Joyce, too, as a prodigious worker." (Kirkus Reviews)

Includes bibliographical references and index

The **Cambridge** companion to Jane Austen; edited by Edward Copeland and Juliet McMaster. Cambridge Univ. Press 1997 251p (Cambridge companions to literature)   **823**

1. Authors 2. Novelists
ISBN 0-521-49517-2; 0-521-49867-8 pa

LC 96-23387

This volume contains a selection of critical essays on the English novelist. "Deirdre Le Faye provides an Austen chronology; Jan Fergus outlines the situation of professional women writers; other essays deal with the novels and letters, and with . . . 'themes' (class, money, religion and politics)." (Times Lit Suppl) Bibliography. Index.

Scholars assess "Jane Austen's works in the contexts of her contemporary world, and of present-day critical discourse. Besides discussions of Austen's novels and letters, there are essays on religion, politics, class consciousness, publishing practices, domestic economy, style in the novels and the significance of her juvenile works. A chronology provides biographical information." Publisher's note

The **Collected** Letters of Thomas Hardy; Further Letters 1861-1927. edited by Michael Millgate and Keith Wilson. Oxford University Press 2012 320 p. $160   **823**

1. Letters
ISBN 0199607753; 9780199607754

LC 77030355

This book, edited by Michael Millgate and Keith Wilson, "contains previously unpublished letters from all periods of [poet Thomas] Hardy's career, his earliest known letter among them. It introduces important new correspondents, throws fresh light on existing correspondences, and richly enhances the reader's understanding of both familiar and hitherto unfamiliar aspects of Hardy's life and work and of the times in which he lived." (Publisher's note)

The **Columbia** history of the British novel; John Richetti, editor; John Bender, Deirdre David, Michael Seidel, associate editors. Columbia Univ. Press 1994 xxix, 1064p $95   **823**

1. English fiction -- History and criticism
ISBN 0-231-07858-7

LC 92-35749

In this chronologically arranged volume, scholars provide 39 essays surveying the history of the British novel. "Some essays are devoted to individual authors (e.g., Austen, Dickens), others to several authors (e.g., Amis, Snow, and Wilson), and still others to such topics as 'The Gothic Novel, 1764-1824.' Each essay has a brief selected bibliography; an appendix includes thumbnail sketches of 100 of the British novelists discussed." Libr J

Conradi, Peter

Iris Murdoch; a life. {by} Peter J. Conradi. Norton 2001 xxix, 706p il $35; pa $19.95   **823**

1. Authors 2. Novelists 3. Philosophers 4. Essayists
ISBN 0-393-04875-6; 0-393-32401-X pa

LC 2001-32972

"Rich footnoting leads the reader to expansions on the narrative as well as to the authority behind the biographer's statements. Scholars need this text, but it will also intrigue lay readers." Libr J

Includes bibliographical references

Cusk, Rachel, 1967-

★ **Aftermath**; on marriage and separation. Rachel Cusk. Farrar, Straus and Giroux 2012 146 p. (alk. paper) $20.00   **823**

1. Marriage 2. Biography 3. Family life 4. Divorce -- Psychological aspects 5. Marriage -- Psychological aspects 6. Authors, English -- 20th century -- Biography
ISBN 0374102139; 9780374102135

LC 2012003807

Author Rachel Cusk looks at "the breakdown of her domestic life. [The book tells the traditional story of] man meets woman . . . [and] create a family . . . [then the] family falls apart . . . [and the] man, woman and children grieve . . . [S]he weaves in figures from ancient Greek drama (Oedipus, Antigone, Agamemnon, Clytemnestra) . . . The last and most unorthodox chapter is told, by Cusk, from the perspective of her au pair Sonia, a scared, scarred girl whom the author abruptly fired when her husband left." (Kirkus)

Davis, Paul B.

★ **Critical** companion to Charles Dickens; a literary reference to his life and work. Rev ed; Facts on File 2007 676p il (Facts on File library of world literature) $75   **823**

1. Authors 2. Novelists
ISBN 0-8160-6407-5; 978-0-8160-6407-6

LC 2006-3026

First published 1998 with title: Charles Dickens A-Z

This "reference contains entries on this writer's works, including the characters in each work, . . . historical and thematic information, and critical discussion. It also includes entries on related people, places, themes, topics, and influences. Additional features include 116 illustrations, a chronology, a bibliography of primary and secondary sources, and much more." Publisher's note

Includes bibliographical references

Dirda, Michael

On Conan Doyle; or, The whole art of storytelling. Princeton University Press 2011 210p (Writers on writers) $19.95   **823**

1. Authors 2. Novelists 3. Mystery writers
ISBN 978-0-691-15135-9; 0-691-15135-0

LC 2011-20674

"Dirda is at his best in his sensitive appreciation of Doyle's style, direct, fluent, and surprisingly flexible as he moves from genre to genre, and in his account of manly civic inspiration as the value Doyle aimed above all to inculcate in his writing . . . . An endearing, well-balanced introduction to a writer the Strand Magazine called 'the greatest natural storyteller of his age.'" Kirkus

Includes bibliographical references

★ The **Facts** on File companion to the British novel. Facts on File 2005 2v (Facts on File library of world literature) set $140   **823**

1. English fiction -- History and criticism
ISBN 0-8160-6377-X; 978-0-8160-6377-2

LC 2004-20914

"This two-volume companion to the British novel contains more than 1000 A-to-Z entries (each averaging several pages in length) on English-writing authors hailing from either the British Isles or the Commonwealth as well as on novels, pertinent literary terms, themes, concepts, influential periodicals, and subgenres." Libr J

"With more than one thousand entries, each with a selected bibliography and a set of very usable appendixes, this work accomplishes much in a compact set." Ref & User Services Quarterly

Includes bibliographical references

Fargnoli, A. Nicholas

Critical companion to James Joyce; a literary companion to his life and work. [by] A. Nicholas Fargnoli, Michael Patrick Gillespie. Rev ed; Facts On File 2006 450p il (Facts on File library of world literature) $65; pa $19.95   **823**

1. Poets 2. Authors 3. Novelists 4. Dramatists 5. Short story writers
ISBN 0-8160-6232-3; 978-0-8160-6232-4; 0-8160-6689-2 pa; 978-0-8160-6689-6 pa

LC 2005-15721

First published 1995 with title: James Joyce A to Z

The authors "divide this reference to the writer's life and work into four parts. Part 1 is a brief biography. Part 2 focuses on individual works (e.g., Dubliners), including its publication date, a brief history, a synopsis, early critical reception, contemporary perspectives, and one or two recommended titles for further reading. The entries in Part 3 cover people (including friends and relatives), places, and ideas related to Joyce. Part 4 contains an appendix, a bibliography of the writer's work, a bibliography of secondary sources, chronologies, family trees, and more. . . . [This is] a great primer for those needing a detailed introduction into Joyce's world." Libr J

Includes bibliographical references

Ford, Paul F.

Companion to Narnia; a complete guide to the magical world of C.S. Lewis's The chronicles of Narnia. foreword by Madeleine L'Engle; illustrated by Lorinda Bryan Cauley. Rev and expanded; HarperSanFrancisco 2005 xxvi, 530p il map pa $16.95 **823**

1. Authors 2. Novelists 3. Theologians 4. Essayists 5. Satirists 6. Literary critics 7. Children's authors
ISBN 0-06-079127-6

First published 1980

C. S. Lewis wrote seven books of fantasy that are collectively called The Chronicles of Narnia. This book "is an encyclopedia of Narnian names and terms and related matters, with . . . footnoted articles, page references to American and British hardcover editions, cross-references, and a running footline for quick location of materials in the alphabet." Choice

Includes bibliographical references

Gordimer, Nadine, 1923-2014

Conversations with Nadine Gordimer; edited by Nancy Topping Bazin and Marilyn Dallman Seymour. University Press of Miss. 1990 xxiv, 321p (Literary conversations series) $46   **823**

1. Authors 2. Novelists 3. Dramatists 4. Essayists 5. Short story writers 6. Nobel laureates for literature
ISBN 0-87805-444-8

LC 90-12556

This is a collection of interviews in which Gordimer talks "about her life as a white South African, about her fiction, and about writers she admires." Booklist

Includes bibliographical references

Head, Dominic

★ The **Cambridge** introduction to modern British fiction, 1950-2000. Cambridge Univ. Press 2002 307p $65; pa $22   **823**

1. English fiction -- History and criticism
ISBN 0-521-66014-9; 0-521-66966-9 pa

LC 2001-43261

"Anyone with an interest in the contemporary novel, not just British fiction, will appreciate this outstanding survey and analysis. . . . The quality of discussion is admirably consistent within and between each chapter, the prose as carefully crafted as the judgments are measured. . . . This book should become a standard reference work for its subject." Choice

Includes bibliographical references

★ **Horror:** another 100 best books; edited by Stephen Jones and Kim Newman; with a foreword by Peter Straub. Carroll & Graf Publishers 2005 456p pa $16.95   **823**

1. Best books 2. Horror fiction -- History and criticism
ISBN 0-7867-1577-4

First published 1988

"Horror fans seeking what to read next will not only find out here; they'll also have their taste and appreciative capacity refined by the intelligent, passionate commentary of the 100 writers who selected these 100 books." Booklist

Hughes, Kathryn

George Eliot; the last Victorian. Cooper Square Press 2001 383p il pa $19.95   **823**

1. Authors 2. Novelists 3. Essayists 4. Authors, English

ISBN 0-8154-1121-9; 978-0-8154-1121-5

LC 2001-28024

First published 1998 in the United Kingdom

In this biography Hughes "shows how George Eliot (nee Mary Anne Evans, 1819-80), in spite of her outwardly anti-Victorian lifestyle, was in fact a true Victorian. . . . A solitary, ascetic child and young woman, she was raised in an upwardly mobile country family. . . . In 1852 she met the married writer and editor George Henry Lewes, with whom she lived until his death in 1878." Libr J

Includes bibliographical references

James, P. D.

Talking about detective fiction. Alfred A. Knopf 2009 198p il $22   **823**

1. Mystery fiction -- History and criticism

ISBN 978-0-307-59282-8

LC 2009-38501

"For crime fiction fans, this master class from one of the leading practitioners of the art will be a real treat." Publ Wkly

Includes bibliographical references

Time to be in earnest; a fragment of autobiography. Knopf 2000 269p hardcover o.p. pa $12.95   **823**

1. Authors 2. Novelists 3. Mystery writers

ISBN 0-345-44212-1 pa

LC 99-57603

"In 1997, on the eve of her 77th birthday noted mystery novelist James . . . decided to keep a diary for the first time ever, recording one year in her life. The result is this 'fragment of autobiography,' a mix of memoir, ruminations on everything from her writing career to Princess Diana's death, and literary criticism." Libr J

Kermode, Frank

Concerning E.M. Forster. Farrar, Straus and Giroux 2009 180p $24   **823**

1. Authors 2. Novelists 3. Essayists 4. Literary critics 5. Short story writers

ISBN 978-0-374-29899-9; 0-374-29899-8

LC 2009-39143

"Overall, Kermode's occasional exasperation with his subject enlivens rather than distorts his eminently fair assessment. Like all good criticism, Concerning EM Forster makes one want to read the books under discussion once more, and it ends on an appropriately affectionate note." Times (London)

Includes bibliographical references

Kiberd, Declan

Ulysses and us; the art of everyday life in Joyce's masterpiece. W.W. Norton & Co. 2009 399p $28.95   **823**

1. Poets 2. Authors 3. Novelists 4. Dramatists 5.

Short story writers

ISBN 978-0-393-07099-6; 0-393-07099-9

LC 2009014101

This "is an ideal introduction [to Ulysses] for the uninitiated—accessible, richly argued, funny and, in a kind of devil's advocacy fashion, begging for rebuttal." Publ Wkly

Includes bibliographical references

King, Dean

Patrick O'Brian; a life revealed. Holt & Co. 2000 397p il hardcover o.p. pa $15   **823**

1. Authors 2. Novelists 3. Biographers 4. Writers on the sea 5. Short story writers

ISBN 0-8050-5977-6 pa

LC 99-48495

"This is exactly the sort of literary biography that O'Brian, the author of the celebrated Aubrey/Maturin naval novels, hoped to avoid. Reluctant to provide facts about himself, and often untruthful when he did so, O'Brian . . . had much in his past that he wanted buried. He walked away from his first marriage, changed his name from Russ to O'Brian, and pretended Anglo-Irish ancestry. King's diligent research yields pleasing details." New Yorker

Includes bibliographical references

Lee, Hermione

★ Virginia Woolf. Knopf 1997 893p il hardcover o.p. pa $20   **823**

1. Authors 2. Novelists 3. Women authors 4. Essayists 5. Authors, English 6. Short story writers

ISBN 0-375-70136-2 pa

LC 97-71155

First published 1996 in the United Kingdom

Lee "re-creates the world Woolf was born into in 1882, a maze of formalities and reticences, and then leads us through changes that, slow in coming but shocking in effect, made all that seem light-years away by the time Woolf was 50. She convinces us that Woolf, contrary to previous assumptions, reveled in a deep intimacy with her husband, Leonard. Finally, she makes a persuasive case for the underlying sanity of this woman as she battled her own madness and shows the brilliant literary uses she made of her instability." N Y Times Book Rev

Includes bibliographical references

Maunder, Andrew

The Facts on File companion to the British short story. Facts on File 2006 528p (Facts on File library of world literature) $75   **823**

1. Short stories -- History and criticism

ISBN 0-8160-5990-X; 978-0-8160-5990-4

LC 2006-6897

More than 450 alphabetically arranged entries cover authors, characters, and major short stories. Literary terms, themes, and motifs are covered. Winners of prizes and awards are noted.

Includes glossary and bibliographical references

Miller, Laura

The magician's book; a skeptic's adventures in Narnia. Little, Brown and Co. 2008 311p $25.99 **823**

1. Authors 2. Novelists 3. Theologians 4. Essayists

5. Satirists 6. Literary critics 7. Children's authors 8. Children's literature -- History and criticism
ISBN 978-0-316-01763-3; 0-316-01763-9

LC 2008-20629

The author explores the meaning and influence of C.S. Lewis' Chronicles of Narnia series while revealing how Lewis's troubled childhood, unconventional love life, and friendship with J. R. R. Tolkien affected his writing.

"Miller's book is itself a welcome bit of magic: part reader's log, part biography, part literary criticism." N Y Times Book Rev

Montillo, Roseanne

★ The **lady** and her monsters; a tale of dissections, attempts to reanimate dead tissue, and the writing of Mary Shelley's Frankenstein. Roseanne Montillo. 1st ed. William Morrow 2013 322 p. ill. (hardcover) $26.99; (ebook) $21.99 **823**
1. Frankenstein's monster (Fictional character) 2. Women and literature -- England -- History -- 19th century
ISBN 9780062025814; 9780062025838; 9780062235886

LC 2012021509

This book, by Roseanne Motillo, "brings to life the . . . science, and real-life horrors behind Mary Shelley's gothic masterpiece, 'Frankenstein.' Montillo recounts how--at the intersection of the Romantic Age and the Industrial Revolution--Shelley's Victor Frankenstein was inspired by actual scientists of the period: curious and daring iconoclasts who were obsessed with the inner workings of the human body and how it might be reanimated after death." (Publisher's note)

"Fraught with suicides, superstitions, natural disasters, and love affairs, the life of Mary Shelley shares much emotionally with the harrowing tale of her great protagonist, Victor Frankenstein. A delicious and enticing journey into the origins of a masterpiece." Pub Wkly

Includes bibliographical references (p. 305-310) and index.

Moore, Wendy

★ **How** to create the perfect wife; Britain's most ineligible bachelor and his enlightened quest to train the ideal mate. Wendy Moore. Basic Books 2013 360 p. (hardcover) $27.99 **823**
1. Wives 2. Marriage 3. Authors, English -- 18th century 4. Marriage -- Great Britain -- History -- 18th century
ISBN 0465065740; 9780465065745

LC 2012048149

This book, by Wendy Moore, tells "tale of one man's mission to groom his ideal mate. [18th-century British writer Thomas] Day adopted two young orphans from the Foundling Hospital and, guided by the writings of Jean-Jacques Rousseau and the principles of the Enlightenment, attempted to teach them to be model wives. His peculiar experiment inevitably backfired--though not before he had taken his theories about marriage, education, and femininity to shocking extremes." (Publisher's note)

Includes bibliographical references and index

Naipaul, V. S. (Vidiadhar Surajprasad), 1932-

Between father and son; selected correspondence of V.S. Naipaul and his family, 1949-1953. edited by Gillon Aitken. Knopf 2000 297p $26; pa $13 **823**
1. Authors 2. Novelists 3. Journalists 4. Essayists 5. Travel writers 6. Radio reporters 7. Nonfiction writers 8. Short story writers 9. Nobel laureates for literature
ISBN 0-375-40730-8; 0-375-70726-3 pa

LC 99-31089

"In 1950, at the age of 17, famous-writer-in-the-making V. S. Naipaul ventured to Oxford University in England on a scholarship supplied by the government of his native Trinidad. He and his father maintained a rich, full correspondence during his time away, and these letters fortunately have been gathered into book form." Booklist

Include bibliographical references

Ngugi wa Thiong'o, 1938-

In the house of the interpreter; a memoir. Ngugi wa'Thiong'o. Pantheon Books 2012 240 p. (hardback) $25.95 **823**
1. Revolutionaries -- Kenya -- Biography 3. Authors, Kenyan -- 20th century -- Biography
ISBN 0307907694; 9780307907691

LC 2012013986

The book by author Ngugi wa Thiong'o presents a collection of his writings. It focuses on the "author's life and times at boarding school--the first secondary educational institution in British-ruled Kenya--in the 1950s, against the backdrop of the tumultuous Mau Mau Uprising for independence and Kenyan sovereignty." Throughout his journey, "he falls victim to the forces of colonialism in the person of a police officer encountered on a bus journey, and he is thrown into jail for six days." (Publisher's note)

Nokes, David

Jane Austen; a life. University of Calif. Press 1998 577p il pa $24.95 **823**
1. Authors 2. Novelists 3. Women authors 4. Authors, English
ISBN 0-520-21606-7; 978-0-520-21606-8

LC 98-15785

First published 1997 by Farrar, Straus & Giroux

"Eschewing the biographer's usual perspective of omniscient foreknowledge in favor of a novelistic perspective of ambiguous immediacy, Nokes allows us to see Austen's talent as a mystery unfolding, not a fact explained. We thus witness the emergence of a personality sufficiently subtle and complex to produce Sense and Sensibility, Pride and Prejudice, and Emma. Readers of Austen's fiction will rejoice at having a biography so carefully nuanced, so refreshingly candid." Booklist

Includes bibliographical references

O'Brien, Edna

James Joyce. Viking 1999 179p (Penguin lives series) $19.95 **823**
1. Poets 2. Authors 3. Novelists 4. Dramatists 5. Short story writers
ISBN 0-670-88230-5

LC 99-23214

O'Brien "tells the story of the aspiring young writer and his downwardly mobile family, his escape to Europe, the constant struggle to scrape together enough money to live on, and finally his relative comfort, thanks to patrons, once Ulysses was published. She also provides thoughtful appreciations of Joyce's major works." Booklist

Includes bibliographical references

Olsen, Kirstin

All things Austen; an encyclopedia of Austen's world. Greenwood Press 2005 2v il maps set $157.95 **823**

1. Authors 2. Novelists 3. Reference books
ISBN 0-313-33032-8

LC 2004-28664

This Jane Austen encyclopedia contains "more than 150 well-designed and well-written A-to-Z articles on such topics as clothing, education, politics, religion, science, business, society, and the military of 18th- and 19th-century England." Libr J

"This well-written and meticulously researched work provides a convenient means for general readers, students, and scholars to gain a better understanding of the social, cultural, and political climate of Austen's time." Booklist

Saler, Michael

As if; modern enchantment and the literary prehistory of virtual reality. Michael Saler. Oxford University Press 2012 x, 283 p.p (pbk. : acid-free paper) $27.95 **823**

1. Virtual reality 2. Imaginary places 3. Books and reading 4. Fantastic, The, in literature 5. Marvelous, The, in literature 6. Virtual reality in literature 7. Imaginary societies in literature
ISBN 0195343174; 9780195343168; 9780195343175

LC 2011010276

This book by Michael Saler was "named one of the 'Best Books of 2012' by the editors of 'The Huffington Post.' . . . It explains how, "beginning in the late nineteenth century, when Sherlock Holmes became the world's first 'virtual reality' character, readers began to colonize imaginary worlds. . . . From Lovecraft's Cthulhu Mythos and Tolkien's Middle-earth to the World of Warcraft and Second Life, 'As If' provides a cultural history that reveals how we can remain enchanted but not deluded in an age where fantasy and reality increasingly intertwine." (Publisher's note)

Includes bibliographical references and index.

Shakespeare, Nicholas

Bruce Chatwin. Talese 2000 618p il $35; pa $18 **823**

1. Authors 2. Novelists 3. Memoirists 4. Travel writers
ISBN 0-385-49829-2; 0-385-49830-6 pa

LC 99-36474

"This life of the author of 'The Songlines', who died of AIDS in 1989, portrays a man, beset with an almost biological lust for loneliness, whose singular genius was for passionate transitory connection." N Y Times Book Rev

Includes bibliographical references

Shields, Carol

Jane Austen. Viking 2001 185p (Penguin lives series) hardcover o.p. pa $13 **823**

1. Authors 2. Novelists 3. Women authors 4. Authors, English
ISBN 0-670-89488-5; 0-14-303516-9 pa

LC 00-43807

"In chronicling her subject's life and personality, Shields emphasizes Austen's keen ability to listen, observe, and capture clearly the social mores of her time and explore human nature in her writing. Shields contends that historical references are behind many of the scenes and characters in Austen's novels, and as a way of more clearly personalizing Austen's experiences or feelings, she interjects commentary regarding writing and publishing that is presumably based on personal experience." Libr J

Smiley, Jane, 1949-

Charles Dickens. Viking 2002 212p (Penguin lives series) $19.95 **823**

1. Authors 2. Novelists 3. Authors, English
ISBN 0-670-03077-5

LC 2001-45607

This "biography examines Dickens' life through his work, starting not with his birth but rather the beginnings of his literary career. After writing short essays for a monthly magazine, Dickens began the serialization of his first novel, The Pickwick Papers. Dickens quickly became both a best-selling novelist and a famous man, who had to contend with both the envy of other authors and, much later on, the very public dissolution of his marriage. . . . Smiley's superb and thoughtful analysis should appeal to anyone familiar with the great author's work." Booklist

Swift, Jonathan

A tale of a tub, and other work; edited with an introduction by Angus Ross and David Woolley. Oxford Univ. Press 1986 xxviii, 237p (The World's classics) pa $8.95 **823**

ISBN 0-19-283593-9

LC 85-5072

A tale of a tub, The battle of the books, and A discourse concerning the mechanical operation of the spirit, were first published together in 1704. The first is an allegorical satire ridiculing the corruptions of religion and learning by extremists and pedants. The second is a mock heroic satire on squabbles concerning the relative merits of ancient and modern authors presented as an account of the battle between ancient and modern books in St James Library. The third ridicules the manner of worship and preaching of religious enthusiasts of the period

Tomalin, Claire

Jane Austen; a life. Knopf 1997 341p il hardcover o.p. pa $14 **823**

1. Authors 2. Novelists 3. Women authors 4. Authors, English
ISBN 0-679-76676-6 pa

LC 97-36887

The author "has produced a portrait of remarkable subtlety. The light Ms. Tomalin casts on her subject is strong but oblique: the profile of the novelist appears surrounded by her friends and neighbours and by her energetic and beloved family." Economist

A **truth** universally acknowledged; 33 great writers on why we read Jane Austen. edited by Susannah Carson; foreword by Harold Bloom. Random House 2009 295p $25   **823**
1. Authors 2. Novelists
ISBN 978-1-4000-6805-0; 1-4000-6805-3
LC 2009-12904

"A collection for both newcomers to the charms of Jane Austen and those longtime 'Janeites'. . . . The writers in this volume explain their own relationship with Austen and together are a kind of invitation for us, whether we're Janeites or not, to understand why we are so in her thrall." Chicago Trib

Includes bibliographical references

Wainaina, Binyavanga

One day I will write about this place. Graywolf Press 2011 256p   **823**
1. Authors 2. Novelists 3. Journalists 4. College teachers 5. Short story writers 6. Biography, Individual
ISBN 1555975917; 9781555975913
LC 2011923190

In this memoir, the Kenyan writer describes "his school days, his mother's religious period, his failed attempt to study in South Africa as a computer programmer, a moving family reunion in Uganda, and his travels around Kenya. The landscape in front of him always claims his main attention, but he also evokes the shifting political scene that unsettles his views on family, tribe, and nationhood. Throughout, reading is his refuge and his solace. And when, in 2002, a writing prize comes through, the door is opened for him to pursue the career that perhaps had been beckoning all along." (Publisher's note)

Weldon, Fay

Auto da Fay. Grove Press 2003 366p il $25; pa $14   **823**
1. Authors 2. Novelists 3. Dramatists 4. Short story writers
ISBN 0-8021-1750-3; 0-8021-4142-0 pa
LC 2002-44685

First published 2002 in the United Kingdom
This "autobiography primarily focuses on her peripatetic childhood and difficult years of single parenthood, concluding in the 1960s with her second marriage and the beginning of her writing career. . . . Filled with warmth, wit, and her trademark irreverence, Weldon's memoir is a vivid and engaging account of a brave and brainy 'lost girl' who found her way." Booklist

Wilson, A. N.

C.S. Lewis; a biography. Norton 1990 334p il hardcover o.p. pa $15.95   **823**
1. Authors 2. Novelists 3. Theologians 4. Essayists 5. Satirists 6. Literary critics 7. Children's authors
ISBN 0-393-32340-4 pa
LC 89-27361

"The mixture presented in Wilson's biography of the life of learning, the college life at Magdalen where he taught, of

domestic drama and bad temper, religion, and sex, is irresistible." N Y Rev Books

Includes bibliographical references

Winterson, Jeanette, 1959-

Why be happy when you could be normal? Jeanette Winterson. Jonathan Cape 2011 230 p. $25   **823**
1. Novelists 2. Autobiographies 3. Adopted children 4. Mother-daughter relationship 5. Women authors -- Biography 6. Authors, English -- 20th century -- Biography
ISBN 0224093452; 0802120105; 9780224093453; 9780802120106
LC 2011507186

Guardian Best Book of 2011
In this book, "author [Jeanette Winterson] ponders her youth and examines how those challenging years changed and shaped her as an adult. Frequently locked out on the doorstep by her abusive, Pentecostal, adoptive mother or often told she was 'a fault to heaven, a fault against the dead, and a fault to nature,' Winterson wondered if she had ever been wanted, by her biological or adoptive mother. . . . At age 16, she was kicked out of the house and forced to live in her car. Books and words brought comfort and led Winterson to Oxford and writing, but she descended into a deep depression when her lover left her. The search for her true identity and her birth mother helped bring her back from the darkness." (Kirkus)

Woolf, Virginia, 1882-1941

Moments of being; edited, with an introduction and notes, by Jeanne Schulkind. 2nd ed; Harcourt Brace Jovanovich 1985 230p pa $14   **823**
1. Authors 2. Novelists 3. Women authors 4. Essayists 5. Authors, English 6. Short story writers
ISBN 0-15-661918-0
LC 85-8521

First published 1976
This volume consists of unpublished autobiographical writings, including several "Reminiscences" written at the start of Woolf's career, a piece entitled "A sketch of the past" written shortly before her suicide, and papers read to the Memoir Club.

Includes bibliographical references

823.5   English fiction -- 1702-1745

Frank, Katherine

Crusoe; Daniel Defoe, Robert Knox and the creation of a myth. Katherine Frank. Bodley Head 2011 338 p.   **823.5**
1. Castaways in literature 2. Crusoe, Robinson (Fictitious character)
ISBN 0224073095; 9780224073097
LC 2011486701

This book "introduces Robert Knox, once a true captive, who survived on his wits and the English practice of making your environment adapt to your needs rather than adjusting to it. . . . As Defoe cherry-picked incidents from different lives, he adapted them to reflect disasters he had suffered. . . .

Frank parallels the lives and adventures of Defoe, Knox and Crusoe, illustrating a deep relationship between author and models. This side-by-side biography of the two men shows similarities between their lives and their attitudes toward disaster, although their personalities and moralities were markedly different. Many have said that Crusoe is much more a self-help book than a novel, while Knox's story is a treatise rather than a travel book." (Kirkus)

Includes bibliographical references and index.

823.8   English fiction -- 1837-1899

Mead, Rebecca ✓
★ **My** life in Middlemarch; Rebecca Mead. CrownCrown Publishers 2014 304 p. $25   **823.8**
1. Creation (Literary, artistic, etc.)
ISBN 0307984761; 9780307984760

LC 2013011477

In this "hybrid work of literary criticism, biography, and memoir," author Rebecca Mead discusses her relationship with the book "Middlemarch" by George Eliot. She " identifies strongly with aspects of Eliot's life and that of the characters in Middlemarch, [and] returns to the novel during various stages of her life: as a young Englishwoman finding her way in New York; in relationships with difficult men; as a stepmother and wife; and eventually as the mother of a son." (Publishers Weekly)

"A rare and remarkable fusion of techniques that draws two women together across time and space." Kirkus

Includes bibliographical references

823.914   English fiction -- 1945-1999

McWilliam, Candia
What to look for in winter. HarperCollins 2012 464p   **823.914**
1. Blind 2. Alcoholism 3. Autobiographies
ISBN 0062094505; 9780062094506

This book is a memoir of "novelist Candia McWilliam [who] began losing her sight, a gradual onset of blindness that seemed like an assault cruelly tailored for someone whose life consisted of reading and writing. Propelled to look inward and into the past, McWilliam embarked on a painful personal voyage through a waste of snows punctuated by shards of ice as she attempted to write her life back. What followed was a flow of memory: her childhood in Edinburgh, her devastating alcoholism, finding and losing her bearings in Cambridge and London, her marriages, her children, and, overshadowing it all, her mother's suicide." (Publisher's note)

824   English essays

Carlyle, Thomas ✓
Sartor resartus; edited with an introduction and notes by Kerry McSweeney and Peter Sabor. Oxford

Univ. Press 1987 xlii, 273p (The World's classics) pa $11.95   **824**
ISBN 0-19-283673-0

LC 87-5753

First published 1833-1834, Sartor resartus contains the germ of Carlyle's philosophy. It purports to be an interpretation of the work of an erudite German professor but is really the story of Carlyle's own fierce spiritual conflict between doubt and faith. It presents a philosophy of clothes, or the outward forms of things

Includes bibliographical references

De Quincey, Thomas
✓The **confessions** of an English opium-eater and other writings. Penguin Books 2003 xliv, 296p pa $14   **824**
1. Drug abuse
ISBN 978-0-14-043901-4; 0-14-043901-3

"Confessions forged a link between artistic self-expression and addiction, paving the way for later generations of literary drug-users from Baudelaire to Burroughs, and anticipating psychoanalysis with its insights into the subconscious. This edition is based on the original serial version of 1821, and reproduces the two 'sequels', 'Suspiria de Profundis' (1845) and 'The English Mail-Coach' (1849). It also includes a critical introduction discussing the romantic figure of the addict and the tradition of confessional literature, and an appendix on opium in the nineteenth century." Publisher's note

Dyer, Geoff
Otherwise known as the human condition; selected essays and reviews, 1989-2010. Graywolf Press 2011 421p il   **824**
1. Criticism
ISBN 1-555-97579-8; 978-1-55597-579-1

LC 2010-937517

This book of essays covers "a broad territory stretching from photographers such as Richard Avedon and William Gedney . . . ; musicians Miles Davis and Def Leppard; writers like D.H. Lawrence, Ian McEwan, and Richard Ford; as well as personal ruminations on, say, reader's block." (Publishers Weekly)

"A grab-bag of critical essays, reportage and personal stories from the irrepressibly curious Dyer. . . . The title of this hefty tome, featuring pieces published in two United Kingdom–only collections, suggests ponderous philosophizing. But though Dyer takes his art seriously, his prose is as relaxed and self-effacing as it is informed. . . . Though the book is wide-ranging, his command is consistent, whether he's writing about Richard Avedon or model airplanes." Kirkus

Includes bibliographical references

James, Clive
As of this writing; the essential essays, 1968-2002. Norton 2003 619p $35   **824**
1. Literature -- History and criticism
ISBN 0-393-05180-3

This collection of "essays dealing with poetry and literature feature[s] pieces on Robert Lowell, D.H. Lawrence, and Solzhenitsyn, while a section on culture and criticism comments on the life and works of Lillian Hellman, Evelyn Waugh and Betrand Russell." Publ Wkly

"James writes with fluent wit, remarkable warmth, deep knowledge, and an exhilarating sense of mission." Booklist

Kermode, Frank

★ **Pieces** of my mind; essays and criticism, 1958-2002. Farrar, Straus & Giroux 2003 466p $26; pa $16 **824**

ISBN 0-8090-7601-2; 0-374-52936-1 pa

LC 2003-54727

The author "parses complicated, even esoteric aspects of story and text, metaphysics and poetry, and the link between social change and the evolution of the novel, yet he is unfailingly clear and cheerfully engaging, classy, and stimulating." Booklist

Includes bibliographical references

O'Faolain, Nuala

A **radiant** life; Nuala O'Faolain; [introduction by Fintan O'Toole; note by Sheridan Hay]. Abrams Image 2011 302p pa $18.95 **824**

1. Catholic Church -- Ireland 2. Women -- Ireland

ISBN 978-0-8109-9806-3; 0-8109-9806-8

LC 2010-37687

"The collection spans two decades and runs the gamut, from feminism to social justice, from pop culture to the elusive fruits of progress. It makes little difference that they spring from a quintessentially Irish voice; they are universal in their appeal. Read more: Book review: Nuala O'Faolain's Irish prose holds universal appeal." Denver Post

Orwell, George, 1903-1950

Essays; selected and introduced by John Carey. Alfred A. Knopf 2002 xlv, 1369p (Everyman's library) $35 **824**

ISBN 978-0-375-41503-6; 0-375-41503-3

"The real reason we read Orwell is because his own fault-line, his fundamental schism, his hybridity, left him exceptionally sensitive to the fissure—which is everywhere apparent–between what ought to be the case and what actually is the case. He says the unsayable." Financial Times

Pratchett, Terry, 1948-

★ A **slip** of the keyboard; collected nonfiction. Terry Pratchett. Doubleday 2014 336 p. **824**

1. Essays 2. Wit and humor

ISBN 9780385538305; 9780804169226

LC 2014011949

"The essays, letters, speeches, and articles feature all the wit and charm of his beloved novels and allow readers a more personal look at Pratchett's life and beliefs. In a mere 336 pages, Pratchett ruminates on the underappreciated role of fantasy fiction and its importance in the literary world; the trick to becoming a successful author (hint: there isn't one); the care and feeding of authors while on book tours; and his work with fellow writer and friend Neil Gaiman." Booklist

Smith, Zadie, 1975-

Changing my mind; occasional essays. Penguin Press 2009 306p $26.95 **824**

ISBN 978-1-59420-237-7; 1-59420-237-0

LC 2009-23419

The author has organized this collection of "essays into sections on reading, being, seeing, feeling, and remembering to create a strong and piquant collection. As the title implies, Smith's thinking evolves before our eyes as she articulates her responses to art and life. . . . Smith is a superb essayist of skill, candor, and caring." Booklist

Includes bibliographical references

Wilde, Oscar, 1854-1900

The **artist** as critic; critical writings of Oscar Wilde. edited by Richard Ellmann. University of Chicago Press 1982 xxviii, 446p pa $36.50 **824**

1. Criticism 2. Literature -- History and criticism

ISBN 978-0-226-89764-6; 0-226-89764-8

LC 82-13361

Wilde's "book reviews and occasional pieces prove that while Wilde could be superbly malicious with fatheads, he was a generous and painstaking critic, quick to find merit and delighted to announce the discovery. It is easy to damn a book amusingly. Wilde could praise amusingly, a rare and difficult trick." Atlantic

827 English humor and satire

The **Oxford** book of humorous prose; William Caxton to P.G. Wodehouse: a conducted tour. [chosen and edited] by Frank Muir. Oxford Univ. Press 1990 xxxiv, 1162p hardcover o.p. pa $21.50 **827**

1. English wit and humor 2. American wit and humor

ISBN 0-19-280379-4 pa

LC 89-9242

"Selections are generally very short, with bridges, often fairly humorous of themselves, by Muir. The humor ranges from the broad to the subtle and, in fact, in any other way that humor might range; there's something in here for everyone." Libr J

828 English miscellaneous writings

Angel, Katherine

Unmastered; a book on desire, most difficult to tell. by Katherine Angel. Farrar, Straus and Giroux 2013 368 p. (alk. paper) $26 **828**

1. Sex 2. Women -- Sexual behavior 3. Desire

ISBN 0374280401; 9780374280406

LC 2012048072

Author Katherine Angel presents a "personal meditation on sex, power, and female desire. It is also a powerful reckoning with our contradictory and deeply entrenched notions of sexuality. Angel embraces the highly charged oppositions—dominance versus submission, liberation versus dependence—and probes the porousness between masculine and feminine, thought and sensation, self and culture, power and pliancy, always reveling in the elusiveness of easy answers." (Publisher's note)

Includes bibliographical references and index

Bradford, Richard

Lucky him: the life of Kingsley Amis. Owen, P. 2001 432p il $44.95   **828**

1. Poets 2. Authors 3. Humorists 4. Novelists 5. Essayists 6. Literary critics 7. Short story writers
ISBN 0-7206-1117-2

LC 2001-431013

This is a biography of the English novelist, best known for such works as Lucky Jim, The old devils, and Difficulties with girls

"The writing is consistently clear and the insights—literary and biographical—are formidable." Publ Wkly

Includes bibliographical references

DeGategno, Paul J.

Critical companion to Jonathan Swift; a literary reference to his life and works. [by] Paul J. DeGategno, R. Jay Stubblefield. Facts on File 2006 474p il (Facts on File library of world literature) $75 **828**

1. Poets 2. Clergy 3. Authors 4. Satirists 5. Pamphleteers 6. Writers on politics
ISBN 0-8160-5093-7; 978-0-8160-5093-2

LC 2005-25470

This "work is divided into five parts. These parts consist of a ten-page biography of satirist Jonathan Swift (1667-1745); a 'Works A-Z' section that includes synopses and commentaries that generally run to several hundred words on virtually all of Swift's poems, essays, and books; a 'Related Entries' section with similar brief articles on persons, topics, and places relevant to Swift studies; appendixes that include a chronology of Swift's life; a . . . bibliography of primary and secondary works; and an index." Libr J

Includes bibliographical references

Huxley, Elspeth

The **flame** trees of Thika; memories of an African childhood. Penguin Bks. 2000 280p pa $15 **828**

1. Authors 2. Novelists 3. Kenya 4. Memoirists
ISBN 0-14-118378-0; 978-0-14-118378-7

LC 99-47965

First published 1959 by Morrow

This is an account of the author's childhood on a coffee plantation in Kenya. She describes the landscape, the Kikuya peoples, the European settlers and the difficulties her parents faced adjusting to life in the bush.

Johnson, Samuel, 1709-1784

Samuel Johnson; the major works. edited with an introduction and notes by Donald Greene. Oxford University Press 2000 xxvii, 840p (Oxford world's classics) pa $18.95 **828**

ISBN 978-0-19-284042-4; 0-19-284042-8

LC 83-17280

"This volume celebrates Johnson's astonishing talent by selecting widely across the full range of his work. It includes 'London' and 'The Vanity of Human Wishes' among other poems, and many of his essays for the Rambler and Idler. The prefaces to his edition of Shakespeare and his fa-

mous Dictionary, together with samples from the texts, are given, as well as selections from A Journey to the Western Islands of Scotland, the Lives of the Poets, and Rasselas in its entirety. There is also a substantial representation of lesser-known prose, and of his poetry, letters, and journals." Publisher's note

Includes bibliographical references

Ker, Ian

G. K. Chesterton; a biography. Ian Ker. Oxford University Press 2011 747 p. ill. $65.00 **828**

1. Intellectuals 2. English authors -- Biography 3. Poets 4. Authors 5. Essayists 6. Novelists 7. Biographers 8. Travel writers 9. Literary critics 10. Short story writers 11. Biography -- Individual
ISBN 0199601283; 9780199601288

LC 2010940318

This book, by Ian Ker, offers a biography of the author G. K. Chesterton. "Remembered as a brilliant creator of nonsense and satirical verse, author of the Father Brown stories, . . . and yet today he is not counted among the major English novelists and poets. However, this . . . biography argues that Chesterton should be seen as the successor of the great Victorian prose writers, Carlyle, Arnold, Ruskin, and above all Newman." (Publisher's note)

Includes bibliographical references and index

Martin, Peter

★ A **life** of James Boswell. Yale Univ. Press 2000 613p $35; pa $18.95 **828**

1. Authors 2. Lawyers 3. Biographers
ISBN 0-300-08489-7; 0-300-09312-8 pa

This is a biography of the diarist and author of The life of Samuel Johnson

"Martin has written the best biography of the greatest biographer in the English language. . . . One of the many virtues of Martin's work is his successful synthesis of Boswell's life story with a keen analysis of Boswell's artistry." Atl Mon

Includes bibliographical references

Mda, Zakes

Sometimes there is a void; memoirs of an outsider. Zakes Mda. Farrar, Straus and Giroux 2012 561 p. **828**

1. Authors, South African 2. South Africa -- Politics and government 3. Authors, South African -- 20th century -- Biography
ISBN 9780374280949

LC 2011020817

In this book, "South African novelist, playwright and poet [Zakes] Mda . . . pens a memoir setting his experiences against the backdrop of a country in turmoil. . . . Although he spent his early years in Soweto, Mda was forced to escape to Lesotho after his father was exiled because of his activism against apartheid. . . . Mda's . . . journeys of romance, rebellion and his search for an artistic calling often kept him feeling like an outsider, a theme repeated throughout the memoir." (Kirkus Reviews)

Meyers, Jeffrey

Orwell; wintry conscience of a generation. Norton 2000 380p il maps hardcover o.p. pa $16.95 **828**

1. Authors 2. Novelists 3. Essayists

ISBN 0-393-32263-7 pa

LC 00-38020

"With wit and acumen, Meyers portrays a complex, eccentric, intelligent, and unbending man hard on family and friends, a writer of singular gifts, and a 'prophetic moralist' whose vision continues to illuminate society's dark side." Booklist

Includes bibliographical references

★ The **New** Oxford book of literary anecdotes. Oxford University Press 2006 385p il hardcover o.p. pa $16.95 **828**

1. Authors, English -- Anecdotes 2. Authors, American -- Anecdotes 3. English literature -- Anecdotes

ISBN 0-19-280468-5; 978-0-19-280468-6; 0-19-954341-0 pa; 978-0-19-954341-0 pa

LC 2005-33698

First published 1975 under the editorship of James Sutherland with title: The Oxford book of literary anecdotes

The editor "has compiled more than 700 anecdotes about English-language writers, from Geoffrey Chaucer to J.K. Rowling. The brief, chronologically-arranged (by subject's birth date) entries offer a glimpse into the personalities and times of these authors." Libr J

Includes bibliographical references

Orwell, George, 1903-1950

★ **Diaries**; George Orwell ; edited by Peter Davison ; introduction by Christopher Hitchens. 1st American ed. Liveright 2012 597 p. **828**

1. Diaries 2. English authors 3. English novelists 4. English literature 5. Authors 6. Essayists 7. Novelists 8. Biography, Individual

ISBN 0871404109; 9780871404107

LC 2012009895

This book, edited by Peter Davison, offers the personal writings of the British author George Orwell. "Written as individual books throughout his career, the eleven surviving diaries collected here record Orwell's youthful travels among miners and itinerant laborers, the fearsome rise of totalitarianism, the horrific drama of World War II, and the feverish composition of his great masterpieces 'Animal Farm' and '1984.'" (Publisher's note)

Includes bibliographical references and index.

Quinn, Edward

Critical companion to George Orwell; a literary reference to his life and work. Facts On File 2009 450p il (Facts on File library of world literature) $75 **828**

1. Authors 2. Novelists 3. Essayists

ISBN 978-0-8160-7091-6

LC 2008-26727

This volume provides a "review of Orwell's life and covers all his novels, nonfiction, and other writings. . . . It is a superb resource for those desiring an introduction to George Orwell, the man and the writer." Booklist

Includes bibliographical references

Sisman, Adam

Boswell's presumptuous task; the making of the life of Dr. Johnson. Penguin 2002 351p il pa $15 **828**

1. Authors 2. Lawyers 3. Biographers

ISBN 978-0-14-200175-2; 0-14-200175-9

First published 2000 in the United Kingdom

James Boswell's The Life of Samuel Johnson was published in 1791, six years after the death of its subject. In this book, Sisman chronicles Boswell's motives for writing his biography and the techniques he adopted.

"Mr. Sisman's book is illuminating both of Boswell's character and of all aspects of his authorship." Economist

Includes bibliographical references

Swift, Graham

Making an elephant; writing from within. Alfred A. Knopf 2009 400p il $26.95 **828**

ISBN 978-0-307-27099-3

LC 2009-14052

This is a collection of the author's "essays, interviews, poetry, and other nonfiction pieces, many of which have previously appeared in various magazines and books. Swift has slightly revised some works and has written new introductions for the pieces. The topics range from autobiography, appreciations of other English colleagues (e.g., Ted Hughes, Caryl Phillips, Kazuo Ishiguro), and . . . stories about the filming of two of his most famous works, Waterland and Last Orders." Libr J

"Out from behind the scrim of fiction, Swift is highly entertaining, at once welcoming and teasing, clever and probing." Booklist

Includes bibliographical references

Thomas, Dylan, 1914-1953

A **child's** Christmas in Wales; with woodcuts by Ellen Raskin. New Directions 2007 51p il pa $9.95 **828**

1. Christmas -- Wales

ISBN 978-0-8112-1731-6; 0-8112-1731-0

LC 2007-24727

First published 1954

The Welsh poet Dylan Thomas recalls the celebration of Christmas with his family and the feelings it evoked in him as a child.

For any season of the year "the language is enchanting and the poetry shines with an unearthly radiance." N Y Times Book Rev

Woolf, Virginia, 1882-1941

The **Virginia** Woolf reader; edited by Mitchell A. Leaska. Harcourt Brace Jovanovich 1984 371p hardcover o.p. pa $16 **828**

ISBN 0-15-693590-2 pa

LC 84-4478

Excerpts from Woolf's "novels form less than 20 percent of a reader whose selections of short stories, essays, letters, and diary entries are excellent. This collection will be useful to those already familiar with Woolf's novels and seeking an introductory selection of her other writings." Libr J

830   German literature and literatures of related languages

★ **Encyclopedia** of German literature; Matthias Konzett, editor. Fitzroy Dearborn Pubs. 2000 2v set $175 **830**
1. Reference books 2. German literature -- Encyclopedias 3. German literature -- Bio-bibliography
ISBN 1-57958-138-2

"Essay-like entries cover three main categories: authors, works (novels, books of poetry, and essays), and topics, the last encompassing everything from literary terms and movements, artistic forums, cities, and historical eras to the key legacy of the Frankfurt School and its members. Rather lengthy lists for further reading are provided with each essay." Libr J

Includes bibliographical references

831   German poetry

Celan, Paul
★ **Poems** of Paul Celan; translated by Michael Hamburger. Rev and expanded; Persea Bks. 2002 xxxiv, 366p $35; pa $18.95 **831**
1. Poetry -- By individual authors
ISBN 0-89255-275-1; 0-89255-276-X pa
LC 2001-59341

First published 1980 with title: Paul Celan: poems
"This bilingual German-English selection culled from [the poet's] nine collections reveals that his is a poetry of darkness: anguish over what life offers and denies; the ever-present shadow of death that shades each breath. . . . Yet it also expresses an undefined, perhaps undefinable, joy." Booklist [review of 1989 edition]

Goethe, Johann Wolfgang von, 1749-1832
Selected poetry; translated with an introduction and notes by David Luke. Penguin Books 2005 xliv, 283p (Penguin classics) pa $16 **831**
1. Poetry -- By individual authors
ISBN 978-0-14-042456-0; 0-14-042456-3
First published 1999 in the United Kingdom
"The introduction gives a thoughtful summary of Goethe's fascinating and problematic life. . . . What Luke triumphantly does is not only to stay close to the original, but also to create a total structure that gives a convincing sense of the overall movement of the poem. . . . Goethe made no secret of his huge debt to Shakespeare; perhaps the English tradition might celebrate the new millennium by learning something from him in return. David Luke's selection makes an excellent starting point." Times Lit Suppl

Maxwell, Glyn, 1962-
One thousand nights and counting; selected poems. Farrar, Straus and Giroux 2011 239p **831**
1. Poetry -- By individual authors
ISBN 9780374226480
LC 2011005176

"The British poet Maxwell's first U.S. selected presents a conversational style that is a constant throughout, as is the setting of England and New England; otherwise, these often surreal and opaque poems range across moods and subjects. The best moments occur when readers can lose themselves in the very long poems, in particular the inventive re-imagining of the story of Noah's Ark, 'Out of the Rain,' and the elegiac 'Letters to Edward Thomas,' in which the speaker waits for a friend who never arrives. . . . Maxwell's poetry can be playful and inventive, beautiful and melancholic, but can also be self-aggrandizing . . . and even pretentious. . . . Yet Maxwell is one of stars of poetry across the pond and a rising presence here; this book should win him new fans." Publ Wkly

Morike, Eduard Friedrich
Mozart's journey to Prague and a selection of poems; [by] Eduard Mörike; translated and with an introduction and notes by David Luke; Scots translations by Gilbert McKay. rev ed; Penguin Books 2003 xl, 216p (Penguin Classics) pa $14 **831**
1. Poetry -- By individual authors
ISBN 978-0-14-044737-8; 0-14-044737-7
LC 2004-298957

First published 1997 in the United Kingdom
A selection of Mörike's most popular romantic and classical folk and fairy-tale poems. Also includes the 1855 novella Mozart's journey to Prague, an imaginary recreation of the journey Mozart made from Vienna to Prague in 1787 to conduct the first performance of Don Giovanni.

Includes bibliographical references

Rilke, Rainer Maria
★ **Duino** elegies; translated by David Young; with an introduction and commentary. W. W. Norton 2006 202p pa $13.95 **831**
1. Poetry -- By individual authors
ISBN 978-0-393-32884-4; 0-393-32884-8
LC 2006-9872

First English translation published 1939; this translation was originally published in Field, Contemporary Poetry and Poetics, issues 5 through 9 and as a Norton paperback edition in 1992
"These elegies, the last great work of the poet, were named for the castle of Duino on the Adriatic, where they were first conceived." New Statesman (1913)

New poems; selected and translated by Edward Snow. rev bilingual ed; North Point Press 2001 329p pa $15 **831**
1. Poetry -- By individual authors
ISBN 0-86547-612-8
LC 2001-42714

In this "translation, Edward Snow renders into believable English the complete text of Rilke's work of early maturity. . . . Maintaining fidelity to Rilke's idiosyncratic and problematic German, Snow does not reproduce his formal structures but does capture the rhythms, tone shifts, and overall feel of the poems to an admirable degree. Bilingual edition." Booklist [review of 1984 edition of New poems (1907)]

★ **Sonnets** to Orpheus; translated by M.D. Herter Norton. W. W. Norton 2006 160p pa $13.95 **831**

1. Poetry -- By individual authors
ISBN 0-393-32885-6

First English translation 1936 in the United Kingdom; this translation first published 1942

"Deeply rooted in the symbolist tradition, the 'Sonnets' collapse the barriers that exist between the inner and the outer world and celebrate the inherently musical quality of language. In his masterful translation of the 'Sonnets', Young captures the fluidity of the original with sensitivity and precision." Libr J

Uncollected poems; selected and translated by Edward Snow. Bilingual ed; North Point Press 1995 265p hardcover o.p. pa $15 **831**

1. Poetry -- By individual authors
ISBN 0-86547-513-X pa

LC 94-24438

"Snow is particularly adept at capturing what one might call the non-Orphic side of Rilke's voice. Even in the most complex and rhetorically charged pieces, however, Snow is careful never to simplify Rilke. . . . Most important of all, these translations . . . let us get beyond the simplifications of the Rilke legend with its cycles of transcendent inspiration and imaginative paralysis." New Repub

Sebald, Winfried Georg, 1944-2001

Across the land and the water; new and selected poems, 1964-2001. W.G. Sebald ; [translated from the German by Iain Galbraith] Random House 2012 166 p. **831**

1. Authors, German 2. German poetry -- Collections 3. World War, 1939-1945 -- Germany -- Poetry
ISBN 9781400068906

LC 2011025272

The book "compiles [W. G. Sebald's] . . . poetic output from his student days through to the last years of his life. . . . Sebald's poems engage . . . with the private archives of Germany's memory of the war. . . . Each poem, in its way, reaches towards the irreducible truth of a large number of individuals, Jewish and non-Jewish, brutally transported from home and out of recognition and existence." (New Statesman)

Includes bibliographical references

832   German drama

Durrenmatt, Friedrich

The visit; a tragi-comedy. translated from the German by Patrick Bowles. Grove Press 1962 109p pa $12 **832**

ISBN 0-8021-3066-6

Characters: 28 men, 6 women, extras. 3 acts. First produced in the United States at the Lunt-Fontaine Theatre, New York City, May 5, 1958

This play "concerns millionaire Claire Zachanassian's return to her small home town where, in her youth, she was

seduced and abandoned by III. She seeks revenge and, to get it, she bribes the entire population: every man, woman and child will be rich for the rest of their lives if they agree to put III to death. After a feeble moral struggle and a travesty of a trial, the people of Güllen condemn and execute the erstwhile lover. In so doing they condemn themselves and Dürrenmatt condemns society as a whole." Cambridge Guide to World Theatre

Goethe, Johann Wolfgang von, 1749-1832

★ **Goethe's** Faust; the original German and a new tr. and introduction by Walter Kaufmann; part one and sections from part two. Anchor Books 1962 503p pa $10.95 **832**

ISBN 978-0-385-03114-1; 0-385-03114-9

Part I first published 1808; Part II 1832

In this epic drama "Mephistopheles makes a bargain with the aged Faust. If Faust is granted one moment of complete contentment, he loses his soul. Faust regains his youth and with Mephistopheles he travels about enjoying every form of earthly pleasure." Haydn. Thesaurus of Book Dig

Lessing, Gotthold Ephraim

Nathan the Wise, Minna von Barnhelm, and other plays and writings; edited by Peter Demetz; foreword by Hannah Arendt. Continuum 1991 xxvii, 335p (German library) hardcover o.p. pa $29.95 **832**

ISBN 0-8264-0706-4; 0-8264-0707-2 pa

LC 91-19344

Contents: Minna von Barnhelm, translated by Kenneth J. Northcott; Emilia Galotti, translated by Anna Johanna Gode von Aesch; The Jews, translated by Ingrid Walsøe-Engel; Nathan the Wise, translated by Bayard Quincy Morgan; Ernst and Falk, translated by William L. Zwiebel; Selections from Lessing's philosophical, theological writings, translated by Henry Chadwick

Schiller, Friedrich

Don Carlos and Mary Stuart; translated with notes by Hilary Collier Sy-Quia; adapted in verse drama by Peter Oswald; with an introduction by Lesley Sharpe. Oxford University Press 2008 xxx, 359p il pa $13.95 **832**

1. Queens 2. Princes
ISBN 978-0-19-954074-7

LC 2008-275155

First published 1996

This volume contains Don Carlos and Mary Stuart, two German historical dramas. "Dating from 1787 and 1800 respectively, one play was written immediately before the French Revolution, the other in its aftermath. These new translations into blank verse are accurate, elegant, and playable. The Introduction, Notes, and Chronology set the plays in their cultural and intellectual background, while a family tree explains the historical relationship between Don Carlos and Mary Stuart." Publisher's note

Includes bibliographical references

The **robbers** [and] Wallenstein; translated with an introduction by F. J. Lamport. Penguin Books 1979 472p (Penguin classics) pa $16   **832**
    ISBN 978-0-14-044368-4; 0-14-044368-1

In The robbers (1782) a man, cheated out of his inheritance by his brother, forms a band of thieves. The Wallenstein trilogy, based on the fall of the German general Count Albrecht von Wallenstein, is comprised of: Wallenstein's camp (1798), The Piccolominis (1799), and Wallenstein's death (1799).

833   German fiction

Sebald, Winfried Georg, 1944-2001
   ★ **On** the natural history of destruction; with essays on Alfred Andersch, Jean Amery, and Peter Weiss. {by} W.G. Sebald; translated by Anthea Bell. Random House 2003 202p $23.95; pa $12.95 **833**
    1. Artists 2. Authors 3. Painters 4. Novelists 5. Dramatists 6. Philosophers 7. Essayists 8. Nonfiction writers 9. Short story writers 10. German literature -- History and criticism 11. World War, 1939-1945 -- Literature and the war
    ISBN 0-375-50484-2; 0-375-75657-4 pa
                          LC 2002-75187

Original German edition, 1999

Stach, Reiner
   ★ **Kafka,** the years of insight; Reiner Stach ; translated by Shelley Frisch. Princeton University Press 2013 720 p. (hardcover) $35   **833**
    1. Tuberculosis 2. Authors, Austrian -- 20th century -- Biography
    ISBN 0691147515; 9780691147512
                          LC 2012042048

This book is part of Reiner Stach's three-part biography of author Franz Kafka. This volume "covers the period from 1916 to 1924, his terminal years." Topics include "his father's disapprobation, his job at the Worker's Accident Insurance Institute, his turbulent courtships with Felice Bauer, Milena Jesenská, and Dora Diamant, and finally his encounter with malignant and fatal tuberculosis." (Library Journal)

Includes bibliographical references and index.

838   German miscellaneous writings

Kleist, Heinrich von
   Selected writings; edited and translated by David Constantine. Hackett Pub. 2004 xxvii, 442p $44; pa $14.95   **838**
    ISBN 978-0-87220-744-8; 0-87220-744-7; 978-0-87220-743-1 pa; 0-87220-743-9 pa
                          LC 2004-54378

"This volume includes the majority of Kleist's writings in English translation. An outstanding representation of his work, this selection offers three plays, eight short stories, five anecdotes, and three essays. Kleist's dramas and stories resonate with complex circumstances and obscure consequences that the characters struggle to sail through. Things are not always what they seem to be; intriguingly, the guilty can look innocent and the innocent guilty. The play The Broken Jug, as well as the stories 'Michael Kohlhaas' and 'The Chilean Earthquake,' depict predicaments of the falsely accused who are denied justice. Constantine . . . does an outstanding job of conveying the beauty of Kleist's literary style while allowing himself some liberties in translation." Libr J

Includes bibliographical references

839   Other Germanic literatures

   ★ **The Sagas** of Icelanders; a selection. preface by Jane Smiley; introduction by Robert Kellogg. Viking 2000 lxvi, 782p il maps (World of the sagas) hardcover o.p. pa $20   **839**
    1. Sagas 2. Old Norse literature
    ISBN 0-14-100003-1 pa
                          LC 99-44111

"The Icelandic Sagas are among the masterpieces of world literature whose composition stretches from about the year 1000 to 1500. Presenting the adventures of Norse and Viking heroes, the sagas are told with ritual simplicity and a realism that anticipate the modern novel." Libr J

Includes bibliographical references

Singer, Isaac Bashevis, 1904-1991
   √ **More** stories from my father's court; translated by Curt Leviant. Farrar, Straus & Giroux 2000 216p hardcover o.p. pa $12   **839**
    1. Authors 2. Novelists 3. Journalists 4. Essayists 5. Jews -- Poland 6. Children's authors 7. Short story writers 8. Nobel laureates for literature
    ISBN 0-374-52798-9 pa
                          LC 00-37583

Sequel to In my father's court

These pieces were first published in Yiddish in the Jewish daily Forward from 1955-1960

These autobiographical sketches depict the workings of the beth din, the rabbinical court that met in the Singer's Warsaw home

"This book is a portrait of the artist as a voyeuristic yeshiva boy, someone who assimilated into his soul the weird contradictions of modern Jewish life and, half chronicler and half creator, spun them into lasting stories." N Y Times Book Rev

839.3   Netherlandish literatures

Prose, Francine
   √ **Anne** Frank; the book, the life, the afterlife. HarperCollins 2009 322p $24.99   **839.3**
    1. Children 2. Creative writing 3. Diarists 4. Holocaust victims 5. Holocaust, 1933-1945 -- Personal narratives
    ISBN 978-0-06-143079-4; 0-06-143079-X
                          LC 2009-17703

"In this definitive, deeply moving inquiry into the life of the young, imperiled artist, and masterful literary exegesis of The Diary of a Young Girl, Prose tells the crushing story of the Frank family, performs a revelatory analysis of Anne's exacting revision of her coming-of-age memoir, and assesses her father's editorial decisions as he edited his murdered daughter's manuscript for publication. . . . Extraordinary testimony to the power of literature and compassion." Booklist

Includes bibliographical references

839.7   Swedish literature

Hammarskjold, Dag

Markings; translated from the Swedish by Leif Sjöberg & W. H. Auden; with a foreword by W. H. Auden. Knopf 1964 xxiii, 221p hardcover o.p. pa $13.95   **839.7**
  1. Spiritual life
  ISBN 0-394-43532-X; 0-307-27742-9 pa; 978-0-307-27742-8 pa

Original Swedish edition, 1963

The author described this account as a sort of white book concerning his negotiations with himself and with God. A record of his inner life, it opens with a poem he wrote around 1925; most of the entries were made during the nineteen forties and fifties—and the book ends with a poem written only a few weeks before his plane crashed.

Prideaux, Sue

Strindberg; a life. Sue Prideaux. Yale University Press 2012 371 p. (cl : alk. paper) $40.00 **839.7**
  1. Dramatists -- Biography 2. Authors, Swedish -- 19th century -- Biography
  ISBN 0300136935; 9780300136937
                                                      LC 2011038050

This book is a biography of the Swedish playwright August Strindberg. "Strindberg (1849-1912) had a miserable childhood and became the devoted father of five children. . . . His plays, murderously claustrophobic scorpion dances of marriage, portray extreme psychological states. He also painted Turneresque pictures, was an expert photographer and gardener, and dabbled fruitlessly in alchemy and the occult." (Booklist)

Includes bibliographical references and index.

Strindberg, August

Strindberg : five plays; translated, with an introduction by Harry G. Carlson. University of Calif. Press 1983 297p hardcover o.p. pa $21.95 **839.7**
  ISBN 978-0-520-04698-6 pa
                                                      LC 82-15882
  Contents: The father; Miss Julie; The dance of death; A dream play; The ghost sonata

Tranströmer, Tomas, 1931-

The **great** enigma. New Directions 2006 xxi, 262p pa $16.95   **839.7**
  ISBN 978-0-8112-1672-2; 0-8112-1672-1
                                                      LC 2006-22551
  This volume "offers the most generous collection of Tranströmer's poems to date. . . . Lean and uncluttered, Ful-

ton's translations in The Great Enigma neither preach nor moralize. They refuse staged psychology and let interiority take shape as mysterious judgments, made by the selection of detail and the juxtaposition of things and times and experiences." Boston Rev

839.8   Danish and Norwegian literatures

Ibsen, Henrik, 1828-1906

★ The **complete** major prose plays; translated [from the Norwegian] and introduced by Rolf Fjelde. New American Library 1978 1143p pa $28 **839.8**
  ISBN 978-0-452-26205-8; 0-452-26205-4
                                                      LC 78-50714
  First published 1978 by Farrar, Straus & Giroux
  Includes bibliographical references
  Contents: Pillars of society; A doll house; Ghosts; An enemy of the people; The wild duck; Rosmersholm; The lady from the sea; Hedda Gabler; The master builder; Little Eyolf; John Gabriel Borkman; When we dead awaken

Jacobsen, Rolf

The **roads** have come to an end now; selected and last poems of Rolf Jacobsen. translated by Robert Bly, Roger Greenwald, and Robert Hedin. Copper Canyon Press 2001 168p pa $16 **839.8**
  ISBN 1-55659-165-9
                                                      LC 2001-4488
  "This bilingual (Norwegian-English) edition of 73 poems demonstrates a poet whose vision of the natural world and humanity's place in it is cosmically penetrative. Jacobsen regards the world as filled with an essential energy, animated by what must be God, and reading his work induces a certain calm ecstasy about everyday existence." Booklist

Wullschlager, Jackie

Hans Christian Andersen; the life of a story teller. University of Chicago Press 2002 489p il map pa $19   **839.8**
  1. Authors 2. Novelists 3. Dramatists 4. Authors, Danish 5. Children's authors 6. Short story writers
  ISBN 0-226-91747-9; 978-0-226-91747-4
                                                      LC 2002-18010
  First published 2000 in the United Kingdom
  "Wullschlager succeeds brilliantly at portraying Andersens inner mind and uncovering his hopes and fears and details the historical context that served to produce such a grand body of literature. . . . [This biography] will be a standard study for years to come." Libr J
  Includes bibliographical references

840.9   French literature -- History and criticism

Becker, Daniel Levin

Many subtle channels; in praise of potential literature. Daniel Levin Becker. Harvard University Press 2012 x, 338 p.p (alk. paper) $27.95 **840.9**
  1. Authorship 2. Intellectuals 3. Literary style 4. Oulipo (Association) 5. Literary form 6. Authors,

American -- 21st century -- Biography
ISBN 0674065778; 9780674065772

LC 2011044577

This book centers on the achievements of "Ouvroir de Littérature Potentielle, or Oulipo, a collective of writers and mathematicians. . . . Since the group's formation in 1960, members of the Oulipo . . . have been concocting . . . intricate [literary] challenges. . . . 'Many Subtle Channels' is Levin Becker's personal history of this literature and his tribute to the people who helped create it, including [Georges] Perec, Jacques Roubaud, Italo Calvino, and Marcel Duchamp." (Bookforum)

841   French poetry

Baudelaire, Charles

Les fleurs du mal; the complete text of The flowers of evil. in a new translation by Richard Howard; illustrated with nine original monotypes by Michael Mazur. Godine 1982 xxxii, 365p il hardcover o.p. pa $18.95   **841**
1. Poetry -- By individual authors
ISBN 978-0-87923-462-1 pa; 0-87923-462-8 pa

LC 81-13283

Original French edition, 1857

"Howard puts the original's rhymed alexandrines primarily into iambic pentameter blank verse, which allows him to capture the immediate, concrete, visceral quality of Baudelaire's imagery." Choice

Poems. Knopf 1993 256p (Everyman's library pocket poets) $12.50   **841**
1. Poetry -- By individual authors
ISBN 0-679-42910-7

LC 93-14363

A representative selection of poetry by the French symbolist.

Beckett, Samuel, 1906-1989

Collected poems in English and French. Grove Press 1977 147p hardcover o.p. pa $13.95   **841**
1. Poetry -- By individual authors
ISBN 978-0-8021-3096-9 pa

LC 77-77855

This work contains poems written by Beckett in English and French along with his translations and bilingual versions of poems by Eluard, Rimbaud, Apollinaire, and Chamfort

Chanson de Roland

★ The **song** of Roland; translated, with an introduction, by W.S. Merwin. Modern Library 2001 137p pa $11.95   **841**
1. Roland (Legendary character)
ISBN 0-375-75711-2

LC 00-48989

"This heroic poem celebrates the mighty feats of Roland, the great French hero in the time of Charlemagne. The medieval legend has replaced and transformed the actual facts of history to a great extent but the epic poem has continued in popularity." Bookman's Manual

Includes bibliographical references

French poetry, 1820-1950, with prose translations; selected, translated, and introduced by William Rees. Penguin Books 1994 xli, 854p (Penguin classics) pa $22   **841**
1. French poetry -- Collections
ISBN 978-0-14-042385-3; 0-14-042385-0

LC 91-127343

First published 1990 in the United Kingdom

"While this anthology contains . . . generous selections from the established giants—Baudelaire, Rimbaud, Mallarmé, Valéry, Apollinaire, Michaux—it also draws attention to interesting 'minor' poets, such as Claudel or Cendrars, whose writing has been vital to the evolution of poetry in France. William Rees gives us an introduction to each poet, his or her life, affinities and aesthetics, and the significant literary movements Romanticism, the Parnassian Movement, Symbolism, Cubism, Surrealism and 'Négritude' are signposted and discussed." Publisher's note

Mallarme, Stephane

Collected poems and other verse; translated with notes by E.H. and A.M. Blackmore; with an introduction by Elizabeth McCombie. Oxford University Press 2006 xxxvii, 282p pa $15.95   **841**
1. Poetry -- By individual authors
ISBN 978-0-19-280362-7; 0-19-280362-X

This collection presents Mallarme's "Poesies in the last arrangement known to have been approved by the author. Prose poems, uncollected verse, and the unique, unclassifiable Un Coup de des. . . (A Dice Throw. . .) are also present, including over 20 items that have never previously been translated. Original spelling, punctuation, and lineation have been preserved throughout." Publisher's note

The **Random** House book of twentieth-century French poetry; with translations by American and British poets; edited by Paul Auster. Random House 1982 xlix, 635p hardcover o.p. pa $26   **841**
1. French poetry -- Collections
ISBN 978-0-394-71748-7 pa; 0-394-71748-1 pa

LC 82-280

This bilingual edition collects the verse of forty-eight poets as translated by eighty-four poets. The volume opens with a section of poems by Guillaume Apollinaire and closes with a group of poems by Philippe Denis. The original and translation appear on facing pages

"This excellent anthology undertakes a double task: to provide a comprehensive view of French poetry in the twentieth century and to show, in the range of translators it offers, the influences of that poetry on American and British poets. . . . Paul Auster has done an excellent job of matching poets and translators." Nation

Includes bibliographical references

Rimbaud, Arthur, 1854-1891

Poems; [selected by Peter Washington] Knopf 1994 288p (Everyman's library pocket poets) $12.50   **841**

1. Poetry -- By individual authors
ISBN 978-0-679-43321-7; 0-679-43321-X

LC 94-2496

A collection of work by the French Symbolist known for his daring images and pioneering prose poems

Verlaine, Paul, 1844–1896

Selected poems; translated by C. F. MacIntyre. University of Calif. Press 1948 xx, 228p il pa $15.95   **841**

1. Poetry -- By individual authors
ISBN 0-520-01298-4

Eighty poems, chosen from Verlaine's first six books. French originals and translations are on facing pages. Contains a preface by the translator

The translator "has done Verlaine a gracious courtesy, and American readers a great kindness. The charm, verbal fireworks, sympathy and nostalgia of this major French poet are Englished with color and convictions." Chicago Sunday Trib

Includes bibliographical references

842   French drama

Beckett, Samuel, 1906-1989

Dramatic works; Paul Auster, series editor; introduction by Edward Albee. Grove Press 2006 509p (Samuel Beckett: the Grove centenary edition) $24.95   **842**

ISBN 978-0-8021-1819-0; 0-8021-1819-4

LC 2005-55078

Camus, Albert, 1913-1960

Caligula & three other plays; translated from the French by Stuart Gilbert; with a preface written specially for this edition and translated by Justin O'Brien. Knopf 1958 302p hardcover o.p. pa $13   **842**

ISBN 978-0-394-70207-0 pa; 0-394-70207-7 pa

"Four of the author's best-known plays, written between 1938 and 1950. 'Caligula,' about the infamous emperor's self-destroying rebellion against fate; 'The Misunderstanding,' about the murder of a man by his ghoulish mother and sister,' 'The Just Assassins,' on the self-questionings of terrorists; and 'State of Siege,' an allegory about the refusal of one individual in a plague-stricken city to compromise with evil." Publ Wkly

Genet, Jean

The **blacks** : a clown show; translated from the French by Bernard Frechtman. Grove Press 1960 128p pa $13   **842**

ISBN 0-8021-5028-4

Original French edition, 1958

"Drama in which a group of bizarrely dressed Negroes give a performance for another group of Negroes who wear white masks and represent the major figures of white society's established authority." McGraw-Hill Ency of World Drama

The **maids** [and] Deathwatch; two plays. with an introduction by Jean-Paul Sartre; translated from the French by Bernard Frechtman. Grove Press 1954 166p hardcover o.p. pa $14   **842**

ISBN 978-0-8021-5056-1 pa; 0-8021-5056-X pa

Deathwatch, a one-act play written 1947 and first produced 1949 "deals with an insignificant criminal who tries to assume the highly desirable and prestigious role of murderer. . . . In 'The Maids (Les bonnes),' produced in 1947, . . . two servant girls have created an elaborate ritual in which they impersonate their mistress and finally murder her symbolically." McGraw-Hill Ency of World Drama

Goldsby, Robert W.

Molière on stage; what's so funny? Robert W. Goldsby. Anthem Press 2012 xx, 202 p.p (pbk. : alk. paper) $39.95   **842**

1. Molière, 1622-1673 -- Dramatic production 2. Molière, 1622-1673 -- Stage history
ISBN 0857284428; 0857284444; 9780857284426; 9780857284440

LC 2012001708

This book by Robert W. Goldsby "takes the reader onstage, backstage and into the audience of Molière's plays, analyzing the performance of his works in both his own time and in ours. . . . This text . . . investigates four key topics. . . : Molière's early experiences that lead to his later theater experiences; his central great plays of love and lust; his comedic genius and his passion for the stage; and the final words and performances of his life." (Publisher's note)

Includes bibliographical references (p. [191]-196) and index

Ionesco, Eugène, 1912-1994

Rhinoceros, and other plays; translated by Derek Prouse. Grove Press 1960 141p pa $10   **842**

ISBN 0-8021-3098-4

Three satirical comedies by a leading dramatist of the "theater of the absurd." In Rhinoceros, one man resists the pressure to conform as everyone about him accepts their transformation into rhinoceroses and he finds himself socially isolated. In The future is in eggs, a couple must produce eggs destined to become intellectuals. The leader is a satire on the mass adulation of political figures in which the leader turns out to be a headless figure

Molière, 1622-1673

The **misanthrope** and other plays. Signet Classics 2005 524p pa $7.95   **842**

ISBN 0-451-52987-1; 978-0-451-52987-9

LC 2006-276841

Contents: The misanthrope; The doctor in spite of himself; The miser; The would-be gentleman; The mischievous machinations of Scapin; The learned women; The imaginary invalid

★ **Tartuffe** and other plays. Signet Classics 2007 xxiv, 408p pa $7.95 **842**
ISBN 978-0-451-53033-2

LC 2007-275593

Contents: The ridiculous precieuses; The school for husbands; The school for wives; The critique of the school for wives; The Versailles impromptu; Tartuffe; Don Juan
Includes bibliographical references

Rostand, Edmond
Cyrano de Bergerac; translated and adapted for the modern stage by Anthony Burgess. Applause Theatre & Cinema Bks. 1998 175p pa $6.95 **842**
1. Poets 2. Authors 3. Soldiers
ISBN 1-55783-230-7

LC 96-2545

A reissue of the title first published 1971 by Knopf
This version was commissioned for production at the Tyrone Guthrie Theater in Minneapolis. It is adapted and translated from the French play originally produced in 1897. Cyrano, the hero, a Gascon poet and swordsman notorious for his long nose, is in love with Roxana

Samuel Beckett's Waiting for Godot; edited and with an introduction by Harold Bloom. New ed; Chelsea House 2008 172p (Modern critical interpretations) $45 **842**
1. Poets 2. Authors 3. Novelists 4. Dramatists 5. Short story writers 6. Nobel laureates for literature
ISBN 978-0-7910-9793-9

LC 2007-49864

First published 1987
Critical interpretations of Beckett's classic tragicomedy illustrating the apparent meaninglessness of life.
Includes bibliographical references

Sartre, Jean Paul, 1905-1980
★ **No** exit, and three other plays. Vintage Bks. 1989 275p pa $12 **842**
ISBN 0-679-72516-4

LC 89-40097

No exit is a modern morality play; The flies is a reworking of the Orestes-Electra story. The third play concerns a young Communist intellectual's attempt to maintain his integrity as party line changes and personal relationships alter perceptions of his murder of a party boss who had fallen out of favor, but whose memory is later rehabilitated. The last play concerns a prostitute's involvement in false charges of rape against a murdered black man and his companion in a town in the American South

843   French fiction

Carter, William C.
Marcel Proust; a life. Yale Univ. Press 2000 946p $45; pa $18.95 **843**
1. Authors 2. Novelists 3. Essayists 4. Literary critics
ISBN 0-300-08145-6; 0-300-09400-0 pa

LC 99-53701

"Excavating biographic details out of such material as untranslated memoirs and recently collected letters, Carter . . . accounts for the daily affairs of this social butterfly-turned-hypochondriac and shut-in. Proust's romances and infatuations, his political action during the Dreyfus affair, and his literary runs-ins with Anatole France and André Gide, as well as larger issues such as his homosexuality, all receive lengthy treatment." Publ Wkly
Includes bibliographical references

Jack, Belinda Elizabeth
George Sand; a woman's life writ large. {by} Belinda Jack. Knopf 2000 395p il hardcover o.p. pa $16 **843**
1. Authors 2. Novelists 3. Dramatists
ISBN 0-679-77918-3 pa

LC 99-40857

"Prodigious author, cross-dresser, lover of Chopin and Alfred de Musset, intimate of (among others) Liszt, Balzac, Dumas (père and fils), Turgenev, and Flaubert (who cried twice at her funeral), Sand was both before her time and quintessentially of it. Jack's nuanced, moving assessment of the writer's early years . . . is the strongest section of this packed life. When Sand moves onto a larger stage, Jack's style becomes breathless, as if she could barely keep up with her flamboyant subject." New Yorker

Severson, Marilyn S.
★ **Masterpieces** of French literature. Greenwood Press 2004 186p (Greenwood introduces literary masterpieces) $45 **843**
1. French literature -- History and criticism
ISBN 0-313-31484-5

LC 2003-59635

Among the novels discussed are Albert Camus's The stranger and The plague, Gustave Flaubert's Madame Bovary, Victor Hugo's The hunchback of Notre Dame and Les Miserables, and Alexander Dumas's The three musketeers
"Students and general readers seeking a thorough understanding of these influential novels will benefit greatly from this outstanding guide." Libr J
Includes bibliographical references

Shattuck, Roger
Proust's way; a field guide to In search of lost time. Norton 2000 xxiv, 290p hardcover o.p. pa $16.95 **843**
1. Authors 2. Novelists 3. Essayists 4. Literary critics
ISBN 0-393-32180-0 pa

LC 99-58472

Shattuck "explains the major settings of the work, summarizes character and plot, and discusses central themes. Shattuck acknowledges that there is no one right interpretation of In Search of Lost Time but succeeds in providing a framework to help readers get through it. He addresses readers coming to the work for the first time." Libr J

Includes bibliographical references

844 French essays

Camus, Albert

★ The **myth** of Sisyphus, and other essays; translated from the French by Justin O'Brien. Knopf 1955 212p hardcover o.p. pa $12.95   **844**

ISBN 0-679-73373-6 pa

Personal reflections on the meaning of life and the philosophical questions surrounding suicide

Resistance, rebellion, and death; translated from the French and with an introduction by Justin O'Brien. Knopf 1961 271p hardcover o.p. pa $13.95   **844**

ISBN 978-0-679-76401-4 pa; 0679764011 pa

"A selection of forthright essays on contemporary world politics, on capital punishment and the relations of the state and the individual, and on art, chosen from the three volumes of 'Actuelles,' published in France between 1950 and 1958." Publ Wkly

Frampton, Saul

When I am playing with my cat, how do I know she is not playing with me? Montaigne and being in touch with life. Pantheon Books 2011 300p $26; ebook $12.99   **844**

1. Judges 2. Authors 3. Essayists

ISBN 978-0-375-42471-7; 978-0-307-37959-7 ebook

LC 2010-43642

The author "renders a rigorous history of ideas in this engaging account of the life and the work of Michel de Montaigne (1533–1592). . . . Frampton tucks a good deal of biography into his tour of the evolution of the essays and the events that inspired them—but his extraordinary achievement is in conveying—and inviting the reader to commune with—Montaigne's unique sensibility and his take on death, sex, travel, friendship, kidney stones, the human thumb, and above all, 'the power of the ordinary and the unremarkable,' the value of the here-and-now.' This scholarly romp through the Renaissance is a jewel." Publ Wkly

Includes bibliographical references

848 French miscellaneous writings

Bair, Deirdre

Simone de Beauvoir; a biography. Summit Bks. 1990 718p il hardcover o.p. pa $31.95   **848**

1. Authors 2. Novelists 3. Dramatists 4. Philosophers 5. Essayists 6. Feminists 7. Biographers 8. Nonfiction writers 9. Short story writers 10. Nobel laureates for literature

ISBN 0-671-74180-2 pa

LC 89-22029

"Bair's biography of the French author, philosopher, and feminist aims to restore the balance between interest in de Beauvoir's personal life—as the lifelong companion of Jean-

Paul Sartre and sometime lover of Nelson Algren—and the question of her achievements as a writer and thinker." Booklist

Includes bibliographical references

Damrosch, Leo

★ **Jean** -Jacques Rousseau; restless genius. Leo Damrosch. Houghton Mifflin Co. 2005 x, 566 p.p ill., map o.p.; (pbk.) $12.00; o.p.   **848**

1. Philosophers 2. Authors 3. Novelists 4. Memoirists 5. Political and social philosophers

ISBN 9780618446964; 9780618872022; 0618446966

LC 2005013579

L.L. Winship/PEN New England Award: Nonfiction (2006)

This book "is [a] . . . single-volume biography of [Jean-Jacques] Rousseau, . . . published in English for the general reader. It . . . illuminate[s] the last decade of his life, a time when his psychological complexity and strangeness came to the fore yet his intellect and creative powers triumphed over his difficult, paranoid temperament. During those ten years, he finished the 'Confessions,' wrote the 'Dialogues,' or 'Rousseau Judge of Jean-Jacques,' which he tried in vain to place in the Notre-Dame cathedral for safekeeping, and began writing 'Reveries of the Solitary Walker.'" (Publisher's note)

"A delight to read, Damrosch comes as close to Rousseau's authentic self as we are likely to get." N Y Times Book Rev

Includes bibliographical references (p. [499]-549) and index.

Gordon, Lois G.

The **world** of Samuel Beckett, 1906-1946; {by} Lois Gordon. Yale Univ. Press 1996 250p il $50; pa $16.95   **848**

1. Poets 2. Authors 3. Novelists 4. Dramatists 5. Short story writers 6. Nobel laureates for literature

ISBN 0-300-06409-8; 0-300-07495-6 pa

LC 95-22851

Gordon "examines the first 40 years of the playwright/novelist's 83-year life, which includes periods in Ireland, where he was born; in Paris, where he spent much of his life; and in London, Germany, and other parts of France. . . . Gordon has been thorough in her research and careful in her presentation." Choice

Includes bibliographical references

Kaplan, Alice

The **collaborator** : the trial & execution of Robert Brasillach; {by} Alice Kaplan. University of Chicago Press 2000 308p $25; pa $15   **848**

1. Authors 2. Novelists 3. Journalists 4. Collaborationists 5. Fascism -- France 6. World War, 1939-1945 -- France 7. France -- Intellectual life -- 20th century 8. Authors, French -- 20th century -- Biography 9. Intellectuals -- France -- Political activity 10. France -- History -- 1940-1945, German occupation 11. World War, 1939-1945 -- Collaborationists -- France 12. Fascism and literature -- France -- History -- 20th century

ISBN 0-226-42414-6; 0-226-42415-4 pa

LC 99-48291

The author considers the trial of French author Robert Brasillach, a Nazi collaborator, who was executed by firing squad in 1945. She explores "the questions posed by the prosecution . . . during the trial. What responsibility do writers bear for their work? When do words become crimes?" (N Y Times Book Rev) Index.

Kaplan details "the life of Robert Brasillach, a prolific and controversial French critic who was executed for treason, at age 35, after France's liberation from the Nazis. A fascist-leaning writer known for his defense of Nazi crimes . . . Brasillach was the only distinguished writer put to death by the postwar French government." Publ Wkly

Includes bibliographical references

Rimbaud, Arthur, 1854-1891

Rimbaud; complete works, selected letters: a bilingual edition. translated with an introduction and notes by Wallace Fowlie; updated, revised and with a foreword by Seth Whidden. University of Chicago Press 2005 xxxvi, 458p il $50; pa $19   **848**
ISBN 978-0-226-71976-4; 0-226-71976-6; 978-0-226-71977-1 pa; 0226719774 pa
LC 2005-41859
First published 1966

In this bilingual edition of Rimbaud's work the original French texts are accompanied by English prose translations. In addition to the complete poetic works there are two prose fragments, a short story in the form of a seminarian's journal, and a selection of letters chosen to illustrate biographical details and Rimbaud's credo as a poet.

Includes bibliographical references

Sartre, Jean-Paul, 1905-1980

We Have Only This Life to Live; Selected Essays, 1939-1975. by Jean-Paul Sartre ; edited by Ronald Aronson and Adrian van den Hoven. Random House Inc 2013 600 p. (paperback) $22.95   **848**
1. Life 2. Literature 3. Modern philosophy
ISBN 1590174933; 9781590174937
LC 2013001043

This collection, by Jean-Paul Sartre, edited by Adrian van den Hoven and Ronald Aronson, presents essays by the author collected between 1939 and 1975. "Here Sartre writes about Faulkner, Bataille, Giacometti, Fanon, the liberation of France, torture in Algeria, existentialism and Marxism, friends lost and found, and much else." (Publisher's note)

Todd, Olivier

Albert Camus; a life. translated by Benjamin Ivry. abr & ed English version; Knopf 1997 434p il $30   **848**
1. Authors 2. Novelists 3. Dramatists 4. Authors, French 5. Essayists 6. Nobel laureates for literature
ISBN 0-679-42855-0
LC 97-2991
Original French edition, 1996

This is a biography of the French novelist, playwright, literary editor, and philosopher.

"Todd's exhaustive biography, which aims—and succeeds—in presenting 'the man' and not just the writer, has been shortened for its English translation, which refers readers to the French edition for notes, sources and bibliography." Publ Wkly

Valery, Paul

Selected writings. New Directions 1950 256p hardcover o.p. pa $12.95   **848**
ISBN 0-8112-0213-5 pa

"Seventeen poems are translated by eighteen translators, including Denis Devlin, Léonie Adams, and C. Day Lewis. . . . The rest of the book is composed of the French love miscellanies, essays, dialogues, and critiques." New Yorker

Voltaire, 1694-1778

The **portable** Voltaire; edited, and with an introduction by Ben Ray Redmen. Viking 1949 569p hardcover o.p. pa $17   **848**
ISBN 0-14-015041-2 pa

The selections from Voltaire's works include: Candide, part one; Three stories: Zadig, Micromegas, and Story of a good Brahmin; Letters, and selections from the Philosophical Dictionary and other works. The editor's introduction gives a biographical sketch of Voltaire.

849   Occitan, Catalan, Franco-Provençal literatures

Pla, Josep

The **Gray** Notebook; Josep Pla ; translated from the Catalan by Peter Bush ; introduction by Valentí Puig. New York Review Books 2013 656 p. (New York Review Books Classics) (alk. paper) $19.95   **849**
1. Diaries 2. Authors, Spanish 3. Authors, Catalan -- 20th century -- Biography
ISBN 1590176715; 9781590176719
LC 2013028497

This book presents the diary of author Joseph Pla, translated by Peter Bush. "Aspiring to be a writer, not a lawyer, he resolved to hone his style by keeping a journal. In it he wrote about his family, local characters, . . . the quips, quarrels, ambitions, and amours of his friends; writers he liked and writers he didn't; and the long . . . walks he would take in the countryside under magnificent skies." (Publisher's note)

"Pla . . . is considered one of the greatest writers of Catalan language, and this beautiful translation lets English readers glory in the quiet strength of his words." Kirkus

850   Literatures of Italian, Dalmatian, Romanian, Rhaetian, Sardinian, Corsican languages

The **Oxford** companion to Italian literature; edited by Peter Hainsworth and David Robey. Oxford Univ. Press 2002 xli, 644p maps $95   **850**
1. Reference books 2. Italian literature -- Dictionaries 3. Italian literature -- Bio-bibliography
ISBN 0-19-818332-1
LC 2001-59301

"A magisterial addition to the Oxford companions to literature, this volume goes far beyond its core subject of Italian literature to cover its substrate and context. . . . An excellent ready-reference companion for readers seeking less an introduction to the summits of the literature . . . but a reminder of relevant details." Choice

Includes bibliographical references

Ruud, Jay

Critical companion to Dante; a literary reference to his life and work. Facts on File 2008 566p il (Facts on File library of world literature) $75   **850**

1. Poets 2. Authors

ISBN 978-0-8160-6521-9

LC 2007-33473

This title covers the works of Dante, including The Divine Comedy, La Vita Nuova, and his philosophical works.

"Ruud has written a useful introductory resource that students and lay readers alike can enjoy." Booklist

Includes bibliographical references

851   Italian poetry

Ariosto, Lodovico

Orlando Furioso/The frenzy of Orlando, part 1; a romantic epic. by Ludovico Ariosto; translated with an introduction by Barbara Reynolds. Penguin Books 1975 827p map (Penguin classics) pa $18   **851**

1. Poetry -- By individual authors

ISBN 978-0-14-044311-0; 0-14-044311-8

LC 75-327748

An English verse translation in the original meter of the epic poem by the sixteenth-century Italian poet, courtier, and statesman, which is based on the adventures of Roland and other knights of Charlemagne in the wars against the Saracens

This translation is "lucid, lively, and eminently readable. . . . The first volume contains one-half (23) of the cantos plus invaluable aids for the reader: a lengthy, informative introduction, a list of characters and devices, maps and genealogical tables, notes for each canto and an index of proper names." Choice

Orlando Furioso/The frenzy of Orlando, part 2; a romantic epic. [by] Ludovico Ariosto; translated with an introduction by Barbara Reynolds. Penguin Books 1977 794p (Penguin Classics) pa $18   **851**

1. Poetry -- By individual authors

ISBN 978-0-14-044310-3; 0-14-044310-X

"The value of this faithful translation is primarily that it helps you with the Italian. It lets you make your way painlessly into the poem. . . . It does not . . . draw attention to itself. Modestly, it points across, to the things going on in the original." Times Lit Suppl

Dante Alighieri, 1265-1321

The **divine** comedy; translated by Allen Mandelbaum; with an introduction by Eugenio Montale; and notes by Peter Armour. Alfred A. Knopf 1995 798p il (Everyman's library) $25   **851**

1. Poetry -- By individual authors

ISBN 978-0-679-43313-2; 0-679-43313-9

LC 95-75206

An epic poem, completed in 1321, in which the poet describes his visionary spiritual journey through Hell, Purgatory and Paradise—guided first by the classical poet Vergil and then by his beloved Beatrice—which results in a purification of his religious faith.

The **Inferno**; translated by Robert Hollander and Jean Hollander; introduction & notes by Robert Hollander. Doubleday 2000 704p hardcover o.p. pa $16.95   **851**

1. Poetry -- By individual authors

ISBN 978-0-385-49698-8 pa; 0-385-49698-2 pa

LC 00-34531

A translation of Dante's poem, in which the Roman poet Virgil guides Dante through the underworld.

"The heart of the Hollanders' edition is the translation itself, which nicely balances the precision required for a much-interpreted allegory and the poetic qualities that draw most readers to the work. The result is a terse, lean Dante with its own kind of beauty. . . . The Hollanders' lines will satisfy both the poetry lover and scholar; they are at once literary, accessible and possessed of the seeming transparence that often characterizes great translations. The Italian text is included on the facing page for easy reference, along with notes drawing on some 60 Dante scholars, several indexes, a list of works cited and an introduction by Robert Hollander." Publ Wkly

Includes bibliographical references

Paradiso; a verse translation by Robert & Jean Hollander; introduction & notes by Robert Hollander. Doubleday 2007 915p $40; pa $19.95   **851**

1. Poetry -- By individual authors

ISBN 978-0-385-50678-6; 0-385-50678-3; 978-1-4000-3115-3 pa; 1-4000-3115-X pa

LC 2007-18070

This is a verse translation of the third volume of Dante's Divine Comedy with the original Italian text on facing pages and an introduction and notes.

"Dante's terza rima is impossible to recreate satisfactorily in English, but the Hollanders have produced a fine verse substitute. . . . Splendid as this new translation is, the endlessly valuable notes are what make this edition supplant all others. The commentary here has evolved not only from extensive research but also from the famous Dante Seminar Hollander has taught at Princeton for many years." Natl Rev

The **portable** Dante; translated, edited, and with an introduction and notes by Mark Musa. Penguin Bks. 1995 xliii, 654p pa $17   **851**

1. Poetry -- By individual authors

ISBN 0-14-243754-9

LC 94-15988

First published 1947

Contains complete verse translations of The Divine comedy and La vita nuova

This book "contains complete verse translations of Dante's two masterworks, The Divine Comedy and La Vita

Nuova, as well as a bibliography, notes, and an introduction by . . . Mark Musa." Publisher's note

Includes bibliographical references

Purgatorio; a verse translation by Jean and Robert Hollander; introduction and notes by Robert Hollander. Doubleday 2003 xxiv, 742p hardcover o.p. pa $18.95 **851**

1. Poetry -- By individual authors

ISBN 978-0-385-49700-8 pa

LC 2002-67100

"To enter Dante's Purgatorio is to step into a charmed world, balanced by the rhythmic interplay of sleep, dreams, light, shadows, smiles, tears, and the reverberations of both solo and choral song. This is the most aesthetically vibrant of Dante's three realms, the one in which the artisanal gestures of poet, painter, and musician prevail. . . . The Hollanders have rendered both the supple lyricism and the rich imagery of the Purgatorio with an admirably informed expertise, preserving the stately economy of Dante's Italian throughout." Literary Rev (Madison, N. J.)

Includes bibliographical references

Montale, Eugenio, 1896-1981

The **collected** poems of Eugenio Montale 1925-1977; translated by William Arrowsmith ; edited by Rosanna Warren. W. W. Norton & Co. 2012 793 p. **851**

1. Italian poetry 2. Poetry -- Collections 3. Modernism in literature

ISBN 0393080633; 9780393080636

LC 2011034993

This poetry collection features works of the 20th-century Nobel Prize-winning writer Eugenio Montale, edited by Rosanna Warren and translated by William Arrowsmith. "Hailed as one of the key poets of the modern era, Eugenio Montale . . . helped to create international Modernism. . . . His poems chart [a] . . . response to the shocks of modernity, fascism, and two world wars." Publisher's note)

Includes bibliographical references and index.

★ **Collected** poems, 1920-1954; translated and annotated by Jonathan Galassi. rev ed; Farrar, Straus & Giroux 2000 625p pa $18 **851**

1. Poetry -- By individual authors

ISBN 0-374-52625-7

LC 00-35456

First published 1997

"It is generally agreed that the core of Montale's work consists of three major collections: Cuttlefish Bones (1925), The Occasions (1939), and The Storm, etc. (1956). Galassi chooses to publish all three together, separating them from a body of work of almost equal length that came later. He defends this decision in a brilliant afterword that offers the best short account I have yet come across of the nature, import, and elusive content of Montale's work." N Y Rev Books {review of 1997 edition}

Includes bibliographical references

Saba, Umberto

Songbook; the selected poems of Umberto Saba. translated by George Hochfield and Leonard Nathan;

introduction, notes, and commentary by George Hochfield. Yale University Press 2009 562p $35 **851**

1. Poetry -- By individual authors

ISBN 978-0-300-13603-6; 0-300-13603-X

LC 2008-17685

"The author of more than fifteen individual books of poetry and a thousand pages of prose, Saba is best known for his Il Canzoniere (The Songbook), a continually revised and augmented collection in poems of his life's work. . . . [This volume] has been handsomely produced by Yale University Press; not among the least of its attractions is how well it fits in the hand. The edition includes, among other work, a generous number of Saba's earliest poems; all fifteen sonnets of his important Autobiografia (1924); several of his experimental works of 1928-29, titled Preludes and Fugues; and a sampling of his late-life poems, including his beautiful sequence Uccelli (Birds) from 1948. . . . Clearly a labor of love, these collaborative versions, presented with the Italian on facing pages, occupied Hochfield and Nathan for more than a decade." Nation

854   Italian essays

Calvino, Italo, 1923-1985

★ **Collection** of Sand; essays. Italo Calvino ; translated by Martin McLaughlin. First U.S. Edition Houghton Mifflin Harcourt"||"Mariner Books 2014 288 p. $13.95 **854**

1. Essays

ISBN 0544146468; 9780544146464

LC 2014001373

This collection of essays, by Italo Calvino, is "the last of his works published during his lifetime. Here he applies his graceful intellect to the delights of the visual world, in essays on subjects ranging from cuneiform and antique maps to Mexican temples and Japanese gardens." (Publisher's note)

"The book offers a delectable array of cognitive insights, ancient history, and Calvino's indispensable voice." Pub Wkly

Eco, Umberto

How to travel with a salmon & other essays; translated from the Italian by William Weaver. Harcourt Brace & Co. 1994 248p il hardcover o.p. pa $15 **854**

ISBN 978-0-15-600125-0 pa; 0-15-600125-X pa

LC 94-10340

"In this collection of parodies, satires and whimsical mini-essays written over the last 30 years, Italian novelist/critic Eco . . . takes readers on a delightful romp through the absurdities of modern life." Publ Wkly

858   Italian miscellaneous writings

Hughes-Hallett, Lucy

Gabriele d'Annunzio; poet, seducer and preacher of war. by Lucy Hughes-Hallett. Alfred A. Knopf 2013 608 p. $35 **858**

1. Nationalists -- Italy -- Biography 2. Fascism --

Italy -- History -- 20th century 3. Poets, Italian -- 20th
century -- Biography 4. Rijeka (Croatia) -- History --
20th century 5. Italy -- Politics and government -- 1914-
1945 6. Militarism -- Italy -- History -- 20th century 7.
Politics and literature -- Italy -- History -- 20th century
8. World War, 1914-1918 -- Territorial questions --
Croatia -- Rijeka
ISBN 0307263932; 9780307263933

LC 2012033943

This book by Lucy Hughes Hallett presents a biography
of "the Italian modernist writer and demagogue" Gabriele
d'Annunzio. "He was a brilliant, scandalous literary celebrity . . . a ruthless seducer of women; an avowed Nietzschean
superman and an effeminate voluptuary who loved fashion,
furnishings, and flowers; and a blood-thirsty militarist who
helped propel Italy into World War I with his pro-war ora-
tory and reveled in the carnage he witnessed at the front."
(Publishers Weekly)
Includes bibliographical references and index

860   Literatures of Spanish, Portuguese, Galician languages

★ The **Cambridge** history of Spanish literature;
edited by David T. Gies. Cambridge University
Press 2004 863p $160   **860**
1. Spanish literature -- History and criticism
ISBN 0-521-80618-6

LC 2004-45601

"The classics of the canon of eleven centuries of Spanish
literature are covered, from Berceo, Cervantes and Calderón
to García Lorca and Martín Gaite, but attention is also paid
to lesser-known writers and works. . . . The volume concludes with a consideration of the influences of film and new
media on modern Spanish literature." Publisher's note
Includes bibliographical references

★ **Concise** encyclopedia of Latin American literature; editor, Verity Smith. Fitzroy Dearborn
Pubs. 2000 xxi, 678p $75   **860**
1. Reference books   2. Latin American literature
-- Encyclopedias 3. Latin American literature -- Bio-
bibliography
ISBN 1-57958-252-4
Based on the Encyclopedia of Latin American literature
(1997)
Contains entries on 50 leading writers and 50 important
works of Latin American and Caribbean literature. Also includes survey articles on the literature of individual countries and topical essays. Bibliographies of primary and secondary sources are listed
Includes bibliographical references

Gonzalez Echevarria, Roberto

The **Cambridge** history of Latin American literature; edited by Roberto González Echevarría and
Enrique Pupo-Walker. Cambridge Univ. Press 1996
3v ea $180   **860**
1. Latin American literature -- History and criticism
ISBN 0-521-34069-1 v1; 0-521-34070-5 v2; 0-521-

41035-5 v3

LC 93-37750

"These volumes span from pre-Columbian times to the
present and include chapters on Latin American writing in
the United States. Some 40 international scholars trace the
development of Latin American literature in essay form. The
bibliography in Volume 3 consumes 455 pages." Libr J
"The editors have added an interdisciplinary dimension
to their work by incorporating the materials and methodologies proper to history. . . . [This] will become a classic in the
field." Choice

861   Spanish poetry

Aleixandre, Vicente

A **longing** for the light; selected poems of Vicente Aleixandre. edited by Lewis Hyde. 2nd ed;
Copper Canyon Press 2007 xxi, 279p pa $18   **861**
1. Poetry -- By individual authors
ISBN 978-1-55659-254-6; 1-55659-254-X

LC 2007-992

First published 1979 by Harper & Row
This "is the only available bilingual Spanish-English
translation of the poetry of Nobel Laureate Vicente Aleixandre. The collection spans the entirety of Aleixandre's
career—from early surrealist work to his complex and fascinating 'dialogues.' It also contains prose interludes, an introduction by editor Lewis Hyde, and a descriptive bibliography." Publisher's note

Borges, Jorge Luis, 1899-1986

★ **Selected** poems; edited by Alexander Coleman. Viking 1999 477p hardcover o.p. pa $20 **861**
1. Poetry -- By individual authors
ISBN 0-14-058721-7 pa

LC 99-10318

"Poetry is the heart of Borges' metaphysical, mythical,
and cosmopolitan oeuvre. . . . Editor Coleman commissioned a wealth of new translations for this unprecedented
and invaluable collection, and the roster of translators includes such luminaries as Robert S. Fitzgerald, W.S. Merwin, Mark Strand, and John Updike." Booklist

Cardenal, Ernesto

Pluriverse; new and selected poems. edited by
Jonathan Cohen; with a foreword by Lawrence Fer-
linghetti; translations from the Spanish by Jonathan
Cohen [et al.] New Directions Pub. 2009 249p pa
$17.95   **861**
1. Poetry -- By individual authors
ISBN 978-0-8112-1809-2 pa; 0-8112-1809-0 pa

LC 2008-40582

"Cardenal, now in his 80s, is a Roman Catholic priest
and was a leading light of the Nicaraguan Sandinistas. One
of his country's most revered figures, Cardenal is these days
being persecuted by President Daniel Ortega, the leader
whose legend Cardenal did much to create and who has
slid now into authoritarian rule. Such tends to be the fate
of the revolutionary writer. Cardenal is political, of course,
and much of the work presented here (translated by many illustrious hands, including Jonathan Cohen, Thomas Merton

and Kenneth Rexroth) deals with the struggle and history of his country and Latin America at large. But he can sing lyrically too. . . . Beautiful." Los Angeles Times Book Rev

Cid

The **poem** of the Cid; translated by Rita Hamilton and Janet Perry; with an introduction and notes by Ian Michael. Penguin 1984 242p map pa $14 **861**

1. Poetry -- By individual authors
ISBN 0-14-044446-7

"The poem is based on the exploits of Rodrigo or Ruy Diaz de Bivar (c.1043-1099), who was known as 'el Cid.' . . . Similar in form to the 'Chanson de Roland,' the poem is notable for its simplicity and directness and for its exact, picturesque detail. Despite the inclusion of much legendary material, the figure of the Cid who is depicted as the model Castilian warrior, is not idealized to an extravagant degree." Reader's Ency. 4th edition

Garcia Lorca, Federico

Collected poems; edited and with an introduction and notes by Christopher Maurer; translated by Francisco Aragon [et al.] Farrar, Straus & Giroux 1991 893p (Poetical works) hardcover o.p. pa $25 **861**

1. Poetry -- By individual authors
ISBN 978-0-374-52691-7; 0-374-52691-5 pa

This bilingual edition of Garcia Lorca's poetry, "which modestly claims not to be 'definitive,' includes every poem written by the acclaimed Spanish poet except Poet in New York. Assembled in the light of recent scholarship, its contents have been rendered into English by newer translators such as Alan S. Trueblood, Catherine Brown, Will Kirkland, and Greg Simon; older translators such as Stephen Spender, Langston Hughes, and Ben Belitt are not represented. Generally, rhyme and assonance are sacrificed to the 'silent counterpoint of poetic meaning,' and old-fashioned diction is avoided." Libr J

Poet in New York; edited and with an introduction and notes by Christopher Maurer; translated by Greg Simon and Steven F. White. Farrar, Straus & Giroux 1988 xxx, 275p il pa $18 **861**

1. New York (N.Y.) -- Poetry
ISBN 978-0-374-52540-8; 0-374-52083-4
LC 87-33154

This "is one of the perplexing classics of twentieth-century poetry. It is a difficult, sometimes bewildered, often hermetic work. It is elusive and enigmatic, mysterious, tortured—a book, to borrow one of the poet's own phrases, 'that can baptize in dark water all who look at it.' Reading it in [this] convincing new translation, . . . one feels the anguished authority and the demonic force and impact of the original. For all its strangeness, Lorca's testament may well be one of the greatest books of poems ever written about New York City." New Yorker

Includes bibliographical references

Neruda, Pablo

★ The **poetry** of Pablo Neruda; edited and with an introduction by Ilan Stavans. Farrar, Straus and Giroux 2003 996p hardcover o.p. pa $20 **861**

1. Poetry -- By individual authors
ISBN 0-374-29995-1; 0-374-52960-4 pa
LC 2002-32548

"Stavans has assembled the most complete anthology of Neruda yet available in English, drawing evenhandedly from the various stages of the poet's long and complex career. Neruda was, it seems, at least half a dozen poets, many of them in competition with the others. Needless to say, there are wonders in these pages that will delight readers unfamiliar with the tumultuously varied planet known as Neruda." Nation

Includes bibliographical references

Paz, Octavio, 1914-1998

★ The **collected** poems of Octavio Paz, 1957-1987; edited & translated by Eliot Weinberger; with additional translations by Elizabeth Bishop [et al.] New Directions 1987 669p il hardcover o.p. pa $26.95 **861**

1. Poetry -- By individual authors
ISBN 978-0-8112-1173-4 pa; 0-8112-1173-8 pa
LC 87-23989

"Dense, weighty, and miraculous, this bilingual edition compresses into one volume all the poems published in book form since 1957. Nearly 200 poems, some newly translated, many new to an English-language edition, conclusively demonstrate Paz's power." Libr J

Includes bibliographical references

The **poems** of Octavio Paz; edited and translated by Eliot Weinberger with additional translations by Elizabeth Bishop, Paul Blackburn, Denise Levertov, Muriel Rukeyser, and Charles Tomlinson. New Directions 2012 606 p. (cloth : acid-free paper) $39.95 **861**

1. Mexican poetry 2. Poetry -- Collections
ISBN 0811220435; 9780811220439
LC 2012016228

This book edited and translated by Eliot Weinberger is "the first retrospective collection of [Octavio] Paz's poetry to span his entire writing career. . . . This edition includes many poems that have never been translated into English before, new translations based on Paz's final revisions, and a . . . capsule biography of Paz by Weinberger, as well as notes on the poems in Paz's own words, taken from various interviews he gave throughout his life." (Publisher's note)

Includes bibliographical references and index.

The **Penguin** book of Spanish verse; introduced and edited by J.M. Cohen; with plain prose translations of each poem. 3rd ed; Penguin 1988 xliii, 596p pa $18 **861**

1. Spanish poetry -- Collections
ISBN 978-0-14-058570-4; 0-14-058570-2
LC 88-166999

First published 1956

More than 300 works by 100 poets reflect nine centuries of poetry in Spain.

Torre, Monica de la

Reversible monuments; contemporary Mexican poetry. edited by Mónica de la Torre and Michael Wiegers. Copper Canyon Press 2002 675p pa $20 **861**

1. Mexican poetry -- Collections
ISBN 1-55659-159-4

LC 2002-6189

This bilingual anthology includes 31 contributors, "most writing in Spanish but some in indigenous languages. Spacious and accommodating, this work presents a generous number of gracefully translated poems by each poet, a felicitous in-depth approach that makes this much more than a sampler, and a sound decision given the poet's propensity for long, dreamy poems. Sensuality is ever-present, as is an intimate connection with nature. . . . This is without doubt a landmark volume." Booklist

Twentieth century Latin American poetry; a bilingual anthology. edited by Stephen Tapscott. University of Tex. Press 1996 xxii, 418p il (Texas Pan American series) hardcover o.p. pa $26.95 **861**

1. Latin American poetry -- Collections
ISBN 0-292-78140-7 pa

LC 95-40288

This anthology "samples the works of more than 75 poets, including such giants as Neruda, Dario, Reyes, Vallejo, Borges and Paz. With original-language versions and translations set side by side, the collection is arranged in order of the poets' dates of birth from José Marti, born in Cuba in 1853, to Marjorie Agosin, born in the U.S. 102 years later. Tapscott's well-conceived and lucid introduction is expanded in concise individual introductions that provide basic information and some evaluation." Publ Wkly

Includes bibliographical references

862 Spanish drama

Calderon de la Barca, Pedro

Life's a dream; a prose translation and critical introduction by Michael Kidd. University Press of Colorado 2004 159p hardcover o.p. pa $13.95 **862**

ISBN 978-0-87081-777-9 pa

LC 2004-10260

17th century Spanish verse play in prose translation. King of Poland tests son, imprisoned from birth because of prophecy, to see if he will become tyrant. Savage at first, Prince later shows true nobility, exposing actual meaning of prophecy.

"Michael Kidd advances the work of two often-exclusive camps of comediantes: scholarship and performance. While his introduction provides ample criticism for the scholar, he successfully presents an accessible script for theatre practitioners looking to enact the story of the play." Bulletin of Hispanic Studies

Includes bibliographical references

Vega, Lope de

Three major plays; translated with an introduction and notes by Gwynne Edwards. Oxford University Press 2008 xli, 300p (Oxford world's classics) pa $14.95 **862**

ISBN 978-0-19-954017-4; 0-19-954017-9

LC 98-26991

Reissue of a title first published 1999

"Fuente Ovejuna , based on Spanish history, and revealing how tyranny leads to rebellion, is perhaps [Vega's] best-known play. The Knight from Olmedo is a moving dramatization of impetuous and youthful passion which ends in death. Punishment without Revenge, Lope's most powerful tragedy, centres on the illicit relationship of a young wife with her stepson and the revenge of a dishonoured husband." Publisher's note

Includes bibliographical references

863 Spanish fiction

Allende, Isabel

My invented country; a nostalgic journey through Chile. translated from the Spanish by Margaret Sayers Peden. HarperCollins Pubs. 2003 199p map $23.95; pa $13.95 **863**

1. Novelists 2. Dramatists 3. Journalists 4. Authors, Chilean 5. Chile 6. Children's authors
ISBN 0-06-054564-X; 0-06-054567-4 pa

LC 2002-191267

"In this memoir-cum-study of her 'home ground,' the author delves into the history, social mores and idiosyncrasies of Chile, where she was raised, showing, in the process, how that land has served as her muse. . . . This is a reflective book, lacking the pull of Allende's fiction but unearthing intriguing elements of the author's captivating history." Publ Wkly

864 Spanish essays

Borges, Jorge Luis, 1899-1986

★ Selected non-fictions; edited by Eliot Weinberger; translated by Esther Allen, Suzanne Jill Levine & Eliot Weinberger. Viking 1999 559p hardcover o.p. pa $20 **864**

ISBN 978-0-14-029011-0 pa; 0-14-029011-7 pa

LC 99-12386

"Shifting effortlessly from Homer to Hitler, from Kafka to King Kong, these hundred and sixty-one essays, appreciations, prologues, and philosophical investigations are dizzying in scope and dazzling in execution. But it is Borges's dogged pursuit of familiar themes—infinity and eternity, reflexivity and recurrence—which gives this collection its unusual unity and depth." New Yorker

Includes bibliographical references

Fuentes, Carlos

Myself with others; selected essays. Farrar, Straus & Giroux 1988 214p $19.95; pa $18   **864**

ISBN 0-374-21750-5; 0-374-52237-5 pa

LC 87-7448

Essays by the Mexican writer on subjects ranging from the cinema of Buñuel to the literary output of Cervantes, Borges and Garcia Marquez

Paz, Octavio, 1914-1998

★ The **labyrinth** of solitude; The other Mexico, Return to the labyrinth of solitude, Mexico and the United States, The philanthropic ogre. Grove Press 1985 398p hardcover o.p. pa $14.50   **864**

1. Mexican national characteristics 2. Mexico -- Civilization

ISBN 978-0-8021-5042-4 pa; 0-8021-5042-X pa

LC 82-47999

The labyrinth of solitude and The other Mexico were first published 1961 and 1972 respectively

In this collection of essays and one interview, Paz explorers the cultural and historical influences on the social behavior of his countrymen

Vargas Llosa, Mario

The **language** of passion; translated by Natasha Wimmer. Farrar, Straus & Giroux 2003 292p $24; pa $14   **864**

ISBN 0-374-18326-0; 0-312-42254-7 pa

LC 2002-37909

"This collection focuses on the essays that appeared during the 1990s, most of which are imbued with a wit and an intellect that make them instantly engaging." Libr J

Includes bibliographical references

868   Spanish miscellaneous writings

Abad, Hector

Oblivion; a memoir. Héctor Abad ; translated from the Spanish by Anne McLean and Rosalind Harvey. Farrar, Straus and Giroux 2012 263 p.   **868**

1. Biography 2. Political activists 3. Father-son relationship 4. Physicians -- Colombia -- Biography 5. Political activists -- Crimes against 6. Colombia -- Politics and government -- 1974- 7. Political activists -- Colombia -- Biography 8. Authors, Colombian -- 20th century -- Biography

ISBN 0374223971; 9780374223977

LC 2011045885

This memoir by Héctor Abad describes the life and work of the author's father "Héctor Abad Gómez, a professor and doctor devoted to his family . . . and committed to a better Colombia. The latter aspiration cost him his life when he was assassinated in 1987." Topics include "Gómez's public health and human rights projects" such as founding "the Colombian Institute of Family Wellbeing, which built aqueducts and sewer systems in villages, rural districts, and cities." (Publishers Weekly)

Biron, Rebecca E.

Elena Garro and Mexico's modern dreams; Rebecca E. Biron. Bucknell University Press 2012 294 p. (Buckell studies in Latin American literature and theory) (cloth : alk. paper) $90   **868**

1. Mexico -- Civilization 2. Modernism in literature 3. Modernism (Literature) -- Mexico 4. National characteristics, Mexican, in literature

ISBN 1611484707; 9781611484700

LC 2012042552

Author Rebecca E. Biron's book focuses on Elena Garro. "The famously scandalous first wife of Nobel Prize winner poet Octavio Paz, and an award-winning author in her own right, Garro constructed a mysterious and often contradictory persona through her very public participation in Mexican political conflicts. . . . Garro's public persona and critical perspective expose the anxieties regarding ethnicity, gender, economic class, and professional identity that define Mexican modernity." (Publisher's note)

Includes bibliographical references and index

869   Literatures of Portuguese and Galician languages

Antunes, Antonio Lobo

The **fat** man and infinity; and other writings. translated with an introduction by Margaret Jull Costa. W. W. Norton & Company 2009 396p il $26.95 **869**

ISBN 978-0-393-06198-7; 0-393-06198-1

LC 2008-41551

This volume "collects the short, impressionistic newspaper columns, or 'cronicas,' that [Antunes] has written for various publications, notably the Portuguese newspaper O Público. Mr. Antunes has played down these columns, referring to them as 'divertissments' written to earn pocket money. But as this book's translator, Margaret Jull Costa, points out, in Portugal these collections 'have enjoyed the kind of popular success his novels never have.' (This book also contains a selection of Mr. Antunes's short stories. . .). Mr. Antunes makes for an unusual newspaper columnist. Jimmy Breslin he's not. His bite-size essays contain no political ruminations and almost nothing about sports, or popular culture, or literary criticism or run-ins with the great and good. Instead they are interior diaries of a kind, most of them imbued with a deep nostalgia for the author's youth." N Y Times Book Rev

Camões, Luis de

★ **Selected** sonnets; edited and translated by William Baer. Bilingual ed; University of Chicago Press 2005 199p il $26   **869**

1. Poetry -- By individual authors

ISBN 0-226-09266-6

LC 2004-58521

Camões "is Portugal's great sonneteer. He published only one sonnet in his lifetime, and many of doubtful authorship crept into the canon during their first century of great popularity. Baer presents 70 in Portuguese and his own English versions, formally faithful to the originals except that in the octaves Baer uses four (abba, cddc) rather than Camoes' two (abba, abba) rhymes. A sketch of Camoes' amazingly adventurous and colorful life, his works, and his reputation precedes the poems." Booklist

870 Latin literature and literatures of related Italic languages

The **Portable** Roman reader; edited, and with an introduction by Basil Davenport. Viking 1951 656p hardcover o.p. pa $18   **870**

1. Latin literature -- Collections

ISBN 0-14-015056-0 pa

This anthology includes selections from Plautus, Terence, Caesar, Virgil, Seneca, Juvenal as well as complete plays by Plautus and Terence and the anonymous poem Vigil of Venus

871 Latin poetry

Horace

The **epistles** of Horace; [translated by] David Ferry. Farrar, Straus, and Giroux 2001 203p hardcover o.p. pa $19   **871**

1. Poetry -- By individual authors

ISBN 978-0-374-52852-7 pa; 0-374-52852-7 pa

LC 00-52746

"Ferry takes his bearings from the great blank verse poets of the last two hundred years, especially Frost, and while he manages to be faithful to the meaning, substance and shades, of the Latin original, Ferry achieves through his historical, cultural, and linguistic cross-pollination something more important and lasting than mere translation: he brings to life new as well as old possibilities for poetry in America now." Harvard Rev

Includes bibliographical references

Virgil

The **eclogues** of Virgil; a translation by David Ferry. Farrar, Straus & Giroux 1999 101p hardcover o.p. pa $14   **871**

1. Poetry -- By individual authors

ISBN 978-0-374-52696-2 pa; 0-374-52696-6 pa

LC 98-52547

The Eclogues "comprise not much more than 800 lines in total, but they may be the most influential collection of short poems by one author ever written. . . . It is a conspicuous merit of Ferry's translations that they have a kind of transparency; he does not intrude his style or his personality between the reader and himself. His versions are rather plain, unfussy, and usually of a quiet dignity." New Republic

872 Latin dramatic poetry and drama

Plautus, Titus Maccius

The **pot** of gold, and other plays; [by] Plautus; tr. by E. F. Watling. Penguin Books 1965 267p (Penguin Classics) pa $12   **872**

ISBN 978-0-14-044149-9; 0-14-044149-2

LC 65-8577

Plautus "romanized many of the plots and characters of New Greek Comedy. Through his plays, he introduced to the non-Greek world characters which have since become part of traditional western European comedy, among them the braggard soldier (in his Miles Gloriosus) and the sly servant (in his Pseudolus)." Benet's Reader's Ency. 4th edition

The **rope,** and other plays; [by] Plautus; tr. by E. F. Watling. Penguin Books 1964 284p (Penguin Classics) pa $12   **872**

ISBN 978-0-14-044136-9; 0-14-044136-0

LC 63-2117

Terence

Terence, the comedies; translations by Palmer Bovie, Constance Carrier, and Douglass Parker; edited by Palmer Bovie. Johns Hopkins Univ. Press 1992 xxi, 398p (Complete Roman drama in translation) hardcover o.p. pa $25   **872**

ISBN 978-0-8018-4354-9 pa; 0-8018-4354-5 pa

LC 91-33984

First published 1974 by Rutgers University Press with title: The complete comedies of Terence

Includes the following plays: The brothers (Adelphoe); The eunuch (Eunouchus); The girl from Andros (Andria); Her husband's mother (Hecyra); Phormio; The self-tormentor (Heautontimorumenos)

Virgil

The **Georgics** of Virgil; a translation. a translation [translated] by David Ferry. Farrar, Straus and Giroux 2005 xx, 202p hardcover o.p. pa $14   **872**

ISBN 978-0-374-16131-0 pa; 0-374-16131-9 pa

LC 2004-20023

"Ferry shows tremendous skill with his taut yet pliant pentameter. He also employs demotic and high lyrical diction with equal finesse. His version contains all the freshness of American speech and all the classical poise of the original: it comes across neither as a curatorial act of conservation nor as a modish remake. . . . This is the best poetry of Ancient Rome, rendered by the best translator of modern America." Poetry (Modern Poetry Association)

873 Latin epic poetry and fiction

Ovid

★ **Metamorphoses**; [by] Ovid; translated and with notes by Charles Martin; introduction by Bernard Knox. W.W. Norton & Co 2004 xxvi, 597p $57; pa $17.95   **873**

ISBN 0-393-05810-7; 0-393-32642-X pa

LC 2003-14491

"A series of tales in Latin verse. . . . Dealing with mythological, legendary, and historical figures, they are written in hexameters, in fifteen books, beginning with the creation of the world and ending with the deification of Caesar and the reign of Augustus." Reader's Ency. 4th edition

Includes bibliographical references

Tales from Ovid; [translated by] Ted Hughes. Farrar, Straus & Giroux 1997 257p hardcover o.p. pa $14 **873**

1. Poetry -- By individual authors

ISBN 0-374-52587-0 pa

LC 97-36061

Hughes retells 24 Greco-Roman myths from Ovid's Latin epic Metamorphoses.

This is "an inspired act of translation that stands as vigorous poetry in its own right." N Y Times Book Rev

Includes bibliographical references

The **Aeneid**; translated by Robert Fitzgerald. Knopf 1992 xxvii,483 (Everyman's library) $20 **873**

1. Poetry -- By individual authors

ISBN 978-0-679-41335-6; 0-679-41335-9

LC 91-58698

This translation first published 1983 by Random House

"Fitzgerald's is so decisively the best modern Aeneid that it is unthinkable anyone will want to use any other version for a long time to come. Latinists, as they read it, will be led to consider their original afresh. Those without Latin are going to find, to their surprise, and I hope their pleasure, that the poem is still as good as anyone ever said it was." N Y Rev Books

874   Latin lyric poetry

Catullus, Gaius Valerius

The **poems** of Catullus; translated by Charles Martin. Johns Hopkins Univ. Press 1990 181p hardcover o.p. pa $19.95 **874**

1. Poetry -- By individual authors

ISBN 978-0-8018-3926-9 pa; 0-8018-3926-2 pa

LC 89-45486

First published 1979 in limited edition by Abattoir Editions, the University of Nebraska at Omaha

"The introduction ranges through Martin's observations on Catullus' place among Roman lyricists, his virtuosity, acuity, irony, and appeal to modern poets. The translations themselves, while open to inevitable quibbling among Latinists, are remarkably true to the versification, denotations, and connotations of the original texts. Martin is particularly adept at shaping the English into approximations of the Latin meters." Choice

Horace

The **odes** of Horace; a translation by David Ferry. Farrar, Straus & Giroux 1997 343p hardcover o.p. pa $28 **874**

1. Poetry -- By individual authors

ISBN 978-0-374-52572-9 pa; 0-374-52572-2 pa

LC 97-9483

"The foremost technician of Rome's Golden Age, Horace (658 B.C.) revolutionized Latin verse. He imported intricate Greek meters, invented the poet as a jeweller of words

and left behind some of the most enduring models of what a short poem should address." Publ Wkly

Ferry "wisely does not try to reproduce Horace's meters in English. . . . And he often rearranges Horace's material to fit the run of his own verse, sometimes to stunning effect. . . . This is a Horace for our times." N Y Rev Books

875   Latin speeches

Cicero, Marcus Tullius, 106-43 B.C.

Political speeches; [by] Cicero; translated with introductions and notes by D.H. Berry. Oxford University Press 2006 xl, 345p map pa $13.95 **875**

1. Speeches 2. Rome -- History

ISBN 978-0-19-283266-5; 0-19-283266-2

LC 2005-20919

"Cicero (106-43 BC) was the greatest orator of the ancient world and a leading politician of the closing era of the Roman republic. This book presents nine speeches which reflect the development, variety, and drama of his political career, among them two speeches from his prosecution of Verres, a corrupt and cruel governor of Sicily; four speeches against the conspirator Catiline; and the Second Philippic , the famous denunciation of Mark Antony which cost Cicero his life. Also included are On the Command of Gnaeus Pompeius , in which he praises the military successes of Pompey, and For Marcellus , a panegyric in praise of the dictator Julius Caesar." Publisher's note

Includes bibliographical references

877   Latin humor and satire

Erasmus, Desiderius

Praise of folly; and, Letter to Maarten Van Dorp, 1515. [by] Erasmus of Rotterdam; translated by Betty Radice; with an introduction and notes by A.H.T. Levi. Penguin Books 1993 lvi, 188p (Penguin classics) pa $13 **877**

ISBN 978-014-044608-1; 0-14-044608-7

LC 94-142502

A "satirical monologue in Latin. . . . Folly praises herself and proclaims her superiority over Wisdom. The author's argument, of course, is 'that it is folly not to see things as they really are; scholars should not abandon ideals just because they cannot be fully realized but should apply their learning and reason as best they can to daily living.'" Reader's Adviser

Juvenal

The **sixteen** satires; translated with an introduction and notes by Peter Green. 3rd ed; Penguin Books 1999 lxviii, 252p (Penguin classics) pa $13 **877**

ISBN 978-0-14-044704-0; 0-14-044704-0

LC 99-987049

First published 1967

"The sixteen 'Satires' of Juvenal, which contain a vivid picture of contemporary Rome under the Empire, have seldom been equalled as biting diatribes. . . . Juvenal's invectives in powerful hexameters, exact and epigrammatic, were aimed at lax and luxurious society, tyranny, criminal excesses, and the immorality of women." Reader's Adviser

878   Latin miscellaneous writings

Caesar, Julius, 100-44 B.C.

The **Gallic** War; with an English translation by H. J. Edwards. Harvard Univ. Press 1958 xxii, 616p il maps $21.50   **878**
    1. Rome -- History
    ISBN 0-674-99080-3
    Caesar's account of his campaign (58-50 B.C.) to bring the province of Gaul (France) under his control.

Cicero, Marcus Tullius, 106-43 B.C.

On the good life; translated with an introduction by Michael Grant. Penguin Books 1971 382p map (Penguin classics) pa $16   **878**
    1. Ethics
    ISBN 978-0-14-044244-1; 0-14-044244-8
                              LC 77-30399
    For "Roman orator and statesman Cicero, 'the good life' was at once a life of contentment and one of moral virtue and the two were inescapably intertwined. This volume brings together a wide range of his reflections upon the importance of moral integrity in the search for happiness. . . . Cicero presents his views upon the significance of friendship and duty to state and family, and outlines a clear system of practical ethics." Publisher's note

Martial

Epigrams; selected and translated by James Michie; introduction by Shadi Bartsch. Modern Library 2002 xxxiv, 199p (Modern Library classics) pa $14.95   **878**
    1. Epigrams
    ISBN 978-0-375-76042-6; 0-375-76042-3
                           LC 2002-22343
    First published 1972
    Michie "has translated a selection of the epigrams—about one tenth of what Martial wrote. He has the text on the facing page—a great advantage if you can read Latin—an Introduction [and] Notes. . . . [He] uses rhyme, and makes his Martial much more like the English idea of an epigram than like the epigrams in the Greek Anthology. There isn't much pure humor in Latin literature (as opposed to waspishness and scurrility) but Martial is often very funny." Encounter (London, England)
    Includes bibliographical references

Suetonius Tranquillus, C.

★ The **twelve** Caesars; {by} Gaius Suetonius Tranquillus; translated by Robert Graves; revised with an introduction by Michael Grant. Penguin Bks. 2003 363p maps pa $14   **878**
    1. Emperors 2. Rome -- History 3. Emperors -- Rome
    ISBN 0-14-044921-3
                          LC 2003-267782
    A reissue with new Chronology and updated further reading of the translation published 1957

"A detailed account of the life and times of the first twelve emperors from Caesar to Domitian." Reader's Ency. 4th edition
Includes bibliographical references

Tacitus, Cornelius

Complete works of Tacitus; translated from the Latin by Alfred John Church and William Jackson Brodribb; edited and with an introduction by Moses Hadas. McGraw-Hill 1964 773p il pa $14.75   **878**
    1. Generals 2. Rome -- History 3. Colonial administrators 4. Germany -- History -- 0-1517
    ISBN 0-07-553639-0; 978-0-07-553639-0
    First published 1942 by Modern Lib.
    Contains: The annals; The history; The life of Cnaeus Julius Agricola; Germany and its tribes; A dialogue on oratory

880   Classical Greek literature and literatures of related Hellenic languages

The **Norton** book of classical literature; edited by Bernard Knox. Norton 1993 866p $29.95   **880**
    1. Greek literature -- Collections
    ISBN 0-393-03426-7
                             LC 92-10378
    "A comprehensive volume of more than 300 pieces of classical literature, primarily Greek but also some Roman." Booklist

★ The **Oxford** companion to classical literature; edited by M.C. Howatson. 3rd ed.; Oxford University Press 2011 un map $65   **880**
    1. Reference books 2. Classical literature -- Dictionaries
    ISBN 978-0-19-954854-5
    First published 1937 under the editorship of Sir Paul Harvey
    This work "covers classical literature from the appearance of the Greeks, around 2200 B.C., to the close of the Athenian philosophy schools in A.D. 529. It includes articles on authors, major works, historical notables, mythological figures, and topics of literary significance. Short summaries of major works, chronologies, charts, and maps are special features." Nichols. Guide to Ref Books for Sch Media Cent. 4th edition

Thorburn, John E.

★ The **Facts** on File companion to classical drama. Facts on File 2005 680p map (Facts on File library of world literature) $71.50   **880**
    1. Reference books 2. Classical drama -- Encyclopedias
    ISBN 0-8160-5202-6
                           LC 2004-16803
    This "compendium covers ancient Greek and Roman drama from the 500s B.C.E. through 100 C.E. Approximately 400 alphabetical entries, ranging in length from one sentence to several pages, delve into plays, authors, characters, settings, genres, themes, theatrical terms, historical events, etc." SLJ
    "It is difficult to think of any other resource quite this thorough that combines all of Greek and Roman drama into a convenient single-volume publication." Libr J
    Includes bibliographical references

881 Classical Greek poetry

7 Greeks; translations by Guy Davenport. New Directions 1995 241p pa $16.95 **881**
    1. Greek literature -- Collections
    ISBN 978-0-8112-1288-5; 0-8112-1288-2
                      LC 95-4227
    Davenport has translated a sampling of seventh- to third-century B.C.E. Greek poetry. "Included among the poems and fragments are lyrics by Archilochos, Sappho, Alkman, and Anakreon; philosophical verse by Herakleitos and Diogenes; and comic dramatic verse by Herondas. Arguing that no translation is final and occasionally offering several versions of the same work, Davenport attempts to capture the tone of the original rather than offering a literal or formal rendition." Libr J

Apollonius

The **voyage** of Argo: the Argonautica; translated with an introd. by E.V. Rieu. 2nd ed; Penguin Books 1971 213p map (Penguin Classics) pa $14 **881**
    1. Argonauts (Greek mythology) 2. Poetry -- By individual authors
    ISBN 978-0-14-044085-0; 0-14-044085-0
    This translation first published 1959
    An epic account of Jason's voyage in quest of the Golden Fleece written in the third century B.C.

882 Classical Greek dramatic poetry and drama

Aeschylus

Aeschylus; edited by David Grene and Richmond Lattimore. University of Chicago Press 1992 352p (Complete Greek tragedies) $55 **882**
    ISBN 978-0-226-30764-0; 0-226-30764-6
    Contents: Agamemnon; Libation bearers; Eumenides; Suppliant maidens; Persians; Seven against Thebes; Prometheus bound

The **Oresteia**; translated by Alan Shapiro and Peter Burian. Oxford University Press 2003 285p (The Greek tragedy in new translations) hardcover o.p. pa $11.95 **882**
    ISBN 978-0-19-513592-3 pa; 0-19-513592-X pa
                      LC 2002-66272
    The only extant Greek dramatic trilogy. "It begins with Agamemnon, which describes Agamemnon's return from the Trojan War and his murder at the hands of his wife Clytemnestra, continues with her murder by their son Orestes in Libation Bearers, and concludes with Orestes' acquittal at a court founded by Athena in Eumenides." Publisher's note
    "The collaboration of poet and scholar . . . produces a language that is easy to read and easy to speak." Libr J
    Includes bibliographical references

Aristophanes

The **complete** plays; the new translations by Paul Roche. New American Library 2005 715p pa $17 **882**
    1. Athens (Greece) -- Drama.
    ISBN 978-0-451-21409-6; 0-451-21409-9
                      LC 2004-56681
    Contents: Acharnians; Knights; Clouds; Wasps; Peace; Birds; Lysistrata; Women at Thesmophoria festival; Frogs; A parliament of women; Plutus (Wealth)

Euripides

Euripides; edited by David Grene and Richmond Lattimore. University of Chicago Press 1992 665p (Complete Greek tragedies) $65 **882**
    ISBN 978-0-226-30766-4; 0-226-30766-2
    First published 1942
    Contents: Alcestis; Medea; Heracleidae; Hippolytus; Cyclops; Heracles; Iphigenia in Tauris; Helen; Hecuba; Andromache; The Trojan women

Euripides [2] edited by David Grene and Richmond Lattimore. University of Chicago Press 1992 314p (Complete Greek tragedies) $44 **882**
    ISBN 978-0-226-30767-1; 0-226-30767-0
    First published 1958
    Contents: Ion; Rhesus; The suppliant women; Orestes; Iphigenia in Aulis; Electra; The Phoenician women; The Bacchae

Selections./English

The **Theban** plays of Sophocles; translated by David R. Slavitt. Yale University Press 2007 237p $28 **882**
    ISBN 978-0-300-11776-9; 0-300-11776-0
                      LC 2006-26965
    Contents: Antigone; Oedipus tyrannos; Oedipus at Colonus
    "This version is meant to be an updated one, and the easy currency of its diction is a great virtue. The natural cadences of its free verse slide smoothly and sometimes beautifully into the ear." Claremont Rev Books
    Includes bibliographical references

Seneca, Lucius Annaeus

Four tragedies, and Octavia; [by] Seneca; tr. with an introduction by E. F. Watling. Penguin Books 1966 318p (Penguin Classics) pa $14 **882**
    ISBN 978-0-14-044174-1; 0-12-044174-3
                      LC 66-8618
    Contents: Phaedra; Oedipus; Thyestes; The Trojan women; Octavia
    "Although their themes are borrowed from Greek drama, these exuberant and often macabre plays focus on action rather than moral concerns and are strikingly different in style from Seneca's prose writing." Publisher's note

Sophocles

Sophocles; edited by David Grene and Richmond Lattimore. University of Chicago Press 1992 466p (Complete Greek tragedies) $50   **882**

ISBN 978-0-226-30765-7; 0-226-30765-4

Contents: Oedipus the King; Oedipus at Colonus; Antigone; Ajax; The women of Trachis; Electra; Philoctetes

883 Classical Greek epic poetry and fiction

Alexander, Caroline

The **war** that killed Achilles; the true story of Homer's Iliad and the Trojan War. Viking 2009 296p map $26.95   **883**

1. Poets 2. Authors 3. Trojan War 4. War in literature
ISBN 978-0-670-02112-3; 0-670-02112-1

LC 2009-20160

"In its bones and sinews, the book is a nobly bold, even rousing, venture, a read-through of the 'Iliad,' from beginning to end, always with a sharp eye to half a century of revealing scholarship, by great Hellenists like Gregory Nagy, Jasper Griffin, M.L. West and many others. The book's best ideas won't be new to readers versed in this work, but it would be hard to find a faster, livelier, more compact introduction to such a great range of recent Iliadic explorations." N Y Times Book Rev

Includes bibliographical references

Homer

The **Iliad**; translated by Robert Fitzgerald. Knopf 1992 xxi, 594p (Everyman's library) $22   **883**

1. Poetry -- By individual authors
ISBN 978-0-679-41075-1; 0-679-41075-9

LC 91-53222

This translation first published 1974 by Anchor Press/Doubleday

Homer's epic of the Trojan War in blank verse

"Fitzgerald has solved virtually every problem that has plagued translators of Homer. The narrative runs, the dialogue speaks, the military action is clear, and the repetitive epithets become useful text rather than exotic relics. Aside from the ability to write poetry, which is basic to the undertaking, Mr. Fitzgerald's success derives from the use of a predominantly Anglo-Saxon vocabulary, a concentration on specific meanings, and an occasional arbitrary, but highly effective, substitution of implication for literal sense." Atlantic

Iliad; translated by Stanley Lombardo; introduction by Sheila Murnaghan. Hackett 1997 516p $37.95; pa $12.95   **883**

1. Poetry -- By individual authors
ISBN 978-0-87220-353-2; 0-87220-353-0; 978-0-87220-352-5 pa; 0-87220-352-2 pa

LC 96-53368

This is a translation from the Greek of the epic poem on the Trojan War

"Lombardo manages to be respectful of Homer's dire spirit while providing on nearly every page some wonderfully fresh refashioning of his Greek. The result is a vivid and sometimes disarmingly hard-bitten reworking of a great classic. . . . Not all of Lombardo's gambles pay off, and his

attention-grabbing colloquialisms sometimes undermine the force of the original. . . . Still, the success of so many of Lombardo's choices more than makes up for the false notes." N Y Times Book Rev

The **Odyssey**; translated by Robert Fagles; introduction and notes by Bernard Knox. Viking 1996 541p $35; pa $16   **883**

1. Poetry -- By individual authors
ISBN 978-0-670-82162-4; 978-0-14-026886-7 pa

LC 96-17280

This is a verse translation of Homer's epic poem

"Fagles' Odyssey is the one to put into the hands of younger, first-time readers, not least because of its paucity of notes, which, though sometimes frustrating, is a sign that translation has been used to do the work of explanation. Altogether, an outstanding piece of work." Booklist

Includes bibliographical references

Odyssey; translated by Stanley Lombardo; introduction by Sheila Murnaghan. Hackett 2000 414p il $37.95; pa $12.95   **883**

1. Poetry -- By individual authors
ISBN 978-0-87220-485-0; 0-87220-485-5; 978-0-87220-484-3 pa; 0-87220-484-7 pa

LC 99-54175

A retelling of Homer's epic that describes the wanderings of Odysseus after the fall of Troy.

Lombardo "has brought his laconic wit and love of the ribald, as well as his clever use of idiomatic American slang, to his version of the 'Odyssey.' His carefully honed syntax gives the narrative energy and a whirlwind pace. The lines, rhythmic and clipped, have the tautness and force of Odysseus' bow." N Y Times Book Rev

Includes bibliographical references

The **Odyssey**; Homer ; translated, with an introduction and notes, by Stephen Mitchell. Atria Books 2013 xlv, 375 p.p map (hdbk.) $35   **883**

1. Greek literature
ISBN 1451674171; 9781451674170

LC 2012050572

This version of Homer's work, translated by Stephen Mitchell, "brings Odysseus and his adventures vividly to life. . . . One-eyed maneating giants; irresistibly seductive sirens; shipwrecks and narrow escapes; princesses and monsters; ghosts sipping blood at the Underworld's portal, desperate for a chance to speak to the living; and the final destruction of all Odysseus's enemies in the banquet hall." (Publisher's note)

"Employing the five-beat, minimally iambic line he used for his translation of The Iliad (2011), Mitchell retells the first, still greatest adventure story in Western literature with the same clarity, sweep, and force." Booklist

Includes bibliographical references

Manguel, Alberto

Homer's The Iliad and The Odyssey; a biography. Atlantic Monthly Press 2008 285p (Books that changed the world) $19.95   **883**

1. Poets 2. Authors 3. Epic poetry
ISBN 978-0-87113-976-4; 0-87113-976-6

First published 2007 in the United Kingdom

A "study of the influence of The Iliad and The Odyssey on Western literature. First describing the two epics and the Homer question, Manguel then compares various translations in English, Spanish, French, and German, a move that brings out the complexities and richness of Homer's language. Does the poet sing of the rage, wrath, anger, rancor, or mania of Achilles? Then, following a more or less chronological progression, Manguel surveys the various shifting interpretations of the epics from Plato and Virgil to the present, including extended discussions of Derek Walcott, Timothy Findley, and Jorge Luis Borges. Highly recommended for general readers." Libr J

884   Classical Greek lyric poetry

Pindar

★ The **complete** odes of Pindar; translated by Anthony Verity; with an introduction and notes by Stephen Instone. Oxford University Press 2007 xxvii, 186p (Oxford world's classics) pa $15.95   **884**
1. Poetry -- By individual authors
ISBN 978-0-19-280553-9; 0-19-280553-3
LC 2006-39673
The Odes (Epinicia) celebrated victories in the great national games, and were accompanied by music, which is lost to us. The fragments represent almost every kind of lyric poem.

"Since Pindar's Epinicia are generally concerned with mythical subjects, reserving praise of the mortal victor for the end of the ode, his works are a fine source of legend." Reader's Ency. 4th edition

Sappho

★ **If** not, winter; fragments of Sappho. translated by Anne Carson. Knopf 2002 397p $27.50; pa $14   **884**
1. Poetry -- By individual authors
ISBN 0-375-41067-8; 0-375-72451-6 pa
LC 2001-50247
"Carson's translation follows Sappho's diction and form . . . closely and includes the Greek original on the facing page. Much of what survives of Sappho are fragments, often just a stray word, phrase, or even a few letters. Like many modern poets, Carson deploys these on the blank page, letting their suggestiveness fill the gaps and create whole lyrics in the imagination of the readers." Libr J

Includes bibliographical references

888   Classical Greek miscellaneous writings

Aristotle, 384-322 B.C.

★ The **basic** works of Aristotle; edited, and with an introduction by Richard McKeon. Random House 1941 xxxix, 1487p $49.95; pa $19.95   **888**
ISBN 0-394-41610-4; 0-375-75799-6 pa
Contains entire texts of the following: Physica; De generatione et corruptione; De anima; Parva naturalia; Metaphysica; Ethica Nicomachea; Politica; De poetica
Includes bibliographical references

Plato

The **collected** dialogues of Plato, including the letters; edited by Edith Hamilton and Huntington Cairns. With introd. and prefatory notes. Princeton University Press 1961 xxv, 1743p (Bollingen series) $49.50   **888**
ISBN 978-0-691-09718-3; 0-691-09718-6
"This elegant edition contains many of the best and most readable English translations of the Dialogues and Letters. . . . Judiciously edited, beautifully printed." Rev of Metaphysics

The **republic**; edited by G.R.F. Ferrari; translated by Tom Griffith. Cambridge Univ. Press 2000 xlviii, 382p (Cambridge texts in the history of political thought) $38; pa $11   **888**
1. Utopias 2. Political science
ISBN 0-521-48173-2; 0-521-48443-X pa
LC 00-24471
Griffith's "aim was to translate the Greek text as if it were a conversation, and he has succeeded admirably. The text does indeed flow like a conversation, with the entire back-and-forth interaction that such exchanges involve. . . . [He] has also written a very useful introduction that places the work in a historical context and provides a glossary that will help readers identify individuals and places mentioned in the work." Libr J

Includes bibliographical references

889   Modern Greek literature

Cavafy, Constantine P.

★ **Collected** poems; [by] C.P. Cavafy; translated, with introduction and commentary, by Daniel Mendelsohn. Alfred A. Knopf 2009 547p $35   **889**
1. Poetry -- By individual authors
ISBN 978-0-375-40096-4; 0-375-40096-6
LC 2008-34718
"Mendelsohn drew together his interests in ancient history, literature, gay life and culture, and beautiful language to produce the finest, most readable version of the modern Greek poet Cavafy (1863-1933) to come along in decades." Publ Wkly

★ The **unfinished** poems; [by] C.P. Cavafy; the first English translation, with introduction and commentary, by Daniel Mendelsohn. Alfred A. Knopf 2009 121p $30   **889**
1. Poetry -- By individual authors
ISBN 978-0-307-26546-3; 0-307-26546-3
LC 2008-34717
Original Greek edition, 1994
This book "contains the first English versions of 30 poems that Cavafy had not finished entirely to his satisfaction when he died. All are in his most developed manner, in which apprehension of the past is so rich and powerful as to expunge mere nostalgia. They are historical vignettes of the declines of Alexander's Hellenistic hegemony, imperial Rome, and the Byzantine Empire; and glowing memories, triggered by news items, drink, or moonlight, of decades-old

homosexual rapture. . . . One could become well informed about centuries of seldom-taught history just by reading the notes, though yet more so by absorbing the poems, as well." Booklist

Elytis, Odysseus

The **collected** poems of Odysseus Elytis; translated by Jeffrey Carson and Nikos Sarris; introduction and notes by Jeffrey Carson. Rev and expanded ed; Johns Hopkins University Press 2005 $60   **889**

    1. Poetry -- By individual authors
    ISBN 0-8018-8045-9

                    LC 2004-13496

First published 1997

"The work of 1979 Nobel Prize winner Elytis (1911-96) has the quality of a cathedral or epic—vast in scope yet richly decorated. This excellent 'complete' collected edition (it omits unpublished poems) testifies to the bountiful, sincere nature of Elytis's voice as patriot and poet. . . . Containing informative annotations, a chronology, an autobiographical essay, and the author's Nobel address, this work is a valuable resource on international poetry." Libr J

Includes bibliographical references

891   East Indo-European and Celtic literatures

Barks, Coleman

Rumi : the big red book; the great masterpiece celebrating mystical love and friendship. the collected translations of Coleman Barks, based on the work of John Moyne ... [et al.] HarperOne 2010 492p $29.95; ebook $14.99   **891**

    1. Poetry -- By individual authors
    ISBN 978-0-06-190582-7; 978-0-06-202078-9 ebook
                    LC 2010-7895

This is "a vast collection centering on Shams Tabrizi, a wandering mystic who transformed Rumi's life. Rumi was already renowned when Shams arrived in Konya, in today's Turkey, having wandered for years searching for someone with a soul as profound as his own with whom to share 'sohbet,' a mystical conversation about God and love. Rumi and Shams inspired each other for several years, until Shams mysteriously disappeared. He lives on in Rumi's searching poems. . . . Richly sensual yet never flowery, Barks' language emphasizes Rumi's embodied spirituality in a book to savor." Booklist

Includes bibliographical references

Firdawsi

★ **Shahnameh**; the Persian book of kings. [by] Abolqasem Ferdowsi; translated by Dick Davis; with a foreword by Azar Nafisi. Viking 2006 xxxvii, 886p il $45   **891**

    ISBN 0-670-03485-1

                    LC 2005-42352

"Unlike Western epics that grasp the events of a single generation, whether of men or angels, Persia's Book of Kings encompasses whole ages of the world, chronicling the stratagems of Kings and heroes as real as Alexander the Great and as legendary as Rostam. . . . Action, myth, and history fairly fly off the page, for Davis renders Ferdowsi's 50,000 sesquipedalian lines of poetry as a prose narrative that here and there erupts into sonnet-sized snatches of verse. The scheme works brilliantly. Repeated for pages on end, Ferdowsi's lines, each longer than an heroic couplet, breed longueurs, but Davis's carefully rendered snatches of the best classic Farsi poetry illuminate the English text like so many Persian miniatures." New Criterion

Frank, Joseph

Dostoevsky. v4 Princeton Univ. Press 1995 523p v4 il hardcover o.p. pa $24.95   **891**

    1. Authors 2. Novelists 3. Authors, Russian 4. Short story writers
    ISBN 0-691-04364-7; 0-691-01587-2 pa

                    LC 94-43403

"This fourth installment in Frank's acclaimed . . . five-volume biography presents an astonishingly vivid, uncanny portrait of Dostoevsky's spiritual, emotional and artistic development during his crucial years abroad." Publ Wkly

Includes bibliographical references

Hafiz

The gift; poems by the great Sufi master. translated by Daniel James Ladinsky. Penguin/Arkana 1999 333p pa $16   **891**

    1. Poetry -- By individual authors
    ISBN 978-0-14-019581-1; 0-14-019581-5

                    LC 99-10920

"Less well known in the U.S. than his Sufi predecessor, Rumi, Hafiz (Shams-ud-din Muhammad) is also worthy of attention, and Ladinsky's free translations should help see that he gets it. Hafiz is so beloved in Iran that he outsells the Koran. Many know his verses by heart and recite them with gusto. And gusto is appropriate to this passionate, earthy poet who melds mind, spirit, and body in each of his usually brief pensees. Ladinsky has deliberately chosen a loose and colloquial tone for this collection, which might grate on the nerves of purists but makes Hafiz come vividly alive for the average reader." Booklist

I am the beggar of the world; landays from contemporary Afghanistan. translated and presented by Eliza Griswold ; photographs by Seamus Murphy. Farrar Straus & Giroux 2014 160 p. illustrations (hardcover) $24   **891**

    1. Afghan literature 2. Poetry -- Collections 3. Poetry -- Women authors -- Collections 4. Folk poetry, Pushto -- Translations into English 5. Pushto poetry -- 20th century -- Translations into English 6. Pushto poetry -- Women authors -- Translations into English
    ISBN 0374191875; 9780374191870

                    LC 2013035179

Translated by Eliza Griswold, with photographs by Seamus Murphy, this book is a "collection of clandestine poems by Afghan women. . . . War, separation, homeland, love-- these are the subjects of landays, which are brutal and spare, can be remixed like rap, and are powerful in that they make no attempts to be literary." (Publisher's note)

"Griswold's selections illustrate the rich potential of this poetic form, at once contemporary and timeless. Murphy's stunning photographs complement the text perfectly." Booklist

Narayan, R. K.

★ The **Ramayana**; a shortened modern prose version of the Indian epic (suggested by the Tamil version of Kamban) introduction by Pankaj Mishra. Penguin Books 2006 157p (Penguin classics) pa $13   **891**
ISBN 0-14-303967-9

LC 2006-45201

First published 1972

A retelling of Prince Rama's courtship of the fourteen-year-old Sita, their exile, Sita's abduction, the search, and the great battle with her abductor Ravana, involving a pantheon of gods, heroes, and evil spirits.

Persian poets; selected and edited by Peter Washington. Knopf 2000 254p (Everyman's library pocket poets) $12.50   **891**
1. Persian poetry -- Collections
ISBN 978-0-375-41126-7

Includes works by Omar, Sanai, Attar, Rumi, Saadi, Hafez, and Jami

Selections/English

The **essential** Rumi; translated by Coleman Barks, with John Moyne, A.A. Arberry, Reynold Nicholson. Harper 1995 302p $23.95; pa $14.95   **891**
1. Poetry -- By individual authors
ISBN 978-0-06-250958-1; 0-06-250958-6; 978-0-06-250959-8 pa; 0-06-250959-4 pa

LC 94-44995

A collection of ecstatic verse by the 13th-century Sufi mystic

Tagore, Rabindranath

Selected poems; translated by William Radice. Penguin Books 2005 202p (Penguin classics) pa $14   **891**
1. Poetry -- By individual authors
ISBN 978-0-14-044988-4

"This collection offers a wide array of Tagore's poems from 1882 to 1941, plus textual notes and other scholarly extras." Libr J

891.6   Celtic literatures

Tain bo Cuailnge

The **Tain**; translated from the Irish epic Tain Bo Cuailnge. [translated] by Thomas Kinsella; with brush drawings by Louis le Brocquy. Oxford University Press 2002 282p il map pa $19.95   **891.6**
ISBN 0-19-280373-5

LC 2002-726950

This translation first published 1969

This Irish epic is the "centerpiece of the eighth-century Ulster cycle of heroic tales. . . . [This] translation is based on the partial texts in two medieval manuscripts, with elements from other versions. This edition includes a group of related stories which prepare for the action of the Tain." Publisher's note

Includes bibliographical references

891.7   Russian literature and related East Slavic literatures

Bartlett, Rosamund

★ **Tolstoy**; 1st U.S. ed. Houghton Mifflin Harcourt 2011 544 p.   **891.7**
1. Biography 2. Novelists 3. Dramatists 4. Authors, Russian 5. Authors 6. Short story writers 7. Writers on religion 8. Biography, Individual
ISBN 9781846681387 Profile Books; 1846681383
Profile Books; 9780151014385

LC 2010050015

This book presents a biography of writer Leo Tolstoy which draws primarily upon Russian scholarship, as well as Tolstoy's "memoirs and correspondences," to narrate his life. "As a cultural historian, Bartlett strives to place the man within his time and milieu. Her Tolstoy in his incarnations as aristocrat, muzhik, czar and other roles is thoroughly Russian, and she uses him to introduce her anglophone readers to sometimes exotic details of Russian life and history. . . . She offers, for instance, a brief history of the family of Tolstoy's wife, the Behrses, who came from a different order of Russian society than the counts and princes from whom Tolstoy descended. . . . There are similar . . . digressions about the Caucasus, Russian Orthodoxy, peasant life, Tolstoyans and other matters." (The Globe and Mail)

Batuman, Elif

The **possessed**; adventures with Russian books and the people who read them. Farrar, Straus and Giroux 2010 296p pa $15   **891.7**
1. Russian literature -- History and criticism
ISBN 978-0-374-53218-5; 0-374-53218-4

LC 2009-25416

In this book, the author "makes you look at Russian literature from a fresh perspective, using an unusual blend of memoir and travelogue as she delves into the lives and personalities of such Russian literary giants as Isaac Babel, Fyodor Dostoevsky and Leo Tolstoy. Many of the chapters are extensions of pieces Batuman first wrote for The New Yorker and n+1 and range geographically from Palo Alto, Calif., where Batuman managed to lose one of Babel's daughters at the local airport, to Uzbekistan, where Batuman spent a few months studying Uzbek. In a sense, the details of Batuman's essays are less significant than the tone. She cruises through minor crises with an air of detached amusement, eye focused on the little absurdities that make travel—and people—fun." Cleveland Plain Dealer

Includes bibliographical references

Brodsky, Joseph

★ **Collected** poems in English, 1972-1999; edited by Ann Kjellberg. Farrar, Straus & Giroux 2000 539p $30; pa $18   **891.7**
1. Poetry -- By individual authors
ISBN 0-374-12545-7; 0-374-52838-1 pa

LC 00-21059

This volume "gathers all the poetry in English Brodsky originally saw through to press in books (or had earmarked for eventual publication), including Russian poems he translated or co-translated. Originally Russian verse from the '60s and '70s gives way to the later, sometimes lighter, work of his last two decades, when he found a second home in the speech of his adoptive country." Publ Wkly

Callow, Philip

Chekhov, the hidden ground; a biography. Dee, I.R. 1998 428p il $30; pa $18.95   **891.7**
1. Authors 2. Dramatists 3. Physicians 4. Short story writers
ISBN 1-56663-187-4; 1-56663-395-8 pa
LC 97-46679

"Callow sees Chekhov as distant in virtually all his relationships, with romantic disillusionment and the search for intimacy recurring themes in his writing. He argues persuasively that while Chekhov's art is resplendent with human emotion, his own life was strangely cold and remote. . . . Not strictly a literary biography, this book is particularly effective in discussing Chekhov's work as it relates to his life." Libr J

Includes bibliographical references

The **Cambridge** history of Russian literature; edited by Charles A. Moser. rev ed; Cambridge Univ. Press 1992 709p hardcover o.p. pa $55 **891.7**
1. Russian literature -- History and criticism
ISBN 0-521-42567-0 pa
LC 91-38275

This volume presents "a survey of Russian literature from the beginnings to this decade, in sufficient but not overwhelming detail.' Ten chapters by specialists elucidate this history from 988 to approximately 1980, with a lengthy bibliography at the end of the volume." Sheehy. Guide to Ref Books. 10th edition. suppl

Chekhov, Anton Pavlovich, 1860-1904

Chekhov; the four major plays. in new translations by Curt Columbus. Ivan R. Dee 2005 294p pa $15.95   **891.7**
ISBN 978-1-56663-626-1; 1-56663-626-4
LC 2004-48612

"Columbus's translation triumphs through its clarity and consistent use of the active voice." Chicago Reader

The **complete** plays; [by] Anton Chekhov; translated, edited, and annotated by Laurence Senelick. W. W. Norton 2006 lx, 1060p pa $22.95   **891.7**
ISBN 978-0-393-04885-8; 0-393-04885-3; 978-0-393-33069-4 pa; 0-393-33069-9 pa
LC 2005-24362

"This volume contains work never previously translated, including the newly discovered farce The Power of Hypnotism, the first version of Ivanov, Chekhov's early humorous dialogues, and a description of lost plays and those Chekhov intended to write but never did." Publisher's note

The **portable** Chekhov; edited and with an introduction by Avrahm Yarmolinsky. Viking 1947 631p hardcover o.p. pa $17   **891.7**
ISBN 0-14-015035-8 pa

This collection contains "two plays, 'The Cherry Orchard' and 'The Boor,' 28 short stories and selections from Chekhov's letters." Publ Wkly

Frank, Joseph

Dostoevsky. v5 Princeton Univ. Press 2002 784p v5 il $60; pa $24.95   **891.7**
1. Authors 2. Novelists 3. Authors, Russian 4. Short story writers
ISBN 0-691-08665-6; 0-691-11569-9 pa
LC 2001-38749

This is the fifth and final volume of Frank's biography of Dostoevsky.

Includes bibliographical references

Malcolm, Janet

Reading Chekhov; a critical journey. Random House 2001 209p hardcover o.p. pa $13.95 **891.7**
1. Authors 2. Dramatists 3. Physicians 4. Short story writers
ISBN 0-375-50668-3; 0-375-76106-3 pa
LC 2001-19585

"The author's pilgrimage to Chekhov's Russia—Moscow, St. Petersburg, the gardens of his villa in Yalta—is a reunion with this most reticent of literary fathers. Malcolm analyzes the transformations that Chekhov grants his redeemable roués and guileless heroines, and illuminates the hidden surreality and waywardness of his realism." New Yorker

Includes bibliographical references

Mandelstam, Osip

The **selected** poems of Osip Mandelstam; translated by Clarence Brown and W.S. Merwin. New York Review Books 2004 167p (New York Review Books classics) pa $14.95   **891.7**
1. Poetry -- By individual authors
ISBN 978-1-59017-091-1; 1-59017-091-1
LC 2004-14656

First published 1974 by Atheneum

"The Brown/Merwin versions represent a sensitive and sensible selection of Mandelstam's poetry. The translations do not attempt to imitate Mandelstam's fluid syntax or subtle sound play. But they are honest representations of Mandelstam's themes and recurrent imagery and many of them, particularly certain of the poems in the section 'Poems of the Thirties,' come across as fine English poems." Libr J

Mayakovsky, Vladimir

Listen! early poems. translated by Maria Enzensberger; with a foreward [sic] by Elaine Feinstein. City Lights Bks. 1991 60p pa $9.95   **891.7**
1. Poetry -- By individual authors
ISBN 978-0-87286-255-5; 0-87286-255-0
LC 91-10330

First published 1987 in the United Kingdom

This collection of the Russian poet's early work has parallel text in Russian and English and is illustrated with some of Mayakovsky's art.

Nabokov, Vladimir Vladimirovich

Lectures on Russian literature; edited with an introduction by Fredson Bowers. Harcourt Brace Jovanovich 1981 324p il hardcover o.p. pa $16 **891.7**
1. Authors 2. Novelists 3. Dramatists 4. Physicians

5. Communism and literature 6. Memoirists 7. Short story writers 8. Writers on religion 9. Russian literature -- History and criticism

ISBN 0-15-602776-3 pa

Companion volume Lectures on literature

This book is "derived from notes Nabokov made for his literature classes at Wellesley and Cornell. Included are chapters on Gogol, Turgenev, Dostoevsky, Tolstoy, Chekhov, and Gorki, as well as several miscellaneous essays on censorship and the art of translation." Libr J

Pushkin, Aleksandr Sergeevich

Eugene Onegin and other poems; translated by Charles Johnston. Knopf 1999 240p (Everyman's library pocket poets) $12.50   **891.7**

1. Poetry -- By individual authors

ISBN 978-0-375-40672-0; 0-375-40672-7

Tale in verse of a rich, bored young man who rather offhandedly destroys his chance at love by killing a friend in a duel and alienating his would-be beloved

Reference guide to Russian literature; editor, Neil Cornwell; associate editor, Nicole Christian. Fitzroy Dearborn Pubs. 1998 xl, 972p $160   **891.7**

1. Reference books 2. Russian literature -- Dictionaries 3. Russian literature -- Bio-bibliography

ISBN 1-88496-410-9

LC 97-169924

A guide to approximately 270 writers and their works "author entries include telegraphic biographical sketches, detailed bibliographies of Russian- and English-language sources and critical studies, and, in many cases, 1000-word entries for specific novels, plays, and stories. There are alphabetical and chronological lists, 13 introductory essays on various aspects of Russian literature, and a Russian/English title index." Libr J

Includes bibliographical references

Akhmatova, A.

Poems; [by] Akhmatova; translated by D.M. Thomas. New expanded ed.; Knopf 2006 6p (Everyman's library pocket poets) $12.50   **891.7**

1. Poetry -- By individual authors

ISBN 978-0-307-26424-4; 0-307-26424-6

LC 2006-297217

First published 1985 in the United Kingdom with title: You will hear thunder

A representative selection of material from all her major works—including "Requiem" commemorating the victims of Stalin's terror.

Terras, Victor

A **history** of Russian literature. Yale Univ. Press 1991 654p $37   **891.7**

1. Russian literature -- History and criticism

ISBN 978-0-300-04971-8; 0-300-04971-4

LC 91-13337

This history of Russian literature begins with a chapter on folklore and then presents a chronological account covering Old Russian literature (eleventh to sixteenth centuries); the seventeenth century; the eighteenth century; the Ro-

mantic period; the age of the novel; the Silver Age, and the Soviet period

"The book's minor shortcomings are overshadowed by its numerous merits; its accuracy, keenness of observation, subtle comments, vivid quotations, erudition. . . . Almost every page of the book invites one to read and re-read Russian literature." Times Lit Suppl

Includes bibliographical references

Tolstaia, Tat'iana

Pushkin's children; writings on Russia and Russians. [by] Tatyana Tolstaya; translated by Jamey Gambrell. Houghton Mifflin 2003 242p pa $15   **891.7**

1. Poets 2. Authors 3. Novelists 4. Presidents 5. Prime ministers 6. Political prisoners 7. Cabinet members 8. Communist leaders 9. Nonfiction writers 10. Short story writers 11. Writers on politics 12. Nobel laureates for peace 13. Nobel laureates for literature 14. Russia -- Politics and government

ISBN 0-618-12500-0

LC 2002-27610

"A collection from a decade of vehement witness to the radical transformations of Russia, with frequent reconsiderations of rulers and people." N Y Times Book Rev

"Tolstaya's essays in this compact, historically significant volume offer a fascinating, highly intelligent analysis of Russian society and politics." Publ Wkly

Tsvetaeva, Marina Ivanovna

Selected poems; [by] Marina Tsvetayeva; translated and introduced by Elaine Feinstein; with literal versions provided by Angela Livingstone . . . [et al.] Penguin Books 1994 131p (Penguin twentieth-century classics) pa $15   **891.7**

ISBN 978-0-14-018759-5; 0-14-018759-6

First published 1971 by Oxford Univ. Press

"As a poet Tsvetayeva impresses with her psychic energy, she is on fire with poetry, and nothing is put in perspective, everything is immediate, emotional in the best sense." N Y Times Book Rev

Volkov, Solomon

Romanov riches; Russian writers and artists under the tsars. translated from the Russian by Antonina W. Bouis. Alfred A. Knopf 2011 285p il $30 **891.7**

1. Emperors 2. Empresses 3. Russian arts 4. Authors, Russian 5. Arts, Russian 6. Artists -- Russia 7. Russia -- History 8. Composers -- Russia 9. Russia -- Kings and rulers 10. Russia -- Intellectual life 11. Russian literature -- History and criticism

ISBN 0-307-27063-7; 978-0-307-27063-4

LC 2010-45132

This is a "cultural history of Russia from the rise of the house of Romanov in 1613 to its downfall at the hands of the Bolsheviks in 1917." (Publisher's note) Index.

"Volkov revitalizes our understanding of rebellious poet Pushkin and offers fresh insights into Tchaikovsky, Dostoevsky, and Turgenev. A thrillingly anecdotal and incisive look at the paradigmatic and paradoxical Romanov world of politics, patronage, and the quest for artistic freedom." Booklist

Includes bibliographical references

Yevtushenko, Yevgeny Aleksandrovich

Selected poems; [by] Yevgeni Yevtushenko; translated by Robin Milner-Gulland and Peter Levi; with an introduction by Robin Milner-Gulland. Penguin Books 2008 90p il (Penguin Classics) pa $14   891.7

1. Poetry -- By individual authors

ISBN 978-0-14-042477-5; 0-14-042477-6

First published 1961

With a "poetic voice that moves effortlessly between social and personal themes, [Yevtushanko] describes his idyllic childhood in Serbia, his impressions of home after a long absence in Moscow, his joy upon discovering the unexpected in a lover, his chance meeting with Hemingway in Copenhagen, and his impressions of war." Publisher's note

"These poems beat and tumble and thrash with life." Daily Telegraph

891.709   Russian literature -- history and criticism

Popoff, Alexandra

The **wives**; The Women Behind Russia's Literary Giants. Alexandra Popoff. Pegasus Books 2012 332 p. $27.95   891.709

1. Wives 2. Authorship 3. Authors, Russian

ISBN 1605983667; 9781605983660

This book, by Alexandra Popoff, explores the "women behind the greatest works of Russian literature. . . . From Sophia Tolstoy to Vera Nabokov, . . . Anna Dostevsky, and Natalya Solzhenitsyn, these women ranged from stenographers and typists to editors, researchers, translators, and even publishers. Living under restrictive regimes, many of these women battled censorship and preserved the writers' illicit archives, often risking their own lives to do so." (Publisher's note)

891.71   Russian poetry

Akhmatova, Anna Andreevna

The **complete** poems of Anna Akhmatova; {by} Anna Akhmatova; translated by Judith Hemschemeyer; edited and with an introduction by Roberta Reeder. Zephyr Press (Somerville) 1990 2v il hardcover o.p. pa $29   891.71

1. Poetry -- By individual authors

ISBN 0-939010-27-5 pa

LC 88-51831

"Anna Akhmatova—the high priestess of Russian poetry—saw her husband shot, her son imprisoned twice by Stalin, her work banned in the 1930's and late 40's. . . . Sonorous, calm, deliberate in movement, her Russian has no English equivalent, but in this admirably restrained and accurate translation, sense and message strike with all the weight of the original." N Y Times Book Rev

Mandelstam, Nadezhda

Hope against hope; a memoir. translated from the Russian by Max Hayward; with an introduction by Clarence Brown and: Nadezhda Mandelstaum (1899-1980): an obituary, by Joseph Brodsky. Modern Lib. 1999 442p pa $23   891.71

1. Authors 2. Memoirists 3. Translators

ISBN 978-0-375-75316-9; 0-375-75316-8

LC 98-47833

"Mandelstam tells the story of her family's experiences of hardship in Soviet Russia under Stalin. What is remarkable about the book is not just its content but also its authorial voice, which, in Max Hayward's deft translation, is so unique and consistent that the reader can get a sense of it by opening the book at random and reading almost any paragraph. Although Hope Against Hope is a painful book to read, one of the things that makes it bearable, apart from its sheer beauty, is a kind of unquenchable spirit and optimism that keeps rising to the surface, compounding the more mysterious consolations of art." Harper's

891.73   Russian fiction

Finn, Peter

The **Zhivago** affair; the Kremlin, the CIA, and the battle over a forbidden book. Peter Finn and Petra Couvee. Pantheon Books 2013 368 p. (hard cover : alkaline paper) $26.95   891.73

1. Cold war 2. Books -- Censorship 3. Dissenters -- Soviet Union -- Biography 4. Prohibited books -- Soviet Union -- History 5. Authors, Russian -- 20th century -- Biography 6. Politics and literature -- Soviet Union -- History 7. Soviet Union -- Foreign relations -- United States 8. United States -- Foreign relations -- Soviet Union 9. Soviet Union -- Politics and government -- 1953-1985 10. United States. Central Intelligence Agency -- History -- 20th century

ISBN 0307908003; 9780307908001

LC 2013033875

This book, by Peter Finn and Petra Couvele, offers "the dramatic story of how a forbidden book in the Soviet Union became a secret CIA weapon in the ideological battle between East and West. . . . The CIA . . . published a Russian-language edition of 'Doctor Zhivago' and smuggled it into the Soviet Union. Copies were devoured in Moscow and Leningrad, sold on the black market, and passed surreptitiously from friend to friend." (Publisher's note)

"Drawing on recently declassified CIA documents, Finn and Couvée present an engaging thriller, in which bureaucratic obstructions and Cold War politics threaten the publication of a controversial masterpiece of world literature." Booklist

Includes bibliographical references and index

Pitzer, Andrea

★ The **Secret** History of Vladimir Nabokov; Andrea Pitzer. W W Norton & Co Inc 2013 352 p. (hardcover) $29.95   891.73

1. Nabokov, Vladimir Vladimirovich, 1899-1977 -- Criticism and interpretation 2. Authors, Russian -- 20th

century -- Biography 3. Authors, American -- 20th century -- Biography.
ISBN 1605984116; 9781605984117

This book, by Andrea Pitzer, discusses the life and work of the Russian novelist Vladimir Nabokov, who "witnessed the horrors of his century, escaping Revolutionary Russia then Germany under Hitler. . . . He repeatedly faced accusations of turning a blind eye to human suffering to write artful tales of depravity. But does one of the greatest writers in the English language really deserve the label of amoral aesthete bestowed on him by so many critics?" (Publisher's note)

"Drawing on new biographical material and her sharp critical senses, Pitzer reveals the tightly woven subtext of the novels, always keen to shine a light where the deception is not obvious. . . . Though no substitute for Brian Boyd's definitive two-volume biography, this is a brilliant examination that adds to the understanding of an inspiring and enigmatic life." Kirkus

891.8   Slavic (Slavonic) literatures

Capek, Karel

R.U.R. and The insect play; by the Brothers Capek. Oxford Univ. Press 1961 179p pa $15.95 **891.8**
ISBN 0-19-281010-3

"R.U.R." is a fantasy in which robots revolt against their human masters. In "The insect play," a dying tramp dreams about insect life

Dimkovska, Lidija

PH neutral history; Lidija Dimkovska ; translated from the Macedonian by Ljubica Arsovska and Peggy Reid. Copper Canyon Press 2012 120 p. (pbk. : alk. paper) $16.00 **891.8**
1. Suicide -- Poetry 2. Nostalgia -- Poetry 3. Macedonia (Republic) -- Folklore -- Poetry
ISBN 1556593759; 9781556593758

LC 2011044017

In this, the "sixth collection of poetry" by "Macedonian poet and novelist Lidija Dimkovska," the author "scrutinizes life's customary and trivial details in a quest for greater meaning." Topics referenced include "religious tenents," "native folklore," and "nostalgia for her youth." Her brother's suicide offers her "reflections on death and its neutralization: life." (Publisher's note)

Havel, Vaclav

The **garden** party and other plays. Grove Press 1993 273p $13.00; pa $14 **891.8**
ISBN 978-0-8021-3307-6; 0-8021-3307-X

LC 93-8656

"Gathered together here for the first time are seven plays that span Havel's career from his early days at the Theater of the Balustrade through the Prague Spring, Charter 77, and the repeated imprisonments that made Havel's name into a rallying cry and propelled him to the leadership of his country." Publisher's note

Herbert, Zbigniew

The **collected** poems, 1956-1998; translated and edited by Alissa Valles; with additional translations by Czeslaw Milosz, and Peter Dale Scott; introduction by Adam Zagajewski. Ecco Press 2007 600p $34.95 **891.8**
1. Poetry
ISBN 978-0-06-078390-7; 0-06-078390-7

LC 2006-40856

Herbert is a "titan of not only Polish poetry, but of twentieth-century European poetry. His celebrated alter ego, Mr. Cogito, ranks as the one of the most original characters in modern poetry. . . . Herbert lived through the Nazi occupation of 1941 and the Soviet occupations of 1939 and 1944 and was an active member of Poland's underground resistance. Decades later, after marshal law was declared in Poland in 1981, Herbert supported the underground opposition to communism and was an important figure in the Solidarity movement. . . . If Herbert is a political poet, he's political in the way Don Quixote is political. He doesn't make us more aware. He makes us more human." Brooklyn Rail

Milosz, Czeslaw

Legends of modernity; essays and letters from occupied Poland, 1942-1943. translated from the Polish by Madeline G. Levine; introduction by Jaroslaw Anders. Farrar, Straus and Giroux 2005 266p $25 **891.8**
1. Polish literature 2. Andrzejewski, Jerzy, 1909-1983 -- Correspondence 3. Authors, Polish -- 20th century -- Correspondence
ISBN 0-374-18499-2

LC 2005-40950

Original Polish edition, 1996

"Written to the young intellectual Jerzy Andrejewski, the letters reveal Milosz's concern about the political climate of the era and the deterioration of religious influence owing to the chaos all across Europe and the rest of the world. . . . The essays explore the ideas of William James, André Gide, Stendhal (Henri Beyle), Honoré de Balzac, and others as they relate to religious faith, reason and rationalism, contradictions, doubting, and believing in a civilized world and its religious institutions. . . . Reading Milosz is a demanding, rewarding, and ultimately powerful experience for the mind and the soul." Libr J

★ **Milosz's** ABCs; translated from the Polish by Madeline G. Levine. Farrar, Straus & Giroux 2001 313p hardcover o.p. pa $14 **891.8**
ISBN 0-374-52795-4 pa

LC 00-42176

"The short prose entries in this quiet book take note of some of the people and places and ideas that contributed to the making of Milosz. The subjects of his sketches range from Alchemy and Curiosity to Rimbaud and Whitman, from childhood friends to Polish intellectuals little known in the West. But what could have been no more than a light memory work becomes almost a registry of gratitude: a meditation on the obligations of having lived a life and the responsibilities inherent in its particulars." New Yorker

Includes bibliographical references

★ **New** and collected poems 1931-2001. Harper-Collins Pubs. 2001 xxi, 776p $45; pa $19.95 **891.8**
1. Poetry
ISBN 0-06-019667-X; 0-06-051448-5 pa

LC 2001-50123

"Milosz has stated repeatedly in his poems his belief in the power of language to rescue from the void all he has seen and all the people he has known in a long life. But beneath this belief, it now appears, was the deeper belief that none of this was possible because of the inadequacy of language to capture reality, though he maintains this always has to be the poet's goal. . . . Throughout his career and throughout this vast collection, Milosz argues with himself about his poetics." N Y Times Book Rev

A roadside dog. Farrar, Straus & Giroux 1998 208p hardcover o.p. pa $14 **891.8**
ISBN 0-374-52623-0 pa

LC 98-14026

This "book is a collection of reflections, a few dreams, some poems, and . . . 'Subjects to Let'—ideas and plots that Milosz, at 87, feels he will never develop and presents for others to flesh out. Two themes recur in many of these little writings: the opposition of the inner life of the mind and emotions and the outer life of the body and communication; and the occasionally paradoxical nature of personality." Booklist

"Milosz makes a wise, wryly humane fin de siècle companion." Publ Wkly

To begin where I am; selected essays. edited and with an introduction by Bogdana Carpenter and Madeline G. Levine. Farrar, Straus & Giroux 2001 462p hardcover o.p. pa $15 **891.8**
1. Poets 2. Authors 3. Novelists 4. Dramatists 5. Philosophers 6. Political prisoners 7. Editors 8. Essayists 9. Translators 10. College teachers 11. Literary critics 12. Short story writers 13. Vilnius (Lithuania) 14. Nobel laureates for literature 15. Political and social philosophers
ISBN 0-374-52859-4 pa

LC 2001-33356

A retrospective of Milosz's "prose works, in which he weaves autobiography and portraits of people, famous and otherwise, who have influenced him into graceful and provocative musings on time, history, religion, science, and art." Booklist

Includes bibliographical references

Sosnowski, Andrzej

Lodgings; selected poems, 1987-2010. translated from the Polish by Benjamin Paloff. Open Letter 2011 163p pa $13.95 **891.8**
1. Poetry
ISBN 978-1-934824-32-0; 1-934824-32-1

LC 2010-52054

With this volume, "translator Benjamin Paloff has made an important contribution to the body of Polish poetry cur-

rently available to readers in English. Complete with a translator's note, a conversation between Sosnowski and Paloff, and poems that span Sosnowski's entire career to date (1987-2010), Lodgings offers an unusual glimpse into a polyphonous, expansive, and chameleonic strain of Polish poetry. The poems included are pulled from nine of Sosnowski's collections . . . , and they are presented, with two exceptions, in their original order." Words without Borders

Szymborska, Wislawa

★ **Monologue** of a dog; new poems. translated from the Polish by Clare Cavanagh and Stanislaw Baranczak; [foreword by Billy Collins] Harcourt 2005 96p $22 **891.8**
1. Poetry
ISBN 0-15-101220-2

LC 2005-16084

Original Polish edition, 2002

This is a collection of poems by the author of Miracle Fair (2001).

In this volume, Nobel laureate Szymborska "invites readers to linger over moments small, earthly, and sometimes life-altering. With characteristically simple language and imagery, wit and irony, she shows us how life can change at any moment. Hers are the politics of the everyday, little observations on the value of life." Libr J

Poems, new and collected, 1957-1997; translated from the Polish by Stanislaw Baranczak and Clare Cavanagh. Harcourt Brace & Co. 1998 273p $27; pa $17 **891.8**
1. Poetry
ISBN 0-15-100353-X; 0-15-601146-8 pa

LC 97-32277

This career-spanning collection by the 1996 Nobel Prize winner includes her Nobel lecture

Szymborska's "work is ultimately wisdom literature, written in a first person that expresses a universal humanity that American poets—lockstep individualists all—haven't dared essay since early in this century." Booklist

Zagajewski, Adam

★ **Without** end; new and selected poems. translations by Clare Cavanagh [et al.] Farrar, Straus & Giroux 2002 285p $30; pa $15 **891.8**
1. Poetry
ISBN 0-374-22096-4; 0-374-52861-6 pa

LC 2001-40252

"Zagajewski's poetic evolution is clearly charted in 'Without End,' a new anthology of his work that is made up of his three English-language collections—'Tremor' (1985), 'Canvas' (1991) and 'Mysticism for Beginners' (1997)—as well as his most recent work and new translations of some early poems. . . . Zagajewski's poems pull us from whatever routine threatens to dull our senses, from whatever might lull us into mere existence. This is an astonishing book." N Y Times Book Rev

Eternal enemies; translated from the Polish by Clare Cavanagh. Farrar, Straus and Giroux 2008 116p **891.8**
1. Poetry
ISBN 0-374-21634-7; 978-0-374-21634-4
LC 2007-42855
This is a collection of poetry by the author of Two Cities (1995), Without End (2002), and A Defense of Ardor (2004).
"Cavanagh's supple translations let the verse sing in American English without making this Polish poet sound too American." Publ Wkly

Unseen hand; translated from the Polish by Clare Cavanagh. Farrar, Straus and Giroux 2011 107p $23 **891.8**
1. Poetry
ISBN 978-0-374-28089-5; 0-374-28089-4
LC 2010-46274
Original Polish edition, 2009
The book "is Adam Zagajewski's sixth book of poetry translated into English. . . . If Szymborska is a poet of imaginary journeys, Zagajewski is a real traveler with a ticket and a suitcase. He even has a poem called 'Self-Portrait in an Airplane.' Many of his poems are about towns and cities in Europe and the United States that he had either lived in or visited. Poetry and travel are allied, Czeslaw Milosz once claimed, since poetry is an expression of wondering at things, landscapes, people, their habits and mores. . . . He compares the impassive river Garonne, flowing in silence, to an Indian brave in plumes of sun; a plane taking off from an airport to a zealous pupil who believes what the old masters told him; the light bulbs hissing in gray hallways at night to the signals of sinking ships." (New York Review of Books)
"The collective calm of these poems creates an odd tension: Within [Zagajewski's] clear, contemplative lines, the indifference of time can always be felt drifting unstoppably by, even as we attempt to scaffold it with history or cage it with memory. . . . [The poems,] translated by the admirably consistent Clare Cavanagh, move through the various locales of Zagajewski's life; from his Polish upbringing in Lvov and the provincial garrison town of Gliwice (to which his family was forced to move shortly after his birth in 1945), to various stints in Krakow, Paris, and Chicago. Markers of place and time are everywhere, but Zagajewski is especially perceptive of the ways the past is channeled through the present — his 'now' tends to carry the authority of an 'always.'" Boston Globe

892 Afro-Asiatic literatures

Amichai, Yehuda
Poems of Jerusalem; and, Love poems; a bilingual edition. Sheep Meadow Press 1992 265p pa $16.95 **892**
1. Poetry -- By individual authors
ISBN 1-87881-819-8
LC 92-31558

Poems of Jerusalem first published 1988 by Perennial Lib.; Love poems first published 1981 by Harper & Row
This work is "actually drawn from eight previous works and boasts an even larger array of translators (including Stephen Mitchell, David Rosenberg, Ted Hughes, and the poet himself). The thematic arrangement deftly emphasizes the Israeli poet's constant preoccupation with both Jerusalem and love." Libr J

The **selected** poetry of Yehuda Amichai; edited and translated from the Hebrew by Chana Bloch and Stephen Mitchell. newly rev & expanded ed; University of Calif. Press 1996 195p pa $16.95 **892**
1. Poetry -- By individual authors
ISBN 0-520-20538-3
LC 96-18580
First published 1986
"Although much of Amichai's poetry focuses on war, he is able to describe its horrors by maintaining a clear distance between himself and his subject. The result is a finely controlled emotional pitch that allows the poet to convey his sense of pain and outrage without pathos or sentimentality. He writes colloquially, in language that is always commensurate with emotional experience." Reader's Ency. 4th edition

Gilgamesh
✓★ **Gilgamesh**; a new English version [by] Stephen Mitchell. Free Press 2004 290p $25; pa $14 **892**
1. Epic poetry
ISBN 0-7432-6164-X; 0-7432-6169-0 pa
LC 2004-50072
"Relying on existing translations (and in places where there are gaps, on his own imagination), Mitchell seeks language that is as swift and strong as the story itself. . . . This wonderful new version of the story of Gilgamesh shows how the story came to achieve literary immortality—not because it is a rare ancient artifact, but because reading it can make people in the here and now feel more completely alive." Publ Wkly
Includes bibliographical references

892.4 Hebrew literature

Amichai, Yehuda
Open closed open; poems. translated from the Hebrew by Chana Bloch and Chana Kronfeld. Harcourt Brace & Co. 2000 184p $25 **892.4**
1. Poetry
ISBN 0-15-100378-5
LC 00-23537
Original Hebrew edition, 1998
Amichai "writes with the casual wisdom and generous humor of a master." Booklist

Shabtai, Aharon

War & love, love & war; new and selected poems. translated by Peter Cole. New Directions 2010
175p pa $15.95   **892.4**
1. Poetry
ISBN 978-0-8112-1890-0; 0-8112-1890-2
LC 2010-10440

"Gritty, controversial and intensely lyrical, this is an excellent collection from one of Israel's most important contemporary poets. Spanning more than three-anda-half decades of writing, it exhibits a wealth of experimentation with
various styles, and a multitude of yearnings and obsessions.
As the title implies, engagement with the Israeli-Palestinian
conflict is one of the book's chief subjects. The real gem,
though, is the closing cycle of poems, which mourns the
passing of Shabtai's wife, Tanya Reinhart." Forward

Includes bibliographical references

892.7   Arabic and Maltese literatures

Anthology of modern Palestinian literature; edited
and introduced by Salma Khadra Jayyusi. Columbia Univ. Press 1992 xxxiii, 744p hardcover o.p.
pa $30.50   **892.7**
1. Arabic literature -- Collections
ISBN 0-231-07508-1; 0-231-07509-X pa
LC 92-5189

"Presented here are translations of poems, stories, and
excerpts from novels, as well as works by Palestinian poets
who write in English. Also included are personal narratives
by Palestinian writers depicting the varied aspects of Palestinian life from the turn of the century to the present. . . .
Biographical sketches introduce the authors, and a chronology of modern Palestinian history provides background for
some of the events and places referred to in the selections.
The introduction by the editor provides a concise but comprehensive political history of Palestinian literature during
the twentieth century." Publisher's note

Includes bibliographical references

Darwish, Mahmud

If I were another; translated from the Arabic by
Fady Joudah. Farrar, Straus and Giroux 2009 201p
$28   **892.7**
1. Poetry -- By individual authors
ISBN 978-0-374-17429-3; 0-374-17429-6
LC 2009-11521

This volume "comprises four nonconsecutive books of
longer poems spanning 1990 to 2005. These works follow
Darwish's poetic development from a historically focused
middle period to the devastatingly personal lyric-epic of
his late style. Formally varied—Rubaiyats alternate with
sprawling freeform poems, in which prose paragraphs meet
both long and short verse lines—Darwish's Sufi-inspired
poetry probes, admires, describes, longs for and questions."
Publ Wkly

Includes bibliographical references

Night and horses and the desert; an anthology of
classical Arabic literature. edited by Robert Irwin. Anchor Books 2001 462p pa $16   **892.7**
1. Arabic literature -- Collections 2. Arabic literature
-- History and criticism
ISBN 0-385-72155-2
LC 2001-53721

First published 2000 by Overlook Press
"The chapter on the Qur'an is perhaps the most essential
as it examines just how vital the dogma of Islam has been
for the Arabic understanding of culture and art. . . . This persuasive work will surely fill in the gap in the study of Arabic
literature in this country." Publ Wkly

Includes bibliographical references

The **Poetry** of Arab women; a contemporary anthology. edited by Nathalie Handal. Interlink Bks.
2000 xxi, 355p pa $22   **892.7**
1. Arabic poetry -- Collections
ISBN 978-1-56656-374-1; 1-56656-374-7
LC 00-58054

"Handal deserves high praise for producing an anthology that mirrors faithfully Arab women's creative role
throughout the last century." Multicultural Rev

894   Literatures of Altaic, Uralic, Hyperborean, Dravidian languages; literatures of miscellaneous languages of south Asia

Pamuk, Orhan

Other colors; essays and a story. translated from
the Turkish by Maureen Freely. Alfred A. Knopf
2007 433p il $27.95   **894**
ISBN 978-0-307-26675-0; 0-307-26675-3
LC 2007-21132

Original Turkish edition, 1999
"Whether he's writing wistfully about Andre Gide as the
hero of Turkish intellectuals . . . or recalling how he used to
collect Coca-Cola cans as a boy, from the trash cans of expat
Americans, Pamuk is taking the world we thought we knew
and making it fresh and alive." N Y Times Book Rev

895.1   Chinese literature

An **Anthology** of Chinese literature; beginnings to
1911. edited and translated by Stephen Owen.
Norton 1996 xlviii, 1212p hardcover o.p. pa
$59.65   **895.1**
1. Chinese literature -- Collections
ISBN 0-393-97106-6 pa
LC 95-11409

"In a book that moves roughly chronologically through
the tradition, Owen gathers texts according to genres,
themes, forms, and other groupings to show the way essential texts build off each other and how the tradition echoes
itself. Included are a range of forms . . . presented . . . {with}
commentary to provide a . . . view of the interplay between
Chinese literature, culture, and history." Publisher's note

Includes bibliographical references

Anthology of modern Chinese poetry; edited and translated by Michelle Yeh. Yale Univ. Press 1993 245p hardcover o.p. pa $21 **895.1**
1. Chinese poetry -- Collections
ISBN 0-300-05947-7 pa

LC 92-16322

"Arranged chronologically, this selection of twentieth-century poetry from China and Taiwan offers a few poems by each of 67 poets born between 1891 and 1963. Its scope is enormous, its range impressive. Editor Yeh's translations are accessible and fluid; her introduction and notes are helpful without being overbearingly scholarly." Booklist
Includes bibliographical references

The Columbia book of Chinese poetry; from early times to the thirteenth century. translated and edited by Burton Watson. Columbia Univ. Press 1984 385p il (Translations from the Oriental classics) $69; pa $27 **895.1**
1. Chinese poetry -- Collections
ISBN 0-231-05682-6; 0-231-05683-4 pa

LC 83-26182

This anthology's "arrangement is historical, beginning with selections from a first millenium BC collection of Chinese verse (the Shih ching), and ending with tz'u lyrics from the Sung period (AD 960-1279). The 12 selections [are] each prefaced with a two- or three-page introduction." Choice
Includes bibliographical references

The Columbia history of Chinese literature; Victor H. Mair, editor. Columbia Univ. Press 2001 xx, 1342p $78 **895.1**
1. Chinese literature -- History and criticism
ISBN 0-231-10984-9

LC 2001-28236

This "history explores a wide range of Chinese literature, from the classics to humor to folk tales to oral traditions, and moves from ancient times to the end of the 20th century. . . . Mair has overseen a host of excellent scholars writing on a vast subject." Libr J
Includes bibliographical references

Mountain home; the wilderness poetry of ancient China. selected and translated by David Hinton. New Directions Pub. 2005 xxi, 295p map pa $17.95 **895.1**
1. Chinese poetry -- Collections
ISBN 978-0-8112-1624-1

LC 2005-869

First published 2002 by Counterpoint
"Translator and scholar Hinton ensures that Western readers will experience this supreme collection of Chinese rivers-and-mountains (shan-shui) poetry at the deepest possible level by succinctly explaining the cosmology inherent in this vital and profoundly influential tradition. The keys to understanding the elegant poetry of such masters as T'ao Ch'ien (365-427), Li Po (701-762), and Lu Yu (1125-1210) are realizing that they perceive no divide between the human and what we call nature, or between being and nonbeing. . . . Oneness with life at its purest is the desired mode for these thoughtful, yet often playful, poets, and dwelling

within these meditative pages is the first step on the way there." Booklist

The New Directions anthology of classical chinese poetry; edited by Eliot Weinberger; translations by William Carlos Williams . . . [et al.] New Directions 2003 xxvii, 242p $24.95; pa $16.95 **895.1**
1. Chinese poetry -- Collections
ISBN 978-0-8112-1540-4; 0-8112-1540-7; 978-0-8112-1605-0 pa; 0-8112-1605-5 pa

LC 2002-156731

The poems are "translated into English by four of the best-known American poets of the 20th century—Ezra Pound, William Carlos Williams, Kenneth Rexroth and Gary Snyder—and an academic scholar/translator called David Hinton, who deserves to be as well known as the others. It is not often that an anthology really demands attention. . . . This poetry means what it says. It feels companionable, and even sexy. It is not excessively—or confusingly—metaphorical. It is not foggy with abstract philosophising. It lacks the shriek of rhetoric; it seems to move, so often, at an agreeable walking pace. It feels spacious. In fact, there seems to be space between the words themselves. It mixes the high and the low with seeming ease. Its temper suggests that there is no unsuitable subject matter for poetry at all." New Statesman

The Shorter Columbia anthology of traditional Chinese literature; Victor H. Mair, editor. Columbia Univ. Press 2000 xxx, 741p map (Translations from the Asian classics) $65; pa $26 **895.1**
1. Chinese literature -- Collections
ISBN 0-231-11998-4; 0-231-11999-2 pa

LC 00-35878

Abridged version of Columbia anthology of traditional Chinese literature, published 1994
This "abridged volume, which, like the original includes selections of Chinese literature from the beginnings to 1919 . . . retains the characteristics of the original in that it is arranged according to genre rather than chronology and interprets 'literature' very broadly to include not just literary fiction, poetry, and drama, but folk and popular literature, lyrics and arias, elegies and rhapsodies, biographies, autobiographies and memoirs, letters, criticism and theory, and travelogues and jokes. It also contains fresh translations by newer voices in the field." Publisher's note
Includes bibliographical references

895.6 Japanese literature

Haiku before haiku; from the Renga masters to Basho. translated, with an introduction, by Steven D. Carter. Columbia University Press 2011 163p (Translations from the Asian classics) $69.50; pa $22.50; ebook $9.99 **895.6**
1. Haiku 2. Renga 3. Japanese poetry
ISBN 978-0-231-15648-6; 978-0-231-15647-9 pa; 978-0-231-52706-4 ebook

LC 2010-37030

"While the rise of the charmingly simple, brilliantly evocative haiku is often associated with the seventeenth-century Japanese poet Matsuo Basho, the form had already flourished for more than four hundred years before Basho even began to write. These early poems, known as hokku, are identical to haiku in syllable count and structure but function differently as a genre. Whereas each haiku is its own constellation of image and meaning, a hokku opens a series of linked, collaborative stanzas in a sequence called renga. . . . [This anthology] presents 320 hokku composed between the thirteenth and early eighteenth centuries, from the poems of the courtier Nijo Yoshimoto to those of the genre's first 'professional' master, Sogi, and his disciples. It features 20 masterpieces by Basho himself." Publisher's note

Includes bibliographical references

Keene, Donald

Five modern Japanese novelists. Columbia Univ. Press 2002 113p $26 **895.6**
1. Japanese literature -- History and criticism
ISBN 0-231-12610-7

LC 2002-73412

In this discussion of the lives and works of five 20th century Japanese novelists, the author recounts personal "anecdotes, telling the stories of their first meetings, and sharing his initial impressions. . . . He [also] mentions their best-known works and discusses some of the controversies surrounding them." Libr J

The author's essays, "part memoir and part literary evaluation, are ideal introductions to their subjects." Booklist

Includes bibliographical references

The **pleasures** of Japanese literature. Columbia Univ. Press 1988 133p il (Companion to Asian studies) $60; pa $19.50 **895.6**
1. Aesthetics 2. Theater -- Japan 3. Japanese literature -- History and criticism
ISBN 0-231-06736-4; 0-231-06737-2 pa

LC 88-18069

The author discusses Japanese aesthetics, poetry, fiction and drama, focusing on works of the premodern period

"If your library has no other introduction to the Japanese classics, nor any need for another, this is the one it ought to include." Booklist

Includes bibliographical references

Seeds in the heart; Japanese literature from earliest times to the late sixteenth century. with a new preface by the author, Donald Keene. Columbia University Press 1999 1265p (History of Japanese literature) pa $37 **895.6**
1. Japanese literature -- History and criticism
ISBN 0-231-11441-9

LC 99-25990

First published 1993 by Holt & Co.

This volume completes the author's history of Japanese literature begun with: World within walls (1977) and Dawn to the West (1984).

"The first half of 'Seeds in the Heart' encompasses everything from the myths, legends, songs and poems of the eighth-century 'Kojiki' ('Record of Ancient Matters') and 'Manyoshu,' a collection of 4,500 poems, to the 'The Tale of

Genji' and later works of fiction. . . . During Japan's middle ages (1185-1600), Buddhism and popular (rather than aristocratic) forms of storytelling and theater generated a repertory of characters and genres that would eventually form the country's first broadly based, national culture. The literature of these centuries has rarely attracted the scholarly attention paid to the earlier 'high' classical tradition. So Mr. Keene's attention to this period makes the second half of 'Seeds in the Heart' especially valuable." N Y Times Book Rev

Includes bibliographical references

Modern Japanese literature; an anthology. compiled and edited by Donald Keene. Grove Press 1960 440p hardcover o.p. pa $15.95 **895.6**
1. Japanese literature -- Collections
ISBN 0-8021-5095-0 pa

"The selections give a representative sampling of the poetry, prose, and drama from the 1870's through the 1940's. Short enlightening notes on the writers or background for the text are added unobtrusively." Booklist

Modern Japanese writers; Jay Rubin, editor. Scribner 2000 434p $130 **895.6**
1. Authors, Japanese 2. Japanese literature -- History and criticism
ISBN 0-684-80598-7

LC 00-63505

"This handbook is a collection of alphabetically arranged articles on 23 twentieth-century Japanese writers and one literary genre, written by noted scholars in the field. Entries are generally around 18 pages in length. Each author entry treats a writer's life and work and is accompanied by a selected bibliography of primary and secondary sources. Most of the writers included have been translated into English, and two of them, Kawabata Yasunari and Oe Kenzaburo, are Nobel Prize winners." Booklist

Includes bibliographical references

One hundred poems from the Japanese; {edited and translated} by Kenneth Rexroth. New Directions 1956 143p hardcover o.p. pa $11.95 **895.6**
1. Japanese poetry -- Collections
ISBN 0-8112-0181-3 pa

A bilingual collection of poems drawn chiefly from the traditional Manyoshu, Kokinshu, and Hyakunin Isshu collections and also containing examples of haiku and other later forms. The translator's introduction provides background information on the history and nature of Japanese poetry

Includes bibliographical references

Waley, Arthur

The **No** plays of Japan; an anthology. Dover Publications 1998 270p pa $12.95 **895.6**
1. No plays
ISBN 978-0-486-40156-0

LC 97-46053

First published 1921 in the United Kingdom; first United States edition published 1922 by Knopf

Contains translation of 20 No plays and summaries of 16 more. In his introduction Mr. Waley gives a brief history of the No drama, its origin, the text of the plays, and the chief playwrights. He also tells about the stage settings, costumes and properties used in the production of these plays. The greatest representation is given to the works of Seami and Zenchiku Ujinobu

896   African literatures

The **Penguin** book of modern African poetry; edited by Gerald Moore and Ulli Beier. 4th ed.; Penguin Books 2007 xxvi, 448p pa $17   **896**
1. African poetry -- Collections
ISBN 978-0-14-042472-0; 0-14-042472-5
First published 1963 in the United Kingdom with title: Modern poetry from Africa
This anthology includes over 200 poems by 67 poets from 23 countries.
Includes bibliographical references

897   Literatures of North American native languages

The **Cambridge** companion to Native American literature; edited by Joy Porter and Kenneth M. Roemer. Cambridge University Press 2005 343p il map hardcover o.p. pa $26.95   **897**
1. Native American literature -- History and criticism
ISBN 978-0-521-52979-2 pa; 0-521-52979-4 pa
LC 2005-44298
Essays organized "by historical and cultural context, by genre, and according to individual authors. Particularly insightful and informative are the tightly written essays on the eight currently best-known Indian writers. Also included are maps, a time line, suggested readings, and a brief series of 40 biobibliographies of notable Native American writers. . . . Readers of this volume should probably already have a working knowledge of the main figures in this increasingly important and respected segment of American literature." Libr J

900   HISTORY

900   History, geography, and auxiliary disciplines

Báez, Fernando
A **universal** history of the destruction of books; from ancient Sumer to modern-day Iraq. translated by Alfred MacAdam. Atlas & Co. 2008 354p il map $25   **900**
1. Censorship 2. Books and reading -- History 3. Libraries -- Destruction and pillage
ISBN 978-1-934633-01-4
LC 2008-932321
Original Spanish edition, 2004
This is a "horrific chronicle of the centuries-long assault on human memory. . . . A sobering reminder of just

how deep-seated is the instinct to destroy other people's truths." Kirkus
Includes bibliographical references

Schweitzer, Albert, 1875-1965
Out of my life and thought; an autobiography. Albert Schweitzer ; foreword by Jimmy Carter ; new foreword by Lachlan Forrow ; translated by Antje Bultmann Lemke. Johns Hopkins University Press 2009 xx, 272 p.p ill. (paperback) $27   **900**
ISBN 0801894123; 9780801894121
LC 2009925674
This book presents Albert Schweitzer's "autobiography, first published in 1933" in which he "discusses his research into primitive Christianity and his search for the historical Jesus; his love of Bach, 'poet and painter in sound'; his fancy for rebuilding old church organs. His philosophy, which he called 'Reverence for Life,' blends mysticism and rationalism, with an impulse to release the 'active ethic' he sees latent in Christianity." (Publishers Weekly)
Includes bibliographical references (p. 257-260) and index

901   Philosophy and theory of history

Hobsbawm, E. J.
On history. New Press (NY) 1997 305p $25; pa $15.95   **901**
1. Historiography
ISBN 1-56584-393-2; 1-56584-468-8 pa
"In these collected pieces—articles, lectures and reviews—Eric Hobsbawm surveys the writings of modern historians with the magisterial gaze of a man who has seen both the rise of Hitler and the fall of Communism. He notes how the discipline has changed in the last century: how social history and economic history have come of age, how modern historians speak of change and forces where Victorians spoke of ideas and progress. He rejects postmodernist claims that history can be freely revised because all facts are merely intellectual constructions." N Y Times Book Rev

MacMillan, Margaret
Dangerous games; the uses and abuses of history. Modern Library 2009 188p $22   **901**
1. Historiography 2. History -- Philosophy
ISBN 978-0-679-64358-6; 0-679-64358-3
First published 2008 in Canada with title: The uses and abuses of history
Explores the ways in which history has been used to influence people and government, focusing on how reportage of past events has been manipulated to justify religious movements and political campaigns. Based on the Joanne Goodman lecture series of the University of Western Ontario.
"This is a must read for anyone who wants to understand the importance of correctly understanding the past." Publ Wkly
Includes bibliographical references

Ortega y Gasset, Jose
The **revolt** of the masses; translated, annotated, and with an introduction by Anthony Kerrigan; edited

by Kenneth Moore; with a foreword by Saul Bellow. University of Notre Dame Press 1985 xxxi, 192p hardcover o.p. pa $13.95 **901**

1. Proletariat 2. Civilization 3. Europe -- Civilization
ISBN 0-393-31095-7

LC 81-40457

Original Spanish edition, 1930; first English translation, 1932

A collection of essays by the Spanish intellectual in which he analyzes the dangers of control of government by the masses. He sees Bolshevism and Fascism as particularly threatening to civilization

Schiffman, Zachary Sayre

The **birth** of the past; Zachary Sayre Schiffman; foreword by Anthony Grafton. Johns Hopkins University Press 2011 xvi, 316 p.p (hardcover : alk. paper) $65.00 **901**

1. History -- Philosophy 2. Civilization, Western 3. Historiography -- Philosophy 4. Historiography -- Western countries 5. Western countries -- Intellectual life
ISBN 1421402785; 9781421402789

LC 2011008229

In this book, author Zachary S. "Schiffman takes readers on a grand tour of historical thinking from antiquity to modernity. He shows how ancient historians could not distinguish between past and present because they conceived of multiple pasts. Christian theologians coalesced these multiple pasts into a single temporal space. . . . French enlighteners . . . engendered a form of social scientific thinking that measured the relations between historical entities." (Publisher's note)

Includes bibliographical references and index.

Spengler, Oswald

The **decline** of the West, volume one; Form and actuality. authorized translation with notes by Charles Frances Atkinson. A. Knopf 1996 various paging $45 **901**

1. History -- Philosophy 2. Civilization -- History
ISBN 0-394-42179-5
First published 1926

The first volume of a work that "reflects the pessimistic atmosphere in Germany after World War I. Spengler maintained that history has a natural development, in which every culture is a distinct organic form that grows, matures, and decays." Reader's Ency. 4th edition

Includes bibliographical references

902 Miscellany of history

Grafton, Anthony

Cartographies of time; a history of the timeline. [by] Daniel Rosenberg and Anthony Grafton. Princeton Architectural Press 2010 272p il $50 **902**

1. Historical chronology 2. History -- Philosophy
ISBN 978-1-56898-763-7; 1-56898-763-3

LC 2008-52892

The authors "aim to provide the first full account of the development of the modern timeline, from its inauspicious beginnings in crude lists and tables, to the glorious, colorful artworks that convey the sweep of time with arresting visual drama. There's more to this story, however. The story of the timeline is also the story of how humanity's perception of time has evolved, and how the various representations of time can tell us much about the personality and proclivity of the era in which it was designed. . . . Rosenberg and Grafton's text is crisp and informative, but the true stars of Cartographies of Time are the numerous illustrations and photographs of the chronologies themselves." PopMatters

Includes bibliographical references.

Grun, Bernard

The **timetables** of history; a historical linkage of people and events. 4th ed.; Simon & Schuster 2005 835p $25 **902**

1. Historical chronology
ISBN 0-7432-7003-7; 978-0-7432-7003-8

LC 2005-49766

Original German edition, 1946; first published in the United States 1975

This chronology "includes material from 4500 BCE to 2004. . . . The information is listed by year in seven columns labeled 'History, Politics', 'Literature, Theater', 'Religion, Philosophy, Learning', 'Visual Arts', 'Music', 'Science, Technology, Growth', and 'Daily Life.' . . . This work is an excellent chronological tool, and should be found in all libraries." Choice

National Geographic concise history of the world; an illustrated timeline. edited by Neil Kagan. National Geographic Society 2005 416p il map $40 **902**

1. Historical chronology
ISBN 0-792-28364-3

LC 2005-52248

This history is organized in time line format and broken up into eight historical eras. Includes maps, sidebars, and illustrations.

Includes bibliographical references

The **timetables** of American history; Laurence Urdang, editor; with an introduction by Henry Steele Commager and a new foreword by Arthur Schlesinger, Jr. Simon & Schuster 2001 534p il pa $24 **902**

1. Historical chronology
ISBN 0-7432-0261-9
First published 1982

Presents information chronologically in tabular form. Each double-page spread has columns for history and politics, the arts, science and technology, and miscellaneous.

902.2 Illustrations, models, miniatures

National Geographic Society (U.S.)

National Geographic visual history of the world; [authors, Klaus Berndl . . . et al.]. National Geographic Society 2005 656p il $35 **902.2**
1. World history
ISBN 0-7922-3695-5

LC 2005-541553

"Over 4,000 illustrations and photographs cover individuals and events from prehistory (the beginning to ca. 4000 BCE) to the contemporary world (1945 to the present). . . . This educational and entertaining volume of social, cultural, and military history will appeal to a wide readership." Choice

Terra Maxima; The Records of Humankind. edited by Wolfgang Kunth. Firefly Books Ltd 2013 576 p. color illustrations $49.95 **902.2**
1. World records 2. Technological innovations
ISBN 1770852425; 9781770852426

LC 2013456556

This book, edited by Wolfgang Kunth, "is comprised of more than 3,000 full-color photographs . . . that showcase the biggest and the best religious, cultural, and technological marvels of the world. The work is broken down into 10 sections: 'Countries and Nations,' 'Languages and Scripts,' 'Faith and Religion,' 'Cities and Metropolises,' 'Urban Megastructures,' 'Transportation and Traffic,' 'Aviation and Space Travel,' 'Art and Culture,' 'Science and Research,' and 'Sports and Leisure.'" (Booklist)

"The emphasis is on the visual, with sumptuous color photographs printed on heavy stock, many appearing on full spreads. The text, while minimal, is nevertheless informative, pointing out interesting historical, architectural, and other details about the structures pictured." LJ

903 Dictionaries, encyclopedias, concordances of history

Berkshire encyclopedia of world history; William H. McNeill, Jerry H. Bentley [and] David Christian, editors. 2nd ed.; Berkshire Pub. Group 2010 6v il map set $875 **903**
1. Reference books 2. World history -- Encyclopedias
ISBN 978-1-933782-65-2

LC 2010021635

First published 2004

"To cover 250,000 years of human history, knowledge from various disciplines is synthesized, summarized, and presented in an easy-to-read fashion. Emphasis is placed on social change and cultural contact over time and place." Booklist

Includes bibliographical references

904 Collected accounts of events

Davis, Lee Allyn

Man -made catastrophes; [by] Lee Davis. rev ed; Facts on File 2002 402p il $60 **904**
1. Disasters
ISBN 0-8160-4418-X

LC 2001-54324

First published 1993

This describes man-made disasters "from the burning of Babylon in 538B.C. to the 2001 terrorist attack on the World Trade Center in New York City. . . . [The entries] are organized by disaster type: air crashes, civil unrest and terrorism, explosions, maritime disasters, nuclear and industrial accidents, railway disasters, and space disasters." Publisher's note

Includes bibliographical references

Hanson, Victor Davis

Carnage and culture; landmark battles in the rise of Western power. Doubleday 2001 492p il hardcover o.p. pa $16 **904**
1. Battles 2. Military history
ISBN 0-385-72038-6 pa

LC 00-65582

The author analyzes nine battles and "maintains that Western nations are the world's best when it comes to waging war. From Salamis in 480 B.C.E. to the Tet offensive in 1968, Western forces have prevailed." Libr J

"This provocative work is likely to engender controversy." Booklist

Includes bibliographical references

907 Education, research, related topics of history

Hamilton, Nigel

★ **Biography**; a brief history. Harvard University Press 2007 345p il $21.95 **907**
1. Biography as a literary form
ISBN 978-0-674-02466-3; 0-674-02466-4

LC 2006-51132

"Hamilton has given readers a thought-provoking look at biography in its various forms; a fascinating and handy reference book for anyone wishing to know more about the history and art of biography." Libr J

Includes bibliographical references (p. 315-21)

Mills, Elizabeth S.

Evidence explained; citing history sources from artifacts to cyberspace. [by] Elizabeth Shown Mills. 2nd ed; Genealogical Pub. Co. 2009 885p $59.95 **907**
1. History -- Sources 2. History -- Research
ISBN 978-0-8063-1806-6

LC 2009-934128

First published 2007

This resource is "indispensable for scholars and accessible enough to meet the needs of amateur genealogists and students." Libr J

Includes bibliographical references

Tuchman, Barbara Wertheim

Practicing history; selected essays. by Barbara W. Tuchman. Knopf 1981 306p hardcover o.p. pa $14.95   **907**

1. Historiography 2. Modern history

ISBN 0-345-30363-6 pa

LC 81-47509

A collection of essays on the nature, methodology and writing of history

908   History with respect to groups of people

Murray, Charles A.

Human accomplishment; the pursuit of excellence in the arts and sciences, 800 B.C. to 1950. [by] Charles Murray. HarperCollins Pubs. 2003 xx, 668p il map pa $24.95   **908**

1. Genius 2. Civilization -- History

ISBN 0-06-019247-X; 978-0-06-092964-0 pa; 0-06-092964-2 pa

LC 2003-47820

This is an "account of human excellence, from the age of Homer to our own time. . . . Murray compiles inventories of the people who have been [considered] essential to the stories of literature, music, art, philosophy, and the sciences—a total of 4,002 men and women from around the world, ranked according to their eminence. The heart of [the book] is a series of . . . descriptive chapters: on the giants in the arts and what sets them apart from the merely great; on the differences between great achievement in the arts and in the sciences; on the meta-inventions, 14 crucial leaps in human capacity to create great art and science; and on the patterns and trajectories of accomplishment across time and geography." Publisher's note

Includes bibliographical references

909   World history

Africana: the encyclopedia of the African and African American experience; editors, Kwame Anthony Appiah, Henry Louis Gates, Jr. 2nd ed; Oxford University Press 2005 5v set $550   **909**

1. Reference books 2. Africa -- Encyclopedias 3. Blacks -- Encyclopedias 4. African diaspora -- Encyclopedias 5. African Americans -- Encyclopedias

ISBN 978-0-19-517055-9; 0-19-517055-5

LC 2004-20222

First published 1999 by Basic Civitas Bks.

This encyclopedia covers "prominent individuals, events, trends, places, political movements, art forms, business and trade, religions, ethnic groups, organizations, and countries on both sides of the ocean. . . . There are articles on contemporary nations of sub-Saharan Africa, ethnic groups from various regions of Africa, African American Academy

award winners, Caribbean musical styles, African religions in Brazil, and European colonial powers." Booklist [review of 1999 edition]

Includes bibliographical references

Aries, Philippe

A History of private life; v2 [Philippe Ariès and Georges Duby, general editors; translated by] Arthur Goldhammer. Belknap Press 1988 650p v2 il hardcover o.p. pa $28   **909**

1. Family life 2. Manners and customs 3. Medieval civilization

ISBN 0-674-40001-1

LC 86-18286

"Spanning the period from the 11th century to the Renaissance and focusing on France and Tuscan Italy, this [second volume] continues the . . . five-volume history of private life from the Roman world to the present. 'Private' is here defined as what medieval people considered intimate, familial, domestic." Libr J

Includes bibliographical references

Boorstin, Daniel J.

The creators. Random House 1992 811p il hardcover o.p. pa $18.95   **909**

1. Arts 2. Civilization 3. Creation (Literary, artistic, etc.)

ISBN 0-394-54395-5; 0-679-74375-8 pa

LC 91-39948

In this volume "Boorstin undertakes an interpretive history of creativity in Western civilization. Packed with shrewd, entertaining profiles of Dante, Goethe, Benjamin Franklin and dozens of others, this stimulating synthesis sets the achievements of individual geniuses into a coherent narrative of humanity's advance from ignorance." Publ Wkly

Includes bibliographical references

Brendon, Piers

★ The **decline** and fall of the British Empire, 1781-1997. Alfred A. Knopf 2008 xxii, 786p il map $37.50   **909**

1. Great Britain -- History 2. Great Britain -- Colonies 3. Great Britain -- Civilization 4. Commonwealth countries -- History

ISBN 978-0-307-26829-7; 0-307-26829-2

LC 2008-14192

First published 2007 in the United Kingdom

"A richly detailed, lucid account of how the British Empire grew and grew—and then, not quite inexorably, fell apart." Kirkus

Includes bibliographical references

Brenner, Frederic

Diaspora : homelands in exile. HarperCollins 2003 2v il map set $100   **909**

1. Jews -- Pictorial works

ISBN 0-06-008778-1

LC 2003-42328

This is a "collection of photographs, taken over the course of 25 years, chronicling Jewish lives, often in declining communities, in every corner of the world, from Azerbaijan and Uzbekistan to Ethiopia and Las Vegas. For anyone, Jewish or otherwise, who generally thinks of Jews in terms of Israel and the United States, the book will be a revelation." Publ Wkly

Includes bibliographical references

Brown, Cynthia Stokes

A **big** history; from the Big Bang to the present. Distributed by W.W. Norton 2007 288p il map $25.95 **909**

1. Human ecology 2. World history
ISBN 978-1-59558-196-9; 1-59558-196-0

LC 2007-6741

"In a multidisciplinary narrative subtly emphasizing the mutual impact of people and planet, Brown covers Earth's history from the big bang through the development of life and the growth of civilization. . . . This exciting saga crosses space and time to illustrate how humans, born of stardust, were shaped—and how they in turn shaped the world we know today." Publ Wkly

Cahill, Thomas

The **gifts** of the Jews; how a tribe of desert nomads changed the way everyone thinks and feels. Talese 1998 291p (Hinges of history) $23.50; pa $14 **909**

1. Jews -- History 2. Judaism -- History 3. Bible -- O.T. -- History of Biblical events
ISBN 0-385-48248-5; 0-385-48249-3 pa

LC 97-45139

In this colloquial look at the influence of the Hebrew Bible on civilization, the author gives "the Jews credit for revolutionizing the concepts of democracy, universal law, monotheism, linear time, personal vocation, destiny, self-improvement and the belief in the equality of all humans. He stumbles on the odd aside and occasionally is surprisingly insensitive. . . Still, his passion and breadth of knowledge are admirable." N Y Times Book Rev

Includes bibliographical references

Sailing the wine-dark sea; why the Greeks matter. Talese 2003 304p (Hinges of history) $27.50; pa $14.95 **909**

1. Greece -- Civilization
ISBN 0-385-49553-6; 0-385-49554-4 pa

LC 2003-50725

This author "begins with a discussion of Homer's Iliad and Odyssey and how these two epic poems relate to the history of Greece. He then focuses on such themes as the Greek alphabet, literature, and political system, and its playwrights, philosophers, and artists. A final chapter examines the effects that Greco-Roman and Judeo-Christian traditions had on each other." Booklist

Includes bibliographical references

The **Cambridge** illustrated history of the Islamic world; edited by Francis Robinson. Cambridge Univ. Press 1996 xxiii, 328p map (Cambridge illustrated history) hardcover o.p. pa $36.99 **909**

1. Islamic countries -- History
ISBN 0-521-43510-2; 0-521-66993-6 pa

LC 95-37562

"Facts about Islam's history and practice are presented, along with its economic, societal, and intellectual structures. Excellent graphics support the text. Maps are extensive and exact." SLJ

Includes bibliographical references

Cliff, Nigel

Holy war. Harper 2011 x, 547 p.p col. ill., maps (chiefly col) **909**

1. Muslims 2. Explorers 3. Christians 4. Trade routes 5. World history -- 15th century
ISBN 978-0-06-173512-7

LC 2011021331

This book presents an historical "interpretation of Vasco da Gama's groundbreaking voyages, seen as a turning point in the struggle between Christianity and Islam." It was the author's intent to demonstrate "that both Vasco da Gama and his archrival, Christopher Columbus, set sail with the clear purpose of launching a Crusade whose objective was to reach the Indies; seize control of its markets in spices, silks, and precious gems from Muslim traders; and claim for Portugal or Spain, respectively, all the territories they discovered. Vasco da Gama triumphed in his mission and drew a dividing line between the Muslim and Christian eras of history -- what we in the West call the medieval and the modern ages." (Publisher's note)

Includes bibliographical references and index.

Cole, Juan

The **New** Arabs; How the Wired and Global Youth of the Middle East Is Transforming It. Juan Cole. Simon & Schuster 2014 384 p. (hardback) $26 **909**

1. Arab Spring, 2010- 2. Youth -- Political activity 3. Arab countries -- Politics and government
ISBN 9781451690392; 1451690398

LC 2014005627

This book, by Juan Cole, "illuminates the role of today's Arab youth--who they are, what they want, and how they will affect world politics. Beginning in January 2011, the revolutionary wave of demonstrations and protests, riots, and civil wars that comprised what many call 'the Arab Spring' shook the world. These upheavals were spearheaded by youth movements, and yet the crucial role they played is relatively unknown." (Publisher's note)

"Cole's deep, nuanced exploration of political and social currents underneath the uprisings shines; he shows Westerners who think the Arab world is divided between corrupt despots and Islamist zealots just how strong and pervasive the tendencies towards liberalism and democracy are." Pub Wkly

Includes bibliographical references and index

★ **Cultures** of the Jews; a new history. edited with an introduction by David Biale. Schocken Bks. 2002 xxxiii, 1196p il $45 **909**

1. Jewish civilization 2. Jews -- History
ISBN 0-8052-4131-0

LC 2002-23008

"The book is split into three main sections: 'Ancient Mediterranean Origins,' 'Diversities of Diaspora,' and 'Modern Encounters.' Within this framework, leading scholars such as Isaiah Gafni, Aron Rodrigue, and Stephen Whit-field contribute broad essays examining the development of Jewish culture in different contexts. Interactions between Jewish and non-Jewish cultures form an important subtext for the essays, as scholars outline the latest thinking about gender, language, religion, drama, and literature in Jewish history. The book pays equal attention to the Sephardic and Ashkenazic experiences and finishes with significant essays on American, European, and non-European Jewries." Choice

"The book is truly one of the most important works on the subject ever published." Booklist

Includes bibliographical references

Daily life through world history in primary documents; Lawrence Morris, general editor. Greenwood Press 2009 3v il map $299.95   909
1. Reference books 2. Civilization -- History -- Sources 3. Manners and customs -- History -- Sources
ISBN 978-0-313-33898-4

LC 2008-8925

"Each of the three volumes . . . begins with a chronology of the era covered as well as a clear, concise historical overview that provides readers with core knowledge of the cultures discussed. The more than 530 entries are grouped into seven categories: domestic, economic, intellectual, material, political, recreational, and religious life." Booklist

Includes bibliographical references

Encyclopedia of Islam and the Muslim world; edited by Richard C. Martin. Macmillan Reference USA 2004 2v il map set $295   909
1. Reference books 2. Islam -- Encyclopedias
ISBN 0-02-865603-2

LC 2003-9964

"A solid choice for libraries needing a general treatment of Islam in sufficient detail." Choice

Includes bibliographical references

Encyclopedia of the developing world; Thomas M. Leonard, editor. Routledge 2005 3v set $625   909
1. Reference books 2. Developing countries -- Encyclopedias
ISBN 1-57958-388-1

LC 2005-49976

The entries "detail developments from 1945 forward. In addition to basic statistical and geographical information, country-focused entries detail history, economy, and political situation. Thematic entries cover people (e.g., Jomo Kenyatta), historical topics (e.g., colonialism), economic and government models (e.g., communism), the environment (e.g., water) and organizations (e.g., WTO)." Libr J

Includes bibliographical references

Fargues, Philippe
The **atlas** of the Arab world; [by] Philippe Fargues & Rafic Boustani. Facts on File 1991 144p il maps $55   909
1. Arab countries
ISBN 0-8160-2346-8

LC 89-675447

"A wealth of information presented in colorful maps, graphs, diagrams, and charts. Arranged by broad cultural topics such as ethnic groups and religions, society, cities, oil and industry, facts not readily available in standard resources are presented and compared." SLJ

Includes bibliographical references

Ferguson, Niall
Empire : the rise and demise of the British world order and the lessons for global power. Basic Books 2003 392p il map hardcover o.p. pa $17.95   909
1. Imperialism 2. Commonwealth countries 3. Great Britain -- Colonies 4. Great Britain -- Foreign relations
ISBN 0-465-02329-0 pa

LC 2003-41469

First published 2002 in the United Kingdom

This book "is ambitious, provocative, and entertaining—a rare hat trick in the genre of historical writing—in its meticulous charting of the rise and fall of the world's largest empire. . . . Ferguson makes a subtle, but impressive, argument that free trade, the English language, and superior education helped improve the lot of those under colonial rule." Natl Rev

Includes bibliographical references

Freeman, Charles
★ **Egypt,** Greece, and Rome; civilizations of the ancient Mediterranean. 2nd ed; Oxford Univ. Press 2004 688p $29.95   909
1. Mediterranean civilization
ISBN 0-19-926364-7

LC 2004-41505

First published 1996

Freeman's "introduction to the ancient Mediterranean adds Egypt to the standard Greco-Roman nexus. Covering an immense variety of material with competence and sensitivity to nuance, Freeman relates the familiar parts of the classical story, but his is no mere rehash of the Persian War or the fall of the Roman Republic. He analytically recounts political events, religious movements, and society, with steady awareness of the fragmented character of the surviving evidence." Booklist [review of 1996 edition]

Includes bibliographical references

Galeano, Eduardo H.
Mirrors; stories of almost everyone. [by] Eduardo Galeano; English translation by Mark Fried. Nation Books 2009 391p il $26.95   909
1. History -- Miscellanea
ISBN 978-1-56858-423-2; 1-56858-423-7

LC 2009-004518

This book contains some 600 meditations on events or persons in history.

"Each entry is an avatar of outrage over the depredations of power against its multifarious victims, those rendered helpless by poverty, religion, race, sexual identity or—as in the vignettes about Galileo and Isaac Babel—the simple accident of being right when the truth defined by the prevailing authority was wrong. . . . As in his previous books, [Galeano] succeeds in capturing the bottomless horror of the state's capacity to inflict pain on the individual, offering as effective an act of political dissent as exists anywhere in contemporary literature." N Y Times Book Rev

Great events from history, The 17th century, 1601-1700; editor, Larissa Juliet Taylor. Salem Press 2005 2v il map set $160   **909**
  1. Reference books 2. World history -- 17th century
ISBN 1-58765-225-0; 978-1-58765-225-7
                 LC 2005-17362
Companion volume to Great lives from history, The 17th century, 1601-1700

Some of the essays in this work were originally published in Chronology of European history, 15,000 B.C. to 1997 (1997) and Great events from history: North American series. Rev. ed. (1997)

This set "offers two to three-page essays that detail the major milestones of the century as well as social developments that were reflective of daily life during the period. The perspective here is international and spans a variety of categories, including religion and theology, cultural and intellectual history, expansion and land acquisition, and natural disasters. A list of key figures involved in each event is provided." SLJ

Includes bibliographical references

Great events from history, The Renaissance & early modern era, 1454-1600; editor, Christina J. Moose. Salem Press 2005 2v il map set $160   **909**
  1. Renaissance 2. Reference books 3. World history -- 15th century 4. World history -- 16th century
ISBN 1-58765-214-5; 978-1-58765-214-1
                 LC 2004-28878
Companion volume to Great lives from history, The Renaissance & early modern era, 1454-1600

Some of the essays were previously published in various works

This collection of essays covers events in the scientific, intellectual, literary, sociological, political and military disciplines that happened worldwide during the Renaissance.

Includes bibliographical references

★ A **Historical** atlas of the Jewish people; from the time of the patriarchs to the present. general editor, Eli Barnavi; English edition editor, Miriam Eliav-Feldon; cartography, Michel Opatowski; new edition revised by Denis Charbit. new ed; Schocken Bks. 2002 321p il maps $45   **909**
  1. Jews -- History -- Maps
ISBN 0-8052-4226-0
                 LC 2003-279553
First published 1992 by Knopf

"Covering three millennia of Jewish history and culture through a combination of concise text, accurate and well-drawn maps, and a sumptuous array of photographs, diagrams, and reproductions of paintings, this atlas succeeds in covering all the main themes of the Jewish experience. The material is arranged chronologically and systematically. . . . The result is a reference that will profit both scholars and lay readers." Libr J [review of 1992 edition]

Hourani, Albert Habib
A **history** of the Arab peoples; with a new afterword by Malise Ruthven. 2nd ed; Belknap Press 2002 xx, 565p il maps hardcover o.p. pa $18.95 **909**
  1. Arab civilization 2. Arab countries -- History
ISBN 0-674-01017-5; 0-674-05819-4 pa
                 LC 2003-269357
First published 1991

This history of the Arab peoples is divided into five parts: The making of a world (seventh-tenth century); Arab Muslim societies (eleventh-fifteenth century); The Ottoman age (sixteenth-eighteenth century); The age of European empires (1800-1939); The age of nation-states (since 1939). Includes a 2002 afterword, genealogies and dynasties

Includes bibliographical references

Johnson, Paul
A **history** of the Jews. Harper & Row 1987 644p hardcover o.p. pa $17   **909**
  1. Jews -- History
ISBN 0-06-091533-1 pa
                 LC 85-42575
This narrative attempts to cover the "interplay between Jewish history and Western history, and between the philosophical, ethical, religious, social and political notions of Judaic culture and those of Western culture." Publisher's note

This "is an absorbing, provocative, well-written, often moving book, an insightful and impassioned blend of history and myth, story and interpretation." Christ Sci Monit

Includes bibliographical references

Kennedy, Hugh
★ The **great** Arab conquests; how the spread of Islam changed the world we live in. Da Capo 2007 421p $27.95   **909**
  1. Islamic civilization 2. Islam -- History
ISBN 0-306-81585-0; 978-0-306-81585-0
                 LC 2008-297360
The author "has produced an extremely readable work chronicling the early Arab conquests to 750 CE. In the flowing narrative style for which he has become known, Kennedy brings together Arab, Byzantine, Armenian, Coptic, and Persian histories, legends, and anecdotes related to Arab expansion into the lands stretching from the Iberian Peninsula to the Sind. . . . Each chapter details the conquest of a given region, intertwining historic reality with legendary tales to provide for very colorful reading." Choice

Includes bibliographical references

Kwarteng, Kwasi
Ghosts of empire; Britain's legacies in the modern world. Kwasi Kwarteng. Perseus Books Group 2012 480 p. (hardcover) $29.99   **909**
  1. Colonization 2. Modern history 3. Great Britain -- Colonies 4. Imperialism -- History 5. Decolonization -- History 6. Great Britain -- Colonies -- History
ISBN 1610391209; 9781610391207
                 LC 2011935845
Author Kwasi Kwarteng presents "a narrative history of the British Empire, one that . . . sees the Empire for what it was: a series of local fiefdoms administered in varying degrees of competence or brutality by a cast of characters as

outsized and eccentric as anything conjured by Gilbert and Sullivan. The truth, as Kwarteng reveals, is that there was no such thing as a model for imperial administration . . . The idiosyncracies of viceroys and soldier-diplomats who ran the colonial enterprise continues to impact the world, from Kashmir to Sudan, Baghdad to Hong Kong." (Publisher's note)

Includes bibliographical references (p. [433]-446) and index

Lamb, David

★ The **Arabs**; journeys beyond the mirage. 2nd Vintage Books ed, rev and updated; Vintage Bks. 2002 348p map pa $15   **909**
1. Arab countries
ISBN 1-4000-3041-2

                       LC 2002-524048
First published 1987 by Random House

The author "explores the Arabs' religious, political, and cultural views, noting the differences and key similarities between the many segments of the Arab world. He explains Arab attitudes and actions toward the West, including the growth of terrorism, and situates current events in a larger historical backdrop that goes back more than a thousand years." Publisher's note

"Intelligent and incisive . . . Mr. Lamb has the first-rate reporter's tools, and he uses them to relate, with compelling detail, who the Arabs are." N Y Times Book Rev

Includes bibliographical references

Mann, Charles C.

1493; uncovering the new world Columbus created. Knopf 2011 535p il map $30.50; ebook $14.99   **909**
1. Explorers 2. Modern history 3. Economic conditions 4. Industrial revolution 5. History, Modern 6. Economic history 7. Ecology -- History 8. Commerce -- History 9. Agriculture -- History 10. America -- Exploration 11. America -- Discovery and exploration
ISBN 978-0-307-26572-2; 0-307-26572-2; 978-0-307-59672-7 ebook

                       LC 2011003408
"Mann traces the subtle, epochal influences of the intercontinental 'Columbian Exchange' of flora, fauna, commodities, and peoples, showing how European honeybees and earthworms remade New World landscapes; how New World corn, potatoes, and fertilizer ignited Eurasian population booms; how Old World diseases prompted an eruption of slavery in the Western Hemisphere; . . . how Latin American silver undermined China's Ming Dynasty; and how the decimation of Indian peoples changed the world's climate. . . . Brilliantly assembling colorful details into big-picture insights, Mann's fresh, challenge to Eurocentric histories puts interdependence at the origin of modernity." Publ Wkly

Includes bibliographical references

Morris, Ian

Why the West rules--for now; the patterns of history, and what they reveal about the future. Farrar, Straus and Giroux 2010 750p il map   **909**
1. East and West 2. Modern civilization 3. Western civilization 4. Civilization, Modern 5. Civilization,

Western 6. Comparative civilization
ISBN 0374290024; 9780374290023

                       LC 2010005702
Morris argues that Western dominance is largely "the result of geography on the everyday efforts of ordinary people as they deal with crises of resources, disease, migration, and climate." (Publisher's note) Bibliography. Index.

"It may seem at first sight a little odd to recommend a history book as a guide to the future. But Morris' new book illustrates perfectly why one really scholarly book about the past is worth a hundred fanciful works of futurology." Foreign Affairs

Includes bibliographical references

Pagden, Anthony

★ **Peoples** and empires; a short history of European migration, exploration, and conquest from Greece to the present. Modern library ed; Modern Lib. 2001 xxv, 206p hardcover o.p. pa $10.95 **909**
1. Colonies 2. World history 3. Immigration and emigration
ISBN 0-679-64096-7; 0-8129-6761-5 pa

                       LC 00-66204
This "overview of European empire building and colonization commences with the diffusion of Greek civilization and traces the subsequent evolution of the ensuing Roman, Spanish, French, and British empires. More interesting than how those empires physically expanded is the insightful discussion on what motivated individual men and entire nations to migrate and conquer." Booklist

Includes bibliographical references

Parker, Geoffrey

Global crisis; war, climate change and catastrophe in the seventeenth century. Geoffrey Parker. Yale University Press 2012 871 p. (cloth : alkaline paper) $40   **909**
1. World history -- 17th century 2. Climate change -- History -- 17th century 3. History, Modern -- 17th century 4. Military history -- 17th century 5. Civil war -- History -- 17th century 6. Disasters -- History -- 17th century 7. Revolutions -- History -- 17th century 8. Climatic changes -- Social aspects -- History -- 17th century
ISBN 0300153236; 9780300153231

                       LC 2012039448
This book "presents a history of the 17th century. . . . Focusing on climate-driven unrest around the world, [Geoffrey] Parker illustrates how events such as drought can drive disease, war, and social change. . . . He traces connections between climate and population and war, factors further influencing attitudes toward education and consumption." (Publishers Weekly)

Includes bibliographical references

Roberts, Callum

The **unnatural** history of the sea. Island Press/ Shearwater Books 2007 435p il map $28   **909**
1. Ocean 2. Commercial fishing 3. Human influence on nature
ISBN 978-1-59726-102-9; 1-59726-102-5

                       LC 2007-1841

"Starting with the eighteenth-century voyages of Vitus Bering, Roberts leads the reader through a wealth of maritime history revealing countless examples of overfishing. . . . Thoughtful, inspiring, devastating, and powerful, Roberts' comprehensive, welcoming, and compelling approach to an urgent subject conveys large problems in a succinct and involving manner. Readers won't be able to put it down." Booklist

Includes bibliographical references

Roberts, J. M.

The **new** history of the world; 4th rev ed; Oxford Univ. Press 2003 1232p il map $40 **909**
1. World history
ISBN 0-19-521927-9

LC 2003-270110

First published 1976 in the United Kingdom with title: The Hutchinson history of the world; first published 1976 in the United States in a slightly different form by Knopf with title: History of the world; this edition first published 2002 in the United Kingdom with title: The New Penguin history of the world

This overview of history from prehistoric times to the effects of the September 11, 2001 attacks is divided into eight sections: Before history--beginnings; The first civilizations; The classical Mediterranean; The age of diverging traditions; The making of the European age; The great acceleration; The end of the Europeans' world; The latest age

Rogan, Eugene

The **Arabs**; a history. Basic Books 2009 553p il map **909**
1. Arab civilization 2. Imperialism -- History 3. Arab countries -- History 4. Nationalism -- Arab countries -- History 5. Arab countries -- Politics and government
ISBN 0465071007; 9780465071005

LC 2009-28575

"Eugene Rogan traces five centuries of Arab history, from the Ottoman conquests through the British and French colonial periods and up to the present age." (Publisher's note) Index.

This "is not a particularly happy story, but it is a fascinating one, and exceedingly well told. [Eugene] Rogan manoeuvres with skilful assurance, maintaining a steady pace through time, and keeping the wider horizon in view even as he makes use of a broad range of judiciously chosen primary sources to enrich the narrative." Economist

Includes bibliographical references

Sachar, Howard Morley

A **history** of the Jews in the modern world; [by] Howard M. Sachar. Knopf 2005 831p hardcover o.p. pa $23 **909**
1. Jews -- History
ISBN 0-375-41497-5; 1-4000-3097-8 pa

LC 2004-48814

The author begins "with an account of the European Jews and anti-Semitism they faced as early as the sixteenth century. . . . He goes on to describe such events as their life in western Europe during the seventeenth and eighteenth centuries, the French Revolution and Jewish questions, the Jews of czarist Russia, their struggle for civil rights in the

1830s and 1840s, and their place in what Sachar labels an emancipated economy." Booklist

This book "relates an immensely complex story with precision and learning." N Y Times Book Rev

Includes bibliographical references

Schama, Simon, 1945-

★ The **story** of the Jews; finding the words : 1000 BC-1492 AD. by Simon Schama. HarperCollins 2014 512 p. ill. (chiefly col.), maps $39.99 **909**
1. Jews -- History
ISBN 0060539186; 9780060539184

This book, by Simon Schama, "details the story of the Jewish experience, tracing it across three millennia, from their beginnings as an ancient tribal people to the opening of the New World in 1492. . . . It takes you to . . . a Jewish kingdom in the mountains of southern Arabia; a Syrian synagogue glowing with . . . wall paintings; [and] the palm groves of the Jewish dead in the Roman catacombs." (Publisher's note)

"Schama has written an unconventional but masterful and deeply felt history of his people, which seamlessly integrates themes of art, religion, and ethnicity as he illustrates how Jews both influenced and were influenced by the other people they lived among for more than 1,500 years." Booklist

Includes bibliographical references (pages 431-465) and index

Tinniswood, Adrian

Pirates of Barbary; corsairs, conquests, and captivity in the seventeenth-century Mediterranean. Riverhead Books 2010 xx, 343p il map $26.95 **909**
1. Pirates 2. North Africa -- History 3. Mediterranean region -- History
ISBN 978-1-59448-774-3

LC 2010-23421

Tinniswood "demonstrates an excellent grasp of obscure sources in crafting a comprehensive synthesis. . . . Throughout, the writing is precise and mordant but also witty, allowing the reader to feel empathy for the rough and absurd lives of these long-ago mariners, and agree with the author's conclusion that whatever the corsairs' faults, a lack of courage was not among them." Kirkus

Includes bibliographical references

Treuer, Anton

Everything you wanted to know about Indians but were afraid to ask; Anton Treuer. Borealis Books 2012 190 p. (pbk. : alk. paper) $15.95 **909**
1. Native Americans 2. Indians -- History 3. Indians in popular culture 4. Indians -- Social life and customs
ISBN 0873518616; 0873518624; 9780873518611; 9780873518628

LC 2011053026

In this book Anton Treuer "endeavors to address misconceptions held by non-natives about the American Indian experience in the United States. He accomplishes his task by posing and answering approximately 125 questions divided into ten categories: 'Terminology,' 'History,' 'Religion, Culture & Identity,' 'Powwow,' 'Tribal Languages,' 'Politics,' 'Economics,' 'Education,' 'Perspectives: Coming to Terms and Future Directions,' and 'Finding Ways to Make a Difference.'" (Library Journal)

Includes bibliographical references and index

Watson, Peter, 1943-

★ The **great** divide; nature and human nature in the old world and the new. Peter Watson. Harper 2012 610 p. $31.99 **909**

1. World history 2. America -- History 3. America -- Civilization 4. Eastern hemisphere -- History 5. Eastern hemisphere -- Civilization

ISBN 0061672459; 9780061672453

Introduction: 15000 BC-AD 1500 : a unique period in human history -- How the first Americans differed from Old World peoples -- How nature differs in the Old World and the New -- Why human nature evolved differently in the Old World and the New -- Conclusion: The shaman and shepherd : the great divide -- Appendix 1: The (never-ending) dispute of the New World -- Appendix 2 (available online): From 100,000 kin groups to 190 sovereign states : some patterns in cultural evolution.

This book by Peter Watson "compares the development of humankind in the Old World and the New between 15,000 BC and AD 1500. Watson identifies three major differences between the two worlds -- climate, domesticable mammals, and hallucinogenic plants -- that combined to produce very different trajectories of civilization in the two hemispheres." The author draws on "knowledge in archaeology, anthropology, geology, meteorology, cosmology, and mythology." (Publisher's note)

Includes bibliographical references and index.

Ideas; a history of thought and invention, from fire to Freud. Peter Watson. HarperCollins 2005 xix, 822 p.p $19.99 **909**

1. Civilization -- History 2. Intellectual life -- History

ISBN 0060935642; 006621064X; 9780060935641

LC 2005050255

This book by Peter Watson presents an "overview of the intellectual development of humans from the discovery of fire up to the beginning of the twentieth century." Topics include "the emergence of language . . . the exploration of the physical world with the Atomists, mathematics, astronomy, literature . . . the rise of Christianity, [and] the rise of the Arabs." (Institute of Public Affairs Review)

Includes bibliographical references (p. [747]-804) and indexes

909.07 General historical periods

Andrea, Alfred J.

Encyclopedia of the crusades. Greenwood Press 2003 xxiii, 356p il, maps $75 **909.07**

1. Reference books 2. Crusades -- Encyclopedias 3. Europe -- Church history -- Encyclopedias

ISBN 0-313-31659-7

LC 2003-48544

This encyclopedia includes "more than 200 entries, each one between approximately 10 lines and four pages in length. . . . The introduction gives the entries some historical context and defines the term crusade for the reader. The

entries are in alphabetical order and include cross-references in bold type to other entries in the book. Many entries also include suggested readings, both primary sources and historical studies. At the end of the work, the author has included a chronology of important dates and events, a 'Basic Crusade Library' of further readings in bibliographic essay style, and a general index. . . . This encyclopedia is recommended for high-school, undergraduate, and public libraries." Booklist

Includes bibliographical references

Asbridge, Thomas

★ The **crusades**; the authoritative history of the war for the Holy Land. [by] Thomas Asbridge. Ecco Press 2010 767p il map **909.07**

1. Crusades 2. Medieval civilization 3. Christianity and other religions 4. Religion and civilization 5. Church history -- 600-1500, Middle Ages

ISBN 9780060787288

Asbridge sets out to "uncover what drove Muslims and Christians alike to embrace the ideals of 'jihad' and crusade, and considers how these holy wars reshaped the medieval world and why they continue to influence events today." (Publisher's note) Index.

"Covering the 200-year period of the Crusades in a single volume is a monumental task, but Asbridge . . . handles it well, presenting an evenhanded view of the actions of Christian and Muslim forces and paying particular attention to the larger-than-life figures of Richard the Lionheart and Saladin. In addition to relating the facts of the expeditions, he explores both the motivations of the Crusaders . . . and the reasons that Christians eventually failed to retain any hold on conquered territory." Libr J

Includes bibliographical references

Burns, Thomas S.

A **history** of the Ostrogoths. Indiana Univ. Press 1984 299p il hardcover o.p. pa $19.95 **909.07**

1. Teutonic peoples 2. Medieval civilization

ISBN 0-253-20600-6 pa

LC 83-49286

This "study of the Ostrogoths . . . explores the interaction between Rome and her eastern Germanic neighbors with the focus on the Ostrogothic experience. Traditional literary sources are looked at with a fresh eye, and new archaeological materials are thoroughly explored." Libr J

Includes bibliographical references

★ The **Crusades**; an encyclopedia. Alan V. Murray, editor. ABC-CLIO 2006 4v il map set $385 **909.07**

1. Reference books 2. Crusades -- Encyclopedias

ISBN 1-57607-862-0; 978-1-57607-862-4

LC 2006-19410

This encyclopedia "surveys all aspects of the crusading movement from its origins in the 11th century to its decline in the 16th century." Publisher's note

Includes bibliographical references

Dictionary of the Middle Ages; Joseph R. Strayer, editor in chief. Scribner 1982 12v + index il maps set $1,625 **909.07**
1. Reference books 2. Middle Ages -- Dictionaries
ISBN 0-684-19073-7

LC 82-5904

ALA RUSA Dartmouth Medal honorable mention (1990)
"Authoritative and modern, this interdisciplinary dictionary spans the years from A.D. 500 to 1500, taking cognizance of the Byzantine, Islamic, and Jewish contributions to medieval life as well as the European. . . . The contents are in alphabetical sequence, some articles providing brief definitions or identifications, others offering extensive background and analysis." Ref Sources: a brief guide

Great events from history, The Middle Ages, 477-1453; editor, Brian A. Pavlac; consulting editors, Byron Cannon, . . . [et al.] Salem Press 2005 2v il map set $160 **909.07**
1. Middle Ages 2. Reference books 3. Medieval civilization
ISBN 1-58765-167-X; 978-1-58765-167-0

LC 2004-16640

Companion volume to Great lives from history, The Middle Ages, 477-1453
Some essays were previously published in Great events from history (1972-1980), Chronology of European history: 15,000 B.C. to 1997 (1997), Great events from history: North American series, revised edition (1997), Great events from history: ancient and medieval series (1972), and Great events from history: modern European series (1973)
This set "offers 322 essays, beginning with Confucianism arrives in Japan (fifth or sixth century) and ending with Fall of Constantinople (May 29, 1453)." Booklist
Includes bibliographical references

The **Oxford** illustrated history of the Crusades; edited by Jonathan Riley-Smith. Oxford Univ. Press 1995 436p il maps hardcover o.p. pa $26.50 **909.07**
1. Crusades
ISBN 0-19-820435-3; 0-19-285428-3 pa

LC 94-24229

Scholars explore the complex religious, economic, and military aspects of the Crusades.
Includes bibliographical references

Phillips, Jonathan
Holy warriors; a modern history of the Crusades. Random House 2010 434p il map $30 **909.07**
1. Crusades 2. Middle East -- History 3. Europe -- Church history 4. Church history -- 600-1500, Middle Ages
ISBN 978-1-4000-6580-6; 1-4000-6580-1

LC 2009-33153

The author "superbly condenses the four centuries of the Crusades into a single, easily accessible volume. . . . The narrative weaves a tragic tapestry, beginning with the bloodily successful First Crusade, through the establishment of the Crusader states, to the failure of subsequent Crusades, the victories of the Muslim 'counter-Crusade,' and the con-

tinuing legacy of religious and cultural hatred that permeates the Holy Land. . . . This is an outstanding summary of centuries of religious strife." Publ Wkly
Includes bibliographical references

909.08 Modern history, 1450/1500-

Aaronovitch, David
Voodoo histories; the role of the conspiracy theory in shaping modern history. Riverhead Books 2010 388p il $26.95 **909.08**
1. Conspiracies
ISBN 978-1-59448-895-5

LC 2009-37018

First published 2009 in the United Kingdom
"The book is an evenhanded, lively, and fascinating look not just at the people who believe these theories but also at the people who promote them: the evidence manipulators, the liars, the con artists, and the almost pathetically gullible and uninformed." Booklist
Includes bibliographical references

Garton Ash, Timothy
★ **Free** world; America, Europe, and the surprising future of the West. Random House 2004 286p il map $24.95; pa $14.95 **909.08**
1. World politics -- 1991-
ISBN 1-400-06219-5; 1-400-07646-3 pa

LC 2004-53862

The author "traces the gradual unravelling of the Atlantic alliance back through the destruction of the Twin Towers in 2001, America's 9/11, to the fall of the Berlin Wall on November 9, 1989, Europe's 9/11. He writes with great insight, balance and yet with passion, too." Times Lit Suppl
Includes bibliographical references

Herman, Arthur
The **idea** of decline in Western history. Free Press 1996 521p pa $23.95 **909.08**
1. Historians 2. Philosophers 3. Western civilization
ISBN 0-684-82791-3; 978-1-4165-7633-4 pa; 1-4165-7633-9 pa

LC 96-36285

"Herman recaps the two-century-long tradition of criticism of Western civilization. . . . He covers two historians most closely identified with predicting decline, Oswald Spengler and Arnold Toynbee, and also brings forth less famous prognosticators of the doom of the West. . . . An accessible survey for the serious nonacademic." Booklist
Includes bibliographical references

Jasanoff, Maya
Edge of empire; lives, culture, and conquest in the East, 1750-1850. Knopf 2005 404p il $27.95 **909.08**
1. Collectors and collecting 2. Great Britain -- Colonies
ISBN 1-4000-4167-8

LC 2004-60221

"In graceful prose and with evocative illustrations, Jasanoff scores her points about conquest, collecting, and cultural crossing, offering a thoughtful and highly subtle study." Libr J

Includes bibliographical references

Kennedy, Paul M., 1945-

The **rise** and fall of the great powers; economic change and military conflict from 1500 to 2000. by Paul Kennedy. Vintage Books 1989 xxv, 677 p.p hardcover o.p. pa $17   **909.08**

1. Modern history 2. Balance of power 3. Economic conditions 4. Economic history 5. Military history, Modern 6. Military readiness -- Economic aspects
ISBN 0-679-72019-7 pa; 0679720197 pa

LC 88040123

"Kennedy's great achievement is that he makes us see our current international problems against a background of empires that have gone under because they were unable to sustain the material cost of greatness; and he does so in a universal historical perspective." N Y Rev Books

Bibliography: p. 625-662

Tuchman, Barbara Wertheim

The **march** of folly; from Troy to Vietnam. [by] Barbara W. Tuchman. Knopf 1984 447p il hardcover o.p. pa $16.95   **909.08**

1. Popes 2. Trojan War 3. Reformation 4. Modern history 5. Vietnam War, 1961-1975 6. Great Britain -- Colonies -- America 7. United States -- History -- 1600-1775, Colonial period
ISBN 0-345-30823-9 pa

LC 83-22206

The author analyzes examples of governmental bumbling including the Trojan horse, the U.S. involvement in Vietnam, and the British loss of the American colonies.

Includes bibliographical references

909.7   Specific historical periods since 1700

Great events from history, The 18th century, 1701-1800; editor John Powell. Salem Press 2006 2v il map set $160   **909.7**

1. Reference books 2. World history -- 18th century
ISBN 978-1-58765-279-0; 1-58765-279-X

LC 2006-5406

Companion volume to Great lives from history, The 18th century, 1701-1800

Some essays previously published in Great events from history: North American series (1997) and Chronology of European history (1997)

"Topics include geopolitical events, social and intellectual issues, scientific developments, philosophy, and the arts. The global coverage emphasizes turning points that redirected and shaped history and helped create the modem world. Essays have an average length of 1600 words. Each one begins with a short summary of the topic and includes dates, locales, categories, key figures, text, significance, further reading, see-also references, and cross-referencing to other essays in this set and in the rest of the series. . . . An informative resource." SLJ

Includes bibliographical references

Winik, Jay

The **great** upheaval; America and the birth of the modern world, 1788-1800. Harper 2007 xx, 659p il map $29.95; pa $17.95   **909.7**

1. Modern history 2. Modern civilization 3. United States -- History -- 1783-1809
ISBN 0-06-008313-1; 978-0-06-008313-7; 0-06-008314-X pa; 978-0-06-008314-4 pa

This narrative history of the concluding decade of the eighteenth century focuses primarily on "the new political world being born in the wake of the American and French revolutions." N Y Times (Late NY Ed)

"An outstandingly wide-ranging account of this vital era in world history." Booklist

Includes bibliographical references

909.8   World history--1800-

Getty Images Inc.

History of the world in photographs; [by] Getty Images; Encyclopedia Britannica. Black Dog & Leventhal 2008 559p il $50   **909.8**

1. Modern history -- Pictorial works
ISBN 978-1-57912-583-7; 1-57912-583-2

"Starting with 1850, this collection of facts and 2,000 photographs chronicles the 150 years since Dickens wrote and the Homestead Act drew hardy families to the western US. Organized by decade, the time line text frames pages with images in the middle. Chronological captions (6,000) mark milestones in science, technology, religion, education, politics, history, business, daily life, and the arts. . . . This resource is enhanced by a companion CD-ROM with another 20,000 images." Choice

This "volume would entice just about anyone to learn about history." Libr J

909.81   World history--19th century, 1800-1899

Great events from history, The 19th century, 1801-1900; editor, John Powell. Salem Press 2006 4v il map set $360   **909.81**

1. Reference books 2. World history -- 19th century
ISBN 978-1-58765-297-4; 1-58765-297-8

LC 2006-19789

Companion volume to Great lives from history, The 19th century, 1801-1900

Some of the essays in this work appeared in various other Salem Press sets

"These volumes cover the world's most important events and developments from 1801 through 1900. . . . Essays address important social and cultural developments in daily life: major literary movements, significant developments in art and music, trends in immigration, and progressive social legislation." Publisher's note

Includes bibliographical references

909.82   World history--20th century, 1900-1999

Cold War; the essential reference guide. James R. Arnold and Roberta Wiener, editors. ABC-CLIO 2012 xxxii, 443 p.p (hardcopy : alk. paper) $89.00   **909.82**
1. International relations 2. Cold war -- Encyclopedias 3. World politics -- 1945-1989 -- Encyclopedias
ISBN 1610690036; 1610690044; 9781610690034; 9781610690041

LC 2011028418

This reference book, edited by James R. Arnold and Roberta Wiener, provides "85 signed alphabetical entries, along with 6 essays discussing the causes and consequences of the Cold War, the growth of technology, evolving East-West relations, proxy wars and military aid, and Ronald Regan and the Cold War. . . . The chronology begins in February 1945 with the Yalta Conference . . . and ends with the official dissolution of the Soviet Union, in December 1991." (Booklist)

Includes bibliographical references and index.

The Columbia history of the 20th century; {edited by} Richard W. Bulliet. Columbia Univ. Press 1998 651p $62; pa $29   **909.82**
1. World history -- 20th century
ISBN 0-231-07628-2; 0-231-07629-0 pa

LC 97-39426

Scholars contribute chapters on topics ranging "from 'Ethnicity and Racism,' to 'Nationalism,' 'Communications,' 'Industry and Business,' and others. The idea is for readers to peruse those chapters that appeal to them. Articles average under 25 pages, so content is quite broad. While the level of scholarship varies a bit, overall quality is good." Libr J

Includes bibliographical references

Dallek, Robert
The **lost** peace; leadership in a time of horror and hope, 1945-1953. Harper 2010 420p il $28.99; ebook $22.99   **909.82**
1. Cold war 2. World politics -- 1945- 3. World War, 1939-1945 -- Peace
ISBN 978-0-06-162866-5; 978-0-06-201671-3 ebook

LC 2010-05727

"In a reinterpretation of the postwar years, historian Robert Dallek examines what drove the leaders of the most powerful nations around the globe—Roosevelt, Churchill, Stalin, Mao, de Gaulle, and Truman—to rely on traditional power politics despite the catastrophic violence their nations had endured." Publisher's note

The author's "interpretation of the thinking and actions of American, Chinese, European, and Soviet leaders is worth the book's reasonable price. This is solid historical scholarship from a master." Libr J

Includes bibliographical references

Emmerson, Charles
1913; in search of the world before the great war. Charles Emmerson. PublicAffairs 2013 544 p. (hardcover) $30   **909.82**
1. World history -- 19th century 2. World War, 1914-

1918 -- Causes 3. Nineteen thirteen, A.D
ISBN 1610392566; 9781610392563; 9781610392570

LC 2013935895

In this book, author Charles Emmerson "surveys a selection of cities around the world as they appeared in 1913. Portraying the European capitals of the next year's belligerent countries, Emmerson strikes a cosmopolitan tone by noting social interconnections linking London to Paris to Berlin to Constantinople. Diarists and travelers populate his narratives, their descriptions lending eyewitness immediacy to his delineation of streetscapes, new architecture, and political issues." (Booklist)

"By staying so tightly focused on this single year, Emmerson is able to reveal causal mechanisms while simultaneously making readers wonder what could have been." Pub Wkly

Includes bibliographical references (p. [495]-501) and index

Nineteen-thirteen

Encyclopedia of conflicts since World War II; edited by James Ciment. 2nd ed; M.E. Sharpe 2007 4v set $439   **909.82**
1. Reference books 2. World politics -- 1945- -- Encyclopedias
ISBN 978-0-7656-8005-1; 0-7656-8005-X

LC 2006-14011

First published 1999

"The illustrations are strong and the maps helpful, and the thumbnail biographies and glossary are useful. A valuable resource for most school and public libraries." SLJ

Includes bibliographical references

Encyclopedia of the Cold War; a political, social, and military history. Spencer C. Tucker, editor. ABC-CLIO 2007 5v il map set $495   **909.82**
1. Reference books 2. Cold war -- Encyclopedias 3. World politics -- 1945- -- Encyclopedias
ISBN 978-1-85109-701-2

LC 2007-9681

This is a "five-volume reference on the defining conflict of the second half of the 20th century, covering all aspects of the Cold War as it influenced events around the world." Publisher's note

"The content gives a broad global view of an anxious period and provides useful background for some of today's conflicts." Booklist

Includes bibliographical references

Gilbert, Martin
History of the twentieth century. Morrow 2001 783p maps hardcover o.p. pa $19.95   **909.82**
1. World history -- 20th century
ISBN 0-06-050594-X pa

LC 2001-32612

Condensed version of the three-volume work first published 1997-1999

The author "chronicles world events year by year, from the dawn of aviation to the flourishing technology age, taking us through World War I to the inauguration of Franklin Roosevelt as president of the United States and Hitler as chancellor of Germany. He continues on to document wars in South Africa, China, Ethiopia, Spain, Korea, Vietnam, and Bosnia, as well as apartheid, the arms race, the moon landing, and the beginnings of the computer age, while interspersing the influence of art, literature, music, and religion." Publisher's note

Great events from history: The 20th century, 1901-1940; editor, Robert F. Gorman. Salem Press 2007 6v il map set $495   **909.82**
   1. Reference books 2. World history -- 20th century
   ISBN 978-1-58765-324-7; 1-58765-324-9
                       LC 2007-1930
Some of the essays in this work originally appeared in various Salem Press publications
   This work "identifies key events that helped to shape the course of the history of the world from 1901 to 1940. In more than 1,000 essays, a plethora of topics are presented, including Canada claiming the Arctic Islands (1901); the plague killing 1.2 million in India (1907); Gertrude Ederle swimming the English Channel (1926); Stalin beginning the Purge Trials (1934); and Germany hosting the 1936 Olympics." Booklist
   Includes bibliographical references

Great events from history: The 20th century, 1941-1970; editor, Robert F. Gorman. Salem Press 2008 6v il map set $495   **909.82**
   1. Reference books 2. World history -- 20th century
   ISBN 978-1-58765-331-5; 1-58765-331-1
                     LC 2007-37204
Some of the essays in this work originally appeared in various Salem Press publications
   The articles in this set "cover everything from the bombing of Pearl Harbor to the celebration of the First Earth Day. Each article lists a locale, key figures, categories, and a summary of events; readers can search for additional information based on categories or key figures. The sixth volume contains a bibliography, personage, subject, category, and geographical indexes and a chronological list of entries. . . . An excellent cross-reference tool." Libr J
   Includes bibliographical references

Great events from history: The 20th century, 1971-2000; editor, Robert F. Gorman. Salem Press 2008 6v il map set $495   **909.82**
   1. Reference books 2. World history -- 20th century
   ISBN 978-1-58765-338-4; 1-58765-338-9
                     LC 2007-51351
Some of the essays originally appeared in other Salem Press sets
   This set "provides extended coverage of 1,083 major events between 1971 and 2000." Publisher's note
   Includes bibliographical references

Hillstrom, Kevin
   ★ The **Cold** War; foreward by Christian Ostermann. Omnigraphics 2006 xx, 536p il (Primary sourcebook series) $65   **909.82**
   1. Cold war 2. World politics -- 1945-1991
   ISBN 0-7808-0934-3; 978-0-7808-0934-5
                     LC 2006-15330

"The wide-ranging scope of documents compiled in this volume will provide AP history and social studies classes with a wealth of information for research and analysis." Libr Media Connect
   Includes glossary and bibliographical references

Huntington, Samuel P.
   The **clash** of civilizations and the remaking of world order. Simon & Schuster 1996 367p il maps hardcover o.p. pa $17   **909.82**
   1. World politics -- 1965- 2. Modern civilization -- 1950-
   ISBN 0-684-84441-9 pa
                     LC 96-31492
Huntington posits "a paradigm for post-Cold War international politics in which the principal source of conflict will be cultural divisions among competing civilizations. Prophesying an assault on Western interests, values, and power from a Confucian-Islamic connection, he . . . {enjoins} Western governments to reconcile themselves to new global realities and {offers} recommendations for prescriptive action." Libr J
   "The Huntington argument that the West should stop intervening in civilizational conflicts it doesn't understand makes a powerful claim that internationalists cannot easily ignore." N Y Times Book Rev

Judt, Tony, 1948-2010
   Reappraisals; reflections on the forgotten twentieth century. Penguin Press 2008 448p bibl f $29.95   **909.82**
   1. Modern history 2. World history -- 20th century
   ISBN 978-1-59420-136-3; 1-59420-136-6
                     LC 2007-30297
The author "writes informatively about Manes Sperber, tenderly about Primo Levi, enthusiastically about Hannah Arendt. . . . [Tony Judt is] not only a historian of the first rank but (in a word we need an equivalent for) a politicologue who gives engagement a good name." N Y Times Book Rev
   Includes bibliographical references and index

Junger, Sebastian
   Fire. Norton 2001 224p $24.95   **909.82**
   1. War 2. Disasters 3. Terrorism 4. World politics -- 1991-
   ISBN 0-393-01046-5
                     LC 2001-45236
This is a collection of previously published magazine articles. "Two {pieces} deal with the dangerous work of firefighting . . . in the American West. . . . {Another} chronicles the author's travels with the anti-Taliban forces in northern Afghanistan a year or so ago, and contains a . . . portrait of Gen. Ahmed Shah Massoud, the Northern Alliance's longtime military leader, who was assassinated . . . by agents reportedly linked to Osama bin Laden." N Y Times (Late N Y Ed)
   The stories are "all told with Junger's unfailing eye for detail, which often lends the pieces a disturbing authenticity." Libr J

Knauer, Kelly

TIME History's Greatest Images; the World's 100 Most Influential Photographs. Time Home Entertainment 2012 154 p. $29.95 **909.82**
  1. World history 2. Photojournalism
  ISBN 1603201971; 9781603201971

This book is a compilation of photographs that "TIME" magazine considers the "most significant and influential photos in history." Here are "scientific breakthroughs, political upheavals and social revolutions, from the first photographs of an embryo in a human womb to the indelible images of America's Civil Rights movement. Here are sailors kissing nurses, a single man defying a Chinese tank, firefighters raising the American flag over the ruins of the World Trade Center." (Publisher's note)

Kurlansky, Mark

1968; the year that rocked the world. Ballantine 2004 xx, 441p il $26.95 **909.82**
  1. Insurgency 2. Radicalism 3. World history -- 1945-
  ISBN 0-345-45581-9

LC 2004-299128

This is an account "of the global, social, and political upheaval, warfare, and assassinations that define one year in a tumultuous decade." Booklist
  Includes bibliographical references

Lukacs, John, 1924-

A short history of the twentieth century; by John Lukacs. The Belknap Press of Harvard University Press 2013 220 p. (hardcover) $24.95 **909.82**
  1. World War, 1939-1945 2. World history -- 20th century 3. History, Modern -- 20th century
  ISBN 9780674725362; 0674725360

LC 2013007948

This book, written by historian John Luckacs, offers a concise history of the twentieth century--its two world wars and cold war, its nations and leaders. The great themes woven through this spirited narrative are . . . the fading of liberalism, the rise of populism and nationalism, the achievements and dangers of technology, and the continuing democratization of the globe." (Publisher's note)
  Includes bibliographical references and index.

Milo, Paul

Your flying car awaits; robot butlers, lunar vacations, and other dead-wrong predictions from the twentieth century. Harper 2009 280p pa $14.99 **909.82**
  1. Forecasting 2. Modern civilization
  ISBN 978-0-06-172460-2

LC 2009-19710

"There was a time when people thought future generations would be living in cities topped by geodesic domes, and that all babies would be born in mechanical incubators, probably after having their DNA selected for better intelligence or physical attractiveness. Milo explains why these and dozens of other predictions never came to fruition in a wide-ranging survey that covers everything from atomic energy (which some scientists predicted would never work out) to Puerto Rican statehood." Publ Wkly

"The book is broken into little sections that are quick and concise but never lacking in detail or depth." PopMatters

National Geographic Society (U.S.)

National Geographic eyewitness to the 20th century. National Geographic Soc. 1998 400p il hardcover o.p. pa $22.95 **909.82**
  1. World history -- 20th century
  ISBN 0-7922-8063-6 pa

LC 98-22756

"Chapters are arranged thematically by decade and open with a six-page essay discussing each era. . . . Most useful of all are the double-page spreads for each year presenting events, people, and themes in short paragraph entries. Brief trends and trivia are listed vertically. A time line appears along the bottom of the pages. Photographs bring the discussions to life and sidebars present interesting developments and people." SLJ

The Oxford history of the twentieth century; edited by Michael Howard and Wm. Roger Louis. Oxford Univ. Press 1998 xxii, 458p il hardcover o.p. pa $26.50 **909.82**
  1. World history -- 20th century
  ISBN 978-0-19-280378-8 pa; 0-19-280378-6 pa

LC 98-12861

"Besides global wars hot and cold, population explosion and urbanization impacted the entire century, as one of 27 articles in Twentieth Century underscores. Embracing nonpolitical topics in areas such as physics, modernism in art, and international economics, this work exposes the interested reader to developments that have affected most people." Booklist
  Includes bibliographical references

Reynolds, David

One world divisible; a global history since 1945. Norton 2000 861p il (Global century series) $35; pa $19.95 **909.82**
  1. World history -- 1945-
  ISBN 0-393-04821-7; 0-393-32108-8 pa

LC 99-33903

This world history focuses on the "concept of state-building, within the contexts of the competing trends of globalization and fragmentation. Writing with great economy but without compromising essential insights, Reynolds brings forth the forces at work—as often as not determined or fanatical individuals—in shaping a country's government and foreign policy. Whether assessing Nasser in Egypt, Jinnah in Pakistan, or Mao in China, Reynolds injects the account with fresh explanations of events." Booklist
  Includes bibliographical references

Summits; six meetings that shaped the twentieth century. Basic Books 2007 544p il map $35 **909.82**
  1. Diplomacy 2. World politics 3. World history -- 20th century
  ISBN 978-0-465-06904-0; 0-465-06904-5

The author provides a "retelling of six pivotal meetings of world leaders in an effort to capture the larger and evolving significance of this diplomatic art form. He argues that modern summitry came of age with Chamberlain and Hitler at Munich in 1938 and was carried forward at Yalta in 1945 and into the Cold War with Kennedy and Khrushchev in 1961, Nixon and Brezhnev in 1972, and Reagan and Gorbachev in 1985." Foreign Affairs

"The author's thorough mastery of his subject is reflected in the fluency and assurance of the writing." Publ Wkly

Includes bibliographical references

Schwartz, Richard Alan

The **1990s**; [by] Richard A. Schwartz. Facts on File 2006 496p il (Eyewitness history) $75 **909.82**
1. United States -- History -- 1989- 2. United States -- Politics and government -- 1989-
ISBN 0-8160-5696-X

LC 2004-28884

This book "provides hundreds of firsthand accounts of the 1990s—including diary entries, letters, speeches, and newspaper accounts—that illustrate how historical events appeared to those who lived through them. Each chapter provides an introductory essay and a chronology of events." Publisher's note

Includes bibliographical references

Tuchman, Barbara Wertheim

The **proud** tower; a portrait of the world before the war, 1890-1914. [by] Barbara W. Tuchman. 1st Ballantine Books ed; Ballantine Books 1996 528p il pa $15.95   **909.82**
1. Composers 2. Socialism 3. Anarchism and anarchists 4. Army officers 5. Europe -- Social conditions 6. World history -- 19th century 7. World history -- 20th century 8. United States -- Social conditions
ISBN 0-345-40501-3

LC 96-96511

First published 1966 by Macmillan

The author describes prewar social conditions in the U.S., France, England and Germany.

Includes bibliographical references

909.83   World history--21st century, 2000-2099

Bergen, Peter L.

The **longest** war; the enduring conflict between America and al-Qaeda. Free Press 2011 xx, 473p il map   **909.83**
1. Terrorism 2. Iraq War, 2003-2011 3. Iraq War, 2003- 4. War on terrorism 5. Al Qaeda (Organization) 6. War on Terrorism, 2001- 7. Terrorism -- United States -- Prevention
ISBN 0743278933; 1439160597; 9780743278935; 9781439160596

LC 2010-15268

"Most histories of the war on terror have been written largely from the American perspective, while this book [aims to] fold into the narrative the perspective of al-Qaeda and allied jihadist groups. . . . This book is first a narrative history of the 'war on terror' based upon a synthesis of . . . available open-source materials, together with my own interviewing and reporting. . . . The book also aspires to provide an analytic net assessment of the 'war on terror' to see what conclusions might now be drawn about what al-

Qaeda and its allied groups accomplished in the first decade of the twenty-first century and where the United States and her partners have succeeded and failed." (Author's note) Bibliography. Index.

This is "a broad, almost stereoscopic account that brings an array of sources together into an illuminating synthesis. . . . If you want a solid, readable history of the Long War, this is a great place to start." Washington Monthly

Includes bibliographical references

Khan, Mahvish Rukhsana

My Guantanamo diary; the detainees and the stories they told me. Public Affairs 2008 302p il $25.95   **909.83**
1. Prisoners of war 2. Afghan War, 2001- 3. War on terrorism 4. Guantánamo Bay Naval Base (Cuba)
ISBN 978-1-58648-498-9

LC 2008-274233

This book "provides a valuable account of what we can now recognize as one of the most shameful episodes in the war on terror. It is hard to read this book without a growing sense of embarrassment and indignation." N Y Times Book Rev

Includes bibliographical references

Mueller, Andrew

I wouldn't start from here; the 21st century and where it all went wrong. Soft Skull Press 2009 464p pa $16.95   **909.83**
1. War 2. Modern history 3. World politics 4. Social conflict
ISBN 978-1-59376-218-6

LC 2008-44091

First published 2007 in Australia

"An erstwhile rock critic, Mueller took the leap into battlefield journalism to investigate the ways in which a chaotic and tenacious concept of nationality can infuse a country's individual citizens with the fervor to kill or die in its defense. Having been wounded and imprisoned in pursuit of this underlying truth through 70 of the world's most volatile regimes, Mueller examines the daily lives of both a new breed of revolutionary and an old guard whose rhetoric is steeped in centuries-old traditions. Peppered with trenchant observations that reflect a nimble, cut-to-the-chase practicality, Mueller's interviews with everyone from terrorist warlords to international peacemakers are refreshingly irreverent yet astute." Booklist

Includes bibliographical references

Reuters; our world now. Reuters. 5th ed. Thames & Hudson 2012 352p. col. ill. (pbk.) $24.95 **909.83**
1. Journalism 2. Photojournalism 3. History, Modern -- 21st century -- Pictorial works 4. Civilization, Modern -- 21st century -- Pictorial works
ISBN 0500289867 2012 edition; 9780500289860 2012 edition

LC 2011933209

This fifth volume in the Our World series from news agency Reuters "captures 2011 in over 350 powerful photos covering the full range of news reporting – politics, commerce, conflict, accidents and disasters, the environment, faith and festivities, entertainment, celebrity and lifestyle. . .

. [C]aptions summarize the story behind each image." (Publisher's note)

910   Geography and travel

Allaby, Michael

The **encyclopedia** of Earth; a complete visual guide. [authors, Michael Allaby ... [et al.]] University of California Press 2008 608p il map $39.95 **910**
1. Reference books 2. Earth sciences -- Encyclopedias
ISBN 978-0-520-25471-8; 0-520-25471-6
LC 2008-6956

This "source includes six main sections. 'Birth' is an overview of Earth's history and evolution; 'Fire' covers its inner workings, structure, and landscape; 'Land' covers rocks, minerals, and habitats; 'Air' covers weather; 'Water' includes information on oceans, rivers, and lakes; and 'Humans' is about humankind's relationship with Earth, including management of its resources. . . . This is a stunning, reasonably priced resource, especially useful for those in need of illustrations or a visual representation of a phenomenon or concept." Choice

Fuller, Gary

The **trivia** lover's guide to the world; geography for the lost and found. Gary Fuller. Rowman & Littlefield Publishers, Inc. 2012 270 p. (pbk. : alk. paper) $16.95 **910**
1. Geography -- Miscellanea
ISBN 1442214031; 9781442214033; 9781442214040
LC 2011051863

In this book on geography for general-interest readers, "using a game-show format and trivia questions, [Gary] Fuller goes beyond short answers to expound on a wide variety of geographic topics. . . . The chapters are arranged around particular themes, which include state capitals, the why and where of various cities, and the links between religion and geography." (Booklist)

Points unknown; a century of great exploration. edited by David Roberts. Norton 2000 608p $29.95 **910**
1. Explorers 2. Voyages and travels 3. Adventure and adventurers
ISBN 0-393-05000-9
LC 00-32915

"A mesmerizing display of the pull adventure exerts." Booklist

Thomas, Nicholas

Cook; the extraordinary voyages of Captain James Cook. Walker & Company 2003 xxxvii, 467p il map $28; pa $18.95 **910**
1. Explorers 2. Naval officers 3. Travel writers
ISBN 0-8027-1412-9; 0-8027-7711-2 pa
LC 2003-57648

"Rich, vivid and deeply provocative, Thomas's work combines premiere adventure story with thorough history and intensive sociology." Publ Wkly

Includes bibliographical references

910.2   Geography--Miscellany; world travel guides

Stellin, Susan

How to travel practically anywhere; the ultimate travel guide. Houghton Mifflin Co. 2006 321p pa $15.95 **910.2**
1. Travel
ISBN 978-0-618-60753-2; 0-618-60753-6
LC 2005-22728

This "guide to travel planning that covers the ins and outs (and ups and downs) of do-it-yourself travel. . . . [The author] offers information and advice on topics that traditional travel guides discuss only minimally: solo travel, travel insurance, last-minute planning, government travel advisories, web fares, home-exchange information, and more; she also includes a helpful section on what to do in an emergency—when you need a doctor or have lost your passport. . . . This comprehensive and well-researched guide is useful for both new and seasoned travelers and is highly recommended for all libraries with travel collections." Libr J

Unesco

World heritage sites; a complete guide to 911 UNESCO world heritage sites. Rev. and updated; Firefly Books 2011 856p il map pa $29.95 **910.2**
1. Historic sites 2. Reference books 3. Historic buildings 4. Unesco -- World Heritage Committee
ISBN 978-1-55407-827-1; 1-55407-827-X
LC 2010-671075

First published 2009

Each site has an entry explaining its historical and cultural significance, with a description and location map.

"UNESCO's World Heritage mission is to encourage the identification, protection, and preservation of cultural and natural heritage around the world considered to be of outstanding value to humanity. This treasure trove of a book reinforces that mission and, through spectacular photographs, shows how remarkable and beautiful our planet truly is. An excellent (and affordable) addition to any library." Libr J

910.285   Computer applications

Bray, Hiawatha

You are here; from the compass to GPS, the history and future of how we find ourselves. Hiawatha Bray. Basic Books 2014 272 p. (hardback) $27.99 **910.285**
1. Navigation 2. Global Positioning System 3. Technological innovations -- Social aspects 4. Geospatial data 5. Electronics in navigation -- History 6. Geographic information systems -- History
ISBN 0465032850; 9780465032853
LC 2014002731

This book, by Hiawatha Bray, "examines the rise of our technologically aided era of navigational omniscience--or how we came to know exactly where we are at all times. In a sweeping history of the development of location technology in the past century, Bray shows how . . . humankind ingeniously solved one of its oldest and toughest problems-

-only to herald a new era in which it's impossible to hide."
(Publisher's note)
Includes bibliographical references and index

910.3   Geography--Dictionaries, encyclopedias, concordances, gazetteers

★ The **Columbia** gazetteer of the world; edited by
Saul B. Cohen. 2nd ed.; Columbia University
Press 2008 3v set $595   **910.3**
1. Gazetteers 2. Reference books
ISBN 978-0-231-14554-1

LC 2008-9181

First published 1952 with title: The Columbia Lippincott
gazetteer of the world
"The 170,000-plus entries cover political, physical, and
special places, including monuments and historic sites. . . .
Historically accurate, this title can be considered a reference
standard." Libr J

The **Oxford** companion to world exploration; David Buisseret, editor in chief. Oxford University
Press 2007 2v il map set $250   **910.3**
1. Exploration
ISBN 0-19-514922-X; 978-0-19-514922-7

LC 2006-27968

"The entries are presented in alphabetical order and cover not only individual explorers, but also some geographic
regions, wars, commercial operations, and religious organizations. . . . This work will become the first stop for students
and general readers who seek either basic information or a
starting point for further reading." Sci Books Films
Includes bibliographical references

Waldman, Carl
Encyclopedia of exploration; [by] Carl Waldman
and Alan Wexler. Facts on File 2004 2v il map
(Facts on File library of world history) set $225 **910.3**
1. Explorers 2. Exploration 3. Voyages and travels
ISBN 0-8160-4678-6

LC 2004-10625

"The first volume is all biographical entries with accompanying appendixes that list explorers by occupation, area(s)
explored, chronology, and the respective explorers' nationality. The second volume has topical entries about all things
related to exploration, such as specific areas, technologies,
and routes." Am Ref Books Annu, 2005
Includes bibliographical references

910.4   Accounts of travel and facilities for travelers

Baggett, Jennifer
The **lost** girls; three friends, four continents,
one unconventional detour around the world. [by]
Jennifer Baggett, Holly C. Corbett, Amanda Pressner. HarperCollins 2010 542p map $24.99; ebook
$11.99   **910.4**
1. Backpacking 2. Voyages and travels 3. Women

-- Travel
ISBN 978-0-06-168906-2; 978-0-06-199347-3 ebook

LC 2009-54294

"Friends Pressner, Baggett, and Corbett were all busy
climbing the corporate ladder of Manhattan media when
they realized that, in their late twenties, they weren't sure
they wanted the golden handcuffs of New York success. Re-
prioritizing, they decide on a rebellious, extreme course of
action: quit their jobs, abandon their boyfriends, and take a
yearlong trip around the world. In this group memoir, the
three take turns chronicling a journey from Peru to Kenya to
Vietnam to Australia, and everywhere in between. . . . [The
authors] provide passionate, vivid descriptions of their far-
flung travels, bolstered by thoughtful insights and genuine
intentions, making this an intensely enjoyable read for fans
of travel writing." Publ Wkly

Bathurst, Bella
The **wreckers**; a story of killing seas and plundered shipwrecks, from the eighteenth century to the
present day. Houghton Mifflin 2005 326p il maps
$25   **910.4**
1. Shipwrecks 2. Great Britain -- Local history
ISBN 0-618-41677-3

LC 2005-45951

The author "explains that 'wreckers' were people who
watched for a ship in distress and stole everything on board
of any value, sometimes also drowning the crew and burning
the boats. . . . Bathurst traveled to eight wrecking 'hot spots'
in Britain in researching the history of wrecking over the last
300 years, its heyday occurring in the eighteenth and nineteenth centuries. . . . The result is an exceptional chronicle
of knavery." Booklist
Includes bibliographical references (p. 309-19)

Bellec, Francois
Unknown lands; the log books of the great ex-
plorers. translated by Lisa Davidson and Elizabeth
Ayre. Overlook Press 2002 213p il map $55 **910.4**
1. Explorers 2. Voyages and travels
ISBN 1-58567-201-7

LC 2001-36800

"Weaving together logs, correspondence, and stories
of the 'ordinary and extraordinary men' who explored the
oceans and unknown lands over five centuries, Bellec offers
a . . . snapshot of the cultural and political circumstances
that set the stage for maritime adventures and New World
discoveries. Eyewitness accounts retold alongside maps and
drawings contribute to an enlightening view of the minds,
hearts, and talents of adventurers such as Columbus, Vasco
de Gama, and James Cook. . . . This is simply a stunning
book." Libr J
Includes bibliographical references

Bergreen, Laurence
Over the edge of the world; Magellan's terrifying
circumnavigation of the globe. Morrow 2003 458p
il maps hardcover o.p. pa $15.95   **910.4**
1. Explorers 2. Voyages around the world
ISBN 0-06-621173-5; 0-06-093638-X pa; 978-0-06-
093638-9 pa

LC 2003-50143

The author "tells a well-rounded story of Magellan, not just that of the romanticized hero but also that of the explorer's darker side. . . . Fascinating reading for history buffs, and a great story that rivals any seagoing adventure." Booklist

Includes bibliographical references

Brandt, Anthony

The **man** who ate his boots; the tragic history of the search for the Northwest Passage. Alfred A. Knopf 2010 441p il map $28.95   **910.4**
 1. Explorers 2. Northwest Passage 3. Arctic regions -- Exploration
 ISBN 978-0-307-26392-6; 0-307-26392-4

LC 2009-38835

The author tells the story of the search for the Northwest Passage, from its beginnings early in the age of exploration through its development into a British national obsession to the final sordid, terrible descent into scurvy, starvation, and cannibalism.

"Often witty in his approach, Brandt makes the absurdity of Arctic exploration and the quest for the Northwest Passage entertaining for the general reader. Highly recommended for fans of British or Arctic exploration history." Libr J

Includes bibliographical references

Chaplin, Joyce E.

★ **Round** about the earth; circumnavigation from Magellan to orbit. Joyce E. Chaplin. Simon & Schuster 2012 535 p. (hardcover) $35   **910.4**
 1. Travel -- History 2. Transportation -- History 3. Voyages around the world -- History
 ISBN 1416596194; 9781416596196; 9781416596202; 9781439100066

LC 2012016459

This book, by Joyce E. Chaplin, offers a "full history of . . . circumnavigation. . . . For almost five hundred years, human beings have been finding ways to circle the Earth. . . . The story begins with the first centuries of circumnavigation, when few survived the attempt. . . . Once continental railroads were built, circumnavigators could traverse sea and land. . . . Finally humans took to the skies to circle the globe in airplanes. Not much later, . . . in orbit." (Publisher's note)

Includes bibliographical references and index.

Cordingly, David

Under the black flag; the romance and the reality of life among the pirates. Random House 1996 296p maps hardcover o.p. pa $15   **910.4**
 1. Pirates
 ISBN 0-679-42560-8; 978-0-8129-7722-6 pa; 0-8129-7722-X pa

LC 95-41414

"This succinct history is full of unexpected revelations about the facts and myths of piracy; a typical seventeenth-century Western pirate vessel, for example, was run democratically long before the French Revolution, and one of the most successful pirates of all time was a nineteenth-century Chinese woman who controlled some fifty thousand seagoing outlaws." New Yorker

Includes bibliographical references

Women sailors and sailors' women; an untold maritime history. Random House 2001 286p il hardcover o.p. pa $14.95   **910.4**
 1. Women 2. Voyages and travels 3. Adventure and adventurers
 ISBN 0-375-75872-0 pa

LC 00-62762

A look at "the lives of the intrepid women who went to sea during the great age of sail. Countless females set sail for reasons of adventure, romance, or duty in the seventeenth, eighteenth, and nineteenth centuries. Included among their numbers were the wives or mistresses of ships' officers, prostitutes, female pirates, and women disguised as male sailors. . . . A significant contribution to both women's history and maritime scholarship." Booklist

Includes bibliographical references

Dana, Richard Henry

Two years before the mast; a personal narrative of life at sea. introduction by Gary Kinder; notes by Duncan Hasell. Modern Library 2001 xxiv, 516p il pa $12.95   **910.4**
 1. Seafaring life 2. Voyages and travels
 ISBN 0-375-75794-5

LC 2001-31243

First published anonymously in 1840

The author "shipped out of Boston in 1834 on the Pilgrim and sailed around the Horn to California on a hide-trading expedition. The book is based on the journal he kept during the voyage. Horrified by the brutal captain's mistreatment of the sailors, and shocked by their lack of legal redress, Dana wrote with a burning indignation that did much to rouse the public to the mariners' plight." HarperCollins Reader's Ency of Am Lit. 2d edition

Fagan, Brian

Beyond the blue horizon; how the earliest mariners unlocked the secrets of the oceans. Brian Fagan. New York 2012 313 p. ill., maps $28   **910.4**
 1. Exploration 2. Ocean travels -- History 3. Seafaring life -- History 4. Sea peoples -- History 5. Navigation, Prehistoric 6. Ocean travel -- History
 ISBN 1608190056; 9781608190058

LC 2011045758

In this book, "historian Brian Fagan tackles . . . the enduring quest to master the oceans, the planet's most mysterious terrain. . . . From the moment when ancient Polynesians first dared to sail beyond the horizon, Fagan . . . explains how our mastery of the oceans changed the course of human history. . . . Fagan reveals how seafaring evolved so that the forbidding realms of the sea gods were transformed from barriers into a nexus of commerce and cultural exchange." (Publisher's note)

Includes bibliographical references and index

Garcia Marquez, Gabriel

The **story** of a shipwrecked sailor; translated from the Spanish by Randolph Hogan. Knopf 1986 106p hardcover o.p. pa $11   **910.4**

1. Survival after airplane accidents, shipwrecks, etc.

ISBN 0-679-72205-X pa

LC 85-45673

Original Spanish edition, 1970

"In 1955 Garcia Marquez was working as a reporter in Colombia. One of his stories was a serialized account of a sailor who was swept overboard with seven other crew members of a Colombian destroyer and who was the only one to survive. This book presents Garcia Marquez' version of the sailor's first-person narrative." Booklist

Heat-Moon, William Least

Here, there, elsewhere; stories from the road. William Least Heat-Moon. Little, Brown and Co. 2013 402 p. $29.99   **910.4**

1. Travel

ISBN 0316110248; 9780316110242

LC 2012953180

This book is a collection of short writings from travel writer William Least Heat-Moon. "Culled from 30 years of magazine articles, these pieces roam across terrain both familiar and exotic. Many find magic in mundane patches of America, from improbably delicious fried-fish stands on Minnesota's Lake Superior shore to oddly idyllic Gulf Coast industrial canals and Seattle's rebel micro-breweries." (Publishers Weekly)

Heyerdahl, Thor

Kon -Tiki; across the Pacific by raft. translated by F.H. Lyon. Washington Square Press 1984 240p map (Enriched classics series) pa $5.99   **910.4**

1. Pacific Ocean 2. Ethnology -- Polynesia 3. Kon-Tiki Expedition (1947)

ISBN 0-671-72652-8

LC 84-42785

Original Norwegian edition, 1948

The "story of the six men who crossed the Pacific from Peru to the Polynesians on a primitive balsa-log raft such as Peruvian natives of the fifth century used, to prove that it was possible that the legendary race that came to Easter Island and the Polynesians could have come from Peru." Wis Libr Bull

Hoffman, Carl

The **lunatic** express; discovering the world -- via its most dangerous buses, boats, trains, and planes. Broadway Books 2010 286p map $24.99   **910.4**

1. Transportation 2. Voyages and travels

ISBN 0-7679-2980-2; 978-0-7679-2980-6

LC 2009-21477

Hoffman "manages to be both brave and compassionate as he lurches on his near-interminable journey from his home turf in the Adams Morgan neighborhood of Washington to the Gobi Desert and back again. He learns enough about himself en route to satisfy the travel-writing theorists, true, and this can be a little tedious. But—more important—he learns along the way a great deal about the habits of the world's peripatetic poor, and he writes about both the process and the people with verve and charity, making this book both extraordinary and extraordinarily valuable." Wall Street J

Junger, Sebastian

★ The **perfect** storm; a true story of men against the sea. Norton 1997 226p il map $23.95; pa $14.95   **910.4**

1. Storms 2. Shipwrecks

ISBN 0-393-04016-X; 0-393-33701-4 pa

LC 96-42412

"With waves as high as a hundred feet and winds so strong that anemometers were torn from their moorings, the storm of the title struck unsuspecting mariners off the coast of Nova Scotia in October, 1991. Junger traces the last voyage of the Andrea Gail—a commercial swordfishing boat that was lost, with all six hands, in the storm—and his account is relentlessly suspenseful." New Yorker

Konstam, Angus

The **history** of pirates. Lyons Press 1999 192p il maps hardcover o.p. pa $19.95   **910.4**

1. Pirates

ISBN 1-58574-516-2 pa

The author "chronicles the evolution of piracy from antiquity to the present. . . . Konstam profiles individual pirates, explores infamous vessels, and compares and contrasts various pirate regions and eras. He does a commendable job of separating fact from fiction." Booklist

Literature of travel and exploration; an encyclopedia. Jennifer Speake, editor. Fitzroy Dearborn 2003 3v il map set $495   **910.4**

1. Voyages and travels

ISBN 1-57958-247-8

LC 2003-5352

"Speake's encyclopedia covers from the classical world to the present and contains over 600 entries, international in scope, in alphabetical order, ranging in length from 1,000 to 5,000 words. Most entries are devoted to the history of people and places related to travel, but some treat travel-related topics, such as trains and airplanes. Entries about people include a brief biography." Choice

"This is a rich introduction to primary sources . . . and an excellent source for further research." Booklist

Includes bibliographical references

Lord, Walter

★ A **night** to remember. Holt & Co. 1955 209p il hardcover o.p. pa $14   **910.4**

1. Shipwrecks 2. Titanic (Steamship)

ISBN 0-03-027615-2; 0-8050-7764-2 pa

A detailed account of "the tragic drama of that terrible night—April 4, 1912—when the 'Titanic,' the unsinkable ship, struck an iceberg and went down in the icy waters of the Atlantic." Libr J

Macleod, Alasdair

Explorers; great tales of adventure and endurance. Royal Geographical Society; [written by Alas-

dair Macleod] DK in association with the Smithsonian Institution 2010 360p il $40 **910.4**
1. Explorers 2. Exploration
ISBN 978-0-7566-6737-5

"The book covers the history of exploration from the discovery of the ancient Egyptians in Nubia to the exploration of space by the Soviet Union and the United States in the 20th century. . . . [It] is a wonderful introduction to the various personalities who, over a period of several thousand years, devoted themselves, to studying the world and revealing its fascinatingly diverse landscapes, conditions, and cultures." Sci Books Films

McPhee, John A.
Looking for a ship. Farrar, Straus & Giroux 1990 241p $18.95; pa $15 **910.4**
1. Seafaring life 2. Stella Lykes (Freighter)
ISBN 0-374-19077-1; 0-374-52319-3 pa

LC 90-3311

In this book McPhee focuses on the "plight of the U.S. merchant marine. Accompanying Second Mate Andy Chase on a 42-day run down the west coast of South America aboard the S.S. Stella Lykes, McPhee provides the reader with stories and tales of modern seafaring life and the problems of making a living as a merchant mariner. . . . An engrossing tale of the sea, with excellent detail and humanity." Libr J

Morris, Jan
Contact! a book of encounters. W. W. Norton & Co. 2010 202p $23.95 **910.4**
1. Voyages and travels
ISBN 978-0-393-07640-0

LC 2009-52193

The author "collects vignettes of encounters with and observations of people from her numerous adventures and assignments. Varying from a few sentences to a few paragraphs, each vignette paints a picture or tells a story that brings a personal touch to the narrative of Morris's life and travels. They range from the humorous to the enchanting and tell us as much about Morris as she tells us of people around the world. This is not a typical travelog that one reads essay by essay but something to pick up and put down as time allows. Readers will appreciate the diversity of the people, from the famous to the relatively unremarkable, from six continents." Libr J

Nootebooms hotel./English
Nomad's hotel; travels in time and space. translated from the Dutch by Ann Kelland; [introduction by Alberto Manguel] Houghton Mifflin Harcourt 2009 242p il pa $13.95 **910.4**
1. Voyages and travels
ISBN 978-0-15-603535-4

LC 2008-20813

First published 2006 in the United Kingdom

The author "surrounds his reader with the sounds, sights, and smells of his wanderings in this lyrical collection written over three decades. From the bone-chilling dampness of winter in the Aran Islands and the insistent bells marking time in the labyrinth of Venice to the endless dry and empty lands of Gambia and Mali, whose people struggle to find

their future, Nooteboom weaves a compelling, perceptive, and yet wondering view of the places he visits. . . . Armchair traveling at its best." Libr J

Read, Piers Paul
★ **Alive**; sixteen men, seventy-two days, and insurmountable odds--the classic adventure of survival in the Andes. Harper Perennial 2005 398p il pa $13.95 **910.4**
1. Survival after airplane accidents, shipwrecks, etc. 2. Andes
ISBN 0-06-077866-0

First published 1974 by Lippincott

The author describes the extraordinary hardships endured by the survivors of a horrific plane crash in the Andes.

Sides, Hampton
★ **In** the kingdom of ice; the grand and terrible polar voyage of the U.S.S. Jeannette. Hampton Sides. Doubleday 2014 480 p. illustrations, maps $28.95 **910.4**
1. Arctic regions -- Exploration 2. United States -- Exploring expeditions 3. Jeannette (Steamer) -- History 4. Shipwrecks -- Arctic Ocean -- History -- 19th century
ISBN 0385535376; 9780385535373

LC 2014004367

This book by Hampton Sides recounts how "James Gordon Bennett . . . funded an official U.S. naval expedition to reach the Pole, choosing as its captain a young officer named George Washington De Long, who had gained fame for a rescue operation off the coast of Greenland. . . . De Long led a team of 32 men deep into uncharted Arctic waters. . . . On July 8, 1879, the USS Jeannette set sail from San Francisco to cheering crowds." (Publisher's note)

"Sides . . . tapped amazing archival material, including diaries, letters, and the ship logs, to render a completely thrilling saga of survival in unbelievably harsh conditions." Booklist

Includes bibliographical references

Turner, Steve
The **band** that played on; the extraordinary story of the 8 musicians who went down with the Titanic. Thomas Nelson 2011 259p $24.99 **910.4**
1. Titanic (Steamship) 2. Musicians -- Biography
ISBN 978-1-59555-219-8; 1-59555-219-7

LC 2010-47182

This is the "first book since the great ship went down to examine the lives of the eight musicians who were employed by the Titanic. What these men did – standing calmly on deck playing throughout the disaster – achieved global recognition. But their individual stories, until now, have been largely unknown. What Turner has uncovered is a narrow but unique slice of history – one more chapter of compelling Titanic lore." Christ Sci Monit

Includes bibliographical references

Wheeler, Sara

The **magnetic** north; notes from the Arctic circle. Farrar, Straus and Giroux 2011 315p il map
$26; ebook $12.99   **910.4**
  1. Arctic regions -- Description and travel
  ISBN 9780374200138; 0374200130; 9781429991940
  ebook
                                              LC 2010-14576
  "With wry humor and extensive research, Wheeler captures a swiftly transforming region with which we all have a
symbiotic relationship." N Y Times Book Rev
  Includes bibliographical references (p. [297]-302)
and index.

Williams, Glyndwr

Arctic labyrinth; the quest for the Northwest Passage. [by] Glyn Williams. University of California
Press 2010 439p il map $34.95   **910.4**
  1. Explorers 2. Northwest Passage 3. Arctic regions
  -- Exploration
  ISBN 978-0-5202-6627-8
                                              LC 2009-35546
  First published 2009 in the United Kingdom
  "If you read one book on the history of the mythic Northwest Passage, read this one. . . . Williams deftly weaves together explorers' logbooks and diaries (published and unpublished) with a lifetime of research, and the result is a
masterpiece." Libr J
  Includes bibliographical references

Voyages of delusion; the quest for the Northwest
Passage. Yale Univ. Press 2003 xx, 467p il maps
$29.95   **910.4**
  1. Northwest Passage 2. Arctic regions -- Exploration
  ISBN 0-300-09866-9
                                              LC 2002-109284
  First published 2002 in the United Kingdom
  "Students of maritime exploration and 18th-century
British politics will find this work engrossing, especially the
detailed notes on sources." Publ Wkly

**910.91   Geography of and travel in areas,
regions, places in general**

Wilkinson, Alec

The **ice** balloon; S.A. Andrée and the heroic age
of arctic exploration. by Alec Wilkinson. Alfred A.
Knopf 2011 239 p.   **910.91**
  1. Balloons 2. Explorers -- Sweden 3. Polar regions --
  Exploration 4. Arctic regions -- Exploration 5. Explorers
  -- Sweden -- Biography 6. Balloon ascensions -- Arctic
  regions 7. Polar regions -- Discovery and exploration 8.
  Arctic regions -- Discovery and exploration
  ISBN 9780307594808
                                              LC 2011025434
  This book explores a 1897 voyage, when "Swedish na-
tional S.A. Andrée and a crew of two attempted to fly from
Spitsbergen to the North Pole and back via hydrogen bal-
loon. [Alec] Wilkinson . . . describes this little-known Arctic
expedition and provides details about late 19th-century bal-

looning. After being aloft for nearly 66 hours while traveling
517 miles, the balloon landed 300 miles short of the pole.
Thus Andrée, Nils Strindberg, and Knut Fraenkel began the
hard work of crossing the Arctic to find land. . . . Andrée's
journal abruptly ends with his landing on White Island after
nearly three months of sledging. No one knows exactly how
or when the men died, a fact that lends greater mystery to
this unusual Arctic expedition." (Libr J)
  Includes bibliographical references (p. [237]-239)

911   Historical geography

Atlas of exploration; cartography by Philip's; foreword by John Hemming. Oxford University Press
2008 256p il map $50   **911**
  1. Reference books 2. Exploration -- Atlases
  ISBN 978-0-19-534318-2
                                              LC 2008-626565
  First published 1998 with title: Oxford atlas
of exploration
  "This atlas describes many of the explorations and participants that changed history and enhanced man's knowledge and perception of the world. . . . The volume is a visual delight, festooned with more than 100 specially drawn
maps and 300 b&w and color photographs, period paintings, and illustrations on the various explorations." Libr
Media Connect

Beck, Warren A.

Historical atlas of the American West; by Warren A. Beck and Ynez D. Haase. University of Okla.
Press 1989 xlii, 78p maps hardcover o.p. pa
$24.95   **911**
  1. Reference books 2. Historical atlases 3. West (U.S.)
  -- Historical geography
  ISBN 0-8061-2456-3
                                              LC 88-40540
  "Defining the West as that part of the United States lying
west of the 100th meridian, Beck and Haase provide a cartographic survey of the history of the region. In addition to
maps illustrating such standard themes as natural resources,
exploration and travel routes, the growth of the transportation network, and Indian tribal lands, the authors have included detailed maps on such topics as the Spanish-Mexican
land grants and the Mt. St. Helens's eruption. . . . This atlas
is an essential purchase for most libraries." Libr J

Hayes, Derek

★ **Historical** atlas of the American West; with
original maps. University of California Press 2009
288p il map   **911**
  1. Reference books 2. Historical atlases 3. West (U.S.)
  -- Historical geography 4. Western states -- Historical
  geography -- Maps
  ISBN 9780520256521
                                              LC 20090279536
  "The West, for the purpose of this atlas, is defined as the
Dakotas, Nebraska, Kansas, Oklahoma, Texas, and all states
west of them, including Alaska, but not Hawai'i. More than
600 maps have been carefully selected and beautifully reproduced in full color. They provide the primary-source docu-

mentation for the historical narrative, written for the general reader, tracing the development of the Western United States from its indigenous inhabitants to European exploration, the migration of settlers, and 20th-century events. . . . A high quality publication at an amazingly low price, this atlas is highly recommended for all public and academic libraries, history buffs, and map enthusiasts." Libr J

Includes bibliographical references

Historical atlas of the United States; with original maps. University of California Press 2007 280p il map $45 **911**

1. Atlases 2. Reference books 3. United States -- Historical geography -- Maps

ISBN 978-0-520-25036-9; 0-520-25036-2

LC 2006-42405

"Hayes has produced an excellent visual history of the land that became the US. The work includes 535 maps gathered from a variety of international collections, coupled with more than 60 other illustrations to chronicle the expansion and development of the nation over the last 500 years." Choice

Includes bibliographical references

Hellmann, Paul T.

★ **Historical** gazetteer of the United States. Routledge 2005 865p $150 **911**

1. Reference books 2. United States -- Gazetteers 3. United States -- Local history -- Dictionaries 4. United States -- Historical geography -- Dictionaries

ISBN 0-415-93948-8

LC 2004-11421

This reference provides "historical records of U.S. cities and towns. Arrangement is alphabetical by state, including the District of Columbia. Each state chapter contains a brief description of major cities, date of incorporation into the U.S., the number of counties, and a rough breakdown of how the state categorizes municipalities, towns, townships, and cities. This is followed by alphabetical entries for significant places. Inclusion is determined more by historical importance (national or regional) than by population. All county seats are included. Entries are in paragraph form and typically begin by noting the country and the part of the state in which the place is located as well as its approximate distance from the state's most important city. Events are listed chronologically ." Booklist

Magocsi, Paul R.

Historical atlas of Central Europe; [by] Paul Robert Magocsi. rev and expanded ed; University of Wash. Press 2002 274p maps (History of East Central Europe) hardcover o.p. pa $45 **911**

1. Atlases 2. Reference books 3. Central Europe -- Historical geography -- Maps

ISBN 0-295-98146-6

LC 2001-27907

First published 1993 with title: Historical atlas of East Central Europe

"The volume is arranged chronologically, with coverage beginning about A.D. 400 (roughly the time of the demise of the Roman Empire) and continuing through the end of the 20th century. The maps and tables provide information

on military affairs; population and population movements; economy; ethnolinguistic distributions; and religious, cultural, and educational institutions. All are extremely well done." SLJ

Thubron, Colin

Shadow of the Silk Road. Harper Collins 2007 363p map $25.95 **911**

1. Asia -- Description and travel

ISBN 978-0-06-123172-8; 0-06-123172-X

LC 2006-52142

First published 2006 in the United Kingdom

"An illuminating account of a breathtaking journey." Booklist

912 Graphic representations of surface of earth and of extraterrestrial worlds

Aczel, Amir D.

The **riddle** of the compass; the invention that changed the world. Harcourt 2001 178p il maps hardcover o.p. pa $13 **912**

1. Compass

ISBN 0-15-100506-0; 0-15-600753-3 pa

LC 00-47153

This book tracks "down the roots of the compass and tells the story of navigation through the ages." Publisher's note

Includes bibliographical references

Atlas A-Z. DK 2012 432 p. $11.95 **912**

1. Atlases 2. Geography

ISBN 0756689775; 9780756689773

LC 2012587235

This book is the updated fifth edition of Dorling Kindersley Publishing's pocket atlas. Readers can "[c]arry the world in [their] pocket[s] with this . . . global guide combining maps, facts, and statistics" about world geography. (Publisher's note)

Atlas of Yellowstone; senior editor, W. Andrew Marcus ; cartographic editor, James E. Meacham ; Yellowstone editor, Ann W. Rodman ; production manager, Alethea Y. Steingisser ; consulting editor, Stuart Allan ; text editor, Ross West. University of California Press"||"University of Oregon 2012 1 atlas (xxi, 274 p.)p ill. (some col.), chiefly col. (cloth : alk. paper) $65 **912**

1. Yellowstone National Park -- Atlases 2. Physical geography -- Yellowstone National Park -- Maps

ISBN 0520271556; 9780520271555

LC 2011037533

This book by W. Andrew Marcus presents an atlas of Yellowstone National Park. "Material ranges from broad overviews to specific details. The 524 maps are presented in five sections: 'Geographic Setting' . . . 'Human Geography' . . . 'Physical Geography' . . . 'Wildlife' . . . and 'Reference Maps.' . . . The atlas also includes 50 color illustrations and more than 260 line illustrations." (Library Journal)

Includes bibliographical references (p. 262-267) and index

Lavin, Stephen J.

Atlas of the great plains; Stephen J. Lavin, Fred M. Shelley, and J. Clark Archer; foreword by David J. Wishart; introduction by John C. Hudson. University of Nebraska Press 2011 335p il $39.95 **912**
1. Atlases 2. Reference books 3. Great Plains -- History -- Maps
ISBN 978-0-8032-1536-8

Lester, Toby

The **fourth** part of the world; the race to the ends of the Earth, and the epic story of the map that gave America its name. Free Press 2009 462p il map $30 **912**
1. Map drawing 2. World maps 3. Cartographers 4. America -- Maps 5. Cartography -- History 6. Voyages and travels -- History 7. Discoveries in geography -- History
ISBN 1416535314; 9781416535317

LC 2009-1230

This "chronicle of the early 16th-century creation of the Waldseemüller map offers insight into how monks, classicists, merchants and other contributors from earlier periods shaped the map's creation and subsequently informed modern worldviews." (Publisher's note)

The book is "history of the centuries-long European fascination with depicting the world in two dimensions." (Reviews in American History).

"In 2003, the Library of Congress paid $10 million for a 1507 map of the world that first used the name 'America' for lands in the New World. It was touted as America's birth certificate. Lester . . . traces the fascinating background to the creation of this map, as Europeans tried to assimilate the discoveries of Columbus, Vespucci, and other explorers into their worldview. . . . Lester provides an engrossing adventure for both general and informed lay readers." Libr J

Includes bibliographical references

★/ **National** Geographic atlas of the world; 9th ed.; National Geographic Society 2010 153p il $175 **912**
1. Atlases 2. Reference books
ISBN 978-1-4262-0634-4
First published 1963

"The National Geographic Society presents more than 80 large-format color maps grouped by continent portraying the world with detailed, digitally painted terrain modeling. Each continent is introduced by satellite, political, and physical maps. Political maps for regions and specific countries follow." Libr J

★ **National** Geographic visual atlas of the world. National Geographic Society 2009 416p il map $100 **912**
1. Atlases 2. Reference books
ISBN 978-1-4262-0332-9

LC 2008-627044

This atlas "has the usual atlas features but emphasizes the more than 850 UNESCO World Heritage Sites. . . . Double-page spreads of regional maps are framed with four to six color photographs of the heritage sites that are indicated on the map. . . . Beautiful color photography and clear topi-

cal material combined with detailed maps of areas not covered as well in other world atlases make the Visual Atlas a recommended purchase. This is a first choice for any library needing a new medium-priced atlas." Booklist

Includes bibliographical references

The **new** atlas of the Arab world. American University in Cairo Press 2010 144p il map $39.50 **912**
1. Atlases 2. Reference books 3. Arab countries -- Maps
ISBN 978-977-416-419-4

This atlas contains maps of the Arab world "showing physical features, political boundaries, towns, and communication networks. In addition, each of the twenty-two countries is the subject of an illustrated essay, with notes and . . . statistics on the geography, population, history and politics, and economy of the country. The countries covered are: Algeria, Bahrain, Comoros, Djibouti, Egypt, Iraq, Jordan, Kuwait, Lebanon, Libya, Mauritania, Morocco, Oman, Palestine, Qatar, Saudi Arabia, Somalia, Sudan, Syria, Tunisia, United Arab Emirates, Yemen." Publisher's note

★ **Oxford** Atlas of the world; [cartography by Philip's] 19th ed. Oxford University Press 2012 448 p. il map (hardcover) $89.95 **912**
1. Atlases 2. Earth -- Maps 3. Physical geography 4. Reference books
ISBN 0199937826; 9780199937820

LC 20100594813

First published 1992. Frequently revised. Variant title: Atlas of the world

This world atlas offers "new census information, dozens of city maps . . . satellite images of Earth, and a geographical glossary." It " provides details on such topics as climate, the greenhouse effect, employment and industry, standards of living, agriculture, population and migration, and global conflicts." (Publisher's note)

"...[U]pdated annually, this large-format resource continues to earn pride of place on the atlas case's top shelf for its combination of currency and eye-widening graphics. The physical, political, and country and regional maps that make up the volume's core are works of art-brilliantly designed for easy comprehension, rendered in bright colors and sharp detail... Atlases are among the quickest reference sources to age, so for classroom or library collections in which students search in vain...this makes a first-rate replacement." SLJ

Oxford new concise world atlas; [cartography by Philip's ; text, Keith Lye]. 3rd ed; Oxford University Press 2010 1 atlas (224 p.) col. ill., col. maps $39.95 **912**
1. Atlases 2. Reference books
ISBN 0195393295; 9780195393293

LC 2009292676

Containing over 100 pages of the most up-to-date topographic and political maps, the New Concise World Atlas also features a unique overview of the planet's human and natural processes in photographs, accessible text, and thematic maps. (Publisher's note)

"This update of the 2006 edition contains 128 pages of full-color, computer-generated maps by Philip's, a division of Octopus Publishing, with detailed and dramatic terrain modeling... This condensed and abridged version of the premium Oxford Atlas of the World offers all libraries outstanding value in an up-to-date, medium-sized atlas for an amazingly low price.—" LJ

Includes index.

Rand McNally Goodes World Atlas; edited by Howard Veregin. Rand McNally 2009 400 p. $45   **912**
1. Maps 2. Atlases
ISBN 0528877542; 9780528877544
This book, edited by Howard Veregin, "features over 250 pages of maps, from definitive physical and political maps to important thematic maps that illustrate the spatial aspects of many important topics. [It] includes 160 pages of new, digitally produced reference maps, as well as new thematic maps on global climate change, sea level rise, CO2 emissions, polar ice fluctuations, deforestation, extreme weather events, infectious diseases, water resources, and energy production." (Publisher's note)

Times comprehensive atlas of the world; 12th ed.; Times Books 2008 various paging il map $285   **912**
1. Atlases 2. Reference books
ISBN 978-0-06-146450-8
First published 1967. Periodically revised
"The classic atlas. Very detailed with listings for most geographic and urban locations. Index gives longitude and latitude as well as map reference. Contains . . . [125] plates and . . . [an] index-gazetteer." Ref Sources for Small & Medium-sized Libr. 6th edition
Includes glossary

913   Geography of and travel in ancient world

Grant, Michael, 1954-
A **guide** to the ancient world; a dictionary of classical place names. Wilson, H.W. 1986 728p maps $105   **913**
1. Reference books 2. Classical dictionaries 3. Mediterranean region -- Gazetteers
ISBN 0-8242-0742-4
LC 86-15785
"This dictionary provides background for about nine hundred places important to an understanding of the cultures of the ancient Greeks, Etruscans, and Romans. . . . The time period covered is from the first millennium B.C. until the fall of the Roman empire in the fifth century A.D. Depending on the subject, a typical entry includes information about history, geography, archaeology, and sometimes art and mythology." Am Ref Books Annu, 1987

914   Geography of and travel in Europe

Baxter, John
The **most** beautiful walk in the world; a pedestrian in Paris. Harper Perennial 2011 298p il pa $14.99   **914**
1. Walking 2. Paris (France) -- Description and travel
ISBN 978-0-06-199854-6; 0-06-199854-0
LC 2010-46259
The author "knows Paris, both the modern, cosmopolitan city of today as well as the 1920s cultural mecca of expat American authors like Ernest Hemingway and F. Scott Fitzgerald. Baxter, in fact, lives in the same Paris building that once was a Jazz Age hangout for literary greats like James Joyce, Ezra Pound, Hemingway, and others. It's also the site of Sylvia Beach's famous bookstore, Shakespeare and Company. . . . [He] takes us on a tour of the city's outdoor cafes, amazing restaurants, cabarets, and gorgeous architecture; he tells us about its history and its unique passion for art. Baxter gives us a Paris that is not just a place but an idea." Boston Globe

Boswell, James
The **journal** of a tour to the Hebrides with Samuel Johnson. Kessinger Publishing 2004 277p pa $28.95   **914**
1. Lexicographers 2. Literary critics 3. Hebrides (Scotland) -- Description
ISBN 978-1-4191-6794-2; 1-4191-6794-4
First published 1785
The renowned biographer here recounts the daily events of a tour which he took in 1773 with Johnson

Bryson, Bill
Notes from a small island. Morrow 1996 324p hardcover o.p. pa $14   **914**
1. Great Britain -- Civilization 2. Great Britain -- Description and travel
ISBN 0-380-72750-1 pa
LC 95-43437
"Before his return to the U.S. after a 20-year residence in England, journalist Bryson . . . embarked on a farewell tour of his adopted homeland. His trenchant, witty and detailed observations of life in a variety of towns and villages will delight Anglophiles." Publ Wkly

Caro, Ina
Paris to the past; traveling through French history by train. W.W. Norton & Co. 2011 381p map $27.95   **914**
1. Historic sites 2. Railroads -- France 3. France -- Description and travel 4. Paris (France) -- Description and travel
ISBN 978-0-393-07894-7; 0-393-07894-9
LC 2011-03060
"One single Paris Metro line can take you through a dazzling panoply of history: the Chateau de Vincennes, Charles V's 14th-century fortress; Francis I's Hotel de Ville; the Place de la Concorde, constructed by Louis V in the mid-18th century; the Palais-Royal, fashioned by Philippe Egalite in the late 18th century; and the 21st-century neighborhood of La Defense. Take another Metro line, Caro dis-

covered gleefully, and you can descend to the period of the Romans, on the Ile-de-la-Cite, then arrive glamorously in the 19th century, at the Opera Garnier. Moreover, you can manage day trips to sites as far away as Tours (90 minutes by TGV) in one day, returning to Paris. In this cheerful, logical, easy-to-follow narrative (which includes favorite restaurants and hotels), Caro builds on previous trips to France and presents her timeline through history chronologically, from the 12th-century Basilica of Saint-Denis, where nearly all of the French kings and queen are buried, to the Gare d'Orsay, now fabulously converted into a museum of 19th-century art." Kirkus

Includes bibliographical references

Kerkeling, Hape

I'm off then; my journey along the Camino de Santiago. translated from the German by Shelley Frisch. Free Press 2009 333p il pa $15   **914**
1. Spain -- Description and travel
ISBN 978-1-416-55387-8; 1-416-55387-8
                      LC 2008-51464

Original German edition, 2006

"Hape Kerkeling, a popular TV talk-show host and cabaret star in his native Germany, cuts loose from the comforts of Düsseldorf and sets off on a hike across the Pyrenees to the grave of St. James at the Cathedral of Santiago de Compostela. Searching for spiritual meaning, this self-described 'couch potato' follows a 1,000-year-old pilgrimage route that lures 100,000 trekkers each year, experiencing almost insufferable heat and physical agony in the process. . . . He skips some of the hardest stretches to hitch rides with local farmers or hop aboard trains, and he avoids fetid pilgrims' hostels whenever possible in favor of the best hotel in town (often not much better). Despite such tactics, this gregarious traveler soon gets into the spirit of things, and his encounters with fellow pilgrims, including a Peruvian shaman with a creepy fondness for 'Mein Kampf,' can be both funny and moving." N Y Times Book Rev

Macfarlane, Robert, 1976-

The **wild** places. Penguin Books 2008 340p map pa $15   **914**
1. Wilderness areas 2. Ireland -- Description and travel
3. Great Britain -- Description and travel
ISBN 978-0-14-311393-5; 0-14-311393-3
                      LC 2008-17162

First published 2007 in the United Kingdom

The author describes his experiences as he "spent a year wandering through remote regions of Britain and Ireland seeking out whatever wild places remain before they vanish." Libr J

"Evocative and well-written, a delight for nature and travel buffs." Kirkus

Includes bibliographical references

Mayes, Frances

A **year** in the world; journeys of a passionate traveller. Broadway Books 2006 xx, 420p map hardcover o.p. pa $15   **914**
1. Europe -- Description and travel
ISBN 0-7679-1005-2; 978-0-7679-1005-7; 978-0-

7679-1006-4 pa; 0-7679-1006-0 pa
                      LC 2005-50831

The trips described in this book "are arranged in calendar order, beginning with a January visit to Andalucia and concluding with a year-end trip to Mantova, Italy. In the months between, Mayes takes a sweltering trip to Greece, reunites with friends in Scotland, and journeys to Fez, Naples, Sicily, Burgundy, Portugal, and more." Libr J

"Befitting her gifts as a poet, Mayes' prose shines with evocative imagery, bringing life to every subject she encounters across her peripatetic year." Booklist

Includes bibliographical references

McGregor, James H. S.

Paris from the ground up. Belknap Press of Harvard University Press 2009 327p il map $29.95 **914**
1. Paris (France) -- History 2. Paris (France) -- Description and travel
ISBN 978-0-674-03316-0; 0-674-03316-7
                      LC 2008-43696

"Readers can use this as a well-researched but accessible history of Paris, tracing the story of the City of Light from its earliest residents, the Gauls and the Parisii, to the present day. Travelers will use chapters on churches, cathedrals, museums, and neighborhoods; those interested in the history of a particular area or landmark will find the index excellent. The many illustrations enhance the text, and the ten historical and contemporary maps help pinpoint attractions both ancient and modern." Libr J

Includes bibliographical references

Starr, William W.

Whisky, kilts, and the Loch Ness Monster; traveling through Scotland with Boswell and Johnson. University of South Carolina Press 2011 223p map $29.95   **914**
1. Authors 2. Lawyers 3. Biographers 4. Lexicographers 5. Literary critics 6. Scotland -- Description and travel
ISBN 978-1-57003-948-5
                      LC 2010020165

The author "is a Samuel Johnson and James Boswell fanatic. He here relates meeting Scots along his travels who drew a blank when asked about Johnson and Boswell, despite the men's whirlwind journey through Scotland in 1773. . . . Starr traces their trek in reverse via car, using their own words as guides and inspiration as he tours the great Scottish sites (and partakes in the great Scottish beverage). . . . Scottish history and travel buffs and Johnson and Boswell enthusiasts will find this fun and inspiring." Libr J

Includes bibliographical references

914.2 England -- geography

Macfarlane, Robert, 1976-

The **old** ways; a journey on foot. Robert Macfarlane. Viking 2012 432 p.   **914.2**
1. Trails 2. Walking 3. Landscapes 4. Natural history 5. Voyages and travels 6. England -- Description and

travel 7. Scotland -- Description and travel
ISBN 9780670025114

LC 2012005887

Includes bibliographical references and index

914.4 France -- geography

Wells, Patricia

The **Food** Lover's Guide to Paris; The Best Restaurants, Bistros, Cafés, Markets, Bakeries, and More. by Patricia Wells ; with Emily Buchanan ; assisted by Susan Herrmann Loomis ; photographs by Gianluca Tamorri. Workman Pub Co 2014 454 p. illustrations $16.95 **914.4**
1. Restaurants 2. French cooking 3. Paris (France) -- Description and travel
ISBN 0761173382; 9780761173380

LC 2014003074

This book, by Patricia Wells, "offers an elegantly written go-to guide to the very best restaurants, cafés, wine bars, and bistros in Paris, as well as where to find the flakiest croissants, earthiest charcuteries, sublimest cheese, most ethereal macarons, and impeccable outdoor markets. . . . Included are 40 recipes from some of her favorite chefs and purveyors and . . .all the practical information: addresses, websites, email, hours, closest métro stop, specialties, and more." (Publisher's note)

"The short and to the point but completely enticing entries are sprinkled with the author's experiences and preferences." LJ

Includes bibliographical references (pages 427-436) and index

914.7 Russia -- geography

Eichar, Donnie

Dead Mountain; the true story of the Dyatlov Pass incident. by Donnie Eichar. Chronicle Books 2013 288 p. illustrations, map (hardback) $24.95 **914.7**
1. Mountaineering 2. Mysterious deaths 3. Hiking -- Russia (Federation) -- Ural Mountains Region 4. Ural Mountains Region (Russia) -- History -- 20th century 5. Mountaineering accidents -- Russia (Federation) -- Ural Mountains Region -- 20th century
ISBN 1452112746; 9781452112749

LC 2013014843

This book, by Donnie Eichar, focuses on how "in February 1959, a group of nine experienced hikers in the Russian Ural Mountains died mysteriously on an elevation known as Dead Mountain. Eerie aspects of the incident--unexplained violent injuries, signs that they cut open and fled the tent without proper clothing or shoes, a strange final photograph taken by one of the hikers, and elevated levels of radiation found on some of their clothes--have led to decades of speculation over what really happened." (Publisher's note)

"Eichar marries the short story of the students' lives with the procedural tale of the official investigation and then integrates his own amateur investigation. . . . [A] well-told and accurate whodunit." Kirkus

915 Geography of and travel in Asia

Belliveau, Denis

In the footsteps of Marco Polo; [by] Denis Belliveau and Francis O'Donnell. Rowman & Littlefield Publishers 2008 280p il map $29.95 **915**
1. Travelers 2. Travel writers 3. Asia -- Description and travel
ISBN 978-0-7425-5683-6; 0-7425-5683-2

LC 2008-23411

"The stunning photographs in this elegant book should please even the most casual reader, while the authors' unpretentious observations will satisfy those who want to know more about a still alien world. A travel/adventure book rather than a study of Marco Polo the man or a history of his travels, this volume deserves many readers. Warmly recommended." Libr J

Includes bibliographical references

Elliot, Jason

Mirrors of the unseen; journeys in Iran. St. Martin's Press 2006 415p il $26.95 **915**
1. Iran -- Description and travel
ISBN 978-0-312-30191-0; 0-312-30191-X

LC 2006-42918

The author discusses his travels in Iran.

"With Iran so central in the news, this is a good read for the armchair traveler and amateur geopolitical strategist alike." Publ Wkly

Feiler, Bruce S.

Walking the Bible; a journey by land through the five books of Moses. by Bruce Feiler. Morrow 2001 451p $26; pa $14.95 **915**
1. Middle East -- Description 2. Bible -- O.T. -- Pentateuch -- Geography
ISBN 0-380-97775-3; 0-380-80731-9 pa

LC 00-56076

"Determined to connect more deeply with his religious roots, Feiler joined an archaeologist in a trek through the Middle East, visiting the sites mentioned in the Pentateuch, the first five books of the Hebrew Bible. A book full of wonder and awe and personal enlightenment." Booklist

Includes bibliographical references

Gargan, Edward A.

A river's tale; a year on the Mekong. Knopf 2002 332p il maps hardcover o.p. pa $14.95 **915**
1. Southeast Asia -- Description and travel
ISBN 0-375-70559-7 pa

LC 2001-38056

"A chronicle of a year-long journey along the nearly 3,000 miles of the Mekong River as it descends from the Tibetan plateau through southern Asia, Gargan's book is a vivid look at the disparate peoples [that] settled the length of the river's path." Publ Wkly

Includes bibliographical references

Grange, Kevin

Beneath blossom rain; discovering Bhutan on the toughest trek in the world. University of Ne-

braska Press 2011 336p il map (Outdoor lives) pa
$19.95   **915**
　　1. Mountaineering 2. Bhutan -- Description and travel
　　ISBN 978-0-8032-3433-8; 0-8032-3433-3
　　　　　　　　　　　　　　　　　LC 2010-28970
　　"For the armchair traveler, Grange does a fine job of
showing readers the nature, history, and landscape of Bhu-
tan, as well as taking us to remote villages and monasteries.
. . He is equally open about what is essentially a personal
search for meaning." Seattle Post-Intelligencer
　　Includes bibliographical references.

Horwitz, Tony
　　Baghdad without a map, and other misadventures
in Arabia. Dutton 1991 276p map hardcover o.p.
pa $16   **915**
　　1. Middle East -- Description and travel
　　ISBN 0-452-26745-5 pa
　　　　　　　　　　　　　　　　　LC 90-46653
　　"Horwitz mixes insight and humor in these observations
that illustrate on an everyday level both the contradictions
and the idiosyncrasies of the Arab world." Booklist

Jubber, Nicholas
　　Drinking arak off an ayatollah's beard; a journey
through the inside-out worlds of Iran and Afghanistan.
Da Capo Press 2010 327p il map pa $15.95   **915**
　　1. Shahnameh (Epic poem) 2. Iran -- Social conditions
　　3. Iran -- Description and travel 4. Afghanistan -- Social
　　conditions 5. Afghanistan -- Description and travel
　　ISBN 978-0-306-81884-4
　　　　　　　　　　　　　　　　　LC 2009-48191
　　"Jubber's account offers a full and satisfying panorama
of the region with its rich paradoxes and complexities in-
tact." Publ Wkly
　　Includes bibliographical references

MacLean, Rory
　　Magic bus; on the hippie trail from Istanbul to
India. Ig Pub. 2009 280p pa $14.95   **915**
　　1. Hippies 2. India -- Description and travel 3.
　　Middle East -- Description and travel 4. Central Asia
　　-- Description and travel
　　ISBN 978-0-9788431-9-9; 0-9788431-9-3
　　　　　　　　　　　　　　　　　LC 2008-45918
　　First published 2006 in the United Kingdom
　　"For a certain breed of independent travelers in the
1960s and '70s, Asia was the Promised Land. For nearly 20
years during those iconic decades, flower children, beat phi-
losophers, and Western wanderers took to the road for the
roughly 6,000-mile journey from Turkey to India. Hundreds
of thousands may have made the trek, though no one has an
exact count. For years after, the trip was nearly impossible to
make through this war-torn area — especially for Westerners. So after parts of the trail reopened in 2002, UK-based
Canadian travel writer Rory MacLean set his sights east. . .
. He recounts his eight-month journey along this epic route.
The book strings together a series of vignettes from his trip
that en masse form a well-rounded and insightful look into
the region." Boston Globe

Matthiessen, Peter
　　The **snow** leopard. Viking 1978 338p hard-
cover o.p. pa $15   **915**
　　1. Zen Buddhism 2. Himalaya Mountains -- Description
　　3. Natural history -- Himalaya Mountains
　　ISBN 0-14-025508-7 pa
　　　　　　　　　　　　　　　　　LC 78-5
　　Companion volume Nine-headed dragon river (1986)
　　This book "is based on the journal Matthiessen kept during his trek with the field biologist George Schaller to the
Crystal Mountain, in upper Nepal, in 1973. The trek took
them 250 miles to the Land of Dolpo, on the Tibetan plateau.
. . . . The purpose: to observe the November rut of the Himalayan blue sheep in order to determine whether this little-
known species is related to the extinct common ancestor of
the goat and the sheep." Saturday Rev
　　Includes bibliographical references

Morris-Suzuki, Tessa
　　To the Diamond Mountains; a hundred-year jour-
ney through China and Korea. Rowman & Littlefield
Publishers 2010 201p il map $34.95   **915**
　　1. Artists 2. Authors 3. Adventurers 4. China --
　　Description and travel 5. China -- Social life and
　　customs 6. Korea (North) -- Description and travel
　　7. Korea (South) -- Description and travel 8. Korea
　　(North) -- Social life and customs 9. Korea (South) --
　　Social life and customs
　　ISBN 978-1-4422-0503-1; 978-1-4422-0505-5 ebook
　　　　　　　　　　　　　　　　　LC 2010023685
　　"Morris-Suzuki, an Australian professor, recently traveled through northeast China and the two Koreas; she was
retracing the route of Emily Kemp, an extraordinary writer,
artist, and intrepid adventurer who wrote about her experiences a century ago. Morris-Suzuki, like her predecessor, is a keen observer and a fine writer; she has combined
the disciplines of history and travel writing in an absorbing analysis of the past, present, and future of this volatile
region." Booklist
　　Includes bibliographical references

Rose, Daniel Asa
　　Larry's kidney; being the true story of how I
found myself in China with my black sheep cousin
and his mail-order bride, skirting the law to get him
a transplant and save his life. William Morrow 2009
305p $25.99   **915**
　　1. Kidneys 2. Transplantation of organs, tissues, etc. 3.
　　China -- Description and travel
　　ISBN 978-0-06-170870-1
　　　　　　　　　　　　　　　　　LC 2009-517312
　　"A satisfying, hysterical page-turner, this will captivate
fans of travel writing and family narratives, with special interest for anyone who's helped a love one through serious
illness." Publ Wkly

Theroux, Paul, 1941-
　　The **great** railway bazaar; by train through Asia.
Houghton Mifflin 1975 342p hardcover o.p. pa
$14.95   **915**
　　1. Railroads -- Asia 2. Asia -- Description and travel
　　ISBN 0-618-65894-7 pa

The author "took a four-month solitary lecture tour of Asia in 1973, traveling by train wherever possible. His route was through Turkey, Iran, India, Southeast Asia, Japan, and back to London via the Soviet Union. He writes of conversations and impressions of the people encountered." Libr J

Riding the iron rooster; by train through China. Paul Theroux. 1st Mariner Books ed.; Houghton Mifflin 2006 480p map pa $7.50 **915**
1. Railroads 2. China -- Description and travel
ISBN 978-0-6186-5897-8
LC 2006028745

First published 1988 by Putnam's

This is an account of the author's yearlong rail journey through China. "For Theroux, traveling is both about people—their thoughts, customs, and peculiarities-and a form of autobiography, and here we learn as much about his own quirks and fancies as we do about the intriguing world of contemporary China." Libr J

Thubron, Colin
To a mountain in Tibet. Harper 2011 227p map $24.99; ebook $19.99 **915**
1. Tibet (China) -- Description and travel
ISBN 978-0-06-176826-2; 978-0-06-206605-3 ebook
LC 2010-43013

"Emotional subtlety and vivid evocations of the people and places are only part of what makes the book so enjoyable. The present-tense narration allows readers make discoveries alongside Thubron, which adds immeasurably to the intimacy and immediacy of the reading experience. A powerful and hauntingly elegiac hybrid of travelogue and memoir." Kirkus

Winchester, Simon
The **river** at the center of the world; a journey up the Yangtze and back in Chinese time. Holt & Co. 1996 xx, 410p maps hardcover o.p. **915**
1. Yangtze River valley (China)
LC 96-12399

In 1994, the author followed the Yangtze's "course from the East China Sea to Tibet by boat, car, train, plane, bus and foot; but this is more than an ordinary account of a traveler's pilgrimage, although it is a must for any visitor to China. Wryly humorous, gently skeptical, immensely knowledgeable as he wends his way along the 3900 miles of the great river, Winchester provides an irresistible feast of detail about the character of the river itself, the landscape, the cities, villages and people along its banks." Publ Wkly

Includes bibliographical references

915.04 Asia -- travel

Polo, Marco, 1254-1323?
The **travels** of Marco Polo; the illustrated edition. Marco Polo, edited by Morris Rossabi, translated by Henry Yule. Sterling Signature 2012 377 p. $40 **915.04**
1. Exploration 2. Mongols -- Hsitory 3. Voyages and travels 4. Asia -- Description and travel -- Early works

to 1800
ISBN 1402796307; 9781402796302
LC 2011051047

This book, written by Marco Polo and edited by Morris Rossabi, "offers the complete text of Polo's travelogue, enhanced with more than 200 images--including illuminated manuscripts, paintings, photographs, and maps. Sidebars and dozens of informative footnotes combine to present Polo and his travels." (Publisher's note)

915.604 Middle east -- travel

Taseer, Aatish
★ **Stranger** to history; a son's journey through Islamic lands. by Aatish Taseer. Canongate 2009 323 p. ill., map $16 **915.604**
1. Islam 2. Islamic civilization 3. Middle East -- Description and travel 4. Fathers and sons 5. Islam -- Middle East
ISBN 155597628X; 1847670717; 9781555976286; 9781847670717
LC 2009483559

This book, by Aatish Taseer, "is the story of the journey [which the author] made to try to understand what it means to be Muslim in the twenty-first century. Starting from Istanbul, Islam's once greatest city, he travels to Mecca, its most holy, and then home through Iran and Pakistan. Ending in Lahore, at his estranged father's home, on the night Benazir Bhutto was killed, it is also the story of Taseer's divided family over the past fifty years." (Publisher's note)

916 Geography of and travel in Africa

Benanav, Michael
Men of salt; across the Sahara with the caravan of white gold. Lyons Press 2006 220p il map $23.95 **916**
1. Salt 2. Sahara Desert -- Description and travel
ISBN 1-59228-772-7; 978-1-59228-772-7
LC 2005-23205

"Even if readers don't find the idea of spending 40 harrowing days with a caravan crossing some of the world's most unforgiving desert as enticing as Benanav does, that doesn't mean they won't quickly devour his thrilling account of that otherworldly journey." Publ Wkly

Includes bibliographical references

Butcher, Tim
Chasing the Devil; a journey through sub-Saharan Africa in the footsteps of Graham Greene. Atlas & Co. 2011 325p il map $26.95 **916**
1. Authors 2. Novelists 3. Essayists 4. Travel writers 5. Short story writers 6. Motion picture critics 7. Liberia -- Description and travel 8. Sierra Leone -- Description and travel
ISBN 978-1-935633-29-7; 1-935633-29-5

First published 2010 in the United Kingdom

"Butcher used Graham Greene's little-known 1935 travel book, Journey Without Maps, as his guide on the 350-

mile trek from Freetown, on the coast of Sierra Leone, to the coast of Liberia." Publ Wkly

Includes bibliographical references

Campbell, James T.

Middle passages; African American journeys to Africa, 1787-2005. [by] James Campbell. Penguin Press 2006 513p il (The Penguin history of American life) $29.95 **916**

1. Africa -- Description and travel
ISBN 1-59420-083-1; 978-1-59420-083-0

LC 2005-58672

"From the repatriation of former slaves in the early years of the United States to the recent heritage tourism featuring Goree Island and other slave-trading sites, Campbell provides an artful reconstruction of the often bittersweet experience of return and reunion." N Y Times Book Rev

Grant, Richard

Crazy river; a journey to the source of the Nile. Free Press 2011 336p pa $15; ebook $9.99 **916**

1. Explorers 2. Travel writers 3. Asian studies specialists 4. Tanzania -- Social conditions 5. East Africa -- Social conditions 6. Middle Eastern studies specialists 7. Tanzania -- Description and travel 8. East Africa -- Description and travel
ISBN 978-1-4391-5414-4 pa; 978-1-4391-5764-0 ebook

LC 2011012168

"The Malagarasi River in Tanzania had not been fully traveled by either Westerners or Africans. So, the tradition of 19th-century British explorers, first and foremost Richard Burton, who became his spectral travel companion, Grant set out to do so. But his adventures on the river—disease and disappointment, danger from crocs, hippos and bandits—became but part of his larger story about what Africa is and how to make sense of it. . . . Dyspeptic, disturbing and brilliantly realized, Grant's account of Africa is literally unforgettable." Kirkus

Langewiesche, William

Sahara unveiled; a journey across the desert. Pantheon Bks. 1996 301p il hardcover o.p. pa $14 **916**

1. Sahara Desert
ISBN 0-679-75006-1 pa

LC 95-48864

"Besides evoking the Sahara's power, majesty, emptiness, heat, beauty and terrors and describing its ecology and meteorology, Langewiesche adds details that may astonish armchair travelers who still think of the desert as populated by camels and Bedouins. . . . He is knowledgeable about the imprint of French colonialism on North African economy and politics, and about Muslim beliefs in practice. Throughout this vivid account, he scatters many charming native folktales." Publ Wkly

Matthiessen, Peter

African silences. Random House 1991 225p maps hardcover o.p. pa $13 **916**

1. Africa -- Description 2. Natural history -- Africa
ISBN 0-679-73102-4 pa

LC 90-52893

"In this account of three trips to Central and Western Africa, Matthiessen reports on the almost total devastation of wildlife in Senegal, Gambia, and the Ivory Coast and describes an expedition searching for the rare Congo peacock and gorillas in the Virunga Mountains of Zaire." Libr J

Tayler, Jeffrey

Angry wind; through Muslim Black Africa by truck, bus, boat, and camel. Houghton Mifflin 2005 252p map $25 **916**

1. Sahel -- Description and travel
ISBN 0-618-33467-X

LC 2004-54066

"This substantial and informative work is no mere travel tale—it is a firsthand account of the author's deeply personal quest for knowledge and understanding of a people and a region that continues to struggle with extreme poverty and unrest." Libr J

Theroux, Paul , 1941-

Dark star safari; overland from Cairo to Cape Town. Houghton Mifflin 2003 472p maps $28 **916**

1. Africa -- Description and travel
ISBN 0-618-13424-7

LC 2002-32710

First published 2002 in the United Kingdom

"Where Theroux sees Africa uncluttered by preconceived notions, his writing can be brilliant. . . . But where Theroux has traveled before—40 years ago, as first a Peace Corps teacher, then a lecturer at Uganda's Makerere University in the golden years just after the country's independence—he sees Africa not for what it is, but for what it might have been." Christ Sci Monit

916.8 Southern Africa -- geography

Theroux, Paul, 1941-

★ Last train to Zona Verde; my ultimate African safari. Paul Theroux. Houghton Mifflin Harcourt 2013 368 p. $27 **916.8**

1. Angola -- Description and travel 2. South Africa -- Description and travel 3. Namibia -- Description and travel
ISBN 061883933X; 9780618839339

LC 2013000388

In this book, by Paul Theroux, the author "sets out on a new journey through the continent he knows and loves best. Theroux first came to Africa as a twenty-two-year-old Peace Corps volunteer. . . . Now he returns, after fifty years on the road, to explore the little-traveled territory of western Africa and to take stock both of the place and of himself." (Publisher's note)

"The acclaimed travel writer and novelist chronicles his journey through Africa as tourist, adventure-seeker, thinker and hopeful critic... Reading this enlightening book won't only open a window into Theroux's mind, it will also impart a deeper understanding of Africa and travel in general." Kirkus

917 Geography of and travel in North America

Ambrose, Stephen E.

★ **Undaunted** courage; Meriwether Lewis, Thomas Jefferson, and the opening of the American West. Simon & Schuster 1996 511p il maps $30; pa $17 **917**
1. Explorers 2. Lewis and Clark Expedition (1804-1806) 3. Territorial governors 4. West (U.S.) -- Exploration
ISBN 0-684-81107-3; 0-684-82697-6 pa
LC 95-37146

This treatment of the Lewis and Clark Expedition "is essentially a biography of Lewis, although the bulk of it is a lively retelling of the journey of the two captains—together with their party of soldiers and frontiersmen, Clark's black slave, York, and the legendary Shoshone Indian woman, Sacagawea, and her infant son—conveyed with passionate enthusiasm by Mr. Ambrose and sprinkled liberally with some of the most famous and vivid passages from the travelers' journals." N Y Times Book Rev
Includes bibliographical references

Beatty, Michael A.

County name origins of the United States. McFarland & Co. 2001 665p $195 **917**
1. United States -- Local history 2. Geographic names -- United States
ISBN 0-7864-1025-6
LC 2001-18034

Arranged alphabetically by state, this study shows "how each county in the United States was named. Dates and circumstances under which counties were named or renamed are provided, including brief biographical, geographical, and other relevant historical information. In cases where name derivations are unknown or disputed, an informed discussion gives probable origins." Libr J
Includes bibliographical references

Bryson, Bill

A **walk** in the woods; rediscovering America on the Appalachian Trail. Broadway Bks. 1998 276p hardcover o.p. pa $14.95 **917**
1. Appalachian region -- Description and travel
ISBN 0-7679-0251-3; 0-7679-0252-1 pa
LC 97-32627

"Bryson's breezy, self-mocking tone may turn off readers who hanker for another 'Into Thin Air' or 'Seven Years in Tibet.' Others, however, may find themselves turning the pages with increasing amusement and anticipation as they discover that they're in the hands of a satirist of the first rank, one who writes (and walks) with Chaucerian brio." N Y Times Book Rev
Includes bibliographical references

The **Columbia** gazetteer of North America; edited by Saul B. Cohen. Columbia Univ. Press 2000 1157p il $156 **917**
1. North America -- Gazetteers
ISBN 0-231-11990-9
LC 00-27512

"This work includes more than 50,000 entries covering every incorporated place and country in the United States, along with many unincorporated places and physical features throughout North America. Arranged alphabetically, each entry includes a pronunciation guide, location information, and longitude and latitude where appropriate. If the listing is a municipality, brief population figures are provided as well. . . . Color maps of the physical regions of North America, along with political maps of the region, are included as reference points." Am Ref Books Annu, 2001

Cronkite, Walter

Around America; a tour of our magnificent coastline. drawings by David Canright. Norton 2001 211p il maps $23.95; pa $13.95 **917**
1. United States -- Local history 2. United States -- Description and travel
ISBN 0-393-04083-6; 0-393-32335-8 pa
LC 00-69563

In this "rumination on the people and places along America's seashores, Cronkite shows his reverence for the country's coastal means of travel. Starting in the Northeast, working south, then circling around to the West Coast, the book reads like a lively but laid-back cruise." Publ Wkly

Duncan, Dayton

Lewis & Clark; the journey of the Corps of Discovery. based on a documentary film by Ken Burns, written by Dayton Duncan; with a preface by Ken Burns and conributions by Stephen E. Ambrose, Erica Funkhouser, William Least Heat-Moon. Knopf 1997 248p il maps $45 **917**
1. Lewis and Clark Expedition (1804-1806) 2. West (U.S.) -- Exploration
ISBN 0-679-45450-0
LC 97-73823

This is a companion volume to PBS television film "Lewis and Clark: The journey of the Corps of Discovery," by Ken Burns.

An "attractive book with a well-written text and an excellent presentation of historic paintings, photographs, maps, and original quotations from various of Lewis and Clark's journals." Sci Books Films

Ferris, Gary W.

Presidential places; a guide to the historic sites of U.S. presidents. [by] Gary Ferris. Blair 1999 284p il pa $15.95 **917**
1. Historic sites 2. Presidents -- United States -- Homes 3. United States -- Description and travel
ISBN 0-89587-176-9
LC 98-50395

This is a "guide to historic places of interest relating to all the American presidents. Included are, among other things, presidential birthplaces, where they lived, where they went to school, the churches they attended, where they are buried, and the monuments, museums, and libraries dedicated to their lives and administrations." Libr J

Includes bibliographical references

Fletcher, Colin

The **man** who walked through time. Vintage Bks. 1989 247p il pa $14.95   **917**

1. Grand Canyon (Ariz.)

ISBN 0-679-72306-4; 978-0-679-72306-6

LC 72-4082

First published 1967 by Knopf

An account of the author's journey on foot through the Grand Canyon National Park.

Frazier, Ian

Great Plains. Farrar, Straus & Giroux 1989 290p il maps hardcover o.p. pa $13   **917**

1. Great Plains -- Description

ISBN 0-312-27850-0 pa

LC 88-31106

The author recounts his experiences and observations traveling in the Western United States

"This is a colorful and engaging blend of travelogue, local color, geography and folklore." Publ Wkly

Gimlette, John

Theatre of fish; travels through Newfoundland and Labrador. Alfred A. Knopf 2005 xxii, 360p il map $25   **917**

1. Atlantic Coast (North America)

ISBN 1-4000-4322-0

LC 2005-44149

"Readers will be fascinated by Newfoundland's and Labrador's bizarre, often tragic pasts and equally strange presents, and they will be glad it was the eloquent Gimlette who made the trip so they don't have to." Publ Wkly

Includes bibliographical references

Heat Moon, William Least

Blue highways; a journey into America. photographs by the author; with a new afterword by the author. Back Bay Bks. 1999 429p il $29.95; pa $14.95   **917**

1. United States -- Description and travel

ISBN 0-316-35391-4; 0-316-35329-9 pa

LC 00-265444

A reissue of the title first published 1982 by Little, Brown

An account of the author's journey across the U.S. in a van taking only secondary roads

Roads to Quoz; an American mosey. Little, Brown and Co. 2008 581p il map $27.99   **917**

1. United States -- Description and travel

ISBN 978-0-316-11025-9; 0-316-11025-6

LC 2008-19375

This is an "account of a series of American journeys into small-town America." N Y Times Book Rev

The author's "journey is as meandering as the Ouachita itself, and readers will relish the experiences he and . . . [his wife] describe along their trip." Libr J

Home ground; language for an American landscape. Barry Lopez, editor; Debra Gwartney, managing editor. Trinity University Press 2006 xxiv, 449p il $29.95   **917**

1. Reference books 2. Americanisms -- Encyclopedias 3. Geographic names -- Encyclopedias

ISBN 978-1-59534-024-5; 1-59534-024-6

LC 2006-19942

This is a "collection of geographical terms from every region of the United States. The 45 contributors, among them Jon Krakauer and Barbara Kingsolver, chose words that Americans use to describe landscape features where they live, then enriched their definitions with literary quotes, comments, irony, and humor. The result is a readable A-to-Z geological and geographical dictionary that surpasses other dictionaries in both scope and coverage." Libr J

Includes bibliographical references

Jenkins, Peter

A **walk** across America. Morrow 1979 288p il maps hardcover o.p. pa $6.99   **917**

1. United States -- Description and travel

ISBN 0-06-095955-X pa

LC 78-10320

This book chronicles the author's journey with his dog from New York to the Gulf of Mexico

Levy, Bernard Henri

American vertigo; traveling America in the footsteps of Tocqueville. [by] Bernard-Henri Lévy; translated by Charlotte Mandell. Random House 2006 308p $24.95   **917**

1. Statesmen 2. American national characteristics 3. Writers on politics 4. Political scientists 5. United States -- Social conditions 6. United States -- Description and travel

ISBN 1-4000-6434-1

LC 2005-44782

The French journalist describes his experiences after The Atlantic Monthly "asked him to hit the road and observe the United States, just as his fellow countryman Alexis de Tocqueville did 173 years ago." N Y Times (Late N Y Ed)

This is "an engaging but often-disturbing portrait of our nation from an eloquent, brutally honest foreigner who wishes our country well." Booklist

McMurtry, Larry

Roads; driving America's great highways. Simon & Schuster 2000 206p hardcover o.p. pa $13   **917**

1. Roads 2. United States -- Description and travel

ISBN 0-684-86885-7 pa

LC 00-27889

In this volume McMurtry provides "reminiscence and commentary on whatever pops up in the windows or in his mind as he crisscrosses the country: enigmatic glances at the Western past, salutes to hundreds of literary and historical figures." N Y Times Book Rev

National Geographic Society (U.S.)

★ **National** Geographic guide to the national parks of the United States; [project manger, Caroline

Hickey] 6th ed.; National Geographic 2009 480p il pa $26 **917**

1. National parks and reserves -- United States
ISBN 978-1-4262-0393-0
First published 1989

This guide provides information on each of the fifty-eight national parks, including things to do, campgrounds and accommodations, and facilities for the disabled.

"You can't do better than this guide. . . . Highly detailed and beautiful, this one is a must for all collections." Libr J

National Geographic guide to the state parks of the United States; 3rd ed.; National Geographic 2008 384p il pa $25 **917**

1. Parks -- United States
ISBN 978-1-4262-0251-3
First published 1997

A guide to more than 200 parks in all 50 states. Each entry provides information on: outstanding scenery and nature; historic and cultural sites; recreational activities; wildlife watching; camping and lodging. 32 maps and 250 color photographs accompany the text.

The **official** guide to America's national parks; editor: Molly Moker. 13th ed; Fodors Travel Pub. 2009 xxxix, 488p il map pa $18.95 **917**

1. National parks and reserves -- United States
ISBN 978-1-4000-1628-0
First published 1979 with title: The complete guide to America's national parks. Periodically revised. Publisher varies

This park visitors' guide also covers national monuments, military parks, seashores and lakeshores, historic sites, and battlefields. Entries are listed by State, and include contact information, activities and facilities, travel directories, and nearby attractions and points of interest.

Includes bibliographical references

Sandoval-Strausz, A. K.

★ **Hotel**; an American history. Yale University Press 2007 375p il map $37.50 **917**

1. Hotels and motels
ISBN 978-0-300-10616-9; 0-300-10616-5
LC 2007-10239

The author "develops social, moral, economic, legal and political connections with originality and insight. His impassioned reading of our 'built environment' is fascinating, his research prodigious. And the subject merits his talent as a historian." N Y Times Book Rev

Includes bibliographical references

Stone, Nathaniel

On the water; discovering America in a rowboat. illustrations by Elizabeth Stone. Broadway Bks. 2002 323p il $21.95; pa $12.95 **917**

1. Boats and boating 2. United States -- Description and travel
ISBN 0-7679-0841-4; 0-7679-0842-2 pa
LC 2002-18489

"Pushing off from New York City's Hudson River, {the author} rowed to the Erie Canal, down to Ohio, onward to the Mississippi, across the Gulf to Key West, and back up

along the coastline of the Atlantic to Maine. It was a 6,000-mile journey, and it took him 10 months to complete. This is the chronicle of his adventure, his voyage into and around America, the story of the people he met and the places he saw. . . . It's a straightforward, crisply written memoir." Booklist

Thoreau, Henry David, 1817-1862

★ **Cape** Cod; photographs by Scot Miller. Ill. ed. of the American classic.; Houghton Mifflin Co. 2008 255p il $35 **917**

1. Cape Cod (Mass.) -- Description and travel
ISBN 978-0-618-75845-6; 0-618-75845-3
LC 2007-42952

First published 1865

This "account is based on the author's experiences during the three short visits to Cape Cod (Oct. 1849; June 1850; July 1855), and includes ten essays on the history and character of the inhabitants, 'The Highland Light,' Nantucket, the sea, the beach, and other aspects of the Cape." Oxford Companion to Am Lit

The **Maine** woods; introduction by Edward Hoagland. Penguin Books 1988 xxxiii, 442p (Penguin nature library) pa $16 **917**

1. Maine -- Description and travel
ISBN 0-14-017013-8
LC 88-3644

First published 1864 by Ticknor & Fields

This account of the author's rambles around the lakes and woods of Maine "records three different excursions: Thoreau's trip to Mount Katahdin (which he called 'Kta-adn'), published in the 'Union Magazine' in 1848; 'Chesuncook,' which appeared in the 'Atlantic Monthly' in the same year; and 'The Allegash and the East Branch,' which is a marvel of precise observation." Herzberg. Reader's Ency of Am Lit

Wallis, Michael

Route 66: the mother road. St. Martin's Griffin 2001 276p il maps $35; pa $19.95 **917**

1. West (U.S.) -- Description and travel
ISBN 0-312-28167-6; 0-312-28161-7 pa
LC 2001-31944

This is a reissue of the title first published 1990

The author examines the highway's history, roadside diners, towns, motels, and people

Includes bibliographical references

Woodger, Elin

Encyclopedia of the Lewis and Clark Expedition; [by] Elin Woodger, Brandon Toropov; foreword by Ned Blackhawk. Facts on File 2004 xxv, 438p il (Facts on File library of American history) $65.00; pa $21.95 **917**

1. Lewis and Clark Expedition (1804-1806) 2. West (U.S.) -- Exploration
ISBN 0-8160-4781-2; 0-8160-4782-0 pa
LC 2003-6120

"Coverage includes information about the people in the expedition party and those encountered, the conditions under which they traveled, the land they traversed, and the plants and animals they observed." Lib Media Connect

"This is a complete, authoritative overview of a fascinating landmark in American history and will be a first purchase for most libraries." SLJ

Includes bibliographical references

917.291   Cuba -- description and travel

Craig, William

Yankee come home; on the road from San Juan Hill to Guantánamo. William Craig. Walker & Co. 2012 437 p. $28.00   **917.291**
1. Spanish-American War, 1898 2. Guantanamo Bay Detention Camp 3. United States -- Foreign relations -- Cuba
ISBN 080271093X; 9780802710932

In this book, "based on his trip to Cuba in 2005, [William] Craig's multipronged account shifts among the events of his journey, thoughts on Cuban culture, an ancestor whom family lore had charging up San Juan Hill in 1898, and his critical views of the history of American-Cuban relations. The Spanish-American War holds these parts together as Craig summarizes Cuban insurrections against the Spanish and the destruction of the 'Maine,' which furnished the American casus belli." (Booklist)

Includes bibliographical references and index.

917.3   Geography of and travel in United States

Gill, A. A.

To America with love; A.A. Gill. Simon & Schuster 2013 256 p. (hardback) $25   **917.3**
1. Cultural critique 2. United States -- Description and travel 3. United States -- Social life and customs
ISBN 1416596216; 9781416596219; 9781439100448
LC 2013019543

This book is Scottish-born A.A. Gill's tribute to America. He "devotes his . . . to defending the country's earnest belief in government by the people, as well as its brashness of character, frank celebration of success, sublime sense of nature, and childish delight in speechifying and hucksterism, among other things." (Publishers Weekly)

918   Geography of and travel in South America

Chatwin, Bruce

In Patagonia; introduction by Nicholas Shakespeare. Penguin Books 2003 204p il map (Penguin classics) pa $15   **918**
1. Patagonia (Argentina and Chile) -- Description and travel
ISBN 0-14-243719-0; 978-0-14-243719-3
LC 2002-45038

First published 1977 in the United Kingdom

This travelogue "captures the exotic characters and scenery Chatwin encountered in the southern tip of South America on a search for an important prehistoric artifact." Booklist

Grann, David

The **lost** city of Z; a tale of deadly obsession in the Amazon. Doubleday 2009 339p il map $27.50   **918**
1. Explorers 2. Amazon River valley
ISBN 978-0-385-51353-1; 0-385-51353-4
LC 2008-17432

Interweaves the story of British explorer Percy Fawcett, who vanished during a 1925 expedition into the Amazon, with the author's own quest to uncover the mysteries surrounding Fawcett's final journey and the secrets of what lies deep in the Amazon jungle.

"A colorful tale of true adventure, marked by satisfyingly unexpected twists, turns and plenty of dark portents." Kirkus
Includes bibliographical references (p. 315-326)

Theroux, Paul, 1941-

The **old** Patagonian express; by train through the Americas. Houghton Mifflin 1979 404p hardcover o.p. pa $15   **918**
1. America -- Description 2. Railroads -- Latin America
ISBN 0-395-52105-X pa
LC 79-15353

The author describes his journey from Boston to Patagonia by train

918.11   Amazon River Region -- Description and travel

Stafford, Ed

Walking the Amazon; 860 days. one step at a time. Ed Stafford. Plume Books 2012 319 p. $16.00   **918.11**
1. Hiking 2. Amazon River 3. Autobiographies 4. Amazon River valley 5. Hiking -- Amazon River Region 6. Amazon River Region -- Description and travel
ISBN 0452298261; 9780452298262
LC 2012010986

In this "memoir . . . about becoming the first person to perambulate the Amazon's entire length, [Ed] Stafford chronicles the countless obstacles he faced, including canoes of armed indigenous peoples, dehydration, sickness, lack of sleep . . . and overwhelming swarms of insects. In addition . . . the author explores his friendship with the longest lasting of his many walking companions, Gadiel 'Cho' Sanchez Rivera." (Kirkus Reviews)

919   Geography of and travel in Australasia, Pacific Ocean islands, Atlantic Ocean islands, Arctic islands, Antarctica and on extraterrestrial worlds

Bryson, Bill

In a sunburned country. Broadway Bks. 2000 307p il maps hardcover o.p. pa $14.95   **919**
1. Australia -- Description and travel
ISBN 0-7679-0386-2 pa
LC 00-25566

In this book, Bryson "chronicles his exploration of Australia, he introduces us to a town that went without electricity until the early 1990s, a former high-ranking politician who hawks his own autobiography to passersby, an assortment of coffee shops and restaurants, . . . a type of giant worm, and the world's most poisonous creature, the box jellyfish." Booklist

Includes bibliographical references

Chatwin, Bruce

The **songlines**. Viking 1987 293p hardcover o.p. pa $13.95 **919**

    1. Australian aborigines 2. Australia -- Description and travel

    ISBN 0-14-009429-6 pa

                LC 86-40512

"This is an important book and a challenging one. . . . It is full of odd characters, bizarre incidents, moments of poetry—some of them comic—that spring as much from the writer's own generosity of spirit as from the richness of things." Times Lit Suppl

Cookman, Scott

  ★ **Ice** blink; the mysterious fate of Sir John Franklin's lost polar expedition. Wiley 2000 244p il maps $24.95; pa $15.95 **919**

    1. Explorers 2. Northwest Passage 3. Naval officers 4. Travel writers 5. Arctic regions -- Exploration

    ISBN 0-471-37790-2; 0-471-40420-9 pa

                LC 99-47620

In this "account of the fabled 1845 Franklin expedition in search of the Northwest Passage, Cookman inculpates a novel malefactor in the tragedy: botulism. In the 1980s, three frozen corpses of expedition members were found and exhumed. . . . Autopsies revealed lead, fingering lead-soldered cans from the provisions. . . . Adventure readers will flock to this fine regaling of the enduring mystery surrounding the best-known disaster in Arctic exploration." Booklist

Includes bibliographical references

Fleming, Fergus

Ninety degrees North; the quest for the North Pole. Grove Press 2002 xxi, 470p il maps $26; pa $15 **919**

    1. North Pole 2. Arctic regions -- Exploration

    ISBN 0-8021-1725-2; 0-8021-4036-X pa

              LC 2002-21469

    Companion volume to Barrow's boys (2000)

    First published 2001 in the United Kingdom

"The book is fascinating for how Fleming renders the haughty, post-Enlightenment brio of the principal adventurers and the extreme, often fatal ends toward which it pushed them." Publ Wkly

Includes bibliographical references

Preston, Diana

A **first** rate tragedy; Robert Falcon Scott and the race to the South Pole. Houghton Mifflin 1998 269p il map hardcover o.p. pa $14 **919**

    1. Explorers 2. South Pole 3. Antarctica -- Exploration 4. British Antarctic ("Terra Nova") Expedition (1910-1913)

    ISBN 0-618-00201-4 pa

                LC 98-47411

"A whole generation was brought up on the legend of Scott of the Antarctic. Diana Preston successfully explains why and how this came about. . . . {She} has written a first-rate book retelling the familiar tale in compulsive terms and adding a thoughtful twist of her own." Times Lit Suppl

Includes bibliographical references

Pyne, Stephen J.

  ★ **Voyager**; seeking newer worlds in the third great age of discovery. Viking 2010 444p il $29.95 **919**

    1. Project Voyager 2. Planets -- Exploration 3. Astronautics -- United States

    ISBN 978-0-670-02183-3; 0-670-02183-0

              LC 2009-46305

"By looking at the mission of Voyager 1 and Voyager 2 and comparing it with past voyages of discovery on Earth, Pyne offers a unique and engrossing history of the Western world's love affair with such journeys. . . . [The author] calls the Voyager mission the hallmark of a 'Third Great Age of Discovery,' similar to ambitious seagoing expeditions in the 16th and 18th centuries. . . . Pyne captures the Western passion for exploration and the lure of the unknown, while relating the fascinating story of two fragile spacecraft continuing after three decades their brave quest across space and time." Publ Wkly

Includes bibliographical references

Solomon, Susan

The **coldest** March. Yale Univ. Press 2001 xxii, 383p il maps hardcover o.p. pa $16.95 **919**

    1. Explorers 2. South Pole 3. Antarctica -- Exploration 4. British Antarctic ("Terra Nova") Expedition (1910-1913)

    ISBN 0-300-08967-8; 0-300-09921-5 pa

              LC 00-54996

"In November 1911, Capt. Robert Falcon Scott and his British team set out to be the first to reach the South Pole. Battling the brutal weather of Antarctica, they reached the pole in January 1912 only to discover that a Norwegian team had beat them there by nearly a month. On their return from the Pole, Scott and four of his companions died in harsh conditions. Ever since, history has not known whether to label them heroes or bunglers. Solomon . . . analyzes all the factors present during Scott's expedition in an attempt to explain that his failure was due not to incompetence but to a combination of unpredictable weather, erroneous choices and bad luck." Libr J

Includes bibliographical references

Theroux, Paul, 1941-

The **happy** isles of Oceania; paddling the Pacific. Houghton Mifflin Co. 2006 528p map pa $15.95 **919**

    1. Oceania -- Description and travel

    ISBN 978-0-618-65898-5; 0-618-65898-X

              LC 2006-28742

    First published 1992 by Putnam

The author "spent 18 months in a one-man collapsible kayak exploring such exotic Pacific islands as New Zealand, Australia, the Soloman and Cook Islands, Fiji, Samoa, Tahiti, Easter Island, and Hawaii. . . . A brilliant storyteller with an eye for the absurd, Theroux takes the reader to little-known places where time seems to have stood still and people lead simple lives totally unrelated to 20th-century America." Libr J

919.8   Arctic islands -- geography

Larson, Edward J.

★ An **empire** of ice; Scott, Shackleton, and the heroic age of Antarctic science. Edward J. Larson. Yale University Press 2011 xiv, 326 p.p ill., maps   **919.8**
1. Explorers 2. Scientific expeditions 3. Antarctica -- Exploration 4. Scientific expeditions/Antarctic regions 5. Antarctic regions/Discovery and exploration 6. Antarctica -- Discovery and exploration -- British
ISBN 0300154089; 9780300154085
LC 2010044396
This book, by Edward J. Larson, "presents a . . . new take on Antarctic exploration. Retold with added information, [it] . . . place[s] the famed voyages of Norwegian explorer Roald Amundsen, his British rivals Robert Scott and Ernest Shackleton, and others in a larger scientific, social, and geopolitical context." (Publisher's note)
Includes bibliographical references (p. 295-315) and index

919.890   Antarctica -- travel

Roberts, David, 1943-

Alone on the ice; the greatest survival story in the history of exploration. David Roberts. W. W. Norton & Company 2013 256 p. (hardcover) $27.95   **919.890**
1. Wilderness survival 2. Antarctica -- Exploration 3. Antarctica -- Discovery and exploration
ISBN 0393083713; 9780393083712
LC 2012037677
This book by David Roberts presents a "portrait of Aussie explorer Douglas Mawson and his arduous trek through some of the most treacherous icy Antarctic terrain. . . . Roberts parallels the courageous achievements of Mawson's team on the 1911-1913 journey along the previously uncharted regions of the landscape with those of his acclaimed peers . . . battling the bitter cold, starvation, and peril to the limits of human endurance." (Publishers Weekly)
Includes bibliographical references and index

92   Individual Biography

Aaron, Hank, 1934-

√ Bryant, Howard. The **last** hero; a life of Henry Aaron. Pantheon Books 2010 600p il $29.95 **92**
1. Baseball players 2. African American athletes 3.

Baseball -- Biography
ISBN 978-0-375-42485-4; 0-375-42485-7
LC 2009-40573
This biography of the baseball player "reveals a multifaceted man, a great American, and an accomplished athlete, in that order. . . . Bryant evokes the apparently distant world marked by cruel segregation, racism, and poverty of the soul, as well as reliving some of the greatest moments of baseball. A most welcome book, most highly recommended." Libr J
Includes bibliographical references

Abdul-Jabbar, Kareem, 1947-

√ ★ Abdul-Jabbar, Kareem. **On** the shoulders of giants; my journey through the Harlem Renaissance. [by] Kareem Abdul-Jabbar with Raymond Obstfeld. Simon & Schuster 2007 274p il hardcover o.p. pa $18.99   **92**
1. Harlem Renaissance 2. Basketball players 3. Nonfiction writers 4. African Americans -- Biography
ISBN 1-4165-3488-1; 978-1-4165-3488-4; 1-4165-3489-X pa; 978-1-4165-3489-1 pa
LC 2006-51776
"By mixing personal anecdotes with traditional research and reporting, . . . [Abdul-Jabbar] acts as a knowledgeable, passionate tour guide through the artistic and social history of one America's most dynamic creative eras." N Y Times Book Rev
Includes bibliographical references

Achebe, Chinua, 1930-2013

√ Achebe, Chinua, 1930-2013. The **education** of a British-protected child; essays. A.A. Knopf 2009 172p $24.95; pa $14.95   **92**
1. Poets 2. Racism 3. Authors 4. Novelists 5. Authors, Nigerian 6. Nigeria 7. Essayists 8. Short story writers 9. Nigeria -- Colonization 10. African literature -- History and criticism
ISBN 978-0-3072-7255-3; 9780307473677
LC 2009017480
This is a collection of essays by the author of Things Fall Apart. In the title piece, Achebe discusses "growing up in colonial Nigeria and inhabiting its 'middle ground,' recalling both his happy memories of reading novels in secondary school and the harsher truths of colonial rule. . . . Politics and history figure in 'What Is Nigeria to Me?,' 'Africa's Tarnished Name,' and 'Politics of the Politicians of Language.' And Achebe's . . . family comes into view in 'My Dad and Me' and 'My Daughters.'" (Publisher's note)
"With African literature emerging as a world force, it's good to have Achebe back after more than 20 years, offering 17 sterling essays." (Library Journal)
Includes bibliographical references

Acheson, Dean, 1893-1971

Chace, James. **Acheson**; the Secretary of State who created the American world. Simon & Schuster 1998 512p hardcover o.p. pa $20   **92**
1. Authors 2. Nonfiction writers 3. Secretaries of state 4. United States -- Foreign relations
ISBN 978-1-416-54865-2; 1-416-54865-3
LC 98-3801

"Dean Acheson was Truman's Secretary of State from 1949 to 1953, and today's world, as Chace shows in this lucid biography, was shaped in no small degree by his efforts." New Yorker

Includes bibliographical references

Adams, Abigail, 1744-1818

✓★ Adams, John. **My** dearest friend; letters of Abigail and John Adams. edited by Margaret A. Hogan and C. James Taylor. Belknap Press of Harvard University Press 2007 508p il map $35   **92**

1. Presidents 2. Vice-presidents 3. Parents of presidents 4. Spouses of presidents 5. Presidents -- United States 6. Presidents' spouses -- United States

ISBN 978-0-674-02606-3; 0-674-02606-3

LC 2007-4380

This collection of correspondence between John and Abigail Adams includes "selection from the entire body of the Adams' correspondence, from their courtship . . . until Abigail left the White House near the end of John's presidential term, reminding him, 'I want to see the list of judges.' . . . This is a treasure, for general readers and scholars alike." Booklist

Holton, Woody. **Abigail** Adams; a life. Free Press 2009 483p il map $30   **92**

1. Presidents 2. Vice-presidents 3. Biography, Individual 4. Parents of presidents 5. Spouses of presidents 6. Presidents' spouses -- United States 7. Women in politics -- United States -- History -- 18th century

ISBN 978-1-4165-4680-1; 1-4165-4680-4

LC 2009016288

This is a "reinterpretation of Adams's life story and of women's roles in the creation of the republic." (Publisher's note) Index.

"Holton's superb biography shows us a three-dimensional Adams as a forward-thinking woman with a mind of her own." Publ Wkly

Includes bibliographical references

Adams, Henry, 1838-1918

Adams, Henry. The **education** of Henry Adams; an autobiography. with a new introduction by Donald Hall. Houghton Mifflin 2000 517p pa $12   **92**

1. Authors 2. Novelists 3. Historians 4. Essayists

ISBN 0-618-05666-1

LC 00-26235

First published 1918

"The book omits any mention of the thirteen years of Adams's marriage and the seven years following his wife's suicide. It does, however, present a vivid picture of the people and places the author knew." Reader's Ency. 4th edition

Adams, John, 1947-

Adams, John. **Hallelujah** junction; composing an American life. Farrar, Straus and Giroux 2008 340p il $26   **92**

1. Composers

ISBN 978-0-374-28115-1; 0-374-28115-7

LC 2008-17922

An eminent composer shares the story of his life, from his childhood and early studies in classical composition to his minimalist and "docu-opera" achievements, in an account that evaluates his professional relationships and the social movements that inspired his creative process

"Readers will enjoy the candor and completeness of the book, which serves as a gateway to an accomplished body of work. Like the author's music: carefully considered, deliberate and often exciting, gathering together many disparate elements of American life." Kirkus

Adams, John, 1735-1826

★ Adams, John. **My** dearest friend; letters of Abigail and John Adams. edited by Margaret A. Hogan and C. James Taylor. Belknap Press of Harvard University Press 2007 508p il map $35   **92**

1. Presidents 2. Vice-presidents 3. Parents of presidents 4. Spouses of presidents 5. Presidents -- United States 6. Presidents' spouses -- United States

ISBN 978-0-674-02606-3; 0-674-02606-3

LC 2007-4380

This collection of correspondence between John and Abigail Adams includes "selection from the entire body of the Adams' correspondence, from their courtship . . . until Abigail left the White House near the end of John's presidential term, reminding him, 'I want to see the list of judges.' . . . This is a treasure, for general readers and scholars alike." Booklist

✓★ Grant, James. **John** Adams; party of one. [by] James L. Grant. Farrar, Straus and Giroux 2005 530p il $30   **92**

1. Presidents 2. Vice-presidents 3. Presidents -- United States

ISBN 0-374-11314-9

LC 2004-10863

The author "is excellent at developing Adams' devotion to liberty, honed by British policies that affronted him and turned him into a revolutionary. In Grant's fine synthesis, Adams on the page is the pious, ambitious, and loving man he was in life." Booklist

Includes bibliographical references

Holton, Woody. **Abigail** Adams; a life. Free Press 2009 483p il map $30   **92**

1. Presidents 2. Vice-presidents 3. Biography, Individual 4. Parents of presidents 5. Spouses of presidents 6. Presidents' spouses -- United States 7. Women in politics -- United States -- History -- 18th century

ISBN 978-1-4165-4680-1; 1-4165-4680-4

LC 2009016288

This is a "reinterpretation of Adams's life story and of women's roles in the creation of the republic." (Publisher's note) Index.

"Holton's superb biography shows us a three-dimensional Adams as a forward-thinking woman with a mind of her own." Publ Wkly

Includes bibliographical references

Adams, John Quincy, 1767-1848

Kaplan, Fred, 1937- **John** Quincy Adams; American visionary. Fred Kaplan. HarperCollins Publishers 2014 672 p. ill. (some col.), col. map $29.99 **92**
1. Presidents -- United States 2. Presidents -- United States -- Biography
ISBN 0061915416; 9780061915413
LC 2013035334
This book, by Fred Kaplan, "brings into focus the . . . life of John Quincy Adams--the little known . . . sixth president of the United States and the first son of John and Abigail Adams. . . . Kaplan draws on a trove of unpublished archival material to trace Adams's evolution from his childhood during the Revolutionary War to his brilliant years as Secretary of State to his time in the White House and beyond." (Publisher's note)
"Kaplan sees not an inadequate man in a position he could not manage. He sees instead a "visionary," who stood for a united American republic free of the divisiveness of slavery." Booklist
Includes bibliographical references and index

Nagel, Paul C. **John** Quincy Adams; a public life, a private life. Harvard University Press 1999 432p il map pa $18.95 **92**
1. Presidents 2. Senators 3. Members of Congress 4. Secretaries of state 5. Presidents -- United States
ISBN 0-674-47940-8
First published 1997 by Knopf
The author traces the life and career of the sixth president of the United States "utilizing diary entries to provide keen insight into this extraordinary man, who often suffered from severe depression. The result is a fascinating psychobiography." Libr J
Includes bibliographical references

Adams, Rachel, 1968-

Adams, Rachel. **Raising** Henry; a memoir of motherhood, disability, and discovery. Rachel Adams. Yale University Press 2013 272 p. (cloth : alk. paper) $26 **92**
1. Down syndrome 2. Mother-son relationship 3. Children with disabilities 4. Parents of children with disabilities
ISBN 0300180004; 9780300180008
LC 2013002096
In this memoir on her experiences raising a child with Down syndrome, author Rachel Adams "chronicles the first three years of Henry's life and her own transformative experience of unexpectedly becoming the mother of a disabled child. . . . Adams untangles the contradictions of living in a society that is more enlightened and supportive of people with disabilities than ever before, yet is racing to perfect prenatal tests to prevent children like Henry from being born." (Publisher's note)
"The author's clear, precise memoir offers an account of her feelings, which run the gamut from shocked dismay to unequivocal acceptance, and the process by which she and her husband arrived at a place of profound love and gratitude for Henry and his differences." Kirkus
Includes bibliographical references

Addams, Jane, 1860-1935

Knight, Louise W. **Jane** Addams; spirit in action. W. W. Norton 2010 334p il $28.95 **92**
1. Authors 2. Philanthropists 3. Hull House (Chicago, Ill.) 4. Essayists 5. Pacifists 6. Social welfare leaders 7. Nobel laureates for peace 8. Chicago (Ill.) -- Social conditions
ISBN 978-0-393-07165-8
LC 2010-20648
"Knight, the author of Citizen (2006), provides the first full-length biography of Jane Addams in 35 years. She carefully traces Addams' philosophical progression as she Addams evolvedfrom a passive reformer into an active collaborator, who tirelessly worked with, not for, others to usher in a new era of democracy and social justice." (Booklist)
Includes bibliographical references

Agassi, Andre 1970-

Agassi, Andre, 1970- **Open**; an autobiography. A. Knopf 2009 385p il $28.95 **92**
1. Tennis 2. Tennis players 3. Tennis -- Biography 4. Biography, Individual
ISBN 0-307-26819-5; 978-0-307-26819-8
LC 2009-24004
This is a memoir by the eight-time Grand Slam championship winner who founded the Andre Agassi Charitable Foundation and the Andre Agassi College Preparatory Academy for underprivileged children in Las Vegas. Agassi discusses his childhood, his relationship with his father, his tennis matches, his addiction in 1997 to crystal meth and his recovery, his rivalries with other players such as Pete Sampras, his fall out of the top 100 ranked players and his return to become the oldest man ever ranked number one, and the final match of his career at the U.S. Open on September 3, 2006.
"By sharing an unvarnished, at times inspiring story in an arresting, muscular style, Agassi may have just penned one of the best sports autobiographies of all time. Check—it's one of the better memoirs out there, period. . . . Fans will devour Agassi's juicy revelations about both himself and other tennis luminaries." Time

Agassiz, Louis, 1807-1873

Irmscher, Christoph. **Louis** Agassiz; creator of American science. Christoph Irmscher. Houghton Mifflin Harcourt 2013 448 p. $35 **92**
1. Natural history -- United States -- History 2. Naturalists -- United States -- Biography 3. Natural history -- United States -- History -- 19th century
ISBN 0547577672; 9780547577678
LC 2012014225
This book, by Christoph Irmscher, is a biography of the scientist Louis Agassiz, sometimes called the "founding father of American science. . . . The irrepressible Louis Agassiz, . . . focused his prodigious energies on the fauna of the New World. Invited to deliver a series of lectures in Boston, he never left, becoming the most famous scientist of his time." (Publisher's note)
"A masterful portrait illuminating the tangled human dynamics of science." Booklist
Includes bibliographical references and index

Agee, James, 1909-1955

Wranovics, John. **Chaplin** and Agee; the untold story of the tramp, the writer, and the lost screenplay. Palgrave Macmillan 2005 256p il $24.95   **92**

1. Poets 2. Actors 3. Authors 4. Novelists 5. Screenwriters 6. Nonfiction writers 7. Motion picture critics 8. Motion picture directors 9. Motion picture producers
ISBN 1-403-96866-7

LC 2004-62807

A "double biography of two of the 20th century's most talented artists. Wranovic's hook is a lost screenplay titled The Tramp's New World, which Agee wrote for Chaplin after the detonation of the atomic bomb over Hiroshima. . . . Using personal correspondence and critical reviews, Wranovics re-creates the fascinating historical backdrop of the Agee/Chaplin friendship, interweaving into the stunning tapestry the colorful lives of such luminaries as Brecht, Auden, Ed Sullivan, and John Huston." Choice

Akhmatova, Anna Andreevna, 1889-1966

★ Feinstein, Elaine. **Anna** of all the Russias; the life of Anna Akhmatova. Knopf 2006 331p il $27.50   **92**

1. Poets 2. Authors
ISBN 1-4000-4089-2; 978-1-4000-4089-6

LC 2005-44542

First published 2005 in the United Kingdom

"In her superb and concise biography, Feinstein brings to life the complex interplay between poetic truth and the ordinary truth of experience in the poet's life and work. . . . Feinstein's poetic sensibility gives her book a distinctive quality, setting it apart from previous biographies." N Y Rev Books

Includes bibliographical references

Al Jundi, Sami, 1962-

Al Jundi, Sami. The **hour** of sunlight; one Palestinian's journey from prisoner to peacemaker. by Sami al Jundi and Jen Marlowe. Nation Books 2010 344p il pa $16.99   **92**

1. Prisoners 2. Palestinian Arabs 3. Israel-Arab conflicts 4. Pacifists
ISBN 978-1-56858-448-5

LC 2010-29340

The authors "trace al Jundi's evolution from Palestinian militant to peacemaker. As teenagers, al Jundi and two friends joined the PLO, but when a bomb exploded as they were building it, one boy was killed, and the other two badly injured—and on the receiving end of Israeli interrogations and torture. Sentenced to a decade in prison, al Jundi dedicates himself to an extensive education program maintained by the prisoners themselves, ultimately committing himself to nonviolence and to bridging the Israeli-Palestinian divide." Publ Wkly

Includes bibliographical references

Albee, Edward, 1928-

Gussow, Mel. **Edward** Albee; a singular journey: a biography. Applause 2001 448p il pa $16.95 **92**

1. Authors 2. Dramatists 3. Dramatists, American
ISBN 978-1-55783-447-8; 1-55783-447-4
First published 1999 by Simon & Schuster

"Albee regained his position as one of America's greatest playwrights with the 1994 production of 'Three Tall Women,' achieving a level of theatrical mastery and critical acclaim that he hadn't seen since 'Who's Afraid of Virginia Woolf' and 'A Delicate Balance,' almost two decades earlier. The years in between were marked by excessive drinking, outrageous behavior, inferior work, and a diminished career, but Gussow, with a light and generous touch, shows us the strengths of an artist whose core of resilience ultimately insured his survival." New Yorker

Includes bibliographical references

Alcott, Amos Bronson, 1799-1888

Matteson, John. **Eden's** outcasts; the story of Louisa May Alcott and her father. W.W. Norton 2007 497p il $29.95   **92**

1. Authors 2. Educators 3. Novelists 4. Philosophers 5. Authors, American 6. Nonfiction writers 7. Young adult authors
ISBN 978-0-393-05964-9

LC 2007-13707

"In his account of Louisa May Alcott and her father, Bronson Alcott, . . . [the author] relies heavily on the journals, letters, and works of both authors to portray their unique lives, also quoting extensively from the writings of famous friends and neighbors like Ralph Waldo Emerson." Libr J

"Matteson's lucid, commanding biography casts new light on an unusual father-daughter bond and a new land at war with itself." Booklist

Includes bibliographical references

Alcott, Louisa May, 1832-1888

Matteson, John. **Eden's** outcasts; the story of Louisa May Alcott and her father. W.W. Norton 2007 497p il $29.95   **92**

1. Authors 2. Educators 3. Novelists 4. Philosophers 5. Authors, American 6. Nonfiction writers 7. Young adult authors
ISBN 978-0-393-05964-9

LC 2007-13707

"Matteson's lucid, commanding biography casts new light on an unusual father-daughter bond and a new land at war with itself." Booklist

Includes bibliographical references

Reisen, Harriet. **Louisa** May Alcott; the woman behind Little women. Henry Holt 2009 362p $26 **92**

1. Authors 2. Novelists 3. Authors, American 4. Young adult authors
ISBN 978-0-8050-8299-9; 0-8050-8299-9

LC 2009-10637

In this biography of the American author, "Reisen analyzes Louisa's great pleasure in writing lucrative pulp fiction, her sacrifices, adventures, and brilliant career. Here . . . is Alcott whole, a trailblazing woman grasping freedom in a time of sexual inequality and war, a survivor of cruel tragedies, a quintessential American writer." Booklist

Includes bibliographical references

Alexandra, Empress, consort of Nicholas II, Em-

peror of Russia, 1872-1918

Massie, Robert K., 1929- **Nicholas** and Alexandra. Ballantine Books 2000 613p il map pa
$18.95   **92**
    1. Monks 2. Emperors 3. Empresses 4. Courtiers 5.
Russia -- History 6. Russia -- Kings and rulers
ISBN 0-345-43831-0; 978-0-345-43831-7

                  LC 99-91507

First published 1967 by Atheneum

This study provides an intimate account of the Romanov
family and the coming of the Russian Revolution. Kerensky,
Lenin and Rasputin are among the personalities profiled.

This book, "solid with research, reads as lightly as a novel, as authoritatively as a textbook. Dialogue and lively description lend a sense of immediacy, but his notes, discreetly
relegated to the back of the book, show how carefully he has
avoided slipping into fiction." Christ Sci Monit

Includes bibliographical references

Ali, Khaliah

Ali, Khaliah. **Fighting** weight; how I achieved
healthy weight loss with banding, a new procedure
that eliminates hunger--forever. [by] Khaliah Ali;
George Fielding, Christine Ren, Lawrence Lindner.
HarperCollins 2007 241p il $22.95   **92**
    1. Weight loss 2. Fashion designers 3. Memoirists
4. Talk show hosts 5. Models (Persons) 6. Stomach
-- Surgery 7. Children of prominent persons
ISBN 0-06-117094-1; 978-0-06-117094-2

                  LC 2007-60870

The author "describes her own lifelong battle with obesity and the effect of her own gastric-banding surgery. . . . Coauthor George Fielding, M.D., who performed Ali's surgery,
explains the process and how it differs from other bariatric
surgeries. . . . A good combination of scientific information
and personal narrative, this title belongs in all public libraries." Libr J

Ali, Muhammad, 1942-

Remnick, David. **King** of the world: Muhammad
Ali and the rise of an American hero. Random House
1998 326p il hardcover o.p. pa $14   **92**
    1. African American athletes 2. Boxers (Persons)
ISBN 0-375-50065-0; 0-375-70229-6 pa

                  LC 98-24539

"This is the best book ever on Muhammad Ali and one of
the best on America in the 1960s." Booklist

Includes bibliographical references

Ali, Nujood

Ali, Nujood. **I** am Nujood, age 10 and divorced;
[by] Nujood Ali, with Delphine Minoui; translated by
Linda Coverdale. Three Rivers Press 2010 188p pa
$12   **92**
    1. Children 2. Child marriage 3. Yemen 4. Abused
persons
ISBN 978-0-307-58967-5; 0-307-58967-6

                  LC 2009-33063

"One of 16 children living in squalor in Yemen, Nujood
was married off at about age 10. Though her husband vowed
he'd wait for sex until she reached puberty, he rapes her on

their first night together. After months of abuse, Nujood
goes to the courthouse, where with heartbreaking naiveté,
she tells a judge she wants a divorce. Supported by the legal
system, Nujood gets her wish." People

Includes bibliographical references

Ali, Taha Muhammad

    ★ Hoffman, Adina. **My** happiness bears no relation to happiness; a poet's life in the Palestinian
century. Yale University Press 2009 454p il map
$27.50   **92**
    1. Poets 2. Authors
ISBN 978-0-300-14150-4

                  LC 2008-37298

This is "the life and incendiary times of Palestinian poet
Taha Muhammad Ali." Kirkus

"An exceptional introduction to a literary world that has,
until now, been little known to English-language readers,
this is highly recommended for all libraries." Libr J

Includes bibliographical references

Alison, Jane

Alison, Jane. The **sisters** antipodes. Houghton
Mifflin Harcourt 2009 276p $23   **92**
    1. Authors 2. Novelists
ISBN 978-0-15-101280-0; 0-15-101280-6

                  LC 2008-14747

The author describes "the strangely definitive reconfiguration of her family when her parents broke up and switched
partners and children with another couple they met in Australia. . . . [This is] a truly unusual, harrowing journey of
identity." Publ Wkly

Allen, Richard, 1760-1831

Newman, Richard S. **Freedom's** prophet; Bishop Richard Allen, the AME Church, and the Black
founding fathers. New York University Press 2008
359p il $34.95   **92**
    1. Slaves 2. Bishops 3. African Methodist Episcopal
Church
ISBN 978-0-8147-5826-7; 0-8147-5826-6

                  LC 2007-43259

"Newman's beautifully written study is not only a firstrate social history of the early Republic and African-American culture and religion, it provides a detailed sketch of
Allen that is sure to become the definitive biography of the
leader." Publ Wkly

Includes bibliographical references

Allende family

    ★ Allende, Isabel. **Paula**; translated from the
Spanish by Margaret Sayers Peden. HarperPerennial
2008 330, 23p pa $14.99   **92**
    1. Authors 2. Novelists 3. Dramatists 4. Journalists
5. Authors, Chilean 6. Children's authors
ISBN 978-0-06-156490-1

First published 1995

Allende "interweaves the story of her own life with the
slow dying of her 28-year-old daughter, Paula." Publ Wkly

Allende, Isabel

★ Allende, Isabel. **Paula**; translated from the Spanish by Margaret Sayers Peden. HarperPerennial 2008 330, 23p pa $14.99 **92**

1. Authors 2. Novelists 3. Dramatists 4. Journalists 5. Authors, Chilean 6. Children's authors

ISBN 978-0-06-156490-1

First published 1995

Allende "interweaves the story of her own life with the slow dying of her 28-year-old daughter, Paula." Publ Wkly

Allende, Isabel. The **sum** of our days; translated from the Spanish by Margaret Sayers Peden. Harper-Collins 2008 320p $26.95 **92**

1. Authors 2. Novelists 3. Dramatists 4. Journalists 5. Authors, Chilean 6. Children's authors

ISBN 978-0-06-155183-3; 0-06-155183-X

LC 2007-33251

"In this sequel to her memoir Paula (1995), about the yearlong coma suffered by her daughter, Chilean novelist Allende tells of the difficult years following Paula's death. . . . Surprisingly candid, frequently funny, and highly aware of her own failings, Allende is a person fully engaged in life, and readers will find her eloquent memoir inspirational reading." Booklist

Al-Maria, Sophia

Al-Maria, Sophia. The **Girl** Who Fell to Earth; A Memoir. HarperCollins 2012 288 p. (paperback) $14.99 **92**

1. Arab Americans 2. Culture conflict

ISBN 006199975X; 9780061999758

In this memoir, "when Sophia Al-Maria's mother sends her away from rainy Washington State to stay with her husband's desert-dwelling Bedouin family in Qatar, she intends it to be a sort of teenage cultural boot camp. What her mother doesn't know is that there are some things about growing up that are universal. In Qatar, Sophia is faced with a new world she'd only imagined as a child. She sets out to find her freedom, even in the most unlikely of places." (Publisher's note)

Altman, Robert, 1925-2006

Zuckoff, Mitchell. **Robert** Altman; the oral biography. Alfred A. Knopf 2009 560p il **92**

1. Motion picture producers and directors 2. Television directors 3. Biography, Individual 4. Motion picture directors 5. Motion picture producers

ISBN 0-307-26768-7; 978-0-307-26768-9

LC 2009-19847

This is a biography of the director of such films as MASH (1970), Nashville (1975), The Player (1992), and Gosford Park (2001). Filmography. Index.

This "is a smart, amusing, lively book, full of anecdotes and a generous step toward perceiving the glorious and perverse ways of Altman himself." New Repub

Includes filmography

Ames, Robert, 1934-1983

Bird, Kai. The **Good** Spy; The Life and Death of Robert Ames. by Kai Bird. Random House Inc 2014 448 p. illustrations $26 **92**

1. Intelligence service -- United States 2. United States. Central Intelligence Agency

ISBN 0307889750; 9780307889751

LC 2013049480

This book, by Kai Bird, is a biography "of CIA agent Robert Ames, one of America's most important assets in the [Middle East] until his life was cut short by the bomb that exploded outside the American Embassy in Beirut in April 1983." (Library Journal)

"A low-key, respectful life of a decent American officer whose quietly significant work helped lead to the Oslo Accords." Kirkus

Includes bibliographical references (pages 403-410) and index

Amis, Kingsley, 1922-1995

Amis, Martin. **Experience**. Hyperion 2000 406p il $23.95; pa $14 **92**

1. Poets 2. Authors 3. Humorists 4. Novelists 5. Essayists 6. Literary critics 7. Short story writers

ISBN 0-7868-6652-7; 0-375-72683-7 pa

LC 00-699777

This is a "portmanteau of personal history, ancestor worship and promiscuous opinionizing, and a piñata of literary gossip that Amis beats with a stick, causing many names to drop. . . . And if we stay put till the last 100 pages, it will break our heart." N Y Times Book Rev

Leader, Zachary. The **life** of Kingsley Amis. Pantheon Books 2007 996p $39.95 **92**

1. Poets 2. Authors 3. Humorists 4. Novelists 5. Essayists 6. Literary critics 7. Short story writers

ISBN 978-0-375-42498-4; 0-375-42498-9

LC 2006-35012

First published 2006 in the United Kingdom

The "great virtue of Leader's biography of Amis is that you do not have to share his high opinion of the subject to benefit from the book's prodigious research and wealth of information so well presented." San Francisco Chronicle

Includes bibliographical references

Amis, Martin

Amis, Martin. **Experience**. Hyperion 2000 406p il $23.95; pa $14 **92**

1. Poets 2. Authors 3. Humorists 4. Novelists 5. Essayists 6. Literary critics 7. Short story writers

ISBN 0-7868-6652-7; 0-375-72683-7 pa

LC 00-699777

This is a "portmanteau of personal history, ancestor worship and promiscuous opinionizing, and a piñata of literary gossip that Amis beats with a stick, causing many names to drop. . . . And if we stay put till the last 100 pages, it will break our heart." N Y Times Book Rev

Andersen, Hans Christian, 1805-1875

Andersen, Jens. **Hans** Christian Andersen: a new life; translated from the Danish by Tiina Nunnally.

Overlook Press 2005 624p il hardcover o.p. pa $22.95   **92**

1. Authors 2. Novelists 3. Dramatists 4. Authors, Danish 5. Children's authors 6. Short story writers
ISBN 1-58567-642-X; 1-58567-737-X pa

LC 2004-65985

The author examines Andersen's "considerable gifts as an oral storyteller; his eccentric, often annoying public habits; his ambivalent sexuality; his bouts of narcissism; his painfully slow transformation from rough-hewn provincial and awkward melodramatist into brilliant, internationally famous writer-celebrity. The biography is best and most moving when it is frank about formerly suppressed aspects of Andersen's life." Booklist

Includes bibliographical references

Anderson, Marian, 1897-1993

Keiler, Allan. **Marian** Anderson; a singer's journey. University of Illinois Press 2002 447p hardcover o.p. pa $21.95   **92**

1. African American singers 2. Opera singers 3. African American women -- Biography
ISBN 0-684-80711-4; 0-252-07067-4 pa

LC 99-43319

First published 2000 by Scribner

The author's "clear, succinct prose, initially lacking narrative coherence, gains strength and momentum as his subject matures from a young and struggling artist into one of the enduring voices of our century." Publ Wkly

Includes discography and bibliographical references

Andoe, Joe

Andoe, Joe. **Jubilee** city; a memoir at full speed. William Morrow 2007 207p il $22.95   **92**

1. Artists 2. Painters
ISBN 978-0-06-124031-7; 0-06-124031-1

In this "memoir, Andoe narrates his journey from his Tulsa childhood through redneck, hard-partying teen years to a highly successful career as a (hard-partying redneck) painter in New York City. While Andoe may not be a professional writer, his humor and offbeat artistic sensibility make up for any lack of prose-writing chops. Through discrete anecdotes that seldom run longer than two pages, Andoe assembles vivid portraits of his family and friends and of the various environments he inhabited-the working-class Tulsa neighborhoods of the 1960s, the high school and college drug culture at the end of the hippie era, and the New York art scene of the 1980s." Publ Wkly

Andrews, Julie

Andrews, Julie. **Home**; a memoir of my early years. Hyperion 2008 339p il $26.95   **92**

1. Actors 2. Singers 3. Children's authors
ISBN 978-0-7868-6565-9; 0-7868-6565-2

LC 2007-48830

"Spanning events from her 1935 birth to the early 1960s, . . . [the author] covers her rise to fame and ends with Walt Disney casting her in Mary Poppins (1963). . . . The heart of her book documents the rehearsals, tryouts and smash 1956 opening of My Fair Lady. Readers will rejoice, since Andrews is an accomplished writer who holds back nothing while adding a patina of poetry to the antics and anecdotes

throughout this memoir of bittersweet backstage encounters and theatrical triumphs." Publ Wkly

Angelou, Maya 1928-2014

★ Angelou, Maya. **I** know why the caged bird sings. Random House 2002 281p $21.95   **92**

1. Poets 2. Actors 3. Singers 4. Dramatists 5. Women authors 6. African American authors 7. Essayists 8. Memoirists 9. Children's authors
ISBN 0-375-50789-2

LC 2001-41914

First published 1969

The first volume in the author's autobiographical series covers her childhood and adolescence in rural Arkansas, St. Louis, and San Francisco.

"Angelou is a skillful writer; her language ranges from beautifully lyrical prose to earthy metaphor, and her descriptions have power and sensitivity." Libr J

Followed by Gather together in my name (1974); Singin' and swingin' and gettin' merry like Christmas (1976); The heart of a woman (1981); All God's children need traveling shoes (1986); A song flung up to heaven (2002)

Angelou, Maya, 1928-2014. **Letter** to my daughter. Random House 2008 166p $25   **92**

1. Poets 2. Actors 3. Singers 4. Dramatists 5. Women authors 6. African American authors 7. Essayists 8. Memoirists 9. Children's authors
ISBN 978-1-4000-6612-4

LC 2008-28843

"A slim volume packed with nourishing nuggets of wisdom." Kirkus

Gillespie, Marcia Ann. **Maya** Angelou; a glorious celebration. [by] Marcia Ann Gillespie, Rosa Johnson Butler and Richard A. Long; foreword by Oprah Winfrey. Doubleday 2008 191p il $30   **92**

1. Poets 2. Actors 3. Singers 4. Dramatists 5. Women authors 6. African American authors 7. Essayists 8. Memoirists 9. Children's authors
ISBN 978-0-385-51108-7

LC 2007-31301

This look at Maya Angelou's life as well as her myriad interests and accomplishments by the people who know her best (longtime friends Marcia Ann Gillespie and Richard Long and niece Rosa Johnson Butler) features over 150 sepia portraits, family photographs, and letters. Includes a bibliography of her works.

"A loving tribute to one of the most renowned authors today, this work is highly recommended." Libr J

Anne Boleyn, Queen, consort of Henry VIII, King of England, 1507-1536

Weir, Alison. The **lady** in the tower; the fall of Anne Boleyn. Ballantine Books 2009 434p il $28   **92**

1. Queens 2. Great Britain -- History -- 1485-1603, Tudors
ISBN 978-0-345-45321-1; 0-345-45321-2

LC 2009-42748

Historian Weir is "well equipped to parse the evidence, ferret out the misconceptions and arrive at sturdy hypotheses about what actually befell Anne. Her command of minutiae is impressive, as is her enthusiasm for even the most minor aspects of Anne's frequently distorted story." N Y Times Book Rev

Includes bibliographical references

Anne, Queen of Great Britain, 1665-1714

Somerset, Anne. **Queen** Anne; the politics of passion. Anne Somerset. Alfred A. Knopf 2013 621 p. illustrations, portraits $35   92

1. Queens -- Great Britain 2. Great Britain -- Kings and rulers 3. Queens -- Great Britain -- Biography 4. Great Britain -- History -- Anne, 1702-1714

ISBN 0307962881; 9780307962881

LC 2012035334

This book, by Anne Somerset, is a biography of British Queen Anne. "She ascended the thrones of England, Scotland and Ireland in 1702, at age thirty-seven, . . . and five years later united two of her realms, England and Scotland, as a sovereign state, creating the Kingdom of Great Britain. She had a history of personal misfortune, overcoming ill health . . . and living through seventeen miscarriages, stillbirths, and premature births in seventeen years." (Publisher's note)

"Anne's natural reserve and her instinct for discretion has led historians to believe that she was weak and dominated by women of stronger character. Somerset's impressive scholarship debunks that belief and shows Anne as a masterful, even authoritative, queen who survived the influence of her 'friends.'" Kirkus

Includes bibliographical references and index

Anthony, Susan B., 1820-1906

Anthony, Susan B. **Failure** is impossible; Susan B. Anthony in her own words. [edited by] Lynn Sherr. Times Bks. 1995 xxviii, 384p il hardcover o.p. pa $23   92

1. Feminism 2. Suffragists 3. Abolitionists

ISBN 0-8129-2718-4

LC 94-29913

This is a collection of Susan B. Anthony's journal entries, correspondence, speeches, interviews, and published writings. The author has arranged the selections by topic and chronologically within topics

Includes bibliographical references

Antonia, Mother

Jordan, Mary. The **prison** angel; Mother Antonia's journey from Beverly Hills to a life of service in a Mexican jail. [by] Mary Jordan and Kevin Sullivan. Penguin Press 2005 237p il $24.95   92

1. Nuns

ISBN 1-59420-056-4

LC 2004-60238

The authors describe the "journey of a woman who, at the age of 50, left the comforts of suburban L.A. to begin a charity mission in Mexico. . . . This is an inspiring story of one woman's compassion and her own journey of spiritual growth." Booklist

Antonius, Marcus, ca. 83-30 B.C.

Goldsworthy, Adrian Keith. **Antony** and Cleopatra; [by] Adrian Goldsworthy. Yale University Press 2010 470p il map $35   92

1. Queens 2. Generals 3. Statesmen 4. Orators 5. Rome -- History 6. Egypt -- History

ISBN 978-0-300-16534-0

LC 2010-929122

"Narrating [Antony] and Cleopatra's parts in the tumultuous end of the Roman Republic, Goldsworthy skillfully integrates the partial and partisan source material into an accessible presentation of a classic tale from classical times." Booklist

Includes bibliographical references

Apana, Chang, 1871-1933

Yunte Huang. **Charlie** Chan; the untold story of the honorable detective and his rendezvous with American history. W.W. Norton 2010 354p il map   92

1. Detectives 2. Chan, Charlie (Fictional character) 3. Biography, Individual

ISBN 0393069621; 9780393069624

LC 2010016653

This is a history of Charlie Chan, the detective feaured in six novels and 47 movies. Huang contends that Charlie Chan is based upon Chang Apana, a real-life Chinese detective on the Honolulu police force. Bibliography. Index.

This "is a terrifically enjoyable and informative book, one that should appeal to both students of racial history and to fans of one of cinema's greatest detectives." Washington Post Book World

Includes bibliographical references

Appleseed, Johnny, 1774-1845

Means, Howard B. **Johnny** Appleseed; the man, the myth, the American story. [by] Howard Means. Simon & Schuster 2011 320p il map $26; ebook $12.99   92

1. Apples 2. Frontier and pioneer life 3. Pioneers 4. Fruit growers

ISBN 978-1-4391-7825-6; 978-1-4391-7827-0 ebook

LC 2011-665

The author attempts to separate "the history from the folklore surrounding one of America's most notable legends, Johnny Appleseed. Born John Chapman in Massachusetts on September 26, 1774, Chapman migrated west in his early twenties, adopting the lifestyle of an itinerant pioneer." Publ Wkly

"Delightfully wry and perceptive, Means' quest to understand Chapman/Appleseed is a captivating achievement in Americana." Booklist

Arana, Marie

Arana, Marie. **American** chica; two worlds, one childhood. Dial Press (NY) 2001 309p hardcover o.p. pa $12.95   92

1. Authors 2. Novelists 3. Editors 4. Memoirists 5. Literary critics

ISBN 0-385-31963-0 pa

LC 00-47529

The author, born to a Peruvian father and an American mother, writes of her childhood in Peru

Arana "blends a journalist's dedication to research with a style that sings with humor. Her memoir is an outstanding contribution to the growing shelf of Latina literature." Publ Wkly

Archimedes, ca. 287-212 B.C.

Hirshfeld, Alan. **Eureka** man; the life and legacy of Archimedes. Walker 2009 242p il map $26   **92**

1. Scientists 2. Mathematicians 3. Writers on science 4. Science -- Greece -- History

ISBN 978-0-8027-1618-7; 0-8027-1618-0

LC 2009-05608

"Thoroughly enjoyable look at the tumultuous life and resounding influence of a genius of antiquity. . . . Hirshfeld writes clearly and with enthusiasm, navigating even the occasional dense mathematical concept with easy-to-understand language and accompanying diagrams." Kirkus

Includes bibliographical references

Arkin, Alan, 1934-

Arkin, Alan. An **improvised** life; a memoir. Da Capo Press 2011 201p $17   **92**

1. Actors 2. Theatrical directors

ISBN 978-0-306-81966-7

LC 2010-45034

"Arkin looks back on his career as an actor, but this memoir forgoes the backstage gossip and star-studded anecdotes readers might expect. In fact, the author largely ignores his accomplishments in favor of charting his inner evolution as an artist, focusing on intellectual and spiritual epiphanies that have shaped his approach to acting. . . . Earnest, intelligent and well-observed—less a celebrity memoir than a serious consideration of the principles of acting and improvisation." Kirkus

Armstrong, Karen, 1944-

Armstrong, Karen. The **spiral** staircase; my climb out of darkness. Knopf 2004 xxii, 305p hardcover o.p. pa $14   **92**

1. Nuns 2. Religious scholars

ISBN 0-375-41318-9; 0-385-72127-7 pa

LC 2003-47550

This "is the story of Armstrong's personal spiritual quest, which led her at age 17 to join a convent. However, she found that her own skeptical nature and the physical constraints of convent life crippled her intellectually and spiritually. . . . After seven years, Armstrong left the convent." SLJ

Armstrong, Lance

Coyle, Daniel. **Lance** Armstrong's war; one man's battle against fate, fame, love, death, scandal, and a few other rivals on the road to the Tour de France. HarperCollins Publishers 2005 326p il $25.95   **92**

1. Athletes 2. Cyclists 3. Olympic athletes

ISBN 0-06-073497-3

LC 2005-279702

This biography focuses particular attention on the American cyclist's preparation for and participation in the 2004

Tour de France, an event that Armstrong won for the sixth time in as many years.

"This work is honest, personal and passionate, with plenty to chew on for fans and novices alike." Publ Wkly

Strickland, Bill. **Tour** de Lance; the extraordinary story of Lance Armstrong's fight to reclaim the Tour De France. Harmony Books 2010 300p il map $25.99   **92**

1. Athletes 2. Cyclists 3. Olympic athletes

ISBN 978-0-307-58984-2

LC 2010-4504

This is "the story of Lance Armstrong's return in 2009, after a three-year absence, to the Tour de France. . . . Strickland, who had access to Armstrong's inner circle, enhances it with an eye for detail and an understanding of its importance in the context of cycling's own physical demands and singular history. He reminds readers, as if they need it, of Armstrong's supremacy and laser dedication in the sport. . . . An irresistible account of a story that needed telling." Booklist

Armstrong, Louis, 1900-1971

Teachout, Terry. **Pops**; a life of Louis Armstrong. Houghton Mifflin Harcourt 2009 475p il $30   **92**

1. Jazz musicians 2. Biography, Individual 3. Jazz -- History and criticism

ISBN 978-0-15-101089-9; 0-15-101089-7

LC 2009-6035

"The author makes an eloquent case for Armstrong's status as a pioneer, not just in jazz but in the broader context of 20th-century art. A rewarding jazz biography and a revealing look at a broad swath of American cultural history." Kirkus

Includes discography and bibliographical references

Armstrong, Neil, 1930-2012

Barbree, Jay. **Neil** Armstrong; A Life of Flight. Jay Barbree. St. Martin's Press 2014 320 p. illustrations $27.99   **92**

1. Astronauts 2. Air pilots -- Biography 3. Project Apollo (U.S.) -- History 4. Space flight to the moon -- History 5. Astronauts -- United States -- Biography

ISBN 125004071X; 9781250040718

LC 2014008696

"Working from 50 years of conversations he had with [astronaut] Neil [Armstrong] . . . , [author Jay] Barbree writes about Neil's three passions--flight, family, and friends. This is the inside story of Neil Armstrong from the time he flew . . . in the Korean War and then flew a rocket plane called the X-15 to the edge of space, to when he saved his Gemini 8 by flying the first emergency return from Earth orbit and then flew Apollo-Eleven to the moon's Sea of Tranquility." (Publisher's note)

"The author paints a detailed and colorful picture of his subject and an unbiased depiction of the period in which he lived, while also demonstrating reverence for Armstrong as a confidant." LJ

Aron, Wendy

Aron, Wendy. **Hide** & seek; how I laughed at depression, conquered my fears and found happiness. Kunati 2008 235p pa $14.95   **92**

1. Authors 2. Dramatists 3. Journalists 4. Depression

(Psychology) 5. Memoirists 6. Television scriptwriters
ISBN 978-1-60164-158-8

LC 2008-14008

"In her efforts to subdue raging depression, TV and stage writer Aron tried to no avail virtually every mainstream and alternative remedy. Her adventures among the lunatic fringe are laugh-out-loud funny. . . . Anyone who has overcome recurring bouts with the blues will relish this comic self-help tale." Libr J

Includes bibliographical references

Atanasoff, John V.

Smiley, Jane. The **man** who invented the computer; the biography of John Atanasoff, digital pioneer. Doubleday 2010 246p il $25.95   **92**
1. Inventors 2. Physicists 3. Mathematicians 4. Computer scientists
ISBN 978-0-385-52713-2; 0-385-52713-6

LC 2010-18887

"Engrossing. Smiley takes science history and injects it with a touch of noir and an exciting clash of vanities." Kirkus
Includes bibliographical references

Athill, Diana

Athill, Diana. **Somewhere** towards the end. W.W. Norton 2009 182p $24.95; pa $13.95   **92**
1. Aging 2. Authors 3. Old age 4. Editors 5. Memoirists 6. Translators 7. Short story writers
ISBN 978-0-393-06770-5; 0-393-06770-X; 978-0-393-33800-3 pa; 0-393-33800-2 pa

LC 2008-41533

First published 2008 in the United Kingdom
The author "offers a spry dispatch on the condition of being elderly. . . . Her perspective is both remorseless and tender as she considers the waning of her sexual desire, the sharpening of her atheist resolve, her increasing preference for nonfiction rather than novels . . . and the truth that, even in her advanced state, much of her time is taken up with caring for those still older. The achievement of Athill's work is its refusal to reduce the specificities of her captivating life to homilies about wisdom." New Yorker

Atkins, Vera, 1908-2000

Helm, Sarah. A **life** in secrets; Vera Atkins and the missing agents of WWII. Nan A. Talese 2006 493p il map hardcover o.p. pa $16   **92**
1. Intelligence service agents 2. World War, 1939-1945 -- Secret service 3. Great Britain -- Special Operations Executive
ISBN 0-385-50845-X; 978-1-4000-3140-5 pa; 1-4000-3140-0 pa

LC 2005-56870

First published 2005 in the United Kingdom
This is a biography of "the highest-ranking female official in the French section of a WWII British intelligence unit that aided the resistance. Atkins sent 400 agents into France, including 39 women she'd personally recruited and supervised. . . . Helm has produced a memorable portrait of a woman who knowingly sent other women to their deaths and a searing history of female courage and suffering during WWII." Publ Wkly

Includes bibliographical references

Atlas, Teddy

Atlas, Teddy. **Atlas**; from the streets to the ring: a son's struggle to become a man. [by] Teddy Atlas and Peter Alson. Ecco 2006 278p il $24.95   **92**
1. Sports trainers
ISBN 0-06-054240-3; 978-0-06-054240-5

LC 2005-52104

The author "traces his circuitous route from Staten Island street thug, emotionally ignored by his doctor father, to renowned [boxing] trainer. . . . It's all here—the good, the bad and the ugly of Teddy Atlas, often rendered in a crude but convincing street language, captured so faithfully and so forcefully by his collaborator, Peter Alson." N Y Times Book Rev

Attila, King of the Huns, d. 453

Kelly, Christopher. The **end** of empire; Attila the Hun and the fall of Rome. W.W. Norton 2009 350p il map $26.95   **92**
1. Huns 2. Tribal leaders 3. Rome -- History
ISBN 978-0-393-06196-3

LC 2009-009072

First published 2008 in the United Kingdom with title: Attila the Hun: barbarian terror and the fall of the Roman Empire
The author "paints an engaging portrait of Attila the Hun's rise to prominence and places the feared warlord in the context of his own time." Libr J

Includes bibliographical references

Audubon, John James, 1785-1851

Rhodes, Richard. **John** James Audubon; the making of an American. Knopf 2004 528p il $30; pa $16   **92**
1. Artists 2. Painters 3. Naturalists 4. Ornithologists 5. Writers on science 6. Biography, Individual 7. Artists -- United States
ISBN 0-375-41412-6; 0-375-71393-X pa

LC 2003-69489

This is a biography of the American ornithologist and painter.
The author "chronicles Audubon's ineluctable sense of mission, phenomenal skills, and triumph over adversity. . . . Rhodes sets Audubon's engrossing tale within the context of the War of 1812, the Louisiana Purchase, the wars against Native Americans (whom Audubon profoundly admired), and the rapid decimation of the American wilderness. . . . Full of passion and discovery, hardship and transcendence, Audubon's story is at once intimate and mythic, and Rhodes' fresh, comprehensive biography will capture the imagination of readers everywhere." Booklist

Includes bibliographical references

Augustus, Emperor of Rome, 63 B.C.-14 A.D.

★ Everitt, Anthony. **Augustus**; the life of Rome's first emperor. Random House 2006 377p il map $26.95   **92**
1. Emperors 2. Rome -- History
ISBN 1-4000-6128-8; 978-1-4000-6128-0

LC 2006-41735

The author's "writing is so crisp and so lively he brings both Rome and Augustus to life in this magnificent work, a must-read for anyone interested in classical times." Booklist

Includes bibliographical references

Aung San Suu Kyi

Wintle, Justin. **Perfect** hostage; a life of Aung San Suu Kyi, Burma's prisoner of conscience. Skyhorse Pub. 2008 464p il map $27.95   92

1. Women political activists 2. Myanmar -- Politics and government 3. National League for Democracy (Burma)

ISBN 978-1-60239-266-3; 1-60239-266-8

LC 2007-51031

This is a biography of the Burmese human rights activist. The author "writes with a snarling wit, firm grasp of Burma's horrors, and penetrating respect for this tenacious and composed prisoner of conscience, detailing her genius for connecting with people, the threats against her life, and her devotion to peace." Booklist

Includes bibliographical references (p. 432-9)

Austen, Jane, 1775-1817

Harman, Claire. **Jane's** fame; how Jane Austen conquered the world. Henry Holt and Co. 2010 277p il $26   92

1. Authors 2. Novelists 3. Women authors 4. Authors, English

ISBN 978-0-8050-8258-6; 0-8050-8258-1

LC 2009-22291

First published 2009 in the United Kingdom

"Engagingly written and full of fascinating bits of information as well as valuable insights, this is a must for any serious Austen reader." Booklist

Includes bibliographical references

Auster, Paul, 1947-

Auster, Paul, 1947- **Report** from the interior; Paul Auster. Henry Holt and Company 2013 352 p. (hardback) $27   92

1. Letters 2. Adolescence 3. Authors, American -- 20th century -- Biography

ISBN 0805098577; 9780805098570

LC 2013002417

Author Paul Auster has divided this book into four parts. The "first is a childhood psychobiography, to the age of 12, recognizing the distortions and holes in memory while discovering the magic of literature. . . . The second consists of exhaustively detailed synopses of two movies that he saw in his midteens, The Incredible Shrinking Man (1957) and was a Fugitive from a Chain Gang (1932)." The third and fourth parts include letters to his wife and a scrapbook. (Kirkus Reviews)

Autry, Gene, 1907-1998

George-Warren, Holly. **Public** cowboy no. 1; the life and times of Gene Autry. Oxford University Press 2007 406p il $28   92

1. Actors 2. Singers 3. Country musicians 4. Cowboys 5. Baseball executives 6. Broadcasting executives

ISBN 978-0-19-517746-6; 0-19-517746-0

LC 2006-36369

This is a biography of the radio performer, singer and actor who performed in rodeos and appeared in such movies as Public Cowboy No.1 (1937) and The Phantom Empire (1935).

"This colorful study is much more than a biography of Autry; it also tells the story of country-western music, singing cowboys, radio and early television, and celebrity." Choice

Includes filmography, discography, and bibliographical references

Avonmore, William Charles Yelverton, Viscount, 1824-1883

Schama, Chloe. **Wild** romance; a Victorian story of a marriage, a trial, and a self-made woman. Walker & Co. 2010 249p il map $24   92

1. Authors 2. Novelists 3. Army officers 4. Great Britain -- Social life and customs

ISBN 978-0-8027-1736-8; 0-8027-1736-5

LC 2009-44758

Schama details the "bigamy trial of William Charles Yelverton, which dominated the front pages of Irish, Scottish, and British newspapers in 1861. Although the story of Yelverton and his first wife, Theresa Longworth, practically tells itself through court documents, letters, and public opinion, Schama adds a journalist's touch in her story development. The latter part of the book deals with Theresa's later life in America as a self-made woman still haunted by her past." Libr J

Includes bibliographical references

Ayers, Nathaniel Anthony

★ Lopez, Steve. The **soloist**; a lost dream, an unlikely friendship, and the redemptive power of music. G. P. Putnam's Sons 2008 273p hardcover o.p. pa $15   92

1. Violinists 2. Homeless persons 3. Homeless 4. Schizophrenics 5. Street entertainers

ISBN 978-0-399-15506-2; 0-399-15506-6; 978-0-425-23836-3 pa; 0-425-23836-9 pa

LC 2007-46314

The true story of Nathaniel Ayers, a musician who becomes schizophrenic and homeless, and his friendship with Steve Lopez, the Los Angeles columnist who discovers and writes about him in the newspaper.

"With self-effacing humor, fast-paced yet elegant prose and unsparing honesty, Lopez tells an inspiring story of heartbreak and hope." Publ Wkly

Baartman, Saartjie

Crais, Clifton C. **Sara** Baartman and the Hottentot Venus; a ghost story and a biography. [by] Clifton Crais and Pamela Scully. Princeton University Press 2009 232p il map $29.95   92

1. Biography, Individual 2. Racism in museum exhibits 3. Museum exhibits -- Moral and ethical aspects

ISBN 9780691135809; 0-691-13580-0

LC 2008-14918

"A member of a small indigenous tribe of herdsmen dubbed the Hottentots by Dutch colonists (but known today by their name Khoikhoi), Baartman was captured in the course of ongoing colonial warfare that effected a genocidal destruction of this peaceful people. Having been enslaved, she was taken to Europe by a member of the family that 'owned' and exhibited her much as an exotic animal might be. . . . [The authors] have done an excellent job not only of telling this rebarbative story but of putting it into the context of its time. This enables them to explain what permitted such an exhibition while at the same time viewing it through our (thankfully) more humane and enlightened lens." Los Angeles Times Book Rev

Includes bibliographical references

★ Holmes, Rachel. **African** queen; the real life of the Hottentot Venus. Random House 2007 161p il $23.95 **92**

1. Entertainers
ISBN 978-1-4000-6136-5; 1-4000-6136-9

LC 2006-45166

"This is a probing look at historical racism and sexual exploitation presented through the life of an extraordinary woman." Booklist

Includes bibliographical references

Bacall, Lauren, 1924-2014

Bacall, Lauren. **By** myself and then some. HarperEntertainment 2005 506p il $26.95 **92**

1. Actors
ISBN 0-06-075535-0

LC 2005-40256

First published 1979 by Knopf with title: Lauren Bacall by myself

In this memoir, the actress describes how she got her start in acting and her relationships with other actors, including Humphrey Bogart.

"Certainly more intelligently written than your average celebrity autobiography, this memoir tells a fascinating story of one woman's journey through life with an intimacy that's sure to engage legions of readers." Booklist

Bach, Johann Sebastian, 1685-1750

Gardiner, John Eliot. **Bach**; music in the castle of heaven. by John Eliot Gardiner. Alfred A. Knopf 2013 672 p. il. (chiefly col.), map, music (hardback) $35 **92**

1. Composers, German 2. Composers -- Biography 3. Composers -- Germany -- Biography
ISBN 0375415297; 9780375415296

LC 2013030398

"Originally published in Great Britain as Music in the castle of heaven, by Allen Lane"--Title page verso

National Book Critics Circle Award Finalist: Biography (2013)

In this book, author John Eliot Gardiner, "takes us . . . into [German composer Johann Sebastian] Bach's works and mind . . . explaining in . . . detail the ideas on which Bach drew, how he worked, how his music is constructed, how it achieves its effects--and what it can tell us about Bach the man." (Publisher's note)

"Although Gardiner celebrates Bach's accomplishments through this dense, demanding but rewarding work, he reminds readers continually that the composer was no saint. . .

. [T]he author's focus is not so much on the man but on the music." Kirkus

Includes bibliographical references and index

★ Geck, Martin. **Johann** Sebastian Bach; life and work. translated from the German by John Hargraves. Harcourt 2006 738p il $40 **92**

1. Composers
ISBN 978-0-15-100648-9; 0-15-100648-2

LC 2006-12390

This book "adds original scholarship to an exhaustive study of other studies of Bach. And although it is often dense with information, it is just as often entertaining: rich in anecdotes and scintillating in its conjectures." N Y Times (Late N Y Ed)

Includes bibliographical references

Baer, Max, 1909-1959

Schaap, Jeremy. **Cinderella** Man; James J. Braddock, Max Baer, and the greatest upset in boxing history. Houghton Mifflin 2005 324p il hardcover o.p. pa $13.95 **92**

1. Boxers (Persons) 2. Boxing -- Biography
ISBN 0-618-55117-4; 0-618-71190-2 pa

LC 2004-66085

The author goes into "detail on the brawny, reserved Braddock, who, at his lowest moments, was reduced to living off government relief and doing grueling work on the Hoboken, N.J., docks. But the story is as much about Max Baer, the lovably clownish and handsome heavyweight Braddock defeated as a 10-to-one underdog. . . . Boxing enthusiasts will be more than satisfied by Schaap's meticulous account, which includes round-by-round details of the fight, as well as profiles of other fighters of the era." Publ Wkly

Includes bibliographical references

Bailey, Blake, 1963-

Bailey, Blake. The **Splendid** Things We Planned; A Family Portrait. by Blake Bailey. W.W. Norton & Co. Inc 2014 288 p. illustrations $25.95 **92**

1. Alcoholism 2. Drug abuse 3. Family life 4. Mental illness 5. Authors, American -- Biography 6. Biographers -- United States -- Biography
ISBN 0393239578; 9780393239577

LC 2013039720

In this book, "biographer [Blake] Bailey tells the story of his own life by chronicling his brother Scott's alcoholism and drug addiction, which causes him to descend into violence and madness. Told in chronological order, starting with the marriage of his straight-laced lawyer father to his bohemian, German-immigrant mother, Bailey's story captures the contradictions and tensions that simmer just below the surface of the family, as they try to live a normal suburban life in Oklahoma." (Publishers Weekly)

A "haunting portrait of more than one tortured soul and a heartfelt probing of the limits of brotherly love." Booklist

Bailey, Elisabeth Tova

Bailey, Elisabeth Tova. The **sound** of a wild snail eating. Algonquin Books of Chapel Hill 2010 190p il $18.95 **92**

1. Snails 2. Authors 3. Essayists 4. Short story writers

5. Biography, Individual
ISBN 978-1-56512-606-0

LC 2010-18603

"A small, short book filled with an enormous amount of natural history and science about snails; also, an acknowledgment of an individual's determination to recover and regain life with humor and insight. Highly recommended." Libr J

Includes bibliographical references

Baker, Russell, 1925-

Baker, Russell, 1925- **Growing** up. New American Library 1983 278p pa $15   **92**
1. Authors 2. Humorists 3. Journalists 4. Essayists 5. Satirists 6. Memoirists
ISBN 0-452-25550-3

First published 1982 by Congdon & Weed

This book "recounts the first 24 years of [Baker's] life as the son of an independent and deep-rooted Virginian family." Natl Rev

Balanchine, George, 1904-1983

Gottlieb, Robert Adams. **George** Balanchine: the ballet maker. HarperCollins\Atlas Books 2004 224p (Eminent lives) $19.95; pa. $13.99   **92**
1. Ballet 2. Dancers 3. Choreographers
ISBN 0-06-075070-7; 9780060750718

LC 2004-48856

"This loving tribute captures Balanchine's legacy: his energy, confidence, lack of pretension and, most important, his joy in creation." Publ Wkly

Includes bibliographical references

★ Teachout, Terry. **All** in the dances: a brief life of George Balanchine. Harcourt 2004 208p $22 **92**
1. Ballet 2. Dancers 3. Choreographers
ISBN 0-15-101088-9

LC 2004-9226

"Balanchine's ballets are modern masterpieces, and Teachout, moving chronologically from work to work, uses them as stepping stones to tell Balanchine's own story. This is highly recommended as a first book on the life and art of George Balanchine for students and the general reader." Publ Wkly

Includes bibliographical references

Balbirer, Nancy

Balbirer, Nancy. **Take** your shirt off and cry; a memoir of near-fame experiences. Bloomsbury 2009 231p pa $16   **92**
1. Actors 2. Memoirists
ISBN 978-1-59691-478-0; 1-59691-478-5

LC 2008-45397

"It is a fact of life seldom discussed in our celebrity-mad media: most actors do not become either rich or famous. Balbirer revels in her failure in this witty, poignant, exceedingly well-written memoir chronicling the ups and downs (mostly downs) of a trained, hardworking actress who always seems on the cusp of greatness but who nevertheless always fails to make the grade." Booklist

Balzac, Honoré de, 1799-1850

Robb, Graham. **Balzac**; a life. Norton 1994 521p il hardcover o.p. pa $15   **92**
1. Authors 2. Novelists 3. Short story writers
ISBN 0-393-31387-5 pa

LC 94-18614

"Balzac's life was more cause for incredulity than anything he wrote, and Robb compellingly sets out the documentable facts against and within the world Balzac created from them. . . . The result is nearly a novel, although Robb does not fictionalize with re-created dialogs and hypothetical events. He has in fact produced an extensive traditional biography . . . not a critical reassessment." Libr J

Includes bibliographical references

Bard, Elizabeth

Bard, Elizabeth. **Lunch** in Paris; a love story, with recipes. Little, Brown and Co. 2010 324p $23.99   **92**
1. Journalists 2. French cooking 3. Art historians 4. Americans -- France 5. Paris (France) -- Description and travel
ISBN 978-0-316-04279-6; 0-316-04279-X

LC 2009-22064

"Falling in love with a Frenchman was not in Elizabeth Bard's master plan, but then he took her to a local canteen: 'Not to minimize Gwendal's many charms, but he was halfway to home base as soon as I cut into that marvelous steak,' she writes. Culture shock set in as she learned to shop and cook in Paris, standing in line here for the best green beans, going there for the best walnuts. I thought the recipes were a cutesy touch until I made a few of them: chicken tagine with two kinds of lemon, spiced apricots, chouquettes. Forget the narrative — you could just buy this as a cookbook." Entertainment Wkly

Baret, Jeanne, 1740-1807

Ridley, Glynis. The **discovery** of Jeanne Baret; a story of science, the high seas, and the first woman to circumnavigate the globe. Crown Publishers 2010 288p il $25; ebook $25   **92**
1. Botanists 2. Explorers 3. Women scientists 4. Voyages around the world
ISBN 978-0-307-46352-4; 978-0-307-46354-8 ebook

LC 2010-16778

This is a biography "of Jeanne Baret. Born in 1740 in France's Loire valley, Baret became an expert 'herb woman' who proved to be indispensable to the ambitious botanist Philibert Commerson, accompanying him as his assistant when Commerson was appointed naturalist for France's first expedition to circumnavigate the globe. But women were forbidden, so Baret dressed as a man. . . . Woven throughout this gripping story are Ridley's piquant insights into eighteenth-century exploration, botany, taxonomy, biopiracy, and sexism. Baret could not have asked for a more exacting and expressive champion. Ridley is incandescent in her passion for the truth." Booklist

Includes bibliographical references

Barnes, Julian, 1946-

Barnes, Julian. **Nothing** to be frightened of. Alfred A. Knopf 2008 243p $24 **92**

1. Death 2. Authors 3. Novelists 4. Essayists 5. Authors, English 6. Television critics 7. Short story writers

ISBN 978-0-307-26963-8; 0-307-26963-9

LC 2008-19603

This is "an elegant memoir and meditation, a deep seismic tremor of a book that keeps rumbling and grumbling in the mind for weeks thereafter." N Y Times Book Rev

Barr, Nevada

Barr, Nevada. **Seeking** enlightenment--hat by hat; a skeptic's path to religion. Putnam 2003 222p $21.95; pa $13 **92**

1. Authors 2. Park rangers 3. Mystery writers

ISBN 0-399-15057-9; 0-425-19603-8 pa

LC 2003-43101

The author "charts the course of her spiritual evolution, how she sought to understand the many aspects of spiritual life, from forgiveness ('a sigh of relief on which the memory of evil is breathed out') to pain ('it is a duty to relieve our own pain') to commitment ('not a contract with the world but with the self'). Barr's account of her transformation from nonbeliever to committed churchgoer—but one who maintains a healthy sense of doubt even as she prays and attends Bible studies—is moving but never saccharine." Booklist

Barthelme, Donald

Daugherty, Tracy. **Hiding** man; a biography of Donald Barthelme. St. Martin's Press 2008 581p il $35 **92**

1. Authors 2. Novelists 3. Authors, American 4. Short story writers

ISBN 978-0-312-37868-4; 0-312-37868-8

LC 2008-29881

"Not dwelling on Barthelme's dark soul or his uneven work, Daugherty has created a convincing narrative from a life that was engaged, passionate and maybe even fulfilled." N Y Times Book Rev

Includes bibliographical references (p. 549-556)

Basie, Count, 1904-1984

Basie, Count. **Good** morning blues: the autobiography of Count Basie; as told to Albert Murray. Da Capo Press 1995 399p il pa $17.95 **92**

1. Pianists 2. Jazz musicians 3. African American musicians 4. Band leaders

ISBN 0-306-81107-3

LC 94-44697

"Basie pays tribute to his colleagues and managers (and to John Hammond for 'discovering' him), but does not hesitate to discuss their weaknesses and short-comings; his language is direct and earthy. Although some of the book reads more like a catalogue or itinerary than an autobiography, it will have strong appeal for jazz buffs and fans of the late bandleader." Publ Wkly

Bass, Rick, 1958-

Bass, Rick. **Why** I came West. Houghton Mifflin Co. 2008 238p $24; pa $14.95 **92**

1. Authors 2. Novelists 3. Geologists 4. Conservationists 5. Literary landmarks 6. Essayists 7. West (U.S.) 8. Authors, American 9. Writers on nature 10. Short story writers

ISBN 978-0-618-59675-1; 0-618-59675-5; 978-0-5472-3771-8 pa; 0-5472-3771-5 pa

LC 2007-30660

Bass "tells the tale of his apprenticeship to literature and the place that has defined his life for the past two decades, Montana's Yaak Valley. Bass looks back to his Houston childhood, Utah college years, and work as an oil geologist in Mississippi, searching for clues to his love-at-first sight response to the Yaak. As he describes his deep immersion in this bountiful land as a hunter, hiker, artist, and environmentalist, he . . . shares his anguish over the clear-cutting of woods, and chronicles the hard work of wilderness advocacy and the virulent hatred it arouses. Versed in paradox, Bass is bracing in his candor about how difficult it will be to change our destructive ways, and incandescent in his reasoned call to preserve the few remaining unspoiled places." Booklist

Baszile, Jennifer, 1969-

Baszile, Jennifer. The **Black** girl next door; a memoir. Simon & Schuster 2009 310p il $25 **92**

1. Historians 2. Memoirists 3. College teachers

ISBN 978-1-4165-4327-5; 1-4165-4327-9

LC 2008-12867

"The Baszile family's move to an exclusive white suburb in Palos Verde, California, was the culmination of the parents' striving for a racially integrated, middle-class life. For their daughters, it meant isolation and coping with the occasional racial slurs that went along with the advantages of suburban life. Their parents veered between an aggressive integration strategy and an equally aggressive strategy to keep their daughters socially connected to other black teens. . . . This is an absorbing look behind the facade of one black family's striving for integration and the American dream." Booklist

Beach, Sylvia

The **letters** of Sylvia Beach; edited by Keri Walsh; with a foreword by Noël Riley Fitch. Columbia University Press 2010 347p il $29.95 **92**

1. Memoirists 2. Shakespeare and Company 3. Booksellers and bookselling -- France -- Paris 4. Paris (France) -- Intellectual life -- 20th century

ISBN 978-0-231-14536-7; 0-231-14535-5

LC 2009-45434

"Beach's story has been told before. . . . [But these letters] have an unvarnished charm all their own. Written to friends, writers, customers and family members, they depict a witty and resourceful woman struggling to keep her business, her writers and her precarious existence afloat." N Y Times Book Rev

Includes bibliographical references

Beah, Ishmael

★ Beah, Ishmael, 1980- A **long** way gone; memoirs of a boy soldier. Farrar, Straus & Giroux 2007 229p map pa $12; $22 **92**

1. Refugees 2. Soldiers 3. Children and war 4. Memoirists 5. Social activists 6. Sierra Leone -- History -- Civil War, 1991- 7. Sierra Leone -- History -- Civil War, 1991-2002

ISBN 0-374-53126-9 pa; 0-374-95191-8; 978-0-374-10523-5; 978-0-374-53126-3 pa

LC 2006-17101

The author writes about his experiences as a recruit in the Sierra Leone Army.

"In 1993, when the author was twelve, rebel forces attacked his home town, in Sierra Leone, and he was separated from his parents. For months, he straggled through the war-torn countryside, starving and terrified, until he was taken under the wing of a Shakespeare-spouting lieutenant in the government army. Soon, he was being fed amphetamines and trained to shoot an AK-47. . . . Beah's memoir documents his transformation from a child into a hardened, brutally efficient soldier who high-fived his fellow-recruits after they slaughtered their enemies—often boys their own age—and who 'felt no pity for anyone.'" New Yorker

Beasley, Sandra

Beasley, Sandra. **Don't** kill the birthday girl; tales from an allergic life. Crown Publishers 2011 229p il $23; ebook $11.99 **92**

1. Poets 2. Authors 3. Food allergy

ISBN 978-0-307-58811-1; 978-0-307-58813-5 ebook

LC 2010043724

"If you didn't have sympathy for this relatively new generation of sufferers, you will after Beasley's book. . . . The emotional stuff is the best—from worrying about kissing boys who may have eaten forbidden foods, to considering the implications of having kids who'll have to wash their hands before hugging their mother." Maclean's

Beatty, Warren, 1937-

Biskind, Peter. **Star**; how Warren Beatty seduced America. Simon & Schuster 2010 627p il $30 **92**

1. Actors 2. Motion picture directors 3. Motion picture producers

ISBN 978-0-7432-4658-3; 0-7432-4658--6

LC 2009-22225

"Biskind brings his historian's acumen to bear on the production of era-defining triumphs like Bonnie and Clyde (1967), Shampoo (1975) and Reds (1981), as well as notorious flops like Ishtar (1987), Love Affair (1994) and Town & Country (2001), and his accounts are full of juicy gossip and intriguing insights into the actor's psychology. . . . A gripping portrait of a difficult talent." Kirkus

Includes bibliographical references

Beaumarchais, Pierre Augustin Caron de, 1732-1799

Lever, Maurice. **Beaumarchais**; a biography. Farrar, Straus and Giroux 2008 411p $35 **92**

1. Authors 2. Dramatists 3. Dramatists, French

ISBN 9780374113285; 0-374-11328-9

LC 2008-55449

"Best known as the author of the comedies that became Mozart's 'The Marriage of Figaro' and Rossini's 'The Barber of Seville,' Beaumarchais was a high-spirited adventurer for whom writing plays was only an 'honest relaxation.' This erudite and wry biography covers the full range of his occupations, including watchmaking, espionage, pamphleteering, and transatlantic trade." New Yorker

Includes bibliographical references

Becker, Suzy

Becker, Suzy. **I** had brain surgery, what's your excuse? an illustrated memoir. Workman Pub 2003 282p il $19.95 **92**

1. Authors 2. Humorists 3. Cartoonists 4. Illustrators 5. Memoirists 6. AIDS activists 7. Social activists 8. Nonfiction writers

ISBN 0-7611-2478-0

LC 2003-60039

Becker "was suffering seizures but didn't tell anyone until a friend witnessed an incident. Eventually, she was scheduled for brain surgery to remove a tumor. Writing with the dry sense of humor that some of us rely on to make it through situations, Becker recalls her reactions to her medical problems, from liking the first doctor who gave her no bad news ('just stress') to the terror of the eventual diagnosis. Her descriptions of the surgery and its dreadful, but temporary, effects on her ability to speak, read, write, and draw make for especially compelling reading. . . . Becker has turned one person's experience into a universal story of family, healing, and the return to creativity." Libr J

Beecher, Henry Ward, 1813-1887

★ Applegate, Debby. The **most** famous man in America; the biography of Henry Ward Beecher. Doubleday 2006 529p il map $27.95 **92**

1. Clergy 2. Nonfiction writers

ISBN 0-385-51396-8; 978-0-385-51396-8

LC 2005-54842

This is a biography of the American clergyman.

"By illuminating Beecher's position in history, Applegate has produced a biography worthy of its subject." N Y Times Book Rev

Includes bibliographical references

Beethoven, Ludwig van, 1770-1827

Morris, Edmund, 1940- **Beethoven** : the universal composer. HarperCollins Publishers 2005 243p (Eminent lives) $21.95; pa $13.99 **92**

1. Composers

ISBN 0-06-075974-7; 978-0-06-075974-2; 9780060759759

LC 2006-274925

This is a biography of the German composer.

The author "clearly admires his subject not only for the work but also for his constant fight against the odds, and

he has written an ideal biography for the general reader."
Publ Wkly

Includes bibliographical references

Suchet, John. **Beethoven**; the man revealed.
John Suchet. Grove Press 2013 xiii, 273 p.p illus-
trations (chiefly color) (hbk.) $30   **92**
 1. Composers, German 2. Composers -- Biography 3.
Composers -- Germany -- Biography
ISBN 080212206X; 9780802122063

LC 2012518710

The Spaniard : in which a momentous life begins -- The
right teacher : this boy could become 'a second Mozart' --
Meeting Mozart : watch out for that boy -- Word spreads :
young Beethoven as kitchen scullion -- Impressing the Viennese : but Haydn feels the wrath of an angry young man
-- My poor hearing haunts me : but there is 'a dear charming
girl who loves me' -- Only my art held me back : in which
Beethoven considers suicide -- Egyptian hieroglyphics : Napoleon is no more than 'a common tyrant' -- O, beloved J!
: musical failure, but will Beethoven succeed in love? -- A
deeply immoral woman : Beethoven holds the most important concert of his life, and is offered a job -- Under cannon
fire : in which Beethoven once again tries his luck at love
-- Immortal beloved : 'my angel, my all, my very self' --
An utterly untamed personality : Beethoven turns again to
his 'poor shipwrecked opera' -- Into the witness box : how
the single letter 'o' ruined Beethoven's life -- A musical gift
from London : how Rossini found Beethoven 'disorderly
and dirty' -- 'I want to be a soldier' : in which Beethoven
gets drunk with friends -- Two pistols and gunpowder : an
invitation to get away from it all -- Frightening the oxen :
'The greatest composer of the century, and you treated him
like a servant!' -- Terminally ill : 'His face was damp, he
spat blood' -- The last master : 'He was an artist, but a man
as well.'

This book, by John Suchet, is a biography of composer
Ludwig von Beethoven. "Suchet illuminates the composer's
difficult childhood, his struggle to maintain friendships and
romances, his ungovernable temper, his obsessive efforts
to control his nephew's life, and the excruciating decline
of his hearing." It also discusses "the landmark events in
Beethoven's career--from his competitive encounters with
Mozart to the circumstances surrounding the creation of
the well-known 'Fur Elise' and 'Moonlight Sonata.'" (Publisher's note)

"For the many readers lacking the proper background in
musical theory, British broadcaster and Beethoven authority Suchet's explanations of Beethoven's music sing to us
almost as if we could hear it." Kirkus

Includes bibliographical references and index

★ Swafford, Jan. **Beethoven**; anguish and tri-
umph : a biography. Jan Swafford. Houghton Mifflin
Harcourt 2014 1104 p. illustrations $40   **92**
 1. Composers, German 2. Composers -- Biography 3.
Composers -- Germany -- Biography
ISBN 061805474X; 9780618054749

LC 2014011681

In this book, music historian Jan Swafford "mines
sources never before used in English-language biographies
to reanimate the revolutionary ferment of Enlightenment-
era Bonn, where Beethoven grew up and imbibed the ideas

that would shape all of his future work. Swafford then tracks
his subject to Vienna, capital of European music, where
Beethoven built his career in the face of critical incomprehension, crippling ill health, romantic rejection, and . . . his
ever-encroaching deafness." (Publisher's note)

"Rich in biographical detail, the volume contains revealing excerpts from many of Beethoven's letters and
from the written observations of his visitors and family; it
also contains detailed analyses of many of his most notable
works." Kirkus

Includes bibliographical references and index

Belafonte, Harry

Belafonte, Harry. **My** song; a memoir. with
Michael Shnayerson. Alfred A. Knopf 2011 469p
il   **92**
 1. Actors 2. Singers 3. African American singers 4.
Social activists
ISBN 9780307272263; 9780307700483

LC 2011014602

The popular singer and former UNICEF Goodwill Ambassador shares the story of his life and career, from his
impoverished childhood in Harlem and Jamaica and his racial barrier-breaking career to his commitment to numerous
civil causes.

The author "covers his public career as an American
entertainment icon (which solidified with his 1956 album,
Calypso) and his interactions with many politicians and celebrities, e.g., Paul Robeson, Poitier, Marlon Brando, and
Robert Kennedy, among many others. How these different
strands interweave—the anger generated by the poverty and
racial discrimination of his early years, the socially conscious reformer, and the well-respected entertainer—make
for a potent memoir of our times." Libr J

Bell, Alexander Graham, 1847-1922

★ Gray, Charlotte. **Reluctant** genius; Alexander Graham Bell and the passion for invention. Arcade Pub. 2006 466p il map $29.95   **92**
 1. Inventors 2. Teachers of the deaf 3.
Telecommunications executives
ISBN 1-55970-809-3; 978-1-55970-809-8

LC 2005-29609

The author "recounts both the inventor of the telephone's creation of the device and the projects he pursued
once his future was secured. . . . Combining the household
history of the Bells with that of Alexander's successive enthusiasms (Helen Keller, kites, airplanes, hydrocraft), Gray
fairly portrays the attractions and exasperations of Bell's
life." Booklist

Includes bibliographical references

Bell, Gertrude Margaret Lowthian, 1868-1926

Howell, Georgina. **Gertrude** Bell; queen of the
desert, shaper of nations. Farrar, Straus and Giroux
2007 481p il map hardcover o.p. pa $16   **92**
 1. Explorers 2. Travelers 3. Archeologists 4.
Archaeologists 5. Women -- Travel
ISBN 978-0-374-16162-0; 0-374-16162-3; 978-0-374-
53135-5 pa; 0-374-53135-8 pa

LC 2006-29994

First published 2006 in the United Kingdom with title: Daughter of the desert

This is a biography of the British archaeologist and author of Desert and the Sown (1907) and Persian Pictures (1928).

"Bell's role in the creation of Iraq and the placement of Faisal upon the throne, is fully detailed. . . . But the strength and delight of Howell's superb biography is in the fullness with which Bell's character is drawn." Publ Wkly

Includes bibliographical references

Bell, Laura, 1954-

Bell, Laura. **Claiming** ground. Alfred A. Knopf 2010 241p $24.95   **92**
1. Shepherds 2. Ranch life 3. Conservationists 4. Wyoming 5. Memoirists
ISBN 978-0-307-27288-1

LC 2009-29644

"After college, a Kentucky girl spends a summer in Wyoming to find herself and regroup. Thirty years later, she's still there. In this memoir, Bell vividly depicts her life out West, starting with her first job herding sheep—an occupation usually done by men. She goes on to write about her life as a ranch hand, masseuse, housewife, stepmother, and forest ranger, mixing work experiences with touching and poignant accounts of family and friends. . . . Bell here turns in satisfying reading for ranching enthusiasts, memoir fanatics, and anyone who likes to get lost in stories about rural life and nature's beauty." Libr J

Belle, Dido Elizabeth, 1761-1804

Byrne, Paula. **Belle**; the slave daughter and the Lord Chief Justice. Paula Byrne. Harper Perennial 2014 304 p. illustrations (paperback) $14.99   **92**
1. Racially mixed people 2. Great Britain -- Race relations 3. Great Britain -- History -- 18th century 4. Slaves -- England -- Biography 5. Nobility -- England -- Biography
ISBN 0062310771; 9780062310774

LC 2014007447

"From . . . biographer Paula Byrne, the . . . tale that inspired the major motion picture 'Belle' (May 2014) starring Tom Wilkinson, Miranda Richardson, Emily Watson, Penelope Wilton, and Matthew Goode--a stunning story of the first mixed-race girl introduced to high society England and raised as a lady. . . . Growing up in his lavish estate, Dido was raised as a sister and companion to her white cousin, Elizabeth." (Publisher's note)

"Byrne brings to this brief history an eye for telling details of daily life, slaveholders' unthinkable cruelty, and the fervent work of a few good men and women who changed their world." Kirkus

Includes bibliographical references

Bellow, Saul, 1915-2005

Bellow, Saul. **Saul** Bellow; letters. edited by Benjamin Taylor. Viking 2010 571p il $35   **92**
1. Authors 2. Novelists 3. Dramatists 4. Authors, American 5. Short story writers 6. Biography, Individual 7. Nobel laureates for literature
ISBN 978-0-670-02221-2; 0-670-02221-7

LC 2010-22395

"Collected for the first time, Bellow's letters offer an alluring backstory to the Chicago-bred imagination that created The Adventures of Augie March, Herzog, Humboldt's Gift and won the Nobel Prize. Like the fiction, the missives can be brilliant, glistening, scathing, boring, funny, generous, probing and always genuinely human. . . . The correspondents throughout are friends, lovers, wives, agents and publishers. Among the dozens of major literary figures with whom Bellow corresponded were William Faulkner, Bernard Malamud, Edmund Wilson, John Berryman, Ralph Ellison, Robert Penn Warren, Philip Roth and Martin Amis. While nothing can substitute for a Bellow novel, Letters offers a strong salve to those who miss his familiar voice. The range of interests, battles fought and art created reflected here is Olympian. Yet the cauldron for much of it was the everyday streets of Chicago." Chicago Sun-Times

Benton, Thomas Hart, 1889-1975

Adams, Henry. **Tom** and Jack; the intertwined lives of Thomas Hart Benton and Jackson Pollock. Bloomsbury Press 2009 405p il $35   **92**
1. Artists 2. Painters 3. Illustrators 4. Lithographers 5. Artists -- United States
ISBN 1-59691-420-3; 978-1-59691-420-9

LC 2009-12309

"In this absorbing, carefully reasoned inquiry into a profound relationship between two painters, Adams reclaims the wrongfully maligned Benton and recalibrates our perception of Pollock and his masterpieces." Booklist

Includes bibliographical references (p. 375-390)

Bergman, Ingrid, 1915-1982

Spoto, Donald. **Notorious**; the life of Ingrid Bergman. Da Capo Press 2001 474p il pa $22 **92**
1. Actors
ISBN 978-0-306-81030-5; 0-306-81030-1

First published 1997 by HarperCollins

The author's "perceptions about Bergman personally and professionally are keen, and the narrative reads like a full-bodied story, not just a listing of professional credits and personal landmarks." Booklist

Includes bibliographical references

Thomson, David, 1941- **Ingrid** Bergman; photo research by Lucy Gray. Faber and Faber, Inc. 2010 113p il (Great stars) pa $14   **92**
1. Actors
ISBN 978-0-86547-934-0

LC 2009-41757

First published 2009 in the United Kingdom

In this biography, the author describes Bergman's "Hollywood-like rise, seemingly both unexpected and preordained, from talented Swedish actress to Hollywood goddess. . . . He reserves his harshest criticism not for her increasingly chaotic private life but for how, after her brilliance in the 1940s—Casablanca, Gaslight, and the Hitchcock masterpieces Spellbound and Notorious, and more—she settled into a kind of unsatisfying mediocrity in the 1950s and 1960s. Thomson speculates that her fortunes faded with her legendary beauty." Booklist

Bernard, Pierre, 1875-1955

Love, Robert. The **Great** Oom; the improbable birth of yoga in America. Viking 2010 402p il **92**

1. Yoga 2. Yogis 3. United States -- Religion
ISBN 067002175X; 9780670021758

LC 2009044784

This book focuses on Pierre Bernard's involvement in the popularization of Yoga in the United States. Bibliography. Index.

A "history of yoga's early days in America. The spiritual discipline that has colonized America's gyms and trendy loft spaces was once a fringe practice, its advocates treated as charlatans and, occasionally, criminals. Yoga's cultural rise is a story of scandal, financial shenanigans, bodily discipline, oversize egos and bizarre love triangles, with a few performing elephants thrown in for good measure. Mr. Love tells his story through the life of one of yoga's earliest promoters, Pierre Bernard—known as the 'Great Oom'—a zany man whose talent for self-invention rivaled that of P.T. Barnum." Wall Street J

Includes bibliographical references

Bernini, Gian Lorenzo, 1598-1680

Mormando, Franco. **Bernini**; his life and his Rome. University of Chicago Press 2011 429p il map pa $35 **92**

1. Artists 2. Sculptors 3. Architects 4. Artists, Italian
ISBN 978-0-226-53852-5; 0-226-53852-4

LC 2011023774

In this biography "of Baroque sculptor Gian Lorenzo Bernini since his death in 1680, . . . Mormando constructs a comprehensive, extraordinarily vivid portrait of the sculptor known as 'the Michelangelo of his age.' . . . Of great interest to general readers seeking a well-researched, highly readable portrait of the sculptor and those interested in the cultural history of baroque Rome." Publ Wkly

Includes bibliographical references

Bernstein, Leonard, 1918-1990

★ Bernstein, Burton. **Leonard** Bernstein; American original; how a modern renaissance man transformed music and the world during his New York Philharmonic years, 1943-1976. [by] Burton Bernstein and Barbara B. Haws. HarperCollins 2008 223p il $29.95 **92**

1. Composers 2. Musicians 3. Conductors (Music) 4. New York Philharmonic 5. Composers -- United States
ISBN 978-0-06-153786-8; 0-06-153786-1

LC 2008-13702

"Essays by nine writers look at various aspects of Bernstein's life and career, placing him in the mid-twentieth-century artistic, social and political contexts he helped to define." Opera News

"A flat-out wonderful book." Booklist

Berr, Hélène, 1921-1945

Berr, Helene. The **journal** of Helene Berr; translated from the French by David Bellos, with an introduction and an essay by David Bellos, and afterword by Mariette Job. Weinstein Books 2008 307p il map $24.95 **92**

1. Diarists 2. Jews -- France 3. Holocaust victims 4. Holocaust, 1933-1945 -- Personal narratives
ISBN 978-1-60286-064-3; 1-60286-064-5

This diary of a young Sorbonne graduate who died at Bergen-Belsen "recounts the experiences and private thoughts of the 21-year-old daughter of a prominent Jewish family as she and those she loved suffered the indignities of life under the Occupation prior to their arrest and ultimate deportation and death. . . . The volume includes useful annotations as well as a postscript that places the plight of French Jewry within historical context." Libr J

Includes bibliographical references

Berra, Yogi, 1925-

★ Barra, Allen. **Yogi** Berra; eternal Yankee. W. W. Norton & Co. 2009 451p il $27.95 **92**

1. Baseball players 2. Baseball coaches 3. Baseball managers 4. Baseball -- Biography 5. New York Yankees (Baseball team)
ISBN 978-0-393-06233-5; 0-393-06233-3

LC 2008-45799

"Barra brings to his sporting version of the Everyman story an encyclopedic knowledge and warm understanding of the game of baseball; meticulous research into business, sociology, and history; and a fluid writing style. . . . Baseball biography taken to a higher level." Booklist

Includes bibliographical references

Berrigan, Sandy

Berrigan, Ted. **Dear** Sandy, hello; letters from Ted to Sandy Berrigan. edited by Sandy Berrigan and Ron Padgett. Coffee House Press 2010 310p il pa $19.95 **92**

1. Poets 2. Authors 3. Poets, American
ISBN 978-1-56689-249-0; 1-56689-249-X

LC 2010-16258

"In addition to the letters, this collection contains never-before-published reproductions from A Book of Poetry for Sandy, featuring Berrigan's cutouts, drawings, photographs of fellow poets and artists, and excerpts from poems that eventually became The Sonnets." Publisher's note

Berrigan, Ted, 1934-1983

Berrigan, Ted. **Dear** Sandy, hello; letters from Ted to Sandy Berrigan. edited by Sandy Berrigan and Ron Padgett. Coffee House Press 2010 310p il pa $19.95 **92**

1. Poets 2. Authors 3. Poets, American
ISBN 978-1-56689-249-0; 1-56689-249-X

LC 2010-16258

"In addition to the letters, this collection contains never-before-published reproductions from A Book of Poetry for Sandy, featuring Berrigan's cutouts, drawings, photographs of fellow poets and artists, and excerpts from poems that eventually became The Sonnets." Publisher's note

Betjeman, John Sir, 1906-1984

Wilson, A. N. **Betjeman**; a life. Farrar, Straus & Giroux 2006 375p il $27 **92**

1. Poets 2. Authors 3. Satirists 4. Poets laureate 5. Architectural historians 6. Historic preservationists
ISBN 978-0-374-11198-4; 0-374-11198-7

LC 2006-930677

Wilson's biography of the British Poet Laureate "is a sharp-edged triumph of honest hero worship. Amazingly, he has found a real-life character whom he can love and admire. . . . Brushing aside hundreds of chatty anecdotes and conversations that might have happened, Wilson has tied his primary source material around a subtle analysis of the ultimate first sources, the poems themselves. This, it is safe to say, should be the final biography." Times Lit Suppl

Bewick, Thomas, 1753-1828

Uglow, Jennifer S. **Nature's** engraver; a life of Thomas Bewick. Farrar, Straus and Giroux 2007 458p il map $30 **92**

1. Artists 2. Woodcuts 3. Illustrators 4. Woodcut artists
ISBN 978-0-374-11236-3; 0-374-11236-3

LC 2006-31878

First published 2006 in the United Kingdom

"Biographies rarely afford a glimpse behind the office door, and it is the image of Bewick at work that is so valuable here. . . . It is hard to imagine a better biographer for this subject than Uglow, with her background in publishing and her knowledge of the North of England and the eighteenth century. It is also hard to imagine a more beautifully produced and illustrated book: scores of Bewick's frameless vignettes float frame-free and captionless throughout, appearing as they would have done in his own time, tale pieces every one." Times Lit Suppl

Includes bibliographical references

Bhutto, Benazir

★ Bhutto, Benazir. **Reconciliation**; Islam, democracy, and the West. HarperCollins 2008 328p $27.95 **92**

1. Prime ministers 2. Islam and politics 3. Political leaders 4. Prime ministers -- Pakistan 5. Pakistan -- Politics and government
ISBN 978-0-06-156758-2; 0-06-156758-2

This "is a book of enormous intelligence, courage and clarity. . . . Washington should arrange to have the portions of the book about Islam republished as a separate volume and translated into several languages. It would do more to win the battle of ideas within Islam than anything an American president could ever say." N Y Times Book Rev

Includes bibliographical references

Bierce, Ambrose, 1842-1914?

Morris, Roy. **Ambrose** Bierce; alone in bad company. Oxford University Press 1998 306p pa $19.95 **92**

1. Authors 2. Journalists 3. Essayists 4. Authors, American 5. Short story writers
ISBN 0-19-512628-9

LC 98-33467

First published 1995 by Crown

"Mr. Morris's disturbing, vividly realized biography brings to life a haunted writer whose private torments mirrored a turbulent era." NY Times Book Rev

Includes bibliographical references

Bilal, Wafaa, 1966-

Bilal, Wafaa. **Shoot** an Iraqi; art, life and resistance under the gun. by Wafaa Bilal and Kari Lydersen. City Lights 2008 177p il pa $16.95 **92**

1. Artists 2. Video artists 3. Performance artists 4. Iraq War, 2003- -- Art and the war
ISBN 978-0-8728-6491-7; 0-8728-6491-X

LC 2008-20487

The creator of 'Domestic Tension,' an unsettling interactive performance piece that speaks to the horrors of life in a conflict zone, reveals his experiences growing up under Saddam Hussein's rule.

"A powerful and demanding read, that is, frankly, a literary punch to the gut." Booklist

Billy, the Kid

Gardner, Mark L. **To** hell on a fast horse; Billy the Kid, Pat Garrett, and the epic chase to justice in the Old West. William Morrow 2010 325p il $26.99 **92**

1. Outlaws 2. Sheriffs
ISBN 978-0-06-136827-1; 0-06-136827-X

LC 2009025467

A "double biography of the iconic western outlaw Billy the Kid and Sheriff Pat Garrett. Maintaining an objective perspective on both men in a narrative closely tied to historic source materials, Gardner's quick-moving story follows events of the civil war in Lincoln County, New Mexico Territory in 1877–78, and the Kid's death-by-shooting at the hands of Garrett in 1881. . . . The final chapters describing Garrett as an old-style lawman in a postfrontier society, with interactions with President Theodore Roosevelt, serve to distinguish this book from other recent Kid biographies." Libr J

Includes bibligraphical references

★ Wallis, Michael. **Billy** the Kid; the endless ride. W.W. Norton & Co. 2007 328p il map $25.95 **92**

1. Outlaws
ISBN 978-0-393-06068-3; 0-393-06068-3

LC 2006-101364

"Drawing on archival sources and interviews as well as documents and secondary works, Wallis digs beneath the surface, clearly identifying what is known or probable and presenting the reasonable alternatives for what is conjecture." Libr J

Includes bibliographical references

Bingham, Hiram, 1875-1956

Heaney, Christopher. **Cradle** of gold; the story of Hiram Bingham, a real-life Indiana Jones, and the search for Machu Picchu. Palgrave Macmillan 2010 285p il $27 **92**

1. Incas 2. Explorers 3. Governors 4. Historians 5.

Senators 6. Machu Picchu (Peru) 7. Peru -- Antiquities
ISBN 0-230-61169-9; 978-0-230-61169-6

LC 2009-38535

"On an archaeological trip to Peru on July 24, 1911, Hiram Bingham, an American explorer and history professor at Yale, happened upon the ruins of the Inca city of Machu Picchu. Although the site was already known to the local native people, Bingham made the Machu Picchu ruins famous and received acclaim as their 'discoverer.' Heaney presents a well-researched and very readable biography of Bingham from his childhood in Hawaii as the son of missionaries, through his education and careers as historian, educator, explorer, and finally politician. He probes the depths of Bingham's work and character, examining setbacks, scandals, and achievements and skillfully unraveling Bingham's role in the controversy that still exists today between the government of Peru and Yale University over the ownership of the Machu Picchu burials and artifacts." Libr J

Includes bibliographical references

Bismarck, Otto, Furst von, 1815-1898

Steinberg, Jonathan. **Bismarck**; Jonathan Steinberg. Oxford University Press 2011 x, 577 p., [16] p. of platesp $34.95   **92**
1. Statesmen -- Germany -- Biography 2. Germany -- Politics and government -- 1866-1918
ISBN 978-0-19-978252-9; 0-19-978252-0; 9780199782529

LC 2010045387

The author of this biography of German Chancellor Otto von Bismarck argues that his subject "remains 'the most remarkable and complex political leader of the nineteenth century' . . . [Jonathan] Steinberg sets out to understand how the man with 'an extraordinary, gigantic self' did it. He reminds readers that Bismarck succeeded only as long as he was indispensable to his royal master and ultimately he fell when Wilhelm II had had enough. Prof. Steinberg also uses his knowledge of nineteenth-century European history . . . to describe the stage on which Bismarck acted. In addition he pays great attention to original sources and Bismarck's collected works." (Contemporary Review) Index.

"This is a beautifully written book that provides a stimulating and enjoyable introduction to the history of modern Europe." New Statesman

Includes bibliographical references (p. [528]-537) and index

Black Elk, 1863-1950

Black Elk. **Black** Elk speaks; being the life story of a holy man of the Oglala Sioux. [as told through] John G. Neihardt; foreword by Vine Deloria, Jr.; with illustrations by Standing Bear; essays by Alexis N. Petri and Lori Utecht. University of Nebraska Press 2004 xxix, 270p il map pa $19.95; pa $14.95 **92**
1. Shamans 2. Oglala Indians 3. Indian leaders 4. Native Americans -- Biography
ISBN 9780803283916; 0-8032-8385-7

LC 2004-12692

A reprint of the title first published 1932 by Morrow

The Indian whose life story this is, was born in 1863. He was a famous warrior and hunter in his youth, and became a practicing medicine man among his people. Of him Nei-

hardt says, "As an indubitable seer, he seemed to represent the consciousness of the Plains Indian more fully than any other I had ever known."

This "is about as near as you can get to seeing life and death, war and religion, through an Indian's eyes." Outlook

Blackburn family

Blackburn, Julia. The **three** of us; a family story. Pantheon Books 2008 313p il $26   **92**
1. Poets 2. Artists 3. Authors 4. Parents 5. Painters 6. Novelists 7. Family life 8. Essayists 9. Biographers
ISBN 978-0-375-42474-8; 0-375-42474-1

LC 2007-50147

Blackburn "recalls her rather chaotic childhood and early adulthood through the lens of her mother's final weeks. Blackburn's father was the poet and scholar Thomas Blackburn; her mother was the painter Rosalie de Meric. Both parents had significant problems, including promiscuity, impulsiveness, and alcohol and prescription-drug abuse." Libr J

This is a "strangely compelling memoir." Publ Wkly

Blackburn, Julia

Blackburn, Julia. The **three** of us; a family story. Pantheon Books 2008 313p il $26   **92**
1. Poets 2. Artists 3. Authors 4. Parents 5. Painters 6. Novelists 7. Family life 8. Essayists 9. Biographers
ISBN 978-0-375-42474-8; 0-375-42474-1

LC 2007-50147

This is a "strangely compelling memoir." Publ Wkly

Blackburn, Lucie, d. 1895

★ Smardz Frost, Karolyn. **I've** got a home in glory land; a lost tale of the Underground Railroad. Farrar, Straus & Giroux 2006 450p il map $30 **92**
1. Slaves 2. Underground railroad 3. Coach drivers
ISBN 978-0-374-16481-2; 0-374-16481-9

LC 2006-64

The author's "fascination with her subject and love of detailed historical documentation are evident in this engrossing look at a couple who defied slavery with their escape and their assistance to other fugitive slaves." Booklist

Includes bibliographical references

Blackburn, Thomas, 1916-1977

Blackburn, Julia. The **three** of us; a family story. Pantheon Books 2008 313p il $26   **92**
1. Poets 2. Artists 3. Authors 4. Parents 5. Painters 6. Novelists 7. Family life 8. Essayists 9. Biographers
ISBN 978-0-375-42474-8; 0-375-42474-1

LC 2007-50147

This is a "strangely compelling memoir." Publ Wkly

Blackburn, Thornton, 1813 or 14-1890

★ Smardz Frost, Karolyn. **I've** got a home in glory land; a lost tale of the Underground Railroad. Farrar, Straus & Giroux 2006 450p il map $30 **92**
1. Slaves 2. Underground railroad 3. Coach drivers
ISBN 978-0-374-16481-2; 0-374-16481-9

LC 2006-64

The author's "fascination with her subject and love of detailed historical documentation are evident in this engrossing look at a couple who defied slavery with their escape and their assistance to other fugitive slaves." Booklist

Includes bibliographical references

Blackjack, Ada, 1898-1983

√ Niven, Jennifer. **Ada** Blackjack; a true story of survival in the Arctic. Hyperion 2003 431p il map $24.95   **92**

1. Explorers 2. Arctic regions -- Exploration 3. Wrangel Island (Russia) -- Exploration

ISBN 0-7868-6863-5

LC 2003-50826

The book "is exhilarating reading." Booklist

Includes bibliographical references

Blackmun, Harry A.

√Greenhouse, Linda. **Becoming** Justice Blackmun; Harry Blackmun's Supreme Court journey. Times Books 2005 268p il $25   **92**

1. Supreme Court justices 2. United States -- Supreme Court

ISBN 0-8050-7791-X

LC 2004-63772

The author's "achievement in her meticulous narrative history is to provide new ammunition for Justice Blackmun's critics as well as his admirers. And readers who are unfamiliar with the inner workings of the court could not hope for a more engrossing introduction." N Y Times (Late N Y Ed)

Blagojevich, Rod R., 1956-

√ Brackett, Elizabeth. **Pay** to play; how Rod Blagojevich turned political corruption into a national sideshow. Ivan R. Dee 2009 247p il $24.95   **92**

1. Governors 2. Political corruption 3. State legislators 4. Members of Congress

ISBN 978-1-56663-834-0

LC 2009-10566

"Blagojevich, the well-coiffed, Elvis-loving former Illinois governor, gained national disrepute for his alleged attempts to sell the vacated U.S. Senate seat of President Barack Obama. . . . Brackett details the long and rocky road that brought Blagojevich to infamy. . . . A thorough and concise look at political corruption and the brazen man behind the scandal." Booklist

Blair, Tony

Blair, Tony. A **journey**; my political life. Alfred A. Knopf 2010 699p il $35; ebook $35   **92**

1. Prime ministers 2. Political leaders 3. Members of Parliament 4. Prime ministers -- Great Britain

ISBN 978-0-307-26983-6; 978-0-307-59487-7 ebook

LC 2010-28262

These are the memoirs of the British Labour Party politician who served as the prime minister of the United Kingdom from 1997 to 2007.

"Without delving too deeply into his personal life, . . . [Blair] gives the reader a good sense of his role not just as a public figure but also as a son, husband, and father. . . . Particulars of British party politics might elude some American

readers, but the narrative keeps flowing. Essential for readers of current British politics." Libr J

Includes bibliographical references

Blunt, Anthony, 1907-1983

√Carter, Miranda. **Anthony** Blunt: his lives. Farrar, Straus & Giroux 2001 590p il $30; pa $18 **92**

1. Spies 2. Art historians 3. Museum administrators

ISBN 0-374-10531-6; 0-312-42146-X pa

LC 2001-50135

In 1979 "the noted British art expert Anthony Blunt was revealed to have been a spy for the Soviet Union. This meticulous book traces Blunt's career: his early school days, his association with the Bloomsbury group, his membership in a 'secret debating society' known as the Apostles, his recruitment into the spy game as a 'talent spotter,' his time spent in MI5 (he started passing documents to the Russians in 1941), and beyond." Booklist

"Thoroughly researched and carefully crafted, this is sure to be the definitive biography." Publ Wkly

Blunt, Judy, 1954-

√ Blunt, Judy. **Breaking** clean. Knopf 2002 303p hardcover o.p. pa $13   **92**

1. Authors 2. Ranchers 3. Memoirists

ISBN 0-375-70130-3 pa

LC 2001-29861

The author chronicles the hardships she endured as a ranch wife, mother, and laborer in rural Montana, and how she left it all, including her marriage, to get herself a college education and become a writer

Blunt has a "keen and poetic awareness, steely candor, and commanding storytelling skills." Booklist

Bogart, Humphrey, 1899-1957

Thomson, David, 1941- **Humphrey** Bogart; photo research by Lucy Gray. Faber and Faber, Inc. 2010 127p il (Great stars) pa $14   **92**

1. Actors

ISBN 978-0-86547-933-3

LC 2009-41758

First published 2009 in the United Kingdom

In this biography, the author "focuses on how long it took the well-bred and educated Bogart to develop his trademark style as the rough-hewn, disillusioned, world-weary, wisecracking, fallen romantic of Casablanca and The Maltese Falcon. He charts Bogart's progress from New York stage performer to featured player in 1930s Hollywood, where he was often cast as a certain kind of feral street rat, to star." Booklist

Bolivar, Simon, 1783-1830

√ Arana, Marie. **Bolivar**; American liberator. Marie Arana. Simon & Schuster 2013 603 p. ill. (chiefly col.), maps (hardcover) $35   **92**

1. Venezuela -- History -- 1810-1830 2. Heads of state -- South America -- Biography 3. South America -- History -- Wars of Independence, 1806-1830

ISBN 1439110190; 9781439110195; 9781439124956

LC 2012034661

In this book, "Peruvian journalist [Marie] Arana . . . chronicles Gen. Simón Bolívar's struggle against the Spanish Empire in the 1810s and '20s through several dizzying cycles of battlefield victory, triumphal procession, demoralizing reversal, and squalid exile, before he finally drove imperial forces out of Venezuela, Colombia, Ecuador, and Peru." (Publishers Weekly)

"Drawing on Bolívar's voluminous correspondence and political writings, Arana assembles a chronological narrative that does justice to both Bolívar's august achievements and his human imperfections. This well-rounded work reveals not just an accomplished military tactician but also an able statesman." LJ

Includes bibliographical references and index

Bolkovac, Kathryn

Bolkovac, Kathryn. The **whistleblower**; sex trafficking, military contractors, and one woman's fight for justice. [by] Kathryn Bolkovac with Cari Lynn. Palgrave Macmillan 2011 240p il map $25; pa $16; ebook $11.99 **92**
1. Whistle blowing 2. Juvenile prostitution 3. Bosnia and Hercegovina 4. Human rights activists 5. United Nations employees
ISBN 978-0-230-10802-8; 978-0-230-11522-4 pa; 978-0-230-11563-7 ebook

LC 2010-23196

"Bolkovac, a veteran of the Lincoln, Neb., police force, was looking for a new challenge, a higher salary and a chance to escape from a bitter divorce. So she signed up with private security company DynCorp to join the peacekeeping mission in Bosnia-Herzegovina after a decade of ethnic violence and civil war. . . . However, Bolkovac soon discovered that DynCorp officials, when not involved in lawlessness themselves, were intent on covering up their employees' patronage of a human-trafficking operation that had taken root in Bosnia."

This story "bristles with disturbing details and heartfelt compassion." Publ Wkly

Bonaparte, Paolina, 1780-1825

Fraser, Flora. **Pauline** Bonaparte; Venus of Empire. Alfred A. Knopf 2009 287p il $28.95 **92**
1. Princesses 2. Patrons of the arts
ISBN 978-0-307-26544-9; 0-307-26544-7

LC 2008-28639

This "narrative by British biographer Fraser . . . fleshes out the privileged and politically unstable world of Pauline, who both commissioned and modeled nearly nude for Canova's symbolic marble statue Venus Victorious as a testament to herself. Pauline's raison d'être was the joyful pursuit of astonishing variety in her love affairs, which Fraser asserts may have been a source of her invalidism throughout her adult life. But her life showcased the dangers in Napoleonic France as well as its pleasures: she faced death from yellow fever and insurrection in French colonial Haiti. Fraser's narrative provides insight into the permissive culture of the French Empire and glimpses into Napoleon as a protective and exasperated older brother while simultaneously engaged in politics, invasions and his eventual fall from power." Publ Wkly

Includes bibliographical references

Bonhoeffer, Dietrich, 1906-1945

Marsh, Charles. **Strange** glory; a life of Dietrich Bonhoeffer. by Charles Marsh. Alfred A. Knopf 2014 528 p. illustrations (hardcover) $35 **92**
1. Clergy 2. Theologians 3. Germany -- History -- 1933-1945
ISBN 0307269817; 9780307269812; 9780307390387

LC 2013045873

This book, by Charles Marsh, offers a biography of "Dietrich Bonhoeffer, the German pastor, theologian, and anti-Hitler conspirator. . . . [I]t was the Nuremberg laws that set Bonhoeffer's earthly life on an ineluctable path toward destruction. His denunciation of the race statutes as heresy and his insistence on the church's moral obligation to defend all victims of state violence, regardless of race or religion, alienated him from what would become the Reich church." (Publisher's note)

"Marsh's portrait is of a spoiled, materialistic, and selfish young man who develops, over time, into a German hero. The writing is clear and concise, the endnotes extensive, and the index generous." LJ

Includes bibliographical references and index

Metaxas, Eric. **Bonhoeffer**; pastor, martyr, prophet, spy: a Righteous Gentile vs. the Third Reich. Thomas Nelson 2010 591p il **92**
1. Spies 2. Clergy 3. Theologians 4. Dissenters 5. Writers on religion 6. Biography, Individual 7. Germany -- History -- 1933-1945
ISBN 1595551387; 1595552464; 9781595551382; 9781595552464 pa

LC 2009013944

This is a biography of the German Lutheran pastor and theologian executed by the Nazis for plotting to overthrow Hitler.

"Insightful and illuminating, this tome makes a powerful contribution to biography, history and theology." Publ Wkly

Includes bibliographical references

Boone, Daniel, 1734-1820

Faragher, John Mack. **Daniel** Boone; the life and legend of an American pioneer. Holt & Co. 1992 429p il maps hardcover o.p. pa $18 **92**
1. Frontier and pioneer life 2. Scouts 3. Pioneers
ISBN 0-8050-3007-7 pa

LC 92-21873

"The popular image of Daniel Boone is that of an unlettered backwoodsman, skilled hunter and Indian fighter. But evidence argues that he was reasonably well educated for his time and place, that he was a landowner, businessman and a respected leader of frontier society. Faragher . . . has sifted through folklore and fact to reconstruct a realistic portrait of Boone and the expanding frontier. . . . Faragher has written an absorbing, definitive biography." Publ Wkly

Includes bibliographical references

Morgan, Robert. **Boone**; a biography. Algonquin Books of Chapel Hill 2007 538p il map $29.95 **92**
1. Frontier and pioneer life 2. Scouts 3. Pioneers
ISBN 978-1-56512-455-4; 1-56512-455-3

LC 2007-14204

A biography of the American pioneer scout.

This is an "absorbing and stirring chronicle of the great frontiersman." Booklist

Includes bibliographical references

Borges, Jorge Luis, 1899-1986

Williamson, Edwin. **Borges,** a life. Viking 2004 416p $34.95 **92**

1. Poets 2. Authors 3. Novelists 4. Essayists 5. Translators 6. Literary critics 7. Short story writers
ISBN 0-670-88579-7

LC 2004-41290

This "is a richly psychological, dynamically intellectual, and deeply affecting portrait of an often anguished and inhibited man who, through heroic perserverance and spiritual conviction, found salvation in writing and transformed literature for all time." Booklist

Includes bibliographical references

Borgia, Lucrezia, 1480-1519

Bradford, Sarah. **Lucrezia** Borgia; life, love, and death in Renaissance Italy. Viking 2004 xxiv, 421p il map $27.95; pa $16 **92**

1. Patrons of the arts
ISBN 0-670-03353-7; 0-14-303595-9 pa

LC 2004-54881

The author "presents Lucrezia as an intelligent noblewoman, powerless to defy her family's patriarchal order, yet an enlightened ruler in her own right as Duchess of Ferrara. . . . As a project designed to distinguish the historical Lucrezia Borgia from the legend, Bradford's readable biography resoundingly succeeds." Publ Wkly

Includes bibliographical references

Born, Max, 1882-1970

Greenspan, Nancy Thorndike. The **end** of the certain world; the Nobel physicist who ignited the quantum revolution. Basic Books 2005 374p il $26.95 **92**

1. Physicists 2. Nobel laureates for physics
ISBN 0-7382-0693-8

LC 2004-21809

"This empathetic work . . . lifts a deserving figure out of semi-obscurity and adds a valuable perspective on the origin of modern physics." Publ Wkly

Includes bibliographical references

Bosch, Carl

Hager, Thomas. The **alchemy** of air; a Jewish genius, a doomed tycoon, and the scientific discovery that fed the world but fueled the rise of Hitler. Harmony Books 2008 316p $24.95; pa $15 **92**

1. Chemists 2. Fertilizers 3. Nobel laureates for chemistry
ISBN 978-0-307-35178-4; 0-307-35178-5; 978-0-307-35179-1 pa; 0-307-35179-3 pa

LC 2008-3192

"A fast-paced account of the early-20th-century quest to develop synthetic fertilizer. . . . Science writing of the first order." Kirkus

Includes bibliographical references

Bourdain, Anthony

Bourdain, Anthony. **Kitchen** confidential; adventures in the culinary underbelly. Updated ed; Harper Perennial 2007 312, 22p pa $15.99 **92**

1. Cooks 2. Authors 3. Novelists 4. Television personalities 5. Memoirists
ISBN 978-0-06-089922-6; 0-06-089922-0

LC 2007-280057

First published 2000

"This is one bitter, nasty, searing, hard-to-swallow piece of work. But if you can choke the thing down, you'll probably wake up grinning in the middle of the night. . . . In a style partaking of Hunter S. Thompson, Iggy Pop and a little Jonathan Swift, Bourdain gleefully rips through the scenery to reveal private backstage horrors little dreamed of by the trusting public. . . . To a world infested with synthesized romance, candlelit illusions and sentimental piety, 'Kitchen Confidential' offers a nice palate-clearing taste of poison." N Y Times Book Rev

Bourdain, Anthony. **Medium** raw; a bloody valentine to the world of food and the people who cook. Ecco Press 2010 281p $26.99 **92**

1. Cooks 2. Authors 3. Novelists 4. Television personalities 5. Memoirists
ISBN 978-0-06-171894-6; 0-06-171894-7

This book mixes personal memoir with travelogues and ruminations on such matters as the degradation of the American hamburger, the dumbing down of the Food Network, the tedium of multicourse tasting menus and the rise of food gurus such as David Chang. . . . Mr. Bourdain is a vivid, bawdy and often foul-mouthed writer. He thrills in the attack, but he is also an enthusiast who writes well about things he holds dear. His detailed reporting on the backroom lives of restaurant employees is terrific. Wall Street J

Bowie, David

Spitz, Marc. **Bowie**; a biography. Crown 2009 429p il $26.99 **92**

1. Actors 2. Singers 3. Rock musicians 4. Songwriters
ISBN 978-0-307-39396-8

LC 2009-16806

For this biography, the author "concentrates on the complex evolution of Bowie's music to deliver an evenhanded, critically thorough, while still reverential life of the Thin White Duke." Publ Wkly

Includes bibliographical references

Bown, Stephen R.

The **last** Viking; the life of Roald Amundsen. Stephen R. Bown. Da Capo Press 2012 xxii, 357 p.p ill., maps (hardcover : alk. paper) $27.50 **92**

1. Explorers -- Norway -- Biography 2. North Pole -- Discovery and exploration -- Norweigian 3. Arctic regions -- Discovery and exploration -- Norweigian
ISBN 0306820676; 9780306820670; 9780306821622

LC 2012012126

This book by Stephen R. Bown is a biography of Roald Amundsen, "a legend of the heroic age of exploration. . . . In 1900, the four great geographical mysteries--the Northwest Passage, the Northeast Passage, the South Pole, and the North Pole--remained blank spots on the globe. Within twenty years Roald Amundsen would claim all four prizes. . . . Féted in his lifetime as an international celebrity, pursued by women and creditors, he died in the Arctic on a rescue mission." (Publisher's note)

Includes bibliographical references and index

Boyd, Gerald

Boyd, Gerald M. **My** Times in black and white; race and power at the New York Times. [by] Gerald M. Boyd; afterword by Robin D. Stone. Lawrence Hill Books 2010 402p il **92**

1. Journalists 2. New York times 3. Newspaper editors 4. Biography, Individual 5. United States -- Race relations

ISBN 1-55652-952-X; 978-1-55652-952-8

LC 2009-35506

This is a memoir of Boyd's experiences as a reporter and editor at The St. Louis Post-Dispatch and The New York Times. Index.

The author "has written a good book filled with ill feeling toward the Times, many of its editors, and a variety of colleagues who turned against him under pressure or simply because they wanted him to fail and be damned. . . . Lovers of newspaper gossip will find it delightfully indiscreet about self-serving treacheries hatched in the newsroom by people simultaneously engaged in high-minded pursuit of all the news that's fit to print." N Y Rev Books

Boylan, Jennifer Finney, 1958-

Boylan, Jennifer Finney. **I'm** looking through you; growing up haunted. Broadway Books 2008 270p il $23.95 **92**

1. Ghosts 2. Authors 3. Novelists 4. Transsexualism 5. Transsexuals 6. Authors, American 7. Short story writers 8. Young adult authors

ISBN 978-0-7679-2174-9; 0-7679-2174-7

LC 2007-19199

The author, a male-to-female transgendered person, "uses the metaphor of 'being haunted' throughout to illustrate not only her boyhood experiences but also the memories that have shaped her as a person as she struggled with her gender identity throughout most of her life. . . . Her writing style is witty, self-deprecating, entertaining, and often poignant, especially when describing family and friends who have passed away. An adventure to read, this is highly recommended for all libraries." Libr J

Boyle, Robert, 1627-1691

Hunter, Michael. **Boyle**; between God and science. Yale University Press 2009 366p il **92**

1. Chemists 2. Physicists 3. Scientists 4. Religion and science 5. Nonfiction writers 6. Writers on science 7. Biography, Individual 8. Religion and science -- England -- History -- 17th century

ISBN 0-300-12381-7; 9780300123814

LC 2009-13997

This is a biography of the seventeenth-century natural philosopher and scientist. Index.

"This painstakingly researched biography of the seventeenth-century scientist Robert Boyle outlines a life in which 'science and theology were truly complementary' but not always in harmony. Best known for Boyle's law, which

established a constant relationship between air's volume and its pressure, Boyle was a moralist from a privileged upbringing whose conception of science—both of its empirical basis and of its transformative potential for mankind—was far ahead of its time." New Yorker

Includes bibliographical references

Bradbury, Ray, 1920-2012

Eller, Jonathan R. **Becoming** Ray Bradbury. University of Illinois Press 2011 324p il $34.95 **92**

1. Authors 2. Novelists 3. Screenwriters 4. Authors, American 5. Children's authors 6. Short story writers 7. Science fiction writers

ISBN 978-0-252-03629-3

LC 2011008562

The author "provides a detailed account of the experiences that shaped Ray Bradbury's life and writing career from his childhood until he embarked on the screenplay for John Huston's Moby Dick in late 1953. . . . Eller's work is thorough and enlightening on the subject of one of science fiction's greatest minds. Highly recommended not just for Bradbury fans but for all students of science fiction." Libr J

Includes bibliographical references

Weller, Sam. The **Bradbury** chronicles; the life of Ray Bradbury. William Morrow 2005 384p il $26.95; pa $15.95 **92**

1. Authors 2. Novelists 3. Screenwriters 4. Authors, American 5. Children's authors 6. Short story writers 7. Science fiction writers

ISBN 0-06-054581-X; 0-06-054584-4 pa

LC 2004-59491

"Weller's research—based on interviews with Bradbury as well as family members and colleagues—is almost exhaustive in its detail, and he does a fine job of presenting the facts of his subject's unique life. The lively, conversational prose brings out the writer's winning personality and turns his struggles and successes into a highly readable story." SLJ

Includes bibliographical references

Braddock, James J., 1906-1974

Schaap, Jeremy. **Cinderella** Man; James J. Braddock, Max Baer, and the greatest upset in boxing history. Houghton Mifflin 2005 324p il hardcover o.p. pa $13.95 **92**

1. Boxers (Persons) 2. Boxing -- Biography

ISBN 0-618-55117-4; 0-618-71190-2 pa

LC 2004-66085

The author goes into "detail on the brawny, reserved Braddock, who, at his lowest moments, was reduced to living off government relief and doing grueling work on the Hoboken, N.J., docks. But the story is as much about Max Baer, the lovably clownish and handsome heavyweight Braddock defeated as a 10-to-one underdog. . . . Boxing enthusiasts will be more than satisfied by Schaap's meticulous account, which includes round-by-round details of the fight, as well as profiles of other fighters of the era." Publ Wkly

Includes bibliographical references

Bradstreet, Anne, 1612?-1672

Gordon, Charlotte. **Mistress** Bradstreet; the untold life of America's first poet. Little, Brown and Co. 2005 337p il map $27.95 **92**

1. Poets 2. Authors 3. Women poets 4. Colonists
ISBN 0-316-16904-8

LC 2004-22702

This is a biography of the colonial poet.

"Written with maximal clarity and communicativeness, this is a vibrant, engaging, realistic portrayal of early colonial Massachusetts and of its fascinating biographical subject." Booklist

Includes bibliographical references

Bragg, Rick

Bragg, Rick. The **prince** of Frogtown. Alfred A. Knopf 2008 255p $24 **92**

1. Authors 2. Journalists 3. Stepfathers 4. Father-son relationship 5. Memoirists
ISBN 978-1-4000-4040-7; 1-4000-4040-X

LC 2007-38884

The author "merges his father's history of severe hardships and simple joys with a tale from the present: his own relationship with his 10-year-old stepson. . . . [This book] is lush with narratives about manhood, fathers and sons, families and the changing face of the rural South." Publ Wkly

Brandeis, Louis Dembitz, 1856-1941

Urofsky, Melvin I. **Louis** D. Brandeis; a life. Pantheon Books 2009 955p il **92**

1. Judges 2. Lawyers 3. Biography, Individual 4. Supreme Court justices 5. United States -- Supreme Court 6. Law -- United States -- History
ISBN 9780375423666

LC 200903992

This is a biography of the American lawyer who was nominated to the Supreme Court in 1916 and served as a justice until his retirement in 1939. Index.

This is a "monumental, authoritative and appreciative biography of the man Franklin D. Roosevelt called 'Isaiah.'" N Y Times Book Rev

Includes bibliographical references

Braun, Eva, 1912-1945

Gortemaker, Heike B. **Eva** Braun; life with Hitler. by Heike B. Görtemaker; translated from the German by Damion Searls. Alfred A. Knopf 2011 324 p. $27.95; ebook $13.99 **92**

1. Women -- Germany -- Biography 2. Mistresses -- Germany -- Biography 3. Germany -- History -- 1933-1945 -- Biography 4. Spouses of heads of state -- Germany -- Biography
ISBN 978-0-307-59582-9; 978-0-307-70139-8 ebook; 9780307595829

LC 2011009551

""This is a Borzoi book"--T.p. verso."||"Originally published in Germany as Eva Braun : Leben mit Hitler, by Verlag C.H. Beck, Munich, in 2010."

This book offers a biography of Adolf Hilter's mistress Eva Braun. "Although by the early-to-mid-Thirties Eva Braun thought that her relationship with Hitler was now on a more established footing, she was soon disillusioned by even longer absences. . . . Görtemaker writes of Eva Braun's 'practically unassailable position at Hitler's side,' even if in the dangerous and byzantine world of the Nazi hierarchy nothing was guaranteed. . . . Hitler . . . appreciate[d] her unquestioning loyalty. . . . Eva Braun . . . probably knew little of the sadism, the squalor, and the horror of the camps. As an impressionable young woman, she had been molded in her opinions during her time in Hitler's presence." (New York Review of Books)

The author "coaxes from history's shadows the woman who for 14 years was the companion, lover and, near the end, wife of Adolf Hitler." Kirkus

Includes bibliographical references

Bray, Willie Reginald, 1879-1939

Tingey, John. The **Englishman** who posted himself and other curious objects. Princeton Architectural Press 2010 175p il $24.95 **92**

1. Autographs 2. Collectors 3. Eccentrics 4. Postal service -- Great Britain
ISBN 978-1-56898-872-6

LC 2009-48612

"The disposition of Bray's collection and how Tingey discovered it add further interest to an already fascinating account. Equally engaging as the narrative are the illustrations." Fine Books & Collections

Includes bibliographical references.

Brecht, Bertolt, 1898-1956

Fuegi, John. **Brecht** and company; sex, politics, and the making of the modern drama. Grove Press 1994 xx, 732p il hardcover o.p. pa $20 **92**

1. Poets 2. Authors 3. Novelists 4. Dramatists 5. Theatrical directors
ISBN 0-8021-3910-8 pa

LC 93-23051

The author "believes Brecht wrote very little in the dramas that made him famous; rather, he systematically plagiarized and 'collaborated' with lovers and colleagues by signing his name to plays they essentially wrote. . . . Fuegi's massive effort examines every aspect of Brecht's career and personality, and ranges from his childhood in Augsburg through his early successes and his exile to his return to East Germany." Booklist

Includes bibliographical references

Brenner, Carl

Brenner, Marie. **Apples** and oranges; my brother and me, lost and found. Farrar, Straus & Giroux 2008 268p il $24; pa $15 **92**

1. Cancer 2. Lawyers 3. Journalists 4. Fruit growers
ISBN 978-0-374-17352-4; 0-374-17352-4; 978-0-312-42880-8 pa; 0-312-42880-4 pa

LC 2008-08929

"In this elegiac memoir, the author, a reporter, applies the same investigative skills that led to her exposé of the tobacco industry and Enron to a more intimate subject: her contentious relationship with her late brother. From an eccentric Jewish Texan family of compulsive record keepers—their father maintained a four-page list of his life's achievements—Marie became a New York liberal, Carl a diehard conservative who abandoned a legal career to farm apples.

As a teenager, he smashed his sister's Joan Baez records; as an adult, given a diagnosis of terminal cancer, he informed her via FedEx. Her attempts to smooth over their differences by mastering the language of fruit (Carl often started conversations, 'I am going to give you a quiz') are at once comic and tinged with regret." New Yorker

Brenner, Marie

Brenner, Marie. **Apples** and oranges; my brother and me, lost and found. Farrar, Straus & Giroux 2008 268p il $24; pa $15 **92**
1. Cancer 2. Lawyers 3. Journalists 4. Fruit growers
ISBN 978-0-374-17352-4; 0-374-17352-4; 978-0-312-42880-8 pa; 0-312-42880-4 pa
LC 2008-08929

"In this elegiac memoir, the author, a reporter, applies the same investigative skills that led to her exposé of the tobacco industry and Enron to a more intimate subject: her contentious relationship with her late brother. From an eccentric Jewish Texan family of compulsive record keepers—their father maintained a four-page list of his life's achievements—Marie became a New York liberal, Carl a diehard conservative who abandoned a legal career to farm apples. As a teenager, he smashed his sister's Joan Baez records; as an adult, given a diagnosis of terminal cancer, he informed her via FedEx. Her attempts to smooth over their differences by mastering the language of fruit (Carl often started conversations, 'I am going to give you a quiz') are at once comic and tinged with regret." New Yorker

Breslin, Ed

Breslin, Ed. **Drinking** with Miss Dutchie; a memoir. Thomas Dunne Books 2011 274p $23.99 **92**
1. Dogs 2. Alcoholism 3. Editors 4. Memoirists 5. Publishing executives
ISBN 978-0-312-61975-6
LC 2010-39302

"Breslin writes about the death of his cherished dog, Miss Dutchie, and how, with her help, he succeeded in overcoming alcoholism. While not a dog-lover himself, in 1994 he bought Dutchie sight-unseen, as a surprise birthday gift for his wife. However, he freely admits that his motives were not entirely pure. 'I got Miss Dutchie to get Lynn off my back about my drinking,' he writes. Breslin had recently quit a decades-long career in publishing in an attempt to write a novel, and he did not expect to be spending his valuable time with a dog. . . . The story revolves around the dog who became the center of the childless couple's life, but the author also writes affectingly about his efforts to overcome addiction to alcohol and nicotine." Kirkus

Breslin, Jimmy

Breslin, Jimmy. **I** want to thank my brain for remembering me; a memoir. Little, Brown 1996 219p hardcover o.p. pa $12.95 **92**
1. Authors 2. Novelists 3. Columnists 4. Nonfiction writers
ISBN 0-316-11879-6 pa
LC 96-10488

"Confronting the possibility of death just past age 65 . . . Breslin memory-surfs through a troubled childhood and a lifetime in various journalistic trenches, from copyboy to columnist. . . . The book is full of family stories, political stories, and classic Breslin street stories, plus lots of details about brain operations from both patient's and surgeon's point of view." Booklist

Brinckle, Gordon, 1915-2007

Messick, Kendall. The **projectionist**. Princeton Architectural Press 2010 159p il $40 **92**
1. Motion picture theaters 2. Motion picture projectionists
ISBN 978-1-56898-933-4
LC 2010-08864

"Marveling at this amazing creation, Kendall knew that he had to photograph not only the theater, but the theater's owner and creator. And fortunately, the timing was perfect. Mr. Brinckle, a very elderly man, was extremely concerned about what would happen to his masterpiece after his passing. Their collaboration has resulted into something quite remarkable." Lenscratch

Brinkley, John Richard, 1885-1942

Brock, Pope. **Charlatan**; America's most dangerous huckster, the man who pursued him, and the age of flimflam. Crown Publishers 2008 324p il **92**
1. Physicians 2. Quacks and quackery 3. Swindlers 4. Broadcasters 5. Biography, Individual 6. Quacks and quackery -- United States
ISBN 0307339882; 9780307339881
LC 2007-10074

This is a biography of John Richard Brinkley. In 1917, Brinkley arrived in "Milford, Kansas. He set up a medical practice and introduced . . . [a] surgical method of using goat glands to restore the fading virility of local farmers. . . . Thousands of paying customers quickly turned 'Dr.' Brinkley into America's richest and most famous surgeon." (Publisher's note)

"Presentation is everything in telling this elaborate, many-faceted story. And Mr. Brock's has three outstanding virtues. First of all, he has a terrific ear for singling out quotations. . . . Second, he is selective. This fast-moving, light-stepping book takes care not to throw in extraneous detail. Third, his own voice is wry enough to compete with the actual Brinkley material, which is saying a great deal." N Y Times (Late N Y Ed)

Includes bibliographical references

Britten, Benjamin, 1913-1976

Powell, Neil, 1948- **Benjamin** Britten; a life for music. by Neil Powell. Henry Holt and Company 2013 528 p. $37 **92**
1. Composers -- Biography 2. Composers -- England -- Biography
ISBN 0805097740; 9780805097740
LC 2012051536

In this biography of "Benjamin Britten, the celebrated British composer . . . [Neil] Powell . . . traces the development of Britten's musical gifts from his childhood and youth in England to his travels to America, his meetings and lifelong friendship with W.H. Auden, and his crucial role in helping to establish the Alderburgh Festival. . . . He probes the genius of Britten's compositions from Sinfonietta . . . to the triptych of Peter Grimes . . . Billy Budd, and Death in Venice." (Publishers Weekly)

Includes bibliographical references and index

Brontë, Charlotte, 1816-1855

Gaskell, Elizabeth Cleghorn. The **life** of Charlotte Bronte; [by] Elizabeth Gaskell; edited with an introduction and notes by Angus Eason. Oxford University Press 2001 xxxvi, 587p (Oxford world's classics) pa $13.95   **92**

1. Poets 2. Authors 3. Novelists 4. Women authors 5. Authors, English

ISBN 0-19-283805-9

First published 1857

"Mrs. Gaskell was herself a popular novelist, who commanded a very wide audience. She brought to bear upon the biography of Charlotte Bronte all those literary gifts which had made the charm of her seven volumes of romance. . . . It is quite certain that Charlotte Bronte would not stand on so splendid a pedestal today but for the single-minded devotion of her accomplished biographer." Clement K. Shorter

Includes bibliographical references

Gordon, Lyndall. **Charlotte** Bronte; a passionate life. Norton 1995 418p il hardcover o.p. pa $17 **92**

1. Poets 2. Authors 3. Novelists 4. Women authors 5. Authors, English

ISBN 0-393-31448-0 pa

First published 1994 in the United Kingdom

The author "dismantles once and for all the image of Charlotte Brontë as a figure of pathos and presents, instead, a courageous survivor, a determined writer, and a woman of volcanic emotion. . . . Gordon, as skilled at literary analysis as at chronicling a life, approaches Brontë's tragic and enduringly relevant story from several angles, carefully identifying all the autobiographical elements of her novels and contrasting her commitment to writing and her independent spirit to her era's strict and pitiless code of behavior for women." Booklist

Includes bibliographical references

Brookhiser, Richard

Brookhiser, Richard. **Right** time, right place; coming of age with William F. Buckley, Jr. and the conservative movement. Basic Books 2009 262p $27.50   **92**

1. Authors 2. Novelists 3. Historians 4. Journalists 5. Conservatism 6. Columnists 7. Biographers 8. National review 9. Magazine editors

ISBN 978-0-465-01355-5; 0-465-01355-4

LC 2009-03073

"Think of a cause you care about deeply. Who's the figure you most admire in that movement? Now picture that person taking you to lunch, when you're 23, and declaring that you – you! – will be his successor. Such was the fantasy that Richard Brookhiser lived as a protégé of National Review editor William F. Buckley Jr., conservatism's standard-bearer for a half-century. Brookhiser was, to put it mildly, a prodigy. He wrote his first magazine cover story at 14. Steep falls often follow such precocious rises. But when Buckley changed his mind and sought a different heir, Brookhiser didn't self-destruct; he just rejiggered his career. Such equa-

nimity means Right Time, Right Place is refreshingly free of spicy score settling and juicy revelations. Instead, readers get tasty morsels of candor caramelized in the searing heat of self-reflection. The result is a psychologically rich personal narrative." Christ Sci Monit

Brown, Carolyn

★ Brown, Carolyn. **Chance** and circumstance; twenty years with Cage and Cunningham. Alfred A. Knopf 2007 645p il $37.50   **92**

1. Poets 2. Authors 3. Dancers 4. Composers 5. Choreographers 6. Essayists

ISBN 978-0-394-40191-1; 0-394-40191-3

LC 2006-48799

The author "traces the trajectory of her modern dance career with that organization during its crawling stages in the 1950s and 1960s, when composer John Cage was musical director and artist Robert Rauschenberg was set and costume designer. Brown documents the company's early struggles for acceptance (it was considered avant-garde), various tours, and eventual world recognition. . . . This book will appeal to modern dance buffs and memoir readers." Libr J

Brown, Claude, 1937-2002

Brown, Claude. **Manchild** in the promised land. Touchstone 1999 415p pa $19.95; pa $14.95   **92**

1. Authors 2. Journalists 3. Essayists 4. Memoirists 5. African Americans -- Biography 6. African Americans -- Harlem (New York, N.Y.)

ISBN 9781451626674; 0-684-86418-5

First published 1965 by Macmillan

This is "the autobiography of a young black man raised in Harlem. It is a realistic description of life in the ghetto. . . . The core of the book concerns the 'plague' of heroin addiction that swept through Harlem in the 1950s taking the lives of many of Brown's contemporaries." Publ Wkly

Brown, Helen Gurley

Scanlon, Jennifer. **Bad** girls go everywhere: the life of Helen Gurley Brown. Oxford University Press 2009 270p il $27.95   **92**

1. Columnists 2. Magazine editors 3. Nonfiction writers

ISBN 978-0-19-534205-5; 0-19-534205-4

LC 2008-30466

This is a biography of Helen Gurley Brown, former editor of Cosmopolitan magazine and author of Sex and the Single Girl (1962), Sex and the Office (1964), and Single Girl's Cookbook (1969).

"Jennifer Scanlon delivers Helen Gurley Brown's 'delightfully knotty life story' in a neat and satisfying package. . . . This is not chick lit but cultural history, the first serious biography of the woman who, in Scanlon's view, 'ushered in and has long continued to define the feminist mainstream.'" Natl Rev

Includes bibliographical references

Brown, James, 1933-2006

Brown, James. **James** Brown, the godfather of soul; by James Brown with Bruce Tucker; new introduction by Bruce Tucker; epilogue by Dave Marsh. Thunder's Mouth Press 1997 352p il pa $14.95 **92**

1. Singers 2. African American singers 3. Soul musicians

ISBN 978-1-56025-115-6; 1-56025-115-8

LC 90-31961

First published 1986 by Macmillan

"Brown's musical career spans four decades and his style defines the genre called soul. He has chronicled his life, from his birth in 1933 through a troubled youth, prison, and the ups and downs of a spiraling career." Libr J

This "is a solid, informative autobiography, and fans will welcome its vast discography." N Y Times Book Rev

Includes discography

Sullivan, James. The **hardest** working man; how James Brown saved the soul of America: live at the Boston Garden, 1968. Gotham Books 2008 244p il $25 **92**

1. Singers 2. African American singers 3. Soul musicians

ISBN 978-1-592-40390-5; 1-592-40390-5

LC 2008-13670

"Sullivan examines James Brown's role in saving Boston from the fires and riots that swept the U.S. after Martin Luther King Jr.'s assassination. Booked into Boston Garden the night of April 5, 1968, Brown agreed to put the show on live local TV to give would-be rioters reason to stay home. Garden management wanted to cancel, doubtless to avoid rioting in the Garden, but Brown and Boston's first black city councillor interceded with Mayor Kevin White to prevent cancellation. Sullivan goes further in crediting Brown for keeping the peace than others have, and so doing, he also examines the Godfather of Soul's life and career in the context of the Civil Rights movement. . . . A good record of a pivotal event and a serviceable Brown bio, to boot." Booklist

Includes bibliographical references

Brown, James, 1957-

Brown, James. The **Los** Angeles diaries; a memoir. Morrow 2003 200p $21.95; pa $12.95 **92**

1. Authors 2. Novelists 3. Short story writers

ISBN 0-06-052151-1; 0-06-052152-X pa

LC 2003-48779

"Brown's revelations have no smugness or self-congratulation; they reek of remorse and desire, passion and futility. . . . The result is a grimly exquisite memoir that reads like a noir novel but grips unrelentingly like the hand of a homeless drunk begging for help." Publ Wkly

Brown, John, 1800-1859

★ Horwitz, Tony. **Midnight** rising; John Brown and raid that sparked the Civil War. Henry Holt and Co. 2011 365p il map $29; ebook $12.99 **92**

1. Abolitionists 2. Pioneers 3. Harpers Ferry (W. Va.) -- History -- John Brown's Raid, 1859

ISBN 978-0-8050-9153-3; 0-8050-9153-X; 978-1-4299-9698-3 ebook; 1-4299-9698-6 ebook

LC 2011015659

The author presents a "narrative of Brown and the raid on Harpers Ferry that in many ways set the stage for Southern secession and civil war. . . . Horwitz's Brown did not die in vain. By recalling the drama that fired the imagination and fears of Brown's time, Midnight Rising calls readers to account for complacency about social injustices today. This is a book for our time." Libr J

Includes bibliographical references

Reynolds, David S. **John** Brown, abolitionist; the man who killed slavery, sparked the Civil War, and seeded civil rights. Alfred A. Knopf 2005 578p il $35 **92**

1. Abolitionists

ISBN 0-375-41188-7

LC 2004-48864

This biography contends "that Brown's most violent acts—his slaughter of unarmed citizens in Kansas, his liberation of slaves in Missouri, and his . . . raid in October 1859, on the federal arsenal at Harpers Ferry, Virginia—were inspired by the slave revolts, guerrilla warfare, and revolutionary Christianity of the day." Publisher's note

"Almost every page forces you to think hard, and in new ways, about American violence, American history, and what used to be called the American character." New Yorker

Includes bibliographical references

Brownfield, Christopher J.

Brownfield, Christopher J. **My** nuclear family; a coming-of-age in America's twenty-first century military. Alfred A. Knopf 2010 314p il $26.95; ebook $26.95 **92**

1. Nuclear submarines 2. Memoirists 3. Naval officers 4. Political scientists 5. Iraq War, 2003- -- Personal narratives

ISBN 978-0-307-27169-3; 978-0-307-59428-0 ebook

LC 2010-11833

This "is not the best book written by an insider about America's post-9/11 military, but it's certainly the most entertaining. It's got a cocky, star-spangled, wide-angle feel, as if a subversive young novelist had decided to rewrite a Tom Clancy thriller after first piloting some nuclear submarines as a gonzo practice drill. . . . This is a book that's going to rattle some cages." N Y Times Book Rev

Includes bibliographical references

Bruni, Frank, 1964-

Bruni, Frank. **Born** round; the secret history of a full-time eater. Penguin Press 2009 354p il $25.95; pa $16 **92**

1. Obesity 2. Food critics

ISBN 978-1-59420-231-5; 1-59420-231-1; 978-0-14-311767-4 pa; 0-14-311767-X pa

LC 2009-09532

"The book does not contain paeans to the glories of locavorism. It's not a tale of bawdy kitchen exploits, or of finding your true self over a bowl of pasta in Rome . . . His memoir tells a story of food addiction, eating disorders, and a lifelong struggle with his voracious appetite . . . Born Round makes for a breezy read. Even at its darkest, it goes down easy." Village Voice

Bryan, William Jennings, 1860-1925

Kazin, Michael. A **godly** hero; the life of William Jennings Bryan. Knopf 2006 374p il hardcover o.p. pa $16.95   **92**

1. Authors 2. Lawyers 3. Political leaders 4. Secretaries of state 5. Presidential candidates
ISBN 0-375-41135-6; 978-0-385-72056-4 pa; 0-385-72056-4 pa

LC 2005-44105

The author "attempts a revisionist portrait of Bryan (1860-1925), whom scholars have long dismissed as a rabid white supremacist, bullying fundamentalist and braying pacifist/isolationist." Publ Wkly

"Kazin is not the first biographer to tackle the Great Commoner, but he is definitely the best writer among them. 'A Godly Hero' is a richly textured narrative with an excellent pace." Christ Sci Monit

Includes bibliographical references

Bryant, Bear

Barra, Allen. The **last** coach: a life of Paul Bear Bryant. W. W. Norton & Co. 2005 xxix, 546p il $26.95   **92**

1. Football 2. Football coaches
ISBN 0-393-05982-0

LC 2005-14609

"Readers will experience an array of emotions—humor, sadness, inspiration, awe—as Barra reveals his subject's contributions to college football and ability to touch and inspire people long after their associations with Bryant ended." Libr J

Includes bibliographical references

Bryson, Bill

Bryson, Bill, 1951- The **life** and times of the thunderbolt kid; a memoir. Broadway Books 2006 270p il $25   **92**

1. Authors 2. Journalists 3. Essayists 4. Linguists 5. Lexicographers 6. Travel writers 7. Nonfiction writers 8. Biography, Individual
ISBN 0-7679-1936-X; 978-0-7679-1936-4

LC 2006-43859

In this book, Bill Bryson "recounts his childhood and teen years. When he was very young, he ran about his town with a towel for a cape, declaring himself the superhero, Thunderbolt Kid. His father wrote for the local paper, his mother worked there as well, leaving their home rather free from 'the domestic arts' (i.e. rather dirty). As he grew up, some of his friends were demonically destructive, while others were skilled at liberating boxcar loads of beer." (Voice of Youth Advocates)

The author "recounts the world of his younger self, buried in comic books in the Kiddie Corral at the local supermarket, resisting civil defense drills at school, and fruitlessly trying to unravel the mysteries of sex. . . . The larger world of 1950s America emerges through the lens of 'Billy's' world, including the dark underbelly of racism, the fight against communism, and the advent of the nuclear age." Libr J

Includes bibliographical references

Buber, Martin, 1878-1965

Friedman, Maurice S. **Encounter** on the narrow ridge: a life of Martin Buber; {by} Maurice Friedman. Paragon House 1991 496p il $22.95; pa $18.95   **92**

1. Authors 2. Zionism 3. Novelists 4. Philosophers 5. Jewish philosophy 6. Essayists 7. Translators 8. Writers on religion
ISBN 1-55778-453-1; 1-55778-596-1 pa

LC 90-44502

This biography (based on the author's three volume Martin Buber's life and work) "traces Buber's career showing the pivotal events in his life as well as the influences of Judaism, Christianity, general philosophical thought, and linguistics on his writings and lectures. Friedman analyzes succinctly, but with great care, Buber's responses to the important events of the 20th century." Libr J

Includes bibliographical references

Buck, Pearl S. (Pearl Sydenstricker), 1892-1973

Spurling, Hilary. **Pearl** Buck in China; journey to The Good Earth. Simon & Schuster 2010 304p il map $27; ebook $12.99   **92**

1. Authors 2. Novelists 3. Short 4. Essayists 5. Memoirists 6. Biographers 7. Authors, American 8. Biography, Individual 9. Nobel laureates for literature
ISBN 978-1-4165-4042-7; 1-4165-4042-3; 978-1-4391-8044-0 ebook; 1-4391-8044-X ebook

LC 2010-07712

Published in the United Kingdom with title: Burying the bones

This is a biography of the American author of The Good Earth (1931).

The author's "account of Buck's 'rootless and fractured existence' provides a fascinating dissection of the tortured relationships between a man of God, the hapless wife sucked into supporting his mission and their increasingly sceptical daughter, Pearl, who, in 1933, publicly turned her back on her late father's church. It is also just as revealing about the no less tortured relationship between the West and China in the early part of the last century." Economist

Includes bibliographical references

Buckley, Bryan

Sielski, Mike. **Fading** echoes; a true story of rivalry and brotherhood from the football field to the fields of honor. Berkley Books 2009 342p il $24.95   **92**

1. School sports 2. Iraq War, 2003-2011 3. Marines 4. Army officers 5. Iraq War, 2003- 6. Football -- Biography 7. Soldiers -- United States
ISBN 978-0-425-22974-3

LC 2009-17001

"Bryan Buckley was the captain of Central Bucks West and [Colby] Umbrell was one of the leaders of Central Bucks East when their teams clashed in their senior year of 1998. Eight years later, both were officers leading men in combat in Iraq, Buckley as a marine and Umbrell as an army ranger. Both were proudly fighting for ideals in which they believed, and only one would come home alive. Sielski . . . chronicles the lives of these two athletes and illustrates how their personalities and values were formed from interactions with family, friends, coaches, and community. In the process, he writes of much broader topics in contemporary American life: dreams, competition, resolve, war, honor, sacrifice, and true heartbreak." Libr J

Includes bibliographical references

Buckley, Christopher Taylor, 1952- ✓

Buckley, Christopher Taylor. **Losing** Mum and Pup; a memoir. [by] Christopher Buckley. Twelve 2009 251p il $24.99; pa $13.99   **92**

1. Authors 2. Humorists 3. Novelists 4. Philanthropists 5. Columnists 6. Socialites 7. Speechwriters 8. Magazine editors 9. Authors, American 10. Spouses of prominent persons

ISBN 978-0-446-54094-0; 0-446-54094-3; 978-0-446-54095-7 pa; 0-446-54095-1 pa

LC 2008-43532

"Christopher Buckley has not written a 'Mommie Dearest' for the Evelyn Waugh set. 'Losing Mum and Pup' is a subtle, fond and, above all, honest chronicle of his celebrated parents. . . . Buckley has pulled off what eludes many writers: he has written candidly but not unkindly about people whose vices and virtues he sees clearly." Newsweek

Buckley, Pat

Buckley, Christopher Taylor. **Losing** Mum and Pup; a memoir. [by] Christopher Buckley. Twelve 2009 251p il $24.99; pa $13.99   **92**

1. Authors 2. Humorists 3. Novelists 4. Philanthropists 5. Columnists 6. Socialites 7. Speechwriters 8. Magazine editors 9. Authors, American 10. Spouses of prominent persons

ISBN 978-0-446-54094-0; 0-446-54094-3; 978-0-446-54095-7 pa; 0-446-54095-1 pa

LC 2008-43532

"Christopher Buckley has not written a 'Mommie Dearest' for the Evelyn Waugh set. 'Losing Mum and Pup' is a subtle, fond and, above all, honest chronicle of his celebrated parents. . . . Buckley has pulled off what eludes many writers: he has written candidly but not unkindly about people whose vices and virtues he sees clearly." Newsweek

Buckley, William F., 1925-2008 ✓

Brookhiser, Richard. **Right** time, right place; coming of age with William F. Buckley, Jr. and the conservative movement. Basic Books 2009 262p $27.50   **92**

1. Authors 2. Novelists 3. Historians 4. Journalists 5. Conservatism 6. Columnists 7. Biographers 8. National review 9. Magazine editors

ISBN 978-0-465-01355-5; 0-465-01355-4

LC 2009-03073

"Think of a cause you care about deeply. Who's the figure you most admire in that movement? Now picture that person taking you to lunch, when you're 23, and declaring that you – you! – will be his successor. Such was the fantasy that Richard Brookhiser lived as a protégé of National Review editor William F. Buckley Jr., conservatism's standard-bearer for a half-century. Brookhiser was, to put it mildly, a prodigy. He wrote his first magazine cover story at 14. Steep falls often follow such precocious rises. But when Buckley changed his mind and sought a different heir, Brookhiser

didn't self-destruct; he just rejiggered his career. Such equanimity means Right Time, Right Place is refreshingly free of spicy score settling and juicy revelations. Instead, readers get tasty morsels of candor caramelized in the searing heat of self-reflection. The result is a psychologically rich personal narrative." Christ Sci Monit

Buckley, Christopher Taylor. **Losing** Mum and Pup; a memoir. [by] Christopher Buckley. Twelve 2009 251p il $24.99; pa $13.99   **92**

1. Authors 2. Humorists 3. Novelists 4. Philanthropists 5. Columnists 6. Socialites 7. Speechwriters 8. Magazine editors 9. Authors, American 10. Spouses of prominent persons

ISBN 978-0-446-54094-0; 0-446-54094-3; 978-0-446-54095-7 pa; 0-446-54095-1 pa

LC 2008-43532

"Christopher Buckley has not written a 'Mommie Dearest' for the Evelyn Waugh set. 'Losing Mum and Pup' is a subtle, fond and, above all, honest chronicle of his celebrated parents. . . . Buckley has pulled off what eludes many writers: he has written candidly but not unkindly about people whose vices and virtues he sees clearly." Newsweek

Buckley, William F. **Miles** gone by; a literary autobiography. [by] William F. Buckley Jr. Regnery Pub. 2004 594p il $29.95; pa $18.95   **92**

1. Authors 2. Novelists 3. Columnists 4. Magazine editors

ISBN 0-89526-089-1; 0-89526-004-2 pa

LC 2004-7170

This "is an elegant book, one of Buckley's best, and the man the reader meets in these pages is the Platonic ideal of a dinner companion, a raconteur whose pomposity is calculated and whose self-deprecation charms." N Y Times Book Rev

Buffalo Bill, 1846-1917

Warren, Louis S. **Buffalo** Bill's America; William Cody and the Wild West Show. Alfred A. Knopf 2005 652p il $30   **92**

1. Entertainers 2. Frontier and pioneer life 3. Scouts 4. Hunters 5. Circus executives 6. Circus performers

ISBN 0-375-41216-6

LC 2004-63280

This is a biography of the American showman.

This book "is well written and exhaustively researched, the weightiest and surely the most ambitious book ever published about Cody and his times." N Y Times Book Rev

Includes bibliographical references

Buffett, Warren E.

Schroeder, Alice D. The **snowball** : Warren Buffett and the business of life; [by] Alice Schroeder. Bantam Books 2008 960p il $35   **92**

1. Capitalists and financiers 2. Financiers

ISBN 978-0-553-80509-3; 0-553-80509-6

LC 2008-17338

A portrait of the life and career of investment guru Warren Buffett

"In a book that is dominated by unstinting descriptions of Buffett's appetites—for profit, women (particularly nurturing maternal types), food (Buffett maintained his and his family's weight by 'dangling money')—it is refreshing that Schroeder keeps her tone free of judgment or awe; Buffett's plain-speaking suffuses the book and renders his public and private successes and failures wonderfully human and universal. . . . Inspiring managerial advice abounds and competes with gossipy tidbits . . . in this rich, surprisingly affecting biography." Publ Wkly

Includes bibliographical references

Bullock-Prado, Gesine, 1970-

Bullock-Prado, Gesine. **Confections** of a closet master baker; one woman's sweet journey from unhappy Hollywood executive to contented country baker. illustrations by Raymond G. Prado. Broadway Books 2009 226p il $24 **92**

1. Baking 2. Bakers 3. Motion picture executives
ISBN 978-0-7679-3268-4

LC 2009-945

The author "chronicles her career change from schmoozing Hollywood production company executive to running a bakery in Montpelier, VT. . . . Memoir lovers will find this a lighthearted, entertaining read filled with humor and acerbic wit; foodies will enjoy the insider's view of running a bakery." Libr J

Bundy, Ted

Rule, Ann. The **stranger** beside me; Updated 20th anniversary ed; Signet 2001 548p il pa $7.99 **92**

1. Criminals 2. Murderers
ISBN 0-451-20326-7; 978-0-451-20326-7
First published 1980 by Norton

This is a biography of Ted Bundy, written by someone who "worked a suicide hotline in Seattle with Ted Bundy, not knowing he was a serial killer." Libr J

Burana, Lily

Burana, Lily. **I** love a man in uniform; a memoir of love, war and other battles. Weinstein Books 2009 352p $23.95 **92**

1. Authors 2. Military spouses 3. Editors 4. Essayists 5. Memoirists 6. Stripteasers
ISBN 978-1-60286-083-4; 1-60286-083-1

This "is a humorous, moving and surprising account of married life in today's military." N Y Times Book Rev

Burbank, Luther, 1849-1926

Smith, Jane S. The **garden** of invention; Luther Burbank and the business of breeding plants. Penguin Press 2009 354p il $25.95 **92**

1. Plant breeding 2. Horticulturists
ISBN 978-1-59420-209-4

LC 2009-1822

This is a biographical study of "Luther Burbank, a man who described himself as an 'evoluter of new plants.'" N Y Times (Late N Y Ed)

"An accessible introduction to an agricultural innovator that gives equal weight to his life of experimentation and what it has meant for society." Kirkus

Includes bibliographical references

Burns, Robert, 1759-1796

Crawford, Robert. The **bard**; Robert Burns, a biography. Princeton University Press 2009 465p $35 **92**

1. Poets 2. Authors
ISBN 978-0-691-14171-8; 0-691-14171-1

LC 2008-937561

"Crawford's Burns, merrily mixing high and low culture, seems eerily contemporary. He shares with great hip-hop artists a genius for catchy, sexy, and memorable rhymes gloriously liberated from the hegemony of standard English." New Yorker

Includes bibliographical references

Burroughs, William S., 1914-1997

Miles, Barry. **Call** Me Burroughs; A Life. Barry Miles. Twelve 2014 736 p. illustrations (hardback) $32 **92**

1. Beat generation 2. American authors 3. Novelists, American -- 20th century -- Biography
ISBN 1455511951; 9781455511952

LC 2013032565

Writer William "Burroughs was the original cult figure of the Beat Movement, and with the publication of his novel 'Naked Lunch,' which was originally banned for obscenity, he became a guru to the 60s youth counterculture. In 'Call Me Burroughs,' biographer and Beat historian Barry Miles presents the first full-length biography of Burroughs to be published in a quarter century." (Publisher's note)

A "dense, detailed, yet wonderfully readable and entertaining narrative that illuminates, without sensationalizing, Burroughs's manifold peculiarities." Pub Wkly

Includes bibliographical references and index

Burton, Isabel, Lady, 1831-1896

Lovell, Mary S. A **rage** to live: a biography of Richard and Isabel Burton. Norton 1998 910p il hardcover o.p. pa $19.95 **92**

1. Authors 2. Explorers 3. Travel writers 4. Asian studies specialists 5. Middle Eastern studies specialists
ISBN 0-393-32039-1 pa

LC 98-29886

This is "a readable narrative of great verve and passion." N Y Rev Books

Includes bibliographical references

Burton, Richard Francis Sir, 1821-1890

Lovell, Mary S. A **rage** to live: a biography of Richard and Isabel Burton. Norton 1998 910p il hardcover o.p. pa $19.95 **92**

1. Authors 2. Explorers 3. Travel writers 4. Asian studies specialists 5. Middle Eastern studies specialists
ISBN 0-393-32039-1 pa

LC 98-29886

This is "a readable narrative of great verve and passion." N Y Rev Books

Includes bibliographical references

Burton, Richard, 1925-1984

Kashner, Sam. **Furious** love; Elizabeth Taylor, Richard Burton, and the marriage of the century. [by]

Sam Kashner and Nancy Schoenberger. Harper 2010 500p il $27.99 **92**

1. Actors

ISBN 978-0-06-156284-6; 0-06-156284-X

LC 2010-06732

"In this dual biography of the two legendary film stars, the authors draw upon new information, including interviews with Elizabeth Taylor and with the Burton family, to capture the famously passionate and tumultuous relationship between the legendary couple. . . . It's a mesmerizing tale, but it's also sad, and sometimes ugly, as the two stars engaged in vicious fights, nursed their jealousies and insecurities, and descended into alcoholism while outwardly living a life of glamour and sophistication." Booklist

Includes bibliographical references

Bush, Barbara, 1925-

Bush, Barbara. **Barbara** Bush; a memoir. Scribner 1994 575p il $25; pa $16 **92**

1. Diplomats 2. Presidents 3. Vice-presidents 4. Members of Congress 5. Parents of presidents 6. Spouses of presidents 7. United Nations officials

ISBN 0-02-519635-9; 0-7432-5447-3 pa

LC 94-13829

The former "First Lady, one of the most popular in modern history, gives the reader a tour through her life story and the parallel universe of the political spouse." NY Times Book Rev

Bush, George, 1924-

Bush, Barbara. **Barbara** Bush; a memoir. Scribner 1994 575p il $25; pa $16 **92**

1. Diplomats 2. Presidents 3. Vice-presidents 4. Members of Congress 5. Parents of presidents 6. Spouses of presidents 7. United Nations officials

ISBN 0-02-519635-9; 0-7432-5447-3 pa

LC 94-13829

The former "First Lady, one of the most popular in modern history, gives the reader a tour through her life story and the parallel universe of the political spouse." NY Times Book Rev

Bush, George. **All** the best, George Bush; my life in letters and other writings. Scribner 1999 640p il $30; pa $16 **92**

1. Diplomats 2. Presidents 3. Vice-presidents 4. Members of Congress 5. Parents of presidents 6. United Nations officials 7. Presidents -- United States

ISBN 0-684-83958-X; 0-7432-0041-1 pa

LC 99-40440

The former president presents his autobiography in the form of annotated letters, memos, journal entries, and speeches written between 1942 and March 1999

This work "is refreshing and, in many ways, will shed more light on the man's personal character and public persona than any memoir or biography could. It offers an intriguing picture of a man who takes fierce pride in his modesty." Publ Wkly

Bush, George W.

Bush, George W. (George Walker), 1946- **Decision** points. Crown Publishers 2010 497p il $35; ebook $14.99 **92**

1. Governors 2. Presidents 3. Baseball executives 4. Biography, Individual 5. Children of presidents 6. Energy industry executives

ISBN 978-0-307-59061-9; 0-307-59061-5; 978-0-307-59062-6 ebook

"Critics on both the left and right are challenged to walk in his shoes, and may come away with a new view of the former president—or at least an appreciation of the hard and often ambiguous choices he was forced to make. . . . Honest, of course, but also surprisingly approachable and engaging." Kirkus

Minutaglio, Bill. **First** son: George W. Bush and the Bush family dynasty. Times Bks. 1999 371p il hardcover o.p. pa $14 **92**

1. Governors 2. Presidents 3. Baseball executives 4. Children of presidents 5. Energy industry executives 6. Presidents -- United States

ISBN 0-609-80867-2 pa

LC 99-16462

In this political biography the "author traces the Bush family history from Prescott to George to First Son. This family dynasty has been of great assistance to George W. as he is called, in his rise in business and politics. While giving surprisingly little attention to George W.'s performance as governor of Texas . . . the author focuses on his development as a young man and emergence into the national political limelight." Libr J

Bush, Laura

Bush, Laura. **Spoken** from the heart. Scribner 2010 456p il $30; ebook $12.99 **92**

1. Teachers 2. Librarians 3. Spouses of presidents 4. Presidents' spouses -- United States 5. United States -- Politics and government -- 2001-

ISBN 978-1-439-15520-2; 1-439-15520-8; 978-1-439-16034-3 ebook; 1-439-16034-1 ebook

LC 2010-13701

This book "reveals Laura Welch Bush to be a beautiful writer, a keen observer and a tender soul who drew on her roots to live a life in the public eye with compassion and grace." Wall Street J

Includes bibliographical references

Byrnes, Thomas, 1842-1910

Conway, J. North. The **big** policeman; the rise and fall of America's first, most ruthless, and greatest detective. Lyons Press 2010 323p il $24.95 **92**

1. Detectives 2. Police officials 3. Police -- New York (N.Y.)

ISBN 978-1-59921-965-3

This is a biography of "Thomas Byrnes, a New York City law enforcer whose career peaked in the 1890s as superintendent of the police force. Impressed by Byrnes' ascent, which began with street-patrol courageousness in the city's 1863 antidraft, antiblack riots, Conway proceeds to Byrnes' successes as a detective, which form the core of the biography. Going case-by-case, . . . Conway combines narrative with explanation of Byrnes' methods of investigation and interrogation. . . . Creating period atmosphere by quoting extensively from newspaper accounts of the sensational crimes Byrnes solved, Conway portrays his subject's cleverness and excesses with a flawed-hero flavor that should draw in true-crime fans." Booklist

Includes bibliographical references

Byron, George Gordon Byron, 6th Baron, 1788-1824

Eisler, Benita. **Byron** --child of passion, fool of fame. Knopf 1999 837p il hardcover o.p. pa $18 **92**
1. Poets 2. Authors
ISBN 0-679-74085-6 pa

LC 98-35261

Eisler's "biography portrays Byron as a restless, brilliant man in thrall: he is, in her view, the puppet of his own extravagant passions and even in his lifetime was so fictionalized and mythologized by others that he found it hard to maintain his own sense of self." Publ Wkly

"This is a splendidly readable biography of a perpetually fascinating genius." Atl Mon

Includes bibliographical references

Bystrolëtov, D. A., 1901-1975

Draitser, Emil. **Stalin's** Romeo spy; the remarkable rise and fall of the KGB's most daring operative: the true life of Dmitri Bystrolyotov. Northwestern University Press 2010 420p il map $35.00 **92**
1. Spies 2. Novelists 3. Russian espionage 4. Translators 5. Political prisoners -- Soviet Union 6. Intelligence service -- Soviet Union -- History
ISBN 0810126648; 9780810126640

LC 2009-44637

This book presents a "biography of one of Soviet Russia's most flamboyant and successful illegals, Dmitry Bystrolyotov." Author Emil Draitser chronicles Bystrolyotov's life from his "youthful adventures around the Black Sea coast, to his pre-WWII travels back and forth across Europe as a 'night of cloak and dagger,' to his term in Norillag, one of the worst of [Joseph] Stalin's slave labor camps." (Russian Life)

"In the 1930s, Dmitri Bystrolyotov moved effortlessly through European capitals, seducing women and collecting secrets for Stalin's Russia—until he was caught in one of Stalin's purges and sent to the Gulag. Emil Draitser tells Bystrolyotov's story." Wall Street J

Includes bibliographical references (p. 407-412) and index.

Cadillac Man

Cadillac Man. **Land** of the lost souls; my life on the streets. Bloomsbury 2009 288p $25 **92**
1. Veterans 2. Homeless persons 3. Homeless
ISBN 978-1-596-914063; 1-596-91406-8

LC 2008-41111

Memoir of a man who became homeless at age 44. Describes his adventures and daily experiences that he recorded in a series of spiral notebooks over fourteen years. He writes about the "indelible characters" who share his New York City streets, including Penny, a young runaway whom he eventually reunites with her family

"A surprising find, Cadillac lets readers in on a rarely seen community, revealing the compassionate hearts that beat even in the most despairing circumstances." Publ Wkly

Caesar, Julius, 100-44 B.C.

★ Goldsworthy, Adrian Keith. **Caesar**; life of a colossus. [by] Adrian Goldsworthy. Yale University Press 2006 583p il map $35 **92**
1. Statesmen 2. Historians 3. Rome -- History
ISBN 978-0-300-12048-6; 0-300-12048-6

LC 2006-922060

This biography draws "together Julius Caesar's personal, political, and military history into a single volume. . . . This is an engaging and well-drawn resource for those who wish to be introduced to the man who was Caesar." Libr J

Includes bibliographical references

Cage, John

★ Brown, Carolyn. **Chance** and circumstance; twenty years with Cage and Cunningham. Alfred A. Knopf 2007 645p il $37.50 **92**
1. Poets 2. Authors 3. Dancers 4. Composers 5. Choreographers 6. Essayists
ISBN 978-0-394-40191-1; 0-394-40191-3

LC 2006-48799

"The author "traces the trajectory of her modern dance career with [the Merce Cunningham Dance Company] during its crawling stages in the 1950s and 1960s, when composer John Cage was musical director and artist Robert Rauschenberg was set and costume designer. Brown documents the company's early struggles for acceptance (it was considered avant-garde), various tours, and eventual world recognition. . . . This book will appeal to modern dance buffs and memoir readers." Libr J

Silverman, Kenneth. **Begin** again; a biography of John Cage. Alfred A. Knopf 2010 483p il $40 **92**
1. Poets 2. Authors 3. Composers 4. Essayists 5. Biography, Individual
ISBN 1-4000-4437-5; 978-1-4000-4437-5

LC 2010-09525

This is a biography of the American "musician, inventor, composer, poet." (Publisher's note) Index.

In this biography of "one of the most influential composers of the 20th century . . . [the author traces Cage's] innovations chronologically—his breakthrough years as a composer of experimental dance and percussion music, his definitive decade inventing chance-derived music as a member of the New York School of artists and musicians in the '50s, and his later development of indeterminate music, the content of which could be created by the performer. . . . Not just an exemplary biography, but a significant contribution to the cultural history of American music." Kirkus

Includes bibliographical references

Cagney, James, 1899-1986

McCabe, John. **Cagney**. Carroll & Graf Pub. 1999 439p il pa $18.95 **92**
1. Actors
ISBN 978-0-7867-0580-1; 0-7867-0580-9
First published 1997 by Knopf

This work "exceeds the typical standards of celebrity biography because McCabe is fully attentive to the many dimensions of his subject's artistry." Commonweal

Includes filmography and bibliographical references

Calcaterra, Regina

Calcaterra, Regina. **Etched** in Sand; A True Story of Five Siblings Who Survived an Unspeakable Childhood on Long Island. HarperCollins 2013 320 p. $15.99   **92**

1. Child abuse 2. Foster children
ISBN 0062218832; 9780062218834

This memoir presents the "true story of a woman surviving domestic abuse as a child, emancipating herself as a teenager, and then becoming a successful attorney. . . . Her story begins with an account of life among 'a scrappy pack of homeless siblings' and narrows to [Regina] Calcaterra's rise to executive director of the New York State Moreland Commission on Utility Preparation and Response." (Publishers Weekly)

Caldwell, Gail, 1951-

★ Caldwell, Gail. **Let's** take the long way home; a memoir of friendship. Random House 2010 190p $23   **92**

1. Friendship 2. Journalists 3. Columnists 4. Memoirists 5. Literary critics
ISBN 978-1-4000-6738-1; 1-4000-6738-3

LC 2009-29384

The author describes "her friendship with Caroline Knapp, the author of the acclaimed Drinking: A Love Story, who died in 2002, seven weeks after being diagnosed with lung cancer." Texas Monthly

"This is a book you'll want to share with your own 'necessary pillars of life,' as Caldwell refers to her nearest and dearest. . . . Her memoir, a tribute to the enduring power of friendship, is a lovely gift to readers." Washington Post

Caldwell, Gail. **New** life, no instructions; a memoir. by Gail Caldwell. Random House 2014 176 p. (alk. paper) $23   **92**

1. Journalists -- United States -- Biography 2. Critics -- United States -- Biography 3. Total hip replacement -- Patients -- Biography
ISBN 1400069548; 9781400069545

LC 2013015486

In this memoir, author Gail Caldwell "confronts . . . the hurdles that life throws her way—in this case, hip surgery while tending to a new pet Samoyed. . . . After the death of her beloved Clementine, in 2008, she tracked down a Samoyed breeder . . . and procured a new puppy, Tula. However, at age 57 and with a 'bum leg,' . . . Caldwell wondered at the wisdom of getting a very muscular, high-octane dog when her leg strength seemed to be diminishing." (Publishers Weekly)

"Readers will enjoy Caldwell's thoughtful, wide-eyed view of the world around her and her musings on how we get our bearings in midlife." Kirkus

Includes bibliographical references and index

Campanella, Roy, 1921-1993

Kashatus, William C. **Jackie** and Campy; the untold story of their rocky relationship and the breaking of baseball's color line. William C. Kashatus. University of Nebraska Press 2014 248 p. illustrations, map (cloth : alk. paper) $24.95   **92**

1. African American baseball players 2. Race discrimination in sports -- History 3. Male friendship -- United States 4. Racism in sports -- United States 5. Discrimination in sports -- United States 6. African American baseball players -- Biography 7. Baseball players -- United States -- Biography
ISBN 0803246331; 9780803246331

LC 2013033133

This book, by William C. Kashatus, focuses on "the first black players to be candidates to break professional baseball's color barrier, Jackie Robinson and Roy Campanella. . . . The two men were divided by . . . [their] differing beliefs about the fight for civil rights. Robinson, the more aggressive and intense of the two, thought Jim Crow should be attacked head-on; Campanella, more passive and easygoing, believed that ability, not militancy, was the key to racial equality." (Publisher's note)

"Kashatus has written a superb narrative of sports, race, and politics in the 1950s and '60s, and also tells of the bittersweet consequences in Jackie and Campy's lives—." Pub Wkly

Includes bibliographical references and index

Campbell, William, 1730?-1778

Harris, J. William. The **hanging** of Thomas Jeremiah; a free Black man's encounter with liberty. Yale University Press 2009 223p il map $27.50   **92**

1. Diplomats 2. Merchants 3. Ship captains 4. Colonial leaders 5. Plantation owners 6. Government officials 7. Colonial administrators 8. Slavery -- United States 9. South Carolina -- Race relations 10. African Americans -- Social conditions
ISBN 978-0-300-15214-2; 0-300-15214-0

LC 2009-15233

This is an "account of nebulous historical figure Thomas Jeremiah. . . . Owner of a fishing company and worth $200,000 in 2009 dollars, . . . [Jeremiah] was probably the richest black man in North America; he was also a slaveowner. That didn't stop him from becoming a scapegoat, accused by patriot leader Henry Laurens—a wealthy plantation owner with hundreds of slaves—of secretly leading a British-sponsored slave insurrection. Though Governor William Campbell, aggrieved by the unlawfulness of Jeremiah's trial, interceded, it didn't stop those determined to hang Jeremiah. . . . Readers will learn much about the darker side of American institutions; students of American history and civil rights will appreciate Harris's impassive approach and thorough standards." Publ Wkly

Includes bibliographical references

Capone, Al, 1899-1947

Balsamo, William. **Young** Al Capone; the untold story of Scarface in New York, 1899-1925. [by]

William Balsamo and John Balsamo. Skyhorse Pub.
2010 270p il $24.95   **92**

1. Mafia 2. Criminals 3. Mobsters 4. Bootleggers
ISBN 978-1-616-08085-3

LC 2010-34682

"Before he became the mythical untouchable 'Scarface,' Alphonse Capone (1899-1947) was a young, cunningly brutal thug schooled by hardboiled criminal minds
in pre-Depression Brooklyn, N.Y. . . . [The authors] revisit
Capone's apprenticeship years in the violent Brooklyn Navy
Yard street gangs and his transformation from a wayward
youth to polished, cold-blooded gangster under the tutelage
of two master mobsters, Johnny Torrio and 'Frankie Yale'
Ioele. . . . With insider facts and spare narrative, the authors
show us not only how Capone got his scarred face; they deliver a scathing portrait of a power-mad predator coming up
through the criminal ranks." Publ Wkly

Eig, Jonathan. **Get** Capone; the real story of
America's legendary gangster. Simon & Schuster
2010 468p il $28   **92**

1. Criminals 2. Organized crime 3. Mobsters 4.
Bootleggers
ISBN 978-1-4165-8059-1; 1-4165-8059-X

LC 2009-33949

The author "rescues the narrative of Al Capone from the
realm of pop melodrama, offering vibrant historical storytelling and a nuanced, enigmatic portrait of Capone and his
Chicago milieu. . . . An impressive, accessible history of a
troubled time." Kirkus

Includes bibliographical references

Capote, Truman, 1924-1984

★ Capote, Truman. **Too** brief a treat; the letters
of Truman Capote. edited by Gerald Clarke. Random
House 2004 487p il $27.95; pa $16   **92**

1. Authors 2. Novelists 3. Nonfiction writers 4. Short
story writers
ISBN 0-375-50133-9; 0-375-70241-5 pa

LC 2004-50313

"Capote's untrammeled personality fairly falls off the
pages of these letters, and rather than being irritating, his
disregard of reticence is especially poignant in this day of
sterile e-mailing. Ideal for devotees to dip into here and there
instead of reading from start to finish." Booklist

Includes bibliographical references

Long, Robert Emmet. **Truman** Capote, enfant
terrible. Continuum 2008 130p $24.95   **92**

1. Authors 2. Novelists 3. Authors, American 4.
Nonfiction writers 5. Short story writers
ISBN 978-0-8264-2763-2; 0-8264-2763-4

LC 2008-4957

Long recounts "Capote's early life, highlighting his
tragic childhood and the relationships the eccentric author
maintained with various members of New York's elite. Long
draws heavily from Capote's unpublished papers and from
Gerald Clarke's Capote: A Biography. This brief sketch,
however, sets the stage for a compelling analysis of the effect of the author's tragic life on the gothic nature of his
prose. Long brilliantly places each piece in the context of the
author's life and of the culture at the time of its release. The

book ends with a retrospective contemplation of Capote's
influence and place in American letters. Each chapter represents a cogent and concise snapshot of Capote's genius in
a specific period, while the entire book becomes a journey
through Capote's life, work, and demons placed within the
context of American literary culture." Libr J

Includes bibliographical references

Caravaggio, Michelangelo Merisi da, 1573-1610

Prose, Francine. **Caravaggio**; painter of miracles.
Atlas Books/HarperCollins 2005 149p il (Eminent
lives) $21.95   **92**

1. Artists 2. Painters 3. Artists, Italian
ISBN 0-06-057560-3

LC 2005-40203

"A contemporary of Shakespeare, Caravaggio was 'belligerent, contemptuous, and competitive,' a revered artist
and a notorious street fighter wanted for murder who died
at 39 under tragic circumstances. Much has been written
about Caravaggio and his dramatic paintings, especially his
daringly earthy depictions of biblical scenes, but somehow
Prose's concentrated interpretation has a stronger impact.
Not only does she cover all the biographical essentials but
she also more clearly and descriptively explicates the pioneering painter's unique perception of the miraculous in everyday life. Prose also reveals, with both subtlety and flourish, how Caravaggio's frank interpretations of violence and
pain, fear and grief, dignity and transcendence are matched
with a brilliant subversion of our sense of reality." Booklist

Carnegie, Andrew, 1835-1919

Nasaw, David. **Andrew** Carnegie. Penguin Press
2006 878p il $35; pa $20   **92**

1. Philanthropists 2. Metal industry executives
ISBN 1-59420-104-8; 0-14-311244-9 pa

LC 2006-44840

This is a biography of the Scottish-born businessman
and philanthropist. Carnegie was the founder of the Carnegie Steel Company which later became U.S. Steel.

"Highly readable despite it's length, 'Andrew Carnegie'
shows signs of prodigious original research on almost every
page." N Y Times (Late N Y Ed)

Includes bibliographical references

Carnegie, Dale, 1888-1955

Watts, Steven. **Self** -help Messiah; Dale Carnegie and success in modern America. by Steven Watts.
Other Press 2013 32 p. $29.95   **92**

1. Self-help techniques 2. Success 3. Conduct of life
4. Orators -- United States -- Biography 5. Teachers
-- United States -- Biography 6. Authors, American --
20th century -- Biography
ISBN 1590515021; 9781590515020

LC 2013003227

This book, by Steven Watts, "tells the story of [Dale]
Carnegie's personal journey and how it gave rise to the
movement of self-help and personal reinvention. His book,
'How to Win Friends and Influence People,' became a best
seller worldwide. Carnegie conceived his book to help
people learn to relate to one another and enrich their lives
through effective communication. His success was extraor-

dinary, so hungry was 1920s America for a little psychological insight." (Publisher's note)

"A fascinating portrait of the father of self-help and incisive analysis of the mercurial era that produced him." Kirkus

Caro, Helga Gerda

★ Seth, Vikram, 1952- **Two** lives; Vikram Seth. HarperCollins 2005 503p ill. (pbk.) $15.95; o.p. **92**
1. Poets 2. Authors 3. Dentists 4. Novelists 5. London (England) -- Biography" 6. East Indians -- England -- London 7. Interracial marriage -- England -- London 8. Authors, English -- 20th century -- Biography 9. Authors, Indic -- Homes and haunts -- England -- London 10. London (England) -- Social life and customs -- 20th century
ISBN 9780060599676; 0060599669

LC 2005052694

In this book, the author presents biographies of "his Shanti Uncle and Aunty Henny. . . . Shanti was Seth's grandfather's brother, a dentist who studied in Berlin, lodging with Fau Caro, whose daughter, Henny was in love with someone else. He left for Britain in 1936. . . . [I]n 1940, as war broke out, he enlisted, served throughout and lost his right arm in combat. . . . Meanwhile, Henny, a German Jew, arrived in Britain weeks before war was declared, leaving her beloved mother and sister behind to death camp murder. . . . Part two of his narrative focuses on Shanti. Part three, Henny's story . . . is based on a trove of remarkable letters she received and wrote. . . . Part four examines their marriage (they didn't marry until seven years after the war), and part five details a family mystery about Shanti's will and Seth's . . . research into these lives." (Publishers Weekly)

"In clear and elegant writing, Seth explores the macrocosm through the microcosm, resulting in a most unusual, worthwhile book." Publ Wkly

Carr, David

Carr, David. The **night** of the gun; a reporter investigates the darkest story of his life, his own. Simon & Schuster 2008 389p il $26; pa $15 **92**
1. Journalists 2. Drug addicts 3. Columnists 4. Memoirists
ISBN 978-1-4165-4152-3; 1-4165-4152-7; 978-1-4165-4153-0 pa; 1-4165-4153-5 pa

LC 2008-12178

Carr "takes a detailed inventory of his years of drug addiction, chronicling the slide from drinking and marijuana use during his teen years in Minneapolis to shooting cocaine and smoking crack while trying to maintain his life as a reporter and the father of twin girls. Carr is meticulous in the investigation of his past, reconstructing events with the aid of police reports, magazine rejection letters, and more than sixty interviews with friends, former dealers, and fellow-addicts. His journalistic skills are on full display as he works to excavate the truth from his often hazy memories. He evinces genuine remorse for his frequently reprehensible behavior and succeeds in creating something more than merely another entry in what he terms the 'growing pile of junkie memoirs.'" New Yorker

Carroll, Diahann

Carroll, Diahann. The **legs** are the last to go; aging, acting, marrying, and other things I learned the hard way. Amistad 2008 271p il $24.95 **92**
1. Actors 2. Singers 3. African American actors 4. African American singers
ISBN 978-0-06-076326-8; 0-06-076326-4

"Carroll looks back on a groundbreaking career: the first black actress to star in her own television show and, more recently, the first black actress to play the role of Norma Desmond in Sunset Boulevard. In between, Carroll has racked up a breathtaking list of achievements on stage, in film, and on television. She's also racked up four failed marriages and a life full of the kind of mistakes a driven woman will make climbing to the top of a show-business career during a period when women and African Americans had few opportunities. Carroll is candid about the trials and tribulations—as well as the joys and triumphs—in her public and private life." Booklist

Carroll, James

Carroll, James. **Practicing** Catholic. Houghton Mifflin Harcourt 2009 385p $28 **92**
1. Authors 2. Priests 3. Novelists 4. Catholic Church 5. Memoirists
ISBN 978-0-618-67018-5; 0-618-67018-1

LC 2008-37386

"This book is both a memoir of former priest and writer Carroll's life and a keen analysis of American Catholicism in the late 20th century. . . . Brilliant prose, historically insightful, and sincere passion remain hallmarks of the author's work." Libr J

Includes bibliographical references

Carroll, Lewis, 1832-1898

Cohen, Morton Norton. **Lewis** Carroll; a biography. by Morton N. Cohen. Knopf 1995 xxiii, 577p il hardcover o.p. pa $14.36 **92**
1. Authors 2. Novelists 3. Mathematicians 4. Children's authors 5. Writers on science
ISBN 0-679-74562-9 pa

LC 95-2663

"Delightfully illustrated with photographs and Carroll's drawings woven throughout, this extraordinary, meticulous biography gives us a sharper and deeper picture of Carroll than any before, presenting a many-sided man." Publ Wkly

Carson, Rachel, 1907-1964

Lytle, Mark Hamilton. The **gentle** subversive; Rachel Carson, Silent spring, and the rise of the environmental movement. Oxford University Press 2007 277p il $23; $12.95 **92**
1. Authors 2. Conservationists 3. Environmental movement 4. College teachers 5. Marine biologists 6. Writers on nature 7. Writers on science 8. Biography, Individual 9. Environmentalism -- History
ISBN 0-19-517246-9; 0-19-517247-7 pa; 978-0-19-517246-1; 978-0-19-517247-8 pa

LC 2006-49350

This book, by Mark Hamilton Lytle, presents a biography of Rachel Carson, an "accomplished marine biologist who worked for many years for the US Fish and Wildlife

Service. In mid-career she gained wide fame as a lyrical popular science writer specializing in studies of the ocean and seashore life. 'Silent Spring' (1962), her final work, won acclaim as a breakthrough book that transformed people's conceptions of the place of science in the natural world." (Choice: Current Reviews for Academic Libraries)

The author "examines the life of Rachel Carson, founder of today's environmental movement and antithesis of the stereotypical 1950s woman. Carson was educated in the sciences, worked full time, and was her family's primary provider and caregiver. Genteel in appearance, she was firmly committed to her goal of preserving nature. Using a lyrical, narrative style, Lytle probes Carson's interests and her purposes in writing a series of wellknown books that include The Sea Around Usand her most famous, Silent Spring." Libr J

Includes bibliographical references

Souder, William. **On** a farther shore; the life and legacy of Rachel Carson. William Souder. 1st ed. Crown Publishing Group 2012 496 p. ill. (hardcover) $30.00; (ebook) $85.00   **92**
1. Biology 2. Women authors 3. Carson, Rachel, 1907-1964 4. Naturalists -- United States -- Biography 5. Environmentalism -- United States -- History 6. Science writers -- United States -- Biography 7. Environmentalists -- United States -- Biography 8. Marine biologists -- United States -- Biography 9. Environmental ethics -- United States -- History 10. Pesticides -- Environmental aspects -- United States -- History
ISBN 030746220X; 9780307462206; 9780307462213; 9780307462220
LC 2012003077
In "this . . . biography, [William] Souder . . . portrays [Rachel] Carson as a woman passionate in friendship, poetic and innovative in her books about the sea, gentle but ambitious, assiduously keeping tabs on her publisher's promotion of her work. A writer since childhood, Carson, inspired by a college professor, developed a love for biology and combined her two passions in a career that included three bestselling books." (Publishers Weekly)

Includes bibliographical references (p. 477-486) and index.

Carter, Jimmy, 1924-

Carter, Jimmy. **Everything** to gain; making the most of the rest of your life. [by] Jimmy and Rosalynn Carter. University of Arkansas Press 1995 176p pa $21.95   **92**
1. Governors 2. Presidents 3. Nobel laureates for peace 4. Presidents -- United States
ISBN 978-1-55728-388-7; 1-55728-388-5
First published 1987 by Random House
"The former president and First Lady alternate first-person reminiscences with sections written jointly to tell the story of their lives after leaving the White House in 1980. Frankly acknowledging the trauma of the lost election, the Carters record their efforts to overcome the difficulties of making a fresh start while deeply in debt, adjusting to

life in a small house in Plains, Ga., and other challenges." Publ Wkly

Carter, Jimmy. **Keeping** faith: memoirs of a president. University of Ark. Press 1995 633p il pa $34.95   **92**
1. Governors 2. Presidents 3. Nobel laureates for peace 4. Presidents -- United States
ISBN 1-55728-330-3
LC 95-9691
A reissue of the title first published 1982 by Bantam Bks.
These memoirs treat such matters as "improving relations with China; enacting energy legislation; negotiating the second Strategic Arms Limitation treaty (SALT II); concluding the Panama Canal treaties; and convincing Menachem Begin and Anwar Sadat to reach agreement at Camp David. Carter also devotes more than a quarter of the book to the frustrations arising from the capture of hostages in Tehran." N Y Rev Books

Carter, Jimmy. **Sharing** good times. Simon & Schuster 2004 174p $21; pa $13   **92**
1. Governors 2. Presidents 3. Nobel laureates for peace 4. Presidents -- United States
ISBN 0-7432-7033-9; 0-7432-7068-1 pa
LC 2004-51351
The author "recalls various occasions in his life that became 'lasting sources of pleasure.' . . . [These remembrances] include his personal reasons for seeing his father as a hero, watching minor and major-league baseball games growing up, his days in the navy, road trips with his wife and children, his entry into politics, taking vacations while in the White House, his famous volunteer work, and even his hobbies." Booklist

Carter, Jimmy **White** House diary. Farrar, Straus and Giroux 2010 570p il $30; ebook $14.99   **92**
1. Biography, Individual 2. Presidents -- United States 3. United States -- Politics and government -- 1974-1989 4. United States -- Politics and government -- 1977-1981
ISBN 978-0-374-28099-4; 978-1-4299-9065-3 ebook
LC 2010-15544
Jimmy Carter, the 39th president of the United States, presents an edited and annotated version of a diary he kept during his term in office.
"That the language is blunt and occasionally a little un-Christian may come as a surprise. . . . But the writings here reflect the Mr. Carter we know: boastful and painfully confessional, sanctimonious and callous, insightful and unself-aware. These are the thoughts of a secular preacher and calculating politician, surrounded by friends and yet often alone." N Y Times (Late N Y Ed)

Zelizer, Julian E. **Jimmy** Carter. Times Books 2010 183p il (American presidents series) $23; ebook $10.99   **92**
1. Governors 2. Presidents 3. Nobel laureates for peace 4. Presidents -- United States 5. United States -- Politics and government -- 1974-1989
ISBN 978-0-8050-8957-8; 978-1-4299-5075-6 ebook
LC 2010-16818

"For general readers, this work offers a fine analysis of the man and his career." Booklist

Includes bibliographical references

Carter, Robert, 1728-1804

Levy, Andrew. The **first** emancipator; the forgotten story of Robert Carter, the founding father who freed his slaves. Random House 2005 310p hardcover o.p. pa $15.95   92

1. Plantation owners 2. Slavery -- United States
ISBN 0-375-50865-1; 0-375-76104-7 pa
                                    LC 2004-54054

"This well-written and thoroughly engaging book will certainly appeal to readers interested in the history of 18th- and 19th-century Virginia, but also to those interested in the history of slavery and racism in America and in historical biography." Publ Wkly

Includes bibliographical references

Carver, Raymond

Sklenicka, Carol. **Raymond** Carver; a writer's life. Scribner 2009 578p il $35   92

1. Poets 2. Authors 3. Authors, American 4. Short story writers
ISBN 978-0-7432-6245-3; 0-7432-6245-X
                                    LC 2009-27291

This is a biography of the American short-story writer and poet.

The author "spoke with nearly everyone in Carver's orbit, making the book a kind of history of American fiction in the '70s and '80s, capturing the crucial writers (Richard Ford, Tobias Wolff, John Cheever) and sea changes in the publishing industry that made Carver such a powerful influence on writers today. The epic biography that Carver deserves." Kirkus

Includes bibliographical references

Cash, Johnny

Hilburn, Robert. **Johnny** Cash; the life. by Robert Hilburn. Little, Brown and Co. 2013 608 p. $32 **92**

1. Musicians -- United States
ISBN 0316194751; 9780316194754
                                    LC 2013941828

In this biography, "drawing upon his personal experience with [musician Johnny] Cash and a trove of never-before-seen material from the singer's inner circle, [author Robert] Hilburn creates [a] . . . deeply human portrait of one of the most iconic figures in modern popular culture - not only a towering figure in country music, but also a seminal influence in rock, whose personal life was far more troubled, and whose musical and lyrical artistry much more profound." (Publisher's note)

"The personal knowledge aided by extensive archival research and always compelling, accessible writing make this an instant-classic music biography with something to offer all generations of listeners." (Kirkus)

Streissguth, Michael. **Johnny** Cash; the biography. Da Capo Press 2006 334p il hardcover o.p. pa $15.95   92

1. Singers 2. Country musicians 3. Songwriters
ISBN 0-306-81368-8; 0-306-81565-6 pa
                                    LC 2006-101191

This is a biography of the country singer and songwriter.

The author "leaves us mightily impressed with the volume of Cash's work and the convictions that animate it, and perhaps even more impressed by Cash's endurance of his own self-destructiveness. . . . Streissguth gives everyone interested in Cash a very satisfying book about him." Booklist

Includes bibliographical references

Thomson, Graeme. The **resurrection** of Johnny Cash; hurt, redemption, and American Recordings. Jawbone 2011 254p il pa $19.95   92

1. Singers 2. Country musicians 3. Songwriters
ISBN 978-1-906002-36-7

This "book focuses on what is, without question, the most spectacular musical comeback of the last 20 years. Cash had been all but dismissed by an increasingly corporate and shallow Nashville, before the unlikely figure of Rick Rubin masterminded a series of stripped-down intimate albums that reestablished his legendary status. It was a rebirth of almost Biblical proportions, the forgotten man in black newly feted by future generations, with the likes of Nick Cave, Trent Reznor, U2, Depeche Mode and Elvis Costello queuing up to have their songs given a fresh lick of statesmanlike paint. . . . One of the difficulties of writing a music biography in modern times is that the internet age makes available all manner of nuts and bolts to fans of any given artist, but though Thomson might not uncover much in the way of previously unknown information his always eloquent writing fills the pages with atmosphere and keen critical assessment." Record Collector

Includes bibliographical references

Cash, Rosanne, 1955-

★ Cash, Rosanne. **Composed**; a memoir. Viking 2010 343p $26.95   92

1. Singers 2. Country musicians 3. Songwriters
ISBN 978-0-670-02196-3
                                    LC 2010-10327

"The moving chapters about Roseanne Cash's glorious career—and the moments of great tenderness and tension with her legendary family—are like exquisite album tracks: Individually they are great reads, but together they add up to something cohesive and powerful. Composed provides no bombshell confessions about her failed marriage to Rodney Crowell or her wonderfully complicated relationship with her dad, Johnny. (Though she does dismiss the biopic Walk the Line as 'an egregious oversimplification of our family's private pain.') Instead, Cash delivers writerly meditations on what it means to be an artist and a public person and, yes, a daughter. Rare is the celebrity memoir that is so full of self-awareness and dignity." Entertainment Wkly

Cassady, Neal

★ Sandison, David. **Neal** Cassady; the fast life of a beat hero. [by] David Sandison and Gra-

ham Vickers. Chicago Review Press 2006 340p il
$24.95   **92**

1. Authors 2. Beat generation 3. Memoirists
ISBN 978-1-55652-615-2; 1-55652-615-6

LC 2006-9112

"Drawing on Cassady's correspondence, interviews with
those who knew him, and previous works by memoirist Carolyn Cassady (the subject's widow), biographer Tom Christopher, and others, Sandison and Vickers portray Cassady as
all too human—a desperate, lost soul who was plagued by
contradictions and sought personal fulfillment and spiritual
salvation. Debunking the mythology that grew up around
Cassady as a result of his appearance in works by Kerouac,
Ken Kesey, and Tom Wolfe, the authors attempt to separate
the life from the legend. They present Cassady as someone
who wanted to be a good husband and father but was unable to conquer his demons, which included sex, drugs,
gambling, and an innate restlessness. Ironically, it was these
very demons that ensured Cassady's place in American literature." Libr J

Includes bibliographical references

Casso, Gaspipe, 1942-

Carlo, Philip. **Gaspipe**; confessions of a Mafia
boss. William Morrow 2008 346p il $25.95   **92**

1. Mafia 2. Criminals 3. Organized crime 4. Mobsters
5. Informers
ISBN 978-0-06-142984-2

LC 2008-2683

"This powerful story is required reading for anyone with
a yen for the Mafia, the criminal underworld and a law enforcement system struggling to keep up." Publ Wkly

Castelli, Leo, 1907-1999

Cohen-Solal, Annie. **Leo** & his circle; the life of
Leo Castelli. Alfred A. Knopf 2010 540p il $35 **92**

1. Art dealers
ISBN 978-1-4000-4427-6; 1-4000-4427-8

LC 2009-34454

First published 2009 in France

This is a biography of the art dealer from Trieste who
came to New York in 1941 and opened his first New York
gallery in 1957. Castelli displayed early work by Andy Warhol, Jasper Johns, Roy Lichtenstein, and Cy Twombly.

This "biography fleshes out not only a fascinating portrait of Castelli but also the excitement of the developing
American art world to which he was so central." Publ Wkly

Includes bibliographical references

Castro, Fidel, 1926-

★ Castro, Fidel. **Fidel** Castro: my life; a spoken
autobiography. [by] Fidel Castro and Ignacio Ramonet; translated by Andrew Hurley. Scribner 2008
723p il map $40   **92**

1. Presidents 2. Communist leaders 3. Cuba -- Politics
and government
ISBN 978-1-4165-5328-1; 1-4165-5328-2

Original Spanish edition, 2006

Ramonet "sat down with Castro over the course of many
hours, engaging him in long, involved discussions about his
revolutionary life (and little about his personal life). The result is, in the words of the interviewer, Castro's 'political

testament, an oral summoning-up of Fidel Castro's life by
Fidel himself at almost eighty.' That rather simple description does not begin to cover the magnitude and significance
of this major document. . . . By itself an incomplete history
of the Cuban Revolution, to be sure, but an important—
the ultimate insider view—contribution to the complete
picture." Booklist

Includes bibliographical references

Coltman, Leycester. The **real** Fidel Castro; with
a foreword by Julia E. Sweig. Yale Univ. Press 2003
335p il map $30; pa $20   **92**

1. Presidents 2. Communist leaders 3. Cuba -- Politics
and government
ISBN 0-300-10188-0; 0-300-10760-9 pa

LC 2003-12942

This biography "offers a fresh assessment of the revolutionary leader. . . . It chronicles the events of Castro's
extraordinary life and explores the contradiction between
the private character and the public reputation." Univ Press
Books for Public and Second Sch Libr, 2004

Includes bibliographical references

Szulc, Tad. **Fidel**; a critical portrait. Post Road
Press 2000 703p map pa $18.95   **92**

1. Presidents 2. Communist leaders 3. Cuba -- Politics
and government
ISBN 978-0-380-80888-5; 0-380-80888-9

First published 1986 by Morrow

The author "devotes the greater part of this book to Castro's early, formative years and the forging and triumph of
his revolutionary movement. The years of Castro's rule after
the Bay of Pigs invasion receive briefer treatment. Well written and very readable." Choice

Includes bibliographical references

**Catharine Parr, Queen, consort of Henry VIII,
King of England, 1512-1548**

Porter, Linda. **Katherine** the queen; the remarkable life of Katherine Parr, the last wife of Henry VIII.
St. Martin's Press 2010 383p il $27.99   **92**

1. Queens 2. Biography, Individual 3. Great Britain --
History -- 1485-1603, Tudors 4. Great Britain -- History
-- Henry VIII, 1509-1547
ISBN 9780312384388

LC 2010035251

In this biography of Katherine Parr, Porter argues that
"Henry VIII's last queen was a more human, complex and
modern figure than has hitherto been realized." (Publisher's
note) Index.

"Although often depicted by the Victorians as a matronly
nurse to an elderly king, Katherine Parr (1512–1548), according to Porter, was a stylish trendsetter of 30, sensual,
confident, dynamic, exceptionally educated and cultured,
and able to perform with aplomb on both an English and international stage. . . . Rich, perceptive, nuanced and creative,
this first full-scale biography gives one of Britain's best but
least-known queens her due." Publ Wkly

Includes bibliographical references

Cather, Willa, 1873-1947

Lee, Hermione. **Willa** Cather; double lives. Pantheon Bks. 1989 410p il hardcover o.p. pa $23 **92**
1. Authors 2. Novelists 3. Western writers 4. Short story writers
ISBN 0-679-73649-2 pa

LC 89-43233

The author's "discussion of Cather's 12 novels and numerous stories is so absorbing that it provokes a rereading of the work, which makes it a valuable critical study." N Y Times Book Rev
Includes bibliographical references

Woodress, James Leslie. **Willa** Cather; a literary life. {by} James Woodress. University of Neb. Press 1987 xx, 583p il hardcover o.p. pa $29.95 **92**
1. Authors 2. Novelists 3. Western writers 4. Short story writers
ISBN 0-8032-9708-4 pa

LC 86-30894

The author "does a fine job of describing Willa Cather's colorful public life and of piecing together the puzzle of her unconventional private life. . . . Mr. Woodress does not try to superimpose on Cather's life any theories—feminist, Freudian, Lacanian, or otherwise. Instead, he recounts in straightforward and lively prose the life of a remarkable woman." N Y Times Book Rev
Includes bibliographical references

Catherine II, the Great, Empress of Russia, 1729-1796

★ Catherine. The **memoirs** of Catherine the Great; a new translation by Mark Cruse and Hilde Hoogenboom. Modern Library 2005 xc, 247p il map $26.95 **92**
1. Empresses 2. Russia -- History 3. Russia -- Kings and rulers
ISBN 0-679-64299-4

LC 2004-61107

Original French edition, 1859
"The memoirs cover the years before Catherine (1729-1796) became empress in 1762." Publ Wkly
This is "a source of major importance and every serious library should own it." Choice

Rounding, Virginia. **Catherine** the Great; love, sex and power. St. Martin's Press 2007 566p il $29.95 **92**
1. Empresses 2. Russia -- History 3. Russia -- Kings and rulers
ISBN 978-0-312-32887-0; 0-312-32887-7

LC 2006-47084

First published 2006 in the United Kingdom
The author "relies on memoirs, private letters and previous monographs as she details how, after dissolution of the unhappy marriage that brought Catherine (1729-1798) to Russia from Germany, the empress juggled her relationships with men as she attempted to thrust Russia into the modern era and make it a European power. . . . [This] work will appeal to Catherine-philes and those interested in women's history." Publ Wkly
Includes bibliographical references

Troyat, Henri. **Catherine** the Great; translated by Joan Pinkham. Dutton 1980 377p il hardcover o.p. pa $16.95 **92**
1. Empresses 2. Russia -- History 3. Russia -- Kings and rulers
ISBN 0-452-01120-5 pa

LC 79-25613

Original French edition, 1977
"Relying heavily on Catherine's own memoirs, plus her correspondence with her Western idolaters-publicists, such as Friedrich Grimm, Voltaire and Diderot, Troyat gives us a portrait the Empress herself might have decreed for posterity." Publ Wkly
Includes bibliographical references

Catlin, George, 1796-1872

Eisler, Benita. The **Red** Man's Bones; George Catlin, Artist and Showman. Benita Eisler. W W Norton & Co Inc 2013 432 p. (hardcover) $29.95 **92**
1. Native Americans in art 2. West (U.S.) -- In art 3. Painters -- United States -- Biography
ISBN 0393066169; 9780393066166

LC 2013013973

Includes bibliographical references and index

Catto, Octavius V., 1839-1871

Biddle, Daniel R. **Tasting** freedom; Octavius Catto and the battle for equality in Civil War America. [by] Daniel R. Biddle [and] Murray Dubin. Temple University Press 2010 616p il $35; e-book $35 **92**
1. Political activists 2. African American athletes 3. African American educators 4. Baseball -- Biography 5. Biography, Individual 6. African Americans -- Biography 7. Pennsylvania -- Race relations 8. Philadelphia (Pa.) -- Race relations -- History 9. Civil rights movements -- Pennsylvania -- Philadelphia 10. African Americans -- Civil rights -- Pennsylvania -- Philadelphia
ISBN 978-1-59213-465-6; 978-1-59213-467-0 e-book

LC 2009049276

This is a biography of 19th-century civil rights activist and baseball player "Octavius Catto of Philadelphia. Catto was a part of the city's black intelligentsia and a vigorous proponent of equal rights. . . . Catto became a martyr to his cause when, at age 32, he was gunned down in Philadelphia's 1871 election-day riot. . . . [The authors] present a clear and compelling portrait of this significant early civil rights activist; they also present a thoughtful assessment of how Catto's efforts relate to the modern black civil rights movement." Choice
Includes bibliographical references

Cayce, Edgar, 1877-1945

Kirkpatrick, Sidney. **Edgar** Cayce; an American prophet. Riverhead Bks. 2000 564p il hardcover o.p. pa $16   **92**
1. Psychics
ISBN 1-57322-896-6 pa

LC 00-27975

This is a "fair, fascinating, and well-researched biography of one of 20th-century America's most famous psychics." Libr J

Chabon, Michael

Chabon, Michael. **Manhood** for amateurs; the pleasures and regrets of a husband, father, and son. Harper 2009 306p $25.99   **92**
1. Authors 2. Fathers 3. Novelists 4. Men -- Psychology 5. Short story writers
ISBN 978-0-06-149018-7; 0-06-149018-0

LC 2009-4749

"For the most part in these pages [Chabon] manages to write about himself, his family and his generation with humor and introspective wisdom. As in his novels, he shifts gears easily between the comic and the melancholy, the whimsical and the serious, demonstrating once again his ability to write about the big subjects of love and memory and regret without falling prey to the Scylla and Charybdis of cynicism and sentimentality." N Y Times (Late N Y Ed)

Chagall, Marc, 1887-1985

★ Wullschlager, Jackie. **Chagall**; a biography. Alfred A. Knopf 2008 582p il $40   **92**
1. Artists 2. Painters 3. Artists, Russian
ISBN 978-0-375-41455-8; 0-375-41455-X

LC 2008-6162

This is a biography of the Russian artist and author of Lithographs (1960), My Life (1960), and The Jerusalem Windows (1962).

"This biography presents Chagall's moving portraits of a vanished age in colors as glowing and haunting as his own canvases." Washington Post Book World

Includes bibliographical references

Chaloner, William, d. 1699

Levenson, Thomas. **Newton** and the counterfeiter; the unknown detective career of the world's greatest scientist. Houghton Mifflin Harcourt 2009 318p $25; pa $14.95   **92**
1. Physicists 2. Mathematicians 3. Counterfeits and counterfeiting 4. Counterfeiters 5. Writers on science
ISBN 978-0-15-101278-7; 0-15-101278-4; 978-0-547-33604-6 pa; 0-547-33604-7 pa

LC 2008-53511

"Levenson demonstrates a surpassing felicity in his brisk treatment of this late-17th-century true-crime adventure. . . . Swift, agile treatment of a little known but highly entertaining episode in a legendary life." Kirkus

Includes bibliographical references

Chambers, Whittaker

Chambers, Whittaker. **Witness**; forewords by William F. Buckley and Robert D. Novak. 50th annivesary ed; Regnery Pub. 2001 808p pa $19.95 **92**
1. Authors 2. Journalists 3. Memoirists 4. Communism -- United States
ISBN 978-0-89526-789-4; 0-89526-789-6
First published 1952 by Random House

Whittaker Chambers' own account of his life, his connection with the Communist Party and his repudiation of it, and his role in the Hiss-Chambers trial.

Champlain, Samuel de, 1567-1635

★ Fischer, David Hackett. **Champlain's** dream. Simon & Schuster 2008 834p il map $40   **92**
1. Explorers 2. America -- Exploration
ISBN 978-1-4165-9332-4; 1-4165-9332-2

LC 2008-16286

The author "offers the definitive biography of an extraordinary and flawed man: Samuel de Champlain (1567-1635): spy, explorer, courtier, soldier and founder and governor of New France (today's Quebec)." Publ Wkly

Includes bibliographical references

Chanel, Coco, 1883-1971

Vaughan, Hal. **Sleeping** with the enemy; Coco Chanel's secret war. Knopf 2011 279p il $27.95; ebook $13.99   **92**
1. Fashion designers 2. Perfumers 3. German espionage 4. Biography, Individual 5. Cosmetics industry executives 6. World War, 1939-1945 -- Secret service
ISBN 978-0-307-59263-7; 978-0-307-95703-0 ebook; 0-7011-8500-7 Chatto & Windus; 978-0-7011-8500-8 Chatto & Windus

LC 2011020430

The author argues "that there were two sides to the elegant Coco Chanel. Using information from French counterintelligence sources as well as other documents hidden for years in French, German, Italian, Soviet, and U.S. archives, he unmasks her activities during the war years; she embarked on a romance with a senior German officer in occupied Paris and cooperated with German military intelligence agents. . . . Engrossing and accessible, this is recommended for general readers interested in fashion celebrity, espionage, or World War II." Libr J

Includes bibliographical references and index

Chaplin, Charlie, 1889-1977

The **essential** Chaplin; perspectives on the life and art of the great comedian. edited with an introduction by Richard Schickel. I.R. Dee 2006 315p $27.50; pa $16.95   **92**
1. Actors 2. Motion picture directors 3. Motion picture producers 4. Motion picture producers and directors -- Biography
ISBN 978-1-56663-682-7; 1-56663-682-5; 978-1-56663-701-5 pa; 1-56663-701-5 pa

LC 2005-37250

"The book's best feature is its organized cacophony, its trace of this astonishingly long and rich body of work and personal travail . . . in some several dozen voices of fading or lasting memory, and with countless aesthetic and ideological grudges beyond the narrow province of the movies. There is much to savor in these essays; and the book might also serve as a worthy companion to a reader's return to Chaplin's films themselves." Va Q Rev

Wranovics, John. **Chaplin** and Agee; the untold story of the tramp, the writer, and the lost screenplay. Palgrave Macmillan 2005 256p il $24.95 **92**
   1. Poets 2. Actors 3. Authors 4. Novelists 5. Screenwriters 6. Nonfiction writers 7. Motion picture critics 8. Motion picture directors 9. Motion picture producers
   ISBN 1-403-96866-7

LC 2004-62807
A "double biography of two of the 20th century's most talented artists. Wranovic's hook is a lost screenplay titled The Tramp's New World, which Agee wrote for Chaplin after the detonation of the atomic bomb over Hiroshima. . . . Using personal correspondence and critical reviews, Wranovics re-creates the fascinating historical backdrop of the Agee/Chaplin friendship, interweaving into the stunning tapestry the colorful lives of such luminaries as Brecht, Auden, Ed Sullivan, and John Huston." Choice

Chapman, Eddie, 1914-1997
  Macintyre, Ben, 1963- **Agent** Zigzag; a true story of Nazi espionage, love, and betrayal. Harmony Books 2007 364p il $25.95 **92**
   1. Thieves 2. Intelligence service agents 3. World War, 1939-1945 -- Secret service
   ISBN 978-0-307-35340-5

LC 2006-101603
This is a biography of Eddie Chapman, a British double agent during World War II.
   "Meticulously researched—relying extensively on recently released wartime files of Britain's Secret Intelligence Service—Macintyre's biography often reads like a spy thriller." Publ Wkly
   Includes bibliographical references

Chapman, Eunice, 1778-1863
  Woo, Ilyon. The **great** divorce; a nineteenth-century mother's extraordinary fight against her husband, the Shakers, and her times. Atlantic Monthly Press 2010 404p $25 **92**
   1. Divorce 2. Shakers 3. Child custody 4. Parental kidnapping 5. Converts 6. Feminists 7. Abusive persons 8. Shakers -- New York (State)
   ISBN 0-8021-1946-8; 978-0-8021-1946-9
This is an account of the divorce, in the early 19th century, of James and Eunice Chapman, and the involvement of the Shaker community in the proceedings. "In 1818, Eunice gained her legislative divorce—the only one ever granted in New York. She also regained her children." (N Y Times Book Rev)
   "Both Eunice's struggle and the Shakers' story fascinate equally while dispelling romanticized myths of utopian societies in the tumultuous postrevolutionary period." Publ Wkly
   Includes bibliographical references

Chapman, James, 1763-1852
  Woo, Ilyon. The **great** divorce; a nineteenth-century mother's extraordinary fight against her husband, the Shakers, and her times. Atlantic Monthly Press 2010 404p $25 **92**
   1. Divorce 2. Shakers 3. Child custody 4. Parental kidnapping 5. Converts 6. Feminists 7. Abusive persons 8. Shakers -- New York (State)
   ISBN 0-8021-1946-8; 978-0-8021-1946-9
This is an account of the divorce, in the early 19th century, of James and Eunice Chapman, and the involvement of the Shaker community in the proceedings. "In 1818, Eunice gained her legislative divorce—the only one ever granted in New York. She also regained her children." (N Y Times Book Rev)
   "Both Eunice's struggle and the Shakers' story fascinate equally while dispelling romanticized myths of utopian societies in the tumultuous postrevolutionary period." Publ Wkly
   Includes bibliographical references

Charlemagne, Emperor, 742-814
  Sypeck, Jeff. **Becoming** Charlemagne; Europe, Baghdad, and the empires of 800 A.D. ECCO 2006 284p il map $25.95 **92**
   1. Emperors 2. Kings and rulers
   ISBN 978-0-060-79706-5; 0-06-079706-1

LC 2006-46460
"This is the story of how one medieval king named Karl was shaped and guided to become the profoundly important Emperor Charlemagne." Libr J
   "An inspired, instantly readable work of popular history." Booklist
   Includes bibliographical references (p. 249-67)

  Wilson, Derek A. **Charlemagne**. Doubleday 2006 226p il map $26; pa $14.95 **92**
   1. Emperors 2. Kings and rulers
   ISBN 0-385-51670-3; 0-307-27480-2 pa

LC 2005-48483
This biography of the Frankish emperor "demonstrates how the empire he built led to the development of the European identity." SLJ
   The author "writes with clarity and passion, and his thesis is food for thought for both general readers and students." Libr J
   Includes bibliographical references

Charles II, King of Great Britain, 1630-1685
  Uglow, Jennifer S. A **gambling** man; Charles II's Restoration game. [by] Jenny Uglow. Farrar, Straus and Giroux 2009 580p il map $35 **92**
   1. Kings 2. Great Britain -- History -- 1660-1688, Restoration
   ISBN 978-0-374-28137-3; 0-374-28137-8

LC 2009-25469
"When Charles II became King of England, in 1660, his task was daunting: to restore the authority of the monarchy while courting a fractious parliament. Uglow's vivid history of the first decade of his reign shows how boldly Charles embraced the openness and experimentation of the Age of Reason." New Yorker
   Includes bibliographical references

Charlotte Augusta, Princess of Great Britain, 1796-1817

Williams, Kate. **Becoming** Queen Victoria; the tragic death of Princess Charlotte and the unexpected rise of Britain's greatest monarch. Ballantine Books 2010 448p il $30; ebook $30 **92**

1. Queens 2. Princesses 3. Great Britain -- Kings and rulers

ISBN 978-0-345-46195-7; 978-0-345-52193-4 ebook

LC 2010-13227

First published 2008 in the United Kingdom with title: Becoming queen

"A lively, juicy read, full of the sordid details of the debauched rule of kings and princes that led to the moralistic rule of a queen focused on creating a royal family that embodied the ideals of a nation. Perfect for fans of royal histories and historical television shows or armchair historians interested in a swift and enjoyable read." Libr J

Includes bibliographical references

Chatwin, Bruce

Under the sun; the letters of Bruce Chatwin. selected and edited by Elizabeth Chatwin and Nicholas Shakespeare. Viking 2011 554p il $35 **92**

1. Authors 2. Novelists 3. Memoirists 4. Travel writers 5. Authors, English 6. Biography, Individual
ISBN 0670022462; 9780670022465

LC 2010-33591

First published 2010 in the United Kingdom

This is a collection of letters by the author of In Patagonia (1977) and The Songlines (1987). "'Under the Sun' contains letters written across four decades, from the time Chatwin was a boy in an English boarding school to letters dictated from his deathbed." (N Y Times (Late N Y Ed)) Index.

"Chatwin's many appreciators will see the compilation in its overall significance as a personal visit with one of their literary heroes, as much as that is possible now." Booklist

Chaucer, Geoffrey, d. 1400

Ackroyd, Peter. **Chaucer**; Peter Ackroyd. 1st ed in the U.S.A; Nan A. Talese/Doubleday 2005 188p il (Ackroyd's brief lives) $19.95 **92**

1. Poets 2. Authors
ISBN 0-385-50797-6

LC 2004-49796

This "account of the life of Geoffrey Chaucer (1343?-1400) [is also] a consideration of his role in shaping England's national identity. The poet is hailed as the 'progenitor of a national style,' and deft literary analysis explicates Chaucer's innovations while acknowledging the influence of other poets. . . . Much is made of Chaucer's position in the royal court, which provided the financial means to live comfortably while writing his verse." Publ Wkly

Includes bibliographical references

Chavez, Cesar, 1927-1993

Pawel, Miriam. The **Crusades** of Cesar Chavez; a biography. Miriam Pawel. St. Martin's Press 2014 560 p. ill (some col), map $35 **92**

1. Hispanic Americans -- History 2. Hispanic Americans

-- Biography 3. Labor movement -- United States
ISBN 1608197107; 9781608197101

This book by Miriam Pawel presents a "biography of the innovative, daring, and persevering activist" Cesar Chavez. "Chavez (1927-93) dropped out of school to work in the fields to support his destitute, homeless family, joining the ranks of California's exploited Mexican American migrant workers. Driven by his social conscience, pragmatic genius, and motivational ardor . . . Chavez created a scrappy and revolutionary labor union for 'the poorest, most powerless workers in the country.'" (Booklist)

"Pawel's clear, accessible prose befits a subject famous for his plain rhetoric, ensuring a broad readership can appreciate this valuable exploration of Chavez's unique legacy." Pub Wkly

Includes bibliographical references and index.

Cheever, John, 1912-1982

Bailey, Blake. **Cheever**; a life. Alfred A. Knopf 2009 770p il $35 **92**

1. Authors 2. Novelists 3. Authors, American 4. Short story writers
ISBN 978-1-4000-4394-1; 1-4000-4394-8

LC 2008-42277

The author "plunges deeply into the murky, sometimes fetid stew of John Cheever's life (1912-82). Beginning with his 1982 appearance at Carnegie Hall to receive the National Medal for Literature (more details appear some 650 pages later), the author proceeds in chronological fashion to tell the story of a deeply needy, difficult man. . . . [This is a] superb work that shows Cheever wrestling with dark angels, but wresting from those encounters some celestial prose." Kirkus

Includes bibliographical references

Chekhov, Anton Pavlovich, 1860-1904

Chekhov, Anton Pavlovich. **Anton** Chekhov's life and thought; selected letters and commentary. translated from the Russian by Michael Henry Heim, in collaboration with Simon Karlinsky; selection, introduction, and commentary by Simon Karlinsky. Northwestern Univ. Press 1997 494p pa $39.95 **92**

1. Authors 2. Dramatists 3. Physicians 4. Short story writers
ISBN 978-0-8101-1460-9; 0-8101-1460-7

LC 96-41240

First published 1973 by Harper & Row with title: Letters of Anton Chekhov

"Karlinsky's extended commentary and detailed notes amount to a first-rate critical biography, with much unfamiliar information and arrows pointing us toward further investigation." Newsweek

Chen, Da, 1962-

Chen, Da. **Colors** of the mountain. Random House 1999 310p hardcover o.p. pa $13 **92**

1. Lawyers 2. Linguists 3. Calligraphers 4. China -- History -- 1949-
ISBN 0-385-72060-2 pa

"Despite the devastating circumstances of his childhood and adolescence, Chen recounts his coming of age with arresting simplicity." Publ Wkly

Chen, Pauline W.

★ Chen, Pauline W. **Final** exam; a surgeon's reflections on mortality. Alfred A. Knopf 2007 267p $23.95 **92**

1. Surgeons 2. Terminal care -- Ethical aspects
ISBN 978-0-307-26353-7; 0-307-26353-3

LC 2006-49361

This collection of essays "follows [the author] over the course of her education, training, and practice as she grapples at . . . with the problem of mortality, and struggles to reconcile the lessons of her training with her innate knowledge of shared humanity, and to separate her ideas about healing from her fierce desire to cure." Publisher's note

"A graceful, precise, and empathetic writer enthralled by her work, Chen imparts much about medical schooling and surgery, too." Booklist

Includes bibliographical references

Cheng, Nien, 1915-2009

Cheng, Nien. **Life** and death in Shanghai. Grove Press 1987 547p hardcover o.p. pa $16 **92**

1. Political prisoners 2. Memoirists 3. China -- History -- 1949-
ISBN 0-14-010870-X pa

LC 86-45254

First published 1986 in the United Kingdom

This "is a volume that belongs on the shelf alongside the writings of Primo Levi, Elie Wiesel, Dith Pran, and other chroniclers of ideological fanaticism, its dehumanizing consequences, and its all too rare resisters." Christ Sci Monit

Chiang, Kai-shek, 1887-1975

Taylor, Jay. The **generalissimo**; Chiang Kai-shek and the struggle for modern China. Belknap Press of Harvard University Press 2009 722p il map $35 **92**

1. Generals 2. Presidents 3. Presidents -- China 4. Presidents -- Taiwan 5. China -- History -- 1912-1949
ISBN 978-0-674-03338-2

LC 2008-40492

This is a biography of the Chinese president who was forced into exile in Taiwan in 1949.

"Taylor's fact-based chronological presentation of Chiang should temper the preexisting opinions of him that history readers may take into reading the book. . . . An important biography, essential to the Chinese history shelves." Booklist

Includes bibliographical references

Chiang, Mei-ling, 1898-2003

Li, Laura Tyson. **Madame** Chiang Kai-Shek; China's eternal first lady. Atlantic Monthly 2006 557p il map $30 **92**

1. Spouses of presidents
ISBN 0-87113-933-2; 978-0-87113-933-7

LC 2005-58858

This is a biography of the wife of former Chinese president Chiang Kai-Shek.

"With access to newly opened files, fluent insights into China's convulsive transformation, and a phenomenal gift for elucidating intricate politics and complicated psyches,

Li brilliantly analyzes a fearless and profoundly conflicted woman of extraordinary force." Booklist

Includes bibliographical references

Pakula, Hannah. The **last** empress; Madame Chiang Kai-Shek and the birth of modern China. Simon & Schuster 2009 787p il map $35 **92**

1. Spouses of presidents 2. China -- History -- 1912-1949
ISBN 978-1-4391-4893-8; 1-4391-4893-7

LC 2009-17576

This is a biography of Soong Mei-ling, who became the wife of the Chinese Nationalist leader Chiang Kai-shek.

"A winning combination of measured, balanced research and critical evaluation—the definitive account of an important figure in 20th-century Chinese politics." Kirkus

Includes bibliographical references

Chiger, Krystyna, 1935-

Chiger, Krystyna. The **girl** in the green sweater; a life in Holocaust's shadow. [by] Krystyna Chiger with Daniel Paisner. St. Martin's Press 2008 272p il $24.95 **92**

1. Holocaust survivors 2. Memoirists 3. Jews -- Ukraine 4. Holocaust, 1933-1945 -- Personal narratives
ISBN 978-0-312-37656-7; 0-312-37656-1

LC 2008-22521

In 1943, with Lvov's 150,000 Jews having been killed, exiled, or forced into ghettos, a group of Polish Jews daringly sought refuge in the city's sewer system. Chiger, the last surviving member of this group, shares one of the most intimate, harrowing, and ultimately triumphant tales of survival to emerge from the Holocaust

"With a powerful story and a keen voice, Chiger's Holocaust survivor's tale is a worthy and memorable addition to the canon." Publ Wkly

Child, Julia

As always, Julia; the letters of Julia Child and Avis DeVoto: food, friendship, and the making of a masterpiece. selected and edited by Joan Reardon. Houghton Mifflin Harcourt Pub. Co. 2010 416p il $26 **92**

1. Cooks 2. Television personalities 3. Editors 4. Cookbook writers 5. Literary critics 6. Biography, Individual
ISBN 9780547417714

LC 2010-25840

This volume presents "the previously unpublished correspondence between the American chef and her unofficial literary agent from 1952 to 1965, offering insight into such events as Julia's early experiences as a new bride in Paris, her support of her diplomat husband and her views on period politics." (Publisher's note) Index.

"Their letters span a wide range of topics, from cookbooks, menus, recipes, and restaurants to Balzac, sex, goose stuffing, gardening, learning languages, the political climate,

Sunday afternoon cocktail parties, and proofreading. Witty, enlightening and entertaining." Publ Wkly

Child, Julia. **My** life in France; [by] Julia Child with Alex Prud'homme. Knopf 2006 317p il $25.95   **92**
1. Cooks 2. Television personalities 3. Cookbook writers
ISBN 1-4000-4346-8; 978-1-4000-4346-0
LC 2005-44727
This is a "memoir of the famous chef's first, formative sojourn in France with her new husband, Paul Child, in 1949. . . . This is a valuable record of gorgeous meals in bygone Parisian restaurants, and the secret arts of a culinary genius." Publ Wkly

Fitch, Noel Riley. **Appetite** for life; the biography of Julia Child. Doubleday 1997 569p il hardcover o.p. pa $16.95   **92**
1. Cooks 2. Television personalities 3. Cookbook writers
ISBN 0-385-49383-5 pa
LC 97-11061
This biography details the private life and professional career of PBS' The French chef, whose Mastering the art of French cooking (1961) revolutionized the American kitchen
"Fitch not only richly details Child's personal life but also effectively places her writing and television shows within the context of work by other cooking luminaries of the time. Entertaining and informative." Libr J
Includes bibliographical references

Chopin, Frédéric, 1810-1849
Eisler, Benita. **Chopin's** funeral. Knopf 2003 230p il $23; pa $13.95   **92**
1. Pianists 2. Composers 3. Classical musicians
ISBN 0-375-40945-9; 0-375-70868-5 pa
LC 2002-73097
"Seeking to untangle the paradoxical relationship between the shy, fragile pianist and the passionate sexual outlaw and novelist George Sand, Eisler's book underscores Chopin's illness and Sand's nursing skills, and sees a mutual attraction arising from their voracious appetite for work." N Y Times Book Rev
"Eisler is a compelling storyteller, sweeping the reader into the exhilarating milieu of Paris in the 1820s and 1830s." Libr J
Includes bibliographical references

Christensen, Kate, 1962-
Christensen, Kate. **Blue** plate special; an autobiography of my appetites. Kate Christensen. Doubleday 2013 368 p. (hardcover : alkaline paper) $26.95   **92**
1. Food -- Psychological aspects 2. Appetite -- Psychological aspects 3. Mothers and daughters -- United States 4. Authors, American -- 21st century -- Biography 5. Women authors, American -- 21st century -- Biography
ISBN 0385536267; 9780385536264
LC 2012048556

In this memoir, "food--eating it, cooking it, reflecting on it--becomes the vehicle for unpacking a life. [Kate] Christensen explores her history of hunger--not just for food but for love and confidence and a sense of belonging . . . starting with her unorthodox childhood in 1960s Berkeley. . . . After a whirlwind adolescent awakening, Christensen strikes out to chart her own destiny within the literary world and the world of men, both equally alluring and dangerous." (Publisher's note)

Churchill, Winston Sir, 1874-1965
D'Este, Carlo. **Warlord**; a life of Winston Churchill at war, 1874-1945. Harper 2008 845p il map $39.95   **92**
1. Statesmen 2. Historians 3. Prime ministers 4. Memoirists 5. Cabinet members 6. Members of Parliament 7. Nobel laureates for literature 8. Prime ministers -- Great Britain
ISBN 978-0-06-057573-1; 0-06-057573-5
LC 2008-9272
A biography of Winston Churchill's military career from his youth through World War II.
"D'Este has produced an outstanding work that should take its rightful place alongside the dozens of other studies of this most remarkable statesman." Libr J
Includes bibliographical references

Herman, Arthur. **Gandhi** and Churchill; the epic rivalry that destroyed an empire and forged our age. Bantam Book 2008 721p il map $30   **92**
1. Authors 2. Statesmen 3. Historians 4. Journalists 5. Prime ministers 6. Essayists 7. Pacifists 8. Memoirists 9. Cabinet members 10. Political leaders 11. Writers on politics 12. Members of Parliament 13. Nobel laureates for literature 14. Great Britain -- Foreign relations -- India 15. India -- Foreign relations -- Great Britain
ISBN 978-0-553-80463-8; 0-553-80463-4
LC 2008-149
"A well-wrought historical narrative that adds significantly to our understanding of both figures." Kirkus
Includes bibliographical references (p. 673-85)

Johnson, Paul. **Churchill**. Viking 2009 181p il $24.95   **92**
1. Statesmen 2. Historians 3. Prime ministers 4. Memoirists 5. Cabinet members 6. Members of Parliament 7. Nobel laureates for literature 8. Prime ministers -- Great Britain 9. Great Britain -- Politics and government -- 20th century
ISBN 978-0-670-02105-5; 0-670-02105-9
LC 2009-08326
"From his beginnings as a youthful war correspondent, to his mature political career, to his hobbies of landscape painting and bricklaying, no aspect of Churchill's life is ig-

nored. . . . An overview of Churchill's life that instructs rather than awes is Johnson's great achievement." New Criterion

Includes bibliographical references

Manchester, William. The **last** lion, Winston Spencer Churchill; visions of glory, 1874-1932. Little, Brown 1983 973p il maps $50 **92**
1. Statesmen 2. Historians 3. Prime ministers 4. Memoirists 5. Cabinet members 6. Biography, Individual 7. Members of Parliament 8. Nobel laureates for literature 9. Prime ministers -- Great Britain 10. Great Britain -- Politics and government -- 20th century
ISBN 0-316-54503-1

LC 82-24972
This first volume of a projected three-volume biography of Churchill covers the life of the British statesman from his birth up to his split with the Conservative party over its policy regarding Indian self-rule.

Includes bibliographical references

Manchester, William. The **last** lion, Winston Spencer Churchill; alone, 1932-1940. Little, Brown 1988 xxvi, 756p il map $50 **92**
1. Statesmen 2. Historians 3. Prime ministers 4. Memoirists 5. Cabinet members 6. Biography, Individual 7. Members of Parliament 8. Nobel laureates for literature 9. Prime ministers -- Great Britain 10. Great Britain -- Foreign relations 11. Great Britain -- Politics and government -- 20th century
ISBN 0-316-54512-0

LC 82-24972
This second volume of a projected three-volume biography of the British statesman "covers the years leading up to the outbreak of World War II." (Time)

This second volume of a projected three-volume biography of the British statesman "covers the years leading up to the outbreak of World War II." Time

Includes bibliographical references

Toye, Richard. **Churchill's** empire; the world that made him and the world he made. Henry Holt 2010 xx, 423p il $32 **92**
1. Statesmen 2. Historians 3. Prime ministers 4. Memoirists 5. Cabinet members 6. Members of Parliament 7. Great Britain -- Colonies 8. Nobel laureates for literature 9. Prime ministers -- Great Britain
ISBN 978-0-8050-8795-6

LC 2010-1427
In this biography, the author "stresses that Churchill (1874-1965), a Victorian aristocrat, assumed white superiority but regularly proclaimed that nonwhites deserved equal rights and, eventually, independence once they discarded their primitive ways and achieved European levels of culture. . . . This work is a valuable contribution to greater understanding of a historical icon." Booklist

Includes bibliographical reference

Churchill, Winston, 1874-1965

★ Manchester, William. The **last** lion, Winston Spencer Churchill; defender of the realm, 1940-

1965. by William Manchester. Little, Brown 2012 1183 p. ill., [32] p. of plates, maps $40 **92**
1. Great Britain -- History 2. World War, 1939-1945 -- Great Britain 3. Great Britain -- Foreign relations -- 20th century 4. Great Britain -- Politics and government -- 20th century
ISBN 9780316547703 (v. 3)

LC 82024972
This book, by William Manchester and Paul Reid, "picks up shortly after Winston Churchill became Prime Minister. . . . Churchill organized his nation's military response and defense; compelled [Franklin Delano Roosevelt] into supporting America's beleaguered cousins, and personified the . . . ethos that helped the Allies win the war, while at the same time adapting . . . his country to the . . . shift of world power from the British Empire to the United States." (Publisher's note)

Includes bibliographies and indexes

Cicero, Marcus Tullius, 106-43 B.C.

Everitt, Anthony. **Cicero**; the life and times of Rome's greatest politician. Random House 2002 359p il maps hardcover o.p. pa $14.95 **92**
1. Statesmen 2. Philosophers 3. Orators 4. Rome -- History
ISBN 0-375-75895-X pa

LC 2001-48531
This "masterful biography draws on Cicero's letters to his friend Atticus to give a clear picture of the famous Roman orator, noting both his brilliance and his faults." Booklist

Includes bibliographical references

Ciezadlo, Annia

Ciezadlo, Annia. **Day** of honey; a memoir of food, love, and war. Free Press 2011 382p $26; pa $12.99 **92**
1. Journalists 2. Women journalists 3. Memoirists 4. Food -- Social aspects 5. Lebanon -- Social life and customs 6. Baghdad (Iraq) -- Social life and customs
ISBN 978-1-4165-8393-6; 1-4165-8393-9; 978-1-4165-8422-3 pa; 1-4165-8422-6 pa

LC 2010-19739
"There are many good reasons to read 'Day of Honey.' It's a carefully researched tour through the history of Middle Eastern food. It's filled with adrenalized scenes from war zones, scenes of narrow escapes and clandestine phone calls and frightening cultural misunderstandings. . . . These things wouldn't matter much, though, if her sentences didn't make such a sensual, smart, wired-up sound on the page." N Y Times Book Rev

Includes bibliographical references

Cixi, Empress dowager of China, 1835-1908

Jung Chang, 1952- **Empress** Dowager Cixi; the concubine who launched modern China. by Jung Chang. Alfred A. Knopf 2013 480 p. ill (some color), map (hardcover) $30 **92**
1. Empresses 2. China -- History -- 19th century 3. China -- History -- 1861-1912 4. Empresses -- China -- Biography 5. China -- Politics and government --

19th century
ISBN 0307271609; 9780307271600; 9780307456700
LC 2013020766

Author Jung Chang "provides a revisionist biography of a controversial concubine who rose through the ranks to become a long-reigning, power- wielding dowager empress during the delicate era when China emerged from its isolationist cocoon to become a legitimate player on the international stage. [He shows how] as Cixi's power and influence grew . . . she radically shifted official attitudes toward Western thoughts, ideas, trade, and technology." (Booklist)

Chang "uses the work of revisionist scholars to paint a largely plausible portrait of a ruthless, farsighted politician who welcomed change and restructured the state." LJ

Includes bibliographical references and index

Clapton, Eric

Clapton, Eric, 1945- **Clapton**; the autobiography. Broadway Books 2007 343p il $26   **92**
1. Singers 2. Guitarists 3. Rock musicians 4. Biography, Individual
ISBN 978-0-385-51851-2; 0-385-51851-X
LC 2007-15482

"As he retraces every step of his career, from the early stints with the Yardbirds and Cream to his solo successes, Clapton also devotes copious detail to his drug and alcohol addictions, particularly how they intersected with his romantic obsession with Pattie Boyd. . . . Both the youthful excesses and the current calm state are narrated with an engaging tone that nudges Clapton's story ahead of other rock 'n' roll memoirs." Publ Wkly

Schumacher, Michael. **Crossroads**; the life and music of Eric Clapton. Citadel Press 2003 420p il pa $15.95   **92**
1. Singers 2. Guitarists 3. Rock musicians
ISBN 978-0-8065-2466-5; 0-8065-2466-9
First published 1995 by Hyperion

The author "chronicles the life and career of the reclusive British blues performer. . . . Schumacher covers a tale of unhappy personal relationships, a failed marriage, drug and alcohol addiction and the tragic death of the performer's infant son, while giving full account of Clapton's significant accomplishments as guitarist and vocalist, his forays into rock and his performances and recordings." Publ Wkly

Clare, John, 1793-1864

Bate, Jonathan. **John** Clare: a biography. Farrar, Straus & Giroux 2003 648p il map $40   **92**
1. Poets 2. Authors
ISBN 0-374-17990-5
LC 2003-44063

This biography "succeeds splendidly . . . not only making generous use of Clare's own wonderful prose and verse but adding historical perspective and a constant, intelligent probing which amount almost to a dialogue with Clare's view of himself." Times Lit Suppl

Includes bibliographical references

Clay, Henry, 1777-1852

Heidler, David Stephen. **Henry** Clay; the essential American. [by] David S. Heidler and Jeanne T. Heidler. Random House 2010 595p il $30   **92**
1. Statesmen 2. Senators 3. Members of Congress 4. Secretaries of state 5. Speakers of the House 6. United States -- Congress 7. Statesmen -- United States 8. United States -- Politics and government -- 1815-1861
ISBN 978-1-4000-6726-8; 1-4000-6726-X
LC 2009-27872

"Anyone wanting to understand political, economic, and social life in the early republic will appreciate the Heidlers' command of sources and balanced treatment of a man too long in the shadow of Andrew Jackson and very much a metaphor for his era." Libr J

Includes bibliographical references

Cleage, Pearl

Cleage, Pearl. **Things** I Should Have Told My Daughter; Lies, Lessons & Love Affairs. Pearl Cleage. Atria Books 2014 320 p. (hardback) $23.99 **92**
1. Motherhood 2. Women authors 3. Self-realization 4. Self-realization in women 5. Women authors, American -- Biography
ISBN 1451664699; 9781451664690; 9781451664706
LC 2013034164

This book, by Pearl Cleage, "reprints journal entries chronicling her tumultuous life in the 1970s and '80s . . . the decades in which she discovered her vocation as a playwright, poet and novelist while remaining deeply engaged in political activism, as a speechwriter for the first black mayor of Atlanta, and as a feminist grappling with marriage, motherhood, divorce and subsequent sexual freedom." (Kirkus Reviews)

Includes bibliographical references and index

Cleland, Max, 1942-

Cleland, Max. **Heart** of a patriot; how I found the courage to survive Vietnam, Walter Reed and Karl Rove. [by] Max Cleland, with Ben Raines. Simon & Schuster 2009 259p il $26   **92**
1. Amputees 2. Veterans 3. Senators 4. Government officials 5. Veterans -- United States 6. State government officials 7. United States -- Congress -- Senate
ISBN 978-1-4391-2605-9
LC 2009-11620

"This heartrending memoir is aimed at former soldiers who have struggled with the trauma of war and at those of us who haven't served in the military but need to understand the personal cost to those who have." Booklist

Includes bibliographical references

Clemente, Roberto, 1934-1972

Maraniss, David. **Clemente**; the passion and grace of baseball's last hero. Simon & Schuster 2006 401p il maps hardcover o.p. pa $15   **92**
1. Baseball players 2. Baseball -- Biography
ISBN 0-7432-1781-0; 978-0-7432-1781-1; 0-7432-9999-X; 978-0-7432-9999-2 pa

LC 2006-42235

The author "has produced a baseball-savvy book sensitive to the social context that made Clemente, a black Puerto Rican, a leading indicator of baseball's future." N Y Times Book Rev

Includes bibliographical references

Santiago, Wilfred. **21**; the story of Roberto Clemente : a graphic novel. Wilfred Santiago. Fantagraphics 2011 148p. chiefly ill. $22.99 **92**

1. Graphic novels 2. Baseball players -- Graphic novels 3. Baseball -- Graphic novels

ISBN 978-1-56097-892-3

This book "is an all-ages graphic biography of baseball star Roberto Clemente: No other baseball player dominated the 1960s like him and no other Latin American player achieved his numbers. '21' chronicles his early days growing up in rural Puerto Rico, the highlights of his career (including the 1960s World Series), the prejudice he faced, his private life and his humanitarian mission." (trplteens.wordpress.com)

"Santiago opens his dazzlingly drawn comics biography of the pioneering Puerto Rican ballplayer on the final game of the 1972 season, with Clemente just one hit shy of joining the 3,000-hit club. Fans will know, of course, that 3,000 would also be his final tally, as he would die in a plane crash delivering relief supplies to the earthquake-rocked Nicaragua that winter. Santiago skitters around formative scenes from Clemente's childhood—striking a complex chord of family, homeland, and a driving passion for baseball—before tracing significant moments from his professional career: staring down racism with the same resolute demeanor with which he faced a high heater, snagging batting championships and fans' hearts many times over, and always looking for ways to honor his heritage." Booklist

Includes bibliographic references.

Cleopatra, Queen of Egypt, d. 30 B.C.

Fletcher, Joann. **Cleopatra** the great; the woman behind the legend. Harpercollins 2011 454p map $27.99 **92**

1. Queens 2. Egypt -- History

ISBN 978-0-06-058558-7

First published 2008 in the United Kingdom

In this biography, the author "argues that Cleopatra's genius as a strategist, which allowed her to restore a fading Egypt to its former glory, is what makes her the 'true heir' to her ancestor Alexander the Great. . . . Those interested in Cleopatra, ancient history, or a well-written and academically sound biography will enjoy this authentic look at a queen of Egypt who managed to be all things to all people—mother, queen, goddess, and whore." Libr J

Includes bibliographical references

Goldsworthy, Adrian Keith. **Antony** and Cleopatra; [by] Adrian Goldsworthy. Yale University Press 2010 470p il map $35 **92**

1. Queens 2. Generals 3. Statesmen 4. Orators 5. Rome -- History 6. Egypt -- History

ISBN 978-0-300-16534-0

LC 2010-929122

"Narrating [Antony] and Cleopatra's parts in the tumultuous end of the Roman Republic, Goldsworthy skillfully integrates the partial and partisan source material into an accessible presentation of a classic tale from classical times." Booklist

Includes bibliographical references

Roller, Duane W. **Cleopatra**; a biography. Oxford University Press 2010 252p il map (Women in antiquity) $24.95 **92**

1. Queens 2. Egypt -- History

ISBN 978-0-19-536553-5; 0-19-536553-4

LC 2009-24061

"Basing this chronicle exclusively on primary sources culled from classical antiquity, the author painstakingly separates myth from reality, discounting . . . [Cleopatra's] undeserved reputation as a seductress and concentrating on her impressive—but often overlooked or minimized—political, military, and administrative achievements. This revisionist portrait of one of the most powerful women in the ancient world adds substance and heft to her exotic legacy." Booklist

Includes bibliographical references

★ Schiff, Stacy. **Cleopatra**; a life. Little, Brown and Co. 2010 368p il map $29.99; ebook $14.99 **92**

1. Queens 2. Egypt -- History 3. Biography, Individual

ISBN 978-0-316-00192-2; 0-316-00192-9; 978-0-316-12180-4 ebook

LC 2010-06988

"It's dizzying to contemplate the thicket of prejudices, personalities and propaganda Schiff penetrated to reconstruct a woman whose style, ambition and audacity make her a subject worthy of her latest biographer. After all, Stacy Schiff's writing is distinguished by those very same virtues." N Y Times Book Rev

Includes bibliographical references

Tyldesley, Joyce A. **Cleopatra**; last queen of Egypt. [by] Joyce Tyldesley. Basic Books 2008 290p il map $27.50 **92**

1. Queens 2. Egypt -- History

ISBN 978-0-465-00940-4; 0-465-00940-9

LC 2008-921307

The author "unscrambles a slew of Ptolemys and Cleopatras who ruled wealthy Egypt from 332 to 30 BCE to tell the story of the dynasty's last and best-remembered queen, Cleopatra VII (c.70-30 BCE). . . . This fascinating and scholarly book belongs in all libraries." Libr J

Includes bibliographical references

Clinton, Bill, 1946-

Branch, Taylor. The **Clinton** tapes; wrestling history with the president. Simon & Schuster 2009 707p $35; pa $20 **92**

1. Governors 2. Presidents 3. Presidents -- United States 4. United States -- Politics and government -- 1989-

ISBN 978-1-4165-4333-6; 1-4165-4333-3; 978-1-4165-4334-3 pa; 1-4165-4334-1 pa

"A history of the Bill Clinton years based on taped interviews with the president while he was in office. . . . As a longtime friend of the family, in 1993 the author agreed to assist in recording what was, in effect, Clinton's secret diary. In 79 informal sessions, held sporadically until 2001,

Clinton talked spontaneously about recent events, aiming to create an unfiltered, on-the-spot record of events for future historians." Kirkus

"Not everyone who begins it will finish Branch's book, yet Clinton's remarks . . . contribute critically to the historical record and accordingly merit a place in most library collections." Booklist

Clinton, Bill. **My** life. Knopf 2004 957p il $35   **92**
1. Governors 2. Presidents 3. Presidents -- United States 4. United States -- Politics and government -- 1989-
ISBN 0-375-41457-6
LC 2004-107564

In this memoir the former president traces his life from his childhood in Arkansas through his time as governor of Arkansas and then focuses on his White House years

"Clinton's memoir has the raw material for a blockbuster book." Publ Wkly

Felsenthal, Carol. **Clinton** in exile; a president out of the White House. William Morrow 2008 386p il $25.95   **92**
1. Governors 2. Presidents 3. Presidents -- United States 4. United States -- Politics and government -- 1989-
ISBN 978-0-06-123159-9; 0-06-123159-2

"Anyone curious, but especially those who remain fans, will enjoy Felsenthal's look at Clinton's post-presidency." Publ Wkly

Maraniss, David. **First** in his class: a biography of Bill Clinton. Simon & Schuster 1995 512p il hardcover o.p. pa $15   **92**
1. Governors 2. Presidents 3. Presidents -- United States
ISBN 0-684-81890-6 pa
LC 94-48245

The author "offers a heavily documented (nearly 400 interviews), unauthorized biography that ends with Clinton's announcement for the presidency. Maraniss writes, 'My goal was for this book to be neither pathography nor hagiography, but a fair-minded examination of a complicated human being and the forces that shaped him and his generation.' He has achieved his goal. . . . All in all, First in His Class is solid journalism that thoughtfully evokes the tumultuous times—desegregation, assassinations, Vietnam—that shaped Clinton." Booklist
Includes bibliographical references

Clinton, Hillary Rodham, 1947-
Bernstein, Carl. A **woman** in charge; the life of Hillary Rodham Clinton. Alfred A. Knopf 2007 628p il $27.95   **92**
1. Lawyers 2. Senators 3. Secretaries of state 4. Spouses of presidents 5. Presidential candidates
ISBN 978-0-375-40766-6; 0-375-40766-9
LC 2007-17472

The author "offers a three-dimensional portrait of a person with enduring strengths (discipline, tenacity, a sustaining religious faith) and weaknesses (excessive secrecy, a tendency to self-righteousness and a habit of nursing grudges). . . . Bernstein almost always finds new facts and telling details. [His] account benefits enormously from remarkably candid on-the-record assessments of both Clintons by intimates such as close friend Jim Blair and Betsey Wright, Clinton's gubernatorial chief of staff in Arkansas." Los Angeles Times Book Rev
Includes bibliographical references

★ Clinton, Hillary Rodham, 1947- **Hard** choices; Hillary Rodham Clinton. Simon & Schuster 2014 656 p. ill. (chiefly color), maps $35   **92**
1. Autobiographies 2. Women politicians 3. United States -- Foreign relations
ISBN 1476751447; 9781476751443
LC 2014407811

This book by Hillary Rodham Clinton discusses how "to her surprise, her former rival for the Democratic Party nomination, newly elected President Barack Obama, asked her to serve in his administration as Secretary of State. This memoir is the story of the four . . . years that followed, and the hard choices that she and her colleagues confronted." (Publisher's note)

"Clinton's calculated mix of soaring rhetoric and tacit realpolitik reveals much, but not everything." Pub Wkly

Close, Chuck, 1940-
Finch, Christopher. **Chuck** Close; life. Prestel 2010 350p il $34.95   **92**
1. Artists 2. Painters 3. Artists -- United States
ISBN 978-3-7913-3677-0

"Focusing on Close's paradigm-altering approaches to portraiture, the author offers an astounding and inspiring story of an artist of uncommon powers." Booklist
Includes bibliographical references

Coates, Ta-Nehisi
Coates, Ta-Nehisi. The **beautiful** struggle. Spiegel & Grau 2008 223p map $22.95; pa $14   **92**
1. Father-son relationship 2. Essayists 3. African Americans -- Social conditions
ISBN 978-0-3855-2036-2; 0-3855-2036-0; 978-0-3855-2746-0 pa; 0-3855-2746-2 pa
LC 2007-52166

"Coates grew up in a tough Baltimore neighborhood, subject to the same temptations as other young black boys. But he had a father in the household, a man steeped in race consciousness and willing to go to any lengths—including beatings—to keep his sons on the right path. With sharp cultural observations and emotional depth, Coates recalls an adolescence of surreptitiously standing on corners eying girls, drinking fifths, and earning reps, mindful of his father's admonition about the Knowledge. . . . A beautifully written, loving portrait of a strong father bringing his sons to manhood." Booklist

Cobain, Kurt, 1967-1994
Cross, Charles R. **Heavier** than heaven: a biography of Kurt Cobain. Hyperion 2001 381p il $24.95; pa $14.95   **92**
1. Singers 2. Guitarists 3. Rock musicians 4. Nirvana

(Musical group)

ISBN 0-7868-6505-9; 0-7868-8402-9 pa

LC 2001-24187

This is a biography of Kurt Cobain, the lead singer of the rock group Nirvana, who committed suicide in 1994 at the age of 27

"Cross followed the Nirvana juggernaut from the beginning, and though he nearly bludgeons the reader with tales of Cobain's debauched excesses, one is still drawn to the artist's forceful personality." Libr J

Cross, Charles R. **Here** we are now; the lasting impact of Kurt Cobain. Charles R. Cross. It Books 2014 192 p. illustration (hardcover) $22.99 **92**
1. Popular culture -- United States 2. Rock musicians -- United States -- Biography 3. Nirvana (Musical group) 4. Rock music -- 1991-2000 -- History and criticism
ISBN 0062308211; 9780062308214; 9780062308221

LC 2013045769

"In 'Here We Are Now: The Lasting Impact of Kurt Cobain,' [author] Charles R. Cross . . . examines the legacy of the Nirvana front man and takes on the question: why does Kurt Cobain still matter so much, 20 years after his death? Kurt Cobain is the icon born of the 90s, a man whose legacy continues to influence pop culture and music. Cross explores the impact Cobain has had on music, fashion, film, and culture, and attempts to explain his lasting and looming legacy." (Publisher's note)

"This short but intriguing book explores the troubled musician as a kind of muse for seemingly unrelated fields (modern hip-hop, medical studies, high-end fashion) as well as a champion for gay and women's rights and racial equality." LJ

Cockburn, Henry, 1982-

Cockburn, Henry. **Henry's** demons; living with schizophrenia: a father and son's story. [by] Patrick Cockburn and Henry Cockburn. Scribner 2011 238p il $25; ebook $11.99 **92**
1. Artists 2. Painters 3. Schizophrenia 4. Father-son relationship 5. Schizophrenics
ISBN 978-1-4391-5470-0; 1-4391-5470-8; 978-1-4391-6035-0 ebook; 1-4391-6035-X ebook

LC 2010-17760

This book focuses on Henry Cockburn's diagnosis of schizophrenia in 2002 at the age of 20. It is narrated in alternating chapters by Henry and his father Patrick, "and Patrick's wife, the academic Janet Montefiore, Henry's mother, also contributes several diary entries." N Y Times (Late N Y Ed)

"This straightforward, unsentimental book, is a bold plea for more research and cutting-edge therapies to combat mental illness." Publ Wkly

Cohen, Leonard, 1934-

Leonard Cohen on Leonard Cohen; interviews and encounters. edited by Jeff Burger. Chicago Review Press 2014 624 p. illustrations (Musicians in Their Own Words) (cloth) $29.95 **92**
1. Singers 2. Composers 3. Singers -- Canada -- Interviews 4. Composers -- Canada -- Interviews 5.

Poets, Canadian -- 20th century -- Interviews

ISBN 1613747586; 9781613747582

LC 2013034568

This book, edited by Jeff Burger, "collects interviews from various sources to present the singular Leonard Cohen in his own voice. The earliest piece is an interview on Canadian television in 1966; the most recent is an article in the Guardian from January of [2014]. Editor Burger divides the book into four parts: the 1960s and 1970s . . . the 1980s . . . the 1990s . . . and the new millennium." (Booklist)

"Burger's discerning editorial hand selects those conversations with Cohen that offer insights into his music." Pub Wkly

Cole, Nat King, 1919?-1965

★ Epstein, Daniel Mark. **Nat** King Cole. Northeastern University Press 2000 437p il pa $20 **92**
1. Singers 2. Pianists 3. Jazz musicians 4. African American singers
ISBN 1-555-53469-4; 978-1-555-53469-1

LC 00-42727

First published 1999 by Farrar, Straus & Giroux

"The biographer sometimes digs too deep into esoterica, spending pages analyzing the lyrics of Straighten Up and Fly Right, for example. But when he recounts the singer's personal struggles, including a shocking 1956 onstage kidnapping attempt by Alabama racists, the human drama is, well unforgettable." Time

Includes bibliographical references

Cole, Natalie

Cole, Natalie. **Angel** on my shoulder; an autobiography. written with Digby Diehl. Warner Bks. 2000 353p il $38 **92**
1. Singers 2. Pop musicians
ISBN 978-0-446-52746-0; 0-446-52746-7

LC 00-61455

In this memoir by the daughter of the late Nat King Cole, the Grammy Award-winning songstress recalls her childhood, her personal battle and victory over drugs and alcohol, and the legal battles with her mother and siblings over her father's estate

"Although she concentrates mostly on the good times, Cole isn't shy about the bad times, which makes this intriguing, engaging, and inspirational life story worthy of attention." Booklist

Coleman, Melissa

Coleman, Melissa. **This** life is in your hands; one dream, sixty acres, and a family undone. HarperCollins 2011 325p il map $25.99; ebook $12.99 **92**
1. Death 2. Authors 3. Farmers 4. Loss (Psychology) 5. Gardeners 6. Columnists 7. Memoirists 8. Farm life -- Maine
ISBN 978-0-06-195832-8; 978-0-06-208735-5 ebook

LC 2010-24942

The author describes her life growing up on an organic farm in Cape Rosier, Me., started by her parents, Eliot and Sue Coleman, followers of "Helen and Scott Nearing, whose books, most notably 'Living the Good Life,' inspired a back-to-land movement predicated on hard work and strict discipline." N Y Times (Late N Y Ed)

"Especially pertinent to those with an interest in self-sufficiency and the locavore movement, this book is packed with historical information beyond the family story. Ultimately, a complex tale of a noble pursuit with tragic consequences." Libr J

Colette, 1873-1954

Thurman, Judith. **Secrets** of the flesh: a life of Colette. Knopf 1999 592p il hardcover o.p. pa $18.95   **92**
1. Authors 2. Novelists 3. Biographers
ISBN 0-345-37103-8 pa
            LC 99-18959
Thurman focuses on the "morally subversive Colette in the social milieu of early-20th-century Paris. . . . {She} does not hesitate to expose the dishonest, selfish, exploitive facets of the feminist icon who wrote articles for Occupation newspapers and sometimes behaved heartlessly toward lovers. Nevertheless, her Colette comes off as an appealing, even heroic, figure." Publ Wkly
Includes bibliographical references

Coltrane, John, 1926-1967

Ratliff, Ben. **Coltrane**; the story of a sound. Farrar, Straus & Giroux 2007 xxi, 250p il hardcover o.p. pa $16   **92**
1. Jazz musicians 2. African American musicians 3. Saxophonists
ISBN 978-0-374-12606-3; 0-374-12606-2; 978-0-312-42778-8 pa; 0-312-42778-6 pa
            LC 2007-4362
This is a biography of the jazz musician.
This is an "engaging study of the jazz saxophonist's artistic influence. . . . Ratliff patiently explicates Coltrane's legend, writing in short, aphoristic bursts, often as elliptically as his subject played tenor saxophone, but never less than lucidly." N Y Times Book Rev
Includes bibliographical references

Columbus, Christopher

Morison, Samuel Eliot. **Admiral** of the ocean sea: a life of Christopher Columbus; maps by Erwin Raisz; drawings by Bertram Greene. Little, Brown 1942 xx, 680p il maps hardcover o.p. pa $28.99 **92**
1. Explorers
ISBN 0-316-58478-9 pa
A condensation of the author's two-volume work with same title also published in 1942 but now o.p.
"An authoritative . . . biography of Columbus which is also decidedly original in its emphasis on the ability of Columbus as seaman and navigator and in the amount of space given to tracing the routes of the voyages and landings." Libr J

Commerson, Philibert, 1727-1773

Ridley, Glynis. The **discovery** of Jeanne Baret; a story of science, the high seas, and the first woman to circumnavigate the globe. Crown Publishers 2010 288p il $25; ebook $25   **92**
1. Botanists 2. Explorers 3. Women scientists 4.

Voyages around the world
ISBN 978-0-307-46352-4; 978-0-307-46354-8 ebook
            LC 2010-16778
This is a biography "of Jeanne Baret. Born in 1740 in France's Loire valley, Baret became an expert 'herb woman' who proved to be indispensable to the ambitious botanist Philibert Commerson, accompanying him as his assistant when Commerson was appointed naturalist for France's first expedition to circumnavigate the globe. But women were forbidden, so Baret dressed as a man. . . . Woven throughout this gripping story are Ridley's piquant insights into eighteenth-century exploration, botany, taxonomy, biopiracy, and sexism. Baret could not have asked for a more exacting and expressive champion. Ridley is incandescent in her passion for the truth." Booklist
Includes bibliographical references

Common (Musician)

Common. **One** day it'll all make sense; a memoir. by Common with Adam Bradley. 1st Atria Books hardcover ed.; Atria Books 2011 305 p. ill. (chiefly col.) $25   **92**
1. Fame 2. Gangs 3. Rap music 4. African Americans -- Chicago (Ill.) 5. African American entertainers -- Biography 6. Rap musicians -- United States -- Biography
ISBN 9781451625875; 9781451625882 pa; 9781451625905
            LC 2011021691
Street Lit Book Award Medal: Adult Non-Fiction (2012)
The author of the book, the hip-hop musician Common, "discusses fame and the deeper meanings of his life. . . . He portrays himself as an openhearted, curious kid, trying to understand the tumult of Chicago's African-American South Side. . . . Common writes frankly about his youthful involvement with gang culture, portrayed as an inevitable rite of passage that became increasingly violent. . . . By 1989, his early demos as Common Sense were drawing industry attention, and he dropped out of college to pursue this calling, over his mother's objections. Much of what follows is a . . . showbiz narrative, moving from hip-hop to film acting." (Kirkus)
Includes bibliographical references and index

Connolly, Kevin Michael, 1985-

Connolly, Kevin Michael. **Double** take; a memoir. HarperStudio 2009 227p il $19.99; pa $14.99   **92**
1. Skiing 2. Athletes 3. Photographers 4. Skateboarding 5. People with disabilities 6. Skiers 7. Athletes with disabilities
ISBN 978-0-06-179153-6; 978-0-06-179152-9 pa
            LC 2009-30496
"An X Games competitive skier and photographer recounts an extraordinary life spent overcoming immense physical limitations. Connolly was born without legs in the summer of 1985, in Helena, Mont. . . . A courageous, immensely rewarding chronicle expressed in arresting words and pictures." Kirkus

Conroy, Frank, 1936-2005

Grimes, Tom. **Mentor;** a memoir. Tin House Books 2010 242p $24.95; pa $16.95 **92**

1. Authors 2. Mentoring 3. Novelists 4. Authorship 5. Dramatists 6. Creative writing 7. Memoirists 8. Biographers 9. Authors, American 10. Short story writers 11. Iowa Writers' Workshop

ISBN 978-0-9825048-8-8; 978-0-9825048-9-5 pa

LC 2010-7124

Grimes discusses his life as a writer, his friendship with Frank Conroy, the director of the Iowa Writers Workshop, the publication of his first book, Season's End, and the effect on Grimes of its poor reception.

"Anyone who dreams of becoming a novelist will need to read Tom Grimes's brutally honest and wonderful Mentor. While there have been plenty of books on how to write, or how to get published, or how to promote your work, as well as a number of triumphalist accounts of 'making it,' this is a story of what it's like to just miss succeeding." Washington Post

Includes bibliographical references

Conway, Jill K., 1934-

Conway, Jill K. **True** north; a memoir. Knopf 1994 250p hardcover o.p. pa $13 **92**

1. Historians 2. College teachers 3. College presidents

ISBN 0-679-74461-4 pa

LC 93-45302

This continuation of the author's memoir begun in The road from Coorain covers "the period from her departure from Australia for the U.S. to enter graduate school in 1960 through her appointment as Smith College president in 1975." Publ Wkly

"Conway analyzes her own experiences in the U.S. and Canada just as thoughtfully and penetratingly as her academic work investigates the lives of several previous generations of American women." Booklist

Cook, James, 1728-1779

Blainey, Geoffrey. **Sea** of dangers; Captain Cook and his rivals in the South Pacific. Ivan R. Dee 2009 322p il map $27.50 **92**

1. Explorers 2. Voyages around the world 3. Ship captains 4. Naval officers 5. Travel writers 6. Oceania -- Exploration

ISBN 978-1-56663-825-8; 1-56663-825-9

LC 2008-52623

This is an "account of the 1768-1771 exploratory voyage of English navigator Capt. James Cook and the contemporaneous voyage of the rival French captain Jean de Surville through the same previously uncharted waters." Publ Wkly

"An excellent work of popular history that recounts the exploits of men who dramatically expanded our knowledge of the globe." Booklist

Includes bibliographical references

Hough, Richard Alexander, 1922-1999. **Captain** James Cook; {by} Richard Hough. Norton 1995 398p il hardcover o.p. pa $18.95 **92**

1. Explorers 2. Naval officers 3. Travel writers

ISBN 0-393-31519-3 pa

LC 94-35998

First published 1994 in the United Kingdom

This is a "narrative of the life of the great 18th-century navigator, explorer, and cartographer." Libr J

"Hough's easygoing, thorough treatment . . . spotlights a proud, determined man." Booklist

Includes bibliographical references

Cooke, Sam

★ Guralnick, Peter. **Dream** boogie; the triumph of Sam Cooke. Little, Brown 2005 750p il $27.95 **92**

1. Singers 2. Soul musicians

ISBN 0-316-37794-5

LC 2005-77

This is a biography of the American singer.

"For those who only know the singer through his pop hits—'You Send Me'; 'Twistin' the Night Away'—the extensive account of his childhood background in gospel music will prove fascinating, and the evocation of the harsh realities faced by African-American musicians touring the South a powerful reminder of just how explosive this music could be." Publ Wkly

Includes discography and bibliographical references

Cooper, Douglas, 1911-1984

Richardson, John. The **sorcerer's** apprentice; Picasso, Provence, and Douglas Cooper. University of Chicago Press 2001 318p il pa $17 **92**

1. Art critics 2. Biographers 3. Art historians

ISBN 0-226-71245-1

First published 1999 by Knopf

Picasso biographer John Richardson "has written a concise account of the first half of his own life and notably of his long relationship as a young man with the Cubist art historian and collector Douglas Cooper. The account concentrates on the dozen years, from early 1949 to the end of 1960, when Richardson lived with Cooper, visiting museums and monuments all over Europe, meeting the great artists and other personalities of the day, and restoring the colonnaded Chateau de Castille in the south of France." NY Times Book Rev

Includes bibliographical references

Cooper, Gary, 1901-1961

Thomson, David, 1941- **Gary** Cooper; photo research by Lucy Gray. Faber and Faber 2010 129p il (Great stars) pa $14 **92**

1. Actors

ISBN 978-0-86547-932-6

LC 2009-41759

First published 2009 in the United Kingdom

In this biography of the actor, "Cooper is presented as a hapless, weak-willed adulterer whose lean body, rugged handsomeness and preternatural stillness translated on camera as a quintessentially American rectitude and heroic stoicism. . . . Thomson is wickedly funny and startlingly poetic in his observations." Kirkus

Cooper, Helene

Cooper, Helene. The **house** at Sugar Beach; in search of a lost African childhood. Simon & Schuster 2008 354p il map $25   **92**
1. Journalists 2. Liberia
ISBN 0-7432-6624-2; 978-0-7432-6624-6

The author traces her childhood in wartorn Liberia and her reunion with a foster sister who had been left behind when her family fled the region.

"A coming-of-age story told with unremitting honesty. With her pedigree and her freedom from internalized racism, Cooper is liberated to enjoy a social universe that is a fluid mix of all things American and African. . . . While Cooper's memoir is mesmerizing in its portrayal of a Liberia rarely witnessed, its description of the psychological devastation—and coping mechanisms—brought on by profound loss is equally captivating." N Y Times Book Rev

Cooper, James Fenimore, 1789-1851

Franklin, Wayne. **James** Fenimore Cooper; the early years. Yale University Press 2007 708p il map $40   **92**
1. Authors 2. Novelists 3. Authors, American
ISBN 978-0-300-10805-7; 0-300-10805-2
LC 2006-31247

"This volume profoundly enriches our understanding of how the young writer helped forge our national mythology in works such as The Last of The Mohicans and The Pioneers." Booklist

Includes bibliographical references

Copernicus, Nicolaus, 1473-1543

Repcheck, Jack. **Copernicus'** secret; how the scientific revolution began. Simon & Schuster 2007 239p il map $25   **92**
1. Astronomers
ISBN 978-0-7432-8951-1; 0-7432-8951-X
LC 2007-24649

This biography "concentrates on the last 12 years of the astronomer's life." N Y Times Book Rev

"The book is fascinating reading, even to those who may be familiar with much of its contents." Choice

Includes bibliographical references

Vollmann, William T. **Uncentering** the Earth; Copernicus and The Revolutions of the Heavenly Spheres. Norton 2006 295p il (Great discoveries) $22.95   **92**
1. Astronomers
ISBN 0-393-05969-3
LC 2005-25864

This is a "meditation on the life and work of astronomer Nicolaus Copernicus (1473-1543). The writer reflects on Copernicus's achievement in pursuing and publishing a heliocentric view of the universe." Libr J

"Readers who want to understand the significance of Copernicus's book in both his own time and ours will find this the next best thing to reading it." Publ Wkly

Coronado, Rodney A., 1966-

Kuipers, Dean. **Operation** Bite Back; Rod Coronado's war to save American wilderness. Bloomsbury 2009 309p il $25   **92**
1. Environmentalists 2. Animal rights movement 3. Animal rights activists
ISBN 1-59691-458-0; 978-1-59691-458-2
LC 2009-6600

This "account of animal rights activist Rod Coronado follows the charismatic Coronado from his introduction to animal protection in the 1980s to his campaign of sabotage against the fur industry, his life in the underground and on reservations among fellow Native Americans, and ultimately his arrests and incarcerations. . . . An important book that will appeal to readers interested in environmental and social issues." Libr J

Corrigan, Kelly, 1967-

Corrigan, Kelly. **Glitter** and Glue; A Memoir. by Kelly Corrigan. Random House Inc 2014 240 p. ill. $26   **92**
1. Travel 2. Nannies 3. Mother-daughter relationship 4. Motherhood 5. Mothers and daughters 6. Sydney (N.S.W.) -- Biography 7. Americans -- Australia -- Sydney (N.S.W.) -- Biography
ISBN 034553283X; 9780345532831
LC 2013041936

This memoir, by Kelly Corrigan, "examines the bond . . . between mothers and daughters. . . . After college, . . . [Corrigan] took off for Australia to see things and do things. . . . In a matter of months, her savings shot, she had a choice: get a job or go home. That's how Kelly met John Tanner, a newly widowed father of two looking for a live-in nanny. . . . Every day she spent with the Tanner kids was a day spent reconsidering her relationship with her mother." (Publisher's note)

"Written in a breezy style with humor and heart, the book reminds us how rewarding it can be to see a parent outside the context of our own needs." Kirkus

Corrigan, Kelly. The **middle** place. Voice/Hyperion 2008 266p il $23.95; pa $14.95   **92**
1. Breast cancer 2. Columnists 3. Cancer patients
ISBN 978-1-4013-0336-5; 978-1-4013-4093-3 pa
LC 2007-15316

The author "was a happily married mother of two young daughters when she discovered a cancerous lump in her breast. She was still undergoing treatment when she learned that her beloved father, who'd already survived prostate cancer, now had bladder cancer. Corrigan's story could have been unbearably depressing had she not made it clear from the start that she came from sturdy stock. . . . Those learning to accept their own adulthood might find strength—and humor—in Corrigan's feisty memoir." Publ Wkly

Cosby, Bill, 1937-

★ Whitaker, Mark. **Cosby**; his life and times. Mark Whitaker. Simon & Schuster 2014 544 p. illustrations   **92**
1. Comedians -- Biography 2. Actors -- United States

-- Biography
ISBN 9781451697971; 9781451697988

LC 2014021330

This book, by Mark Whitaker, is the "first major biography of an American icon, comedian Bill Cosby. Based on extensive research and in-depth interviews with Cosby and more than sixty of his closest friends and associates, it is a frank, fun and fascinating account of his life and historic legacy." (Publisher's note)

Includes bibliographical references and index

Cosell, Howard, 1918-1995

Bloom, John. **There** you have it; the life, legacy, and legend of Howard Cosell. University of Massachusetts Press 2010 220p il $80; pa $24.95 **92**
1. Lawyers 2. Television personalities 3. Television broadcasting of sports 4. Sportscasters
ISBN 978-1-55849-836-5; 1-55849-836-2; 978-1-55849-837-2 pa; 1-55849-837-0 pa

LC 2010037284

This is a "biography of the lawyer-turned-sports journalist whose brash style and penchant for social commentary changed the way American sporting events are reported." Publisher's note

"Many of the contradictions of his character and the finer intricacies of his legacy are teased out in this carefully observed portrait." Publ Wkly

Includes bibliographical references

Ribowsky, Mark. **Howard** Cosell. W.W. Norton & Co. 2011 477p il $29.95 **92**
1. Sports 2. Lawyers 3. Television personalities 4. Sportscasters
ISBN 978-0-393-08017-9; 0-393-08017-X

LC 2011-27501

This book offers a biography of "Howard Cosell, of ABC, who died in 1995, [and] was [a] . . . famous television sports announcer. . . . He was a star for three decades, and during his early-1970s heyday, which coincided with the maximum reach of network television, he was a ubiquitous figure in American culture. . . . [The book attempts to elucidate] the interplay among Cosell's life story, the stories he covered, and the institutional rise of televised sports . . . [and larger claims] about American culture. . . . [The author examines how] Cosell became a star by covering a bigger star, Muhammad Ali, the great heavyweight boxer, [as well as other aspects of his career.]" (N Y Review of Books)

"The sportscaster Howard Cosell erupted onto the national stage in the 1960s and quickly became a pop-culture icon. His raspy, heavily New York-accented voice, a sharp mind, an expansive vocabulary and a photographic memory were packaged into a larger-than-life and sometimes abrasive figure. Whether his audience loved him, hated him or loved to hate him, they tuned in, and he turned them on. He was impossible to ignore. . . . Mr. Ribowsky's book is an entertaining read and a thought-provoking portrayal of the multifaceted Howard Cosell in all his glory and enmity. It is based on voluminous, well-sourced research into print and electronic material, coupled with numerous interviews with Cosell's contemporaries." Wall Street J

Includes bibliographical references

Cousteau, Jacques Yves, 1910-1997

Matsen, Bradford. **Jacques** Cousteau; the sea king. [by] Brad Matsen. Pantheon Books 2009 296p il $27.95 **92**
1. Authors 2. Oceanography 3. Divers 4. Naval officers 5. Oceanographers 6. Nonfiction writers
ISBN 978-0-375-42413-7; 0-375-42413-X

LC 2009-11640

This biography "places Cousteau's films, books, and fame into the context of the rest of his life—ambitions, childhood, family relationships, friendships, and disagreements. . . . Readers who dive, who are interested in ecology or the oceans, or who simply recognize the name Cousteau, will want to read this full, well-rounded portrait of one of the world's greatest explorers and conservationists. Highly recommended." Libr J

Includes bibliographical references

Cox, Lynne

Cox, Lynne. **Swimming** to Antarctica; tales of a long-distance swimmer. Knopf 2004 323p $24.95 **92**
1. Women athletes 2. Swimmers
ISBN 0-375-41507-6

LC 2003-47577

The author "has swum the Mediterranean, the three-mile Strait of Messina, under the ancient bridges of Kunning Lake, [and] below the old summer palace of the emperor of China in Beijing. . . . She writes about the ways in which these swims . . . became vehicles for personal goals." Publisher's note

"Cox is a pleasure. . . . Many passages are grip-the-page exciting, whether she's dodging Antarctic icebergs or Nile River sewage." Booklist

Coxeter, H. S. M. (Harold Scott Macdonald), 1907-2003

★ Roberts, Siobhan. **King** of infinite space; Donald Coxeter, the man who saved geometry. Walker & Co. 2006 399p il $27.95 **92**
1. Mathematicians 2. College teachers
ISBN 0-8027-1499-4; 978-0-8027-1499-2

LC 2006-497355

This is the story of geometer H. S. M. "Donald" Coxeter's "life, his work, and his interactions with mathematicians, scientists, and artists of his time. . . . The author carefully weaves a lot of mathematical details into her work, but not so much that it becomes burdensome to the historical focus of the book." Sci Books Films

Includes bibliographical references

Craddock, Ida C., 1857-1902

Schmidt, Leigh Eric. **Heaven's** bride; the unprintable life of Ida C. Craddock, American mystic, scholar, sexologist, martyr, and madwoman. Basic Books 2010 335p il **92**
1. Mysticism 2. Occultists 3. Sex researchers 4. Biography, Individual
ISBN 9780465002986

LC 2010-929343

This is a biography of the American freethinker. Index.

The author "delineates the life of Philadelphia-born self-styled religion scholar and sexologist Ida Craddock (1857–1902), who navigated two important currents in late-19th-century America: the campaign for 'moral purity' waged by a righteous Protestant majority, and a spirit of liberalism and spiritualism as advocated by women's-rights activists, intellectuals and free-thinkers. . . . A colorful contextual study of Craddock and her teeming era." Kirkus

Includes bibliographical references

Crais, Clifton C.

Crais, Clifton. **History** lessons; a memoir of madness, memory, and the brain. Clifton Crais. The Overlook Press 2014 272 p. (alk. paper) $26.95 **92**
1. Amnesia 2. Autobiographies 3. Collective memory 4. Autobiographical memory 5. New Orleans (La.) -- Biography 6. Historians -- United States -- Biography
ISBN 1468303686; 9781468303681
LC 2014002373

"Born in Louisiana to a soon-to-be absent father and an alcoholic mother--who tried to drown him in a bathtub when he was three--[author] Clifton Crais spent his childhood . . . living with relatives too old or infirmed to care for him, or rambling on his own through New Orleans. . . . Crais examines the science of memory and forgetting, from the ways in which experience shapes the developing brain to . . . chronic childhood amnesia . . . from which he suffers." (Publisher's note)

"The ambiguities of a life only half recalled are fully illuminated in this chronicle of trying to understand what has been forgotten.—" LJ

Crane, Kathleen, 1951-

Crane, Kathleen. **Sea** legs; tales of a woman oceanographer. Westview Press 2003 318p il map hardcover o.p. pa $16 **92**
1. Oceanography 2. Women scientists 3. Oceanographers
ISBN 0-8133-4004-7; 0-8133-4285-6 pa
LC 2003-1690

"Crane chronicles the relentless adversity she faced in becoming a world-class oceanographer with a modest matter-of-factness that almost camouflages the high caliber of her achievements. . . . She was the first to postulate the existence of the now famous deep-sea hot springs. . . . Crane's experiences are diverse, dramatic, and important; her understanding of international affairs and environmental realities laudable and moving; and her triumphs over personal sorrows and illness impressive and inspiring." Booklist

Includes bibliographical references

Crazy Horse, Sioux Chief, ca. 1842-1877

McMurtry, Larry. **Crazy** Horse. Viking 1999 148p (Penguin lives series) hardcover o.p. pa $14 **92**
1. Oglala Indians 2. Native Americans -- Biography
ISBN 0-670-88234-8; 0-14-303480-4 pa
LC 98-26644

"Though essentially a loner and devoid of political ambition, Crazy Horse was a respected military tactician, equally feared and admired for the strength and the intensity of his convictions. Rather than merely attempting to sort out fact from fiction, McMurtry incorporates conjecture and legend into this philosophical portrait of both the man and the myth." Booklist

Powers, Thomas. The **killing** of Crazy Horse. Alfred A. Knopf 2010 568p il map $30 **92**
1. Oglala Indians 2. Biography, Individual 3. Dakota Indians -- Wars
ISBN 978-0-375-41446-6; 0-375-41446-0
LC 2010-16842

"With the Great Sioux War as background and context, . . . Powers recounts the final months and days of Crazy Horse's life." (Publisher's note) Bibliography. Index.

"Despite the title, this beautifully written and absorbing work is less about the death of Crazy Horse and more about the personality and life of the Native American icon. It is also an insightful and scrupulously fair examination of the culture of Plains Indian bands and their interaction with advancing white civilization in the nineteenth century." Booklist

Includes bibliographical references

Crick, Francis, 1916-2004

Ridley, Matt. **Francis** Crick; discoverer of the genetic code. Atlas Books 2006 213p (Eminent lives) $19.95 **92**
1. Genetics 2. Scientists 3. Biochemists 4. Nobel laureates for physiology or medicine
ISBN 0-06-082333-X; 978-0-06-082333-7
LC 2005-55878

This "biography examines the paired strands of Crick's life and work." N Y Times Book Rev

"A briskly written essential for the DNA shelf." Booklist

Includes bibliographical references

Crosby, Bing, 1904-1977

Giddins, Gary. **Bing** Crosby: a pocketful of dreams: the early years, 1903-1940. Little, Brown 2001 728p il $30; pa $17.95 **92**
1. Actors 2. Singers
ISBN 0-316-88188-0; 0-316-88645-9 pa
LC 00-44403

This "work chronicles Crosby's life as well as his singing, recording, radio, and film careers up to 1940, the year of the first of his popular 'Road' movies with Bob Hope." Libr J

"Giddins has contributed a landmark study of popular singing in the first half of the twentieth century." Booklist

Includes bibliographical references

Crowell, Rodney, 1950-

★ Crowell, Rodney. **Chinaberry** sidewalks. Alfred A. Knopf 2011 259p il $24.95 **92**
1. Singers 2. Country musicians 3. Songwriters
ISBN 978-0-307-59420-4
LC 2010-35996

"Crowell is among the best storytellers to emerge from Nashville. Up to now, he told his stories in song, but with this heartfelt memoir, he can now be called a writer of the first order. Houston, where Crowell grew up in the 1950s and early 1960s, was a city full of characters found in stereotypical country songs: hard-drinking fathers and longsuffering mothers singing along to the beer-soaked ballads of Hank Williams. But this is not fiction; Crowell actually lived the life, soaking up its exhilarating and disturbing atmosphere. Crowell is unsparingly honest, yet there is an admirable restraint here, too." Booklist

Crystal, Billy ✓

Crystal, Billy, 1948- **Still** foolin' 'em; where i've been, where i'm going, and where the hell are my keys? by Billy Crystal. Henry Holt and Company 2013 288 p. (hardback) $28   **92**

1. Aging 2. American wit and humor 3. Comedians -- United States -- Biography
ISBN 0805098208; 9780805098204

LC 2013012238

Author and comedian Billy Crystal "outlines the absurdities and challenges that come with growing old, from insomnia to memory loss to leaving dinners with half your meal on your shirt. Crystal not only catalogues his physical gripes, but offers a road map to his 77 million fellow baby boomers who are arriving at this milestone age with him. He also looks back at the most powerful and memorable moments of his long and storied life." (Publisher's note)

"Avoiding the trappings—excess schmaltz, laundry list of famous friends, boozy party log—of so many celebrity memoirs, Crystal delivers a funny and genuinely moving chronicle of his life inside and outside Hollywood." Pub Wkly

Culkin, Jennifer

Culkin, Jennifer. A **final** arc of sky; a memoir of critical care. Beacon Press 2009 237p $24.95   **92**

1. Nurses 2. Authors 3. Nursing 4. Essayists
ISBN 978-0-8070-7285-1

LC 2008-46810

"It's clear that Culkin has little use for cheap sentiment. However, this memoir time and again shares with us her efforts to make meaning of the pain and fear and loss that is intrinsic to her line of work. . . . The author gets even more personal when she shares stories from her own family. With unflinching honesty, she talks about how she coped with the decline of her father's health; what she did at the deathbed of her mother; and how she came to terms with her own MS diagnosis. 'A Final Arc of Sky' tackles that toughest of subjects—our own mortality—with grit, compassion, and humor." Bellingham Herald

Includes bibliographical references

Cummings, E. E. (Edward Estlin), 1894-1962 ✓

★ Sawyer-Laucanno, Christopher. **E.E.** Cummings; a biography. Sourcebooks 2004 606p il $29.95; pa $16.95   **92**

1. Poets 2. Authors
ISBN 1-570-71775-3; 1-4022-0594-5 pa

LC 2004-12234

This biography of poet and artist e.e. cummings draws parallels between cummings' private life and his work.

This "is a responsible, adept, and necessary contribution to the body of secondary work about one of America's greatest poets." Christ Sci Monit

Cunningham, Merce

✓★ Brown, Carolyn. **Chance** and circumstance; twenty years with Cage and Cunningham. Alfred A. Knopf 2007 645p il $37.50   **92**

1. Poets 2. Authors 3. Dancers 4. Composers 5. Choreographers 6. Essayists
ISBN 978-0-394-40191-1; 0-394-40191-3

LC 2006-48799

The author "traces the trajectory of her modern dance career with that organization during its crawling stages in the 1950s and 1960s, when composer John Cage was musical director and artist Robert Rauschenberg was set and costume designer. Brown documents the company's early struggles for acceptance (it was considered avant-garde), various tours, and eventual world recognition. . . . This book will appeal to modern dance buffs and memoir readers." Libr J

Curie, Marie, 1867-1934

✓Brian, Denis. The **Curies**; a biography of the most controversial family in science. Wiley 2005 438p il $30   **92**

1. Chemists 2. Physicists 3. Nobel laureates for physics
ISBN 0-471-27391-0

LC 2005-7001

This book "follows five generations of the Sklodowska-Curie-Joliot family. Beginning before Marie Sklodowska and Pierre Curie meet, Brian details their courtship and 11-year marriage, bringing the reader to the Curie dinner table and into the converted garden shed (replete with a leaking roof) where the Curies' work on polonium and radium transformed physics and won them two Nobel prizes. . . . Extremely well-done and highly recommended." Publ Wkly

Includes bibliographical references

✓Dry, Sarah. **Curie**; with an essay by Sabine Seifert. Haus 2003 170p il (Life & times) pa $15.95 **92**

1. Chemists 2. Physicists 3. Women scientists 4. Chemists -- France 5. Chemists -- Poland 6. Women chemists -- France 7. Women chemists -- Poland 8. Nobel laureates for physics
ISBN 1-904341-29-2

This is a biography of the first woman to win two Nobel Prizes, one for physics and the other for chemistry

"Concise and engaging, this amply illustrated history of Madame Curie . . . makes an excellent introduction to the feminist icon and scientific pioneer. Dry does an excellent job of delineating the major events of Curie's life, including her early education in the underground schools of the 19th-century Polish resistance movement, her heady intellectual courtship with Pierre Curie in France, and later their discovery of radioactivity in 1898. Sidebars on topics such as the invention of the laboratory, and the inclusion of Seifert's essay on Irène Joliot-Curie, Marie Curie's less famous daughter and co-worker, make this pocket sized book especially comprehensive, and a wonderful introduction to a fascinating and inspiring career." Publ Wkly

Includes bibliographical references

✓Quinn, Susan. **Marie** Curie; a life. Addison-Wesley 1996 509p il pa $21   **92**

1. Chemists 2. Physicists 3. Women scientists 4.

Nobel laureates for physics
ISBN 0-201-88794-0; 978-0-201-88794-5

LC 96-167

First published 1995 by Simon & Schuster

This a biography of the Polish-born scientist who was twice the recipient of the Nobel Prize for her work with radium.

"A well-written, evenhanded story of dedication, disappointment, tragedy, and extraordinary achievement." Booklist

Includes bibliographical references

Curie, Pierre, 1859-1906

Brian, Denis. The **Curies**; a biography of the most controversial family in science. Wiley 2005 438p il $30 **92**

1. Chemists 2. Physicists 3. Nobel laureates for physics
ISBN 0-471-27391-0

LC 2005-7001

This book "follows five generations of the Sklodowska-Curie-Joliot family. Beginning before Marie Sklodowska and Pierre Curie meet, Brian details their courtship and 11-year marriage, bringing the reader to the Curie dinner table and into the converted garden shed (replete with a leaking roof) where the Curies' work on polonium and radium transformed physics and won them two Nobel prizes. . . . Extremely well-done and highly recommended." Publ Wkly

Includes bibliographical references

Da Ponte, Lorenzo, 1749-1838

Bolt, Rodney. The **librettist** of Venice; the remarkable life of Lorenzo Da Ponte, Mozart's poet, Casanova's friend, and Italian opera's impresario in America. Bloomsbury Pub. 2006 428p il $29.95 **92**

1. Poets 2. Authors 3. Librettists
ISBN 1-59691-118-2

LC 2006-5713

"Reading Bolt's lively narrative of Da Ponte's life from the ghetto of Venice to the sparkling opera houses of Europe is pure pleasure." Publ Wkly

Dahl, Roald

Sturrock, Donald. **Storyteller**; the authorized biography of Roald Dahl. Simon & Schuster 2010 655p il $30 **92**

1. Authors 2. Authors, English 3. Children's authors 4. Short story writers
ISBN 978-1-4165-5082-2; 1-4165-5082-8

LC 2010-07175

"In this authorized biography of Dahl, Sturrock, the artistic director of the Roald Dahl Foundation, reveals a life marked by tragedy: the early deaths of Dahl's father and sister, his son's tragic accident, the death of a daughter at seven, and the debilitating stroke of his wife, Patricia Neal, at age 39...This carefully researched and unflinching portrait of an immensely complicated and talented writer will appeal to Dahl's fans and other serious readers of biography." (Library Journal)

Includes bibliographical references

Dalai Lama II, 1476-1542

Mullin, Glenn H. The **second** Dalai Lama; his life and teachings. translated, edited, introduced, and annotated by Glenn H. Mullin. Snow Lion Publications 2005 270p pa $16.95 **92**

1. Buddhism
ISBN 1-55939-233-9

LC 2005-281580

The author "has divided his book into three parts: a general introduction to Tibetan religious history and the lineage of the Dalai Lamas, a biography of the Second Dalai Lama (1475-1541), particularly noted for his POETRY, and a selection in 25 chapters of his mystical poems, translated and commented on by Mullin." LJ

Dalai Lama XIV, 1935-

★ Bstan-'dzin-rgya-mtsho, Dalai Lama XIV, 1935- **Freedom** in exile; the autobiography of the Dalai Lama. HarperCollins Pubs. 1990 288p il maps hardcover o.p. pa $15 **92**

1. Buddhism 2. Tibet (China) 3. Buddhist leaders 4. Political leaders 5. Nobel laureates for peace
ISBN 0-06-098701-4

LC 89-46523

"The Dalai Lama's story is, in part, a chapter in the 2,500-year history of Buddhism as well as a testament to the 'mendacity and barbarity' of Communist China. He shares the details of his amazing life, a glimpse at some of the mysteries of Tibetan Buddhism, and his unshakable belief in the basic good of humanity." Booklist

★ Iyer, Pico. The **open** road; the global journey of the fourteenth Dalai Lama. Bloomsbury 2008 288p $24 **92**

1. Buddhist leaders 2. Political leaders 3. Nobel laureates for peace
ISBN 978-0-307-26760-3; 0-307-26760-1

LC 2007-43991

"The combination of Iyer's exacting observations, incisive analysis, and frank respect for the unknowable results in a uniquely internalized, even empathic portrait of one of the world's most embraced and least understood guiding lights." Booklist

Includes bibliographical references

Talty, Stephan. **Escape** from the land of snows; the young Dalai Lama's harrowing flight to freedom and the making of a spiritual hero. Crown Publishers 2010 320p map $26; ebook $26 **92**

1. Escapes 2. Tibet (China) 3. Buddhist leaders 4. Political leaders 5. Nobel laureates for peace
ISBN 978-0-307-46095-0; 978-0-307-46097-4 ebook

LC 2010-19827

This is a "narrative about the current Dalai Lama's 14-day escape from Chinese-occupied Tibet in 1959. . . . [The author] uses this remarkable historical event to tell the greater story of Tibet's transformation from a veiled kingdom to a world cause, and the Dalai Lama's coming of age from a teenage king and living god to an international spiritual leader. The author effectively gives the reader an introductory lesson in Tibetan history and a sense of the Tibetan people while maintaining the pace of an adventure tale." Kirkus

Includes bibliographical references

Dampier, William, 1652-1715

Preston, Diana. A **pirate** of exquisite mind: explorer, naturalist, and buccaneer: the life of William Dampier; {by} Diana and Michael Preston. Walker & Company 2004 372p il map $27 **92**
ISBN 0-8027-1425-0

LC 2003-62197

"Dampier's adventures and observations ignited the imagination of a generation, but today his name is largely unknown. This exhaustive biography . . . won't make Dampier famous again, but it will give readers a clear understanding of one of the most well-traveled men in history." Publ Wkly

Includes bibliographical references

Danticat, Edwidge, 1969-

★ Danticat, Edwidge. **Brother,** I'm dying. Alfred A. Knopf 2007 272p hardcover o.p. pa $15 **92**
1. Authors 2. Novelists 3. Dramatists 4. Women authors 5. Editors 6. Essayists 7. Children's authors 8. Short story writers
ISBN 978-1-4000-4115-2; 1-4000-4115-5; 978-1-4000-3430-7 pa; 1-4000-3430-2 pa

LC 2007-06887

The author "has written a fierce, haunting book about exile and loss and family love, and how that love can survive distance and separation, loss and abandonment and somehow endure, undented and robust." N Y Times (Late NY Ed)

Danticat, Edwidge. **Create** dangerously; the immigrant artist at work. Princeton University Press 2010 189p (Toni Morrison lecture series) $19.95 **92**
1. Authors 2. Novelists 3. Dramatists 4. Women authors 5. Editors 6. Essayists 7. Children's authors 8. Short story writers 9. Biography, Individual 10. Haiti -- Social conditions
ISBN 0-691-14018-9; 978-0-691-14018-6

LC 2010-10302

This is Danticat's "new collection of essays, adapted and updated from the Toni Morrison Lecture she gave in 2008 at Princeton University, and expanded with her writing for The New Yorker, The Progressive and other publications." (N Y Times Book Rev) Index.

This "tender . . . book about loss and the unquenchable passion for homeland makes us remember the powerful material from which most fiction is wrought: it comes from childhood, and place. No matter her geographic and temporal distance from these, Danticat writes about them with the immediacy of love." N Y Times Book Rev

Includes bibliographical references

Danton, Georges Jacques, 1759-1794

Lawday, David. The **giant** of the French Revolution; Danton, a life. Grove Press 2010 294p il map $27.50 **92**
1. Revolutionaries 2. France -- History -- 1789-1799, Revolution
ISBN 978-0-8021-1933-9

"This is the best biography of Danton to be written since Hilaire Belloc's over 100 years ago. Both the scholar and the general reader will find this biography an informative and lively read." Libr J

Includes bibliographical references

Darling, Ron, 1960-

Darling, Ron. The **complete** game; reflections on baseball, pitching, and life on the mound. by Ron Darling, with Daniel Paisner. Alfred A. Knopf 2009 272p $24.95 **92**
1. Baseball players 2. Baseball -- Biography
ISBN 978-0-307-26984-3; 0-307-26984-1

LC 2008-55706

Darling, "the stalwart ex-Mets starter and incumbent Mets broadcaster . . . offers pitches and outcomes (but no box scores) from ten selected games in his career, including a successful World Series start against the Red Sox at Fenway Park in 1986, a gruesome windy-day thumping suffered at Wrigley Field, and his celebrated extra-inning near-no-hitter back when he was pitching for Yale. Among them are enough oddities and thrilling turns of baseball to make a reader glad to be here and—well, not out there." New Yorker

Darnley, Henry Stewart, Lord, 1545-1567

Weir, Alison. **Mary,** Queen of Scots, and the murder of Lord Darnley. Ballantine Bks. 2003 670p il map $27.95; pa $16.95 **92**
1. Queens 2. Princes 3. Scotland -- History -- 16th century
ISBN 0-345-43658-X; 0-8129-7151-5 pa

LC 2002-34467

"No stone is left unturned in {Weir's} investigation, and despite its detail, her book is as dramatic as witnessing firsthand the most riveting court case." Booklist

Darnton, John

Darnton, John. **Almost** a family; a memoir. Alfred A. Knopf 2011 347p il $27.95; ebook $13.99 **92**
1. Authors 2. Journalists 3. Father-son relationship 4. Authors, American
ISBN 978-0-307-26617-0; 978-0-307-59524-9 ebook

LC 2010-16835

"In this unsentimental narrative, Darnton vividly chronicles the high-water era of classic journalism and his stints as a Times correspondent in Africa and Solidarity-era Poland, but what drives his memoir are the pursuit of the fullest possible picture of his father's death, the story of his mother's alcoholism and sobriety, and most of all, the quest for deeply buried facts about his parents and their relationship." Publ Wkly

Darrow, Clarence, 1857-1938

Farrell, John A. **Clarence** Darrow; attorney for the damned. Doubleday 2011 561p il $32.50; ebook $15.99 **92**
1. Lawyers 2. Memoirists 3. Writers on law 4. State legislators
ISBN 978-0-385-52258-8; 0-385-52258-4; 978-0-385-53451-2 ebook

LC 2010-46273

This is a biography of the American lawyer who defended John Scopes, Nathan Leopold and Richard Loeb.

"Farrell gleans from previously undisclosed material to offer a completely engaging portrait of a flawed man of noble ideals." Booklist

Includes bibliographical references

McRae, Donald. The **last** trials of Clarence Darrow. William Morrow 2009 422p il $26.99 **92**
1. Lawyers 2. Memoirists 3. Writers on law 4. State legislators
ISBN 978-0-06-116149-0; 0-06-116149-7
LC 2008-51237
Published in the United Kingdom with title: The old devil: Clarence Darrow, the world's greatest trial lawyer
"Darrow's long affair with journalist Mary Field Parton frames a vivid retelling of his three most famous court cases: defending an evolutionist against the church; a black physician accused of killing a member of a lynch mob; and Leopold and Loeb, two wealthy teenagers who killed a younger boy for fun. Viewed through Field Parton's eyes, Darrow's flawed brilliance is compelling." Guardian
Includes bibliographical references

Darst, Jeanne
Darst, Jeanne. **Fiction** ruined my family. Riverhead Hardcover 2011 303p $25.95 **92**
1. Authors 2. Novelists, American 3. Performance artists
ISBN 978-1-59448-814-6
LC 2011027830
"Perfectly balanced in tone, this is one of the few truly funny memoirs that can also talk about the love, frustration, and deep despair that only relatives can bring out. With highly quotable moments; a keeper." Libr J

Darwin, Charles, 1809-1882
Browne, Janet. **Charles** Darwin; v1 a biography. Princeton Univ. Press 1996 605p v1 il pa $25.95 **92**
1. Naturalists 2. Travel writers 3. Writers on science
ISBN 0-691-02606-8
LC 95-53319
First published 1995 by Knopf
This first volume of a two-part biography of Darwin focuses on his early years, leading up to his marriage and his moving out of London to the countryside of Kent.
The author "captures the spirit of a quietly revolutionary scientist whose ingrained Victorian prejudices were at odds with his radical ideas." Publ Wkly
Includes bibliographical references
Followed by Charles Darwin: The power of place (2002)

Browne, Janet. **Charles** Darwin. v2 Knopf 2002 591p v2 il $37.50 **92**
1. Naturalists 2. Travel writers 3. Writers on science
ISBN 0-679-42932-8
This second volume of Browne's biography of Darwin begins "a year before the publication of On the Origin of Species, with the arrival of a package from Alfred Russel Wallace, whose own ideas on natural selection virtually mirrored Darwin's, forcing him to go public. . . . Browne's

subject is monumental, but her writing style is never overburdened by the weight. Rather, her prose is elegant in its clarity of thought, her craftsmanship impeccable in the way it weaves a coherent whole from the innumerable threads of thought, experience and persona that comprised this colossal life." Publ Wkly
Includes bibliographical references

Desmond, Adrian J. **Darwin**; [by] Adrian Desmond & James Moore. W.W. Norton & Co. 1994 808p il pa $23.95 **92**
1. Naturalists 2. Travel writers 3. Writers on science
ISBN 0-393-31150-3; 978-0-393-31150-1
First published 1991 in the United Kingdom
"No other biography of Darwin has anywhere near the density of detail this book has. This rich tapestry, supplemented with 91 fine illustrations, is intended to provide the basis for relating Darwin the creative scientist to his social and political milieu." N Y Times Book Rev
Includes bibliographical references

Desmond, Adrian J. **Darwin's** sacred cause; how a hatred of slavery shaped Darwin's views on human evolution. [by] Adrian Desmond & James Moore. Houghton Mifflin Harcourt 2009 484p il map $30 **92**
1. Slavery 2. Evolution 3. Naturalists 4. Travel writers 5. Writers on science
ISBN 978-0-547-05526-8; 0-547-05526-9
LC 2008-43482
This "book reinterprets much of . . . [Darwin's] life work as having been motivated by an altruistic humanitarian vision and an equally intense abhorrence of slavery. . . . Well researched, likely to be controversial (some will call it revisionist history), this book provides another enlightening glimpse into a life of seemingly infinite complexity." Libr J
Includes bibliographical references

★ Quammen, David. The **reluctant** Mr. Darwin; an intimate portrait of Charles Darwin and the making of his theory of evolution. Atlas Books/Norton 2006 304p (Great discoveries) hardcover o.p. pa $14.95 **92**
1. Naturalists 2. Travel writers 3. Writers on science
ISBN 0-393-05981-2; 978-0-393-05981-6; 0-393-32995-X pa; 978-0-393-32995-7 pa
LC 2006-9864
The author "concentrates on how Darwin privately developed his theory of evolution and reluctantly made his ideas public when [Alfred] Wallace began to publish similar theories." Libr J
"This often slyly witty book stands out among the flood of books being published for Darwin's bicentenary." Publ Wkly
Includes bibliographical references

Thomson, Keith Stewart. The **young** Charles Darwin; [by] Keith Thomson. Yale University Press 2009 276p il $28 **92**
1. Naturalists 2. Travel writers 3. Writers on science
ISBN 978-0-300-13608-1; 0-300-13608-0

"Thomson's writing style is fluid and engaging and his grasp of the Darwinian literature encyclopedic. His scholarly thoroughness is balanced by his very human appreciation for a very human scientist." Choice

Includes bibliographical references

David, King of Israel

Pinsky, Robert. The **life** of David. Schocken 2005 209p (Jewish encounters) $19.95   **92**

1. Kings

ISBN 0-8052-4203-1

LC 2005-41696

The author "considers the peculiarities, paradoxes, and timeless significance of David's often baffling story from his golden days as a handsome upstart confronting King Saul in 'gangsterish' encounters to David's wild years as a desert Robin Hood and ascension to the throne. . . . Witty, frank, skeptical, and clearly moved by mercurial David's chutzpah and losses, Pinsky brings remarkable lucidity, depth, and creativity to his dynamic and poetic reading of a legendary figure who has become emblematic of both destructive and heroic aspects of human nature." Booklist

Davis, Bette, 1908-1989

Thomson, David, 1941- **Bette** Davis; photo research by Lucy Gray. Faber and Faber 2010 128p il (Great stars) pa $14   **92**

1. Actors

ISBN 978-0-86547-931-9

LC 2009-41760

First published 2009 in the United Kingdom

"Chronicling Davis' life and evolution in Hollywood, Thomson illustrates how changes in her often-disappointing private life (she had a habit of marrying the wrong men) influenced and often deepened her onscreen persona. Reading of how Davis bounced from one bad movie to the next in the early years of her career, it's hard not to share Thomson's enthusiasm for her talent, drive, and will. And it is hard not to feel Thomson's disappointment when Davis' major, artistic breakthroughs (The Little Foxes, All About Eve) are followed by lapses into forgettable mediocrity (The Man Who Came to Dinner, Payment on Demand)." Booklist

Includes filmography and bibliographical references

Davis, Clive

Davis, Clive, 1932- The **soundtrack** of my life; Clive Davis with Anthony DeCurtis. Simon & Schuster 2013 608 p. ill. (some col.) $30   **92**

1. Executives 2. Music industry 3. Popular music -- United States 4. Rock music -- United States -- History and criticism 5. Popular music -- United States -- History and criticism 6. Sound recording executives and producers -- United States -- Biography

ISBN 1476714789; 9781476714783

LC 2013560241

Lambda Literary Awards Finalist: Bisexual Nonfiction (2014)

This book presents a memoir of author Clive Davis's career in the music industry. "Born into a working-class family in Brooklyn, he won scholarships to New York University and Harvard Law School and eventually landed a job as legal counsel for Columbia Records. He was handed the presidency of the company by chance, and it was then he learned he had 'ears': the ability to spot talent and create hit records." (Library Journal)

"Revealing, entertaining account of the fortunes--almost always waxing--of the music mogul." Kirkus

Davis, Miles

Cook, Richard. **It's** about that time; Miles Davis on and off record. Oxford University Press 2007 373p il $27   **92**

1. Jazz musicians 2. African American musicians 3. Band leaders 4. Flugelhornists 5. Trumpet players

ISBN 978-0-19-532266-8; 0-19-532266-5

LC 2006-50694

"Cook's thoughtful, illuminating criticism and boundless knowledge of his subject make this a rich and satisfying read for jazz aficionados and novices alike." Publ Wkly

Includes discography and bibliographical references

Davis, Miles. **Miles,** the autobiography; {by} Miles Davis with Quincy Troupe. Simon & Schuster 1989 431p il hardcover o.p. pa $15   **92**

1. Jazz musicians 2. African American musicians 3. Band leaders 4. Flugelhornists 5. Trumpet players

ISBN 0-671-72582-3 pa

LC 89-19652

"The legendary jazz musician Miles Davis . . . takes us on a historical journey that begins with his growing up in the mid-1920s in East St. Louis, then moves on to New York City in the 1940s, where he was a student at the Julliard School of Music, and to his encounters with other jazz greats like Charlie Parker, Dizzy Gillespie, Billie Holiday, Herbie Hancock, and George Duke." Libr J

Dawidoff, Nicholas

Dawidoff, Nicholas. The **crowd** sounds happy; a story of love, madness, and baseball. Pantheon Books 2008 271p $24.95   **92**

1. Authors 2. Sportswriters 3. Nonfiction writers 4. Baseball -- Biography

ISBN 978-0-375-40028-5; 0-375-40028-1

LC 2007-30525

In this memoir, the author describes how his love of baseball helped him through rough periods of his youth, including his father's descent into mental illness.

"Essential reading for anyone who wishes a balm for heartbreaks in youth, torn family life, love, and seventh-game losses." Libr J

Dawkins, Richard, 1941-

Dawkins, Richard, 1941- An **Appetite** for Wonder; The Making of a Scientist. HarperCollins 2013 304 p. $27.99   **92**

1. Atheism 2. Scientists -- Biography

ISBN 0062225790; 9780062225795

"In the first volume of a projected two-volume memoir, evolutionary biologist and ethologist [Richard] Dawkins . . . looks back on his life from childhood through the publication of his first and most famous book, 'The Selfish Gene,' in 1976. . . . Ultimately, this is a self-portrait of a . . . man whose radical positions are the logical outgrowth of his skeptical, science-based approach. . . . . His memoir is more about science than atheism, although both topics crop up." (Library Journal)

Day, Doris, 1924-

Kaufman, David. **Doris** Day; the untold story of the girl next door. Virgin Books 2008 626p il $29.95; pa $19.95   **92**

   1. Actors 2. Singers

   ISBN 978-1-90526-430-8; 1-90526-430-5; 978-0-75351-809-0 pa; 0-75351-809-0 pa

                  LC 2008-9410

This is a biography of the actor who starred in such films as Love Me or Leave Me (1955), The Man Who Knew Too Much (1956), and Pillow Talk (1959).

   "Readers, especially fans of the star, will thoroughly enjoy this meaty, well-written, entertaining look at the surprisingly tumultuous life of an American icon." Booklist

   Includes bibliographical references

De Kooning, Willem, 1904-1997

Swan, Annalyn. **De** Kooning: an American master; [by] Mark Stevens and Annalyn Swan. Knopf 2004 731p il $35   **92**

   1. Artists 2. Painters

   ISBN 1-4000-4175-9

                LC 2004-48297

This is a biography of the twentieth-century painter and a study of his work

   This is a "sweeping, authoritative biography. . . . The elusiveness of its subject makes the achievements of 'De Kooning' that much more dazzling. This is a book that traces de Kooning's history, puts him on Freud's couch, plumbs the mysteries of his cryptic and ever-changing work and follows the arc of modern art through much of the 20th century, fusing all these elements into a remarkably lucid narrative." N Y Times (Late N Y ed)

   Includes bibliographical references

De Meric, Rosalie, 1916-1999

Blackburn, Julia. The **three** of us; a family story. Pantheon Books 2008 313p il $26   **92**

   1 Poets 2. Artists 3. Authors 4. Parents 5. Painters 6. Novelists 7. Family life 8. Essayists 9. Biographers

   ISBN 978-0-375-42474-8; 0-375-42474-1

                LC 2007-50147

This is a "strangely compelling memoir." Publ Wkly

De Mille, Cecil B., 1881-1959

★ Eyman, Scott. **Empire** of dreams; the epic life of Cecil B. DeMille. Simon & Schuster 2010 579p il $35; ebook $16.99   **92**

   1. Motion picture producers and directors 2. Motion picture directors 3. Motion picture producers

   ISBN 978-0-7432-8955-9; 0-7432-8955-2; 978-1-4391-8041-9 ebook; 1-4391-8041-5 ebook

                LC 2010-27710

This is a biography of the film director and producer Cecil B. DeMille, whose movies include King of Kings and The Ten Commandments.

"Eyman's evocative prose and exhaustive research makes this an engaging and authoritative biography." Publ Wkly

   Includes bibliographical references

DeVoto, Avis

As always, Julia; the letters of Julia Child and Avis DeVoto: food, friendship, and the making of a masterpiece. selected and edited by Joan Reardon. Houghton Mifflin Harcourt Pub. Co. 2010 416p il $26   **92**

   1. Cooks 2. Television personalities 3. Editors 4. Cookbook writers 5. Literary critics 6. Biography, Individual

   ISBN 9780547417714

                LC 2010-25840

This volume presents "the previously unpublished correspondence between the American chef and her unofficial literary agent from 1952 to 1965, offering insight into such events as Julia's early experiences as a new bride in Paris, her support of her diplomat husband and her views on period politics." (Publisher's note) Index.

   "Their letters span a wide range of topics, from cookbooks, menus, recipes, and restaurants to Balzac, sex, goose stuffing, gardening, learning languages, the political climate, Sunday afternoon cocktail parties, and proofreading. Witty, enlightening and entertaining." Publ Wkly

Dean, James, 1931-1955

Alexander, Paul. **Boulevard** of broken dreams; the life, times, and legend of James Dean. Plume 1997 312p il pa $16   **92**

   1. Actors

   ISBN 978-0-452-27840-0; 0-452-27840-6

   First published 1994 by Viking

   "The interesting thing about James Dean is the fact that, almost 40 years after his death, he remains an icon of American pop culture. In the last chapter of this tell-all biography, Alexander takes a stab at accounting for Dean's continuing popularity, but his real interest throughout the book is in the actor's sex life. Although he devotes some attention to Dean's work as an actor and to his heterosexual liaisons, Alexander's contribution to the Dean legend is to label him as homosexual." Booklist

★ Gehring, Wes D. **James** Dean: rebel with a cause. Indiana Historical Society Press 2005 303p il (Indiana biography series) $19.95   **92**

   1. Actors

   ISBN 0-87195-181-9

                LC 2005-41440

This is a "study of Dean's entire life and an appreciation of his rightful place in film history. Gehring makes the point that audiences have confused the actor with his troubled-teenager roles, and he counters that misimpression with a fuller portrait." Booklist

   Includes filmography and bibliographical references

Deen, Paula H., 1947-

Deen, Paula H. **Paula** Deen; it ain't all about the cookin' [by] Paula Deen, with Sherry Suib Cohen. Simon & Schuster 2007 287p il $25; pa $14　**92**

1. Cooks　2. Southern cooking　3. Television personalities　4. Restaurateurs　5. Cookbook writers
ISBN 978-0-7432-9285-6; 0-7432-9285-5; 978-1-4391-6335-1 pa; 1-4391-6335-9 pa

LC 2006-53501

"Deen talks about everything from her decades-long battle with agoraphobia and her troubled first marriage to the hard work that went into building her first business, The Bag Lady, and the professional and personal successes that followed. A few of Deen's recipes . . . are sprinkled among her stories, which offer a sample of the distinctively Southern cooking that is the foundation of Deen's life and career. This wonderfully nourishing book will have readers laughing, crying, and hungry for more." Libr J

Delany, Bessie

Delany, Sadie. **Having** our say; the Delany sisters' first 100 years. [by] Sarah and A. Elizabeth Delany; with Amy Hill Hearth. Kodansha Int. 1993 210p il pa $17; $20　**92**

1. Dentists　2. Centenarians　3. Science teachers　4. Nonfiction writers　5. United States -- Race relations　6. African American women -- Biography
ISBN 9780385312523; 1-56836-010-X

LC 93-23890

"The Delany sisters' story is a collective meditation on American life since Sadie's birth in 1889 and Bessie's in 1891 in Raleigh, North Carolina. . . . The sisters migrated to New York City's Harlem in the 1910s and in the 1950s to the suburb of Mt. Vernon, New York. The assertive Bessie battled racism and sexism as the only black female member of her Columbia University Dental School class in the 1920s. The more reticent Sadie became the first black domestic science teacher in the New York City high schools." Libr J

"The combination of the two voices, beautifully blended by Ms. Hearth, evokes an epic history, often cruel and brutal, but always deeply humane in their spirited telling of it." N Y Times Book Rev

Delany, Mary Granville Pendarves, 1700-1788

Peacock, Molly, 1947- The **paper** garden; an artist begins her life's work at 72. Bloomsbury USA 2010 397p il $30　**92**

1. Artists　2. Collage　3. Women artists　4. Flowers in art　5. Artists, British　6. Creation (Literary, artistic, etc.)　7. Biography, Individual　8. Creative ability in old age
ISBN 978-1-60819-523-7; 1-60819-523-6

"The author entwines the story of Delany with private reflections on her own life as an artist and a woman. As Peacock undertook her eccentric quest to discover the life of the woman who created the beautiful paper mosaics that she so admired, she discovered resonant parallels. . . . A lyrical, meditative rumination on art and the blossoming beauty of self that can be the gift of age and love." Kirkus

Includes bibliographical references

Delany, Sadie

Delany, Sadie. **Having** our say; the Delany sisters' first 100 years. [by] Sarah and A. Elizabeth Delany; with Amy Hill Hearth. Kodansha Int. 1993 210p il pa $17; $20　**92**

1. Dentists　2. Centenarians　3. Science teachers　4. Nonfiction writers　5. United States -- Race relations　6. African American women -- Biography
ISBN 9780385312523; 1-56836-010-X

LC 93-23890

"The Delany sisters' story is a collective meditation on American life since Sadie's birth in 1889 and Bessie's in 1891 in Raleigh, North Carolina. . . . The sisters migrated to New York City's Harlem in the 1910s and in the 1950s to the suburb of Mt. Vernon, New York. The assertive Bessie battled racism and sexism as the only black female member of her Columbia University Dental School class in the 1920s. The more reticent Sadie became the first black domestic science teacher in the New York City high schools." Libr J

"The combination of the two voices, beautifully blended by Ms. Hearth, evokes an epic history, often cruel and brutal, but always deeply humane in their spirited telling of it." N Y Times Book Rev

Delbridge, Melissa J.

Delbridge, Melissa J. **Family** Bible. University of Iowa Press 2008 143p (Sightline books: the Iowa series in literary nonfiction) $23.95　**92**

1. Authors　2. Memoirists　3. Tuscaloosa (Ala.)　4. Short story writers
ISBN 978-1-58729-651-2; 1-58729-651-9

LC 2007-43968

A collection of autobiographical essays about growing up in 1960s Tuscaloosa, Alabama

"Melissa's daddy was a charmer, a Kirk Douglas lookalike who loved to fish and hunt and to go away for the weekend pretending to be fishing and hunting at the 'River Bend Hunting Club' while actually seeing other women. This naturally drove Momma crazy and, sadly, she took it out on Melissa. Momma took her kids from the house in the middle of the night, moved across town, and, when she left Melissa's father for good, 'remarried fast enough to cause a lot of high talk.' . . . The relationship between Delbridge's parents and then the toxic mess that constituted her home with her stepdad, identified as a local exterminator magnate and ex-Marine, are staples in memoir, but the story is gracefully told, without self-pity. . . . Much of this volume is, as one might expect, about Delbridge's own sexual awakening, and you know it will be out of the ordinary, even melodramatic." Tuscaloosa News

Deming, Barbara, 1917-1984

Duberman, Martin B. A **saving** remnant; the radical lives of Barbara Deming and David McReynolds. New Press 2011 298p il $27.95　**92**

1. Poets　2. Authors　3. Feminism　4. Radicalism　5. Political activists　6. Political prisoners　7. Essayists　8. Pacifists　9. Political leaders　10. Socialist leaders
ISBN 978-1-59558-323-9; 1-59558-323-8

LC 2010-45060

"As radical left-wing writers and activists, Deming and McReynolds were immersed in the issues of nonviolence, nuclear disarmament, civil rights and the Vietnam War. Both remained dedicated to peaceful protest, even in the face of legal repercussions. Though naturally frail, Deming picketed and marched her way through the 1960s, and was frequently imprisoned. In 1963, several weeks after taking part in the March on Washington, McReynolds was thrown into a North Carolina jail for eating at a whites-only restaurant with black acquaintants. Two years later, he was one of the first men in the nation to publicly burn his draft card. Duberman . . . tells us that the two were friends and 'often worked together politically,' though we rarely see them interact. The book's parallel narratives intersect in a meaningful way only when its subjects disagree, most notably on the issues of a gay rights movement and feminism. . . . The author makes use of letters, private papers, diaries and recent interviews with McReynolds. (Deming died of ovarian cancer in 1984.) The result is an intimate study, written in straightforward prose." N Y Times Book Rev

Includes bibliographical references

Dempsey, Jack, 1895-1983

Kahn, Roger. A **flame** of pure fire: Jack Dempsey and the roaring '20s. Harcourt Brace & Co. 1999 474p il hardcover o.p. pa $15   **92**

1. Boxers (Persons)
ISBN 0-15-601414-9 pa

LC 99-15382

This biography details the life and career of heavyweight boxer William Harrison "Jack" Dempsey

"In graceful and fluid prose, Kahn presents the con men, gangsters, prostitutes and starlets who inhabited the turbulent, Prohibition-era story of Jack Dempsey." Publ Wkly

Includes bibliographical references

Descartes, René, 1596-1650

Grayling, A. C. **Descartes** : the life and times of a genius. Walker 2006 303p il map $27   **92**

1. Authors 2. Philosophers 3. Mathematicians
ISBN 978-0-8027-1501-2; 0-8027-1501-X

First published 2005 in the United Kingdom with title: Descartes : the life of René Descartes and its place in his times

"As Newton was to physics, so Descartes was to philosophy, moving it from superstition and religion to science and reason. They are the founding fathers of the modern world. Grayling's life of Descartes is set firmly in the age of the Counter-Reformation and the Thirty Years War, which are evoked in a lively, almost novelistic style of which Descartes would certainly have approved. This propels the narrative forward and illuminates the philosophy for a lay readership." Times (London)

★ Watson, Richard A. **Cogito** ergo sum: the life of Rene Descartes; {by} Richard Watson. Godine 2002 375p $35   **92**

1. Authors 2. Philosophers 3. Mathematicians
ISBN 1-56792-184-1

LC 2001-40858

"For all of his puckish delight in a juicy anecdote, Watson recognizes and carefully explicates the cultural centrality of Descartes' intellectual legacy. That legacy ensures numerous readers sure to praise a biographer who delivers

both the philosopher's cerebral doctrines and his unmistakably human conduct." Booklist

Includes bibliographical references

DiMaggio, Joe

Kennedy, Kostya. **56**; Joe DiMaggio and the last magic number in sports. Sports Illustrated Books 2011 367p il por $26.95   **92**

1. Baseball players 2. Baseball -- Biography 3. New York Yankees (Baseball team)
ISBN 9781603201773; 1603201777

Recounts Joe DiMaggio's streak during the summer of 1941 and how it found its way into countless lives.

"From the private world inhabited only by DiMaggio and his new bride to Newark barbershops, the playgrounds of Queens, and the streets of DiMaggio's hometown, San Francisco, Kennedy humanizes an immortal accomplishment." Publ Wkly

Includes bibliographical references (p. 351-357) and index.

Diaghilev, Serge, 1872-1929

Scheijen, Sjeng. **Diaghilev**; a life. translated by Jane Hedley-Prôle and S.J. Leinbach. Oxford University Press 2010 552p il   **92**

1. Ballet dancers 2. Theatrical producers 3. Biography, Individual
ISBN 0199751498; 9780199751495

LC 2010-02205

Original Dutch edition, 2009; first English translation published 2009 in the United Kingdom

This is a "biography of Serge Diaghilev, founder and impresario of the Ballets Russes." (Publisher's note) Bibliography. Index.

"The parade of great dancers, composers, and artists through Diaghilev's life give this book the sweep of a Russian novel with a fascinating, brilliant, and complex protagonist who, according to the author, lived a very public life, but kept his most intimate feelings hidden." Publ Wkly

Includes bibliographical references

Diana, Princess of Wales, 1961-1997

★ Brown, Tina. The **Diana** chronicles. Doubleday 2007 542p $27.50   **92**

1. Princesses
ISBN 978-0-385-51708-9; 0-385-51708-4

This is a biography of Diana, Princess of Wales.

"Like scraping barnacles off an old hulk, Tina Brown has taken the story of Princess Diana, hosed off layers of hearsay and myth, sifted through tons of accumulated legend, and presented us with a fresh and vividly perceptive portrait." Times Lit Suppl

Includes bibliographical references

Dickens, Charles, 1812-1870

Charles Dickens and the great theatre of the world; by Simon Callow. Random House Inc. 2012 xiii, 370 p.p (pbk.) $16   **92**

1. Drama 2. Theater 3. Biography 4. Novelists, English -- 19th century -- Biography
ISBN 034580323X; 9780345803238

LC 2012014287

With this book, actor and director Simon Callow provides a "biography that explores the central importance of the theatre to the life of [Charles Dickens]. . . . From his early years as a child entertainer in Portsmouth to his reluctant retirement . . . just before his death, Dickens was [a man] obsessed with the stage . . . who wrote, acted in and stage-managed plays." (Publisher's note)

Douglas-Fairhurst, Robert. **Becoming** Dickens; the invention of a novelist. Belknap Press of Harvard University Press 2011 389p il $29.95   **92**
1. Authors 2. Novelists 3. Novelists, English 4. Biography, Individual
ISBN 978-0-674-05003-7; 0-674-05003-7
LC 2011004219
The author discusses "Charles Dickens' early life before, and as, he established himself as a novelist, explaining how he was uncertain as to which career path to follow and describing the many struggles he had early on." (Publisher's note) "Concentrating on Dickens's early career, this . . . biography takes us through the 1830s and the completion of 'Oliver Twist,' his second novel." (New York Times Book Review)
Includes bibliographical references

★ Slater, Michael. **Charles** Dickens. Yale University Press 2009 696p il $35   **92**
1. Authors 2. Novelists 3. Authors, English
ISBN 978-0-300-11207-8; 0-300-11207-6
LC 2009-26834
This "biography actually feels somewhat austere: Slater sticks to the known Gradgrindian facts, emphasizes the writing and public performances, seldom goes in for much scene-painting or gratuitous anecdote, and refuses to speculate unduly without evidence. . . . For anybody who wants to know more about this dynamo of Victorian letters, Michael Slater's superb biography is the one to read." Washington Post Book World
Includes bibliographical references (p. 624-626)

Tomalin, Claire. **Charles** Dickens: a life. Penguin Press 2011 527 p. ill., maps $35   **92**
ISBN 978-1-59420-309-1; 1-59420-309-1
LC 2011031466
The book presents a biography of author Charles Dickens, with topics including "the familiar story of the idyllic childhood years in Kent . . . the terrible experience of being forced to work in a blacking factory rather than go to school . . . a rapid, improbable journey from obscure clerk to diligent reporter and sketch-writer . . . [and] Dickens' moral and physical decline as he abandoned his wife . . . to pursue and ultimately seduce [actress Nelly Ternan]." (History Today)
This work chronicles the life of Charles Dickens, "from the challenges he faced as the imprisoned son of a profligate father, his rise to one of England's foremost novelists, and the personal demons that challenged his relationships." Publisher's note

Dickinson, Amy

Dickinson, Amy. The **mighty** queens of Freeville; a mother, a daughter, and the town that raised them. Hyperion Books 2009 225p $22.99   **92**
1. Authors 2. Journalists 3. Advice columnists
ISBN 978-1-4013-2285-4; 1-4013-2285-9
LC 2008-26525
"In the summertime of 2002, after spending months living off of her credit cards between freelance writing jobs, Dickinson sent in an audition column to the Chicago Tribune and became the paper's replacement for the late Ann Landers. Here, Dickinson traces her own personal history, as well as the history of her mother's family whose members make up the Mighty Queens of Freeville, N.Y., the small town where Dickinson was raised, and where she raised her own daughter between stints in London; New York City; Washington, D.C.; and Chicago. Dickinson writes with an honesty that is at once folksy and intelligent, and brings to life all of the struggles of raising a child (Dickinson was a single mother) and the challenges and rewards of having a supportive extended family." Publ Wkly

Dickinson, Emily, 1830-1886

★ Gordon, Lyndall. **Lives** like loaded guns; Emily Dickinson and her family's feuds. Viking 2010 491p il $32.95   **92**
1. Poets 2. Authors 3. Poets, American
ISBN 978-0-670-02193-2; 0-670-02193-8
LC 2009-46311
The author argues that "it wasn't heartbreak that kept the poet sequestered, . . . it was epilepsy, a then-uncontrollable and shameful malady. With one stroke, Gordon recasts Dickinson's entire oeuvre. She then reveals the outrageous treachery of the poet's esteemed brother, Austin, who held his unmarried sisters, wife Susan, and their children hostage to his passion for his ambitious mistress, Mabel Loomis Todd, whose scheming husband encouraged the affair. . . . A jolting and utterly intriguing watershed achievement." Booklist
Includes bibliographical references

Habegger, Alfred. **My** wars are laid away in books; the life of Emily Dickinson. Random House 2001 764p il hardcover o.p. pa $16.95   **92**
1. Poets 2. Authors
ISBN 0-8129-6601-5 pa
LC 2001-19429
"Weaving together a chronologically integrated reading of Emily Dickinson's poetry and correspondence, Habegger has written the most complete and satisfying biography to date of a poet long shrouded in myth and illusion." Booklist
Includes bibliographical references

Wineapple, Brenda. **White** heat; the friendship of Emily Dickinson and Thomas Wentworth Higginson. Alfred A. Knopf 2008 416p il $27.95   **92**
1. Poets 2. Clergy 3. Authors 4. Memoirists 5. Poets, American 6. Social reformers
ISBN 1-4000-4401-4; 978-1-4000-4401-6
LC 2008-11770
This is an account of the friendship between the poet Emily Dickinson and the reformer Thomas Wentworth Higginson, author of Army Life in a Black Regiment (1869).

"A moving portrait of two unalike but kindred spirits who did indeed 'Dare [to] see a Soul at the "White Heat.""" Kirkus

Includes bibliographical references

Didion, Joan

Didion, Joan, 1934- **Blue** nights. Alfred A. Knopf 2011 188p $25; ebook $12.99   **92**
1. Novelists, American 2. Biography, Individual
ISBN 978-0-307-26767-2; 0-307-26767-9; 978-0-307-70051-3 ebook

LC 2011013582

This work "shares the author's frank observations about her daughter, Quintana Roo, as well as her own thoughts and fears about having children and growing old, in a personal account that discusses such topics as her daughter's wedding and her feelings of failure as a parent." (Publisher's note)

"In December 2003, Didion's husband, fellow writer John Gregory Dunne, died of a heart attack while only daughter Quintana Roo lay hospitalized with a bout of pneumonia that had led to septic shock. Quintana recovered to attend the services but died of a hematoma in 2005. . . . Here, Didion focuses on her daughter, recalling Quintana's life while asking herself the questions parents inevitably ask about what they did wrong and what important clues they missed." Libr J

★ Didion, Joan, 1934- The **year** of magical thinking. Knopf 2005 227p $23.95   **92**
1. Authors 2. Novelists 3. Journalists 4. Essayists 5. Screenwriters 6. Nonfiction writers 7. Biography, Individual
ISBN 1-4000-4314-X

LC 2005-45132

"Several days before Christmas 2003, John Gregory Dunne and Joan Didion saw their only daughter, Quintana, fall ill with what seemed at first flu, then pneumonia, then complete septic shock. She was put into an induced coma and placed on life support. Days later—the night before New Year's Eve—the Dunnes were just sitting down to dinner after visiting the hospital when John Gregory Dunne suffered a massive and fatal coronary. In a second, [a] . . . partnership of forty years was over. Four weeks later, their daughter pulled through. Two months after that, arriving at LAX, she collapsed and underwent six hours of brain surgery at UCLA Medical Center to relieve a massive hematoma. This book is Didion's attempt to make sense of the 'weeks and then months that cut loose any fixed idea I ever had about death, about illness . . . about marriage and children and memory . . . about the shallowness of sanity, about life itself.'" (Publisher's note)

The author "chronicles the year following the death of her husband, fellow writer John Gregory Dunne, from a massive heart attack on December 30, 2003, while the couple's only daughter, Quintana, lay unconscious in a nearby hospital suffering from pneumonia and septic shock. . . . This is an indispensable addition to Didion's body of work and a lyrical, disciplined entry in the annals of mourning literature." Publ Wkly

Dillard, Annie

Dillard, Annie. An **American** childhood. Harper & Row 1987 255p hardcover o.p. pa $14   **92**
1. Poets 2. Authors 3. Essayists 4. Literary critics 5. Writers on nature
ISBN 0-06-091518-8 pa

LC 87-45042

In this autobiography, Dillard presents as account of her life from her childhood in Pittsburgh until her entrance into college

"Dillard's luminous prose painlessly captures the pain of growing up in this wonderful evocation of childhood. . . . The events of childhood often loom larger than life; the magic of Dillard's writing is that she sets down typical childhood happenings with their original immediacy and force." Publ Wkly

Diller, Phyllis, 1917-2012

Diller, Phyllis. **Like** a lampshade in a whorehouse; my life in comedy. [by] Phyllis Diller with Richard Buskin. J.P. TarcherPenguin 2005 266p il $24.95; pa $14.95   **92**
1. Comedians
ISBN 1-585-42396-3; 1-585-42476-5 pa

LC 2004-58520

This is an autobiography by the American comedian.

"Brash comedy and a surprising bitterness fuel this unsparing account of Diller's drive to make it big." Publ Wkly

Dillinger, John, 1903-1934

Gorn, Elliott J. **Dillinger's** wild ride; the year that made America's public enemy number one. Oxford University Press 2009 268p il $24.95   **92**
1. Criminals
ISBN 978-0-19-530483-1; 0-19-530483-7

LC 2008-48150

"A solid, unromanticized account. . . . [The author] relies on newspaper accounts and government documents (and, thankfully, no reconstructed dialogue) to plot the movements of a criminal who, 75 years after his death, still reverberates in the American consciousness." Publ Wkly

Includes bibliographical references

Dinesen, Isak, 1885-1962

★ Thurman, Judith. **Isak** Dinesen; the life of a storyteller. St. Martin's Press 1982 495p il hardcover o.p. pa $18   **92**
1. Authors 2. Novelists 3. Memoirists 4. Short story writers
ISBN 0-312-13525-4 pa

LC 82-5573

This biography traces Dinesen's life from her childhood in Denmark through her years in Kenya and her return to Denmark to focus on her literary career

"With great insight and a novelist's gift for nuance and narrative sweep, Thurman shows the extraordinary degree to which Dinesen's life and art meshed. In addition, Thurman's sensitive criticism of Dinesen's work reveals exceptional artistry in its own right." Booklist

Includes bibliographical references

Dirac, Paul Adrien Maurice, 1902-1984

★ Farmelo, Graham. The **strangest** man; the hidden life of Paul Dirac, mystic of the atom. Basic Books 2009 539p il $29.95 **92**

1. Physicists 2. Nobel laureates for physics

ISBN 978-0-465-01827-7

This is a biography of the British theoretical physicist Paul Dirac.

"This biography is a gift. It is both wonderfully written . . . and a thought-provoking meditation on human achievement, limitations and the relations between the two." N Y Times Book Rev

Includes bibliographical references (p. 439-508)

Diski, Jenny

Diski, Jenny. The **Sixties**. Picador 2009 148p (Big ideas/small books) pa $14 **92**

1. Authors 2. Novelists 3. Counter culture 4. Authors, English 5. Great Britain -- Social life and customs

ISBN 978-0-312-42721-4; 0-312-42721-2

The author "recalls (sometimes hilariously) her experience of the '60s, but her emphasis is on the culture's ideas— about drugs, sex, education, mental illness and, to a lesser extent, politics. Very little of what she says is new, but she says it with intelligence, wit, an eye for detail and an extraordinary ability to laugh at her young self while respecting that self's hopes and efforts. . . . She leaves you with plenty to think about, and wanting more." N Y Times Book Rev

Dixon, Willie

Inaba, Mitsutoshi, 1964- **Willie** Dixon; preacher of the blues. Scarecrow Press 2011 xxxi, 445p il (African American cultural theory and heritage) $55; ebook $57.99 **92**

1. Singers 2. Blues musicians 3. African American musicians 4. Blues music -- History and criticism

ISBN 978-0-8108-6993-6; 978-0-8108-6994-3 ebook

LC 2009033237

"This exhaustive biography and analysis of Dixon's music, the most comprehensive study of Dixon's life and work available, features extensive references, many details drawn from interviews, an analysis of Dixon's composition and studio methods, and a complete discography. Inaba . . . tells the story of Dixon's life, from his 1915 birth in Vicksburg, Mississippi, through his childhood in an impoverished area blemished further by racism, to his adulthood in Chicago as a boxer and musician. . . . From the Big Three Trio to Dixon's highly productive years with Chess Records to finally, his own Blues Factory studio, Inaba traces and comments on the significance of Dixon's lasting imprint on music." Publ Wkly

Includes discography and bibliographical references

Dodd, William Edward, 1869-1940 √

Larson, Erik. **In** the garden of beasts; love, terror, and an American family in Hitler's Berlin. Crown 2011 448p il map $26 **92**

1. Diplomats 2. Historians 3. National socialism 4. National socialism -- Germany 5. Germany -- History -- 1933-1945 6. Germany -- Social conditions -- 1933-

1945

ISBN 978-0-307-40884-6; 0-307-40884-1

LC 2010045402

This is an account of the experiences of William Dodd and his family in Berlin. Dodd, formerly a professor of history, served as the American ambassador to Germany from 1933 to 1937. Index.

Larson describes the "experiences of U.S. ambassador to Germany William E. Dodd and his family in Berlin in the early years of Hitler's rule. Dodd had been teaching history at the University of Chicago when he was summoned by FDR to the German ambassadorship. Larson, using lots of archival as well as secondary-source research, focuses on Dodd's first year in Berlin and, using Dodd's diary, chillingly portrays the terror and oppression that slowly settled over Germany in 1933. Dodd quickly realized the Nazis' evil intentions; his daughter Martha, in her mid-20s, was initially smitten by the courteous SS soldiers surrounding her family, but over time she, too, became disenchanted with the brutality of the regime. Along the way Larson provides portraits based on primary-source impressions of Hermann Göring, Joseph Goebbels, Heinrich Himmler, and Hitler himself. He also traces the Dodds' lives after their time in Germany." Libr J

Includes bibliographical references

Dokoupil, Anthony, 1946-

Dokoupil, Tony. The **last** pirate; a father, his son, and the golden age of marijuana. Tony Dokoupil. Doubleday 2014 272 p. (alk. paper) $26.95 **92**

1. Drug traffic 2. Autobiographies 3. Marijuana industry 4. Drug trade -- United States 5. Marijuana industry -- United States 6. Editors -- United States -- Biography 7. Journalists -- United States -- Biography

ISBN 0385533462; 9780385533461; 9780385533478

LC 2013034094

"As he relates his father's rise from hey-man hippie dealer to multi-ton smuggler extraordinaire, [author] Tony Dokoupil tells the larger history of marijuana and untangles the controversies still stirring furious debate today. He blends superb reportage with searing personal memories, presenting a probing chronicle of pot-smoking, drug-taking America from the perspective of the generation that grew up in the aftermath of the Great Stoned Age." (Publisher's note)

"Dokoupil's sharp eye for detail makes for a lively and often moving narrative full of cinematic scenes and snappy dialogue. Dokoupil draws on his experience as a reporter to deliver an unflinching and detailed look at a criminal family's life." Pub Wkly

Dokoupil, Tony

Dokoupil, Tony. The **last** pirate; a father, his son, and the golden age of marijuana. Tony Dokoupil. Doubleday 2014 272 p. (alk. paper) $26.95 **92**

1. Drug traffic 2. Autobiographies 3. Marijuana industry 4. Drug trade -- United States 5. Marijuana industry -- United States 6. Editors -- United States -- Biography 7. Journalists -- United States -- Biography

ISBN 0385533462; 9780385533461; 9780385533478

LC 2013034094

"As he relates his father's rise from hey-man hippie dealer to multi-ton smuggler extraordinaire, [author] Tony Dokoupil tells the larger history of marijuana and untangles the controversies still stirring furious debate today. He blends superb reportage with searing personal memories, presenting a probing chronicle of pot-smoking, drug-taking America from the perspective of the generation that grew up in the aftermath of the Great Stoned Age." (Publisher's note)

"Dokoupil's sharp eye for detail makes for a lively and often moving narrative full of cinematic scenes and snappy dialogue. Dokoupil draws on his experience as a reporter to deliver an unflinching and detailed look at a criminal family's life." Pub Wkly

Domino, Fats, 1928-

Coleman, Rick. **Blue** Monday; Fats Domino and the lost dawn of rock 'n' roll. Da Capo 2006 364p il map hardcover o.p. pa $15.95   **92**
1. Singers 2. Pianists 3. Rock musicians 4. African American musicians
ISBN 0-306-81491-9; 978-0-306-81531-7 pa; 0-306-81531-1 pa

Coleman has crafted a "biography of Fats Domino, drawing on new interviews with the pianist himself. From his childhood in New Orleans through the early days of rock'n'roll, when he endured travel difficulties in the segregated South and frequent riots at his concerts, Fats remained a shy but demanding performer and personality. A homesick father who seemed to cherish his family, Fats was also a hard-drinking womanizer, and Coleman tells his story with compassion and honesty up to Fats's survival of Hurricane Katrina in his Ninth Ward home. His argument that rock'n'roll sprung from Fats and the New Orleans sound is hard to dispute, as Fats was playing long before others now credited with starting the revolution. Despite the occasional slips into fandom, this is an essential purchase for any library collecting the history of rock'n'roll." Libr J

Includes bibliographical references

Donaldson, Ross I.

Donaldson, Ross I. The **Lassa** ward; one man's fight against one of the world's deadliest diseases. St. Martin's Press 2009 270p $24.95; pa $14.99   **92**
1. Physicians 2. Lassa fever 3. Sierra Leone 4. Textbook writers
ISBN 978-0-312-37700-7; 0-312-37700-2; 978-0-312-37701-4 pa; 0-312-37701-0 pa
LC 2008-43923

"This book is a wild and extraordinary memoir of . . . [the author's] 2003 summer in Sierra Leone as a naïve medical student studying Lassa fever (a close cousin of the Ebola virus). Donaldson gives passionate and powerful reportage on a struggling clinic treating villagers and refugees from neighboring war-torn Liberia suffering from the devastating and often fatal illness." Publ Wkly

Doolittle, James Harold, 1896-1993

Glines, Carroll V. **I** could never be so lucky again; an autobiography. by General James H. "Jimmy" Doolittle, with Carroll V. Glines. Bantam Bks. 1991 574p il hardcover o.p. pa $7.99   **92**
1. Generals 2. Air pilots 3. Air force officers 4. United States -- Army Air Forces
ISBN 0-553-07807-0; 0-553-58464-2 pa
LC 91-3353

In this "memoir, World War II flying ace Doolittle . . . recalls his sterling military career and the importance of his family." Booklist

"The book recalls vividly Doolittle's days as an aviation pioneer—and retells the exciting story of the Tokyo raid." Publ Wkly

Includes bibliographical references

Dornstein, David Scott, 1963-1988

Dornstein, Ken. The **boy** who fell out of the sky; a true story. Random House 2006 304p il $23.95; pa $13.95   **92**
1. Travelers 2. Pan Am Flight 103 Bombing Incident, 1988 3. Murder victims
ISBN 0-375-50359-5; 0-375-70769-7 pa
LC 2005-42683

"Dornstein's account of his relationship with his brother and of his own self-examination is a startlingly honest, completely absorbing look at loss and brotherly love." Booklist

Includes bibliographical references

Dostoyevsky, Fyodor, 1821-1881

Frank, Joseph. **Dostoevsky**. v1 Princeton University Press 1976 401p v1 il hardcover o.p. pa $24.95   **92**
1. Authors 2. Novelists 3. Authors, Russian 4. Short story writers
ISBN 0-691-06260-9; 0-691-01355-1 pa

This first volume of a five volume biography of Dostoyevsky traces his life from his boyhood to 1849. His writings are discussed in relation to influences and themes which recur in his greatest works.

Includes bibliographical references

Frank, Joseph. **Dostoevsky**. v2 Princeton Univ. Press 1983 320p v2 il hardcover o.p. pa $24.95 **92**
1. Authors 2. Novelists 3. Authors, Russian 4. Short story writers
ISBN 0-691-06576-4; 0-691-01422-1 pa
LC 83-11216

In this second of a five-volume biography of Dostoyevsky, Frank focuses on the Russian author's arrest, imprisonment, and exile for his socialist activities. Special attention is given to his book, The House of The Dead.

Includes bibliographical references

★ Frank, Joseph. **Dostoevsky**; a writer in his time. edited by Mary Petrusewicz. Princeton University Press 2009 959p il $35   **92**
1. Authors 2. Novelists 3. Authors, Russian 4. Short story writers
ISBN 978-0-691-12819-1
LC 2009-1418

An abridged edition of the author's five volume work published 1976-2002

"Frank displays a brilliant command of Dostoyevsky's heroic endeavors, and his biography reads readily, especially for such a scholarly work." Libr J

Includes bibliographical references and index

Doty, Mark

Doty, Mark, 1953- **Dog** years; a memoir. HarperCollins Publishers 2007 215p $23.95 **92**
1. Poets 2. Authors 3. Dogs 4. Essayists
ISBN 0-06-117100-X; 978-0-06-117100-0

LC 2006-46491

"In a memoir, the poet Mark Doty meditates on grief and the death of his dogs." (N Y Times Book Rev)

The author "celebrates the 16 lovely years his two beloved 70-pound Labs, Beau and Arden, gave him. . . . Against a backdrop of devastating human loss, both personal (the death of his partner) and public (9/11), Doty bears witness to the inexorable decline of his beloved retrievers. . . . Poignant, intelligent, and quite simply superb." Libr J

Doughty, Caitlin

Doughty, Caitlin. **Smoke** gets in your eyes; and other lessons from the crematory. Caitlin Doughty. W W Norton & Co Inc. 2014 272 p. (hardcover) $24.95 **92**
1. Cremation 2. Autobiographies 3. Undertakers and undertaking 4. Undertakers and undertaking -- Anecdotes 5. Undertakers and undertaking -- United States -- Biography
ISBN 0393240231; 9780393240238

LC 2014017294

This book describes how author Caitlin Doughty "took a job at a crematory, turning morbid curiosity into her life's work. Thrown into a profession of gallows humor and vivid characters (both living and very dead), Caitlin learned to navigate the secretive culture of those who care for the deceased. 'Smoke Gets in Your Eyes' tells an unusual coming-of-age story full of bizarre encounters and unforgettable scenes." (Publisher's note)

"Not shying away from candid descriptions of corpses, cremation, and putrefaction, Doughty— . . . details postmortem proceedings not to repulse but to reveal our modern society's 'death denial.'" Booklist

Includes bibliographical references

Douglas, Helen Gahagan, 1900-1980

Denton, Sally. The **pink** lady; the many lives of Helen Gahagan Douglas. Bloomsbury Press 2009 240p il $26 **92**
1. Actors 2. Singers 3. Members of Congress 4. United States -- Congress -- House
ISBN 978-1-59691-480-3; 1-59691-480-7

LC 2009-08148

This is a "biography of the Broadway star turned California Democratic Congresswoman. . . . [The author] does a handsome job exploring Helen Gahagan's early life as an actress and singer as well as her later political activism . . . [and] displays a solid grasp of the ignominious politics of McCarthy-era America. Eye-opening, entertaining portrait of a fascinating proto-feminist." Kirkus

Includes bibliographical references (p. [215]-223) and index.

Douglas, Marjory Stoneman *Online*

Davis, Jack E. An **Everglades** providence; Marjory Stoneman Douglas and the American environmental century. University of Georgia Press 2009 758p il map $34.95 **92**
1. Authors 2. Novelists 3. Conservationists 4. Nature conservation 5. Centenarians 6. Everglades (Fla.) 7. Writers on nature 8. Short story writers 9. Biography, Individual 10. Everglades (Fla.) -- Environmental conditions
ISBN 0-8203-3071-X; 978-0-8203-3071-6

LC 2008-49073

This book presents a biography of Marjory Stoneman Douglas, "a suffragist, a lifetime feminist and supporter of the ERA, a champion of social justice, and an author of diverse literary talent. She came of age literally and professionally during the American environmental century, the century in which Americans mobilized an unprecedented popular movement to counter the equally unprecedented liberties they had taken in exploiting, polluting, and destroying the natural world." (Publisher's note)

This is "both a portrait of one of the 20th century's most important environmental figures and a history of Florida's Everglades. The long-lived Douglas (1890-1998) is best known for the classic The Everglades: River of Grass and her tireless efforts to preserve that region. But she was also a lifelong feminist and social activist who worked to advance human rights. . . . In addition to the rich detail and documentation of Douglas's life, Davis offers an impressive look at America during Douglas's lifetime and the growth of America's environmental movement." Libr J

Includes bibliographical references

Douglass, Frederick, 1818-1895

Douglass, Frederick, 1818-1895. **Narrative** of the life of Frederick Douglass, an American slave; written by himself; edited with an introduction by Houston A. Baker, Jr. Penguin Bks 1982 159p il pa $10 **92**
1. Slaves 2. Authors 3. Abolitionists 4. Memoirists 5. African Americans -- Biography
ISBN 0-14-039012-X

LC 82-5371

Originally published 1845 by the Boston Antislavery office

"Frederick Douglass became famous as a slave who escaped to the North and spent his lifetime in the abolitionist movement. His 'Narrative,' one of three autobiographical works written by the self-taught slave, is the story of his life up to his escape to freedom." Libr J

Includes bibliographical references

Doyle, Arthur Conan Sir, 1859-1930

★ Doyle, Arthur Conan. **Arthur** Conan Doyle; his life in letters. edited by Jon Lellenberg, Daniel Stashower & Charles Foley. Harper Press 2007 706p il $37.95 **92**
1. Authors 2. Novelists 3. Authors, Scottish 4. Mystery writers
ISBN 978-1-59420-135-6; 1-59420-135-8

LC 2007-14692

This volume presents the selected correspondence of the British author at various points during his life.

"This will be essential reading for all fans of Conan Doyle and his sleuth." Publ Wkly

Stashower, Daniel. **Teller** of tales: the life of Arthur Conan Doyle. Holt & Co. 1999 472p il hardcover o.p. pa $16 **92**
1. Authors 2. Novelists 3. Authors, Scottish 4. Mystery writers
ISBN 0-8050-6684-5 pa

LC 98-35059

"Stashower has done an admirable job in creating both a general, well-researched biography of a complex literary giant and in providing insights into the origins and apparent contradictions of his later beliefs." Publ Wkly
Includes bibliographical references

Drewe, John
Salisbury, Laney. **Provenance**; how a con man and a forger rewrote the history of modern art. [by] Laney Salisbury and Aly Sujo. Penguin Press 2009 327p $26.95; pa $16 **92**
1. Painters 2. Criminals 3. Impostors and imposture 4. Swindlers 5. Art dealers 6. Art forgers 7. Art -- Forgeries
ISBN 978-1-59420-220-9; 978-0-14-311740-7 pa

LC 2009-3552

"Tautly written and assiduously researched . . . [this book] has the pace and suspense of a good thriller, and a colorful international cast." Wall Street J
Includes bibliographical references

Drinan, Robert F.
Schroth, Raymond A. **Bob** Drinan; the controversial life of the first Catholic priest elected to Congress. Fordham University Press 2011 393p il **92**
1. Lawyers 2. Priests 3. College deans 4. College teachers 5. Members of Congress 6. Biography, Individual 7. Catholic Church -- Clergy 8. United States -- Congress -- House 9. Catholic Church -- United States -- History 10. United States -- Politics and government -- 1969-1974 11. United States -- Politics and government -- 1974-1977 12. United States -- Politics and government -- 1977-1981
ISBN 9780823233045; 9780823233069

LC 2010033726

This is a biography of the Jesuit priest and law professor who served as Democratic congressman from Massachusetts for ten years. Father Drinan demonstrated against the Vietnam War and ran as an anti-war candidate, called for the impeachment of Richard Nixon, and was a strong supporter of the civil rights movement. He believed that abortion was morally wrong but should not be illegal. Father Drinan withdrew his candidacy for Congress in 1980 when Pope John Paul II requested it, based on the principle that priests should not hold political office. Bibliography. Index.

"In 1970, the Jesuit priest Robert Drinan was elected to Congress after famously running as an antiwar candidate; he served for a decade, opposing the encroachment of U.S. military forces into Cambodia and actively calling for President Nixon's impeachment. Schroth's . . . biography carefully and lovingly chronicles Drinan's life and work, from his childhood and youth in Massachusetts through his devel-

opment into a passionate advocate for civil rights and ecumenical dialogue, especially between Christians and Jews, and as a moral architect for change in America. . . . Schroth's loving tribute to Drinan restores the late priest-legislator's thoughtful and forceful voice to contemporary religious life." Publ Wkly
Includes bibliographical references

Du Bois, W. E. B. (William Edward Burghardt), 1868-1963
★ Lewis, David Levering. **W.E.B.** Du Bois; a biography. Henry Holt and Co. 2009 893p hardcover o.p. pa $25 **92**
1. Authors 2. Novelists 3. Historians 4. Editors 5. Essayists 6. Sociologists 7. Nonfiction writers 8. Civil rights activists 9. African Americans -- Biography 10. African Americans -- Civil rights
ISBN 978-0-8050-8769-7; 0-8050-8769-9; 978-0-8050-8805-2 pa; 0-8050-8805-9 pa

LC 2008-696

Condensed and updated edition of a 2 volume set, first published 1993-2000

This is a biography of the African American scholar who helped bring forth the civil rights movement.
Includes bibliographical references

Dubus, Andre, 1959-
Dubus, Andre, 1959- **Townie**; a memoir. [by] Andre Dubus III. W. W. Norton & Co. 2011 387p $25.95 **92**
1. Authors 2. Novelists 3. Authors, American 4. Short story writers 5. Biography, Individual
ISBN 978-0-393-06466-7; 0-393-06466-2

LC 2010038029

This is a memoir by the author of Bluesman (1993) and The Garden of Last Days (2008). "Young Andre and his siblings, two sisters and a brother, grew up in a series of Massachusetts mill towns after their father left their mother for one of his . . . young students." (N Y Times (Late N Y Ed))

"The author grew up poor in Massachusetts mill towns, the oldest of four children of the celebrated short-story writer Andre Dubus (1936–1999), who abandoned the family in 1968 to pursue a young student. Beautifully written and bursting with life, the book tells the story of a boy struggling to express his 'hurt and rage,' first through violence aimed at school and barroom bullies and ultimately through the power of words." Kirkus

Dukakis, Olympia
Dukakis, Olympia. **Ask** me again tomorrow; a life in progress. [by] Olympia Dukakis with Emily Heckman. HarperCollins Pubs. 2003 211p il $25.95; pa $13.95 **92**
1. Actors
ISBN 0-06-018821-9; 0-06-093409-3 pa

LC 2003-49909

"Students of the theater will be interested in her views on acting. All in all, this is a satisfying look into the personal and professional life of a theater actor." Libr J
Includes bibliographical references

Dunne, John Gregory, 1932-2003

★ Didion, Joan, 1934- The **year** of magical thinking. Knopf 2005 227p $23.95 **92**
1. Authors 2. Novelists 3. Journalists 4. Essayists 5. Screenwriters 6. Nonfiction writers 7. Biography, Individual
ISBN 1-4000-4314-X

LC 2005-45132

"Several days before Christmas 2003, John Gregory Dunne and Joan Didion saw their only daughter, Quintana, fall ill with what seemed at first flu, then pneumonia, then complete septic shock. She was put into an induced coma and placed on life support. Days later—the night before New Year's Eve—the Dunnes were just sitting down to dinner after visiting the hospital when John Gregory Dunne suffered a massive and fatal coronary. In a second, [a] . . . partnership of forty years was over. Four weeks later, their daughter pulled through. Two months after that, arriving at LAX, she collapsed and underwent six hours of brain surgery at UCLA Medical Center to relieve a massive hematoma. This book is Didion's attempt to make sense of the 'weeks and then months that cut loose any fixed idea I ever had about death, about illness . . . about marriage and children and memory . . . about the shallowness of sanity, about life itself.'" (Publisher's note)

The author "chronicles the year following the death of her husband, fellow writer John Gregory Dunne, from a massive heart attack on December 30, 2003, while the couple's only daughter, Quintana, lay unconscious in a nearby hospital suffering from pneumonia and septic shock. . . . This is an indispensable addition to Didion's body of work and a lyrical, disciplined entry in the annals of mourning literature." Publ Wkly

Durrell, Gerald M., 1925-1995

Botting, Douglas. **Gerald** Durrell; the authorized biography. Carroll & Graf Pubs. 1999 xx, 644p il $29.95; pa $16.95 **92**
1. Authors 2. Novelists 3. Naturalists 4. Conservationists 5. Children's authors 6. Writers on science
ISBN 0-7867-0655-4; 0-7867-0796-8 pa

LC 00-268642

A biography of the naturalist, writer, and founder of the Jersey Zoo

"Given full access to Durrell's personal and professional papers, Botting clearly admires his subject yet presents an evenhanded account." Libr J

Includes bibliographical references

Dylan, Bob, 1941-

Dylan, Bob, 1941- **Chronicles**. v1 Simon & Schuster 2004 293p v1 il $24 **92**
1. Singers 2. Folk musicians 3. Rock musicians 4. Songwriters 5. Biography, Individual
ISBN 0-7432-2815-4

LC 2004-564

This is the first installment of a projected three-volume autobiography by the American singer and songwriter.

"This book will stand as a record of a young man's self-education, as contagious in its frank excitement as the letters of John Keats and as sincere in its ramble as Jack Kerouac's

On the Road, to which Dylan frequently refers. A person of Dylan's stature could have gotten away with far less; that he has been so thoughtful in the creation of this book is a measure of his talents, and a gift to his fans." Publ Wkly

Epstein, Daniel Mark. The **ballad** of Bob Dylan; a portrait. Harper 2011 496p il $27.99 **92**
1. Singers 2. Folk musicians 3. Songwriters
ISBN 978-0-06-180732-9; 0-06-180732-X

LC 2011-282607

The author "tells the songwriter's story through a series of concerts and albums, beginning with an appearance in Washington, D.C., in 1963. He cleverly pits the young Mr. Dylan's self-styled orphan-hobo persona against the real-life son of middle-class Jewish parents from Hibbing, Minn. When a Newsweek article in 1963 spills the beans about his actual origins, the fiction and the reality collide, and Mr. Dylan is devastated, railing at his managers for talking to the press. . . . [The author] is one of the better stylists to tackle the Dylan story. Still, like many intellectuals who write about Mr. Dylan, he errs on the side of idolatry. . . . Mr. Epstein takes us next to concerts at Madison Square Garden in 1974, Tanglewood in 1997 and Aberdeen in 2009. His meticulous set lists chart Mr. Dylan's changes from folk, to electric, to Christian and trace the high and low points of the Rolling Thunder Review (which featured Joan Baez, Ramblin' Jack Elliott and others in 1975-76) and the Never-Ending Tour (that is, Mr. Dylan's crowded performance schedule since 1988)." Wall Street J

Rogovoy, Seth. **Bob** Dylan; prophet, mystic, poet. Scribner 2009 324p $26 **92**
1. Singers 2. Folk musicians 3. Rock musicians 4. Songwriters
ISBN 978-1-4165-5915-3; 1-4165-5915-9

The author "explores the influence of the Bible, the Talmud, and the Kabbalah on Dylan's songwriting, uncovering references to these texts in each of Dylan's 33 studio albums, up through 2009's Together Through Life. Rogovoy's research adds fresh insight into iconic songs such as 'Blowin' in the Wind,' 'Like a Rolling Stone,' and 'Forever Young,' providing a deeper understanding of Dylan's Jewish influences. Chronological album-by-album and song-by-song analyses make up the book's core, and Rogovoy gives just enough biographical context to argue convincingly that Judaism strongly influences Dylan's life and lyrics." Libr J

Includes bibliographical references (p. 291-296)

Spitz, Bob. **Dylan**; a biography. with a discography by Jeff Friedman. Norton 1991 664p il pa $19.95 **92**
1. Singers 2. Folk musicians 3. Rock musicians 4. Songwriters
ISBN 0-393-30769-7

LC 88-12912

First published 1989 by McGraw-Hill

"Lamenting the impenetrable mythology that surrounds singer/songwriter Bob Dylan . . . Spitz accomplishes his demystification through a sometimes fanciful reconstruction of Dylan's life, replete with sordid examples of his reputedly capricious personality. Although the relevance of such treatment is questionable and his often lurid prose will be objectionable to some, Spitz gives a fascinating portrayal of one of the most influential and complex figures in popular music." Choice

Includes discography and bibliographical references

Wilentz, Sean. **Bob** Dylan in America. Doubleday 2010 400p il $28.95 **92**

1. Singers 2. Folk musicians 3. Songwriters
ISBN 978-0-385-52988-4; 0-385-52988-0

LC 2009-47636

"Dylan, of course, has been the subject of other biographies and has published the first book in what he intends as a multi-volume autobiography. Wilentz's book stands apart from these in the lucidity of its prose, the rigor of its research and convincing originality of the place he assigns his subject in the context of American cultural history. Fans looking for a recording-by-recording, concert-by-concert account of the singer and songwriter's career would do better looking elsewhere, though there's plenty of truly fine analysis of the most significant songs and recordings. Where Wilentz excels is in teasing out the origins of Dylan's artistic impulses, the context in which they arose and flowered, the multiple sources of his art." Los Angeles Times

Includes bibliographical references

Yaffe, David. **Bob** Dylan; like a complete unknown. Yale University Press 2011 171p il $19.95 **92**

1. Singers 2. Folk musicians 3. Songwriters
ISBN 978-0-300-12457-6; 0-300-12457-0

LC 2011-920627

"Not for the neophyte, but fascinating for obsessives who think they know everything and want to know more." Kirkus
Includes bibliographical references

Brown, Donald. **Bob** Dylan; American troubadour. Donald Brown. Rowman & Littlefield Publishers, Inc. 2014 308 p. (Tempo : a Rowman & Littlefield music series on rock, pop, and culture) (cloth : alk. paper) $40 **92**

1. Musicians -- United States
ISBN 0810884208; 9780810884205; 9780810884212

LC 2013044394

This biography, by Daniel Brown, "follows [Bob] Dylan chronologically through his career, from young troubadour in Greenwich Village who unwittingly became the spokesman of a generation through his controversial electric transformation to the 'rural glory' of the Basement Tapes to his richly creative Blood on the Tracks period to his born-again phase to his current renaissance as a rock elder and cultural force." (Booklist)

"While it covers familiar territory, the book's strength is a thorough assessment of Dylan's career, album by album, song by song." LJ

Includes bibliographical references, discography, and index

Dyson, Freeman J.

Schewe, Phillip F. **Maverick** Genius; The Pioneering Odyssey of Freeman Dyson. Phillip F. Schewe. St Martins Pr 2013 352 p. $27.99 **92**

1. Physicists -- Biography 2. Mathematicians --

Biography
ISBN 0312642350; 9780312642358

Author Phillip F. Schewe presents a biography of Freeman J. Dyson. "Schewe examines the life of a man whose accomplishments have shaped our world in many ways," focusing on theoretical physics "from quantum physics to national defense, from space to biotechnology . . . Many of his [Dyson's] colleagues, including Nobelists Steven Weinberg and Frank Wilczek, as well as his wives and his children, Esther and George Dyson, have been interviewed for this book." (Publisher's note)

Eakins, Thomas, 1844-1916

Kirkpatrick, Sidney. The **revenge** of Thomas Eakins; [by] Sidney D. Kirkpatrick. Yale University Press 2006 565p il (The Henry McBride series in modernism and modernity) $39.95 **92**

1. Artists 2. Painters 3. Sculptors 4. Art teachers
ISBN 0-300-10855-9

LC 2005-27935

This is a "portrait of Thomas Eakins, the controversial Philadelphia portrait artist whose 'failure to abide by the artistic trends that defined his times' resulted in work that was richly interesting and highly controversial. . . . Kirkpatrick gives Eakins convincing depth that reminds readers of the ways biography can enhance appreciation of art." Publ Wkly
Includes bibliographical references

Earhart, Amelia, 1898-1937

Winters, Kathleen C. **Amelia** Earhart; the turbulent life of an American icon. Palgrave Macmillan 2010 242p il map $25 **92**

1. Air pilots 2. Missing persons 3. Women air pilots 4. Memoirists
ISBN 978-0-230-61669-1

LC 2010-20026

"This book reveals a flawed heroine who was frequently reckless and lacked basic navigation skills, but who was also a canny manipulator of mass media. Winters details how Earhart and her husband, publisher George Putnam, worked to establish her as an international icon, even as other spectacular pilots went unnoticed." Publisher's note

"With erudite analysis of everything from Earhart's flying to her marriage and longtime financial support of her parents and sister, Winters proves there is still much to learn about this American icon." Booklist
Includes bibliographical references

Earp, Wyatt, 1848-1929

Barra, Allen. **Inventing** Wyatt Earp; his life and many legends. Carroll & Graf Pubs. 1998 432p hardcover o.p. pa $15.95 **92**

1. Sheriffs
ISBN 0-7867-0685-6 pa

This is a "biographical and historical study of the legend of Wyatt Earp as it occurs in text and film." Libr J

"Barra is at his best in describing the efforts of assorted Hollywood icons, including John Ford, John Sturges, and Kevin Costner, to depict the 'real' Earp." Booklist

Tefertiller, Casey. **Wyatt** Earp; the life behind the legend. Wiley 1997 403p $45; pa $19.95   **92**
1. Sheriffs
ISBN 0-471-18967-7; 0-471-28362-2 pa
LC 97-2932
This is an account "of the storied life of lawman Wyatt Earp—a villain and a hero in Tombstone, Arizona, both before and after his death in 1929. Portrayed by novelists, historians, and filmmakers, the Earp brothers—especially Wyatt—became the stuff of legends. Attempting to uncover what really happened in Tombstone, Tefertiller draws on newspaper articles and personal accounts by Earp's friends, enemies, and acquaintances." Libr J
"An engrossing, satisfying inspection of a quintessential figure in American popular culture." Booklist
Includes bibliographical references

Ebadi, Shirin

Ebadi, Shirin. **Iran** awakening; a memoir of revolution and hope. [by] Shirin Ebadi with Azedeh Moaveni. Random House 2006 232p il map hardcover o.p. pa $14.95   **92**
1. Lawyers 2. Human rights activists 3. Iran -- History -- 1979- 4. Nobel laureates for peace
ISBN 1-4000-6470-8; 978-1-4000-6470-0; 978-0-8129-7528-4 pa; 0-8129-7528-6 pa
LC 2005-55255
This is a memoir by the Iranian lawyer and human right activist.
This book "offers the chance to understand Iran's tumultuous recent history, seen through the eyes of a supremely courageous Islamic woman." Christ Sci Monit
Includes bibliographical references

Ebert, Roger

Ebert, Roger, 1942-2013. **Life** itself; a memoir. Grand Central Pub. 2011 436p il $27.99; ebook $12.99   **92**
1. Autobiographies 2. Motion picture industry 3. Motion pictures -- History and criticism 4. Writers on film 5. Motion picture critics
ISBN 978-0-446-58497-5; 978-0-446-58498-2 ebook
LC 2011022442
The book presents an autobiography by newspaper film reviewer Roger Ebert. It is "an episodic tour of Ebert's memory cabinet, one three-or-four page jot at a time, from his upbringing and his college opportunities to his days as a cub reporter in Chicago, his decision to quit drinking and join AA in 1979, [and] his screenwriting with Russ Meyer. . . . [Ebert] spends many chapters recalling the dinners and interviews he had with Martin Scorsese, Werner Horzog, Robert Mitchum, Woody Allen etc. Naturally, he also ruminates at length about his testy relationship with TV co-host Gene Siskel." (Sight & Sound)
"Ebert illuminates and assesses his life with the same insight and clarity that mark his acclaimed movie reviews." Booklist

Eckford, Elizabeth, 1942-

Margolick, David. **Elizabeth** and Hazel; two women of Little Rock. Yale University Press 2011 310p il $26   **92**
1. School integration 2. Arkansas -- Race relations 3. Little Rock (Ark.) -- Race relations 4. Central High School (Little Rock, Ark.) 5. School integration -- Arkansas -- Little Rock -- History -- 20th century
ISBN 978-0-300-14193-1; 0-300-14193-9
LC 2011-14101
"When Elizabeth Eckford braved the gauntlet of white hecklers leading to the newly desegregated Central High School in Little Rock, Arkansas, in 1957, photographers captured her image and that of the angry young white woman behind her. Elizabeth, the stoic, and Hazel Bryan, the tormentor, were frozen as icons. Elizabeth was part of the Little Rock Nine, the black teens who became the targets of race hatred as well as national and international inspirations. . . . Margolick draws on interviews and press reports of the time to present a very nuanced analysis of how Elizabeth and Hazel were affected by the scene that made them famous. . . . A complex look at two women at the center of a historic moment." Booklist
Includes bibliographical references

Edelman, Marian Wright, 1939-

Edelman, Marian Wright. **Lanterns**; a memoir of mentors. HarperPerennial 2000 xxi, 208p il pa $14   **92**
1. Mentoring 2. Social welfare leaders 3. Children's rights advocates
ISBN 0-06-095859-6
LC 00-33430
First published 1999 by Beacon Press
"Throughout this absorbing memoir, Edelman's voice resounds with spirituality, a reliance on her faith, and a belief in equality." Booklist
Includes bibliographical references

Edge, Rosalie

Furmansky, Dyana Z. **Rosalie** Edge, hawk of mercy; the activist who saved nature from the conservationists. [by] Dyana Z. Furmansky; with a foreword by Bill McKibben & an afterword by Roland C. Clement. University of Georgia Press 2009 312p il $28.95   **92**
1. Suffragists 2. Conservationists 3. Feminists
ISBN 978-0-8203-3341-0; 0-8203-3341-7
LC 2009-8551
The book discusses "Mabel Rosalie Barrow Edge (1877–1962) [who was] . . . a conservation activist . . . [and t]he founder of the Emergency Conservation Committee (ECC). . . . Using previously unavailable primary sources, Dyana Z. Furmansky offers an engaging portrait of Edge as activist while piecing together the story of Edge as a daughter, wife, mother, friend, and colleague. . . . Furmansky notes that Edge's writings, public testimony, and sometimes-assertive personal style inspired others to see and care about nature as she did. Furmansky looks for clues to Edge's commitment to nature in her privileged New York childhood, in her experiences abroad, and in her engagement with the suffrage movement. Edge's activism began after she read a 1929

pamphlet called 'Crisis in Conservation,' written in part by Willard Van Name, who would become Edge's mentor and financial backer. This pamphlet inspired Edge to found the ECC." (Journal of American History)

A biography of the conservationist and suffragette who "founded the Hawk Mountain Sanctuary and fought hard for the Olympic National Park. Clearly relishing every moment of Edge's remarkable life, Furmansky vividly enriches environmental history with her inspiring portrait of this indomitable champion of the wild." Booklist

Includes bibliographical references

Edison, Thomas A. (Thomas Alva), 1847-1931

★ Israel, Paul. **Edison**; a life of invention. Wiley 1998 552p il $50; pa $18.95 **92**
1. Inventors
ISBN 0-471-52942-7; 0-471-36270-0 pa

LC 98-10105

This biography focuses on Edison's technical work, experiments, and business dealings

"Dozens of facsimiles of his original drawings are reproduced, which fortify the impression of Edison's meticulousness, as do Israel's accounts of his business ventures." Booklist

Includes bibliographical references

Edward VII, King of Great Britain, 1841-1910

√ ★ Ridley, Jane. The **heir** apparent; a life of Edward VII, the playboy prince. Jane Ridley. Random House Inc 2013 752 p. (alk. paper) $35 **92**
1. Great Britain -- Kings and rulers 2. Great Britain -- Kings and rulers -- Biography 3. Great Britain -- History -- Edward VII, 1901-1910
ISBN 1400062551; 9780812994759; 9781400062553

LC 2013002597

This biography, by Jane Ridley, "chronicles the . . . life of Queen Victoria's firstborn son. . . . Born Prince Albert Edward . . . the future King Edward VII had a . . . reputation for debauchery. . . . Yet by the time he died . . . he had proven himself a deft diplomat, hardworking head of state, and the architect of Britain's modern constitutional monarchy." (Publisher's note)

Includes bibliographical references and index

Edwards, Jonathan, 1703-1758

√ Marsden, George M. **Jonathan** Edwards; a life. Yale Univ. Press 2003 xx, 615p $35; pa $19.95 **92**
1. Clergy 2. Theologians 3. Congregationalism 4. College presidents 5. Writers on religion
ISBN 0-300-09693-3; 0-300-10596-7 pa

LC 2002-013611

"Clearly sympathetic to his subject without ever becoming an outright apologist for either his character or his theology, Marsden . . . writes with such verve that he has given us not only the definitive biography but also a narrative that reads like a novel—that most appropriate art form for examining the interior drama of the soul." Commonweal

Includes bibliographical references

Ehrenreich, Barbara

√ Ehrenreich, Barbara, 1941- **Living** with a Wild God; a nonbeliever's search for the truth about ev-

erything. Barbara Ehrenreich. Twelve 2014 256 p. (hardback) $26 **92**
1. American authors 2. Self-realization 3. Religion -- Philosophy 4. Self-actualization (Psychology) -- Biography
ISBN 145550176X; 9781455501762

LC 2013038766

In this memoir, author Barbara Ehrenreich "recounts her quest–beginning in childhood–to find 'the Truth' about the universe and everything else: What's really going on? Why are we here? In middle age, she rediscovered the journal she had kept during her tumultuous adolescence, which records an event so strange, so cataclysmic, that she had never, in all the intervening years, written or spoken about it to anyone." (Publisher's note)

"A powerful, honest account of a lifelong attempt to understand that will please neither theists nor atheists." Kirkus

Einstein, Albert, 1879-1955

Einstein, Albert. **Einstein** on politics; his private thoughts and public stands on nationalism, Zionism, war, peace, and the bomb. edited by David E. Rowe and Robert Schulmann. Princeton University Press 2007 xxxiv, 523p il $29.95 **92**
1. Politics 2. Physicists 3. Nobel laureates for physics
ISBN 978-0-691-12094-2; 0-691-12094-3

LC 2006-100303

This is a collection of excerpts from Albert Einstein's writings on politics and other social topics.

"Powerful in its personal and political disclosures, this is an essential primary source." Booklist

Includes bibliographical references

√ Folsing, Albrecht. **Albert** Einstein; a biography. translated from the German by Ewald Osers. Viking 1997 882p il hardcover o.p. pa $20 **92**
1. Physicists 2. Nobel laureates for physics
ISBN 0-14-023719-4 pa

LC 96-26341

This biography traces "Einstein's life from early childhood through his final years at Princeton's Institute for Advanced Study. It gives equal detail to his technical accomplishments and personal life, including his role as an international spokesman for Zionism and pacifism. It also includes a more honest picture of his relationships with women." Libr J

Includes bibliographical references

√ ★ Isaacson, Walter. **Einstein** : his life and universe. Simon & Schuster 2007 xxii, 675p il hardcover o.p. pa $17.95 **92**
1. Physicists 2. Nobel laureates for physics
ISBN 978-0-7432-6473-0; 0-7432-6473-8; 978-0-7432-6474-7 pa; 0-7432-6474-6 pa

LC 2006-51264

This book tells the story of the German-American physicist's life.

"This is a warm, insightful, affectionate portrait with a human and immensely charming Einstein at its core." N Y Times (Late N Y Ed)

Includes bibliographical references

Eire, Carlos M. N., 1951-

Eire, Carlos M. N. **Learning** to die in Miami; confessions of a refugee boy. [by] Carlos Eire. Free Press 2010 307p $26 **92**

1. Cuban refugees 2. Cuban Americans 3. Memoirists 4. Miami (Fla.) 5. College teachers 6. Religious scholars 7. Writers on religion 8. Biography, Individual
ISBN 978-1-4391-8190-4; 1-4391-8190-X

LC 2009052286

Continues Waiting for snow in Havana (2003)

The author, a professor of history and religious studies at Yale, continues the memoir begun with Waiting for Snow in Havana (2003). In the present volume he writes about his introduction to America in 1962, when he was eleven.

The author "takes readers on his personal journey, beginning in 1962 when he and his brother arrived in Florida as part of Operation Peter Pan—an evacuation of 14,000 Cuban children whose parents arranged for their relocation to the United States, away from Castro. Eire's prose engages us throughout as we learn of the challenges he faced as he assimilated to his new world. . . . Readers of memoir and immigrant stories will appreciate Eire's journey and celebrate his accomplishments." Libr J

Eire, Carlos M. N. **Waiting** for snow in Havana; confessions of a Cuban boy. {by} Carlos Eire. Free Press 2003 383p il hardcover o.p. pa $15 **92**

1. Memoirists 2. Havana (Cuba) 3. College teachers 4. Religious scholars 5. Operation Peter Pan 6. Writers on religion
ISBN 0-7432-1965-1; 978-0-7432-4641-5; 0-7432-4641-1 pa

LC 2002-73875

"From 1960 through 1962, some fourteen thousand Cuban children were airlifted—unaccompanied—to the United States by Operation Pedro (Peter) Pan. Once here, they were farmed out to CIA-funded refugee camps, then to foster homes. Many never saw their island parents again. Carlos Eire, now a Yale professor of history and religious studies, was a Peter Pan. {This memoir} tells mostly of Eire's privileged boyhood during the pre-Castro 1950s." Commonweal

Eisenhower, Dwight D. (Dwight David), 1890-1969

Ambrose, Stephen E. **Eisenhower**; soldier and president. Simon & Schuster 1990 635p il hardcover o.p. pa $18 **92**

1. Generals 2. Presidents 3. College presidents 4. Presidents -- United States
ISBN 0-671-74758-4 pa

LC 90-9701

Condensed version of a two volume work published 1983-1984

"Tracing Eisenhower's family background, education, military and political careers, and influence as elder statesman, the author chronicles Eisenhower's triumphs and failures and at the same time provides a vivid picture of the off-duty Ike. . . . This is the definitive one-volume biography of Eisenhower." Publ Wkly

Includes bibliographical references

Eisenhower, David. **Going** home to glory; a memoir of life with Dwight D. Eisenhower, 1961-1969. [by] David Eisenhower with Julie Nixon Eisenhower. Simon & Schuster 2010 323p il $28; ebook $14.99 **92**

1. Generals 2. Presidents 3. College presidents 4. Presidents -- United States
ISBN 1-4391-9090-9; 1-4391-9095-X ebook; 978-1-4391-9090-6; 978-1-4391-9095-1 ebook

LC 2010-27707

The authors "present an amiable and insightful memoir of the ex-president's retirement years. . . . [David Eisenhower's] mixture of personal memories and research produces a fine addition to the history of both Eisenhower and the '60s." Kirkus

Includes bibliographical references

Korda, Michael. **Ike**; an American hero. HarperCollins 2007 779p il map $34.95 **92**

1. Generals 2. Presidents 3. College presidents 4. Presidents -- United States
ISBN 978-0-06-075665-9; 0-06-075665-9

LC 2006-52856

This is a biography of the American president and World War II general.

"With a sure touch on Ike's Kansas boyhood, marriage to Mamie, and prewar army mentors, Korda . . . successfully reintroduces the Eisenhower personality that was so popular privately, militarily, and politically." Booklist

Includes bibliographical references

Eisner, Will, 1917-2005

Andelman, Bob. **Will** Eisner, a spirited life. M Press 2005 375p il pa $14.95 **92**

1. Authors 2. Cartoonists 3. Comic book writers 4. Publishing executives
ISBN 1-59582-011-6

LC 2005-26326

This is a biography of the American cartoonist and comic book publisher.

"Besides verifying Eisner's impact on nearly every artist who drew comics in his wake, Andelman shows that Eisner's influence extends to such film directors as Spielberg and Tarantino." Booklist

Schumacher, Michael. **Will** Eisner; a dreamer's life in comics. Bloomsbury 2010 359p il $28 **92**

1. Authors 2. Cartoonists 3. Comic book writers 4. Publishing executives
ISBN 978-1-60819-013-3

LC 2010-11283

"Born in 1917, Will Eisner, now known as the father of the graphic novel, grew up in the Bronx poor but resourceful. . . . [The author] zeroes in on the essence of Eisner's success: his rare ability to unite art (he inherited his phenomenal gift for drawing from his immigrant artist father) with practicality (his mother's specialty). . . . Propelled by Eisner's geyserlike energy and output, Schumacher keenly chronicles

Eisner's brilliant career within a lively history of American comics and creates an inspiring portrait of a perpetually diligent and innovative artist whose belief in comics as fine art fueled a new and fertile creative universe." Booklist

Includes bibliographical references

Eliot, T. S. (Thomas Stearns), 1888-1965

★ Gordon, Lyndall. **T.S.** Eliot; an imperfect life. Norton 1999 721p $35; pa $18.95 **92**

1. Poets 2. Authors 3. Dramatists 4. Editors 5. Essayists 6. Literary critics 7. Nobel laureates for literature

ISBN 0-393-04728-8; 0-393-32093-6 pa

LC 98-46864

First published 1998 in the United Kingdom

"Gordon's book is the most authoritative life of Eliot thus far, and is certain to spark new controversies." Publ Wkly

Includes bibliographical references

Elizabeth I, Queen of England, 1533-1603

Hibbert, Christopher. The **virgin** queen: Elizabeth I, genius of the Golden Age. Perseus Books 1992 287p il map pa $22 **92**

1. Queens 2. Great Britain -- Kings and rulers 3. Great Britain -- History -- 1485-1603, Tudors

ISBN 978-0-201-60817-5; 0-201-60817-0

First published 1990 in the United Kingdom; First United States edition published 1991 by Addison-Wesley

This "biography is essentially personal rather than political history. . . . There are many biographies of Elizabeth, and more than a few good ones, but Hibbert's is solid and sure to charm. . . . A reliable and highly readable choice." Libr J

Includes bibliographical references

Strachey, Lytton. **Elizabeth** and Essex; a tragic history. Harcourt Brace & Co. 1928 296p il hardcover o.p. pa $14 **92**

1. Queens 2. Generals 3. Courtiers 4. Conspirators 5. Royal favorites 6. Great Britain -- Kings and rulers 7. Great Britain -- History -- 1485-1603, Tudors

ISBN 0-15-602761-5 pa

The story "begins where the conventional biography recedes, when the queen at fifty-three falls in love with a lad of twenty—a favorite whom she forgives again and again and sends at last to the scaffold." Chicago Public Libr

Includes bibliographical references

Elizabeth II, Queen of Great Britain, 1926-

Pimlott, Ben. The **Queen** : a biography of Elizabeth II. Wiley 1997 651p il hardcover o.p. pa $24.95 **92**

1. Queens 2. Great Britain -- History -- 1952-

ISBN 0-471-28330-4 pa

LC 97-21270

First published 1996 in the United Kingdom

The author explores "the role of the queen and how the events of the past few decades have changed it. Is the monarch just a figurehead, or are there specific governmental actions she can take? How did the royal family lose its privacy, along with much public respect? Pimlott tackles these ques-

tions and other historical, psychological, and sociological issues surrounding the queen and her family." Libr J

Includes bibliographical references

Elkin, Stanley, 1930-1995

Dougherty, David C. **Shouting** down the silence: a biography of Stanley Elkin. University of Illinois Press 2010 281p il $40 **92**

1. Authors 2. Novelists 3. Authors, American 4. Short story writers

ISBN 978-0-252-03508-1; 0-252-03508-9

LC 2009-24341

"The life of a writer often celebrated by critics and admired by fellow novelists but who never achieved the popular acclaim and wealth he felt he deserved. . . . Elkin stayed married to the same woman, remained a professor at the same school—Washington University in St. Louis, though he had numerous visiting gigs elsewhere—stayed devoted to his early literary mentors and to his craft, continuing to labor on his fiction and essays until multiple sclerosis and a troubled heart finally felled him. Dougherty proceeds in traditional fashion. After mentioning each new major work, he pauses for summary and analysis. . . . Though sometimes admiring rather than analytical, a thoroughly reliable portrait of a neglected novelist." Kirkus

Ellington, Duke, 1899-1974

Teachout, Terry. **Duke**; a life of Duke Ellington. Terry Teachout. Gotham Books 2013 496 p. $30 **92**

1. Jazz musicians -- United States -- Biography

ISBN 1592407498; 9781592407491

LC 2013011138

This book presents a biography of musician Duke Ellington. "The grandson of a slave, he dropped out of high school to become one of the world's most famous musicians, a showman of incomparable suavity who was as comfortable in Carnegie Hall as in the nightclubs where he honed his style. He wrote some fifteen hundred compositions, many of which . . . remain beloved standards, and he sought inspiration in an endless string of transient lovers." (Publisher's note)

Ellison, Ralph

★ Rampersad, Arnold. **Ralph** Ellison; a biography. Alfred A. Knopf 2007 657p il $35 **92**

1. Authors 2. Novelists 3. Essayists 4. Literary critics 5. Short story writers

ISBN 978-0-375-40827-4; 0-375-40827-4

LC 2006-26464

"As the first scholar granted complete access to the Ellison papers, Rampersad introduces us to people and places that reveal the total range of Ellison's sensibilities. . . . Through elegant and lively prose, Rampersad reveals sides of Ellison that are disturbing and instructive." Charlotte Observer

Includes bibliographical references

Eminem

Bozza, Anthony. **Whatever** you say I am; the life and times of Eminem. Crown Pubs. 2003 278p il $23; pa $12.95 **92**

1. Actors 2. Rap music 3. Songwriters 4. Rap

musicians 5. Recording producers
ISBN 1-400-05059-6; 1-400-05380-3 pa
LC 2003-8923

"It is Bozza's relationship with Eminem that lends credibility to this bio, as well as his ability to fold personal reminiscence into longer analytical sections on Eminem's life, the Detroit rap scene and pop culture. Bozza's unprecedented access to Mathers then and now has given rise to one of the only fully honest accounts of the now brilliant star." Publ Wkly

Includes bibliographical references

Engels, Friedrich, 1820-1895

Hunt, Tristram. **Marx's** general; the revolutionary life of Friedrich Engels. Metropolitan Books 2009 430p il $32　　　　　**92**
1. Political and social philosophers
ISBN 978-0-8050-8025-4; 0-8050-8025-2
LC 2009-03845

This is a biography of Friedrich Engels, Karl "Marx's best friend and closest ally [and] the co-author of 'The Communist Manifesto.'" N Y Times (Late N Y Ed)

"A useful and well-done study of Engels and the radical epoch he helped create." Booklist

Includes bibliographical references

Equiano, Olaudah, 1745-1797

★ Carretta, Vincent. **Equiano,** the African; biography of a self-made man. University of Georgia Press 2005 xxiv, 436p il map $29.95　　**92**
1. Slaves 2. Abolitionists 3. Memoirists
ISBN 0-8203-2571-6
LC 2005-11898

This "biography tells the story of the former slave Olaudah Equiano. . . . [Equiano authored the] 1789 autobiography, The Interesting Narrative of the Life of Olaudah Equiano, or Gustavus Vassa, the African. . . . [The Narrative] includes the earliest firsthand description by a slave of the . . . Middle Passage from Africa to the Americas." Publisher's note

"This is a thoroughly rich, engrossing, and well-researched portrait of an exceptional man and the cause he championed." Booklist

Includes bibliographical references

Erdrich, Louise

Erdrich, Louise. **Books** and islands in Ojibwe country. National Geographic Soc. 2003 143p il map (National Geographic directions) $20　　**92**
1. Poets 2. Authors 3. Novelists 4. Ojibwa Indians 5. Essayists 6. Children's authors 7. Short story writers
ISBN 0-7922-5719-7
LC 2003-45906

"Fans of Erdrich's bestselling fiction will recognize her signature combination of the sacred and the ordinary in this lively traveler's memoir, and many will enjoy the rare glimpse of her personal life as well as the physical facts of her journey from her home in Minneapolis to the lakes and islands of her Ojibwe ancestors in Ontario and Minnesota." Booklist

Erikson, Erik H. (Erik Homburger), 1902-1994

Friedman, Lawrence Jacob. **Identity's** architect; a biography of Erik H. Erikson. Harvard University Press 2000 592p il pa $19.95　　**92**
1. Authors 2. Essayists 3. Psychoanalysts
ISBN 978-0-674-00437-5; 0-674-00437-X
First published 1999 by Scribner

"Friedman's biography is lucidly written, extensively researched and covers both Erikson's rise to celebrity in the 1950s and 1960s and the attacks on his reputation from feminist and New Left critics in the 1970s." Publ Wkly

Includes bibliographical references

Ertegun, Ahmet M.

Greenfield, Robert. The **last** sultan; the life and times of Ahmet Ertegun. Simon & Schuster 2011 429p il map $30; ebook $14.99　　**92**
1. Music industry 2. Sound recordings 3. Soccer executives 4. Atlantic Records (Firm) 5. Recording industry executives
ISBN 978-1-4165-5838-5; 1-4165-5838-1; 978-1-4391-9862-9 ebook; 1-4391-9862-4 ebook
LC 2011-28507

"The eternal music-biz question—what exactly do record-label executives do?—is explored in this sprightly bio of the legendary Atlantic Records cofounder. Journalist Greenfield . . . finds Mephistophelian traits in the Turkish-American impresario—a preternaturally suave, persuasive schmoozer, Ertegun commits his share of cheats, betrayals and payola—but Greenfield credits him with creative midwifery of the rock 'n' roll revolution. We see Ertegun scouting R&B pioneers, spotting potential hits amid the dross, singing backup on the pathbreaking 'Shake, Rattle and Roll,' matchmaking super-group Crosby, Stills, Nash, and Young, and introducing Bianca and Mick. . . . A vivid saga of the an industry in its salad days, and of the unholy but fertile union of money and music." Publ Wkly

Includes bibliographical references

Esfandiari, Haleh, 1940-

Esfandiari, Haleh. **My** prison, my home; one woman's story of captivity in Iran. Ecco/HarperCollins 2009 230p il $25.99　　**92**
1. Political prisoners 2. Middle Eastern studies specialists 3. Iran -- Foreign relations -- United States 4. United States -- Foreign relations -- Iran
ISBN 978-0-06-158327-8; 0-06-158327-8

"Esfandiari, born in Tehran in 1940, had been living in the U.S. with her Jewish husband since 1980 when she returned to Tehran in December 2006 to visit her aging mother. On the eve of her departure for the U.S. she was picked up for interrogation—and ended up spending four months in solitary confinement in the dreaded Evin Prison, drawing worldwide attention. In her remarkable memoir, Esfandiari tells the story of her education, her evolution from an apolitical student to an ardent feminist and staunch supporter for the rights of Iranian women, and her many accomplishments, including serving as director of the Woodrow Wilson Center's Middle East Program." Booklist

Essex, Robert Devereux, 2nd Earl of, 1566-1601

Strachey, Lytton. **Elizabeth** and Essex; a tragic history. Harcourt Brace & Co. 1928 296p il hardcover o.p. pa $14   **92**

1. Queens 2. Generals 3. Courtiers 4. Conspirators 5. Royal favorites 6. Great Britain -- Kings and rulers 7. Great Britain -- History -- 1485-1603, Tudors

ISBN 0-15-602761-5 pa

The story "begins where the conventional biography recedes, when the queen at fifty-three falls in love with a lad of twenty—a favorite whom she forgives again and again and sends at last to the scaffold." Chicago Public Libr

Includes bibliographical references

Eteraz, Ali

Eteraz, Ali. **Children** of dust; a memoir of Pakistan. HarperOne 2009 337p $25.99   **92**

1. Muslims 2. Radicalism 3. Journalists 4. Islamic fundamentalism 5. Bloggers 6. Memoirists 7. Writers on politics 8. Writers on religion

ISBN 978-0-06-156708-7

LC 2009-9666

The author "opens his memoir with a vivid description of his father promising Allah that if God bestowed him with a son, that boy 'will become a great leader and servant of Islam.' The rest of the book finds Eteraz, whose given name is Abir ul Islam (which translates as 'Perfume of Islam') trying to come to terms with his father's mannat, or covenant, and understand the role that Islam will play in his life as well as the role he will play for Islam. . . . A gifted writer and scholar, Eteraz is able to create a true-life Islamic bildungsroman as he effortlessly conveys his coming-of-age tale while educating the reader. When his religious awakening finally occurs, his catharsis transcends the page." Publ Wkly

Evans, Harold

Evans, Harold. **My** paper chase; true stories of vanished times: an autobiography. Little, Brown and Co. 2009 515p il $27.99   **92**

1. Journalists 2. Magazine editors 3. Newspaper editors 4. Publishing executives 5. Sunday times (London, England)

ISBN 978-0-316-03142-4

LC 2009-15541

This is a memoir by the British journalist. Evans discusses his early life in Manchester, his National Service tour of duty in the R.A.F, his editorships at the Northern Echo and subsequently at the Sunday Times, where he campaigned to win compensation for the victims of Thalidomide, his relationship with Rupert Murdoch, and his second career in American publishing.

This "refreshing memoir . . . jettisons hand-wringing over the 'vanished times' of its melancholy subtitle for one man's unquenchable enthusiasm. . . . [This] is the Gospel of Evans, and the gospel makes juicy copy." Christ Sci Monit

Includes bibliographical references

Evans, Walker, 1903-1975

Rathbone, Belinda. **Walker** Evans; a biography. Houghton Mifflin 1995 358p il hardcover o.p. pa $15   **92**

1. Photographers

ISBN 0-6180-5672-6 pa

LC 95-3711

This is a biography of the photographer whose "documentary studies of the rural South during the Depression evoke the dark side of the American dream." Publ Wkly

"Rathbone does a superb job of describing Evans' elusive personality and unique vision." Booklist

Includes bibliographical references

Evers, Medgar Wiley, 1925-1963

Evers, Medgar Wiley. The **autobiography** of Medgar Evers: a hero's life and legacy revealed through his writings, letters, and speeches; edited by Myrlie Evers-Williams and Manning Marable. Basic Civitas Books 2005 xxiv, 352p il $26; pa $14 **92**

1. Civil rights activists

ISBN 0-465-02177-8; 0-465-02178-6 pa

LC 2006-296327

This is a collection of "Evers's unpublished papers and personal collections as well as [his widow] Evers-Williams's recollections. The resulting text resurrects the life, intellectual output, and creative legacy of the slain civil rights hero." Libr J

Includes bibliographical references

Evert, Chris

Howard, Johnette. The **rivals**; Chris Evert vs. Martina Navratilova: their epic duels and extraordinary friendship. Broadway Books 2005 296p il $24.95   **92**

1. Tennis players 2. Tennis -- Biography

ISBN 0-7679-1884-3

LC 2004-61918

In sixteen years, Chris Evert and Martina Navratilova met on the tennis court eighty times—sixty times in finals. . . . [This book examines] the intertwined lives of these [athletes]." Publisher's note

"This work makes a fine contribution to the history of women in sports." Publ Wkly

Faraday, Michael, 1791-1867

Hirshfeld, Alan. The **electric** life of Michael Faraday. Walker & Co. 2006 258p il $24   **92**

1. Chemists 2. Physicists 3. Writers on science

ISBN 0-8027-1470-6

LC 2005-25533

In this biography of the English scientist, the author "explains Faraday's status as one of the most inspirational and significant figures of science. . . . A vibrant portrayal that emphasizes Faraday's qualities of wonder, acuity, and diligence, which propelled him to greatness." Booklist

Includes bibliographical references

Farmer, Paul, 1959-

Kidder, Tracy. **Mountains** beyond mountains; the quest of Dr. Paul Farmer, a man who would cure the world. by Tracy Kidder ; adapted for young people by Michael French. Delacorte Press 2013 288 p. hardcover o.p. (hardcover trade) $16.99 **92**

1. Physicians 2. Access to health care 3. Human rights -- Juvenile literature 4. Right to health -- Juvenile literature 5. Poor -- Medical care -- Juvenile literature 6. Physicians -- Biography -- Juvenile literature 7. Missionaries, Medical -- Biography -- Juvenile literature

ISBN 0385743181; 9780307980885; 9780375990991; 9780385743181

LC 2012024905

This book is a study of Paul Farmer, an American doctor who opened a healthcare center for the poor in Haiti. "By Farmer's decree, no patient can be turned away. But medical aid alone is not enough. He also emphasizes the need to eliminate problems that contribute to illness: dirty water, inadequate nutrition, poor sanitation, illiteracy. . . . Encouraged by the success of his clinic, Farmer wants to replicate it as 'a laboratory for the world.'" (Christian Science Monitor)

This is a "portrait of Paul Farmer (MacArthur 'genius' grant, 1993), a driven, dedicated, rigidly idealistic doctor who commutes between Harvard and Haiti, where he works . . . to relieve the suffering of some of the poorest people on earth." N Y Times Book Rev

Includes bibliographical references

Farrand, Beatrix, 1872-1959

Tankard, Judith B. **Beatrix** Farrand; private gardens, public landscapes. Monacelli Press 2009 240p il $60 **92**

1. Garden design 2. Landscape architecture 3. Landscape architects

ISBN 978-1-58093-227-1; 1-58093-227-4

LC 2009-17705

"This book brings to life the gardens of a nascent and grand American landscape style, influenced by European gardens, modified for the nouveaux riches. You might want to get out a magnifying glass to view Farrand's meticulous plans, a trove of inspiration." N Y Times Book Rev

Includes bibliographical references

Farrington, Tim

Farrington, Tim. A **hell** of mercy; a meditation on depression and the dark night of the soul. HarperOne 2009 117p pa $18.95 **92**

1. Authors 2. Novelists 3. Depression (Psychology)

ISBN 978-0-06-082518-8; 0-06-082518-9

The author "offers a wry, almost stream-of-consciousness musing about his struggles with depression throughout a large part of his life. Bordering on a devotional of sorts, the book includes frequent quotations from John of the Cross and many other spiritual writers. Farrington also fills his book with funny anecdotes and jokes that illustrate points he is making. Ultimately, this is a personal diary of one man's journey to the other side of the black chasm of depression." Libr J

Fatsis, Stefan

Fatsis, Stefan. A **few** seconds of panic; a 5-foot-8, 170-pound, 43-year-old sportswriter plays in the NFL. Penguin Press 2008 340p il hardcover o.p. pa $16 **92**

1. Journalists 2. Nonfiction writers 3. Football -- Biography 4. National Football League

ISBN 978-1-59420-178-3; 978-0-14-311547-2 pa

LC 2008-2919

For this book, the author attended "the Denver Broncos' training camp in hopes of learning 'one very specific athletic skill'—that is, placekicking—and not to become an NFL-caliber kicker, but to become a 'credible one.' . . . It's an incredibly fascinating read for football fans, squashing the notion that the life of an NFL player is always glamorous." Publ Wkly

Includes bibliographical references

Faulkner, William, 1897-1962

★ Parini, Jay. **One** matchless time; a life of William Faulkner. HarperCollins Publishers 2004 492p il $29.95; pa $14.95 **92**

1. Authors 2. Novelists 3. Screenwriters 4. Short story writers 5. Nobel laureates for literature

ISBN 0-06-621072-0; 0-06-093555-3 pa

LC 2004-42891

The author "offers a portrait of a man always trying to invent a new mask for himself as well as the portrait of an artist consumed by a desire to tell about the South and its class struggles, its depravity, and its captivity to the double bonds of land and history. Parini examines each of Faulkner's novels, from Soldier's Pay to The Reivers, and connects the Snopses, Sutpens, and Compsons of Faulkner's mythic Yoknapatawpha County foibles, his insecurities, and his inestimable literary achievement." Libr J

Includes bibliographical references

Federico, Meg

Federico, Meg. **Welcome** to the departure lounge; adventures in mothering mother. Random House 2009 191p $25 **92**

1. Humorists 2. Caregivers 3. Aging parents 4. Mother-daughter relationship

ISBN 978-1-4000-6795-4; 1-4000-6795-2

One can read Meg Federico's "account of caring for her difficult mother, Addie (and her mother's beyond-difficult new husband, Walter) during Addie's last 18 months, and laugh all the way through in a there-but-for-the-grace-of-God way. From its opening, when Addie, 81 and unconscious on a hospital gurney, wakes up long enough to yell, 'I demand an autopsy,' to 82-year-old Walter's fascination with mail-order sex aids, the book reads like a geriatric version of a 1930s screwball comedy. Federico is a humour columnist, and her story is skilfully told, but in the end (no pun intended), it's no laughing matter. Flowing not very far beneath the surface humour, and made palatable by the laughs, are some dead serious issues that, one way or another, most of us will someday face." Macleans

Feiffer, Jules

Feiffer, Jules. **Backing** into forward; a memoir. Nan A. Talese-Doubleday 2010 440p il $30 **92**

1. Artists 2. Authors 3. Novelists 4. Dramatists 5. Cartoonists 6. Illustrators 7. Satirists 8. Authors,

American 9. Children's authors
ISBN 978-0-385-53158-0

LC 2009-21933

This is an autobiography by the American syndicated cartoonist.

"Feiffer is masterful at self-analyzing the skinny Jewish kid from the Bronx who grew up during the Depression, whose sister was a Communist, and whose distant cousin Roy Cohn was a Red-baiter, while he himself was full of insecurities but fortunate enough to 'luck into the zeitgeist.'... He offers social commentary and memorable moments from career and family life as he moved from cartooning to screen and playwriting, to authoring children's books, all the while maintaining a wry perspective that shows in the cartoons interspersed throughout this wonderful memoir." Booklist

Fermor, Patrick Leigh

Cooper, Artemis. **Patrick** Leigh Fermor; an adventure. Artemis Cooper. New York Review Books 2013 480 p. illustrations, map (hardback) $30　**92**
1. Soldiers -- Great Britain -- Biography 2. Travel writers -- Great Britain -- Biography
ISBN 159017674X; 9781590176740

LC 2013020807

Originally published: Great Britain : John Murray (Publishers), 2012

This book offers a biography of Sir Patrick Leigh Fermor, who "explored eastern Europe, fell in love with a Romanian princess and lived with her in a Balkan idyll until the outbreak of war.... He was commissioned in the intelligence corps and sent to the Middle East. After escaping from a defeated Greece he returned to Crete to help organise the resistance and made his name with the capture and evacuation to Egypt of a German general." (Economist)

Cooper "uses not only Fermor's published stories but also letters, interviews, and journals to write this authorized biography that shows the big picture without ever apologizing for her subject's faults." LJ

Includes bibliographical references (pages 401-430) and index

Fey, Tina, 1970-

Fey, Tina, 1970- **Bossypants**. Little, Brown and Co. 2011 277p il $26.99　**92**
1. Actors 2. Comedians 3. Autobiographies 4. American wit and humor 5. Screenwriters 6. Biography, Individual 7. Television scriptwriters
ISBN 978-0-316-05686-1

LC 2011002415

In this book, comedian "Tina Fey's story can be told. From her youthful days as a vicious nerd to her tour of duty on 'Saturday Night Live'; from her passionately halfhearted pursuit of physical beauty to her life as a mother eating things off the floor; from her one-sided college romance to her nearly fatal honeymoon -- from the beginning of this paragraph to this final sentence, Tina Fey reveals all, and proves what we've all suspected: you're no one until someone calls you bossy." (Publisher's note)

"Perhaps best known to mass audiences for her writing and performances on Saturday Night Live, Fey's most inventive work is likely her writing for the critically acclaimed TV show 30 Rock, in which she stars alongside Alec Baldwin and fellow SNL alum Tracy Morgan. In typical self-dep-

recating style, the author traces her awkward childhood and adolescence, rise within the improv ranks of Second City and career on the sets of SNL and 30 Rock." Kirkus

Feynman, Richard Phillips, 1918-1988

Gleick, James. **Genius** : the life and science of Richard Feynman. Pantheon Bks. 1992 532p hardcover o.p. pa $16　**92**
1. Authors 2. Physicists 3. Writers on science 4. Nobel laureates for physics
ISBN 0-679-74704-4 pa

LC 92-6577

"Although it would be hard to relate personal stories about Feynman more engagingly than Feynman himself did in What Do You Care What Other People Think? the late Nobelist could not hope for better than his biographer here delivers—a portrait in which the physicist remains a person and is not reduced to an icon of science." Publ Wkly
Includes bibliographical references

Krauss, Lawrence Maxwell. **Quantum** man; Richard Feynman's life in science. [by] Lawrence M. Krauss. W.W. Norton 2011 350p il (Great discoveries) $24.95　**92**
1. Authors 2. Physicists 3. Writers on science 4. Nobel laureates for physics
ISBN 978-0-393-06471-1; 0-393-06471-9

LC 2010-45512

"This book is highly recommended for readers who want to get to know one of the preeminent scientists of the 20th century." Publ Wkly
Includes bibliographical references

Mlodinow, Leonard. **Feynman's** rainbow; a search for beauty in physics and life. Warner Bks. 2003 171p il $21; pa $13.95　**92**
1. Authors 2. Physicists 3. Writers on science 4. Nobel laureates for physics
ISBN 0-446-53045-X; 0-446-69251-4 pa

LC 2002-31137

In this memoir "of a stint as a postdoctoral colleague of Feynman's at Caltech, the aging physicist ... cracks wise, crashes parties, works on his physics at a strip joint and needles stuffed-shirt academics.... Mlodinow's accessible style manages to convey Feynman's cantankerous appeal as well as some of the weirdness of theoretical physics without overtaxing lay readers." Publ Wkly

Ottaviani, Jim. **Feynman**; written by Jim Ottaviani; art by Leland Myrick; coloring by Hilary Sycamore. 1st ed. First Second 2011 262 p. chiefly ill. (some col.) (hardcover) $29.99; (paperback) $19.99; (prebind) $33.99　**92**
1. Atomic bomb 2. Nobel Prizes 3. Musicians -- Biography 4. Biography, Individual 5. Physicists -- Graphic novels
ISBN 1596432594; 9781596432598; 9781596438279; 9781451722406

LC 2010036260

Author Jim Ottaviani presents a "graphic novel biography ... [of] Nobel-winning quantum physicist, adventurer, musician, world-class raconteur, and one of the greatest minds of the twentieth century: Richard Feynman . . . [The book] tells the story of the great man's life from his childhood in Long Island to his work on the Manhattan Project and the Challenger disaster." (Publisher's note)

"This is a fascinating look at the life of an eccentric genius, a man who worked on the Manhattan Project, won a Nobel Prize, was the first great physicist to teach freshmen classes, and was the investigator into the cause of the Challenger explosion who discovered the problem was the 0-rings. This work was so entertaining it was difficult to put down." Voice Youth Advocates

Fillmore, Millard, 1800-1874

Finkelman, Paul. **Millard** Fillmore. Times Books 2011 171p (American presidents series) $23; ebook $10.99   **92**

1. Presidents 2. Vice-presidents 3. Members of Congress 4. Presidents -- United States 5. United States -- Politics and government -- 1815-1861
ISBN 978-0-8050-8715-4; 978-1-4299-2301-9 ebook
LC 2010-47174

The author "describes Millard Fillmore's nearly forgotten presidency by rigidly contrasting him with Abraham Lincoln, another self-made man who wrestled with racial and regional tensions as president. . . . This book is an enlightening view into the often overlooked beginnings of the Civil War, which history buffs and students alike will find enjoyable." Publ Wkly

Includes bibliographical references

Fischer, Bobby, 1943-2008

Brady, Frank. **Endgame**; Bobby Fischer's remarkable rise and fall--from America's brightest prodigy to the edge of madness. Crown 2010 402p il $25.99   **92**

1. Chess 2. Chess players
ISBN 978-0-307-46390-6; 0-307-46390-7
LC 2010-33840

"Brady's insightful biography of the legendary chess player focuses more on Fischer's life as a chess champion than on his much-publicized legal troubles and alleged psychological breakdowns. Brady first became friends with Fischer at a chess tournament when they were both children, and he combines a traditional biography with a personal memoir. . . . Brady is uniquely qualified to write this book. Not only is he a seasoned biographer and someone who knew Fischer on a personal level; he's also an accomplished chess player himself, able to convey the game's intricacies to the reader in a clear, uncomplicated manner." Booklist

Fisher, Carrie

Fisher, Carrie, 1956- **Wishful** drinking. Simon & Schuster 2008 163p il $21   **92**

1. Actors 2. Authors 3. Novelists 4. Memoirists 5. Short story writers 6. Biography, Individual
ISBN 1-439-10225-2; 978-1-439-10225-1

This is a memoir by the author of Postcards From the Edge (1987), which became a film in 1990.

In this "memoir, Carrie Fisher—actress, novelist and self-described daughter of 'Hollywood inbreeding'—writes about her tumultuous life as showbiz royalty. In Wishful Drinking, Fisher discusses her bipolar disorder, addictions and divorce—and still manages to laugh." NPR

Flaubert, Gustave, 1821-1880

Brown, Frederick. **Flaubert**; a biography. Little, Brown 2006 628p il $35   **92**

1. Authors 2. Novelists 3. Short story writers
ISBN 0-316-11878-8
LC 2005-17036

This is a biography of the nineteenth-century French novelist.

The author "has put together a judicious work that sticks to the record and relies on expertly chosen passages from Flaubert's brilliant letters and the works of his contemporaries to develop a convincing portrait, brushstroke by brushstroke." N Y Times (Late N Y Ed)

Includes bibliographical references

Fleming, Victor, 1883-1949

Sragow, Michael. **Victor** Fleming; an American movie master. Pantheon 2008 645p il $40   **92**

1. Motion picture directors 2. Motion picture producers and directors -- Biography
ISBN 978-0-375-40748-2; 0-375-40748-0
LC 2008-15255

Fleming "was the director MGM tapped to take over two thorny, unwieldy and expensive projects—'The Wizard of Oz' and 'Gone With the Wind'—and make them into enormous successes. Had he never completed those two epics, Fleming's other cinematic triumphs had already sealed his reputation. They included 'The Virginian,' 'Red Dust,' 'Mantrap,' 'Bombshell' and 'Captains Courageous.' . . . Mr. Sragow deftly takes us through the twists and turns of Fleming's life, with a vital sense of time and place. We learn much not only about Fleming, but also about his contemporaries and the Hollywood they lived in." Washington Times

Includes bibliographical references and filmography

Flynn, Nick, 1960-

Flynn, Nick. **Another** bullshit night in Suck City; a memoir. W.W. Norton & Co 2004 347p il $23.95   **92**

1. Poets 2. Authors
ISBN 0-393-05139-0
LC 2004-11796

This "memoir describes the years poet Flynn . . . spent, in his late 20s, working at one of the city's homeless shelters, where his path crisscrossed with his down-and-out father's. . . . Although it's depressing, the book never seems hopeless, because readers know the author has succeeded at doing what his father only pretended to do: write, and write well." Publ Wkly

Foner, Moe, 1915-2002

Foner, Moe. **Not** for bread alone; a memoir. by Moe Foner with Dan North; foreword by Ossie Davis. Cornell Univ. Press 2002 142p $25   **92**

1. Labor leaders 2. Health care personnel
ISBN 0-8014-4061-0
LC 2002-5100

Foner's "memoir is a unique window into the evolution of 1199 SEIU from its origins as a tiny conglomeration of drugstore employees into the country's largest healthcare union." Libr J

Includes bibliographical references

Ford, Henry, 1863-1947

Watts, Steven. The **people's** tycoon; Henry Ford and the American century. Knopf 2005 614p il $30   **92**

1. Antisemitism 2. Philanthropists 3. Automobile executives

ISBN 0-375-40735-9

LC 2004-48594

"Steven Watts is intelligent, thorough and engaging . . . in telling the story of an American who not only was influential but remains unavoidable to this day." N Y Times Book Rev

Includes bibliographical references

Forster, E. M. (Edward Morgan), 1879-1970

Moffat, Wendy. A **great** unrecorded history; a new life of E.M. Forster. Farrar, Straus and Giroux 2010 480p il $32.50   **92**

1. Authors 2. Novelists 3. Essayists 4. Authors, English 5. Literary critics 6. Short story writers

ISBN 978-0-374-16678-6; 0-374-16678-1

LC 2009-29504

In this "well-written, intelligent and perceptive biography of Forster . . . [the author attemps] to draw a picture of a figure who was sensitive, sensuous and kind, an artist who possessed a keen, plain sort of wisdom and lightness of touch that make him, to this day, an immensely influential novelist, almost a prophet. She uses the sources for our knowledge of Forster's sexuality, including letters and diaries, without reducing the mystery and sheer individuality of Forster, without making his sexuality explain everything." N Y Times Book Rev

Includes bibliographical references

Fort, Charles, 1874-1932

Steinmeyer, Jim. **Charles** Fort; the man who invented the supernatural. J. P. Tarcher/Penguin 2008 332p il $24.95   **92**

1. Supernatural 2. Parapsychology 3. Curiosities and wonders 4. Parapsychologists 5. Writers on science

ISBN 978-1-58542-640-9; 1-58542-640-7

LC 2008-5961

"Steinmeyer is an elegant and unobtrusive author who shows us an entirely fascinating, shy, and witty man. . . . This book is not to be missed." Libr J

Includes bibliographical references

Fosdick, Sarah Graves, 1825-1871

Brown, Daniel. The **indifferent** stars above; the harrowing saga of a Donner Party bride. [by] Daniel James Brown. William Morrow 2009 337p il $25.99   **92**

1. Donner party 2. Overland journeys to the Pacific 3. Pioneers 4. Frontier and pioneer life -- California

ISBN 978-0-06-134810-5; 0-06-134810-4

LC 2008-40646

"In April 1846, as young newlywed Sarah Graves departed her Illinois home on a journey to California, she could not foresee the misery and horror that awaited her. After numerous delays on their difficult westward path, she and her family found themselves dangerously behind schedule as winter loomed, and they decided to join an ill-fated wagon train under the leadership of George Donner. Ending up snowbound and starving in the Sierra Nevada range, the Donner party descended into cannibalism. . . . Never melodramatic or maudlin, Brown's work gracefully balances graphic depictions of extreme privation with humanizing glimpses of the emigrants' everyday hopes and fears." Libr J

Includes bibliographical references

Fosse, Bob, 1927-1987

★ Wasson, Sam. **Fosse**; by Sam Wasson. Houghton Mifflin Harcourt 2013 672 p. $32   **92**

1. Choreographers 2. Choreographers -- United States -- Biography

ISBN 0547553293; 9780547553290

LC 2013026082

This book, by Sam Wasson, presents a biography of choreographer and director Bob Fosse. "Fosse revolutionized nearly every facet of American entertainment, forever marking Broadway and Hollywood with his iconic style--hat tilted, fingers splayed--that would influence generations of performing artists. Yet in spite of Fosse's innumerable achievements, no accomplishment ever seemed to satisfy him, and offstage his life was shadowed in turmoil and anxiety." (Publisher's note)

Foster, Stephen Collins, 1826-1864

Emerson, Ken. **Doo** -dah!: Stephen Foster and the rise of American popular culture. Da Capo Press 1998 400p il pa $16.50   **92**

1. Composers 2. Songwriters

ISBN 0-306-80852-8

LC 98-15480

First published 1997 by Simon & Schuster

The author "explores the roots of early popular music while tracing the tragic life of composer Stephen Collins Foster. . . . He also aims his spotlight at other musical personalities of the period, and provides further illumination of how Foster's songs have been incorporated into popular contemporary melodies. . . . Emerson's exhaustive research . . . has been meticulously worked into a vivid portrait of 19th-century America." Publ Wkly

Includes discography and bibliographical references

Fowler, Ruth

Fowler, Ruth. **No** man's land; a memoir. Viking Penguin 2008 265p $24.95   **92**

1. Striptease 2. Journalists 3. Memoirists 4. New York (N.Y.)

ISBN 978-0-670-01939-7; 0-670-01939-9

LC 2007-40509

"Welsh-born, Cambridge-educated Fowler . . . recreates her dizzying descent into New York's demimonde as a strip-club dancer." Publ Wkly

"Eyebrow-raising revelations about the sex industry abound in this sharp, racy, and relentlessly candid tale." Booklist

Fox, Michael J.

Fox, Michael J. **Always** looking up; the adventures of an incurable optimist. Hyperion 2009 279p il $25.99   **92**

1. Actors 2. Parkinson's disease -- Personal narratives
ISBN 978-1-4013-0338-9

LC 2008-55129

An autobiography of the actor and Parkinson's disease sufferer.

Fox, Michael J. **Lucky** man; a memoir. Hyperion 2002 304p $22.95; pa $12.95   **92**

1. Actors 2. Parkinson's disease -- Personal narratives
ISBN 0-7868-6764-7; 0-7868-8874-1 pa

In this autobiography the actor discusses his professional career in feature films and television. He also "writes of the last 10 years, during which--with the unswerving support of his wife, family, and friends--he has dealt with his illness. He talks about what Parkinson's has given him: the chance to appreciate a wonderful life and career, and the opportunity to help search for a cure and spread public awareness of the disease." Publisher's note

Fragoso, Margaux, 1979-

Fragoso, Margaux. **Tiger,** tiger; a memoir. Farrar, Straus and Giroux 2011 322p $26.00   **92**

1. Poets 2. Authors 3. Adult child sexual abuse victims 4. Memoirists 5. Child sexual abuse 6. Short story writers
ISBN 0374277621; 9780374277628

LC 2010-39058

This is the author's "memoir of her 15-year relationship with Peter Curran, whom she met at a public pool in Union City, N.J., when she was 7 and he was 51." (N Y Times Book Rev)

"In this gut-wrenching memoir of sexual abuse, Fragoso . . . explores with unflinching honesty the ways in which pedophiles can manipulate their way into the lives of children. Fragoso met Peter Curran at a public pool in Union City, N.J., in 1985 when she was seven and he was 51. He seemed harmless, and invited Fragoso and her mother back to his house. This marked the beginning of Curran and Fragoso's 15-year relationship, which ended when Curran committed suicide at age 66. . . . Using her own diaries and the myriad letters, diaries, and photographs Curran left behind, Fragoso eloquently depicts psychological and sexual abuse in disturbing detail." Publ Wkly

Francis, Pope, 1936-

Cool, Michel. **Francis,** a new world pope; Michel Cool ; translated by Regan Kramer. William B. Eerdmans Publishing Company 2013 viii, 120 p.p illustrations (pbk. : alk. paper) $14   **92**
ISBN 0802871003; 9780802871008

LC 2013020717

Author Michel Cool "surveys Pope Francis's journey to the papacy, his convictions, his personality, his writings, and the challenges he faces in his new office--governance of the church, new evangelization actor in secularized societies, and poverty, among many others." (Publisher's note)

"An intelligent and prudent guide to the new pope, Cool's book urges a modest optimism about Francis's leadership." LJ

Includes bibliographical references and index

Francis, of Assisi, Saint, 1182-1226

Martin, Valerie. **Salvation** : scenes from the life of St. Francis. Knopf 2001 268p hardcover o.p. pa $13   **92**

1. Saints 2. Writers on religion
ISBN 0-375-70883-9 pa

LC 00-44361

"This portrait will be most interesting to readers who are already familiar with the basic facts of Francis's life and remain open to exploring a new, gritty interpretation of them." Publ Wkly

Includes bibliographical references

Frank family

Gies, Miep. **Anne** Frank remembered; the story of the woman who helped to hide the Frank family. [by] Miep Gies and Alison Leslie Gold. Simon & Schuster trade pbk. ed.; Simon and Schuster Paperbacks 2009 264p il pa $15   **92**

1. Holocaust, 1933-1945 2. Amsterdam (Netherlands) 3. Netherlands -- History -- 1940-1945, German occupation
ISBN 978-1-4165-9885-5; 1-4165-9885-5

LC 2009294295

First published 1987

"A memoir by the courageous Dutch woman who helped hide the Frank family, this book augments the Anne Frank story. Perceptive characterizations, with insight into life in Amsterdam during the Nazi occupation." SLJ

Frank, Anne, 1929-1945

Barnouw, David. The **diary** of Anne Frank: the critical edition; rev Critical ed; Doubleday 2003 851p il $75   **92**

1. Children 2. Diarists 3. Holocaust victims 4. Jews -- Netherlands 5. Holocaust, 1933-1945 6. World War, 1939-1945 -- Jews 7. Netherlands -- History -- 1940-1945, German occupation
ISBN 0-385-50847-6

LC 2003-269527

First published 1989

This volume brings together "the three known versions of Frank's diary—the original, a self-edited version . . . {and} another edited by her father. It also contains . . . handwriting and paper analyses, new documentation regarding the Frank family's arrest, and . . . information about the diary's troubled publication history." Libr J {review of 1989 edition}

Includes bibliographical references

★ Frank, Anne. The **diary** of a young girl: the definitive edition; edited by Otto H. Frank and Mirjam Pressler; translated by Susan Massotty. Doubleday 1995 340p $29.95; pa $6.99   **92**

1. Children 2. Diarists 3. Holocaust victims 4. Jews -- Netherlands 5. Holocaust, 1933-1945 6. World War,

1939-1945 -- Jews 7. Netherlands -- History -- 1940-1945, German occupation

ISBN 0-385-47378-8; 0-553-57712-3 pa

LC 94-41379

"This new translation of Frank's famous diary includes material about her emerging sexuality and her relationship with her mother that was originally excised by Frank's father, the only family member to survive the Holocaust." Libr J

Jacobson, Sidney. **Anne** Frank; the Anne Frank House authorized graphic biography. [by] Sid Jacobson and Ernie Colón. Hill and Wang 2010 152p il $30; pa $16.95   **92**

1. Children 2. Graphic novels 3. Biographical graphic novels 4. Diarists 5. Holocaust victims 6. Jews -- Netherlands -- Graphic novels 7. Holocaust, 1933-1945 -- Graphic novels 8. World War, 1939-1945 -- Jews -- Graphic novels

ISBN 978-0-8090-2684-5; 978-0-8090-2685-2 pa

LC 2010-5776

"Panel arrangements effectively show simultaneous events happening in the life of the family and in the world, while brief 'snapshots' provide enough historical information to make motives, fears, and expectations sensible to anyone unfamiliar with the Holocaust's machinery. More than simply poignant, this biography elucidates the complex emotional aspects of living a sequestered adolescence as a brilliant, budding writer." Booklist

Includes bibliographical references

Müller, Melissa, 1967- **Anne** Frank; the biography. by Melissa Muller ; translated by Rita and Robert Kimber. 2nd U.S. ed. Metropolitan Books/Henry Holt and Company 2013 480 p. hardcover o.p. (hardcover) $35   **92**

1. Children 2. Amsterdam (Netherlands) -- Biography 3. Jewish children in the Holocaust -- Biography 4. Jews -- Netherlands -- Amsterdam -- Biography 5. Holocaust, Jewish (1939-1945) -- Netherlands -- Amsterdam -- Biography

ISBN 0805087311; 9780805087314

LC 2013000297

This biography of Anne Frank "was originally published in 1998, but this expanded edition takes into account diary entries that had previously been redacted by Anne's father [Otto], as well as recently discovered letters from Otto to relatives in the United States and unpublished documents provided to [Melissa] Müller during interviews with those who knew Anne and her family." (Publishers Weekly)

"Müller includes a family tree; a family history; and considerable insight into the character, personality, and quality of life of Anne's parents, relatives, and friends. Interviews with many of these surviving people give a clearer idea of the situation and Anne's reactions to it." SLJ

Frank, Otto, 1889-1980

Lee, Carol Ann. The **hidden** life of Otto Frank. Morrow 2003 411p il hardcover o.p. pa $13.95 **92**

1. Holocaust survivors 2. Holocaust, 1933-1945 3.

Parents of prominent persons

ISBN 0-06-052083-3 pa

LC 2002-38941

Lee offers a portrait of Anne Frank's father and seeks to settle the question of who betrayed the Frank family to the Nazis

Includes bibliographical references

Frankl, Viktor E.

★ Frankl, Viktor E. (Viktor Emil), 1905-1997. **Man's** search for meaning; part one translated by Ilse Lasch; foreword by Harold S. Kushner; afterword by William J. Winslade. Beacon Press 2006 165p pa $13   **92**

1. Psychologists 2. Holocaust, 1933-1945 -- Personal narratives

ISBN 0-8070-1427-3; 978-0-8070-1427-1

LC 2006-287144

Original German edition, 1946

"Between 1942 and 1945 Frankl labored in four different camps, including Auschwitz, while his parents, brother, and pregnant wife perished. Based on his own experience and the experiences of others he treated later in his practice, Frankl argues that we cannot avoid suffering but we can choose how to cope with it, find meaning in it, and move forward with renewed purpose. Frankl's theory—known as logotherapy, from the Greek word logos ('meaning')—holds that our primary drive in life is not pleasure, as Freud maintained, but the discovery and pursuit of what we personally find meaningful." Publisher's note

Franklin, Benjamin, 1706-1790

Brands, H. W. The **first** American: the life and times of Benjamin Franklin. Doubleday 2000 759p hardcover o.p. pa $17   **92**

1. Authors 2. Diplomats 3. Inventors 4. Statesmen 5. Scientists 6. Writers on science 7. Members of Congress 8. Statesmen -- United States

ISBN 0-385-49540-4 pa

LC 00-27930

"Brands fills in disparate pockets of history (the importance of Cotton Mather in Boston, the intellectual enthusiasms of the Royal Society in London) with readable, unobtrusive scholarship. Perhaps he took as his model his unassuming subject, who treated his extraordinary achievements in fields as diverse as science and diplomacy as if they were ordinary. Franklin emerges as a man with a passion to add to human happiness." New Yorker

Includes bibliographical references

★ Franklin, Benjamin. The **autobiography** of Benjamin Franklin; introduction by Lewis Leary. Simon & Schuster 2004 143p pa $10.95   **92**

1. Authors 2. Diplomats 3. Inventors 4. Statesmen 5. Scientists 6. Writers on science 7. Members of Congress 8. Statesmen -- United States

ISBN 0-7432-5506-2

LC 2003-54477

Written between 1771 and 1788

"Franklin's account of his life, written for his son William. . . . During the Revolutionary War, the manuscript was put aside. . . . Franklin later more than doubled the length . . .

but still took the story only to 1757-1759, ending before the period of his greatest public service. Still, the book remains the first undisputed classic of American literature and one of the most interesting autobiographies in English." Benet's Reader's Ency of Am Lit

★ Franklin, Benjamin. **Not** your usual founding father; selected readings from Benjamin Franklin. edited by Edmund S. Morgan. Yale University Press 2006 303p il map hardcover o.p. pa $16   **92**
1. Authors 2. Diplomats 3. Inventors 4. Statesmen 5. Scientists 6. Writers on science 7. Members of Congress 8. Statesmen -- United States
ISBN 0-300-11394-3; 978-0-300-11394-5; 0-300-12688-3 pa; 978-0-300-126884 pa
LC 2006-45706
The editor "explains that this anthology differs from the typical selections of writings by founders, which showcase themes of revolution, war, and political philosophy. Here Morgan pursues the man himself, particularly Franklin's fascination with the curiosities of human behavior. . . . Franklin's humane solicitude and observational acuity surface in varied places (on ship, in Parisian salons) and in varied formats (personal letters, published satires) in such a way that readers encounter directly Franklin's seeming simplicity, which actually masked a deep complexity and which continually makes him the most interesting founder." Booklist

Isaacson, Walter. **Benjamin** Franklin; an American life. Simon & Schuster 2003 590p il $30; pa $16.95   **92**
1. Authors 2. Diplomats 3. Inventors 4. Statesmen 5. Scientists 6. Writers on science 7. Members of Congress 8. Statesmen -- United States
ISBN 0-684-80761-0; 0-7432-5807-X pa
LC 2003-50463
This "is a thoroughly researched, crisply written, convincingly argued chronicle that is also studded with little nuggets of fresh information." N Y Times Book Rev
Includes bibliographical references

★ Lepore, Jill. **Book** of ages; the life and opinions of Jane Franklin. Jill Lepore. Alfred A. Knopf 2013 464 p. $27.95   **92**
1. Boston (Mass.) -- Biography 2. Women -- United States -- Social conditions -- 18th century
ISBN 0307958345; 9780307958341
LC 2013001012
This book on Jane Franklin Mecom by Jill Lepore tells "the story of Benjamin Franklin's youngest sister . . . using only a few of her letters and a small archive of births and deaths." (Kirkus Reviews) "Jane's surviving letters are . . . the correspondence of a smart, witty, hardworking woman who 'loved best books about ideas,' reveled in gossip, expressed 'impolite' opinions on religion and politics, and

shared piquant observations of the struggle for American independence." (Booklist)
Includes bibliographical references

Morgan, Edmund Sears. **Benjamin** Franklin; {by} Edmund S. Morgan. Yale Univ. Press 2002 339p il $24.95; pa $16   **92**
1. Authors 2. Diplomats 3. Inventors 4. Statesmen 5. Scientists 6. Writers on science 7. Members of Congress 8. Statesmen -- United States
ISBN 0-300-09532-5; 0-300-10162-7 pa
LC 2002-1143
"The general reader will find this book to be a well-written, thoughtful appreciation of one of the Founding Fathers who did the most to shape his era and our own." Libr J
Includes bibliographical references

Franklin, Rosalind, 1920-1958
Maddox, Brenda. **Rosalind** Franklin: the dark lady of DNA. HarperCollins Pubs. 2002 380p il $29.95; pa $15.95   **92**
1. DNA 2. Chemists 3. Biologists 4. Geochemists
ISBN 0-06-018407-8; 0-06-098508-9 pa
LC 2002-68898
The author "does an excellent job of revisiting Franklin's scientific contributions . . . while revealing Franklin's complicated personality." Libr J
Includes bibliographical references

Franzen, Jonathan
Franzen, Jonathan. The **discomfort** zone; a personal history. Farrar, Straus & Giroux 2006 195p $22   **92**
1. Authors 2. Novelists
ISBN 978-0-374-29919-4; 0-374-29919-6
LC 2006-2700
This is a memoir by the author of The Corrections.
"For those who admire the razor-sharp jabs Franzen makes at himself and anyone else standing too close, 'The Discomfort Zone' is both a delicious read and a clever showcase for Franzen's talents." Christ Sci Monit

Fraser, Laura
Fraser, Laura. **All** over the map. Harmony Books 2010 271p $24; ebook $24   **92**
1. Journalists 2. Single women 3. Women authors
ISBN 978-0-307-45063-0; 0-307-45063-5; 978-0-307-45091-3 ebook; 0-307-45091-0 ebook
LC 2009-45251
"The title is an apt description of both Fraser's travels—which include jaunts to Italy, Provence, and Rwanda described in evocative, lush prose—and her frame of mind over the course of the eight years that her winning coming-of-middle-age memoir spans." Booklist

Freeman, Walter J.
★ El-Hai, Jack. The **lobotomist**; a maverick medical genius and his tragic quest to rid the world of

mental illness. J. Wiley 2005 362p il $27.95; pa
$16.95 **92**

1. Neurologists 2. College teachers
ISBN 0-471-23292-0; 0-470-09830-9 pa

LC 2004-14946

El-Hai chronicles the life and professional career of the
American neuroscientist who pioneered the use of lobotomy
in the treatment of mental illness.

"This is a well-written, thoroughly researched book, a
fascinating story that deserves to be considered as the definitive biography of a physician who went from fame to infamy
as 'the most scorned physician of the twentieth century.'"
Sci Books Films

Includes bibliographical references

Freud, Sigmund, 1856-1939

Gay, Peter. **Freud**; a life for our time. with a new
foreword. Norton 2006 810p il pa $21.95 **92**
1. Psychoanalysts 2. Writers on medicine
ISBN 0-393-32861-9

LC 2006-283026

First published 1988

"The book is beautifully written. Gay's approach is to
try to understand Freud and his alliances and environment
rather than to worship or challenge him." Choice

Includes bibliographical references

Friedan, Betty, 1921-2006

Friedan, Betty. **Life** so far. Simon & Schuster
2000 399p il hardcover o.p. pa $17 **92**
1. Authors 2. Feminism 3. Feminists 4. Nonfiction
writers 5. Organization officials
ISBN 0-684-80789-0; 978-0-7432-9986-2 pa; 0-7432-
9986-8 pa

LC 00-23920

In this memoir, "Friedan reminisces over a life of so-
cial activism that has included helping to found the National
Organization for Women, the National Abortion and Repro-
ductive Rights Action League, and the National Women's
Political Caucus, as well as writing the pivotal The Feminine
Mystique." Libr J

Friedman, Milton, 1912-2006

Ebenstein, Alan O. **Milton** Friedman; a biography. [by] Lanny Ebenstein. Palgrave Macmillan
2007 286p $27.95 **92**
1. Economists 2. College teachers 3. Nobel laureates
for economic sciences
ISBN 1-4039-7627-9; 978-1-4039-7627-7

LC 2006-52023

The author "creates a picture of Milton Friedman, one
of the leading economists and political philosophers of the
twentieth century, as not just a revered economic theorist but
also a public intellectual. Ebenstein begins with Friedman's
childhood and early career, moving through his long tenure
as an economist at the University of Chicago, and completes
the book with a picture of Friedman as a renowned public
figure. . . . Ebenstein's attention to detail and copious quotes
from others who knew Friedman well make for an engaging picture of one of America's most important economic
theorists." Booklist

Includes bibliographical references

Fuller, Alexandra, 1969-

Fuller, Alexandra. **Don't** let's go to the dogs tonight; an African childhood. Random House 2002
301p il hardcover o.p. pa $13.95 **92**
1. Authors 2. Zimbabwe 3. Memoirists
ISBN 0-375-50750-7; 0-375-75899-2 pa

LC 2001-41752

"Fuller grew up in Rhodesia (now Zimbabwe) during
the civil war, and she watched her parents fight against the
local Africans to keep their farm. In a memoir powerful in
its frank straightforwardness, she neither apologizes for nor
champions her family's views and actions. Instead she gives
us an honest, moving portrait of one family struggling to
survive tumultuous times." Booklist

Followed by Cocktail hour under the tree of forgetfulness (2011)

Fuller, Margaret, 1810-1850

★ Marshall, Megan. **Margaret** Fuller; a new
American life. Megan Marshall. Houghton Mifflin Harcourt 2013 496 p. illustrations (hardback)
$30 **92**
1. Feminism 2. Women authors 3. Feminists -- United
States -- Biography 4. Authors, American -- 19th
century -- Biography
ISBN 0547195605; 9780547195605

LC 2012042179

Pulitzer Prize: Biography (2014)

This book, by Megan Marshall, presents a biography of
American writer and intellectual Margaret Fuller. "Though
organized around places Fuller lived, the book's real driving
force is her relationships, from the perfectionist father who
gave her a thirst for education early on to the circle of academics and radicals over whom Fuller exerted her influence,
among them Ralph Waldo Emerson." (Publishers Weekly)

"A magnificent biography of a revolutionary thinker,
witness, and writer." Booklist

Includes bibliographical references and index.

Fuller, R. Buckminster, 1895-1983

Lorance, Loretta. **Becoming** Bucky Fuller. MIT
Press 2009 284p il $29.95 **92**
1. Engineers 2. Inventors 3. Architects 4. Writers on
science 5. Mechanical engineers
ISBN 978-0-262-12302-0; 0-262-12302-9

LC 2008-29418

The author is the "first to compare systematically the
authorized biography with the actual documents in Fuller's
scrapbooks. Her focus is the critical interlude between 1927
and 1930, when Fuller conceived the Dymaxion House and
first presented it to the public. Her chief insight is that if
Fuller was a futurist prophet, it was only inadvertently. He
should rather be seen as a failed entrepreneur who recast
himself as a bold visionary only after the Dymaxion project collapsed ignominiously. . . . In the end, her revisionist
Fuller is not terribly different from the one we have always
had before us—a vivid example of the inventor/salesman/
messiah type that America seems to produce every generation or so." Wall Street J

Includes bibliographical references

Gabriel, Sarah, 1961-

Gabriel, Sarah. **Eating** pomegranates; a memoir of mothers, daughters, and the BRCA gene. Scribner 2010 259p $25   **92**

1. Journalists 2. Breast cancer
ISBN 978-1-4391-4819-8; 1-4391-4819-8

LC 2009-49524

First published 2009 in the United Kingdom
"Gabriel shares an estimable gift for memoir and introspection in this forceful account of the breast cancer caused by a potentially fatal inheritance, the BRCA Gene, from her mother and her mother's mother before her and so on. . . . Raw grace is in evidence here as Gabriel lives to speak to realities to which all too many women can relate." Booklist

Galento, Tony, 1910-1979

Monninger, Joseph. **Two** Ton; one fight, one night: Tony Galento vs. Joe Louis. Steerforth Press 2006 208p il $19.95   **92**

1. Boxers (Persons)
ISBN 978-1-58642-115-1; 1-58642-115-8

LC 2006-12828

Th author offers a detailed "description of the 1939 heavyweight title fight between Joe Louis and Orange, New Jersey native 'Two Ton' Tony Galento. Monninger's real achievement is not the tale of the fight itself, but rather of the circumstances that lead up to it, and its explanation of how one chunky, heavyset bartender with a far-from-average left hook could rise to fight for the world championship." BrickCityBoxing.com

Galilei, Galileo, 1564-1642

Heilbron, J. L. **Galileo**. Oxford University Press 2010 508p il $34.95   **92**

1. Astronomers 2. Writers on science 3. Astronomy -- History 4. Biography, Individual 5. Italy -- Intellectual life 6. Science -- Italy -- History
ISBN 978-0-19-958352-2; 0-19-958352-8

This "will no doubt become the standard, comprehensive biography. . . . In one of his most inventive sections, [Heilbron] creates a Galilean dialogue on issues of algebra and geometry. Though not easy to read, it brilliantly expresses the ambiguities and blind alleys as Galileo wrestled with the conceptual difficulty of introducing a nongeometrical quantity—time itself— into the proportions." N Y Times Book Rev

Includes bibliographical references

Shea, William R. **Galileo** in Rome; the rise and fall of a troublesome genius. [by] William R. Shea and Mariano Artigas. Oxford University Press 2003 226p il hardcover o.p. pa $15.95   **92**

1. Astronomers 2. Religion and science 3. Writers on science
ISBN 0-19-516598-5; 0-19-517758-4 pa

LC 2003-4247

In recounting the story of Galileo's conflict with the Roman Catholic Church over his heliocentric theory, this book "promotes the idea that Galileo himself contributed to his fate. . . . Structuring their narrative around the several journeys Galileo made from Florence to Rome, Shea and Artigas identify numerous friendly suggestions given to him by supporters to tone things down. . . . In recounting the actual people with whom Galileo fenced, as well as the theological doctrines involved, the authors demythologize the man. Their criticism makes Galileo as interesting a figure as ever." Booklist

Includes bibliographical references

Sobel, Dava. **Galileo's** daughter; a historical memoir of science, faith, and love. Walker & Co. 1999 420p $27   **92**

1. Nuns 2. Astronomers 3. Writers on science 4. Children of prominent persons
ISBN 0-8027-1343-2

LC 99-23885

"Sobel has a remarkable ability to explain technical subjects without being simplistic or pedantic. There is a tremendous amount of fascinating detail in this work, and yet it reads as smoothly and compellingly as fiction." Libr J

Includes bibliographical references

Gandhi, Mahatma, 1869-1948

Gandhi, Rajmohan. **Gandhi**; the man, his people, and the empire. University of California Press 2008 xv, 738p il map $34.95   **92**

1. Authors 2. Journalists 3. Essayists 4. Pacifists 5. Memoirists 6. Political leaders 7. Writers on politics 8. India -- Politics and government
ISBN 978-0-520-25570-8; 0-520-25570-4

LC 2007-40986

First published 2006 in India with title: Mohandas: a true story of a man, his people, and an empire
The author exhibits a deep "understanding of the social and political landscape of India, of the cleavages of caste and religion, and of the dynamics of the dominant Congress Party (to which Gandhi had a lifelong allegiance). Rajmohan takes us at a leisurely pace through the broad sweep of Gandhi's personal and public life." Times Lit Suppl

Includes bibliographical references (p. 703-708)

★ Guha, Ramachandra, 1958- **Gandhi** before India; Ramachandra Guha. Alfred A. Knopf 2014 672 p. illustrations, maps $35   **92**

1. India -- History -- 20th century 2. Statesmen -- India -- Biography 3. South Africa -- Politics and government -- 1836-1909 4. East Indians -- South Africa -- Politics and government
ISBN 0385532296; 9780385532297

LC 2013025014

This biography "takes us from Mohandas Gandhi's birth in 1869 through his upbringing in Gujarat, his two years as a student in London, and his two decades as a lawyer and community organizer in South Africa." Author Ramachandra Guha "makes clear that Gandhi's work in South Africa--far from being a mere prelude to his accomplishments in India--was profoundly influential on his evolution as a political thinker, social reformer, and beloved leader." (Publisher's note)

"This first volume in a two-part biography of Gandhi from Guha . . . . proves itself an essential work for its bold purpose, extensive research, and engaging prose." Pub Wkly

Includes bibliographical references and index

Herman, Arthur. **Gandhi** and Churchill; the epic rivalry that destroyed an empire and forged our age. Bantam Book 2008 721p il map $30   **92**

1. Authors 2. Statesmen 3. Historians 4. Journalists 5. Prime ministers 6. Essayists 7. Pacifists 8. Memoirists 9. Cabinet members 10. Political leaders 11. Writers on politics 12. Members of Parliament 13. Nobel laureates for literature 14. Great Britain -- Foreign relations -- India 15. India -- Foreign relations -- Great Britain

ISBN 978-0-553-80463-8; 0-553-80463-4

LC 2008-149

"A well-wrought historical narrative that adds significantly to our understanding of both figures." Kirkus

Includes bibliographical references (p. 673-85)

Lelyveld, Joseph. **Great** soul; Mahatma Gandhi and his struggle with India. Alfred A. Knopf 2011 425p il map $28.95; ebook $14.99   **92**

1. Authors 2. Journalists 3. Essayists 4. Pacifists 5. Memoirists 6. Political leaders 7. Statesmen -- India 8. Writers on politics 9. Biography, Individual 10. India -- Politics and government 11. India -- Politics and government -- 1919-1947

ISBN 978-0-307-26958-4; 978-0-307-59536-2 ebook

LC 2010-34252

"Mr. Lelyveld has restored human depth to the Mahatma, the plaster saint, allowing his flawed human readers to feel a little closer to his lofty ideals of nonviolence and universal brotherhood." N Y Times (Late N Y Ed)

Includes bibliographical references

García Lorca, Federico, 1898-1936

Gibson, Ian. **Federico** Garcia Lorca: a life. Pantheon Bks. 1989 xxii, 551p il hardcover o.p. pa $18   **92**

1. Poets 2. Authors 3. Dramatists 4. Theatrical directors

ISBN 0-679-77401-7 pa

LC 88-28871

Loosely based on the two-volume Spanish work published 1985-1987

This is a biography of the Spanish writer who was assassinated during the Spanish Civil War

"Gibson's sense of place is equalled by his sense of person. His re-creation of the teeming artistic talent and the café life of Spain in the 1930s is superb. So effective is Gibson's account of Lorca's vitality and fecundity that along with admiration for the poet's opulent talent, he provokes a fierce outrage at his ultimate fate." Times Lit Suppl

Includes bibliographical references

García Márquez, Gabriel, 1928-

Garcia Marquez, Gabriel. **Living** to tell the tale; translated by Edith Grossman. Knopf 2003 483p maps $26.95; pa $14.95   **92**

1. Authors 2. Novelists 3. Journalists 4. Short story

writers 5. Nobel laureates for literature

ISBN 1-4000-4134-1; 1-4000-3454-X pa

LC 2003-58924

"Garcia Márquez tells the entrancing story of his remarkable family, chronicles the turbulence of his troubled country, Colombia, and offers a piquant portrait of himself as a struggling young writer. A resplendent memoir written with compassion and artistry." Booklist

★ Martin, Gerald. **Gabriel** Garcia Marquez; a life. Alfred A. Knopf 2009 642p il map   **92**

1. Authors 2. Novelists 3. Journalists 4. Authors, Colombian 5. Short story writers 6. Nobel laureates for literature

ISBN 978-0-307-27177-8

LC 200903806

First published 2008 in the United Kingdom

This is a biography of the Colombian novelist and author of One Hundred Years of Solitude (1967) and Love in the Time of Cholera (1985).

"This superbly researched biography is nothing short of a tour de force. . . . This work not only details the life of a great writer but also provides considerable insight into life in Latin America." Libr J

Includes bibliographical references

Garcia, Jerry

Jackson, Blair. **Garcia**; an American life. Viking 1999 497p hardcover o.p. $18   **92**

1. Singers 2. Guitarists 3. Rock musicians 4. Grateful Dead (Musical group)

ISBN 978-0-14-029199-5; 0-14-029199-7

LC 99-28775

"Jackson has written a wonderful account of the beginnings of the band . . . in the mid-1960's, their relationship with Ken Kesey and his Merry Pranksters, their embrace of psychedelic drugs and the adoration and obsession of Deadheads throughout the country." N Y Times Book Rev

Includes bibliographical references

Gardner, Chris

Gardner, Chris. The **pursuit** of happyness; [by] Chris Gardner with Quincy Troupe and Mim Eichler Rivas. Amistad 2006 302p il map $25.95   **92**

1. Securities brokers

ISBN 978-0-06-074486-1; 0-06-074486-3

LC 2005-57203

The author "recounts his 'long walk to Wall Street,' a journey that took him from a childhood in the ghettos of Milwaukee to an enormously successful career as a stockbroker in New York city." Libr J

Gardner, Martin, 1914-2010

Gardner, Martin, 1914-2010. **Undiluted** hocuspocus; the autobiography of Martin Gardner. Martin Gardner, with a foreword by Persi Diaconis and an afterword by James Randi. Princeton University Press 2013 288 p. illustrations (hardcover : acid-free paper) $24.95   **92**

1. Magicians 2. Mathematicians -- Biography 3. Magicians -- United States -- Biography 4. Journalists -- United States -- Biography 5. Science writers --

United States -- Biography 6. Mathematical recreations -- United States -- History -- 20th century 7. Science -- Social aspects -- United States -- History -- 20th century 8. Mathematics -- Social aspects -- United States -- History -- 20th century

ISBN 0691159912; 9780691159911

LC 2013016324

In this autobiography, author Martin Gardner "gives [a] look into his diverse life and interests outside the cultural mainstream, from religion, science fiction, and poetry to magic, chess, and learning to play the saw. After leading a double life as an amateur magician and philosophy major . . . Gardner was determined to make a living as a writer. He . . . eventually landed in New York City, where his Mathematical Games column in Scientific American ran for more than 25 years." (Publishers Weekly)

"Fans of Martin Gardner will find this posthumously published autobiography fascinating and will forgive the sometimes rambling, less polished style of the prose." LJ

Garrett, Pat F. (Pat Floyd), 1850-1908

Gardner, Mark L. **To** hell on a fast horse; Billy the Kid, Pat Garrett, and the epic chase to justice in the Old West. William Morrow 2010 325p il $26.99 **92**

1. Outlaws 2. Sheriffs

ISBN 978-0-06-136827-1; 0-06-136827-X

LC 2009025467

A "double biography of the iconic western outlaw Billy the Kid and Sheriff Pat Garrett. Maintaining an objective perspective on both men in a narrative closely tied to historic source materials, Gardner's quick-moving story follows events of the civil war in Lincoln County, New Mexico Territory in 1877–78, and the Kid's death-by-shooting at the hands of Garrett in 1881. . . . The final chapters describing Garrett as an old-style lawman in a postfrontier society, with interactions with President Theodore Roosevelt, serve to distinguish this book from other recent Kid biographies." Libr J

Includes bibligraphical references

Gates, Henry Louis

Gates, Henry Louis. **Colored** people; a memoir. [by] Henry Louis Gates, Jr. Knopf 1994 216p hardcover o.p. pa $13 **92**

1. Authors 2. Philologists 3. College teachers 4. Literary critics 5. Social scientists 6. Nonfiction writers

ISBN 0-679-73919-X pa

LC 93-12256

"As Gates traces his evolution from 'Negro' to Afro-wearing 'black,' he also traces the evolution of Piedmont (and, by extension, of much of America) at a time when the relationship between the races was being redefined." Newsweek

Gatzoyiannis, Eleni

Gage, Nicholas. **Eleni**. Random House 1983 470p hardcover o.p. pa $14.95 **92**

1. Martyrs 2. Murder victims 3. Parents of prominent persons 4. Greece -- History -- 1900-1999 (20th century)

ISBN 0-394-52093-9; 978-0-345-41043-6 pa; 0-345-41043-2 pa

LC 82-42803

"The separate strands lead to an intensely moving climax, making Eleni one of the rare books in which the power of art re-creates the full historical truth." NY Rev Books

Gauguin, Paul, 1848-1903

Gayford, Martin. The **yellow** house; Van Gogh, Gauguin, and nine turbulent weeks in Arles. Little, Brown and Co. 2006 339p il $24.99 **92**

1. Artists 2. Painters

ISBN 978-0-316-76901-3; 0-316-76901-0

LC 2006-10538

"Though it is impossible to entirely understand what motivated these two great artists during their weeks together in Arles, these pages deliver as close and vivid an image as may be possible." Publ Wkly

Includes bibliographical references

Gehrig, Lou, 1903-1941

Eig, Jonathan. **Luckiest** man; the life and death of Lou Gehrig. Simon & Schuster 2005 420p il $26; pa $15 **92**

1. Baseball players 2. Baseball -- Biography

ISBN 0-7432-4591-1; 0-7432-6893-8 pa

LC 2004-59137

This is a biography of the first baseman for the New York Yankees.

The author "has done a superb job of digging out the real Gehrig from behind the legend, and the mask of his own modesty." N Y Times Book Rev

Includes bibliographical references

Robinson, Ray. **Iron** horse: Lou Gehrig in his time. Norton 1990 300p il pa $14.95 **92**

1. Baseball players 2. Baseball -- Biography

ISBN 978-0-393-32882-0 pa; 0-393-32882-1 pa

LC 89-29272

"Playing in the considerable shadow of Babe Ruth, Lou Gehrig's accomplishments as baseball's 'Iron Horse' include a legendary record of 2,130 consecutive games played. . . . Robinson's narrative not only traces Gehrig's life and career but also provides an insightful look at baseball in the 1920s and the Depression years." Libr J

Gehry, Frank

Isenberg, Barbara. **Conversations** with Frank Gehry. Alfred A. Knopf 2009 290p il map $40 **92**

1. Architects

ISBN 978-0-307-26800-6; 0-307-26800-4

LC 2008-47616

This book "brings together in one book a series of candid interviews that the accomplished Isenberg recorded between 2004 and 2008, embracing Gehry's entire life and career, comprising a kind of verbal autobiography. . . . This very accessible, readable volume will be a gold mine for scholars and the general public for generations." Libr J

Gelb, Arthur, 1924-2014

Gelb, Arthur. **City** room. Putnam 2003 664p
$29.95; pa $17.95 **92**

1. Newspaper editors 2. New York Times Company
ISBN 0-399-15075-7; 0-425-19831-6 pa

LC 2003-43154

This is a "memoir of life at The New York Times by one
who spent nearly 50 years there, rising from copy boy to
managing editor; {the author} has the power to evoke whole
generations of change in the news business, reaching back
to the glorious postwar years of manual typewriters, chain
smokers, and all-nighters." N Y Times Book Rev

Gell-Mann, Murray, 1929-

Johnson, George. **Strange** beauty: Murray Gell-
Mann and the revolution in twentieth-century physics. Knopf 1999 434p il hardcover o.p. pa $15 **92**

1. Physicists 2. Nuclear physics 3. College teachers 4.
Writers on science 5. Nobel laureates for physics
ISBN 0-679-75688-4 pa

LC 99-19952

This is a biography of the American physicist who was
awarded the Nobel prize in 1969 for his work on the interaction of elementary particles and their classification

"While it is necessarily dense in parts, this book is free
of mathematics and is accessible to the advanced lay reader."
Libr J

Includes bibliographical references

Geronimo, Apache Chief, 1829-1909

Debo, Angie. **Geronimo**; the man, his time, his
place. University of Okla. Press 1976 xx, 480p il
maps (Civilization of the American Indian series)
hardcover o.p. pa $24.95 **92**

1. Apache Indians
ISBN 0-8061-1333-2; 0-8061-1828-8 pa

LC 76-13858

The author "interviewed people who knew Geronimo,
who fought with him and lived with him in captivity. She has
written a colorful narrative of revenge and raids, of escape,
pursuit and surrender. . . . Her portrait of Geronimo the old
celebrity is touching, and a tribute to an exceptional leader."
Publ Wkly

Includes bibliographical references

Gershwin, George, 1898-1937

★ Pollack, Howard. **George** Gershwin; his life
and work. University of California Press 2006 884p
il $39.95 **92**

1. Composers
ISBN 978-0-520-24864-9; 0-520-24864-3

LC 2006-17926

"This engaging biography is also a tour de force of
scholarship." Booklist

Includes bibliographical references

Ghahramani, Zarah, 1981-

Ghahramani, Zarah. **My** life as a traitor; [by]
Zarah Ghahramani , with Robert Hillman. Farrar,
Straus and Giroux 2008 242p $23 **92**

1. Political prisoners 2. Dissenters 3. Memoirists 4.

Women -- Iran
ISBN 978-0-374-21730-3; 0-374-21730-0

LC 2007-17983

"This compelling book is a coming-of-age story in
which the author examines her beliefs and emotions while
she tells of a country in turmoil." SLJ

Gibson, Margaret Dunlop, 1843-1920

Soskice, Janet Martin. The **sisters** of Sinai; how
two lady adventurers discovered the hidden Gospels.
[by] Janet Soskice. Alfred A. Knopf 2009 316p
$27.95 **92**

1. Twins 2. Travelers 3. Biblical scholars 4. Biography,
Individual 5. Bible -- N.T. -- Syriac 6. Bible -- N.T.
-- Gospels
ISBN 978-1-4000-4133-6; 1-4000-4133-3;
1400041333; 9781400041336

LC 2009011098

This is a biography of Agnes and Margaret Smith, sisters
"whose travels to St. Catherine's Monastery in the Sinai desert resulted in the . . . discovery of one of the oldest manuscripts of the Gospels ever found. . . . The Sinai Palimpsest,
or Lewis Codex, as it came to be called, would prove to date
to the late fourth century; the translation it preserved . . .
[dated] from the late second century A.D." (N Y Times Book
Rev) Bibliography. Index.

This book "is by turns a rattling adventure yarn—thick
with roving Bedouin and ancient tombs—and a testament to
the power of perseverance." Washington Post Book World

Includes bibliographical references

Gielgud, John Sir, 1904-2000

Gielgud, John. An **actor** and his time. Applause
Theatre Bk. Pubs. 1997 333p $21.95; pa $16.95 **92**

1. Actors 2. Theatrical directors 3. Theatrical producers
ISBN 1-55783-299-4; 1-55783-415-6 pa

LC 97-31701

First published 1979 in the United Kingdom

This autobiography chronicles Gielgud's work in the
theatre and motion pictures. Includes his personal reminiscences of Ellen Terry, Sarah Bernhardt, Mrs. Patrick Campbell, Bernard Shaw and Ralph Richardson, among others

Gielgud "proves himself to be a storyteller of the highest order, making this essential reading for theater lovers."
Libr J

Giffels, David

Giffels, David. **All** the way home; building a
family in a falling-down house. William Morrow
2008 314p $25.95 **92**

1. Houses 2. Authors 3. Essayists 4. Columnists 5.
Memoirists 6. Television scriptwriters
ISBN 978-0-06-136286-6; 0-06-136286-7

LC 2007-39267

Journalist Giffels "settles on a rundown, soon to be condemned early–20th century mansion, but when he arrives at
the mansion to begin his work—aided eventually by scores
of workers—he finds leaks in several areas of the roof,
crumbling brick, dry-rotted wood, warped floors, vermin
droppings and nests, as well as a beautiful old staircase, a
fireplace in the bedroom and gorgeous brass hinges and other fixtures. Convinced that he can recover the former glory

of this house with a little elbow grease and perseverance, Giffels sets out on his mission—fueled by the strains of R.E.M. and the Clash—to renovate the house one room at a time. . . . Sometimes humorous, Giffels's memoir comments sadly on one man's stubbornness and selfishness (even his wife's miscarriages don't stop him from his work) in his quest to make a house a home." Publ Wkly

Gilbert, Elizabeth, 1969-

Gilbert, Elizabeth, 1969- **Eat,** pray, love; one woman's search for everything across Italy, India and Indonesia. Viking 2006 334p $24.95   **92**

> 1. Authors 2. Novelists 3. Journalists 4. Short story writers 5. Biography, Individual
> ISBN 0-670-03471-1
>
>   LC 2005-42435

"In order to give herself the time and space to find out who she really was and what she really wanted, [the author] got rid of her belongings, quit her job, and undertook a year-long journey around the world—all alone. Eat, Pray, Love is the . . . chronicle of that year." (Publisher's note)

"A probing, thoughtful title with a free and easy style, this work seamlessly blends history and travel for a very enjoyable read." Libr J

Gilkey, John, 1968-

Bartlett, Allison Hoover. The **man** who loved books too much; the true story of a thief, a detective, and a world of literary obsession. Riverhead Books 2009 274p $24.95   **92**

> 1. Thieves 2. Book collecting
> ISBN 978-1-59448-891-7; 1-59448-891-6
>
>   LC 2009-21324

"This excellent tale of people's intimate, complex, and sometimes dangerous relationships to books will be relished by readers, writers, and collectors who are passionate about books as well as fans of true crime stories." Libr J

Gillies, Isabel, 1970-

Gillies, Isabel. **Happens** every day; an all-too-true story. Scribner 2009 261p il $25   **92**

> 1. Actors
> ISBN 978-1-4391-1007-2; 1-4391-1007-7
>
>   LC 2008-51362

"Isabel Gillies had a wonderful life -- a handsome, intelligent, loving husband; two glorious toddlers; a beautiful house; the time and place to express all her ebullience and affection and optimism. Suddenly, that life was over. Her husband, Josiah, announced that he was leaving her and their two young sons." Publisher's Note

Gillies "has created an evenhanded account of a horribly difficult time in her life, which she has probed for meaning and mined for a great story." Libr J

Ginsberg, Allen, 1926-1997

Ginsberg, Allen. The **letters** of Allen Ginsberg; edited by Bill Morgan. DaCapo Press 2008 468p $30   **92**

> 1. Poets 2. Authors 3. Poets, American
> ISBN 978-0-30681-463-1; 0-30681-463-3
>
>   LC 2008-11054

"Morgan, Ginsberg's biographer (I Celebrate Myself) and archivist, studied 3700 letters left behind by the poet, selecting 165 of the most significant for this edition; over 125 appear here for the first time. Always intelligent, sometimes gossipy, and occasionally cranky and impatient, Ginsberg is accurately reflected in these letters taken together. Correspondents include Ginsberg's father, Louis, and brother, Eugene; the poet's longtime companion, Peter Orlovsky; fellow Beat writers Jack Kerouac, William Burroughs, and Gregory Corso; and a host of friends and acquaintances." Libr J

Includes bibliographical references

★ **Jack** Kerouac and Allen Ginsberg; the letters. edited by Bill Morgan and David Stanford. Viking 2010 500p $35   **92**

> 1. Poets 2. Authors 3. Novelists 4. Beat generation 5. Biography, Individual
> ISBN 0-670-02194-6; 978-0-670-02194-9
>
>   LC 2010-03213

These two hundred letters commence "in 1944 while Ginsberg was a student at Columbia University and continues until shortly before Kerouac's death in 1969." (Publisher's note) Index.

"At times loving, at others blistering, sarcastic, often uncomfortably self-lacerating and intimate, these 200 letters, collected in a heroic editorial effort by Ginsberg biographer Morgan and independent editor Stanford, cover the years 1944-1963, the most fertile in the creative lives of Kerouac and Ginsberg. . . . Throughout, the sometimes sporadic letter writing is filled with fragments of works in progress and pungent observations on the authors and publishing people who influenced them, from Dante and Gide to Malcolm Cowley and Sterling Lord. There also is plenty of gossip about Peter Orlovsky, William Burroughs, and others in the circle." Publ Wkly

Morgan, Bill. **I** celebrate myself; the somewhat private life of Allen Ginsberg. Viking 2006 702p il $29.95   **92**

> 1. Poets 2. Authors 3. Beat generation
> ISBN 0-670-03796-6
>
>   LC 2006-50045

"Relying heavily on Ginsberg's journals and letters, as well as interviews with close friends, [Morgan] creates here a detailed, revealing portrait of Ginsberg as a gifted poet and flawed human being driven by a fierce hunger for love and an insatiable thirst for fame. This most exhaustive biography to date chronicles Ginsberg's life from cradle to grave, but a major theme is Ginsberg's love life especially his relationship with Peter Orlovsky. Although he became an icon for gay liberation, Ginsberg tended to fall in love with straight men like Jack Kerouac, Neal Cassady, and Orlovsky, which, of course, led to a good deal of rejection and frustration. Morgan's is the first life of Ginsberg to explore this curious paradox in any depth. Cleverly designed, his book includes marginal references to the poems Ginsberg was working on at the time. A monumental work." Libr J

Giuliani, Rudolph W.

Kirtzman, Andrew. **Rudy** Giuliani; emperor of
the city. Morrow 2000 333p il hardcover o.p. pa
$13.95   **92**

1. Mayors 2. Lawyers 3. District attorneys 4.
Presidential candidates 5. New York (N.Y.) -- Politics
and government

ISBN 0-06-009389-7 pa

This political biography follows Giuliani from 1989
when he first set out to capture New York's City's mayoralty
to his withdrawal from the 2000 senate race for medical and
personal reasons

Siegel, Frederick F. The **prince** of the city; Giuliani, New York, and the genius of American life.
[by] Fred Siegel, with Harry Siegel. Encounter
Books 2005 386p $26.95   **92**

1. Mayors 2. Lawyers 3. District attorneys 4.
Presidential candidates 5. New York (N.Y.) -- Politics
and government

ISBN 1-594-03084-7

LC 2005-40127

This is a "narrative of Giuliani's eight years (1994-2001)
as New York's chief elected executive. The account engagingly portrays how Giuliani made things happen, ranging
from Giuliani the man to Giuliani the politician to Giuliani
the policy innovator." Choice

Includes bibliographical references

Glavine, Tom, 1966-

Feinstein, John. **Living** on the black; two pitchers, two teams, one season to remember. Little,
Brown 2008 525p il $26.99   **92**

1. Baseball players 2. Baseball -- Biography 3. New
York Mets (Baseball team) 4. New York Yankees
(Baseball team)

ISBN 978-0-316-11391-5; 0-316-11391-3

LC 2007-50618

The author presents a yearlong look at the lives of
pitchers Mike Mussina of the New York Yankees and Tom
Glavine of the New York Mets during the 2007 MLB season.

"Feinstein achieves a double play fans should savor for
its scrupulous look at what life is like for the 21st-century
major leaguer." Christ Sci Monit

Goddard, Robert Hutchings, 1882-1945

★ Clary, David A. **Rocket** man; Robert H. Goddard and the birth of the space age. Hyperion 2003
324p il $24.95   **92**

1. Rocketry 2. Physicists 3. Aerospace engineers 4.
Aeronautical engineers

ISBN 0-7868-6817-1

LC 2002-27321

In this biography Goddard emerges "as a paradoxical
man who relentlessly promoted his work, winning hundreds of thousands of dollars in Guggenheim grants, while
shunning offers to collaborate with other scientists. Clary
presents a clear and relatively straightforward narrative of
his subject's life. . . . Readers who come to this generally
well-written biography with some knowledge of Goddard's
significance will find much of interest to fill out their knowl-

edge of this complex and fascinating scientist for whom
NASA's Goddard Space Center is named." Publ Wkly

Includes bibliographical references

Godwin, Gail, 1937-

Godwin, Gail. The **making** of a writer; v2 edited by Rob Neufeld. Random House 2011 319p v2
$26   **92**

1. Authors 2. Novelists 3. Authors, American 4.
Nonfiction writers 5. Short story writers

ISBN 978-1-4000-6433-5; 1-4000-6433-3

"Beginning in London, where Godwin had fled after a
divorce and professional disappointment, the entries chart
the gradual evolution of the themes and prose style in her fiction. . . . In addition to offering valuable glimpses of a writer
pursuing her craft, Godwin's journals are candid reflections
of her emotional swings (she worries about 'my perversity in
human relationships') and the tumultuous romantic liaisons
that reflect her search for a lifetime partner." Publ Wkly

Godwin, Gail. The **making** of a writer; journals,
1961-1963. edited by Rob Neufeld. Random House
2006 333p hardcover o.p. pa $16.95   **92**

1. Authors 2. Novelists 3. Authors, American 4.
Nonfiction writers 5. Short story writers

ISBN 1-4000-6432-5; 0-8129-7469-7 pa

LC 2005-44929

"The text begins in 1961 after Godwin, 24, has departed
North Carolina for a job at the Miami Herald—a job from
which she is soon fired. At the same time, she is married
and divorced. She records her relationships and observations
throughout with humor and humility, which results in a vivid
portrait of Godwin's daily life and her relentless pursuit of a
career as a writer." Libr J

Includes bibliographical references

Godwin, Peter

Godwin, Peter. **When** a crocodile eats the sun; a
memoir of Africa. Little, Brown and Co. 2007 344p
il map $24.99   **92**

1. Journalists 2. Zimbabwe 3. Zimbabwe -- History 4.
Biography, Individual

ISBN 0-316-15894-1; 978-0-316-15894-7

LC 2006-27973

First published 2006 in South Africa

This book is a memoir of the author's family's life in
Zimbabwe under the Mugabe regime.

"In 1996 when his father suffers a heart attack, Godwin
returns to Africa and sparks the central revelation of the
book—the father is Jewish and has hidden it from Godwin
and his siblings. As his father's health deteriorates, so does
Zimbabwe. [Robert] Mugabe, self-proclaimed president for
life, institutes a series of ill-conceived land reforms that
throw the white farmers off the land they've cultivated for
generations and consequently throws the country's economy
into free fall. . . . This is a tour de force of personal journalism and not to be missed." Publ Wkly

Includes bibliographical references

Goethe, Johann Wolfgang von, 1749-1832

Armstrong, John. **Love,** life, Goethe; lessons
of the imagination from the great German poet. 1st

American ed.; Farrar, Straus and Giroux 2007 482p il $30 **92**

1. Poets 2. Authors 3. Novelists 4. Dramatists 5. Essayists 6. Nonfiction writers 7. Writers on science
ISBN 978-0-374-29968-2; 0-374-29968-4

LC 2006-34072

First published 2006 in the United Kingdom

"Armstrong's thoughtful analysis of Goethe's life and works enables readers to fully appreciate the great German poet as an eminently human genius striving for growth and wholeness." Booklist

Includes bibliographical references

Gogh, Vincent van, 1853-1890

Gayford, Martin. The **yellow** house; Van Gogh, Gauguin, and nine turbulent weeks in Arles. Little, Brown and Co. 2006 339p il $24.99 **92**

1. Artists 2. Painters
ISBN 978-0-316-76901-3; 0-316-76901-0

LC 2006-10538

"Though it is impossible to entirely understand what motivated these two great artists during their weeks together in Arles, these pages deliver as close and vivid an image as may be possible." Publ Wkly

Includes bibliographical references

Goldberg, Jeffrey

★ Goldberg, Jeffrey. **Prisoners**; a Muslim and a Jew across the Middle East divide. Knopf 2006 316p $25 **92**

1. Journalists 2. Israel-Arab conflicts 3. Political leaders
ISBN 0-375-41234-4; 978-0-375-41234-9

LC 2006-41026

This is a "memoir of the author, an American-bred Zionist, and his 15-year relationship with a Palestinian insurgent. . . . Goldberg lived in Israel as a college student, sharpening the contradictory emotions shared by many of his American peers and eventually watching his former certainty crumble under the weight of military service at Ketziot, an Israeli prison. Grounded in his relationship with a prisoner, Goldberg's book travels from Long Island to Afghanistan as he struggles to understand Israeli-Palestinian violence. . . . Like the warring nationalisms it presents, his book is complex and deeply affecting." Publ Wkly

Goodall, Jane, 1934-

★ Goodall, Jane. **Beyond** innocence; an autobiography in letters: the later years. edited by Dale Peterson. Houghton Mifflin 2001 418p il $28; pa $15 **92**

1. Women scientists 2. Primatologists 3. Writers on nature 4. Nonfiction writers
ISBN 0-618-12520-5; 0-618-25734-9 pa

LC 00-54124

In this "volume of Goodall's letters, a lively portrait is formed through her missives as the young woman rose to the height of her scientific contributions and fame. She became a mother, divorced her first husband, married her second, and lost him to cancer. She was also the first to observe cannibalism in chimps, lost many of her study troop during a polio epidemic, and weathered the kidnapping of a group of

her students. . . . This illuminating glimpse into the mind, emotions, and philosophy of an important scientist who also happens to be a celebrated figure will be requested in all libraries." Booklist

Goodall, Jane. **Reason** for hope; a spiritual journey. {by} Jane Goodall with Phillip Berman. Warner Bks. 1999 282p $26.95; pa $14.95 **92**

1. Women scientists 2. Primatologists 3. Writers on nature 4. Nonfiction writers
ISBN 0-446-52225-2; 0-446-67613-6 pa

LC 99-25611

Primatologist Goodall "offers this autobiography as a meditation on how her spiritual beliefs evolved in response to major events of her lifetime, including her childhood in World War II-era England; early days at Gombe with the chimpanzees; rearing her only child, Grub; divorce, remarriage, and the loss of her second husband to cancer, and the turning point in her career when she dedicated herself to the plight of chimpanzees held in captivity for biomedical research." Libr J

Peterson, Dale. **Jane** Goodall: the woman who redefined man. Houghton Mifflin 2006 740p il $24.95; pa $17.95 **92**

1. Women scientists 2. Primatologists 3. Writers on nature 4. Nonfiction writers
ISBN 978-0-395-85405-1; 0-395-85405-9; 978-0-547-05356-1 pa; 0-547-05356-8 pa

LC 2006-6050

The author "details the life of the woman who revolutionized primate studies." Publ Wkly

Peterson "vividly and significantly enriches our understanding of Goodall as a scientist, spiritual thinker, and humanist." Booklist

Includes bibliographical references

Gordon, Anna, d. 2002

Gordon, Mary. **Circling** my mother. Pantheon Books 2007 254p $24 **92**

1. Authors 2. Novelists 3. Authors, American 4. Legal secretaries 5. Short story writers 6. Parents of prominent persons
ISBN 978-0-375-42456-4; 0-375-42456-3

LC 2006-102?

This is "is a moving, affecting work on the tug between mother and daughter, between w... the changing world around them." Publ...

Gordon, M...

...on, Mary. **Circling** my mother. Pantheon ...ooks 2007 254p $24 **92**

1. Authors 2. Novelists 3. Authors, American 4. Legal secretaries 5. Short story writers 6. Parents of prominent persons
ISBN 978-0-375-42456-4; 0-375-42456-3

LC 2006-102286

Mary Gordon's "memoir centers on her mother's . . . religious life and her deep respect for priests." N Y Times Book Rev

This is "is a moving, affecting work on the tug-of-war between mother and daughter, between women and the changing world around them." Publ Wkly

Gore, Al, 1948-

Zelnick, Bob. **Gore**: a political life. Regnery Pub. 1999 384p $29.95; pa $16.95　　　**92**
1. Vice-presidents 2. Conservationists 3. Senators 4. Members of Congress 5. Presidential candidates 6. Nobel laureates for peace
ISBN 0-89526-326-2; 0-89526-241-X pa
LC 99-194035

Zelnick examines the life and career of Al Gore, the former senator from Tennessee and Vice President of the United States

The author provides "a useful and comprehensive survey of the highs and lows of Gore's political career." NY Times Book Rev

Gorky, Arshile, 1904-1948

Spender, Matthew. **From** a high place; a life of Arshile Gorky. University of California Press 2000 417p il pa $21.95　　　**92**
1. Artists 2. Painters 3. Artists -- United States
ISBN 0-520-22548-1; 978-0-520-22548-0
LC 00-28715

First published 1999 by Knopf
"Spender, a sculptor and writer and the husband of Gorky's daughter, provides a personal and intimate biography of the Armenian American abstract expressionist." Libr J

Includes bibliographical references

Gorokhova, Elena

Gorokhova, Elena. A **mountain** of crumbs; a memoir. Simon & Schuster 2010 308p il $26　　**92**
1. Linguists 2. Memoirists 3. College teachers 4. Soviet Union -- History 5. Saint Petersburg (Russia)
ISBN 978-1-4391-2567-0; 1-4391-2567-8
LC 2009-474

In this memoir, Elena Gorokhova discusses growing up in Leningrad, her love of languages and her eventual move to the United States.

"Gorokhova vividly evokes the bleak years of the latter half of the 20th century in Russia, when the Great Patriotic War was followed by the Cold War and food shortages were the norm. . . . Articulate, touching and hopeful." Kirkus

Gould, Glenn, 1932-1982

Hafner, Katie. A **romance** on three legs; Glenn Gould's obsessive quest for the perfect piano. Bloomsbury 2008 259p il $24.99; pa $16　　**92**
1. Pianos 2. Pianists 3. Composers 4. Steinway & Sons
ISBN 978-1-59691-524-4; 1-59691-524-2; 978-1-59691-525-1 pa; 1-59691-525-0 pa
LC 2007-48808

This book discusses pianist Glenn Gould and a "particular piano, a Steinway concert grand known as CD 318. . . . A Romance on Three Legs is the story of Gould's love for this piano." Publisher's note

"When Gould was paired with the right composer, Bach especially, he could make you wonder if he was altogether human. And reading Hafner on Gould is sometimes as much fun as listening to him play. And that's saying a lot." Newsweek

Includes bibliographical references

Goya, Francisco, 1746-1828

Blackburn, Julia. **Old** man Goya. Pantheon Bks. 2002 239p il $23; pa $13　　　**92**
1. Artists 2. Etchers 3. Painters 4. Printmakers
ISBN 0-375-40611-5; 0-375-70579-1 pa
LC 2002-280534

The author "focuses on the second half of Goya's long and amazingly productive life, beginning with the devastating illness that left him deaf at age 47. . . . {She} not only empathetically imagines the sea change caused by Goya's abrupt sensory loss, and convincingly assesses its impact on his work, she also conjures up the artists's mise-en-scène, from the frenetic streets of Madrid to the sanctuary of the studio, the bizarreness of the court of Charles IV, the horrors of famine and war, Goya's long marriage, and, after his wife's death, late-life relationship with a much younger woman. . . . {This is a} vital, inventively participatory portrait of a master portraitist and observer of life." Booklist

Includes bibliographical references

Graham, Billy, 1918-

Graham, Billy. **Just** as I am; the autobiography of Billy Graham. HarperSanFrancisco 1997 xxiii, 760p il maps hardcover o.p. pa $18　　　**92**
1. Clergy 2. Evangelists 3. Inspirational writers
ISBN 0-06-063387-5; 0-06-063392-1 pa
LC 97-605

"In this memoir, Graham looks back at age 78 on his lifetime of personal relationships, ministry, leadership, and experiences. He chronicles such events and stories as his boyhood in North Carolina, his first steps in ministry, details of evangelistic trips and revivals, and meetings with world and local leaders. . . . All libraries would do well to stock this readable title by an important national figure." Libr J

Grandmaster Flash, 1958-

Grandmaster Flash. The **adventures** of Grandmaster Flash; my life, my beats. by Grandmaster Flash with David Ritz. Broadway Books 2008 258p il $22.95　　　**92**
1. Hip-hop 2. Musicians 3. Rap musicians 4. Disc jockeys (Club)
ISBN 978-0-7679-2475-7; 0-7679-2475-4
LC 2007-48224

"Grandmaster Flash is best known in conjunction with the Furious Five, the first hip-hop artists inducted into the Rock and Roll Hall of Fame. But before the fame, Joseph Robert Saddler was born into an abusive family in the Bronx. His evolution from a kid spinning records in the streets to hip-hop stardom is an inspiring story filled with heartbreak, determination, and perseverance." Libr J

Includes discography and bibliographical references

Grant, Lee, 1927-

Grant, Lee, 1927- **I** Said Yes to Everything; A Memoir. Lee Grant. Penguin Group USA 2014 368 p. ill. (some col.) $28.95   **92**
1. Autobiographies 2. Actresses -- Biography 3. Actors -- United States -- Biography 4. Motion picture producers and directors -- Biography
ISBN 039916930X; 9780399169304

LC 2014011916
This autobiography tells how "actress Lee Grant spent her youth accumulating more experiences than most people have in a lifetime: from student at the famed Neighborhood Playhouse to member of the legendary Actors Studio; from celebrated Broadway star to Vogue 'It Girl.' . . . Finding reserves of strength she didn't know she had, Grant took action against anti-Communist witch hunts in the arts." (Publisher's note)

"Grant doesn't make us read between the lines here; it's all right there, on the page. . . . An excellent show-business autobiography." Booklist

Grant, Ulysses S. (Ulysses Simpson), 1822-1885

Bunting, Josiah. **Ulysses** S. Grant; [by] Josiah Bunting III. Times Books 2004 xx, 180p (American presidents series) $20   **92**
1. Generals 2. Presidents 3. United States -- History -- 1861-1865, Civil War
ISBN 0-8050-6949-6

LC 2004-47889
"This superb book should support those who are gradually moving Grant from the lower to the upper half of rankings of chief executives." Publ Wkly
Includes bibliographical references

★ Catton, Bruce, 1899-1978. **Grant** moves south; with maps by Samuel H. Bryant. Little, Brown 1960 564p maps hardcover o.p. pa $24.99   **92**
1. Generals 2. Presidents 3. United States -- History -- 1861-1865, Civil War -- Campaigns
ISBN 0-316-13244-6 pa
"Grant's development as a man and leader is brilliantly shown in this reconstruction of his Mississippi campaign." Booklist
Includes bibliographical references

Catton, Bruce, 1899-1978. **Grant** takes command; with maps by Samuel H. Bryant. Little, Brown 1969 556p maps hardcover o.p. pa $24.99   **92**
1. Generals 2. Presidents 3. United States -- History -- 1861-1865, Civil War -- Campaigns
ISBN 0-316-13240-3 pa
This sequel to Grant moves south "takes up Ulysses S. Grant's career just after his capture of Vicksburg in 1863. . . . It carries the action right up to Richmond and Lee's surrender at Appomattox." Publ Wkly
Includes bibliographical references

Flood, Charles Bracelen. **Grant** and Sherman; the friendship that won the Civil War. Farrar, Straus and Giroux 2005 460p il map $27   **92**
1. Generals 2. Presidents 3. Memoirists 4. Secretaries of war 5. United States -- History -- 1861-1865, Civil War
ISBN 0-374-16600-5

LC 2005-04170
The author "underscores the powerful bond formed between Ulysses S. Grant and William Tecumseh Sherman and tells the story of a friendship that would influence both the politics and the military operations of the Civil War. . . . One of the big-profile history books of the season and highly recommended for all history-minded readers." Booklist
Includes bibliographical references

Flood, Charles Bracelen. **Grant's** final victory; Ulysses S. Grant's heroic last year. Da Capo Press 2011 288p il   **92**
1. Generals 2. Presidents 3. Presidents -- United States
ISBN 9780306820281; 9780306820564

LC 2011020263
The author "writes movingly of the last months of Ulysses S. Grant's life, 1884–85, when, in the wake of financial ruin from a failed investment and suffering from terminal throat cancer, he labored to complete his memoirs (which would be published by Mark Twain) so that his family might once again prosper after his death. . . . Those who like presidential or post-Civil War history will especially enjoy this book, aimed at general readers, with its compelling portrait of a well-known historical figure." Libr J
Includes bibliographical references

Korda, Michael. **Ulysses** S. Grant: the unlikely hero. Atlas Books\HarperCollins 2004 161p (Eminent lives) $19.95   **92**
1. Generals 2. Presidents 3. United States -- History -- 1861-1865, Civil War
ISBN 0-06-059015-7

LC 2004-46125
The author "freshly characterizes his man without psychologizing an unpromising subject. . . . This is a highly readable, accurate study of the man." Publ Wkly
Includes bibliographical references

Grealy, Lucy, 1963-2002

Patchett, Ann. **Truth** & beauty; a friendship. HarperCollins Publishers 2004 257p hardcover o.p. pa $13.95   **92**
1. Poets 2. Authors 3. Novelists 4. Women authors 5. Memoirists
ISBN 0-06-057214-0; 0-06-057215-9 pa

LC 2003-67586
"As young writers. Patchett and Lucy Grealy began an intense friendship that lasted until Grealy's tragic death. With intimacy, gracy, and humor, Patchett's memoir captures Lucy's exuberance and her roller-coaster struggles with disfigurement and depression." Booklist

Green, C.

Wild, David. **Everybody's** brother; CeeLo Green, Big Gipp, David Wild. Grand Central Pub. 2013 288 p. (hardcover) $28   **92**
1. Biography 2. Rap musicians
ISBN 1455516678; 9781455516674; 9781619696358
LC 2013942951

Author CeeLo Green presents an autobiography. "This story begins in The Dirty South, where South Atlanta's native son transformed himself into the Abominable SHOWman. Along the way, innocence was lost; farther down the path, his parents passed on. Yet he still found family at the Dungeon with the likes of Goodie Mob, Outkast, L.A. Reid, and Lauryn Hill. Then one day he teamed up with Danger Mouse and everything went 'Crazy.' The book "is the untold story of CeeLo Green's rise from the streets of Atlanta to the top of the charts." (Publisher's note)

Greenberg, Michael, 1952-

Greenberg, Michael. **Beg,** borrow, steal; a writer's life. Other Press 2009 217p $19.95 **92**

1. Authors 2. Journalists 3. Essayists 4. Columnists 5. Memoirists 6. Literary critics 7. Short story writers
ISBN 978-1-59051-341-5

LC 2009-17790

"The short pieces in 'Beg, Borrow, Steal' are in the tradition of the literary-journalistic essays that Europeans call feuilletons. Although flexible, this form requires skill and concision, and Michael Greenberg uses it brilliantly. Personal experience is at the center of each piece, but none is solipsistic; the tone is understated and ironic, and every essay contains a hard-won glimmer of insight." Washington Post Book World

Greenberg, Sally, 1981-

Greenberg, Michael. **Hurry** down sunshine. Other Press 2008 234p $22 **92**

1. Mentally ill 2. Manic-depressive illness
ISBN 978-1-59051-191-6; 1-59051-191-3

LC 2008-2674

Greenberg presents a memoir of his daughter Sally, who began experiencing psychiatric problems at the age of fifteen.

"In its detail, depth, richness, and sheer intelligence, Hurry Down Sunshine will be recognized as a classic of its kind." New York Rev Books

Greene, Belle da Costa, 1883-1950

Ardizzone, Heidi. An **illuminated** life; Belle da Costa Greene's journey from prejudice to privilege. W. W. Norton & Co. 2007 580p il $35 **92**

1. Librarians 2. African American women 3. African American librarians 4. Bibliographers 5. Morgan Library & Museum (New York, N.Y.)
ISBN 978-0-393-05104-9; 0-393-05104-8

LC 2007-04967

This is a biography of the first director of the Morgan Library.

"Ardizzone more than succeeds in portraying a vivid figure who rose to the top in a segregated, paternalistic world yet suffered loneliness and was haunted by personal demons. A valuable work for students of early 20th-century culture as well as for librarians, feminists, and students of race relations." Libr J

Includes bibliographical references

Greene, Graham, 1904-1991

Greene, Graham. **Graham** Greene; a life in letters. edited by Richard Greene. W. W. Norton & Company 2008 446p il $35 **92**

1. Authors 2. Novelists 3. Essayists 4. Travel writers 5. Short story writers 6. Motion picture critics
ISBN 978-0-393-06642-5; 0-393-06642-8

LC 2008-40452

First published 2007 in the United Kingdom

"Greene is presented in these letters through the five main preoccupations of his life: Roman Catholicism, politics, love, travel and . . . the processes of writing and publishing. . . . This well-thought-out collection newly reveals a remarkable activist-writer." Publ Wkly

Includes bibliographical references

Sherry, Norman. The **life** of Graham Greene. v3 Viking 2004 800p v3 $39.95 **92**

1. Authors 2. Novelists 3. Essayists 4. Travel writers 5. Short story writers 6. Motion picture critics
ISBN 0-670-0342-9

"In the final volume of this definitive life of Greene . . . {Sherry} chronicles years during which Greene turned almost everything—politics, romance, literature, and religion—into reasons for conflict. . . . Nor did Greene's religious faith—eaten away by doubt and self-accusation—provide much late-life serenity or assurance. In narrating Greene's unending struggles, Sherry candidly confronts the author's deplorable lapses in craft and judgment. But, in the end, he delivers a writer who triumphed in his truth-seeking artistry and who even experienced the unexpected final beauty of peace on his Swiss deathbed. Greene's many readers will cherish this poignant and detailed concluding volume to a masterful portrait." Booklist

Greenlaw, Lavinia, 1962-

Greenlaw, Lavinia. The **importance** of music to girls. Farrar, Straus and Giroux 2008 195p $23; pa $15 **92**

1. Poets 2. Authors 3. Novelists 4. Women authors 5. Music appreciation
ISBN 978-0-374-17454-5; 978-0-312-42837-2 pa

LC 2008-925188

First published 2007 in the United Kingdom

The author "brings her youth to life in this book. And whether it's madrigal singers rehearsing in the living room or metal blasting from the radio in a car full of partying teenagers, readers will hear the accompanying soundtrack wafting off the pages." Washington Post

Greenspan, Alan

Greenspan, Alan. The **age** of turbulence; adventures in a new world. Penguin Press 2007 531p il $35 **92**

1. Economists 2. Bankers 3. Government officials 4. Presidential advisers 5. Regulatory agency officials
ISBN 978-1-59420-131-8

LC 2007-13169

"The former U. S. Federal Reserve Board chair relates his life story, focusing on lessons learned in government service, particularly post-9/11. He also includes political anecdotes, asserts his faith in market capitalism, and shares his predictions for the world of 2030." Libr J

Includes bibliographical references

Martin, Justin. **Greenspan**; the man behind money. Perseus Bks. 2000 284p il hardcover o.p. pa $17.50 **92**

1. Economists 2. Bankers 3. Government officials 4. Presidential advisers 5. Regulatory agency officials 6. Federal Reserve System (U.S.) -- Board of Governors

ISBN 0-7382-0524-9 pa

In this biography the author "shows how Alan Greenspan's early experiences have shaped his tenure as chairman of the Federal Reserve Board." N Y Times Book Rev

Includes bibliographical references

Grennan, Conor

Grennan, Conor. **Little** princes; one man's promise to bring home the lost children of Nepal. William Morrow 2011 294p il map $25.99; ebook $20.99 **92**

1. Orphanages 2. Nepal 3. Child benefactors

ISBN 978-0-06-193005-8; 0-06-193005-9; 978-0-06-204243-9 ebook; 0-06-204243-2 ebook

Describes how the author's three-month service as a volunteer at the Little Princes Orphanage in wartorn Nepal became a commitment for advocacy and reform when he discovered that many of his young charges were victims rescued from human traffickers.

"If you've never believed in miracles, this book could convince you otherwise. . . . Like the children he writes about, Grennan has boundless resilience and determination, in addition to self-effacing humor and tunnel-vision devotion. He's also a good writer." Christ Sci Monit

Grey, Zane, 1872-1939

Pauly, Thomas H. **Zane** Grey; his life, his adventures, his women. University of Illinois Press 2005 385p il map $34.95 **92**

1. Authors 2. Novelists 3. Western writers 4. Biography, Individual

ISBN 0-252-03044-3; 978-0-252-03044-4

LC 2005-9413

This is a biography of the "author of westerns like 'Riders of the Purple Sage,' 'The Light of Western Stars' and 'Code of the West.'" (N Y Times Book Rev) Index.

The author "offers an honest exploration of the complex author. . . . A solid, entertaining read." Choice

Includes bibliographical references

Grimes, Tom, 1954-

Grimes, Tom. **Mentor**; a memoir. Tin House Books 2010 242p $24.95; pa $16.95 **92**

1. Authors 2. Mentoring 3. Novelists 4. Authorship 5. Dramatists 6. Creative writing 7. Memoirists 8. Biographers 9. Authors, American 10. Short story writers 11. Iowa Writers' Workshop

ISBN 978-0-9825048-8-8; 978-0-9825048-9-5 pa

LC 2010-7124

Grimes discusses his life as a writer, his friendship with Frank Conroy, the director of the Iowa Writers Workshop, the publication of his first book, Season's End, and the effect on Grimes of its poor reception.

"Anyone who dreams of becoming a novelist will need to read Tom Grimes's brutally honest and wonderful Mentor. While there have been plenty of books on how to write, or how to get published, or how to promote your work, as well as a number of triumphalist accounts of 'making it,' this is a story of what it's like to just miss succeeding." Washington Post

Includes bibliographical references

Grogan, John, 1957-

Grogan, John. The **longest** trip home; a memoir. William Morrow 2008 334p il $25.95 **92**

1. Journalists 2. Memoirists

ISBN 978-0-06-171324-8; 0-06-171324-4

LC 2008-25913

This is the author's "hilarious and touching memoir of his childhood in suburban Detroit." Publ Wkly

Groom, Kelle

Groom, Kelle. **I** wore the ocean in the shape of a girl; a memoir. Free Press 2011 238p $23 **92**

1. Poets 2. Authors 3. Alcoholism 4. Bereavement 5. Essayists 6. Memoirists 7. Poets, American 8. Magazine editors 9. Short story writers

ISBN 978-1-4516-1668-2

LC 2010048931

"Groom's stunning memoir reads more like poetry than prose and leaves the 'brain singing with neurons like a city at night.' Precise diction and punchy syntax coupled with raw subject matter give birth to an intense narrative containing some matter-of-fact passages almost too grueling to accept." Booklist

Includes bibliographical references

Grove, Andrew S., 1936-

Tedlow, Richard S. **Andy** Grove; the life and times of an American. Portfolio 2006 512p $29.95 **92**

1. Intel Corp. 2. College teachers 3. Electronics industry executives

ISBN 978-1-591-84139-5; 1-591-84139-9

LC 2006-49829

The author "presents the story of Andy Grove, a penniless Hungarian immigrant who became an icon of twentieth-century corporate America. Grove joined Intel in 1968 at its founding, and while he was CEO from 1987 to 1998, 'market capitalization increased from $4.3 billion to $197.6 billion, a compound annual growth rate of 42% and a total increase of almost 4,500%.' Grove led the company with Intel's 386 microprocessor, which became the industry standard. Tedlow describes Grove, Time magazine's 1997 man of the year, as an extraordinary manager, author, and significant player in the fights against prostate cancer and Parkinson's disease. With unique access to Grove and Intel's internal resources and documents, Tedlow claims objectivity, telling the truth as he sees it in this laudatory narrative, although he also confirms his close ties to the subject." Booklist

Groves, Leslie R., 1896-1970

Norris, Robert S. **Racing** for the bomb: General Leslie R. Groves, the Manhattan Project's indispensable man. Steerforth Press 2002 xxi, 722p hardcover o.p. pa $24.95 **92**

1. Generals 2. Manhattan Project 3. Computer industry executives
ISBN 1-58642-067-4 pa

LC 2001-57629

This is a biography of the military engineer in charge of the Manhattan Project, which developed the atomic bomb

This "work will not only serve scholars and general readers equally well but also take its place among the handful of best books about the birth of the atomic age." Booklist

Includes bibliographical references

Guevara, Che, 1928-1967

Anderson, Jon Lee. **Che** Guevara; a revolutionary life. Grove Press 1997 814p il maps hardcover o.p. pa $20 **92**

1. Physicians 2. Revolutionaries
ISBN 0-8021-3558-7 pa

LC 97-3993

This is a "biography of the life and death of the larger-than-life revolutionary Ernesto 'Che' Guevara, the Argentine doctor who joined with Castro to overturn Fulgencio Batista's reign in Cuba. . . . This book, with its 89 photographs, will be an invaluable addition to the literature of American revolutionaries." Booklist

Includes bibliographical references

Guevara, Ernesto Che. **Diary** of a combatant; from the Sierra Maestra to Santa Clara, Cuba, 1956-58. Ernesto Che Guevara ; edited by María del Carmen Ariet. Ocean Press 2011 368 p. ill., map, facsim. $23.95 **92**

1. Diaries 2. Cuba -- History -- 1958-1959, Revolution
ISBN 0987077945; 9780987077943

LC 2011943989

This book is a translation of the diary "Ernesto Che Guevara kept during the guerrilla war in Cuba when he joined the struggle to overthrow the Batista dictatorship that led to the 1959 revolution. . . . [It was] meticulously transcribed by his widow, Aleida March. . . . Other features of this new book are fifty-eight unpublished photos from Che's personal archive and unpublished letters (including correspondence between Che and Fidel)." (Publisher's note)

"Editor Ariet has included a useful chronology and a most helpful biographical glossary, detailing many of the names Che introduces in these diaries." LJ

Includes bibliographical references

Guggenheim, Peggy, 1898-1979

★ Gill, Anton. **Art** lover; a biography of Peggy Guggenheim. HarperCollins Pubs. 2002 480p il $29.95; pa $15.95 **92**

1. Art collectors 2. Patrons of the arts
ISBN 0-06-019697-1; 0-06-095681-X pa

LC 2001-51731

Guggenheim "was known as much for her sexual exploits as for her championing of modern art, a fact Gill .

. . examines with candor, sensitivity, and mellifluous grace." Booklist

Includes bibliographical references

Gunther, John, 1929-1947

★ Gunther, John. **Death** be not proud; a memoir. Harper & Row 1949 261p il hardcover o.p. pa $13.95 **92**

1. Sick 2. Cancer 3. Brain -- Tumors
ISBN 0-06-123097-9

A memoir of John Gunther's seventeen-year-old son, who died after a series of operations for a brain tumor. Not only a tribute to a remarkable boy but an account of a brave fight against disease

Guthrie, Woody, 1912-1967

Klein, Joe. **Woody** Guthrie; a life. Knopf 1980 475p il pa $17 **92**

1. Singers 2. Folk musicians 3. Memoirists 4. Songwriters 5. Musicians -- United States
ISBN 0-385-33385-4 pa

LC 80-7634

"The author incorporates into his text a great deal of information sifted from Guthrie's voluminous unpublished writings. . . . He also uses information from historical sources, published works, and hundreds of interviews to place Guthrie in a social and historical perspective. The result of all this research is . . . a very interesting and personal biography." Libr J

Gödel, Kurt

Goldstein, Rebecca. **Incompleteness**; the proof and paradox of Kurt Godel. Rebecca Goldstein. W.W. Norton 2005 296p il (Great discoveries) $22.95 **92**

1. Mathematicians
ISBN 0-393-05169-2

LC 2004-23052

The author "explains the philosophical vision that inspired Gödel's mathematics, and reveals the ironic twist that led to radical misinterpretations of his theorems by the trendier intellectual fashions of the day, from positivism to postmodernism." Publisher's note

This "is a stimulating exploration of both the power and the limitations of the human intellect." Publ Wkly

Includes bibliographical references

Haber, Fritz, 1868-1934

Hager, Thomas. The **alchemy** of air; a Jewish genius, a doomed tycoon, and the scientific discovery that fed the world but fueled the rise of Hitler. Harmony Books 2008 316p $24.95; pa $15 **92**

1. Chemists 2. Fertilizers 3. Nobel laureates for chemistry
ISBN 978-0-307-35178-4; 0-307-35178-5; 978-0-307-35179-1 pa; 0-307-35179-3 pa

LC 2008-3192

"A fast-paced account of the early-20th-century quest to develop synthetic fertilizer. . . . Science writing of the first order." Kirkus

Includes bibliographical references

Habsburg-Lothringen, Wilhelm, 1895-1949

Snyder, Timothy. The **Red** Prince; the secret lives of a Habsburg archduke. Basic Books 2008 344p il map $27.95   **92**
1. Spies 2. Princes
ISBN 978-0-465-00237-5; 0-465-00237-4
LC 2008-2783

"As a scion of the Austrian imperial family, [Wilhelm von Habsburg] had many of the predictable aristocratic attributes, including a grasp of several languages, skill at swordplay, and a sense that he was entitled to command and rule others. Yet he turned his back on his family and a life of comfortable exile to engage in a series of dangerous escapades until his death, in a Soviet prison hospital in 1948. Along the way, von Habsburg led Ukrainian nationalists in a futile fight to establish an independent state, fought the Nazis, plotted against the Soviets, and managed to acquire a diverse collection of sexual conquests. Snyder portrays him as a restless spirit with dreams of grandeur who was attractive, even charismatic, without being particularly admirable." Booklist

Includes bibliographical references

Hadfield, Chris, 1959-

Hadfield, Chris, 1959- An **astronaut's** guide to life on earth; what going to space taught me about ingenuity, determination, and being prepared for anything. Col. Chris Hadfield. Little, Brown and Co. 2013 304 p. ill. (some col.) $28   **92**
1. Astronauts 2. Outer space -- Exploration
ISBN 0316253014; 9780316253017
LC 2013943519

Author and astronaut Chris Hadfield "takes readers deep into his years of training and space exploration to show how to make the impossible possible. Through eye-opening, entertaining stories filled with the adrenaline of launch, the mesmerizing wonder of spacewalks, and the measured, calm responses mandated by crises, he explains how conventional wisdom can get in the way of achievement-and happiness." (Publisher's note)

"The author emphasizes that becoming an astronaut involved developing physical capabilities and technical skills through tireless practice and a fanatic attention to detail. . . . A page-turning memoir of life as a decorated astronaut." Kirkus

Hadrian, Emperor of Rome, 76-138

Everitt, Anthony. **Hadrian** and the triumph of Rome. Random House 2009 xxix, 392p il map $30   **92**
1. Emperors 2. Rome -- History 3. Emperors -- Rome
ISBN 978-1-4000-6662-9; 1-4000-6662-X
LC 2009-05683

"Emperor from 117 to 138 A.D., Hadrian styled himself princeps, or first among equals, and his reversal of his predecessors' expansionist policies contributed to an era of prosperity and relative calm. He was unapologetically Hellenic, a poet and a dabbler in magic, and he kept in his retinue a young male lover whom he later deified. If Hadrian is indeed an enigma, it's because so few accounts of his life have survived, and this is where Everitt—whose books rely heavily on primary sources—runs into difficulty. One gets a clear and compelling sense of Hadrian's times, but the Emperor himself remains tantalizingly unknowable." New Yorker

Includes bibliographical references

Hajratwala, Minal

Hajratwala, Minal. **Leaving** India; my family's journey from five villages to five continents. Houghton Mifflin Harcourt 2009 430p il $26   **92**
1. Poets 2. Authors 3. Journalists 4. Gujarati Americans 5. Children of immigrants 6. Immigration and emigration 7. East Indians 8. Performance artists
ISBN 978-0-618-25129-2; 0-618-25129-4
LC 2008-36079

"At times the writer's many threads are confusing, and the narrative could have been more tightly edited; nevertheless, 'Leaving India' is a rich, entertaining and illuminating story." San Francisco Chron

Includes bibliographical references

Hall, Meredith

Hall, Meredith. **Without** a map; a memoir. Beacon Press 2007 221p $24.95   **92**
1. Authors 2. Essayists 3. Memoirists 4. College teachers 5. Authors, American
ISBN 978-0-8070-7273-8; 0-8070-7273-7
LC 2006-27507

"The year: 1965. The place: a small, insular New Hampshire community where church and home life are dominant forces. When Hall becomes pregnant at 16, she is shunned by family members and friends she's known throughout her school years. After traveling to the Middle East and suffering the indignities of loneliness and poverty, which include selling her own blood, she returns to the United States and creates a new life out of her still-palpable grief. . . . The message of redemptive compassion makes this a worthwhile and moving read." Libr J

Halsted, William Stewart, 1852-1922

Imber, Gerald. **Genius** on the edge; the bizarre story of William Stewart Halsted, the father of modern surgery. Kaplan Pub. 2010 389p il $25.95 **92**
1. Surgeons 2. Drug abuse 3. Writers on medicine
ISBN 978-1-60714-627-8; 1-60714-627-4
LC 2009-35525

This biography of William Halsted is in "many ways . . . a history of medicine/surgery in America. Halsted was very influential in bringing aseptic techniques to surgery and introduced the residency training system. He used his knowledge of anatomy to improve surgical technique. He performed the first successful hernia repair and radical mastectomy for breast cancer. Early in his career Halsted became addicted to cocaine while experimenting with the drug for use as a local anesthetic. Treatment at the time, involved substituting morphine for cocaine. Halsted spent 40 years of his life struggling with his addiction to both cocaine and morphine. . . . You don't need to be a surgeon to appreciate this book. You only need to have a love of history." Better Health

Hamilton, Alexander, 1757-1804

Brookhiser, Richard. **Alexander** Hamilton, American. Free Press 1999 240p il hardcover o.p. pa $14   **92**

1. Statesmen 2. Secretaries of the treasury 3. United States -- Politics and government -- 1783-1809
ISBN 0-684-86331-6 pa

LC 98-46846

This is a biography of the Secretary of the Treasury. Brookhiser discusses Hamilton's life, from his "teenage years in St. Croix and youth in Manhattan, through his formative years as Washington's aide during the Revolutionary War, to his role in the writing of the Constitution and the Federalist Papers, to his later careers as Secretary of the Treasury, lawyer, politician, and journalist." Natl Rev

Includes bibliographical references

★ Chernow, Ron. **Alexander** Hamilton. Penguin Press 2004 818p il $35   **92**

1. Statesmen 2. Secretaries of the treasury 3. United States -- Politics and government -- 1783-1809
ISBN 1-594-20009-2

LC 2003-65641

"Chernow makes fresh contributions to Hamiltoniana: no one has discovered so much about Hamilton's illegitimate origins and harrowed youth; few have been so taken by Hamilton's long-suffering, loving wife, Eliza. . . . This is a fine work that captures Hamilton's life with judiciousness and verve." Publ Wkly

Includes bibliographical references

Randall, Willard Sterne. **Alexander** Hamilton; a life. HarperCollins Pubs. 2003 476p il map $32.50; pa $15.95   **92**

1. Statesmen 2. Secretaries of the treasury 3. United States -- Politics and government -- 1783-1809
ISBN 0-06-019549-5; 0-06-095466-3 pa

LC 2002-68674

The author focuses on "Hamilton's fortune-marked rise to fame, which was sealed when the ambitious aide-de-camp of Washington pleaded for, and got, the assignment to lead the final assault at the Battle of Yorktown. . . . Randall's vigorous prose captures shows the compass of Hamilton's life and his role in making the U.S. a going concern." Booklist

Includes bibliographical references

Hamilton, Gabrielle, 1965-

Hamilton, Gabrielle. **Blood,** bones & butter; the inadvertent education of a reluctant chef. Random House 2011 291p $26   **92**

1. Cooks 2. Restaurateurs 3. Biography, Individual
ISBN 978-1-4000-6872-2; 1-4000-6872-X; 978-1-58836-931-4 ebook; 1-58836-931-5 ebook

LC 2010-17518

This book recounts how "when [Gabrielle] Hamilton was growing up, her parents would throw enormous parties for their friends and neighbors. Cooking for more than one hundred people was a common event in her family life. As she grew up, she sought to recreate the challenge and joy of feeding all those people and, unsurprisingly, she became a world-class chef. Her journey to owning her own New York City restaurant was not smooth, and took her all over the world." (Voice of Youth Advocates)

Though this book "is rhapsodic about food—in every variety, from the humble egg-on-a-roll sandwich served by Greek delis in New York to more esoteric things like 'fried zucchini agrodolce with fresh mint and hot chili flakes'— the book is hardly just for foodies. Ms. Hamilton . . . is as evocative writing about people and places as she is at writing about cooking." N Y Times (Late N Y Ed)

Hammer, Armand, 1898-1990

Epstein, Edward Jay. **Dossier**; the secret history of Armand Hammer. Carroll & Graf 1999 418p il pa $15.95   **92**

1. Art dealers 2. Art collectors 3. Energy industry executives
ISBN 978-0-7867-0677-8; 0-7867-0677-5
First published 1996 by Random House

The author employs a "wealth of primary sources he tapped in Soviet archives and elsewhere. . . . It is hard to imagine a sharper picture of how a tycoon is both born and made and how the power game is played." N Y Times Book Rev

Includes bibliographical references

Hammond, John, 1910-1987

Prial, Dunstan. The **producer**; John Hammond and the soul of American music. Farrar, Straus and Giroux 2006 347p il $27   **92**

1. Recording industry executives
ISBN 978-0-374-11304-9; 0-374-11304-1

LC 2005-12666

The author "brings Hammond to life in clear, insightful prose and places him and figures such as Dylan, Franklin, and Springsteen in the proper historical context." Libr J

Includes discography and bibliographical references

Handel, George Frideric, 1685-1759

Harris, Ellen T. **George** Frideric Handel; a life with friends. Ellen T. Harris. W. W. Norton & Company 2014 496 p. illustrations (hardcover) $37.95   **92**

1. Composers -- Biography
ISBN 0393088952; 9780393088953

LC 2014008148

This book, by Ellen T. Harris, is "[a]n intimate portrait of [George Frideric] Handel's life and inner circle. . . . Harris has spent years tracking down the letters, diaries, personal accounts, legal cases, and other documents connected to these bequests. The result is a tightly woven tapestry of London in the first half of the eighteenth century, one that interlaces vibrant descriptions of Handel's music with stories of loyalty, cunning, and betrayal." (Publisher's note)

A "readable tale of one of the world's most enigmatic musicians and composers." Pub Wkly

Includes bibliographical references, discography,

and index

Hogwood, Christopher. **Handel**; chronological table by Anthony Hicks. Rev ed; Thames & Hudson 2007 324p map pa $21.95 **92**
1. Composers
ISBN 978-0-500-28681-4; 0-500-28681-7
LC 2006-909559
First published 1984 in the United Kingdom
The author "addresses his book to the serious layman. The composer's comings and goings are documented as accurately as possible, and Mr. Hogwood has added terse critical commentary about the music in sophisticated language but without musical examples." N Y Times Book Rev
Includes bibliographical references

Handy, W. C. (William Christopher), 1873-1958
Robertson, David. **W.C.** Handy; the life and times of the man who made the blues. Alfred A. Knopf 2009 286p il $27.95 **92**
1. Composers 2. Blues music 3. Blues musicians 4. Music publishers
ISBN 978-0-307-26609-5; 0-307-26609-5
LC 2008-45983
The author "casts overdue light on Handy's essential role in establishing the blues as a popular art, and he does this, much to his credit, without resorting to dubious claims that Handy was the first or the best of the blues' multiple progenitors. A mark of both the evenhandedness of his scholarship and the delicacy of his writing is Robertson's resistance to the idea of Handy as the Father of the Blues — a notion that Handy himself advanced and exploited deftly during his lifetime." N Y Times Book Rev
Includes bibliographical references

Hansberry, Lorraine, 1930-1965
Hansberry, Lorraine. **To** be young, gifted, and Black; Lorraine Hansberry in her own words. adapted by Robert Nemiroff; with drawings and art by Lorraine Hansberry; introduction by James Baldwin; and a new preface by Jewell Handy Gresham Nemiroff. 1st Vintage Books ed; Vintage Books 1995 xxx, 261p il pa $8.95; pa $13.95 **92**
1. Authors 2. Dramatists 3. Essayists 4. Newspaper editors 5. Nonfiction writers 6. Dramatists, American 7. African American women -- Biography
ISBN 9780451531780; 0-679-76415-1
LC 96-119999
First published 1969 by Prentice-Hall
Work on this book and on the script for the play of the same title, which was presented at New York's Cherry Lane Theatre in 1969, "proceeded concurrently, each drawing upon the experiences and creative discoveries of the other, but ultimately diverging quite drastically." Postscript

Hardy, Thomas, 1840-1928
Tomalin, Claire. **Thomas** Hardy. Penguin Group 2006 xxv, 486p il map $35 **92**
1. Poets 2. Authors 3. Novelists 4. Short story writers
ISBN 1-59420-118-8; 978-1-59420-118-9
LC 2007-295886

"A priceless resource for the general reader and the Victorian scholar." Booklist
Includes bibliographical references

Hari, Daoud
Hari, Daoud. The **translator**; a tribesman's memoir of Darfur. Random House 2008 204p hardcover o.p. pa $13 **92**
1. Refugees 2. Memoirists 3. Guides (Persons) 4. Sudan -- History -- Darfur conflict, 2003-
ISBN 978-1-4000-6744-2; 1-4000-6744-8; 978-0-8129-7917-6 pa; 0-8129-7917-6 pa
LC 2007-42308
In this memoir, the author recounts his life in Darfur, Sudan before and after the conflict in 2003.
"Those with the courage to join Hari's odyssey may find this a life-changing read." Publ Wkly

Harrison, Benjamin, 1833-1901
Calhoun, Charles W. **Benjamin** Harrison. Times Books 2005 206p il (American presidents series) $20 **92**
1. Presidents 2. Senators 3. Presidents -- United States
ISBN 0-8050-6952-6; 978-0-8050-6952-5
LC 2004-63778
The author "dusts off an almost thoroughly forgotten chief executive, known primarily for serving between Cleveland's two terms, to disclose a harbinger of the modern, activist president. . . . One of the most revelatory entries in the American Presidents series." Booklist
Includes bibliographical references

Hart, Moss, 1904-1961
Bach, Steven. **Dazzler**; the life and times of Moss Hart. Da Capo 2002 462p il pa $20 **92**
1. Authors 2. Dramatists 3. Dramatists, American
ISBN 0-306-81135-9; 978-0-306-81135-7
First published 2001 by Knopf
This biography of the actor, director, and playwright chronicles "Hart's life, his early successes, his artistic missteps in middle age, and his later-life triumphs in the 1950s and 1960s." Booklist
"In narrating its subject's life, Dazzler is both gossipy and credible, a relatively rare and laudable combination." New Leader
Includes bibliographical references

Harvey, Fred
Fried, Stephen. **Appetite** for America; how visionary businessman Fred Harvey built a railroad hospitality empire that civilized the Wild West. Bantam Books 2010 518p il map $27 **92**
1. Restaurants 2. Restaurateurs 3. Cookery, American 4. Fred Harvey Company 5. Biography, Individual 6. West (U.S.) -- History 7. Railroads -- Western States -- History 8. Southwestern States -- History -- 19th century
ISBN 978-0-553-80437-9; 0-553-80437-5
LC 2009-47790
This is a biography of Fred Harvey, whose Harvey House restaurants were located at railroad depots across America. Bibliography. Index.

"A sturdy, detailed work of history that will appeal to business readers as well as aficionados of railroading and the Old West." Kirkus

Includes bibliographical references (p. 483-488)

Hatshepsut, Queen of Egypt

Ryan, Donald P. **Beneath** the sands of Egypt; adventures of an unconventional archaeologist. William Morrow 2010 286p il $26.99; ebook $12.99   **92**
1. Queens 2. Archeologists 3. College teachers 4. Egypt -- Antiquities 5. Excavations (Archeology) -- Egypt
ISBN 978-0-06-173282-9; 0-06-173282-6; 978-0-06-200280-8 ebook; 0-06-200280-5 ebook
LC 2010-20355

"Ryan, the archaeologist who rediscovered tomb KV 60 in the Valley of the Kings (later identified as the final resting place of the pharoah Hatshepsut), takes us through his life, career, and numerous expeditions. It's a thrilling book, not because it's full of Indiana Jones heroics but because Ryan's enthusiasm for what he does (more dirt-sifting than bullwhip-wielding) is manifested on every page; and . . . he catches us up in his excitement, makes us wish we weren't just reading about this stuff but were actually doing it. . . . This wonderful adventure story should be must reading for anyone aspiring to become an archaeologist, but even those of us who harbor no such dreams will be aching to get a little dirt under our fingernails." Booklist

Haubner, Shozan Jack

Haubner, Shozan Jack. **Zen** confidential; confessions of a wayward monk. Shozan Jack Haubner. Shambhala 2013 240 p. (pbk.) $14.95   **92**
1. Monks 2. Buddhism 3. Zen Buddhism 4. Wit and humor 5. Zen Buddhists -- United States -- Biography 6. Buddhist monks -- United States -- Biography
ISBN 1611800331; 9781611800333
LC 2012048993

"These hilarious essays on life inside and outside a Zen monastery make up the spiritual memoir of Shozan Jack Haubner, a Zen monk who didn't really start out to be one. Raised in a conservative Catholic family, Shozan went on to study philosophy (becoming de-Catholicized in the process) and to pursue a career as a screenwriter and stand-up comic in the clubs of L.A." (Publisher's note)

Hauerwas, Stanley, 1940-

Hauerwas, Stanley, 1940- **Hannah's** child; a theologian's memoir. W.B. Eerdmans Pub. Co. 2010 287p $24.99   **92**
1. Authors 2. Theologians 3. College teachers 4. Writers on religion 5. Biography, Individual
ISBN 978-0-8028-6487-1; 0-8028-6487-2
LC 2009-44729

This is an autobiography by the son of a Texas bricklayer who now teaches theological ethics at Duke University's Divinity School. His title refers to the Biblical Hannah, mother of Samuel, who promised God that if He allowed her to conceive a son in her old age, the child would be dedicated to God's service.

"Fans of Christian memoirs will be pleased with Hauerwas's frank yet poignant style, and those who are simply

fans of the memoir genre will find the book's careful blend of faith and scholarship easily accessible and far from didactic." Publ Wkly

Havel, Václav, 1936-2011

Havel, Vaclav. **To** the castle and back; translated from the Czech by Paul Wilson. Knopf 2007 383p $27.95; pa $15.95   **92**
1. Authors 2. Dramatists 3. Presidents 4. Essayists 5. Dissenters 6. Czech Republic -- Politics and government 7. Czechoslovakia -- Politics and government
ISBN 978-0-307-26641-5; 0-307-26641-9; 978-0-307-33845-2 pa; 0-307-38845-X pa
LC 2007-4413

Original Czech edition, 2006

The book "gives Havel's account of his journey from dissident-in-chief to head of state during the Velvet Revolution of 1989—and the turmoil that followed. Hardly a conventional memoir, its three intermixed narratives are at first as disorienting as his role reversal—which dismayed his wife Olga as much as himself. . . . These selections are by turns obscure, funny, insightful, poignant, and peevish. . . . Living in truth was what [Havel] preached as a dissident, and it is what he preached as president. . . . Whatever his political shortcomings in office, at least in this, the Czechs were privileged to have Havel as president." Commonweal

Hawa Abdi, 1947-

Abdi, Hawa. **Keeping** hope alive; one woman, 90,000 lives changed. Hawa Abdi with Sarah J. Robbins. Grand Central Pub. 2013 272 p. (hardcover) $26.99   **92**
1. Refugees -- Somalia 2. Somalia -- Biography 3. Gynecologists -- Somalia -- Biography 4. Women gynecologists -- Somalia -- Biography 5. Human rights workers -- Somalia -- Biography 6. Women human rights workers -- Somalia -- Biography
ISBN 1455503762; 9781455503766; 9781619696389
LC 2012041781

This book presents a memoir by physician Haw Abdi, "who, along with her daughters, has kept 90,000 of her fellow citizens safe, healthy, and educated for over 20 years in Somalia." The author "is the founder of a massive camp for internally displaced people located a few miles from war-torn Mogadishu, Somalia. Since 1991, when the Somali government collapsed . . . she has dedicated herself to providing help for people whose lives have been shattered by violence and poverty." (Publisher's note)

Hawking, Stephen, 1942-

Hawking, S. W. (Stephen W.), 1942- **My** brief history; Stephen Hawking. Bantam Books 2013 144 p. illustrations $22   **92**
1. Cosmology 2. Black holes (Astronomy) 3. Physicists -- Biography
ISBN 0345535286; 9780345535283
LC 2013027938

In this autobiography, Stephen Hawking "opens up about the challenges that confronted him following his diagnosis of ALS at age twenty-one. Tracing his development as a thinker, he explains how the prospect of an early death urged him onward through numerous intellectual breakthroughs, and talks about the genesis of his masterpiece 'A Brief History of Time'". (Publisher's note)

"Hawking says it all with charm, intermingling his personal life with abstruse theoretical physics in nontechnical language. Revealing the power of mind over body, this is an enjoyable, entertaining, and inspiring work." Choice

Hawthorne, Nathaniel, 1804-1864

Miller, Edwin Haviland. **Salem** is my dwelling place: a life of Nathaniel Hawthorne. University of Iowa Press 1991 596p il hardcover o.p. pa $24.95 **92**

1. Authors 2. Novelists 3. Short story writers
ISBN 0-87745-332-2; 0-87745-381-0 pa

LC 91-14543

This is a biography of the 19th century American novelist

"Psychologically probing (but free of all jargon), Miller's elegantly written study gives us a fresh, sympathetic picture of an immensely complex, repressed man. . . . A masterful work, wholly satisfying." Libr J

Includes bibliographical references

★ Wineapple, Brenda. **Hawthorne** : a life. Alfred A. Knopf 2003 xii, 509 p.p il $30 **92**

1. Authors 2. Novelists 3. Short story writers
ISBN 0-375-40044-3; 9780812972917

LC 2002-192485

In this biography Wineapple discusses the "public controversies that shaped [Hawthorne's] world: the Whig triumphs that cost him his customhouse job and forced him into writing; the critical exchanges that heartened him with praise for his work . . . and wounded him with disparagement; and the Civil War battles that drove him to despair—and into political disrepute as a copperhead." Booklist

Includes bibliographical references (p. 473-486) and index.

Haydn, Joseph, 1732-1809

Geiringer, Karl. **Haydn** : a creative life in music; by Karl Geiringer in collaboration with Irene Geiringer. 3rd rev & enl ed; University of Calif. Press 1982 403p il hardcover o.p. pa $21.95 **92**

1. Composers
ISBN 0-520-04317-0 pa

LC 82-2821

First published 1946

The author is "one of the few scholars who have devoted themselves almost exclusively to the study of this great master. He has not only collected all the new data that have cast light on Haydn research . . . he has also contributed many valuable observations and ideas." Saturday Rev

Includes bibliographical references

Haydn; edited by David Wyn Jones; consultant editor Otto Biba. Oxford Univ. Press 2002 xxi, 515p il map (Oxford composer companions) $75 **92**

1. Composers
ISBN 0-19-866216-5

LC 2002-510033

"This volume will be useful to persons who need quick, specific information about Haydn, his works, and 18th-century style." Choice

Hazan, Marcella

Hazan, Marcella. **Amarcord,** Marcella remembers; the remarkable life story of the woman who started out teaching science in a small town in Italy, but ended up teaching America how to cook Italian. Gotham Books 2008 307p il $27.50 **92**

1. Cooks 2. Italian cooking 3. Cookbook writers 4. Cooking teachers
ISBN 978-1-59240-388-2; 1-59240-388-3

LC 2007-46197

This is a memoir by the author of The Classic Italian Cook Book (1973) and More Classic Italian Cooking (1978).

"Hazan has selected the best stories from her own life to present Amarcord with all the warmth and humor of a long meal in famiglia made from the choicest ingredients. . . . If you've never been [to] Italy, the time spent with Hazan will have you planning your next vacation faster than you can say manicotti." Christ Sci Monit

Hearst, William Randolph, 1863-1951

Whyte, Kenneth. The **uncrowned** king; the sensational rise of William Randolph Hearst. Counterpoint 2009 546p il $30 **92**

1. Publishers and publishing 2. Newspaper editors 3. Newspaper executives
ISBN 978-1-58243-467-4; 1-58243-467-0

LC 2008-47442

"A very worthwhile reexamination of the rise of a flawed but accomplished man." Booklist

Includes bibliographical references (p. 505-511)

Hefner, Hugh

Watts, Steven. **Mr.** Playboy; Hugh Hefner and the American dream. Wiley 2008 529p il $29.95 **92**

1. Magazine executives
ISBN 9780471690597; 0-4716-9059-7

LC 2008-9572

"This is not a gossip book but a well-documented biography written with access to Hefner's over 1800 scrapbooks, the company archives, and interviews. Watts finds Hefner comparable to the subjects of his other books about Henry Ford and Walt Disney in that all were major contributors to aspects of the American dream." Libr J

Includes bibliographical references

Heisenberg, Werner, 1901-1976

Cassidy, David C., 1945- **Beyond** uncertainty; Heisenberg, quantum physics, and the bomb. David C. Cassidy. Bellevue Literary Press 2009 480 p. $27 **92**

1. Physicists 2. Biography, Individual 3. Nobel laureates for physics 4. Physicists -- Germany -- Biography 5. World War, 1939-1945 -- Science -- Germany 6. Atomic bomb -- Germany -- History -- 20th century
ISBN 978-1-934137-13-0; 1-934137-13-8; 1934137138; 9781934137130

LC 2008039885

This is a biography "of the German wunderkind Werner Heisenberg (1901–1976), who won the 1932 Nobel Prize in physics for revolutionizing the nascent field of quantum physics, first with his matrix interpretation of quantum mechanics, then with his famous uncertainty principle. . . . Exhaustively detailed yet eminently readable, this is an important book." Publ Wkly

Includes bibliographical references (p. [411]-456) and index

Hell, Richard

Hell, Richard. **I** Dreamed I Was a Very Clean Tramp; an autobiography. Richard Hell. HarperCollins 2013 304 p. $25.99   **92**
1. Autobiography 2. Rock musicians -- United States -- Biography
ISBN 0062190830; 9780062190833

In this autobiography, punk rocker "[Richard] Hell takes us on a journey through his youth in Lexington, Ky., his boredom with school, his attempts at running away, his to move to New York in the 1970s, and his struggles with drug addiction. . . . Hell's memoir spills over with recollections of his times with Andrew Wylie . . . and rock critic Lester Bangs. In 1976, the Voidoids debuted at CBGB; the following year, Hell descended into drug addiction. " (Publishers Weekly)

Heller, Erica

Heller, Erica. **Yossarian** slept here; when Joseph Heller was dad, the Apthorp was home, and life was a catch-22. Simon & Schuster 2011 272p il $25; ebook $11.99   **92**
1. Authors 2. Novelists 3. Journalists 4. Copywriters 5. Novelists, American 6. Short story writers 7. Biography, Individual 8. Children of prominent persons
ISBN 978-1-4391-9768-4; 1-4391-9768-7; 978-1-4391-9770-7 ebook; 1-4391-9770-9 ebook
LC 2011-08283

The daughter of author Joseph Heller shares the story of her childhood, marked by her father's fame, her parents' acrimonious divorce, and their unconventional parenting choices.

"An affectionate family scrapbook crafted with a bittersweet blend of humor and pathos." Kirkus

Heller, Joseph

Daugherty, Tracy. **Just** one catch; a biography of Joseph Heller. St. Martin's Press 2011 548p il $35   **92**
1. Authors 2. Novelists 3. Authors, American 4. Short story writers 5. Biography, Individual
ISBN 978-0-312-59685-9; 0-312-59685-5
LC 2011-20749

This biography offers "countless insightful, amusing anecdotes from Heller's childhood, military service and postpublication notoriety as a celebrated literary figure. But the writing, publishing and ensuing aftermath of Catch-22 is the clear focal point of Daugherty's book. Lacking the self-assured swagger of Norman Mailer and the countercultural sway of the Beats, Heller was a long-frustrated and surprising emergent on the literary scene. A reluctant participant in the burgeoning Madison Avenue advertising world of the 1950s, Heller seemed a figure unlikely to publish a work of such unimpeachable influence. Published when Heller was 39, Catch-22 represents the high-water mark of his career and to some extent his personal life—it is as if everything

prepublication was prologue and everything that followed was postscript. Heller wrote copiously throughout the remainder of his life but never attained those heights again, critically or commercially. Nonetheless, Daugherty persuasively endorses the view of Heller as a pivotal figure in American letters." Time Out N Y

Includes bibliographical references

Heller, Erica. **Yossarian** slept here; when Joseph Heller was dad, the Apthorp was home, and life was a catch-22. Simon & Schuster 2011 272p il $25; ebook $11.99   **92**
1. Authors 2. Novelists 3. Journalists 4. Copywriters 5. Novelists, American 6. Short story writers 7. Biography, Individual 8. Children of prominent persons
ISBN 978-1-4391-9768-4; 1-4391-9768-7; 978-1-4391-9770-7 ebook; 1-4391-9770-9 ebook
LC 2011-08283

The daughter of author Joseph Heller shares the story of her childhood, marked by her father's fame, her parents' acrimonious divorce, and their unconventional parenting choices.

"An affectionate family scrapbook crafted with a bittersweet blend of humor and pathos." Kirkus

Hellman, Lillian, 1906-1984

Hellman, Lillian. **Pentimento**. Little, Brown 1973 297p hardcover o.p. pa $14.95   **92**
1. Authors 2. Dramatists 3. Memoirists 4. Dramatists, American
ISBN 0-316-35288-8 pa

This continuation of An unfinished woman—a memoir (1969) offers sketches of events and people from the author's past. She reminisces about her childhood in the South, some of her eccentric relatives including Cousin Bethe and Uncle Willy, Julia, her childhood friend who was trapped by the Nazis, Dashiell Hammett, who was her lover, and her experiences in the theater

"Pentimento is valuable as a picture of a woman and writer in the making." New Repub

Martinson, Deborah. **Lillian** Hellman; a life with foxes and scoundrels. Counterpoint 2005 448p il $27.95   **92**
1. Authors 2. Dramatists 3. Memoirists 4. Dramatists, American
ISBN 1-58243-315-1
LC 2005-16616

The author describes the details of the playwright's "life, from her demanding temperament to her gutsy politics and legendary relationship with Dashiel Hammett." Booklist

This is "a richly thorough, sometimes somber, and fairly objective portrait of an enigmatic individual." Libr J

Includes bibliographical references

Hemingway, Ernest, 1899-1961

★ Hendrickson, Paul. **Hemingway's** boat; everything he loved in life, and lost, 1934-1961. Alfred A. Knopf 2011 531p il $30; ebook $14.99   **92**
1. Poets 2. Authors 3. Novelists 4. Journalists 5. Authors, American 6. Short story writers 7. Nobel

laureates for literature
ISBN 9781400041626; 1400041627; 9780307700537
ebook

LC 2011003398

The author frames "the last 27 years of Hemingway's over-dissected life with his yacht, Pilar. Outlasting marriages and relationships with friends and family, the 38' Brooklyn-built fishing machine was the lasting love of his life. Hendrickson has come neither to praise nor to bury his subject, but to give him a fair shot. . . . Hendrickson brings fresh meat to the table, delivering one of the most satisfying Hemingway assessments in many years. A delight for Ernesto's numerous fans." Libr J

Includes bibliographical references and index.

Lynn, Kenneth S. **Hemingway**. Harvard University Press 1995 702p il pa $27 **92**
1. Poets 2. Authors 3. Novelists 4. Journalists 5. Authors, American 6. Short story writers 7. Nobel laureates for literature
ISBN 0-674-38732-5; 978-0-674-38732-4

LC 95-129513

First published 1987 by Simon and Schuster

"Taking as his premise Hemingway's glib assertion that the only analyst he relied upon was his 'portable Corona Number 3,' Lynn tracks the exploration of a disordered inner world as Hemingway sought to find some sort of resolution to the agony of his personal conflicts through 'his cunningly wrought fiction.' The man who emerges from Lynn's biography is a vastly more complex and compelling figure than the white-bearded, pontificating 'Papa' of myth." Publ Wkly

Includes bibliographical references

Reynolds, Michael S. **Hemingway** : the homecoming; [by] Michael Reynolds. W.W. Norton 1999 xxiii, 264p il map pa $14.95 **92**
1. Poets 2. Authors 3. Novelists 4. Journalists 5. Authors, American 6. Short story writers 7. Nobel laureates for literature
ISBN 0-393-31981-4

First published 1992 by Blackwell with title: Hemingway: the American homecoming

This third volume of a five-volume study of Hemingway's life begun with The young Hemingway (1998) and Hemingway: the Paris years (1999) "covers 1926-29, a transitional period that marked the conclusion of Hemingway's artistic apprenticeship and the cooling of many literary friendships; the end of one marriage and the beginning of another; the suicide of his father; and the writing of The Sun Also Rises, Men Without Women, A Farewell to Arms, and an ultimately abandoned novel." Libr J

Includes bibliographical references

Reynolds, Michael S. **Hemingway** : the Paris years; [by] Michael Reynolds. W.W. Norton 1999 402p il map pa $18.95 **92**
1. Poets 2. Authors 3. Novelists 4. Journalists 5. Authors, American 6. Short story writers 7. Nobel laureates for literature
ISBN 0-393-31879-6

First published 1989 by Blackwell

In this second volume of a five-volume biography of Hemingway begun with The young Hemingway (1998), the author "locates Hemingway in an American sociocultural context wherein he rejects middle-class restraints and aspires to identity as hero and self-reliant frontiersman (soldier, bullfighter, hunter, lover). The genius of the book lies in a graceful and informative linkage between literary creation and biographical incident." Libr J

Includes bibliographical references

Reynolds, Michael S. The **young** Hemingway; [by] Michael Reynolds. W. W. Norton 1998 291p il pa $15.95 **92**
1. Poets 2. Authors 3. Novelists 4. Journalists 5. Authors, American 6. Short story writers 7. Nobel laureates for literature
ISBN 0-393-31776-5

First published 1986 in the United Kingdom

"This incisive, well-written biography . . . will prove useful at almost every readership level, from general reader to scholar." Choice

Includes bibliographical references

Henderson, Artis

Henderson, Artis. **Unremarried** widow; a memoir. Artis Henderson. Simon & Schuster 2013 272 p. (hardcover : alk. paper) $25 **92**
1. Widows 2. Military spouses 3. Bereavement 4. Helicopter pilots -- Iraq 5. Husband and wife -- United States 6. War widows -- United States -- Biography 7. Military spouses -- United States -- Biography 8. Iraq War, 2003-2011 -- Personal narratives, American 9. Iraq War, 2003-2011 -- Women -- United States -- Biography
ISBN 1451649282; 9781451649284; 9781451649291

LC 2013008799

In this memoir, "Artis Henderson was a free-spirited young woman with dreams of . . . becoming a writer. Marrying a conservative Texan soldier and becoming an Army wife was never part of her plan, but when she met Miles, Artis threw caution to the wind. . . . On November 6, 2006, the . . . helicopter carrying Miles crashed in Iraq. . . . Artis recounts not only the . . . love story she shared with Miles, . . . but also reveals how Miles's death mirrored her father's death in a plane crash." (Publisher's note)

"[Henderson's] willingness to reveal the complexities of her marriage as well as the raw emotion of her loss makes for a compelling page-turner." Booklist

Includes bibliographical references and index

Henderson, Bill, 1941-

★ Henderson, Bill. **All** my dogs; a life. drawings by leslie Moore. David R. Godine 2011 145p $19.95 **92**
1. Dogs 2. Authors 3. Novelists 4. Editors 5. Memoirists 6. Publishing executives
ISBN 978-1-56792-435-0; 1-56792-435-2

LC 2010-49824

"This is a lovely little volume, gentle in tone and a bit artless, telling the story of a life through the dogs who attended it. Bill Henderson, the founder of Pushcart Press and its better-known progeny, the annual Pushcart Prize, hasn't written his account as an instructional, or a confessional, or even a celebration. Rather, it's a meditation on the grace notes both dogs and people bring to a life—a hybrid 'mutt memoir,' as he calls it. . . . This small, kind book is steeped with an earnest sort of fondness all the way through—the back matter even points out that it's set in Minion, which means 'faithful companion.' The accompanying line drawings by Leslie Moore, appealing portraits of each dog recreated from photos and Henderson's desriptions, add a nice touch." Open Letters Monthly

Hendrix, Jimi

★ Cross, Charles R. **Room** full of mirrors; a biography of Jimi Hendrix. Hyperion 2005 384p il $24.95; pa $15.99   92
    1. Singers 2. Guitarists 3. Rock musicians
    ISBN 1-401-30028-6; 0-7868-8841-5 pa
                                    LC 2005-46362
The author's "narrative, based on more than 300 interviews, describes Hendrix as thoughtful and craving some semblance of order to his life, even as it became steeped in drug use." Publ Wkly
"Admirably comprehensive and well referenced, this is the Hendrix biography to acquire if you can acquire only one." Booklist
Includes bibliographical references

Hennessey, Patrick, 1982-

Hennessey, Patrick. The **Junior** Officers' Reading Club; killing time and fighting wars. Riverhead Books 2010 310p il map pa $16   92
    1. Army officers 2. Soldiers -- Great Britain 3. Iraq War, 2003- -- Personal narratives 4. Afghan War, 2001- -- Personal narratives 5. Great Britain -- Army -- Grenadier Guards -- Battalion, 1st
    ISBN 978-1-59448-479-7; 1-59448-479-1
                                    LC 2010-17134
First published 2009 in the United Kingdom
"Oxford graduate Hennessey decided he wanted to do something exciting, so he went to Sandhurst, England's Royal Military Academy, and then to Bosnia, Iraq, and, ultimately, Afghanistan as a lieutenant and platoon leader in the Grenadier Guards. There he found what he was looking for, and this voluble, kinetic, and often funny book recounts his experiences. . . . The book's pace, never leisurely, accelerates in Afghanistan, as Hennessey vividly describes near-constant battle with Taliban fighters and confronts his reactions: exhaustion, fear, grief, fellowship, confusion, and what he calls the 'rapture' of war. All wars generate fine books. This may be one of the best to come out of the war in Afghanistan." Booklist

Hensley, William L., 1941-

Hensley, William L. **Fifty** miles from tomorrow; a memoir of Alaska and the real people. [by] William L. Iggiagruk Hensley. Farrar, Straus and Giroux 2008 256p il map $24   92
    1. Inupiat 2. Eskimo leaders 3. State legislators
    ISBN 978-0-374-15484-4; 0-374-15484-8
                                    LC 2008-31409
The author "manages to make fresh an old narrative of people who arise just as their culture is being erased—be they 'Braveheart' Scotsmen or outback Aborigines. His

book is also bright and detailed, moving along at a clip most sled dogs would have trouble keeping up with." N Y Times Book Rev

Henson, Jim

Jones, Brian Jay. **Jim** Henson; the biography. Brian Jay Jones. Ballantine Books 2013 608 p. (hardback) $35   92
    1. Muppet show (Television program) 2. Sesame Street (Television program) 3. Puppeteers -- United States -- Biography 4. Television producers and directors -- United States -- Biography
    ISBN 0345526112; 9780345526113
                                    LC 2013024039
This book explores "the life of Muppets creator Jim Henson (1936-1990) . . . explaining how Henson grew up to become a daring puppeteer and scriptwriter, how he managed to attract so much remarkable talent to his side, and how his stressful business relationship with the Disney Company might have aggravated the bacterial infection that weakened the normally healthy Henson, who died at age 53 while trying to negotiate the planned Disney purchase of the franchise." (Kirkus Reviews)
Includes bibliographical references and index

Hepburn, Audrey, 1929-1993

Walker, Alexander. **Audrey**; her real story. St. Martin's Press 1995 319p il hardcover o.p. pa $16.95   92
    1. Actors
    ISBN 0-312-18046-2 pa
                                    LC 94-33716
The author "recounts his subject's childhood in war-torn Europe and her early stage and film career. . . . Both the narrative and the writing itself become more lively as he discusses the heyday of her career, her sometimes turbulent love life and her work with Third World children for UNICEF." Publ Wkly

Hepburn, Katharine, 1907-2003

Berg, A. Scott. **Kate** remembered. Putnam 2003 370p il $25.95; pa $15   92
    1. Actors
    ISBN 0-399-15164-8; 0-425-19909-6 pa
                                    LC 2003-545232
In this posthumous biography, the author reveals "details about such pivotal events as the death of her brother by hanging, her relationships with powerful men like Howard Hughes and John Ford, and her slow, sad decline. . . . Berg's writing is so intimate that readers may feel they are hiding behind a curtain as they listen to the stories he elicits from his subject. Kate herself comes across pretty much the way she did on screen: bossy, courageous, and self-involved." Booklist

Hepburn, Katharine. **Me**; stories of my life. Knopf 1991 420p il hardcover o.p. pa $15.95 92
    1. Actors
    ISBN 0-345-41009-2
                                    LC 90-50805
This book "sounds just like its author—lots of cropped sentences, dashes, Hepburnian phrasing. But it's not a full-

dress autobiography; as the subtitle proclaims, this is a collection of stories. . . . Still, fans will not be disappointed. Beginning with her early years . . . and concluding with her relationship with Tracy, Hepburn delivers all kinds of wry moments and, of course, a most interesting cast of characters." Booklist

Leaming, Barbara. **Katharine** Hepburn. Limelight Eds. 2000 549p il $23.95 **92**
1. Actors
ISBN 0-87910-293-4

LC 00-25227

A reissue of the title first published 1995 by Crown

This biography begins with a "portrait of the entire Hepburn clan, stressing the effect of the suicides that ran through Kate's maternal and paternal families. This is, in fact, a family biography, with at least half the book devoted to Hepburn's grandmother and mother. . . . By the time Kate enters the story, readers will be thoroughly caught up in a tale that already has delivered a full measure of intrigue, romance, and scandal. The book has been prodigiously researched (Leaming's source notes make fascinating reading on their own), and her access to various, previously unavailable papers not only makes possible the family history, but also paves the way for startling new revelations about Hepburn's life." Booklist {review of 1995 edition}

Mann, William J. **Kate** : the woman who was Hepburn. H. Holt 2006 xxviii, 621p il $30 **92**
1. Actors
ISBN 978-0-8050-7625-7; 0-8050-7625-5
This is a biography of the American actress.
"This will surely be the definitive version of Hepburn's life for decades to come, as it is an outstanding example of painstaking research matched with splendid writing." Publ Wkly
Includes bibliographical references

Herod I, King of Judea, 73 B.C.-4 B.C.
Vermès, Géza, 1924-2013. The **True** Herod; by Geza Vermes. Bloomsbury USA Academic 2014 216 p. ill. (chiefly col.), col. map $35 **92**
ISBN 0567575446; 9780567575449
In this book, author Geza Vermes "provides a new portrait of Herod [the Great]. Vermes examines Herod's legacy as a political leader, and a potentate, a man of culture, and an all-round smooth operator. Vermes opens up the fascinating character of Herod, from his sizable and fragile ego to his devastation at the execution of his beloved wife, an execution that Herod ordered himself." (Publisher's note)
"Vermes not only gives context for Herod's negative reputation but also provides a fresh perspective for appreciating admirable accomplishments (for example, renovating the Jerusalem temple) and qualities (loyalty, savvy political instincts, fondness for the learned Jews of his time)." LJ
Includes bibliographical references and index

Herr, Norma Kurap, 1926-2007
★ Bartok, Mira. The **memory** palace; by Mira Bartok. Free Press 2011 305p. ill. $25; ebook $11.99 **92**
1. Pianists 2. Mentally ill 3. Schizophrenia 4.

Homeless 5. Schizophrenics
ISBN 978-1-4391-8331-1; 1-4391-8331-7; 978-1-4391-8333-5 ebook; 1-4391-8333-3 ebook

LC 201008399

National Book Critics Circle Award: Autobiography (2011)
Bartók is a painter and the author of children's books. "'The Memory Palace' begins in the final days of her mother's life, when Bartók finds out that the woman she has not seen in 17 years is dying and decides to go to her." (N Y Times Book Rev)
This is "personal narrative about growing up with a brilliant but schizophrenic mother. The book is comprised of two intertwining narratives. One concerns artist Bartók's mother, Norma Herr, and her struggle with mental illness. The other examines the author's midlife struggle with a traumatic brain injury. . . . Richly textured, compassionate and heartbreaking." Kirkus

Herriot, James
Herriot, James. **All** creatures great and small; 20th anniversary ed; St. Martin's Press 1992 442p $21.95; pa $13.95 **92**
1. Authors 2. Veterinarians 3. Veterinary medicine 4. Memoirists
ISBN 0-312-08498-6; 0-312-33085-5 pa

LC 92-18975

First published 1972
The first volume of Herriot's autobiographical account of the practice of veterinary medicine in Yorkshire, England in the 1930s
Followed by All things bright and beautiful (1974), All things wise and wonderful (1977), and The Lord God made them all (1981)

Herriot, James. **All** things bright and beautiful. St. Martin's Press 1974 378p $19.95 **92**
1. Authors 2. Veterinarians 3. Veterinary medicine 4. Memoirists
ISBN 0-312-02030-9
A continuation of Herriot's reminiscences of pre-World War II Yorkshire

Herriot, James. **All** things wise and wonderful. St. Martin's Press 1977 432p $18.95; pa $7.99 **92**
1. Authors 2. Veterinarians 3. Veterinary medicine 4. Memoirists
ISBN 0-312-02031-7; 0-312-96655-5 pa

LC 77-76640

This installment of Herriot's memoirs focuses on his RAF service during the war

Herriot, James. The **Lord** God made them all. St. Martin's Press 1981 373p $17.95 **92**
1. Authors 2. Veterinarians 3. Large print books 4. Veterinary medicine 5. Memoirists
ISBN 0-312-49834-9

LC 80-29097

This volume deals with post-war changes in veterinary medicine and Herriot's trips to Russia and Turkey

Herschel, Caroline Lucretia, 1750-1848

Lemonick, Michael D. The **Georgian** star; how William and Caroline Herschel revolutionized our understanding of the cosmos. W.W. Norton 2009 199p il map (Great discoveries) $23.95; pa $14.95 **92**

1. Astronomers
ISBN 978-0-393-06574-9; 0-393-06574-X; 978-0-393-33709-9 pa; 0-393-33709-X pa

LC 2008-29820

A tribute to the scientific contributions of William Herschel and his pioneering sister, Caroline, describes their establishment of surveying techniques that are still in use, Caroline's cataloging of nebulae, and William's discovery of infrared radiation.

"A rewarding account of two scientists who not only made great discoveries but enjoyed world recognition during their long, eventful lives." Kirkus

Includes bibliographical references

Herschel, William Sir, 1738-1822

Lemonick, Michael D. The **Georgian** star; how William and Caroline Herschel revolutionized our understanding of the cosmos. W.W. Norton 2009 199p il map (Great discoveries) $23.95; pa $14.95 **92**

1. Astronomers
ISBN 978-0-393-06574-9; 0-393-06574-X; 978-0-393-33709-9 pa; 0-393-33709-X pa

LC 2008-29820

A tribute to the scientific contributions of William Herschel and his pioneering sister, Caroline, describes their establishment of surveying techniques that are still in use, Caroline's cataloging of nebulae, and William's discovery of infrared radiation.

"A rewarding account of two scientists who not only made great discoveries but enjoyed world recognition during their long, eventful lives." Kirkus

Includes bibliographical references

Hersh, Seymour M.

Miraldi, Robert. **Seymour** Hersh; scoop artist. Robert Miraldi. Potomac Books, An Imprint of the University of Nebraska Press 2013 415 p. (cloth : alk. paper) $34.95 **92**

1. Journalism -- United States 2. Journalists -- United States -- Biography 3. United States -- Foreign relations -- 1989- 4. United States -- Foreign relations -- 1945-1989 5. United States -- Politics and government -- 1989- 6. United States -- Politics and government -- 1945-1989
ISBN 1612344755; 9781612344751

LC 2013023619

This book, by Robert Miraldi, offers a biography of the investigative reporter Seymour Hersh. "From his exposé of the My Lai massacre in 1969 to his revelations about torture at Abu Ghraib prison in 2004, Hersh has consistently captured the public imagination, spurred policymakers to reform, and drawn the ire of presidents. . . . This . . . biography captures a . . . successful career of important exposés and outstanding accomplishments." (Publisher's note)

"A deep biographical treatment of the Pulitzer Prize–winning journalist who is the scourge of those in power. . . . Hersh comes across as a good guy of limited patience when approached by fellow journalists and as a bulldog with sharp teeth when in his reporter mode." Kirkus

Includes bibliographical references and index

Hershey, Milton Snavely, 1857-1945

D'Antonio, Michael. **Hershey**; Milton S. Hershey's extraordinary life of wealth, empire, and utopian dreams. Simon & Schuster 2006 305p il hardcover o.p. pa $15 **92**

1. Food industry executives
ISBN 0-7432-6409-6; 0-7432-6410-X pa

LC 2005-51581

This is a "look at the man who brought America the five-cent chocolate bar and founded a utopian village." Publ Wkly

"While some look at Hershey and see either a beneficent angel or a willful tyrant, it is the great charm of D'Antonio's book that he will not plunk entirely for one judgment or the other. It's the man he's after, not the god." N Y Times Book Rev

Includes bibliographical references

Higashida, Naoki, 1992-

Naoki Higashida. The **reason** I jump; the inner voice of a thirteen-year-old boy with autism. by Naoki Higashida ; translated by KA Yoshida and David Mitchell. Random House 2013 176 p. illustrations (acid-free paper) $22 **92**

1. Autism 2. Children with autism 3. Autistic people -- Psychology 4. Autistic people -- Japan -- Biography
ISBN 0812994868; 9780812994865

LC 2012045703

In this book, "a 13-year-old Japanese author illuminates his autism from within. . . . The book takes the form of a series of straightforward questions followed by answers. . . . He describes the difficulty of expressing through words what the brain wants to say, the challenge of focusing and ordering experience, the obsessiveness of repetition, the comfort found in actions that others might find odd, and the frustration of being the source of others' frustration." (Kirkus Reviews)

A "a mixture of invaluable anecdotal information, practical advice and whimsical self-expression." Pub Wkly

Higginson, Thomas Wentworth, 1823-1911

Wineapple, Brenda. **White** heat; the friendship of Emily Dickinson and Thomas Wentworth Higginson. Alfred A. Knopf 2008 416p il $27.95 **92**

1. Poets 2. Clergy 3. Authors 4. Memoirists 5. Poets, American 6. Social reformers
ISBN 1-4000-4401-4; 978-1-4000-4401-6

LC 2008-11770

This is an account of the friendship between the poet Emily Dickinson and the reformer Thomas Wentworth Higginson, author of Army Life in a Black Regiment (1869).

"A moving portrait of two unalike but kindred spirits who did indeed 'Dare [to] see a Soul at the "White Heat."'" Kirkus

Includes bibliographical references

Highsmith, Patricia, 1921-1995

Schenkar, Joan. The **talented** Miss Highsmith; the secret life and serious art of Patricia Highsmith. St. Martin's Press 2009 684p il $40   **92**
1. Authors 2. Novelists 3. Mystery writers 4. Authors, American
ISBN 978-0-312-30375-4

LC 2009-18363

"It is hard to imagine a more thoroughly fact-filled or energetic biography than 'The Talented Miss Highsmith' or one more determined to examine the deepest recesses of its complicated subject. Ms. Schenkar's presentation is cubist, off-putting at first, featuring separated essays that isolate various topics. The dislocation can be confusing, yet one soon comes to accept the method as a way of mining the many veins of a very strange life." Wall Street J
Includes bibliographical references

Hijazi, Rafiq

★ Goldberg, Jeffrey. **Prisoners**; a Muslim and a Jew across the Middle East divide. Knopf 2006 316p $25   **92**
1. Journalists 2. Israel-Arab conflicts 3. Political leaders
ISBN 0-375-41234-4; 978-0-375-41234-9

LC 2006-41026

This is a "memoir of the author, an American-bred Zionist, and his 15-year relationship with a Palestinian insurgent. . . . Goldberg lived in Israel as a college student, sharpening the contradictory emotions shared by many of his American peers and eventually watching his former certainty crumble under the weight of military service at Ketziot, an Israeli prison. Grounded in his relationship with a prisoner, Goldberg's book travels from Long Island to Afghanistan as he struggles to understand Israeli-Palestinian violence. . . . Like the warring nationalisms it presents, his book is complex and deeply affecting." Publ Wkly

Hilburn, Robert

Hilburn, Robert. **Cornflakes** with John Lennon; and other tales from a rock 'n' roll life. Rodale 2009 208p il $24.99   **92**
1. Journalists 2. Music critics 3. Rock musicians -- Anecdotes
ISBN 978-1-59486-921-1; 1-59486-921-9

LC 2009-26604

"Fans of Springsteen, Dylan and U2 will be thrilled to find multiple chapters devoted to their idols, who are clearly Hilburn's favorites as well. . . . The most intriguing sections, however, are the glimpses into the private lives of a who's who of popular music in the 20th century. . . . A must-read for pop-music lovers." Kirkus

Hill, Joe, 1879-1915

Adler, William M. The **man** who never died; the life, times, and legacy of Joe Hill, American labor icon. Bloomsbury 2011 435p il $30   **92**
1. Poets 2. Authors 3. Folk musicians 4. Songwriters 5. Revolutionaries 6. Biography, Individual 7. Industrial Workers of the World
ISBN 978-1-59691-696-8; 1-59691-696-6

LC 2011009821

This is a biography of the poet, songwriter and labor activist who was executed in 1915. Index.
"Presenting Hill as man and symbol, Adler contributes vitally to labor history." Booklist
Includes bibliographical references

Hilleman, Maurice R., 1919-2005

Offit, Paul A. **Vaccinated**; one man's quest to defeat the world's deadliest diseases. Smithsonian Books/Collins 2007 254p $26.95   **92**
1. Biologists 2. Vaccination 3. Microbiologists
ISBN 978-0-06-122795-0; 0-06-122795-1

LC 2006-53054

"This book leaves one with a great appreciation for the work of the Salks and Sabins of the world, and it makes one want to lead a movement to enshrine Maurice Hilleman in the pantheon of American pop heroes." Choice
Includes bibliographical references

Himmler, Heinrich, 1900-1945

Breitman, Richard. The **architect** of genocide; Himmler and the final solution. University Press of New England 1992 335p (The Tauber Institute for the Study of European Jewry) pa $30   **92**
1. Heads of state 2. National socialism 3. Nazi leaders 4. Germany -- Politics and government -- 1933-1945
ISBN 0-87451-596-3; 978-0-87451-596-1

LC 92-53857

First published 1991 by Knopf
"This engrossing, detailed study constitutes a powerful refutation of revisionist scholars who claim that Hitler did not plan the Final Solution in advance but instead improvised it out of either military or political frustration." Publ Wkly
Includes bibliographical references

Hinton, Milt, 1910-2000

Hinton, Milt. **Playing** the changes; Milt Hinton's life in stories and photographs. [by] Milt Hinton, David G. Berger, and Holly Maxson; foreword by Clint Eastwood; preface by Dan Morganstern. Vanderbilt University Press 2008 364p il $75   **92**
1. Photographers 2. Jazz musicians 3. Bassists
ISBN 978-0-8265-1574-2; 0-8265-1574-6

LC 2007-30389

First published 1988 with title: Bass line
"More than just a biography and more than a photography book. This is an excellent selection for any library music collection. It opens up the world of jazz as well as a time in African-American history that isn't always pleasant to remember." Univ Press Books for Public and Second Sch Libr, 2009
Includes discography, filmography, and bibliographical references

Hirohito, Emperor of Japan, 1901-1989

★ Bix, Herbert P. **Hirohito** and the making of modern Japan. HarperCollins Pubs. 2000 800p il maps hardcover o.p. pa $18   **92**
1. Emperors 2. Japan -- Politics and government
ISBN 0-06-093130-2 pa

LC 99-89427

"In 1945, fearing that the Japanese would resist American occupation unless the Emperor ordered them to obey, General MacArthur colluded with Hirohito in maintaining that the sovereign had been powerless to control Japan's military leaders. . . . {Bix}, uses newly available sources to argue that Hirohito was a war criminal. An imperialist whose policies reflected his belief in the racial superiority of the Japanese, Hirohito governed by manipulation for almost two decades, and used the threat of Soviet Communism to justify domestic repression and soaring military budgets. The author's virtuoso scholarship and accessible narrative invite us into Hirohito's world." New Yorker
Includes bibliographical references

Hirsi Ali, Ayaan, 1969-

Hirsi Ali, Ayaan. **Infidel**. Free Press 2007 353p il $26; pa $15   **92**
1. Refugees 2. Muslim women 3. Feminists 4. Memoirists 5. Members of Parliament
ISBN 0-7432-8968-4; 978-0-7432-8968-9; 0-7432-8969-2 pa; 978-0-7432-8969-6 pa

LC 2006-49762

"A Somali by birth and a recently elected member of the Dutch Parliament, Ms. Hirsi Ali had waged a personal crusade to improve the lot of Muslim women. Her warnings about the dangers posed to the Netherlands by unassimilated Muslims made her Public Enemy No. 1 for Muslim extremists, a feminist counterpart to Salman Rushdie. The circuitous, violence-filled path that led Ms. Hirsi Ali from Somalia to the Netherlands is the subject of 'Infidel,' her brave, inspiring and beautifully written memoir." N Y Times (Late N Y Ed)

Hitchcock, Alfred, 1899-1980

Chandler, Charlotte. **It's** only a movie; Alfred Hitchcock, a personal biography. Simon & Schuster 2005 349p il $26   **92**
1. Motion picture directors
ISBN 0-7432-4508-3

LC 2004-52559

The author reveals "several insights into Hitchcock's technical genius, creative worldview and personality. . . . Chandler allows her sources to reminisce at great length, and they tend to tell fascinating stories." Publ Wkly
Includes filmography

Spoto, Donald. **Spellbound** by beauty; Alfred Hitchcock and his leading ladies. Harmony Books 2008 xxiii, 324p il $25.95   **92**
1. Motion picture producers and directors 2. Motion picture directors
ISBN 978-0-307-35130-2; 0-307-35130-0

LC 2008-08922

The third volume in a trilogy exploring the life and work of the legendary director examines Hitchcock's life in terms of his relationships with the actresses in his films, including Ingrid Bergman, Grace Kelly, Kim Novak, and Tippi Hedren, in a study of his films, rise to fame and power, artistic legacy, unconventional marriage, and obsessions.

"Relying on hours of personal interviews with both Hitchcock and his various players, Spoto shines an admiring yet unflinching light on one of the most celebrated directors in history." Publ Wkly
Includes bibliographical references

Hitchens, Christopher, 1949-2011

Hitchens, Christopher, 1949-2011. **Hitch** -22; a memoir. Twelve 2010 435p il $26.99   **92**
1. Authors 2. Journalists 3. Essayists 4. Writers on politics 5. Biography, Individual
ISBN 978-0-446-54033-9

LC 2009051959

This is an autobiography by the British journalist. Christopher Hitchens is the author of For the Sake of Argument: Essays and Minority Reports (1993); Blood, Class, and Nostalgia (1990); Blood, Class, and Empire (2004), and God is Not Great (2007). Index.

Few authors can rile as easily as Hitchens does, but even his detractors might find it difficult to put down a book so witty, so piercing, so spoiling for a fight. He makes you want to be as good a reader as he is a writer. Booklist

Hitler, Adolf, 1889-1945

Breitman, Richard. The **architect** of genocide; Himmler and the final solution. University Press of New England 1992 335p (The Tauber Institute for the Study of European Jewry) pa $30   **92**
1. Heads of state 2. National socialism 3. Nazi leaders 4. Germany -- Politics and government -- 1933-1945
ISBN 0-87451-596-3; 978-0-87451-596-1

LC 92-53857

First published 1991 by Knopf
"This engrossing, detailed study constitutes a powerful refutation of revisionist scholars who claim that Hitler did not plan the Final Solution in advance but instead improvised it out of either military or political frustration." Publ Wkly
Includes bibliographical references

Bullock, Alan. **Hitler** and Stalin; parallel lives. Knopf 1992 1081p il maps hardcover o.p. pa $25   **92**
1. Heads of state 2. Nazi leaders 3. Communist leaders 4. Political leaders 5. Soviet Union -- Politics and government 6. Germany -- Politics and government -- 1933-1945
ISBN 0-679-72994-1 pa

LC 91-52711

First published 1991 in the United Kingdom
"The twentieth century cannot be understood without close examination of the work of Stalin and Hitler. It is particularly important to note what their regimes and aims had in common and where they differed. Alan Bullock has put us all in his debt by placing their actions side by side, in

enormous detail, and in chronological sequence to make the comparison easy." Times Lit Suppl

Includes bibliographical references

Cornwell, John. **Hitler's** pope: the secret history of Pius XII. Viking 1999 430p il hardcover o.p. pa $15   **92**
1. Popes 2. Heads of state 3. Nazi leaders
ISBN 0-14-029627-1 pa

LC 99-28311

"Relying on exclusive access to Vatican and Jesuit archives, . . . {the author} argues that through a 1933 Concordat with Hitler, Pope Pius XII facilitated the dictator's rise—and, ultimately, the Holocaust." Libr J

Includes bibliographical references

★ Hitler, Adolf. **Mein** Kampf; translated by Ralph Manheim. Houghton Mifflin 1943 xxi, 694p $40; pa $22   **92**
1. Heads of state 2. National socialism 3. Nazi leaders
4. Germany -- Politics and government -- 1918-1933
ISBN 0-395-95105-4; 0-395-92503-7 pa

"Hitler's steady rise to power was interrupted only by the Beer Hall Putsch (1923), an unsuccessful attempt to overthrow the Weimar Republic. . . . During the nine months of imprisonment that followed he wrote 'Mein Kampf' (1924; tr. 'My struggle,' 1940). This book contained autobiographical and reflective passages, rife with hysterical anti-Semitism and paranoia, as well as the program he intended to implement; for the West it was a warning that went unheeded." Reader's Ency. 3d edition

Kershaw, Ian. **Hitler**; a biography. W.W. Norton 2008 1029p il map $39.95   **92**
1. Heads of state 2. Nazi leaders
ISBN 978-0-393-06757-6; 0-393-06757-2

LC 2008-37294

This abridgment of the author's two-volume biography on Hitler "retains two themes of Kershaw's full-scale original: analyzing the political support the demagogue mustered from the populace and key institutional centers of Germany on his ascent to and exercise of power; and the decisive personal role of Hitler in instigating World War II and genocide. The narrative Kershaw constructs on this foundation is a superb organization and expression of Hitler's chronological arc that plummeted the world into catastrophe and moral trauma, a trajectory informed by Kershaw's attention to rationalizations by which people in and outside Germany, whether leaders or led, buried doubts about Hitler until his power was unrestrained, impossible to stop but by war or assassination. Manifestly, Kershaw constitutes core-collection material." Booklist

Includes bibliographical references

Kershaw, Ian. **Hitler,** 1889-1936: hubris. Norton 1999 xxx, 845p il $35; pa $21.95   **92**
1. Heads of state 2. Nazi leaders 3. Germany -- Politics and government -- 1918-1933 4. Germany -- Politics and government -- 1933-1945
ISBN 0-393-04671-0; 0-393-32035-9 pa

LC 98-29569

"Kershaw provides an examination based on a number of archival sources not used by previous biographers. . . . More than a chronicle of Hitler's life, this is an analysis of the major historiographical issues, the circumstances that shaped his personality, and the historical events that enabled Hitler to rise to power." Libr J

Includes bibliographical references

Toland, John. **Adolf** Hitler. Anchor Bks. (NY) 1992 xx, 1035p il pa $24   **92**
1. Heads of state 2. National socialism 3. Nazi leaders
4. Germany -- Politics and government -- 1933-1945
ISBN 0-385-42053-6

LC 91-31242

A reissue of the title first published 1976

This biography is based on more than 250 interviews with people acquainted with Hitler and materials from U.S. and British archives

"In the course of detailed and painstaking investigations {Toland} has disposed of a number of myths." N Y Times Book Rev

Includes bibliographical references

Hoffa, Jimmy, b. 1913

Russell, Thaddeus. **Out** of the jungle; Jimmy Hoffa and the remaking of the American working class. Temple University Press 2003 272p il (Labor in crisis) pa $21.95   **92**
1. Missing persons 2. Labor leaders 3. Trucking executives 4. International Brotherhood of Teamsters, Chauffeurs, Warehousemen and Helpers of America
ISBN 1-592-13027-5; 978-1-592-13027-6

LC 2002-43556

First published 2001 by Knopf

In this chronicle of the life and career of Hoffa, "the author presents new interpretations of how the Depression, the New Deal, World War II, and Robert F. Kennedy's crusade against organized crime affected not only Hoffa and the Teamsters but also the American labor movement as a whole." Publisher's note

"Russell makes good use of a range of primary-source materials plus period newspaper accounts and other materials to highlight this story." Libr J

Includes bibliographical references

Holiday, Billie, 1915-1959

★ Blackburn, Julia. **With** Billie. Pantheon Books 2005 354p $25   **92**
1. Singers 2. Blues musicians 3. African American singers
ISBN 0-375-40610-7

LC 2004-58661

This "oral biography of Billie Holiday is based on interviews that researcher Linda Kuehl did in the late 1970s with more than 150 people who knew and worked with the singer. . . . Rather than her recordings, the emphasis is on the events and issues surrounding the music. . . . This is in many ways a joyful portrait of a woman determined to go her own way but, in the end, unable to fulfill her own dreams." Libr J

Includes bibliographical references

Clarke, Donald. **Billie** Holiday; wishing on the moon. Da Capo 2002 468p il pa $21   **92**

1. Singers 2. Blues musicians 3. African American singers

ISBN 0-306-81136-7; 978-0-306-81136-4

First published 1994 by Viking with title: Wishing on the moon: the life and times of Billie Holiday

This biography "not only chronicles every phase of Holiday's ascent from the streets of Baltimore to the stages of New York's hottest nightclubs and most prestigious concert halls, but also documents every significant recording session, performance, and tour. . . . Clarke's portrait embraces every facet of Holiday's paradoxical nature, from her fierceness to her vulnerability, her childlikeness to her innate elegance and amazing strength." Booklist

Griffin, Farah Jasmine. **If** you can't be free, be a mystery; in search of Billie Holiday. Ballantine Books 2002 240p il pa $14.95   **92**

1. Singers 2. Blues musicians 3. African American singers

ISBN 978-0-345-44973-3; 0-345-44973-8

First published 2001 by Free Press

"While Griffin's book isn't the last word on Holiday, it does prove to be an excellent antidote to the often ridiculous material that has been written about Lady Day over the years." Libr J

Includes bibliographical references

★ Holiday, Billie. **Lady** sings the blues; [Billie Holiday with William Dufty] 50th anniversary ed.; Harlem Moon 2006 231p il pa $15.95   **92**

1. Singers 2. Blues musicians 3. African American singers

ISBN 978-0-7679-2386-6; 0-7679-2386-3

LC 2007-271682

First published 1956 by Doubleday

"A hard, bitter and unsentimental book, written with brutal honesty and having much to say not only about Billie Holiday, the person, but about what it means to be poor and black in America." N Y Her Trib Books

Includes discography

O'Meally, Robert G. **Lady** Day; the many faces of Billie Holiday. [by] Robert O'Meally; produced by Toby Byron/Multiprises. Da Capo Press 1991 207p il pa $20   **92**

1. Singers 2. Blues musicians 3. African American singers

ISBN 978-0-306-80959-0; 0-306-80959-1

First published 1991 by Arcade

"Narcotics, jail, sexual abuse, and prejudice are often our first associations concerning the life of the great jazz singer, but this biography recalls only Holiday as artist. O'Meally . . . puts her tragedy and talent into perspective, and what emerges is a critique of a singer. The book's first section is

outstanding in this regard, employing stories, quotes, and interviews in describing Holiday's technique." Libr J

Includes discography and bibliographical references

Hollenbeck, Don, 1905-1954

Ghiglione, Loren. **CBS's** Don Hollenbeck; an honest reporter in the age of McCarthyism. Columbia University Press 2008 330p il $29.95   **92**

1. Journalists 2. Radio reporters 3. Television reporters

ISBN 978-0-231-14496-4; 0-231-14496-2

LC 2008-10686

The author "presents Hollenbeck as a hardworking reporter and a complex personality who struggled with some of the most difficult issues of his time." Booklist

"Ghiglione's attention to detail and use of numerous personal interviews make this both a compelling biography and a rich contextual history of the McCarthy era." Libr J

Includes bibliographical references (p. 289-316)

Holman, James, 1786-1857

Roberts, Jason. A **sense** of the world; how a blind man became history's greatest traveler. HarperCollins Publishers 2006 382p il $26.95; pa $14.95   **92**

1. Blind 2. Naval officers 3. Travel writers

ISBN 0-00-716106-9; 978-0-00-716106-5; 0-00-716126-3 pa; 978-0-00-716126-3 pa

LC 2005-58166

The author "narrates the life of a 19th-century British naval officer who was mysteriously blinded at 25, but nevertheless became the greatest traveler of his time. . . . Roberts does Holman justice, evoking with grace and wit the tale of this man once lionized as 'The Blind Traveler.'" Publ Wkly

Includes bibliographical references

Homes, A. M.

Homes, A. M. The **mistress's** daughter. Viking 2007 238p il $24.95   **92**

1. Authors 2. Novelists 3. Short story writers

ISBN 978-0-670-03838-1; 0-670-03838-5

LC 2006-41354

"Before A. M. Homes was born, she was put up for adoption. Her birth mother was a twenty-two-year-old single woman who was having an affair with a much older married man with children of his own. The Mistress's Daughter is the story of what happened when, thirty years later, her birth parents came looking for her." Publisher's note

"Though the quest seems, at times, overwrought as Homes searches for meaning and connection where there may not be any, the writing is consistently controlled and knowing. . . . Though Homes gives away some of her mystery with this book, she will gain further respect as a writer." Seattle Times

Honig, Donald

Honig, Donald. The **fifth** season; tales of my life in baseball. Ivan R. Dee 2009 287p $26.95   **92**

1. Authors 2. Novelists 3. Historians 4. Sportswriters 5. Mystery writers 6. Short story writers 7. Baseball -- Biography

ISBN 978-1-56663-810-4; 1-56663-810-0

LC 2008-36471

"Honig gives us a lyrical account of growing up in New York City besotted with baseball, his own abbreviated pitching career, and his passion for the greats and near-greats of the game. This nuanced, pitch-perfect memoir will make readers appreciate the nuances and permutations of the game itself. Stats, salary statistics, and free-agent greed are (thankfully) absent, replaced by warm recitations of bygone games and now-departed characters both on the field and off." Libr J

Hood, Ann, 1956-

Hood, Ann. **Comfort**; a journey through grief. W. W. Norton & Co. 2008 188p $19.95   **92**
   1. Death 2. Authors 3. Novelists 4. Bereavement 5. Loss (Psychology) 6. Short story writers
   ISBN 978-0-393-06456-8

LC 2008-1310

"Ann Hood has written about her little girl's death. Grace died on April 18, 2002, from a virulent form of strep. She was 5 years old. One morning she was there and the next she was gone, leaving her tights on the floor and her leopard-print rain boots in the hall and her hat with the pompom on a hook by the door. . . . What makes this book so different from other such memoirs is that it seems to be taking place in real time. Hood doesn't cut us any slack. Even Joan Didion, grieving the loss of her husband and her daughter's illness in 'The Year of Magical Thinking,' held back from the brink, retreated into her vast intellect. Hood will not retreat." Los Angeles Times Book Rev

Hooks, Bell

Hooks, Bell. **Belonging**; a culture of place. Routledge 2008 230p $95; pa $19.95   **92**
   1. Home 2. Poets 3. Authors 4. Dramatists 5. Women authors 6. African American authors 7. Kentucky 8. Essayists 9. Feminists 10. Memoirists 11. Social critics 12. College teachers 13. Children's authors 14. Nonfiction writers
   ISBN 978-0-415-96815-7; 978-0-415-96816-4 pa

LC 2008-21846

The author "writes about the solace she found as a girl in the hills of Kentucky, her long years away, and her return, which has inspired a fresh look at the self-reliant communities of black Appalachians and their nurturing connection to the land." Booklist

Includes bibliographical references

Hooks, Bell. **Wounds** of passion; a writing life. Holt & Co. 1997 xxiii, 260p hardcover o.p. pa $13   **92**
   1. Poets 2. Authors 3. Dramatists 4. Essayists 5. Feminists 6. Memoirists 7. Social critics 8. College teachers 9. Children's authors 10. Nonfiction writers
   ISBN 0-8050-5722-6 pa

LC 97-23506

In this continuation of the author's autobiography, Hooks chronicles "her rigorous education, both in a long, complicated relationship with a fellow writer and as a college and graduate student, experiences that led her away from poetry (her first literary love) to groundbreaking prose that expressed her feminist convictions and views on the status of black women in America." Booklist

Hoover, Herbert, 1874-1964

Leuchtenburg, William Edward. **Herbert** Hoover; [by] William E. Leuchtenburg. Times Books 2009 186p (American presidents series) $22   **92**
   1. Presidents 2. Philanthropists 3. Secretaries of commerce 4. Presidents -- United States 5. United States -- Politics and government -- 1919-1933
   ISBN 978-0-8050-6958-7; 0-8050-6958-5

LC 2008-26456

This is a biography of the American president.

"A veteran historian of this period, Leuchtenburg brings vivid prose and strong opinions to this richly insightful biography of a president whose impressive business acumen served him poorly." Publ Wkly

Includes bibliographical references (p. 167-172)

Hope, Bob, 1903-2003

Quirk, Lawrence J. **Bob** Hope: the road well-traveled. Applause Theatre Bk. Pubs. 1998 327p il hardcover o.p. pa $14.95   **92**
   1. Actors 2. Comedians
   ISBN 1-55783-353-2; 1-55783-450-4 pa

LC 98-87957

"Quirk recaps Hope's life and surveys his relationships with myriad entertainment personalities. . . . This is a good, solid Hollywood bio by a veteran Tinseltown observer." Booklist

Includes filmography and bibliographical references

Hopkins, Lightnin', 1912-1982

Govenar, Alan B. **Lightnin'** Hopkins; his life and blues. Chicago Review Press 2010 334p il $28.95   **92**
   1. Singers 2. Guitarists 3. Blues music 4. Blues musicians 5. African American musicians 6. Songwriters
   ISBN 978-1-55652-962-7

LC 2009-48798

In this "biography of the prolific and influential blues icon Sam 'Lightnin'' Hopkins, . . . [the author] presents important new research and employs neglected primary sources to offer an accessible critical analysis of Hopkins's artistic achievement buttressed by generous quotations from his lyrics. . . . [This] biography of an important figure in blues history is an essential purchase for anyone interested in American popular music or African American culture." Libr J

Includes discography and bibliographical references

Hopper, Grace, 1906-1992

★ Beyer, Kurt W. **Grace** Hopper and the invention of the information age. MIT Press 2009 398p il (Lemelson Center studies in invention and innovation) $27.95   **92**
   1. Admirals 2. Computer scientists 3. Computer programming 4. Biography, Individual 5. COBOL (Computer program language)
   ISBN 978-0-262-01310-9

LC 2008-44229

This is a biography of the computer programmer who "abandoned academia to serve her country in the Navy after Pearl Harbor. . . . Hopper made herself 'one of the boys' in

Howard Aiken's wartime Computation Laboratory at Harvard, then moved on to the Eckert and Mauchly Computer Corporation. . . . . Hopper's greatest technical achievement was to create the tools that would allow humans to communicate with computers in terms other than ones and zeroes." (Publisher's note) Index.

"In Beyer's fascinating mix of biography and technological history, Grace Hopper comes vividly to life as a navy admiral who launched the art of computer programming." Booklist

Includes bibliographical references

Horne, Lena

Gavin, James. **Stormy** weather; the life of Lena Horne. Atria 2009 598p il $27; pa $16   **92**
1. Actors 2. Singers 3. African American women 4. African American singers
ISBN 978-0-7432-7143-1; 0-7432-7143-2; 978-0-7432-7144-8 pa; 0-7432-7144-0 pa
LC 2009-08170
This is a biography of the American singer who has appeared in the films Stormy Weather and Cabin in the Sky (both 1943) and on Broadway in Jamaica (1957) and The Lady and Her Music (1981).

Horne "has had a life so rich in ups and downs as to make page after page eventful and suspenseful. This all the more so since the book is also two books in one: a thorough and fluent biography and a history of the slow social rise of black people despite crippling discrimination and stinging humiliations—a history in which Horne's story is embedded." N Y Times Book Rev

Includes discography, filmography, and bibliographic references

Houdini, Harry, 1874-1926

Steinmeyer, Jim. The **last** greatest magician in the world; Howard Thurston versus Houdini & the battles of the American wizards. Jeremy P. Tarcher/Penguin, a member of Penguin Group 2011 377p il $26.95   **92**
1. Magicians 2. Nonfiction writers
ISBN 978-1-58542-845-8
LC 2010-35384
This is a "an engaging full-length biography of the man Orson Welles called 'the master.' . . . Tracing the magician's rise to fame, this volume neatly juggles his marriages and his magic with his triumphs, travails, showmanship, and marketing ballyhoo." Publ Wkly

Houghton family

Leaming, Barbara. **Katharine** Hepburn. Limelight Eds. 2000 549p il $23.95   **92**
1. Actors
ISBN 0-87910-293-4
LC 00-25227
A reissue of the title first published 1995 by Crown
This biography begins with a "portrait of the entire Hepburn clan, stressing the effect of the suicides that ran through Kate's maternal and paternal families. This is, in fact, a family biography, with at least half the book devoted to Hepburn's grandmother and mother. . . . By the time Kate enters the story, readers will be thoroughly caught up in a tale that

already has delivered a full measure of intrigue, romance, and scandal. The book has been prodigiously researched (Leaming's source notes make fascinating reading on their own), and her access to various, previously unavailable papers not only makes possible the family history, but also paves the way for startling new revelations about Hepburn's life." Booklist {review of 1995 edition}

Houze, David, 1965-

★ Houze, David. **Twilight** people; one man's journey to find his roots. University of California Press 2006 329p il $24.95   **92**
1. Apartheid 2. Journalists 3. Memoirists 4. African Americans -- Civil rights
ISBN 0-520-24398-6; 978-0-520-24398-9
LC 2005-35322
This "graceful memoir is a sensitive look into racial history in Africa and America, as well as a riveting personal narrative." Publ Wkly

Includes bibliographical references

Howe, Ben Ryder

Howe, Ben Ryder. **My** Korean deli; risking it all for a convenience store. Henry Holt and Co. 2010 304p $25   **92**
1. Korean Americans 2. Convenience stores 3. Editors 4. Small business owners
ISBN 978-0-8050-9343-8; 0-8050-9343-5
LC 2010-24962
The author's "wife Gab bought (with the money the couple had saved for a down payment on their first house) her hardworking Korean parents a deli in Brooklyn as a gesture of thanks for all their self-sacrifice. What follows is a series of both comic and tragic vignettes that will leave the reader as surprised as the author about how emotionally invested you can get in a deli. . . . [Howe] delivers a smartly written narrative about love, literature, and the lengths one goes to for family, which turns out to be epically far." Maclean's

Howe, Louis M., 1871-1936

Fenster, J. M. **FDR's** shadow; Louis Howe, the force that shaped Franklin and Eleanor Roosevelt. [by] Julie M. Fenster. Palgrave Macmillan 2009 248p il $27   **92**
1. Diplomats 2. Governors 3. Presidents 4. People with disabilities 5. Columnists 6. Philatelists 7. Humanitarians 8. Social activists 9. Government officials 10. Presidential advisers 11. Spouses of presidents 12. United Nations officials
ISBN 0-230-60910-4; 978-0-230-60910-5
LC 2009-39965
This is a "portrait of a once-famous, now nearly forgotten figure in 20th-century American politics. Louis Howe (1871-1936) met Franklin Roosevelt in 1911, when Howe was a newspaper reporter and FDR a freshly minted New York state senator. They became fast friends, and Howe proved to be a pivotal figure in Roosevelt's life and career. . . . An insightful look at a complex relationship that has been largely lost to history." Kirkus

Includes bibliographical references

Hoyle, Fred

Mitton, Simon. **Conflict** in the cosmos; Fred Hoyle's life in science. Joseph Henry Press 2005 401p il $27.95 **92**

1. Authors 2. Novelists 3. Astronomers 4. Writers on science 5. Science fiction writers
ISBN 0-309-09313-9

LC 2004-30638

The author "sheds light on both the scientist and the science through research and his own experiences with Hoyle's colleagues, students, and the man himself. . . . This excellent biography brings Hoyle to life while explaining, in language clear enough for the amateur enthusiast, the work that made him great." Libr J
Includes bibliographical references

Hughes, Langston, 1902-1967

Marshall, Paule. **Triangular** road; a memoir. BasicCivitas Books 2009 165p il $23 **92**

1. Poets 2. Authors 3. Novelists 4. Dramatists 5. African American authors 6. Essayists 7. Short story writers 8. Young adult authors 9. African Americans -- Intellectual life
ISBN 978-0-465-01359-3

LC 2008-36671

This is a memoir by the author of Praisesong for the widow (1983).
"Though fiction may have pride of place in . . . [the author's] heart, 'Triangular Road' reveals a strong gift for self-scrutiny made all the more revealing by quiet humor and what appears to be complete honesty." Washington Post

Rampersad, Arnold. The **life** of Langston Hughes Volume I: 1902-1941; I, too, sing America. 2nd ed; Oxford University Press 2002 478p il hardcover o.p. pa $33 **92**

1. Poets 2. Authors 3. Novelists 4. Dramatists 5. African American authors
ISBN 0-19-515160-7; 0-19-514642-5 pa
First published 1986
This is the first volume of a two-volume set chronicling the life of the Harlem Renaissance poet and author.
Includes bibliographical references

Hughes, Robert

★ Hughes, Robert. **Things** I didn't know; a memoir. Knopf 2006 395p $27.95 **92**

1. Art critics 2. Nonfiction writers
ISBN 1-4000-4444-8; 978-1-4000-4444-3

LC 2006-40968

This is a memoir by the author of Heaven and Hell in Western Art (1968), The Shock of the New, and The Culture of Complaint (1993).
"Hughes's vivid ruminations and sharp-eyed insights combine in bold, definitive strokes to yield a rich portrait of the art expert." Publ Wkly

Humbert, Agnès, 1894-1963

Humbert, Agnes. **Resistance**; a woman's journal of struggle and defiance in occupied France. Bloomsbury 2008 370p il $26 **92**

1. Art historians 2. Underground leaders 3. World War, 1939-1945 -- Personal narratives 4. World War, 1939-1945 -- Prisoners and prisons 5. World War, 1939-1945 -- Underground movements 6. France -- History -- 1940-1945, German occupation
ISBN 978-1-59691-559-6; 1-59691-559-5

LC 2008-16603

Original French edition, 1946
"Humbert's firsthand account of her work for the resistance in occupied Paris and her subsequent arrest and deportation to a forced-labor camp in Germany is an invaluable addition to works highlighting the role of women during wartime." Publ Wkly
Includes bibliographical references

Hurston, Zora Neale, 1891-1960

Boyd, Valerie. **Wrapped** in rainbows; the life of Zora Neale Hurston. Scribner 2003 527p il $30 **92**

1. Authors 2. Novelists 3. Dramatists 4. African American authors 5. Memoirists 6. Folklorists 7. Short story writers 8. African American women -- Biography
ISBN 0-684-84230-0

LC 2002-17011

This is a biography of the folklorist and author of Their Eyes Were Watching God (1937), Tell My Horse (1938), Dust Tracks on a Road (1942) and Seraph on the Suwanee (1948)
"As the author adeptly and passionately analyzes Hurston's revolutionary books, intense spirituality, and myriad adventures, Hurston emerges in all her splendor—not only smarter, tougher, and more dazzlingly alive than most people but also freer." Booklist
Includes bibliographical references

★ Hurston, Zora Neale. **Dust** tracks on a road; an autobiography. with a foreword by Maya Angelou. 1st Harper Perennial Modern Classic ed; Harper Perennial Modern Classics 2006 308p il pa $13.95 **92**

1. Authors 2. Novelists 3. Dramatists 4. African American authors 5. Memoirists 6. Folklorists 7. Short story writers 8. African American women -- Biography
ISBN 0-06-085408-1; 978-0-06-085408-9

LC 2005-52616

First published 1942 by Lippincott
The author describes her wanderings in and out of schools and jobs as a young girl, finishing her course work at Barnard, and beginning her life's work.
Includes bibliographical references

Hurston, Zora Neale. **Zora** Neale Hurston: a life in letters; collected and edited by Carla Kaplan. Doubleday 2002 880p il $40; pa $19.95 **92**

1. Authors 2. Novelists 3. Dramatists 4. African American authors 5. Memoirists 6. Folklorists 7. Short story writers 8. African American women --

Biography
ISBN 0-385-49035-6; 0-385-49036-4 pa
LC 00-65671

A collection of over 500 letters by the Harlem Renaissance author

These letters reveal "a gifted yet complex personality at once humorous, cynical, and analytical." Libr J

Includes bibliographical references

Hussein, King of Jordan, 1935-1999

Ashton, Nigel. **King** Hussein of Jordan; a political life. [by] Nigel Ashton. Yale University Press 2008 431p il map $35   **92**
1. Kings 2. Jordan -- History 3. Biography, Individual 4. Jordan -- Kings and rulers 5. Jordan -- Politics and government 6. Jordan -- Politics and government -- 1952-1999
ISBN 0-300-09167-2; 978-0-300-09167-0
LC 2008-10803

This is a biography of King Hussein of Jordan, who "reigned for nearly half a century, from his grandfather's assassination in 1953 to his own death in 1999." (Publisher's note) Bibliography. Index.

With "unprecedented access to the late king's entire correspondence and more than two dozen interviews . . . Ashton reveals Hussein's longstanding covert contact with Israel and his clandestine communications with Israelis in the immediate aftermath of the 1967 war to suggest the possibilities and missed opportunities (including by the U.S.) for a peaceful settlement in the Palestinian-Israeli conflict." Publ Wkly

Includes bibliographical references (p. 371-378)

Huston, John, 1906-1987

Meyers, Jeffrey. **John** Huston; courage and art. Crown Archetype 2011 475p il $30; ebook $14.99   **92**
1. Motion picture producers and directors 2. Screenwriters 3. Motion picture directors
ISBN 978-0-307-59067-1; 978-0-307-59069-5 ebook
LC 2010047642

"By balancing the flamboyant life with the landmark works of legendary movie director John Huston, . . . Meyers reveals how a flawed man produced nearly flawless and indelible films." Booklist

Includes filmography and bibliographical references

Hustvedt, Siri

Hustvedt, Siri. The **shaking** woman; or, A history of my nerves. Henry Holt 2010 224p $23 **92**
1. Authors 2. Novelists
ISBN 978-0-8050-9169-4; 0-8050-9169-6
LC 2009-15385

Hustvedt "investigates the reason(s) she suddenly began shuddering violently while delivering a memorial talk about her father, more than two years after his death. The author pursues her symptoms with Javertian devotion. . . She read voraciously, attended lectures on brain science, visited a variety of medical and psychological specialists, underwent examinations and MRIs and took drugs. She also ruminated excessively. The result is a narrative that is alternately transparent and scientifically dense, frustrating and satisfying,

conclusive and vague. . . . Self-absorption can be grating in memoirs by lesser writers; in Hustvedt's capable hands, it opens a door to revelation." Kirkus

Ian, Janis, 1951-

Ian, Janis. **Society's** child; my autobiography. Jeremy P. Tarcher/Penguin 2008 xxii, 361p il $26.95   **92**
1. Singers
ISBN 9781585426751
LC 2008-17130

This is a memoir by the American folk singer.

"Fans will love the book, of course, but many nonfans, too, should find this painfully candid memoir hard to put down." Booklist

Includes bibliographical references

Ice-T

Ice-T. **Ice**; a memoir of gangster life and redemption--from South Central to Hollywood. [by] Ice-T and Douglas Century. One World Books 2011 251p il $25; ebook $12.99   **92**
1. Actors 2. Rap music 3. African American musicians 4. Rap musicians
ISBN 978-0-345-52328-0; 978-0-345-52330-3 ebook
LC 2010-41069

"A fascinating and inspiring story about an African American orphan who beat the odds to become successful, this memoir will appeal to fans of hip-hop and popular culture." Booklist

Irving, Henry Sir, 1838-1905

Holroyd, Michael. A **strange** eventful history; the dramatic lives of Ellen Terry, Henry Irving and their remarkable families. Farrar Straus Giroux 2009 620p $40   **92**
1. Actors
ISBN 978-0-374-27080-3; 0-374-27080-5
LC 2008-48330

First published 2008 in the United Kingdom

"Holroyd's sweeping group biography traces the lives of Ellen Terry and Henry Irving, two stars of the Victorian theatre, and their descendants. Terry was 'embodied sunshine,' beloved for her naturalness and grace onstage. In 1878, when she was thirty-one, she began a professional (and perhaps amorous) partnership with Irving, the despotic actor-manager of the Lyceum Theatre, in London. . . . The pair rose to international fame performing melodramas and Shakespeare abridgments. Both had children who attempted careers in the theatre, and the second half of the book dwells on their struggles amid their parents' decline." New Yorker

Ishi

★ Kroeber, Theodora. **Ishi** in two worlds; a biography of the last wild Indian in North America. University of Calif. Press 1976 262p il $50; pa $16.95   **92**
1. Yana Indians 2. Linguistic informants
ISBN 0-520-00674-7; 0-520-22940-1 pa
First published 1961

An account "of the life of the sole survivor of a California Indian tribe. The author, wife of the famed anthropologist, reconstructs the decimation of Ishi's {Yana} people and his reluctant entry in 1911 into the world of his conquerors." Booklist

Ivan IV, the Terrible, Czar of Russia, 1530-1584

De Madariaga, Isabel. **Ivan** the Terrible; first tsar of Russia. Yale University Press 2005 xxi, 484p il map $35   **92**
1. Emperors
ISBN 0-300-09757-3
LC 2004-29807
This is a biography of the Russian tsar.
This "is a persuasively argued, widely researched and impressively authoritative work that casts new light on the Tsar, his reign, and Russia in the sixteenth century." Times Lit Suppl
Includes bibliographical references

Ivers, Peter

Frank, Josh. **In** heaven everything is fine; the unsolved life of Peter Ivers and the lost history of New wave theatre. [by] Josh Frank with Charlie Buckholtz. Free Press 2008 327p il $25   **92**
1. Comedians 2. Rock musicians 3. Television personalities 4. Songwriters 5. National Lampoon, Inc.
ISBN 978-1-4165-5120-1; 1-4165-5120-4
LC 2008-2943
In this chronicle of Ivers' life, the authors examine his influence upon "such contemporaries and friends . . . as National Lampoon cofounder Doug Kenney, John Belushi, and David Lynch. . . . An appreciative look at a figure peripheral to a clutch of now-aging major stars." Booklist
Includes bibliographical references

Jackson, Andrew, 1767-1845

★ Brands, H. W. **Andrew** Jackson; his life and times. Doubleday 2005 620p il map $35   **92**
1. Generals 2. Presidents 3. Presidents -- United States
ISBN 0-385-50738-0; 978-0-385-50738-7
LC 2005-42178
This is a biography of the seventh president of the United States.
This book "is a bracing, human portrait of both a remarkable man and of American democracy as it was transformed from a 'government of the people' into a 'government by the people.'" Publ Wkly
Includes bibliographical references

Burstein, Andrew. The **passions** of Andrew Jackson. Knopf 2003 xxi, 292p il map $25; pa $15   **92**
1. Generals 2. Presidents 3. Presidents -- United States
ISBN 0-375-41428-2; 0-375-71404-9 pa
LC 2002-16258
Burstein "explains his subject's imperious personality in relation to the uncertainties of frontier life in the Old Southwest and guides the reader through the 'politics of memory,' or what people have chosen to remember. The author succeeds in illuminating the strengths and weakness of his subject, whose forceful, at times bullying personality represent-

ed the temperament of many early 19th-century Americans. This captivating, richly documented work fills a niche even within the crowded field of Jackson studies. A worthwhile purchase for academic and large public libraries." Libr J
Includes bibliographical references

Meacham, Jon. **American** lion; Andrew Jackson in the White House. Random House 2008 483p il $30   **92**
1. Generals 2. Presidents 3. Presidents -- United States
ISBN 978-1-4000-6325-3; 1-4000-6325-6
LC 2008-23466
The author "looks past the theatrics and posturing to the essential elements of Jackson's many showdowns. Mr. Meacham . . . dispenses with the usual view of Jackson as a Tennessee hothead and instead sees a cannily ambitious figure determined to reshape the power of the presidency during his time in office (1829 to 1837). Case by case, Mr. Meacham dissects Jackson's battles and reinterprets them in a revealing new light." N Y Times (Late N Y Ed)
Includes bibliographical references

Remini, Robert Vincent. **Andrew** Jackson; [by] Robert V. Remini; foreword by General Wesley K. Clark. Palgrave Macmillan 2008 204p il map (Great generals series) $21.95   **92**
1. Generals 2. Presidents 3. Presidents -- United States
ISBN 0-230-60015-8; 978-0-230-60015-7
LC 2008-394
This is a "study of Jackson from a military perspective. Remini maintains a birth-to-death narrative while keeping the focus on Jackson's fundamental existence as a soldier. The result is a fine introduction based on years of advanced knowledge on the subject, distilled by Remini into a very good read." Libr J
Includes bibliographical references

Wilentz, Sean. **Andrew** Jackson. Times Books 2005 195p (American presidents series) $20   **92**
1. Generals 2. Presidents 3. Presidents -- United States
ISBN 0-8050-6925-9
LC 2005-52857
The author "shows that our complicated seventh president was a central figure in the development of American democracy. . . . It is rare that historians manage both Wilentz's deep interpretation and lively narrative." Publ Wkly
Includes bibliographical references

Jackson, Michael, 1958-2009

★ Greenburg, Zack O'Malley. **Michael** Jackson, Inc; the rise, fall and rebirth of a billion-dollar empire. Zack O'Malley Greenburg. Atria Books 2014 293 p. $26   **92**
1. Music industry 2. Musicians -- United States 3. Popular music -- Economic aspects -- United States
ISBN 1476705968; 9781476705965
LC 2013045449
"'Michael Jackson, Inc.' reveals the incredible rise, fall, and rise again of Michael Jackson's fortune--driven by the unmatched perfectionism of the King of Pop. 'Forbes' senior editor Zack O'Malley Greenburg uncovers never-before-told stories from interviews with more than 100 people, includ-

ing music industry veterans Berry Gordy, John Branca, and Walter Yetnikoff; artists 50 Cent, Sheryl Crow, and Jon Bon Jovi; and members of the Jackson family." (Publisher's note)

"A quick-moving yet comprehensive narrative of the singer's career, downfall and unlikely post-mortem second act." Kirkus

Includes bibliographical references and index

Jackson, Stonewall, 1824-1863

Gwynne, S. C. **Rebel** Yell; The Violence, Passion, and Redemption of Stonewall Jackson. S. C. Gwynne. Simon & Schuster 2014 688 p. illustrations, maps, portraits $35   **92**

1. Confederate States of America -- History 2. United States -- History -- 1861-1865, Civil War
ISBN 1451673280; 9781451673289

LC 2014010046

This book, by S. C. Gwynne, is an "account of how Civil War general Thomas 'Stonewall' Jackson became a great and tragic American hero. . . . In April 1862 Jackson was merely another Confederate general in an army fighting what seemed to be a losing cause. By June he had engineered perhaps the greatest military campaign in American history and was one of the most famous men in the Western world. He had, moreover, given the Confederate cause what it had recently lacked--hope." (Publisher's note)

"Gwynne presents Jackson's eccentric personality in biographical episodes that he injects into the arc of Jackson's Civil War campaigns and battles. . . . [The] technique succeeds, thanks to his spry prose and cogent insight, in revealing Jackson's character." Booklist

Includes bibliographical references (pages 577-634) and index

Jacobs, Harriet A., 1813-1897

Yellin, Jean Fagan. **Harriet** Jacobs: a life. Basic Civitas Books 2004 394p il map $27.50; pa $16.95   **92**

1. Slaves 2. Authors 3. Domestics 4. Memoirists
ISBN 0-465-09288-8; 0-465-09289-6 pa

LC 2003-17256

Yellin "presents the first full biography of a woman who began life in slavery and survived the Civil War to become a politically and socially active citizen." Booklist

"This scholarly account, woven in a reader friendly fashion, restores 'an heroic woman who lived in an heroic time' to history and to us." Publ Wkly

Includes bibliographical references

Jaffrey, Madhur

Jaffrey, Madhur. **Climbing** the mango trees; a memoir of a childhood in India. Knopf 2006 297p il $25   **92**

1. Actors 2. Cookbook writers
ISBN 1-4000-4295-X; 978-1-4000-4295-1

LC 2006-45255

First published 2005 in the United Kingdom

This is the memoir by the Indian actress and cookbook author.

The author's "taste memories sparkle with enthusiasm, and her talent for conveying them makes the book relentlessly appetizing." N Y Times Book Rev

James, Eloisa

★ James, Eloisa. **Paris** in love; a memoir. Eloisa James. Random House 2012 x, 260 p.p   **92**

1. Autobiographies 2. Women -- Biography 3. Americans -- France 4. Paris (France) -- Description and travel 5. Life change events 6. Authors, American -- Biography 7. Cancer -- Patients -- Biography 8. Self-actualization (Psychology) 9. Quality of life -- France -- Paris 10. Women authors, American -- Biography 11. Americans -- France -- Paris -- Biography
ISBN 9780679604440; 9781400069569; 0679604448; 1400069564

LC 2011040662

This expatriate memoir by Eloisa James tells how "in 2009, [the] . . . author . . . sold her house, took a sabbatical from her job as a Shakespeare professor, and moved her family to Paris. [The story} chronicles her joyful year . . . [w]ith no classes to teach, no committee meetings to attend, no lawn to mow or cars to park, Eloisa revels in the ordinary pleasures of life . . . She copes with her Italian husband's notions of quality time; her two hilarious children, ages eleven and fifteen, as they navigate schools—not to mention puberty—in a foreign language; and her mother-in-law Marina's raised eyebrow in the kitchen (even as Marina overfeeds Milo, the family dog)." (Publisher's note)

James, Etta, 1938-2012

James, Etta. **Rage** to survive; the Etta James story. [by] Etta James with David Ritz. Da Capo Press 2003 288p il pa $18   **92**

1. Singers 2. Blues musicians 3. Songwriters 4. Soul musicians 5. Singers -- United States
ISBN 0-306-81262-2; 978-0-306-81262-0

First published 1995 by Villard Books

"Born to a 14-year-old mother and raised by surrogate parents, blues and R&B star James started singing gospel in church at five, was discovered at 14 and had a rapid rise to fame. Nevertheless, her story is a disturbing saga of drug addiction, jail sentences for writing bad checks and stealing prescription drugs, involvements with the wrong men and anger at a disruptive and unstable mother who has refused to reveal who her daughter's father is." Publ Wkly

"With a supporting cast resembling the roster of the Rock Hall of Fame, this autobiography reads as its author sings-rough, gritty, and brutally honest." Libr J

Discography

James, Henry, 1843-1916

Portrait of a novel; Henry James and the making of an American masterpiece. Michael Gorra. W.W. Norton & Co. Inc. 2012 416 p. (hardcover) $29.95   **92**

1. Travel 2. Criticism 3. Fictional characters 4. American fiction -- European influences 5. Authors, American -- 19th century -- Biography 6. Authors, American -- 20th century -- Biography
ISBN 0871404087; 9780871404084

LC 2012013838

In this book, Michael Gorra looks at writer Henry James "combining elements of biography, criticism, and travelogue in re-creating the dramatic backstory of James's masterpiece, 'Portrait of a Lady.' . . . Traveling to Florence, Rome, Paris, and England, Gorra sheds new light on James's family, the European literary circles . . . in which James made his name, and the psychological forces that enabled him to create this most memorable of female protagonists." (Publisher's note)

Includes bibliographical references and index.

James, William, 1842-1910

Richardson, Robert D. **William** James; in the maelstrom of American modernism: a biography. Houghton Mifflin 2006 622p il $30   **92**

1. Philosophers 2. Psychologists 3. Writers on science
ISBN 978-0-618-43325-4; 0-618-43325-2

LC 2005-37776

This is a biography of the psychologist and philosopher. The author's "enthusiasm for what he calls 'the matchless incandescent spirit' of William James is contagious." Publ Wkly

Includes bibliographical references (p. 586-9)

Jamison, Kay R.

Jamison, Kay R. **Nothing** was the same; a memoir. by Kay Redfield Jamison. Alfred A. Knopf 2009 208p $25   **92**

1. Bereavement 2. Psychiatrists 3. Psychologists 4. Hodgkin's disease 5. Manic-depressive illness 6. College teachers
ISBN 978-0-307-26537-1; 0-307-26537-4

LC 2009-11096

"The great gift Jamison offers here, beyond her honesty and the beauty of her writing, is perspective: a clear-eyed view of illness and death, sanity and insanity, love and grief. . . . Jamison seems to be telling the truth, no matter how difficult it may be, in a way that avoids self-pity and inspires courage." Washington Post Book World

Janabi, Kamel Sachet Aziz

Steavenson, Wendell. The **weight** of a mustard seed; the intimate story of an Iraqi General and his family during thirty years of tyranny. Collins Pub. Group 2009 288p $24.99   **92**

1. Generals 2. Iraq -- Politics and government
ISBN 978-0-06-172178-6; 0-06-172178-6

LC 2008-24402

This is "a masterly and elegantly told story that weaves together the Iraqi past and present." N Y Times Book Rev

Jang, Jin-sung

Jang Jin-sung. **Dear** Leader; poet, spy, escapee? : a look inside North Korea. Jang Jin-sung ; translated by Shirley Lee. 37 Ink/Atria Books 2014 368 p. (hardback) $27.99   **92**

1. Poets 2. Autobiographies 3. Korea (North) -- Biography 4. Propaganda -- Korea (North) 5. Poets -- Korea (North) -- Biography 6. Political refugees -- Korea (North) -- Biography 7. Korea (North) -- Politics and government -- 1994-2011
ISBN 147676655X; 9781476766553

LC 2014010236

This memoir tells how "[a]s North Korea's State Poet Laureate, Jang Jin-sung led a charmed life. With food provisions . . . , a travel pass, access to strictly censored in-

formation, and audiences with Kim Jong-il himself, his life in Pyongyang seemed safe and secure. But this privileged existence was about to be shattered. When a strictly forbidden magazine he lent to a friend goes missing, Jang Jin-sung must flee for his life." (Publisher's note)

"A defector of Kim Jong-il's rarefied inner circle reveals the desperate, despicable machinations of North Korea's police state." Kirkus

Jefferson, Thomas, 1743-1826

Bernstein, Richard B. **Thomas** Jefferson; [by] R.B. Bernstein. Oxford University Press 2003 253p il hardcover o.p. pa $15.95   **92**

1. Architects 2. Presidents 3. Vice-presidents 4. Essayists 5. Presidents -- United States
ISBN 0-19-516911-5; 978-0-19-518130-2 pa; 0-19-518130-1 pa

LC 2003-5556

The author "provides a . . . view not of Jefferson the politician, but of the man whose ideas changed the world and provided the US with a sense of purpose. This short biography provides a judicious synthesis of the prevailing scholarship on the third president and explores more deeply his views on government and union, slavery (revealing what is known about the Sally Hemings affair and what cannot yet be determined), and debt. . . . Its concise form, limited notes, and evenhanded style will appeal to general readers seeking insight into an incredibly complex historical figure." Choice

Includes bibliographical references

Hitchens, Christopher. **Thomas** Jefferson: author of America. HarperCollins Publishers 2005 188p (Eminent lives) $19.95   **92**

1. Architects 2. Presidents 3. Vice-presidents 4. Essayists 5. Presidents -- United States
ISBN 0-06-059896-4

LC 2005-296593

"Beginning with his aristocratic upbringing, . . . this biography explores both the private and public aspects of Jefferson's life, from his political philosophies to his affair with his slave Sally Hemings. . . . This opinionated, lively narrative sheds light not only on Jefferson's complex personality but on the politics of his time, making it both a fascinating character study and an excellent review of early American history." Publ Wkly

Randall, Willard Sterne. **Thomas** Jefferson; a life. HarperPerennial 1994 708p pa $20   **92**

1. Architects 2. Presidents 3. Vice-presidents 4. Essayists 5. Presidents -- United States
ISBN 0-06-097617-9

LC 94-14363

First published 1993 by Holt & Co.

"Randall's substantial, balanced biography will be valuable for general readers who seek a one-volume work on one of the leading Founding Fathers." Libr J

Includes bibliographical references

Jenkins, Charles Robert

Jenkins, Charles Robert. The **reluctant** communist; my desertion, court-martial, and forty-year imprisonment in North Korea. with Jim Frederick.

University of California Press 2008 xxxvi, 192p il $24.95; pa $15.95 **92**

1. Defectors 2. Korea (North) 3. Military deserters 4. Military desertion -- United States
ISBN 978-0-520-25333-9; 0-520-25333-7; 978-0-520-25999-7 pa; 0-520-25999-8 pa

LC 2007-33315

This "book is one of the most important and devastating accounts of life inside a totalitarian society to appear in many years." Commentary

Jeremiah, Thomas, d. 1775

Harris, J. William. The **hanging** of Thomas Jeremiah; a free Black man's encounter with liberty. Yale University Press 2009 223p il map $27.50 **92**

1. Diplomats 2. Merchants 3. Ship captains 4. Colonial leaders 5. Plantation owners 6. Government officials 7. Colonial administrators 8. Slavery -- United States 9. South Carolina -- Race relations 10. African Americans -- Social conditions
ISBN 978-0-300-15214-2; 0-300-15214-0

LC 2009-15233

This is an "account of nebulous historical figure Thomas Jeremiah. . . . Owner of a fishing company and worth $200,000 in 2009 dollars, . . . [Jeremiah] was probably the richest black man in North America; he was also a slaveowner. That didn't stop him from becoming a scapegoat, accused by patriot leader Henry Laurens—a wealthy plantation owner with hundreds of slaves—of secretly leading a British-sponsored slave insurrection. Though Governor William Campbell, aggrieved by the unlawfulness of Jeremiah's trial, interceded, it didn't stop those determined to hang Jeremiah. . . . Readers will learn much about the darker side of American institutions; students of American history and civil rights will appreciate Harris's impassive approach and thorough standards." Publ Wkly

Includes bibliographical references

Joan, of Arc, Saint, 1412-1431

Pernoud, Regine. **Joan** of Arc: her story; Régine Pernoud, Marie-Véronique Clin; translated and revised by Jeremy duQuesnay Adams; edited by Bonnie Wheeler. St. Martin's Griffin 1999 xxii, 304p il map hardcover o.p. pa $16.95 **92**

1. Saints 2. Christian saints 3. France -- History -- 1328-1589, House of Valois
ISBN 0-312-21442-1; 0-312-22730-2 pa

LC 98-45059

Original French edition, 1986

This work "traces the appearance of Joan as a documented historical character rather than adhering to a standard chronological sequence. Informing the narrative is a novel interpretation of Joan as a political prisoner. Moving beyond the narrative, the American translator . . . has added a series of appendixes containing valuable contextual material. . . . These materials discuss key historical events, provide biographical information on Joan's contemporaries, and discuss Joan's afterlife in history, literature, folklore, art, and iconography." Libr J

Includes bibliographical references

Jobs, Steve, 1955-2011

★ Isaacson, Walter. **Steve** Jobs. Simon & Schuster 2011 656p il por **92**

1. Executives 2. Biography, Individual 3. Apple Computer, Inc. -- History 4. Businesspeople -- United States -- Biography 5. Computer engineers -- United States -- Biography
ISBN 9781451648546; 1451648537; 9781451648539; 9781451648553; 1451648553 ebook

LC 2011045006

This is a biography of the former CEO of Apple, Inc.

This book discusses the "basic outlines of [Steve] Jobs' career. . . . He was the co-creator of the personal computer. . . . [A]gainst the backdrop of [Jobs's] abrasive personality, [Walter] Isaacson's book offers an overriding message . . . he was a creative genius whose profound understanding of consumer appetites allowed him to create technology that no one else imagined or even thought feasible." (Commentary)

This "is an encyclopedic survey of all that Mr. Jobs accomplished, replete with the passion and excitement that it deserves." N Y Times Book Rev

Includes bibliographical references and index.

John Paul II, Pope, 1920-2005

Cornwell, John. The **pontiff** in winter; triumph and conflict in the reign of John Paul II. Doubleday 2004 336p il $24.95; pa $14.95 **92**

1. Popes
ISBN 0-385-51484-0; 0-385-51485-9 pa

LC 2004-58306

The author "argues that John Paul's mystical view of history and conviction that his mission has been divinely established are central to understanding his pontificate." Publisher's note

Includes bibliographical references

Flynn, Raymond. **John** Paul II; a personal portrait of the pope and the man. St. Martin's Press 2001 204p il hardcover o.p. pa $14.95 **92**

1. Popes
ISBN 0-312-28328-8 pa

LC 00-45965

Flynn, the "former mayor of Boston and ex-ambassador to the Vatican, tells us . . . what his book is not: It is not a biography, or an analysis. . . . Flynn views it, rather, as a profile based on his own experiences with Pope John Paul II, dating back to a 1969 visit to Boston of then-Cardinal Karol Wojtyla." Natl Rev

O'Connor, Garry. **Universal** Father: a life of John Paul II. Bloomsbury 2005 436p il map $24.95 **92**

1. Popes
ISBN 1-59691-096-8

"The text is divided into four distinct phases of Pope John Paul II's life: '1920-1946,' '1946-1978,' '1978-1990,' and '1990-2005.' Each phase balances fact with anecdotal evidence, which lends the biography both credibility and charm. . . . This timely and remarkable biography will be sought after by serious readers." Libr J

Weigel, George. **Witness** to hope: the biography of Pope John Paul II. Cliff St. Bks. 1999 992p il $35; pa $20   **92**
1. Popes
ISBN 0-06-018793-X; 0-06-093286-4 pa

LC 99-26340

Weigel "focuses on John Paul's trademark ideas: Christian humanism, the inner connection between freedom and truth, and culture as the driving force of history. As a guide to the pope's thought, Witness to Hope is invaluable." Publ Wkly

Includes bibliographical references

Johnson, Andrew, 1808-1875

Gordon-Reed, Annette. **Andrew** Johnson. Times Books/Henry Holt and Company 2011 166p il (American presidents series) $23   **92**
1. Governors 2. Presidents 3. Vice-presidents 4. Members of Congress 5. Presidents -- United States 6. United States -- Politics and government -- 1865-1898
ISBN 978-0-8050-6948-8

LC 2010-32595

"Andrew Johnson rose from humble beginnings in the South to serve as Lincoln's second vice president, thus becoming President just as the Civil War was ending. He showed none of his predecessor's political finesse and is often viewed as among the worst to hold the office. . . . [The author] argues that the nation went from the best President to the worst during this most crucial period of its history. This slim study does cover Johnson from birth to death (1808–75), but the focus is assuredly on his presidency." Libr J
Includes bibliographical references

Johnson, Harriet McBryde

Johnson, Harriet McBryde. **Too** late to die young; nearly true tales from a life. Henry Holt and Co. 2005 261p $23; pa $14   **92**
1. Lawyers 2. Human rights activists
ISBN 0-8050-7594-1; 0-312-42571-6 pa

LC 2004-54007

In this memoir, the wheelchair-bound lawyer and activist describes her battles for disability rights.

"From her first demonstration against the MDA telethon to her celebrated debate with Peter Singer of Harvard, who has stated that killing a disabled infant is not morally equivalent to killing a person, this lady pulls no punches. An entertaining look at an activist who insists on living life her way, disability or no." Libr J

Johnson, Jack, 1878-1946

★ Ward, Geoffrey C. **Unforgivable** blackness; the rise and fall of Jack Johnson. Knopf 2004 492p il $26.95   **92**
1. Boxers (Persons)
ISBN 0-375-41532-7

LC 2004-48524

The author "brings us back into Johnson's life and times with exquisitely rendered details, and the fight scenes themselves are gripping: fights so bloody that referees have to change shirts midbout, for instance, and a manager who pulls a gun on his fighter to keep him from quitting. The authoritative biography of Johnson for sure, but also one of the best boxing books in recent memory." Booklist
Includes bibliographical references

Johnson, Lyndon B. (Lyndon Baines), 1908-1973

Caro, Robert A. **Master** of the senate. Knopf 2002 xxiv, 1167p il (The years of Lyndon Johnson) $35; pa $19.95   **92**
1. Presidents 2. Vice-presidents 3. Senators 4. Members of Congress 5. Presidents -- United States 6. United States -- Politics and government -- 20th century
ISBN 0-394-52836-0; 0-394-72095-4 pa

LC 2002-282796

The third entry in Mr. Caro's multi-volume biography of the thirty-sixth president of the United States, this installment covers Johnson's Senate career.

"Mr. Caro has written a panoramic study of how power plays out in the legislative arena. Combining the best techniques of investigative reporting with majestic storytelling ability, he has created a vivid, revelatory institutional history as well as a rich hologram of Johnson's character." N Y Times (Late N Y Ed)

Includes bibliographical references

Caro, Robert A. **Means** of ascent. Knopf 1990 xxxiv, 506p il (The years of Lyndon Johnson) $45; pa $20   **92**
1. Presidents 2. Vice-presidents 3. Senators 4. Members of Congress 5. Presidents -- United States 6. United States -- Politics and government -- 20th century
ISBN 0-394-52835-2; 0-679-73371-X pa

LC 90-201544

"Caro has written a brilliant but disturbing book that Johnson admirers will intensely dislike. It throws a merciless spotlight on its subject. Readers are asked to reexamine the distinction between political means and ends. Caro examines what he perceives to be Johnson's deepest weaknesses: his lust for power and wealth; his mean spiritedness; his perversity to exploit the difficulties of others and then revel in his own brazen dishonesty. One looks in vain for a redeeming sign of decency in the LBJ of this volume." Christ Sci Monit

Includes bibliographical references

Peters, Charles. **Lyndon** B. Johnson. Times Books 2010 199p (American presidents series) $23   **92**
1. Presidents 2. Vice-presidents 3. Senators 4. Members of Congress 5. Presidents -- United States 6. United States -- Politics and government -- 1945-
ISBN 978-0-8050-8239-5

LC 2009-45612

"Peters describes Johnson's Texas childhood, his years in Congress, his frustrating years as Kennedy's vice president, and the triumphs and failures of his presidency (1963-68). . . . This book is aimed at general readers who want a brief account of this controversial President. . . . Its intended audience will not be disappointed with this fast-moving story." Libr J

Includes bibliographical references

Woods, Randall Bennett. **LBJ**; architect of American ambition. [by] Randall B. Woods. Free Press 2006 1007p il $35   **92**
1. Presidents 2. Vice-presidents 3. Senators 4. Members of Congress 5. Presidents -- United States 6. United States -- Politics and government -- 20th century
ISBN 978-0-684-83458-0; 0-684-83458-8

LC 2006-41259

This is a biography of the 36th president of the United States.

The author "has produced an excellent biography that fully deserves a place alongside the best of the Johnson studies yet to appear." N Y Times Book Rev

Includes bibliographical references

Johnson, Robert, 1911-1938

★ Wald, Elijah. **Escaping** the delta; Robert Johnson and the invention of the blues. Amistad 2004 342p $24.95; pa $14.95   **92**
1. Singers 2. Guitarists 3. Blues music 4. Blues musicians 5. African American musicians 6. Songwriters
ISBN 0-06-052423-5; 0-06-052427-8 pa

LC 2003-52287

The author "writes better than anyone else ever has about the blues. If you read only one book about blues—maybe ever—read this one." Booklist

Includes bibliographical references

Johnson, Samuel, 1709-1784

Boswell, James. The **life** of Samuel Johnson; with an introduction by Claude Rawson. Random House 1992 liii, 127p il (Everyman's library) $30   **92**
1. Lexicographers 2. Literary critics
ISBN 0-679-41717-6

LC 92-52915

First published 1791

"The most famous biography in the English language. It is an intimate and minute delineation of the great lexicographer's life, character and person, enlivened with small-talk, gossip and bits of familiar correspondence. It is also an admirable portrayal of the society of which Johnson was the outstanding figure." Pratt Alcove

Includes bibliographical references

Martin, Peter. **Samuel** Johnson; a biography. Harvard University Press 2008 608p il $35   **92**
1. Lexicographers 2. Literary critics
ISBN 978-0-674-03160-9; 0-674-03160-1

LC 2008-11327

This "biography of the English essayist, lexicographer, and literary personality . . . emphasizes aspects of Johnson not covered by any previously published biographies . . . notably Johnson's deep depressions; his liberal views on women writers, slavery, and poverty (he was not the complete Tory that others have painted him); and Johnson as a writer whose works deserve to be better known by the general pub-

lic. Martin covers all the well-known facts and accomplishments of Johnson's life, and he emphasizes the turbulent times in which Johnson lived and the intriguing people he knew. Scholarly but written in an engaging manner and featuring many quotations from Johnson and his friends and acquaintances, this [is a] new portrait of a complex, multifaceted writer and thinker." Libr J

Includes bibliographical references (p. 565-572)

Meyers, Jeffrey. **Samuel** Johnson; the struggle. Basic Books 2008 528p il $35   **92**
1. Lexicographers 2. Authors, English 3. Literary critics
ISBN 978-0-465-04571-6; 0-465-04571-5

LC 2008-12302

This biography "departs from a strict chronology to narrate significant events and their meaning for Johnson. A central concern involves one of Johnson's darkest secrets, which Meyers says other biographers have evaded: his masochistic sexuality at the hands of his confidante Mrs. Hester Thrale. The biography also speculates on other aspects of Johnson's sex life, both during his marriage to a much older woman and after her death. But Meyers's book is balanced and accomplishes much else." Publ Wkly

Includes bibliographical references

Johnson, Scott C

Johnson, Scott C. The **Wolf** and the Watchman; A Father, a Son, and the CIA. Scott C. Johnson. W W Norton & Co Inc 2013 320 p. (hbk.) $26.95 **92**
1. Father-son relationship 2. Intelligence service -- United States 3. Journalists -- United States -- Biography 4. Fathers and sons -- United States -- Biography 5. Intelligence officers -- United States -- Biography 6. United States. Central Intelligence Agency -- Officials and employees -- Biography
ISBN 0393239802; 9780393239805

LC 2013005130

In this book, journalist Scott C. Johnson describes how he discovered that "his father was a spy, one of the CIA's most trusted officers. At first the secret was thrilling. But over time Scott began to have doubts. . . . When Scott embarked on a career as a foreign correspondent, he found himself returning to many of the troubled countries of his youth. . . . [There] he came face to face with his father's murky past--and his own complicity in it." (Publisher's note)

"A former Newsweek foreign correspondent reviews his often perplexing experiences as the son of a CIA operative..The author does not obey a strict chronology. After 10 chapters that deliver us to 2001, Johnson returns to Mexico City in 1968, wondering if or how his father was involved in the deadly violence that occurred there just before the Olympics...They took some road trips, and en route, we learn about some of the missions and adventures of Johnson père, though he says he resents interrogations. Nonetheless, the author kept pushing him to impart as much family and professional history as possible, trying to understand a man with such a deadly past who nonetheless both professes and demonstrates a profound love for his son. Gripping, emotional depictions of the conflicts that rage in the interior and exterior worlds of a spy—and of a journalist." (Kirkus)

Johnson-Sirleaf, Ellen

Johnson-Sirleaf, Ellen. **This** child will be great; memoir of a remarkable life by Africa's first woman president. HarperCollins 2009 353p il $26.99 **92**
1. Economists 2. Presidents 3. Cabinet members 4. Political leaders 5. Presidents -- Liberia 6. Nobel laureates for peace
ISBN 978-0-06-135347-5
"An inspiring inside look at a nation struggling to rebuild itself and the woman now behind those efforts." Booklist
Includes bibliographical references

Jones, John Paul, 1747-1792

Morison, Samuel Eliot. **John** Paul Jones; a sailor's biography. with an introduction by James C. Bradford; charts and diagrams by Erwin Raisz. Naval Inst. Press 1989 xxvi, 537p il (Classics of naval literature) hardcover o.p. pa $24.95 **92**
1. Naval officers 2. United States -- Naval history
ISBN 1-55750-410-5 pa
LC 89-13423
A reissue with a new introduction of the title first published 1959 by Little, Brown
"Morison has destroyed the myth of John Paul Jones but has left us a more human, more understandable character." Best Sellers
Includes bibliographical references

Jones, Judith

Jones, Judith. The **tenth** muse; my life in food. Alfred A. Knopf 2007 290p il $24.95 **92**
1. Cooks 2. Editors
ISBN 0-307-26495-5; 978-0-307-26495-4
LC 2007-6789
This is a memoir of the author's career in publishing. "Judith Jones is senior editor and vice president at Alfred A. Knopf, where she has worked since 1957." Publisher's note
The author "recounts experiences that food and book lovers will admire and envy." Booklist
Includes bibliographical references

Jones, Malcolm, 1952-

Jones, Malcolm. **Little** boy blues; a crash course in growing up. Pantheon Books 2010 228p il map $24.95 **92**
1. Journalists 2. Magazine editors
ISBN 978-0-307-37772-2; 0-307-37772-5
LC 2009-17838
"In the background of this memoir, the South also complicates the child's horizon, with its own coded vocabulary, reprimanding glances and generations clinging to a crumbling way of life. . . . With all the hype, marketing and lying that the genre's been subjected to in recent years, I had forgotten that it is also the most vulnerable, intimate form a writer can employ. Often, this gets covered over in supportspeak: the way a writer's memories turn into a way to help alleviate the pain of others suffering from similar memories. Jones is far too good a writer to indulge in messianic messages." PopMatters

Jones, Quincy, 1933-

Jones, Quincy. **Q** : the autobiography of Quincy Jones. Doubleday 2001 412p il $26; pa $15.95 **92**
1. Composers 2. Conductors (Music) 3. Music arrangers 4. Recording producers
ISBN 0-385-48896-3; 0-7679-0510-5 pa
LC 2001-28151
"With some chapters written by Jones, and others by his family and friends . . . this (auto)biography full of behind-the-scenes anecdotes has an improvisational feel that suits its subject: a jazz musician and superstar composer. . . . Jones has composed a life story that gives much more than the typical celebrity memoir." Publ Wkly
Includes discography and filmography

Joplin, Scott, 1868-1917

Berlin, Edward A. **King** of ragtime: Scott Joplin and his era. Oxford Univ. Press 1994 334p il hardcover o.p. pa $21.50 **92**
1. Pianists 2. Composers 3. Jazz musicians
ISBN 0-19-510108-1 pa
LC 93-28318
"Essential in any library concerned with American music." Booklist
Includes bibliographical references

Jordan, Michael, 1963-

Lazenby, Roland. **Michael** Jordan; the life. Roland Lazenby. Little Brown & Co 2014 720 p. ill. (some col.) $30 **92**
1. African American baseball players 2. Basketball players -- United States -- Biography
ISBN 0316194778; 9780316194778
LC 2014932746
In this biography about basketball player Michael Jordan, "basketball journalist Roland Lazenby . . . draws on his personal relationships with Jordan's coaches; countless interviews with Jordan's friends, teammates, and family members; and interviews with Jordan himself to provide the first truly definitive study of Michael Jordan: the player, the icon, and the man." (Publisher's note)
"Lazenby's thoroughly enjoyable biography is an impressive portrait of a man consumed by his competitive ambitions." LJ
Includes bibliographical references and index

Joyce, James, 1882-1941

Ellmann, Richard. **James** Joyce; new and rev ed; Oxford Univ. Press 1982 887p il hardcover o.p. pa $27.50 **92**
1. Poets 2. Authors 3. Novelists 4. Dramatists 5. Short story writers
ISBN 0-19-503381-7 pa
LC 81-22455
First published 1959
This "is a vast undertaking and continuing achievement—massive, masterly, and definitive, rich in anecdote and detail. It is also extremely readable; the easy, often sympathetic style communicates gracefully not only facts but analysis." Choice
Includes bibliographical references

Juan Carlos I, King of Spain, 1938-

Preston, Paul. **Juan** Carlos; steering Spain from dictatorship to democracy. W. W. Norton 2004 608p $35 **92**

1. Kings 2. Spain -- History -- 1975-
ISBN 0-393-05804-2

LC 2004-47435

This biography explores the life of the Spanish monarch

Preston "supplies a much-needed, serious, comprehensive, and absolutely dynamic biography of el rey, impressively researched and deeply probing." Booklist

Includes bibliographical references

Judas Iscariot

★ Gubar, Susan. **Judas**; a biography. W. W. Norton & Co. 2009 453p il $27.95 **92**

1. Apostles
ISBN 978-0-393-06483-4; 0-393-06483-2

LC 2008-42967

An account of the story of the New Testament's archvillain and his history over the past 2000 years in which Gubar links Christian anti-Semitism with Christianity's attempt to grapple with transcendent evil.

"An exhaustive, beautifully written cultural history of our favorite wrongdoer, Gubar's work is an immensely rewarding and crucially important book." Libr J

Includes bibliographical references

Judt, Tony, 1948-2010

Judt, Tony, 1948-2010. The **memory** chalet. Penguin Press 2010 226p $25.95 **92**

1. Historians 2. Modern civilization 3. Authors, English 4. College teachers 5. Nonfiction writers 6. World history -- 20th century
ISBN 978-1-59420-289-6; 1-59420-289-3

LC 2010-283600

The book "is a memoir . . . [consisting of] essay[s that] bring . . . the smallest details of personal experience into the larger frame of history. Judt's youthful love of a London bus route becomes a reflection on public civility. . . . Judt takes us from the postwar London of his childhood through Paris, Prague, and points east to New York, where he found his home. Judt [discusses] . . . everything from fast cars to radical politics and, finally, the devastating illness that took his life. This book, composed when Judt was paralyzed and unable physically to write, found its shape in the ordered rooms of a Swiss Chalet of the mind: a warm refuge in the closing darkness of his final years." (Publisher's note)

This "is a book that stands above the gimmickry and canned nostalgia of most memoirs both in its authenticity and its urgency. Writing literally kept Judt alive: The Memory Chalet was an effort to get everything onto the page before dying. It is a beautiful book that invites the reader into the most intimate spaces of his mind, which chugged briskly along even as his body was a train lifting slowly off the tracks." Washington Monthly

Jurgensen, Dalia

Jurgensen, Dalia. **Spiced**; a pastry chef's true stories of trials by fire, afterhours exploits, and what really goes on in the kitchen. Putnam 2009 274p il $24.95 **92**

1. Cooks
ISBN 978-0-399-15561-1; 0-399-15561-9

LC 2008-46364

Jurgensen's "book takes readers on a culinary adventure through her rise as a pastry chef at New York's best restaurants while attending culinary school. The highlights include her experiences at Martha Stewart Living Television, when she accidentally melted her glasses while making macaroons. A quick read, this book will appeal to those interested in chef stories and what happens behind the scenes in the kitchen." Libr J

K-Doe, Ernie

Sandmel, Ben. **Ernie** K-Doe; the R&B emperor of New Orleans. by Ben Sandmel ; edited by Sarah Doerries. Historic New Orleans Collection 2012 304 p. ill. (The Louisiana musicians biography series) $39.95 **92**

1. Musicians 2. Rhythm and blues musicians -- United States -- Biography
ISBN 0917860608; 9780917860607

LC 2011040576

This book is a biography of New Orleans, Louisiana musician Ernest Kador Jr., aka Ernie K-Doe, known for his hit song "Mother-in-Law." Filled "with anecdotes, candid photos, and interviews from those who knew K-Doe best, [Ben] Sandmel charts the mercurial performer's rise, fall, and redemption before his death in 2001." (Publishers Weekly)

Discography: p""||"Includes bibliographical references and index

Kael, Pauline, 1919-2001

Kellow, Brian. **Pauline** Kael; a life in the dark. Viking 2011 417p il $27.95 **92**

1. Motion pictures 2. Writers on film 3. Motion picture critics
ISBN 978-0-670-02312-7; 0-670-02312-4

LC 2011-21798

This book by Brian Kellow presents a biography of film critic Pauline Kael. "She first came to some prominence as a movie maven in San Francisco, where she selected programs for an art house and opined on films for listener-supported radio. She was already 50 when she began writing for the New Yorker, but those two decades of her life take up roughly 75 percent of Kellow's book," which "tell[s] her story mostly through her most famous (and notorious) reviews." (Kirkus Reviews)

"During her glory years at The New Yorker from 1968 to 1991, Pauline Kael enlivened the quiet art of analyzing movies with a lusty noise that echoes in certain movie-festival hallways a decade after her death. . . . [Kellow] brings two unassailable strengths to a bio that's bound to be catnip for both Kael's fans and her naysayers. First, he is impressively thorough in his research. He ferrets out illuminating information about Kael's childhood as the daughter of Polish Jewish chicken farmers in California, her never-quite-satisfactory romantic relationships with men, her dependence on the daughter she raised as a single mother, her financial struggles, and (most juicily) her oil-and-water clashes with The New Yorker's painfully genteel editor William Shawn.

As for Kellow's second strength, it's an elegantly simple one: He's a movie lover but not a professional critic. Kael had many axes to grind, but Kellow appears to have none." Entertainment Wkly

Kafka, Franz, 1883-1924

★ Kafka, die Jahre der Entscheidungen/English. **Kafka,** the decisive years; the decisive years. translated from the German by Shelley Frisch. 1st U.S. ed.; Harcourt 2005 581p il $35   **92**
1. Poets 2. Authors 3. Novelists 4. Short story writers
ISBN 0-15-100752-7

LC 2005-14554

Original German edition, 2002
This first of a projected three-volume biography focuses on Kafka's life from 1910 to 1915, during which he wrote "The Metamorphosis" and The Trial.
"Essential reading for all Kafka devotees." Booklist
Includes bibliographical references

Murray, Nicholas. **Kafka**. Yale University Press 2004 440p il $30   **92**
1. Poets 2. Authors 3. Novelists 4. Short story writers
ISBN 0-300-10631-9

LC 2004-107048

This biography "relates Kafka's brief life, trying valiantly to depict a more normal Kafka, a man who lived in society with good friends, enjoyed sex, had wide-ranging intellectual interests and became enamored of Judaism. In Murray's account, Kafka's employer valued him highly, and under the imprint of no less a figure than Kurt Wolff, he experienced some literary success. Despite Murray's best efforts to contain Kafka's idiosyncrasies, though, the writer remains the tormented soul who created out of his personal anxieties and agonies some of the most acclaimed works of the 20th century." Publ Wkly
Includes bibliographical references

Kaganovich family

Laskin, David. The **Family**; Three Journeys into the Heart of the Twentieth Century. David Laskin. Viking Adult 2013 400 p. $32   **92**
1. Jews 2. Genealogy 3. World history -- 20th century 4. Jews -- Belarus -- Biography 5. Valozhyn (Belarus) -- Biography 6. Jews, Belarusian -- Palestine -- Biography 7. Jews, Belarusian -- United States -- Biography
ISBN 067002547X; 9780670025473

LC 2013017047

Author David Laskin presents a "work of twentieth century history through the riveting story of one extraordinary Jewish family. In tracing the roots of . . . his own family . . . Laskin honors the traditions, the lives, and the choices of his ancestors: revolutionaries and entrepreneurs, scholars and farmers, tycoons and truck drivers." (Publisher's note)
Includes bibliographical references (pages 341-371) and index

Kahlo, Frida, 1907-1954

Kahlo, Frida. The **diary** of Frida Kahlo; an intimate self-portrait. introduction by Carlos Fuentes; essay and commentaries by Sarah M. Lowe; [project director, Claudia Madrazo; editor, Phyllis Freeman; translators, Barbara Crow de Toledo and Ricardo Pohlenz] 2005 ed.; Harry N. Abrams 2005 295p il $24.95   **92**
1. Artists 2. Painters 3. Artists, Mexican
ISBN 0-8109-5954-2

LC 2006-284768

First published 1995
"Sprinkled with irony, black humor, even gaiety . . . this volume is a testament to Kahlo's resilience and courage." Publ Wkly
Includes bibliographical references

Kambalu, Samson, 1975-

Kambalu, Samson. The **jive** talker; an artist's genesis: a memoir. Free Press 2008 320p $24   **92**
1. Artists
ISBN 978-1-4165-5931-3; 1-4165-5931-0

LC 2008-26784

"Artist Kambalu recounts his long journey from poverty in Malawi to fame in the London art world. The 'jive talker' was his father, a hospital administrator whose career ups and downs set the mood for the entire family even as they endured the political fortunes of Malawi under Life President Hastings Banda. Kambalu senior died of AIDS in 1995, bequeathing his family memories of his odd assortment of books and love of words." Booklist

Kamkwamba, William, 1987-

Kamkwamba, William. The **boy** who harnessed the wind; William Kamkwamba and Bryan Mealer. William Morrow 2009 273 p. (hbk.) $25.99; pa $14.99   **92**
1. Windmills -- Malawi 2. Malawi -- Rural conditions 3. Water-supply, Rural -- Malawi 4. Rural electrification -- Malawi 5. Electric power production -- Malawi 6. Mechanical engineers -- Malawi -- Biography
ISBN 0-06-173032-7; 0-06-173033-5 pa; 0061730327; 978-0-06-173032-0; 978-0-06-173033-7 pa; 9780061730320

LC 2010275963

Autobiography of a teenager in Malawi who builds a windmill and brings electricity to his village.
"This exquisite tale strips life down to its barest essentials, and once there finds reason for hopes and dreams, and is especially resonant for Americans given the economy and increasingly heated debates over health care and energy policy." Publ Wkly

Kane, Elisha Kent, 1820-1857

McGoogan, Kenneth. **Race** to the Polar Sea; the heroic adventures of Elisha Kent Kane. [by] Ken McGoogan. Counterpoint 2008 380p il map $28   **92**
1. Explorers 2. Physicians 3. Travel writers 4. Arctic regions -- Exploration
ISBN 978-1-58243-440-7; 1-58243-440-9

LC 2008-12045

This is a biography of the American explorer who discovered the Humboldt Glacier.
"With his access to previously unknown Kane logbooks, McGoogan makes an impressive case for the bravery and

importance of the explorer who first identified the Greenland ice sheet." Publ Wkly

Includes bibliographical references

Kantner, Seth, 1965-

Kantner, Seth. **Shopping** for porcupine; a life in arctic Alaska. Milkweed Editions 2008 240p il $28; pa $18   **92**

1. Authors 2. Novelists 3. Photographers 4. Alaska 5. Trappers 6. Fishermen 7. Arctic regions 8. Authors, American 9. Young adult authors

ISBN 978-1-57131-301-0; 978-1-57131-311-9 pa

LC 2007-46477

"Crafted with the precision and verve acquired by living off the land, this is a powerful and important book of remembrance, protest, and warning." Booklist

Karp, Brianna, 1985-

Karp, Brianna. The **girl's** guide to homelessness; a memoir. Harlequin 2011 344p pa $16.95   **92**

1. Office workers 2. Homeless persons 3. Homeless

ISBN 978-0-373-89235-8

LC 2010044201

"Sexually and emotionally abused by her parents, Karp left home ASAP. Self-sufficiency delighted her; she adored her job and beach cottage. She lost both to the recession and moved into a trailer she parked in a Walmart lot while using free Starbucks wi-fi and her laptop to apply for jobs. She began blogging about her situation, documenting her struggles with homelessness and trying to regain stability. Candidly humorous, Karp's memoir is sharp and insightful, reminding readers just how perilous the security of a permanent address can be and offering tips on what to do if it is lost." Libr J

Karr, Mary

Karr, Mary. **Lit**; a memoir. Harper 2009 386p $25.99; pa $14.95   **92**

1. Poets 2. Authors 3. Alcoholics 4. Essayists 5. Memoirists 6. Poets, American 7. College teachers

ISBN 978-0-06-059698-9; 0-06-059698-8; 978-0-06-059699-6 pa; 0-06-059699-6 pa

LC 2009-24810

The author reveals how, shortly after giving birth to a child she adored, she drank herself into the same numbness that nearly devoured her charismatic but troubled mother, reaching the brink of suicide before a spiritual awakening led her to sobriety.

Karr "has written a book that lassos you, hogties your emotions and won't let you go. It's a memoir that . . . explores the subjectivity of memory even as it chronicles with searching intelligence, humor and grace the author's slow, sometimes exhilarating, sometimes painful discovery of her vocation." N Y Times (Late N Y Ed)

Kazan, Elia

Schickel, Richard. **Elia** Kazan; a biography. HarperCollins 2005 xxxi, 510p il $29.95   **92**

1. Authors 2. Novelists 3. Memoirists 4. Theatrical directors 5. Motion picture directors

ISBN 0-06-019579-7

LC 2005-43344

This is "the life story of the distinguished stage and screen director. No mere page turner, this is a page devourer, generating the kind of suspense that is usually the province of the playwright or novelist." N Y Times Book Rev

Includes bibliographical references

Kazin, Alfred, 1915-1998

Cook, Richard M., 1941- **Alfred** Kazin's journals; selected and edited by Richard M. Cook. Yale University Press 2011 598p $45   **92**

1. Biography, Individual

ISBN 978-0-300-14203-7; 0-300-14203-X

LC 2010-45254

The literary critic's "passions — for sex, for novels, for ideas, for talk, for city life — spill from 'Alfred Kazin's Journals,' edited by his biographer, Richard M. Cook. This is a remarkable book, easily one of the great diaries and moral documents of the past American century. What it lacks in cohesiveness it makes up in its frankness, its quick-pivoting angularities. Kazin dismisses his journal at one point as a 'disorderly pile of shavings.' That disorder only adds to its amplitude." N Y Times Book Rev

Includes bibliographical references

Keaton, Buster, 1895-1966

Meade, Marion. **Buster** Keaton; cut to the chase. 1st Da Capo Press ed.; Da Capo Press 1997 440p il pa $18   **92**

1. Actors 2. Motion picture directors

ISBN 0-306-80802-1

LC 97-17745

First published 1995 by HarperCollins

The author "paints a moving and loving portrait of a comic genius, mechanical thinker, and superb athlete. The book provides the context of family and friends, (including Charlie Chaplin and Fatty Arbuckle) behind Keaton's career, and in doing so adds flesh and humanity to the funny bones and gags that have entertained and marveled audiences for decades. A remarkably gentle and insightful story of a silent comic riddle." Choice

Includes filmography and bibliographical references

Keller, Helen, 1880-1968

Herrmann, Dorothy. **Helen** Keller; a life. University of Chicago Press 1999 394p il pa $22   **92**

1. Deaf 2. Blind 3. Authors 4. Memoirists 5. Humanitarians 6. Inspirational writers 7. Social welfare leaders

ISBN 0-226-32763-9; 978-0-226-32763-1

LC 99-23242

First published 1998 by Knopf

The author "takes us beyond the image of Helen Keller portrayed in The Miracle Worker to unearth a passionate, politically radical woman whose inspiration and teacher, Annie Sullivan, is equally fiery and brilliant. Herrmann brings us into the every day lives of the famous pair, but the story is hardly mundane. . . . Herrmann gives us fascinating details via archives and unpublished memoirs to show how society's view of disabled people was greatly shaped by Keller and Sullivan." Libr J

Includes bibliographical references

Keller, Helen. **Helen** Keller: selected writings; edited by Kim E. Nielsen; consulting editor, Harvey J. Kaye. New York University Press 2005 317p il (History of disability series) $35   **92**
1. Deaf 2. Blind 3. Authors 4. Memoirists 5. Humanitarians 6. Inspirational writers 7. Social welfare leaders
ISBN 0-8147-5829-0

LC 2004-28974

This is a collection "of Keller's personal letters, political writings, speeches, and excerpts of her published materials from 1887 to 1968." Univ Press Books for Public and Second Sch Libr, 2006

Includes bibliographical references

★ Keller, Helen. The **story** of my life; edited and with a preface by James Berger. The restored ed.; Modern Library 2003 xlvi, 343p il hardcover o.p. pa $9.95   **92**
1. Deaf 2. Blind 3. Authors 4. Memoirists 5. Humanitarians 6. Inspirational writers 7. Social welfare leaders
ISBN 0-679-64287-0; 0-8129-6886-7 pa

LC 2002-40971

First published 1903

This biography of the inspirational Keller contains accounts of her home life and her relationship with her devoted teacher Anne Sullivan.

Includes bibliographical references

Kennan, George Frost, 1904-2005

Kennan, George Frost. **Sketches** from a life. W. W. Norton 2000 365p pa $14.95   **92**
1. Authors 2. Diplomats 3. Historians 4. Centenarians 5. Nonfiction writers 6. United States -- Foreign relations
ISBN 978-0-393-32139-5; 0-393-32139-8

First published 1989 by Pantheon

"This is a collection of very private reflections spanning some 60 years of foreign service in Nazi Germany, the Baltic states, the Low Countries, the Soviet Union, as well as nonofficial travels covering the entire globe. Kennan has marvelous insight into his ever-changing surroundings—an insight that is always sharp, sometimes melancholy, and punctuated frequently by dry, Midwestern wit." Libr J

Includes bibliographical references

Thompson, Nicholas. The **hawk** and the dove; Paul Nitze, George Kennan, and the history of the Cold War. Henry Holt 2009 403p il $27.50   **92**
1. Authors 2. Cold war 3. Diplomats 4. Statesmen 5. Historians 6. Centenarians 7. Nonfiction writers 8. Government officials 9. Biography, Individual 10. Secretaries of the navy 11. United States -- Officials and employees 12. United States -- Foreign relations -- 1945-1989 13. National security -- United States -- History -- 20th century 14. Anti-communist movements

-- United States -- History -- 20th century
ISBN 0805081429; 9780805081428

LC 2009-09225

This biography of Nitze and Kennan focuses on their "careers as statesmen, policy makers and public intellectuals." (N Y Times Book Rev) Index.

This book "does an inspired job of telling the story of the Cold War through the careers of two of its most interesting and important figures." Washington Monthly

Includes bibliographical references

Kennedy family

Taraborrelli, J. Randy. **After** Camelot; an intimate history of the Kennedy family, 1968 to the present. J. Randy Taraborrelli. Grand Central Pub. 2012 602 p.   **92**
1. Kennedy family 2. Presidents' spouses -- United States 3. Presidents -- United States -- Family
ISBN 9780446553902

LC 2011029518

For this book, which "document[s] America's "royal family," . . . [J. Randy Taraborrelli] conducted interviews with [Kennedy] family members and their intimates, such people as Eunice Kennedy Shriver, Oleg Cassini, Robert McNamara, Pierre Salinger, Arthur Schlesinger Jr., and numerous confidential sources. He also relied heavily on the 40 years of personal correspondence between Jackie Kennedy and Lady Bird Johnson. . . . [The book offers] a . . . view of family dynamics in crises both public and private: financial negotiations before Jackie's marriage to Onassis; family interference in Pat Kennedy and Peter Lawford's troubled marriage; Ted Kennedy's bad behavior at Chappaquiddick, and his support of Caroline's abortive Senate run to carry on the "family dynasty."" (Publishers Weekly)

Includes bibliographical references and index

Kennedy, Edward Moore, 1932-2009

English, Bella. **Last** lion; the fall and rise of Ted Kennedy. Simon & Schuster 2009 464p il $28 **92**
1. Senators 2. Siblings of presidents 3. Presidential candidates 4. United States -- Congress -- Senate
ISBN 978-1-4391-3817-5; 1-4391-3817-6

LC 2008-50491

"A respectful but not stuffy . . . [biography] of Edward Kennedy, the playboy of legendary appetites turned senior statesman. . . . A balanced, nuanced, warts-and-all portrait." Kirkus

Includes bibliographical references

★ Kennedy, Edward Moore. **True** compass; a memoir. [by] Edward M. Kennedy. Twelve 2009 532p il $35   **92**
1. Senators 2. Siblings of presidents 3. Presidential candidates 4. United States -- Congress -- Senate
ISBN 978-0-446-53925-8; 0-446-53925-2

This autobiography by the former senator from Massachusetts was published posthumously.

"Mr. Kennedy's conversational gifts as a storyteller and his sense of humor . . . shine through here, as does his old-school sense of public service and his hard-won knowledge, in his son Teddy Jr.'s words, that 'even our most profound losses are survivable.'" N Y Times (Late N Y Ed)

Includes bibliographical references

Kennedy, John F. (John Fitzgerald), 1917-1963

Clarke, Thurston. **JFK's** last hundred days; the transformation of a man and the emergence of a great president. Thurston Clarke. The Penguin Press 2013 448 p. (hardcover) $29.95 **92**

1. United States -- Politics and government -- 1961-1974 2. Change (Psychology) -- Case studies 3. Presidents -- United States -- Biography 4. Political leadership -- United States -- Case studies 5. United States -- Politics and government -- 1961-1963

ISBN 159420425X; 9781594204258

LC 2012047456

"This . . . look at J.F.K.'s last 100 days makes the case that had he survived that fateful November afternoon, his political star would've only continued to rise in a seemingly assured second term. [Thurston] Clarke . . . contends that Kennedy's successful resolution of the Cuban Missile Crisis, as well as his popular stances on civil rights, lunar exploration, arms reduction, and tax cuts would've overshadowed his romantic scandals, [and] tensions relating to Vietnam." (Publishers Weekly)

Includes bibliographical references and index

Dallek, Robert. **Let** every nation know; John F. Kennedy in his own words. [by] Robert Dallek and Terry Golway. Sourcebooks MediaFusion 2006 289p il $29.95; pa $19.95 **92**

1. Presidents 2. Senators 3. Members of Congress 4. Presidents -- United States 5. United States -- Politics and government -- 1961-1974

ISBN 1-4022-0647-X; 978-1-4022-0647-4; 1-4022-0922-3 pa; 978-1-4022-0922-2 pa

LC 2005-37973

"The voice of John F. Kennedy is burned into the brains of people of a certain age. But younger citizens may not be familiar with his ideas and the distinctive way in which he expressed himself. There have been past recordings of JFK's presidential speeches, but this unique package pairs a CD of the speeches with a collection of essays on them by historians Golway and Dallek (the latter wrote his own JFK book, An Unfinished Life, 2003). The result is nothing short of terrific..." (Booklist)

Includes bibliographical references

Mahoney, Richard D. **Sons** and brothers: the days of Jack and Bobby Kennedy. Arcade Pub. 1999 441p il $27.95; pa $14.95 **92**

1. Diplomats 2. Presidents 3. Senators 4. Financiers 5. Attorneys general 6. Members of Congress 7. Parents of presidents 8. Siblings of presidents 9. Presidential candidates 10. Regulatory agency officials 11. United States -- Politics and government -- 1961-1974

ISBN 1-55970-480-2; 1-55970-534-5 pa

LC 99-25681

"Writing in a steady, almost relentlessly elegiac tone, Mahoney proves that the lives and deaths of John F. and

Robert F. Kennedy remain as compelling now as they were throughout the turbulent 1960s." Publ Wkly

Includes bibliographical references

Sorensen, Theodore C., 1928-2010. **Counselor**; a life at the edge of history. [by] Ted Sorensen. HarperCollins 2008 556p il $27.95 **92**

1. Lawyers 2. Presidents 3. Senators 4. Members of Congress 5. Government officials 6. Biography, Individual 7. Presidential advisers 8. United States -- Politics and government -- 20th century

ISBN 0-06-079871-8; 978-0-06-079871-0

LC 2007-47328

This is a memoir by President Kennedy's advisor and speechwriter. Index.

"This book is instantly essential for any student of the period. It fills gaps in the historical record; it vividly conveys life inside the administration; and it generously dishes anecdotes." Washington Post Book World

Kennedy, Joseph P., 1888-1969

Mahoney, Richard D. **Sons** and brothers: the days of Jack and Bobby Kennedy. Arcade Pub. 1999 441p il $27.95; pa $14.95 **92**

1. Diplomats 2. Presidents 3. Senators 4. Financiers 5. Attorneys general 6. Members of Congress 7. Parents of presidents 8. Siblings of presidents 9. Presidential candidates 10. Regulatory agency officials 11. United States -- Politics and government -- 1961-1974

ISBN 1-55970-480-2; 1-55970-534-5 pa

LC 99-25681

"Writing in a steady, almost relentlessly elegiac tone, Mahoney proves that the lives and deaths of John F. and Robert F. Kennedy remain as compelling now as they were throughout the turbulent 1960s." Publ Wkly

Includes bibliographical references

Kennedy, Robert F., 1925-1968

Clarke, Thurston. The **last** campaign; Robert F. Kennedy and 82 days that inspired America. Thurston Clarke. Henry Holt 2008 321p il $25; pa $15 **92**

1. Senators 2. Attorneys general 3. Siblings of presidents 4. Presidential candidates 5. United States -- Politics and government -- 20th century

ISBN 978-0-8050-7792-6; 0-8050-7792-8; 978-0-8050-9022-2 pa; 0-8050-9022-3 pa

LC 2007-45880

In this account of Robert F. Kennedy's run for president, Clarke "follows on Bobby's heels as he plunged headlong into his campaign, from Kansas and Indiana to Oregon and California, throwing off his brother's mantle and becoming at last his own man. He spoke passionately, almost recklessly, inciting crowds to frenzy with his idealistic speeches about the moral shame of Vietnam, the needs of the poor and minorities and the responsibility of each American. Incorporating accounts by a gamut of reporters, politicians, family and 'Honorary Kennedys,' as well as extracts from Bobby's own stunning stump speeches, Clarke compellingly recreates this 'huge, joyous adenture.'" Kirkus

Includes bibliographical references

Mahoney, Richard D. **Sons** and brothers: the days of Jack and Bobby Kennedy. Arcade Pub. 1999 441p il $27.95; pa $14.95   **92**

1. Diplomats 2. Presidents 3. Senators 4. Financiers 5. Attorneys general 6. Members of Congress 7. Parents of presidents 8. Siblings of presidents 9. Presidential candidates 10. Regulatory agency officials 11. United States -- Politics and government -- 1961-1974

ISBN 1-55970-480-2; 1-55970-534-5 pa

LC 99-25681

"Writing in a steady, almost relentlessly elegiac tone, Mahoney proves that the lives and deaths of John F. and Robert F. Kennedy remain as compelling now as they were throughout the turbulent 1960s." Publ Wkly

Includes bibliographical references

Schlesinger, Arthur M. (Arthur Meier), 1917-2007. **Robert** Kennedy and his times; {by} Arthur M. Schlesinger, Jr. Houghton Mifflin 1978 1066p il hardcover o.p. pa $17.95   **92**

1. Senators 2. Attorneys general 3. Siblings of presidents 4. Presidential candidates 5. United States -- Politics and government -- 20th century

ISBN 978-0-618-21928-5 pa; 0-618-21928-5 pa

LC 78-8469

"A highly sympathetic and readable political biography covering in depth Robert Kennedy's tenure in public life. At times extremely partisan, at times dispassionate, Schlesinger's study effectively captures Kennedy's impact on national politics and the main currents of American politics during the 1950s and 1960s." Choice

Includes bibliographical references

Kenney, David Ngaruri, 1973-

Kenney, David Ngaruri. **Asylum** denied; a refugee's struggle for safety in America. [by] David Ngaruri Kenney and Philip G. Schrag. University of California Press 2008 352p il map $40; pa $17.95   **92**

1. Refugees 2. Political refugees 3. Kenya 4. Immigrants -- United States

ISBN 978-0-520-25510-4; 0-520-25510-0; 978-0-520-26159-4 pa; 0-520-26159-3 pa

LC 2007-48703

"One cannot read this book without experiencing rage, disbelief, and an overwhelming sense of sadness over the inhumanity Kenney suffered, both in Kenya and in this country. Still, it is also an inspiring story of human courage, heartfelt friendships, and unrelenting devotion to fighting the good fight. . . . This account should be required reading for anyone who has contact with immigrants in America. It should also be on the reading list of anyone who cares about the preservation of human rights and human dignity in our world." Calif Lawyer

Includes bibliographical references

Kerouac, Jack, 1922-1969

★ **Jack** Kerouac and Allen Ginsberg; the letters. edited by Bill Morgan and David Stanford. Viking 2010 500p $35   **92**

1. Poets 2. Authors 3. Novelists 4. Beat generation 5. Biography, Individual

ISBN 0-670-02194-6; 978-0-670-02194-9

LC 2010-03213

These two hundred letters commence "in 1944 while Ginsberg was a student at Columbia University and continues until shortly before Kerouac's death in 1969." (Publisher's note) Index.

"At times loving, at others blistering, sarcastic, often uncomfortably self-lacerating and intimate, these 200 letters, collected in a heroic editorial effort by Ginsberg biographer Morgan and independent editor Stanford, cover the years 1944–1963, the most fertile in the creative lives of Kerouac and Ginsberg. . . . Throughout, the sometimes sporadic letter writing is filled with fragments of works in progress and pungent observations on the authors and publishing people who influenced them, from Dante and Gide to Malcolm Cowley and Sterling Lord. There also is plenty of gossip about Peter Orlovsky, William Burroughs, and others in the circle." Publ Wkly

Kerouac, Jack. **Selected** letters, 1940-1956; edited with an introduction and commentary by Ann Charters. Viking 1995 xxvi, 629p hardcover o.p. pa $16.95   **92**

1. Authors 2. Novelists

ISBN 0-14-023444-6 pa

LC 94-12911

The editor "made two very wise decisions here: she supplied continuity and context for the letters, and she included significant letters from the correspondents. The frustration of the long-rejected writer is doubly felt by the reader, since this selection ends on the eve of the big Beat breakthrough." Choice

Includes bibliographical references

Khrushchev, Nikita Sergeevich, 1894-1971

Nikita Khrushchev; edited by William Taubman, Sergei Khrushchev, and Abbott Gleason; translated by David Gehrenbeck, Eileen Kane, and Alla Bashenko. Yale Univ. Press 2000 391p $45   **92**

1. Heads of state 2. Communist leaders 3. Political leaders 4. Soviet Union -- Politics and government

ISBN 0-300-07635-6

LC 99-51323

A collection of essays re-evaluating aspects of Khrushchev's political career. Topics include his rise to power and his domestic, foreign, and military policy. Two essays compare Khrushchev and Gorbachev

Includes bibliographical references and index

Taubman, William. **Khrushchev**; the man and his era. Norton 2003 p. cm   **92**

1. Heads of state 2. Communist leaders 3. Political leaders 4. Heads of state -- Soviet Union -- Biography

ISBN 0-393-05144-7

LC 2002-26404

Includes bibliographical references and index

Kilgore, Bernard, 1908-1967

Tofel, Richard J. **Restless** genius; Barney Kilgore, The Wall Street journal, and the invention of modern journalism. St. Martin's Press 2009 271p il $25.95　　　**92**

1. Journalists 2. Wall Street journal 3. Newspaper executives
ISBN 978-0-312-53674-9; 0-312-53674-7
LC 2008-29880

"What makes this work especially appealing is the incorporation of the many letters Kilgore wrote to his father, giving the reader a glimpse into this esteemed newsman's way of thinking about his newspaper and the news of the day." Libr J

Includes bibliographical references

Kim, Jong-il, 1942-2011

Jang Jin-sung. **Dear** Leader; poet, spy, escapee? : a look inside North Korea. Jang Jin-sung ; translated by Shirley Lee. 37 Ink/Atria Books 2014 368 p. (hardback) $27.99　　　**92**

1. Poets 2. Korea (North) 3. Autobiographies 4. Korea (North) -- Biography 5. Propaganda -- Korea (North) 6. Poets -- Korea (North) -- Biography 7. Political refugees -- Korea (North) -- Biography 8. Korea (North) -- Politics and government -- 1994-2011
ISBN 147676655X; 9781476766553
LC 2014010236

This memoir tells how "[a]s North Korea's State Poet Laureate, Jang Jin-sung led a charmed life. With food provisions . . . , a travel pass, access to strictly censored information, and audiences with Kim Jong-il himself, his life in Pyongyang seemed safe and secure. But this privileged existence was about to be shattered. When a strictly forbidden magazine he lent to a friend goes missing, Jang Jin-sung must flee for his life." (Publisher's note)

"A defector of Kim Jong-il's rarefied inner circle reveals the desperate, despicable machinations of North Korea's police state." Kirkus

Kimball, Kristin

Kimball, Kristin. The **dirty** life; on farming, food, and love. Scribner 2010 276p $25; ebook $11.99　　　**92**

1. Authors 2. Farmers 3. Journalists 4. Organic farming 5. Farm life -- New York (State)
ISBN 978-1-4165-5160-7; 978-1-4391-8714-2 ebook

"A hearty, chromatic account of a meaningful accomplishment in farming, 'that dirty concupiscent art.'" Kirkus

King, Clarence, 1842-1901

Sandweiss, Martha A. **Passing** strange; a Gilded Age tale of love and deception across the color line. Penguin Press 2009 370p il $27.95　　　**92**

1. Geologists 2. Travel writers 3. Passing (Identity) 4. Writers on science 5. Government officials 6. Biography, Individual 7. United States -- Race relations 8. African Americans -- Race identity 9. Racially mixed people -- Race identity
ISBN 978-1-59420-200-1
LC 2008-34886

The book tells the story of "Clarence King (1842–1901), the eminent nineteenth-century geologist . . . [and] mapper of the American West . . . [who] successfully avoided military service in the Civil War and chose instead to cultivate his manliness in the rugged life of a western explorer." In particular the book looks at his travels across the color line in the U.S. and how "for the last thirteen years of his life he led a double life in Brooklyn as James Todd, a light-skinned African American Pullman porter." (Journal of American History)

Sandweiss's "great accomplishment is to have explored not only how the 19th-century explorer and scientist Clarence King reinvented himself but also why that reinvention was so singularly American. Best of all are Ms. Sandweiss's insights into what King's deception and its consequences really mean." N Y Times (Late N Y Ed)

Includes bibliographical references

King, Martin Luther, Jr., 1929-1968

Burns, Rebecca. **Burial** for a King; Martin Luther King Jr.'s funeral and the week that transformed Atlanta and rocked the nation. Scribner 2011 244p il $25; ebook $11.99　　　**92**

1. Clergy 2. Nonfiction writers 3. Civil rights activists 4. Nobel laureates for peace 5. Atlanta (Ga.) -- Race relations 6. United States -- Race relations
ISBN 978-1-4391-3054-4; 978-1-4391-4309-4 ebook
LC 2010-29980

This is a "recreation of the aftermath of Martin Luther King Jr.'s assassination. . . . [The author] provides a snapshot of a still-segregated nation poised between uneasy reconciliation and violent chaos. Using terse language and precise, straightforward descriptions . . . she views the crisis and aftermath of King's death in Memphis through multiple points of view, beginning with the traumatic center of his family and closest associates in Atlanta. . . . A pertinent, you-are-there historical page-turner with a strong moral message." Kirkus

Flowers, Arthur. **I** see the promised land; a life of Martin Luther King Jr. [text by] Arthur Flowers, [illustrations by] Manu Chitrakar, [design by] Guglielmo Rossi. Groundwood Books/House of Anansi Press 2013 154 p. il $16.95　　　**92**

1. Clergy 2. Graphic novels 3. Biographical graphic novels 4. Nonfiction writers 5. Civil rights activists 6. Nobel laureates for peace 7. African Americans -- Civil rights -- Graphic novels
ISBN 1554983282; 9781554983285

This book is an illustrated biography of civil rights activist Martin Luther King Jr. by African American novelist and performance poet Arthur Flowers. "He weaves the entire history of the enslavement of black Americans into King's story, refers to unspecified gods taking an interest in affairs, and comments on King's speeches." (School Library Journal)

"A myth-making take on King's life that has both emotional and intellectual impact, the Flowers/Chitrakar collaboration supplies fresh color and richness to the oft-told history of this game-changer. . . . Designed for adults but fine for teens and up; recommended for all libraries." Libr J

Jackson, Troy. **Becoming** King; Martin Luther King, Jr. and the making of a national leader. introduction by Clayborne Carson. University Press of Kentucky 2008 248p (Civil rights and the struggle for Black equality in the twentieth century) $35 **92**
1. Clergy 2. Nonfiction writers 3. Civil rights activists 4. Nobel laureates for peace 5. African Americans -- Civil rights
ISBN 978-0-8131-2520-6; 0-8131-2520-0
LC 2008-25041
"The author's comprehensive analysis of King's sermons before, during and after the boycott artfully depicts a man in transition, from naive do-gooder to world-changer. Jackson's treatment of Montgomery in the post-boycott era offers new insight into the void in leadership and the fractious infighting among the movement's luminaries after King departed the scene. An informed investigation of the struggles that defined a time and place-and the man who gave them a voice." Kirkus
Includes bibliographical references (p. 229-239) and index.

Young, Andrew. An **easy** burden; the civil rights movement and the transformation of America. foreword by Quincy Jones. Baylor University Press 2008 550p il pa $29.95 **92**
1. Clergy 2. Mayors 3. Nonfiction writers 4. Members of Congress 5. Civil rights activists 6. United Nations officials 7. Nobel laureates for peace 8. United States -- Race relations 9. African Americans -- Civil rights
ISBN 978-1-602580-73-2
LC 2007-49679
First published 1996 by HarperCollins Pubs.
This memoir focuses on Young's early life as a middle-class African American growing up in segregated New Orleans, his call to the ministry, and his years working with Dr. King and the Southern Christian Leadership Conference.

Kipling, Rudyard, 1865-1936

Gilmour, David. The **long** recessional: the imperial life of Rudyard Kipling. Farrar, Straus & Giroux 2002 351p il maps $26; pa $15 **92**
1. Poets 2. Authors 3. Novelists 4. Memoirists 5. Children's authors 6. Short story writers 7. Nobel laureates for literature
ISBN 0-374-18702-9; 0-374-52896-9 pa
LC 2002-100585
This biography focuses on Kipling's social and political views in relation to the British Empire, especially as expressed in his fiction and poetry
The author "offers a brief, sympathetic, well-informed, and highly readable account of Kipling." Libr J
Includes bibliographical references

Ricketts, Harry. **Rudyard** Kipling; a life. Carroll & Graf Pubs. 2000 434p il hardcover o.p. pa $16 **92**
1. Poets 2. Authors 3. Novelists 4. Memoirists 5. Children's authors 6. Short story writers 7. Nobel laureates for literature
ISBN 0-7867-0830-1 pa
First published 1999 in the United Kingdom with title: The unforgiving minute: a life of Rudyard Kipling
This work "succeeds in disentangling some of the political muddle of Kipling's life. Ricketts' literary analysis is competent, if unsophisticated. Most valuably, he traces the debt to Browning and the many other resonant literary allusions in Kipling's work, thus undermining the charges of philistinism . . . levelled against it." New Statesman (Engl)

Kirshenblatt, Mayer, 1916-2009

Kirshenblatt, Mayer. **They** called me Mayer July; painted memories of a Jewish childhood in Poland before the Holocaust. [by] Mayer Kirshenblatt, Barbara Kirshenblatt-Gimblett. University of California Press 2007 411p il (S. Mark Taper Foundation imprint in Jewish studies) $39.95 **92**
1. Artists 2. Painters 3. Holocaust survivors 4. Memoirists 5. Jews -- Poland
ISBN 978-0-520-24961-5
LC 2006-36182
"Kirshenblatt's illustrated memoir of growing up as a Jew in pre-World War II Poland reads like an episodic novel as he introduces the reader to village life and the myriad of unusual and interesting characters." Univ Press Books for Public and Second Sch Libr, 2008
Includes bibliographical references

Kissinger, Henry, 1923-

Dallek, Robert. **Nixon** and Kissinger; partners in power. HarperCollins Publishers 2007 740p il $32.50 **92**
1. Presidents 2. Vice-presidents 3. Senators 4. College teachers 5. Nonfiction writers 6. Members of Congress 7. Writers on politics 8. Secretaries of state 9. Presidential advisers 10. Nobel laureates for peace 11. United States -- Foreign relations 12. International relations specialists
ISBN 978-0-06-072230-2; 0-06-072230-4
LC 2006-52100
A look "behind the scenes at this quintessential pair of power brokers and their lasting influence, for good and ill, on the political stage." Bookmarks Magazine
Includes bibliographical references

Knapp, Caroline

★ Caldwell, Gail. **Let's** take the long way home; a memoir of friendship. Random House 2010 190p $23 **92**
1. Friendship 2. Journalists 3. Columnists 4. Memoirists 5. Literary critics
ISBN 978-1-4000-6738-1; 1-4000-6738-3
LC 2009-29384
"This is a book you'll want to share with your own 'necessary pillars of life,' as Caldwell refers to her nearest and dearest. . . . Her memoir, a tribute to the enduring power of friendship, is a lovely gift to readers." Washington Post

Knight, Bobby

Knight, Bobby. **Knight** : my story; [by] Bob Knight with Bob Hammel. Thomas Dunne Bks. 2002 387p il $25.95; pa $14.95 **92**

1. Basketball coaches 2. Basketball -- Biography

ISBN 0-312-28257-5; 0-312-31117-6 pa

LC 2001-48990

"College hoops fans can learn more about the game from this book than from most instructional guides." Publ Wkly

Koenigswarter, Pannonica de, Baroness, 1913-1988

Kastin, David. **Nica's** dream; the life and legend of the jazz baroness. W. W. Norton 2011 336p il $26.95 **92**

1. Patrons of the arts 2. Jazz music -- History and criticism

ISBN 978-0-393-06940-2

LC 2011013213

"Kastin succeeds in bringing the surprisingly selfeffacing Nica to blazing life while also capturing the transcendent synergy among now-iconic jazz musicians, beat writers, and abstract painters, a creative cosmos profoundly enriched by the passion, largesse, and daring of the incomparable baroness." Booklist

Includes discography and bibliographical references

Koestler, Arthur, 1905-1983

Scammell, Michael. **Koestler**; the literary and political odyssey of a twentieth-century skeptic. Random House 2009 xxi, 689p il **92**

1. Authors 2. Novelists 3. Journalists 4. Essayists 5. Authors, English

ISBN 0-394-57630-6; 978-0-394-57630-5

LC 2008-51108

"Although he wrote more than 30 books, Koestler is today known primarily, perhaps exclusively, as the author of 'Darkness at Noon,' his gripping short novel of Stalinist coercion. The biographer Michael Scammell wants to put Koestler's multifaceted intelligence back on display and to show that something more than frivolity or opportunism lay behind his ever-shifting preoccupations and allegiances. As a source of information, 'Koestler,' the work of two decades, will never be surpassed. As an argument for the man's importance, however, it must contend with the eccentricity of Koestler's preoccupations and—although Scammell does not always seem to realize it—his vices."

"Although he wrote more than 30 books, Koestler is today known primarily, perhaps exclusively, as the author of 'Darkness at Noon,' his gripping short novel of Stalinist coercion. The biographer Michael Scammell wants to put Koestler's multifaceted intelligence back on display and to show that something more than frivolity or opportunism lay behind his ever-shifting preoccupations and allegiances. As a source of information, 'Koestler,' the work of two decades, will never be surpassed. As an argument for the man's importance, however, it must contend with the eccentricity of Koestler's preoccupations and—although Scammell does not always seem to realize it—his vices." N Y Times Book Rev

Includes bibliographical references

Kramer, Clara, 1927-

Kramer, Clara. **Clara's** war; one girl's story of survival. [by] Clara Kramer with Stephen Glantz. Ecco 2009 339p il $25.99 **92**

1. Holocaust survivors 2. Memoirists 3. Jews -- Poland 4. Holocaust, 1933-1945 -- Personal narratives

ISBN 978-0-06-172860-0; 0-06-172860-8

First published 2008 in the United Kingdom

ALA RUSA Sophie Brody Award Honor Book (2010)

"Based on her wartime diary, which she kept while hiding in a basement in Poland, Kramer's book vividly recalls the tensions within her hidden community after the Nazis overtook the town of Zolkiew in 1942. Of particular interest are revelations about the family who hid the Kramers, particularly how an anti-Semitic Polish householder demonstrated great courage in shielding Jews in his basement." Libr J

Krasner, Lee, 1908-1984

Levin, Gail, 1948- **Lee** Krasner; a biography. William Morrow 2011 546p il $30; ebook $23.99 **92**

1. Artists 2. Painters 3. Women artists 4. Biography, Individual 5. Artists -- United States

ISBN 978-0-06-184525-3; 0-06-184525-6; 978-0-06-207462-1 ebook; 0-06-207462-8 ebook

LC 2010-46347

This is a "full-length treatment of the talented and tenacious painter.... Levin piles up adequate evidence to assure Krasner's place in the American abstract expressionist pantheon. Detailed and meticulously researched, this is essential reading for those who want to know more about protofeminist artist Krasner, New York-based action/abstract expressionist painting, and the postwar NYC art scene." Libr J

Kreuger, Ivar, 1880-1932

Partnoy, Frank. The **match** king; Ivar Kreuger, the financial genius behind a century of Wall Street scandals. PublicAffairs 2009 272p $26.95; pa $15.95 **92**

1. Swindlers and swindling 2. Capitalists and financiers 3. Financiers 4. Kreuger & Toll, Inc. 5. Manufacturing executives

ISBN 978-1-58648-743-0; 1-58648-743-4; 978-1-58648-812-3 pa; 1-58648-812-0 pa

The author "delivers a thrilling account of the grandfather of all Ponzi and Madoff schemes—Ivar Kreuger (1880-1932), who made his fortune in the 1920s by raising money from American investors to lend to European governments in exchange for match monopolies.... A fascinating depiction of a man and his era." Publ Wkly

Includes bibliographical references (p. 230-235)

Kubrick, Stanley

LoBrutto, Vincent. **Stanley** Kubrick; a biography. Da Capo Press 1999 579p pa $20 **92**

1. Motion picture directors 2. Motion picture producers and directors -- Biography

ISBN 0-306-80906-0

LC 98-47434

First published 1996 by Fine, D.I.

"For the true film buff, there's an astonishing amount of technical information, but there's also a good deal of illuminating backstage human interest." Publ Wkly

Includes filmography and bibliographical references

Kurosawa, Akira, 1910-1998

Kurosawa, Akira. **Something** like an autobiography; translated by Audie E. Bock. Knopf 1982 205p il hardcover o.p. pa $15   **92**

1. Motion picture industry 2. Motion picture directors
ISBN 0-394-71439-3 pa

LC 81-48100

These are the memoirs of the Japanese filmmaker, covering his life up to 1951-52, when his film Rashomon won international awards

This "is a fascinating, moving record of one man's pursuit of excellence in a single art." N Y Times Book Rev

Kurson, Robert, 1963-

Kurson, Robert. **Crashing** through; a story of risk, adventure, and the man who dared to see. Random House 2007 306p il $25.95   **92**

1. Authors 2. Journalists 3. Nonfiction writers
ISBN 978-1-4000-6335-2; 1-4000-6335-3

LC 2007-3092

The book "becomes most interesting when the flaws in Mr. May's new eyesight become apparent. He makes wondrous discoveries of things blind people never hear about—shadows, freckles, the movement and transparency of running water—but has more difficulty with the cognitive aspects of pattern recognition. He can see facial features but cannot decipher facial expressions. . . . Eventually the joy of sight fades for him and the investigatory challenges begin." N Y Times (Late N Y Ed)

La Tour du Pin Gouvernet, Henriette Lucie Dillon, marquise de, 1770-1853

Moorehead, Caroline. **Dancing** to the precipice: Lucie de la Tour du Pin and the French Revolution. HarperCollins 2009 480p il $27.99   **92**

1. Memoirists 2. France -- Social life and customs 3. United States -- Social life and customs
ISBN 978-0-7011-7904-5; 0-7011-7904-X

"In 1820, at the age of forty-nine, Lucie Dillon, the Marquise de la Tour du Pin, started writing her memoirs, an endeavor that went on for thirty years and produced one of the great monuments of French history. Lucie began life as an aristocrat, débuting at Versailles at the age of eleven; at the beginning of the Terror, as friends and relatives fell to the guillotine, she fled France with her husband and children. Resilient and resourceful, the family thrived on a farm in upstate New York, where Lucie churned butter, traded with Indians, and played hostess to Talleyrand. A return to France brought Lucie and her husband into Napoleon's inner circle; in later years, following an exile in London, they found favor with the restored Bourbon monarchy. Moorehead's biography, drawing on a trove of previously unpublished correspondence, captures the rhythm of the radical contrasts in her subject's life." New Yorker

Includes bibliographical references

Lacks, Henrietta

★ Skloot, Rebecca, 1972- The **immortal** life of Henrietta Lacks. Crown Publishers 2010 369p il $26   **92**

1. Cancer 2. Homemakers 3. Human experimentation in medicine 4. Cancer patients 5. African American women -- Biography
ISBN 978-1-4000-5217-2

LC 2009-31785

"A thorny and provocative book about cancer, racism, scientific ethics and crippling poverty, 'The Immortal Life of Henrietta Lacks' also floods over you like a narrative dam break, as if someone had managed to distill and purify the more addictive qualities of 'Erin Brockovich,' 'Midnight in the Garden of Good and Evil' and 'The Andromeda Strain.' More than 10 years in the making, it feels like the book Ms. Skloot was born to write." N Y Times Book Rev

Includes bibliographical references

Lafayette, Marie Joseph Paul Yves Roch Gilbert du Motier, marquis de, 1757-1834

Gaines, James R. **For** liberty and glory; Washington, Lafayette, and their revolutions. W.W. Norton & Co. 2007 533p il map $29.95   **92**

1. Generals 2. Statesmen 3. Presidents 4. France -- History -- 1789-1799, Revolution 5. United States -- History -- 1775-1783, Revolution
ISBN 0-393-06138-8; 978-0-393-06138-3

LC 2007-22449

Gaines examines the relationship between George Washington and the Marquis de Lafayette.

This is a "fresh and engaging new look at the pair. . . . Gaines has a dry sense of humor and an appreciation for human foibles. . . . The American founding fathers, in particular, come across as extraordinary men with ordinary obsessions and—surprise!—senses of humor." Christ Sci Monit

Includes bibliographical references

Laffite, Jean, 1780?-1825?

Davis, William C. The **pirates** Laffite; the treacherous world of the corsairs of the Gulf. Harcourt 2005 706p il map $28   **92**

1. Pirates
ISBN 0-15-100403-X

LC 2004-29150

"This is an excellent examination of interesting, tough men who knew how to survive in an interesting, tough age." Booklist

Includes bibliographical references

Laffite, Pierre, d. 1826?

Davis, William C. The **pirates** Laffite; the treacherous world of the corsairs of the Gulf. Harcourt 2005 706p il map $28   **92**

1. Pirates
ISBN 0-15-100403-X

LC 2004-29150

This is a study of "Jean and Pierre Laffite, [brothers whose] lives were intertwined with . . . [a] colorful period in New Orleans' history, the era from just after the Louisiana Purchase through the War of 1812. Labeled as corsairs and buccaneers for methods that bordered on piracy, the brothers ran a privateering cooperative that provided contraband goods to a hungry market." Publisher's note

"This is an excellent examination of interesting, tough men who knew how to survive in an interesting, tough age." Booklist

Includes bibliographical references

Lamarr, Hedy, 1913-2000

Rhodes, Richard. **Hedy's** folly; the life and breakthrough inventions of Hedy Lamarr, the most beautiful woman in the world. Doubleday 2011 261p il $26.95; ebook $13.99 **92**

1. Actors

ISBN 978-0-385-53438-3; 978-0-385-53439-0 ebook

LC 2011021746

"Here's a recipe that might surprise you: take a silver-screen sex goddess (Hedy Lamarr), an avant-garde composer (George Antheil), a Hollywood friendship, and mutual technological curiosity, and mix well. What results is a patent for spread-spectrum radio, which has impacted the development of everything from torpedoes to cell phones and GPS technologies. This surprising and long-forgotten story is brought to life . . . [by Rhodes,] who deftly moves between Nazi secrets, scandalous films, engineering breakthroughs, and musical flops to weave a taut story that straddles two very different worlds—the entertainment industry and wartime weaponry—and yet somehow manages to remain a delectable read."

"Here's a recipe that might surprise you: take a silver-screen sex goddess (Hedy Lamarr), an avant-garde composer (George Antheil), a Hollywood friendship, and mutual technological curiosity, and mix well. What results is a patent for spread-spectrum radio, which has impacted the development of everything from torpedoes to cell phones and GPS technologies. This surprising and long-forgotten story is brought to life . . . [by Rhodes,] who deftly moves between Nazi secrets, scandalous films, engineering breakthroughs, and musical flops to weave a taut story that straddles two very different worlds—the entertainment industry and wartime weaponry—and yet somehow manages to remain a delectable read." Libr J

Includes bibliographical references

Shearer, Stephen Michael. **Beautiful**; the life of Hedy Lamarr. Thomas Dunne Books 2010 464p il $29.99 **92**

1. Actors

ISBN 978-0-312-55098-1; 0-312-55098-7

LC 2010-13058

This biography chronicles "the life of Hollywood legend Hedy Lamarr, from her cosseted childhood in an assimilated Jewish family in Austria to her early breaks in Max Reinhardt's internationally famous theater company; her scandalous, career-launching nude scene in the Czech film Ecstasy; her tortured first marriage to Jewish Nazi arms manufacturer Friedrich Mandl (dubbed an 'honorary Aryan' by the Third Reich); and her daring escape from the sadistic Mandl and Nazi Germany to Los Angeles and MGM. . . . One finishes the book feeling that one has read a complete portrait of Hedy Lamarr, actor and inventor, a biography that reveals, with drama and wit, how much more there was

to this complex, brilliant woman than her ethereal natural beauty." Booklist

Includes bibliographical references

Lancaster, Burt, 1913-1994

Buford, Kate. **Burt** Lancaster; an American life. Da Capo Press 2001 447p il pa $20 **92**

1. Actors 2. Motion picture producers

ISBN 978-0-306-81019-0; 0-306-81019-0

First published 2000 by Knopf

"Lancaster's decades-long political involvement with liberal causes (and his constant run-ins with the House Un-American Activities Committee in the 1950s) are a central theme in this well-researched and engaging biography, which also details the artist's acting career, his turns as a producer and his personal life." Publ Wkly

Includes filmography and bibliographical references

Landry, Tom

Ribowsky, Mark. The **last** cowboy; a life of Tom Landry. Mark Ribowsky. Liveright Publishing Corporation 2014 720 p. (hardcover) $29.95 **92**

1. Football coaches 2. Dallas Cowboys (Football team) 3. Dallas Cowboys (Football team) -- History 4. Football coaches -- United States -- Biography

ISBN 9780871403339

LC 2013034731

Author Mark Ribowsky presents a biography of professional football coach Tom Landry. He "begins amid the dusty roads of Mission, Texas, where Tom Landry's childhood played out like a homespun American fable. It then takes us to the war-torn skies over western Europe, where the straight-A student and high school football star piloted a B-17 through thirty harrowing, at times near-fatal, missions. And finally back to a booming Texas, where he continued his faithful march toward gridiron immortality." (Publisher's note)

"Tom Landry spent 40 years in professional football, most notably 29 years as the original coach of the oft-celebrated Dallas Cowboys. Landry was one of the most innovative and influential coaches in NFL history, essentially inventing his own offensive and defensive systems that spread throughout the league...Although Ribowsky (Howard Cosell) is gratuitously snarky about Landry's religious and political beliefs at times, he recounts Landry's life honestly, avoiding both distortion and hagiography while portraying a stoic, flawed man of honor... Nonetheless, this is a triumph of extensive research and interviews. It will be welcomed by all football fans." (Library Journal)

Includes bibliographical references and index

Lang, Lang, 1982-

Lang, Lang. **Journey** of a thousand miles; my story. [by] Lang Lang with David Ritz. Spiegel & Grau 2008 239p il $24.95 **92**

1. Pianists 2. Classical musicians

ISBN 978-0-385-52456-8

LC 2008-732

An autobiography of the Chinese classical piano prodigy.

"Lang tells the story of his childhood without self-pity or bitterness, making his success, and the book itself, all the more satisfying." N Y Times Book Rev

Lange, Dorothea, 1895-1965

Gordon, Linda. **Dorothea** Lange; a life beyond limits. W.W. Norton 2009 xxiii, 536p il $35   **92**

1. Women photographers 2. Biography, Individual 3. Photography -- History -- United States

ISBN 978-0-393-05730-0; 0-393-05730-5

LC 2009-19639

This is a biography of the American photographer who worked for the Historical Section of the Farm Security Administration (FSA) during the Depression.

"Gordon's elegant biography is testament to Lange's gift for challenging her country to open its eyes." N Y Times Book Rev

Includes bibliographical references

Larsen, Nella

Hutchinson, George. **In** search of Nella Larsen; a biography of the color line. Belknap Press of Harvard University Press 2006 611p il $39.95   **92**

1. Nurses 2. Authors 3. Novelists 4. Short story writers

ISBN 0-674-02180-0; 978-0-674-02180-8

LC 2005-58129

This is a biography of the author of Quicksand (1928) and Passing (1929).

The author "has produced what must be the definitive biography of Larsen. It's hard to think of a stone he hasn't looked under in his quest to establish the facts, correct mistakes and trace her private life. But Hutchinson's biography also manages to be an insightful reconsideration of a much-studied period in American literature and black cultural history." Nation

Includes bibliographical references

Laskin, David, 1953-

Laskin, David. The **Family**; Three Journeys into the Heart of the Twentieth Century. David Laskin. Viking Adult 2013 400 p. $32   **92**

1. Jews 2. Genealogy 3. World history -- 20th century 4. Jews -- Belarus -- Biography 5. Valozhyn (Belarus) -- Biography 6. Jews, Belarusian -- Palestine -- Biography 7. Jews, Belarusian -- United States -- Biography

ISBN 067002547X; 9780670025473

LC 2013017047

Author David Laskin presents a "work of twentieth century history through the riveting story of one extraordinary Jewish family. In tracing the roots of . . . his own family . . . Laskin honors the traditions, the lives, and the choices of his ancestors: revolutionaries and entrepreneurs, scholars and farmers, tycoons and truck drivers." (Publisher's note)

Includes bibliographical references (pages 341-371) and index

Latus, Amy, 1965-2002

Latus, Janine. **If** I am missing or dead. Simon & Schuster 2007 309p il $25   **92**

1. Journalists 2. Abused women 3. Memoirists 4. Abused persons 5. Murder victims 6. Social activists

ISBN 978-0-7432-9653-3; 0-7432-9653-2

LC 2006-52313

"When journalist Latus's younger sister Amy vanishes at age 37 in 2002, authorities find a chiller of a note in Amy's desk: 'If I am missing or dead . . . question Ron.' Ron Ball is Amy's ex-con boyfriend, and when Amy's body is found, something shatters in Latus. A victim of abuse herself, Latus tunnels back to her difficult suburban childhood to decode why two smart, talented sisters might be so starving for love that they would risk their lives to get it. Latus's book unfolds like a gripping novel, getting at the brutal heart of darkness that underscores domestic violence." People

Latus, Janine, 1959-

Latus, Janine. **If** I am missing or dead. Simon & Schuster 2007 309p il $25   **92**

1. Journalists 2. Abused women 3. Memoirists 4. Abused persons 5. Murder victims 6. Social activists

ISBN 978-0-7432-9653-3; 0-7432-9653-2

LC 2006-52313

"When journalist Latus's younger sister Amy vanishes at age 37 in 2002, authorities find a chiller of a note in Amy's desk: 'If I am missing or dead . . . question Ron.' Ron Ball is Amy's ex-con boyfriend, and when Amy's body is found, something shatters in Latus. A victim of abuse herself, Latus tunnels back to her difficult suburban childhood to decode why two smart, talented sisters might be so starving for love that they would risk their lives to get it. Latus's book unfolds like a gripping novel, getting at the brutal heart of darkness that underscores domestic violence." People

Laurens, Henry, 1724-1792

Harris, J. William. The **hanging** of Thomas Jeremiah; a free Black man's encounter with liberty. Yale University Press 2009 223p il map $27.50   **92**

1. Diplomats 2. Merchants 3. Ship captains 4. Colonial leaders 5. Plantation owners 6. Government officials 7. Colonial administrators 8. Slavery -- United States 9. South Carolina -- Race relations 10. African Americans -- Social conditions

ISBN 978-0-300-15214-2; 0-300-15214-0

LC 2009-15233

This is an "account of nebulous historical figure Thomas Jeremiah. . . . Owner of a fishing company and worth $200,000 in 2009 dollars, . . . [Jeremiah] was probably the richest black man in North America; he was also a slaveowner. That didn't stop him from becoming a scapegoat, accused by patriot leader Henry Laurens—a wealthy plantation owner with hundreds of slaves—of secretly leading a British-sponsored slave insurrection. Though Governor William Campbell, aggrieved by the unlawfulness of Jeremiah's trial, interceded, it didn't stop those determined to hang Jeremiah. . . . Readers will learn much about the darker side of American institutions; students of American history and civil rights will appreciate Harris's impassive approach and thorough standards." Publ Wkly

Includes bibliographical references

Laveau, Marie, 1794-1881

Ward, Martha Coonfield. **Voodoo** queen; the spirited lives of Marie Laveau. by Martha Ward. University Press of Mississippi 2004 246p il map $26   **92**

1. Witches 2. Voodooism

ISBN 1-578-06629-8

LC 2003-18292

"Spiritual leaders Marie Laveau, mother and daughter, reigned in New Orleans between the 1820s and 1880s. Through their story, Ward offers fresh perspective on Creole culture and voodoo." Booklist

Including bibliographical references

Lawrence, D. H. (David Herbert), 1885-1930

Worthen, John. **D.H.** Lawrence; the life of an outsider. Counterpoint 2005 xxvi, 518p il $29.95 **92**

1. Poets 2. Authors 3. Novelists 4. Dramatists 5. Essayists 6. Short story writers

ISBN 1-58243-341-0

"Using as a unifying theme Lawrence's perpetual status as an outsider, both in working-class Nottinghamshire and in the English literary world, Worthen gives us the full sweep of this groundbreaking writer's utterly unconventional, often torturous, and occasionally rhapsodic life." Booklist

Includes bibliographical references

Worthen, John. **D.H.** Lawrence, the early years, 1885-1912. Cambridge Univ. Press 1991 626p il (The Cambridge biography¿D.H. Lawrence, 1885-1930) hardcover o.p. pa $30 **92**

1. Poets 2. Authors 3. Novelists 4. Dramatists 5. Essayists 6. Short story writers

ISBN 0-521-43772-5 pa

LC 90-23423

This "first volume of Cambridge's three-volume life of Lawrence, . . . takes the young writer through his elopement with Frieda. . . . This persuasive biography is compulsive good reading from cover to cover. A major event in modern literary studies." Libr J

Includes bibliographical references

Lawrence, Sarahlee

Lawrence, Sarahlee. **River** house; a memoir. Tin House Books 2010 272p pa $16.95 **92**

1. Farmers 2. Rafting (Sports) 3. Adventure and adventurers

ISBN 978-0-9825691-3-9

LC 2010-7702

"Handy with tools and rafts, a good neighbor, and a mighty fine horsewoman, Lawrence is also adept with language, writing with arresting lucidity and a driving need to understand her father, her legacy, the land, community, work, and herself. A true adventure story of rare dimension." Booklist

Lawrence, T. E. (Thomas Edward), 1888-1935

★ Brown, Malcolm. **T.E.** Lawrence. New York University Press 2003 160p il map (Historic lives) $21.95 **92**

1. Authors 2. Soldiers 3. Archaeologists 4. Travel writers

ISBN 0-8147-9920-5

LC 2003-51387

This biography is part "adventure story, part modern morality tale, and places special emphasis on the years of the desert war the period that both made Lawrence and broke him. It also shows how the once haloed figure surrounded by hero-worship has increasingly come to be seen as a man of our time, to whom countless people can relate, not because he acquired what we now call celebrity status, but because he was prepared to relinquish it." Publisher's note

"The book is a major literary work." Publ Wkly

Includes bibliographical references

Korda, Michael, 1933- **Hero**; the life and legend of Lawrence of Arabia. Harper 2010 762p il map $34.99 **92**

1. Authors 2. Soldiers 3. Archaeologists 4. Travel writers 5. Biography, Individual 6. Soldiers -- Great Britain 7. World War, 1914-1918 -- Middle East 8. World War, 1914-1918 -- Campaigns -- Turkey 9. World War, 1914-1918 -- Campaigns -- Middle East

ISBN 978-0-06-171261-6

LC 2010-33189

This is a biography of T. E. Lawrence, the "British scholar, adventurer, soldier, and hero who became a myth in his lifetime." (Publisher's note) Index.

"This magisterial biography of British soldier and adventurer T.E. Lawrence celebrates a life spent subverting authority in the most glamorous—and bizarre—ways. . . . [The author] gives a rousing, lucid account of Lawrence's leadership of the Arab revolt against the Ottoman Empire during WWI and his diplomatic championing of Arab nationalism. But it's Lawrence's artistic bent . . . and his magnetic but tortured soul that take center stage." Publ Wkly

Includes bibliographical references

Le Moyne de Morgues, Jacques, ca. 1533-1588

Harvey, Miles. **Painter** in a savage land; the strange saga of the first European artist in North America. Random House 2008 xx, 338p il map $27 **92**

1. Artists 2. Artists, French 3. America -- Exploration

ISBN 978-1-4000-6120-4; 1-4000-6120-2

LC 2007-39105

"This book doubles as a narrative of Harvey's own expedition to discover more about his subject and the story of Le Moyne's works in the centuries after his death—and their sad fate at the hands of a New York antiquities dealer. Harvey's volume hits the sweet spot for both adventure buffs and history fans." Publ Wkly

Includes bibliographical references

LeMieux, Richard

LeMieux, Richard. **Breakfast** at Sally's; one homeless man's inspirational journey. Skyhorse 2008 433p il $24.95 **92**

1. Homeless persons 2. Homeless 3. Memoirists

ISBN 978-1-60239-293-9; 1-60239-293-5

LC 2008-24420

"Former successful businessman Richard LeMieux has lived better than the average American, but descended, through economic and personal failures, to homelessness for almost two years. Writing of life on the streets with his dog, Willow, he introduces a cast of characters from his experiences. . . . This inspirational political and social memoir can offer readers hope for a renewal of faith—in God and humanity. All public libraries will want this book for their collections." Libr J

Leadbelly, 1885-1949

Wolfe, Charles K. The **life** and legend of Leadbelly; [by] Charles Wolfe and Kip Lornell. Da Capo Press 1999 333p il pa $16.95　　　　92

1. Singers 2. Guitarists 3. Blues music 4. African American musicians 5. Songwriters 6. Accordionists
ISBN 978-0-306-80896-8; 0-306-80896-X
First published 1992 by HarperCollins

"Drawing on a variety of primary and secondary sources, including numerous interviews, Wolfe and Lornell attempt to separate fact from fiction. . . . Photographs, informative notes, and a full discography are valuable additions." Choice

Includes discography and bibliographical references

Lear, Norman

Lear, Norman. **Even** This I Get to Experience; Norman Lear. Penguin Group USA 2014 448 p. illustrations, portraits $32.95　　　　92

1. Autobiographies 2. Comedy television programs
ISBN 1594205728; 9781594205729

LC 2014032903

This memoir by Norman Lear describes how "Lear led a charmed life throughout postwar Hollywood's golden years, befriending the likes of Carl Reiner and Mel Brooks; writing and directing Frank Sinatra, Robert Redford, Dick Van Dyke, and Martha Raye; becoming the highest paid comic writer in the country while working for Jerry Lewis and Dean Martin. Not to mention, Lear flew some fifty bombing missions over Germany with the Fifteenth Air Force." (Publisher's note)

"A big-hearted, richly detailed chronicle of comedy, commitment and a long life lived fully." Kirkus

Leary, Timothy, 1920-1996

Greenfield, Robert. **Timothy** Leary; a biography. Harcourt, Inc. 2006 689p il $28　　　　92

1. Psychologists 2. College teachers 3. Social reformers
ISBN 0-15-100500-1; 978-0-15-100500-0

LC 2005-30154

This is a biography of LSD guru and counterculture icon Timothy Leary.

"A veritable who's who of the age of Aquarius and a real page-turner, Greenfield's cornerstone portrait of the acidhead who would be king brilliantly illuminates the paradoxes of the psychedelic age." Booklist

Leavitt, Henrietta Swan, 1868-1921

Johnson, George. **Miss** Leavitt's stars; the untold story of the woman who discovered how to measure the universe. W. W. Norton 2005 162p il (Great discoveries) $22.95　　　　92

1. Astronomers 2. Photometrists
ISBN 0-393-05128-5

LC 2005-02823

This is a biography of the American astronomer whose research concerned the measuring of distance in space.

This book is "a fine tribute to a remarkable woman of science." Publ Wkly

Includes bibliographical references

Ledyard, John, 1751-1789

Gifford, Bill. **Ledyard**; in search of the first American explorer. Harcourt 2007 331p il map $25　　　　92

1. Explorers 2. Travel writers
ISBN 978-0-15-101218-3; 0-15-101218-0

LC 2006-17064

This book "makes an important contribution to the existing literature through its personal approach to Ledyard's life. Few of Ledyard's letters and journals remain . . . but, by using most of what's available and tracking down details through his own travels, the author paints a fascinating portrait of the man he calls the 'archetype of the restless American wanderer.'" N Y Times Book Rev

Lee, Gypsy Rose, 1914-1970

Abbott, Karen. **American** rose; a nation laid bare: the life and times of Gypsy Rose Lee. Random House 2010 422p il $26; ebook $12.99　　　　92

1. Actors 2. Novelists 3. Striptease 4. Stripteasers
ISBN 978-1-4000-6691-9; 978-0-679-60456-3 ebook

LC 2010-15081

"Imaginative and engaging, Abbott's biography of the celebrated stripper, who died in 1970 at age 59, also proves a well-informed look at the evolution of musical theater in the early 20th century." Publ Wkly

Includes bibliographical references

Lee, Harper

Mills, Marja. The **Mockingbird** Next Door; Life with Harper Lee. Marja Mills. The Penguin Press 2014 288 p. illustrations (hardback) $27.95　　　　92

1. Alabama 2. American authors 3. Alabama -- Biography 4. Authors, American -- 20th century -- Biography
ISBN 1594205191; 9781594205194

LC 2013039938

This book, by Marja Mills, is a memoir recounting her friendship with "To Kill a Mockingbird" author Harper Lee. "Journalists have trekked to her hometown of Monroeville, Alabama, where . . . Lee, known to her friends as Nelle, has lived with her sister, Alice, for decades, trying and failing to get an interview with the author. But in 2001, the Lee sisters opened their door to Chicago Tribune journalist Marja Mills. It was the beginning of a long conversation--and a great friendship." (Publisher's note)

Lee, Robert E. (Robert Edward), 1807-1870

Korda, Michael, 1933- **Clouds** of Glory; The Life and Legend of Robert E. Lee. Michael Korda. HarperCollins 2014 640 p. illustrations, maps $40　　　　92

1. Command of troops 2. United States -- History -- 1861-1865, Civil War
ISBN 0062116290; 9780062116291

LC 2014415636

This book, by Michael Korda, is a "historical biography of General Robert E. Lee. . . . [It] analyzes Lee's command during the Civil War and explores his responsibility for the fatal stalemate at Antietam, his defeat at Gettysburg . . . and ultimately, his failed strategy for winning the war. As Korda shows, Lee's dignity, courage, leadership, and modesty

made him a hero on both sides of the Mason-Dixon Line."
(Publisher's note)

Korda "examines the life of Robert E. Lee from start to
finish, illuminating not just the man, but his extended family
and the society which produced him." Pub Wkly

Includes bibliographical references and index

Leiber, Jerry, 1933-2011

Leiber, Jerry. **Hound** dog; the Leiber & Stoller
autobiography. [by] Jerry Leiber and Mike Stoller
with David Ritz. Simon & Schuster 2009 322p il
$25   **92**
1. Composers 2. Lyricists 3. Songwriters 4. Rock
music -- History and criticism
ISBN 978-1-4165-5938-2; 1-4165-5938-8
LC 2008-47821

"Collaboration is a messy business. So is autobiography.
But it shouldn't be forgotten that Leiber and Stoller were
among the pioneers who helped bring black and white musical forms together. It has been a historically fraught process,
but the collision of cultures is probably what has given such
energy and tension to American music. Hound Dog is an important part of that story." N Y Times Book Rev

Includes bibliographical references

Lelyveld, Joseph

Lelyveld, Joseph. **Omaha** blues; a memory loop.
Farrar, Straus and Giroux 2005 226p il $22; pa
$14   **92**
1. Newspaper editors 2. Nonfiction writers
ISBN 0-374-22590-7; 0-312-42510-4 pa
LC 2004-12362

In this autobiographical narrative, the American newspaper editor reflects on his childhood.

This "is a worldly, graceful book; there is a great deal to
admire in it and to be moved by." New Leader

Lemon, Alex

Lemon, Alex. **Happy**; a memoir. Scribner 2010
292p $25   **92**
1. Poets 2. Authors 3. Poets, American 4. Brain
-- Diseases
ISBN 978-1-4165-5023-5; 1-4165-5023-2
LC 2009-27293

The author, a poet, "was a carefree, hard partying, base-
ball-playing college student at Macalester College in Minnesota in 1997 when he suffered a stroke and later two brain
bleeds. Readers are swept along on his rough ride during the
next two years, through his nasty travails of frenetic drug
and alcohol use, terribly misguided attempts to cope with his
deteriorating and frightening condition. . . . Lemon offers a
raw and honest narration of his college life, his relationships
with girlfriends and family members, especially his loving
and quirky mother. . . . [This] is a voltaic narrative that is
alternately horrifying and touching." Publ Wkly

Lenin, Vladimir Ilyich, 1870-1924

Pomper, Philip. **Lenin's** brother; the origins of
the October Revolution. W.W. Norton & Co. 2010
276p il $24.95   **92**
1. Heads of state 2. Revolutionaries 3. Communist
leaders 4. Political leaders 5. Soviet Union -- History

-- 1917-1921, Revolution
ISBN 978-0-393-07079-8
LC 2009-27390

"In 1887, the future leader of the Russian revolution,
Vladimir Ulyanov (later Lenin), was 17 when his 21-year-
old brother was hanged for his role in a bungled attempt to
assassinate Czar Alexander III. Historians consider this the
seminal event that launched Lenin's career as a revolutionary. . . . [The author] delivers an absorbing and surprisingly
detailed account of Alexander Ulyanov's short life and even
shorter career (four months) as a terrorist." Publ Wkly

Includes bibliographical references

Lennon, John, 1940-1980

Greenberg, Keith Elliot. **December** 8, 1980; the
day John Lennon died. Backbeat Books 2010 240p
il $24.99   **92**
1. Singers 2. Rock musicians 3. Songwriters
ISBN 978-0-87930-963-3
LC 2010-31425

"Greenberg's definitive and unforgettable inquiry into
John Lennon's death illuminates the cruel mysteries of madness, and, more resonantly, all the qualities that made Lennon such an exceptional and compelling artist." Booklist

Includes bibliographical references

Norman, Philip. **John** Lennon; the life. Ecco
HarperCollins 2008 851p il $34.95; pa $19.99 **92**
1. Singers 2. Rock musicians 3. Songwriters
ISBN 978-0-06-075401-3; 0-06-075401-X; 978-0-06-
075402-0 pa; 0-06-075402-8 pa
LC 2008-4684

This is a biography of the singer-songwriter and author of In His Own Write (1964), A Spaniard in the Works
(1965), and Lennon Remembers (1971).

This work's "ambitious range proves to be its strength,
enveloping you in ways that a quicker read could not. . . .
[This] is a gift of a book, heartfelt and heart-rending." Christ
Sci Monit

Riley, Tim. **Lennon**; the man, the myth, the
music--the definitive life. Hyperion 2011 765p il
$35   **92**
1. Singers 2. Rock musicians 3. Songwriters 4.
Biography, Individual
ISBN 978-1-4013-2452-0; 1-4013-2452-5
LC 2011-15657

"Here is Lennon in the fullness of his diffracted personality, across the spectrum of his phases and faces. Leather
John, mugging sailors in Hamburg — 'A Lennon punch
felled him to his knees' — is superseded by Beatle John,
mugging for the world's press. . . . Beatle John contains
both 'Ed Sullivan' John, yodeling harmonies and bending
his knees in awkward demi-pliés, and 'Revolver' John, acidhead, sleepyhead, drug dormouse, singing in that cold little
cocoon voice (Riley calls it 'timefrozen') about floating
downstream and not wanting to be woken up. Then there's
'Imagine' John, the drooping sage. And finally, of course,
John the martyr." N Y Times Book Rev

Includes bibliographical references and discography

Lenz, Frank, d. 1894

Herlihy, David V. The **lost** cyclist; the epic tale of an American adventurer and his mysterious disappearance. [by] David V. Herlihy. Houghton Mifflin Harcourt 2010 326p il map **92**

1. Cycling 2. Photographers 3. Cyclists 4. Murder victims 5. Retail personnel 6. Biography, Individual
ISBN 0-547-19557-5; 0-547-52198-7 pa; 978-0-547-19557-5; 978-0-547-52198-5 pa

LC 2009-28857

This is a biography of "Frank Lenz, a 24-year-old wheelman [who] departed New York in 1892 to round the globe. . . . [Lenz disappeared in] eastern Turkey, in the midst of a Turkish and Kurdish campaign that would kill some 10,000 Armenian civilians." (N Y Times Book Rev) Index.

"This well-researched and stylishly written book puts Lenz back in the public eye as well as offering readers a look at the very early days of modern cycling." Booklist

Leonardo, da Vinci, 1452-1519

Aquino, Lucia. **Leonardo** Da Vinci; preface by Mario Pomilio; [translation, Miriam Hurley] Rizzoli 2005 173p il (Art classics) pa $9.95 **92**

1. Artists 2. Painters 3. Scientists 4. Artists, Italian 5. Writers on science
ISBN 978-0-8478-2677-3; 0-8478-2677-5

LC 2004-099908

This book "features a literary introduction and . . . description of a selection of the artist's masterpieces. . . . [It also includes] a visual chart with captions as to the whereabouts of each painting and a . . . bibliography." Publisher's note

Includes bibliographical references

White, Michael. **Leonardo**; the first scientist. St. Martin's Press 2000 370p il $27.95; pa $16.95 **92**

1. Artists 2. Painters 3. Scientists 4. Artists, Italian 5. Writers on science
ISBN 0-312-20333-0; 0-312-27026-7 pa

The author "focuses on the scientific creations of da Vinci, emphasizing his notebooks, which had been lost for 200 years and only portions of which have been recovered. White describes how da Vinci's personal life affected his scientific discoveries and predictions, and vice versa." Booklist

Leonowens, Anna Harriette, 1831-1915

Landon, Margaret. **Anna** and the King of Siam; illustrated by Margaret Ayer. Harper & Row 1944 391p il map hardcover o.p. pa $14.95 **92**

1. Kings 2. Governesses 3. Thailand -- Social life and customs
ISBN 0-06-095488-4 pa

Anna Leonowens' experiences at the Siamese court in the 1860's. From her experiences she wrote two books, "The English governess at the Siamese court," and "The romance of the harem." The author has put these two books into one story with additions to make a complete tale.

Lessing, Doris May, 1919-

★ Lessing, Doris May. **Under** my skin; volume one of my autobiography, to 1949. {by} Doris Less-

ing. HarperCollins Pubs. 1994 419p il hardcover o.p. pa $15 **92**

1. Authors 2. Novelists 3. Dramatists 4. Essayists 5. Short story writers 6. Nobel laureates for literature
ISBN 0-06-092664-3 pa

LC 94-20051

"In this immediate, vivid, beautifully paced memoir, Doris Lessing sets the individual against history, the personal against the general, and shows, by the example of her own life set down honestly, how biography and fiction mesh, how fiction transmutes the personal to the general, how the particular experience illuminates the universe." London Rev Books

Levi, Primo, 1919-1987

Angier, Carole. The **double** bond: Primo Levi, a biography. Farrar, Straus & Giroux 2002 xxvi, 898p il $40; pa $20 **92**

1. Poets 2. Authors 3. Chemists 4. Novelists 5. Holocaust survivors 6. Essayists 7. Memoirists 8. Short story writers
ISBN 0-374-11315-7; 0-374-52898-5 pa

This is a biography of the Italian Jewish chemist and writer. Levi was the author of The Periodic Table, Survival in Auschwitz, The Drowned and the Saved and Other People's Trades

"Angier's long, gripping narrative of Levi's time in Auschwitz synthesizes the best of his memoirs, poetry, fiction, essays, and scientific writing. . . . A compelling biography and a must for all Holocaust collections." Booklist

Includes bibliographical references

Levi, Primo, 1919-1987. The **periodic** table; translated from the Italian by Raymond Rosenthal. Schocken Bks. 1984 233p hardcover o.p. pa $12 **92**

1. Poets 2. Authors 3. Chemists 4. Novelists 5. Holocaust survivors 6. Essayists 7. Memoirists 8. Short story writers
ISBN 0805210415 pa; 0-8052-1041-5 pa

LC 84-5453

Original Italian edition, 1975

"This curious memoir, organized in 21 chapters from Argon to Zinc, ransacks the periodic table of the elements for strained metaphors as it traces one adolescent's search for identity. Levi ironically portrays himself as a young aspiring chemist eager to fathom nature's secrets."

"This curious memoir, organized in 21 chapters from Argon to Zinc, ransacks the periodic table of the elements for strained metaphors as it traces one adolescent's search for identity. Levi ironically portrays himself as a young aspiring chemist eager to fathom nature's secrets." Publ Wkly

Lewin, W. H. G. (Walter H. G.)

★ Goldstein, Warren. **For** the love of physics; from the end of the rainbow to the edge of time--a journey through the wonders of physics. [by] Walter Lewin and Warren Goldstein. Free Press 2011 302p il $26; ebook $12.99 **92**

1. Physicists 2. Physics -- Study and teaching 3. Colleges and universities -- Faculty
ISBN 978-1-4391-0827-7; 978-1-4391-2354-6 ebook

LC 2010-47737

"MIT's Lewin is deservedly popular for his memorable physics lectures . . . and this quick-paced autobiography-cum-physics intro fully captures his candor and lively teaching style. . . . [This text] glows with energy and should please a wide range of readers." Publ Wkly

Lewis, Agnes Smith, 1843-1926

Soskice, Janet Martin. The **sisters** of Sinai; how two lady adventurers discovered the hidden Gospels. [by] Janet Soskice. Alfred A. Knopf 2009 316p $27.95 **92**

1. Twins 2. Travelers 3. Biblical scholars 4. Biography, Individual 5. Bible -- N.T. -- Syriac 6. Bible -- N.T. -- Gospels

ISBN 978-1-4000-4133-6; 1-4000-4133-3; 1400041333; 9781400041336

LC 2009011098

This is a biography of Agnes and Margaret Smith, aisters "whose travels to St. Catherine's Monastery in the Sinai desert resulted in the . . . discovery of one of the oldest manuscripts of the Gospels ever found. . . . The Sinai Palimpsest, or Lewis Codex, as it came to be called, would prove to date to the late fourth century; the translation it preserved . . . [dated] from the late second century A.D." (N Y Times Book Rev) Bibliography. Index.

This book "is by turns a rattling adventure yarn—thick with roving Bedouin and ancient tombs—and a testament to the power of perseverance." Washington Post Book World

Includes bibliographical references

Lewis, C. S. (Clive Staples), 1898-1963

McGrath, Alister. **C.** S. Lewis; a life : eccentric genius, reluctant prophet. Alister McGrath. Tyndale House Publishers 2013 350 p. (hc) $24.99 **92**

1. Authors -- Biography 2. Christian literature 3. Authors, English -- 20th century -- Biography

ISBN 9781414339351; 1414339356

LC 2012033140

This book, by Alister McGrath, is a biography of the 20th century Christian author and apologist Clive Staples Lewis. "After thoroughly examining recently published Lewis correspondence, Alister challenges some of the previously held beliefs about the exact timing of Lewis's shift from atheism to theism and then to Christianity. [The author] paints a portrait of an eccentric thinker who became an inspiring, though reluctant, prophet for our times." (Publisher's note)

Includes bibliographical references and index

Lewis, Jerry, 1926-

Lewis, Jerry. **Dean** & me; a love story. Doubleday 2005 340p il $26.95 **92**

1. Actors 2. Singers 3. Comedians 4. Television personalities 5. Motion picture directors

ISBN 0-7679-2086-4

LC 2005-49682

"This is a wild, joyous book, but also a heartbreaking one." N Y Times Book Rev

Li, Charles N., 1940-

Li, Charles N. The **bitter** sea; coming of age in a China before Mao. HarperCollins Publishers 2008 283p il hardcover o.p. pa $14.99 **92**

1. Anthropologists 2. Linguists 3. College teachers 4. China -- History -- 1949-

ISBN 978-0-06-134664-4; 0-06-134664-0; 978-0-06-170954-8 pa; 0-06-170954-9 pa

LC 2007-25697

The author, "who had an extraordinary life growing up in pre-Communist China, shares his story of betrayal, loss, hope, and triumph in this lyrical account. . . . This brilliant memoir is as much about modern Chinese history as it is about familial relationships." Libr J

Li, Leslie, 1945-

Li, Leslie. **Daughter** of heaven; a memoir with earthly recipes. Arcade Pub. 2005 274p $25; pa $13.95 **92**

1. Chinese cooking

ISBN 1-55970-768-2; 1-55970-800-X pa

LC 2004-23452

The book centers on the author's "relationship with her father and Nai-nai, her grandmother, who lands in New York City for an extended visit. . . . In stories and in the nearly 20 recipes (including Drunken Chicken and Cantonese Fried Rice), Li reveals the tale of an Asian woman caught between many different worlds and times and places." Booklist

Lincoln, Abraham, 1809-1865

Burlingame, Michael. **Abraham** Lincoln; a life. Johns Hopkins University Press 2008 2v il set $125 **92**

1. Lawyers 2. Presidents 3. State legislators 4. Members of Congress 5. Biography, Individual 6. Presidents -- United States

ISBN 0-8018-8993-6; 978-0-8018-8993-6

LC 2007-52919

In this 2-volume set on U.S. President Abraham Lincoln, "volume 1 covers Lincoln's early childhood, his experiences as a farm boy in Indiana and Illinois, his legal training, and the political ambition that led to a term in Congress in the 1840s. In volume 2, [Michael] Burlingame examines Lincoln's life during his presidency and the Civil War, narrating . . . the crisis over Fort Sumter and Lincoln's own battles with relentless office seekers, hostile newspaper editors, and incompetent field commanders." (Publisher's note)

The author "has produced the finest Lincoln biography in more than 60 years. . . . Future Lincoln books cannot be written without it, and from no other book can a general reader learn so much about Abraham Lincoln." Publ Wkly

Includes bibliographical references

Carwardine, Richard. **Lincoln** : a life of purpose and power. Knopf 2006 394p il map $27.50 **92**

1. Lawyers 2. Presidents 3. State legislators 4. Members of Congress 5. Presidents -- United States 6. United States -- History -- 1861-1865, Civil War

ISBN 1-4000-4456-1

LC 2005047230

First published 2003 in the United Kingdom

This book "is not only analytical and smart, it's also delightfully readable—and it will surely emerge as one of the most important Lincoln books to be published this decade." Publ Wkly

Includes bibliographical references

Donald, David Herbert. **Lincoln**. Simon & Schuster 1995 714p il maps hardcover o.p. pa $20   **92**
1. Lawyers 2. Presidents 3. State legislators 4. Members of Congress 5. Presidents -- United States
ISBN 0-684-80846-3; 0-684-82535-X pa
LC 95-4782
This biography examines: "Lincoln's relationship with his father; his romance with Ann Rutledge; his bouts of 'hypo,' which amounted at times almost to clinical depression; his marriage; his political ambition; his attitudes toward slavery and black people; his relations with radical Republicans during the Civil War; the mistakes and successes of his wartime leadership." Atl Mon

Includes bibliographical references

★ Goodwin, Doris Kearns, 1943- **Team** of rivals; the political genius of Abraham Lincoln. Simon & Schuster 2005 916p il map $35   **92**
1. Lawyers 2. Governors 3. Presidents 4. Senators 5. Attorneys general 6. State legislators 7. Members of Congress 8. Secretaries of state 9. Biography, Individual 10. Supreme Court justices 11. Presidential candidates 12. Presidents -- United States 13. Secretaries of the treasury 14. United States -- Politics and government -- 1861-1865
ISBN 0-684-82490-6
LC 2005-44615
"The knowledge gained here about these three significant figures who well attended Lincoln gain for the reader an even keener appreciation of the rare individual that he was." Booklist

Includes bibliographical references

Holzer, Harold. **Lincoln** president-elect; Abraham Lincoln and the great secession winter 1860-1861. Simon & Schuster 2008 623p il $30   **92**
1. Lawyers 2. Presidents 3. State legislators 4. Members of Congress 5. Presidents -- United States
ISBN 978-0-7432-8947-4; 0-7432-8947-1
LC 2008-21520
"This excellent study fills a gap about which not much has been written in Lincoln's presidential career." Choice

Includes bibliographical references

Keneally, Thomas. **Abraham** Lincoln. Viking 2003 183p (Penguin lives series) hardcover o.p. pa $14   **92**
1. Lawyers 2. Presidents 3. State legislators 4. Members of Congress 5. Presidents -- United States 6. United States -- History -- 1861-1865, Civil War
ISBN 0-670-03175-5; 0-14-311475-1 pa
LC 2003-268078
"Keneally's Lincoln is a self-actuated farm boy made good by self-discipline, savvy instincts, wit, the wisdom acquired from courtrooms, friendships, and political huckster-

ing—and luck . . . [The author] recounts Lincoln's early missteps in romance, business, and politics and his self-doubts and depression as his star dimmed several times, and he concedes Lincoln's erratic course toward emancipation and a successful strategy for Union victory during the Civil War . . . This is an epic compressed into a tightly written biography that all Americans might read with profit. Keneally's occasional tendency to let folklore stand as fact notwithstanding, there is no better brief introduction to Lincoln and his American dream." Libr J

Kunhardt, Philip B. **Looking** for Lincoln; the making of an American icon. [by] Philip B. Kunhardt III, Peter W. Kunhardt and Peter W. Kunhardt, Jr.; foreword by David Herbert Donald; introduction by Doris Kearns Goodwin. Alfred A. Knopf 2008 494p il $50   **92**
1. Lawyers 2. Presidents 3. State legislators 4. Members of Congress 5. Presidents -- United States
ISBN 978-0-307-26713-9; 0-307-26713-X
LC 2008-14193
Sequel to: Lincoln: an illustrated biography
"The Kunhardts' book represents a visual and literary feast for all devotees of the sacred national idol that is Lincoln." Publ Wkly

Includes bibliographical references

The Lincoln anthology; great writers on his life and legacy from 1860 to now. edited by Harold Holzer. Library of America 2009 964p il $40   **92**
1. Lawyers 2. Presidents 3. State legislators 4. Members of Congress 5. Presidents -- United States
ISBN 978-1-59853-033-9; 1-59853-033-X
LC 2008-934337
This "is a solid compilation of work on Abraham Lincoln from a diverse selection of writers in various genres, celebrating his extensive legacy and providing insight from a number of angles and time periods." Publ Wkly

Includes bibliographical references

Lind, Michael. **What** Lincoln believed; the values and convictions of America's greatest president. Doubleday 2005 358p $27.95   **92**
1. Lawyers 2. Presidents 3. State legislators 4. Members of Congress 5. Presidents -- United States
ISBN 0-385-50739-9
LC 2004-41333
"Some readers may not recognize their own cherished Lincoln in Lind's well-researched and reasoned book. Yet it adds a valuable perspective to the vast arena of Lincoln scholarship." Christ Sci Monit

Includes bibliographical references

★ McPherson, James M. **Abraham** Lincoln. Oxford University Press 2009 79p $12.95   **92**
1. Lawyers 2. Presidents 3. State legislators 4. Members of Congress 5. Presidents -- United States
ISBN 978-0-19-537452-0; 0-19-537452-5
LC 2008-35623
"McPherson, America's leading authority on Lincoln and his times, demonstrates his complete command of his subject in this concise but remarkably rich and perceptive

biography. . . . This little book is bigger than its pages and should be in every library, schoolhouse, and home." Libr J

Includes bibliographical references

★ McPherson, James M. **Tried** by war; Abraham Lincoln as commander in chief. Penguin Press 2008 329p il map hardcover o.p. pa $17   **92**

1. Lawyers 2. Presidents 3. State legislators 4. Members of Congress 5. Presidents -- United States 6. United States -- History -- 1861-1865, Civil War 7. United States -- Politics and government -- 1861-1865
ISBN 978-1-594-20191-2; 1-594-20191-9; 978-0-14-311614-1 pa; 0-14-311614-2 pa

LC 2008-25229

Evaluates Lincoln's talents as a commander in chief in spite of limited military experience, tracing the ways in which he worked with, or against, his senior commanders to defeat the Confederacy and reshape the presidential role.

This book "is a perfect primer, not just for Civil War buffs or fans of Abraham Lincoln, but for anyone who wishes to understand the evolution of the president's role as commander in chief." N Y Times Book Rev

Includes bibliographical references

★ Our Lincoln; new perspectives on Lincoln and his world. edited by Eric Foner. W.W. Norton 2008 336p il   **92**

1. Lawyers 2. Presidents 3. State legislators 4. Members of Congress 5. Presidents -- United States 6. United States -- History -- 19th century 7. United States -- History -- Civil War, 1861-1865 8. United States -- Politics and government -- 1861-1865
ISBN 0-393-06756-4; 9780393067569

LC 2008-17096

"Twelve essays present the ideas of recent historians on Lincoln's evolving views on race, religion, and civil liberties, his military leadership, his family, photographs and portraits of Lincoln, and the use of his memory in the 21st century." (Publisher's note) Index.

Historians "collectively situate Lincoln's ideas, interests, and policies and the meanings various people from abolitionists to neo-Confederates have found in Lincoln, from the microscopic to a wider historical context of politics, culture, and memory. Essays explore such topics as presidential leadership, civil liberties, citizenship and rights, democratic politics, mass-produced imagery, African colonization, antislavery, race, religion, family life, writing sensibilities and style, and the need to claim Lincoln for one's own cause. The eloquent and compelling results show how and why Lincoln was both a man of his time and a man for all time." Libr J

Includes bibliographical references

Pinsker, Matthew. **Lincoln's** sanctuary; Abraham Lincoln and the Soldiers' Home. Oxford University Press 2003 256p il maps hardcover o.p. pa $17.95   **92**

1. Lawyers 2. Presidents 3. State legislators 4. Members of Congress 5. Presidents -- United States 6. United States Soldiers' and Airmen's Home (Washington, D.C.)
ISBN 0-19-516206-4; 978-0-19-517985-9 pa; 0-19-

517985-4 pa

LC 2003-1215

The author "follows the War President to his 'retreat' at the Soldiers' Home away from the daily noise, posturing, and politicking of the capital and finds there a serenity that allowed Lincoln to relax with his family, think through issues, conduct secret meetings with allies and enemies, and reinvigorate his resolve. . . . Through Pinsker's probing inquiry into sources heretofore surprisingly underused, the ever elusive private Lincoln comes into new light. A book for our time and for all libraries." Libr J

Sandburg, Carl. **Abraham** Lincoln: The prairie years and The war years; illustrated ed; Harcourt Brace Jovanovich 1970 640p il maps hardcover o.p. pa $26   **92**

1. Lawyers 2. Presidents 3. Frontier and pioneer life 4. State legislators 5. Members of Congress 6. Presidents -- United States 7. United States -- History -- 1861-1865, Civil War
ISBN 0-15-602752-6 pa
First published 1954

A condensation of the two volumes of "The prairie years" (1926) and the four volumes of "The war years" (1939). The author has taken advantage of material made available since the original volumes were published to include in this edition of his lifetime study of Lincoln

"A biography that as a whole is superior to the longer life. This one volume has a form which the six lacked. It is a tighter and tidier book. It retains the superb qualities of the original work without the faults of the latter." Saturday Rev

Includes bibliographical references

Shenk, Joshua Wolf. **Lincoln's** melancholy; how depression challenged a president and fueled his greatness. Houghton Mifflin 2005 350p $25   **92**

1. Lawyers 2. Presidents 3. State legislators 4. Members of Congress 5. Presidents -- United States
ISBN 0-618-55116-6

LC 2005-9653

This book "argues that Abraham Lincoln's lifelong depression was responsible for his becoming one of America's greatest presidents." N Y Times Book Rev

"An estimable contribution to the Lincoln literature." Booklist

Includes bibliographical references

Symonds, Craig L. **Lincoln** and his admirals; Abraham Lincoln, the U.S. Navy, and the Civil War. Oxford University Press 2008 430p il $27.95   **92**

1. Lawyers 2. Presidents 3. State legislators 4. Military officials 5. Members of Congress 6. Government officials 7. Newspaper executives 8. United States -- Navy 9. Secretaries of the navy 10. State government officials 11. Presidents -- United States 12. United States -- History -- 1861-1865, Civil War -- Naval operations
ISBN 978-0-19-531022-1; 0-19-531022-5

LC 2008-4251

"For scholars and the general reader alike, an insightful and highly readable treatment of a neglected dimension of Lincoln's wartime leadership." Kirkus

Includes bibliographical references (p. 407-416)

★ Van Sciver, Noah. The **Hypo**; The Melancholic Young Lincoln. Noah Van Sciver. Fantagraphics 2012 192 p. chiefly ill. $24.99   **92**

1. Depression (Psychology) 2. Biographical graphic novels

ISBN 1606996193; 9781606996195

This graphic novel, by Noah Van Sciver, "is based on [Abraham] Lincoln's battle with depression. . . . [It] follows the twenty-something Abraham Lincoln as . . . a rising Whig in the state's legislature as he arrives in Springfield, IL to practice law. . . . But, as time passes and uncertainty creeps in, young Lincoln is forced to battle a dark cloud of depression brought on by a chain of defeats and failures culminating into a nervous breakdown that threatens his life and sanity." (Publisher's note)

"A thoroughly engaging graphic novel that seamlessly balances investigation and imagination." Pub Wkly

White, Ronald C. **A.** Lincoln; a biography. Random House Pub. Group 2009 796p il map $35   **92**

1. Lawyers 2. Presidents 3. State legislators 4. Members of Congress 5. Presidents -- United States 6. United States -- Politics and government -- 1861-1865

ISBN 978-1-4000-6499-1

LC 2008-28840

In this biography, the author "follows the familiar trajectory of the 16th President's life; what's unique is his insight into the moral and intellectual framework of Lincoln's thinking. . . . An exceptional work that belongs in every public and academic library." Libr J

Includes bibliographical references (p. [745]-764) and index.

White, Ronald C. The **eloquent** president: a portrait of Lincoln through his words; [by] Ronald C. White, Jr. Random House 2005 xxiii, 448p il $26.95; pa $15.95   **92**

1. Lawyers 2. Presidents 3. State legislators 4. Members of Congress 5. Presidents -- United States

ISBN 1-400-06119-9; 0-8129-7046-2 pa

LC 2004-50766

The author "traces Lincoln's evolving rhetoric over the course of his presidency in a series of highly detailed critical essays. He follows Lincoln from the cautious, lawyerly text of the First Inaugural to the soaring, triumphant poetics of the Gettysburg Address." Publ Wkly

Includes bibliographical references

Lincoln, Mary Todd, 1818-1882

Baker, Jean H. **Mary** Todd Lincoln; a biography. Norton 1987 429p il hardcover o.p. pa $17.95 **92**

1. Spouses of the presidents 2. Spouses of presidents

ISBN 0-393-30586-4 pa

LC 86-23757

The author "portrays Mrs. Lincoln as a woman tortured by a series of family bereavements and thwarted from developing her natural talents by a patriarchal society that brand-ed as 'unwomanly' her involvement in her husband's political career. Ms. Baker establishes her first argument with a lengthy investigation of Mary Todd's early family history in Lexington, Ky., and sustains the second by enlarging upon such topics as 19th-century domesticity, childbirth, mourning customs, spiritualism and America's deplorable insanity laws." NY Times Book Rev

Includes bibliographical references

Clinton, Catherine. **Mrs.** Lincoln; a life. HarperCollins 2009 415p il $26.99   **92**

1. Spouses of presidents 2. Presidents' spouses -- United States

ISBN 978-0-06-076040-3; 0-06-076040-0

The author "sifts through the many criticisms of Mary Lincoln to offer a sensitive reassessment that debunks unjust attacks and reveals Mrs. Lincoln's many strengths—charitableness, devotion to family and nation, unwavering love and encouragement for her beleaguered husband—alongside the mental illness and flaws of temperament for which she is better known. . . . Written in a style that will appeal to the general reader, Clinton's book features sufficient nuance to satisfy scholars looking for a greater interpretation of the life of this controversial historical figure." Libr J

Includes bibliographical references

Lindbergh, Anne Morrow, 1906-2001

Hertog, Susan. **Anne** Morrow Lindbergh; a biography. Talese 1999 561p il hardcover o.p. pa $17   **92**

1. Poets 2. Authors 3. Novelists 4. Diarists 5. Essayists 6. Memoirists 7. Spouses of prominent persons

ISBN 0-385-72007-6 pa

LC 99-28759

After her marriage to Charles Lindbergh, Anne Morrow "soon recognized the difficulty of reconciling her literary ambitions with accompanying her husband as copilot, navigator and radio operator. After the tragic kidnapping and death of their first child, which they blamed in part on dogged press coverage of their personal life, the Lindberghs moved abroad. They became embroiled with the leaders of Nazi Germany, according to Hertog, because Charles believed that the democratic system was weak and ineffectual. . . . This sympathetic portrayal of Anne as a wife, mother, poet and feminist may well find a readership more interested in a talented woman's creative struggle than in the oft-told Lindbergh story." Publ Wkly

Includes bibliographical references

Lindbergh, Reeve. **Under** a wing; a memoir. Delta Trade Paperbacks 1999 223p il pa $15   **92**

1. Poets 2. Authors 3. Generals 4. Novelists 5. Air pilots 6. Diarists 7. Essayists 8. Memoirists 9. Air force officers 10. Children's authors 11. Spouses of prominent persons 12. Children of prominent persons

ISBN 978-0-385-33444-0; 0-385-33444-3

First published 1998 by Simon & Schuster

From the "perspective of a woman in her early fifties, the youngest child of aviator and American hero Charles Lindbergh and beloved writer Anne Morrow Lindbergh tellingly reflects on the foibles, as well as the strength of character of those two well-known figures." Booklist

"A rare memoir whose goal is not to expose but finally to understand." Libr J

Winters, Kathleen C. **Anne** Morrow Lindbergh; first lady of the air. Palgrave Macmillan 2006 241p il map $24.95 **92**
1. Poets 2. Authors 3. Novelists 4. Diarists 5. Essayists 6. Memoirists 7. Spouses of prominent persons
ISBN 978-1-4039-6932-3; 1-4039-6932-9
LC 2006-43290
This book focuses on Anne Morrow Lindbergh's career as an aviator. "She was one of the earliest female pilots, as well as the first American female glider pilot, and a radio operator. . . . Winters shows in great detail that Lindbergh accomplished this under the glare of an unremitting spotlight, and in the company of an often-demanding spouse. That the author is able to bring something new to the Lindbergh story is impressive, and she does it through both technical explanations of Lindbergh's accomplishments and Anne's own words about her flying exploits, marriage, and writing." Booklist
Includes bibliographical references

Lindbergh, Charles, 1902-1974

Kessner, Thomas. The **flight** of the century; Charles Lindbergh & the rise of American aviation. Oxford University Press 2010 313p il map (Pivotal moments in American history) **92**
1. Generals 2. Air pilots 3. Memoirists 4. Air force officers 5. Biography, Individual 6. Aeronautics -- United States -- History
ISBN 0-19-532019-0; 978-0-19-532019-0
LC 2010-06082
Thomas Kessner's book examines "how and why Lindbergh elicited so much popular excitement and what his status as an international hero meant for the development of aviation." (J Am Hist) Index.
"In May 1927 at the age of 25, the 'Lone Eagle' flew from New York to Paris, a startling accomplishment that made the awkward, reticent aviator the world's best-known person. But Lindbergh lived until 1974, and two elements were added to his legacy — he was the father whose tiny son was kidnapped and slain by Bruno Hauptmann, and, much worse for his reputation, he was the fascist-tinged advocate of U.S. neutrality before World War II. . . . [Kessner's book] aims to balance the equation. His book recaps Lindbergh's epochal flight and carries it forward, discussing his subsequent role in the aviation boom that followed. While there is nothing particularly earth-shattering about what he has written, Kessner's fresh perspective breathes new life into Lindbergh's tale." Philadelphia Inquirer
Includes bibliographical references and index

Lindbergh, Reeve. **Under** a wing; a memoir. Delta Trade Paperbacks 1999 223p il pa $15 **92**
1. Poets 2. Authors 3. Generals 4. Novelists 5. Air pilots 6. Diarists 7. Essayists 8. Memoirists 9. Air force officers 10. Children's authors 11. Spouses of prominent persons 12. Children of prominent persons
ISBN 978-0-385-33444-0; 0-385-33444-3
First published 1998 by Simon & Schuster

"A rare memoir whose goal is not to expose but finally to understand." Libr J

Lindbergh, Reeve

Lindbergh, Reeve. **Under** a wing; a memoir. Delta Trade Paperbacks 1999 223p il pa $15 **92**
1. Poets 2. Authors 3. Generals 4. Novelists 5. Air pilots 6. Diarists 7. Essayists 8. Memoirists 9. Air force officers 10. Children's authors 11. Spouses of prominent persons 12. Children of prominent persons
ISBN 978-0-385-33444-0; 0-385-33444-3
First published 1998 by Simon & Schuster
"A rare memoir whose goal is not to expose but finally to understand." Libr J

Lindhout, Amanda

★ Corbett, Sara. A **house** in the sky; a memoir. Amanda Lindhout, Sara Corbett. Scribner 2013 373 p. (paperback) $16 **92**
1. Somalia 2. Hostages 3. Somalia -- History -- 1991- 4. Hostages -- Somalia -- Biography 5. Journalists -- Canada -- Biography
ISBN 1451645619; 9781451645606; 9781451645613
LC 2013016015
In this book, "Canadian journalist [Amanda] Lindhout gives . . . [an] account of her 459-day captivity at the hands of Somali Islamist rebels. . . . Convinced war-torn Somalia would be the 'hurricane' to make her career, in August 2008, at age 25, she . . . set off to view a displaced-persons' camp but was instead carjacked by a group of kidnappers. . . . Her captors moved her frequently from hideout to hideout, and she . . . was raped and tortured." (Publishers Weekly)
Includes bibliographical references and index

Linné, Carl von, 1707-1778

Blunt, Wilfrid. **Linnaeus,** the compleat naturalist; with an introduction by William T. Stearn. Princeton Univ. Press 2002 264p il maps $35 **92**
1. Botanists 2. Writers on science
ISBN 0-691-09636-8
First published 1971 by Viking with title: The compleat naturalist: a life of Linnaeus
This biography traces the Swedish scientist's life from his days as a poor student at Lund University through his scientific achievements and academic career at Uppsala
Includes bibliographical references

Lispector, Clarice, 1925-1977

Moser, Benjamin. **Why** this world; a biography of Clarice Lispector. Oxford University Press 2009 479p il $29.95 **92**
1. Authors 2. Novelists 3. Journalists 4. Women authors 5. Short story writers 6. Biography, Individual
ISBN 0-19-538556-X; 978-0-19-538556-4
LC 2008-55639
This is a biography of the Brazilian novelist.
"Lispector makes a difficult, often lurid subject, and Moser's account of her life is riveting—he draws extensively on previously untranslated letters and criticism (he does the translations himself, from Yiddish, German, French

and Portuguese); at times the book reads like a gothic horror story." Nation

Includes bibliographical references

Lithgow, John, 1945-

Lithgow, John, 1945- **Drama**; an actor's education. John Lithgow. Harper 2011 p. cm. $26.99; $12.99   92

1. Actors -- United States -- Biography

ISBN 978-0-06-173497-7; 978-0-06-209773-6 ebook; 9780061734977

LC 2011008172

"More than the run-of-the-mill 'And then I met . . . And then I was in . . .' actor's autobiography, this is both a memoir full of emotion and a cautionary tale." Libr J

Lively, Penelope, 1933-

Lively, Penelope. A **house** unlocked. Grove Press 2002 225p il $23; pa $13   92

1. Authors 2. Novelists 3. Children's authors 4. Short story writers

ISBN 0-8021-1712-0; 0-8021-4007-6 pa

LC 2001-55745

First published 2001 in the United Kingdom

"The British novelist Penelope Lively spent her early childhood in Egypt, but it was her school holidays at Golsoncott—a manor house that her grandparents bought in the wilds of Somerset, in 1923—that shaped her life. In this slim, beguiling book, Lively describes the contents and customs of the house. . . . By meticulously tracing the provenance of these objects, she re-creates the life they once furnished." New Yorker

Includes bibliographical references

Lobdell, William

Lobdell, William. **Losing** my religion; how I lost my faith reporting on religion in America--and found unexpected peace. Collins 2009 291p $25.99   92

1. Journalists 2. Bloggers

ISBN 978-0-06-162681-4; 0-06-162681-3

LC 2008-24010

"Lobdell's spiritual journey fascinates, not least on account of the irony of his trajectory from agnosticism to belief to atheism while covering religion. It's a story that may raise eyebrows among believers and nonbelievers alike." Booklist

Includes bibliographical references

Lobo, Julio, 1898-1983

Rathbone, John Paul. The **sugar** king of Havana; the rise and fall of Julio Lobo, Cuba's last tycoon. Penguin Press 2010 304p il map $27.95   92

1. Sugar 2. Businessmen 3. Cuba -- History 4. Agribusiness executives

ISBN 978-1-59420-258-2; 1594202583

LC 2010-13790

"An exceptionally rich portrait not only of an empire and its progenitor but Cuba itself, and the economic legacy of Castro's revolution, the loss of capital, and the end of Cuba's 'great age of sugar.'" Publ Wkly

Includes bibliographical references

Lockwood, Belva Ann, 1830-1917

Norgren, Jill. **Belva** Lockwood; the woman who would be president. New York University Press 2007 311p il $40; pa $22   92

1. Lawyers 2. Suffragists 3. Lecturers 4. Biography, Individual 5. Presidential candidates 6. Women in politics -- United States

ISBN 0-8147-5834-7; 0-8147-5851-7 pa; 978-0-8147-5834-2; 978-0-8147-5851-9 pa

LC 2006-34486

This is a biography of Belva Lockwood, a lawyer and suffragist who twice ran for president. Index.

"Those with interests in women's, political, social, and cultural history will enjoy Lockwood." Choice

Includes bibliographical references

Lomax, Alan, 1915-2002

Szwed, John F. **Alan** Lomax; the man who recorded the world. Viking 2010 438p $29.95   92

1. Authors 2. Folk music 3. Folklorists 4. Musicologists 5. Writers on music 6. Biography, Individual

ISBN 978-0-670-02199-4

LC 2010-15332

This is a biography of the American folklorist and ethnomusicologist.

This "biography is a worthy testament to Lomax's passions and ideals, which gifted the world some of the most important American recordings ever made." New Statesman

Includes bibliographical references

Lombardi, Vince

Maraniss, David. **When** pride still mattered: a life of Vince Lombardi. Simon & Schuster 1999 541p il hardcover o.p. pa $16   92

1. Football coaches 2. Green Bay Packers (Football team)

ISBN 0-684-77018-5 pa

LC 99-37859

"From Lombardi's formative years as a player and coach at Fordham University through assistantships with West Point and the Giants and, finally, to his tenure as head coach of the Packers, Maraniss presents a portrait of a complicated human being who was a great teacher but a mediocre listener, an effective psychologist despite being rife with flaws." Publ Wkly

Includes bibliographical references

London, Jack, 1876-1916

Adam, Philip. **Jack** London, photographer; [by] Jeanne Campbell Reesman, Sara S. Hodson, & Philip Adam. University of Georgia Press 2010 271p il $49.95   92

1. Authors 2. Novelists 3. Photographers 4. Authors, American 5. Short story writers

ISBN 978-0-8203-2967-3

LC 2010005973

"This book will be of great appeal to a broad range of audiences interested in history, American literature, and photography." Libr J

Includes bibliographical references

Labor, Earle. **Jack** London; an American life. Earle Labor. Farrar Straus & Giroux 2013 480 p. (hardback) $30   **92**

1. American authors -- Biography 2. Authors, American -- 19th century -- Biography 3. Authors, American -- 20th century -- Biography

ISBN 0374178488; 9780374178482

LC 2012050948

This book presents a biography of writer Jack London. "Born in San Francisco in 1876 to an impoverished single mother, London . . . took up factory work to support his household while still a child, and by age 18 had worked as an oyster pirate, sailor, and rail-riding hobo. Omnivorous reading and sporadic education fueled his desire to write, and a year spent surviving the Yukon Gold Rush (1897-1898) provided him with inspiration for his earliest nonfiction and fiction." (Publishers Weekly)

Includes bibliographical references and index

Long, Huey Pierce, 1893-1935

Hair, William Ivy. The **Kingfish** and his realm: the life and times of Huey P. Long. Louisiana State Univ. Press 1991 406p il map hardcover o.p. pa $21.95   **92**

1. Governors 2. Senators 3. State government officials 4. Louisiana -- Politics and government

ISBN 0-8071-2124-X pa

LC 91-18546

This is a biography of the man who was governor of Louisiana from 1928 to 1932 and senator from 1932 until his assassination in 1935

"Written with passion and mordant wit, the book is literally hard to put down; the Kingfish seems to stimulate good writing. Overall, {this} is one of the more convincing negative biographies of recent years." Rev Am Hist

Includes bibliographical references

Longworth, Alice Roosevelt, 1884-1980

Cordery, Stacy A. **Alice**; Alice Roosevelt Longworth, from White House princess to Washington power broker. Viking 2007 590p il $32.95   **92**

1. Socialites 2. Children of presidents

ISBN 978-0-670-01833-8

LC 2006-103087

This is a biography of Alice Roosevelt Longworth, the Washington hostess and author of Crowded Hours (1933).

The author "pens an authoritative, intriguing portrait of a first daughter who broke the mold." Publ Wkly

Includes bibliographical references (p. [555]-572) and index.

Louis XIV, King of France, 1638-1715

Fraser, Antonia. **Love** and Louis XIV; the women in the life of the Sun King. Nan A. Talese/Doubleday 2006 xxviii, 388p il $32.50   **92**

1. Kings

ISBN 978-0-38550984-8; 0-385-50984-7

LC 2006-44674

This is an account of Louis XIV's relationships with his wife and his mistresses.

"One of the most enveloping popular histories of the current publishing season." Booklist

Includes bibliographical references

Louis, Joe, 1914-1981

Roberts, Randy. **Joe** Louis; hard times man. Yale University Press 2010 308p il $27.50   **92**

1. African American athletes 2. Boxing -- History 3. Boxing -- Biography 4. Biography, Individual

ISBN 978-0-300-12222-0

LC 2010-15422

In this biography of the American boxer, "Roberts handles the boxing action with professional aplomb, and he knows when to cut away to tell us something of consequence and when to return to the ring. The author ably chronicles Louis's rise from Alabama cotton fields to the cavernous Yankee Stadium, where celebrities glittered in the ringside seats for his big fights; the development of the mass media (boxing was enormously popular on radio); Louis's career in the U.S. Army; and his sad decline, amid unpayable debts and mental illness. All legendary athletes should hope for treatment by such capable, compassionate hands." Kirkus

Includes bibliographical references and index

Loy, Myrna

Leider, Emily W. **Myrna** Loy; the only good girl in Hollywood. [by] Emily W. Leider. University of California Press 2011 411p il $34.95   **92**

1. Actors

ISBN 978-0-520-25320-9; 0-520-25320-5

LC 2011-11571

"Loy's gifts are easy to enjoy, hard to describe. She's been lucky in attracting an even-tempered sympathetic biographer like Ms. Leider, whose book, like the best of its genre, sends you back to the films." Wall Street J

Includes bibliographical references

Luce, Clare Boothe, 1903-1987

Morris, Sylvia Jukes. **Rage** for fame: the ascent of Clare Boothe Luce. Random House 1997 561p il hardcover o.p. pa $27   **92**

1. Authors 2. Diplomats 3. Dramatists 4. Members of Congress 5. Writers on politics

ISBN 0-8129-9249-0 pa

LC 96-43084

This first of a projected two-volume biography "describes how the future congresswoman and second wife of Time magazine founder Henry Luce, bedded her way upward while career-climbing in New York journalism and writing a stage mega-hit, The Women. . . . By 1942—at age 39—she turned to politics and was elected a Republican representative from Connecticut." Publ Wkly

Includes bibliographical references

Luce, Henry Robinson, 1898-1967

★ Brinkley, Alan. The **publisher**; Henry Luce and his American century. Alfred A. Knopf 2010 531p il $35 **92**

1. Journalists 2. Publishers and publishing 3. Magazine editors 4. Magazine executives

ISBN 978-0-679-41444-5; 0-679-41444-4

LC 2009-38834

"In this superb biography Alan Brinkley . . . has told the curiously depressing story of a brilliant man who got everything wrong, including so many of the things that mattered most to him. Mr Brinkley has an eye for both the telling detail and the broad sweep of Luce's role as the man who saw the need for a national news magazine and foresaw the American century." Economist

Includes bibliographical references

Lukas, Christopher

Lukas, Christopher. **Blue** genes; a memoir of loss and survival. Doubleday 2008 248p il $24.95 **92**

1. Depression (Psychology) 2. Television directors 3. Television producers 4. Television scriptwriters

ISBN 978-0-385-52520-6; 0-385-52520-6

LC 2008-6648

In this memoir, "Lukas shatters the silence surrounding the long history of suicide in his Hungarian-German-Jewish family, especially that of his older brother, J. Anthony Lukas (Tony). Depression and what is now diagnosed as bipolar disorder hounded various family members, most notably the brothers' beautiful college-educated actress mother, Elizabeth, whose deepening depression . . . led her to cut her own throat in 1941, when the boys were just six and eight. Lukas writes with the reassuring sagacity of hindsight, knowing the negative long-term effects of his mother's mental illness on his brother especially. . . . In clear, forceful prose, the author attempts to make sense of these calamities and assert a life-affirming purpose." Publ Wkly

Luther, Martin, 1483-1546

Bainton, Roland Herbert. **Here** I stand: a life of Martin Luther. Abingdon Press 1950 422p il music hardcover o.p. pa $7 **92**

1. Reformation 2. Theologians 3. Social reformers 4. Religious leaders 5. Writers on religion 6. Europe -- Church history

ISBN 0-687-16895-3 pa

This biography of Martin Luther interprets his work, writings, and lasting contributions. It recreates the spiritual setting of the sixteenth century and shows Luther's place within it

Includes bibliographical references

Erikson, Erik H. **Young** man Luther; a study in psychoanalysis and history. Norton 1958 288p hardcover o.p. pa $13.95 **92**

1. Reformation 2. Theologians 3. Social reformers 4. Religious leaders 5. Writers on religion 6. Europe -- Church history

ISBN 0-393-31036-1 pa

"This study of Martin Luther as a young man was planned as a chapter in a book on emotional crises in late adolescence and early adulthood. But Luther proved too bulky a man to be merely a chapter." Preface

Oberman, Heiko Augustinus. **Luther** : man between God and the Devil; {by} Heiko A. Oberman; translated by Eileen Walliser-Schwarzbart. Yale Univ. Press 1990 xx, 380p il hardcover o.p. pa $20 **92**

1. Reformation 2. Theologians 3. Social reformers 4. Religious leaders 5. Writers on religion 6. Europe -- Church history

ISBN 978-0-300-10313-7 pa; 0-300-10313-1 pa

LC 89-5747

Original German edition, 1982

The author "posits that to understand Luther the reformer is to first realize he was a medieval man for whom Satan was as real as God and human. By placing Luther back into the context of his own age, Oberman strips away any simplistic, post-Enlightenment notions of Luther as the savior of humanity from the darkest obscurantism of the Catholic Church. . . . A triumph of scholarship that brings Luther to life in all of his furious, outspoken, and violent passion." Booklist

Includes bibliographical references

Wilson, Derek A. **Out** of the storm; the life and legacy of Martin Luther. [by] Derek Wilson. St. Martin's Press 2008 399p il $29.95 **92**

1. Reformation 2. Theologians 3. Social reformers 4. Religious leaders 5. Writers on religion 6. Europe -- Church history

ISBN 978-0-312-37588-1; 0-312-37588-3

LC 2007-39331

This is a "biography of the man who, more than any other, precipitated the Protestant Reformation." Libr J

"A nuanced portrait of a perplexing titan." Booklist

Includes bibliographical references

Luxenberg, Steve

Luxenberg, Steve. **Annie's** ghosts; a journey into a family secret. Hyperion Books 2009 401p il $24.99 **92**

1. Newspaper editors

ISBN 978-1-4013-2247-2; 1-4013-2247-6

LC 2008-55661

"In 1995, the author learned that his aging mother had a sister she had never mentioned. . . . After his mother's death a few years later, he learned that the sister's name was Annie and she was buried with his grandparents in Michigan. . . . As Luxenberg slowly uncovers Annie's story, he realizes that by exposing one ghost, he exposes thousands; by discovering one secret, he discovers those of his entire family." Kirkus

"Part memoir, part mystery, part history of the mental-health movement, . . . [this] is a fascinating account of a life lived in the shadows." Booklist

Includes bibliographical references

Lynn, Loretta

Lynn, Loretta. **Still** woman enough; a memoir.
{by} Loretta Lynn with Patsi Bale Cox. Hyperion
2002 244p il $24.95; pa $7.99   **92**

1. Singers 2. Country musicians 3. Songwriters
ISBN 0-7868-6650-0; 0-7868-8987-X pa

In this sequel to Coal miner's daughter, "Lynn mostly
focuses on her marriage and the trials and pleasures of
Nashville stardom, including fond recollections of friends
like Conway Twitty and Tammy Wynette. . . . Though her
grammar may make purists flinch . . . Lynn's literary voice is
as natural and endearing as her songs." Publ Wkly

Maathai, Wangari, 1940-2001

Maathai, Wangari. **Unbowed**; a memoir. [by]
Wangari Muta Maathai. Knopf 2006 314p il hardcover o.p. pa $15   **92**

1. Biologists 2. Conservationists 3. Environmentalists
4. Kenya 5. Nobel laureates for peace 6. Green Belt
Movement (Kenya)
ISBN 0-307-26348-7; 978-0-307-26348-3; 0-307-
27520-5 pa; 978-0-307-27520-2 pa

LC 2006-44729

"Nobel Peace Prize winner Maathai tells the unforgettable story of her Kenya girlhood, struggles as a biologist
and professor, and founding of the Green Belt Movement to
restore Kenya's decimated forests and provide women with
work." Booklist

MacArthur, Douglas, 1880-1964

Frank, Richard B. **MacArthur**; foreword by
Wesley K. Clark. Palgrave Macmillan 2007 224p
(Great generals series) hardcover o.p. pa $12.95 **92**

1. Generals
ISBN 1-4039-7658-9; 978-1-4039-7658-1; 0-230-
61397-7 pa; 978-0-230-61397-3 pa

This biography of the World War II general is an "assessment of both the man and the soldier, covering the failures
and triumphs in an assured and dispassionate tone. . . . A
good starting point for generalists." Libr J

Perry, Mark. The **most** dangerous man in America; the making of Douglas MacArthur. Mark Perry.
Basic Books 2014 416 p. illustrations (hardcover)
$29.99   **92**

1. Generals 2. United States -- Military history 3.
United States. Army -- Biography 4. Generals -- United
States -- Biography 5. United States -- History, Military
-- 20th century
ISBN 0465013287; 9780465013289; 9780465080670
LC 2014004629

"At times, even his admirers seemed unsure of what to
do with General Douglas MacArthur. . . . In 'The Most Dangerous Man in America,' celebrated historian Mark Perry
examines how this paradox of a man overcame personal and
professional challenges to lead his countrymen in their darkest hour. As Perry shows, Franklin Roosevelt and a handful
of MacArthur's subordinates made this feat possible, taming
MacArthur, making him useful, and finally making him victorious." (Publisher's note)

"While much has been written on the general topic,
Perry is strong on discussing MacArthur's relationship with
FDR as well as his fellow officers in the Pacific." LJ
Includes bibliographical references and index

MacLeish, Archibald, 1892-1982

MacLeish, Archibald. **Archibald** MacLeish: re-
flections; edited by Bernard A. Drabeck and Helen
E. Ellis; foreword by Richard Wilbur. University of
Mass. Press 1986 291p il $40; pa $18.95   **92**

1. Poets 2. Authors 3. Essayists 4. Librarians of
Congress
ISBN 0-87023-511-7; 0-87023-623-7 pa

LC 85-28912

"In this genial, relaxed book we have a golden view of
the candidly retrospective statesman-poet in his old age as
he really was, with most pretension and all rhetoric abandoned." N Y Times Book Rev
Includes bibliographical references

Macfadden, Bernarr, 1868-1955

Adams, Mark. **Mister** America; how muscular
millionaire Bernarr Macfadden transformed the nation through sex, salad, and the ultimate starvation
diet. Harper 2009 292p il $25.99   **92**

1. Bodybuilding 2. Physical fitness 3. Fitness experts
4. Magazine executives
ISBN 978-0-06-059475-6

LC 2008-18705

This is a "biography of pioneering health-and-fitness
guru Bernarr Macfadden. . . . A funny, informative history
of a true American eccentric and the national preoccupation
with health and fitness." Kirkus

Machiavelli, Niccolò, 1469-1527

Viroli, Maurizio. **Niccolo's** smile: a biography
of Machiavelli; translated from the Italian by Antony
Shugaar. Farrar, Straus & Giroux 2000 271p maps
hardcover o.p. pa $13   **92**

1. Authors 2. Statesmen 3. Dramatists 4. Writers on
politics 5. Political and social philosophers
ISBN 0-374-52800-4 pa

LC 00-29380

This biography of the Italian political philosopher traces
his life "from respected secretary of the Florentine republic,
dispatched on crucial diplomatic missions to Europe's most
illustrious courts, to forgotten commoner. . . . Viroli provides
a detailed, historical background for Machiavelli's personal
triumphs and woes. But the strength of this work lies in his
ceaseless concentration on Machiavelli the man, who comes
alive on each page." Publ Wkly
Includes bibliographical references

Madison, Dolley, 1768-1849

Allgor, Catherine. A **perfect** union; Dolley
Madison and the creation of the American nation.
Henry Holt & Co. 2006 493p il $30   **92**

1. Biography, Individual 2. Spouses of presidents
ISBN 0-8050-7327-2; 978-0-8050-7327-0

LC 2005-55127

This is a biography of the First Lady. Allgor argues that while Dolley Madison's "gender prevented her from openly playing politics, those very constraints of womanhood allowed her to construct an American democratic ruling style, and to achieve her husband [James's] political goals." (Publisher's note) Index.

"In this evocative study a remarkable woman, creator of the 'first lady' role, comes vividly to life. " N Y Times Book Rev

Includes bibliographical references

Madison, James, 1751-1836

Cheney, Lynne V., 1941- **James** Madison; a life reconsidered. Lynne Cheney. Viking Adult 2014 576 p. illustrations (hardback) $36   **92**
1. Presidents -- United States 2. Statesmen -- United States -- Biography 3. United States -- Politics and government -- 1783-1865
ISBN 0670025194; 9780670025190

LC 2013047837

This biography of U.S. president James Madison, by Lynne Cheney, "explores the astonishing story of a man of vaunted modesty. . . . Among the Founding Fathers, Madison was a true genius of the early republic. Outwardly reserved, Madison was the intellectual driving force behind the Constitution and crucial to its ratification. His visionary political philosophy and rationale for the union of states--so eloquently presented in The Federalist papers--helped shape . . . America." (Publisher's note)

"Cheney conclusively demonstrates through the historical record that Madison, in word and deed, was a primary figure in shaping early American development." Pub Wkly

Includes bibliographical references and index

Mahler, Gustav, 1860-1911

Lebrecht, Norman. **Why** Mahler? how one man and ten symphonies changed our world. Pantheon Books 2010 326p $27.95   **92**
1. Composers 2. Conductors (Music)
ISBN 978-0-375-42381-9; 0-375-42381-8

LC 2010-06034

"This is music history, criticism, and biography at its best. A treasure trove for Mahler fans, this is also likely to convert even the most obstinate detractor. Highly recommended for all music lovers." Libr J

Includes bibliographical references

Mailer, Norman, 1923-2007

Lennon, J. Michael. **Norman** Mailer; a double life. J. Michael Lennon. Simon & Schuster 2013 928 p. $40   **92**
1. American novelists 2. Journalists -- United States -- Biography 3. Authors, American -- 20th century -- Biography
ISBN 1439150192; 9781439150191

LC 2013005097

In this biography of Norman Mailer, author J. Michael Lennon depicts his subject "as a dual-natured personality: a passive observer and an activist, a family man and a philanderer,. . . . While Lennon treats readers to accounts of Mailer's celebrity and his relations with stars such as Muhammad Ali . . . he also explores the writer's seamier side,

including his stabbing of Adele Morales, his second wife, and his support of Jack Abbott, who committed murder after being paroled." (Library Journal)

"Detailed and anecdotal without being gossipy . . . and a must-read for students and admirers of Mailer's work." Kirkus

Includes bibliographical references and index

Mailer, Norris Church. A **ticket** to the circus; a memoir. Random House 2010 416p il $26   **92**
1. Artists 2. Authors 3. Novelists 4. Essayists 5. Authors, American 6. Spouses of prominent persons
ISBN 978-1-4000-6794-7; 1-4000-6794-4

LC 2009-33941

This memoir by Norris Church Mailer focuses on her marriage of thirty-three years to Norman Mailer.

The author adds "a fat new sheaf to the public dossier on her late husband, Norman Mailer, and tells an involving coming-of-age story to boot. . . . The book will be of interest to anyone who works in a university marriage lab. It also shows that Norman wasn't the only talented raconteur in the family." N Y Times Book Rev

Mailer, Norris Church

Mailer, Norris Church. A **ticket** to the circus; a memoir. Random House 2010 416p il $26   **92**
1. Artists 2. Authors 3. Novelists 4. Essayists 5. Authors, American 6. Spouses of prominent persons
ISBN 978-1-4000-6794-7; 1-4000-6794-4

LC 2009-33941

This memoir by Norris Church Mailer focuses on her marriage of thirty-three years to Norman Mailer.

The author adds "a fat new sheaf to the public dossier on her late husband, Norman Mailer, and tells an involving coming-of-age story to boot. . . . The book will be of interest to anyone who works in a university marriage lab. It also shows that Norman wasn't the only talented raconteur in the family." N Y Times Book Rev

Majorana, Ettore

Magueijo, Joao. A **brilliant** darkness; the extraordinary life and disappearance of Ettore Majorana, the troubled genius of the nuclear age. Basic Books 2009 280p il $27.50   **92**
1. Physicists 2. Nuclear physics
ISBN 978-0-465-00903-9; 0-465-00903-4

LC 2009-37678

The author "paints the life of a twenty something math prodigy who joined Enrico Fermi, Emilio Segre, and the other 'Via Panisperna Boys' who in 1934 discovered nuclear fusion. The author could have easily fallen into the jargon of his profession to describe the work of a fellow scientist, but he does not. His clear explanation of Majorana's insight into nuclear physics, often accompanied with drawings and illustrations, will appeal to a wide audience." Libr J

Includes bibliographical references

Malamud, Bernard, 1914-1986

Smith, Janna Malamud. **My** father is a book; a memoir of Bernard Malamud. Houghton Mifflin 2006 292p $24   **92**
1. Authors 2. Novelists 3. Short story writers 4.

Biography, Individual
ISBN 0-618-69166-9; 978-0-618-69166-1

LC 2005-24736

"On the twentieth anniversary of Bernard Malamud's death, Janna Malamud Smith explores her father's private, unpublished letters and journals to remember the life of [the writer]." (Publisher's note)

"Analytical without being acrimonious, honest without wallowing in self-preening exposure, this is a wise, generous book full of insights on what it's like to be a writer and to be a writer's daughter." Christ Sci Monit

Includes bibliographical references

Malcolm X, 1925-1965

Carson, Clayborne. **Malcolm** X: the FBI file; introduction by Spike Lee; edited by David Gallen. Carroll & Graf Pubs. 1991 514p il hardcover o.p. pa $13.95   **92**
1. Black Muslim leaders 2. Civil rights activists 3. United States -- Federal Bureau of Investigation
ISBN 0-88184-758-5 pa

LC 91-26697

"This is a collection of declassified documents from the FBI surveillance of the orator and religious (later political) leader that, with historian Carson's studious commentary, focuses less on Malcolm's relation to the FBI and more on that to the larger civil rights movement. These excerpts . . . follow his travels and speeches, media interviews and FBI interviews, oftentimes including transcripts as written or summarized by Gallen and Carson." Booklist

★ Malcolm X. The **autobiography** of Malcolm X; with the assistance of Alex Haley; introduction by M. S. Handler; epilogue by Alex Haley; afterword by Ossie Davis. Ballantine Bks. 1992 500p $25; pa $15   **92**
1. Black Muslims 2. Black Muslim leaders 3. Civil rights activists 4. African Americans -- Biography
ISBN 0-345-37975-6; 0-345-37671-4 pa

LC 92-52659

First published 1965 by Grove Press
Based on tape-recorded conversations with Alex Haley, this account of the life of the Black Muslim leader was completed shortly before his murder

Alex Haley "did his job with sensitivity and with devotion. . . . {The book} will have a permanent place in the literature of the Afro-American struggle." N Y Rev Books

★ Marable, Manning. **Malcolm** X; a life of reinvention. Manning Marable. Viking 2011 594 p., [16] p. of platesp ill. $30   **92**
1. Black Muslims 2. Black Muslim leaders 3. Civil rights activists 4. African Americans -- Biography 5. African Americans -- Civil rights
ISBN 978-0-670-02220-5; 0-670-02220-9

LC 2010025768

Pulitzer Prize: History (2012)
This "biography of Malcolm X draws on new research to trace his life from his troubled youth through his involvement in the Nation of Islam, his activism in the world of Black Nationalism, and his assassination." (Publisher's note) Glossary. Bibliography. Index.

This is an "account of the 'lives' of Malcolm X (1925–65), including his years as a street hustler in Boston and Harlem, his time in prison where voracious reading led to his transformation into a the devout follower of Elijah Muhammad's Nation of Islam (NOI), his rise as the NOI's chief minister, and, finally, his split from Elijah Muhammad and his acceptance of all people who would work for African American human and economic rights." Libr J

Perry, Bruce. **Malcolm**; the life of a man who changed black America. Station Hill Press 1991 542p il hardcover o.p. pa $14.95   **92**
1. Black Muslim leaders 2. Civil rights activists
ISBN 0-88268-121-4 pa

LC 90-23350

"Perry traces Malcolm X's footsteps from birth in 1925 to death in 1965, using several hundred interviews to fill in detail and correct the autobiography Alex Haley edited. Probing what he labels as the deep-seated and hidden causes that made Malcolm who and what he was, Perry produces a portrait of an emotionally abused and abandoned boy who grew to manipulate his fearful helplessness into emotional and political power." Libr J

Includes bibliographical references

Mandela, Nelson, 1918-2013

Mandela, Nelson. **Long** walk to freedom: the autobiography of Nelson Mandela. Little, Brown 1994 558p il hardcover o.p. pa $16.95   **92**
1. Presidents 2. Political prisoners 3. Political leaders 4. Human rights activists 5. Nobel laureates for peace 6. South Africa -- Race relations 7. South Africa -- Politics and government
ISBN 0-316-54818-9 pa

LC 94-79980

This book "provides important new evidence to the forty-year story of apartheid, as seen by its most formidable opponent. And there is enough candour to provide insights into the nature of leadership." Times Lit Suppl

Mandela, Nelson, 1918-2013. **Conversations** with myself. Farrar Straus & Giroux 2010 454p il map $28   **92**
1. Presidents 2. Political prisoners 3. Political leaders 4. Biography, Individual 5. Human rights activists 6. Apartheid -- South Africa 7. Nobel laureates for peace 8. Presidents -- South Africa 9. South Africa -- Race relations 10. South Africa -- Politics and government 11. South Africa -- Politics and government -- 20th century
ISBN 978-0-374-12895-1; 0-374-12895-2

LC 2010-933174

This "is a moving account of Mandela's struggle and a testament to his triumph." Publ Wkly

Includes bibliographical references

Mandela, Nelson, 1918-2013. **In** his own words; edited by Kader Asmal, David Chidester, [and] Wilmot James. Little, Brown 2003 558p il $28.95   **92**
1. Presidents 2. Political prisoners 3. Political leaders 4. Human rights activists 5. Nobel laureates for peace 6. South Africa -- Race relations 7. South Africa --

Politics and government
ISBN 0-316-11019-1

LC 2004-107807

"This collection of Mandela's speeches shows why he remains a universal hero. . . . This volume will be in great demand for the personal drama, the history, and, yes, for the inspiring moral values." Booklist

Sampson, Anthony. **Nelson** Mandela; the authorized biography. Knopf 1999 xxvi, 672p hardcover o.p. pa $19 **92**
1. Presidents 2. Political prisoners 3. Political leaders 4. Human rights activists 5. Nobel laureates for peace 6. South Africa -- Race relations 7. South Africa -- Politics and government
ISBN 0-679-78178-1 pa

LC 99-18498

Sampson traces "the course of Nelson Mandela's life, from his birth in 1918 in the Transkei region of South Africa, to his retirement from the presidency in 1999, at the end of his first and only term." Commonwealth
"While not neglecting the personality of the man, Mr. Sampson has concentrated on the politics, and, for an authorised life, it can be treated as definitive." Economist
Includes bibliographical references

Smith, David James. **Young** Mandela. Little, Brown 2010 405p il **92**
1. Apartheid 2. Presidents 3. Political prisoners 4. Anti-apartheid movement 5. Political leaders 6. Biography, Individual 7. Human rights activists 8. African National Congress 9. Nobel laureates for peace 10. South Africa -- Politics and government
ISBN 0-316-03548-3; 978-0-316-03548-4

LC 2010-31883

This is an account of Mandela's life from boyhood through the early 1960s. Bibliography. Index.
"No hagiography, Smith's measured study qualifies, lends nuance to, and even contradicts the mythology around Mandela's background and formative influences." Publ Wkly
Includes bibliographical references

Manet, Édouard, 1832-1883

Brombert, Beth Archer. **Edouard** Manet; rebel in a frock coat. University of Chicago Press 1997 505p il pa $19.95 **92**
1. Artists 2. Painters 3. Artists, French
ISBN 0-226-07544-3; 978-0-226-07544-0

LC 97-3321

First published 1996 by Little, Brown
"To recount Manet's life, as Brombert has done in this elegant biography, is to tell the story of an enormously influential artist struggling to paint what he called 'the spirit of contemporaneity' while remaining committed to the conservative institutions of civil life—the very same institutions that shunned him." New Yorker
Includes bibliographical references

Mankiller, Wilma

Mankiller, Wilma. **Mankiller** : a chief and her people; {by} Wilma Mankiller and Michael Wallis. St. Martin's Press 1993 xxiv, 292p il hardcover o.p. pa $14.95 **92**
1. Cherokee Indians
ISBN 0-312-20662-3 pa

LC 93-25698

"A must-read for everyone interested in, specifically, the history of Native Americans and women and, in general, tales of exceptional people." Booklist

Mann, Thomas, 1875-1955

Kurzke, Hermann. **Thomas** Mann; life as a work of art: a biography. translated by Leslie Willson. Princeton Univ. Press 2002 581p il $35 **92**
1. Authors 2. Novelists 3. Essayists 4. Short story writers 5. Nobel laureates for literature
ISBN 0-691-07069-5

LC 2002-23665

This biography of the German author focuses on "Mann's homosexuality, his relations to Jews and Judaism, the canny construction of the persona of Great Author, and how Mann transformed everything around him into art." Libr J
"A major achievement in literary biography." Booklist

Mansfield, William Murray, Earl of, 1705-1793

Byrne, Paula. **Belle**; the slave daughter and the Lord Chief Justice. Paula Byrne. Harper Perennial 2014 304 p. illustrations (paperback) $14.99 **92**
1. Racially mixed people 2. Great Britain -- Race relations 3. Great Britain -- History -- 18th century 4. Slaves -- England -- Biography 5. Nobility -- England -- Biography 6. Illegitimate children -- England -- Biography 7. Racially mixed people -- England -- Biography 8. England -- Race relations -- History -- 18th century 9. Antislavery movements -- England -- History -- 18th century
ISBN 0062310771; 9780062310774

LC 2014007447

"From . . . biographer Paula Byrne, the . . . tale that inspired the major motion picture 'Belle' (May 2014) starring Tom Wilkinson, Miranda Richardson, Emily Watson, Penelope Wilton, and Matthew Goode--a stunning story of the first mixed-race girl introduced to high society England and raised as a lady. . . . Growing up in his lavish estate, Dido was raised as a sister and companion to her white cousin, Elizabeth." (Publisher's note)
"Byrne brings to this brief history an eye for telling details of daily life, slaveholders' unthinkable cruelty, and the fervent work of a few good men and women who changed their world." Kirkus
Includes bibliographical references

Mantle, Mickey, 1931-1995

★ Leavy, Jane. The **last** boy; Mickey Mantle and the end of America's childhood. HarperCollins Publishers 2010 456p il $27.99 **92**
1. Baseball players 2. Baseball -- History 3. Baseball -- Biography 4. Biography, Individual 5. New York Yankees (Baseball team)
ISBN 978-0-06-088352-2; 0-06-088352-9

This is a biography of the New York Yankees center fielder. Bibliography. Index.

"This is unlike any biography on the sports shelf. Leavy, in exploring her own ambivalent feelings toward Mantle, permits readers to experience the same confusing emotions that many of those around him felt: proud to bask in his reflected glory but too intimidated to confront him. . . . A masterpiece of sports biography." Booklist

Mao Zedong, 1893-1976

Chang, Jung. **Mao** : the unknown story; [by] Jung Chang, Jon Halliday. Knopf 2005 814p il $35 **92**
1. Heads of state 2. Communist leaders 3. Political leaders 4. China -- Politics and government
ISBN 0-679-42271-4

LC 2004-63826

"This is a magisterial work. . . . This biography supplies substantial . . . information and presents it all in a stylish way that will put it on bedside tables around the world." N Y Times Book Rev

Includes bibliographical references

Mapplethorpe, Robert

★ Smith, Patti, 1946- **Just** kids. Ecco 2010 278p il $27; pa $16 **92**
1. Rock musicians 2. Poets, American 3. Biography, Individual
ISBN 978-0-06-621131-2; 0-06-621131-X; 978-0-06-093622-8 pa; 0-06-093622-3 pa

The author writes about her relationship with the photographer Robert Mapplethorpe in the late 1960s and 1970s.

This "is one of the best books ever written on becoming an artist—not the race for online celebrity and corporate sponsorship that often passes for artistic success these days, but the far more powerful, often difficult journey toward the ecstatic experience of capturing radiance of imagination on a page or stage or photographic paper." Washington Post

Maraniss, David

Maraniss, David. **Into** the story; a writer's journey through life, politics, sports and loss. Simon & Schuster 2010 283p il $26 **92**
1. Journalists 2. Biographers
ISBN 978-1-4391-6002-2; 1-4391-6002-3

LC 2009-42338

"In this collection of previously published articles and excerpts from his books, . . . [the author] ranges over topics from the death of his sister and the deaths of strangers on September 11 to the political fortunes of Barack Obama, Bill Clinton, and Al Gore and the timeless contributions to sports of legendary figures like Vince Lombardi, Muhammad Ali, and Roberto Clemente. . . . Maraniss's lively sketches illuminate the lives of significant cultural and political figures and intimately capture various moments that define modern American cultural history." Publ Wkly

Maravich, Pete, 1947-1988

★ Kriegel, Mark. **Pistol**; the life of Pete Maravich. Free Press 2007 381p il $27; pa $15 **92**
1. Basketball players
ISBN 978-0-7432-8497-4; 0-7432-8497-6; 978-0-

7432-8498-1 pa; 0-7432-8498-4 pa

LC 2006-51526

This is a biography of the basketball player who played at Louisiana State University before joining the N.B.A.

The author "skillfully pulls off the balancing act required of good sports biography. It plays large historical forces (segregation, the rise of televised sports) against the individual magic of its subject." New York

Includes bibliographical references

Maria Celeste, 1600-1634

Sobel, Dava. **Galileo's** daughter; a historical memoir of science, faith, and love. Walker & Co. 1999 420p $27 **92**
1. Nuns 2. Astronomers 3. Writers on science 4. Children of prominent persons
ISBN 0-8027-1343-2

LC 99-23885

"Sobel has a remarkable ability to explain technical subjects without being simplistic or pedantic. There is a tremendous amount of fascinating detail in this work, and yet it reads as smoothly and compellingly as fiction." Libr J

Includes bibliographical references

Marie Antoinette, Queen, consort of Louis XVI, King of France, 1755-1793

Lever, Evelyne. **Marie** Antoinette; the last queen of France. translated from the French by Catherine Temerson. Farrar, Straus & Giroux 2000 357p il hardcover o.p. pa $16.95 **92**
1. Queens 2. France -- History -- 1589-1789, Bourbons
ISBN 0-312-28333-4 pa

LC 00-28763

The author examines "the opulent Versailles subculture and the queen whose royal excesses served as a major catalyst for the revolutionary upheaval of 1789. Through the skillful use of memoirs and other primary documents, Lever creates an empathic picture of Louis XVI's headstrong wife." Libr J

Includes bibliographical references

Marion, Robert

Marion, Robert. **Genetic** rounds; a doctor's encounters in the field that has revolutionized medicine. Kaplan Pub. 2009 275p $24.95 **92**
1. Physicians 2. Medical genetics 3. Pediatricians
ISBN 978-1-60714-460-1

LC 2009-19110

The author "aims to give readers insight into the experiences and role of clinical geneticists. In his practice, Marion must deliver the devastating news to parents that their child has a genetic disease that often may have no cure." Libr J

This is "a straightforward, and often poignant, collection of true stories. Particularly compelling are several stories that describe the pain and pathos of life for some individuals with genetic disorders." Am J Human Genetics

Maris, Roger, 1934-1985

Clavin, Thomas. **Roger** Maris; baseball's reluctant hero. [by] Tom Clavin and Danny Peary. Simon & Schuster 2010 422p il $26.99 **92**

1. Baseball players 2. Baseball -- Biography 3. New York Yankees (Baseball team)

ISBN 978-1-4165-8928-0; 1-4165-8928-7

LC 2009-39722

The authors "trace the dramatic arc of Maris's life, from his boyhood in Fargo through his early pro career in the Cleveland Indians farm program, to his World Series championship years in New York and beyond. At the center is the exciting story of the 1961 season and the ordeal Maris endured as an outsider in Yankee pinstripes, unloved by fans who compared him unfavorably to their heroes Ruth and Mantle, relentlessly attacked by an aggressive press corps who found him cold and inaccessible, and treated miserably by the organization." Publisher's note

Includes bibliographical references

Marlowe, Christopher, 1564-1593

★ Honan, Park. **Christopher** Marlowe; poet & spy. Oxford University Press 2005 421p il $32.50 **92**

1. Authors 2. Dramatists 3. Dramatists, English 4. Great Britain -- History -- 1485-1603, Tudors

ISBN 0-19-818695-9

LC 2005-19761

This is a biography of the sixteenth-century English dramatist.

The author "sheds light on the much-speculated (and previously erroneously reported) aspects of Marlowe's life without neglecting its more ordinary features (his stable two-parent upbringing, his diligent scholarship at Cambridge) or destroying the poet's aura of intrigue." Publ Wkly

Includes bibliographical references

Nicholl, Charles. The **reckoning**; the murder of Christopher Marlowe. University of Chicago Press 1995 413p il pa $33 **92**

1. Authors 2. Dramatists 3. Dramatists, English 4. Great Britain -- History -- 1485-1603, Tudors

ISBN 0-226-58024-5; 978-0-226-58024-1

First published 1992 in the United Kingdom

The author argues that the Elizabethan playwright, who is believed to have been stabbed in a dispute over the bill ('recknynge') at Eleanor Bull's victualling house in 1593, was in fact murdered with government complicity as part of a plot against Sir Walter Raleigh.

"A remarkable piece of scholarship, this work carefully reconstructs the events leading up to the murder with all the excitement and suspense of a modern mystery novel; at the same time it vividly conveys the energy and color of Elizabethan England." Libr J

Includes bibliographical references

Marshall, Paule, 1929-

Marshall, Paule. **Triangular** road; a memoir. BasicCivitas Books 2009 165p il $23 **92**

1. Poets 2. Authors 3. Novelists 4. Dramatists 5. African American authors 6. Essayists 7. Short story writers 8. Young adult authors 9. African Americans

-- Intellectual life

ISBN 978-0-465-01359-3

LC 2008-36671

This is a memoir by the author of Praisesong for the widow (1983).

"Though fiction may have pride of place in . . . [the author's] heart, 'Triangular Road' reveals a strong gift for self-scrutiny made all the more revealing by quiet humor and what appears to be complete honesty." Washington Post

Marshall, Thurgood, 1908-1993

Rowan, Carl Thomas. **Dream** makers, dream breakers; the world of Justice Thurgood Marshall. [by] Carl T. Rowan. Welcome Rain 2002 475p il pa $18.95 **92**

1. Judges 2. Lawyers 3. Solicitors general 4. Civil rights activists 5. Supreme Court justices 6. United States -- Supreme Court 7. National Association for the Advancement of Colored People

ISBN 978-1-56649-235-5; 1-56649-235-1

First published 1993 by Little, Brown

The author "offers a no-holds barred account of one of the most influential and controversial figures in American law and jurisprudence of this century. His work brings to life Marshall, the Surpreme Court, U.S. law and modern America itself. Particularly effective is Rowan's account of the innovative legal arguments Marshall and his colleagues employed to win the now-famous Brown v. Board of Education case of 1954." Libr J

Includes bibliographical references

Martin, Dean

Lewis, Jerry. **Dean** & me; a love story. Doubleday 2005 340p il $26.95 **92**

1. Actors 2. Singers 3. Comedians 4. Television personalities 5. Motion picture directors

ISBN 0-7679-2086-4

LC 2005-49682

The author "recounts his professional and personal relationship with his former show business partner, the late Dean Martin." Libr J

"This is a wild, joyous book, but also a heartbreaking one." N Y Times Book Rev

Martin, Luther, 1744-1826

Kauffman, Bill. **Forgotten** founder, drunken prophet; the life of Luther Martin. ISI Books 2008 202p $25 **92**

1. Lawyers 2. Members of Congress 3. Law enforcement officials 4. State government officials 5. United States -- Constitutional Convention (1787) 6. United States -- Politics and government -- 1783-1809

ISBN 978-1-933859-73-6; 1-933859-73-3

LC 2008-928223

Kauffman "tells the story of Luther Martin, one of America's less-remembered founding fathers. A livid Anti-Federalist, Martin has gone down in the annals of 18th century America as little more than a footnote. He was accused of being an absolute boor, drinking to excess, rambling in speech with incessant monotony, and having an altogether prickly disposition. Kauffman takes up the cross of giving Martin a fair shake, not by defending the man but just by telling his story. . . . Never the explicit apologist, Kauffman delicately and humorously weaves a more complete portrait of Martin. Furthermore, Kauffman's writing is well-founded upon a towering bibliography that Kauffman adroitly parses." PopMatters

Includes bibliographical references

Martin, Roger H., 1943-

Martin, Roger H. **Racing** Odysseus; a college president becomes a freshman again. University of California Press 2008 262p $24.95   **92**
  1. Higher education 2. Biography, Individual 3. Education, Higher -- United States 4. St. John's College (Annapolis, Md.)
  ISBN 978-0-520-25541-8; 0-520-25541-0
                                    LC 2007-51017
Martin "examines a number of experiences uncommon to 61-year-old college presidents. On a sabbatical after horrific treatments for cancer, he enrolled as a freshman at St. John's College in Maryland, studied classics, joined the crew team, prepared for a major race, and learned to connect with his 18-year-old classmates. He notes the follies of the students, as well as his own, and offers perceptive and affectionate insights into the challenges of growing up in today's complicated world. Education is his profession, and as he carefully observes the impact of the Great Books curriculum at St. John's, he sees the relevance of the Greek classics to our own time." Libr J

Includes bibliographical references

Martin, Steve, 1945-

Martin, Steve. **Born** standing up; a comic's life. Scribner 2007 209p il $25   **92**
  1. Actors 2. Comedians 3. Novelists 4. Dramatists 5. Memoirists 6. Screenwriters
  ISBN 978-1-4165-5364-9; 1-4165-5364-9
                                    LC 2007-27143
This is an autobiography by the comedian and author of Shopgirl (2000).

This book "does a sharp-witted job of breaking down the step-by-step process that brought [the author] from Disneyland, where he spent his version of a Dickensian childhood as a schoolboy employee, to both the pinnacle of stardom and the brink of disaster. . . . Even for readers already familiar with Mr. Martin's solemn side, [this] is a surprising book: smart, serious, heartfelt and confessional without being maudlin." N Y Times (Late NY Ed)

Marton, Endre, 1910-2005

Marton, Kati. **Enemies** of the people; my family's journey to America. Simon & Schuster 2009 272p il $26   **92**
  1. Authors 2. Journalists 3. Political prisoners 4. Hungary -- History 5. Nonfiction writers
  ISBN 978-1-4165-8612-8; 1-4165-8612-1
                                    LC 2009-14480
"An American journalist trolls the archives of the Hungarian secret police (AVO) to piece together her parents' imprisonment in and flight from Hungary in the mid-1950s. . . . The author's probing work effectively renders an enormously unsettled, painful time of shifting allegiances and political

treachery. . . . A dark, compelling narrative of secrecy and betrayal." Kirkus

Includes bibliographical references

Marton, Ilona, 1912-2004

Marton, Kati. **Enemies** of the people; my family's journey to America. Simon & Schuster 2009 272p il $26   **92**
  1. Authors 2. Journalists 3. Political prisoners 4. Hungary -- History 5. Nonfiction writers
  ISBN 978-1-4165-8612-8; 1-4165-8612-1
                                    LC 2009-14480
"An American journalist trolls the archives of the Hungarian secret police (AVO) to piece together her parents' imprisonment in and flight from Hungary in the mid-1950s. . . . The author's probing work effectively renders an enormously unsettled, painful time of shifting allegiances and political treachery. . . . A dark, compelling narrative of secrecy and betrayal." Kirkus

Includes bibliographical references

Marton, Kati

Marton, Kati. **Enemies** of the people; my family's journey to America. Simon & Schuster 2009 272p il $26   **92**
  1. Authors 2. Journalists 3. Political prisoners 4. Hungary -- History 5. Nonfiction writers
  ISBN 978-1-4165-8612-8; 1-4165-8612-1
                                    LC 2009-14480
"An American journalist trolls the archives of the Hungarian secret police (AVO) to piece together her parents' imprisonment in and flight from Hungary in the mid-1950s. . . . The author's probing work effectively renders an enormously unsettled, painful time of shifting allegiances and political treachery. . . . A dark, compelling narrative of secrecy and betrayal." Kirkus

Includes bibliographical references

Marx, Groucho, 1891-1977

Kanfer, Stefan. **Groucho** : the life and times of Julius Henry Marx. Knopf 2000 465p il hardcover o.p. pa $15   **92**
  1. Comedians 2. Television personalities 3. Game show hosts
  ISBN 0-375-70207-5 pa
                                    LC 99-54002
"Plagued by nagging financial insecurities, partly realized literary ambitions, and difficult, unsatisfying relations with his wives, lovers, and daughters, Groucho was a 'depressive clown,' notes Kanter. . . . The book also details Groucho's ambivalent relations with his son, Arthur; his brothers; New Deal liberals; intellectuals and collaborators like S. J. Perelman; and his custodian, Erin Fleming." Libr J

Includes bibliographical references

Marx, Jenny

Gabriel, Mary. **Love** and capital; Karl and Jennie Marx and the birth of a revolution. Little, Brown and Company 2011 lviii, 707p il   **92**
  1. Marxism 2. Writers on politics 3. Spouses of

prominent persons 4. Political and social philosophers
ISBN 0-316-06611-7; 978-0-316-06611-2
LC 2010-44021
An "account of the lives of Karl Marx and his wife, Jenny von Westphalen. . . . Tracing their tumultuous lives from Prussia, via Paris to Brussels and finally London, Gabriel tells the story of a woman who forswore the comforts of her noble upbringing to raise a family in often very straitened circumstances with a man committed in both his life and letters to social justice and the emancipation of the working class. Equally at home with the details of Marxist theory and revolutionary Europe as she is with the private lives of Karl and Jenny, the author dazzles most with her fascinating accounts of the lives of the Marx children." Publ Wkly
Includes bibliographical references

Marx, Karl, 1818-1883
Gabriel, Mary. **Love** and capital; Karl and Jennie Marx and the birth of a revolution. Little, Brown and Company 2011 lviii, 707p il   **92**
1. Marxism 2. Writers on politics 3. Spouses of prominent persons 4. Political and social philosophers
ISBN 0-316-06611-7; 978-0-316-06611-2
LC 2010-44021
An "account of the lives of Karl Marx and his wife, Jenny von Westphalen. . . . Tracing their tumultuous lives from Prussia, via Paris to Brussels and finally London, Gabriel tells the story of a woman who forswore the comforts of her noble upbringing to raise a family in often very straitened circumstances with a man committed in both his life and letters to social justice and the emancipation of the working class. Equally at home with the details of Marxist theory and revolutionary Europe as she is with the private lives of Karl and Jenny, the author dazzles most with her fascinating accounts of the lives of the Marx children." Publ Wkly
Includes bibliographical references

Mary, Blessed Virgin, Saint
Hazleton, Lesley. **Mary** : a flesh-and-blood biography of the Virgin Mother. Bloomsbury 2004 246p $24.95   **92**
1. Saints
ISBN 1-582-34236-9
LC 2003-17403
Hazleton "takes readers through an impressive array of historical, cultural, literary, and spiritual topics. . . . This book is an easy read, and Hazleton's stream-of-consciousness style is intriguing." Libr J
Includes bibliographical references

Mary, Queen of Scots, 1542-1587
Fraser, Antonia. **Mary** Queen of Scots; illustrated abridged ed; Delacorte Press 1978 208p il hardcover o.p. pa $19.95   **92**
1. Queens 2. Scotland -- History -- 16th century 3. Great Britain -- History -- 1485-1603, Tudors
ISBN 0-380-31129-X pa
LC 78-703
A condensation of the title first published 1969

A look at the tragic life of Mary Stuart, the 16th century Catholic ruler of Protestant Scotland, and her incessant struggle with political and religious opponents
Includes bibliographical references

Weir, Alison. **Mary,** Queen of Scots, and the murder of Lord Darnley. Ballantine Bks. 2003 670p il map $27.95; pa $16.95   **92**
1. Queens 2. Princes 3. Scotland -- History -- 16th century
ISBN 0-345-43658-X; 0-8129-7151-5 pa
LC 2002-34467
The author "sets out to prove that contrary to supposition Mary, Queen of Scots, was innocent of the murder of her husband, Lord Darnley." Libr J
"No stone is left unturned in {Weir's} investigation, and despite its detail, her book is as dramatic as witnessing first-hand the most riveting court case." Booklist

Maryam Jameelah, 1934-2012
Baker, Deborah. The **convert**; a tale of exile and extremism. Graywolf Press 2011 246p il $23   **92**
1. Converts 2. Muslim women 3. Biography, Individual
ISBN 1-55597-582-8; 978-1-55597-582-1
This is a biography of the Islamic polemicist Maryam Jameelah. Jameelah was "born as Margaret Marcus in 1934 in New Rochelle, N.Y." (N Y Times Book Rev)
This "is a cogent, thought-provoking look at a radical life and its rippling consequences." Publ Wkly
Includes bibliographical references

Mason, George, 1725-1792
★ Broadwater, Jeff. **George** Mason, forgotten founder. University of North Carolina Press 2006 329p il $34.95   **92**
1. Statesmen 2. Essayists 3. Colonial leaders 4. Plantation owners
ISBN 978-0-8078-3053-6; 0-8078-3053-4
LC 2006-10729
"Because Mason left little evidence of his private life, there are blurred edges in the portrait that Broadwater paints, but overall this is an exemplary biography: sympathetic but dispassionate, thorough but not cluttered, convincing in its interpretations and arguments. It leaves no doubt that Mason deserves to be returned to the esteem and reputation he enjoyed during his lifetime, but in no way is it hagiography." Washington Post Book World
Includes bibliographical references

Massery, Hazel Bryan, 1942-
Margolick, David. **Elizabeth** and Hazel; two women of Little Rock. Yale University Press 2011 310p il $26   **92**
1. School integration 2. Arkansas -- Race relations 3. Little Rock (Ark.) -- Race relations 4. Central High School (Little Rock, Ark.) 5. School integration -- Arkansas -- Little Rock -- History -- 20th century
ISBN 978-0-300-14193-1; 0-300-14193-9
LC 2011-14101
"When Elizabeth Eckford braved the gauntlet of white hecklers leading to the newly desegregated Central High School in Little Rock, Arkansas, in 1957, photographers

captured her image and that of the angry young white woman behind her. Elizabeth, the stoic, and Hazel Bryan, the tormentor, were frozen as icons. Elizabeth was part of the Little Rock Nine, the black teens who became the targets of race hatred as well as national and international inspirations. . . . Margolick draws on interviews and press reports of the time to present a very nuanced analysis of how Elizabeth and Hazel were affected by the scene that made them famous. . . . A complex look at two women at the center of a historic moment." Booklist

Includes bibliographical references

Masters, Jarvis

Masters, Jarvis. **That** bird has my wings; the autobiography of an innocent man on death row. [by] Jarvis Jay Masters. HarperOne 2009 281p $24.99 **92**

1. Prisoners 2. African Americans -- Biography
ISBN 978-0-06-173045-0; 0-06-173045-9

LC 2009-22124

The author, "who has been imprisoned on San Quentin's death row since 1990 and become a devout Buddhist, recalls the neglect, abuse and cycle of crime and hopelessness that relegated him to prison by age 19." Publ Wkly

"A heartbreaking memoir; the brutal conditions of Masters's boyhood will be difficult for some readers to take, but his ultimate message of hope and reconciliation is moving and inspiring." Libr J

Matisse, Henri

Spurling, Hilary. **Matisse** the master; a life of Henri Matisse, the conquest of colour, 1909-1954. Knopf 2005 xxi, 511p il $40 **92**

1. Artists 2. Painters
ISBN 0-679-43429-1

LC 2004-51074

Companion volume to The unknown Matisse
"Spurling's rich, flexible style is well attuned to the rigors and flights of Matisse's creative life." Publ Wkly
Includes bibliographical references

Spurling, Hilary. The **unknown** Matisse; v1 a life of Henri Matisse. Knopf 1998 xxv, 480p v1 il $40 **92**

1. Artists 2. Painters
ISBN 0-679-43428-3

LC 97-46816

In this first volume of the author's biography of the French artist, Spurling focuses on Matisse's training as an art student in Paris

This volume "makes for a gripping read and reveals much about the artist's early development." Publ Wkly
Includes bibliographical references

Maugham, W. Somerset (William Somerset), 1874-1965

Hastings, Selina. The **secret** lives of Somerset Maugham; a biography. Random House 2010 626p il **92**

1. Authors 2. Novelists 3. Dramatists 4. Travel writers 5. Authors, English 6. Short story writers 7.

Biography, Individual
ISBN 978-1-4000-6141-9

LC 2009-35797

This is a biography of the English novelist and playwright. "This steady-eyed biography of an extraordinary, extravagant, generous and bitter artist will not only fascinate its readers but encourage some to go to his work for the first time." Times Lit Suppl

Includes bibliographical references (p. 599-602)

Mauldin, Bill, 1921-2003

DePastino, Todd. **Bill** Mauldin; a life up front. W.W. Norton 2008 370p il $27.95 **92**

1. Cartoonists
ISBN 978-0-393-06183-3; 0-393-06183-3

LC 2007-40494

This is a biography of the author of What's Got Your Back Up? (1961), I've Decided I Want My Seat Back (1965), and The Brass Ring (1971). During World War II, Mauldin was a cartoonist who depicted the daily lives of soldiers for the G.I. newspaper Stars and Stripes.

"Thoroughly researched and sprightly written, DePastino's balanced biography is a solid introduction to an American original. Classic Mauldin cartoons are an entertaining bonus." Publ Wkly

Includes bibliographical references

Maxwell, William, 1908-2000

What there is to say we have said; the correspondence of Eudora Welty and William Maxwell. edited by Suzanne Marrs. Houghton Mifflin Harcourt 2011 499p il $35 **92**

1. Authors 2. Novelists 3. Magazine editors 4. Short story writers
ISBN 0547376499; 9780547376493; 978-0-547-37649-3; 0-547-37649-9

LC 2010-42105

"Letters between writers often have a lot of shop talk of interest to other writers and literary cultists, but this collection yields broader pleasures, too. In addition to being stellar writers, Welty and Maxwell were also accomplished critics, and one of the joys of the book is eavesdropping on their assessments of authors as varied as John Updike and Virginia Woolf, Anton Chekhov and Charles Dickens, William Faulkner and E. M. Forster. Welty and Maxwell also shared an intense love of gardening – so much so that Marrs was forced, in the book's index, to include an extensive listing of various varieties of roses. . . . As these letters show, Welty and Maxwell regarded domestic life not as a tedious distraction from the writing desk, but as a crucial source of insight. . . . The title of the collection comes from Maxwell's conclusion, as he and Welty faced their mortality, that 'what there is to say we have said, in one way or the other. You know how much we love you.' That love, a source of sustenance and strength between two great writers, is also a bright tonic for the readers of this volume." Christ Sci Monit

Includes bibliographical references

Mayakovsky, Vladimir, 1893-1930

Night wraps the sky; writings by and about Maya-kovsky. edited by Michael Almereyda. Farrar, Straus and Giroux 2008 xxvii, 272p il $27 **92**

1. Poets 2. Authors 3. Dramatists

ISBN 978-0-374-28135-9; 0-374-28135-1

LC 2007-46662

"The book further explores Mayakovsky's relationships with Lili Brik and Tatiana Yakovleva, explains his propa-ganda work, and addresses his mixture of the surreal, the lyric, and the sarcastic; the text is generously illustrated with photographs of Mayakovsky's friends and contemporaries and artworks of the times." Libr J

Mayer, Louis B. (Louis Burt), 1885-1957

★ Eyman, Scott. **Lion** of Hollywood; the life and legend of Louis B. Mayer. Simon & Schuster 2005 596p il $35 **92**

1. Motion picture executives

ISBN 0-7432-0481-6

LC 2005-42472

This is a "biography of Louis B. Mayer, the chief of Metro-Goldwyn-Mayer—MGM—the biggest and most successful film studio of Hollywood's Golden Age." Pub-lisher's note

"Eyman's extensive knowledge of old Hollywood, his scrupulous research and his refusal to indict the often-pillo-ried Mayer make this biography an often revelatory delight." Publ Wkly

Includes bibliographical references

Mayes, Frances

Mayes, Frances. **Under** magnolia; a Southern memoir. Frances Mayes. Crown Publishers 2014 336 p. illustrations (hardback) $26 **92**

1. Bildungsromans 2. Autobiographies 3. Southern States 4. Authors, American -- 20th century -- Biography

ISBN 0307885917; 9780307885913

LC 2013042448

"'Under Magnolia' is a . . . moving ode to family and place, and a . . . meditation on the ways they define us. . . . With acute sensory language, [author Frances] Mayes rel-ishes the sweetness of the South, the smells and tastes at her family table, the fragrance of her hometown trees, and writes an unforgettable story of a girl whose perspicacity and dawning self-knowledge lead her out of the South and into the rest of the world, and then to a profound return home." (Publisher's note)

"With her trademark skill for capturing the essence of place and time, Mayes candidly reveals a youth riddled with psychological abuse and parental neglect that, nev-ertheless, ignited a fiery passion for adventure and self-discovery." Booklist

Includes bibliographical references

Mays, Willie, 1931-

Hirsch, James S. **Willie** Mays; the life, the leg-end. authorized by Willie Mays. Scribner 2010 628p il $30 **92**

1. Baseball players 2. Baseball -- History 3. Baseball -- Biography 4. Biography, Individual 5. New York

Giants (Baseball team)

ISBN 978-1-4165-4790-7; 1-4165-4790-8

LC 2009-49214

"This is a superb baseball book, but it's also a riveting narrative of Mays' life and times, ranging from his penchant for fancy suits to urban development in New York City to the giddy cult of celebrity. In the mid-1950s, Willie Mays was as famous as anyone in the country, gracing the cover of Time and other magazines and appearing on numerous tele-vision shows. More impressive — and what distinguishes this book from the run-of-the-mill sports biography — is Hirsch's extensive and cogent take on race relations and the civil-rights movement both within and outside of baseball." Seattle Times

Includes bibliographical references

Mbeki, Thabo, 1942-

Gevisser, Mark. A **legacy** of liberation; Thabo Mbeki and the future of the South African dream. Palgrave Macmillan 2009 376p il $29.95 **92**

1. Presidents 2. Political leaders 3. Government officials 4. South Africa -- Politics and government

ISBN 978-0-230-61100-9; 0-230-61100-1

LC 2008-50763

Abridged version of a book first published 2007 in South Africa with title: Thabo Mbeki: the dream deferred

This is a biography of South Africa's second president. Gevisser "traces Mbeki's family back several generations, from colonial dispossession through the struggle for libera-tion. . . . Mbeki's life story has the makings of a gripping tale. . . . Gevisser writes well, particularly when he is wit-ness to an event, when his narrative leaps off the page." N Y Times Book Rev

Includes bibliographical references (p. [346]-365) and index

McBride, James

McBride, James. The **color** of water; a black man's tribute to his white mother. Riverhead Bks. 1996 228p il pa $14; $23.95 **92**

1. Authors 2. Novelists 3. Journalists 4. Memoirists 5. Parents of prominent persons

ISBN 1-57322-578-9 pa; 1-57322-022-1

LC 95-37243

"Told with humor and clear-eyed grace, McBride's memoir is not only a terrific story, it's a subtle contribution to the current debates on race and identity. . . . The sheer strength of spirit, pain and humor of McBride and his mother as they wrestled with different aspects of race and identity is vividly told." Nation

McCain, John S., 1936-

McCain, John S. **Faith** of my fathers; {by} John McCain with Mark Salter. Random House 1999 349p $25 **92**

1. Prisoners of war 2. Senators 3. Members of Congress 4. Presidential candidates

ISBN 0-375-50191-6

LC 99-13496

"McCain examines the lives of his grandfather and fa-ther—both four-star admirals—and shows how their lessons helped him through his years as a prisoner of war in Vietnam." Booklist

This is a "serious, utterly engrossing account of faith, fathers and military tradition." Publ Wkly

McCain, John S. (John Sidney), 1911-1981

McCain, John S. **Faith** of my fathers; {by} John McCain with Mark Salter. Random House 1999 349p $25   **92**

1. Prisoners of war 2. Senators 3. Members of Congress 4. Presidential candidates
ISBN 0-375-50191-6

LC 99-13496

This is a "serious, utterly engrossing account of faith, fathers and military tradition." Publ Wkly

McCartney, Paul

Sounes, Howard. **Fab**; an intimate life of Paul McCartney. Da Capo Press 2010 634p il $29.95 **92**

1. Singers 2. Rock musicians 3. Beatles 4. Songwriters
ISBN 978-0-306-81783-0

LC 2010-936124

"Divided into two equally large sections—'With the Beatles' and 'After the Beatles'—Fab covers all the highlights of McCartney's life and long career: his early days in Liverpool; his meeting with John Lennon; the craziness of Beatlemania; his solo albums; the creation and collapse of his post-Beatles band, Wings; his marriage to Linda Eastman; his last meetings with Lennon; his drug bust in Japan; his forays into classical music; his disastrous second marriage to Heather Mills. . . . Sounes is often brutally honest, offering a full portrait—warts and all—of one of the most famous men of the modern era. A must for Beatles and McCartney fans." Booklist

Includes bibliographical references

McClellan, George Brinton, 1826-1885

Sears, Stephen W. **George** B. McClellan; the young Napoleon. Da Capo Press 1999 482p il map pa $16.95   **92**

1. Generals 2. Governors 3. Presidential candidates 4. United States -- History -- 1861-1865, Civil War
ISBN 0-306-80913-3

LC 98-33277

First published 1988 by Ticknor & Fields

This biography of the Civil War general "covers both the awkward character traits that led to McClellan's incompetence and the battlefield actions that he regularly bungled. In addition to its merit as Civil War history, the book is of great interest as the portrait of an intelligent man working at what he failed to realize was the wrong profession." Atlantic

Includes bibliographical references

McCourt family

★ McCourt, Frank, 1930-2009. **Angela's** ashes; a memoir. Scribner 1996 364p il pa $14; $25 **92**

1. Authors 2. Irish Americans 3. Memoirists 4. High school teachers 5. Biography, Individual
ISBN 0-684-84267-X pa; 0-684-87435-0

LC 96-5335

This is a memoir by a New York City high school teacher. "Born to Irish immigrants in Depression-era Brooklyn,

McCourt's mother (Angela) and father . . . return to family in Ireland. . . . A baby sister dies in Brooklyn, and two more brothers die in Ireland. . . . {McCourt suffers from} afflictions brought on by the starvation and squalor in his family's . . . Limerick slum, including a bout of typhoid." (Commonweal)

"Frank McCourt, a teacher, grandfather and occasional actor, was born in New York City, but grew up in the Irish town of Limerick during the grim 1930's and 40's before he came back here as a teen-ager. His recollections of childhood are mournful and humorous, angry and forgiving." N Y Times Book Rev

McCourt, Alphie

McCourt, Alphie. A **long** stone's throw. Sterling & Ross Publishers 2008 267p $24.95   **92**

1. Irish Americans 2. Memoirists 3. Restaurateurs 4. Business managers 5. Immigrants -- United States
ISBN 978-0-9814535-5-2; 0-9814535-5-4

LC 2008-32672

"Alphie is the youngest of the four McCourt brothers and the third—after Frank and Malachy—to pen a memoir about his life in Ireland and the U.S. . . . McCourt always finds irony in life and his tales of the bar and restaurant business and its clientele are laugh-out-loud funny. Sensitive, lyrical, funny, stubborn, impetuous, McCourt writes with a steady hand, a joyful heart, and an Irishman's sense of life's absurdities." Publ WKly

McCourt, Frank 1930-2009.

★ McCourt, Frank. **Angela's** ashes; a memoir. Scribner 1996 364p il pa $14; $25   **92**

1. Authors 2. Irish Americans 3. Memoirists 4. High school teachers 5. Biography, Individual
ISBN 0-684-84267-X pa; 0-684-87435-0

LC 96-5335

This is a memoir by a New York City high school teacher. "Born to Irish immigrants in Depression-era Brooklyn, McCourt's mother (Angela) and father . . . return to family in Ireland. . . . A baby sister dies in Brooklyn, and two more brothers die in Ireland. . . . {McCourt suffers from} afflictions brought on by the starvation and squalor in his family's . . . Limerick slum, including a bout of typhoid." (Commonweal)

"Frank McCourt, a teacher, grandfather and occasional actor, was born in New York City, but grew up in the Irish town of Limerick during the grim 1930's and 40's before he came back here as a teen-ager. His recollections of childhood are mournful and humorous, angry and forgiving." N Y Times Book Rev

McCourt, Frank. **Teacher** man; a memoir. Scribner 2005 258p $26   **92**

1. Authors 2. Irish Americans 3. Memoirists 4. High school teachers
ISBN 0-7432-4377-3

LC 2005-54113

"Full of gritty specifics, never preachy, often hilarious, McCourt's . . . book thrusts you right into the hormones-and-catcalls chaos of the classroom—where learning is not just a mystery but a flat-out miracle." Newsweek

McCourt, Frank. **'Tis**; a memoir. Scribner 1999 367p hardcover o.p. pa $14   **92**
1. Authors 2. Irish Americans 3. Memoirists 4. High school teachers
ISBN 0-684-86574-2 pa

LC 99-31280

Sequel to Angela's ashes
This volume "takes McCourt from his arrival in America and subsequent service in the Korean War through the mid-1980s. . . . This memoir features a mesmerizing narrative fraught with sufferings. It triumphs by effecting a genuinely comic meditation upon human frailty, grace and possibility." Publ Wkly

McCourt, James, 1941-

McCourt, James. **Lasting** City; the Anatomy of Nostalgia. James McCourt. Liveright Pub. Corporation 2013 336 p. (hardcover) $26.95   **92**
1. Autobiographies 2. Irish Americans 3. New York (N.Y.) -- 20th century
ISBN 0871404583; 9780871404589

LC 2013031496

This memoir by James McCourt is "an operatic recollection that braids a nostalgic portrait of old-Irish New York with a boy's funny, gutter-snipe precocity and hardly innocent coming-of-age in the 1940s and '50s. . . . Mating fact with fantasy, or fantasy with fact, McCourt takes us from his deeply moving bedside account of his mother Catherine's death to its traumatic aftermaths." (Publisher's note)
"[L]ess autobiography than a powerful work of creative nonfiction. . . . Intensely personal, unabashedly playful, and brilliantly inventive in its own gorgeous spotlight." Booklist

McCracken, Elizabeth

McCracken, Elizabeth. An **exact** replica of a figment of my imagination; a memoir. Little, Brown and Co. 2008 184p $19.99   **92**
1. Authors 2. Novelists 3. Librarians 4. Bereavement 5. Miscarriage 6. Essayists 7. Short story writers 8. Biography, Individual
ISBN 978-0-316-02767-0; 0-316-02767-7

LC 2008-5032

This is a memoir by the American novelist. "Two years ago [Elizabeth McCracken] was living in a remote part of France, working on her novel, and waiting for the birth of her first child. This book is about what happened next. In her ninth month of pregnancy, she learned that her baby boy had died. How do you deal with and recover from this kind of loss? . . . McCracken considers the nature of love and grief [here]." (Publisher's note)
"McCracken has succeeded in writing a beautiful, precise and heartbreaking account without sentimentality or pity." Publ Wkly

McDaniel, Hattie, 1895-1952

Jackson, Carlton. **Hattie** : the life of Hattie McDaniel. Madison Bks. 1989 220p il hardcover o.p. pa $12.95   **92**
1. Actors
ISBN 1-56833-004-9 pa

LC 89-30903

"For those of us who knew her only as 'Mammy' in Gone with the Wind, Hattie McDaniel's life story holds lots of surprises. She was also a singer, songwriter, and radio, stage, and TV performer. With an anecdotal style, the author clears up a lot of errors concerning her career." Booklist
Includes bibliographical references

Watts, Jill. **Hattie** McDaniel; black ambition, white Hollywood. Amistad 2005 352p il hardcover o.p. pa $14.95   **92**
1. Actors
ISBN 0-06-051490-6; 0-06-051491-4 pa

LC 2005-42126

"Watts is both sympathetic and honest: we pity McDaniel and her unenviable position, but at the same time, see how her intense careerism drove her often to accommodate rather than challenge film industry racism. . . . Watts' research is extensive, her writing clear and accessible, and her book a thorough, engaging, intelligent piece of historical scholarship." Women's Rev of Books

McKenney, Eileen, d. 1940

Meade, Marion. **Lonelyhearts**; the screwball world of Nathanael West and Eileen McKenney. Houghton Mifflin Harcourt 2010 392p il map $28   **92**
1. Authors 2. Novelists 3. Screenwriters 4. Authors, American 5. Spouses of prominent persons
ISBN 978-0-15-101149-0

LC 2009-13285

"West and McKenney died young in a car crash in 1940—too soon for him to know that his lacerating novels, especially The Day of the Locust (1939), would become American classics; too soon for his new wife, Eileen, to claim her life for her own after her sister, Ruth, co-opted it to write her best-seller, My Sister Eileen (1938). . . . [The author] tells the trenchant and secret-laden life stories of West (born Nathan Weinstein in New York) and Ohioan McKenney in a ravishingly atmospheric yet propulsive narrative." Booklist
Includes bibliographical references

McKinley, William, 1843-1901

★ Phillips, Kevin P. **William** McKinley; {by} Kevin Phillips. Times Bks. 2003 188p (American presidents series) $20   **92**
1. Governors 2. Presidents 3. Members of Congress 4. United States -- Politics and government -- 1898-1919
ISBN 0-8050-6953-4

LC 2003-50701

Phillips portrays a "'surprisingly modern McKinley' who honored Booker T. Washington and competently directed the Spanish-American War by cable and telephone; 'the egalitarian who ran with the Grangers and promoted women's rights, the "people's candidate" who beat the Eastern bosses, the man who wouldn't have a lobbyist in his cabinet, the cautious reformer who was on the verge of leading a fight to curb the trusts, reform the tariff system and reenact a progressive income tax.'" N Y Times Book Rev

"This little work of rehabilitation should help set McKinley's reputation right." Publ Wkly

Includes bibliographical references

McLuhan, Marshall, 1911-1980

Coupland, Douglas. **Marshall** McLuhan; you know nothing of my work! Atlas & Co. 2010 216p $24　　**92**

1. Authors 2. Mass media 3. Sociologists 4. Literary critics 5. Nonfiction writers 6. Television critics

ISBN 978-1-935633-16-7

This is a biography of the Canadian mass media specialist.

"The book rewards by refusing to slip into the numbing vortex of academic discourse, taking a fizzy, pop-culture approach to explaining a deep thinker, one who ended up popularized almost in spite of himself." N Y Times Book Rev

McMullen, William, 1824-1901

Biddle, Daniel R. **Tasting** freedom; Octavius Catto and the battle for equality in Civil War America. [by] Daniel R. Biddle [and] Murray Dubin. Temple University Press 2010 616p il $35; e-book $35 **92**

1. Political activists 2. African American athletes 3. African American educators 4. Baseball -- Biography 5. Biography, Individual 6. African Americans -- Biography 7. Pennsylvania -- Race relations 8. Philadelphia (Pa.) -- Race relations -- History 9. Civil rights movements -- Pennsylvania -- Philadelphia 10. African Americans -- Civil rights -- Pennsylvania -- Philadelphia

ISBN 978-1-59213-465-6; 978-1-59213-467-0 e-book

LC 2009049276

This is a biography of 19th-century civil rights activist and baseball player "Octavius Catto of Philadelphia. Catto was a part of the city's black intelligentsia and a vigorous proponent of equal rights. . . . Catto became a martyr to his cause when, at age 32, he was gunned down in Philadelphia's 1871 election-day riot. . . . [The authors] present a clear and compelling portrait of this significant early civil rights activist; they also present a thoughtful assessment of how Catto's efforts relate to the modern black civil rights movement." Choice

Includes bibliographical references

McMurtry, Larry

McMurtry, Larry. **Books**; a memoir. Simon & Schuster 2008 259p $24　　**92**

1. Authors 2. Novelists 3. Booksellers and bookselling 4. Essayists 5. Authors, American 6. Short story writers

ISBN 978-1-416-58334-9; 1-416-58334-3

LC 2008-10565

This is an account of the author's experiences "during his four decades in the antiquarian book trade." N Y Times (Late N Y Ed)

"A pleasant amble in Bookland and a treat for the bookishly inclined." Kirkus

McPherson, Aimee Semple, 1890-1944

Epstein, Daniel Mark. **Sister** Aimee: the life of Aimee Semple McPherson. 1993 475p il hardcover o.p. pa $18　　**92**

1. Evangelists

ISBN 0-15-600093-8 pa

LC 92-23324

This is a biography of the American evangelist and faith healer

"Any secular treatment of a subject who claims divine inspiration must sooner or later confront The Question: did God actually speak to her? Epstein's hedge is that Sister Aimee believed He did. . . . On the whole, however, the book is a lively read. That it is neither hagiography nor exposé is its strength as well as its weakness. Sister Aimee emerges as an unlikely yet compelling heroine." Natl Rev

Includes bibliographical references

McReynolds, David, 1929-

Duberman, Martin B. A **saving** remnant; the radical lives of Barbara Deming and David McReynolds. New Press 2011 298p il $27.95　　**92**

1. Poets 2. Authors 3. Feminism 4. Radicalism 5. Political activists 6. Political prisoners 7. Essayists 8. Pacifists 9. Political leaders 10. Socialist leaders

ISBN 978-1-59558-323-9; 1-59558-323-8

LC 2010-45060

"As radical left-wing writers and activists, Deming and McReynolds were immersed in the issues of nonviolence, nuclear disarmament, civil rights and the Vietnam War. Both remained dedicated to peaceful protest, even in the face of legal repercussions. Though naturally frail, Deming picketed and marched her way through the 1960s, and was frequently imprisoned. In 1963, several weeks after taking part in the March on Washington, McReynolds was thrown into a North Carolina jail for eating at a whites-only restaurant with black acquaintances. Two years later, he was one of the first men in the nation to publicly burn his draft card. Duberman . . . tells us that the two were friends and 'often worked together politically,' though we rarely see them interact. The book's parallel narratives intersect in a meaningful way only when its subjects disagree, most notably on the issues of a gay rights movement and feminism. . . . The author makes use of letters, private papers, diaries and recent interviews with McReynolds. (Deming died of ovarian cancer in 1984.) The result is an intimate study, written in straightforward prose." N Y Times Book Rev

Includes bibliographical references

McTell, Blind Willie, 1898?-1959

Gray, Michael. **Hand** me my travelin' shoes; in search of Blind Willie McTell. Chicago Review Press 2009 432p il $26.95　　**92**

1. Blind 2. Singers 3. Guitarists 4. Blues music 5. Blues musicians 6. Songwriters

ISBN 978-1-55652-975-7

LC 2009-22329

First published 2007 in the United Kingdom

"Less a conventional biography than a mixture of history, travelogue and detective story, Gray paints an evocative portrait of an artist who defied blues stereotypes." Kirkus

Includes bibliographical references

Mead, Margaret, 1901-1978

Mead, Margaret. **Blackberry** winter; my earlier years. with a new introduction by Nancy Lutkehaus. Kodansha International 1995 305p il (Kodansha globe) pa $15   **92**

1. Anthropologists 2. Curators 3. Writers on science
ISBN 1-568-36069-X; 978-1-568-36069-0

LC 95-13302

First published 1972 by Morrow

"About one-third of Mead's autobiography covers the years before she became an anthropologist and another third her field work in Samoa, in New Guinea, among the Omaha Indians, and in Bali. . . . The concluding chapters . . . describe in subjective detail her role as mother and grandmother." Choice

Includes bibliographical references

Mecom, Jane, 1712-1794

★ Lepore, Jill. **Book** of ages; the life and opinions of Jane Franklin. Jill Lepore. Alfred A. Knopf 2013 464 p. $27.95   **92**

1. Boston (Mass.) -- Biography 2. Women -- United States -- Social conditions -- 18th century
ISBN 0307958345; 9780307958341

LC 2013001012

This book on Jane Franklin Mecom by Jill Lepore tells "the story of Benjamin Franklin's youngest sister . . . using only a few of her letters and a small archive of births and deaths." (Kirkus Reviews) "Jane's surviving letters are . . . the correspondence of a smart, witty, hardworking woman who 'loved best books about ideas,' reveled in gossip, expressed 'impolite' opinions on religion and politics, and shared piquant observations of the struggle for American independence." (Booklist)

Includes bibliographical references

Meeink, Frank, 1975-

Meeink, Frank. **Autobiography** of a recovering skinhead; Frank Meeink's story. as told to Jody M. Roy. Hawthorne Books 2010 350p pa $10   **92**

1. White supremacy movements 2. Memoirists 3. Gang members 4. Social activists 5. White supremacists 6. Motivational speakers
ISBN 978-0-9790188-2-4

LC 2009-27527

"Before he was out of his teens, Meeink, a member of a group of white supremacists, was behind prison bars. But by the time he was released on parole, he was a changed man, having cast off his hatred; he became a public speaker, sharing his experiences, helping others to understand the nature of hatred and to find ways to combat it. . . . Stories of personal redemption don't get much more interesting than this one, and the gritty first-person narrative . . . draws the reader into Meeink's story, giving it an immediacy and a visceral intensity that makes us feel as though we've lived a bit of his life. Readers should be warned that the book is unflinchingly straightforward: some of the language is quite raw, and some of the imagery quite graphic." Booklist

Melinek, Judy

Mitchell, T. J. **Working** stiff; two years, 262 bodies, and the making of a medical examiner. Judy Melinek, MD and T.J. Mitchell. First Scribner hardcover ed Scribner 2014 272 p. (hardback) $25 **92**

1. Forensic sciences 2. Medical jurisprudence 3. Forensic pathologists -- New York (State) -- New York -- Biography 4. Medical examiners (Law) -- New York (State) -- New York -- Biography
ISBN 1476727252; 9781476727257; 9781476727264

LC 2014017610

This book, by Judy Melinek and T. J. Mitchell, offers a "memoir of a young forensic pathologist's 'rookie season' as a NYC medical examiner, and the cases--hair-raising and heartbreaking and impossibly complex--that shaped her as both a physician and a mother. . . . [It] offers a firsthand account of daily life in one of America's most arduous professions, and the unexpected challenges of shuttling between the domains of the living and the dead." (Publisher's note)

"Though some sections call for a strong stomach, armchair detectives and would-be forensic pathologists will find Melinek's well-written account to be inspiring and engaging." Pub Wkly

Mellon, Andrew William, 1855-1937

★ Cannadine, David. **Mellon**; an American life. A.A. Knopf 2006 779p il $35   **92**

1. Philanthropists 2. Financiers 3. Art collectors 4. Secretaries of the treasury
ISBN 0-679-45032-7; 978-0-679-45032-0

LC 2006-45116

This is a "biography of Andrew Mellon, the powerful American financier, secretary of the treasury, and art collector. . . . Cannadine's recounting of Mellon's public career make this a worthy contribution to our understanding of the man and his era." Booklist

Includes bibliographical references

Melville, Herman, 1819-1891

Delbanco, Andrew. **Melville**; his world and work. Knopf 2005 xxiii, 415p il map $30   **92**

1. Authors 2. Novelists 3. Authors, American
ISBN 0-375-40314-0

LC 2005-40919

"This is sure to elicit new appreciation for Melville's work and could well be the best one-volume biography for some time to come." Libr J

Includes bibliographical references

Mencken, H. L. (Henry Louis), 1880-1956

Rodgers, Marion Elizabeth. **Mencken**; the American iconoclast. Oxford University Press 2005 662p il $35   **92**

1. Authors 2. Essayists 3. Philologists 4. Social critics 5. Literary critics 6. Newspaper editors
ISBN 0-19-507238-3

LC 2005-47786

The author offers a "look at the 'bad boy of Baltimore' who grew to international fame and influence." Booklist

"This is a meticulous portrait of one of the most original and complicated men in American letters." Publ Wkly
Includes bibliographical references

Teachout, Terry. The **skeptic** : the life of H.L. Mencken. HarperCollins Pubs. 2002 410p il $29.95; pa $15.95 **92**
1. Authors 2. Essayists 3. Philologists 4. Social critics 5. Literary critics 6. Newspaper editors
ISBN 0-06-050528-1; 0-06-050529-X pa
LC 2002-24953
This is "an engrossing, sympathetic biography." Booklist
Includes bibliograpical references

Mendeleev, Dmitri I.

★ Gordin, Michael D. A **well** -ordered thing: Dmitrii Mendeleev and the shadow of the periodic table. Basic Books 2004 364p il $30 **92**
1. Chemists 2. Periodic law
ISBN 0-465-02775-X
LC 2003-25533
"This is not a chronological biography of the man; rather, it is a work that shows Mendeleev as an important part of the changes that occurred in Russia during the days between the freeing of the serfs in 1861 and the crumbling of tsarist power in 1905." Sci Books & Films
Includes bibliographical references

Mendelsohn, Daniel, 1960-

Mendelsohn, Daniel. The **lost**; a search for six of six million. photographs by Matt Mendelsohn. HarperCollins Publishers 2006 512p il $27.95 **92**
1. Journalists 2. Classicists 3. College teachers 4. Literary critics 5. Holocaust, 1933-1945
ISBN 0-06-054297-7
LC 2006-41096
The author describes his efforts to find out what happened to his uncle Shmiel Jager, his wife and four daughters, who lived in the Polish town of Bolechow, and perished during the Holocaust.
"Mr. Mendelsohn, an evocative, ruminative writer, brings to life the vanished world not just of prewar Poland but also of his childhood and his extended family." N Y Times (Late N Y Ed)

Mendelssohn, Felix, 1809-1847

Mercer-Taylor, Peter Jameson. The **life** of Mendelssohn; [by] Peter Mercer-Taylor. Cambridge Univ. Press 2000 238p il (Musical lives) hardcover o.p. pa $34.99 **92**
1. Composers
ISBN 0-521-63025-8; 0-521-63972-7 pa
LC 99-58441
A study of "the composer and his music, family history, cultural setting, and creative aspirations. . . . The book contains no musical examples but plentiful allusions to monumental works in the Western art music tradition. . . . The author describes pieces in ways music lovers can appreciate and places the composer in the context of his times for historians who seek breadth in biographies. The bibliographic essay . . . guides readers to other sources." Libr J

"The book is well written, carefully produced, and a pleasure to read." Choice

Merman, Ethel, 1908 or 9-1984

Flinn, Caryl. **Brass** diva; the life and legends of Ethel Merman. University of California Press 2007 542p il $34.95; pa $18.95 **92**
1. Actors 2. Singers
ISBN 978-0-520-22942-6; 0-520-22942-8; 978-0-520-26022-1 pa; 0-520-26022-8 pa
LC 2007-29515
This is a biography of the singer and musical comedy star who appeared in the shows Girl Crazy (1930), Annie Get Your Gun (1946), and Gypsy (1959).
"A definitive all-inclusive piece of work that has been masterfully put together." Univ Press Books for Public and Second Sch Libr, 2008
Includes bibliographical references, discography, and filmography

Merton, Thomas, 1915-1968

★ Merton, Thomas. The **seven** storey mountain; Fiftieth anniversary edition; Harcourt Brace & Co. 1998 467p $35; pa $16 **92**
1. Monks 2. Poets 3. Authors 4. Nonfiction writers 5. Writers on religion
ISBN 0-15-100413-7; 0-15-601086-0 pa
LC 98-198169
First published 1948. This edition includes an introduction by Merton's editor, Robert Giroux, and a reader's note by biographer and Thomas Merton Society Founder Fr. William Shannon. Libr J
"The autobiography of a poet who became a convert to Catholicism and at the age of 26 after a full and traveled world career as student and teacher, entered a Trappist monastery." Publ Wkly

Micheaux, Oscar, 1884-1951

McGilligan, Patrick. **Oscar** Micheaux; the great and only; the life of America's first great Black filmmaker. HarperCollins Publishers 2007 402p il $29.95 **92**
1. Authors 2. Novelists 3. Screenwriters 4. Motion picture directors
ISBN 978-0-06-073139-7; 0-06-073130-7
LC 2007-60735
"One of the fascinating side streets in American film is the history of 'race pictures,' celluloid productions by black artists for black audiences during those decades when Jim Crow laws enforced segregation. The mainstay of race pictures was Oscar Micheaux (18841951), an intrepid filmmaker-novelist-entrepreneur whose career spanned four decades and who made more than 40 movies. . . . McGilligan's prose style may be pedestrian, but he organizes his biographical materials into a lively, readable tale." N Y Times Book Rev

Michelangelo Buonarroti, 1475-1564

Unger, Miles J. **Michelangelo**; a life in six masterpieces. Miles J. Unger. Simon & Schuster 2014 416 p. illustrations, map (hardback) $29.95   **92**

1. Artists, Italian 2. Artists -- Biography
ISBN 9781451678741; 1451678746

LC 2013045778

In this biography of the artist Michelangelo, author "Miles Unger narrates the astonishing life of this driven and difficult man through six of his greatest masterpieces. Each work expanded the expressive range of the medium, from the Pietà Michelangelo carved as a brash young man, to the apocalyptic Last Judgment, the work of an old man tested by personal trials." (Publisher's note)

"Unger highlights Michelangelo's singular achievement without glossing over the defects in his mercurial character—or obscuring the corruption and violence pervading his Renaissance world. A masterful portrait of a dauntingly complex figure." Booklist

Includes bibliographical references and index

Miletich, Patrick Jay, 1968-

Wertheim, L. Jon. **Blood** in the cage; mixed martial arts, Pat Miletich, and the furious rise of the UFC. Houghton Mifflin Harcourt 2009 251p il $25   **92**

1. Martial arts 2. Sportswriters 3. Ultimate Fighting Championship (Organization)
ISBN 978-0-618-98261-5; 0-618-98261-2

LC 2008-36764

"MMA has yet to find its great scribe, its Liebling, Pierce Egan or Norman Mailer, but it is young. Until that new bard of bloodshed comes along, 'Blood in the Cage' will stand as a worthy introduction to the birth of something both awful and beautiful." Salon

Mill, John Stuart, 1806-1873

Mill, John Stuart. **Autobiography**; edited with an introduction by John M. Robson. Penguin Bks. 1989 234p pa $8.95   **92**

1. Economists 2. Philosophers 3. Essayists 4. Writers on politics
ISBN 0-14-043316-3

LC 91-103446

Written 1873

"A human document of unusual interest. Mill, a noble spirit educated by a narrow-minded pedant, shut off from all normal contact, developed an egotism that makes this book so completely an autobiography that besides his father and [his] wife he seems to exist alone in a world of which he has both center and circumference." Pratt Alcove

Includes bibliographical references

Millay, Edna St. Vincent, 1892-1950

Milford, Nancy. **Savage** beauty: the life of Edna St. Vincent Millay. Random House 2001 550p il $29.95; pa $14.95   **92**

1. Poets 2. Authors 3. Dramatists
ISBN 0-394-57589-X; 0-375-76081-4 pa

LC 2001-18598

"In 1923, Edna St. Vincent Millay became the first woman to win the Pulitzer Prize for poetry. To write her biography, Milford . . . persuaded Millay's younger sister and sole heir, Norma, to give her access to hundreds of Millay's personal papers, letters, and notebooks. Selecting from 'this extraordinary collection,' Milford meticulously integrates Millay's major poems, letters received and sent, reactions of friends, and comments from extensive interviews with Norma into an orderly and affecting narrative." Libr J

Includes bibliographical references

Miller, Arthur, 1915-2005

Bigsby, Christopher. **Arthur** Miller; 1915-1962. [by] Christopher Bigsby. Harvard University Press 2009 739p il $35   **92**

1. Authors 2. Dramatists 3. Screenwriters 4. Dramatists, American
ISBN 978-0-674-03505-8; 0-674-03505-4

LC 2009-2489

First published 2008 in the United Kingdom

This is a biography of the American playwright.

"A richly detailed, revealing look at the making of a playwright and a man." Kirkus

Includes bibliographical references

Gottfried, Martin. **Arthur** Miller; his life and work. Da Capo Press 2003 484p il hardcover o.p. pa $18   **92**

1. Authors 2. Dramatists 3. Screenwriters
ISBN 0-306812-14-2; 0-306813-77-7 pa

LC 2004-298989

"[The author] discusses the importance of Miller's marriages, his immense and uninterrupted popularity in Great Britain, the erosion and resurrection of his reputation in the US, his involvement with Hollywood, and his political activities, especially with the director Elia Kazan and the House Committee on Un-American Activities." Choice

This is "an uncomfortable, challenging work, forbidding us any bien-pensant ease, and we should be grateful for it." Times Lit Suppl

Includes bibliographical references

Miller, Kimberly Rae

Miller, Kimberly Rae. **Coming** clean; Kimberly Rae Miller. New Harvest/Houghton Mifflin Harcourt 2013 272 p.   **92**

1. Compulsive hoarding 2. Parent-child relationship 3. Authors -- United States -- Biography
ISBN 9780544025837

LC 2013010483

In this memoir, author Kim Miller relates the story of a childhood lived "behind the closed doors of her family's idyllic Long Island house, navigating between teetering stacks of aging newspapers, broken computers, and boxes upon boxes of unused junk festering in every room--the product of her father's painful and unending struggle with hoarding." (Publisher's note)

Miller, Lee, 1907-1977

★ Burke, Carolyn. **Lee** Miller; a life. Knopf 2005 426p il $35   **92**

1. Photographers 2. Models (Persons)
ISBN 0-375-40147-4

LC 2004-43844

This is a biography of the model and photographer.

This "sympathetic tribute sheds further light on the lives of this highly original, often misunderstood woman." Economist

Includes bibliographical references

Miller, Sue

Miller, Sue. The **story** of my father; a memoir. Knopf 2003 173p il $22.50; pa $12.95   **92**
1. Authors 2. Novelists 3. Memoirists 4. Short story writers
ISBN 0-375-41479-7; 0-345-45544-4 pa
LC 2002-69460

"A familiar but still touching story of a parent's descent into Alzheimer's disease; the deeper Miller's father sinks into confusion, the more powerfully candid her writing becomes." N Y Times Book Rev

Millner, Caille, 1979-

Millner, Caille. The **golden** road; notes on my gentrification. Penguin Press 2007 248p $22.95 **92**
1. Journalists
ISBN 978-1-59420-109-7; 1-59420-109-9
LC 2006-51010

The author "uses her own story to explore geographic and personal notions of place and the effects of change on both. The product of a troubled family and raised in Latino and Caucasian neighborhoods, she searches for her identity as a black woman, a search complicated by her parents' efforts to succeed in white America and their determination that their children do the same. . . . In quietly mesmerizing prose informed throughout by an attitude of wry objectivity, Millner makes her life thus far compelling reading and an outstanding addition to a crowded field." Libr J

Mills, Marja

Mills, Marja. The **Mockingbird** Next Door; Life with Harper Lee. Marja Mills. The Penguin Press 2014 288 p. illustrations (hardback) $27.95   **92**
1. American authors 2. Alabama -- Biography 3. Authors, American -- 20th century -- Biography
ISBN 1594205191; 9781594205194
LC 2013039938

This book, by Marja Mills, is a memoir recounting her friendship with "To Kill a Mockingbird" author Harper Lee. "Journalists have trekked to her hometown of Monroeville, Alabama, where . . . Lee, known to her friends as Nelle, has lived with her sister, Alice, for decades, trying and failing to get an interview with the author. But in 2001, the Lee sisters opened their door to Chicago Tribune journalist Marja Mills. It was the beginning of a long conversation--and a great friendship." (Publisher's note)

Milton, John, 1608-1674

Campbell, Gordon. **John** Milton; life, work, and thought. [by] Gordon Campbell [and] Thomas N. Corns. Oxford University Press 2008 488p il map $39.95   **92**
1. Blind 2. Poets 3. Authors 4. Essayists 5. Great Britain -- History -- 1603-1714, Stuarts
ISBN 978-0-19-928984-4; 0-19-928984-0
LC 2008-300712

This biography "draws chiefly on documentary evidence and an easy familiarity with the 17th-century English scene. As a prodigy scholar, pamphleteer, government translator on the international stage and the blind . . . bard of the Bible, Milton found himself astride a world of hardening views, as it spiraled in political and spiritual transition. . . . The authors set Milton's imaginative life against this backdrop, stretching from Shakespeare, to whom Milton's father may have been loosely connected, to Dryden's ingenious staging of Paradise Lost in couplets. With nearly 100 pages of notes and bibliography, this is a no-nonsense contribution to our understanding of a genius who, in many ways, is hardly remote from our times." Publ Wkly

Includes bibliographical references (p. 446-472)

Hawkes, David. **John** Milton; a hero for our time. Counterpoint 2010 354p $28   **92**
1. Blind 2. Poets 3. Authors 4. Poets, English 5. Essayists
ISBN 978-1-58243-437-7; 1-58243-437-9
LC 2009-53998

"Hawkes writes with little academic jargon, and his style is lively and entertaining. Political and religious history enthusiasts will find this excellent and challenging." Libr J

Includes bibliographical references

Min, Anchee, 1957-

★ Anchee Min. The **Cooked** Seed; A Memoir. Anchee Min. St. Martin's Press 2013 368 p. $26 **92**
1. Immigrants -- United States 2. China -- History -- 1949-1976 3. Chinese -- United States -- Biography 4. Chinese American authors -- Biography 5. Immigrants -- United States -- Biography
ISBN 1596916982; 9781596916982
LC 2013015953

This book is an "examination of the legacy of Mao Zedong's Cultural Revolution," in which author Anchee Min offers a "contrast between American and Chinese attitudes about human worth and dignity. Raised in Shanghai in a hardscrabble family of four children and educated parents who were denounced as 'bourgeois,' Min was plucked as a teenager from a labor camp in 1974" to appear in propaganda films. At 27, she came to the U.S. (Publishers Weekly)

Includes bibliographical references and index

Min, Anchee. **Red** Azalea. Anchor Books 2006 306p pa $13   **92**
1. Actors 2. Artists 3. Authors 4. Novelists 5. Photographers 6. Memoirists 7. China -- History -- 1949-
ISBN 978-1-4000-9698-5; 1-4000-9698-7
LC 2006-271433

First published 1994 by Pantheon Bks.

"In this memoir of growing up in China during the Cultural Revolution, sexual freedom becomes a powerful political as well as literary statement." N Y Times Book Rev

Minnelli, Vincente, 1910-1986

Levy, Emanuel. **Vincente** Minnelli; Hollywood's dark dreamer. St. Martin's Press 2009 448p il $35   **92**
1. Motion picture producers and directors 2. Motion

picture directors
ISBN 978-0-312-32925-9; 0-312-32925-3

LC 2008-28751

"Relying mostly on secondary sources, Levy traces [Minnelli's] career from early days as a stage designer in New York to arrival at MGM and his most fruitful period, the 1950s, when his films were box office and critical successes, to his frustrating final decades after the collapse of the studio system. . . . Levy provides some valuable insight into the life of a genuine artist who struggled—frequently successfully—to inject a higher aesthetic into popular entertainment." Booklist

Includes bibliographical references

Mitchell, Andrea

Mitchell, Andrea. **Talking** back--to presidents, dictators, and assorted scoundrels. Viking 2005 414p il $25.95 **92**

1. Television reporters 2. Spouses of prominent persons

ISBN 0-670-03403-7

LC 2005-42279

In this "memoir, Mitchell recalls her climb to the top of her profession, including stints at NBC Nightly News, Today, and Meet the Press." Booklist

This "is a collection of good stories, inside dope and real-life quandaries, all from someone still eager enough to compare herself to Nancy Drew and Brenda Starr." Am Journalism Rev

Mitchell, Joan

Albers, Patricia. **Joan** Mitchell; lady painter: a life. Alfred A. Knopf 2011 xxi, 514p il ebook $21.99; $40 **92**

1. Artists 2. Painters 3. Women artists 4. Abstract expressionism 5. Biography, Individual 6. Artists -- United States

ISBN 978-0-307-59598-0 ebook; 978-0-375-41437-4

LC 2011-00457

This is a "biography of the abstract expressionist painter who came of age in the 1950s, '60s, and '70s." (Publisher's note) Index.

This is a "biography of Joan Mitchell (1925–92), a major 20th-century American artist. . . . This significant biography covers all aspects of Mitchell's life, including her synesthesia, eidetic memory, alcoholism, troubled relationships, and art. Filled with intimate details of her complex personality and unconventional lifestyle, this is a conscientiously objective yet sympathetic portrait of the 'lady painter' and the social and cultural contexts in which she became a successful artist in the male-dominated Parisian and New York art worlds." Libr J

Includes bibliographical references

Mithridates VI Eupator, King of Pontus, ca. 132-63 B.C.

Mayor, Adrienne. The **Poison** King; the life and legend of Mithridates, Rome's deadliest enemy. Princeton University Press 2009 448p il map $29.95 **92**

1. Kings and rulers 2. Kings 3. Rome -- History 4. Black Sea region -- History 5. Mediterranean region

-- History
ISBN 9780691126838

LC 2009-15050

This is "a reappraisal of Mithradates's character and a detailed account of his scientific pursuits, notably his in-depth studies of poison. . . . [The author places] him in his proper context as a Greco-Persian ruler following in the footsteps of his purported ancestor Alexander the Great. The most compelling aspect of this book is Mayor's engaging style. A true storyteller, she makes Mithradates's world come alive." Libr J

Includes bibliographical references

Moaveni, Azadeh, 1976-

Moaveni, Azadeh. **Honeymoon** in Tehran; two years of love and danger in Iran. Random House 2009 340p $26 **92**

1. Authors 2. Journalists 3. Iranian Americans 4. Women journalists 5. Memoirists

ISBN 978-1-4000-6645-2; 1-4000-6645-X

The Iranian-American author describes her return to Iran as a reporter for 'Time' magazine, her marriage to an Iranian man, the repressive Iranian society and its impact, and her family's decision to leave Iran.

"This perfect blend of political commentary and social observation is an excellent choice for readers interested in going beyond the headlines to gain an in-depth understanding of twenty-first-century Iran." Booklist

Includes bibliographical references

Moaveni, Azadeh. **Lipstick** jihad; a memoir of growing up Iranian in America and American in Iran. Public Affairs 2005 249p $25; pa $13 **92**

1. Authors 2. Journalists 3. Iran 4. Memoirists

ISBN 1-58648-193-2; 1-58648-378-1 pa

LC 2004-43184

"Moaveni, an Iranian-American who grew up in California, decided to embark on a journey in spring 2000 to rediscover her Iranian heritage. In this account, she . . . conveys the tensions she observed between the fundamentalist mullahs and younger Iranians, who are pushing for a more Westernized, modern Iran. . . . A charming and informative memoir." Libr J

Modigliani, Amedeo, 1884-1920

Secrest, Meryle. **Modigliani**; a life. Alfred A. Knopf 2011 387p il $35; ebook $17.99 **92**

1. Artists, Italian 2. Biography, Individual

ISBN 978-0-307-26368-1; 978-0-307-59547-8 ebook

LC 2010-45357

This "is an enjoyable read for all, and a most welcome contribution to Modigliani scholarship." Publ Wkly

Mongkut, King of Siam, 1804-1868

Landon, Margaret. **Anna** and the King of Siam; illustrated by Margaret Ayer. Harper & Row 1944 391p il map hardcover o.p. pa $14.95 **92**

1. Kings 2. Governesses 3. Thailand -- Social life and customs

ISBN 0-06-095488-4 pa

Anna Leonowens' experiences at the Siamese court in the 1860's. From her experiences she wrote two books, "The

English governess at the Siamese court," and "The romance of the harem." The author has put these two books into one story with additions to make a complete tale.

Monk, Thelonious, 1917-1982

★ Kelley, Robin D. G., 1962- **Thelonious** Monk; the life and times of an American original. Free Press 2009 588p il $30   **92**
1. Pianists 2. Jazz musicians 3. African American musicians 4. Jazz 5. Biography, Individual
ISBN 0-684-83190-2; 978-0-684-83190-9
                                           LC 2009-08526
This is a biography of the jazz musician and composer. Discography. Videography. Index.

The author "knows music, especially Monk's music, and his descriptions of assorted studio and live dates, along with what Monk is up to musically throughout, are handled expertly. . . . Likewise, the characters in Monk's life and career are well served. . . . The 'genius of modern music' has gotten the passionate, and compassionate, advocate he deserves." N Y Times Book Rev

Includes discography, videography, and bibliographical references

Monroe, James, 1758-1831

Unger, Harlow G. The **last** founding father; James Monroe and a nation's call to greatness. [by] Harlow Giles Unger. Da Capo Press 2009 388p il map $26   **92**
1. Presidents 2. Secretaries of state 3. Presidents -- United States 4. United States -- Politics and government -- 1783-1865
ISBN 978-0-306-81808-0
                                           LC 2009-26195
"A worthy attempt to rescue Monroe from obscurity for a mainstream audience." Kirkus
Includes bibliographical references (p. 371-376)

Monroe, Marilyn, 1926-1962

★ Taraborrelli, J. Randy. The **secret** life of Marilyn Monroe. Grand Central Pub. 2009 560p il $26.99   **92**
1. Actors
ISBN 978-0-446-58082-3
                                           LC 2008-44704
For this biography, the author "delves beneath the legend of Marilyn Monroe to uncover the stark facts of the life and times of a singularly vulnerable woman woefully unequipped to deal with the quotidian business of 'normal' life, much less the pressures of a Hollywood career and international celebrity. . . . A painful and engrossing account of the profoundly damaged personality at the heart of the world's greatest sex symbol." Kirkus
Includes filmography

Montaigne, Michel de, 1533-1592

Bakewell, Sarah. **How** to live, or, A life of Montaigne in one question and twenty attempts at an an-

swer. Other Press 2010 389p il map $25; ebook $19.99   **92**
1. Judges 2. Authors 3. Authors, French 4. Essayists
ISBN 978-1-59051-425-2; 978-1-59051-426-9 ebook
                                           LC 2010-26896
"In a wide-ranging intellectual career, Michel de Montaigne found no knowledge so hard to acquire as the knowledge of how to live this life well. By casting her biography of the writer as 20 chapters, each focused on a different answer to the question How to live? Bakewell limns Montaigne's ceaseless pursuit of this most elusive knowledge. Embedded in the 20 life-knowledge responses, readers will find essential facts—when and where Montaigne was born, how and whom he married, how he became mayor of Bordeaux, how he managed a public life in a time of lethal religious and political passions. . . . Because Montaigne's capacious mirror still captivates many, this insightful life study will win high praise from both scholars and general readers." Booklist
Includes bibliographical references

Mooney, Jonathan

Mooney, Jonathan. The **short** bus; a journey beyond normal. H. Holt 2007 272p hardcover o.p. pa $14.99   **92**
1. Students with disabilities 2. Memoirists 3. Social activists 4. Motivational speakers
ISBN 978-0-8050-7427-7; 0-8050-7427-9; 978-0-8050-8804-5 pa; 0-8050-8804-0 pa
                                           LC 2006-52588
The author's "target audience is not policy makers but his fellow misfits, and his boundless empathy will surely console those who also face the worst that cruel schoolchildren and the educational bureaucracy have to offer." N Y Times Book Rev

Mooney, Paul

Mooney, Paul. **Black** is the new white; a memoir. Simon Spotlight Entertainment 2009 264p il $24.99   **92**
1. Actors 2. Comedians 3. Screenwriters 4. Television scriptwriters 5. United States -- Race relations
ISBN 978-1-4165-8795-8; 1-4165-8795-0
                                           LC 2009-19572
"Paul Mooney recalls the day he became Richard Pryor's shadow partner. It was 1968, and the two young comics were sitting in a Hollywood greasy spoon, with Pryor nursing another hangover, so Mooney lightened the mood with an off-the-cuff, X-rated one-liner that made his buddy convulse. . . . [This book] is Mooney's unvarnished memoir of that friendship. At a time when comedians—even African American icons such as Bill Cosby—never talked about race, Pryor (aided and abetted by Mooney) dared to confront the elephant in the room. Mooney, who has also written for 'In Living Color' and 'Chappelle's Show,' also traces his own path from humble Deep South roots to a comedy elder statesman known for his incisive riffs on racism." Los Angeles Times book Rev

Moore, Honor, 1945-

Moore, Honor. The **bishop's** daughter; a memoir. W. W. Norton & Co. 2008 365p il $25.95; pa $16.95 **92**

1. Poets 2. Authors 3. Bishops 4. Dramatists 5. Essayists 6. Memoirists 7. Literary critics

ISBN 978-0-393-05984-7; 978-0-393-33536-1 pa

LC 2008-01337

This is "a generous and thought-provoking chronicle of public altruism and private betrayal, high ideals and forbidden desire, love and forgiveness." Booklist

Includes bibliographical references

Moore, Marianne, 1887-1972

Molesworth, Charles. **Marianne** Moore; a literary life. Northeastern University Press 1991 xxii, 472p il pa $16.95 **92**

1. Poets 2. Authors 3. Essayists 4. Poets, American

ISBN 1-555-53115-6

LC 91-13570

First published 1990 by Atheneum Pubs.

"Molesworth charts the growth of a major modernist through careful critical readings of her poetry and prose, her work as an editor of the Dial, and an examination of Moore as an active, social New York literary figure whose colleagues and admirers included T.S. Eliot and Ezra Pound." Publ Wkly

Includes bibliographical references

Moore, Mary Tyler

Moore, Mary Tyler. **Growing** up again; life, love, and oh yeah, diabetes. St. Martin's Press 2009 216p il $24.95 **92**

1. Actors 2. Diabetes

ISBN 978-0-312-37631-4; 0-312-37631-6

LC 2008-37579

"While working on The Dick Van Dyke Show, . . . [the author] was diagnosed with juvenile (Type 1) diabetes and quickly discovered that managing the disease is a full-time job. . . . Moore details the daily challenges she faces to maintain healthy blood sugar levels. . . . Moore's humor, authoritative information, and honest evaluation of her own experiences with diabetes make this work essential for diabetes and consumer health collections." Libr J

Moore, Michael

Rapoport, Roger. **Citizen** Moore; the life and times of an American iconoclast. RDR 2006 310p il $15.95 **92**

1. Screenwriters 2. Social critics 3. Magazine editors 4. Nonfiction writers 5. Motion picture directors 6. Motion picture producers and directors -- Biography

ISBN 1-57143-163-2; 9781571431639 pa

In this biography of the controversial filmmaker, the author "compares Moore to Upton Sinclair and Ralph Nader, chronicling the filmmaker's early activism, community organizing, radio and theater career, and involvement in alternative journalism. . . . In this engaging profile, Rapoport portrays the quirks and complexities of a man whose life is as fascinating as his films." Booklist

Moore, Paul, 1919-2003

Moore, Honor. The **bishop's** daughter; a memoir. W. W. Norton & Co. 2008 365p il $25.95; pa $16.95 **92**

1. Poets 2. Authors 3. Bishops 4. Dramatists 5. Essayists 6. Memoirists 7. Literary critics

ISBN 978-0-393-05984-7; 978-0-393-33536-1 pa

LC 2008-01337

This is "a generous and thought-provoking chronicle of public altruism and private betrayal, high ideals and forbidden desire, love and forgiveness." Booklist

Includes bibliographical references

Moore, Wes, 1975-

Moore, Wes, 1978- The **other** Wes Moore; the story of one name and two fates. [by] Wes Moore; afterword by Tavis Smiley. Spiegel & Grau 2010 233p il $25 **92**

1. Prisoners 2. Murderers 3. Memoirists 4. Army officers 5. Baltimore (Md.) 6. African Americans -- Biography

ISBN 978-0-385-52819-1

LC 2009-41663

"In 2000, Wes Moore had recently been named a Rhodes Scholar in his final year of college at Johns Hopkins University when he read a newspaper article about another Wes Moore who was on his way to prison. It turned out that the two of them had much in common, both young black men raised in inner-city neighborhoods by single mothers. Stunned by the similarities in their names and backgrounds and the differences in their ultimate fates, the author eventually contacted the other Wes Moore and began a long relationship. . . . The author examines eight years in the lives of both Wes Moores to explore the factors and choices that led one to a Rhodes scholarship, military service, and a White House fellowship, and the other to drug dealing, prison, and eventual conversion to the Muslim faith, with both sharing a gritty sense of realism about their pasts." Booklist

Moore, Westley W.

Moore, Wes, 1978- The **other** Wes Moore; the story of one name and two fates. [by] Wes Moore; afterword by Tavis Smiley. Spiegel & Grau 2010 233p il $25 **92**

1. Prisoners 2. Murderers 3. Memoirists 4. Army officers 5. Baltimore (Md.) 6. African Americans -- Biography

ISBN 978-0-385-52819-1

LC 2009-41663

"In 2000, Wes Moore had recently been named a Rhodes Scholar in his final year of college at Johns Hopkins University when he read a newspaper article about another Wes Moore who was on his way to prison. It turned out that the two of them had much in common, both young black men raised in inner-city neighborhoods by single mothers. Stunned by the similarities in their names and backgrounds and the differences in their ultimate fates, the author eventually contacted the other Wes Moore and began a long relationship. . . . The author examines eight years in the lives of both Wes Moores to explore the factors and choices that led one to a Rhodes scholarship, military service, and a White House fellowship, and the other to drug dealing, prison, and eventual conversion to the Muslim faith, with both sharing a gritty sense of realism about their pasts." Booklist

Morante, Elsa, d. 1985

Tuck, Lily. **Woman** of Rome: a life of Elsa Morante. HarperCollins 2008 263p il $25.95   **92**
1. Poets 2. Authors 3. Novelists 4. Women authors 5. Authors, Italian 6. Short story writers
ISBN 978-0-06-147256-5; 0-06-147256-5
LC 2007-44647
"Written with a charming personal touch . . . that warms the narrative to a fine glow, this is a vital biography bringing to American audiences a writer most will have previously known little about." Booklist
Includes bibliographical references (p. 245-246)

Morgan, J. Pierpont (John Pierpont), 1837-1913

Strouse, Jean. **Morgan**; American financier. HarperPerennial 2000 796p il pa $18   **92**
1. Businesspeople 2. Bankers 3. Financiers 4. Book collectors
ISBN 0-06-095589-9; 978-0-06-095589-2
LC 99-87598
First published 1999 by Random House
"Strouse is in full command of Pierpont Morgan's personal life, his financial operations, his collecting, and his benefactions, and presents a rich, vivid picture of the background against which they took place. . . . She has written a magnificent biography, which illuminates her subject and his world." N Y Rev Books
Includes bibliographical references

Morris, Tom, 1821-1908

Cook, Kevin. **Tommy's** honor; the story of old Tom Morris and young Tom Morris, golf's founding father and son. Gotham Books 2007 327p il $27.50   **92**
1. Golf 2. Golfers
ISBN 978-1-59240-297-7; 1-59240-297-6
LC 2007-8165
"In Cook's telling, the story of Tom Morris, winner of golf's first Open Championship in 1860, and his son, Tommy, who won the Open three years in a row, becomes a compelling saga of near-Homeric proportions." Booklist
Includes bibliographical references

Morris, Tom, 1851-1875

Cook, Kevin. **Tommy's** honor; the story of old Tom Morris and young Tom Morris, golf's founding father and son. Gotham Books 2007 327p il $27.50   **92**
1. Golf 2. Golfers
ISBN 978-1-59240-297-7; 1-59240-297-6
LC 2007-8165
"In Cook's telling, the story of Tom Morris, winner of golf's first Open Championship in 1860, and his son, Tommy, who won the Open three years in a row, becomes a compelling saga of near-Homeric proportions." Booklist
Includes bibliographical references

Morrison, Jim, 1943-1971

Hopkins, Jerry. **No** one here gets out alive; by Jerry Hopkins and Daniel Sugerman. Warner Bks. 1980 387p il hardcover o.p. pa $7.99   **92**
1. Singers 2. Rock musicians 3. Songwriters 4. Doors (Musical group)
ISBN 0-446-60228-0 pa
LC 79-26611
This biography of rock musician Jim Morrison gives "an idea of how profoundly Morrison, as lyricist and lead singer of the Doors, affected the youth of America in the late 1960s. . . . The book includes a list of the Doors' records, books, and films." Booklist

Moses, Robert, 1888-1981

Caro, Robert A. The **power** broker: Robert Moses and the fall of New York. Knopf 1974 1246, xxxivp il $50; pa $21.95   **92**
1. Urban planners 2. Local government officials 3. State government officials
ISBN 0-394-48076-7; 0-394-72024-5 pa
This is a biographical critique of the man who in four decades as a public official "built most of the parks, bridges and highways in and around New York City." Newsweek
Includes bibliographical references

Mowat, Farley

King, James. **Farley** : the life of Farley Mowat. Steerforth Press 2002 397p il $27.95   **92**
1. Authors 2. Historians 3. Ethnologists 4. Children's authors 5. Nonfiction writers
ISBN 1-58642-055-0
LC 2002-151149
The author "recounts Mowat's life from his experience in college to his service in World War II and his work in the Northwest Territories as a student biologist. The emerging portrait is of a man whose evolution as both an environmentalist and an artist was profound, an activist who has never backed away from a controversy. The exploration of Mowat's life is detailed but never boring." Libr J
Includes bibliographical references

Mowat, Farley. **Born** naked. Houghton Mifflin 1994 256p il maps hardcover o.p. pa $13   **92**
1. Authors 2. Historians 3. Naturalists 4. Authors, Canadian 5. Ethnologists 6. Children's authors 7. Nonfiction writers
ISBN 0-395-73528-9
LC 93-23702
First published 1993 in Canada
"There are no dull pages here; every man, woman, child, and animal mentioned even casually makes an impression. . . . Highly recommended to all those who like good writing." Libr J

Moyers, William C.

Moyers, William C. **Broken** : my story of addiction and redemption; [by] William Cope Moyers with Katherine Ketcham. Viking 2006 372p il $25.95 **92**
1. Journalists
ISBN 0-670-03789-3; 978-0-670-03789-6
LC 2006-41378

This is an autobiography of "the prodigal son of Bill Moyers, the exemplary broadcast journalist, [who] wrecked a bright career at CNN and deserted his family in 1994, hitting bottom as a 'thirty-five-year-old crack addict.'" Publ Wkly

The author's "gripping account of his struggles with alcohol and crack addiction will have readers rooting for him from the very beginning." Libr J

Mozart, Wolfgang Amadeus, 1756-1791

Einstein, Alfred. **Mozart**; his character, his work. translated by Arthur Mendel and Nathan Broder. Oxford Univ. Press 1945 492p il music hardcover o.p. pa $22.50   **92**
1. Composers
ISBN 0-19-500732-8 pa
The author's "examination of the events of Mozart's life in relation to his character, and even more, his analysis of the sources, models, and methods of the musician's creative processes are penetrating and illuminating." Christ Sci Monit

Solomon, Maynard. **Mozart**; a life. HarperCollins Pubs. 1995 640p il hardcover o.p. pa $22.95 **92**
1. Composers
ISBN 0-06-019046-9; 978-0-06-088344-7 pa; 0-06-088344-8 pa

LC 94-42277

"The author explores Mozart's life and works with a wealth of facts that were culled from 18th-century sources as well as from the most recent scholarship. Mozart and his family emerge in a new light from this mass of well-chosen detail through Solomon's own convincing interpretation of events and relationships. Appropriate musical and pictorial examples, which will appeal to both scholarly and casual readers, accompany the text." Libr J
Includes bibliographical references

Muir, John, 1838-1914

★ Heacox, Kim. **John** Muir and the ice that started a fire; how a visionary and the glaciers of Alaska changed America. Kim Heacox. Lyons Press 2014 264 p. illustrations, map (hardback) $25.95 **92**
1. Alaska 2. Glaciers 3. Nature conservation 4. Glaciers -- Alaska 5. Climatic changes -- Alaska 6. Nature conservation -- Alaska
ISBN 0762792426; 9780762792429

LC 2013050235

This book, by Kim Heacox, "takes two of the most compelling elements in the narrative of wild America, John Muir and Alaska, and combines them into a brisk and engaging biography. . . . The book also offers an environmental caveat on global climate change and the glaciers' retreat alongside a beacon of hope: Muir shows us how one person changed America, helped it embrace its wilderness, and in turn, gave us a better world." (Publisher's note)

"The book is an engaging and informative look at Muir and his life's work, as well as a timely call to action that poses difficult questions to the reader and the philosophies that underpin modern life." Pub Wkly
Includes bibliographical references and index

Muir, John. The **story** of my boyhood and youth; with a foreword by Vernon Carstensen. University of Wisconsin Press 1965 227p hardcover o.p. pa $17.95   **92**
1. Authors 2. Naturalists 3. Writers on nature
ISBN 0-299-03654-5 pa

LC 65-14539

First published 1913 by Houghton Mifflin
"The naturalist's childhood in a strict Presbyterian home in Scotland, his boyhood experiences of the privations and out-of-door delights of pioneer life on a Wisconsin farm, and his shifts and contrivances while earning his way through the state university." Cleveland Public Libr

Worster, Donald. A **passion** for nature; the life of John Muir. Oxford University Press 2008 535p il map $34.95   **92**
1. Authors 2. Naturalists 3. Writers on nature
ISBN 978-0-19-516682-8; 0-19-516682-5

LC 2008-1441

The author "draws on John Muir's (1838-1914) correspondence and writings to offer an enlightening biography of the influential naturalist. . . . Competently documented, this all-inclusive biography explains the life and times of a figure known to all who love nature and will appeal to general readers and anyone interested in the early roots of today's green movement and its founding fathers." Libr J
Includes bibliographical references (p. 494-508)

Munch, Edvard, 1863-1944

Prideaux, Sue. **Edvard** Munch; behind the Scream. Yale University Press 2005 391p il map $35   **92**
1. Artists 2. Painters
ISBN 0-300-11024-3

LC 2005-12040

Prideaux's "treatment is very effective and her writing, cohesive, clear, and often compelling." Libr J
Includes bibliographical references

Murdoch, Rupert

Wolff, Michael. The **man** who owns the news; inside the secret world of Rupert Murdoch. Broadway Books 2008 446p $29.95   **92**
1. Mass media 2. Businessmen 3. Newspaper executives 4. Publishing executives 5. Broadcasting executives 6. Motion picture executives
ISBN 978-0-385-52612-8; 0-385-52612-1

LC 2008-37414

This biography of the Australian media entrepreneur describes how Rupert Murdoch came to own various companies, including The Wall Street Journal as well as its parent company, Dow Jones.

"There's lots of good material. . . . Perhaps most instructive, Wolff has melded interview and observation into what might be called a plausible theory of Murdoch." LA Times
Includes bibliographical references (p. 430-434)

Murray, Liz

Murray, Liz. **Breaking** night; a memoir of forgiveness, survival, and my journey from homeless to Harvard. Hyperion 2010 334p il $24.99   **92**

1. Students 2. Homeless persons 3. Children of drug addicts 4. Homeless 5. Motivational speakers

ISBN 978-0-7868-6891-9; 0-7868-6891-0

LC 2010-13679

This is a memoir by Liz Murray. "Murray grew up with drug-addicted parents but survived . . . and landed a place at Harvard." N Y Times Book Rev

"Neither sensationalizing nor soliciting pity, Murray's generous account of and caring attitude toward her past are not only uplifting, but also a fascinating lesson in the value of dedication." Booklist

Murrow, Edward R.

Edwards, Bob. **Edward** R. Murrow and the birth of broadcast journalism; {by} Robert A. Edwards. Wiley 2004 174p (Turning points) $19.95   **92**

1. Journalists 2. Radio reporters 3. Government officials 4. Television reporters 5. Television news anchors

ISBN 0-471-47753-2

LC 2003-21223

"The author chronicles Murrow's innovations in radio and television broadcasting, including live radio reports of the war in progress in Europe in 1940; exposure of the despotism of Senator Joseph McCarthy on CBS in 1953; the powerful television documentary Harvest of Shame on the deplorable conditions of migrant workers in the U.S.; and the first in-depth television news program, See It Now. . . . Edwards brings to life the early days of radio and television and the innovations that Murrow sparked. . . . Readers interested in journalism will enjoy this slim book." Booklist

Includes bibliographical references

Sperber, Ann M. **Murrow,** his life and times; {by} A. M. Sperber; with a preface by Neil Hickey. Fordham Univ. Press 1998 xxvi, 795p il $35; pa $25   **92**

1. Journalists 2. Radio reporters 3. Government officials 4. Television reporters 5. Television news anchors

ISBN 0-8232-1881-3; 0-8232-1882-1 pa

LC 98-52507

A reissue of the title first published 1986 by Freundlich Bks.

This "ambitious exploration of Murrow's life places his story in the foreground of what is, as well, a panorama of the years 1935-65." N Y Times Book Rev

Includes bibliographical references

Mussina, Mike, 1968-

Feinstein, John. **Living** on the black; two pitchers, two teams, one season to remember. Little, Brown 2008 525p il $26.99   **92**

1. Baseball players 2. Baseball -- Biography 3. New York Mets (Baseball team) 4. New York Yankees (Baseball team)

ISBN 978-0-316-11391-5; 0-316-11391-3

LC 2007-50618

The author presents a yearlong look at the lives of pitchers Mike Mussina of the New York Yankees and Tom Glavine of the New York Mets during the 2007 MLB season.

"Feinstein achieves a double play fans should savor for its scrupulous look at what life is like for the 21st-century major leaguer." Christ Sci Monit

Myatt, John

Salisbury, Laney. **Provenance**; how a con man and a forger rewrote the history of modern art. [by] Laney Salisbury and Aly Sujo. Penguin Press 2009 327p $26.95; pa $16   **92**

1. Painters 2. Criminals 3. Impostors and imposture 4. Swindlers 5. Art dealers 6. Art forgers 7. Art -- Forgeries

ISBN 978-1-59420-220-9; 978-0-14-311740-7 pa

LC 2009-3552

The authors "present the story of what Scotland Yard called 'the biggest art fraud of the twentieth century.' In 1996, British con man John Drewe was convicted of forgery and theft, among other charges. Sujo and Salisbury . . . delineate how he wormed his way into some of the most tightly controlled art archives in the world. His scam—aided by the initially reluctant work of forger John Myatt—spanned ten years, hundreds of forged paintings and dozens of art galleries across the globe." Kirkus

"Tautly written and assiduously researched . . . [this book] has the pace and suspense of a good thriller, and a colorful international cast." Wall Street J

Includes bibliographical references

Nafisi, Azar

Nafisi, Azar. **Reading** Lolita in Tehran; a memoir in books. Random House 2003 347p $23.95; pa $11.16   **92**

1. Books and reading 2. Memoirists 3. Women -- Iran 4. College teachers 5. Literary critics

ISBN 0-375-50490-7; 0-8129-7106-X pa

LC 2002-36724

"In 1997 Iran, Nafisi formed an illicit book group whose syllabus provided the perfect framework for appraising life before and after the Islamic Revolution—and afforded her female students what little freedom they knew. Through impassioned discussions of Nabokov, James, and Fitzgerald, she details her teaching career and the obstacles her students faced. Her seamless blend of literary criticism and memoir begets a whole new genre." Libr J

★ Nafisi, Azar. **Things** I've been silent about; memories. Random House 2008 336p il $27   **92**

1. Memoirists 2. Women -- Iran 3. College teachers 4. Literary critics

ISBN 978-1-4000-6361-1; 1-4000-6361-2

LC 2008-482096

This is the author's "account of growing up under a chilly, tyrannical parent in a changing Iran. . . . An immensely rewarding and beautifully written act of courage, by turns amusing, tender and obsessively dogged." Kirkus

Naipaul, V. S. (Vidiadhar Surajprasad), 1932-

French, Patrick. The **world** is what it is; the authorized biography of V.S. Naipaul. Knopf 2008 554p il $30 **92**

1. Authors 2. Novelists 3. Journalists 4. Essayists 5. Travel writers 6. Radio reporters 7. Nonfiction writers 8. Short story writers 9. Nobel laureates for literature

ISBN 978-1-4000-4405-4; 1-4000-4405-7

LC 2008-6988

This authorized study of Nobel laureate V.S. Naipaul examines his difficult early life as a child of Indian parents in colonial Trinidad, his Oxford education, the depression that marked his life in England, his complex personal life and romantic relationships, and his pursuit of becoming a great writer.

This book "is a prodigious achievement, a wonderful biography, a justification for the art of biography itself." Times Lit Suppl

Includes bibliographical references

Naipaul, V. S. **Reading** & writing; a personal account. New York Review of Bks. 2000 64p $16.95 **92**

1. Authors 2. Novelists 3. Journalists 4. Essayists 5. Travel writers 6. Radio reporters 7. Nonfiction writers 8. Short story writers 9. Nobel laureates for literature

ISBN 0-940322-38-2

LC 99-49615

Naipaul writes about his experiences growing up as an Indian living in Trinidad, his travels in India, his education at Oxford, and his struggles as a young writer in London

The author "elegantly expresses hard-earned wisdom about literature and culture, the political stakes of history and the relationship between the writer and the world." N Y Times Book Rev

Napoleon I, Emperor of the French, 1769-1821

Schom, Alan. **Napoleon** Bonaparte; a life. HarperCollins Pubs. 1997 xxii, 888p hardcover o.p. pa $23.95 **92**

1. Emperors 2. France -- Kings and rulers

ISBN 0-06-092958-8 pa

LC 97-5805

"Schom's judgments have all the more impact for being brief and infrequent. What really interests him is telling the story of the man who made universal rules for others but recognized none for himself. He tells it straightforwardly and well; and not, thankfully, at the multi-volume length he believes the subject still really requires." Times Lit Suppl

Includes bibliographical references

Nash, Ogden, 1902-1971

Parker, Douglas M. **Ogden** Nash; the life and work of America's laureate of light verse. with a foreword by Dana Gioia. Ivan R. Dee 2005 316p il $27.50 **92**

1. Poets 2. Authors 3. Humorists 4. Children's authors

ISBN 1-566-63637-X

LC 2004-59912

"Parker's is a useful, highly readable biography of one of America's best-loved poets." Publ Wkly

Includes bibliographical references

Navasky, Victor S.

Navasky, Victor S. A **matter** of opinion. Farrar, Straus and Giroux 2005 458p $27 **92**

1. Authors 2. Journalists 3. Magazine editors 4. Nation (Periodical)

ISBN 0-374-29997-8

LC 2004-59395

"Anybody who has ever dreamed of starting a magazine, or worried that the country is losing the ability to speak seriously to itself, should read 'A Matter of Opinion.'" N Y Times Book Rev

Navratilova, Martina, 1956-

Howard, Johnette. The **rivals**; Chris Evert vs. Martina Navratilova: their epic duels and extraordinary friendship. Broadway Books 2005 296p il $24.95 **92**

1. Tennis players 2. Tennis -- Biography

ISBN 0-7679-1884-3

LC 2004-61918

"In sixteen years, Chris Evert and Martina Navratilova met on the tennis court eighty times—sixty times in finals. . . . [This book examines] the intertwined lives of these [athletes]." Publisher's note

"This work makes a fine contribution to the history of women in sports." Publ Wkly

Needham, Joseph, 1900-1995

Winchester, Simon. The **man** who loved China; the fantastic story of the eccentric scientist who unlocked the mysteries of the Middle Kingdom. HarperCollins Publishers 2008 316p il map $27.95 **92**

1. Scientists 2. Biochemists 3. Science historians 4. Writers on science 5. Biography, Individual 6. Science -- China -- History

ISBN 978-0-06-088459-8; 0-06-088459-2

LC 2007-40516

The author "explores Needham's fascinating and sometimes controversial personal life, his travels to China, and especially the significance and topicality of his scholarship on the early accomplishments of Chinese science and technology. . . . Essential for all libraries." Libr J

Includes bibliographical references

Neel, Alice, 1900-1984

Hoban, Phoebe. **Alice** Neel; the art of not sitting pretty. St. Martin's Press 2010 500p il $35 **92**

1. Artists 2. Painters 3. Women artists

ISBN 978-0-312-60748-7; 0-312-60748-7

LC 2010-35781

"This biography of the American painter is also a "cultural history of the artistic and political scene in 20th-century New York." Publ Wkly

"Judicious and ardent, Hoban has created a galvanizing portrait of a 'rebel artist' who remained true to her humanist convictions." Booklist

Includes bibliographical references

Nehru, Jawaharlal, 1889-1964

Brown, Judith M. **Nehru** : a political life. Yale University Press 2003 407p il $35   **92**
1. Prime ministers 2. Nonfiction writers 3. Prime ministers -- India
ISBN 0-300-09279-2

LC 2003-5807

"This compelling biography, the most complete and penetrating account of Nehru yet written, casts new light on both the public and private man. It also offers insights into the history of India's nationalist movement and the complexities of constructing a new nation state in the aftermath of imperial rule." Univ Press Books for Public and Second Sch Libr, 2004

Includes bibliographical references

Nelson, Horatio Nelson, Viscount, 1758-1805

Hibbert, Christopher. **Nelson**; a personal history. Addison-Wesley 1994 472p il hardcover o.p. pa $22   **92**
1. Admirals
ISBN 0-201-40800-7 pa

LC 94-39545

The book "succeeds admirably in presenting a vivid and intimate picture of Nelson and Lady Hamilton together, helped by numerous and apt illustrations, half of them in colour. . . . The result is essentially a book of domestic detail, told with charm and perception." Times Lit Suppl

Includes bibliographical references

Sugden, John. **Nelson** : a dream of glory, 1758-1797. Henry Holt 2004 943p il map $35   **92**
1. Admirals
ISBN 0-8050-7757-X

LC 2004-54057

"This first of a projected two-volume study covers the least familiar period of Nelson's life, from childhood through his rise to international fame in 1797. . . . Sugden's account of Nelson's early career certainly bids fair to fill the gaps, ranging from the future admiral's first years to the disastrous action off Tenerife. . . . Sugden has done well here." Libr J

Includes bibliographical references (p. 883-906)

Nelson, Paul

Avery, Kevin. **Everything** is an afterthought; the life and writings of Paul Nelson. Fantagraphics Books 2011 xxvi, 497p il $29.99   **92**
1. Journalists 2. Music critics 3. Writers on music 4. Rock music -- History and criticism
ISBN 978-1-60699-475-7

"Seamlessly incorporating the perspectives of Nick Tosches, Robert Christgau, and Jann Wenner, Avery has crafted both a cautionary tale and a celebration of a noir-influenced writer who deserves a place alongside Lester Bangs for his ability to live, always, in the music. Devotees of folk, establishment rock 'n' roll, and pulp fiction will rue not having discovered Nelson sooner." Libr J

Includes bibliographical references

Nelson, Willie

★ Patoski, Joe Nick. **Willie** Nelson; an epic life. Little, Brown 2008 567p il $27.99; pa $16.99 **92**
1. Singers 2. Country musicians 3. Songwriters
ISBN 978-0-316-01778-7; 0-316-01778-7; 978-0-316-01779-4 pa; 0-316-01779-5 pa

LC 2007-44984

A biography of the country music singer and songwriter.

"This impressive, entertaining chronicle of Willie Nelson's life is replete with exactly what you'd expect—honky-tonk, long nights on the open road, whiskey, womanizing and weed—but . . . [the author] looks beyond country music trappings to find the funny, talented, determined man who became an unlikely icon." Publ Wkly

Includes discography and bibliographical references

Nemat, Marina

Nemat, Marina. **Prisoner** of Tehran; a memoir. Free Press 2007 306p $26   **92**
1. Political prisoners 2. Memoirists 3. Iran -- History -- 1979-
ISBN 1-4165-3742-2; 978-1-4165-3742-7

LC 2006-50191

Nemat was sixteen when she was arrested in Iran in early 1982 for political protests against the new fundamentalist regime. This is an account of her prison experiences.

The author's "story is not so much a political history lesson than it is a memoir of faith and love, a protest against violence that cannot be silenced. . . . Her persistence in standing for goodness is a lesson for us all." Christ Sci Monit

Neruda, Pablo, 1904-1973

★ Feinstein, Adam. **Pablo** Neruda; a passion for life. Bloomsbury 2004 497p il $32.50; pa $18.95   **92**
1. Poets 2. Authors 3. Diplomats 4. Novelists 5. Nobel laureates for peace 6. Nobel laureates for literature
ISBN 1-582-34410-8; 1-582-34594-5 pa

LC 2004-715

"Feinstein undoubtedly researched every existent source and found new ones, and the result is a detailed and accurate biography. . . . This is a necessary book, with many beautiful photos." Publ Wkly

Includes bibliographical references

Urrutia, Matilde. **My** life with Pablo Neruda; {translated by} Alexandra Giardino. Stanford University Press 2004 318p $27.95   **92**
1. Poets 2. Authors 3. Diplomats 4. Novelists 5. Nobel laureates for peace 6. Nobel laureates for literature
ISBN 0-8047-5009-2

LC 2004-8535

Original Spanish edition, 1986

"Urrutia, Neruda's third wife, provides a . . . biography from her particular vantage. Her purpose is twofold: to present her Pablo as the exuberant, warm, and loving individual he was and to inform readers of the menace imposed by Chilean dictator Pinochet, who was responsible for the assassination of elected president Allende, Neruda's close friend. Urrutia's account is highly selective but well worth reading for another perspective on this great man." Libr J

Newman, Paul, 1925-2008

Levy, Shawn. **Paul** Newman; a life. Harmony Books 2009 490p il $29.99; pa $16   **92**
1. Actors 2. Motion picture directors 3. Automobile racing drivers
ISBN 978-0-307-35375-7; 0-307-35375-3; 978-0-307-35376-4 pa; 0-307-35376-1 pa
LC 2009-11220

This is a behind-the-scenes examination of the actor's life, from his merry pranks on the set to his lasting romance with Joanne Woodward to the devastating impact of his son's death from a drug overdose

"An illuminating look at one of the true greats, full of humor and intelligent analysis—highly recommended." Kirkus
Includes bibliographical references

Newton, Isaac Sir, 1642-1727

Fara, Patricia. **Newton** : the making of genius. Columbia Univ. Press 2002 347p il $83.50; pa $23   **92**
1. Physicists 2. Scientists 3. Mathematicians 4. Writers on science
ISBN 0-231-12806-1; 0-231-12807-X pa
LC 2003-265510

This "social history examines the reasons behind Isaac Newton's canonization as scientific genius. . . . Fara contributes to Newton's biography by focusing on the roots of Newton's apotheosis. She examines how idealized portraits propagated Newton's public image, and how the marketing of Newtonian images outside academic circles commercialized science in the same way Einstein's face sells today. Throughout, Fara, . . . effectively employs the words and imagery of religious discourse to characterize the idealization and commercialization of Newton in the service of emerging secular politics and culture." Publ Wkly
Includes bibliographical references

Gleick, James. **Isaac** Newton. Pantheon Bks. 2003 272p il hardcover o.p. pa $13   **92**
1. Physicists 2. Scientists 3. Mathematicians 4. Writers on science
ISBN 0-375-42233-1; 1-4000-3295-4 pa
LC 2002-192696

This "is now the biography of choice for the interested layman. Gleick copes with the complex tapestry of Newton's interests by teasing them apart into individual chapters, assembled into a smooth chronological flow. . . . Newton the man emerges from the shadows." N Y Times Book Rev
Includes bibliographical references

Levenson, Thomas. **Newton** and the counterfeiter; the unknown detective career of the world's greatest scientist. Houghton Mifflin Harcourt 2009 318p $25; pa $14.95   **92**
1. Physicists 2. Mathematicians 3. Counterfeits and counterfeiting 4. Counterfeiters 5. Writers on science
ISBN 978-0-15-101278-7; 0-15-101278-4; 978-0-547-33604-6 pa; 0-547-33604-7 pa
LC 2008-53511

"Levenson demonstrates a surpassing felicity in his brisk treatment of this late-17th-century true-crime adventure. . . . Swift, agile treatment of a little known but highly entertaining episode in a legendary life." Kirkus
Includes bibliographical references

Westfall, Richard S. The **life** of Isaac Newton. Cambridge Univ. Press 1993 328p il hardcover o.p. pa $16   **92**
1. Physicists 2. Scientists 3. Mathematicians 4. Writers on science
ISBN 0-521-47737-9 pa
LC 92-33777

In this book the author has "reduced his longer 1980 biography of Newton (Never at Rest) to a size that is more suitable for general audiences. The result is a work whose faults lie only in the paucity of source materials that all Newton biographers face. . . . Westfall's book comes as close to presenting the man as the impersonal evidence allows without undue extrapolation." Sci Books Films
Includes bibliographical references

Nicholas II, Emperor of Russia, 1868-1918

Ferro, Marc. **Nicholas** II; the last of the tsars. translated by Brian Pearce. Oxford Univ. Press 1993 305p il map hardcover o.p. pa $19.95   **92**
1. Emperors 2. Russia -- History 3. Russia -- Kings and rulers
ISBN 0-19-509382-8 pa
LC 92-41440

"The last Tsar, as this fluently written biography makes abundantly clear, was largely to blame for the demise of the monarchy. Ferro is concerned to illuminate the personality of the Tsar, his relationship with his wife and Rasputin and to look again at the circumstances surrounding his death." Hist Today
Includes bibliographical references

Massie, Robert K., 1929- **Nicholas** and Alexandra. Ballantine Books 2000 613p il map pa $18.95   **92**
1. Monks 2. Emperors 3. Empresses 4. Courtiers 5. Russia -- History 6. Russia -- Kings and rulers
ISBN 0-345-43831-0; 978-0-345-43831-7
LC 99-91507

First published 1967 by Atheneum

This study provides an intimate account of the Romanov family and the coming of the Russian Revolution. Kerensky, Lenin and Rasputin are among the personalities profiled.

This book, "solid with research, reads as lightly as a novel, as authoritatively as a textbook. Dialogue and lively description lend a sense of immediacy, but his notes, discreetly relegated to the back of the book, show how carefully he has avoided slipping into fiction." Christ Sci Monit
Includes bibliographical references

Nightingale, Florence, 1820-1910

Bostridge, Mark. **Florence** Nightingale; the making of an icon. Farrar, Straus and Giroux 2008 646p il $35 **92**

1. Nurses 2. Nonfiction writers
ISBN 978-0-374-15665-7; 0-374-15665-4

LC 2008-31424

Bostridge presents a "well-researched, and comprehensive biography of Nightingale, drawing heavily on letters, diaries, and other primary sources in a successful effort to create a balanced and authentic portrait of the woman, not the myth. Beginning with moving depictions of Nightingale's struggles to be allowed to pursue her calling despite her family's objections, Bostridge skillfully illuminates the spiritual and philosophical motivations that drove Nightingale's impassioned and lifelong dedication to the causes of nursing and public health reform." Libr J

Includes bibliographical references

Nitze, Paul H.

Thompson, Nicholas. The **hawk** and the dove; Paul Nitze, George Kennan, and the history of the Cold War. Henry Holt 2009 403p il $27.50 **92**

1. Authors 2. Cold war 3. Diplomats 4. Statesmen 5. Historians 6. Centenarians 7. Nonfiction writers 8. Government officials 9. Biography, Individual 10. Secretaries of the navy 11. United States -- Officials and employees 12. United States -- Foreign relations -- 1945-1989 13. National security -- United States -- History -- 20th century 14. Anti-communist movements -- United States -- History -- 20th century
ISBN 0805081429; 9780805081428

LC 2009-09225

This biography of Nitze and Kennan focuses on their "careers as statesmen, policy makers and public intellectuals." (N Y Times Book Rev) Index.

This book "does an inspired job of telling the story of the Cold War through the careers of two of its most interesting and important figures." Washington Monthly

Includes bibliographical references

Nixon, Richard M. (Richard Milhous), 1913-1994

Black, Conrad M. **Richard** M. Nixon; a life in full. [by] Conrad Black. PublicAffairs 2007 1152p il $40 **92**

1. Presidents 2. Vice-presidents 3. Senators 4. Nonfiction writers 5. Members of Congress 6. Presidents -- United States
ISBN 978-1-58648-519-1; 1-58648-519-9

LC 2007-34530

This is a biography of the thirty-seventh president.

"Black's superb volume, incorporating much new research, is an important and worthy addition to the literature." Publ Wkly

Includes bibliographical references

Dallek, Robert. **Nixon** and Kissinger; partners in power. HarperCollins Publishers 2007 740p il $32.50 **92**

1. Presidents 2. Vice-presidents 3. Senators 4. College teachers 5. Nonfiction writers 6. Members of Congress 7. Writers on politics 8. Secretaries of state

9. Presidential advisers 10. Nobel laureates for peace 11. United States -- Foreign relations 12. International relations specialists
ISBN 978-0-06-072230-2; 0-06-072230-4

LC 2006-52100

A look "behind the scenes at this quintessential pair of power brokers and their lasting influence, for good and ill, on the political stage." Bookmarks Magazine

Includes bibliographical references

Niyizonkiza, Deogratias, 1970-

Kidder, Tracy. **Strength** in what remains. Random House 2009 277p $26; pa $16 **92**

1. Genocide 2. Refugees 3. Students 4. Burundi
ISBN 978-1-4000-6621-6; 1-4000-6621-2; 978-0-8129-7761-5 pa; 0-8121-7761-0 pa

LC 2008-44865

This "book is the story of a young medical student from Burundi who barely survives the civil war and genocide during which many members of his family are killed. He spends months on the run in jungles and makeshift refugee camps, and finally manages to flee to New York City." N Y Times (Late N Y Ed)

"This profoundly gripping, hopeful and crucial testament is a work of the utmost skill, sympathy and moral clarity." Publ Wkly

Includes bibliographical references

Norris, Kathleen, 1947-

Norris, Kathleen. **Acedia** & me; a marriage, monks, and a writer's life. Riverhead Books 2008 334p $25.95 **92**

1. Poets 2. Apathy 3. Authors 4. Melancholy 5. Monasticism and religious orders 6. Inspirational writers
ISBN 978-1-59448-996-9

LC 2008-10150

In this memoir, the author examines the medieval concept of acedia or soul-weariness "in the light of theology, psychology, monastic spirituality, the healing powers of religious practice, and Norris's own experience." Publisher's note

"The result of Norris's decades-long meditation on acedia is peaceful, graceful prose, amplified by word histories and gentle humor." Christ Today

Includes bibliographical references

Norris, Michele, 1961-

Norris, Michele. The **grace** of silence; a memoir. Pantheon Books 2010 185p il $24.95; ebook $24.95 **92**

1. Journalists 2. Women journalists 3. Radio reporters 4. Television reporters 5. United States -- Race relations 6. African American women -- Biography
ISBN 978-0-307-37876-7; 978-0-307-37946-7 ebook

LC 2010-19285

"In examining her personal roots for this memoir, African American Norris . . . found some skeletons in her family's closet. For example, she discovered that in the early 20th century her grandmother had dressed as Aunt Jemina to pitch pancake flour to the wives of white farmers in the Midwest. Using her skills as an investigative reporter, Norris also pieces together details of an incident in 1946 when her father was shot by a white policeman in Birmingham, AL. . . . Norris's family history offers Americans of all races a moving and revealing account of the obstacles facing several generations of middle-class African Americans in the pre-Civil Rights era." Libr J

Includes bibliographical references

Northup, Solomon, 1808-1863

★ Northup, Solomon. **Twelve** years a slave; Solomon Northup ; introduction by Ira Berlin ; general editor Henry Louis Gates, Jr. Penguin Books 2012 xxxvi, 240 p.p ill., music (Penguin Classics) (pbk.) $16
92

1. Slaves -- United States -- 19th century 2. Slaves' writings, American 3. African Americans -- Biography 4. Slaves -- United States -- Biography 5. Slavery -- Louisiana -- History -- 19th century 6. Plantation life -- Louisiana -- History -- 19th century
ISBN 0143106708; 9780143106708

LC 2012012550

This autobiographical book "recounts how Solomon Northup, born a free man in New York, was lured to Washington, D.C., in 1841 with the promise of fast money, then drugged and beaten and sold into slavery. He spent the next twelve years of his life in captivity on a Louisiana cotton plantation. After his rescue, Northup published this . . . detailed account of slave life." (Publisher's note)

Includes bibliographical references and index

Novacek, Michael J.

Novacek, Michael J. **Time** traveler; in search of dinosaurs and ancient mammals from Montana to Mongolia. {by} Michael Novacek. Farrar, Straus & Giroux 2002 368p il $26; pa $15
92

1. Curators 2. Paleontologists
ISBN 0-374-27880-6; 0-374-52876-4 pa

LC 2001-40438

"The author first describes the youthful experiences that inspired him to become a paleontologist. . . . Then Novacek launches into his various expeditions. . . . Interweaving his adventures with explanations of where his finds fit into the geologic past, Novacek has combined the comedic with the informative in this entertaining survey of his career." Booklist

Includes bibliographical references

Nudelman, Meyer

Nuland, Sherwin B. **Lost** in America; a journey with my father. Knopf 2003 209p $24; pa $12
92

1. Authors 2. Surgeons 3. Factory workers 4. Writers on medicine
ISBN 0-375-41294-8; 0-375-75722-1 pa

LC 2002-40795

This is a "memoir about becoming an assimilated second-generation American from a home dominated by his angry, altogether unassimilable Orthodox Jewish father." N Y Times Book Rev

"Written with enormous empathy, yet without a hint of sentimentality, Nuland's memoir is both heartbreaking and breathtaking." Publ Wkly

Nuland, Sherwin B.

Nuland, Sherwin B. **Lost** in America; a journey with my father. Knopf 2003 209p $24; pa $12
92

1. Authors 2. Surgeons 3. Factory workers 4. Writers on medicine
ISBN 0-375-41294-8; 0-375-75722-1 pa

LC 2002-40795

"Written with enormous empathy, yet without a hint of sentimentality, Nuland's memoir is both heartbreaking and breathtaking." Publ Wkly

Nureyev, Rudolf, 1938-1993

★ Kavanagh, Julie. **Nureyev**; the life. Pantheon Books 2007 782p il $37.50
92

1. Ballet dancers
ISBN 978-0-375-40513-6; 0-375-40513-5

LC 2006-38137

In this biography of the Russian ballet dancer, the author "chronicles Nureyev's many tempestuous relationships, including his legendary work with Margot Fonteyn and his formative affair with the outstanding Danish dancer Erik Bruhn. . . . Kavanagh's consummate biography will stand as a pillar in dance history." Booklist

Includes bibliographical references

Nusseibeh, Sari

David, Anthony. **Once** upon a country; a Palestinian life. [by] Sari Nusseibeh, with Anthony David. Farrar, Straus and Giroux 2007 542p il $27.50
92

1. Philosophers 2. Palestinian Arabs 3. Israel-Arab conflicts 4. Political leaders 5. College presidents 6. Biography, Individual
ISBN 0-374-29950-1; 978-0-374-29950-7

LC 2006-13272

This is an autobiography by "Sari Nusseibeh, a Palestinian intellectual and public figure." (N Y Times (Late N Y Ed))

"This is a rare book, one written by a partisan in the struggle over Palestine who nevertheless recognizes—and bravely records—the moral and political failures of his own people." Los Angeles Times

Includes bibliographical references

O'Brien, Edna

O'Brien, Edna, 1930- **Country** Girl; A Memoir. by Edna O'Brien. Little, Brown and Co. 2013 x, 357 p.p ill. (hardcover) $27.99
92

1. Authors 2. Women authors -- Biography 3. Women authors, Irish -- 20th century -- Biography
ISBN 031612270X; 9780316122702

LC 2012047510

This memoir, written by Edna O'Brien, starts "with [her] birth in a grand but deteriorating house in Ireland, [and] moves through convent school to elopement, divorce, single-motherhood, the wild parties of the [1960s] in London, and encounters with Hollywood giants, pop stars, and literary titans. There is love and unrequited love, and the glamour of trips to America as an acclaimed writer hosted by Jackie Onassis and Hillary Clinton." (Publisher's note)

"While O'Brien overly devotes her time to cataloguing the notable actors, writers, and politicians of her acquaintance, the accounts of her childhood and her descriptions of Ireland soar with a lyricism reminiscent of Joyce." LJ

O'Connor, Flannery

Cash, Jean W. **Flannery** O'Connor: a life. University of Tenn. Press 2002 356p il $30; pa $24.95   **92**

1. Authors 2. Novelists 3. Short story writers
ISBN 1-572-33192-5; 1-572-33305-7 pa
LC 2002-250

"Cash analyzes the woman behind the myth, introducing an extraordinarily intelligent human being noted for her keen sense of humor, intellectual versatility, and tremendous capacity for friendship. This intimate chronicle of a major literary talent will appeal to both students and scholars." Booklist

Includes bibliographical references

★ Gooch, Brad. **Flannery**; a life of Flannery O'Connor. Little, Brown and Co. 2009 448p il $30   **92**

1. Authors 2. Novelists 3. Women authors 4. Authors, American 5. Short story writers 6. Biography, Individual
ISBN 978-0-316-00066-6; 0-316-00066-3
LC 2008-28504

This biography of writer Flannery O'Connor, by Brad Gooch, focuses on "O'Connor's significant friendships--with Robert Lowell, Elizabeth Hardwick, Walker Percy, and James Dickey among others--and her deeply felt convictions, as expressed in her communications with Thomas Merton, Elizabeth Bishop, and Betty Hester. . . . O'Connor's capacity to live fully--despite the chronic disease that eventually confined her to her mother's farm in Georgia" is also discussed. (Publisher's note)

"Gooch comfortably traces her fiction to its real-life roots in a meticulous yet seemingly effortless writing style, resulting in the definitive biography as well as providing the impetus for general readers to return to O'Connor's timeless fiction." Booklist

Includes bibliographical references

O'Connor, Flannery. The **habit** of being; letters. edited and with an introduction by Sally Fitzgerald. Farrar, Straus & Giroux 1979 617p hardcover o.p. pa $20   **92**

1. Authors 2. Novelists 3. Short story writers
ISBN 0-374-52104-2 pa
LC 78-11559

This collection includes letters to friends in the literary establishment: Robert Lowell and Elizabeth Hardwick, Caroline Gordon Tate, Robert and Sally Fitzgerald and others

O'Connor, Sandra Day

Biskupic, Joan. **Sandra** Day O'Connor; how the first woman on the Supreme Court became its most influential justice. Ecco 2005 419p il $26.95   **92**

1. Supreme Court justices
ISBN 0-06-059018-1
LC 2005-52103

The author "offers an insightful biography of perhaps the most influential associate justice in recent history." Libr J

Includes bibliographical references

O'Dell, Chris, 1947-

O'Dell, Chris. **Miss** O'Dell; my hard days and long nights with the Beatles, the Stones, Bob Dylan, Eric Clapton, and the women they loved. [by] Chris O'Dell with Katherine Ketcham. Touchstone 2009 403p il $26   **92**

1. Music industry 2. Hypnotists 3. Memoirists 4. Drug abuse counselors 5. Rock musicians -- Anecdotes
ISBN 978-1-416-59093-4; 1-416-59093-5
LC 2009-14555

"An irresistible memoir of one of the lesser lights of a major constellation of rock stars and their satellites." Kirkus

O'Keeffe, Georgia, 1887-1986

Drohojowska-Philp, Hunter. **Full** bloom; the art and life of Georgia O'Keeffe. W.W. Norton 2004 630p hardcover o.p. pa $21.95   **92**

1. Artists 2. Painters 3. Biography, Individual
ISBN 0-393-05853-0; 0-393-32741-8 pa
LC 2003-26071

This is a biography of the American painter.

"O'Keeffe lived a long, adventurous, and profoundly productive life, and Drohojowska-Philp charts her triumphs over adversity in an involving, revelatory biography that attains the grand scope and depth her subject deserves." Booklist

Includes bibliographical references

O'Malley, Walter Francis, 1903-1979

D'Antonio, Michael. **Forever** blue; the true story of Walter O'Malley, baseball's most controversial owner, and the Dodgers of Brooklyn and Los Angeles. Riverhead Books 2009 355p il $25.95   **92**

1. Baseball executives 2. Baseball -- Biography 3. Brooklyn Dodgers (Baseball team) 4. Los Angeles Dodgers (Baseball team)
ISBN 978-1-59448-856-6; 1-59448-856-8
LC 2008-46311

"This is a wonderfully readable, insightful, and—for anyone interested in baseball history—important biography of the man who forever changed the course of the game in America." Booklist

Includes bibliographical references

O'Reilly, Bill

O'Reilly, Bill. A **bold** fresh piece of humanity. Broadway Books 2008 256p il $26   **92**

1. Journalists 2. Talk show hosts 3. Television reporters 4. Television moderators
ISBN 978-0-7679-2882-3; 0-7679-2882-2
LC 2008-25510

This is a memoir by the broadcaster and author of The O'Reilly Factor (2000), The No Spin Zone (2001), and Who's Looking Out For You? (2003).

O'Rourke, Barbara Kelly, d. 2008

O'Rourke, Meghan. The **long** goodbye; a memoir. Riverhead Books 2011 306p $25.95   **92**
1. Poets 2. Authors 3. Bereavement 4. Mother-daughter relationship 5. Essayists 6. Cancer patients 7. Poets, American 8. Magazine editors 9. Biography, Individual 10. Mothers and daughters
ISBN 978-1-59448-798-9

LC 2010047948

"The raw feelings, the inevitable self-pity over each person's own loss, and their futile wishes to somehow make Mother's last days not be her last days will likely feel all too close to home for many who have suffered similarly. . . . Every tear-stained page is not a road map, but rather a lovely gift from a fellow traveler." Booklist

Includes bibliographical references

O'Rourke, Meghan

O'Rourke, Meghan. The **long** goodbye; a memoir. Riverhead Books 2011 306p $25.95   **92**
1. Poets 2. Authors 3. Bereavement 4. Mother-daughter relationship 5. Essayists 6. Cancer patients 7. Poets, American 8. Magazine editors 9. Biography, Individual 10. Mothers and daughters
ISBN 978-1-59448-798-9

LC 2010047948

"The raw feelings, the inevitable self-pity over each person's own loss, and their futile wishes to somehow make Mother's last days not be her last days will likely feel all too close to home for many who have suffered similarly. . . . Every tear-stained page is not a road map, but rather a lovely gift from a fellow traveler." Booklist

Includes bibliographical references

O'Shea, James

O'Shea, James. The **deal** from hell; how moguls and Wall Street plundered great American newspapers. PublicAffairs 2011 395p $28.99   **92**
1. Journalists 2. Los Angeles times 3. Newspaper editors 4. Newspaper executives 5. Newspapers -- United States 6. Cooperative organization administrators
ISBN 978-1-58648-791-1; 978-1-58648-865-9 ebook

LC 2011009204

In this book, James O'Shea "details the development, events, and aftermath of the Tribune Company's 2007 purchase by investor Sam Zell. . . . O'Shea suggests the 'deal from hell' resulted from executive malpractice that unnecessarily jeopardized the financial and journalistic status quo of a declining--but profitable--mass-media conglomerate." (Choice: Current Reviews for Academic Libraries)

The author "recounts the events leading to the dissolution of several major American newspapers in this gripping story of a troubled industry. Told from the 'front-row,' O'Shea shows how ill-advised mergers, mismanagement, acquisitive Wall Street execs, and the Tribune Company's eventual bankruptcy filing crippled an industry. . . . For those who want an inside look at what makes American journalism work (and not work), O'Shea offers a unique and valuable perspective." Publ Wkly

Includes bibliographical references

Oates, Joyce Carol, 1938-

★ Oates, Joyce Carol. The **journal** of Joyce Carol Oates: 1973-1982; edited by Greg Johnson. Ecco 2007 509p il $29.95   **92**
1. Poets 2. Authors 3. Novelists 4. Women authors 5. Essayists 6. Authors, American 7. Children's authors 8. Short story writers
ISBN 978-0-06-122798-1; 0-06-122798-6

LC 2007-29378

This is a collection of diaries from the period when Oates published Do With Me What You Will (1973), Bellefleur (1980), and other works.

"This journal immerses the reader in a complex, searching, imaginative personality—an artist who continues to refine her search for literary expression." Publ Wkly

Includes bibliographical references

Oates, Joyce Carol, 1938- A **widow's** story; a memoir. Ecco 2011 415p il $27.99   **92**
1. Poets 2. Widows 3. Authors 4. Novelists 5. Bereavement 6. Loss (Psychology) 7. Essayists 8. Biographers 9. Magazine editors 10. Authors, American 11. Children's authors 12. Short story writers 13. Biography, Individual 14. Spouses of prominent persons
ISBN 9780062015532

This is an account of the novelist's loss of her "husband of 47 years, Raymond J. Smith. . . . He collaborated with his wife in founding The Ontario Review as well as Ontario Review Books." (N Y Times (Late N Y Ed))

"In a narrative as searing as the best of her fiction, Oates describes the aftermath of her husband Ray's unexpected death from pneumonia. Scattershot moments stand out — the day she cancels their 30-year subscription to The New York Times, unable to bear the sight of his favorite paper; her fury at the tulips, harbingers of spring, pushing through the snow ('Too soon! This is too soon!'); the night she weans herself from Lorazepam. A Widow's Story is the painful, scorchingly angry journey of a woman struggling to live in a house 'from which meaning has departed, like air leaking from a balloon.'" Entertainment Wkly

Obama, Barack, 1961-

Alter, Jonathan. The **promise**; President Obama, year one. Simon & Schuster 2010 458p il $28; ebook $12.99   **92**
1. Lawyers 2. Presidents 3. Senators 4. State legislators 5. Nobel laureates for peace 6. Presidents -- United States 7. United States -- Politics and government -- 2001- 8. United States -- Politics and government -- 2009-
ISBN 978-1-4391-0119-3; 978-1-4391-5408-3 ebook

LC 2010-20438

"Alter's writing is sharp. His tone is breezy and engaging but appropriate to the subject matter. No deep, dark secrets are revealed, but readers will come away from this book with a good idea of how the Obama administration understands itself." Commonweal

Includes bibliographical references

Mendell, David. **Obama**; from promise to power. Amistad 2007 406p il $25.95; pa $14.95   **92**
1. Lawyers 2. Presidents 3. Racially mixed people 4. Senators 5. State legislators 6. Nobel laureates for peace 7. Presidents -- United States 8. African Americans -- Biography 9. United States -- Congress -- Senate
ISBN 978-0-06-085820-9; 0-06-085820-6; 978-0-06-085821-6 pa; 0-06-085821-4 pa
This is a biography of President Barack Obama
The author "draws on interviews with Obama, his wife, family, friends, aides, and rivals, as well as his own extensive coverage since Obama's days in the Illinois Senate, to offer a nuanced, compelling look at a man of idealism and ambition intent on making history." Booklist
Includes bibliographical references

★ Obama, Barack. **Dreams** from my father; a story of race and inheritance. Crown Publishers 2007 442p $25.95   **92**
1. Presidents 2. Racially mixed people 3. Senators 4. State legislators 5. Nobel laureates for peace 6. Presidents -- United States 7. African Americans -- Biography
ISBN 978-0-307-38341-9

LC 2007-271892
First published 1995 by Times Books
This is the autobiography of the Illinois senator who would later become the 44th president of the United States.
The author "offers an account of his life's journey that reflects brilliantly on the power of race consciousness in America. . . . Obama writes well; his account is sensitive, probing, and compelling." Choice [review of 1995 edition]

★ Remnick, David, 1958- The **bridge**; the life and rise of Barack Obama. Alfred A. Knopf 2010 656p il $29.95   **92**
1. Presidents 2. Racially mixed people 3. Senators 4. State legislators 5. Biography, Individual 6. Nobel laureates for peace 7. Presidents -- United States 8. African Americans -- Biography 9. United States -- Politics and government -- 2001-2009
ISBN 978-1-4000-4360-6; 1-4000-4360-3

LC 2010-922697
This is a biography of the 44th president of the United States.
Writing with emotional precision and a sure knowledge of politics, Mr. Remnick situates Mr. Obama's career firmly within a historical context. He puts Mr. Obama's life and political philosophy in perspective with the civil rights movement that shaped his imagination, as well as the power politics of Chicago, and the politics of race as it has been played out, often nastily, on the state and national stages. N Y Times (Late N Y Ed)
Includes bibliographical references (p. [617]-623) and index

Oher, Michael, 1986-
★ Lewis, Michael. The **blind** side; evolution of a game. W.W. Norton 2006 299p $24.95   **92**
1. College sports 2. Football players 3. Biography, Individual 4. Football -- Biography 5. College sports -- United States
ISBN 0-393-06123-X; 978-0-393-06123-9

LC 2006-23509
Michael Oher, the young man at the center of this story, "will one day be among the most highly paid athletes in the National Football League. When we first meet him, he is one of thirteen children by a mother addicted to crack; he does not know his real name, his father, his birthday, or any of the things a child might learn in school—such as, say, how to read or write. Nor has he ever touched a football. What changes? He takes up football, and school, after a rich, Evangelical, Republican family plucks him from the . . . streets. Their love is the first great force that alters the world's perception of the boy, whom they adopt. The second force is the evolution of professional football itself into a game where the quarterback must be protected at any cost. Our protagonist turns out to be the priceless combination of size, speed, and agility necessary to guard the quarterback's greatest vulnerability: his blind side." (Publisher's note)
The author "describes the NFL's ever-growing obsession with left tackles as a means to counter defenders who seem to grow bigger, stronger, and more vicious each season. He juxtaposes that narrative with the unlikely story of [football player] Michael Oher. . . . The book works on three levels. First as a shrewd analysis of the NFL; second, as an expose of the insanity of big-time college football recruiting; and, third, as a moving portrait of the positive effect that love, family, and education can have in reversing the path of a life that was destined to be lived unhappily and, most likely, end badly." Booklist

Ol' Dirty Bastard, 1969-2004
Lowe, Jaime. **Digging** for dirt; the life and death of ODB. Faber and Faber 2008 273p $25   **92**
1. Rap music 2. African American musicians 3. Rap musicians
ISBN 978-0-8654-7969-2; 0-8654-7969-0

LC 2008-29144
"As one of Wu Tang Clan, Russell Jones became known for his off-kilter raps and odd stage mannerisms. Like bandmates Method Man and Ghostface Killah, he also had a solo career as Ol' Dirty Bastard (ODB) that placed two number-one albums on the rap charts, and his duet with Mariah Carey, 'Fantasy,' brought mainstream success. Simply put, life was good. As time went by, though, he devolved into a more and more disturbed state, and some of his entertaining traits came to suggest mental-health issues. . . . Seemingly unable to avoid incarceration for a variety of offenses, he died of 'heart failure after cerebral hemorrhaging,' arguably caused by years of drug and other abuse. Lowe tells ODB's tale admirably thoroughly, making this a must-have profile of a singular personality and another sad casualty in rap history." Booklist

Ollestad, Norman, 1968-
Ollestad, Norman. **Crazy** for the storm; a memoir of survival. Ecco 2009 272p il $25.99   **92**
1. Aircraft accidents 2. Father-son relationship 3.

Memoirists
ISBN 978-0-06-176672-5; 0-061-76672-0

LC 2008-53675

"In the winter of 1979, the 11-year-old Ollestad survived a plane crash in which his father and his father's girlfriend were killed. Alternating with young Norman's nine-hour trek to safety are scenes from the year preceding the crash, when the boy took a surfing trip with his father through the jungle along Mexico's Pacific coast. The flashbacks sections are the most fascinating parts of the book, and Ollestad ably captures the contrast between his charismatically cool father, Norman Sr., and his bullying stepfather-to-be, Nick. . . . [He] presents a captivating account of high-altitude disaster that nicely dovetails with his coming-of-age story in '70s California. Deep and resonant." Kirkus

Onassis, Jacqueline Kennedy, 1929-1994

Bowles, Hamish. **Jacqueline** Kennedy; the White House Years: selections from the John F. Kennedy Library and Museum. {compiled and edited by} Hamish Bowles; with essays by Arthur Schlesinger, Jr., Hamish Bowles, and James Wagner. Bulfinch Press 2001 198p il $50   **92**
1. Editors 2. Socialites 3. Spouses of presidents
ISBN 0-8212-2745-9

LC 00-66237

The selections "examine in detail different aspects of Jackie's life, including the inauguration, her White House style, her travels, and her hats, as well as other topics. . . . Viewers can expect a sense of nostalgia, a swelling of pride, and a tightening of the throat. A time line of Jackie's life is appended." Booklist

Davis, John H. **Jacqueline** Bouvier; an intimate memoir. [by] John Davis. Wiley 1996 208p il $24.95; pa $14.95   **92**
1. Editors 2. Socialites 3. Spouses of presidents
ISBN 0-471-12945-3; 0-471-24944-0 pa

LC 96-4332

"Davis is an engaging writer, and although many of the facts of his story will be known by Kennedy aficionados, there is a wistful sweetness to his writing that captures both the woman and the era of privileged upbringings." Booklist

Oppenheimer, Frank, 1912-1985

Cole, K. C. **Something** incredibly wonderful happens; Frank Oppenheimer and the world he made up. Houghton Mifflin Harcourt 2009 396p il $27   **92**
1. Physicists 2. College teachers 3. Biography, Individual 4. Museum administrators
ISBN 978-0-15-100822-3; 0-15-100822-1

LC 2008052954

This is a biography of the physicist and young brother of J. Robert Oppenheimer.

"In a thought-provoking and pleasant manner, Cole's much-welcomed book shines a new light on a remarkable man and scientist. Readers interested in good popular science biographies will enjoy this." Libr J

Includes bibliographical references

Oppenheimer, J. Robert, 1904-1967

Bernstein, Jeremy. **Oppenheimer**; portrait of an enigma. Dee, I.R. 2004 223p il $25   **92**
1. Physicists 2. College teachers 3. Government officials
ISBN 1-566-63569-1

LC 2003-66652

The author "recounts Oppenheimer's eclectic life as it evolved in the US through his education and service at several prestigious institutions. . . . The book is not a review of Oppenheimer's contributions to physics or the development of the atomic bomb; rather, it provides insight into the human side of a brilliant individual, all things considered. Of course, his leadership of the Manhattan Project, and his persecution by Congress for alleged communist sympathies, defined Oppenheimer's career. Bernstein provides personalized insights into both." Choice

Includes bibliographical references

★ Bird, Kai. **American** Prometheus; the triumph and tragedy of J. Robert Oppenheimer. [by] Kai Bird and Martin J. Sherwin. Knopf 2005 721p il hardcover o.p. pa $18.95   **92**
1. Physicists 2. College teachers 3. Government officials
ISBN 0-375-41202-6; 0-375-72626-8 pa

LC 2004-61535

The authors explore Oppenheimer's life "from his youth as a child prodigy through his radical political activities in the 1930s, and on to the Manhattan Project and its political fallout. The humanity of the troubled man behind the porkpie hat emerges on every page of this unquestionably definitive account." Booklist

Includes bibliographical references

★ Monk, Ray. **Robert** Oppenheimer; a life inside the center. Ray Monk. 1st American ed. Doubleday 2013 xvi, 825 p.p (hardback) $37.50   **92**
1. Atomic bomb -- History 2. Physicists -- Biography 3. Physicists -- United States -- Biography 4. Atomic bomb -- United States -- History -- 20th century 5. Physicists -- United States -- Intellectual life -- 20th century
ISBN 0385504071; 9780385504072

LC 2012046045

This book by Ray Monk is a biography of physicist Robert Oppenheimer. "As a young professor at Berkeley, the wealthy, cultured Oppenheimer finally came into his own as a physicist and also began a period of support for Communist activities. . . . He was chosen to lead the Manhattan Project and develop . . . the atomic bomb. Upon its creation, Oppenheimer . . . refused to help create the far more powerful hydrogen bomb, bringing the wrath of McCarthyite suspicion upon him." (Publisher's note)

Includes bibliographical references and index

Orwell, George, 1903-1950

★ Taylor, David J. **Orwell** : the life; {by} D.J. Taylor. Holt & Co. 2003 466p il $30; pa $17 **92**
1. Authors 2. Novelists 3. Essayists
ISBN 0-8050-7473-2; 0-8050-7693-X pa

LC 2003-41747

"Starting with a . . . description of Orwell's funeral in 1950, Taylor . . . presents the years in India, the 'down and out' adventures, fighting in Spain, Orwell's work with the BBC during the war, and his final great novels. Taylor breaks the chronological flow with nine brief, interpretive essays (e.g., on Orwell's face, voice, and paranoia). . . . Taylor's book is a fresh and compelling life of the man he calls 'a light glinting in the darkness.'" Libr J

Includes bibliographical references

Osama bin Laden

Randal, Jonathan C. **Osama** : the making of a terrorist; {by} Jonathan Randal. Knopf 2004 339p $26.95   **92**

1. Terrorism 2. Terrorists
ISBN 0-375-40901-7

LC 2004-46522

The author's "meticulous account of the emergence and spread of the terror virus is less a biography of the strange, desiccated Saudi Arabian terrorist who heads Al Qaeda than a map of the world that produced him and his fellow Islamists. This is the biography of a hatred: deep, detailed, and depressing." N Y Times Book Rev

Includes bibliographical references

Scheuer, Michael. **Osama** bin Laden; [by] Michael Scheuer. Oxford University Press 2011 278p $19.95   **92**

1. Terrorists 2. Biography, Individual
ISBN 978-0-19-973866-3; 0-19-973866-1

LC 2010-21715

The author "offers a serious and nonideological treatment and analysis of bin Laden's thinking. Unlike many Western analysts who dismiss bin Laden as simplistic, uncouth, and incompetent, Scheuer portrays him as a patient, devout, and talented, albeit ruthless, leader who remains a formidable enemy of the West. . . . This informative book is one of the most detailed biographical sketches of bin Laden available in the West and is useful for both the general public and specialists." Libr J

Includes bibliographical references

Osborne, John, 1929-1994

Heilpern, John. **John** Osborne; the many lives of the angry young man. Alfred A. Knopf 2007 527p il $35   **92**

1. Authors 2. Dramatists
ISBN 978-0-375-40315-6; 0-375-40315-9

LC 2006-46575

First published 2006 in the United Kingdom

"Heilpern draws on Osborne's bleak private notebooks to generate acute readings of his often autobiographical plays. Sympathy for the man and admiration for the work don't blind Heilpern to his subject's outsized flaws. Osborne had a talent for invective and could be cruelly intolerant in matters large and small. He threatened theatre critics with physical violence by way of anonymous seaside postcards. Stung by his teenage daughter's indifference to high culture, he damned her as 'criminally commonplace' and never spoke to her again. Without excusing such 'breathtaking abuse,' Heilpern makes a compelling case for Osborne as a

necessary 'truthteller' and 'unyielding advocate of individualism in conformist times.'" New Yorker

Includes bibliographical references

Osbourne, Ozzy

Osbourne, Ozzy. **I** am Ozzy; [by] Ozzy Osbourne with Chris Ayres. Grand Central Publishing 2010 391p $26.99   **92**

1. Singers 2. Rock musicians 3. Black Sabbath (Musical group)
ISBN 978-0-446-56989-7

LC 2009-937230

"Osbourne offers the most detail about growing up and the Black Sabbath years – no surprise as you'd expect decades of drug use have nearly wiped clean those later years. He discusses his youth in England, his brief stint in jail, how a flier posted in a music store – 'Ozzy Zig Needs a Gig' – led to the eventual formation of Black Sabbath, his relationship with his wives and children, his own health scares, and The Osbournes television show. The book is written with Osbourne's wit and sense of humor as he shares laugh-out-loud tales of practical jokes while touring around the world and recording inside a castle. There's even a look at the sensitive side when he discusses the death of guitarist Randy Rhodes and his wife's (Sharon's) battle with cancer." Creative Loafing

Owens, Jesse, 1913-1980

Schaap, Jeremy. **Triumph**; the untold story of Jesse Owens and Hitler's Olympics. Houghton Mifflin 2007 272p il $24; pa $14.95   **92**

1. African American athletes 2. Olympic games, 1936 (Berlin, Ger.) 3. Olympic athletes 4. Runners (Athletes)
ISBN 978-0-618-68822-7; 0-618-68822-6; 978-0-618-91910-9 pa; 0-618-91910-4 pa

LC 2006-26926

"Schaap's chronicle of Jesse Owens's journey to and glorious triumph at the 1936 Berlin Olympics is snappy and dramatic, with an eye for the rousing climax." Publ Wkly

Includes bibliographical references

Oz, Amos

Oz, Amos. A **tale** of love and darkness; translated from the Hebrew by Nicholas de Lange. Harcourt 2004 538p $26   **92**

1. Authors 2. Novelists 3. Essayists 4. Short story writers
ISBN 0-15-100878-7

LC 2004-7302

This is "the story of a boy growing up in the wartorn Jerusalem of the forties and fifties, in a small apartment crowded with books in twelve languages and relatives speaking nearly as many. . . . When Oz was twelve and a half years old, his mother committed suicide, a tragedy that was to change his life. He leaves the constraints of the family and the community of dreamers, scholars, and failed businessmen and joins a kibbutz, changes his name, marries, has children, and finally becomes a writer as well as an active participant in the political life of Israel." Publisher's note

"A powerful story of the making of a writer . . . Oz's panoramic memoir enhances the history of literature and of Israel, and the literature of examined lives." Booklist

Paddleford, Clementine, 1900-1967

Alexander, Kelly. **Hometown** appetites; the story of Clementine Paddleford, the forgotten food writer who chronicled how America ate. by Kelly Alexander and Cynthia Harris; foreward by Coleman Andrews. Gotham Books 2008 318p il $27.50 **92**

1. Columnists 2. Food critics 3. Magazine editors
ISBN 978-1-592-40389-9; 1-592-40389-1

LC 2008-15264

This biography explores "Paddleford's career as food writer from 1936 to 1966 at the New York Herald Tribune. . . . The authors make an upbeat case for reconsidering Paddleford's achievement in this enjoyable read, and include a slew of her comfort recipes." Publ Wkly

Includes bibliographical references

Paige, Satchel, 1906-1982

Fox, William Price. **Satchel** Paige's America. University of Alabama Press 2005 142p pa $16.95 **92**

1. Baseball players 2. Baseball -- Biography
ISBN 0-8173-5189-2

LC 2004-18911

This biography is based upon the author's conversations with the legendary baseball pitcher as he spent a week following him around Kansas City, MO, in 1970.

This is "a lively, moving, and often hilarious tale of an encounter 30 years ago and of a life richly led." Libr J

Tye, Larry. **Satchel**; the life and times of an American legend. Random House 2009 392p il **92**

1. Baseball players 2. African American athletes 3. Baseball -- Biography 4. Biography, Individual 5. Negro leagues -- History
ISBN 0812977971; 1400066514; 9780812977974; 9781400066513

LC 2008-44858

A biography of the Negro League pitcher Satchel Paige "evaluates the role of discrimination in limiting his career, covering such topics as his near-defeat of a young Joe DiMaggio, the Jim Crow biases that prevented his signing with the big leagues until he was in his forties, and his [legacy]." (Publisher's note)

This is a "discerning, empathetic and hype-free [biography]. . . . While Paige's life has become the stuff of legend, its particulars are not easily verified. . . . Yet 'Satchel' makes a cool, clear, tenacious effort to find the real Paige behind all [the] hyperbole." N Y Times (Late N Y Ed)

Includes bibliographical references

Paine, Thomas, 1737-1809

Collins, Paul. The **trouble** with Tom: the strange afterlife and times of Thomas Paine. Bloomsbury 2005 278p map hardcover o.p. pa $15 **92**

1. Essayists 2. Pamphleteers 3. Writers on politics 4. Writers on religion 5. Political and social philosophers
ISBN 1-58234-502-3; 1-58234-613-5 pa

LC 2005-45240

The author "traces the bizarre story of Thomas Paine's remains through nearly two centuries of American and English history. . . . Part travelogue, part memoir and part historical mystery, this book reads like a wry, witty novel and offers a delicious twist at the end." Publ Wkly

Includes bibliographical references

Palin, Michael

Palin, Michael, 1943- **Halfway** to Hollywood; diaries 1980-1988. Thomas Dunne Books 2011 622p il $32.50 **92**

1. Actors 2. Authors 3. Comedians 4. Humorists 5. Screenwriters 6. Biography, Individual 7. Television scriptwriters 8. Monty Python (Comedy troupe)
ISBN 0312682026; 9780312682026

First published 2009 in the United Kingdom

This second volume of diaries by the Monty Python comedian traces the years during which the troupe completed their final performances together. Index.

Palmer, Arnold, 1929-

Palmer, Arnold. A **golfer's** life; {by} Arnold Palmer with James Dodson. Ballantine Bks. 1999 420p il hardcover o.p. pa $15 **92**

1. Golfers
ISBN 0-345-41482-9 pa

LC 98-51681

Palmer's "immense popularity is widely credited with rescuing professional golf in the late 1950s and 1960s. Written with humor and candor, the book recounts Palmer's friendships and rivalries with the greats of the game, his enduring marriage to Winnie Palmer, his legendary triumphs and disasters, and his battle against cancer." Libr J

Papp, Joseph

★ Turan, Kenneth. **Free** for all; Joe Papp, the Public, and the greatest theater story ever told. [by] Kenneth Turan and Joseph Papp; with the assistance of Gail Merrifield Papp. Doubleday 2009 592p il $39.95 **92**

1. Theatrical producers and directors 2. Theatrical directors 3. Theatrical producers 4. Joseph Papp Public Theater (New York, N.Y.)
ISBN 978-0-7679-3168-7

LC 2008-50887

"A wonderful book that clearly and powerfully shows that Papp's own story was the most enduring drama he ever produced." Kirkus

Paracelsus, 1493-1541

Webster, Charles. **Paracelsus**; medicine, magic and mission at the end of time. Yale University Press 2008 326p il $40 **92**

1. Alchemy 2. Physicians 3. Alchemists 4. Writers on science
ISBN 978-0-300-13911-2; 0-300-13911-X

LC 2008-27973

In this consideration of the "Renaissance doctor, alchemist, and theologian, Webster draws on nonscientific writings by Paracelsus that have been made widely available only in the past few decades. . . . [Paracelsus] orbited a wealthy and powerful class of physicians, but his unorthodox views made him a virtual 'vagrant' among his peers. He broke from the millennia-old theory of the humors, developing new medical theories based upon a mystical vision of man as a microcosm of the universe, and an alchemically informed notion of the intrinsic properties of certain metals. Webster paints Paracelsus as a 'religious and social controversialist,' and argues that the diverse strands of his thought were unified by his belief that the end of time was near, when, he imagined, the demise of physical suffering would obviate the need for medical intervention." New Yorker

Includes bibliographical references and index.

Parker, Charlie, 1920-1955

Crouch, Stanley, 1945- **Kansas** City lightning; the rise and times of Charlie Parker. by Stanley Crouch. Harper 2013 384 p. $27.99 **92**
1. Jazz musicians 2. Jazz musicians -- United States -- Biography
ISBN 0062005596; 9780062005595
LC 2013015773

This book, by Stanley Crouch, "is the first installment in . . . [a] portrait of one of the most talented and influential musicians of the twentieth century, from Stanley Crouch, one of the foremost authorities on jazz and culture in America. Drawing on interviews with peers, collaborators, and family members, 'Kansas City Lightning' recreates Parker's Depression-era childhood; his early days navigating the Kansas City nightlife." (Publisher's note)

Parker, Dorothy, 1893-1967

Meade, Marion. **Dorothy** Parker; what fresh hell is this? Penguin 1989 459p il pa $20 **92**
1. Poets 2. Authors 3. Humorists 4. Dramatists 5. Essayists 6. Screenwriters 7. Authors, American 8. Short story writers
ISBN 0-14-011616-8; 978-0-14-011616-8
LC 88-23782

First published 1988 by Villard Books

"The author has written a disturbing story of a writer whose life was marked by endless disturbances and self-depreciation, and who left behind no correspondence, manuscripts, or private papers. Under the circumstances, Ms. Meade has brilliantly reconstructed her subject's life. . . . The book is a tribute to a woman who left her mark on the literary history of her times and whose coruscating wit is still remembered." West Coast Rev Books

Includes bibliographical references

Parker, Quanah, Comanche Chief, 1845?-1911

Gwynne, S. C. **Empire** of the summer moon; Quanah Parker and the rise and fall of the Comanches, the most powerful Indian tribe in American history. Scribner 2010 371p il map $27.50 **92**
1. Comanche Indians 2. West (U.S.) -- History 3. Comanche Indians -- Wars 4. Western States -- History 5. Comanche Indians -- History 6. Frontier and pioneer life -- West (U.S.) 7. Frontier and pioneer life -- Western States
ISBN 978-1-4165-9105-4; 1-4165-9105-2
LC 2009049747

The author "tracks one of the U.S.'s longest-running military conflicts in this . . . history of the war against the Comanche Indians on the high plains of Texas and Colorado." Publ Wkly

"A welcome contribution to the history of Texas, Westward expansion and Native America." Kirkus

Includes bibliographical references

Parravani, Cara

Parravani, Christa, 1978- **Her**; a memoir. Christa Parravani. Henry Holt & Co 2013 320 p. $26 **92**
1. Twins 2. Sisters 3. Rape victims 4. Loss (Psychology) 5. Twins -- United States -- Biography 6. Sisters -- United States -- Biography
ISBN 0805096531; 9780805096538
LC 2012029499

In this memoir, author Christa Parravani "deconstructs the intense bonds between identical twins, the trauma of her sister's death and her battle against similar self-destruction. . . . Plagued by unstable and abusive father figures and poverty, [Christa and Cara] still managed to attend prestigious colleges, begin careers as artists and embark on marriages. But following a rape while out walking her dog, [Cara] began a terrifying descent into drugs and self-destruction." (Kirkus Reviews)

A "finely wrought achievement of grace, emotional honesty, and self-possession." Pub Wkly

Parravani, Christa

Parravani, Christa, 1978- **Her**; a memoir. Christa Parravani. Henry Holt & Co 2013 320 p. $26 **92**
1. Twins 2. Sisters 3. Rape victims 4. Loss (Psychology) 5. Twins -- United States -- Biography 6. Sisters -- United States -- Biography
ISBN 0805096531; 9780805096538
LC 2012029499

In this memoir, author Christa Parravani "deconstructs the intense bonds between identical twins, the trauma of her sister's death and her battle against similar self-destruction. . . . Plagued by unstable and abusive father figures and poverty, [Christa and Cara] still managed to attend prestigious colleges, begin careers as artists and embark on marriages. But following a rape while out walking her dog, [Cara] began a terrifying descent into drugs and self-destruction." (Kirkus Reviews)

A "finely wrought achievement of grace, emotional honesty, and self-possession." Pub Wkly

Parsons, Jack, 1914-1952

Pendle, George. **Strange** angel; the otherworldly life of rocket scientist John Whiteside Parsons. Harcourt 2005 350p il $25; pa $15 **92**
1. Scientists
ISBN 0-15-100997-X; 0-15-603179-5 pa
LC 2004-10666

"Marshaling a cast of characters ranging from Robert Millikan to L. Ron Hubbard, Pendle offers a fascinating glimpse into a world long past, a story that would make a compelling work of fiction if it weren't so astonishingly true." Publ Wkly

Includes bibliographical references

Pascal, Blaise, 1623-1662

Connor, James A. **Pascal's** wager; the man who played dice with God. HarperSanFrancisco 2006 224p il $24.95   **92**

1. Theologians 2. Mathematicians 3. Writers on religion

ISBN 978-0-06-076691-7; 0-06-076691-3

LC 2006-43489

This biography of the mathematician and theologian focuses on his Jansenist religious beliefs.

This book "should interest readers drawn to the crossroads of religion and science." Booklist

Includes bibliographical references

Patchett, Ann

Patchett, Ann, 1963- **This** Is the Story of a Happy Marriage; Ann Patchett. HarperCollins 2013 320 p. $27.99   **92**

1. Opera 2. Divorce 3. Human-animal relationship

ISBN 0062236679; 9780062236678

This is an essay collection from award-winning author Ann Patchett. She explores "some of the milestones of her life, such as her deep love for her dog, Rose (not to be confused with the desire for a baby), learning from scratch how to love opera in order to write her bestseller 'Bel Canto,' preparing with her ex-cop father's guidance for the grueling L.A. Police Academy exams ('The Wall'), . . . and her painful but merciful segue from divorce to remarriage." (Publishers Weekly)

Patel, Eboo, 1975-

Patel, Eboo. **Acts** of faith; the story of an American Muslim, the struggle for the soul of a generation. Beacon Press 2010 195p pa $14   **92**

1. Multiculturalism 2. Sociologists 3. Youth leaders 4. Religious leaders 5. Writers on religion 6. Organization officials 7. Muslims -- United States

ISBN 978-0-8070-0622-1; 0-8070-0622-X

LC 2010-537438

First published 2007

The author, "a founder of the Interfaith Youth Core, traces the personal journey that led to the group's formation and introduces readers to its philosophy." Kirkus

Includes bibliographical references

Paterniti, Michael

Paterniti, Michael. The **telling** room; a tale of love, betrayal, revenge, and the world's greatest piece of cheese. by Michael Paterniti. The Dial Press 2013 xii, 349 p.p (hbk. : alk. paper) $27   **92**

1. Cheese 2. Spain -- Description and travel 3. Spain -- Social life and customs 4. Guzmán (Spain) -- Biography 5. Cheesemaking -- Spain -- Guzmán -- History 6. Cheesemakers -- Spain -- Guzmán -- Biography

ISBN 0385337000; 9780385337007

LC 2013001430

This book, by Michael Paterniti, is "equal parts mystery and memoir, travelogue and history. A moving exploration of happiness, friendship, and betrayal, 'The Telling Room' introduces us to Ambrosio Molinos de las Heras, . . . a Spanish cheesemaker [who tells] compelling tale about a piece of cheese. An unusual piece of cheese. Made from an old family recipe, Ambrosio's cheese was reputed to be among the finest in the world, and was said to hold mystical qualities." (Publisher's note)

Includes bibliographical references and index

Paterson, Katherine

Paterson, Katherine. **Stories** of my life; by Katherine Paterson. Dial Books for Young Readers 2014 320 p. illustrations (hardcover) $17.99   **92**

1. Autobiographies 2. Women authors -- Biography 3. Children's stories -- Authorship 4. Authors, American -- 20th century -- Biography

ISBN 0803740433; 9780803740433

LC 2013042628

Author Katherine "Paterson's tales reveal details about her life from her childhood with missionary parents, to living as a single woman in Japan, to raising four children in suburban Maryland with her minister husband. . . . Filled with personal photos and letters, this . . . history from a legendary writer lets fans in on the making of literary classics." (Publisher's note)

"Written in a conversational style, these 'kitchen sink stories' will perhaps be received best by professional adults and readers who grew up with her books; much of what she recounts is about the distant past, courtship, and motherhood. What absolutely shines through is Paterson's warm, self-effacing humor, and the extraordinary humility of a writer who has won two National Book Awards, two Newbery Medals, and the Hans Christian Andersen Medal." Pub Wkly

Patterson, Floyd

Levy, Alan Howard. **Floyd** Patterson; a boxer and a gentleman. [by] Alan H. Levy. McFarland & Co. 2008 289p il pa $35   **92**

1. African American athletes 2. Boxers (Persons) 3. Boxing -- Biography

ISBN 978-0-7864-3950-8; 0-7864-3950-5

LC 2008-32250

This is a "biography of the man who was the youngest world heavyweight champion in boxing history as well as the first boxer to regain the championship after losing it. . . . This book is not only an excellent study of Patterson but a superior source on professional boxing from the mid-1950s through the mid-1970s." Libr J

Includes bibliographical references

Patton, George S. (George Smith), 1885-1945

D'Este, Carlo. **Patton**; a genius for war. HarperCollins Pubs. 1995 977p il maps hardcover o.p. pa $21   **92**

1. Generals 2. Army officers

ISBN 0-06-092762-3 pa

LC 95-38433

In this biography of the World War II general the author "provides new information from family archives and other sources about Patton's ancestry, childhood and pre-WW II military career. . . . The account of Patton's campaigns from North Africa through Sicily, Normandy and the Ardennes enables the reader to understand why the general is regarded as one of the great military leaders. This is a major biography of a major American military figure." Publ Wkly

Includes bibliographical references

★ Showalter, Dennis E. **Patton** and Rommel; men of war in the twentieth century. [by] Dennis Showalter. Berkley Caliber 2005 441p $24.95   **92**
1. Generals 2. World War, 1939-1945 3. Marshals 4. Army officers
ISBN 0-425-19346-2

LC 2004-57464

This is a "parallel biography of George Patton and Erwin Rommel. The research is thorough, the quality of the writing superb. . . . [The author] ranks as a scholar who has done them justice, making two complex men and a vast panorama of military history remarkably accessible for experts and lay readers alike." Publ Wkly

Paul, Alan, 1966-
Paul, Alan. **Big** in China; my unlikely adventures raising a family, playing the blues, and becoming a star in Beijing. HarperCollins Pub. 2011 282p $25.99; ebook $20.99   **92**
1. Journalists 2. Blues musicians 3. Bloggers 4. Columnists 5. Memoirists 6. Beijing (China)
ISBN 978-0-06-199315-2; 978-0-06-206582-7 ebook
"A rollicking, inspiring narrative with plenty of memorable characters and scenes." Libr J

Pelosi, Nancy, 1940-
Pelosi, Nancy. **Know** your power; a message to America's daughters. with Amy Hill Hearth. Doubleday 2008 180p $23.95; pa $14.95   **92**
1. Women politicians 2. Members of Congress 3. Speakers of the House 4. Politicians -- United States
ISBN 978-0-385-52586-2; 0-385-52586-9; 978-0-7679-2944-8 pa; 0-7679-2944-6 pa

LC 2008-20607

"In this graceful personal and political history, Pelosi describes growing up as the daughter of a congressman in an Italian-American Catholic world . . . and her burgeoning political interest. . . . Pelosi's book is a simply crafted acknowledgment of the support of her family, mentors and helpful colleagues without rhetorical flourishes, insider scandal or intimate revelations—a gentle account from a tough politician." Publ Wkly

Perelman, Grigori
Gessen, Masha. **Perfect** rigor; a genius and the mathematical breakthrough of the century. Houghton Mifflin Harcourt 2009 242p $26   **92**
1. Mathematicians
ISBN 978-0-15-101406-4; 0-15-101406-X

LC 2009-14742

"The story of Russian mathematical prodigy Grigory Perelman, who solved a problem that had stumped everyone for a century—then walked away from his chosen field. . . . [The author] paints a fascinating picture of the Soviet math establishment and of the mind of one of its most singular products. An engrossing examination of an enigmatic genius." Kirkus

Includes bibliographical references

Perkins, Frances, 1882-1965
Downey, Kirstin. The **woman** behind the New Deal; the life of Frances Perkins, FDR's Secretary of Labor and his moral conscience. Nan A. Talese 2009 458p il $35   **92**
1. Cabinet officers 2. College teachers 3. Secretaries of labor 4. State government officials 5. United States -- Dept. of Labor
ISBN 978-0-385-51365-4; 0-385-51365-8

LC 2008-23208

A biography of "one of FDR's confidants and the first female secretary of labor in U.S. history. . . . Like many biographers, Downey . . . is enamored of her subject. But her fascination serves her well, allowing her to construct an intriguing catalog of Perkins's achievements and explore the influences that held sway in her life, a psychological approach lacking in previous Perkins biographies. Here Perkins's triumphs and tragedies are compiled into a compelling narrative that never loses its scholarly touch." Libr J

Includes bibliographical references

Perry, Michael, 1964-
Perry, Michael. **Coop**; a year of poultry, pigs, and parenting. Harper 2009 352p il $25.99   **92**
1. Authors 2. Farmers 3. Farm life 4. Humorists 5. Essayists 6. Memoirists 7. Marketing executives
ISBN 978-0-06-124043-0

LC 2008-43832

The author's "essays chronicle a year on 37 acres of land with his wife, daughters and titular menagerie of livestock. . . . But these luminous pieces meander back to his childhood on the hardscrabble Wisconsin dairy farm where his parents, members of a tiny fundamentalist Christian sect, raised him and dozens of siblings and foster-siblings, many of them disabled. . . . Perry writes vividly about rural life; peck at any sentence . . . and you'll find a poetic evocation of barnyard grace." Publ Wkly

Peter, Jason, 1974-
Peter, Jason. **Hero** of the underground; a memoir. [by] Jason Peter with Tony O'Neill. St. Martin's Press 2008 289p $24.95; pa $14.95   **92**
1. Heroin 2. Drug abuse 3. Football players 4. Football -- Biography
ISBN 978-0-312-37576-8; 0-312-37576-X; 978-0-312-56103-1 pa; 0-312-56103-2 pa

LC 2008-12364

A former NFL player traces his journey from professional athlete to drug addict after injuries ended his career, describing the range of physical, psychological, and legal dilemmas that affected his perception of reality and nearly ended his life.

"Avoiding self-help urgings and self-congratulations, Peter (who is now clean) and O'Neill have crafted an unflinching look at the dark side of a life devoted to pleasure." Publ Wkly

Pham, Thong Van
★ Pham, Andrew X. The **eaves** of heaven; a life in three wars. by Andrew X. Pham, on behalf of

my father, Thong Van Pham. Harmony Books 2008
301p $24.95   **92**

> 1. Refugees 2. Vietnamese Americans 3. Vietnam
> -- History

ISBN 978-0-307-38120-0; 0-307-38120-X

LC 2007-33894

"In a narrative set between the years of 1940 and 1976,
Pham . . . recounts the story of his once wealthy father,
Thong Van Pham, who lived through the French occupation of Indochina, the Japanese invasion during WWII, and
the Vietnam War. . . . For those not familiar with Vietnamese history, Pham does an admirable job of recounting the
complex cast of characters and the political machinations of
the various groups vying for power over the years. In the
end, he also gracefully delivers a heartfelt family history."
Publ Wkly

Includes bibliographical references

Piaf, Édith, 1915-1963

Burke, Carolyn. **No** regrets; the life of Edith
Piaf. Alfred A. Knopf 2011 282p il $27.95   **92**

> 1. Singers

ISBN 978-0-307-26801-3; 0-307-26801-2

LC 2010-35229

The author "focuses on the internationally renowned
French vocalist and lyricist best known for the song 'La Vie
en Rose.' Piaf is commonly associated with la chanson ré-
aliste, realistic songs that speak to the underprivileged. . . .
Burke's contextual detail and attention to research will appeal to scholars, and her masterful storytelling will engage
readers." Libr J

Includes bibliographical references

Pickford, Mary, 1893-1979

Whitfield, Eileen. **Pickford**; the woman who
made Hollywood. University Press of Ky. 1997
441p il $27.50   **92**

> 1. Actors

ISBN 0-8131-2045-4

LC 97-29312

"Silent screen star Mary Pickford was 'America's
Sweetheart,' capturing the imagination of the public as 'Little Mary,' the adolescent with spunk. She married swash-
buckler Douglas Fairbanks, and with Charlie Chaplin and
D.W. Griffith they formed United Artists, the first production
company run by people who acted and directed. . . . Though
it does include delicious anecdotes from those who were
there, this is not simply a typical celebrity biography but a
'biography' of the times." Libr J

Includes bibliographical references

Pinter, Harold, 1930-2008

Fraser, Antonia. **Must** you go? my life with Harold Pinter. Nan A. Talese/Doubleday 2010 328p il
$28.95; ebook $28.95   **92**

> 1. Authors 2. Dramatists 3. Dramatists, English 4.
> Screenwriters 5. Authors, English 6. Nobel laureates
> for literature

ISBN 978-0-385-53250-1; 978-0-385-53251-8 ebook

LC 2010-7374

Harold Pinter's widow, the biographer, historian and
novelist Antonia Fraser, recalls their years together from

1975 until the playwright's death of cancer on Christmas
Eve in 2008.

The author "simultaneously creates a tender portrait of an
exciting marriage, and a deliciously detailed account of living in the thick of creativity and fame." Entertainment Wkly

Pirsig, Robert M., 1928-

Pirsig, Robert M. **Zen** and the art of motorcycle
maintenance; an inquiry into values. Morrow 1974
412p $26; pa $13.95   **92**

> 1. Authors 2. Novelists 3. Essayists

ISBN 0-688-00230-7; 0-06-083987-2 pa

A collection of the author's philosophical musings inspired by a motorcycle trip with his son

Pius XII, Pope, 1876-1958

Cornwell, John. **Hitler's** pope: the secret history
of Pius XII. Viking 1999 430p il hardcover o.p. pa
$15   **92**

> 1. Popes 2. Heads of state 3. Nazi leaders

ISBN 0-14-029627-1 pa

LC 99-28311

"Relying on exclusive access to Vatican and Jesuit archives, . . . {the author} argues that through a 1933 Concordat with Hitler, Pope Pius XII facilitated the dictator's
rise—and, ultimately, the Holocaust." Libr J

Includes bibliographical references

Plimptom, George

George, being George; George Plimpton's life as
told, admired, deplored, and envied by 200 friends,
relatives, lovers, acquaintances, rivals, and a few un-
appreciative observers. edited by Nelson W. Aldrich,
Jr. Random House 2008 423p il $30   **92**

> 1. Authors 2. Journalists 3. Essayists 4. Sportswriters
> 5. Magazine editors

ISBN 978-1-4000-6398-7; 1-4000-6398-1

LC 2007-46215

"George Plimpton (1927–2003) wore many hats: writer, Paris Review editor, actor, boxing fanatic, toastmaster,
prankster, fireworks enthusiast, urban cyclist. In the oral
history George, Being George, Nelson W. Aldrich Jr. skillfully weaves together more than 200 voices into a coherent
account of Plimpton's prismatic existence. . . . The contributors—who include literary luminaries Norman Mailer, Gore
Vidal and Peter Matthiessen—report on Plimpton's life with
varying degrees of grandiosity and nuance." Time Out N Y

Plummer, Christopher

Plummer, Christopher. **In** spite of myself; a
memoir. Knopf 2009 648p il $29.95   **92**

> 1. Actors

ISBN 978-0-679-42162-7; 0-679-42162-9

LC 2008-31229

The author is "an enchanting observer of the showbiz
cavalcade, drawing vivid thumbnails of everyone from Laurence Olivier to Lenny Bruce and tossing off witty anecdotes
. . . like the most effortless ad libs. The result is a sparkling
star turn from a born raconteur for whom all the world is
indeed a stage." Publ Wkly

Poe, Edgar Allan, 1809-1849

Ackroyd, Peter. **Poe**; a life cut short. Nan A. Talese/Doubleday 2008 205p il (Ackroyd's brief lives) $21.95   **92**

1. Poets 2. Authors 3. Essayists 4. Authors, American 5. Short story writers

ISBN 978-0-385-50800-1; 0-385-50800-X

LC 2008-18244

Explores Poe's literary accomplishments and legacy against the background of his erratic, dramatic, and sometimes sordid life, including his marriage to his thirteen-year-old cousin and his much-written-about problems with gambling and alcohol.

This "readable account should appeal to Poe devotees and newcomers alike." Publ Wkly

Includes bibliographical references

Silverman, Kenneth. **Edgar** A. Poe; mournful and never-ending remembrance. HarperCollins Pubs. 1991 564p il hardcover o.p. pa $18   **92**

1. Poets 2. Authors 3. Essayists 4. Short story writers

ISBN 0-06-092331-8 pa

LC 90-56397

The author explains "how Poe's early life influenced his work. He details Poe's turbulent career as poet, short story writer, and editor . . . and traces his literary development through bouts of alcoholism and hallucinations and disputes with literary rivals. An excellent addition to the literature that furthers understanding of America's gothic tale-teller." Libr J

Includes bibliographical references

Poitier, Sidney

Goudsouzian, Aram. **Sidney** Poitier; man, actor, icon. University of North Carolina Press 2004 480p il $29.95   **92**

1. Actors 2. Motion picture directors

ISBN 0-8078-2843-2

LC 2003-19372

The author "traces Poitier's journey from life as the son of a poor Bahamian farmer to celebrity status in the States as a trailblazing actor who has received as much criticism as praise for his portrayal of dignified and stoical black men." Booklist

Includes bibliographical references

★ Poitier, Sidney. The **measure** of a man; a spiritual autobiography. HarperSanFrancisco 2007 299p il $25.95; pa $14.95   **92**

1. Actors 2. Motion picture directors 3. Actors -- United States -- Biography

ISBN 978-0-06-135791-6; 0-06-135791-X; 978-0-06-135790-9 pa; 0-06-135790-1 pa

A reissue of the title first published 2000

"Poitier attempts to unravel for himself his own remarkable life story, looking at early life experiences, his family, and various themes that he believes have contributed to his success. Measure is not a chronological autobiography; the book emphasizes themes that have shaped his life. . . . Poitier's tale is an affirmation of the value of morality and personal integrity in leading a successful, fulfilling life." Booklist

Polk, James K. (James Knox), 1795-1849

Borneman, Walter R. **Polk**; the man who transformed the presidency and America. Random House 2008 422p il map $30   **92**

1. Governors 2. Presidents 3. Members of Congress 4. Speakers of the House 5. Presidents -- United States

ISBN 978-1-4000-6560-8

LC 2007-14040

The author "presents a birth-death biography of Polk. . . . Borneman has a pleasing style and makes fine use of primary sources that all demonstrate why Polk is habitually ranked as one of the ten best presidents by historians." Libr J

Includes bibliographical references

Merry, Robert W., 1946- A **country** of vast designs; James K. Polk, the Mexican War, and the conquest of the American continent. Simon & Schuster 2009 576p il map   **92**

1. Governors 2. Presidents 3. Members of Congress 4. Biography, Individual 5. Speakers of the House 6. Presidents -- United States 7. United States -- Territorial expansion 8. United States -- Territorial expansion -- History 9. United States -- Politics and government -- 1815-1861 10. United States -- Politics and government -- 1841-1845 11. United States -- Politics and government -- 1845-1849 12. United States -- Politics and government -- 1845-1861

ISBN 0743297431; 9780743297431

LC 2009024131

This is a biography of the eleventh president of the United States. Bibliography. Index.

"Merry's chronicle is filled with excellent insights into the critical events and fine portrayals of a cast of statesmen, warriors, and scheming rogues. . . . [This is] an outstanding addition to American history collections." Booklist

Includes bibliographical references (p. 543-550)

Pollock, Jackson, 1912-1956

Adams, Henry. **Tom** and Jack; the intertwined lives of Thomas Hart Benton and Jackson Pollock. Bloomsbury Press 2009 405p il $35   **92**

1. Artists 2. Painters 3. Illustrators 4. Lithographers 5. Artists -- United States

ISBN 1-59691-420-3; 978-1-59691-420-9

LC 2009-12309

"In this absorbing, carefully reasoned inquiry into a profound relationship between two painters, Adams reclaims the wrongfully maligned Benton and recalibrates our perception of Pollock and his masterpieces." Booklist

Includes bibliographical references (p. 375-390)

Solomon, Deborah. **Jackson** Pollock; a biography. Cooper Square Press 2001 287p il pa $17.95   **92**

1. Artists 2. Painters 3. Abstract expressionism 4. Artists -- United States

ISBN 978-0-8154-1182-6; 0-8154-1182-0

LC 2001-28915

First published 1987 by Simon and Schuster

A biography of the American abstract expressionist painter.

"A concisely written biography; the footnotes indicate solid research." Libr J

Includes bibliographical references

Polo, Marco, 1254-1323?

Bergreen, Laurence. **Marco** Polo; from Venice to Xanadu. Knopf 2007 415p il map $28.95; pa $16.95   **92**

1. Explorers 2. Travelers 3. Voyages and travels 4. Travel writers 5. China -- Description and travel

ISBN 978-1-4000-4345-3; 1-4000-4345-3; 978-1-4000-7880-6 pa; 1-4000-7880-6 pa

LC 2007-21860

This is a biography of the Venetian explorer.

The author "gives a full-blooded rendition of Polo's astonishing journey. It is richly researched and vividly conveyed." Washington Post Book World

Includes bibliographical references (p. 383-391)

Pomus, Doc, 1925-1991

Halberstadt, Alex E. **Lonely** avenue; the unlikely life and times of Doc Pomus. Da Capo Press 2007 254p il $26   **92**

1. Singers 2. Blues musicians 3. Songwriters

ISBN 978-0-306-81300-9; 0-306-81300-9

"Throughout this book Halberstadt sketches a broad canvas of characters, Pomus's friends and enemies along with a gallery of rogues, malcontents, hustlers, knaves, acquaintances, colleagues, and hangers-on. . . . There's some guesswork here; Halberstadt had access to Pomus' notebooks and done interviews with some of Doc's contemporaries, but there are also moments of revelation and introspection that can only be ventured. Halberstadt exercises this license faithfully and believably." PopMatters

Pop, Iggy, 1947-

Trynka, Paul. **Iggy** Pop; open up and bleed. Broadway Books 2007 371p il $23.95; pa $14.95   **92**

1. Singers 2. Rock musicians 3. Punk rock music 4. Songwriters

ISBN 978-0-7679-2319-4; 978-0-7679-2320-0 pa

LC 2006-30216

"Drawing from original interviews with Iggy (né James Newell Osterberg Jr.) and his countless accomplices over the years, Trynka . . . has constructed a comprehensive portrait of the seemingly indestructible rock provocateur, one that touches all the familiar bases in recounting Iggy's riotous ascent from suburban Michigan schoolboy to frontman of the Stooges to solo artist with an intermittently transcendent career to composer of a drug-inspired hit song that became the jingle for a luxury cruise line." N Y Times Book Rev

Includes bibliographical references

Potter, Beatrix, 1866-1943

★ Lear, Linda J. **Beatrix** Potter; a life in nature. [by] Linda Lear. Allen Lane/Penguin 2007 583p il $30   **92**

1. Artists 2. Authors 3. Illustrators 4. Children's authors

ISBN 9780312369347; 0-312-36934-4

LC 2006-51245

This is a biography of the children's author.

This "is a meticulously researched and brilliantly recreated life that . . . is endlessly fascinating and often illuminating. It is altogether a remarkable achievement." Booklist

Includes bibliographical references (p. 541-544)

Pound, Ezra, 1885-1972

Tytell, John. **Ezra** Pound; the solitary volcano. Anchor Press 1987 368p il hardcover o.p. pa $19   **92**

1. Poets 2. Authors 3. Literary critics

ISBN 0-385-19870-1 pa

LC 86-25912

"In this incisive interpretative biography, based on interviews with those who knew him and a mass of published and unpublished Poundiana, Tytell examines the circumstances behind the poems and thereby generates new understanding of the man." Publ Wkly

Includes bibliographical references

Powell, Colin L., 1937-

De Young, Karen. **Soldier** : the life of Colin Powell. Knopf 2006 610p il $28.95   **92**

1. Generals 2. Secretaries of state 3. Statesmen -- United States

ISBN 1-400-04170-8

LC 2006-45288

This biography ranges "from Powell's Bronx childhood and meteoric rise through the military ranks to his formative roles in Washington's corridors of power and his controversial tenure as secretary of state." Publisher's note

This is a "diligent, sympathetic, but not uncritical full-scale biography." N Y Rev Books

Includes bibliographical references

Powell, Colin L. **My** American journey; [by] Colin L. Powell, with Joseph E. Persico. Random House 1995 643p il $26.95; pa $14.95   **92**

1. Generals 2. Secretaries of state 3. Statesmen -- United States

ISBN 0-679-43296-5; 0-345-46641-1 pa

LC 95-17119

"This is the 'story so far,' as General Powell tells it, from the Bronx to Vietnam to the White House, from the common to the regal. His account is one of . . . extremes, tales that span from peeling potatoes with the Soviet General Staff to conversing with the Queen of England." Libr J

This "is an endearing and well-written book. It will make you like Colin Powell." N Y Times Book Rev

Powers, J. F. (James Farl), 1917-1999

Suitable accommodations; an autobiographical story of family life : the letters of J. F. Powers, 1942-1963. edited by Katherine A. Powers. Fararr, Straus & Giroux 2013 480 p. illustrations (hardcover) $35   **92**

1. Letters 2. American authors 3. Authors, American -- 20th century -- Correspondence

ISBN 0374268061; 9780374268060

LC 2013010997

This book, edited by Katherine A. Powers, presents a "collection of letters from the late J. F. Powers. . . . Beginning in prison, where Powers spent more than a year as a conscientious objector, the letters move on to his courtship, marriage, comically unsuccessful attempt to live in the woods, life in the Midwest and in Ireland, an unorthodox view of the Catholic Church, and an increasingly bizarre search for 'suitable accommodations,' which included three full-scale emigrations to Ireland." (Publisher's note)

Presley, Elvis, 1935-1977

★ Guralnick, Peter. **Careless** love: the unmaking of Elvis Presley. Little, Brown 1999 767p il $27.95; pa $17.95   **92**

1. Actors 2. Singers 3. Rock musicians

ISBN 0-316-33222-4; 0-316-33297-6 pa

LC 98-25778

This second and concluding volume of Guralnick's biography of the rock star covers "Elvis's hitch in the army through his death in 1977. . . . The breadth of Guralnick's research is nothing short of amazing, and his lyrical narrative presents an empathetic portrait of a man struggling with drugs, sex, family, personal eccentricities, money, and the delicate web of relationships surrounding any famous figure." Libr J

Includes bibliographical references

Preston, Katherine, 1984-

Preston, Katherine. **Out** with it; how stuttering helped me find my voice. Katherine Preston. Atria Books 2013 244 p. (hardback) $24   **92**

1. Stutterers 2. Speech disorders 3. Stutterers -- Biography 4. Stutterers -- Rehabilitation

ISBN 1451676581; 9781451676587; 9781451676594

LC 2012048984

This book is a memoir by Katherine Preston about her "struggle to come to terms with her stuttering." She began stuttering around the age of 7, and the book starts there, . . . capturing the mix of abject terror and curious observation that childhood stuttering can create. . . . She chronicles her many interviews with fellow stutterers--people bullied, people strengthened, and people driven from those they care about." (Kirkus Reviews)

Price, George

Harman, Oren Solomon. The **price** of altruism; George Price and the search for the origins of kindness. W.W. Norton 2010 451p il $27.95   **92**

1. Altruism 2. Genetics 3. Scientists 4. Geneticists

ISBN 978-0-393-06778-1; 0-393-06778-5

LC 2010-11934

This is a biography of the scientist "whose quest to fathom the mysteries of altruism . . . [ended with his] suicide in a squatter's flat, among the vagabonds to whom he gave all his possessions." Publisher's note

This book "puts Price's work into a wide scientific and social context, showing real insight into its importance and genuine sympathy for the tale of his life." New Sci

Includes bibliographical references

Price, Reynolds, 1933-2011

Price, Reynolds. **Ardent** spirits; leaving home, coming back. Scribner 2009 408p il $35   **92**

1. Authors 2. Novelists 3. Essayists 4. College

teachers 5. Short story writers

ISBN 978-0-7432-9189-7; 0-7432-9189-1

LC 2009-2376

In this memoir, Price "takes up where his 1989 Clear Pictures left off—with a young Price heading for England on a Rhodes scholarship, a young man lighting into new and unfamiliar territories and the lessons he learns about literature, life and love. Covering the years 1955 to 1961, Price chronicles the challenges of living in a strange place, his emotional insecurities and his anxieties about his ability to complete the thesis on Milton, his adventures in Europe with a close friend and his eventual return to his alma mater, Duke University, to teach writing and literature. Along the way, Price recalls his friendships with Stephen Spender, Cyril Connolly, W.H. Auden and his brief encounters with Jean-Paul Sartre and J.R.R. Tolkien. . . . [Price] powerfully articulates the strength of memory in shaping our lives and gracefully draws us into a literary life lived fully." Publ Wkly

Priestley, Joseph, 1733-1804

Johnson, Steven, 1968- The **invention** of air; a story of science, faith, revolution, and the birth of America. Riverhead Books 2008 254p il $25.95 **92**

1. Clergy 2. Chemists 3. Scientists 4. Writers on science 5. Biography, Individual

ISBN 1-59448-852-5; 978-1-59448-852-8

LC 2008-46101

This "portrait of scientist and theologian Joseph Priestley evaluates his friendships with such Founding Fathers as Benjamin Franklin and Thomas Jefferson while citing his role in the nation's intellectual development and the founding of the Unitarian Church." (Publisher's note) Bibliography. Index.

"What enlivens the book is that Johnson does not simply describe the system within which Priestley and his contemporaries hashed out the features of classical science; he sets it against other, later systems for comprehending physical reality, showing laymen how far we have come from the classical age of science." N Y Times Book Rev

Includes bibliographical references

Pritchett, V. S. (Victor Sawdon), 1900-1997

Treglown, Jeremy. **V.S.** Pritchett: a working life. Random House 2005 334p $25.95   **92**

1. Authors 2. Novelists 3. Literary critics 4. Short story writers

ISBN 0-375-50853-8

LC 2004-53857

This biography follows the life and career of the English writer, who for most of the century ennobled the ordinary and whose two tumultuous marriages fueled his art

"Treglown's genial and sympathetic biography effectively expands . . . awareness of the life and career of this greatly accessible and warmhearted writer of fiction, travel literature, and criticism. . . . This is a biography as open-minded and unpretentious as Pritchett's own writing." Booklist

Includes bibliographical references

Prokofiev, Sergey, 1891-1953

★ Nice, David. **Prokofiev** : from Russia to the West, 1891-1935. Yale Univ. Press 2003 390p il music $35   **92**
1. Composers
ISBN 0-300-09914-2
"Part 1 chronicles Prokofiev's childhood, family relationships, and training at the St. Petersburg Conservatoire, while Part 2 covers his concert tours in America, France, and Germany and prodigious compositional output, beginning with the fairy tale opera, The Love of Three Oranges. . . . Nice embeds many musical examples in the body of the text and writes cogently about them. . . . Overall, the writing is fluid and unencumbered by excessive analytical detail, and at times witty. . . . Throughout, the composer's outsized personality and compositional brilliance shine through." Libr J
Includes discography and bibliographical references

Prophet, Elizabeth Clare

Prophet, Erin L. **Prophet's** daughter; my life with Elizabeth Clare Prophet inside the Church Universal and Triumphant. Lyons Press 2009 286p il $24.95   **92**
1. Religious leaders 2. Writers on religion
ISBN 978-1-5992-1425-2; 1-5992-1425-3
LC 2008-33760
"Prophet pulls the curtain back on the highest levels of life inside a cult, documenting her life inside as the daughter of cult leader Elizabeth Clare Prophet, of the Church Universal and Triumphant, from her birth through 1990, when the Church's long-awaited apocalypse failed to materialize. Without judgment or reservation, but a remarkably clear-eyed view built on more than 10 years on the outside, Prophet's account reveals cult life through the complex relationship with her charismatic, manipulative mother—a figure of equal reverence and alarm. . . . Prophet's intense tale is sure to stick with readers long after they make it through." Publ Wkly

Prophet, Erin L.

Prophet, Erin L. **Prophet's** daughter; my life with Elizabeth Clare Prophet inside the Church Universal and Triumphant. Lyons Press 2009 286p il $24.95   **92**
1. Religious leaders 2. Writers on religion
ISBN 978-1-5992-1425-2; 1-5992-1425-3
LC 2008-33760
"Prophet pulls the curtain back on the highest levels of life inside a cult, documenting her life inside as the daughter of cult leader Elizabeth Clare Prophet, of the Church Universal and Triumphant, from her birth through 1990, when the Church's long-awaited apocalypse failed to materialize. Without judgment or reservation, but a remarkably clear-eyed view built on more than 10 years on the outside, Prophet's account reveals cult life through the complex relationship with her charismatic, manipulative mother—a figure of equal reverence and alarm. . . . Prophet's intense tale is sure to stick with readers long after they make it through." Publ Wkly

Proulx, Annie

Proulx, Annie. **Bird** cloud; a memoir. Scribner 2011 234p il map $26; ebook $12.99   **92**
1. Authors 2. Novelists 3. Journalists 4. Women authors 5. Editors 6. Nonfiction writers 7. Short story writers 8. Wyoming -- Description and travel
ISBN 978-0-7432-8880-4; 978-1-4391-7171-4 ebook
"Proulx bought a 640-acre nature preserve by the North Platte River in Wyoming and started building her dream house, a project that took years and went hundreds of thousands of dollars over budget. In her bustling account, Proulx salivates over the prospect of a Japanese soak tub, polished concrete floor, solar panels, and luxe furnishings that often turn into pricey engineering fiascoes. . . . [This] is a fine evocation of place that becomes a meditation on the importance of a home, however harsh and evanescent." Publ Wkly
Includes bibliographical references

Pryor, Richard, 1940-2005

Henry, David. **Furious** cool; Richard Pryor and the world that made him. by David Henry and Joe Henry. Algonquin Books 2013 400 p. $25.95   **92**
1. Comedians -- Biography 2. Comedians -- United States -- Biography 3. Motion picture actors and actresses -- United States -- Biography
ISBN 1616200782; 9781616200787
LC 2013019665
In this biography of Richard Pryor, authors David Henry and Joe Henry "bring him to life both as a man and as an artist, providing an in-depth appreciation of his talent and his lasting influence, as well as an . . . examination of the world he lived in and the influences that shaped both his persona and his art." (Publisher's note)
"A beautifully written account of the troubled life of a manic genius." Booklist
Includes bibliographical references

Mooney, Paul. **Black** is the new white; a memoir. Simon Spotlight Entertainment 2009 264p il $24.99   **92**
1. Actors 2. Comedians 3. Screenwriters 4. Television scriptwriters 5. United States -- Race relations
ISBN 978-1-4165-8795-8; 1-4165-8795-0
LC 2009-19572
"Paul Mooney recalls the day he became Richard Pryor's shadow partner. It was 1968, and the two young comics were sitting in a Hollywood greasy spoon, with Pryor nursing another hangover, so Mooney lightened the mood with an off-the-cuff, X-rated one-liner that made his buddy convulse. . . . [This book] is Mooney's unvarnished memoir of that friendship. At a time when comedians—even African American icons such as Bill Cosby—never talked about race, Pryor (aided and abetted by Mooney) dared to confront the elephant in the room. Mooney, who has also written for 'In Living Color' and 'Chappelle's Show,' also traces his own path from humble Deep South roots to a comedy elder statesman known for his incisive riffs on racism." Los Angeles Times book Rev

Puccini, Giacomo, 1858-1924

Berger, William. **Puccini** without excuses; a refreshing reassessment of the world's most popular composer. Vintage Books 2005 471p pa $16   **92**

1. Opera 2. Composers

ISBN 978-1-4000-7778-6; 1-4000-7778-8

LC 2005-46157

The author "sets Puccini within his times before discussing the circumstances of each opera's premiere and famous interpreters of the roles, providing character lists and synopses and fleshing all this out with musical commentary. Chapters on opera production and the genre's relation to film are useful. . . Berger's lucid yet hardly dispassionate views are designed to elicit strong reactions, so this is not the first place one should go for an unbiased introduction to the composer's oeuvre. But the author's grounding information is helpful for the novice, and he refers to some of the current authoritative sources." Libr J

Pulitzer, Joseph, 1847-1911

Morris, James McGrath. **Pulitzer**; a life in politics, print, and power. Harper 2010 558p il $29.99   **92**

1. Journalists 2. Members of Congress 3. Newspaper executives

ISBN 978-0-06-079869-7; 0-06-079869-6

LC 2009-27501

This is an "excellent book: a thorough, possibly definitive biography of the man who shaped the modern newspaper more than anyone else." Washington Post

Includes bibliographical references

Pushkin, Aleksandr Sergeevich, 1799-1837

★ Binyon, T. J. **Pushkin** : a biography. Knopf 2003 xxix, 727p il maps $35; pa $20   **92**

1. Poets 2. Authors 3. Novelists 4. Short story writers

ISBN 1-4000-4110-4; 1-4000-7652-8 pa

LC 2003-112113

The author argues that Pushkin's "political views and rebellious temper were a continual source of trouble, inviting criticism and condemnation his entire life and eventually ending it in 1837 when he was fatally wounded in a duel with George D'Anthes. . . . A stunning achievement, this thorough biography is sure to become the definitive account of Pushkin's life for years to come and will appeal to the scholar and general reader alike." Libr J

Includes bibliographical references

Putin, Vladimir

Putin, Vladimir. **First** person: an astonishingly frank self-portrait; by Russia's president Vladimir Putin with Nataliya Gevorkyan, Natalya Timakova, and Andrei Kolesnikov; translated by Catherine A. Fitzpatrick. PublicAffairs 2000 206p il pa $15 **92**

1. Presidents 2. Prime ministers

ISBN 1-58648-018-9

LC 00-132549

This volume is "the product of some 24 hours of interviews with Putin conducted by three Russian journalists, with brief comments from other sources, including Putin's family, friends, teachers, and some associates. . . . The approach is chronological , describing Putin as son, schoolboy,

university student, young intelligence specialist, spy, democrat, bureaucrat, family man, and politician." Booklist

Qazwini, Hassan

Qazwini, Hassan. **American** crescent; A Muslim cleric on the power of his faith, the struggle against prejudice, and the future of Islam and America. Random House 2007 282p il $26.95   **92**

1. Islamic leaders 2. Muslims -- United States

ISBN 978-1-4000-6454-0; 1-4000-6454-0

LC 2007-10345

This "a useful book, especially for American readers who are unfamiliar with Islam or who wonder how Muslim Americans and Arab-Americans can be integrated into American life." N Y Times Book Rev

Includes bibliographical references

Quasthoff, Thomas

Quasthoff, Thomas. The **voice**; a memoir. recorded by Michael Quasthoff; translated from the German by Kirsten Stoldt Wittenborn. Pantheon 2008 241p $24.95   **92**

1. Singers 2. Classical musicians

ISBN 978-0-375-42406-9; 0-375-42406-7

LC 2007-39089

"Bass-baritone Quasthoff recounts his remarkable experience overcoming severe physical disability to become one of the world's most celebrated classical singers. . . . Playful and humorous in tone, this inspirational story prompts admiration for the author's intellect and integrity, rather than facile tears for his condition." Kirkus

Includes discography

Queenan, Joe

Queenan, Joe. **Closing** time; a memoir. Viking 2009 338p $26.95   **92**

1. Authors 2. Father-son relationship 3. Adult children of alcoholics 4. Essayists 5. Satirists 6. Social critics 7. Authors, American 8. Biography, Individual 9. Motion picture critics 10. Irish American families -- Pennsylvania -- Philadelphia

ISBN 978-0-670-02063-8; 0-670-02063-X

LC 2008-34567

"Unsentimental and brutally honest, Queenan's memoir captures the pathos of growing up in a difficult family and somehow getting beyond it." Publ Wkly

Queller, Jessica, 1969-

Queller, Jessica. **Pretty** is what changes; impossible choices, the breast cancer gene, and how I defied my destiny. Spiegel & Grau 2008 247p $24.95 **92**

1. Breast cancer 2. Surgical patients 3. Television scriptwriters 4. Cancer -- Genetic aspects

ISBN 978-0-385-52040-9; 0-385-52040-9

LC 2008-4303

The author tells her story—from her mother's death from ovarian cancer and her positive testing for the breast cancer gene BRCA-1 to her decision to have a double mastectomy and remove her ovaries.

This "story is seamless and gripping; readers will be rooting for Queller and her heroic decision to confront her genetic destiny." Publ Wkly

Quiñones-Hinojosa, Alfredo

Quiñones-Hinojosa, Alfredo. **Becoming** Dr. Q; my journey from migrant farm worker to brain surgeon. with Mim Eichler Rivas. University of California Press 2011 317p il $27.50 **92**

1. Surgeons 2. Migrant labor 3. Mexican Americans 4. Neurologists 5. Neurosurgeons

ISBN 978-0-520-27118-0; 0-520-27118-1

LC 2011011531

"When the callow Quiñones-Hinojosa, or Dr. Q, made up his mind to pursue a better life and, especially, an education in the U.S., no border or barrier could have kept him from his destiny: a fate that led eventually to his becoming a Johns Hopkins University neurosurgeon, professor, and brain-cancer research scientist. Indeed, the brash teenager left all that was familiar in his native Mexico and, with less than $70 in his pocket, climbed the fence. In fact, he scaled it twice because he was caught the first time and sent back. . . . Quiñones-Hinojosa's story is gripping, inspiring, and just plain awesome." Booklist

Rabin, Yitzhak, 1922-1995

Shalom, friend: the life and legacy of Yitzhak Rabin; the Jerusalem Report staff; edited by David Horovitz; prologue by Hirsch Goodman. Newmarket Press 1996 314p il maps $24.95 **92**

1. Prime ministers 2. Cabinet members 3. Political leaders 4. Nobel laureates for peace

ISBN 1-55704-287-X

LC 96-5146

"This is a collaborative effort by more than a dozen writers and editors of the Jerusalem Report, a prestigious Israeli newsmagazine, all of whom had close personal and professional knowledge of the former prime minister, assassinated in November 1995. Their views are supplemented by numerous, interviews with knowledgeable people." Libr J

Includes bibliographical references

Rand, Ayn, 1905-1982

Heller, Anne Conover. **Ayn** Rand and the world she made; [by] Anne C. Heller. Nan A. Talese/Doubleday 2008 567p il $35 **92**

1. Authors 2. Novelists 3. Philosophers 4. Women authors 5. Authors, American 6. Nonfiction writers 7. Objectivism (Philosophy)

ISBN 978-0-385-51399-9

LC 2008-27638

This is a biography of the author of Atlas Shrugged and The Fountainhead.

The author "has delivered a thoughtful, flesh-and-blood portrait of an extremely complicated and self-contradictory woman, coupling this character study with literary analysis and plumbing the quirkier depths of Rand's prodigious imagination." N Y Times (Late N Y Ed)

Includes bibliographical references

Rand, Ayn. **Journals** of Ayn Rand; edited by David Harriman; foreword by Leonard Peikoff. Dutton 1997 727p il hardcover o.p. pa $22 **92**

1. Authors 2. Novelists 3. Philosophers 4. Nonfiction writers

ISBN 0-452-27887-2 pa

LC 97-12737

"This work offers almost everything the author ever wrote to herself. As intriguing yet sometimes numbing as her fiction, the book, which covers the years from 1927 to the mid-1970s, contains her first philosophical stabs, notes on her novels, HUAC testimony against alleged Hollywood communists, and her unfinished projects." Publ Wkly

Rao, Cheeni

Rao, Cheeni. **In** Hanuman's hands; a memoir of recovery and redemption. HarperOne 2009 399p $25.99 **92**

1. Authors 2. Dramatists 3. Drug addicts 4. East Indian Americans 5. Editors 6. Memoirists 7. Short story writers

ISBN 978-0-06-073662-0; 0-06-073662-3

LC 2008-55421

"It is the rapture of . . . [the author's] language; his hallucinatory, world-bridging storytelling; and his high-wire variations on the timeless struggles between truth and deception, good and evil, that make this journey to hell and back all-consuming and profound." Booklist

Rasputin, Grigori Yefimovich, 1871-1916

Massie, Robert K., 1929- **Nicholas** and Alexandra. Ballantine Books 2000 613p il map pa $18.95 **92**

1. Monks 2. Emperors 3. Empresses 4. Courtiers 5. Russia -- History 6. Russia -- Kings and rulers

ISBN 0-345-43831-0; 978-0-345-43831-7

LC 99-91507

First published 1967 by Atheneum

This study provides an intimate account of the Romanov family and the coming of the Russian Revolution. Kerensky, Lenin and Rasputin are among the personalities profiled.

This book, "solid with research, reads as lightly as a novel, as authoritatively as a textbook. Dialogue and lively description lend a sense of immediacy, but his notes, discreetly relegated to the back of the book, show how carefully he has avoided slipping into fiction." Christ Sci Monit

Includes bibliographical references

Rather, Dan 1931-

Diehl, Digby. **Rather** outspoken; my life in the news. Dan Rather with Digby Diehl. Grand Central Pub. 2012 vi, 309 p.p (regular edition) $27.99 **92**

1. CBS Inc. 2. Television broadcasting of news 3. Television journalists -- United States -- Biography

ISBN 1455502413; 9781455502417; 9781455513468

LC 2011052227

This book by Dan Rather presents an "investigation of how the news media has become dangerously intertwined with politics and corporate interests." It focuses on "the circumstances behind his firing from CBS News, where he had worked as a reporter since 1962. . . . In between, he provides . . . portraits of the presidents he has interviewed . . . and expresses concern for the future of independent media in an industry that is increasingly kowtowing to the almighty bottom line." (Kirkus Reviews)

Reagan, Ronald, 1911-2004

Buckley, William F. The **Reagan** I knew; [by] William F. Buckley, Jr. Basic Books 2008 279p il $25 **92**

1. Actors 2. Governors 3. Presidents 4. Presidents -- United States

ISBN 978-0-465-00926-8; 0-465-00926-3

LC 2008-32557

"The correspondence, which spans the period 1965–98 (with one final letter, written in 2005), seems on the surface to be concerned almost entirely with mundane matters: thank-you letters written after a get-together, apologies for missed birthdays, etc. But look beneath the surface, and you'll find a revealing portrait of two men: Reagan, a driven political contender who never gave up his decency or his sense of family, and Buckley, a tireless Reagan booster who used his many public forums to promote Reagan's political agenda." Booklist

Reagan, Ron. **My** father at 100. Viking 2011 228p il $25.95 **92**

1. Actors 2. Governors 3. Presidents 4. Presidents -- United States

ISBN 978-0-670-02259-5; 0-670-02259-4

LC 2010-45833

The son of Ronald and Nancy Reagan presents an assessment of his father's life that features his childhood observations of the qualities that rendered the future fortieth president a powerful leader.

A "nuanced and satisfying portrait is provided by Ron Reagan in My Father at 100. . . . [This work] is most poignant in its description of the author's search for his father's approval, forever just out of reach." Time

★ Reagan, Ronald. **Reagan**; a life in letters. edited, with an introduction and commentary by Kiron K. Skinner, Annelise Anderson, {and} Martin Anderson; with a foreword by George P. Shultz. Free Press 2003 934p $35; pa $18.95 **92**

1. Actors 2. Governors 3. Presidents 4. Presidents -- United States

ISBN 0-7432-1966-X; 0-7432-1967-8 pa

LC 2003-49249

"This volume consists of a sampling of the former president's copious outpouring of personal letters, from his childhood to the onset of Alzheimer's after the presidency. The editors . . . arrange the letters thematically, introduce each chapter with a brief commentary, and introduce each letter with a sentence or two of explanation. The editors have done an admirable job in compiling these documents. Their commentary is exactly as it might have been had Ronald Reagan been able to produce this volume himself." Choice

Includes bibliographical references

Reagan, Ronald, 1911-2004. The **Reagan** diaries; edited by Douglas Brinkley. HarperCollins 2007 767p il $35; pa $19.99 **92**

1. Biography, Individual 2. Presidents -- United States 3. United States -- Politics and government -- 1974-1989 4. United States -- Politics and government -- 1981-1989

ISBN 978-0-06-087600-5; 0-06-087600-X; 978-0-06-

155833-7 pa; 0-06-155833-8 pa

"There is a kind of touching banality to many of the entries, as though Reagan were just another CEO writing about corporate life at the top, albeit corporate life that revolved around nuclear and hostage negotiations. Edited by Douglas Brinkley . . . , the book shows a Reagan almost sweetly amazed by small trappings of office. . . . Reading these diaries, Americans will find it easier to understand how Reagan did what he did for so long: by steady work, and a steadfast commitment to the job at hand." Newsweek

Reeve, Christopher, 1952-2004

Reeve, Christopher. **Still** me. Random House 1998 309p il hardcover o.p. pa $7.99 **92**

1. Actors 2. People with disabilities 3. People with physical disabilities 4. Physically handicapped

ISBN 0-345-43241-X pa

LC 98-10223

This autobiography begins with Reeve's "riding accident and relates in almost slow-motion detail what happened before and after the near-fatal spill in 1995. His remembrances then move back and forth in time. Reeve's early life, his complex relationships, and his career are juxtaposed against the life he leads now as filmmaker, husband and father, and spokesman for those with spinal-cord injuries." Booklist

Reichl, Ruth

Reichl, Ruth. **Comfort** me with apples; more adventures at the table. Random House 2001 302p $24.95; pa $13.95 **92**

1. Memoirists 2. Food critics 3. Magazine editors

ISBN 0-375-50195-9; 0-375-75873-9 pa

LC 00-53355

Sequel to Tender at the bone (1998)

"In this second installment of her memoirs, {Reichl} retraces her route from married life on a commune in late-seventies Berkeley to her first job as a food critic, dining at expensive restaurants in Los Angeles with her glamorous editor. . . . Reichl writes with gusto, and her story has all the ingredients of a modern fairy tale: hard work, weird food, and endless curiosity." New Yorker

Reichl, Ruth. **Garlic** and sapphires. Penguin Press 2005 333p $24.95 **92**

1. Memoirists 2. Food critics 3. Magazine editors

ISBN 1-594-20031-9

LC 2004-51362

This is "an account of the various disguises [the author] donned so she would not be recognized as restaurant critic of the New York Times." Libr J

"Reichl's ability to experience meals in such a dramatic way brings an infectious passion to her memoir. Reading this work . . . ensures that the next time readers sit down in a restaurant, they'll notice things they've never noticed before." Publ Wkly

Reiner, Jon

Reiner, Jon. The **man** who couldn't eat; a memoir. Gallery 2011 313p $25; ebook $11.99 **92**

1. Sick 2. Inflammatory bowel diseases

ISBN 978-1-4391-9246-7; 1-4391-9246-4; 978-1-

4391-9254-2 ebook; 1-4391-9254-5 ebook

LC 2011005441

"Reiner's self-pitiless account stands out for the irony of a foodie being unable to eat, the sheer magnitude of the torment endured, the courage to stare down unrelenting pain, the honest introspection into how suffering made the author insufferable and rocked his family and, above all, his refreshingly snide attitude toward his disease. . . . An inspiring, incredible tale. " Kirkus

Reinhardt, Django, 1910-1953

Dregni, Michael. **Django** : the life and music of a Gypsy legend. Oxford University Press 2004 326p il $35; pa $16.95 **92**

1. Guitarists 2. Jazz musicians

ISBN 0-19-516752-X; 0-19-530448-9 pa

LC 2004-6214

This "biography does its complex subject justice. And even when Dregni dallies overlong on some byways, his immersion in the period's history enriches his storytelling and our understanding. The panoramic results present Django Reinhardt as he has never been seen." N Y Times Book Rev

Includes bibliographical references

Rembrandt Harmenszoon van Rijn, 1606-1669

Schama, Simon. **Rembrandt's** eyes. Knopf 1999 640p il $50; pa $35 **92**

1. Artists 2. Etchers 3. Painters 4. Drafters

ISBN 0-679-40256-X; 0-375-70981-9 pa

LC 99-19971

Schama's prose unfurls the life of Rembrandt in all its pathos. From prodigy to pauper, the troubled genius of 17th century Dutch painting is intricately conceived as he rises and falls in a world of war, plague and stolid bourgeois comfort. . . . Schama's book is a marvel of storytelling: sometimes heart pounding, always sympathetic and coolly reasoned. Seamlessly joining social history and art, what a triumph of scholarship and imagination." Time

Rhodes, William Reginald

Rhodes, William R. **Banker** to the world; leadership lessons from the front lines of global finance. [by] William R. Rhodes. McGraw-Hill 2011 xxxiii, 249p $25; ebook $25 **92**

1. Leadership 2. Decision making 3. Banks and banking 4. International finance 5. Bankers 6. Biography, Individual 7. Banks and banking, International

ISBN 978-0-07-170425-0; 0-07-170425-6; 978-0-07-170424-3 ebook; 0-07-170424-8 ebook

LC 2010032040

This book "should be required reading not only for other bankers, but also for Washington's would-be reformers of Wall Street, and most of all for the ordinary lay citizen dismayed by the persisting panic that has gripped us since 2007." Am Spectator

Includes bibliographical references

Rice, Anne, 1941-

Rice, Anne. **Called** out of darkness; a spiritual confession. Alfred A. Knopf 2008 245p $24 **92**

1. Authors 2. Novelists 3. Women authors 4. Spiritual life 5. Catholic Church 6. Authors, American

ISBN 0-307-26827-6; 978-0-307-26827-3

LC 2008-20192

This memoir by the author of Interview With the Vampire (1976) focuses on Rice's return to Catholicism.

"As plainly written as a Quaker spiritual journal, Rice's confession of faith will impress many who wouldn't think of reading vampire romances—and possibly many who read little else." Booklist

Includes bibliographical references

Rice, Condoleezza, 1954-

Rice, Condoleezza, 1954- **Extraordinary**, ordinary people; a memoir of family. Crown Publishers 2010 342p il **92**

1. College teachers 2. Government officials 3. Political scientists 4. Secretaries of state 5. Biography, Individual 6. Presidential advisers 7. College administrators 8. Statesmen -- United States 9. African American women -- Biography

ISBN 978-0-307-58787-9; 978-0-307-71960-7 ebook

LC 2010-21645

"The personal story of the former Secretary of State traces her childhood in segregated Alabama, describes the influence of people who shaped her life, and pays tribute to her parents' characters and sacrifices." (Publisher's note) Index.

"Rice's graceful memoir is a personal, multigenerational look into her own, and our country's, past. With vivid and heartfelt writing, Rice, U.S. secretary of state under George W. Bush, looks back on her grandparents and parents, then moves forward through her own life up to the 2000 election. . . . Readers will perceive Rice's emotion in relating her story, yet her portrayal seems fair and unbiased." Libr J

Richard, Mark, 1955-

Richard, Mark, 1955- **House** of prayer no. 2; a writer's journey home. Nan A. Talese/Doubleday 2011 201p $23.95 **92**

1. Authors 2. Novelists 3. Authorship 4. Authors, American 5. Short story writers 6. Biography, Individual 7. Southern States -- Description and travel

ISBN 0-385-51302-X; 978-0-385-51302-9

LC 2010-06317

An "account of growing up in the 1960s South, living with a disability, becoming a writer and finding faith. Richard's book attests to the power of words (and the Word) in shaping a life, while at the same time challenging some dearly held beliefs about memoir as a genre." N Y Times Book Rev

Richards, Keith

★ Richards, Keith. **Life**; [by] Keith Richards with James Fox. Little, Brown 2010 564p il $29.99; ebook $14.99 **92**

1. Guitarists 2. Rock musicians 3. Rolling Stones

ISBN 978-0-316-03438-8; 978-0-316-12856-8 ebook

This autobiography of the Rolling Stones guitarist "is way more than a revealing showbiz memoir. It is also a high-def, high-velocity portrait of the era when rock 'n' roll came of age, a raw report from deep inside the counterculture maelstrom of how that music swept like a tsunami over Britain and the United States. It's an eye-opening all-nighter in the studio with a master craftsman disclosing the alchemical secrets of his art. And it's the intimate and moving story of one man's long strange trip over the decades, told in dead-on, visceral prose without any of the pretense, caution or self-consciousness that usually attend great artists sitting for their self-portraits." N Y Times Book Rev

Richardson, John, 1924-

Richardson, John. The **sorcerer's** apprentice; Picasso, Provence, and Douglas Cooper. University of Chicago Press 2001 318p il pa $17   **92**
1. Art critics 2. Biographers 3. Art historians
ISBN 0-226-71245-1
First published 1999 by Knopf

Picasso biographer John Richardson "has written a concise account of the first half of his own life and notably of his long relationship as a young man with the Cubist art historian and collector Douglas Cooper. The account concentrates on the dozen years, from early 1949 to the end of 1960, when Richardson lived with Cooper, visiting museums and monuments all over Europe, meeting the great artists and other personalities of the day, and restoring the colonnaded Chateau de Castille in the south of France." NY Times Book Rev

Includes bibliographical references

Richter, Charles F., 1900-1985

Hough, Susan Elizabeth. **Richter's** scale; measure of an earthquake, measure of a man. Princeton University Press 2007 335p il $27.95   **92**
1. Scientists 2. Seismologists 3. College teachers
ISBN 978-0-691-12807-8; 0-691-12807-3
LC 2006-16480

"The discussions of the effects of earthquakes on land, structures, and people and the intense search for an understanding of the complex, underlying science will be of interest to many. Readers with substantially different levels of scientific knowledge will find the book comprehensible and interesting." Sci Books Films

Includes bibliographical references (p. 231-240)

Rickey, Branch, 1881-1965

Breslin, Jimmy. **Branch** Rickey. Viking 2010 147p (Penguin lives series) $19.95   **92**
1. Baseball managers 2. Baseball executives 3. Baseball -- Biography 4. Biography, Individual 5. Brooklyn Dodgers (Baseball team)
ISBN 0-670-02249-7; 978-0-670-02249-6
LC 2010-35008

This is a biography of Branch Rickey, the president and general manager of the Brooklyn Dodgers, who, in 1947, brought Jackie Robinson to the team.

"Breslin reveals much about the development of baseball, the Dodgers' last years in Brooklyn, and the struggle to overcome the national pastime's racism while tracing the life, deeds, and some (but not all) of Branch Rickey's warts. A breezy read, this 'Penguin Life' is nonetheless insightful, humorous, and biting at times as it traces how the man dubbed 'the Mahatma' by sportswriters emerged from obscurity as an Idaho lawyer to develop the baseball farm system, multiple MLB winners, Vero Beach spring training,

the scientific teaching of skills, and the MLB expansion that brought New York the Mets." Libr J

Includes bibliographical references

Ride, Sally

Sherr, Lynn. **Sally** Ride; America's first woman in space. Lynn Sherr. Simon & Schuster 2014 400 p. illustrations (hardcover) $28   **92**
1. Women astronauts 2. Women -- Biography 3. Astronauts -- United States -- Biography
ISBN 1476725764; 9781476725765; 9781476725772
LC 2013039647

This book is "The definitive biography of Sally Ride, America's first woman in space, with exclusive insights from Ride's family and partner, by [journalist Lynn Sherr] who covered NASA during its transformation from a test-pilot boys' club to a more inclusive elite. . . . Sally Ride made history as the first American woman in space." (Publisher's note)

"This is an intimate and enormously appealing biography of a fascinating woman, a triumph of research and sensitivity that lives up to its subject." Booklist

Includes bibliographical references and index

Rideau, Wilbert

Rideau, Wilbert. **In** the place of justice; a story of punishment and deliverance. Alfred A. Knopf 2010 366p il map $26.95   **92**
1. Thieves 2. Prisoners 3. Journalists 4. Murderers 5. Louisiana State Penitentiary
ISBN 978-0-307-26481-7; 0-307-26481-5
LC 2009038526

"In 1961, after a bungled bank robbery, Rideau was convicted of murder at the age of 19 and received a death sentence that was later commuted to life in prison at Louisiana's Angola penitentiary, then the most violent in the nation. Against all expectations, his own included, he turned his up-to-then cursed life around, becoming editor of the prison newsmagazine, the Angolite, and an NPR correspondent who published nationally acclaimed articles on prison violence, rape and sexual slavery, and the cruelty of the electric chair. Rideau frames his 44-year fight to get his conviction reduced to manslaughter and win parole (he succeeded in 2005) as a black man's struggle against a racist criminal justice establishment. . . . Rideau's story is a compelling reminder that rehabilitation should be the focus of a penal system." Publ Wkly

Riefenstahl, Leni, 1902-2003

Bach, Steven. **Leni** : the life and work of Leni Riefenstahl. A.A. Knopf 2007 368p il $30   **92**
1. Actors 2. Centenarians 3. Motion picture directors 4. Motion picture producers
ISBN 978-0-375-40400-9; 0-375-40400-7
LC 2006-49323

This is a biography of the filmmaker.

This "is a lively, incisive look at a compelling and somewhat appalling figure who demonstrated that beauty isn't always truth." Publ Wkly

Includes bibliographical references

Trimborn, Jurgen. Leni Riefenstahl; translated from the German by Edna McCown. Faber & Faber 2007 351p il $30   **92**

1. Actors 2. Centenarians 3. Motion picture directors 4. Motion picture producers
ISBN 978-0-374-18493-3; 0-374-18493-3

LC 2006-13263

Original German edition, 2002

This is a biography of the German filmmaker whose work includes Triumph of the Will, a propaganda film for Hitler, and Ölympia, a documentary of the 1936 Olympics in Berlin

Trimborn "interviewed Riefenstahl in 1997, when he was twenty-five, having already spent six years of 'intensive labor' on the project, and he briefly entertained the quixotic hope of writing a definitive book with her blessing and collaboration. Unwilling to misrepresent himself as a hagiographer, he was doomed to fail, though his disappointment does not seem to have warped his fair-mindedness. . . . [The author's] aim was to correct the murky published record and the 'attitudes' of his compatriots. One has to admire the sniperlike precision with which he takes out fugitive falsehoods that have lived under cover for a century." New Yorker

Riis, Jacob A. (Jacob August), 1849-1914

Buk-Swienty, Tom. The **other** half; the life of Jacob Riis and the world of immigrant America. translated from the Danish by Annette Buk-Swienty. W.W. Norton & Co. 2008 331p il $27.95   **92**

1. Journalists 2. Memoirists 3. Photojournalists 4. Social reformers
ISBN 978-0-393-06023-2; 0-393-06023-3

LC 2008-22853

The author "examines the life and impact of Progressive reformer and muckraker Jacob Riis (1849-1914), arguably the inventor of photojournalism." Libr J

This "biography is superb—not only as an instructive tale for today's journalists, but as a remarkable immigrant saga for readers from all vocations." Columbia J Rev

Includes bibliographical references and index

Rimbaud, Arthur, 1854-1891

White, Edmund. **Rimbaud**; the double life of a rebel. Atlas & Company 2008 192p $24   **92**

1. Poets 2. Authors 3. Poets, French
ISBN 978-1-934633-15-1

"Included in this literary biography are White's superb translations of works he is discussing. . . . This is a disturbing and original portrait of a man White sees as a fallen angel who misbehaved even in hell." Publ Wkly

Ripken, Cal, Jr.

Ripken, Cal. The **only** way I know; [by] Cal Ripken, Jr., and Mike Bryan. Viking 1997 326p il hardcover o.p. pa $12.95   **92**

1. Baseball players 2. Baseball -- Biography 3.

Baltimore Orioles (Baseball team)
ISBN 0-670-87193-1; 0-14-026626-7 pa

LC 97-9159

"Cal Junior chronicles his moves through the minor leagues and into the majors in great detail, always pointing out what he learned at each step of the journey and who taught it to him. There are some great baseball anecdotes—especially involving fiery Oriole skipper Earl Weaver—and plenty of the behind-the-scenes detail." Booklist

Rivera, Diego, 1886-1957

Marnham, Patrick. **Dreaming** with his eyes open; a life of Diego Rivera. University of California Press 2000 350p il pa $29.95   **92**

1. Artists 2. Painters 3. Artists, Mexican
ISBN 0-520-22408-6; 978-0-520-22408-7

LC 99-44964

First published 1998 by Knopf

"For the browsing public as well as specialists in European, Latin American, and American modern art, this book is not to be overlooked." Libr J

Includes bibliographical references

Rivera, Mariano, 1969-

Rivera, Mariano, 1969- The **closer**; Mariano Rivera, Wayne Coffey. Little, Brown & Co. 2014 280 p. ill. (some col.) (hardcover) $28   **92**

1. Baseball pitchers
ISBN 0316400734; 9780316400732; 9780316405621; 9780316277617

LC 2014934754

In this memoir, relief pitcher Mariano Rivera "his extraordinary story of survival, love, and baseball. . . . The thirteen-time All-Star discusses his drive to win; the secrets behind his legendary composure; the story of how he discovered his cut fastball; the untold, pitch-by-pitch account of the ninth inning of Game 7 in the 2001 World Series; and why the lowest moment of his career became one of his greatest blessings." (Publisher's note)

"[I]n this entertaining, admirably subdued autobiography, the glory is God's: Rivera's story brims with examples of his faith.

Robbins, Jerome

★ Vaill, Amanda. **Somewhere**; the life of Jerome Robbins. Broadway Books 2006 675p il $40   **92**

1. Dancers 2. Choreographers 3. Theatrical directors
ISBN 0-7679-0420-6; 978-0-7679-0420-9

LC 2006-48960

This is a biography of the choreographer of such works as Afternoon of a Faun, On the Town, Gypsy, West Side Story, and Fiddler on the Roof.

"The book is essential reading for lovers of theater and dance." Publ Wkly

Includes bibliographical references

Robbins, Tom, 1932-

Robbins, Tom, 1932- **Tibetan** Peach Pie; A True Account of an Imaginative Life. Tom Robbins. HarperCollins 2014 28 p. $27.99   **92**

1. Autobiographies 2. American authors
ISBN 006226740X; 9780062267405

In this memoir by Tom Robbins, "we travel with Tommy Rotten--his mother's pet name for him--from his birth in Statesville, N.C., through his youth in Virginia--including a stint at Hargrave Military Academy--his meteorological training in the military, and his peripatetic pursuit of language and wonder. . . . Along the way, Robbins offers flashes of enlightenment into the writing of each of his novels." (Publishers Weekly)

"Each piece stands on its own, but when read side by side they develop into a powerful argument about magic and the necessity of imaginative, interior worlds." LJ

Robeson, Eslanda Goode, 1896-1965

Ransby, Barbara. **Eslanda**; the large and unconventional life of Mrs. Paul Robeson. Barbara Ransby. Yale University Press 2013 424 p. (cloth : alk. paper) $35   **92**
1. Harlem Renaissance   2. African American anthropologists -- Biography 3. Women anthropologists -- United States -- Biography
ISBN 0300124341; 9780300124347

LC 2012022359

In this book, Barbara Ransby "details the accomplishments, struggles and impact of Eslanda Cardozo Goode Robeson. . . . Ransby outlines Essie's early life and family history, delves into the high points of her married life in Harlem, and recounts her growing awareness and tenacious engagement in the numerous political causes she supported." (Kirkus)

Includes bibliographical references and index

Robeson, Paul, 1898-1976

Ransby, Barbara. **Eslanda**; the large and unconventional life of Mrs. Paul Robeson. Barbara Ransby. Yale University Press 2013 424 p. (cloth : alk. paper) $35   **92**
1. Harlem Renaissance   2. African American anthropologists -- Biography 3. Women anthropologists -- United States -- Biography
ISBN 0300124341; 9780300124347

LC 2012022359

In this book, Barbara Ransby "details the accomplishments, struggles and impact of Eslanda Cardozo Goode Robeson. . . . Ransby outlines Essie's early life and family history, delves into the high points of her married life in Harlem, and recounts her growing awareness and tenacious engagement in the numerous political causes she supported." (Kirkus)

Includes bibliographical references and index

Robeson, Paul. **Here** I stand; with a preface by Lloyd L. Brown and a new introduction by Sterling Stuckey. Beacon Press 1988 xxxvi, 121p hardcover o.p. pa $14   **92**
1. Actors 2. Singers 3. Football players 4. Civil rights activists 5. African Americans -- Civil rights
ISBN 0-8070-6445-9 pa

LC 87-47882

First published 1958 by Othello Associates

"Combining a narrative of his life and travels with commentary on history and the events of his time, [the author] relates the fight against segregation to social progress for all

Americans, white and black, claiming that 'white supremacy' disenfranchises and impoverishes white workers and white farmers as well as black." Libr J

Robespierre, Maximilien, 1758-1794

Scurr, Ruth. **Fatal** purity; Robespierre and the French Revolution. Metropolitan Books 2006 408p il map $30   **92**
1. Revolutionaries 2. Political leaders 3. France -- History -- 1789-1799, Revolution
ISBN 978-0-8050-7987-6; 0-8050-7987-4

LC 2005-57694

This is a biography of the French revolutionary.

This "is quite the calmest and least abusive history of the Revolution you will ever read. It works well as a general history of the years 1789-94, besides being a succinct guide to one of its dominant figures." London Rev Books

Includes bibliographical references

Robinson, Jackie, 1919-1972

Falkner, David. **Great** time coming: the life of Jackie Robinson, from baseball to Birmingham. Simon & Schuster 1995 382p il hardcover o.p. pa $18.95   **92**
1. Baseball players 2. Army officers
ISBN 0-684-82348-9 pa

LC 94-44876

This is a biography of the baseball player and civil rights activist. In addition to covering Robinson's professional career, the book focuses attention on his life after baseball

"Falkner has written a very balanced account—neither muckraking nor fawning—of a fascinating and complex figure, one whose importance and interest reaches well beyond his exploits as an athlete." Christ Sci Monit

Includes bibliographical references

Kashatus, William C. **Jackie** and Campy; the untold story of their rocky relationship and the breaking of baseball's color line. William C. Kashatus. University of Nebraska Press 2014 248 p. illustrations, map (cloth : alk. paper) $24.95   **92**
1. African American baseball players 2. Race discrimination in sports -- History 3. Male friendship -- United States 4. Racism in sports -- United States 5. Discrimination in sports -- United States 6. African American baseball players -- Biography 7. Baseball players -- United States -- Biography
ISBN 0803246331; 9780803246331

LC 2013033133

This book, by William C. Kashatus, focuses on "the first black players to be candidates to break professional baseball's color barrier, Jackie Robinson and Roy Campanella. . . . The two men were divided by . . . [their] differing beliefs about the fight for civil rights. Robinson, the more aggressive and intense of the two, thought Jim Crow should be attacked head-on; Campanella, more passive and easygoing, believed that ability, not militancy, was the key to racial equality." (Publisher's note)

"Kashatus has written a superb narrative of sports, race, and politics in the 1950s and '60s, and also tells of the bittersweet consequences in Jackie and Campy's lives—." Pub Wkly

Includes bibliographical references and index

Robinson, Sugar Ray, 1921-1989

★ Haygood, Wil. **Sweet** thunder; the life and times of Sugar Ray Robinson. Alfred A. Knopf 2009 461p il $27.95   **92**

1. Boxers (Persons) 2. Boxing -- Biography

ISBN 978-1-4000-4497-9

LC 2009-5534

This "book is certainly one of the best biographies of a boxer ever written . . . [and] an important contribution to both sports literature and African American studies." Washington Post Book World

Includes bibliographical references

Robison, John Elder, 1957-

Robison, John Elder. **Look** me in the eye; my life with Asperger's. Crown Publishers 2007 288p $25.95   **92**

1. Photographers 2. Asperger's syndrome 3. Mechanics (Persons) 4. Restorers 5. Memoirists

ISBN 978-0-307-39598-6; 0-307-39598-7

LC 2007-13139

In this memoir, the author describes growing up with Asperger's syndrome (which went undiagnosed until he was 40 years old), dealing with an alcoholic father and a mentally unstable mother, and developing an affinity for machines that would eventually lead him to a career restoring classic cars.

"Robison's memoir is must reading for its unblinking (as only an Aspergian can) glimpse into the life of a person who had to wait decades for the medical community to catch up with him." Booklist

Includes bibliographical references

Rockefeller, John D. (John Davison), 1839-1937

Chernow, Ron. **Titan** : the life of John D. Rockefeller, Sr. Random House 1998 xxii, 774p il $30; pa $18   **92**

1. Philanthropists 2. Energy industry executives

ISBN 0-679-43808-4; 0-679-75703-1 pa

LC 97-33117

"This book is a triumph of the art of biography. Unflaggingly interesting, it brings John D. Rockefeller Sr. . . to life through sustained narrative portraiture of the large-scale, 19th-century kind." N Y Times Book Rev

Includes bibliographical references

Rockne, Knute, 1888-1931

Robinson, Ray. **Rockne** of Notre Dame; the making of a football legend. Oxford Univ. Press 1999 290p il hardcover o.p. pa $16.95   **92**

1. Football coaches 2. Notre Dame Fighting Irish (Football team)

ISBN 0-19-515792-3 pa

LC 99-13712

"After a childhood sketch, Robinson briefly touches on Rockne's playing career before devoting most of the book to a game-by-game description of Rockne's 12 years as coach, during which his Notre Dame teams, with the help of Rockne's motivational techniques and coaching tactics, won an astounding 105 games while losing only 12. To Robinson's credit, the book is cleanly written and mainly free of sports jargon." Publ Wkly

Rodgers, Jimmie, 1897-1933

Mazor, Barry. **Meeting** Jimmie Rodgers; how America's original roots music hero changed the pop sounds of a century. Oxford University Press 2009 376p il $27.95   **92**

1. Singers 2. Country musicians 3. Songwriters 4. Country music -- History and criticism

ISBN 978-0-19-532762-5

LC 2008-41924

"This is a fine addition to the literature on Rodgers. . . . [The author] traces Rodgers's influence through the 20th century and into the 21st not only on country music but also on popular music of many other genres and on media such as film. Whereas Rodgers's influence on country artists could be expected, his influence on people as diverse as Rick Nelson, George Harrison, and Louis Armstrong might not. A book for both music researchers and fans." Choice

Includes bibliographical references

Rodriguez, Richard, 1944-

Rodriguez, Richard. **Hunger** of memory; the education of Richard Rodriguez: an autobiography. Bantam trade pbk. ed.; Bantam Books 2004 212p pa $15   **92**

1. Poets 2. Authors 3. Television personalities 4. Essayists 5. Memoirists 6. Mexican Americans -- Biography

ISBN 0-553-38251-9

LC 2004-269979

First published 1982 by Godine

An account "of the coming of age of a person of Mexican descent and culture in American society and the inevitable transition in the private life of his family. Rodriguez focuses on his educational experiences, from his parochial elementary school . . . to his university years and subsequent experience as an educator." Libr J

Rodríguez, Richard. **Darling**; a spiritual autobiography. by Richard Rodriguez. Viking 2013 256 p. illustrations $26.95   **92**

1. Sex 2. Religion 3. Autobiographies 4. United States -- Religion 5. Christian pilgrims and pilgrimages -- Israel 6. Catholic Church -- United States -- Biography

ISBN 0670025305; 9780670025305

LC 2013017046

In this book, author Richard Rodriguez "examin[es] his continuing belief in God and in the Catholic Church in the context of his life as a gay man in the early years of the twenty-first century, years, he says, that have been defined by religious extremism, rising public atheism, and what he calls 'digital distraction.' And, yet, in the wake of September 11, Rodriguez found himself searching for commonality rather than difference between the 'religions of the desert'." (Booklist)

"With compassion and profundity of vision, Rodriguez offers a compelling view of modern spirituality that is as multifaceted as it is provocative." Kirkus

Roiphe, Anne Richardson, 1935-

Roiphe, Anne Richardson. **Art** and madness; a memoir of lust without reason. [by] Anne Roiphe. Nan A. Talese/Doubleday 2011 220p il $24.95 **92**

1. Authors 2. Novelists 3. Women authors 4. Essayists 5. Authors, American 6. Biography, Individual

ISBN 9780385531641

LC 2010-28051

This book recounts the lost years of Anne Roiphe's twenties, when the author put her dreams of becoming a writer on hold to devote herself to the magnetic but coercive male artists of the period.

"Roiphe's narrative moves in punchy, spare episodes, nonchronologically and erratically, veering from past to present tense, and requiring effort on the part of the reader. Yet she is a masterly writer: her work presents vivid, priceless snapshots of the roiling era of Communist hysteria, faddish homosexuality, male privilege, and the heartbreaking fragility of talented men and their dreams of fame." Publ Wkly

Roiphe, Anne Richardson. **Epilogue**; a memoir. [by] Anne Roiphe. Harper 2008 214p il $24.95 **92**

1. Widows 2. Authors 3. Novelists 4. Bereavement 5. Women authors 6. Essayists 7. Authors, American

ISBN 978-0-06-125462-8; 0-06-125462-2

LC 2008-34530

The author "tells an unflinching and unsentimental story of widowhood's stupefying disquiet, of surviving love and living on." Publ Wkly

Romm, Robin, 1975-

Romm, Robin. The **mercy** papers; a memoir of three weeks. Scribner 2009 213p $22 **92**

1. Authors 2. Hospices 3. Mother-daughter relationship 4. College teachers 5. Short story writers

ISBN 978-1-4165-6788-2; 1-4165-6788-7

LC 2008-10601

In this book Robin Romm focuses on the final weeks of her mother Jackie's life.

"A piercing, heartbreaking reminder that 'loss doesn't end.'" Kirkus

Rommel, Erwin, 1891-1944

★ Showalter, Dennis E. **Patton** and Rommel; men of war in the twentieth century. [by] Dennis Showalter. Berkley Caliber 2005 441p $24.95 **92**

1. Generals 2. World War, 1939-1945 3. Marshals 4. Army officers

ISBN 0-425-19346-2

LC 2004-57464

This is a "parallel biography of George Patton and Erwin Rommel. The research is thorough, the quality of the writing superb. . . . [The author] ranks as a scholar who has done them justice, making two complex men and a vast panorama of military history remarkably accessible for experts and lay readers alike." Publ Wkly

Roosevelt family

McCullough, David G. **Mornings** on horseback; {by} David McCullough. Simon & Schuster 1981 445p il hardcover o.p. pa $16 **92**

1. Governors 2. Presidents 3. Vice-presidents 4. Nobel laureates for peace 5. Presidents -- United States

ISBN 0-671-44754-8 pa

LC 81-1697

This biography follows Theodore Roosevelt from his childhood to his defeat for mayor of New York and marriage to Edith Carow in 1886.

"Based on diligent and thorough research, with emphasis on family, physical ailments, and friends, and written with verve and color, this is a stimulating book that will appeal to the general reader." Libr J

Includes bibliographical references

Roosevelt, Curtis

Roosevelt, Curtis. **Too** close to the sun; growing up in the shadow of my grandparents, Franklin and Eleanor. PublicAffairs 2008 302p il $29.95 **92**

1. Diplomats 2. Governors 3. Presidents 4. People with disabilities 5. Grandparent-grandchild relationship 6. Columnists 7. Philatelists 8. Humanitarians 9. Social activists 10. Spouses of presidents 11. College administrators 12. United Nations officials 13. Presidents -- United States 14. Presidents' spouses -- United States

ISBN 978-1-5864-8554-2; 1-5864-8554-2

LC 2008-33994

Offers a portrait of this celebrated president and his wife as experienced by the grandson of FDR, who recounts what it was like to come of age under constant media attention and public scrutiny in their formidable shadows

"No one alive today knew Franklin and Eleanor quite as well as Curtis, their eldest grandson, and his sister. Thus this splendid, intimate memoir represents an invaluable addition to the literature of the Roosevelt era." Publ Wkly

Includes bibliographical references

Roosevelt, Eleanor, 1884-1962

Cook, Blanche Wiesen. **Eleanor** Roosevelt. v2 Viking 1999 686p v2 hardcover o.p. pa $20 **92**

1. Diplomats 2. Columnists 3. Humanitarians 4. Social activists 5. Spouses of presidents 6. United Nations officials 7. Presidents' spouses -- United States

ISBN 0-14-017894-5 pa

"Cook is unafraid to take on difficult issues . . . thus rendering the biography not simply a riveting read but also a profoundly moving and wise account of how history has been shaped by the intricacies of the human heart, mind and spirit." Publ Wkly

Includes bibliographical references

Fenster, J. M. **FDR's** shadow; Louis Howe, the force that shaped Franklin and Eleanor Roosevelt. [by] Julie M. Fenster. Palgrave Macmillan 2009 248p il $27 **92**

1. Diplomats 2. Governors 3. Presidents 4. People with disabilities 5. Columnists 6. Philatelists 7. Humanitarians 8. Social activists 9. Government officials 10. Presidential advisers 11. Spouses of

presidents 12. United Nations officials
ISBN 0-230-60910-4; 978-0-230-60910-5

LC 2009-39965

This is a "portrait of a once-famous, now nearly forgotten figure in 20th-century American politics. Louis Howe (1871-1936) met Franklin Roosevelt in 1911, when Howe was a newspaper reporter and FDR a freshly minted New York state senator. They became fast friends, and Howe proved to be a pivotal figure in Roosevelt's life and career. . . . An insightful look at a complex relationship that has been largely lost to history." Kirkus

Includes bibliographical references

Goodwin, Doris Kearns. **No** ordinary time; Franklin and Eleanor Roosevelt: the home front in World War II. Simon & Schuster 1994 759p il hardcover o.p. pa $18 **92**
1. Diplomats 2. Governors 3. Presidents 4. People with disabilities 5. Columnists 6. Philatelists 7. Humanitarians 8. Social activists 9. Spouses of presidents 10. United Nations officials 11. United States -- History -- 1933-1945 12. World War, 1939-1945 -- United States
ISBN 0-684-80448-4 pa

LC 94-28565

"This is a nearly day-by-day account of the doings of Franklin and Eleanor Roosevelt during the Second World War. While Eleanor was championing the rights of female munitions workers and of Negroes in segregated Army barracks, her husband was making and breaking policy." New Yorker

Includes bibliographical references

Roosevelt, Curtis. **Too** close to the sun; growing up in the shadow of my grandparents, Franklin and Eleanor. PublicAffairs 2008 302p il $29.95 **92**
1. Diplomats 2. Governors 3. Presidents 4. People with disabilities 5. Grandparent-grandchild relationship 6. Columnists 7. Philatelists 8. Humanitarians 9. Social activists 10. Spouses of presidents 11. College administrators 12. United Nations officials 13. Presidents -- United States 14. Presidents' spouses -- United States
ISBN 978-1-5864-8554-2; 1-5864-8554-2

LC 2008-33994

Offers a portrait of this celebrated president and his wife as experienced by the grandson of FDR, who recounts what it was like to come of age under constant media attention and public scrutiny in their formidable shadows

"No one alive today knew Franklin and Eleanor quite as well as Curtis, their eldest grandson, and his sister. Thus this splendid, intimate memoir represents an invaluable addition to the literature of the Roosevelt era." Publ Wkly

Includes bibliographical references

Roosevelt, Franklin D. (Franklin Delano), 1882-1945

Brands, H. W. **Traitor** to his class; the privileged life and radical presidency of Franklin Delano Roosevelt. Doubleday 2008 888p il $35 **92**
1. Governors 2. Presidents 3. People with disabilities

4. Philatelists 5. Presidents -- United States
ISBN 978-0-385-51958-8; 0-385-51958-3

LC 2008-15164

This is a study of Franklin D. Roosevelt's life and career. "A thoroughly readable, scrupulously fair assessment of the one president who could inspire a Mt. Rushmore makeover." Kirkus

Includes bibliographical references

Fenster, J. M. **FDR's** shadow; Louis Howe, the force that shaped Franklin and Eleanor Roosevelt. [by] Julie M. Fenster. Palgrave Macmillan 2009 248p il $27 **92**
1. Diplomats 2. Governors 3. Presidents 4. People with disabilities 5. Columnists 6. Philatelists 7. Humanitarians 8. Social activists 9. Government officials 10. Presidential advisers 11. Spouses of presidents 12. United Nations officials
ISBN 0-230-60910-4; 978-0-230-60910-5

LC 2009-39965

This is a "portrait of a once-famous, now nearly forgotten figure in 20th-century American politics. Louis Howe (1871-1936) met Franklin Roosevelt in 1911, when Howe was a newspaper reporter and FDR a freshly minted New York state senator. They became fast friends, and Howe proved to be a pivotal figure in Roosevelt's life and career. . . . An insightful look at a complex relationship that has been largely lost to history." Kirkus

Includes bibliographical references

Fried, Albert. **F.D.R.** and his enemies. St. Martin's Press 1999 261p hardcover o.p. pa $15.95 **92**
1. Governors 2. Presidents 3. People with disabilities 4. Philatelists 5. Presidents -- United States 6. United States -- Politics and government -- 1933-1945
ISBN 0-312-23827-4 pa

LC 98-56141

The author "examines Roosevelt's conflict with and victory over varied critics, including Al Smith, Huey Long, Charles Lindbergh, and Charles Coughlin. Fried convincingly asserts that Roosevelt defeated his critics primarily because he was a superb pragmatist who refused to be hindered by an ideological straightjacket." Booklist

Includes bibliographical references

Goodwin, Doris Kearns. **No** ordinary time; Franklin and Eleanor Roosevelt: the home front in World War II. Simon & Schuster 1994 759p il hardcover o.p. pa $18 **92**
1. Diplomats 2. Governors 3. Presidents 4. People with disabilities 5. Columnists 6. Philatelists 7. Humanitarians 8. Social activists 9. Spouses of presidents 10. United Nations officials 11. United States -- History -- 1933-1945 12. World War, 1939-1945 -- United States
ISBN 0-684-80448-4 pa

LC 94-28565

"This is a nearly day-by-day account of the doings of Franklin and Eleanor Roosevelt during the Second World War. While Eleanor was championing the rights of female munitions workers and of Negroes in segregated Army

barracks, her husband was making and breaking policy."
New Yorker

Includes bibliographical references

Roosevelt, Curtis. **Too** close to the sun; growing up in the shadow of my grandparents, Franklin and Eleanor. PublicAffairs 2008 302p il $29.95 **92**

1. Diplomats 2. Governors 3. Presidents 4. People with disabilities 5. Grandparent-grandchild relationship 6. Columnists 7. Philatelists 8. Humanitarians 9. Social activists 10. Spouses of presidents 11. College administrators 12. United Nations officials 13. Presidents -- United States 14. Presidents' spouses -- United States

ISBN 978-1-5864-8554-2; 1-5864-8554-2

LC 2008-33994

Offers a portrait of this celebrated president and his wife as experienced by the grandson of FDR, who recounts what it was like to come of age under constant media attention and public scrutiny in their formidable shadows

"No one alive today knew Franklin and Eleanor quite as well as Curtis, their eldest grandson, and his sister. Thus this splendid, intimate memoir represents an invaluable addition to the literature of the Roosevelt era." Publ Wkly

Includes bibliographical references

Smith, Jean Edward. **FDR**. Random House 2007 858p il $35 **92**

1. Governors 2. Presidents 3. People with disabilities 4. Philatelists 5. Presidents -- United States

ISBN 978-1-4000-6121-1; 1-4000-6121-0

LC 2006-43087

Smith's "FDR is at once a careful, intelligent synopsis of the existing Roosevelt scholarship (the sheer bulk of which is huge) and a meticulous reinterpretation of the man and his record. Smith pays more attention to Roosevelt's personal life than have most previous biographers. He is openly sympathetic yet ready to criticize when that is warranted, and to do so in sharp terms; he conveys the full flavor and import of Roosevelt's career without ever bogging down in detail." Washington Post Book World

Includes bibliographical references

Roosevelt, Theodore, 1858-1919

Brinkley, Douglas. The **wilderness** warrior; Theodore Roosevelt and the crusade for America. Harper 2009 940p il map $34.99 **92**

1. Nature conservation 2. Conservation of natural resources 3. Biography, Individual 4. Presidents -- United States 5. Wilderness areas -- United States 6. Conservation of natural resources -- United States -- History -- 20th century

ISBN 978-0-06-056528-2; 0-06-056528-4

This biography of the 26th president of the United States focuses on his interests and activities on behalf of conservation and nature.

This "book is divided into four sections dealing respectively with the origins and early careers of both men, the parallel presidencies of Theodore Roosevelt (US) and Woodrow Wilson (Princeton), the election of 1912, and WW I." Choice

The author "has absorbed a huge amount of research, but encyclopedic inclusiveness and repetition occasionally mar narrative movement. . . . But this book has Rooseveltian energy. It is largehearted, full of the vitality of its subject and a palpable love for the landscape it describes." N Y Times Book Rev

Includes bibliographical references

Cooper, John Milton. The **warrior** and the priest: Woodrow Wilson and Theodore Roosevelt; [by] John Milton Cooper, Jr. Belknap Press 1983 442p il hardcover o.p. pa $20.95 **92**

1. Governors 2. Presidents 3. Vice-presidents 4. College presidents 5. Nobel laureates for peace 6. Presidents -- United States 7. United States -- Politics and government -- 1898-1919

ISBN 0-674-94751-7 pa

LC 83-6021

The author's "distinctions are sharp, his insights original, his judgments balanced and his narrative unfailingly graceful." N Y Times Book Rev

Includes bibliographical references

DiSilvestro, Roger L. **Theodore** Roosevelt in the Badlands; a young politician's quest for recovery in the American West. Walker & Co. 2011 352p il map $27 **92**

1. Governors 2. Presidents 3. Ranch life 4. Vice-presidents 5. Nobel laureates for peace 6. Frontier and pioneer life -- North Dakota

ISBN 978-0-8027-1721-4

LC 2010-44297

"Focused on TR in his twenties, DiSilvestro's work elaborates on the future president's days devoted to hunting and ranching in the Dakota Territory. . . . With its sources fully researched and capably integrated, DiSilvestro's account definitively fills in this part of TR's story." Booklist

Includes bibliographical references

McCullough, David G. **Mornings** on horseback; {by} David McCullough. Simon & Schuster 1981 445p il hardcover o.p. pa $16 **92**

1. Governors 2. Presidents 3. Vice-presidents 4. Nobel laureates for peace 5. Presidents -- United States

ISBN 0-671-44754-8 pa

LC 81-1697

This biography follows Theodore Roosevelt from his childhood to his defeat for mayor of New York and marriage to Edith Carow in 1886.

"Based on diligent and thorough research, with emphasis on family, physical ailments, and friends, and written with verve and color, this is a stimulating book that will appeal to the general reader." Libr J

Includes bibliographical references

★ Morris, Edmund, 1940- **Colonel** Roosevelt. Random House 2010 766p il map $35; ebook $35 **92**

1. Biography, Individual 2. Presidents -- United States 3. United States -- Politics and government -- 1909-1913 4. United States -- Politics and government --

1913-1921
ISBN 978-0-375-50487-7; 0-375-50487-7; 978-0-679-60415-0 ebook; 0-679-60415-4 ebook

LC 2010-5890

Sequel to Theodore Rex (2001)

"Mr. Morris has addressed the toughest and most frustrating part of Roosevelt's life with the same care and precision that he brought to the two earlier installments. And if this story of a lifetime is his own life's work, he has reason to be immensely proud." N Y Times (Late N Y Ed)

Includes bibliographical references

★ Morris, Edmund. The **rise** of Theodore Roosevelt; Modern Library pa. ed; Modern Lib. 2001 xxxiv, 920p il pa $17.95 **92**

1. Governors 2. Presidents 3. Vice-presidents 4. Nobel laureates for peace 5. Presidents -- United States

ISBN 0-375-75678-7

LC 2001-30520

A reissue of the title first published 1979 by Coward, McCann & Geoghegan

This first volume of a three volume study of the life and times of Theodore Roosevelt "covers Roosevelt's life up to the age of 42, when an assassin's bullet elected him the youngest president in the nation's history." Booklist

Includes bibliographical references

Followed by Theodore Rex (2001) and Colonel Roosevelt (2010)

O'Toole, Patricia. **When** trumpets call; Theodore Roosevelt after the White House. Simon & Schuster 2005 494p il hardcover o.p. pa $16 **92**

1. Governors 2. Presidents 3. Vice-presidents 4. Nobel laureates for peace 5. Presidents -- United States

ISBN 0-684-86477-0; 0-684-86478-9 pa

LC 2004-62590

The author "adeptly revisits this story, uncovering previously unexploited material and presenting a fuller and more sympathetic account. . . . O'Toole has written the definitive account of TR's postpresidential years." Libr J

Includes bibliographical references

Root, Joan, d. 2006

Seal, Mark. **Wildflower**; a story of love, murder, and the woman who tried to save Kenya. Random House 2009 232p il $26 **92**

1. Conservationists 2. Motion picture producers

ISBN 978-1-4000-6736-7; 1-4000-6736-7

LC 2008-51106

This is a "biography of the conservationist and wildlife filmmaker Joan Root, who was brutally murdered in her home on Lake Naivasha, Kenya, a region she was trying to save from poachers and environmental ruin." Publ Wkly

"This is a great story built from many interviews of friends and family and from Root's extensive diaries and letters. What an adventure! What an example!" Libr J

Rose, Pete, 1941-

Kennedy, Kostya. **Pete** Rose; An American Dilemma. Kostya Kennedy. Time Home Entertainment Inc. 2014 352 p. illustrations $26.95 **92**

1. Sports betting 2. Rose, Pete, 1941- 3. Major League

Baseball 4. Baseball players -- Biography

ISBN 1618930966; 9781618930965

LC 2013949234

This book on former professional baseball player Pete Rose presents a "consideration of Rose's place in baseball history 25 years after his ban from Major League Baseball (MLB) and from Hall of Fame consideration because he bet on baseball games. The narrative shifts between Rose's past--with anecdotes from family, friends, and former teammates--to his present life working the autograph circuit and filming a reality show with his young fiancée." (Library Journal)

"This is a wonderful biography as well as a thoughtful examination of a moral quandary." Booklist

Includes bibliographical references and index

Rosenblatt, Roger

Rosenblatt, Roger. **Making** toast; a family story. Ecco 2010 166p $21.99 **92**

1. Authors 2. Bereavement 3. Journalists 4. Grandparent-grandchild relationship 5. Essayists 6. Authors, American 7. Nonfiction writers 8. Political commentators

ISBN 978-0-06-182593-4; 0-06-182593-X

"A 38-year-old pediatrician named Amy Solomon collapsed on her treadmill at home. She died of what was discovered to be a rare, undiagnosed heart defect. The day she died, Amy's parents—Roger and Ginny Rosenblatt—drove from their house on Long Island to their daughter's home in Bethesda, Md. The Rosenblatts have been there ever since, helping their son-in-law take care of three children, who were 6, 4, and 1 when their mother died. Now, Roger Rosenblatt has written about this reconfigured family in an exquisite, restrained little memoir filled with both hurt and humor." NPR

Ross, Barney, 1909-1967

Century, Douglas. **Barney** Ross. Schocken Books 2006 215p il (Jewish encounters) $19.95 **92**

1. Boxers (Persons)

ISBN 0-8052-4223-6; 978-0-8052-4223-2

LC 2005-49939

This is a biography of the American boxer.

"This is an excellent story of a man and his times. And proof positive that time does not relinquish its hold over men or monuments." N Y Times Book Rev

Includes bibliographical references

Ross, Betsy, 1752-1836

Miller, Marla R. **Betsy** Ross and the making of America. Henry Holt 2010 467p il map $30 **92**

1. Dressmakers 2. Needleworkers 3. Biography, Individual 4. Flags -- United States 5. Philadelphia (Pa.) -- History -- 18th century 6. Philadelphia (Pa.) -- History -- 19th century 7. United States -- History -- 1775-1783, Revolution

ISBN 0-8050-8297-2; 978-0-8050-8297-5

LC 2009-35385

This is a biography of the flag-maker Betsy Ross and a portrait of Revolutionary War-era Philadelphia. Index.

"This first-rate biography of Ross (1752–1836) is authoritative and engrossing and goes a long way toward re-

covering the history of early American women and work."
Publ Wkly

Includes bibliographical references

Rossini, Gioacchino, 1792-1868

Servadio, Gaia. **Rossini**; a life. Carroll & Graf
Publishers 2003 244p il $26   **92**

1. Composers
ISBN 0-7867-1195-7

LC 2003-43563

The author "traces the history of Rossini—a man who
exchanged ideas with Richard Wagner and in Paris salons
kept company with Victor Hugo, Honore de Balzac, and Eugene Delacroix—from a difficult, impoverished childhood
through his complicated relationships with his divas, to his
battles with nervous illnesses. She sets Rossini's life, too,
against the sweep of European history in an age defined and
betrayed by Napoleon." Publisher's note

"This is a deeply rewarding book, written with real personality and much scholarship." Publ Wkly

Includes bibliographical references

Roth, Henry, 1906-1995

Kellman, Steven G. **Redemption** : the life of
Henry Roth. W.W. Norton 2005 371p il $25.95 **92**

1. Authors 2. Novelists 3. Essayists 4. Short story
writers
ISBN 0-393-05779-8

LC 2005-11979

The author "traces Roth's fascinating career from his
birth in Galicia, Austria-Hungary, to his final years in New
Mexico. He focuses on his experience of New York's Lower
East Side and Jewish and Irish Harlem. . . . This biography
should be included in all public library and academic collections." Libr J

Includes bibliographical references

Roth, Joseph, 1894-1939

Roth, Joseph, 1894-1939. **Joseph** Roth; Joseph
Roth; translated and edited by Michael Hofmann. W.
W. Norton 2012 xvii, 551p $39.95   **92**

1. Authors 2. Novelists 3. Journalists 4. Authors,
Austrian 5. Short story writers
ISBN 978-0-393-06064-5

LC 2011032677

This book "contains 457 letters [by writer Joseph Roth],
only a small number of which are to family or close friends
or comment on his novels as he was writing them. Most are
to fellow writers . . . or to translators and colleagues at The
Frankfurter Zeitung and other newspapers for which Roth
wrote essays, reviews, and sketches." He discusses "his personal affairs, . . . and, most of all, his unending financial
woes." Other topics include "Nazism, . . . Jewishness, . . .
[and] the Soviet Union." (New York Times)

Includes bibliographical references

Rothschild, Charlotte, 1819-1884

Weintraub, Stanley. **Charlotte** and Lionel; a
Rothschild love story. Free Press 2003 316p il
hardcover o.p. pa $22.95   **92**

1. Bankers 2. Members of Parliament 3. Spouses of
prominent persons
ISBN 0-7432-2686-0; 978-1-4165-7332-6; 1-4165-
7332-1 pa

LC 2002-29994

The author profiles one of the Victorian era's "oddly
(given their Jewishness and British anti-Semitism) quintessential couples. Lionel Rothschild, scion of the British
branch of the famed banking family, married his beautiful
German wife, Charlotte, in 1836, when she was 16 (he was
a decade older). The bride was, following family custom,
also Lionel's cousin and would mature into a sparkling salo-
niste and hostess whose dinner invitations, Weintraub notes,
were preferred over those from Buckingham Palace. . . .
Weintraub offers an enticing inside look at a storied family that played a central public role in Victorian England."
Publ Wkly

Includes bibliographical references

Rothschild, Lionel Nathan, Baron, 1808-1879

Weintraub, Stanley. **Charlotte** and Lionel; a
Rothschild love story. Free Press 2003 316p il
hardcover o.p. pa $22.95   **92**

1. Bankers 2. Members of Parliament 3. Spouses of
prominent persons
ISBN 0-7432-2686-0; 978-1-4165-7332-6; 1-4165-
7332-1 pa

LC 2002-29994

The author profiles one of the Victorian era's "oddly
(given their Jewishness and British anti-Semitism) quintessential couples. Lionel Rothschild, scion of the British
branch of the famed banking family, married his beautiful
German wife, Charlotte, in 1836, when she was 16 (he was
a decade older). The bride was, following family custom,
also Lionel's cousin and would mature into a sparkling salo-
niste and hostess whose dinner invitations, Weintraub notes,
were preferred over those from Buckingham Palace. . . .
Weintraub offers an enticing inside look at a storied family that played a central public role in Victorian England."
Publ Wkly

Includes bibliographical references

Rousseau, Jean-Jacques, 1712-1778

Cranston, Maurice. **Jean** -Jacques: the early life
and work of Jean-Jacques Rousseau, 1712-1754.
University of Chicago Press 1991 382p il map pa
$23   **92**

1. Authors 2. Novelists 3. Memoirists 4. Political and
social philosophers
ISBN 0-226-11862-2

LC 90-45994

First published 1983 by Norton

"Cranston presents Rousseau's work in the context of
his life. He proceeds impartially but not dispassionately; his
scholarship is impeccable but not obtrusive. The result is a
most readable narrative that has something for readers at all
levels of sophistication." Choice

Includes bibliographical references

Cranston, Maurice. The **solitary** self: Jean-
Jacques Rousseau in exile and adversity; with a fore-

word by Sanford Lakoff. University of Chicago Press
1997 247p il $35; pa $20 **92**
    1. Authors 2. Novelists 3. Memoirists 4. Political and
social philosophers
    ISBN 0-226-11865-7; 0-226-11866-5 pa
                    LC 96-12922
"This final volume in Cranston's definitive trilogy
chronicles Rousseau's last turbulent years as an outcast in
England and Neuchatel, after the burning of %Emile and the
order for his arrest. . . . This is a scholarly yet ingratiating
portrayal of a man whose last years found him battling sci-
atica and Voltaire, enjoying botany and Boswell. Cranston's
authoritative work has given us an invaluable account of the
paradoxical life of an emotionally devoted yet tactlessly demanding man." Booklist
Includes bibliographical references

Rousseau, Jean-Jacques. **Confessions**; edited and
introduced by P. N. Furbank. Knopf 1992 2v in 1
$20 **92**
    1. Authors 2. Novelists 3. Memoirists 4. Political and
social philosophers
    ISBN 0-679-40998-X
                    LC 91-53194
First Everyman's library edition, 1931
"An autobiography by Jean-Jacques Rousseau. The
twelve volumes, written between 1766 and 1770, were published posthumously (I-VI, 1781; VII-XII, 1788). In this
work, Rousseau 'frankly and sincerely' reveals the details
of his erratic and rebellious life. Scholars find, however, that
his unconscious motivation was to justify himself in the eyes
of his supposedly numerous persecutors." Reader's Ency.
4th edition

Rudd, Mark, 1947-

Rudd, Mark. **Underground**; my life with SDS
and the Weathermen. William Morrow 2009 324p il
map $25.99 **92**
    1. Teachers 2. Radicalism 3. Youth leaders 4.
Revolutionaries 5. Weathermen (Organization) 6.
Students for a Democratic Society
    ISBN 978-0-06-147275-6; 0-06-147275-1
"Even those who condemn Rudd's work in history can
be grateful for Rudd's work of history. 'Underground' is
honest and funny, passionate and contrite, meticulously researched and deeply philosophical: an essential document
on the '60s." Washington Post Book World

Rudnick, Paul

Rudnick, Paul. **I** shudder; and other reactions
to life, death, and New Jersey. Harper 2009 318p
$23.99 **92**
    1. Authors 2. Humorists 3. Novelists 4. Dramatists
5. Screenwriters 6. Dramatists, American
    ISBN 978-0-06-178018-9; 0-06-178018-9
                    LC 2009-36459
This is the author's "collection of uproariously self-deprecating essays about being gay and Jewish in suburban New
Jersey and downtown Manhattan, and about his career as a
playwright and script doctor in Hollywood and on Broadway." N Y Times Book Rev

Rupert, Prince, Count Palatine, 1619-1682

Spencer, Charles Edward Maurice Spencer.
Prince Rupert; the last cavalier. [by] Charles Spencer. Weidenfeld and Nicolson 2007 430p il $37.95;
pa $19.95 **92**
    1. Princes 2. Admirals 3. Generals 4. Great Britain
-- History -- 1642-1660, Civil War and Commonwealth
    ISBN 978-0-297-84610-9; 0-297-84610-8; 978-0-
7538-2401-6 pa; 0-7538-2401-9 pa
"This delightful book could change the nonspecialist
reader's perception of the English Civil War era as tedious
while impressing those already familiar with it. . . . highly
recommended for any college, high school, or public library." Libr J
Includes bibliographical references

Rushdie, Salman

  ★ Rushdie, Salman, 1947- **Joseph** Anton; a
memoir. Salman Rushdie. Random House 2012 xii,
636 p.p (acid-free paper) $30 **92**
    1. Fatwas -- Personal narratives 2. Authors, Indic
-- Great Britain -- Biography 3. Blasphemy (Islam)
-- History -- 20th century 4. Authors, English -- 20th
century -- Biography 5. Freedom of the press -- History
-- 20th century 6. Islam and literature -- History --
20th century 7. Protective custody -- Great Britain --
Personal narratives
    ISBN 0812992784; 9780679643883; 9780812992786
                    LC 2012372283
This memoir describes author Salman Rushdie's time
under police protection after Iranian leader Ayatollah Kho-
meini issued a death sentence against the author following
the publication of his novel "The Satanic Verses." The book
answers questions like "How do a writer and his family live
with the threat of murder for more than nine years? How
does he go on working? . . . How does despair shape his
thoughts and actions, . . . how does he learn to fight back?"
(Publisher's note)

Russo, Richard, 1949-

Elsewhere; Richard Russo. Alfred A. Knopf
2012 246 p. $25.95 **92**
    1. Biography 2. Authors -- Family life 3. Parent-
child relationship 4. Gloversville (N.Y.) -- Biography
5. Novelists, American -- Biography
    ISBN 0307959538; 9780307959539
                    LC 2012016354
Author Richard Russo presents a book that chronicles
his life. When he went to college, "his mother joined him
as they drove to Arizona, and she'd rarely be far from him
in the decades that followed. Russo describes how his life
decisions were often limited by the need to accommodate
his mother's particular needs and, later, debilitating illness
. . . He explores how her options were limited as a single
mother in the '60s, as a product of a manufacturing culture
that collapsed before her eyes, and as a woman who needed
to define herself through other men." (Kirkus Reviews)

Russo, Vito, 1946-1990

Schiavi, Michael. **Celluloid** activist; the life and
times of Vito Russo. [by] Michael Schiavi. Universi-

ty of Wisconsin Press 2011 361p il $29.95; e-book
$14.95 **92**

1. Gay activists 2. Film historians 3. Gay rights
activists 4. ACT UP (Organization) 5. Motion picture
critics 6. Homosexuality in motion pictures 7. Gay and
Lesbian Alliance Against Defamation
ISBN 978-0-299-28230-1; 978-0-299-28233-2 e-book

LC 2010-44627

A biography of the "man who wrote The Celluloid Closet: Homosexuality in the Movies, commonly regarded as the
foundational text of gay and lesbian film studies and one of
the first to be widely read. But Russo was much more than a
pioneering journalist and author. A founding member of the
Gay and Lesbian Alliance Against Defamation (GLAAD)
and cofounder of the AIDS Coalition to Unleash Power
(ACT UP), Russo lived at the center of the most important
gay cultural turning points in the 1960s, 1970s, and 1980s."
Publisher's note

"Conventionally academic but complex portrait of an
undeservedly obscure gay author and activist." Kirkus
Includes bibliographical references

Ruth, Babe, 1895-1948

Creamer, Robert W. **Babe**; the legend comes to
life. Simon & Schuster 1974 443p il hardcover o.p.
pa $14 **92**

1. Baseball players 2. Baseball -- Biography
ISBN 0-671-76070-X pa

This biography covers Babe Ruth's personal life and his
sports career.

Rutherford, Ernest, 1871-1937

Reeves, Richard. A **force** of nature; the frontier
genius of Ernest Rutherford. W. W. Norton & Co.
2008 207p il (Great discoveries) $23.95 **92**

1. Physicists 2. Nobel laureates for chemistry
ISBN 978-0-393-05750-8; 0-393-05750-X

LC 2007-33184

The author "re-introduces Ernest Rutherford, one of the
founding geniuses of nuclear physics. . . . This biography
does an outstanding job of capturing the excitement and
almost breathless pace of physics research in the 20th century's first four decades." Publ Wkly
Includes bibliographical references

Ryan, Donald P., 1957-

Ryan, Donald P. **Beneath** the sands of Egypt; adventures of an unconventional archaeologist. William
Morrow 2010 286p il $26.99; ebook $12.99 **92**

1. Queens 2. Archeologists 3. Archaeologists 4.
College teachers 5. Egypt -- Antiquities 6. Excavations
(Archeology) -- Egypt
ISBN 978-0-06-173282-9; 0-06-173282-6; 978-0-06-
200280-8 ebook; 0-06-200280-5 ebook

LC 2010-20355

"Ryan, the archaeologist who rediscovered tomb KV 60
in the Valley of the Kings (later identified as the final resting place of the pharoah Hatshepsut), takes us through his
life, career, and numerous expeditions. It's a thrilling book,
not because it's full of Indiana Jones heroics but because
Ryan's enthusiasm for what he does (more dirt-sifting than
bullwhip-wielding) is manifested on every page; and . . . he

catches us up in his excitement, makes us wish we weren't
just reading about this stuff but were actually doing it. . . .
This wonderful adventure story should be must reading for
anyone aspiring to become an archaeologist, but even those
of us who harbor no such dreams will be aching to get a little
dirt under our fingernails." Booklist

Sabbag, Robert

Sabbag, Robert. **Down** around midnight; a
memoir of crash and survival. Viking 2009 214p
$25.95 **92**

1. Journalists 2. Aircraft accidents 3. Survival
after airplane accidents, shipwrecks, etc. 4. Authors,
American
ISBN 978-0-670-02102-4

LC 2008-46688

"On June 17, 1979, Air New England flight 248 crashed
into the woods on Cape Cod. The pilot died but the copilot
and eight passengers survived. . . . [This is Sabbag's] account of what exactly happened on that foggy night. . . . He
reconnects with the other survivors and their rescuers for the
first time in thirty years." Publisher's note

"A remarkably powerful, human story not merely of a
plane crash but of the impact that one brief moment can have
on an entire life." Booklist

Sacagawea, b. 1786

★ Clark, Ella Elizabeth. **Sacagawea** of the Lewis and Clark expedition; {by} Ella E. Clark and Margot Edmonds. University of Calif. Press 1979 171p
il hardcover o.p. pa $16.95 **92**

1. Lewis and Clark Expedition (1804-1806) 2.
Interpreters 3. Guides (Persons)
ISBN 0-520-05060-6 pa

LC 78-65466

"Sacagawea, the Shoshone Indian woman who accompanied the Lewis and Clark expedition, has been a regional
heroine and a feminist celebrity for most of this century. But,
as these writers show, her role as 'the guide' was more fic-
tive than actual. . . . Based on careful interpretation of the
explorer's journals, this revisionist study does a good job of
redefining her actual contributions." Booklist
Includes bibliographical references

Said, Kurban, 1905-1942

Reiss, Tom. The **Orientalist**; solving the mystery of a strange and a dangerous life. Random House
2005 xxvii, 433p il $25.95; pa $14.95 **92**

1. Authors 2. Novelists 3. Historians 4. Biographers
ISBN 1-4000-6265-9; 0-8129-7276-7 pa

LC 2004-50928

This is a biography of Lev Nussimbaum, a Jew from
Baku who wrote in Germany under the pseudonyms Essad
Bey and Kurban Said.

The author "takes the reader through his own search for
the truth; through the twists of 20th-century history in Russia and Germany, and hence though the life-story itself. This
would be hard work if the interweaving of biography, investigation and geopolitics were not so elegant." Economist
Includes bibliographical references

Saldana, Stephanie

Saldana, Stephanie. The **bread** of angels; a journey to love and faith. Doubleday 2010 309p $24.95; pa $15 **92**

1. Christianity and other religions 2. Spiritual biography 3. Biography, Individual 4. Islam -- Relations -- Christianity 5. Christianity and other religions -- Islam 6. Damascus (Syria) -- Description and travel

ISBN 978-0-385-52200-7; 0-385-52200-2; 978-0-307-28046-6 pa; 0-307-28046-2 pa

LC 2009-16852

This book "operates on several levels: as a spiritual testament and journey of faith; as a Western woman's positive encounter with Islam; as a writer's successful quest to find poetry and beauty even in the midst of war; and as a love story, told with novelistic suspense and a refreshing humor that keeps the romanticism of her story as grounded in reality as possible. . . . This is the type of memoir, recounting a journey to the depths of the soul, that makes the personal universal." America

Salinger, J. D. (Jerome David), 1919-2010

Beller, Thomas. **J.D.** Salinger; the escape artist. Thomas Beller. New Harvest 2014 160 p. (Icons) (hardback) $20 **92**

1. American authors -- Biography 2. Authors, American -- 20th century -- Biography

ISBN 0544261992; 9780544261990

LC 2013045583

In this book, author Thomas Beller "gives us a sense of life at 'The New Yorker' . . . and a portrait of editor Gus Lobrano, whose relationship with [writer J. D.] Salinger has rarely been written about. He visits Salinger's summer camp and the apartment buildings where the author lived. He reads the famous works with obsessive attention, finding in them an image of his own life experience." (Publisher's note)

"Beller's prose is conversational and intimate, and his admiration for his subject is evident." LJ

Includes bibliographical references

★ Slawenski, Kenneth. **J.D.** Salinger; a life. Random House 2011 450p il $27; ebook $27 **92**

1. Authors 2. Novelists 3. Authors, American 4. Short story writers

ISBN 978-1-4000-6951-4; 978-0-679-60479-2 ebook

LC 201008926

First published 2010 in the United Kingdom

This biography is "a highly informative effort to assess the arc of Salinger's career, the themes of his fiction, and his influence on 20th-century American literature. . . . Slawenski describes Salinger's three marriages, records his contentious relationships with his publishers, his special relationship with the New Yorker, and Slawenski's assiduous research allows him to identify and assess many obscure and unpublished stories. In total, an invaluable work that sheds fascinating light on the willfully elusive author." Publ Wkly

Includes bibliographical references

Salk, Jonas, 1914-1995

Kluger, Jeffrey. **Splendid** solution: Jonas Salk and the conquest of polio. G.P. Putnam's Sons 2004 373p il hardcover o.p. pa $15 **92**

1. Physicians 2. Poliomyelitis 3. Microbiologists 4. Writers on medicine

ISBN 0-399-15216-4; 0-425-20570-3 pa

LC 2004-50527

"Can't-put-it-down medical-science history." Booklist

Includes bibliographical references

Sampson, Deborah, 1760-1827

★ Young, Alfred Fabian. **Masquerade** : the life and times of Deborah Sampson, Continental soldier; [by] Alfred F. Young. Knopf 2004 417p il map $26.95; pa $16 **92**

1. Soldiers 2. Women soldiers 3. Memoirists 4. United States -- History -- 1775-1783, Revolution

ISBN 0-679-44165-4; 0-679-76185-3 pa

LC 2003-47549

This is a biography of a woman "who fought in the American Revolution as Robert Shurtliff. . . . [Deborah Sampson served] for seventeen months during the period between the British surrender at Yorktown and the signing of the final treaty." Publisher's note

This book "makes a valuable contribution to American women's history. It offers nuggets of insight about an array of historical topics. . . . What's more, it tells a terrific story." Rev Am Hist

Includes bibliographical references

Samuelsson, Marcus

Chambers, Veronica. **Yes,** chef; a memoir. Marcus Samuelsson. Random House Inc 2012 319 p. ill. (pbk) $16 **92**

1. Cooks 2. Family life 3. Swedish Americans -- Biography 4. Cooks -- United States -- Biography 5. African American cooks -- United States -- Biography

ISBN 9780385342612; 0385342616; 9780385342605; 9780440338819

LC 2011042220

James Beard Foundation Award: Writing and Literature (2013)

In this memoir, the author Marcus Samuelsson, was "born in Ethiopia, . . . placed in an orphanage after his mother died from tuberculosis, and the Samuelsson family adopted him and his sister. After becoming a famous chef, the author sought out his roots in multiple visits to his birth country. During one of those visits, he reconnected with his father, and he has kept in touch with his birth family since then. In rich detail, the author tracks his rise as a chef." (Kirkus Reviews)

"This distinctive and compelling memoir has all the elements of a good story: humor, travel, and a young individual overcoming obstacles via a passionate calling." LJ

Sand, George, 1804-1876

Eisler, Benita. **Naked** in the marketplace; the lives of George Sand. Counterpoint 2006 308p $26.95   **92**

1. Authors 2. Novelists 3. Dramatists
ISBN 978-1-58243-349-3; 1-58243-349-6

LC 2006-21684

This is a biography of the French writer.

"Eisler's portrait of this woman of many firsts brings Sand and her boldly improvised life forward more vividly than ever before." Booklist

Includes bibliographical references

Harlan, Elizabeth. **George** Sand. Yale University Press 2004 376p il $35   **92**

1. Authors 2. Novelists 3. Dramatists
ISBN 0-300-10417-0

LC 2004-10315

"Sand, née, Aurore Dupin, left her husband and two children in provincial France and successfully launched herself as a self-supporting writer in Paris, donning men's clothing to ease passage into the professional world and taking a pseudonym to protect her aristocratic family's name. Sand took on many lovers, among them poet Alfred de Musset and composer Frédéric Chopin. Yet despite Sand's outward daring, as Harlan shows, she obsessed over her identity, as both a woman and an aristocrat. . . . Harlan sensitively analyzes the gaps and idiosyncrasies in her subject's heavily self-edited correspondence, autobiography and novels to uncover a fresh portrait of this volatile, imaginative woman of letters." Publ Wkly

Includes bibliographical references

Sanders, Scott R. (Scott Russell), 1945-

Sanders, Scott R. A **private** history of awe; [by] Scott Russell Sanders. North Point Press 2006 322p hardcover o.p. pa $15   **92**

1. Authors 2. Novelists 3. Essayists 4. College teachers 5. Children's authors 6. Short story writers
ISBN 0-86547-693-4; 978-0-86547-693-6; 978-0-86547-734-6 pa; 0-86547-734-5 pa

LC 2005-14236

The author "uses autobiography as a vehicle for far-reaching reflections on nature and humankind. . . . Sanders' thoughtful reflections on the cycles of life, the flashpoints of awe, and our quest for meaning are quietly revelatory." Booklist

Includes bibliographical references

Sanger, Margaret, 1879-1966

Baker, Jean H. **Margaret** Sanger. Hill and Wang 2011 349p il $35   **92**

1. Nurses 2. Birth control 3. Women's rights 4. Essayists 5. Feminists 6. Memoirists 7. Social activists 8. Family planning advocates
ISBN 978-0-8090-9498-1

LC 2011008439

This biography of Margaret Sanger "seeks to clear the noted birth-control pioneer's name of the charges of elitism and racism, which have darkened her reputation in recent years. . . . It was the death of a young woman from a self-induced abortion that impelled her to take up the cause of women's rights to contraception. . . . [The author] acknowledges Sanger's support of eugenics but asserts that Sanger was being pragmatic, requiring allies and finding many in the then-popular eugenics movement." (Kirkus Reviews)

"Baker relates Sanger's crusade with unfailing precision as she recounts Sanger's years as a nurse, when she mended the damage caused by self-induced abortions and listened to the pitiful plights of young women enchained by the relentless cycle of childbirth. Sanger distributed pamphlets on contraception, risking imprisonment on account of their legally designated obscenity; opened the first legal family planning clinic in 1940; and at the culmination of her career, in the 1960s, promoted use of the birth control pill. Connecting the details of each battle Sanger won and lost, Baker recreates the train of events in an arduous, iconic, and controversial journey. A moving biography chronicling the hard-fought struggle for women to gain control of their reproductive destiny." Booklist

Sartre, Jean Paul, 1905-1980

Sartre, Jean Paul. The **words**; translated from the French by Bernard Frechtman. Vintage 1981 255p pa $11.95   **92**

1. Authors 2. Novelists 3. Dramatists 4. Philosophers 5. Authors, French 6. Essayists 7. Nonfiction writers 8. Short story writers 9. Nobel laureates for literature
ISBN 0-394-74709-7; 978-0-394-74709-5

First published 1964 by Braziller

The French existentialist writer "examines the formation of his character during his childhood years, which were passed in a completely adult world between his widowed mother and her parents. The central event of his childhood was the discovery of the world of words, of language." Libr J

Savonarola, Girolamo, 1452-1498

Martines, Lauro. **Fire** in the city; Savonarola and the struggle for Renaissance Florence. Oxford University Press 2006 336p il map $30   **92**

1. Monks 2. Martyrs 3. Writers on religion 4. Florence (Italy) -- History
ISBN 0-19-517748-7; 978-0-19-517748-0

LC 2005-31802

"This absorbing account . . . captures Savonarola's brilliance as well as the exciting and dangerous days of Renaissance Florence." Publ Wkly

Includes bibliographical references

Sayrafiezadeh, Saïd

Sayrafiezadeh, Saïd. **When** skateboards will be free; a memoir of a political childhood. Dial Press 2009 287p $22; pa $15   **92**

1. Authors 2. Socialism 3. Dramatists 4. Memoirists 5. Biography, Individual 6. Socialist Workers' Party (U.S.)
ISBN 0-385-34068-0; 0-385-34069-9 pa; 978-0-385-34068-7; 978-0-385-34069-4 pa

LC 2008-51096

The author presents a memoir "of growing up with (and without) his parents, ardent members of the Socialist Workers Party." (N Y Times (Late N Y Ed))

Schön, Jan Hendrik

Reich, Eugenie Samuel. **Plastic** fantastic; how the biggest fraud in physics shook the scientific world. Palgrave Macmillan 2009 266p $26.95 **92**
1. Physicists 2. Fraud in science 3. Biography, Individual
ISBN 0230224679; 9780230224674; 0-230-22467-9; 978-0-230-22467-4

LC 2008-51801

This is the story of Bell Laboratories "physicist Jan Hdn-rik Schön who faked the discovery of a new superconductor made from plastic." (Publisher's note) Index.

"A compelling look inside big science at one of its least admirable moments." Kirkus

Includes bibliographical references

Scheeres, Julia, 1967-

Scheeres, Julia. **Jesus** land; a memoir. Counterpoint 2005 356p $23; pa $14 **92**
1. Adoption 2. Siblings 3. Child abuse 4. Journalists 5. Christian life 6. Memoirists 7. United States -- Race relations
ISBN 1-58243-338-0; 1-58243-354-2 pa

LC 2005-14816

The author writes about her "bond with the boy her fundamentalist family adopted and abused." N Y Times Book Rev

"Tinged with sadness yet pervaded by a sense of triumph, Scheeres's book is a crisply written and earnest examination of the meaning of family and Christian values." Publ Wkly

Schiaparelli, Elsa, 1890-1973

Volk, Patricia. **Shocked**; my mother, Schiaparelli, and me. Patricia Volk. Alfred A. Knopf 2013 304 p. ill. (some col.) (hardcover) $26.95 **92**
1. Femininity 2. Beauty, Personal 3. Mothers and daughters -- United States 4. Fashion designers -- France -- Paris -- Biography
ISBN 9780307962102; 0307962105

LC 2012034922

This book by Patricia Volk presents a "study of two very different but very glamorous women--her mother, Audrey, an upper-class New York domestic goddess with the looks and manners of Grace Kelly, and genius haute couture European artist Elsa Schiaparelli, whose book, art, and (yes) perfume forever change the course of young Volk's life." (Library Journal)

"[T]he narrative that emerges from Volk's deft interweaving of lives is as sharp-eyed as it is wickedly funny." Kirkus
Includes bibliographical references

Schickler, David

Schickler, David. The **Dark** Path; A Memoir. David Schickler. Penguin Group USA 2013 336 p. $27.95 **92**
1. Religious life 2. Man-woman relationship 3. Catholic authors -- Biography
ISBN 159448645X; 9781594486456

LC 2013017000

Since he was a young boy, Schickler . . . grappled with twin desires, to become a Catholic priest and to revel in the company of women. . . . Full of pathos and humor, Schick-

ler's memoir explores just what it means to feel love and have faith." Booklist

Schiff, Dorothy, 1903-1989

Nissenson, Marilyn. The **lady** upstairs; Dorothy Schiff and the New York Post. St. Martin's Press 2007 500p il $29.95 **92**
1. New York post 2. Newspaper executives
ISBN 978-0-312-31310-4; 0-312-31310-1

LC 2006-53087

This "is Marilyn Nissenson's carefully documented and revealing account of Schiff's nearly four decades of ownership. It's an admiring but not uncritical story of a woman who at her best 'was feisty rather than cowed, personally diffident but professionally forceful,' and who, although married four times, ended up wedded mainly to the paper itself." Columbia J Rev

Includes bibliographical references

Schindler, Oskar, 1908-1974

Crowe, David. **Oskar** Schindler; the untold account of his life, wartime activities, and the true story behind the list. [by] David M. Crowe. Westview Press 2004 766p il $30 **92**
1. Humanitarians 2. Manufacturing executives
ISBN 0-8133-3375-X

LC 2004-13879

This biography of the businessman who saved over 1100 Jews during the Holocaust "covers both the prewar and the postwar periods through Schindler's death and the death of his wife." Libr J

This book "is essential in understanding one of the most extraordinary figures from the Holocaust." Booklist
Includes bibliographical references

Schlesinger, Arthur M., 1917-2007

Schlesinger, Arthur M. (Arthur Meier), 1917-2007. **Journals** : 1952-2000; edited by Andrew Schlesinger and Stephen Schlesinger. Penguin Press 2007 894p $40 **92**
1. Authors 2. Historians 3. Biographers 4. Nonfiction writers 5. Government officials 6. Historians -- United States 7. United States -- History -- 1945-
ISBN 978-1-594-20142-4

The distinguished political historian's journals provide an intimate history of postwar America, the writer's contributions to multiple presidential administrations, and his relationships with numerous cultural and intellectual figures.

This book "contains juicy morsels on every one of its [pages]. . . . The book contains not just his witty apercus, but those of hundreds of A-list friends, some of whom are still alive and will blanch at seeing private lunches in print. The presidential scuttlebutt is prime. . . . The private score-settling is fun reading." Newsweek

Schriever, Bernard A., 1910-2005

Sheehan, Neil. A **fiery** peace in a cold war; Bernard Schriever and the ultimate weapon. Random House 2009 534p il $32 **92**
1. Cold war 2. Generals 3. Nuclear weapons 4.

Ballistic missiles 5. Air force officers
ISBN 978-0-679-42284-6

LC 2009-02247

The author "has written the best kind of biography, one that tells history through a central character. . . . The real story is of the bureaucratic hand-to-hand combat that let to . . . [the ICBM] finally taking flight. . . . Crafting an engrossing five-hundred-page account of a bureaucratic tussle is no easy task. Yet Sheehan makes it work." Columbia J Rev

Includes bibliographical references (p. [501]-509) and index.

Schultz, Philip, 1945-

Schultz, Philip. **My** dyslexia. W. W. Norton & Co. 2011 120p $21.95   **92**

1. Poets 2. Authors 3. Dyslexia 4. Poets, American 5. College teachers
ISBN 978-0-393-07964-7

LC 2011015859

The author "tackles his struggle with dyslexia—a condition he only learned he had when his son was diagnosed. Schultz paints a precise and compelling picture of how his brain works, how he sees himself, and how he thinks others have seen him throughout his life. . . . His affecting prose will inspire compassion and leave readers with an understanding not only of dyslexia, but of the lifelong challenges that someone with disabilities may face." Publ Wkly

Schulz, Charles M.

★ Michaelis, David. **Schulz** and Peanuts; a biography. Harper 2007 655p il $34.95   **92**

1. Cartoonists 2. Peanuts (Comic strip)
ISBN 978-0-06-621393-4; 0-06-621393-2

This is a biography of the cartoonist and author of Happiness is a Warm Puppy (1962), The Charlie Brown Dictionary (1973), Peanuts Jubilee (1975), Snoopy's Tennis Book (1979), and Things I Learned After It Was Too Late (1981).

"It is Mr. Michaelis's achievement in these pages that he leaves us with both a shrewd appreciation of Schulz's minimalist art and a sympathetic understanding of Schulz the man." N Y Times (Late N Y Ed)

Includes bibliographical references

Scott, Dred, ca. 1795-1858

VanderVelde, Lea. **Mrs.** Dred Scott; a life on slavery's frontier. Oxford University Press 2009 480p il map $34.95   **92**

1. Slaves 2. Biography, Individual 3. Slavery -- United States 4. Spouses of prominent persons 5. United States -- Supreme Court 6. Slaves -- Legal status, laws, etc. 7. Slaves -- United States -- Biography
ISBN 0-19-536656-5; 978-0-19-536656-3

LC 2008-27920

This is a "biography of Harriet Scott, wife of Dred Scott, and the story of the family's flight for freedom." (Publisher's note) Bibliography. Index.

"Through Harriet Scott's life, the author is able to create a valuable portrait of the development of slavery on the U.S. frontier during an era in which that scourge was leading the country toward civil war. Despite the wealth of historical knowledge presented, the heart of this well-researched work is the tragic tale of how a loving family's effort to gain their freedom was brutally rejected by Supreme Court justices bent on maintaining the institution of slavery at all costs." Libr J

Includes bibliographical references (p. 443-466)

Scott, Harriet Robinson

VanderVelde, Lea. **Mrs.** Dred Scott; a life on slavery's frontier. Oxford University Press 2009 480p il map $34.95   **92**

1. Slaves 2. Biography, Individual 3. Slavery -- United States 4. Spouses of prominent persons 5. United States -- Supreme Court 6. Slaves -- Legal status, laws, etc. 7. Slaves -- United States -- Biography
ISBN 0-19-536656-5; 978-0-19-536656-3

LC 2008-27920

This is a "biography of Harriet Scott, wife of Dred Scott, and the story of the family's flight for freedom." (Publisher's note) Bibliography. Index.

"Through Harriet Scott's life, the author is able to create a valuable portrait of the development of slavery on the U.S. frontier during an era in which that scourge was leading the country toward civil war. Despite the wealth of historical knowledge presented, the heart of this well-researched work is the tragic tale of how a loving family's effort to gain their freedom was brutally rejected by Supreme Court justices bent on maintaining the institution of slavery at all costs." Libr J

Includes bibliographical references (p. 443-466)

Scott, Wendell, 1921-1990

Donovan, Brian. **Hard** driving: the Wendell Scott story; the odyssey of NASCAR'S first Black driver. Steerfort Press 2008 311p il hardcover o.p. pa $16.99   **92**

1. Automobile racing 2. African American athletes 3. Automobile racing drivers
ISBN 978-1-58642-144-1; 978-1-58642-160-1 pa

LC 2008-24287

For this biography, the author "interviewed Scott extensively over the last 14 months of his life. He also interviewed more than 200 other individuals, including Scott's widow and children. The result is the gripping story of a fascinating, brave man who deserves serious recognition for his solitary accomplishment. . . . A must-read for NASCAR fans." Booklist

Includes bibliographical references

Sediqi, Kamela, 1977-

Lemmon, Gayle Tzemach. The **dressmaker** of Khair Khana; five sisters, one remarkable family, and the woman who risked everything to keep them safe. Harper 2011 256p   **92**

1. Dressmaking 2. Businesswomen 3. Taliban 4. Afghanistan 5. Dressmakers
ISBN 978-0-06-173237-9

LC 2010-20774

This book "is a fascinating window on Afghan life under the Taliban and a celebration of women the world over who support their loved ones with tenacity, inventiveness and sheer guts." People

Includes bibliographical references

Seeger, Pete

★ Dunaway, David King. **How** can I keep from singing? the ballad of Pete Seeger. Trade paperback ed.; Villard 2008 xxx, 512p il pa $18   **92**

1. Singers 2. Folk musicians 3. Songwriters

ISBN 978-0-345-50608-5

LC 2007-41814

A reprint of the title first published 1981 by McGraw-Hill

"The focus of Seeger's life has been on using music as a force for social change. . . . But he is perhaps best known as the major banjo-playing folksinger who pioneered the folk music revival that flowered in the 1960s. This excellent book provides a well-written and extensively researched account, not only of Seeger's life, but also of the social and political movements of the times in which he lived. An extensive bibliography and discography add to the book's usefulness." Libr J

Includes discography and bibliographical references

Wilkinson, Alec. The **protest** singer; an intimate portrait of Pete Seeger. Alfred A. Knopf 2009 151p il $22.95; pa $14   **92**

1. Singers 2. Folk musicians 3. Songwriters

ISBN 978-0-307-26995-9; 978-0-307-39098-1 pa

LC 2008-54387

The author "draws on interviews with Seeger and others to present a seamless chronicle of his life and music, vivifying his passion for humanity, love of the environment, and deep curiosity about music." Libr J

Semmelweis, Ignác Fülöp, 1818-1865

Nuland, Sherwin B., 1930-2014. The **doctors'** plague; germs, childbed fever, and the strange story of Ignac Semmelweis. Norton 2003 191p il (Great discoveries) $21.95; pa $13.95   **92**

1. Physicians 2. Writers on medicine 3. Puerperal septicemia

ISBN 0-393-05299-0; 0-393-32625-X pa

LC 2003-11412

This is an account of the work of the 19th-century obstetrician Ignas Semmelweis. "Semmelweis is remembered for the now-commonplace notion that doctors must wash their hands before examining patients. . . . With deaths from childbed fever exploding, Semmelweis discovered that doctors themselves were spreading the disease. While his simple reforms worked immediately, they also threatened the medical establishment." (Publisher's note)

Includes bibliographical references

Senna, Danzy

Senna, Danzy. **Where** did you sleep last night? a personal history. Farrar, Straus and Giroux 2009 200p il $23   **92**

1. Authors 2. Novelists 3. Racially mixed people 4. Authors, American

ISBN 978-0-374-28915-7; 0-374-28915-8

LC 2008-43413

The author examines "the pasts of her parents. . . . The author's white mother came from an aristocratic family; her black father's background was a mystery." N Y Times Book Rev

This "is a haunting, introspective meditation on race and family ties that tackles the tricky questions involved in constructing identity." Publ Wkly

Seth, Shanti Behari

★ Seth, Vikram, 1952- **Two** lives; Vikram Seth. HarperCollins 2005 503p ill. (pbk.) $15.95; o.p. **92**

1. Poets 2. Authors 3. Dentists 4. Novelists 5. London (England) -- Biography" 6. East Indians -- England -- London 7. Interracial marriage -- England -- London 8. Authors, English -- 20th century -- Biography 9. Authors, Indic -- Homes and haunts -- England -- London 10. London (England) -- Social life and customs -- 20th century

ISBN 9780060599676; 0060599669

LC 2005052694

In this book, the author presents biographies of "his Shanti Uncle and Aunty Henny. . . . Shanti was Seth's grandfather's brother, a dentist who studied in Berlin, lodging with Fau Caro, whose daughter, Henny was in love with someone else. He left for Britain in 1936. . . . [I]n 1940, as war broke out, he enlisted, served throughout and lost his right arm in combat. . . . Meanwhile, Henny, a German Jew, arrived in Britain weeks before war was declared, leaving her beloved mother and sister behind to death camp murder. . . . Part two of his narrative focuses on Shanti. Part three, Henny's story . . . is based on a trove of remarkable letters she received and wrote. . . . Part four examines their marriage (they didn't marry until seven years after the war), and part five details a family mystery about Shanti's will and Seth's . . . research into these lives." (Publishers Weekly)

"In clear and elegant writing, Seth explores the macrocosm through the microcosm, resulting in a most unusual, worthwhile book." Publ Wkly

Seton, Elizabeth Ann, Saint, 1774-1821

Barthel, Joan. **American** saint; the life of Elizabeth Seton. Joan Barthel. Thomas Dunne Books 2014 304 p. illustrations (hardback) $26.99   **92**

1. Religious biography 2. Christian saints -- Biography 3. Christian saints -- United States -- Biography

ISBN 0312571623; 9780312571627

LC 2013030995

In this biography of Elizabeth Seton, author Joan Barthel "tells the . . . story of a woman whose life featured wealth and poverty, passion and sorrow, love and loss. Elizabeth was born into a prominent New York City family in 1774. . . . When Elizabeth and her wealthy husband Will sailed to Italy in a doomed attempt to cure his tuberculosis, she and her family were quarantined. . . . And when Elizabeth later became a Catholic, she was so scorned that people talked of burning down her house." (Publisher's note)

"A biography of the first American saint. . . offering a rounded portrait of an ambitious woman who struggled mightily to fulfill the tenets of her faith: to be obedient, merciful and good." Kirkus

Includes bibliographical references and index

Seuss, Dr.

Morgan, Judith. **Dr.** Seuss & Mr. Geisel; a biography. [by] Judith & Neil Morgan. Da Capo Press 1996 345p il pa $18.50   **92**
1. Artists 2. Authors 3. Humorists 4. Illustrators 5. Authors, American 6. Children's authors
ISBN 0-306-80736-X; 978-0-306-80736-7
LC 96-19313
First published 1995 by Random House
"Fans of The Cat in the Hat, The Grinch Who Stole Christmas and other classics may be surprised to learn that Dr. Seuss was terrified of children and had none of his own, and that writing verse was a supreme effort for him. While children's literature is Ted Geisel's principal claim to fame, his creative life was multifarious, including an apprenticeship with film director and army major Frank Capra during WWII and stints in advertising. The authors deftly evoke the settings where Geisel lived and worked." Publ Wkly

Sewall, Samuel, 1652-1730

LaPlante, Eve. **Salem** witch judge; the life and repentance of Samuel Sewall. HarperSanFrancisco 2007 352p il map $25.95   **92**
1. Judges 2. Diarists 3. Colonial leaders 4. Massachusetts -- History -- 1600-1775, Colonial period
ISBN 978-0-06-078661-8; 0-06-078661-2
LC 2007-18392
"In 1692, Salem magistrate Samuel Sewall (1652-1730), along with several others, presided over the conviction and execution of 20 people accused of witchcraft. Five years and much soul-searching later, Sewall publicly repented of his part in the witch trials. . . . [The author] richly narrates his life in its cultural and religious setting." Publ Wkly
Includes bibliographical references

Shabazz, Betty

Rickford, Russell John. **Betty** Shabazz: a remarkable story of survival and faith before and after Malcolm X; foreword by Myrlie Evers-Williams. Sourcebooks 2003 xxii, 633p il $35   **92**
1. Civil rights activists 2. Spouses of prominent persons 3. African Americans -- Civil rights
ISBN 1-4022-0171-0
LC 2002-003447
"Just as the achievements of her husband, Malcolm X, were overshadowed by those of Martin Luther King Jr., Betty Shabazz's accomplishments have been overshadowed by those of King's widow. {The author} corrects that imbalance with this penetrating biography." Booklist
Includes bibliographical references

Shalev, Meir

Shalev, Meir. **My** Russian grandmother and her American vacuum cleaner; a memoir. translated from the Hebrew by Evan Fallenberg. Schocken Books 2011 $25.95   **92**
1. Authors, Israeli
ISBN 978-0-8052-4287-4
"Shalev delivers a punchy family memoir that examines his relationship with his grandmother. Grandma Tonia, whoas a young woman immigrated to Israel and married, is obsessed with cleanliness. When her husband's oldest brother sends an American vacuum cleaner from Los Angeles, however, she locks it in the bathroom, where it lives 'in dark and lonely confinement wrapped in its white shroud and as clean as the day it was born, untainted by dust.' . . . This memoir composed of a series of engaging anecdotes, mostly about Shalev's training in 'Grandma Tonia's University of Cleaning,' grants readers a glimpse into the zany aspects of immigrant culture and acclimation." Booklist

Sharon, Ariel

Hefez, Nir. **Ariel** Sharon; a life. [by] Nir Hefez and Gadi Bloom; translated from the Hebrew by Mitch Ginsburg. Random House 2006 490p il $29.95   **92**
1. Generals 2. Prime ministers 3. Cabinet members 4. Political leaders
ISBN 1-4000-6587-9; 978-1-4000-6587-5
LC 2006-49144
This is a biography of the Israeli prime minister.
"This revealing and engrossing biography adds a great deal to our understanding of the man." Booklist
Includes bibliographical references

Shaw, Artie, 1910-2004

Nolan, Tom. **Three** chords for beauty's sake: the life of Artie Shaw. W.W. Norton 2010 430p il $29.95   **92**
1. Jazz musicians 2. Band leaders 3. Clarinetists
ISBN 978-0-393-06201-4; 0-393-06201-5
LC 2010-06301
In this biography of the swing clarinetist-bandleader Nolan, "who interviewed Shaw and many of his band mates and intimates, appraises his difficult subject with a cool eye. His briskly written work lauds the musician's instrumental virtuosity and ambitious conceptions, but the author cuts Shaw no slack about his many personal failings—his arrogance, anger, selfishness, egocentricity and his horrific relationships with parents, wives and children. It's a multidimensional portrait of a brilliant yet self-absorbed autodidact who could never find happiness or satisfaction, even when his greatest fantasies of fame and success were realized. An exemplary work of jazz biography." Kirkus
Includes bibliographical references

Shawn, Allen

Shawn, Allen. **Wish** I could be there; notes from a phobic life. Viking 2007 267p $24.95   **92**
1. Composers 2. Agoraphobia
ISBN 0-670-03842-3; 978-0-670-03842-8
LC 2006-41368
The author "probes the causes of his long struggle with agoraphobia—a fear of certain spaces which makes it difficult to 'move forward in the world without knowing already what lies ahead'—in this vividly written combination of memoir and scientific inquiry." New Yorker
Includes bibliographical references

Sheehan, Jason

★ Sheehan, Jason. **Cooking** dirty; a story of life, sex, love and death in the kitchen. Farrar, Straus and Giroux 2009 355p $26; pa $15   **92**

1. Cooks 2. Food critics

ISBN 978-0-374-28921-8; 0-374-28921-2; 978-0-374-53227-7 pa; 0-374-53227-3 pa

LC 2008-47158

"Sheehan's memoir is emphatically not about 'the glam end of cooking' or celebrity chefs, but about 'a straight blue-collar gig,' where the kitchens are staffed by the kind of guys who get off on the fact that the work is insanely grueling. . . . The war stories are as profane and outrageous as you'd expect, and Sheehan finds just the right balance between bravado and humility." Publ Wkly

Sheehy, Gail

Sheehy, Gail. **Daring**; My Passages: a Memoir. Gail Sheehy. William Morrow 2014 416 p. illustrations (some color) $29.99   **92**

1. Women journalists 2. Journalism -- United States -- History 3. Journalists -- United States -- Biography

ISBN 0062291696; 9780062291691

LC 2014034090

This memoir, by Gail Sheehy, is "a chronicle of her trials and triumphs as a groundbreaking 'girl' journalist in the 1960s. . . . [It] is the story of the unconventional life of a writer who dared . . . to walk New York City streets with hookers and pimps to expose violent prostitution; to march with civil rights protesters in Northern Ireland as British paratroopers opened fire; to seek out Egypt's president Anwar Sadat when he was targeted for death after making peace with Israel." (Publisher's note)

"Sheehy gives readers a distinct glimpse into some of the most important events of the last 40 years. . . . Her perspective on the women's movement and the decline of print journalism is especially compelling." LJ

Shelley, Mary Wollstonecraft, 1797-1851

Seymour, Miranda. **Mary** Shelley. Grove Press 2001 655p il $35; pa $20   **92**

1. Authors 2. Novelists 3. Women authors 4. Authors, English

ISBN 0-8021-1702-3; 0-8021-3948-5 pa

LC 2001-35094

First published 2000 in the United Kingdom

"A convincing and memorable portrait." Booklist

Includes bibliographical references

Shen, Aisling Juanjuan, 1974-

Shen, Aisling Juanjuan. A **tiger's** heart; the story of a modern Chinese woman. Soho Press 2009 309p $24   **92**

1. Memoirists 2. Financial analysts 3. Immigrants -- United States 4. Yangtze River valley (China) 5. Chinese Americans -- Biography

ISBN 978-1-56947-586-7; 1-56947-586-5

LC 2009-5426

"Like a suspense novel, this book is impossible to put down. All readers interested in China, as well as memoir fans (especially of success stories), must read this astonishing title." Libr J

Shepard, Sadia

Shepard, Sadia. The **girl** from foreign; a search for shipwrecked ancestors, forgotten histories, and a sense of home. Penguin Press 2008 364p il map $25.95; pa $16   **92**

1. Memoirists 2. Jews -- India 3. Motion picture directors

ISBN 978-1-59420-151-6; 978-0-14-311577-9 pa

LC 2008-3912

A young Muslim-Christian woman travels to an insular Jewish community in India to unlock her family's secret history.

"A readable account that gives a vivid taste of life in present-day India as well as a poignant glimpse of complicated family relations." Kirkus

Includes bibliographical references

Sherman, William T. (William Tecumseh), 1820-1891

Fellman, Michael. **Citizen** Sherman; a life of William Tecumseh Sherman. University Press of Kansas 1997 486p il pa $19.95   **92**

1. Generals 2. Memoirists 3. Secretaries of war 4. United States -- History -- 1861-1865, Civil War

ISBN 978-0-7006-0840-9; 0-7006-0840-0

First published 1995 by Random House

"This superb biography gives as full a portrait of nineteenth-century family dynamics as of the dynamics of the battlefield. Fellman's Sherman is not a lovable man, but he is a complete one." New Yorker

Includes bibliographical references

Flood, Charles Bracelen. **Grant** and Sherman; the friendship that won the Civil War. Farrar, Straus and Giroux 2005 460p il map $27   **92**

1. Generals 2. Presidents 3. Memoirists 4. Secretaries of war 5. United States -- History -- 1861-1865, Civil War

ISBN 0-374-16600-5

LC 2005-04170

The author "underscores the powerful bond formed between Ulysses S. Grant and William Tecumseh Sherman and tells the story of a friendship that would influence both the politics and the military operations of the Civil War. . . . One of the big-profile history books of the season and highly recommended for all history-minded readers." Booklist

Includes bibliographical references

Woodworth, Steven E. **Sherman**; [foreword by Wesley K. Clark] Palgrave Macmillan 2009 198p il map (Great generals series) $21.95   **92**

1. Generals 2. Memoirists 3. Secretaries of war 4. United States -- History -- 1861-1865, Civil War

ISBN 0-230-61024-2; 978-0-230-61024-8

LC 2008-22060

This is a biography of the Civil War general.

"An excellent brief life of a major and controversial figure." Booklist

Includes bibliographical references

Shulman, Alix Kates

Shulman, Alix Kates. **To** love what is; a marriage transformed. Farrar, Straus and Giroux 2008 160p $22   **92**

1. Love 2. Authors 3. Marriage 4. Novelists 5. Feminists
ISBN 978-0-374-27815-1; 0-374-27815-6
LC 2008-21504

"A fall from a loft bed left author Shulman's 75-year-old husband with traumatic brain injury and utterly dependent on his wife, as she recounts in this deeply affecting memoir of their ordeal together. . . . Carving out time for herself and her writing kept her from having a nervous breakdown, and while her hope at times flagged, Shulman's devotion never faltered, as demonstrated by her candid account." Publ Wkly

Shuster, Joe

Ricca, Brad. **Super** boys; the amazing adventures of Jerry Siegel and Joe Shuster: the creators of Superman. Brad Ricca. St Martins Pr 2013 432 p. $27.99   **92**

1. Superman (Fictional character) 2. Superman (Fictitious character) 3. Cartoonists -- United States -- Biography 4. Comic books, strips, etc. -- United States -- History and criticism
ISBN 0312643802; 9780312643805
LC 2013004046

This biography of Superman creators Jerry Siegel and Joe Shuster, by Brad Ricca, "reveals the real-life model for Lois Lane . . . and the model for Superman himself (Johnny Weissmuller, who played Tarzan). At the center of the story, of course, is Siegel and Shuster's decision to sell the Superman rights to Action Comics for a pittance--a choice they lamented the rest of their lives. The pair endured poverty, bad marriages, bad health, and a lack of recognition for their work." (Publishers Weekly)

"Ricca's comprehensive biography reveals the turmoil and creative genius that led to our most enduring superhero, the Man of Steel." Pub Wkly

Includes bibliographical references (pages 403-406) and index

Sickles, Daniel E., 1825-1914

★ Keneally, Thomas. **American** scoundrel: the life of the notorious Civil War General Dan Sickles. Talese 2002 397p $27.50; pa $15   **92**

1. Generals 2. Diplomats 3. Members of Congress
ISBN 0-385-50139-0; 0-385-72225-7 pa
LC 2001-43078

"A frequently spellbinding recitation of the career of a totally awful politician, crook, adulterer and murderer who was no good as a general either." N Y Times Book Rev

Siegel, Jerry, 1914-1996

Ricca, Brad. **Super** boys; the amazing adventures of Jerry Siegel and Joe Shuster: the creators of Superman. Brad Ricca. St Martins Pr 2013 432 p. $27.99   **92**

1. Superman (Fictional character) 2. Superman (Fictitious character) 3. Cartoonists -- United States -- Biography 4. Comic books, strips, etc. -- United States

-- History and criticism
ISBN 0312643802; 9780312643805
LC 2013004046

This biography of Superman creators Jerry Siegel and Joe Shuster, by Brad Ricca, "reveals the real-life model for Lois Lane . . . and the model for Superman himself (Johnny Weissmuller, who played Tarzan). At the center of the story, of course, is Siegel and Shuster's decision to sell the Superman rights to Action Comics for a pittance--a choice they lamented the rest of their lives. The pair endured poverty, bad marriages, bad health, and a lack of recognition for their work." (Publishers Weekly)

"Ricca's comprehensive biography reveals the turmoil and creative genius that led to our most enduring superhero, the Man of Steel." Pub Wkly

Includes bibliographical references (pages 403-406) and index

Silko, Leslie, 1948-

Silko, Leslie, 1948- The **turquoise** ledge; [by] Leslie Marmon Silko. Viking 2010 319p $25.95 **92**

1. Poets 2. Authors 3. Novelists 4. Women authors 5. Sonoran Desert 6. College teachers 7. Authors, American 8. Short story writers 9. Biography, Individual
ISBN 0-670-02211-X; 978-0-670-02211-3
LC 2010-12128

This book "combines memoir and family history and reflections on the beings and creatures that . . . [Marmo sees] on her daily walks through the arroyos and ledges of the Sonoran desert in Arizona." (Publisher's note)

"Silko draws on her Laguna Pueblo, Cherokee, Mexican, and European ancestry and extended family in this richly veined eco-memoir of desert life, spiritual forces, close bonds with animals, and environmental destruction." Booklist

Silone, Ignazio, 1900-1978

Pugliese, Stanislao G. **Bitter** spring; a life of Ignazio Silone. Farrar, Straus and Giroux 2009 426p il $35   **92**

1. Authors 2. Novelists 3. Authors, Italian 4. Essayists
ISBN 978-0-374-11348-3; 0-374-11348-3
LC 2008-50410

This is a biography of the Italian writer. Silone wrote three novels set in his birthplace, Pescina. Fontamara . . . was followed by Bread and Wine and The Seed Beneath the Snow. N Y Times Book Rev

The author a mature account of a life that produced some of the twentieth century's most powerful and widely translated literary art and political commentary. . . . A much-needed work of literary and political scholarship. Booklist

Includes bibliographical references (p. 387-397)

Simone, Nina

Cohodas, Nadine. **Princess** Noire; the tumultuous reign of Nina Simone. Pantheon Books 2010 449p il $30   **92**

1. Singers 2. Pianists 3. Jazz musicians 4. African American singers 5. African American musicians 6. Songwriters 7. Soul musicians 8. Biography, Individual
ISBN 0-307-37899-3 ebook; 0-375-42401-6; 978-0-

307-37899-6 ebook; 978-0-375-42401-4

LC 2009-22252

This is a biography of the singer. Discography. Bibliography. Index.

"Looking at every aspect of Simone's work, from stage decorum to audience interaction, the author offers many rich insights into her subject's conflicted emotional world. Throughout, she nurtures the reader's empathy for the artist but takes care to avoid unfounded speculation on racism or gender bias. In fact, this is a 360-degree profile of Simone, offering solid critical insights at every turn." Choice

Includes discography and bibliographical references

Sinatra, Frank, 1915-1998

Kaplan, James, 1951- **Frank**; the voice. Doubleday 2010 786p il $35; ebook $35   **92**
1. Actors 2. Singers 3. Biography, Individual
ISBN 0-385-51804-8; 0-385-53364-0 ebook; 978-0-385-51804-8; 978-0-385-53364-5 ebook

LC 2009-31046

This biography covers the life of the American singer and actor from his birth in 1915 to his comeback in 1954 in the film From Here to Eternity. Index.

"Kaplan's enthralling tale of an American icon serves as an introduction of 'old blue eyes' to a new generation of listeners while winning the hearts of Sinatra's diehard fans." Publ Wkly

Includes bibliographical references

Santopietro, Tom. **Sinatra** in Hollywood. Thomas Dunne Books 2008 530p il $29.95   **92**
1. Actors 2. Singers
ISBN 978-0-312-36226-3; 0-312-36226-9

LC 2008-24941

"Striving for honest critiques and a witty, encyclopedic coverage, Santopietro begins with Sinatra's 1935 short subjects; dances through the grandiose 1940s MGM musicals; documents Sinatra's professional and personal despair and decline in such giant turkey disasters as The Kissing Bandit (1948); and analyzes his Oscar-winning comeback in From Here to Eternity (1953). . . . This mammoth movie compendium, filled with forgotten facts, 53 b&w photos and a detailed filmography, is certain to satisfy Sinatra's legions of fans." Publ Wkly

Includes bibliographical references

Sirhan, Kamilah, d. 2001

Hikayati sharhun yatul./English. The **locust** and the bird; my mother's story. translated from the Arabic by Roger Allen. Pantheon Books 2009 302p il $24.95   **92**
1. Muslim women 2. Parents of prominent persons
ISBN 978-0-307-37820-0; 0-307-37820-9

LC 2008-54683

"Al-Shaykh's poignant family history, narrated in the voice of her mother, Kamila, transports us to Beirut in the nineteen-thirties. At eleven, the beautiful and strong-willed Kamila is illiterate, her family penniless. She falls in love with the handsome Muhammad, but at fourteen is married off to an older man. . . . Later, Kamila runs away with Muhammad, abandoning her daughters. Al-Shaykh writes in the prologue that this book is largely an attempt to come to terms with that decision. Through telling her mother's story, she learns to appreciate the sacrifices demanded of so many Arab women in their bid for freedom." New Yorker

Sitting Bull, Dakota Chief, 1831-1890

Utley, Robert Marshall. **Sitting** Bull: the life and times of an American patriot; by Robert M. Utley. Henry Holt 2008 464p il pa $18   **92**
1. Dakota Indians
ISBN 978-0-8050-8830-4; 0-8050-8830-X

A reissue with a new preface by the author of the title first published 1993

"This book is well written, strongly documented, and fairly reasoned to satisfy even specialists within the field. It surpasses all previous biographies of Sitting Bull." Choice

Includes bibliographical references

Yenne, Bill. **Sitting** Bull. Westholme 2008 379p il map $29.95   **92**
1. Dakota Indians
ISBN 978-1-59416-060-8; 1-59416-060-0

In this biography, the author "captures the extraordinary life of Plains Indian leader Sitting Bull while providing new insight into the nomadic culture of the Lakota." Publ Wkly

Includes bibliographical references

Skinner, B. F. (Burrhus Frederic), 1904-1990

Bjork, Daniel W. **B.F.** Skinner; a life. American Psychological Assn. 1997 298p il pa $19.95   **92**
1. Psychologists
ISBN 1-55798-416-6

LC 96-40385

A reissue of the title first published 1993 by Basic Bks.

This is a biography of the psychologist known for his utopian novel Walden Two, his book Beyond freedom and dignity, and his behaviorist theories

"Bjork places Skinner squarely in the context of the US social, technological, and political history. . . . Although heavily documented, Bjork's book is very readable because documentation is in endnotes. A handsome, well-indexed work, with an excellent bibliography." Choice

Skloot, Floyd

Skloot, Floyd. The **wink** of the zenith; the shaping of a writer's life. University of Nebraska Press 2008 231p $24.95   **92**
1. Poets 2. Authors 3. Novelists 4. Essayists
ISBN 978-0-8032-1119-3; 0-8032-1119-8

LC 2008-3674

"Novelist and poet Skloot was struck by a brain virus in 1988, which left him unable to write novels. The memoir form 'saved' him, and in his latest he ponders the proclivities and circumstances that led him to become a writer. . . . [This book is] wise, thoughtful, and gently humorous." Booklist

Slowinski, Joseph, 1962-2001

James, Jamie. The **snake** charmer; a life and death in pursuit of knowledge. Hyperion 2008 260p il $24.95   **92**
1. Snakes 2. Curators 3. Herpetologists
ISBN 978-1-4013-0213-9; 1-4013-0213-0

LC 2007-48987

James recounts "the gritty and sad story of Joe Slowinski, a flamboyant and well-known herpetologist who died in Burma in 2001, aged 38, from the poisonous bite of a krait snake. . . . This book is both a tribute to Slowinski's spirit and scientific accomplishments, and a cautionary tale about the dangers of an overly passionate ambition." Publ Wkly

Smith, Alfred Emanuel, 1873-1944

Finan, Christopher M. **Alfred** E. Smith, the happy warrior. Hill & Wang 2002 396p il $26; pa $16   **92**
1. Governors 2. Political leaders 3. State legislators 4. Presidential candidates 5. United States -- Politics and government
ISBN 0-8090-3033-0; 0-8090-1632-X pa
LC 2002-19476
This is a biography of the "governor of New York and the first Catholic candidate for president, trounced by Herbert Hoover in the 1928 election amidst a torrent of anti-Catholic bigotry." Booklist
"Finan writes well, but for an occasional lapse into anachronism." NY Times Book Rev
Includes bibliographical references

Smith, Joseph, 1805-1844

Barnes, Jane. **Falling** in love with Joseph Smith; my search for the real prophet. Jane Barnes. Jeremy P. Tarcher/Penguin 2012 294 p. $25.95   **92**
1. Faith 2. Mormons 3. Church of Jesus Christ of Latter-day Saints 4. Conversion
ISBN 1585429252; 9781585429257
LC 2012018119
This book is an "account of a female intellectual's passion for Mormon prophet Joseph Smith and her near-conversion to the faith." Jane Barnes "developed an especially profound fascination with Smith. Her interest manifested first as a treatment for a PBS documentary about Smith's life, then evolved into a full-blown love for the man and his work." She explored the Mormon faith and learned of her family's connections to it. (Kirkus Reviews)

Brodie, Fawn McKay. **No** man knows my history: the life of Joseph Smith, the Mormon prophet; by Fawn M. Brodie. 2nd ed rev and enl; Knopf 1971 499, xxp il hardcover o.p. pa $18   **92**
1. Mormons 2. Mormon leaders
ISBN 0-679-73054-0 pa
First published 1945
Taking as her title a phrase from a sermon by Joseph Smith himself, the author has attempted to discover as much of the truth concerning Joseph Smith and the beginnings of Mormonism, as can be found in an intensive research into documents, diaries, unpublished manuscripts, etc.
Includes bibliographical references

Bushman, Richard L. **Joseph** Smith; rough stone rolling. [by] Richard Lyman Bushman, with the assistance of Jed Woodworth. Knopf 2005 740p il map $35; pa $18.95   **92**
1. Mormons 2. Mormon leaders
ISBN 1-4000-4270-4; 1-4000-7753-2 pa
LC 2004-61613
In this biography of the founder of the Mormon church, the author "stresses the boy seer's thoroughly ordinary origins—born to a hard-pressed New England farm family and denied all but the rudiments of a formal education—to emphasize the marvel of the religious revolution he brought about. . . . A deft portrait of a deeply controversial figure." Booklist
Includes bibliographical references

Remini, Robert Vincent. **Joseph** Smith. Viking 2002 190p (Penguin lives series) $19.95   **92**
1. Mormons 2. Mormon leaders
ISBN 0-670-03083-X
LC 2001-56762
"A masterful evenhanded précis that will engross history and religion readers alike." Booklist
Includes bibliographical references

Smith, Patti

★ Smith, Patti, 1946- **Just** kids. Ecco 2010 278p il $27; pa $16   **92**
1. Rock musicians 2. Poets, American 3. Biography, Individual
ISBN 978-0-06-621131-2; 0-06-621131-X; 978-0-06-093622-8 pa; 0-06-093622-3 pa
The author writes about her relationship with the photographer Robert Mapplethorpe in the late 1960s and 1970s.
This "is one of the best books ever written on becoming an artist—not the race for online celebrity and corporate sponsorship that often passes for artistic success these days, but the far more powerful, often difficult journey toward the ecstatic experience of capturing radiance of imagination on a page or stage or photographic paper." Washington Post

Smith, Raymond J.

Oates, Joyce Carol, 1938- A **widow's** story; a memoir. Ecco 2011 415p il $27.99   **92**
1. Poets 2. Widows 3. Authors 4. Novelists 5. Bereavement 6. Loss (Psychology) 7. Essayists 8. Biographers 9. Magazine editors 10. Authors, American 11. Children's authors 12. Short story writers 13. Biography, Individual 14. Spouses of prominent persons
ISBN 9780062015532
This is an account of the novelist's loss of her "husband of 47 years, Raymond J. Smith. . . . He collaborated with his wife in founding The Ontario Review as well as Ontario Review Books." (N Y Times (Late N Y Ed))
"In a narrative as searing as the best of her fiction, Oates describes the aftermath of her husband Ray's unexpected death from pneumonia. Scattershot moments stand out — the day she cancels their 30-year subscription to The New York Times, unable to bear the sight of his favorite paper; her fury at the tulips, harbingers of spring, pushing through the snow ('Too soon! This is too soon!'); the night she weans herself from Lorazepam. A Widow's Story is the painful, scorchingly angry journey of a woman struggling to live in

a house 'from which meaning has departed, like air leaking from a balloon.'" Entertainment Wkly

Smithson, James, 1765-1829

Ewing, Heather P. The **lost** world of James Smithson; science, revolution, and the birth of the Smithsonian. [by] Heather Ewing. Bloomsbury 2007 432p il map $29.95 **92**
1. Chemists 2. Geologists 3. Scientists 4. Philanthropists 5. Smithsonian Institution -- History
ISBN 978-1-59691-029-4; 1-59691-029-1

This is a biography of the British chemist who founded the Smithsonian Institution in Washington, DC.

The author "provides a readable and informative perspective on late Enlightenment chemistry, backing it up with extensive archival research and forays into secondary literature on science." Times Lit Suppl

Includes bibliographical references

Snetsinger, Phoebe, 1931-1999

★ Gentile, Olivia. **Life** list; a woman's quest for the world's most amazing birds. Bloomsbury USA 2008 345p il $26 **92**
1. Bird watching 2. Bird watchers 3. Biography, Individual
ISBN 1-59691-169-7; 978-1-59691-169-7
LC 2008-27036

This is a biography of birder Phoebe Snetsinger. Index.

Gentile describes Phoebe Snetsinger as a "frustrated stay-at-home wife and mother during the 1950s and 1960s who began birding to escape the boredom of suburban life. When she was diagnosed with terminal cancer at age 49, she decided to travel the world in search of birds while her health allowed. Each trip became a short-term goal for Phoebe and let her focus on birds instead of the cancer. She did this for 18 years, traveling between two and ten months a year, despite two cancer recurrences, injuries, assaults, kidnapping, and other difficulties. Phoebe eventually amassed a life list of 8,674 species, or 85 percent of living birds then known." Libr J

Includes bibliographical references

Sneum, Thomas, 1917-2007

Ryan, Mark. **Hornet's** sting; the amazing untold story of World War II spy Thomas Sneum. Skyhorse Pub. 2009 386p il map $24.95 **92**
1. Spies 2. World War, 1939-1945 -- Secret service
ISBN 978-1-6023-9710-1
LC 2009-6210

Sneum's "real-life exploits include all the key elements of any good spy story: sex, danger, and intrigue. . . . Readers will find the book hard to put down." Libr J

Includes bibliographical references

Socrates

★ Hughes, Bettany. The **hemlock** cup; Socrates, Athens, and the search for the good life. Alfred A. Knopf 2011 484p il map $35 **92**
1. Philosophers 2. Athens (Greece) -- History
ISBN 978-1-4000-4179-4; 1-4000-4179-1
LC 2010-45486

"For decades, while his city underwent war and hardship and defeat and civil war and political restructuring, Socrates settled himself in the agora and talked of inner things, the essence of things. Some of his words were taken down by acolytes such as Plato and Xenophon; some of his mannerisms were mocked by playwrights such as Aristophanes; the master himself, a man Hughes claims 'we can all benefit from getting to know a little better,' wrote nothing, but his recorded dialogues, his 'Socratic method' of relentless questioning, have become indispensable pieces of our Western mental furniture. Hughes revisits all of this with the panache of a born explainer, enthusiastically filling out the world of ancient Athens. . . . She takes readers through the torturous birth and early crises of Athenian democracy, and she's refreshingly evenhanded about the resentment such a democracy might feel toward somebody like Socrates." Washington Post

Includes bibliographical (p. 438-472) references

Johnson, Paul, 1928- **Socrates**; a man for our times. Viking 2011 208p $25.95 **92**
1. Philosophers
ISBN 978-0-670-02303-5
LC 2011019767

"A succinct, useful exploration of life in ancient Athens and of the great philosopher's essential beliefs." Kirkus

Includes bibliographical references

Snyder, John

★ **Hill** of Beans; coming of age in the last days of the Old South. John Snyder. Natl Book Network 2011 256 p. $24.00 **92**
1. Family life 2. Southern States -- History 3. Great Depression, 1929-1939
ISBN 098306220X; 9780983062202

In this memoir, "[John] Snyder documents growing up in the Carolinas during the Great Depression . . . . Presenting remembrances from three geographic locations that shaped his young life, Snyder explores Cedar Mountain, N.C. . . . ; Greenville, S.C. . . . ; and the Snyder family farm in Walhalla, S.C. . . . Snyder also . . . profiles a wide range of family and friends—most notably his father, a hard man given to arcane phrases . . . and his Aunt Bess." (Publishers Weekly)

Includes bibliographical references and index.

Solomon, Dorothy Allred

Solomon, Dorothy Allred. **Predators,** prey, and other kinfolk; growing up in polygamy. Norton 2003 399p $24.95 **92**
1. Mormons 2. Polygamy 3. Teachers 4. Memoirists
ISBN 0-393-04946-9
LC 2003-1044

This is the memoir of "the only daughter of a polygamous, fundamentalist Mormon. . . . The twenty-eighth of 48 children, she was instilled, as were her many brothers, by her father with the sense of the family's difference, which the world beyond its circle, even most other Mormons (the church officially abolished polygamy in 1890), wouldn't welcome." Booklist

The author "provides a remarkably balanced account of the contradictions and pressures she experienced both from within her family and from the surrounding culture." Libr J

Includes bibliographical references

Sondheim, Stephen

Sondheim, Stephen, 1930- **Finishing** the hat; collected lyrics (1954-1981) with attendant comments, principles, heresies, grudges, whines and anecdotes. Knopf 2010 445p il $39.95   **92**

1. Songs 2. Musicals 3. Composers 4. Lyricists 5. Biography, Individual 6. Musical theater -- History 7. Popular music -- Writing and publishing

ISBN 0-679-43907-2; 978-0-679-43907-3

LC 2010-11056

"Along with the lyrics for all of his productions from 1954 to 1981—including West Side Story, Company, Follies, A Little Night Music, and Sweeney Todd—Sondheim discusses his relationship with his mentor, Oscar Hammerstein II, and his collaborations with . . . Leonard Bernstein, Arthur Laurents, Ethel Merman, Richard Rodgers, Angela Lansbury, Hal Prince, and [others]. . . . Sondheim [also seeks to] analyze his work and dissect his own songs as well as those of others." (Publisher's note) Index.

"There's so much more to 'Finishing the Hat' than witty, profound and groundbreaking lyrics. In chapters and annotations every budding lyricist and musical fan will relish, Sondheim covers everything from the history of musical theater and views of major lyricists to stories about the making of his shows and lessons in the craft of lyric writing. . . . The 80-year-old Sondheim, not surprisingly, turns out to be a remarkable writer, even when no rhymes are in sight. He's at turns funny and poignant, ornery and instructive. His honesty often stings, especially in analytical sidebars that detail the varied flaws of such heralded lyric-writing comrades as Noel Coward, Ira Gershwin, Lorenz Hart, Alan Jay Lerner and (heresy!) even Oscar Hammerstein II, his mentor." Cleveland Plain Dealer

Includes bibliographical references

Sonnenberg, Susanna

Sonnenberg, Susanna. **Her** last death; a memoir. Scribner 2008 273p $24   **92**

1. Authors 2. Journalists 3. Columnists

ISBN 978-0-7432-9108-8; 0-7432-9108-5

LC 2007-3515

Sonnenberg's memoir illuminates her resolve to forge her independence, to become a woman capable of trust and to be a good mother to her own children after being raised by a mother who was a compulsive liar and a drug user.

"A heartbreaking yet wickedly entertaining portrait of a magically seductive, immensely flawed mother who fails dramatically as a parent and of a daughter who learns to trust and love others despite an orphanlike upbringing marked by disillusion." Libr J

Sontag, Susan, 1933-2004

Sontag, Susan. **Reborn**; journals and notebooks, 1947-1963. edited by David Rieff. Farrar, Straus and Giroux 2008 318p $24   **92**

1. Authors 2. Novelists 3. Women authors 4. Essayists 5. Literary critics 6. Authors, American 7. Short story

writers

ISBN 978-0-374-10074-2; 0-374-10074-8

LC 2008-34247

"As a psychic collage, Reborn is far more fascinating than the sum of its parts: lists of errands, scraps of dialogue, notes on the breakup of a marriage. An essential tension animates almost every page. Sontag's theoretical mind always wants to be totalizing—to sum up, distill, command. But journal entries are, like the lives they document, provisional, incomplete, ragged. The resulting clash—with its canceled insights, non sequiturs, and self-critical marginalia—often reads like a brilliant pomo bildungsroman: A Portrait of the Theorist As a Young Woman," New York

Sorensen, Theodore C., 1928-2010

Sorensen, Theodore C., 1928-2010. **Counselor**; a life at the edge of history. [by] Ted Sorensen. HarperCollins 2008 556p il $27.95   **92**

1. Lawyers 2. Presidents 3. Senators 4. Members of Congress 5. Government officials 6. Biography, Individual 7. Presidential advisers 8. United States -- Politics and government -- 20th century

ISBN 0-06-079871-8; 978-0-06-079871-0

LC 2007-47328

This is a memoir by President Kennedy's advisor and speechwriter. Index.

"This book is instantly essential for any student of the period. It fills gaps in the historical record; it vividly conveys life inside the administration; and it generously dishes anecdotes." Washington Post Book World

Soto, Jock

Marshall, Leslie. **Every** step you take; a memoir. with Leslie Marshall. Harper 2011 271p il $24.99; ebook $11.99   **92**

1. Ballet dancers

ISBN 978-0-06-173238-6; 978-0-06-209798-9 ebook

LC 2011012725

"Acclaimed dancer Soto—a principal for the New York City Ballet for 20 years (1985–2005)—writes about his career, his Native American heritage, his homosexuality, his passion for cooking, his struggles to find a family and his discovery of love. . . . A powerful story, affectionately told, about the demands and dimensions of personal and professional success." Kirkus

Soyinka, Wole

★ Soyinka, Wole. **You** must set forth at dawn; a memoir. Random House 2006 499p map $26.95 **92**

1. Poets 2. Authors 3. Novelists 4. Dramatists 5. Essayists 6. Memoirists 7. Nobel laureates for literature

ISBN 0-375-50365-X; 978-0-375-50365-8

"By turns panoramic and intimate, ruminative and politically resolute, Soyinka's memoir is a dense but intriguing conversation between a writer and his times." Publ Wkly

Spark, Muriel

Stannard, Martin. **Muriel** Spark; the biography. W.W. Norton & Co. 2010 xxvi, 627p il $35   **92**

1. Authors 2. Novelists 3. Women authors 4. Authors,

Scottish 5. Biographers 6. Short story writers
ISBN 978-0-393-05174-2

LC 2009-47982

First published 2009 in the United Kingdom

This is "among the richest and most satisfying literary biographies of our time: not only a portrait of the artist herself but also a rendering of her literary and social context and a judicious examination of her works." Wall Street J

Includes bibliographical references

Speaker, Tris, 1888-1958

Gay, Timothy M. **Tris** Speaker; the rough-and-tumble life of a baseball legend. University of Nebraska Press 2005 314p il $27.95   **92**

1. Baseball players 2. Baseball managers
ISBN 0-8032-2206-8

LC 2005-16975

This is a "look at the Hall of Fame center fielder, whose colorful personality and remarkable talent were overshadowed by contemporaries like Ty Cobb and Cy Young. . . . Gay has insured the righting of history with this biography. A worthwhile read for any sports fan." Publ Wkly

Spector, Phil

★ Brown, Mick. **Tearing** down the wall of sound; the rise and fall of Phil Spector. Knopf 2007 452p il $26.95; pa $16.95   **92**

1. Record producers 2. Songwriters 3. Music arrangers 4. Recording producers
ISBN 978-1-4000-4219-7; 1-400-04219-4; 978-1-4000-7661-1 pa; 1-4000-7661-7 pa

LC 2007-4819

This is a biography of the record producer and songwriter. "Stacked with incredible anecdotes, Brown's entertaining and nuanced portrait lifts the fog of myth and outright falsehood (including Spector's own) that have obscured the celebrity producer (like an enormous, gravity-defying wig) through the years." Publ Wkly

Includes bibliographical references

Speer, Albert, 1905-1981

Fest, Joachim C. **Speer** : the final verdict; {by} Joachim Fest; translated from the German by Ewald Osers and Alexandra Dring. Harcourt 2002 419p il $30; pa $15   **92**

1. Architects 2. War criminals 3. National socialism 4. Memoirists 5. Nazi leaders 6. Germany -- Politics and government -- 1933-1945
ISBN 0-15-100556-7; 0-15-602874-3 pa

LC 2002-6074

"This is a valuable, important biography, but perhaps it is an effort to explain the unexplainable." Booklist

Includes bibliographical references

Sereny, Gitta. **Albert** Speer; his battle with truth. Knopf 1995 757p il hardcover o.p. pa $25   **92**

1. Architects 2. War criminals 3. National socialism 4. Memoirists 5. Nazi leaders 6. Germany -- Politics and government -- 1933-1945
ISBN 0-679-76812-2 pa

LC 94-19764

The author of this biography of the Nazi war criminal "conducted intensive and protracted interviews with Speer . . . and many of the people who were close to him. Along with the interviews and analysis are good descriptions of what was happening in Germany throughout the Third Reich. Sereny's clear and concise prose makes this book suitable for both the scholar and the lay reader. She has produced what will become one of the standard works in Holocaust studies." Libr J

Includes bibliographical references

Spender, Stephen, 1909-1995

Sutherland, John. **Stephen** Spender; a literary life. Oxford University Press 2005 627p il $40 **92**

1. Poets 2. Authors 3. Novelists 4. Essayists 5. Memoirists 6. Biographers 7. Literary critics 8. Short story writers
ISBN 0-19517-816-5

LC 2004-09727

"Stephen Spender was one of a generation of Oxford-educated English writers, including W. H. Auden and Christopher Isherwood, who sought to revolutionize literature in the 1930s. In this official account of his life . . . emphasis is appropriately placed on the 1930s, when Spender came to prominence writing prose, short stories, criticism, and journalism in addition to his politically charged poetry. He was as experimental in life as in art, as evidenced by his bisexuality and his loyalty to left-wing Socialist causes." Libr J

Stalin, Joseph, 1879-1953

Bullock, Alan. **Hitler** and Stalin; parallel lives. Knopf 1992 1081p il maps hardcover o.p. pa $25   **92**

1. Heads of state 2. Nazi leaders 3. Communist leaders 4. Political leaders 5. Soviet Union -- Politics and government 6. Germany -- Politics and government -- 1933-1945
ISBN 0-679-72994-1 pa

LC 91-52711

First published 1991 in the United Kingdom

"The twentieth century cannot be understood without close examination of the work of Stalin and Hitler. It is particularly important to note what their regimes and aims had in common and where they differed. Alan Bullock has put us all in his debt by placing their actions side by side, in enormous detail, and in chronological sequence to make the comparison easy." Times Lit Suppl

Includes bibliographical references

Conquest, Robert. **Stalin**; breaker of nations. Viking 1991 346p il hardcover o.p. pa $14.95   **92**

1. Dictators 2. Heads of state 3. Communist leaders 4. Political leaders 5. Soviet Union -- Politics and government
ISBN 0-14-016953-9 pa

LC 91-28782

"Intended for the general reader, [this work] provides a superb portrait of the man who terrorized his country for 30 years. . . . Briskly written, authoritative yet not pedantic,

filled with interesting incidents and anecdotes, [it] makes for fascinating reading." N Y Times Book Rev
Includes bibliographical references

★ Montefiore, Sebag. **Stalin** : the court of the red tsar; by Simon Sebag Montefiore. Knopf 2004 xxvii, 785p il map $30   **92**
1. Dictators 2. Heads of state 3. Communist leaders 4. Political leaders 5. Soviet Union -- History
ISBN 1-400-04230-5
LC 2003-27390
First published 2003 in the United Kingdom
"In the relentless detail, the mood-setting descriptions of the leader's surroundings, the sketches of the people around him and in Stalin's own words, pranks and tempers, Montefiore gives us not only the most intimate view of the general secretary that we have to date but a rounded and complex portrait of a man who could go from charming to lethal in the space of a few seconds." Nation
Includes bibliographical references

★ Montefiore, Sebag. **Young** Stalin; [by] Simon Sebag Montefiore. Knopf 2007 xxxii, 460p il map $30   **92**
1. Dictators 2. Heads of state 3. Communist leaders 4. Political leaders 5. Soviet Union -- History
ISBN 1-4000-4465-0; 978-1-4000-4465-8
LC 2007-29220
Stalin "is brilliantly brought to life in this superb biography." Hist Today
Includes bibliographical references

Pringle, Peter. The **murder** of Nikolai Vavilov; the story of Stalin's persecution of one of the great scientists of the twentieth century. Simon & Schuster 2008 370p il $26   **92**
1. Botanists 2. Heads of state 3. Communist leaders 4. Plant geneticists 5. Political leaders
ISBN 978-0-7432-6498-3; 0-7432-6498-3
LC 2008-03510
This is a biography of the Russian botanist and geneticist who was starved to death in a Soviet prison in 1943.
This "is a must-read to grasp the ultimate, disastrous effect of politics trumping science." Sci Books Films
Includes bibliographical references

Radzinsky, Edvard. **Stalin**; the first in-depth biography based on explosive new documents from Russia's secret archives. translated by H.T. Willetts. Doubleday 1996 607p il hardcover o.p. pa $16.95   **92**
1. Dictators 2. Heads of state 3. Soviet Union 4. Communist leaders 5. Political leaders
ISBN 0-385-47954-9 pa
LC 95-4495
For this biography of the Soviet ruler the author "has examined mountains of rare archival sources and interviewed many who lived through decades of Stalinist (mis)rule. The result is the best general biography of Stalin to date. Radzinsky strips away layer after layer of myth, falsehood, and

enigma to produce a riveting portrait of a man whose primary role model was Ivan the Terrible." Libr J
Includes bibliographical references

Service, Robert. **Stalin**; a biography. Belknap Press of Harvard University Press 2005 715p il map $29.95   **92**
1. Dictators 2. Heads of state 3. Communist leaders 4. Political leaders 5. Soviet Union -- History
ISBN 0-674-01697-1
LC 2004-61115
This book covers Stalin's life "from his early, troubled years in a small town in Georgia to the pinnacle of power in the Kremlin. . . . By providing such a rich and complex portrait of the dictator and the Soviet system, Service humanizes Stalin without ever diminishing the extent of the atrocities he unleashed upon the Soviet population." Publ Wkly
Includes bibliographical references

Stanley, Henry M. (Henry Morton), 1841-1904
Jeal, Tim. **Stanley**; the impossible life of Africa's greatest explorer. Yale University Press 2007 570p il map $38   **92**
1. Explorers 2. Journalists 3. Travel writers
ISBN 978-0-300-12625-9; 0-300-12625-5
LC 2007-923548
This is a biography of the explorer.
"There have been many biographies of Stanley, but Jeal's is the most felicitous, the best informed, the most complete and readable and exhaustive." N Y Times Book Rev
Includes bibliographical references

Stanley, Ralph, 1927-
Stanley, Ralph. **Man** of constant sorrow; my life and times. [by] Ralph Stanley with Eddie Dean. Gotham Books 2009 452p $27.50   **92**
1. Bluegrass music 2. Banjo players 3. Bluegrass musicians
ISBN 978-1-592-40425-4
LC 2009-21920
A memoir by the bluegrass singer and banjo player.
"Unashamedly old-fashioned, opinionated and prickly, . . . [the author is] at his best recalling his backwoods upbringing, the vicissitudes of the bluegrass road, the murder of one of his lead singers, regional Democratic politics, the power of gospel music and old-time religion and the fast-vanishing South of his boyhood. An often tart yet affecting music memoir." Kirkus

Stanton, Elizabeth Cady, 1815-1902
Ginzberg, Lori D. **Elizabeth** Cady Stanton; an American life. Hill and Wang 2009 254p il $25 **92**
1. Feminism 2. Suffragists 3. Women -- Suffrage
ISBN 978-0-8090-9493-6; 0-8090-9493-2
LC 2008-54395
The author "makes a convincing case for Stanton as the founding philosopher of the American women's rights movement in a lively voice that enhances her eccentric subject. . . . Ginzberg has created a vibrant portrait of a key, often misrepresented figure in American history." Am Hist
Includes bibliographical references

Stanton, Tom

Stanton, Tom. **Road** to Cooperstown; a father, two sons, and the journey of a lifetime. Thomas Dunne Bks. 2003 260p il $24.95; pa $13.95 **92**
1. Artists 2. Painters 3. Baseball -- Biography 4. National Baseball Hall of Fame and Museum
ISBN 0-312-30350-5; 0-312-33118-5 pa

LC 2003-40862

Companion volume to The final season

The author "examines family, fatherhood, life and, of course, baseball while on a road trip that was a lifetime in the making." Publ Wkly

Staples, Mavis

Kot, Greg. **I'll** take you there; Mavis Staples, the Staple Singers, and the march up freedom's highway. Greg Kot. Scribner 2014 320 p. illustrations (hardback) $26 **92**
1. Staple Singers 2. Gospel musicians -- United States -- Biography
ISBN 1451647859; 9781451647853; 9781451647860

LC 2013032633

This book, by Greg Kot, is a biography of "Mavis Staples--lead singer of the Staple Singers and a major figure in the music that shaped the civil rights era. From her love affair with Bob Dylan, to her creative collaborations with Prince, to her recent revival alongside Wilco's Jeff Tweedy, this . . . account shows Mavis as you've never seen her before. . . . Readers will also hear from Prince, Bonnie Raitt, David Byrne, Marty Stuart, Ry Cooder, Steve Cropper, and many other individuals." (Publisher's note)

"Kot's effort remains clear and respectful and takes us deep into the golden age of Mavis and her marvelously talented group." Pub Wkly

Includes bibliographical references, discography, and index

Steffens, Lincoln, 1866-1936

Steffens, Lincoln. The **autobiography** of Lincoln Steffens; foreword by Thomas C. Leonard. Heyday Books 2005 882p il (California legacy book) pa $21.95 **92**
1. Authors 2. Journalists 3. Essayists 4. Biographers 5. Social reformers 6. Writers on politics
ISBN 1-59714-016-3

LC 2005-27009

First published 1931 by Harcourt Brace & Co.

The life of an American reporter, journalist, student of ethics and politics.

"Here is a textbook on journalism; a treasure house for the historian of that wave of social idealism that shook the United States from 1900 to 1917; a casebook for the psychologist of political types. Above all it is the vivid diary of a bold and humane pilgrim." Survey

Stein, Gertrude, 1874-1946

Malcolm, Janet. **Two** lives; Gertrude and Alice. Yale University Press 2007 229p il $25 **92**
1. Poets 2. Authors 3. Novelists 4. Essayists 5. Memoirists 6. Literary critics 7. Authors, American 8.

Private secretaries
ISBN 978-0-300-12551-1; 0-300-12551-8

LC 2007-12085

This book examines the "relationship between Gertrude Stein and Alice B. Toklas." N Y Times Book Rev

"This is a vital addition to Stein criticism as well as an important work that critiques the political responsibility of the artist (even a genius) to the larger world." Publ Wkly

Includes bibliographical references

Stein, Gertrude. The **autobiography** of Alice B. Toklas. Modern Lib. 1993 342p hardcover o.p. pa $13 **92**
1. Poets 2. Authors 3. Novelists 4. Essayists 5. Memoirists 6. Literary critics 7. Authors, American 8. Private secretaries 9. Paris (France) -- Intellectual life
ISBN 0-679-60081-7; 0-679-72463-X pa

LC 93-15339

First published 1933 by Harcourt Brace & Co.

"The book is really Stein's autobiography, presented as though written by her secretary, Alice Toklas. The book provoked a rejoinder from various Parisian artists and writers, Testimony Against Gertrude Stein (1935). . . . For the average reader, however, Stein's book holds much fascination in its views of Parisian life and personalities, and the whole is offered in a genuinely witty style." Benet's Reader's Ency of Am Lit

Steinberg, Neil

Steinberg, Neil. **Drunkard**; a hard-drinking life. Dutton 2008 270p $24.95; pa $15 **92**
1. Journalists 2. Nonfiction writers 3. Alcoholics -- Rehabilitation
ISBN 978-0-5259-5065-3; 0-5259-5065-6; 978-0-4522-9543-8 pa

LC 2007-51603

"Forced by the court into rehab, Steinberg chronicles his journey to sobriety, following a circuitous route that included plenty of stops in local watering holes along the way. . . . Frank, funny, and insightful, Steinberg writes the book of his life." Booklist

Steinem, Gloria

Heilbrun, Carolyn G. The **education** of a woman; the life of Gloria Steinem. Ballantine Books 1996 450p il pa $23 **92**
1. Authors 2. Feminism 3. Journalists 4. Feminists 5. Memoirists 6. Magazine editors
ISBN 0-345-40621-4; 978-0-345-40621-7

First published 1995 by Dial Press

"The portrait that results is nuanced and thoughtful. . . . Heilbrun's goal is at once to understand how Steinem became the woman she is, and what her life can teach us about childhood and family, self and society. Slow at the start, but Heilbrun soon captures readers' interest and imagination." Booklist

Includes bibliographical references

Steinke, Darcey

Steinke, Darcey. **Easter** everywhere; a memoir. Bloomsbury USA 2007 225p $24.95 **92**

1. Authors 2. Novelists 3. College teachers
ISBN 978-1-582-34530-7; 1-582-34530-9

LC 2006-31637

"This book is an excellent account of a writer going head-to-head with the divine and finding some inner quiet— even in the darkest corners of her imagination." Time Out New York

Stern, Jessica, 1958-

Stern, Jessica. **Denial**; a memoir of terror. Ecco Press 2010 300p $24.99; ebook $11.99 **92**

ISBN 978-0-06-162665-4; 978-0-06-200011-8 ebook

A scientist and expert on terrorism and post-traumatic stress disorder describes her own journey through trauma and its lingering effects after repressing and disassociating her own ordeal as the victim of an unsolved sexual assault as a teenager.

"Though the narrative continually threatens to spiral into stream-of-consciousness ramblings, Stern always manages to hold it together, thus lending a sense of the floating dissociation she often feels while still holding the narrative together as a cohesive whole. She successfully unearths difficult emotional terrain without sinking into utter subjectivity and maintains an orderly progression without becoming clinical. A disturbing, captivating memoir." Kirkus

Includes bibliographical references

Steward, Samuel M., 1909-1993

Spring, Justin. **Secret** historian; the life and times of Samuel Steward, professor, tattoo artist, and sexual renegade. Farrar, Straus and Giroux 2010 478p il $32.50; ebook $16.99 **92**

1. Authors 2. Novelists 3. Tattoo artists 4. College teachers 5. Authors, American 6. Short story writers 7. Biography, Individual
ISBN 0-374-28134-3; 1-4299-3294-5 ebook; 978-0-374-28134-2; 978-1-4299-3294-3 ebook

LC 2009-43086

This book is "drawn from the secret diaries and journals of novelist, poet, and university professor Samuel M. Steward." (Publisher's note) Index.

"This is a rich and exuberant biography of a man who deserves to be better known, as well as a rare window on gay life in an era known mostly for its furtiveness and repression." Economist

Includes bibliographical references

Stoller, Mike, 1933-

Leiber, Jerry. **Hound** dog; the Leiber & Stoller autobiography. [by] Jerry Leiber and Mike Stoller with David Ritz. Simon & Schuster 2009 322p il $25 **92**

1. Composers 2. Lyricists 3. Songwriters 4. Rock music -- History and criticism
ISBN 978-1-4165-5938-2; 1-4165-5938-8

LC 2008-47821

"Collaboration is a messy business. So is autobiography. But it shouldn't be forgotten that Leiber and Stoller were among the pioneers who helped bring black and white musi-

cal forms together. It has been a historically fraught process, but the collision of cultures is probably what has given such energy and tension to American music. Hound Dog is an important part of that story." N Y Times Book Rev

Includes bibliographical references

Stone, I. F. (Isidor Feinstein), 1907-1989

Guttenplan, D. D. **American** radical; the life and times of I. F. Stone. Farrar, Straus and Giroux 2009 570p il $35 **92**

1. Authors 2. Journalists 3. Magazine editors
ISBN 978-0-374-18393-6; 0-374-18393-7

LC 2009-09667

This is a biography of the American journalist who published I.F. Stone's Weekly from 1953 until 1971.

"Guttenplan's lively biography brings back to life a man whose work has often been forgotten but whose writing and life provide a model for the kind of freethinking journalism missing in society today." Publ Wkly

Includes bibliographical references (p. [483]-538) and index. (BLCM)

★ MacPherson, Myra. **All** governments lie; the life and times of rebel journalist I.F. Stone. Scribner 2006 564p il hardcover o.p. pa $20 **92**

1. Authors 2. Journalists 3. Magazine editors
ISBN 978-0-684-80713-3; 0-684-80713-0; 978-1-4165-5679-4 pa; 1-4165-5679-6 pa

LC 2006-42389

"This biography interweaves his life and journalism within the context of the social and political era, providing an engaging overview of a complex man who challenged his contemporaries. Many of the political issues Stone confronted will resonate with today's readers." Libr J

Includes bibliographical references

Stone, Robert, 1937-

Stone, Robert. **Prime** green; remembering the sixties. Ecco 2007 229p il $25.95 **92**

1. Authors 2. Novelists 3. Screenwriters 4. United States -- History -- 1961-1974
ISBN 0-06-019816-8; 978-0-06-019816-9

LC 2006-46351

The author "is a born storyteller, with a wonderful feel for place and character that vividly evokes the cultural gulf America crossed in that decade." Publ Wkly

Stowe, Harriet Beecher, 1811-1896

Hedrick, Joan D. **Harriet** Beecher Stowe; a life. Oxford Univ. Press 1994 507p il hardcover o.p. pa $19.95 **92**

1. Authors 2. Novelists 3. Abolitionists 4. Children's authors 5. Nonfiction writers 6. Short story writers
ISBN 0-19-509639-8 pa

LC 93-16610

This biography "brings to life not just the complex and fascinating woman and writer but also the 19th-century America that shaped her and was in turn shaped by her. Hedrick manages to weave into his immensely readable biography a history teeming with the domestic detail of the famous

Beecher clan, the settling of the West, and the impact of the Civil War and the abolition movement." Libr J

Includes bibliographical references

Stravinsky, Igor, 1882-1971

Walsh, Stephen. **Stravinsky** : a creative spring; Russia and France, 1882-1934. University of California Press 2002 698p il pa $25.95   **92**

1. Composers

ISBN 978-0-520-22749-1; 0-520-22749-2

LC 2002-23256

First published 1999 by Knopf

"In this reference-oriented biography, Walsh uses diaries, press clippings, and other materials to probe in detail the life of a man kept very busy with effectively dividing his time between performance, composition, family, and mistress." Booklist

Includes bibliographical references

Walsh, Stephen. **Stravinsky** : the second exile; France and America, 1934-1971. Stephen Walsh. Alfred A. Knopf 2006 709p il $40   **92**

1. Composers

ISBN 0-375-40752-9

LC 2005-47231

Sequel to Stravinsky: a creative spring

"This is essential reading for musicologists and other music enthusiasts who wish to delve into the life and mind of perhaps the greatest composer of the 20th century." Libr J

Includes bibliographical references

Streb, Elizabeth

Streb, Elizabeth. **Streb**; how to become an extreme action hero. foreword by Anna Deavere Smith & introduction by Peggy Phelan. Feminist Press 2010 201p il pa $18.95   **92**

1. Dance 2. Dancers 3. Choreographers 4. Human locomotion

ISBN 978-1-55861-656-1

LC 2009-52614

"In this dizzying, inspirational self-help memoir, choreographer and performer Streb details her lifelong exploration of movement, the body, and time while providing brief lessons in math and practical philosophy. . . . In her explanations and experiments, including an unprotected and unrehearsed dive through glass, Streb gives readers news ways to consider the body and its movement, from 'the mechanical measurement of the legs, arms, torso, neck, hips, feet, shoulders, ankles, and knees' to 'the alchemic processes of the neurological systems.' Accompanied by full-color and black-and-white photographs, Streb's riveting prose should provoke and inspire philosophy students, dancers, and athletes of all kinds." Publ Wkly

Includes bibliographical references

Streisand, Barbra

Mann, William J. **Hello,** gorgeous; becoming Barbra Streisand. William J. Mann. Houghton Mifflin Harcourt 2012 576 p. (hardback) $30.00   **92**

1. Fame 2. Singers 3. Singers -- United States --

Biography

ISBN 0547368925; 9780547368924

LC 2012016364

In this book, "[b]estselling biographer [William J.] Mann . . . chronicles the . . . series of events as [Barbra] Streisand 'gate-crashed her way to fame.' Mann tightens the focus in this . . . volume to just the early, formative years of her career, choosing 1964 as his cutoff point. . . . The marketing of Streisand and the men in her life are key themes throughout." (Publishers Weekly)

Includes bibliographical references and index.

Stringer, Caverly

Stringer, Caverly. **Sleepaway** school; stories from a boy's life. [by] Lee Stringer. A Seven Stories Press 1st ed; Seven Stories Press 2004 227p $21.95; pa $13.95   **92**

1. Authors 2. Homeless 3. Memoirists 4. African Americans -- Biography

ISBN 1-58322-478-5; 1-58322-701-6 pa

LC 2004-3610

"In more than 30 connected true stories, Stringer portrays his boyhood as a poor, black foster child coincidentally growing up in a wealthy white neighborhood after he was sent to a school for troubled boys—mostly white, middle-class boys." Booklist

The author "deftly tells a believable, candid and vivid tale of a person scarred by his past." Publ Wkly

Strouse, Charles

Strouse, Charles. **Put** on a happy face; a Broadway memoir. Union Square Press 2008 326p il $19.95   **92**

1. Composers 2. Musicians 3. Composers -- United States

ISBN 978-1-4027-5889-8; 1-4027-5889-8

LC 2008-300247

"Three-time Tony Award–winning composer Strouse is best known for the musical Annie and his All in the Family theme, 'Those Were the Days.' While wary of the ghosts that appear, he summons up memories of a career that spans decades, beginning with his Manhattan boyhood, study at Rochester's Eastman School of Music, touring the South with Butterfly McQueen and early collaborations with lyricist Lee Adams. . . . Although he covers his film scores and music for TV commercials, the book's best chapters center on the staging struggles of Annie and Applause, plus breaking racial barriers with Sammy Davis Jr. in Golden Boy. . . . Detailing desperate rewrites, insecurities of theater people, footlight failures and humiliations, as well as theatrical triumphs, Strouse's superb backstage memoir deserves a standing ovation." Publ Wkly

Stuart, Granville, 1834-1918

Milner, Clyde A. **As** big as the West; the pioneer life of Granville Stuart. [by] Clyde A. Milner II and Carol A. O'Connor. Oxford University Press 2009 430p il map $34.95   **92**

1. Miners 2. Diplomats 3. Merchants 4. Frontier and pioneer life 5. Montana 6. Pioneers 7. Ranchers

ISBN 978-0-19-512709-6; 0-19-512709-9

A biography of "Granville Stuart (1834-1918), a Gold Rush miner, Montana cattle baron and hanging-hungry vigilante as well as a master of languages, a U.S. ambassador to Paraguay and Uruguay, and the author of an intriguing autobiography, Forty Years on the Frontier." Publ Wkly

"In fully revealing Stuart's fascinating and complex life, Milner and O'Connor illuminate the conflicting realities of the frontier." Libr J

Includes bibliographical references and index

Stuart, Jeb, 1833-1864

Wert, Jeffry D. **Cavalryman** of the lost cause; a biography of J.E.B. Stuart. Simon & Schuster 2008 496p il map $32; pa $18   **92**

1. Generals 2. Confederate States of America -- Army 3. United States -- History -- 1861-1865, Civil War
ISBN 978-0-7432-7819-5; 0-7432-7819-4; 978-0-7432-7824-9 pa; 0-7432-7824-0 pa

LC 2007-51552

This is a chronicle of the life of "the controversial cavalry leader of the Army of Northern Virginia until his death in combat in 1864. Wert's thoughtful account of Stuart's role at Gettysburg eventuates in a balanced analysis of a well-conceived reconnaissance-in-force. . . . This is a portrait of a Stuart more complex and, indeed, more attractive than either his friends or his enemies have painted in at least a generation." Booklist

Includes bibliographical references

Stuart, Sarah Payne

Stuart, Sarah Payne. **Perfectly** miserable; guilt, God and real estate in a small town. Sarah Payne Stuart. Riverhead Hardcover 2014 320 p. illustrations (hardback) $27.95   **92**

1. Autobiographies 2. Mother-daughter relationship 3. American literature -- New England 4. Authors, American -- 20th century -- Biography 5. Authors, American -- 21st century -- Biography
ISBN 1594631816; 9781594631818

LC 2013048095

"At eighteen, Sarah Payne Stuart fled her mother and all the other disapproving mothers of her too perfect hometown of Concord, Massachusetts, only to return years later when she had children of her own. Whether to defy the previous generation or finally earn their approval and enter their ranks, she hurled herself into upper-crust domesticity. . . . When Stuart's own mother dies, she realizes that there is no one left to approve or disapprove." (Publisher's note)

Sullivan, Ed, 1902-1974

Maguire, James. **Impresario**; the life and times of Ed Sullivan. Billboard Books 2006 344p il $24.95   **92**

1. Television personalities 2. Columnists
ISBN 0-8230-7962-7; 978-0-8230-7962-9 ISBN-13

The author "has written a fascinating biography and meticulously recorded the birth of TV, the heyday of newspaper columnists and the glamour of New York." Publ Wkly

Surville, Jean François de, 1717-1770

Blainey, Geoffrey. **Sea** of dangers; Captain Cook and his rivals in the South Pacific. Ivan R. Dee 2009 322p il map $27.50   **92**

1. Explorers 2. Voyages around the world 3. Ship captains 4. Naval officers 5. Travel writers 6. Oceania -- Exploration
ISBN 978-1-56663-825-8; 1-56663-825-9

LC 2008-52623

"An excellent work of popular history that recounts the exploits of men who dramatically expanded our knowledge of the globe." Booklist

Includes bibliographical references

Swift, Jonathan, 1667-1745

★ Damrosch, Leo. **Jonathan** Swift; his life and his world. Leo Damrosch. Yale University Press 2013 573 p. illustrations, maps (The Lewis Walpole Series in Eighteenth-Century Culture and History) (clothbound : alk. paper) $35   **92**

1. Authors, Irish 2. Authors, Irish -- 18th century -- Biography
ISBN 0300164998; 9780300164992

LC 2013013063

Pulitzer Prize Finalist: Biography or Autobiography (2014)

"In this . . ." biography, Leo Damrosch draws on discoveries made over the past thirty years to tell the story of [Jonathan] Swift's life anew. Probing holes in the existing evidence, he takes seriously some daring speculations about Swift's parentage, love life, and various personal relationships and shows how Swift's public version of his life--the one accepted until recently--was deliberately misleading." (Publisher's note)

"A rich and rewarding portrait of an irreplaceable genius." Kirkus

Includes bibliographical references and index

Sycamore, Mattilda Bernstein

Sycamore, Mattilda Bernstein. The **end** of San Francisco; Mattilda Bernstein Sycamore. City Lights 2012 192 p. $15.95   **92**

1. Gays 2. San Francisco (Calif.) 3. Gays -- United States 4. Lesbians -- United States -- Identity 5. Lesbians -- United States -- Biography
ISBN 087286572X; 9780872865723

LC 2012046897

Lamba Literary Awards - Transgender Nonfiction Winner (2014)

In this memoir, "gender-ambiguous author and activist [Mattilda Bernstein Sycamore] reflects on her halcyon days as a wild child in San Francisco. . . . She writes of becoming . . . seduced by the gender fluidity of San Francisco's house music-powered club scene circa 1992 and participation in AIDS activism with ACT-UP. Her efforts to create a San Francisco counterculture with political activist movement Gay Shame only reiterated how much she'd outgrown the Bay Area." (Kirkus Reviews)

Sylvester II, Pope, ca. 945-1003

Brown, Nancy Marie. The **abacus** and the cross; the story of the pope who brought the light of science to the Dark Ages. Basic Books 2010 310p il map $27.95 **92**

1. Popes 2. Religion and science 3. Biography, Individual

ISBN 9780465009503; 0465009506

LC 2010-36361

"As readably knowledgeable about Gerbert's political fortunes as about his intellectual influence, Brown is a lively narrator and interesting interpreter of Gerbert's life and world. This portrait gives both the science and the history audiences something to talk about." Booklist

Includes bibliographical references and index.

Taft, Helen Herron, 1861-1943

Anthony, Carl Sferrazza. **Nellie** Taft; the unconventional first lady of the ragtime era. 1st ed; William Morrow 2005 534p il $29.95; pa $15.95 **92**

1. Spouses of presidents

ISBN 0-06-051382-9; 0-06-051383-7 pa

LC 2004-52553

"This lively biography provides an illuminating glimpse into the life of an until-now underappreciated First Lady." Booklist

Includes bibliographical references

Tallchief, Maria

Tallchief, Maria. **Maria** Tallchief; America's prima ballerina. [by] Maria Tallchief with Larry Kaplan. University Press of Florida 2005 368p pa $19.95 **92**

1. Ballet dancers 2. Dance teachers 3. Osage Indians -- United States -- Biography.

ISBN 0-8130-2846-9; 978-0-8130-2846-0

LC 2005-42211

First published 1997 by Henry Holt

In this memoir Tallchief focuses "on her remembrances of her years with choreographer George Balanchine. . . . She met Balanchine at the start of her career, when she was with the Ballet Russe de Monte Carlo and Balanchine was about to form a company that would become a precursor to the New York City Ballet. Tallchief subsequently became Balanchine's wife, muse, and prima ballerina, and, though the marriage was short-lived, their artistic partnership endures in Balanchine's works created for Tallchief. She also writes about other stars, but the memoir sparkles when she recalls the subtlety and detail of a movement or the beauty of a musical phrase." Libr J

Tammet, Daniel, 1979-

Tammet, Daniel. **Born** on a blue day; inside the extraordinary mind of an autistic savant: a memoir. Free Press 2007 226p il $24; pa $14 **92**

1. Autism 2. Asperger's syndrome 3. Savants (Savant syndrome) 4. Mental calculators

ISBN 1-4165-3507-1; 978-1-4165-3507-2; 1-4165-4901-3 pa; 978-1-4165-4901-7 pa

LC 2006-41331

First published 2006 in the United Kingdom

This "first-person account offers a window into the mind of a high-functioning, 27-year-old British autistic savant with Asperger's syndrome." Publ Wkly

This "autobiography is as fascinating as Benjamin Franklin's and John Stuart Mill's, both of which are, like his, about the growth of a mind." Booklist

Taylor, Barbara Brown

Taylor, Barbara Brown. An **altar** in the world; a geography of faith. HarperOne 2008 216p $24.99 **92**

1. Clergy 2. Spiritual life 3. Religious scholars 4. Writers on religion

ISBN 978-0-06-137046-5

LC 2008-18303

The author, a preacher, gives an "account of her personal spiritual journey while counseling readers on how to encounter the sacred in everyday life, describing how to render a typical routine more relevant and sharing recommendations for intensive prayer and meditation." Publisher's note

"Taylor is one of those rare people who truly can see the holy in everything. Since everyone should know such a person, those who don't can—no, must—read this book, with its friendly reminders of everyday sacred." Publ Wkly

Taylor, Elizabeth, 1932-2011

Kashner, Sam. **Furious** love; Elizabeth Taylor, Richard Burton, and the marriage of the century. [by] Sam Kashner and Nancy Schoenberger. Harper 2010 500p il $27.99 **92**

1. Actors

ISBN 978-0-06-156284-6; 0-06-156284-X

LC 2010-06732

"In this dual biography of the two legendary film stars, the authors draw upon new information, including interviews with Elizabeth Taylor and with the Burton family, to capture the famously passionate and tumultuous relationship between the legendary couple. . . . It's a mesmerizing tale, but it's also sad, and sometimes ugly, as the two stars engaged in vicious fights, nursed their jealousies and insecurities, and descended into alcoholism while outwardly living a life of glamour and sophistication." Booklist

Includes bibliographical references

Taylor, Major, 1878-1932

Balf, Todd. **Major**; a Black athlete, a White era, and the fight to be the world's fastest human being. Crown Publishers 2008 306p il $24; pa $13.95 **92**

1. Bicycle racing 2. African American athletes 3. Cyclists

ISBN 978-0-307-23658-6; 0-307-23658-7; 978-0-307-23659-3 pa; 0-307-23659-5 pa

LC 2007-20747

The author "chronicles the life of the unlikeliest of stars in the early years of cycling: Marshall 'Major' Taylor. Taylor was an incomparable athlete, poet and celebrity, but he was also a black man living during a time when the scars of the Civil War and slavery were still fresh in the minds of Americans. Balf . . . does great work presenting the complex nature of Taylor's life, including his upbringing in poverty in Indianapolis, the years he was treated as a son by a rich white family, the fans who both worshipped and vilified him and his close relationships with his white trainer and promoter." Publ Wkly

Includes bibliographical references

Teferra, Haregewoin

Greene, Melissa Fay. **There** is no me without you; one woman's odyssey to rescue Africa's children. Bloomsbury Pub. 2006 472p il $25.95   **92**
1. Orphans 2. AIDS (Disease) 3. Ethiopia 4. Relief workers 5. Child benefactors
ISBN 978-1-59691-116-1; 1-59691-116-6

                    LC 2006-14088

This book chronicles "the odyssey of Haregewoin Teferra, who took in AIDS orphans. . . . In telling her story, journalist Greene who had adopted two Ethiopian children before meeting Teferra, juggles political history, medical reportage and personal memoir. . . . Greene takes a very close look at what appears to be the fringe of an important social event and illuminates the entire subject." Publ Wkly
Includes bibliographical references

Teller, Edward, 1908-2003

★ Goodchild, Peter. **Edward** Teller, the real Dr Strangelove. Harvard University Press 2004 xxv, 469p il $29.95   **92**
1. Physicists 2. Writers on science
ISBN 0-674-01669-6

                    LC 2004-54257

This is a biography of "the 'father of the hydrogen bomb,' a witness against J. Robert Oppenheimer in the latter's security hearing, and, finally, an ardent promoter of the Cold War arms race. . . . {The author} studied a wide range of primary and secondary sources and interviewed many people on both sides of the controversies that swirled around Teller. The result is a remarkably well-balanced study of a notoriously prickly and opinionated person." Libr J
Includes bibliographical references

Teller, Edward. **Memoirs**; a twentieth-century journey in science and politics. {by} Edward Teller with Judith Shoolery. Perseus Bks. 2001 628p il hardcover o.p. pa $18.95   **92**
1. Physicists 2. Writers on science
ISBN 0-7382-0778-0 pa

This memoir, by the nuclear physicist who worked to develop the hydrogen bomb, recounts his origins in the scientific community in Germany prior to the Nazi takeover and describes his "work on safe proliferation of nuclear energy, the so-called Stars Wars defense system and the early detection of earth-crossing objects. . . . Readers can enjoy these panoramic and beautifully written recollections of one of the great scientific, if controversial, figures of all time." Publ Wkly
Includes bibliographical references

Teresa, Mother, 1910-1997

Spink, Kathryn. **Mother** Teresa; a complete authorized biography. by Kathryn Spink. HarperOne 2011 336 p. ill. $15.99   **92**
1. Nuns 2. Nobel Prizes 3. Missions -- India 4. Christian missionaries 5. Biography, Individual 6. Missionaries of Charity
ISBN 0062026143; 9780062026149

                    LC 2011001621

"Spink's biography benefits from her own 18-year involvement with the work of the Missionaries of Charity Order as well as from the intimate relationship she developed over the years with Mother Teresa. . . . A final chapter in the book provides glimpses of Mother Teresa's affection for Princess Diana, a brief description of Mother Teresa's funeral and a short account of the election of Sister Nirmal as her successor." (Publ Wkly)

Terkel, Studs, 1912-2008

Terkel, Studs, 1912-2008. **Touch** and go; a memoir. [by] Studs Terkel, with Sydney Lewis. New Press 2007 269p il $24.95   **92**
1. Authors 2. Historians 3. Talk show hosts 4. Authors, American 5. Television moderators
ISBN 978-1-59558-043-6; 1-59558-043-3

                    LC 2007-18673

"Terkel's memoir is . . . a medley of all the extraordinary characters he's encountered through his career, from the adult loners of his youth in Chicago's Wells-Grand Hotel, to New Deal politicians. Terkel details his long journey through law school, the air force, theater, radio, early television, sports commentary, jazz criticism and oral history. . . . Americans might get to know their collective past a lot better if all history lessons were as absorbing and entertaining as this one." Publ Wkly

Terry, Ellen Dame, 1847-1928

Holroyd, Michael. A **strange** eventful history; the dramatic lives of Ellen Terry, Henry Irving and their remarkable families. Farrar Straus Giroux 2009 620p $40   **92**
1. Actors
ISBN 978-0-374-27080-3; 0-374-27080-5

                    LC 2008-48330

First published 2008 in the United Kingdom

"Holroyd's sweeping group biography traces the lives of Ellen Terry and Henry Irving, two stars of the Victorian theatre, and their descendants. Terry was 'embodied sunshine,' beloved for her naturalness and grace onstage. In 1878, when she was thirty-one, she began a professional (and perhaps amorous) partnership with Irving, the despotic actor-manager of the Lyceum Theatre, in London. . . . The pair rose to international fame performing melodramas and Shakespeare abridgments. Both had children who attempted careers in the theatre, and the second half of the book dwells on their struggles amid their parents' decline." New Yorker

Tesla, Nikola, 1856-1943

Carlson, W. Bernard. **Tesla**; inventor of the electrical age. W. Bernard Carlson. Princeton University Press 2013 xiii, 500 p.p ill. (hardcover) $29.95 **92**
1. Electricity -- History 2. Inventors -- United States -- Biography 3. Electrical engineers -- United States -- Biography
ISBN 0691057761; 9780691057767

                    LC 2012049608

This book, by W. Bernard Carlson, presents a biography of the inventor Nikola Tesla, "a major contributor to the electrical revolution . . . at the turn of the twentieth century. His inventions, patents, and theoretical work formed the basis of modern AC electricity, and contributed to the development of radio and television. . . . An astute self-promoter and gifted showman, he cultivated a public image of the eccentric genius." (Publisher's note)

"Carlson provides not only a more detailed explanation of Tesla's science but also a . . . focused psychological account of Tesla's inventive process." Booklist

Includes bibliographical references and index

Thomas, Abigail, 1941-

Thomas, Abigail. A **three** dog life. Harcourt 2006 182p $22   **92**

1. Authors 2. Novelists 3. Short story writers

ISBN 978-0-15-101211-4; 0-15-101211-3

LC 2005-33782

In this memoir, the author focuses on her "third husband, Rich, who flounders in a miasmic present after a hit-and-run in their Manhattan neighborhood shatters his skull, destroys his short-term memory and consigns him to permanent brain trauma." Publ Wkly

"Thomas has elevated what could be, at best, an overemotional sermon or, at worst, a grim romp in self-pity to a high plain of true inspiration." Booklist

Thomas, Dylan, 1914-1953

Lycett, Andrew. **Dylan** Thomas: a new life. Overlook Press 2004 434p il $35   **92**

1. Poets 2. Authors

ISBN 1-58567-541-5

First published 2003 in the United Kingdom

"Other biographies . . . have ably recounted the essential details of Thomas's life, but Lycett here provides a wealth of useful detail, bringing the Welsh poet's life story up to date." Libr J

Includes bibliographical references

Thompson, Hunter S., 1937-2005

McKeen, William. **Outlaw** journalist; the life and times of Hunter S. Thompson. W. W. Norton 2008 428p il $27.95; pa $16.95   **92**

1. Authors 2. Novelists 3. Journalists 4. Satirists 5. Columnists 6. Nonfiction writers

ISBN 978-0-393-06192-5; 0-393-06192-2; 978-0-393-33545-3 pa; 0-393-33545-3 pa

LC 2008-13214

This is a biography of the journalist and author of Hell's Angels (1967), Fear and Loathing in Las Vegas (1972), The Great Shark Hunt (1979) and Generation of Swine (1988).

"The book does justice to the legend that was Thompson. The thorough reporting lends insight to a writer who was as much a personality as a scribe." Am Journalism

Includes bibliographical references

★ Wenner, Jann S. **Gonzo**; the life of Hunter S. Thompson. by Jann S. Wenner & Corey Seymour; introduction by Johnny Depp. Little, Brown 2007 467p il $28.99   **92**

1. Authors 2. Novelists 3. Journalists 4. Satirists 5. Columnists 6. Nonfiction writers

ISBN 978-0-316-00527-2; 0-316-00527-4

LC 2007-11693

This oral biography is a "look at the turbulent life of Gonzo journalism pioneer Hunter S. Thompson (1937-2005). . . . This fine, fond biography amuses, inspires, outrages and haunts at all the right moments—and sometimes all at once." Publ Wkly

Thomson, David, 1941-

Thomson, David, 1941- **Try** to tell the story; a memoir. Alfred A. Knopf 2009 214p $23.95   **92**

1. Authors 2. Novelists 3. Father-son relationship 4. Biographers 5. Film historians 6. World War, 1939-1945 -- Personal narratives

ISBN 978-0-375-41213-4; 0-375-41213-1

LC 2008-19605

"In the heart of this haunting, eloquent memoir, as might be expected, [Thomson] gets rhapsodic when recalling the films that left an indelible impression on him: Red River, Meet Me in St. Louis, Citizen Kane, East of Eden. While following a film critic in the making, we also see the changing cultural landscape of the 1940s and 1950s through his eyes." Publ Wkly

Thoreau, Henry David, 1817-1862

Sullivan, Robert. The **Thoreau** you don't know; what the prophet of environmentalism really meant. Collins 2009 354p $25.99   **92**

1. Authors 2. Naturalists 3. Essayists 4. Pacifists 5. Authors, American 6. Writers on nature 7. Nonfiction writers

ISBN 978-0-06-171031-5; 0-06-171031-8

LC 2008-34495

The author "endeavors to free Henry David Thoreau from his calcified reputation as a cantankerous hermit and nature worshipper. Sounding like your favorite teacher who manages to make history fun and relevant, Sullivan vibrantly portrays the sage of Walden as a geeky, curious, compassionate fellow of high intelligence and deep feelings who loved company, music, and long walks." Booklist

Thorndike, Joseph Jacobs, 1913-2005

Thorndike, John. The **last** of his mind; a year in the shadow of Alzheimer's. Swallow Press 2009 243p il $24.95   **92**

1. Alzheimer's disease 2. Magazine editors

ISBN 978-0-8040-1122-8; 0-8040-1122-2

LC 2009-26118

"A brave, moving story of a son's devotion to his dying father. . . . Thorndike's prose is serenely beautiful and his patience in caring for an Alzheimer's patient is extremely admirable. An affecting work of emotional honesty and forgiveness." Kirkus

Thorpe, Jim, 1888-1953

Buford, Kate. **Native** American son; the life and sporting legend of Jim Thorpe. Alfred A. Knopf 2010 479p il $35   **92**

1. Athletes 2. Biography, Individual 3. Native Americans -- Biography

ISBN 978-0-375-41324-7; 0-375-41324-3

LC 2010012815

This biography of the Native American athlete covers topics ranging "from the disastrous divvying up of Native American land that young Jim witnessed in 1890s Oklahoma; to Thorpe's stellar performances in football, baseball, and track and field; to the stripping of his 1912 Olympics medals because he was paid to play baseball for two summers; and, finally, to the makeshift life he cobbled together after his playing days ended. Buford imparts a sense of the incandescent skills Thorpe applied to his sports, and the discrimination and self-destruction that shadowed him throughout his life." Booklist

Includes bibliographical references

★ Crawford, Bill. **All** American; the rise and fall of Jim Thorpe. John Wiley & Sons, Inc 2004 284p il $24.95 **92**

1. Athletes 2. Decathletes 3. Pentathletes 4. Olympic athletes 5. Native Americans -- Biography

ISBN 0-471-55732-3

LC 2004-14376

This "terse, punchy biography of sports legend Thorpe (1888–1953) illuminates the current debate over the exploitation of unpaid college athletes by moneymaking, headline-grabbing educational institutions." Publ Wkly

Includes bibliographical references

Thurston, Howard, 1869-1936

Steinmeyer, Jim. The **last** greatest magician in the world; Howard Thurston versus Houdini & the battles of the American wizards. Jeremy P. Tarcher/Penguin, a member of Penguin Group 2011 377p il $26.95 **92**

1. Magicians 2. Nonfiction writers

ISBN 978-1-58542-845-8

LC 2010-35384

This is a "an engaging full-length biography of the man Orson Welles called 'the master.' . . . Tracing the magician's rise to fame, this volume neatly juggles his marriages and his magic with his triumphs, travails, showmanship, and marketing ballyhoo." Publ Wkly

Timerman, Jacobo, 1923-1999

Timerman, Jacobo. **Prisoner** without a name, cell without a number; translated from the Spanish by Toby Talbot. University of Wisconsin Press 2002 164p (The Americas) pa $17.95 **92**

1. Journalists 2. Political prisoners 3. Newspaper executives

ISBN 978-0-299-18244-1; 0-299-18244-4

First published 1981 by Knopf

The author, "an outspoken Zionist and formerly a newspaper publisher in Buenos Aires, relates his 30-month political incarceration—torture and isolation in a clandestine prison, then detention in an official penal institution—which preceded his expulsion from Argentina in 1979." Publ Wkly

Tirone Smith, Mary-Ann, 1944-

★ Tirone Smith, Mary-Ann. **Girls** of tender age; a memoir. Free Press 2006 285p il map $24 **92**

1. Authors 2. Novelists 3. Memoirists 4. Young adult authors

ISBN 0-7432-7977-8

LC 2005-51376

This memoir, an "unsentimental view of life in a post-World War II working-class family, is interspersed with the story of Bob Malm, a serial pedophile who brutally murdered a fifth-grade classmate of hers in December 1953. . . . . This poignant memoir belongs in all collections." Libr J

Includes bibliographical references

Titian, ca. 1488-1576

Hudson, Mark. **Titian**; the last days. Walker 2009 304p il $27 **92**

1. Artists 2. Painters 3. Artists, French

ISBN 978-0-8027-1076-5; 0-8027-1076-X

"At the time of his death—from plague, in Venice in 1576—Titian had been one of the most celebrated artists in Europe for most of the century, the revered portrait painter of popes, emperors, and kings. But in his final works, as plague swept Venice, Titian, then in his mid-eighties, began confronting darker themes, including his own mortality. Hudson focusses his book on this group of paintings, now largely lost, and discusses Titian's career with humor, enlivening a potentially staid subject." New Yorker

Tocqueville, Alexis de

Epstein, Joseph. **Alexis** De Tocqueville; democracy's guide. Atlas Books 2006 208p (Eminent lives) $21.95 **92**

1. Statesmen 2. Writers on politics 3. Political scientists

ISBN 0-06-059898-0; 978-0-06-059898-3

LC 2006-47175

The author provides an "examination of the man, his works, his influence, his times and what we can learn from Democracy in America. . . . As an introduction to the man and a primer for his works, Epstein's book is admirable." Publ Wkly

Toklas, Alice B.

Malcolm, Janet. **Two** lives; Gertrude and Alice. Yale University Press 2007 229p il $25 **92**

1. Poets 2. Authors 3. Novelists 4. Essayists 5. Memoirists 6. Literary critics 7. Authors, American 8. Private secretaries

ISBN 978-0-300-12551-1; 0-300-12551-8

LC 2007-12085

"This is a vital addition to Stein criticism as well as an important work that critiques the political responsibility of the artist (even a genius) to the larger world." Publ Wkly

Includes bibliographical references

Stein, Gertrude. The **autobiography** of Alice B. Toklas. Modern Lib. 1993 342p hardcover o.p. pa $13 **92**

1. Poets 2. Authors 3. Novelists 4. Essayists 5. Memoirists 6. Literary critics 7. Authors, American 8. Private secretaries 9. Paris (France) -- Intellectual life

ISBN 0-679-60081-7; 0-679-72463-X pa

LC 93-15339

First published 1933 by Harcourt Brace & Co.

"The book is really Stein's autobiography, presented as though written by her secretary, Alice Toklas. The book provoked a rejoinder from various Parisian artists and writers, Testimony Against Gertrude Stein (1935). . . . For the average reader, however, Stein's book holds much fascination in its views of Parisian life and personalities, and the whole is offered in a genuinely witty style." Benet's Reader's Ency of Am Lit

Torre, Joe, 1940-

Torre, Joe. The **Yankee** years; [by] Joe Torre and Tom Verducci. Doubleday 2009 502p il $26.95 **92**
1. Baseball players 2. Baseball managers 3. Baseball -- Biography 4. New York Yankees (Baseball team)
ISBN 978-0-385-52740-8; 0-385-52740-3
LC 2008-52628
Joe Torre, who was manager of the New York Yankees from 1996 to 2007, focuses on the team's circumstances beginning with their loss of the seventh game of the 2001 World Series.

"This is an interesting and fast read and, for those who are not aficionados of baseball, the clash of powerful personalities and drama are more than sufficient to merit attention. Baseball enthusiasts, while undoubtedly familiar with the characters and events, will find the quick review of 12 years of Yankee history enjoyable for its details, particularly as the men's words flesh out the drama behind the sports pages." USA Today

Toulouse-Lautrec, Henri de, 1864-1901

Frey, Julia. **Toulouse** -Lautrec; a life. Phoenix 1995 597p il pa $27.50 **92**
1. Artists 2. Painters 3. Lithographers 4. Artists, French
ISBN 1-85799-363-2; 978-1-85799-363-9
First published 1994 by Viking
"The author chronicles Toulouse-Lautrec's transformation from a pampered invalid into one of the most radical of the fin de siecle artists. . . . Her sensitive, eloquent, and richly illustrated biography has brought the real Toulouse-Lautrec out from behind the scrim of myth." Booklist
Includes bibliographical references

Toussaint Louverture, 1743?-1803

★ Bell, Madison Smartt. **Toussaint** Louverture; a biography. Pantheon Books 2007 333p map $27 **92**
1. Generals 2. Revolutionaries
ISBN 978-0-375-42337-6; 0-375-42337-0
LC 2006-45848
This is a biography of the Haitian leader.
"This is the best biography of Toussaint yet, in large part because Bell does not shy away from the man's contradictions." N Y Times Book Rev
Includes bibliographical references

Tracy, Spencer, 1900-1967

Curtis, James. **Spencer** Tracy; a biography. Alfred A. Knopf 2011 1001p il $39.95; ebook $19.99 **92**
1. Actors 2. Biography, Individual
ISBN 978-0-307-26289-9; 978-0-307-59522-5 ebook
LC 2011014719
This is a biography of the actor. Bibliography. Index.
The author "presents an exhaustive and exhausting biography of the legendary Hollywood star, famed for his uncanny naturalism and authority on camera and best remembered for the series of films he made with longtime companion Katharine Hepburn. . . . A monumental, definitive biography of one of the finest film actors in the history of the medium." Kirkus
Includes bibliographical references and index

Trebincevic, Kenan, 1980-

Shapiro, Susan. The **Bosnia** list; a memoir of war, exile, and return. Kenan Trebincevic and Susan Shapiro. Penguin Books 2014 336 p. illustrations, map (paperback) $16 **92**
1. Muslims 2. Bosnia and Hercegovina 3. Yugoslav War, 1991-1995 4. Bosnian Americans -- Biography 5. Brčko (Bosnia and Hercegovina) -- Biography 6. Escapes -- Bosnia and Hercegovina -- History -- 20th century 7. Bosnia and Hercegovina -- Ethnic relations -- History -- 20th century 8. Yugoslav War, 1991-1995 -- Bosnia and Hercegovina -- Personal narratives
ISBN 0143124579; 9780143124573
LC 2013035345
In this memoir, author Kenan Trebincevic "blends his childhood experience of Bosnia's tragedy with a return to his original home in Brcko after nearly 20 years in the United States. The titular list is of goals the author intends to accomplish. They include seeking out surviving friends and relatives as well as confronting Serbs guilty of crimes against Trebincevi's defenceless Muslim family." (Library Journal)
"An engaging memoir of war trauma and the redemption to be found in confronting it." Kirkus
Includes bibliographical references and index

Trebing, Katie, 2002-

Whitehouse, Beth. The **match**; savior siblings and one family's battle to heal their daughter. Beacon Press 2010 255p $24.95; pa $16 **92**
1. Sick 2. Fertilization in vitro 3. Procurement of organs, tissues, etc. 4. Bone marrow -- Transplantation
ISBN 978-0-8070-7286-8; 0-8070-7286-9; 978-0-8070-0121-9 pa; 0-8070-0121-X pa
LC 2009035949
The author "tracks Stacy and Steve Trebing and their decision to create a baby boy selected as an embryo as a genetic match for a sister suffering from Diamond-Blackfan anemia, a rare and fatal disease." Publ Wkly

Trillin, Alice, 1938-2001

Trillin, Calvin. **About** Alice. Random House 2007 78p $14.95 **92**
1. Television producers
ISBN 1-4000-6615-8; 978-1-4000-6615-5
LC 2006-45573
This book is a "love letter to Trillin's wife, Alice, who died in 2001 at the age of 63 while awaiting a heart transplant, after a battle with lung cancer 25 years previously had left her heart weakened by radiation." N Y Times Book Rev
"This succinct account of Alice's upbringing, their meeting, their romance, their family, and her career beyond that of Trillin's helpmeet, offers glimpses into a multifaceted character." Booklist

Trotsky, Leon, 1879-1940

★ Service, Robert, 1947- **Trotsky**; a biography. Belknap Press of Harvard University Press 2009 600p il map $35 **92**

1. Revolutionaries 2. Communist leaders 3. Political leaders 4. Nonfiction writers 5. Biography, Individual 6. Soviet Union -- History 7. Communism -- Soviet Union 8. Soviet Union -- Foreign relations
ISBN 0-674-03615-8; 978-0-674-03615-4

LC 2009-25417

This biography discusses Trotsky's "relations with the leaders he was trying to unify; his attempt to disguise his political closeness to Stalin; and his role in the early 1920s as the progenitor of political and cultural Stalinism." (Publisher's note) Index.

"Thick and intensely researched but a pleasure to read, . . . [this] should remain the definitive work for some time. . . . This is a thoughtful, rewarding and essential contribution to 20th-century history." Publ Wkly
Includes bibliographical references

Truman, Harry S., 1884-1972

Dallek, Robert. **Harry** S. Truman; Robert Dallek. Times Books 2008 xviii, 183p.p (American presidents series) $22 **92**

1. Presidents 2. Vice-presidents 3. Senators 4. Presidents -- United States
ISBN 978-0-8050-6938-9

LC 2008-10193

This is a biography of the 33rd president.

This book is "the best starting point for knowledge of Truman's life and for an astute assessment of his career." Publ Wkly
Includes bibliographical references

Trump, Donald J.

Slater, Robert. **No** such thing as over-exposure; inside the life and celebrity of Donald Trump. Prentice Hall 2005 xxiv, 247p $24.95 **92**

1. Hotel executives 2. Airline executives 3. Real estate developers 4. Construction industry executives
ISBN 0-13-149734-0

LC 2004-116294

Donald Trump "is not so easily understood, but this book goes a long way toward defining him." Booklist
Includes bibliographical references

Tubman, Harriet, 1820?-1913

Humez, Jean McMahon. **Harriet** Tubman; the life and the life stories. [by] Jean M. Humez. University of Wisconsin Press 2004 471p il (Wisconsin studies in autobiography) hardcover o.p. pa $21.95 **92**

1. Abolitionists 2. Underground railroad 3. African American women -- Biography
ISBN 0-299-19120-6; 0-299-19124-9 pa

LC 2003-5676

In this volume the author "includes a collection of Tubman's autobiographical stories culled from rare early publications and manuscript sources. This book will become an important resource for scholars, historians, and general readers interested in slavery, the Underground Railroad, the Civil War, and African American women." Univ Press Books for Public and Second Sch Libr, 2004
Includes bibliographical references

Larson, Kate Clifford. **Bound** for the promised land; Harriet Tubman, portrait of an American hero. Ballantine Bks. 2003 xxi, 402p il map $26.95; pa $14.95 **92**

1. Abolitionists 2. Underground railroad 3. African American women -- Biography
ISBN 0-345-45627-0; 0-345-45628-9 pa

LC 2004-297886

"Using a clear writing style, Larson does an excellent job of placing Tubman in the context of her times." SLJ
Includes bibliographical references

Turing, Alan Mathison, 1912-1954

Copeland, B. Jack. **Turing**; Pioneer of the Information Age. by Jack Copeland. Oxford Univ Press 2013 224 p. $21.95 **92**

1. Mathematicians -- Biography 2. Turing, Alan Mathison, 1912-1954 3. Mathematicians -- Great Britain -- Biography
ISBN 0199639795; 9780199639793

LC 2012289154

Author Jack Copeland presents an "introduction to . . . scientist [Alan Turing] and his work. Copeland describes Alan Turing's revolutionary ideas about Artificial Intelligence and his pioneering work on Artificial Life, his all-important code-breaking work during World War II, and his contributions to mathematics, philosophy, and the foundations of computer science." (Publisher's note)
Includes bibliographical references and index

Leavitt, David. The **man** who knew too much; Alan Turing and the invention of the computer. W. W. Norton 2006 319p il (Great discoveries) $22.95 **92**

1. Mathematicians
ISBN 0-393-05236-2

LC 2005-18034

This is a biography of the British mathematician.

The author "succeeds in drawing a wonderfully vivid picture of his shy, dry, brilliant hero." Natl Rev
Includes bibliographical references

Turner, Ted, 1938-

Auletta, Ken. **Media** man; Ted Turner's improbable empire. Norton 2004 205p il $22.95 **92**

1. Philanthropists 2. Boat racers 3. Baseball executives 4. Broadcasting executives
ISBN 0-393-05168-4

LC 2004-12215

The author "describes how Turner's upbringing by a domineering father and his marriage to and later divorce from actress and radical Jane Fonda influenced his life and career. He also shows how Turner revolutionized TV by turning a tiny Atlanta station into a national cable powerhouse." Libr J
Includes bibliographical references

Turner, Tina

Turner, Tina. **I,** Tina; {by} Tina Turner, with Kurt Loder. Morrow 1986 236p il pa $6.99 **92**
1. Singers 2. Rhythm and blues musicians
ISBN 0-380-70097-2 pa

LC 86-16455

"Kurt Loder has edited I, Tina nicely, letting {Turner's} narrative take center stage, punctuating it with the voices of friends, colleagues, and family." Nation

Tuttle, Elizabeth

Chamberlain, Ava. The **notorious** Elizabeth Tuttle; marriage, murder, and madness in the family of Jonathan Edwards. Ava Chamberlain. New York University Press 2012 xiii, 257 p.p ill., maps (North American religions) (hardcover) $27.95; (ebook) $27.95 **92**
1. Connecticut -- Biography 2. Families -- Mental health 3. Murder -- Connecticut -- History -- 17th century 4. Divorce -- Connecticut -- History -- 17th century
ISBN 0814723721; 9780814723722; 9780814723739; 9780814723746

LC 2012010671

This book, by Ava Chamberlain, is part of the "North American Religions" series. "Who was Elizabeth Tuttle? In most histories, . . . she is a minor villain in the story of Jonathan Edwards, . . . the . . . American theologian of the colonial era. . . . Ava Chamberlain unearths a fuller history of Elizabeth Tuttle . . . in which anxious patriarchs struggle to govern . . . , unruly women disobey . . . , mental illness tears families apart, and loved ones die sudden deaths." (Publisher's note)

Includes bibliographical references (p. 201-245) and index.

Twain, Mark, 1835-1910

Loving, Jerome. **Mark** Twain; the adventures of Samuel L. Clemens. University of California Press 2010 491p il $34.95 **92**
1. Authors 2. Humorists 3. Novelists 4. Essayists 5. Satirists 6. Memoirists 7. Travel writers 8. Authors, American 9. Short story writers 10. Biography, Individual
ISBN 978-0-520-25257-8

LC 2009-15366

The author "serves up a balanced literary biography of a crowded life—'to renew our acquaintance with this familiar stranger in our literature and culture.' Many of the best chapters include sensitive appraisals of The Adventures of Huckleberry Finn, The Tragedy of Pudd'nhead Wilson, and the anonymously published Personal Recollections of Joan of Arc, with The Adventures of Tom Sawyer put in a different context as possibly the most overrated work of American fiction when considered as adult literature. . . . [This] is a solid contribution to literary interpretation of the man who infused American literature with what has been called 'tragic laughter.'" Publ Wkly

Includes bibliographical references

Powers, Ron. **Mark** Twain; a life. Free Press 2005 722p il $35 **92**
1. Authors 2. Humorists 3. Novelists 4. Essayists 5. Satirists 6. Memoirists 7. Travel writers 8. Short story writers
ISBN 0-7432-4899-6

LC 2005-48816

The author "develops topics neglected by other Twain biographers: the writer's genuinely mean late treatment of his bumbling brother, Orion; the negative impact of advancing technology on Twain's capacity for visual description; and his principled determination, late in life, to repay every cent he owed his creditors." Libr J

"A masterful biography of interest to both general readers and academics." Booklist

Includes bibliographical references

Shelden, Michael. **Mark** Twain; man in white: the grand adventure of his final years. Random House 2010 xxxix, 484p il $30 **92**
1. Authors 2. Humorists 3. Novelists 4. Essayists 5. Satirists 6. Memoirists 7. Travel writers 8. Authors, American 9. Short story writers
ISBN 978-0-679-44800-6; 0-679-44800-4

LC 2009-19719

The author "tells the story of Twain's last 40 months, richly detailing fresh facts new to most readers and fleshing out the conventional Twain biography to make the man's life complete. . . . This superb biography, told in a nonacademic tone, is saturated with sadness, but every reader will be grateful that, finally, Mark Twain appears before us, warts and all." Libr J

Includes bibliographical references

★ Twain, Mark, 1835-1910. **Autobiography** of Mark Twain; v1 The Complete and Authoritative Edition. Harriet Elinor Smith, editor; associate editors: Benjamin Griffin, Victor Fischer, Michael B. Frank, Sharon K. Goetz, Leslie Myrick. University of California Press 2010 736 p. ill. (The Mark Twain papers) (hbk.) $45.00 **92**
1. Autobiographies 2. Authors, American -- 19th century -- Biography
ISBN 0520267192; 9780520267190 (alk. paper)

LC 2009047700

This is "the first of a projected three-volume edition of the complete, uncensored autobiography. The book became an immediate bestseller and was hailed as the capstone of the life's work of America's favorite author." It includes text that was not to be published until the 100th anniversary of Twain's death. (Publisher's note)

"Laced with Twain's unique blend of humor and vitriol, the haphazard narrative is engrossing, hugely funny, and deeply revealing of its author's mind." Pub Wkly

Includes bibliographical references (p. 681-712)

and index

Twain, Mark, 1835-1910. **Autobiography** of Mark Twain; v2 The Complete and Authoritative Edition. Harriet Elinor Smith, editor; associate editors: Benjamin Griffin, Victor Fischer, Michael B. Frank, Sharon K. Goetz, Leslie Myrick. University of California Press 2010 736 p. ill. (The Mark Twain papers) (hbk.) $45.00   92

1. Autobiographies 2. Authors, American -- 19th century -- Biography
ISBN 0520272781; 9780520272781

LC 2009047700

This second volume of Mark Twain's autobiography "continues the writer's formula of random dictation, allowing readers to read forward and backward to find Twain's varied cultural illuminations. The pretense of narrating his own life allowed Twain to ransack 50 years of American culture to enlarge on the nature of humanity." (Choice Reviews)

"Twain traveled extensively and befriended many luminaries, and his colorful experiences give the book the same Dickensian scope as the first volume, and presents a vivid picture of America in the 19th century and Twain's indelible mark on it." Pub Wkly

Includes bibliographical references and index

Tye, Laurene, 1931-1989

Tye, Diane. **Baking** as biography; a life story in recipes. McGill-Queen's University Press 2010 268 p il   92

1. Baking 2. Homemakers 3. Eating customs 4. Women -- Canada 5. Biography, Individual 6. Food -- Social aspects 7. Canada -- Social life and customs
ISBN 978-0-7735-3724-8; 978-0-7735-3725-5 pa

Diane Tye uses her mother's recipe collection as a focus for this memoir and study of Maritime culture. Index

"Using her mother's recipes as a framework, Tye . . . explores Canadian women's roles from 1930 to 1980. She recalls her mother as a minister's wife who didn't care for baking yet consistently produced an abundance of sweets for her family, church, and community. Her succinct recipes range from simple (biscuits and oatcakes) to 'exotic' (anything involving JELL-O, Dream Whip, or canned pie filling). . . . Because this book blends memoir, biography, culinary history, and research, it should appeal to both scholars and readers who enjoy historical or intellectual food writing." Libr J

Includes bibliographical references

Tyler, John, 1790-1862

★ Crapol, Edward P. **John** Tyler; the accidental president. University of North Carolina Press 2006 332 p il map $37.50   92

1. Governors 2. Presidents 3. Vice-presidents 4. Senators 5. Members of Congress
ISBN 978-0-8078-3041-3; 0-8078-3041-0

LC 2005-37963

In this biography of the former U.S. president, the author "argues that Tyler was in fact a terrifically strong president who helped strengthen the executive branch. . . . This bal-

anced, fascinating volume will introduce a new generation of readers to an oft-ignored president." Publ Wkly

Includes bibliographical references

May, Gary. **John** Tyler. Times Books/Henry Holt and Co. 2008 183 p (American presidents series) $22   92

1. Governors 2. Presidents 3. Vice-presidents 4. Senators 5. Members of Congress 6. Presidents -- United States
ISBN 978-0-8050-8238-8; 0-8050-8238-7

LC 2008-18131

This biography of the American president focuses on "Tyler's controversial presidency, which saw him set aside his dedication to the Constitution to gain his two great ambitions: Texas and a place in history." Publisher's note

Includes bibliographical references

Uhlberg, Myron

Uhlberg, Myron. **Hands** of my father; a hearing boy, his deaf parents, and the language of love. Bantam Books 2009 232 p il $23   92

1. Deaf 2. Authors 3. Children's authors
ISBN 978-0-553-80688-5; 0-553-80688-2

LC 2008-25628

A memoir about growing up the son of deaf parents in 1940s Brooklyn

"Uhlberg's emotions toward his family, and especially his father, run the gamut from embarrassment to anger to a deep and abiding love. Sections titled 'Memorabilia' pepper the narrative, and many black-and-white photographs are scattered throughout this rich, textured portrait of the deaf community on Coney Island at a turbulent time in U.S. history." SLJ

Ulianov, Aleksandr, 1886-1887

Pomper, Philip. **Lenin's** brother; the origins of the October Revolution. W.W. Norton & Co. 2010 276 p il $24.95   92

1. Heads of state 2. Revolutionaries 3. Communist leaders 4. Political leaders 5. Soviet Union -- History -- 1917-1921, Revolution
ISBN 978-0-393-07079-8

LC 2009-27390

"In 1887, the future leader of the Russian revolution, Vladimir Ulyanov (later Lenin), was 17 when his 21-year-old brother was hanged for his role in a bungled attempt to assassinate Czar Alexander III. Historians consider this the seminal event that launched Lenin's career as a revolutionary. . . . [The author] delivers an absorbing and surprisingly detailed account of Alexander Ulyanov's short life and even shorter career (four months) as a terrorist." Publ Wkly

Includes bibliographical references

Umbrell, Colby, 1981-2007

Sielski, Mike. **Fading** echoes; a true story of rivalry and brotherhood from the football field to the fields of honor. Berkley Books 2009 342 p il $24.95   92

1. School sports 2. Iraq War, 2003-2011 3. Marines 4. Army officers 5. Iraq War, 2003- 6. Football --

Biography 7. Soldiers -- United States
ISBN 978-0-425-22974-3

LC 2009-17001

"Bryan Buckley was the captain of Central Bucks West and [Colby] Umbrell was one of the leaders of Central Bucks East when their teams clashed in their senior year of 1998. Eight years later, both were officers leading men in combat in Iraq, Buckley as a marine and Umbrell as an army ranger. Both were proudly fighting for ideals in which they believed, and only one would come home alive. Sielski . . . chronicles the lives of these two athletes and illustrates how their personalities and values were formed from interactions with family, friends, coaches, and community. In the process, he writes of much broader topics in contemporary American life: dreams, competition, resolve, war, honor, sacrifice, and true heartbreak." Libr J

Includes bibliographical references

Umrigar, Thrity N.

Umrigar, Thrity N. **First** darling of the morning; selected memories of an Indian childhood. Harper Perennial 2008 294, 18p pa $14.95 **92**
1. Authors 2. Novelists 3. Journalists 4. Essayists 5. Bombay (India) 6. Literary critics 7. Authors, American
ISBN 978-0-06-145161-4; 0-06-145161-4
First published 2004 in India

In this memoir, the author "alternates between sweet and biting accounts of her middle-class Parsi upbringing in 1960s and 1970s Bombay. With a mixture of rawness and warmth, she recalls moments from her tumultuous childhood through her teenage years, and finally into her early 20s when she leaves India for the U.S. . . . Umrigar's memoir is colorful and moving." Publ Wkly

Ung, Chou

★ Ung, Loung. **Lucky** child; a daughter of Cambodia reunites with the sister she left behind. HarperCollins Publishers 2005 268p il $24.95; pa $13.95 **92**
1. Homemakers 2. Cambodian Americans 3. Memoirists 4. Social activists 5. Cambodia -- History -- 1975-
ISBN 0-06-073394-2; 0-06-073395-0 pa

LC 2004-54346

Sequel to First they killed my father

In this "memoir, Ung picks up where her first . . . left off, with the author escaping a devastated Cambodia in 1980 at age 10 and flying to her new home in Vermont. . . . She and her eldest brother, with whom she escaped, left behind their three other siblings. This book is alternately heart-wrenching and heartwarming, as it follows the parallel lives of Loung Ung and her closest sister, Chou, during the 15 years it took for them to reunite." Publ Wkly

Includes bibliographical references

Ung, Loung, 1970-

★ Ung, Loung. **Lucky** child; a daughter of Cambodia reunites with the sister she left behind. HarperCollins Publishers 2005 268p il $24.95; pa $13.95 **92**
1. Homemakers 2. Cambodian Americans 3.

Memoirists 4. Social activists 5. Cambodia -- History -- 1975-
ISBN 0-06-073394-2; 0-06-073395-0 pa

LC 2004-54346

Sequel to First they killed my father

In this "memoir, Ung picks up where her first . . . left off, with the author escaping a devastated Cambodia in 1980 at age 10 and flying to her new home in Vermont. . . . She and her eldest brother, with whom she escaped, left behind their three other siblings. This book is alternately heart-wrenching and heartwarming, as it follows the parallel lives of Loung Ung and her closest sister, Chou, during the 15 years it took for them to reunite." Publ Wkly

Includes bibliographical references

Ungern-Sternberg, Roman, 1885-1921

Palmer, James. The **bloody** white baron; the extraordinary story of the Russian nobleman who became the last khan of Mongolia. Basic Books 2009 274p $26.95 **92**
1. Generals 2. Soviet Union -- History -- 1917-1921, Revolution
ISBN 978-0-465-01448-4; 0-465-01448-8

LC 2008-937254

First published 2008 in the United Kingdom

"What makes 'The Bloody White Baron' so exceptional is Palmer's lucid scholarship, his ability to make perfect sense of the maelstrom of a forgotten war. This is a brilliant book." N Y Times Book Rev

Includes bibliographical references

Updike, John

Begley, Adam. **Updike**; Adam Begley. Harper 2014 576 p. illustrations (hardback) $29.99 **92**
1. American authors 2. American literature -- History and criticism 3. Authors, American -- 20th century -- Biography
ISBN 0061896454; 9780061896453

LC 2013039246

This biography of John Updike "explores the stages of the writer's pilgrim's progress: his beloved home turf of Berks County, Pennsylvania; his escape to Harvard; his brief, busy working life as the golden boy at The New Yorker; his family years in suburban Ipswich, Massachusetts; his extensive travel abroad; and his retreat to another Massachusetts town, Beverly Farms, where he remained until his death in 2009." (Publisher's note)

"Begley draws on deep research and interviews with the author and his circle to chart his early influences—in particular his ambitious mother, Linda—and rigorously explore the heavily autobiographical dimensions of his fiction and poetry." Pub Wkly

Includes bibliographical references and index

Van Buren, Martin, 1782-1862

Widmer, Edward L. **Martin** Van Buren; [by] Ted Widmer. Times Bks. 2005 189p (American presidents series) $20 **92**
1. Presidents 2. Vice-presidents 3. Secretaries of state 4. Presidents -- United States
ISBN 0-8050-6922-4

LC 2004-53652

This is a "portrait of our eighth president, who, Widmer says, created the modern political party system." Publ Wkly

The author "keenly evokes the environment that enabled Van Buren to thrive. . . . Widmer also lends a certain dignity to Van Buren's post-presidential attempts to resolve the sectional crisis." N Y Times Book Rev

Includes bibliographical references

Van Vechten, Carl, 1880-1964

★ White, Edward. The **Tastemaker**; Carl Van Vechten and the Birth of Modern America. Edward White. Farrar, Straus & Giroux 2014 400 p. illustrations (hardback) $30 **92**

1. Photographers -- Biography 2. American authors -- Biography 3. Photographers -- United States -- Biography 4. Authors, American -- 20th century -- Biography

ISBN 0374201579; 9780374201579

LC 2013034003

A biography by Edward White, "'The Tastemaker' explores the many lives of Carl Van Vechten, the most influential cultural impresario of the early twentieth century: a patron and dealmaker of the Harlem Renaissance, a photographer who captured the era's icons, and a novelist who created some of the Jazz Age's most salacious stories." (Publisher's note)

"In orderly chapters, White tackles this complicated, multifaceted, tremendously fascinating and contradictory subject. . . . A vigorous, fully fleshed biography of an important contributor to American culture." Kirkus

Includes bibliographical references and index

Van Zandt, Townes, 1944-1997

Kruth, John. **To** live's to fly; the ballad of the late, great Townes Van Zandt. Da Capo 2007 326p il $26 **92**

1. Singers 2. Guitarists 3. Folk musicians 4. Country musicians 5. Songwriters

ISBN 978-0-306-81553-9; 0-306-81553-2

This is "the first biography of legendary Texas singer/songwriter Townes Van Zandt (1944-97). In his struggle for recognition among a wider public, Van Zandt wrestled for years with depression and alcoholism while writing songs—e.g., 'Pancho and Lefty' and 'Be Here To Love Me'—that today are revered by the elite of Texas and Nashville songwriters as well as by a cult group of fans. Through access to Van Zandt's friends, family members, and fellow musicians, Kruth provides an intimate and unflinching look at the singer's life." Libr J

Vanderbilt, Cornelius, 1794-1877

Renehan, Edward J. **Commodore**; the life of Cornelius Vanderbilt. [by] Edward J. Renehan Jr. Basic Books 2007 xx, 364p il $27.50 **92**

1. Businessmen 2. Financiers 3. Railroad executives 4. Shipping executives

ISBN 978-0-465-00255-9; 0-465-00255-2

LC 2007-22392

This is a "look at Cornelius Vanderbilt (1794-1877), who rose from nothing to amass one of the great fortunes in American history (more than $158 billion in 2005 dollars) in the burgeoning steamship and railroad industries." Publ Wkly

"A warts and more warts portrait of a brilliantly successful, genuinely despicable man." Kirkus

Includes bibliographical references

★ Stiles, T. J. The **first** tycoon; the epic life of Cornelius Vanderbilt. Alfred A. Knopf 2009 719p $37.50 **92**

1. Businessmen 2. Railroads -- History 3. Biography, Individual 4. Steamboats -- History

ISBN 978-0-375-41542-5; 0-375-41542-4

LC 2008-47879

National Book Award Finalists (2009)

This is a biography of the American steamship and railroad magnate.

"This is a mighty—and mighty confident—work, one that moves with force and conviction and imperious wit through Vanderbilt's noisy life and times. . . . This is state-of-the-art biography, crisper and more piquant than a 600-page book has any right to be." N Y Times (Late N Y Ed)

Includes bibliographical references

Varmus, Harold

Varmus, Harold. The **art** and politics of science. W.W. Norton 2009 315p il $24.95 **92**

1. Scientists 2. Nobel Prizes 3. Microbiologists 4. College teachers 5. Government officials 6. Public health officials 7. National Institutes of Health (U.S.) 8. Nobel laureates for physiology or medicine

ISBN 978-0-393-06128-4; 0-393-06128-0

LC 2008-42963

"Varmus offers a plain-spoken and fascinating story of his path from graduate student in English literature to the forefront of biomedical research. His journey to the highest echelons of the scientific establishment is as interesting for its incidental details as for its glimpse into the process of modern biomedical science." Washington Post

Includes bibliographical references

Vavilov, N. I. (Nikolai Ivanovich), 1887-1943

Pringle, Peter. The **murder** of Nikolai Vavilov; the story of Stalin's persecution of one of the great scientists of the twentieth century. Simon & Schuster 2008 370p il $26 **92**

1. Botanists 2. Heads of state 3. Communist leaders 4. Plant geneticists 5. Political leaders

ISBN 978-0-7432-6498-3; 0-7432-6498-3

LC 2008-03510

This is a biography of the Russian botanist and geneticist who was starved to death in a Soviet prison in 1943.

This "is a must-read to grasp the ultimate, disasterous effect of politics trumping science." Sci Books Films

Includes bibliographical references

Vespucci, Amerigo, 1451-1512

★ Fernandez-Armesto, Felipe. **Amerigo**; the man who gave his name to America. Random House 2007 231p il map $24.95; pa $15 **92**

1. Explorers 2. America -- Exploration

ISBN 978-1-4000-6281-2; 1-4000-6281-0; 978-0-

8129-7298-6 pa; 0-8129-7298-8 pa

LC 2006-51739

First published 2006 in the United Kingdom

The author chronicles the life and times of the explorer and navigator Amerigo Vespucci

"A well-connected Florentine wheeler-dealer who settled in Seville, Vespucci began by outfitting Columbus's ships and later made voyages of his own. . . . Fernandez-Armesto accepts that Amerigo Vespucci made two voyages to north eastern South America, one in 1499 and another in 1501-02. But the evidence is maddeningly vague on exactly where he went, what he did, and even in what capacity he served (he is unlikely to have been the commander, as he claimed). Faced by such unreliable sources, Fernandez-Armesto sticks to what can be said of Vespucci with confidence, and wisely opts to paint a rich portrait of the times rather than speculate about details that may never be known." Times Lit Suppl

Includes bibliographical references

Victoria, Queen of Great Britain, 1819-1901

Erickson, Carolly. **Her** little majesty: the life of Queen Victoria. Simon & Schuster 1997 304p il hardcover o.p. pa $19.95   **92**

1. Queens 2. Great Britain -- History -- 19th century
ISBN 0-7432-3657-2 pa

LC 96-35041

This is a biography of the British monarch

"Erickson has a knack for plucking pithy quotes, and the essentials of the queen's life are often deftly set out." Publ Wkly

Includes bibliographical references

Hibbert, Christopher. **Queen** Victoria; a personal history. Basic Bks. 2000 557p il hardcover o.p. pa $21   **92**

1. Queens 2. Great Britain -- History -- 19th century
ISBN 0-306-81085-9 pa

LC 2001-269136

Hibbert explores the life and reign of the British monarch based on "primary sources, particularly the 60 million words of Victoria's letters and journals. As a result, he renders Victoria and her familial and political relationships with deliciously gossipy and often touching intimacy." N Y Times Book Rev

Includes bibliographical references

Williams, Kate. **Becoming** Queen Victoria; the tragic death of Princess Charlotte and the unexpected rise of Britain's greatest monarch. Ballantine Books 2010 448p il $30; ebook $30   **92**

1. Queens 2. Princesses 3. Great Britain -- Kings and rulers
ISBN 978-0-345-46195-7; 978-0-345-52193-4 ebook

LC 2010-13227

First published 2008 in the United Kingdom with title: Becoming queen

"A lively, juicy read, full of the sordid details of the debauched rule of kings and princes that led to the moralistic rule of a queen focused on creating a royal family that embodied the ideals of a nation. Perfect for fans of royal his-

tories and historical television shows or armchair historians interested in a swift and enjoyable read." Libr J

Includes bibliographical references

Vidal, Gore, 1925-2012

Vidal, Gore. **Point** to point navigation; a memoir, 1964 to 2006. Doubleday 2006 277p il $26 **92**

1. Authors 2. Novelists 3. Dramatists 4. Essayists
5. Screenwriters
ISBN 0-385-51721-1; 978-0-385-51721-8

LC 2006-11644

"The memoir is a perfect encapsulation of Vidal's outsized personality—and readers' reactions will be determined by how they already feel about him." Publ Wkly

Vieira de Mello, Sergio, 1948-2003

Power, Samantha. **Chasing** the flame; Sergio Vieira de Mello and the fight to save the world. Penguin Press 2008 622p il $32.95 **92**

1. Diplomats 2. United Nations 3. United Nations officials
ISBN 978-1-594-20128-8

LC 2007-30978

This is a biography of the career diplomat who "died in a terrorist attack on UN Headquarters in Iraq in 2003." Publisher's note

"Strongly argued, lacerating, and utterly human, this invaluable history will be a catalyst for soul searching and debate." Booklist

Includes bibliographical references

Volk, Audrey Morgen

Volk, Patricia. **Shocked**; my mother, Schiaparelli, and me. Patricia Volk. Alfred A. Knopf 2013 304 p. ill. (some col.) (hardcover) $26.95 **92**

1. Femininity 2. Beauty, Personal 3. Mothers and daughters -- United States 4. Fashion designers -- France -- Paris -- Biography
ISBN 9780307962102; 0307962105

LC 2012034922

This book by Patricia Volk presents a "study of two very different but very glamorous women--her mother, Audrey, an upper-class New York domestic goddess with the looks and manners of Grace Kelly, and genius haute couture European artist Elsa Schiaparelli, whose book, art, and (yes) perfume forever change the course of young Volk's life." (Library Journal)

"[T]he narrative that emerges from Volk's deft interweaving of lives is as sharp-eyed as it is wickedly funny." Kirkus

Includes bibliographical references

Volk, Patricia

Volk, Patricia. **Shocked**; my mother, Schiaparelli, and me. Patricia Volk. Alfred A. Knopf 2013 304 p. ill. (some col.) (hardcover) $26.95 **92**

1. Femininity 2. Beauty, Personal 3. Mothers and daughters -- United States 4. Fashion designers -- France -- Paris -- Biography
ISBN 9780307962102; 0307962105

LC 2012034922

This book by Patricia Volk presents a "study of two very different but very glamorous women--her mother, Audrey, an upper-class New York domestic goddess with the looks and manners of Grace Kelly, and genius haute couture European artist Elsa Schiaparelli, whose book, art, and (yes) perfume forever change the course of young Volk's life." (Library Journal)

"[T]he narrative that emerges from Volk's deft interweaving of lives is as sharp-eyed as it is wickedly funny." Kirkus

Includes bibliographical references

Volpe, Joseph

Volpe, Joseph. The **toughest** show on earth; my rise and reign at the Metropolitan Opera. [by] Joseph Volpe with Charles Michener. Knopf 2006 304p il $25.95   **92**

1. Music administrators 2. Metropolitan Opera (New York, N.Y.)

ISBN 0-307-26285-5; 978-0-307-26285-1

LC 2005-57932

This is a memoir by the "general manager of New York's Metropolitan Opera since 1990. . . . This enthralling book provides an insider's view of a complex and fascinating institution." Libr J

Includes bibliographical references

Volpe, Lou

Sokolove, Michael. **Drama** high; the incredible true story of a brilliant teacher, a struggling town, and the magic of theater. by Michael Sokolove. Riverhead Hardcover 2013 352 p. ill (hardback) $27.95   **92**

1. College and school drama 2. Performing arts -- Study and teaching 3. English teachers -- Pennsylvania -- Levittown -- Biography 4. High school teachers -- Pennsylvania -- Levittown -- Biography 5. Theater -- Producers and directors -- Pennsylvania -- Levittown -- Biography

ISBN 1594488223; 9781594488221

LC 2013019393

In this book, author Michael Sokolove "chronicles the [Harry S Truman High School] drama director [Lou Volpe's] last school years and follows a group of student actors as they work through riveting dramas both on and off the stage. This is a story of an economically depressed but proud town finding hope in a gifted teacher and the magic of theater." (Publisher's note)

"During the season Sokolove spends at Truman, Volpe and his kids put on the play Good Boys and True and the musical Spring Awakening—both of which address teen sexuality, angst, and reckless behavior. Volpe pushes his student actors hard, but for most of them, being in one of his productions is transformative. Many alums go on to pursue careers in theater or the arts. A powerful look at the way a dynamic and dedicated teacher can change lives." (Booklist)

Voltaire, 1694-1778

★ Pearson, Roger. **Voltaire** almighty; a life in pursuit of freedom. Bloomsbury 2005 xxxii, 447p il $35   **92**

1. Poets 2. Authors 3. Novelists 4. Dramatists 5. Philosophers 6. Essayists

ISBN 978-1-58234-630-4; 1-58234-630-5

LC 2005-53027

This is a biography of the French philosopher.

The author "has composed a lively and thorough account of the illustrious philosophe's chaotic life." Choice

Includes bibliographical references

Von Braun, Wernher, 1912-1977

Biddle, Wayne. **Dark** side of the moon; Wernher von Braun, the Third Reich, and the space race. W.W. Norton 2009 220p il map $25.95   **92**

1. Rocketry 2. Scientists 3. Aerospace engineers 4. NASA officials

ISBN 978-0-393-05910-6; 0-393-05910-3

LC 2009-15572

The author "intertwines the rise of Hitler and Nazi Germany with scientist Wernher von Braun and his role in the creation of Germany's deadly V-1 and V-2 rockets, and his postwar apotheosis as a leader of the United States space program." Publ Wkly

"A stern, prosecutorial portrait of the famous German American rocketeer." Booklist

Includes bibliographical references

★ Neufeld, Michael J. **Von** Braun; dreamer of space, engineer of war. A.A. Knopf 2007 587p il $35; pa $19.95   **92**

1. Rocketry 2. Scientists 3. Aerospace engineers 4. NASA officials

ISBN 978-0-307-26292-9; 0-307-26292-8; 978-0-307-38937-4 pa; 0-307-38937-5 pa

LC 2007-5711

This is a "biography of Wernher von Braun, chief rocket engineer of the Third Reich—creator of the . . . V2 rocket—who became one of the fathers of the U.S. space program." Publisher's note

This "is a meticulously researched and technically accurate biography of von Braun." N Y Rev Books

Includes bibliographical references

Vonnegut, Kurt, 1922-2007

Shields, Charles J. **And** so it goes: Kurt Vonnegut: a life. Henry Holt and Co. 2011 513p il $30 **92**

1. Authors 2. Novelists 3. Journalists 4. Biographers 5. Authors, American 6. Short story writers 7. Science fiction writers

ISBN 978-0-8050-8693-5

LC 2010-45173

"Kurt Vonnegut had a chip on his shoulder when it came to the critics. Despite being one of the most popular writers of his generation, he routinely complained that his work was overlooked, or miscast as high-concept, middle-brow fiction. The publication of Charles J. Shields's fascinating new biography . . . probably won't put this beef to rest, at least among his loyalists. But it does provide a definitive and disturbing account of the late author, whose ambition and talent transformed him from an obscure science fiction writer to a countercultural icon." Boston Globe

Includes bibliographical references

Vreeland, Diana

Stuart, Amanda Mackenzie. **Empress** of Fashion; A Life of Diana Vreeland. HarperCollins 2012 419 p. $35   **92**

1. Fashion

ISBN 0061691747; 9780061691744

This book is a biography of fashion editor Diana Vreeland by Amanda Mackenzie Stuart. Mackenzie describes how Vreeland's "creation of an idealized image she called the Girl, coupled with a creative flair 'and the development of an idiosyncratic way with words,' propelled Vreeland into becoming one of the most influential tastemakers in American fashion." (Publishers Weekly)

Waits, Tom, 1949-

Hoskyns, Barney. **Lowside** of the road; a life of Tom Waits. Broadway Books 2009 xxix, 609p il $29.95   **92**

1. Actors 2. Singers 3. Rock musicians 4. Blues musicians 5. Songwriters

ISBN 978-0-7679-2708-6; 0-7679-2708-7

This "book lights up and whirls like one of the greasy carnival rides in Mr. Waits's own sprawling oeuvre . . . Mr. Hoskyns rummaged through Mr. Waits's interviews, pored through the historical record and talked to those who were willing to speak. Thus his unauthorized biography mirrors, in some ways, Mr. Waits's own junkyard aesthetic. Mr. Hoskyns picks up what shards of Mr. Waits's life he can find and holds them to the light, turning them eagerly in his hands." N Y Times Book Rev

Wallace, Alfred Russel, 1823-1913

Slotten, Ross A. The **heretic** in Darwin's court; the life of Alfred Russel Wallace. Columbia University Press 2004 602p il maps $77.50; pa $25 **92**

1. Naturalists 2. Writers on science

ISBN 0-231-13010-4; 0-231-13011-2 pa

LC 2003-68833

"With a narrative of almost 500 pages, the biography was clearly a labor of love for the author, who is a medical doctor and a Wallace enthusiast. Although some readers may find the amount of material overwhelming, it is quite accessible to general audiences." Sci Books Films

Includes bibliographical references

Wallace, Danny, 1976-

Wallace, Danny. **Friends** like these; my world-wide quest to find my best childhood friends, knock on their doors, and ask them to come out and play. with illustrations by Daniel Wallace. Little, Brown 2009 402p il $24.99   **92**

1. Humorists 2. Friendship 3. Television producers 4. Television scriptwriters

ISBN 978-0-316-04277-2

LC 2009-6616

First published 2008 in the United Kingdom

The author "describes how impending adulthood—he was about to turn 30—made him wonder what had happened to the friends he hung out with years ago. He did what any impulsive fella would do: he hauled out an old address book and started making calls. . . . A well-told, often laugh-out-loud-funny story that will ring true for anyone who's stared an approaching birthday in the face and not liked what they saw." Booklist

Wallace, David Foster

Every love story is a ghost story; a life of David Foster Wallace. D.T. Max. Viking 2012 x, 356 p.p $27.95   **92**

1. Suicide 2. Literary style 3. Depression (Psychology) 4. Novelists, American -- 20th century -- Biography

ISBN 0670025925; 9780670025923

LC 2012008488

Author D. T. Max's "book begins with [author David Foster] Wallace's childhood and ends with his suicide, detailing both the highs (his marriage to Karen Green) and lows (his string of breakdowns that began in college). There is the mutating public and critical opinion of his work, his troubled history with women, and his tendency to roam for much of his life while he struggled to balance writing and relationships, and writing and well-being." (Publishers Weekly)

Includes bibliographical references and index.

Wallach, Eli, 1915-2014

Wallach, Eli. The **good,** the bad, and me; in my anecdotage. Harcourt 2005 312p il $25; pa $16 **92**

1. Actors

ISBN 0-15-101189-3; 0-15-603169-8 pa

LC 2004-23121

The author "tells his story, from a Brooklyn childhood as the only Jew in an Italian neighborhood, through Actors Studio days with Brando and others, and on to his long and illustrious career on both stage and screen. . . . This compelling memoir shows the full range of a remarkable actor's life." Booklist

Walls, Jeannette

★ Walls, Jeannette. The **glass** castle; a memoir. Scribner 2005 288p $25; pa $14   **92**

1. Authors 2. Novelists 3. Memoirists 4. Gossip columnists

ISBN 0-7432-4753-1; 0-7432-4754-X pa

LC 2004-58907

The author "describes a childhood spent careering across the country, from California to West Virginia, in a succession of ever more rattletrap cars, in pursuit of increasingly implausible get-rich-quick schemes." Time

"Shocking, sad, and occasionally bitter, this gracefully written account speaks candidly, yet with surprising affection, about parents and about the strength of family ties—for both good and ill." Booklist

Walsh, Bill, 1931-2007

Harris, David. The **genius**; how Bill Walsh reinvented football and created an NFL dynasty. Random House 2008 385p il $26   **92**

1. Football coaches 2. Football -- Biography 3. San Francisco 49ers (Football team)

ISBN 978-1-4000-6665-0; 1-4000-6665-4

LC 2008-16566

This is a biography of the "head coach and general manager of the San Francisco Forty Niners." Publisher's note

"Walsh was one of the NFL's greatest coaches, and Harris' book does him justice." Booklist

Includes bibliographical references

Walsh, Mikey

Gypsy boy; my life in the secret world of the Romany Gypsies. Mikey Walsh. Thomas Dunne Books/ St. Martin's Press 2012 278 p.   **92**

1. Gay men -- Biography 2. England -- Ethnic relations 3. Gypsies -- England -- Biography 4. England -- Social life and customs 5. Romanies -- England -- Biography 6. Young gay men -- England -- Biography 7. Romanies -- England -- Social life and customs

ISBN 9780312622084; 9781250011978

LC 2011038168

This memoir, a "number-one best-seller in the UK following its 2009 release," was written "under a pseudonym to protect . . . [author Mikey] Walsh [who] has ongoing concerns for his safety after leaving the highly secretive Romany Gypsy community 15 years ago. . . . He claims his ultraviolent father once put a contract out on his life. He was born into a roving caravan of outsiders, brutally abused as a child (both physically by his father and sexually by an uncle), and never received any formal education growing up. He is also gay." (Booklist)

Walters, Barbara, 1931-

Walters, Barbara. **Audition**; a memoir. Alfred A. Knopf 2008 612p il $29.95   **92**

1. Women journalists 2. Talk show hosts 3. Television news anchors

ISBN 978-0-307-26646-0; 0-307-26646-X

LC 2008-05843

This is a memoir by the television newscaster.

"Alternating between tales of her personal struggles, professional achievements and insider anecdotes about the celebrities and world leaders she's interviewed, this mammoth memoir's energy never flags." Publ Wkly

Walton, Sam

Walton, Sam. **Sam** Walton, made in America; my story. by Sam Walton with John Huey. Bantam Books 1992 346p il pa $7.99   **92**

1. Businessmen 2. Retail executives 3. Wal-Mart Stores, Inc.

ISBN 0-553-56283-5; 978-0-553-56283-5

First published 1992 by Doubleday

The founder of Wal-Mart Stores, the largest retail chain in the world, recounts how he made his fortune.

"Readers will enjoy the folksy narrative of the small-town millionaire who revolutionized retail distribution. . . . Coauthor Huey does a fine job of incorporating candid testimonials from family members and associates." Libr J

Warburg, Siegmund George Sir, 1902-1982

Ferguson, Niall, 1964- **High** financier; the lives and time of Siegmund Warburg. Penguin Press 2010 548p il pa $22; $35   **92**

1. Banks and banking 2. Bankers 3. SBC Warburg (Firm) 4. Biography, Individual 5. Banks and banking

-- Great Britain -- History -- 20th century

ISBN 978-0-14-311940-1 pa; 978-1-59420-246-9

LC 2010-18353

This is a biography of the founder of the investment bank S. G. Warburg and Company. Index.

"Ferguson draws a richly vivid portrait of this unusual banker, an intellectual who read the Latin and Greek classics in the original and preferred Nietzsche to newspapers." N Y Times Book Rev

Includes bibliographical references

Ward, Jesmyn

Ward, Jesmyn. **Men** We Reaped; A Memoir. by Jesmyn Ward. Bloomsbury USA 2013 272 p. $26   **92**

1. Death 2. Grief 3. Poverty -- United States 4. African American men -- Mississippi 5. Rural poor -- Mississippi -- Biography 6. African American women authors -- Biography

ISBN 160819521X; 9781608195213

LC 2013013600

In this memoir, author Jesmyn Ward tells how she "grew up in poverty in rural Mississippi. She writes powerfully about the pressures this brings, on the men who can do no right and the women who stand in for family in a society where the men are often absent. She bravely tells her story, revisiting the agonizing losses of her only brother and her friends." (Publisher's note)

Includes bibliographical references and index

Ward, Samuel, 1814-1884

Jacob, Kathryn Allamong. **King** of the lobby; the life and times of Sam Ward, man-about-Washington in the Gilded Age. Johns Hopkins University Press 2010 212p il $40   **92**

1. Lobbying 2. Lobbyists 3. United States -- Politics and government -- 1861-1865 4. United States -- Politics and government -- 1865-1898

ISBN 978-0-8018-9397-1; 0-8018-9397-6

LC 2009-9807

This is a "biography of Sam Ward, scion of a New York banking family, '49er, spendthrift and lobbyist. Ward earned the title 'King of the Lobby' by applying savoir faire, gastronomy and a genius for social combinations to the hitherto crude process of influencing votes in Congress." Publ Wkly

The author's "trim and surprising biography of Sam Ward . . . will not change most people's view of what is essentially a hustler's profession. But she brilliantly shows how, in the hands of a master, lobbying can be lifted to the level of art." Wall Street J

Includes bibliographical references

Wareham, Dean

Wareham, Dean. **Black** postcards; a rock & roll romance. Penguin Press 2008 324p il $25.95   **92**

1. Singers 2. Guitarists 3. Rock musicians 4. Luna (Musical group) 5. Galaxie 500 (Musical group)

ISBN 978-1-59420-155-4; 1-59420-155-2

LC 2007-35280

"In this collection of over 50 sequential autobiographical essays, . . . [the author] takes us from his childhood in New Zealand, through his formative years exploring New York

City's punk scene, to his adult life in Cambridge, MA, where he becomes a notable figure in the alternative music scene. Wareham documents in great detail the history of his two bands, Galaxy 500 and Luna. . . . Fans of Wareham's bands and such bands as Bongwater, Cocteau Twins, R.E.M., and the Velvet Underground, as well as anyone with an interest in American and European alternative music, will find this to be an insightful and entertaining read." Libr J

Warhol, Andy, 1928?-1987

★ Scherman, Tony. **Pop**; the genius of Andy Warhol. [by] Tony Scherman and David Dalton. HarperCollins 2009 509p il $40 **92**
1. Artists 2. Pop art 3. Artists -- United States 4. Motion picture directors
ISBN 978-0-06-621243-2; 0-06-621243-X
LC 2009-24815
This biography covers the artist's career and personal life through 1968.
"Not only is . . . [this book] well written and researched, it manages to unearth details that reframe the debate about Warhol's real importance as an artist." Bookforum
Includes bibliographical references

Warren, Elizabeth 1949-

Warren, Elizabeth, 1949- A **fighting** chance; Elizabeth Warren. Metropolitan, Henry Holt & Co. 2014 384 p. illustrations (chiefly color) (hardcover) $28 **92**
1. Autobiographies 2. Politicians' writings 3. Middle class -- United States 4. Legislators -- United States -- Biography 5. United States. Congress. Senate -- Biography 6. Women legislators -- United States -- Biography 7. United States -- Politics and government -- 2009-
ISBN 1627790527; 9781627790529
LC 2014000776
This book by Elizabeth Warren tells the "story of the two-decade journey that taught her how Washington really works--and really doesn't. . . . She fought for better bankruptcy laws for ten years and lost. She tried to hold the federal government accountable during the financial crisis but became a target of the big banks. . . . Finally, at age 62, she decided to run for elective office and won the most competitive--and watched--Senate race in the country." (Publisher's note)
"Warren emerges as a committed advocate with real world sensibility, who tasted tough economic times at an early age and did not forget its bitterness." Pub Wkly
Includes bibliographical references and index

Washington, Booker T., 1856-1915

Harlan, Louis R. **Booker** T. Washington: the making of a black leader, 1856-1901. Oxford Univ. Press 1972 379p il hardcover o.p. pa $21.50 **92**
1. Slaves 2. Authors 3. Educators 4. African American educators 5. Memoirists 6. Nonfiction writers 7. Tuskegee Institute 8. Civil rights activists 9. African Americans -- Biography
ISBN 0-19-501915-6 pa
This book "covers Washington's life from his birth as a slave in western Virginia up to [the year 1901, when he

dined] with Theodore Roosevelt at the White House, an event signifying white recognition of Washington as the chief spokesman for black interests in the period before World War I." Libr J

Harlan, Louis R. **Booker** T. Washington: the wizard of Tuskegee, 1901-1915. Oxford Univ. Press 1983 548p il hardcover o.p. pa $24.95 **92**
1. Slaves 2. Authors 3. Educators 4. African American educators 5. Memoirists 6. Nonfiction writers 7. Tuskegee Institute 8. Civil rights activists 9. African Americans -- Biography
ISBN 0-19-504229-8 pa
LC 82-14547
This is the second and concluding volume of a life of the black educator and founder of Tuskegee Institute.
"Having avoided the pitfalls of white guilt and black rage and the temptation to judge the past by standards of the present, Mr. Harlan deserves honors for his remarkable achievement." N Y Times Book Rev
Includes bibliographical references

Norrell, Robert J. **Up** from history; the life of Booker T. Washington. Belknap Press of Harvard University Press 2009 508p il $35 **92**
1. Slaves 2. Authors 3. Educators 4. African American educators 5. Memoirists 6. Nonfiction writers 7. Tuskegee Institute 8. Biography, Individual 9. Civil rights activists 10. African Americans -- Biography 11. Race discrimination -- History
ISBN 067403211X; 9780674032118; 978-0-674-03211-8; 0-674-03211-X
LC 2008-32599
This is a biography of the educator who founded the Tuskegee Institute and wrote the memoir Up From Slavery (1901). Index.
This "is in all respects an exemplary book, scrupulously fair to its subject and thus to the reader as well." Washington Post Book World
Includes bibliographical references

Smock, Raymond W. **Booker** T. Washington; black leadership in the age of Jim Crow. [by] Raymond W. Smock. Ivan R. Dee 2009 223p il (Library of African-American biography) $26 **92**
1. Slaves 2. Authors 3. Educators 4. African American educators 5. Memoirists 6. Nonfiction writers 7. Tuskegee Institute 8. Civil rights activists 9. African Americans -- Biography
ISBN 978-1-56663-725-1; 1-56663-725-2
LC 2009-3277
The author "examines Washington's legacy and how he came to be alternately lauded and lambasted for his practical approach to racism following Reconstruction: to build a school to prepare blacks to occupy the unchallenged place set aside for them in the Jim Crow South. . . . This is a nuanced portrait of an enigmatic man of enduring contribution to black leadership." Booklist
Includes bibliographical references

★ Washington, Booker T. **Up** from slavery; edited with an introduction and notes by William L.

Andrews. Oxford University Press 2008 xxvii, 196p (Oxford world's classics) pa $9.95 **92**

1. Slaves 2. Authors 3. Educators 4. African American educators 5. Memoirists 6. Nonfiction writers 7. Tuskegee Institute 8. Civil rights activists 9. African Americans -- Biography
ISBN 978-0-19-955239-9

LC 2008-279129

First published 1901

"The classic autobiography of the man who, though born in slavery, educated himself and went on to found Tuskegee Institute." N Y Public Libr

Includes bibliographical references

Washington, George, 1732-1799

Brookhiser, Richard. **Founding** father: rediscovering George Washington. Free Press 1996 230p hardcover o.p. pa $14 **92**

1. Generals 2. Presidents 3. Presidents -- United States
ISBN 0-684-83142-2 pa

LC 95-50650

"Brookhiser's slim, graceful volume is readable in one sitting. His style is muscular and discursive, yet unaffectedly erudite." Christ Sci Monit

Includes bibliographical references

Chernow, Ron. **Washington**; a life. Penguin Press 2010 xxi, 904p il $40 **92**

1. Biography, Individual 2. Presidents -- United States 3. United States -- Politics and government -- 1775-1783 4. United States -- Politics and government -- 1783-1809
ISBN 978-1-59420-266-7

LC 2010-19154

Chernow "has done justice to the solid flesh, the human frailty and the dental miseries of his subject—and also to his immense historical importance. . . . This is a magnificently fair, full-scale biography. Its judgments are lapidary." Economist

Includes bibliographical references

★ Ellis, Joseph J. **His** Excellency; George Washington. Knopf 2004 320p il hardcover o.p. pa $15 **92**

1. Generals 2. Presidents 3. Presidents -- United States
ISBN 1-4000-4031-0; 1-4000-3253-9 pa

LC 2004-46576

The author "offers a magisterial account of the life and times of George Washington, celebrating the heroic image of the president whom peers like Jefferson and Madison recognized as 'their unquestioned superior' while acknowledging his all-too-human qualities." Publ Wkly

Includes bibliographical references

Flexner, James Thomas. **George** Washington and the new nation, 1783-1793. Little, Brown 1969 466p il map (His George Washington) $42 **92**

1. Generals 2. Presidents 3. Presidents -- United States
ISBN 0-316-28600-1

LC 78-117042

This third volume of a four-volume biography of Washington focuses on the period between the end of the Revolutionary War through his first term as president.

Includes bibliographical references

Flexner, James Thomas. **George** Washington: anguish and farewell 1793-1799. Little, Brown 1972 554p il (His George Washington) $45 **92**

1. Generals 2. Presidents 3. Presidents -- United States
ISBN 0-316-28602-8

LC 72-6875

This final volume of a four-volume biography of Washington covers his second term as president, his retirement, and death.

Includes bibliographical references

Flexner, James Thomas. **George** Washington: the forge of experience, 1732-1775. Little 1965 390p il map (His George Washington) $40 **92**

1. Generals 2. Presidents 3. Presidents -- United States
ISBN 0-316-28597-8

LC 65-21361

The author "covers forty-three years of Washington's life in this volume, the first in a series of four . . . [that carries] Washington through the Revolutionary War and on to the end of his life." Publisher's note

Includes bibliographical references

Gaines, James R. **For** liberty and glory; Washington, Lafayette, and their revolutions. W.W. Norton & Co. 2007 533p il map $29.95 **92**

1. Generals 2. Statesmen 3. Presidents 4. France -- History -- 1789-1799, Revolution 5. United States -- History -- 1775-1783, Revolution
ISBN 0-393-06138-8; 978-0-393-06138-3

LC 2007-22449

Gaines examines the relationship between George Washington and the Marquis de Lafayette.

This is a "fresh and engaging new look at the pair. . . . Gaines has a dry sense of humor and an appreciation for human foibles. . . . The American founding fathers, in particular, come across as extraordinary men with ordinary obsessions and—surprise!—senses of humor." Christ Sci Monit

Includes bibliographical references

Johnson, Paul. **George** Washington: the Founding Father. HarperCollins Publishers 2005 126p (Eminent lives) $19.95 **92**

1. Generals 2. Presidents 3. Presidents -- United States
ISBN 0-06-075365-X

LC 2004-52907

This is a biography of the first president of the United States.

The author "submits a beautifully cogent, enthrallingly perceptive, and . . . startlingly fresh take on the ultimate American icon." Booklist

Includes bibliographical references

Washington, Martha, 1731-1802

Brady, Patricia. **Martha** Washington; an American life. Viking 2005 276p il $24.95; pa $15 **92**

1. Spouses of presidents 2. Presidents' spouses --

United States

ISBN 0-670-03430-4; 0-14-303713-7 pa

LC 2004-61242

In this book, the original first lady "is depicted as a very human but true heroine who remained steadfast through personal adversity and the uncertainties of war and revolution." Libr J

"Brady's splendid biography offers a compelling new portrait of this passionate, committed founding mother who has unjustly been obscured by others, such as Abigail Adams." Publ Wkly

Includes bibliographical references

Waters, Ethel, 1896-1977

Bogle, Donald. **Heat** wave; the life and career of Ethel Waters. HarperCollins 2011 624p il $26.99 **92**

1. Actors 2. Singers 3. African American singers 4. Biography, Individual

ISBN 0-06-124173-3; 978-0-06-124173-4

LC 2010-29230

This is a biography of the actress and singer Ethel Waters, who starred in the film Cabin in the Sky (1943). Bibliography. Index.

"In this powerful biography, Bogle recovers the rich fullness of singer Ethel Waters's life (1896–1977). In vivid though often exhausting detail, Bogle traces Waters's rise from the poverty of her surroundings in Chester, Pa., through her early musical successes in Harlem in the 1920s and 1930s to her film and Broadway career and her later religious conversion as her health declined." Publ Wkly

Includes bibliographical references

Waters, John, 1946-

Waters, John. **Role** models. Farrar, Straus and Giroux 2010 304p il $25 **92**

1. Motion picture producers and directors 2. Screenwriters 3. Motion picture directors

ISBN 978-0-374-25147-5; 0-374-25147-9

LC 2009-42211

"The famed cult-film director recalls the famous—and not-so-famous—people he has idolized over the years. . . . In this consistently charming and witty collection of essays, he fondly remembers the many artists he has admired throughout his life, from stars, such as Little Richard, to such near-unknown figures as the 1960s Baltimore stripper Lady Zorro. . . . An impressive, heartfelt collection by a true American iconoclast." Kirkus

Includes bibliographical references

Waters, John. **Carsick**; John Waters. Farrar Straus & Giroux 2014 336 p. illustrations (hardcover) $26 **92**

1. Hitchhiking 2. Autobiographies 3. Hitchhiking -- United States 4. United States -- Description and travel 5. United States -- Social life and customs -- 21st century -- Humor 6. Motion picture producers and directors -- United States -- Biography

ISBN 0374298637; 9780374298630

LC 2013034093

In this book, author "John Waters is putting his life on the line. Armed with wit, a pencil-thin mustache, and a card-

board sign that reads 'I'm Not Psycho,' he hitchhikes across America from Baltimore to San Francisco, braving lonely roads and treacherous drivers. But who should we be more worried about, the delicate film director with genteel manners or the unsuspecting travelers transporting the Pope of Trash?" (Publisher's note)

"For more than half of this account of his 2012 cross-country journey . . . [Waters] imagines what lies in store, with dueling full-length novellas that spin best and worst case scenarios. . . . [A] sweet and funny ride." Kirkus

Watson, James D., 1928-

Watson, James D. **Avoid** boring people; lessons from a life in science. Alfred A. Knopf 2007 347p il $26.95 **92**

1. Scientists 2. College teachers 3. Molecular biologists 4. Nobel laureates for physiology or medicine

ISBN 978-0-375-41284-4; 0-375-41284-0

LC 2007-15675

"In this memoir, Watson shows by example how to get to the top and stay there. Spanning his boyhood interest in birds to his resignation from Harvard University in 1976 to his leadership of Cold Spring Harbor Laboratory, Watson's reminiscences encompass his claim to fame—cocredit for deducing DNA's structure in 1953—but focus on his ambition and his conduct of academic politics. . . . In angular and opinionated prose, Watson proves as engaging as ever." Booklist

Includes bibliographical references

Watson, James D. **Genes,** girls, and Gamow; after the double helix. Knopf 2002 xxix, 259p il $26; pa $14 **92**

1. College teachers 2. Molecular biologists 3. Nobel laureates for physiology or medicine

ISBN 0-375-41283-2; 0-375-72715-9 pa

LC 2001-38543

"In 1953, Watson, then 25, and colleague Francis Crick discovered the structure of DNA. . . . Here Watson . . . gives a detailed, journal-writer's account of the aftermath, recalling . . . his younger self's professional and—equally pressing—amorous ambitions. . . . Reading Watson is a delight, an opportunity to breathe the rarefied air of his generation's greatest scientists and to crash a faculty cocktail party or two along the way." Publ Wkly

Wayne, John, 1907-1979

Eyman, Scott. **John** Wayne: the life and legend; the life and legend. Scott Eyman. Simon & Schuster 2014 672 p. illustrations (hardback) $32.50 **92**

1. Actors -- United States -- Biography 2. Motion picture actors and actresses -- United States -- Biography

ISBN 1439199582; 9781439199589

LC 2013032604

Author Scott Eyman "interviewed [John] Wayne, as well as many family members, and he has drawn on previously unpublished reminiscences from friends and associates of the Duke in this biography, as well as documents from his production company that shed light on Wayne's business affairs. He traces Wayne from his childhood to his stardom in Stagecoach and dozens of films after that." (Publisher's note)

"Insightful, exhaustive and engrossing—a definitive portrait of the man and the legend." Kirkus

Includes bibliographical references and index

Weisskopf, Michael

Weisskopf, Michael. **Blood** brothers; among the soldiers of Ward 57. H. Holt 2006 301p il hardcover o.p. pa $15　　**92**

1. Journalists　2. Iraq War, 2003- -- Personal narratives

ISBN 978-0-8050-7860-2; 0-8050-7860-6; 978-0-8050-8660-7 pa; 0-8050-8660-9 pa

LC 2006-43382

The author, "an embedded journalist on assignment for Time magazine, was riding through the streets of Baghdad in the back of a Humvee when a small, dark object landed on the seat beside him. For reasons he still finds inexplicable, he picked it up. He was trying to toss it away when it exploded, obliterating his right hand and inflicting serious shrapnel wounds on him and several men riding with him. . . . He recounts the struggles of three other amputees, as well as his own, as they try to put their lives back together. " N Y Times Book Rev

"Weisskopf recognizes his own experience in that of the soldiers, making for a wonderful story of tragedy and recovery." Libr J

Includes bibliographical references

Welles, Orson, 1915-1985

Thomson, David, 1941- **Rosebud** : the story of Orson Welles. Knopf 1996 463p il hardcover o.p. pa $16　　**92**

1. Actors　2. Radio directors　3. Theatrical directors　4. Theatrical producers　5. Motion picture directors　6. Motion picture producers

ISBN 0-679-77283-9 pa

LC 95-44216

In this examination of Welles, "Thomson trots out the myths and reinterprets them in Welles' favor, which he fits into his ingenious conceit of Welles as the antihero Kane. . . . Throughout, Thomson is engaging and humorous, particularly in working with another masterful conceit. On a controversial interpretation or on an exquisite insight, the publisher enters the narrative and converses with the author. Prettily done. Thomson summarizes that Welles was, at once, 'magnificent and a poor bastard.' And this is, at once, a brilliant and maddening inquiry." Booklist

Includes bibliographical references

Wellington, Arthur Wellesley, Duke of, 1769-1852

Hibbert, Christopher. **Wellington**; a personal history. Perseus Books 1999 460p il map pa $22　**92**

1. Generals　2. Statesmen　3. Prime ministers　4. Great Britain -- History -- 19th century

ISBN 0-7382-0148-0; 978-0-7382-0148-1

First published 1997 in the United Kingdom by HarperCollins

"Altogether, Wellington does not quite pass the 'niceness' test. . . . He was a difficult man, a major military figure, a minor Prime Minister and in sum a historically important legend. Hibbert skillfully brings out all these characteristics." N Y Times Book Rev

Includes bibliographical references

Wells-Barnett, Ida B., 1862-1931

★ Giddings, Paula. **Ida** : a sword among lions; Ida B. Wells and the campaign against lynching. Amistad 2008 800p il $35　　**92**

1. Authors　2. Lynching　3. Journalists　4. Women political activists　5. Essayists　6. Nonfiction writers　7. Newspaper executives　8. Civil rights activists　9. African Americans -- Civil rights　10. African American women -- Biography

ISBN 978-0-06-051921-6; 0-06-051921-5

"An iconic figure in American history, Wells was not always celebrated by her contemporaries for her groundbreaking activism because of her assertive politics and difficult personality. . . . Giddings offers a look at how Wells' own self-assertion affected her relationships with family, friends, colleagues, and the broader American public as she evolved as a woman and an activist. . . . With meticulous research, including Wells' own diary, Giddings brings to life one of the most fascinating women in American history, giving readers a real feel for the texture and context of Wells' life." Booklist

Includes bibliographical references

Welty, Eudora, 1909-2001

Marrs, Suzanne. **Eudora** Welty: a biography. Harcourt 2005 652p il $28　　**92**

1. Authors　2. Novelists　3. Authors, American　4. Short story writers

ISBN 0-15-100914-7

LC 2004-30490

This book "belongs on the shelf beside its subject's own work. Neither hagiography nor pathography, it is, you feel, the thoroughly respectful and straightforward biography its honest, modest, intensely private subject would have wanted." N Y Times Book Rev

Includes bibliographical references

Waldron, Ann. **Eudora**; a writer's life. Doubleday 1998 398p il hardcover o.p. pa $23　　**92**

1. Authors　2. Novelists　3. Authors, American　4. Short story writers

ISBN 0-385-47648-5 pa

LC 98-5708

This is a biography of the writer from Mississippi

"Waldron's biography of Welty is the first to be written and, until the definitive treatment arrives, will satisfy readers curious to know details about the life of this much loved figure." Booklist

Includes bibliographical references

Welty, Eudora. **One** writer's beginnings. Harvard Univ. Press 1984 104p il (William E. Massey, Sr. lectures in the history of American civilization) hardcover o.p. pa $12　　**92**

1. Authors　2. Novelists　3. Authors, American　4. Short story writers

ISBN 0-674-63925-1; 0-674-63927-8 pa

LC 83-18638

A series of lectures in which the author reflects on her Southern heritage and her early artistic influences.

What there is to say we have said; the correspondence of Eudora Welty and William Maxwell.

edited by Suzanne Marrs. Houghton Mifflin Harcourt 2011 499p il $35 **92**

1. Authors 2. Novelists 3. Magazine editors 4. Short story writers

ISBN 0547376499; 9780547376493; 978-0-547-37649-3; 0-547-37649-9

LC 2010-42105

"Letters between writers often have a lot of shop talk of interest to other writers and literary cultists, but this collection yields broader pleasures, too. In addition to being stellar writers, Welty and Maxwell were also accomplished critics, and one of the joys of the book is eavesdropping on their assessments of authors as varied as John Updike and Virginia Woolf, Anton Chekhov and Charles Dickens, William Faulkner and E. M. Forster. Welty and Maxwell also shared an intense love of gardening – so much so that Marrs was forced, in the book's index, to include an extensive listing of various varieties of roses. . . . As these letters show, Welty and Maxwell regarded domestic life not as a tedious distraction from the writing desk, but as a crucial source of insight. . . . The title of the collection comes from Maxwell's conclusion, as he and Welty faced their mortality, that 'what there is to say we have said, in one way or the other. You know how much we love you.' That love, a source of sustenance and strength between two great writers, is also a bright tonic for the readers of this volume." Christ Sci Monit

Includes bibliographical references

West, Jerry, 1938-

Lazenby, Roland. **Jerry** West; the life and legend of a basketball icon. ESPN Books; Ballantine Books 2010 xxi, 422p il $28 **92**

1. Basketball players 2. Basketball executives 3. Basketball -- Biography 4. Los Angeles Lakers (Basketball team)

ISBN 978-0-345-51083-9; 0-345-51083-6

LC 2009-43777

The life of the basketball great from his hardscrabble West Virginia youth to his pro career with the Los Angeles Lakers from 1960 to 1974

"Sports biographies tend to careen between breathless hagiography and the slyly salacious. Lazenby . . . has produced something of a different order — a first-rate piece of narrative nonfiction whose subject happens to be a star athlete. His biography of West is, by turns, smart, beautifully reported, well-written and psychologically shrewd. It also manages to put both the NBA and individual players in a telling social and historical context without straying into didacticism." PopMatters

Includes bibliographical references

West, Nathanael, 1903-1940

Meade, Marion. **Lonelyhearts**; the screwball world of Nathanael West and Eileen McKenney. Houghton Mifflin Harcourt 2010 392p il map $28 **92**

1. Authors 2. Novelists 3. Screenwriters 4. Authors, American 5. Spouses of prominent persons

ISBN 978-0-15-101149-0

LC 2009-13285

"West and McKenney died young in a car crash in 1940—too soon for him to know that his lacerating novels,

especially The Day of the Locust (1939), would become American classics; too soon for his new wife, Eileen, to claim her life for her own after her sister, Ruth, co-opted it to write her best-seller, My Sister Eileen (1938). . . . [The author] tells the trenchant and secret-laden life stories of West (born Nathan Weinstein in New York) and Ohioan McKenney in a ravishingly atmospheric yet propulsive narrative." Booklist

Includes bibliographical references

Wharton, Edith, 1862-1937

Lee, Hermione. **Edith** Wharton. Alfred A. Knopf 2007 869p il $35 **92**

1. Authors 2. Novelists 3. Nonfiction writers 4. Short story writers

ISBN 978-0-375-40004-9; 0-375-40004-4

LC 2006-48795

"Marked by an elegant literary style that does justice to its subject and a clear, compassionate eye for detail, [this] is not only the best book on its subject, but one of the finest literary biographies to appear in recent years." Atlanta Journal-Constitution

Includes bibliographical references

White, Bill

White, Bill. **Uppity**; my untold story about the games people play. [by] Bill White with Gordon Dillow; foreword by Willie Mays. Grand Central Pub. 2011 303p il $26.99 **92**

1. Baseball players 2. African American athletes 3. Sportscasters 4. Baseball executives 5. Baseball -- Biography 6. Sport association executives 7. United States -- Race relations

ISBN 9780446555258; 0446555258

LC 2010-38025

"During his 13 years as a player, [Bill White] won All-Star recognition and frequent Gold Gloves as a slick-fielding, power-hitting first baseman, though he was never the flamboyant type who would call attention to himself. Then he embarked on an 18-year career as a broadcaster, memorably providing a balance to the more unpredictable Phil Rizzuto as announcers for the New York Yankees. He capped his career by serving five years as president of the National League. . . . Whatever his level of involvement, White approached baseball as a career through which he made his living rather than a sport he loved, an attitude that is likely to ruffle sentimentalists. . . . He describes the abuse he took from redneck fans during minor league days when he was one of the few black players on a team, through his battles with the white tycoons who exerted increasing control over the industry before he resigned as league president. Yet his account is otherwise color blind as it separates the heroes of White's life (Willie Mays, Bing Devine, Johnny Keane and others in addition to Rizzuto) from the villains." Kirkus

White, E. B. (Elwyn Brooks), 1899-1985

Elledge, Scott. **E.** B. White; a biography. Norton 1984 400p il hardcover o.p. pa $21.95 **92**

1. Poets 2. Authors 3. Humorists 4. Novelists 5. Essayists 6. Satirists 7. Authors, American 8.

Children's authors

ISBN 0-393-30305-5 pa

LC 83-4032

This biography "follows White from his birth in Mount Vernon, N.Y. to his . . . octogenarian retreat in Maine." Libr J

The author is "fair, respectful, thorough, entertaining, skillful and unpedantic. He has performed a splendid exercise in scholarship and literary analysis, and the result is fun." N Y Times Book Rev

Includes bibliographical references

White, E. B. **Letters** of E.B. White; originally collected and edited by Dorothy Lobrano Guth. Rev. ed.; Harper Collins 2006 713p il $35 **92**

1. Poets 2. Authors 3. Humorists 4. Novelists 5. Essayists 6. Satirists 7. Authors, American 8. Children's authors

ISBN 978-0-06-075708-3; 0-06-075708-6

LC 2006-43490

First published 1976

This collection of letters by the essayist, poet, novelist and author of several classic children's books is chronologically arranged. Written between the years 1908 when White was nine and 1985 when he died, they concern his relationships with his wife, Katherine White and his family and friends, which include Harold Ross, James Thurber, Robert Benchley, Alexander Woollcott and others.

White, Edmund, 1940-

White, Edmund. **City** boy; my life in New York during the 1960s and 70s. Bloomsbury USA 2009 297p $26 **92**

1. Authors 2. Gay men 3. Novelists 4. Memoirists 5. Biographers 6. Authors, American 7. Short story writers 8. New York (N.Y.) -- Intellectual life

ISBN 978-1-596-91402-5; 1-596-91402-5

LC 2009-12493

This memoir is a "tour of gay life in New York City before and after the Stonewall riots in 1969." N Y Times (Late N Y Ed)

The author "weaves erotic encounters and long-ago literati into a vast tapestry of Manhattan memories. . . . This is a brilliant recreation of an era, rich in revels, revolutions and 'leather boys leading the human tidal wave.'" Publ Wkly

Wiesenthal, Simon

Segev, Tom. **Simon** Wiesenthal; the life and legends. Doubleday 2010 482p il $35; ebook $35 **92**

1. Authors 2. Architects 3. Holocaust survivors 4. Nazi 5. Essayists 6. Memoirists 7. Nazi hunters 8. Jewish leaders 9. Jews -- Austria 10. Biography, Individual

ISBN 978-0-385-51946-5; 978-0-385-53371-3 ebook

LC 2009-53480

The book is a biography about "Simon Wiesenthal, . . . the survivor of a succession of concentration camps, . . . [and] the Nazi hunter who tracked down Adolf Eichmann and brought to justice such [war criminals] . . . as Franz Stangl, the commandant of Treblinka, . . . and Hermine Braunsteiner." The author recounts how Wiesenthal "talked his way into jobs with the American military—an army war crimes unit and the local bureau of the counterintelligence

corps—and became the head of local refugee groups, . . . as well as a representative of the Joint Distribution Committee, a Jewish relief organization working with DPs. The American connection, which involved identifying and apprehending war criminals, led directly to his life's work: creating a database of Nazi criminals, tracking them down, and bringing them to justice." (New York Review of Books)

"The man who emerges from this text is ultimately more complex, and indeed likable, than the mythologized figure. Segev's study should be the standard for many years." Libr J

Includes bibliographical references

Wilberforce, William, 1759-1833

Hague, William Jefferson. **William** Wilberforce; the life of the great anti-slave trade campaigner. HarperCollins 2008 582p il $35 **92**

1. Abolitionists 2. Philanthropists 3. Essayists 4. Writers on religion 5. Members of Parliament

ISBN 978-0-15-101267-1; 0-15-101267-9

LC 2007-45981

First published 2007 in the United Kingdom

Hague describes how Wilberforce, "dedicating his political life to moral causes . . . decided on two: 'the reformation of manners,' as he confided to his diary, and the abolition of African slavery. Wilberforce's campaign against vice had scant historical effect, but that against slavery in British realms arguably prodded the Western world toward abolition. Why Wilberforce's effort (trade in slaves was banned in 1807; abolition occurred in 1834) followed a tortuous path becomes understandable as Hague explains the parliamentary practicalities that Wilberforce faced. Incorporating Wilberforce's domestic life, Hague's effort is a well-rounded portrait of the pioneering British abolitionist." Booklist

Wilde, Oscar, 1854-1900

Ellmann, Richard. **Oscar** Wilde. Knopf 1988 680p il hardcover o.p. pa $19.95 **92**

1. Poets 2. Authors 3. Novelists 4. Dramatists 5. Lecturers

ISBN 0-394-75984-2 pa

LC 87-45354

First published 1987 in the United Kingdom

"Wilde's life epitomizes the classic formula for a tragic history, the man who, by hubris, falls from greatness. In Mr. Ellmann's hands, the story becomes as compelling as fiction while never deviating from the facts. Humour and elegance illuminate the accounts of Wilde's family, his friends and the enemies he earned." Economist

Includes bibliographical references

Wilder, Billy, 1906-2002

Sikov, Ed. **On** Sunset Boulevard: the life and times of Billy Wilder. Hyperion 1998 675p il hardcover o.p. pa $17.95 **92**

1. Screenwriters 2. Motion picture directors

ISBN 0-7868-8503-3 pa

LC 98-23504

"Sikov has painted as good a portrait of Billy Wilder, the man, the artist, the showman, the self-promoter, the profitably prescient art collector and the successful businessman, as we are likely to get from the outside." N Y Times Book Rev

Includes filmography

Wilder, Laura Ingalls, 1867-1957

Anderson, William T. **Laura** Ingalls Wilder country; text by William Anderson; color photography by Leslie A. Kelly. HarperPerennial 1990 119p il hardcover o.p. pa $24.95   92

1. Authors 2. Novelists 3. Western writers 4. Children's authors 5. Young adult authors 6. Literary landmarks -- United States
ISBN 0-06-097346-3 pa

LC 89-46512

"Contemporary and period photographs of the places in the Laura Ingalls Wilder books have been combined with a narrative about the actual historical settings." Horn Book

Wilkinson, James, 1757-1825

Linklater, Andro. An **artist** in treason; the extraordinary double life of General James Wilkinson. Walker 2009 392p il map $27   92

1. Spies 2. Generals 3. Territorial governors 4. United States -- Politics and government -- 1783-1865
ISBN 978-0-8027-1720-7

LC 2009-19184

A profile of the Continental Army general explores his career with the Spanish secret service, his protection by four presidents in spite of his treasonous acts, and his role in foiling Aaron Burr's conspiracy to break up the Union.

The author "lucidly details the general's often tangled affairs, but he also uses his story to illuminate the personal feuds, political struggles, and international entanglements that helped shape the young United States. He manages to tell this story of skullduggery and self-interest without wagging his finger in high moral dudgeon at Wilkinson's betrayals. In fact, at times the wily double-crosser almost comes across as sympathetic—but never as someone to trust." Am Heritage

Includes bibliographical references and index.

Willan, Anne

Friedman, Amy. **One** souffle at a time; a memoir of food and France. Anne Willan ; with Amy Friedman. St. Martin's Press 2013 320 p. ill. (hardcover) $27.99   92

1. Cooks 2. French cooking 3. Cooking, French
ISBN 0312642172; 9780312642174; 9781466837027
LC 2013004043

IACP Cookbook Award (2014)

In this book, chef Anne Willan "tells her story and the story of the food-world greats--including Julia Child, James Beard, Simone Beck, Craig Claiborne, Richard Olney, and others--who changed how the world eats and who made cooking fun. She writes about how a sturdy English girl from Yorkshire made it not only to the stove, but to France, and how she overcame the exceptionally closed male world of French cuisine to found and run her school." (Publisher's note)

"A charming, if not revelatory, portrait of a woman determined to bring French cuisine to a wider audience, with emphasis on traditional, accessible recipes that respect the intellectual side of cookery." Kirkus

Williams, Art, Jr.

Kersten, Jason. The **art** of making money; the story of a master counterfeiter. Gotham Books 2009 292p $26   92

1. Criminals 2. Counterfeits and counterfeiting 3. Counterfeiters
ISBN 978-1-59240-446-9

LC 2009-9407

"A young smalltime crook with a meticulous eye for artistic detail and an addiction to the thrill of crime crafts millions in high-quality phony bills in Kersten's account of counterfeiter Art Williams Jr." Publ Wkly

This "absorbing account reads like crime fiction, offering an understanding of modern counterfeiting that will appeal to readers of that genre as well as those who like true crime." Libr J

Williams, Hank, 1923-1953

Escott, Colin. **Hank** Williams; the biography. {by} Colin Escott with George Merritt and William MacEwen. Little, Brown 1994 307p il hardcover o.p. pa $19.99   92

1. Singers 2. Country musicians 3. Songwriters
ISBN 0-316-24938-6 pa

LC 93-48092

A look at the career of the influential country singer/songwriter. Williams' self-destructive behavior and turbulent personal life are also examined

Includes discography and bibliographical references

★ Hemphill, Paul. **Lovesick** blues; the life of Hank Williams. Viking 2005 207p $23.95   92

1. Singers 2. Country musicians 3. Songwriters
ISBN 0-670-03414-2

LC 2004-65113

This is a biography of the country singer.

"This is the finest work of literature about Williams yet written." Booklist

Williams, Roger, 1604?-1683

Gaustad, Edwin Scott. **Roger** Williams; [by] Edwin S. Gaustad. Oxford University Press 2005 150p il (Lives and legacies) $17.95   92

1. Clergy 2. Puritans 3. Colonial leaders 4. Writers on religion 5. United States -- History -- 1600-1775, Colonial period
ISBN 0-19-518369-X

LC 2004-25246

This is a biography of "the founder of Rhode Island and of the first Baptist Church in America." Publisher's note

The author "provides not just an excellent introduction to the man but a deep analysis of his largely unacknowledged influence on our political and cultural life." Reason

Williams, Ted, 1918-2002

Bradlee, Benjamin C., 1921-2014. The **kid**; the immortal life of Ted Williams. Ben Bradlee, Jr. Little Brown & Co 2013 864 p. illustrations $35   **92**

1. Baseball players -- United States -- Biography

ISBN 0316614351; 9780316614351

LC 2013028253

This book, by Ben Bradlee, Jr., offers a biography of the baseball player Ted Williams. "Born in 1918 in San Diego, Ted would spend most of his life disguising his Mexican heritage. During his 22 years with the Boston Red Sox, Williams electrified crowds across America--and shocked them, too: His notorious clashes with the press and fans threatened his reputation. Yet while he was a God in the batter's box, he was profoundly human once he stepped away from the plate." (Publisher's note)

"Sprawling, entertaining life of the baseball great, renowned as a sports hero while leading a life as checkered as Babe Ruth's or Ty Cobb's." Kirkus

Includes bibliographical references and index

Linn, Edward. **Hitter** : the life and turmoils of Ted Williams; {by} Ed Linn. 1993 437p il hardcover o.p. pa $16   **92**

1. Baseball players 2. Baseball managers 3. Boston Red Sox (Baseball team)

ISBN 0-15-600091-1 pa

LC 92-41870

"Linn's book is not a typical game-by-game baseball biography, but a series of snapshots of Williams's career. The {author} . . . touches on the many high points, but does not neglect Williams's warts, including his constant battle with Boston baseball writers. The product of an unhappy childhood, Williams formed close friendships with the 'underdogs,' and gave unsparingly of himself to a charity for combatting cancer in children." Libr J

Williams, Tennessee, 1911-1983

Leverich, Lyle. **Tom**; the unknown Tennessee Williams. Norton 2007 644p il pa $35   **92**

1. Authors 2. Novelists 3. Dramatists 4. Short story writers 5. Dramatists, American

ISBN 978-0-393-31663-6; 0-393-31663-7

First published 1995 by Crown

This is the first installment of a projected two-volume biography of the American dramatist. Coverage begins with Williams' birth in 1911 and extends to the opening of The Glass Menagerie in 1945.

"The book is a tremendous accomplishment, and Leverich is an appealing biographer: modest, thorough, balanced, and passionate. In prose that is clear—if not scintillating—he bushwhacks a path through a morass of gossip and myth, and prepares the way for a more subtle interpretation of the man and his plays." New Yorker

Spoto, Donald. The **kindness** of strangers: the life of Tennessee Williams. Da Capo Press 1997 409p il pa $18.50   **92**

1. Authors 2. Novelists 3. Dramatists 4. Short story writers

ISBN 0-306-80805-6

LC 97-8428

First published 1985 by Little, Brown

"Based on hundreds of interviews with those who knew him and on other previously unpublished material, {the author} presents a portrait of Tennessee Williams which is both respectful and sensitive." Wilson Libr Bull

Includes bibliographical references

Williams, William Carlos, 1883-1963

Leibowitz, Herbert A. **Something** urgent I have to say to you: the life and works of William Carlos Williams; [by] Herbert Leibowitz. Farrar, Straus and Giroux 2011 496p il $40   **92**

1. Poets 2. Authors 3. Physicians 4. Essayists 5. Short story writers

ISBN 978-0-374-11329-2; 0-374-11329-7

LC 2010-46548

"In the 50s when Williams first became popular, convention said critics did not cross boundaries to conjecture on psychological motivations. This book is very much a product of a new century where all is transparent; and if Williams broke taboos in writing, Leibowitz does in reporting. . . . Leibowitz is quick to attribute Williams's writing to his tortured sexuality. The poet's pull between duty and a libidinous fantasy world is well known but never before used so relentlessly as capital. This also makes the book as readable as fiction, something bound to get it off the shelf and into the reader's hands. Leibowitz tackles the poetry through the man, not the other way around. . . . In the second half of the book, Leibowitz's comparison of Williams's book Spring and All to T.S. Eliot's The Waste Land is a brilliant analysis. Also, the careful reasoning behind Williams's In the American Grain is a contribution to literary thought. Another real bonus is that this biography tracks the Little Magazine movement in America nicely." Washington Independent Rev of Books

Includes bibliographical references

Wills, Garry, 1934-

Wills, Garry. **Outside** looking in; adventures of an observer. Viking 2010 195p $25.95   **92**

1. Authors 2. Historians 3. Journalists 4. Essayists 5. Social critics 6. College teachers

ISBN 978-0-670-02214-4

LC 2010-05323

"Wills's curiosity and personal integrity shine through this intellectual memoir that is both intimate and journalistic. Readers who have followed Wills's writing career will welcome these reflections on his life and the world around him." Libr J

Includes bibliographical references

Wilson, Diane

Wilson, Diane. **Holy** roller; growing up in the church of knock down drag out, or, How I stopped loving a blue-eyed Jesus: a childhood memoir. Chelsea Green Pub. 2008 210p il $24.95   **92**

1. Conservationists 2. Environmentalists 3. Fishermen

ISBN 978-1-933392-82-0; 1-933392-82-7

LC 2008-21199

"Churchgoing was more than an occasional Sunday morning outing; it was a 24/7 occupation overseen by a grandmother who judged every aspect of life according to a strict and literal interpretation of the scriptures. In Wilson's provocative memoir of life in the Texas Bible Belt of the 1950s, snake-handling preachers, fitful parishioners speaking in tongues, and money-hungry radio evangelists share equal billing with corrupt game wardens, outlaw fishermen, and less-than-devout male relatives whose 'backsliding' ways give their womenfolk immense cause for concern. Through a vividly kaleidoscopic voice that captures the intensity of fanatical religious rapture with pitch-perfect accuracy, Wilson exuberantly animates a feverish time, a frenetic place, and its fiery people." Booklist

Wilson, Diane. An **unreasonable** woman; a true story of shrimpers, politicos, polluters and the fight for Seadrift, Texas. foreword by Kenny Ausubel. Chelsea Green 2005 400p map $27.50; pa $18 **92**

1. Conservationists 2. Environmental protection 3. Fishermen
ISBN 1-931498-88-1; 978-1-931498-88-3; 1-933392-27-4 pa; 978-1-933392-27-1 pa

LC 2005-9894

"With the discovery that her 'piddlin' little county on the Gulf Coast' led the nation in toxic emissions, shrimper Wilson, a mother of five, found herself embarking on a voyage of discovery and activism that would strain her marriage and stretch her horizons. A David up against big-time chemical Goliaths, Wilson is a gifted storyteller, rendering dialogue and pacing plot turns as a novelist might." Publ Wkly

Wilson, Woodrow, 1856-1924

★ Berg, A. Scott. **Wilson**; A. Scott Berg. G.P. Putnam's Sons 2013 832 p. $40 **92**

1. Presidents -- United States 2. Presidents -- United States -- Biography 3. United States -- Politics and government -- 1913-1921
ISBN 0399159215; 9780399159213

LC 2013009339

This book is a biography of the United States' 28th president, Woodrow Wilson. Author A. Scott Berg "is generally sympathetic to the man (he puts much emphasis on Wilson's love for his two wives and characterizes him as a passionate lover as well as a determined leader), while taking a more critical stand against his racial views and policies, his handling of the League of Nations, and of the secrecy that surrounded his late-presidency illness." (Publishers Weekly)

Cooper, John Milton. The **warrior** and the priest: Woodrow Wilson and Theodore Roosevelt; [by] John Milton Cooper, Jr. Belknap Press 1983 442p il hardcover o.p. pa $20.95 **92**

1. Governors 2. Presidents 3. Vice-presidents 4. College presidents 5. Nobel laureates for peace 6. Presidents -- United States 7. United States -- Politics and government -- 1898-1919
ISBN 0-674-94751-7 pa

LC 83-6021

This "book is divided into four sections dealing respectively with the origins and early careers of both men, the parallel presidencies of Theodore Roosevelt (US) and Woodrow Wilson (Princeton), the election of 1912, and WW I." Choice

The author's "distinctions are sharp, his insights original, his judgments balanced and his narrative unfailingly graceful." N Y Times Book Rev
Includes bibliographical references

Cooper, John Milton. **Woodrow** Wilson; a biography. Alfred A. Knopf 2009 702p il $35 **92**

1. Governors 2. Presidents 3. College presidents 4. Biography, Individual 5. Nobel laureates for peace 6. Presidents -- United States 7. United States -- Politics and government -- 1898-1919 8. United States -- Politics and government -- 1913-1921 9. United States -- Politics and government -- 1919-1933
ISBN 978-0-307-26541-8

LC 2009-19097

This is a biography of the twenty-eighth president of the United States. Index.

"Cooper exhibits complete command of his materials, a sure knowledge of the man and a nuanced understanding of a presidency almost Shakespearean in its dimensions." Kirkus

Includes bibliographical references (p. [601]-668) and index.

Winkfield, Jimmy, 1882-1974

Drape, Joe. **Black** maestro; the epic life of an American legend. Morrow 2006 280p il $24.95 **92**

1. Jockeys
ISBN 0-06-053729-9; 978-0-06-053759-6

LC 2006-41939

This is a biography of "Jimmy Winkfield, the last black jockey to win the Kentucky Derby. . . . This well-researched biography of Jimmy Winkfield and the larger chapter of America his life highlights is a valuable and entertaining read." Publ Wkly

Winters, Richard

Alexander, Larry. **Biggest** brother; the life of Major D. Winters, the man who led the Band of Brothers. NAL Caliber 2005 287p il $24.95 **92**

1. Veterans 2. World War, 1939-1945 3. Army officers
ISBN 0-451-21510-9

LC 2004-27330

This is "the story of what distinguished Easy Company from other first-class field units: its leadership, in the person of Major Richard Winters, its commander. . . . Alexander is especially good at showing how Winters' sense of responsibility developed as a student, an enlistee, in OCS, and as an officer. He also gives a detailed picture of the army of 60-plus years ago, and the process that turned thousands of young civilians into the men who beat the Germans." Booklist

Wizenberg, Molly

Wizenberg, Molly. A **homemade** life; stories and recipes from my kitchen table. illustrations by Camilla Engman. Simon & Schuster 2009 320p il $25 **92**

1. Cooking 2. Women authors 3. Bloggers 4. Food critics
ISBN 1-4165-5105-0; 978-1-4165-5105-8

LC 2008-36430

"When Molly Wizenberg's father died of cancer, everyone told her to go easy on herself, to hold off on making any major decisions for a while. But when she tried going back to her apartment in Seattle and returning to graduate school, she knew it wasn't possible to resume life as though nothing had happened. So she went to Paris, a city that held vivid memories of a childhood trip with her father. . . . She was supposed to be doing research for her dissertation, but more often, she found herself peering through the windows of chocolate shops. . . . Molly's blog Orangette started out merely as a pleasant pastime. But it wasn't long before her writing and recipes developed [a following]. . . . In A Homemade Life: Stories and Recipes from My Kitchen Table, Molly Wizenberg recounts a life with the kitchen at its center." (Publisher's note) Recipe index.

This "delightful . . . book will undoubtedly be gobbled up like a tin of Christmas cookies." Libr J

Wodehouse, P. G. (Pelham Grenville), 1881-1975

McCrum, Robert. **Wodehouse**; a life. Norton 2004 530p il $27.95 **92**

1. Authors 2. Humorists 3. Novelists 4. Dramatists 5. Short story writers

ISBN 0-393-05159-5

LC 2004-18562

The author "takes the reader from Wodehouse's school days at Dulwich to his successful work as a Broadway lyricist and a master storyteller of Edwardian times who gave us Bertie Wooster and Jeeves to his darkest hour during World War II and final years of semi-exile in America. He offers his most spirited and convincing analysis in countering accusations that Wodehouse knowingly collaborated with the Nazis. . . . This work is thoroughly researched and well written; it will please Wodehouse aficionados and general readers alike." Libr J

Includes bibliographical references

Wolff, Tobias, 1945-

★ Wolff, Tobias. **This** boy's life: a memoir. Atlantic Monthly Press 1989 288p hardcover o.p. pa $14 **92**

1. Authors 2. Novelists 3. Memoirists 4. College teachers 5. Authors, American 6. Nonfiction writers 7. Short story writers

ISBN 0-871-13248-6; 0-8021-3668-0 pa

LC 88-17600

The novelist and short story writer "offers an engrossing and candid look into his childhood and adolescence in his first book of nonfiction. In unaffected prose he recreates scenes from his life that sparkle with the immediacy of narrative fiction. The result is an intriguingly guileless book, distinct from the usual reflective commentary of autobiography." Libr J

Wollstonecraft, Mary, 1759-1797

Gordon, Lyndall. **Vindication**; a life of Mary Wollstonecraft. HarperCollins 2005 562p il $29.95 **92**

1. Authors 2. Novelists 3. Essayists 4. Feminists 5. Writers on politics

ISBN 0-06-019802-8

LC 2005-40237

The author "tackles this formidable woman with grace, clarity and much new research. . . . Gordon relates Woll-

stonecraft's story with the same potent mixture of passion and reason her subject personified." N Y Times Book Rev

Includes bibliographical references

Wood, Grant, 1891-1942

Evans, R. Tripp. **Grant** Wood; a life. Alfred A. Knopf 2010 402p il $37.50; ebook $37.50 **92**

1. Artists 2. Painters 3. Artists -- United States

ISBN 978-0-307-26629-3; 978-0-307-59433-4 ebook

LC 2010-18019

"Evans transforms our view of painter Grant Wood and his all-American paintings, including American Gothic, in a revelatory and heartrending biography of an artist forced to conceal his homosexuality." Booklist

Includes bibliographical references

Wooden, John, 1910-2010

Davis, Seth. **Wooden**; a coach's life. Seth Davis. Times Books 2014 608 p. illustrations (hardback) $35 **92**

1. College basketball 2. Basketball coaches -- United States -- Biography

ISBN 0805092803; 9780805092806

LC 2013020209

This book, by Seth Davis, offers a biography of the University of California, Los Angeles basketball coach John Wooden. "His UCLA teams reached unprecedented heights in the 1960s and '70s capped by a run of ten NCAA championships in twelve seasons and an eighty-eight-game winning streak. . . . Davis shows how hard Wooden strove for success, . . . only to discover that reaching new heights brought new burdens and frustrations." (Publisher's note)

"Davis has avoided stultifying, game-by-game detail (but does offer genuinely exciting accounts of several key games) and has provided a multidimensional, nearly cradle-to-grave portrait of a highly successful and revered coach and teacher, in the process delivering a history of the evolution of college basketball and profiles of many of its stars." Booklist

Includes bibliographical references (pages 327-565) index

Woodhull, Victoria C., 1838-1927

Goldsmith, Barbara. **Other** powers; the age of suffrage, spiritualism, and the scandalous Victoria Woodhull. HarperPerennial 1999 531p il pa $16 **92**

1. Feminism 2. Suffragists 3. Spiritualism 4. Feminists 5. Women -- Suffrage 6. Presidential candidates

ISBN 0-06-095332-2

LC 98-33315

First published 1998 by Knopf

"Victoria Woodhull was a charismatic and notorious figure in the struggle for women's rights in the years following the Civil War. She was the first woman to address Congress and the first woman to run for president. Goldsmith . . . has successfully woven together a history of Woodhull's life with the lives of the powerful she touched." Libr J

Includes bibliographical references

Woods, Tiger, 1975-

Callahan, Tom. **In** search of Tiger; a journey through golf with Tiger Woods. Crown 2003 245p il $23.95; pa $14 **92**

1. Golfers

ISBN 0-609-60943-2; 1-4000-5140-1 pa

LC 2002-11350

The author "examines Tiger's early years, how he got to the top of his game and his vision for the future. Anecdotes and insider insights highlight portraits of major Tiger victories. . . . This is a comprehensive examination of the man, his talent, his competition and the world of professional golf, a must-read for fans and players alike." Publ Wkly

Woolf, Leonard, 1880-1969

★ Glendinning, Victoria. **Leonard** Woolf; a biography. Simon & Schuster 2006 498p il $30 **92**

1. Authors 2. Editors 3. Essayists 4. Memoirists 5. Writers on politics 6. Publishing executives

ISBN 978-0-7432-4653-8; 0-7432-4653-5

LC 2006-49784

This is a biography of the publisher and author of Empire and Commerce in Africa (1920), Village in the Jungle (1926), After the Deluge (1931), Quack, Quack! (1935), Barbarians Within and Without (1939), Sowing (1960), Growing (1961), Beginning Again (1964), Downhill All the Way (1967), and The Journey Not the Arrival Matters (1969).

"Glendinning's generous biography does not ignore that Woolf could be grumpy and was too often cheeseparing, but her account does justice to his range of passions, his literary and political contributions and, above all, his human goodness—he was a man who knew how to live." New Statesman

Includes bibliographical references

Woolf, Virginia, 1882-1941

Briggs, Julia. **Virginia** Woolf: an inner life. Harcourt 2005 527p il $30 **92**

1. Authors 2. Novelists 3. Women authors 4. Essayists 5. Authors, English 6. Short story writers

ISBN 0-15-101143-5

LC 2005-16048

"That this book is a must for Woolf fans goes without saying, but it is also a must for anyone interested in the nature of female consciousness at its most self-aware and the workings of artistic sensibility at their most illuminating." Publ Wkly

Includes bibliographical references

Gordon, Lyndall. **Virginia** Woolf, a writer's life. Norton 1985 341p il hardcover o.p. pa $14.95 **92**

1. Authors 2. Novelists 3. Women authors 4. Essayists 5. Authors, English 6. Short story writers

ISBN 0-393-32205-X pa

LC 84-25424

First published 1984 in the United Kingdom

"Gordon combines literary criticism with biographical investigation in her life of Virginia Woolf. . . . Using the major novels To the Lighthouse and The Waves, Gordon explores in detail the autobiographical ramifications of these works as she traces Woolf's childhood, marriage, and literary career." Booklist

Includes bibliographical references

Woolf, Virginia. A **moment's** liberty: the shorter diary; abridged and edited by Anne Olivier Bell; introduction by Quentin Bell. Harcourt Brace Jovanovich 1990 516p hardcover o.p. pa $20 **92**

1. Authors 2. Novelists 3. Essayists 4. Authors, English 5. Short story writers

ISBN 0-15-161894-1; 0-15-661912-1 pa

LC 90-33428

An abridged edition of the five volumes of Woolf's Diary, published 1977-1984

"The diaries here may appeal to a larger audience, not least because each year represented is prefaced by a wonderfully succinct overview. Here are Woolf's superbly drawn portraits of Max Beerbohm, T.S. Eliot, John Maynard Keynes, Katherine Mansfield—and her occasionally acerbic remarks on what they said and did. But the diaries are also a repository for luminous thoughts on birds and weather, the pleasures of walking or listening to music." Publ Wkly

Woolman, John, 1720-1772

Slaughter, Thomas P. The **beautiful** soul of John Woolman, apostle of abolition. Hill and Wang 2008 464p il map **92**

1. Clergy 2. Authors 3. Abolitionists 4. Diarists 5. Essayists 6. Quaker leaders 7. Biography, Individual 8. Slavery and the church -- Society of Friends

ISBN 0-8090-9514-9; 978-0-8090-9514-8

LC 2008-22765

This is a biography of the New Jersey Quaker abolitionist. Index.

"Any understanding of the history of social reform in America begins with Woolman, and understanding Woolman begins here." Kirkus

Includes bibliographical references and index

Worden, Alfred M., 1932-

French, Francis. **Falling** to Earth; an Apollo 15 astronaut's journey. [by] Al Worden with Francis French. Smithsonian Books 2011 300p il **92**

1. Astronauts 2. Apollo project 3. Space flight to the moon 4. Air force officers 5. Biography, Individual 6. Apollo 15 (Spacecraft)

ISBN 1-58834-309-X; 978-1-58834-309-3

LC 2011003440

"Worden is eloquent, witty, and brutally honest, still in awe of the company he kept and the history he belongs to. A solid addition to space-literature collections."

"Worden is eloquent, witty, and brutally honest, still in awe of the company he kept and the history he belongs to. A solid addition to space-literature collections." Booklist

Includes bibliographical references

Wordsworth, Dorothy, 1771-1855

Wilson, Frances. The **ballad** of Dorothy Wordsworth; a life. Farrar, Straus and Giroux 2009 316p il map $30 **92**

1. Poets 2. Authors 3. Diarists 4. Poets laureate 5.

Travel writers 6. Authors, English
ISBN 978-0-374-10867-0; 0-374-10867-6

LC 2008-41263

First published 2008 in the United Kingdom

"Ms. Wilson focuses primarily on the years 1800-3, when Dorothy, then in her late 20s and early 30s, lived with her brother in the Lake District of England and kept her famous Grasmere Journals, which were not published in full until 1958. They were crucial years, not just for her but also for her brother, who was still writing some of his most important poems, and for Samuel Coleridge, who moves in and out of this book like the third magpie in a bustling nest. Ms. Wilson's decision to limit her scope was a small bit of genius. She's written a succinct yet roomy book, one that moves along with novelistic buoyancy and grace." N Y Times Book Rev

Includes bibliographical references

Wordsworth, William, 1770-1850

Wilson, Frances. The **ballad** of Dorothy Wordsworth; a life. Farrar, Straus and Giroux 2009 316p il map $30 **92**

1. Poets 2. Authors 3. Diarists 4. Poets laureate 5. Travel writers 6. Authors, English
ISBN 978-0-374-10867-0; 0-374-10867-6

LC 2008-41263

First published 2008 in the United Kingdom

"Ms. Wilson focuses primarily on the years 1800-3, when Dorothy, then in her late 20s and early 30s, lived with her brother in the Lake District of England and kept her famous Grasmere Journals, which were not published in full until 1958. They were crucial years, not just for her but also for her brother, who was still writing some of his most important poems, and for Samuel Coleridge, who moves in and out of this book like the third magpie in a bustling nest. Ms. Wilson's decision to limit her scope was a small bit of genius. She's written a succinct yet roomy book, one that moves along with novelistic buoyancy and grace." N Y Times Book Rev

Includes bibliographical references

Wright, Frank Lloyd, 1867-1959

★ Huxtable, Ada Louise. **Frank** Lloyd Wright. Lipper\Viking 2004 251p il (Penguin lives series) $19.95 **92**

1. Architects 2. Nonfiction writers
ISBN 0-670-03342-1

LC 2004-46477

"The eventfulness of the extraordinary life and the refreshing intelligence and craft of the author make this book a pleasure to read. That I found myself on occasion arguing with the text only proves the provocative quality of Huxtable's exploration." N Y Times Book Rev

Secrest, Meryle. **Frank** Lloyd Wright; a biography. University of Chicago Press 1998 634p il pa $20 **92**

1. Architects 2. Nonfiction writers
ISBN 0-226-74414-0

LC 97-51590

First published 1992 in the United Kingdom; first United States edition published 1993 by Knopf

A portrait of a "complex, often contradictory architect. . . . Secrest writes with authority and compassion about Wright's long and turbulent career. Her exhaustive scholarship provides fresh insights into Wright's personality." Libr J

Includes bibliographical references

Wright, Orville, 1871-1948

Wright, Orville. **How** we invented the airplane; an illustrated history. edited with an introduction and commentary by Fred C. Kelly; additional text by Alan Weissman. Dover Publs. 1988 87p il pa $9.95 **92**

1. Inventors 2. Aeronautics -- History 3. Aircraft industry executives
ISBN 0-486-25662-6

LC 87-33037

First published 1953 by D. McKay

This "account by the two inventors . . . covers experiments, discovery of aeronautical principles, construction of planes and motors, first flights, and much more. Also included is a later account written by both brothers." Publisher's note

Includes bibliographical references

Wright, Richard, 1908-1960

★ Wright, Richard. **Black** boy; (American hunger): a record of childhood and youth. foreword by Edward P. Jones. 60th anniversary ed., 1st ed.; HarperCollinsPublishers 2005 419p $24.95; pa $14.95 **92**

1. Authors 2. Novelists 3. Dramatists 4. African American authors 5. Essayists 6. Nonfiction writers 7. Short story writers 8. African Americans -- Social conditions
ISBN 0-06-083400-5; 978-0-06-083400-5; 0-06-113024-9 pa; 978-0-06-113024-3 pa

LC 2005-52698

First published 1945 by World Publishing Company

This autobiographical work concludes with Wright "newly arrived in Chicago in 1927 as a fugitive from the white South that never knew him. [It] relates his nomadic life in Tennessee, Arkansas, and Mississippi, abandoned by his father and with his mother working at menial jobs or incapacitated by illness." Benet's Reader's Ency of Am Lit

Includes bibliographical references

Wright, Wilbur, 1867-1912

Wright, Orville. **How** we invented the airplane; an illustrated history. edited with an introduction and commentary by Fred C. Kelly; additional text by Alan Weissman. Dover Publs. 1988 87p il pa $9.95 **92**

1. Inventors 2. Aeronautics -- History 3. Aircraft industry executives
ISBN 0-486-25662-6

LC 87-33037

First published 1953 by D. McKay

This "account by the two inventors . . . covers experiments, discovery of aeronautical principles, construction of planes and motors, first flights, and much more. Also included is a later account written by both brothers." Publisher's note

Includes bibliographical references

Wyatt, Richard Jed, 1939-2002

Jamison, Kay R. **Nothing** was the same; a memoir. by Kay Redfield Jamison. Alfred A. Knopf 2009 208p $25   **92**

1. Bereavement 2. Psychiatrists 3. Psychologists 4. Hodgkin's disease 5. Manic-depressive illness 6. College teachers

ISBN 978-0-307-26537-1; 0-307-26537-4

LC 2009-11096

"The great gift Jamison offers here, beyond her honesty and the beauty of her writing, is perspective: a clear-eyed view of illness and death, sanity and insanity, love and grief. . . . Jamison seems to be telling the truth, no matter how difficult it may be, in a way that avoids self-pity and inspires courage." Washington Post Book World

Wyeth, Andrew, 1917-2009

Wyeth, Andrew. **Andrew** Wyeth; autobiography. [by] Andrew Wyeth and Thomas Hoving. Bulfinch Press 1999 168p il $29.99   **92**

1. Artists 2. Painters 3. Artists -- United States

ISBN 978-0-8212-2569-1; 0-8212-2569-3

First published 1995

This "volume reproduces 138 tempera, drybrush & watercolor paintings & pencil studies by Andrew Wyeth." Publisher's note

"Each painting is accompanied by commentary from the artist that lends insight into his life and character. Several nude studies are included." Booklist [review of 1995 edition]

Includes bibliographical references

Wyeth, N. C. (Newell Convers), 1882-1945

Michaelis, David. **N.C.** Wyeth; a biography. Perennial 2003 555p il pa $27.95   **92**

1. Artists 2. Painters 3. Illustrators 4. Artists -- United States

ISBN 0-06-008926-1; 978-0-06-008926-9

LC 2003-42876

First published 1998 by Knopf

"Michaelis's work is an outstanding example of the biographer's art. Integrating Wyeth's complex personal and psychological life with his artistic oeuvre, Michaelis creates a portrait of both the artist and the man." Libr J

Includes bibliographical references

Wynette, Tammy, 1942-1998

McDonough, Jimmy. **Tammy** Wynette; tragic country queen. Viking 2010 432p il $27.95   **92**

1. Singers 2. Country musicians

ISBN 978-0-670-02153-6; 0-670-02153-9

LC 2009-42565

"Mr. McDonough is crazy about Wynette but also detached enough to see her clearly, writing with obvious respect for both her life and art. . . . You 'bookish types,' as Mr. McDonough describes his readers, will surely want to listen to her sing on the basis of this book's recommendations. With an emphatic sense of her place in country music—at the top of the heap, casting a shadow big enough to obscure today's woefully synthetic assembly-line singers—he combines a love of her overlooked and minor classics with a compelling big-picture life story. His opinions

are often corroborated by the colorfully authentic voices of those who knew her well and marveled at her moxie." N Y Times (Late N Y Ed)

Includes bibliographical references

Yang, Kao Kalia, 1980-

Kao Kalia Yang. The **latehomecomer**; a Hmong family memoir. Coffee House Press 2008 277p il pa $14.95   **92**

1. Authors 2. Refugees 3. Hmong Americans 4. Memoirists

ISBN 978-1-56689-208-7

LC 2007-46386

The author, "of the Southeast Asian Hmong people, was born in a refugee camp in Thailand in 1980. Her family was forced to flee the Pathet Lao, of Laos, who singled out the Hmong in retribution for their aiding the Americans during the Vietnam War. With no homeland to return to and not necessarily welcome in Thailand, Yang's family took the opportunity to come to the United States and make a new life. . . . Yang chronicles her family's journey." Libr J

"By the end of this moving, unforgettable book . . . readers will delight at how intimately they have become part of this formerly strange culture." Publ Wkly

Yelverton, Thérèse, Viscountess Avonmore, 1832?-1881

Schama, Chloe. **Wild** romance; a Victorian story of a marriage, a trial, and a self-made woman. Walker & Co. 2010 249p il map $24   **92**

1. Authors 2. Novelists 3. Army officers 4. Great Britain -- Social life and customs

ISBN 978-0-8027-1736-8; 0-8027-1736-5

LC 2009-44758

Schama details the "bigamy trial of William Charles Yelverton, which dominated the front pages of Irish, Scottish, and British newspapers in 1861. Although the story of Yelverton and his first wife, Theresa Longworth, practically tells itself through court documents, letters, and public opinion, Schama adds a journalist's touch in her story development. The latter part of the book deals with Theresa's later life in America as a self-made woman still haunted by her past." Libr J

Includes bibliographical references

Young, Andrew, 1932-

Young, Andrew. An **easy** burden; the civil rights movement and the transformation of America. foreword by Quincy Jones. Baylor University Press 2008 550p il pa $29.95   **92**

1. Clergy 2. Mayors 3. Nonfiction writers 4. Members of Congress 5. Civil rights activists 6. United Nations officials 7. Nobel laureates for peace 8. United States -- Race relations 9. African Americans -- Civil rights

ISBN 978-1-602580-73-2

LC 2007-49679

First published 1996 by HarperCollins Pubs.

This memoir focuses on Young's early life as a middle-class African American growing up in segregated New Orleans, his call to the ministry, and his years working with Dr. King and the Southern Christian Leadership Conference.

Young, Brigham

★ Turner, John G. **Brigham** Young, pioneer prophet; The Belknap Press of Harvard University Press 2012 500 p. (alk. paper) $35.00   92

1. Biography 2. Religious life 3. Church of Jesus Christ of Latter-day Saints -- Presidents -- Biography
ISBN 0674049675; 9780674049673

LC 2012015555

Author John G. Turner tells the story of "Brigham Young, [who] was Joseph Smith's lieutenant in spreading the newly coined doctrine of Mormonism and his successor on Smith's murder." Turner chronicles "Young's rise in the early hierarchy. . . . The author looks at the various strains of Protestantism, 'ecstatic' and otherwise, that fed into early Mormonism, drawing particularly on Methodism in the British Isles, where Young worked as one of the church's first missionaries." (Kirkus Reviews)

Includes bibliographical references and index

Yousafzai, Malala, 1997-

Lamb, Christina. **I** am Malala; The Girl Who Stood Up for Education and Was Shot by the Taliban. Malala Yousafzai. Little, Brown and Co. 2013 viii, 327 p.p (hardcover) $26.00   92

1. Terrorism 2. Women -- Pakistan 3. Girls -- Education
ISBN 0316322407; 9780316322409

LC 2013941811

Amelia Bloomer Project (2014)

This memoir, by Malala Yousafzai, "is the . . . tale of a family uprooted by global terrorism, of the fight for girls' education, of a father who, himself a school owner, championed and encouraged his daughter to write and attend school, and of . . . parents who have a . . . love for their daughter in a society that prizes sons." (Publisher's note)

"On October 9, 2012, the teenaged Yousafzai was very nearly assassinated by members of the Taliban who objected to her education and women's rights activism in Pakistan. Currently, she lives in England, under threat of execution by the Taliban if she returns home. Lamb, who has been reporting from Pakistan for 26 years and was named Foreign Correspondent of the Year five times, helps Yousafzai tell her hugely significant story." (Library Journal)

Zappa, Frank

Zappa, Frank. The **real** Frank Zappa book; [by] Frank Zappa, with Peter Occhiogrosso. Poseidon Press 1989 352p il hardcover o.p. pa $14   92

1. Composers 2. Guitarists 3. Rock musicians 4. Songwriters 5. Recording producers
ISBN 0-671-70572-5 pa

LC 89-3470

"The outspoken Zappa, one of the most inventive and controversial artists of the past 20 years, is frank, often disgusting, and always entertaining in describing his life. . . . Zappa also relates his opinions about the music performing and recording industries, but then rattles on about a myriad of things: church, drugs, yuppies, politics." Libr J

Zeitoun, Abdulrahman

Eggers, Dave, 1970- **Zeitoun**. McSweeney's 2009 351p il $24   92

1. Hurricane Katrina, 2005 2. Contractors 3. House painters 4. New Orleans (La.) 5. Muslims -- United States 6. New Orleans (La.) -- History 7. Arab Americans -- Social conditions 8. Hurricane Katrina, 2005 -- Social aspects
ISBN 978-1-934781-63-0; 1-934781-63-0

When Hurricane Katrina struck New Orleans, Abdulrahman Zeitoun, a prosperous Syrian-American and father of four, chose to stay through the storm to protect his house and contracting business. In the days after the storm, he traveled the flooded streets in a secondhand canoe, passing on supplies and helping those he could. A week later, on September 6, 2005, Zeitoun abruptly disappeared. . . . [Eggers's book] explores Zeitoun's roots in Syria, his marriage to Kathyan American who converted to Islamand their children. Publisher's note

This book is a more powerful indictment of America's dystopia in the Bush era than any number of well-written polemics. N Y Times Book Rev

Includes bibliographical references

Zellner, Robert, 1939-

Zellner, Robert. The **wrong** side of Murder Creek; a White southerner in the freedom movement. [by] Bob Zellner, with Constance Curry; foreword by Julian Bond. NewSouth Books 2008 351p il $27.95   92

1. Historians 2. Civil rights demonstrations 3. College teachers 4. Civil rights activists 5. Southern States -- Race relations 6. Student Nonviolent Coordinating Committee
ISBN 978-1-58838-222-1; 1-58838-222-2

LC 2008-25962

"Zellner's memoir focuses on his experiences as a civil rights activist from 1960 to 1967. He tells a story that is sometimes horrific, always interesting, and ultimately inspirational about a white Southerner's commitment to racial justice. . . . This powerful portrait of a courageous man is highly recommended." Libr J

Zevon, Warren

Zevon, Crystal. **I'll** sleep when I'm dead; the dirty life and times of Warren Zevon. foreword by Carl Hiassen. Ecco Press 2007 452p il $26.95; pa $15.95   92

1. Singers 2. Rock musicians 3. Songwriters
ISBN 978-0-06-076345-9; 0-06-076345-0; 978-0-06-076349-7 pa; 0-06-076349-3 pa

LC 2006-52138

"Interweaving the remembrances of Zevon's many friends with entries from his own journals, Crystal, his widow, presents an intimate look at Zevon's wild life of drugs, women, and music. Among others, Jackson Browne, Linda Ronstadt, Bruce Springsteen, Carl Hiaasen, Stephen King, and the Everly Brothers, with whom Zevon got his start, share reminiscences. . . . All pop music collections need this book." Libr J

Zhao Ziyang, 1919-2005

Prisoner of the state; the secret journal of premier Zhao Ziyang. translated and edited by Bao Pu, Renee Chiang and

Adi Ignatius; foreword by Roderick MacFarquhar. Simon and Schuster 2009 306p il $26 **92**

1. Prime ministers 2. Cabinet members 3. Communist leaders 4. Biography, Individual 5. China -- Politics and government 6. China -- Politics and government -- 1976-2002 7. China -- History -- Tiananmen Square Incident, 1989
ISBN 1-4391-4938-0; 978-1-4391-4938-6

This "memoir produced from tapes the former Chinese premier recorded in secrecy during his sixteen years of house arrest discusses his efforts to stop the Tiananmen Square massacre and the need for China to adopt democratic reforms." (Publisher's note)

"Until the appearance of this posthumous work, not a single voice of dissent had ever emerged from the [Chinese Communist] party's inner circle . . . . Fascinating." Economist

Ziegfeld, Florenz, 1869-1932

Mordden, Ethan. **Ziegfeld**; the man who invented show business. St. Martin's Press 2008 335p il **92**

1. Theatrical producers and directors 2. Theatrical producers 3. Biography, Individual
ISBN 0312375433; 9780312375430

LC 2008028746

This is a biography of the impresario whose Ziegfeld Follies showcased such performers as Fanny Brice, Will Rogers, Eddie Cantor, W.C. Fields, and Marilyn Miller. Index.

"In his witty, well-researched biography of the great producer Florenz Ziegfeld, Mordden discusses Ziegfeld's extraordinary eye for talent and transforming approach to staging musicals." Booklist

Includes bibliographical references

Ziegesar, Peter von

Von Ziegesar, Peter. The **looking** glass brother; Peter von Ziegesar. St. Martin's Press 2013 336 p. (hardback) $25.99 **92**

1. Brothers 2. Mentally ill 3. Authors -- United States -- Biography
ISBN 0312592981; 9780312592981

LC 2013004049

In this memoir, Peter von Ziegesar describes his relationship with his mentally ill stepbrother, also named [Little] Peter. They had been out of touch for decades "when Little Peter surfaced in New York City just before Big Peter's first child was born. As Big Peter tried to figure out how to help recalcitrant and homeless Little Peter, he began facing his own fraught past." (Booklist)

Zierman, Addie

Zierman, Addie. **When** we were on fire; a memoir of obsessive faith. Addie Zierman. Convergent Books 2013 256 p. $14.99 **92**

1. Christians 2. Christian life 3. Autobiographies 4. Christian biography -- United States
ISBN 1601425457; 9781601425454

LC 2013022552

In this memoir, author Addie Zierman "grows up in an average, Bible-studying, Christian family but as a teenager, her zeal for being the perfect, evangelical Christian girl reaches a new level, one that disturbs even her parents. Falling in love with a rigid, similarly zealous, boy named Chris who is

bound for mission work doesn't hurt these faith pursuits, and is in fact the reason behind her newfound obsessions with purity and perfect devotion to Jesus." (Publishers Weekly)

Zine, Edward E.

Murphy, Terry Weible. **Life** in rewind; the story of a young courageous man who persevered over OCD and the Harvard doctor who broke all the rules to help him. with Michael A. Jenike and Edward E. Zine. HarperCollins 2009 242p il $24.99 **92**

1. Mentally ill 2. Obsessive-compulsive disorder
ISBN 978-0-06-156153-5; 0-06-156153-3

LC 2008-51240

"Murphy, mother of an OCD patient, recounts the . . . tale of Ed Zine, a man so mired in obsessive-compulsive behavior that he was trapped for six years in his squalid basement, compelled to perform an endless series of rituals meant to stop time and the inevitability of death. . . . Murphy traces Zine's illness from its roots in childhood trauma (his mother's death from cancer) through its full flower, shortly after high school graduation, when it began to take over his life. Unable to get Zine out of his house, leading OCD expert Jenike made the three-hour trip from his Boston office to Zine's Cape Cod home once a week. The bond between them developed slowly and with difficulty, but ultimately proved deeper than either suspected. . . . A passionate, faithful narrative from a reporter who understands the stakes and the people behind them, this is a fascinating, hopeful read." Publ Wkly

920 Collective biography

Abdul-Jabbar, Kareem

Black profiles in courage; a legacy of African American achievement. [by] Kareem Abdul-Jabbar and Alan Steinberg; foreword by Henry Louis Gates, Jr. Morrow 1996 xxiv, 232p il hardcover o.p. pa $13 **920**

1. Slaves 2. Authors 3. Children 4. Explorers 5. Inventors 6. Abolitionists 7. Sheriffs 8. Colonists 9. Dissenters 10. Memoirists 11. Murder victims 12. Revolutionaries 13. Writers on science 14. Civil rights activists 15. African Americans -- Biography
ISBN 0-688-13097-6; 0-380-81341-6 pa

LC 96-26245

The authors have provided "interesting and nuanced accounts of heroic African Americans whose accomplishments changed U.S. history. . . . Although Abdul-Jabbar is highly critical of past and present racism in the U.S., he gives credit to the abolitionist movement and leaders such as William Lloyd Garrison for their efforts toward ending slavery." Publ Wkly

Includes bibliographical references

Acocella, Joan Ross

Twenty -eight artists and two saints; essays. [by] Joan Acocella. Pantheon Books 2007 524p il $30   **920**

1. Artists 2. Art -- 20th century
ISBN 978-0-375-42416-8; 0-375-42416-4

LC 2006-47266

"Like every great critic, Acocella is subjective, uncompromising. She has a distinct point of view, a refreshingly not-fashionable one—she salutes Sunday-school virtues!—and writes from her conviction that beneath its hectic, irresponsible, even intoxicated surface, art makes singularly unglamorous demands: integrity, sacrifice, discipline." N Y Times Book Rev

Adams, Maureen B.

Shaggy muses; the dogs who inspired Virginia Woolf, Emily Dickinson, Edith Wharton, Elizabeth Barrett Browning, and Emily Bronte. Ballantine Books 2007 299p il $24.95   **920**

1. Dogs 2. Poets 3. Authors 4. Novelists 5. Essayists 6. Nonfiction writers 7. Short story writers
ISBN 978-0-345-48406-2; 0-345-48406-1

LC 2006-101291

"Despite their different personalities and backgrounds, these writers all had in common dogs that provided stability and consistency in their lives. Each chapter is a minibiography of an author emphasizing and offering anecdotes about the deep bond she shared with her dog. By using diaries, letters, illustrations, and sometimes passages from these women's writings, Adams provides a unique perspective of her subjects as pet owners. A recurrent theme is the comfort the dogs provided. . . . From this unusual vantage point, Adams succeeds in linking these writers' lives in various ways." Libr J

Includes bibliographical references

African American lives; edited by Henry Louis Gates, Jr. and Evelyn Brooks Higginbotham. Oxford University Press 2004 xxvi, 1025p $55 **920**

1. African Americans -- Biography
ISBN 0-19-516024-X

LC 2003-23640

This compilation offers "biographies of 611 African-Americans over more than four centuries, beginning with Esteban, the first African known to have set foot in North America, up through writers, academics, artists, activists and more of today. A few of these profiles have been written by notable names—Gerald Early on Muhammad Ali, Clayborne Carson on Martin Luther King Jr. and Malcolm X, John Szwed on Miles Davis—though most are by lesser-known contributors." Publ Wkly

"This work opens multiple fresh vistas on proper African American history. . . . Essential for any serious African American collection." Libr J

Includes bibliographical references

Almanac of Famous People; A Comprehensive Reference Guide to More Than 40,000 Famous and Infamous Newsmakers from Biblical Times to the Present. edited by Kristin Mallegg. 10th ed. Gale / Cengage Learning 2011 2887 p. (hardcover) $280   **920**

1. Celebrities -- Encyclopedias
ISBN 1414445482; 9781414445489

This reference book offers "biographical information on more than 30,000 famous individuals and groups." Entries provide the "subject's best-known name, complete name, nickname, [and] name of group," "dates and places of birth and death," and "nationality and occupation. Most entries include citations to sources that provide additional biographical information." (Publisher's note)

Angelo, Bonnie

★ **First** families; the impact of the White House on their lives. Morrow 2005 336p il hardcover o.p. pa $15.95   **920**

1. White House (Washington, D.C.) 2. Presidents -- United States -- Family
ISBN 0-06-056356-7; 0-06-056358-3 pa

LC 2005-41474

The author "takes readers inside the lives of the presidential families." Libr J

"Relying heavily on the recollections and memoirs of presidential family members, White House staff, and D.C. journalists, this chatty slice of Americana is chock-full of fun First Family facts." Booklist

Includes bibliographical references

Anthony, Carl Sferrazza

America's first families; an inside view of 200 years of private life in the White House. Touchstone 2000 411p il hardcover o.p. pa $18   **920**

1. White House (Washington, D.C.) 2. Presidents -- United States -- Family
ISBN 0-684-86442-8 pa

LC 00-64936

"Anthony's book records the behind-the-scene lives of American presidents and their families with photographs, drawings, and letters from newspapers, library archives, and private collections." Booklist

"This close-up look at the lives of White House residents offers an intimate and objective perspective on the fish-bowl life most First Families have experienced." Libr J

Includes bibliographical references

Baker, John F.

The **Washingtons** of Wessyngton Plantation; stories of my family's generational journey to freedom. Atria 2009 419p il $26; (pa) $16   **920**

1. Slavery 2. Plantation life
ISBN 978-1-4165-6740-0; 1-4165-6740-2; 9781416567417

LC 2008-18742

"When Baker was in a seventh-grade social studies class, he saw a photograph of four African Americans in a textbook. Baker later learned from his grandmother that the three men and one woman were ancestors, former slaves of the Washington family of Tennessee. . . . Based on the papers of the Washington family, U.S. census records, period newspaper accounts, interviews with 11 family members, and DNA evidence, Baker's book traces his family from its origin in West Africa through enslavement in Virginia and

Tennessee, the Civil War, emancipation and sharecropping, and departure from the rural South for the urban North. He also provides a detailed account of life on the Wessyngton Plantation, once the largest tobacco plantation in the United States. Historians will find this book useful for its examination of rural life in the 19th-century South, and general readers will find a moving story of a family achieving freedom." Libr J

Includes bibliographical references

Ball, Edward

The **sweet** hell inside; the rise of an elite Black family in the segregated South. Perennial 2002 384p il pa $13.95   **920**
1. African Americans -- Biography
ISBN 978-0-06-050590-5; 0-06-050590-7
First published 2001 by Morrow
"The Harlestons of South Carolina were descended from a slave woman and her master, the start of a line of fair-skinned blacks who rose to prominence in the state through commerce, social service, and the arts. . . . [The author] was approached by Edwina Harleston Whitlock, a distant black relative (a sixth cousin, twice removed), to take a storehouse of genealogical material she had about her family and to write its history. The result is a stunning look at a fascinating family and the history of blacks in the U.S. from the 1800s to the 1960s." Booklist
Includes bibliographical references

Barrett, Paul M.

American Islam; the struggle for the soul of a religion. Farrar, Straus & Giroux 2006 304p $25 **920**
1. Islam 2. Biography, Collective 3. Muslims -- United States 4. United States -- Ethnic relations
ISBN 0-374-10423-9; 978-0-374-10423-8
LC 2006-11404
The author presents profiles of seven American Muslims. They include Khaled Abou El Fadi, an Egyptian-born law professor and Islamic scholar at UCLA; Osama Siblani, a secular Lebanese Shiite who publishes a weekly newspaper in Dearborn, Mich.; Siraj Wahhaj, an African American prayer leader, formerly a member of the Nation of Islam, now a Sunni; and "Asra Nomani, a colleague of Mr. Barrett's from The Wall Street Journal, who . . . [criticized] the way American mosques demean women." (N Y Times (Late N Y Ed)) Bibliography. Index.
"In the post-9/11 world Muslims have frequently been stereotyped as monolithically murderous. . . . The heated debates among Muslims themselves about violence committed under the banner of Islam are often drowned out in the fray. Paul M. Barrett's timely and engaging new book brings some of those voices in the United States to life." N Y Times (Late N Y Ed)
Includes bibliographical references

Bell, Eric Temple

★ **Men** of mathematics; [by] E. T. Bell. Simon & Schuster 1937 xxi, 592p il hardcover o.p. pa $18   **920**
1. Authors 2. Physicists 3. Astronomers 4. Theologians 5. Philosophers 6. Mathematicians 7. Essayists 8. Logicians 9. Memoirists 10. College

teachers 11. Writers on science 12. Writers on religion
ISBN 0-671-62818-6 pa
This volume looks at the lives and contributions of 35 pioneers of modern mathematics.

Benfey, Christopher E. G.

A **summer** of hummingbirds; love, art, and scandal in the intersecting worlds of Emily Dickinson, Mark Twain, Harriet Beecher Stowe, and Martin Johnson Heade. [by] Christopher Benfey. Penguin Press 2008 287p il $25.95   **920**
1. Poets 2. Artists 3. Authors 4. Painters 5. Humorists 6. Novelists 7. Abolitionists 8. Women in literature 9. Essayists 10. Satirists 11. Memoirists 12. Travel writers 13. Children's authors 14. Nonfiction writers 15. Short story writers 16. United States -- History -- 1865-1898 17. American literature -- History and criticism
ISBN 978-1-594-20160-8; 1-594-20160-9
LC 2007-36512
"Benfey's subtitle neatly conveys the fascinating and sometimes tortuous complexities of this literary/historical snapshot of post–Civil War America. . . . Benfey finds a common connection among these diverse characters through, improbably, hummingbirds, an intense interest in which seems to have taken hold of artists and writers throughout the late nineteenth century. Benfey's eclectic and original approach brings this period and these personalities vividly to life. He presents sensitive critiques of literature and art alongside tales of illicit love and broken, bent, or triumphant lives, all of which makes for compelling reading for specialist and nonspecialist alike." Booklist

Berkin, Carol

Civil War wives; the lives and times of Angelina Grimke Weld, Varina Howell Davis, and Julia Dent Grant. Alfred A. Knopf 2009 361p il $28.95   **920**
1. Authors 2. Abolitionists 3. Feminists 4. Nonfiction writers 5. Spouses of presidents 6. Spouses of prominent persons 7. Women -- United States -- Biography 8. United States -- History -- 1861-1865, Civil War -- Women
ISBN 978-1-4000-4446-7
LC 2009-19476
"Biography of three important women from the Civil War era. . . . Angelina Grimke Weld, who married abolitionist agitator Theodore Weld, was an outspoken proponent of abolition, racial equality and women's rights; Varina Howell Davis had a sharp mind and an independent streak that helped her fight for the freedom of her husband, Confederate President Jefferson Davis, after his postwar imprisonment; Julia Dent Grant found contentment in her domestic role as wife to Ulysses S. Grant and mother to four children." Kirkus
"This finely nuanced, absorbing account makes an important contribution to both Civil War literature and the history of American women." Booklist
Includes bibliographical references (p. 317-345)

Black Firsts: 4,000 Ground-breaking and Pioneering Historical Events; edited by Jessie Carney

Smith. 3rd ed. Visible Ink Press 2012 833 p. $24.95 **920**

1. World records 2. African Americans -- History 3. African Americans -- History -- Miscellanea. 4. World records -- United States -- Miscellanea.

ISBN 9781578593699

LC 2012034407

"Achievements, pride, and accomplishments involving people, places, and events in black history are gathered in Black Firsts: 4,000 Ground-Breaking and Pioneering Events. This new edition collects and celebrates the thousands of world-moving people and hard-to-find facts and accomplishments that have helped shape society and culture. It recognizes and honors both renowned and lesser-known barrier-breaking trailblazers in all fields - arts, entertainment, business, civil rights, education, government, invention, journalism, religion, science, sports, music, and more." (Publisher's note)

"The third edition of this invaluable resource of African American achievements updates the previous edition, from 2003 to the present day. Events are arranged into categories such as arts and entertainment; government (local, state, and federal); science and medicine; and education, with subheadings within each category. These firsts are listed in chronological order and range from a couple of sentences to almost a full page. Contemporary achievements are included as well as previously undiscovered firsts from the pre–Revolutionary War era. More than 350 photos are included. Recommended for anyone from elementary-school age to adults who are interested in African American history." (Booklist)

Boller, Paul F.

Presidential wives; {by} Paul F. Boller, Jr. 2nd, rev ed; Oxford Univ. Press 1998 553p pa $17.95 **920**

1. Presidents' spouses -- United States

ISBN 0-19-512142-2

LC 98-3480

First published 1988

This collection covers every First Lady from Martha Washington to Hillary Rodham Clinton. The author devotes a chapter to each of his subjects featuring a biographical essay followed by anecdotes

Includes bibliographical references (p. 491-542) and index

Bond, Jenny

Who the hell is Pansy O'Hara? the fascinating stories behind 50 of the world's best-loved books. [by] Jenny Bond & Chris Sheedy. Penguin Books 2008 318p pa $13 **920**

1. Authorship 2. Authors, English 3. Authors, American

ISBN 978-0-14-311364-5; 0-14-311364-X

LC 2007-39840

"From Stephen King's childhood fascination with gruesome comics to the famous family name behind Peter Benchley, . . . Bond and Sheedy light up some intriguing angles on many popular authors. Journalists in Australia, the authors deliver their 50 profiles with reportorial vigor, moving quickly through each profile while highlighting the salient and salacious details of, for example, the role played by Mary Shelley's literary legacy (daughter of two leading British writers) and her free-love husband (poet Percy Shelley) in the genesis of Frankenstein. . . . Between the engaging information and the range of popular texts (Pride and Prejudice, The Origin of Species, The War of the Worlds, In Cold Blood, Lolita, Roots, The Cat in the Hat, The Da Vinci Code), this affectionate literary history should appeal to many readers." Publ Wkly

Includes bibliographical references

Booknotes (Television program)

Booknotes : life stories; notable biographers on the people who shaped America. {complied by} Brian Lamb. Times Bks. 1999 xxiii, 471p il hardcover o.p. pa $16.95 **920**

1. Biography

ISBN 0-8129-3339-7 pa

LC 98-41374

"Lamb, host of C-SPAN's Booknotes, has compiled an anthology of interviews focusing on the lives of 75 prominent people from the 1700s to the present. The result is chatty and informal." Libr J

Borneman, Walter R., 1952-

The **admirals**; Nimitz, Halsey, Leahy, and King-- the five-star admirals who won the war at sea. Walter R. Borneman. Little, Brown and Co. 2012 559 p. ill., maps $29.99 **920**

1. World War, 1939-1945 -- Naval operations 2. United States. Navy -- Biography 3. World War, 1939-1945 -- Biography 4. Admirals -- United States -- Biography 5. United States. Navy -- History -- 20th century 6. Naval art and science -- History -- 20th century 7. World War, 1939-1945 -- Naval operations, American

ISBN 0316097845; 9780316097840

LC 2011032394

This book, by historian Walter R. Borneman, tells the story of the "[o]nly four men in American history [who] have been promoted to the five-star rank of Admiral of the Fleet: William Leahy, Ernest King, Chester Nimitz, and William Halsey. . . . Drawing upon journals, ship logs, and other primary sources, he brings an incredible historical moment to life, showing us how the four admirals revolutionized naval warfare forever with submarines and aircraft carriers." (Publisher's note)

"Borneman deftly manipulates multiple narrative strands and a wealth of detail. He vividly fleshes out the numerous vain, ambitious men vying for power at the top and examines their important decisions and lasting ramifications." Kirkus

Includes bibliographical references and index

Brightman, Carol

Sweet chaos; the Grateful Dead's American adventure. Pocket 1999 356p il pa $17 **920**

1. Singers 2. Guitarists 3. Rock musicians 4. Grateful Dead (Musical group)

ISBN 0-671-01117-0

First published 1998 by Clarkson Potter

"Brightman's is an engrossing treatment of the Dead and their times. . . . She offers fresh perspectives and insights and captures the flavor of the band." Booklist

Includes bibliographical references

Brighton, Terry

Patton, Montgomery, Rommel; masters of war. Crown Forum 2009 426p il map $30   **920**
1. Generals 2. Marshals 3. Army officers 4. World War, 1939-1945 -- Biography
ISBN 978-0-307-46154-4
First published 2008 in the United Kingdom with title: Masters of battle
"Brighton shows how during the period between the wars, each refined his skills, which included reading one another's published treatises on the subject of mobile warfare. The author pulls no punches in revealing their flaws as well. Very highly recommended." Libr J
Includes bibliographical references

Brynner, Rock

★ **Empire** & odyssey; the Brynners in Far East Russia and beyond. Steerforth Press 2006 331p il map $29.95   **920**
1. Actors 2. Industrialists
ISBN 1-58642-102-6; 978-1-58642-102-1
LC 2005-36507
The author "chronicles the lives of four generations of his own family, beginning with his great-grandfather, Jules Bryner, a Swiss who eventually settled in Vladivostok, where he was greatly responsible for establishing its importance in the Russian Far East. Next, he covers Jules's son Boris, a major industrialist, and then Boris's son, the author's father, actor Yul Brynner. He concludes, full circle, with his own odyssey to Vladivostok in 2003. . . . [This is] a fascinating tale of a fascinating family." Libr J
Includes bibliographical references

Burns, Ken, 1953-

★ The **Roosevelts**; An Intimate History. by Geoffrey C. Ward and Ken Burns. Random House Inc 2014 576 p. illustrations $60   **920**
ISBN 0307700232; 9780307700230
LC 2014019251
In this companion book to the PBS series, authors Geoffrey C. Ward and Ken Burns "present an intimate history of three extraordinary individuals from the same extraordinary family--Theodore, Eleanor, and Franklin Delano Roosevelt. . . . All the history the Roosevelts made is here, but this is primarily an intimate account, the story of three people who overcame obstacles that would have undone less forceful personalities." (Publisher's note)
"Starting with Teddy's asthma-plagued youth and ending with Eleanor's death in 1962, every aspect of their lives and legacies is touched upon. Hundreds of photos, newspaper clippings, and accompanying captions flesh out the story, which expands to cover their friends and family, enemies, and (alleged) lovers." Pub Wkly
Includes bibliographical references and index

Cannon, John

The **kings** & queens of Britain; [by] John Cannon and Anne Hargreaves. 2nd ed., rev; Oxford University Press 2009 404p il map (Oxford paperback reference) pa $19.99   **920**
1. Reference books 2. Great Britain -- History 3. Great

Britain -- Kings and rulers
ISBN 978-0-19-955922-0; 0-19-955922-8
LC 2009-278738
First published 2001
This book "details the pedigree, birth order, and political legacies of 600 English, Irish, and Welsh regents. . . . Studded with informative black-and-white artifact illustrations, maps, portraits, and family trees, this [is an] extensive quick-reference " Libr J
Includes bibliographical references

Carey, Charles W.

American inventors, entrepreneurs & business visionaries; [by] Charles W. Carey, Jr. Rev. ed; Facts On File 2010 xxi, 455p il (Facts on File library of American history) $95   **920**
1. Inventors 2. Businesspeople 3. Reference books 4. United States -- Biography
ISBN 978-0-8160-8146-2; 978-1-4381-3336-2 ebook
LC 2009-54269
First published 2002
"This biographical dictionary includes profiles of more than 300 individuals who have made significant and lasting contributions to American industry dating from the Colonial era to the present. Each entry addresses the subject chronologically through his or her life, focusing on major professional achievements as well as personal triumphs and tragedies. . . . The book paints a fascinating portrait of American ingenuity. A well-written biographical dictionary that will appeal to anyone interested in the history of American invention and entrepreneurialism." Libr J
Includes bibliographical references

Caroli, Betty Boyd

First ladies; from Martha Washington to Michelle Obama. Rev. and updated ed.; Oxford University Press 2010 xxii, 437p il pa $17.95   **920**
1. Presidents' spouses -- United States
ISBN 978-0-19-539285-2; 0-19-539285-X
LC 2010-14673
First published 1987
In addition to profiling each woman who has served as First Lady the author examines the ways the role has evolved over the years.
Includes bibliographical references

Carr, Jonathan

The **Wagner** clan; the saga of Germany's most illustrious and infamous family. Grove Atlantic 2007 409p $27.50; pa $16.95   **920**
ISBN 978-0-87113-975-7; 0-87113-975-8; 978-0-8021-4399-0 pa; 0-8021-4399-7 pa
"Richard Wagner was many things—composer, philosopher, philanderer, failed revolutionary, and virulent anti-Semite—and his descendants have carried on his complex legacy. Here, biographer Jonathan Carr retraces the path of the renowned composer and his descendants, showing how its history and that of Europe are intertwined." Publisher's note

"Carr's sprightly, fluent narrative places the family in its historical and intellectual context without reducing it to the symbolic effigy it has often become." Publ Wkly

Includes bibliographical references

Carroll, Sean B.

★ **Brave** genius; two remarkable friends and their unlikely journey from the French resistance to the Nobel prize. Sean B. Carroll. Crown Publishers 2013 576 p. $28   **920**

1. World War, 1939-1945 -- France 2. Nobel Prize winners -- France -- Biography 3. France -- Intellectual life -- 20th century 4. Molecular biologists -- France -- Biography 5. Authors, French -- 20th century -- Biography 6. Authors, Algerian -- 20th century -- Biography 7. World War, 1939-1945 -- Underground movements -- France 8. Politics and culture -- France -- History -- 20th century

ISBN 0307952339; 9780307952332; 9780307952349
LC 2012050707

Author Sean B. Carroll tells how "writer Albert Camus and budding scientist Jacques Monod were quietly pursuing ordinary, separate lives in Paris. After the German invasion and occupation of France, each joined the Resistance to help liberate the country [and] after the war . . . they became friends. [He] tells the story of how each man endured the most terrible episode of the twentieth century and then blossomed into extraordinarily creative and engaged individuals." (Publisher's note)

"A rare chronicle of valiant thinkers fighting political oppression and transcending professional boundaries." Booklist

Includes bibliographical references

Castor, Helen

She -wolves; the women who ruled England before Elizabeth. Harper/Collins 2011 480p il map $27.99; ebook $19.99   **920**

1. Queens 2. Great Britain -- Kings and rulers 3. Monarchy -- Great Britain -- History 4. Great Britain -- History -- Elizabeth, 1558-1603

ISBN 978-0-06-143076-3; 978-0-06-206578-0 ebook
LC 2010013263

The author "recounts the lives of six women who exercised—or tried to exercise—political power in England prior to Elizabeth I: Matilda, granddaughter of William the Conqueror; Eleanor of Aquitaine; Isabella of France; Margaret of Anjou; Jane Grey; and Mary Tudor. . . . Readers of popular history of British royals will enjoy their immensely human stories and applaud the indomitable will of these strong protofeminists." Libr J

Includes bibliographical references

Chernow, Ron

The **Warburgs**; the twentieth-century odyssey of a remarkable Jewish family. Random House 1993 820p il hardcover o.p. pa $21   **920**

1. Bankers

ISBN 0-679-74359-6 pa
LC 93-16599

The author "chronicles the saga of {one} of the world's most powerful and oldest banking families. In telling this monumental tale of the Warburgs, Chernow offers a pan-

oramic view of nearly 500 years of world history, concentrating on the role of Jews in German business, culture, and politics from the time of Kaiser Wilhelm to that of Adolf Hitler. He also explains how the Warburgs extended their influence to America by marrying into two influential families." Booklist

Includes bibliographical references

Chick, Steve

Spray paint the walls; the story of Black Flag. IPG/PM 2011 403p il pa $19.95   **920**

1. Punk rock music 2. Black Flag (Musical group)

ISBN 978-1-60486-418-2

This is a history of seminal punk band Black Flag.

"For a plunge into SST lore, this is the book to grab for summer's enervating heat. Don't expect newfound testimonies that will upset the Black Flag brand, but do expect a fascinating and eventful journey into the heart of damaged territory." PopMatters

Includes discography and bibliographical references

Clay, Catrine

King, Kaiser, Tsar; three royal cousins who led the world to war. Walker & Company 2007 416p il $26.95; pa $16.99   **920**

1. Emperors 2. Kings and rulers 3. World War, 1914-1918 4. Kings

ISBN 0-8027-1623-7; 978-0-8027-1623-1; 0-8027-1677-6 pa; 978-0-8027-1677-4 pa

This is a "biography of not one but three significant men. King George V of England, Kaiser Wilhelm II of Germany, and Tsar Nicholas II of Russia (familiarly known as Georgie, Willy, and Nicky) were more than just the leaders of three of the most powerful countries in the world in the early 20th century—they were cousins who had grown up together, played together, and attended family functions together. . . . [The author] provides an intimate look inside the lives of these boys as they grew into manhood and became king, kaiser, and tsar, bringing new pleasures and details to a well-known subject." Libr J

Includes bibliographical references

Cohen, Rich

Sweet and low; a family story. Farrar, Straus and Giroux 2006 272p il $25   **920**

1. Food industry executives 2. Cumberland Packing Corporation

ISBN 0-374-27229-8; 978-0-374-27229-6
LC 2005-15730

The author tells the "story of an American family and its patriarch, a short-order cook named Ben Eisenstadt who, in the years after World War II, invented the sugar packet and Sweet'N Low, converting his Brooklyn cafeteria into a factory and amassing the great fortune that would destroy his family." Publisher's note

This "is a story peopled with eccentrics and naifs and scoundrels, and a story recounted with uncommon acuity and wit." N Y Times (Late N Y Ed)

Coll, Steve

The **Bin** Ladens; an Arabian family in the American century. Penguin Press 2008 671p il $35 **920**
1. Saudi Arabia -- History
ISBN 978-1-59420-164-6

LC 2007-42748

This "book not only gives us the most psychologically detailed portrait of the brutal 9/11 mastermind yet, but in telling the epic story of Osama bin Laden's extended family, it also reveals the crucial role that his relatives and their relationship with the royal house of Saud played in shaping his thinking, his ambitions, his technological expertise and his tactics." N Y Times (Late N Y Ed)
Includes bibliographical references

Contemporary black biography, v68; profiles from the international black community. Gale Res. 2008 275p il $124 **920**
1. African Americans -- Biography
ISBN 978-1-4144-3275-5; 1-4144-3275-5

Started publication 1992. Editors vary

"Included in each volume are biographies of innovators in the black global community who are currently living and/or who have had a lasting impact on society. Every field of endeavor imaginable is represented, from science, politics, and creative arts to sports. . . . This . . . title will be useful for its coverage of current people in the news who are not as easy to find elsewhere." Booklist

Dance, Stanley

The **world** of Count Basie. Da Capo Press 1985 xxi, 399p il pa $18 **920**
1. Singers 2. Pianists 3. Guitarists 4. Jazz musicians 5. Drummers 6. Flutists 7. Trombonists 8. Band leaders 9. Clarinetists 10. Saxophonists 11. Trumpet players
ISBN 0-306-80245-7

LC 85-12901

A reprint of the title first published 1980 by Scribner

This book "consists of numerous tape-recorded and edited interviews with musicians and vocalists associated with Basie, and each gets to tell his own story. Many overlap and there are interesting confirmations and disputes over details. The language has been polished (and no doubt in some cases cleaned up), but Dance does not noticeably impose his own views on others. There are good photographs." Choice
Includes discography and bibliographical references

Davis, Peter G.

The **American** opera singer; the lives and adventures of America's great singers in opera and concert, from 1825 to the present. Doubleday 1997 626p il hardcover o.p. pa $19.95 **920**
1. Singers
ISBN 0-385-42174-5 pa

LC 97-9123

"Davis tells anecdotes and presents essential details of his subjects' personal lives in biographical sketches ranging from a paragraph to several pages in length." Booklist
Includes bibliographical references

De Lisle, Leanda

The **sisters** who would be queen; Mary, Katherine, and Lady Jane Grey: a Tudor tragedy. Ballantine Books 2009 xxx, 350p il $30 **920**
1. Queens 2. Courtiers 3. Great Britain -- Kings and rulers 4. Great Britain -- History -- 1485-1603, Tudors
ISBN 978-0-345-49135-0

LC 2009-31074

First published 2008 in the United Kingdom

This is a biography of the Grey sisters, "who were victimized in the notoriously vicious Tudor power struggle and whose heirs would otherwise probably be ruling England today." Publisher's note
Includes bibliographical references

De Waal, Edmund

The **hare** with amber eyes; a family's century of art and loss. Farrar, Straus and Giroux 2010 354p il map $26 **920**
1. Art collections 2. Bankers 3. Art collectors 4. Magazine executives 5. Patrons of the arts
ISBN 978-0-374-10597-6

LC 2010-25539

"From a hard and vast archival mass of journals, memoirs, newspaper clippings and art-history books, Mr de Waal has fashioned, stroke by minuscule stroke, a book as fresh with detail as if it had been written from life, and as full of beauty and whimsy as a netsuke from the hands of a master carver." Economist

Denlinger, Elizabeth Campbell

Before Victoria; extraordinary women of the British Romantic era. by Elizabeth Campbell Denlinger; foreword by Lyndall Gordon. Columbia University Press 2005 188p il $41.50 **920**
1. Women -- Great Britain 2. Great Britain -- History -- 19th century
ISBN 0-231-13630-7

LC 2004-59267

This book "offers portraits of a group of women who were scientists, artists, writers, poets, philanthropists and reformers during the Romantic Era and details how their accomplishments changed the social and economic landscape for women." Univ Press Books for Public and Second Sch Libr, 2006
Includes bibliographical references

Dinnage, Rosemary

★ **Alone!** alone!: lives of some outsider women. New York Review Books 2004 296p $24.95 **920**
1. Women authors 2. Women -- Biography
ISBN 1-590-17069-5

LC 2003-27805

The subjects of this volume of biographical essays include: Gwen John, Stevie Smith, Barbara Pym, Simone Weil, Clementine Churchill, Ottoline Morrell, Dora Russell, Giuseppina Verdi, Olive Schreiner, Helena Blavatsky and Annie Besant; Marie Stopes, Enid Blyton, Angela Brazil, Isak Dinesen, Rebecca West, Margaret Oliphant, Alice James and Katherine Mansfield

"The book is dutifully footnoted and academically solid yet is also beautifully written, marked with great feeling and

vivid flashes of insight. It cannot fail to enrich a collection."
Libr J

Dray, Philip

Capitol men; the epic story of Reconstruction
through the lives of the first Black congressmen.
Houghton Mifflin Co. 2008 463p il $30   **920**
1. Reconstruction (1865-1876) 2. African Americans
-- Biography 3. United States -- Congress -- House 4.
United States -- Politics and government -- 1865-1898
ISBN 978-0-618-56370-8; 0-618-56370-9
LC 2008-11292

This book presents profiles of such 19th-century politi-
cians as "P.B.S. Pinchback of Louisiana; Richard Cain of
South Carolina; Hiram Revels of Mississippi; and Robert
Smalls of South Carolina." N Y Times Book Rev

"A welcome addition to the literature of the Civil War
and Reconstruction Era, and important for students of the
civil-rights movement and its origins." Kirkus

Includes bibliographical references

Duberman, Martin B., 1930-

Hold tight gently; Michael Callen, Essex Hemp-
hill, and the Battlefield of AIDS. Martin Duberman.
New Press, The 2014 368 p. illustrations (hardback)
$27.95   **920**
1. Gay men 2. AIDS (Disease) 3. Gay artists -- United
States -- Biography 4. Gay singers -- United States
-- Biography 5. HIV-positive persons -- United States
-- Biography 6. AIDS (Disease) -- Patients -- United
States -- Biography
ISBN 1595589457; 9781595589453
LC 2013039158

In this book, historian Martin Duberman "attempts to
revive AIDS awareness by detailing the early years of the
epidemic, particularly the period of 1981-1995. He sets
the details within a framework constructed around the experiences of two men: white singer/activist Michael Callen and black poet/cultural worker Essex Hemphill, both
of whom lived with AIDS for years and died at age 38."
(Publishers Weekly)

"This combination of cautionary tale, history, and dual
biography of compelling, if obscure, artist-activists is fluidly
written." LJ

Includes bibliographical references and index

Emling, Shelley

Marie Curie and her daughters; the private lives
of science's first family. Shelley Emling. 1st ed. Palgrave Macmillan 2012 xx, 219 p.p ill. (hardback)
$26.00   **920**
1. Mothers and daughters 2. Women chemists --
Biography 3. Women journalists -- Biography 4.
Women philanthropists -- Biography 5. Women
scientists -- Family relationships
ISBN 0230115713; 9780230115712
LC 2012005625

In this book, Shelley Emling "tells the story of science
icon Marie Sklodowska Curie . . . . Emling writes here of
Curie's later years and of her relationships with her daughters . . . . Curie's trips to the United States and her relationship with magazine editor and socialite Missy Meloney, who

started a fund to buy radium for Curie, are covered here in
both personal and professional terms." (Library Journal)
Includes bibliographical references and index.

Englehart, Murray

AC /DC; maximum rock and roll. [by] Murray Engleheart with Arnaud Durieux. Morrow 2007
488p il $25.95   **920**
1. Rock musicians 2. AC\DC (Musical group)
ISBN 0-06-113391-4; 978-0-06-113391-6
LC 2007-295661

This is a "biography of the wildly successful Australian
rockers. Covering everything from guitarist Angus Young's
first record purchase (Club A Go-Go by the Yardbirds) to
the band's induction into the Rock and Roll Hall of Fame
and all points in between, this book is a godsend for fans."
Publ Wkly

Includes discography

Evans, Harold

They made America; [by] Harold Evans, with
Gail Buckland and David Lefer. Little, Brown 2004
496p $40; pa $18.95   **920**
1. Inventors 2. Inventions
ISBN 0-316-27766-5; 0-316-01385-4 pa
LC 2003-65954

The author "profiles 70 of America's leading inventors,
entrepreneurs and innovators, some better known than others. Along with such obvious choices as Henry Ford, Thomas Edison and the Wright brothers, Evans profiles Lewis
Tappan (an abolitionist who dreamed up the idea of credit
ratings), Gen. Georges Doriot (pioneer of venture capital)
and Joan Ganz Cooney, of the Children's Television Workshop." Publ Wkly

Farris, Scott

Almost president; the men who lost the race
but changed the nation. Lyons Press 2012 339p il
$24.95   **920**
1. Presidents -- United States -- Election 2. United
States -- Politics and government
ISBN 978-0-7627-6378-8
LC 2011033001

When the author "lost a 1998 race for Wyoming's at-
large congressional district, he was prompted to examine the
role losers play in democracy. Farris notes that some unsuccessful White House aspirants have had a far greater impact
on American history than many who became president. . .
. Moving chronologically through 184 years, he finds past/
present linkages as he profiles Henry Clay, Stephen Douglas,
William Jennings Bryan, Al Smith, Thomas E. Dewey, Barry
Goldwater, George McGovern, Ross Perot, Al Gore, John
Kerry, and John McCain. . . . Documenting changes in the
face of America and the impact of such issues as race, religion, and workplace reform on elections, Farris writes with a
lively flair, skillfully illustrating his solid historical research
with revelatory anecdotes and facts." Publ Wkly

Includes bibliographical references

Feather, Leonard

From Satchmo to Miles; new foreword by the author. Da Capo Press 1984 258p il (Roots of jazz) hardcover o.p. pa $16   **920**

1. Blind 2. Singers 3. Pianists 4. Composers 5. Jazz musicians 6. Blues musicians 7. African American musicians 8. Band leaders 9. Saxophonists 10. Pop musicians 11. Flugelhornists 12. Trumpet players 13. Recording producers
ISBN 0-306-80302-X pa

LC 83-15223

First published 1972 by Stein & Day

A collection of profiles of jazz musicians including Count Basie, Lester Young, Oscar Peterson, Ray Charles, Don Ellis, Duke Ellington, Billie Holiday, Ella Fitzgerald, Louis Armstrong, Dizzy Gillespie, Norman Granz, Miles Davis and Charlie Parker.

Feldman, Burton

112 Mercer Street; Einstein, Russell, Godel, Pauli, and the end of innocence in science. edited and completed by Katherine Williams. Arcade Pub. 2007 243p $26   **920**

1. Physicists 2. Scientists 3. Philosophers 4. Mathematicians 5. Essayists 6. Logicians 7. Nonfiction writers 8. Nobel laureates for physics 9. Nobel laureates for literature
ISBN 978-1-55970-704-6; 1-55970-704-6

LC 2007-1194

"During the winter of 1943–1944, Albert Einstein met weekly with three other aging geniuses—philosopher Bertrand Russell, mathematician Kurt Gödel and physicist Wolfgang Pauli—in the study of his home at 112 Mercer Street in Princeton, N.J. . . . What the authors present are illuminating biographical sketches of these men and their earlier, groundbreaking work." Publ Wkly

Includes bibliographical references

Feldman, Noah

Scorpions; the battles and triumphs of FDR's great Supreme Court justices. Twelve 2010 513p il $30   **920**

1. Judges 2. Lawyers 3. Governors 4. Presidents 5. People with disabilities 6. Senators 7. Philatelists 8. Attorneys general 9. Government officials 10. Biography, Collective 11. Presidential advisers 12. Supreme Court justice 13. Supreme Court justices 14. Judges -- United States 15. Regulatory agency officials 16. United States -- Supreme Court
ISBN 978-0-446-58057-1; 0-446-58057-0

LC 2010-07788

The book discusses the period of U.S. Supreme Court history in which "FDR had promised the next Supreme Court seat to Joe Robinson, the Senate majority leader who led the fight for the court-packing bill in Congress. As the plan was collapsing in the Senate, the exhausted Robinson died of a heart attack. Roosevelt nominated Senator Hugo Black for the seat. He was able to appoint eight more justices, including Felix Frankfurter, William O. Douglas, and Robert Jackson, who with Black are generally recognized to be among the Court's greatest judges. These four are the subjects of Noah Feldman's 'Scorpions.' . . . Feldman's .

. . book is . . . focused on the members of the Court and their decisions; . . . but also takes more time to explain each judge's distinctive theories of the Constitution and the role of judges in interpreting it." (New York Review of Books)

The author argues "that the 'distinctive constitutional theories' of Roosevelt's four greatest justices, all of whom began as New Deal liberals—Hugo Black, William O. Douglas, Felix Frankfurter, and Robert Jackson—have continued to 'cover the whole field of constitutional thought' up to the present day. . . . This is a first-rate work of narrative history that succeeds in bringing the intellectual and political battles of the post-Roosevelt Court vividly to life." Publ Wkly

Includes bibliographical references

Finkbeiner, Ann K.

The **Jasons**; the secret history of science's postwar elite. [by] Ann Finkbeiner. Viking 2006 304p hardcover o.p. pa $15   **920**

1. Physicists 2. Scientists 3. Jason (Organization)
ISBN 978-0-670-03489-5; 0-670-03489-4; 978-0-14-303847-4 pa; 0-14-303847-8 pa

LC 2005-43471

"The Jasons is a small and elite group of scientists—once consisting almost exclusively of physicists, but now more ecumenical—who since 1960 have helped the government find solutions to particularly difficult technical problems, mostly having to do with defense. During the Cold War, the Jasons were a hush-hush organization, much like the National Security Agency. Today, they labor not so much in secret as in obscurity-which, one learns from Finkbeiner's book, is the way most Jasons prefer it. . . . By focusing on some of the more colorful Jasons, Finkbeiner shines a spotlight on the activities of the group as a whole." American Scientist

Flanders, Judith

A **circle** of sisters; Alice Kipling, Georgiana Burne-Jones, Agnes Poynter and Louisa Baldwin. W.W. Norton & Co. 2005 xxiii, 392p $27.95   **920**

1. Poets 2. Authors 3. Novelists 4. Short story writers 5. Parents of prominent persons 6. Spouses of prominent persons
ISBN 0-393-05210-9

LC 2004-65415

This is a collective biography of the McDonald sisters, two of whom grew up to marry Edward Burne-Jones and Edward Poynter, while the other two became the mothers of Rudyard Kipling and prime minister Stanley Baldwin.

"Offering perceptive commentary on the prescribed role of women in Victorian society to be mere helpmeets, Flanders' attentive, scholarly accuracy is enhanced by piquant observations that demonstrate both her professional talent and personal take on the lives of these remarkable, but unremarked upon, women." Booklist

Includes bibliographical references

Fraser, Antonia

The **wives** of Henry VIII. Knopf 1993 479p il hardcover o.p. pa $18.95   **920**

1. Queens 2. Kings 3. Great Britain -- History -- 1485-1603, Tudors
ISBN 978-0-394-58538-3; 978-0-679-73001-9 pa;

0-679-73001-X pa

LC 92-52950

First published 1992 in the United Kingdom with title: The six wives of Henry VIII

This work examines the lives of the six women—Catherine of Aragon, Anne Boleyn, Jane Seymour, Anna of Cleves, Katherine Howard, and Catherine Parr—who became Queens of England between 1509 and 1547. The author discusses their marriages to Henry VIII

"Fraser's readable style, empathy for her subjects, and piquant use of historical details and anecdotes make this a satisfying addition to the history shelves." Libr J

Includes bibliographical references

Fraser, Flora

Princesses; the six daughters of George III. Knopf 2005 478p il hardcover o.p. pa $16.95 **920**

1. Queens 2. Princesses 3. Kings 4. Great Britain -- Kings and rulers

ISBN 0-679-45118-8; 1-4000-9669-5 pa

First published 2002 in the United Kingdom

This "is a rich and richly hued Regency tale. . . . Fraser is splendidly at home in the 18th century, adroit at teasing history out from between guarded lines." N Y Times Book Rev

Includes bibliographical references

Gigante, Denise

The **Keats** brothers; Denise Gigante. Belknap Press of Harvard University Press 2011 ix, 499p.p ill., maps **920**

1. Brothers 2. Poets, English

ISBN 9780674048560

LC 2011014487

This book examines the impact of "George [Keats]'s 1818 move to the western frontier of the United States," which "created in John [Keats] an abysm of alienation and loneliness that would inspire the poet's most plangent and sublime poetry. [Author] Denise Gigante's account of this emigration places John's life and work in a transatlantic context . . . while revealing the emotional turmoil at the heart of some of the most lasting verse in English." (Publisher's note)

Gordon-Reed, Annette

★ The **Hemingses** of Monticello; an American family. W.W. Norton & Co. 2008 798p il map $35 **920**

1. Slaves 2. Architects 3. Presidents 4. Vice-presidents 5. Essayists 6. Mistresses 7. African Americans -- Biography

ISBN 978-0-393-06477-3

LC 2008-14642

The author tells the story of the Hemingses, an American slave family and their close blood ties to Thomas Jefferson.

"This is a masterpiece brimming with decades of dedicated research and dexterous writing." Libr J

Includes bibliographical references

Gould, Jonathan

Can't buy me love; the Beatles, Britain, and America. Harmony Books 2007 661p il $27.50 **920**

1. Rock musicians 2. Beatles

ISBN 978-0-307-35337-5; 0-307-35337-0

LC 2007-13240

"Gould's combination group biography, cultural history, and musical criticism artfully places the Beatles in their time and social context while examining with great skill how they became an international phenomenon comparable only to themselves." Booklist

Includes bibliographical references

Grant, Colin

The **natural** mystics; Marley, Tosh, and Wailer. W. W. Norton 2011 305p il $26.95 **920**

1. Singers 2. Reggae music 3. Songwriters 4. Percussionists 5. Reggae musicians 6. Wailers (Musical group)

ISBN 0-393-08117-6; 9780393081176

LC 2011-12323

This is a history of the Jamaican reggae group, the Wailers. Bibliography. Index.

"This history of the Wailers, among the first acts to bring reggae to a worldwide audience in the 1970s, doesn't function like most music biographies. Grant . . . resists assembling detailed family trees for the band's prime movers, Bob Marley, Peter Tosh and Bunny Wailer. Nor does he obsess over discography or even dwell much on the musical shifts the trio made as it evolved from playful, syncopated ska to emotionally intense Rastafarian reggae. Instead of writing from a critical remove, Grant freely injects the story with first-person asides about his experiences with interviewees. All these tactics are assets, because they help the author avoid stock band-history patter and instead drill into the broader cultural life of 20th-century Jamaica." Kirkus

Includes bibliographical references

Grant, Gail Milissa

At the elbows of my elders; one family's journey toward civil rights. Missouri History Museum 2008 251p il $24.95 **920**

1. Undertakers 2. African Americans -- Biography 3. United States -- Race relations 4. African Americans -- Civil rights

ISBN 978-1-8839-8266-9; 1-8839-8266-9

LC 2008-24219

"Grant's father, a lawyer and civil rights activist in St. Louis in the 1950s, was among the less well known resisters of segregation, eventually working with more prominent figures, from Thurgood Marshall to Ralph Bunche and A. Phillip Randolph, to fight racial inequities in St. Louis. Grant recalls a long line of family resisters, middle-class business owners who were always on the forefront of the racial divide, challenging Jim Crow laws and practices while sustaining the social and economic underpinnings of the segregated black community. . . . This is a fascinating look at the struggles of one black family that mirrored the national struggle for civil rights." Booklist

Includes bibliographical references

Groom, Winston

The **aviators**; Eddie Rickenbacker, Jimmy Doo-
little, Charles Lindbergh, and the epic age of flight.
Winston Groom. National Geographic 2013 464 p.
(hardback : alkaline paper) $30   **920**
    1. Air pilots -- Biography 2. World War, 1939-1945
-- Aerial operations 3. Heroes -- United States --
Biography 4. Air pilots -- United States -- Biography
5. Air pilots, Military -- United States -- Biography
6. United States -- History, Military -- 20th century 7.
Aeronautics -- United States -- History -- 20th century 8.
Aeronautics, Military -- United States -- History -- 20th
century
    ISBN 1426211562; 9781426211560
             LC 2013015171
This book, by Winston Groom, "tells the saga of three
. . . aviators--Charles Lindbergh, Eddie Rickenbacker, and
Jimmy Doolittle. . . . [Their] adventures take us from . . .
World War I through . . . World War II and beyond, including . . . military raids and survival-at-sea. . . . Groom's . . .
narrative tells their intertwined stories--from broken homes
to Medals of Honor." (Publisher's note)
    "A gripping document of a brilliant era in our history and
a few of the men who helped make it so." Kirkus
    Includes bibliographical references and index

Gross, Michael

Rogues' gallery; the secret history of the moguls
and the money that made the Metropolitan Museum.
Broadway Books 2009 545p $29.95   **920**
    1. Art -- Collectors and collecting 2. Metropolitan
Museum of Art (New York, N.Y.) -- History
    ISBN 978-0-7679-2488-7; 0-76792488-6
             LC 2008-41480
This is a "history of the Metropolitan Museum of Art in
New York, not around its more than two million artworks . . .
but around the handful of men (and rare women) who have
run what may be America's pre-eminent cultural institution.
The Met's gatekeepers are the 'rogues' of the book's title."
N Y Times Book Rev
    "A deft rendering of the down-and-dirty politics of the
art world." Kirkus
    Includes bibliographical references

The **Grove** book of opera singers; edited by Laura
    Macy. Oxford University Press 2008 626p il
    $39.95   **920**
    1. Opera 2. Singers
    ISBN 978-0-19-533765-5; 0-19-533765-4
             LC 2008-17065
This "volume offers biographical and professional information about more than 1,500 opera singers active from the
sixteenth through the twenty-first centuries. . . . Each brief
article includes birthplace and date, education details, date
of professional debut, and important subsequent appearances at major opera houses. Many entries also provide names
of influential figures, a general description of the singer's
voice quality, critical reception, comparisons to other singers, or other personal information. Color and black-and-
white photos and indexes of opera titles and roles are also
included." Booklist

    "A useful and comprehensive tool for novice and experi-
enced opera researchers alike." Libr J

Haley, Alex

    ★ **Roots**; the saga of an American family: the
30th anniversary edition. Vanguard Books 2007
899p pa $15.95   **920**
    1. African American families. 2. African Americans
-- Biography.
    ISBN 978-1-59315-449-3; 1-59315-449-6
             LC 2007-8822
    First published 1976 by Doubleday
    This book details Haley's "search for the genealogical
history of his family. He describes his trip to Gambia, the
African homeland of his ancestors, and recounts the lives of
his forebears." Benet's Reader's Ency of Am Lit

Hardesty, Von

Black wings; courageous stories of African
Americans in aviation and space history. HarperCollins Publishers 2007 180p il $21.95   **920**
    1. African American pilots 2. African American
astronauts
    ISBN 978-0-06-126138-1
             LC 2007-21270
    "This book companion to the Smithsonian National Air
and Space Museum exhibit of the same name offers a look
at the little-known and long-neglected history of black pioneers in aviation. . . . [Along with] the Tuskegee Airmen,
Hardesty profiles barnstormers, including the Blackbirds;
William J. Powell, founder of an aviation club; military flyers, including Benjamin O. Davis Jr.; and astronauts Guy
Bluford, Ronald McNair, and Mae Jemison. This is an inspiring look at the adventurous individuals who pushed
against the limits of racial discrimination to realize their
passion for flying." Booklist
    Includes bibliographical references

Hargittai, Istvan

The **Martians** of science; five physicists who
changed the twentieth century. Oxford University
Press 2006 xxiv, 313p il map $34.50   **920**
    1. Physicists 2. Mathematicians 3. College teachers
4. Writers on science 5. Mathematics teachers 6.
Aeronautical engineers 7. Nobel laureates for physics
    ISBN 978-0-19-517845-6; 0-19-517845-9
             LC 2005-29427
    This is a "presentation of the lives of five scientists
(physicists and engineers) from Hungary who went to Germany and then to the United States. They . . . [are] Theodore
von Karman, Leo Szilard, Eugene P. Wigner, John von Neumann, and Edward Teller. . . . [This book is an] extremely
valuable account of the lives of these five brilliant and interesting Hungarian physicists." Sci Books Films
    Includes bibliographical references

Haskins, James

    African American religious leaders; [by] Jim
Haskins and Kathleen Benson. Wiley 2008 162p il
(Black stars) lib bdg $24.95   **920**
    1. African Americans -- Religion 2. African Americans

-- Biography
ISBN 978-0-471-73632-5; 0-471-73632-5

LC 2007-27347

"It's great to have all these figures between two covers, and even a sampling of the entries captures the importance of religion, and its leaders, in African American life." Booklist

Includes bibliographical references

Heller, Nancy

Women artists; an illustrated history. 4th ed.; Abbeville Press 2003 312p il $39.95   **920**

1. Women artists
ISBN 978-0-7892-0768-5; 0-7892-0768-0

LC 2004-269241

First published 1987

"Organized in six chapters by century, the survey provides brief biographical information, some critical analysis and context, and at least one color plate of the work of 125 women artists who lived and worked in Europe or North America. . . . An excellent resource." SLJ

Includes bibliographical references

Hibbert, Christopher

The **House** of Medici; its rise and fall. Morrow 1975 364p il maps hardcover o.p. pa $16   **920**

1. Bankers 2. Political leaders 3. Florence (Italy) -- History
ISBN 0-688-05339-4 pa

First published 1974 in the United Kingdom with title: The rise and fall of the House of Medici

This book is concerned with "heads of the Medici family {who} directed the government of the Florentine state from 1434, with Cosimo's return from exile, until the death of the Grand Duke Giovanni Gastone in 1737." Times Lit Suppl

Includes bibliographical references

Hutchison, Kay Bailey

American heroines; the spirited women who shaped our country. 1st ed; William Morrow 2004 384p il $24.95; pa $14.95   **920**

1. Women -- United States -- Biography
ISBN 0-06-056635-3; 0-06-056636-1 pa

LC 2004-56677

The author "presents female pioneers in fields as varied as government, business, education and healthcare, who overcame the resistance and prejudice of their times and accomplished things that no woman—and sometimes no man—had done before." Publisher's note

"Hutchinson's lively, personal writing makes this an accessible and important volume." Booklist

James, Clive

Cultural amnesia; necessary memories from history and the arts. W.W. Norton & Co. 2007 xxxii, 876p il $35   **920**

1. Artists 2. Musicians 3. Philosophers 4. Intellectuals 5. Intellectual life 6. Western civilization
ISBN 978-0-393-06116-1; 0-393-06116-7

LC 2006-36398

"Containing over 100 original essays, organized by quotations from A to Z, Cultural Amnesia . . . [covers] thinkers,

humanists, musicians, artists, and philosophers of the twentieth century." Publisher's note

The author "not only preserves culture and nurtures humanism but also revitalizes the beauty and power of the English language." Booklist

Kane, Joseph Nathan

★ **Facts** about the presidents; a compilation of biographical and historical information. Joseph Nathan Kane, Janet Podell [editors] 8th ed; Wilson, H.W. 2009 720p $150   **920**

1. Reference books 2. Presidents -- United States
ISBN 9780824210878

LC 2008056016

First published 1959

The main part of this work provides an individual chapter on each President, from Washington through Barack Obama, presenting such information as family, education, election, Vice President, main events and accomplishments of his administration, and First Lady. Part two contains tables and lists presenting comparative data on all the Presidents

Kennedy, John F.

★ **Profiles** in courage. HarperCollins Pubs. 2003 xxii, 245p $19.95; pa $13.95   **920**

1. Judges 2. Courage 3. Lawyers 4. Governors 5. Statesmen 6. Presidents 7. Senators 8. Army officers 9. Political leaders 10. State legislators 11. Members of Congress 12. Newspaper executives 13. Secretaries of state 14. Territorial governors 15. Supreme Court justices 16. Presidential candidates 17. Secretaries of the interior 18. Politicians -- United States
ISBN 0-06-053062-6; 0-06-085493-6 pa

LC 2003-40676

A reissue of the title first published 1956

This series of profiles of Americans who took courageous stands at crucial moments in public life includes John Quincy Adams, Daniel Webster, Thomas Hart Benton, Sam Houston, Edmund G. Ross, Lucius Q. C. Lamar, George Norris, Robert A. Taft and others.

Includes bibliographical references

Kimball, George

Four kings; Leonard, Hagler, Hearns, Duran, and the last great era of boxing. [foreword by Pete Hamill] McBooks Press 2008 339p il $22.95; pa $16.95   **920**

1. Boxers (Persons) 2. Olympic athletes 3. Boxing -- Biography
ISBN 978-1-59013-162-6; 1-59013-162-2; 978-1-59013-238-8 pa; 1-59013-238-6 pa

LC 2008-13825

The author "resurrects Sugar Ray Leonard, Marvin Hagler, Thomas Hearns, and Roberto Duran from the mists of memory, re-creating the nine bouts the middleweights fought against one another in the 1980s. A great boxing book." Booklist

Includes bibliographical references

Kingston, Maxine Hong

China men. Knopf 1980 308p hardcover o.p.
pa $13.95   **920**
1. Chinese Americans -- Biography
ISBN 0-679-72328-5 pa

LC 79-3469

This book "paints a rich picture of the writer's male family members, but those portraits of her grandfathers, father, and brothers are interspersed with fascinating bits of historical data. . . . The whole is held together by pieces of folklore that one feels compelled to go back to and reread." Libr J

Kreisler, Harry

Political awakenings; conversations with history.
New Press; distributed by Perseus Distribution 2010
286p pa $17.95   **920**
1. Political activists 2. World history -- 1945- 3. World politics -- 1945-
ISBN 978-1-59558-340-6

LC 2009-36808

"As the director of the Institute of International Studies at the University of California at Berkeley, Kreisler has spent 25 years interviewing hundreds of well-regarded economists, politicians, activists, and artists. In this fascinating collection, he offers 20 of those interviews, focusing on the common theme of how their ideas and perspectives were formulated. . . . Interviews are organized under topical headings, including protest and change, environmental issues, imperialism, resistance through the arts, and human rights." Booklist

Laskin, David

The **long** way home; an American journey from Ellis Island to the Great War. Harper 2010 xxiv,
386p il $26.99   **920**
1. Soldiers -- United States 2. Immigrants -- United States 3. World War, 1914-1918 -- Biography
ISBN 978-0-06-123333-3

LC 2009-28191

The author follows "the lives of 12 American doughboys who had been born in Europe and who then returned there to fight for their adopted country in World War I. It's an imaginative concept, and Laskin mines family legends and official documents to tell the stories of these ordinary foot soldiers from Italy and Ireland, Poland and Russia, Slovakia and Norway." Washington Post
Includes bibliographical references

Lattin, Don

The **Harvard** Psychedelic Club; how Timothy Leary, Ram Dass, Huston Smith, and Andrew Weil killed the fifties and ushered in a new age for America. HarperCollins Publishers 2010 256p il $24.99   **920**
1. Physicians 2. Hallucinogens 3. Psychologists 4. Counter culture 5. Yogis 6. College teachers 7. Social reformers 8. Harvard University 9. Nonfiction writers 10. Religious scholars 11. Writers on medicine 12. Writers on religion 13. Alternative medicine practitioners
ISBN 978-0-06-165593-7; 0-06-165593-7

LC 2009-26323

"Mr. Lattin does a lovely, gently humorous job of setting the scene and bringing these men together. . . . This groovy story unfurls . . . like a ready-made treatment for a sprawling, elegiac and crisply comic movie, let's say Robert Altman by way of Wes Anderson." N Y Times (Late N Y Ed)
Includes bibliographical references

Leamer, Laurence

The **Kennedy** men; 1901-1963: the laws of the father. Perennial 2002 882p il pa $19.95   **920**
1. Diplomats 2. Presidents 3. Senators 4. Financiers 5. Political leaders 6. Members of Congress 7. Parents of presidents 8. Regulatory agency officials
ISBN 978-0-06-050288-1; 0-06-050288-6
First published 2001 by Morrow

This is a biography of Joseph P. Kennedy and his sons from the beginning of the last century through the assassination of John F. Kennedy.

"Leamer's writing is impressive throughout, regularly catching the reader up with a felicitous phrase or a surprising insight." Booklist
Includes bibliographical references

Life stories; profiles from The New Yorker. edited by David Remnick. Random House 2000 480p hardcover o.p. pa $15.95   **920**
1. Biography -- 20th century 2. United States -- Biography
ISBN 0-375-50355-2; 0-375-75751-1 pa

LC 99-53712

An assemblage of 25 biographical profiles spanning the years 1927 to 1999 "with subjects ranging from Ernest Hemingway and Marlon Brando to a fake prince, a pair of eccentric mathematicians, and Biff the show dog." Booklist

Lliteras, D. S.

Flames and Smoke Visible; A Fire Fighter's Tale. by D. S. Lliteras. Square One Publishers 2013 224p. (paperback) $17.95   **920**
1. Fire fighters 2. Fire fighting
ISBN 1937907090; 9781937907099

In this book, veteran and firefighter D.S. Lliteras writes of his experience as a uniformed member of a fire department in Norfolk, Va. He writes of the hazards, challenges, and camaraderie of the job. . . . When the author suffered a heart attack, he weighed the sum and total of his life, devaluating his family and work experiences, replaying highlights of rescuing a man from a burning car and delivering a baby to grateful parents." (Publishers Weekly)

Louvin, Charlie, 1927-2011

Satan is real; the ballad of the Louvin Brothers. Charlie Louvin and Benjamin Whitmer. itBooks 2012 297 p. $22.99   **920**
1. Brothers 2. Musicians
ISBN 0062069039; 9780062069030

This book tells "[t]he tempestuous history of country music's Louvin Brothers, recalled by the younger musical sibling [Charlie]. . . . Here, Charlie . . . recounts the twosome's rise from hardscrabble beginnings in Alabama's cotton country to national fame. Basically self-taught, the brothers were reared on church singing before they launched an uphill professional career in the '40s. Louvin maps the pair's arduous journey through small-town radio gigs and endless regional touring." (Kirkus)

Louvish, Simon

Monkey business; the lives and legends of the Marx brothers: Groucho, Chico, Harpo, Zeppo with added Gummo. St. Martin's Press 2000 471p il hardcover o.p. pa $13.95 **920**
1. Comedians
ISBN 0-312-28382-2 pa

LC 00-302623

First published 1999 in the United Kingdom

In addition to Groucho, the author "expands the canvas to appraise the contributions of the other brothers, plus Margaret Dumont, a regular target of the brothers' mayhem. . . . Louvish does a solid job of separating fact from fiction and includes a family tree and a discussion of the FBI's file on the group." Libr J

Mackrell, Judith

Flappers; Six Women of a Dangerous Generation. Judith Mackrell. Sarah Crichton Books 2014 480 p. illustrations $28 **920**
1. Women's movement 2. Nineteen twenties 3. Women -- United States -- Biography 4. Sex role -- United States -- History -- 20th century 5. Sex customs -- United States -- History -- 20th century 6. Popular culture -- United States -- History -- 20th century
ISBN 0374156085; 9780374156084

LC 2013035397

Originally published: Great Britain : Macmillan, 2013

This book by Judith Mackrell profiles "six women, Zelda Fitzgerald, Diana Cooper, Nancy Cunard, Tallulah Bankhead, Josephine Baker and Tamara de Lempicka, whose careers as drinking, smoking, jazzing party creatures reached their critical mass in 1925. . . . Mackrell draws an analogy between the experimental freedoms of the Roaring Twenties and those of the Swinging Sixties." (Times Literary Supplement)

"Avidly researched and deeply inquisitive, Mackrell's prodigious group portrait is spectacularly dramatic and thought-provoking." Booklist

Includes bibliographical references and index

Maki, Allan

Football's greatest stars; additional research and writing by George Johnson; with a foreword by Thurman Thomas. Firefly Books 2008 216p il $35 **920**
1. Athletes 2. Football -- Biography 3. National Football League
ISBN 978-1-55407-389-4; 1-55407-389-8

"This book attempts to profile the top 50 stars of the last 50 years of professional football. . . . The 50 selections are divided into two sections, Top 20 and Next 30, and are arranged alphabetically within those groupings. . . . The profiles themselves are knowledgably written but take a back seat to the well-chosen illustrations—135 color photographs mixed with scores of black-and-white ones in a very striking layout. . . . In short, a beautiful if not essential book that would be at home in any public library." Libr J

Includes bibliographical references

Malone, John Williams

It doesn't take a rocket scientist; great amateurs of science. {by} John Malone. Wiley 2002 232p $24.95 **920**
1. Clergy 2. Authors 3. Chemists 4. Novelists 5. Architects 6. Physicists 7. Presidents 8. Scientists 9. Astronomers 10. Vice-presidents 11. Essayists 12. Geneticists 13. Photometrists 14. Microbiologists 15. Writers on science 16. Short story writers 17. Science fiction writers
ISBN 0-471-41431-X

LC 2003-269159

This examines the lives and work of ten amateur scientists, including Gregor Mendel, David H. Levy, Henrietta Swan Leavitt, Joseph Priestley, Michael Faraday, Grote Reber, Arthur C. Clarke, Thomas Jefferson, Susan Hendrickson, and Felix d'Herelle

Includes bibliographical references

Marias, Javier

★ **Written** lives; translated from the Spanish by Margaret Jull Costa. New Directions 2006 200p il $22.95 **920**
1. Authors
ISBN 0-8112-1611-X

LC 2005-15033

Original Spanish edition, 2000

This book features "portraits of Rimbaud, Turgenev, Rilke, Giuseppe Tomasi di Lampedusa, Robert Louis Stevenson, Isak Dinesen, Djuna Barnes and a dozen other literary eminences. . . . [Though the author] acknowledges the artistic greatness of his chosen writers, he prefers to point out and relish their personal oddities, all those quirks, eccentricities and obsessions that make them neurotically and sometimes pitiably human. . . . This is a delightful volume." Washington Post Book World

Marton, Kati

The **great** escape; nine Jews who fled Hitler and changed the world. Simon & Schuster 2006 271p il $27 **920**
1. Authors 2. Novelists 3. Physicists 4. Journalists 5. Photographers 6. Mathematicians 7. Jewish refugees 8. Essayists 9. Jews -- Hungary 10. College teachers 11. Photojournalists 12. Writers on science 13. Mathematics teachers 14. Motion picture directors 15. Motion picture producers 16. Nobel laureates for physics
ISBN 978-0-7432-6115-9; 0-7432-6115-1

LC 2006-49162

"Cast out of the cafes of cosmopolitan Budapest by the war, each of the nine extraordinary and ambitious men portrayed in this account would become a household name by the end of the twentieth century: Manhattan Project physicists Leo Szilard, Edward Teller, and Eugene Wigner; computer inventor John von Neuman; writer Arthur Koestler . . . ; filmmakers Alexander Korda (The Third Man) and Michael Curtiz (Casablanca); New York photographer Andre Kertesz; and D-Day photographer Robert Capa." Booklist

"By looking at these nine lives—salvaged, and crucial—Marton provides a moving measure of how much was lost." New Yorker

Includes bibliographical references

Hidden power; presidential marriages that shaped our recent history. Pantheon Bks. 2001 414p il hardcover o.p. pa $14 **920**

1. Presidents -- United States 2. Presidents' spouses -- United States

ISBN 0-385-72188-9 pa

This book provides a "survey of a dozen First Couples, from Edith and Woodrow Wilson to Laura and George Bush. Marton mixes some good history with a lot of pop marriage psychology to show the part that patience, tolerance, insight, determination, sex and occasionally even love have played in the pursuit and exercise of presidential power." Time

Includes bibliographical references

Matteson, John

The **lives** of Margaret Fuller; John Matteson. W. W. Norton & Co. 2012 384p. **920**

1. Feminism 2. Women authors 3. Feminists -- United States -- Biography 4. Women authors, American -- 19th century -- Biography

ISBN 9780393068054

LC 2011040432

This book offers a biography of "writer and a fiery social critic, Margaret Fuller (1810–1850). . . . She became the leading female figure in the transcendentalist movement, wrote a celebrated column of literary and social commentary for Horace Greeley's newspaper, and served as the first foreign correspondent for an American newspaper. . . , In 1848 she joined the fight for Italian independence and, the following year, reported on the struggle." (Publisher's note)

Includes bibliographical references and index.

Matuz, Roger

Reconstruction era: biographies; Lawrence W. Baker, project editor. UXL 2004 xxiv, 246p il (Reconstruction Era reference library) $60 **920**

1. Reconstruction (1865-1876)

ISBN 0-7876-9218-2

LC 2004-17300

This "volume covers political and military leaders as well as activists, artists, writers, and more. Among them are Louisa May Alcott, Frederick Douglass, Ulysses S. Grant, and Zebulon Vance. Within each biographical entry are cross-references to other individuals covered in this volume." Booklist

Includes bibliographical references

McBrien, Richard P.

Lives of the popes; the pontiffs from St. Peter to John Paul II. HarperOne 2006 522p il pa $19.95 **920**

1. Popes 2. Papacy

ISBN 978-0-06-087807-8; 0-06-087807-X

A reissue of the title first published 1997

McBrien offers "plenty of historical facts and sobering, valuable judgments." N Y Times Book Rev

Includes bibliographical references

The **Mitfords;** letters between six sisters. edited by Charlotte Mosley. Harper 2007 xxi, 834p il $39.95 **920**

1. Eccentrics

ISBN 978-0-06-137364-0; 0-06-137364-8

"The lost art of letter writing is splendidly portrayed in this massive volume of correspondence among the six Mitford sisters: Nancy, Pamela, Diana, Unity, Jessica, and Deborah. . . . Arranged chronologically covering the years 1925-2002, they include footnotes identifying people, places, and activities. In introductions to each of the nine sections of letters, Mosley provides a synopsis of the major events in each sister's life as well as thoughtful commentary and analysis." Libr J

Includes bibliographical references

Mordden, Ethan

Love song; the lives of Kurt Weill and Lotte Lenya. Ethan Mordden. St. Martin's Press 2012 x, 334 p.p (hardcover) $29.99 **920**

1. Singers -- Biography 2. Composers -- Biography

ISBN 0312676573; 9780312676575; 9781250017574

LC 2012028287

This book by Ethan Mordden is "a dual biography [of composer Kurt Weill and actress Lotte Lenya] that unfolds against the background of the tumultuous twentieth century. . . . The romance of Weill, the Jewish cantor's son, and Lenya, the Viennese coachman's daughter, changed the history of Western music. With Bertolt Brecht, they created one of the definitive works of the twentieth century, The Threepenny Opera, a smash that would live on in musical theatre history." (Publisher's note)

Morgan, Edmund Sears

★ **American** heroes; profiles of men and women who shaped early America. [by] Edmund S. Morgan. W.W. Norton & Co. 2009 278p il $27.95 **920**

1. Heroes and heroines 2. United States -- History -- 1783-1809 3. United States -- History -- 1775-1783, Revolution 4. United States -- History -- 1600-1775, Colonial period

ISBN 978-0-393-07010-1; 0-393-07010-7

LC 2009-714

"From a body of work stretching back seven decades, . . . [the author] selects 17 essays on characters large and small who illuminate early American history." Kirkus

"This book is a perfect gem. . . . Both specialists and general readers will find this book both authoritative and fun to read." Libr J

Morgan, Robert, 1944-

Lions of the West; heroes and villains of the westward expansion. Algonquin Books of Chapel Hill 2011 xxiii, 497p il map $29.95; ebook $28.95 **920**

1. West (U.S.) -- History 2. West (U.S.) -- Biography 3. United States -- Territorial expansion

ISBN 978-1-56512-626-8; 978-1-61620-119-7 ebook

LC 2011023832

This is a "collection of biographical sketches of 10 men largely limited to the pivotal roles each played in America's westward expansion. Included are four U.S. presidents, Thomas Jefferson, Andrew Jackson, James K. Polk, and

John Quincy Adams; orchardist and naturalist John 'Johnny Appleseed' Chapman; frontier legends Davy Crockett and Kit Carson; statesmen Sam Houston and Nicholas Trist; and General Winfield Scott. . . . This collective biography provides a digestible introduction to American expansion, Manifest Destiny, and the larger-than-life men who led the inexorable charge westward." Booklist

Includes bibliographical references

Morris, Charles R.

The **surgeons**; life and death in a top heart center. W.W. Norton 2007 317p $24.95; pa $15.95   **920**

1. Heart -- Surgery 2. Columbia University Medical Center (New York, N.Y.)

ISBN 978-0-393-06562-6; 0-393-06562-6; 978-0-393-33400-5 pa; 0-393-33400-7 pa

LC 2007-24227

Morris "embedded himself for six months in the elite cardiac surgery center at Columbia-Presbyterian hospital in New York City. Unlike some noncardiac surgeries where music blares in the operating room, an aortic valve replacement for a retired pharmacy executive, says Morris, is a solemn affair, the calm briefly interrupted only when the patient fibrillates, his heart muscle fibers fluttering irregularly. . . . The reserved Craig Smith, the unit's head, who gained national fame when he performed a quadruple bypass on former President Clinton, impresses readers with his skill and deep concern for his patients. From detailing the workings of the heart's chambers and valves to the bald economics of cardiac surgery—including Smith's income ($1.5 million in 2004), the hospital's billing and collection procedures and forecasts on universal health insurance—Morris masterfully breaks down complex jargon, procedures and policies for a lay audience." Publ Wkly

Includes bibliographical references

Morrow, Lance

The **best** year of their lives; Kennedy, Johnson, and Nixon in 1948: learning the secrets of power. Basic Books 2005 xl, 312p $26   **920**

1. Presidents 2. Vice-presidents 3. Senators 4. Nonfiction writers 5. Members of Congress 6. United States -- Politics and government -- 1945-1953

ISBN 0-465-04723-8

LC 2005-1836

"The book succeeds in drawing together three fascinating characters into an illuminating historical intersection. You don't have to agree with all of Morrow's interpretations to be entertained by his lively treatment of three crucial figures during an important time in American history." N Y Times Book Rev

Includes bibliographical references

Mortimer, Gavin

The **great** swim. Walker & Company 2008 325p il map $24.95   **920**

1. Women athletes 2. Marathon swimming 3. United States -- History -- 1919-1933

ISBN 978-0-8027-1595-1; 0-8027-1595-8

LC 2008-256

Draws on primary sources, diaries, and family interviews to document the story of four American athletes who

in 1926 became the first women to swim the English Channel, in an account that also cites the media frenzy that surrounded their achievement.

"The book can be read as the story of a sporting competition or as an exploration of our timeless fascination with celebrity. Either way, it's an absorbing and inspirational saga in the Seabiscuit mold." Booklist

Includes bibliographical references

Nelson, James Carl

The **remains** of Company D; a story of the Great War. St. Martin's Press 2009 363p il map $25.99   **920**

1. Soldiers 2. Veterans 3. Centenarians 4. Soldiers -- United States 5. World War, 1914-1918 -- Personal narratives 6. United States -- Army -- Infantry Regiment, 28th

ISBN 978-0-312-55100-1; 0-312-55100-2

LC 2009-16931

"This outstanding book paints the portrait of a small military unit, in this case, Company D of the Twenty-eighth Infantry Regiment in World War I. . . . Nelson orients the narrative around his grandfather, who lived to 101 despite serious wounds and awakened Nelson's interest in WWI by what he did not say about his experiences. Nelson set out to tell the Company D story from official records and the documents and reminiscences left behind by dozens of other veterans. . . . [The author] writes so clearly about the background, especially trench warfare, that even readers with minimal WWI knowledge will feel educated as well as fascinated." Booklist

Includes bibliographical references

The **Norton** book of American autobiography; edited and introduced by Jay Parini and with a preface by Gore Vidal. Norton 1999 711p $32.50   **920**

1. Autobiography 2. United States -- Biography

ISBN 0-393-04677-X

LC 98-43398

"Parini has compiled over 60 selections from autobiographies and memoirs published since the 17th century. . . . {He} includes works by such diverse writers as Henry David Thoreau, U.S. Grant, Gertrude Stein, Malcom X, Mary McCarthy, and Richard Rodriguez. . . . The selections are arranged chronologically, and each is prefaced by an introduction on its author and its merit." Libr J

Includes bibliographical references

O'Brien, Geoffrey

The **fall** of the house of Walworth; a tale of madness and murder in gilded age America. Henry Holt and Co. 2010 337p il $30   **920**

1. Authors 2. Lawyers 3. Homicide 4. Novelists 5. Mental illness 6. Murderers 7. Murder victims 8. Saratoga Springs (N.Y.) 9. Historic preservationists

ISBN 978-0-8050-8115-2; 0-8050-8115-1

LC 2010-00394

The author "turns a telescopic lens on the moral and economic collapse of the Walworths, a socially prominent Saratoga Springs, New York, clan. While tracing the rise and fall of the Walworths over the course of the nineteenth century, he also exposes signs of insanity festering in various family members across several generations. The downward spiral of this once-proud family culminates in 1873 when 18-year-old Frank Walworth calmly and deliberately shot and killed his father. O'Brien makes the most of this gripping saga by steeping the narrative in descriptive Gilded Age details." Booklist

Includes bibliographical references

Persico, Joseph E.

Franklin and Lucy; President Roosevelt, Mrs. Rutherfurd, and the other remarkable women in his life. Random House 2008 443p il $28; pa $18 **920**
1. Diplomats 2. Governors 3. Presidents 4. People with disabilities 5. Archivists 6. Columnists 7. Philatelists 8. Humanitarians 9. Social activists 10. Private secretaries 11. Parents of presidents 12. Spouses of presidents 13. United Nations officials 14. Presidents -- United States 15. Spouses of prominent persons 16. Presidents' spouses -- United States
ISBN 978-1-4000-6442-7; 1-4000-6442-2; 978-0-8129-7496-6 pa; 0-8129-7496-4 pa
LC 2007-36851
The author "engagingly and eloquently narrates the tangled relationships between Franklin and the various women to whom he became close. . . . Persico offers what will prove an important, lasting addition to the literature of the Roosevelts." Publ Wkly

Includes bibliographical references

Plutarch

Plutarch : the lives of the noble Grecians and Romans; the Dryden translation; edited and revised by Arthur Hugh Clough. Modern Lib. 1992 2v ea $23.95 **920**
1. Rome -- Biography 2. Greece -- Biography
ISBN 0-679-60008-6 v1; 0-679-60009-4 v2
LC 92-50223
First Modern Library edition published 1932

This work is "arranged mainly in pairs in which a Greek and a Roman are contrasted. His subjects, who include Demosthenes and Cicero, were statesmen or generals. In the process of writing about them, he invents dialogue and describes the emotions of the personages involved." Reader's Ency. 4th edition

Povey, Glenn

Echoes : the complete history of Pink Floyd. Chicago Review Press 2010 388p il $39.95 **920**
1. Rock musicians 2. Pink Floyd (Musical group)
ISBN 978-1-56976-313-1; 1-56976-313-5
First published 2007 in the United Kingdom

"Long time fans will find Echoes a pleasure to read as well as to look at. For the most part, the book has the knowing and reverential feeling of liner notes. But occasionally some mordant humor comes through. . . . A congenital defect of tribute volumes is that they tend to recite band lore that you already know about. For the most part, Povey avoids this tendency and digs up some of the strange bypaths of the band's long history." PopMatters

Includes discography and bibliographical references

Rappaport, Helen

The **Romanov** sisters; the lost lives of the daughters of Nicholas and Alexandra. Helen Rappaport. St. Martin's Press 2014 448 p. illustrations (hardback) $27.99 **920**
1. Princesses -- Russia -- Biography -- Sources 2. Sisters
ISBN 1250020204; 9781250020208
LC 2014003159
This book, by Helen Rappaport, presents biographical material on "the four captivating Russian Grand Duchesses--Olga, Tatiana, Maria and Anastasia Romanov. . . . [The book] sets out to capture the joy as well as the insecurities and poignancy of those young lives against the backdrop of the dying days of late Imperial Russia, World War I and the Russian Revolution." (Publisher's note)

"A gossipy, revealing story of the doomed Russian family's fairy tale life told by an expert in the field." Kirkus

Includes bibliographical references and index

Ritter, Lawrence S.

The **glory** of their times; the story of the early days of baseball told by the men who played it. new enl ed; Morrow 1984 360p il hardcover o.p. pa $14.95 **920**
1. Baseball -- Biography
ISBN 0688112730 pa
LC 84-221549
First published 1966 by Macmillan

A collection of 26 oral histories of baseball's early days by veteran players

Roberts, Cokie

★ **Founding** mothers; the women who raised our nation. William Morrow 2004 xx, 359p il $24.95; pa $14.95 **920**
1. Women -- United States -- History
ISBN 0-06-009025-1; 0-06-009026-X pa
LC 2004-042873
"Focusing mainly on the wives, daughters, sisters, and mothers of the Founding Fathers, this . . . title chronicles the adventures and contributions of numerous women of the era between 1740 and 1797." SLJ

"In addition to telling wonderful stories, Roberts also presents a very readable, serviceable account of politics—male and female—in early America. If only our standard history textbooks were written with such flair!" Publ Wkly

Ladies of liberty; the women who shaped our nation. William Morrow 2008 481p il $26.95; pa $15.99 **920**
1. Women -- United States -- History 2. Women -- United States -- Biography 3. United States -- History -- 1783-1865
ISBN 978-0-06-078234-4; 0-06-078234-X; 978-0-06-078235-1 pa; 0-06-078235-8 pa
"While Roberts' aim is to see the period from her subjects' point of view, she is not uncritical; for instance, Roberts casts blame on Mrs. Adams's uncompromising partisanship 'in the undoing of her husband.' With a little-seen perspective and fascinating insight into the culture of the day, this is popular history done right." Publ Wkly

Roiphe, Katie

Uncommon arrangements; seven portraits of married life in London literary circles, 1910-1939. Dial Press 2007 343p il $26 **920**

1. Marriage 2. Women authors 3. Authors, English

ISBN 978-0-385-33937-7; 0-385-33937-2

LC 2007-11798

"Seven 'modern' partnerships move through the book, all in (or near) the world of art and letters, including those of Vanessa and Clive Bell, Katherine Mansfield and John Middleton Murry, H.G. and Jane Wells, Radclyffe Hall and Una Troubridge, Vera Brittain and George Catlin. In different but always striking ways, each looked to transform the terms of intimacy." Salon.com

"Roiphe is at her most insightful—and funniest—in showing us where the declared credo of her characters collides with reality. . . . Often these unorthodox unions endured only because someone was willing to knuckle under." N Y Times Book Rev

Rubin, Louis Decimus

My father's people; a family of Southern Jews. {by} Louis D. Rubin Jr. Louisiana State Univ. Press 2002 139p il $22.50 **920**

ISBN 0-8071-2808-2

LC 2002-454

The author "tells the stories of Hyman and Fannie Rubin, his grandparents, and their seven children. . . . Rubin's descriptions are affectionate, yet he doesn't gloss over their flaws, and as a result, those he knows best come alive for readers." Publ Wkly

Salley, Columbus

The black 100; a ranking of the most influential African-Americans, past and present. Columbus Salley. rev ed; Kensington Publishing Corp. 1999 384p il pa $18.95 **920**

1. African Americans -- Biography

ISBN 978-0-8065-1550-2; 0-8065-1550-3

LC 98-47713

A reprint of the title first published 1993 by Carol Publishing Group

The author profiles 100 black men and women and ranks them, based upon his subjective evaluation of their contributions to black American society. They include Dr. Martin Luther King, Jr., Malcolm X, Zora Neale Hurston, Paul Robeson, Muhammad Ali, Arthur Ashe, Toni Morrison, Oprah Winfrey, and August Wilson

Includes bibliographical references

Schiff, Karenna Gore

Lighting the way; nine women who changed modern America. Miramax Books/Hyperion 2006 528p il $25.95; pa $17.95 **920**

1. Women -- United States -- Biography

ISBN 1-4013-5218-9; 1-4013-6015-7 pa

LC 2005-56247

The author "profiles nine women who helped change the course of history by overcoming injustice in their own lives." Libr J

"This is an inspirational collection of biographies of women of various social, ethnic, and racial backgrounds fighting for social justice." Booklist

Includes bibliographical references

Schonberg, Harold C.

The great pianists; rev and updated; Simon & Schuster 1987 525p il hardcover o.p. pa $18 **920**

1. Pianists 2. Composers 3. Musicians 4. Statesmen 5. Prime ministers 6. Conductors (Music) 7. Classical musicians

ISBN 0-671-63837-8 pa

LC 87-341

First published 1963

Beginning with the Bach family, the author describes the personal lives and careers of outstanding pianists from the eighteenth century to the present

Scott-Heron, Gil, 1949-2011

The last holiday; Gil Scott Heron. Grove Press 2012 384p. **920**

1. Music industry 2. Autobiographies 3. African American musicians

LC 97808802129017

"This [book, a posthumously published memoir,] is a . . . testament to the career and achievements of [African-American musician and writer] Gil Scott-Heron. But it is also a . . . personal account of his growing up in the South, a . . . portrait of Stevie Wonder, and a . . . narrative vehicle for Scott-Heron's . . . insights into the music industry, the civil rights movement, modern America, governmental hypocrisy, and our wider place in the world." (Publisher's note)

Sifters: Native American women's lives; edited by Theda Perdue. Oxford Univ. Press 2001 260p (Viewpoints on American culture) $55; pa $19.95 **920**

1. Native American women

ISBN 0-19-513080-4; 0-19-513081-2 pa

LC 00-39950

"From Pocahontas, a Powhatan woman of the seventeenth century, to Ada Deer, the Menominee woman who headed the Bureau of Indian Affairs in the 1990s, the essays span four centuries. Each one recounts the experiences of women from vastly different cultural traditions. . . . Contributors focus on the ways in which different women have fashioned lives that remain firmly rooted in their identity as Native women." Publisher's note

Includes bibliographical references

Singer, Mark

Character studies; encounters with the curiously obsessed. Houghton Mifflin 2005 256p hardcover o.p. pa $13.95 **920**

1. Actors 2. Educators 3. Magicians 4. Eccentrics and eccentricities 5. Collectors 6. Book collectors 7. Hotel executives 8. Airline executives 9. Purchasing managers 10. Real estate developers 11. Motion picture directors 12. Construction industry executives

ISBN 0-618-77363-0 pa

LC 2004-62757

This is a "mix of . . . [the author's] portraits from The New Yorker, gathered in book form for the first time. In the essays he trains his skills on the likes of Martin Scorsese and Donald Trump; The Wednesday Group, the self-selected intelligentsia of El Paso; well-known bibliophile Michael Zinman; high-powered women who decide to quit the fast track; and Richard Seiverling, a Tom Mix fan determined to preserve the memory of the movie cowboy. It's quite a cast of characters, and Singer lavishly gives them all their due." Libr J

Smith, Andrew

Moondust; in search of the men who fell to earth. Fourth Estate 2005 372p il $24.95; pa $14.95 **920**

1. Astronauts 2. Apollo project

ISBN 0-00-71554-17; 978-0-00-715541-5; 0-00-715542-5 pa; 978-0-00-715542-2 pa

LC 2005-40081

This book describes the lives of nine astronauts after they walked on the moon.

"In an artful blend of memoir and popular history, Smith makes flesh-and-blood people out of icons and reveals the tenderness of his own heart." Publ Wkly

Includes bibliographical references

Spera, Keith

Groove interrupted; loss, renewal, and the music of New Orleans. St. Martin's Press 2011 260p $26.99 **920**

1. Musicians 2. Hurricane Katrina, 2005 3. Music -- New Orleans (La.)

ISBN 978-0-312-55225-1; 0-312-55225-4

LC 2011-10122

This look at the music community "of New Orleans is a collection of profiles of individual musicians who all had their ability to make music threatened after Hurricane Katrina in 2005. . . . many of the stories presented here had their origin in Spera's articles written before and after Katrina. All of them show how artists as varied as blues guitarist Clarence 'Gatemouth' Brown, jazz trumpeter Terence Blanchard, heavy metal singer Phil Anselmo of Pantera, and New Orleans legends Fats Domino and Allen Toussaint tried 'to make sense of the storm through music, comforting themselves and uplifting those around them.' Some of the finest profiles—and there is no weak one in the book—detail a combination of sadness and joy, such as Aaron Neville's triumphant return to the city after the death of his wife to close out the 2008 New Orleans Jazz & Heritage Festival." Publ Wkly

Spitz, Bob

★ The **Beatles** : the biography. Little, Brown 2005 983p il hardcover o.p. pa $17.99 **920**

1. Rock musicians 2. Beatles

ISBN 0-316-80352-9; 0-316-01331-5 pa

LC 2005-3838

This "beautifully written chronicle breathes new life into the familiar story of the Liverpool boys who conquered the world and became . . . the most influential entertainers of the past century. The author's passion for his subject, and for every nuance of every scene, electrifies even the most familiar moments in the legend." N Y Times Book Rev

Includes discography and bibliographical references

Stark, Steven D.

Meet the Beatles; a cultural history of the band that shook youth, gender, and the world. HarperEntertainment 2005 344p il $26.95; pa $14.95 **920**

1. Rock musicians 2. Beatles

ISBN 0-06-000892-X; 0-06-000893-8 pa

LC 2004-59794

In this biography of the Beatles, the author focuses "as much on the cultural trends that produced the Beatles—and the trends they created—as on the Fab Four themselves. . . . Throughout, Stark is sharp and insightful, even when he wades into the psychoanalytic waters of the John/Yoko and Paul/Linda relationships." Publ Wkly

Stolen voices; young people's war diaries from World War I to Iraq. edited with commentaries by Zlata Filipovic and Melanie Challenger; foreword by Olara A. Otunnu. Penguin 2007 xxiii, 293p il pa $14 **920**

1. Children and war

ISBN 978-0-14-303871-9; 0-14-303871-0

The editors have "compiled 14 diaries that were kept by children during wartime, from World War I to Iraq. Their poignant voices will break your heart." Libr J

Strathern, Paul

The **artist,** the philosopher, and the warrior; the intersecting lives of da Vinci, Machiavelli, and Borgia and the world they shaped. Bantam Books 2009 xxiii, 456p il map $30 **920**

1. Artists 2. Authors 3. Painters 4. Statesmen 5. Dramatists 6. Scientists 7. Renaissance 8. Heads of state 9. Writers on science 10. Writers on politics 11. Italy -- History -- 0-1559 12. Political and social philosophers

ISBN 978-0-553-80752-3

LC 2009-6950

Strathern "does for Machiavelli and da Vinci what he does for Borgia: creates a flesh-and-blood portrait for each that defies historical stereotype. Using his novelist's eye and a historian's sweep, Strathern conveys the emotional subtleties that animated their lives. It's no small feat that he makes you care deeply for these complex figures who lived half a millennium ago." Washington Post

Includes bibliographical references

Strauss, Neil

Everyone loves you when you're dead; journeys into fame and madness. It Books 2011 507p il pa $16.99 **920**

1. Celebrities 2. Rock musicians

ISBN 978-0-06-154367-8

LC 2010-52255

"By his own count, the author has conducted some 3,000 interviews with the famous, not-so-famous, used-to-be-famous and ought-to-be-famous denizens of popular culture. Here he brings together the best of these interviews in loosely and at times bizarrely connected chapters. All the well-knowns are here, including Madonna, Lady Gaga, David Bowie, The Who, Kenny G, Led Zeppelin, Puffy Combs and Bo Diddley. . . . Gonzo interviewing at its best." Kirkus

Szegedy-Maszák, Marianne

I kiss your hands many times; hearts, souls, and wars in Hungary. Marianne Szegedy-Maszak. Spiegel & Grau, an imprint of The Random House Publishing Group 2013 400 p. $27   **920**
1. Holocaust, 1939-1945 2. World War, 1939-1945 -- Hungary 3. Hungary -- Biography 4. Jews -- Hungary -- Biography 5. Holocaust, Jewish (1939-1945) -- Hungary 6. Hungarians -- United States -- Biography
ISBN 0385524854; 9780385524858; 9780679645221
LC 2012043179

"This . . . family history weaves together the lives of journalist [Marianne] Szegedy-Maszák's parents . . . with the fate of their native Hungary during and after WWII. The author's father, Aladár, was a Gentile civil servant in the Hungarian Foreign Ministry, whereas her mother, Hanna, came from a family of Jewish industrialists who converted to Christianity. Aladár and Hanna's romance . . . continues to grow even after Aladár is shipped off to the Dachau concentration camp." (Publishers Weekly)
Includes bibliographical references

Terkel, Studs, 1912-2008

My American century. New Press 1997 xxiii, 532p hardcover o.p. pa $14.95   **920**
1. United States -- Biography
ISBN 1-56584-469-6 pa
LC 96-52779

This volume gathers "the introductions Terkel wrote for his eight oral-history books (and the fiftieth anniversary edition of Steinbeck's The Grapes of Wrath) with 40-odd interviews: Terkel's conversations with gangsters and grandmothers, authors and executives, photographers and farmers, cabbies and crusaders. . . . A superb introduction to Terkel's work (or to oral history) and a trip down memory lane for his fans." Booklist

Thomas, Robert McG.

52 McGs; the best obituaries from legendary New York Times writer Robert McG. Thomas Jr. edited by Chris Calhoun; foreword by Thomas Mallon. Scribner 2001 192p il hardcover o.p. pa $14.95   **920**
1. Obituaries
ISBN 1-4165-9827-8 pa
LC 2001-42952

Thomas chose "as his subjects unsung characters who had died in unremarkable ways. His obituaries, which became known simply as McG.s, focused on such marginal celebrities as the inventor of Kitty Litter, a traveling goat man, and a champion duckpins player." Libr J
"This highly browsable collection of 52 obits shows Thomas at his deadline best." Publ Wkly

Tillyard, Stella K.

A royal affair; George III and his scandalous siblings. [by] Stella Tillyard. Random House 2006 xxiv, 352p il $26.95   **920**
1. Kings 2. Great Britain -- Kings and rulers
ISBN 978-1-4000-6371-0; 1-4000-6371-X
LC 2006-45130

This biography examines the life of King George III of Great Britain and his siblings.
"This riveting account reminds us that in the past, the misdemeanors of royals had serious, not simply gossip-rag, implications." Booklist
Includes bibliographical references

Tinniswood, Adrian

The Verneys; a true story of love, war, and madness in seventeenth-century England. Riverhead Books 2007 569p il map $35   **920**
1. Great Britain -- History -- 1603-1714, Stuarts
ISBN 978-1-59448-948-8; 1-59448-948-3
LC 2007-911

"The letters of the Verney family survive as the largest and most continuous collection of personal correspondence from seventeenth-century Britain, and Tinniswood draws on them to produce a lively, almost novelistic account of an aristocratic family. . . Their stories range from the outrageous—Sir Francis Verney, who 'turned Turk' and became a pirate along the Barbary Coast; 'Mad' Mary Verney, whose husband's philandering drove her to zelotypia, or morbid jealousy—to the more familiar and heartrending: a father and son separated by political allegiances during civil war; a patriarch who worries about his children's financial security. Tinniswood's portraits are intimate, compelling, and deftly situated within the broader historical period, so that the turbulence of the seventeenth century is rendered as a human drama." New Yorker
Includes bibliographical references

Tomkins, Calvin

Lives of the artists. Henry Holt 2008 254p $26   **920**
1. Art -- 20th century 2. Artists -- Biography
ISBN 978-0-8050-8872-4; 0-8050-8872-5
LC 2008-13121

This is "a collection of New Yorker profiles published over the last ten years or so." Bookforum
"Tomkins is a ruthless observer. . . . Books that trade on content that originally appeared in the New Yorker have become a small industry, but not all are as intimate as this one." Publ Wkly

Unferth, Deb Olin

Revolution; Deb Olin Unferth. Henry Holt 2011 208p.   **920**
1. Authors 2. Novelists 3. Revolutions 4. Autobiographies 5. Nicaragua -- Politics and government 6. College teachers 7. Short story writers 8. Biography, Individual
ISBN 978-0-8050-9323-0; 0-8050-9323-0
LC 201023471

The author writes about "the year she ran away from college with her . . . boyfriend and followed him to Nicaragua to join the Sandinistas." (Publisher's note)

Vowell, Sarah

Assassination vacation. Simon & Schuster 2005 258p il hardcover o.p. pa $14   **920**
1. United States -- Local history 2. United States -- Description and travel 3. Presidents -- United States -- Assassination
ISBN 0-7432-6003-1; 0-7432-6004-X pa
LC 2004-59134
The author "takes readers on a pilgrimage of sorts to the sites and monuments that pay homage to Lincoln, Garfield and McKinley, visiting everything from grave sites and simple plaques (like the one in Buffalo that marks the place where McKinley was shot) to places like the National Museum of Health and Medicine, where fragments of Lincoln's skull are on display." Publ Wkly
"[Vowell] has done her homework, providing lucid descriptions of the murders and agile summations of the scholarly assessments of each era." America

Waller, Maureen

Sovereign ladies; the six reigning queens of England. St. Martin's Press 2007 554p il $29.95; pa $19.95   **920**
1. Queens 2. Great Britain -- Kings and rulers
ISBN 978-0-312-33801-5; 0-312-33801-5; 978-0-312-38608-5 pa; 0-312-38608-7 pa
LC 2007-16181
First published 2006 in the United Kingdom
This is a "glossy, deeply detailed . . . comparative examination of the six queens who have ruled England in their own right." Kirkus
Includes bibliographical references

Walsh, Jim

The **Replacements** : all over but the shouting; an oral history. MBI Pub. Co. and Voyageur Press 2007 304p il $21.95   **920**
1. Rock musicians 2. Replacements (Musical group)
ISBN 978-0-7603-3062-3; 0-7603-3062-X
LC 2007-22576
"In this loving, appropriately ramshackle tribute to one of the most beloved rock-and-roll bands of the 1980s, Walsh gives his subjects the oral history treatment, assembling a wide range of associates, friends and famous fans to put their memories on the record." Publ Wkly
Includes bibliographical references

Ward-Royster, Willa

How I got over; Clara Ward and the world-famous Ward Singers. {by} Willa Ward-Royster; as told to Toni Rose; foreword by Horace Clarence Boyer. Temple Univ. Press 1997 263p hardcover o.p. pa $24.95   **920**
1. Gospel music 2. Clara Ward Singers
ISBN 1-56639-489-9; 978-1-56639-490-1 pa; 1-56639-490-2 pa
LC 96-5943

"Ward-Royster relates the rise of her family's world-renowned gospel group, formed by her mother and headlined by her sister. . . . The book contains details on everything from successful performances on the stage of the Apollo, major TV variety shows, and international tours to top sales of hit recordings and friendships with such luminaries as Mahalia Jackson." Libr J

Warner, Ezra J.

Generals in blue; lives of the Union commanders. Louisiana State Univ. Press 1964 xxiv, 679p il $39.95   **920**
1. Generals 2. United States -- History -- 1861-1865, Civil War -- Biography
ISBN 0-8071-0822-7
This book contains biographical sketches of the 583 men who attained the rank of general during the Civil War years. A photograph of each man is also included
Includes bibliographical references

Generals in gray; lives of the Confederate commanders. Louisiana State Univ. Press 1959 xxvii, 420p il $39.95   **920**
1. Generals 2. Confederate States of America -- Biography 3. United States -- History -- 1861-1865, Civil War -- Biography
ISBN 0-8071-0823-5
"Biographical sketches of the Confederate generals; concise outlines of their military careers, also giving dates of birth and death and places of burial. The product of ten years of research, much of it done in interviews with descendants. Illustrated with 425 portraits." Publ Wkly
Includes bibliographical references

Waugh, Alexander

Fathers and sons; the autobiography of a family. Nan A. Talese 2007 472p il $27.50   **920**
1. Authors 2. Authors, English
ISBN 978-0-385-52150-5; 0-385-52150-2
LC 2007-5239
First published 2004 in the United Kingdom
"The scion of an illustrious—and fabulously eccentric—English literary dynasty referees four generations of father-son antagonisms in this scintillating family memoir. Waugh . . . focuses on the fraught relationship between his great-grandfather, prominent critic and publisher Arthur Waugh, and Arthur's son, the famous novelist Evelyn. . . . If this tome were merely an excuse to reprint some of Evelyn's hilarious jottings, it would be well worth the price, but it's also an absorbing study of how writers process their most painfully formative experiences." Publ Wkly
Includes bibliographical references

The **House** of Wittgenstein; a family at war. Doubleday 2009 333p il $28.95   **920**
1. Metal industry executives
ISBN 978-0-385-52060-7; 0-385-52060-3
LC 2008-33312
Waugh "tells the story of the downfall of the wealthy Wittgenstein family. He follows the intellectually and musically gifted Wittgenstein children as history conspires to rob them of one of Europe's largest fortunes. Waugh weaves the

family's story around that of the fourth son, Paul: losing his arm in the Great War, Paul gained international acclaim as a left-handed concert pianist; at that time, his brother Ludwig's notoriety was limited to a small circle at Cambridge. With the rise of the Nazis, the Wittgenstein siblings were declared racially Jewish and held hostage for their wealth—a peril that ratchets up the book's tension and contributes to the already tragic atmosphere haunting the family. Waugh sifted through letters and journals held in archives and private collections for this masterfully researched work that brings the characters of this previously untold story to life. He moves seamlessly among historical circumstance, personal relations, and the world of classical composition and performance." Libr J

Includes bibliographical references (p. 315-21)

Waxman, Sharon

Rebels on the backlot; six maverick directors and how they conquered the Hollywood studio system. 1st ed; W. Morrow 2005 386p il $25.95; pa $14.95   **920**

1. Actors 2. Screenwriters 3. Video directors 4. Motion picture directors 5. Motion pictures -- Production and direction

ISBN 0-06-054017-6; 0-06-054018-4 pa

LC 2004-59269

This is the author's "study of six boundary-breaking young directors who revolutionized 1990s filmmaking and still represent a refreshing alternative to 'cookie cutter scripts and cheap MTV imagery.' Her full-blooded profiles introduce Quentin Tarantino (Pulp Fiction), Paul Thomas Anderson (Boogie Nights), David Fincher (Fight Club), Steven Soderbergh (Traffic), David O. Russell (Three Kings) and Spike Jonze (Being John Malkovich). . . . Their stories make for compelling reading." Publ Wkly

Includes bibliographical references

Weber, Nicholas Fox, 1947-

The **Bauhaus** group; six masters of modernism. Alfred A. Knopf 2009 521p il $40   **920**

1. Artists 2. Painters 3. Architects 4. Artists, German 5. Avant-garde (Aesthetics) 6. Bauhaus 7. Weavers 8. Printmakers 9. Art teachers 10. Textile artists 11. Furniture designers 12. Biography, Collective 13. Avant-garde (Aesthetics) -- Germany -- History -- 20th century

ISBN 978-0-307-26836-5; 0-307-26836-5

LC 2009-28729

The author presents a "group portrait of the immeasurably influential Bauhaus artists Gropius, Klee, Kandinsky, van der Rohe, and Anni and Josef Albers." Booklist

"A rigorously researched and often fascinating history that morphs into memoir." Kirkus

Includes bibliographical references

Weintraub, Stanley

15 stars; Eisenhower, MacArthur, Marshall: three generals who saved the American century. Free Press 2007 541p il $30   **920**

1. Generals 2. Statesmen 3. Presidents 4. College presidents 5. Secretaries of state 6. Secretaries of defense 7. Nobel laureates for peace

ISBN 978-0-7432-7527-9; 0-7432-7527-6

LC 2007-16018

This is an account of the intertwined "careers of Eisenhower, Marshall, and MacArthur." N Y Times Book Rev

The author "provides a detailed and absorbing gloss on the relationships among three extraordinary leaders." Libr J

Includes bibliographical references

Weller, Sheila

Girls like us; Carole King, Joni Mitchell, and Carly Simon--and the journey of a generation. Atria Books 2008 584p il $27.95; pa $17   **920**

1. Singers 2. Folk musicians 3. Rock musicians 4. Women musicians 5. Songwriters

ISBN 978-0-743-49147-1; 0-743-49147-5; 978-0-743-49148-8 pa; 0-743-49148-3 pa

LC 2007-43445

This is a biography of the singer-songwriters Carole King, Joni Mitchell, and Carly Simon.

"A must-read for any fan of these artists, this bio will prove an absorbing, eye-opening tour of rock (and American) history for anyone who's appreciated a female musician in the past thirty years." Publ Wkly

Wiencek, Henry

The **Hairstons**; an American family in black and white. St. Martin's Press 1999 xx, 361p il map hardcover o.p. pa $14.95   **920**

1. Slavery -- United States 2. United States -- Race relations 3. African Americans -- Southern States

ISBN 0-312-25393-1 pa

LC 98-44014

Wiencek tells the "story of the Hairston family, the largest slaveholders in the South and one of the wealthiest families in the U.S. Wiencek details the race mixing that occured between master and slave and the family's efforts to keep its dark-skinned members enslaved and to maintain wealth only for its white members. A fascinating book that explores the complexity of family and racial relationships in the U.S." Booklist

Includes bibliographical references

Wolff, Daniel

★ **How** Lincoln learned to read; twelve great Americans and the educations that made them. Bloomsbury 2009 345p $26   **920**

1. United States -- Biography 2. Education -- United States -- History

ISBN 978-1-59691-290-8; 1-59691-290-1

LC 2008-24695

"This provocative book is not only an important addition to the history of education in America, but also a valuable contribution to the history and understanding of the country's ideas and culture." SLJ

Includes bibliographical references

Xinran

China witness; voices from a silent generation. translated from Chinese by Nicky Harman, Julia

Lovell and Esther Tyldesley. Pantheon Books 2009
434p il map $28.95 **920**
1. China -- Biography
ISBN 978-0-375-42547-9; 0-375-42547-0

LC 2008-35840

First published 2008 in the United Kingdom

The author, "traveling across the expanse of the Chinese Republic over the years, sought out those who had witnessed the rise of communism more than half a century ago. The result is this stirring, startlingly honest account of life under Chairman Mao and the current reformers revamping the socialist state." Publ Wkly

920.003 Dictionaries, encyclopedias, concordances of biography as a discipline

★ The **African** American national biography; editors in chief, Henry Louis Gates, Jr., Evelyn Brooks-Higginbotham. Oxford University Press 2008 8v il set $995 **920.003**
1. Reference books 2. African Americans -- Biography -- Dictionaries
ISBN 978-0-19-516019-2

LC 2007-44671

"A supplement to the 24-volume American National Biography . . . [this biographical encyclopedia] records the contributions of more than 4,000 African Americans— slaves, architects, entertainers, dentists, political leaders, artists, poets, and activists. . . . [This] is a major . . . standard reference work that most libraries of any size will want to have." Booklist
Includes bibliographical references

American statesmen; secretaries of state from John Jay to Colin Powell. edited by Edward S. Mihalkanin. Greenwood Press 2004 xxxv, 571p $99.95 **920.003**
1. Reference books 2. Statesmen -- United States -- Dictionaries
ISBN 0-313-30828-4

LC 2004-10871

For a fuller review, see: Booklist, Feb. 15, 2005

This biographical dictionary features "65 biographical essays on each of the secretaries of state plus two important interim secretaries. . . . Each essay blends biographical information, early life, education, and influences; career information, appointment, and relations with the president and Congress; and a review of the major issues and accomplishments during the secretary's tenure in office." Am Ref Books Annu, 2005
Includes bibliographical references

American writers; a collection of literary biographies. Leonard Unger, editor in chief. Scribner 1974 4v + supplement I-IV set $1845 **920.003**
1. Reference books 2. Authors, American -- Dictionaries 3. American literature -- History and criticism
ISBN 0-684-80586-3

"Signed essays on the life and works of selected American authors; selective bibliographies by and about each author. The basic set (1974. 4 v.) contains 97 essays origi-

nally published in the University of Minnesota pamphlets on American writers series; some have been revised and updated. Each of the 2-v. supplements covers 29 writers not included in the parent series; the supplements give greater attention to women and minorities." Guide to Ref Books. 11th edition
American writers: selected authors; a three volume set containing sixty-four essays from the parent publication is available $325 (ISBN 0-684-80604-5)

Ancell, R. Manning
The **biographical** dictionary of World War II generals and flag officers; the U.S. Armed Forces. {by} R. Manning Ancell with Christine M. Miller. Greenwood Press 1996 706p $130.95 **920.003**
1. World War, 1939-1945 -- Biography
ISBN 0-313-29546-8

LC 95-50450

"The nearly 2,400 entries, which, according to the preface, represent 99 percent of the total number who served, are listed in alphabetical order in six chapters: 'Army,' 'Army Air Force,' 'National Guard,' 'Navy,' 'Marine Corps,' and 'Coast Guard.' . . . The volume concludes with two appendixes (state-by-state and service-by-service summary of birthplaces and birth dates; generals and flag officers who died during World War II) and an alphabetical index to all biographees." Booklist
Includes bibliographical references

Attwater, Donald
The **Penguin** dictionary of saints; {by} Donald Attwater, with Catherine Rachel John. 3rd ed; Penguin Bks. 1995 381p pa $15.95 **920.003**
1. Reference books 2. Christian saints -- Dictionaries
ISBN 0-14-051312-4

LC 96-165638

First published 1965

"Information includes classification of saints (martyr, confessor, and so on); date of existence; their circumstances in becoming a saint; and their feast day. It also provides a glossary and lists of further reading, some patron saints, some emblems that identify specific saints, and feast days in the order that they arrive within the calendar year." Am Ref Books Annu, 1997

Bader, Philip
★ **African** -American writers; revised by Catherine Reef. Rev. ed; Facts On File 2010 340p il (A to Z of African Americans) $49.50 **920.003**
1. Reference books 2. African American authors -- Dictionaries 3. American literature -- African American authors -- Bio-bibliography
ISBN 978-0-8160-8141-7

LC 2010-05463

First published 2004

This book "profiles popular and prominent African-American writers across many genres of literature. Each entry in this . . . resource provides a biographical profile, concentrating on the major literary works and accomplishments of each author as well as an outline of his or her contributions to American literature." Publisher's note
Includes bibliographical references

Baile de Laperriere, Charles

Who's who in art; Charles Baile de Laperrière, editor. 33rd ed; Hilmarton Manor Press 2008 1128p $175   **920.003**

1. Reference books 2. Artists, British -- Dictionaries

ISBN 978-0-9047-2242-0; 0-9047-2242-2

Biennial. First published 1927 by Art Trade Press. Subtitle varies

"Includes primarily British artists, designers, craftsmen, critics, writers, teachers, collectors, and curators, with appendixes of monograms and signatures, and obituary, and acronyms. Includes a list of academies, groups, and societies." Guide to Ref Books. 11th edition

★ **Biographical** encyclopedia of artists; Sir Lawrence Gowing, general editor. Facts on File 2005 4v il set $260   **920.003**

1. Reference books 2. Artists -- Biography -- Encyclopedias

ISBN 0-8160-5803-2

LC 2005-40500

First published 1983 by Prentice-Hall as volume two of Encyclopedia of visual art

"The artists covered include Laurie Anderson, Frank Gehry, Anselm Kiefer, Jan Vermeer, and Andy Warhol. . . . A visual chronology of artists by country and era functions as an index to artists, and an alphabetical artist/subject index concludes the work." Libr J

Includes bibliographical references

★ **Black** women in America; Darlene Clark Hine, editor in chief. 2nd ed; Oxford University Press 2005 3v il set $325   **920.003**

1. Reference books 2. African American women -- Dictionaries

ISBN 0-19-515677-3

LC 2005-1532

First published 1993 by Carlson Pub.

"The essays offer fascinating glimpses into black women's economic, social, and political contributions, even at the grassroots level, and explore issues such as spirituality, domestic servitude, and mixed-race identity in terms of how they have shaped history." SLJ

Includes bibliographical references

Butler, Alban

★ **Butler's** Lives of the saints. Christian Classics 1956 4v set $149.95; pa set $109.95 **920.003**

1. Reference books 2. Christian saints -- Dictionaries

ISBN 0-87061-045-7; 0-87061-137-2 pa

A reprint of the four volume set published 1956 by Kenedy; New edition of a work first published 1756-1759. The calendar arrangement is retained, but the number of entries has almost doubled and many of the entries have been rewritten in whole or part

"The biographies of the saints and beati are arranged by their feast days with each of the four volumes containing three months. . . . Each volume has a table of contents arranged by the days of the month with a list of the feasts for each day." Booklist

Colby, Vineta

World authors, 1975-1980; editor, Vineta Colby. Wilson, H.W. 1985 829p il (Authors series) $140   **920.003**

1. Reference books 2. Authors -- Dictionaries 3. Literature -- Bio-bibliography

ISBN 0-8242-0715-7

LC 85-10045

This work profiles the lives and works of 379 writers

Contemporary women artists; editors, Laurie Collier Hillstrom, Kevin Hillstrom; with a preface by Lucy R. Lippard. St. James Press 1999 760p $175   **920.003**

1. Reference books 2. Women artists -- Dictionaries

ISBN 1-558-62372-8

LC 99-10053

This work "covers 350 women artists, mostly US painters and sculptors. Entries are helpfully indexed by nationality and medium and include photographers, performance and video artists, ceramicists, filmmakers, textile artists, and weavers from countries in Latin America and western and eastern Europe." Choice

Includes bibliographical references

Drew, Bernard A.

100 most popular nonfiction authors; biographical sketches and bibliographies. Libraries Unlimited 2007 438p il (Popular authors series) $65 **920.003**

1. Reference books 2. Authors -- Dictionaries 3. Literature -- Bio-bibliography

ISBN 978-1-59158-487-2

LC 2007-19949

"The authors, chosen by means of consultations with librarians, are those whose impact has been seen mostly in the last half century, among them Diane Ackerman, John Krakauer, David McCullough, and Cornel West. Entries are headed by author's birth year and birthplace, and, if applicable, date of death, and by signature work and primary genres." Booklist

Includes bibliographical references

Encyclopedia of women's autobiography; edited by Victoria Boynton and Jo Malin; Emmanuel S. Nelson, advisory editor. Greenwood Press 2005 2v set $249.95   **920.003**

1. Autobiography 2. Reference books 3. Women -- Biography -- Encyclopedias

ISBN 0-313-32737-8

LC 2005-8526

The contents "range from autobiographies of individuals (e.g., Adrienne Rich, Sojourner Truth, Isak Dinesen) to those of specific ethnicities or nationalities (e.g., African American Women's Autobiography) to important genres and terms (e.g., Captivity/Prison Narrative, Diary, Feminism, and Voice)." Choice

This set's "encyclopedic and culturally diverse nature should appeal to a wide audience and provide a valuable starting point for further research." Libr J

Includes bibliographical references

Encyclopedia of world biography; 2nd ed; Gale Res. 1998 17v il set $1787   **920.003**
1. Reference books 2. Biography -- Dictionaries
ISBN 0-7876-2221-4

LC 97-42327

First published 1973 with title: McGraw-Hill encyclopedia of world biography

Presents brief biographical sketches which provide vital statistics as well as information on the importance of the person listed. Volumes 1-16 are arranged alphabetically; volume 17 is the index

Farmer, David Hugh
The **Oxford** dictionary of saints; 5th ed; Oxford University Press 2004 xxiv, 579p map pa $16.95   **920.003**
1. Reference books 2. Christian saints -- Dictionaries
ISBN 978-0-19-860949-0; 0-19-860949-3 pa

LC 2005-272790

A reissue of the title first published 1978

This biographical dictionary profiles the lives, cults, and artistic associations of over 1,000 saints, from the famous to the obscure. An appendix on pilgrimage sights in Europe is also included

"Even those who do not believe in the saints . . . will be able to enjoy and to profit from this splendid book." Economist

Includes bibliographical references

Friedman, Ian C.
Latino athletes. Facts on File 2007 278p il (A to Z of Latino Americans) $44   **920.003**
1. Reference books 2. Athletes -- Dictionaries 3. Hispanic Americans -- Dictionaries
ISBN 978-0-8160-6384-0; 0-8160-6384-2

LC 2006-16901

"Gymnast Trent Dimas, mountain biker Juli Furtado, and speed skater Derek Parra are among the 176 athletes profiled in this volume. . . . Following the entries, athletes are listed by sport, year of birth, and ethnicity or country of origin." Booklist

Includes bibliographical references

Friedwald, Will
A **biographical** guide to the great jazz and pop singers. Pantheon Books 2010 811p $45 **920.003**
1. Reference books 2. Singers -- Dictionaries 3. Jazz music -- Dictionaries 4. Popular music -- Dictionaries 5. Jazz music -- Bio-bibliography 6. Popular music -- Bio-bibliography
ISBN 978-0-375-42149-5; 0-375-42149-1

LC 2009-44405

The author "celebrates 200-odd performers of jazz and pop standards, from the mid-20th-century titans—Louis Armstrong, Bing Crosby, Ella Fitzgerald, Frank Sinatra—to latter-day acolytes like Diana Krall and Harry Connick Jr., with a raft of unjustly obscure singers in between. . . . Friedwald is all about the music; he primly shies away from his subjects' scandal-prone personal lives, but accords each a substantial career retrospective, selected discography and wonderfully pithy interpretive essay. . . . Friedwald's exu-

berant medley is that rarest of things: music criticism that actually makes you sit up and listen." Publ Wkly

Garraty, John Arthur
★ **American** national biography; general editors, John A. Garraty, Mark C. Carnes. Oxford Univ. Press 1999 24v set $2,095   **920.003**
1. Reference books 2. United States -- Biography -- Dictionaries
ISBN 0-19-520635-5

LC 98-20826

ALA RUSA Dartmouth Medal (1999)

"ANB defines 'American' broadly as a person whose significance, achievement, fame, or influence occurred during residence within what is now the US, or whose life or career directly influenced the course of US history. Subjects must have died before 1996. . . . Subjects are arranged alphabetically. The typical entry, 750 to 7,500 words in length, proceeds chronologically, following the major personal and professional events of the subject's life, birth to death. The concluding paragraph attempts to assess the subject's contributions from today's perspective. A brief bibliography after each entry, not meant to be comprehensive, lists major sources, including locations of archives and collections of personal papers." Choice

Includes bibliographical references

Gates, Alexander E.
A to Z of earth scientists. Facts on File 2002 336p il (Notable scientists) $45   **920.003**
1. Earth sciences 2. Reference books 3. Scientists -- Dictionaries
ISBN 0-8160-4580-1

LC 2002-14616

This "profiles the lives of 192 people who devoted their careers to the disciplines and subdisciplines of the earth sciences during the 18th century to the present. . . . Entries appear in alphabetic order under the name by which the scientist is most commonly known. Also included are birth date, date of death (if applicable), nationality, and earth science specialty. An essay containing more personal data, including an emphasis on the scientist's main work and contributions to the field follows this information." Am Ref Books Annu, 2003

Includes bibliographical references

Great lives from history
Great lives from history, The 17th century, 1601-1700; editor, Larissa Juliet Taylor. Salem Press 2005 2v il set $160   **920.003**
1. Reference books 2. Biography -- Dictionaries 3. World history -- 17th century
ISBN 1-58765-222-6; 978-1-58765-222-6

LC 2005-17804

Companion volume to Great events from history, The 17th century, 1601-1700

First published as part of the Great lives from history series, published 1987-1995 under the editorship of Frank N. Magill; previously published as half of volume 4 of Dictionary of world biography, published 1998-1999

This "is a collection of biographical essays, ranging from three to five pages in length and documenting the lives of those individuals who helped to shape the history of the 17th century. The coverage is also global and includes both well-known and lesser-known figures." SLJ

Includes bibliographical references

Great lives from history, The 18th century, 1701-1800; editor, John Powell; editor, first edition, Frank N. Magill. Salem Press 2006 2v il map set $160   **920.003**
1. Reference books 2. Biography -- Dictionaries 3. World history -- 18th century
ISBN 978-1-58765-276-9; 1-58765-276-5
LC 2006-5336
Companion volume to Great events from history, The 18th century, 1701-1800

First published as part of the Great lives from history series, published 1987-1995 under the editorship of Frank N. Magill; previously published as half of volume 4 of Dictionary of world biography, published 1998-1999

"The alphabetically listed subjects encompass 36 areas of expertise and include John Newbery, Pontiac, Qianlong, Hannah More, Pius IV, Paul Revere, and Shah Wali Allah, among others. Each article is approximately three pages long and lists the subject's major accomplishments, important dates, and areas of achievement. . . . A well-written, useful set." SLJ

Includes bibliographical references

Great lives from history, The 19th century, 1801-1900; editor, John Powell. Salem Press 2006 4v il map set $360   **920.003**
1. Reference books 2. Biography -- Dictionaries 3. World history -- 19th century
ISBN 978-1-58765-292-9; 1-58765-292-7
LC 2006-20187
Companion volume to Great events from history, The 19th century, 1801-1900

First published as part of the Great lives from history series, published 1987-1995 under the editorship of Frank N. Magill; previously published as volumes 5 and 6 of Dictionary of world biography, published 1998-1999

"A total of 737 essays covering 757 major figures including 123 on women make up the set. . . . Major world leaders appear here, as well as the giants of religious faith who dominated the century: monarchs, presidents, popes, philosophers, writers, social reformers, educators, and military leaders who left their imprint on political as well as spiritual institutions." Publisher's note

Includes bibliographical references

Great lives from history: the 20th century, 1901-2000; editor, Robert F. Gorman. Salem Press 2008 10v il set $795   **920.003**
1. Reference books 2. Biography -- Dictionaries 3. World history -- 20th century
ISBN 978-1-58765-345-2
LC 2008-17125
First published as part of the Great lives from history series, published 1987-1995 under the editorship of Frank N. Magill; previously published as volumes 7-9 of Dictionary of world biography, published 1998-1999

"This ten-volume set offers 1,330 . . . biographies of major personages in world history (many still living) from 1901-2000. . . . The personages covered are identified with one or more of the following regions: Africa, Asia, Australia, Caribbean, Europe, Latin America, Middle East, North America, South America, and Southeast Asia." Publisher's note

Includes bibliographical references

Great lives from history, The ancient world, prehistory-476 C.E; editor, Christina A. Salowey. Salem Press 2004 2v il, maps set $160   **920.003**
1. Ancient history 2. Reference books 3. Biography -- Dictionaries
ISBN 1-587-65152-1; 978-1-58765-164-9
LC 2004-705
Companion volume to Great events from history, The ancient world, prehistory-476 C.E

First published as part of the Great lives from history series, published 1987-1995 under the editorship of Frank N. Magill; previously published as volume 1 of Dictionary of world biography, published 1998-1999

This "set provides three-to-six-page biographies on major personages from the ancient world. Arranged alphabetically, each article gives basic information such as when and where the individual was born and also where and when he or she died, a description of his or her early life and life's work, the significance of the individual, an annotated bibliography, and related entries in both this set and in the . . . [Great events from history] set." Ref & User Services Quarterly

Includes bibliographical references

Great lives from history, the Middle Ages, 477-1453; editor, Shelley Wolbrink. Salem Press 2005 2v il map set $160   **920.003**
1. Reference books 2. Middle ages -- Biography 3. Biography -- Dictionaries
ISBN 1-58765-164-5; 978-1-58765-164-9
LC 2004-16696
Companion volume to Great events from history, the Middle Ages, 477-1453

First published as part of the Great lives from history series, published 1987-1995 under the editorship of Frank N. Magill; previously published as volume 2 of Dictionary of world biography, published 1998-1999

These "volumes focus on the people throughout the world from after the Fall of Rome, in 476 C.E., to 1453. Coverage is worldwide. . . . Each entry begins with ready-reference information, followed by a summary of the person's life, a paragraph or two on 'Significance,' a list of further readings, and cross-references to entries both within the set and within the [Great events in history] companion set." Booklist

Includes bibliographical references

Great lives from history, the Renaissance & early modern era, 1454-1600; editor, Christina J. Moose. Salem Press 2005 2v il map set $160   **920.003**
1. Renaissance 2. Reference books 3. Biography --

Dictionaries
ISBN 1-58765-211-0; 978-1-58765-211-0
LC 2004-28875
Companion volume to Great events from history, the Renaissance & early modern era, 1454-1600

First published as part of the Great lives from history series, published 1987-1995 under the editorship of Frank N. Magill; previously published as volume 3 of Dictionary of world biography, published 1998-1999

"This two-volume work offers biographies of 338 historical figures in entries that range from two to five pages in length. A publisher's note in volume 1 explains the set's format and use. All the biographies include name, nationality or ethnicity, historical role, dates, and area(s) of achievement; description of early life, work, and significance; an annotated bibliography; and cross-references." Choice
Includes bibliographical references

Great lives from history: Notorious lives; editor, Carl L. Bankston III. Salem Press 2007 3v il set $252   **920.003**
1. Criminals 2. Dictators 3. Terrorists 4. War criminals 5. Reference books 6. Political corruption 7. Biography -- Dictionaries
ISBN 978-1-58765-320-9
LC 2006-32935
"The scope and depth of coverage make it a valuable resource for not just biographies but for criminal justice and popular culture as well." Booklist
Includes bibliographical references

Hamilton, Neil A.
Presidents; a biographical dictionary. Ian C. Friedman, reviser. 3rd ed; Facts on File 2010 496p il (Facts on File library of American history) $85; pa $19.95   **920.003**
1. Reference books 2. Presidents -- United States -- Dictionaries
ISBN 978-0-8160-7708-3; 978-0-8160-8247-6 pa
LC 2009-10191
First published 2001
This book "contains biographies and portraits of all presidents, a . . . chronology of the life of each president, and suggested further reading about each president." Publisher's note
Includes bibliographical references

Havlice, Patricia Pate
Index to artistic biography. Scarecrow Press 1973 2v set $135   **920.003**
1. Reference books 2. Artists -- Biography 3. Biography -- Indexes
ISBN 0-8108-0540-5
The first two volumes list some 70,000 artists' biographies found in sixty-four reference works. The first supplement covers seventy titles and lists around 47,000 names. The second supplement covers 131 titles published from 1980 through 1999

★ **Holy** people of the world; a cross-cultural encyclopedia. Phyllis G. Jestice, editor. ABC-CLIO 2004 3v il set $285   **920.003**
1. Reference books 2. Religious biography -- Encyclopedias
ISBN 1-576-07355-6
LC 2004-22606
"More than 1,000 of the 1,183 entries are biographical sketches of men and women from a variety of religious traditions, including African religions, Amerindian religions, Bahaism, Buddhism, Christianity, Hinduism, Islam, Judaism, Shinto, and Sikhism. There are also survey articles that address aspects of holy people across religious traditions." Booklist
"This edition deserves to become well-worn by the time a second appears." Libr J
Includes bibliographical references

Jaques Cattell Press
Who's who in American politics 2007-2008; [prepared by Marquis Who's Who] 21st ed.; Marquis Who's Who 2007 xxxvi, 1960p $314.10 **920.003**
1. Reference books 2. Politicians -- United States -- Dictionaries
ISBN 978-0-8379-6918-3
Biennial. First published 1967 by Bowker
"Biographical directory of political leaders in the Congress, the executive branch of the federal government, state legislatures, state executive branches, mayors of cities with populations over 50,000, national and state party chairs, national party committee members, county chairs, and state supreme court justices. Entries are arranged by state, then alphabetically by name. Indexed by name." Ref Sources for Small & Medium-sized Libr. 6th edition

Kelly, J. N. D.
The **Oxford** dictionary of Popes; with new material by Michael Walsh. Updated [ed]; Oxford University Press 2006 349p pa $21.43 **920.003**
1. Reference books 2. Popes -- Dictionaries
ISBN 978-0-19-861433-3; 0-19-861433-0
LC 2006-277841
First published 1986
"An excellent source of information, arranged chronologically with an alphabetical index. Includes popes, antipopes, and an appendix on Pope Joan." Ref Sources for Small & Medium-sized Libr. 6th edition
Includes bibliographical references

Krismann, Carol
★ **Encyclopedia** of American women in business; from colonial times to the present. [by] Carol H. Krisman. Greenwood Press 2004 692p 2v set $175   **920.003**
1. Reference books 2. Businesswomen -- Encyclopedias 3. Women executives -- Encyclopedias
ISBN 0-313-32757-2
LC 2004-56065
The author "presents the stories of 327 businesswomen who have succeeded as entrepreneurs, executives, or business owners in profit-making enterprises from Colonial times to this day. . . . In addition to the biographies, the

book contains entries for work-related issues like old-boys network, office romance, and diversity as well as profiles of agencies related to women. . . . This excellent reference book is wonderfully readable and should encourage readers to conduct further research of the women profiled." Libr J

Includes bibliographical references

Kuhlman, Erika A.

A to Z of women in world history; [by] Erika Kuhlman. Facts on File 2002 452p il (Facts on File library of world history) $49.50   **920.003**
1. Reference books 2. Women -- Biography -- Dictionaries
ISBN 0-8160-4334-5

LC 2001-54327

"The 260 women who are profiled here have not only made a mark on their own cultures but have also 'influenced other women from diverse cultures and different historical periods pursuing the same goals.'. . . Entries are organized first under 14 areas of accomplishment, from 'Adventurers and Athletes' to 'Writers.'. . . Entries are generally around two pages in length, and each offers suggestions for further reading. . . . A to Z of Women in World History is a good place to start for researchers who are taking a sphere-of-activity approach to women's history. This highly readable volume is recommended." Booklist

Includes bibliographical references

Mandel, David

Who's who in the Jewish Bible. Jewish Publication Society 2007 xx, 422p pa $30   **920.003**
1. Reference books 2. Bible -- O.T. -- Biography -- Dictionaries
ISBN 978-0-8276-0863-4; 0-8276-0863-2

LC 2007-27288

"Using only the Bible as its basis, this encyclopedia catalogues 3,000 characters from A to Z. General readers and students interested in past Jewish life will find this work most useful as a quick reference for information and a starting point for research." Booklist

Includes bibliographical references

Martinez Wood, Jamie

Latino writers and journalists. Facts on File 2007 294p il (A to Z of Latino Americans) $44   **920.003**
1. Reference books 2. Hispanic Americans -- Dictionaries 3. American literature -- Hispanic American authors -- Bio-bibliography
ISBN 0-8160-6422-9; 978-0-8160-6422-9

LC 2006-17394

This book "brings together 150 writers identified as Latino Americans. Approximately one-third of the profiles are accompanied by photographs." Booklist

Includes bibliographical references

Millar, David

★ The **Cambridge** dictionary of scientists; [by] David Millar [et al.] 2nd ed; Cambridge Univ. Press 2002 464p il hardcover o.p. $99; pa $34.99 **920.003**
1. Reference books 2. Scientists -- Dictionaries
ISBN 0-521-80602-X; 0-521-00062-9 pa

LC 2002-512240

First published 1996 as a revision of: Chambers concise dictionary of scientists

"The alphabetically organized, illustrated biographical dictionary . . . [covers] over 1,500 key scientists . . . from 40 countries. Physics, chemistry, biology, geology, astronomy, mathematics, medicine, meteorology and technology are all represented and special attention is paid to pioneer women." Publisher's note

Monush, Barry

★ **Screen** world presents the encyclopedia of Hollywood film actors; v1 edited by Barry Monush. Applause Theatre and Cinema Bks. 2003 1200p v1 il $35   **920.003**
1. Reference books 2. Actors -- Dictionaries 3. Motion pictures -- Biography -- Dictionaries
ISBN 1-557-83551-9

LC 2002-152728

"The first of a projected two-volume set, this encyclopedia provides biographical profiles of actors who worked in Hollywood between 1915 and 1965 . . . . [The author] includes all Oscar-winning actors as well as performers who became prominent in film before the late 1960s. . . . Entries are arranged in alphabetical order (Bud Abbott and Lou Costello to George Zucco), include vital statistics, and note any higher-education institution the actor attended. . . . This is an item that academic libraries and specialized film libraries will want to add. It would also no doubt find an audience in public libraries." Booklist

Musicians & composers of the 20th century; editor Alfred W. Cramer. Salem Press 2009 5v il set $399   **920.003**
1. Reference books 2. Music -- Bio-bibliography 3. Musicians -- Dictionaries
ISBN 978-1-58765-512-8

LC 2009-2980

"The work covers 614 composers, performers, and teachers, chosen for musical influence as well as fame. All major genres are covered, from classical to rap, along with many subgenres, such as rockabilly, atonal, and funk. . . . This work provides valuable, basic information on the topic as well as multiple, easy-access routes to it. Highly recommended." Libr J

Includes bibliographical references

New dictionary of scientific biography; Noretta Koertge, editor in chief. Scribner's 2008 8v il set $995   **920.003**
1. Reference books 2. Scientists -- Dictionaries
ISBN 978-0-684-31320-7

LC 2007-31384

First published 1970-1980 in 16 volumes with title: Dictionary of scientific biography

This biographical dictionary "contains thousands of biographies of mathematicians and natural scientists from all countries and from all historical periods." Publisher's note

Includes bibliographical references

Newton, David E.

Latinos in science, math, and professions. Facts on File 2007 274p il (A to Z of Latino Americans) $44 **920.003**

1. Reference books 2. Scientists -- Dictionaries 3. Mathematicians -- Dictionaries 4. Hispanic Americans -- Dictionaries

ISBN 978-0-8160-6385-7; 0-8160-6385-0

LC 2006-16769

Among the figures profiled in this biographical dictionary "are sociology expert Maxine Baca Zinn; Ellen Ochoa, the first Latina in space; and research entomologist Fernando E. Vega." Libr J

Includes bibliographical references

Notable American women; a biographical dictionary completing the twentieth century. Susan Ware, editor; Stacy Braukman, assistant editor. Belknap Press 2004 xxx, 729p $45 **920.003**

1. Reference books 2. Women -- United States -- Biography 3. United States -- Biography -- Dictionaries

ISBN 0-674-01488-X

LC 2004-48859

This volume includes "stars of the golden ages of radio, film, dance, and television; scientists and scholars; politicians and entrepreneurs; authors and aviators; civil rights activists and religious leaders; Native American craftspeople and world-renowned artists. Women from a broad spectrum of ethnic , class, political, religious, and sexual identities are all acknowledged." Publisher's note

Includes bibliographical references

Notable American women: the modern period; a biographical dictionary. edited by Barbara Sicherman {et al.} Harvard Univ. Press 1980 xxii, 773p hardcover o.p. pa $41.50 **920.003**

1. Reference books 2. Women -- United States -- Biography 3. United States -- Biography -- Dictionaries

ISBN 0-674-62733-4 pa

LC 80-18402

This set provides "1 1/2- to 2-page biographies and references for 442 American women. Women were chosen from science, business, and engineering as well as from such traditional fields as education, entertainment, and social work, with a wide variety of career patterns, philosophical outlooks and personal styles' represented. . . . Entries describe the life and personality of the individual, evaluate her career, and place it in an historical context. Special emphasis is given to the conflicting demands of her public and personal lives." Choice

Notable black American men, book I; Jessie Carney Smith, editor. Gale Res. 1998 xxxiv, 1365p il $150 **920.003**

1. Reference books 2. United States -- Biography -- Dictionaries 3. African Americans -- Biography -- Dictionaries

ISBN 0-7876-0763-0

LC 98-38166

Companion to Notable black American women

This work, the first volume of a two-volume biographical dictionary, "profiles 500 men, from poet Jupiter Hammon (b.

1711) to Tiger Woods. . . . Each entry begins with birth and death dates and a few words describing the subject's major fields of endeavor, followed by a biographical essay, a list of references, and, in some cases, a note on collections of source material." Booklist

Includes bibliographical references

Notable black American men, book II; Jessie Carney Smith, editor. Thomson Gale 2007 xxiv, 827p il $193 **920.003**

1. Reference books 2. United States -- Biography -- Dictionaries 3. African Americans -- Biography -- Dictionaries

ISBN 0-7876-6493-6; 978-0-7876-6493-0

LC 2006-21193

Covering "prominent newsmakers as well as lesser-known individuals, . . . [this second volume of a two-volume work] offers full biographical entries, portraits, addresses for living listees and recommended sources for further study." Publisher's note

Includes bibliographical references

Notable black American women, book I; Jessie Carney Smith, editor. Gale Res. 1992 xlvii, 1334p il $203 **920.003**

1. Reference books 2. African American women -- Dictionaries 3. United States -- Biography -- Dictionaries

ISBN 0-8103-4749-0

LC 91-35074

This first volume of a three-volume biographical encyclopedia "documents the achievements of 500 African-American women who have made significant contributions to American culture from the colonial era to the present. . . . Subjects include women active in all fields of endeavor, from education, science, and the arts, to business, law and politics. . . . Authoritative and entertaining at the same time." Am Libr

Notable black American women, Book III; Jessie Carney Smith, editor. Gale 2003 lxxviii, 881p il $165 **920.003**

1. Reference books 2. African American women -- Dictionaries 3. United States -- Biography -- Dictionaries

ISBN 0-7876-6494-4

In this third volume of a three-volume biographical dictionary, "narrative biographical essays . . . discuss each woman's significant achievements and the public response to those achievements. . . . [This book] features 300 contemporary and historical women, including Sarah Allen, Alicia Keys, Ruth Simmons and . . . more." Publisher's note

Includes bibliographical references

Notable native Americans; Sharon Malinowski, editor; George H.J. Abrams, consulting editor and author of foreword. Gale Res. 1995 xliv, 492p il $105 **920.003**

1. Reference books 2. Native Americans -- Dictionaries

ISBN 0-8103-9638-6

LC 94-36202

This is a "compilation of biographical and bibliographical information on more than two hundred and sixty-five notable Native North American men and women throughout history, from all fields of endeavor. . . . Approximately thirty percent of the entries focus on historical figures and seventy percent on contemporary or twentieth-century individuals. Signed narrative essays, ranging from one to three pages in length, include Indian names and their English translations as well as name variants." Preface

Oakes, Elizabeth H.
★ **A to Z of chemists**. Facts on File 2002 276p il $45   **920.003**
1. Chemists 2. Reference books 3. Scientists -- Dictionaries
ISBN 0-8160-4579-8
LC 2002-68685
"This title includes 152 biographies of chemists, including 23 women. . . . The entries run between 750 and 1200 words (one to one and one-half pages apiece). They all begin with a summary of the subject's major contribution, followed by a chronological biography of their personal and professional life. Appendixes list the birthplace and country of activity of the chemists as well as a chart of their life spans." Libr J
Includes bibliographical references

American writers. Facts on File 2004 430p il (American biographies) $65   **920.003**
1. Reference books 2. Authors, American -- Dictionaries 3. American literature -- Bio-bibliography
ISBN 0-8160-5158-5
LC 2003-15743
"The volume has alphabetically arranged entries for approximately 260 authors from a variety of genres—poetry, fiction, drama, essay, and autobiography. Each . . . entry contains a short biography, critical analysis, and a bibliography of works about the author in both printed and Web formats. . . . [This book] offers a convenient introduction and is a worthwhile purchase." Booklist
Includes bibliographical references

Otfinoski, Steven
Latinos in the arts. Facts on File 2007 277p il (A to Z of Latino Americans) $44   **920.003**
1. Reference books 2. Actors -- Dictionaries 3. Artists -- Dictionaries 4. Musicians -- Dictionaries 5. Hispanic Americans -- Dictionaries
ISBN 978-0-8160-6394-9; 0-8160-6394-X
LC 2006-16900
"This volume profiles more than 178 individuals in the performing and visual arts 'who were born in the United States or who settled here permanently,' among them Marc Anthony, Cameron Diaz, Carmen Miranda, Tito Punete, and Shakira. Each entry concludes with a list of 'Further Reading' . . . and, in many cases, 'Further Listening' and 'Further Viewing.'" Booklist
Includes bibliographical references

Pendergast, Tom
★ **U** -X-L graphic novelists; [by] Tom Pendergast and Sara Pendergast; Sarah Hermsen, project editor. U-X-L/Thomson Gale 2007 lxii, 634p 3v il set $181   **920.003**
1. Reference books 2. Cartoonists -- Dictionaries 3. Graphic novels -- Dictionaries
ISBN 1-4144-0440-9; 978-1-4144-0440-0
LC 2006-13711
The three volumes include 75 alphabetically-arranged articles that profile authors, illustrators, and author-illustrators, and include European, American, and Japanese creators. The introduction provides some history of graphic novels, and there is a separate essay on manga.
"This accessible and readable survey of a timely topic should generate considerable attention in school library media center and public library collections. Well researched and documented, with subject and language appropriate for its intended audience, this set is highly recommended." Booklist
Includes bibliographical references

Rich, Mari
★ **World** authors, 2000-2005; editors, Jennifer Curry, David Ramm, Mari Rich, Albert Rolls. Wilson, H. W. 2007 800p il (Authors series) $170 **920.003**
1. Reference books 2. Authors -- Dictionaries 3. Literature -- Bio-bibliography
ISBN 978-0-8242-1077-9
This book "covers some 300 novelists, poets, dramatists, essayists, scientists, biographers, and other authors whose books [were] published 2000 through 2005." Publisher's note

Schneider, Dorothy
★ **First** ladies; a biographical dictionary. [by] Dorothy Schneider, Carl J. Schneider. 3rd ed; Facts on File 2010 436p il (Facts on File library of American history) $85   **920.003**
1. Reference books 2. Presidents' spouses -- United States -- Dictionaries
ISBN 978-0-8160-7724-3
LC 2009-9047
First published 2001
This book "covers all the women who have held this esteemed 'office' since the founding of the United States. . . . Arranged chronologically by term of presidency, each biographical entry includes a . . . biography emphasizing each first lady's life during the presidency, as well as a chronology, appendixes, and suggestions for further reading." Publisher's note
Includes bibliographical references

The **Scribner** encyclopedia of American lives; Kenneth T. Jackson, editor in chief; Karen Markoe, general editor; Arnold Markoe, executive editor. Scribner 1998 8v il set $768   **920.003**
1. Reference books 2. United States -- Biography -- Dictionaries
ISBN 0-684-31292-1
LC 98-33793
"Scribner envisions SEAL as the continuation of the Dictionary of American Biography (DAB). . . . Selection criteria are that the biographees made significant contributions to American life and culture. . . . An appreciable number of women and people of color are recognized. All biographies

are signed contributions by 332 scholars." Libr J [review of first two volumes]

The **Scribner** encyclopedia of American lives, The 1960s; William L. O'Neill, volume editor. Scribner 2003 2v il set $250   **920.003**
1. Reference books 2. United States -- Biography -- Dictionaries
ISBN 0-684-80666-5

LC 2002-12581

"The two alphabetically arranged volumes in SEAL 1960s contain biographical sketches, usually between 1,000 and 2,000 words, of 647 figures who 'defined the decade, or who were influential at the time.' Americans from different races, socioeconomic groups, classes, and regions of the U.S. are included, along with the occasional person of another nationality who had long periods of residence in the U.S. and was an influence on American culture. The signed entries, written by scholars, begin with a brief summary of the person's chronology and important accomplishments. This is followed by a narrative of the subject's life. . . . In many cases, a black-and-white photograph accompanies the narrative, which concludes with an assessment of the subject's overall contribution and a brief bibliography listing a few key sources. . . . Recommended for all high-school, public, and academic libraries wanting complete SEAL coverage or libraries wanting to supplement their collection of 1960s resources with a purely biographical approach." Booklist
Includes bibliographical references

Shipp, Steve
Latin American and Caribbean artists of the modern era; a biographical dictionary of more than 12,700 persons. McFarland & Co 2002 864p il $115   **920.003**
1. Reference books 2. Latin American art 3. Artists -- Dictionaries
ISBN 0-7864-1057-4

LC 2002-13828

"All entries include expected information such as birth date and place and artist's medium, and longer entries also feature biographical sketches, including education and influences, as well as lists of collections, exhibits, and titles. . . . A good starting point for further research." Libr J
Includes bibliographical references

St. James guide to Hispanic artists; profiles of Latino and Latin American artists. editor, Thomas Riggs. St. James Press 2002 xx, 682p il $195 **920.003**
1. Hispanic American art 2. Artists -- United States
ISBN 1-55862-470-8

LC 2001-41935

This "guide profiles some 375 of the most prominent Hispanic artists of the past century. The entries include basic biographical information, critical commentary, and lists of exhibitions, publications, and collections holding their works." Libr J
Includes bibliographical references and indexes

Wakeman, John
World authors, 1950-1970; a companion volume to Twentieth century authors. edited by John Wakeman; editorial consultant: Stanley J. Kunitz. Wilson, H.W. 1975 1594p il (Authors series) $160 **920.003**
1. Reference books 2. Authors -- Dictionaries 3. Literature -- Bio-bibliography
ISBN 0-8242-0419-0

This volume includes 959 "authors who came into prominence between 1950 and 1970. . . . Authors were chosen for literary importance or outstanding popularity." Wilson Libr Bull

World authors, 1970-1975; editor, John Wakeman; editorial consultant, Stanley J. Kunitz. Wilson, H.W. 1980 894p il (Authors series) $140 **920.003**
1. Reference books 2. Authors -- Dictionaries 3. Literature -- Bio-bibliography
ISBN 0-8242-0641-X

LC 79-21874

This volume provides biographical or autobiographical sketches for 348 of the most influential and popular men and women of letters who have come into prominence between 1970 and 1975

Waldrup, Carole Chandler
The **vice** presidents; biographies of the 45 men who have held the second highest office in the United States. McFarland & Co. 1996 271p il hardcover o.p. pa $39.95   **920.003**
1. Vice-presidents -- United States
ISBN 0-7864-0179-6; 978-0-7864-2611-9 pa; 0-7864-2611-X pa

LC 96-30538

This work "presents biographical portraits of the 45 individuals who have theoretically been 'a heartbeat from the presidency.' These portraits are presented in chronological order of service, from John Adams to Albert Gore Jr." Am Ref Books Annu, 1997

"Well-written with clear, precise language and vocabulary, this informative book will be useful in either the reference section or with the collective biographies." Book Rep
Includes bibliographical references

Who was who in America; with world notables. Marquis Who's Who 1942 23v set $999.95 **920.003**
1. Reference books 2. United States -- Biography -- Dictionaries
ISBN 978-0-8379-0282-1

"Includes sketches removed from 'Who's who in America' because of death of the biographee; date of death and, often, interment location is added." Guide to Ref Books. 11th edition

★ **Who's** who 2008; an annual biographical dictionary. 160th ed.; A. & C. Black 2007 2574p $325   **920.003**
1. Reference books 2. Great Britain -- Biography -- Dictionaries
ISBN 978-0-7136-8555-8; 0-7136-8555-7
Annual. First published 1849

"The pioneer work of the who's who type and still one of the most important. Until 1897, it was the handbook of titled and official classes and included lists of names rather than biographical sketches. . . . It is principally British, but a few prominent names of other nationalities are included. Biographies are reliable and fairly detailed; they give main facts, addresses, often telephone numbers and in case of authors, lists of works." Guide to Ref Books. 11th edition

Who's who among African Americans; 21st ed.; Gale Res. 2008 1477p $275   **920.003**
1. Reference books 2. African Americans -- Biography -- Dictionaries
ISBN 978-1-4144-0020-4; 1-4144-0020-9
First published 1976 by Educational Communications with title: Who's who among black Americans. Biennial schedule after 5th edition
"Short entries focusing on career achievements and positions. Indexes list entries by place of birth and profession." N Y Public Libr Book of How & Where to Look It Up

Who's who in America, 2008; 62nd ed.; Marquis Who's Who 2007 2v set $710.10   **920.003**
1. Reference books 2. United States -- Biography -- Dictionaries
ISBN 978-0-8379-7011-0; 0-8379-7011-3
Annual. First published 1899
"The standard dictionary of contemporary biography, containing concise biographical data, prepared according to established practices, with addresses and, in the case of authors, lists of works. . . . Each edition is thoroughly revised, new biographies added, and others dropped. For names of persons dropped because of death, see 'Who was who in America'." Guide to Ref Books. 11th edition

★ Who's who in American art, 2008; 28th ed.; Marquis Who's Who 2007 1550p $267.30   **920.003**
1. Reference books 2. Artists -- United States -- Dictionaries
ISBN 978-0-8379-6307-5; 0-8379-6307-9
Companion volume to American art directory
Biennial. First published 1936 by American Federation of Arts as part of American art annual
"Profiles representatives of all segments of the art world including artists, administrators, and librarians. Entries give vital statistics, professional education and training, commissions and exhibitions, and membership in art societies. Includes geographic and professional classification indexes and cumulative necrology." N Y Public Libr Book of How & Where to Look It Up

Who's who in British history; beginnings to 1901. general editor, Geoffrey Treasure; authors and contributors, Ian Dawson {et al.} Fitzroy Dearborn Pubs. 1998 2v maps set $325   **920.003**
1. Reference books 2. Great Britain -- Biography -- Dictionaries
ISBN 1-884964-90-7
"The length of entries varies from many pages (Henry VIII) to a column for most persons. . . . The choice of entries (ending with 1901) reflects the traditional emphasis of history teaching, with heavy representation of statemen, royalty, military persons, diplomats, major writers, and leading ladies of the stage and aristocracy." Choice
Includes bibliographical references

★ Who's who in finance and business 2008-2009; 36th ed; Marquis Who's Who 2007 1,100 $349   **920.003**
1. Reference books 2. Business -- Biography -- Dictionaries
ISBN 978-0-8379-0356-9
Biennial. First published 1936 with title: Who's who in commerce and industry. Continues Who's who in finance and industry
"Gives international coverage of businessmen. Includes index of firms with references to personnel for whom sketches are included." Guide to Ref Books. 11th edition

★ Who's who of American women 2007; 26th ed; Marquis Who's Who 2006 1,700 $305   **920.003**
1. Reference books 2. Women -- United States -- Biography 3. United States -- Biography -- Dictionaries
ISBN 0-8379-0434-X
Biennial. First published for 1958/1959
"This title provides information on women who are successful in a variety of professions, including business, government, education, art and culture, and those who have received prestigious honors or have been selected for honorary institutions. The biographical data are provided by the women themselves so the quality varies. In general it includes name, occupation, birth date, education, career history, publications, professional activities, awards, and home and office addresses. This has long been a standard source in many public and academic libraries." Am Ref Books Annu, 2003

Women in world history; a biographical encyclopedia. Anne Commire, editor, Deborah Klezmer, associate editor. Gale Res. 1999 17v set $1,495   **920.003**
1. Reference books 2. Women -- Biography 3. Women -- History -- Encyclopedias
ISBN 0-7876-3736-X
LC 99-24692
ALA RUSA Dartmouth Medal (2001)
"The editors researched wives, daughters, mothers, and other women who were not documented in traditional, male-oriented sources, especially history books. . . . Some entries are only a sentence or two because of lack of information, but the majority include most or all of the following: dates, if known, or time of flourishing; an identifying summary of life and achievements; a personal profile with vital statistics and names of family members; events in the life of the biographee; vitae listing such things as works for authors or winning records for athletes; a quotation by or about the individual; and bibliographical references." Booklist
Includes bibliographical references

World explorers and discoverers; editor, Richard E. Bohlander; consultants, John L. Allen {et al.} Macmillan 1991 531p il maps $110   **920.003**
1. Reference books 2. Explorers -- Dictionaries
ISBN 978-0-02-897445-3; 0-02-897445-X
LC 91-23156
"Over 300 explorers and discoverers are featured in this attractive compilation that covers exploration from ancient

times to the present and includes such notable moderns as Jacques Cousteau and Edmund Hillary." Am Libr

Yount, Lisa
★ **A to Z of biologists**. Facts on File 2003 390p il (Notable scientists) $45   **920.003**
1. Biologists 2. Reference books 3. Scientists -- Dictionaries
ISBN 0-8160-4541-0

LC 2002-13816

"Each profile focuses on a particular biologist's research and contributions to the field and his or her effect on scientists whose work followed. Their lives and personalities are also discussed through incidents, quotations, and photographs. The profiles are culturally inclusive and span a range of biologists from ancient times to the present day." Publisher's note

Includes bibliographical references

920.009   Ethnic and national groups

Great lives from history: Latinos--Volume 2; editors, Carmen Tafolla and Martha P. Cotera. Salem Press 2012 3 v., xxvi, 1058 p.p ill. (set) $395   **920.009**
1. Latinos (U.S.) 2. Hispanic Americans -- Biography -- Encyclopedias
ISBN 9781587658112; 9781587658129; 9781587658136; 1587658100; 9781587658105

LC 2011043168

The authors "[Carmen] Tafolla, an award-winning author of Chicana literature for children and adults, . . . and librarian and activist [Martha P.] Cotera, . . . provide brief biographical essays covering 518 figures from Latino history." Among those profiled are actor Desi Arnaz, football player Tony Romo, and actress Rita Hayworth. (Library Journal)

Includes bibliographical references and indexes

McCullough, David G., 1933-
★ The **greater** journey; [by] David McCollough. Simon & Schuster 2011 558p. ill. (some col.), maps $37.50; ebook $19.99   **920.009**
1. Artists 2. Paris (France) -- History 3. Intellectuals -- United States 4. Paris (France) -- Intellectual life 5. Authors, American 6. Americans -- France 7. Biography, Collective 8. Paris (France) -- Intellectual life -- 19th century 9. Americans -- France -- Paris -- History -- 19th century
ISBN 978-1-4165-7176-6; 1-4165-7176-0; 978-1-4165-7689-1 ebook; 9781416571766; 9781416576891; 1416576894

LC 2010053001

In this book, "award-winning historian [David] McCullough . . . [tells the story of] a cluster of aspiring young people such as portraitist George Healy and lawyer Charles Sumner, eager to expand their horizons [in Paris] in the 1830s. . . . [The book] include[s] numerous other visitors over an entire eventful century. . . . [N]ovelist James Fenimore Cooper, widowed schoolteacher Emma Hart Willard and young medical student Oliver Wendell Holmes Sr. all knew their education was not complete without a stint in the

medieval capital. For many of these American rubes, exposure to the fine arts, old-world architecture, fashion, fine dining, museums and teaching hospitals proved transformative, and the knowledge they gained would define their professional lives back in America." (Kirkus)

An "account of young Americans, driven by wanderlust, setting out in search of greener Parisian pastures. Well-known figures such as James Fenimore Cooper, Oliver Wendell Holmes Sr., and Mary Cassat, and long-forgotten entities like Elizabeth Blackwell and William Wells Brown, all walked along the Avenue des Champs-Élysées, went to the Musée du Louvre, ate wonderful meals, and became inspired. Their life-changing adventures played a vital role in transforming the course of US history." Christ Sci Monit

Includes bibliographical references (p. 519-537) and index.

920.073   Biography--United States

McCarthy, Andrew
The **longest** way home; one man's quest for the courage to settle down. Andrew McCarthy. Free Press 2012 273 p.   **920.073**
1. Self-realization 2. Voyages and travels 3. Self-actualization (Psychology) 4. Travel -- Psychological aspects 5. Actors -- United States -- Biography 6. Travel writers -- United States -- Biography 7. Motion picture producers and directors -- United States -- Biography
ISBN 1451667485; 9781451667486; 9781451667516

LC 2012010509

This book, by Andrew McCarthy, is a travel memoir. "Unable to commit to his fiancee of nearly four years, . . . Andrew . . . sets out to look for answers. Hobbling up the . . . slopes of Mt. Kilimanjaro, dodging . . . passengers aboard an Amazonian riverboat, and trudging through . . . Costa Rican rain forests--Andrew takes us on exotic trips to some of the world's most beautiful places, but his real journey is one of the spirit." (Publisher's note)

920.71   Men

Gates, Henry Louis
Thirteen ways of looking at a black man. Random House 1997 xxvii, 226p hardcover o.p. pa $12   **920.71**
1. Actors 2. Authors 3. Dancers 4. Singers 5. Generals 6. Novelists 7. Dramatists 8. Choreographers 9. Football players 10. Essayists 11. Memoirists 12. Screenwriters 13. Sportscasters 14. Literary critics 15. Music historians 16. Social activists 17. Short story writers 18. Young adult authors 19. Black Muslim leaders 20. Secretaries of state 21. African Americans -- Biography
ISBN 0-679-77666-4 pa

LC 96-33138

A "collection of essays about contemporary African Americans. . . . Each essay focuses on a noted cultural figure: James Baldwin, Albert Murray, Bill T. Jones, Colin Powell, O. J. Simpson, Louis Farrakhan, Harry Belafonte, and Anatole Broyard; however, the effect of each essay goes beyond its primary subject by illuminating society at large." Booklist

"Mr. Gates's strong suit is finding the common man in uncommon figures, without losing sight of the ways in which race, class and personal experience have shaped each life." N Y Times Book Rev

920.72 Women

Cohen, Lisa

All we know; three lives. Lisa Cohen. Farrar, Straus and Giroux 2012 429 p. ill. (alk. paper) $30.00   **920.72**

1. Women -- Biography 2. Biography -- 20th century 3. Women intellectuals -- Biography 4. Socialites -- United States -- Biography 5. Women fashion designers -- England -- Biography 6. Modernism (Aesthetics) -- History -- 20th century 7. Women authors, American -- 19th century -- Biography

ISBN 0374176493; 9780374176495

LC 2011041055

This collective biography examines the lives of "Esther Murphy (1897-1962) . . . Mercedes de Acosta (1893-1968) . . . and feminist Madge Garland (1898-1990). . . .They knew each other well from social circles, and none of them had simple lives. [Lisa] Cohen . . . delineates the . . . biographical matters of ancestry, parents, schooling, marriages, affairs, friendships, breakups, work, and death. . . . [A] three-part inquiry into the meaning of failure, style, and sexual identity." (Publishers Weekly)

Includes bibliographical references (p. [359]-406) and index

Ware, Susan

Letter to the world; seven women who shaped the American century. Norton 1998 xxiv, 344p il $25.95   **920.72**

1. Actors 2. Dancers 3. Diplomats 4. Journalists 5. Choreographers 6. Anthropologists 7. Golfers 8. Curators 9. Hurdlers 10. Columnists 11. High jumpers 12. Humanitarians 13. Opera singers 14. Dance teachers 15. Javelin throwers 16. Olympic athletes 17. Social activists 18. Women -- Biography 19. Writers on science 20. Spouses of presidents 21. United Nations officials

ISBN 0-393-04652-4

LC 97-45923

The author "considers the lives of seven women who had an exceptional impact on 20th-century American culture and society's perception of the role of women: Eleanor Roosevelt, Dorothy Thompson, Margaret Mead, Katharine Hepburn, Babe Didrikson Zaharias, Martha Graham, and Marian Anderson. In addition to focusing on outstanding achievements in their chosen fields, Ware looks at their often unconventional private lives." Libr J

Includes bibliographical references

929   Genealogy, names, insignia

Baxter, Angus

In search of your European roots; a complete guide to tracing your ancestors in every country in Europe. 3rd ed; Genealogical 2001 315p pa $18.95   **929**

1. Genealogy

ISBN 0-8063-1657-8

LC 00-136383

First published 1985

This work covers the various types of genealogical records available in approximately 30 European countries. Archival resources from the national to local level are described. Also included are telephone numbers, e-mail addresses, fax numbers, and URL's for various European archives and organizations

Includes bibliographical references

Bentley, Elizabeth Petty

Directory of family associations; {by} Elizabeth Petty Bentley, & Deborah Ann Carl. 4th ed; Genealogical 2001 320p $34.95   **929**

1. Genealogy

ISBN 0-8063-1679-9

LC 2001-131456

First published 1991

Contains information on approximately 6,000 family name associations in the United States; lists addresses, phone numbers, contact persons, and publications (if any)

★ The **genealogist's** address book; state and local resources: with special resources including ethnic and religious organizations. 6th ed.; Genealogical Pub. Co. 2009 799p $69.95   **929**

1. Genealogy

ISBN 978-0-8063-1796-0

First published 1991. Periodically revised

This is a source for "fax, phone, web addresses, and contact names for genealogical, historical, and religious societies across the United States. Bentley . . . judiciously divides contact information into three subject segments. The first organizes genealogical and historical associations alphabetically, initially by state, then county, and finally by society name. Essential for genealogists and regional historians." Libr J

Croom, Emily Anne

The **genealogist's** companion and sourcebook; 2nd ed; Betterway Bks. 2003 454p il map pa $19.99   **929**

1. Genealogy

ISBN 1-55870-651-8

LC 2003-50017

First published 1994

This how-to genealogy handbook seeks to explore "collections and libraries within the U.S. and the records that may be found within them. . . . In addition to covering government records, cemetery records, newspapers, city directories, and other sources, there are chapters of African American and Native American genealogy. . . . Because the volume is easy reading and instructive at the same time, it will be a very popular choice for public libraries." Booklist {review of 1994 edition}

Includes bibliographical references

Franklin, John Hope

★ **In** search of the promised land; a Black family and the Old South. [by] John Hope Franklin, Loren Schweninger. Oxford University Press 2005 286p il map (New narratives in American history) $23; pa $13.95 **929**

    1. Slavery -- United States 2. United States -- Race relations 3. African Americans -- Southern States

    ISBN 0-19-516087-8; 0-19-516088-6 pa

                 LC 2004-61666

The authors trace "the history of the Thomas-Rapier family during the antebellum and Civil War eras. Starting with matriarch Sally Thomas, born a slave in 1787, the book enables readers to distinguish the various complex modes within which slavery operated. The resulting family history also traces the evolution of race relations in diverse locations from New Orleans to New York City, Canada, Minnesota, and the Caribbean." Libr J

Includes bibliographical references

Greenwood, Val D.

The **researcher's** guide to American genealogy; 3rd ed; Genealogical 2000 662p il $29.95 **929**

    1. Genealogy 2. Archives -- United States

    ISBN 0-8063-1621-7

                 LC 99-73349

  First published 1973

"This classic textbook for the more experienced researcher gives detailed answers to questions about primary records, including vital, census, probate, land, court (including adoption), church, military, cemetery, and wills. Completely updated, it remains the outstanding text and reference book in American genealogy and the benchmark against which others must be judged." Libr J {review of 1990 edition}

Includes bibliographical references

Kemp, Thomas Jay

International vital records handbook; 5th ed.; Genealogical Publishing Co. 2009 587p pa $49.95 **929**

    1. Registers of births, etc.

    ISBN 978-0-8063-1793-9

             LC 2008-940022

First published 1988 with title: Vital records handbook

"The book is divided into these three major segments. The first offers approved-form facsimiles for the request of U.S. state-issued documents. The second segment covers request forms issued in U.S. Territories. The third details various procedures and forms necessary to attain official documents in foreign countries. . . . A crucial, time-saving resource." Libr J

Includes bibliographical references

Virtual roots 2.0; a guide to genealogy and local history on the World Wide Web. rev and updated; Scholarly Resources 2003 311p $75; pa $29.95 **929**

    1. Genealogy 2. World Wide Web

    ISBN 0-8420-2922-2; 0-8420-2923-0 pa

             LC 2002-154366

  First published 1997

The more than 1,000 "Web sites in this directory are arranged into four primary categories—general subjects, U.S., international, and family associations—each of which is further subdivided by topic, state, country, or family name. Web site entries include organization name, address, telephone number(s), Internet and e-mail addresses, and, where appropriate, other Web links that open even more doorways." Booklist {review of 1997 edition}

Includes bibliographical references

Kovacs, Diane K.

Genealogical research on the Web. Neal-Schuman 2002 194p (Neal-Schuman netguide series) pa $59.95 **929**

    1. Genealogy -- Internet resources

    ISBN 1-55570-430-1

             LC 2001-59644

"The first section of this book . . . addresses the basics of using the Internet for genealogical research. Next is a discussion of the top 10 genealogical tools on the Internet, followed by a chapter on networking with other genealogists. . . . Each chapter ends with a tutorial composed of several activities, typically involving visits to Web sites. . . . This is one work that serves a variety of users as well as uses and should be of interest wherever genealogists are to be found." Booklist

Includes bibliographical references

Melnyk, Marcia Yannizze

Family history 101; a beginner's guide to finding your ancestors. [by] Marcia D. Yannizze Melnyk. Family Tree Books 2005 138p il pa $16.99 **929**

    1. Genealogy

    ISBN 1-558-70706-9

             LC 2004-58111

"The author provides information on recording data, surfing the Web in search of relevant information, separating facts from fiction, and accessing the most likely places to locate records. . . . Novices wondering where and how to undertake the task will appreciate having the fundamentals succinctly laid out for them." Booklist

Includes bibliographical references

Moore, Dahrl Elizabeth

The **librarian's** genealogy notebook; a guide to resources. American Lib. Assn. 1998 142p il map pa $35 **929**

    1. Genealogy

    ISBN 0-8389-0744-X

             LC 98-19110

"Moore shows librarians how to mine their own libraries for reference sources that might already be available, offers useful advice on obtaining information from external sources, and also includes general sources to which libraries may want to provide access or own." Publisher's note

Includes bibliographical references

Roberts, Ralph

Genealogy via the Internet; tracing your family roots quickly and easily: computerized genealogy in plain English. 2nd ed; Alexander Bks. 2003 288p il $24.95   **929**

1. Genealogy -- Internet resources
ISBN 1-57090-129-5
First published 1998

The author "explains about personal computers, the basics of genealogy and how to go about combining the two for online searching. He provides several pages of possible web sites a searcher might explore, and an index for easy location of topics." Book Rep {review of 1998 edition}

Includes bibliographical references

929.20973   Family histories--United States

Well, François

Family trees; a history of genealogy in America. François Weil. Harvard University Press 2013 320 p. (hardcover) $27.95   **929.20973**

1. Genealogy 2. United States -- Social conditions 3. National characteristics, American 4. Genealogy -- United States -- History 5. Genealogy -- Social aspects -- United States
ISBN 0674045831; 9780674045835

LC 2012044769

This book is a survey of genealogy in America, which has become easier with the advent of the Internet. "The author enumerates four growth stages in the endeavor," looking at colonial America, the late 18th-century, after the Civil War and modern day. François Weil "explains how the proliferation of genealogy-focused Web sites and DNA testing has transformed the pursuit into a lucrative commercial venture." (Publishers Weekly)

Includes bibliographical references and index

929.4   Personal names

Ciuraru, Carmela

Nom de plume; a (secret) history of pseudonyms. Harper 2011 xxiv, 343p $24.99   **929.4**

1. Authors 2. Pseudonyms
ISBN 978-0-06-173526-4

LC 2010-53603

The author "tells the stories of some of literature's most famous pen names by weaving in details about these secretive, often eccentric writers' lives and works to examine their decision to use pen names. From Lewis Carroll (born Charles Dodgson) to Mark Twain (Samuel Clemens) and Victoria Lucas (Sylvia Plath), one chapter is devoted to each with so much detail that the authors under discussion seem to become characters in Ciuraru's book. . . . For anyone who

creates — writers, artists and performers — the book will enthrall. It's as much a meditation on the creative process as it is a tell-all about their names and the intrigue, branding or mind games that created them." Associated Press

Includes bibliographical references

Delahunty, Andrew

Oxford dictionary of nicknames. Oxford University Press 2003 229p $29.95; pa $24   **929.4**

1. Nicknames
ISBN 0-19-860539-0; 0-19-860948-5 pa

LC 2004-273526

"This volume is a treasure trove of popular linguistic creativity. From the Hanging Judge to Hanoi Jane, and from Queen Dick to the Queen of Hearts, it makes for delightful bathroom browsing with just a dab of history and culture." Publ Wkly

★ **Dictionary** of American family names; Patrick Hanks, editor. Oxford Univ. Press 2003 3v set $295   **929.4**

1. Personal names -- United States
ISBN 0-19-508137-4

LC 2003-3844

This is a "guide to 70,000 of the most frequently found surnames in the United States. Based on an 88.7 million-name sample culled from a commercial telephone database, the entries indicate the frequency of the name within the sample, plus an explanation of the name." Libr J

"This set will be useful for genealogists, historians, and others curious about their family roots." SLJ

Includes bibliographical references

Latham, Edward

A **dictionary** of names, nicknames, and surnames of persons, places, and things. Omnigraphics 1990 334p $48   **929.4**

1. Nicknames 2. Reference books 3. Names -- Dictionaries 4. Personal names -- Dictionaries
ISBN 1-55888-901-9

LC 89-26513

A reissue of the title first published 1904 by Dutton

Compiled as a supplement to the "ordinary dictionaries of biography, geography, mythology, etc. {wherein} a person or place is often alluded to by means of a surname or nickname without any clue being given to the reader, who does not happen to be aware of the actual name of the person or place." Preface

929.9   Forms of insignia and identification

Leepson, Marc

Flag : an American biography. Thomas Dunne Books/St. Martin's Press 2005 334p il $24.95; pa $14.95   **929.9**

1. Flags -- United States
ISBN 978-0-312-32308-0; 0-312-32308-5; 978-0-312-32309-7 pa; 0-312-32309-3 pa

LC 2004-65920

"From reverence to kitsch, Americans' attitudes to their flag and its mythology have changed over the years, and

Leepson does a creditable job of recounting those changes." Publ Wkly

Includes bibliographical references

Minahan, James

The **complete** guide to national symbols and emblems. Greenwood Press 2010 2v il set $180 **929.9**

1. Reference books 2. Signs and symbols 3. National emblems -- Encyclopedias 4. National characteristics -- Encyclopedias

ISBN 978-0-313-34496-1; 978-0-313-34497-8 ebook

LC 2009-36963

"This set is an impressive compilation of material that should be quite useful for anyone looking for current information about flags, anthems, athletic teams, cuisines, and such. The 200-plus entries cover independent nations of the world and some dependent states and territories that seek greater visibility, such as Wallonia (an autonomous region within Belgium) and Puerto Rico. Volume 1 covers Asia and Oceania, Central and South America, and Europe. Volume 2 covers the Middle East and North Africa, North America and the Caribbean, and sub-Saharan Africa. National flags and coats of arms are shown in color." Booklist

Includes bibliographical references

Shearer, Benjamin F.

State names, seals, flags, and symbols; a historical guide. [by] Benjamin F. Shearer and Barbara S. Shearer. 3rd ed, rev and expanded; Greenwood Press 2001 495p il $73.95 **929.9**

1. Reference books 2. Seals (Numismatics) 3. Flags -- United States 4. Geographic names -- United States

ISBN 0-313-31534-5

LC 2001-23525

First published 1987

"Chapters on mottoes, flowers, trees, birds, songs, holidays, and license plates are just a sampling of what is covered, and the format is such that the concisely written material can be found as expeditiously as possible. Even though the book is touted predominantly as a reference tool, the information provided makes fascinating and enlightening reading." Libr J [review of 1994 edition]

Includes bibliographical references

Testi, Arnaldo

Capture the flag; the Stars and Stripes in American history. translated by Noor Giovanni Mazhar. New York University Press 2010 165p il $22.95 **929.9**

1. Patriotism 2. American national characteristics 3. Flags -- United States

ISBN 978-0-8147-83221; 0-8147-8322-8

LC 2009-39278

Original Italian edition, 2003

"From our July 4th celebrations to the iconic images from 9/11, the American flag is an all-pervasive, definitive symbol of American national identity. . . . [Testi] provides readers with an engaging and fresh perspective that can only be provided by an outsider standing above the fray. Whether discussing the evolution of flag etiquette or its relationship to the U.S. Constitution, Testi deftly explores the shifting cultural meanings of the American symbol, from 1776

through the growth of the American empire to the contentious debates occurring today." Libr J

Includes bibliographical references

Znamierowski, Alfred, 1940-

The **World** Encyclopedia of Flags; The definitive guide to international, flags, banners, standards and ensigns, with over 1400 illustration. by Alfred Znamierowski. Lorenz Books 2013 256 p. $16.99 **929.9**

1. Flags

ISBN 0754826295; 9780754826293

This book, by Alred Znamierowski, presents "a directory of flags and a fascinating history of their development and usage, featuring over 600 flags including military signs, royal standards, civic flags, ensigns and national flags, expertly illustrated throughout." (Publisher's note)

930 History of ancient world (to ca. 499)

Beard, Mary, 1955-

Confronting the classics; traditions, adventures, and innovations. Mary Beard. Liveright Publishing Corporation, a Division of W. W. Norton & Company 2013 320 p. (hardcover) $28.95 **930**

1. Classical education 2. Classical civilization 3. Classical antiquities 4. Civilization, Classical

ISBN 0871407167; 9780871407160

LC 2013016133

"This collection comprises a decade's worth of [Mary] Beard's . . . book reviews, mostly from the 'Times Literary Supplement' and the 'New York Review of Books,' plus one lecture not previously published. . . . The work follows a chronological arrangement, with the first section on ancient Greece, the next on early Rome, the third on Imperial Rome, and so forth, with later pieces focusing on the classicists themselves across the subsequent centuries." (Library Journal)

Includes bibliographical references and index

The **Cambridge** ancient history. Cambridge Univ. Press 1970 il maps set $3500 **930**

1. Ancient history

ISBN 978-0-521-85073-5

Original 12 volume set published 1923-1939 with 5 volumes of plates

"An excellent reference history. Each chapter has been written by a specialist, with full bibliographies at the end of each volume." Guide to Ref Books. 11th edition

Cantor, Norman F.

Antiquity : the civilization of the ancient world. HarperCollins Pubs. 2003 240p map $24.95; pa $13.95 **930**

1. Ancient civilization

ISBN 0-06-017409-9; 0-06-093098-5 pa

LC 2003-42317

"Cantor's work provides the beginning classicist with an enticing yet sturdy foundation for further exploration." Booklist

Includes bibliographical references

★ **Encyclopedia** of the ancient world; editor, Thomas J. Sienkewicz. Salem Press 2002 3v il maps set $341   **930**
1. Reference books   2. Ancient civilization -- Encyclopedias
ISBN 0-89356-038-3

LC 2001-49896

This reference work encompasses "not only Greece and Rome but also 'the civilizations, cultures, traditions, monuments and artifacts, significant wars and battles, and important personages of the rest of the world: Europe (outside Greece and Rome), Africa, the Americas, Asia, and Oceania.' The time span is from prehistory to approximately 700 C.E." Booklist

Includes bibliographical references

Felch, Jason

Chasing Aphrodite; the hunt for looted antiquities at the world's richest museum. [by] Jason Felch and Ralph Frammolino. Houghton Mifflin Harcourt 2011 375p il $28.00   **930**
1. Cultural property 2. Classical antiquities 3. J. Paul Getty Museum 4. Archaeological thefts 5. Classical antiquities -- Italy 6. Cultural property -- Repatriation -- Italy 7. Classical antiquities -- Destruction and pillage
ISBN 0151015015; 9780151015016

LC 2010-25835

In 1976 "oil billionaire J. Paul Getty left his estate to the museum that bears his name, which was suddenly the wealthiest collecting institution in the world—one whose problem was how to spend rather than raise money. The founder's narrow interests had determined the museum's collecting areas, one of which was Greek and Roman art. The stage was set for trouble, and the trouble is described in fascinating detail in 'Chasing Aphrodite,' an account of the Getty's travails in collection-building by Los Angeles Times reporters Jason Felch and Ralph Frammolino. In 2005, longtime Getty curator Marion True would be indicted by authorities in Rome for traffic in illicit antiquities; not long after, in a related controversy, she was forced to resign. The reporters covered these events, as well as the museum's agreements to repatriate works acquired before and during Ms. True's tenure. They were given access by unidentified sources to the museum's archives, and in this book they document a museum administration often motivated by ambition but eventually also by stirrings of conscience." Wall Street J

Includes bibliographical references and index

Great events from history, The ancient world, prehistory-476 C.E. editor, Mark W. Chavalas; consulting editors, Mark S. Aldenderfer . . . [et al.] Salem Press 2004 2v il map set $160   **930**
1. Ancient history 2. Reference books
ISBN 1-58765-155-6; 978-1-58765-155-7

LC 2004-1360

Companion volume to Great lives from history, The ancient world, prehistory-476 C.E.

Some essays previously published in Great events from history (1972-1980), Chronology of European history, 15,000 B.C. to 1997 (1997), and Great events from history, North American series (1997)

"Articles are arranged chronologically, beginning around 25,000 B.C.E. with the San Peoples, who created the first discernible art in Africa, and ends on September 4, 476 C.E. with the fall of Rome, when the last Roman emperor, Romulus Augustulus, was deposed. Articles cover the entire world, with special attention paid to non-European areas. . . . All articles maintain the same structure and give the locale of the event, its category, a summary of the event, its significance, an annotated list of further readings, and cross references to related events." Ref & User Services Quarterly

Includes bibliographical references

Kapuscinski, Ryszard

Travels with Herodotus; translated from the Polish by Klara Glowczewska. Alfred A. Knopf 2007 275p $25   **930**
1. Historians 2. Voyages and travels
ISBN 9781400043385; 1-400-04338-5

LC 2006-39565

Original Polish edition, 2004

The late author offers an "account of his beginnings as a journalist and an homage to the ancient-Greek historian whom Cicero dubbed the 'father of history.'. . . Kapuscinski was working for a Polish newspaper in the mid-1950s when his editor dispatched him to India and, as a parting gift, gave him a copy of Herodotus's Histories. The book spurred the young Kapuscinski's imagination and virtually altered his view of time, space, and the contours of the past. It would become a decisive influence, he tells us, an introduction to politics, foreign places, the nature of tyranny, and the savagery of conflict between peoples, the stuff that became his subject matter." Bookforum

"A work of art: so eloquent, so simple, that you find yourself marveling at its prose, its gentle observation and the rhythm of the words. And you find yourself applauding such good translation as well." Washington Post Book World

Kemp, Barry

The **city** of Akhenaten and Nefertiti; Amarna and its people. Barry Kemp. Thames & Hudson 2012 320 p. (hardcover) $45   **930**
1. Egypt -- History 2. Egypt -- Antiquities 3. Tell el-Amarna (Egypt)
ISBN 0500051739; 9780500051733

LC 2011945993

This book by Barry Kemp describes the history of "the ancient site of Tell el-Amarna in Middle Egypt, [which] was the capital city of the heretic pharaoh Akhenaten and his chief consort, Nefertiti. Occupied for just sixteen or so years in the fourteenth century BC, the city lay largely abandoned and forgotten until excavations over the last hundred years brought it back into prominence." (Publisher's note)

930.1 Archaeology

Beneath the seven seas; adventures with the Intitute of Nautical Archaeology. edited by George

F. Bass. Thames & Hudson 2005 256p il maps
$39.95 **930.1**
1. Archeology 2. Shipwrecks 3. Underwater
exploration
ISBN 978-0-500-05136-8; 0-500-05136-4
LC 2005-900862
This book features "accounts by many distinguished archaeologists associated with the INA [Institute of Nautical
Archaeology]. They tell of the discovery, excavation, and
preservation of more than 40 shipwrecks—and one sunken
city—the world over, from ancient times through the Byzantine, medieval, and Renaissance eras and on through World
War II. . . . This book will appeal to general readers and
specialists alike in nautical archaeology." Libr J
Includes bibliographical references

Ceram, C. W.
Gods, graves, and scholars; the story of archaeology. translated from the German by E. B. Garside
and Sophie Wilkins. 2nd rev and substantially enl
ed; Knopf 1967 441p il maps hardcover o.p. pa
$11.16 **930.1**
1. Mayas 2. Aztecs 3. Archeology 4. Hieroglyphics
5. Babel, Tower of 6. Cuneiform inscriptions 7.
Rosetta stone inscription 8. Kings 9. Crete (Greece)
10. Egypt -- Antiquities
ISBN 0-394-74319-9 pa
Original German edition, 1949; first English language
edition, 1951
"The story of Champollion and the reading of the Rosetta Stone, the decipherment of the inscriptions on the
monument of Darius the Great, Leonard Woolley's famous
excavations at Ur, and John Lloyd Stephens' discovery of
the ruins of a great Mayan city are . . . told in this book."
Doors to More Mature Read
Includes bibliographical references

Childs, Craig Leland
Finders keepers; a tale of archaeological plunder
and obsession. Little, Brown and Co. 2010 274p
$24.99 **930.1**
1. Archeologists -- Ethics
ISBN 978-0-316-06642-6; 0-316-06642-7
LC 2009-51921
"Childs treks the canyon-incised Colorado Plateau in
search of pre-Columbian artifacts. Their legal regulation
collides with collectors' obsessions to possess them. Childs,
though, does not remove what he finds, an ethic that vies
with other precepts for the proper preservation of antiquities.
For every stand he takes on archaeological morality in this
narrative mix of his backcountry experiences and conversations with collectors, curators, dealers, and an occasional
looter, Childs engages their justifications for taking custody
of ancient objects. . . . Alternating romantic and practical
moods, Childs hunts virtue as much as baskets in this engaging discourse." Booklist
Includes bibliographical references

Hunt, Patrick
Ten discoveries that rewrote history. Plume 2007
226p pa $27.95 **930.1**
1. Antiquities 2. Ancient civilization 3. Archeology

-- History
ISBN 978-0-452-28877-5; 0-452-28877-0
LC 2007-19808
The author "has produced a wonderful volume of of ar-
chaeological history. In doing so, he has provided a seldom
seen look at some of the most important scientific develop-
ments in the field." Sci Books Films
Includes bibliographical references

Kersel, Morag M.
U.S. cultural diplomacy and archaeology; soft
power, hard heritage. by Christina Luke and Morag
M. Kersel. Routledge 2012 169 p. (Routledge stud-
ies in archaeology) (alk. paper) $125 **930.1**
1. Historic preservation 2. Cultural policy -- United
States 3. United States -- Foreign relations 4. United
States -- Relations 5. United States -- Cultural policy
6. Power (Social sciences) -- United States 7. Historic
preservation -- Political aspects 8. Archaeology --
Political aspects -- United States 9. Cultural property
-- Protection -- Political aspects
ISBN 0415645492; 9780415645492
LC 2012022434
This book, by Christina Luke and Morag Kersel, attempts to "evaluate museums and their roles in presenting
the past at national and international levels, contextualizing the practical and diplomatic processes of archaeological research within the realm of cultural heritage. [It draws]
from analyses and discussion of several U.S. governmental
agencies' treatment of international cultural heritage and its
funding, the history of diplomacy-entangled research centers
abroad, and the necessity of archaeologists' involvement in
diplomatic processes." (Publisher's note)
Includes bibliographical references and index

MacGregor, Neil, 1946-
A **history** of the world in 100 objects; Neil Mac-
Gregor. Viking 2011 xxvi, 707 p. p col. ill., maps
$45 **930.1**
1. Antiques 2. Art objects 3. World history 4. Material
culture 5. Ceremonial objects 6. Archaeology, Medieval
7. Classical antiquities 8. Antiquities, Prehistoric
ISBN 0670022705; 1846144132; 9780670022700;
9781846144134
LC 2011021769
The book by Neil MacGregor is the result of "a joint
project between the [British M]useum and the British Broadcasting Corporation's Radio Four. . . . In this project, . . .
one hundred objects from the museum's enormous holdings
[were be chosen]. . . . The book . . . is . . . a compilation of
the one hundred objects, arranged more or less chronologically, . . . each with essay and commentary as edited for final
broadcast format." (New York Review of Books)
Includes bibliographical references (p. 671-678)
and index

The **Oxford** companion to archaeology; editor in
chief, Brian M. Fagan; editors, Charlotte Beck [et

al.] Oxford Univ. Press 1996 xx, 844p il maps $75 **930.1**
1. Reference books 2. Archeology -- Dictionaries
ISBN 0-19-507618-4

LC 96-30792

"In addition to broad discussions of specific civilizations such as Islamic, Olmec, and African, there are entries on theories (post processual), ethics, processes (lithics), dating techniques, pop culture (archaeology in film and television), specific sites and site management, plantation archaeology, and human evolution." Booklist

Ryan, William B. F.

Noah's flood; the new scientific discoveries about the event that changed history. [by] William Ryan and Walter Pitman; illustrations by Anastasia Sotiropoulos; maps by William Haxby. Simon & Schuster 1999 319p il maps hardcover o.p. pa $14 **930.1**
1. Floods
ISBN 0-684-81052-2; 0-684-85920-3 pa

LC 98-45384

This is "an interesting and provocative story . . . that incorporates archeology, oceanography, biblical studies, anthropology (not to mention archeobotany, paleopathology and archeozoology) and, one must conclude, a healthy portion of imagination." N Y Times Book Rev
Includes bibliographical references

Van Tilburg, JoAnne

Among stone giants; the life of Katherine Routledge and her remarkable expedition to Easter Island. foreword by Andrew Tatham. Scribner 2003 351p il $26 **930.1**
1. Easter Island 2. Archaeologists
ISBN 0-7432-4480-X

LC 2002-42751

This is a "biography of Katherine Routledge, an Englishwoman who was the first to attempt a methodical archaeological study of Easter Island." N Y Times Book Rev
Includes bibliographical references

932 Egypt to 640

Aldred, Cyril

Akhenaten : King of Egypt. Thames & Hudson 1988 320p il hardcover o.p. pa $26.95 **932**
1. Kings 2. Egypt -- Antiquities
ISBN 0-500-27621-8 pa

LC 87-51153

Aldred "ranges over archaeology, art-history, morbid pathology, social and political history and the evolution of ideas. This is a book to which one will return, and gain each time one does so." Times Lit Suppl
Includes bibliographical references

★ **Ancient** Nubia; African Kingdoms on the Nile. Edited by Marjorie M. Fisher, Peter Lacovara, Salima Ikram, and Sue D'Auria; with photographs by Chester Higgins Jr. American University in Cairo Press 2012 368 p. (hardcover) $59.95 **932**
1. Nubia 2. Archeology 3. Egypt -- History
ISBN 9774164784; 9789774164781

This work "brings the ancient unknown kingdom of Nubia alive through essays and . . . photos. Part 1 opens with maps a chronology as well as a list of Kushite rulers. In 18 essays, contributors from around the globe provide facts and insights on the architecture, culture, customs, geography, and general history of the region, which stretched from Sudan through northern Egypt. . . . Part 2 is a gazetteer of 48 excavated archaeological sites, with illustrations." (Booklist)

Brier, Bob

The **murder** of Tutankhamen; a true story. Berkley Books 2005 xx, 264p il pa $14 **932**
1. Kings 2. Egypt -- History
ISBN 0-425-20690-4; 978-0-425-20690-4

LC 2005-41085

First published 1998 by Putnam
"Brier obviously knows his subject and is impassioned by it. Readers who enjoy history or true-crime stories will be intrigued by this work." SLJ
Includes bibliographical references

Bunson, Margaret R.

Encyclopedia of ancient Egypt; rev ed; Facts on File 2002 462p il maps $70 **932**
1. Reference books 2. Egypt -- Civilization -- Encyclopedias
ISBN 0-8160-4563-1

LC 2002-3550

First published 1991
This work consists of "alphabetically arranged entries covering Egypt from around 3200 B.C. to the fall of the New Kingdom in 1070 B.C. There are several broad entries such as Egypt, Agriculture, and Religion. The bulk of the book, however, consists of specific entries for kings and queens, gods and goddesses, cities, important documents, etc." Booklist [review of 1991 edition]

David, A. Rosalie

Handbook to life in ancient Egypt; [by] Rosalie David. rev ed; Facts on File 2003 417p il map (Facts on File library of world history) $50 **932**
1. Egypt -- Civilization
ISBN 0-8160-5034-1

LC 2002-35229

First published 1998
This covers such topics as the geography of Ancient Egypt, society and government, religion, funerary beliefs and customs, architecture, trade and transport, the army and navy, economy and industry, and everyday life.
Includes bibliographical references

Dreyfus, Renee

Hatshepsut : from queen to Pharaoh; edited by Catharine H. Roehrig with Renée Dreyfus and Cath-

leen A. Keller. Yale University Press 2005 339p il map $65 **932**
1. Queens 2. Egypt -- History 3. Egypt -- Civilization
ISBN 0-300-11139-8

LC 2005-20286

The editors "offer a magnificent portrait of this remarkable woman and all aspects of Egyptian life in the 18th Dynasty, from religion and politics to art and jewelry." Publ Wkly

Includes bibliographical references

Hawass, Zahi A.

Hidden treasures of ancient Egypt; unearthing the masterpieces of Egyptian history. [by] Zahi Hawass; photographs by Kenneth Garrett. National Geographic Society 2004 256p il $35 **932**
1. Egyptian art 2. Egypt -- Antiquities 3. Excavations (Archeology) -- Egypt
ISBN 0-7922-6319-7

LC 2004-44845

The author "narrates the past 150 years of excavation, from the colonial period—when Westerners overwhelmed the ranks of those recovering the nation's treasures—through Egypt's independence and the present era of international cooperation. . . . This breathtaking glimpse at the country's archeological wealth should excite curious and adventurous minds worldwide." Publ Wkly

★ **Tutankhamun** and the golden age of the pharaohs; [by] Zahi Hawass; photographs by Kenneth Garrett. National Geographic Books 2005 285p il map $35 **932**
1. Kings 2. Egypt -- Antiquities
ISBN 0-7922-3873-7

LC 2005-41678

This companion to an exhibition displaying about 130 items found in the tombs of Tutankhamun and other kings from the same dynasty "describes the physical and symbolic attributes of each object and explains its purpose in the afterlife. . . . An arrestingly visual album destined for high demand." Booklist

Includes bibliographical references

Lepre, J. P.

The **Egyptian** pyramids; a comprehensive, illustrated reference. McFarland & Co. 1990 341p il hardcover o.p. pa $35 **932**
1. Pyramids 2. Egypt -- Antiquities
ISBN 0-89950-461-2; 0-7864-2955-0 pa

LC 89-43623

This "study of the pyramids built during the reigns of 42 different pharaohs, incorporates details pertaining to the history of each of the pharaohs who constructed a pyramid, concise chronological listings of the pyramids, relevant textual studies from the ancient Egyptian sources, and a review of the material remains associated with the pyramids." Choice

Includes bibliographical references

Mertz, Barbara

Temples, tombs, & hieroglyphs; a popular history of ancient Egypt. 2nd ed., 1st William Morrow ed.; William Morrow 2007 xxvi, 324p il map $26.95 **932**
1. Queens 2. Hieroglyphics 3. Egyptian language 4. Kings 5. Syria 6. Egypt -- Antiquities 7. Egypt -- Civilization 8. Thebes (Egypt: Extinct city)
ISBN 978-0-06-125276-1; 0-06-125276-X

LC 2007-29118

First published 1964 by Coward-McCann

This is an "introduction to the history of ancient Egypt and Egyptology. . . . Mertz gives special attention to such topics as the kingship (yes) of Queen Hatshepsut, the exploits of Thutmose III, and the Amarna Period with its intriguing players Akhenaten, Nefertiti, and Tutankhamen. Presenting both pros and cons of current theories, Mertz also explains in simple language archaeological techniques such as carbon 14 dating and historical chronology. . . . [This is] an excellent introduction for patrons interested in the land of the pharaohs." Libr J

The **Oxford** encyclopedia of ancient Egypt; Donald B. Redford, editor in chief. Oxford Univ. Press 2001 3v set $450 **932**
1. Reference books 2. Egypt -- Antiquities -- Encyclopedias 3. Egypt -- Civilization -- Encyclopedias
ISBN 0-19-510234-7

LC 99-54801

ALA RUSA Dartmouth Medal (2002)

This reference work covers "archaeology, biography, history, language, social history, and more. . . . [It features] essays from more than 250 contributors from various countries and scholarly pursuits, all with solid academic credentials. . . . One is not likely to encounter another work of this magnitude on a subject of such universal interest for some time." Booklist

Includes bibliographical references

Romer, John

A **history** of ancient Egypt; from the first farmers to the Great Pyramid. John Romer. Thomas Dunne Books 2013 512 p. (hardcover) $29.99 **932**
1. Archeology 2. Egypt -- History 3. Egypt -- History -- To 332 B.C
ISBN 1250030110; 9781250030115

LC 2013012485

This book, "the first of John Romer's promised two-volume history of ancient Egypt, . . .takes us from the earliest farming communities in northeast Africa, to the building of the Great Pyramid of King Khufu. . . . The evidence he looks at goes well beyond the written sources . . . to archaeological evidence . . . which allows him to explore pre-unification Egypt in some detail." (History Today)

Includes bibliographical references and index

Tyldesley, Joyce A.

Nefertiti; Egypt's sun queen. {by} Joyce Tyldesley. Viking 1999 232p il $27.95; pa $14.95 **932**
1. Queens 2. Egypt -- History
ISBN 0-670-86998-8; 0-14-025820-5 pa

LC 98-35469

"Born in approximately 1350 B.C., Nefertiti was the wife of Akhenaten, an eighteenth-dynasty pharaoh who initiated a radical religious revolution in his kingdom. . . .

Adored by the masses, Nefertiti was elevated to semidivine status and adopted a dynamic political and cultural role. . . . Tyldesley manages to do an admirable job re-creating the exquisite opulence of palace life and piecing together Nefertiti's early public years." Booklist

Includes bibliographical references

Verner, Miroslav

The **pyramids**; the mystery, culture, and science of Egypt's great monuments. translated from the German by Steven Rendall. Grove Press 2001 495p il map hardcover o.p. pa $17.50   **932**

1. Pyramids 2. Egypt -- Antiquities
ISBN 0-8021-3935-3 pa

LC 2001-35084

In this study, the author "focuses on research of the last decade and excavations over the past 20 years. Verner divides his book into chapters according to pharaonic dynasty, spotlighting individual pharaohs' pyramids. He not only explains the layout of each pyramid but also presents various theories on how each pyramid was built and tells stories about the people that were buried there." Booklist

Includes bibliographical references

Wilkinson, Toby

★ The **rise** and fall of ancient Egypt; [by] Toby Wilkinson. Random House 2011 611p il map $35   **932**

1. Egypt -- History 2. Egypt -- History -- 332-30 B.C.
3. Egypt -- History -- To 332 B.C.
ISBN 978-0-553-80553-6; 0-553-80553-3

LC 2009-47322

The author "offers a revisionist view of the ugly life hidden by the splendors and dazzling treasures of pharaonic Egypt. He shows in rich detail that it was a brutal society where life was cheap, royal power absolute and established through fear and coercion. . . . This is a penetrating and authoritative overview of a violent ancient civilization often revered by contemporary scholars and enthusiasts." Publ Wkly

Includes bibliographical references

932.0072   Egypt to 640--Research

Noël Hume, Ivor

Belzoni; the giant archaeologists love to hate. Ivor Noel Hume. University of Virginia Press 2011 301 p. ill. (some col.), maps $34.95   **932.0072**

1. Archeologists -- Biography 2. Egypt -- Antiquities
3. Egyptologists -- Biography 4. Egypt -- Description and travel 5. Excavations (Archeology) -- Egypt
ISBN 0813931401; 9780813931401

LC 2011000693

This book by Ivor Noel Hume presents a biography of "Giovanni Belzoni (1778-1824) . . . one of the most controversial figures in in the history of Egyptian archaeology. . . . The book includes . . . accounts of Belzoni's . . . productive, and physically brutal, expeditions, as well as a . . . portrait of his wife, Sarah, who suffered the hardships of the Egyptian deserts and later bore the brunt of the disillusionment that

came with the declining popular perception of her husband." (Publisher's note)

Includes bibliographical references (p. [289]-292) and index

933   Palestine to 70

Burleigh, Nina

Unholy business; a true tale of faith, greed, and forgery in the holy land. Smithsonian Books 2008 271p $27.50   **933**

1. Forgery 2. Engineers 3. Entrepreneurs 4. Antiquarians 5. Israel -- Antiquities
ISBN 978-0-06-145845-3

LC 2008-23425

"In 2002, the James Ossuary, an ancient limestone box for bones with an inscription on it that said 'James, son of Joseph, brother of Jesus' was publicized as the first real physical evidence of Jesus Christ's existence. The plot thickened when the ossuary went on tour, creating lots of publicity, a book by advocate Hershel Shanks, and a Discovery Channel documentary. Then the ossuary's owner, Oded Golan, and his antique-dealer associates were charged with forgery. . . . Whether or not readers believe the ossuary is authentic, they will thoroughly enjoy this book." Libr J

Goodman, Martin

Rome and Jerusalem; the clash of ancient civilizations. Alfred A. Knopf 2007 598p il map $35 **933**

1. Jews -- Rome 2. Jews -- History
ISBN 978-0-375-41185-4; 0-375-41185-2

LC 2007-5267

This is a "history of the titanic struggle between the Roman and Jewish worlds that led to the destruction of Jerusalem." Publisher's note

"For scholars of Roman and Jewish history as well as well-informed general readers, this work provides a definitive account." Booklist

Includes bibliographical references

Korb, Scott

Life in year one; what the world was like in first-century Palestine. Riverhead Books 2010 241p $25.95   **933**

1. Palestine 2. Jews -- History 3. Bible -- History
ISBN 978-1-59448-899-3

LC 2010-146

The author "calls his retrospective 'a lively romp through the land of Palestine,' circa 5 B.C.E.–70 C.E., but the picture he draws from archeology, ancient historical accounts, and religious texts is anything but lighthearted. . . . Korb's vivid, breezy prose makes accessible a mountain of scholarship that illuminates the past." Publ Wkly

Includes bibliographical references

935 Mesopotamia to 637 and Iranian Plateau to 637

Kriwaczek, Paul

Babylon; Mesopotamia and the birth of civilization. Paul Kriwaczek. Thomas Dunne Books/St. Martin's Press 2012 310 p. **935**
1. Tigris River 2. Euphrates River 3. Iraq -- History 4. Ancient civilization 5. Babylon (Extinct city) 6. Iraq -- History -- To 634 7. Iraq -- Civilization -- To 634 8. Iraq -- Politics and government 9. Babylon (Extinct city) -- History 10. Babylon (Extinct city) -- Civilization 11. Babylon (Extinct city) -- Politics and government
ISBN 9781250000071; 9781429941068
LC 2012003104
This book is an "overview of the rich, ancient civilizations that flourished in the land between the two rivers. . . . The ancient simmering conflict of the Fertile Crescent boils down to the question: "Should the Tigris-Euphrates Valley be mastered from the west or the east"? . . .. The need to organize systems of irrigation in Eridu . . . spawned an "urban revolution," with the invention of cities and all that came with them: division of labor, social classes, engineering, the arts, education, numbers and law, to mention a few. . . . The author keeps close to biblical readings for comparative accounts of the Flood and the succession of kings of the city-states to the founder of the first true empire, Sargon." (Kirkus)
Includes bibliographical references and index

936 Europe north and west of Italian Peninsula to ca. 499

★ **Ancient** Europe 8000 B.C.-A.D. 1000; encyclopedia of the Barbarian world. Peter Bogucki & Pam J. Crabtree, editors-in-chief. Thomson/Gale 2004 2v il, maps set $280 **936**
1. Ancient history 2. Reference books 3. Europe -- History -- Encyclopedias
ISBN 0-684-80668-1
LC 2003-15251
"The 212 articles are arranged in seven sections. The first provides a general overview, while the remainder cover major periods from Mesolithic hunters to the Middle Ages." Libr J
"Any public and academic library that has a clientele interested in European archeology or the featured historical period covered will find this a valuable purchase." Booklist
Includes bibliographical references

Cunliffe, Barry

The **ancient** Celts. Penguin Books 1999 324p il map pa $21.95 **936**
1. Celts
ISBN 0-14-025422-6
First published 1997 by Oxford Univ. Press
This is a "survey of the origins of the Celts and their expansion during the Iron Age through their largely successful subjection by the Romans. . . . [Cunliffe] has written a readable and informative book with many attractive illustrations." Libr J
Includes bibliographical references

Hill, Rosemary

Stonehenge. Harvard University Press 2008 242p il map (Wonders of the world) $19.95 **936**
1. Stonehenge (England) 2. Megalithic monuments -- Great Britain
ISBN 9780674031326; 0674031326
LC 2008-12024
"Many books seek to tell 'the truth about Stonehenge,' ranging from exact measurements of its various stones to theories about its original use. Hill's is less concerned with some inarguable truth than with the history of various interpretations of Stonehenge." Booklist
Hill's "book is a treasure: stylish, thoughtful, miraculously condensed, and as full of knowledge as a megalith is full of megalith." Sunday Times (London)
Includes bibliographical references (p. 211-222)

936.2 England to 410 and Wales to 410

Pearson, Mike Parker

Stonehenge; a new understanding : solving the mysteries of the greatest stone age monument. by Mike Parker Pearson. The Experiment 2013 432 p. (hardcover) $27.50 **936.2**
1. Stonehenge (England) 2. Excavations (Archeology) 3. England -- Antiquities 4. Megalithic monuments -- England
ISBN 1615190791; 9781615190799
LC 2012047688
This book, by Mike Parker Pearson, "changes the way we think about [Stonehenge] correcting previously erroneous dating, filling gaps in our knowledge about its builders and how they lived, clarifying the monument's significance both celestially and as a burial ground, and contextualizing Stonehenge . . . within the broader landscape of the Neolithic Age." (Publisher's note)
"Renowned archaeologist Pearson . . . presents the findings of the most ambitious and scientifically informed investigation of Stonehenge thus far. . . . Filled with maps, drawings, photographs and diagrams, the book details the group's findings in a well-organized, absorbing manner." Kirkus
Includes bibliographical references and index

937 Italian Peninsula to 476 and adjacent territories to 476

Allan, Tony

Life, myth, and art in Ancient Rome. J. Paul Getty Museum 2005 144p il pa $19.95 **937**
1. Roman art 2. Roman mythology 3. Rome -- Antiquities 4. Rome -- Civilization
ISBN 0-89236-821-7
LC 2004-114326
This is an "illustrated guide to the cultural and political heritage of ancient Rome, including the enduring legacy of its art and architecture, the engineering innovations of its

vast system of roads and aqueducts, the . . . myths of its gods and goddesses, and the power of its emperors and legions." Publisher's note

Includes bibliographical references

Beard, Mary, 1955-

The **fires** of Vesuvius; Pompeii lost and found. Belknap Press of Harvard University Press 2008 360p il map $26.95; pa $17.95 **937**

1. Pompeii (Extinct city)

ISBN 978-0-674-02976-7; 0-674-02976-3; 978-0-674-04586-6 pa; 0-674-04586-6 pa

LC 2008-27513

"The eruption of Mt. Vesuvius in 79 A.D. preserved a uniquely rich sample of Roman life. Buried among the ruins of Pompeii are frescoes, graffiti ('Atimetus got me pregnant'), campaign ads, and housewares; the victims themselves left hollows in the lava that, when cast in plaster, yield details as fine as the imprint of one man's eyebrows. In this lively survey, Beard, a classicist at Cambridge, tempers erudition with a skepticism toward interpretive overreach. " New Yorker

Includes bibliographical references

Berry, Joanne

The **complete** Pompeii. Thames & Hudson 2007 256p il map $40 **937**

1. Pompeii (Extinct city)

ISBN 978-0-500-05150-4; 0-500-05150-X

LC 2007-922095

This book "covers the origins and evolution of the city, the daily life of its residents, the geography of the region, and the eruption of Mt. Vesuvius, as well as a history of the excavation of the site. Easy to read and with full color pictures of the excavation, along with maps, time lines, diagrams, and vivid art reproductions, this book gives a broad and comprehensive introduction to the Pompeian world. . . . High school libraries should be advised that there is a section on eroticism that contains visually and verbally explicit sexual material." Libr J

Includes bibliographical references

Bunson, Matthew

Encyclopedia of ancient Rome; Matthew Bunson. 3rd ed. Facts On File 2012 xxxvii, 788 p.p ill., maps (acid-free paper) $95.00 **937**

1. Rome -- Antiquities 2. Rome -- Civilization 3. Rome -- History -- Encyclopedias 4. Rome -- History -- Empire, 30 B.C.-476 A.D. -- Encyclopedias

ISBN 0816082170; 9780816082179

LC 2011038366

This encyclopedia, by Matthew Bunson, "provides . . . coverage of the people, places, events, and ideas of ancient Rome. Each entry . . . reflect[s] recent advances in archaeology, historical and literary criticism, and social analysis. In addition, the scope . . . include[s] the entire history of ancient Rome, from the first founding of the city . . . to the final collapse of Roman power in the fifth century CE." (Publisher's note)

"A superb source of detailed, engaging information on the ever fascinating and often perplexing ancient Roman civilization, Bunson's work is a handy reference for classics students and enthusiasts alike." LJ

Includes bibliographical references (p. 757-760) and index

Encyclopedia of the Roman Empire; rev ed; Facts on File 2002 636p il maps $75 **937**

1. Reference books 2. Rome -- History -- Encyclopedias

ISBN 0-8160-4562-3

LC 2001-53253

First published 1994

This reference work provides information on the key places, people, events, and culture of Roman history, from the reign of Julius Caesar to the fall of the last Roman emperor in 476 A.D.

"An excellent ready-reference source." Booklist [review of 1994 edition]

Includes bibliographical references

The **Cambridge** illustrated history of the Roman world; edited by Greg Woolf. Cambridge University Press 2003 384p il map (Cambridge illustrated history) $45 **937**

1. Rome -- History

ISBN 0-521-82775-2

LC 2004-298480

This book explores such topics as "religion, Rome's relationship with Greece, warfare and Empire, and science and culture." Publisher's note

Includes bibliographical references

Everitt, Anthony

The **rise** of Rome; the making of the world's greatest empire. Anthony Everitt. 1st ed. Random House 2012 xxxii, 478 p., [8] p. of platesp col. ill., maps (ebook) $85.00; (hardcover : alk. paper) $30.00 **937**

1. Rome -- History 2. Rome -- Politics and government 3. Rome -- History -- Empire, 284-476 4. Rome -- History -- Empire, 30 B.C.-284 A.D

ISBN 1400066638; 9780679645160; 9781400066636; 0679645160

LC 2011048318

This book by Anthony Everitt examines the history of "Rome and its . . . ascent from an obscure agrarian backwater. . . . He chronicles the clash between patricians and plebeians that defined the politics of the Republic. He shows how Rome's . . . strategy of offering citizenship to her defeated subjects was instrumental in expanding the reach of her burgeoning empire. And he outlines the corrosion of constitutional norms that accompanied Rome's . . . expansion." (Publisher's note)

Includes bibliographical references (p. [423]-426) and index.

Fowler, Brenda

Iceman; uncovering the life and times of a prehistoric man found in an alpine glacier. University of Chicago Press ed; University of Chicago Press 2001 315p il pa $15 **937**

1. Mummies 2. Prehistoric peoples 3. Italy --

Antiquities
ISBN 0-226-25823-8

LC 2001-27805

First published 2000 by Random House

"In September 1991, hikers in the Alps discovered a well-preserved frozen corpse; nearby lay a stone ax and swatches of leather and fur. The man turned out to have died in the early Bronze Age, making him an incalculable treasure for students of early human beings. Fowler . . . offers a brisk and easy-to-follow narrative, first of the great discovery, then of the personal and political struggles for control of the frozen body." Publ Wkly

Includes bibliographical references

Freisenbruch, Annelise

Caesars' wives; sex, power, and politics in the Roman Empire. Free Press 2010 xxvi, 337p il $28; ebook $14.99   **937**

1. Empresses 2. Women -- Rome 3. Rome -- History
ISBN 978-1-4165-8303-5; 1-4165-8303-3; 978-1-4165-8357-8 ebook; 1-4165-8357-2 ebook

LC 2010-19368

"Providing well-chosen, scintillating details—e.g., enemies being boiled alive, familial bonds savagely snapped in an instant—alongside careful historical analysis, the author breathes new life into these overlooked subjects. . . . A captivating look at imperial Rome's roots in the making of the modern stateswoman " Kirkus

Includes bibliographical references

Gibbon, Edward

★ The **decline** and fall of the Roman empire; Edward Gibbon; edited, abridged, and with a critical introduction by Hans-Friedrich Mueller; introduction by Daniel J. Boorstin; illustrations by Giovanni Battista Piranesi. Modern Library paperback ed.; Modern Library 2003 xxxvii, 1258p il map pa $15.95   **937**

1. Rome -- History 2. Byzantine Empire
ISBN 0-375-75811-9

LC 2002-32585

First published 1776-1788 in the United Kingdom with title: The history of the decline and fall of the Roman Empire

"In this substantial history of the Roman Empire, Gibbon bridges the abyss between the ancient and the modern world. It is the one historical work of the eighteenth century that is still accepted as authoritative. It covers thirteen centuries of history, during which time paganism was breaking down and Christianity was taking its place." Reader's Adviser

Includes bibliographical references

Goldsworthy, Adrian Keith

How Rome fell; death of a superpower. [by] Adrian Goldsworthy. Yale University Press 2009 531p il map $32.50   **937**

1. Rome -- History
ISBN 978-0-300-13719-4; 0-300-13719-2

In this history of the Roman Empire's decline, the author "concludes that fear of usurpation turned the increasingly militarized empire into a vast vehicle for each Roman ruler's self-preservation—and that this internal flaw, rather than the

external threats, deserves prime blame for the decline and fall." N Y Times Book Rev

"This richly rewarding work will serve as an introduction to Roman history, but will also provide plenty of depth to satisfy the educated reader." Publ Wkly

Includes bibliographical references

Grant, Michael, 1954-

Collapse and recovery of the Roman Empire. Routledge 1999 123p $34.95   **937**

1. Rome -- History 2. Emperors -- Rome
ISBN 0-415-17323-X

LC 98-8222

"Grant examines the causes for the near disintegration of the empire in the mid-third century A.D., including the problems of imperial succession, Germanic encroachments on the frontiers, and chronic conflicts with the Persians in the East. . . . This work is a worthy and necessary addition to both academic and public library collections on classical history." Booklist

Includes bibliographical references

O'Connell, Robert L.

The **ghosts** of Cannae; Hannibal and the darkest hour of the Roman republic. Random House 2010 310p map $27   **937**

1. Generals 2. Punic Wars, 264 B.C.-146 B.C. 3. Rome -- History 4. Punic Wars, 264-146 B.C.
ISBN 978-1-4000-6702-2; 1-4000-6702-2

LC 2009-40006

"The distinctive edge of The Ghosts of Cannae is Robert L. O'Connell's consistently professional instinct for the behavior of men and units on the battlefield. He is able to put himself and his reader on the ground at Cannae, gagging in the heat of a southern Italian midsummer, assailed by an overload from every one of the five senses." N Y Times Book Rev

Includes bibliographical references

The **Oxford** history of the Roman world; edited by John Boardman, Jasper Griffin, Oswyn Murray. Oxford Univ. Press 1991 518p il maps hardcover o.p. pa $17.95   **937**

1. Rome -- History
ISBN 0-19-280203-8

LC 91-11763

This "work tells the story of the rise of Rome from its origins as a cluster of villages to the foundation of the Roman Empire by Augustus, to its consolidation in the first two centuries CE. It also discusses aspects of the later Empire and its influence on Western civilization." Publisher's note

Includes bibliographical references

Pellegrino, Charles R.

★ **Ghosts** of Vesuvius; a new look at the last days of Pompeii, how the towers fell, and other strange connections. [by] Charles Pellegrino. 1st ed; W. Morrow 2004 489p il map $25.95; pa $15.95   **937**

1. Pompeii (Extinct city) 2. Excavations (Archeology)

-- Italy

ISBN 0-380-97310-3; 0-06-075100-2 pa

LC 2003-71055

"In August A.D. 79, Mt. Vesuvius erupted and famously buried the city of Pompeii and, less famously, the city of Herculaneum. From this node of history, Pellegrino goes off on a . . . search for the connections and ruptures that have shaped not only human civilization but the very course of life on Earth and the universe at large. . . . This is a book to be savored, reread and passed along to future generations." Publ Wkly

Includes bibliographical references

Woolf, Greg

Rome; an empire's story. Greg Woolf. Oxford University Press 2012 xiii, 366 p.p ill., maps (hardcover) $29.95   **937**
1. Imperialism 2. Rome -- History 3. Imperialism -- History -- To 1500 4. Rome -- History -- Empire, 30 B.C.-476 A.D. 5. Rome -- Politics and government -- 30 B.C.-476 A.D.

ISBN 019977529X; 9780199775293

LC 2011037613

This book, by Greg Woolf, explores the imperial history of Rome. The book "recounts how this mammoth empire was created, how it was sustained in crisis, and how it shaped the world of its rulers and subjects. . . . Woolf provides . . . retellings . . . from the height of territorial expansion under the emperors Trajan and Hadrian to the founding of Constantinople and the barbarian invasions which resulted in Rome's ultimate collapse." (Publisher's note)

Includes bibliographical references (p. [327]-356) and index.

938   Greece to 323

Adkins, Lesley

Handbook to life in ancient Greece; [by] Lesley Adkins and Roy A. Adkins. Updated ed; Facts on File 2005 514p il map (Facts on File library of world history) $70   **938**
1. Greece -- Civilization

ISBN 0-8160-5659-5

LC 2004-47105

This book covers "all aspects of ancient Greek life—from the beginnings of the Minoan civilization in Crete to the final defeat by the Roman world in 30 BCE." Publisher's note

Includes bibliographical references

★   **Ancient** Greece; edited by Thomas J. Sienkewicz. Salem Press 2007 3v il map (Magill's choice) set $207   **938**
1. Reference books 2. Greece -- History -- Encyclopedias

ISBN 1-58765-281-1; 978-1-58765-281-3

LC 2006-16525

Some of the essays in this work appeared in various other Salem Press sets

This is a "comprehensive examination of Greek civilization and its impact on Western history, 'from its earliest archaeological remains until the Battle of Actium in 31

B.C.E.' . . . [The essays included] cover art, daily life and customs, government, literature, medicine and science, war, the role of women, and mythology. Biographical entries profile statesmen, artists, writers, scientists, and philosophers, and relevant entries probe battles, philosophical movements, and types of literature." SLJ

Includes bibliographical references

Burckhardt, Jacob

The Greeks and Greek civilization; translated by Sheila Stern; edited with an introduction by Oswyn Murray. St. Martin's Press 1998 449p hardcover o.p. pa $16.95   **938**
1. Greece -- Civilization

ISBN 0-312-24447-9 pa

LC 98-30107

Translation of selected lectures on ancient Greece delivered by the German cultural historian in the 1870s

"These lectures provide not only a rich overview of Burckhardt's learning but a precious glimpse into the intellectual world of the late nineteenth century. . . . Here his topics range from the importance of the 'agon' in forging individualism to the pessimism and violence that underlay much of Greek culture." New Yorker

Includes bibliographical references

★   **The Cambridge** dictionary of classical civilization; edited by Graham Shipley . . . [et al.] Cambridge University Press 2006 xliv, 966p il map $180   **938**
1. Reference books 2. Classical civilization -- Dictionaries

ISBN 0-521-48313-1; 978-0-521-48313-1

LC 2006-299203

The "entries and more than 500 illustrations focus on social, economic, and cultural aspects of these civilizations from the mid-eighth century BCE to the end of the fifth century." Booklist

Includes bibliographical references

Cartledge, Paul

Ancient Greece; a history in eleven cities. Oxford University Press 2009 261p il map $19.95 **938**
1. Greece -- Civilization 2. Greece -- History -- 0-323

ISBN 978-0-19-923338-0

LC 2009-26999

"Aiming for a general audience, Cartledge achieves a fast-paced, highly engaging romp through ancient Greece. An excellent choice for anyone seeking an introduction to the topic; for all its readability, this book doesn't skimp on the research." Libr J

Includes bibliographical references

Great moments in Greek archaeology; academic coordinator, Panos Valavanis; translated by David Hardy; foreword by Angelos Delivorrias; essays by George F. Bass . . . [et al.] The J. Paul Getty Museum 2007 379p il $75   **938**
1. Greece -- Antiquities 2. Excavations (Archeology) -- Greece

ISBN 978-0-89236-910-2; 0-89236-910-8

LC 2007-16609

"This magnificently illustrated book with essays by leading scholars—frequently the excavators themselves—tells the story of Greek archaeological discoveries, capturing the excitement and rendering details accessible to a wide audience." Libr J

Includes bibliographical references

Green, Peter

The **Hellenistic** age; a history. Modern Library 2007 xxxiii, 199p map (Modern Library chronicles) hardcover o.p. pa $14   **938**
  1. Hellenism 2. Greece -- History 3. Mediterranean region -- History
  ISBN 978-0-679-64279-4; 0-679-64279-X; 978-0-8129-6740-1 pa; 0-8129-6740-2 pa
          LC 2006-46657

Tis study "traces the unfolding of Hellenistic civilization in a linear fashion, while at the same time drawing connections between successive alterations in the political, economic and social landscape of the Hellenistic East and the appearance of new cultural and intellectual perspectives. . . . [The book] provides an interesting and well-written overview of a historical period that Green aptly describes as covering 'some of the most crucial and transformational history of the ancient world. . . . The changes are lasting and fundamental.' If only for this, students of world history are in Green's debt." Philadelphia Inquirer

Includes bibliographical references

Herodotus, ca. 484 B.C.-425 B.C.

The **Histories**; Herodotus ; translated by Tom Holland ; introduction and notes by Paul Cartledge. Viking Adult 2014 880 p. maps (hbk.) $40   **938**
  1. Ancient history 2. Greece -- History -- 0-323 3. History, Ancient 4. Greece -- History -- To 146 B.C
  ISBN 0670024899; 9780670024896
          LC 2012474647

This book by Herodotus, translated by Tom Holland, "is the earliest surviving work of nonfiction and a thrilling narrative account of (among other things) the war between the Persian Empire and the Greek city-states in the fifth century BC." This edition includes "an introduction and notes by Professor Paul Cartledge, a translator's preface, an index of significant persons and places, maps, and a supplementary index." (Publisher's note)

"This ancient Greek historian could easily be called the father of humor. . . ; he irreverently describes events, players and their countless harebrained schemes." Kirkus

Includes bibliographical references (pages 745-746) and indexes

★ The **landmark** Herodotus; the Histories: a new translation. a new translation by Andrea L. Purvis with maps, annotations, appendices, and encyclopedic index; edited by Robert B. Strassler; with an introduction by Rosalind Thomas. Pantheon Books 2007 lxiv, 953p $45   **938**
  1. History, Ancient 2. Greece -- History 3. Greece -- History -- To 146 B.C.
  ISBN 978-0-375-42109-9; 0-375-42109-2; 0375421092; 9780375421099
          LC 2007024149

This is a new translation of Herodotus' Histories. Indexes.

"A major theme of the Histories is the way in which time can effect surprising changes in the fortunes and reputations of empires, cities, and men; all the more appropriate, then, that Herodotus' reputation has once again been riding very high. In the academy, his technique, once derided as haphazard, has earned newfound respect, while his popularity among ordinary readers will likely get a boost from the publication of perhaps the most densely annotated, richly illustrated, and user-friendly edition of his Histories ever to appear: 'The Landmark Herodotus,' edited by Robert B. Strassler and bristling with appendices, by a phalanx of experts, on everything from the design of Athenian warships to adent units of liquid measure." New Yorker

Includes bibliographical references

Higgins, Charlotte

It's all Greek to me; from Homer to the Hippocratic Oath, how ancient Greece has shaped our world. Harper 2010 229p il map $16.99   **938**
  1. Greece -- Civilization
  ISBN 978-0-06-180400-7; 0-06-180400-2
          LC 2010-06737

First published 2008 in the United Kingdom

"The book has plenty of useful aspects, perhaps most notably in the rich back matter, comprising an alphabet, map, timeline, key to important Greek gods and notables and a sampling of Greek sayings and words (and root words) that still inhabit our language (tantalizing, Draconian). Anyone reading The Iliad or any other of the Greek classic texts for the first time would do well to keep the section bookmarked. Higgins covers Homer, the playwrights, the historians, the nascent scientists and the philosophers, and she gives special attention to the warriors, wars and other aspects of the ancient world that continue to make us uncomfortable—e.g., homosexuality, women's rights, slavery. Periodically, she pauses to offer mini-disquisitions on topics as varied as the plots of The Iliad and The Odyssey, the architecture of the Parthenon and the uneven verisimilitude of the 2007 film 300." Kirkus

Includes bibliographical references

Kagan, Donald

The **Peloponnesian** War. Viking 2003 xxvii, 511p il map $29.95; pa $15   **938**
  1. Greece -- History -- 431-404 B.C., Peloponnesian War
  ISBN 0-670-03211-5; 0-14-200437-5 pa
          LC 2002-193377

This is a study of "the conflict between Athens and Sparta in the fifth century B.C.E. . . . {Kagan's} primary source is, of course, Thucydides' epic history, but {he} draws on Aristotle, Xenophon, and others to provide an objective, nuanced perspective on the military drama. And it's quite a drama: the clash of democracy and oligarchy, the testing of great leaders, the innovative military tactics, and the unprecedented human cost." Booklist

Includes bibliographical references

Thucydides; the reinvention of history. Viking 2009 257p map $26.95   **938**
  1. Historians 2. Historiography 3. Greece --

Historiography 4. Greece -- Intellectual life -- To 146 B.C. 5. Greece -- History -- 431-404 B.C., Peloponnesian War 6. Greece -- History -- Peloponnesian War, 431-404 B.C.

ISBN 0670921296; 9780670021291

LC 2009-08368

Kagan argues that "The Peloponnesian War differs significantly from other accounts offered by Thucydides' contemporaries and stands as the first modern work of political history." (Publisher's note) Index.

"Kagan's utter mastery is on display in this vigorous, elegantly written, provocative book." PopMatters

Includes bibliographical references

★ The **Landmark** Xenophon's Hellenika; a new translation. translation by John Marincola; with maps, annotations, appendices, and encyclopedic index edited by Robert B. Strassler; with an introduction by David Thomas. Pantheon Books 2009 lxxxii, 579p il map $40 **938**

1. Greece -- History -- To 146 B.C. 2. Greece -- History -- 431-404 B.C., Peloponnesian War 3. Greece -- History -- Peloponnesian War, 431-404 B.C.

ISBN 9780375422553

LC 2009-20970

This is a new translation "of the Hellenika, the major primary source for the events of the final seven years and aftermath of the Peloponnesian War. Hellenika covers the years between 411 and 362 B.C.E.." (Publisher's note) Glossary. Bibliography. Index.

"The Hellenika is often messy: Athens and Sparta are the primary players, but Corinth and Thebes constantly jump into the fray, and Persia, Sparta's sometime ally, is always lurking at the periphery. All this can be confusing, and one of the more impressive things about the Landmark edition is how much it tries—and succeeds—in making the texts of ancient Greece accessible to contemporary audiences. The extensive footnotes are both informative and readable. . . . Side notes, meanwhile, offer a running plot summary, in case the casual reader neglects to follow, say, the hostilities between Agesilaos and Phleious. The maps generously sprinkled across these pages are uniformly clear, showing both battle maneuvers and shifting geopolitical alliances. And the appendix is a veritable treasure trove of secondary material." New Criterion

Includes bibliographical references and index

Lane Fox, Robin

The **classical** world; an epic history from Homer to Hadrian. Basic Books 2006 656p il map $35 **938**

1. Classical civilization 2. Rome -- Civilization 3. Greece -- Civilization

ISBN 978-0-465-02496-4; 0-465-02496-3

LC 2006-20247

First published 2005 in the United Kingdom

A "portrait of Greek and Roman culture over a period of roughly 900 years. Although he utilizes a broadly chronological approach, Fox goes well beyond the usual, dreary narrative of battles, dynastic changes, and political conflicts that often characterize surveys of the period. Instead, Fox focuses on the gradual development and transformation of various cultural aspects of Greek and Roman societies, and

he discusses in often fascinating detail topics that are normally given short shrift in general histories." Booklist

The **Oxford** classical dictionary; general editors, Simon Hornblower and Antony Spawforth ; assistant editor, Esther Eidinow. 4th ed; Oxford University Press 2012 lv, 1592 p **938**

1. Classical dictionaries 2. Classical civilization -- Dictionaries

ISBN 0199545561; 9780199545568

LC 2012009579

First published 1949 under the editorship of M. Cary and others

This reference book "offers nearly 1600 pages of entries that detail important topics of the Classical world from agriculture to war, social history to science, biography to religion. . . . Two focus areas are new to this edition: anthropology and reception, an area of study that examines how a Classical idea or concept affected various societies during different periods of history, depending on the context of the people reading the narrative, viewing the art . . . etc." (Library Journal)

"A scholarly dictionary, with signed articles, covering biography, literature, mythology, philosophy, religion, science, geography, etc. Most of the articles are brief, but there are some longer survey articles, e.g. Rome, music, scholarship, etc." Guide to Ref Books. 11th edition

Includes bibliographical references

Sacks, David

Encyclopedia of the ancient Greek world; editorial consultant, Oswyn Murray; revised by Lisa R. Brody. Rev ed; Facts on File 2005 xx, 412p il map (Facts on File library of world history) $75 **938**

1. Reference books 2. Greece -- History -- Encyclopedias

ISBN 0-8160-5722-2

LC 2004-56429

First published 1995

This encyclopedia covers "ancient Greece, from the dawning of Minoan civilization to the conquest of Rome—2000 years of a remarkable civilization that left an indelible imprint on human history. . . . This is a first-rate purchase for libraries on a topic of endless inquiry and fascination." SLJ

Includes bibliographical references

Thucydides

The **history** of the Peloponnesian War; Rev ed; Penguin Group 1954 648p map (Penguin classics) pa $15 **938**

1. Greece -- History -- 431-404 B.C., Peloponnesian War

ISBN 978-0-14-044039-3; 0-14-044039-9

Thucydides' "chosen subject was the Peloponnesian War, which covered 27 years of his own lifetime, 431-404 B.C., and in which he fought as a commander of the Athenian troops in Thrace. His ideal of history is said to have been first accuracy, and then relevancy. . . . He rarely digressed. His history is unfinished, breaking off in the middle of the year 411 B.C." Reader's Adviser

The **landmark** Thucydides; a comprehensive guide to the Peloponnesian War. edited by Robert

B. Strassler; introduction by Victor Davis Hanson. A newly revised edition of the Richard Crawley translation with maps, annotations, appendices, and e Free Press 1996 xxxiii,713 $45; pa $25 **938**

1. Greece -- History -- 431-404 B.C., Peloponnesian War

ISBN 978-1-416-59087-3; 0-684-82790-5

LC 96-24555

"Strassler, an unaffiliated scholar of classical studies, has remedied many of the flaws of Richard Crawley's 1874 translation of The Peloponnesian War. He has added descriptive paragraph-by-paragraph synopses, topic headers on every page, numerous maps keyed to the adjoining text, explanatory footnotes, an extensive index, an excellent introduction by Victor Davis Hanson . . . , and 11 appendixes (by various scholars) on politics, warfare, and society in the Greece of the fifth century B.C.E." Libr J

939　Other parts of ancient world

★ **Civilizations** of the Ancient Near East; Jack M. Sasson, editor in chief; John Baines, Gary Beckman, Karen S. Rubinson, associate editors. Hendrickson Publishers 2000 4v in 2 il map set $169.95 **939**

1. Middle East -- Civilization

ISBN 1-56563-607-4

LC 00-63144

First published 1995 by Scribner

The author "outlines the path the legend took through medieval, Renaissance and modern society. The bulk of this . . . book is devoted to archeological efforts to prove the truth of Homer's epic and confirm that Troy was actually at Hissarlik. Mr. Wood also describes the history and archeology of Mycenae." N Y Times Book Rev [review of 1985 edition]

This "work concentrates on the Near East, broadly defined to include a region from Northeast Africa to India, Pakistan, and Burma, with principal focus on the core areas of Egypt, Syro-Palestine, Mesopotamia, and Anatolia. The time span ranges from the third millennium B.C.E., when writing was invented, to 330 B.C.E., when Alexander triumphed over the Persian Empire. The 189 contributors from five continents and 16 countries include some of the world's finest scholars." Libr J [review of 1995 edition]

Includes bibliographical references

Wood, Michael

In search of the Trojan War. University of Calif. Press 1998 288p il pa $19.95 **939**

1. Bronze Age 2. Trojan War 3. Troy (Extinct city) 4. Turkey -- Antiquities

ISBN 0-520-21599-0

LC 98-4958

First published 1985 by Facts on File

"This is a first-rate book. . . . The book makes a readable and clear approach to some of the knottiest problems of Bronze Age archaeology." Choice [review of 1985 edition]

Includes bibliographical references

940　History of Europe

Eastern Europe; an introduction to the people, lands, and culture. edited by Richard Frucht. ABC-CLIO 2004 3v set $285 **940**

1. Central Europe 2. Eastern Europe 3. Balkan Peninsula

ISBN 1-57607-800-0

LC 2004-22300

"Clearly written essays, which average 50-plus pages, examine cultural, political, and economic developments in addition to geography and history. Each one concludes with an evaluation of the challenges facing the country, a selective bibliography, and a chronology. Short essays, set off from the text, add additional information on relevant figures, topics, and events." SLJ

Includes bibliographical references

940.1　Europe--Early history to 1453

English, Edward D.

Encyclopedia of the medieval world. Facts on File 2004 2v il map (Facts on File library of world history) set $150 **940.1**

1. Reference books 2. Middle Ages -- Encyclopedias

ISBN 0-8160-4690-5

LC 2003-27825

This encyclopedia "covers the time period from the late antique world to about 1500 C.E and includes events, people, institutions, and culture in western and eastern Europe, Scandinavia, North Africa, Byzantium, and the Near East. The 2,000 entries discuss significant people, art, politics, literature, religion, economics, law, science, and warfare in an A-Z format." Booklist

Includes bibliographical references

Freeman, Charles

The **closing** of the Western mind; the rise of faith and the fall of reason. Knopf 2003 xxiii, 432p il map $32.50; pa $16.95 **940.1**

1. Hellenism 2. Western civilization 3. Europe -- Intellectual life 4. Europe -- History -- 476-1492 5. Church history -- 30-600, Early church

ISBN 1-400-04085-X; 1-400-03380-2 pa

LC 2002-44821

"This is one of the best books to date on the development of Christianity. . . . Beautifully written and impressively annotated, this is an indispensable read for anyone interested in the roots of Christianity and its implications for our modern worldview." Choice

Includes bibliographical references

Gies, Frances

Life in a medieval village; [by] Frances and Joseph Gies. Harper & Row 1990 257p il maps hardcover o.p. pa $14.95 **940.1**

1. Middle Ages 2. Medieval civilization

ISBN 0-06-016215-5; 0-06-092046-7 pa

LC 89-33759

"Elton, England, is the focal point of the authors' efforts to portray the everyday life and social structure of the High Middle Ages. After giving a brief summary of Elton's origins and development in the Roman and Anglo-Saxon periods, the book examines just how the residents lived and worked within the feudal structure at the beginning of the fourteenth century." Booklist

Includes bibliographical references

Gies, Joseph

Life in a medieval city; [by] Joseph and Frances Gies. HarperPerennial 1981 274p il map pa $13.95   **940.1**

1. Middle Ages 2. Medieval civilization
ISBN 0-06-090880-7
First published 1969 by Crowell
"A portrait of a medieval city [Troyes], a flourishing settlement of a type not known in Europe before the Middle Ages." Cincinnati Public Libr

Includes bibliographical references

Herlihy, David

The **black** death and the transformation of the west; edited and with an introduction by Samuel K. Cohn, Jr. Harvard Univ. Press 1997 117p hardcover o.p. pa $12   **940.1**

1. Plague 2. Renaissance 3. Medieval civilization 4. Europe -- History -- 476-1492
ISBN 0-674-07613-3 pa

LC 96-54637

These "essays redefine the historical study of the Black Death. . . . Herlihy's contention is that we can learn from this 'devastating natural disaster': for example, parallels can be drawn to today's pandemic of AIDS, especially in the resultant bigotries that both engendered. Cohn introduces the lectures, admirably setting the scene. This book, which opens a new chapter on the history and implications of the plague, is essential for all readers of medieval history." Libr J

Includes bibliographical references

Knights; in history and in legend. chief consultant Constance Brittain Bouchard. Firefly Books 2009 304p il map $40   **940.1**

1. Knights and knighthood 2. Military art and science -- History
ISBN 978-1-55407-480-8
The history of knights, from their everyday lives to their clothing, training, heraldry and orders, as well as their role in literature and film, and the decline of traditional knighthood.
"Aimed at history and art history lovers, this work would be excellent reading for medieval history enthusiasts and should be welcomed as a library reference resource." Libr J

Includes bibliographical references

The **New** Cambridge medieval history; edited by Paul Fouracre . . . [et al.] Cambridge Univ. Press 2005 7v in 8 il maps set $1600   **940.1**

1. Middle Ages 2. Medieval civilization
ISBN 978-0-521-85360-6; 0-521-85360-5
This set replaces the Cambridge medieval history, published 1929-1967

"An excellent reference history, written by specialists, with full bibliographies at the end of each volume." Guide to Ref Books. 11th edition [entry for Cambridge medieval history]

★ The **Oxford** history of medieval Europe; edited by George Holmes. Oxford Univ. Press 2001 395p il maps pa $16.95   **940.1**

1. Europe -- History -- 476-1492
ISBN 0-19-280133-3

LC 2002-281715

This is an abridged edition of The Oxford illustrated history of medieval Europe, published 1988
This compact edition covers such subjects as the chivalric code of knights, popular festivals, new art forms, the Black Death, the fall of Rome, and the emergence of the Reformation

Includes bibliographical references

Reston, James

The **last** apocalypse; Europe at the year 1000 A.D. Doubleday 1998 299p il map hardcover o.p. pa $14.95   **940.1**

1. Europe -- History -- 476-1492
ISBN 0-385-48336-8 pa

LC 97-18812

"Reston's seemingly encyclopedic knowledge of the tenth century, combined with his disarming interpretations of the period's events, makes for fascinating reading." Booklist

Includes bibliographical references

Wickham, Chris

★ The **inheritance** of Rome; a history of Europe from 400 to 1000. Viking 2009 650p il map (The Penguin history of Europe) $35   **940.1**

1. Middle Ages 2. Medieval civilization 3. Rome -- Civilization
ISBN 978-0-670-02098-0

LC 2009-15169

The author "lays out, in 23 chapters, 600 years of early medieval political, social, economic and religious history. He begins with a . . . description of the culture and belief systems of the late Roman Empire and the crises that led to its dissolution, then goes on to cover post-Roman Western Europe between 550 and 750, the Byzantine and Arab empires between 550 and 1000, and Carolingian and post-Carolingian Europe between 750 and 1000." Times Higher Ed

"Wickham's achievement contributes richly to our picture of this often narrowly understood period." Publ Wkly

Includes bibliographical references

940.2 Europe--1453-

Adkin, Mark

The **Trafalgar** companion; a guide to history's most famous sea battle and the life of Admiral Lord Nelson. Aurum Press 2005 560p il map $75 **940.2**

1. Admirals 2. Trafalgar (Spain), Battle of, 1805
ISBN 1-84513-018-9
"Beginning with a prologue that describes the wounding and death of Vice-Admiral Horatio Nelson, the book intro-

duces readers to the history of the campaign from 1802 to 1805 and to . . . information about the men and ships of the Royal Navy, in alternate chapters. . . . It will long stand as the definitive one-volume study of Great Britain's foremost naval hero and his times." Choice

Includes bibliographical references

Barbero, Alessandro

The **Battle**; a new history of Waterloo. Walker & Company 2005 340p il map $28; pa $16   **940.2**

  1. Waterloo, Battle of, 1815

  ISBN 0-8027-1453-6; 978-0-8027-1453-4; 0-8027-1500-1 pa; 978-0-8027-1500-5 pa

  Original Italian edition, 2003

The author's "narrative flows smoothly, making readers feel part of the battle's events. The chapters are short—never more than a few pages—and they pull the reader along with the action." Choice

Includes bibliographical references (p. 318-324)

Barzun, Jacques

From dawn to decadence; 500 years of Western cultural life, 1500 to the present. HarperCollins Pubs. 2000 877p hardcover o.p. pa $20   **940.2**

  1. Western civilization 2. Europe -- Civilization 3. Europe -- Intellectual life

  ISBN 0-06-092883-2 pa

                    LC 99-16194

"Encyclopedic without being discontinuous, the book hardly seems as long, as carefully constructed or as densely packed as it is. Though the ideas it explains are often complicated, the explanations it offers are limpidly clear, sparkling with biographical anecdote and counter-canonical observations." N Y Times Book Rev

Includes bibliographical references

Blanning, T. C. W.

★ The **pursuit** of glory; Europe, 1648-1815. [by] Tim Blanning. Viking 2007 xxvii, 707p il map (The Penguin history of Europe) $39.95   **940.2**

  1. Europe -- Civilization 2. Europe -- History -- 1492-1789 3. Europe -- History -- 1789-1815

  ISBN 978-0-670-06320-8; 0-670-06320-7

                LC 2006-37324

This is an "account of Europe from the end of the Thirty Years' War to the Battle of Waterloo." Publisher's note

The author "thoroughly covers the politics and endless wars of the period. . . . 'The Pursuit of Glory' is history writing at its glorious best." N Y Times (Late N Y Ed)

Includes bibliographical references

Blom, Philipp

The **vertigo** years; Europe 1900-1914. Basic Books 2008 466p il $29.95   **940.2**

  1. Europe -- History -- 1871-1918 2. Europe -- History -- 20th century 3. Europe -- Civilization -- 20th century

  ISBN 0-465-01116-0; 978-0-465-01116-2

              LC 2008-935053

Blom examines the period between 1900 and the outbreak of the First World War, as cities grew, "education changed the outlook of millions; mass-produced items transformed daily life; industrial laborers demanded a share of political power; and women sought to change their place in society." (Publisher's note) Bibliography. Index.

"Blom's engrossing history begins with an invitation: 'Imagine yourself looking at the years 1900 to 1914 without the long shadows of the future darkening their historical present.' His imaginative recreation of this period argues that speed—both literal and figurative—came to typify and, ultimately, define modern life. This was the age that gave rise not only to Futurism and Vorticism but also to car racing and the electric chair. Precipitate change also ushered in an age of uncertainty and attraction to the seeming stability of the past. The book's strength is also its charm—a multifaceted, panoramic approach animated by vivacious narration of individual stories." New Yorker

Includes bibliographical references

Coote, Stephen

Napoleon and the Hundred Days. DaCapo Press 2005 308p il $27.50   **940.2**

  1. Emperors 2. France -- History -- 1799-1815

  ISBN 0-306-81408-0

              LC 2004-65505

  First published 2004 in the United Kingdom

This history "of the 100 days between Napoleon's escape from Elba and his capitulation after Waterloo uses the period as a lens through which to examine his character in general. . . . This accessible work is reminiscent of the finest classical Roman histories and biographies." Publ Wkly

Includes bibliographical references

Esdaile, Charles J.

Napoleon's wars; an international history, 1803-1815. [by] Charles Esdaile. Viking 2008 621p il map $35   **940.2**

  1. Emperors 2. Europe -- History -- 1789-1815 3. France -- History -- 1799-1815

  ISBN 978-0-670-02030-0; 0-670-02030-3

  First published 2007 in the United Kingdom

"Recapturing the flux of international diplomacy and Napoléon's congenital rejection of compromise, Esdaile persuasively places the diplomatic foundation to popular military histories about the Napoleonic wars." Booklist

Includes bibliographical references (p. 567-602)

Europe 1789 to 1914; encyclopedia of the age of industry and empire. Merriman and Jay Winter, editors in chief. Charles Scribner's Sons 2006 5v il map (Scribner library of modern Europe) set $595   **940.2**

  1. Reference books 2. Europe -- Civilization -- Encyclopedias 3. Europe -- History -- 1789-1900 -- Encyclopedias 4. Europe -- History -- 1871-1918 -- Encyclopedias

  ISBN 0-684-31359-6; 978-0-684-31359-7

              LC 2006-7335

This encyclopedia covers "the time period between the onset of the French Revolution to the outbreak of World War I." Publisher's note

Includes bibliographical references

Gies, Joseph

Life in a medieval castle; [by] Joseph and Frances Gies. Harper & Row 1979 272p il pa $14.95 **940.2**

1. Castles 2. Feudalism 3. Middle Ages 4. Knights and knighthood 5. Hunting -- Great Britain

ISBN 0-06-090674-X

LC 79-103901

First published 1974 by Crowell

Using Chepstow Castle on the Welsh border as a model, the authors provide "descriptions of the medieval world where the castle was household, feudal center, and military target, and by concentrating on Anglo-Norman examples illustrate what existence was like as the dark ages began to brighten." Booklist

Includes glossary and bibliographical references

Greenblatt, Stephen

★ The swerve; [by] Stephen Greenblatt. W.W. Norton 2011 356p il $26.95 **940.2**

1. Poets 2. Renaissance 3. Philosophers 4. Modern civilization 5. Civilization, Modern 6. Science, Renaissance 7. Philosophy, Renaissance

ISBN 0393064476; 9780393064476

LC 2011019765

National Book Award: Nonfiction (2011)

Pulitzer Prize: General Nonfiction (2012)

The book presents a history of the "ancient Roman philosophical epic, On the Nature of Things, by Lucretius - a beautiful poem of the most dangerous ideas: that the universe functioned without the aid of gods, that religious fear was damaging to human life, and that matter was made up of very small particles in eternal motion, colliding and swerving in new directions." According to the author, "the copying and translation of this ancient book - the greatest discovery of the greatest book-hunter of his age - fueled the Renaissance, inspiring artists such as Botticelli and thinkers such as Giordano Bruno; shaped the thought of Galileo and Freud, Darwin and Einstein; and had a revolutionary influence on writers such as Montaigne and Shakespeare and even Thomas Jefferson." (books.wwnorton.com)

"A fascinating, intelligent look at what may well be the most historically resonant book-hunt of all time." Booklist

Includes bibliographical references (p. [309]-335) and index.

Hobsbawm, E. J.

The age of revolution 1789-1848. Vintage Books 1996 356p il map pa $15.95 **940.2**

1. Industries -- History 2. Europe -- History -- 1789-1900

ISBN 978-0-679-77253-8; 0-679-77253-7

First published 1962 by World Pub. Co.

"This book traces the transformation of the world between 1789 and 1848 insofar as it was due to what is here called the 'dual revolution'—the French Revolution of 1789 and the contemporaneous (British) Industrial Revolution." Preface

Includes bibliographical references

King, David

Vienna, 1814; how the conquerors of Napoleon made love, war, and peace at the Congress of Vienna. Harmony Books 2008 434p il $27.50 **940.2**

1. Congress of Vienna (1814-1815) 2. Europe -- History -- 1789-1815 3. Europe -- Politics and government

ISBN 978-0-307-33716-0; 0-307-33716-2

LC 2007-24680

"The conquerors of Napoleon were in a festive mood when they met in Vienna in the fall of 1814 to decide the fate of Europe. . . . [The author] does a superb job of evoking the bedazzling social scene that served as the backdrop to the Congress of Vienna. His characterizations of such luminaries as Czar Alexander, Metternich, Talleyrand, and Castlereagh are lucid and thoroughly grounded in primary sources. . . . This is a worthy contribution to the study of a critical historical event long neglected by historians." Libr J

Includes bibliographical references

Lieven, D. C. B.

Russia against Napoleon; the true story of the campaigns of War and Peace. [by] Dominic Lieven. Viking 2010 617p il map $35.95 **940.2**

1. Emperors 2. Russia -- History 3. Europe -- History -- 1789-1815 4. Napoleonic Wars, 1800-1815 -- Campaigns -- Russia

ISBN 978-0-670-02157-4

LC 2009-42564

First published 2009 in the United Kingdom

"Lieven's book is lucid, engaging and reflects his deep love for Russia. This is a fascinating, exhaustively researched work, an elegant handling of a welter of confusing sources and a vital account of Russia from 1807 to 1814 that is unlikely to be bettered." Hist Today

Includes bibliographical references

Manchester, William

A world lit only by fire; the medieval mind and the Renaissance: portrait of an age. Little, Brown 1992 318p il maps hardcover o.p. pa $15.95 **940.2**

1. Explorers 2. Renaissance

ISBN 0-316-54556-2 pa

LC 91-39928

The author covers "the tumultuous span from the Dark Ages to the dawn of the Renaissance. He delineates an age when invisible spirits infested the air, when tolerance was seen as treachery and 'a mafia of profane popes desecrated Christianity.' Besides re-creating the arduous lives of ordinary people, . . . {Manchester] peoples his tapestry with such figures as Leonardo, Machiavelli, Lucrezia Borgia, Erasmus, Luther, Henry VIII and Anne Boleyn." Publ Wkly

Includes bibliographical references

Mostert, Noel

The line upon a wind; the great war at sea, 1793-1815. W.W. Norton & Co. 2008 xxv, 774p il map $35 **940.2**

1. Naval history 2. Seafaring life 3. Europe -- History -- 1789-1900 4. France -- History -- 1799-1815

ISBN 978-0-393-06653-1; 0-393-06653-3

LC 2007-39313

First published 2007 in the United Kingdom

"This is a vast, fast-moving chronicle that ranges across great distances while examining a host of characters, both well known and relatively obscure. Mostert does justifiably place great emphasis on Admiral Nelson and the critical battle at Trafalgar. He also offers useful and interesting descriptions of less-prominent aspects of the wars, including conflicts with the Barbary pirates and the British struggles against the rise of American naval power. This is an outstanding survey of a prolonged struggle that helped shape world history." Booklist

Includes bibliographical references (p. 748-752)

O'Brien, Michael

Mrs. Adams in winter; a journey in the last days of Napoleon. Farrar, Straus and Giroux 2010 364p il map $27 **940.2**

1. Presidents 2. Senators 3. Members of Congress 4. Secretaries of state 5. Spouses of presidents 6. Europe -- History -- 1789-1815 7. Europe -- Description and travel

ISBN 978-0-374-21581-1; 0-374-21581-2

LC 2009-25437

The author "pursues Louisa Adams's 40-day trek through a Europe in the process of transformation. The Mrs. Adams in question is not to be confused with Abigail Adams, the Colonial matriarch and wife of the second president. Rather, Louisa Catherine Adams was her London-born daughter-in-law, the wife to Abigail's son John Quincy Adams. . . . O'Brien's narrative is richly contextual, encompassing not only the great personalities of the age, whom Mrs. Adams met, but penetrating the secrets of a complicated marriage. A wide-sweeping historical survey and original intellectual journey." Kirkus

Includes bibliographical references

Pagden, Anthony

The **Enlightenment**; and why it still matters. Anthony Pagden. 1st ed. Random House 2013 xx, 501 p.p ill. (ebook) $85.00; (hardcover) $30.00 **940.2**

1. Enlightenment

ISBN 1400060680; 9780679645313; 9781400060689

LC 2012043848

This book, by Anthony Pagden, "takes a fresh look at the revolutionary intellectual movement that laid the foundation for the modern world. Liberty and equality. Human rights. Freedom of thought and expression. Belief in reason and progress. The value of scientific inquiry. These are just some of the ideas that were conceived and developed during the Enlightenment, and which changed forever the intellectual landscape of the Western world." (Publisher's note)

Includes bibliographical references (pages   ) and index

Pocock, Tom

The **terror** before Trafalgar; Nelson, Napoleon and the secret war. Naval Institute Press 2005 255p il map pa $16.95 **940.2**

1. Admirals 2. Emperors 3. Europe -- History -- 1789-1815

ISBN 978-1-5911-4681-0; 1-5911-4681-X

LC 2004-58185

First published 2003 by Norton

The author "retells the story of the four years in which the French confidently prepared to invade Britain, overrun its army, take out its armaments and replace the government with something easier to control. . . . Pocock's little book . . . gives a chilling insight into ineffectual undercover operations and groundbreaking weaponry: rockets, torpedos, submarines, airships and the construction of an undersea tunnel, all so far ahead of their time that none turned out in the end to be much use in practical terms to either side." N Y Times Book Rev

Includes bibliographical references

Pope, Stephen

★ **Dictionary** of the Napoleonic wars. Facts on File 2000 572p $71.50 **940.2**

1. Reference books 2. Europe -- History -- 1789-1815 -- Dictionaries

ISBN 0-8160-4243-8

LC 99-48829

Pope "has produced more than 1000 alphabetical entries, supplemented by 30 maps, detailing nearly every aspect of Napoleonic warfare. From broad subjects such as strategy, tactics, diplomacy, and propaganda to specific battles, treaties, weapons, naval warfare, and myriad colorful personalities, the book offers a wealth of succinct information." Libr J

The **Renaissance;** an encyclopedia for students. [edited by] Paul F. Grendler. Charles Scribner's Sons 2003 4v set $395 **940.2**

1. Reference books 2. Renaissance -- Encyclopedias

ISBN 0-684-31281-6

LC 2003-15672

Adaptation of Encyclopedia of the Renaissance, published 1999

This encyclopedia includes articles on various aspects of social, cultural, and political history such as literature, government, warfare, and technology, plus maps, charts, definitions, and chronology

"Researchers should find their needs more than satisfied by this appealing and student-friendly resource." SLJ

Renaissance Society of America

Encyclopedia of the Renaissance; Paul F. Grendler, editor in chief. Scribner 1999 6v set $750 **940.2**

1. Reference books 2. Renaissance -- Encyclopedias

ISBN 0-684-80514-6

LC 99-48290

ALA RUSA Dartmouth Medal (2000)

This set covers "aspects of the Renaissance from the origins of humanism in Italy (ca. 1350) through 1750. . . . The encyclopedia's strength lies in its scholarship and in the comprehensiveness and diversity of its scope." Booklist

Reston, James

Defenders of the faith; Charles V, Suleyman the Magnificent, and the battle for Europe, 1520-1536. Penguin Press 2009 xxi, 407p il map $29.95 **940.2**

1. Emperors 2. Holy Roman Empire 3. Sultans 4. Turkey -- History -- Ottoman Empire, 1288-1918

ISBN 978-1-59420-225-4

LC 2008-54655

The author focuses on "Ottoman sultan Suleyman the Magnificent's attempted Islamic conquest of Austria and Hungary, which culminated in battles at Vienna in 1529 and 1532." Booklist

"Fast-paced and engaging, this is excellent reading for popular audiences." Libr J

Includes bibliographical references

Roberts, Andrew

Waterloo : June 18, 1815; the battle for modern Europe. HarperCollins 2005 143p il maps (Making history) $21.95; pa $12.95   **940.2**
1. Waterloo, Battle of, 1815
ISBN 0-06-008866-4; 0-06-076215-2 pa
LC 2005-282517

This is a study of the defeat of Napoleon's army at the Battle of Waterloo in June, 1815.

The author "instills an appreciation for Waterloo as a horrific experience saturated with alternative possible outcomes. A must for the military shelf." Booklist

Includes bibliographical references (p. 135-136)

Talty, Stephan

The **illustrious** dead; the terrifying story of how typhus killed Napoleon's greatest army. Crown Publishers 2009 315p map $27   **940.2**
1. Typhus 2. Emperors 3. Europe -- History -- 1789-1815 4. France -- History -- 1799-1815
ISBN 978-0-307-39404-0
LC 2008-50646

The author "examines how typhus became the primary killer in Napoleon's disastrous 1812 invasion of Russia." Kirkus

"Talty delivers a breezy, popular account of a gruesome campaign, emphasizing the equally gruesome epidemic that accompanied it." Publ Wkly

Includes bibliographical references

Vincent, Edgar

Nelson; love & fame. Yale Univ. Press 2003 640p il map $35; pa $19.95   **940.2**
1. Admirals 2. Great Britain -- Royal Navy
ISBN 0-300-09797-2; 0-300-10260-7 pa
LC 2002-14566

"Nelson is a masterly biography, cool and sharp in long shots, intimately persuasive in close focus, at all times difficult to put down and as timely as it is suggestive in its implications." N Y Times Book Rev

Includes bibliographical references

Wells, C. M.

Sailing from Byzantium; how a lost empire shaped the world. Colin Wells. Delacorte Press 2006 xxx, 335p map $22   **940.2**
1. Byzantine Empire
ISBN 0-553-80381-6
LC 2006-42665

The author "considers how Byzantium, the Eastern, Greek-language Roman Empire of the Middle Ages, influenced three successor civilizations Western Europe, Islam, and the eastern Slavic world of the Balkans and Russia. . . .

This history is a needed reminder of the debt that three of our major civilizations owe to Byzantium." Libr J

Includes bibliographical references

Wilson, Ellen Judy

★ **Encyclopedia** of the Enlightenment; Peter Hanns Reill, consulting editor; Ellen Judy Wilson, principal author. rev ed; Facts on File 2004 670p $75   **940.2**
1. Reference books 2. Europe -- Intellectual life 3. Philosophy -- Encyclopedias 4. Enlightenment -- Encyclopedias
ISBN 0-8160-5335-9
LC 2003-22973

First published 1996

This reference provides a "review of the important ideas, people, and events that shaped the world during the Enlightenment. [It] covers the major changes in science, education, philosophy, art and architecture, and politics which took place during the 17th and 18th centuries and led to the birth of the modern era. . . . The biographical entries cover such notables as Robespierre, Schiller, Fielding, Kant, and Voltaire. . . . Larger public, school, and academic libraries looking for a comprehensive overview of the subject for the student or interested reader will find this a valuable and accessible resource." Libr J

Includes bibliographical references

Wilson, Peter H.

The **Thirty** Years War; Europe's tragedy. Belknap Press of Harvard University Press 2009 xxii, 996p il map $35   **940.2**
1. Thirty Years' War, 1618-1648
ISBN 978-0-674-03634-5
LC 2009-11266

For this "narrative of the 1618-48 wars that devastated central Europe, historian Wilson advances three theses: the wars were not inevitable, were not primarily about religion, and were mostly about the constitution of the Holy Roman Empire." Booklist

This "is a history of prodigious erudition that manages to corral the byzantine complexity of the Thirty Years War into a coherent narrative." Wall Street J

Includes bibliographical references

Zamoyski, Adam

Rites of peace; the fall of Napoleon and the Congress of Vienna. HarperColins 2007 634p il map $29.95   **940.2**
1. Congress of Vienna (1814-1815) 2. Europe -- History -- 1789-1815
ISBN 0-06-077518-1; 978-0-06-077518-6

"This sequel to Zamoyski's . . . Moscow 1812 (2004) shifts from military to diplomatic affairs surrounding the defeat of Napoleonic France and the disposal of its empire. Zamoyski narrates their course from 1813, when Russia's Alexander I decided to continue the war rather than settle with Napoleon, to 1815 and the latter's final Waterloo." Booklist

This "book is old-fashioned, impressively detailed diplomatic history." Economist

Includes bibliographical references

940.3   World War I, 1914-1918

Audoin-Rouzeau, Stephane

14 -18, understanding the Great War; {by} Stéphane Audoin-Rouzeau and Annette Becker; translated from the French by Catherine Temerson. Hill & Wang 2002 280p $24; pa $14   **940.3**
   1. World War, 1914-1918
   ISBN 0-8090-4642-3; 0-8090-4643-1 pa
                                                LC 2002-111422
Original French edition, 2000
   "The authors take an anthropological approach to the cataclysm that engulfed Europe in 1914 and examine three significant aspects of the war: violence, crusade, and mourning. . . . Supported by contemporary documentation, this unique work will become a classic study." Libr J
   Includes bibliographical references

Burg, David F.

Almanac of World War I; [by] David F. Burg and L. Edward Purcell; introduction by William Manchester. University Press of Ky. 1998 320p il maps hardcover o.p. pa $22   **940.3**
   1. World War, 1914-1918
   ISBN 0-8131-2072-1; 0-8131-9087-8 pa
                                                LC 98-26625
   "The bulk of the text is arranged chronologically by year and date, listing almost daily occurrences from 1914 through 1918. . . . The work is international in scope, covering political and military happenings from around the world. . . . There is really nothing comparable to this volume." Booklist
   Includes bibliographical references

Carter, Miranda

George, Nicholas, and Wilhelm; three royal cousins and the road to World War I. Alfred A. Knopf 2010 498p il map $30   **940.3**
   1. Emperors 2. Kings 3. Biography, Individual 4. World War, 1914-1918 -- Causes 5. Europe -- Politics and government -- 1871-1918
   ISBN 978-1-4000-4363-7; 1-4000-4363-8
                                                LC 2009-37690
First published 2009 in the United Kingdom with title: The three emperors
   In the years before World War I, the great European powers were ruled by three first cousins: King George V, Kaiser Wilhelm II, and Tsar Nicholas II. Carter uses the cousins' correspondence and a host of historical sources to tell their tragicomic stories.
   The author "writes with lusty humour at times, has a fresh clarifying intelligence when unravelling knotty problems of ancien régime life and a sharp eye for telling details about people's gestures, temper, appearance and attitudes. . . . This is traditional narrative history with a 21st-century zing—a real corker of a book." Hist Today
   Includes bibliographical references

Clark, Christopher

The **sleepwalkers**; how Europe went to war in 1914. Christopher Clark. Harper 2013 697 p. $29.99   **940.3**
   1. Europe -- History -- 1871-1918 2. World War, 1914-1918 -- Causes 3. World War, 1914-1918 -- Diplomatic history 4. Europe -- Politics and government -- 1871-1918
   ISBN 006114665X; 9780061146657
                                                LC 2012038473
   In this book on the origins of World War I, author Christopher Clark "posits a bad brew of diplomatic contingencies and individual agency as the cause. . . . Clark . . . begins by describing the interactions of Serbia and Austria-Hungary, which sparked the conflict. He presents the former as a 'raw and fragile democracy' whose 'turbulent' politics challenged a neighboring empire held together by habit. Indeed, the instability across Europe further polarized alliance networks." (Publishers Weekly)
   Includes bibliographical references and index

The **Encyclopedia** of World War I; a political, social, and military history. ABC-CLIO 2005 5v il map set $485   **940.3**
   1. Reference books 2. World War, 1914-1918 -- Encyclopedias
   ISBN 1-85109-420-2
                                                LC 2005-22937
   This set opens with "four essays discussing the origins, outbreak, overview, and legacy of the war. They are followed by alphabetical entries on virtually every aspect of the conflict, including battles, people, military equipment and strategies, and social and political changes associated with it." SLJ
   Includes bibliographical references

Englund, Peter

★ The **beauty** and the sorrow; an intimate history of the First World War. translated by Peter Graves. Alfred A. Knopf 2011 540p il $35   **940.3**
   1. World War, 1914-1918 -- Personal narratives
   ISBN 978-0-307-59386-3; 0-307-59386-X
                                                LC 2011-20828
Original Swedish edition, 2009
   This work "threads together the wartime experiences of 20 more or less unremarkable men and women, on both sides of the war, from schoolgirls and botanists to mountain climbers, doctors, ambulance drivers and clerks. A few of these people will become heroes. A few will become prisoners of war, or lose limbs, go mad or die. . . . Mr. Englund's book is a deviation from standard history books. It is a corrective too to the notion that World War I was only about the dire trench warfare on the Western Front. . . . [It] expertly pans across other theaters of war: the Alps, the Balkans, the Eastern Front, Mesopotamia, East Africa." N Y Times Book Rev
   Includes bibliographical references

Gilbert, Martin

The **First** World War; a complete history. Holt & Co. 1994 xxiv, 615p il maps hardcover o.p. pa $25   **940.3**

1. World War, 1914-1918

ISBN 0-8050-1540-X; 0-8050-7617-4 pa

LC 94-27268

This work "covers WW I on all major fronts—domestic, diplomatic, military—as well as such bloody preludes as the Armenian massacre of 1915." Publ Wkly

"What Mr. Gilbert seeks to do, and frequently succeeds in doing, is to humanize, indeed to personalize, World War I. His effort and accomplishment make this a rewarding and significant book." N Y Times Book Rev

Includes bibliographical references

Grant, R. G.

World War I; The Definitive Visual History : from Sarajevo to Versailles. R. G. Grant. Dk Pub. 2014 360 p. ill. (some color), color maps $40 **940.3**

1. Weapons -- History 2. World War, 1914-1918

ISBN 1465419381; 9781465419385

LC 2013387827

"Written by historian R. G. Grant, and created by DK's award-winning editorial and design team, World War I charts the . . . war. . . . Using illustrated timelines, detailed maps, and personal accounts, readers will see the oft-studied war in a new light. Key episodes are set clearly in the wider context of the conflict, in-depth profiles look at the key generals and political leaders, and full-color photo galleries showcase . . . weapons, inventions, and new technologies." (Publisher's note)

"This is a broad, moving, informative account of the war that's perfect for both the young, budding historian and the well-versed WWI reader." Pub Wkly

Hastings, Max

Catastrophe 1914; Europe goes to war. by Max Hastings. Alfred A. Knopf 2013 672 p. (hardback) $35   **940.3**

1. Europe -- History -- 1871-1918 2. World War, 1914-1918 -- Causes 2. Europe -- History -- July Crisis, 1914

ISBN 0307597059; 9780307597052; 9780307743831

LC 2013027865

Author Max Hastings "traces the path to [World War I] making clear why Germany and Austria-Hungary were primarily to blame, and describes the gripping first clashes in the West, where the French army marched into action. Hastings gives us frank assessments of generals and political leaders. He argues passionately against the contention that the war was not worth the cost, maintaining that Germany's defeat was vital to the freedom of Europe." (Publisher's note)

"...After many accounts of World War II, the veteran military historian tries his hand, with splendid results. Most readers will be familiar with many of the facts...Who's to blame? Hastings loves Barbara Tuchman's 1962 classic The Guns of August but agrees that her verdict—everything got out of hand; it was no one's fault—is passé. Hastings shows modest respect for the German school, which blames Germany; historian Sean McMeekin, who emphasizes Russia's role; and even Niall Ferguson, who believes that Britain should have remained neutral. He concludes that national leaders (mediocrities all, with a few frank dimwits) focused with paranoid intensity on selfish interests, that stupidity trumped malevolence, and that German paranoia won by a nose...Readers accustomed to Hastings' vivid battle descriptions, incisive anecdotes from all participants, and shrewd, often unsettling opinions will not be disappointed. Among the plethora of brilliant accounts of this period, this is one of the best." (Kirkus)

Includes bibliographical references (pages 595-603) and index

Hochschild, Adam

To end all wars; a story of loyalty and rebellion, 1914-1918. Houghton Mifflin Harcourt 2011 xx, 448p map $28; ebook $28   **940.3**

1. Pacifism 2. Soldiers -- Great Britain 3. World War, 1914-1918 -- Great Britain 4. World War, 1914-1918 -- Social aspects 5. World War, 1914-1918 -- Psychological aspects 6. World War, 1914-1918 -- Conscientious objectors

ISBN 978-0-618-75828-9; 0-618-75828-3; 978-0-54754-921-7 ebook; 0-54754-921-0 ebook

LC 2010-25836

Hochschild focuses "on the British experience. Moving from the western front to the home front, he counterposes two story lines: . . . one about those who opposed the war, the other about the warriors and politicians who carried it out." Bookforum

"An ambitious narrative that presents a teeming worldview through intimate, human portraits." Kirkus

Includes bibliographical references=

MacMillan, Margaret

Paris 1919; six months that changed the world. Random House 2002 560p $35; pa $16.95   **940.3**

1. Governors 2. Presidents 3. College presidents 4. Treaty of Versailles 5. Nobel laureates for peace 6. World War, 1914-1918 -- Peace 7. Germany -- History -- 1918-1933 8. Paris Peace Conference (1919-1920)

ISBN 0-375-50826-0; 0-375-76052-0 pa

LC 2002-23707

First published 2001 in the United Kingdom with title: Peacemakers

The author examines the Paris Peace Conference of 1919. Economist John Maynard Keynes blamed "the failure of the conference on the vindictiveness of the French in general and of Clemenceau in particular. Margaret MacMillan . . . argues that the conference has been blamed for many disasters that were, in fact, determined either by events that took place before it began or by later troubles." (Economist) Index.

"MacMillan's lucid prose brings her participants to colorful and quotable life, and the grand sweep of her narrative encompasses all the continents the peacemakers vainly carved up." Publ Wkly

Includes bibliographical references

McMeekin, Sean

★ The **Berlin** -Baghdad express; the Ottoman Empire and Germany's bid for world power. The

Belknap Press of Harvard University Press 2010 460p il map **940.3**
1. Jihad 2. Railroads 3. Geopolitics 4. World War, 1914-1918 5. Germany -- Foreign relations -- Turkey 6. Turkey -- Foreign relations -- Germany
ISBN 0-0674-05739-2; 978-0-674-05739-5

LC 2010019199

"Germany saw the ambitious Berlin-to-Baghdad railway as a powerful tool to win World War I. But the doomed project wasn't completed until 1940. The railway debacle provides a colorful backdrop for historian McMeekin's look at the Great War from the German-Turk perspective; as a cast of ruthless characters illustrate Germany's attempt to topple what was then the largest Middle East power: the British Empire." N Y Post

Includes bibliographical references

★ **July** 1914; countdown to war. Sean McMeekin. Basic Books, a member of the Perseus Books Group 2013 xviii, 461 p.p ill. (hardcover) $29.99 **940.3**
1. Austria -- History 2. World War, 1914-1918 -- Causes 3. Europe -- History -- July Crisis, 1914
ISBN 0465031455; 9780465031450

LC 2012049777

This book is a "political history of the weeks between the assassination of Austria's Archduke Franz Ferdinand and the beginning of World War I. . . . Relying on extensive research in numerous archives, as well as diaries and correspondence from key national leaders, [Sean] McMeekin examines the intricacies of Austrian politics and diplomacy." (Publishers Weekly)

Includes bibliographical references and index.

Slotkin, Richard, 1942-
Lost battalions; the Great War and the crisis of American nationality. Richard Slotkin. H. Holt 2005 639p il maps **940.3**
1. Minorities -- United States 2. African American soldiers -- History 3. World War, 1914-1918 -- United States 4. United States -- Army -- Infantry Regiment, 369th 5. United States -- Army -- Infantry Division, 77th -- Joint Assault Signal Company, 292nd
ISBN 0-8050-4124-9

LC 2005-46312

Slotkin "follows the Negro soldiers of the 369th and the Jewish, Italian, and other immigrants of the 77th into conflict." (Publisher's note) Index.

Stone, Norman
★ **World** War One. Basic Books 2009 226p il map $25 **940.3**
1. World War, 1914-1918
ISBN 978-0-465-01368-5; 0-465-01368-6
First published 2007 in the United Kingdom
The author presents a narrative history of the First World War.

"Stone is as unconventional as he is brilliant, and this provocative interpretation of the Great War combines impressive command of the literature with a telling eye for

relevant facts and a sensitive ear for telling epigrams." Publ Wkly

Includes bibliographical references

Strachan, Hew
The **First** World War. Viking 2004 364p il maps hardcover o.p. pa $16 **940.3**
1. World War, 1914-1918
ISBN 0-14-303518-5 pa; 0-670-03295-6

LC 2003-62191

This book examines "the causes, the major campaigns, and the consequences of the First World War." (Publisher's note) Index.

"Readers already familiar with the sequence of events in strict order will benefit most. But all readers will eventually be gripped, and even the most seasoned ones will praise the insights and the original choice of illustrations." Publ Wkly

Includes bibliographical references

Tuchman, Barbara Wertheim
★ The **guns** of August; [by] Barbara W. Tuchman; [with a new foreword by Robert K. Massie] 1st Ballantine Books ed; Ballantine 1994 xxiv, 511p il, maps pa $14 **940.3**
1. World War, 1914-1918
ISBN 0-345-38623-X

LC 93-90461

First published 1962 by Macmillan
A history of the negotiations that preceded World War I and the course of the war's first month.

Includes bibliographical references

The **Zimmermann** telegram. Ballantine Books 1985 244p il pa $14 **940.3**
1. World War, 1914-1918 -- Causes
ISBN 0-345-32425-0

LC 84-91737

First published 1958 by Macmillan
The author discusses the German plan to induce Mexico to attack the U.S. during World War I.

Includes bibliographical references

The **United** States in the First World War; an encyclopedia. editor, Anne Cipriano Venzon; consulting editor, Paul L. Miles. Garland 1995 xx, 830p maps (Garland reference library of the humanities) $155; pa $45 **940.3**
1. Reference books 2. World War, 1914-1918 -- Encyclopedias
ISBN 0-8240-7055-0; 0-8153-3353-6 pa

LC 95-1782

"Biography, economics, civil rights, women's issues, foreign relations, battles, armaments, and conferences are among the topics included. Arrangement is alphabetical, and most articles are brief—between one column and a page. . . . Most articles include brief bibliographies. There are six maps, but no other illustrations." Libr J

Woodward, David R.

World War I almanac. Facts On File 2009 554p il map (Almanacs of American wars) $95   **940.3**
 1. Almanacs 2. Reference books 3. World War, 1914-1918
 ISBN 978-0-8160-7134-0; 978-1-4381-1896-3 ebook
LC 2008-41575

This almanac covers "all geographic areas affected by the conflict and all belligerents. The day-by-day chronicle, with topical headings within each date, forms the main section of the Almanac. The chronology spans 1871-1923. It includes the main events of the war and its aftermath, including major battles, domestic politics, the Russian Revolution, the periods of American neutrality (1914-17), belligerency on the side of the Allies (1917-18), the Paris Peace Conference, and President Wilson's battle for the League of Nations." Choice

This book "would be a welcome addition to public, school, and academic libraries where a student needs to find basic information quickly." Booklist

Includes glossary and bibliographical references

World War I; a history. edited by Hew Strachan. Oxford Univ. Press 1999 356p il maps hardcover o.p. pa $28.95   **940.3**
 1. World War, 1914-1918
 ISBN 0-19-820614-3; 978-0-19-289325-3 pa; 0-19-289325-4 pa
LC 97-44997

First published 1998 in the United Kingdom with title: The Oxford illustrated history of the First World War

"Strachan has commissioned 20 historians to summarize present thought about the July 1914 crisis, the military course of the war, the social and economic strains it exerted in all the belligerents, and its conclusion in revolutions and treaties. . . . Readers will find this comprehensive work a captivating introduction to the Great War." Booklist

Includes bibliographical references

940.4   Military history of World War I

Anderson, Scott, 1959-

Lawrence in Arabia; war, deceit, imperial folly and the making of the modern Middle East. Scott Anderson. Doubleday 2013 592 p. $28.95   **940.4**
 1. Middle East -- History 2. Great Britain. Army -- Biography 3. Middle East -- History -- 1914-1923 4. Soldiers -- Great Britain -- Biography 5. World War, 1914-1918 -- Campaigns -- Turkey 6. World War, 1914-1918 -- Campaigns -- Middle East
 ISBN 038553292X; 9780385532921
LC 2012049719

In this biography of Lawrence of Arabia, Scott Anderson "reasons that 'Lawrence was both eyewitness to and participant in some of the most pivotal events leading to the creation of the modern Middle East . . . a corner of the earth where even the simplest assertion is dissected and parsed and argued over.' Too many biographers of Lawrence, he suggests, have let political biases and academic hobbyhorses overshadow their work." (Publishers Weekly)

Includes bibliographical references

Dallas, Gregor

1918 : war and peace. Overlook Press 2001 616p $40; pa $19.95   **940.4**
 1. World War, 1914-1918 -- Peace
 ISBN 1-58567-157-6; 1-58567-319-6 pa
LC 2001-21104

The author discusses how the First World War ended. He examines "how the ceasefire was arranged, who the major participants were, and how the general population learned about the armistice." Libr J

Dallas "provides a meticulously detailed and intensive study of the years 1918-1919." Publ Wkly

Includes bibliographical references

Dyer, Geoff

The **missing** of the Somme; Geoff Dyer. Vintage Books 2011 176p.   **940.4**
 1. Memory 2. Veterans 3. World War, 1914-1918
 ISBN 9780307742971; 9780307743237
LC 2002327412

This book offers an "exploration of the meaning and formal remembrance of British participation in World War I. . . . [Author Geoff] Dyer argues that our perceptions of the WWI are shaped by impressions of the war presented through the literature and public statuary (and, to a lesser degree, photography) produced within 15 years of the Armistice. The dominant theme of these cultural works is . . . sacrifice as a virtue in itself and its formal remembrance, and he believes this was evident even in works produced at the very beginning of the war. . . . Dyer intertwines the story of his travels with two friends to visit monuments and military cemeteries of the Western Front with . . . observations on statuary by Charles Sargeant Jagger, the poetry of Wilfred Owen and the literary criticism of Paul Fussell, among others." (Kirkus)

Eisenhower, John S. D.

Yanks : the epic story of the American Army in World War I; {by} John S. D. Eisenhower with Joanne Thompson Eisenhower. Free Press 2001 353p il maps hardcover o.p. pa $16   **940.4**
 1. United States -- Army 2. World War, 1914-1918 -- Campaigns
 ISBN 0-684-86304-9; 0-7432-2385-3 pa
LC 2001-23124

"This history focuses entirely on the challenges, victories, sacrifices . . . and long-term consequences of the American Expeditionary Force (AEF) in Europe during World War I." Libr J

"This is an important work that should help alter the historical picture of the American role in the conflict." Booklist

Includes bibliographical references

Farwell, Byron

Over there; the United States in the Great War, 1917-1918. Norton 1999 336p $27.95; pa $15.95   **940.4**
 1. World War, 1914-1918 -- United States
 ISBN 0-393-04698-2; 0-393-32028-6 pa
LC 98-35705

This history of American intervention in World War I focuses primarily on the military aspects of the war but also discusses its social and economic impact

"This title does provide good coverage on the intervention in Russia and the role of women in the war, notably the 'Hello Girls.' " Libr J

Includes bibliographical references

Harries, Meirion

The **last** days of innocence; America at war, 1917-1918. {by} Meirion and Susie Harries. Random House 1997 573p il hardcover o.p. pa $16 **940.4**
1. World War, 1914-1918 -- United States
ISBN 0-679-74376-6 pa
LC 96-21756
"This is an excellent study of US participation in WWI. The research is in far greater depth than the usual 'popular history,' the analysis is sharp and informative, and the writing is clear and a pleasure to read. The authors strike an even balance between necessity for condensation and the accuracy that comes from detailed treatment." Choice

Includes bibliographical references

Hart, Peter

The **Somme**; the darkest hour on the Western Front. Pegasus Books 2008 589p il map $35; pa $17.95 **940.4**
1. World War, 1914-1918 -- Campaigns -- France
ISBN 978-1-60598-016-4; 1-60598-016-1; 978-1-60598-081-2 pa; 1-60598-081-1 pa
First published 2005 in the United Kingdom

This is an "account of the Somme offensive. . . . [The author evokes] the horrors of combat on the western front, skillfully blending these personal accounts with strategic considerations of a battle that slaughtered nearly a million French, German, and British soldiers. . . . Military history at its best." Libr J

Includes bibliographical references

Herwig, Holger H.

The **Marne,** 1914; the opening of World War I and the battle that changed the world. Random House 2009 391p il map $28 **940.4**
1. World War, 1914-1918 -- Campaigns -- France
ISBN 9781400066711; 1-4000-6671-9
LC 2009-5687
This fine history of World War I's opening battle argues persuasively that it was decisive in setting the pattern for the war, a pattern that made World War II inevitable. . . . Herwig's research has been exhaustive, including of archives long since thought destroyed that help him fill in a great many details about the German side. . . . As fine an addition to scholarly World War I literature as has been seen in some time. Booklist

Includes bibliographical references

Lawrence, T. E.

Seven pillars of wisdom; a triumph. Doubleday 1935 672p il maps hardcover o.p. pa $19.95 **940.4**
1. Arabs 2. Bedouins 3. Wahhabis 4. World War, 1914-1918 -- Middle East
ISBN 0-385-41895-7 pa
"Not only a history of the Arab revolt during the {First} World War, but a commentary on the national character-

istics, and political policies of Arabs, Turks and British." Cleveland Public Libr

Liddell Hart, Basil Henry

The **real** war, 1914-1918; with twenty-five maps. by B. H. Liddell Hart. Little, Brown 1930 508p maps hardcover o.p. pa $23.99 **940.4**
1. World War, 1914-1918
ISBN 0-316-52505-7 pa
A short history of World War I in which the action of the book ranges wherever Germany and the Allies locked in combat: Poland, Mesopotamia, Gallipoli, Caporetto, Baghdad, the North Sea, and the Mediterranean

Includes bibliographical references

Lussu, Emilio, 1890-1975

A **soldier** on the southern front; the classic Italian memoir of World War I. Emilio Lussu. Rizzoli Ex Libris 2014 278 p. (alk. paper) $26.95 **940.4**
1. Autobiographies 2. World War, 1914-1918 -- Campaigns -- Italy 3. World War, 1914-1918 -- Personal narratives
ISBN 0847842789; 9780847842780
LC 2013943440
Written by Emilio Lussu, translated by Gregory Conti, this memoir is "a rediscovered Italian masterpiece chronicling the author's experience as an infantryman, newly translated and reissued to commemorate the centennial of World War I. . . . A classic in Italy but virtually unknown in the English-speaking world, it reveals . . . the almost farcical side of the war as seen by a Sardinian officer fighting the Austrian army on the Asiago plateau in northeastern Italy." (Publisher's note)

A "compelling read that enters the mind of a man at the front, exposed daily to terrible scenes and decisions that change who he is." LJ

Massie, Robert K.

Castles of steel; Britain, Germany, and the winning of the Great War at sea. Random House 2003 865p il map pa $17.95; $35 **940.4**
1. Germany -- Kriegsmarine 2. Great Britain -- Royal Navy 3. World War, 1914-1918 -- Naval operations
ISBN 0-345-40878-0 pa; 0-679-45671-6
LC 2003-41373
Focusing on Britain's Grand Fleet and Germany's High Seas Fleet, Massie examines the role of sea power in determining the outcome of the First World War. Index.

The author "makes a coherent if long narrative out of a sequence of events familiar to students of naval history but probably not to many other potential readers." Publ Wkly

Millman, Chad

The **detonators**; the secret plot to destroy America and an epic hunt for justice. Little, Brown 2006 330p il map $24.99 **940.4**
1. Sabotage 2. World War, 1914-1918 -- United States
ISBN 978-0-316-73496-7; 0-316-73496-9
LC 2005-24401
"In 1916, a group of German agents blew up an ammunition warehouse on Black Tom Island in New York Harbor near the Jersey shore. The explosion destroyed thousands of

tons of munitions destined for France, shattered windows all over lower Manhattan, and triggered a 23-year legal battle. . . . [The author describes] the sabotage ring's effects. His story then shifts to the legal battle, after World War I, to assess the damages and determine whether Germany's Weimar Republic was responsible." Libr J

"With its obvious contemporary resonance, Millman's able account of an earlier foreign attack on America should draw the espionage audience and more." Booklist

Includes bibliographical references

Mosier, John

The **myth** of the Great War; a new military history of World War I. HarperCollins Pubs. 2001 381p il hardcover o.p. pa $14.95   **940.4**

1. World War, 1914-1918 -- Campaigns
ISBN 0-06-019676-9; 0-06-008433-2 pa

LC 00-46103

"After dissecting the major campaigns on the western front, Mosier concludes that Germany's ultimate defeat was the direct result of the influx of American soldiers into France in 1917 and 1918. . . . This is revisionist history that convincingly smashes the myths that Allied governments, leaders, and propagandists worked so hard to promulgate. Mosier's masterful account is a welcome addition." Booklist

Includes bibliographical references

Neiberg, Michael

★ **Fighting** the Great War; a global history. [by] Michael S. Neiberg. Harvard University Press 2005 xx, 395p il map $27.95   **940.4**

1. World War, 1914-1918
ISBN 0-674-01696-3

LC 2004-54330

In this history of World War I, the author "develops military explanations for its continuation in the face of apparent futility." Booklist

"Readers interested in a general overview of WW I can do no better than Neiberg's excellent account." Choice

Includes bibliographical references

Ousby, Ian

The **road** to Verdun; World War I's most momentous battle and the folly of nationalism. Doubleday 2002 393p il maps $30; pa $16   **940.4**

1. World War, 1914-1918 -- Campaigns
ISBN 0-385-50393-8; 0-385-72173-0 pa

LC 2002-19475

This is a study of the Battle of Verdun which "killed 700,000 French and German soldiers, 10% of all those killed in the war. Yet a sense of glory was maintained, however inappropriately, amid the gore: the road leading to the battlefield was called the Sacred Way, and the French General Neville gained immortality by his brave statement, 'They {the Germans} shall not pass.'" Publ Wkly

Paice, Edward

World War I: the African Front. Pegasus 2008 xxxix, 488p il map $35   **940.4**

1. World War, 1914-1918 -- Campaigns -- East Africa
ISBN 978-1-933648-90-3

This "history of the World War I African campaigns focuses on the Allied efforts—ultimately unsuccessful and at great human cost—to root out a stubborn German colonial force." Libr J

"An authoritative summing-up of a grim, complex and little-known part of World War I." Kirkus

Includes bibliographical references

Philpott, William

Three armies on the Somme; the first battle of the twentieth century. [by] William Philpott. Alfred A. Knopf 2010 631p il map $35; ebook $35 **940.4**

1. Germany -- Heer 2. France -- Armée 3. Great Britain -- Army 4. World War, 1914-1918 -- Campaigns -- France
ISBN 978-0-307-26585-2; 978-0-307-59372-6 ebook

LC 2010-4070

First published 2009 in the United Kingdom with title: Bloody victory

"The Battle of the Somme is branded in British memory as the exemplar of WWI: a months-long cataclysm that, at the cost of monumental casualties, repelled the Germans from a few square miles of shell-blasted French countryside. This account by a descendant of an artillerist in the battle has two aims: to narrate the battle from its initial strategic concept to its sputtering-out in late 1916 and to refute historical and popular opinion about the battle. . . . Comprehensive research and convention-bucking argument qualify Philpott for the WWI shelf." Booklist

Includes bibliographical references

Sacco, Joe

The **Great** War; July 1, 1916 : the first day of the Battle of the Somme : an illustrated panorama. Joe Sacco. W.W. Norton & Co. Inc. 2013 54 p. $35   **940.4**

1. World War, 1914-1918 2. Great Britain -- Military history 3. World War, 1939-1945 -- Campaigns -- France 4. Somme, 1st Battle of the, France, 1916 5. Somme, 1st Battle of the, France, 1916 -- Comic books, strips, etc
ISBN 0393088804; 9780393088809

LC 2013010710

This art book by Joe Sacco presents "a single continuous panorama, eight inches tall and twenty-four feet long," which "illustrates, in minutely detailed black-and-white drawings, events just before and during a summer day when the British army suffered morethan fifty-seven thousand dead and wounded, its greatest single-day loss. . . . An accompanying booklet" presents a "brief account of the day by Adam Hoschchild." (Bookforum)

July 1, 1916
First day of the Battle of the Somme

Scott, R. Neil

★ **Many** were held by the sea; the tragic sinking of HMS Otranto. R. Neil Scott. Rowman & Littlefield 2012 249 p. (cloth : alk. paper) $35.00 **940.4**

1. World War, 1914-1918 -- Naval operations 2. Kashmir (Troopship) 3. Otranto (Troopship) 4. Shipwrecks -- Scotland -- Islay 5. World War, 1914-1918 -- Naval operations, British 6. World War, 1914-

1918 -- Casualties -- Great Britain 7. Transports -- Great Britain -- History -- 20th century 8. World War, 1914-1918 -- Transportation -- Great Britain 9. Marine accidents -- Great Britain -- History -- 20th century
ISBN 1442213426; 9781442213425; 9781442213449
LC 2012003033
This book by R. Neil Scott tells the story of a 1918 disaster in which the "HMS Kashmir rammed HMS Otranto off Islay, Scotland. . . . On board were 372 British officers and sailors and 701 American soldiers. . . . The Kashmir managed to back away and follow the harsh wartime order . . . to continue on her prescribed course rather than stop and take on survivors. Thus it was that . . . the severely damaged Otranto was left dead in the water with more than a thousand souls aboard." (Publisher's note)
Includes bibliographical references and index

Thompson, Mark

The **white** war; life and death on the Italian front, 1915-1919. Basic Books 2009 454p il map $30 **940.4**
1. World War, 1914-1918 -- Campaigns -- Italy
ISBN 978-0-465-01329-6; 0-465-01329-5
First published 2008 in the United Kingdom
"Penetrating study of one of the forgotten fronts of the Great War. . . . A much-needed addition to the literature of World War I." Kirkus
Includes bibliographical references

Wawro, Geoffrey

A **mad** catastrophe; the outbreak of World War I and the collapse of the Habsburg Empire. Geoffrey Wawro. Basic Books 2014 472 p. illustrations, maps (hardback) $29.99 **940.4**
1. Austria -- History 2. Hungary -- History 3. World War, 1914-1918 4. World War, 1914-1918 -- Causes 5. Austria -- History -- Franz Joseph I, 1848-1916 6. World War, 1914-1918 -- Campaigns -- Balkan Peninsula 7. World War, 1914-1918 -- Campaigns -- Galicia (Poland and Ukraine)
ISBN 0465028357; 9780465028351
LC 2013039393
"The Austro-Hungarian army that marched east and south to confront the Russians and Serbs in the opening campaigns of World War I had a glorious past but a pitiful present. . . . As prizewinning historian Geoffrey Wawro explains in 'A Mad Catastrophe,' the doomed Austrian conscripts were an unfortunate microcosm of the Austro-Hungarian Empire itself--both equally ripe for destruction." (Publisher's note)
"Wawro's authoritative account is a damning analysis of an empire and a people unready for war." Pub Wkly
Includes bibliographical references and index

Weber, Thomas

Hitler's first war; Adolf Hitler, the men of the List Regiment, and the First World War. Oxford University Press 2010 450p il $34.95 **940.4**
1. Heads of state 2. Nazi leaders 3. Soldiers -- Germany 4. World War, 1914-1918 5. Biography, Individual 6. World War, 1914-1918 -- Germany 7. World War, 1914-1918 -- Campaigns 8. Germany -- Heer -- Bayerisches

Reserve-Infanterie-Regiment 16
ISBN 0199233209; 9780199233205
"Hitler claimed that his years as a soldier in the First World War were the most formative years of his life. However, for the six decades since his death in the ruins of Berlin, Hitler's time as a soldier on the Western Front has remained a blank spot. . . . [Weber's book] looks at what really happened to Private Hitler and the men of the Bavarian List Regiment of which he was a member." (Publisher's note) Index.
"A triumph of original research in a very stony field. The conclusion that might be drawn is that Hitler was far more of the opportunist than is generally supposed. He made things up as he went along, including his own past." Wall Street J
Includes bibliographical references

940.5 Europe--1918-

Europe since 1914; encyclopedia of the age of war and reconstruction. John Merriman and Jay Winter, editors in chief. Charles Scribner's Sons/ Thomson Gale 2006 5v il map (Scribner library of modern Europe) set $595 **940.5**
1. Reference books 2. Europe -- Civilization -- Encyclopedias 3. Europe -- History -- 20th century -- Encyclopedias
ISBN 0-684-31365-0; 978-0-684-31365-8
LC 2006-14427
This encyclopedia "details European history from the Bolshevik Revolution to the European Union, linking it to the history of the rest of the world." Publisher's note
Includes bibliographical references

Linenthal, Edward Tabor

Preserving memory; the struggle to create America's Holocaust Museum. [by] Edward T. Linenthal. Columbia University Press 2001 xxiv, 336p il pa $18.50 **940.5**
1. Holocaust, 1933-1945 2. United States Holocaust Memorial Museum
ISBN 0-231-12407-4
LC 2001-37168
First published 1995 by Viking
The author "describes the 15-year effort to create a national museum commemorating the Holocaust. He begins with the creation in May 1978 of the President's Commission on the Holocaust during the Carter administration. He then covers issues related to the location, design, and construction of the museum building. Linenthal's most significant contribution is the chapter on defining and representing the horror of the Holocaust." Libr J
Includes bibliographical references

Mak, Geert

★ **In** Europe; travels through the twentieth century. translated from the Dutch by Sam Garrett. Pantheon 2007 876p map $35 **940.5**
1. Europe -- Description and travel 2. Europe -- History -- 20th century
ISBN 0-375-42495-4; 978-0-375-42495-3
LC 2007-9260

Original Dutch edition, 2004

This book recounts the author's travels through Europe and examines the history of European countries, particularly focusing on the the effects of the Treaty of Rome.

"Mak's brilliant compendium is difficult to define—is it a history book, a travelogue, a memoir?—but stands out as a remarkable, insightful, exhilarating exposition on that peculiar continent across the Atlantic." Publ Wkly

Sachar, Howard Morley

Dreamland; Europeans and Jews in the aftermath of the Great War. {by} Howard M. Sachar. Knopf 2002 385p map hardcover o.p. pa $15   **940.5**

1. Jews -- Europe 2. Europe -- History -- 1918-1945
ISBN 0-375-70829-4 pa

LC 2001-38471

An overview of Jewish life in Europe during the three decades before the Holocaust

"This scholarly analysis provides a completely original slant on the much-studied interwar period." Booklist

Includes bibliographical references

Talty, Stephan

Agent Garbo; the brilliant, eccentric secret agent who tricked Hitler and saved D-Day. Stephan Talty. Houghton Mifflin Harcourt 2012 301 p.   **940.5**

1. Spies 2. Normandy (France), Attack on, 1944 3. World War, 1939-1945 -- Secret service 4. Spies -- Great Britain -- Biography 5. World War, 1939-1945 -- Secret service -- Great Britain
ISBN 0547614810; 9780547614816

LC 2012005470

This book by Stephan Talty tells the story of "Juan Pujol, the Spanish hotel manager who, in January 1941, waltzed into the British Embassy in Madrid and announced that he wanted to help the Allied war effort. . . . Turned down by the British, Pujol came up with a stunningly audacious plan: he would approach the Germans, offer his services as a spy, gather intelligence, and then go back to the British, operating as a double agent. And here's the thing: it worked." (Booklist)

Includes bibliographical references (pages [281]-283) and index

940.53   World War II, 1939-1945

Ackerman, Diane, 1948-

★ The **zookeeper's** wife. W.W. Norton 2007 368p il $24.95   **940.53**

1. Zoos 2. Jews -- Poland 3. Holocaust, 1933-1945 4. World War, 1939-1945 -- Jews -- Rescue
ISBN 978-0-393-06172-7; 0-393-06172-8

LC 2007-12635

This is an account of how the director of the Warsaw Zoo and his wife, Jan and Antonina Zabinski, respectively, saved 300 Jews during World War II.

"An exemplary work of scholarship and an 'ecstasy of imagining,' Ackerman's affecting telling of the heroic Zabinskis' dramatic story illuminates the profound connec-

tion between humankind and nature, and celebrates life's beauty, mystery, and tenacity." Booklist

Includes bibliographical references

Allied Forces/Supreme Headquarters/Psychological Warfare Division/Intelligence Team

The **Buchenwald** report; translated, edited, and with an introduction by David A. Hackett; foreword by Frederick A. Praeger. Westview Press 1995 397p map hardcover o.p. pa $29   **940.53**

1. Buchenwald (Germany: Concentration camp) 2. Holocaust, 1933-1945 -- Personal narratives
ISBN 0-8133-1777-0; 0-8133-3363-6 pa

LC 94-39714

"This seminal document, published here in its entirety for the first time, is a report compiled for the Allied Army from interviews with the inmates of the Buchenwald concentration camp, located near Weimar, Germany in April 1945, shortly after the camp's liberation. . . . It is immediate, direct, and, as the product of the testimony of many people, more inclusive and wide-ranging than any single individual's personal testament. A classic of Holocaust literature that should be in any library that covers European history." Libr J

Includes bibliographical references

Arrington, Leonard J.

Japanese Americans, from relocation to redress; edited by Roger Daniels, Sandra C. Taylor, Harry H.L. Kitano; contributions by Leonard J. Arrington {et al.} rev & updated ed; University of Wash. Press 1991 xxi, 242p il pa $25   **940.53**

1. World War, 1939-1945 -- Reparations 2. Japanese Americans -- Evacuation and relocation, 1942-1945
ISBN 0-295-97117-7

LC 91-2892

First published 1986 by University of Utah Press

A collection of essays on Japanese Americans focusing on their wartime relocation and their efforts to seek reparations.

Includes bibliographical references

Berenbaum, Michael

The **world** must know; the history of the Holocaust as told in the United States Holocaust Memorial Museum. Arnold Kramer, editor of photographs. 2nd ed; United States Holocaust Memorial Museum 2006 xxi, 250p il pa $29.95   **940.53**

1. Holocaust, 1933-1945 2. United States Holocaust Memorial Museum
ISBN 0-8018-8358-X

First published 1993 by Little, Brown

"Visually evocative and unsettling, the book, supplemented with a useful bibliography, is an excellent choice for those with little acquaintance of the subject or those needing a concise synopsis." Libr J [review of 1993 edition]

Includes bibliographical references

Berthon, Simon

Warlords; an extraordinary recreation of World War II through the eyes and minds of Hitler, Roosevelt, Churchill, and Stalin. [by] Simon Berthon

and Joanna Potts. Da Capo Press 2006 358p il
$24.95   **940.53**

> 1. Governors 2. Statesmen 3. Historians 4. Presidents
> 5. Heads of state 6. Prime ministers 7. People
> with disabilities 8. Memoirists 9. Nazi leaders 10.
> Philatelists 11. Cabinet members 12. Communist
> leaders 13. Political leaders 14. Members of Parliament
> 15. Nobel laureates for literature 16. World War, 1939-
> 1945 -- Diplomatic history
>
> ISBN 0-306-81467-6

LC 2005-432583

First published 2005 in the United Kingdom

This book focuses "on the day-to-day actions of Hitler,
Stalin, Churchill, and Roosevelt as they grapple with the
war's events and plot strategy. . . . For anyone interested in
how these four leaders engaged in the war, here is a great
place to start." Libr J

Includes bibliographical references

Beschloss, Michael R.

★ The **conquerors** : Roosevelt, Truman, and the
destruction of Hitler's Germany, 1941-1945; {by}
Michael Beschloss. Simon & Schuster 2002 377p il
maps $26.95; pa $15   **940.53**

> 1. Governors 2. Presidents 3. Vice-presidents 4.
> People with disabilities 5. Reconstruction (1939-1951)
> 6. Senators 7. Philatelists 8. World War, 1939-1945
> -- Germany 9. Germany -- Foreign relations -- United
> States 10. United States -- Foreign relations -- Germany
>
> ISBN 0-684-81027-1; 0-7432-4454-0 pa

LC 2002-30331

"As German forces were driven back in 1943-45, American leaders were anxious that in 20 years, just as it had done
after its defeat in 1918, a vengeful Germany would start
another world war. To prevent this, two schools of thought
flowed through DC's salons of power: punishment or rehabilitation. . . . Beschloss covers the meeting-by-meeting, me-
mo-by-memo political battle between the two approaches.
. . . Beschloss' comprehensive research and narration into
every nuance opens a significant perspective on bureaucratic
politics' effect on the Germany that eventually formed in the
early cold war." Booklist

Includes bibliographical references

Buruma, Ian

Year zero; 1945 and the aftermath of war. Ian
Buruma. Penguin Press 2013 384 p. $29.95 **940.53**

> 1. World history -- 1945- 2. World politics -- 1945- 3.
> World War, 1939-1945 -- Influence 4. History, Modern
> -- 1945-1989 5. World War, 1939-1945 -- Peace
>
> ISBN 1594204365; 9781594204364

LC 2013007702

This book by Ian Buruma "explores the nascent social
and political forces that later influenced the Cold War and
post-colonial movements. . . . Starting with a world ruined
by war, Buruma moves . . . from describing the elation of
victory and the desire for revenge to the Allies' attempts to
reform societies by eliminating all traces of militarism or
fascism and establishing a European welfare state, as destroyed cities are rebuilt and fallen nations reimagined."
(Publishers Weekly)

"Insightful meditation on the world's emergence from
the wreckage of World War II.

Buruma... offers a vivid portrayal of the first steps toward normalcy in human affairs amid the ruins of Europe
and Asia. The end of hostilities left landscapes of rubble
and eerie silence and an economic collapse that gave rise
to countless black markets. There was widespread hunger
and misery... Many of the displaced were afraid to go home,
fearful that their homes were gone or that they would be regarded as strangers. Buruma re-creates the emotions of the
time: the joy that lipstick brought to emaciated women in
Bergen-Belsen; the wild abandon and eroticism of the liberation; and the desire for vengeance, sometimes officially
encouraged, as in Russian road signs that said, "Soldier, you
are in Germany. Take revenge on the Hitlerites." ...Recount-
ing the occupations of Germany and Japan and life in the
Allied nations, Buruma finds that the war was a great leveler, eliminating inequalities in Great Britain and rooting
out feudal customs and habits in Japan...An authoritative,
illuminating history/memoir." (Kirkus)

Includes bibliographical references and index

Carley, Michael Jabara

1939; the alliance that never was and the coming
of World War II. Dee, I.R. 1999 xxv, 321p maps
$28.95   **940.53**

> 1. World War, 1939-1945 -- Causes 2. World War,
> 1939-1945 -- Diplomatic history
>
> ISBN 1-56663-252-8

LC 99-24873

Carley "asserts that reflexive and extreme anti-Communist paranoia on the part of British and French politicians
and diplomats prevented a very achievable alliance against
Hitler." Booklist

The author "provides a detailed and fascinating perspective on one of the major causes of World War II." Libr J

Includes bibliographical references (p. {299}-308)
and index

Churchill, Winston, 1874-1965

Closing the ring. Houghton Mifflin 1951 749p
maps (Second World War) hardcover o.p. pa
$18   **940.53**

> 1. World War, 1939-1945 2. World War, 1939-1945
> -- Great Britain
>
> ISBN 0-395-41059-2 pa

"'Closing the Ring' sets forth the year of conflict from
June 1943 to June 1944. Aided by the command of the
oceans, the mastery of the U-boats, and our ever growing
superiority in the air, the Western Allies were able to conquer Sicily and invade Italy, with the result that Mussolini
was overthrown and the Italian nation came over to our
side." Preface

The **gathering** storm. Houghton Mifflin 1948
784p maps (Second World War) hardcover o.p. pa
$19   **940.53**

> 1. World War, 1939-1945 2. World War, 1939-1945
> -- Great Britain
>
> ISBN 0-395-41055-X pa

The first volume of Churchill's monumental history of the Second World War describes the days between the false peace and Hitler's near-victory just before Dunkirk

The **grand** alliance. Houghton Mifflin 1950 903p maps (Second World War) hardcover o.p. pa $18 **940.53**
1. World War, 1939-1945 2. World War, 1939-1945 -- Great Britain
ISBN 0-395-41057-6 pa
This volume begins with the German drive in the East, covers the War in Africa and describes the entrance into the war of Russia and, after Pearl Harbor, the United States

The **hinge** of fate. Houghton Mifflin 1950 1000p maps (Second World War) hardcover o.p. pa $18 **940.53**
1. World War, 1939-1945 2. World War, 1939-1945 -- Great Britain
ISBN 0-395-41058-4 pa
Describing events leading to the invasion of Sicily, warfare in Africa, the discouragingly slow job of reconquest in Europe, meetings with Roosevelt, and efforts at collaboration with Stalin, this volume covers the period from January 1942 to May 1943

Their finest hour. Houghton Mifflin 1949 751p maps (Second World War) hardcover o.p. pa $19 **940.53**
1. World War, 1939-1945 2. World War, 1939-1945 -- Great Britain
ISBN 0-395-41056-8 pa
This volume starts with the problems confronting Churchill as he assumed the office of Prime Minister in 1940 and continues with accounts of the Battle of Britain, the Battle of France and Dunkirk

Triumph and tragedy. Houghton Mifflin 1953 800p maps (Second World War) hardcover o.p. pa $18 **940.53**
1. World War, 1939-1945 2. World War, 1939-1945 -- Great Britain
ISBN 0-395-41060-6 pa
The concluding volume of Churchill's history of World War II begins with D-Day and covers campaigns leading to the defeat of Germany and Japan

Clendinnen, Inga
Reading the Holocaust. Cambridge Univ. Press 1999 227p il map $69; pa $19.99 **940.53**
1. Holocaust, 1933-1945 -- Historiography
ISBN 0-521-64174-8; 0-521-01269-4 pa
LC 98-53636
In this reexamination of the Holocaust Clendinnen "first considers the problematic nature of eyewitness accounts, then turns to an unflinching inquiry into the Nazi mentality and finally takes on the tough question of artistic representation. . . . This slim, powerful book forces a reader to reexamine almost all the assumptions we've accepted since the Holocaust occurred." N Y Times Book Rev
Includes bibliographical references

Cohen, Rich
The **avengers**. Knopf 2000 261p il hardcover o.p. pa $13 **940.53**
1. Poets 2. Authors 3. Underground leaders 4. Holocaust, 1933-1945 5. World War, 1939-1945 -- Underground movements
ISBN 0-375-70529-5 pa
LC 00-21062
Cohen chronicles the resistance efforts of a small group of European Jews during the Second World War. Attention is focused primarily on the activities of three individuals: Rozka Korczak, Vitka Kempner, and Abba Kovner
"Cohen is a skilled writer. His language is spare and muscular, his descriptions evocative, his technique suspenseful." N Y Times Book Rev

Collingham, Lizzie
The **taste** of war; World War II and the battle for food. Lizzie Collingham. Penguin Press 2012 xv, 634 p.p il map $36 **940.53**
1. Strategy 2. World War, 1939-1945 -- Food supply 3. Starvation -- History -- 20th century 4. Food habits -- History -- 20th century 5. Food supply -- History -- 20th century 6. Food security -- History -- 20th century 7. War and society -- History -- 20th century 8. Nutrition policy -- History -- 20th century
ISBN 1594203296; 9781594203299
LC 2011043783
This book examines "the fundamental role that food played in the planning, conduct, and course of the Second World War." Author Lizzie Collingham "explicates how Italy's plans for colonizing Ethiopia and further infiltrating Libya, Japan's expansion into Manchuria and China, and Germany's drive into Russia and the Ukraine were in essence 'battle[s] for Food.'" (Atlantic Monthly)
Includes bibliographical references (p. 581-620) and index

Colors of confinement; rare Kodachrome photographs of Japanese American incarceration in World War II. edited by Eric L. Muller ; with photographs by Bill Manbo. Univ. of North Carolina Pr."||"in ass. w/the Ctr. for Documentary Studies at Duke Univ. 2012 122 p. ill. (some col.) (Documentary arts and culture) (cloth : alk. paper) $35 **940.53**
1. World War, 1939-1945 -- Pictorial works 2. World War, 1939-1945 -- Prisoners and prisons, American 3. Japanese Americans -- Evacuation and relocation, 1942-1945 4. Heart Mountain Relocation Center (Wyo.) -- Pictorial works 5. World War, 1939-1945 -- Concentration camps -- Wyoming -- Pictorial works 6. Japanese Americans -- Evacuation and relocation, 1942-1945 -- Pictorial works
ISBN 0807835730; 9780807835739
LC 2011052817
This book, edited by Eric L. Muller, as part of the "Documentary Arts and Culture" series, with photographs by Bill Manbo, presents images of the Japanese American internments of World War II. "In 1942, Bill Manbo . . . and his family were forced . . . into the Japanese American internment camp at Heart Mountain in Wyoming. While there,

Manbo documented . . . his family's struggle to maintain a normal life under the harsh conditions of racial imprisonment." (Publisher's note)

Includes bibliographical references and index

Cooke, Alistair

American home front, 1941-1942. Atlantic Monthly 2006 xx, 327p il $24 **940.53**

1. United States -- Social conditions 2. World War, 1939-1945 -- United States 3. United States -- Description and travel 4. United States -- Social life and customs

ISBN 978-0-87113-939-9; 0-87113-939-1

LC 2005-58860

"Crisscrossing the American continent from east to west and north to south, stopping in diners and bus stations and newly humming industrial plants, Mr. Cooke brings to life an America stepping into the unknown, committing its muscle and blood to an enterprise that most citizens could barely articulate, in places most of them had never heard of." N Y Times (Late N Y Ed)

Costigliola, Frank

Roosevelt's lost alliances; how personal politics helped start the Cold War. Frank Costigliola. Princeton University Press 2012 533 p. $35.00 **940.53**

1. World politics -- 1945-1991 2. Cold war 3. United States -- Foreign relations 4. World War, 1939-1945 -- Diplomatic history 5. Soviet Union -- Foreign relations -- United States 6. United States -- Foreign relations -- Soviet Union 7. Great Britain -- Foreign relations -- United States 8. United States -- Foreign relations -- Great Britain

ISBN 069112129X; 9780691121291

LC 2011025271

Author Frank Costigliola "describes the functional alliance among the big three--Roosevelt, Churchill, and Stalin--during World War II and how, after Roosevelt's death, it was undermined. . . . Churchill is presented as an unchanging warrior and colonialist, whereas Stalin is portrayed" as "a 'realist' who, despite his brutality, sought secure borders, internal order, modernization, and respect. . . . FDR is pictured as being in reasonable health at Yalta and not bamboozled by Stalin." (Library Journal)

Includes bibliographical references.

Dallas, Gregor

1945; the war that never ended. Yale University Press 2005 xx, 739p il map $40; pa $22 **940.53**

1. World War, 1939-1945

ISBN 0-300-10980-6; 978-0-300-10980-1; 0-300-11988-7 pa; 978-0-300-11988-6 pa

LC 2005-926051

"The book begins with the death of Adolf Hitler, followed by a history of WW II in Europe, omitting the struggle in Asia. The author argues that the movement of armies determined European life for the next two generations. . . . Dallas's history is not for beginners, but it will be a very important addition to every collection on WW II in Europe." Choice

Includes bibliographical references

Daniels, Roger

Prisoners without trial; Japanese Americans in World War II. Rev. ed.; Hill and Wang 2004 162p il (Critical issue series) pa $12 **940.53**

1. World War, 1939-1945 -- United States 2. Japanese Americans -- Evacuation and relocation, 1942-1945

ISBN 0-8090-7896-1

LC 2004-47328

First published 1993

An account of "the relocation of Japanese Americans during World War II, an injustice prompted not by military necessity but by political and racial motivations. The purpose of this volume is to tell the story in light of the redress legislation enacted in 1988." Libr J [review of 1993 edition]

Includes bibliographical references

Dawidowicz, Lucy S.

The **war** against the Jews, 1933-1945; 10th anniversary ed; Bantam Books 1986 xxxx, 466p il pa $19 **940.53**

1. Jews -- Europe 2. Holocaust, 1933-1945

ISBN 978-0-553-34532-2; 0-553-34532-X

LC 85-48051

A reissue with new introduction and supplementary bibliography of the title first published 1975 by Holt, Rinehart & Winston

"One of the best histories of the mass murder of Jews in World War II. Argues for the centrality of anti-Semitism in Hitler's program." Reader's Adviser

Includes bibliographical references

Dobbs, Michael

Six months in 1945; FDR, Stalin, Churchill, Truman, and the birth of the modern world. by Michael Dobbs. 1st ed. Alfred A. Knopf 2012 418 p. (hardcover) $28.95 **940.53**

1. Cold war 2. World War, 1939-1945 -- Peace 3. World War, 1939-1945 -- Diplomatic history 4. World politics -- 1945-1955 5. Cold War -- Diplomatic history 6. Soviet Union -- Foreign relations -- United States 7. United States -- Foreign relations -- Soviet Union

ISBN 030727165X; 9780307271655

LC 2012021747

This book, by Michael Dobbs, provides an "account of the pivotal six-month period spanning the end of World War II, the dawn of the nuclear age, and the beginning of the Cold War. When Roosevelt, Stalin, and Churchill met in Yalta in February 1945, . . . victory was imminent. The Big Three wanted to draft a blueprint for a lasting peace--but instead set the stage for a forty-four-year division of Europe into Soviet and western spheres of influence." (Publisher's note)

Includes bibliographical references and index

Dower, John W.

★ **Ways** of forgetting, ways of remembering; Japan in the modern world. John W. Dower. New Press 2012 336 p. (hardcover : alk. paper) $26.95 **940.53**

1. Propaganda 2. American essays 3. Japan -- History 4. Japan -- History -- 1945- 5. World War, 1939-1945 -- Japan 6. World War, 1939-1945 -- Influence 7. Japan -- Social conditions -- 1945 8. Japan -- Politics and government -- 1945 9. Japan -- History -- 1945-

-- Historiography   10.   World War, 1939-1945 -- Japan
-- Historiography   11.   World War, 1939-1945 -- Social
aspects -- Japan   12.   Social change -- Japan -- History --
20th century   13.   Collective memory -- Japan -- History
-- 20th century
ISBN 1595586180;   9781595586186

LC 2011033861

This book "brings together a number of [John W. Dower's] essays written between 1993 and 2007. . . . Most deal with Japan since WWII, although Dower . . . invokes much earlier history." Particular focus is given to "national hypocrisy and the misuses of history and memory, American as well as Japanese. His topics include Japanese racism along with the enthusiasm with which Japan went to war. . . . Essays on Hiroshima round out the volume." (Publishers Weekly)

Includes bibliographical references and index

Dwork, Deborah
★ **Holocaust** : a history; {by} Deborah Dwork,
Robert Jan Van Pelt.   Norton   2002   xx, 444p   il
$27.95; pa $15.95   **940.53**
1. Jews -- Germany   2. Holocaust, 1933-1945   3.
Germany -- Politics and government -- 1933-1945
ISBN 0-393-05188-9; 0-393-32524-5 pa

LC 2002-23565

"The authors examine such issues as the historic relationship between Jews, gentiles, and Germans; World War I and its consequences; National Socialism in the Weimar Republic; the Third Reich and its anti-Semitic measures; worldwide refugee policies that became a disaster for the Jews; and Jewish and gentile life under German occupation. They also examine the efforts by Allied nations to help the Jews. . . . This is a monumental work of impeccable scholarship." Booklist

Includes bibliographical references

Encyclopedia of Jewish life before and during the
Holocaust; edited by Shmuel Spector and Geoffrey Wigoder.   New York Univ. Press   2001   3v   il
maps   set $99   **940.53**
1. Reference books   2. Jews -- Europe   3. Holocaust,
1933-1945 -- Encyclopedias
ISBN 0-8147-9356-8

"Each entry provides vital information on the town's Jewish inhabitants on the eve of German occupation, gives the dates of Jewish roundups and mass executions and estimates how many Jews from that community survived the war." Publ Wkly

Eisner, Peter
The **Pope's** Last Crusade; How an American Jesuit Helped Pope Pius XI's Campaign to Stop Hitler.
HarperCollins   2013   352 p. $27.99   **940.53**
1. Holocaust, 1939-1945   2. Catholic Church --
Relations -- Judaism
ISBN 0062049143; 9780062049148

This book by Peter Eisner offers an account of the "efforts by the Vatican to counter the Nazis before WWII. . . . According to Eisner, the Vatican's track record [regarding the Holocaust] might have been different if Pius XI had lived to deliver a speech in 1939 condemning the German regime" that was "based on the thinking of the Rev. John

LaFarge, an American . . . whom Pius XI had commissioned to write a papal encyclical on" church action against racism. (Publishers Weekly)

Encyclopedia of the Holocaust; Schmuel Spector,
Robert Rozett, editors.   Facts on File   2000   528p
il $93.50   **940.53**
1. Reference books   2. Holocaust, 1933-1945 --
Encyclopedias
ISBN 0-8160-4333-7

LC 00-30917

Following several introductory essays are "alphabetical entries on people, places, events, organizations, laws, and concepts. The language is clear, but more important is the authenticity of the information and the refusal to surrender to a simplification of issues. There are ample good-quality, black-and-white photographs, some unfamiliar, and also maps and tables. A detailed chronology and a thematic bibliography conclude the volume." SLJ

Includes bibliographical references

★ **Encyclopedia** of World War II; a political, social
and military history.   Spencer C. Tucker, editor,
Priscilla Mary Roberts, editor   volume 5.   ABC-CLIO   2004   5v   il map   set $485   **940.53**
1. Reference books   2. World War, 1939-1945 --
Encyclopedias
ISBN 1-576-07999-6

LC 2004-23745

"The 1,465 alphabetically arranged articles provide an international perspective on people; key battles, campaigns, and events; military equipment and strategy; countries; and other relevant topics. . . . Country entries not only cover the main Allied and Axis powers but also such countries as Afghanistan, Brazil, Estonia, Iraq, Mexico, New Zealand, and Somalia as well as world regions. . . . An excellent resource for high-school, public, and academic libraries." Booklist

Includes bibliographical references

Epstein, Eric Joseph
Dictionary of the Holocaust; biography, geography, and terminology.   [by] Eric Joseph Epstein
and Philip Rosen; foreword by Henry R. Huttenbach.
Greenwood Press   1997   416p $67.95   **940.53**
1. Reference books   2. Holocaust, 1933-1945 --
Dictionaries
ISBN 0-313-30355-X

LC 97-8779

The nearly 2,000 alphabetically arranged entries cover people, places and events related to the Holocaust. "Among the personalities profiled here are Dietrich Bonhoeffer, Anne Frank, Primo Levi, Oskar Schindler, Harry S. Truman, and Elie Wiesel. Place entries include references to well-known locations, the number of prewar Jewish inhabitants, the date of liberation, and the number of Jews left after liberation. Entries dealing with concentration camps are generally the longest and identify camps by location, type, when opened and liberated, nationalities incarcerated, numbers murdered, other victimization, and camp commandants. Among the terms that are defined are many foreign expressions." Booklist

Evans, Richard J.

Lying about Hitler; history, Holocaust, and the David Irving trial. [by] Richard Evans. Basic Bks. 2001 318p hardcover o.p. pa $16.95   **940.53**
1. Trials 2. Historians 3. College teachers 4. Holocaust, 1933-1945 -- Historiography
ISBN 0-465-02152-2; 0-465-02153-0 pa
LC 00-140130
Evans's "superb [book], . . . is never less than absorbing. A sure-footed writer, he allows the story to tell itself, eschewing rhetorical flourishes in favor of a clinical dissection of Irving's works and statements." Natl Rev
Includes bibliographical references

★ The **Third** Reich at war. Penguin Press 2009 926p il map $40   **940.53**
1. Germany -- History -- 1933-1945 2. World War, 1939-1945 -- Germany
ISBN 978-1-59420-206-3
LC 2008-44765
First published 2008 in the United Kingdom
This is a "very readable, well-paced account that is fully familiar with the huge amount of specialist scholarship in this field but never gets bogged down by excessive detail." Hist Today
Includes bibliographical references

Faber, David

Munich, 1938; appeasement and World War II. Simon & Schuster 2009 520p il $30   **940.53**
1. World War, 1939-1945 -- Causes 2. Munich Four-Power Agreement (1938) 3. World War, 1939-1945 -- Diplomatic history 4. Europe -- Politics and government -- 1918-1945
ISBN 978-1-4391-3233-3
LC 2008-44896
"The 1938 Munich Conference has been referred to as the Great Betrayal, virtually guaranteeing the start of war in Europe the following year. In return for Hitler's empty promises of peace, the British and French governments acquiesced to his demand to annex the Sudetenland, a largely German-speaking region of Czechoslovakia. The appeasement emboldened Hitler and led directly to the German-Soviet nonaggression pact and their joint invasion of Poland. Faber's account of the preparation for and actual unfolding of the conference is comprehensive, engrossing, and depressing, like viewing a slow-motion train wreck. . . . He does a masterful job of recounting the political maneuvers and infighting within both the British and German camps." Booklist
Includes bibliographical references

Fortunoff Video Archive for Holocaust Testimonies

Witness; voices from the Holocaust. edited by Joshua M. Greene and Shiva Kumar in consultation with Joanne Weiner Rudof; foreword by Lawrence L. Langer; in association with the Fortunoff Video

Archive for Holocaust Testimonies, Yale University. Free Press 2000 xxx, 270p il $26; pa $15 **940.53**
1. Holocaust, 1933-1945 -- Personal narratives
ISBN 0-684-86525-4; 0-684-86526-2 pa
LC 99-58401
In this companion to the PBS series the editors "have woven together the testimonies of 27 individuals into an unforgettable narrative of the Holocaust: starting with pre-WWII Jewish life, they go on to describe the war's outbreak, ghettos, resistance and hiding, death camps, death marches, liberation and life after the Holocaust." Publ Wkly
Includes bibliographical references

Friedlander, Saul

Nazi Germany and the Jews. vl HarperCollins Pubs. 1997 436p vl hardcover o.p. pa $19.95 **940.53**
1. Jews -- Germany 2. Holocaust, 1933-1945 3. Jews -- Persecutions 4. Germany -- History -- 1933-1945
ISBN 0-06-019042-6; 0-06-092878-6 pa
LC 96-21915
"Not the least impressive aspect of Friedländer's book is the skill with which he juxtaposes different levels of reality within an overall chronological frame, moving from high-level Nazi debates on Jewish policy to the routine brutalities of the SA and SS, and from the perceptions of the average German citizen to those of the victims." N Y Rev Books
Includes bibliographical references

The **years** of extermination; Nazi Germany and the Jews, 1939-1945. HarperCollins Publishers 2007 xxvi, 870p $39.95   **940.53**
1. Jews -- Germany 2. Holocaust, 1933-1945 3. Jews -- Persecutions 4. Germany -- History -- 1933-1945
ISBN 0-06-019043-4; 978-0-06-019043-9
LC 2006-48982
The second part of a two-part series starting with Nazi Germany and the Jews: vl: The years of persecution, 1933-1939 (1997)
"This is a masterful synthesis that draws on a lifetime of learning and research." Publ Wkly
Includes bibliographic references

Gilbert, Martin

Holocaust journey; traveling in search of the past. Columbia Univ. Press 1997 480p il $60; pa $20.95   **940.53**
1. Concentration camps 2. Jews -- Europe 3. Holocaust, 1933-1945
ISBN 0-231-10964-4; 0-231-10965-2 pa
LC 97-15895
The author chronicles "a tour of Holocaust sites that he conducted with a dozen students and friends; the text of documents they studied at each stop is included. Gilbert not only describes their itinerary and the problems of conducting a tour but integrates the history of European Jewry into his

narrative. He then details the specific events of the Holocaust associated with each location." Libr J

Includes bibliographical references

Kristallnacht; prelude to destruction. HarperCollins Publishers 2006 314p il map (Making history) hardcover o.p. pa $14.99   **940.53**

1. Jews -- Persecutions 2. Germany -- History -- 1933-1945

ISBN 0-06-057083-0; 978-0-06-057083-5; 0-06-112135-5 pa; 978-0-06-112135-7 pa

LC 2005-58169

This is "an account of the Night of Broken Glass, which was unleashed against the Jewish communities across Germany on November 10, 1938. . . . A powerful account of the helplessness of the Jews." Booklist

Includes bibliographical references

★ The **Routledge** atlas of the Holocaust; 4th ed.; Routledge 2009 286p map $120; pa $30.95 **940.53**

1. Atlases 2. Reference books 3. Holocaust, 1933-1945 -- Maps

ISBN 978-0-415-48481-7; 0-415-48481-2; 978-0-415-48486-2 pa; 0-415-48486-3 pa

LC 2008-43844

First published 1982 in the United Kingdom with title: The Dent atlas of the Holocaust

The author uses "maps, text, and photographs to document Hitler's attempt to destroy Europe's Jews. . . . Commentary offers statistical information, historical background, and something about the people of the area. Archival photographs bring the events to life. . . . This small but effective work demonstrates the magnitude of the Nazi terror by bringing it down to a personal level." Am Ref Books Annu, 2003 [review of 2002 edition]

Includes bibliographical references

The **Second** World War; a complete history. Holt & Co. 1989 846p il maps hardcover o.p. pa $25   **940.53**

1. World War, 1939-1945

ISBN 0-8050-1788-7 pa

LC 89-11129

The author begins this study "with the invasion of Poland. Gilbert's flowing narrative is spiced with anecdotal details culled from diaries, memoirs and official documents. He is especially skillful at interweaving summaries of military strategy with vignettes of civilian suffering—the genocide of the Jews is never far from view." Newsweek

Includes bibliographical references

Goldhagen, Daniel

Hitler's willing executioners; ordinary Germans and the Holocaust. [by] Daniel Jonah Goldhagen. Knopf 1996 622p il maps hardcover o.p. pa $16   **940.53**

1. Antisemitism 2. National socialism 3. Holocaust, 1933-1945 4. Germany -- History -- 1933-1945

ISBN 0-679-44695-8; 0-679-77268-5 pa

LC 95-38591

The author "endeavors to show that the common apologia for the Germans—that Hitler 'brainwashed' them—is

nonsense and that most Germans gave their active assent to genocide. An ordinary German commander, for example, might feel himself bound by a strict code of conduct yet not be at all averse to murdering Jews. The book ends with a detailed notes section and an appendix that explains the correct methodology for studying the Nazi period." Libr J

A **moral** reckoning; the role of the Catholic Church in the Holocaust and its unfulfilled duty of repair. [by] Daniel Jonah Goldhagen. Knopf 2002 362p il hardcover o.p. pa $16   **940.53**

1. Popes 2. Antisemitism 3. Holocaust, 1933-1945 4. Catholic Church -- Relations -- Judaism

ISBN 0-375-41434-7; 0-375-71417-0 pa

LC 2002-16264

This is "a landmark work. . . . This volume is recommended for all libraries and essential for those supporting a Holocaust studies program." Libr J

Includes bibliographical references

Goldsmith, Martin

The **inextinguishable** symphony; a true story of music and love in Nazi Germany. Wiley 2000 346p il hardcover o.p. pa $15.95   **940.53**

1. Drummers 2. Jews -- Germany 3. Holocaust, 1933-1945

ISBN 0-471-35097-4; 0-471-07864-6 pa

LC 00-25955

Goldsmith's "weaving together of cultural and personal history constitutes a gripping tale of persecution, intrigue, and love and an insider's—or two insiders'—view of a dark time." Booklist

Includes bibliographical references

Groom, Winston

★ **1942**; the year that tried men's souls. Atlantic Monthly Press 2005 459p il maps $27.50   **940.53**

1. World War, 1939-1945

ISBN 0-8711-3889-1

LC 2004-62779

In this military history of one year during World War II, the author "delivers the traditional worshipful portrait of General MacArthur while admitting he made several key blunders that doomed the Philippines in the year's early months. . . . He adds that brains and luck win more battles than courage, providing a perfect illustration in Midway, fought in June 1942. . . . Groom has written a page-turner; readers needing an introduction will love it." Publ Wkly

Includes bibliographical references

Guttenplan, D. D.

The **Holocaust** on trial. Norton 2001 328p il hardcover o.p. pa $15.95   **940.53**

1. Trials 2. Historians 3. College teachers 4. Holocaust, 1933-1945 -- Historiography

ISBN 0-393-32292-0 pa

LC 2001-30370

The author chronicles the "libel trial in Britain brought by historian David Irving. Irving, widely viewed as an apologist for Hitler, sued American scholar Deborah Lipstadt, whose Denying the Holocaust (1993) had labeled Irving as a right-wing extremist. . . . Interspersing essayistic diversions, the author presents a thoughtful work as well as a courtroom thriller." Booklist

Includes bibliographical references

Herman, Arthur

Freedom's forge; how American business produced victory in World War II. Arthur Herman. Random House 2012 xiv, 413 p.p   **940.53**
1. Economic policy -- United States 2. Industrial mobilization -- United States 3. Manufacturing industries -- United States 4. United States -- Economic conditions -- 1933-1945 5. World War, 1939-1945 -- Economic aspects -- United States 6. United States -- Economic policy -- 1933-1945 7. Industrial management -- United States -- History -- 20th century 8. Industrial mobilization -- United States -- History -- 20th century 9. Manufacturing industries -- Military aspects -- United States -- History -- 20th century
ISBN 1400069645; 9780679604631; 9781400069644
      LC 2011040661

In this book, "the author argues . . . against the conventional wisdom that America's rearmament [during World War II] took place under the guidance of a competent federal government. . . . The production of the flood of war materiel that drowned the Axis was achieved by the voluntary cooperation of businesses driven as much by the profit motive as by patriotism, solving problems through their own ingenuity rather than waiting for government directives." (Kirkus Reviews)

Includes bibliographical references (p. [387-399]) and index

Hoffman, Eva

After such knowledge; memory, history and the legacy of the Holocaust. Public Affairs 2004 301p $25; pa $14   **940.53**
1. Holocaust, 1933-1945
ISBN 1-586-48046-4; 0-586-48304-8 pa
      LC 2003-66443

The author "focuses on the consciousness and experience of the Holocaust's second generation—the children of survivors. . . . The book considers such diverse concepts as how the 'trauma' of the Holocaust is constructed, the role of emigration and national identity in shaping the second generation's narratives of their lives. . . . Hoffman writes with a subdued but vibrant passion." Publ Wkly

Includes bibliographical references

The Holocaust encyclopedia; Walter Laqueur, editor; Judith Tydor Baumel, associate editor. Yale Univ. Press 2001 xxxix, 765p il maps $60   **940.53**
1. Reference books 2. Holocaust, 1933-1945 -- Encyclopedias
ISBN 0-300-08432-3
      LC 00-106567

This "encyclopedia provides fresh and lengthy articles on such topics as antisemitism, historiography, Jewish women, memorials, and resistance, just to brush the surface." Choice

Includes bibliographical references

Horwitz, Gordon J.

Ghettostadt; Lodz and the making of a Nazi city. The Belknap Press of Harvard University Press 2008 395p il map   **940.53**
1. Holocaust, 1933-1945 2. Jews -- Persecutions 3. ¿ódz (Poland) 4. ¿ódz (Poland) -- Ethnic relations 5. Holocaust, Jewish (1939-1945) -- Poland -- ¿ódz 6. Jews -- Persecutions -- Poland -- ¿ódz -- History
ISBN 0-674-02799-X; 978-0-674-02799-2
      LC 2007-50934

The author discusses how the Nazis transformed Lodz, whose population was more than one-third Jewish, into a new German city called Litzmannstadt. Index.

"The Nazis' use of bureaucracy to achieve their genocidal aims comes through clearly in this historical tour de force. The Nazis attempted to 're-engineer' the Polish city of Lodz, home to more than 230,000 Jews (one-third of the city's population) before the war, into a model—and Judenfrei—German city embodying health and beauty they called Litzmannstadt. This required forcing the Jews into a ghetto with the help of Jewish leaders, especially the . . . reportedly lascivious industrialist Chaim Rumkowski. . . . With a graceful style rare in academic history, Horwitz . . . marshals a host of primary sources to highlight the gradual destruction of the ghetto." Publ Wkly

Includes bibliographical references

Huchthausen, Peter A.

Shadow voyage; the extraordinary wartime escape of the legendary SS Bremen. Wiley 2005 260p il $24.95   **940.53**
1. World War, 1939-1945 -- Naval operations
ISBN 0-471-45758-2
      LC 2004-14948

"This book will interest not only World War II buffs but also anyone drawn to tales of the sea." Libr J

Includes bibliographical references

Karski, Jan

★ **Story** of a secret state; my report to the world. Jan Karski ; foreword by Madeleine Albright. Georgetown University Press 2013 464 p. (hbk. : alk. paper) $26.95   **940.53**
1. World War, 1939-1945 -- Poland 2. World War, 1939-1945 -- Personal narratives 3. Poland -- History -- Occupation, 1939-1945 4. World War, 1939-1945 -- Personal narratives, Polish
ISBN 1589019830; 9781589019836
      LC 2012037549

This book, by Jan Karski, is a memoir of a diplomat who served during "World War II and the Holocaust. With elements of a spy thriller, documenting his experiences in the Polish Underground, and as one of the first accounts of the systematic slaughter of the Jews by the German Nazis, this volume is a remarkable testimony of one man's courage and a nation's struggle for resistance against overwhelming oppression." (Publisher's note)

Includes bibliographical references and index

Keegan, John

The **Second** World War. Penguin Books 2005
608p il map pa $22 **940.53**
1. World War, 1939-1945
ISBN 0-14-303573-8; 978-0-14-303573-2
LC 2005-274899
First published 1989 in the United Kingdom
This military and stategic history contains sections
covering the Eastern and Western fronts and the war in
the Pacific.
"Keegan accompanies his narrative with a series of set
battlepieces, of strategic analyses, and of 'themes of war'...
. The book is beautifully ordered and ... a pleasure to read."
New Statesman Soc
Includes bibliographical references

Kershaw, Ian

Hitler, the Germans, and the final solution. Yale
University Press 2008 394p $35; pa $22 **940.53**
1. Heads of state 2. National socialism 3. Nazi leaders
4. Holocaust, 1933-1945 5. Germany -- Ethnic relations
6. Germany -- History -- 1933-1945
ISBN 978-0-300-12427-9; 978-0-300-15127-5 pa
LC 2007-940635
This "history of Hitler's rise to power—14 essays ar-
ranged in four sections—offers a comprehensive view of the
destructive force of the Nazi leadership and of the attitudes
and behavior of Germans in the persecution of the Jews...
. This is a precise and sensitive account of an aspect of the
Holocaust." Booklist
Includes bibliographical references

Klein, Maury

A **call** to arms; mobilizing America for World
War II. by Maury Klein. 1st U.S. ed. Bloomsbury
2013 912 p. (hardcover) $40.00 **940.53**
1. Military weapons 2. World War, 1939-1945 3.
United States -- Armed forces 4. Military history 5.
United States -- Economic policy -- 1933-1945 6.
World War, 1939-1945 -- Economic aspects -- United
States 7. Industrial mobilization -- United States
-- History -- 20th century 8. United States -- Armed
Forces -- Mobilization -- History -- 20th century
ISBN 1596916079; 9781596916074
LC 2012039497
This book, written by Maury Klein, examines U.S. ef-
forts to "create, outfit, transport, and supply huge armies,
navies, and air forces" for World War II. It looks at how
American productivity, "American industry, and Ameri-
can workers, won World War II [and how it] [n]ot only ...
determine[d] the outcome of the war, but it transformed the
American economy and society." (Publisher's note)
Includes bibliographical references and index.

Kochanski, Halik

The **Eagle** Unbowed; Poland and the Poles in
the Second World War. Halik Kochanski. Harvard
University Press 2012 624 p. $35 **940.53**
1. Poland -- History -- 1918-1945 2. World War, 1939-
1945 -- Poland 3. Poland -- Social conditions -- 1918-
1945 4. Poland -- Politics and government -- 1918-1945

5. World War, 1939-1945 -- Social aspects -- Poland
ISBN 0674068149; 9780674068148
LC 2012026952
This book by Halik Kochanski offers an "English-lan-
guage history of Poland at war" from the Polish perspective.
"She ranges from the fatal weaknesses of pre-war Poland
(divided, cash-strapped and isolated) to the humiliation of
Britain's victory parade in 1946 when organizers invited
Fijians and Mexicans, but not Poles.... For Poles the war
was three-sided. The Western allies were duplicitous and the
Soviets for the most part as bad as the Nazis." (Economist)
Includes bibliographical references (pages 694-715)
and index

Koker, David

At the edge of the abyss; a concentration camp
diary, 1943-1944. David Koker ; edited by Robert
Jan van Pelt ; translated from the Dutch by Michiel
Horn and John Irons. Northwestern University Press
2012 xii, 396 p.p **940.53**
1. Diaries 2. Jews -- Biography 3. World War, 1939-
1945 -- Prisoners and prisons 4. Vught (Concentration
camp) 5. Prisoners of war -- Netherlands -- Biography
6. World War, 1939-1945 -- Personal narratives, Dutch
ISBN 0810126362; 9780810126367
LC 2011026584
The book presents the diary of David Koker from 1943-
1944. "During his time in the Vught concentration camp, the
21-year-old David recorded on an almost daily basis his observations, thoughts, and feelings. He mercilessly probed the
abyss that opened around him and, at times, within himself.
David's diary covers almost a year, both charting his daily
life in Vught as it developed over time and tracing his spiritual evolution as a writer. Until early February 1944, David
was able to smuggle some 73,000 words from the camp to
his best friend Karel van het Reve, a non-Jew." (Amazon)
Includes bibliographical references

Kruk, Herman

The **last** days of the Jerusalem of Lithuania;
chronicles from the Vilna ghetto and the camps, 1939-
1944. edited and introduced by Benjamin Harshav;
translated by Barbara Harshav. Yivo Inst. for Jewish
Res. 2002 732p il maps $45 **940.53**
1. Jews -- Lithuania 2. Holocaust, 1933-1945 3. World
War, 1939-1945 -- Underground movements
ISBN 0-300-04494-1
LC 2002-16736
This a collection of Kruk's journals and other writings
from the Jewish ghetto of Vilna and a labor camp in Estonia
This "is a major addition to Holocaust literature and
Jewish history. In 1961 a Yiddish edition of the Vilna diaries
was published. This larger new edition has been painstak-
ingly assembled from those diaries and other documents and
writings by Kruk that were widely scattered and only found
since the 1961 edition; Harshav has also added a wealth of
new footnotes." Publ Wkly
Includes bibliographical references

Langer, Lawrence L.

Admitting the Holocaust; collected essays. Oxford Univ. Press 1995 202p hardcover o.p. pa $14.95   **940.53**
1. Poets 2. Authors 3. Novelists 4. Dramatists 5. Holocaust, 1939-1945, in literature 6. Essayists 7. Short story writers 8. Holocaust, 1933-1945 9. Nobel laureates for literature 10. Holocaust, 1933-1945, in literature
ISBN 0-19-510648-2 pa
LC 94-13368
"A horribly bleak, undeniably important book." Booklist
Includes bibliographical references

Lewy, Guenter

★ The **Nazi** persecution of the gypsies. Oxford Univ. Press 2000 306p il hardcover o.p. pa $24.95   **940.53**
1. Gypsies 2. National socialism 3. World War, 1939-1945 -- Atrocities
ISBN 0-19-512556-8; 0-19-514240-3 pa
LC 98-52545
The author "begins with a brief history of the maltreatment of Gypsies all over Europe, from the fifteenth century onward; then, by dint of exhaustive research, Lewy documents the horrors of their expulsions, detentions, deportations, and deaths during the systematic madness of the Holocaust." Booklist
Includes bibliographical references

Lifton, Robert Jay

The **Nazi** doctors; medical killing and the psychology of genocide. Basic Bks. 1986 561p hardcover o.p. pa $23   **940.53**
1. Physicians 2. War criminals 3. Concentration camps 4. Murderers 5. Nazi leaders 6. Holocaust, 1933-1945 7. World War, 1939-1945 -- Atrocities
ISBN 0-465-04905-2 pa
LC 85-73874
"How could German physicians trained as scientist-healers carry out Nazi orders for mass killings? . . . Lifton, an American Jewish physician, seeks answers through interviews with surviving doctors, family members, and victims and by painstakingly gleaning Holocaust archives." Sci Books Films
Includes bibliographical references

Lipstadt, Deborah E.

Denying the Holocaust; the growing assault on truth and memory. with a new preface by the author. Plume 1994 278p pa $16   **940.53**
1. Antisemitism 2. Holocaust, 1933-1945 -- Historiography
ISBN 0-452-27274-2; 978-0-452-27274-3
LC 93-45586
First published 1993 by Free Press

"Lipstadt has written a disturbing book that deserves a wide readership." Libr J
Includes bibliographical references

★ **History** on trial; my day in court with David Irving. Ecco 2005 xxi, 346p il $25.95; pa $14.95   **940.53**
1. Trials 2. Historians 3. Holocaust, 1933-1945 -- Historiography
ISBN 0-06-059376-8; 0-06-059377-6 pa
LC 2004-57533
"No one who cares about historical truth, freedom of speech or the Holocaust will avoid a sense of triumph from Gray's decision—or a sense of dismay that British libel laws allowed such intimidation by Irving of a historian and a publisher in the first place." Publ Wkly
Includes bibliographical references

Lukacs, John

Five days in London, May 1940. Yale Univ. Press 1999 236p $19.95; pa $11.95   **940.53**
1. Diplomats 2. Statesmen 3. Historians 4. Prime ministers 5. Memoirists 6. Cabinet members 7. Government officials 8. Members of Parliament 9. Colonial administrators 10. Nobel laureates for literature 11. World War, 1939-1945 -- Great Britain 12. World War, 1939-1945 -- Diplomatic history 13. Great Britain -- Politics and government -- 20th century
ISBN 0-300-08030-1; 0-300-08466-8 pa
LC 99-27583
This work focuses on the "chaotic few days during which, according to the author, Hitler came closest to winning the war. . . . Lukacs concentrates on the struggle within the British War Cabinet, which pitted the Prime Minister, Winston Churchill, against the Foreign Secretary, Lord Halifax, a Tory idol and a friend of the King. The point of contention was Halifax's belief that England should attempt to negotiate a general European settlement with Hitler. Churchill's stubborn refusal won out. The author's equally stubborn digging uncovered a stunning amount of defeatism and intrigue against Churchill by contemporary statesmen." New Yorker
Includes bibliographical references

Maitland, Leslie

Crossing the borders of time; a true story of war, exile, and love reclaimed. Leslie Maitland. Other Press 2012 494 p.   **940.53**
1. Love stories 2. Jews -- France 3. Jewish refugees -- Biography 4. World War, 1939-1945 -- Jews 5. Immigrants -- United States -- Biography 6. First loves -- France -- Biography 7. Jewish refugees -- United States -- Biography 8. World War, 1939-1945 -- Jews -- France -- Biography 9. World War, 1939-1945 -- Refugees -- France -- Biography
ISBN 1590514963; 9781590514962
LC 2011047110
This book focuses on "love lost in Alsace during World War II, rediscovered 50 years later in New Jersey. . . . [Author Leslie] Maitland's mother Janine, along with her German-speaking parents, sister and brother, originally fled in 1938 from Freiburg,. . . . The family then landed in Lyon,

where Janine . . . reignited a friendship with a dashing Catholic law student, Roland Arcieri. After falling in love during their brief time together, Janine was yanked away again with her family." (Kirkus Reviews)

Includes bibliographical references (p. 489-492)

Mazower, Mark

Hitler's empire; how the Nazis ruled Europe. Penguin Press 2008 xl, 725p il map   **940.53**
1. National socialism 2. Europe -- History -- 1918-1945 3. Germany -- History -- 1918-1945 4. Germany -- History -- 1933-1945 5. World War, 1939-1945 -- Germany
ISBN 1-594-20188-9; 978-1-594-20188-2
LC 2008-26997

This is an account of how the Nazis designed, maintained, and ultimately lost their European empire. (Publisher's note) Index.

The author's compelling analysis of the contradictions underpinning the Nazis' dream of Lebensraum impressively demonstrates that the Nazis were destined to lose World War II. But he soberly reminds us that, inefficient as the Nazis may have been at running an empire, they were brutally effective at suppressing resistance to it. New Leader

Includes bibliographical references

Mortimer, Gavin

The longest night; the bombing of London on May 10, 1941. Berkley Caliber 2005 356p il $24.95   **940.53**
1. World War, 1939-1945 -- Great Britain 2. World War, 1939-1945 -- Aerial operations
ISBN 0-425-20557-6
LC 2005-45281

"This account is given special power and poignancy by using the recollections of surviving men and women who endured that terrible night. An outstanding addition to World War II collections." Booklist

The New York Times complete World War II, 1939-1945; the coverage from the battlefields to the home front. edited by Richard Overy. Black Dog & Leventhal Pub 2013 611 p. $40   **940.53**
1. World War, 1939-1945 2. Newspapers -- United States
ISBN 1579129447; 9781579129446

This book, edited by Richard Overy, features "hundreds of . . . articles from the archives of the 'Times'—including firsthand accounts of major events and little-known anecdotes. . . . The book covers the biggest battles of the war, from the Battle of the Bulge to the Battle of Iwo Jima, as well as moving stories from the home front and profiles of noted leaders and heroes such as Winston Churchill and George Patton." (Publisher's note)

"This is a book to lose yourself in, to witness the war transmuted into print for the masses of readers living through it and anxious to follow its twists and turns." LJ

Nicholas, Lynn H.

★ Cruel world; the children of Europe in the Nazi web. A.A. Knopf 2005 632p il maps $35; pa $17.95   **940.53**
1. Children and war 2. Holocaust, 1933-1945 3. World War, 1939-1945 -- Children
ISBN 0-679-45464-0; 0-679-77663-X pa
LC 2004-57745

This is an account of the lives of children in Europe during the Holocaust and World War II.

The author "has put together a well-written, compelling history that makes us look at the war era anew." Publ Wkly

Includes bibliographical references

Nossiter, Adam

★ The Algeria Hotel; France, memory, and the Second World War. Houghton Mifflin 2001 302p il maps $26   **940.53**
1. World War, 1939-1945 -- France 2. France -- History -- 1940-1945, German occupation
ISBN 0-395-90245-2
LC 00-69458

"The rationalizations that let the French dispose of the past are the subject of this sensitive book, which covers the trial of a former cabinet minister, the Vichy memory hole and the interpretation of a Nazi atrocity." N Y Times Book Rev

Includes bibliographical references

Olson, Lynne

Those angry days; Roosevelt, Lindbergh, and America's fight over World War II, 1939-1941. by Lynne Olson. Random House Inc. 2013 576 p. (hardcover) $30.00; (ebook) $85.00   **940.53**
1. World War, 1939-1945 -- United States 2. United States -- Military policy 3. World War, 1939-1945 -- Diplomatic history 4. United States -- Foreign relations -- 1933-1945 5. United States -- Politics and government -- 1933-1945 6. Isolationism -- United States -- History -- 20th century 7. Intervention (International law) -- History -- 20th century 8. Political culture -- United States -- History -- 20th century
ISBN 9781400069743; 1400069742; 9780679604716
LC 2012025381

This book, by Lynne Olson, offers an "account of the debate over American intervention in World War II. . . . At the center of this controversy stood the two most famous men in America: President Franklin D. Roosevelt, who championed the interventionist cause, and aviator Charles Lindbergh, who as unofficial leader and spokesman for America's isolationists emerged as the president's most formidable adversary." (Publisher's note)

Includes bibliographical references (p. [509]-518) and index.

Overy, R. J.

Why the Allies won; {by} Richard Overy. Norton 1996 396p il maps hardcover o.p. pa $17.95 **940.53**
1. Strategy 2. World War, 1939-1945
ISBN 0-393-31619-X pa
LC 95-52444

"Eschewing the belief that the Allies won solely because of their prodigious production of weapons and equipment,

Mr. Overy points out that in the early stages of the war, before the Allies were fully mobilized, the Axis countries held the production advantage, yet failed to achieve victory because Germany's management of supply logistics was far inferior to that of the Allies—frequently as a result of Hitler's wrongheaded interference. . . . Assiduously researched and concisely written, this is a highly perceptive study." N Y Times Book Rev

Includes bibliographical references

Pick, Hella

Simon Wiesenthal; a life in search of justice. Northeastern Univ. Press 1996 349p il $35 **940.53**
1. Authors 2. Architects 3. Holocaust survivors 4. Essayists 5. Memoirists 6. Nazi hunters 7. Jewish leaders
ISBN 1-55553-273-X

LC 96-11808

This biography "has interesting things to say about forgiveness, including an extraordinary hallucinogenic encounter with a dying SS officer, and conveys a broadly sympathetic picture of a man capable of distinguishing between individuals and their political rhetoric." Times Lit Suppl

Includes bibliographical references

Pivnik, Sam

Survivor; Auschwitz, the Death March and My Fight for Freedom. Sam Pivnik. St. Martin's Press 2013 320 p. (hardcover) $26.99 **940.53**
1. Holocaust, 1939-1945
ISBN 125002952X; 9781250029522

This book, by Sam Pivnik, presents a memoir of a Jewish Holocaust survivor. "On fourteen occasions he should have been killed, but luck, his physical strength, and his determination not to die all played a part in Sam Pivnik living to tell his . . . story. In 1939, . . . Pivnik's life changed forever when the Nazis invaded Poland. He survived the two ghettoes . . . , six months [in] Auschwitz . . . , [and] the brutal Fürstengrube mining camp." (Publisher's note)

Plokhy, S. M.

Yalta; the price of peace. [by] S.M. Plokhy. Viking 2010 xxviii, 451p il map **940.53**
1. Yalta Conference (1945) 2. World politics -- 1945-1991 3. World War, 1939-1945 -- Peace 4. World War, 1939-1945 -- Diplomatic history
ISBN 978-0-670-02141-3

LC 2009-26833

Plokhy "has produced a colorful and gripping portrait of the three aging leaders at their historic encounter." Wall Street J

Includes bibliographical references

Rees, Laurence

Auschwitz : a new history; Laurence Rees. Public Affairs 2005 xxii, 327p il $30; pa $16 **940.53**
1. Holocaust, 1933-1945 2. Auschwitz (Poland: Concentration camp)
ISBN 1-586-48303-X; 1-586-48357-9 pa

LC 2004-43196

For this history of the concentration camp, the author "interviewed 100 former Nazi perpetrators and survivors

from the camp and drew on hundreds of interviews conducted for his previous research on the Third Reich, many with former members of the Nazi Party. . . . This is a significant contribution to our understanding of the intricacies of Nazi racial and ethnic policy that resulted in this ultimate abomination." Booklist

Includes bibliographical references

Reporting World War II. Library of Am. 1995 2v ea $35 **940.53**
1. World War, 1939-1945 2. Reporters and reporting
ISBN 1-883011-04-3 v1; 1-883011-05-1 v2

LC 94-45463

This "collection of some 200 entries by nearly 90 writers, drawn from newspapers, magazine articles, broadcast transcripts and book excerpts, recalls WW II campaigns and battles in all theaters but pays attention to the home front as well. It begins with an excerpt from William L. Shirer's Berlin Diary and ends with one from John Hersey's Hiroshima. . . . This is a treasure trove of war reporting, featuring writing of the highest order." Publ Wkly

Reynolds, David

In command of history; Churchill fighting and writing the Second World War. by David Reynolds. Random House 2005 xxiv, 631p il $35 **940.53**
1. Statesmen 2. Historians 3. Prime ministers 4. Memoirists 5. Cabinet members 6. Members of Parliament 7. Nobel laureates for literature 8. World War, 1939-1945 -- Historiography
ISBN 0-679-45743-7

LC 2004-51087

"Packed with detail and vivid characterizations . . . [this book is] a different take on one of the few men capable of both making history and writing it." Publ Wkly

Includes bibliographical references

Rosenfeld, Oskar

In the beginning was the ghetto; 890 days in Lodz. edited and with an introduction by Hanno Loewy; translated from the German by Brigitte M. Goldstein. Northwestern Univ. Press 2002 xxxviii, 313p $40 **940.53**
1. Łódz (Poland) 2. Jews -- Poland 3. Holocaust, 1933-1945 -- Personal narratives
ISBN 0-8101-1488-7

LC 2001-6691

Original German edition, 1994

These entries from Rosenfeld's diary "contain vivid descriptions of daily life in the ghetto, including details about deportations, forced labor, hunger, diseases, cold, terror, and the struggle to maintain human dignity. . . . This book is one of the most important and lasting works documenting the horrors of the Holocaust." Booklist

Includes bibliographical references

Rosenzveig, Charles H.

The **World** reacts to the Holocaust; David S. Wyman, editor; Charles H. Rosenzveig, project direc-

tor. Johns Hopkins Univ. Press 1996 xxiii, 981p
$80   **940.53**
   1. Holocaust, 1933-1945
   ISBN 0-8018-4969-1

                       LC 96-15395
This is a "country-by-country chronicle of the impact of
the Holocaust on world history. Covering 22 countries and
the United Nations, the volume carefully traces the contentions and controversies involved in coming to terms with the
events leading up to the Holocaust, from prewar attitudes
and perceptions to the political, economic, and cultural legacies in the 1990s." Univ Press Books for Public and Second
Sch Libr
   Includes bibliographical references

Shephard, Ben

   The **long** road home; the aftermath of the Second
World War. Alfred A. Knopf 2011 489p map $35;
ebook $35   **940.53**
   1. World War, 1939-1945 -- Refugees 2. World War,
1939-1945 -- Forced repatriation 3. United Nations
Relief and Rehabilitation Administration
   ISBN 978-1-4000-4068-1; 978-1-4000-4068-1 ebook
                       LC 2010-23894
First published 2010 in the United Kingdom
   The book examines the experience of "roughly eleven
million foreigners stranded in Germany [after World War II],
often in ghastly conditions, after surviving years of hard labor and imprisonment in labor camps, concentration camps,
death camps, and POW camps. . . . The Allied armies, chiefly the Americans, Soviets, and British, were faced with the
kind of catastrophe left in the wake of most wars, but the
scale in 1945 was unprecedented. . . . Shephard describes .
. . the . . . confrontation of well-fed people from a relatively
secure world with human beings who had indeed been reduced to a state that seemed lower than animals." (New York
Review of Books)
   "Ben Shephard's account of this demanding and important subject is a triumph. He has unearthed new and moving
testimony by former DPs and has burrowed into official and
personal papers without ever letting his deep scholarship get
in the way of the riveting story he has to tell." Hist Today
   Includes bibliographical references

Smith, Lyn

   Remembering, voices of the holocaust; a new
history in the words of the men and women who survived. [foreword by Laurence Rees] Carroll & Graf
2006 351p il map $27   **940.53**
   1. Holocaust, 1933-1945 -- Personal narratives
   ISBN 0-7867-1640-1

                    LC 2006-284769
First published 2005 in the United Kingdom
   The author, "who has recorded the experiences of survivors for London's Imperial War Museum, weaves together
more than 100 accounts to construct a narrative of Nazi
persecutions from the first anti-Semitic measures in 1933
through the liberation of the concentration camps. . . . This
is an extraordinary work of scholarship and a reminder of
the power of individual stories, which can bring home the

horrors of WWII more forcefully than abstract numbers."
Publ Wkly
   Includes bibliographical references

Spiegelman, Art

   Maus; a survivor's tale. Pantheon Bks. 1996 2v
in 1 il $35   **940.53**
   1. Graphic novels 2. Biographical graphic novels 3.
Holocaust, 1933-1945 -- Graphic novels
   ISBN 0-679-40641-7

                       LC 96-32796
   A combined edition of Maus (1986) and Maus II (1991)
   Awards: 1992 Pulitzer Prize Special Award; Eisner
Award for Best Graphic Album: Reprint for Maus II; Harvey Award for Best Graphic Album of Previously Published
Work (for Maus II); 1993 Los Angeles Times Book Prize for
Fiction (for Maus II)
   In this work "Spiegelman takes the comic book to a new
level of seriousness, portraying Jews as mice and Nazis as
cats. Depicting himself being told about the Holocaust by
his Polish survivor father, Spiegelman not only explores the
concentration-camp experience, but also the guilt, love, and
anger between father and son." Rochman. Against borders

Stargardt, Nicholas

   Witnesses of war; children's lives under the Nazis. Distributed by Random House 2006 493p il
map $30; pa $16.95   **940.53**
   1. World War, 1939-1945 -- Children
   ISBN 1-4000-4088-4; 978-1-4000-4088-9; 1-4000-
3379-9 pa; 978-1-4000-3379-9 pa
                       LC 2005-50409
First published 2005 in the United Kingdom
   This is "a sharp and taut account of misery." Publ Wkly
   Includes bibliographical references

Takaki, Ronald T.

   Double victory; a multicultural history of America in World War II. [by] Ronald Takaki. Little, Brown
2000 282p il hardcover o.p. pa $19.99   **940.53**
   1. United States -- Race relations 2. World War, 1939-
1945 -- United States
   ISBN 0-316-83155-7; 0-316-83156-5 pa
                       LC 99-40374

   Amelia Bloomer Project (2014)
   "Takaki discusses the experiences of African Americans,
Indians, Chicanos, Asian Americans from several nations,
German and Italian Americans, and Jewish Americans. .
. . Despite Jim Crow, internment camps, neglected slums,
barrios, reservations, and rejection of Jewish refugees, the
nation's not-quite-Americans fought bravely in World War
II." Booklist
   Includes bibliographical references

United States Holocaust Memorial Museum

   The **Holocaust** and history; the known, the un-
known, the disputed, and the reexamined. edited by
Michael Berenbaum and Abraham J. Peck. Indiana
Univ. Press 1998 836p $58.71; pa $35   **940.53**
   1. Holocaust, 1933-1945
   ISBN 0-253-33374-1; 0-253-21529-3 pa
                       LC 97-40030

"Papers collected here originated at a 1993 conference organized by the US Holocaust Memorial Museum's Research Institute. . . . The 50 contributors treat the subject from every conceivable angle: the role of antisemitism and racism; the politics of 'racial hygiene'; Nazi leadership and bureaucracy; the complicity of 'ordinary' people; the experiences of Gypsies, homosexuals, and blacks; the concentration camps; the Holocaust as reflected in international relations; the response of Jews, rescuers, and survivors. Recognizing the passionately controversial nature of the field, the editors have opted for variety over unanimity." Choice

The **United** States Holocaust Memorial Museum encyclopedia of camps and ghettos, 1933-1945; v 2 Geoffrey P. Megargee, general editor; Martin Dean, volume editor. Indiana University Press 2012 2096 p. v 2 ill., maps (hardcover) $295.00 **940.53**
1. Jewish ghettos 2. Concentration camps 3. Holocaust, 1939-1945 -- Encyclopedias 4. World War, 1939-1945 -- Prisoners and prisons 5. Concentration camps -- Europe -- Encyclopedias 6. Jewish ghettos -- Europe, Eastern -- Encyclopedias 7. World War, 1939-1945 -- Jews -- Europe -- Encyclopedias 8. World War, 1939-1945 -- Concentration camps -- Europe -- Encyclopedias
ISBN 0253353289; 0253355990; 9780253355997; 2008037382

LC 2008037382

This book "offers a[n] . . . account of how the Nazis conducted the Holocaust throughout . . . Poland and the Soviet Union. It covers more than 1,150 sites, including both open and closed ghettos. Regional essays outline the patterns of ghettoization in 19 German administrative regions. Each entry discusses key events in the history of the ghetto; living and working conditions; activities of the Jewish Councils . . . and details of the ghetto's liquidation." (Publisher's note)

Includes bibliographical references and indexes.

Weinberg, Gerhard L.

★ A **world** at arms; a global history of World War II. 2nd ed; Cambridge University Press 2005 xxix, 1178p map $65; pa $25.99 **940.53**
1. World War, 1939-1945
ISBN 0-521-85316-8; 978-0-521-85316-3; 0-521-61826-6 pa; 978-0-521-61826-7 pa

LC 2005-41954

First published 1994

"Weinberg's unrivaled command of archival sources combine with a smooth writing style to produce a definitive one-volume history of World War II." Libr J [review of 1994 edition]

Includes bibliographical references

Weiss, Helga, 1929-

Helga's diary; a young girl's account of life in a concentration camp. Helga Weiss ; translated by Neil Bermel ; Introduction by Francine Prose. 1st American ed. W.W. Norton & Co Inc. 2013 256 p. (hardcover) $24.95 **940.53**
1. Concentration camps -- Juvenile literature 2. Terezin (Czechoslovakia: Concentration camp) 3. Prague (Czech Republic) -- Biography 4. Theresienstadt (Concentration camp) -- Juvenile literature 5. Jews -- Czech Republic -- Prague -- Biography -- Juvenile literature 6. Jewish children in the Holocaust -- Czech Republic -- Biography -- Juvenile literature 7. Holocaust, Jewish (1939-1945) -- Czech Republic -- Prague -- Personal narratives -- Juvenile literature
ISBN 0393077977; 9780393077971

LC 2013003775

Helga Weiss "begins her diary as a frightened eight-year-old in a bomb shelter . . . . The scene sets the tone of fear and confusion that will dominate her life for the next several years, the bulk of which she spends in the Jewish ghetto, Terezín. Her writings describe both the torturous physical circumstances of daily life, as well as the psychological toll wrought by ceaseless anxiety, degradation, and survivor's guilt." (Publishers Weekly)

Includes bibliographical references.

Weller, George

Weller's war; a legendary foreign correspondent's saga of World War II on five continents. edited by Anthony Weller. Crown Publishers 2009 644p il map $30 **940.53**
1. World War, 1939-1945 -- Campaigns 2. World War, 1939-1945 -- Personal narratives
ISBN 978-0-307-40655-2; 0-307-40655-5

The author "wrote for the Chicago Daily News for 35 years, achieving fame for his widely ranging dispatches from the many fronts of World War II. He was captured by the Gestapo in Greece, escaped from Java on a boat strafed by Japanese fighters, marched with Belgian colonial troops fighting Italian colonial troops in Ethiopia, and slogged through swamps with Americans and Australians locked in grim struggles in New Guinea. Weller's war reporting won him the Pulitzer Prize in 1943. Here, his son assembles many of his dispatches, which add tremendously to our understanding of the war at ground level, the people's war." Libr J

Weyr, Thomas

The **setting** of the pearl; Vienna under Hitler. by Thomas Weyr. Oxford University Press 2005 352p il map $30 **940.53**
1. Vienna (Austria) 2. World War, 1939-1945 -- Austria
ISBN 0-19-514679-4

LC 2004-18295

"This is a superbly written work and an excellent addition to World War II collections." Booklist

Includes bibliographical references

A **woman** in Berlin; eight weeks in the conquered city: a diary. by Anonymous; translated by Philip Boehm. Metropolitan Books/Henry Holt 2005 261p $23 **940.53**
1. Berlin, Battle of, 1945 2. World War, 1939-1945 -- Women 3. World War, 1939-1945 -- Personal narratives
ISBN 0-8050-7540-2

LC 2005-41984

Original German edition, 2003; Expurgated edition translated by James Stern published 1954 by Harcourt, Brace

This "is one of the most important documents to emerge from World War II." N Y Times Book Rev

"The author of this diary was a 34-year-old journalist, now deceased, who consistently refused to reveal her identity publicly. . . . [This] account covers the period from late April to mid-June 1945, beginning with the massive Soviet bombardment of Berlin and ending with the opening weeks of the Soviet occupation." Booklist

World War II; an encyclopedia of quotations. compiled and edited by Howard J. Langer. Greenwood Press 1999 449p il $83.95   **940.53**
1. Quotations 2. World War, 1939-1945 -- Quotations
ISBN 0-313-30018-6

LC 98-26436

This is a collection of 1,554 "quotations dealing with World War II. . . . The first 12 chapters are arranged by type of person quoted . . . and then alphabetically by name. A typical entry has a short introductory paragraph providing biographical and historical information including birth and death years of persons. The remaining chapters cover other sources, including movies and songs." Booklist

Yellin, Emily
Our mothers' war; American women at home and at the Front during World War II. Free Press 2004 447p il hardcover o.p. pa $14   **940.53**
1. World War, 1939-1945 -- Women
ISBN 0-7432-4514-8; 0-7432-4516-4 pa

LC 2004-40496

"Yellin reveals all of the responsibilities held by women, including helping to manufacture aircraft, ships, and other munitions; and, in the process, outproducing all of America's allies and enemies, by far. Readers see war brides who worked hard to maintain the morale of their husbands while surviving long separation, fear, and shortages of virtually everything necessary to support a family. . . . [This book] is an important book because the role played by women in World War II has been regularly ignored." SLJ
Includes bibliographical references

Zuccotti, Susan
Père Marie-Benoît and Jewish rescue; how a French priest together with Jewish friends saved thousands during the Holocaust. Susan Zuccotti. Indiana University Press 2013 280 p. (cloth : alkaline paper) $35   **940.53**
1. World War, 1939-1945 -- Jews -- Rescue 2. Marseille (France) -- Biography 3. Priests -- France -- Marseille -- Biography 4. Capuchins -- France -- Marseille -- Biography 5. Marseille (France) -- History -- 20th century 6. Holocaust, Jewish (1939-1945) -- France -- Marseille 7. Jews -- France -- Marseille -- History -- 20th century 8. World War, 1939-1945 -- Jews -- Rescue -- France -- Marseille 9. Righteous Gentiles in the Holocaust -- France -- Marseille -- Biography
ISBN 0253008530; 9780253008534

LC 2012047187

Here, Susan Zuccotti offers an account "of the life of Capuchin priest Père Marie-Benoît and his successful efforts to save thousands of Jews." Her "approach begins before Marie-Benoît's birth in 1895, with a review of the geography and history of the region in France where he was born. She then moves on to profile the courageous priest in

the trenches of the First World War, . . . and afterward during his high-level religious studies in Rome after the war." (Publishers Weekly)
Includes bibliographical references and index

Under his very windows; the Vatican and the Holocaust in Italy. Yale Univ. Press 2000 408p il $29.95; pa $16.95   **940.53**
1. Popes 2. Jews -- Italy 3. Holocaust, 1933-1945 4. Catholic Church -- Relations -- Judaism
ISBN 0-300-08487-0; 0-300-09310-1 pa

LC 00-43307

Zuccotti's "aim is to show that whatever help was given to the Jews by the Catholic Church during the war resulted almost entirely from spontaneous acts by courageous individuals—priests, monks and nuns, and occasionally prelates—and not from any interventions by the Vatican. . . . Zuccotti makes her case strongly. . . . This is a serious and well-researched book." N Y Times Book Rev
Includes bibliographical references (p.) and index

940.54   Military history of World War II

Alperovitz, Gar
The **decision** to use the atomic bomb and the architecture of an American myth; {by} Gar Alperovitz with the assistance of Sanho Tree {et al.} Knopf 1995 843p hardcover o.p. pa $18   **940.54**
1. United States -- Foreign relations 2. World War, 1939-1945 -- United States 3. Hiroshima (Japan) -- Bombardment, 1945
ISBN 0-679-76285-X pa

LC 95-8778

"Alperovitz is the dean of revisionist scholars who argue that the nuclear bombing of Japan was unnecessary and that America bears a hefty responsibility for the cold war. . . . His main and probably most controversial contention is that certain documents pertaining to the decision were doctored, some by none other than Truman himself. Further, Alperovitz sees James Byrnes, Truman's Mephistophelian secretary of state, as a furtive player who nixed such alternative plans as modifying the unconditional-surrender demand and encouraging a Russian declaration of war." Booklist
Includes bibliographical references

Ambrose, Stephen E., 1936-2002
★ **Band** of brothers; E Company, 506th Regiment, 101st Airborne from Normandy to Hitler's Eagle's Nest. [by] Stephen Ambrose. Simon & Schuster 2001 333p il maps $25; pa $16   **940.54**
1. World War, 1939-1945 -- Europe 2. United States -- Army -- Parachute Infantry Regiment, 506th -- Company E
ISBN 0-7432-1638-5; 0-7432-2454-X pa

LC 2001-20134

A reissue of the title first published 1992
"Here is the story of the daring E Company, which began the war by parachuting into France on D-Day and ended it by capturing Eagle's Nest, Hitler's outpost in Bavaria." Libr J

"Moving, poignant, and uplifting, this book is highly recommended for medium and large World War II collections." Booklist

Includes bibliographical references

Citizen soldiers; the U.S. Army from the Normandy beaches to the Bulge to the surrender of Germany, June 7, 1944-May 7, 1945. Simon & Schuster 1997 512p il maps hardcover o.p. pa $17 **940.54**
1. World War, 1939-1945 -- Campaigns -- France
ISBN 0-684-84801-5 pa
LC 97-23876
This continuation of D-Day focuses on the front-line experiences of American soldiers who fought in northwestern Europe in the war's last years
"These events have all been well documented, but in Ambrose's capable hands, the bloody and dramatic battles fought in northwest Europe in 1944-45 come alive as never before." N Y Times Book Rev

Includes bibliographical references

D -Day, June 6, 1944; the climactic battle of World War II. Simon & Schuster 1994 655p il maps $30; pa $17 **940.54**
1. Normandy (France), Attack on, 1944 2. World War, 1939-1945 -- Campaigns -- France
ISBN 0-671-88403-4; 0-684-80137-X pa
LC 93-40353
This is an account of the Allied invasion of Normandy in 1944. The author argues "that the invasion represented a triumph of the old United States Army, whose officers had transformed millions of civilians into a cohesive, highly trained and motivated mass army that, backed by a united nation, won with relative ease." (Christ Sci Monit) Index.
"Mr. Ambrose wonderfully illuminates the mind of the very young soldier of any nation anywhere who has never been in fighting before." N Y Times Book Rev

Includes bibliographical references

The **victors**; Eisenhower and his boys, the men of World War II. Simon & Schuster 1998 396p hardcover o.p. pa $16 **940.54**
1. Generals 2. Presidents 3. College presidents 4. United States -- Army 5. World War, 1939-1945 -- Campaigns
ISBN 0-684-85629-8 pa
LC 98-37808
"The author is a master of letting his subjects tell the story, of standing back and allowing the large lessons to unfold. The result is history with lasting impact." SLJ

Includes bibliographical references

The **wild** blue; the men and boys who flew the B-24s over Germany 1944-45. Simon & Schuster 2001 299p il $26; pa $16 **940.54**
1. Air pilots 2. B-24 bomber 3. Senators 4. Members of Congress 5. Government officials 6. Presidential candidates 7. World War, 1939-1945 -- Aerial operations
ISBN 0-7432-0339-9; 0-7432-2309-8 pa
LC 2001-20563

Ambrose presents profiles of American pilots who flew B-24 bombers focusing on the Dakota Queen piloted by future senator and presidential candidate George McGovern
"Ambrose's narrative flows smoothly, even as he manages to cover each man's story." Libr J

Includes bibliographical references

Atkinson, Rick
★ An **army** at dawn; the war in North Africa, 1942-1943. Holt & Co. 2002 681p il maps (The liberation trilogy) $30; pa $16 **940.54**
1. Africa, North -- History, Military 2. World War, 1939-1945 -- North Africa 3. World War, 1939-1945 -- Campaigns -- North Africa 4. World War, 1939-1945 -- Campaigns -- Africa, North
ISBN 0-8050-6288-2; 0-8050-7448-1 pa
LC 2002-24130
This is the first volume of a projected World War II trilogy.
This "volume covers the conception of Operation Torch through the German surrender in Tunisia in May 1943. . . . An exemplary work that feeds anticipation of the succeeding volumes." Booklist

Includes bibliographical references
Followed by The day of battle (2007)

★ The **day** of battle; the war in Sicily and Italy, 1943-1944. H. Holt 2007 791p il map (The liberation trilogy) $35; pa $17 **940.54**
1. World War, 1939-1945 -- Campaigns -- Italy
ISBN 978-0-8050-6289-2; 0-805-06289-0; 978-0-8050-8861-8 pa; 0-8050-8861-X pa
LC 2007-7653
"The second volume of . . . [the author's] 'Liberation' trilogy, which began with the Pulitzer Prizewinning An Army at Dawn: The War in North Africa, 1942–1943, this is probably the most eagerly awaited World War II book of the year. Atkinson's clear prose, perceptive analysis, and grasp of the personalities and nuances of the campaigns make his book an essential purchase." Libr J

Includes bibliographical references

The **guns** at last light; the war in Western Europe, 1944-1945. Rick Atkinson. Henry Holt and Co. 2013 877 p. ill. (The liberation trilogy) $40 **940.54**
1. Generals 2. Soldiers 3. World War, 1939-1945 4. World War, 1939-1945 -- Campaigns -- Western Front
ISBN 0805062904; 9780805062908
LC 2012034312
This book concludes Rick Atkinson's series about World War II. "Peopling the pages [of the book] are German, British, French, Canadian, and (primarily) American generals and common soldiers. Excerpts from the letters of dead soldiers on both sides, as well as from the diaries of captain generals, fill out the story." (Publishers Weekly)
"[L]ively, occasionally lyric prose brings the vast theater of battle, from the beaches of Normandy deep into Germany, brilliantly alive." Pub Wkly

Includes bibliographical references (pages 813-841) and index

Ballard, Robert D.

Return to Midway; {by} Robert D. Ballard and Rick Archbold; principal photography by David Doubilet. . . . National Geographic Soc. 1999 191p il maps $40 　　　　**940.54**

　　1. Shipwrecks 2. Midway, Battle of, 1942 3. World War, 1939-1945 -- Naval operations

　　ISBN 0-7922-7500-4

　　　　　　　　　　　　　　　　LC 99-10831

In this narrative, Ballard "intersperses chapters on the Battle of Midway with a fascinating account of his search for the U.S.S. Yorktown, which was sunk by a Japanese destroyer on June 7, 1942. Period photographs from the battle are combined with those of the Yorktown as she rests today, and paintings by marine artist Ken Marschall add detail to complete the record. The lively narrative is punctuated with two Japanese and two American oral history accounts of the battle." Libr J

　　Includes bibliographical references

Bayly, C. A.

Forgotten armies; the fall of British Asia, 1941-1945. [by] Christopher Bayly and Tim Harper. Belknap Press of Harvard University Press 2005 xxxiii, 555p il maps $29.95; pa $18.95 　　**940.54**

　　1. World War, 1939-1945 -- Asia 2. Great Britain -- Colonies -- Asia

　　ISBN 0-674-01748-X; 0-674-02219-X pa

　　　　　　　　　　　　　　　LC 2004-54300

This "study is by far the most comprehensive to date, an excellent survey for those interested in both WW II and the denouement of British imperialism in Asia." Choice

　　Includes bibliographical references

Beevor, Antony

D -day; the Battle for Normandy. Viking 2009 591p il map $32.95 　　　　　　**940.54**

　　1. Normandy (France), Attack on, 1944

　　ISBN 978-0-670-02119-2

　　　　　　　　　　　　　　　LC 2009-23574

The author "presents an account of the Normandy invasion that . . . [examines] the experiences of soldiers and French civilians, . . . the heavy casualties suffered on all fronts and the ways in which the war influenced relations between America and Europe." Publisher's note

This "is a vibrant work of history that honors the sacrifice of tens of thousands of men and women." Time

　　Includes bibliographical references

The **fall** of Berlin 1945. Viking 2002 xxxvii, 489p il maps $29.95; pa $16 　　　　**940.54**

　　1. Berlin, Battle of, 1945 2. World War, 1939-1945 -- Germany

　　ISBN 0-670-03041-4; 0-14-200280-1 pa

　　　　　　　　　　　　　　　LC 2002-510674

The author "relies on material from American, German, British, French, and Swedish archives and documents from former Soviet files, making the book an invaluable and meticulous account." Booklist

　　Includes bibliographical references (p. 466-475) and index

Beevor, Antony, 1946-

The **Second** World War; Antony Beevor. Little, Brown & Co 2012 xii, 863 p.p 　　　　**940.54**

　　1. Military history 2. World War, 1939-1945 3. Europe -- History -- 1918-1945

　　ISBN 0316023744; 9780316023740

　　　　　　　　　　　　　　　LC 2012007028

In this book on World War II Anthony Beevor describes how "the war was set in motion by a single person--Adolf Hitler--and its extension reflected specific decisions by specific people, and its course changed lives across the globe in ways impossible to predict. . . . And from heads of state to front-line riflemen, from field marshals to teenaged girls, Beevor's protagonists exercise choice in the context of 'the greatest man-made disaster in history.'" (Publishers Weekly)

　　Includes bibliographical references and index.

Bishop, Patrick

The **Hunt** for Hitler's Warship; Patrick Bishop. Perseus Distribution Services 2013 416 p. (hardcover) $27.95 　　　　　　**940.54**

　　1. Warships 2. World War, 1939-1945 -- Naval operations

　　ISBN 1621570037; 9781621570035

This book, by Patrick Bishop, discusses the Allied efforts to sink "the Tirpitz, Hitler's mightiest warship, a 52,000-ton behemoth. . . . Patrick Bishop tells the epic story of the men who would not rest until the Tirpitz lay at the bottom of the sea. In November of 1944, . . . a raid as audacious as any Royal Air Force operation of the war was launched, under the command of one of Britain's greatest but least-known war heroes, Wing Commander Willie Tait." (Publisher's note)

Blair, Clay

Hitler's U-boat war; the hunted, 1942-1945. Random House 1998 xxviii, 909p 2v il map hardcover o.p. pa $19.95 　　　　**940.54**

　　1. World War, 1939-1945 -- Atlantic Ocean 2. World War, 1939-1945 -- Naval operations -- Submarine

　　ISBN 0-6794-5742-9

　　　　　　　　　　　　　　　LC 96-2275

This is a history of the German submarine campaign against Allied forces during the Second World War

This is "the most thorough study of the U-Boat campaign available; it includes a massive amount of detailed statistics." Libr J {review of volume 1}

　　Includes bibliographical references

Bradley, James

Flags of our fathers; [by] James Bradley with Ron Powers. Bantam Bks. 2000 376p $24.95; pa $14 　　　　　　　　　　**940.54**

　　1. Iwo Jima, Battle of, 1945 2. Photojournalists 3. United States -- Marine Corps

　　ISBN 0-553-11133-7; 0-553-38415-5 pa

　　　　　　　　　　　　　　　LC 00-25803

This is the "story of the most famous photograph to come out of World War II, the flag-raising on Mount Suribachi during the Battle of Iwo Jima in February 1945. Bradley is the son of one of the six men immortalized in that remarkable photo, and his gripping narrative, vivid descriptions, and heartfelt style make this a powerful story of courage, humility, and tragedy." Libr J

Includes bibliographical references

Breitman, Richard

Official secrets; what the Nazis planned, what the British and Americans knew. Hill & Wang 1998 325p hardcover o.p. pa $22 **940.54**
1. Holocaust, 1933-1945 2. World War, 1939-1945 -- Atrocities 3. Germany -- Politics and government -- 1933-1945

ISBN 0-8090-3819-6; 0-8090-0184-5 pa

LC 98-7997

Breitman sheds new light on "evidence that Britain's top intelligence analysts knew, as early as September 1941, that the Germans were systematically carrying out mass murder of Jews in Nazi-occupied Soviet territories and planning their liquidation in the lands they conquered." Publ Wkly

This "is a remarkable study, concise yet carefully nuanced." N Y Times Book Rev

Includes bibliographical references

Brokaw, Tom

An **album** of memories; personal histories from the greatest generation. Random House 2001 314p il maps $29.95; pa $14.95 **940.54**
1. United States -- History -- 1933-1945 2. World War, 1939-1945 -- Personal narratives

ISBN 0-375-50581-4; 0-375-76041-5 pa

LC 2001-273436

This volume "gathers letters written to Brokaw by Americans who lived through the Depression and World War II and, in some cases, letters written by their children. Brokaw provides a brief introduction and a time line for each chapter; these cover the Depression, the war in Europe and in the Pacific, and the wartime 'home front,' closing with 'Reflections.' The book is lavishly illustrated with reproductions of photographs, drawings, documents, and other memorabilia of the era." Booklist

Burgin, R. V.

Islands of the damned; a Marine at war in the Pacific. [by] R.V. Burgin with William Marvel. New American Library 2010 296p il $24.95 **940.54**
1. World War, 1939-1945 -- Pacific Ocean 2. World War, 1939-1945 -- Personal narratives

ISBN 978-0-451-22990-8

LC 2009-40454

"As this well-written, excellently detailed personal narrative makes clear, some Marines who fought alongside him did not make it home alive. They and thousands more died amid war's confusing and unspeakable horrors. Sometimes they were killed by the enemy, sometimes by friendly fire, sometimes by accidents, and sometimes by shocking, split-second decisions where one life was sacrificed to save others. . . . Time is thinning the ranks of America's Pacific War veterans. But Islands of the Damned is a taut, engrossing, haunting book that will help keep their accomplishments and enormous sacrifices alive." Dallas Morning News

Burleigh, Michael

Moral combat; good and evil in World War II. Harper 2011 xxi, 650p il map $29.95 **940.54**
1. World War, 1939-1945 -- Ethical aspects

ISBN 978-0-06-058097-1; 0-06-058097-6

First published 2010 in the United Kingdom

"No-one with an interest in the Second World War should be without this book; and indeed nor should anyone who cares about how our world has come about." Daily Telegraph

Includes bibliographical references

Caddick-Adams, Peter

Monte Cassino; ten armies in Hell. Peter Caddick-Adams. Oxford University Press 2013 432 p. $29.95 **940.54**
1. World War, 1939-1945 -- Italy 2. Cassino, Battle of, Cassino, Italy, 1944

ISBN 0199974640; 9780199974641

LC 2012030395

This book, by Peter Caddick-Adams, examines the World War II Battle of Monte Cassino. "Waged deep in the Italian mountains beneath a medieval monastery, it was an astonishingly brutal encounter, grinding up ten armies in conditions as bad as the Eastern Front at its worst. . . . Military historian Peter Caddick-Adams provides a vivid account of how an array of men . . . fought the most lengthy and devastating engagement of the Italian campaign in an ancient monastery town." (Publisher's note)

Includes bibliographical references and index

Conant, Jennet

A **covert** affair; Julia Child and Paul Child in the OSS. Simon & Schuster 2011 395p il $28 **940.54**
1. Cooks 2. Artists 3. Diplomats 4. Intelligence service 5. Anticommunist movements 6. Television personalities 7. Senators 8. Cookbook writers 9. Spouses of prominent persons 10. World War, 1939-1945 -- Secret service 11. United States -- Office of Strategic Services 12. United States -- Politics and government -- 1945-1953 13. World War, 1939-1945 -- Secret service -- United States 14. Anti-communist movements -- United States -- History -- 20th century

ISBN 978-1-4391-6352-8; 978-1-4391-6850-9 ebook

LC 2011-02875

This is an "account of Julia and Paul Child's experiences as members of the Office of Strategic Services (OSS) in the Far East during World War II." (Publisher's note) Index.

"Paul and Julia Child are merely supporting players in this book about the Office of Strategic Services in World War II and the McCarthy witch hunts that followed. Despite this blatant marketing ploy, the book is a well-researched and well-written account of this period in American history." Seattle Times

Includes bibliographical references

The **irregulars**; Roald Dahl and the British spy ring in wartime Washington. Simon & Schuster 2008 xx, 393p il $27.95 **940.54**
1. Authors 2. Children's authors 3. Short story writers 4. Intelligence service -- Great Britain 5. World War,

1939-1945 -- Secret service
ISBN 978-0-7432-9458-4; 0-7432-9458-0
                                                LC 2008-12483
Conant tells the story of young writer Roald Dahl who
is assigned by His Majesty's Government to Washington,
D.C. as a diplomat to gather intelligence about America's
isolationist circles. In the course of his "spying," he meets or
works closely with David Ogilvy, Ian Fleming, and the great
spymaster William Stephenson (aka Intrepid).

"Entertaining social history that also reveals a little-
known aspect of an important literary figure's life." Kirkus
Includes bibliographical references

Costello, John

The **Pacific** War. Quill 1982 742p il
$21.95   **940.54**
    1. World War, 1939-1945 -- Pacific Ocean
    ISBN 0-688-01620-0; 978-0-688-01620-3
                                                LC 82-15054
First published 1981 by Rawson, Wade
A "history of World War II as it was played out in the Pacific theater. . . . Emphasizing the role played by Allied intelligence sources during the early period of the war, Costello
analyzes the actual battles from Pearl Harbor to the atomic
bombing of Japan." Booklist
Includes bibliographical references

Daws, Gavan

Prisoners of the Japanese; POWs of World War
II in the Pacific. Morrow 1994 462p il map hardcover o.p. pa $19.95   **940.54**
    1. Prisoners of war 2. World War, 1939-1945 -- Pacific
    Ocean 3. World War, 1939-1945 -- Prisoners and prisons
    ISBN 0-688-11812-7; 0-688-14370-9 pa
                                                LC 93-49363
"Daws offers a well-written thoroughly researched account of these POWs. . . . An exceptionally worthwhile addition to the literature on the war in the Pacific." Booklist
Includes bibliographical references

Dunnigan, James F.

The **Pacific** War encyclopedia; {by} James F.
Dunnigan and Albert A. Nofi. Facts on File 1998 2v
il maps set $137.50   **940.54**
    1. Reference books 2. World War, 1939-1945 --
    Encyclopedias
    ISBN 0-8160-3439-7
                                                LC 97-15634
This work "is lively as well as informative, and . . . will
be attractive to military buffs while still useful to more serious researchers." Libr J

Frank, Richard B.

★ **Downfall**; the end of the Imperial Japanese
Empire. Penguin 2001 484p il map pa $18 **940.54**
    1. Japan -- History -- 1868-1945 2. World War, 1939-
    1945 -- Japan 3. World War, 1939-1945 -- Aerial
    operations
    ISBN 0-14-100146-1
First published 1999 by Random House
"Weaving together the strands of military and diplomatic
events, Frank contends that absent the bombings of Hiro-

shima and Nagasaki the war would have continued for at
least several more months, at a cost in Japanese and Allied
civilian and combatant lives far in excess of the admittedly
awful toll that the atomic bombs exacted. A powerful work
of history." Libr J
Includes bibliographical references

Fussell, Paul

Wartime : understanding and behavior in the
Second World War. Oxford Univ. Press 1989 330p
il $35; pa $16.95   **940.54**
    1. World War, 1939-1945 -- Propaganda 2. World War,
    1939-1945 -- Great Britain 3. World War, 1939-1945
    -- United States
    ISBN 0-19-503797-9; 0-19-506577-8 pa
                                                LC 89-2875
"Fussell's version of the war doesn't, perhaps, exactly
'balance the scales,' but it is a useful corrective. Nobody
who reads it will come away thinking about the war compla-
cently." New Repub
Includes bibliographical references

Giangreco, D. M.

Hell to pay; Operation Downfall and the invasion
of Japan, 1945-47. Naval Institute Press 2009 xxiii,
362p il map $36.95   **940.54**
    1. World War, 1939-1945 -- Campaigns -- Japan
    ISBN 978-1-59114-316-1
                                                LC 2009-27766
"Illustrative of just how much the war with Japan was a
close-run thing, this is essential reading." Libr J
Includes bibliographical references

Glass, Charles

The **deserters**; a hidden history of World War
II. Charles Glass. The Penguin Press 2013 400 p.
(hardcover) $27.95   **940.54**
    1. Military desertion 2. World War, 1939-1945
    3. Military policy -- United States 4. Combat --
    Psychological aspects 5. World War, 1939-1945
    -- Desertions 6. Military deserters -- History -- 20th
    century 7. World War, 1939-1945 -- Psychological
    aspects 8. Desertion, Military -- History -- 20th century
    ISBN 1594204284; 9781101617816; 9781594204289
                                                LC 2012046881
This book follows three World War II soldiers court-
martialed for desertion. "Tracking in detail the wartime
biographies of three privates in the infantry—Tennessee
farm boy Alfred Whitehead, Brooklyner Steve Weiss and
Britisher John Bain—the author constructs a frame for his
much broader . . . discussion of military personnel policy."
(Kirkus Reviews)
Includes bibliographical references and index

The **good** war; an oral history of World War Two.
[edited by] Studs Terkel. New Press 1997 589p
pa $16.95   **940.54**
    1. World War, 1939-1945 -- Personal narratives
    ISBN 1-56584-343-6
                                                LC 2003-389322
First published 1984 by Pantheon Bks.

In a series of interviews Terkel depicts how WWII affected the lives of average Americans.

Grayling, A. C.

Among the dead cities; the history and moral legacy of the WWII bombing of civilians in Germany and Japan. Walker & Co. 2006 361p il maps $25.95   **940.54**
1. World War, 1939-1945 -- Ethical aspects 2. World War, 1939-1945 -- Aerial operations
ISBN 0-8027-1471-4

LC 2005-58597

"Was it wrong for the Allies to bomb German and Japanese civilians in World War II? In this book, . . . [the author] attends to one of the twentieth-century's largest unexploded moral conundrums. . . . Grayling's book builds careful, generous cases for and against the bombing, admitting as evidence both the experience of the bombed as well as the bombers." Booklist

Includes bibliographical references

Ham, Paul

Hiroshima Nagasaki; the real story of the atomic bombings and their aftermath. Paul Ham. Doubleday 2012 ix, 629 p.p ill. (some color), maps (hbk.) $35   **940.54**
1. Atomic bomb -- History 2. Nagasaki (Japan) -- Bombardment, 1945 3. Hiroshima (Japan) -- Bombardment, 1945 4. Atomic bomb victims -- Japan 5. World War, 1939-1945 -- Japan -- Nagasaki-shi 6. World War, 1939-1945 -- Japan -- Hiroshima-shi 7. Atomic bomb -- Government policy -- United States -- History -- 20th century 8. Nagasaki-shi (Japan) -- History -- Bombardment, 1945 -- Moral and ethical aspects 9. Hiroshima-shi (Japan) -- History -- Bombardment, 1945 -- Moral and ethical aspects
ISBN 1250047110; 9781448126279; 1448126274; 9781250047113

LC 2012515240

"In this harrowing history of the Hiroshima and Nagasaki bombings, Paul Ham argues against the use of nuclear weapons, drawing on extensive research and hundreds of interviews to prove that the bombings had little impact on the eventual outcome of the Pacific War. More than 100,000 people were killed instantly by the atomic bombs. . . . Many hundreds of thousands more succumbed to their horrific injuries later, or slowly perished of radiation-related sickness." (Publisher's note)

"A valuable contribution to the literature of World War II that asks its readers to rethink much of what they've been taught about America's just cause." Kirkus

Includes bibliographical references and index

Hamilton, Nigel, 1944-

The **mantle** of command; FDR at war, 1941-1942. Nigel Hamilton. Houghton Mifflin Harcourt 2014 528 p. illustrations, maps (hardcover) $30   **940.54**
1. Strategy 2. World War, 1939-1945 -- United States 3. World War, 1939-1945 -- Campaigns 4. Command of troops -- United States -- Case studies 5. World War, 1939-1945 -- United States -- Biography 6. United

States -- Foreign relations -- Great Britain
ISBN 0547775245; 9780544227842; 9780547775241

LC 2013045586

"Based on years of archival research and interviews with the last surviving aides and Roosevelt family members, Nigel Hamilton offers a definitive account of FDR's masterful--and underappreciated--command of the Allied war effort. Hamilton takes readers inside FDR's White House Oval Study--his personal command center--and into the meetings where he battled with Churchill about strategy and tactics and overrode the near mutinies of his own generals and secretary of war." (Publisher's note)

"Though it's a weighty tome, and is based extensively on Roosevelt's own notes, Hamilton keeps a brisk pace throughout to produce what will likely be seen as a definitive volume on this aspect of Roosevelt's career." Pub Wkly

Includes bibliographical references and index

Hastings, Max

Armageddon : the battle for Germany, 1944-45. A.A. Knopf 2004 584p il maps $30   **940.54**
1. World War, 1939-1945
ISBN 0-375-41433-9

LC 2004-46468

The author "tells the grim tale of the final collapse of the Third Reich. It does so from the viewpoints of the upper millstone (the Western Allies), the lower millstone (the Russians) and the grain being ground in between (the Germans). The research includes previously untapped Russian archives (particularly in the accounts of Soviet veterans) and leads to a gripping and horrifying story that serious students of military history will find almost impossible to put down." Publ Wkly

Includes bibliographical references

Inferno; by Max Hastings. Alfred A. Knopf 2011 xx, 729 p.p [48] p. of plates ill maps   **940.54**
1. Military history 2. World War, 1939-1945 3. Military art and science -- History
ISBN 9780307273598

LC 2011013890

'This book "offers an account of the [Second World] war that concentrates on the lived experience of the men and women who took part in it. On almost every page there is . . . material from interviews, diaries, letters, memoirs and personal documents of many kinds. . . . This is at its core very much a military history, despite the space devoted to the experiences of civilians. . . . [Author Max] Hastings argues that the navies of the United Kingdom and the United States were their best fighting forces; he thinks the armies of the two Allied powers were mostly no match for the ruthless fighting prowess of the Germans and Japanese, whose willingness to sacrifice themselves contrasted with the care taken by Allied generals to minimize casualties among their own men. Red Army troops behaved in a manner not unlike that of the Germans, their reckless disregard for their own

safety driven on by the knowledge that the Soviet secret police would shoot them if they hesitated." (N Y Times)

Includes bibliographical references and index.

Retribution; the battle for Japan, 1944-45. Alfred A. Knopf 2008 615p il map $35   **940.54**
1. World War, 1939-1945 -- Japan
ISBN 978-0-307-26351-3; 0-307-26351-7
LC 2007-34202

First published 2007 in the United Kingdom with title:
Nemesis

This chronicle of the final year of the Pacific war discusses such topics as the events leading to Allied victory,
Japan's war against China, and the decision to bomb Hiroshima and Nagasaki.

"Encompassing the British, Chinese, and Soviet roles
in vanquishing Japan, Hastings is both comprehensive and
finely acute in this masterful interpretive narrative." Booklist

Includes bibliographical references

Haynes, Fred

The **lions** of Iwo Jima; [by] Fred Haynes and
James A. Warren. Henry Holt 2008 272p il map
$26; pa $17   **940.54**
1. Iwo Jima, Battle of, 1945 2. World War, 1939-1945
-- Personal narratives 3. United States -- Marine Corps
-- Marines, 28th
ISBN 978-0-8050-8325-5; 0-8050-8325-1; 978-0-
8050-9017-8 pa; 0-8050-9017-7 pa
LC 2007-42245

"The account focuses on the experience of Combat Team
28, a unit of 4,500 marines; their best-known accomplishment was the raising of the flag atop Mount Suribachi. However, that event, immortalized by the classic photograph,
occurred only four days into the monthlong battle. Ahead
lay a cauldron of merciless slaughter, with marines inching
forward against Japanese troops entrenched in a series of
interlocking caves and tunnels. The authors capture the horror of their advance as close-range combat in confined areas
became the norm. This is a disturbing, sometimes sickening
chronicle, but the harsh face of war in the Pacific theater has
rarely been portrayed so effectively." Booklist

Includes bibliographical references

Hersey, John

Hiroshima; a new edition with a final chapter
written forty years after the explosion. Knopf 1985
196p il $26; pa $6.50   **940.54**
1. Atomic bomb 2. World War, 1939-1945 -- Japan 3.
Hiroshima (Japan) -- Bombardment, 1945
ISBN 0-394-54844-2; 0-679-72103-7 pa
LC 85-40346

First published 1946

An account of the aftermath of the first atomic bomb as
reflected in the lives of six survivors

Hicks, George

The **comfort** women; Japan's brutal regime
of enforced prostitution in the Second World War.
Norton 1995 303p il maps hardcover o.p. pa
$14.95   **940.54**
1. Comfort women 2. Sino-Japanese Conflict, 1937-

1945 3. World War, 1939-1945 -- Women 4. World
War, 1939-1945 -- Atrocities
ISBN 0-393-03807-6; 0-393-31694-7 pa
LC 95-2162

The author begins his "report with a historical survey
of wartime sexual exploitation of women, then narrows
the focus to the 'comfort women' system developed by the
Japanese. The copious testimony of victims is shockingly
graphic. . . . This significant addition to 'the poor record
of mankind to womankind, especially in war,' properly approaches the subject as a human-rights issue tied to the rise
of feminism in Asia." Publ Wkly

Includes bibliographical references

Hillenbrand, Laura, 1967-

Unbroken. Random House 2010 473p il map
$27; ebook $27   **940.54**
1. Veterans 2. Prisoners of war 3. Evangelists 4.
Olympic athletes 5. Air force officers 6. Runners
(Athletes) 7. Biography, Individual 8. World War,
1939-1945 -- Aerial operations 9. World War, 1939-
1945 -- Prisoners and prisons
ISBN 978-1-4000-6416-8; 1-4000-6416-3; 978-0-679-
60375-7 ebook; 0-679-60375-1 ebook
LC 2010017517

This is an account of Army Air Force bomber Louis
Zamperini's plane crash in 1943 and his abuse as a Japanese
prisoner of war.

"Hillenbrand's triumph is that in telling Louie's story . .
. she tells the stories of thousands whose suffering has been
mostly forgotten. She restores to our collective memory this
tale of heroism, cruelty, life, death, joy, suffering, remorse-
lessness, and redemption." Publ Wkly

Includes bibliographical references

Holland, James

Battle of Britain; five months that changed history, May-October 1940. St. Martin's Press 2011
677p il map $40; ebook $19.99   **940.54**
1. Britain, Battle of, 1940
ISBN 978-0-312-67500-4; 978-1-4299-1941-8 ebook
LC 2010-40646

First published 2010 in the United Kingdom

"This massive volume is informative, enthralling, and
moving—often all three at once. It effectively combines narrative and analysis to tell the story of the confrontation between the Luftwaffe and RAF Fighter Command from May
through October 1940." Booklist

Includes bibliographical references

Hornfischer, James D.

Ship of ghosts; the story of the USS Houston,
FDR's legendary lost cruiser, and the epic saga of
her survivors. Bantam Books 2006 530p il map
$26   **940.54**
1. Houston (Cruiser) 2. World War, 1939-1945 -- Naval
operations
ISBN 0-553-80390-5; 978-0-553-80390-7
LC 2006-47530

This book "recounts the exploits of the Houston, mainstay of the skimpy Allied fleet opposing the Japanese onslaught in the war's early days, until her sinking in a des-

perate battle with overwhelming Japanese forces in the Java Sea in 1942. . . . The narrative then shifts gears to follow the Houston's several hundred survivors through Japanese POW camps in Southeast Asia, focusing on the labor camps on the Burma-Thailand railway (glamorized in the movie Bridge on the River Kwai). . . . [This is] a gripping, well-told memorial to Greatest Generation martyrdom." Publ Wkly

Includes bibliographical references

Hotta, Eri

Japan 1941; countdown to infamy. by Eri Hotta. Alfred A. Knopf 2013 352 p. (hardcover) $27.95 **940.54**

1. World War, 1939-1945 -- Japan 2. Japan -- Politics and government 3. Pearl Harbor (Oahu, Hawaii), Attack on, 1941 4. War -- Decision making 5. Pearl Harbor (Hawaii), Attack on, 1941 6. Japan -- Politics and government -- 1926-1945 7. Japan -- Military policy -- History -- 20th century 8. Military planning -- Japan -- History -- 20th century

ISBN 0307594017; 9780307594013

LC 2013014781

In this book, author Eri Hotta presents his attempt "to examine the lead up to the attack on Pearl Harbor from a Japanese perspective [and] portrays the dilemma faced by the Japanese government and military in 1941. She indicts American policy makers for their failure to understand Japan's views [and] condemns U.S. demands that Japan withdraw from China." (Booklist)

Includes bibliographical references and index

Iwo Jima; World War II veterans remember the greatest battle of the Pacific. [edited by] Larry Smith. W.W. Norton 2008 xxiv, 345p il map $26.95; pa $17.95 **940.54**

1. Iwo Jima, Battle of, 1945 2. World War, 1939-1945 -- Personal narratives

ISBN 978-0-393-06234-2; 0-393-06234-1; 978-0-393-33491-3 pa; 0-393-33491-0 pa

LC 2008-1301

This is "a superb collection of 22 oral histories from Iwo Jima veterans, including two Medal of Honor winners, a Navajo 'Code-Talker,' the last surviving flag raiser from the first flag raising on Mount Suribachi, a war correspondent, and an African American marine who served in an ammo company." Libr J

Jones, Michael K.

The **retreat**; Hitler's first defeat. [by] Michael Jones. Thomas Dunne Books/St. Martin's Press 2010 xxi, 328p il map $27.99 **940.54**

1. World War, 1939-1945 -- Campaigns -- Soviet Union

ISBN 978-0-312-62819-2

LC 2010-34784

First published 2009 in the United Kingdom

"Fluently written with good sourcing, this book covers both sides of a vast conflict that dwarfed any other in Western Europe." Libr J

Includes bibliographical references

Jordan, Jonathan W.

Brothers, rivals, victors; Eisenhower, Patton, Bradley, and the partnership that drove the Allied conquest in Europe. New American Library 2011 654p il map $28.95 **940.54**

1. Generals 2. Presidents 3. Army officers 4. College presidents 5. United States -- Army 6. World War, 1939-1945 -- Europe 7. World War, 1939-1945 -- Campaigns -- Europe

ISBN 0451232127; 9780451232120

LC 2010-34841

This book explores the "relationships of Dwight Eisenhower, George Patton, and Omar Bradley." (N Y Times Book Rev) Glossary. Bibliography. Index.

"Dwight D. Eisenhower, George S. Patton and Omar N. Bradley, the three outstanding American commanders in North Africa and Europe from 1942 to 1945, were, if not exactly 'brothers in arms,' at least friends, even if their friendship was often disrupted by envy, backbiting and disagreements over strategy. . . . This is not really a work of military history. Readers who want a rounded description of the war in Europe should look elsewhere. What Jordan gives us is the war as Eisenhower, Bradley and Patton saw it. Indeed, German generals and a whole range of major Allied figures, including Alan Brooke and Harold Alexander, get limited treatment. At his worst, Jordan can sound parochial. . . . Where Jordan does excel is in his diligent use of quotations to capture exactly what the three men thought of one another, and to show how each went out of his way to strike the image of a 'fighting general.' " N Y Times Book Rev

Includes bibliographical references

Kaplan, Alice Yaeger

The **interpreter**; [by] Alice Kaplan. University of Chicago Press 2007 240p il map pa $15 **940.54**

1. Authors 2. Veterans 3. Novelists 4. Trials (Homicide) 5. African American soldiers 6. Army officers 7. World War, 1939-1945 -- African Americans

ISBN 978-0-226-42425-5; 0-226-42425-1

LC 2006-35822

First published 2005 by Free Press

This is an "account of the trials of two American soldiers accused of murdering French citizens in the waning days of World War II. One of the accused soldiers, a black man named James Hendricks, was sentenced to death, while the other, George Whittington, a white who had been proclaimed a war hero, was acquitted. French political novelist Louis Guilloux served as an interpreter at these trials, and Kaplan draws from Guilloux's diaries as well as from a novel he based upon the trials. . . . Inventive, moving, and beautifully written, this is a major contribution to investigative history." Libr J

Includes bibliographical references

Katz, Robert

The **battle** for Rome; the Germans, the allies, the partisans and the Pope, September 1943-June 1944. Simon & Schuster 2003 418p il map $28; pa $16 **940.54**

1. World War, 1939-1945 -- Italy

ISBN 0-7432-1642-3; 0-7432-5808-8 pa

LC 2003-45677

"This narrative history describes the Eternal City at a key time of struggle—the dark year of German occupation between the overthrow of Mussolini in 1943 and liberation by the Allies in 1944. Four parties wrestle for Rome: the ruthless yet wary German occupiers, the Holy See in self-preservation mode, a gutsy band of patriotic students with homemade explosives, and the U.S. Fifth Army under Mark Clark.... This is challenging research presented fluidly, and Katz's fascination with a key moment for a fascinating city shines through." Booklist

Includes bibliographical references

Kennedy, Paul M., 1945-

Engineers of victory; the problem solvers who turned the tide in the Second World War. Paul Kennedy. Random House 2013 464 p. (alk. paper) $30   **940.54**

1. World War, 1939-1945 -- Campaigns 2. Germany -- Armed Forces -- Organization 3. World War, 1939-1945 -- Naval operations 4. World War, 1939-1945 -- Aerial operations 5. Bombing, Aerial -- History -- 20th century 6. Amphibious warfare -- History -- 20th century 7. World War, 1939-1945 -- Amphibious operations 8. World War, 1939-1945 -- Campaigns -- Pacific Area 9. Germany -- Armed Forces -- History -- World War, 1939-1945 10. Naval convoys -- Atlantic Ocean -- History -- 20th century

ISBN 1400067618; 9781400067619; 9781588368980

LC 2012024284

This book by Paul Kennedy "provides a new and unique look at how World War II was won." The book is a "nuts-and-bolts account of the strategic factors that led to Allied victory. Kennedy reveals how the leaders' grand strategy was carried out by the ordinary soldiers, scientists, engineers, and businessmen responsible for realizing their commanders' visions of success." (Publisher's note)

Includes bibliographical references and index

Kershaw, Alex

Escape from the deep; the epic story of a legendary submarine and her courageous crew. Da Capo Press 2008 270p il map $26; pa $15.95   **940.54**

1. Tang (Ship) 2. World War, 1939-1945 -- Pacific Ocean 3. World War, 1939-1945 -- Naval operations 4. World War, 1939-1945 -- Prisoners and prisons

ISBN 978-0-306-81519-5; 0-306-81519-2; 978-0-306-81790-8 pa; 0-306-81790-X pa

LC 2008-298762

Details the history of the U.S. Navy submarine Tang in the Pacific theater of World War II, the explosion that led to its sinking, the ordeal of its surviving crew members and their capture by the Japanese, followed by months of brutal captivity.

The author "has researched exhaustively, including interviewing the last two living survivors, and written compactly the portrait of nine Americans who rose to heroism and of a ship that well deserved its status . . . as a legend in the naval history of World War II." Booklist

Includes bibliographical references

Keuning-Tichelaar, An

Passing on the comfort; the war, the quilts, and the women who made a difference. [by] An Keuning-Tichelaar and Lynn Kaplanian-Buller. Good Books 2005 186p il pa $14.95   **940.54**

1. Quilts 2. World War, 1939-1945 -- Personal narratives

ISBN 1-561484-82-2

LC 2005-01932

This is the "narrative of a Dutch resistance operation during WWII conducted by Keuning-Tichelaar and her husband, Herman, a Mennonite minister. With the support of their townspeople, the two young newlyweds sheltered and saved the lives of Jewish adults and children, and others in danger from the Nazis. As part of a relief effort, quilts were created by women in North American Mennonite circles and sent to the Netherlands. Beautifully illustrated with 19 color photographs of the quilts, this book describes in an understated voice the harrowing events and the daily acts of courage that Keuning-Tichelaar undertook. When, decades later, coauthor Kaplanian-Buller, a U.S. citizen living in Amsterdam, found the old quilts, she persuaded An to share her story." Publ Wkly

Includes bibliographical references

Korda, Michael

With wings like eagles; a history of the Battle of Britain. Harper 2009 322p il map $25.95   **940.54**

1. Britain, Battle of, 1940 2. Great Britain -- Royal Air Force 3. World War, 1939-1945 -- Aerial operations

ISBN 978-0-06-112535-5; 0-06-112535-0

LC 2008-09293

This "is a skillful, absorbing, often moving contribution to the popular understanding of one of the few episodes in history to live on untarnished and undiminished in the collective memory and to deserve the description 'heroic.'" Washington Post

Includes bibliographical references (p. 303-305)

Leckie, Robert, 1920-2001

Okinawa; the last battle of World War II. Viking 1995 220p il hardcover o.p. pa $13.95   **940.54**

1. World War, 1939-1945 -- Campaigns -- Okinawa Island

ISBN 0-670-84716-X; 0-14-017389-7 pa

LC 94-39145

In this history of the Battle of Okinawa "Leckie supplies an accessible historical overview of a perplexing war tactic, the kamikaze attack." Booklist

Lee, Bruce

Marching orders; the untold story of World War II. Da Capo Press 2001 608p map pa $24 **940.54**

1. Cryptography 2. World War, 1939-1945 -- Japan 3. World War, 1939-1945 -- Secret service

ISBN 978-0-306-81036-7; 0-306-81036-0

First published 1995 by Crown

"Many of the mysteries that have eluded historians since the end of the war are much clarified. . . . This is the most significant publication about World War II since the recent series of books on the Ultra revelations and should be purchased by all libraries." Libr J

Includes bibliographical references

Lewis, Damien

The **Dog** Who Could Fly; The Incredible True Story of a WWII Airman and the Four-legged Hero Who Flew at His Side. Damien Lewis. Pocket Books 2014 304 p. illustrations $26 **940.54**
1. Dogs 2. World War, 1939-1945 -- Aerial operations
ISBN 1476739145; 9781476739144

LC 2014015567

This book by Damien Lewis "is the true account of a German shepherd who was adopted by the Royal Air Force during World War II, joined in flight missions, and survived everything from crash-landings to parachute bailouts--ultimately saving the life of his owner and dearest friend. . . . Airman Robert Bozdech stumbled across the tiny German shepherd--whom he named Ant--after being shot down on a daring mission over enemy lines." (Publisher's note)

A "heartwarming and well-paced man-and-his-dog story. . . . Lewis has captured the spirit of the era and told the story using Bozdech's manuscript as source material without making it maudlin or sentimental." Pub Wkly

Includes bibliographical references

Liebling, A. J.

World War II writings. Library of America 2008 1089p map (The library of America) $40 **940.54**
1. World War, 1939-1945 -- Campaigns 2. World War, 1939-1945 -- Personal narratives
ISBN 978-1-59853-018-6

LC 2007-938791

"The war brought out the best in [Liebling]. Here he . . . relied on straightforward observation, delivered in a style less mannered than Hemingway's, less sentimental than Ernie Pyle's, less excitable than Michael Herr's. It's the kind of writing that looks easy, except that very few war correspondents have ever done it so well." N Y Times Book Rev

Includes bibliographical references

Lifton, Robert Jay

Hiroshima in America; a half century of denial. [by] Robert Jay Lifton & Greg Mitchell; with a new afterword by the authors. Avon Books 1996 427p il pa $18.95 **940.54**
1. Atomic bomb 2. Hiroshima (Japan) -- Bombardment, 1945
ISBN 978-0-380-72764-3; 0-380-72764-1

First published 1995 by Putnam with title: Hiroshima in America: fifty years of denial

Lifton and Mitchell examine "the reaction of the American people to the bombing of Hiroshima in 1945 and its domestic aftermath. The authors examine what they perceive to be a conspiracy by the government to mislead and suppress information about the actual bombing, Truman's decision to drop the bomb, and the birth and mismanagement of the beginning of the nuclear age." Libr J

Includes bibliographical references

Lineberry, Cate

The **secret** rescue; Cate Lineberry. Little, Brown and Co. 2013 320 p. $27 **940.54**
1. Nurses 2. World War, 1939-1945 3. Special forces

(Military science) -- United States
ISBN 0316220221; 9780316220224

LC 2013934814

This book looks at the Medical Air Evacuation Transport Squadron during World War II. Cate Lineberry "looks in particular at the 807th MAETS, consisting of 25 female nurses, 24 medics and other enlisted men from all over the country. They were assembled at Bowman Field in Louisville, Ky., for training before being shipped off in mid-August 1943." When they were forced down over enemy territory, there "ensued many weeks of near-comical confusion" before a rescue took place. (Kirkus Reviews)

Lukacs, John D.

Escape from Davao; the forgotten story of the most daring prison break of the Pacific war. Simon & Schuster 2010 xiii, 433p il $27.99 **940.54**
1. Davao City (Philippines) 2. Soldiers -- United States 3. World War, 1939-1945 -- Philippines 4. World War, 1939-1945 -- Prisoners and prisons 5. World War, 1939-1945 -- Underground movements
ISBN 978-0-7432-6278-1; 0-7432-6278-6

LC 2010-03238

The author "is a gifted stylist and storyteller. He doesn't flinch at the grim or the gruesome. . . . At bottom, 'Escape From Davao' is a morality tale, not unlike the war movies of the 1940s and '50s, about pluck, luck, courage, comradeship, Yankee humor, ingenuity, and religious faith." Pittsburgh Post-Gazette

Includes bibliographical references

Macintyre, Ben, 1963-

Double cross; the true story of the D-day spies. Ben Macintyre. Crown 2012 399 p. ill., maps **940.54**
1. Spies 2. World War, 1939-1945 3. Normandy (France), Attack on, 1944 4. Spies -- Europe -- Biography 5. World War, 1939-1945 -- Deception 6. World War, 1939-1945 -- Secret service 7. World War, 1939-1945 -- Military intelligence 8. Espionage -- Europe -- History -- 20th century 9. Deception (Military science) -- History -- 20th century 10. World War, 1939-1945 -- Campaigns -- France -- Normandy
ISBN 9780307888754; 9780307888761

LC 2012003089

This book looks at the "deceit operation [that] was aimed at convincing the Nazis that Calais and Norway, not Normandy, were the targets of the 150,000-strong [D-Day] invasion force. The deception involved every branch of Allied wartime intelligence - the Bletchley Park code-breakers, MI5, MI6, SOE, Scientific Intelligence, the FBI and the French Resistance. But at its heart was the 'Double Cross System', a team of double agents controlled by the secret Twenty Committee." The squad comprised "a bisexual Peruvian playgirl, a tiny Polish fighter pilot, a Serbian seducer, a wildly imaginative Spaniard with a diploma in chicken farming, and a hysterical Frenchwoman whose obsessive love for her pet dog very nearly wrecked the entire deception," as well as a "sixth spy." (Publisher's note)

Includes bibliographical references (p. [383]-386)

and index.

Operation Mincemeat; how a dead man and a bizarre plan fooled the Nazis and assured an allied victory. Harmony Books 2010 400p il $25.99 **940.54**
1. Lawyers 2. Intelligence service agents 3. World War, 1939-1945 -- Secret service
ISBN 978-0-307-45327-3; 0-307-45327-8

LC 2009-47562

A "true WWII tale that reads like something by Ian Fleming. In fact, two of Fleming's fellow British intelligence officers hatched the title operation. They dressed a corpse in uniform and arranged for it to wash up on a Nazi-friendly stretch of the Spanish coast bearing a suitcase with false war plans. Against all odds, Operation Mincemeat succeeded — and helped convince the Germans that the Allies planned to invade Sardinia and Greece in 1943 instead of their real target, Sicily. Relying on a cache of once-classified documents, Macintyre provides the fullest account yet of this curious episode and enlivens his yarn with quirky details." Entertainment Wkly

Includes bibliographical references

Manchester, William
Goodbye, darkness; a memoir of the Pacific War. Little, Brown 1980 401p il hardcover o.p. pa $16.95 **940.54**
1. World War, 1939-1945 -- Pacific Ocean 2. World War, 1939-1945 -- Personal narratives
ISBN 0-316-50111-5 pa

LC 80-17310

This memoir arises from a 1978 trip the author made "to Pacific battlefields, seeking to exorcise three decades of nightmares dating to wartime days as a Marine Corps sergeant. . . . First tracing his family background, youth, enlistment, training, and embarkation from San Diego, Manchester unravels a memoir featuring historical reconstruction, disjointed flash-forwards, shocking vignettes, {and} redoubtable vocabulary." Choice

McKay, Sinclair
The **secret** lives of codebreakers; the men and women who cracked the Enigma code at Bletchley Park. Sinclair McKay. Penguin Group 2012 vi, 338 p.p (paperback) $16.00 **940.54**
1. Cryptography 2. World War, 1939-1945 -- Great Britain 3. World War, 1939-1945 -- Military intelligence 4. World War, 1939-1945 -- Cryptography 5. Bletchley Park (Milton Keynes, England) -- History 6. Great Britain. Government Communications Headquarters -- History 7. World War, 1939-1945 -- Electronic intelligence -- Great Britain
ISBN 0452298717; 9780452298712

LC 2012018408

This book by Sinclair McKay looks at the staff of "the Government Code & Cypher School, where [during World War II] British experts deciphered German communications, including those encrypted by the Enigma coding machine. . . . McKay presents a sociological history of the scientists, engineers, and other academics . . . thrown together at Bletch-

ley Park with debutantes and ordinary workers, all with a common goal." (Library Journal)

Includes bibliographical references and index.

Megellas, James
All the way to Berlin; a paratrooper at war in Europe. Presidio Press 2003 xxi, 309p il maps $25.95 **940.54**
1. World War, 1939-1945 -- Europe 2. World War, 1939-1945 -- Campaigns 3. World War, 1939-1945 -- Personal narratives
ISBN 0-89141-784-2

LC 2002-192563

This is the author's account of "the September 1944 assault across the Waal River. . . . The attrition Megellas witnessed over months on the front line, at Anzio and in the Battle of the Bulge, shapes his narrative, but his observations about the craft of killing lend it a distinctive tone. . . . Strongly put and unsentimental, this memoir is a must for the World War II collection." Booklist

Merridale, Catherine
★ **Ivan's** war; life and death in the Red Army, 1939-1945. Metropolitan Books 2006 426p il map $30 **940.54**
1. Soviet Union -- Red Army 2. World War, 1939-1945 -- Soviet Union
ISBN 0-8050-7455-4

LC 2005-50457

The author discusses the life of the ordinary Russian soldier during World War II.

Merridale "succeeds admirably in fashioning a compelling portrait, helped immensely by her talent as a writer." Foreign Affairs

Includes bibliographical references

Miller, Nathan
War at sea; a naval history of World War II. Oxford University Press 1996 592p il map pa $29.95 **940.54**
1. World War, 1939-1945 -- Naval operations
ISBN 0-19-511038-2

LC 96-31787

First published 1995 by Scribner

The author "relates the history of the last great sea war for the general reader, from the sinking of the passenger ship Athenia on September 2, 1939, to the surrender ceremony aboard the USS Missouri on September 2, 1945." Publ Wkly

"Miller's research—primarily on the Royal Navy—and a reading of hundreds of pertinent monographs has enabled him to fashion a briskly paced narrative that will both inform and entertain." Choice

Includes bibliographical references

Moses, Sam
At all costs; how a crippled ship and two American merchant mariners turned the tide of World War II. Random House 2006 335p il $25.95 **940.54**
1. World War, 1939-1945 -- Naval operations 2. World War, 1939-1945 -- Mediterranean Sea
ISBN 1-4000-6318-3

LC 2006-40425

This is a "retelling of the story of Operation Pedestal, one of the most desperate convoy battles of World War II." Booklist

"The remarkable heroism that won the day, as well as Moses' thorough retelling, makes this an exciting, imperative read for anyone interested in WWII." Publ Wkly

Includes bibliographical references

Mulley, Clare

The **Spy** Who Loved; The Secrets and Lives of Christine Granville. Clare Mulley. St. Martin's Press 2013 xix, 426 p.p (hbk.) $26.99   **940.54**

1. Spies -- Great Britain -- Biography 2. Women spies -- Great Britain -- Biography 3. World War, 1939-1945 -- Secret service -- Great Britain

ISBN 9781250030320; 1250030323; 1447201183; 9781447201182

LC 2013010210

A biography of "the UK's first female secret agent." The author "meticulously mined private archives, conducted personal interviews, and consulted previously published and unpublished sources in order to give the reader a balanced account of the woman behind the legend." LJ

Includes bibliographical references (pages [363]-411) and index

Murphy, David E.

What Stalin knew; the enigma of Barbarossa. Yale University Press 2005 xxii, 310p il maps $30; pa $18   **940.54**

1. Heads of state 2. Communist leaders 3. Political leaders 4. Soviet Union -- Politics and government 5. World War, 1939-1945 -- Campaigns -- Soviet Union

ISBN 0-300-10780-3; 0-300-11981-X pa

LC 2004-65916

This is an account of Soviet intelligence regarding the German invasion in 1941.

"Murphy's well-researched account offers both a meticulous reconstruction of an intelligence epic and a window into the tragedy of Stalin's despotism." Publ Wkly

Includes bibliographical references

Neiberg, Michael

The **blood** of free men; the liberation of Paris, 1944. Michael Neiberg. Basic Books, A Member of the Perseus Books Group 2012 309 p. (hardcover : alk. paper) $28.99   **940.54**

1. World War, 1939-1945 -- France -- Paris 2. World War, 1939-1945 -- Campaigns -- France -- Paris

ISBN 0465023991; 9780465023998

LC 2012016282

This book by Michael Neiber focuses on Paris, France during World War II. "As the Allies struggled inland from Normandy in August of 1944, the fate of Paris hung in the balance. Other jewels of Europe . . . were, or would soon be, reduced to rubble during attempts to liberate them. But Paris endured, thanks to a fractious cast of characters, from Resistance cells to Free French operatives to an unlikely assortment of diplomats, Allied generals, and governmental officials." (Publisher's note)

Includes bibliographical references and index.

Neitzel, Sönke, 1968-

Soldaten; On Fighting, Killing, and Dying: The Secret WWII Transcripts of German POWs. Sönke Neitzel and Harald Welzer ; translated from the German by Jefferson Chase. Alfred A. Knopf 2012 x, 437 p.p $30.50   **940.54**

1. World War, 1939-1945 -- Prisoners and prisons, German 2. Eavesdropping -- Great Britain 3. World War, 1939-1945 -- Anecdotes 4. Soldiers -- Germany -- Attitudes -- Sources 5. Prisoners of war -- Germany -- Attitudes -- Sources 6. World War, 1939-1945 -- Prisoners and prisons, British 7. Prisoners of war -- Great Britain -- Attitudes -- Sources 8. Germany -- Armed Forces -- History -- 20th century -- Sources 9. World War, 1939-1945 -- Military intelligence -- Great Britain

ISBN 0307958124; 9780307958129

LC 2012005744

This book, by Sönke Neitzel and Herald Welzer, "closely examines. . . recorded interrogations of German POWs. . . and the casual, pitiless brutality omnipresent in them, from a historical and psychological perspective. What factors led to the degradation of the soldiers' sense of awareness and morality? How much did their social environments affect their interpretation of the war and their actions during combat? . . . [An] unflinching narrative of wartime experience emerges." (Publisher's note)

Includes bibliographical references (p. [397]-412)

Nelson, Craig

The **first** heroes; the extraordinary story of the Doolittle Raid--America's first World War II victory. Viking 2002 430p il $27.95; pa $15   **940.54**

1. Generals 2. Air force officers 3. World War, 1939-1945 -- Japan 4. United States -- Army Air Forces 5. World War, 1939-1945 -- Aerial operations

ISBN 0-670-03087-2; 0-14-200341-7 pa

LC 2002-28092

"The most interesting part of the book is the harrowing story of survival as crew members are forced to ditch their planes on the Asian mainland. This is a thrilling real-life saga that both informs and inspires." Booklist

Includes bibliographical references

Norman, Elizabeth M.

★ **Tears** in the darkness; the story of the Bataan Death March and its aftermath. [by] Michael Norman and Elizabeth M. Norman. Farrar, Straus, and Giroux 2009 463p il $30   **940.54**

1. Prisoners of war 2. World War, 1939-1945 -- Atrocities 3. World War, 1939-1945 -- Prisoners and prisons 4. World War, 1939-1945 -- Campaigns -- Philippines 5. Prisoners of war -- Philippines -- Bataan (Province) 6. World War, 1939-1945 -- Prisoners and prisons, Japanese

ISBN 0-374-27260-3; 978-0-374-27260-9

LC 2008-47163

"For the first four months of 1942, U.S., Filipino, and Japanese soldiers fought what was America's first major land battle of World War II, the battle for the tiny Philippine peninsula of Bataan. It ended with the surrender of 76,000 Filipinos and Americans, the single largest defeat in American military history. The defeat, though, was only the beginning, as Michael and Elizabeth M. Norman [argue in this] . . . book. From then until the Japanese surrendered in August 1945, the prisoners of war suffered an ordeal of unparalleled cruelty and savagery: forty-one months of captivity, starvation rations, dehydration, hard labor, deadly disease, and torture." (Publisher's note) Index.

This book "is authoritative history. Ten years in the making, it is based on hundreds of interviews with American, Filipino and Japanese combatants. But it is also a narrative achievement. The book seamlessly blends a wide-angle view with the stories of many individual participants." N Y Times (Late N Y Ed)

Includes bibliographical references

Olson, Lynne

Citizens of London; the Americans who stood with Britain in its darkest, finest hour. Random House 2010 471p il $28   **940.54**
1. Diplomats 2. Governors 3. Radio reporters 4. Government officials 5. Television reporters 6. Television news anchors 7. World War, 1939-1945 -- Diplomatic history 8. Great Britain -- Foreign relations -- United States 9. United States -- Foreign relations -- Great Britain
ISBN 978-1-4000-6758-9

The story of how the United States forged its wartime alliance with Britain, told from the perspective of three key American players in London: Edward R. Murrow, Averell Harriman, and John Gilbert Winant.

A nuanced history that captures the intensity of life in a period when victory was not a foregone conclusion. Kirkus
Includes bibliographical references

The **Pacific** War; from Pearl Harbor to Hiroshima. editor, Daniel Marston. Pbk. ed.; Osprey Pub. 2010 272p il map pa $19.95   **940.54**
1. World War, 1939-1945 -- Campaigns -- Pacific Ocean
ISBN 978-1-84908-382-9

LC 2010-292672
First published 2005 with title: The Pacific war companion

"These essays on the Pacific theater of WW II, written by a group of international scholars representing Australia, Great Britain, Japan, and the US, cover the wellknown events at Pearl Harbor, the Coral Sea, and Midway; MacArthur's push to the Philippines; Nimitz's island campaign in the central Pacific; Okinawa; and the dropping of the atomic bomb on Hiroshima and Nagasaki. . . . A chronology, detailed maps, and photographs greatly enhance this excellent volume on the Pacific phase of WW II." Choice
Includes bibliographical references

Patton, George S.

War as I knew it; by George S. Patton, Jr.; annotated by Paul D. Harkins. Houghton Mifflin 1947 425p il maps hardcover o.p. pa $18   **940.54**
1. World War, 1939-1945 -- Campaigns
ISBN 0-395-73529-7 pa

An account of the General's WWII European campaigns from the fight for Sicily to the conquest of Germany based on a series of "open letters" written to his wife

Pleshakov, Konstantin

★ **Stalin's** folly; the tragic first ten days of World War II on the Eastern Front. [by] Constantine Pleshakov. Houghton Mifflin 2005 326p il map $26   **940.54**
1. Heads of state 2. Communist leaders 3. Political leaders 4. World War, 1939-1945 -- Europe
ISBN 0-618-36701-2

LC 2004-65133
This is an account of the German invasion of the Soviet Union in 1941.
This book "belongs in every World War II collection." Libr J
Includes bibliographical references

Prange, Gordon William

At dawn we slept; the untold story of Pearl Harbor. {by} Gordon W. Prange in collaboration with Donald M. Goldstein and Katherine V. Dillon. Viking 1991 889p il hardcover o.p.   **940.54**
1. Pearl Harbor (Oahu, Hawaii), Attack on, 1941
LC 91-50176
First published 1981 by McGraw-Hill
The author "offers a comprehensive account of Japanese preparations for the attack, the origins and extent of American unpreparedness, and the aftermath of the attack on both sides." Booklist
Includes bibliographical references

Read, Anthony

The **fall** of Berlin; [by] Anthony Read and David Fisher. Da Capo Press 1995 513p il map pa $18.50   **940.54**
1. Berlin, Battle of, 1945 2. Germany -- History -- 1933-1945 3. World War, 1939-1945 -- Germany
ISBN 0-306-80619-3; 978-0-306-80619-3
LC 94-47998
First published 1992 in the United Kingdom
A description of "the bombing of Berlin by the British and Americans and how the Russian Army fought its way toward and through Berlin in 1945. The authors intend no startling new interpretations or profound analysis. Instead, they offer vignettes, often based on diaries, to describe life in Berlin late in the war. They also retell the story of fanatical Nazi leaders and of the Wehrmacht's desperate efforts to defend the city. The result is a highly readable and, at the same time, sophisticated and reliable narrative history." Libr J
Includes bibliographical references

Revelli, Nuto

Mussolini's death march; eyewitness accounts of Italian soldiers on the Eastern Front. Benvenuto Revelli ; translated and with an introduction by John Penuel. University Press of Kansas 2013 xxxiii, 540 p.p (Modern war studies) (cloth : alkaline paper) $45   **940.54**
1. World War, 1939-1945 -- Italy 2. World War, 1939-1945 -- Prisoners and prisons 3. Soldiers -- Italy -- Biography 4. Italy. Regio Esercito. Alpini -- Biography 5. World War, 1939-1945 -- Campaigns -- Soviet Union 6. World War, 1939-1945 -- Campaigns -- Eastern Front

7. World War, 1939-1945 -- Personal narratives, Italian
8. Soviet Union -- History -- German occupation, 1941-1944
ISBN 0700619089; 9780700619085

LC 2012045427

For this book, Nuto Revelli "interviewed 43 surviving mountain troops transported to Russia and marched to the Don River where, during the ice-cold winter of 1942-43, they were quickly decimated. The vast majority later starved or froze to death in various labor camps alongside millions of Germans, Croatians, Romanians, Hungarians, and occasional Finns." (Choice)

Includes bibliographical references (pages 509-521) and index

Roberts, Andrew

The **storm** of war; a new history of the Second World War. HarperCollins 2011 lvi, 712p il map $29.99 **940.54**
1. World War, 1939-1945
ISBN 978-0-06-122859-9; 0-06-122859-1
First published 2009 in the United Kingdom
"In general, histories of the Second World War in the English language can be divided sharply into those written by Americans, which downplay the British role in the war, and those written by British historians, which downplay the role of the Americans (and also give less space and attention to the Pacific theater than the European theater). Roberts has managed to write a book that both strives and succeeds in giving more or less equal time to both, and also manages to include enough about events in China and the war on the Eastern Front to give the reader a well-balanced and excitingly written account of the whole war. . . . His scholarship is superb, and the 'packaging' of the book, with very good illustrations and ample first-class maps, makes it a real pleasure to read." Daily Beast
Includes bibliographical references

Roberts, Andrew, 1963-

Masters and commanders; how four titans won the war in the West, 1941-1945. HarperCollins 2009 xl, 673p il map $35 **940.54**
1. Generals 2. Governors 3. Statesmen 4. Historians 5. Presidents 6. Prime ministers 7. People with disabilities 8. Marshals 9. Memoirists 10. Philatelists 11. Cabinet members 12. Secretaries of state 13. Members of Parliament 14. Secretaries of defense 15. Nobel laureates for peace 16. Great Britain -- War Cabinet 17. Nobel laureates for literature 18. World War, 1939-1945 -- Campaigns 19. Strategy -- History -- 20th century 20. World War, 1939-1945 -- Military intelligence 21. World War, 1939-1945 -- Personal narratives, British 22. World War, 1939-1945 -- Personal narratives, American
ISBN 0-06-122857-5; 978-0-06-122857-5
First published 2008 in the United Kingdom with subtitle: how Roosevelt, Churchill, Marshall and Alanbrooke won the war in the West
Roberts contends that various events "of the Second World War turned on the personalities and relationships between two political masters—Winston Churchill and Franklin D. Roosevelt—and the military commanders of their armed forces—the Chief of the Imperial General Staff,

General Sir Alan Brooke, and the US Army Chief of Staff, General George C. Marshall. In reconstructing the debates between these four principals and . . . [other] senior Allied figures, Roberts draws upon the private papers of . . . contemporaries and on verbatim accounts of Churchill's War Cabinet meetings." (Publisher's note)

Roberts examines the "history of the four men responsible for final decisions: FDR, Churchill, and their top military advisors, George Marshall and Alan Brooke, respectively. Both to humanize the pressure on figures now memorialized in bronze and to serve as Clio's arbiter of impassioned disagreements over the optimal strategy to defeat Nazi Germany, Roberts examines how arguments played out amongst the quartet and those in their orbit. . . . Roberts reinforces his reputation for high-quality military history with this comprehensive synthesis of primary sources about the fundamental strategic decisions of WWII." Booklist

Roberts, Geoffrey

Stalin's general; the life of Georgy Zhukov. Geoffrey Roberts. Random House 2012 375 p. (alk. paper) $30 **940.54**
1. Biography 2. National socialism 3. Soviet Union -- History -- 1939-1945 4. World War, 1939-1945 -- Soviet Union 5. Marshals -- Soviet Union -- Biography
ISBN 1400066921; 9780679645177; 9781400066926

LC 2011040663

Author Geoffrey Roberts presents a "biography of the ruthless Red Army general who defeated the Nazis and then spent decades alternately disgraced and rehabilitated in Soviet Russia. . . . As [Georgy] Zhukov, a rising cavalry commander in the rapidly modernizing Red Army, managed to escape being a victim of the army purges of 1937-38 and was then appointed on his first important mission for Stalin: to 'conduct a purge' of the Japanese from the Mongolian-Manchurian border in 1939." (Kirkus Reviews)

Includes bibliographical references and index.

Rooney, Andrew A.

My war; [by] Andy Rooney. PublicAffairs 2000 333p il $20; pa $14 **940.54**
1. Authors 2. Humorists 3. Journalists 4. World War, 1939-1945 -- Personal narratives
ISBN 1-58648-010-3; 1-58648-159-2 pa

LC 00-59228

First published 1995 by Random House

The author "relates how he became a notable combat journalist in WW II, a war he calls 'the ultimate experience for anyone in it.' For the Army newspaper Stars and Stripes, he covered the air war over Germany, the D-Day invasion of Normandy and the Allied drive into Germany. Rooney's simple, ruminative style . . . grips the reader as he describes famous events of the war." Publ Wkly

Scott-Clark, Cathy

The **Amber** Room; the fate of the world's greatest lost treasure. [by] Catherine Scott-Clark & Adrian Levy. Walker & Co. 2004 386p il $26 **940.54**
1. Art thefts 2. World War, 1939-1945 -- Destruction and pillage
ISBN 0-8027-1424-2

LC 2004-49625

The authors "tell an exciting, intense, and surprising story. It is filled with episodes of cold-war intrigue, cynicism, amoral betrayal, and bureaucratic stalling that degenerates into absurdity." Booklist

Includes bibliographical references

Sebag-Montefiore, Hugh

Enigma : the battle for the code. Wiley 2000 422p il hardcover o.p. pa $16.95   **940.54**
1. Cryptography 2. World War, 1939-1945 -- Secret service

ISBN 0-471-40738-0; 0-471-49035-0 pa

LC 00-43920

This is the story of the German Enigma code.

"Describing the breaking of the German naval code during World War II, is both engrossing and exciting. Much of the information presented here is based on recently declassified documents." Booklist

Includes bibliographical references

Sheftall, Mordecai G.

Blossoms in the wind; the human legacy of the Kamikaze. [by] M.G. Sheftall. NAL Caliber 2005 480p il $24.95   **940.54**
1. Kamikaze airplanes 2. World War, 1939-1945 -- Aerial operations

ISBN 0-451-21487-0

LC 2004-27356

This account of the "design, training, and execution [of Japanese suicide missions] includes interviews with the families of dead pilots and, harder to reach, pilots who survived the missions." Booklist

Includes bibliographical references

Sides, Hampton

Ghost soldiers; the forgotten epic story of World War II's most dramatic mission. Doubleday 2001 342p il maps $24.95   **940.54**
1. World War, 1939-1945 -- Prisoners and prisons 2. United States -- Army -- Ranger Battalion, 6th 3. World War, 1939-1945 -- Campaigns -- Philippines

ISBN 0-385-49564-1

LC 2001-17337

"The author's excellent grasp of human emotions and bravery makes this a compelling book hard to put down." Publ Wkly

Smyth, Denis

Deathly deception; the real story of Operation Mincemeat. Oxford University Press 2010 xx, 367p il   **940.54**
1. Lawyers 2. Intelligence service agents 3. World War, 1939-1945 -- Secret service

ISBN 978-0-19-923398-4

LC 2010-923437

"When the Allies decided to invade Sicily in summer 1943, they floated the body of a British military officer ashore in German-friendly Spain with the hope that the documents he carried would influence the Germans to believe that the Greek islands or Sardinia would be the Allies' actual target—and the ruse appeared to work. . . . [This is an] administrative history of both sides."

"This superlative and almost unexpurgated account of Operation Mincemeat will enthrall serious students of WWII." Booklist

Includes bibliographical references

Snyder, Timothy

Bloodlands; Europe between Hitler and Stalin. Basic Books 2010 524p map $29.95   **940.54**
1. Genocide 2. Massacres 3. Heads of state 4. Nazi leaders 5. Eastern Europe 6. Communist leaders 7. Political leaders 8. Genocide -- Europe 9. Holocaust, 1933-1945 10. Soviet Union -- History 11. Holocaust, Jewish (1939-1945) 12. Germany -- History -- 1933-1945 13. World War, 1939-1945 -- Atrocities 14. Soviet Union -- History -- 1917-1936 15. Eastern Europe -- History -- 1918-1945

ISBN 978-0-465-00239-9; 0-465-00239-0

LC 2010-16816

The book "tr[ies] to explain mass violence in parts of Eastern Europe in the twentieth century. . . . Snyder deals with territories that were ruled for some time by both Nazi Germany and the USSR from 1930 to 1953. He covers most of today's Poland and Ukraine (the focus of his interest), Belarus, the three Baltic countries, and the most western strip of Russia. . . . Snyder gives a[n] . . . account of political history. . . . [He] places . . . emphasis on the exploitation of the countryside and enforced hunger, which claimed half of the fourteen million victims in the 'bloodlands.' Economically speaking, he emphasizes the extraction of resources by imperialists as the cause of mass starvation." (American Historical Review)

"Mr. Snyder's book is revisionist history of the best kind: in spare, closely argued prose, with meticulous use of statistics, he makes the reader rethink some of the best-known episodes in Europe's modern history." Economist

Includes bibliographical references

Spector, Ronald

Eagle against the sun; the American war with Japan. {by} Ronald H. Spector. Free Press 1985 589p il hardcover o.p. pa $18   **940.54**
1. World War, 1939-1945 -- Japan 2. World War, 1939-1945 -- United States 3. World War, 1939-1945 -- Campaigns -- Pacific Ocean

ISBN 0-394-74101-3 pa

LC 84-47888

While "policy, strategy and military operations are emphasized . . . Mr. Spector makes a real attempt to give readers some idea of what the war was like for the men and women who fought it. It is here that the book is at its best." N Y Times Book Rev

Includes bibliographical references

Stinnett, Robert B.

Day of deceit; the truth about FDR and Pearl Harbor. Free Press 1999 386p il maps hardcover o.p. pa $16   **940.54**
1. Governors 2. Presidents 3. People with disabilities 4. Pearl Harbor (Oahu, Hawaii), Attack on, 1941 5. Philatelists 6. Intelligence service -- United States

ISBN 0-7432-0129-9 pa

LC 99-38402

The author addresses the question of whether the U.S. had knowledge of the impending Japanese attack on Pearl Harbor

"Although Stinnett's accusatory light doesn't definitively fall on FDR, it illuminates fishy aspects of the case. . . . Whether the result of simple dereliction or sinister dereliction of duty, Pearl Harbor holds fewer secrets because of Stinnett's research." Booklist

Includes bibliographical references

Takaki, Ronald T.

Hiroshima; why America dropped the atomic bomb. [by] Ronald Takaki. Little, Brown 1995 193p il $28; pa $14.95 **940.54**
  1. Atomic bomb 2. World War, 1939-1945 -- United States 3. Hiroshima (Japan) -- Bombardment, 1945
  ISBN 0-316-83122-0; 0-316-83124-7 pa
                                LC 95-13546
This study of the bombings of Hiroshima and Nagasaki focuses on the psychological motivations of the American decision-makers, especially Harry Truman.

"Right or wrong, the study is a provocative addition to the unresolved debate over the dropping of the atomic bombs." Publ Wkly

Includes bibliographical references

Thomas, Evan

★ **Sea** of thunder; four commanders and the last great naval campaign, 1941-1945. Simon & Schuster 2006 415p il map $27 **940.54**
  1. World War, 1939-1945 -- Naval operations 2. World War, 1939-1945 -- Campaigns -- Pacific Ocean
  ISBN 978-0-7432-5221-8; 0-7432-5221-7
                           LC 2006-47511
This is an "account of the Battle of Leyte Gulf, October 1944, one of history's largest naval battles, where Admiral William 'Bull' Halsey, the commander of the U.S. Third Fleet, and his commander, Ernest Evans, met the forces of Japanese admirals Takeo Kurita and Matome Ugaki. . . . Thomas paints compelling portraits of these men, offering insight into their characters and actions throughout the war in the Pacific." Libr J

Includes bibliographical references

Toll, Ian W.

Pacific crucible; war at sea in the Pacific, 1941-1942. Ian W. Toll. W.W. Norton 2011 xxxvi, 597p il map $35 **940.54**
  1. United States -- Naval history 2. World War, 1939-1945 -- Naval operations 3. Pearl Harbor (Oahu, Hawaii), Attack on, 1941 4. World War, 1939-1945 -- Campaigns -- Pacific Ocean
  ISBN 978-0-393-06813-9; 0-393-06813-7
                          LC 2011028907
In this book, "[p]rize-winning freelance naval historian [Ian W.] Toll . . . chronicles one of the U.S. Navy's finest performances of WWII in this . . . narrative of the months following the . . . attacks on Pearl Harbor. Eyewitness accounts and . . . research in American and Japanese print and archival sources" form the book's basis. (Publishers Weekly)

"The author makes vast quantities of technological and tactical concepts intelligible to all but the rankest beginner—

for whom this book is not remotely suitable. A particular gift of the author is intelligent character portraits: Yamamoto, MacArthur, Halsey, and Nimitz (clearly one of the author's favorites). Add to all these other attributes a thorough scholarly apparatus, and it is difficult to think of a recent book on this subject that is of such consistently outstanding value." Booklist

Includes bibliographical references and index

Weale, Adrian

Army of evil; a history of the SS. Adrian Weale. NAL Caliber 2012 xiii, 459 p.p $28.95 **940.54**
  1. Waffen-SS 2. World War, 1939-1945 -- Germany 3. World War, 1939-1945 -- Regimental histories 4. National Socialism 5. Waffen-SS -- History 6. Germany -- Politics and government -- 1933-1945 7. World War, 1939-1945 -- Regimental histories -- Germany 8. Nationalsozialistische Deutsche Arbeiter-Partei. Schutzstaffel
  ISBN 0451237919; 9780451237910
                          LC 2012014170
This book by Adrian Weale presents a "look at the formation of the Schutzstaffeln (aka the SS), from [Adolf] Hitler's early private bodyguards to Heinrich Himmler's elite extermination squads. Weale . . . plots the evolution of the SS as the embodiment and implementation of the Nazi racist ideology. . . . Weale delineates the consolidation of Himmler's power, including the implementation of the concentration camp system . . . as the SS soldiers evolved into instruments of genocide." (Kirkus Reviews)

Includes bibliographical references (p. 433-440) and index

Zuckoff, Mitchell

Frozen in Time; An Epic Story of Survival and a Modern Quest for Lost Heroes of World War II. Mitchell Zuckoff. HarperCollins 2013 384 p. (hardcover) $28.99 **940.54**
  1. Rescue work 2. Arctic regions
  ISBN 0062133438; 9780062133434
This book, by Mitchell Zuckoff, tells of how "on November 5, 1942, a US cargo plane slammed into the Greenland Ice Cap." Several subsequent rescue attempts themselves crashed. This book "tells the story of these crashes and the fate of the survivors, bringing vividly to life their battle to endure 148 days of the brutal Arctic winter, until an expedition headed by famed Arctic explorer Bernt Balchen brought them to safety." (Publisher's note)

"Zuckoff's...complex narrative involves the fates of three downed missions to Greenland in late 1942, juxtaposed with the events of the modern-day search effort, led by an exploration company in August 2012 and joined by the author. As a result of the many competing strands and characters, some confusion in the details ensues--though maps and a cast of characters are included to help orient readers... An exhaustively layered but exciting account involving characters of enormous courage and stamina." Kirkus

Lost in Shangri-la. HarperCollins 2011 xii, 384p.p ill. $26.99 **940.54**
  1. Primitive societies 2. Survival after airplane accidents, shipwrecks, etc. 3. New Guinea 4. Aircraft

accidents -- New Guinea 5. Primitive societies -- New Guinea 6. World War, 1939-1945 -- Missing in action 7. World War, 1939-1945 -- Aerial operations, American 8. World War, 1939-1945 -- Search and rescue operations
ISBN 978-0-06-198834-9; 0-06-198834-0

LC 201034508

L.L. Winship/PEN New England Award: Nonfiction (2012)

This book describes "how three World War II sightseers survived a crash in remote New Guinea." (N Y Times Book Rev) Bibliography. Index.

"On May 13, 1945, an American transport plane carrying 24 servicemen and women crashed into a mountain in the tropical jungles of Dutch New Guinea (now Papua), leaving three survivors. Learning about the event while researching another subject, the author recognized the ingredients of a terrific tale: a beautiful young WAC, a hidden valley reminiscent of the Shangri-La in James Hilton's Lost Horizon, primitive tribal people and a daring air rescue. In this well-crafted book, Zuckoff turns the long-forgotten episode into an unusually exciting narrative. Drawing on the young WAC survivor Margaret Hastings' diary as well as journals and interviews, the author hones in on life at the U.S. military base in Hollandia, on the northern coast of uncharted New Guinea; a soldier's chance discovery a year earlier of Baliem Valley, a verdant area about 150 miles into the interior, with its hundreds of native villages surrounded by gardens; and the doomed flight of officers and enlisted personnel out on a joy ride to view this much-talked-about land of Stone Age people from the air." Kirkus

Includes bibliographical references and index.

940.55   Europe--1945-1999

Judt, Tony

Postwar; a history of Europe since 1945. Penguin Press 2005 878p il maps $39.95   **940.55**
1. Europe -- History -- 1945-
ISBN 1-59420-065-3

LC 2005-52126

This is a "historical overview of today's Europe from the end of World War II through the economic, social, cultural, and political changes and continuities of the last 60 years." Libr J "This is the best history we have of Europe in the postwar period and not likely to be surpassed for many years." Publ Wkly

Includes bibliographical references

Lowe, Keith

Savage continent; Europe in the aftermath of World War II. St. Martin's Press 2012 460 p. $30.00   **940.55**
1. Europe -- History -- 1945- 2. Reconstruction (1939-1951) 3. World War, 1939-1945 -- Occupied territories
ISBN 1250000203; 9781250000200

LC 2011279703

Includes bibliographical references and index.

This book offers an "account of the violent and vengeful aftermath of the Second World War in Europe. . . . The aftermath was in part a product of inherited political tensions and ideological conflicts from before 1939 but chiefly a consequence of the massive destruction, displacement and criminality unleashed by Hitler's invasion of Poland and, perhaps more important, the Anglo-French decision to resist it." (New Statesman)

Mazower, Mark

Dark   continent: Europe's twentieth century. Knopf 1999 487p il maps hardcover o.p. pa $16   **940.55**
1. Europe -- History -- 20th century
ISBN 0-679-75704-X pa

LC 98-15886

The author's "relative unconcern with international and great-power politics probably accounts for a rather intra-European perspective . . . just as it contributes to some exaggeration of the points of comparison and convergence in East and West European economic history. . . . But these are minor defects, the price to be paid for a confident and unconventional work of historical interpretation." N Y Times Book Rev

Includes bibliographical references

941   British Isles

Burns, William E.

A **brief** history of Great Britain. Facts On File 2010 xxiv, 296p il map (Brief history) $49.50; pa $19.95   **941**
1. Great Britain -- History
ISBN 978-0-8160-7728-1; 978-0-8160-8124-0 pa

LC 2009-8217

This book "narrates the history of Great Britain from the earliest times to the 21st century, covering the entire island—England, Wales, and Scotland—as well as associated archipelagos such as the Channel Islands, the Orkneys, and Ireland as they have influenced British history. The central story of this volume is the development of the British kingdom, including its rise and decline on the world stage." Publisher's note

Includes bibliographical references

The **Columbia** companion to British history; edited by Juliet Gardiner & Neil Wenborn. Columbia Univ. Press 1997 840p maps $63   **941**
1. Reference books 2. Great Britain -- History -- Encyclopedias
ISBN 0-231-10792-7

LC 96-23774

First published 1995 in the United Kingdom with title: The History today companion to British history

This reference work contains "more than 4,500 dictionary entries that not only cover political and constitutional history, but also provide information on social, economic, religious, military, naval, legal, and cultural history. . . . The entries . . . {cover topics such as} blasphemy, divorce, and homosexuality, as well as the historical events and rulers that are standard for any encyclopedia. In addition, the encyclopedia seems to be strong on entries for Scotland and Ireland." Booklist

Farquhar, Michael

Behind the palace doors; five centuries of sex, adventure, vice, treachery, and folly from royal Britain. Random House Trade Paperbacks 2011 307p pa $15; ebook $11.99 **941**

1. Great Britain -- Kings and rulers
ISBN 978-0-8129-7904-6 pa; 978-0-679-60453-2 ebook

LC 2010-21116

The author "probes 500 years of monarchical mishaps and misdeeds, screaming headlines and gleeful attacks by cartoonists. He uncloaks secrets, schemes, scandals, blood-soaked sheets, public humiliations, intrigues, and adultery. Illustrated with lineage charts and chronologically organized, chapters cover the houses of Tudor, Stuart, Hanover, Saxe-Coburg-Gotha, and Windsor. . . . [His] style is a breezy pleasure throughout." Publ Wkly

Includes bibliographical references.

Fraser, Rebecca

★ The **story** of Britain; from the Romans to the present: a narrative history. Norton 2005 829p il map $35 **941**

1. Great Britain -- History
ISBN 0-393-06010-1

LC 2004-26049

First published 2003 in the United Kingdom with title: A people's history of Britain

The author's "narrative advances with the emphasis on the roles of a litany of historical icons, from Queen Boudica to Margaret Thatcher. For those readers who are primarily interested in the 'who, what, when, where, why' of British history, this is a valuable general study." Booklist

Includes bibliographical references

Guy, John

The **Children** of Henry VIII. Oxford University Press 2013 272 p. (hardcover) $27.95 **941**

1. Great Britain -- History -- 1485-1603, Tudors
ISBN 0192840908; 9780192840905

This book by John Guy looks at "the heirs of Henry VIII. . . . Rather than attempt the massive undertaking of covering in depth the histories of Edward, Mary, and Elizabeth, Guy has chosen to give the most salient details regarding the monarchs . . . present[ing] an overall picture of their lives and upbringings under Henry's rule and during their later reigns. His particular focus is on how their relationships with each other--and . . . their father--affected them." (Library Journal)

Lacey, Robert

Great tales from English history; the truth about King Arthur, Lady Godiva, Richard the Lionheart, and more. Little, Brown and Co. 2004 254p maps $22.95 **941**

1. Great Britain -- History
ISBN 0-316-10910-X

LC 2003-115660

First published 2003 in the United Kingdom

"This volume begins in 7150 BC with the life and death of Cheddar Man and ends in 1381 with Wat Tyler and the Peasants' Revolt." Publisher's note

Includes bibliographical references

Great tales from English history [2] Joan of Arc, the princes in the Tower, Bloody Mary, Oliver Cromwell, Sir Isaac Newton, and more. Little, Brown and Co. 2005 271p il map $23.95 **941**

1. Great Britain -- History
ISBN 0-316-10924-X

LC 2004-63351

First published 2004 in the United Kingdom

The author's "second volume on English history opens in 1348, the year of the Black Plague, which wiped out half of England's five million people, and proceeds through the astonishing scientific discoveries of Sir Isaac Newton in 1687. . . . Lacey's animated prose, energetic storytelling and spirited approach to British history bring the past to life." Publ Wkly

Includes bibliographical references

★ **Great** tales from English history [3] Captain Cook, Samuel Johnson, Queen Victoria, Charles Darwin, Edward the Abdicator, and more. Little, Brown and Co. 2006 305p $23.99 **941**

1. Great Britain -- History
ISBN 978-0-316-11459-2; 0-316-11459-6

LC 2006-931723

"The third volume in Lacey's series of edifying and entertaining stories from English history abounds in fascinating profiles. Industrial and agricultural pioneers such as Jethro Tull, James Hargreaves and Isambard Kingdom Brunel abide alongside human rights protestors such as Thomas Clarkson, who founded the British antislavery movement; feminist philosopher Mary Wollstonecraft; and journalist Annie Besant, who initiated a successful 1888 match girls' strike." Publ Wkly

Includes bibliographical references

The **Oxford** history of Britain; edited by Kenneth O. Morgan. Rev ed, New ed; Oxford University Press 2010 821p map pa $18.95 **941**

1. Great Britain -- History
ISBN 978-0-19-957925-9; 0-19-957925-3

LC 2010279308

Text based on The Oxford illustrated history of Britain, published 1984. This version first published 2001

This "volume tells the story of Britain and its people over two thousand years, from the coming of the Roman legions to the present day." Publisher's note

Includes bibliographical references

Schama, Simon

A **history** of Britain. Hyperion 2000 3v ea $40 **941**

1. Great Britain -- History
ISBN 0-7868-6675-6 v1; 0-7868-6752-3 v2; 0-7868-6899-6 v3

LC 00-61442

Schama "writes wonderfully, in an easygoing yet elegant manner, with an eye for the telling aesthetic detail, and

throughout brimming with intelligence and passion." N Y
Times Book Rev

Includes bibliographical references

Tompson, Richard S.

★ **Great** Britain: a reference guide from the Renaissance to the present. Facts on File 2003 552p il
(European nations series) $85 **941**

1. Great Britain -- History

ISBN 0-8160-4474-0

LC 200219

This guide contains "an introductory overview of British history, Renaissance to the present; a narrative history; a
historical dictionary, topical and biographical; a chronology;
appendixes (maps, genealogies of English royal houses, lists
of English sovereigns from 899, and prime ministers from
1721). The work concludes with an unannotated bibliography, arranged in sections for bibliogaphies, dictionaries and
encyclopedias, general works, surveys, and topics." Choice

941.06 House of Stuart and Commonwealth periods, 1603-1714

Long, James

The **plot** against Pepys; [by] James Long & Ben
Long. Overlook Press 2008 322p il $27.95 **941.06**

1. Trials 2. Diarists 3. Military officials 4. Government
officials 5. Members of Parliament 6. Great Britain --
History -- 1603-1714, Stuarts

ISBN 978-1-59020-069-8; 1-59020-069-1

First published 2007 in the United Kingdom

"The book is packed with marvellous asides that add
colour to an already kaleidoscopic cavalcade of crass credulousness, court drama and crookery. . . . I couldn't put it
down, and there aren't many books on the seventeenth century you can say that about." Hist Today

Includes bibliographical references

Pepys, Samuel

★ The **diary** of Samuel Pepys; edited and with
a preface by Richard Le Gallienne; introduction by
Robert Louis Stevenson. Modern Lib. 2001 xxxv,
310p $22; pa $15.95 **941.06**

1. Diarists 2. Military officials 3. Government officials
4. Members of Parliament

ISBN 0-679-64221-8; 0-8129-7071-3 pa

LC 00-54817

An abridged edition of Pepys' eleven-volume diary,
originally written between 1660 and 1669.

Tomalin, Claire

Samuel Pepys; the unequalled self. Knopf 2002
xxiii, 470p il $30; pa $16.95 **941.06**

1. Diarists 2. Military officials 3. Government officials
4. Members of Parliament 5. Great Britain -- Social life
and customs 6. Great Britain -- History -- 1603-1714,
Stuarts

ISBN 0-375-41143-7; 0-375-72553-9 pa

LC 2002-75701

"Tomalin mines the diary, and she also expands upon the
characters and events, great and small, that affected Pepys'
life and livelihood to bring the man and his milieu to life—
pungently as well as vibrantly." Booklist

Includes bibliographical references

941.07 Period of House of Hanover, 1714-1837

Brewer, John

The **pleasures** of the imagination; English culture in the eighteenth century. University of Chicago
Press 2000 721p il pa $20 **941.07**

1. Great Britain -- Civilization 2. Great Britain
-- Intellectual life 3. Great Britain -- Social life and
customs

ISBN 0-226-07419-6; 978-0-226-07419-1

LC 99-57059

First published 1997 by Farrar, Straus and Giroux

"A remarkable feat of scholarship, this volume will quickly establish itself as an indispensable reference." Booklist

Includes bibliographical references

Foreman, Amanda

Georgiana, Duchess of Devonshire. Random
House 2000 454p hardcover o.p. pa $15.95 **941.07**

1. Socialites 2. Spouses of prominent persons

ISBN 0-375-75383-4 pa

LC 99-23580

Georgiana "was the society leader of her day. Daughter
of the fabulously wealthy Earl Spencer (and ancestor of the
late princess of Wales) and married to the even more wealthy
duke of Devonshire, Georgiana was watched, adored, and
imitated. But she evolved herself into more than just a fashionable hostess; she got involved in Whig politics, to an extent unprecedented for women. . . . The tenor of the subject's
time and place—in this instance, aristocratic Britain in the
late 1700s and early 1800s—is both colorfully and meaningfully realized." Booklist

Includes bibliographical references

McLynn, Frank

1759 : the year Britain became master of the
world. Atlantic Monthly Press 2004 422p il map
$26 **941.07**

1. Seven Years' War, 1756-1763 2. Great Britain --
Colonies 3. Great Britain -- Foreign relations

ISBN 0-87113-881-6

LC 2004-57397

First published 2004 in the United Kingdom

1759 "was the fourth [year] in the Seven Years War, a
struggle between France and England for global dominance
that was fought worldwide. McLynn focuses on the deadly
conflict, contrasting the two nations' differing wartime policies and showing how the combination of Britain's maritime
prowess and sheer good luck helped it emerge triumphant,
albeit by a narrow margin. . . . Splendidly narrated, with balanced insights into the Native American aspect of the French
and Indian Wars, McLynn's book will enthrall all lovers of
history told well." Publ Wkly

Includes bibliographical references

Norman, Jesse

    Edmund Burke; the first conservative. by Jesse Norman. Basic Books, A Member of the Perseus Books Group 2013 325 p. ill. ports, maps (hardcover) $27.99   **941.07**

    1. Political philosophy 2. Orators -- Great Britain -- Biography 3. Statesmen -- Great Britain -- Biography 4. Political scientists -- Great Britain -- Biography 5. Great Britain -- Politics and government -- 1760-1820

    ISBN 0465058973; 9780465058976

                       LC 2013935334

    This book, written by Jesse Norman, presents a biography of Edmund Burke "an 18th-century Irish philosopher and statesman [and] champion of human rights and the Anglo-American constitutional tradition, and a lifelong campaigner against arbitrary power. As Norman reveals, Burke was often ahead of his time, anticipating the abolition of slavery and arguing for free markets, equality for Catholics in Ireland, and responsible government in India." (Publisher's note)

    Includes bibliographical references (p. [299]-305) and index.

941.08   Period of Victoria and House of Windsor, 1837-

The Cambridge illustrated history of the British Empire; edited by P.J. Marshall. Cambridge Univ. Press 1996 400p il maps $55; pa $35   **941.08**

    1. Imperialism 2. Great Britain -- Colonies 3. Commonwealth countries -- History

    ISBN 0-521-43211-1; 0-521-00254-0 pa

                       LC 95-14535

    "This book examines the experience of colonialism in North America, India, Africa, Australia and the Caribbean, giving a brief history of the British imperial territories and looking at slavery, trade, religion, art, transportation, and the development of new ideas." Book Rep

    Includes bibliographical references

McKillop, A. B.

    The **spinster** & the prophet; H.G. Wells, Florence Deeks, and the case of the plagiarized text. Four Walls Eight Windows 2002 477p il $26.95   **941.08**

    1. Authors 2. Novelists 3. Historians 4. Plagiarism 5. Historiography 6. Feminists 7. Writers on science 8. Writers on politics 9. Science fiction writers

    ISBN 1-56858-236-6

                       LC 2002-71292

    "When, in 1920, Florence Deeks finally received her rejected manuscript—a feminist history of the world—from Macmillan after eight months, she couldn't understand why it appeared in such bad condition. . . . Later that year, when she read H.G. Wells's new book, The Outline of History, published by Macmillan, she felt a chill. There were so many similarities to her own work: shared themes, organization, word choice, even the same mistakes. Florence made a dramatic decision—she would sue Wells and his publisher for plagiarism. . . . The author handles the dual story line bril-

liantly, weaving together two opposing characters into one altogether gripping tale of literary theft." Publ Wkly

    Includes bibliographical references

Vallone, Lynne

    Becoming Victoria. Yale Univ. Press 2001 256p il $26.95   **941.08**

    1. Queens 2. Great Britain -- History -- 19th century

    ISBN 0-300-08950-3

                       LC 00-68561

    "Analyzing Victoria's girlhood diaries, drawings and fiction, as well as records of her education and scores of accounts of her childhood, Valone . . . constructs a revisionist account of the princess's youthful persona but also traces the process by which Victoria was molded into the 'right' kind of adult: capable of assuming the throne and also a clear embodiment of all that was womanly and pure. . . . Well-researched, and with sophisticated cultural criticism, this sound scholarship will engage the interest of academics and nonacademics alike." Publ Wkly

    Includes bibliographical references

941.081   British Isles--Reign of Victoria, 1837-1901

Encyclopedia of the Victorian era; James Eli Adams, editor in chief; Tom Pendergast, Sara Pendergast, editors. Grolier Academic Reference 2004 4v il map set $499   **941.081**

    1. Great Britain -- Civilization 2. Great Britain -- History -- 19th century

    ISBN 0-7172-5860-2

                       LC 2003-57101

    "Entries ranging in length from a few paragraphs to several pages are written by experts, treat topics from William Acton to zoological gardens, and seek to encompass the important issues, people, and events of the Victorian era. . . . While predictable figures such as Queen Victoria and Benjamin Disraeli appear, so too do social history topics such as the sporting life, penny dreadfuls, and cholera." Choice

    Includes bibliographical references

Jenkins, Roy

    Gladstone; a biography. Random House 1997 xxvii, 698p il hardcover o.p. pa $16.95   **941.081**

    1. Statesmen 2. Prime ministers 3. Great Britain -- Politics and government -- 19th century

    ISBN 0-8129-6641-4 pa

                       LC 96-49632

    First published 1995 in the United Kingdom

    This "book is a very decent try at an immensely difficult subject, encompassing an enormous amount of material. Lord Jenkins goes through the sources with commendable zeal. He also writes well." N Y Times Book Rev

    Includes bibliographical references

Murphy, Paul Thomas

    Shooting Victoria; madness, mayhem, and the rebirth of the British monarchy. Paul Thomas Murphy. Pegasus Books 2012 669 p. $35.00   **941.081**

    1. Victoria, Queen of Great Britain, 1819-1901 --

Assassination attempts

ISBN 9781605983547; 1605983543

This book on various attempts to assassinate Queen Victoria of England "recounts . . . how these deluded subjects managed to channel their mental instability or optimistic naïveté into assassination attempts with barely functioning pistols or stout canes. . . . [Paul Thomas] Murphy . . . weaves their life stories in with the reactions of Victoria and Albert and other notables as the government struggled to define a policy for punishing assassins." (Publishers Weekly)

Summerscale, Kate

Mrs. Robinson's disgrace; the private diary of a Victorian lady. Kate Summerscale. Bloomsbury 2012 xvi, 303 p.p geneal. tables $26.00   **941.081**

1. Diaries 2. Divorce 3. Great Britain -- History -- Victoria, 1837-1901

ISBN 1608199134; 9781608199136

LC 2012451243

This book considers the experience of Victorian woman "Isabella Robinson [who] defended herself in the newly created English divorce court over a mislaid diary filled with passionate erotic entries, philosophical musings, and complaints against her husband. . . . In two sections, the book first describes Isabella's flowery, coy memories of [her lover] . . . ; the second part focuses on her trial on an adultery charge and the scrambling of her male friends to preserve their reputations." (Publishers Weekly)

Includes bibliographical references and index

Wilson, A. N.

The **Victorians**. Norton 2003 724p il $35; pa $17.95   **941.081**

1. Great Britain -- Civilization 2. Great Britain -- History -- 19th century

ISBN 0-393-04974-4; 0-393-32543-1 pa

LC 2002-33809

First published 2002 in the United Kingdom

"Even to fastidious readers, Wilson's failings are minor, and the colorful tapestry he presents of a smoky world peopled with the likes of Carlyle, Mill, Marx, Ruskin, and Darwin can hardly fail to enthrall. Both professional scholars and laypeople will love to relax with this book, although some knowledge of the age is a must." Choice

Includes bibliographical references

941.084   British Isles, 1936-1945

Clarke, Peter

Mr. Churchill's profession; the statesman as author and the book that defined the 'special relationship' Peter Clarke. 1st US ed. Bloomsbury Press 2012 xix, 347 p.p ill. (alk. paper) $30.00   **941.084**

1. Politicians' writings 2. Prime ministers -- Great Britain 3. Great Britain -- History -- 20th century 4. Prime ministers -- Great Britain -- Biography

ISBN 1608193721; 9781608193721

LC 2011044274

This book "traces the making of the . . . work that occupied [Winston] Churchill for a quarter century, his four-volume 'History of the English-Speaking Peoples.' Churchill signed the contract for 'History' in 1932, at a time when his political career seemed over. His . . . return to power when the Nazis swept across Europe meant the book went uncompleted until the 1950s. But long before he took office, the . . . project was shaping his worldview, his speeches, and his leadership." (Publisher's note)

Includes bibliographical references (p.318 -331) and index

941.085   British Isles, 1945-1999

Junor, Penny

The **Firm** : the troubled life of the House of Windsor. Thomas Dunne Books 2005 xxi, 442p il $25.95   **941.085**

1. Queens 2. Kings 3. Great Britain -- Kings and rulers

ISBN 0-312-35274-3

LC 2005-45528

"Readers of this interesting and occasionally jaw-dropping look at the world's most famous dysfunctional family will find plenty to engage them." Libr J

Includes bibliographical references

Kynaston, David

Austerity Britain; 1945-51. Walker & Co. 2008 692p il (Tales of a new Jerusalem) $45   **941.085**

1. Great Britain -- Social conditions 2. Great Britain -- History -- 1945-1952 3. Great Britain -- Politics and government -- 20th century

ISBN 978-0-8027-1693-4; 0-8027-1693-8

First published 2007 in the United Kingdom

"Drawing on a remarkable array of diaries, letters, memoirs, and surveys, Kynaston assembles a polyphonic history of a pivotal time." New Yorker

Includes bibliographic references

Family Britain, 1951-1957. Walker & Co 2010 776p il $47.50   **941.085**

1. Great Britain -- History -- 1952- 2. Great Britain -- Social conditions 3. Great Britain -- Politics and government -- 20th century

ISBN 978-0-8027-1797-9

"Picking up where the much-lauded Austerity Britain, 1945-1951 (2008) left off, Kynaston's latest presents a panoramic view of a transformative period. . . . Leading us on an immersive tour of headlines and correspondence, diaries and sociological studies, Kynaston narrates moments and motifs both great and small, among them the Festival of Britain, Council housing, the queen's coronation, pub culture, Kingsley Amis, smog, labor strikes, skiffle, the 'colour bar,' grammar schools, football, the Suez Crisis, young Mick Jagger, and the BBC." Booklist

Includes bibliographical references

Moore, Charles

★ **Margaret** Thatcher; The Authorized Biography: From Grantham to the Falklands. Charles Moore. Knopf 2013 896 p. (hbk.) $35   **941.085**

1. Prime ministers -- Great Britain -- Biography 2. Conservative Party (Great Britain) -- Biography 3. Women prime ministers -- Great Britain -- Biography 4.

Great Britain -- Politics and government -- 1979-1997
ISBN 0307958949
9780307958945

LC 2013020670

This "authorized biography of Margaret Thatcher reveals . . . the early life, rise to power, and first years as prime minister of the woman who transformed Britain and the world in the late twentieth century. [Author Charles] Moore has had unique access to all of Thatcher's private and governmental papers, and interviewed her and her family extensively for this book." (Publisher's note)

Includes bibliographical references and index

941.1   Scotland

Devine, T. M.

The **Scottish** nation 1700-2000. Viking 1999 xxiii, 695p il maps hardcover o.p. pa $20   **941.1**
1. Scotland -- History
ISBN 0-14-100234-4 pa

LC 99-29866

"The author divides the book into chronological periods to cover Scottish economic, military, and social history; regional differences in the Highlands and Lowlands; and the development of Scottish identity." Libr J

Includes bibliographical references

Herman, Arthur

How the Scots invented the modern world; the true story of how western Europe's poorest nation created our world & everything in it. Crown 2001 392p $25.95; pa $14.95   **941.1**
1. Scottish national characteristics 2. Scotland -- Civilization
ISBN 0-609-60635-2; 0-609-80999-7 pa

LC 2001-28951

"This is a worthwhile book for the general reader." Publ Wkly

Includes bibliographical references (p. 362-376) and index

Nicolson, Adam

Sea room: an island life in the Hebrides. North Point Press 2002 391p il maps $27; pa $14 **941.1**
1. Hebrides (Scotland) -- Social life and customs
ISBN 0-86547-636-5; 0-86547-667-5 pa

LC 2002-19816

First published 2001 in the United Kingdom

"Magnificent and poetic, this is a literary and ecological masterpiece." Booklist

Includes bibliographical references

941.5   Ireland

The **Encyclopedia** of Ireland; edited by Brian Lalor; foreword by Frank McCourt. Yale University Press 2003 xxxvii, 1218p il map $65   **941.5**
1. Reference books 2. Ireland -- Encyclopedias
ISBN 0-300-09442-6

LC 2003-103834

This encyclopedia contains alphabetically arranged entries from Abbey Theatre to Zozimus, a nineteenth-century balladeer. Coverage includes art, cinema, current events, fashion, food, history, Irish language, literature, music, politics, religion, sports, and biographies of a wide range of famous people of Irish descent, including St. Brigid, Éamon de Valera, John F. Kennedy, Bono, Eugene O'Neill, Mary Robinson, and William Butler Yeats

"This wonderful reference work will delight researchers and lovers of Ireland and the Irish." Choice

★ **Encyclopedia** of Irish history and culture; James S. Donnelly Jr., editor in chief; Karl S. Bottigheimer . . . [et al.], associate editors. Macmillan Reference USA 2004 2v il map set $270 **941.5**
1. Reference books 2. Ireland -- Encyclopedias
ISBN 0-02-865902-3

LC 2004-5353

"The A-Z entries are preceded by a chronology and followed by a selection of almost 150 primary documents ranging from the Confession of St. Patrick (c. 450) to the Belfast/Good Friday Agreement (1998). . . . Providing the latest in scholarship, entries are well written and cover the gamut of historical, social, and cultural topics." Booklist

Includes bibliographical references

Ferriter, Diarmaid

The **transformation** of Ireland. Overlook Press 2005 884p $37.50   **941.5**
1. Ireland -- History
ISBN 1-58567-681-0

LC 2005-49849

First published 2004 in the United Kingdom

"This book isn't a political history of 20th-century Ireland; it's more a chronicle of the social reaction to the events that shaped that century. . . . [The author] has written an informative, funny, at times derisive book that takes a fresh approach to 20th-century Ireland." Publ Wkly

Includes bibliographical references

The **Oxford** illustrated history of Ireland; edited by R.F. Foster. Oxford University Press 2001 382p il map pa $29.95   **941.5**
1. Ireland -- History
ISBN 0-19-289323-8

First published 1989

This illustrated history includes "six essays by Irish scholars, five covering chronological periods in Irish history and the sixth a . . . discussion of the interplay between Irish literature and history." Libr J

Includes bibliographical references

Parks, Tim

Italian ways; on and off the rails from Milan to Palermo. Tim Parks. W W Norton & Co Inc 2013 288 p. (hardcover) $25.95   **941.5**
  1. Railroad travel -- Italy 2. Italy -- Description and travel 3. Italy -- Social life and customs
ISBN 0393239322; 9780393239324

                     LC 2013011386

In this book, author Tim Parks "pokes affectionate fun at his fellow train travelers and surveys a rapidly changing Italian landscape. . . . Here, he chronicles his adventures on the nation's rails. . . . Train travel in Italy is the ultimate leveler, Parks finds, and it provides a microcosm of what is transpiring in the society as a whole since globalization has taken root. His observations mingle travelogue, history and memoir, spanning the years from 2005 to the present." (Kirkus Reviews)

State, Paul F.

A **brief** history of Ireland. Facts On File 2009 xxiv, 408p il map (Brief history) $49.50; pa $19.95   **941.5**
  1. Ireland -- History
ISBN 978-0-8160-7516-4; 0-8160-7516-6; 978-0-8160-7517-1 pa; 0-8160-7517-4 pa

                     LC 2008-29243

The author "opens this vibrant reference with an introduction to Ireland's landscape, people, economics, natural resources, and current government. Following this essay-style overview are 11 chronologically organized chapters. Each is devoted to a significant historical watershed, tracing events from Ireland's prehistory to its contemporary prosperity. Appendixes provide at-a-glance portraits of Northern Ireland and the Irish Republic, including a list of presidents, prime ministers, and a time line of notable dates." Libr J

  Includes bibliographical references

941.501   Early history to 1086

Cahill, Thomas

How the Irish saved civilization; the untold story of Ireland's heroic role from the fall of Rome to the rise of medieval Europe. {by} Thomas Cahill. Talese 1995 246p il maps $27.50; pa $12.95   **941.501**
  1. Medieval civilization 2. Learning and scholarship 3. Ireland -- Civilization
ISBN 0-385-41848-5; 0-385-41849-3 pa

                     LC 94-28130

"Highly literate and affectionate, if somewhat rambling and indulgent. . . . As a freewheeling, witty popular history of Irish Christianity in the Dark Ages, this will amuse and enlighten." Libr J

  Includes bibliographical references

941.508   Ireland, 1800-

Kelly, John

The **graves** are walking; the great famine and the saga of the Irish people. John Kelly. Henry Holt and Co. 2012 397 p.   **941.508**
  1. Famines -- Ireland 2. Ireland -- History 3. Ireland -- Immigration and emigration 4. Ireland -- History -- Famine, 1845-1852 5. Famines -- Ireland -- History -- 19th century 6. Irish -- Migrations -- History -- 19th century 7. Ireland -- Emigration and immigration -- History -- 19th century
ISBN 080509184X; 9780805091847

                     LC 2012011493

This book, by John Kelly, offers an "account of . . . the Great Irish Potato Famine. . . . It started in 1845, . . . [a] perfect storm of bacterial infection, political greed, and religious intolerance. . . . But even more extraordinary . . . were its political underpinnings, and [the author] . . . provides . . . analysis on the role that Britain's nation-building policies played in exacerbating the devastation by attempting to use the famine to reshape Irish society and character." (Publisher's note)

  Includes bibliographical references and index

941.6   Northern Ireland; Donegal, Monaghan, Cavan counties of Republic of Ireland

Campbell, Julieann

Setting the truth free; the inside story of the Bloody Sunday Justice Campaign. Julieann Campbell. Liberties Press 2012 219 p. ill. (some col.) (pbk.) $24.95   **941.6**
  1. Civil rights demonstrations 2. Northern Ireland -- History 3. Bloody Sunday, Derry, Northern Ireland, 1972 4. Bloody Sunday Justice Campaign 5. Londonderry (Northern Ireland) -- History -- 20th century 6. Massacres -- Northern Ireland -- Londonderry -- History -- 20th century
ISBN 1907593373; 9781907593376

                     LC 2012379691

In this book about the "1972 Bloody Sunday massacre during a peaceful civil rights march in Derry, Northern Ireland .. . . [Julieann] Campbell, an Irish journalist . . . niece of the first person slain on that tragic day . . . [and] the press officer for the campaign to find justice for those killed and wounded, not only tells the tale of her murdered 17-year-old uncle, Jackie Duddy, but also details the planning of the march, the . . . slaughter by the British troops, and the traumatic remembrances of the survivors. . . . A need to seek justice, as Campbell writes, motivated the Irish community to protest and pressure the British government to launch a real inquiry into the shootings." (Publishers Weekly)

Coogan, Tim Pat

The **troubles**; Ireland's ordeal, 1966-1996, and the search for peace. Palgrave 2002 589p il map pa $22.95   **941.6**
  1. Northern Ireland
ISBN 978-0-312-29418-2; 0-312-29418-2
  First published 1995 in the United Kingdom

In this political history the author "examines all parties to the struggle. . . . He reconstructs the past 30 years, from the 1969 marching and riots to the H-Block protests, the MacBride Principles, the Anglo-Irish agreement, and the recent paramilitary cease-fire. Coogan traces the current peace process, stalled by Great Britain's insistence that the IRA hand in its weapons, to the 1979 visit of Pope John Paul II." Libr J

Includes bibliographical references

942   England and Wales

Ackroyd, Peter

London : the biography. Talese 2001 xxvi, 801p il $45; pa $18.95   **942**
1. London (England) -- History
ISBN 0-385-49770-9; 0-385-49771-7 pa
LC 2001-27153
First published 2000 in the United Kingdom
"A sweeping, highly readable account of London's colorful and complicated history." Libr J
Includes bibliographical references

Thames; the biography. Nan A. Talese/Doubleday 2008 481p il map $40   **942**
1. Thames River (England) 2. London (England) -- History
ISBN 978-0-385-52623-4; 0-385-52623-7
LC 2008-02864
First published 2007 in the United Kingdom
"Eschewing standard organization, Ackroyd jumps from today's posh London banks to Roger Bacon's observatory at Grandpont to Dickens's 'deathlike and mysterious' waterway. We learn about the riverbank's many species of willow (white, weeping, crack, cane osier), and about the Retribution and the Belliqueux, eighteenth-century prison boats that each held hundreds of men. . . . A survey of the many ways in which the river can kill notes that most Thames suicides remain 'anonymous and unlamented.' Not every tidbit will appeal to every reader, but the book demands to be read as it was written, according to one's fancy." New Yorker
Includes bibliographical references

Cartwright, Justin

Oxford revisited. Bloomsbury 2009 223p pa $18   **942**
1. Oxford (England) 2. University of Oxford
ISBN 978-1-59691-093-5; 1-59691-093-3
First published 2008 in the United Kingdom with title: This secret garden
"A South African-born novelist who graduated from Oxford University in the 1960s, Cartwright returns to the medieval campus nearly four decades later on a combination nostalgic tour and journalistic inquiry. Seeking to define the university's greatness, Cartwright offers erudite meditations on everything from the solidity of its buildings . . . to the fiercely individualistic lives of its students. . . . He offers sharply observed homages to the thinkers and writers—Isaiah Berlin, J. R. R. Tolkien, Charles Dodgson—who shaped Oxford's discourse, and maps out the university's peculiar mix of silly rituals and sublime intellectual life. In addition,

the book retraces Cartwright's own journey from callow teenager to confident young scholar-athlete." N Y Times Book Rev

Gott, Richard

Britain's empire; resistance, repression and revolt. Richard Gott. Verso Books 2011 vii, 568 p.p $34.95   **942**
1. Imperialism 2. Resistance to government 3. Great Britain -- Colonies 4. Imperialism -- History 5. Great Britain -- Civilization 6. Commonwealth countries -- History 7. Great Britain -- Colonies -- History 8. Government, Resistance to -- Commonwealth countries -- History 9. Government, Resistance to -- Great Britain -- Colonies -- History
ISBN 1844677389; 9781844677382
LC 2011456112
This book, by Richard Gott, offers a "history of the foundation of the British empire, . . . punctur[ing] the still widely held belief that the British Empire was a . . . civilizing enterprise of great benefit to its subject peoples. Instead, [it] reveals a history of systemic repression . . . and . . . military dictatorship. . . . [But w]herever Britain tried to plant its flag, there was resistance. From Ireland to India, from the American colonies to Australia." (Publisher's note)
Includes bibliographical references and index.

Hollis, Leo

London rising; the men who made modern London. Walker & Co. 2008 390p il map $27.99 **942**
1. Authors 2. Architects 3. Economists 4. Physicians 5. Physicists 6. Philosophers 7. Diarists 8. Essayists 9. Biographers 10. College teachers 11. Members of Parliament 12. London (England) -- History 13. Political and social philosophers 14. St. Paul's Cathedral (London, England)
ISBN 978-0-8027-1632-3; 0-8027-1632-6
LC 2008-000179
"London in the mid-17th century remained a medieval city. The civil war, a plague that claimed 100,000 lives and the Great Fire of 1666 would have been sufficient to send it back to the Dark Ages. Instead, London was transformed into a modern metropolis. . . . Hollis controls the narrative by focusing on the five figures who best represent the spirit of the age. John Locke, the philosopher, outlined a daring theory of universal natural rights; social observer John Evelyn grappled with the specific meaning of Englishness; real estate developer and speculator Nicholas Barbon rebuilt the center of London (with designs by the scientific polymath Robert Hooke); and lastly, Christopher Wren, who created St. Paul's Cathedral, eternal symbol of the glittering city." Publ Wkly
Includes bibliographical references

Medieval England; an encyclopedia. editors: Paul E. Szarmach, M. Teresa Tavormina, Joel T. Rosentha. Garland 1998 lxiv, 882p il maps $155 **942**
1. Reference books 2. Medieval civilization -- Encyclopedias 3. Great Britain -- History -- Encyclopedias
ISBN 0-8240-5786-4
LC 97-35523

"Containing more than 700 entries by more than 300 international scholars, the volume encompasses the fields of Old English and Middle English language and literature, music and liturgy, history, and history of art. . . . The A-Z entries are supported by lists of kings and queens of England, archbishops of Canterbury and York, and popes, 590-1502, as well as a glossary of musical and liturgical terms." Booklist

Nicolson, Juliet

The **perfect** summer; England 1911, just before the storm. Grove Press 2007 290p il $25; pa $15　　　　　　　　　　　　　　　　　　**942**
　1. Great Britain -- Social conditions　2. Great Britain -- History -- 20th century　3. Great Britain -- Social life and customs
　ISBN 0-8021-1846-1; 978-0-8021-1846-2; 0-8021-4367-9 pa; 978-0-8021-4367-9 pa
　　　　　　　　　　　　　　　　LC 2006-48854
First published 2006 in the United Kingdom
"With her sparkling social history about Edwardian society on the brink of World War I, Nicolson has created the perfect beach reading for Anglophiles." Christ Sci Monit
Includes bibliographical references

Taylor, A. J. P.

English history, 1914-1945. Oxford Univ. Press 1965 xxvii, 708p maps (Oxford history of England) $194.50　　　　　　　　　　　　　　　　**942**
　1. World War, 1914-1918 -- Great Britain　2. World War, 1939-1945 -- Great Britain　3. Great Britain -- History -- 20th century
　ISBN 0-19-821715-3
A study of the political, economic, and social changes in England over a thirty year span.

942.01　　England--Early history to 1066

Goodrich, Norma Lorre

King Arthur. Harper & Row 1989 406p il map pa $17　　　　　　　　　　　　　　　**942.01**
　1. Kings　2. Great Britain -- History -- 0-1066
　ISBN 0-06-097182-7; 978-0-06-097182-3
　　　　　　　　　　　　　　　　LC 85-22558
First published 1986 by Watts
The author examines historical and literary materials relating to Arthur as both an actual and legendary figure.
Includes bibliographical references

King Arthur in legend and history; edited by Richard White; foreword by Allan Massie. Routledge 1998 xxv, 570p il maps hardcover o.p. pa $34.95　　　　　　　　　　　　　　　　**942.01**
　1. Kings　2. Great Britain -- History -- 0-1066
　ISBN 0-415-92063-9 pa
　　　　　　　　　　　　　　　　LC 97-47726
First published 1997 in the United Kingdom
"This book is a compilation of source material excerpted primarily from longer works. . . . The documents themselves are arranged in roughly chronological and geographical order, ranging from Gildas (c. 548) to The Buik of the Chronicles of Scotland (1535). The anthology presents both historical and literary works and draws from French and German as well as English sources." Libr J
Includes bibliographical references

942.02　　England--Norman period, 1066-1154

Morris, Marc

★ The **Norman** Conquest; The Battle of Hastings and the Fall of Anglo-saxon England. by Marc Morris. W W Norton & Co Inc 2013 464 p. $32　　　　　　　　　　　　　　　　**942.02**
　1. Hastings (East Sussex, England), Battle of, 1066　2. Great Britain -- History -- 1066-1154, Norman period
　ISBN 1605984515; 9781605984513
This book by Marc Morris "explains why the Norman Conquest was the most significant cultural and military episode in English history. It explain[s] why England was at once so powerful and yet so vulnerable to William the Conqueror's attack; why the Normans, in some respects less sophisticated, possessed the military cutting edge; how William's hopes of a united Anglo-Norman realm unraveled, dashed by English rebellions, Viking invasions, and the insatiable demands of his fellow conquerors." (Publisher's note)

942.03　　England--Period of House of Plantagenet, 1154-1399

Guy, John

Thomas Becket; warrior, priest, rebel : a nine-hundred-year-old story retold. John Guy. Random House 2011 424 p.　　　　　　　　　　　**942.03**
　1. Biography　2. Christian saints　3. Christianity and politics　4. Great Britain -- History -- 1066-1154, Norman period　5. Statesmen -- Great Britain -- Biography　6. Christian saints -- England -- Biography　7. Christian martyrs -- England -- Biography　8. Great Britain -- History -- Henry II, 1154-1189 -- Biography
　ISBN 1400069076; 9780679603412; 9781400069071
　　　　　　　　　　　　　　　　LC 2011042794
This book by John Guy presents a biography "of Thomas Becket (1118–1170), the man who refused to subordinate the power of the church to the power of the state, and was martyred for it. . . . Distilling and disputing materials from several previous Becket biographies, Guy traces his subject's development from a handsome, superficial, and socially ambitious youth to a mature man who rose intellectually, morally, and politically to become lord chancellor to Henry II. In 1162, he was named archbishop of Canterbury, a position he accepted reluctantly, knowing that his honest exercise of the office as a defender of liberty and as one who would assert the church's power to cancel unjust state laws would bring him into conflict with Henry." (Publishers Weekly)
Includes bibliographical references and index.

Jones, Dan

★ The **Plantagenets**; the warrior kings and queens who made England. Dan Jones. Viking 2013 xxv, 534 p.p (hardcover) $36   **942.03**

1. Great Britain -- Kings and rulers 2. Great Britain -- History -- 1154-1399, Plantagenets 3. Great Britain -- Kings and rulers -- Biography 4. Great Britain -- History -- Plantagenets, 1154-1399 5. Great Britain -- Politics and government -- 1154-1399
  ISBN 0670026654; 9780670026654

                     LC 2012039998

First published in Great Britain in 2012.

This book, by Dan Jones, examines how "the first Plantagenet king inherited a blood-soaked kingdom from the Normans and transformed it into an empire stretched at its peak from Scotland to Jerusalem. . . . We meet . . . Eleanor of Aquitaine, . . . her son, Richard the Lionheart, . . . and King John, a tyrant who was forced to sign Magna Carta. . . . This is the era of chivalry, . . . the Black Death, the founding of Parliament, . . . and the Hundred Year's War." (Publisher's note)

"The great battles against the Scots and French and the subjugation of the Welsh make for thrilling reading but so do the equally enthralling struggles over succession, the Magna Carta, and the Provisions of Oxford...Written with prose that keeps the reader captivated throughout accounts of the span of centuries and the not-always-glorious trials of kingship, this book is at all times approachable, academic, and entertaining." Booklist

Includes bibliographical references and index

Ormrod, W. Mark

Edward III; W. Mark Ormrod. Yale University Press 2012 xx, 721 p.p (cl : alk. paper) $45.00 **942.03**

1. Great Britain -- Kings and rulers -- Biography 2. Great Britain -- History -- Edward III, 1327-1377 3. Great Britain -- Politics and government -- 1327-1377
  ISBN 0300119100; 9780300119107

                     LC 2011013536

In this biography of Edward III of England, it was the author's intent to demonstrate "that Edward's personality and ambitions remained absolutely at the heart of English royal policy for at least forty years, and that his skills as a politician shaped a unique political culture that brought about a long period of domestic stability within England." (Times Literary Supplement)

Includes bibliographical references and index.

Weir, Alison

Eleanor of Aquitaine; a life. Ballantine Bks. 2000 xxi, 441p il maps $28; pa $15.95   **942.03**

1. Queens
  ISBN 0-345-40540-4; 0-345-43487-0 pa

                     LC 99-54785

First published 1999 in the United Kingdom with title Eleanor of Aquitaine: by the wrath of God, Queen of England

A biography of the twelfth-century queen, first of France, then of England, the consort of Henry II and mother of Richard the Lionhearted

"In approaching as complex a subject as feudalism, Weir wears her learning lightly and has a pleasant habit of anticipating all the questions of a curious reader." Publ Wkly

Includes bibliographical references

942.04   England--Period of Houses of Lancaster and York, 1399-1485

Gristwood, Sarah

Blood sisters; the women behind the Wars of the Roses. Sarah Gristwood. Basic Books, A Member of the Perseus Books Group 2013 432 p. (hard cover : alk. paper) $29.99   **942.04**

1. Courts and courtiers 2. Queens -- Great Britain 3. Great Britain -- History -- 1455-1485, Wars of the Roses 4. Great Britain -- History -- Henry VII, 1485-1509 5. Great Britain -- History -- Wars of the Roses, 1455-1485
  ISBN 0465018319; 9780465018314

                     LC 2012044813

This book, by historian Sarah Gristwood, examines the female dynamics behind the War of the Roses. "While the events of this turbulent time are usually described in terms of the male leads who fought and died seeking the throne, a handful of powerful women would prove just as decisive as their kinfolks' clashing armies. . . . Gristwood traces the rise and rule of the seven most critical women in the wars." (Publisher's note)

Includes bibliographical references and index

Weir, Alison

The **Wars** of the Roses. Ballantine Bks. 1995 462p il hardcover o.p. pa $15.95   **942.04**

1. Great Britain -- History -- 1455-1485, War of the Roses
  ISBN 0-345-39117-9; 0-345-40433-5 pa

"No history collection should do without this perfectly focused and beautifully unfolded account." Booklist

942.05   England--Period of House of Tudor, 1485-1603

Ackroyd, Peter, 1949-

Tudors; The History of England from Henry VIII to Elizabeth I. by Peter Ackroyd. Thomas Dunne Books 2013 512 p. (History of England) $29.99   **942.05**

1. England 2. Great Britain -- History -- 1485-1603, Tudors 3. Great Britain -- History -- Tudors, 1485-1603
  ISBN 1250003628; 9781250003621

                     LC 2013024573

This book, the "second title in [Peter Ackroyd's] projected six-volume history of England," focuses on "the 16th-century religious reformation that began, as a dynastic matter, with Henry VIII's divorce from Katherine of Aragon in 1533. . . . The Reformation in England was marked by upheaval and bloodshed, as the Tudors imposed religious changes upon an initially reluctant populace." (Publishers Weekly)

Includes bibliographical references (pages 473-481)

and index

Fletcher, Catherine

The **divorce** of Henry VIII; the untold story from inside the Vatican. Catherine Fletcher. Palgrave Macmillan 2012 xxiv, 266 p.p ill., map (hardcover) $28   **942.05**

1. Great Britain -- Foreign relations 2. Catholic Church -- Foreign relations 3. Reformation -- England 4. Catholic Church -- Foreign relations -- Great Britain 5. Great Britain -- Foreign relations -- Catholic Church 6. Great Britain -- Politics and government -- 1509-1547 7. Church and state -- Great Britain -- History -- 16th century

ISBN 0230341519; 9780230341517

LC 2011050335

This book, by historian Catherine Fletcher, explores the history and politics of the formation of the Church of England from Vatican archive sources. "In 1533 . . . Henry VIII decided to divorce his wife of twenty years. . . . But getting his freedom involved a terrific web of intrigue. . . . Henry's man in Rome was a wily Italian diplomat named Gregorio Casali who drew no limits on skullduggery including kidnapping, bribery and theft to make his king a free man." (Publisher's note)

Includes bibliographical references and index

Lipscomb, Suzannah

★ A **Journey** Through Tudor England; Hampton Court Palace and the Tower of London to Stratford-upon-avon and Thornbury Castle. by Suzannah Libscomb. 1st ed. W W Norton & Co Inc 2013 336 p. (hardcover) $26.95   **942.05**

1. Great Britain -- Description and travel 2. Great Britain -- History -- 1485-1603, Tudors

ISBN 1605984604; 9781605984605

This is "a guidebook that introduces readers to the history of the [Tudor] period through 50 of 'the best and most interesting' buildings associated with Tudor royalty. Each chapter tells the story of how a specific building served as the physical backdrop to the lives of those who inhabited it or to a particularly important visit from a famous personage." (Publishers Weekly)

Meyer, G. J.

The **Tudors**; the complete story of England's most notorious dynasty. Delacorte Press 2010 xxvi, 612p il map $30   **942.05**

1. Queens 2. Kings 3. Great Britain -- Kings and rulers 4. Great Britain -- History -- 1485-1603, Tudors

ISBN 978-0-385-34076-2

LC 2009-40032

"History buffs will savor Meyer's cheeky, nuanced, and authoritative perspective on an entire dynasty, and his study brims with enriching background discussions, ranging from class structure and the medieval Catholic Church to the Tudor connection to Spanish royalty." Publ Wkly

Includes bibliographical references

Mortimer, Ian

The **time** traveler's guide to Elizabethan England; Ian Mortimer. Viking 2013 416 p. (hardcover) $27.95   **942.05**

1. Great Britain -- Social conditions -- History 2. Great Britain -- History -- 1558-1603, Elizabeth 3. England -- Social conditions -- 16th century 4. Great Britain -- History -- Elizabeth, 1558-1603 5. England -- Social life and customs -- 16th century

ISBN 0670026077; 9780670026074

LC 2013001566

In this book, British historian Ian Mortimer offers an "account of life during Queen Elizabeth's 1558-1603 reign. The average Elizabethan paid little attention to politics but a great deal to domestic technology. Thus, bricks and clear glass became cheaper." Topic include the advent of chimneys, Elizabethan professionals, bathing habits, and personal hygiene. (Kirkus Reviews)

Includes bibliographical references and index

Ronald, Susan

Heretic queen; Queen Elizabeth I and the wars of religion. Susan Ronald. St. Martin's Press 2012 350 p. (hardcover) $27.99   **942.05**

1. Religious tolerance 2. War -- Religious aspects 3. Great Britain -- History -- 1485-1603, Tudors 4. Reformation -- England 5. England -- Church history -- 16th century 6. Great Britain -- History -- Elizabeth, 1558-1603

ISBN 0312645384; 9780312645380; 9781250015211

LC 2012010248

In this "companion volume to 'Pirate Queen,' [Susan] Ronald's 2007 study of . . . England's Elizabeth I, the author sets the Elizabethan age within the context of the Catholic-Protestant wars of religion" of "the latter half of the 16th century. Elizabeth had witnessed the religious divisions that marked the reigns of" Henry VIII, Edward VI, and Mary I, "so upon her ascension to the throne in 1558 she was eager to grant a measure of religious tolerance to her subjects." (Publishers Weekly)

Includes bibliographical references and index

Starkey, David

Six wives: the queens of Henry VIII. HarperCollins Pubs. 2003 xxvii, 852p il hardcover o.p. pa $16.95   **942.05**

1. Queens 2. Great Britain -- History -- 1485-1603, Tudors

ISBN 0-694-01043-X; 0-06-000550-5 pa

The author covers each of Henry's six wives, "their personalities, their place in the family networks and religious currents at court and the overall patterns of the king's infatuations and disillusionments." Publ Wkly

"Solidly researched and delightfully told, this is highly recommended." Libr J

Includes bibliographical references

Weir, Alison

Henry VIII; the king and his court. Ballantine Bks. 2001 632p il $28; pa $16.95   **942.05**

1. Kings 2. Great Britain -- History -- 1485-1603,

Tudors

ISBN 0-345-43659-8; 0-345-43708-X pa

LC 2001-116042

In this biography of the Tudor king, the author "examines the minutiae of his daily life and gives prominence to the background players of his court. . . . At times, the weighty detail and numerous characters will make the work inaccessible; however, as a scholarly study it is a significant achievement." Libr J

Includes bibliographical references

The **life** of Elizabeth I. Ballantine Bks. 1998 532p il hardcover o.p. pa $15.95   **942.05**

1. Queens 2. Great Britain -- History -- 1485-1603, Tudors

ISBN 0-345-42550-2 pa

LC 98-34917

This is a biography of "Elizabeth Tudor, the second of the three surviving children of the great English king Henry VIII." Booklist

"Weir brings a fine sense of selection and considerable zest to her portrait of the self-styled Virgin Queen." Publ Wkly

Includes bibliographical references

The **six** wives of Henry VIII. Grove Weidenfeld 1992 643p il hardcover o.p. pa $15   **942.05**

1. Kings 2. Great Britain -- History -- 1485-1603, Tudors

ISBN 0-8021-3683-4 pa

LC 91-29522

First published 1991 in the United Kingdom

This is a collective biography of the wives of the Tudor king of England

"Wonderfully detailed, extensively researched. . . . The narrative is free flowing, humorous, informative, and readable." SLJ

Includes bibliographical references

942.06   England--House of Stuart and Commonwealth periods to present, 1603-

Fraser, Antonia

Faith and treason; the story of the Gunpowder Plot. Doubleday 1996 xxxv, 347p il hardcover o.p. pa $16   **942.06**

1. Gunpowder plot, 1605 2. Conspirators 3. Revolutionaries 4. Great Britain -- History -- 1603-1714, Stuarts

ISBN 0-385-47190-4 pa

LC 96-21709

"A small group of Roman Catholics planned to blow up Parliament on its opening day in 1605, when the Protestant King James and his older son would be present, and to proclaim the nine-year-old princess Elizabeth queen, raise her as a Catholic, and so restore Catholicism as the state religion. . . . The Gunpowder Plot was both cruel and crackpot, but Fraser does a wonderful job of conveying to the modern reader just why a few Catholics felt that it was justified and also was likely to succeed." New Yorker

Includes bibliographical references

Trevelyan, George Macaulay

The **English** Revolution, 1688-1689; [by] G. M. Trevelyan. Oxford University Press 1965 136p pa $30   **942.06**

1. Great Britain -- History -- 1688, Revolution

ISBN 978-0-19-500263-8; 0-19-500263-6

First published 1938 in the United Kingdom

This study covers not only the revolution itself but also the events of the reign of James II, which led up to it and the political changes which followed.

Includes bibliographical references

942.1   London (England)

Jones, Nigel

Tower; an epic history of the Tower of London. Nigel Jones. St. Martin's Press 2012 464 p. (hardcover) $35.00   **942.1**

1. Great Britain -- History 2. London (England) -- History 3. Prisons -- England -- London -- History 4. Tower of London (London, England) -- History 5. Fortification -- England -- London -- History 6. London (England) -- Buildings, structures, etc

ISBN 0312622961; 9780312622961; 9781250018144

LC 2012028273

The book presents a history of the Tower of London in which the author "seeks to conjure the many characters that have lived, been imprisoned and perished within its walls. His concern is not so much with the building itself: he pays only fleeting attention to its architectural development. Instead, he is interested in the 'great actors in the dramas of English history' who trod its passages." These include "Henry VII . . . Simon de Montfort . . . Elizabeth I . . . [and] Sir Walter Raleigh". (TLS)

Includes bibliographical references and index

942.9   Wales

Morris, Jan

A **writer's** house in Wales. National Geographic Soc. 2002 143p (National Geographic directions) $25   **942.9**

1. Wales

ISBN 0-7922-6523-8

LC 2001-44731

The author "reflects on her home in Wales, its beautiful setting and the nature of being Welsh. . . . This slim and charming volume offers a crisp account of the turbulent history of the Welsh and their battle to maintain their language and culture in the shadow of their more powerful neighbor." Publ Wkly

942.901 Historical periods

Charles-Edwards, T. M.

Wales and the Britons, 350-1064; by T.M. Charles-Edwards. Oxford University Press 2013 xx, 795 p.p (The history of Wales) $185 **942.901**
1. Wales -- History 2. Great Britain -- History -- 0-1066 3. Wales -- History -- To 1063
ISBN 0198217315; 9780198217312

LC 2012376060

This book, by T.M. Charles-Edwards, "provides a detailed history of Wales in the period in which it was created out of the remnants of Roman Britain. It thus begins in the fourth century, with accelerating attacks from external forces, and ends shortly before the Norman Conquest of England. The narrative history is interwoven with chapters on the principal sources, the social history of Wales, the Church, the early history of the Welsh language, and its early literature, both in Welsh and in Latin." (Publisher's note)

Includes bibliographical references (p. [680]-739) and index

943 Germany and neighboring central European countries

Coy, Jason Philip

A **brief** history of Germany; [by] Jason P. Coy. Facts on File 2011 288p il map (Brief history) $49.50; pa $19.95 **943**
1. Germany -- History
ISBN 978-0-8160-8142-4; 978-0-8160-8329-9 pa

LC 2010-23139

This book provides an "account of the events, people, and special customs and traditions that have shaped Germany from ancient times to the present." Publisher's note
Includes bibliographical references

Craig, Gordon Alexander

The **Germans**; [by] Gordon A. Craig. Meridian 1991 361p il pa $18 **943**
1. Antisemitism 2. Heads of state 3. Nazi leaders 4. Germany -- History 5. Germany -- Civilization
ISBN 0-452-01085-3; 978-0-452-01085-7

LC 91-12814

First published 1982 by Putnam

This work examining the social history of Germany contains "chapters on religion, money, Germans and Jews, women, professors and students, romantics, literature and society, soldiers, Berlin—and an appendix called 'The Awful German Language.'" Publisher's note
Includes bibliographical references

Fulbrook, Mary

★ A **concise** history of Germany; 2nd ed; Cambridge University Press 2004 277p il, maps (Cambridge concise histories) hardcover o.p. pa $22 **943**
1. Princes 2. Statesmen 3. Heads of state 4. Prime ministers 5. National socialism 6. Nazi leaders 7.

Germany -- History
ISBN 0-521-83320-5; 0-521-54071-2 pa

LC 2004-271599

First published 1990 in the United Kingdom

This history of Germany "spans the early Middle Ages to the present day. . . . Mary Fulbrook explores the interrelationships between social, political and cultural factors in the light of the latest scholarly controversies." Publ Wkly
Includes bibliographical references

Gay, Peter

My German question; growing up in Nazi Berlin. Yale Univ. Press 1998 208p il $40; pa $11.95 **943**
1. Historians 2. National socialism 3. Jews -- Germany 4. College teachers 5. Nonfiction writers 6. Jews -- Persecutions 7. Germany -- Politics and government -- 1933-1945
ISBN 0-300-07670-3; 0-300-08070-0 pa

LC 98-26686

"A searching, sensitive portrait of Gay's youth, as crystalline as memory can be made." Booklist

Gay, Ruth

The **Jews** of Germany; a historical portrait. with an introduction by Peter Gay. Yale Univ. Press 1992 297p il maps hardcover o.p. pa $35 **943**
1. Jews -- Germany
ISBN 0-300-05155-7; 0-300-06052-1 pa

LC 91-30235

This is a history of Germany's Jews from the first century to the Holocaust.

"Illustrated sumptuously with paintings, photographs and excerpts from letters and historical documents, . . . this affirming history survives the sad end of the centuries-old German Jewish way of life." N Y Times Book Rev

Gorra, Michael Edward

The **bells** in their silence; travels through Germany. {by} Michael Gorra. Princeton University Press 2004 211p $24.95 **943**
1. Germany -- Description and travel
ISBN 0-691-11765-9

Gorra's "account of his travels through Germany is shaped—perhaps even haunted—by figures from the past: historical, literary, personal. A captivating, unique work of synthesis." Booklist
Includes bibliographical references

MacDonogh, Giles

Frederick the Great; a life in deed and letters. St. Martin's Press 2000 436p il hardcover o.p. pa $16.95 **943**
1. Kings
ISBN 0-312-27266-9 pa

LC 00-24799

First published 1999 in the United Kingdom

"Both general readers and those with a strong background in European history will find great value in this outstanding biography." Booklist
Includes bibliographical references

Moorhouse, Roger

Berlin at war. Basic Books 2010 432p il
$29.95 **943**

1. Berlin (Germany) -- History 2. World War, 1939-1945 -- Germany

ISBN 978-0-465-00533-8

LC 2010-907169

"Election results in the fading days of the Weimar Republic indicate that Berliners were not particularly sympathetic to Hitler or his movement. Yet Berlin endured horrible physical destruction, deprivation, and death. This included intense Allied bombings by day and night, and a siege and eventual ravaging by the Russian army. . . . [Moorhouse] begins with an almost idyllic scene as huge crowds in Berlin witness the celebration of Hitler's birthday in April 1939; at the time, of course, Germany seemed to have achieved its foreign-policy goals without firing a shot. As the fortunes of Germany and Berlin deteriorate, Moorhouse uses the testimonies of a variety of Berliners to describe some memorable scenes and struggles.This is a hard, unrelenting saga of the effects of total warfare on citizens just hoping to survive." Booklist

Includes bibliographical references

Watson, Peter, 1943-

The **German** genius; Europe's third renaissance, the second scientific revolution, and the twentieth century. Harper 2010 964p il $35 **943**

1. Germany -- Civilization 2. Germany -- Intellectual life

ISBN 0060760222; 9780060760229

LC 2010-06738

This is a "cultural history of German ideas and influence, from 1750 to the present day." (Publisher's note) Index.

This is "a panoramic review of German cultural and intellectual development from 1750 to the present. Examining the contributions of literally hundreds of German thinkers and doers and mapping the conceptual connections between them, the author demonstrates the breadth, volume, and influence of German output in philosophy, science, industry, art, literature, and all forms of scholarly activity. But Watson's true focus is the cultural crucible, forged in the eighteenth and nineteenth centuries and informed by notions of Bildung and inwardness, that gave rise to such accomplishments but also set the stage for the evil actions of the Third Reich. To some extent an effort to untether our understanding of German history from the conflicts of the twentieth century, this study is also a reminder that our modern Western worldview has deep German roots." Booklist

Includes bibliographical references

943.08   Germany since 1866

Craig, Gordon Alexander

Germany, 1866-1945; by Gordon A. Craig. Oxford Univ. Press 1978 825p (Oxford history of modern Europe) hardcover o.p. pa $41.95 **943.08**

1. Germany -- History

ISBN 0-19-502724-8 pa

LC 78-58471

"An impressive . . . survey of modern German history, this book is an indispensable reference." New Statesman (1913)

Includes bibliographical references

Evans, Richard J.

★ The **coming** of the Third Reich; a history. Penguin Press 2004 622p il map hardcover o.p. pa $18 **943.08**

1. National socialism 2. Germany -- History -- 1866-1918 3. Germany -- History -- 1918-1933

ISBN 1-594-20004-1; 0-14-303469-3 pa

LC 2003-63205

First published 2003 in the United Kingdom

"This is a first-rate narrative history that informs and educates and may inspire readers to delve even deeper into the subject." Booklist

Includes bibliographical references

Stern, Fritz Richard

Five Germanys I have known; [by] Fritz Stern. Farrar, Straus & Giroux 2006 546p il map $30 **943.08**

1. Germany -- History

ISBN 978-0-374-15540-7; 0-374-15540-2

LC 2006-60

In this "memoir, Stern looks back over the 'five Germanys' his generation has seen—the Weimar Republic, Nazi tyranny, the post-1945 Federal Republic, the Soviet-controlled German Democratic Republic and, lastly, the reunited Germany of the present—and explains how he came to reconcile himself with his birth country (which his Jewish family fled in 1938) as it has come to terms with its new place in today's more cohesive and peaceful Europe. . . . The book's intriguing structure makes it a wonderful combination of history, memoir, analysis and even poetry." Publ Wkly

943.085   Period of Weimar Republic, 1918-1933

Haffner, Sebastian

Defying Hitler; a memoir. translated from the German by Oliver Pretzel. Farrar, Straus & Giroux 2002 309p il $24; pa $14 **943.085**

1. Germany -- History -- 1918-1933

ISBN 0-374-16157-7; 0-312-42113-3 pa

LC 2002-17058

"In August 1938 a young German lawyer and journalist with the . . . name of Raimund Pretzel arrived in England. . . . Pretzel, a non-Jew, was fleeing to join and marry a Jewish woman pregnant with their first child. . . . Choosing a new name—Sebastian Haffner—to keep the Nazis from retaliating against his relatives, he went on to a . . . career as a journalist and historian in England, where he died in 1999. Afterward, while perusing his father's papers, Oliver Pretzel . . . found a . . . typescript in German. It was Haffner's unfinished memoir about his early years, begun in 1939, that sought through autobiography to understand how Hitler came to power." New Leader

943.086   Germany--Period of Third Reich, 1933-1945

Album of the damned; snapshots from the Third Reich. Academy Chicago Publishers 2008 408p il $50   **943.086**
1. Germany -- History -- 1933-1945 2. World War, 1939-1945 -- Pictorial works
ISBN 978-0-89733-576-8; 0-89733-576-7

"Photographed almost exclusively by amateurs — both soldiers and civilians — the pictures in Album of the Damned center on the daily life within the Third Reich, both at home and on the battlefield. . . . Garson assembled the exclusively black-and-white photos from private collections around the world, including many captured by the Soviets that only became available after the fall of the Soviet Union. . . . Critics might maintain that by focusing on showing how Nazis were 'human,' attention is diverted from their crimes against humanity. But it's impossible to thumb through the book on any page and not see the ghosts of the six million floating around every photo. A narrative that snakes through the book provides an overview of the time period and background on what's taking place in the photos." Jerusalem Post

Ayçoberry, Pierre

The **social** history of the Third Reich; 1933-1945. translated from the French by Janet Lloyd. New Press 2000 380p $30; pa $15.95   **943.086**
1. National socialism 2. Germany -- Social conditions 3. Germany -- Politics and government -- 1933-1945
ISBN 1-56584-549-8; 1-56584-635-4 pa
LC 99-14059

"In examining the actions of individuals and social groups, {the author} illustrates that German citizens' response to the Nazi regime varied wildly. Some resisted bravely; others saw an opportunity for advancement. Most people sought merely to survive. In fact, what is extremely unsettling is how so many could maintain a semblance of normalcy in their lives. Ayçoberry does not attempt to answer the unanswerable questions posed by the Nazi era, but his disturbing, brutally honest, and scrupulously fair work may be a landmark in the field." Booklist
Includes bibliographical references

Bascomb, Neal

Hunting Eichmann; how a band of survivors and a young spy agency chased down the world's most notorious Nazi. Houghton Mifflin Harcourt 2009 390p il map $26   **943.086**
1. War criminals 2. Nazi leaders 3. Secret service -- Israel
ISBN 978-0-618-85867-5; 0-618-85867-9
LC 2008-35757

The author recounts the pursuit, capture, and abduction of Nazi war criminal Adolf Eichmann. "Bascomb spread a wide net in researching the 15-year hunt, and he fills his book with previously unknown or neglected details, utilizing the remembrances of former Mossad agents, German and American intelligence operatives, and Argentine Nazi sympathizers who tried to find Eichmann after his seizure. .

. . This is an outstanding account of a sustained and worthy manhunt." Booklist
Includes bibliographical references

Burleigh, Michael

The **Third** Reich; a new history. Hill & Wang 2000 xxv, 965p il maps hardcover o.p. pa $18   **943.086**
1. Germany -- History -- 1933-1945
ISBN 0-8090-9326-X pa
LC 00-31838

This account of Germany under National Socialism "focuses on the moral breakdown that gave Hitler control of an industrial society, which then, along with the rest of the world, suffered the catastrophic consequences." Publ Wkly
"This brilliant and unique view of a great tyranny is an important addition to our understanding of the first half of the twentieth century." Booklist
Includes bibliographical references

Evans, Richard J.

★ The **Third** Reich in power, 1933-1939. Penguin Press 2005 941p il map hardcover o.p. pa $20   **943.086**
1. National socialism 2. Germany -- History -- 1933-1945
ISBN 1-594-20074-2; 0-14-303790-0 pa
LC 2005-52128

This "is a major achievement. No other recent synthetic history has quite the range and narrative power of Evans's work." Publ Wkly
Includes bibliographical references

Fischer, Klaus P.

Nazi Germany; a new history. Continuum 1995 734p il hardcover o.p. pa $32.95   **943.086**
1. Heads of state 2. National socialism 3. Nazi leaders 4. Germany -- History -- 1933-1945
ISBN 0-8264-0906-7 pa
LC 94-41796

This is an "analysis of the Third Reich from its late-19th-century origins to its apocalyptic collapse." Libr J
"An indispensable, compellingly readable political, military and social history of the Third Reich." Publ Wkly
Includes bibliographical references

Fleming, Gerald

Hitler and the final solution; with an introduction by Saul Friedlander. University of Calif. Press 1984 xxxvi, 219p il hardcover o.p. pa $18.95   **943.086**
1. Heads of state 2. Nazi leaders 3. Holocaust, 1933-1945
ISBN 0-520-06022-9 pa
LC 83-24352

Original German edition, 1982
This work attempts to prove "that the Final Solution was deliberately designed and personally willed and ordered by Hitler. Fleming reveals the elaborate precautions taken not only to disguise the nature of the operation but also to ensure that it could not be connected with Hitler." Publisher's note
Includes bibliographical references

Fritzsche, Peter

Life and death in the Third Reich. Belknap Press of Harvard University Press 2008 368p **943.086**
1. National socialism 2. Holocaust, 1933-1945 3. Germany -- Ethnic relations 4. Collective memory -- Germany 5. Holocaust, Jewish (1939-1945) 6. Germany -- History -- 1933-1945 7. Holocaust, Jewish (1939-1945) -- Germany
ISBN 0-674-02793-0; 0-674-03465-1 pa; 978-0-674-02793-0; 978-0-674-03465-5 pa

LC 2007-40552

This is a sequel to the author's Germans into Nazis (1998). In this study, Fritzsche seeks to explain the success of the ideology of Nazism. He argues that "its basic appeal lay in the Volksgemeinschaft—a 'people's community' that appealed to Germans to be part of a great project to redress the wrongs of the Versailles treaty, make the country strong and vital, and rid the body politic of unhealthy elements. The goal was to create a new national and racial self-consciousness among Germans. For Germany to live, others—especially Jews—had to die. . . . Fritzsche examines the efforts of Germans to adjust to new racial identities, to believe in the necessity of war, to accept the dynamic of unconditional destruction—in short, to become Nazis." (Publisher's note) Index.

"This book combines a compelling historical narrative with a thought-provoking analysis and will be of much interest to scholars in the field as well as a more general readership." Times Higher Ed

Includes bibliographical references

Johnson, Eric A.

What we knew; terror, mass murder and everyday life in Nazi Germany: an oral history. [by] Eric A. Johnson and Karl-Heinz Reuband. Basic Books 2005 xxiii, 434p $27.50 **943.086**
1. Holocaust, 1933-1945 2. Germany -- History -- 1933-1945
ISBN 0-465-08571-7

"The authors posit that 'far from living in a state of constant fear and discontent, most Germans led happy and even normal lives in Nazi Germany.' They believe that the Holocaust could not have been possible without the complicity of the majority of the German population. . . . This scholarly work is a major contribution to the understanding of life in Nazi Germany and a compelling narrative that is certain to be the standard work on the subject." Booklist

Includes bibliographical references

Kershaw, Ian

Hitler, 1936-1945: nemesis. Norton 2000 832p hardcover o.p. pa $25 **943.086**
1. Dictators 2. Heads of state 3. National socialism 4. Nazi leaders 5. Germany -- Politics and government -- 1933-1945
ISBN 0-393-04994-9; 0-393-32252-1 pa

"The second volume of Kershaw's biography of Hitler covers the period from the Anschluss with Austria to 1945. . . . By 1938, Hitler's word was the equivalent of written law. After 1936, Hitler also came to believe his own propaganda. . . . Without any reasonable restraint, he led Germany inexo-

rably to destruction. . . . Kershaw's two volumes will probably be the standard source for many years." Libr J

Klemperer, Victor

★ **I** will bear witness; a diary of the Nazi years, 1933-1941. translated by Martin Chalmers. Random House 1998 556p hardcover o.p. pa $15.95 **943.086**
1. Holocaust survivors 2. Diarists 3. Germany -- History -- 1933-1945
ISBN 0-375-75378-8 pa

LC 98-15429

"Klemperer, a professor at the University of Dresden, was a Jew by birth. He managed to survive the war, living relatively unscathed with his Aryan wife in Dresden. After his death in 1960, a former student discovered his wartime diaries, and this is the first volume to be published in the U.S." Booklist

"Never has the isolation of living in a world that wishes one's people dead been rendered with greater pathos. Every act of cruelty as well as every gesture of kindness is scrupulously recorded." Nation

Nelson, Anne

Red Orchestra; the story of the Berlin underground and the circle of friends who resisted Hitler. Random House 2009 388p il $27 **943.086**
1. National socialism 2. Rote Kapelle (Resistance group) 3. World War, 1939-1945 -- Underground movements
ISBN 978-1-4000-6000-9; 1-4000-6000-1

LC 2008-23465

The author "documents the wartime journey of Greta Kuckhoff, a young German, and her valiant colleagues who formed a potent resistance to the Hitler regime in its glory days. . . . Nelson's riveting book speaks proudly of Greta . . . and all of the nearly three million Germans who resisted Hitler's iron will, and gives the reader a somber view of hell from the inside." Publ Wkly

Includes bibliographical references

Ortner, Helmut

The lone assassin; the epic true story of the man who almost killed Hitler. Helmut Ortner ; translated by Ross Benjamin. Skyhorse Pub. 2012 183 p. (hardcover : alk. paper) $24.95 **943.086**
1. World War, 1939-1945 -- Underground movements 2. Germany -- History -- 1933-1945
ISBN 1616083832; 9781616083830

LC 2011049214

"In this book . . . author [Helmut] Ortner . . . lays out the story of Georg Elser, the carpenter who attempted to assassinate [Adolf] Hitler in 1939, courtesy of a bomb in the Munich Beer Hall. . . . Ortner examines Elser's life as well as covering the conditions that led to Hitler's rise to power, including the 1923 failed coup that made the Munich Beer Hall so symbolic to the Nazi regime." (Publishers Weekly)

Parssinen, Terry M.

The **Oster** conspiracy of 1938; the unknown story of the military plot to kill Hitler and avert World

War II. {by} Terry Parssinen. HarperCollins Pubs. 2003 xxii, 232p il map $27.95; pa $13.95 **943.086**
1. Generals 2. Heads of state 3. Nazi leaders 4. Underground leaders 5. Germany -- Politics and government -- 1933-1945
ISBN 0-06-019587-8; 0-06-095525-2 pa
LC 2002-68896
"A fascinating, blow-by-blow account of a seemingly feasible but failed attempt to prevent World War II. . . . Even knowing the outcome, readers feel suspense and hope as events unfold; alternate history buffs and history students alike will gain new insight into the past and into human character from this tragic story." SLJ
Includes bibliographical references

Pool, James
Hitler and his secret partners; contributions, loot and rewards, 1933-1945. Pocket Bks. 1997 415p il hardcover o.p. pa $14   **943.086**
1. Heads of state 2. Nazi leaders 3. Germany -- Politics and government -- 1933-1945 4. World War, 1939-1945 -- Destruction and pillage
ISBN 0-671-76082-3 pa
LC 97-15506
The author examines the way German industrialists and financiers backed Hitler and how the Nazis received material support from abroad. Pool alleges that Henry Ford, Edward VIII and Joe Kennedy assisted the Nazi regime
This book "is a reminder that the worst-kept secret of WWII is that so many malefactors emerged little the worse." Publ Wkly
Includes bibliographical references

Rosenbaum, Ron
Explaining Hitler; the search for the origins of his evil. HarperPerennial 1999 444p pa $16 **943.086**
1. Heads of state 2. National socialism 3. Nazi leaders 4. Germany -- Politics and government -- 1933-1945
ISBN 0-06-095339-X; 978-0-06-095339-3
LC 99-25965
First published 1998 by Random House
This book examines interpretations of Hitler made by his contemporaries and by historians.
"In this brilliantly skeptical inventory of the world's Hitler-thinking, Rosenbaum analyzes not only the multiple Hitler theories but also the agendas and fantasies that the theorizers bring to their subject." Time
Includes bibliographical references

Shirer, William L.
The rise and fall of the Third Reich; a history of Nazi Germany. with a new afterword by the author. Simon & Schuster 1990 1249p hardcover o.p. pa $25   **943.086**
1. Heads of state 2. Nazi leaders 3. Germany -- History -- 1933-1945 4. World War, 1939-1945 -- Germany
ISBN 0-671-72868-7 pa
LC 90-221762
First published 1960
This is a comprehensive, documented history of Germany from the beginning of the Nazi party in 1918 to the World War II defeat of Germany in 1945. Here is a detailed

account of the events, and the leading figures of the Nazi era, especially Adolf Hitler
Includes bibliographical references

Speer, Albert
Inside the Third Reich; memoirs. translated from the German by Richard and Clara Winston; introduction by Eugene Davidson. Simon & Schuster 1997 596p il pa $18   **943.086**
1. Heads of state 2. Nazi leaders 3. Germany -- History -- 1933-1945 4. World War, 1939-1945 -- Germany
ISBN 0-684-82949-5; 978-0-684-82949-4
Original German edition, 1969
The author, Hitler's "architect and later his armaments minister, was in the dictator's inner circle for almost 12 years. . . . After the war Speer used the enforced leisure of his 20 prison years as a war criminal to plan and write these memoirs." Libr J
Includes bibliographical references

Tubach, Frederic C.
German voices; memories of life during Hitler's Third Reich. [by] Frederic C. Tubach with Sally Patterson Tubach. University of California Press 2011 273p il $26.95   **943.086**
1. National socialism 2. Germany -- History -- 1933-1945 3. World War, 1939-1945 -- Germany 4. Germany -- Social life and customs
ISBN 978-0-520-26964-4; 0-520-26964-0
LC 2010-51218
"Tubach approaches his mission with a nice, unobtrusive blend of sympathetic warmth and scholarly detachment. . . . The best recommendation I can make—and it is a warm one—is that readers go into German Voices prepared to treat it as one facet of a larger investigation into the phenomenon that was the Third Reich—as a uniquely accessible, honest and frequently thought-provoking window enabling some valuable ground-level insight into the much larger evil behavior that prevailed—until it imploded." PopMatters
Includes bibliographical references

Turner, Henry Ashby
Hitler's thirty days to power; January 1933. {by} Henry Ashby Turner, Jr. Addison-Wesley 1996 255p il hardcover o.p. pa $16   **943.086**
1. Heads of state 2. National socialism 3. Nazi leaders 4. Germany -- Politics and government -- 1918-1933
ISBN 0-201-32800-3 pa
LC 96-20012
The author explores "the fateful 30 days before Hitler became chancellor of Germany in January 1933. Although many of the facts are known, this study reveals that the Nazi dictator did not come to power as the result of 'impersonal forces.' The slender, analytical volume indicates that rather, at a time of mortal peril for Germany—and the world—intrigue was the order of the day in Berlin. . . . Students of German history and extremist movements should enjoy this fast-paced narrative." Publ Wkly
Includes bibliographical references

943.087 Germany--1945-1990

Bessel, Richard

Germany 1945; from war to peace. HarperCollins 2009 522p il map $28.99 **943.087**
1. Reconstruction (1939-1951) 2. World War, 1939-1945 -- Peace 3. Germany -- History -- 1945-1990 4. World War, 1939-1945 -- Germany
ISBN 978-0-06-054036-4; 0-06-054036-2

This is an account of the German home front during the last months of the war. Bessel also writes about the country's path to economic recovery in the second half of 1945.

The author "does an excellent job of evoking the blasted landscape of a conquered Germany—the homelessness and the hunger, the rubble and the mass rape." New Yorker
Includes bibliographical references

Brenner, Michael

After the Holocaust; rebuilding Jewish lives in postwar Germany. translated from the German by Barbara Harshav. Princeton Univ. Press 1997 196p il $47.50; pa $19.95 **943.087**
1. Holocaust survivors 2. Jews -- Germany 3. Germany -- History -- 1945-1990
ISBN 0-691-02665-3; 0-691-00679-2 pa
LC 97-1149
Original German edition, 1995

This introduction to German Jewry since 1945 consists of two essays by Brenner and 15 short autobiographical statements by Jewish communal, religious, and cultural leaders

"If the middle section of interviews seems redundant, it is only because Brenner has covered the material so well and so succinctly elsewhere." Publ Wkly
Includes bibliographical references

Darnton, Robert

Berlin journal, 1989-1990. Norton 1991 352p il hardcover o.p. pa $12.95 **943.087**
1. Berlin (Germany) 2. Germany (East) -- Politics and government
ISBN 0-393-31018-3 pa
LC 90-19745

"Darnton spent parts of 1989 and 1990 in Germany, witnessing the end of that country's division into East and West as the Berlin Wall fell. . . . {He} focuses more on events and aftereffects in East Germany as experienced by ordinary citizens, rather than trying to write a definitive study. Darnton talks with workers, bureaucrats, and government officials and describes what was happening and what the people understood about these momentous events." Booklist

Reeves, Richard

Daring young men; the heroism and triumph of the Berlin Airlift, June 1948-May 1949. Simon & Schuster 2010 316p il map $28 **943.087**
1. Air pilots 2. Air pilots -- Biography 3. Air pilots, Military -- History 4. Berlin (Germany) -- History -- Blockade, 1948-1949
ISBN 978-1-4165-4119-6; 1-4165-4119-5
LC 2009-15333

"'The American people will not allow the German people to starve,' Colonel Frank Howley, one of the top American commanders in Berlin, said in June, 1948, after the Soviets cut off all supply routes except an air corridor to the Western sectors of the city. But when the blockade began, as Reeves notes in his appealing account, almost no one believed that food and fuel for an urban population of more than two million could be delivered by air, and many American officials thought the question was how Berlin could be abandoned with the least embarrassment. Ten and a half months and a quarter-million American and British flights later—an unmatched act of politico-logistical bravado—the Soviets abandoned their blockade." New Yorker
Includes bibliographical references

Taylor, Frederick

Exorcising Hitler; the occupation and denazification of Germany. [by] Frederick Taylor. Bloomsbury Press 2011 xxxvii, 438p il $30 **943.087**
1. Nazi leaders 2. Denazification 3. Heads of state 4. Germany -- History -- 1945-1955 5. Germany -- History -- 1945-1990 6. Reconstruction (1939-1951) -- Germany 7. Germany -- Politics and government -- 1945-1990
ISBN 1-59691-536-6; 978-1-59691-536-7
LC 2010-46282

This is a "history of the birth of democracy in the ruins of Hitler's Germany." (Publisher's note) It "chronicles the bitter endgame of war, the murderous Nazi resistance, the vast displacement of people in Central and Eastern Europe, and the nascent cold war struggle between Soviet and Western occupiers". (New York Times Book Review)

This is a "history of the birth of democracy in the ruins of Hitler's Germany." Publisher's note
Includes bibliographical references

943.71 Czech Republic

Albright, Madeleine Korbel, 1937-

Prague winter; a personal story of remembrance and war, 1937-1948. Madeleine Albright with Bill Woodward. HarperCollins 2012 x, 467 p.p $29.99 **943.71**
1. Czechoslovakia -- History -- 1918-1968 2. World War, 1939-1945 -- Personal narratives 3. Prague (Czech Republic) -- Biography 4. Czechoslovakia -- History -- 1938-1945 5. World War, 1939-1945 -- Czechoslovakia 6. World War, 1939-1945 -- Czech Republic -- Prague 7. Prague (Czech Republic) -- History -- 20th century 8. Jewish families -- Czech Republic -- Prague -- Biography
ISBN 0062030310; 9780062030313
LC 2011049416

This book by Madeleine Albright chronicles her personal "experiences, and those of her family . . . [during] the years of 1937 to 1948. . . . The book takes readers from the Bohemian capital . . . to the bomb shelters of London, from the desolate prison ghetto of Terezin to the highest councils of European and American government. Albright reflects on her discovery of her family's Jewish heritage many decades after the war, [and] on her Czech homeland's tangled history." (Publisher's note)
Includes bibliographical references and index.

Demetz, Peter

Prague in black and gold; scenes from the life of a European city. Hill & Wang 1997 411p maps hardcover o.p. pa $15   **943.71**
    1. Prague (Czech Republic) -- History
    ISBN 0-8090-1609-5 pa

                LC 96-52216

The author presents an "account of the city's history and culture by focusing on epic events as well as heroes, villains and martyrs throughout the millennia of its existence. . . . A highly literate panorama of a focal point of European culture." Publ Wkly

Includes bibliographical references

943.8 Poland

The Chronicle of the Lodz ghetto, 1941-1944; edited by Lucjan Dobroszycki; translated by Richard Lourie {et al.} Yale Univ. Press 1984 lxviii, 551p il hardcover o.p. pa $37   **943.8**
    1. Jews -- Poland 2. Holocaust, 1933-1945 3. Lodz (Poland) -- Social conditions
    ISBN 0-300-03924-7 pa

                LC 84-3614

"This English edition comprises about one fourth of the original surviving German and Polish manuscript. Day-by-day entries of one to ten pages recorded events and living conditions from January 1941 to the ghetto's liquidation in July 1944. The chronicle was composed by a team of writers, employees of the Jewish ghetto administration." Libr J

"The record is made more profoundly melancholic by the restrained archivist style employed by the chroniclers." New Statesman (1913)

943.9 Hungary

Michener, James A.

The **bridge** at Andau. Fawcett Crest 1983 277p pa $6.99   **943.9**
    1. Hungarian refugees 2. Hungary -- History -- 1956, Revolution
    ISBN 978-0-449-21050-5; 0-449-21050-2
    First published 1957 by Random House

"The heroism, horror and tragedy of the 1956 Hungarian revolt is revealed through interviews with many refugees who crossed the bridge at Andau to freedom." Cleveland Public Libr

944 France and Monaco

Baldwin, Rosecrans

Paris, I love you but you're bringing me down; Rosecrans Baldwin. Farrar, Straus and Giroux 2012 286 p.   **944**
    1. Autobiographies 2. Americans -- France 3. Paris (France) -- Description and travel 4. Paris (France) -- Biography 5. Couples -- France -- Paris -- Biography 6. Americans -- France -- Paris -- Biography 7. Paris (France) -- Social life and customs
    ISBN 0374146683; 9780374146689

                LC 2011045886

This expatriate memoir by Rosecrans Baldwin presents an account of his time living in Paris, France. "Baldwin discovered some very French things about office life in Paris: You have to eat lunch, because the company docks a portion of your pay and returns it to you as meal coupons. . . . It's virtually impossible to get fired. . . . The author also discovered that French banks seem never to have heard of credit cards, and although he and wife qualified as legal residents for health-insurance coverage, the cards permitting them to actually use the insurance didn't arrive until a month before they left. Nonetheless, despite tight finances and loud construction work around their apartment, Baldwin fell in love just like everyone else." (Kirkus)

Buckley, Veronica

The **secret** wife of Louis XIV; Francoise d'Aubigne, Madame de Maintenon. Farrar, Straus and Giroux 2009 498p il map $35   **944**
    1. Kings 2. Royal favorites 3. France -- History -- 1589-1789, Bourbons
    ISBN 978-0-374-15830-9; 0-374-15830-4

                LC 2008-16210

This is a biography of "the Marquise de Maintenon, mistress of Louix XIV." Publisher's note

This is "a lively, sympathetic portrayal of the woman who, against all odds, succeeded in taming the royal tomcat." N Y Times Book Rev

Includes bibliographical references

Fraser, Antonia

Marie Antoinette; the journey. Talese 2001 xxii, 512p il $35; pa $16.95   **944**
    1. Queens 2. France -- History -- 1589-1789, Bourbons
    ISBN 0-385-48948-X; 0-385-48949-8 pa

                LC 2001-23493

The author portrays the Austrian-born Queen consort of Louis XVI of France as "neither heroine nor villain, but a young wife and mother who, in her journey into maturity, finds herself caught in a deadly vise." Publ Wkly

"A well-researched biography that may cause one to rethink the role in which history has cast Marie Antoinette." Libr J

Includes bibliographical references

Gordon, Mary

★ **Joan** of Arc. Viking 2000 xxv, 180p (Penguin lives series) $19.95   **944**
    1. Saints 2. Christian saints 3. France -- History -- 1328-1589, House of Valois
    ISBN 0-670-88537-1

                LC 99-55678

"This biography rehearses the well-known highlights in Joan's short life: the voices she heard who charged her with the mission to save France, her participation in the Battle of Orléans and the coronation of King Charles VII; her trial by an ecclesiastical court, where she was charged with witchcraft, heresy and idolatry. . . . The strength of this 'biographical meditation' lies in the penultimate chapter, in which Gordon investigates the numerous re-creations of Joan on stage and screen." Publ Wkly

Includes bibliographical references

Horne, Alistair

★ **La** belle France; a short history. Knopf 2005 485p il map $30 **944**

1. France -- History

ISBN 1-4000-4140-6

LC 2004-42329

First published 2004 in the United Kingdom with title: Friend or foe: an Anglo-Saxon history of France

"This compelling narrative belongs in any public library needing an excellent, current one-volume history of France." Booklist

Includes bibliographical references

Seven ages of Paris. Knopf 2002 448p $35; pa $16 **944**

1. Paris (France)

ISBN 0-679-45481-0; 1-4000-3446-9 pa

LC 2002-29653

The author traces "the history of Paris through seven periods, beginning in the 12th century and ending with the death of Charles de Gaulle in 1969. . . . Each section includes fascinating insights into the social and cultural life of the age, fashions in clothing, architectural developments, leading personalities, and lifestyles of rich and poor alike. With the verve of a master storyteller, Horne captures Parisians' 'zest for living.'" Libr J

Includes bibliographical references

Jones, Colin

Paris; biography of a city. Colin Jones. Viking 2005 xxv, 566p il map $29.95 **944**

1. Paris (France)

ISBN 0-670-03393-6

LC 2004-53608

First published 2004 in the United Kingdom

"Moving from prehistoric tribal habitation through Roman times, medieval uncertainty and splendor, early modern religious wars, Enlightenment, revolution, and two world wars, Jones examines how rulers, economy, religion and violence have shaped the city. . . . Anyone who loves Paris will find connections and revelations here, a Paris of the mind that resonates through the centuries." Publ Wkly

Includes bibliographical references

Jonnes, Jill

Eiffel's tower; and the World's Fair where Buffalo Bill beguiled Paris, the artists quarreled, and Thomas Edison became a count. Viking 2009 354p il map $27.95 **944**

1. Structural engineers 2. Eiffel Tower (Paris, France) 3. Exposition Universelle de 1889 (Paris, France)

ISBN 978-0-670-02060-7; 0-670-02060-5

LC 2008-49839

"Not long after Gustave Eiffel, an engineer and builder of railway bridges, won the contract to build a centerpiece attraction for the 1889 World's Fair, he faced a barrage of criticism of its design as well as financial, architectural, mechanical, and political obstacles to its construction. Jonnes

. . . captures the verve and personality of the Belle Epoque as Paris struggled to show the world its glory. . . . [She also] details the iconic figures who added to the allure of the fair—James McNeill Whistler, Paul Gauguin, Thomas Edison, Annie Oakley, and Buffalo Bill—and the excitement and ambitions of the era." Booklist

Includes bibliographical references

Kaplan, Alice

Dreaming in French; the Paris years of Jacqueline Bouvier Kennedy, Susan Sontag, and Angela Davis. Alice Kaplan. University of Chicago Press 2012 x, 289 p.p **944**

1. Paris (France) -- History 2. Foreign students -- France 3. Women -- United States -- Biography 4. Women -- United States -- Intellectual life 5. Students, Foreign -- France -- Paris -- Biography 6. United States -- Civilization -- French influences

ISBN 0226424383; 9780226424385

LC 2011026598

This book by Alice Kaplan offers a biographical account of the "transformative Parisian experiences of three strikingly different young women: Jacqueline Bouvier Kennedy, Susan Sontag, and Angela Davis. . . . In her comparisons of the three women's experiences, . . . she argues . . . about the impact of Paris on the rest of their lives: Bouvier's, aesthetic; Sontag's, intellectual; and Davis's, political." (Choice: Current Reviews for Academic Libraries)

Includes bibliographical references and index

Karnow, Stanley

Paris in the fifties; illustrations by Annette Karnow. Times Bks. 1997 352p il hardcover o.p. pa $14 **944**

1. French national characteristics 2. France -- Politics and government 3. Paris (France) -- Social life and customs

ISBN 0-8129-3137-8 pa

LC 97-18521

"Not content with simply ensconcing himself in the Time bureau offices, . . . Karnow created a personal life for himself and took in all that Paris and the provinces had to offer. And now he offers this succulent book, which Francophiles will devour." Booklist

Lever, Evelyne

Madame de Pompadour; translated from the French by Catherine Temerson. Farrar, Straus & Giroux 2002 310p il $26; pa $16.95 **944**

1. Royal favorites 2. France -- History -- 1589-1789, Bourbons

ISBN 0-374-11308-4; 0-312-31050-1 pa

LC 2002-22811

Original French edition, 2000

"Lever has crafted a detailed and fascinating portrait of the woman who pretty well ran France from 1745 to 1764." Publ Wkly

Includes bibliographical references

Paris was ours; thirty-two writers reflect on the City of Light. edited by Penelope Rowlands. Al-

gonquin Books of Chapel Hill 2011 279p pa
$15.95   **944**
   1. Paris (France) -- Description and travel
ISBN 978-1-56512-953-5; 1-56512-953-9

                              LC 2010-30560
In this anthology "Penelope Rowlands culled 32 essays,
stories and poems, some original, some previously published, from writers who include professors, single mothers,
gay men, a homeless woman, a wealthy Iranian and a poor
young Cuban. The collection takes some of the shine off
Paris but not the allure — not unlike the pull of a troubled
but passionate lover who could never be more than a fling.
. . . Ultimately, the writers fall in love with Paris, a city that
embraces sorrow, depression, snarkiness, human frailty and
living in the moment no matter the menial task that entails.
In dismantling the dream of Paris, they reveal an infinitely
more complex city and people." Minneapolis Star Tribune

Riding, Alan
   And the show went on; cultural life in Nazi-
occcupied Paris. Alfred A. Knopf 2010 399p il map
$28.95   **944**
   1. Popular culture -- France 2. World War, 1939-1945
-- France 3. France -- Social life and customs 4. Paris
(France) -- Intellectual life 5. France -- History -- 1940-
1945, German occupation
ISBN 978-0-307-26897-6; 0-307-26897-7

                              LC 2010-16841
"This engrossing work, rich in detail, should appeal to
French historians and serious readers interested in 20th-cen-
tury cultural history." Libr J
   Includes bibliographical references

Robb, Graham
   Parisians; an adventure history of Paris. W.W.
Norton & Co. 2010 475p il map $28.95   **944**
   1. Paris (France) -- History
ISBN 978-0-393-06724-8; 0-393-06724-6

                              LC 2009-54279
Part history, part travelog, part Ripley's Believe It or
Not!, this creative historical geography takes us on a tour
of Paris via a series of chronologically arranged vignettes
stretching from the eve of the Revolution of 1789 to the present. . . . The book records a series of moments and meetings
when characters both obscure and famous interacted with
key landmarks like the Palais Royal, Notre Dame, or Place
de la Concorde. Robb . . . recreates the drama and turmoil
of key events like the bloody horrors of the Commune, De
Gaulle's triumphant 1944 entry into Paris, or the tumultuous
student demonstrations of May 1968. Libr J
   Includes bibliographical references

Tuchman, Barbara Wertheim
   A **distant** mirror; the calamitous 14th century.
{by} Barbara W. Tuchman. Knopf 1978 xx, 677p il
maps hardcover o.p. pa $17.95   **944**
   1. Plague 2. Crusades 3. Medieval civilization 4.
Women -- Europe 5. World history -- 14th century 6.
Church history -- 600-1500, Middle Ages 7. France --
History -- 1328-1589, House of Valois 8. Great Britain

-- History -- 1154-1399, Plantagenets
ISBN 0-345-34957-1 pa

                              LC 78-5985
The author traces the history of the fourteenth century by
following the career of a "feudal lord, Enguerrand de Coucy
VII, the seigneur of some 150 towns and villages in Picardy.
He was born in 1340, and he died in captivity in 1397, hav-
ing been made a prisoner by the Turks." Time
   Includes bibliographical references

Williams, Charles
   The **last** great Frenchman; a life of General de
Gaulle. Wiley 1995 544p il $30; pa $19.95   **944**
   1. Generals 2. Statesmen 3. Presidents 4. Prime
ministers
ISBN 0-471-11711-0; 0-471-18071-8 pa

                              LC 94-42881
The author offers "appraisals of de Gaulle's career as
soldier, politician and head of state. Williams contrasts the
infuriatingly obstinate public figure with the private man,
emotional and affectionate in the bosom of his family. Especially interesting is the account of de Gaulle's tender relationship with his retarded daughter. . . . The author also
sheds light on de Gaulle's determined anti-Americanism
during his final years." Publ Wkly
   Includes bibliographical references

Yalom, Marilyn
   How the French invented love; nine hundred
years of passion and romance. HarperCollins 2012
416 p. $15.99   **944**
   1. Cultural critique 2. French literature 3. Love in
literature
ISBN 0062048317; 9780062048318
This book offers author Marilyn Yalom's literary investigation into "how the French manage their romances, marriages, affairs, and obsession with love and sex." She "argues that it's not only gender-specific traits and roles that
are socially constructed, but love, too. For example, 'Les
liaisons dangereuses' . . . is still on the list of required reading in French high schools." (Publishers Weekly)

944.04   France since 1789

Burke, Edmund
   ★ **Reflections** on the Revolution in France; edited by J.C.D. Clark. Stanford Univ. Press 2001 446p
$65; pa $29.95   **944.04**
   1. France -- History -- 1789-1799, Revolution
ISBN 0-8047-3923-4; 978-0-8047-3923-8; 0-8047-
4205-7 pa; 0-8047-4205-4 pa

                              LC 00-63732
First published 1790
   "A treatise by Edmund Burke, written in the form of a
letter to a Frenchman. It attacks the leaders and principles
of the French Revolution for their violence and excesses,
and urges reform, rather than rebellion, as a means of correcting social and political abuses." Benet's Reader's Ency.
4th edition
   Includes bibliographical references

Lefebvre, Georges
The **French** Revolution. Columbia Univ. Press 1962 2v hardcover o.p. v1 pa $32; v2 pa $32 **944.04**
1. France -- History -- 1789-1799, Revolution
ISBN 0-231-08598-2 v1 pa; 0-231-08599-0 v2 pa
Original French edition, 1930; this translation is based on 1957 reprintings
An account of the political, military, social, economic and intellectual aspects of the French Revolution.
Includes bibliographical references

944.04092   France since 1789--Biography

McPhee, Peter
Robespierre; a revolutionary life. Peter McPhee. Yale University Press 2012 299 p. (cloth : alk. paper) $40 **944.04092**
1. Statesmen -- France -- Biography 2. Revolutionaries -- France -- Biography 3. France -- History -- Revolution, 1789-1799 4. France -- Politics and government -- 1789-1799 5. France -- History -- Reign of Terror, 1793-1794
ISBN 0300118112; 9780300118117
LC 2011027640
This book provides a "treatise on the life of one of France's most notorious revolutionaries. Maximilien Robespierre (1758-1794) . . . [became] a leader of the leftist Jacobins in the revolutionary National Convention. . . . Robespierre began his career as an opponent of capital punishment but ended it obsessed with omnipresent treasonous conspiracies and meting out death without trial to perceived enemies of the state . . . . [Author Peter] McPhee . . . strives to rehabilitate Robespierre somewhat, arguing that the sanguinary excesses of the period were necessary to sustain the revolution against attacks from without and within, and that Robespierre's role in them was later exaggerated by other deputies seeking to minimize their own culpability." (Kirkus)
Includes bibliographical references

Reiss, Tom
★ The **Black** Count; glory, revolution, betrayal, and the real Count of Monte Cristo. Tom Reiss ; [maps by David Lindroth Inc.] Crown Trade 2012 ix, 414 p.p maps (hardcover) $27 **944.04092**
1. Generals -- France -- Biography 2. France. Armée -- Biography 3. France -- History, Military -- 1789-1815
ISBN 030738246X; 9780307382467; 9780307952950
LC 2012017633
Pulitzer Prize: Biography (2013)
This book by Tom Reiss, which won the Pulitzer Prize for biography presents the story of "General Alex Dumas, . . . the son of a black slave--who rose higher in the white world than any man of his race. . . . Born in Saint-Domingue (now Haiti), Alex Dumas was briefly sold into bondage but made his way to Paris where he was schooled as a sword-fighting member of the French aristocracy. Enlisting as a private, he rose to command armies at the height of the Revolution." (Publisher's note)
Includes bibliographical references (p. [341]-403) and index

944.05   Period of First Empire, 1804-1815

Johnson, Paul
★ **Napoleon**. Viking 2002 190p (Penguin lives series) hardcover o.p. pa $13 **944.05**
1. Emperors 2. France -- Kings and rulers
ISBN 0-670-03078-3; 0-14-303745-5 pa
LC 2001-45605
Johnson "presents a concise appraisal of Napoleon's career and a precise understanding of his enigmatic character. The author views Napoleon, not as an 'idea man' whose ideology was the ladder by which he propelled himself to heights of power, but as an opportunist who took advantage of a series of events and situations he could manipulate into achieving supreme control." Booklist
Includes bibliographical references

Schom, Alan
One hundred days; Napoleon's road to Waterloo. Oxford University Press 1993 398p pa $45 **944.05**
1. Emperors 2. Waterloo, Battle of, 1815
ISBN 978-0-19-508177-0; 0-19-508177-3
LC 93-11787
First published 1992 by Atheneum
This is an account of "Napoleon's escape from Elba in February 1815 and his return . . . to France. Rallying the nation behind him, he mustered his army and marched off to meet Wellington at Waterloo. . . . This is a first-class reconstruction of Napoleon's final campaign." Publ Wkly
Includes bibliographical references

944.081   Period of Third Republic, 1870-1945

Bredin, Jean-Denis
The **affair**; the case of Alfred Dreyfus. translated from the French by Jeffrey Mehlman. Braziller 1986 628p il hardcover o.p. pa $19.95 **944.081**
1. Antisemitism 2. Army officers 3. France -- Politics and government -- 1815-1914
ISBN 0-8076-1175-1 pa
LC 85-22374
Original French edition, 1983
"That Bredin manages to be both passionate and exact is his first outstanding virtue. He is admirably free of the baroque conspiracy theories that sprout so luxuriantly on both sides of this case." N Y Rev Books
Includes bibliographical references

Brown, Frederick
For the soul of France; culture wars in the age of Dreyfus. Alfred A. Knopf 2010 304p il $28.95 **944.081**
1. French national characteristics 2. Nationalism -- France 3. France -- History -- 1815-1914
ISBN 978-0-307-26631-6; 0-307-26631-1
LC 2009-30912
"Brown recounts the history of France, following its 1789 revolution, as an ongoing contest between the champions and foes of the Enlightenment. . . . The humiliating defeat of the Franco-Prussian War of 1870-71 was followed by the economic crash of 1882 and the Panama Company brib-

ery scandal of 1893, both of which were reputedly executed by Jewish masters. . . . In 1894, an opportunity for revenge presented itself in the person of Alfred Dreyfus, a 34-year-old Jewish army officer. Accused of espionage on the flimsiest of evidence—fabrications, and forgeries—Dreyfus was twice tried and convicted. Dreyfus was eventually freed in 1906, one year after a law requiring the separation of church and state had passed. Secularism seemed to hold sway. But, as Brown demonstrates in his brilliant study, religious fervor and bellicose patriotism combined in World War I to shift the balance yet again." Boston Globe

Includes bibliographical references

Derfler, Leslie

★ The **Dreyfus** affair. Greenwood Press 2002 xxii, 167p il (Greenwood guides to historic events, 1500-1900) $44.95   **944.081**
1. Antisemitism 2. Army officers 3. France -- Politics and government -- 1815-1914
ISBN 0-313-31791-7

LC 2001-38365

"Following a chronology is a 'Historical Overview' containing several chapters of background and analysis. These chapters provide context for what is commonly known as the Dreyfus affair, discuss how anti-Semitism and socialism played into and were affected by the affair, and summarize how the affair has been viewed through history. The next section is an A-Z collection of biographies of almost 20 key individuals. . . . Primary documents comprise the next chapter and most documents are accompanied by short explanations. . . . This guide is useful for researchers who need more information than they can find in an encyclopedia." Booklist

Includes bibliographical references

Glass, Charles

Americans in Paris; life and death under Nazi occupation. Penguin Press 2010 524p il map **944.081**
1. Americans -- France 2. World War, 1939-1945 -- France 3. Paris (France) -- Intellectual life 4. France -- History -- 1940-1945, German occupation
ISBN 1594202427; 9781594202421

LC 2009-39650

First published 2009 in the United Kingdom

"Despite occasional excesses of detail, Americans in Paris is a much richer book than its title suggests, and for anyone interested in France during this period it is a fascinating treat." Telegraph (London)

Includes bibliographical references

Read, Piers Paul, 1941-

The **Dreyfus** affair; the scandal that tore France in two. Piers Paul Read. Bloomsbury Press 2012 408 p.   **944.081**
1. Treason 2. Scandals 3. Antisemitism 4. France -- History -- 1815-1914 5. France -- Intellectual life -- 19th century 6. Scandals -- France -- History -- 19th century 7. France -- History -- Third Republic, 1870-1940 8. France -- Politics and government -- 1870-1940 9. Trials (Treason) -- Political aspects -- France 10. Antisemitism -- France -- History -- 19th century 11.

Religion and politics -- France -- History -- 19th century
ISBN 1608194329; 9781608194322

LC 2011034456

This historical work by Piers Paul Read reviews the Dreyfus Affair. "Captain Alfred Dreyfus was a rising star in the French artillery command. . . . However, Dreyfus had enemies as a result of his ambition. . . . On the basis of flimsy evidence, Dreyfus was placed under arrest for the crime of high treason. Not long afterward, he was sentenced to spend the rest of his life on the legendary, lethal Devil's Island. The saga of Dreyfus's many trials . . . the fight to free him, and the intrigues on both sides, is a . . . story rife with heroes and villains. . . . The anti-Semitism and deceit on display in the Dreyfus case was an ominous prelude to the Holocaust and the long, bloody twentieth century to come." (Publisher's note)

Includes bibliographical references and index.

944.083   Period of Fifth Republic, 1958-

Mayle, Peter

Encore Provence; new adventures in the south of France. Knopf 1999 226p   **944.083**
1. Authors 2. Humorists 3. Provence (France) 4. Children's authors 5. Nonfiction writers 6. Provence (France) -- Social life and customs
ISBN 0679441247; 0679762698

LC 99-62335

Mayle, the author of A Year in Provence (1990) and Toujours Provence (1991), discusses his experiences after "he and his wife returned to Provence after an absence of four years." (Booklist)

Mayle's "book is all about the renewal of his acquaintance with the land he so loves. Essays range widely over Provençal life. . . . His observations and commentaries are laced with humor but encompass true respect and admiration for his adopted homeland." Booklist

White, Edmund

The **flaneur**; a stroll through the paradoxes of Paris. Bloomsbury Pub. 2001 211p maps $16.95   **944.083**
1. Paris (France) -- Description and travel
ISBN 1-58234-135-4

LC 00-46812

"White defines the flâneur of his title as an 'aimless stroller who loses himself in the crowd, who has no destination and goes wherever caprice or curiosity direct his or her step.' White assumes the role of flâneur to perambulate the narrow streets and grand boulevards of Paris, to gather impressions of people and places." Booklist

"White is richly informed, and his evocative writing should appeal to both armchair travelers and visitors to Paris." Libr J

944.084   France, 2000-

Chirac, Jacques, 1932-
My life in politics; Jacques Chirac ; edited by Catherine Spencer. Palgrave Macmillan 2012 352 p.   **944.084**
1. France -- Politics and government 2. Presidents -- France -- Biography 3. France -- Politics and government -- 1958-
ISBN 0230340881; 9780230340886
LC 2012018097
This book by "[t]wo-time president of France, mayor of Paris, and international politician" Jacques Chirac "covers the full scope of Chirac's political career of more than 50 years. . . . As mayor of Paris, Chirac was famed for his success in beautifying the City of Lights and keeping it whole during the heady days of the 1968 riots. As president in the 1990s and early 2000s, Chirac took controversial steps to privatize the economy and plan the European Union." (Publisher's note)

945   Italy, San Marino, Vatican City, Malta

Berendt, John
The **city** of falling angels; a Venice story. Penguin Press 2005 414p $25.95; pa $15   **945**
1. Venice (Italy) -- Social life and customs
ISBN 1-59420-058-0; 1-59420-061-0 pa
LC 2005-47661
The author describes some of his encounters with contemporary Venetians. The starting point for his travels was the investigation of the fire which destroyed La Fenice opera house in 1996.
Berendt "delivers an urbane, beautifully fashioned book with much exotic charm. . . . [The author] makes erudite, inquisitive, nicely skeptical company as he leads the reader through the shadows of what was heretofore better known as a tourist attraction." N Y Times (Late N Y Ed)

Bosworth, R. J. B.
Mussolini's Italy; life under the dictatorship, 1915-1945. Penguin 2006 xxvi, 692p il map $35   **945**
1. Heads of state 2. Fascism -- Italy 3. Italy -- History -- 1914-1945
ISBN 1-59420-078-5
LC 2005-52127
First published 2005 in the United Kingdom
Bosworth "combines prodigious research with a clear writing style that will appeal to all readers interested in the Italy of Il Duce." Libr J
Includes bibliographical references

Clark, Robert
Dark water; flood and redemption in the city of masterpieces. Doubleday 2008 354p il $26   **945**
1. Floods 2. Florence (Italy)
ISBN 978-0-7679-2648-5; 0-7679-2648-X
LC 2008-1695
This is an account of the Florence flood of 1966.

The author "tells an enthralling true story in a way that makes it read like a novel." Economist
Includes bibliographical references

Crowley, Roger
★ **City** of fortune; how Venice ruled the seas. Roger Crowley. Random House 2011 xxix, 432 p.p (alk. paper) $32.00   **945**
1. Venice (Italy) 2. Italy -- History 3. Medieval civilization 4. Venice (Italy) -- Commerce -- History 5. Venice (Italy) -- History -- 697-1508 6. Merchants -- Italy -- Venice -- History 7. Mediterranean Region -- Commerce -- History 8. Venice (Italy) -- Economic conditions -- To 1797
ISBN 1400068207; 9780679644262; 9781400068203
LC 2011005529
Author Roger Crowley "narrate[s] the rise and apogee of the empire acquired by Venice [Italy] between 1000 and 1500 . . . [It discusses] . . . the collective nature of the medieval Venetian state, its organisation and its awe-inspiring effectiveness [and] . . . draws the substantive difference between Venice and Genoa in their centuries-long struggle for commercial and economic dominance." (History Today)
Includes bibliographical references (p. [407]-415) and index

Frieda, Leonie
The **Deadly** Sisterhood; A Story of Women, Power, and Intrigue in the Italian Renaissance, 1427-1527. Leonie Frieda. HarperCollins 2013 xi, 403 p.p (hardcover) $32.50   **945**
1. Renaissance 2. Women -- Biography 3. Italy -- History -- 0-1559
ISBN 0061563080; 9780061563089
This book, by Leonie Frieda, provides a biography of "eight women whose lives . . . encompass the spectacle, opportunity, and depravity of Italy's Renaissance. Lucrezia Turnabuoni, Clarice Orsini, Beatrice d'Este, Isabella d'Este, Caterina Sforza, Giulia Farnese, Isabella d'Aragona, and Lucrezia Borgia shared the riches of their birthright: wealth, political influence, and friendship, but none were not exempt from personal tragedies, exile, and poverty." (Publisher's note)

Hazzard, Shirley
The **ancient** shore; dispatches from Naples. [by] Shirley Hazzard and Francis Steegmuller. University of Chicago Press 2008 129p il $18; pa $13   **945**
1. Italy -- Description and travel
ISBN 978-0-2263-2201-8; 0-2263-2201-7; 978-0-226-32202-5 pa; 0-226-32202-5 pa
LC 2008-15420
"Born in Australia, Shirley Hazzard first moved to Naples as a young woman in the 1950s to take up a job with the United Nations. It was the beginning of a long love affair with the city. . . . [This volume collects some of] Hazzard's writings on Naples, along with a . . . New Yorker essay by her late husband, Francis Steegmuller." Publisher's note
"Much larger than all its parts, this book does full justice to a place, and a time, where 'nothing was pristine, except the light.'" Bookforum

Hibbert, Christopher

The **Borgias** and their enemies; 1431-1519. Harcourt, Inc. 2008 328p $26 **945**

1. Kings 2. Italy -- History

ISBN 978-0-15-101033-2; 0-15-101033-1

LC 2008-03076

"Lucrezia Borgia, on hearing that her father, Pope Alexander VI, was choosing her third husband, noted that her first two had been 'very unlucky.' Luck had little to do with it, as Hibbert shows in this vivid chronicle of the notoriously corrupt Renaissance family. One husband was killed on the orders of her brother Cesare, whose ruthlessness made him the model for Machiavelli's 'The Prince'; the other was discarded after ceasing to be politically useful to the Pope. Hibbert ably traces the web of alliances through which the Spanish-born Alexander hoped to secure his hold on Italy and his family's place in power." New Yorker

Includes bibliographical references

Hughes, Robert

Rome; a cultural, visual, and personal history. Alfred A. Knopf 2011 498p il $35 **945**

1. Rome -- History

ISBN 978-0-307-26844-0; 0-307-26844-6

LC 2011-14600

The author "gives us a guided tour through the city in its many incarnations, excavating the geologic layers of its cultural past and creating an indelible portrait of a city in love with spectacle and power . . . The reader need not agree with Mr. Hughes's acerbic assessments or even be interested in Rome as a destination on the map to relish this volume, so captivating is his narrative. Although his book is a biography of Rome, it is also an acutely written historical essay informed by his wide-ranging knowledge of art, architecture and classical literature, and a thought-provoking meditation on how gifted artists (like Bernini and Michelangelo) and powerful politicians and church leaders (like Augustus, Mussolini and Pope Sixtus V) can reshape the map and mood of a city." n Y times Book Rev

Includes bibliographical references

Keahey, John

Seeking Sicily; a cultural journey through myth and reality in the heart of the Mediterranean. Thomas Dunne Books/St. Martin's Press 2011 312p il $27.99; ebook $14.99 **945**

1. Sicily (Italy) -- Description and travel 2. Sicily (Italy) -- Social life and customs

ISBN 978-0-312-59705-4; 978-1-4299-9067-7 ebook

LC 2011026786

The author "takes a meandering and inspiring tour through the history, culture, and landscape of Sicily, an island that has been a crossroads for the various peoples of the Mediterranean for millennia. . . . Keahey's thoroughly researched book will inspire any traveler to look past the Sicily of the traditional tourist's guide and appreciate its diverse, layered, and sometimes dark history." Libr J

Includes bibliographical references

Leon, Donna

My Venice and Other Essays; by Donna Leon. Pgw 2013 240 p. $26 **945**

1. Venice (Italy)

ISBN 0802120369; 9780802120366

This book, by Donna Leon, presents "over fifty . . . essays that range from battles over garbage in the canals to the troubles with rehabbing Venetian real estate. She shares episodes from her life in Venice, explores her love of opera, and recounts tales from in and around her country house in the mountains. With pointed observations and humor, she also explores her family history and former life in New Jersey, and the idea of the Italian man." (Publisher's note)

Levey, Michael

Florence; a portrait. Harvard Univ. Press 1996 xxix, 498p il hardcover o.p. pa $22.95 **945**

1. Florence (Italy) -- History

ISBN 0-674-30658-9 pa

LC 95-31215

"If at times the detail overwhelms the big picture, the 150 illustrations (50 in color) and Levey's excellent artistic counsel make this a worthy guide for anyone seriously seeking Florence." Publ Wkly

Includes bibliographical references

Madden, Thomas F.

Venice; a new history. Thomas F. Madden. Viking 2012 xi, 446 p.p (hbk. : alk. paper) $35 **945**

1. Venice (Italy) -- History

ISBN 0670025429; 9780670025428

LC 2012005304

This book on the history of Venice by Thomas Madden "trac[es] an arc from the city's humble origins as a lagoon refuge to its apex as a vast maritime empire and Renaissance epicenter to its rebirth as a modern tourist hub. Madden explores all aspects of Venice's . . . achievements . . . its role as an economic powerhouse and birthplace of capitalism, its popularization of opera, the stunning architecture of its watery environs, and more." (Publisher's note)

Includes bibliographical references and index.

Mayes, Frances

Under the Tuscan sun; at home in Italy. Chronicle Bks. 1996 280p $22.95 **945**

1. Italian cooking 2. Tuscany (Italy) -- Social life and customs

ISBN 0-8118-0842-4

LC 96-15137

"Casual and conversational, {Ms. Mayes's} chapters are filled with craftsmen and cooks, with exploratory jaunts into the countryside—but what they all boil down to is an intense celebration of what she calls 'the voluptuousness of Italian life.' Occasionally, this leads to the sort of gushy observations you might expect from a besotted lover. But more often it produces an appealing and very vivid snapshot imagery." N Y Times Book Rev

Taylor, Benjamin

Naples declared; a walk around the bay. Benjamin Taylor. G.P. Putnam's Sons 2012 240 p. **945**

1. Local history 2. Naples (Italy) 3. City and town life

4. Naples (Italy) -- History 5. Naples, Bay of (Italy) -- History 6. City and town life -- Italy -- Naples 7. Naples (Italy) -- Description and travel 8. Naples (Italy) -- Social life and customs 9. Naples, Bay of (Italy) -- Description and travel

ISBN 0399159177; 9780399159176

LC 2011049450

This book by Benjamin Taylor provides a description of Naples, Italy with "discussions of history, philosophy, religion, art, culture, literature, [and] customs. The book meanders between past and present, wanders in stream-of-thought fashion through the Naples streets, delves . . . into the city's stories, lives, and lore, and drops in for conversations with locals . . ." (Library Journal) "[including] present-day encounters with a fervently communist doctor, with a chain-smoking student of Faulkner, and with novelist Shirley Hazzard." (Kirkus)

Includes bibliographical references and index

945.091 Reign of Victor Emmanuel III, 1900-1946

Bosworth, R. J. B.

Mussolini. Oxford Univ. Press 2002 584p il hardcover o.p. pa $14.95   **945.091**
1. Heads of state 2. Fascism -- Italy 3. Italy -- Politics and government

ISBN 0-340-73144-3; 0-340-80988-4 pa

LC 2002-283267

This is "the definitive study of the Italian dictator and belongs in every public and academic library with a strong European history collection." Libr J

Includes bibliographical references

Corner, Paul

The **Fascist** Party and popular opinion in Mussolini's Italy; by Paul Corner. Oxford University Press 2012 302 p. (hbk.) $125   **945.091**
1. Public opinion 2. Fascism -- Italy 3. Fascism -- Italy -- History 4. Fascism -- Italy -- Public opinion 5. Partito nazionale fascista (Italy) 6. Public opinion -- Italy -- History -- 20th century

ISBN 0198730691; 9780198730699

LC 2012462711

Focusing on fascism in Italy, author Paul Corner "argues that 'real existing Fascism', as lived by a large part of the population, was in fact an increasingly negative experience and reflected few of those colourful and attractive features of fascist propaganda which have induced more favourable interpretations of the regime. Distinguishing clearly between the fascist project and its realisation, Corner examines the ways in which the fascist party asserted itself at the local level." (Publisher's note)

946 Spain, Andorra, Gibraltar, Portugal

Kamen, Henry

Philip of Spain. Yale Univ. Press 1997 384p il maps hardcover o.p. pa $18.95   **946**
1. Kings 2. Spain -- History

ISBN 0-300-07081-0; 0-300-07800-5 pa

LC 96-52421

"Kamen's prose is lucid, succinct, and thorough. . . . In humanizing a man too often viewed as a cardboard tyrant, Kamen has made a valuable contribution to European historiography." Booklist

Includes bibliographical references

Kurlansky, Mark

The **Basque** history of the world. Penguin 2001 387p il map pa $15   **946**
1. Basque Provinces (France and Spain)

ISBN 978-0-14-029851-2; 0-14-029851-7

First published 1999 by Walker & Co.

"This book traces the history of the Basques from their mysterious origins to their politically fraught existence in this century. . . . Kurlansky shows how Basques, famed for their geographic and linguistic isolation, have played significant roles in world history-as mercenaries in ancient Greece, whalers in the Middle Ages, explorers in the Americas, and even cautious supporters of modern European integration." New Yorker

Lowney, Chris

A **vanished** world; medieval Spain's golden age of enlightenment. Free Press 2005 320p il map $26   **946**
1. Spain -- Civilization

ISBN 0-7432-4359-5

LC 2004-56362

This is a history of Spain between the Muslim conquest in 711 and the driving of Muslims from Iberia in 1492, during which the author argues there was a tentative peace between Christians, Muslims, and Jews.

The author "successfully brings the story of medieval Spain to a wider audience and draws out of this rich history important lessons for the post-9/11 world." Christ Sci Monit

Includes bibliographical references

Spain: a history; edited by Raymond Carr. Oxford Univ. Press 2000 318p il hardcover o.p. pa $19.95   **946**
1. Spain -- History

ISBN 0-19-820619-4; 978-0-19-280236-1 pa; 0-19-280236-4 pa

LC 99-42639

The essays in this volume present a journey through Spain's "entire history: from its prehistoric settlement through Roman, Visigothic, and Islamic rule, and from its golden age of exploration to the Spanish Civil War in the 1930s, Franco's resulting rule, the monarchy's reestablishment, Basque separatists, and modern Spain's political unrest." Booklist

Includes bibliographical references

Tremlett, Giles

Ghosts of Spain; travels through Spain and its secret past. Walker 2007 386p $26.95 **946**

1. Spain -- Description and travel 2. Spain -- Social life and customs
ISBN 0-8027-1574-5; 978-0-8027-1574-6

First published 2006 in the United Kingdom

An "examination of the Franco years and their legacy make a somber backdrop for an otherwise cheery tale. Having summoned the ghosts, [the author] moves along to offer a guided tour of modern Spain, making stops at the usual journalistic destinations. The educational system, politics, health care, child rearing and the national character are dealt with in well-organized chapters that move the reader briskly along. . . . A highly informative, well-written introduction to post-Franco Spain." N Y Times (Late N Y Ed)

946.081 Period of Second Republic, 1931-1939

Lewis, Norman

The **tomb** in Seville; crossing Spain on the brink of civil war. introduction by Julian Evans. Carroll & Graf 2005 150p $20; pa $14.95 **946.081**

1. Spain -- Description and travel
ISBN 0-7867-1439-5; 0-7867-1687-8 pa

First published 2003 in the United Kingdom

"Reading the author's account of his travels in a country on the brink of war is almost as satisfying as being there." Booklist

946.083 Reign of Juan Carlos I, 1975-

Stewart, Chris

Driving over lemons; an optimist in Andalucia. Pantheon Bks. 2000 248p il maps hardcover o.p. pa $13,95 **946.083**

1. Spain -- Description
ISBN 978-0-375-41028-4; 978-0-375-70915-9 pa; 0-375-70915-0 pa

LC 99-56675

"The ability to write hilarious travelogues featuring excruciating scenes of discomfort may well be a {British} national characteristic. It's certainly possessed by Chris Stewart." N Y Times Book Rev

947 Russia and neighboring east European countries

Borrero, Mauricio

★ **Russia** : a reference guide from the Renaissance to the present. Facts on File 2004 497p il map (European nations series) $85 **947**

1. Reference books 2. Russia -- History -- Dictionaries
ISBN 0-8160-4454-6

LC 2003-60547

Alphabetically arranged entries cover "influential individuals, significant places, important policies . . . {and} var-

ious moments that have profoundly impacted the historical development of the country and its people." Publisher's note

Includes bibliographical references

Drakulic, Slavenka

Cafe Europa; life after communism. Penguin Books 1999 213p pa $14 **947**

1. Eastern Europe -- Social conditions 2. Eastern Europe -- Politics and government
ISBN 978-0-14-027772-2; 0-14-027772-2

First published 1996 in the United Kingdom; first United States edition published 1997 by Norton

The author of these pieces is "at once critical of a culture that remains bleakly conformist in the aftermath of Communist rule and empathetic for its having known nothing else. With consistent equanimity, she examines the frustrating plight of the novice Balkan democracies. On a more quotidian level, too, she finds that much is wanting, measured against Western standards of richesse, congeniality, and even taxi service. Owing largely to Drakulic's knack for drawing humor from an abundance of anecdotes—whether about a toothpaste monopoly or the bureaucratic cartwheels required to purchase a vacuum cleaner—these essays read like stories." New Yorker

Erickson, Carolly

Great Catherine. St. Martin's Griffin 1995 392p pa $18.95 **947**

1. Empresses 2. Russia -- History 3. Russia -- Kings and rulers
ISBN 0-312-13503-3

LC 95-22619

First published 1994 by Crown

"Erickson's fluid, captivating portrait of Catherine the Great reads like a first-rate historical novel." Booklist

Figes, Orlando, 1959-

The **Crimean** War; a history. Metropolitan Books 2010 576p il map $35; e-book $16.99 **947**

1. Crimean War, 1853-1856
ISBN 978-0-8050-7460-4; 0-8050-7460-0; 978-1-4299-9724-9 e-book; 1-4299-9724-9 e-book

LC 2010-23152

Published in the United Kingdom with title: Crimea

This "is a complex tale, told vividly by Mr Figes. Perhaps it should serve as a healthy cold shower for any modern civilisational warrior who sets out to present the course of history as a simple tug-of-war between Christianity and Islam." Economist

Includes bibliographical references

Hosking, Geoffrey A.

★ **Russia** and the Russians; a history. {by} Geoffrey Hosking. Belknap Press 2001 718p il map $35; pa $18.95 **947**

1. Russia -- History 2. Soviet Union -- History
ISBN 0-674-00473-6; 0-674-01114-7 pa

LC 00-65085

"This is a high-quality overview, suitable for all libraries." Booklist

Russia : people and empire, 1552-1917; {by} Geoffrey Hosking. Harvard Univ. Press 1997 548p maps $33; pa $15.16   **947**
1. Russian national characteristics 2. Russia -- History
ISBN 0-674-78118-X; 0-674-78119-8 pa
        LC 97-5069
The author explores the question "of how and why the Russians never developed a sense of nation. He argues that the Russian monarchy and aristocracy were always more interested in building an expansive empire than in promoting the belief in nationhood, something understood by the powerless peasantry. The expensive and inefficient bureaucracy that emerged over the centuries weighed against any possibility of community, and in the end this tottering edifice was unable to withstand the cataclysm of World War I. Hosking has brought a powerful intellect and great erudition to this work." Libr J
Includes bibliographical references

King, David

Red star over Russia; a visual history of the Soviet Union from the revolution to the death of Stalin: posters, photographs and graphics from the David King collection. Abrams 2009 345p il $50   **947**
1. Russian art 2. Soviet Union -- History -- Pictorial works
ISBN 978-0-8109-8279-6; 0-8109-8279-X
In this survey "the graphics used to promote the workers' paradise deserve admiration. But the rest of this extraordinarily illustrated book provides witness to the corrosive effects of ham-handed propaganda, and to the role of state-sanctioned imagery in demeaning and subjugating the arts. Red Star Over Russia is a mammoth collection of rare Soviet applied art and photographs . . . organized not into individual chapters, but into pages and spreads devoted to a range of themes addressed in graphic and photographic materials, including 'Political Abstraction,' 'Urban Proletariat' and 'Workers of the World, Unite.' Prominent artists like El Lissitzky and Gustav Klutsis are featured." N Y Times Book Rev

Kotkin, Stephen

Uncivil society; 1989 and the implosion of the communist establishment. with a contribution by Jan T. Gross. Modern Library 2009 197p il map (Modern Library chronicles) $24   **947**
1. Soviet Union -- Social conditions 2. Eastern Europe -- Social conditions 3. Soviet Union -- Politics and government 4. Eastern Europe -- Politics and government
ISBN 978-0-679-64276-3; 0-679-64276-5
      LC 2009-12903
"Combining scholarship with sparkling prose, the authors recount a thoroughly satisfying historical struggle in which the good guys won." Publ Wkly
Includes bibliographical references

Massie, Robert K., 1929-

Catherine the Great; portrait of a woman. Robert K. Massie. Random House 2011 xiii, 625p ill. (some col.), maps   **947**
1. Biography 2. Empresses 3. Russia -- Kings and rulers
ISBN 9780679456728; 9781588360441
      LC 2011015279
Presents a reconstruction of the eighteenth-century empress's life that covers her efforts to engage Russia in the cultural life of Europe, her creation of the Hermitage, and her numerous scandal-free romantic affairs.
"Massie delivers a fascinating account of dog-eat-dog politics in 18th-century Europe and the larger-than-life Russian empress who gave as good as she got." Kirkus
Includes bibliographical references

Massie, Suzanne

Land of the firebird; the beauty of old Russia. Hearttree 1980 493p il pa $32   **947**
1. Russian art 2. Russia -- Civilization
ISBN 978-0-9644184-1-7; 0-9644184-1-X
First published 1980 by Simon & Schuster
The author's intent "is to give 'a sense of the whole, now-vanished culture of old Russia . . . to describe that beauty which the Russians once knew how to create, what they loved, and admired and how they once lived and rejoiced.'" N Y Times Book Rev
Includes bibliographical references

Pleshakov, Konstantin

There is no freedom without bread! 1989 and the civil war that brought down communism. [by] Constantine Pleshakov. Farrar, Straus, and Giroux 2009 289p $26   **947**
1. Communism 2. Berlin Wall (1961-1989) 3. Poland -- Politics and government 4. Soviet Union -- Politics and government 5. Eastern Europe -- Politics and government
ISBN 978-0-374-28902-7; 0-374-28902-6
      LC 2009-10185
The author's "explanation of the 1989 collapse respects the complexity of Eastern Europe, yet his account is both clear and beautifully lyrical. His greatest strength lies in not being burdened by doctrine; he finds worth in communists and in Reagan. . . . Pleshakov writes history with a human face." Washington Post Book World
Includes bibliographical references

Polonsky, Rachel

Molotov's magic lantern; travels in Russian history. Farrar, Straus and Giroux 2011 390p map $27; ebook $14.99   **947**
1. Diplomats 2. Authors, Russian 3. Communism and literature 4. Cabinet members 5. Communist leaders 6. Soviet Union -- Intellectual life 7. Moscow (Russia) -- Description and travel 8. Russia (Federation) -- Description and travel
ISBN 978-0-374-21197-4; 978-1-4299-7490-5 ebook
      LC 2010-23037
Polonsky "has produced a spectacular and enjoyable display of intellectual fireworks for the general reader. . . . Her

finely drawn literary travelogues on Taganrog, Murmansk, Vologda, Irkutsk and other places depict squalor, pomp, misery, exhilaration, heroism and brutishness, each cameo framed in its historical, cultural and physical context. . . . She has a knack for putting herself into other people's shoes with empathy and skill. . . . The author has grit, charm and style—and a gift for traveller's tales." Economist

Riasanovsky, Nicholas V.
A **history** of Russia; 8th ed; Oxford University Press 2011 various paging il map pa $64.95   **947**
1. Russia -- History 2. Soviet Union -- History
ISBN 978-0-19-534197-3
LC 2010-23174
First published 1963
This narrative history includes discussions of economics, social organization, religion, and culture.
Includes bibliographical references

Sebestyen, Victor
Revolution 1989; the fall of the Soviet empire. Pantheon Books 2009 xxi, 451p il $30   **947**
1. Soviet Union -- Politics and government 2. Eastern Europe -- Politics and government
ISBN 978-0-375-42532-5; 0-375-42532-2
LC 2009-23045
"Numerous books have come out that attempt to synthesize the compelling story of the fall of communism, but Revolution 1989 comes closest to being the essential volume. Sebestyen's elegant narrative lays out in crisp episodes what was happening in Russia, Bulgaria, East Germany, Hungary, Czechoslovakia, and Afghanistan throughout the tumultuous 1980s. His portrait of Gorbachev is particularly sharp—and asks us to reconsider the Soviet leader's surprising role 20 years ago. As a refugee from Hungary in 1956, Sebestyen brings a personal touch to these historic moments." Daily Beast
Includes bibliographical references

Volkov, Solomon
St. Petersburg; a cultural history. translated by Antonina W. Bouis. Free Press 1995 598p il hardcover o.p. pa $26.50   **947**
1. Poets 2. Authors 3. Dancers 4. Composers 5. Dramatists 6. Choreographers 7. Essayists 8. Nobel laureates for literature 9. Saint Petersburg (Russia) -- History
ISBN 0-684-83296-8 pa
LC 95-24116
Four of Volkov's "six very long chapters revolve around figures representative of certain periods or trends in the evolution of the St. Petersburg myth: Akhmatova, Balanchine, Shostakovich and Brodsky. Aspects of these central biographical and cultural portraits lead him . . . into countless mini-biographies of related figures." N Y Times Book Rev

Warnes, David
Chronicle of the Russian tsars; the reign-by-reign record of the rulers of imperial Russia. Thames & Hudson 1999 224p il $34.95   **947**
1. Russia -- History 2. Russia -- Kings and rulers
ISBN 0-500-05093-7
LC 98-61289
The introduction provides a "historical overview of how Tsarism came into being. The succeeding chapters are divided by major political events and social upheaval. . . . The reign of each tsar is analyzed within this framework, highlighting major events, but also giving abundant personal details such as marriages, children, etc." SLJ
Includes bibliographical references (p. 218-219) and index

947.0009 Eastern Europe--Historical periods

Applebaum, Anne
★ **Iron** curtain; the crushing of Eastern Europe, 1945-1956. Anne Applebaum. Doubleday 2012 xxxvi, 566 p.p (hardcover) $35.00   **947.0009**
1. Communism -- Russia 2. Soviet Union -- Social conditions 3. Communist countries -- Social conditions 4. Europe, Eastern -- Relations -- Soviet Union 5. Soviet Union -- Relations -- Europe, Eastern 6. Communist countries -- Politics and government 7. Europe, Eastern -- Social conditions -- 20th century 8. Communism -- Europe, Eastern -- History -- 20th century 9. Europe, Eastern -- Politics and government -- 1945-1989 10. Political culture -- Europe, Eastern -- History -- 20th century 11. Political persecution -- Europe, Eastern -- History -- 20th century 12. Communism -- Social aspects -- Europe, Eastern -- History -- 20th century
ISBN 9780385515696; 0385515693
LC 2012022086
In this book, "journalist Anne Applebaum delivers a . . . history of how Communism took over Eastern Europe after World War II." She "describes how the Communist regimes of Eastern Europe were created and what daily life was like once they were complete. She draws on newly opened East European archives, interviews, and personal accounts translated for the first time to portray . . . the dilemmas faced by millions of individuals." (Publisher's note)
Includes bibliographical references and index.

947.08   Russia since 1855

Kurth, Peter
Tsar : the lost world of Nicholas and Alexandra; photographs by Peter Christopher. Little, Brown 1995 229p il hardcover o.p. pa $29.95   **947.08**
1. Emperors 2. Empresses 3. Russia -- History
ISBN 0-316-50787-3; 0-316-55788-9 pa
LC 95-12820
In text and photographs, this volume examines the lives of Tsar Nicholas II, the Empress Alexandra, and the Russian Imperial family.
"A large format and a profusion of illustrations ostensibly mark it a picture book; instead it is a remarkably com-

prehensive overview of the reign of the last czar and his consort. . . . Kurth sensitively documents the imperial family's suffering as prisoners of the Bolsheviks and their eventual execution." Booklist

Includes bibliographical references

Massie, Robert K., 1929-

The **Romanovs**; the final chapter. Random House 1995 308p il hardcover o.p. pa $14.95   **947.08**
1. Emperors 2. Empresses 3. Forensic anthropology 4. Impostors 5. Royal pretenders 6. Russia -- Kings and rulers
ISBN 0-394-58048-6; 0-345-40640-0 pa

LC 95-4718

This book "is divided into three major parts. The first segment—by far the most fascinating and original—focuses on the complex scientific process used in identifying the Romanovs' remains. . . . The second part concerns the various impostors who have claimed to be members of the Russian imperial family. . . . [The] third segment [is] a report on those Romanov émigrés—close relatives of the Czar's—who survived the Bolsheviks' persecution." N Y Times Book Rev

Includes bibliographical references

Pipes, Richard

The **Russian** Revolution. Knopf 1990 xxiv, 944p il maps hardcover o.p. pa $25   **947.08**
1. Russia -- History
ISBN 0-679-73660-3 pa

LC 89-35129

This is a "massive, wonderfully vivid, gripping chronicle. . . . No other book so brilliantly clarifies the inner dynamics of the Russian Revolution." Publ Wkly

Includes bibliographical references

947.084   Russia (Soviet Union)--1917-1991

Amis, Martin

Koba the dread; laughter and the twenty million. Hyperion 2002 306p il $24.95   **947.084**
1. Heads of state 2. Communist leaders 3. Political leaders 4. Soviet Union -- Politics and government
ISBN 0-7868-6876-7

"Amis create{s} a compelling narrative, summarizing vast amounts of information and presenting it in a lucid, accessible form." New York Times

Brent, Jonathan

Stalin's last crime; the plot against the Jewish doctors, 1948-1953. {by} Jonathan Brent and Vladimir P. Naumov. HarperCollins 2003 399p $26.95; pa $14.95   **947.084**
1. Heads of state 2. Communist leaders 3. Political leaders 4. Jews -- Persecutions
ISBN 0-06-019524-X; 0-06-093310-0 pa

LC 2002-191930

"This book points out suspicious inconsistencies in official accounts of Stalin's death and fingers chief of secret police Beria as a likely assassin. . . . Brent and Naumov link Stalin's famously anti-Semitic 'Doctors' Plot,' in which Jewish doctors were unjustly accused of conspiring to murder

important politicians, to the ridiculous 'plan of the internal blow,' another alleged conspiracy of officials supposedly aiding an American plan to nuke the Kremlin itself. The authors argue that these Stalin-engineered plots were to be used by the paranoid dictator as justification for nuclear war. Tales of Stalin's paranoia are nothing new, but rarely are his subtle, yet relentless, machinations laid out in such intricate detail." Booklist

Includes bibliographical references

Competing voices from the Russian Revolution; edited by Michael C. Hickey. Greenwood 2011 xiii, 599p ill. (alk. paper) $65.00   **947.084**
1. History -- Sources 2. World War, 1914-1918 3. Russia -- History -- 1917-1921, Revolution 4. Social conflict -- Soviet Union -- History -- Sources 5. Soviet Union -- History -- Revolution, 1917-1921 -- Sources 6. Soviet Union -- Politics and government -- 1917-1936 -- Sources 7. Soviet Union -- History -- Revolution, 1917-1921 -- Personal narratives 8. Soviet Union -- History -- Revolution, 1917-1921 -- Social aspects -- Sources
ISBN 9780313385230; 0313385238; 9780313385247; 0313385246

LC 2010039676

This book "presents documents that underscore the . . . public discussion about key events and issues during the 1917 Russian Revolution, one of the pivotal events in modern history. . . . [T]he documents . . . clarify the issues while revealing the broad range of ways in which Russians understood the events unfolding around them. Focusing on public rhetoric and debate in Russia from the outbreak of World War I in 1914 through the dissolution of the Constituent Assembly in January 1918, the documents present the views not only of key political figures, but also of ordinary men and women—mothers, soldiers, factory workers, peasants, students, businesspeople, and educated professionals." (Publisher's note)

Includes bibliographical references (p. 583-588) and index.

Figes, Orlando

A **people's** tragedy; the Russian Revolution, 1891-1924. Viking 1997 xx, 923p hardcover o.p. pa $25   **947.084**
1. Soviet Union -- History -- 1917-1921, Revolution
ISBN 0-14-024364-X pa

LC 96-36761

First published 1996 in the United Kingdom

The author has "produced an engagingly written and well-researched book that will leave few readers with any doubts that the Bolsheviks, and especially their leader, Lenin, were ruthless killers, willing to sacrifice millions of lives for the sake of power and their own personal ambitions." N Y Times Book Rev

Includes bibliographical references

★ The **whisperers**; private life in Stalin's Russia. Metropolitan Books 2007 xxxviii, 739p il map $35   **947.084**
1. Communism -- Soviet Union 2. Soviet Union --

Social conditions
ISBN 978-0-8050-7461-1; 0-8050-7461-9
LC 2007-24223
"This is a humbling monument to the evil and endurance of Russia's Soviet past and, implicitly, a guide to its present." Economist
Includes bibliographical references

Gellately, Robert
Stalin's curse; battling for communism in war and Cold War. by Robert Gellately. Knopf 2013 496 p. $32.50   **947.084**
1. Communism -- Russia 2. Communism -- Europe -- History -- 20th century 3. Soviet Union -- Politics and government -- 1936-1953
ISBN 0307269159; 9780307269157
LC 2012028768
Author Robert Gellately presents an "account based on newly released Russian documentation that reveals Joseph Stalin's true motives--and the extent of his enduring commitment to expanding the Soviet empire--during the years in which he seemingly collaborated with Franklin D. Roosevelt, Winston Churchill, and the capitalist West." (Publisher's note)
Includes bibliographical references and index

Hochschild, Adam
The **unquiet** ghost; Russians remember Stalin. Houghton Mifflin 2003 304p il map pa $14.95   **947.084**
1. Heads of state 2. Communist leaders 3. Political leaders 4. Soviet Union -- History
ISBN 978-0-618-25747-8; 0-618-25747-0
First published 1994 by Viking
In this look at Stalin's legacy the author "visits the ruins of the old prison camps of Kazakhstan and Kolyma, digs through the K.G.B. archives and spends a night at Stalin's seaside retreat. Most important, he interviews camp survivors, camp guards and the children of both. The questions he asks are of universal significance. . . . By asking these questions while traveling through today's Russia, Mr. Hochschild effectively places Stalinism in a modern context." N Y Times Book Rev
Includes bibliographical references

McMeekin, Sean
History's greatest heist; the looting of Russia by the Bolsheviks. Yale University Press 2009 302p il $38   **947.084**
1. Public finance 2. Soviet Union -- Politics and government
ISBN 9780300135589
LC 2008-22100
"After the October Revolution, the Bolsheviks were enmeshed in a civil war and desperate for funds for everything from guns and boots for soldiers to a luxury car for Lenin. In theory, they had at their disposal the riches of the deposed Tsar, including one of the world's great reserves of gold. But the gold was the security for Russia's national debt, and most of Europe didn't recognize the new regime or its right to the treasury anyway. . . . What followed, McMeekin writes, was a 'gold-laundering boom,' involving art-thieving

commissars, double-dealing smugglers, and a surprisingly nefarious cast of Swedes." New Yorker
Includes bibliographical references

Medvedev, Roy Aleksandrovich
★ **Let** history judge; the origins and consequences of Stalinism. {by} Roy Medvedev. rev and expanded ed; Columbia Univ. Press 1989 xxi, 903p $104; pa $35   **947.084**
1. Heads of state 2. Communist leaders 3. Political leaders 4. Soviet Union -- Politics and government
ISBN 0-231-06350-4; 0-231-06351-2 pa
LC 89-758
Original Russian edition copyrighted 1967; first United States edition published 1972 by Knopf
"Never have Stalin's crimes against humanity been more forcefully or more thoroughly documented than in . . . {this book, which} distills firsthand testimonies of the mass arrests, torture, imprisonment and executions that befell millions of innocent Soviet citizens." Publ Wkly
Includes bibliographical references

Pipes, Richard
A **concise** history of the Russian Revolution. Knopf 1995 431p il maps hardcover o.p. pa $16   **947.084**
1. Russia -- History
ISBN 0-679-74544-0 pa
LC 95-3127
A one volume condensation of the author's The Russian Revolution and Russia under the Bolshevik regime
"Forcefully showing why the 70-year-old Communist experiment failed {Pipes} provides the nonacademic reader with accurate historical events in a highly readable format." Libr J
Includes bibliographical references

Russia under the Bolshevik regime. Vintage Books 1995 587p il map pa $21   **947.084**
1. Heads of state 2. Revolutionaries 3. Communist leaders 4. Political leaders 5. Soviet Union -- History
ISBN 978-0-679-76184-6; 0-679-76184-5
First published 1994 by Knopf
"In this sequel to The Russian Revolution Pipes persuasively argues that Lenin's one-party dictatorship, through its terrorizing, suppression of the press, censorship and monopolistic control of cultural organizations, set the stage for Stalin's genocidal totalitarianism. . . . Pipes shows how both Hitler and Mussolini drew on Lenin's tyrannical methods, and he perceptively analyzes the mindset of Western fellow-travelers who wove fantasies of the U.S.S.R. as an egalitarian Eden while rationalizing its evils." Publ Wkly
Includes bibliographical references

Reed, John
Ten days that shook the world. Penguin Books 2007 368p (Penguin classics) pa $12   **947.084**
1. Soviet Union -- History -- 1917-1921, Revolution
ISBN 978-0-14-144212-9; 0-14-144212-3
First published 1919 by International Pubs.
"A reportorial, firsthand, and sympathetic account of the November Revolution in Russia (1917). . . . After prefa-

tory explanation of political groups and other organizations, and of the background of the uprising, the work tells with graphic detail of the fall of the provisional government, the revolution and counterrevolution, the solidifying of power, and the resultant congress." Oxford Companion to Am Lit. 5th edition

Service, Robert

A **history** of twentieth-century Russia. Harvard Univ. Press 1998 xxxiii, 653p il maps $32.50; pa $20.95   **947.084**

1. Soviet Union -- History 2. Russia (Federation) -- History

ISBN 0-674-40347-9; 0-674-40348-7 pa

LC 97-37440

First published 1997 in the United Kingdom

"A perceptive, judicious appraisal." Booklist

Includes bibliographical references

Lenin --a biography. Harvard Univ. Press 2000 xxv, 561p il maps $38.95; pa $19.95   **947.084**

1. Heads of state 2. Revolutionaries 3. Communist leaders 4. Political leaders

ISBN 0-674-00330-6; 0-674-00828-6 pa

LC 00-21394

This biography focuses "on Lenin the man. It draws on a wealth of new material to provide a subtle and complex portrait. . . . In particular, Service's account adds much to our knowledge of Lenin's early years and his final years as a man cut down by a series of strokes. . . . It is lucidly written, sharply observed, full of good sense, packed with vivid anecdote and, above all, succeeds—where so many have failed—in creating a Lenin who is believably human." Hist Today

Includes bibliographical references

Volkogonov, Dmitrii Antonovich

Lenin; a new biography. {by} Dmitri Volkogonov; translated and edited by Harold Shukman. Free Press 1994 xxxix, 529p il $30   **947.084**

1. Heads of state 2. Revolutionaries 3. Communist leaders 4. Political leaders

ISBN 0-02-933435-7

LC 94-31752

A condensed English version of the two-volume Russian edition published in 1994

"The author draws heavily on newly declassified KGB archives that he oversees as special assistant to President Boris Yeltsin. . . . Volkogonov's narrative is indispensable for understanding the Bolshevik coup, their crushing of the democratic opposition and the tragic aftermath." Publ Wkly

Includes bibliographical references

947.085   Russia (Soviet Union)--1953-1991

Carlson, Peter

K blows top; a Cold War comic interlude starring Nikita Khrushchev, America's most unlikely tourist. PublicAffairs 2009 327p il $26.95   **947.085**

1. Cold war 2. Heads of state 3. Communist leaders 4. Political leaders 5. Soviet Union -- Foreign relations

-- United States 6. United States -- Foreign relations -- Soviet Union

ISBN 9781586484972; 1-58648-497-4

LC 2008-39090

Recounts Khrushchev's 1959 trip across America against the backdrop of the Cold War and a capitalist America living under the shadow of the hydrogen bomb.

"Drawing on contemporary news reports, modern interviews, and memoirs written by some of the participants, [this is] . . . a story about a poorly educated but extraordinarily powerful man who became, for a brief time, a pop-culture icon. . . . A fine example of popular history at its most engaging—anecdotal but informative and written with great feeling for the comedic side of current events." Booklist

Includes bibliographical references

Gorbachev, Mikhail

On my country and the world; {by} Gorbachev. Columbia Univ. Press 1999 300p $50; pa $17.95   **947.085**

1. World politics -- 1965- 2. Soviet Union -- Politics and government 3. Russia (Federation) -- Politics and government

ISBN 0-231-11514-8; 0-231-11515-6 pa

LC 99-31273

The former Soviet leader presents an analysis of his country's Communist past and an account of his role in government in the 1980s. Gorbachev also includes ideas for political change

Gorbachev is "fresh and candid in its initial section on the pluses and minuses of the Revolution of 1917." Nation

Remnick, David

★ **Lenin's** tomb; Russia and the fall of Communism. Random House 1993 576p hardcover o.p. pa $15.95   **947.085**

1. Soviet Union -- Politics and government

ISBN 0-679-75125-4 pa

LC 92-56841

"This book is a record of almost four years beginning in 1988 when David Remnick, a Washington Post reporter, was assigned to Moscow. . . . He argues convincingly that what did in the old Soviet leadership, right down through Mikhail Gorbachev, was its unending assault not only on people but on memory. By making a secret of history, it made its people increasingly distracted, and desperate, until they overthrew it." N Y Times Book Rev

Satter, David

Age of delirium; the decline and fall of the Soviet Union. Yale University Press 2001 424p pa $30   **947.085**

1. Soviet Union -- History

ISBN 0-300-08705-5; 978-0-300-08705-5

First published 1996 by Knopf

The author "appraises the Russians by writing about the travails of average people in the last decade of Soviet rule. Objects of the Communist ideology's enforced unanimity, his subjects include dissidents sent to psychiatric wards, persecuted religious people, a TASS journalist learning how to write the party line, and miners exploited by the workers' state. . . . An insightful from-the-ground-up view of typical Russians whom the top-down politicians are now courting." Booklist

Stokes, Gale

The **walls** came tumbling down; the collapse of communism in Eastern Europe. Oxford Univ. Press 1993 319p hardcover o.p. pa $31.95   **947.085**
1. Communism 2. Eastern Europe -- Politics and government
ISBN 0-19-506644-8; 0-19-506645-6 pa
LC 92-44862

This book "can be recommended as a coherent, well-written history that defines its time frame well, provides sound coverage, makes prudent judgments, and wears its analysis lightly. . . . Stokes's overview traces the ebb and flow of personalities and events in a manner that is both accessible to lay readers and informative to scholars." Libr J

947.086   -1991

Baker, Peter

Kremlin rising; Vladimir Putin's Russia and the end of revolution. [by] Peter Baker and Susan Glasser. Scribner 2005 453p il $27.50   **947.086**
1. Russia (Federation) -- Politics and government
ISBN 0-743-26431-2
LC 2005-44157

The authors chronicle the transformation of contemporary Russia under President Vladimir Putin.

"Well written, well reported and well organized, the book consists of freestanding chapters that touch on the most important events and trends in contemporary Russia, from the war in Chechnya to the spread of AIDS and the dire state of the Russian judicial system." N Y Times (Late N Y Ed)

Includes bibliographical references

Brent, Jonathan

Inside the Stalin archives; discovering the new Russia. Atlas & Company 2008 335p il $26 **947.086**
1. Heads of state 2. Communist leaders 3. Political leaders 4. Russia (Federation) 5. Archives -- Soviet Union
ISBN 978-0-9777-4333-9; 0-9777-4333-0

This work, which draws upon the author's fifteen years of unprecedented access to high-level Soviet Archives, "reveals as much about the grim realities of post-Soviet life and bureaucracy as it does about the archives themselves. Equipped with little Russian and few contacts, but with an almost palpable sense of decency and honest intentions that illuminate his book, Brent explains for the general reader as well as for specialists how he went about his work in the new Russia." N Y Times Book Rev

Lieven, Anatol

Chechnya; tombstone of Russian power. with photographs by Heidi Bradner. Yale Univ. Press 1998 436p il $55; pa $28   **947.086**
1. Chechnya (Russia)
ISBN 0-300-07398-4; 0-300-07881-1 pa
LC 98-84479

"The book is a great, ostentatiously erudite festival of ideas, sometimes brilliant, sometimes dubious, but never less than interesting." N Y Times Book Rev

Meier, Andrew

Black earth; a journey through Russia after the fall. Norton 2003 511p il map $28.95; pa $15.95   **947.086**
1. Russia (Federation)
ISBN 0-393-05178-1; 0-393-32641-1 pa
LC 2003-6562

"After talking to scores of people—from survivors of the Aldy massacre to a harrowed Russian lieutenant colonel who runs the body-collection point closest to the Chechen battleground—Meier paints in this heartbreaking book a devastating picture of contemporary life in a country where, as one man put it, people have 'lived like the lowest dogs for more than eighty years.'" Publ Wkly

Includes bibliographical references

Politkovskaya, Anna

A **Russian** diary; a journalist's final account of life, corruption, and death in Putin's Russia. translated by Arch Tait; foreword by Scott Simon. Random House 2007 369p map $25.95   **947.086**
1. Presidents 2. Prime ministers 3. Russia (Federation) -- Politics and government
ISBN 1-4000-6682-4; 978-1-4000-6682-7
LC 2007-296943

These are the journals kept by the Russian journalist who was killed in Moscow in 2006.

This is a "brilliant . . . portrayal of Russian life during the middle years of Putin's rule." New York Rev Books

Remnick, David

Resurrection; the struggle for a new Russia. Random House 1997 398p hardcover o.p. pa $15   **947.086**
1. Russia (Federation) -- Politics and government
ISBN 0-375-75023-1 pa
LC 96-47360

In this companion volume to Lenin's tomb, "Remnick concentrates on the post-Soviet scene and its prospects. . . . Chaotic uncertainty, massive corruption, and crime are notoriously present, yet the possibility of a different, better life also beckons. . . . This is an interesting, highly informative portrait of a country struggling toward a fateful future." Libr J

Includes bibliographical references

Richards, Susan

Lost and found in Russia; lives in a post-Soviet landscape. Other Press 2010 544p pa $15.95; ebook $15.95   **947.086**
1. Russia (Federation) -- Description and travel 2. Russia (Federation) -- Social life and customs
ISBN 978-1-59051-348-4 pa; 978-1-59051-369-9 ebook
First published 2010 in the United Kingdom

"During many trips from 1992 to 1998, Richards . . . traveled to visit friends in Russia, particularly in the southwestern towns of Saratov and Marx. . . . She fashions the narrative around the friends she met and lived with closely. Vera, follower of the Vissarion cult, was an inhabitant of Saratov, once called the Athens of the Volga, now a forsaken place closed to foreigners because of its military industry (presently defunct). In Marx, once the nexus of the Russian Germans, Richards stayed with Anna, a tensely coiled journalist—a pravednik, or 'truth bearer'—who had been punished for her honest writing; the volatile couple Natasha and Igor, lured to the dead-end town by Gorbachev's promise of a German homeland, now mostly unemployed and alcoholic; and the couple Misha and Tatiana, marooned in Marx after their engineering training, who became thriving entrepreneurs and part of the rising Russian middle class. . . . Other trips took her through Siberia and the Crimea to view the residues of Russian Orthodoxy, the Old Believers and folksy spiritualism. A patiently crafted glimpse 'through a crack in the wardrobe' of the devastation wrought on Russian society during the turbulent post-Communist '90s." Kirkus

Treisman, Daniel

The **return**; Russia's journey from Gorbachev to Medvedev. Free Press 2011 523p il $30; ebook $14.99 **947.086**

1. Russia (Federation) -- Politics and government
ISBN 978-1-4165-6071-5; 1-4165-6071-8; 978-1-4516-0574-7 ebook; 1-4516-0574-9 ebook; 1416560718; 1451605749 ebook; 978141656071-5; 9781451605747 ebook

LC 2010011520

"The politics and economics of post-Communist Russia occupy this survey of the past two decades. Treisman . . . works commentary about Russia's successive leaders—Gorbachev, Yeltsin, Putin, and Medvedev—into the problems they confronted. . . . Encompassing foreign policy and Russian public opinion, Treisman's knowledgeable presentation is a reliable current-affairs source for Russia's economic revival and reassertion in international affairs." Booklist

947.5 Caucasus

Baiev, Khassan

The **Oath**; a surgeon under fire. [by] Khassan Baiev; with Ruth and Nicholas Daniloff. Walker & Co. 2003 376p il $26 **947.5**

1. Chechnya (Russia)
ISBN 0-8027-1404-8

LC 2003-52502

The author "is modest, which only adds to his heroism. But more than that, he has humanized the Chechens, whom others have portrayed as terrorists. Russian president Vladimir Putin has tried to equate Russia's fight against the Chechens with the U.S. battle against al-Qaida. Those who read this stirring memoir will be hard-pressed to see the situation so simply." Publ Wkly

Seierstad, Asne

The **angel** of Grozny; orphans of a forgotten war. translated by Nadia Christensen. Basic Books 2008 340p $25.95 **947.5**

1. Chechnya (Russia) -- History -- 1994- (Civil War)
ISBN 978-0-465-01122-3; 0-465-01122-5

LC 2008-925222

In the early hours of New Year's 1994, Russian troops invaded the Republic of Chechnya, plunging the country into a prolonged and bloody conflict that continues to this day. A foreign correspondent in Moscow at the time, Asne Seierstad traveled regularly to Chechnya to report on the war, describing its affects on those trying to live their daily lives amidst violence.

"Seierstad's searing, evocative recounting brings Chechnya to life, especially the unimaginable suffering and strength of the Chechen people. Powerful, painful, and raw, . . . [this] is essential reading." Booklist

947.7 Ukraine

King, Charles

Odessa; genius and death in a city of dreams. W.W. Norton & Co. 2011 336p il map $27.95 **947.7**

1. Jews -- Ukraine 2. Odessa (Ukraine) 3. Odessa (Ukraine) -- History 4. Jews -- Ukraine -- Odessa -- History 5. Odessa (Ukraine) -- Politics and government
ISBN 9780393070842; 0-393-07084-0

LC 2010-38000

This is a "finely written and evocative portrait of the city. . . . [Its] detail, coupled with a fine feel for the sweep of history . . . makes this book a worthy tribute to one of Europe's greatest and least-known cities." Economist

Includes bibliographical references

947.98 Estonia

Theroux, Alexander

Estonia : a ramble through the periphery. Fantagraphics Books 2011 351p il $29.99 **947.98**

1. Estonia -- Description and travel
ISBN 978-1-60699-465-8; 1-60699-465-4

Theroux "follows his wife, Sarah, to [Estonia] in 2008, where she paints on her Fulbright grant scenes of its stolid towns. Brother of the equally waspish travel writer Paul, Alexander Theroux, meanwhile, skulks, fulminates, studies, and walks wherever he can, soaking up the frigid atmosphere of its people. . . . He deploys bombast, overkill, and ridicule to pepper his perennial pop-up targets of greed, lassitude, and stupidity. He includes here his caustic if characteristic habit of lists, ruminations, and rants. For all his predilection for careful observation of how people look, sound, and move, he inflates, if maybe in sly self-deprecation, the impact others have on him—rather than vice versa. . . . Full of endnotes, translating many phrases he quotes in their original languages, and graced by a few of the couple's photos and Sarahs plein air oil paintings, this provides a suitably quirky introduction to Theroux as an essayist and critic." PopMatters

948   Scandinavia

Ferguson, Robert

The **Vikings**; a history. Viking 2009 450p il
map   **948**
1. Vikings 2. Europe -- History -- 476-1492
ISBN 978-0-670-02079-9

LC 2009-26818

"Ferguson's scholarly study requires close attention, but
the intellectual rewards are plentiful. Provides a significant
deepening of our knowledge of the Vikings." Kirkus
Includes bibliographical references

The Oxford illustrated history of the Vikings; edited
by Peter Sawyer. Oxford Univ. Press 1997 298p
il maps hardcover o.p. pa $27.50   **948**
1. Vikings
ISBN 0-19-820526-0; 0-19-285434-8 pa

LC 97-16649

This illustrated collection of articles includes discussion of the Vikings' impact on England, Iceland, Greenland,
Russia, and the Frankish and Danish Empires; Viking ships
and ship-building; Viking religion; and the ways in which
Vikings have been portrayed throughout history. Significant
archaeological finds are featured.
Includes bibliographical references

Roesdahl, Else

The **Vikings**; translated by Susan M. Margeson
and Kirsten Williams. 2nd ed; Penguin Books 1998
324p il map pa $17   **948**
1. Vikings
ISBN 0-14-025282-7; 978-0-14-025282-8
Original Danish edition, 1987
A survey of Viking civilization from c.750-c.1050.
"About one-third of the book deals with Viking expansion into Russia, Normandy, the British Isles, Iceland,
Greenland, etc. . . . Most of the book surveys the geography,
people, society, religion, art, etc., of the Vikings' Scandinavian homelands." Libr J
Includes bibliographical references

948.97   Finland

Beach, Hugh

A **year** in Lapland; guest of the reindeer herders.
with a new afterword by the author. University of
Washington Press 2001 242p il map pa $25 **948.97**
1. Sami (European people) 2. Lapland
ISBN 0-295-98037-0; 978-0-295-98037-9

LC 00-47936

First published 1993 by Smithsonian Institution Press
The author "tells of his first year among the Saami reindeer herders of Swedish Lapland. His narrative interweaves
adventure, descriptions of the harsh beauty of the landscape,
supernatural tales and ancient myths. Beach also explores
topics of change in the lives of the herders brought on by
laws requiring village groups to move and by adaptations to
new items such as rubber boots, seaplanes, and appliances."
Libr J

Edwards, Robert

The **Winter** War; Russia's invasion of Finland,
1939-1940. Pegasus Books 2008 319p il map
$27.95   **948.97**
1. Russo-Finnish War, 1939-1940 2. World War, 1939-
1945 -- Finland
ISBN 978-1-933648-50-7
First published 2006 in the United Kingdom
"A brisk, efficient account of one of the most overlooked episodes of World War II. . . . Highly readable and
informative." Kirkus
Includes bibliographical references

949.12   Iceland

Johanneson, Gudni Thorlacius

The **history** of Iceland; Guðni Thorlacius Jóhan-
nesson. Greenwood 2013 xv, 172 p.p (The Greenwood Histories of the Modern Nations) (hardcopy :
acid-free paper) $58   **949.12**
1. Iceland -- History
ISBN 0313376204; 9780313376207

LC 2012031759

This book divides the "history of Iceland into seven sections chronicling events and conditions in the country from
874 through mid-2012. . . . The author enlivens his coverage with . . . stories, such as one of an early chronicler who
marveled that the midnight sun was so bright that lice could
easily be picked out of clothing." (Booklist)
Includes bibliographical references (pages 157-160)
and index

949.2   Netherlands

Schama, Simon

The **embarrassment** of riches; an interpretation
of Dutch culture in the Golden Age. Knopf 1987
698p il maps hardcover o.p. pa $23   **949.2**
1. Netherlands -- Civilization
ISBN 0-679-78124-2 pa

LC 86-45418

"Delving into customs, beliefs, popular art and quirks
of behavior, Schama has fashioned a tour de force, a profound, unconventional and rewarding portrait of a people."
Publ Wkly
Includes bibliographical references

Shorto, Russell

Amsterdam; a history of the world's most lib-
eral city. Russell Shorto. Doubleday 2013 368 p.
$28.95   **949.2**
1. Liberalism 2. Netherlands -- History 3. Amsterdam
(Netherlands) -- History 4. Liberalism -- Netherlands
-- Amsterdam -- History
ISBN 0385534574; 9780385534574

LC 2013003544

Author Russell Shorto's book presents a history of the
city of Amsterdam. "Weaving in his own experiences of
his adopted home, Shorto provides" a "story of Amsterdam

from the building of its first canals in the 1300s, through its brutal struggle for independence, its golden age as a vast empire, to its complex present in which its cherished ideals of liberalism are under siege." (Publisher's note)

Includes bibliographical references

949.5 Greece

Brownworth, Lars

Lost to the West; the forgotten Byzantine Empire that rescued Western civilization. Crown Publishers 2009 329p map $26; pa $15   **949.5**

1. Byzantine Empire

ISBN 978-0-307-40795-5; 978-0-307-40796-2 pa

"Brownworth delivers just enough of the big picture for interested readers to pursue specific events in greater detail. An energetic look at a still-misunderstood period in late antiquity." Kirkus

Includes bibliographical references

Clogg, Richard

A **concise** history of Greece; 2nd ed; Cambridge Univ. Press 2002 291p il maps (Cambridge concise histories) $53; pa $19   **949.5**

1. Greece -- History

ISBN 0-521-80872-3; 0-521-00479-9 pa

LC 2002-725551

First published 1992

This is an illustrated introduction to the history of modern Greece from the late eighteenth century to the present

Includes bibliographical references

Mazower, Mark

Salonica, city of ghosts; Christians, Muslims, and Jews, 1430-1950. Knopf 2005 490p il maps $35   **949.5**

1. Thessalonike (Greece)

ISBN 0-375-41298-0

LC 2004-57690

First published 2004 in the United Kingdom

This is a history of the Greek city.

The author's "graceful, evocative prose, his deft attention to details and his empathetic presentation of all sides of the story add up to a magnificent tale of this unique city." Publ Wkly

Includes bibliographical references

Norwich, John Julius

Byzantium : the apogee. Knopf 1991 xxiv, 389p il map $49.95   **949.5**

1. Byzantine Empire

ISBN 0-394-53779-3

LC 91-53119

This is the second volume of a three-volume narrative history of the Byzantine Empire. "Beginning with Charlemagne's coronation in 800 A.D. and the resulting split in the Christian world, Norwich traces the return of iconoclasm, political intrigues, military campaigns, atrocities, and alliances, ending with the fateful battle at Nanzikert from

which the Empire never recovered. . . . [The author] deftly brings to life the frozen icons of the history books." Libr J

Includes bibliographical references

Byzantium : the decline and fall. Knopf 1995 xxxvii, 488p il maps $49.95   **949.5**

1. Byzantine Empire

ISBN 0-679-41650-1

This final volume of the author's three volume narrative history chronicles the last four centuries of the Byzantine Empire.

Includes bibliographical references

Byzantium : the early centuries. Knopf 1989 407p il $49.95   **949.5**

1. Byzantine Empire

ISBN 0-394-53778-5

LC 88-45508

First published 1988 in the United Kingdom

This is the first of a three-volume narrative history of the Byzantine Empire. It traces Byzantium's history "from the birth of Constantine c.274 to the coronation of Charlemagne on Christmas Day 800." Libr J

Includes bibliographical references

949.6 Balkan Peninsula

Pamuk, Orhan

Istanbul; memories and the city. translated from the Turkish by Maureen Freely. Knopf 2005 384p il $26.95   **949.6**

1. Istanbul (Turkey)

ISBN 1-400-04095-7

LC 2004-61537

Original Turkish edition, 2003

The novelist writes about his life as a resident of Istanbul.

"The author mingles 'personal memoir with cultural history', and a fascinating read it is too for anyone who has even the slightest acquaintance with this fabled bridge between east and west." Economist

949.7 Serbia, Croatia, Slovenia, Bosnia and Hercegovina, Montenegro, Macedonia

Di Giovanni, Janine

Madness visible; a memoir of war. Knopf 2003 285p map hardcover o.p. pa $14   **949.7**

1. Kosovo (Serbia)

ISBN 0-375-41073-2; 978-0-375-72455-8 pa; 0-375-72455-9 pa

LC 2002-44820

This "narrative of the 1999 war in Kosovo, NATO's campaign against Serbia, and the ouster of Milosevic offers an unbiased view of the enormous suffering of Yugoslav Albanians and Serbs following the genocidal rage of the Belgrade regime against the Kosovo Liberation Army's (KLA) drive for an independent Kosovo. . . . This exciting work is highly recommended for all libraries." Libr J

Includes bibliographical references

Rieff, David

Slaughterhouse; Bosnia and the failure of the West. Simon & Schuster 1995 240p hardcover o.p. pa $18.95   **949.7**

1. Yugoslav War, 1991-1995 2. Bosnia and Hercegovina
ISBN 0-684-81903-1 pa

LC 94-40148

This account of the war in the former Yugoslavia grew out of Rieff's travels in the region from 1992 through 1994

"Slaughterhouse is perhaps the most powerful, passionate, and penetrating dissection of a Westerner of the ongoing Bosnian tragedy." Booklist

Rohde, David

Endgame; the betrayal and fall of Srebrenica, Europe's worst massacre since World War II. Westview Press 1998 450p il pa $20   **949.7**

1. Yugoslav War, 1991-1995 2. Srebrenica (Bosnia and Hercegovina)
ISBN 0-8133-3533-7; 978-0-8133-3533-9

LC 98-26127

First published 1997 by Farrar, Straus & Giroux

"Rohde argues that the fall of Srebrenica could have been prevented, but he is ultimately unable to explain the 'collective failure' of the United States, the United Nations, and NATO in stopping the massacre. His investigation is carefully documented by over 300 footnotes. This is an important and revealing book." Libr J

Includes bibliographical references

West, Richard

Tito; and the rise and fall of Yugoslavia. Carroll & Graf Pubs. 1995 436p il hardcover o.p. pa $15.95   **949.7**

1. Heads of state 2. Communist leaders 3. Political leaders 4. Yugoslavia -- Politics and government
ISBN 0-7867-0332-6 pa

LC 95-10404

First published 1994 in the United Kingdom

This biography "describes Tito's rise to power, his creation of the Partisan Army during the Axis occupation, his consolidation of southern Slavs after the war and establishment of a Communist Yugoslavia, the break with Stalin in 1948, Tito's subsequent rivalry with the Soviet bloc and his leadership of nonaligned states. . . . The book also clarifies the present three-way conflict among Serbs, Croats and Muslims." Publ Wkly

Includes bibliographical references

949.702 Yugoslavia, 1918-1991

Maass, Peter

Love thy neighbor; a story of war. Knopf 1996 305p hardcover o.p. pa $14   **949.702**

1. Yugoslav War, 1991-1995 2. Bosnia and Hercegovina
ISBN 0-679-76389-9 pa

LC 95-39250

This book on the Yugoslav conflict is based on Maass's experiences as the Washington Post's reporter in Bosnia

"Maass was only in Bosnia for about a year, from 1992 to 1993, but he saw a great deal. And he displays extraordinary sensitivity to the ambiguities of his position." Nation

Includes bibliographical references

949.703 Period as sovereign nations, 1991-

Clark, Wesley K.

★ **Waging** modern war; Bosnia, Kosovo, and the future of combat. PublicAffairs 2001 xxxi, 479p il map hardcover o.p. pa $18   **949.703**

1. Yugoslav War, 1991-1995 2. Kosovo (Serbia) -- History
ISBN 1-58648-139-8 pa

LC 01-19717

This is an account of the former Supreme Allied Commander's experiences during the Kosovo crises. "Clark tells a story of frustration with NATO allies, who had to approve each operation and target selection, and with U.S. policymakers as he tried to formulate a strategy that would achieve his military goals." Libr J

949.71 Serbia

McAllester, Matthew

Beyond the Mountains of the Damned; the war inside Kosovo. New York Univ. Press 2002 227p il $30; pa $17.95   **949.71**

1. Kosovo (Serbia) -- History
ISBN 0-8147-5660-3; 0-8147-5661-1 pa

LC 2001-4370

This is an account of the war in Kosovo. McAllester "tells the story of Pec, Kosovo's most destroyed city and the site of the earliest and worst atrocities of the war, through the lives of two men—one Serb and one Kosovar." Publisher's note

"McAllester's spare, understated prose . . . is potent, as is his exploration of the human side of geopolitics and war." Publ Wkly

Includes bibliographical references

950 History of Asia

Fallows, James M.

Looking at the sun; {by} James Fallows. Pantheon Bks. 1994 517p hardcover o.p. pa $15   **950**

1. East Asia
ISBN 0-679-76162-4 pa

LC 93-38367

The author discusses the "culture, government and economic development of 11 East Asian nations. . . . Mr. Fallows's central thesis is that Western societies, especially the United States, 'have been using the wrong mental tools to classify, shape and understand the information they receive about Asia.'" N Y Times Book Rev

"A fascinating, fresh, and potentially controversial contemplation of the global market." Booklist

Higham, Charles

Encyclopedia of ancient Asian civilizations; [by] Charles F.W. Higham. Facts on File 2004 xxi, 440p il map (Facts on File library of world history) $85 **950**

1. Reference books 2. Asia -- Civilization -- Encyclopedias
ISBN 0-8160-4640-9

LC 2003-48513

This "volume 'concentrates on civilizations that arose east of the Caspian Sea,' from modern Afghanistan and the Aral Sea south to India and Sri Lanka and east to Japan, Korea, and the islands of Southeast Asia. The years covered range from 3000 B.C.E. through the 15th century." SLJ

"This is a good beginning point for research, especially in regard to archaeological excavations." Booklist

Includes bibliographical references

Levinson, David

Encyclopedia of modern Asia; {by} David Levinson, Karen Christensen. Scribner 2002 6v il maps set $695 **950**

1. Reference books 2. Asia -- Encyclopedias
ISBN 0-684-80617-7

LC 2002-8712

This "set is alphabetically arranged by topic. Volume 6 provides the index for the set. . . . The topics cover the 33 Asian countries' geography, economics, politics, human rights, cultures and languages, and biographies. Sidebars derived from primary source materials and black-and-white illustrations are interspersed throughout the text." Am Ref Books Annu, 2003

Includes bibliographical references

Mishra, Pankaj

From the ruins of empire; the intellectuals who remade Asia. Pankaj Mishra. Farrar, Straus and Giroux 2012 368 p. ill. (alk. paper) $27.00 **950**

1. Intellectuals
ISBN 0374249598; 9780374249595

LC 2012940483

"Originally published in 2012 by Allen Lane, an imprint of Penguin Books, Great Britain as From the ruins of empire : the revolt against the West and the remaking of Asia"--Title page verso.

This book "looks at how, between about 1870 and 1940, 'some of the most intelligent and sensitive people in the East responded to the encroachments of the West (both physical and intellectual) on their societies.' In particular, he focuses on Jamal al-Din al-Afghani and Liang Qichao, intellectuals and political activists." (Publishers Weekly)

Includes bibliographical references (pages 311-340) and index.

951 China and adjacent areas

Atwood, Christopher Pratt

Encyclopedia of Mongolia and the Mongol empire; [by] Christopher P. Atwood. Facts on File 2004

678p il map (Facts on File library of world history) $85 **951**

1. Mongolia
ISBN 0-8160-4671-9

LC 2003-61696

"Coverage is good for all time periods, and the encyclopedia as a whole makes a sound case for the enormous influence of Mongolian civilization on the history of the Far East, the Indian subcontinent, and Eastern Europe." Booklist

Includes bibliographical references

Berkshire encyclopedia of China; modern and historic views of the world's newest and oldest global power. Berkshire Pub. Group 2009 5v il map set $675 **951**

1. Reference books 2. China -- Civilization -- Encyclopedias 3. China -- Social life and customs -- Encyclopedias
ISBN 978-0-9770159-4-8; 0-9770159-4-7

LC 2009-7589

"Arranged alphabetically, the nearly 1000 articles cover an . . . array of subjects as they relate to China. Among those explored are the country's history (both ancient and modern), politicians, architecture, food, international relations, and medicine." Libr J

Includes bibliographical references

Bstan-'dzin-rgya-mtsho, Dalai Lama XIV, 1935-

My Tibet; text by His Holiness the fourteenth Dalai Lama of Tibet; photographs and introduction by Galen Rowell. University of Calif. Press 1990 162p il hardcover o.p. pa $34.95 **951**

1. Buddhism 2. Tibet (China) -- Pictorial works
ISBN 0-520-08948-0 pa

LC 90-10868

This is "a volume of photographs taken in recent years by Galen Rowell, with a text drawn from interviews with the Dalai Lama or essays written previously by him." N Y Times Book Rev

The **Cambridge** history of China; general editors, Denis Twitchett and John K. Fairbank. Cambridge Univ. Press 1978 12v v1 $205; v3 $205; v6 $178; v7 $205; v8 $178; v9 $178; v10 $195; v11 $205; v12 $205; v13 $205; v14 $180; v15 $195 **951**

1. China -- History
ISBN 0-521-24327-0 v1; 0-521-21446-7 v3; 0-521-24331-9 v6; 0-521-24332-7 v7; 0-521-24333-5 v8; 0-521-24334-3 v9; 0-521-21447-5 v10; 0-521-22029-7 v11; 0-521-23541-3 v12; 0-521-24338-6 v13; 0-521-24336-X v14; 0-521-24337-3 v15

LC 76-29852

"An important series for scholars, this is also a valuable reference tool for general collections." Libr J

Includes bibliographical references

Chetham, Deirdre

Before the deluge; the vanishing world of the Yangtze's Three Gorges. Palgrave 2002 xxiii, 296p il map hardcover o.p. pa $17.95 **951**

1. Yangtze River valley (China) 2. China -- Social life and customs

ISBN 1-4039-6428-9 pa

LC 2002-16939

The author "paints a pulsating picture of the great river, the countryside, the people and their occupations, the amazingly fluid political philosophies and the sheer endurance of all parties, past and present, involved with the overwhelming project." Publ Wkly

Includes bibliographical references

Dalle, Eric

Facts about China; edited by Xiao-bin Ji; contributors, Eric Dalle. Wilson, H.W. 2003 751p map $105 **951**

1. China

ISBN 0-8242-0961-3

LC 2001-45510

This "reference source covers all major topics regarding the People's Republic of China. Part 1 includes chapters on its geography and climate, peoples and language, systems of thought and belief, health and medicine, arts, entertainment and sports, literature, science and technology, economy and trade, and institutions (government and other) of Chinese society. Part 2 provides a chronology of important events in Chinese history; part 3, an alphabetical list of common Chinese concepts, important figures and events; and part 4, information and advice for future travelers." Choice

Includes bibliographical references

DeWoskin, Rachel

Foreign babes in Beijing; behind the scenes of a new China. W. W. Norton 2005 332p $24.95; pa $13.95 **951**

1. China -- Social life and customs

ISBN 0-393-05902-2; 0-393-32859-7 pa

LC 2005-939

The author recounts her experiences living in China in the 1990s, where she had a starring role in the soap opera "Foreign Babes in Beijing."

"Ms DeWoskin's portrait of the complexities of urban China is not uncritical. But her book is written with enormous warmth for its people. And it is all the better for avoiding neat conclusions." Economist

Dong, Stella

Shanghai, 1842-1949; the rise and fall of a decadent city. Morrow 2000 318p il hardcover o.p. pa $15 **951**

1. Shanghai (China)

ISBN 0-06-093481-6 pa

LC 99-41902

An "account of a city legendary for decadence, violence, and greedy imperialism. Dong meticulously details the European commercial interests that deliberately promoted opium trafficking and exploited the land and people of Shanghai with every conceivable vice for nearly 100 years." Booklist

Encyclopedia of modern China; David Pong, editor in chief. Charles Scribner's Sons/Gale, Cengage Learning 2009 4v il map set $520 **951**

1. Reference books 2. China -- Civilization -- Encyclopedias

ISBN 978-0-684-31566-9; 978-0-684-31571-3 ebook

LC 2009-3279

"Covering the period 1800 to the present, this attractive and authoritative set includes 936 entries and sidebars by nearly 500 authors. . . . There are main entries for each province (including a map and a box containing key data), major cities, important people, Chinese relations with countries from Australia to Vietnam, and hundreds of miscellaneous subjects." Booklist

Includes bibliographical references

Fairbank, John King

★ **China**; a new history. [by] John King Fairbank and Merle Goldman. 2nd enl. ed.; Belknap Press of Harvard University Press 2006 560p il map pa $24 **951**

1. China -- History

ISBN 0-674-01828-1; 978-0-674-01828-0

LC 2005-53695

First published 1992

Fairbank covers the history of China from paleolithic cultures of 400,000 B.C. up to 1989. Goldman adds a chapter on events in the post-Mao period and an epilogue on China at the beginning of the 21st century.

Includes bibliographical references

The **great** Chinese revolution: 1800-1985. Harper & Row 1986 396p maps hardcover o.p. pa $16 **951**

1. China -- History

ISBN 0-06-039057-3; 0-06-039076-X pa

LC 86-665

"The book is never pedantic, but gathers together a lifetime of scholarship plus a true gift for presentation of complex issues and a fine eye for telling illustration." Libr J

Includes bibliographical references

Hessler, Peter

★ **Oracle** bones; a journey between China's past and present. HarperCollins 2006 491p il $26.95; pa $15.99 **951**

1. China -- Civilization 2. China -- Description and travel

ISBN 0-06-082658-4; 0-06-082659-2 pa

LC 2005-52607

The author "has a marvelous sense of the intonations and gestures that give life to the moment; he knows when to join in the action and when simply to wait for things to happen. Today's China could have been made for him." N Y Times Book Rev

Includes bibliographical references

Meyer, Michael J.

The **last** days of old Beijing; life in the vanishing backstreets of a city transformed. [by] Michael Mey-

er. Walker & Company 2008 355p il map $25.99; pa $16 **951**
1. Beijing (China)
ISBN 978-0-8027-1652-1; 0-8027-1652-0; 978-0-8027-1750-4 pa; 0-8027-1750-4 pa

LC 2008-15546

This is a "revealing portrait of urban change, and the consequences of China's unquenchable thirst for modernization." Kirkus
Includes bibliographical references

Palmer, James
Heaven cracks, earth shakes; James Palmer. Basic Books, a member of the Perseus Books Group 2012 ix, 273p.p ill. **951**
1. Earthquakes 2. China -- History -- 1949-1976
ISBN 9780465014781; 9780465023493

LC 2011934180

In this book, "Beijing-based author [James] Palmer . . . lays out the devastation wrought by 10 years of the Cultural Revolution, and how over the space of a few months the Chinese people managed to rebound and move forward. The year was scarred irrevocably by three events: the death in January of the people's beloved prime minister Zhou En-lai; the earthquake in Tangshan, which had been predicted several days before yet warnings ignored, flattening the coal-mining town in the space of 23 seconds and killing more than 650,000 people; and Mao's death in September, which set off a power struggle between the Gang of Four, led by Mao's widow, Jiang Qing, and the supporters of Deng Xiaoping." (Kirkus)
Includes bibliographical references (p. 261-264) and index.

Platt, Stephen R.
Autumn in the Heavenly Kingdom; China, the West, and the epic story of the Taiping Civil War. by Stephen R. Platt. Alfred A. Knopf 2012 468 p. **951**
1. Manchus 2. China -- Foreign relations 3. Europeans -- China -- History 4. Christian missionaries -- History 5. China -- History -- 1850-1864, Taiping Rebellion 6. Manchus -- History -- 19th century 7. China -- Relations -- Western countries 8. Western countries -- Relations -- China 9. Americans -- China -- History -- 19th century 10. Europeans -- China -- History -- 19th century 11. China -- History -- Taiping Rebellion, 1850-1864 12. Ethnic conflict -- China -- History -- 19th century 13. China -- Ethnic relations -- History -- 19th century 14. Visitors, Foreign -- China -- History -- 19th century 15. China -- History -- Taiping Rebellion, 1850-1864 -- Participation, Foreign
ISBN 9780307271730

LC 2011035137

The book is author Stephen R. Platt's account of "[t]he cataclysmic Taiping rebellion. . . . In 1837 a peasant named Hong Xiuquan announced that he was Jesus' younger brother, sent to rid China of 'devils' including its weak, corrupt, ethnically foreign Manchu rulers. His charisma attracted a vast following that by the 1850s had conquered a large area, the Taiping Heavenly Kingdom, with a capital at Nanjing." (Publishers Weekly)
Includes bibliographical references

Prager, Emily
Wuhu diary; on taking my adopted daughter back to her hometown in China. Random House 2001 238p il hardcover o.p. pa $13 **951**
1. Adoption 2. China -- Description and travel
ISBN 0-385-72199-4 pa

LC 2001-19104

"For anyone considering multicultural adoption or already involved in one, this compelling work offers encouragement and an example of how to help an adopted child get acquainted with her roots and build her sense of self. For others, it provides a wonderful view of a part of China seldom written about." Libr J

Preston, Diana
The **Boxer** Rebellion; the dramatic story of China's war on foreigners that shook the world in the summer of 1900. Walker & Co. 2000 xxvii, 436p il maps $28 **951**
1. China -- History
ISBN 0-8027-1361-0

LC 00-39243

"Preston's account, compiled from the many letters, diaries, and memoirs by European survivors of the siege, captures an odd strain of mordant humor." N Y Times Book Rev
Includes bibliographical references and index

Schell, Orville
Virtual Tibet; searching for Shangri-la from the Himalayas to Hollywood. Metropolitan Bks. 2000 340p $26; pa $15 **951**
1. Tibet (China)
ISBN 0-8050-4381-0; 0-8050-4382-9 pa

LC 99-88146

Schell examines romanticized visions of Tibet in Western travel accounts and films
The author is a "seasoned traveler in China, . . . and his book has the bracing air about it of disenchantment. The fact that he was a bit of a seeker once himself, mesmerized by the idea of Tibet, and of Communist China, makes him the perfect chronicler of such afflictions in others." N Y Rev Books

★ **Wealth** and power; Orville Schell & John Delury. Random House Inc 2013 496 p. $30 **951**
1. China -- Social conditions 2. China -- Politics and government 3. China -- History -- 20th century -- Biography 4. China -- History -- 21st century -- Biography 5. China -- Politics and government -- 20th century 6. China -- Politics and government -- 21st century
ISBN 0679643478; 9780679643470

LC 2013002596

In this book, the authors "track the intellectual and political pursuit of fuqiang, or wealth and power, by Chinese thinkers and leaders in response to the humiliations heaped upon their country by Western powers, beginning with the Opium Wars of the mid-19th century. The work comprises chronologically ordered minibiographies, . . . with long sections devoted to Mao Zedong and Deng Xiaoping." (Publishers Weekly)
Includes bibliographical references and index

Spence, Jonathan D.

The **Chan's** great continent; China in Western minds. Norton 1998 279p hardcover o.p. pa $14.95   **951**

1. China -- Civilization
ISBN 0-393-31989-X pa

LC 98-10823

"Spence's book will appeal not only to those interested in history and literature, but to anyone looking for a perspective on contemporary discourse about China." Publ Wkly
Includes bibliographical references

God's Chinese son; the Taiping Heavenly Kingdom of Hong Xiuquan. Norton 1996 400p il maps hardcover o.p. pa $15.95   **951**

1. Revolutionaries 2. Religious leaders 3. China -- History -- 1850-1864, Taiping Rebellion
ISBN 0-393-31556-8 pa

LC 95-17245

"In 1836, twenty-two-year-old Hong Xiuquan failed the civil-service examinations in Canton and came across some Christian tracts. When he later fell sick and had visions, he became convinced that he was the Christian God's second son, destined to rule a 'heavenly kingdom' on earth. Many were attracted to Hong's egalitarian policies—despite his enforced separation of the sexes—and his sect prospered. But its attempts to overthrow the Qing dynasty resulted in unprecedented bloodshed: twenty million people died before the uprising was defeated, in 1864. Spence's present-tense narrative is riveting." New Yorker
Includes bibliographical references

The **search** for modern China. Norton 1990 xxv, 876p il maps hardcover o.p. pa $27.70   **951**

1. China -- History
ISBN 0-393-30780-8 pa

LC 89-9241

Spence's "own sense of China's past is so vivid, his understanding so sure and his writer's skill so powerful that the reader apprehends distant events as if they were contemporary." New Statesman (1913)
Includes bibliographical references

Treason by the book; {by} Jonathan Spence. Viking 2001 300p map $24.95; pa $14   **951**

1. China -- History 2. China -- Politics and government
ISBN 0-670-89292-0; 0-14-200041-8 pa

LC 00-43805

"Spence's story of emperor, officials, and conspirators is both rousingly unlikely and highly informative." Libr J

Tsering Shakya

The **dragon** in the land of snows; a history of modern Tibet since 1947. Columbia Univ. Press 1999 574p il $32.50   **951**

1. Tibet (China)
ISBN 0-231-11814-7

LC 99-14020

"Drawing on Tibetan, Chinese, British, Indian and American sources, Shakya weaves an authoritative and easily readable narrative. 'The Dragon in the Land of Snows'

is likely to be the definitive history of modern Tibet for a generation or more." N Y Times Book Rev
Includes bibliographical references

951.04   China--Period of Republic, 1912-1949

Chang, Iris

★ The **rape** of Nanking; the forgotten holocaust of World War II. Penguin 1998 290p il pa $16   **951.04**

1. Sino-Japanese Conflict, 1937-1945 2. Nanjing (Jiangsu Province, China) massacre, 1937
ISBN 0-14-027744-7; 978-0-14-027744-9

LC 97-24137

First published 1997 by Basic Books

"Chang's book is a memorial to the victims of Nanking, a damning indictment of Japanese political historiography, a valuable addition to Pacific war literature, and a literary model of how to speak about the unspeakable." Booklist
Includes bibliographical references

Sun Shuyun

The **Long** March; the true history of Communist China's founding myth. Doubleday 2007 270p il map $26   **951.04**

1. Heads of state 2. Communist leaders 3. Political leaders 4. China -- History -- 1912-1949
ISBN 978-0-385-52024-9; 0-385-52024-7

First published 2006 in the United Kingdom

"In 1934, surrounded by Chiang Kai-shek's forces in the south, Mao's Red Army marched more than eight thousand miles to a new base, in the northwest. The march, completed by only a fifth of the original army, was a defeat in all ways but one: it returned Mao from the political wilderness to power. Mao transformed the march into the founding myth of modern China and, in doing so, created a new narrative around victories that never happened. Shuyun, a Chinese-born BBC documentary producer, retraces the route and interviews the few remaining survivors, in an account that shows the human cost of Mao's revisionism." New Yorker

951.05   China--Period of People's Republic, 1949-

August, Oliver

Inside the red mansion; on the trail of China's most wanted man. Houghton Mifflin Company 2007 268p map $26   **951.05**

1. Smugglers 2. Commercial agents 3. China -- Description and travel
ISBN 978-0-618-71498-8; 0-618-71498-7

LC 2006-26930

"In 1999, China's Public Enemy No. 1 was 'Fatty' Lai Changxing, an illiterate rice farmer turned real-estate and shipping mogul who fled the country, accused of heading a multibillion-dollar smuggling ring. This account . . . casts Lai's rise and fall as a cautionary tale of boomtown China. The author tours the remains of Lai's empire—a film studio built as a replica of the Forbidden City; a posh brothel where he bribed Party officials with the company of 'Miss Temporarys'—but he reserves his most vivid prose for the 'fakers and fortune seekers, oddballs and outlaws' he meets along the way." New Yorker

Becker, Jasper

The **Chinese**. Oxford University Press 2002 493p il map pa $21.95 **951.05**
1. China -- Social conditions 2. China -- Economic conditions
ISBN 0-19-514940-8
First published 2000 by Free Press
This "is a captivating and enlightening read for anyone interested in Asian or cultural studies." Booklist [review of 2000 edition]
Includes bibliographical references

Buruma, Ian

Bad elements; Chinese rebels from Los Angeles to Beijing. Random House 2001 xxv, 367p hardcover o.p. pa $15 **951.05**
1. Dissent 2. Human rights 3. China -- Politics and government
ISBN 0-679-78136-6 pa
LC 2001-19365
The author interviews Chinese dissidents in the United States, Asia, and Europe "to find out what happened to them and how they feel about the future of human rights in China. Buruma's study is both engaging and deeply informed." Libr J
Includes bibliographical references

Chang, Jung

Wild swans; three daughters of China. Simon & Schuster 1991 524p il hardcover o.p. pa $15 **951.05**
1. Women -- China 2. China -- History
ISBN 0-7432-4698-5 pa
LC 91-20696
The author "tells the harrowing life stories of her maternal grandmother, her mother, and herself. Their tales span a period of radical change in China that has touched every aspect of life." Booklist

Chen, Da

Sounds of the river; a memoir. HarperCollins Pubs. 2002 307p hardcover o.p. pa $12.95 **951.05**
1. Lawyers 2. Linguists 3. Calligraphers 4. China -- History -- 1949-
ISBN 0-06-095872-3 pa
LC 2001-39215
"Da Chen once again describes his past with fondness and buoyancy." N Y Times Book Rev

Dikötter, Frank

Mao's great famine; the history of China's most devastating catastrophe, 1958-1962. Walker & Co. 2010 420p il map $30 **951.05**
1. Food supply 2. Heads of state 3. Famines -- China 4. Communist leaders 5. Political leaders 6. Food supply -- China 7. Economic policy -- China 8. China

-- Economic policy -- 1949-1976
ISBN 978-0-8027-7768-3; 0-8027-7768-6
LC 2010-13141
This book on the 1958-1962 famine in China "focuses on describing and conveying to the reader the stark effects of the famine at the local level. . . . [T]he first two . . . parts retrace major events of the Great Leap Forward disaster and famine. . . stressing the crucial role of the Lushan Conference." Other chapters depict "survival strategies, repressive violence . . . the various ways in which people died, and the places where most deaths occurred." (China Perspectives)
The author parses this study of the Great Leap Forward into three "components: Mao Zedong's bloody-minded resolve to implement the accelerated collectivization of the countryside, and the stifling of all opposition; the effects of these devastating policies on agriculture, industry, trade, housing and nature; and the catastrophic human toll ('at least 45 million people died unnecessarily between 1958 and 1962')." Kirkus
Includes bibliographical references and index

Fallows, James M.

Postcards from Tomorrow Square; reports from China. [by] James Fallows. Vintage Books 2009 262p pa $14.95 **951.05**
1. China -- History -- 1976-
ISBN 978-0-307-45624-3; 0-307-45624-2
LC 2008-28083
"In this series of articles, Fallows reports on interesting trends and personalities in China—ambitious entrepreneurs and the rise in popularity of reality shows on state-run television. Despite the Western view of a powerful, single-minded China, Fallows presents a portrait of a huge and complex nation with such a vast range of ages and regional, geographic, and cultural differences that it defies simple definition." Booklist

Fang Lizhi

Bringing down the Great Wall; writings on science, culture, and democracy in China. introduction by Orville Schell; editor and principal translator, James H. Williams. Norton 1992 336p pa $10.95 **951.05**
1. Human rights 2. China -- Politics and government
ISBN 0-393-30885-5; 978-0-393-30885-3
LC 90-53064
First published 1990 by Knopf
"A comprehensive selection of the written (and spoken) words of the witty, passionate, tenacious and articulate Chinese scientist and dissident who at present is living in the United States." N Y Times Book Rev
Includes bibliographical references

Kemenade, Willem van

China, Hong Kong, Taiwan, Inc. translated from the Dutch by Diane Webb. Knopf 1997 444p hardcover o.p. pa $16 **951.05**
1. Taiwan 2. Hong Kong (China) 3. China -- Politics and government
ISBN 0-679-77756-3 pa
LC 97-71923

This is an "analysis of China's recent past and reflections on its future direction. Van Kemenade explores the anticipated political and economic fallout from the mainland's absorption of capitalist Hong Kong . . . and the possibility of its eventual takeover of Taiwan. He projects a foreseeable confrontation with Japan over Asian hegemony, ethnic and economic upheavals on China's 'wild' western border that abuts former Soviet republics and a political backlash from the fast-growing middle class, which in its pursuit of wealth seems no longer loyal to socialist ideals." Publ Wkly

Leibovitz, Liel

Fortunate sons; the 120 Chinese boys who came to America, went to school, and revolutionized an ancient civilization. [by] Liel Leibovitz & Matthew Miller. W.W. Norton 2011 319p il $26.95   **951.05**
  1. Educators 2. China -- History 3. Education -- China 4. China -- Politics and government
  ISBN 978-0-393-07004-0; 0-393-07004-2
                 LC 2010-37724
"A curious, little-known episode of Sino-American history vividly told." Kirkus
Includes bibliographical references

Levine, Steven I.

★ **Mao**; the real story. Alexander V. Pantsov with Steven I. Levine. 1st Simon & Schuster hardcover Simon & Schuster 2012 xix, 755 p.p $35   **951.05**
  1. Communism -- China 2. China -- Politics and government 3. Heads of state -- China -- Biography 4. China -- Politics and government -- 1949-1976
  ISBN 1451654472; 9781451654479; 9781451654493
                 LC 2011053113
This book offers a biography of Communist leader Mao Zedong. It relates "how Mao, who joined the Communist Party in 1920, fought his way . . . to its leadership in the 1930s. . . . Taking power in 1949, Mao established a Stalinist autocracy featuring purges, massive social upheaval, and disastrous economic policies. . . . [Alexander V.] Pantsov reveals that Mao took pains to remain a faithful follower until Stalin's 1952 death." (Publishers Weekly)
Includes bibliographical references and index

Lord, Bette Bao

Legacies : a Chinese mosaic. Knopf 1990 245p hardcover o.p. pa $19   **951.05**
  1. China -- Politics and government 2. China -- Social life and customs
  ISBN 0-449-90620-5 pa
                 LC 89-43452
The author lived in China from 1985 to 1989. Her book is based on interviews with Chinese people, including an actress, a teacher, a veteran of the Long March, an artist, a journalist, a peasant, an entrepreneur and a Communist Party cadre, who recount their experiences of persecution during the Cultural Revolution. The author also describes her own experiences and her family history
"A vivid and startling mosaic of the political struggles that foreshadowed the Tiananmen Square uprising." Time

Ma Jian

Red dust; a path through China. translated from the Chinese by Flora Drew. Pantheon Bks. 2001 324p maps hardcover o.p. pa $14   **951.05**
  1. China -- Description and travel
  ISBN 0-385-72023-8 pa
                 LC 2001-21575
"Faced with imprisonment, Jian fled to the Chinese countryside, eventually making his way to Tibet. His journey is presented as a combination travelogue and a narrative of sheer poetry and spirituality." Booklist

Mexico, Zachary

China underground. Soft Skull Press 2009 306p pa $16.95   **951.05**
  1. China -- Social life and customs
  ISBN 978-1-59376-223-0; 1-59376-223-2
                 LC 2008-45319
"Through encounters with sundry artists, musicians, students, bar owners, gangsters, prostitutes, and slackers, Mexico assembles a compelling portrait of China's contemporary youth culture and the limits of Communist control. The book's subjects include a twenty-seven-year-old self-taught disaster photographer from the coal country in Shenyang; a twenty-nine-year-old mobster in Qingdao; a twenty-two-year-old Hendrixian Uighur guitar player making a splash in Shanghai; a Beijing university student who wishes that the system encouraged less rote memorization and more original thought; and an investigative journalist who no longer publishes himself, instead leading Western reporters to controversial stories." New Yorker

Pan, Philip P.

★ **Out** of Mao's shadow; the struggle for the soul of a new China. Simon & Schuster 2008 349p il map $28; pa $16   **951.05**
  1. China -- History -- 1949- 2. China -- Social conditions
  ISBN 978-1-4165-3705-2; 1-4165-3705-8; 978-1-4165-3706-9 pa; 1-4165-3706-6 pa
                 LC 2008-11550
The author examines contemporary China, "looking at both the growing personal freedom its citizens now enjoy and the Communist Party's continued monopoly on power." N Y Times (Late N Y Ed)
This is "one of the most revealing books about China since it opened up to the outside world in the 1970s." N Y Rev Books
Includes bibliographical references

Pomfret, John

Chinese lessons; five classmates and the story of the new China. H. Holt 2006 315p il map $26   **951.05**
  1. China
  ISBN 978-0-8050-7615-8; 0-8050-7615-8
                 LC 2006-41211
"As a twenty-year-old exchange student from Stanford University, John Pomfret spent a year at Nanjing University in China. His fellow classmates were among those who survived the twin tragedies of Mao's rule—the Great Leap Forward and the Cultural Revolution. . . . Pomfret went on to a career in journalism, spending the bulk of his time in

China. After attending the twentieth reunion of his class, he decided to reacquaint himself with some of his classmates. Chinese Lessons is their story and his own." Publisher's note

This "is a highly personal, honest, funny and well-informed account of China's hyperactive effort to forget its past and reinvent its future." N Y Times Book Rev

Salzman, Mark

Iron & silk. Random House 1987 211p hardcover o.p. pa $12.95 **951.05**
1. Martial arts 2. China -- Description and travel
ISBN 0-394-55156-7; 0-394-75511-1 pa

LC 86-11846

The author tells of his two years teaching English to medical students in China's Hunan Province following his graduation from Yale University in 1982.

This book is "not so much a treatise on modern Chinese mores as a series of telling vignettes. . . . [The author] describes his encounter with Pan Qingfu, the country's foremost master of wushu, the traditional Chinese martial art." Time

Schoppa, R. Keith

The **Columbia** guide to modern Chinese history. Columbia Univ. Press 2000 356p il map (Columbia guides to Asian history) $49 **951.05**
1. China -- History
ISBN 0-231-11276-9

LC 99-53420

This narrative overview of Chinese history focuses on five areas: domestic politics, society, the economy, culture, and relations with the outside world. Contains approximately 500 annotated entries for further research in English as well as electronic resources and films. A chronology, excerpts from primary documents, and numerous graphs and tables are appended
Includes bibliographical references

Short, Philip

Mao; a life. Holt & Co. 2000 782p il maps hardcover o.p. pa $20 **951.05**
1. Heads of state 2. Communist leaders 3. Political leaders 4. China -- Politics and government
ISBN 0-8050-6638-1 pa

LC 99-41839

This biography "takes Mao from his 1893 birth in the village of Shaoshan to school in Changsha, where he trained to be a teacher, and then into revolutionary activity, the long fight with Chiang Kai-shek, and leadership of the most populous nation on Earth." Booklist
Includes bibliographical references

Spence, Jonathan D.

Mao Zedong; {by} Jonathan Spence. Viking 1999 188p map (Penguin lives series) $19.95 **951.05**
1. Heads of state 2. Communist leaders 3. Political leaders 4. China -- Politics and government
ISBN 0-670-88669-6

LC 99-27739

"This specialist's book for nonspecialists concisely recounts the life of the Communist leader who revolutionized China. Ideas travel fast: Mao, a peasant son born in 1893,

was able to read Darwin and Marx in translation and add Western ideas to his heritage of classical Chinese thought, and Spence helps us understand why he eventually embraced Communism. What is less clear is why a gifted, high-minded youth became a ruthless, crackpot tyrant." New Yorker
Includes bibliographical references

Vogel, Ezra F.

Deng Xiaoping and the transformation of China; Ezra F. Vogel. Belknap Press of Harvard University Press 2011 xxiv, 876p ill. **951.05**
1. Communism -- China 2. China -- Economic conditions 3. China -- Politics and government 4. Biography, Individual
ISBN 978-0-674-05544-5; 0-674-05544-6; 9780674062832

LC 2011006925

Lionel Gelber Prize (Canada) (2012)

This book, a 2012 Lionel Gelber Prize winner, offers a biography of Chinese politician Deng Xiaoping. "Deng was the pragmatic yet disciplined driving force behind China's radical transformation in the late twentieth century. He confronted the damage wrought by the Cultural Revolution, dissolved Mao's cult of personality, and loosened the economic and social policies that had stunted China's growth. Obsessed with modernization and technology, Deng opened trade relations with the West, which lifted hundreds of millions of his countrymen out of poverty. Yet at the same time he answered to his authoritarian roots, most notably when he ordered the crackdown in June 1989 at Tiananmen Square. . . . In the fifty years of his tumultuous rise to power, he endured accusations, purges, and even exile before becoming China's preeminent leader from 1978 to 1989 and again in 1992. When he reached the top, Deng saw an opportunity to creatively destroy much of the economic system he had helped build for five decades as a loyal follower of Mao— and he did not hesitate." (Publisher's note)
Includes bibliographical references and index

Wong, Jan

A **comrade** lost and found; a Beijing story. Houghton Mifflin Harcourt 2009 322p map $25 **951.05**
1. Beijing (China) -- Description and travel
ISBN 978-0-15-101342-5; 0-15-101342-X

LC 2008-23788

First published 2007 in Canada with title Beijing confidential: a tale of comrades lost and found

Wong spent a year in Beijing on a foreign exchange program during the cultural revolution. In this "book, she recounts her return to the city in an effort to find a former classmate she betrayed with grave consequences. . . . Wong is a gifted storyteller, and hers is a deeply personal and richly detailed eyewitness account of China's journey to glossy modernity." Booklist

Wu, Harry

Bitter winds; a memoir of my years in China's Gulag. {by} Harry Wu and Carolyn Wakeman. Wiley 1993 290p il $35; pa $19.95   **951.05**
1. Political prisoners 2. China -- Politics and government
ISBN 0-471-55645-9; 0-471-11425-1 pa
LC 93-15799
In this "memoir, Wu recalls his 19 years in Chinese labor camps. Though a middle-class college student, he was initially a patriotic Communist, but he soon ran afoul of the thought police. Hoping to flee the country in 1959, he was denounced as an 'enemy of the revolution.' The book . . . focuses primarily on Wu's first decade as a prisoner struggling against starvation, seeing others succumb and learning a brutal survival ethic from fellow inmates. It is an intimate story of bravery and tragedy." Publ Wkly

Troublemaker; one man's crusade against China's cruelty. [by] Harry Wu, with George Vecsey. NewsMax.com Book 2002 326p il pa $24.95 **951.05**
1. Human rights 2. Political prisoners 3. China -- Politics and government
ISBN 0-9704029-9-6; 978-0-9704029-9-8
LC 2004-273145
First published 1996 by Times Books
"Denounced in China as a 'traitor' and 'spy,' Wu is hailed as a hero in the West and has received many human rights awards. This book meticulously unveils the dramatic story of his 'crusade' against the Chinese government. . . . An interesting but disturbing book." Libr J

951.249   Taiwan (Formosa) and adjacent islands

Copper, John F.

Taiwan; nation-state or province? John F. Copper. Westview Press 2013 xiii, 259 p.p ill., maps (pbk. : alk. paper) $36   **951.249**
1. Taiwan 2. Taiwan -- International status
ISBN 0813346924; 9780813346922; 9780813346939
LC 2012031338
This book, by John Copper, focuses on Taiwan. The "country's culture, history, and geography are explored in detail, allowing readers a chance to see how people live. . . . Sidebars highlight especially interesting people, places, and events [and] recipes give readers the opportunity to experience foreign cuisine first-hand." (Publisher's note)
"[A] comprehensive yet concise introduction to Taiwan." Choice
Includes bibliographical references (p. 237-246) and index

951.9   Korea

Brady, James

The **coldest** war; a memoir of Korea. St. Martin's Griffin 2000 248p il map pa $15.95   **951.9**
1. Korean War, 1950-1953 -- Personal narratives
ISBN 978-0-312-26511-3; 0-312-26511-5
First published 1990 by Orion Bks.

"From November 1951 to July 1952, the author was a marine lieutenant who frequently found himself called upon to fight and kill Chinese and North Korean soldiers on the battlefields of Korea. His memoir of that experience is a well-crafted piece told in a voice that skillfully mixes the sardonic insight of an older man looking back on a highly extraordinary episode of his past with the naivete of the young warrior he once was." Booklist

Breen, Michael

The **Koreans**; who they are, what they want, where their future lies. St. Martin's Press 1999 276p hardcover o.p. pa $14.95   **951.9**
1. Korean national characteristics 2. Korea -- History
ISBN 0-312-32609-2 pa
LC 99-45599
First published 1998 in the United Kingdom
In this survey of Korea's culture, the author "probes such diverse topics as the status of civil liberties, generational social strains within families, and the massive corruption that permeates Korean society. He writes with a snappy, readable style." Booklist
Includes bibliographical references

Cumings, Bruce, 1943-

★ **Korea's** place in the sun; a modern history. Updated ed; W. W. Norton 2005 542p il map pa $16.95   **951.9**
1. Korea -- History
ISBN 0-393-32702-7; 0-393-31681-5
LC 2006-276040
First published 1997
This history of Korea from 1860 focuses primarily on the post-1945 period
"Mr. Cumings has pored over the historical documents and he argues intelligently. His book is important precisely because he marshals considerable evidence to challenge conventional understanding." N Y Times Book Rev
Includes bibliographical references

The **Korean** War; a history. Modern Library 2010 288p il map (Modern Library chronicles)   **951.9**
1. Korean War, 1950-1953 2. Korean War, 1950-1953 -- United States
ISBN 0-679-64357-5; 978-0-679-64357-9
LC 2010005629
This is a "revisionist history of America's intervention in Korea." (N Y Times (Late N Y Ed)) Index.
A "revisionist history of America's intervention in Korea. Beneath its bland title, Mr. Cumings's book is a squirm-inducing assault on America's moral behavior during the Korean War, a conflict that he says is misremembered when it is remembered at all. It's a book that puts the reflexive anti-Americanism of North Korea's leaders into sympathetic historical context. . . . [Cumings] mows down a host of myths about the war in his short new book, which is a distillation of his own scholarship and that of many other historians." N Y Times (Late N Y Ed)
Includes bibliographical references

Edwards, Paul M.

Korean War almanac. Facts on File 2006 592p il map (Almanacs of American wars) $85   **951.9**
1. Korean War, 1950-1953
ISBN 0-8160-6037-1

LC 2005-9374

First published 1990 under the authorship of Harry G. Summers

This book "contains a day-by-day chronology of the events and the people involved in this important war." Publisher's note

Includes bibliographical references

The **encyclopedia** of the Korean War; a political, social, and military history. Spencer C. Tucker, volume editor; Paul G. Pierpaoli, Jr., associate editor and editor, documents volume; Jinwung Kim, Xiaobing Li, James I. Matray, assistant editors. 2nd ed.; ABC-CLIO 2010 3v il map set $295   **951.9**
1. Reference books 2. Korean War, 1950-1953 -- Encyclopedias
ISBN 978-1-85109-849-1; 1-85109-849-6; 978-1-85109-850-7 ebook; 1-85109-850-X ebook

LC 2010-681

First published 2000

A resource on the confrontation that became the first shooting war of the Cold War, the first limited conflict of the Atomic Age, and the war that led to a dramatic escalation of the national security state while foreshadowing U.S. involvement in Vietnam.

"This is an excellent source for high-school, academic, and public libraries." Booklist

Includes glossary and bibliographical references

Halberstam, David

★ The **coldest** winter; America and the Korean War. Hyperion 2007 719p map $35   **951.9**
1. Korean War, 1950-1953
ISBN 1-401-30052-9; 978-1-401-30052-4

LC 2007-1635

In this history of the Korean War, the author presents a "narrative of the political decisions and miscalculations on both sides. . . . At the heart of the book are the individual stories of the soldiers on the front lines who were left to deal with the consequences of the dangerous misjudgements and competing agendas of powerful men." Publisher's note

"Alive with the voices of the men who fought, Halberstam's telling is a virtuoso work of history." Publ Wkly

Includes bibliographical references

Oberdorfer, Don

The **two** Koreas; a contemporary history. New ed; Basic Bks. 2001 521p il map pa $21   **951.9**
1. Korea -- History
ISBN 0-465-05162-6

LC 2001-43486

First published 1997 by Addison-Wesley

This is a study of North and South Korean politics and an analysis of U.S. policy from the 1970s to the present

Includes bibliographical references

Peterson, Mark

A **brief** history of Korea; [by] Mark Peterson with Phillip Margulies. Facts On File 2010 328p il map (Brief history) $49.50   **951.9**
1. Korea -- History
ISBN 978-0-8160-5085-7

LC 2009-18889

This book "covers the history of Korea from the origins of the Korean people in prehistoric times to the economic and political situation in North and South Korea today." Publisher's note

Includes bibliographical references

951.904   Korea, 1945-1999

Hickey, Michael

The **Korean** War; the West confronts communism. Overlook Press 2000 397p il maps $35   **951.904**
1. Korean War, 1950-1953 2. United Nations -- Armed Forces -- Korea
ISBN 1-58567-035-9

LC 00-27692

First published 1999 in the United Kingdom

An "analysis of both the military and political factors that caused the war and the conduct on all sides. . . . The author does not mince words when criticizing General MacArthur and other UN commanders. Using declassified documents as well as regimental and personal diaries, he wades through political intrigue and military disasters and triumphs to give us a memorable account." Libr J

Includes bibliographical references

951.93   North Korea (People's Democratic Republic of Korea)

Demick, Barbara

Nothing to envy; ordinary lives in North Korea. Spiegel & Grau 2009 314p il map   **951.93**
1. Koreans 2. Korea (North) 3. Korea (North) -- Social conditions 4. Korea (North) -- Economic conditions
ISBN 0-385-52390-4; 978-0-385-52390-5

LC 2009-22420

This book "follows the lives of six ordinary North Koreans, including a female doctor, a pair of star-crossed lovers, a factory worker and an orphan." (N Y Times (Late N Y Ed))

"A fascinating and deeply personal look at the lives of six defectors from the repressive totalitarian regime of the Republic of North Korea, in which Demick . . . draws out details of daily life that would not otherwise be known to Western eyes because of the near-complete media censorship north of the arbitrary border drawn after Japan's surrender ending WWII." Publ Wkly

Includes bibliographical references

Hassig, Ralph

The **hidden** people of North Korea; everyday life in the hermit kingdom. [by] Ralph Hassig and

Kongdan Oh. Rowman & Littlefield Publishers 2009
300p il $39.95 **951.93**
1. Heads of state 2. Korea (North) 3. Communist
leaders 4. Korea (North) -- Social conditions 5.
Political culture -- Korea (North) 6. Korea (North) --
Economic conditions 7. Korea (North) -- Politics and
government
ISBN 978-0-7425-6718-4; 0-7425-6718-4
LC 2009-29786

The authors "gather behind-the-curtain research to expose day-to-day life, and the powers that control it, in North
Korea, a developed nation where meat is a luxury and the
Internet doesn't exist for anyone but the dictator. . . . The
uninformed will find much that's fascinating and shocking:
a nation of castes and concentration camps, replete with a
politics of fear that rivals the worst Orwell could imagine."
Publ Wkly

Includes bibliographical references

951.9304 North Korea (People's Democratic Republic of Korea), 1945-1994

Lankov, Andrei
The **real** North Korea; life and politics in the failed
Stalinist utopia. Andrei Lankov. Oxford University
Press 2013 304 p. (hardcover) $27.95 **951.9304**
1. Korea (North) -- Social conditions 2. Korea (North)
-- Politics and government 3. Korea (North) -- Foreign
relations 4. Korea (North) -- Politics and government
-- 1994-
ISBN 0199964297; 9780199964291
LC 2012046992

This first half of this book by Andrei Lankov "provides an overview of North Korea's past history, and discusses how it has changed in the years since the famine of
the 1990s. The second half predicts that the North Korean
regime will ultimately collapse, then discusses likely outcomes of this event." (Library Journal)

Includes bibliographical references and index

952 Japan

The **Cambridge** encyclopedia of Japan; editors,
Richard Bowring, Peter Kornicki. Cambridge
Univ. Press 1993 400p il maps $70 **952**
1. Reference books 2. Japan -- Civilization --
Encyclopedias
ISBN 0-521-40352-9
LC 92-8167

This volume is divided "into eight categories: geography, history, language, thought and religion, arts and crafts,
society, politics, and the economy. Each of these categories
is further divided into 7-11 subjects that deal with numerous
topics, such as the physical structure of the country, climate,
education, family, judicial system, cinema, products, foreign
policy, and important historical figures." Am Ref Books
Annu, 1994

Jansen, Marius B.
★ The **making** of modern Japan. Belknap Press
2000 871p il maps $35; pa $18.95 **952**
1. Japan -- History
ISBN 0-674-00334-9; 0-674-00991-6 pa
LC 00-41352

"Jansen has produced what is sure to become the standard narrative history of modern Japan. . . . In every way
this is a remarkable book . . . and no reference collection on
Japan can pretend to be complete without it." Choice

Includes bibliographical references

McClain, James L.
Japan, a modern history. Norton 2001 632p il
maps $35; pa $31.25 **952**
1. Japan -- History
ISBN 0-393-04156-5; 0-393-97720-X pa
LC 2001-34545

"This is a well-written, well-researched, and easily readable survey of the modern history of a fascinating and important nation." Booklist

Includes bibliographical references

Perez, Louis G.
The **history** of Japan; 2nd ed.; Greenwood Press
2009 266p map (Greenwood histories of the modern
nations) $49.95 **952**
1. Reference books 2. Japan -- History
ISBN 978-0-313-36442-6
LC 2008-52242

First published 1998

This history covers prehistoric and early feudal Japan to
the 21st Century. Cultural aspects examined include theater
and cinema, marriage customs, and youth culture as well as
the women's movement and political scandals.

"With its essential chronology, term glossary, and premier list, the volume serves as both engaging read and
quick-reference." Libr J

Includes bibliographical references

Reischauer, Edwin O.
Japan; the story of a nation. 4th ed.; McGraw-
Hill 1990 401p il map pa $68.75 **952**
1. Japan -- History
ISBN 0-07-557074-2; 978-0-07-557074-5
LC 89-12418

First published 1970 by Knopf

This history of the Japanese people from their origins
to the present examines their civilization, cultural heritage,
militarism, and economy.

Includes bibliographical references

The **Japanese** today; change and continu-
ity. Belknap Press 1988 426p il maps $25; pa
$12.50 **952**
1. Feudalism 2. Japan 3. Education -- Japan 4.
Agriculture -- Japan
ISBN 0-674-47181-4; 0-674-47182-2 pa
LC 87-14904

First published 1977 with title: The Japanese

The author "shows how change within continuity has
been the most enduring characteristic of the Japanese ex-

perience—throughout the nation's history. He analyzes and explains in detail the government, education, business, and social structure of the country in modern times." Christ Sci Monit

Includes bibliography

Smith, Patrick L.

Japan; a reinterpretation. Pantheon Bks. 1997 385p hardcover o.p. pa $14   **952**

1. Japan -- History 2. Japan -- Civilization
ISBN 0-679-74511-4 pa

LC 96-39220

This study focuses on events after World War II. Smith examines the U.S. role in post-war Japan, and the social structure of Japanese society

"In his sweeping analysis of the country's history, economy, politics and culture, Smith has produced a new startlingly clear-sighted vision of the often misunderstood Japanese." Publ Wkly

Includes bibliographical references

952.03   Japan--1868-1945

Buruma, Ian

Inventing Japan, 1853-1964. Modern Lib. 2003 194p hardcover o.p. pa $12.95   **952.03**

1. Japan -- History
ISBN 0-679-64085-1; 0-8129-7286-4 pa

LC 2002-26346

"Buruma traces the remarkable metamorphosis that transformed an isolated island shogunate into an expansive military empire and then into a pacified and prosperous democracy. . . . An excellent introductory study." Booklist

Includes bibliographical references

Gordon, Andrew

The **modern** history of Japan. Oxford University Press 2003 384p il $35; pa $29.95   **952.03**

1. Japan -- History
ISBN 0-19-511060-9; 0-19-511061-7 pa

LC 2002-70916

The author examines "Japan's political, economic, social, and cultural inventions of its modernity in evolving international contexts, incorporating inside viewpoints and debates. Beyond identifying the national stages (feudalism, militarism, democracy), the author innovatively emphasizes how labor unions, cultural figures, and groups in society (especially women) have been affected over time and have responded." Libr J

Includes bibliographical references and index

Keene, Donald

Emperor of Japan: Meiji and His world, 1852-1912. Columbia Univ. Press 2002 922p il $82.50; pa $27.95   **952.03**

1. Emperors 2. Japan -- History -- 1868-1945
ISBN 0-231-12340-X; 0-231-12341-8 pa

LC 2001-28826

This is a "biography-cum-history of Emperor Meiji and his times. . . . Meiji's reign saw Japan become fully industrialized under a brand new constitution, and with new eco-

nomic and educational systems adopted. Despite the book's massive scale, Keene's graceful writing holds the reader's interest throughout." Booklist

Includes bibliographical references

Pleshakov, Konstantin

The **Tsar's** last armada; the epic journey to the Battle of Tsushima. {by} Constantine Pleshakov. Basic Bks. 2002 xx, 396p il maps hardcover o.p. pa $17.50   **952.03**

1. Russo-Japanese War, 1904-1905
ISBN 0-465-05792-6 pa

LC 2001-52532

This is an account of events leading to the Russo-Japanese War and the defeat of the Russian fleet in the Tsushima Straits in 1905

"A compulsively readable account told from the Russian viewpoint." Booklist

Includes bibliographical references

Seagrave, Sterling

The **Yamato** dynasty; the secret history of Japan's Imperial family. Broadway Bks. 2000 394p il hardcover o.p. pa $23   **952.03**

1. Emperors 2. Japan -- Kings and rulers 3. Japan -- Politics and government
ISBN 0-7679-0497-4 pa

LC 99-49888

This "history of Japan from the mid-19th century to the present weaves together an iconoclastic historical narrative with a mostly caustic view of Japan's imperial family. The Seagraves depict modern Japan as a country consistently dominated by a closed financial oligarchy in league with politicians, bureaucrats, the imperial family, and underworld bosses." Libr J

Includes bibliographical references

952.04   Japan, 1945-1999

Dower, John W.

Embracing defeat; Japan in the wake of World War II. by John Dower. Norton 1999 676p il $29.95; pa $17.95   **952.04**

1. Japan -- History -- 1945-1952, Allied occupation
ISBN 0-393-04686-9; 0-393-32027-8 pa

LC 98-22133

"Dower demonstrates an impressive mastery of voluminous sources, both American and Japanese, and he deftly situates the political story within a rich cultural context." Publ Wkly

Includes bibliographical references

★ **Encyclopedia** of contemporary Japanese culture; edited by Sandra Buckley. Routledge 2001 xxix, 634p $315; pa $80   **952.04**

1. Reference books 2. Japan -- Civilization -- Encyclopedias
ISBN 0-415-14344-6; 0-415-48152-X pa

LC 2001-19655

This reference includes "more than 750 topical and bio-graphical entries exploring the 'lived experience of every-day Japanese life' for the postwar period. . . . [It includes] articles on minorities in Japan and the Japanese Diaspora in the Americas. Most notably . . . [this] features excellent coverage of Japanese women and consistently introduces critical feminist perspectives that are rarely seen in other reference works on Japan. . . . [This] is eminently readable . . . an ideal reference tool." Am Ref Books Annu, 2003

Includes bibliographical references

Richie, Donald

The **Japan** journals, 1947-2004; edited by Leza Lowitz. Stone Bridge Press 2004 494p il $29.95   **952.04**

1. Japan -- Civilization

ISBN 1-88065-691-4

LC 2004-16239

"The material in this volume was extracted and organized by Lowitz from previously unpublished sporadic diaries and jottings. They give a running commentary on Japan's rise from wartime destitution into the rich society of the 1980s boom, then its development into overbuilt and washed out postmodern complacency. There is some personal trivia, but most entries are alert and sometimes surprising glimpses of modern Japanese writers and filmmakers." Libr J

953   Arabian Peninsula and adjacent areas

Krane, Jim

City of gold; Dubai and the dream of capitalism. St. Martin's Press 2009 356p il map $27.99   **953**

1. Dubai (United Arab Emirates)

ISBN 9780312535742

LC 2009-13188

The author "traces the historical roots and economic and political changes of 'a small Arab village that grew into a big city' and profiles the members of the ruling royal fam-ily—Sheikh Rashid, Sheikh Zayed, and Sheikh Moham-med—whose vision brought Dubai to where it is today. . . . This landmark work is recommended to those interested in the history, politics, and economics of the Middle East; an excellent choice for anyone who wishes to learn more about Dubai." Libr J

Includes bibliographical references

Theroux, Peter

Sandstorms : days and nights in Arabia. Norton 1990 281p hardcover o.p. pa $13.95   **953**

1. Arab countries -- Description

ISBN 0-393-30797-2 pa

LC 89-28609

The author "recounts his experiences in the Middle East of the 1980s. The author went to Egypt to teach English and wound up chronicling the disappearance of Lebanon's Shia Iman Moussa Sadr. But Sandstorms is the human side of an American in Arabia. . . . Theroux's Arabia is rough but unde-niably real, poignant and elemental." Libr J

953.8   Saudi Arabia

House, Karen Elliott

On Saudi Arabia; its people, past, religion, fault lines--and future. Karen Elliott House. 1st ed. Alfred A. Knopf 2012 x, 308 p.p ill., map (hardcover) $28.95   **953.8**

1. Saudi Arabia -- History 2. Saudi Arabia -- Politics and government 3. Saudi Arabia -- Religion 4. Saudi Arabia -- Civilization 5. Saudi Arabia -- Social life and customs

ISBN 0307272168; 9780307272164

LC 2012018977

This book, by Pulitzer Prize-winning reporter Karen El-liott House, "explores all facets of life in . . . [Saudi Arabia]: its tribal past, its complicated present, its precarious future. Through observation, anecdote, extensive interviews, and analysis Karen Elliot House navigates the maze in which Saudi citizens find themselves trapped and reveals the mys-terious nation that is the world's largest exporter of oil, criti-cal to global stability, and a source of Islamic terrorists." (Publisher's note)

Includes bibliographical references (p. 281-289)

Lacey, Robert

Inside the Kingdom; kings, clerics, modernists, terrorists, and the struggle for Saudi Arabia. Viking 2009 404p il map $27.95   **953.8**

1. Saudi Arabia -- Social conditions

ISBN 978-0-670-02118-5; 0-670-02118-0

LC 2009-08367

Sequel to The kingdom (1982)

The author's "eye for sweeping trends and the telling de-tail combined with the depth, breadth and evenhandedness of his research makes for an indispensable guide." Publ Wkly

Includes bibliographical references

Wynbrandt, James

A **brief** history of Saudi Arabia; foreword by Fawaz A. Gerges. 2nd ed; Facts On File 2010 364p il map (Brief history) $49.50; pa $19.95   **953.8**

1. Saudi Arabia -- History

ISBN 978-0-8160-7876-9; 978-0-8160-8250-6 pa

LC 2010-5466

First published 2004

This history of Saudi Arabia covers "pre-Islamic Arabia; Bedouin society and culture; the birth and spread of Islam; the development of and philosophy behind Wahhabism; the origins of House Saud; Saudi Arabia's role in the Middle East; Saudi Arabia's relationship to the United States; the battle between conservative and progressive elements in the monarchy today; [and] the reign of King Abdullah." Pub-lisher's note

Includes glossary and bibliographical references

954 India and neighboring south Asian countries

Dalrymple, William
White Mughals; love and betrayal in the eighteenth-century India. Viking 2003 xlvii, 459p il map $34.95; pa $16 **954**
1. British -- India
ISBN 0-670-03184-4; 0-14-200412-X pa
LC 2002-191082
James Kirkpatrick was the Resident of the East India Company in Hyderabad. This book documents his marriage to Khair-un-Nissa, a Mughal aristocrat
This "book, ambitious in scope and rich in detail, demonstrates that a century before Kipling's 'never the twain'— and two centuries before neocons and radical Islamists trumpeted the clash of civilizations—the story of the Westerner in Muslim India was one not of conquest but of appreciation, adaptation, and seduction." New Yorker
Includes bibliographical references

Hardy, Justine
In the valley of mist; Kashmir: one family in a changing world. Free Press 2009 209p il map $25 **954**
1. Jammu and Kashmir (India)
ISBN 978-1-4391-0289-3; 1-4391-0289-9
LC 2008-55093
The author "channels the story of Kashmir's dark transformation from an idyllic place . . . of beauty and freedom to a realm of chaos and bloodshed through the lives of one family, the Dars. . . . Hardy's intimate and dramatic chronicle clarifies and humanizes Kashmir's torments, which are of grave global consequence." Booklist

Lapierre, Dominique
The **City** of Joy. Warner Books 1991 528p il pa $7.99 **954**
1. Calcutta (India) -- Social conditions
ISBN 0-446-35556-9
Original French edition, 1985
An account of life in the most squalid of Calcutta's slums, Anand Nagar (The City of Joy). The author focuses on the lives of a rickshaw driver, a Polish Catholic priest, an American doctor and an Assamese nurse.

McLeod, John
The **history** of India. Greenwood Press 2002 xx, 223p (Greenwood histories of the modern nations) $39.95 **954**
1. Mogul Empire 2. India -- History -- 1526-1765
ISBN 0-313-31459-4
LC 2002-276829
The author presents "in broad outlines some of the major events and episodes that make up India's history. . . . This is a useful compilation of important facts relating to Indian history. Its strength lies primarily in the last six chapters in which brief narratives of the struggle for independence and post-independence India down to the close of the twentieth century are nicely presented. All in all, this is a book that

all libraries should have." Recomm Ref Books for Small & Medium-sized Libr & Media Cent, 2003
Includes bibliographical references

Mehta, Suketu
★ **Maximum** city; Bombay lost and found. Alfred A. Knopf 2004 542p $27.95 **954**
1. Bombay (India)
ISBN 0-375-40372-8
LC 2004-48969
The author "explores various aspects of Bombay life, from setting up residence to exploring the hugely successful domestic film industry; from detailing Bombay's sex industry to profiling the reasons behind India's own 'September 11,' the 1993 riots and bombings that exposed a vast enmity between extremist Hindus and Muslims. . . . Mehta delivers a fresh and unblinking look at contemporary Bombay." Booklist

Miller, Sam
Delhi; adventures in a megacity. St. Martin's Press 2010 291p il map $25.99 **954**
1. India -- Social life and customs 2. Delhi (India) -- Description and travel
ISBN 978-0-312-61237-5
LC 2010-13043
First published 2009 in the United Kingdom
The author "presents a highly entertaining and witty account of a walking tour of Delhi. He describes 12 walks that begin in the center of the city and proceed outward to the satellite towns at the outskirts. Miller's portrayal of the changing landscape and street life is engrossing." Libr J

Rashid, Ahmed
Descent into chaos; the US and the failure of nation building in Pakistan, Afghanistan, and Central Asia. Viking 2008 lviii, 484p il map $27.95; pa $18 **954**
1. Pakistan -- Politics and government 2. Afghanistan -- Politics and government 3. Central Asia -- Foreign relations -- United States 4. United States -- Foreign relations -- Central Asia
ISBN 978-0-670-01970-0; 0-670-01970-4; 978-0-14-311557-1 pa; 0-14-311557-X pa
LC 2008-02949
"While Iraq continues to attract most of American media and military might, Rashid argues that Pakistan and Afghanistan are where the conflict will finally be played out and that these failing states pose a greater threat to global security than the Middle East." N Y Times Book Rev
This is a "lucid, insightful, and highly readable tome on the existent and emergent threats in Central Asia." Choice
Includes bibliographical references

Roy, Arundhati
Walking with the comrades. Penguin Books 2011 220p il map pa $15 **954**
1. Terrorism 2. Atrocities 3. Guerrillas 4. Social conflict 5. India -- Politics and government
ISBN 978-0-14-312059-9
LC 2011039307

The author "exposes the violent contradictions of India's economic miracle in this blistering critique of the Indian government's campaign against the Maoist insurgents in the country's central tribal lands encompassing several states. Roy, who recounts time spent on the move with a cadre of rebels, argues forcefully that Operation Green Hunt— launched by the state under the rubric of the threat of terrorism—is an all-out war to remove indigenous communities from lands already promised to corporations eager to exploit their extremely valuable resources. . . . Informed, impassioned, at times strident, and fleet and fascinating when describing life on the ground among the rebels, Roy's prose will both rouse and ruffle." Publ Wkly

Includes bibliographical references

Sen, Amartya Kumar

The **argumentative** Indian; writings on Indian history, culture, and identity. [by] Amartya Sen. Farrar, Straus and Giroux 2006 xx, 409p il   **954**

1. India -- Civilization
ISBN 0-374-10583-9

LC 2005-49460

The author "addresses the many aspects of Indian identity, from the Vedas (the sacred Hindu scriptures) to nuclear weapons, in order to build evidence for an inclusive, humane vision of India's potential." Libr J

"Sen's lucid reasoning and thoroughgoing humanism . . . ensure a lively and commanding defense of diversity and dialogue." Publ Wkly

Includes bibliographical references

Walsh, Judith E.

A **brief** history of India; 2nd ed.; Facts On File, Inc. 2010 414p il map (Brief history) $49.50; pa $19.95   **954**

1. India -- History
ISBN 978-0-8160-8143-1; 978-0-8160-8362-6 pa

LC 2010-26316

First published 2006
Includes bibliographical references

Wolpert, Stanley A.

A **new** history of India; 7th ed; Oxford University Press 2004 530p il map $63.95; pa $43   **954**

1. Mogul Empire
ISBN 0-19-516677-9; 0-19-516678-7 pa

LC 2003-53589

First published 1977. Periodically revised

A comprehensive survey of Indian history from its early beginnings to the present. Includes discussion of the assassination of Rajiv Gandhi; violence in Kashmir, Punjab, and Assam; and the effects of rural development

Includes bibliographical references

954.03   India--Period of British rule, 1785-1947

Chadha, Yogesh

Gandhi; a life. Wiley 1998 546p il hardcover o.p. pa $19.95   **954.03**

1. Authors 2. Journalists 3. Essayists 4. Pacifists 5. Memoirists 6. Political leaders 7. Writers on politics

8. India -- Politics and government
ISBN 0-471-35062-1 pa

LC 97-37406

First published 1997 in the United Kingdom with title: Rediscovering Gandhi

"Chadha reexamines Gandhi's life with an eye to restoring its complications and contradictions, noting that 'to suppress his weaknesses would be to undermine his strengths.' And he succeeds in his mission, presenting the great leader not as a holy man but as a humanist and politician." Booklist

Includes bibliographical references

Wolpert, Stanley A.

★ **Gandhi's** passion; the life and legacy of Mahatma Gandhi. [by] Stanley Wolpert. Oxford Univ. Press 2001 308p il hardcover o.p. pa $17.95 **954.03**

1. Authors 2. Journalists 3. Essayists 4. Pacifists 5. Memoirists 6. Political leaders 7. Writers on politics 8. India -- Politics and government
ISBN 0-19-513060-X; 0-19-515634-X pa

LC 00-45298

"From his pampered childhood to his ascetic final years, the text follows the Mahatma ('Great Soul') on a paradoxical pilgrimage in which the deliberate acceptance of suffering endowed him with the power he needed to challenge the leading politicians of Europe, Africa, and Asia." Booklist

Includes bibliographical references

954.04   India--1947-1971

French, Patrick

India; a portrait. Alfred A. Knopf 2011 398p il $30   **954.04**

1. India -- History -- 1947-
ISBN 978-0-307-27243-0; 0-307-27243-5

LC 2011-03921

This work "combines deep research about the country's history with a series of vignettes culled from French's street-level reporting. Taken together, his reading of seminal texts and his interviews with politicians, pimps, businessmen, laborers, farmers, scholars and people from all levels of India's caste system result in a fittingly vigorous and colorful book about what it means to live in India six decades after the nation freed itself from British rule." San Francisco Chron

Includes bibliographical references

Guha, Ramachandra

India after Gandhi; the history of the world's largest democracy. Ecco 2007 893p il map $34.95   **954.04**

1. India -- History -- 1947-
ISBN 978-0-06-019881-7; 0-06-019881-8

LC 2006-52180

This book documents India's transformation from a colonial state to independence.

The author "builds his story by making us witnesses of events as they occur, drawing on contemporary accounts. His voluminous account may seem daunting, but it is crucial for the understanding of modern India. . . . Guha is patient in his approach, gentle in his criticism, exasperated by what he does not like, and eclectic in drawing on evidence that supports his argument." New Statesman

Includes bibliographical references

Tharoor, Shashi

India; from midnight to the millennium. Arcade Pub. 1997 392p map hardcover o.p. pa $15.95 **954.04**

1. India -- History

ISBN 1-55970-384-9; 978-1-55970-803-6 pa; 1-55970-803-4 pa

LC 97-8376

This is an "economic, political, and sociological study of India since independence in 1947, considering such issues as centralization vs. federalism and pluralism vs. fundamentalism." Libr J

"Each telling anecdote illuminates some aspect of Indian culture, from politics to religion, creating a mosaic that reflects India's endless variations on the theme of life." Booklist

Nehru : the invention of India. Arcade Pub 2003 282p $24.95; pa $13.95 **954.04**

1. Prime ministers 2. Nonfiction writers 3. Prime ministers -- India

ISBN 1-559-70697-X; 1-559-70737-2 pa

LC 2003-58274

The author touches "on key points in Nehru's life: his English education, the importance of guidance he received from his father and Gandhi, his prison years during the drive for independence, and his administration of the new Indian republic. He neatly pulls together the essence of Nehru's beliefs in democratic institution building, pan-Indian secularism, Socialist democratic economy, and the foreign policy of nonalignment. . . . If readers could choose only one narrative about Nehru, this would suffice." Libr J

Includes bibliographical references

954.05 India--1971-

Deb, Siddhartha

The beautiful and the damned; Siddhartha Deb. Faber and Faber, Inc. 2011 253p. **954.05**

1. Journalism 2. Globalization 3. Cultural critique 4. India -- Social conditions 5. India -- Civilization -- 21st century 6. India -- Social conditions -- 21st century 7. India -- Economic conditions -- 21st century 8. India -- Politics and government -- 21st century

ISBN 9780865478732; 0865478627; 9780865478626

LC 2011024408

This book "examines India's many contradictions through various individual . . . perspectives. . . . [Author Siddhartha] Deb introduces the reader to an unforgettable group of Indians, including a Gatsby-like mogul in Delhi whose hobby is producing big-budget gangster films that no one sees; a wiry, dusty farmer named Gopeti whose village is plagued by suicides and was the epicenter of a riot; and a sad-eyed waitress named Esther who has set aside her dual degrees in biochemistry and botany to serve Coca-Cola to arms dealers at an upscale hotel called Shangri La." (Publisher's note)

Giridharadas, Anand

India calling; an intimate portrait of a nation's remaking. Times Books/Henry Holt and Co. 2011 273p $25; ebook $11.99 **954.05**

1. Journalists 2. India -- Civilization 3. Social change -- India 4. India -- Social conditions 5. India -- Civilization -- 1947- 6. India -- Description and travel 7. India -- Social life and customs 8. India -- Social conditions -- 1947- 9. National characteristics, East Indian

ISBN 0-8050-9177-7; 1-4299-5062-5 ebook; 978-0-8050-9177-9; 978-1-4299-5062-6 pa

LC 2010-18447

The author, who is "an American, traces his parents' journey from India." (N Y Times Book Rev) Index.

This "is a fine book, elegant, self-aware and unafraid of contradictions and complexity. Giridharadas captures fundamental changes in the nature of family and class relationships and the very idea of what it means to be an Indian." N Y Times Book Rev

Mishra, Pankaj

★ Temptations of the West; how to be modern in India, Pakistan, Tibet, and beyond. Farrar, Straus & Giroux 2006 323p $25 **954.05**

1. South Asia -- Description and travel

ISBN 0-374-17321-4; 978-0-374-17321-0

LC 2006-11987

"It is impossible in a short form to do justice to the density and complexity of . . . [the author's] arguments, to his comprehensive illustrations, to his scathing demolition of the comfort zones of both East and West, and to the intrepid and endlessly questioning spirit which lies behind his book." N Y Rev Books

954.9 Other jurisdictions

Napoli, Lisa

Radio Shangri-La; what I learned in the happiest kingdom on earth. Crown Publishers 2010 xx, 277p $25 **954.9**

1. Bhutan -- Description and travel

ISBN 978-0-307-45302-0; 978-0-307-45304-4 ebook

LC 2009-49176

"The author provides a readable account of her life-changing decision to leave the comforts of her cosmopolitan Los Angeles life and serve as a volunteer at Kuzoo FM 90, a radio station for young people in the remote Himalayan kingdom of Bhutan. Disillusioned with her love life and fed up with her job as a public-radio commentator, Napoli took a chance on a mysterious stranger's offer of unpaid work in a country where '[b]eing, not having' and '[h]appiness above wealth' were the prevailing national philosophies. . . . The author's authentic voice and light, pleasant cultural insights make for a refreshingly uplifting book." Kirkus

Includes bibliographical references

954.91   Pakistan

Gull, Imtiaz

The **most** dangerous place; Pakistan's lawless frontier. Viking 2010 xxx, 282p map   **954.91**
1. Terrorism 2. Taliban 3. Al Qaeda (Organization)
ISBN 0-670-02225-X; 978-0-670-02225-0

LC 2010-01898

First published 2009 in India with title: The al Qaeda connection

Gul "tracks the Taliban and al-Qaeda insurgents into the mountainous tribal regions to investigate the tangle of perilous allegiances. The destabilized Afghanistan-Pakistan border region is constantly in the news as the Obama administration attempts to flush out the militants using the area as a base to train soldiers and launch terrorist attacks. In a dense, timely study, the author investigates the complicated makeup of these groups. . . . Informational rather than didactic, Gul's insider take will serve as an excellent resource."

Gul "tracks the Taliban and al-Qaeda insurgents into the mountainous tribal regions to investigate the tangle of perilous allegiances. The destabilized Afghanistan-Pakistan border region is constantly in the news as the Obama administration attempts to flush out the militants using the area as a base to train soldiers and launch terrorist attacks. In a dense, timely study, the author investigates the complicated makeup of these groups. . . . Informational rather than didactic, Gul's insider take will serve as an excellent resource." Kirkus

Includes bibliographical references

Inskeep, Steve

Instant city; life and death in Karachi. Penguin Press 2011 284p il map $27.95   **954.91**
1. Karachi (Pakistan) -- Social conditions 2. Karachi (Pakistan) -- Description and travel
ISBN 978-1-59420-315-2; 1-59420-315-6

LC 2011020673

Analyzes the growing metropolis of Karachi, Pakistan, including the importance of regional stability to American security interests, the terrorist bombing of a Shia religious procession, and the challenging religious, ethnic, and political divides.

"This is an intimate book about a megacity, and Inskeep succeeds by keeping his ambitions modest. By trying to understand the horrific event of one particular day, he keeps his narrative well paced and full of small surprises. The book sparkles when Inskeep takes an unexpected turn and follows a stranger, or when he tracks down a new trend to illuminate a new facet of the city." Publ Wkly

Includes bibliographical references

Lieven, Anatol

Pakistan; a hard country. PublicAffairs 2011 558p il $35   **954.91**
1. Pakistan -- History 2. Pakistan -- Social conditions 3. Pakistan -- Politics and government 4. Pakistan -- Politics and government -- 1988-
ISBN 978-1-61039-021-7; 1-61039-021-0

LC 2011-921821

"Lieven breaks down his study by specific region; considers the structures of justice, religion, the military and politics in turn; and, finally, in a skillful, insightful synthesis, addresses the history of and issues concerning the Taliban, both Pakistani and Afghani. A well-reasoned, welcome resource for Western 'experts' and lay readers alike." Kirkus

Schmidle, Nicholas

To live or to perish forever; two tumultuous years in Pakistan. Henry Holt and Co. 2009 254p il map $25   **954.91**
1. Pakistan -- Description and travel 2. Pakistan -- Politics and government
ISBN 978-0-8050-8938-7; 0-8050-8938-1

LC 2008-48373

"Schmidle offers a gripping, grim account of his two years as a journalism fellow in Pakistan, where his travels took him into the most isolated and unfriendly provinces, and into the thick of interests and beliefs that impede that nation's peace and progress. . . . Schmidle has, with this effort, established himself as a fresh, eloquent and informed contributor to the ongoing dialogue regarding Pakistan, terrorism and the strategic importance of engaging Central Asia in efforts toward peace and stability." Publ Wkly

954.93   Sri Lanka

Deraniyagala, Sonali

Wave; Sonali Deraniyagala. Alfred A. Knopf 2013 240 p. (hardcover) $24   **954.93**
1. Grief 2. Indian Ocean earthquake and tsunami, 2004 3. Bereavement 4. Parents -- Death 5. Children -- Death 6. Widows -- Biography 7. Indian Ocean Tsunami, 2004 8. Disaster victims -- Sri Lanka -- Biography
ISBN 0307962695; 9780307962690

LC 2012040980

This book offers author Sonali Deraniyagala's experience coping with the loss of her parents, husband, and two young sons, who perished in the "Indian Ocean tsunami that broke loose on December 26, 2004" and "killed something like 230,000 people." This is "an account of her coping with her grief while also celebrating the memories of those she loved. . . . She ranges over her childhood in Colombo, meeting her English husband at Cambridge, and the birth of her children." (Library Journal)

955   Iran

Follett, Ken

On wings of eagles. New American Library 1984 415p il pa $7.99   **955**
1. Iran hostage crisis, 1979-1981
ISBN 0-451-16353-2; 978-0-451-16353-0
First published 1983 by Morrow

The author "recounts the efforts of successful Texas industrialist Ross Perot to rescue from a Teheran jail two senior corporate executives arrested during the anti-American and revolutionary period in Iran in 1979." Libr J

Housden, Roger

Saved by beauty; an American romantic in Iran. Broadway Books 2011 290p map $24; ebook $11.99 **955**

1. Iran -- Description and travel 2. Iran -- Social life and customs

ISBN 978-0-307-58773-2; 978-0-307-58775-6 ebook

LC 2011003323

The author "documents his travels to Iran in late 2008 and early 2009. The narrative flows seamlessly as the author visits Tehran, paradise gardens in Shiraz, the Pasargadae archaeological site where Cyrus the Great is buried, Persepolis, the Jewish quarter in Yazd, Esfaha-n, Sanandaj, Mashhad, Neysha-bur, Tu-s, Kermanshah, Ahvaz, and Turkey's Bursa and Konya, as well as surrounding settlements, plains, deserts, and mountainous areas. . . . Poetry lovers and adventurers alike will appreciate this work." Libr J

Mackey, Sandra

The **Iranians**; Persia, Islam, and the soul of a nation. W. Scott Harrop, research assistant. Dutton 1996 xxii, 426p maps hardcover o.p. pa $15.95 **955**

1. Iran -- Politics and government

ISBN 04-522-7563-6 pa

LC 95-44135

The author presents "information on Iranian civilization from Cyrus the Great to the present. Throughout this turbulent history of invasions and conquerors, the Persian soul, with its foundations in the Zoroastrian concept of justice overlaid with Shia Islam, has steadfastly endured. Since many Westerners had little familiarity with Iran until the overthrow of the Shah in 1979, this very readable book provides a perspective on what led up to those events, what is happening in Iran today, and how the current situation is likely to affect the future of Iran and its relationship with the West." Libr J

Majd, Hooman

The **Ayatollah** begs to differ; the paradox of modern Iran. Doubleday 2008 272p il $24.95 **955**

1. Iran -- Description and travel 2. Iran -- Politics and government

ISBN 978-0-385-52334-9; 0-385-52334-3

LC 2008-4648

The son of an Iranian diplomat and the grandson of an ayatollah grew up in exile, yet he also remained closely attached to his homeland. Majd's reports on his travels throughout Iran try to explain the economic, political, and social forces that lie at its heart, and to show the paradoxes of the Iranian character that have baffled Americans.

The author's "witty and captivating book makes it possible for a nonexpert to appreciate the multiple layers of sociocultural factors that define today's Iran." Libr J

Includes bibliographical references

Peterson, Scott

Let the swords encircle me; Iran--a journey behind the headlines. Simon & Schuster 2010 732p il $32; ebook $16.99 **955**

1. Iran -- History -- 1979- 2. Iran -- Social conditions 3. Iran -- Politics and government 4. Iran -- Foreign relations -- United States 5. United States -- Foreign relations -- Iran

ISBN 978-1-4165-9728-5; 978-1-4165-9739-1 ebook

LC 2010-17761

"Reading 'Let the Swords Encircle Me' is like taking a seminar on modern Iran with a patient guide who knows and loves both Iran and the US, and wants only for them to reconcile. The book's deep understanding of the nuances and many shades of Iran are valuable." Christ Sci Monit

Includes bibliographical references

Wright, Robert A.

Our man in Tehran; the true story behind the secret mission to save six Americans during the Iran Hostage Crisis and the foreign ambassador who worked with the CIA to bring them home. [by] Robert Wright. Other Press ed.; Other Press 2011 xxvi, 406p il $25.95; ebook $25.95 **955**

1. Escapes 2. Diplomats 3. Iran hostage crisis, 1979-1981 4. Iran -- Foreign relations -- United States 5. United States -- Foreign relations -- Iran

ISBN 978-1-59051-413-9; 978-1-59051-414-6 ebook

LC 2010-20376

First published 2010 in Canada

"Much of Iran's relationship with the West—and their mutual antipathy—stems from the muddled events of a single day: November 4, 1979, when Iranian militants overran the U.S. embassy in Tehran, launching a 444-daylong hostage drama. What's often forgotten is that six Americans evaded their would-be captors and were protected and eventually extracted from Iran by Canadian diplomats. In this fascinating account of spycraft and compassion, Wright . . . puts newly unclassified documents to excellent use in recounting how Canadian ambassador Ken Taylor hid the Americans who had slipped out a side door and gathered intelligence for the U.S. government." Publ Wkly

Includes bibliographical references

955.05 Iran--1906-2005

Abrahamian, Ervand

The **coup**; 1953, the CIA, and the roots of modern U.S.-Iranian relations. Ervand Abrahamian. The New Press 2013 277 p. (hardcover) $26.95 **955.05**

1. Iran -- History -- 1941-1979 2. United States. Central Intelligence Agency 3. Great Britain -- Foreign relations -- Iran 4. Iran -- Foreign relations -- Great Britain 5. Iran -- Foreign relations -- United States 6. Iran -- History -- Coup d'état, 1953 7. United States -- Foreign relations -- Iran 8. Iran -- Politics and government -- 1941-1979 9. United States. Central Intelligence Agency -- History -- 20th century 10. Petroleum industry and trade -- Political aspects -- Iran -- History -- 20th century 11. Petroleum industry and trade -- Political aspects -- United States -- History -- 20th century

ISBN 1595588264; 9781595588265

LC 2012031402

This book, by Ervand Abrahamian, profiles how "in August 1953, the U.S. Central Intelligence Agency orchestrated the swift overthrow of Iran's democratically elected leader and installed Muhammad Reza Shah Pahlavi in his place.

Over the next twenty-six years, the United States backed the unpopular, authoritarian shah. . . . The blowback was almost inevitable, as this new and revealing history of the coup and its consequences shows." (Publisher's note)

Includes bibliographical references and index

Baglio, Matt

Argo; how the CIA and Hollywood pulled off the most audacious rescue in history. Antonio J. Mendez and Matt Baglio. Viking 2012 viii, 310 p.p $26.95 **955.05**

1. Iran -- History 2. United States -- History 3. United States -- Foreign relations -- Iran 4. Iran Hostage Crisis, 1979-1981 5. Canada -- Foreign relations -- Iran 6. Iran -- Foreign relations -- Canada 7. United States. Central Intelligence Agency 8. Diplomats -- United States -- History -- 20th century

ISBN 0670026220; 9780670026227

LC 2012014991

In this book, Antonio J. Mendez tells the story of "November 4, 1979, [when] Iranian militants stormed the American embassy in Tehran and captured dozens of American hostages. . . . Disguising himself as a Hollywood producer, and supported by [under]cover CIA operatives . . . Mendez traveled to Tehran under the guise of scouting locations for a fake science fiction film called 'Argo.' While pretending to find the perfect film backdrops, Mendez and a colleague succeeded in contacting the escapees, and smuggling them out of Iran." (Publisher's note)

Includes bibliographical references and index.

Wright, Robin

The last great revolution; turmoil and transformation in Iran. Knopf 2000 xxiv, 339p il hardcover o.p. pa $14 **955.05**

1. Iran -- Politics and government

ISBN 0-375-40639-5; 0-375-70630-5 pa

LC 99-27798

The author "talks to journalists, educators, politicians, entertainers, and others to present a picture of the cultural and political changes in Iran: the softening of cultural restrictions, the empowerment of women, and the modernization of industry and the economy." Booklist

Includes bibliographical references

956 Middle East (Near East)

Armenian Golgotha; translated by Peter Balakian with Aris Sevag. Alfred A. Knopf 2009 509p il map $35 **956**

1. Genocide 2. Armenian massacres, 1915-1923 3. Priests 4. Genocide -- Turkey 5. Biography, Individual 6. Armenian massacres, 1915-1923 -- Personal narratives

ISBN 0-307-26288-X; 978-0-307-26288-2

LC 2008-39957

This is a first-person account of the Armenian massacre. Chronology. Glossary. Bibliography. Index.

"On the night of April 24, 1915, Grigoris Balakian, an Armenian priest, and more than two hundred other Armenian politicians and intellectuals were arrested in Constantinople. Soon, Armenians across Turkey were massacred or forced to join a death march to the desert of Der Zor. Balakian walked among the displaced for months before he fled, disguising himself variously as a German engineer, a soldier, and a worker in the vineyards; he began this book while in hiding. (It was published in Armenian in 1922 and in 1959; the translator is Balakian's great-nephew.) Both a memoir and an attempt at a history of the genocide, it assumes considerable familiarity with Ottoman politics, but remains fascinating firsthand testimony to a monumental crime." New Yorker

Includes bibliographical references

Barr, James

A line in the sand. W. W. Norton & Co. 2012 xii, 450 p ill. 12 p. of plates **956**

1. Diplomats 2. Middle East 3. World War, 1914-1918 4. Sykes-Picot Agreement 5. France -- Foreign relations -- Great Britain 6. Great Britain -- Foreign relations -- France 7. Middle East -- Foreign relations -- 20th century 8. Middle East -- Politics and government -- 1914-1945

ISBN 1-84737-453-0 Simon & Schuster; 978-1-84737-453-0 Simon & Schuster; 9780393070651 W.W. Norton & Co. 2012; 0393070654 W.W. Norton & Co., 2012

LC 2011038037

"In 1916, in the middle of the First World War, two men secretly agreed to divide the Middle East between them. Sir Mark Sykes was a visionary politician; François Georges-Picot a diplomat with a grudge. The deal they struck, which was designed to relieve tensions that threatened to engulf the Entente Cordiale, drew a line in the sand from the Mediterranean to the Persian frontier. Territory north of that stark line would go to France; land south of it, to Britain. . . . Their pact survived the war to form the basis for the postwar division of the region into five new countries Britain and France would rule. The creation of Britain's mandates of Palestine, Transjordan and Iraq, and France's in Lebanon and Syria, made the two powers uneasy neighbours for the following thirty years. . . . [This book] tells the story of the . . . era when Britain and France ruled the Middle East. It [aims to] explain . . . how the old antagonism between these two powers inflamed the . . . modern rivalry between the Arabs and the Jews, and ultimately led to war between the British and the French in 1941 and between the Arabs and the Jews in 1948." (Publisher's note)

Includes bibliographical references and index.

Churchill, Buntzie Ellis

Notes on a century; reflections of a Middle East historian. Bernard Lewis ; with Buntzie Ellis Churchill. Viking 2012 388 p. **956**

1. Autobiographies 2. International relations 3. Middle East -- Politics and government 4. Middle East -- Historiography 5. Middle East -- History -- 20th century 6. Middle East -- History -- 21st century 7. Middle East specialists -- Great Britain -- Biography

ISBN 0670023531; 9780670023530

LC 2011049267

This memoir by political consultant and historian Bernard Lewis provides the author's personal reflections on his international career and his views on the major themes of world politics spanning "World War II, up through the Arab Spring. . . . Lewis . . . was the first to warn of a coming 'clash of civilizations,' a term he coined in 1957, and has led [a] life, as much a political actor as a scholar of the Middle East." (Publisher's note)

Includes bibliographical references and index.

Congressional Quarterly, Inc.

★ The **Middle** East; 11th ed; CQ Press 2007 xix, 663p il map $70; pa $46.95   956

1. Middle East -- Politics and government

ISBN 978-0-87289-368-9; 0-87289-368-5; 978-0-87289-369-6 pa; 0-87289-369-3 pa

LC 2007-19956

First published 1974. Periodically revised

Covers topics such as oil, Islam, the Arab-Israeli conflict, the Persian Gulf, and the arms trade in the Middle East. Also presents profiles of Middle Eastern nations and twentieth-century leaders and includes documents such as UN resolutions and peace treaties

Includes bibliographical references

de Bellaigue, Christopher

Rebel land; unraveling the riddle of history in a Turkish town. Penguin Press 2010 270p il map $25.95   956

1. Genocide 2. Armenian massacres, 1915-1923 3. Turkey -- History

ISBN 978-1-59420-252-0; 1-59420-252-4

First published 2009 in the United Kingdom

This is "a revealing and stunning examination of Turkey's past and present that also poses interesting questions about ethnic and national identity." Booklist

Includes bibliographical references

Encyclopedia of the modern Middle East & North Africa; Philip Mattar, editor in chief. 2nd ed; Macmillan Reference USA 2004 4v il map set $475   956

1. Reference books 2. Middle East -- Encyclopedias 3. North Africa -- Encyclopedias

ISBN 0-02-865769-1

LC 2004-5650

First published 1996

"For current, accurate, and non-partisan information on the Middle East and North Africa, this excellent reference set . . . will answer basic questions and serve as a starting point for research on the region." Libr Media Connect

Includes bibliographical references

Finkel, Caroline

★ **Osman's** dream; the story of the Ottoman Empire, 1300-1923. Basic Books 2006 660p il map   956

1. Turkey -- History 2. Turkey -- History -- Ottoman Empire, 1288-1918

ISBN 0465023967; 9780465023967

First published 2005 in the United Kingdom

This is a history "of the Ottoman Empire from its origins in the thirteenth century through its destruction on the battlefields of World War I." (Publisher's note)

This is a history "of the Ottoman Empire from its origins in the thirteenth century through its destruction on the battlefields of World War I." Publisher's note

Includes bibliographical references

Friedman, Thomas L.

From Beirut to Jerusalem. Farrar, Straus & Giroux 1989 541p il maps $32   956

1. Jewish-Arab relations 2. Lebanon -- History 3. Israel -- Politics and government 4. Middle East -- Politics and government

ISBN 0-374-15895-9

LC 92-148666

First published 1989

The author presents an account of the political situation in the Middle East as he witnessed it in his years as a reporter in Lebanon and Jerusalem

"When recounting his frequently harrowing experiences in that troubled region, Friedman can be absolutely riveting; similarly, his historical insights, his explanation of the root causes of the Arab-Israeli conflict, and his impressions of people and places in the Holy Land never fail to fascinate." Booklist

Herzog, Chaim

The **Arab** -Israeli wars; war and peace in the Middle East from the 1948 War of Independence to the present. updated by Shlomo Gazit; introduction by Isaac Herzog and Michael Herzog. 2nd ed, rev and updated; Vintage Books 2005 476p il pa $16.95   956

1. Jewish-Arab relations

ISBN 1-4000-7963-2

LC 2005-280207

First published 1982 by Random House

This book traces "the Arab-Israeli wars and military conflicts from the 1948 War of Independence through the 1973 Yom Kippur War." Libr J

Includes bibliographic references

Hiro, Dilip

The **essential** Middle East; a comprehensive guide. Dilip Hiro. 1st Carroll & Graf ed.; Carroll & Graf 2003 639p il map pa $17.95   956

1. Middle East

ISBN 0786712694

LC 2003055293

First published 1996 by St. Martin's Press with title: A dictionary of the Middle East

"In more than 1,000 alphabetically arranged entries, varying in length from a few lines to a few pages, Hiro covers more than 150 personalities in politics, business, culture, and religion; places of religious and cultural significance; oil and other minerals; political and religious sects; economic infrastructure; and political and religious ideologies." Booklist

Lewis, Bernard, 1916-

The **Middle** East; a brief history of the last 2,000 years. Scribner 1995 433p il hardcover o.p. pa $16 　　**956**

1. Middle East -- History

ISBN 0-684-80712-2; 0-684-83280-1 pa

LC 96-4384

"Lewis has chosen to accentuate the social, economic, and cultural changes that have occurred over 20 centuries. He ranges from seemingly trivial concerns (changes in dress and manners in an Arab coffeehouse) to earth-shaking events (the Mongol conquest of Mesopotamia) in painting a rich, varied, and fascinating portrait of a region that is steeped in traditionalism while often forced by geography and politics to accept change." Booklist

Includes bibliographical references

What went wrong? Western impact and Middle Eastern response. Oxford Univ. Press 2002 180p il $23 　　**956**

1. Middle East -- History

ISBN 0-19-514420-1

LC 2001-36214

"Like many of Lewis's previous writings on this subject . . . this book will undoubtedly generate significant debate and disagreement among scholars regarding the author's analysis of Islamic responses to modernity and Westernization." Libr J

Includes bibliographical references

Meyer, Karl E.

Kingmakers; the invention of the modern Middle East. [by] Karl E. Meyer and Shareen Blair Brysac. Norton 2008 507p il map $27.95 　　**956**

1. Middle East -- History

ISBN 978-0-393-06199-4; 0-393-06199-X

LC 2008-07378

The authors "have written a timely and engrossing study of the men and women who were instrumental in giving birth to some of the nations, institutions, and chronic problems of the area." Booklist

Includes bibliographical references

Morris, Benny

Righteous victims; a history of the Zionist-Arab conflict, 1881-1998. Knopf 1999 751p hardcover o.p. pa $18 　　**956**

1. Israel-Arab conflicts 2. Jewish-Arab relations

ISBN 0-679-74475-4 pa

LC 98-42774

Morris traces the history of Arab-Israeli conflicts and examines major events and their aftereffects

"The author displays a remarkable grasp of the history of the Zionist-Arab conflict and an analytical style that is devoid of the polemics that have characterized so many books on this subject." Libr J

Includes bibliographical references

Sela, Avraham

The **Continuum** political encyclopedia of the Middle East; Avraham Sela, editor. rev and updated ed; Continuum 2002 944p maps $175 　　**956**

1. Middle East -- History 2. Middle East -- Politics and government

ISBN 0-8264-1413-3

LC 2001-8542

First published 1999 with title: The political encyclopedia of the Middle East

This "contains entries on countries ranging from Afghanistan to Yemen; political movements and leaders; major foreign nations that impact this area, such as the United States and Russia; religions and religious movements; and regional topics of concern including 'Oil,' 'Terrorism,' 'Water Politics,' and 'Women, Gender and Politics.'. . . Alphabetical entries range from a few paragraphs to lengthy commentaries. . . . Large libraries serving older students will find this a useful . . . source of objective information on the history and issues affecting the contemporary Middle East." SLJ

Includes bibliographical references

Wallach, Janet

Desert queen; the extraordinary life of Gertrude Bell: adventurer, adviser to kings, ally of Lawrence of Arabia. Talese 1996 xxv, 419p hardcover o.p. pa $15.95 　　**956**

1. Explorers 2. Travelers 3. Archeologists 4. Archaeologists 5. Women -- Travel

ISBN 0-385-47408-3; 978-1-4000-9619-0 pa; 1-4000-9619-7 pa

LC 95-44868

"High-spirited, outspoken, and self-reliant, . . . {Bell} was the first woman to earn a degree in history at Oxford, a skilled mountain climber and equestrienne, and an avid and fearless traveler who found her spiritual home in the deserts of Iraq and Arabia. . . . Fluent in Arabic and on good terms with powerful men, Bell became an invaluable asset to British intelligence and was drafted as a spy during World War I. . . . Wallach . . . brings the resolute Bell and her complex world vividly to life." Booklist

Includes bibliographical references

956.04　　Middle East--1945-1980

MacFarquhar, Neil

The **media** relations department of Hizbollah wishes you a happy birthday; unexpected encounters in the changing Middle East. PublicAffairs 2009 387p il map $26.95; pa $15.95 　　**956.04**

1. Middle East -- Description and travel 2. Middle East -- Politics and government

ISBN 978-1-58648-635-8; 978-1-58648-811-6 pa

LC 2009-2004

The author "offers something fresh and unexpected for readers steeped in a decade of news reports about suicide bombers, absolutist imams and tyrannical despots. . . . [This book] is MacFarquhar's effort to write a funny (yet penetrating) account about real Arabs—and a few Persians—struggling against long odds to bring their societies into the modern age. . . . For those who care about the Middle East and want to start listening to weak but growing voices calling for reform and modernization on local rather than Western terms, MacFarquhar's account is a fine place to begin." N Y Times Book Rev

Includes bibliographical references

Oren, Michael

Six days of war; June 1967 and the making of the modern Middle East. {by} Michael B. Oren. Oxford Univ. Press 2002 446p il $30   **956.04**
1. Israel-Arab War, 1967
ISBN 0-19-515174-7

         LC 2001-58823

This is a history of the June 1967 Arab-Israeli War

"What makes this book important is the breadth and depth of the research. Oren draws on archives, newly declassified documents, memoirs and interviews from Israel, America, Britain and what was then the Soviet Union." N Y Times Book Rev

Includes bibliographical references and index

Sacco, Joe

Footnotes in Gaza. Metropolitan Books 2009 418p il $29.95   **956.04**
1. Graphic novels 2. Massacres -- Graphic novels 3. Israel-Arab conflicts -- Graphic novels
ISBN 978-0-8050-7347-8; 0-8050-7347-7

         LC 2009-28433

"Cartoonist and journalist Joe Sacco is the world's foremost creator of 'comics journalism'—a contemporary field he basically invented. . . . [This] book, whose 'footnotes' refer both to facts and metaphorically to history's forgotten people, is about two massacres of Palestinians in the Gaza Strip in November 1956. . . . Very little has been written about either event. Sacco conducted extensive research of U.N. documents and other materials, and additionally set out to interview as many eyewitnesses as he could track down. This is really the heart of this moving, precisely drawn work." Time Out N Y

Includes bibliographical references

Shlaim, Avi

The **iron** wall; Israel and the Arab world since 1948. Norton 1999 704p il hardcover o.p. pa $17.95   **956.04**
1. Israel-Arab conflicts 2. Jewish-Arab relations 3. Israel -- Foreign relations
ISBN 0-393-32112-6 pa

         LC 99-23121

"A thorough analysis of Israel's relationships with the West as well as its neighbors from a controversial but thoughtful point of view." Booklist

Includes bibliographical references

Israel and Palestine; reappraisals, revisions, refutations. Verso 2009 392p map $34.95   **956.04**
1. Palestinian Arabs 2. Israel-Arab conflicts 3. Arab-Israeli conflict 4. Israel -- Politics and government
ISBN 978-1-84467-366-7

         LC 2009-455813

This volume presents "reflections on the causes and consequences of the Israel-Palestine conflict, by the author of

The Iron Wall [2000]. . . . Israel and Palestine assesses the impact of key political and intellectual figures, including Yasir Arafat and Ariel Sharon, Edward Said and Benny Morris; it also reexamines the United States' . . . role in the conflict, and explores [what Shlaim views as] the many missed opportunities for peace and progress in the region." (Publisher's note) Index.

The author, "an Israeli army veteran and international relations professor at Oxford University, offers a penetrating critique of Zionism in these reviews and essays collected from the last 30 years. He focuses on the three main watersheds—Israel's establishment, the Six Day War of 1967 and the Oslo Accords of 1993 and offers valuable commentary on current scholarship." Publ Wkly

Includes bibliographical references

Wright, Lawrence

★ **Thirteen** Days in September; Carter, Begin, and Sadat at Camp David. Lawrence Wright. Random House Inc"||"Alfred A. Knopf 2014 368 p. illustrations, maps $27.95   **956.04**
1. Egypt -- History 2. Arab countries -- Foreign relations -- Israel 3. Camp David Agreements (1978) 4. Israel-Arab War, 1973 -- Peace 5. United States -- Foreign relations -- 1977-1981
ISBN 0385352034; 9780385352031

         LC 2013497329

This book by Lawrence Wright is a "day-by-day account of the 1978 Camp David conference, when President Jimmy Carter persuaded Israeli prime minister Menachem Begin and Egyptian president Anwar Sadat to sign the first peace treaty in the modern Middle East, one which endures to this day. . . . Wright draws vivid portraits of other fiery personalities who were present at Camp David—including Moshe Dayan, Osama el-Baz, and Zbigniew Brzezinski." (Publisher's note)

"The author alternates among each day's events, biographical sketches of the central and supporting players, and insightful sociopolitical essays on the three leaders and their countries as he explains the process that led to a Nobel Peace Prize for Sadat and Begin and laid the foundation for the subsequent Oslo Accords." LJ

Includes bibliographical references and index

956.05 Middle East (Near East)--1980-

Hider, James

The **spiders** of Allah; travels of an unbeliever on the frontline of holy war. St. Martin's Griffin 2009 323p pa $14.95   **956.05**
1. Religion and politics 2. Religious fundamentalism 3. Terrorism -- Religious aspects 4. Middle East -- Description and travel 5. Middle East -- Politics and government
ISBN 978-0-312-56585-5; 0-312-56585-2

         LC 2009-7378

"A British journalist's firsthand account of fanaticism and bloodshed in the Middle East. . . . [The author] loosely examines the ways in which radical Islam and fundamentalist Christianity have continually warped and damaged an already difficult situation. . . . The author's dense, vivid descriptions, frequently steeped in irony and humor, make for a slow but powerful read." Kirkus

Miller, Aaron David

The **much** too promised land; America's elusive search for Arab-Israeli peace. Bantam Books 2008 407p $26; pa $16   **956.05**

1. Israel-Arab conflicts 2. Middle East -- Foreign relations -- United States 3. United States -- Foreign relations -- Middle East

ISBN 978-0-553-80490-4; 0-553-80490-1; 978-0-553-38414-7 pa; 0-553-38414-7 pa

LC 2007-38982

The author presents advice on Mideast policy after having been a participant in diplomatic efforts made by the administrations of Presidents Carter, Clinton, and George W. Bush.

This is "an indispensable guide to the recent history of American peacemaking efforts in the defining conflict of the Middle East." Bookforum

Includes bibliographical references

Pope, Hugh

Dining with al-Qaeda; three decades exploring the many worlds of the Middle East. Thomas Dunne Books/St. Martin's Press 2010 332p il map $26.99   **956.05**

1. Middle East -- Description and travel 2. Middle East -- Politics and government

ISBN 978-0-312-38313-8

Pope's "criticisms of the invasion and of Israel may grate some readers, but those interested in the interpersonal rather than the international will enjoy Pope's bold curiosity in meeting people all over the Middle East." Booklist

Sadat, Jehan

My hope for peace. Free Press 2009 208p map $25   **956.05**

1. Presidents 2. Islam and politics 3. Israel-Arab conflicts 4. Nobel laureates for peace

ISBN 978-1-4165-9219-8; 1-4165-9219-9

LC 2008-32100

"Widow of the assassinated Egyptian president Anwar Sadat, Jehan Sadat . . . fashions a gracious plea for better understanding between the East and West, especially in terms of the fundamentals of Islam and the derailed Middle East peace process. . . . Sadat provides an important, insistent voice for continued advancement in peace and social justice." Publ Wkly

Includes bibliographical references

Said, Edward W.

The **end** of the peace process; Oslo and after. Pantheon Bks. 2000 345p $27.50; pa $14   **956.05**

1. Israel-Arab conflicts 2. Jewish-Arab relations

ISBN 0-375-40930-0; 0-375-72574-1 pa

LC 99-44765

The author provides "analysis of the pitfalls of the Oslo agreement. Most of the essays in this collection have appeared in Cairo's al-Ahram Weekly and al-Hayat, London's Arabic-language daily. Each essay is Said's reflection on a dimension of the Palestinian predicament. . . . He is as criti-cal of the corruption, incompetence, and authoritarianism of the Palestinian Authority as he is of American and Israeli postures." Libr J

Shavit, Ari, 1957-

My promised land; Ari Shavit. Spiegel & Grau 2013 464 p.   **956.05**

1. Zionism 2. Israel -- History 3. Israel-Arab conflicts 4. Israel -- Politics and government 5. Arab-Israeli conflict

ISBN 9780385521703; 9780812984644

LC 2012046122

In this book, "Israeli journalist [Ari] Shavit . . . presents a history of and meditation on Zionism's successes and failures. . . .He traces the rise and demise of the kibbutzim, the 1948 displacement of Palestinians, the shock of 1967's Six-Day War victory, and the near defeat in the 1973 Yom Kippur War." He asks, "Can Israel fully integrate its Arab citizens, do justice to the Palestinians, and assure security in the face of looming military and demographic threats? " (Library Journal)

Stack, Megan

Every man in this village is a liar; an education in war. [by] Megan K. Stack. Doubleday 2010 257p $26.95   **956.05**

1. War and civilization 2. War on terrorism 3. Middle East -- Description and travel

ISBN 978-0-385-52716-3; 0-385-52716-0

LC 2009-34473

"As a 25-year-old correspondent for the Los Angeles Times, Stack covered Afghanistan in the days immediately following 9/11, then traveled to other outposts in the war on terror, from Iraq to Iran, Libya, and Lebanon. In a disquieting series of essays, Stack now takes readers deep into the carnage where she was exposed to the insanity, innocence, and inhumanity of wars with no beginning, middle, or end. Her soaring imagery sears itself into the brain, in acute and accurate tales that should never be forgotten by the wider world, and yet always are." Booklist

Wright, Robin

Dreams and shadows; the future of the Middle East. Penguin Press 2008 464p map $26.95 **956.05**

1. Middle East -- Politics and government

ISBN 1-59420-111-0; 978-1-59420-111-0

LC 2007-46267

"Absorbing accounts of brave activists are interwoven with relevant context and history in clear, vivid language. These elements make the book an engaging read, and a useful one for people who want to better understand this important part of the world." Christ Sci Monit

Includes bibliographical reference

956.1 Turkey

Goodwin, Jason

Lords of the horizons; a history of the Ottoman Empire. Holt & Co. 1999 351p il map hardcover o.p. pa $15 **956.1**

1. Turkey -- History -- Ottoman Empire, 1288-1918
ISBN 0-312-42066-8 pa

LC 98-41601

"A history of distinctive originality, Goodwin's account imbibes deeply of traveler's impressions and seeks to see and describe, rather than explain and judge. A valuable synthesis." Booklist

Includes bibliographical references

Kinzer, Stephen

Crescent and star; Turkey between two worlds. Farrar, Straus & Giroux 2001 252p hardcover o.p. pa $14 **956.1**

1. Turkey -- Politics and government
ISBN 0-374-52866-7 pa

LC 2001-23298

The author "gives a concise introduction to Turkey: Kemal Atatürk's post-WWI establishment of the modern secular Turkish state; the odd makeup of contemporary society, in which the military enforces Atatürk's reforms. In stylized but substantive prose, he devotes chapters to the problems he sees plaguing Turkish society: Islamic fundamentalism, frictions regarding the large Kurdish minority and the lack of democratic freedoms." Publ Wkly

Mango, Andrew

The **Turks** today; Andrew Mango. 1st ed; Overlook Press 2004 292p map $29.95; pa $17.95 **956.1**

1. Turkey -- History
ISBN 1-585-67615-2; 1-585-67756-6 pa

LC 2004-58339

"This fascinating and timely survey is both a political history and a cultural examination of a diverse, dynamic society." Booklist

Includes bibliographical references

956.6 Eastern Turkey

Akcam, Taner

A **shameful** act; the Armenian genocide and the question of Turkish responsibility. translated by Paul Bessemer. Metropolitan Books 2006 483p map $30 **956.6**

1. Genocide 2. Armenian massacres, 1915-1923
ISBN 0-8050-7932-7; 978-0-8050-7932-6

LC 2005-58401

Original Turkish edition, 1999

"This groundbreaking and lucid account by a prominent Turkish scholar speaks forcefully to all." Publ Wkly

Includes bibliographical references

Balakian, Peter

★ The **burning** Tigris; the Armenian genocide and America's response. HarperCollins 2003 xx, 475p il $26.95; pa $14.95 **956.6**

1. Genocide 2. Armenian massacres, 1915-1923
ISBN 0-06-019840-0; 0-06-055870-9 pa

LC 2003-44986

"The book's real power derives from the eyewitness accounts of the genocide itself. The sheer volume of outsiders' testimony that Balakian compiles, and the horrifying similarity of their observations of men, women and children beaten, tortured, burned to death in churches or sent out into the desert to starve, is an overwhelmingly convincing retort to genocide deniers." N Y Times Book Rev

Includes bibliographical references

956.7 Iraq

Allawi, Ali A.

The **occupation** of Iraq; winning the war, losing the peace. Yale University Press 2007 xxiv, 518p il map $28 **956.7**

1. Iraq War, 2003-2011 2. Iraq War, 2003- 3. Iraq -- Politics and government
ISBN 978-0-300-11015-9; 0-300-11015-4

LC 2006-39445

This "scholarly yet immensely readable exposition of Iraqi society and politics will likely become the standard reference on post-9/11 Iraq." Publ Wkly

Includes bibliographical references

Atkinson, Rick

Crusade; the untold story of the Persian Gulf War. Houghton Mifflin 1993 575p il maps hardcover o.p. pa $17 **956.7**

1. Persian Gulf War, 1991
ISBN 0-395-71083-9 pa

LC 93-14388

The author provides an "account of the actions and utterances of those who directed and fought in the Persian Gulf War. He also provides a thorough analysis of diplomatic and political aspects of the conflict. Rich in pertinent details, the powerful narrative leaps nimbly from Washington to Riyadh, from Baghdad to Kuwait City, and to various battle sites across the sands. Expectedly, the book's dominant personality is General H. Norman Schwarzkopf." Publ Wkly

Includes bibliographical references

In the company of soldiers; a chronicle of combat. H. Holt 2004 319p il maps $25; pa $14 **956.7**

1. Iraq War, 2003-2011 2. Iraq War, 2003- 3. United States -- Army -- Airborne Division, 101st
ISBN 0-8050-7561-5; 0-8050-7773-1 pa

LC 2003-67607

This is an eyewitness account of the war in Iraq. "In the spring of 2003, the author accompanied combat units to Iraq. He spent two months embedded with the 101st Airborne Division's headquarters staff, sharing their daily experiences from initial deployment out of Fort Campbell, KY, to overseas staging areas in Kuwait, and ultimately bearing witness to the unit's march on Baghdad. His view of the war was from a vantage point that permitted scrutiny of strategy, planning, and decision making at the senior command level." SLJ

Baker, James A.

★ The **Iraq** Study Group report; James A. Baker, III, and Lee H. Hamilton, co-chairs; [by] Lawrence S. Eagleburger . . . [et al.] Vintage Books 2006 142p map pa $10.95 **956.7**

1. Iraq War, 2003-2011 2. Iraq War, 2003- 3. War on terrorism 4. Military policy -- United States
ISBN 0-307-38656-2; 978-0-307-38656-4

LC 2006-474152

This book was "delivered by the Iraq Study Group to the Bush administration and simultaneously and inexpensively published for the general public. And there is no excuse for any public library, large or small, not to own a copy." Booklist

Bogdanos, Matthew

Thieves of Baghdad; one marine's passion for ancient civilizations and the journey to recover the world's greatest stolen treasures. [by] Matthew Bogdanos with William Patrick. Bloomsbury 2005 302p il map $25.95; pa $15.95 **956.7**

1. Iraq -- Antiquities 2. Iraq War, 2003- -- Destruction and pillage
ISBN 1-58234-645-3; 1-59691-146-8 pa

LC 2005-27652

Bogdanos "cuts through politics and hyperbole to tell an engrossing story abundant with history, colored by stories of brave Iraqis and Americans, and shaded with hope for the future." Publ Wkly

Includes bibliographical references

Campbell, Donovan

Joker one; a Marine platoon's story of courage, sacrifice, and brotherhood. Random House 2009 313p map hardcover o.p. pa $16.00 **956.7**

1. Memoirists 2. Marine corps officers 3. Beverage industry executives 4. Iraq War, 2003- -- Campaigns 5. United States -- Marine Corps 6. Iraq War, 2003- -- Personal narratives
ISBN 0812979567; 1400067731; 9780812979565 pa; 9781400067732

LC 2008-23896

This is an account of the seven-month street, to street, house to house battle fought in Ramadi by Marine platoon "Joker One" and the platoon's commander, Lt. Campbell.

This is "a harrowing narrative of [the author's] time as an infantry officer in Ramadi from March to September of 2004. . . . Campbell is a gifted writer who describes his own marines with deep care and attention." Washington Post

Chatterjee, Pratap

Halliburton's army; how a well-connected Texas oil company revolutionized the way America makes war. Nation Books 2009 284p $26.95 **956.7**

1. Halliburton Co. -- History
ISBN 978-1-56858-392-1

LC 2008-45876

This book "delves into the nebulous world of the Houston-based Halliburton corporation, tracing the company to its roots. . . . The author details the military contracting that largely funded the company through WWII and into the present-day war in Iraq, intertwining the company's history with the biographies of Dick Cheney, Donald Rumsfeld and other officials in the Bush administration. . . . Chatterjee keeps the pace of the narrative at a quick clip and nimbly marshals his extensive evidence to reveal—without sanctimony or stridency—Halliburton's record of corruption, political manipulation and human rights abuses." Publ Wkly

Includes bibliographical references

Cockburn, Patrick

The **occupation**. Norton 2006 229p map $24.95; pa $16.95 **956.7**

1. Iraq War, 2003-2011 2. Iraq War, 2003-
ISBN 1-84467-100-3; 978-1-84467-100-7; 1-84467-164-X pa; 978-1-84467-164-9 pa

LC 2006-19472

The author "takes the reader through the often bewildering array of forces and personalities that are shaping developments in post-Saddam Iraq and makes them comprehensible to Western readers. . . . Cockburn's account of the evolving conflict, the emergence of the resistance movement, the increasingly sectarian nature of the conflict, and the jockeying for power among the Shia, Sunni, and Kurdish communities is informed by his keen personal observations and understanding of the complexities and horrors of daily life in Iraq." Libr J

Includes bibliographical references

Danner, Mark

Torture and truth; America, Abu Ghraib, and the war on terror. New York Review Books 2004 580p il pa $19.95 **956.7**

1. Iraq War, 2003-2011 2. Political prisoners 3. Iraq War, 2003- 4. Abu Ghraib (Baghdad, Iraq: Prison)
ISBN 1-590-17152-7

LC 2004-22408

This is "a book of permanent value for the study of the Iraq war and of how apparently reasonable policies can be swept away by intense pressure, political or military, to produce a particular result." Publ Wkly

Etherington, Mark

Revolt on the Tigris; the Al-Sadr uprising and the governing of Iraq. Cornell University Press 2005 252p il maps $25 **956.7**

1. Iraq War, 2003-2011 2. Iraq War, 2003-
ISBN 0-8014-4451-9

LC 2005-49675

"Anyone seriously interested either in the future of that beleaguered nation or the possibilities of intelligent diplomacy would do well to read this firsthand account." Publ Wkly

Includes bibliographical references

Feuer, Alan

Over there; from the Bronx to Baghdad. Counterpoint 2005 283p $24   **956.7**

1. Iraq War, 2003- -- Personal narratives
ISBN 1-58243-327-5; 978-1-58243-327-1

LC 2004-27149

The author describes the events that occured after he "was bustled off to the Middle East to cover the invasion of Iraq. . . . This is one war memoir that demands to be read." Booklist

Filkins, Dexter

★ The **forever** war. Alfred A. Knopf 2008 368p il $25   **956.7**

1. Iraq War, 2003-2011 2. Iraq War, 2003-
ISBN 0-307-26639-7; 978-0-307-26639-2

LC 2008-11761

An account of the wars in Afghanistan and Iraq since the 1990s.

This is "wonderfully written and carefully researched [book]. . . . Filkins's gripping account gives readers a clear, though disturbing, view of what's happening on the ground in Iraq. And he has put himself in the middle of this madness to deliver a stunning and illuminating story." Christ Sci Monit

Includes bibliographical references

Finkel, David

The **good** soldiers. Sarah Crichton Books 2009 287p il $26   **956.7**

1. Iraq War, 2003-2011 2. Iraq War, 2003- 3. United States -- Army 4. Counterinsurgency -- Iraq 5. Soldiers -- United States 6. Iraq War, 2003- -- Campaigns 7. Soldiers -- United States -- Biography
ISBN 0-374-16573-4; 978-0-374-16573-4

LC 2009-19391

This is an account of the Iraq "war as experienced on the ground . . . by members of an Army battalion sent to Baghdad during the surge in 2007." (N Y Times (Late N Y Ed))

"Finkel's keen firsthand reportage, its grit and impact only heightened by the literary polish of his prose, gives us one of the best accounts yet of the American experience in Iraq." Publ Wkly

Frederick, Jim

Black hearts; one platoon's descent into madness in Iraq's triangle of death. Harmony Books 2010 439p il map $26   **956.7**

1. War crimes 2. Iraq War, 2003- -- Atrocities 3. United States -- Army -- Airborne Division, 101st
ISBN 978-0-307-45075-3; 0-307-45075-9

LC 2009-35537

"Frederick recounts the events leading up to and following the rape and murder of 14-year-old Iraqi Abeer al-Janabi and the subsequent murder of her family—parents Qassim and Fakhriah and six-year-old sister Hadeel—committed by members of one U.S. Army deployment in Iraq's 'Triangle of Death.'" Publ Wkly

Includes bibliographical references

Ghareeb, Edmund A.

Historical dictionary of Iraq; [by] Edmund A. Ghareeb; with the assistance of Beth K. Dougherty. Scarecrow Press 2004 lxxvi, 459p map (Historical dictionaries of Asia, Oceania, and the Middle East) $85   **956.7**

1. Iraq -- History
ISBN 0-8108-4330-7

LC 2003-11526

"This work should be a required purchase in academic, public, and even some high-school libraries." Booklist

Includes bibliographical references

Gordon, Michael R.

The **generals'** war; the inside story of the conflict in the Gulf. by Michael R. Gordon and Bernard E. Trainor. Little, Brown 1994 551p il map hardcover o.p. pa $18.95   **956.7**

1. Persian Gulf War, 1991
ISBN 0-316-32100-1 pa

LC 94-27144

"This cogent analysis provides several disturbing answers worthy of our attention." Libr J

Includes bibliographical references

Gordon, Michael R., 1951-

The **endgame**; the inside story of the struggle for Iraq, from George W. Bush to Barack Obama. Michael R. Gordon and Bernard E. Trainor. Pantheon Books 2012 xix, 779 p.p $35   **956.7**

1. Iraq War, 2003-2011 2. Iraq -- Politics and government 3. Iraq -- Foreign relations -- United States 4. United States -- Foreign relations -- Iraq 5. Insurgency -- Iraq 6. Iraq -- Ethnic relations 7. Iraq -- Relations -- United States 8. United States -- Relations -- Iraq 9. Iraq -- Politics and government -- 21st century 10. United States -- Armed Forces -- Iraq -- History 11. Iraq War, 2003-2011 -- Political aspects -- United States
ISBN 0307377229; 9780307377227

LC 2012024746

This book by Michael R. Gordon and Bernard E. Trainor presents a "chronicle of the Iraq War, emphasizing military maneuvers and Iraqi participation at all levels." It offers a "record of the nine years of conflict between the 'inside-out' versus 'outside-in' strategies of the U.S. government in dealing with Iraqi intransigence and conversion to democracy. . . . The authors take great pains to delineate the makeup of the Iraqi government in the prickly transition to sovereignty." (Kirkus Reviews)

Includes bibliographical references and index.

Gourevitch, Philip

Standard operating procedure; [by] Philip Gourevitch and Errol Morris. Penguin Press 2008 286p il $25.95   **956.7**

1. Prisoners of war 2. Iraq War, 2003-2011 3. Iraq War, 2003- 4. Abu Ghraib (Baghdad, Iraq: Prison)
ISBN 978-1-59420-132-5

LC 2008-10215

"This deft piece of reportage will stir readers' anger, at both the actions and the consequences. . . . A thorough, terrifying account of an American-made 'bedlam.'" Publ Wkly

Haass, Richard

War of necessity: war of choice; a memoir of two Iraq wars. by Richard N. Haass. Simon & Schuster 2009 336 p. $27   **956.7**

> 1. Iraq War, 2003- -- Causes 2. Persian Gulf War, 1991 -- Causes 3. United States -- Military policy 4. Iraq War, 2003- -- Political aspects 5. Persian Gulf War, 1991 -- Political aspects 6. Middle East -- Foreign relations -- United States 7. United States -- Foreign relations -- Middle East
> ISBN 978-1-4165-4902-4; 1-4165-4902-1; 1416549021; 9781416549024
>   LC 2009004495
> "A unique perspective on how war policy was formed by two very different presidents." Kirkus
> Includes bibliographical references and index

Kelly, Michael

Martyrs' Day; chronicle of a small war. 2nd Vintage Books ed; Vintage Bks. 2001 365p pa $14   **956.7**

> 1. Persian Gulf War, 1991 -- Personal narratives
> ISBN 1-4000-3036-6
>   LC 2002-524049
> First published 1993 by Random House
> "This eyewitness account differs from the many other books on the Persian Gulf War in that it deals primarily with the human-interest elements rather than military matters. Kelly, a journalist who traveled extensively in the countries that were affected by the Gulf conflict, chronicles the vagaries of the war and its impact on the lives of the people in a revealing and disturbing text." Libr J

Kennedy, Hugh

When Baghdad ruled the Muslim world; the rise and fall of Islam's greatest dynasty. Da Capo Press 2005 xxv, 326p il map hardcover o.p. pa $18.95   **956.7**

> 1. Islamic civilization 2. Baghdad (Iraq)
> ISBN 0-306-81435-8; 978-0-306-81435-8; 0-306-81480-3 pa; 978-0-306-81480-8 pa
>   LC 2006-295518
> First published 2004 in the United Kingdom with title: The Court of the Caliphs
> The author "has written an informative and sobering lesson for those who idolize the past." Choice
> Includes bibliographical references

Mansoor, Peter R.

Baghdad at sunrise; a Brigade Commander's war in Iraq. foreword by Donald Kagan and Frederick Kagan. Yale University Press 2008 xxvii, 376p il map (Yale library of military history) $28   **956.7**

> 1. Iraq War, 2003- -- Personal narratives
> ISBN 978-0-300-14069-9; 0-300-14069-X
>   LC 2008-07366

"This is a unique contribution to the burgeoning literature on the Iraq war. . . . The critique is balanced, perceptive and merciless." Publ Wkly
Includes bibliographical references

Miller, T. Christian

Blood money; wasted billions, lost lives, and corporate greed in Iraq. Little, Brown 2006 334p il map $24.99; pa $14.99   **956.7**

> 1. Governors 2. Presidents 3. Iraq War, 2003-2011 4. Iraq War, 2003- 5. Baseball executives 6. Children of presidents 7. Energy industry executives 8. United States -- Politics and government -- 2001-
> ISBN 0-316-16627-8; 978-0-316-16627-0; 0-316-16628-6 pa; 978-0-316-16628-7 pa
>   LC 2006-15074
> This is an "account of how the Bush administration has mismanaged the Iraq war and reconstruction. Miller focuses on the bungling of government spending and private contracts, some $30 billion committed to rebuilding Iraq, a greater sum than for the Marshall Plan. . . . Readers interested in understanding the political and economic dynamics behind the faltering campaign in Iraq will appreciate this investigation." Booklist
> Includes bibliographical references

Mills, Dan

Sniper one; on scope and under siege with a sniper team in Iraq. St. Martin's Press 2008 xxvi, 349p il map $26.95   **956.7**

> 1. Iraq War, 2003- -- Personal narratives
> ISBN 978-0-312-53126-3; 0-312-53126-5
>   LC 2008-20438
> First published 2007 in the United Kingdom
> "When a battalion of the Prince of Wales' Royal Regiment landed in Iraq in 2004, Mills commanded the 18 men of the sniper platoon. His gripping combat narrative covers how the platoon did more than its share of the fighting during the months when the Iraqis virtually besieged the battalion." Booklist

Murray, Williamson

The **Iraq** war; a military history. by Williamson Murray and Robert H. Scales, Jr. Belknap Press of Harvard University Press 2003 312p il map $29.95; pa $20   **956.7**

> 1. Iraq War, 2003-2011 2. Iraq War, 2003- 3. United States -- Armed forces
> ISBN 0-674-01280-1; 0-674-01968-7 pa
> This is a military history of the 2003 American-led war against Iraq
> "Williamson Murray and Robert Scales, both American military academics, have produced a superlative record of the invasion—part history, part critique and part doctrinal template for the future. Technical and operational aspects are explained clearly without losing the depth required to make this a serious study." Economist
> Includes bibliographical references

Operation homecoming; Iraq, Afghanistan, and the Home Front, in the words of U.S. troops and their families. preface by Dana Gioia; edited by An-

drew Carroll. Updated ed.; University of Chicago Press 2008 xxviii, 408p il pa $16 **956.7**
1. Iraq War, 2003- -- Personal narratives 2. Afghan War, 2001- -- Personal narratives
ISBN 978-0-226-09499-1; 0-226-09499-5

LC 2007-48835

First published 2006 by Random House

This book was created as part of a National Endowment for the Arts-funded project that "brought together some of the nation's most distinguished writers, including Tobias Wolff and Marilyn Nelson, and the men and women (and their spouses) fighting in the Middle East. The result is an incredibly wide range of opinions and emotions about U.S. policy in the Middle East, the war on terrorism, and the duties and responsibilities of citizens and the military. In 100 pieces of poetry, essays, letters, e-mails, plays, and journal entries, soldiers recall the awful thrill in the threat of killing or being killed, the deaths of buddies, and the cultural and psychological adjustments to a strange land." Booklist

Packer, George
The **assassins'** gate; America in Iraq. Farrar, Straus & Giroux 2005 467p hardcover o.p. pa $15 **956.7**
1. Iraq War, 2003-2011 2. Iraq War, 2003- 3. Iraq -- Politics and government 4. United States -- Politics and government -- 2001-
ISBN 0-374-29963-3; 0-374-53055-6 pa

LC 2005-11521

This "book rests on three main pillars: analysis of the intellectual origins of the Iraq war, summary of the political argument that preceded and then led to it, and firsthand description of the consequences on the ground. . . . The Iraq debate has long needed someone who is both tough-minded enough, and sufficiently sensitive, to register all its complexities. In George Packer's work, this need is answered." Publ Wkly
Includes bibliographical references

Polk, William Roe
★ **Understanding** Iraq; the whole sweep of Iraqi history, from Genghis Khan's Mongols to the Ottoman Turks to the British mandate to the American occupation. [by] William R. Polk. HarperCollins 2005 221p map $22.95; pa $13.95 **956.7**
1. Iraq -- History
ISBN 0-06-076468-6; 0-06-076469-4 pa

LC 2005-281319

The author presents an account of the history of Iraq, from the Dark Ages to the American occupation that began in 2003.
This is "a sober and informed account of Iraq's history, culminating in a compelling critique of the U.S. intervention there." Foreign Affairs
Includes bibliographical references

Raddatz, Martha
The **long** road home; a story of war and family. Putnam 2007 310p il map hardcover o.p. pa $15 **956.7**
1. Soldiers -- United States 2. United States -- Army

-- Cavalry, 1st 3. Iraq War, 2003- -- Personal narratives
ISBN 0-399-15382-9; 978-0-399-15382-2; 0-425-21934-8 pa; 978-0-425-21934-8 pa

LC 2006-37332

This "account has grit and high drama. . . . Sometimes the level of detail is astonishing." N Y Times (Late N Y Ed)

Ricks, Thomas E.
Fiasco : the American military adventure in Iraq. Penguin Press 2006 482p il map hardcover o.p. pa $16 **956.7**
1. Iraq War, 2003-2011 2. Iraq War, 2003 3. Iraq War, 2003-
ISBN 0-14-303891-5 pa; 1-59420-103-X; 978-0-14-303891-7 pa; 978-1-59420-103-5

LC 2006-45357

This book is "not a political rant nor is it shrill. But in its low-key, extraordinarily well-sourced, highly-detailed portrait of the run-up to and conduct of the war it is devastating." Christ Sci Monit
Includes bibliographical references

Rosen, Nir
Aftermath; following the bloodshed of America's wars in the Muslim world. Nation Books 2010 587p map $35 **956.7**
1. Islam and politics 2. Iraq War, 2003-2011 3. Iraq War, 2003- 4. Iraq -- Politics and government 5. Middle East -- Strategic aspects
ISBN 978-1-56858-401-0; 9781568584010

LC 2010023467

This is "a scathing study of U.S. policy in the region— with a focus on the 2003 invasion of Iraq and its aftermath. Rosen argues that the 'brutal' occupation inflicted daily violence and humiliation on civilians, 'divided Iraqis against one another,' catalyzed a devastating civil war, and reinvigorated regional sectarianism. . . . [This book is] a provocative indictment of American policy and policy makers." Publ Wkly
Includes bibliographical references

Seierstad, Asne
A **hundred** and one days; a Baghdad journal. translated by Ingrid Christophersen. Basic Books 2005 321p il maps hardcover o.p. pa $14 **956.7**
1. Iraq War, 2003- -- Personal narratives
ISBN 0-465-07600-9; 0-465-07601-7 pa
First published 2005 in the United Kingdom

The author "writes about her stay as a reporter for Scandinavian, Dutch, and German media in Baghdad in the days before the war in Iraq through the fall of Baghdad. . . . Seierstad puts a human face to and provides insight into the mosaic of the people of Iraq, the Bath party supporters, the dissidents, and the average person caught in the nightmare of the Saddam regime and the horrors of war." SLJ

Shadid, Anthony
Night draws near; Iraq's people in the shadow of America's war. Picador 2006 507p map pa $15 **956.7**
1. Iraq War, 2003-2011 2. Iraq War, 2003-
ISBN 978-0-312-42603-3; 0-312-42603-8

First published 2005 by Holt & Co.

"Evenhanded and keenly observed, containing just enough (and no more) of the author to suggest a decent man worthy of our trust, . . . [this book] is written for the inexpert but has fresh material for scholars." Economist

Includes bibliographical references

Sheeler, Jim

Final salute; a story of unfinished lives. Penguin Press 2008 280p il $25.95   **956.7**

1. Death 2. Bereavement 3. Iraq War, 2003-2011 4. Iraq War, 2003- 5. Military personnel -- United States
ISBN 978-1-59420-165-3; 1-59420-165-X

LC 2007-44130

This is a "tribute to the soldiers who have died in Iraq and their devastated families. The author spent two years shadowing Maj. Steve Beck, a marine in charge of casualty notification, as he delivered the news of battlefield death to families. Sheeler puts readers in Beck's shoes as he walks up to houses, delivers the knock on the door so dreaded by military families and tries to comfort distraught spouses and parents. . . . Sheeler's book is a devastating account of the sacrifices military families make and should be required reading for all Americans." Publ Wkly

Skiba, Katherine M.

Sister in the Band of Brothers; embedded with the 101st Airborne in Iraq. University Press of Kansas 2005 257p il (Modern war studies) $29.95   **956.7**

1. Iraq War, 2003- -- Personal narratives 2. United States -- Army -- Airborne Division, 101st
ISBN 0-7006-1382-X

LC 2004-26475

The author "was the only woman embedded with the 101st Airborne when the United States invaded Iraq in 2003. She has written a fascinating memoir of her time within the training with other reporters, waiting to invade Iraq and spending the first few months of the war with soldiers in Iraq." Univ Press Books for Public and Second Sch Libr, 2006

Stewart, Rory

★ The **prince** of the marshes; and other occupational hazards of a year in Iraq. Harcourt, Inc. 2006 396p il $25   **956.7**

1. Diplomats 2. Nonfiction writers 3. Iraq -- Social conditions 4. Iraq -- Description and travel 5. Iraq -- Politics and government
ISBN 0-15-101235-0; 978-0-15-101235-0

LC 2006-06905

"In August 2003, at the age of thirty, Rory Stewart took a taxi from Jordan to Baghdad. A Farsi-speaking British diplomat who had recently completed an epic walk from Turkey to Bangladesh, he was soon appointed deputy governor of Amarah and then Nasiriyah, provinces in the remote, impoverished marsh regions of southern Iraq. He spent the next eleven months negotiating hostage releases, holding elections, and splicing together some semblance of an infrastructure for a population of millions. . . . The Prince of the Marshes tells the story of Stewart's year." (Publisher's note) Chronology.

"In 2003, Stewart, a former British diplomat, joined the Coalition Provisional Authority in Iraq and was posted to the southern province of Maysan, where he found himself the de-facto governor of a restive populace whose allegiances were split among fifty-four political parties, twenty major tribes, and numerous militias. Stewart's account of his attempts to placate the various local figures who continually threaten to kill each other, or him, is both shrewd and self-deprecating." New Yorker

Tripp, Charles

A **history** of Iraq; 3rd ed.; Cambridge University Press 2007 xxiii, 357p il map $70; pa $24.99 **956.7**

1. Iraq -- History
ISBN 978-0-521-87823-4; 978-0-521-70247-8 pa

LC 2007-282451

First published 2000

This book traces the political history of Iraq from the Ottoman Empire to the fall of Saddam Hussein and the American occupation.

Includes bibliographical references

What was asked of us; an oral history of the Iraq War by the soldiers who fought it. [compiled by] Trish Wood. Little, Brown and Co. 2006 309p il map pa $14.99   **956.7**

1. Iraq War, 2003- -- Personal narratives
ISBN 978-0-316-01670-4; 0-316-01670-5; 978-0-316-01671-1 pa; 0-316-01671-3 pa

LC 2006-930963

"Colloquial, coarse and compelling, these narratives flash with humor, horror, nihilism and poesy." Publ Wkly

Woodward, Bob

★ **Plan** of attack. Simon & Schuster 2004 467p il map hardcover o.p. pa $14   **956.7**

1. Iraq War, 2003-2011 2. Iraq War, 2003- 3. United States -- Politics and government -- 2001-
ISBN 0-7432-5547-X; 0-7432-5548-8 pa

LC 2004-351204

The author "delivers an engrossing blow-by-blow of the run-up to war in Iraq. . . . With this book, Woodward . . . has delivered his most important and impressive work in years. Ultimately, this first-class work of contemporary history will be remembered for shedding needed light on the Iraq War." Publ Wkly

Wright, Evan

Generation kill; Devil Dogs, Iceman, Captain America, and the new face of American war. G.P. Putnam's Sons 2004 354p il maps hardcover o.p. pa $15   **956.7**

1. Iraq War, 2003- -- Personal narratives
ISBN 0-399-15193-1; 0-425-20040-X pa

LC 2004-44682

The author discusses his experiences when embedded with the First Marine Division in Iraq. This book is based on a series of articles that originally appeared in Rolling Stone.

This "account is a personality-driven, readable and insightful look at the Iraq War's first month from the Marine grunt's point of view." Publ Wkly

956.704   Iraq--1979-

Ballard, John R.

From   Kabul to Baghdad and back; the U.S. at war in Afghanistan and Iraq. by John R. Ballard, David W. Lamm, and John K. Wood. Naval Institute Press 2012 xxvi, 369 p., [8] p. of platesp ill., maps (hardcover) $42.95; (ebook) $42.95   **956.704**
1. Afghan War, 2001- 2. Iraq War, 2003-2011 3. Strategy 4. War on Terrorism, 2001-2009 5. Afghan War, 2001- -- Campaigns 6. Iraq War, 2003-2011 -- Campaigns 7. United States -- History, Military -- 21st century 8. United States -- Military policy -- History -- 21st century
ISBN 1612510221; 9781612510224; 9781612511689 pdf

LC 2012026125

This book offers an assessment of the U.S. wars in Afghanistan and Iraq. The authors "compare and contrast the key strategic decisions of the wars, assessing the successes and failures of strategic operations and analyzing the impact of the Iraq War on the war in Afghanistan. They criticize the decision to give NATO the lead in Afghanistan and to duplicate an Iraq War-style surge there." (Library Journal)
Includes bibliographical references (p. 351-356) and index.

Castner, Brian

The **long** walk; a story of war and the life that follows. Brian Castner. Doubleday 2012 222 p.   **956.704**
1. Autobiographies 2. Ordnance disposal units 3. Post-traumatic stress disorder 4. Iraq War, 2003-2011 -- Personal narratives 5. Ordnance disposal units -- Iraq 6. Ordnance disposal units -- United States 7. United States. Air Force -- Officers -- Biography 8. Iraq War, 2003-2011 -- Personal narratives, American 9. Iraq War, 2003-2011 -- Veterans -- United States -- Biography
ISBN 0385536208; 9780385536202

LC 2011052419

This memoir by Brian Castner describes his life during and after the Iraq War. "[A]s the commander of an Explosive Ordnance Disposal unit in Iraq . . . [d]ays and nights he and his team . . . would . . . engage in . . . disarming the deadly improvised explosive devices that had been discovered. . . . When Castner returned home to his wife and family, he began a struggle with . . . an unshakable feeling of fear and confusion and survivor's guilt that he terms The Crazy." (Publisher's note)
Includes bibliographical references and index.

Chandrasekaran, Rajiv

Imperial life in the emerald city; inside Iraq's green zone. Rajiv Chandrasekaran. Alfred A. Knopf 2006 x, 320p maps (alk. paper) $25.95   **956.704**
1. Iraq 2. Iraq War, 2003-2011 3. Political corruption 4. United States -- Politics and government 5. Iraq War, 2003- 6. Iraq -- Coalition Provisional Authority 7. United States -- Politics and government -- 2001- 8. United States -- Politics and government -- 2001-2009
ISBN 1400044871 ; 9781400044870

LC 2006041014

BBC Samuel Johnson Prize for Non-Fiction (2007)
This book discusses "the Green Zone in Baghdad, headquarters for the American occupation in Iraq, . . . [and provides a] portrait of the Green Zone and the Coalition Provisional Authority (which ran Iraq's government from April 2003 to June 2004) that becomes a metaphor for the [U.S.] administration's larger failings in Iraq. An insular, often blinkered approach to decision making; a reluctance to listen to experts; Pollyannaish expectations leading to inadequate allocations of resources and staff; a willful ignorance of Iraqi culture and history; and an obliviousness to realities on the ground: all are on unfortunate display in the Emerald City." (New York Times)
"This is a clearly written, blessedly undidactic book. It should be read by anyone who wants to understand how things went so badly wrong in Iraq." N Y Times Book Rev
Includes bibliographical references (p. [303]-306) and index.

Clancy, Tom

Into the storm; a study in command. {by} Tom Clancy with Fred Franks, Jr. Putnam 1997 531p il maps hardcover o.p. pa $16.95   **956.704**
1. Persian Gulf War, 1991
ISBN 0-425-16308-3 pa

LC 96-38068

This history of the Persian Gulf War focuses on the command of General Frederick M. Banks
Includes bibliographical references

Hornfischer, James D.

Service; a Navy SEAL at war. Marcus Luttrell ; with James D. Hornfischer. Little, Brown and Co. 2012 xv, 364 p.p (hardcover) $27.99   **956.704**
1. War 2. Soldiers -- United States 3. Voluntary military service 4. Afghan War, 2001- -- Campaigns 5. Iraq War, 2003-2011 -- Campaigns 6. Afghan War, 2001- -- Personal narratives, American 7. United States. Navy. SEALs -- Officers -- Biography 8. Iraq War, 2003-2011 -- Personal narratives, American
ISBN 0316185361; 9780316185363

LC 2012904468

Author Marcus "Luttrell chronicles his missions preserving democracy for America . . . During their time in Iraq, his SEAL combat brothers killed perceived enemies, suffered countless wounds, and died at a rapid pace, making the narrative occasionally difficult to follow. In some chapters, battle tactics predominate, and the sentences are quick and graphic . . . Luttrell explains why some men answer the call of war no matter the risk to themselves or their loved ones. The author seeks to explain the honor of military service to . . . readers who have never experienced it." (Kirkus)
Includes bibliographical references.

Kamber, Michael

Photojournalists on war; the untold stories from Iraq. Michael Kamber ; foreword by Dexter Filkins. University of Texas Press 2012 300 p. ill. (chiefly col.), col. map (cl. : alk. paper) $65   **956.704**
1. Photojournalism 2. War photography 3. Iraq War, 2003-2011 4. Photojournalists -- Interviews 5.

Photojournalism -- Iraq -- History -- 21st century
ISBN 0292744080; 9780292744080

LC 2012026258

This book "presents a . . . new visual and oral history of America's nine-year conflict in the Middle East. Michael Kamber interviewed photojournalists from . . . news organizations, including Agence France-Presse, the Associated Press, the Guardian, the Los Angeles Times, Magnum, Newsweek, the New York Times, Paris Match, Reuters, Time, the Times of London, VII Photo Agency, and the Washington Post, to create . . . [a] comprehensive collection of eyewitness accounts of the Iraq War." (Publisher's note)

"The visuals hold center stage: the book brings to life the suffering of those affected by this war, giving the viewer powerful and disturbing (and frequently graphic) reminders of the war's physical and psychological destruction." LJ

Mackey, Sandra

The **reckoning**; Iraq and the legacy of Saddam Hussein. Norton 2002 415p il maps $27.95; pa $16.95   **956.704**
1. Presidents 2. Iraq -- Politics and government
ISBN 0-393-05141-2; 0-393-32428-1 pa%

LC 2002-16611

The author offers a "history of Iraq and its early Mesopotamian civilization with . . . biographies of all of its historical figures through the ages, shedding perspective on the current regime of Saddam Hussein and looking ahead to what an Iraq without Hussein might resemble. . . . An extremely thorough appraisal." Booklist

Includes bibliographical references

Maraniss, David

They marched into sunlight; war and peace in Vietnam and America, October 1967. Simon & Schuster 2003 592p il map hardcover o.p. pa $16   **956.704**
1. Vietnam War, 1961-1975
ISBN 0-7432-1780-2; 0-7432-6104-6 pa

LC 2003-52885

This is a "narrative by a reporter who juxtaposes a ghastly little battle in Vietnam with an antiwar and anti-Dow demonstration at the University of Wisconsin, Madison, on the same day; it captures moral ambiguity everywhere, without stereotyping or condescension." N Y Times Book Rev

Includes bibliographical references

Newell, Clayton R.

Historical dictionary of the Persian Gulf War, 1990-1991. Scarecrow Press 1998 lix, 363p maps (Historical dictionaries of war, revolution, and civil unrest) $65   **956.704**
1. Persian Gulf War, 1991
ISBN 0-8108-3511-8

LC 98-18944

The author attempts "to help the reader understand the Gulf War and its background. He includes several pages of abbreviations and acronyms along with pages of maps, all . . . describing what happened and why during the 1991 conflict. There is . . . a 30-page introduction that describes the political developments that led up to the war and a much-needed chronology of events. . . . The dictionary entries av-

erage about a paragraph and cover the war's personalities as well as its combat equipment." Libr J

Schwartz, Richard Alan

Encyclopedia of the Persian Gulf War. McFarland & Co. 1998 216p il maps hardcover o.p. pa $45   **956.704**
1. Reference books 2. Persian Gulf War, 1991 -- Encyclopedias
ISBN 0-7864-0451-5; 0-7864-4103-8 pa

LC 97-51886

"Beginning with a seven-page overview, this encyclopedia presents alphabetically arranged entries that describe the conflict, including key figures, places, battles, diplomacy, and more." SLJ

Includes bibliographical references

Swofford, Anthony

Jarhead : a Marine's chronicle of the Gulf War and other battles. Scribner 2003 260p hardcover o.p. pa $15   **956.704**
1. United States -- Marine Corps 2. Persian Gulf War, 1991 -- Personal narratives
ISBN 0-7432-3535-5; 0-7432-8721-5 pa

LC 2002-30866

This book offers "an unflinching portrayal of the loneliness and brutality of modern warfare and sophisticated analyses of—and visceral reactions to—its politics." Publ Wkly

Walker, J. B.

Nightcap at dawn; American soldiers' counterinsurgency in Iraq. Skyhorse Pub 2012 555 p. $16.95   **956.704**
1. Counterinsurgency 2. Iraq War, 2003-2011 3. Military personnel -- United States
ISBN 1616086173; 9781616086176

This book's "narrative is comprised of candid e-mails assembled once the group [of American soldiers] returned to American soil and encompasses much more than its original intent to detail 'the simple charms of soldiering.' With exacting scrutiny, many of the unnamed authors share the stark realities and myriad complications of counterinsurgency efforts." (Kirkus)

956.94   Palestine; Israel

Armstrong, Karen

Jerusalem; one city, three faiths. Knopf 1996 xxi, 471p il maps hardcover o.p. pa $17.95 **956.94**
1. Jerusalem -- History
ISBN 0-679-43596-4; 0-345-39168-3 pa

LC 96-75888

Armstrong's "overarching theme, that Jerusalem has been central to the experience and 'sacred geography' of Jews, Muslims and Christians and thus has led to deadly struggles for dominance, is a familiar one, yet she brings to her sweeping, profusely illustrated narrative a grasp of sociopolitical conditions seldom found in other books." Publ Wkly

Bregman, Ahron

A **history** of Israel. Palgrave Macmillan 2002 xx, 320p map (Palgrave essential histories) $70; pa $21.95 **956.94**

1. Israel -- History

ISBN 0-333-67631-9; 0-333-67632-7 pa

LC 2002-72304

This book "examines Israel's turbulent history from the first Zionist Congress in 1897 to the present day. The driving themes of this . . . account are Jewish immigration, war, and attempts to forge peace between Israelis, Arabs, and Palestinians. " Publisher's note

"Bregman takes into account all the major issues involving Israel's history." Booklist

Includes bibliographical references and index

Carroll, James, 1943-

Jerusalem, Jerusalem; how the ancient city ignited our modern world. Houghton Mifflin Harcourt 2011 418p $20 **956.94**

1. Jerusalem

ISBN 978-0-547-19561-2; 0-547-19561-3

LC 2010-43034

"Carroll examines the enigma that is Jerusalem—the holiest and most blood-soaked spot on earth. . . . While various religions flourished all over the ancient world, it was in Jerusalem that God emerged. Not just a god, but God, one who recognizes how both the need for violence and the hatred of violence reside within the human spirit. These conflicting impulses are the subthemes that propel Carroll's story across the ages, through Jerusalem's wreckages and rebirths, as the three Abrahamic religions claim the city as its own. Carroll's writing is so compelling, so beautifully constructed, that, ironically, the book can be a very slow read. There is something on almost every page that makes the reader want to stop and contemplate." Booklist

Includes bibliographical references

Cesarani, David

Major Farran's hat; the untold story of the struggle to establish the Jewish state. Da Capo Press 2009 290p il map $26 **956.94**

1. Terrorism 2. Palestine 3. Army officers 4. Kidnap victims 5. Murder victims 6. Revolutionaries 7. Political leaders 8. Government officials 9. Newspaper executives

ISBN 978-0-306-81845-5

This book "provides a neat, if briskly presented, history of British involvement in Palestine and the international power politics involved. . . . [It] is a piece of contemporary history with bite and verve." Times Higher Ed

Includes bibliographical references

Cohen, Rich

Israel is real. Farrar, Straus, and Giroux 2009 383p map $27; pa $16 **956.94**

1. Jews -- History 2. Israel -- Description and travel

ISBN 978-0-374-17778-2; 0-374-17778-3; 978-0-312-42976-8 pa; 0-312-42976-2 pa

LC 2008-49223

The author explains "the history of a people and its religion from the time Zealots revolted against their Roman occupiers to the rise of the Zionists, who helped build the current republic. . . . A must-read for those who want to understand the context of the modern Jewish state." Kirkus

Includes bibliographical references

Collins, Larry

O Jerusalem! {by} Larry Collins and Dominique Lapierre. Simon & Schuster 1972 637p il maps hardcover o.p. pa $17 **956.94**

1. Israel-Arab War, 1948-1949 2. Jerusalem -- History -- 1948, Siege

ISBN 0-671-66241-4 pa

This is an account of the struggle for the city of Jerusalem during the Israel-Arab War of 1948

Includes bibliographical references

Farsoun, Samih K.

Palestine and the Palestinians; {by} Samih K. Farsoun with Christina E. Zacharia. Westview Press 1997 375p maps hardcover o.p. pa $29 **956.94**

1. Palestinian Arabs 2. Israel-Arab conflicts

ISBN 0-8133-2773-3 pa

LC 97-21954

This study of the Palestinian peoples covers their economic and social conditions, their political activity and national aspirations

"This is an excellent introduction to the modern history of the Palestinians, the transformations of their troubled land, and the prospects of both." Choice

Includes bibliographical references

Gilbert, Martin

Jerusalem in the twentieth century. Wiley 1996 412p il maps $30; pa $16.95 **956.94**

1. Jerusalem 2. Palestine -- History

ISBN 0-471-16308-2; 0-471-28328-2 pa

LC 96-18458

"Gilbert's history is heavily Zionist. . . . Nonetheless, despite his tilt, Gilbert is well worth reading. He has an unrivalled ability to tell a story through the eyes of (some of) those taking part and his book is good popular history." London Rev Books

Includes bibliographical references

Gorenberg, Gershom

The **accidental** empire; Israel and the birth of the settlements, 1967-1977. Times Books 2006 454p il map $30 **956.94**

1. West Bank 2. Gaza Strip 3. Israel -- Politics and government

ISBN 0-8050-7564-X; 978-0-8050-7564-9

LC 2005-52988

This is an account of the settler movement in Israel, beginning with the aftermath of the 1967 war.

This is "an absorbing narrative with extensive references to archives, private papers, oral histories, books and articles." Nation

Includes bibliographical references

★ How Israelis and Palestinians negotiate; a cross-cultural analysis of the Oslo peace process. edited

by Tamara Cofman Wittes. United States Institute
of Peace Press 2005 160p $40; pa $12 **956.94**
1. Palestinian Arabs 2. Israel-Arab conflicts 3. Cross-
cultural studies 4. Israeli national characteristics
ISBN 1-929223-64-1; 1-929223-63-3 pa
LC 2004-65759
"Five essays by leading scholars focus on the concept
of culture and the role it plays in the success and failure of
the Middle East peace process. Both Israeli and Palestinian
cultures are assessed and explained as a context to understand snags and successes from Oslo II to the Camp David
accords. This small volume is very accessible to high school
readers and should generate interest in understanding the
larger issues which continue to add to the instability of the
region." Univ Press Books for Public and Second Sch Libr,
2006
Includes bibliographical references

Laqueur, Walter
A **history** of Zionism; with a new preface by the
author. Schocken Bks. 1989 xxii, 639p il hardcover
o.p. pa $16.95   **956.94**
1. Zionism
ISBN 0-8052-1149-7 pa
LC 88-38221
A reissue with new introduction of the title first published 1972 by Holt, Rinehart & Winston
The author examines the history of Zionism over the past
three centuries from its European roots to the establishment
of the state of Israel
Includes bibliographical references

LeBor, Adam
City of oranges; an intimate history of Arabs and
Jews in Jaffa. W.W. Norton 2007 xxxviii, 424p il
map pa $14.95   **956.94**
1. Israel-Arab conflicts
ISBN 0-393-32984-4; 978-0-393-32984-1
LC 2007-2389
First published 2006 in the United Kingdom
LeBor presents interviews with Arab and Jewish fami-
lies in Jaffa, Israel.
"Those looking for a well-rounded and truly human in-
sight into the conflict will enjoy this account." Publ Wkly
Includes bibliographical references

Miller, Jennifer
★ **Inheriting** the Holy Land; an American's
search for hope in the Middle East. Ballantine Books
2005 xxxiii, 261p map $24.95; pa $14.95 **956.94**
1. Israel-Arab conflicts
ISBN 0-345-46924-0; 978-0-345-46924-3; 0-345-
46925-9 pa; 978-0-345-46925-0 pa
LC 2004-66349
The author "is the daughter of one of the chief American
negotiators in the Israeli-Palestinian conflict and a longtime
participant in the Seeds of Peace program, bringing together
Israeli and Palestinian children. Using the many contacts
that she has made, from the highest leaders to the children on
the street, Miller explores . . . the many different viewpoints
and preconceptions of the people involved in the conflict,

not excluding her own. . . . This is a superb book on a crucial
issue of our time." SLJ
Includes bibliographical references

Montefiore, Sebag
Jerusalem; the biography. [by] Simon Sebag
Montefiore. Knopf 2011 638p il map $35 **956.94**
1. Jerusalem -- History
ISBN 978-0-307-26651-4; 0-307-26651-6

Sachar, Howard Morley
A **history** of Israel; from the rise of Zionism
to our time. [by] Howard M. Sachar. 3rd ed, rev
and updated; Knopf 2007 xxii, 1270p map pa
$39.95   **956.94**
1. Zionism 2. Israel -- History
ISBN 978-0-375-71132-9; 0-375-71132-5
LC 2006-101970
First published in two volumes 1976-1987
This is a history of the state of Israel. "When first published in 1976, this truly monumental history was hailed as
a definitive work. . . . As extraordinarily stimulating as the
first edition." Booklist
Includes bibliographical references

Shipler, David K.
Arab and Jew; wounded spirits in a promised
land. rev ed; Penguin Bks. 2002 xxxix, 565p maps
pa $17   **956.94**
1. Palestinian Arabs 2. Israel-Arab conflicts 3. Jewish-
Arab relations 4. Israel -- Social conditions
ISBN 0-14-200229-1
LC 2001-54862
First published 1986 by Times Bks.
The author examines the stereotypes that Arabs and Jews
have of one another and "the origins of the prejudices that
have been intensified by war, terrorism, and nationalism. . .
. Shipler examines the process of indoctrination that begins
in schools; he discusses the far-ranging effects of socioeco-
nomic differences, historical conflicts between Islam and
Judaism, attitudes about the Holocaust, and much more."
Publisher's note
Includes bibliographical references and index

Timmerman, Kenneth R.
Preachers of hate; Islam and the war on Amer-
ica. Crown Publishers 2003 370p $25.95; pa
$14.95   **956.94**
1. Israel-Arab conflicts
ISBN 1-4000-4901-6; 1-4000-5373-0 pa
LC 2003-11455
The author "examines the politics that demonize Is-
rael—and, increasingly, the U.S.—for failures of domestic
policy in many Arab nations." Booklist
Includes bibliographical references

Tolan, Sandy

The **lemon** tree; an Arab, a Jew, and the heart of the Middle East. Bloomsbury Pub. 2006 362p $24.95 **956.94**

1. Israel-Arab conflicts
ISBN 1-58234-343-8; 978-1-58234-343-3

LC 2005-30360

The author "captures the Arab-Israeli struggle in this story of a house and the two families, first Palestinian and then Jewish, who successively lived in it. . . . This wonderful human story vividly depicts the depths of attachment to contested ground." Libr J

956.940 Palestine; Israel -- 1948-

Bar-On, Mordechai

Moshe Dayan; Israel's controversial hero. Mordechai Bar-On. 1st ed. Yale University Press 2012 xii, 247 p.p photograph (alk. paper) $25 **956.940**

1. Soldiers -- Israel 2. Israel -- Politics and government 3. Generals -- Israel -- Biography 4. Statesmen -- Israel -- Biography 5. Arab-Israeli conflict -- Biography
ISBN 0300149417; 9780300149418

LC 2012000595

"In this . . . biography [of Israeli leader Moshe Dayan], Mordechai Bar-On . . . offers a . . . view of Dayan's private life, public career, and political controversies, set against an . . . analysis of Israel's political environment from pre-Mandate Palestine through the early 1980s. . . . Drawing on . . . Israeli archives, accounts by Dayan and members of his circle, and firsthand experiences, Bar-On reveals Dayan as a man unwavering in his devotion to Zionism and . . . Israel." (Publisher's note)

Includes bibliographical references (p. 219-236) and index

Horovitz, David Phillip

A **little** too close to God; the thrills and panic of a life in Israel. {by} David Horovitz. Knopf 2000 311p $27.50 **956.940**

1. Israeli national characteristics 2. Israel -- Social conditions 3. Israel -- Politics and government
ISBN 0-375-40381-7

The author, editor of the Jerusalem Report, argues "that in recent years the conservative Netanyahu government and the continued influence of extreme Orthodox Jews have done little except complicate daily life in Israel and prevent serious peace negotiations from taking place. He presents a highly informative history and current-events narrative in a manner that makes it personal and relevant to Jews and non-Jews alike." Libr J

La Guardia, Anton

War without end; Israelis, Palestinians, and the struggle for a promised land. St. Martin's Griffin 2003 xxii, 436p il map pa $16.95 **956.940**

1. Zionism 2. Palestinian Arabs 3. Israel-Arab conflicts 4. Israeli national characteristics
ISBN 0-312-31633-X

LC 2003-41288

First published 2001 in the United Kingdom with title: Holy Land, unholy war: Israelis and Palestinians

"This is fundamentally an examination of two wounded peoples, neither of whom seems capable of surmounting national myths and past hatreds to forge a new future. La Guardia is evenhanded in his criticism of both Israeli and Palestinian leaders, but he does not spare ordinary people. . . . This is an absorbing but heartbreaking examination of a seemingly endless tragedy that continues to unfold before our eyes." Booklist [review of 2002 edition]

Includes bibliographical references

Lozowick, Yaacov

Right to exist; a moral defense of Israel's wars. Doubleday 2003 326p map $26; pa $15 **956.940**

1. Israel-Arab conflicts
ISBN 0-385-50905-7; 1-4000-3243-1 pa

LC 2003-48477

The author "asserts that Israel is now, as before, struggling against opponents whose goal is the eventual destruction of the Jewish state. In examining the entire history of the Zionist enterprise, he illustrates both the moral justification of that enterprise and of the wars Israelis have been compelled to fight to preserve their independence. . . . {This} is an eloquent and necessary justification of Israel's right to defend itself." Booklist

Rubin, Barry

Israel; an introduction. Barry Rubin. Yale University Press 2012 ix, 340 p.p (paperback : alk. paper) $30.00 **956.940**

1. Israel
ISBN 0300162308; 9780300162301

LC 2011028927

This book presents a "survey of the many . . . facets of Israeli history, society, government, economics and culture . . . Such issues include existential insecurity, ongoing Palestinian conflict, fluid borders, diverse immigrant population, living with daily terrorist violence and the sense of being 'misunderstood by outside observers.' . . . [Barry Rubin] reminds readers that Jews even in exile acted as a 'national people, arguably the first such in history,' and thus the establishment of Israel was 'the continuation of a long historical process,' not merely the result of the Holocaust." (Kirkus)

Includes bibliographical references and index

Shilon, Avi

Menachem Begin; a life. Avi Shilon ; translated from the Hebrew by Danielle Zilberberg and Yoram Sharett. Yale University Press 2012 545 p. (clothbound : alk. paper) $40 **956.940**

1. Prime ministers -- Israel 2. Israel -- Politics and government 3. Prime ministers -- Israel -- Biography 4. Revisionist Zionists -- Israel -- Biography 5. Israel -- Politics and government -- 20th century
ISBN 0300162359; 9780300162356

LC 2012012189

Author Avi Shilon discusses Menachem Begin. "The book presents a detailed new portrait of Israel's founding leader. Among the many topics Avi Shilon holds up to new light are Begin's antagonistic relationship with David Ben-Gurion, his controversial role in the 1982 Lebanon War, his unique leadership style, the changes in his ideology over the years, and the mystery behind the total silence he maintained at the end of his career." (Publisher's note)

Includes bibliographical references and index

956.95   Jordan and West Bank

Grossman, David

The **yellow** wind; translated from the Hebrew by Haim Watzman; {with a new afterword by the author} Picador 2002 222p map pa $13   **956.95**

1. Palestinian Arabs 2. Jewish-Arab relations 3. West Bank

ISBN 0-312-42098-6

LC 2002-67325

Original Hebrew edition, 1987; this translation first published 1988

"Grossman was assigned to report for a weekly newspaper on life for both occupied and occupier on the West Bank during the 20th anniversary of its conquest. With an eye and ear for revealing detail, he argues that the Jews are now doing to Palestinians what has been done to them through the ages." Libr J

Shehadeh, Raja

Palestinian walks; forays into a vanishing landscape. Scribner 2008 xxii, 200p il map pa $15   **956.95**

1. Israel-Arab conflicts 2. West Bank -- Description and travel

ISBN 978-1-4165-6966-4; 1-4165-6966-9

First published 2007 in the United Kingdom

The author "spent most of his adult life as a lawyer trying to prevent Jewish settlement development in the West Bank. In this work, he recounts his thoughts during six walks into the surrounding Ramallah wilderness between 1978 and 2006. . . . He reveals his anger and pain as he muses on history, his life, his failures, political turmoil, and the unique natural beauty of a beloved land that is succumbing to development and access restrictions. . . . This compelling but unsettling story, which provides insight into the endless woes of a troubled region, is highly recommended for general libraries and Middle Eastern collections." Libr J

Winslow, Philip C.

Victory for us is to see you suffer; in the West Bank with the Palestinians and the Israelis. Beacon Press 2007 xxiii, 224p map $24.95   **956.95**

1. Israel-Arab conflicts 2. West Bank

ISBN 978-0-8070-6906-6; 0-8070-6906-X

LC 2007-13411

The author "depicts the universal cost of Israel's occupation of Palestinian lands in excruciatingly human terms in a memoir detailing 30 months spent on the West Bank with the United Nations Relief and Works Agency (UNRWA)." Publ Wkly

Includes bibliographical references

957   Siberia (Asiatic Russia)

Frazier, Ian

Travels in Siberia. Farrar, Straus and Giroux 2010 529p il map $30   **957**

1. Siberia (Russia) -- Description and travel

ISBN 978-0-374-27872-4; 0-374-27872-4

LC 2010-05784

"Frazier records several visits [to Siberia]: a summer's trip via cantankerous automobile across the entire region, in the company of a couple of local companions; a winter's journey by train and car, during which the car sometimes used frozen waterways for roads; and a return visit to see the effects of the emerging Russian energy industry. . . . The contrasts are stark—one day, he walked through the ruins of a remote, frozen Soviet-era prison camp and later saw a ballet in St. Petersburg—and the writing is consistently rich. A dense, challenging, dazzling work that will leave readers exhausted but yearning for more." Kirkus

Includes bibliographical references

Thubron, Colin

In Siberia. HarperCollins Pubs. 2000 287p hardcover o.p. pa $14   **957**

1. Siberia (Russia) -- Description and travel

ISBN 0-06-095373-X pa

LC 99-41346

"Thubron elegantly encompasses both awe-inspiring landscapes and their dark histories as well as immersing himself in local eccentricities." Times Lit Suppl

958   Central Asia

Hanks, Reuel R.

★ **Central** Asia; a global studies handbook. ABC-CLIO 2005 xvii, 467p il map (Global studies) $55   **958**

1. Central Asia

ISBN 1-85109-656-6

LC 2005-14716

"The superb text makes accessible, whether for reports or general reading, former Silk Road lands that may play increasingly important roles—think of oil-rich Kazakhstan—in the world's economy." SLJ

Includes bibliographical references

958.1   Afghanistan

Ansary, Mir Tamim

West of Kabul, East of New York; an Afghan American story. Farrar, Straus & Giroux 2002 292p hardcover o.p. pa $13   **958.1**

1. Islamic civilization 2. Afghanistan -- Social conditions

ISBN 0-374-28757-0; 0-312-42151-6 pa

The author, an Afghan American, reflects on his dual heritage. In light of the events of September 11, he focuses particular attention on the relationship between Islam and the West.

"While Ansary's political insights can be detached or perhaps purposefully aloof his descriptions of having lived in and identified alternately with the West and the Islamic world are utterly compelling." Publ Wkly

Chayes, Sarah

★ The **punishment** of virtue; inside Afghanistan after the Taliban. Penguin Press 2006 386p il map hardcover o.p. pa $16   **958.1**
   1. Afghan War, 2001-
   ISBN 1-59420-096-3; 978-0-14-311206-8 pa; 0-14-311206-6 pa

                LC 2006-43499

This is an eyewitness account of conditions "in Afghanistan in the wake of the defeat of the Taliban." Publisher's note

The author's "hands-on experience as a deeply immersed reporter and activist gives her lucid analysis and prescriptions a practical scope and persuasive authority." Publ Wkly

   Includes bibliographical references

Coll, Steve

Ghost wars; the secret history of the CIA, Afghanistan, and bin Laden, from the Soviet invasion to September 10, 2001. Penguin Press 2004 695p maps $29.95; pa $16   **958.1**
   1. Terrorists 2. Afghanistan 3. United States -- Central Intelligence Agency
   ISBN 1-594-20007-6; 0-14-303466-9 pa

                LC 2003-58593

This is a "history of the CIA's role in Afghanistan, including its covert program against Soviet troops from 1979 to 1989, and examines the rise of the Taliban, the emergence of bin Laden, and the secret efforts by CIA officers and their agents to capture or kill bin Laden in Afghanistan after 1998." Publisher's note

The author "has given us what is certainly the finest historical narrative so far on the origins of Al Qaeda in the post-Soviet rubble of Afghanistan." N Y Times Book Rev

   Includes bibliographical references

Dalrymple, William

Return of a king; the battle for Afghanistan, 1839-42. William Dalrymple. 1st ed. Alfred A. Knopf 2013 xxix, 515 p.p ill. (some col.), maps (hardcover) $30   **958.1**
   1. Afghan War, 2001- 2. Afghanistan -- History -- British Intervention, 1838-1842 3. Afghanistan -- History, Military -- 19th century 4. British -- Afghanistan -- History -- 19th century
   ISBN 0307958280; 9780307958280

                LC 2012040998

This book, by William Dalrymple, "gives us the . . . account yet of the spectacular first battle for Afghanistan: the British invasion of the remote kingdom in 1839. . . . But Dalrymple takes us beyond the bare outline of this infamous battle, and . . . illuminates the uncanny similarities between the West's first disastrous entanglement with Afghanistan and the situation today." (Publisher's note)

   Includes bibliographical references (pages 493-497) and index.

Elliot, Jason

An **unexpected** light; travels in Afghanistan. St. Martin's Press 2001 473p map hardcover o.p. pa $18   **958.1**
   1. Afghanistan -- Description and travel
   ISBN 0-312-28846-8 pa

                LC 2001-50036

This "is an account of Elliot's two visits to Afghanistan. The first occurred when he joined the mujaheddin circa 1979 and was smuggled into Soviet-occupied Afghanistan; the second happened nearly ten years later, when he returned to the still war-torn land. The skirmishes that Elliot painstakingly describes here took place between the Taliban and the government of Gen. Ahmad Shah Massoud in Kabul. . . . Elliot traveled widely in the hinterland, visiting Faizabad in the north and Herat in the west. The result is some of the finest travel writing in recent years." Libr J

Ewans, Martin

Afghanistan; a short history of its people and politics. HarperCollins Pubs. 2002 244p il maps hardcover o.p. pa $13.95   **958.1**
   1. Afghanistan -- History
   ISBN 0-06-050508-7 pa

                LC 2002-17342

"Ewans shows how centuries of invasions, fierce tribal rivalries, and powerful dynasties led to the creation of an Afghan empire during the eighteenth century. . . . The ruling Afghan dynasty was overthrown by a communist coup in the 1970s, which was answered in turn by a Soviet invasion in 1979. Roughly a decade later, the Soviet Union was forced to withdraw and left Afghanistan with a civil war that was to tear apart the nation's last remnants of religious and ethnic unity. It was into this climate that the Taliban was born." Publisher's note

"This is a fascinating story and the best book-length examination of Afghanistan's history we're likely to have for some time." Booklist

   Includes bibliographical references

Feifer, Gregory

The **great** gamble; the Soviet war in Afghanistan. Harper 2009 326p il map $27.99   **958.1**
   1. Afghanistan -- History -- Soviet occupation, 1979-1989
   ISBN 978-0-06-114318-2; 0-06-114318-9

                LC 2008-22594

This is a history of the Soviet Union's 1979-1989 war in Afghanistan. "Taking advantage of his skills, experience, and contacts . . . as a foreign correspondent, Feifer's narrative relies greatly on the experiences of those involved on all sides of the conflict—from Soviet political and military insiders to various participants in the mujahideen resistance and even former CIA operatives—but he leans most heavily on the poignant stories of Soviet veterans. Fortunately for the reader, Feifer's research also includes a prudent mix of combat analyses, contemporary reports, and historical studies that inform a balanced treatment of his complex subject." Open Letters

   Includes bibliographical references

Fitzgerald, Paul

Invisible history; Afghanistan's untold story. by Paul Fitzgerald and Elizabeth Gould. City Lights Books 2009 389p map pa $18.95   **958.1**

1. Afghanistan -- History

ISBN 978-0-87286-494-8; 0-87286-494-4

LC 2008-20486

The authors "seek to clarify and contextualize the current situation in conflict-torn Afghanistan with this comprehensive history. The material covers events starting in ancient antiquity, but puts a heavy emphasis on the second half of the 20th century through the end of 2007. The work concludes with analysis and strategy recommendations for the incoming American President and is supplemented by an appendix of historical maps." Middle East Journal

Includes bibliographical references

Junger, Sebastian

War. Twelve 2010 287p map $26.99   **958.1**

1. Afghan War, 2001- -- Personal narratives 2. United States -- Army -- Airborne Brigade, 173rd

ISBN 978-0-446-55624-8

LC 2009-49493

"The war in Afghanistan contains brutal trauma but also transcendent purpose in this riveting combat narrative. Junger spent 14 months in 2007-2008 intermittently embedded with a platoon of the 173rd Airborne brigade in Afghanistan's Korengal Valley, one of the bloodiest corners of the conflict. . . . Junger experiences everything they do—nerve-racking patrols, terrifying roadside bombings and ambushes, stultifying weeks in camp when they long for a firefight to relieve the tedium. . . . The result is an unforgettable portrait of men under fire." Publ Wkly

Includes bibliographical references

Rashid, Ahmed

Taliban; militant Islam, oil and fundamentalism in Central Asia. 2nd ed; Yale University Press 2010 319p map pa $17.95   **958.1**

1. Islam and politics 2. Islamic fundamentalism 3. Taliban 4. Afghanistan -- Politics and government

ISBN 978-0-300-16368-1; 0-300-16368-1

LC 2009-938249

First published 2000

The author explains "the Taliban's rise to power, its impact on Afghanistan and the region, its role in oil and gas company decisions, and the effects of changing American attitudes toward the Taliban. He also describes the new face of Islamic fundamentalism and explains why Afghanistan has become the world center for international terrorism." Publisher's note

Includes bibliographical references

Schroen, Gary C.

First in; an insider's account of how the CIA spearheaded the war on terror in Afghanistan. Presidio Press/Ballantine Books 2005 $25.95; pa $14.95   **958.1**

1. Afghanistan 2. United States -- Central Intelligence Agency

ISBN 0-89141-872-5; 0-89141-875-X pa

LC 2005-43171

The author describes his experiences after he "was tapped to lead the effort to establish contact with the Northern Alliance in the days following 9/11; the 35-year CIA veteran commanded the first American team on the ground in Afghanistan. . . . Schroen delivers what he advertises: a powerful account that takes the reader inside war councils and 19th-century- style cavalry charges in the months just after 9/11." Publ Wkly

Seierstad, Asne

The **bookseller** of Kabul; translated by Ingrid Christophersen. Little, Brown 2003 287p $19.95; pa $12.95   **958.1**

1. Afghanistan 2. Women -- Afghanistan

ISBN 0-316-73450-0; 0-316-15941-7 pa

LC 2003-54643

The author "entered Kabul with Northern Alliance soldiers after they ousted the Taliban. She took the rare opportunity to live with and write a book about the extended family of Sultan Khan, bookseller and entrepreneur. The result, organized around events in the lives of individual members of Khan's large clan . . . provides appropriate information about recent Afghani history, a glimpse from the inside at an Islamic family, and an understanding of the harshness and difficulty of the daily grind in Afghanistan—both under the Taliban and after the U.S. antiterrorist campaign." Booklist

Shah, Saira

The **storyteller's** daughter. Knopf 2003 253p $24; pa $13.95   **958.1**

1. Afghanistan

ISBN 0-375-41531-9; 1-4000-3147-8 pa

LC 2004-295126

The author "weaves oral traditions with history to describe life as an Afghani raised in the West but with solid roots in the East. . . . We learn about Shah's documentary work in Afghanistan, the power of myth through which Afghanistan's tradition is born, the brave work of peoples and organizations such as the Revolutionary Association of the Women of Afghanistan (RAWA), and the West's (and even East's) misconceptions regarding Muslim teachings. . . . This rare personal and historic account of the region is a great addition to public and academic libraries." Libr J

Wahab, Shaista

★ A **brief** history of Afghanistan; [by] Shaista Wahab and Barry Youngerman. 2nd ed; Facts on File 2010 354p il map (Brief history) $49.50; pa $19.95   **958.1**

1. Afghanistan -- History

ISBN 978-0-8160-8218-6; 978-0-8160-8219-3 pa; 978-1-4381-0819-3 ebook

LC 2010-19656

First published 2006

This history of Afghanistan "examines this country's isolation and how it found itself involved in 30 years of war and anarchy. . . . [It] explores the culture and politics of the Pashtun tribes whose homeland extends across much of Afghanistan and northern Pakistan, as well as the Taliban insurgency and the relationship between local leaders and the central government in Kabul." Publisher's note

Includes bibliographical references

West, Bing

The **wrong** war; grit, strategy, and the way out of Afghanistan. [by] Bing West. Random House 2011 307p il map $28 **958.1**
1. Afghan War, 2001-
ISBN 978-1-4000-6873-9; 1-4000-6873-8
LC 2010043107

West argues that "the central premise of counterinsurgency doctrine holds that if the Americans sacrifice on behalf of the Afghan government, then the Afghan people will risk their lives for that same government in return. They will fight the Taliban. . . . This isn't happening. . . . [The author contends that] the Afghans are waiting to see who prevails, but prevailing is impossible without their help." (N Y Times Book Rev) Bibliography. Index.

This is "a crushing and seemingly irrefutable critique of the American plan in Afghanistan. It should be read by anyone who wants to understand why the war there is so hard." N Y Times Book Rev

Includes bibliographical references

Zoya

Zoya's story; an Afghan woman's struggle for freedom. {by} Zoya with John Follain and Rita Cristofari. HarperCollins Pubs. 2002 239p $24.95; pa $12.95 **958.1**
1. Afghanistan 2. Women -- Afghanistan
ISBN 0-06-009782-5; 0-06-009783-3 pa

"After both her parents were killed by the Mujahideen, Zoya took up her mother's work in the Revolutionary Association of the Women of Afghanistan and, with her grandmother, journeyed to Pakistan, where she could receive an education. A few years later, Zoya returned to Afghanistan, where she witnessed public executions but also saw heartening displays of courage. A stirring memoir by an uncompromisingly brave woman." Booklist

958.104 Afghanistan--1919-

Anderson, Jon Lee

The **lion's** grave; dispatches from Afghanistan. photographs by Thomas Dworzak. Grove Press 2002 244p il $23; pa $13 **958.104**
1. Afghanistan
ISBN 0-8021-1723-6; 0-8021-4025-4 pa
LC 2002-70659

In this "account, which includes his diary entries. Anderson recounts the arduous task of developing sources and reporting on the complexities of a nation caught up in its own ethnic and religious conflicts and its place in the new war on terrorism." Booklist

Chandrasekaran, Rajiv

Little America; the war within the war for Afghanistan. Rajiv Chandrasekaran. Alfred A. Knopf 2012 368 p. ill., maps $27.95 **958.104**
1. Taliban 2. Bureaucracy 3. Afghan War, 2001- 4. Afghanistan -- Strategic aspects 5. Internal security -- Afghanistan 6. United States -- Military policy 7. United States -- Politics and government -- 2009- 8.

Afghan War, 2001- -- Political aspects -- United States
ISBN 0307957144; 9780307957146
LC 2012010354

This book offers journalist Rajiv Chandrasekaran's coverage of the U.S. surge in Afghanistan. "He found the effort sabotaged not only by Afghan and Pakistani malfeasance but by infighting and incompetence within the American government. . . . Along the way, we meet an Army general whose experience as the top military officer in charge of Iraq's Green Zone couldn't prepare him for the bureaucratic knots of Afghanistan . . . and a war-seasoned diplomat frustrated in his push for a scaled-down but long-term American commitment." (Publisher's note)

Includes bibliographical references and index

Corwin, Phillip

Doomed in Afghanistan; a UN officer's memoir of the fall of Kabul and Najibullah's escape, 1992. Rutgers Univ. Press 2003 xx, 241p il $28 **958.104**
1. Presidents 2. Communist leaders 3. United Nations -- Afghanistan 4. Afghanistan -- History -- Soviet occupation, 1979-1989
ISBN 0-8135-3171-3
LC 2002-24831

This book "focuses on the period after the Soviets left the country in 1988, when the UN was given the task of establishing a broad-based regime that would have included the communists. Thanks to the intrigues of the US and its clients, Pakistan and Saudi Arabia, the UN team, of which the author was a member, failed to effect the escape of Najibullah, the leftist president of Afghanistan, from Kabul. As a result, there could be no broad-based coalition that might have prevented the rise of the Taliban and the country's decline into barbarism. . . . This engaging and sympathetic essay enables readers to understand the country's tragic recent past and the failure of diplomacy . . . which paved the way for civil war and the rise of 'Islamic fundamentalism.'" Choice

Includes bibliographical references

Eichstaedt, Peter

Above the din of war; Afghans speak about their lives, their country, and their future--and why America should listen. by Peter Eichstaedt. Lawrence Hill Books 2013 304 p. col. ill., map (hardcover) $26.95 **958.104**
1. Afghan War, 2001- 2. Afghanistan -- Social conditions 3. Afghanistan -- Politics and government 4. Public opinion -- Afghanistan 5. Postwar reconstruction -- Afghanistan -- Public opinion 6. Afghanistan -- Politics and government -- 2001- -- Public opinion 7. Afghanistan -- Social conditions -- 21st century -- Public opinion
ISBN 161374515X; 9781613745151
LC 2012045820

In this book, "journalist [Peter] Eichstaedt . . . .) delivers from Afghanistan a dismal report on that country's continued disintegration and decline and the failure of U.S. efforts to prevent it. . . . Eichstaedt interviewed Afghans from all walks of life: government officials, Taliban leaders, shopkeepers, mullahs, would-be suicide bombers, victims of self-immolation and others." (Kirkus Reviews)

Gezari, Vanessa M.

The **tender** soldier; a true story of war and sacrifice. by Vanessa M. Gezari. Simon & Schuster 2013 336 p. $25   **958.104**

   1. Social sciences 2. Afghan War, 2001- 3. Afghanistan -- Social conditions   4.   Applied anthropology -- Afghanistan 5. United States. Army. Human Terrain System 6. Anthropologists -- United States -- Biography 7. Counterinsurgency -- Afghanistan -- De Maywand Kārīz 8. Applied anthropology -- United States -- Moral and ethical aspects 9. Social sciences -- Research -- United States -- Moral and ethical aspects 10. Afghan War, 2001- -- Campaigns -- Afghanistan -- De Maywand Kārīz

ISBN 1439177392; 9781439177396

                          LC 2013001090

This book, by Vanessa M. Gezari, looks at the U.S. "Pentagon's controversial attempt to bring social science to the battlefield, a program, called the Human Terrain System.... Gezari follows ... three idealists from the hope that brought them to Afghanistan through the events of the fateful day when one is gravely wounded, an Afghan is dead, and a proponent of cross-cultural engagement is charged with his murder." (Publisher's note)

Includes bibliographical references

Giunta, Salvatore A., 1985-

Living with honor; by Salvatore A. Giunta ; with Joe Layden. Threshold Books 2012 304 p. $26   **958.104**

   1. Afghan War, 2001- 2. Soldiers -- United States 3. Medal of Honor -- Biography 4. Soldiers -- United States -- Biography 5. Afghan War, 2001- -- Personal narratives, American   6.   Afghan War, 2001- -- Campaigns -- Afghanistan -- Korangal Valley

ISBN 1451691467; 9781451691467; 9781451691504; 9781451691535

                          LC 2012030594

In the book by Salvatore A. Giunta, "this hero . . . tells us the story of the fateful day in Afghanistan that led to his receiving the" Medal of Honor. "Stationed with the 173rd Airborne Brigade near the Afghanistan-Pakistan border in the Korengal Valley . . . Giunta and his company were ambushed by Taliban insurgents . . . Discovering two rebels carrying away a U.S. soldier, Giunta killed one insurgent and wounded the other, and immediately provided aid to the injured soldier." (Publisher's note)

Maurer, Kevin

No easy day; the autobiography of a Navy SEAL : the firsthand account of the mission that killed Osama Bin Laden. Mark Owen ; with Kevin Maurer. Dutton 2012 xiii, 316 p.p $26.95   **958.104**

   1. Afghan War, 2001- -- Personal narratives 2. Special forces (Military science) -- United States 3. Qaida (Organization)   4.   United States. Navy. SEALs -- Biography 5. United States. Navy -- Commando troops -- Biography

ISBN 0525953728; 9780525953722

                          LC 2012371921

This book, by Mark Owen with Kevin Mauer, offers a "first-person account of the planning and execution of the Bin Laden raid from a Navy Seal" who was present on the mission. The book follows "Owen and the other handpicked members of the twenty-four-man team as they train[ed] for the biggest mission of their lives." It provides a "narrative of the assault, beginning with the helicopter crash . . . straight through to the radio call confirming Bin Laden's death." (Publisher's note)

Includes bibliographical references.

Omar, Qais Akbar

★ A **fort** of nine towers; an Afghan family story. by Qais Akbar Omar. 1st ed. Farrar, Straus and Giroux 2013 396 p. maps (hardcover) $27.00 **958.104**

   1. Family 2. Afghanistan -- Social conditions 3. Afghanistan -- Biography 4. Afghanistan -- Social conditions -- 20th century

ISBN 0374157642; 9780374157647

                          LC 2012034566

In this book, author Qais Akbar Omar presents a coming-of-age memoir about his experiences in Afghanistan during the Afghan Civil War. "With rockets falling around them, Omar's family fled, leaving behind everything they owned to take shelter in an old fort. As the violence escalated, Omar's father decided he must take his children out of the country to safety. Omar recounts terrifyingly narrow escapes and absurdist adventures, as well as moments of intense joy and beauty." (Publisher's note)

Wahab, Saima, 1974-

In my father's country; an Afghan woman defies her fate. Saima Wahab. 1st ed. Crown Publishers 2012 346 p. (hardcover) $25.00; (ebook) $75.00   **958.104**

   1. Refugees 2. Afghan American women -- Biography 3. Postwar reconstruction -- Afghanistan 4. Women translators -- Afghanistan -- Biography 5. Afghanistan -- Social conditions -- 21st century

ISBN 9780307884947; 9780307884961

                          LC 2011039456

This is Pashtun refugee Saima Wahab's memoir. At age five, "Wahab began her life on the run after her father was taken from their Kabul home by KGB agents during the Soviet occupation of Afghanistan." Ultimately educated in America, Wahab "was hired by the U.S. military in 2004 to help coordinate efforts in Afghanistan." (Kirkus)

958.4   Turkestan

Girardet, Edward

Killing the cranes; Edward Girardet. Chelsea Green Pub. Co. 2011 xiv, 417p.p   **958.4**

   1. Journalists 2. Afghan War, 2001- 3. Afghanistan -- History 4. Afghanistan -- History -- Soviet occupation, 1979-1989

ISBN 9781603583428

                          LC 2011014661

This book presents a "personal account of Afghanistan and its people from 1979 to the present. . . . During his long career, Girardet has met, befriended and been threatened by many key figures in Afghanistan's recent history, including Gulbuddin Hekmatyar, Ahmed Shah Massoud and even the recently assassinated Osama bin Ladin. . . . The author is concerned that corruption, criminality and religious fundamentalism have undermined the country's potential, especially since the 1990s. With a long-view perspective, Girardet puts forward a view of a culture based on generosity and openness, a culture which he thinks has been wronged by misguided association with the fighting qualities of guerrillas and terrorists." (Kirkus)

Robbins, Christopher

Apples are from Kazakhstan; the land that disappeared. Atlas Books 2008 296p il map $24 **958.4**
1. Kazakhstan
ISBN 0-9777433-8-1; 978-0-9777433-8-4

LC 2008-299516

First published 2007 in the United Kingdom with the title: In search of Kazakhstan

A "delightful and masterful travelog reveals . . . a country rich in history, natural beauty, and, perhaps most important, tolerance. . . . [The author] manages to make this an overall hopeful book by combining grave topics with less grave ones and adding a good dose of wit." Libr J

959   Southeast Asia

Somers Heidhues, Mary F.

Southeast Asia: a concise history. Thames & Hudson 2000 192p il maps hardcover o.p. pa $18.95   **959**
1. Southeast Asia -- History
ISBN 0-500-28303-6 pa

LC 99-66014

This "history ranges from Southeast Asia's prehistoric times to the most recent political developments in Indonesia. Heidhues . . . divides her study into seven well-balanced chapters, touching on the political history, economics, society, and culture of Burma, Thailand, Cambodia, Vietnam, Malaysia, Singapore, Brunei, Indonesia, and the Philippines." Libr J

★ **Southeast** Asia; a historical encyclopedia from Angkor Wat to East Timor. edited by Ooi Keat Gin. ABC-CLIO 2004 3v il map set $285 **959**
1. Southeast Asia
ISBN 1-576-07770-5

LC 2004-4813

The countries covered in this book include "Myanmar (Burma), Thailand (Siam), Laos, Cambodia, Vietnam, Malaysia, Singapore, Brunei, the Philippines, Indonesia, and East Timor. This A-Z aims to help students and researchers grasp the fragmented region through 800 detailed articles on archaeology, politics, culture, economic transformation, and more." Libr J
Includes bibliographical references

959.1   Myanmar

Aung San Suu Kyi

Freedom from fear, and other writings; edited with an introduction by Michael Aris; foreword to the first edition by Vaclav Havel, foreword to the second edition by Archbishop Desmond Tutu. rev ed; Penguin Bks. 1995 xxxi, 374p il pa $14.95   **959.1**
1. Myanmar -- Politics and government
ISBN 0-14-025317-3

LC 96-902734

First published 1991

This is a collection of essays, letters, speeches, and other writings by the Burmese opposition leader, Winner of the 1991 Nobel Peace Prize

"Mrs. Aung San Suu Kyi's excellent book offers inspiration to many other peoples in the region as much as it reflects Myanmar's own desire for change." N Y Times Book Rev {review of 1991 edition}
Includes bibliographical references

Larkin, Emma

Everything is broken; a tale of catastrophe in Burma. Penguin Press 2010 271p map $25.95 **959.1**
1. Cyclones 2. Disaster relief 3. Myanmar
ISBN 978-1-59420-257-5; 1-59420-257-5

LC 2010-04029

"Larkin is such a facile observer and writer, she tempts comparisons to Orwell, and certainly ranks with Ryszard Kapuscinski as a lyric writer of reportage." Cleveland Plain Dealer

Thant Myint-U

The **river** of lost footsteps; histories of Burma. Farrar, Straus & Giroux 2006 361p il map $25; pa $15   **959.1**
1. Myanmar
ISBN 978-0-374-16342-6; 0-374-16342-1; 978-0-374-53116-4 pa; 0-374-53116-1 pa

LC 2006-09199

The author "tells the story of modern Burma, in part through a telling of his own family's history." Publisher's note

"This readable, reflective history will support revived interest in Burma." Booklist
Includes bibliographical references

Where China meets India; Burma and the new crossroads of Asia. Farrar, Straus and Giroux 2011 361p map $27   **959.1**
1. Myanmar -- Description and travel 2. China -- Foreign relations -- Myanmar 3. India -- Foreign relations -- Myanmar 4. Myanmar -- Foreign relations -- China 5. Myanmar -- Foreign relations -- India
ISBN 978-0-374-29907-1; 0-374-29907-2

LC 2011024406

In the book, "Thant Myint-U advances the . . . argument for changing Western policy [regarding Burma]: isolation is useless because Burma is . . . becoming a bridge between two rising global giants. Writing of his travels through the borderlands of China, India and Burma, Thant Myint-U hopes to demonstrate how this region of Asia, home to more than 600 million people, is integrating, and how Burma will be at the center of it." (Nation)

Focusing "on his home country of Burma, and the area encompassed by a diameter of 1,000 miles drawn from the city of Mandalay on the edge of the Shan Plateau, Thant suggests that this corner of the world (with a population of 600 million) is destined to become a bridge between Bengal, Bangladesh, India's North Eastern Provinces, and China's Yunnan province." Publ Wkly

Includes bibliographical references

959.3 Thailand

Krauss, Erich

Wave of destruction; the stories of four families and history's deadliest tsunami. Rodale 2006 244p il map $24.95 **959.3**

1. Tsunamis 2. Survival after airplane accidents, shipwrecks, etc. 3. Thailand
ISBN 1-59486-378-4

LC 2005-24531

The author provides an "account of four families in a Thai village devastated by the tsunami of December 26, 2004. . . . Passionately told, this tragic story portrays the full human cost of natural devastation." Publ Wkly

Osborne, Lawrence

Bangkok days. North Point Press 2009 271p il $25 **959.3**

1. Bangkok (Thailand) -- Description and travel
ISBN 978-0-86547-732-2; 0-86547-732-9

LC 2008-44741

Osborne "provides a raunchy account of the nightlife and bars and bargirls of Thailand's capital. In particular, he delves into the lives of a motley band of aging, libertine Westerners (Farangs) living in his apartment complex and explores the city in their company. Their tragicomic lives are compelling, and Osborne provides some extraordinary anecdotes." Libr J

Wyatt, David K.

★ **Thailand** : a short history; 2nd ed; Yale Univ. Press 2003 352p il maps pa $20 **959.3**

1. Thailand -- History
ISBN 0-3000-8475-7
First published 1984

This volume provides a general history of Thailand beginning with the migrations of the Tai peoples from southern China, examining the social and economic changes to the present

Includes bibliographical references

959.6 Cambodia

Brinkley, Joel, 1952-2014

Cambodia's curse; the modern history of a troubled land. PublicAffairs 2011 386p il $27.99 **959.6**

1. Heads of state 2. Communist leaders 3. Political leaders 4. Democracy -- Cambodia 5. Cambodia --

History -- 1979- 6. Cambodia -- Social conditions 7. Cambodia -- Politics and government 8. Cambodia -- Politics and government -- 1979-
ISBN 978-1-58648-787-4; 1-58648-787-6

LC 2010-44806

"Brinkley cuts a clear narrative path through the bewildering, cynical politics and violent social life of one of the worlds most brutalized and hard-up countries." Foreign Affairs

Includes bibliographical references

Dunlop, Nic

The **lost** executioner; a journey to the heart of the killing fields. Walker & Co. 2006 326p il map $24 **959.6**

1. Murderers 2. Evangelists 3. Khmer Rouge 4. Executioners 5. Cambodia -- History -- 1975-
ISBN 0-8027-1472-2
First published 2005 in the United Kingdom

This is an "account of the Khmer Rouge, the Cambodian Communist regime responsible for more than two million deaths between 1975 and 1979. Armed with a black-and-white photograph of Comrade Duch—Pol Pot's chief executioner—Dunlop traveled to the war-ravaged country to probe the dark depths of a once-studious young boy and dedicated teacher who became one of the twentieth-century's most notorious mass murderers. . . . Dunlop's interviews with former Khmer Rouge members are both wrenching and revelatory." Booklist

Includes bibliographical references

Kiernan, Ben

The **Pol** Pot regime; race, power, and genocide in Cambodia under the Khmer Rouge, 1975-79. 2nd ed; Yale Univ. Press 2002 xxiii, 477p il map (Yale Nota bene) pa $19.95 **959.6**

1. Atrocities 2. Communism -- Cambodia 3. Cambodia -- Politics and government
ISBN 0-300-09649-6

LC 2002-100979

First published 1996

This is an account of "the Cambodian catastrophe; the significant internal resistance to the Khmer Rouge; and the racialist and totalitarian attitudes by which Pol Pot's regime justified the death, by starvation and disease as well as torture and murder, of some 1.5 million of their 8 million countrymen." Booklist {review of 1996 edition}

Includes bibliographical references

Ung, Loung

First they killed my father; a daughter of Cambodia remembers. HarperCollins Pubs. 2000 240p il hardcover o.p. pa $13.95 **959.6**

1. Cambodia -- History -- 1975-
ISBN 0-06-019332-8; 0-06-085626-2 pa

LC 99-34707

The author's father was a "high-ranking government official in Phnom Penh. She was only five when the Khmer Rouge stormed the city and her family was forced to flee. They sought refuge in various camps, hiding their wealth and education, always on the move and ever fearful of being betrayed. After 20 months, Ung's father was taken away, never to be seen again. Her story of starvation, forced labor, beatings, attempted rape, separations, and the deaths of her family members is one of horror and brutality." SLJ

959.604   -1949

Bizot, Francois

The **gate**; translated from the French by Euan Cameron; with a preface by John Le Carré. Knopf 2003 275p $24; pa $14   **959.604**

1. Atrocities 2. Communism -- Cambodia 3. Cambodia -- History -- 1970-1975, Civil War

ISBN 0-375-41293-X; 0-375-72723-X pa

LC 2002-69428

Original French edition, 2000

The author, who was "seized by Cambodian rebels in 1971, recalls peculiar daily chat sessions over politics and philosophy with his chief captor, an obviously dangerous man who later ran one of the Khmer Rouge's ghastliest killing fields." N Y Times Book Rev

Bizot's "tale of his experiences, both in the camp and as translator at the gate of the French embassy, leaves readers with haunting images of the doomed." Booklist

Him, Chanrithy

When broken glass floats; growing up under the Khmer Rouge. Norton 2000 330p il map hardcover o.p. pa $13.95   **959.604**

1. Refugees 2. Memoirists 3. Interpreters 4. Cambodia -- History 5. Political refugees -- Cambodia 6. Political atrocities -- Cambodia 7. Political refugees -- United States 8. Cambodia -- Politics and government -- 1975-1979

ISBN 0-393-32210-6 pa

LC 99-58417

This is an account of the author's experiences as a child in Cambodia under the Khmer Rouge. Him "watched {her} father hauled away to be killed, saw {her} mother and several siblings die by execution, starvation and disease. After the Khmer Rouge's downfall, {she} eventually escaped to Thailand and then to the United States." (N Y Times Book Rev)

Him "was 10 in 1975 when the Khmer Rouge overtook her country in what she calls the time of broken glass. Feeling a survivor's responsibility to do so, Him vividly recalls the brutality of the camps, the strict social control, and alienation from family that the Khmer Rouge enforced." Booklist

Kamm, Henry

Cambodia : report from a stricken land. Arcade Pub. 1998 xxiv, 262p il maps $25.95   **959.604**

1. Cambodia -- History

ISBN 1-55970-433-0

LC 98-22707

This is an account of events in Cambodia since the 1970s. Kamm argues that these "events were man-made and avoidable, the consequence of cynical and callous decisions by rival Cambodian leaders and by foreign powers, including the United States. . . . Guiltiest by far were the Khmer Rouge, who made Cambodia a killing field while their . . .

regime under Pol Pot held power between 1975 and 1979." N Y Times Book Rev

"Sober yet passionate, Kamm's well-informed survey is an excellent introduction to a country that the world has all but abandoned." Libr J

959.7   Vietnam

Sachs, Dana

The **house** on Dream Street; memoir of an American woman in Vietnam. Seal Press 2003 357p pa $15.95   **959.7**

1. Vietnam -- Description and travel

ISBN 1-580-05100-6

LC 2003-57299

First published by Algonquin Bks in 2000

This is an American journalist's account of her visits to Vietnam. "Her memoir covers the time from her initial plunge into the country, as a touring backpacker in 1989, to her triumphant return in 1998 with . . . [her] husband and son." Publ Wkly

959.704   Vietnam--1945-

Anderson, David L.

★ The **Columbia** guide to the Vietnam War. Columbia Univ. Press 2002 308p maps (Columbia guides to American history and cultures) $47; pa $22.50   **959.704**

1. Vietnam War, 1961-1975

ISBN 0-231-11492-3; 0-231-11493-1 pa

LC 2002-20143

"Anderson's guide successfully compresses the copiously documented, labyrinthine history of the Vietnamese conflict into a single economical volume. In five parts, the guide's narrative and encyclopedia sections provide a fascinating survey of the war, while the remaining elements of the work link modern researchers to a host of richly documented resources. . . . The guide will become an important resource for those seeking a historical overview as well as direction for further research. Strongly recommended." Choice

Includes bibliographical references

Berman, Larry, 1951-

No peace, no honor; Nixon, Kissinger, and betrayal in Vietnam. Free Press 2001 334p $27.50; pa $14   **959.704**

1. Presidents 2. Vice-presidents 3. Vietnam War, 1961-1975 4. Senators 5. College teachers 6. Nonfiction writers 7. Members of Congress 8. Writers on politics 9. Secretaries of state 10. Presidential advisers 11. Nobel laureates for peace 12. International relations specialists 13. United States -- Politics and government -- 1961-1974

ISBN 0-684-84968-2; 0-7432-2349-7 pa

LC 2001-23904

"In the endless flow of assessments, reassessments and re-reassessments of the war in Vietnam, a study occasionally appears that goes beyond a rehash of the polemics that have marked that tragic experience. Larry Berman's 'No Peace, No Honor' belongs in that select category." N Y Times Book Rev

Includes bibliographical references

Bissell, Tom

The **father** of all things; a Marine, his son, and the legacy of Vietnam. Pantheon Books 2007 407p il $25   **959.704**
1. Veterans 2. Vietnam War, 1961-1975 3. Marine corps officers 4. Vietnam -- Description and travel
ISBN 978-0-375-42265-2; 0-375-42265-X
LC 2006-49427

"In 2003, Bissell travelled to Vietnam with his father, who had fought there nearly four decades before. Their relationship was uneasy: as a child, Bissell once reported his father to an abuse hotline (after an unusually physical game of rock, paper, scissors), and, at the age of twenty-nine, he still felt 'diminished' in the man's presence; meanwhile, his father, only half joking, called him a Communist. In this ambitious, uneven book, Bissell chronicles their pilgrimage to former battlefields and seeks to reconcile his personal 'mythology,' as the son of a Vietnam veteran, with the larger context of 'the only war in which the United States failed to enact its will.' Bissell writes with conviction, and his prose, if sometimes swashbuckling, has moments of startling beauty." New Yorker

Includes bibliographical references

Caputo, Philip

★ A **rumor** of war; with a twentieth anniversary postscript by the author. Henry Holt and Co. 1996 xxi, 356p pa $15   **959.704**
1. Vietnam War, 1961-1975 -- Personal narratives
ISBN 0-8050-4695-X
LC 96-19314
First published 1977 by Holt, Rinehart & Winston

These are "the combat recollections of a very young Marine officer in Vietnam in 1965-1966. Caputo later became a newspaperman. . . . He remembers himself as a patriotic youngster, eager to prove his manhood, and then . . . he takes us through his step-by-step discovery that war and manhood and their interrelation are more complicated than he had dreamed." New Yorker

Duiker, William J.

Ho Chi Minh; by William Duiker. Hyperion 2000 695p il maps $35; pa $16.95   **959.704**
1. Heads of state 2. Communist leaders 3. Political leaders
ISBN 0-7868-6387-0; 0-7868-8701-X pa
LC 00-26757

In this biography the author "examines Ho's life primarily in the context of his political activity in Paris, Moscow, southern China, and Vietnam, occasionally spiced with anecdotes of Ho's highly secretive personal life. . . . Duiker handles the complicated political and diplomatic issues with ease, and his narrative, though it sometimes strays from Ho's life to fill in the bigger picture, never bogs down." Booklist

Includes bibliographical references

Ellsberg, Daniel

Secrets : a memoir of Vietnam and the Pentagon papers. Viking 2002 498p il $29.95; pa $16   **959.704**
1. Vietnam War, 1961-1975 2. Pentagon Papers
ISBN 0-670-03030-9; 0-14-200342-5 pa
LC 2002-16874

Ellsberg recalls how he leaked "the Pentagon Papers, which documented U.S. foreign-policy failures and deceit in Vietnam from 1945 to 1968. . . . Ellsberg's autobiographical account provides insight into the disturbing abuses of presidential power that plagued the Vietnam/Watergate era." Libr J

Includes bibliographical references

The encyclopedia of the Vietnam War; a political, social, and military history. Spencer C. Tucker, editor. 2nd ed.; ABC-CLIO 2011 4v il map set $395   **959.704**
1. Reference books 2. Vietnam War, 1961-1975 -- Encyclopedias
ISBN 978-1-85109-960-3; 978-1-85109-961-0 ebook
LC 2011007604
First published 1998

"Written to provide multidimensional perspectives into the conflict, . . . [this encyclopedia] covers not only the American experience in Vietnam, but also the entire scope of Vietnamese history, including the French experience and the Indochina War, as well as the origins of the conflict, how the United States became involved, and the extensive aftermath of this prolonged war." Publisher's note

Includes bibliographical references

FitzGerald, Frances

Fire in the lake; the Vietnamese and the Americans in Vietnam. Little, Brown 1972 491p maps hardcover o.p. pa $16.95   **959.704**
1. Vietnam War, 1961-1975 2. Vietnam -- Politics and government
ISBN 0-316-15919-0 pa

This book looks at the effects American intervention had on the Vietnamese social and intellectual landscape.

Includes bibliographical references

Frankum, Ronald B.

Historical dictionary of the war in Vietnam; Ronald B. Frankum, Jr. Scarecrow Press 2011 672p (Historical dictionaries of war, revolution, and civil unrest) $99; ebook $99   **959.704**
1. Vietnamese Conflict, 1961-1975
ISBN 978-0-8108-6796-3; 978-0-8108-7956-0 ebook; 9780810867963 (cloth : alk. paper); 9780810879560 (ebook)
LC 2010052321
First published 1999

This book "contains approximately 700 entries that provide a balanced view, beginning with the start of the First Indochina War, in 1946, through the fall of Saigon, in 1975. The main portion of the book is, appropriately, the dictionary entry section. From one or two-paragraph definitions for terms such as Napalm, Nixon Doctrine, and Viet Cong to multipage descriptions for entries such as Air war, Ho Chi

Minh, and Tet Offensive, 1968, Frankum's writing is consistently straightforward and accurate, and the topics he includes are appropriate." Booklist

Includes bibliographical references.

Glasser, Ronald J.

365 days. Braziller 1971 292p hardcover o.p. pa $14.95 **959.704**

1. Vietnam War, 1961-1975 -- Medical care 2. Vietnam War, 1961-1975 -- Personal narratives

ISBN 0-8076-1527-7 pa

The author, a military doctor who was stationed in Japan, recounts his experiences treating wounded American military personnel during the Vietnam War

Goldstein, Donald M.

The **Vietnam** War: the story and photographs; by Donald M. Goldstein, Katherine V. Dillon, and J. Michael Wenger. Brassey's 1997 179p il maps hardcover o.p. pa $19.95 **959.704**

1. Vietnam War, 1961-1975

ISBN 1-57488-210-4 pa

LC 97-11574

This history of the Vietnam War "proceeds both chronologically and thematically, beginning with the French colonial era and the Indochina War, then covering successive stages of the U.S. involvement. The text is sufficiently detailed, clear, and balanced to serve as a narrative introduction to the subject, but the real strength lies in the photographs. They cover the subject with admirable thoroughness. . . . They do not include too many chestnuts, and they adequately cover the Vietnamese, the navy, and other subjects relatively neglected in the literature thus far." Booklist

Includes bibliographical references

Hendrickson, Paul

The **living** and the dead; Robert McNamara and five lives of a lost war. Knopf 1996 427p il hardcover o.p. pa $15 **959.704**

1. Vietnam War, 1961-1975 2. Bankers 3. Secretaries of defense 4. International organization officials

ISBN 0-679-7811-X pa

LC 96-7445

"Exhaustively researched, probing, important contribution to the annals of American history." Publ Wkly

Includes bibliographical references

Hershberg, James G.

Marigold; the lost chance for peace in Vietnam. James G. Hershberg. Stanford University Press 2011 960 p. $39.50 **959.704**

1. Vietnam War, 1961-1975 2. Vietnam War, 1961-1975 -- Peace 3. Vietnam War, 1961-1975 -- Diplomatic history 4. United States -- Foreign relations -- 1963-1969

ISBN 0804778841; 9780804778848

LC 2011034990

This book by James Hershberg "presents the . . . in-depth story of one of the Vietnam War's last great mysteries: the secret Polish-Italian peace initiative, codenamed 'Marigold,' that sought to end the war, or at least to open direct talks between Washington and Hanoi, in 1966. . . . This book uses new evidence from long hidden communist sources to show that Warsaw was authorized by Hanoi to open direct contacts and that Hanoi had committed to entering talks with Washington." (Publisher's note)

Includes bibliographical references and index

Inside the Pentagon papers; edited by John Prados and Margaret Pratt Porter. University Press of Kansas 2004 248p (Modern war studies) $29.95 **959.704**

1. Vietnam War, 1961-1975 2. Pentagon Papers

ISBN 0-7006-1325-0

LC 2004-1961

The editors "reexamine the secret government papers that blew the whistle on the Vietnam War, led to the federal attempts to restrain the press and ultimately resulted in President Richard Nixon's resignation. . . . Volumes about these issues abound, but Prados and Porter offer a concise look at those pivotal events and their long-term effects." Publ Wkly

Includes bibliographical references

Kaiser, David E.

American tragedy; Kennedy, Johnson, and the origins of the Vietnam War. {by} David Kaiser. Harvard Univ. Press 2000 566p il $36; pa $18.95 **959.704**

1. Presidents 2. Vice-presidents 3. Vietnam War, 1961-1975 4. Senators 5. Members of Congress 6. United States -- Politics and government -- 1961-1974

ISBN 0-674-00225-3; 0-674-00672-0 pa

LC 99-52925

"The first-rate research is complemented by an intriguing model of intergenerational policy-making." Libr J

Includes bibliographical references

Karnow, Stanley

Vietnam; a history. 2nd rev & updated ed; Penguin Bks. 1997 768p il maps pa $17.95 **959.704**

1. Vietnam War, 1961-1975 2. Vietnam -- History

ISBN 0-14-026547-3

First published 1983

A summation "of over two centuries of conflict in Indochina. Chronicling a tragic history, Karnow presents a balanced and sympathetic view of Vietnamese aspirations and the mishaps that led to American involvement in a 'war nobody won.'" Voice Youth Advocates [review of 1983 edition]

Includes bibliographical references

Kissinger, Henry, 1923-

Ending the Vietnam War; a history of America's involvement in and extrication from the Vietnam War. Touchstone 2002 640p map pa $18 **959.704**

1. Vietnam War, 1961-1975

ISBN 0-7432-1532-X

LC 2002-17996

"Readers interested in the Vietnam period but unfamiliar with Kissinger's previous books will find this new volume worthwhile. . . . Kissinger's account of America's venture in Vietnam and his role in that shipwreck is factually accurate, eminently informed and masterfully crafted." Publ Wkly

Includes bibliographical references

Lair, Meredith H.

Armed with abundance; consumerism & soldiering in the Vietnam War. Meredith H. Lair. University of North Carolina Press 2011 xviii, 295 p.p ill., map (cloth : alk. paper) $34.95   **959.704**

1. Soldiers -- United States -- Recreation 2. Vietnam War, 1961-1975 -- Social aspects 3. Lifestyles -- United States -- History -- 20th century 4. United States. Army -- History -- Vietnam War, 1961-1975 5. United States -- Moral conditions -- History -- 20th century 6. United States. Army -- Military life -- History -- 20th century 7. Soldiers -- United States -- Social life and customs -- 20th century 8. Consumption (Economics) -- Social aspects -- United States -- History -- 20th century

ISBN 0807834815; 9780807834817

LC 2011022140

This book, by Meredith Lair, "focuses on the noncombat experiences of U.S. soldiers in Vietnam, redrawing the landscape of the war so that swimming pools, ice cream, visits from celebrities, and other 'comforts' share the frame with combat. . . . Relying on memoirs, military documents, and G.I. newspapers, Lair finds that consumption and satiety, rather than privation and sacrifice, defined most soldiers' Vietnam deployments." (Publisher's note)

Includes bibliographical references and index

Langguth, A. J.

Our Vietnam; the war, 1954-1975. Simon & Schuster 2000 766p il maps hardcover o.p. pa $20   **959.704**

1. Vietnam War, 1961-1975 2. Vietnam -- Politics and government

ISBN 0-7432-1231-2 pa

LC 00-57384

The author tells the story of the Vietnam War "mainly through the actions of key personalities. Each of his chapters is titled for one of the principal characters, . . . among them presidents and other . . . American officials of the era, as well as figures like Daniel Ellsberg, who leaked the Pentagon Papers. The list also includes the names of . . . Vietnamese leaders on both sides." N Y Times Book Rev

This book "is unique in its perspective of the major players on both sides." Booklist

Includes bibliographical references

Lind, Michael

Vietnam, the necessary war; a reinterpretation of America's most disastrous military conflict. Free Press 1999 314p $25; pa $14   **959.704**

1. Vietnam War, 1961-1975 2. United States -- Foreign relations

ISBN 0-684-84254-8; 0-684-87027-4 pa

LC 99-28449

"Lind's arguments, if not always persuasive, are always provocative." Publ Wkly

Includes bibliographical references

Logevall, Fredrik

★ **Embers** of War; The Fall of an Empire and the Making of America's Vietnam. Fredrik Logevall. Random House 2012 xxii, 839 p.p ill.   **959.704**

1. France -- Colonies 2. Vietnam War, 1961-1975 3. Indochinese War, 1946-1954 4. United States -- Foreign relations -- Vietnam 5. United States -- Politics and government -- 1961-1974

ISBN 0375504427; 9780375504426

LC 2011034971

Pulitzer Prize: History (2013)

This book examines "the [Vietnam] war's roots in the U.S. reaction to the French colonial experience." Discussing "the global changes wrought by WWII, the beginning of the cold war, and America's new role as the pre-eminent power in Asian and world affairs . . . [Fredrik] Logevall makes" the "case that America's Vietnam involvement replicated the French experience: the U.S. was fighting against an anticolonialist revolution and giving the Democratic Republic of Vietnam legitimacy." (Publishers Weekly)

Includes bibliographical references and index.

Mann, Robert

A **grand** delusion; America's descent into Vietnam. Basic Bks. 2000 821p il $35; pa $22 **959.704**

1. Vietnam War, 1961-1975 2. Vietnam -- Politics and government 3. United States -- Politics and government -- 20th century

ISBN 0-465-04369-0; 0-465-04370-4 pa

LC 00-49824

This account of the United States involvement in the Vietnam War focuses on the political causes and "collision of personalities throughout the White House, Congress, and elsewhere during that era. Mann's history concentrates on seven American leaders in the halls of power rather than on the battlefield." Libr J

Includes bibliographical references and index

McCloud, Bill

What should we tell our children about Vietnam? University of Okla. Press 1989 155p hardcover o.p. pa $14.95   **959.704**

1. Vietnam War, 1961-1975

ISBN 0-8061-3240-X pa

LC 89-40218

"President Bush, William Westmoreland, Gary Trudeau, and Philip Caputo are among some of the best known of 128 individuals who gave their views when McCloud, a junior high school teacher and veteran, wrote to ask them what young people should understand about the war." Booklist

Includes bibliographical references

McNamara, Robert S.

In retrospect; the tragedy and lessons of Vietnam. Vintage Bks. 1996 518p il map pa $16.95 **959.704**

1. Vietnam War, 1961-1975

ISBN 0-679-76749-5; 978-0-679-76749-7

First published 1995 by Times Books

"Former defense secretary McNamara seeks 'to put Vietnam in context' and counter 'the cynicism and even contempt with which so many people view our political institutions and leaders.' . . . He identifies 'eleven major causes for our disaster in Vietnam' and six points when the U.S. could legitimately have withdrawn. Certainly not the last word on this still-controversial subject but an essential acquisition for most libraries." Booklist

Includes bibliographical references

Miller, Edward

Misalliance; Ngo Dinh Diem, the United States, and the fate of South Vietnam. Edward Miller. Harvard University Press 2013 419 p. (hardcover : alk. paper) $39.95   **959.704**
1. Vietnam -- Foreign relations -- United States 2. Vietnam (Republic) -- Politics and government 3. United States -- Foreign relations -- Vietnam (Republic) 4. Vietnam (Republic) -- Foreign relations -- United States
ISBN 0674072987; 9780674072985

LC 2012035332
This book is a "reassessment of former South Vietnamese leader Ngo Dinh Diem and his relationship with the US. . . . Miller takes a . . . transnational approach by utilizing Vietnamese and foreign language sources and presenting an analysis that is much more Vietnamese centered. . . . The author argues that it was, in fact, the politics of nation building that shaped the evolution and ultimate collapse of the US alliance with Diem." (Choice)
Includes bibliographical references and index

Moore, Harold G.

We are soldiers still; a journey back to the battlefields of Vietnam. [by] Harold G. Moore and Joseph L. Galloway. Harper 2008 248p il $24.95; pa $14.99   **959.704**
1. Vietnam -- Description and travel 2. Vietnam War, 1961-1975 -- Personal narratives
ISBN 978-0-06-114776-0; 0-06-114776-1; 978-0-06-114777-7 pa; 0-06-114777-X pa

LC 2008-11034
Sequel to We were soldiers once¿and young (1992)
"A worthy and wise successor to one of the best books ever about combat in Vietnam." Kirkus

We were soldiers once--and young; Ia Drang: the battle that changed the war in Vietnam. [by] Harold G. Moore and Joseph L. Galloway. Random House 1992 412p il maps $26.95; pa $7.50   **959.704**
1. Vietnam War, 1961-1975 -- Personal narratives
ISBN 0-679-41158-5; 0-345-47264-0 pa

LC 92-53642
"On Nov. 14, 1965, the 1st Battalion of the 7th Cavalry, commanded by Col. Moore and accompanied by UPI reporter Galloway, helicoptered into Vietnam's remote Ia Drang Valley and found itself surrounded by a numerically superior force of North Vietnamese regulars. Moore and Galloway here offer a detailed account, based on interviews with participants and on their own recollections, of what happened during the four-day battle." Publ Wkly
Includes bibliographical references
Followed by We are soldiers still (2008)

Morgan, Ted

Valley of death; the tragedy at Dien Bien Phu that led America into the Vietnam War. Random House 2010 722p il map $35   **959.704**
1. Indochinese War, 1946-1954 2. Dien Bien Phu, Battle of, 1954 3. United States -- Foreign relations --

Vietnam 4. Vietnam -- Foreign relations -- United States
ISBN 978-1-4000-6664-3

LC 2009-19714
"This absorbing account of the prelude, battle, and aftermath that ended the 'first Viet Nam War' is a sad tale of misconception, missed opportunities, and massive blunders by French and even American military and civilian officials. . . . This is a superb chronicle of a sad and avoidable conflict that led to an even more destructive one." Booklist
Includes bibliographical references

Napoli, Philip F.

Bringing it all back home; oral histories of New York's Vietnam veterans. by Philip F. Napoli. 1st ed. Hill and Wang 2012 254 p., [8] p. of platesp ill. (hardcover) $27   **959.704**
1. Oral history 2. Vietnam War, 1961-1975 -- Veterans 3. New York (N.Y.) -- Biography 4. Vietnam War, 1961-1975 -- New York (State) -- New York 5. Vietnam War, 1961-1975 -- Personal narratives, American 6. Vietnam War, 1961-1975 -- Veterans -- New York (State) -- New York -- Interviews
ISBN 0809073188; 9780809073184

LC 2012034731
For this book, Philip F. Napoli "spent six years conducting extensive interviews with more than 200 Vietnam vets who either grew up in New York City or who currently live there. The result of those 600 hours of recordings is a readable chronicle that uses the personal histories of the soldiers (in the interviewees' transcribed words) to tell the human story of the American war in Vietnam." (Publishers Weekly)
Includes bibliographical references.

Sallah, Michael

Tiger Force; a true story of men and war. [by] Michael Sallah and Mitch Weiss. Little, Brown 2006 403p il map $25.95   **959.704**
1. Vietnam War, 1961-1975 2. United States -- Army -- Infantry Regiment, 327th -- Battalion, 1st
ISBN 0-316-15997-2; 978-0-316-15997-5

LC 2005-20921
"In 1967, the Tiger Force platoon of the 101st Airborne went on a seven-month-long rampage through South Vietnam's central highlands that left dead more than 325 civilians, mostly children, women, and old men. . . . [This] is a searing narrative, difficult to read yet difficult to put down, about Tiger Force's descent into a leaderless and ruthless unit, in which, as one of the ex-soldiers puts it to the authors, the objective was to 'kill anything that moves.'" Libr J
Includes bibliographical references

Sheehan, Neil

A bright shining lie: John Paul Vann and America in Vietnam. Random House 1988 861p il hardcover o.p. pa $18   **959.704**
1. Vietnam War, 1961-1975 2. Army officers
ISBN 0-679-72414-1 pa

LC 87-43330
The author "tells the story of the war through the focus of John Paul Vann, an army officer who faced down South Vietnamese politicians and American generals to expose the corruption that undermined our efforts and later was Presi-

dent Nixon's civilian adviser in Vietnam until he was killed in a helicopter crash in 1972. It is a dramatic device that lets Mr. Sheehan bring the very palpable feel of the war to us with passionate power." N Y Times Book Rev

Includes bibliographical references

Shultz, Richard H.

The **secret** war against Hanoi; Kennedy and Johnson's use of spies, saboteurs, and covert warriors in North Vietnam. {by} Richard H. Shultz, Jr. HarperCollins Pubs. 1999 408p il hardcover o.p. pa $15   **959.704**

    1. Subversive activities 2. Vietnam War, 1961-1975 -- Secret service 3. United States -- Politics and government -- 1961-1974 4. United States -- Military Assistance Command, Vietnam -- Studies and Observations Group

    ISBN 0-06-093253-8 pa

                        LC 99-44524

"Organized in a military entity euphemistically named the Studies and Observation Group (SOG), the covert war, it was hoped, would annoy Hanoi enough to force it to scale back its war in the south. . . . Schultz was given access to SOG archives and veterans and has produced a professional volume on how SOG originated and operated over its eight-year existence." Booklist

Includes bibliographical references

Stur, Heather Marie

Beyond combat; women and gender in the Vietnam War era. Heather Marie Stur. Cambridge University Press 2011 xiii, 263 p.p (hardback) $90   **959.704**

    1. Gender role 2. Masculinity 3. Vietnam War, 1961-1975 -- Social aspects 4. Women -- United States -- History -- 20th century 5. Vietnam War, 1961-1975 -- Women 6. Women -- Vietnam -- History -- 20th century 7. Sex role -- Vietnam -- History -- 20th century 8. Vietnam War, 1961-1975 -- Participation, Female 9. Masculinity -- Vietnam -- History -- 20th century 10. Sex role -- United States -- History -- 20th century 11. Masculinity -- United States -- History -- 20th century

    ISBN 0521127416; 0521762758; 9780521127417; 9780521762755

                        LC 2011015050

This book, by Heather Marie Stur, "investigates how the Vietnam War both reinforced and challenged the gender roles . . . of . . . Cold War ideology. . . . Encounters between Americans and Vietnamese were shaped by . . . images used to . . . justify American intervention . . . . Stur also examines the . . . ideas about masculinity [that] shaped the American GI experience in Vietnam and . . . how some American[s] . . . returned from Vietnam to challenge homefront . . . norms." (Publisher's note)

Includes bibliographical references and index.

The **Vietnam** War; editor, Mark Lawrence; introduction by David K. Shipler. Fitzroy Dearborn Pubs.

2001 2v il maps (New York Times 20th century in review) set $150   **959.704**

    1. Vietnam War, 1961-1975

    ISBN 1-57958-368-7

                      LC 2002-726953

Articles and photos from The New York Times trace "the origins, the strategies, the successes, the failures, and the bitter legacy of this war for the United States, Vietnam, and the world." Publisher's note

"A must-have for all libraries." Recomm Ref Books for Small & Medium-sized Libr & Media Cent, 2003

Willbanks, James H.

Vietnam War almanac. Facts On File 2008 590p il map (Almanacs of American wars) $95   **959.704**

    1. Reference books 2. Vietnam War, 1961-1975

    ISBN 978-0-8160-7102-9; 0-8160-7102-0

                      LC 2008-6881

Contains a "day-by-day chronology of the events and people involved in the Vietnam War . . . [and] also features an A-to-Z biographical dictionary of the key figures involved in the conflict." Publisher's note

Includes bibliographical references

959.8   Indonesia and East Timor

Taylor, Jean Gelman

   ★ **Indonesia** : peoples and histories. Yale University Press 2003 420p il maps hardcover o.p. pa $24   **959.8**

    1. Indonesia

    ISBN 0-300-09709-3; 0-300-10518-5 pa

                    LC 2002-152348

This is "an account of Indonesia from the earliest migrations and settlements in the archipelago to the collapse of yet another government just a few years ago. While basically historical in design, this is no ordinary history. The book is one great historical essay . . . that allows the historian's search for the past to wander into social, religious, artistic, and anthropological byways." Choice

Includes bibliographical references

959.9   Philippines

Jones, Gregg

Honor in the dust; Theodore Roosevelt, war in the Philippines, and the rise and fall of America's imperial dream. Gregg Jones. New American Library 2012 xvi, 430 p.p (hbk.) $26.95   **959.9**

    1. Philippenes -- History -- Philippine American War, 1899-1902 2. Philippines -- Annexation to the United States 3. Philippines -- History -- Philippine American War, 1899-1902 -- Atrocities 4. Philippines -- History -- Philippine American War, 1899-1902 -- Campaigns -- Philippines -- Samar 5. Philippines -- History -- Philippine American War, 1899-1902 -- Political aspects -- United States

    ISBN 0451229045; 9780451229045

                    LC 2011033386

This book by Gregg Jones is the story of how "an up-and-coming Theodore Roosevelt set out to transform the U.S. into a major world power. The Spanish-American War would forever change America's standing in global affairs, and drive the young nation into its own imperial showdown in the Philippines. . . . [Jones] captures an era brimming with American optimism and confidence as the nation expanded its influence abroad." (Publisher's note)

Includes bibliographical references (p. 382-420) and index

Karnow, Stanley

In our image; America's empire in the Philippines. Random House 1989 494p il maps hardcover o.p. pa $27 **959.9**

1. Philippines -- History
ISBN 0-345-32816-7 pa

LC 88-42676

A history of American involvement in the Philippines from 1898 to the present

The author's "treatment of the indecisiveness of President McKinley over the issue of empire and of the egotistical General MacArthur make the work a definite purchase for libraries. . . . Those who love swashbuckling history will enjoy this work." Libr J

Includes bibliographical references

960   History of Africa

Encyclopedia of African history; Kevin Shillington, editor. Fitzroy Dearborn 2004 3v il map set $395 **960**

1. Reference books 2. Africa -- Encyclopedias
ISBN 1-579-58245-1

LC 2004-16779

"The scope of the coverage encompasses the entire continent, including North Africa, and features all historical periods, with special attention to recent events. Most entries are given 1000 words, though major topics, such as regional surveys, stretch to 3000-4000 words. Topics range from art to anthropology to economics, but emphasis is placed on biographies and country studies, both pre- and postcolonial. . . . Simply put, this is an essential reference resource for students of African history." Libr J

Includes bibliographical references

★ Encyclopedia of African history and culture; Willie F. Page, editor. rev ed; Facts on File 2005 5v il map set $425 **960**

1. Reference books 2. Africa -- Encyclopedias
ISBN 0-8160-5199-2

LC 2004-22929

First published 2001

This set "fulfills its information and education goals and is highly recommended for high-school, public, and academic libraries." Booklist

Includes bibliographical references

Falola, Toyin

★ Key events in African history; a reference guide. Greenwood Press 2002 xxiii, 347p il maps $64.95; pa $25 **960**

1. Africa -- History
ISBN 0-313-31323-7; 0-313-36122-3 pa

LC 2001-58644

"Falola surveys the . . . history of the African continent by focusing on 36 pivotal events that either caused or led to significant changes and developments in African social, political, and cultural life from around 40,000 B.C.E. to the collapse of apartheid in the 1990s. . . . Following a detailed time line of historical events, each topic is highlighted in an individual chapter including cross-references, historical and political maps, illustrations, a notes section, and a suggested list for further reading." Booklist

Includes bibliographical references

Gates, Henry Louis

Wonders of the African world; [by] Henry Louis Gates, Jr. Knopf 1999 275p il map hardcover o.p. pa $24.95 **960**

1. Africa -- Civilization
ISBN 0-375-40235-7; 0-375-70948-7 pa

LC 99-18496

"Gates writes with concentration and clarity, and anticipates the questions that arise in the wary reader's mind, delivering the answers at just the right time." N Y Times Book Rev

Includes bibliographical references

Lefkowitz, Mary R.

Not out of Africa; how Afrocentrism became an excuse to teach myth as history. [by] Mary Lefkowitz. Basic Bks. 1996 222p il map hardcover o.p. pa $19 **960**

1. Africa -- Historiography 2. History -- Study and teaching
ISBN 0-465-09837-1; 0-465-09838-X pa

LC 95-49109

"The book is a case study in historical methods, the value and limits of scholarship, and the preciousness of hard-bitten reason and objectivity. The book is also lucid and accessible." Christ Sci Monit

Includes bibliographical references

Meredith, Martin

Born in Africa; by Martin Meredith. 1st ed.; PublicAffairs 2011 xxiv, 230p ill. **960**

1. Africa 2. Anthropology 3. Human origins
ISBN 9781586486631 pa; 9781610391054

LC 2010043985

This book presents an "account of human evolution and the fiercely competitive anthropologists who are unearthing our ancestors' remains and arguing over what they mean. . . . [It] describe[s] the nuts-and-bolts of field research, the meaning of the often headline-producing findings and the ever-changing variety of species who split off from the common ancestors of chimpanzees and hominids." (Kirkus)

"Scientists . . . have firmly established Africa as the birthplace not only of humankind but of modern humans. They have revealed how early technology, language ability, and artistic endeavour all originated in Africa; and they have shown how small groups of Africans spread out from Africa in an exodus sixty thousand years ago to populate the rest of the world." (Publisher's note)

Includes bibliographical references (p. 199-218) and index.

Middleton, John

Africa : an encyclopedia for students; John Middleton, editor. Scribner 2002 4v il maps set $395   **960**

1. Reference books 2. Africa -- Encyclopedias

ISBN 0-684-80650-9

LC 2001-49348

A comprehensive look at the continent of Africa and the countries that comprise it, including peoples and cultures, the land and its history, art and architecture, and daily life

New encyclopedia of Africa; John Middleton, editor in chief; Joseph C. Miller, editor. Charles Scribner's Sons 2008 5v il map set $625   **960**

1. Reference books 2. Africa -- Encyclopedias

ISBN 978-0-684-31454-9

LC 2007-21746

First published 1997 with title: Encyclopedia of Africa, south of the Sahara

This encyclopedia "covers the entire continent, from the Europe-facing shores of the Mediterranean to the commercial bustle of Cape Town. The set addresses the . . . history of African cultures from the pharaohs and the ancient civilizations of the south through the colonial era to the emergence of 53 independent countries." Publisher's note

Includes bibliographical references

Pakenham, Thomas

The **scramble** for Africa; the White man's conquest of the dark continent from 1876 to 1912. Avon 1992 xxv, 738p il map pa $22.95   **960**

1. Africa -- History

ISBN 0-380-71999-1

First published 1991 by Random House

This book is an account of the colonization and conquest of Africa by five European nations—Great Britain, France, Belgium, Germany, and Italy.

This is a "sweeping narrative, refreshingly old fashioned in its appreciation of the fact that imperialism did have some virtues, which offers as good an introduction to the 'scramble' as has ever been written." Libr J

Includes bibliographical references

Soyinka, Wole, 1934-

Of Africa; Wole Soyinka. Yale University Press 2012 199 p. (cloth : alk. paper) $24   **960**

1. Africa -- History 2. Africa -- Civilization

ISBN 0300140460; 9780300140460

LC 2012013544

In this book 1986 Nobel Laureate Wole Soyinka "argues that the abuse of Africa and Africans (i.e., the slave trade) belongs in company with the Holocaust and Hiroshima in the museum of human inhumanity. . . . He offers anecdotal accounts of non-Western medical achievements and paeans to a more accepting, less intrusive, nonviolent set of

spiritual beliefs encompassed by the Yoruba deity Orisa." (Kirkus Reviews)

961.204   Libya--1952-2011

Chorin, Ethan

Exit the colonel; the hidden history of the Libyan revolution. Ethan Chorin. PublicAffairs 2012 viii, 374 p.p map (hardcover) $29.99; (ebook) $29.99   **961.204**

1. Libya -- History -- Civil War, 2011-

ISBN 1610391713; 9781610391719; 9781610391726 pdf

LC 2012021266

This book, by, Ethan Chorin, "goes . . . beyond recent reporting on the Arab Spring to link the Libyan uprising to a flawed reform process, egregious human rights abuses, regional disparities, and inconsistent stories spun by Libya and the West to justify the Gaddafi regime's 'rehabilitation.'. . . [The book] is based upon extensive interviews with senior US, EU, and Libyan officials, and with rebels and loyalists." (Publisher's note)

Includes bibliographical references (p. 347-354) and index

962   Egypt, Sudan, South Sudan

Goldschmidt, Arthur

A **brief** history of Egypt. Facts on File 2008 294p il map (Brief history) $45; pa $19.95   **962**

1. Egypt -- History

ISBN 978-0-8160-6672-8; 0-8160-6672-8; 978-0-8160-7333-7 pa; 0-8160-7333-3 pa

LC 2007-7374

The author "explores Egypt's broad political, economic, social, and cultural developments, covering roughly 6,000 years of history." Publisher's note

Includes glossary and bibliographical references

Jeal, Tim

Explorers of the Nile; the triumph and tragedy of a great Victorian adventure. Yale 2011 510p il map $32.50   **962**

1. Explorers 2. East Africa -- History 3. Central Africa -- History 4. Nile River -- Exploration

ISBN 978-0-300-14935-7

LC 2011933872

In this book on Victorian "efforts to find the source of the [Nile River]," the author focuses on a "quintet of great Victorian explorers," namely David Livingstone, Henry Morton Stanley, John Hanning Speke, Richard Burton, and Samuel Baker. "He recreates the mosquito-infested journeys and reveals the complex personal relationships, as Livingtone's early ventures to Lake Nyasa give way to the rivalry between Burton and Speke, who ventured north to Lakes Tanganyika, Victoria and Albert." Details on "the geopolitical consequences of finding the source of the Nile" are also presented. (History Today)

"Jeal's judicious account is a must-read for anyone hoping to understand the internal dynamics of modern state-building in central Africa." Booklist

Includes bibliographical references

Morrison, Dan

The **black** Nile; one man's amazing journey through peace and war on the world's longest river. Viking 2010 307p il map $26.95   **962**

1. Canoes and canoeing 2. War and civilization 3. Nile River -- Social conditions 4. Nile River -- Description and travel

ISBN 978-0-670-02198-7

LC 2010-4709

A foreign correspondent traces the four-thousand-mile plank-board boat journey he took with an inexperienced childhood friend along the Nile River from Lake Victoria to the Mediterranean Sea.

"Morrison's account transcends the travel genre to provide authentic and timely information on a complicated part of the world." Libr J

Stothard, Peter

Alexandria; The Last Nights of Cleopatra. Penguin Group USA 2013 400 p. $26.95   **962**

1. Alexandria (Egypt) 2. Egypt -- Description and travel

ISBN 1468303708; 9781468303704

In this book, "when Peter Stothard, editor of the 'Times Literary Supplement,' finds himself stranded in Alexandria in the winter of 2010 after his flight to South Africa has been cancelled, he sets out to explore a nation on the brink of revolution. Guided by two native Egyptians, Stothard traces his own life-long interest in the history of Cleopatra, and his repeated failure to write the book about her that he had always wanted to." (Publisher's note)

Strathern, Paul

Napoleon in Egypt; Bantam hardcover ed; Bantam Books 2008 480p il map $30   **962**

1. Emperors 2. Egypt -- History -- 1798-1801, French occupation

ISBN 978-0-553-80678-6; 0-553-80678-5

LC 2008-28135

First published 2007 in the United Kingdom

"Strathern's skillful use of memoir and other primary sources brings to life one of the most fascinating campaigns in military history." Libr J

Includes bibliographical references (p. 429-460)

Thompson, Jason

★ A **history** of Egypt; from earliest times to the present. Anchor Books 2008 382p il map pa $17   **962**

1. Egypt -- History

ISBN 978-0-307-47352-3

First published 2008 by American University in Cairo Press

The author "has masterfully undertaken the daunting task of presenting the 5000-year history of Egypt to the general reader, with each period given its due attention. Thompson captures the surprising continuity in Egyptian civiliza-

tion despite the great cultural currents that have impacted the people over the millennia. . . . Thompson's compact, comprehensive, and balanced history of all periods of Egyptian civilization will serve a wide range of readers seeking to understand this enduring nation and people." Libr J

Includes bibliographical references

962.05   Egypt since 1922

Khalil, Ashraf

Liberation Square; Ashraf Khalil. St. Martin's Press 2012 x, 324p.p   **962.05**

1. Revolutions 2. Political corruption 3. Egypt -- History -- 1970- 4. Egypt -- History -- Protests, 2011 5. Egypt -- Politics and government -- 21st century

ISBN 9781250006691; 9781429962445

LC 2011038194

This book covers "the rise and fall of Hosni Mubarak's dictatorship. . . . The . . . combination of judicial corruption and police brutality began to awake significant opposition, and the tipping point was the brutal beating death of Khalid Saieed in Alexandria on June 6, 2010. . . . [Author Ashraf] Khalil's discussion of the role of the Internet and social media . . . [shows] how large numbers of people were organized to achieve specific objectives--for example, converging on Cairo's squares and other public areas. The author . . . examines how the opposition to Egypt's paramilitary police gained strength, and how American diplomacy contributed to the cause. Khalil closes with the battle for Tahrir Square and the overthrow of the dictatorship." (Kirkus)

962.4   Sudan and South Sudan

Deng, Benson

They poured fire on us from the sky; the true story of three lost boys from Sudan. [by] Benson Deng, Alephonsion Deng, Benjamin Ajak; with Judy Bernstein. Public Affairs 2005 xxiii, 311p map hardcover o.p. pa $13.95   **962.4**

1. Refugees 2. Sudan

ISBN 1-58648-269-6; 1-58648-388-9 pa

LC 2005-42566

"This collection is moving in its depictions of unbelievable courage." Publ Wkly

963   Ethiopia and Eritrea

Shah, Tahir

In search of King Solomon's mines. Little, Brown 2003 240p il map $24.95; pa $13.95 **963**

1. Ethiopia -- Description and travel

ISBN 1-55970-641-4; 1-55970-724-0 pa

First published in 2002 in the United Kingdom

This is an account of the author's search for "the mysterious mines of Ophir, where King Solomon, the Bible's wisest king, was supposed to have buried a fortune in gold. . . . According to his reckoning, the mines should be in modern-day Ethiopia, so he set out on an adventure of a lifetime with a shifty bookseller named (no kidding) Ali Baba. Along the way, readers are treated to his accounts of everything from the California gold rush to a sadistic Sultan." Libr J

Includes bibliographical references

964   Morocco, Ceuta, Melilla, Western Sahara, Canary Islands

Shah, Tahir

The **Caliph's** house; Tahir Shah. Bantam Books 2006 349p il $22   **964**

1. Morocco -- Description and travel
ISBN 0-553-80399-9

LC 2005-53656

"Shah's picture of Moroccan society, its deeply held Islamic faith, its primitive superstition, and its raucous economy makes for endlessly fascinating reading." Booklist

965   Algeria

Macey, David

Frantz Fanon; a biography. Picador 2001 640p maps $40; pa $20   **965**

1. Diplomats 2. Psychiatrists 3. Revolutionaries 4. Algeria -- History 5. Writers on medicine 6. Algeria -- Biography 7. Political and social philosophers 8. Intellectuals -- Algeria -- Biography 9. Psychiatrists -- Algeria -- Biography 10. Revolutionaries -- Algeria -- Biography
ISBN 0-312-27550-1; 0-312-30042-5 pa

LC 2001-21807

A biography "of the psychiatrist from Martinique who propagandized for Algerian independence in the 1950's and sought to justify violence not only as a tactic but also as therapy for the oppressed." N Y Times Book Rev

"Macey's writing and research is rich with historical context and personal information that both Fanon loyalists and general readers will appreciate." Libr J

Includes bibliographical references

Morgan, Ted

My battle of Algiers; by Ted Morgan. Collins/Smithsonian 2006 284p maps $24.95   **965**

1. Algeria -- History -- 1954-1962, Revolution
ISBN 0-06-085224-0

LC 2005-52160

The author "recalls his service as a young officer in France's bitter war in Algeria. . . . Anyone interested in the origins of modern terrorist tactics will benefit from his recollections." Publ Wkly

965.04   Algeria--1900-1962

Camus, Albert, 1913-1960

Algerian chronicles; Albert Camus ; translated by Arthur Goldhammer ; with an introduction by Al-

ice Kaplan. Harvard University Press 2013 240 p. (hardcover) $21.95   **965.04**

1. Algeria -- History 2. Algeria -- History -- Revolution, 1954-1962   3.   Algeria -- Social conditions -- 20th century 4. Algeria -- Politics and government -- 20th century
ISBN 0674072588; 9780674072589

LC 2012036100

This book is "the first English translation of [Albert Camus'] 'Chroniques Algériennes' (1958)." It includes his "reportage of the 1939 famine in Kabylia" as well as other observations "fixed historically in the French-Algerian war." Camus' struggles "with the concept and conflicts of colonialism" are shared. (Publishers Weekly)

Includes bibliographical references and index.

965.046   Algeria--Period of Revolution, 1954-1962

Evans, Martin

Algeria; France's undeclared war. Martin Evans. Oxford University Press 2012 xxi, 457 p.p (hardcover) $35.00   **965.046**

1. Torture 2. Nationalism 3. War and civilization 4. Algeria -- Foreign relations 5. France -- Colonies -- Africa 6. France -- Foreign relations -- 1945- 7. Algeria -- Foreign relations -- France 8. France -- Foreign relations -- Algeria
ISBN 0192803506; 9780192803504

LC 2012371069

Author "Martin Evans argues that it was the Socialist led Republican Front, in power from January 1956 until May 1957, which was the defining moment in the [Algerian revolutionary] war [of 1954-1962 . . . [and] underlines the conflict of values between the Republican Front and Algerian nationalism, explaining how this clash produced patterns of thought and action, such as the institutionalization of torture and the raising of pro-French Muslim militias, which tragically polarized choices and framed all subsequent stages of the conflict." (Publisher's note)

Includes bibliographical references (p. [415]-429) and index

966.68   Côte d'Ivoire (Ivory Coast)

Erdman, Sarah

Nine hills to Nambonkaha; two years in the heart of an African village. Holt & Co. 2003 322p $23; pa $14   **966.68**

1. Ivory Coast 2. Peace Corps (U.S.)
ISBN 0-8050-7381-7; 0-312-42312-8 pa

LC 2003-44955

The author "spent two years as a Peace Corps worker in the small town of Nambonkaha, Ivory Coast, at the end of the last decade. Erdman, who acted as a health-care worker and instructor, is surprised to find herself called upon to help women in labor, surrounded by curious children who want to learn to read, and honored with gifts from the chief. She also faces the challenge of trying to meld medical knowledge with traditional sorcery, as the village denizens believe most illness and misfortune is caused by witchcraft rather than infection." Booklist

"This is an engrossing, well-told tale certain to appeal to armchair travelers and to anyone—especially women—considering international volunteer work." Publ Wkly

966.705 Ghana--1957-

Mahama, John Dramani, 1958-
My first coup d'etat and other true stories from the lost decades of Africa; John Dramani Mahama. Bloomsbury 2012 318 p. $25.00 **966.705**
1. Revolutions 2. Ghana -- History 3. Ghana -- Biography 4. Ghana -- History -- 1957- 5. Vice-presidents -- Ghana -- Biography 6. Ghana -- History -- Coup d'état, 1966
ISBN 1608198596; 9781608198597
LC 2011053052
In "this memoir, [vice president of Ghana John Dramani] Mahama, the son of a member of parliament, recounts how [African] affairs of state became real in his young mind on the day in 1966 when no one came to collect him from boarding school—the government had been overthrown, his father arrested, and his house confiscated. . . . Mahama unspools Ghana's recent history via . . . personal anecdotes." (Publishers Weekly)

966.905 Nigeria--1960-

Maier, Karl
This house has fallen; midnight in Nigeria. PublicAffairs 2000 xxxvii, 327p hardcover o.p. pa $18 **966.905**
1. Nigeria -- Politics and government
ISBN 0-8133-4045-4 pa
LC 00-28199
The author "explores the promise and paradox of Nigeria. {He} . . . recounts the history of this nation cobbled together from British colonial interests in its formative years and dominated by international oil interests in more recent years." Booklist
Includes bibliographical references

967 Central Africa and offshore islands

French, Howard W.
A continent for the taking; the tragedy and hope of Africa. Howard W. French. 1st ed Vintage Books 2005 280 p. il, map pbk $15.95 **967**
1. Africa -- History -- 1960- 2. Africa -- Politics and government 3. Africa, Sub-Saharan -- Description and travel 4. Africa, Sub-Saharan -- Social conditions -- 1960- 5. Africa, Sub-Saharan -- Politics and government -- 1960- 6. Africa, Sub-Saharan -- Foreign relations -- United States 7. United States -- Foreign relations -- Africa, Sub-Saharan
ISBN 1400030277; 9781400030279
LC 2003058920

Originally published: Knopf, 2004.
This book, by Howard W. French, is an "account of some of Africa's most devastating recent history--from the fall of Mobutu Sese Seko, to Charles Taylor's arrival in Monrovia, to the genocide in Rwanda and the Congo that left millions dead. . . . French searches deeply into the causes of today's events, illuminating the debilitating legacy of colonization and the abiding hypocrisy and inhumanity of both Western and African political leaders." (Publisher's note)
"[A] sobering and much-needed portrait of a land that merits, and requires, our attention." Kirkus
Includes bibliographical references (p. {259}-263) and index

967.5 Democratic Republic of the Congo, Rwanda, Burundi

Hochschild, Adam
★ **King** Leopold's ghost; a story of greed, terror, and heroism in Colonial Africa. Houghton Mifflin 1998 366p il map hardcover o.p. pa $15 **967.5**
1. Atrocities 2. Belgium -- Colonies 3. Congo (Republic) -- History
ISBN 0-395-75924-2; 0-618-00190-5 pa
LC 98-16813
"Hochschild's impressively researched history records the roles of the famous and obscure, missionaries, journalists, opportunists, politicians, and royalty in this long-forgotten drama." Booklist
Includes bibliographical references

967.51 Democratic Republic of the Congo

Stearns, Jason K.
Dancing in the glory of monsters; the collapse of the Congo and the great war of Africa. PublicAffairs 2011 380p $28.99 **967.51**
1. Genocide 2. Massacres 3. Congo (Republic) 4. Massacres -- Congo (Democratic Republic) 5. Congo (Democratic Republic) -- History -- 1997- 6. Political violence -- Congo (Democratic Republic)
ISBN 978-1-58648-929-8; 1-58648-929-1
LC 2010-43075
This book does not tell "the story of the Rwanda genocide in 1994, in which 800,000 people—almost all civilians—were massacred by their ethnic rivals in the space of a hundred days. That great atrocity is now relatively well known. Instead, this book tells of the war that broke out in the same region two years later, and that was in many ways its consequence. . . . As the Rwandan invaders penetrated into the eastern Congo, atrocities broke out. The Rwandans murdered the Hutus who had not fled. . . . Robert Mugabe of Zimbabwe and Eduardo Dos Santos of Angola pulled their troops out of the war, warning Kabila to negotiate for peace. . . . As well as 'big men' actors, [Jason K.] Stearns questioned many survivors of battle and massacre." (New York Review of Books)
A "look at the war that began in Congo in 1996 and that eventually involved nine countries and 20 different rebel movements, resulting in the deaths of more than five mil-

lion people. In sheer brutality, this mostly unremarked upon cataclysm ranks with the two world wars, the Great Leap Forward and the Cambodia genocide. . . . Mr. Stearns has spoken to everyone—villagers, child soldiers, Mobutu's commanders, Kabila's ministers, Rwandan intelligence officers. In these conversations he found gold, bringing clarity—and humanity—to a place that usually seems inexplicable and barbaric. "Dancing in the Glory of Monsters" is riveting and certain to become essential reading for anyone looking to understand Central Africa." Wall Street J

Sundaram, Anjan

Stringer; a reporter's journey in the Congo. Anjan Sundaram. Doubleday 2014 265 p. $25.95 **967.51**
1. Journalism 2. Congo (Democratic Republic) 3. Congo (Democratic Republic) -- Description and travel 4. Congo (Democratic Republic) -- Social conditions -- 21st century
ISBN 0385537751; 9780345806321; 9780385537759; 9780385537766
LC 2013000980
Author Anjan "Sundaram exchanged mathematics for journalism, starting out as a stringer in dangerous Congo with little in the way of experience or contacts. This memoir sees him struggling to learn his craft while battling malaria, isolation, financial woes, and the tendency of editors to send in name reporters when a big story breaks. In addition, Sundaram offers an intensely rendered account of the immeasurable sadness of Congo through the tumultuous 2006 elections. " (Library Journal)
"The author skillfully captures the smallest details of life in a destitute land, blending the sordid history of Congo with his battle to forge a career in a troubled and forsaken country." Pub Wkly

967.571 Rwanda

Gourevitch, Philip

We wish to inform you that tomorrow we will be killed with our families; stories from Rwanda. Farrar, Straus & Giroux 1998 355p hardcover o.p. pa $15 **967.571**
1. Genocide 2. Rwanda -- Politics and government
ISBN 0-374-28697-3; 0-312-24335-9 pa
LC 98-22132
This work is "readable and moving, Gourevitch is an impassioned and thoughtful observer. But this is not a work that gives much pleasure or comfort. Nor are its arguments fool-proof, its evidence complete, or its documentation thorough. . . . Still Gourevitch does struggle to come close to a great mystery of evil, and he makes us attend to great crimes." Commonweal

Hatzfeld, Jean

The **antelope's** strategy; living in Rwanda after the genocide. a report by Jean Hatzfeld; translated from the French by Linda Coverdale. Farrar, Straus and Giroux 2009 242p map $25 **967.571**
1. Genocide 2. Hutu (African people) 3. Tutsi (African people) 4. Rwanda
ISBN 978-0-374-27103-9; 0-374-27103-8
LC 2008-52489
Original French edition, 2007
The author "follows up Machete Season (2005), an account of the Hutu slaughter of Tutsi in Rwanda, with a report seven years later of the process of reconciliation between the two ethnic groups. Hatzfeld went back to interview those among the 40,000 killers who had been released by the government after serving time and those who were survivors of the attempted genocide." Publ Wkly
This "is a book that illustrates vividly the thorny realities that accompany survival and appeasement." Washington Post

Machete season; the killers in Rwanda speak: a report. translated from the French by Linda Coverdale; preface by Susan Sontag. Farrar, Straus and Giroux 2005 253p il maps hardcover o.p. pa $14 **967.571**
1. Genocide 2. Hutu (African people) 3. Tutsi (African people) 4. Rwanda
ISBN 0-374-28082-7; 0-312-42503-1 pa
LC 2004-61600
Original French edition, 2003
"Steering clear of politics, this important book succeeds in offering the reader some grasp of how such unspeakable acts unfolded." Publ Wkly

967.6 Uganda and Kenya

Beard, Peter H.

The **end** of the game; the last word from paradise. [by] Peter Beard; [foreword by Paul Theroux] Taschen 2008 280p il $39.99 **967.6**
1. Hunting 2. East Africa -- Description and travel
ISBN 978-3-83650-530-7; 3-83650-530-4
First published 1965 by Viking; updated 1977 and published by Doubleday
"This landmark book, with a chilling (and acerbic) new introduction by travel writer and novelist Paul Theroux, contains photographs many of them shocking that reveal the sad situation of African wildlife, and most particularly the elephant. Beard mourns the end of a continent from a diverse and interdependent ecosystem to a land suffocated by cement, wire, walls and ditches (not to mention war)." Stuart News (Stuart, Florida)

Chretien, Jean-Pierre

★ The **great** lakes of Africa; two thousand years of history. translated by Scott Straus. Zone Books 2003 504p map $36 **967.6**
1. Rwanda 2. Uganda 3. Burundi 4. East Africa
ISBN 1-89095-134-X
LC 2002-191001
"This is an impressive and important book surveying 2,000 years of history. . . . The preeminence accorded Rwanda and Burundi . . . leads to the book's most significant contribution: to demonstrate that the region's recent interrelated conflicts claiming over four million lives are not based

on ancient, unchanging 'ethnic' cleavages, most notably between Tutsi and Hutu." Choice

Includes bibliographical references

Rice, Andrew

The **teeth** may smile but the heart does not forget; murder and memory in Uganda. Metropolitan Books/ Henry Holt and Co. 2009 363p il map $26   **967.6**
1. Generals 2. Atrocities 3. Presidents 4. Uganda 5. Murderers 6. Murder victims 7. Government officials 8. Children of prominent persons
ISBN 978-0-8050-7965-4; 0-8050-7965-3

LC 2008-41984

"At the core of the book is an unsolved disappearance: Eliphaz Laki, a local leader with ties to the anti-Amin opposition, vanished in the early days of the Amin regime. When his son, Duncan, uncovered a clue to his father's disappearance 30 years later, the investigation eventually implicated Amin's second-in-command, Maj. Gen. Yusuf Gowon. With Amin living out his years safely in Saudi Arabia, the trial of Gowon forced Uganda to confront its brutal past. Treating the Lakis' story as a microcosm of Uganda's own, the author weaves together the family's search for truth and justice with Uganda's history." Publ Wkly

967.62   Kenya

Anderson, David M.

Histories of the hanged; the dirty war in Kenya and the end of the empire. [by] David Anderson. Norton 2005 406p il map $25.95; pa $15.95   **967.62**
1. Kenya 2. Mau Mau 3. Great Britain -- Colonies -- Africa
ISBN 0-393-05986-3; 0-393-32754-X pa

LC 2004-24804

This "history of the last days of the British Empire in Kenya focuses on the colonial judicial system, which sent over 1,000 native Kenyans to the gallows between 1952 and 1959, during the state of emergency triggered by the Mau Mau insurrection. . . . This is vital reading for any student of British colonial and African history." Publ Wkly

Includes bibliographical references

Dinesen, Isak

★ **Out** of Africa and Shadows on the grass. Vintage Bks. 1989 462p pa $13.95   **967.62**
1. Kenya
ISBN 0-679-72475-3

LC 89-40144

Out of Africa is a recording of the author's life on a Kenya coffee plantation. Shadows on the grass consists of four short essays which present the author's recollections of her servants in Africa

967.730   Somalia--1960-

Bowden, Mark

Black Hawk down; a story of modern war. Atlantic Monthly Press 1999 386p il maps $25; pa $13.95   **967.730**
1. Somalia 2. United States -- Army -- Task Force Ranger
ISBN 0-87113-738-0; 0-14-028850-3 pa

LC 98-46688

The author describes "both sides of the October 1993 raid into the heart of Mogadishu, Somalia, a raid that quickly became the most intensive close combat Americans have engaged in since the Vietnam War. But Bowden's gripping narrative of the fighting is only a framework for an examination of the internal dynamics of America's elite forces and a critique of the philosophy of sending such high-tech units into combat with minimal support." Publ Wkly

Fergusson, James

The **world's** most dangerous place; inside the outlaw state of Somalia. James Fergusson. Da Capo Press 2013 432 p. (hardcover) $27.50   **967.730**
1. Violence 2. Somalia -- Social conditions
ISBN 0306821176; 9780306821172

LC 2013933566

This book "investigates the civil war, foreign interventions and mass starvation of Somalia. . . . The vast majority of Somalians is illiterate, desperately poor and so committed to genetic ties within their particular geographic clan that pulling together as a nation seems hopeless. Many of the peacekeeping soldiers are from Uganda, ironic given that nation's recent bouts of sectarian violence." (Kirkus)

968   Republic of South Africa and neighboring southern African countries

Thompson, Leonard Monteath

A **history** of South Africa; {by} Leonard Thompson. 3rd ed; Yale Univ. Press 2001 xxiv, 358p il maps hardcover o.p. pa $17.95   **968**
1. South Africa -- History
ISBN 0-300-08776-4 pa

LC 00-32101

First published 1990

This is an exploration of South Africa's "history, from the earliest known human inhabitation of the region to the present, focusing primarily on the experiences of its black inhabitants." Publisher's note

Includes bibliographical references

968.04   South Africa--1814-1910

Meredith, Martin

Diamonds, gold, and war; the British, the Boers, and the making of South Africa. PublicAffairs 2007 570p il map $35   **968.04**
1. South African War, 1899-1902 2. South Africa --

History 3. Great Britain -- Colonies -- Africa
ISBN 978-1-58648-473-6; 1-58648-473-7

LC 2007-34540

A history of the tumultuous period leading up to the 1910 founding of the modern state of South Africa explores how the discovery of vast diamond and gold deposits led to a fierce struggle between the British and the Boers for control of the region.

"Meredith thoroughly involves us in this gripping history. Highly recommended for all libraries." Libr J

Includes bibliographical references (p. 540-550)

968.06   South Africa--Period as Republic, 1961-

Carlin, John

Playing the enemy; Nelson Mandela and the game that made a nation. Penguin 2008 274p il $24.95 **968.06**

1. Presidents 2. Rugby football 3. Political prisoners 4. Rugby 5. Political leaders 6. Human rights activists 7. Nobel laureates for peace
ISBN 978-1-59420-174-5; 1-59420-174-9

LC 2008-298721

"Deftly sketched characters make up both an audience for the big game and a gallery of South Africa, through which Carlin will recount the absorbing story of a country emerging from its cruelly absurd racist experiment." N Y Times Book Rev

Includes bibliographical references

Duke, Lynne

Mandela, Mobutu, and me; a newswoman's African journey. Doubleday 2003 294p $24 **968.06**

1. Generals 2. Presidents 3. Political prisoners 4. Political leaders 5. Human rights activists 6. Nobel laureates for peace 7. South Africa -- Politics and government
ISBN 0-385-50398-9

LC 2002-73365

The author covers "some of the bloodier postcolonial wars of southern Africa as well as one of the most constructive struggles: the shaping of a postapartheid government. Her interviews with Mandela and Mobutu 'bookend' . . . conversations with common folk: township women struggling for clean water, AIDS nurses battling superstitious villagers and even a quiet old Zulu man impressed to meet his 'first foreign black folk.' A consummate journalist, Duke gives readers concise but thorough background briefings on a country's relevant history before cutting to the chase: who's taken control now, why, and what that means for the balance of power. . . . She deftly combines solid information and personal perspective to produce a powerful, readable chronicle." Publ Wkly

Mandela, Nelson

Mandela; an illustrated autobiography. Little, Brown 1996 208p il map $29.95 **968.06**

1. Presidents 2. Political prisoners 3. Political leaders 4. Human rights activists 5. Nobel laureates for peace 6. South Africa -- Race relations 7. South Africa --

Politics and government
ISBN 0-316-55038-8

LC 96-77497

"The photos, from a variety of archives and journalistic sources, ably illustrate Mandela and, even more so, the South Africa around him." Libr J

Tutu, Desmond

No future without forgiveness; [by] Desmond Mpilo Tutu. Doubleday 1999 287p hardcover o.p. pa $15.95 **968.06**

1. South Africa -- Race relations 2. South Africa -- Commission for Truth and Reconciliation
ISBN 0-385-49690-7 pa

LC 99-34451

The author reflects on his role "as chairman of the Truth and Reconciliation Commission. Tutu speaks frankly of . . . the struggle that preceded it and of the betrayals and jubilations of this unique commission. The TRC's work was unprecedented not only in its emphasis on restorative over retributive justice but in the spirituality that permeated its work, the bulk of which constituted hearings from the 'victims' and 'perpetrators' of apartheid." Publ Wkly

Includes bibliographical references

The **rainbow** people of God; the making of a peaceful revolution. edited by John Allen. Doubleday 1994 xxii, 281p il hardcover o.p. pa $15.95 **968.06**

1. Sermons 2. South Africa -- Race relations
ISBN 0-385-48374-0 pa

LC 94-16011

This collection of Tutu's "speeches, letters, and sermons—from the time of the 1976 Soweto Uprising, through the long years of repression and defiance, up to the triumph of the democratic election—serves as an immediate contemporary history of South Africa. Tutu's media secretary, John Allen, provides a general historical introduction and a connecting narrative that places the individuals pieces in dramatic context." Booklist

Includes bibliographical references

Waldmeir, Patti

Anatomy of a miracle; the end of apartheid and the birth of the new South Africa. Rutgers University Press 1998 289p pa $22.95 **968.06**

1. South Africa -- Race relations 2. South Africa -- Politics and government
ISBN 0-8135-2582-9; 978-0-8135-2582-2

LC 98-15628

First published 1997 by W.W. Norton

Waldmeir traces the political and personal struggles that ultimately contributed to the dismantling of apartheid in South Africa

"Although Mandela attributes greatness to de Klerk for his courage, it is Mandela's own character that dominates this history. . . . Engrossing in its sweep, this account also describes the obstacles facing the regime." Publ Wkly

Includes bibliographical references

968.91   Zimbabwe

Lamb, Christina

House of stone; the true story of a family divided in war-torn Zimbabwe. Lawrence Hill Books 2007 290p il map   **968.91**
1. Farmers 2. Nannies 3. Zimbabwe -- Race relations
ISBN 978-1-55652-735-7; 1-55652-735-7

LC 2007-19814

"Through the parallel accounts of two people in Zimbabwe, one a poor black maid, one a rich white farmer, . . . Lamb tells the compelling story of a country ravaged first by colonial settlers and now by brutal civil war. . . . The anguished personal detail, true to the changing viewpoints, makes for a gripping read." Booklist

Rogers, Douglas

The **last** resort; a memoir of Zimbabwe. Harmony Books 2009 309p map $24.99   **968.91**
1. Resorts 2. Zimbabwe
ISBN 978-0-307-40797-9; 0-307-40797-7

"A nuanced, funny, and heartbreaking story of one community's experience of survival in Mugabe's Zimbabwe." New Yorker

970   History of North America

Morgan, Ted

Wilderness at dawn; the settling of the North American continent. Simon & Schuster 1993 541p il maps hardcover o.p. pa $20   **970**
1. North America -- History 2. Canada -- History -- 0-1763 (New France) 3. United States -- History -- 1600-1775, Colonial period
ISBN 0-671-88237-6 pa

LC 93-2628

Morgan "tells a good story, emphasizing the ordinary people who did the actual settlement. . . . A useful survey of the colonial frontier." Libr J

Includes bibliographical references

970.004   North American native peoples

America in 1492; the world of the Indian peoples before the arrival of Columbus. edited and with an introduction by Alvin Josephy, Jr.; developed by Frederick E. Hoxie. Knopf 1992 477p il maps hardcover o.p. pa $20   **970.004**
1. America -- Antiquities 2. America -- Exploration 3. Native Americans -- History 4. Native Americans -- Antiquities
ISBN 0-394-56438-3; 0-679-74337-5 pa

LC 90-26222

These essays depict "the diverse lives of the approximately 75 million people living in the Americas around the turn of the fifteenth century. Geography guides the first section. . . . Another section focuses on languages, spiritual beliefs and customs, art, and 'systems of knowledge.'" Booklist

Includes bibliographical references

American Indians; consulting editor, Harvey Markowitz. Salem Press 1995 3v il maps (Ready reference) set $331   **970.004**
1.   Reference books   2.   Native Americans -- Encyclopedias   3.   Native Americans -- Mexico -- Encyclopedias
ISBN 0-89356-757-4

LC 94-47633

"This set contains 1,129 articles ranging in length from 200 to 3,000 words. The entries cover a wide range of persons, tribes, organizations, cultural and historical events, and contemporary issues of U.S., Canadian, and some Mesoamerican Indian groups. Individual entries appear for 275 North American tribes. Entries are arranged alphabetically and are illustrated with 250 black-and-white photographs, maps, charts, tables, and drawings." Booklist

Bragdon, Kathleen J.

The **Columbia** guide to American Indians of the Northeast. Columbia Univ. Press 2001 292p il maps (Columbia guides to American Indian history and culture) $53.50; pa $25.50   **970.004**
1. Native Americans
ISBN 0-231-11452-4; 0-231-11453-2 pa

LC 2001-47341

This handbook "includes not only a broad overview of the history of Native Americans in the Northeast but also a partially annotated listing of materials for further research including published primary sources, oral traditions, films, and Internet sites." Libr J

Includes bibliographical references

Brown, Dee Alexander

★ **Bury** my heart at Wounded Knee; an Indian history of the American West. [by] Dee Brown. Thirtieth anniversary ed; Holt & Co. 2001 487p il hardcover o.p. pa $16   **970.004**
1. Generals 2. Civil engineers 3. Government officials 4. West (U.S.) -- History 5. Native Americans -- Wars 6. Native Americans -- West (U.S.)
ISBN 0-8050-6634-9; 0-8050-6669-1 pa

LC 00-40958

First published 1970

This is an account of the experience of the American Indian during the white man's expansion westward.

Includes bibliographical references

Bruchac, Joseph

Our stories remember; American Indian history, culture, & values through storytelling. Fulcrum 2003 192p map pa $16.95   **970.004**
1. Storytelling 2. Native Americans -- History
ISBN 1-555-91129-3

LC 2002-151236

"This important volume includes a wealth of traditional stories and solid information." SLJ

Includes bibliographical references

Deloria, Vine

Custer died for your sins; an Indian manifesto. by Vine Deloria, Jr. University of Oklahoma Press 1988 278p pa $19.95   **970.004**
1. Native Americans
ISBN 0-8061-2129-7
                            LC 87-40561
First published 1969 by Macmillan
The author examines how anthropologists, missionaries, and government agencies have mistreated American Indians.

Documents of American Indian diplomacy; treaties, agreements, and conventions, 1775-1979. {compiled by} Vine Deloria, Jr., and Raymond J. DeMallie; with a foreword by Daniel K. Inouye. University of Okla. Press 1999 2v (Legal history of North America) set $125   **970.004**
1. Treaties 2. Native Americans -- Government relations
ISBN 0-8061-3118-7
                            LC 98-45365
This is a collection of hundreds of treaties and agreements made by American Indian nations with the Continental Congress, England, Spain, and other foreign countries, the Confederacy, the Republic of Texas, railroad companies, other Indian nations, and the U.S. government, with chapter introductions which put them in historical and political context
"A must for all libraries." Libr J
Includes bibliographical references

Encyclopedia of Native American wars and warfare; general editors, William B. Kessel, Robert Wooster. Facts on File 2005 398p il map $75; pa $21.95   **970.004**
1. Reference books 2. Native Americans -- Wars -- Encyclopedias
ISBN 0-8160-3337-4; 0-8160-6430-X pa
                            LC 00-56200
"This encyclopedia offers readers a wide range of information about Native American history in North America after 1492." Choice
Includes bibliographical references

Fenton, William Nelson

The **Great** Law and the Longhouse; a political history of the Iroquois Confederacy. {by} Willam N. Fenton. University of Okla. Press 1998 xxii, 786p il map (Civilization of the American Indian series) $75   **970.004**
1. Iroquois Indians -- History
ISBN 0-8061-3003-2
                            LC 97-19842
"If a library has only one book about the Iroquois . . . it should be this title." Libr J
Includes bibliographical references

Fowler, Loretta

The **Columbia** guide to American Indians of the Great Plains. Columbia Univ. Press 2003 283p il maps (Columbia guides to American Indian history and culture) $53.50; pa $26.50   **970.004**
1. Native Americans -- Great Plains
ISBN 0-231-11700-0; 0-231-11701-9 pa
                            LC 2002-73708
"This work is divided into four parts: a general survey of the history and cultures of the native peoples of the region; alphabetically arranged entries focusing on individuals, places, and events; a chronology; and a listing of resources for further research that includes published primary sources, oral traditions, films, and Internet sites. . . . Highly recommended." Libr J
Includes bibliographical references

Harmon, Alexandra

Indians in the making; ethnic relations and Indian identities around Puget Sound. University of Calif. Press 1998 393p il maps (American crossroads) hardcover o.p. pa $21.95   **970.004**
1. Washington (State) -- History 2. Native Americans -- Northwest Coast of North America
ISBN 0-520-22685-2 pa
                            LC 98-17665
The author "examines how both the federal government and the native peoples of western Washington were constantly redefining Indian identity to their advantage over a 150-year period. Harmon's examination of the native fishing rights controversy of the 1960s and 1970s is particularly useful." Libr J
Includes bibliographical references

Hendricks, Steve

The **unquiet** grave; the FBI and the struggle for the soul of Indian country. Thunder's Mouth Press 2006 490p il map $27.95   **970.004**
1. Educators 2. Dissenters 3. Indian leaders 4. Social activists 5. American Indian Movement 6. Native Americans -- Government relations 7. United States -- Federal Bureau of Investigation
ISBN 1-56025-735-0; 978-1-56025-735-6
The author tells "the story of the American Indian Movement (AIM) to reclaim civil and treaty rights. . . . Bracketed by the 1976 murder of AIM activist Anna Mae Aquash and the 2004 trial related to it, Hendricks's swift narrative is riddled with judicial travesties, coverups, vigilantism, COINTELPRO-style tactics, mounting paranoia and lawlessness on both sides, as activists and ordinary American Indians confront the devastating neglect and outright hostility of government authorities." Publ Wkly
Includes bibliographical references

Iverson, Peter

We are still here; American Indians in the twentieth century. Davidson, H. 1998 255p il (American history series) pa $14.95   **970.004**
1. Native Americans
ISBN 0-88295-940-9
                            LC 97-38321
The author "begins at Wounded Knee and tells the stories of Indian communities throughout the United States,

including not only political leaders and activists, but also professionals, artists, soldiers and athletes." Publisher's note

Includes bibliographical references

Johansen, Bruce E.

The **Native** peoples of North America; a history. Praeger 2005 2v il set $99.95   **970.004**
1. Native Americans -- History
ISBN 0-275-98159-2

LC 2004-28732

This is a history of "cultures indigenous to North America from their earliest origins to the present. . . . Encompassing not only traditional historical records but also oral histories and biographical sketches, these two volumes will undoubtedly become an integral part of Native American history, an increasingly popular field." Booklist

Includes bibliographical references

Johnson, Michael

Encyclopedia of native tribes of North America; color plates by Richard Hook. 3rd ed; Firefly Books 2007 320p il map $49.95   **970.004**
1. Reference books 2. Native Americans -- Encyclopedias
ISBN 978-1-55407-307-8; 1-55407-307-3

First published 1993 in the United Kingdom with title: The native tribes of North America

"The volume is organized into ten regionally based culture areas (Northwestern Woodlands, Southeastern Woodlands, Plains and Prairie, Plateau, Great Basin, California, Southwest, Northwest Coast, Subarctic, and Arctic); each area is introduced with general information on language, subsistence, religion, culture, and history. . . . The rich illustrations and supplemental sections make this volume worthwhile." Choice

Includes bibliographical references

Josephy, Alvin M.

The **Nez** Perce Indians and the opening of the Northwest; {by} Alvin M. Josephy, Jr. Houghton Mifflin 1997 xx, 705p il map pa $19   **970.004**
1. Nez Percé Indians 2. Pacific Northwest
ISBN 0-395-85011-8

LC 96-54278

First published 1965 by Yale University Press

This history of the Nez Perce tribe traces its contact with white settlers from Lewis and Clark to Chief Joseph and war in 1877

Includes bibliographical references

McLoughlin, William Gerald

After the Trail of Tears; the Cherokees' struggle for sovereignty, 1839-1880. {by} William G. McLoughlin. University of N.C. Press 1993 439p maps hardcover o.p. pa $21.95   **970.004**
1. Cherokee Indians
ISBN 0-8078-4433-0 pa

LC 93-18532

The author "recounts the tragedy that continued to afflict the Cherokee Nation after their forced removal from their traditional home to Oklahoma during the 1820s and 1830s. In Oklahoma the Cherokee Nation set out to reconstruct

their society, reestablishing their newspaper, which published in the Cherokee language, and governing themselves according to a constitution modeled on that of the United States. . . . McLoughlin vividly depicts the conflicts between 'full-bloods,' who sought to live by more traditional ways, and Cherokees of mixed ancestry who favored assimilation into the dominant culture." Publ Wkly

Includes bibliographical references

McReynolds, Edwin C.

The **Seminoles**. University of Okla. Press 1957 397p il maps (Civilization of the American Indian series) hardcover o.p. pa $21.95   **970.004**
1. Seminole Indians
ISBN 0-8061-1255-7 pa

"This is almost strictly a military and political history, in great detail, spiced with a few incidents which reveal the courageous character of the Seminoles, and stressing their relations with the Creeks." Libr J

Includes bibliographical references

Milton, Giles

Big Chief Elizabeth; the adventures and fate of the First English Colonists in America. Farrar, Straus & Giroux 2000 358p il maps hardcover o.p. pa $14   **970.004**
1. Queens 2. Native Americans 3. Virginia -- History 4. America -- Exploration 5. Great Britain -- Colonies -- America
ISBN 0-312-42018-8 pa

LC 00-31522

"Nearly 500 years ago, a small group of white men landed on the shores of North America and named it Virginia (for the Virgin Queen [Elizabeth]). Their purpose was to capture some natives and bring them to England to learn their language and everything else they could about the country they wished to colonize. . . . [Milton] chronicles the century-long battle to establish a permanent settlement in Virginia." Christ Sci Monit

Includes bibliographical references

Native America in the twentieth century; an encyclopedia. edited by Mary B. Davis; assistant editors, Joan Berman, Mary E. Graham, Lisa A. Mitten. Garland 1994 xxxvii, 787p il maps (Garland reference library of social science) hardcover o.p. pa $50   **970.004**
1. Reference books 2. Native Americans -- Encyclopedias
ISBN 0-8153-2583-5 pa

LC 94-768

This volume offers "tribal-specific information on the art, daily life, economic development, and religion of 20th-century American Indians and Alaskan Natives and the government policy that affects them." Libr J

★ **Native** American testimony; a chronicle of Indian-white relations from prophecy to the present, 1492-2000. edited by Peter Nabokov; with a foreword by Vine Deloria, Jr. Rev and updated

ed; Penguin Bks. 1999 xxiii, 506p il maps pa
$16.95   **970.004**
1. Native Americans -- History -- Sources 2. Native
Americans -- Government relations
ISBN 0-14-028159-2

First published 1978 by Crowell with subtitle: An anthology of Indian and white relations, first encounter
to dispossession

"A collection of primary-source material, grouped by
key issues that arose during 500 years of Indian and white
encounters in North America. Nabokov uses traditional narratives, old government transcripts, reservation newspapers,
and firsthand interviews to highlight this chronological volume. Photographs appear throughout." SLJ {review of 1991
edition}

Includes bibliographical references

Osborn, William M.

The **wild** frontier; atrocities during the Ameri-
can-Indian War from Jamestown Colony to Wounded
Knee. Random House 2000 363p hardcover o.p. pa
$19   **970.004**
1. Frontier and pioneer life 2. Native Americans --
Wars 3. Native Americans -- Government relations
ISBN 0-375-75856-9 pa

LC 00-27171

"Characterizing the years between 1622 and 1890 as
the era of the American-Indian War, Osborn provides a balanced analysis of the vicious atrocities committed by white
settlers and Native Americans during the prolonged period
of westward expansion. . . . Laden with stark, unsparing
descriptions . . . the detailed narrative retains an admirable
objectivity." Booklist

Includes bibliographical references

Perdue, Theda

The **Columbia** guide to American Indians of the
Southeast; [by] Theda Perdue and Michael D. Green.
Columbia Univ. Press 2001 325p il maps (Columbia guides to American Indian history and culture)
$53.50; pa $27.50   **970.004**
1. Native Americans -- Southern States
ISBN 0-231-11570-9; 0-231-11571-7 pa

LC 2001-35338

"The first half of the text focuses on the history and culture of the region's native groups. This includes not only the
Mississippian Moundbuilder cultures that arose between
800 and 1000 C.E. but also well-known native groups such
as the Cherokee and Creeks. . . . Immediately following the
survey are alphabetically arranged entries focusing on individuals, places, and events. The final two sections are a chronology and a listing of resources for further research, which
include published primary sources, oral traditions, films, and
Internet sites. . . . An essential purchase for all libraries collecting books about Native Americans." Libr J

Includes bibliographical references

Philip, Neil

The **great** circle; a history of the First Nations.
foreword by Dennis Hastings. Clarion Books 2006
153p il map $25   **970.004**
1. Native Americans
ISBN 978-0-618-15941-3; 0-618-15941-X

LC 2005032743

"Philip takes on a huge challenge here: to present a unified narrative that explains the complex and confrontational
relationships between Native Americans and white settlers.
. . . He pulls it off, however, thanks to solid research, an
engaging writing style, and a talent for making individual
stories serve the whole. . . . Top marks, too, for the volume's
photographs and historical renderings, which so intensely illustrate the pages." Booklist

Includes bibliographical references

Pritzker, Barry

A **Native** American encyclopedia; history,
culture, and peoples. [by] Barry M. Pritzker. Oxford Univ. Press 2000 591p il hardcover o.p. pa
$29.95   **970.004**
1. Reference books 2. Native Americans --
Encyclopedias
ISBN 0-19-513897-X; 0-19-513877-5 pa

LC 99-53677

First published 1998 by ABC-CLIO as a two-volume set
with title: Native Americans

"Organized geographically, each section begins with an
introduction to the area and its original inhabitants. Tribal
entries follow, with some smaller related groups discussed
together. Each article includes sections on location, population, language, history, religion, government, customs,
dwellings, diet, key technology, trade, notable arts, transportation, dress, and war/weapons. A contemporary section follows, with information on government/reservations,
economy, legal status, and daily life." Libr J [review of 1998
edition]

Includes bibliographical references

Rajtar, Steve

Indian war sites; a guidebook to battlefields,
monuments, and memorials, state by state with
Canada and Mexico. McFarland & Co. 1999 330p
$39.95   **970.004**
1. Native Americans -- Wars
ISBN 0-7864-0710-7

LC 99-25893

This is a "reference to hundreds of conflicts, both major and minor, between American Indians and Europeans.
Divided alphabetically by state and then chronologically
within each, entries include name and date, a nonspecific
location (e.g., Spring River), a brief description, and bibliographic sources. If the battle was a part of a larger war Rajtar
also gives the name of the war; and if there is a monument,
he tells its location and briefly describes what's there." Libr J

Includes bibliographical references

Richter, Daniel K.

Facing east from Indian country; a Native history of early America. Harvard Univ. Press 2001 317p il maps $27.50; pa $15.95 **970.004**
1. Native Americans
ISBN 0-674-00638-0; 0-674-01117-1 pa

LC 2001-24997

The author "recasts early American history from the Native American point of view and in doing so illuminates as much about the Europeans as about the original Americans. . . . Exploring the varying complexities of different native people's relationships with England, France and Spain, he argues that the Native Americans were safer during the colonial era than after the Revolution. . . . Gracefully written and argued, Richter's compelling research and provocative claims make this an important addition to the literature for general readers of both Native American and U.S. studies." Publ Wkly
Includes bibliographical references and index

Robbins, Catherine C.

All Indians do not live in teepees (or casinos) University of Nebraska Press 2011 385p il map $26.95 **970.004**
1. Native Americans -- Social life and customs
ISBN 978-0-8032-3973-9; 0-8032-3973-4

LC 2011011320

"A solid, insightful overview of the way American Indians live now." Kirkus
Includes bibliographical references

Roberts, David

Once they moved like the wind; Cochise, Geronimo, and the Apache wars. Simon & Schuster 1993 368p il hardcover o.p. pa $22 **970.004**
1. Apache Indians 2. Native Americans -- Wars
ISBN 0-671-70221-1; 0-671-88556-1 pa

LC 93-7112

"The book is history at its most engrossing." Publ Wkly
Includes bibliographical references

Waldman, Carl

Atlas of the North American Indian; 3rd ed; Facts on File 2009 450p il map (Facts on file library of American history) $85; pa $24.95 **970.004**
1. Atlases 2. Reference books 3. Native Americans
ISBN 978-0-8160-6858-6; 0-8160-6858-5; 978-0-8160-6859-3 pa; 0-8160-6859-3 pa

LC 2008-40736

First published 1985
"This is a very well-designed book, a bargain for any library." Voice Youth Advocates [review of 2000 edition]
Includes glossary and bibliographical references

Encyclopedia of Native American tribes; 3rd rev ed; Facts on File 2006 xxiv, 360p il map (Facts on File library of American history) $75; pa $21.95 **970.004**
1. Reference books 2. Native Americans -- Encyclopedias
ISBN 978-0-8160-6273-7; 0-8160-6273-0; 978-0-

8160-6274-4 pa; 0-8160-6274-9 pa

LC 2006-12529

First published 1988
"This well-written and easily accessible encyclopedia of a good starting point for research on Native American tribes." Libr Media Connect
Includes bibliographical references

Weatherford, J. McIver

Native roots; how the Indians enriched America. [by] Jack Weatherford. Fawcett 1992 310p il map pa $13.95 **970.004**
1. Native Americans
ISBN 978-0-449-90713-9; 0-449-90713-9
First published 1991 by Crown
"A valuable corrective to the sentimentality with which we regard the first U.S. settlers and developers." Booklist
Includes bibliographical references

Wilson, James

The **earth** shall weep; the history of Native Americans. Atlantic Monthly Press 1999 xxix, 466p maps hardcover o.p. pa $16 **970.004**
1. Native Americans
ISBN 0-8021-3680-X pa

LC 99-13098

"Employing elegiac prose and steady narrative momentum, Wilson has written a richly informative history that places Native Americans 'at the center of the historical stage.'" Publ Wkly
Includes bibliographical references

Woodard, Colin

American nations; a history of the eleven rival regional cultures of North America. Viking 2011 371p map $30 **970.004**
1. Multiculturalism 2. Regionalism -- North America 3. North America -- Race relations
ISBN 978-0-670-02296-0

LC 2011015196

The author's "take on American history identifies the original cultural settlements that became the United States, and proceeds with the thesis that these regional and cultural divisions are responsible for clashes stretching back to Revolutionary times. The 11 nations don't follow state or even country territory lines, but rather the paths taken by the earliest settlers of these areas; while later immigrants added to the mix, they didn't change the fundamental culture. . . . The book's compelling explanations and apt descriptions will fascinate anyone with an interest in politics, regional culture, or history." Publ Wkly
Includes bibliographical references

970.01   North America--Early history to 1599

Adovasio, J. M.

The **first** Americans; in pursuit of archaeology's greatest mystery. {by} J.M. Adovasio with Jake

Page. Random House 2002 328p il maps hardcover
o.p. pa $14.95   **970.01**
1. America -- Antiquities 2. Native Americans -- Origin
ISBN 0-375-75704-X pa

LC 2002-69766

"Readers get a lively, close-up view of how archaeologists study America's original discoverers." Booklist
Includes bibliographical references

Archaeology of prehistoric native America; an encyclopedia. editor, Guy Gibbon; associate editors,
Kenneth M. Ames [et al.] Garland 1998 lxxvii,
941p il map (Garland reference library of the hu-
manites) $205   **970.01**
1. Reference books 2. North America -- Antiquities
-- Encyclopedias 3. Native Americans -- Antiquities --
Encyclopedias
ISBN 0-8153-0725-X

LC 98-11443

This encyclopedia includes alphabetically arranged en-
tries covering North American prehistory and archaeology.
"This superb reference source . . . has no equal in its cov-
erage of Native American cultures in North America prior to
European contact." Libr J
Includes bibliographical references

Dillehay, Tom D.
★ The **settlement** of the Americas; a new prehistory. {by} Thomas D. Dillehay. Basic Bks. 2000
xxi, 371p il hardcover o.p. pa $22   **970.01**
1. America -- Antiquities 2. America -- Exploration
ISBN 0-465-07669-6 pa

LC 00-27572

This "is a seminal work in the field that is accessible to
lay readers." Libr J
Includes bibliographical references

Horwitz, Tony
★ A **voyage** long and strange; rediscovering the
new world. Henry Holt and Co. 2008 445p il map
$27.50   **970.01**
1. Explorers 2. America -- Exploration
ISBN 978-0-8050-7603-5; 0-8050-7603-4

LC 2007-45883

"Realizing that his knowledge of American history between Columbus's discovery and Plymouth Rock over 100
years later was sketchy at best, . . . [the author] sets out to
educate himself with his own explorations. He intertwines
his experiences retracing the early conquistadors, adventurers, and entrepreneurs through such regions as Newfoundland, the Dominican Republic, and the American South,
Southwest, and New England with thoroughly researched
accounts of the territories themselves, the natives who were
historically affected, and the motives of the explorers. . . .
This readable and vastly entertaining history travelog is
highly recommended for public libraries." Libr J
Includes bibliographical references

Mann, Charles C.
1491; new revelations of the Americas before Columbus. Knopf 2005 465p il maps   **970.01**
1. Indians -- Origin 2. Indians -- History 3. America
-- Antiquities 4. Native Americans -- History
ISBN 1-4000-3205-9 pa; 1-4000-4006-X

LC 2005-42178

This is a portrait "of the Americas before the arrival of
the Europeans in 1492." (Publisher's note) Index.
"Mann navigates adroitly through the controversies. He
approaches each in the best scientific tradition, carefully sifting the evidence, never jumping to hasty conclusions, giving
everyone a fair hearing—the experts and the amateurs; the
accounts of the Indians and their conquerors. And rarely is
he less than enthralling." N Y Times Book Rev
Includes bibliographical references

National Museum of Natural History (U.S.)
Vikings : the North Atlantic saga; edited by William W. Fitzhugh and Elisabeth I. Ward. Smithsonian
Institution Press 2000 432p il maps hardcover o.p.
pa $34.95   **970.01**
1. Vikings 2. America -- Exploration
ISBN 1-56098-970-X; 1-56098-995-5 pa

LC 99-57983

This book is "well designed, heavily illustrated and almost encyclopedic in scope and detail." Publ Wkly
Includes bibliographical references

Schneider, Paul
Brutal journey: the epic story of the first crossing of North America. Holt 2006 366p il maps
$26   **970.01**
1. Explorers 2. America -- Exploration
ISBN 978-0-8050-6835-1; 0-8050-6835-X

LC 2005-50246

"Equally able in his dramatizations of the privations and
brutalities suffusing this extraordinary tale, Schneider scores
big with fans of historical (mis)adventure." Booklist
Includes bibliographical references

Schobinger, Juan
★ The **ancient** Americans; a reference guide to
the art, culture, and history of pre-Columbian North
and South America. translation, Carys Evans-Cor-
rales; consultant, Susan Kart. Sharpe, M.E. 2000 2v
il maps set $159   **970.01**
1. Native American art 2. Rock drawings, paintings,
and engravings 3. America -- Antiquities 4. Native
Americans -- Antiquities
ISBN 0-7656-8034-3

LC 00-56280

Original Spanish language edition, 1997
This reference "surveys the entire Western Hemisphere
prior to the arrival of Europeans in the Americas. This copiously illustrated work is especially notable for its numerous
full-color plates of Native American rock art." Libr J
Includes bibliographical references

971 Canada

Gray, Charlotte
Gold diggers; striking it rich in the Klondike. Counterpoint 2010 413p il map $29.95   **971**
1. Gold mines and mining 2. Klondike River valley (Yukon) -- Gold discoveries 3. Frontier and pioneer life -- Klondike River valley (Yukon)
ISBN 978-1-58243-611-1

LC 2010-17805

This is "an enchanting recitation of lives—and deaths—in the Klondike during the gold rush over 100 years ago. Combining a keen eye for detail and firsthand histories of contemporary witnesses, Gray sets forth the lives of six 'stampeders,' including Jack London (who almost died in the wild before writing so wonderfully of those who did), Mountie Sam Steele, business wiz Belinda Mulrooney, highborn journalist Flora Shaw, devoted Jesuit priest William Judge, and, most of all, Bill Haskell, a simple soul who left America with a dream of exploration and riches." Libr J
Includes bibliographical references

MacDonald, Laura M.
Curse of the Narrows. Walker & Co. 2005 355p il maps $26   **971**
1. Explosions 2. Halifax (N.S.)
ISBN 0-8027-1458-7

LC 2005-44255

This "book captures in vivid detail the history of this catastrophe." Booklist
Includes bibliographical references

Mowat, Farley
High latitudes; an Arctic journey. foreword by Margaret Atwood. Steerforth Press 2003 300p map pa $15.95   **971**
1. Arctic regions 2. Natural history -- Canada
ISBN 1-58642-061-5

LC 2002-151151

First published 2002 in Canada
"In 1966, Mowat's publisher, Jack McClelland, sent Mowat into northern Canada to research an illustrated volume on the region. This book is the tale of that journey. Hopscotching by creaky plane from one isolated settlement to another, Mowat witnesses the devastation being wrought on the native peoples by encroaching white men, lured by a mirage of the north's supposedly limitless minerals and the raw beauty of the land and its people. A cavalcade of vivid, fiction-worthy characters fills these pages. . . . Voiced with a passionate sense of justice, this work is stirring reading from the bard of the Canadian north." Publ Wkly

Riendeau, Roger E.
★ A brief history of Canada; [by] Roger Riendeau. 2nd ed; Facts on File 2007 444p il map (Brief history) $45   **971**
1. Canada -- History
ISBN 978-0-8160-6335-2

LC 2006-47130

First published 2000
This is a history of Canada "beginning with the exploration of the Northern American frontier and continuing through the rise and fall of the French and British empires to the foundations of Canadian nationhood and the present day." Publisher's note
Includes bibliographical references

972 Mexico, Central America, West Indies, Bermuda

Coe, Michael D.
The Maya; Michael D. Coe. 7th ed fully rev and expanded; Thames and Hudson 2005 272p il map (Ancient peoples and places) pa $22.50   **972**
1. Mayas
ISBN 978-0-500-28505-3; 0-500-28505-5
First published 1966 by Praeger
An illustrated survey of the Maya civilization, focusing on the achievements of the Classic Period, A.D. 300-900
Includes bibliographical references

Diaz del Castillo, Bernal
The discovery and conquest of Mexico, 1517-1521; translated by A.P. Maudslay. Da Capo Press 2003 478p il map pa $24   **972**
1. Mexico -- History
ISBN 0-306-81319-X; 978-0-306-81319-1
First published 1956 by Farrar, Straus & Giroux
"The memoirs of an old man, who began to write of his experiences half a century after they occurred and completed his account at the age of 84, they are not free from minor inaccuracies, but they are the most reliable narrative that exists." Chicago Sunday Trib

Foster, Lynn V.
★ A brief history of Mexico; 4th ed; Facts On File 2009 324p il map (Brief history) $49.50; pa $19.95   **972**
1. Mexico -- History
ISBN 978-0-8160-7405-1; 978-0-8160-7406-8 pa

LC 2009-18298

First published 1997
An overview of Mexican history covering pre-Columbian civilizations and contemporary indigenous cultures. Language, art, religion, politics and economics are discussed. A chronology and bibliography are included.
Includes bibliographical references

Henderson, Timothy J.
The Mexican Wars for Independence. Hill and Wang 2009 xxiii, 246p il map $27.50   **972**
1. Mexico -- History
ISBN 978-0-8090-9509-4; 0-8090-9509-2

LC 2008-48141

"A solid overview of a decidedly difficult time and place, and a lucid introduction for those unfamiliar with Mexican history." Kirkus
Includes bibliographical references

Kirkwood, Burton

The **history** of Mexico; 2nd ed.; Greenwood Press/ABC-CLIO 2010 258p il map (Greenwood histories of the modern nations) $49.95 **972**

1. Mexico -- History

ISBN 978-0-313-36601-7; 0-313-36601-2

LC 2009036964

First published 2000

A historical survey of Mexico and its people from the arrival of the first humans in the Western Hemisphere to the first decade of the 21st century. Topics range from Mexico's cultural past to more current issues such as the war on drugs and the North American Free Trade Agreement.

Includes bibliographical references

Meyer, Michael C.

★ The **course** of Mexican history; [by] Michael C. Meyer, William L. Sherman, Susan M. Deeds. 8th ed.; Oxford University Press 2007 688p il map hardcover o.p. pa $64.95 **972**

1. Mexico -- History

ISBN 0-19-517835-1; 978-0-19-517835-7; 0-19-517836-X pa; 978-0-19-517836-4 pa

LC 2006-51741

A chronologically arranged survey of the political, economic, social, and cultural history of Mexico, ranging from the pre-Columbian period to the present.

Includes bibliographical references

The **Oxford history** of Mexico; edited by Michael C. Meyer and William H. Beezley. Oxford Univ. Press 2000 709p il maps $45 **972**

1. Mexico -- History

ISBN 0-19-511228-8

LC 99-56044

The editors "have compiled 20 previously unpublished essays by experts who explore Mexico from precolonial times to the present. . . . Examining the country with new and different approaches, the contributors challenge traditional historical concepts on a variety of issues." Libr J

Includes bibliographical references

Prescott, William Hickling

History of the conquest of Mexico. Modern Lib. 1998 xxvi, 1005p hardcover o.p. pa $17.95 **972**

1. Aztecs 2. Explorers 3. Mexico -- History 4. Colonial administrators

ISBN 0-375-75803-8 pa

LC 98-10173

First published 1843 in three volumes

This is a history of the subjugation of the Aztec people by Hernan Cortez and his soldiers between 1519 and 1522.

Smith, Michael Ernest

The **Aztecs**; [by] Michael E. Smith. 2nd ed; Blackwell 2003 367p il maps (Peoples of America) hardcover o.p. pa $29.95 **972**

1. Aztecs 2. Mexico -- Antiquities

ISBN 0-631-23015-7; 0-631-23016-5 pa

LC 2001-6950

First published 1996

The author "summarizes the results of archaeological research conducted largely in the past 30 years into the everyday lives of ordinary people in the villages, hamlets, and farmsteads from many regions of central Mexico. His method permits a fresh view of such topics as agricultural methods, population size, market system, relations between city-states and the empire, and even human sacrifice. Smith carries his social account of these people through transformation under Spanish rule and their legacy in modern Mexico." Libr J [review of 1996 edition]

Includes bibliographical references

Townsend, Richard F.

The **Aztecs**; 3rd ed; Thames & Hudson 2009 256p il map (Ancient peoples and places) pa $24.95 **972**

1. Aztecs

ISBN 978-0-500-28791-0

LC 2008-908216

First published 1992

"Examines the history of these accomplished people through a review of the monuments and artifacts they left behind; exploring how their water-control projects worked, the purposes of their ceremonial centers, and the way they built their incredible ancient structures that still stand today." Publisher's note

Includes bibliographical references

972.08 Mexico since 1867

Fuentes, Carlos

A **new** time for Mexico; translated from the Spanish by Marina Gutman Castañeda and the author. University of Calif. Press 1997 226p pa $16.95 **972.08**

1. Mexico -- Politics and government

ISBN 0-520-21183-9

LC 97-8427

First published 1996 by Farrar, Straus, & Giroux

In these essays "Fuentes calls on Mexican president Ernesto Zedillo to take definitive steps toward a full democracy—electoral reform; equal access of candidates to the media; independent, aggressive labor unions; and, above all, true separation between the ruling party and the government. . . . Offering lapidary, lyrical meditations on Mexico as a land of continual metamorphosis, Fuentes nostalgically reminisces about his home in Veracruz, whose port his father defended against a Yankee invasion in 1914." Publ Wkly

Katz, Friedrich

The **life** and times of Pancho Villa. Stanford Univ. Press 1998 985p hardcover o.p. pa $30.95 **972.08**

1. Outlaws 2. Revolutionaries 3. Mexico -- History

ISBN 0-8047-3046-6 pa

LC 97-47271

The author "traces Pancho Villa's rise from relatively obscure outlaw to national leader of the Mexican Revolution (1910-20) and his subsequent decline to guerrilla leader. . . .{This} is likely to be the definitive account of Villa for years to come." Libr J

Includes bibliographical references

Lewis, Oscar

★ The **children** of Sanchez; autobiography of a Mexican family. Random House 1961 xxxi, 499p hardcover o.p. pa $17   **972.08**

1. Family 2. Poor -- Mexico City (Mexico) 3. Mexico City (Mexico) -- Social conditions

ISBN 0-394-70280-8 pa

"Oscar Lewis has made something brilliant and of singular significance, a work of such unique concentration and sympathy." N Y Times Book Rev

Womack, John

Zapata and the Mexican Revolution. Knopf 1969 435p il hardcover o.p. pa $17   **972.08**

1. Revolutionaries 2. Mexico -- History

ISBN 0-394-70853-9 pa

The author reconstructs the "history of the agrarian revolution in southern Mexico from the late Diaz period to about 1920. The work is well written {and} carefully conceived." Choice

972.8   Other parts of Middle America

Perez-Brignoli, Hector

A **brief** history of Central America; translated by Ricardo B. Sawrey A. and Susana Stettri de Sawrey. University of Calif. Press 1989 223p maps hardcover o.p. pa $18.97   **972.8**

1. Central America -- History

ISBN 0-520-06832-7 pa

                   LC 89-31889

This book presents the economic, political and cultural history of Guatemala, Honduras, El Salvador, Nicaragua and Costa Rica, the five national states of Central America

"For interested laypersons, this is an excellent introduction with an accurate sense of the region." Libr J

Includes bibliographical references

972.81   Guatemala

Coe, Michael D.

Royal cities of the ancient Maya; Michael D. Coe ; photographs by Barry Brukoff. Vendome Press 2012 224 p. $50   **972.81**

1. Mayas -- History 2. Cities and towns -- HIstory 3. Maya architecture 4. Mayas -- Antiquities 5. Central America -- Antiquities

ISBN 0865652848; 9780865652842

              LC 2011051139

This book presents the "history of Mayan civilization as seen through the development and decline of its many impressive city-states." It offers "glimpses, through dated stone monuments, into the hereditary lines of dynastic kings who ruled Mayan city-states and frequently did battle with each other." (Library Journal)

Includes bibliographical references

Goldman, Francisco

The **art** of political murder; who killed the Bishop? Grove Press 2007 396p il map $25   **972.81**

1. Bishops 2. Trials (Homicide) 3. Murder victims 4. Human rights activists 5. Guatemala -- Politics and government

ISBN 978-0-8021-1828-8; 0-8021-1828-3

This book "is a tour de force, not just for . . . [the author's] reportorial tenacity . . . but because his novelist's eye and his deep understanding of Guatemalan society take you places no other reporter could." Nation

Includes bibliographical references

972.87   Panama

McCullough, David G.

★ The **path** between the seas; the creation of the Panama Canal, 1870-1914. [by] David McCullough. Simon & Schuster 1977 698p il maps hardcover o.p. pa $18   **972.87**

1. Diplomats 2. Governors 3. Physicians 4. Presidents 5. Panama Canal 6. Vice-presidents 7. Army officers 8. Public health officials 9. Nobel laureates for peace

ISBN 0-671-24409-4

              LC 76-57967

"Not only is this a well-told story of the building of the Panama Canal but it also supplies welcome background for the . . . debate on the canal's role in inter-American relations." Booklist

Includes bibliographical references

972.9   West Indies (Antilles) and Bermuda

Kincaid, Jamaica, 1946-

A **small** place. Farrar, Straus & Giroux 1988 81p hardcover o.p. pa $11   **972.9**

1. Antigua and Barbuda 2. Antigua (Antigua and Barbuda)

ISBN 0-374-52707-5 pa

              LC 88-376

The author of Annie John addresses foreign visitors to her country, the island of Antigua. In this essay, she discusses the poverty and political corruption of the island, which she views as a legacy of British colonialism and also as a result of an economy controlled by tourism.

Von Tunzelmann, Alex

Red heat; conspiracy, murder, and the Cold War in the Caribbean. Henry Holt 2011 449p il $30; ebook $14.99   **972.9**

1. Generals 2. Physicians 3. Presidents 4. Revolutionaries 5. Haiti -- History 6. Communist leaders 7. Political leaders 8. Cuba -- History -- 1959- 9. Caribbean region -- History 10. Dominican Republic -- History 11. Haiti -- History -- 1934-1986 12. Caribbean region -- History -- 1945- 13. Dominican Republic -- History -- 1930-1961 14. Caribbean region -- Foreign relations -- United States 15. United States

-- Foreign relations -- Caribbean region
ISBN 978-0-8050-9067-3; 978-1-4299-6673-3 ebook
LC 2010-37585

"Three dictators, circa 1960—Castro in Cuba, François Duvalier in Haiti, and Rafael Trujillo in the Dominican Republic—are the principals in von Tunzelmann's political history. Recounting alarms that trio set off in Washington, she ponders how well the Eisenhower and Kennedy administrations understood situations on the islands of Cuba and Hispaniola. Not very realistically, runs the tenor of von Tunzelmann's narrative. . . . Punctuated by accounts of such major incidents as the Bay of Pigs, the assassination of Trujillo, the Cuban missile crisis, and LBJ's 1965 intervention in the Dominican Republic, von Tunzelmann's diligent work will widen the eyes of cold war buffs." Booklist

Includes bibliographical references

972.91   Cuba

Cooke, Julia

The **other** side of paradise; life in the new Cuba. Julia Cooke. Seal Press 2014 248 p. (paperback) $17   **972.91**
1. Havana (Cuba) 2. Cuba -- Social life and customs 3. Havana (Cuba) -- Biography 4. Cuba -- History -- 1990- -- Biography 5. Cuba -- Politics and government -- 1990- 6. Young adults -- Cuba -- Havana -- Biography 7. Havana (Cuba) -- Social conditions -- 21st century 8. Havana (Cuba) -- Social life and customs -- 21st century 9. Social change -- Cuba -- Havana -- History -- 21st century
ISBN 1580055311; 9781580055314
LC 2013044413

This book by Julia Cook describes how "[t]his last generation of Cubans raised under Fidel Castro animate life in a waning era of political stagnation as the rest of the world beckons: waiting out storms at rummy hurricane parties and attending raucous drag cabarets, planning ascendant music careers and black-market business ventures, trying to reconcile the undefined future with the urgent today." (Publisher's note)

"An absorbing and educational read about contemporary Cuba, the love of its people for their country, and their hope for opportunity." LJ

Includes bibliographical references

Guillermoprieto, Alma

Dancing with Cuba; a memoir of the revolution. translated from the Spanish by Esther Allen. Pantheon 2004 290p $25; pa $13   **972.91**
1. Cuba -- Description and travel
ISBN 0-375-42093-2; 0-375-72581-4 pa
LC 2003-44200

"Guillermoprieto vividly and purposefully recounts her acute discomfort with the strained and ludicrous rhetoric of the revolution, her sorrow over Castro's catastrophic failures, her astonishment at the great valor of Cuba's people, and her gradual recognition of her true calling as a journalist." Booklist

Martinez-Fernandez, Luis

Encyclopedia of Cuba; people, history, culture. edited by Luis Martinez-Fernández [et al.] Greenwood Press 2003 2v il maps set $174.95   **972.91**
1. Reference books 2. Cuba -- Encyclopedias
ISBN 1-57356-334-X
LC 2002-70030

"The editors intend this work to be a non-politicized look at Cuban people, politics, history, and culture. Chapters cover topics such as history, government, and popular culture. Within each chapter, entries are in alphabetical order. An excellent introduction to a colorful and important nation." Booklist

Includes bibliographical references

Perez, Louis A.

Cuba; between reform and revolution. Oxford University Press 2006 442p il map (Latin American histories) $77.95; pa $34.95   **972.91**
1. Cuba -- History
ISBN 0-19-517911-0; 978-0-19-517911-8; 0-19-517912-9 pa; 978-0-19-517912-5 pa
LC 2004-65477

First published 1988

"A narrative history that emphasizes the antecedents of the Cuban revolution and concludes with an analysis of Fidel Castro's successes and failures." N Y Public Libr Book of How & Where to Look It Up [entry for 1988 edition]

Includes bibliographical references

Rasenberger, Jim

The **brilliant** disaster; JFK, Castro, and America's doomed invasion of Cuba's Bay of Pigs. Scribner 2011 460p il   **972.91**
1. Presidents 2. Senators 3. Communist leaders 4. Members of Congress 5. Cuba -- History -- 1961, Invasion 6. Cuba -- Foreign relations -- United States 7. United States -- Foreign relations -- Cuba
ISBN 978-1-4165-9650-9
LC 2011-4178

"On Apr., 17, 1961, a CIA-trained brigade of 1,400 Cuban exiles, mostly students and former soldiers, made an unsuccessful amphibious assault on the Bay of Pigs, in southern Cuba, hoping to spur a popular revolt and overthrow the Castro regime. Fifty years later, Rasenberger . . . succeeds admirably in offering a nuanced view of the entire botched operation, from its planning in two U.S. administrations to the Cuban armed forces' quick defeat of the exiles, whose attack lacked air cover and the element of surprise." Kirkus

Includes bibliographical references

Suchlicki, Jaime

Cuba; from Columbus to Castro and beyond. {by} Jaime Suchlicki. 5th ed; Brassey's 2002 285p pa $24.95   **972.91**
1. Cuba -- History
ISBN 1-57488-436-0
LC 2002-3953

First published 1997

A summary of Cuba's development, with emphasis on the twentieth century and the factors that led to the Cuban revolution

Includes bibliographical references

Symmes, Patrick

The **boys** from Dolores; Fidel Castro's schoolmates from revolution to exile. Pantheon Books 2007 352p $26.95   **972.91**

1. Presidents 2. Communist leaders 3. Colegio de Dolores (Cuba) 4. Cuba -- Description and travel
ISBN 978-0-375-42283-6; 0-375-42283-8

LC 2006-30323

"The author writes of Castro's schoolmates from Dolores, the private Jesuit academy in Santiago de Cuba on the island's eastern end, and he visits several of them. . . . Among the Dolores students were Castro's brothers Raul and Ramon and a future star in North American television, Desi Arnaz. But it is Cuban intellectuals like Lundy Aguilar to whom Symmes turns for insights into Cuba before and after Castro's revolution. The result is a remarkable account of the country and its people." Libr J

972.910   Cuba--1899-

Gimbel, Wendy

Havana dreams; a story of Cuba. Knopf 1998 234p il hardcover o.p. pa $13   **972.910**

1. Defectors 2. Presidents 3. Mistresses 4. Socialites 5. Cuba -- History 6. Communist leaders 7. Children of prominent persons
ISBN 0-679-75070-3 pa

LC 98-14571

Gimbel "succeeds in showing the complexity of family relationships resulting from the Cuban revolution, which extends into two countries." Libr J

Includes bibliographical references

March, Aleida

Remembering Che; my life with Che Guevara. Aleida March ; [translated by Pilar Aguilera] Ocean Press 2012 viii, 168 p.p ill.   **972.910**

1. Cuba -- History -- 1958-1959, Revolution 2. Cuba -- History -- 1990- 3. Cuba -- History -- 1959-1990 4. Revolutionaries -- Latin America -- Biography 5. Revolutionaries' spouses -- Latin America -- Biography
ISBN 0987077937; 9780987077936; 9780987077998
LC 2011943980

Author Aleida March "evokes the memories of her partner, Ernesto Che Guevara. She describes their great romance and life together from the days when they first met as fellow guerrillas in Cuba's revolutionary war up to the tragic moment when she learned of Che's assassination in Bolivia less than a decade later. . . . She also describes her efforts to raise her four children as ordinary children despite their father's legendary status in Cuba and abroad." (Publisher's note)

Includes bibliographical references

Quirk, Robert E.

Fidel Castro. Norton 1993 898p il maps hardcover o.p. pa $19.95   **972.910**

1. Presidents 2. Communist leaders 3. Cuba -- Politics and government
ISBN 0-393-31327-1 pa

LC 92-39300

"Quirk's richly detailed, psychologically acute portrait reveals more about Castro's unique personality and character than do previous biographies." Publ Wkly

Includes bibliographical references

972.94   Haiti

Dubois, Laurent

Haiti; the aftershocks of history. Laurent Dubois. 1st ed.; Henry Holt and Co. 2012 p. cm. $32 **972.94**

1. Haiti -- History
ISBN 978-0-8050-9335-3

LC 2011020162

Includes bibliographical references

Laferriee, Dany

The **World** Is Moving Around Me; A Memoir of the Haiti Earthquake. Dany Laferrière ; translated by David Homel. Arsenal Pulp Press 2013 192 p. $15.95   **972.94**

1. Natural disasters 2. Haiti Earthquake, Haiti, 2010
ISBN 1551524988; 9781551524986

LC 2012517880

This book by Dany Laferriere "is an eyewitness account of the [January 12, 2010 earth]quake and its aftermath. In a series of vignettes, Laferrière reveals the shock, rage, and grief experienced by those around him, the acts of heroism he witnessed, and his own sense of survivor guilt. This book is not only the chronicle of a natural disaster; it is also a personal meditation about the responsibility and power of the written word." (Publisher's note)

---

973   United States

American Association for State and Local History

Directory of historical organizations in the United States and Canada; 15th ed.; American Assn. for State & Local Hist. 2002 1358p pa $149.95   **973**

1. Reference books 2. United States -- History -- Societies -- Directories
ISBN 0-7591-0002-0

First published 1956 with title: Directory of historical societies and agencies in the United States and Canada. Periodically revised

This publication "lists historical societies geographically, giving mailing address, number of members, museums, hours and size of library, publication program, etc." Ref Sources for Small & Medium-sized Libr. 5th edition

The **American** experience; the history and culture of the United States through speeches, letters, essays, articles, poems, songs, and stories. edited by

Erik Bruun and Jay Crosby. Black Dog & Leventhal Publishers 2012 894 p. $22.95   **973**
1. Popular culture -- United States 2. United States -- History -- Sources
ISBN 1579129072; 9781579129071

This book presents "569 primary documents, organized chronologically, cover[ing] elements of American history from 1763 to the present. Originally published in hardcover as 'Our Nation's Archive: The History of the United States in Documents' (1999), this update cuts about one-third of the initial volume's documents but adds recent events, from the 9/11 terrorist attacks through the Obama administration, ending with the text of the bill repealing collective bargaining in Wisconsin." (Booklist)

The **American** presidency; edited by Alan Brinkley and Davis Dyer. Houghton Mifflin Co 2004 572p il pa $19.95   **973**
1. Presidents -- United States 2. United States -- Politics and government
ISBN 0-618-38273-9
LC 2003-62513

An updated version of The reader's companion to the American presidency (2000)

This work assesses "how presidents shape and define culture and society and, at the same time, reflect them. . . . {This} can serve as a beginning point for research and should engage casual readers as well as students of the American presidency." Choice
Includes bibliographical references

Americans at war; society, culture, and the homefront. John P. Resch, Editor in Chief. Macmillan Reference USA 2005 4v il set $395   **973**
1. War and civilization 2. United States -- Civilization 3. United States -- Military history
ISBN 0-02-865806-X
LC 2004-17314

This book "delivers well-written articles and would make an excellent addition to high-school, academic, and public libraries." Booklist
Includes bibliographical references

Appleby, Joyce Oldham
Inheriting the revolution; the first generation of Americans. {by} Joyce Appleby. Belknap Press 2000 322p il hardcover o.p. pa $16   **973**
1. United States -- Social conditions 2. United States -- History -- 1783-1865
ISBN 0-674-00236-9; 0-674-00663-1 pa
LC 99-49787

The author "deals with two themes in this book: the historical experience of the generation after the American Revolution and conflicts within American identity." N Y Times Book Rev

"This book provides a splendid introduction to the period for students and general readers." Libr J
Includes bibliographical references

Ashby, Ruth
The **great** american documents; Volume 1, 1620-1830 Ruth Ashby ; illustrated by Ernie Colón ; edito-

rial consultant Russell Motter. Hill and Wang 2014 160 p. col. ill. (hardcover) $40   **973**
1. United States -- History -- Sources 2. United States -- Politics and government -- Sources
ISBN 0809094606; 9780809094608
LC 2013956401

Written by Ruth Ashby and illustrated by Ernie Colón, "'The Great American Documents: Volume 1' introduces as series narrator none other than Uncle Sam, who walks us through twenty essential documents. Each document gets a chapter, in which Uncle Sam explains its key passages, its origins, how it came to be written, and its impact. This graphic primer is an indispensable resource for students and anyone else who wants the facts of American history close at hand." (Publisher's note)

"Colon uses well-designed, full-color panel layouts to eloquently blend charts and other informative graphics with straightforward images of events, clothing, and customs as well as clear, concise metaphors, all with an eye toward promoting a solid understanding of the basic facts and their impact." Booklist
Includes bibliographical references

Berger, Joseph
The **pious** ones; the world of Hasidim and their battles with America. Joseph Berger. Harper Perennial 2014 384 p. (paperback) $15.99   **973**
1. Ethnic relations 2. Jews -- New York (N.Y.) 3. Hasidim -- Social conditions 4. New York (N.Y.) -- Ethnic relations 5. Hasidim -- New York (State) -- New York -- Social conditions 6. Jews -- New York (State) -- New York -- Social life and customs
ISBN 0062123343; 9780062123343; 9780062123350
LC 2014011724

In this book, "journalist Joseph Berger takes us inside the notoriously insular world of the Hasidim to explore their origins, beliefs, and struggles--and the social and political implications of their expanding presence in America. . . . Berger traces their origins in eighteenth-century Eastern Europe, illuminating their dynamics and core beliefs that remain so enigmatic to outsiders." (Publisher's note)

"Through Berger's solid research and approachable writing, readers will gain a clear, well-rounded understanding of who the Hasidim are, where they came from and where they are going as a people." Kirkus

Boller, Paul F.
Presidential inaugurations; {by} Paul F. Boller, Jr. Harcourt 2001 298p $25; pa $14   **973**
1. Presidents -- United States -- Inauguration 2. Washington (D.C.) -- Social life and customs
ISBN 0-15-100546-X; 0-15-600759-2 pa
LC 00-49893

The author "examines the events and controversies surrounding Presidential inaugurations. . . . Written with elegance and wit, this is a wonderful addition to the very thin literature available on Presidential inaugurations." Libr J
Includes bibliographical references

Boorstin, Daniel J.

The **Americans** : The democratic experience.
Random House 1973 717p hardcover o.p. pa
$19   **973**
1. Advertising 2. American art 3. Americanisms 4.
Higher education 5. Automobile industry 6. United
States -- Civilization 7. Cities and towns -- United
States 8. United States -- Social conditions 9. United
States -- Economic conditions
ISBN 0-394-71011-8 pa
Concluding volume of the author's trilogy which began
with The Americans: The colonial experience and continued
with The Americans: The national experience
This volume is concerned with the democratization of
the national character over the past hundred years and the
growth of technology
Includes bibliographical references

The **Americans** : The national experience. Ran-
dom House 1965 517p hardcover o.p. pa $16 **973**
1. Americanisms 2. Federal government 3. Heroes
and heroines 4. American national characteristics
5. America -- Exploration 6. African Americans --
Religion 7. United States -- Civilization 8. United
States -- Intellectual life 9. Constitutional history --
United States 10. Colleges and universities -- United
States
ISBN 0-394-70358-8 pa
This is the second volume of the author's trilogy
A cultural interpretation of American history, this book
traces "the roots of contemporary American life to the years
between the Revolution and the Civil War." Booklist
Includes bibliographical references

Hidden history; selected and edited by Daniel J.
Boorstin and Ruth F. Boorstin. Vintage Books 1989
332p pa $15   **973**
1. United States -- Civilization
ISBN 978-0-679-72223-6; 0-679-72223-8
First published 1987 by Harper & Row
"A collection of essays and abridgments from [Boorst-
in's] books that investigates certain overlooked or disregarded corners of history. . . . History engagingly written, deeply
felt, widely appealing." Booklist

Bracks, Lean'tin

African American almanac; 400 years of triumph,
courage and excellence. Lean'tin Bracks. Visible Ink
Press 2012 xiii, 543 p.p ill. (pbk.) $22.95   **973**
1. Almanacs 2. African Americans -- History 3. African
Americans -- Encyclopedias 4. African Americans --
Biography -- Encyclopedias 5. African Americans --
Biography 6. African Americans -- Intellectual life 7.
African Americans -- Social life and customs
ISBN 1578593239; 9781578593231
LC 2011038636
This reference book by Lean'tin Bracks "chronicles the
African American experience from the arrival of the first Af-
ricans to North America in the early 1600s to the present
day," including an almanac of topics such as Civil Rights,
politics, and music, as well as biographies of various notable

African Americans. "Bracks also gives context to less documented areas of African American history." (Booklist)
"This mostly excellent overview of African American
contributions to the United States will be a welcome addition to school, public, and community college libraries.—"
LJ
Includes bibliographical references (p. 469-477)
and index

Churchill, Winston

The **great** republic; a history of America. edited
by Winston S. Churchill. Random House 1999 454p
hardcover o.p. pa $15.95   **973**
1. United States -- History
ISBN 0-375-50320-X; 978-0-375-75440-1 pa; 0-375-
75440-7 pa
LC 99-28511
"The first half of the volume offers an old-fashioned narrative history of America's political development, from the
age of exploration to the 1880s. The second half reprints articles that Churchill penned for English publications on such
themes as Prohibition, the muckracking of Upton Sinclair,
and the death of Franklin Delano Roosevelt." Libr J
Includes bibliographical references

Commager, Henry Steele

The **American** mind; an interpretation of American thought and character since the 1880's. Yale Univ.
Press 1950 476p hardcover o.p. pa $14.95   **973**
1. Authors 2. Lawyers 3. Economics 4. Sociology
5. Economists 6. Journalism 7. Pragmatism 8.
Philosophers 9. Psychologists 10. Law teachers 11.
Sociologists 12. Social critics 13. College teachers 14.
Authors, American 15. Nonfiction writers 16. Writers
on science 17. Law -- United States 18. Supreme Court
justices 19. United States -- Religion 20. United States
-- Civilization 21. National characteristics, American
22. United States -- Intellectual life 23. United States
-- Economic conditions 24. United States -- Politics and
government
ISBN 0-300-00046-4 pa

Cornelison, Pam

★ The **great** American history fact-finder; the
who, what, where, when, and why of American history. [by] Pam Cornelison and Ted Yanak. 2nd ed, updated and expanded; Houghton Mifflin 2004 608p
il, maps pa $14.95   **973**
1. Reference books 2. United States -- History --
Dictionaries
ISBN 0-618-43941-2
LC 2004-47480
First published 1993 with authors' names in reverse order
This book provides "information about significant persons as well as political, legal, sporting, and cultural events
in American history. Entries are alphabetically arranged,
and related entries cross-referenced. . . . Besides an index,
there are suggested readings and information on the states,
presidents, vice presidents, population, Supreme Court, Articles of Confederation, Declaration of Independence, and US
Constitution (with signers and nonsigners). This is a good
quick reference." Choice

Curtis, Nancy C.

Black heritage sites; an African American odyssey and finder's guide. American Lib. Assn. 1996 677p il $75 **973**

1. Historic sites 2. African Americans -- History
ISBN 0-8389-0643-5

LC 95-5788

This "guide locates significant places in African-American history and supplies . . . recent addresses, phone numbers, and visitors' information. . . . Organized by region, a historical essay introduces each section, presenting the culture and history in that area." Publisher's note

Daily life through American history in primary documents; Randall M. Miller, general editor. Greenwood 2012 1099 p. **973**

1. Archives -- United States 2. United States -- History -- Sources 3. United States -- History -- Chronology 4. United States -- Social life and customs 5. United States -- Social life and customs -- Sources
ISBN 161069032X; 1610690338; 9781610690324; 9781610690331

LC 2011040023

In this history book, "four volumes are organized chronologically and then thematically and present the 'many small things that made up Americans' daily life.' Volumes are 'The Colonial Period through the American Revolution,' 'The American Revolution to the Civil War,' 'The Civil War to World War I,' and 'World War I to the Present.' Each volume begins with a time line of selected events and a lengthy historical-overview essay describing significant themes, events, and concerns of the period. This is followed by about 100 primary documents that illustrate daily life." (Booklist)
Includes bibliographical references and index

Duberman, Martin

Howard Zinn; a life on the left. Martin Duberman. New Press"||"Distributed by Perseus Distribution 2012 p. cm. **973**

1. Historians -- United States -- Biography
ISBN 9781595586780

LC 2012017592

This biography of historian Howard Zinn by Martin Duberman, a "bestselling author . . . political activist . . . lecturer, and one of America's most recognizable and admired progressive voices," details Zinn's life "from the battlefields of World War II to the McCarthy era, the civil rights and the antiwar movements, and beyond." (Publisher's note)
Includes bibliographical references and index

Encyclopedia of American cultural and intellectual history; edited by Mary Kupiec Cayton and Peter W. Williams. Scribner 2000 3v il set $400 **973**

1. Reference books 2. United States -- Civilization -- Encyclopedias 3. United States -- Intellectual life -- Encyclopedias
ISBN 0-684-80561-8

LC 2001-20005

Art movements, education and academia, the counterculture, the sciences, domestic life, social classes, Hollywood, and post-structuralism are among the topics covered.

Each article includes illustrations, boxed biographies, or documentary excerpts

★ **Encyclopedia** of American historical documents; edited by Susan Rosenfeld. Facts on File 2004 3v (Facts on File library of American history) set $300 **973**

1. United States -- History -- Sources
ISBN 0-8160-4995-5

LC 2003-51610

"Each section begins with an overview of the period and each document is introduced with commentary on when and why it was created and its significance, then and now. Entries include material 'with resonance for the 21st century' that represents turning points in U.S. history, and documents of a controversial nature. Students can read Supreme Court justices' opinions, presidential announcements and inaugural addresses, excerpts from noteworthy books that influenced American thought and action, and speeches of women and people of color. . . . Students and teachers will welcome this mammoth resource." SLJ
Includes bibliographical references

Encyclopedia of American history; Gary B. Nash, general editor. Rev. ed.; Facts on File 2010 11v il map (Facts on File library of American history) set $1,150 **973**

1. Reference books 2. United States -- History -- Encyclopedias
ISBN 978-0-8160-7136-4

LC 2008-35422

First published 2003

This encyclopedia provides a "presentation of the political, social, economic, and cultural events that have shaped the land and the nation." Publisher's note
Includes bibliographical references

The **Encyclopedia** of American political history; edited by Paul Finkelman, Peter Wallenstein. CQ Press 2001 xxxii, 494p il map $140 **973**

1. Reference books 2. United States -- Politics and government -- Encyclopedias
ISBN 1-56802-511-4

LC 00-66812

This reference tool covers "significant events, people {and} concepts in U.S. political history. Organized alphabetically, the 225 entries vary in length from a few paragraphs to several pages. The book opens with a descriptive time line of political events and ends with an appendix of acronyms and abbreviations used in U.S. history." Libr J
Includes bibliographical references

Encyclopedia of rural America; the land and people. Gary A. Goreham, editor. 2nd ed; Grey House Pub. 2008 2v il map set $250 **973**

1. Reference books 2. United States -- Geography -- Encyclopedias 3. Country life -- United States -- Encyclopedias 4. United States -- Rural conditions -- Encyclopedias
ISBN 978-1-59237-115-0; 1-59237-115-9

First published 1997 by ABC-CLIO

"This encyclopedia covers a broad range of topics, such as agriculture, the arts, economics, the environment, health, humanities, and political and social science. The . . . alphabetically arranged entries, from addiction to worker's compensation, are listed in the front of each volume for handy reference." Booklist [review of 1997 edition]

Includes bibliographical references

Encyclopedia of the new American nation; the emergence of the United States, 1754-1829. Paul Finkelman, editor in chief. Thomson Gale 2005 3v il map set $395   **973**
1. Reference books 2. United States -- History -- 1783-1865 -- Encyclopedias 3. United States -- History -- 1775-1783, Revolution -- Encyclopedias 4. United States -- History -- 1600-1775, Colonial period -- Encyclopedias
ISBN 0-684-31346-4

LC 2005-17783

The timeframe covered in this encyclopedia of major political events and figures "is roughly from 1754 (beginning of the Seven Years' War) to the inauguration of President Andrew Jackson (1829). Woven among this set of political markers and milestones are entries outlining the cultural development of the new nation, including entries on art, music, literature, dress and daily life." Publisher's note

The editor and contributors "have produced a wonderful reference source." Ref & User Services Quarterly

Includes bibliographical references

Encyclopedia of U.S. political history. CQ Press 2009 7v il map set $1200   **973**
1. Reference books 2. Political science -- Encyclopedias 3. United States -- Politics and government -- Encyclopedias
ISBN 978-0-87289-320-7

LC 2010-2253

"An impressive work remarkable for its breath and scope, this encyclopedia covers U.S. political history chronologically from the year 1500 to the present day. . . . Written in a vivid and accessible yet scholarly manner, this wonderful synthesis of history and political science will greatly benefit students, lovers of political history, and academics alike." Libr J

Includes bibliographical references

Eyewitness to America; 500 years of America in the words of those who saw it happen. edited by David Colbert. Pantheon Bks. 1997 xxx, 599p hardcover o.p. pa $16.95   **973**
1. United States -- History -- Sources
ISBN 0-679-44224-3; 0-679-76724-X pa

LC 96-24150

This volume contains a "panorama of first-person accounts of moments in the country's story that stretch from an October 10, 1492, diary entry by one of Columbus's crewmen to a 1994 e-mail message from Bill Gates. The nearly 300 entries tend to be short, preceded by informative introductions. The result is a feeling for history that is both immediate and dramatic." Publ Wkly

Includes bibliographical references

Feiler, Bruce S.
America's prophet; Moses and the American story. [by] Bruce Feiler. William Morrow 2009 352p il $26.99   **973**
1. Prophets 2. Biblical characters 3. United States -- History
ISBN 978-0-06-057488-8

An exploration of how the story of Moses has influenced American history traces the biblical figure's role in inspiring change, from the Pilgrims' journey and the visions of the Founding Fathers to the ideologies of the civil rights movement.

The author's argument is "an eye-opening contention, beautifully argued. . . . Fascinating and thought-provoking." Booklist

Includes bibliographical references and index

Grande, Reyna
The **distance** between us; a memoir. Reyna Grande. Atria Books 2012 336 p. (hardcover) $25.00   **973**
1. Poor 2. Novelists 3. Immigrants -- United States 4. Mexican Americans -- Biography 5. Los Angeles (Calif.) -- Biography 6. Immigrants -- United States -- Biography 7. Mexican American women authors -- Biography 8. Abused children -- United States -- Biography 9. Mexico -- Emigration and immigration -- Social aspects 10. Mexican Americans -- California -- Los Angeles -- Biography 11. United States -- Emigration and immigration -- Social aspects
ISBN 1451661770; 9781451661774; 9781451661781; 9781451661804

LC 2012001634

This book presents a memoir by "award-winning novelist . . . [Reyna] Grande. . . . Four-year-old Grande and her two siblings lived with their cruel grandmother after both parents departed for the U.S. in search of work. . . . Eight years later her father returned and reluctantly agreed to take his children to the States. . . . Surrounded by family turmoil, Grande discovered a love of writing . . . and went on to become the first person in her family to graduate from college." (Publishers Weekly)

★   The **Greenwood** encyclopedia of American regional cultures;   William Ferris, consulting editor. Greenwood Press 2004 8v il map set $699.95   **973**
1. Reference books 2. United States -- Civilization -- Encyclopedias 3. United States -- Social life and customs -- Encyclopedias
ISBN 0-313-33266-5

This "set explores the history and culture of U.S. regions from the Atlantic to the Pacific. The essay-long articles examine at length each region's art, ethnicity, fashion, film, folklore, food, literature, religion, sports, and more." Libr J

Includes bibliographical references

The **Greenwood** library of American war reporting; David A. Copeland, general editor. Greenwood Press 2005 8v il set $995	**973**
1. United States -- Military history -- Sources
ISBN 0-313-33435-8

LC 2005-10122

"Beginning with 1753 and ending in April 2004 with photographs depicting the mistreatment of Iraqi prisoners at Abu Ghraib, these volumes offer primary documents, mainly newspaper and magazine articles and radio and television transcripts. Indispensable to the study of war reporting and the most definitive . . . reference work available on the subject." Booklist
Includes bibliographical references

Gregorian, Vartan

The **road** to home; my life and times. Simon & Schuster 2003 354p il hardcover o.p. pa $15	**973**
1. Library directors 2. College presidents 3. Foundation officials
ISBN 0-684-80834-X; 978-0-7432-5565-3; 0-7432-5565-8 pa

LC 2003-45566

In this "memoir, Gregorian explains how he went from a childhood in a poor section of Tabriz, Iran, to become president of the New York Public Library and, later, the president of Brown University." Publ Wkly

Hofstadter, Richard

The **American** political tradition, and the men who made it; with a foreword by Christopher Lasch. 25th anniversary ed; Knopf 1973 xxxiii, 378p hardcover o.p. pa $14	**973**
1. Authors 2. Lawyers 3. Generals 4. Governors 5. Statesmen 6. Architects 7. Presidents 8. Abolitionists 9. Philanthropists 10. Vice-presidents 11. People with disabilities 12. Orators 13. Essayists 14. Philatelists 15. Political leaders 16. State legislators 17. College presidents 18. Secretaries of war 19. Members of Congress 20. Secretaries of state 21. Presidential candidates 22. Secretaries of commerce 23. Nobel laureates for peace 24. United States -- Politics and government
ISBN 0-679-72315-3 pa
First published 1948

This volume contains twelve essays, ten of which analyze the political careers of Lincoln, Jefferson, Jackson, Calhoun, Wendell Phillips, Bryan, Theodore Roosevelt, Wilson, Hoover and Franklin D. Roosevelt.
Includes bibliographical references

Kammen, Michael G.

In the past lane; historical perspectives on American culture. {by} Michael Kammen. Oxford Univ. Press 1997 277p il hardcover o.p. pa $25	**973**
1. United States -- Civilization 2. United States -- Historiography 3. Popular culture -- United States
ISBN 0-19-513091-X pa

LC 97-21613

These essays "range from the influence of the personal experiences of prominent historians on their work to the changing attitudes toward the 'unique' aspects of American

history as reflected in the views of historians, past and present. For professional historians or serious students of history, Kammen's essays provide an excellent opportunity to gauge how those who chronicle our past both influence and are influenced by national and personal experiences." Booklist
Includes bibliographical references

Lepore, Jill

★ The **mansion** of happiness; a history of life and death. Jill Lepore. 1st ed. Alfred A. Knopf 2012 xxxiii, 282 p.p $27.95	**973**
1. Life 2. Death 3. Popular culture 4. United States -- Intellectual life 5. United States -- Social conditions 6. United States -- Social life and customs 7. Popular culture -- United States -- History 8. Politics and culture -- United States -- History 9. Life -- Social aspects -- United States -- History 10. Death -- Social aspects -- United States -- History 11. Happiness -- Social aspects -- United States -- History 12. Life (Biology) -- Social aspects -- United States -- History 13. Life cycle, Human -- Social aspects -- United States -- History
ISBN 0307592995; 9780307592996

LC 2011050566

In this book Jill Lepore examines "the history of American ideas about life and death. . . . Lepore starts . . . with the story of a seventeenth-century Englishman who had the idea that all life begins with an egg and ends it with an American who, in the 1970s, began freezing the dead. . . . Investigating the surprising origins of the stuff of everyday life . . . Lepore argues that the age of discovery, Darwin, and the Space Age turned ideas about life on earth topsy-turvy." (Publisher's note)
Includes bibliographical references and index.

The **story** of America; essays on origins. Jill Lepore. Princeton University Press 2012 viii, 416 p.p (acid-free paper) $27.95	**973**
1. United States -- History 2. Democracy -- United States -- History 3. United States -- Politics and government 4. United States -- History -- Sources 5. United States -- Politics and government -- Sources
ISBN 069115399X; 9780691153995

LC 2012016854

In this book, "Jill Lepore investigates American origin stories . . . to show how American democracy is bound up with the history of print. . . . Part civics primer, part cultural history, 'The Story of America' excavates the origins of everything from the paper ballot and the Constitution to the I.O.U. and the dictionary. . . . From past to present, Lepore argues, Americans have wrestled with the idea of democracy by telling stories." (Publisher's note)
Includes bibliographical references and index.

Loewen, James W.

Lies across America; what our historic sites get wrong. Simon & Schuster 2007 464p pa $16	**973**
1. Monuments 2. Historic sites
ISBN 978-0-7432-9629-8; 0-7432-9629-X
First published 1999 by New Press

"The book consists of 95 brief commentaries on specific sites from Alaska to Florida to Maine, sandwiched between essays that offer advice on how to interpret what you read or are told at historic sites." N Y Times Book Rev [review of 1999 edition]

Marcus, Greil

The **shape** of things to come; prophecy and the American voice. Farrar, Straus & Giroux 2006 320p $25 **973**

1. American national characteristics 2. Nationalism -- United States 3. United States -- Civilization

ISBN 978-0-374-10438-2; 0-374-10438-7

LC 2005-33139

Marcus "posits that the United States of America is a cultural construction, grounded in the Declaration of Independence and the Constitution. Without those bedrocks, Marcus believes, the nation would be 'little more than a collection of buildings and people who have no special reason to speak to each other, and nothing to say.' Marcus builds his own erudite vision upon John Winthrop's 1630 speech 'A Modell of Christian Charity,' Abraham Lincoln's second inaugural address in 1865, Martin Luther King Jr.'s 1963 exhortation from the steps of the Lincoln Memorial in Washington, the later novels of Philip Roth, the films of David Lynch and the music of David Thomas with his band Pere Ubu. More than most books, Marcus's latest tour de force is quite likely to divide readers into two camps: those who find it brilliant and those who find it baffling." Publ Wkly

Merry, Robert W., 1946-

Where they stand; the American presidents in the eyes of voters and historians. Robert W. Merry. Simon & Schuster 2012 xxii, 298 p.p ill. (hardcover) $28.00 **973**

1. Presidents -- United States 2. Presidents -- United States -- Rating 3. Presidents -- United States -- Election 4. Presidents -- United States -- History 5. Presidents -- Rating of -- United States 6. Presidents -- United States -- Biography 7. United States -- Politics and government 8. Political leadership -- United States -- History

ISBN 1451625405; 9781451625400; 9781451625424; 9781451625431

LC 2011039883

In this book on "the ranking of U.S. presidents by historians and political scientists . . . [Robert W.] Merry . . . looks at these academic rankings, examines their correlation with the electorate's original judgement, and shows what this correlation tells us about the presidency and how presidents succeed or fail. Discussions about the truly great, the failures, those in between, and some commentary by Merry on the five most recent presidents" are also presented. (Library Journal)

Includes bibliographical references (p. 251-281) and index

Morison, Samuel Eliot

A **concise** history of the American Republic; {by} Samuel Eliot Morison, Henry Steele Commager, William E. Leuchtenburg. 2nd ed; Oxford

Univ. Press 1983 765p il maps hardcover o.p. pa $58.95 **973**

1. United States -- History

ISBN 0-19-503180-6 pa

LC 82-3621

First published 1977

Includes bibliographical references

The **growth** of the American Republic; {by} Samuel Eliot Morison, Henry Steele Commager, and William E. Leuchtenburg. 7th ed; Oxford Univ. Press 1980 2v il maps ea $59.95 **973**

1. United States -- History

ISBN 0-19-502593-8 v1; 0-19-502594-6 v2

LC 79-52432

First published 1930 in a single volume

A history of the United States that deals with military, political, economic, social, literary and spiritual aspects of the nation's development

"A good general history, well-written." Sheehy. Guide to Ref Books. 10th edition

Morris, Edmund, 1940-

This living hand; and other essays. Edmund Morris. Random House 2012 xx, 497 p.p ill. (acid-free paper) $32 **973**

1. Authorship 2. Literature 3. American essays 4. Literature -- History and criticism 5. Music 6. Biography 7. Biography -- Authorship 8. United States -- Biography 9. Presidents -- United States

ISBN 0812993128; 9780679644668; 9780812993127

LC 2012013612

This is a collection of essays by Pulitzer Prize and National Book Award winner Edmund Morris. He "begins with a 1972 essay . . . in which he recounts his time as a schoolboy in Kenya. . . . In other pieces, Morris laments the disappearance of snow on Mount Kilimanjaro; probes the psyche of South African writer Nadine Gordimer; explains his passion for writing biographies; . . . and bemoans the loss of the physical pleasure of writing with pen and ink or typewriter." (Kirkus)

The **New** encyclopedia of American scandal; George Childs Kohn, editor. Facts on File 2001 455p il (Facts on File library of American history) $71.50; pa $24.95 **973**

1. United States -- History -- Miscellanea

ISBN 0-8160-4225-X; 0-8160-4420-1 pa

LC 00-34099

First published 1989 under the authorship of George C. Kohn with title: Encyclopedia of American scandal

This compendium includes "more than 450 people and incidents from the 1600s to the present, surveying episodes of graft, bribery, deception, and outrage by people in high places. Although the tragic, career-derailing impact of historic humiliations cannot be denied, this frank book entertains as well as informs." Choice

Includes bibliographical references

New York Public Library

The **New** York Public Library American history desk reference; 2nd ed; Hyperion 2003 576p il maps pa $21.95 **973**

1. Reference books 2. United States -- History -- Dictionaries
ISBN 0-7868-6847-3

LC 2003-56655

First published 1997 by Macmillan

"{This is a} well-designed, convenient-size volume filled with lists, charts, tables, and short articles. . . . {This} volume should be {a} useful ready-reference compilation for public and academic libraries." Booklist {review of 1997 edition}

Includes bibliographical references

Olson, James Stuart

Encyclopedia of the industrial revolution in America; {by} James S. Olson; technical editor: Robert L. Shadle. Greenwood Press 2002 xxv, 313p il $69.95 **973**

1. Reference books 2. Industrial revolution -- Encyclopedias
ISBN 0-313-30830-6

LC 00-52129

This encyclopedia offers "coverage of the economic, political, and social developments of the Industrial Revolution in the United States from 1750 to 1920. . . . Highlights of the work include . . . entries on developments in water and rail transportation, agriculture, manufacturing, mass production, the labor movement, big government, and the key inventions that changed the American economy." Publisher's note

"A well-organized and comprehensive ready reference." Voice Youth Advocates

Includes bibliographical references

The **Oxford** companion to United States history; editor in chief, Paul S. Boyer; editors, Melvyn Dubofsky {et al.} Oxford Univ. Press 2001 xliv, 940p il maps $75 **973**

1. Reference books 2. United States -- History -- Dictionaries
ISBN 0-19-508209-5

LC 00-55801

First published 1966 under the authorship of Thomas A. Johnson with title: The Oxford companion to American history

This reference work contains 1,400 alphabetically arranged signed entries. See and see also references are provided. Coverage starts with the colonial period and examines notable men and women and major events in U.S. history

Includes bibliographical references

Prothero, Stephen

The **American** Bible; how our words unite, divide, and define a nation. Stephen Prothero. 1st ed. HarperOne 2012 vii, 533 p.p (hardback) $29.99 **973**

1. American national characteristics 2. United States -- Politics and government 3. American literature -- History and criticism 4. Group identity in literature 5. United States -- Civilization 6. National characteristics, American 7. Language and culture -- United States 8. Nationalism and literature -- United States 9. National characteristics, American, in literature 10. Literature and society -- United States -- History 11. Rhetoric -- Political aspects -- United States -- History 12. Speeches, addresses, etc., American -- History and criticism
ISBN 0062123432; 9780062123435

LC 2012005054

In this book, Stephen Prothero has "assembl[ed] a version of the American canon: 'Not the books I revere but those that Americans themselves have made sacred.' His scripture comprises a set of essays, speeches and fiction that, in his judgment, have largely influenced the United States' self-image. By recovering their teachings, he believes, we can heal the divisiveness and self-interest that ail our politics." (Washington Post)

Includes bibliographical references (p. 491-510) and index.

Remini, Robert Vincent

Short history of the United States; [by] Robert V. Remini. HarperCollins Publishers 2008 373p il map $27.95 **973**

1. United States -- History
ISBN 978-0-06-083144-8; 0-06-083144-8

LC 2007-34811

The author "deftly wraps his expertise and deep knowledge of his subject in stripped-down prose that provides everything a casual (or bewildered) reader needs to know about the United States from the first English colonists until the beginning of 2008." Publ Wkly

Includes bibliographical references

Reynolds, David, 1952-

America, empire of liberty; a new history of the United States. Basic Books 2009 563p map **973**

1. United States -- History
ISBN 9780465015009

LC 2009-17831

This is "a one-volume history of the United States, from the mound-builders of the 11th century to the challenges facing President Barack Obama. . . . Mr. Reynold's book provides an entertaining and fair-minded introduction to American history." Economist

Includes bibliographical references

Said, Edward W.

Out of place; a memoir. Knopf 1999 295p il $26.95; pa $14 **973**

1. Authors 2. Essayists 3. Social critics 4. Literary critics 5. Writers on politics
ISBN 0-394-58739-1; 0-679-73067-2 pa

LC 99-31106

In this memoir Said offers an "account of his intellectual and moral development. At the heart of Said's story is the sense of dislocation experienced by a boy whose father was a Palestinian-born American citizen, whose mother was Lebanese, and who was raised in Egypt under the colonial rule of the British. This is the moving tale of a man who is always an outsider." Publ Wkly

Schlesinger, Arthur M. (Arthur Meier), 1917-2007

The **cycles** of American history; {by} Arthur M. Schlesinger, Jr. Houghton Mifflin 1986 498p hardcover o.p. pa $16   **973**
1. United States -- History 2. United States -- Foreign relations 3. United States -- Politics and government
ISBN 0-395-95793-1 pa

LC 86-7706

"For this volume, Schlesinger has revised and updated papers, reviews, and essays that have appeared in various forms over the past quarter-century. . . . Each of the 14 essays that make up the book offers a fresh, demanding, and lively argument about important issues in American intellectual, political, or diplomatic history." Choice
Includes bibliographical references

The **disuniting** of America; reflections on a multicultural society. rev & enl ed; Norton 1998 208p $21.95; pa $12.95   **973**
1. Multiculturalism 2. Multicultural education 3. United States -- Civilization 4. United States -- Historiography
ISBN 0-393-04580-3; 0-393-31854-0 pa

LC 97-25124

First published 1992

The author argues against radical multiculturalism, bilingual education, and the influence of ethnic, political, and religious pressure groups on the teaching of history. Includes an epilogue that assesses the impact of radical multiculturalism and radical monoculturalism on the Bill of Rights and concludes with an annotated reading list of titles essential for understanding the American experience
Includes bibliographical references

Shenkman, Richard

Legends, lies & cherished myths of American history. HarperPerennial 1989 213p il pa $13 **973**
1. Legends -- United States 2. United States -- History
ISBN 978-0-06-097261-5; 0-06-097261-0
First published 1988 by Morrow
The author "debunks a host of popular myths associated with U.S. history. From the Founding Fathers to the Reagan presidency, heretofore undisputed facts are exposed as fiction. Misquotes, misinterpretations, and downright fabrications are all duly recorded in an amusing and illuminating fashion. An irresistible browsing item." Booklist
Includes bibliographical references

Stark, Peter

The **last** empty places; a past and present journey through the blank spots on the American map. Ballantine Books 2010 325p il map $26   **973**
1. Wilderness areas 2. United States -- Local history 3. United States -- Description and travel
ISBN 978-0-345-49537-2; 0-345-49537-3

LC 2010-09942

Stark writes "about exploring Maine's northern woods and the St. John River, the forests and glens of western Pennsylvania, the vast empty deserts of southeast Oregon and the High Desert of New Mexico, deep within the Gila Wilderness. Often he takes his family with him, and we get to read about the trials and tribulations of tents, backpacks, river crossings, switchbacks, towering cliffs and shadowy canyons. At the same time he intersperses his journeys with historical tales and horrors. . . . Stark keeps his writing sharp and clear and, wonderfully, does not slip into celebration of some mystical state of oneness with nature." Providence J
Includes bibliographical references

State by state; a panoramic portrait of America. edited by Matt Weiland & Sean Wilsey. Ecco 2008 xxxi, 572p il map $29.95   **973**
1. United States
ISBN 978-0-06-147090-5; 0-06-147090-2

LC 2008-300642

"Taking as their inspiration the state guides published by the Federal Writers' Project during and shortly after the Great Depression, Weiland and Wilsey assembled 50 of America's finest writers and asked them to contribute essays on the same general theme: why my state is special—or not. The result is a funny, moving, rousing collection, greater than the sum of its excellent parts, a convention of literary super-delegates, each one boisterously nominating his or her piece of the Republic." N Y Times Book Rev

Steinbeck, John

Travels with Charley; in search of America. Viking 1962 246p hardcover o.p. pa $14   **973**
1. United States -- Civilization 2. United States -- Description and travel
ISBN 0-670-72508-0; 0-14-200070-1 pa
The Nobel laureate recounts his impressions and observations of America gathered during a trip through forty states in the company of his French poodle Charley

Steltenkamp, Michael F.

Black Elk, holy man of the Oglala. University of Okla. Press 1993 xxiii, 211p il maps hardcover o.p. pa $17.95   **973**
1. Shamans 2. Oglala Indians 3. Indian leaders
ISBN 0-8061-2988-3 pa

LC 93-22089

This "is the story of Black Elk's later years, when the holy man converted to Roman Catholicism and worked actively as a catechist, converting the Lakota to his new religion." Antioch Rev
Includes bibliographical references

Virga, Vincent

Eyes of the nation; a visual history of the United States. by Vincent Virga and curators of the Library of Congress; historical commentary by Alan Brinkley. Knopf 1997 399p il $75   **973**
1. United States -- History -- Pictorial works
ISBN 0-679-44330-4

LC 97-36603

This visual history "showcases more than 500 illustrations, manuscripts, engravings, prints, movie stills and other artifacts stretching back to the 15th century. The accompanying text by the historian Alan Brinkley rolls through the high and low points of the nation's history, but it is the captions that sparkle the brightest, adding context while offering surprising information." N Y Times Book Rev

Walker, Jesse

The **United** States of paranoia; a conspiracy theory. Jesse Walker. Harper 2013 448 p. $25.99 **973**

1. Paranoia 2. Conspiracies 3. United States -- Civilization 4. National characteristics, American 5. Political culture -- United States 6. Conspiracy theories -- United States 7. United States -- Politics and government 8. Paranoia -- Social aspects -- United States 9. Paranoia -- Political aspects -- United States
ISBN 0062135554; 9780062135551

LC 2013011426

In this book, Jesse Walker offers an analysis of conspiracy theories in the U.S., dividing them into five types: "those dealing with the perceived enemy within (e.g., militia and hate groups); the enemy outside (e.g., al-Qaeda); the enemy above (e.g., the Illuminati); and the enemy below (e.g., the Occupy movement). The fifth category relates to theories of a so-called benevolent conspiracy, which assume that someone or something is working for the betterment of humanity." (Publishers Weekly)

Wetterau, Bruce

Congressional Quarterly's desk reference on the Presidency. CQ Press 2000 311p il (Desk reference series) $49.95   **973**

1. Presidents -- United States
ISBN 1-56802-589-0

LC 00-63024

Over 500 questions and answers on the organization, procedures, and history of the office and on the presidents and their wives. Topics covered include scandals, elections, the White House, and the executive branch
Includes bibliographical references

Wills, Garry

A **necessary** evil; a history of American distrust of government. Simon & Schuster 1999 365p hardcover o.p. pa $15   **973**

1. Resistance to government 2. United States -- Politics and government
ISBN 0-684-87026-6 pa

LC 99-35879

This "analysis of the distorted mythology that has grown up around government in the U.S. takes on hot-button issues from the Second Amendment and term limits to the idea that the Founders sought to create an inefficient government. Provocative and enlightening." Booklist
Includes bibliographical references

Winchester, Simon

The **Men** Who United the States; America's Explorers, Inventors, Eccentrics and Mavericks, and the Creation of One Nation, Indivisible. HarperCollins 2013 480 p. $29.99   **973**

1. Exploration 2. United States -- History 3. Infrastructure (Economics)
ISBN 0062079603; 9780062079602

This book by Simon Winchester "profiles a huge cast of eclectic characters who helped transform America from a cluster of colonies to a unified nation through the taming of the wilderness and the expansion of the country's infrastructure. The . . . narrative is . . . organized into five sections-

-each corresponds to one of the classical elements (wood, earth, water, fire, metal) and focuses on a different phase of American exploration or development." (Publishers Weekly)

Zimmermann, Warren

First great triumph; how five Americans made their country a world power. Farrar, Straus & Giroux 2002 562p il $30; pa $15   **973**

1. Poets 2. Lawyers 3. Admirals 4. Diplomats 5. Governors 6. Statesmen 7. Historians 8. Presidents 9. Vice-presidents 10. Spanish-American War, 1898 11. Senators 12. Biographers 13. Secretaries of war 14. Secretaries of state 15. Nobel laureates for peace 16. United States -- History -- 1898-1919
ISBN 0-374-17939-5; 0-374-52893-4 pa

LC 2002-25015

The author credits five men "for the vision, determination and political skill that first gave the United States its global ambition. His book is a history of the American rise to power and a collective biography of [his] five heroes: Theodore Roosevelt, the assistant secretary of the Navy and later president; Alfred T. Mahan, the naval strategist; Senator Henry Cabot Lodge of Massachusetts; Secretary of State John Hay; and the first American colonial administrator, Elihu Root." N Y Times (Late N Y Ed)
Includes bibliographical references

973.03   United States--Encyclopedias

Encyclopedia of women and American politics; edited by Lynne E. Ford. Facts On File 2008 xx, 636 p.p (hc : alk. paper) $85   **973.03**

1. Feminism -- History 2. Women political activists 3. Women -- Political activity 4. Women in politics -- United States -- Encyclopedias 5. Women legislators -- United States -- Encyclopedias 6. United States -- Politics and government -- Encyclopedias
ISBN 0816054916; 9780816054916

LC 2007004331

Author Lynne E. Ford discusses "the role of women throughout America's political history. . . . [The book] contains more than 500 entries covering the people, events, and terms involved in the history of women and politics. . . . [The] encyclopedia also provides a biography for every woman who has served in the U.S. House of Representatives, the Senate, and the Supreme Court. Broad topics, such as sexual harassment, are cross-referenced with key events and people who are relevant to the topic." (Publisher's note)
Includes bibliographical references and index.

973.04   Native peoples--United States

Alvarez, Alex

Native America and the question of genocide; Alex Alvarez. Rowman & Littlefield Publishers, Inc. 2014 222 p. (Studies in genocide: religion, history, and human rights) (cloth : alk. paper) $40   **973.04**

1. Genocide 2. Native Americans -- United States 3. United States -- Social policy 4. United States -- Race relations 5. Genocide -- United States -- History 6.

United States -- Politics and government 7. Indians of North America -- Violence against 8. Indians of North America -- Social conditions 9. Indians, Treatment of -- North America -- History
ISBN 1442225815; 9781442225817; 9781442225824
LC 2013048466
"Did Native Americans suffer genocide? This controversial question lies at the heart of 'Native America and the Question of Genocide.' After reviewing the various meanings of the word genocide, author Alex Alvarez examines a range of well-known examples . . . to determine where genocide occurred and where it did not. The book explores the destructive beliefs of the European settlers, and then looks at topics including disease, war, and education through the lens of genocide." (Publisher's note)

"In his sensitive treatment of this difficult issue, Alvarez strikes a balance between scholarly pragmatism and a humanist's empathy for the victims of this immense tragedy." Booklist
Includes bibliographical references and index

973.09   Presidents--United States

Chronology of the U.S. presidency; Mathew Manweller, editor. ABC-CLIO 2012 4 v. xxii, 1556 p.p (hbk. : acid-free paper) $399.00 **973.09**
1. Cabinet officers 2. United States -- History 3. Presidents -- United States 4. Presidents -- United States -- Biography 5. Presidents -- United States -- History -- Chronology 6. United States -- Politics and government -- Chronology
ISBN 1598846450; 9781598846454; 9781598846461
LC 2011053314
This book looks at the 44 U.S. presidents. "Entries begin with a portrait of the president and contain a biographical sketch of both the man himself and the First Family, information on each member of the cabinet, a chronology of significant term events, and primary-source materials." (Library Journal)
Includes bibliographical references and index.

Freedman, Eric
Presidents and Black America; a documentary history. Stephen A. Jones, Eric Freedman. CQ Press 2011 xxxiv, 546 p.p (cloth : alk. paper) $145 **973.09**
1. African Americans 2. Presidents -- Attitudes 3. Presidents -- United States 4. African Americans -- Political activity 5. United States -- Race relations -- History 6. African Americans -- Attitudes -- History -- Sources 7. Presidents -- United States -- Racial attitudes -- Sources 8. Presidents -- Relations with African Americans -- History -- Sources
ISBN 1608710084; 9781608710089
LC 2011032618
This reference book "features a mixture of primary source material with introductory essays outlining each president's views on blacks in America. . . . . The work is arranged in chronological order, with each chapter covering a president. . . . Chapters open with an introductory essay. . . . One can clearly see how the successive Republican presidencies of Harding, Coolidge, and Hoover turned American

blacks . . . to the Democratic party of Franklin Roosevelt." (Booklist)
Includes bibliographical references and index.

Nowlan, Robert A.
The **American** presidents, Washington to Tyler; what they did, what they said, what was said about them, with full source notes. Robert A. Nowlan. McFarland & Co. 2012 x, 450 p.p (softcover : alk. paper) $55 **973.09**
1. Presidents -- United States 2. Presidents -- United States -- Biography 3. United States -- Politics and government -- 1789-1815 4. United States -- Politics and government -- 1815-1861
ISBN 0786463368; 9780786463367
LC 2011039072
This book is an "account of each of the first 10 men who held the highest office in the United States. Within each chapter is a thorough account of the man's term, including major events in foreign affairs, primary-source documents by and about him, and, in some cases, how he was viewed by his contemporaries and other presidents." (School Library Journal)

"This book—the first volume in what the author states will be a multivolume set on all the American presidents—covers the life of the first 10 presidents...ch chapter is devoted to a president, covering his time in office, domestic policy and foreign policy, family background, family life, religious beliefs, his life before and after the presidency, and a "Miscellanea" section featuring trivia and interesting facts.Black-and-white illustrations are included. The chapter notes and the reference section at the end of the book provide exhaustive and comprehensive sources that the reader can use to find out more about each president. This book is suitable for advanced high-school students, academic libraries, and history buffs." (Booklist)
Includes bibliographical references (p. 388-439) and index

★ The **presidency** A to Z; Gerhard Peters, editor ; John T. Woolley, editor. 5th ed. CQ Press 2012 xix, 715 p.p ill. (hardcover) $125 **973.09**
1. Presidents -- United States -- Biography 2. Presidents -- United States -- Encyclopedias
ISBN 1608719081; 9781608719082
LC 2012023290
This book, by Gerhard Peters, presents a dictionary of the U.S. presidency. The book is a "tool for understanding the presidency, both historically and today and for appraising how it and the executive branch have responded to the challenges facing the nation. It provides readers with quick information and in-depth background on the presidency through a comprehensive encyclopedia of over 300 easy-to-read entries." (Publisher's note)

"At over 700 pages and also available online, this core title. . . provid[es] a comprehensive encyclopedic treatment of the U.S. presidency. . . . A recommended purchase for all libraries and a required one for those with earlier editions, which it supplants." LJ
Includes bibliographical references (p. 684-690) and index.

973.2   United States--Colonial period, 1607-1775

Anderson, Fred

The **crucible** of war; the Seven Years' War and
the fate of empire in British North America, 1754-
1766. with illustrations from the William L. Clem-
ents Library. Knopf 2000 862p il hardcover o.p. pa
$21   **973.2**
   1. Seven Years' War, 1756-1763 2. United States --
History -- 1600-1775, Colonial period
   ISBN 0-375-70636-4 pa

                            LC 99-18512

The author "demonstrates that the conflict was more
than just a peripheral squabble that anticipated the American
Revolution. Not only did the war decisively alter relations
among the French, the English and the Native American
allies of the two powers, who for decades had played the
English and French off one another to their own advantage,
but just as critical, argues Anderson, the war also changed
the character of British imperialism, with the mother country
trying to reshape the terms of empire and the colonists' place
in it." Publ Wkly

The **dominion** of war; empire and liberty in
North America, 1500-2000. [by] Fred Anderson and
Andrew Cayton. Viking 2005 520p il maps $27.95;
pa $16   **973.2**
   1. United States -- Military history 2. United States
-- Territorial expansion
   ISBN 0-670-03370-7; 0-14-303651-3 pa

The authors provide an "account of the U.S. rise to
global preeminence over five centuries. Central to their thesis is the assertion that military conflict has been essential
in determining the cultural and political evolution of North
America. . . . Anderson and Cayton have provided a well-
written and important reinterpretation of our past." Booklist
   Includes bibliographical references

Bailyn, Bernard

★ The **barbarous** years; the peopling of British
North America : the conflict of civilizations, 1600-
1675. Bernard Bailyn. Alfred A. Knopf 2012 614 p.
$35   **973.2**
   1. Colonization 2. Immigration and emigration 3.
Great Britain -- Colonies -- America 4. United States
-- History -- 1600-1775, Colonial period 5. Canada
-- History -- To 1763 (New France) 6. North America
-- Civilization -- 17th century 7. Immigrants -- North
America -- History -- 17th century 8. United States
-- History -- Colonial period, ca. 1600-1775 9. Great
Britain -- Colonies -- America -- History -- 17th century
   ISBN 0394515706; 9780394515700

                      LC 2012034223

This book, by Bernard Bailyn, presents an account of the
17th century colonial migrations to North America. "They
moved . . . from different social backgrounds and cultures
. . . and circumstances. . . . They came hoping to re-create if not to improve these diverse lifeways in a remote .
. . environment. But their stories are mostly of confusion,
failure, violence, and the loss of civility as they sought to

normalize abnormal situations and recapture lost worlds."
(Publisher's note)
   Includes bibliographical references and index.

The **peopling** of British North America; an introduction. Knopf 1986 177p hardcover o.p. pa
$12   **973.2**
   1. United States -- History -- 1600-1775, Colonial period
   ISBN 0-394-75779-3 pa

                          LC 85-82144

In this introductory volume of a projected multivolume
work, the author "gives first airing to his overall argument
on settling patterns in history. Though designed to introduce
the subsequent volumes, this superbly articulate study is understandable on its own." Booklist
   Includes bibliographical references

Boorstin, Daniel J.

The **Americans** : The colonial experience. Random House 1958 434p hardcover o.p. pa $15 **973.2**
   1. Puritans 2. Americanisms 3. Society of Friends 4.
American national characteristics 5. Georgia -- History
6. Law -- United States 7. United States -- Civilization
8. United States -- Intellectual life 9. Colleges and
universities -- United States 10. United States -- History
-- 1600-1775, Colonial period
   ISBN 0-394-70513-0 pa

The first volume of the author's trilogy entitled:
The Americans
   "This study of colonial America attempts to show that it
was not merely an offshoot of the mother country, but a new
civilization. . . . The author centers his highly informative
work on colonial education, the special qualities of American speech, and the growth of a distinct culture." Booklist
   Includes bibliographical references

Demos, John

The **unredeemed** captive; a family story from
early America. Knopf 1994 315p maps hardcover
o.p. pa $14   **973.2**
   1. Clergy 2. Mohawk Indians 3. Massachusetts --
History -- 1600-1775, Colonial period
   ISBN 0-679-75961-1 pa

                         LC 93-23907

John Williams, "a Puritan minister, and his family were
captured in 1704 in their Massachusetts home by a group
of Frenchmen and Native Americans, and forced to march
to Canada. Although he and four of his children were later
released, his wife died on the march and his daughter, Eunice, became a convert to Catholicism and married a Native
American. Despite the ongoing attempts of her father and
brother to persuade Eunice to return to Massachusetts, she
would agree only to brief visits and lived in a Native American settlement until her death at the age of 95." Publ Wkly
   This "is a lively introduction to an authentically multicultural colonial North America." N Y Times Book Rev

Fowler, William M.

Empires at war; the French & Indian War and the
struggle for North America, 1754-1763. [by] William

M. Fowler, Jr. Walker & Company 2005 xxv, 332p il maps $27; pa $15 **973.2**

1. United States -- History -- 1755-1763, French and Indian War

ISBN 0-8027-1411-0; 0-8027-7737-6 pa

LC 2004-43064

In this history of the French and Indian War, the author "glances occasionally at the European and Caribbean theaters of this 'first world war,' but concentrates on the North American operations that determined Britain's victory over France in the struggle for imperial supremacy. . . . The result is a judicious, well-paced and engaging introduction to a turning point in American and world history." Publ Wkly

Includes bibliographical references

Goetzmann, William H.

Beyond the Revolution; a history of American thought from Paine to pragmatism. Basic Books 2009 456p $35 **973.2**

1. American philosophy 2. United States -- Intellectual life

ISBN 978-0-465-00495-9; 0-465-00495-4

LC 2008-25590

"It's conventional to spin American history as a story of unfolding freedom, a quest to perfect our founding ideals, but Beyond the Revolution introduces something of a countervailing narrative. The country was as free and limitless as it would ever want to be right after the founding, Mr. Goetzmann contends, and the task since then has been to find a workable frame to harness that freedom. . . . [This book argues that] the entire frenzy of American enterprise from the founding to the present can be understood as an effort to invent, peddle, connive or discern, a model for how to choose and what to value in country where anything is possible." N Y Observer

Includes bibliographical references (p. 403-436)

Hawke, David Freeman

Everyday life in early America. Harper & Row 1988 195p il (Everyday life in America) hardcover o.p. pa $13 **973.2**

1. United States -- Social life and customs 2. United States -- History -- 1600-1775, Colonial period

ISBN 0-06-091251-0 pa

LC 87-17667

The author "provides enlightening and colorful descriptions of early Colonial Americans and debunks many widely held assumptions about 17th century settlers." Publ Wkly

Includes bibliographical references

Lepore, Jill

The **name** of war; King Philip's War and the origins of American identity. Knopf 1998 xxviii, 337p il maps hardcover o.p. pa $15 **973.2**

1. King Philip's War, 1675-1676 2. Native Americans -- Wars 3. Great Britain -- Colonies -- America

ISBN 0-375-70262-8 pa

LC 97-2820

"This is a powerful book that doesn't shy away from depicting the sheer horror of what must be termed a race war." Booklist

Includes bibliographical references

Philbrick, Nathaniel

★ **Mayflower**; a story of courage, community, and war. Viking 2006 461p il $29.95; pa $16 **973.2**

1. Pilgrims (New England colonists) 2. Massachusetts -- History -- 1600-1775, Colonial period

ISBN 0-670-03760-5; 978-0-670-03760-5; 978-0-14-311197-9 pa; 0-14-311197-3 pa

LC 2005-58470

The author "has written a judicious, fascinating work of revisionist history. 'Mayflower' is a surprise-filled account of what are supposed to be some of the best-known events in this country's past but are instead an occasion for collective amnesia." N Y Times (Late N Y Ed)

Includes bibliographical references

Remini, Robert Vincent

The **Battle** of New Orleans; {by} Robert V. Remini. Viking 1999 226p il maps hardcover o.p. pa $14 **973.2**

1. New Orleans (La.), Battle of, 1815

ISBN 0-14-100179-8 pa

LC 99-19837

This "book establishes the War of 1812 historically as our second War of Independence, and describes its climactic battle in the maze of cypress swamps and bayous along the winding Mississippi. Remini, . . . unforgettably portrays individuals on both sides, and provides good maps to help us follow the action." New Yorker

Includes bibliographical references

Schultz, Eric B.

King Philip's War; the history and legacy of America's forgotten conflict. {by} Eric B. Schultz, Michael J. Tougias. Countryman Press 1999 416p il maps hardcover o.p. pa $18.95 **973.2**

1. King Philip's War, 1675-1676 2. Native Americans -- Government relations 3. New England -- History -- 1600-1775, Colonial period

ISBN 0-88150-483-1 pa

LC 99-23481

The first part of this volume provides a "chronological retelling of the war. The second part, organized geographically and the heart of the volume, takes readers through New England to various sites associated with the conflict. . . . The third part offers three contemporary narratives reflecting the significance of the war on the people of the era. Useful maps assist the reader throughout." Libr J

Includes bibliographical references

Woodward, Hobson

A **brave** vessel; the true tale of the castaways who rescued Jamestown and inspired Shakespeare's The tempest. Viking 2009 268p il map $25.95 **973.2**

1. Poets 2. Authors 3. Dramatists 4. Shipwrecks 5. Seafaring life 6. Bermuda 7. Colonists 8. Sea Venture (Ship) 9. Jamestown (Va.) -- History

ISBN 978-0-670-02096-6

LC 2008-51325

"A skillfully written history of the trials of some the earliest American colonists." Kirkus

Includes bibliographical references

973.3   United States--Periods of Revolution and Confederation, 1775-1789

Allen, Danielle

Our Declaration; A Reading of the Declaration of Independence in Defense of Equality. Danielle Allen. W W Norton & Co Inc 2014 288 p. illustrations $27.95   **973.3**

1. Freedom   2. United States. Declaration of independence 3. Equality -- United States 4. United States. Declaration of Independence -- Criticism, Textual
ISBN 087140690X; 9780871406903

              LC 2014009825

"Troubled by the fact that so few Americans actually know what it says, Danielle Allen . . . set out to explore the arguments of the Declaration, reading it with both adult night students and University of Chicago undergraduates. Keenly aware that the Declaration is riddled with contradictions--liberating some while subjugating slaves and Native Americans--Allen and her students nonetheless came to see that the Declaration makes a coherent and riveting argument about equality." (Publisher's note)

"As if conducting a friendly conversation, sentence by sentence, [Allen] takes readers through all the text's words, and she proves a patient, informed and friendly guide." Kirkus

Includes bibliographical references and index

The **American** Revolution: writings from the War of Independence. Library of Am. 2001 878p $40   **973.3**

1. United States -- History -- 1775-1783, Revolution
ISBN 1-88301-191-4

              LC 00-45373

This collection includes "over 120 pieces by more than 70 Revolution-era writers from both sides of the War of Independence. The book begins with Paul Revere's personal account of his famous ride in April 1775 and ends with a description of George Washington's resignation from the command of the Continental Army in December 1783. . . . At the book's end one can find a long section that includes a chronology, biographical sketches of the authors, and other notes on the texts." Libr J

"This work will serve as a marvelous research tool for specialists, but general readers with an interest in American history will also find fascinating gems." Booklist

Includes bibliographical references

Archer, Richard

As if an enemy's country; the British occupation of Boston and the origins of revolution. Oxford University Press 2010 284p il map (Pivotal moments in American history) $24.95   **973.3**

1. Boston (Mass.) -- History 2. United States -- History -- Revolution, 1775-1783 3. Boston (Mass.) -- History -- Colonial period, ca. 1600-1775 4. United States -- History -- 1775-1783, Revolution -- Causes
ISBN 978-0-19-538247-1; 0-19-538247-1

              LC 2009-39919

Archer "utilizes a wealth of primary sources, from diaries to depositions, to provide an edifying account of the 17-month British occupation of Boston from October 1768

to the winter of 1770. . . . The uniqueness of Archer's superbly crafted tale lies in his discussion of how the politics of nonimportation polarized the elite of Boston society on the eve of revolution. Combining engaging prose and a wealth of interesting characters, Archer has provided students and general enthusiasts alike with a concise, appealing work of first-rate scholarship." Libr J

Includes bibliographical references and index

Becker, Carl

The **Declaration** of Independence; a study in the history of political ideas. Knopf 1942 286p hardcover o.p. pa $11   **973.3**

1. Architects 2. Presidents 3. Vice-presidents 4. Essayists 5. United States -- Declaration of Independence 6. United States -- Politics and government -- 1775-1783, Revolution
ISBN 0-394-70060-0 pa

A reprint, with a new preface, of a book first published 1922 by Harcourt Brace & Co.

"A study of the Declaration, the philosophy that lay behind it, the history of its several drafts, an estimate of its literary quality." Wis Libr Bull

Includes bibliographical references

Beeman, Richard R.

Our lives, our fortunes and our sacred honor; the forging of American independence, 1774-1776. Richard R. Beeman. Basic Books, A Member of the Perseus Books Group 2013 528 p. (hardcover) $29.99   **973.3**

1. United States -- History 2. United States -- Politics and government 3. United States. Continental Congress, 1774 4. Statesmen -- United States -- Biography 5. Revolutionaries -- United States -- Biography 6. United States. Continental Congress -- History 7. United States -- History -- Revolution, 1775-1783 8. United States -- Politics and government -- To 1775 9. United States -- Politics and government -- 1775-1783 10. United States -- History -- Revolution, 1775-1783 -- Biography
ISBN 046502629X; 9780465026296; 9780465037827

              LC 2013001875

This book by Richard B. Beeman "examines the . . . period between the meeting of the Continental Congress on September 5, 1774 and the . . . decision for independence in July of 1776. Beeman brings to life a cast of characters, including the . . . passionate John Adams, Adams much-misunderstood foil John Dickinson, the fiery political activist Samuel Adams, and the relative political neophyte Thomas Jefferson, and . . . reveals their path from subjects of England to citizens of a new nation." (Publisher's note)

Includes bibliographical references and index

Blumrosen, Alfred W.

Slave nation; how slavery united the colonies & sparked the American Revolution. [by] Alfred W. Blumrosen and Ruth G. Blumrosen; introduction by Eleanor Holmes Norton. Sourcebooks 2005 336p il map $24.95   **973.3**

1. Slavery -- United States 2. African Americans -- History 3. United States -- History -- 1775-1783,

Revolution -- Causes
ISBN 1-4022-0400-0

LC 2004-27271

The authors "use the Somerset case of 1772, which freed all slaves in Britain, to illustrate how the price of freedom from English rule ensured continued bondage for slaves in the American South. The Blumrosens argue that Southerners feared that the ruling might be extended to the entire empire and therefore joined the move to win independence from Britain. . . . This well-researched book is sure to be controversial." Libr J

Includes bibliographical references

Bobrick, Benson

Angel in the whirlwind; the triumph of the American Revolution. Penguin Bks. 1998 553p map pa $18 **973.3**
1. United States -- History -- 1775-1783, Revolution
ISBN 0-14-027500-2; 978-0-14-027500-1

LC 97-11320

First published 1997 by Simon & Schuster

"Many of the stories are familiar—Paul Revere's ride, Arnold's descent into infamy—but the book's strength lies in its many lesser-known details on the battlefield and beyond. . . . Though the format demands only brief treatment of complicated issues, what emerges is a highly impressive show of exhaustive research and engaging storytelling." Publ Wkly

Includes bibliographical references

Breen, T. H.

American insurgents, American patriots; the revolution of the people. Hill and Wang 2010 337p $27 **973.3**
1. United States -- History -- 1775-1783, Revolution 2. United States -- Militia -- History -- Revolution, 1775-1783 3. United States -- History -- Revolution, 1775-1783 -- Social aspects 4. United States -- History -- Revolution, 1775-1783 -- Committees of safety
ISBN 978-0-8090-7588-1; 0-8090-7588-1

LC 2009-42496

Breen "uses correspondence, diaries, outtakes from clergy sermons and newspaper reports to build a mosaic representation of the popular mood, and the escalating willingness to take up arms. . . . [The] book shows an energetic and necessarily untidy process of invention on the part of a people, and captures well its improvisatory nature." Chicago Trib

Includes bibliographical references and index

Cohen, I. Bernard

Science and the founding fathers; science in the political thought of Jefferson, Franklin, Adams and Madison. Norton 1995 368p il hardcover o.p. pa $15.95 **973.3**
1. Authors 2. Diplomats 3. Inventors 4. Statesmen 5. Architects 6. Presidents 7. Scientists 8. Vice-presidents 9. Political science 10. Senators 11. Essayists 12. Writers on science 13. Members of Congress 14. Secretaries of state 15. Science -- United States -- History
ISBN 0-393-31510-X pa

LC 94-26731

The author "analyzes how Thomas Jefferson, Benjamin Franklin, John Adams, and James Madison incorporated their scientific beliefs and knowledge into their political lives. Cohen examines each man's scientific education and then searches for examples of how that knowledge was expressed in their published works. He looks closely at phrases from the Declaration of Independence and the Constitution and shows that they have a Newtonian basis." Libr J

Davis, William C.

Battle at Bull Run; a history of the first major campaign of the Civil War. Louisiana State University Press 1981 298p il map pa $19.95 **973.3**
1. Bull Run, 1st Battle of, 1861
ISBN 978-0-8071-0867-3; 0-8071-0867-7
First published 1977 by Doubleday

In this account of the war's first major engagement Davis' "sketches of the commanders, which will particularly delight Civil War enthusiasts, delve into the officer's backgrounds and unusual characteristics and include critical appraisals of their leadership capabilities. In addition, Davis includes fascinating human interest stories about the troops." Libr J

Includes bibliographical references

Draper, Theodore

A **struggle** for power; the American Revolution. Times Bks. 1996 544p hardcover o.p. pa $13.56 **973.3**
1. United States -- History -- 1775-1783, Revolution
ISBN 0-679-77642-7 pa

LC 95-11605

This is an "elegantly written, masterful study. . . . Drawing freely on period pamphlets, letters, petitions, travelogues and assembly minutes, [the author] vividly evokes the populist discontent, intellectual gymnastics and mob violence that led to revolution." Publ Wkly

Includes bibliographical references

Dunn, Susan

Sister revolutions; French lightning, American light. Faber & Faber 1999 258p il hardcover o.p. pa $14 **973.3**
1. France -- History -- 1789-1799, Revolution 2. United States -- History -- 1775-1783, Revolution
ISBN 0-571-19989-5 pa

LC 99-18178

"The American Revolution, according to Dunn, was more peaceful and practical, in part because its leaders were both intellectuals and men of political experience. The French Revolution, on the other hand, veered into extravagant abstractions because its leaders were intellectuals with little or no previous political experience. This book is clearly written and should appeal particularly to undergraduate students and members of the general public." Choice

Includes bibliographical references

Egerton, Douglas R.

Death or liberty; African Americans and revolutionary America. Oxford University Press 2009 342p il map $29.95 **973.3**
1. Slavery -- United States 2. African Americans --

History 3. United States -- History -- 1775-1783, Revolution

ISBN 978-0-19-530669-9; 0-19-530669-4

LC 2008-27862

The author "traverses the rise and the debatable inevitability of slavery in the United States between the end of the Seven Years' War (1763) and Jefferson's election (1800), arguing that the 'division of the Republic into free wage labor sections and proslavery regions did not have to happen that way.'" Publ Wkly

Includes bibliographical references and index

Ellis, Joseph J.

American creation; triumphs and tragedies at the founding of the republic. A. A. Knopf 2007 283p   **973.3**

1. United States -- History -- 1783-1809 2. United States -- History -- 1775-1783, Revolution 3. United States -- Politics and government -- 1783-1809 4. United States -- Politics and government -- 1775-1783, Revolution

ISBN 978-0-307-26369-8; 0-307-26369-X

LC 2007-5273

The author "selects 'certain propitious moments' from the American Revolution and early republic, dramatizes them, and analyzes their crucial ramifications for America's future. . . . A history bound for phenomenal popularity." Booklist

Includes bibliographical references

★ Revolutionary summer; the birth of American independence. by Joseph J. Ellis. 1st ed. Alfred A. Knopf 2013 xiii, 219 p., 8 unnumbered pages of platesp col. ill., map (hardcover) $26.95   **973.3**

1. Founding Fathers of the United States 2. United States -- History -- 1775-1783, Revolution 3. United States -- History -- Revolution, 1775-1783

ISBN 0307701220; 9780307701220

LC 2012026140

This book, by Pulitzer-winning historian Joseph Ellis, discusses "the summer months of 1776 . . . in the story of our country's founding. . . . The Continental Congress and the Continental Army were forced to make decisions on the run, improvising as history congealed around them. . . . Ellis . . . examines the most influential figures in this propitious moment . . . [and] weaves together the political and military experiences as two sides of a single story." (Publisher's note)

Includes bibliographical references (pages 189-208) and index.

Ferling, John E.

Setting the world ablaze; Washington, Adams, and Jefferson and the American Revolution. {by} John Ferling. Oxford Univ. Press 2000 xxiv, 392p il maps hardcover o.p. pa $19.95   **973.3**

1. Generals 2. Architects 3. Presidents 4. Vice-presidents 5. Essayists 6. United States -- History -- 1775-1783, Revolution

ISBN 0-19-515084-8 pa

LC 99-89686

In this history Ferling profiles "the three men who were, in his view, the most important leaders of the American Revolution. Thomas Jefferson was the 'pen,' John Adams the 'tongue,' and George Washington the 'sword.' Ferling's command of the material is sure-footed, though not everyone will agree with his views." Libr J

Includes bibliographical references

Fischer, David Hackett

Paul Revere's ride. Oxford Univ. Press 1994 445p il maps $37.50; pa $19.95   **973.3**

1. Concord (Mass.), Battle of, 1775 2. Lexington (Mass.), Battle of, 1775 3. Artisans 4. Metalworkers 5. Revolutionaries

ISBN 0-19-508847-6; 0-19-509831-5 pa

LC 93-25739

"Fischer's solid study of Paul Revere and his infamous ride debunks the myths surrounding the event, reconstructing the circumstances leading to the Battle of Lexington and Concord. Fischer's extensive use of primary sources affords an intimate glimpse of the participants' thoughts and feelings." Booklist

Includes bibliographical references

Washington's crossing. Oxford University Press 2004 564p il maps (Pivotal moments in American history) $35; pa $16.95   **973.3**

1. Generals 2. Presidents 3. United States -- History -- 1775-1783, Revolution -- Campaigns

ISBN 0-19-517034-2; 0-19-518159-X pa

LC 2003-19858

The author describes how "Washington, his officers, and their men turn the early military defeats of Long Island and New York City into victory at Trenton and Princeton. The opening chapter is devoted to the painting Washington Crossing the Delaware. Then the author discusses the British, Hessian, and American military units that were involved in these campaigns and gives background on their officers. This is Fischer's strong suit: he tells stories and gives details that bring history alive. . . . In the hands of such a thorough researcher and talented writer, this is powerful stuff." SLJ

Includes bibliographical references

Fleming, Thomas J.

Washington's secret war; the hidden history of Valley Forge. [by] Thomas Fleming. Smithsonian Books/Collins 2005 384p il map $27.95; pa $14.95   **973.3**

1. Generals 2. Presidents 3. United States -- Continental Army 4. United States -- History -- 1775-1783, Revolution -- Campaigns

ISBN 0-06-082962-1; 0-06-087293-4 pa

LC 2005-52157

The author "writes of the trials and tribulations of George Washington as he led the Continental Army during the infamous Valley Forge winter of 1777-78. . . . Fleming's point is that he was not simply fighting the elements and attacks by the nearby British; he was also reckoning with members of the Continental Congress and fellow army officers who deemed him inadequate." Libr J

"Fleming has provided an original and provocative reinterpretation of a critical period in the struggle for independence." Booklist

Includes bibliographical references

Foner, Eric

Tom Paine and Revolutionary America; Updated ed; Oxford University Press 2005 xxxvi, 326p $71.50; pa $34.95 **973.3**

1. Essayists 2. Pamphleteers 3. Writers on politics 4. Writers on religion 5. Political and social philosophers 6. United States -- Social conditions 7. United States -- Economic conditions -- 1775-1783, Revolution 8. United States -- Politics and government -- 1775-1783, Revolution

ISBN 0-19-517486-0; 0-19-517485-2 pa

LC 2004-54799

First published 1976

The author examines the roots of Paine's thought within the social, economic and political context of colonial America

Includes bibliographical references

Fowler, William M.

American crisis; George Washington and the dangerous two years after Yorktown, 1781-1783. Walker & Co. 2011 340p il map $28 **973.3**

1. Generals 2. Presidents 3. United States -- History -- 1775-1783, Revolution

ISBN 978-0-8027-1706-1; 0-8027-1706-3

The author "artfully records the dangerous situation in the United States during the time between Cornwallis's surrender at Yorktown in 1781 and the evacuation of British troops from New York two years later. Drawing from a wealth of letters, he describes General Washington's skill as a leader, his humble and respectful character, and his noble motives in fighting to keep the army organized and disciplined. . . . This well-documented and highly readable account will engage and enrich scholars and general readers alike." Libr J

Includes bibliographical references

Gould, Eliga H.

Among the powers of the earth; the American Revolution and the making of a new world empire. Eliga H. Gould. Harvard University Press 2012 301 p., [22] p. of platesp ill., maps (alk. paper) $45 **973.3**

1. Imperialism 2. United States -- Foreign relations 3. United States -- History -- 1775-1783, Revolution 4. United States -- Territorial expansion 5. United States -- Foreign relations -- 1775-1783 6. United States -- Foreign relations -- 1783-1815 7. United States -- International status -- History 8. United States -- History -- Revolution, 1775-1783 -- Influence

ISBN 0674046080; 9780674046085

LC 2011035333

This book by Eliga Gould was named a "Library Journal" Best Book of 2012. "In this reappraisal of the American Revolution . . . Gould argues that the nation's founding was far from a straightforward bid for liberty and independence. Even as Americans strove to be free from . . . imperialism, they sought the recognition of Europe's imperial powers -- and the authority to become colonizers in their own right and rule a New World empire." (Publisher's note)

Includes bibliographical references and index

Hibbert, Christopher

Redcoats and rebels; the American Revolution through British eyes. Norton 1990 xx, 375p il maps hardcover o.p. pa $18.95 **973.3**

1. United States -- History -- 1775-1783, Revolution

ISBN 0-393-02895-X; 0-393-32293-9 pa

LC 90-31753

"Mr. Hibbert has an eye for the telling anecdote and the graphic quotation, and his bibliography indicates that he has consulted a wealth of manuscript material as well as research published during the last 30 years that illuminates what lay behind the British defeat." N Y Times Book Rev

Hogeland, William

Declaration; the nine tumultuous weeks when America became independent, May 1-July 4, 1776. Simon & Schuster 2010 273p il $26; ebook $12.99 **973.3**

1. United States -- Continental Congress 2. United States -- Declaration of Independence 3. United States -- History -- 1775-1783, Revolution -- Causes 4. United States -- Politics and government -- 1775-1783, Revolution

ISBN 978-1-4165-8409-4; 1-4165-8409-9; 978-1-4165-8425-4 ebook

LC 2010-3239

The author "forges a compelling narrative from the dozens of intricate political imbroglios that culminated with the signing of the Declaration of Independence. By casting a light on the daily interests of colonial Americans, particularly those whose homes and businesses patterned the spaces of bustling 18th-century Philadelphia, the author animates the discontents of the soon-to-be independent citizenry. With charming detail, the narrative brings together the diverse political players working during the nine weeks prior to the signing of the Declaration. These included rural militias, landed aristocrats, city merchants and immigrants, all of whom found a voice in Philadelphia." Kirkus

Includes bibliographical references

Howard, Hugh

Houses of the founding fathers; original photography by Roger Straus III. Artisan 2007 354p il $50 **973.3**

1. Statesmen -- United States 2. Politicians -- United States 3. United States -- Local history 4. Historic buildings -- United States

ISBN 978-1-57965-275-3; 1-57965-275-1

LC 2006-48015

"A prolific and popular architecture writer specializing in Colonial and early American historic preservation, teams up with veteran architecture photographer . . . to offer a sumptuously illustrated American history primer-cum-historic house tour. . . . A pleasantly flowing text interweaves historic events, details of daily life, personal anecdotes, and architectural insights into descriptions of the homes built and occupied by the era's upper social stratum." Libr J

Includes bibliographical references

Jasanoff, Maya

Liberty's exiles; Maya Jasanoff. Alfred A. Knopf 2011 xvi, 460.p.p col. ill., maps $30   **973.3**
1. Refugees 2. American Loyalists 3. American loyalists 4. Great Britain -- Colonies 5. United States -- History -- 1775-1783, Revolution 6. United States -- History -- Revolution, 1775-1783
ISBN 978-1-4000-4168-8; 1-4000-4168-6; 978-0-307-59530-0 e-book

LC 201023514

National Book Critics Circle Award: General Nonfiction (2011)

This book offers a "global history of the [American] loyalist exodus to Canada, the Caribbean, Sierra Leone, India, and beyond. . . . [Loyalists discussed include] Elizabeth Johnston, a young mother from Georgia, who led her growing family to Britain, Jamaica, and Canada, questing for a home; black loyalists . . . and Mohawk Indian leader Joseph Brant, who tried to find autonomy for his people in Ontario." (Publisher's note)

The author "examines the effects of the American Revolution on those whose loyalty to the Crown compelled them to flee the new United States." Kirkus

Includes bibliographical references and index.

Ketchum, Richard M.

Saratoga; turning point of America's Revolutionary War. Holt & Co. 1997 545p il maps hardcover o.p. pa $18   **973.3**
1. Saratoga Campaign, 1777
ISBN 0-8050-6123-1 pa

LC 97-2773

A "narrative account of the Saratoga campaign of 1777. . . . Ketchum provides the full political context within which the fighting took place while penning dozens of colorful portraits of the principal characters. The author also succeeds in his goal of telling the story from the perspective of the participants, illustrating what the American Revolution in upstate New York meant for soldiers and civilians alike." Libr J

Includes bibliographical references

Lockhart, Paul Douglas

The **whites** of their eyes; Bunker Hill, the first American Army, and the emergence of George Washington. Harper 2011 414p il map $27.99   **973.3**
1. Generals 2. Presidents 3. Bunker Hill (Boston, Mass.), Battle of, 1775 4. United States -- Continental Army 5. United States -- Military history 6. United States -- History -- 1775-1783, Revolution
ISBN 978-0-06-195886-1; 0-06-195886-7

LC 2010-43033

"Lockhart's shrewd, well-judged interpretation corrects myths about the battle and the men who fought it while doing full justice to their achievement in creating an army—and a nation—out of chaos." Publ Wkly

Includes bibliographical references

Maier, Pauline

American scripture; making the Declaration of Independence. Knopf 1997 xxi, 304p hardcover o.p. pa $14   **973.3**
1. United States -- Declaration of Independence 2.

United States -- Politics and government -- 1775-1783, Revolution
ISBN 0-679-77908-6 pa

LC 97-2769

"In the spring of 1776, with a British invasion fleet on its way, the Second Continental Congress appointed a committee to compose a statement explaining America's decision to seek independence. Thomas Jefferson was the principal drafter of the statement, but Maier makes it clear that his task was to express the sentiments of the Congress, not his personal views, and she shows that when the congressmen edited his draft they improved it greatly (rather than 'mangling' it, as Jefferson ever after maintained). The Declaration of Independence is, she argues, a profoundly collective document, both in its origins and in our still-evolving interpretation of its self-evident truths." New Yorker

McCullough, David G.

1776; [by] David McCullough. Simon & Schuster 2005 386p il map $32   **973.3**
1. United States -- History -- 1775-1783, Revolution
ISBN 0-7432-2671-2

LC 2005-42505

The author provides "account of the year that began with the humiliating British abandonment of Boston and ended with Washington's small but symbolically important triumph at Trenton. In between, McCullough recounts the American disaster at Brooklyn and the demoralizing retreat across New Jersey." Booklist

"This is a narrative tour de force, exhibiting all the hallmarks the author is known for: fascinating subject matter, expert research and detailed, graceful prose." Publ Wkly

Includes bibliographical references

Middlekauff, Robert

★ The **glorious** cause; the American Revolution, 1763-1789. Rev. and expanded ed.; Oxford University Press 2004 736p il map (Oxford history of the United States) $37.50   **973.3**
1. United States -- History -- 1775-1783, Revolution
ISBN 0-19-516247-1

LC 2004-16295

First published 1982

"Beginning with the French and Indian War and continuing to the election of George Washington as first president, Robert Middlekauff offers a . . . history of the conflict between England and America." Publisher's note

"This is narrative history at its best, written in a conversational and engaging style." Libr J

Includes bibliographical references

Morgan, Edmund Sears

The **birth** of the Republic, 1763-89; 3rd ed; University of Chicago Press 1992 206p (Chicago history of American civilization) hardcover o.p. pa $13   **973.3**
1. United States -- History -- 1783-1809 2. United States -- History -- 1775-1783, Revolution
ISBN 0-226-53756-0; 0-226-53757-9 pa

LC 92-8871

First published 1956

A brief study of the American revolutionary period from 1763 to 1789.

Includes bibliographical references

Nelson, James L.

With fire & sword; the battle of Bunker Hill and the beginning of the American Revolution. Thomas Dunne Books 2011 364p il map $27.99; ebook $14.99 **973.3**

1. Bunker Hill (Boston, Mass.), Battle of, 1775 2. United States -- History -- 1775-1783, Revolution -- Causes

ISBN 978-0-312-57644-8; 978-1-4299-6807-2 ebook
LC 2010-40653

"This rousing history rescues Bunker Hill from its folkloric shroud and presents it as one of the revolution's more significant and dramatic battles. . . . Nelson's gripping portrait of the battle caps a lively chronicle of the early days of the rebellion in Massachusetts and of the revolutionaries' scramble to establish a government and organize an army as they edged uneasily toward independence." Publ Wkly

Includes bibliographical references

Paul, Joel R.

Unlikely allies; how a merchant, a playwright, and a spy saved the American Revolution. [by] Joel Richard Paul. Riverhead Books 2009 405p il $25.95 **973.3**

1. Spies 2. Authors 3. Diplomats 4. Dramatists 5. Transvestites 6. Saratoga Campaign, 1777 7. Secret service -- United States 8. United States -- History -- 1775-1783, Revolution

ISBN 978-1-59448-883-2; 1-59448-883-5
LC 2009-34986

The author "examines three critical but forgotten characters of the American Revolution. The merchant is American Silas Deane, a Connecticut man sent to France by Congress to broker an alliance and arms treaty for the Continental Army. The playwright is a Frenchman named Pierre-Augustin Caron de Beaumarchais, author of The Barber of Seville, who saw the Revolution as an opportunity for profit. The spy is the colorful Chevalier d'Eon, who worked for Louis XV, and threatened to provoke war with England after Louis XVI came to power, using old letters that outlined a plan to invade London." Publ Wkly

"A rip-roaring account of the American Revolution, told from a fresh, and undeniably offbeat, perspective." Booklist

Includes bibliographical references (p. 384-396)

Philbrick, Nathaniel

Bunker Hill; A City, a Siege, a Revolution. Nathaniel Philbrick. Viking Adult 2013 400 p. (hardcover) $32.95 **973.3**

1. Boston (Mass.) -- History 2. Bunker Hill (Boston, Mass.), Battle of, 1775 3. United States -- History -- 1775-1783, Revolution

ISBN 0670025445; 9780670025442
LC 2013001534

This book, by Nathaniel Philbrick, profiles the history of the Battle of Bunker Hill. "After the Boston Tea Party, British and American soldiers and Massachusetts residents have warily maneuvered around each other until April 19, [1775]

when violence finally erupts. . . . In June, . . . skirmishes give way to outright war in the Battle of Bunker Hill. It would be the bloodiest battle of the Revolution to come, and the point of no return for the rebellious colonists." (Publisher's note)

Includes bibliographical references and index

Phillips, Kevin, 1940-

1775; a good year for revolution. Kevin Phillips. Viking 2012 656 p. $36 **973.3**

1. Great Britain -- History 2. United States -- History -- 1775-1783, Revolution 3. United States -- Foreign relations -- Great Britain 4. United States. Continental Congress 5. Concord (Mass.), Battle of, 1775 6. Fort Ticonderoga (N.Y.) -- Capture, 1775 7. Lexington (Mass.), Battle of, 1775 8. Boston (Mass.) -- History 9. United States -- History -- Revolution, 1775-1783 10. United States -- Politics and government -- 1775-1783

ISBN 0670025127; 9780670025121
LC 2012001786

Author Kevin Phillips looks at "the myth that 1776 was the watershed year of the American Revolution. He suggests that the great events and confrontations of 1775--Congress's belligerent economic ultimatums to Britain . . . and the new provincial congresses and hundreds of local committees that quickly reconstituted local authority in Patriot hands--achieved a sweeping Patriot control of territory and local government that Britain was never able to overcome." (Publisher's note)

Includes bibliographical references and index.

Rakove, Jack

Revolutionaries; a new history of the invention of America. [by] Jack Rakove. Houghton Mifflin Harcourt 2010 487p $30 **973.3**

1. Statesmen -- United States 2. United States -- Intellectual life 3. United States -- History -- 1775-1783, Revolution 4. United States -- History -- Revolution, 1775-1783 5. United States -- Intellectual life -- 18th century 6. United States -- Politics and government -- 1775-1783 7. Revolutionaries -- United States -- History -- 18th century 8. United States -- Politics and government -- 1775-1783, Revolution

ISBN 978-0-618-26746-0
LC 2009-47557

The author "reflects on how a group of lawyers and planters came to wage the American Revolution. Instead of focusing on the battlefield, the author examines what might be called a revolution of the mind—that is, how the early Founding Fathers' ideas developed and took hold. . . . An ambitious, intelligent exploration into the intellectual underpinnings of the Revolution." Kirkus

Includes bibliographical references

Raphael, Ray

★ A people's history of the American Revolution; how common people shaped the fight for independence. 1st Perennial ed; Perennial 2002 506p pa $13.95 **973.3**

1. United States -- History -- 1775-1783, Revolution

ISBN 0-06-000440-1
LC 2002-16992

First published 2001 by New Press

This volume "collects the experiences of ordinary people during the American Revolution and sutures them into a story. And that story is that the rebellion and war inescapably influenced everyone—farmers, townspeople, women, Indians, free blacks and enslaved blacks, plutocrats and proletarians." Booklist

"Moving from broad overviews to stories of small groups or individuals, Raphael's study is impressive in both its sweep and its attention to the particular." Publ Wkly

Includes bibliographical references

Thomas, Evan

★ **John** Paul Jones; sailor, hero, father of the American Navy. Simon & Schuster 2003 383p il hardcover o.p. pa $16　　**973.3**

1. Naval officers 2. United States -- Naval history
ISBN 0-7432-0583-9; 978-0-7432-5804-3; 0-7432-5804-5 pa

LC 2003-42411

"The complex portrait is rendered with nautical precision—the author knows his topsail from his topgallant—and a lively eye for such details as the Enlightenment virtues espoused by Freemasonry or the proper way to kiss a French lady in the eighteenth century." Publ Wkly

Includes bibliographical references

Tuchman, Barbara Wertheim

The **first** salute; [by] Barbara W. Tuchman. Knopf 1988 347p il maps hardcover o.p. pa $16.95　　**973.3**

1. United States -- History -- 1775-1783, Revolution
ISBN 0-394-55333-0; 0-345-33667-4 pa

LC 88-45216

"The book is a tightly woven narrative, ingeniously structured. It is not a blow-by-blow account of the conflict; familiarity with issues and events is assumed. Instead, Tuchman takes a specific incident and through it elucidates the course and outcome of the war." Christ Sci Monit

Includes bibliographical references

Unger, Harlow Giles

American tempest; how the Boston Tea Party sparked a revolution. [by] Harlow Giles Unger. Da Capo Press 2011 288p il map $26　　**973.3**

1. Boston Tea Party, 1773 2. United States -- History -- 1775-1783, Revolution -- Causes
ISBN 978-0-306-81962-9; 0-306-819627

LC 2010-47734

"As Unger makes clear, the true impact of the Boston Tea Party came from Britain's ill-advised overreaction to the symbolic act of vandalism. It was exactly the response [Sam] Adams had dreamed of, with an enraged British government closing the port of Boston, sending more troops, imposing martial law, and requiring permits for any large Boston meetings. These 'Coercive Acts,' along with Adams's constant drumbeat of anti-British propaganda, helped unify the colonies around the idea of independence. Unger ends the book with British soldiers marching out to Lexington and Concord hoping to arrest Adams and Hancock (who, tipped off by Paul Revere, had fled). The rest, as they

say, is history, and Unger has brought it to life brilliantly." Boston Globe

Includes bibliographical references

Weintraub, Stanley

Iron tears; America's battle for freedom, Britain's quagmire, 1775-1783. Free Press 2005 375p il maps $28　　**973.3**

1. United States -- History -- 1775-1783, Revolution
ISBN 0-7432-2687-9

LC 2004-56363

The author "examines the possibility that the British lost the war because of protest and lack of support at home. . . . The British failure to win a war against ill-trained but determined guerrilla forces in often unpredictable circumstances and weather appears now as an eerie harbinger of modern conflicts such as the Vietnam War. Weintraub's fast-paced narrative and impeccable historical research provide a stimulating challenge to conventional histories of the Revolutionary War that focus exclusively on the heroism of American forces." Publ Wkly

Includes bibliographical references

Wood, Gordon S.

The **radicalism** of the American Revolution. Knopf 1992 447p hardcover o.p. pa $16　　**973.3**

1. United States -- Social life and customs 2. United States -- History -- 1775-1783, Revolution 3. United States -- Politics and government -- 1775-1783, Revolution
ISBN 0-679-73688-3 pa

LC 91-19719

"Under the broad categories of monarchy, republicanism, and democracy, Wood explains how the US was transformed from a society that took for granted a nonworking elite and a dependent servile underclass to one in which the free-standing individualist, who worked for a living, became the norm. . . . {A} readable book based on hundreds of primary and secondary sources." Choice

Includes bibliographical references

973.331　American Revolution-- Operations of 1775

Borneman, Walter R., 1952-

American spring; Lexington, Concord, and the road to revolution. Walter R. Borneman. Little Brown & Co 2014 480 p. illustrations, maps, portraits (hardcover) $30　　**973.331**

1. United States -- History -- 1775-1783, Revolution
ISBN 0316221023; 9780316221016; 9780316221023

LC 2014932742

Includes bibliographical references and index

This book, by Walter R. Borneman, "look[s] at the American Revolution's first months. . . . [It] follows a fledgling nation from Paul Revere's little-known ride of December 1774 and the first shots fired on Lexington Green through the catastrophic Battle of Bunker Hill, culminating with a Virginian named George Washington taking command of colonial forces on July 3, 1775." (Publisher's note)

"Taking advantage of massive documentation, Borneman delivers a gripping, almost moment-by-moment account of the nasty exchanges and bloody retreat of British troops followed by hundreds and then thousands of militia who camped around Boston and laid siege." Kirkus

973.4 United States--Constitutional period, 1789-1809

Brookhiser, Richard
America's first dynasty; the Adamses, 1735-1918. Free Press 2002 244p il $25; pa $14 **973.4**
1. Authors 2. Diplomats 3. Novelists 4. Historians 5. Presidents 6. Vice-presidents 7. Senators 8. Essayists 9. Political leaders 10. Members of Congress 11. Secretaries of state
ISBN 0-684-86881-4; 0-684-86864-4 pa
LC 2001-51276
An "account of the lives of John, John Quincy, Charles Francis and Henry, four generations of men often brilliant but often shortsighted as well: two presidents, one diplomat and, finally, a historian who felt he had failed the ancestors." N Y Times Book Rev
Includes bibliographical references

Burstein, Andrew
Madison and Jefferson; [by] Andrew Burstein and Nancy Isenberg. Random House 2010 809p il map $35; e-book $35 **973.4**
1. Architects 2. Presidents 3. Vice-presidents 4. Essayists 5. Members of Congress 6. Secretaries of state 7. Presidents -- United States 8. United States -- Politics and government -- 1783-1865 9. United States -- Politics and government -- 1775-1783, Revolution
ISBN 978-1-4000-6728-2; 978-0-679-60410-5 e-book
LC 2010-5884
This "dual biography promotes Madison from junior partner to full-fledged colleague of the 'more magnetic' Jefferson. According to the authors, Madison's popular image peaked in 1789 as 'father of the Constitution.' But Burstein . . . and Isenberg . . . see him as a canny, effective politician for four decades, from the Continental Congress through his two terms as America's fourth president. . . . An important, thoughtful, and gracefully written political history from the viewpoint of the young nation's two most intellectual founding fathers." Publ Wkly
Includes bibliographical references and index

Cerami, Charles A.
Jefferson's great gamble; the remarkable story of Jefferson, Napoleon and the men behind the Louisiana Purchase. Sourcebooks 2003 309p il $22.95; pa $14.95 **973.4**
1. Emperors 2. Architects 3. Presidents 4. Vice-presidents 5. Louisiana Purchase 6. Essayists
ISBN 1-57071-945-4; 1-40220-240-7 pa
LC 2002-153440
In this history of the Louisiana Purchase, the author gives a "retelling of the long and tangled negotiations between a team of Americans (chiefly Thomas Jefferson, Robert Livingston, James Madison, and James Monroe) and a rival team of Frenchmen (chiefly Napoleon and his adviser, Talleyrand)." Libr J
"Anyone wanting to read the story of a momentous turning point in American history, a story of diplomatic maneuvering and international politics, will be hard-pressed to find a better version than this." Publ Wkly
Includes bibliographical references

Ellis, Joseph J.
American sphinx: the character of Thomas Jefferson. Knopf 1997 365p $29.95; pa $15 **973.4**
1. Architects 2. Presidents 3. Vice-presidents 4. Essayists
ISBN 0-679-44490-4; 0-679-76441-0 pa
LC 96-26171
This biography focuses on "various important junctures of Jefferson's life (his tenures as minister to France, secretary of state, and, of course, president, among others) and major aspects of his personal consciousness (from his conduct of romance to his attitude toward slavery)." Booklist
"Penetrating Jefferson's placid, elegant facade, this extraordinary biography brings the sage of Monticello down to earth without either condemning or idolizing him." Publ Wkly

Founding brothers; the revolutionary generation. Knopf 2000 288p $26.95; pa $14 **973.4**
1. Authors 2. Generals 3. Diplomats 4. Inventors 5. Statesmen 6. Architects 7. Presidents 8. Scientists 9. Vice-presidents 10. Essayists 11. Writers on science 12. Members of Congress 13. Secretaries of state 14. United States -- Biography 15. Presidents -- United States 16. Secretaries of the treasury 17. United States -- History -- 1783-1809 18. United States -- Politics and government -- 1783-1809
ISBN 0-375-40544-5; 0-375-70524-4 pa
LC 99-59304
This study looks at the intertwined lives of "Benjamin Franklin, Thomas Jefferson, John Adams, Alexander Hamilton, James Madison and Aaron Burr. . . . As Ellis sees it, the founding brethren not only 'created the American republic' but 'held it together throughout the volatile and vulnerable early years by sustaining their presence until national habits and customs took root.'" NY Times Book Rev
"Ellis' essays are angled, fascinating, and perfect for general-interest readers." Booklist
Includes bibliographical references

Gordon-Reed, Annette
Thomas Jefferson and Sally Hemings; an American controversy. University Press of Va. 1997 xx, 288p hardcover o.p. pa $14.95 **973.4**
1. Slaves 2. Architects 3. Presidents 4. Vice-presidents 5. Essayists 6. Mistresses
ISBN 0-8139-1833-2 pa
LC 96-34550
"Hemings, a slave who was one-quarter African, was also a half sister of Jefferson's deceased wife, and she lived at Monticello for many years. In this understated, brilliant study an African-American law professor examines the al-

legation that Jefferson was the father of Hemings' children."
New Yorker

Includes bibliographical references

Hamilton, Alexander

Writings. Library of Am. 2001 1108p $40 **973.4**
1. United States -- Politics and government -- 1783-
1809 2. United States -- Politics and government --
1775-1783, Revolution
ISBN 1-931082-04-9

LC 2001-23043

"The text consists of more than 170 letters, speeches,
essays, reports, and memoranda written between 1769 and
1804, including all of Hamilton's material presented in
The Federalist. This additionally sports several conflicting
eyewitness accounts of Hamilton's lethal duel with Aaron
Burr." Libr J

Includes bibliographical references

Hogeland, William

★ The **Whiskey** Rebellion; George Washington, Alexander Hamilton, and the frontier rebels who
challenged America's newfound sovereignty. Scribner 2006 302p map $26.95; pa $16 **973.4**
1. Whiskey Rebellion, Pa., 1794
ISBN 978-0-7432-5490-8; 0-7432-5490-2; 978-0-
7432-5491-5 pa; 0-7432-5491-0 pa

LC 2005-56340

"Soon after Americans ousted inequitable British taxation, Secretary of Finance Alexander Hamilton, hatched a
plan to put the new nation on steady financial footing by
imposing the first American excise tax, on whiskey makers. The tax favored large distillers over small farmers with
stills in the mountains of Pennsylvania, Maryland and Virginia, and the farmers fomented their own new revolution—
a challenge to the sovereignty of the new government and
the power of the wealthy eastern seaboard. In a fast-paced,
blow-by-blow account of this 'primal national drama,' journalist Hogeland energetically chronicles the skirmishes that
made the Whiskey Rebellion from 1791 to 1795 a symbol of
the conflict between republican ideals and capitalist values."
Publ Wkly

Includes bibliographical references

Kranish, Michael

Flight from Monticello; Thomas Jefferson at war.
Michael Kranish. Oxford University Press 2010 xii,
388 p.p **973.4**
1. Statesmen 2. Architects 3. Presidents 4. Vice-
presidents 5. Governors -- Virginia -- Biography 6.
Presidents -- United States -- Biography 7. Virginia
-- History -- Revolution, 1775-1783 8. Virginia --
Politics and government -- 1775-1783 9. United States
-- Politics and government -- 1783-1809
ISBN 0195374622; 9780195374629 (acid-free paper)

LC 2009018156

This is an account of Jefferson's life during the period
when he served as governor of Virginia. He became governor "in 1779 and had to face repeated invasions of his state
by British forces." (Newsweek) Index.

"Crisply written and well documented, this book is popular history at its best and will appeal to a wide readership.
Highly recommended." Libr J

Includes bibliographical references (p. [371]-373)

Kukla, Jon

A **wilderness** so immense; the Louisiana Purchase and the destiny of America. Knopf 2003 430p
il map $30; pa $16 **973.4**
1. Louisiana Purchase
ISBN 0-375-40812-6; 0-375-70761-1 pa

LC 2002-27395

Kukla discusses the "struggles in the 1780's and 90's
for unimpeded use of the {Mississippi} river and its south-
ernmost port {New Orleans}. . . . So alarmed by westward
expansion were some new Englanders in the 1780's that they
started a separatist movement. . . . After the {Louisiana} Purchase in {1803}, Jeffersonian Republicans rejoiced in the
ties that would bind East and West." N Y Times Book Rev

"This judicious, aptly illustrated work will gratify all
its readers. Rarely does a work of history combine grace of
writing with such broad authority." Publ Wkly

Includes bibliographical references

The **Louisiana** Purchase; a historical and geographical encyclopedia. Junius P. Rodriguez, editor.
ABC-CLIO 2002 xxxv, 513p il maps $95 **973.4**
1. Louisiana Purchase 2. United States -- History --
1783-1809
ISBN 1-57607-188-X

LC 2002-3228

"The reasons for as well as the immediate and historical repercussions of the purchase are explored in nearly
300 articles written by 85 distinguished scholars. Coverage
includes native peoples, noteworthy personalities, and geographical areas associated with a land acquisition that nearly
doubled the size of our nation. An extensive bibliography, 49
pertinent documents, a chronology, and an index round out
this excellent volume." Libr J

Includes bibliographical references

McCullough, David G., 1933-

John Adams; {by} David McCullough. Simon &
Schuster 2001 751p il maps $35; pa $18.95 **973.4**
1. Presidents 2. Vice-presidents 3. Large print books
4. Presidents -- United States 5. United States --
Politics and government -- 1775-1783 6. United States
-- Politics and government -- 1783-1809 7. United
States -- Politics and government -- 1797-1801 8.
United States -- Politics and government -- 1775-1783,
Revolution
ISBN 0-684-81363-7; 0-7432-2313-6 pa

LC 2001-27010

This is a biography of the second president of the United
States. Index.

"This is a wonderfully stirring biography; to read it
is to feel as if you are witnessing the birth of a country
firsthand." Booklist

Includes bibliographical references

Meacham, Jon

★ **Thomas** Jefferson; the art of power. Jon Meacham. 1st ed. Random House 2012 448 p. (acid-free paper) $35 **973.4**

1. Presidents -- United States -- Biography 2. United States -- Politics and government -- 1783-1809

ISBN 1400067669; 9780679645368; 9781400067664

LC 2012013700

In this book, author Jon Meacham "claims that previous . . . scholars have not grasped the authentic [Thomas] Jefferson . . . a power-hungry, masterful, pragmatic leader who was not above being manipulative to achieve his goal: an enduring, democratic republic defined by him. A brilliant philosopher whose lofty principles were sometimes sidelined for more realistic goals, Meacham's Jefferson, neither idol nor rogue, is a complex mortal with serious flaws and contradictions." (Library Journal)

Includes bibliographical references and index.

Miller, John Chester

The **Federalist** era, 1789-1801; by John C. Miller. Waveland Press 1998 304p il pa $16.95 **973.4**

1. Statesmen 2. Architects 3. Presidents 4. Vice-presidents 5. Essayists 6. Federal Party (U.S.) 7. Secretaries of the treasury 8. United States -- History -- 1783-1809

ISBN 978-1-57766-031-6; 1-57766-031-5

First published 1960 by Harper & Row

A chronicle of the administrations of George Washington and John Adams, concentrating on the politics and diplomacy.

Includes bibliographical references

Purcell, Sarah J.

The **early** national period; [by] Sarah Purcell. Facts on File 2004 420p il map (Eyewitness history) $75 **973.4**

1. United States -- History -- 1783-1865

ISBN 0-8160-4769-3

LC 2003-14969

"The introduction to each section summarizes major events and provides excerpts from primary resources including speeches, letters, newspaper accounts, diary entries, and advertisements." SLJ

"A serious history student will find this book invaluable." Libr Media Connect

Includes bibliographical references

Randall, Willard Sterne

George Washington; a life. Holt & Co. 1997 548p hardcover o.p. pa $18 **973.4**

1. Generals 2. Presidents 3. United States -- History 4. Presidents -- United States

ISBN 0-8050-5992-X pa

LC 97-19125

"Chronicling less the adaptive leader of the struggling rebellion or the persuasive conciliator of the infant republic, Randall . . . portrays instead the vain, restless, ambitious provincial who got 'tremendously lucky'. . . . Altogether human, Randall's demythologized Washington comes vividly to life." Publ Wkly

Includes bibliographical references

Staloff, Darren

Hamilton, Adams, Jefferson; the politics of enlightenment and the American founding. Hill & Wang 2005 419p $30 **973.4**

1. Statesmen 2. Architects 3. Presidents 4. Enlightenment 5. Vice-presidents 6. Essayists 7. Secretaries of the treasury

ISBN 0-8090-7784-1; 978-0-8090-7784-7

LC 2005-40433

The author "provides a biographical and intellectual comparison among three major early American statesmen. He shows how the personal experiences and regional cultural traditions of each man shaded his interpretation of the European Enlightenment." Libr J

"Staloff has created a work that is a must-read for any serious scholar of US history." Choice

Includes bibliographical references

Steele, Brian

Thomas Jefferson and American nationhood; Brian Steele, University of Alabama, Birmingham. Cambridge University Press 2012 xiii, 321 p.p $99 **973.4**

1. Political science 2. United States -- Politics and government 3. HISTORY -- United States -- 19th Century 4. United States -- Politics and government -- Philosophy

ISBN 1107020700; 9781107020702

LC 2012013662

This book "emphasizes the centrality of nationhood to Thomas Jefferson's thought and politics, envisioning Jefferson as a cultural nationalist whose political project sought the alignment of the American state system with the will and character of the nation. Jefferson believed that America was the one nation on earth able to realize in practice universal ideals to which other peoples could only aspire." (Publisher's note)

Includes bibliographical references and index

Stewart, David O.

American emperor; Aaron Burr's challenge to Jefferson's America. Simon & Schuster 2011 xx, 410p il map $30; ebook $14.99 **973.4**

1. Architects 2. Presidents 3. Vice-presidents 4. Essayists 5. Presidents -- United States -- Election -- 1800 6. United States -- Politics and government -- 1783-1809

ISBN 978-1-4391-5718-3; 978-1-4391-6032-9 ebook

LC 2011002647

Traces the career of the third U.S. vice president and would-be secession leader, discussing his acrimonious relationship with Thomas Jefferson; his ambitious vision of expansion; and his historical, self-defended trial for treason.

"A persuasive, engaging examination of the post-political career of a shadowy and much-maligned figure from the era of the Founders." Kirkus

Includes bibliographical references

Vidal, Gore

Inventing a nation: Washington, Adams, Jefferson. Yale University Press 2003 224p $22; pa $14   **973.4**
1. Generals 2. Architects 3. Presidents 4. Vicepresidents 5. Essayists
ISBN 0-300-10171-6; 0-300-10592-4 pa
                              LC 2003-015612
Vidal offers "characteristically brilliant and acerbic reflections on power and personality. . . . This entertaining and enlightening reappraisal of the Founders is a must for buffs of American civilization and its discontents." Booklist

Washington, George, 1732-1799

★ **George** Washington's diaries; an abridgment. Dorothy Twohig, editor. University Press of Va. 1999 xxxi, 453p il $65; pa $22.95   **973.4**
1. Generals 2. Presidents 3. Presidents -- United States
ISBN 0-8139-1856-1; 0-8139-1857-X pa
                              LC 98-11681
"Culled from the six volumes of The Diaries of George Washington completed in 1979, this selection of entries . . . reveals the lifelong preoccupations of the public and private man." Publisher's note
Includes bibliographical references

★ **Writings**. Library of Am. 1997 xxiii, 1149p $40   **973.4**
1. Virginia -- History 2. United States -- Politics and government -- 1783-1809 3. United States -- Politics and government -- 1775-1783, Revolution
ISBN 1-883011-23-X
                              LC 96-9665
This "selection of Washington's letters, speeches, diary entries, maxims and military orders reveals a writer of surprising versatility and a statesman consciously involved with the forging of our national character." Publ Wkly

Wiencek, Henry

★ An **imperfect** god; George Washington, his slaves, and the creation of America. Farrar, Straus and Giroux 2003 404p il map $26; pa $15   **973.4**
1. Generals 2. Presidents 3. Presidents -- United States
ISBN 0-374-17526-8; 0-374-52951-5 pa
                              LC 2003-6984
"This work of stylish scholarship and genealogical investigation makes Washington an even greater and more human figure than he has seemed before." Publ Wkly
Includes bibliographical references

★ **Master** of the mountain; Thomas Jefferson and his slaves. Henry Wiencek. Farrar, Straus and Giroux 2012 352 p. ill. maps, geneal. tables (alk. paper) $28.00   **973.4**
1. Slavery -- United States 2. United States -- History -- 1775-1865 3. Monticello (Va.) -- History 4. Slaves -- Virginia -- Albemarle County -- History 5. Plantation life -- Virginia -- Albemarle County -- History
ISBN 0374299560; 9780374299569
                              LC 2011052231

In this book, Henry Wiencek "explores the economic calculus behind [Thomas] Jefferson's gradual cooling toward emancipation and eventual acceptance of human capital as a great 'investment opportunity.' Wiencek argues . . . that Jefferson not only failed to follow the advice and example of his peers . . . and embrace emancipation but was in fact a 'pioneer in the monetizing of slaves' and went to great lengths to impose 'his own reality' on his 'little familial empire.'" (Library Journal)
"Wiencek's insightful and engaging account is recommended to both the illustrious Virginian's detractors and to his devotees." LJ
Includes bibliographical references (p.305-315) and index.

Wills, Garry

Henry Adams and the making of America. Houghton Mifflin 2005 467p hardcover o.p. pa $15.95   **973.4**
1. Authors 2. Novelists 3. Historians 4. Essayists 5. United States -- Historiography
ISBN 0-618-13430-1; 0-618-87266-3 pa
                              LC 2005-40305
"Those unfamiliar with Adams' historical writings will find Wills a helpful and accessible guide; those who know Adams already will enjoy revisiting his histories with this knowledgeable and learned companion." Foreign Affairs
Includes bibliographical references

Wood, Gordon S., 1933-

★ **Empire** of liberty; a history of the early Republic, 1789-1815. Oxford University Press 2009 778p il map (Oxford history of the United States) $35   **973.4**
1. United States -- Civilization 2. National characteristics, American 3. United States -- Civilization -- 1783-1865 4. United States -- Politics and government -- 1783-1809 5. United States -- Politics and government -- 1783-1865
ISBN 978-0-19-503914-6
                              LC 2009-10762
"Skillfully traversing seminal topics such as slavery, westward expansion, social leveling, diplomacy, evangelicalism, the arts and sciences, and the transformation of the American legal system, Wood's authoritative and compelling narrative presents a picture of early Americans engaged in pursuit of cultural, social, and economic self-discovery. . . . [This is] a brilliant, definitive, and thought-provoking historical synthesis; sure to become indispensable to any study of the era." Libr J
Includes bibliographical references

Zacks, Richard

The **pirate** coast; Thomas Jefferson, the first marines, and the secret mission of 1805. Hyperion 2005 432p il map $25.95; pa $15.95   **973.4**
1. Diplomats 2. Architects 3. Presidents 4. Vicepresidents 5. Essayists 6. Army officers 7. United States -- History -- 1801-1805, Tripolitan War 8. Jefferson, Thomas, 1743-1826
ISBN 1-401-30003-0; 1-401-30849-X pa
                              LC 2004-60635

The focus of this book "is on the long-forgotten William Eaton, dispatched by Jefferson to lead a column of troops, including eight U.S. marines, overland from Egypt to Tripoli to overthrow the Bashaw, or Pasha." Libr J

"This is the book that Captain Eaton has long deserved." Publ Wkly

Includes bibliographical references

973.5 United States--1809-1845

Broadwater, Jeff

James Madison; a son of Virginia & a founder of the nation. Jeff Broadwater. University of North Carolina Press 2012 xvi, 266 p.p **973.5**
1. Presidents -- United States 2. Founding Fathers of the United States 3. Statesmen -- United States -- Biography 4. Presidents -- United States -- Biography 5. United States -- Politics and government -- 1789-1815 6. United States -- Politics and government -- 1809-1817
ISBN 9780807835302

LC 2011035946

In this biography of U.S. President James Madison, professor "[Jeff] Broadwater specifically provides readers with a detailed account of Madison's attempts to secure religious freedom in his native Virginia, his relationship with his charismatic wife Dolley Madison (sometimes referred to as 'Lady Presidentess'), and his ongoing struggle with his ideas about slavery." (Publishers Weekly)

Includes bibliographical references and index.

Collins, Gail

William Henry Harrison; Gail Collins. Times Books/Henry Holt and Co. 2012 xviii, 153 p.p **973.5**
1. War of 1812 2. Presidents -- United States -- Biography 3. Governors -- Indiana -- Biography 4. United States -- History -- 1783-1865 5. Presidents -- United States -- Election -- 1840 6. United States -- Politics and government -- 1841-1845
ISBN 9780805091182

LC 2011018976

This book offers a biography of U.S. former president William Henry Harrison. "Despite the legendary 1840 campaign featuring a 'log cabin, hard cider' frontiersman with humble origins, Harrison was born on a Virginia plantation, built himself a mansion as governor of the rough Indiana frontier territory, and avoided alcohol. His fame rested on two victories: the 1811 battle of Tippecanoe against the Shawnee Indians, and the 1813 Battle of the Thames during the War of 1812, in which the Indian leader Tecumseh was killed. For decades afterward, he struggled as a farmer and Ohio politician; he lost the 1836 presidential election but won four years later." (Publishers Weekly)

Includes bibliographical references and index

Cook, Jane Hampton

American phoenix; John Quincy and Louisa Adams, the War of 1812, and the exile that saved American independence. Jane Hampton Cook. Thomas Nelson 2013 x, 502 p.p ill. (some col.) (hardcover) $26.99 **973.5**
1. Diplomats -- United States -- Biography 2. Presidents -- United States -- Biography 3. Russia -- Foreign relations -- United States 4. United States -- Foreign relations -- Russia 5. United States -- History -- War of 1812 -- Peace 6. Presidents' spouses -- United States -- Biography 7. United States -- History -- War of 1812 -- Biography 8. United States -- History -- War of 1812 -- Diplomatic history
ISBN 1595555412; 9781595555410

LC 2012039898

This is a "dual biography of John Quincy and Louisa Adams during the former's service as United States envoy to Russia (1809-1814) and throughout his negotiations with Britain that produced the Treaty of Ghent and ended the War of 1812." Jane Hampton Cook "draws heavily from diaries and voluminous correspondences to render the couple's daily and inner struggles." (Publishers Weekly)

Includes bibliographical references and index

Daughan, George C.

1812 : the Navy's war; George C. Daughan. Basic Books 2011 xxix, 491p il map $32.50 **973.5**
1. War of 1812 2. United States -- Navy -- History
ISBN 978-0-465-02046-1; 978-0-465-02808-5 ebook

LC 2011020923

This book provides an account of "the U.S. Navy's surprising performance in the war that finally reconciled the British to America's independence. . . . If the U.S. Navy . . . didn't win the War of 1812, it probably kept the nation from losing. The . . . exploits of outstanding officers like Isaac Hull, David Porter, Stephen Decatur and Oliver Hazard Perry earned new respect for America's fleet; victories by the Essex, the Hornet and the Constitution . . . set off national celebrations. Daughan supplies . . . the big picture-the dismal struggles of both armies, Napoleon's off-stage machinations that determined so much of the war's progress, the outcome of domestic political squabbles upon which the navy's survival depended . . . but he focuses on the personalities, ships and battles that prevented the British from suffocating the infant nation's maritime ambitions." (Kirkus)

"Daughan narrates the story of the War of 1812, focusing on the tiny, 20-ship U.S. Navy. In doing so, from the poorly conducted chase of HMS Belvidera by Commodore John Rogers in June 1812 to the capture of HMS Penguin by USS Hornet in March 1815, Daughan also traces the development of the U.S. Navy." Libr J

Includes bibliographical references

Encyclopedia of the United States in the nineteenth century; Paul Finkelman, editor in chief. Scribner 2001 3v il maps set $400 **973.5**
1. Reference books 2. United States -- History -- 19th century -- Encyclopedias
ISBN 0-684-80500-6

LC 00-45811

In this historical overview: "population, politics and government, economy and work, society and culture, religion, social problems and reform, everyday life, and foreign policy are explored in more than 600 A-to-Z articles. Complete with more than 400 illustrations and maps, this set includes . . . {a} year-by-year chronology, original documents {and} tables." Publisher's note

Giles Unger, Harlow

John Quincy Adams; Harlow Giles Unger. Da Capo Press 2012 xv, 364 p.p ill., map (hardcover : alk. paper) $27.50   **973.5**
  1. Statesmen -- United States -- Biography 2. Presidents -- United States -- Biography 3. United States -- Politics and government -- 1789-1815   4. United States -- Politics and government -- 1825-1829
  ISBN 030682129X; 9780306821295; 9780306821301
                                              LC 2012009399

This book, by Harlow Giles Unger, offers a biography of the U.S. president John Quincy Adams. "He fought for Washington, served with Lincoln, witnessed Bunker Hill, and sounded the clarion against slavery on the eve of the Civil War. He negotiated an end to the War of 1812, . . . and won the Supreme Court decision that freed the African captives of 'The Amistad.' He served his nation as minister to six countries, secretary of state, senator, congressman, and president." (Publisher's note)

Includes bibliographical references (p. 339-348) and index.

Groom, Winston

Patriotic fire; Andrew Jackson and Jean Laffite at the Battle of New Orleans. Alfred A. Knopf 2006 xxiv, 292p il map $26   **973.5**
  1. Pirates 2. Generals 3. Presidents 4. New Orleans (La.), Battle of, 1815
  ISBN 1-4000-4436-7; 978-1-4000-4436-8
                                              LC 2005-51001

"This is a beautifully written and exciting work of popular history." Booklist
Includes bibliographical references

Howe, Daniel Walker

★ What hath God wrought; the transformation of America, 1815-1848. Oxford University Press 2007 904p il map (Oxford history of the United States) $35   **973.5**
  1. Social change -- United States 2. United States -- History -- 1815-1861 3. United States -- Foreign relations -- 1815-1861 4. United States -- Politics and government -- 1815-1861
  ISBN 978-0-19-507894-7; 0-19-507894-2
                                              LC 2007-12370

The author "narrates a crucial period in U.S. history— a time of territorial growth, religious revival, booming industrialization, a recalibrating of American democracy and the rise of nationalist sentiment. . . . Supported by engaging prose, Howe's achievement will surely be seen as one of the most outstanding syntheses of U.S. history published this decade." Publ Wkly
Includes bibliographical references

Langguth, A. J., 1933-2014

Driven West; Andrew Jackson and the Trail of Tears to the Civil War. Simon & Schuster 2010 466p il map $30; ebook $14.99   **973.5**
  1. Generals 2. Presidents 3. Trail of Tears, 1838-1839

  4. United States -- History -- 1815-1861 5. Indians of North America -- Relocation
  ISBN 978-1-4165-4859-1; 1-4165-4859-9; 978-1-4391-9327-3 ebook; 1-4391-9327-4 ebook
                                              LC 2010-20455

Langguth argues "that the passage of the Indian Removal Act of 1830, Jackson's breaking of Indian treaties and his support of the Southern states, especially Georgia, in resisting a Supreme Court ruling in favor of the Cherokees were 'salvos . . . fired in the nation's first civil war'." (N Y Times Book Rev) Bibliography. Index.

"A disturbing reconsideration of a key period of history and a powerful indictment of its main actors." Kirkus
Includes bibliographical references

Lincoln, Abraham 1809-1865

★ Speeches and writings, 1832-1858; speeches, letters, and miscellaneous writings: the Lincoln Douglas debates. Library of Am. 1989 898p $35 **973.5**
  1. Lincoln-Douglas debates, 1858 2. United States -- Politics and government -- 1815-1861
  ISBN 0-940450-43-7
                                              LC 88-82723

Based on the "eight volumes of 'The Collected Works of Abraham Lincoln,' edited by Roy P. Basler, Marion Dolores Pratt and Lloyd A. Dunlap, the present . . . [volume contains] all seven of the Lincoln-Douglas debates, as well as the . . . speeches, before and after the debates, that attacked the repeal of the Missouri Compromise of 1820 and 'squatter sovereignty' in the territories." N Y Times Book Rev
Includes bibliographical references

Miller, William Lee

Arguing about slavery; the great battle in the United States Congress. Knopf 1996 577p hardcover o.p. pa $17   **973.5**
  1. Presidents 2. Senators 3. Members of Congress 4. Secretaries of state 5. Slavery -- United States 6. United States -- Congress 7. United States -- Politics and government -- 1815-1861
  ISBN 0-679-76844-0 pa
                                              LC 95-35075

"Miller lays out the arcane workings of the proceedings with admirable detail, clarity, and verve." Christ Sci Monit
Includes bibliographical references

Oates, Stephen B.

The **approaching** fury; voices of the storm, 1820-1861. Buz Wyeth, editor. HarperCollins Pubs. 1997 495p hardcover o.p. pa $15   **973.5**
  1. United States -- History -- 1815-1861 2. United States -- History -- 1861-1865, Civil War -- Causes
  ISBN 0-06-092885-9 pa
                                              LC 96-31965

Companion volume to The whirlwind of war
"Taken on its own terms, this book powerfully re-creates some of the momentous events that produced the catastrophe of 1861. Mr. Oates succeeds in bringing his characters alive and in creating highly dramatic scenes for them to act out." N Y Times Book Rev
Includes bibliographical references

Remini, Robert Vincent

John Quincy Adams; [by] Robert V. Remini. Times Bks. 2002 172p (American presidents series) $20 **973.5**

1. Presidents 2. Senators 3. Members of Congress 4. Secretaries of state 5. Presidents -- United States 6. United States -- Politics and government -- 1783-1865 ISBN 0-8050-6939-9

LC 2002-24210

The author's "judicious, eloquent survey of the sixth president's life and career intends not to proffer new and explosive ideas but to fashion recent scholarship into a highly readable overview for the general reader." Booklist

Includes bibliographical references

Reynolds, David S.

Waking giant; America in the age of Jackson. Harper 2008 466p il $29.95 **973.5**

1. Generals 2. Presidents 3. United States -- History -- 1815-1861 ISBN 978-0-06-082656-7

LC 2007-51751

This is "a terrific introduction of succinct length to . . . a time when the foundations of much of modern America were laid." N Y Times (Late N Y Ed)

Includes bibliographical references

Smith, Gene Allen

The **slaves'** gamble; choosing sides in the War of 1812. Gene Allen Smith. Palgrave Macmillan 2013 272 p. $27 **973.5**

1. War of 1812 2. Slavery -- United States ISBN 0230342086; 9780230342088

LC 2012045726

This book by Gene Allen Smith explains that "in the [19th] century's first two decades, the [United States] waged war against Britain, Spain, and various Indian tribes. Slaves played a role in the military operations, and the different sides viewed them as a potential source of manpower. While surprising numbers did assist the Americans, the wars created opportunities for slaves to find freedom among the Redcoats, the Spaniards, or the Indians." (Publisher's note)

Includes bibliographical references and index.

Smith, Myron J.

The **CSS** Arkansas; a Confederate ironclad on western waters. Myron J. Smith, Jr. McFarland & Co. 2011 viii, 351 p.p ill. (softcover : alk. paper) $35.00 **973.5**

1. Arkansas (Confederate ram) 2. United States -- History -- 1861-1865, Civil War -- Naval operations 3. United States -- History -- Civil War, 1861-1865 -- Naval operations, Confederate 4. Mississippi River Valley -- History -- Civil War, 1861-1865 -- Naval operations, Confederate ISBN 0786447265; 9780786447268

LC 2011023403

This book by Myron J. Smith discusses the CSS Arkansas, an ironclad ship used in the fleet of the Confederate States of America. "The makeshift CSS Arkansas . . . gave the South a surge of confidence when it launched in 1862. For 28 days of summer, the ship engaged in five battles with Union warships, falling victim in the end only to her own primitive engines. The saga of the CSS Arkansas represents the last significant Rebel naval activity in the war's Western theater." (Publisher's note)

Includes bibliographical references and index.

Taylor, Alan

The **civil** war of 1812; American citizens, British subjects, Irish rebels, & Indian allies. Alfred A. Knopf 2010 620p il map $35; e-book $35 **973.5**

1. War of 1812 2. Ontario -- History -- War of 1812 3. United States -- History -- War of 1812 4. Northern boundary of the United States -- History ISBN 978-1-4000-4265-4; 1-4000-4265-8; 978-0-307-59459-4 e-book

LC 2010-12783

In this book, Alan "Taylor examines themes pertinent to the period and the war [of 1812], blending narrative with analysis. He sees this upheaval, and the earlier American Revolution, as part of an anglophone civil war that defined America, Canada, and the British Empire in the nineteenth century. It was a peculiar type of civil war, to be certain, as it involved more than one state and more than one culture. . . . Many Canadians were in fact displaced American loyalists who hoped to undo the revolution. . . . Taylor draws on the conceptual frameworks created in the burgeoning field of borderlands history to construct his study. He uses this approach to situate the character of the war along the American-Canadian border, which he sees as central to the entire conflict." (American Historical Review)

"Instead of a traditional narrative of the war from its beginnings in June 1812 to its end in early 1815, [this] book is structured topically. . . . Such a neat and methodical organization helps Taylor bring the confused and chaotic events of the war under control. It also allows him to present an enormous amount of material—on persons, events, and stories—without overwhelming the reader. And the amount of material is enormous." N Y Rev Books

Includes bibliographical references

Tocqueville, Alexis de

Democracy in America; with an introduction by Alan Ryan. Knopf 1994 lxxii, 434, xi, 394p (Everyman's library) $27 **973.5**

1. Democracy 2. American national characteristics 3. United States -- Social conditions 4. United States -- Politics and government ISBN 978-0-679-43134-3; 0-679-43134-9

LC 94-1752

First part originally published in France, 1835; the second in 1840

Based partly on the French author's observations of American political and social conditions during a visit in 1831-1832. "It remains the best philosophical discussion of Democracy illustrated by the experience of the United States, up to the time when it was written, which can be found in any language." Pratt Alcove

Includes bibliographical references

Vogel, Steve

Through the perilous fight; six weeks that saved the nation. Steve Vogel. Random House Inc 2013 560 p. (acid-free paper) $30   **973.5**
1. War of 1812 2. Baltimore, Battle of, Baltimore, Md., 1814 3. Maryland -- History -- War of 1812 -- Campaigns 4. United States -- History -- War of 1812 -- Campaigns 5. Washington (D.C.) -- History -- Capture by the British, 1814
ISBN 1400069130; 9780679603474; 9781400069132

                   LC 2012039797

This book is a "chronicle of the critical closing months of the War of 1812—specifically, the British attacks on Washington and Baltimore." Steve Vogel "begins in the summer of 1814 with the British planning their attack. They were eager for payback after the American invasion of Canada two years earlier. Vogel focuses on Rear Adm. George Cockburn—a figure he revisits throughout—who was especially intent on capturing and torching Washington." (Kirkus Reviews)

Includes bibliographical references and index

Wilentz, Sean

The **rise** of American democracy; Jefferson to Lincoln. Norton 2005 xxiii, 1044p il $35   **973.5**
1. Democracy 2. Democracy -- United States 3. United States -- Politics and government -- 1783-1865
ISBN 0-393-05820-4

                   LC 2004-29466

Wilentz traces the evolution of democratic principles in the United States from the American Revolution to the Civil War. Index.

This "is a magnificent chronicle, the life of an idea that, although it is mentioned nowhere in the Constitution, nevertheless slowly elbowed its way into the heart of American life.... Wilentz shows what [the] fight has cost, and why it's worth it." Newsweek

Includes bibliographical references

Wills, Garry

James Madison. Times Bks. 2002 xx, 184p (American presidents series) $20   **973.5**
1. Presidents 2. Members of Congress 3. Secretaries of state 4. Presidents -- United States
ISBN 0-8050-6905-4

                   LC 2002-19692

The author "maintains that Madison possessed qualities that served him well early in his career but proved to be a handicap during his Presidency. . . . Written with flair, this clear and balanced account is based on a sure handling of the material." Libr J

Includes bibliographical references

973.6   United States--1845-1861

Bordewich, Fergus M.

America's great debate; Henry Clay, Stephen A. Douglas, and the compromise that preserved the Union. Fergus M. Bordewich. Simon & Schuster 2012 x, 480 p.p   **973.6**
1. Debates and debating 2. Slavery -- United States

-- History 3. United States -- History -- 1861-1865, Civil War 4. United States -- Politics and government -- 1861-1865 5. Compromise of 1850 6. Slavery -- United States -- History -- 19th century 7. United States -- Politics and government -- 1815-1861 8. United States -- History -- Civil War, 1861-1865 -- Causes
ISBN 1439124604; 9781439124604; 9781439141687

                   LC 2011029547

In this book, "Historian [Fergus M.] Bordewich . . . recounts the amazing story of the cliffhanging compromise hammered out in both houses of Congress in 1850 that pitted the rival pro- and antislavery factions against each other and saved the country, temporarily, from dissolution. . . . Bordewich portrays a colorful cast of characters--Democrats, Whigs, Free Soilers and abolitionists--whose passionate rhetoric attained lyrical heights and brought the debate about America's very identity to the forefront. Chief architect Henry Clay . . . warned his colleagues of the dire consequences of disunion. . . . Warring factions . . . threatened to defeat the omnibus bill, until the rhetorical arm-wringing by . . . Stephen A. Douglas squeezed a compromise and the necessary passage." (Kirkus)

Includes bibliographical references (p. [403]-463) and index

Dusinberre, William

Slavemaster president; the double career of James Polk. Oxford Univ. Press 2003 258p il map $35   **973.6**
1. Governors 2. Presidents 3. Members of Congress 4. Speakers of the House 5. Slavery -- United States 6. Presidents -- United States
ISBN 0-19-515735-4

                   LC 2002-74852

This book focuses on "Polk's management of his slaves and his public positions on slavery and related issues. The author suggests that Polk's policies were critical to the development of the secessionist movement in the South and that these policies derived from his personal financial interests. . . . Dusinberre's research also expands our understanding of the management of plantations. Essential reading for anyone wanting greater insight into the factors that led to the Civil War, this work is highly recommended." Libr J

Includes bibliographical references

Guelzo, Allen C.

Lincoln and Douglas; the debates that defined America. Simon & Schuster 2008 xxvii, 383p il map $26   **973.6**
1. Lawyers 2. Presidents 3. Lincoln-Douglas debates, 1858 4. Senators 5. Political leaders 6. State legislators 7. Members of Congress 8. Presidential candidates 9. United States -- Politics and government -- 1815-1861
ISBN 978-0-7432-7320-6; 0-7432-7320-6

                   LC 2007-44254

"This Lincoln-Douglas rendition will engage every interest in Civil War and black history." Booklist

Includes bibliographical references

Wineapple, Brenda

Ecstatic nation; confidence, crisis, and compromise, 1848-1877. Brenda Wineapple. Harper 2013 736 p. $35   **973.6**

1. United States -- History 2. Slavery -- United States -- History 3. United States -- History -- 1849-1877 4. Reconstruction (U.S. history, 1865-1877) 5. United States -- History -- Civil War, 1861-1865 6. Slavery -- United States -- History -- 19th century 7. United States -- History -- Civil War, 1861-1865 -- Causes 8. Antislavery movements -- United States -- History -- 19th century 9. United States -- Territorial expansion -- History -- 19th century

ISBN 0061234575; 9780061234576

LC 2012051538

Author Brenda Wineapple's book focuses on the history of the U.S. and discusses people "such as P. T. Barnum, Walt Whitman, George Armstrong Custer, Horace Greeley, and Jefferson Davis." The book discusses "slavery through the devastations of the Civil War and its aftermath. It explores the terrible complexities of Reconstruction and the fledgling hope that women would share equally in a new definition of American citizenship, and it traces the lust for land and the lure of its beauty from a frenzied rush to riches to the displacement of Indians." (Publisher's note)

Includes bibliographical references and index

973.7 Administration of Abraham Lincoln, 1861-1865

Abbott, Karen

Liar, Temptress, Soldier, Spy; Four Women Undercover in the Civil War. by Karen Abbott. HarperCollins Publishers 2014 368 p. illustrations, map $27.99   **973.7**

1. American espionage 2. Women -- United States -- History 3. United States -- History -- 1861-1865, Civil War

ISBN 0062092898; 9780062092892

LC 2014013602

In this book, author Karen Abbott "illuminates . . . little known aspects of the Civil War: the stories of four courageous women--a socialite, a farmgirl, an abolitionist, and a widow--who were spies. . . . Using a wealth of primary source material and interviews with the spies' descendants, Abbott seamlessly weaves the adventures of these four heroines throughout the tumultuous years of the war." (Publisher's note)

"Remarkable, brave lives rendered in a fluidly readable, even romantic history lesson." Kirkus

Includes bibliographical references and index

Ash, Stephen V.

Firebrand of liberty; the story of two Black regiments that changed the course of the Civil War. W.W. Norton & Co. 2008 282p il map $25.95   **973.7**

1. African American soldiers 2. United States -- Army -- South Carolina Volunteers, 1st 3. United States -- History -- 1861-1865, Civil War -- Campaigns 4. United States -- Army -- South Carolina Volunteers, 2nd

(1863-1864)

ISBN 978-0-393-06586-2; 0-393-06586-3

LC 2008-2503

"The titular firebrand in this revealing history is not an individual but a curious and ambitious project: the establishment, in March 1863, of a permanent Union outpost in Florida to serve as a haven for fugitive slaves and to 'help ignite the destruction of Southern slavery from within.' In readable prose and relying exclusively on primary sources, historian Ash . . . tells the little-known but crucial story of how 900 newly freed slaves, under the leadership of white abolitionist officers, captured Jacksonville." Publ Wkly

Includes bibliographical references (p. [256]-265) and index.

Berg, Scott W.

★ **38** nooses; Lincoln, Little Crow, and the beginning of the frontier's end. Scott W. Berg. Pantheon Books 2012 384 p. $27.95   **973.7**

1. Native Americans -- Wars 2. United States -- History -- 1775-1865 3. Native Americans -- Government relations -- History 4. Dakota Indians -- Relocation 5. Dakota Indians -- Wars, 1862-1865 6. Dakota Indians -- Government relations -- History -- 19th century 7. Executions and executioners -- United States -- History -- 19th century

ISBN 0307377245; 9780307377241

LC 2012002807

Author Scott W. Berg discusses "events within the larger context of the Civil War, the history of the Dakota people, and the subsequent United States-Indian wars. . . . In August 1862, after decades of broken treaties, increasing hardship, and relentless encroachment on their lands, a group of Dakota warriors convened a council at the tepee of their leader, Little Crow. . . . So began six weeks of intense conflict along the Minnesota frontier as the Dakotas clashed with settlers and federal troops, all the while searching for allies in their struggle." (Publisher's note)

Includes bibliographical references and index.

Blanton, DeAnne

They fought like demons; women soldiers in the American Civil War. {by} DeAnne Blanton and Lauren M. Cook. Louisiana State Univ. Press 2002 277p il (Conflicting worlds) $29.95   **973.7**

1. Women soldiers 2. United States -- History -- 1861-1865, Civil War

ISBN 0-8071-2806-6

LC 2002-4441

"The authors reconstruct the reasons why women entered the armed forces: many were simply patriotic, while others followed their husbands or lovers and yet others yearned to break free from the constraints that Victorian society had laid on them as women. Blanton and Cook detail women soldiers in combat, on the march, in camp and in the hospital, where many were discovered after getting sick. Some even wound up in grim prisons kept by both sides, while a few hid pregnancies and were only discovered after giving birth. . . . Solid research by the authors, including a look at the careers of a few women soldiers after the war, makes this a compelling book that belongs in every Civil War library." Publ Wkly

Includes bibliographical references

Blight, David W.

American oracle. Belknap Press of Harvard University Press 2011 314p $27.95   **973.7**

1. United States -- History -- 1861-1865, Civil War -- Historiography

ISBN 978-0-674-04855-3

LC 2011006653

This book by David W. Blight "examines how we handled the centennial [of the U.S. Civil War,] which occurred at the infancy of the civil rights movement, and the persistent questioning about all the elements that were at the heart of the nation-rending civil conflict." It focuses on "the works of four writers -- Robert Penn Warren, southern-born novelist; Bruce Catton, historian and journalist; Edmund Wilson, literary critic; and James Baldwin, northern-born essayist and race critic." (Booklist)

This "book is a set of critical reflections on the racial attitudes and historical views of four great American writers—James Baldwin, Bruce Catton, Robert Penn Warren, and Edmund Wilson (and in an epilogue, Ralph Ellison)—around the time of the Civil War centennial 50 years ago." Publ Wkly

Includes bibliographical references

Blount, Roy

★ **Robert** E. Lee; a Penguin life. [by] Roy Blount, Jr. Lipper/Viking Bk. 2003 210p (Penguin lives series) $19.95; pa $13   **973.7**

1. Generals 2. College presidents 3. Confederate States of America -- Army 4. United States -- History -- 1861-1865, Civil War

ISBN 0-670-03220-4; 0-14-303866-4 pa

LC 2002-32423

This is a biography of "the famous Southern general admired for his military leadership but also scorned for defending the Confederacy. Blount's concise writing keeps his biography trim and succinct, and his admiration for the subject allows for enjoyable reading." Booklist

Includes bibliographical references

Boatner, Mark Mayo

The **Civil** War dictionary; by Mark Mayo Boatner III; maps and diagrams by Allen C. Northrop and Lowell I. Miller. 1st Vintage Civil War Library ed.; Vintage Civil War Library 1991 974p il map pa $24   **973.7**

1. Reference books 2. United States -- History -- 1861-1865, Civil War -- Encyclopedias

ISBN 0-679-73392-2; 978-0-679-73392-8

LC 91-50013

First published 1959 by McKay

"With more than 4,000 entries . . . this dictionary remains the most comprehensive and consistently accurate reference tool on the American Civil War. In addition to the biographical sketches there are entries relating to campaigns and battles, naval engagements, weapons, issues and inci-

dents, military terms and definitions, politics, literature, and statistics." Choice

Includes bibliographical references

Bordewich, Fergus M.

★ **Bound** for Canaan; the epic story of the underground railroad, America's first integrated civil rights movement. Fergus M. Bordewich. Amistad 2005 540p il map $27.95; pa $14.95   **973.7**

1. Underground railroad 2. Slavery -- United States

ISBN 0-06-052430-8; 0-06-052431-6 pa

LC 2004-52082

The author "covers six decades of the Underground Railroad, from its inchoate beginnings to its height, when it boasted a complex network of individuals determined to eliminate slavery from a nation proclaiming to be the land of liberty." Libr J

"The men and women of this remarkable account will remain with readers for a long time to come." Publ Wkly

Includes bibliographical references

Boritt, G. S.

The **Gettysburg** gospel; the Lincoln speech that nobody knows. Simon & Schuster 2006 415p il $28   **973.7**

1. Presidents 2. State legislators 3. Members of Congress

ISBN 978-0-7432-8820-0; 0-7432-8820-3

LC 2006-50578

"The author sets the speech in its contemporary context and, most interestingly, demonstrates that it was not only minimally noticed by Lincoln's peers and the press at the time but was virtually forgotten to history until the 20th century. He addresses many of the myths surrounding the address, such as that Lincoln wrote it in haste on the train to Gettysburg. In fact, it went through a number of careful revisions. He includes images of the known copies of the handwritten address, broadsides and programs relating to the dedication ceremony at Gettysburg, selections of photos from the era, and a line-byline analysis of the various drafts of the address. Boritt's narrative style will appeal to lay readers . . . , while his extensive research and insightful conclusions will appeal to scholars." Libr J

Catton, Bruce, 1899-1978

A **stillness** at Appomattox. Doubleday 1953 438p maps hardcover o.p. pa $14.95   **973.7**

1. Appomattox Campaign, 1865 2. United States -- History -- 1861-1865, Civil War -- Campaigns

ISBN 0-385-04451-8 pa

Concluding volume of trilogy which began with Mr. Lincoln's army (1951) and Glory road (1952). This final volume of the author's study of the Army of the Potomac covers the period from early 1864 to April, 1865

The author's "approach is judicious, his interpretation unbiased and his coverage comprehensive." N Y Times Book Rev

Includes bibliographical references

The **Causes** of the Civil War; edited by Kenneth M. Stampp. 3rd rev ed; Simon & Schuster 1991 255p pa $14   **973.7**
1. Nationalism 2. State rights 3. Slavery -- United States 4. Southern States -- Economic conditions 5. United States -- History -- 1861-1865, Civil War -- Causes 6. United States -- History -- 1861-1865, Civil War -- Sources
ISBN 0-671-75155-7
LC 91-36819
First published 1959 by Prentice-Hall
This book integrates the conclusions of various post-war historians with the thoughts of contemporary commentators like Jefferson Davis, Horace Greeley, and Lincoln. Political, cultural and economic aspects are emphasized
Includes bibliographical references

Center for the National Archives Experience
Discovering the Civil War; by the National Archives Experience's ¿Discovering the Civil War¿ Exhibition Team with a message from David S. Ferriero, Archivist of the United States; foreword by Ken Burns. D. Giles Ltd. 2010 208p il map $44.95 **973.7**
1. United States -- History -- 1861-1865, Civil War
ISBN 978-1-904832-91-1
LC 2010-27924
"Created to accompany the major National Archives Civil War exhibit that mined our national trove of photographs, manuscripts, maps, ephemera, realia, and more, this book is spectacular in its presentation of the wide array of seemingly mundane but surprisingly revealing sources from both the well known and the obscure. . . . The intelligent framing of issues (e.g., government controls, technological and scientific innovation) for each chapter will invite readers to consider many questions about war and society, war making, and the economy of war." Libr J
Includes bibliographical references

★ The **Civil** War; the first year told by those who lived it. edited by Brooks D. Simpson, Stephen W. Sears, Aaron Sheehan-Dean. Library of America 2011 xxv, 814p map $37.50 **973.7**
1. United States -- History -- 1861-1865, Civil War -- Sources 2. United States -- History -- Civil War, 1861-1865 -- Sources 3. United States -- History -- 1861-1865, Civil War -- Personal narratives
ISBN 978-1-59853-088-9; 1-59853-088-7
LC 2010-931718
"Drawing on diaries, letters, speeches, newspaper reports and editorials, memoirs, songs, poems, and other sources, the editors bring together a rich variety of voices relating or remembering the crisis of the Union from Lincoln's election in 1860 through the first year of war. . . . Readable and riveting, this 'you are there' collection makes real the sense of urgency that gripped Americans as the nation came apart and as the war began, 175 years ago. An excellent primer on why the Civil War mattered to those living it." Libr J
Includes bibliographical references

The **Civil** War: a visual history; [produced in association with the Smithsonian Institution] DK Publishing 2011 360p il map $40 **973.7**
1. United States -- History -- 1861-1865, Civil War -- Pictorial works
ISBN 978-0-7566-7185-3
"Drawing on Smithsonian Institution collections, this fact-filled and richly illustrated history brings the war fully to life, along with time lines, sidebars on particular issues, chapter introductions, lengthy captions, and detailed maps. The emphasis throughout is on the military. Multiple examples of weapons, supplies, uniforms, camp life necessities, transport, and battle scenes dominate and show the variety, complexity, and prolixity of making war. Espionage, the home front, and politics get a nod, but this book is for those wanting to smell the sulfur and hear the thunder of guns." Libr J

Clinton, Catherine
Harriet Tubman: the road to freedom. Little, Brown 2004 272p hardcover o.p. pa $14.95 **973.7**
1. Abolitionists 2. Underground railroad 3. African American women -- Biography
ISBN 0-316-14492-4; 0-316-15594-2 pa
LC 2003-56185
"Clinton turns sobriquets into meaningful descriptors of a unique person. In her hands, a familiar legend acquires human dimension with no diminution of its majesty and power." Publ Wkly
Includes bibliographical references

Colaiaco, James A.
Frederick Douglass and the Fourth of July. Palgrave Macmillan 2006 247p hardcover o.p. pa $16.95 **973.7**
1. Slaves 2. Authors 3. Abolitionists 4. Memoirists 5. Slavery -- United States
ISBN 1-4039-7033-5; 1-4039-8072-1 pa
LC 2005-51520
"Colaiaco's careful study recaptures Douglass' reputation as one of America's greatest orators." Booklist
Includes bibliographical references

Cooper, William J.
Jefferson Davis, American. Knopf 2000 757p il maps $35; pa $18 **973.7**
1. Statesmen 2. Senators 3. Political leaders 4. Secretaries of war 5. Confederate States of America 6. United States -- History -- 1861-1865, Civil War
ISBN 0-394-56916-4; 0-375-72542-3 pa
LC 00-62006
In this biography of the president of the Confederacy, the author traces Davis' political career and personal life, including his days at West Point, as Secretary of War in the Mexican War, and as U.S. senator from Mississippi
"In the already cluttered field of Civil War history, Cooper's is the definitive biography; readers will be particularly pleased to discover the compelling power of his narrative." Publ Wkly
Includes bibliographical references

Craughwell, Thomas J.

Stealing Lincoln's body. Belknap Press of Harvard University Press 2007 250p il $24.95 **973.7**

1. Presidents 2. Grave robbing 3. Counterfeits and counterfeiting 4. State legislators 5. Members of Congress

ISBN 978-0-674-02458-8; 0-674-02458-3

LC 2006-50842

"Summoning the raw spirit of crime novels and horror stories, as well as the forensic detail of a coroner's inquest, Thomas J. Craughwell has turned the eerie final chapter of the Lincoln story into a guilty pleasure." Washington Post Book World

Includes bibliographical references

Daniel, Larry J.

Shiloh; the battle that changed the Civil War. Simon & Schuster 1997 430p il map hardcover o.p. pa $14 **973.7**

1. Shiloh (Tenn.), Battle of, 1862

ISBN 0-684-83857-5 pa

LC 96-51539

The author "has crafted a superbly researched volume that will appeal to both the beginning Civil War reader as well as those already familiar with the course of fighting in the wooded terrain bordering the Tennessee River." Publ Wkly

Includes bibliographical references

Davis, Burke

Sherman's march. Random House 1980 335p il maps hardcover o.p. pa $14 **973.7**

1. Generals 2. Bentonville (N.C.), Battle of, 1865 3. Memoirists 4. Secretaries of war 5. United States -- History -- 1861-1865, Civil War -- Campaigns

ISBN 0-394-75763-7 pa

LC 79-5550

The author "reconstructs Sherman's infamous, but vastly consequential march through Georgia and the Carolinas, which sent the Confederacy into its death throes. Basing his narrative on eyewitness accounts, Davis brings the event down to a personal level." Booklist

Includes bibliographical references

To Appomattox; nine April days, 1865. Burford Books 2002 433p map pa $18.95 **973.7**

1. Appomattox Campaign, 1865 2. United States -- History -- 1861-1865, Civil War

ISBN 1-580-80097-1; 978-1-580-80097-6

LC 2001-56744

First published 1959 by Rinehart

"The story of the last nine days of the Civil War from the march on Richmond to the surrender at Appomattox. Quotations from diaries, letters, newspapers and military reports create a sense of immediacy as the reader follows each day's events in the city, in the Confederate camp, and with the Union Army." Publ Wkly

Includes bibliographical references

Davis, William C.

An **honorable** defeat; the last days of the Confederate government. Harcourt 2001 496p il maps $30; pa $16 **973.7**

1. Generals 2. Statesmen 3. Vice-presidents 4. Senators 5. Political leaders 6. Secretaries of war 7. Presidential candidates 8. Confederate States of America

ISBN 0-15-100564-8; 0-15-600748-7 pa

LC 00-46143

Davis "knows his two principal players well, and a marvelous supporting cast of politicians and soldiers helps him to fashion a story rich in pathos and humor." N Y Times Book Rev

Includes bibliographical references

Detzer, David

Allegiance; Fort Sumter, Charleston, and the beginning of the Civil War. Harcourt 2001 367p $27 **973.7**

1. Charleston (S.C.) -- History 2. Fort Sumter (Charleston, S.C.) 3. United States -- History -- 1861-1865, Civil War -- Causes

ISBN 0-15-100641-5

LC 00-50570

"The central figure in this drama is Maj. Robert Anderson, commander of the Union garrison in Charleston Harbor. . . . Detzer's writing style brings the reader into close contact with soldiers, civilians and politicians as they struggle to solve the fate of Anderson and his men." Publ Wkly

Includes bibliographical references

Egerton, Douglas R.

Year of meteors; Stephen Douglas, Abraham Lincoln, and the election that brought on the Civil War. Bloomsbury Press 2010 399p il $29 **973.7**

1. Presidents -- United States -- Election -- 1860 2. United States -- Politics and government -- 1815-1861 3. United States -- Politics and government -- 1857-1861 4. United States -- History -- 1861-1865, Civil War -- Causes 5. United States -- History -- Civil War, 1861-1865 -- Causes

ISBN 978-1-59691-619-7

LC 2010-4965

In this book on the causes of the U.S. Civil War, Douglas R. Egerton "asserts that the reason strains evolved into full-scale hostilities was the result of actions by a relatively few men. Egerton views the election of [Abraham] Lincoln, which seemed inconceivable at the beginning of 1860, as the trigger for secession. He suggests that to some extent the election was the result of what amounted to a conspiracy on the part of Southern radicals." (Booklist)

The author "examines the importance of race in the presidential election of 1860, when a relatively unknown candidate came from behind to be elected to the nation's highest office. Following the fortunes of Democrat Stephen Douglas, Republican Abraham Lincoln, and a host of others significant to the election, Egerton highlights the central role played by race in the dynamics of political party, sectionalism, and politics generally in the election after which the nation was plunged into Civil War. . . . Heavily documented, relying on substantial primary and manuscript sources, this book sheds new light on an often researched topic. All those with an interest in the importance of race in the nation's history will want to acquire this highly readable work." Libr J

Includes bibliographical references and index.

Eicher, David J.

The **longest** night; a military history of the Civil War. foreword by James M. McPherson; maps by Lee Vande Visse. Simon & Schuster 2001 990p maps $40; pa $22   **973.7**

1. United States -- History -- 1861-1865, Civil War -- Campaigns

ISBN 0-684-84944-5; 0-684-84945-3 pa

LC 2001-34153

An account of battles and military strategies in the Civil War

"Civil War buffs and military history scholars will find Eicher's superb analyses and original insights into oft-neglected theaters of operations extremely valuable. An important work that will be an essential component of Civil War collections." Booklist

Includes bibliographical references

★ **Encyclopedia** of the American Civil War; a political, social, and military history. David S. Heidler and Jeanne T. Heidler, editors; foreword by James W. McPherson; David J. Coles, associate editor; Gary W. Gallagher, James M. McPherson, Mark E. Neely, Jr., editorial board. ABC-CLIO 2000 5v il maps set $425   **973.7**

1. Reference books 2. United States -- History -- 1861-1865, Civil War -- Encyclopedias

ISBN 1-57607-066-2

LC 00-11195

ALA RUSA Dartmouth Medal honorable mention (2001)

"The editors have compiled a comprehensive source that provides a first-stop reference on broad areas or specific topics on the Civil War. The contemporary photographs and lithographs bring the human element into the encyclopedia, a type of reference known more for facts and figures than emotions. The primary-source-documents volume brings obscure resources together, which will further illumine the period for students."—"Outstanding Reference Sources." American Libraries, May 2001

Includes bibliographical references

Faust, Drew Gilpin

Mothers of invention; women of the slaveholding South in the American Civil War. University of N.C. Press 1996 326p il $37.50; pa $19.95 **973.7**

1. Women -- Southern States 2. United States -- History -- 1861-1865, Civil War -- Women

ISBN 0-8078-2255-8; 0-8078-5573-1 pa

LC 95-8896

Based on journals, letters and memoirs, this is an "analysis of the impact of secession, invasion and conquest on Southern white women. Antebellum images based on helplessness and dependence were challenged as women assumed an increasing range of social and economic responsibilities. . . . Faust's provocative analysis of a complex subject merits a place in all collections of U.S. history." Publ Wkly

Includes bibliographical references

This republic of suffering; death and the American Civil War. Alfred A. Knopf 2008 346p il $27.95   **973.7**

1. Death 2. United States -- History -- 1861-1865, Civil War

ISBN 978-0-375-40404-7; 0-375-40404-X

LC 2007-14658

The author "surveys the many ways the Civil War generation coped with the trauma: the concept of the Good Death—conscious, composed and at peace with God; the rise of the embalming industry; the sad attempts of the bereaved to get confirmation of a soldier's death, sometimes years after war's end; the swelling national movement to recover soldiers' remains and give them decent burials; the intellectual quest to find meaning—or its absence—in the war's carnage. . . . The result is an insightful, often moving portrait of a people torn by grief." Publ Wkly

Includes bibliographical references

Fellman, Michael

The **making** of Robert E. Lee. Johns Hopkins Univ. Press 2003 360p il pa $19.95   **973.7**

1. Generals 2. College presidents 3. United States -- History -- 1861-1865, Civil War

ISBN 0-8018-7411-4

LC 2002-43290

First published 2000 by Random House

"Struggling to subdue his ambitions and passions in a peacetime military career whose monotony was only momentarily breached by the Mexican American War and at Harpers Ferry, Lee found in the Civil War a chance to express himself fully. In a study rich with discussions of Lee's religious beliefs and political opinions, the author skewers previous efforts to detach Lee from slavery, racism, and the mentality of the Lost Cause. Sure to arouse debate, this book challenges and delights." Libr J

Includes bibliographical references

Ferguson, Andrew

Land of Lincoln; adventures in Abe's America. Atlantic Monthly Press 2007 279p il $24   **973.7**

1. Lawyers 2. Presidents 3. State legislators 4. Members of Congress 5. United States -- Description and travel

ISBN 978-0-871-13967-2; 0-871-13967-7

LC 2006-52634

An "offbeat tour of Lincoln shrines, statues, cabins and museums. The 16th president comes in many forms, and every one, it seems, has a following, right down to Lincoln the chief executive officer, dispenser of corporate leadership tips. . . . Along with the silly statues, the bogus exhibits and Abe's get-rich-quick tips, Mr. Ferguson includes some genuinely touching, if strange, examples of Lincoln love. . . . The Land of Lincoln turns out to be a big place: bigger than Illinois, bigger even than the United States, stranger than anyone would have thought. Mr. Ferguson maps it expertly, with an understated Midwestern sense of humor that

Lincoln, master of the funny story, would have been the first to appreciate." N Y Times (Late N Y Ed)

Foner, Eric

The **fiery** trial; Abraham Lincoln and American slavery. W.W. Norton 2010 426p il map $29.95   **973.7**
1. Presidents 2. State legislators 3. Members of Congress 4. Biography, Individual 5. Slavery -- United States 6. Slaves -- Emancipation -- United States
ISBN 978-0-393-06618-0; 0-393-06618-5
LC 2010-23425

The book presents "a sustained argument for [U.S. President Abraham] Lincoln's growth into greatness." (London Review of Books) It presents the "history of Lincoln and the end of slavery in America" with a particular focus on "his capacity for moral and political growth through real engagement with allies and critics alike . . . Although 'naturally anti-slavery' . . . Lincoln . . . holds to the position that the Constitution protects the institution in the original slave states. But the political landscape is transformed in 1854 when the Kansas-Nebraska Act makes the expansion of slavery a national issue. . . . Lincoln navigates the dynamic politics . . . taking measured steps, often along a path forged by abolitionists and radicals in his party . . . As president of a divided nation and commander in chief at war . . . Lincoln finally embraces what he calls the Civil War's 'fundamental and astounding' result: the immediate, uncompensated abolition of slavery and recognition of blacks as American citizens." (books.wwnorton.com)

The author "explores the evolution—from frontier lawyer to Great Emancipator—of Lincoln's thought about and response to slavery. The book . . . showcases Foner's engaging style and insight, while keeping a tight focus on Lincoln in his own historical context. [This work] explains how a man who was more skilled politician than reformer came to issue one of the most sweeping, consequential edicts in American history." Am Scholar

Includes bibliographical references

Foote, Shelby

The **Civil** War; a narrative. Random House 1958 3v maps set $165; pa $75   **973.7**
1. United States -- History -- 1861-1865, Civil War
ISBN 0-394-49517-9; 0-394

"In objectivity, in range, in mastery of detail, in beauty of language and feeling for the people involved, this work surpasses anything else on the subject." New Repub

Includes bibliographical references

Ford, Lacy K.

Deliver us from evil; the slavery question in the old South. Oxford University Press 2009 673p $34.95   **973.7**
1. Slavery -- United States 2. Southern States -- History 3. Southern States -- Race relations 4. Slavery -- United States -- History
ISBN 0-19-511809-X; 978-0-19-511809-4
LC 2008-47533

This book focuses "on the period from the drafting of the federal consitution in 1787 through the age of Jackson. . . . [Ford] examines the political, intellectual, economic , and

social thought of leading white southerners." (N Y Times Book Rev) Index.

This book provides "an intricate, textured argument about the intellectual, social, and political interests shaping 'the slavery question,' as well as a reminder that Southern white commitment to a hardened proslavery position was not preordained or one-dimensional. Essential for all students of this subject." Libr J

Includes bibliographical references

Foreman, Amanda

A **world** on fire; Britain's crucial role in the American Civil War. Random House 2011 958p il map $35   **973.7**
1. United States -- History -- 1861-1865, Civil War
2. Great Britain -- Foreign relations -- United States
3. United States -- Foreign relations -- Great Britain
4. United States -- History -- Civil War, 1861-1865 -- Participation, British 5. United States -- History -- Civil War, 1861-1865 -- Foreign public opinion, British
ISBN 0-375-50494-X; 978-0-375-50494-5
First published 2010 in the United Kingdom

Amanda Foreman tells the "story of the American Civil War and the major role played by Britain and its citizens in that struggle. . . . Between 1861 and 1865, thousands of British citizens volunteered for service on both sides of the Civil War. From the first cannon blasts on Fort Sumter to Lee's surrender at Appomattox, they served as officers and infantrymen, sailors and nurses, blockade runners and spies." (Publisher's note)

"Ranging from the drawing rooms of Washington and London to the battlefields of Gettysburg and Antietam, to the high seas, and to Confederate and Union home fronts, Foreman has written a diplomatic, military, and social kaleidoscope of the Civil War. She superbly conveys the horror, pathos, and chaos of battle, the political and moral ambiguities, and the devotion of those who fought. She has also restored an international dimension missing from many histories. The fall of Fort Sumter in April 1861 set off a furious diplomatic contest between North and South for the favors of Great Britain, then the world's superpower. Britain had a tangle of economic interests in the United States; it was bound to the South by cotton, which kept the British textile industry spinning, and British investors held millions in stocks and securities." Boston Globe

Fredrickson, George M.

Big enough to be inconsistent; Abraham Lincoln confronts slavery and race. Harvard University Press 2008 156p (The W.E.B. Du Bois lectures) $19.95   **973.7**
1. Lawyers 2. Presidents 3. State legislators 4. Members of Congress 5. Slavery -- United States 6. African Americans -- Civil rights
ISBN 978-0-674-02774-9; 0-674-02774-4
LC 2007-34018

The author "wades into a controversial arena: was Lincoln a heroic emancipator or a racist who didn't care about slaves at all? Stating that in between 'pathological' racism and egalitarianism lies a spectrum of possibilities, Fredrickson says that Lincoln is not easily classified. . . . This brief book will be widely discussed by historians and will provide nonacademic readers a lucid introduction to some of the most heated debates about the 16th president." Publ Wkly

Includes bibliographical references

Fredriksen, John C.

Civil War almanac. Facts on File, Inc. 2007 858p il map (Almanacs of American wars) $85   **973.7**

  1. United States -- History -- 1861-1865, Civil War

  ISBN 0-8160-6459-8; 978-0-8160-6459-5

                        LC 2006-29985

First published 1983 under the editorship of John Stewart Bowman

This book contains a "day-by-day chronology of the events and people of this monumental war, along with an A-to-Z dictionary offering biographical information on leading military and political figures involved in the conflict." Publisher's note

Includes bibliographical references

Freeman, Douglas Southall

Lee; an abridgment in one volume, by Richard Harwell, of the four-volume R. E. Lee. with a new foreword by James M. McPherson. Scribner 1991 xxiii, 601p il maps hardcover o.p. pa $18   **973.7**

  1. Generals 2. College presidents 3. United States -- History -- 1861-1865, Civil War

  ISBN 0-684-82953-3 pa

                        LC 91-20088

First published 1961

"Students of history will continue to want and to use the original four-volume work but most general readers will find this abridgment more convenient and adequate to their interest. All footnotes and all of the appendix have been omitted as well as details of Civil War action that are not necessary to show the main course of Lee's life and action." Booklist

Furgurson, Ernest B.

Chancellorsville, 1863; the souls of the brave. Knopf 1992 405p il maps hardcover o.p. pa $16   **973.7**

  1. Chancellorsville (Va.), Battle of, 1863

  ISBN 0-679-72831-7 pa

                        LC 91-47059

"Mr. Furgurson has written what should become the standard account of the battle. He is especially good at discussing both larger tactical issues and the experiences of ordinary soldiers. He is also evenhanded." N Y Times Book Rev

Includes bibliographical references

Freedom rising; Washington in the Civil War. Knopf 2004 463p il hardcover o.p. pa $16 **973.7**

  1. Lawyers 2. Presidents 3. State legislators 4. Washington (D.C.) 5. Members of Congress 6. United States -- History -- 1861-1865, Civil War

  ISBN 0-375-40454-6; 0-375-70409-4 pa

                    LC 2004-40820

"Furgurson paints a compelling portrait of a dynamic, rapidly evolving city on edge. . . . This is a well-written and informative account of a city and its citizens passing through a traumatic national ordeal." Booklist

Includes bibliographical references

Not war but murder; Cold Harbor, 1864. Knopf 2000 328p il maps hardcover o.p. pa $14   **973.7**

  1. Cold Harbor (Va.), Battle of, 1864

  ISBN 0-679-78139-0 pa

                        LC 99-37147

The author's "engagement with the people he writes about comes through in every line, making one of the most wrenching incidents of the war grimly immediate." Publ Wkly

Includes bibliographical references

Gallagher, Gary W.

The **Confederate** War. Harvard Univ. Press 1997 218p il hardcover o.p.   **973.7**

  1. Confederate States of America 2. United States -- History -- 1861-1865, Civil War

                        LC 97-2495

This book "is the best thing that has happened to Confederate historiography in many years. Gallagher has a more thorough command of the sources for Confederate history than any other historian I have read and he brings that mastery to bear in a concise, hard-hitting book." NY Rev Books

Includes bibliographical references

The **union** war. Harvard University Press 2011 215p il $27.95   **973.7**

  1. United States -- History -- 1861-1865, Civil War 2. United States -- History -- Civil War, 1861-1865 3. United States -- Politics and government -- 1861-1865 4. Popular culture -- United States -- History -- 19th century

  ISBN 978-0-674-04562-0; 0-674-04562-9

                    LC 2010-51977

In this book, "Gary Gallagher argues . . . that Northerners, ranging from President Lincoln all the way down to the conscripts in the Army of the Potomac, didn't fight the Civil War to free the slaves or to topple white supremacy in the South. Instead, they fought for the Union, an admittedly diffuse concept, Gallagher admits, but nevertheless their central animating principle." (Times Literary Supplement)

"Gallagher offers not so much a history of wartime patriotism as a series of meditations on the meaning of the Union to Northerners, the role of slavery in the conflict and how historians have interpreted (and in his view misinterpreted) these matters." N Y Times Book Rev

Includes bibliographical references

Gienapp, William E.

Abraham Lincoln and Civil War America; a biography. Oxford Univ. Press 2001 239p il maps hardcover o.p. pa $24.95   **973.7**

  1. Presidents 2. State legislators 3. Members of Congress 4. Presidents -- United States 5. United States -- History -- 1861-1865, Civil War

  ISBN 0-19-515099-6; 0-19-515100-3 pa

                    LC 2001-50056

This biography focuses on the American president's leadership during the Civil War.

"In spite of the book's size, its discriminating history of Lincoln's life is surprisingly rich, and the narrative of his presidency and the unfolding of the war is crisp and coherent." Bookmarks

Includes bibliographical references

Goldfield, David R.

★ **America** aflame; how the Civil War created a nation. [by] David Goldfield. Bloomsbury Press 2011 632p il $35   **973.7**

1. United States -- History -- 1861-1865, Civil War -- Causes 2. United States -- History -- Civil War, 1861-1865 -- Causes 3. United States -- History -- Civil War, 1861-1865 -- Campaigns 4. United States -- History -- Civil War, 1861-1865 -- Influence 5. United States -- History -- Civil War, 1861-1865 -- Social aspects 6. United States -- History -- Civil War, 1861-1865 -- Religious aspects

ISBN 978-1-59691-702-6; 1-59691-702-4

LC 2010-25241

"A provocatively written, scrupulously researched, and well-framed consideration of evangelical religion's questionable role in the antebellum, Civil War, and Reconstruction periods of our history." Libr J

Includes bibliographical references

Goodheart, Adam

★ **1861**; the Civil War awakening. 1st ed.; Alfred A. Knopf 2011 481p il $28.95   **973.7**

1. United States -- Intellectual life 2. United States -- Politics and government -- 1861-1865 3. United States -- History -- 1861-1865, Civil War -- Causes

ISBN 978-1-4000-4015-5; 1-4000-4015-9

LC 2010-51326

"Goodheart leads us on a journey through the frenzied, frightening months between Abraham Lincoln's election to the presidency in 1860 — followed with breakneck speed by the secession of the Confederate States and the outbreak of war — and July 4, 1861, when President Lincoln delivered his first message to Congress, laying out the case not only for the necessity of war, but for a more democratic vision of the United States. The election of Lincoln and the secession crisis is, of course, familiar terrain. But Goodheart's version is at once more panoramic and more intimate than most standard accounts, and more inspiring. This is fundamentally a history of hearts and minds, rather than of legislative bills and battles." N Y Times Book Rev

Gopnik, Adam

Angels and ages; a short book about Darwin, Lincoln, and modern life. Alfred A. Knopf 2009 211p $24.95   **973.7**

1. Presidents 2. Naturalists 3. Modern civilization 4. Travel writers 5. State legislators 6. Writers on science 7. Members of Congress

ISBN 978-0-307-27078-8; 0-307-27078-5

LC 2008-36224

"The book is worth reading . . . for the author's unquestioned skill as a craftsman and the light he sheds on what has become, for many, settled history." Bookmarks

Groom, Winston

Shiloh, 1862; the first great and terrible battle of the civil war. Winston Groom. National Geographic Books 2012 446 p.   **973.7**

1. Shiloh (Tenn.), Battle of, 1862 2. Tennessee -- History -- 1861-1865, Civil War 3. United States -- History -- 1861-1865, Civil War -- Campaigns 4. Shiloh, Battle of, Tenn., 1862 5. Tennessee -- History -- Civil War, 1861-1865 -- Campaigns 6. United States -- History -- Civil War, 1861-1865 -- Campaigns

ISBN 9781426208744

LC 2012372339

This book "presents Shiloh, fought on April 6-7 in western Tennessee, as a turning point in the [U.S. Civil War]." (Kirkus) "[Winston] Groom . . . compels the reader to appreciate the enormous toll to both sides owing to advanced arms, outmoded battle tactics, and poor generalship. Although Groom lays responsibility on both sides, he especially blames General [Ulysses] Grant and General [William] Sherman . . . for failure to fortify positions, properly reconnoiter, read the signs of enemy advances, and have a battle plan in case of attack. . . . Groom sees Shiloh as a learning experience for Grant, who finally understood that no single battle, no matter how costly or geographically significant, could end the rebellion: the Union could be restored only through the total conquest of the South." (Libr J)

Includes bibliographical references (p. 409-419) and index

Vicksburg, 1863. Alfred A. Knopf 2009 482p il $30   **973.7**

1. Vicksburg (Miss.) -- Siege, 1863 2. United States -- History -- 1861-1865, Civil War -- Campaigns

ISBN 978-0-307-26425-1

LC 2008-45984

The author "recalls the Union's campaign against Vicksburg, Miss., 'the Gibraltar of the West.'" Kirkus

"Rarely has the story of such a lengthy and complicated campaign been told with such clarity and grace." Washington Post

Includes bibliographical references

Guelzo, Allen C.

Gettysburg; the last invasion. by Allen C. Guelzo. 1st ed. Alfred A. Knopf 2013 xix, 632 p., 16 unnumbered pages of platesp ill., maps (hardcover) $35   **973.7**

1. Gettysburg (Pa.), Battle of, 1863 2. United States -- History -- 1861-1865, Civil War 3. Gettysburg, Battle of, Gettysburg, Pa., 1863

ISBN 0307594084; 9780307594082

LC 2012047013

The book offers an account of the battle of Gettysburg. Though "the battle site was not inevitable, the actual battle was . . . . The Union had reason to be concerned, but, as [Allen C.] Guelzo documents, their foe was scattered and divided, with rivalries and miscommunication . . . keeping James Longstreet from attacking, J.E.B. Stuart from arriving on the battlefield in time, and the much-disliked George Pickett from enjoying a better fate than being cannon fodder." (Kirkus Reviews)

Includes bibliographical references (pages 483-599)

and index.

Harper, Judith E.

Women during the Civil War; an encyclopedia. Routledge 2003 472p il map $170; pa $59.95 **973.7**
1. Reference books 2. United States -- History -- 1861-1865, Civil War -- Women -- Encyclopedias
ISBN 0-415-93723-X; 0-415-95574-2 pa

LC 2003-7181

"The 128 entries range in length from 400 to 4000 words, and include biographies of women from all regions of the U.S. Well-known figures such as Harriet Tubman, Clara Barton, Louisa May Alcott, and Mary Todd Lincoln are represented but so too are African-American sculptor Edmonia Lewis, poet Lucy Larcom, and Emma LeConte. . . . As well as biographies, there are superb thematic entries on women living in the West, prostitutes, industrial workers, family life, and invasion and occupation. . . . This encyclopedia is a welcomed addition to reference collections." SLJ

Includes bibliographical references

Hearts touched by fire; the best of battles and leaders of the Civil War. edited with an introduction by Harold Holzer; with contributions by James M. McPherson ... [et al.] Modern Library 2011 xxiii, 1230p il map $38 **973.7**
1. United States -- History -- 1861-1865, Civil War -- Personal narratives
ISBN 978-0-679-64364-7

An anthology of excerpts from the four-volume classic "Battles and Leaders of the Civil War" features firsthand recollections by the Civil War's commanders and subordinates on both sides, with commentary by such leading scholars as James McPherson and Joan Waugh.

Horwitz, Tony

Confederates in the attic; dispatches from the unfinished Civil War. Pantheon Bks. 1998 406p map hardcover o.p. pa $14.95 **973.7**
1. United States -- History -- 1861-1865, Civil War
ISBN 0-679-75833-X pa

LC 97-26759

According to Horwitz's "chronicle of his tour of the Old South, many people have yet to make peace with the past. In a South Carolina town, whites relate to Horwitz their pride in the 'lost cause,' even equating southern valor with the courage of Martin Luther King; a black preacher explains that affection for the 'cause' strikes him as an endorsement of slavery. Esteemed Civil War scholar Shelby Foote strives to explain the origins of the Klan as the reaction to a perceived foreign occupation." Booklist

This "is the work of a skilled journalist looking at how—and why—the War Between the States continues to live in so many issues still with us." Libr J

Howard, David

Lost rights; the misadventures of a stolen American relic. Houghton Mifflin Harcourt 2009 344p $26 **973.7**
1. Theft 2. Manuscripts 3. United States -- Constitution

-- 1st-10th amendments
ISBN 978-0-618-82607-0; 0-618-82607-6

LC 2009-18046

"The tale pulsates with dynamic personalities greatly affected by their connection to one of the rarest, most influential and valuable documents in American history. Howard has produced a marvelously compelling read." Publ Wkly

Includes bibliographical references

Hyslop, Stephen G.

Atlas of the Civil War; a comprehensive guide to the tactics and terrain of battle. edited by Neil Kagan; narrative by Stephen G. Hyslop; introduction by Harris J. Andrews. National Geographic Society 2009 255p il map $40 **973.7**
1. Reference books 2. Historical atlases 3. United States -- History -- 1861-1865, Civil War -- Maps
ISBN 978-1-4262-0347-3

LC 2008-35066

"Arranged chronologically, this atlas combines period photographs and illustrations, rare period maps and modern cartography, with just enough narrative to explain the two-page spread devoted to each subject (the majority being about particular battles or campaigns). . . . The text also features numerous sidebars throughout, offering micro-timelines, biographies, and images showing the human side of the war. All of these special features make this large-format atlas a superior choice for Civil War buffs as well as those new to the subject." Libr J

Katz, Harry L.

Civil War sketch book; drawings from the battlefront. Harry L. Katz and Vincent Virga ; with a preface by Alan Brinkley. W.W. Norton & Co Inc. 2012 xxv, 251 p.p col. ill. (hardcover) $50 **973.7**
1. United States -- History -- 1861-1865, Civil War -- Pictorial works 2. United States -- History -- 1861-1865, Civil War -- Personal narratives 3. Drawing, American -- 19th century 4. United States -- History -- Civil War, 1861-1865 -- Art and the war 5. United States -- History -- Civil War, 1861-1865 -- Pictorial works
ISBN 0393072207; 9780393072204

LC 2011044004

In this book, Harry L. Katz and Vincent Virga "look at the illustrators—including Winslow Homer and Thomas Nast—who covered the war for popular newspapers of the time . . . by traveling with the troops and sketching among the dead and wounded as well as bullets, fire, and the general chaos of the battlefield. . . . The book's text, which follows the chronology of the war, includes selections from the artists' letters, logbooks, diaries, and other firsthand accounts." (Library Journal)

Includes bibliographical references and index

Keegan, John

The **American** Civil War; a military history. Alfred A. Knopf 2009 396p il map $35 **973.7**
1. Military geography -- United States 2. United States -- History -- 1861-1865, Civil War -- Campaigns
ISBN 978-0-307-26343-8; 0-307-26343-6

LC 2009-19469

This book provides accounts of Civil War battles, "from Sumter to Shiloh, from Antietam to Chickamauga, to William Tecumseh Sherman's march to the sea." N Y Times (Late N Y Ed)

The author "provides the single best one-volume assessment of the military character and conduct of America's ordeal by fire." Libr J

Includes bibliographical references

Klein, Maury

Days of defiance; Sumter, secession, and the coming of the Civil War. Knopf 1997 496p il hardcover o.p. pa $16   973.7

1. United States -- History -- 1861-1865, Civil War

ISBN 0-679-76882-3 pa

LC 96-39156

This is "a study of the months between Abraham Lincoln's election and the outbreak of hostilities at Fort Sumter on April 12, 1861." New Leader

"With a novelist's skill, Klein has crafted an engrossing portrait of the nation's descent into chaos and war." Publ Wkly

Includes bibliographical references

Krauthamer, Barbara

Envisioning emancipation; Black Americans and the end of slavery. Deborah Willis and Barbara Krauthamer. Temple University Press 2013 223 p. ill. (cloth : alk. paper) $35   973.7

1. Slaves -- Emancipation 2. Slavery -- United States 3. African Americans -- Portraits 4. Documentary photography -- United States 5. Historiography and photography -- United States 6. African Americans -- History -- 1863-1877 -- Pictorial works 7. United States -- History -- Civil War, 1861-1865 -- African Americans -- Pictorial works

ISBN 1439909857; 9781439909850

LC 2012032600

This book is a collection "of nearly 150 photographs reaching from the mid-19th to the early 20th century" that are meant to help readers "contemplate not only the history of slavery and emancipation but also our continued ties to that history and its legacies." Subjects include the "escaped slave Dolly pictured on a reward notice, a group gathered for a 1916 slave reunion, Emancipation Day celebrations, fugitives fording a river, chimney sweeps, family groups, and penal slavery crews." (Publishers Weekly)

Includes bibliographical references and index

Leonard, Elizabeth D.

All the daring of the soldier; women of the Civil War armies. Norton 1999 368p il hardcover o.p. pa $22.95   973.7

1. Women soldiers 2. United States -- Army 3. Confederate States of America -- Army 4. United States -- History -- 1861-1865, Civil War

ISBN 978-0-393-04712-7; 0-393-04712-1; 978-0-393-33547-7 pa; 0-393-33547-X pa

LC 98-52304

The author presents "stories of dozens of women who served in both the Union and Confederacy during the Civil War. Some were spies, but many more adopted men's

names, dressed in men's clothes and lived and fought and died alongside mostly unsuspecting men." Publ Wkly

Includes bibliographical references

Levine, Bruce

The **fall** of the house of Dixie; how the Civil War remade the American South. Bruce Levine. Random House 2013 xix, 439 p., [16] p. of platesp ill., map $30   973.7

1. Confederate States of America -- History 2. United States -- History -- 1861-1865, Civil War 3. Confederate States of America 4. Confederate States of America -- Social conditions 5. Confederate States of America -- Economic conditions 6. Elite (Social sciences) -- Southern States -- History -- 19th century 7. Slavery -- Social aspects -- Southern States -- History -- 19th century 8. Slavery -- Economic aspects -- Southern States -- History -- 19th century

ISBN 1400067030; 9780679645351; 9781400067039

LC 2011048310

In this book Bruce Levine tells the "story of how [the American Civil War] upended the economic, political, and social life of the old South, utterly destroying the Confederacy and the society it represented and defended. Told through the words of the people who lived it, 'The Fall of the House of Dixie' illuminates the way a war undertaken to preserve the status quo became a second American Revolution whose impact on the country was as strong and lasting as that of our first." (Publishing note)

Includes bibliographical references (p. [377]-415) and index.

Lincoln, Abraham, 1809-1865

Lincoln on war; edited and with an introduction by Harold Holzer. Algonquin Books of Chapel Hill 2011 xxvi, 304p il $24.95; ebook $24.95   973.7

1. United States -- History -- 1861-1865, Civil War -- Sources

ISBN 978-1-56512-378-6; 978-1-61620-060-2 ebook

LC 2010-44569

"A wisely chosen, expertly arranged collection." Kirkus

★ **Speeches** and writings, 1859-1865; speeches, letters, and miscellaneous writings, presidential messages and proclamations. Library of Am. 1989 xxxiii, 787p $35   973.7

1. United States -- Politics and government -- 1861-1865

ISBN 0-940450-63-1

LC 89-45349

This volume is based upon The Collected Works of Abraham Lincoln. It includes public statements, business letters, "poems, personal letters, telegrams to generals in the field, and other [writings]." Libr J

Includes bibliographical references

Lubet, Steven

John Brown's spy; the adventurous life and tragic confession of John E. Cook. Steven Lubet. Yale University Press 2012 325 p. (cloth : alk. paper) $28   973.7

1. Harpers Ferry (W. Va.) -- History -- John Brown's

Raid, 1859
ISBN 0300180497; 9780300180497

LC 2012019509

This book by Steven Lubet tells the story "of John E. Cook, the person John Brown trusted most with the details of his plans to capture the Harper's Ferry armory in 1859. Cook was a poet, a marksman, a boaster, a dandy, a fighter, and a womanizer--as well as a spy. In a life of only thirty years, he studied law in Connecticut, fought border ruffians in Kansas, served as an abolitionist mole in Virginia, [and] took white hostages during the Harper's Ferry raid." (Publisher's note)

Includes bibliographical references and index

Marten, James

Civil War America; voices from the home front. ABC-CLIO 2003 346p il $85 **973.7**
1. United States -- History -- 1861-1865, Civil War -- Personal narratives
ISBN 1-576-07237-1

LC 2002-154377

"Marten offers a view of the war through the eyes of diverse noncombatants. Four parts of this five-part work each deal with Southerners, Northerners, children, and African Americans . . . Part five, 'Aftermaths,' includes descriptions of the postwar lives of veterans, orphans, and ex-slaves, and concludes with a chapter on the Civil War stories by Ambrose Bierce. Readers will find Marten's overarching theme of change—both immediate and long-range—revelatory and instructional." SLJ

Includes bibliographical references

Masur, Louis P.

The **Civil** War: a concise history. Oxford University Press 2011 118p il $18.95 **973.7**
1. United States -- History -- 1861-1865, Civil War
ISBN 978-0-19-974048-2

LC 2010-19460

The author provides "a concise but compelling narrative of the Civil War era, packing in the critical information to track the trajectory of secession, war, emancipation, and Reconstruction. He focuses on the political and the military, with Lincoln, Jefferson Davis, and the generals especially getting their due." Libr J

Includes bibliographical references

McPherson, James M.

Abraham Lincoln and the second American Revolution. Oxford Univ. Press 1991 173p hardcover o.p. pa $16.95 **973.7**
1. Presidents 2. State legislators 3. Members of Congress 4. United States -- History -- 1861-1865, Civil War
ISBN 0-19-507606-0 pa

LC 90-6885

The author "examines Lincoln's role in the transformation wrought by the Civil War—the liberation of four million slaves, the overthrow of the social and political order of the South." Publ Wkly

Includes bibliographical references

Battle cry of freedom; the Civil War era. Oxford Univ. Press 1988 904p il maps (Oxford history of the United States) $47.50; pa $18.95 **973.7**
1. United States -- History -- 1861-1865, Civil War
ISBN 0-19-503863-0; 0-19-516895-X pa

LC 87-11045

A narrative history of events from the Mexican War through Appomattox. The author describes military campaigns, tactics and leaders. How the war changed the American political, social and economic landscape is explored

This volume "is comprehensive yet succinct, scholarly without being pedantic, eloquent but unrhetorical. It is compellingly readable." N Y Times Book Rev

Includes bibliographical references

Drawn with the sword; reflections on the American Civil War. Oxford Univ. Press 1996 258p $45; pa $18.95 **973.7**
1. Authors 2. Lawyers 3. Generals 4. Novelists 5. Statesmen 6. Presidents 7. Abolitionists 8. Vice-presidents 9. Orators 10. State legislators 11. Children's authors 12. Nonfiction writers 13. Secretaries of war 14. Members of Congress 15. Short story writers 16. Secretaries of state 17. Glory (Motion picture) 18. Emancipation Proclamation (1863) 19. United States -- History -- 1861-1865, Civil War
ISBN 0-19-509679-7; 0-19-511796-4 pa

LC 95-38107

"These pieces provide a lively reminder that the best scholarship is also often a pleasure to read." N Y Times Book Rev

For cause and comrades; why men fought in the Civil War. Oxford Univ. Press 1997 237p $25; pa $15.95 **973.7**
1. Soldiers -- United States 2. United States -- History -- 1861-1865, Civil War
ISBN 0-19-509023-3; 0-19-512499-5 pa

LC 96-24760

"Volumes have been written on the causes of the Civil War, but less has been written on what caused soldiers to risk their lives on the battlefield. McPherson . . . fills the gap. After studying thousands of letters and diaries, he discusses what really led soldiers to enlist, what kept them in the army, and what led them to the front lines." Libr J

Includes bibliographical references

Hallowed ground; a walk at Gettysburg. Crown Publishers 2003 144p map (Crown Journeys series) $16 **973.7**
1. Gettysburg (Pa.), Battle of, 1863
ISBN 0-609-61023-6

LC 2002-35154

"If it were only a pointer to the physical ground and commemorative markers, this guide would be ordinary, but McPherson so articulately injects reminders—as of a free black farmer who fled the approaching battle lest Confederates enslave him—of what the Civil War was about as to display the crystalline style that has made him one of our finest Civil War historians." Booklist

★ **This** mighty scourge; perspectives on the Civil War. Oxford University Press 2007 260p $28 **973.7**
1. Presidents 2. State legislators 3. Members of Congress 4. United States -- History -- 1861-1865, Civil War
ISBN 0-19-531366-6

LC 2006-35523

These essays "stand as a remarkably elegant and clarifying narrative exploration of the most basic questions concerning the Civil War, issues over which scholars and activists still contend. . . 'This Mighty Scourge,' in fact, is an exemplary exercise in the contribution a great historian and eloquent writer can make to a people's understanding of themselves." Los Angeles Times

Nolan, Alan T.
Lee considered; General Robert E. Lee and Civil War history. University of N.C. Press 1991 231p il $29.95; pa $16.95 **973.7**
1. Generals 2. College presidents 3. United States -- History -- 1861-1865, Civil War
ISBN 0-8078-1956-5; 0-8078-4587-6 pa

LC 90-48296

"Nolan uses sources cleverly to build his case and adroitly pits this new 'truth' against the words of Lee's historically staunchest promoters." Booklist
Includes bibliographical references

Oakes, James
Freedom national; the destruction of slavery in the United States, 1861-1865. James Oakes. W. W. Norton & Co. 2013 608 p. (hardcover) $29.95 **973.7**
1. Slavery -- United States 2. Slaves -- Emancipation -- United States 3. United States -- History -- 1861-1865, Civil War 4. Slavery -- United States -- History 5. United States -- History -- Civil War, 1861-1865 6. Antislavery movements -- United States -- History 7. United States. President (1861-1865 : Lincoln). Emancipation Proclamation
ISBN 0393065316; 9780393065312

LC 2012035601

This book by James Oakes "shows how deftly [Abraham] Lincoln and congressional Republicans pursued antislavery throughout the [American Civil] war, pragmatic in policy but steadfast on principle. . . . As the devastating war continued with slavery still entrenched, Republicans embraced a more aggressive military emancipation, triggered by the Emancipation Proclamation. Finally it took a constitutional amendment on abolition to achieve the Union's primary goal in the war." (Publisher's note)
Includes bibliographical references and index

Paludan, Phillip S.
The **presidency** of Abraham Lincoln; {by} Phillip Shaw Paludan. University Press of Kan. 1994 xx, 384p (American presidency series) $29.95; pa $15.95 **973.7**
1. Presidents 2. State legislators 3. Members of Congress 4. United States -- Politics and government

-- 1861-1865
ISBN 0-7006-0671-8; 0-7006-0745-5 pa

LC 93-46830

The author "traces the year-by-year chronology of a Presidency engaged with recruiting, placating, appeasing and coercing the various and competing factions of the war years, and sees in Lincoln 'a commitment to the political-constitutional system that would itself move the nation toward its highest ambitions.' . . . Equally interesting is Mr. Paludan's depiction of how the war transformed the national Government, not only establishing the foundations for the Gilded Age but more subtly strengthening and enriching the role of government." NY Times Book Rev
Includes bibliographical references

Perry, James M.
Touched with fire; five presidents and the Civil War battles that made them. PublicAffairs 2003 335p il map $26; pa $16 **973.7**
1. Generals 2. Governors 3. Presidents 4. Senators 5. Members of Congress 6. Presidents -- United States 7. United States -- History -- 1861-1865, Civil War
ISBN 1-586-48114-2; 1-586-48290-4 pa

LC 2003-46625

"All chief executives during the Gilded Age volunteered for the Union in the Civil War (excluding Grover Cleveland, who paid for a substitute). Perry here recounts their war records with an eye to the subsequent electoral advertising of their bravery and patriotism. . . . Perry, a wry storyteller, delivers the regimental-level detail that buffs crave while dusting events with the skepticism that presidential electoral campaigning invites." Booklist
Includes bibliographical references

Pitch, Anthony
They have killed Papa dead! the road to Ford's Theatre, Abraham Lincoln's murder, and the rage for vengeance. Steerforth Press 2008 493p il $29.95 **973.7**
1. Presidents 2. State legislators 3. Members of Congress 4. Presidents -- United States -- Assassination 5. United States -- Politics and government -- 1861-1865
ISBN 978-1-5864-2158-8; 1-5864-2158-1

LC 2008-43222

The author presents "new evidence that Lincoln was under genuine threat as early as the eve of his first inauguration, not just after his second one. The result is a fast-moving telling of the multiple plots on Lincoln's life, the implementation of the successful one, its complex aftermath and the way it threw the nation into deep mourning and despair. . . . A real page-turner about real history." Publ Wkly
Includes bibliographical references

Rable, George C.
God's almost chosen peoples; a religious history of the American Civil War. University of North Carolina Press 2010 586p il (Littlefield history of the Civil War era) $35 **973.7**
1. United States -- History -- 1861-1865, Civil War -- Religious aspects
ISBN 978-0-8078-3426-8; 0-8078-3426-2

LC 2010-23646

This book offers a history of the religious aspects of the U.S. Civil War, with "archival research and . . . [a] reading that reaches beyond the war's marquee names to exhume the voices and jottings of ministers, diarists, and combatants, who never fail to remark the presence (or absence) of God in the proceedings. Indeed, the stated occasion for [George C.] Rable's study is the notion that most of the war's actors would judge the scant 'attention to religion' in 'the grand and sweeping narratives of the sectional crisis' to be 'a curious omission.' . . . Rable responds to this curiosity with a religious narrative of the conflict . . . that showcases a war among and between rival interpretations of God's providential guidance." (Journal of Religion)

"Rable draws upon newspapers, sermons, diaries, letters, and journals to show that many people on both sides of the conflict turned to faith to help explain the war's causes, course, and consequences. Rable demonstrates that both Northerners and Southerners tried to make sense of the brutal war by thumbing through their Bibles, listening to their preachers, and interpreting battles as a fulfillment of a divine plan. . . . Because of its thorough research and its chronicle of the lives of ordinary people, Rable's engrossing study of the role of religion in the Civil War will stand as the definitive religious history of America's most divisive conflict." Publ Wkly

Includes bibliographical references and index

Roper, Robert
Now the drum of war; Walt Whitman and his brothers in the Civil War. Walker & Co. 2008 421p il $28 **973.7**
1. Poets 2. Authors 3. Essayists 4. Army officers 5. United States -- History -- 1861-1865, Civil War
ISBN 978-0-8027-1553-1; 0-8027-1553-2

This is a "history of the Civil War by means of a family portrait, presenting the war through the eyes and words of the Whitman family. . . . The book provides a simultaneous historical perspective on the war and on an exceptional family, giving general readers and students a vivid depiction of both and a deeper understanding of one of America's greatest poets." Libr J

Includes bibliographical references and index

Sears, Stephen W.
★ **Chancellorsville**. Houghton Mifflin 1996 593p hardcover o.p. pa $17 **973.7**
1. Generals 2. Chancellorsville (Va.), Battle of, 1863
ISBN 0-395-87744-X pa
LC 96-31220

In this history of the campaign that ended in Chancellorsville, the author argues that "a chain of errors, assumptions, and communications failures combined with the genuine brilliance and good luck of the Confederates to lead to a stinging if indecisive Union defeat." Booklist

Includes bibliographical references

★ **Gettysburg**. Houghton Mifflin 2003 623p il map $30; pa $17 **973.7**
1. Gettysburg (Pa.), Battle of, 1863
ISBN 0-395-86761-4; 0-618-48538-4 pa
LC 2002-191259

This is an "assessment of the battle of Gettysburg and the events leading up to it. . . . Sears examines several turning points during the battle's buildup and three-day duration. The resulting insights add to the excellent and dramatic narrative flow. . . . For all Civil War collections and academic libraries." Libr J

Includes bibliographical references

★ **Landscape** turned red; the Battle of Antietam. Houghton Mifflin 2003 431p il pa $17 **973.7**
1. Antietam (Md.), Battle of, 1862
ISBN 978-0-618-34419-2; 0-618-34419-5
First published 1983 by Ticknor & Fields

This "account of the Battle of Antietam, the bloodiest day of the Civil War, is wide-ranging, detailed, and copiously documented. Stephen Sears . . . describes the tension-filled days preceding September 17, 1862, especially the political climate of Union pessimism and Confederate optimism. . . . The battle itself is then exhaustively recounted." Booklist

★ **To** the gates of Richmond; the peninsula campaign. Mariner 2001 468p il map pa $17 **973.7**
1. Peninsular Campaign, 1862
ISBN 978-0-618-12713-9; 0-618-12713-5
First published 1992 by Ticknor & Fields

"The campaign on the peninsula between the James and York rivers in Virginia in the spring of 1862 was McClellan's major strategic effort and the first major Union offensive in the East. . . . Sears does an outstanding job in making intelligible an extremely complex campaign." Booklist

Includes bibliographical references

Slotkin, Richard, 1942-
Long Road to Antietam; how the Civil War became a revolution. Richard Slotkin. Liveright Publishing Corporation 2012 512 p. (hardcover) $32.95 **973.7**
1. Emancipation Proclamation 2. United States -- History -- 1861-1865, Civil War 3. Antietam, Battle of, Md., 1862 4. United States. President (1861-1865 : Lincoln). Emancipation Proclamation
ISBN 0871404117; 9780871404114
LC 2012007795

This book looks at the germination of the U.S. Civil War which "became a revolution in summer 1862, when Lincoln acknowledged that peaceful compromise was at that point impossible and thoroughly committed himself to war. First up in this new strategy: the Emancipation Proclamation. As Lincoln clashed with ambitious general George McClellan, the country started on the bloody road to Antietam." (Library Journal)

Includes bibliographical references and index

No quarter; the Battle of the Crater, 1864. Random House 2009 411p il map $28 **973.7**
1. Petersburg (Va.) -- History -- Siege, 1864-1865 2. United States -- History -- 1861-1865, Civil War -- Campaigns
ISBN 978-1-4000-6675-9; 1-4000-6675-1
LC 2008-36260

"By 1864, the North and South had settled into a positional war around Richmond and Petersburg, VA, with trenches, cannon, disease, and delay. Gen. Grant decided to try a mine, digging under a portion of the fortifications and cramming the tunnel with explosives. It was the largest explosion ever seen at the time—and led to a crushing Union defeat, with 4500 dead. There have been lots of books about the Crater, but the eminent Slotkin does a respectable job. Civil War history enthusiasts will want this." Libr J

Includes bibliographical references

Snodgrass, Mary Ellen

★ The **Underground** Railroad; an encyclopedia of people, places, and operations. Sharpe Reference 2007 2v il map set $199   **973.7**

1. Reference books 2. Underground railroad -- Encyclopedias 3. Slavery -- United States -- Encyclopedias

ISBN 978-0-7656-8093-8

LC 2007-9199

The author "has compiled an important and extensively researched encyclopedia of the Underground Railroad. Beginning with a concise, informative general introduction, this ambitious two-volume set neatly identifies the key people, places, documents, organizations, and publications of the Underground Railroad movement, along with significant actions, events, and ideas underlying it in the US and Canada. Offering photographs, bookplates, sketches, and handbills, the set is visually attractive." Choice

Includes bibliographical references

Stout, Harry S.

Upon the altar of the nation : a moral history of the American Civil War. Viking 2006 552p il $29.95   **973.7**

1. United States -- History -- 1861-1865, Civil War

ISBN 0-670-03470-3

LC 2005-42420

The author "examines the evolving rhetoric of warfare, both Northern and Confederate, within the rubric of 'the just war' theory of conflict." Publ Wkly

"Impeccably sourced and highly engaging, the book will surely be controversial—the best histories often are." Booklist

Includes bibliographical references

Swanson, Mark

Atlas of the Civil War, month by month; major battles and troop movements. maps by Mark Swanson, with Jacqueline D. Langley. University of Georgia Press 2004 141p il map $39.95   **973.7**

1. Reference books 2. Historical atlases 3. United States -- History -- 1861-1865, Civil War -- Maps

ISBN 0-8203-2658-5

LC 2004-12264

This Civil War atlas depicts "multiple aspects of the war's action in a month-by-month sequence from April 1861 to June 1865. . . . An absolute must for Civil War studies." Univ Press Books for Public and Second Sch Libr, 2006

Includes bibliographical references

Thomas, Emory M.

Robert E. Lee; a biography. Norton 1995 472p il maps pa $17.95   **973.7**

1. Generals 2. College presidents 3. United States -- History -- 1861-1865, Civil War

ISBN 0-393-31631-9 pa

LC 95-10522

"Civil War historian Thomas presents Lee as neither an icon nor a flawed figure, but rather as a man who made the best of his lot, whose comic vision of life ultimately shaped him into an individual who was both more and less than his legend." Publ Wkly

Includes bibliographical references

Tobin, Jacqueline

Hidden in plain view; the secret story of quilts and the underground railroad. [by] Jacqueline L. Tobin and Raymond G. Dobard. Doubleday 1999 208p il map hardcover o.p. pa $14   **973.7**

1. Quilts 2. Ciphers 3. Underground railroad

ISBN 0-385-49137-9; 0-385-49767-9 pa

LC 98-49804

The authors present the "theory that slaves created quilts coded with patterns to help one another flee to freedom." N Y Times Book Rev

This is "a needed and valuable contribution to the literature of African American culture." Libr J

Includes bibliographical references

Trudeau, Noah Andre

Like men of war; black troops in the Civil War, 1862-1865. Little, Brown 1998 xxii, 548p il maps hardcover o.p. pa $18   **973.7**

1. African American soldiers 2. United States -- History -- 1861-1865, Civil War

ISBN 0-316-85325-9; 0-316-85344-5 pa

LC 97-15380

A "study of the battlefield experiences of black Union regiments. Some 60 maps help the reader make sense of famous engagements (Fort Wagner and the Crater) and notorious incidents (Fort Pillow) in which black soldiers fought, as well as scores of lesser-known clashes. Rich archival research is integrated into a lively narrative that places the raising and deployment of black regiments in broader contexts. This book will become a basic source of information on the subject." Libr J

Includes bibliographical references

Von Drehle, David

Rise to greatness; Abraham Lincoln and America's most perilous year. David Von Drehle. Henry Holt and Co. 2012 480 p. $30.00   **973.7**

1. Military history 2. United States -- History -- 1861-1865, Civil War 3. United States -- History -- Civil War, 1861-1865 4. United States -- Politics and government -- 1861-1865 5. Political leadership -- United States -- History -- 19th century

ISBN 080507970X; 9780805079708

LC 2012013053

In this book, "[David] Von Drehle . . . asserts that 1862 was the transformative year [of the U.S. Civil War] that led directly to the ultimate Union triumph. . . . [V]on Drehle illustrates Lincoln's transformation into a great political and war leader, who learned to manage and effectively utilize the talents of his advisors and decisively assumed the role of commander in chief, dismissing McClellan and beginning the advancement of fighting officers, especially Grant." (Booklist)

Includes bibliographical references and index.

Walters, Kerry

The **Underground** Railroad; a reference guide. Kerry Walters. ABC-CLIO 2012 x, 223 p.p ill. (hardcover : acid-free paper) $58.00; (ebook) $58.00 **973.7**

1. Abolitionists 2. Slavery -- United States -- History 3. Underground railroad -- Encyclopedias 4. Underground railroad 5. Fugitive slaves -- United States -- History 6. Antislavery movements -- United States -- History -- 19th century

ISBN 1598846477; 9781598846478; 9781598846485

LC 2011041517

"This book, part of the Guides to Historic Events in America series, brings into perspective what the Underground Railroad did and how it operated. This guide begins with a chronology from 1690 to 1870, followed by an introduction that attempts to separate the legends from the reality of the times. Subsequent chapters cover the major aspects of slavery and the Underground Railroad." (Booklist)

Includes bibliographical references and index.

Ward, Andrew

★ The **slaves'** war; the Civil War in the words of former slaves. Houghton Mifflin Co. 2008 386p il $28 **973.7**

1. Slavery -- United States 2. Freedmen -- United States 3. Slaves -- Southern States -- Biography 4. United States -- History -- Civil War, 1861-1865 -- Social aspects 5. United States -- History -- Civil War, 1861-1865 -- African Americans 6. United States -- History -- 1861-1865, Civil War -- Personal narratives

ISBN 0-618-63400-2; 978-0-618-63400-2

LC 2008-1532

Collected from "interviews, diaries, letters, and memoirs, here is the Civil War as seen from not only battlefields, capitals, and camps, but also slave quarters, kitchens, roadsides, farms, towns, and swamps." (Publisher's note) Index.

The author "has provided a . . . narrative that gives voice to the experiences and attitudes of slaves who endured the conflict. Ward utilizes testimonials, diaries, and letters, and organizes them in chronological order from the months before the commencement of hostilities to the aftermath of the surrender at Appomattox. . . . This is a work that will interest both scholars and general readers." Booklist

Includes bibliographical references

Ward, Geoffrey C.

The **Civil** War; an illustrated history. {by} Geoffrey C. Ward with Ken Burns and Ric Burns. Knopf 1990 425p il maps $75; pa $29.95 **973.7**

1. United States -- History -- 1861-1865, Civil War

ISBN 0-394-56285-2; 0-679-74277-8 pa

LC 89-43475

The authors aim to "present the war as the central defining event of American history and of the lives of those Americans caught up in it. In four separate, additional essays, professional historians briefly discuss the causes of the war, emancipation, the politics of the war, and its long-term meaning." Libr J

"A companion to a nine-part Public Broadcasting System documentary, this superbly designed book easily stands on its own." N Y Times Book Rev

Includes bibliographical references

Wert, Jeffry D.

Mosby's Rangers. Simon & Schuster 1990 384p il hardcover o.p. pa $14 **973.7**

1. United States -- History -- 1861-1865, Civil War 2. Confederate States of America -- Army -- Virginia Cavalry Battalion, 43rd

ISBN 0-671-74745-2 pa

LC 90-37917

In this "history of Mosby's Rangers, one of the most successful irregular army units to operate during the Civil War, Wert details the guerrilla group's exploits which provided Jeb Stuart and Robert E. Lee with valuable intelligence on the enemy's movements." Booklist

"Well-researched, objectively written, this is a first-class history." Publ Wkly

Includes bibliographical references

White, Ronald C.

★ **Lincoln's** greatest speech; the second inaugural. {by} Ronald C. White Jr. Simon & Schuster 2002 254p il hardcover o.p. pa $14 **973.7**

1. Lawyers 2. Presidents 3. State legislators 4. Members of Congress 5. Presidents -- United States -- Inaugural addresses

ISBN 0-7432-1299-1 pa

LC 2001-54234

"White breaks down the speech phrase by phrase, then integrates it according to its rhetorical framework of past, present, and future. He seeks sources for the speech's ideas in Lincoln's ambiguous stance toward organized religion, in the sermons of preachers he listened to, and in his Bible-reading habit. . . . Must-have Lincolnalia." Booklist

Includes bibliographical references

Wiley, Bell Irvin

The **life** of Billy Yank; the common soldier of the Union. with a foreword by James I. Robertson, Jr. Updated ed.; Louisiana State University Press 2008 454p il pa $21.95 **973.7**

1. United States -- Army -- Military life 2. United States -- History -- 1861-1865, Civil War

ISBN 978-0-8071-3375-0; 0-8071-3375-2

LC 2008-24243

First published 1952 by Bobbs-Merrill

"The soldiers' own writings—their letters and diaries—are . . . used as chief source for a picture of the response of the Union men to the call to arms, their training, army life, reactions to Southerners they encountered, opinions of Negroes, and comments on their Reb counterparts." Booklist

Includes bibliographical references

The **life** of Johnny Reb; the common soldier of the Confederacy. Updated ed.; Louisiana State University Press 2008 444p il pa $21.95   **973.7**

1. United States -- History -- 1861-1865, Civil War 2. Confederate States of America -- Army -- Military life

ISBN 978-0-8071-3325-5

LC 2007-33859

First published 1943 by Bobbs-Merrill

"Composite biography of the ordinary soldier of the Confederacy—his behavior in camp and under fire, his food, clothing, weapons, religion, amusements, attitude toward women, and so on. Taken mostly from firsthand accounts in letters, diaries, and records." New Yorker

Includes bibliographical references

Williams, David

★ **Bitterly** divided; the South's inner Civil War. David Williams. New Press 2008 310p ill., ports. (hbk.) o.p.; (pbk.) $14; (hbk.) o.p.   **973.7**

1. Social conflict 2. Southern States -- History 3. Secession -- Southern States 4. Confederate States of America 5. United States -- History -- 1861-1865, Civil War 6. Social conflict -- Southern States -- History -- 19th century

ISBN 1-59558-108-1; 978-1595584755; 9781595581082

LC 2007045285

In this book, author and "historian David Williams lays bare the myth of a united confederacy, revealing that the South was in fact fighting two civil wars--an external one that we know so much about and an internal one about which there is scant literature and virtually no public awareness. . . . [The book] shows that from the Confederacy's very beginnings white Southerners were as likely to have opposed secession as supported it, and they undermined the Confederate war effort at nearly every turn. In just one of many telling examples in . . . narrative history, Williams shows that when planters grew too much cotton and tobacco and exempted themselves from the draft, plain folk called the conflict a 'rich man's war' and rioted. Many formed armed anti-Confederate bands. Southern blacks, in what W.E.B. DuBois called 'a general strike against the Confederacy,' resisted in increasingly overt ways, escaped by the thousands, and forced a change in the war's direction that led to emancipation." (Publisher's note)

"Williams marshals abundant evidence to demonstrate that the Confederacy also lost an internal civil war during 1861-65. . . . This firm repudiation of the myth of the solid Confederate South is absolutely essential Civil War reading." Booklist

Includes bibliographical references (p. [275]-291) and index

Wills, Garry

Lincoln at Gettysburg; the words that remade America. Simon & Schuster 1992 317p hardcover o.p. pa $14   **973.7**

1. Presidents 2. State legislators 3. Members of Congress

ISBN 0-671-86742-3 pa

LC 92-3546

The author "argues that in the Gettysburg Address Abraham Lincoln, with consummate skill, changed the Constitution from within, making the hope it embodies triumph over its words by insinuating the ringing affirmation of equality from the Declaration of Independence into people's minds as the foundation of the American Government." N Y Times Book Rev

This is a "tour de force that will cause much discussion and argument." Libr J

Includes bibliographical references

Woodworth, Steven E.

Atlas of the Civil War; by Steven Woodworth and Kenneth J. Winkle; foreword by James M. McPherson. Oxford University Press 2004 400p il map $75   **973.7**

1. Reference books 2. Historical atlases 3. United States -- History -- 1861-1865, Civil War -- Maps

ISBN 0-19-522131-1

LC 2004-53112

"Richly illustrated, this publication will be wanted by all types of libraries. . . . The text entries are useful, while the maps and illustrations are both informative and eye-catching." Choice

973.7075   Civil War--Collections

Holzer, Harold

The **Civil** War in 50 objects; Harold Holzer and the New-York Historical Society ; with an introduction by Eric Foner. Viking 2013 416 p. (hardcover) $36   **973.7075**

1. United States -- Antiquities 2. United States -- History -- 1861-1865, Civil War 3. New-York Historical Society 4. United States -- History -- Civil War, 1861-1865 -- Museums 5. United States -- History -- Civil War, 1861-1865 -- Anecdotes 6. United States -- History -- Civil War, 1861-1865 -- Antiquities 7. United States -- History -- Civil War, 1861-1865 -- Collectibles

ISBN 067001463X; 9780670014637

LC 2013001532

This book, by Harold Holzer, explores the U.S. Civil War through a set of preserved objects "from a soldier's diary with the pencil still attached to John Brown's pike, the Emancipation Proclamation, a Confederate Palmetto flag, and the leaves from Abraham Lincoln's bier. . . . Lincoln scholar Harold Holzer sheds new light on the war by examining fifty objects from the New-York Historical Society's acclaimed collection." (Publisher's note)

Includes bibliographical references and index

973.709   Biography

Leaders of the American Civil War; a biographical and historiographical dictionary. edited by

Charles F. Ritter and Jon L. Wakelyn. Greenwood Press 1998 xxxiv, 465p $85 **973.709**
1. Reference books 2. United States -- History -- 1861-1865, Civil War -- Biography -- Dictionaries
ISBN 0-313-29560-3

LC 98-12156

This dictionary "includes 47 articles on outstanding military and civilian Union and Confederate leaders as well as entries for other significant figures, including Frederick Douglass, Clara Barton, Dorothea Dix, and even Walt Whitman." Libr J

Includes bibliographical references

Masur, Louis P.
Lincoln's Hundred Days; The Emanicpation Proclamation and the War for the Union. Louis P. Masur. Harvard Univ Pr 2012 viii, 358 p.p ill. **973.709**
1. Slaves -- Emancipation 2. Slavery -- United States 3. Emancipation Proclamation 4. United States -- History -- 1861-1865, Civil War 5. Slaves -- Emancipation -- United States 6. United States -- Politics and government -- 1861-1865 7. United States. President (1861-1865 : Lincoln). Emancipation Proclamation
ISBN 0674066901; 9780674066908

LC 2012009044

This book by Louis P. Masur "seeks to restore the document's [Emancipation Proclamation] reputation by exploring its evolution.... [Masur] portray[s] the daily struggles and enormous consequences of the president's efforts as Lincoln led a nation through war and toward emancipation [and] ... presents a ... portrait of Lincoln as a complex figure who ... followed his conviction in directing America toward a terrifying and thrilling unknown." (Publisher's note)

Includes bibliographical references and index

Moody, Wesley
Demon of the lost cause; Sherman and Civil War history. by Wesley Moody. Univ of Missouri Press 2011 190 p. (hardcover) $30.00 **973.709**
1. Mythology 2. United States -- History -- 1861-1865, Civil War 3. Generals 4. Memoirists 5. Secretaries of war
ISBN 0826219454; 9780826219459

Author Wesley Moody "reveals the machinations behind the [Union general William Tecumseh] Sherman myth and the reasons behind the acceptance of such myths, no matter who invented them. In the case of Sherman's own myth-making, Moody postulates that his motivation was to secure a military position to support his wife and children ... In tracing Sherman's ever-changing reputation, Moody sheds light on current and past understanding of the Civil War through the lens of one of its most controversial figures." (Publisher's note)

Stahr, Walter
Seward; Lincoln's indispensable man. by Walter Stahr. Simon & Schuster 2012 720 p. $32.50; (hardcover) $32.50 **973.709**
1. Legislators 2. Statesmen -- United States 3. Statesmen -- United States -- Biography 4. United States. Dept. of State -- Biography 5. Cabinet officers -- United States -- Biography 6. United States -- Foreign

relations -- 1861-1865 7. United States -- Politics and government -- 1861-1865
ISBN 9781439127940; 1439121168; 9781439121160; 9781439121184

LC 2011052984

This book presents a biography of William Henry Seward, U.S. Secretary of State under President Abraham Lincoln. "Seward was New York governor and senator, then a rival for Lincoln's place on the 1860 presidential ticket, finally senior cabinet officer.... Among other things, he kept Britain out of the Civil War, then negotiated the acquisition of Alaska for the U.S." (Publishers Weekly)

Includes bibliographical references and index

973.713   The South and secession

McPherson, James M., 1936-
Embattled rebel; Jefferson Davis as commander in chief. James M. McPherson. The Penguin Press 2014 352 p. ill. (some col.), maps $32.95 **973.713**
1. Confederate States of America -- History 2. United States -- History -- 1861-1865, Civil War 3. Confederate States of America -- Politics and government 4. Presidents -- Confederate States of America -- Biography 5. United States -- History -- Civil War, 1861-1865 -- Biography 6. United States -- History -- Civil War, 1861-1865 -- Campaigns
ISBN 1594204977; 9781594204975

LC 2014005403

"A seasoned Civil War historian examines the beleaguered president of the Confederacy. Did Jefferson Davis (1807/1808-1889) get a bum rap? Pulitzer Prize and two-time Lincoln Prize winner McPherson ... reveals the degree of vitriol unleashed against the president of the Confederacy from fellow Southerners who accused him of arrogance and malice due to the fact that he could not marshal the wherewithal to win the war." (Kirkus Reviews)

"Despite the biography's dry, yet light presentation and relatively singular focus, Davis is most redeemed not by justifications for his decisions, but through an empathetic, simple understanding of his motives: namely, an admirable (if in hindsight horribly misguided) passion for the Confederacy." Pub Wkly

Includes bibliographical references and index

973.73   Civil War--Operations

Johnson, Martin P.
Writing the Gettysburg Address; Martin P. Johnson. University Press of Kansas 2013 336 p. illustrations (hardback) $34.95 **973.73**
1. American speeches 2. Gettysburg (Pa.), Battle of, 1863
ISBN 070061933X; 9780700619337

LC 2013020162

Author Martin P. Johnson tells the "story of how [Abraham] Lincoln wrote the Gettysburg Address. Johnson guides readers on Lincoln's emotional and intellectual journey to the speaker's platform, revealing that Lincoln himself experienced writing the Gettysburg Address as an eventful process that was filled with the possibility of failure, but which he knew resulted finally in success." (Publisher's note)

"Johnson's meticulous and well-grounded detective work brings new understanding of the speech, its speaker, and our responses to his words--then and over the last 150 years." LJ

Includes bibliographical references and index

973.8   United States--Reconstruction period, 1865-1901

Algeo, Matthew

The **president** is a sick man; wherein the supposedly virtuous Grover Cleveland survives a secret surgery at sea and vilifies the courageous newspaperman who dared expose the truth.   Chicago Review Press 2011 255p il $24.95   **973.8**
1. Mayors 2. Governors 3. Journalism 4. Presidents 5. Journalists 6. District attorneys 7. United States -- Politics and government -- 1865-1898
ISBN 978-1-56976-350-6; 1-56976-350-X
LC 2010-44639

"Incredibly, shortly after his second term began in 1893, Cleveland boarded a friend's yacht and sailed into the Long Island Sound where surgeons, in a makeshift operating theater, cut away cancerous tissue in his mouth and part of his jawbone. . . . Cancer was virtually taboo in Cleveland's day. He didn't want to lose public confidence or become a spectacle like former President Grant, who had died from cancer. Also, Cleveland was in a contentious political struggle over whether the U.S. should return to the gold standard to back its money (his position), or continue with a policy that also accepted silver, the view of his vice president, Adlai Stevenson. Cleveland feared that should he become incapacitated, Stevenson would assume power and sway the country's financial direction. The yacht's crew and surgeons kept mum, except for a dentist serving as anesthetist, who told a fellow doctor. Word found its way to Philadelphia Press reporter E.J. Edwards, who confirmed enough of the tale to print it. Cleveland's circle squatted on the scoop and undermined the reporter's reputation. . . . Only decades later would one of the surgeons tell all in an article, and make amends to Edwards for the harm done to him." Milwaukee J Sentinel
Includes bibliographical references

Connell, Evan S.

★ **Son** of the Morning Star. North Point Press 1984 441p il hardcover o.p. pa $18   **973.8**
1. Generals 2. Little Bighorn, Battle of the, 1876 3. Army officers
ISBN 0-86547-160-6; 0-86547-510-5 pa
LC 84-60681

This book is "impressive in its massive presentation of information, and in the conclusions it draws about the probable events that led to the fracas on the banks of the Little Bighorn. But its strength lies in the way the author has shaped his material." N Y Times Book Rev
Includes bibliographical references

Diner, Steven J.

A **very** different age; Americans of the progressive era. Hill & Wang 1997 320p hardcover o.p. pa $14   **973.8**
1. Progressivism (United States politics) 2. United States -- History -- 20th century
ISBN 0-8090-1611-7 pa
LC 97-3801

The author examines the "social, economic, political, and other changes experienced by Americans during the first two decades of the 20th century. . . . The writing is succinct and fluid. . . . This rewarding social history is an excellent book for both experienced historians and novices." Libr J
Includes bibliographical references

Donovan, Jim

A **terrible** glory; Custer and the Little Bighorn-- the last great battle of the American West. [by] James Donovan. Little, Brown and Co. 2008 528p il map $26.99; pa $16.99   **973.8**
1. Generals 2. Little Bighorn, Battle of the, 1876 3. Army officers
ISBN 978-0-316-15578-6; 0-316-15578-0; 978-0-316-06747-8 pa; 0-316-06747-4 pa
LC 2007-26156

The author "collects the multiple threads that led to the 1876 massacre at Little Big Horn. . . . Exhaustive research, lively prose and fresh interpretation make for a valuable addition to literature on this otherwise well-trodden historical event." Publ Wkly
Includes bibliographical references (p. [487]-511) and index

Douglass, Frederick, 1818-1895

★ **Autobiographies**. Library of Am. 1994 1126p $35; pa $13.95   **973.8**
1. Slaves 2. Authors 3. Abolitionists 4. Memoirists 5. African Americans -- Biography
ISBN 0-940450-79-8; 1-883011-30-2 pa
LC 93-24168

"This one volume containing Douglass's seminal works is highly recommended for black history collections." Libr J
Includes bibliographical references

My bondage and my freedom; edited with an introduction and notes by John David Smith. Penguin Bks. 2003 lx, 366p (Penguin Classics) pa $12 **973.8**
1. Slaves 2. Authors 3. Abolitionists 4. Memoirists 5. African Americans -- Biography
ISBN 0-14-043918-8
LC 2002-28992

First published 1855 by Orton & Mulligan
In this autobiography Douglass tells of his life as a slave and his early years in the abolitionist movement.
Includes bibliographical references

Encyclopedia of the Gilded Age and Progressive Era; edited by John D. Buenker and Joseph Buenker. M.E. Sharpe 2005 3v il set $299   **973.8**
1. Reference books 2. United States -- History -- 1865-1898 -- Encyclopedias 3. United States -- History --

1898-1919 -- Encyclopedias
ISBN 0-7656-8051-3

LC 2003-24653

This set focuses "on a period between 1870 and 1920, when the United States emerged as an urban and industrial world power. Some 900 A-Z entries cover key individuals, events, and organizations of the times, and 17 essays discuss broad themes like the economy, politics, religion, and pop culture." Libr J

Includes bibliographical references

Foner, Eric

Forever free; the story of emancipation and Reconstruction. illustrations edited and with commentary by Joshua Brown. Knopf 2005 xxx, 268p il $27.50; pa $15 **973.8**

1. Reconstruction (1865-1876) 2. Slavery -- United States 3. United States -- Politics and government -- 1865-1898

ISBN 0-375-40259-4; 978-0-375-40259-3; 0-375-70274-1 pa; 978-0-375-70274-7 pa

LC 2005-40706

This "is an invaluable and timely book about a subject central to U.S. history and still of obvious significance today—slavery, the Civil War, emancipation, Reconstruction, and both the immediate aftermath and longer-term consequences of those things." Rev Am Hist

Includes bibliographical references

★ **Reconstruction**; America's unfinished revolution, 1863-1877. HarperCollins Pubs. 1988 xxvii, 690p il maps hardcover o.p. pa $23.95 **973.8**

1. Reconstruction (1865-1876) 2. United States -- History -- 1865-1898

ISBN 0-06-093716-5 pa

LC 87-45615

"Incorporating much eyewitness material, this book emphasizes the centrality of the Black experience. The book also examines the themes of race and class, the remodeling of Southern society, and the national context. A complete, modern, scholarly text." N Y Public Libr Book of How & Where to Look It Up

Includes bibliographical references

Franklin, John Hope

Reconstruction after the Civil War; 2nd ed; University of Chicago Press 1994 265p (Chicago history of American civilization) hardcover o.p. pa $16 **973.8**

1. Reconstruction (1865-1876) 2. United States -- History -- 1865-1898

ISBN 0-226-26079-8 pa

LC 94-27366

First published 1961

This is an "account of American life in a time of great challenge, unfamiliar problems, and uncertain leadership. Discusses the Radicals' effort to secure racial justice in the South, the fact that corruption existed not only in the South, and that some worthwhile measures emerged from 'carpetbag' legislatures." Guide to Read in Am Hist {review of 1961 edition}

Includes bibliographical references

Graff, Henry F.

Grover Cleveland. Times Bks. 2002 154p il (American presidents series) $20 **973.8**

1. Mayors 2. Governors 3. Presidents 4. District attorneys 5. Presidents -- United States

ISBN 0-8050-6923-2

LC 2002-20315

A biography of the only American president to serve two nonconsecutive terms

This "volume is a valuable addition to the literature on the Presidency and is a compelling argument for taking Cleveland seriously as a President." Libr J

Includes bibliographical references

Grant, Ulysses S.

Memoirs and selected letters; personal memoirs of U.S. Grant, selected letters, 1839-1865. Library of Am. 1990 2v in 1 il maps $35 **973.8**

1. Generals 2. Presidents 3. United States -- History -- 1861-1865, Civil War

ISBN 0-940450-58-5

LC 90-60013

This volume includes Grant's personal memoirs, first published in 1885 and 175 letters written between 1839 and 1865

Includes bibliographical references

Grumet, Bridget Hall

Reconstruction era: primary sources; Lawrence W. Baker, project editor. UXL 2004 xxv, 228p il (Reconstruction Era reference library) $60 **973.8**

1. Reconstruction (1865-1876)

ISBN 0-7876-9219-0

LC 2004-17309

This book "contains 19 complete or partial documents, such as the Fourteenth Amendment of the U.S. Constitution and Rutherford B. Hayes' inaugural address. Each document is accompanied by an introduction, keys to reading the document, a discussion of subsequent events related to the document, and other material." Booklist

Includes bibliographical references

Howes, Kelly King

Reconstruction era: almanac; Lawrence W. Baker, project editor. UXL 2004 xxxvii, 228p il map (Reconstruction Era reference library) $60 **973.8**

1. Reconstruction (1865-1876)

ISBN 0-7876-9217-4

LC 2004-17301

This book "covers the political and social aspects of Reconstruction, including carpetbaggers and scalawags, amnesty for white Southerners, 'Black Codes,' the impeachment of President Johnson, the rise of the Ku Klux Klan, attempts to restore the old order in the South and much more." Publisher's note

Includes bibliographical references

Lears, T. J. Jackson

Rebirth of a nation; the making of modern America, 1877-1920. [by] Jackson Lears. Harper-Collins 2009 418p il $27.99   **973.8**

1. United States -- History -- 1865-1898 2. United States -- History -- 1898-1919

ISBN 978-0-06-074749-7; 0-06-074749-8

"A fascinating cultural history. . . . [This] is a major work by a leading historian at the top of his game—at once engaging and tightly argued. Like the best histories, it is also a book that speaks to our own time." N Y Times Book Rev

McFarland, Philip

Mark Twain and the Colonel; Samuel L. Clemens, Theodore Roosevelt, and the arrival of a new century. Philip McFarland. Rowman & Littlefield Publishers, Inc. 2012 499 p. (cloth : alk. paper) $28.00   **973.8**

1. Biography 2. United States -- Civilization -- 1865-1918

ISBN 1442212268; 9781442212268; 9781442212282
                                        LC 2011051861

In this book, "[Philip] McFarland . . . presents [satirist Mark Twain and U.S. President Theodore Roosevelt] as dynamic foils, indicative of the social and political growing pains of the country. Differences in background and beliefs abounded: Roosevelt was an expansionist; Twain was a staunch anti-imperialist. McFarland doesn't shy away from the complex notions each man had of the other." (Publishers Weekly)

Includes bibliographical references and index.

McMurtry, Larry, 1936-

Custer; Larry McMurtry. Simon & Schuster 2012 pages cm   **973.8**

1. Little Bighorn, Battle of the, 1876 2. United States. Army -- Biography 3. Generals -- United States -- Biography 4. Little Bighorn, Battle of the, Mont., 1876 5. Indians of North America -- Wars -- Great Plains 6. United States -- History -- Civil War, 1861-1865

ISBN 9781451626209

                                        LC 2012012374

Author Larry McMurtry presents a biography of George Armstrong Custer. "On June 25, 1876, General George Armstrong Custer and his 7th Cavalry attacked a large Lakota Cheyenne village on the Little Bighorn River in Montana Territory. He lost not only the battle but his life--and the lives of his entire cavalry. 'Custer's Last Stand' was a spectacular defeat that shocked the country and grew quickly into a legend that has reverberated in our national consciousness to this day." (Publisher's note)

Includes bibliographical references.

Millard, Candice

The **destiny** of the republic; Candice Millard. Doubleday 2011 x, 319 p., [16] p. of platesp ill.   **973.8**

1. United States -- History -- 1865-1898 2. Presidents -- United States -- Assassination 3. Presidents -- United States -- Biography 4. Medicine -- United States -- History -- 19th century 5. United States -- Politics and government -- 1881-1885 6. Political culture -- United

States -- History -- 19th century 7. Power (Social sciences) -- United States -- History -- 19th century 8. Presidents -- Medical care -- United States -- History -- 19th century 9. Medical instruments and apparatus -- United States -- History -- 19th century

ISBN 9780307939654; 0385535007; 9780385526265; 9780385535007

                                        LC 2011001549

This book explores U.S. history during the presidency and assassination of U.S. president James Garfield. "As [the author] . . . builds to the president's fatal encounter with his assassin, she details the intra-party struggle among Republicans that led to Garfield's surprise 1880 nomination. . . . During the nearly three excruciating months Garfield lay dying, Alexander Graham Bell . . . scrambled to perfect his induction balance (a metal detector) in time to locate the lead bullet lodged in the stricken president's back. Meanwhile, Garfield's medical team persistently failed to observe British surgeon Joseph Lister's methods of antisepsis—the American medical establishment rejected the idea of invisible germs as ridiculous—a neglect that almost surely killed the president." (Kirkus)

Includes bibliographical references (p. 313-323) and index

Miller, Scott

The **President** and the assassin; McKinley, terror, and empire at the dawn of the American century. Random House 2011 422p il   **973.8**

1. Governors 2. Presidents 3. Anarchism and anarchists 4. Murderers 5. Anarchists 6. Members of Congress 7. Anarchism -- United States -- History 8. United States -- Social conditions -- 1865-1918 9. United States -- Politics and government -- 1865-1898 10. United States -- Politics and government -- 1897-1901 11. United States -- Politics and government -- 1898-1919 12. United States -- Territorial expansion -- History -- 19th century

ISBN 1-4000-6752-9; 978-1-4000-6752-7

                                        LC 2010-38857

"Miller examines the social, economic and political forces that underlay the transformation of the U.S. after the Civil War from a feeble newcomer in world affairs to the global power we know today in a way that keeps you learning and turning pages at the same time. Rewarding as it is to be able to grasp at last such late 19th-century mysteries as the monetary debates that have befuddled college students ever since, what makes the book compelling is neither the narrative nor the explanations but the sense of familiarity that pervades it all. Indeed, so many of the circumstances and events of the earlier time have parallels in our own that the experience of reading it is practically eerie." Oregonian

Includes bibliographical references (p. [385]-403) and index

Philbrick, Nathaniel

★ The **last** stand; Custer, Sitting Bull, and the Battle of the Little Bighorn. Viking 2010 466p il map $30   **973.8**

1. Generals 2. Dakota Indians 3. Little Bighorn, Battle of the, 1876 4. Army officers 5. Dakota Indians --

Wars, 1876 6. Little Bighorn, Battle of the, Mont., 1876
ISBN 978-0-670-02172-7

LC 2009-47209

The author "writes a lively narrative that brushes away
the cobwebs of mythology to reveal the context and realities of Custer's unexpected 1876 defeat at the hands of his
Indian enemies under Sitting Bull, and the character of each
leader. Judicious in his assessments of events and intentions,
Philbrick offers a rounded history of one of the worst defeats
in American military history, a story enhanced by his minute
examination of the battle's terrain and interviews with descendants in both camps." Publ Wkly

Includes bibliographical references

Rauchway, Eric

Murdering McKinley; the making of Theodore
Roosevelt's America. Hill & Wang 2003 250p il
$25; pa $14   **973.8**
    1. Governors 2. Presidents 3. Vice-presidents 4.
Murderers 5. Anarchists 6. Members of Congress 7.
Nobel laureates for peace 8. United States -- Politics
and government -- 1898-1919
    ISBN 0-8090-7170-3; 0-8090-1638-9 pa

LC 2003-40666

The author "uses a search for the motive of President
William McKinley's assassin as a means to comment on the
Progressive Era and show how Theodore Roosevelt manipulated the emotions of rage and despair after the tragic event to
give it meaning, thereby advancing his own political vision.
. . . Novel in its conception and well written, the book is
appropriate for public as well as academic libraries." Choice

Includes bibliographical references

Sandoz, Mari

   ★ The **Battle** of the Little Bighorn. Lippincott
1966 191p maps (Great battles of history series)
hardcover o.p. pa $12.95   **973.8**
    1. Generals 2. Little Bighorn, Battle of the, 1876 3.
Army officers
    ISBN 0-397-00410-9; 0-8032-9100-0 pa

"An account of the United States Army expedition
against the Sioux Nation with emphasis on the political motives and ambitions of General Custer." Publ Wkly

Includes bibliographical references

Schlereth, Thomas J.

Victorian America; transformations in everyday life, 1876-1915. HarperCollins Pubs. 1991
363p (Everyday life in America) hardcover o.p. pa
$15   **973.8**
    1. United States -- Social life and customs
    ISBN 0-06-092160-9 pa

LC 89-46555

The author surveys the objects, events, experiences,
products and tastes that comprised what he terms America's
Victorian culture (1876-1915) and shows how its values
shaped modern life.

"What a wonderful book. . . . Schlereth is no wry compiler of trivia. His analysis of social context reveals truly profound, intangible transformations in how and where Americans spent their time during four pivotal decades." Booklist

Includes bibliographical references

Smith, Jean Edward

Grant. Simon & Schuster 2001 781p il $35; pa
$20   **973.8**
    1. Generals 2. Presidents 3. United States -- History
-- 1861-1865, Civil War
    ISBN 0-684-84926-7; 0-684-84927-5 pa

LC 00-53794

This biography surveys the career and achievements
of the 18th U.S. president, from his days at West Point to
the Civil War campaigns and his subsequent elevation to
the presidency

"While he acknowledges Grant's failure to rein in his
'friends' and cabinet members as president, Smith convincingly illustrates how Grant's backbone and political skills
were used to advance the cause of former slaves in the South.
This is an outstanding and long overdue reevaluation of the
life and career of a great American." Booklist

Includes bibliographical references

Thomas, Evan

The **war** lovers; Roosevelt, Lodge, Hearst, and
the rush to empire, 1898. Little, Brown and Co. 2010
471p il $29.99   **973.8**
    1. Governors 2. Presidents 3. Vice-presidents
4. Spanish-American War, 1898 5. Senators 6.
Biographers 7. Newspaper editors 8. Political leaders
9. Members of Congress 10. Newspaper executives 11.
Speakers of the House 12. Nobel laureates for peace
13. Spanish-American War, 1898 -- Causes 14. United
States -- Territorial expansion 15. United States --
Politics and government -- 1897-1901 16. United States
-- Politics and government -- 1898-1919 17. Business
and politics -- United States -- History -- 19th century
    ISBN 0-316-00409-X; 978-0-316-00409-1

LC 2009-43616

This book focuses on the "Spanish American War and
[on the involvement of] Roosevelt, Lodge, Hearst, McKinley, William James, and Thomas Reed." (Publisher's
note) Index.

The author's multifaceted portraits lend the book a
sweeping, almost cinematic quality. A lively, well-rounded
look at politics and personalities in late-19th-century America. Kirkus

Includes bibliographical references

Utley, Robert Marshall

Custer : cavalier in buckskin; {by} Robert M.
Utley. rev ed; University of Okla. Press 2001 176p
il map $29.95; pa $17.95   **973.8**
    1. Generals 2. Army officers 3. West (U.S.) -- History
4. Native Americans -- Wars
    ISBN 0-8061-3347-3; 0-8061-3387-2 pa

LC 2001-27356

First published 1988 with title: Cavalier in buckskin

The author offers theories and facts regarding the mythology surrounding Custer, telling how he promoted himself as
an American hero in an effort to increase his rank in the army.

This "is a fair and full-bodied account that cogently interprets the facts, provides the proper psychological analysis,
and offers solid grounding for the development of the considerable myth." Booklist {review of 1988 edition}

Includes bibliographical references

Wall, Joseph Frazier

Andrew Carnegie. University of Pittsburgh Press 1989 1137p il hardcover o.p. pa $22.50   **973.8**
   1. Philanthropists 2. Metal industry executives
   ISBN 0-8229-5904-6 pa

                   LC 88-38160

A reissue of the title first published 1970 by Oxford University Press

This biography follows Carnegie from his boyhood in Scotland through his emigration to America, his rise in the business world, and his early ventures in oil, railroads, telegraphy, and the iron and steel industries
   Includes bibliographical references

Welch, James

Killing Custer; the Battle of the Little Bighorn and the fate of the Plains Indians. by James Welch with Paul Stekler. Norton 1994 320p il hardcover o.p. pa $14.95   **973.8**
   1. Little Bighorn, Battle of the, 1876 2. Native Americans -- Wars
   ISBN 0-393-32939-9 pa

                   LC 94-5617

"Welch produced this history of the Indian wars of the northern plains as a by-product of his work scripting a television documentary on the Battle of the Little Bighorn. In addition to military history, it contains long sections describing the life of the Plains Indians, accounts of contemporary Indian radical groups, and Welch's reactions while visiting the various historic sites in the area." Libr J
   Includes bibliographical references

Wert, Jeffry D.

Custer; the controversial life of George Armstrong Custer. Simon & Schuster 1996 462p il maps hardcover o.p. pa $20   **973.8**
   1. Generals 2. Army officers
   ISBN 0-684-81043-3; 0-684-83275-5 pa

                   LC 96-7290

"Focusing on Custer's Civil War actions, Wert methodically examines a man often considered an enigma in American history. Clear writing and excellent use of primary source materials demonstrate how history should be written." Booklist

West, Elliott

The **last** Indian war; the Nez Perce story. Oxford University Press 2009 397p il map (Pivotal moments in American history)   **973.8**
   1. Nez Percé War, 1877 2. Big Hole, Battle of the, 1877 3. Nez Percé Indians -- Wars, 1877 4. Nez Percé Indians -- History -- 19th century
   ISBN 9780195136753

                   LC 2008051382

This is an account of the 1877 war between the Nez Perce Indians and the United States government. Chronology. Index.

The author "uses the story of the Nez Percé War of 1877 and its origins and aftermath to illuminate the era of expansion and consolidation between 1845 and 1877 that forged the American identity, a period he calls the 'Greater Reconstruction.' . . . This well-written book is an excellent place

to start in understanding the Nez Percé War and is highly recommended for all libraries." Libr J
   Includes bibliographical references (p. 325-328) and index.

973.9   United States--1901-

American decades. Gale Res. 1994 11v set $1495   **973.9**
   1. United States -- Civilization 2. United States -- History -- 20th century
   ISBN 0-7876-5076-5

"A series of volumes covering the twentieth century by decades. . . . Fun to browse, each volume is divided into 13 sections covering topics such as the arts, government and politics, lifestyles and social trends, medicine and health, and sports. Each section opens with a chronology and overview and closes with short biographies, deaths, and a bibliography of important books published in the decade. Sidebars highlight events and prominent individuals." Am Libr

American decades primary sources; Cynthia Rose, project editor. Gale 2004 10v il map set $1495   **973.9**
   1. United States -- Civilization 2. United States -- History -- 20th century -- Sources
   ISBN 0-7876-6587-8

                   LC 2002-8155

Companion set to American decades published 1994-2000

"A treasure trove of more than 2,000 primary sources on U.S. history and culture, ranging from speeches and literary works to graphs and architectural drawings. Although many of the sources might be found on the Internet, they lack the organization and context provided here." Booklist

Caro, Robert A.

The **path** to power. Knopf 1982 xxiii, 882p il (The years of Lyndon Johnson) $49.95; pa $19.95   **973.9**
   1. Presidents 2. Vice-presidents 3. Senators 4. Members of Congress 5. Presidents -- United States 6. United States -- Politics and government -- 20th century
   ISBN 0-394-49973-5; 0-679-72945-3 pa

                   LC 90-201781

This volume, the first volume of a projected four-volume biography of Lyndon B. Johnson, "follows him from the Hill Country to New Deal Washington, from his boyhood through the years of the Depression to his debut as Congressman, his . . . defeat in his first race for the Senate, and his attainment, nonetheless, at age 31, of the national power for which he hungered." Publisher's note
   Includes bibliographical references

Cooke, Alistair

Letter from America, 1946-2004. Knopf 2004 xx, 503p il $35   **973.9**
   1. United States -- Social life and customs 2. United States -- Politics and government -- 20th century
   ISBN 1-4000-4402-2

                   LC 2004-304550

"Arranged into chapters by decades, these commentaries reveal not only Cooke's mastery of clear prose but also the range of American topics that caught his interest, from politics to culture. . . . A book for appreciators of American culture in the second half of the previous century as well as those who relish the essay in either oral or written form." Booklist

Galbraith, John Kenneth
Name -dropping; from F.D.R. on. Houghton Mifflin 1999 194p $26; pa $14   **973.9**
1. Lawyers 2. Diplomats 3. Governors 4. Statesmen 5. Architects 6. Presidents 7. War criminals 8. Prime ministers 9. Vice-presidents 10. People with disabilities 11. Editors 12. Senators 13. Columnists 14. Memoirists 15. Socialites 16. Nazi leaders 17. Philatelists 18. Humanitarians 19. Social activists 20. Nonfiction writers 21. Members of Congress 22. Government officials 23. Spouses of presidents 24. Advertising executives 25. Presidential candidates 26. United Nations officials 27. Politicians -- United States 28. United States -- Politics and government -- 20th century
ISBN 0-395-82288-2; 0-618-15453-1 pa
    LC 99-20070
The author "reminisces about important figures with whom he has been involved in his long and distinguished life in the public arena. Among the brief portraits are those of Franklin and Eleanor Roosevelt, Harry Truman, JFK, LBJ, Nehru, and others. More than the self-effacing title indicates, this book offers important insights into the people and times on which its author reflects. Galbraith writes with a wit, style, and elegance few can match." Libr J

Gould, Lewis L.
The **modern** American presidency; foreword by Richard Norton Smith. 2nd ed., rev. and updated.; University Press of Kansas 2009 318p il $34.95; pa $17.95   **973.9**
1. Presidents -- United States
ISBN 978-0-7006-1683-1; 0-7006-1683-7; 978-0-7006-1684-8 pa; 0-7006-1684-5 pa
    LC 2009-20161
First published 2003
"Gould traces the decline of the party system, the increasing importance of the media and its role in creating the president-as-celebrity, and the growth of the White House staff and executive bureaucracy. He also shows us a succession of chief executives who increasingly have known less and less about the business of governing the country, observing that most would have had a better historical reputation if they had contented themselves with a single term." Publisher's note
Includes bibliographical references

Grose, Peter
Gentleman spy; the life of Allen Dulles. University of Mass. Press 1996 641p il pa $19.95 **973.9**
1. Lawyers 2. Diplomats 3. Government officials 4. Intelligence service officials 5. United States -- Central

Intelligence Agency
ISBN 1-55849-044-2; 978-1-55849-044-4
    LC 96-19010
First published 1994 by Houghton Mifflin
This biography of the CIA director under Eisenhower and Kennedy "renders the interplay of person and public event and allows readers to enter the dark world of US-sponsored terror and covert paramilitary operations. . . . Grose sets forth in fascinating and often unfamiliar detail the spectacular CIA covert operations: in Iran, Guatemala, Indonesia; the U2 incident; the Bay of Pigs." Choice

Menand, Louis
The **Metaphysical** Club. Farrar, Straus & Giroux 2001 546p il $30; pa $15   **973.9**
1. Educators 2. Metaphysics 3. Philosophers 4. Psychologists 5. Logicians 6. Writers on science 7. Supreme Court justices 8. United States -- Intellectual life
ISBN 0-374-19963-9; 0-374-52849-7 pa
    LC 00-66279
In this book Menand "provides a panorama of American post-Civil War thought . . . focusing on the lives and thinking of 'four giants': William James, Charles Sanders Peirce, Oliver Wendell Holmes Jr., and John Dewey. . . . The 'club' of the title, with the four giants as its core, actually only existed for about nine months in 1872, but its members influenced the culture for decades to come." Booklist
"Menand brings rare common sense and graceful, witty prose to his richly nuanced reading of American intellectual history." N Y Times Book Rev
Includes bibliographical references

Morgan, Ted
Reds : McCarthyism in twentieth-century America. Random House 2003 685p $35; pa $16.95 **973.9**
1. Anticommunist movements 2. Senators 3. Communism -- United States 4. United States -- Politics and government -- 20th century
ISBN 0-679-44399-1; 0-812-97302-X pa
    LC 2003-46509
"Senator Joseph McCarthy's demagogic career is just part of this sweeping account of anti-Communist purges and Communist espionage." N Y Times Book Rev
Includes bibliographical references

Slotkin, Richard
Gunfighter nation; the myth of the frontier in twentieth-century America. University of Oklahoma Press 1998 850p pa $32.95   **973.9**
1. Popular culture -- United States 2. Frontier and pioneer life -- West (U.S.)
ISBN 0-8061-3031-8; 978-0-8061-3031-6
    LC 97-32043
First published 1992 by Atheneum
"On the premise that myth is spread by mass media, Slotkin examines numerous elements of popular culture ranging from James Fenimore Cooper's Hawkeye in The last of the Mohicans to John Wayne's Green Berets film to demonstrate how the myth affects American perceptions regarding foreign and domestic issues." Libr J
Includes bibliographical references

St. James encyclopedia of popular culture; editors, Tom Pendergast and Sara Pendergast; with an introduction by Jim Cullen. St. James Press 1999 5v il set $695   **973.9**
1. Reference books 2. United States -- Civilization -- Encyclopedias 3. Popular culture -- United States -- Encyclopedias
ISBN 1-55862-400-7

                   LC 99-46540

This is an "overview of popular culture in twentieth-century America with a particular emphasis on the second half of the century. In more than 2,700 entries, the nearly 450 contributors attempt to cover the major personalities, productions, products, events, and developments from film, music, print culture, social life, sports, television and radio, art, and performances (which include theater, dance, stand-up comedy, and other live performances). . . . The entries seldom sink to trivialization. They are generally thoughtful and well written, providing information and insight. . . . The editors have done a masterful job of providing something for nearly everyone." Am Ref Books Annu, 2001
Includes bibliographical references

Tintori, Karen
   Trapped : the 1909 Cherry Mine disaster. Simon & Schuster 2002 273p il $25; pa $14   **973.9**
1. Coal mines and mining -- Accidents
ISBN 0-7434-2194-9; 0-7434-2195-7 pa

                 LC 2002-104596

"On November 13, 1909, a fire trapped 480 coal miners . . . 400 feet below ground in a mine at Cherry, Illinois. Only 221 escaped. . . . Tintori describes the life-and-death struggle of the miners below ground and the terror of the women and children gathered at the mine's entrance. . . . Tintori's graphic account of this tragedy is a sad but gripping story." Booklist

973.9092   United States--1901---biography

Nasaw, David
   ★ The **patriarch**; the remarkable life and turbulent times of Joseph P. Kennedy. David Nasaw. Penguin Press 2012 xxiv, 868 p.p ill. $40   **973.9092**
1. Presidents -- United States -- Family 2. Ambassadors -- United States -- Biography 3. Politicians -- United States -- Biography 4. Businesspeople -- United States -- Biography
ISBN 1594203768; 9781594203763

                 LC 2012027315

In this biography, "[David] Nasaw takes on Joseph P. Kennedy, businessman, Hollywood mogul, founding chair of the Securities and Exchange Commission, U.S. ambassador to Britain, and, of course, father to our 35th President. He had exclusive access to Kennedy's papers and addresses some longstanding questions." (Library Journal)
Includes bibliographical references (p. [793]-834) and index

973.91   United States--1901-1953

Allen, Frederick Lewis
   Only yesterday; an informal history of the 1920's. Wiley 1997 285p (Wiley investment classics) $21.95   **973.91**
1. United States -- Social conditions 2. United States -- History -- 1919-1933 3. United States -- Economic conditions -- 1919-1933
ISBN 0-471-18952-9

                 LC 97-19930

A reissue of the title first published 1931 by Harper and Brothers
"An account of the years from the spring of 1919 to . . . {1931}. It is a kaleidoscopic picture of American politics, society, manners, morals, and economic conditions." Booklist
Includes bibliographical references

Beam, Alex
   A **great** idea at the time; the rise, fall, and curious afterlife of the Great Books. PublicAffairs 2008 245p il $24.95   **973.91**
1. Books and reading 2. United States -- Intellectual life 3. Great books of the Western world (Franklin Center, Pa.)
ISBN 978-1-58648-487-3; 1-58648-487-7

                 LC 2008-33115

This is a "look at the marketing phenomenon and cultural-icon status of the Great Books of Western Civilization, a 54-volume collection compiled by university-affiliated academics. . . . Beam's book will have readers looking at volumes in the series from a whole new perspective owing to its witty handling of popular culture." Libr J
Includes bibliographical references (p. 223-228) and index

Brands, H. W.
   ★ **Woodrow** Wilson. Times Books 2003 169p il (American presidents series) $20   **973.91**
1. Governors 2. Presidents 3. College presidents 4. Nobel laureates for peace 5. Presidents -- United States
ISBN 0-8050-6955-0

                 LC 2002-41393

The author "presents Wilson as a moralistic, idealistic intellectual who came to the presidency well versed in domestic policy but sadly lacking in knowledge and experience of international affairs, a leader who ultimately sacrificed his health and his presidential legacy in a doomed battle with Sen. Henry Cabot Lodge to have the League of Nations ratified. . . . Brands's brief, skillful life of the President is recommended for all public libraries." Libr J
Includes bibliographical references

Burns, James MacGregor
   The **three** Roosevelts; patrician leaders who transformed America. by James MacGregor Burns & Susan Dunn. Atlantic Monthly Press 2001 678p il $37.50; pa $18   **973.91**
1. Diplomats 2. Governors 3. Presidents 4. Vice-presidents 5. People with disabilities 6. Columnists 7. Philatelists 8. Humanitarians 9. Social activists 10. Spouses of presidents 11. United Nations officials 12.

Nobel laureates for peace 13. United States -- Politics and government -- 20th century

ISBN 0-87113-780-1; 0-8021-3872-1 pa

LC 00-60896

Burns and Dunn "present an analysis of the Roosevelts that {aims to} establish the connections among their careers, ideas and values. . . . Theodore, Franklin and Eleanor not only changed the very nature of American society, {the authors argue}, they also altered the history of the rest of the world." America

Burns and Dunn "succeed in approaching their subjects with grace, respect and insight. In the end, they do great justice to three remarkable lives." Publ Wkly

Includes bibliographical references

Davis, Deborah

Guest of honor; Booker T. Washington, Theodore Roosevelt, and the White House dinner that shocked a nation. by Deborah Davis. Atria Books 2012 x, 308 p.p **973.91**

1. Presidents -- United States -- Biography 2. United States -- Race relations -- History 3. United States -- Politics and government -- 1898-1919 4. United States -- Social conditions -- 1865-1918 5. United States -- Politics and government -- 1901-1909 6. United States -- Race relations -- History -- 20th century

ISBN 1439169810; 9781439169810; 9781439169827; 9781439169834

LC 2012009045

This book is a "portrayal of the . . . oppressive racial attitudes prevalent at the turn of the twentieth century. As [Deborah] Davis indicates, even many so-called Progressives adhered to pseudoscientific doctrines of social Darwinism and Anglo-Saxon racial superiority Given that context, the unprecedented dinner invitation extended by President Teddy Roosevelt to preeminent black educator Booker T. Washington assumed great importance. Davis first expends considerable effort in drawing parallels between the two men . . . showing both as intense strivers. . . . When she gets to the meeting itself and the reactions to it, she . . . provid[es a] . . . snapshot of the prejudices and schisms in American society a century ago." Booklist

Includes bibliographical references (p.[285]-295) and index

Dickstein, Morris

Dancing in the dark; a cultural history of the Great Depression. W. W. Norton 2009 598p il $29.95 **973.91**

1. Great Depression, 1929-1939 2. Popular culture -- United States 3. United States -- History -- 1919-1933 4. United States -- History -- 1933-1945 5. United States -- Social life and customs

ISBN 978-0-393-07225-9

LC 2009-17389

A cultural history of the 1930s explores the anxiety, despair, and optimism of the period while evaluating such factors as the Dust Bowl migrations, "screwball comedy," and swing band music to evaluate how period culture provided a dynamic lift to the country's morale.

"Whether discussing Citizen Kane or Porgy and Bess, the poetry of Langston Hughes, William Carlos Williams or Robert Frost, Faulkner's unique achievement and odd relation to the period, the films of Cary Grant or the elegance and energy of Art Deco, Dickstein always has something smart and lively to say. His scintillating commentary illuminates an important dimension of a decade too often considered only in political or economic terms. It's hard to imagine a more astute, more graceful guide to a remarkably creative period." Kirkus

Includes bibliographical references

Egan, Timothy

★ The **big** burn; Teddy Roosevelt and the fire that saved America. Houghton Mifflin Harcourt 2009 324p il map $27 **973.91**

1. Governors 2. Presidents 3. Forest fires 4. Vice-presidents 5. Conservationists 6. Forest conservation 7. Nature conservation 8. Foresters 9. Nobel laureates for peace 10. United States -- Forest Service 11. Forest conservation -- United States 12. Forest fires -- United States -- History 13. National parks and reserves -- United States 14. Forest conservation -- United States -- History 15. Nature conservation -- United States -- History 16. National parks and reserves -- United States -- History

ISBN 978-0-618-96841-1; 0-618-96841-5

LC 2009-21881

"This is history that is well researched, vividly set into the context of the early twentieth century, and written with such skill in character development and pacing that readers will be lost in a vivid reimagining of those surreal days in 1910 when an ecological event unfolded with the spectacle of a modern summer blockbuster." Orion

Includes bibliographical references (p. [287]-305) and index.

Goldberg, Ronald Allen

America in the forties; Ronald Allen Goldberg ; foreword by John Robert Greene. Syracuse University Press 2012 xiii, 213 p.p (pbk. : alk. paper) $19.95 **973.91**

1. Cold war 2. United States -- Military history 3. United States -- Foreign relations 4. Nineteen forties 5. United States -- History -- 1933-1945 6. United States -- History -- 1945-1953 7. World War, 1939-1945 -- United States 8. United States -- Social conditions -- 1945- 9. United States -- Social conditions -- 1933-1945

ISBN 0815632657; 0815632924; 9780815632658; 9780815632924

LC 2011036927

Author Ronald Allen Goldberg "argues that the decade of the 1940s was . . . a period marked by war, sacrifice, and profound social changes . . . in American history . . . [He] traces the entire decade . . . through the conflicts with Europe and Japan, to the start of the Cold War and the dawn of the atomic age . . . Goldberg chronicles US heroic accomplishments during World War II and the early Cold War, showing how these . . . achievements helped lay the foundation for the country's current role in economic and military affairs worldwide." (Syracuse University Press)

Includes bibliographical references and index

Goodwin, Doris Kearns, 1943-

★ The **Bully** Pulpit; Theodore Roosevelt, William Howard Taft, and the Golden Age of Journalism. Doris Kearns Goodwin. Simon & Schuster 2013 848 p. illustrations $40   **973.91**

1. Journalism -- United States -- History 2. United States -- Politics and government -- 1901-1909 3. United States -- Politics and government -- 1909-1913 4. Republican Party (U.S. : 1854-) -- History -- 20th century 5. Press and politics -- United States -- History -- 20th century 6. Progressivism (United States politics) -- History -- 20th century

ISBN 141654786X; 9781416547860

LC 2013032709

Andrew Carnegie Medal for Excellence in Nonfiction (2014)

This book, by Doris Kearns Goodwin, examines "the friendship of two very different Presidents, [Theodore] Roosevelt and William Howard Taft. . . . Though the book is primarily concerned with the intervening private lives of two politicians, a prominent second narrative emerges as Goodwin links both presidents' fortunes to the rise of 'muckraking' journalism, specifically the magazine 'McClure's' and its influence over political and social discussion." (Publishers Weekly)

"By shining a light on a little-discussed President and a much-discussed one, Goodwin manages to make history very much alive and relevant." Pub Wkly

Includes bibliographical references (pages 753-867) and index

Hagedorn, Ann

Savage peace; hope and fear in America, 1919. Simon & Schuster 2007 543p il $30   **973.91**

1. United States -- Race relations 2. United States -- History -- 1919-1933

ISBN 978-0-7432-4371-1; 0-7432-4371-4

LC 2006-51258

Hagedorn "weaves numerous threads of history together to provide a clear vision of American society at the dawn of the modern age. This is not the dull history of academia: Her writing is concise, colorful and compelling." PopMatters

Includes bibliographical references (p. [499]-510) and index.

Hofstadter, Richard

The **age** of reform from Bryan to F.D.R. Knopf 1955 328, xxp hardcover o.p. pa $12.95   **973.91**

1. United States -- Politics and government -- 20th century

ISBN 0-394-70095-3 pa

This analysis of the reform movements in American politics from 1890-1940 reviews: The agrarian uprising that found its expression in the Populist movement of the 1890's; The Progressive movement from about 1900-1914; The New Deal of the 1930's. Emphasis is placed upon the ideas of the leading political reformers.

Includes bibliographical references

Kennedy, David M.

★ **Freedom** from fear; the American people in depression and war, 1929-1945. Oxford Univ. Press

1999 936p il maps (Oxford history of the United States) $39.95; pa $22.50   **973.91**

1. United States -- History -- 1919-1933 2. United States -- History -- 1933-1945

ISBN 0-19-503834-7; 0-19-514403-1 pa

LC 98-49580

This narrative history of the United States spans the period from the Great Depression to the end of the Second World War

"Rarely does a work of historical synthesis combine such trenchant analysis and elegant writing. For its scope, its insight and its purring narrative engine, Kennedy's book will stand for years to come as the definitive account of the critical decades of the American century." Publ Wkly

Includes bibliographical references

Lingeman, Richard

The **noir** forties; the American people from victory to Cold War. Richard Lingeman. Nation Books 2012 432 p. (hardcover : alk. paper) $29.99 **973.91**

1. United States -- History -- 1945-1953 2. United States -- Social conditions -- 1945- 3. United States -- Intellectual life -- 20th century 4. Film noir -- United States -- History and criticism 5. United States -- Politics and government -- 1945-1953 6. Social change -- United States -- History -- 20th century 7. Social psychology -- United States -- History -- 20th century 8. Film noir -- Social aspects -- United States -- History -- 20th century

ISBN 1568584369; 9781568584362; 9781568586908

LC 2012024868

The author "inquires into America's shift from New Deal liberalism to conservatism through the lenses of America's late-1940s cultural and political scenes. . . . Lingeman eventually devises an end-point of sorts with the ascendance of anticommunism, the blacklisting of Hollywood figures, and the exhaustion of film noir's creativity. A work that never resolves whether it's film history, political history, or lamentation for liberalism, Lingeman's survey becomes everything by turns." Booklist

Includes bibliographical references and index

Millard, Candice

The **river** of doubt; Theodore Roosevelt's darkest journey. Doubleday 2005 416p il map $26 **973.91**

1. Governors 2. Presidents 3. Vice-presidents 4. Amazon River valley 5. Nobel laureates for peace 6. Roosevelt-Rondon Scientific Expedition (1913-1914)

ISBN 0-385-50796-8

LC 2005-46541

This is an account of the Amazon expedition Theodore Roosevelt undertook in 1912, with his son Kermit and the Brazilian explorer Col. Candido Rondon.

The author "turns this incredible story into one that easily matches an Indiana Jones screen adventure." Libr J

Includes bibliographical references

Miller, Nathan

New world coming; the 1920s and the making of modern America. Da Capo Press 2004 433p pa $19.95   **973.91**

1. Authors 2. Novelists 3. Screenwriters 4. Short

story writers 5. United States -- History -- 1919-1933
ISBN 978-0-306-81379-5; 0-306-81379-3

LC 2004-56140

First published 2003 by Scribner

The author "illuminates the United States as it existed under presidents Harding, Coolidge and Hoover, using the life of F. Scott Fitzgerald, with all its peaks and valleys during the 1920s, as the backbone of his narrative. . . . In addition to events in the arts and sciences, Miller details bitter labor struggles, the rise of the reconstituted Ku Klux Klan and Prohibition. . . . This volume comprises an excellent chronicle of that turbulent, troubled and tempestuous decade called 'the roaring '20s.'" Publ Wkly

Includes bibliographical references

Moore, Lucy

Anything goes; a biography of the roaring twenties. Overlook Press 2010 352p il $25.95   **973.91**
1. United States -- History -- 1919-1933
ISBN 978-1-59020-313-2

LC 2009-46437

First published 2008 in the United Kingdom

"Rather than presenting her material as an extended survey of the period, Moore focuses on a single Jazz Age trope per chapter, resulting in easily digestible takes on prohibition and the high-spirited criminal culture it engendered; the explosion in popularity of jazz music; the evolution of the flapper; the emergence of Hollywood as creator of a national cultural consciousness; the financial scandals of the Harding presidency; the Sacco/Vanzetti and Scopes trials; the resurgence of the Ku Klux Klan; the Algonquin round table and the founding of the New Yorker; Charles Lindbergh's historic trans-Atlantic flight; the spectacular boxing career of Jack Dempsey; and the financial devastation of the Wall Street crash that ended the party and ushered in the Great Depression. . . . Snappy, vivid account of America's most glittering decade." Kirkus

Includes bibliographical references

Morris, Edmund

★ **Theodore** Rex. Random House 2001 772p il map $35; pa $16.95   **973.91**
1. Governors 2. Presidents 3. Vice-presidents 4. Nobel laureates for peace 5. Presidents -- United States
ISBN 0-394-55509-0; 0-8129-6600-7 pa

LC 2001-19366

"The second entry in Morris's . . . three-volume life of Theodore Roosevelt focuses on the presidential years 1901 through early 1909." Publ Wkly

"Morris excels at placing TR in the context of his time, showing how he out maneuvered powerful but ossified opponents from the Gilded Age and trumped isolationists by averting war, in the process winning the first Nobel Peace Prize." Libr J

Includes bibliographical references

Followed by Colonel Roosevelt (2010)

Pietrusza, David

1920 : the year of the six presidents. Carroll & Graf 2007 533p il $28.95   **973.91**
1. Presidents -- United States -- Election -- 1920
ISBN 978-0-78671-622-7; 0-7867-1622-3

"Six men—a sitting president, former president, and four eventual presidents—competed in the 1920 presidential election. . . . [The author] contends that this election marked the birth of modern American politics. . . . The many issues and forces that swirled during that time, from the fear of Communists and Socialists and the terrorism they allegedly perpetrated to technological advances and Prohibition, make for a fascinating and compelling tale of an often-overlooked election in our history." Libr J

Includes bibliographical references

Schlesinger, Arthur M. (Arthur Meier), 1917-2007

The **crisis** of the old order, 1919-1933; [by] Arthur M. Schlesinger, Jr. Houghton Mifflin 2003 557p (Age of Roosevelt) pa $17   **973.91**
1. Governors 2. Presidents 3. People with disabilities 4. Philatelists 5. United States -- History -- 1919-1933
ISBN 0-618-34085-8

LC 2003-47884

First published 1957

This is the first of three volumes which interpret the political, economic, social, and intellectual life of the United States during the time when Franklin D. Roosevelt was in office. This volume covers the years preceding his first term

Includes bibliographical references

Followed by The coming of the New Deal, and The politics of upheaval

A **life** in the twentieth century; innocent beginnings, 1917-1950. [by] Arthur M. Schlesinger, Jr. Houghton Mifflin 2000 557p il $28.95; pa $15   **973.91**
1. Authors 2. Historians 3. Biographers 4. Nonfiction writers 5. Government officials 6. Historians -- United States
ISBN 0-395-70752-8; 0-618-21925-0 pa

LC 00-61322

This first volume of Schlesinger's autobiography covers the author's life through the publication of The Age of Jackson and The Vital Center.

Schlesinger's "autobiography, skillfully interweaving the personal and the historical, is elegantly simple and marvellously clear. Complex thoughts are set forth with a lucidity that conceals the depth of the intellectual analysis. Wit, humour and the resources of a natural storyteller sweep the reader along." Economist

Shlaes, Amity

Coolidge; Amity Shlaes. Harper 2013 viii, 565 p., [14] p. of platesp ill. $35   **973.91**
1. United States -- History -- 1919-1933 2. United States -- Economic conditions -- 1919-1933 3. Presidents -- United States -- Biography 4. United States -- Politics and government -- 1923-1929
ISBN 0061967556; 9780061967559

LC 2012032098

In this biography of U.S. President Calvin Coolidge, "[Amity] Shlaes shows that the mid-1920s was . . . a triumphant period that established our modern way of life. . . Coolidge's discipline and composure, Shlaes reveals, represented not weakness but strength. . . . Coolidge proved unafraid to take on the divisive issues of this crucial period:

reining in public-sector unions, unrelentingly curtailing spending, and rejecting funding for new interest groups." (Publisher's note)

Includes bibliographical references and index

The **forgotten** man; a new history of the Great Depression. by Chuck Dixon (Adapter), Amity Shlaes (Author), Paul Rivoche (Illustrator) HarperCollins 2014 293 p. il $19.99   **973.91**
1. New Deal, 1933-1939 2. Great Depression, 1929-1939 3. New Deal, 1933-1939 -- Graphic novels 4. Great Depression, 1929-1939 -- Graphic novels 5. Depressions -- 1929 -- United States 6. Presidents --United States -- Policies 7. Economic stabilization -- United States -- History -- 20th century
ISBN 0061967645; 9780061967641

This graphic novel, adapted from Amity Shlaes' history text by Chuck Dixon and illustrated by Paul Rivoche, "brings to life one of the most devastating periods in . . . [U.S.] history—the Great Depression—through the lives of American people, from politicians and workers to businessmen, farmers, and ordinary citizens." (Publisher's note)

"Reminding readers that the reputedly do-nothing Hoover pulled hard on the fiscal levers (raising tariffs, increasing government spending), Shlaes nevertheless emphasizes that his enthusiasm for intervention paled against the ebullient FDR's glee in experimentation. She focuses closely on the influence of his fabled Brain Trust, her narrative shifting among Raymond Moley, Rexford Tugwell, and other prominent New Dealers. Businesses that litigated their resistance to New Deal regulations attract Shlaes' attention, as do individuals who coped with the despair of the 1930s through self-help, such as Alcoholics Anonymous cofounder Bill Wilson. The book culminates in the rise of Wendell Willkie, and Shlaes' accent on personalities is an appealing avenue into her skeptical critique of the New Deal." Booklist

Includes bibliographical references

Smith, Hedrick

Who stole the American dream? Hedrick Smith. Random House 2012 xxxi, 557 p.p   **973.91**
1. American dream 2. Middle class -- United States 3. United States -- Politics and government 4. Public interest -- United States 5. Divided government -- United States 6. Income distribution -- United States 7. Polarization (Social sciences) -- United States 8. United States -- Politics and government -- 1989- 9. Middle class -- Political activity -- United States 10. Middle class -- United States -- Economic conditions 11. United States -- Politics and government -- 1945-1989 12. Political culture -- United States -- History -- 20th century 13. Political culture -- United States -- History -- 21st century
ISBN 1400069661; 9780679604648; 9781400069668
                                        LC 2012005865

This book, by Pulitzer Prize winner Hedrick Smith, offers an "account of how, over the past four decades, the American Dream has been dismantled. . . . Smith reveals how pivotal laws and policies were altered while the public wasn't looking, how Congress often ignores public opinion, why moderate politicians got shoved to the sidelines, and

how Wall Street often wins politically by hiring over 1,400 former government officials as lobbyists." (Publisher's note)

Includes bibliographical references (p. [527]-538) and index

Starobin, Paul

After America; narratives for the next global age. Viking 2009 358p $26.95   **973.91**
1. International relations 2. United States -- Civilization 3. United States -- Foreign relations
ISBN 978-0-670-02094-2
                                        LC 2008-46685

This "is a narrative of extraordinary range and contemporary relevance." Publ Wkly

Includes bibliographical references

Terkel, Studs, 1912-2008

★ **Hard** times; an oral history of the great depression. Norton 2000 462p pa $14.95   **973.91**
1. Great Depression, 1929-1939 2. United States -- Social conditions 3. United States -- Economic conditions -- 1919-1933 4. United States -- Economic conditions -- 1933-1945
ISBN 1-56584-656-7
                                        LC 2003-389318

A reissue of the title first published 1970 by Pantheon Bks. "Persons of all ages, occupations, and classes scattered across the U.S. remember what they experienced or were told about the economic crisis of the 1930's. The result is a social document of immense interest." Booklist

973.917   Administration of Franklin Delano Roosevelt, 1933-1945

The **40s;** the story of a decade. The New Yorker ; edited by Henry Finder with Giles Harvey ; introduction by David Remnick. Random House Inc 2014 720 p. illustrations (acid-free paper) $30   **973.917**
1. Nineteen forties 2. New York (N.Y.) -- Intellectual life 3. United States -- In literature 4. New Yorker (New York, N.Y. : 1925) 5. United States -- History -- 1933-1945 6. United States -- History -- 1945-1953 7. United States -- Social customs -- 1945- 8. United States -- Social customs -- 1933-1945 9. United States -- Social life and customs -- 20th century
ISBN 0679644792; 9780679644798; 9780679644804
                                        LC 2013047082

"The 1940s were when 'The New Yorker' came of age. A magazine that was best known for its humor and wry social observation would extend itself, offering the first in-depth reporting from Hiroshima and introducing American readers to the fiction of Vladimir Nabokov and the poetry of Elizabeth Bishop. In this . . . book, . . . contributions from the . . . writers who graced [the magazine's] pages throughout the decade are placed in history by the magazine's current writers." (Publisher's note)

"Readers are certain to enjoy the beautiful writing, clever thinking and insightful thoughts across a vast range of topics." Kirkus

Cook, Blanche Wiesen

Eleanor Roosevelt. v1 Penguin Bks. 1993 587p
v1 il pa $18   **973.917**
1. Diplomats 2. Columnists 3. Humanitarians 4.
Social activists 5. Spouses of presidents 6. United
Nations officials 7. Presidents' spouses -- United States
ISBN 0-14-009460-1

LC 87040632

First published 1992
This first volume of a two-volume biography of Eleanor Roosevelt "spans the years from Eleanor's birth to her
husband Franklin Delano's inauguration." Publisher's note
Includes bibliographical references

Fullilove, Michael

Rendezvous with destiny; how Franklin D.
Roosevelt and five extraordinary men took Ameri-
ca into the war and into the world. Michael Fulli-
love. The Penguin Press 2013 480 p. (hardcover)
$29.95   **973.917**
1. World War, 1939-1945 -- United States 2. World
War, 1939-1945 -- Diplomatic history 3. United States
-- Foreign relations -- 1933-1945
ISBN 1594204357; 9781594204357

LC 2012047003

This book by Michael Fullilove looks at the lead-up to
the U.S. entry in to World War II. President Franklin D. Roosevelt "had to jump some big hurdles: he had to convince
his fellow Americans of the necessity of getting involved,
and he had to support Britain's efforts to keep Hitler from
overwhelming the U.K.'s skies and shores. In 1940, Roosevelt enlisted five capable men to cross the Atlantic to visit,
negotiate, observe the war-weary British, and assess how the
U.S. could help." (Publishers Weekly)
Includes bibliographical references and index

Golay, Michael

★ **America** 1933; the Great Depression, Lorena
Hickok, Eleanor Roosevelt, and the shaping of the
New Deal. by Michael Golay. Free Press 2013 336
p. $26.99   **973.917**
1. Great Depression, 1929-1939 2. United States --
History -- 1919-1933 3. Depressions -- 1929 -- United
States 4. United States -- History -- 1933-1945 5.
United States -- Social conditions -- 1918-1945 6.
United States -- Economic conditions -- 1918-1945 7.
Investigative reporting -- United States -- History -- 20th
century
ISBN 143919601X; 9781439196014

LC 2012041139

In this book, author Michael Golay "writes of the 1933-
34 cross-country trip undertaken by Lorena Hickok to
evaluate and report to the new Federal Emergency Relief
Administration (FERA) on how the Great Depression was
impacting ordinary families. . . . She had been an Associated
Press reporter; her friendship with Eleanor Roosevelt (ER)
helped her to create FERA reports that captured President
Roosevelt's attention. Golay focuses here on the grinding
poverty that Hickok witnessed." (Library Journal)
Includes bibliographical references and index

Jackson, Robert Houghwout

That man: an insider's portrait of Franklin D.
Roosevelt; [by] Robert H. Jackson; edited and introduced by John Q. Barrett; with a foreword by William
E. Leuchtenburg. Oxford University Press 2003 xxviii, 290p il hardcover o.p. pa $17.95   **973.917**
1. Governors 2. Presidents 3. People with disabilities
4. Philatelists 5. Presidents -- United States 6. United
States -- Politics and government -- 1933-1945
ISBN 0-19-516826-7; 0-19-517757-6 pa

LC 2003-9275

This "is a lively, revealing and suddenly relevant book.
Jackson's memoir sheds new light—not always flattering—
on important events and on a president who too often appears only in silhouette." N Y Times Book Rev
Includes bibliographical references

Katznelson, Ira

Fear itself; the New Deal and the origins of our
time. Ira Katznelson. Liveright Publishing Corporation 2013 512 p. (hardcover) $29.95   **973.917**
1. New Deal, 1933-1939 2. United States -- Economic
conditions -- 1919-1933 3. World politics, 1933-1945
4. United States -- Politics and government -- 1933-
1945 5. Political culture -- United States -- History --
20th century
ISBN 0871404508; 9780871404503

LC 2012041794

Author Ira Katznelson looks at the New Deal in this
book. "Rather than seeing [Franklin D. Roosevelt]'s brain-
child as simply a great experiment in economic recovery and
the enlargement of government responsibility, Katznelson
emphasizes three often neglected aspects of that extraordinary era"--fear, pressure from Nazi and Soviet regimes, and
the "southern cage." (Publishers Weekly)
Includes bibliographical references and index

Leuchtenburg, William Edward

Franklin D. Roosevelt and the New Deal, 1932-
1940; {by} William E. Leuchtenburg. Harper &
Row 1963 393p il (New American nation series)
hardcover o.p. pa $16   **973.917**
1. Governors 2. Presidents 3. New Deal, 1933-1939 4.
People with disabilities 5. Philatelists 6. United States
-- History -- 1933-1945
ISBN 0-06-133025-6 pa

This treatment of Roosevelt's first two terms in office
emphasizes the economic crisis and New Deal reforms.
The author shows how social forces influenced government action: the San Francisco strike in 1934, the careers of
Huey Long and Father Coughlin, the sharecroppers' revolt,
and unemployment
This book "is comprehensive, logically organized, and
written with clarity and detachment." Am Hist Rev
Includes bibliographical references

Moe, Richard

Roosevelt's second act; the election of 1940 and
the politics of war. Richard Moe. Oxford University
Press 2013 392 p. $29.95   **973.917**
1. World War, 1939-1945 -- United States 2. Presidents

-- Term of office -- United States 3. Presidents -- United States -- Election -- 1940 4. United States -- Foreign relations -- 1933-1945 5. United States -- Politics and government -- 1933-1945
ISBN 0199981914; 9780199981915

LC 2013004529

This book by Richard Moe looks at the "the lead-up to the U.S. election of 1940 and war in Europe. . . . Moe aims to get inside FDR's head and delineate the president's decision-making process step by step. From 'shifting gears' from trying to jump-start the crippled economy in his first term to focusing on German aggression and bolstering England in his second, Roosevelt never let himself be pinned down." (Kirkus Reviews)

Includes bibliographical references and index

Schlesinger, Arthur M. (Arthur Meier), 1917-2007

The **coming** of the New Deal, 1933-1935; {by} Arthur M. Schlesinger, Jr. Houghton Mifflin 2003 669p (Age of Roosevelt) pa $17   **973.917**
1. Governors 2. Presidents 3. New Deal, 1933-1939 4. People with disabilities 5. United States -- History -- 1933-1945
ISBN 0-618-34086-6

LC 2003-47859

First published 1959

"This second volume of 'The Age of Roosevelt' continues the work begun with 'The Crisis of the Old Order, 1919-1933'. . . . The dramatic story of how representative democracy began the battle to conquer economic collapse is followed through the first two years of the New Deal." Libr J

Includes bibliographical references
Followed by The politics of upheaval

The **politics** of upheaval, 1935-1936; {by} Arthur M. Schlesinger, Jr. Houghton Mifflin 2003 749p (Age of Roosevelt) pa $17   **973.917**
1. Governors 2. Presidents 3. New Deal, 1933-1939 4. People with disabilities 5. United States -- History -- 1933-1945
ISBN 0-618-34087-4

LC 2003-47889

First published 1960

This third volume of The age of Roosevelt "concentrates on the turbulent concluding years of Franklin D. Roosevelt's first term." Publisher's note

Includes bibliographical references

Simon, James F.

FDR and Chief Justice Hughes; the president, the Supreme Court, and the epic battle over the New Deal. James F. Simon. Simon & Schuster 2012 461 p. $28   **973.917**
1. New Deal, 1933-1939 2. Presidents -- United States 3. United States -- Foreign relations 4. United States. Supreme Court -- Biography 5. United States -- Politics and government -- 1933-1945 6. Executive power -- United States -- History -- 20th century 7. Political questions and judicial power -- United States -- History -- 20th century
ISBN 9781416573289; 9781416573296;

9781416578895

LC 2011028825

Author James F. Simon focuses on "the struggle between FDR and Chief Justice Charles Evans Hughes that decided the fate of the New Deal. . . . In 1936, FDR was reelected by a landslide and the exasperated president proposed legislation to relieve, he said, the overburdened and elderly justices of their heavy workload. He proposed the appointment of an additional justice for each sitting member over seventy years old. . . . The proposal would have permitted the president to stack the Court with justices favorable to the New." (Publisher's note)

Includes bibliographical references and index.

973.918   Administration of Harry S. Truman, 1945-1953

Donald, Aida D.

Citizen soldier; a life of Harry S. Truman. Aida D. Donald. Basic Books 2012 xvi, 265 p.p (hardcover : alk. paper) $26.99   **973.918**
1. Soldiers -- United States -- Biography 2. Presidents -- United States -- Biography 3. United States -- Politics and government -- 1945-1953
ISBN 046503120X; 9780465031207

LC 2012025583

This book by Aida D. Donald is a biography of former U.S. President Harry S. Truman. "When Franklin Roosevelt passed away in April 1945, Truman unexpectedly found himself at the helm of the American war effort--and in command of the atomic bomb, the most lethal weapon humanity had ever seen. Truman's decisive leadership during the remainder of World War II and the period that followed reshaped American politics, economics, and foreign relations." (Publisher's note)

Includes bibliographical references and index

McCullough, David G., 1933-

Truman; {by} David McCullough. Simon & Schuster 1992 1117p il $40; pa $22   **973.918**
1. Presidents 2. Vice-presidents 3. Senators 4. Biography, Individual
ISBN 0-671-45654-7; 0-671-86920-5 pa

LC 92-5245

This is a biography of the thirty-third president of the United States. Bibliography. Index.

This biography of the 33rd president "not only conveys in rich detail Truman's accomplishments as a politician and statesman, but also reveals the character and personality of this constantly-surprising man—as schoolboy, farmer, soldier, merchant, county judge, senator, vice president and chief executive. The book relates how Truman overcame the stigma of business failure and debt . . . and acquired a reputation for honesty, reliability and common sense." Publ Wkly

Includes bibliographical references

973.92   United States--1953-2001

American empire, 1945-2000; the rise of a global power, the democratic revolution at home. Joshua Freeman. Viking 2012 512 p.   **973.92**
1. United States -- History -- 1945- 2. United States -- Foreign relations 3. United States -- Politics and government -- 1945- 4. United States -- Economic conditions -- 20th century 5. United States -- Foreign relations -- 1989- 6. United States -- Economic conditions -- 1945- 7. United States -- Foreign relations -- 1945-1989 8. United States -- Politics and government -- 1989- 9. United States -- Politics and government -- 1945-1989
ISBN 0670023787; 9780670023783

LC 2011049263

In this book, author Joshua B. Freeman examines a postwar dominant America . . . . Covering the glory years of 1945-2000, Freeman . . . turns his critical eye on America's turbulent internal affairs, delving into Truman's contested Fair Deal reforms, the McCarthy communist witch-hunts, Eisenhower's cautious civil rights record, LBJ's ambitious Great Society programs, Nixon's Watergate disgrace, the return of "corporate capitalism" and Reagan conservatism. Freeman deals with the Clinton administration's economic policies . . . followed by the Republican victory in 2000. Though at its peak, America's power exceeded that of the Roman and British empires in cultural, economic, military, and political terms, the nation's postwar dreams were never completely fulfilled, says Freeman. (Publishers Weekly)
Includes bibliographical references and index

Bloom, Allan David

The **closing** of the American mind. Simon & Schuster 1987 392p hardcover o.p. pa $14 **973.92**
1. Higher education 2. United States -- Intellectual life
ISBN 0-671-65715-1 pa

LC 86-24768

This is the author's assessment of liberal arts education today. "In essence, he argues that over the last 25 years the academy has all but abandoned the intellectual and moral principles that have traditionally informed and given substance to liberal education, becoming prey to the enthusiasms—increasingly politicized—of the moment." N Y Times Book Rev

Duffy, Michael

★ The **presidents** club; inside the world's most exclusive fraternity. Nancy Gibbs and Michael Duffy. Simon & Schuster 2012 vii, 641 p.p   **973.92**
1. Interpersonal relations 2. Presidents -- United States 3. United States -- Politics and government -- 1945- 4. Presidents -- United States -- History 5. Ex-presidents -- United States -- History
ISBN 1439127700; 9781439127704

LC 2011042047

This book "chart[s] the zigzag arc of relationships among the men who have occupied the White House since the mid 20th century. . . . [T]he authors present numerous instances of presidents warming to their predecessors. . . . Sometimes mutual admiration was already in place (Truman and Eisenhower--though it later disintegrated); sometimes,

antipathy (Clinton and Bush II). But almost always the sitting presidents found in their predecessors some solace, willing ears and sound advice." (Kirkus)
Includes bibliographical references.

Frank, Thomas

The **wrecking** crew; how conservatives rule. Metropolitan Books 2008 369p il $25   **973.92**
1. Conservatism 2. Republican Party (U.S.) 3. United States -- Politics and government
ISBN 978-0-8050-7988-3; 0-8050-7988-2

LC 2008-15802

The author offers his assessment of the conservative Republican approach to government.
This "is a useful introduction to a world of pricey lobbyists, crackpot theorists, bought legislators and hapless government. And, in part through these very caricatures, the book gets at some essential questions about politics and markets in a democratic society." Nation
Includes bibliographical references

Frum, David

How we got here; the 70's: the decade that brought you modern life (for better or worse) Basic Bks. 2000 xxiv, 418p il hardcover o.p. pa $18.95   **973.92**
1. United States -- Civilization -- 1970-
ISBN 0-465-01496-5 pa

The author "aims 'to describe—and to judge' the transformation of American values during the '70s. Surveying politics, legal cases and opinion polls as well as popular culture, he links what he sees as America's loss of faith in government, the rise of 'sourness and cynicism' and the culture of licentiousness and divorce, among other social changes, to events in that decade." Publ Wkly
Includes bibliographical references

Gregory, Ross

Cold War America, 1946 to 1990; Richard Balkin, general editor. Facts on File 2003 670p il map (Almanacs of American life) $105   **973.92**
1. Cold war 2. United States -- History -- 1945- 3. United States -- Social conditions
ISBN 0-8160-3868-6

LC 2001-51136

"This is a treasure trove of statistical information documenting the enormous changes in American life from 1945 to 1990. . . . Found herein are data on everything from the population by sex . . . region, and race, business formations and failures, bull and bear markets, and operations of the postal service to the federal debt, high school seniors and drugs, executions by gender and race, and recipients of National Book Awards and Pulitzer Prizes. . . . Enhancing the work's appeal are photographs throughout the text and an exhaustive index." Am Ref Books Annu, 2003
Includes bibliographical references

Halberstam, David

The **fifties**. Villard Bks. 1993 800p il hardcover o.p. pa $17.95   **973.92**
1. Popular culture -- United States 2. United States -- Social life and customs 3. United States -- Politics and

government -- 20th century
ISBN 0-449-90933-6 pa

LC 92-56815

This is a social history of the United States during the 1950s

The author's "sources are secondary and derivative, but his instinct for the revealing anecdote, his ear for the memorable quote, and his awesome powers of organization add up to a variegated overview that moves seamlessly between the serious shenanigans of Chief Justice Earl Warren and the frivolous ones of . . . Grace Metalious." Natl Rev

Includes bibliographical references

Hayden, Tom

The **long** sixties; from 1960 to Barack Obama. Paradigm Publishers 2009 272p $26.95 **973.92**

1. Lawyers 2. Presidents 3. Social change 4. Social movements 5. Senators 6. State legislators 7. Nobel laureates for peace 8. United States -- Social conditions 9. United States -- History -- 1961-1974

ISBN 978-1-59451-739-6; 1-59451-739-8

"With elements of a new Rules for Radicals and knowing takes on such old New Left moments as The Port Huron Statement, Hayden's book could be a worthy foundational document." Kirkus

Includes bibliographical references

Hodgson, Godfrey

The **gentleman** from New York: Daniel Patrick Moynihan: a biography. Houghton Mifflin 2000 452p il $38 **973.92**

1. Diplomats 2. Senators 3. Nonfiction writers 4. Political scientists 5. United Nations officials

ISBN 0-395-86042-3

LC 00-38921

"A cold war liberal, more of a regular Democrat than a reformer, Moynihan will no doubt be remembered as one of the smarter, more thoughtful elected officials of the late twentieth century. Others will probably produce more critical biographies, but, for now, Hodgson has supplied a fairly balanced overview." Booklist

Includes bibliographical references

Holmes, David L.

The **faiths** of the postwar presidents; from Truman to Obama. David L. Holmes ; introduction by Martin E. Marty. University of Georgia Press 2012 pxiii, 396 p.p $29.95 **973.92**

1. Presidents -- United States -- Religion 2. Presidents -- United States -- Biography 3. Christianity and politics -- United States

ISBN 0820338621; 9780820338620

LC 2011029959

This book, by David L. Holmes, "looks at the role of faith in the lives of the twelve presidents who have served since the end of World War II. Holmes examines not only the beliefs professed by each president but also the variety of possible influences on their religious faith, such as their upbringing, education, and the faith of their spouse." (Publisher's note)

Includes bibliographical references (p. 321-378) and index

Huchthausen, Peter A.

America's splendid little wars; a short history of U.S. military engagements, 1975-2000. Viking 2003 254p il, maps $25.95; pa $15 **973.92**

1. Intervention (International law) 2. United States -- Military history

ISBN 0-670-03232-8; 0-14-200465-0 pa

LC 2002-38025

This is "a review of America's conflicts since the fall of Saigon in 1975. Each of the 15 chronologically arranged conflicts has its own chapter, and they are also grouped by presidential administration, with the author demonstrating how U.S. foreign policy changed during each administration. The author does an excellent job of describing the circumstances surrounding the different conflicts, including eyewitness testimony and solid research to tell each story. . . . This book should appeal to subject specialists and casual readers alike." Libr J

Includes bibliographical references and index

King, Martin Luther

The **trumpet** of conscience; [by] Martin Luther King, Jr. Beacon Press 2010 80p (King legacy series) $22; pa $12 **973.92**

1. United States -- Social conditions

ISBN 978-0-8070-0071-7; 0-8070-0071-X; 978-0-8070-0170-7 pa; 0-8070-0170-8 pa

LC 2010007881

First published 1968 by Harper & Row

"In November and December 1967, Dr. Martin Luther King, Jr., delivered five lectures for the renowned Massey Lecture Series of the Canadian Broadcasting Corporation. The collection was immediately released as a book under the title Conscience for Change, but after King's assassination in 1968, it was republished as The Trumpet of Conscience. The collection . . . is his final testament on racism, poverty, and war. Each oration in this volume encompasses a distinct theme, . . . addressing issues of equality, conscience and war, the mobilization of young people, and nonviolence." Publisher's note

Kirkpatrick, Rob

1969; the year everything changed. Skyhorse Pub. 2009 302p $24.95 **973.92**

1. United States -- Social conditions 2. United States -- History -- 1961-1974 3. United States -- Civilization -- 1945- 4. United States -- Social life and customs

ISBN 978-1-60239-366-0

LC 2008-43073

The author "asserts that 1969 was the birth of modern America and sets out to relate how this incredible year reflected deep underlying changes in American culture. The book is divided into four parts that roughly outline the year, including 'sexual revolutions of springtime' and 'the apocalyptic standoffs at year's end.' A riveting look at a pivotal year." Booklist

Includes bibliographical references

Klosterman, Chuck

Eating the dinosaur. Scribner 2009 245p $25 **973.92**

1. Sports 2. Consumption (Economics) 3. Popular

culture -- United States 4. United States -- Civilization
-- 1970-
ISBN 978-1-4165-4420-3; 1-4165-4420-8

LC 2009-18719

"Klosterman delivers his findings like earth-shattering epiphanies, letting the layers of subtle humor and irony fill in any gaps in logic. The result is a collection as much about the author and his way of thinking as it is about his topics. In both cases, the author is unique. Funny, irreverent and fascinating-Klosterman at his best." Kirkus

Kort, Michael
The **Columbia** guide to the Cold War. Columbia Univ. Press 1998 366p (Columbia guides to American history and cultures) $60; pa $19.50 **973.92**
1. Cold war 2. United States -- History -- 1945- 3. United States -- Foreign relations
ISBN 0-231-10772-2; 0-231-10773-0 pa

LC 98-7154

The author begins "with a narrative survey of the Cold War which explains some of the historiographical debates that have occupied historians for more than 50 years. Following this section is a mini-encyclopedia consisting of one- or two-page essays on a wide range of Cold War topics. The book concludes with a concise chronology and a comprehensive bibliography of books, films, novels, journal articles, and archival sources. Finally . . . Kort points out some of the relevant current websites and CD-ROM products." Libr J

Kuralt, Charles
Charles Kuralt's America. Anchor Books 1996 279p il pa $14.95 **973.92**
1. United States -- Description and travel 2. United States -- Social life and customs
ISBN 0-385-48510-7; 978-0-385-48510-4

LC 96-18992

First published 1995 by Putnam

"Kuralt is not in search of crises or epiphanies; he values nature and good food, neighborliness and craftsmanship, quaintness and quirkiness. Though no literary match for American chroniclers like Calvin Trillin, the effable Kuralt does, in un-fancy style, convey his enthusiasm and his engagement." Publ Wkly

On the road with Charles Kuralt. Fawcett 1986 363p il pa $19 **973.92**
1. United States -- Description and travel 2. United States -- Social life and customs
ISBN 0-449-00740-5; 978-0-449-00740-2

First published 1985 by Putnam

"As a CBS reporter specializing in 'soft' news, Kuralt has been roaming around the U.S. since 1967 in search of 'just plain folks.' Some 100 of the television interviews that resulted from that search have been transcribed for this collection. Loosely organized by themes emphasizing the individuality, altruism, and humor that characterize small town and rural Americans, the interviews and anecdotes are consistently entertaining." Booklist

Lifton, Robert Jay, 1926-
Witness to an extreme century; a memoir. Free Press 2011 xv, 428 p.p il **973.92**
1. Authors 2. Psychiatrists 3. Autobiographies 4. College teachers 5. Nonfiction writers 6. Biography, Individual
ISBN 9781416590767; 9781416597186 ebook; 978-1-4165-9076-7; 978-1-4165-9718-6 ebook

LC 2010046148

This book presents "a memoir of [American psychiatrist Robert J.] Lifton's life and career." It "is a work of intellectual autobiography. . . . At bottom, [it] is a book about scholarship and activism, and the links between the two. . . . [Lifton's] passions include disarmament and social justice, and he possesses a firm belief in the virtues of the autonomous intellect. The enemy is what he calls 'totalism,' by which he means systems of political or religious belief that seek to stamp out the possibility for independent thought. . . . Lifton has tried throughout his life to develop and apply a morally and politically consistent standard for humane behavior to his own nation as well as to others. In doing so, he became an outspoken critic of the Vietnam War, developing a close relationship in the early 1970s with antiwar Vietnam veterans, whom he served as both clinician and advocate." (N Y Times)

Marling, Karal Ann
As seen on TV; the visual culture of everyday life in the 1950s. Harvard Univ. Press 1994 328p il map $27.50; pa $20.50 **973.92**
1. Television broadcasting 2. Popular culture -- United States 3. United States -- Social life and customs
ISBN 0-674-04882-2; 0-674-04883-0 pa

LC 94-2814

"Marling highlights the impact of television's first influential decade. From Mamie Eisenhower's apparel to the aesthetics of food advertising and cookbooks, she {aims to} demonstrate the extent to which Americans began to measure their personal lives against what was seen on television." Christ Sci Monit

"A nostalgic, informative and sometimes funny view of 1950's American culture." Publ Wkly

Includes bibliographical references

Morrow, Lance
Second drafts of history; essays. Lance Morrow. Basic Books 2006 323p $26.95 **973.92**
1. United States -- Social conditions 2. United States -- Politics and government -- 1989-
ISBN 0-4650-4750-5

LC 2005-17092

"Loosely arranged by subject, these essays cover the gamut of human experience, seen through Morrow's practiced yet unjaundiced point of view. Whether offering a fact-laden piece on the AIDS epidemic or a personal meditation on the Jonesboro, Ark., school shootings, Morrow manages—without becoming sentimental—to evoke the spirit of a collective America. . . . Since Morrow is a weekly columnist, the news of the day is often the primary subject." Publ Wkly

Patterson, James T.

Grand expectations; the United States, 1945-1974. James T. Patterson. Oxford Univ. Press 1996 xviii, 829p ill., maps (pbk.) $27.95; o.p.   **973.92**
1. United States -- History -- 1945- 2. United States -- Economic conditions 3. United States -- Politics and government -- 1945-
ISBN 9780195117974; 019507680X
LC 9513878
Bancroft Prize (1996)
In this book, author "James T. Patterson['s] . . . work . . . weaves [together] the major political, cultural, and economic events of . . . America from 1945 through Watergate. . . . [The book explores events from] the bloody campaigns in Korea and . . . McCarthyism to the assassinations of the Kennedys and Martin Luther King, to the Vietnam War, Watergate, and Nixon's resignation. Patterson . . . portray[s] the . . . [economic] growth after World War II . . . as well as the resultant buoyancy of spirit reflected in everything from streamlined toasters, to big, flashy cars, to the soaring, butterfly roof of TWA's airline terminal in New York. . . . [A]n important thread running through the book is a . . . depiction of the civil rights movement--from the electrifying Brown v. Board of Education decision, to the violent confrontations in Little Rock, Birmingham, and Selma, to the landmark civil rights acts of 1964 and 1965." (Publisher's note)
Includes bibliographical references (p. 791-802) and index.

Restless giant; the United States from Watergate to Bush v. Gore. James T. Patterson. Oxford University Press 2005 xii, 448p ill., maps $45   **973.92**
1. United States -- History -- 1945- 2. United States -- Politics and government -- 1945- 3. United States -- History -- 1969-
ISBN 019512216X; 9780195122169
LC 2005016711
This book provides an "assessment of the twenty-seven years between the resignation of Richard Nixon and the election of George W. Bush in a . . . narrative that . . . weaves together social, cultural, political, economic, and international developments. . . . [Author James T.] Patterson describes how America began facing bewildering developments in places such as Panama, Somalia, Bosnia, and Iraq, and discovered that it was far from easy to direct the outcome of global events, and at times even harder for political parties to reach a consensus over what attempts should be made. At the same time, domestic issues such as the persistence of racial tensions, high divorce rates, alarm over crime, and urban decay led many in the media to portray the era as one of decline." (Publisher's note)
Includes bibliographical references and index.

Pietrusza, David

1960 : LBJ vs. JFK vs. Nixon; the epic campaign that forged three presidencies. Union Square Press 2008 xx, 523p il $24.95   **973.92**
1. Presidents 2. Vice-presidents 3. Senators 4. Nonfiction writers 5. Members of Congress 6. Presidents -- United States -- Election -- 1960
ISBN 978-1-402-76114-0
LC 2009-291219

"The 1960 presidential campaign season was dominated by the personalities of three men, each of whom became president. . . . Pietrusza chronicles their roles and character in a stirring, hard-edged political saga." Booklist
Includes bibliographical references

Postwar America; an encyclopedia of social, political, cultural, and economic history. James Ciment, editor. M.E. Sharpe 2006 4v il set $399   **973.92**
1. Reference books 2. United States -- Civilization -- Encyclopedias
ISBN 0-7656-8067-X; 978-0-7656-8067-9
LC 2004-13120
"A-Z entries address specific persons, groups, concepts, events, geographical locations, organizations, and cultural and technological phenomena. Sidebars highlight primary source materials, items of special interest, statistical data, and other information; and Cultural Landmark entries chronologically detail the music, literature, arts, and cultural history of the era. Bibliographies covering literature from the postwar era and about the era are also included, as well as illustrations and specialized indexes." Publisher's note
Includes bibliographical references

Rather, Dan

The **American** dream; stories from the heart of our nation. Morrow 2001 xxii, 266p hardcover o.p. pa $12.95   **973.92**
1. American national characteristics 2. United States -- Social conditions 3. United States -- Social life and customs
ISBN 0-688-17892-8; 0-06-093770-X pa
LC 2001-30031
In this book Rather tells stories of individual Americans and their dreams. He "groups his material into chapters that focus on elements of our national aspirations: liberty, enterprise, pursuit of happiness, family, fame, education, innovation, and 'giving back.' The Americans that Rather describes are a diverse group but, he urges, their stories are an inspirational reminder of the power of the nation's fundamental ideas to motivate a wide range of people." Booklist

Schwartz, Richard Alan

Cold War culture; media and the arts, 1945-1990. [by] Richard A. Schwartz. Facts on File 1998 376p il (Cold War America) $60.50; pa $24.95   **973.92**
1. United States -- Civilization 2. Popular culture -- United States
ISBN 0-8160-3104-5; 0-8160-4264-0 pa
LC 96-29642
This work "covers the various influences on American culture during the years 1945 to 1990. Schwartz organizes Cold War culture alphabetically within the following broad categories: art, cartoons, consumer goods, dance, film, games and toys, television and theater. . . . This reference source is easy to read and hard to put down as a browsing item." SLJ
Includes bibliographical references

Shelley, Fred M.

★ **Atlas** of American politics, 1960-2000; [by] Fred M. Shelley [et al.] CQ Press 2002 242p maps $156.25 **973.92**

   1. United States -- Politics and government -- Maps

   ISBN 1-56802-665-X

                      LC 2001-18267

This work "examines U.S. government and politics at the congressional district, state, and national levels from a combined historical, geographical, and political perspective. More than 200 maps from a variety of government and private sources show the relationship between the nation's geography and its political life. . . . This book provides a unique look at U.S. politics during the last 40 years and will be useful to students and researchers from the high-school level up." Booklist

Includes bibliographical references

Sirota, David

Back to our future; how the 1980s explains the world we live in now--our culture, our politics, our everything. Ballantine Books 2011 276p $25; ebook $12.99 **973.92**

   1. Popular culture -- United States 2. United States -- Social conditions 3. United States -- Civilization -- 1970-

   ISBN 978-0-345-51878-1; 0-345-51878-0; 978-0-345-51880-4 ebook

                      LC 2010-41627

"The scope of the author's period knowledge is indisputable, and he parlays his experience as a Democratic strategist into politically charged discussions about the anti-governmental preaching on The A-Team, Ronald Reagan's questionable approach to Vietnam veterans and the bulletproof vigor of movies like Rambo, Red Dawn and Top Gun. . . . A sharp, dizzying history lesson that packs a punch." Kirkus

Includes bibliographical references.

Wheen, Francis

Strange days indeed; the golden age of paranoia. Public Affairs 2010 344p $26.95 **973.92**

   1. Paranoia 2. Presidents 3. Prime ministers 4. Vice-presidents 5. Senators 6. Nonfiction writers 7. Members of Congress 8. Members of Parliament 9. World politics -- 1945-1991

   ISBN 978-1-58648-845-1; 1-58648-845-7

                      LC 2009-941854

First published 2009 in the United Kingdom

"A hugely entertaining book that makes you laugh, think, and look over your shoulder—sometimes all at the same time." Booklist

Includes bibliographical references

Woodward, Bob

Shadow; five presidents and the legacy of Watergate. Simon & Schuster 1999 592p il hardcover o.p. pa $16 **973.92**

   1. Actors 2. Diplomats 3. Governors 4. Presidents 5. Vice-presidents 6. Watergate Affair, 1972-1974 7. Senators 8. Nonfiction writers 9. Members of Congress 10. Parents of presidents 11. United Nations officials 12. Nobel laureates for peace 13. Presidents -- United

States 14. United States -- Politics and government -- 1989- 15. United States -- Politics and government -- 1974-1989

   ISBN 0-684-85263-2 pa

                      LC 99-37045

Woodward examines the long-term effect of the Watergate Affair on the presidencies of Gerald Ford, Jimmy Carter, Ronald Reagan, George Bush, and Bill Clinton

The author is an "effective investigative journalist. These skills are on full display in Shadow. . . . {The book} is most interesting as a reconstruction of the many scandals that have troubled the Clinton Administration." Nation

Includes bibliographical references

973.92092   United States--1953-2001--biography

Busch, Benjamin, 1968-

Dust to dust; a memoir. Benjamin Busch. HarperCollins Publishers 2012 309 p. ill. (alk. paper) $26.99 **973.92092**

   1. Autobiographies 2. Iraq War, 2003-2011 3. Iraq War, 2003-2011 -- Biography 4. Madison County (N.Y.) -- Biography 5. Actors -- United States -- Biography 6. Iraq War, 2003-2011 -- Personal narratives, American 7. United States. Marine Corps -- Officers -- Biography

   ISBN 0062014846; 9780062014849

                      LC 2012009518

In this memoir, Benjamin Busch, son of the novelist Frederick Busch, "intersperses stories of growing up in North Carolina, rural New York, and California with his harrowing and life-defining experiences on the sports field and on the battlefields of Iraq. While his father experienced the world through language and had an intellectual relationship with the physical universe, Busch gains comprehension of his environment by throwing himself against it." (Publishers Weekly)

973.921   Administration of Dwight David Eisenhower, 1953-1961

Branch, Taylor

★ **Parting** the waters: America in the King years, 1954-63. Simon & Schuster 1988 1064p il hardcover o.p. pa $22 **973.921**

   1. Clergy 2. Nonfiction writers 3. Civil rights activists 4. Nobel laureates for peace 5. African Americans -- Civil rights 6. United States -- History -- 1953-1961

   ISBN 0-671-46097-8; 0-671-68742-5 pa

                      LC 88-24033

This history of the American civil rights movement from 1954 to 1963 focuses on the life of Dr. Martin Luther King.

The author "has searched out the hidden reality and often tragic human drama of the King years. On his best pages, the past, miraculously, seems to spring back to life. King himself appears human, all too human. Yet when the reader is done, his remarkable virtues and ordinary vices seem of a piece, the component parts of a coherent, towering personality." Newsweek

Includes bibliographical references

Eisenhower, Susan

Mrs. Ike; memories and reflections on the life of Mamie Eisenhower. Capital Bks. 2002 398p il (Capital classics) pa $16.95   **973.921**
1. Spouses of presidents 2. Presidents' spouses -- United States
ISBN 1-931868-04-2; 978-1-931868-04-4
       LC 2002-31378
First published 1996 by Farrar, Straus & Giroux
"Enhanced by unpublished letters . . . this work is a good attempt at exploring a woman of another time who lived in a different state of grace." Libr J
Includes bibliographical references

Frank, Jeffrey

Ike and Dick; portrait of a strange political marriage. Jeffrey Frank. Simon & Schuster 2013 448 p. (hardcover) $30   **973.921**
1. Presidents -- United States -- Biography 2. Nixon, Richard M. (Richard Milhous), 1913-1994 3. United States -- Politics and government -- 1945-1989
ISBN 1416587012; 9781416587019; 9781416588207
       LC 2012015138
Author Jeffrey Frank's book on the "1952 presidential election focuses on Republican vice presidential candidate" Richard Nixon. "Easily winning the Republican presidential nomination, Eisenhower left the choice of a running mate to advisers, who picked Nixon: a first-term senator, he was much younger, politically astute, and possessing suitably fierce anticommunist credentials." (Publishers Weekly)
Includes bibliographical references and index

Johnson, Haynes Bonner

The **age** of anxiety; McCarthyism to terrorism. [by] Haynes Johnson. Harcourt 2005 609p il $26   **973.921**
1. Anticommunist movements 2. Senators 3. War on terrorism
ISBN 0-15-101062-5; 978-0-15-101062-2
       LC 2005-13117
The author "offers an engrossing account of the career of red-baiting demagogue Joseph McCarthy and a chilling description of his legacy for today." Publ Wkly
Includes bibliographical references

Smith, Jean Edward

Eisenhower; in war and peace. by Jean Edward Smith. Random House 2012 950 p. (hbk : alk. paper) $40.00   **973.921**
1. Biography 2. Presidents -- United States -- Biography 3. Generals 4. Presidents 5. College presidents 6. Presidents -- United States 7. United States. Army -- Biography 8. United States -- Politics and government -- 1953-1961
ISBN 9781400066933; 140006693X; 9780679644293
       LC 2011008605
This book presents a biography of former U.S. President Dwight D. Eisenhower. Jean Edward Smith "provides . . . insight into Ike's . . . apprenticeship under Douglas MacArthur in Washington and the Philippines. Then the whole panorama of World War II unfolds, with Eisenhower's . . . generalship forging the Allied path to victory. . . . Domesti-

cally, Eisenhower reduced defense spending, balanced the budget, constructed the interstate highway system, and provided social security coverage for millions who were self-employed." (Publisher's note)
Includes bibliographical references

Thomas, Evan

★ **Ike's** bluff; President Eisenhower's secret battle to save the world. Evan Thomas. Little, Brown and Co. 2012 496 p. $29.99   **973.921**
1. Generals 2. Presidents -- United States 3. Cold war -- Diplomatic history 4. United States -- Foreign relations -- 1953-1961 5. National security -- United States -- History -- 20th century 6. Nuclear warfare -- Government policy -- United States -- History -- 20th century 7. Nuclear weapons -- Government policy -- United States -- History -- 20th century
ISBN 0316091049; 9780316091046; 9780316224161
       LC 2012019640
In this book about U.S. President Dwight Eisenhower, Evan Thomas makes a "case for the way that Eisenhower, the World War II Allied forces' supreme commander and one of the greatest shoo-ins in American electoral history, brought his military instincts form the battlefield to the White House . . . Eisenhower's combination of courage, petulance and cunning are hard qualities to reconcile." (New York Times)
Includes bibliographical references and index.

Wicker, Tom

Dwight D. Eisenhower. Times Bks. 2002 158p (American presidents series) $20   **973.921**
1. Generals 2. Presidents 3. College presidents 4. Presidents -- United States 5. United States -- Politics and government -- 1953-1961
ISBN 0-8050-6907-0
       LC 2002-20397
This volume "holds Eisenhower's accomplishments up against the two major issues of his time: the cold war and civil rights. Wicker . . . likes the man more than his policies." N Y Times Book Rev
This work "captures the key events of the Eisenhower presidency in a way that is highly accessible and intellectually compelling." Libr J
Includes bibliographical references

Shooting star: the brief arc of Joe McCarthy. Harcourt 2006 212p $22   **973.921**
1. Senators
ISBN 978-0-15-101082-0; 0-15-101082-X
       LC 2005-20990
This is a biography of the Senator from Wisconsin who led the House Committee on Un-American Activities and was censured by the Senate in 1954.
"This perceptive, well-written book should have wide appeal." Choice
Includes bibliographical references

973.922 Administration of John Fitzgerald Kennedy, 1961-1963

Brinkley, Alan

John F. Kennedy; Alan Brinkley. 1st ed. Times Books 2012 xviii, 202 p.p $23   973.922
1. Biography 2. Kennedy family 3. United States -- Politics and government 4. Presidents -- United States -- Biography 5. United States -- Politics and government -- 1961-1963
ISBN 0805083499; 9780805083491
LC 2011043747

Author Alan Brinkley discusses John F. Kennedy, suggesting that "he left an enormous legacy as a charismatic leader and a glamorous symbol of hope and purpose long after his death." Brinkley describes Kennedy as "the handsome, unscholarly, self-indulgent son of Joseph Kennedy, whose enormous wealth and ambition cleared his path through Massachusetts and then national politics." The book features Kennedy's experiences "as a [president,] congressman and senator, [describing his views on] . . . military spending . . . [and] civil rights." (Kirkus Reviews)
Includes bibliographical references and index

Bugliosi, Vincent

Reclaiming history; the assassination of President John F. Kennedy. W.W. Norton & Co. 2007 xlv, 1612p il $49.95   973.922
1. Presidents 2. Conspiracies 3. Senators 4. Murderers 5. Members of Congress
ISBN 978-0-393-04525-3; 0-393-04525-0
LC 2007-01545

The author argues that Lee Harvey Oswald was the lone assassin of John F. Kennedy.
"Destined to be the most significant challenge (save the Warren Report) to conspiracy theories, Bugliosi's study will provoke controversy and debate." Booklist
Includes bibliographical references

Coleman, David G.

The **fourteenth** day; JFK and the aftermath of the Cuban Missile Crisis. David G. Coleman. 1st ed. W.W. Norton & Co. 2012 192 p. (hardcover) $25.95   973.922
1. United States -- History -- 1961-1974 2. United States -- Foreign relations -- Soviet Union 3. United States -- Foreign relations -- 1961-1963 6. Soviet Union -- Foreign relations -- United States 4. United States -- Politics and government -- 1961-1963
ISBN 0393084418; 9780393084412
LC 2012025397

In this book on the aftermath of the 1962 Cuban Missile Crisis, "[David G.] Coleman . . . reveals that the possibility of a U.S.-USSR war did not end . . . when . . . [John F.] Kennedy lifted the naval blockade. The author draws on Kennedy's 260 hours of secret White House tapes and presidential and foreign relations records to offer a narrative covering from October 29, 1962, through February 1963, when tensions subsided and relations between the two superpowers began to improve." (Library Journal)
Includes bibliographical references and index.

Dallek, Robert

An **unfinished** life: John F. Kennedy, 1917-1963. Little, Brown 2003 838p il $30; pa $17.95 973.922
1. Presidents 2. Senators 3. Members of Congress 4. Presidents -- United States 5. United States -- Politics and government -- 1961-1974
ISBN 0-316-17238-3; 0-316-90792-8 pa
LC 2002-116388

This is a biography of the thirty-fifth president of the United States
The author "has written the most accessible, balanced, and scholarly biography yet of JFK. . . . It is the Kennedy biography against which others will be measured." Libr J
Includes bibliographical references

Dobbs, Michael

★ **One** minute to midnight; Kennedy, Khrushchev, and Castro on the brink of nuclear war. Alfred A. Knopf 2008 426p $28.95   973.922
1. Cuban Missile Crisis, 1962
ISBN 978-1-4000-4358-3; 1-4000-4358-1
LC 2007-52250

The author discusses the Cuban Missile Crisis of 1962.
This book "is filled with . . . insights that will change the views of experts and help inform a new generation of readers." N Y Times Book Rev
Includes bibliographical references

Freedman, Lawrence

Kennedy's wars; Berlin, Cuba, Laos, and Vietnam. Oxford Univ. Press 2000 xx, 528p il hardcover o.p. pa $18.95   973.922
1. Presidents 2. Vietnam War, 1961-1975 3. Cuban Missile Crisis, 1962 4. Senators 5. Members of Congress 6. Berlin Wall (1961-1989) 7. Military policy -- United States 8. United States -- Foreign relations
ISBN 0-19-513453-2; 0-19-515243-3 pa
LC 99-87898

The author examines how President Kennedy's "time in office was occupied with a series of confrontations with communism. . . . {He contends that} in each of the four cases under review Kennedy resisted pressure from his staff and advisers, not to mention from the Pentagon, to take drastic action, . . . and that he left the cold war in a far less dangerous state than he found it." Economist
"Lawrence's book is an excellent treatment of U.S. foreign policy during this dynamic era and an insightful portrait of John F. Kennedy as a leader." Libr J
Includes bibliographical references

Fursenko, A. V.

One hell of a gamble; Khrushchev, Castro, and Kennedy, 1958-1964. {by} Aleksandr Fursenko and Timothy Naftali. Norton 1997 420p il hardcover o.p. pa $15.95   973.922
1. Cuban Missile Crisis, 1962 2. Soviet Union -- Foreign relations -- United States 3. United States -- Foreign relations -- Soviet Union
ISBN 0-393-31790-0 pa
LC 97-1022

For this diplomatic history of the Cuban Missile Crisis, the authors were granted "permission to review Krushchev's papers; they were also able to draw on archival material from other official Soviet sources." N Y Times Book Rev

Includes bibliographical references

Gitlin, Todd

The **sixties**; years of hope, days of rage. Bantam Bks. 1987 513p hardcover o.p. pa $19.95 **973.922**

1. Students -- Political activity 2. United States -- Social conditions 3. United States -- History -- 1961-1974

ISBN 0-553-37212-2 pa

LC 87-47575

"Though ex-SDS leader Gitlin occasionally falls prey to the self-indulgence that snares most sixties' commentators, his analysis of the decade's politics is thought-provoking and clearheaded. Rather than singing the familiar hymn of praise to youthful idealism, Gitlin carefully dissects why the activist spirit developed when it did and what its legacy has been." Am Libr

Includes bibliographical references

Halberstam, David

The **best** and the brightest; foreword by John McCain. Modern Library ed; Modern Lib. 2001 xxviii, 780p $24.95; pa $16,95   **973.922**

1. Authors 2. Generals 3. Diplomats 4. Educators 5. Statesmen 6. Presidents 7. Vice-presidents 8. Bankers 9. Senators 10. Army officers 11. College teachers 12. Nonfiction writers 13. Members of Congress 14. Foundation officials 15. Government officials 16. Political scientists 17. Secretaries of state 18. Presidential advisers 19. Secretaries of defense 20. Nobel laureates for peace 21. International organization officials 22. United States -- Foreign relations -- Vietnam 23. Vietnam -- Foreign relations -- United States 24. United States -- Politics and government -- 1961-1974

ISBN 0-679-64099-1; 0-449-90870-4 pa

LC 2001-31261

A reissue of the title first published 1972

"The author describes analytically rather than narratively, how the Kennedy-Johnson intellectual (McNamara, Bundy, Rusk, Ball, Taylor, et al.) men praised as 'the best and the brightest' men of this century, became the architects of the disastrous American policy of Indochina." Libr J

Includes bibliographical references

Hill, Clint

Five days in November; Clint Hill and Lisa McCubbin. Gallery Books 2013 256 p. (hardback) $30   **973.922**

1. Kennedy, John F. (John Fitzgerald), 1917-1963 -- Assassination 2. United States. Secret Service -- Officials and employees -- Biography

ISBN 1476731497; 9781476731490; 9781476731506

LC 2013019272

Author Clint Hill presents a book of photographs pertaining to the day that President John F. Kennedy was assassinated. Through the pictures, "we witness three-year-old John Kennedy Jr.'s pleas to come to Texas with his parents and the rapturous crowds of mixed ages and races that greeted the Kennedys at every stop in Texas. We stand beside a shaken Lyndon Johnson as he is hurriedly sworn in as the new president. We experience the first lady's steely courage when she insists on walking through the streets of Washington, D.C., in her husband's funeral procession." (Publisher's note)

Mrs. Kennedy and me; Clint Hill ; with Lisa McCubbin. Gallery Books 2012 viii, 343 p.p   **973.922**

1. Bodyguards -- Biography 2. Secret service -- United States 3. Presidents' spouses -- United States 4. Presidents -- United States -- Assassination 5. Presidents' spouses -- Protection -- United States 6. United States. Secret Service -- Officials and employees -- Biography

ISBN 1451648448; 9781451648447; 9781451648461

LC 2011051017

This book is a "memoir of guarding First Lady Jacqueline Kennedy through the young and sparkling years of the Kennedy presidency and the dark days following the assassination. Secret Service Special Agent [Clint] Hill . . . first met a young and pregnant soon-to-be First Lady in November 1960. For the next four years Hill would seldom leave her side. Theirs would be an odd relationship of always-proper formality combined with deep intimacy crafted through close proximity and mutual trust and respect. . . .When the bullet ripped into the president's brain with Hill not five feet away, he remained with her, through the public and private mourning. . . . Soon after, both would go on with their lives, but Hill would . . . never stop feeling he could have done more to save the president." (Kirkus)

Kaiser, David E.

The **road** to Dallas; the assassination of John F. Kennedy. [by] David Kaiser. Belknap Press of Harvard University Press 2008 509p il map $35 **973.922**

1. Presidents 2. Senators 3. Members of Congress

ISBN 978-0-674-02766-4; 0-674-02766-3

LC 2007-27305

The author argues that "the events of November 22, 1963, cannot be understood without fully grasping the two larger stories of which [he believes] they were a part: the U.S. government's campaign against organized crime, which began in the late 1950s and accelerated dramatically under Robert Kennedy; and the . . . quest of two administrations—along with a cadre of private interest groups—to eliminate Fidel Castro." Publisher's note

"This is a deeply disturbing look at a national tragedy, and Kaiser's sober tone and reasoned analysis may well convince some in the Oswald-was-alone-nut camp." Publ Wkly

Includes bibliographical references

Kennedy, Caroline, 1957-

Jacqueline Kennedy; foreword by Caroline Kennedy; introduction and annotations by Michael Beschloss. Hyperion 2011 xxxii, 368 p.p 8 sound discs   **973.922**

1. Interviews 2. Presidents' spouses -- United States 3. United States -- History -- 1953-1961 4. Presidents -- United States -- Biography 5. Presidents' spouses -- United States -- Interviews 6. United States -- Politics and government -- 1961-1963

ISBN 9781401324254 ; 1401324258

LC 2012372265

This book, accompanied by a set of 8 compact discs (CDs), presents "seven historic interviews" by U.S. First Lady Jacqueline Kennedy "about her life with John F. Kennedy" (JFK). Recorded in 1964, "shortly after President . . . Kennedy's assassination," the interviews discuss JFK's political career and his views on various subjects, "including his thoughts and feelings about his brothers Robert and Ted, and his take on world leaders past and present." (Publisher's note) Other topics include JFK's reading habits, U.S. relations with Cuba, and Kennedy's relationship with her husband.

Includes bibliographical references and index.

Kennedy, Robert F., 1925-1968

Make gentle the life of this world; the vision of Robert F. Kennedy. edited and with an introduction by Maxwell Taylor Kennedy. Broadway Books 1999 188p il pa $15　　　**973.922**
  1. Quotations
  ISBN 0-7679-0371-4

LC 98-55988
First published 1998 by Harcourt Brace & Co.
This is a collection of quotations by Robert F. Kennedy and the authors who inspired him
"Chapters are arranged by issues that were most important to Kennedy and remain timely today—the responsibilities of citizens to their government, the tragedy of poverty in the midst of plenty, the importance of dissent in a democratic society, and work as the solution for the welfare crises. The book's haunting photos convey Kennedy's spirit as successfully as the words." Libr J
Includes bibliographical references

Thirteen days; a memoir of the Cuban missile crisis. with introductions by Robert S. McNamara and Harold Macmillan. Norton 1969 224p il hardcover o.p. pa $12.95　　　**973.922**
  1. Cuban Missile Crisis, 1962　2. Soviet Union -- Foreign relations -- United States　3. United States -- Foreign relations -- Soviet Union　4. United States -- Politics and government -- 1961-1974
  ISBN 0-393-31834-6 pa
A behind-the-scenes account of the Cuban Missile Crisis of 1962. Includes reproductions of pertinent documents and speeches by both President Kennedy and Nikita Khrushchev.

Leaming, Barbara

Mrs. Kennedy; the missing history of the Kennedy years. Free Press 2001 406p il $25; pa $14　　　**973.922**
  1. Editors　2. Socialites　3. Spouses of presidents
  ISBN 0-684-86209-3; 0-7432-2749-2 pa

LC 2001-40442
"Asserting that Jacqueline Kennedy's role in shaping her husband's presidency has been under-examined, Leaming . . . offers a corrective in this intimate look at a very private woman. Initially inclined to keep herself as much in the background as possible, says Leaming, Jacqueline Kennedy became an increasingly visible and vocal first lady as she realized how effective she could be as an image maker. It's in this capacity that Leaming convincingly depicts her

as being instrumental in shaping the course of her husband's administration." Publ Wkly
Includes bibliographical references

Matthews, Chris

Kennedy & Nixon; the rivalry that shaped postwar America. {by} Christopher Matthews. Simon & Schuster 1996 377p il hardcover o.p. pa $14　　　**973.922**
  1. Presidents　2. Vice-presidents　3. Senators　4. Nonfiction writers　5. Members of Congress　6. United States -- Politics and government -- 20th century
  ISBN 0-684-83246-1 pa

LC 96-15677
This exploration of the rift between Kennedy and Nixon "shows how these two anti-New Dealers, anti-Communists, and freshmen members of Congress in 1946 became enemies as their political careers advanced." Libr J
Includes bibliographical references

Minutaglio, Bill

Dallas 1963; Bill Minutaglio, Steven L. Davis. Twelve 2013 336 p. (hardcover) $28　　　**973.922**
  1. Conspiracies　2. Kennedy, John F. (John Fitzgerald), 1917-1963 -- Assassination
  ISBN 9781455522095; 9781455522118; 9781619692794

LC 2013939303
Author Bill Minutaglio's book focuses on the assassination of President John F. Kennedy. "Beginning with the campaign for Kennedy's election and set against a nation in transition, Bill Minutaglio and Steven L. Davis ingeniously explore the swirling forces that led numerous friends and aides to warn the president against stopping in Dallas on his fateful trip to Texas." (Publisher's note)
Includes bibliographical references (pages 341-362) and index

Posner, Gerald L.

Case closed; Lee Harvey Oswald and the assassination of JFK. [by] Gerald Posner. Anchor Books 2003 608p il pa $17.95　　　**973.922**
  1. Presidents　2. Senators　3. Murderers　4. Members of Congress
  ISBN 1-400-03462-0; 978-1-400-03462-8

LC 2003-283539
First published 1993
In this book Posner argues that Lee Harvey Oswald was solely responsible for the assassination of President Kennedy and that none of the theories alleging conspiracy is valid.
"One of the strongest and most important features of the book, indeed, is Posner's painstaking dissection of each and every one of the competing conspiracy theories. None of them stands up under scrutiny." Natl Rev
Includes bibliographical references

Reeves, Richard

President Kennedy; profile of power. Simon & Schuster 1993 798p il hardcover o.p. pa $22　　　**973.922**
  1. Presidents　2. Senators　3. Members of Congress　4. Biography, Individual　5. Presidents -- United States　6.

United States -- Politics and government -- 1961-1974
ISBN 0-671-89289-4 pa

LC 93-24805

This is an account "of John F. Kennedy's three years as president, with an emphasis on leadership techniques." (Choice) "Each chapter presents a different day in the administration. . . . The Berlin Wall, the Cuban Missile Crises, Vietnam, and the diplomacy of arms reduction illustrate how Kennedy was constrained by the unshakable Cold War fear of monolithic communism." (Library Journal)

"Reeves doesn't try to soft-pedal the distasteful, but his account of the Kennedy presidency is resolutely matter of fact and not an indictment." Time

Includes bibliographical references

Stoll, Ira

JFK, conservative; Ira Stoll. Houghton Mifflin Harcourt 2013 288 p. $27   **973.922**
1. Conservatism -- United States -- History 2. United States -- Politics and government -- 1961-1974 3. United States -- Politics and government -- 1961-1963 4. Conservatism -- United States -- History -- 20th century
ISBN 0547585985; 9780547585987

LC 2013001595

It was the author's intent to demonstrate that "John F. Kennedy's priorities as president . . . were not to promote large government and federally funded social programs but to seek tax reductions, maintain a strong department of defense, fight communism, and reduce federal spending. . . . [Ira] Stoll posits that Ronald Reagan is the true inheritor of the Kennedy legacy because . . . he advocated the same priorities as JFK and made similar fiery, anticommunist speeches." (Library Journal).

Includes bibliographical references and index

Swanson, James L.

End of Days; The Assassination of John F. Kennedy. James L. Swanson. HarperCollins 2013 416 p. illustrations, map $29.99   **973.922**
1. Kennedy, John F. (John Fitzgerald), 1917-1963 -- Assassination
ISBN 0062083481; 9780062083487

LC 2013498445

This book, by James L. Swanson, on the assassination of U.S. President John F. Kennedy "follows the event hour-by-hour, from the moment Lee Harvey Oswald conceived of the crime three days before its execution, to his own murder two days later at a Dallas Police precinct at the hands of Jack Ruby, a two-bit nightclub owner." (Publisher's note)

"Drawing on the decades of technological advances that have deepened the knowledge of the assassination, the author presents the stunning unfolding of the event in punchy, poignant vignettes, following one character after another to the inexorable conclusion." Kirkus

Includes bibliography and index

Thomas, Evan

★ **Robert** Kennedy; his life. Simon & Schuster 2000 509p il hardcover o.p. pa $15   **973.922**
1. Senators 2. Attorneys general 3. Siblings of presidents 4. Presidential candidates 5. United States

-- Politics and government -- 20th century
ISBN 0-7432-0329-1 pa

LC 00-41995

This biography "reveals a very human Kennedy struggling to come to terms with his brother's assassination, his role in wiretapping Martin Luther King Jr., and his fatal decision to take on Eugene McCarthy and Hubert Humphrey in the 1968 Democratic primary." Libr J

"A solid, judicious life of a politician whose tragic death inspired a generation of what-if history." Booklist

Includes bibliographical references

**973.923   Administration of Lyndon Baines
Johnson, 1963-1969**

Branch, Taylor, 1947-

★ **At** Canaan's edge; America in the King years, 1965-68. Simon & Schuster 2006 1039p il hardcover o.p.   **973.923**
1. Clergy 2. Nonfiction writers 3. Civil rights activists 4. Civil rights movements 5. Nobel laureates for peace 6. African Americans -- Civil rights 7. United States -- History -- 1961-1969 8. United States -- History -- 1961-1974 9. African Americans -- Civil rights -- History -- 20th century 10. Civil rights movements -- United States -- History -- 20th century
ISBN 0-684-85712-X; 0-684-85713-8 pa

LC 2005-40177

This is "the third and final volume of Taylor Branch's . . . history of the life and times of King." (N Y Times (Late N Y Ed)) Index.

In this history that follows the life of Martin Luther King "from the protest at Selma and the 1966 Meredith March through King's expanding political concern for the poor to his 1968 assassination in Memphis, Tenn., Branch gives us not only the civil rights leader's life but also the rapidly changing pulse of American culture and politics. . . . This magisterial book is a fitting tribute to a magisterial man." Publ Wkly

Includes bibliographical references

Busby, Horace W.

The **thirty** -first of March; an intimate portrait of Lyndon Johnson's final days in office. [by] Horace Busby; with a preface by Scott Busby and an introduction by Hugh Sidey. Farrar, Straus and Giroux 2005 250p il $24; pa $14   **973.923**
1. Presidents 2. Vice-presidents 3. Senators 4. Members of Congress 5. United States -- Politics and government -- 1961-1974
ISBN 0-374-27574-2; 0-374-53021-1 pa

This book "covers the 20 years during which Busby served as a trusted advisor and speechwriter for Johnson. This previously unpublished manuscript was discovered by Busby's son after his father's death in 2000. . . . This is an engrossing and important contribution to our understanding of a compelling political personality." Booklist

Caro, Robert A., 1935-

★ The **passage** of power; Robert A. Caro. Alfred A. Knopf 2012 xix, 712 p.p **973.923**
1. Biography 2. Presidents -- United States -- Biography 3. United States -- Politics and government -- 1945- 4. United States -- Politics and government -- 1963-1969
ISBN 0679405070; 9780679405078

LC 2012010752

This fourth book of Robert A. Caro's series on Lyndon Baines Johnson (LBJ) "chronicles LBJ's life from 1958 to the passage of the Civil Rights Act, in July 1964. It follows Johnson as he . . . seeks the Democratic presidential nomination in 1960; as he is outmaneuvered by John F. Kennedy; as he" cultivates himself to be the "most powerful Senate majority leader in American history" and finally "as he has the presidency thrust upon him following Kennedy's murder." (Atlantic Monthly)

Includes bibliographical references and index.

The **Columbia** guide to America in the 1960s; David Farber and Beth Bailey, editors. Columbia Univ. Press 2001 508p il map (Columbia guides to American history and cultures) $60; pa $25 **973.923**
1. United States -- Social conditions 2. United States -- History -- 1961-1974
ISBN 0-231-11372-2; 0-231-11373-0 pa

LC 00-65577

This reference work includes "a dictionary, an extensive annotated bibliography, a chronology of the era, and statistical information [and] two extraordinary bonuses: a section 'Debating the Sixties,' which includes ten essays by prominent historians . . . and an excellent 77-page history of the 1960s. This book is a fine addition to any library's collection." Choice

Includes bibliographical references

Gillette, Michael L.

Lady Bird Johnson; an oral history. Michael L. Gillette. Oxford University Press 2012 400 p. illustrations (hardback : alk. paper) $29.95 **973.923**
1. United States -- History 2. Presidents' spouses -- United States -- Biography 3. United States -- Politics and government -- 1945-1989
ISBN 0199908087; 9780199908080

LC 2012011580

For this book, Michael L. Gillette, "former director of the LBJ Library's oral history program, has selected and edited these interviews" with former U.S. First Lady Lady Bird Johnson. The histories "cover the first lady's life from her birth in 1912 through [Lyndon B.] Johnson's presidency, thus throwing light on a more than half a century of American history." (Publishers Weekly)

Includes bibliographical references and index

Patterson, James T.

The **eve** of destruction; how 1965 transformed America. James T. Patterson. Basic Books 2012 344 p. (hardcover : alk. paper) $28.99 **973.923**
1. Vietnam War, 1961-1975 2. United States -- History -- 1961-1974 3. Civil rights -- United States -- History 4. United States -- Politics and government -- 1961-1974

5. United States -- History -- 1961-1969 6. Vietnam War, 1961-1975 -- United States 7. United States -- Social conditions -- 1960-1980 8. United States -- Politics and government -- 1963-1969
ISBN 0465013589; 9780465013586; 9780465033485

LC 2012033786

In this book, James T. Patterson "asserts that 1965 was 'a pivotal year in American life.' He sets the stage with a picture of 'buoyant and confident' white America in late 1964, before addressing the 'shifts of mood . . . politics, culture, and foreign policies' that many found unsettling and divisive. . . . The bulk of his attention is turned toward the civil rights movement . . . the Great Society programs of President Johnson and the escalation of the Vietnam War." (Publishers Weekly)

Risen, Clay

A **nation** on fire; America in the wake of the King assassination. John Wiley & Sons 2009 292p il $25.95 **973.923**
1. Riots 2. Clergy 3. Nonfiction writers 4. Civil rights activists 5. Nobel laureates for peace 6. United States -- Race relations 7. African Americans -- Social conditions
ISBN 978-0-470-17710-5

LC 2008-26789

"When Martin Luther King was murdered on April 4, 1968, riots erupted in 125 cities and resulted in 39 deaths, 2600 injuries, and 21,000 arrests. Risen . . . [presents a] narrative describing the chaos and fear that gripped Americans, as their homes, businesses, and cities went up in flames during the weeks after the assassination." Libr J

The author "has crafted a crucial addition to civil rights history, sure to absorb anyone interested in the times, the movement or MLK Jr." Publ Wkly

Includes bibliographical references

Taking charge; the Johnson White House tapes, 1963-1964. edited and with commentary by Michael R. Beschloss. Simon & Schuster 1997 591p il hardcover o.p. pa $16 **973.923**
1. Presidents 2. Vice-presidents 3. Senators 4. Members of Congress 5. United States -- Politics and government -- 1961-1974
ISBN 0-684-84792-2 pa

LC 97-26749

This book is a "selection of conversations taped by Lyndon B. Johnson during the first nine months of his Presidency—beginning on the day of the Kennedy assassination and continuing through the close of the Democratic National Convention in 1964. . . . There are no stunning revelations and no recorded moments of epochal importance. But 'Taking Charge' is a riveting book nevertheless. This is partly because it has been superbly edited and annotated by the historian Michael R. Beschloss, who has made everything—even the most arcane references—accessible to ordinary readers." N Y Times Book Rev

The **Times** were a changin' the sixties reader. edited by Irwin Unger and Debi Unger. Three Riv-

ers Press (NY) 1998 355p hardcover o.p. pa
$16   **973.923**
1. United States -- History -- 1961-1974
ISBN 0-609-80337-9 pa
                                      LC 97-39844

"The broad range of viewpoints and the easy access to
such an array of primary sources make the book a powerful
adjunct for study of the sixties, as well as an interesting book
for browsing." Book Rep

Witcover, Jules
The **year** the dream died; revisiting 1968
in America. Warner Bks. 1997 544p $25; pa
$16   **973.923**
1. United States -- History -- 1961-1974
ISBN 0-446-51849-2; 0-446-67471-0 pa
                                      LC 96-42017

Political columnist Witcover reviews "the tumultuous
year in which the nation came 'unglued.' Nixon and Agnew
vie for the villain's role, although neither would have been
significant, contends the author, had LBJ not eroded his
Kennedy legacy by escalating American involvement in
Vietnam. . . . This backward look is enriched by the 20/20
hindsight of surviving participants, some still prominent in
public life." Publ Wkly

973.924   Administration of Richard Milhous Nixon, 1969-1974

Abuse of power; the new Nixon tapes. edited with
an introduction and commentary by Stanley I.
Kutler. Free Press 1997 xxiii, 675p hardcover
o.p. pa $30.95   **973.924**
1. Presidents 2. Vice-presidents 3. Watergate Affair,
1972-1974 4. Senators 5. Nonfiction writers 6.
Members of Congress 7. United States -- Politics and
government -- 1961-1974
ISBN 0-684-85187-3 pa
                                      LC 97-32096

"This is an edited collection of transcripts of President
Nixon's Watergate-related conversations made available under a 1974 Congressional directive covering tapes related
to 'abuse of governmental power.' More than 90 percent of
the volume covers the year after the June 1972 break-in and
focuses on Watergate." Choice

Bernstein, Carl
All the president's men; {by} Carl Bernstein,
Bob Woodward. Simon & Schuster 1999 349p il
hardcover o.p. pa $14   **973.924**
1. Watergate Affair, 1972-1974 2. Washington post
ISBN 0-684-86355-3; 0-671-89441-2 pa
                                      LC 98-54773

A reissue of the title first published 1974
The two Washington Post reporters whose investigative
journalism first revealed the Watergate scandal tell the way it
happened from the first suspicions, through the trail of false
leads, lies, secrecy, and high-level pressure, to the final moments when they were able to put the pieces of the puzzle together and write the series that won the Post a Pulitzer Prize

Dean, John W. (John Wesley), 1938-
The **Nixon** Defense; What He Knew and When
He Knew It. John W. Dean. Viking 2014 416 p.
$35   **973.924**
1. Watergate Affair, 1972-1974 2. Nixon, Richard M.
(Richard Milhous), 1913-1994
ISBN 0670025364; 9780670025367
                                      LC 2014020821

In this book, author and former White House Counsel
John W. Dean "connects the dots between what we've come
to believe about Watergate and what actually happened. . .
. [He] draws on his own transcripts of almost a thousand
conversations, a wealth of Nixon's secretly recorded information, and more than 150,000 pages of documents in the
National Archives and the Nixon Library to provide the definitive answer to the question: What did President Nixon
know and when did he know it?" (Publisher's note)

"[O]ne of the best and fullest accounts of the Watergate
cover-up, one that conveys in Nixon's own voice the casual
criminality of his troubled presidency." Pub Wkly

Includes bibliographical references (pages 661-719)
and index

Emery, Fred
Watergate; the corruption of American politics
and the fall of Richard Nixon. Touchstone 1994 xvi,
559p il pa $25.95   **973.924**
1. Presidents 2. Vice-presidents 3. Watergate Affair,
1972-1974 4. Senators 5. Nonfiction writers 6.
Members of Congress
ISBN 0-684-81323-8
                                      LC 95-12511

First published 1994 by Times Bks.
"In addition to an introductory section on the cast of
characters involved, Emery provides a detailed examination of the Committee To Reelect the President (CRP) and
its dirty tricks: wiretapping, money laundering campaigns,
and the infamous burglary of Democratic National Committee headquarters. Unlike much of the psychopersonal material that has come out on Nixon, Emery's book focuses
on the tough political problems, documenting the need for
impeachment and ultimately endorsing it. Riveting reading
that is based on an unprecedented combing of the primary
sources." Libr J
Includes bibliographical references

Feldstein, Mark
Poisoning the press; Richard Nixon, Jack Anderson, and the rise of Washington's scandal culture.
[by] Mark Feldstein. Farrar, Straus and Giroux 2010
461p il $30; ebook $14.99   **973.924**
1. Press -- Government policy 2. Political culture --
Washington (D.C.) 3. Presidents -- United States -- Press
relations 4. United States -- Politics and government --
1961-1974 5. United States -- Politics and government
-- 1969-1974 6. Political culture -- United States --
History -- 20th century 7. Press and politics -- United
States -- History -- 20th century
ISBN 978-0-374-23530-7; 978-1-4299-7897-2 ebook
                                      LC 2010-10272

"This fast-moving narrative will fascinate readers of recent American political and journalism history." Libr J

Includes bibliographical references

Glasser, Joshua M.

The **eighteen** -day running mate; McGovern, Eagleton, and a campaign in crisis. Joshua M. Glasser. Yale University Press 2012 381 p. ill. (hardcover) $26   **973.924**

1. United States -- Politics and government -- 1961-1974 2. Presidents -- United States -- Election -- 1972 3. United States -- Politics and government -- 1969-1974

ISBN 0300176295; 9780300176292

LC 2012002582

This book, by Joshua M. Glasser, examines the brief 1972 U.S. vice-presidential campaign of Thomas Eagleton with Democratic nominee George McGovern. "Within days of Eagleton's nomination, a pair of anonymous phone calls brought to light his history of hospitalizations . . . and past treatment with electroshock therapy. The revelation rattled the campaign and placed McGovern's organization under intense public and media scrutiny." (Publisher's note)

Includes bibliographical references and index

Killen, Andreas

1973 nervous breakdown; Watergate, Warhol, and the birth of post-sixties America. Bloomsbury 2006 312p $24.95   **973.924**

1. United States -- Civilization -- 1970-

ISBN 1-59691-059-3; 978-1-59691-059-1

LC 2005-23661

This "is a high-definition snapshot, both nostalgic and perceptive, of a transitional time." Libr J

Includes bibliographical references

Kissinger, Henry, 1923-

Years of renewal. Simon & Schuster 1999 1151p il maps hardcover o.p. pa $24   **973.924**

1. College teachers 2. Nonfiction writers 3. Writers on politics 4. Secretaries of state 5. Presidential advisers 6. Nobel laureates for peace 7. United States -- Foreign relations 8. International relations specialists

ISBN 0-684-85572-0 pa

LC 98-41038

This concluding volume of Kissinger's memoirs "starts with Nixon's resignation and continues through the two years of the Ford administration. . . . As Kissinger explains China policy, Soviet policy, Middle East diplomacy and various crises (in Cyprus, Angola and elsewhere), his insight extends not only to explanations of policy but also to accounts of bureaucratic infighting and turf battles—as well as to relations between the executive branch and Congress." Publ Wkly

"Statecraft defies simple solutions, and one of the merits of Kissinger's memoir—especially this somber and reflective third volume—is that he so rarely provides them." N Y Times Book Rev

Includes bibliographical references

Olson, Keith W.

Watergate; the presidential scandal that shook America. University Press of Kansas 2003 220p il $35; pa $15.95   **973.924**

1. Watergate Affair, 1972-1974

ISBN 0-7006-1250-5; 0-7006-1251-3 pa

LC 2002-38058

The author describes "the White House-approved break-in at Democratic National Committee headquarters in Washington's Watergate complex and its aftermath—most importantly, the dramatic proceedings of the Senate Watergate Committee. . . . {This} book provides an excellent, compact narrative of a crucial moment in the history of the American presidency." Publ Wkly

Includes bibliographical references

Packer, George

★ The **unwinding**; an inner history of the new America. George Packer. Farrar Straus & Giroux 2013 448 p. (hardcover) $27   **973.924**

1. Economics -- History 2. United States -- Economic conditions 3. Crises -- United States 4. United States -- Biography 5. Social problems -- United States 6. United States -- History -- 1969- 7. Celebrities -- United States -- Biography 8. Politicians -- United States -- Biography 9. United States -- Social conditions -- 1980- 10. United States -- Politics and government -- 1989-

ISBN 0374102414; 9780374102418

LC 2013004431

In this book, George Packer "charts the erosion of the social compact that kept the country stable and middle class. Readers experience three decades of change via the personal histories of an Ohio factory worker, a Washington political operative, a North Carolinian small businessman, and an Internet billionaire. Their lives follow the ups and downs of a changing country, where manufacturing jobs vanish, businesses thrive and fail, and political fortunes crest and recede." (Publishers Weekly)

Includes bibliographical references (pages 431-434)

Perlstein, Rick

The **Invisible** Bridge; The Fall of Nixon and the Rise of Reagan. by Rick Perlstein. Simon & Schuster 2014 800 p. illustrations (some color) $37.50   **973.924**

1. Conservatism -- United States 2. United States -- History -- 20th century 3. Nixon, Richard M. (Richard Milhous), 1913-1994

ISBN 1476782415; 9781476782416

LC 2014381509

This book, by Rick Perlstein, is a "portrait of America on the verge of a nervous breakdown in the tumultuous political and economic times of the 1970s. In January of 1973 Richard Nixon announced the end of the Vietnam War and prepared for a triumphant second term--until televised Watergate hearings revealed his White House as little better than a mafia den." Ronald Reagan was "inventing the new conservative political culture we know now." (Publisher's note)

"Although the book only goes up to Reagan's loss of the 1976 Republican nomination to President Gerald Ford, the scope of the work never feels limited. . . . A compelling, astute chronicle of the politics and culture of late-20th-century America." Kirkus

★ **Nixonland**; the rise of a president and the fracturing of America. Scribner 2008 881p il **973.924**

1. Presidents 2. Vice-presidents 3. Senators 4. Nonfiction writers 5. Members of Congress 6. Presidents -- United States 7. United States -- Politics and government -- 1961-1974 8. United States -- Politics and government -- 1969-1974 9. United States -- Politics and government -- 1974-1977

ISBN 0743243021; 074324303X; 9780743243025; 9780743243032 pa

LC 20080273706

This book focuses on U.S. President Richard Nixon, from the "tumultuous years of 1965, on the eve of the Watts Riot, through Nixon's landslide victory in 1972. [Rick] Perlstein has twin objectives. First, he develops a . . . narrative about how Richard Nixon . . . came to epitomize and personify the values of the 'silent majority.' Second, Nixon's ability to exploit voters' anxieties about race, poverty, law and order, and patriotism has produced bitter partisan divisions." (Choice: Current Reviews for Academic Libraries)

This "is an exceptionally broad and thorough social, cultural and political history of eight tumultuous years. . . . It sings with outstanding storytelling and insight." Washington Monthly

Includes bibliographical references

Reeves, Richard

President Nixon; alone in the White House. Simon & Schuster 2001 702p il $35; pa $16 **973.924**

1. Presidents 2. Vice-presidents 3. Senators 4. Nonfiction writers 5. Members of Congress 6. Presidents -- United States 7. United States -- Politics and government -- 1961-1974

ISBN 0-684-80231-7; 0-7432-2719-0 pa

LC 2001-34417

This narrative "is chronological, from Nixon's inauguration in January 1969 to April 1973, when he realized that he had lost control over the Watergate scandals. . . . In between are Vietnam and crime in the streets, affirmative action and the end of the gold standard, Chile and the antiballistic missile treaty, the opening to China and, of course, Watergate. A fascinating study of the brilliant, profoundly flawed man elected to lead the nation through a troubled time." Booklist

Includes bibliographical references

Reston, James

The **conviction** of Richard Nixon; the untold story of the Frost/Nixon interviews. Harmony Books 2007 207p $22 **973.924**

1. Presidents 2. Vice-presidents 3. Watergate Affair, 1972-1974 4. Senators 5. Talk show hosts 6. Nonfiction writers 7. Members of Congress 8. Television producers 9. Presidents -- United States

ISBN 978-0-307-39420-0; 0-307-39420-4

LC 2007-1238

"In 1977, three years after his resignation, Richard Nixon returned to the public eye in a series of interviews with British television journalist David Frost, for which Nixon received $1 million. Figuring his political and lawyerly skills were more than a match for Frost's interrogation, Nixon instead found himself doing exactly what his successor, Gerald Ford, had tried to prevent with a presidential pardon: publicly admitting that he had broken the law. Reston Jr. was one of the aides Frost hired to help him plan his line of attack; this book, written at the time of the interviews, is being published for the first time now. . . . Reston's passion for finding the chinks in Nixon's armor makes for fascinating reading." Publ Wkly

Shriver, Mark K., 1964-

A **good** man; rediscovering my father, Sargent Shriver. Mark K. Shriver. Henry Holt and Co. 2012 x, 273 p., [16] p. of platesp ill. (some col.) (audiobook) &29.99; (hbk.) $24.00 **973.924**

1. Autobiographies 2. Father-son relationship 3. Fathers and sons -- United States 4. Fathers -- United States -- Biography 5. Politicians -- United States -- Biography

ISBN 9781427221452; 0805095306; 9780805095302

LC 2011050028

In this memoir by Mark Kennedy Shriver, "the son of . . . Sargent Shriver and Eunice Kennedy Shriver reflects on his father's towering achievements. . . . Shriver struggled mightily his whole life under the shadow of a benevolent, famous father. . . . 'Sarge' was a hard act to follow. His slipping into Alzheimer's during his last years strained . . . yet also transformed and deepened the son's appreciation of his father's accomplishments and his own shortcomings." (Kirkus Reviews)

"A fairly straightforward, rueful memoir in which the author achieves frank self-acceptance." Kirkus

Woodward, Bob

The **final** days; {by} Bob Woodward, Carl Bernstein. Simon & Schuster 1976 476p il hardcover o.p. pa $16 **973.924**

1. Presidents 2. Vice-presidents 3. Watergate Affair, 1972-1974 4. Senators 5. Nonfiction writers 6. Members of Congress 7. United States -- Politics and government -- 1961-1974

ISBN 0-7432-7406-7 pa

The title refers to the final days of the Nixon Presidency. The authors have "constructed a two-part narrative, the first half covering the period from April 30, 1973—the day John Dean was fired as White House counsel—until late July 1974, and the second half covering the last two weeks in detail." N Y Times Book Rev

Zinn, Howard, 1922-2010

The **historic** unfullfilled promise; Howard Zinn ; introduction by Mathew Rothschild. City Lights Books 2012 250 p. $16.95 **973.924**

1. Military policy -- United States 2. United States -- Economic conditions 3. United States -- Politics and government 4. World politics -- 20th century 5. United States -- History -- 1969- 6. United States -- Foreign relations -- 1989- 7. United States -- Foreign relations -- 1981-1989 8. United States -- Politics and government -- 1989- 9. United States -- Politics and government

-- 1981-1989

ISBN 087286555X; 9780872865556

LC 2012007955

This book by Howard Zinn collects "the dozens of articles he penned for 'The Progressive' magazine from 1980 to 2009." Topics include "the Barack Obama White House, the sorry state of US government and politics, the tragic futility of US military actions in Afghanistan and Iraq, or the plight of working people in an economy rigged to benefit the rich and powerful." (Publisher's note)

Includes index.

973.925   Administration of Gerald Rudolph Ford, 1974-1977

Schulman, Bruce J.

The **seventies**; the great shift in American culture, society, and politics. Da Capo 2002 334p pa $17.95   **973.925**

1. United States -- Civilization -- 1970-

ISBN 0-306-81126-X; 978-0-306-81126-5

First published 2001 by Free Press

Schulman explores developments in American politics and culture during "the years between Woodstock and Reagan. . . . 'The great shift' [he sees] is away from the public-spirited universalism that gave America the New Deal and the civil rights movement, and toward the sovereignty of the free market and private life." N Y Times Book Rev

"This is an important contribution to modern American social history and the literature of popular culture." Publ Wkly

Includes bibliographical references

973.926   Administration of Jimmy (James Earl) Carter, 1977-1981

Carter, Jimmy

An **hour** before daylight; memories of my rural boyhood. Simon & Schuster 2001 284p il hardcover o.p. pa $15   **973.926**

1. Governors 2. Presidents 3. Nobel laureates for peace 4. Presidents -- United States 5. Georgia -- Social life and customs

ISBN 0-7432-1193-6; 0-7432-1199-5 pa

LC 00-48248

In this memoir, the thirty-ninth president of the United States remembers his childhood in rural Georgia.

This "is social and agricultural history as plain and honest as one of the tables the author makes in his workshop—an American classic." New Yorker

Morris, Kenneth Earl

Jimmy Carter, American moralist; {by} Kenneth E. Morris. University of Ga. Press 1996 397p il $29.95; pa $19.95   **973.926**

1. Governors 2. Presidents 3. Nobel laureates for peace 4. Presidents -- United States

ISBN 0-8203-1862-0; 0-8203-1949-X pa

LC 96-6350

The author asserts that "the Carter family is not quite the downhome, folksy clan of campaign advertising; they were actually rural gentry perched atop their county's segregated social pyramid. Members of the family were internally estranged, according to Morris, and Jimmy was a loner—a persona confirmed at Annapolis, where he left no discernible impression besides good grades. Yet Carter surmounted these aspects of himself and his background to become a gregarious integrationist, an indefatigable campaigner, and after a 1966 electoral defeat, a born-again Christian." Booklist

Includes bibliographical references

973.927   Administration of Ronald Reagan, 1981-1989

Brokaw, Tom

The **time** of our lives; past, present, promise. Random House 2011 xxii, 291p il $26; ebook $12.99   **973.927**

1. Social problems 2. American national characteristics 3. United States -- Social conditions 4. United States -- Politics and government -- 1989-

ISBN 978-1-4000-6458-8; 978-0-679-64392-0 ebook

LC 2011022825

"At this troubled point in the nation's history, . . . Brokaw offers a perspective from his own life and career. Drawing on interviews and observations, he ponders how the U.S. has come to a point where the country is suffering from eroding confidence, a financial crisis, declining education, and fears about China's progress. . . . Through the prism of his family and career, Brokaw looks back on the Great Depression, the civil rights era, the Cold War, and more recent history and looks forward to the future for his grandchildren and the nation. With commonsense values, he appeals to Americans to recommit to family and community, increase civic engagement, and make sacrifices in an effort to ensure some security for generations to come. An engaging recollection of the achievements of the past, the realities of the present, and the promise of the future." Booklist

D'Souza, Dinesh

Ronald Reagan; how an ordinary man became an extraordinary leader. Free Press 1997 292p hardcover o.p. pa $13   **973.927**

1. Actors 2. Governors 3. Presidents 4. Presidents -- United States 5. United States -- Politics and government -- 1974-1989

ISBN 0-684-84823-6 pa

LC 97-31396

The author's "provocative argument for Reagan's greatness opens a necessary and complicated debate." Commentary

Includes bibliographical references

FitzGerald, Frances

Way out there in the blue; Reagan, Star Wars, and the end of the Cold War. Simon & Schuster 2000 592p hardcover o.p. pa $17   **973.927**

1. Actors 2. Cold war 3. Governors 4. Presidents 5. Strategic Defense Initiative 6. United States -- Politics

and government -- 1974-1989
ISBN 0-7432-0023-3 pa

LC 99-59913

Fitzgerald offers a history of U.S. missile-defense programs over the last two decades, focusing particular attention on the Strategic Defense Initiative (SDI) supported by President Reagan

"Explaining the Star Wars saga, Fitzgerald delivers all the information that any nonexpert could absorb." Booklist

Includes bibliographical references

Glenn, John

John Glenn; a memoir. [by] John Glenn with Nick Taylor. Bantam Bks. 1999 422p il $27; pa $7.99   **973.927**
1. Astronauts 2. Senators 3. United States -- Congress -- Senate
ISBN 0-553-11074-8; 0-553-58157-0 pa

LC 99-42672

This is Glenn's account of how a "small-town Ohio boy weathers the Depression nurtured by conservative patriotic values, marries his high school sweetheart, flies combat missions in two wars, is selected as one of the original Mercury astronauts, becomes an instant national hero as the first American to orbit the earth, is elected to the Senate, and, after serving for four terms . . . returns to space aboard the Shuttle at age 77." Libr J

The **Iran**-Contra scandal; the declassified history. edited by Peter Kornbluh and Malcolm Byrne. New Press 1993 xxxiii, 412p hardcover o.p. pa $24.95   **973.927**
1. Iran-Contra Affair, 1985-1990
ISBN 1-56584-047-X pa

LC 92-53732

This volume contains "one hundred documents concerning the Iran-Contra Scandal, covering the period from Reagan's original presidential finding of Dec. 1, 1981 to Bush's grant of executive clemency of Dec. 24, 1992. With a helpful chronology of key events and a glossary of major participants, the volume sets forth with contextual introductions the documents, the paper trail of this major controversy in contemporary American politics." Libr J

Includes bibliographical references

Johnson, Haynes Bonner

Sleepwalking through history; America in the Reagan years. {by} Haynes Johnson. Norton 1991 524p il hardcover o.p. pa $15.95   **973.927**
1. Actors 2. Governors 3. Presidents 4. United States -- History -- 1974-1989 5. United States -- Politics and government -- 1974-1989
ISBN 0-393-32434-6 pa

LC 90-38623

This is a study of American politics, history, and culture during the 1980s

The author "concentrates on major events like the Iran-contra affair and the Wall street scene, and briefly touches on other domestic scandals. . . . Not the definitive history of the 1980s, but recommended as an important book by an important author." Libr J

Includes bibliographical references

Mann, James

The **rebellion** of Ronald Reagan; a history of the end of the Cold War. [by] James Mann. Viking 2009 396p il   **973.927**
1. Actors 2. Cold war 3. Governors 4. Presidents 5. Cold War 6. Cabinet members 7. Communist leaders 8. Nobel laureates for peace 9. Soviet Union -- Foreign relations -- United States 10. United States -- Foreign relations -- Soviet Union 11. Political leadership -- United States -- History -- 20th century
ISBN 0670020540; 9780670020546

LC 2008029029

In this book, journalist James Mann "details the battles [U.S. President Ronald] Reagan waged against critics like former president Richard Nixon and members of his own cabinet to forge an alliance with Gorbachev that resulted in the end of the Cold War. Like most 'Reagan revisionists,' Mann understands that the Soviet leader was the major catalyst in ending the Cold War." Included is a "discussion of the Nixon-Reagan relationship and the role that consultant Suzanne Massie played in Reagan's policy." (Choice: Current Reviews for Academic Libraries)

Ronald Reagan did not win the Cold War, nor was he just historically lucky, as two contrasting viewpoints would sometimes have it. Instead, . . . [the author writes,] after a career of hard line anticommunism Reagan proved more flexible and visionary than many other leaders of American foreign policy and more opportunistic and insightful into the motives of Mikhail Gorbachev when the Soviet leader signaled change in the USSR's own conventional hard-line position. . . . Mann bases his argument upon impressive original research, including interviews with principals who range from George Shultz, to Colin Powell, to Helmut Kohl, to Nancy Reagan. Libr J

Includes bibliographical references

Ratnesar, Romesh

Tear down this wall; a city, a president, and the speech that ended the Cold War. Simon & Schuster 2009 229p $27   **973.927**
1. Actors 2. Cold war 3. Governors 4. Presidents 5. American speeches 6. Cabinet members 7. Communist leaders 8. Berlin Wall (1961-1989) 9. Nobel laureates for peace 10. Soviet Union -- Foreign relations -- United States 11. United States -- Foreign relations -- Soviet Union
ISBN 978-1-4165-5690-9

LC 2009-24213

Drawing on interviews with Reagan administration officials, journalists, historians, and eyewitnesses, the author focuses on Ronald Reagan's June 1987 speech at the Brandenburg Gate and his historic challenge to Mikhail Gorbachev to tear down the Berlin Wall.

"This book may be read with pleasure by many, from trained historians to curious general readers. Generally objective in its approach, it will yet lead readers to understand why Reagan is remembered fondly by many and why both he and Gorbachev were key figures in this significant element of 20th-century history." Libr J

Includes bibliographical references

Reagan, Ronald

Reagan, in his own hand; edited, with an introduction and commentary by Kiron K. Skinner, Annelise Anderson, Martin Anderson; with a foreword by George P. Schultz. Free Press 2001 xxvi, 549p il $30; pa $16   **973.927**

   1. United States -- Politics and government -- 1989-
ISBN 0-7432-0123-X; 0-7432-1938-4 pa

                            LC 00-66304

"A collection of . . . manuscripts is presented here, just as Reagan wrote them, including his corrections and notes. With a few exceptions, they are very short radio commentaries delivered during the pre-presidential period (1975-1979), focusing mostly on foreign policy and the economy." Publ Wkly

Reeves, Richard

President Reagan: the triumph of imagination. Simon & Schuster 2005 571p il $30   **973.927**

   1. Actors 2. Governors 3. Presidents 4. United States -- Politics and government -- 1974-1989
ISBN 0-7432-3022-1

                      LC 2005-54198

This is an examination of the Reagan presidency.

This book "is a compelling read, fast-paced and scrupulously fair. . . . Anybody who is interested in Reagan's extraordinary presidency needs to reckon with Reeves." N Y Times Book Rev

Includes bibliographical references

Wilber, Del Quentin

Rawhide down; the near assassination of Ronald Reagan. Henry Holt and Co. 2011 305p il   **973.927**

   1. Actors 2. Governors 3. Presidents 4. Presidents -- United States -- Assassination
ISBN 0-805-09346-X; 978-0-8050-9346-9

                      LC 2010-49808

"On March 30, 1981, President Reagan walked out of a hotel in Washington, D.C. and was shot by a would-be assassin. For years, few people knew the truth about how close the president came to dying. . . . [Now, drawing on] new interviews, Del Quentin Wilber tells the [story]." (Publisher's note)

"A welcome addition to the literature of the Reagan era—and, for that matter, of political violence." Kirkus

Includes bibliographical references

973.928 Administration of George Bush, 1989-1993

Parmet, Herbert S.

George Bush; the life of a Lone Star Yankee. with a new introduction by the author. Transaction Pubs. 2001 576p il (American presidents) pa $29.95   **973.928**

   1. Diplomats 2. Presidents 3. Vice-presidents 4. Members of Congress 5. Parents of presidents 6. United Nations officials 7. Presidents -- United States
ISBN 0-7658-0730-0; 978-0-7658-0730-4

                      LC 00-42597

First published 1997 by Scribner

This biography of the forty-first president of the United States details his "climb up the business and political ladder in Texas . . . [then focuses on his] first runs for office, in 1964, when he faced a problem that dogged him his entire career: convincing right-wing Republicans that he was a true-blue Goldwater conservative. But he wasn't, and Parmet astutely analyzes both the contributors to and the forces within the Republican Party with which the unideological Bush had to contend." Booklist

Includes bibliographical references

Schell, Jonathan

Writing in time; a political chronicle. Moyer Bell 1997 303p hardcover o.p. pa $14.95 **973.928**

   1. United States -- Politics and government -- 1989-
ISBN 1-55921-295-0 pa

                      LC 96-8516

This volume "traces the 1992 Presidential campaign, the election and President Clinton's first term through Jonathan Schell's columns for Newsday. This chronicle is a distinctly partisan one: Schell's views of the White House and its wannabes are seen strictly from the left. But the author's eye for issues and motives is so sure that even those who detest his opinions will find 'Writing in Time' a lively refresher course on five years of American history." N Y Times Book Rev

Woodward, Bob

The **commanders.** Simon & Schuster 1991 398p il hardcover o.p. pa $16   **973.928**

   1. Diplomats 2. Presidents 3. Vice-presidents 4. Persian Gulf War, 1991 5. Members of Congress 6. Parents of presidents 7. United Nations officials 8. United States -- Dept. of Defense 9. United States -- Foreign relations
ISBN 0-671-41367-8; 0-7432-3475-8 pa

                      LC 91-13037

This book discusses "top-level White House [and] Pentagon decisionmaking, first in the attack on Panama, and then in the 5½ months of diplomatic and especially military maneuvering that preceded the [1991] war with Iraq." Christ Sci Monit

973.929 Administration of Bill Clinton, 1993-2001

Applebome, Peter

Dixie rising; how the South is shaping American values, politics, and culture. Harcourt Brace 1997 393p il pa $14   **973.929**

   1. Southern States -- Civilization 2. Southern States -- Politics and government
ISBN 0-15-600550-6; 978-0-15-600550-0

                      LC 97-27787

First published 1996 by Times Books

The author explores the "contradictions of the modern South. Not only does the South exercise disproportionate political power (Dixie now claims leadership of Congress as well as the White House); most of our serious conflicts over race and religion continue to play out dramatically in the old Confederacy. Applebome's unusual historical literacy helps him understand a region drenched in the tradition and legends of the Civil War, racist demagoguery and the battles over integration." Publ Wkly

Includes bibliographical references

Chafe, William H.

Bill and Hillary; the politics of the personal. William H. Chafe. 1st ed. Farrar Strauss and Giroux 2012 x, 387 p.p (hardcover : alk. paper) $28.00   **973.929**
1. Married people 2. Presidents -- United States -- Biography 3. Presidents' spouses -- United States -- Biography 4. United States -- Politics and government -- 1993-2001

ISBN 0809094657; 9780809094653

LC 2011041302

This book offers a "portrait of how the dynamic between Bill and Hillary Clinton affected their achievements in public life. Both fiercely ambitious super-achievers from dysfunctional families, their personalities were complementary (he charming and brilliant, she disciplined and demanding)." They worked as a team, which "caused controversy when he was Arkansas governor and threatened disaster when he became president in 1992." (Publishers Weekly)

Includes bibliographical references and index.

Clinton, Hillary Rodham, 1947-

Living history. Simon & Schuster 2003 562p il $28; pa $16   **973.929**
1. Lawyers 2. Senators 3. Secretaries of state 4. Spouses of presidents 5. Presidential candidates

ISBN 0-7432-2224-5; 0-7432-2225-3 pa

LC 2003-276264

"This book is important not because of the history Senator Clinton records, but because of the history she doesn't record, and what that airbrushing tells us about the history she aspires to shape." N Y Times Book Rev

Gormley, Ken

The **death** of American virtue; Clinton vs. Starr. Crown Publishers 2010 789p il $35   **973.929**
1. Judges 2. Lawyers 3. Governors 4. Presidents 5. Political ethics 6. Misconduct in office 7. Interns 8. Senators 9. Law teachers 10. Presidential aides 11. Government officials 12. Secretaries of state 13. Spouses of presidents 14. Presidential candidates 15. Clothing industry executives 16. Whitewater Inquiry, 1993-2000 17. Special prosecutors -- United States 18. Misconduct in office -- United States 19. Governmental investigations -- United States

ISBN 0-307-40944-9; 978-0-307-4094-4

The author presents an analysis of the events leading up to the impeachment trial of President William Jefferson Clinton, from Ken Starr's initial Whitewater investigation through the Paula Jones sexual harassment suit to the Monica Lewinsky affair. . . . [The book includes material from interviews with] Bill Clinton, Ken Starr, Monica Lewinsky, Paula Jones, [and] Susan McDougal. (Publisher's note) Index.

For those wishing to understand exactly what happened during this confusing, dismal time, Gormley's informed reporting and evenhanded analysis is the place to start. The entire nightmare vividly recalled. Kirkus

Includes bibliographical references

McDougal, Susan

The **woman** who wouldn't talk; {by} Susan McDougal with Pat Harris; introduction by Helen Thomas. Carroll & Graf Pubs. 2003 384p il $25; pa $14   **973.929**
1. Governors 2. Prisoners 3. Presidents 4. Real estate developers 5. Spouses of prominent persons

ISBN 0-7867-1128-0; 0-7867-1302-X pa

LC 2002-192705

"In the 1996 Whitewater investigation, McDougal was indicted for fraud over a $300,000 loan, claiming that only her ex-husband, Jim McDougal, knew the money's intended purpose. Kenneth Starr, head of the Office of the Independent Counsel investigating Whitewater, offered her leniency if she would implicate President Clinton and Hillary Clinton. McDougal refused to testify, she writes, because she didn't want her statements about the Clintons' innocence twisted into perjury by the Starr Commission. She spent the next 21 months in prison on a charge of civil contempt. McDougal has written an engaging, sometimes gossipy, insightful biography, notable for its accounts of her different trials and more so for the depiction of life in women's prisons." Libr J

Reich, Robert B.

Locked in the cabinet. Knopf 1997 338p hardcover o.p. pa $15   **973.929**
1. United States -- Dept. of Labor 2. United States -- Politics and government -- 1989-

ISBN 0-375-70061-7 pa

LC 97-71921

The author writes about his tenure as Secretary of Labor in the first Clinton administration

"Reich has an acid pen, and he is by turns witty, churlish, and plain vulgar. . . . The specificity of detail in this book adds up not only to an absorbing accounting of failed service in the Cabinet but also to a powerful indictment of the Clinton Presidency." New Leader

Stephanopoulos, George

All too human; a political education. Little, Brown 1999 456p $32; pa $14.95   **973.929**
1. Governors 2. Presidents 3. Presidents -- United States 4. United States -- Politics and government -- 1989-

ISBN 0-316-92919-0; 0-316-93016-4 pa

LC 99-13817

This is a political memoir by a former senior advisor to President Clinton

"A fascinating if controversial insiders account of life inside the Clinton pressure cooker administration during its early years." Libr J

Includes bibliographical references

Toobin, Jeffrey R.

A **vast** conspiracy; the real story of the sex scandal that nearly brought down a president. 1st

Touchstone ed.; Simon & Schuster 2000 422p pa
$20 **973.929**

1. Governors 2. Presidents 3. United States -- Politics
and government -- 1989-
ISBN 0-7432-0413-1; 978-0-7432-0413-2

LC 00-59524

First published 1999 by Random House

"Even for those who disagree with [Toobin's] assessment, the book is still hugely entertaining. There are plenty
of scandal pellets to be found scattered throughout the analysis." Christ Sci Monit

Includes bibliographical references

973.93   United States--2001-

Caputo, Philip

The **longest** road; overland in search of America
from Key West to the Arctic Ocean. by Philip Caputo.
Henry Holt and Company 2013 352 p. $28 **973.93**

1. Travel writing 2. United States -- Social conditions 3.
United States -- Biography 4. National characteristics,
American 5. United States -- Description and travel
6. United States -- Social conditions -- 21st century 7.
United States -- Social life and customs -- 21st century
ISBN 0805094466; 9780805094466

LC 2012050451

In this book author Philip Caputo takes a "journey across
America, Airstream in tow, and asks everyday Americans
what unites and divides a country as endlessly diverse as it
is large. What he found is a story [designed to] entertain and
inspire readers as much as it informs them about the state
of today's United States, the glue that holds us all together,
and the conflicts that could cause us to pull apart." (Publisher's note)

Schama, Simon

The **American** future; a history. Ecco 2009
400p il $29.99 **973.93**

1. American national characteristics 2. United States
-- History 3. United States -- Civilization
ISBN 978-0-06-053923-8; 0-06-053923-2

LC 2009-358875

First published 2008 in the United Kingdom

Schama "has begun wandering through the literature of
the American past to snap up unconsidered trifles. The result
is a book of mixed genre-history, memoir and journalism-
and none the worse for that. In four successive chapters,
Schama considers the American relationship to war, religion, immigration and prosperity. Within each, he moves
between historical narratives and vignettes from the contemporary scene, usually involving his own presence. So the
book's architecture is crisp, even as its rationale is mysterious." Times Lit Suppl

Shorris, Earl

The **politics** of heaven; America in fearful times.
Norton 2007 371p $25.95 **973.93**

1. Conservatism 2. Christian fundamentalism 3.
Christianity and politics 4. United States -- Politics and

government -- 2001-
ISBN 978-0-393-05963-2; 0-393-05963-4

LC 2007-12726

The author "offers a historical perspective on religion in
the U.S., from Calvinist doctrine marrying religion and capitalism to the conservative modern-day gospels as preached
by Billy Graham and Jerry Falwell. Drawing on research
and interviews with political figures and advisors, academics, and theologians, Shorris examines the confluence of history, philosophy, experiences, and 'elemental feelings' that
have gained enough momentum to become a movement of
the fearful . . . Shorris eloquently offers a penetrating and
unsettling look at American fear birthed by the horrors of
the atom bomb and nurtured by 9/11 that promises to have an
enduring impact on global and domestic policy for generations to come.." Booklist

973.931   Administration of George W. Bush, 2001-2009

Bernstein, Richard

Out of the blue; the story of September 11, 2001,
from Jihad to Ground Zero. {by} Richard Bernstein
and the staff of the New York Times. Times Bks.
2002 287p il hardcover o.p. pa $15 **973.931**

1. Terrorism 2. September 11 terrorist attacks, 2001
ISBN 0-8050-7240-3; 0-8050-7410-4 pa

LC 2002-20396

This account of the September 11, 2001 terrorist attacks
focuses "on the personal—the victims, the perpetrators and
heroes whose lives became tangled in catastrophe. . . . It uses
these stories as a jumping-off point for a comprehensive
look at the terror attacks—the reactions of New Yorkers,
the nation and the world; the criticism of U.S. government
agencies; the lingering effects of the tragedy. While some
of this information has been published elsewhere, it has not
been gathered so comprehensively—nor has it been written
so well." Publ Wkly

Brill, Steven

After : how America confronted the September
12 era. Simon & Schuster 2003 723p $29.95; pa
$16 **973.931**

1. September 11 terrorist attacks, 2001
ISBN 0-7432-3709-9; 0-7432-3710-2 pa

LC 2003-42727

The author presents a "narrative of how Americans responded to personal, social, political, and economic upheavals during the year following {September 11th, 2001}. . . .
Stories of selected ordinary people serve as examples of the
traumas and life-altering experiences endured by so many
Americans." Libr J

This "book gives a sophisticated demonstration of the
strengths and weaknesses of 21-century commercial democracy under pressure." N Y Times Book Rev

Includes bibliographical references

Bruni, Frank

Ambling into history: the unlikely odyssey of George W. Bush. HarperCollins Pubs. 2002 278p hardcover o.p. pa $12.95   **973.931**

    1. Governors 2. Presidents 3. Baseball executives 4. Children of presidents 5. Energy industry executives 6. Presidents -- United States

    ISBN 0-06-093782-3 pa

The author, who covered Bush's 2000 presidential campaign for the New York Times, focuses on Bush's personality and mannerisms as well as his basic interactions with family, friends, and the public.

    "Given [Bruni's] familiarity with Bush, one would expect his book to contain revealing insights, and this superb, incisive, and surprising account does not disappoint." Booklist

    Includes bibliographical references

Buchanan, Patrick

Where the right went wrong; how neoconservatives subverted the Reagan revolution and hijacked the Bush presidency. [by] Patrick J. Buchanan. Thomas Dunne Books 2004 264p $24.95; pa $14.95   **973.931**

    1. Conservatism 2. War on terrorism 3. Economic policy -- United States 4. United States -- Politics and government -- 2001-

    ISBN 0-312-34115-6; 0-312-34116-4 pa

                  LC 2004-558171

This is a critique of the present-day conservative movement in the United States

    "Whether or not one agrees with [his] conclusions, Buchanan's book is provocative and will certainly ruffle feathers on both sides of the party line." Publ Wkly

Clarke, Richard A.

Against all enemies; inside America's war on terror. Free Press 2004 304p $27; pa $14   **973.931**

    1. September 11 terrorist attacks, 2001 2. War on terrorism 3. Al Qaeda (Organization)

    ISBN 0-7432-6024-4; 0-7432-6045-7 pa

                  LC 2004-273844

    "Richard A. Clarke knows too much, and 'Against All Enemies' is too good to be ignored. . . . It is a rarity among Washington-insider memoirs—it's a thumping good read." N Y Times Book Rev

Corn, David

The **lies** of George W. Bush; mastering the politics of deception. Crown 2003 337p $24; pa $12.95   **973.931**

    1. Governors 2. Presidents 3. Baseball executives 4. Children of presidents 5. Energy industry executives 6. United States -- Politics and government -- 2001-

    ISBN 1-4000-5066-9; 1-400-05067-7 pa

                  LC 2003-18347

The author chronicles "the lies, falsehoods, and misrepresentations of President George W. Bush. . . . He also shows that Bush committed them for a reason, engaging in 'strategic lying' in an effort to cover up his past and pave his way to governance. . . . From lies about his arrest and National Guard records, to environmental and energy concerns, to the war against Iraq, Corn has painstakingly unearthed a bill of particulars against the President that is as damaging as it is thorough." Libr J

Dowd, Maureen

Bushworld; enter at your own risk. G.P. Putnam's Sons 2004 523p $25.95; pa $15   **973.931**

    1. Governors 2. Presidents 3. Baseball executives 4. Children of presidents 5. Energy industry executives 6. United States -- Politics and government -- 2001-

    ISBN 0-399-15258-X; 0-425-20276-3 pa

                  LC 2004-48798

The author "is scorching in her analysis of the Bushes, putting them 'on the couch,' as they have contemptuously labeled efforts to delve into their relationship. . . . Bush detractors will love Dowd's sharp analysis, but even his fans should acknowledge her wit." Booklist

Draper, Robert

★ **Dead** certain; the presidency of George W. Bush. Free Press 2007 463p il $28   **973.931**

    1. Governors 2. Presidents 3. Baseball executives 4. Children of presidents 5. Energy industry executives 6. Presidents -- United States

    ISBN 978-0-7432-7728-0; 0-7432-7728-7

                  LC 2007-23471

The author sets out to tell "the story of the Bush White House from the inside, with a special emphasis on how the very personality of this strong-willed president has affected the outcome of events." Publisher's note

    This book gives "the reader an intimate sense of the president's personality and how it informs his decision making." N Y Times (Late N Y Ed)

    Includes bibliographical references

Eichenwald, Kurt

500 days; secrets and lies in the terror wars. by Kurt Eichenwald. 1st Touchstone hardcover ed. Touchstone 2012 xxiii, 611 p.p (hardcover) $30.00; (paperback) $18.00   **973.931**

    1. International relations 2. Terrorism -- Prevention 3. September 11 terrorist attacks, 2001 4. War on Terrorism, 2001-2009 5. World politics -- 21st century 6. September 11 Terrorist Attacks, 2001

    ISBN 1451669380; 9781451669381; 9781451674132; 9781451669398

                  LC 2012001214

    This book offers an "episodic reconstruction of the fallout from 9/11 in the highest spheres of terrorist strategy. Former 'New York Times' reporter [Kurt] Eichenwald . . . chronicles the entire post-9/11 year-and-a-half spectacular, demonstrating literally how the anti-terrorist hysteria in the United States, and the hatred of America and general global paranoia, forged the 'trauma that haunts the world to this day.'" (Kirkus Reviews)

    Includes bibliographical references (p. [525]-576) and index.

Farmer, John J.

The **ground** truth; the untold story of America under attack on 9/11. [by] John Farmer. Riverhead Books 2009 388p $26.95   **973.931**

1. Terrorism 2. September 11 terrorist attacks, 2001
ISBN 978-1-59448-894-8; 1-59448-894-0

LC 2009-23297

The author "presents a dismaying catalogue of incompetence and dissembling before and after the attack on the World Trade Center and the Pentagon. The author makes excellent use of declassified primary-source documents from 9/11—including transcriptions of frantic last-minute phone calls of air-traffic controllers—to demonstrate how a massively funded national-security system, a relic of the Cold War, failed to counter a small band of terrorists. . . . An important systematic brief on how an elaborately constructed national-defense system was penetrated, and why lessons of that day for disaster response remain dimly understood." Kirkus

Includes bibliographical references

Franks, Tommy

American soldier; [by] Tommy Franks, with Malcolm McConnell. Regan Bks. 2004 590p il map $27.95; pa $16.95   **973.931**

1. Generals
ISBN 0-06-073158-3; 0-06-077954-3 pa

LC 2004-558617

"The real value of 'American Soldier' . . . is not what it says about the war on terror, but what it reveals about Tommy Franks. . . . The chapter on Vietnam, where Franks spent a year in brutal combat as a field artillery officer, is a cleareyed, mordant memoir." N Y Times Book Rev

Friedman, Thomas L.

Longitudes and attitudes; exploring the world after September 11. Farrar, Straus & Giroux 2002 383p $23   **973.931**

1. Terrorism 2. September 11 terrorist attacks, 2001
3. United States -- Foreign relations 4. United States -- Politics and government -- 1989-
ISBN 0-374-19066-6

LC 2002-74321

"Unapologetically pro-American, Friedman's deliberation on what changed on September 11 outside of the U.S. ultimately centers on the strength of American society and our place in the world." Publ Wkly

Includes bibliographical references

Hersh, Seymour M.

★ **Chain** of command; the road from 9/11 to Abu Ghraib. HarperCollins 2004 394p map $25.95; pa $14.95   **973.931**

1. Iraq War, 2003-2011 2. September 11 terrorist attacks, 2001 3. Iraq War, 2003- 4. War on terrorism 5. Abu Ghraib (Baghdad, Iraq: Prison)
ISBN 0-06-019591-6; 0-06-095537-6 pa

"This sobering book is the closest anyone without a security clearance will get to operatives in the inner sanctums of America's intelligence, military, political and diplomatic worlds." Publ Wkly

Kaplan, Robert D.

Imperial grunts; the American military on the ground. Random House 2005 421p maps $27.95   **973.931**

1. Soldiers -- United States 2. Military policy -- United States
ISBN 1-4000-6132-6

LC 2004-61466

The author argues that "America is no less an imperial power than Britain and Rome in their times . . . one that is backed by the same sort of enforcers. To illustrate, he travels to seven nations and describes how American troops are, if not ruling the world, working to persuade it to follow our lead." Publ Wkly

Kaplan's "on-the-ground reportage makes for riveting reading." N Y Times (Late N Y Ed)

Includes bibliographical references

Kessler, Ronald

The **CIA** at war; inside the secret campaign against terror. St. Martin's Press 2003 362p il $27.95; pa $15.95   **973.931**

1. War on terrorism 2. United States -- Central Intelligence Agency
ISBN 0-312-31932-0; 0-312-31933-9 pa

LC 2003-58487

The author "takes us from the formation of the CIA as an outgrowth of World War II OSS intelligence activities, when most agents were East Coast Ivy League elites focused on cold war scrimmages, through the current war on terror, where the enemy is often unknown and the agency elite are somewhat more diverse. Through numerous interviews with both agents and operatives, Kessler brings to life a world generally described only in fiction." Booklist

Includes bibliographical references

Koltz, Tony

★ **It** worked for me; in life and leadership. Colin Powell with Tony Koltz. 1st ed. Harper 2012 xii, 283 p.p (hardcover) $27.99; (paperback) $27.99; (ebook) $21.99   **973.931**

1. Leadership 2. Iraq War, 2003-2011 3. African American generals -- Biography 4. Leadership -- United States 5. United States -- Politics and government -- 1993-2001 -- Quotations, maxims, etc
ISBN 0062135120; 9780062135124; 9780062184061; 9780062135148

LC 2012002970

This autobiography continues the life story of Colin Powell. "The author rose in the military to become 'the first black Army officer to have a four-star troop command.' . . . He describes how . . . his military training also prepared him for his role in government. . . . Powell reviews his profound disagreements with Defense Secretary Donald Rumsfeld and Vice President Dick Cheney on the handling of the war in Iraq, while taking full responsibility for mistakes made on his watch." (Kirkus Reviews)

Mayer, Jane

The **dark** side; the inside story of how the war on terror turned into a war on American ideals. Doubleday 2008 392p il $27.50   **973.931**

1. September 11 terrorist attacks, 2001 2. War on terrorism 3. United States -- Politics and government -- 2001-

ISBN 978-0-385-52639-5; 0-385-52639-3

LC 2008-299452

This is an account of how the Bush administration has fought the war on terror.

This is a "brilliantly researched and deeply unsettling book." N Y Times Book Rev

Includes bibliographical references (p. 361-369)

Miller, John

The **cell** : inside the 9/11 plot and why the FBI and CIA failed to stop it; {by} John Miller and Michael Stone, with Chris Mitchell. Hyperion 2002 336p $24.95; pa $13.95   **973.931**

1. Terrorism 2. September 11 terrorist attacks, 2001 3. Intelligence service -- United States 4. United States -- Central Intelligence Agency 5. United States -- Federal Bureau of Investigation

ISBN 0-7868-6900-3; 0-7868-8782-6 pa

LC 2002-27322

The authors analyze the circumstances inside and outside the United States that culminated in the September 11 terrorist attack. Included is an account of Miller's face-to-face meeting with Osama bin Laden in Afghanistan in 1998.

This is a "frightening and important book." Publ Wkly

National Commission on Terrorist Attacks Upon the United States

★ The **9** /11 Commission report; final report of the National Commission on Terrorist Attacks Upon the United States. Norton 2004 567p il $19.95; pa $10   **973.931**

1. Terrorism 2. September 11 terrorist attacks, 2001 3. War on terrorism 4. Qaida (Organization) 5. National security -- United States

ISBN 0-393-06041-1; 0-393-32671-3 pa

LC 2004-57564

This work aims to describe how the terrorist attacks of September 11, 2001 occurred and to provide recommendations for the prevention of future attacks.

This book "reads like a Shakespearean drama. . . . This multi-author document produces an absolutely compelling narrative intelligence, one with clarity, a sense of shared mission and an overriding desire to do something about the situation." Publ Wkly

Includes bibliographical references

Noonan, Peggy

A **heart,** a cross & a flag; America today. Free Press 2003 270p (Wall Street journal book) hardcover o.p. pa $19.95   **973.931**

1. American national characteristics 2. September 11 terrorist attacks, 2001 3. War on terrorism 4. United States -- Politics and government -- 2001-

ISBN 0-7432-5005-2; 978-0-7432-5048-1; 0-7432-

5048-6

LC 2003-48336

"Noonan's essays are thoughtful, introspective, and deeply patriotic. Although she is devastated by the horror of 9/11, her spirits are lifted by the heroism and kindness she sees in her fellow New Yorkers, from the firemen who bravely raced into the doomed towers to the people who turned out to cheer on the rescue workers and firemen who toiled in the wreckage." Booklist

Ramo, Joshua Cooper

The **age** of the unthinkable; why the new world disorder constantly surprises us and what we can do about it. Little, Brown and Company 2009 279p $25.99   **973.931**

1. World politics -- 1991- 2. Military policy -- United States 3. United States -- Foreign relations

ISBN 978-0-316-11808-8; 0-316-11808-7

LC 2009-00854

This is "a fascinating look at various aspects of today's complicated world and how interconnecting systems often come to bear in unexpected ways." Libr J

Includes bibliographical references

Soufan, Ali H.

★ The **black** banners; the inside story of 9/11 and the war against Al-Qaeda. [by] Ali H. Soufan; with Daniel Freedman. W.W. Norton & Co. 2011 xxvi, 572p il map $26.95   **973.931**

1. Terrorism 2. September 11 terrorist attacks, 2001 3. War on terrorism 4. Al Qaeda (Organization) 5. War on Terrorism, 2001- 6. Terrorism -- United States -- Prevention

ISBN 978-0-393-07942-5; 0-393-07942-2

LC 2011026938

A former FBI special agent offers an insider's account of how the September 11th attacks could have been prevented, as well as his role in the war on terror.

"The best and most original book published in the West on al-Qaeda, this is highly recommended." Libr J

Includes bibliographical references

Spiegelman, Art

In the shadow of no towers. Pantheon Books 2004 il $19.95   **973.931**

1. Graphic novels 2. September 11 terrorist attacks, 2001 -- Graphic novels

ISBN 0-375-42307-9

LC 2004-43870

The author "provides a hair-raising and wry account of his family's frantic efforts to locate one another on September 11 as well as a morbidly funny survey of his trademark sense of existential doom. . . . This is a powerful and quirky work of visual storytelling by a master comics artist." Publ Wkly

Suskind, Ron

The **one** percent doctrine; deep inside America's pursuit of its enemies since 9/11. Simon & Schuster 2006 367p $27   **973.931**

1. Terrorism 2. War on terrorism 3. United States

-- Politics and government -- 2001-
ISBN 0-7432-7109-2; 978-0-7432-7109-7

LC 2006-279373

"Relying on . . . access to former and current government officials, this book [seeks to] . . . reveal for the first time how the U.S. government—from President Bush on down—is frantically improvising to fight a new kind of war." Publisher's note

The **torture** papers; the road to Abu Ghraib. edited by Karen J. Greenberg, Joshua L. Dratel; introduction by Anthony Lewis. Cambridge University Press 2005 xxxiv, 1249p il $30   **973.931**
1. Iraq War, 2003-2011 2. Iraq War, 2003- 3. Abu Ghraib (Baghdad, Iraq: Prison)
ISBN 0-521-85324-9
"A gripping and alarming read about the use of government power." Choice
Includes bibliographical references

Woodward, Bob
   State of denial. Simon & Schuster 2006 560p il hardcover o.p. pa $16   **973.931**
1. Governors 2. Presidents 3. Iraq War, 2003-2011 4. Iraq War, 2003- 5. Baseball executives 6. Children of presidents 7. Energy industry executives
ISBN 0-7432-7223-4; 978-0-7432-7223-0; 0-7432-7224-2 pa; 978-0-7432-7224-7 pa

LC 2006-285190

This is a critique of the Bush administration's handling of the war in Iraq.
"If journalism is the first page of history, then Woodward's opus will be required reading for any would-be historians of the time." Publ Wkly
Includes bibliographical references

Wright, Lawrence
   The **looming** tower; Al Qaeda and the road to 9/11. Knopf 2006 469p map $27.95   **973.931**
1. Terrorism 2. September 11 terrorist attacks, 2001 3. Al Qaeda (Organization)
ISBN 0-375-41486-X

LC 2006-41032

This book "is not just a detailed, heart-stopping account of the events leading up to 9/11, written with style and verve, and carried along by villains and heroes that only a crime novelist could dream up. It's an education, too . . . a thoughtful examination of the world that produced the men who brought us 9/11, and of their progeny who bedevil us today." N Y Times Book Rev
The author "goes back—way back—to 1948 to dissect the personal influences and political radicalization that would lead to al Qaeda's attack on America." Libr J
Includes bibliographical references

973.932   Administration of Barack Obama, 2009-

Balz, Daniel J.
   The **battle** for America, 2008; the story of an extraordinary election. [by] Dan Balz and Haynes Johnson. Viking Press 2009 415p $29.95   **973.932**
1. Presidents -- United States -- Election -- 2008 2. United States -- Politics and government -- 2001-
ISBN 978-0-670-02111-6; 0-670-02111-3

LC 2009-17129

This is an account of the 2008 American presidential campaign and election.
"Although we all know how things turned out, the authors know how to work a cliffhanger, and, as they effectively demonstrate, things could have turned out differently at any number of turns. Essential for watchers of politics and a model for similar electoral analyses in the future." Kirkus
Includes bibliographical references

Berry, Mary Frances
   Power in words; the stories behind Barack Obama's speeches, from the state house to the White House. [by] Mary Frances Berry, Josh Gottheimer; foreword by Ted Sorensen. Beacon Press 2010 xxxiii, 267p $24.95   **973.932**
1. American speeches 2. Presidents -- United States -- Election -- 2008 3. United States -- Politics and government -- 2001-
ISBN 978-0-8070-0104-2

LC 2010004085

Collection of 18 of Obama's most memorable speeches between 2002 and 2008, each introduced by Berry and Gottheimer with political analysis, historical context, and commentary from the speechwriters.
"A book to savor and return to for subsequent readings." Kirkus
Includes bibliographical references

Frank, Justin A.
   Obama on the couch; inside the mind of a president. Justin A. Frank. 1st Free Press hardcover ed.; Free Press 2011 256p $26   **973.932**
1. Lawyers 2. Presidents 3. Senators 4. State legislators 5. Nobel laureates for peace 6. Presidents -- United States 7. United States -- Politics and government -- 2009-
ISBN 978-1-4516-2063-4; 978-1-4516-2065-8 ebook

LC 2011025377

"As in his previous book, Bush on the Couch, psychiatrist Frank analyzes Obama by reviewing his speeches, memoirs, and behaviors. Frank delves into Obama's youth—his reconciliation of his biracial identity, non-traditional upbringing, and travels—to paint a detailed portrait of a president who is charismatic, well-intentioned, and the ultimate consensus builder. . . . While the text becomes repetitive, it may satisfy readers curious about the psychology of their leadership." Publisher's Weekly
Includes bibliographical references

Kantor, Jodi
The **Obamas**; Jodi Kantor. Little, Brown and Co. 2012 viii, 359 p.p $16 **973.932**
1. Presidents -- United States -- Family 2. White House (Washington, D.C.) 3. Presidents -- United States -- Biography
ISBN 0316098760; 9780316098755; 9780316098762
LC 2011940240
This book profiles the marriage of U.S. President Barack Obama and his wife Michelle. Author Jodi Kantor, "a 'New York Times' Washington correspondent, offers a prolonged peek behind the curtain at the evolving role of the Obama marriage as a driver of White House East and West Wing sensibility." (AudioFile)
Includes bibliographical references (p. 343-347) and index

Maraniss, David
★ **Barack** Obama; the story. David Maraniss. Simon & Schuster 2012 xxiii, 641 p.p $32.50 **973.932**
1. Children -- Travel 2. Presidents -- United States 3. Hawaii -- Biography 4. Presidents -- United States -- Biography
ISBN 1439160406; 9781439160404; 9781439160411; 9781439167533
LC 2011052983
This book offers a biography of Barack Obama, "the 44th president [of the United States,] through the age of 27." Topics include the "confluence of Kenya and Kansas in Obama's veins," "the legacy of his father's keen intellect, his mother's self-possession, social conscience, and anthropologist's neutrality, and Obama's cosmopolitan childhood spent bouncing between Hawaii and Indonesia." (Publishers Weekly)
Includes bibliographical references (p. 607-609) and index

Sunstein, Cass R. (Cass Robert), 1954-
Simpler; The Future of Government. Cass R. Sunstein. Simon & Schuster 2013 240 p. $26 **973.932**
1. Economics 2. Political science 3. United States -- Economic policy -- 2009- 6. United States -- Politics and government -- 2009-
ISBN 1476726590; 9781476726595
LC 2012048234
This book, written by Cass R. Sunstein, discusses simpler government. "Behavioral economics has influenced business and politics. Sunstein [shows] why Americans are better off as a result, and what the future has in store. Backed by historic executive orders ensuring transparency and accountability, simpler government can be found in new initiatives that save money and time, improve health, and lengthen lives. [The book attempts to] transform what you think government can and should accomplish." (Publisher's note)
Includes bibliographical references and index

Swarns, Rachel L.
★ **American** tapestry; the story of the black, white, and multiracial ancestors of Michelle Obama. Rachel L. Swarns. Amistad 2012 391 p., [8] p. of platesp ill. (some col.) $27.99 **973.932**
1. Genealogy 2. United States -- Race relations 3. African American families 4. African Americans --

Biography 5. Racially mixed people -- United States -- Biography
ISBN 0061999865; 9780061999864
LC 2012454035
This book traces the ancestry of U.S. First Lady Michelle Obama. "'New York Times' reporter [Rachel L.] Swarns traces the threads, some not previously known to Michelle Obama herself . . . to black, white, Native American, and multiracial family members. . . . Swarns presents the complicated story of race in the U.S. through the prism of one family's history. . . . A central figure is Melvinia, a young slave girl who gave birth to mixed-race children." (Publishers Weekly)
Includes bibliographical references (p. [357]-367) and index

Taibbi, Matt
Griftopia; bubble machines, vampire squids, and the long con that is breaking America. Spiegel & Grau 2010 252p $26 **973.932**
1. Despotism 2. Political corruption 3. Global Financial Crisis, 2008-2009 4. United States -- Politics and government -- 2001-
ISBN 978-0-385-52995-2; 978-0-385-52997-6 ebook
LC 2010-15067
This is a study of the causes and consequences of the 2008 financial crisis.
"Taibbi's glib prose is punctuated with just enough irreverence and wit to allow him to appeal to more casual readers while providing sufficient detail to satisfy those looking for a serious discussion of the high-level manipulation of the economy. Recommended for anyone interested in understanding the economy and how it got that way." Libr J

974 Specific states of United States

★ The **Encyclopedia** of New England; the culture and history of an American region. edited by Burt Feintuch and David H. Watters; foreword by Donald Hall. Yale University Press 2005 xxiii, 1564p il map $65 **974**
1. Reference books 2. New England -- Encyclopedias
ISBN 0-300-10027-2
LC 2005-10353
For a fuller review, see: Booklist, Nov. 15, 2005
This "work aims to serve as an authoritative resource of information about people, places, events, culture, and ideas of the region. . . . [This is] a valuable tool for students, researchers, and casual readers alike." Libr J
Includes bibliographical references

Macdonald, Cameron
The **endangered** species road trip; a summer's worth of dingy motels, poison oak, ravenous insects, and the rarest species in North America. by Cameron MacDonald. Pgw 2013 216 p. $17.95 **974**
1. Travel 2. Rare animals
ISBN 155365935X; 9781553659358
In this book, author Cameron MacDonald discusses his "road trip of a lifetime to observe North America's rarest species. MacDonald offers fascinating details about the nat-

ural history of the endangered species he seeks, as well as threats like overpopulation, commercial fishing, and climate change that are driving them towards extinction." (Publisher's note)

"Documenting the ongoing simplification of North America's ecologies could be grim work . . . but MacDonald's comedic sense and his engaging style are addictive and the resulting tale is intensely charming." Pub Wkly

Vowell, Sarah

The **wordy** shipmates. Riverhead Books 2008 254p map $25.95 **974**
1. Puritans 2. Pilgrims (New England colonists) 3. New England -- History -- 1600-1775, Colonial period
ISBN 978-1-59448-999-0; 1-59448-999-8
LC 2008-30491
"Focusing on the Puritans who settled in 1692 in the Massachusetts Bay Colony, Vowell laments their image as 'boring killjoys' when in fact they were 'fascinating killjoys.' A book dense with detail, insight, and humor." Booklist

"A book dense with detail, insight, and humor." Booklist

974.4   Massachusetts

Bradford, William

Of Plymouth Plantation, 1620-1647; the complete text, with notes and an introduction by Samuel Eliot Morison. Knopf 1952 xliii, 448p maps $25 **974.4**
1. Pilgrims (New England colonists) 2. Massachusetts -- History -- 1600-1775, Colonial period
ISBN 0-394-43895-7
Written between 1630 and 1650; first published 1856 with title: History of Plymouth Plantation
"The opening book sketches the origin of the Separatist movement, the flight from England to Holland, the settlement at Leiden, the plans for the settlement in New England, and the Mayflower voyage. The second book, which includes the major part of the history, is in the form of annals from 1620 to 1646, and describes every aspect of the life of the Pilgrims. Besides being a primary historical source, the work has artistic value because of its dignified, sonorous style, deriving from the Geneva Bible." Oxford Companion to Am Lit. 5th edition

Bremer, Francis J.

John Winthrop; America's forgotten founding father. Oxford University Press 2003 478p il hardcover o.p. pa $21.95 **974.4**
1. Clergy 2. Government officials 3. Colonial administrators
ISBN 0-19-514913-0; 978-0-19-517981-1 pa; 0-19-517981-1 pa
LC 2002-38143
"Bremer's definitive biography gracefully portrays Winthrop as a man of his time, whose influence in the new colony grew out of his own struggles to establish his identity before he left England." Publ Wkly
Includes bibliographical references

Bunker, Nick

★ **Making** haste from Babylon; the Mayflower Pilgrims and their world: a new history. Alfred A. Knopf 2010 489p il map $30 **974.4**
1. Pilgrims (New England colonists) 2. Mayflower (Ship) 3. Pilgrims (New Plymouth Colony) 4. Massachusetts -- History -- New Plymouth, 1620-1691 5. Massachusetts -- History -- 1600-1775, Colonial period
ISBN 978-0-307-26682-8; 0-307-26682-6
LC 2009038520
This is an "account of the Mayflower project and the first decade of the Plymouth Colony." (Publisher's note)
"Never before has such a comprehensive and thoroughly researched study of the subject appeared. . . . [This book] scoops up every relevant character and links all to the basic tale of indomitable courage, religious faith, commercial ambition, international rivalry, and domestic politics. The results are stunning. Certain to be the dominating work on the Pilgrims for decades." Publ Wkly
Includes bibliographical references

Cliff, Nigel

The **Shakespeare** riots; revenge, drama, and death in nineteenth-century America. Random House 2007 312p il $26.95 **974.4**
1. Poets 2. Actors 3. Authors 4. Dramatists 5. Riots -- New York (N.Y.) 6. Astor Place (New York, N.Y.) 7. New York (N.Y.) -- Social life and customs
ISBN 9780345486943; 0-345-48694-3
LC 2006-49139
"Cliff argues persuasively that 'the Astor Place riot,' as it came to be known, marked a turning point in America's search for a national identity. . . . [This] is an intriguing, thought-provoking book." Washington Post Book World
Includes bibliographical references

Corbett, Christopher

Poker bride; the first Chinese in the Wild West. Atlantic Monthly Press 2010 218p il $24 **974.4**
1. Pioneers 2. Chinese Americans -- History 3. California -- Gold discoveries
ISBN 978-0-8021-1909-4; 0-8021-1909-3
This book mixes a "mystery-wrapped story with the larger picture of Chinese immigration into the American West. The central story concerns a young Chinese woman sold by her family in 1872 into indentured prostitution. She turns up as a concubine in Idaho, is said then to have been won by another man in a poker game, and became Polly Bemis, the winner's legal, beloved wife in the remote wilderness of Idaho. Polly emerged into public view only in 1923, a tiny old woman on horseback, her identity and story known only to a few old-timers. Corbett wisely sets Bemis's life into the context of Chinese immigration, gold-country anti-Chinese prejudice, and life in the mining communities." Publ Wkly
Includes bibliographical references

East, Elyssa

Dogtown; death and enchantment in a New England ghost town. Free Press 2009 291p map $26 **974.4**

1. Dogtown (Mass.)

ISBN 978-1-4165-8704-0; 1-4165-8704-7

LC 2009-17197

"A true-crime story, an art appreciation course and an American history lesson stitched together, and it succeeds as all three. . . . Plaudits to East for exploring the relationship of the land to artists, as well as to the people who live upon it, in this case for generations." N Y Times Book Rev

Francis, Richard

Fruitlands; the Alcott family and their search for utopia. Yale University Press 2010 321p il $30 **974.4**

1. Authors 2. Utopias 3. Educators 4. Journalists 5. Philosophers 6. Communal living 7. Transcendentalism 8. Social reformers 9. Nonfiction writers 10. Biography, Collective 11. Fruitlands Colony (Mass.) 12. Fruitlands (Harvard, Mass.)

ISBN 978-0-300-14041-5; 0-300-14041-X

LC 2010-19705

The book "examin[es] . . . the complicated intellectual and emotional entanglements not just between Fruitlands' titular 'heads,' New Englander Amos Bronson Alcott and Englishman Charles Lane, but . . . the many people with whom they interacted before and during the community's brief seven-month existence, from June to December 1843. . . . Francis begins his examination of Fruitlands a few years earlier with the failure and collapse of Bronson Alcott's infamous Temple School in Boston, and the controversial educator's subsequent vilification. . . . Alcott's fall from grace as an innovative and progressive educator was accompanied by his nearly simultaneous apotheosis overseas among the English Transcendentalists. Francis devotes the first third of the book to this crucial period of cross-cultural germination . . . The second two-thirds of Francis's study examines the months immediately preceding the utopian experiment fourteen miles west of Concord, day-to-day life at Fruitlands itself, and its demise in December 1843." (American Historical Review)

"Though obviously sympathetic to the Fruitlands experiment, Mr. Francis gives us enough facts to let us draw our own conclusions. . . . Along the way he adumbrates the ways in which idealism can slide into megalomania." Wall Street J

Includes bibliographical references

Kidder, Tracy

Home town. Washington Square Press 2000 432p pa $14.95 **974.4**

1. City and town life 2. Northampton (Mass.)

ISBN 978-0-671-78521-5; 0-671-78521-4

First published 1999 by Random House

This "acutely observed, crisply written, and utterly absorbing documentary proves that there is nothing on this spinning earth more amazing and full of grace than everyday life." Booklist

Includes bibliographical references

Manegold, Catherine

Ten Hills Farm; the forgotten history of slavery in the North. [by] C.S. Manegold. Princeton University Press 2010 317p il map $29.95 **974.4**

1. Slaves -- Massachusetts 2. Massachusetts -- History 3. Slavery -- Massachusetts 4. Slavery -- United States 5. Slave trade -- Massachusetts

ISBN 978-0-691-13152-8; 0-691-13152-X

LC 2009030875

This book tells the story "of five generations of slave owners in colonial New England. Settled in 1630, . . . Ten Hills Farm, a six-hundred-acre estate just north of Boston, passed from the Winthrops to the Ushers, to the Royalls—all . . . dynasties tied to the Native American and Atlantic slave trades." (Publisher's note) Index.

"Full of rich historical detail, this is a story that needed to be told." Kirkus

Includes bibliographical references

Masur, Louis P.

The **soiling** of Old Glory; the story of a photograph that shocked America. Bloomsbury Press 2008 224p il $24.95 **974.4**

1. Demonstrations 2. Photojournalism 3. Busing (School integration) 4. Boston (Mass.) -- Race relations

ISBN 978-1-59691-364-6; 1-59691-364-9

LC 2007-31215

"On April 5, 1976, an antibusing rally in Boston grew violent when African American lawyer Ted Landsmark was attacked by some of the protesters. News photographer Stanley Forman captured the ruckus on film; one photo gained international attention and is the subject of this . . . study by Masur. . . . Masur writes descriptively about the photo while creating an ethnographic history of 1970s Boston, with diversions into the political and cultural uses of the American flag and the history of photojournalism in the United States. He also describes the aftermath of the photo's front-page publication. . . . A compelling story; highly recommended for all high school, public, and academic libraries." Libr J

Includes bibliographical references

Nugent, Rory

Down at the docks. Pantheon Books 2009 290p $24.95 **974.4**

1. Commercial fishing 2. New Bedford (Mass.)

ISBN 978-0-375-42064-1; 0-375-42064-9

LC 2008-20104

The author "describes his sometime home of New Bedford, Massachusetts. Long famous for whaling—Melville set sail from there—the city remains a major fishing port and produces the most valuable annual catch of any in the country. But in the past two decades consolidation and legislation have shackled what Nugent eulogizes as the fleet's 'frontier mentality.' This canny self-reliance took a variety of forms; Nugent documents two kinds of insurance fraud and a 'night menu' of drugs smuggled to supplement the legitimate catch. Nugent strings together his subjects' boasts, banter, and laments into an engagingly anecdotal social history, fleshed out by strokes of fine description." New Yorker

Schama, Simon

Dead certainties; unwarranted speculations. Knopf 1991 333p hardcover o.p. pa $16   **974.4**

1. Generals 2. Historians 3. Physicians 4. Historiography 5. Murder victims 6. Horticulturists
ISBN 0-679-73613-1 pa

LC 90-52902

This exploration of the nature of historical writing consists of two stories. The first one "is concerned with the battlefield death of James Wolfe, British commander in the North American campaign of the Seven Years' War; the second with the murder ninety years later of a Harvard Medical School professor, George Parkman." New Repub

974.5   Rhode Island

Barry, John M.

Roger Williams and the creation of the American soul; church, state, and the birth of liberty. John M. Barry. Viking 2012 464 p.   **974.5**

1. Puritans 2. Religion and politics -- United States 3. United States -- History -- 1600-1775, Colonial period 4. United States -- History -- 17th century 5. United States -- Civilization -- 17th century
ISBN 0670023051; 9780670023059

LC 2011032995

This book by John M. Barry offers a "look at how Roger Williams shaped the nature of religion, political power, and individual rights in America. . . . Americans have [always] wrestled with . . . two concepts that define the nature of the nation: the proper relation between church and state and between a free individual and the state. These debates began with the extraordinary thought and struggles of Roger Williams. . . . This is a story . . . set against Puritan America and the English Civil War. Williams's interactions with King James, Francis Bacon, Oliver Cromwell, and his mentor Edward Coke set his course, but his fundamental ideas came to fruition in America, as Williams, though a Puritan, collided with John Winthrop's vision of his 'City upon a Hill.'" (Publisher's note)

Includes bibliographical references (p. 427-438) and index

974.7   New York

★ **After** the fall; edited by Mary Marshall Clark ... [et al.] New Press 2011 xxiii, 263 p.p $26.95 **974.7**

1. September 11 terrorist attacks, 2001 -- Personal narratives
ISBN 978-1-59558-647-6; 9781595586476

LC 2011012833

This book was produced by "Columbia University's Oral History Research Office, headed by [the book's editor,] Mary Marshall Clark, [who] went to work immediately after September 11, 2001, and has now issued a selection from its hundreds of interviews with those most directly involved—first responders, victims' families, residents of lower Manhattan. . . . The interviews make clear the distance between those who will go on distressfully reliving their experience

forever and those of us who were merely bystanders." (Columbia Journalism Review)

"The Columbia Center for Oral History (CCOH) is committed to building 'repositories of living memory,' and after 9/11 began to gather narratives from a variety of New York survivors and witnesses, eventually collecting over 600 histories. The skilled interviewers . . . are trained in oral history methods and richly summon forth from interviewees the repercussions of the attack on individuals, families, and communities. Those interviewed reflect a variety of perspectives, including both professional and unskilled workers in the Twin Towers, neighbors, first responders, and many of New York's immigrant groups, including Muslims." Libr J

Anasi, Robert

The **last** bohemia; scenes from the life of Williamsburg, Brooklyn. Robert Anasi. Farrar, Straus and Giroux 2012 240 p. (alk. paper) $15.00 **974.7**

1. Brooklyn (New York, N.Y.) 2. New York (N.Y.) -- Social conditions 3. New York (N.Y.) -- Description and travel 4. New York (N.Y.) -- Social life and customs 5. Bohemianism -- New York (State) -- New York 6. Social change -- New York (State) -- New York 7. City and town life -- New York (State) -- New York 8. Williamsburg (New York, N.Y.) -- Social conditions 9. Williamsburg (New York, N.Y.) -- Description and travel 10. Williamsburg (New York, N.Y.) -- Social life and customs
ISBN 0374533318; 9780374533311

LC 2011051267

This memoir about Brooklyn, New York focuses on the "eternal clash between authenticity, art, and real estate development." Author "[Robert] Anasi witnessed Williamsburg's progress in the 1990s and 2000s from crime-ridden working-class neighborhood overshadowed by crumbling factories . . . to edgy arts scene and hipster mecca to end-stage self-parody as an unaffordably upscale 'Bohemian theme park.'" (Publishers Weekly)

Bloom, Ken

Broadway; its history, people, and places: an encyclopedia. 2nd ed; Routledge 2003 679p il $95   **974.7**

1. Theater -- New York (N.Y.)
ISBN 0-415-93704-3

LC 2003-2692

First published 1991

"Following a brief historical overview, . . . {the author} presents 394 alphabetical entries with multiple cross references for easy browsing. The most substantial entries cover theaters, playwrights, composers, directors, performers, and producers, with a special emphasis on composers and lyricists. . . . Bloom adds a touch of atmosphere with entries on critics, restaurants, publicity stunts, nightclubs, and other periphery characters and incidents that are so much a part of the Great White Way. As much a storyteller as a chronicler, he uses anecdotes and a plethora of black-and-white photographs, many never before published, to produce an entertaining as well as an informative work. Highly recommended for all theater collections." Libr J

Includes bibliographical references

Burns, Cherie

The **great** hurricane-1938. Atlantic Monthly
Press 2005 240p il $24   **974.7**

1. Hurricanes 2. Northeastern States
ISBN 0-8711-3893-X

LC 2005-41211

The author discusses the hurricane of September 1938,
which affected the northeastern United States from Long Island to Providence, Rhode Island.

The author "has dug up old newspaper accounts and
local histories to reconstruct the terror and destruction that
accompanied the 1938 hurricane. Those who suffered the
most, of course, did not survive to tell their tales. Nearly 700
people died, and about 63,000 were left homeless. . . . Survivor's stories, however, give ample feeling for the power of
the rain, tide, and wind." Nat Hist

Burrows, Edwin G.

Gotham; a history of New York City to 1898.
{by} Edwin G. Burrows and Mike Wallace. Oxford
Univ. Press 1998 xxiv, 1383p il maps hardcover o.p.
pa $29.95   **974.7**

1. New York (N.Y.) -- History
ISBN 0-19-514049-4 pa

LC 97-39308

This history "begins with the Indian settlements and the
subsequent seizure of the city by the Dutch in 1626 and continues up to the consolidation of the five boroughs in 1898.
The authors . . . cover an extraordinary range of topics, including religion, race, gender and class, architecture, society
and the arts, noted personalities, sports and the special customs immigrants brought with them." America

Includes bibliographical references

Dwyer, Jim

102 minutes; the untold story of the fight to survive inside the Twin Towers. [by] Jim Dwyer and
Kevin Flynn. Times Books 2005 322p il $26; pa
$15   **974.7**

1. September 11 terrorist attacks, 2001 2. World Trade
Center terrorist attack, 2001
ISBN 0-8050-7682-4; 0-8050-8032-5 pa

LC 2004-55321

Dwyer and Flynn have "given us a fitting tribute to the
people caught up in one of the great dramas of our time.
And for people still haunted by the events of that day, reading '102 Minutes' provides a cathartic release." N Y Times
Book Rev

★ The **encyclopedia** of New York State; editor in
chief, Peter Eisenstadt; managing editor, Laura-
Eve Moss; foreword by Carole F. Huxley. 1st ed.;
Syracuse University Press 2005 xxviii, 1921p il
map $95   **974.7**

1. Reference books 2. New York (State) -- Encyclopedias
ISBN 0-8156-0808-X

LC 2005-1032

"The alphabetically arranged entries include all cities,
towns, and counties (more than 1,500), with an additional

3,000-plus entries for information on a wide range of topics.
. . . This ambitious project is a definite success." Booklist

Includes bibliographical references

Friend, David

Watching the world change; the stories behind
the images of 9/11. Farrar, Straus and Giroux 2006
435p il $30   **974.7**

1. Documentary photography 2. World Trade Center
(New York, N.Y.) 3. September 11 terrorist attacks,
2001 -- Pictorial works
ISBN 978-0-374-29933-0; 0-374-29933-1

LC 2005-36158

In this "analysis of how images of 9/11 and the 'war on
terror' have altered our understanding of power, world politics, religion and identity, . . . [the author] successfully merges reportage and analysis as he interprets the images of falling towers, panic in Manhattan streets and prisoners at Abu
Ghraib that have been burned into our brains." Publ Wkly

Includes bibliographical references

Gage, Beverly

The **day** Wall Street exploded; a story of America in its first age of terror. Oxford University Press
2009 400p il   **974.7**

1. Bombings 2. Terrorism 3. Wall Street (New York,
N.Y.) 4. Terrorism -- New York (N.Y.) 5. Terrorism
-- United States -- History
ISBN 0-19-514824-X; 978-0-19-514824-4

LC 2008022074

This is an account of the "1920 terrorist attack on Wall
Street—why it happened [and] how it shaped American politics." (Publisher's note) Index.

"Gage has performed a real service, both in presenting
such a complicated case in such a fair and balanced way and
in reminding readers how large a space terrorism once occupied on the political landscape." San Francisco Chron

Includes bibliographical references

Gill, Jonathan

Harlem; the four hundred year history from
Dutch village to capital of black America. Grove
Press 2011 520p il map $29.95   **974.7**

1. New York (N.Y.) -- Harlem
ISBN 978-0-8021-1910-0

"Comprehensive and compassionate—an essential text
of American history and culture." Kirkus

Includes bibliographical references

Goodman, Matthew

The **Sun** and the moon; the remarkable true account of hoaxers, showmen, dueling journalists, and
lunar man-bats in nineteenth-century New York. Basic Books 2008 350p il $26; pa $15   **974.7**

1. Fraud 2. Journalism 3. Moon 4. New York sun
(Newspaper: 1833-1950)
ISBN 978-0-465-00257-3; 0-465-00257-9; 978-0-465-
01900-7 pa; 0-465-01900-5 pa

LC 2008-23617

"These incredible events occurred during a great democratization of media, with affordable news for all and the seeds
of pop culture beginning to take root. To read The Sun and

the Moon is to enter a world of aeronauts, automaton chess players, and glorious lunar temples. It is the old New York of P.T. Barnum brought into incredible focus and Goodman's research couldn't be more comprehensive." PopMatters

Includes bibliographical references

Griswold, Mac

★ The **Manor**; Three Centuries at a Slave Plantation on Long Island. Mac Griswold. Farrar Straus & Giroux 2013 304 p. $28   **974.7**

1. Plantations 2. Slavery -- United States 3. Long Island (N.Y.) -- History 4. Long Island (N.Y.) -- Biography 5. Shelter Island (N.Y.) -- History 6. Sylvester Manor Plantation Site (N.Y.) 7. Slavery -- New York (State) -- Long Island -- History 8. Plantations -- New York (State) -- Long Island -- History 9. Excavations (Archaeology) -- New York (State) -- Long Island 10. Plantation life -- New York (State) -- Long Island -- History 11. Plantation owners -- New York (State) -- Long Island -- Biography

ISBN 0374266298; 9780374266295

LC 2013005463

This book is Mac Griswold's exploration of a 1652 plantation house on Long Island. She uncovers the histories of "those who lived in it or passed through its grounds: Native Americans, generation after generation of Sylvesters (the original owners), and—most surprisingly, considering that the Sylvesters were Quakers—the family's slaves." (Publishers Weekly)

Includes bibliographical references and index

Homberger, Eric

The **historical** atlas of New York City; a visual celebration of nearly 400 years of New York City's history. Alice Hudson, cartographic consultant. Holt & Co. 1994 192p il maps (Henry Holt reference book) hardcover o.p. pa $22   **974.7**

1. New York (N.Y.) -- History

ISBN 0-8050-6004-9 pa

LC 94-18992

This is an "encyclopedic overview of the history of New York City. . . . Detailed color maps abound, accompanied by a running commentary of major historical and cultural eras. Many of the most detailed maps are rendered schematically for easier reading. Each period treated features historical photos and illustrations along with accompanying map(s). . . . A visual delight." Libr J

Khan, Yasmin Sabina

Enlightening the world; the creation of the Statue of Liberty. Cornell University Press 2010 231p il $24.95   **974.7**

1. Artists 2. Sculptors 3. National monuments 4. Statue of Liberty (New York, N.Y.) 5. France -- Foreign relations -- United States 6. United States -- Foreign relations -- France

ISBN 978-0-8014-4851-5; 0-8014-4851-4

LC 2009035711

This is "a lucid account connecting France's widespread grief over Abraham Lincoln's 1865 assassination with that country's own struggles to establish a lasting democracy. Khan shows how Édouard-René Lefebvre de Laboulaye, a

legal scholar and celebrant of French-American friendship, led others to design and construct what was officially called Liberty Enlightening the World. . . . An important book for general audiences." Publ Wkly

Includes bibliographical references

Langewiesche, William

American ground, unbuilding the World Trade Center. North Point Press 2002 205p $22; pa $13   **974.7**

1. September 11 terrorist attacks, 2001 2. World Trade Center (New York, N.Y.)

ISBN 0-86547-582-2; 0-86547-675-6 pa

LC 2002-75153

First published as a three part series of articles in Atlantic Monthly

"This is a genuinely monumental story, told without melodrama, an intimate depiction of ordinary Americans reacting to grand-scale tragedy at their best—and sometimes their worst." Publ Wkly

Lepore, Jill

New York burning; liberty, slavery, and conspiracy in an eighteenth-century Manhattan. Alfred A. Knopf 2005 323p il maps $26.95   **974.7**

1. Slavery -- United States 2. New York (N.Y.) -- History

ISBN 1-4000-4029-9

LC 2004-57625

"In this first-rate social history, Lepore not only adroitly examines the case's travesty, questioning whether such a conspiracy ever existed, but also draws a splendid portrait of the struggles, prejudices and triumphs of a very young New York City in which fully 'one in five inhabitants was enslaved.'" Publ Wkly

Includes bibliographical references

MacColl, Gail

To marry an English Lord; by Gail MacColl and Carol McD. Wallace. Workman Pub. 1989 x, 403 p.p ill. (pbk.) $15.95; o.p.   **974.7**

1. Marriage 2. Nobility 3. Great Britain -- History 4. Women -- Social conditions 5. Women -- United States -- History 6. England -- Social life and customs

ISBN 9780761171959; 0894809393

LC 85040529

This book traces how "[f]rom the Gilded Age until 1914, more than 100 American heiresses invaded Britannia and swapped dollars for titles--just like Cora Crawley, Countess of Grantham, the first of the Downton Abbey characters Julian Fellowes was inspired to create [for the television program] after reading 'To Marry An English Lord.' Filled with . . . personalities, . . . anecdotes, grand houses, and . . . period details--plus photographs, illustrations, quotes, and the finer points of Victorian and Edwardian etiquette--'To Marry An English Lord' is [a] social history." (Publisher's note)

McCourt, Malachy

A **monk** swimming. Hyperion 1998 290p
$23.95; pa $14   **974.7**
1. Actors
ISBN 0-7868-6398-6; 0-7868-8414-2 pa
       LC 97-46720
The author recounts stories of his "serendipitous success
as an actor and a bar owner after arriving in New York penniless and uneducated." Booklist
"The memoir, which covers ground through 1963, will
have readers smiling and laughing constantly." Publ Wkly

Singing my him song. HarperCollins Pubs. 2000
242p hardcover o.p. pa $14   **974.7**
1. Actors
ISBN 0-06-095548-1 pa
       LC 00-59774
In this sequel to A monk swimming, "McCourt tells us
the rest of his story; how he got from there to here, how
he went from living the headlong and heedless life of a
world-class drunk to becoming a sober, loving father and
grandfather, still happily married after thirty-five years."
Publisher's note

Miller, Donald L.

★ **Supreme** city; How Jazz Age Manhattan
gave birth to modern America. Donald L. Miller.
Simon & Schuster 2014 784 p. illustrations, map
$37.50   **974.7**
1. Manhattan (New York, N.Y.) 2. New York (N.Y.)
-- History 3. New York (N.Y.) -- History -- 20th century
4. New York (N.Y.) -- Politics and government -- 1898-
1951 5. New York (N.Y.) -- Social life and customs
-- 20th century
ISBN 1416550194; 9781416550198
       LC 2013020154
This book, by Donald L. Miller, "is the story of Manhattan's growth and transformation in the 1920s and the brilliant people behind it. . . . As mass communication emerged,
the city moved from downtown to midtown through a series
of engineering triumphs--Grand Central Terminal . . . the
Holland Tunnel, and the modern skyscraper. In less than ten
years Manhattan became the social, cultural, and commercial hub of the country. The 1920s was the Age of Jazz and
the Age of Ambition." (Publisher's note)
"Conveying the panoramic sweep of the era with wit,
illuminating details, humor, and style, Miller illustrates how
Midtown Manhattan became the nation's communications,
entertainment, and commercial epicenter." Pub Wkly
Includes bibliographical references and index

New York Historical Society

The **encyclopedia** of New York City; edited by
Kenneth T. Jackson. 2nd ed; New-York Historical
Society 2010 1561p il map $65   **974.7**
1. Reference books 2. New York (N.Y.) -- Encyclopedias
ISBN 978-0-300-11465-2; 0-300-11465-6
       LC 2010-31294
First published 1995
This encyclopedia "amasses the collective knowledge
on New York City into a volume small enough to pick up
and hold and large enough to satisfy the scholars, students,

and enthusiasts native to New York or just passing through.
. . . [Entries] describe and contextualize the people, places,
events, and phenomena that tell the story of New York City."
Libr J

Schecter, Barnet

★ The **devil's** own work; the Civil War draft
riots and the fight to reconstruct America. Barnet
Schecter. Walker & Co. 2005 434p il $28   **974.7**
1. Riots 2. United States -- History -- 1861-1865, Civil
War -- Draft resisters
ISBN 0-8027-1439-0
       LC 2005-18089
"Copiously researched and highlighted with a wealth of
period commentary, his lucid narrative colorfully recreates a
historical watershed and offers a rich exploration of the Civil
War's unfinished business." Publ Wkly
Includes bibliographical references

Schneider, Paul

The **Adirondacks**; a history of America's first
wilderness. Holt & Co. 1997 368p il maps hardcover o.p. pa $16   **974.7**
1. Adirondack Mountains (N.Y.) -- History
ISBN 0-8050-5990-3 pa
       LC 96-39844
The author presents a "history of New York State's Adirondack region. He relates here the life and lore of these
scenic mountains and lakes (Whiteface, Mt. Marcy, Fulton
Chain Lakes) from the region's earliest inhabitants (Haude-
nosaunce/Iroquois) through the advent of Henry Hudson
(1609), the Revolutionary War, abolitionists (John Brown),
19th-century homesteaders, Hudson River School artists, tuberculosis patients to Melville Dewey's Lake Placid Club,
the Adirondack Mountain Club, and the present environmental conservation efforts." Libr J

Smith, Dennis

A **decade** of hope; stories of grief and endurance
from 9/11 families and friends. [by] Dennis Smith
with Deirdre Smith. Viking 2011 364p $26.95 **974.7**
1. September 11 terrorist attacks, 2001 -- Personal
narratives
ISBN 978-0-670-02293-9
       LC 2011023325
The author, "a former firefighter, collects 25 moving personal narratives in this significant addition to the literature
of September 11. Featuring notable figures such as NYPD
Commissioner Ray Kelly and Congressman Peter King
alongside rescue workers and victims' family members and
loved ones, Smith's interviewees offer their experiences of
that tragic day, illustrating how the pain and losses are still
acutely felt. . . . With restraint and pathos, Smith's book provides powerful tribute and testimony." Publ Wkly

Strausbaugh, John

The **Village**; 400 Years of Beats and Bohemi-
ans, Radicals and Rogues, a History of Greenwich
Village. HarperCollins 2013 640 p. (hardcover)
$29.99   **974.7**
1. Bohemianism -- New York (N.Y.) 2. Greenwich
Village (New York, N.Y.) -- History 3. Greenwich

Village (New York (N.Y.) -- Social life and customs
ISBN 0062078194; 9780062078193

In this book, author John Strausbaugh "traces the history of [Greenwich Village, New York City] . . . from its early settlement in the 1600s to the present day. He examines its role in the arts within the context of broader issues and periods such as Prohibition, World War II, McCarthyism, organized crime, and gay liberation. Among the writers, artists, and musicians discussed are Amy Lowell, Maxwell Bodenheim, Norman Mailer, Allen Ginsberg . . . and Edward Albee." (Library Journal)

Taylor, Alan

The **divided** ground; Indians, settlers and the northern borderland of the American Revolution. Alfred A. Knopf 2006 542p il maps $35; pa $16.95   **974.7**

1. Iroquois Indians -- History 2. New York (State) -- History 3. United States -- History -- 1775-1783, Revolution
ISBN 0-679-45471-3; 1-4000-7707-9 pa

LC 2005-43582

"Taylor's exquisite writing and thorough research in both Canadian and US archives and manuscript collections make this a major work." Choice

Includes bibliographical references

Tribble, Scott

A **colossal** hoax; the giant from Cardiff that fooled America. Rowman & Littlefield Publishers, Inc. 2009 311p il   **974.7**

1. Cardiff giant 2. Impostors and imposture
ISBN 0-7425-6050-3; 978-0-7425-6050-5

LC 2008-25178

"Tribble tells the tale of the 1869 'discovery' of a tenfoot giant reputed to be either a petrified Biblical-era man or an ancient statue fashioned by pre-American Indian inhabitants of North America. The story focuses on huckster George Hull, who commissioned the fake fossil's carving out of gypsum and planted it for profit derived from paid viewings by a gullible public. . . . After exposure, the giant had an afterlife at fairs and museums; he is still on display as an example of American innocence and humbug. Engagingly written in a thorough treatment that this popular culture phenomenon has not usually received." Libr J

Includes bibliographical references

Von Drehle, Dave

★ **Triangle** : the fire that changed America. Atlantic Monthly Press 2003 340p il hardcover o.p. pa $14   **974.7**

1. Fires 2. Factories 3. Clothing industry 4. New York (N.Y.) 5. Triangle Shirtwaist Company, Inc.
ISBN 0-87113-874-3; 0-8021-4151-X pa

LC 2003-41835

"Von Drehle's engrossing account, which emphasizes the humanity of the victims and the theme of social justice, brings on of the pivotal and most shocking episodes of American labor history to life." Publ Wkly

Includes bibliographical references

Ward, Geoffrey C.

A **disposition** to be rich; how a small-town pastor's son ruined an American president, brought on a Wall Street crash, and made himself the best-hated man in the United States. by Geoffrey C. Ward. Alfred A. Knopf 2012 418 p.   **974.7**

1. Financial crises 2. Capitalists and financiers 3. United States -- Biography 4. Swindlers and swindling -- United States -- History 5. New York (N.Y.) -- Biography 6. Rochester (N.Y.) -- Biography 7. Children of clergy -- New York (State) -- Biography 8. Swindlers and swindling -- United States -- Biography 9. Capitalists and financiers -- United States -- Biography 10. Financial crises -- United States -- History -- 19th century 11. Ponzi schemes -- New York (State) -- New York -- History -- 19th century
ISBN 0679445307; 9780679445302

LC 2011035140

This book by Geoffrey C. Ward looks at "American financial swindler . . . Ferdinand Ward. . . . The secret of his success was the classic pyramid scheme, which entailed paying off earlier investors with proceeds from newer ones. . . . In 1884, it all came crashing down . . . ruining countless individuals . . . and arguably contributing to the Panic of 1884. Ward went to prison but never acknowledged responsibility." (Library Journal)

Includes bibliographical references

White, Shane

Stories of freedom in Black New York. Harvard Univ. Press 2002 260p il $27.95   **974.7**

1. Authors 2. Painters 3. Diplomats 4. Architects 5. Dramatists 6. Journalists 7. Essayists 8. Local government officials 9. African Company (Theater company) 10. New York (N.Y.) -- Race relations 11. African Americans -- New York (N.Y.) 12. New York (N.Y.) -- Intellectual life
ISBN 0-674-00893-6

LC 2002-68540

The author "makes a persuasive case for the company's cultural importance, particularly as a forerunner of the Harlem Renaissance that was still a century away." Publ Wkly

Includes bibliographical references

974.71   New York (N.Y.)

Gopnik, Adam

Through the children's gate; a home in New York. Alfred A. Knopf 2006 318p $25   **974.71**

1. Home -- Social aspects -- New York (State) -- New York 2. New York (N.Y.) -- Description and travel 3. New York (N.Y.) -- Social life and customs
ISBN 1-4000-4181-3; 978-1-4000-4181-7

LC 2006-45260

"Gopnik writes about returning to New York after five years in Paris." (N Y Times Book Rev)

"You don't have to be a New Yorker or even necessarily an enthusiast of the city to be alternately amused, touched, and charmed by Gopnik's well-crafted pieces." Christ Sci Monit

974.8   Pennsylvania

Pennsylvania: a history of the Commonwealth; edited by Randall M. Miller and William Pencak. Pennsylvania State Univ. Press 2002 xxxi, 654p il maps $49.95; pa $29.95   **974.8**
1. Pennsylvania -- History
ISBN 0-271-02213-2; 0-271-02214-0 pa
      LC 2002-5457

"More than half of this book is an unusual and inspired hybrid of history and nine other disciplines from geography to literature. . . . The editors profess to discover the sources of Pennsylvania's greatness and significance but also expose its faults and declining significance in the 20th century. They succeed at both." Choice

974.9   New Jersey

Wolff, Daniel
    4th of July, Asbury Park; a history of the promised land. Bloomsbury 2005 277p hardcover o.p. pa $14.95   **974.9**
1. Singers 2. Rock musicians 3. Songwriters 4. Asbury Park (N.J.)
ISBN 1-58234-509-0; 1-59691-114-X pa
      LC 2004-26965

This is a "history of the New Jersey resort town where [Bruce] Springsteen, after graduating from Freehold High School and briefly attending Ocean County Community College, served his rock 'n' roll apprenticeship." N Y Times Book Rev

The author "creates popular history at its best. Springsteen fans will love it, and so will anyone interested in American social history." Booklist
Includes bibliographical references

975   Southeastern United States (South Atlantic states)

Blount, Roy
    Long time leaving; dispatches from up South. [by] Roy Blount, Jr. Knopf 2007 383p $25   **975**
1. Southern States -- Humor 2. Southern States -- Civilization
ISBN 978-0-307-26618-7; 0-307-26618-4
      LC 2007-6799

In this collection of essays, the author "focuses on his own dueling loyalties across [what he sees as] the great American divide, North vs. South." Publisher's note
"This delightful collection is not only fun and funny but insightful as well." Libr J

Bragg, Rick
    Ava's man. Knopf 2001 259p $25; pa $13 **975**
1. Southern states
ISBN 0-375-41062-7; 0-375-72444-3 pa
      LC 2001-32677

In this account of his maternal grandfather's life as a roofer and bootlegger in Appalachia, the author "creates a

soulful, poignant portrait of working-class Southern life." Publ Wkly

Cash, Wilbur Joseph
    The **mind** of the South; with a new introduction by Bertram Wyatt-Brown. Vintage Bks. 1991 xliv, 444p pa $16   **975**
1. Southern States -- Civilization
ISBN 0-679-73647-6
      LC 91-50042

First published 1941 by Knopf
A psychological, cultural, and social history of the old South

Dent, Tom
    Southern journey; a return to the civil rights movement. University of Georgia Press 2001 400p pa $18.95   **975**
1. African Americans -- Civil rights 2. Southern States -- Race relations
ISBN 0-8203-2291-1; 978-0-8203-2291-9
      LC 00-61990

First published 1997 by Morrow
"Dent compellingly reveals that ordinary Southerners fundamentally changed the region and are poised to make more substantive changes." Libr J
Includes bibliographical references

Lemann, Nicholas
    Redemption : the last battle of the Civil War. Farrar, Straus and Giroux 2006 257p $24   **975**
1. African Americans -- Segregation 2. Southern States -- Race relations
ISBN 978-0-374-24855-0; 0-374-24855-9
      LC 2006-91

This book "offers a vigorous, necessary reminder of how racist reaction bred an American terrorism that suppressed black political activity and crushed Reconstruction in the South." N Y Times Book Rev
Includes bibliographical references

975.3   District of Columbia (Washington)

Bordewich, Fergus M.
    Washington : the making of the American capital. Amistad 2008 367p map $27.95; pa $15.99 **975.3**
1. Washington (D.C.)
ISBN 978-0-06-084238-3; 0-06-084238-5; 978-0-06-084239-0 pa; 0-06-084239-3 pa
      LC 2007-52053

The author explains "how the city's site was chosen and how political scheming, personal conflicts, and greed almost doomed the project of designing and constructing a capital city from scratch. Two themes are woven throughout his narrative: the important but often overlooked role played by slaves and former freed slaves and the constant North-South debate at the root of the bitter dispute over the capital's locale. . . . Bordewich introduces readers to the key players: George Washington, Thomas Jefferson, African American surveyor Benjamin Banneker, intractable and ill-fated architect and city planner Maj. Pierre Charles L'Enfant, the city's triumvirate of commissioners, and a host of pernicious financial speculators." Libr J

Includes bibliographical references

Gugliotta, Guy

Freedom's cap; Guy Gugliotta. Hill and Wang 2012 viii, 486 p.p **975.3**
1. Capitols 2. Historic buildings -- United States 3. United States -- History -- 1815-1861 4. United States -- History -- 1849-1877 5. Washington (D.C.) -- Buildings, structures, etc. 6. United States Capitol (Washington, D.C.) -- History
ISBN 9780809046812

LC 2011025750
This book takes place in "Washington [in the] 1850s. . . . [Author Guy Gugliotta provides an] account of the transformation of the U. S. Capitol from a[n] . . . inadequate . . . structure into today's massive marble symbol of democracy. . . . The author begins in the mid-1850s with the issue of Thomas Crawford's statue, 'Freedom,' now perched atop the Capitol dome. The . . . contest that Gugliotta outlines was between Army engineer Montgomery C. Meigs and architect Thomas Ustick Walter, both of whom would, at times, have control of the project. Both had ferocious work ethics, as well as enormous egos. . . . Gugliotta . . . includ[es] stories about marble quarries and ironworks; John Brown (whom he labels a terrorist); Presidents Fillmore, Pierce, Buchanan and Lincoln; and the many artisans and artists, principally Constantino Brumidi." (Kirkus)

Includes bibliographical references and index

Katharine Graham's Washington; {compiled by} Katharine Graham. Knopf 2002 813p il $30; pa $16.95 **975.3**
1. Washington (D.C.)
ISBN 0-375-41471-1; 1-4000-3059-5 pa

LC 2002-111640
"The late newspaper publisher's posthumous legacy is a delightful and insightful anthology of writings on the city that formed so much of her personality and her professional life. She draws from her personal collection of writings by a range of writers, many of them personal friends." Booklist

Lusane, Clarence

The **Black** history of the White House. City Lights Books 2011 575p il (Open Media series) **975.3**
1. Slavery -- United States 2. White House (Washington, D.C.) 3. United States -- Race relations 4. Presidents -- United States -- Staff 5. African Americans -- Washington (D.C.)
ISBN 978-0-8728-6532-7

LC 2010-36925
The author "offers a comprehensive and well-documented account of African Americans who have graced the White House as builders, slaves, servants, entertainers, policy professionals, and finally as the nation's First Family. . . . This is an important work of historical scholarship, bringing together chronicles of the African Americans who have played major roles in the annals of the presidential mansion." Libr J

Includes bibliographical references

Monkman, Betty C.

★ The **White** House; its historic furnishings and first families. principal photography by Bruce White. Abbeville Press 2000 320p il $65 **975.3**
1. White House (Washington, D.C.)
ISBN 0-7892-0624-2

LC 00-27085
"Monkman, the White House curator, documents the furnishings and decorative objects as well as the metamorphoses of White House interiors. The impact of the presidents and first ladies is particularly intriguing." Libr J

Includes bibliographical references

White House Historical Association

The **White** House; actors and observers. edited by William Seale. Northeastern Univ. Press 2002 xxii, 214p il $40 **975.3**
1. Presidents -- United States 2. White House (Washington, D.C.)
ISBN 1-55553-547-X

LC 2002-9087
This is "a pictorial history of the presidential residence. Accompanied by a succession of essays presented at a symposium honoring the 200th anniversary of the White House, this stunning collection of paintings, drawings, and photographs chronicles two centuries of presidential life. . . . This irresistible gallery of pictures will appeal to scholars and browsers alike." Booklist

Includes bibliographical references

975.5 Virginia

Fox, James

Five sisters; the Langhornes of Virginia. Simon & Schuster 2000 496p il $30; pa $16 **975.5**
1. Members of Parliament 2. Spouses of prominent persons
ISBN 0-684-80812-9; 0-7432-0042-X pa

LC 99-41815
First published 1998 in the United Kingdom with title: The Langhorne sisters

"Irene Langhorne, the last great Southern belle, moved North in 1895, when she married Charles Dana Gibson, creator of the Gibson girl. In her wake, three younger sisters (her elder, Lizzie, was already married) burst onto the glittering society stage. Nancy, the most famous, married Waldorf Astor and threw herself into English political activism; Phyllis, the author's grandmother, was more introverted; Nora, with 'a heart like a hotel,' repeatedly led the family to the brink of scandal. Fox brings intimacy to these semi-public personalities, elevating a century's gossip and legend into absorbing history." New Yorker

Includes bibliographical references

Furgurson, Ernest B.

Ashes of glory; Richmond at war. Knopf 1996 419p il maps hardcover o.p. pa $16 **975.5**
1. Richmond (Va.) -- History 2. United States -- History -- 1861-1865, Civil War -- Campaigns
ISBN 0-679-74660-9 pa

LC 95-49591

The author "tells the story of a city that between 1861 and 1865 epitomized the experience of the Civil War as a revolutionary one. Capital of a state that had long opposed secession, Richmond now became the symbol of Southern independence. It also remained a center of clandestine Unionism that hosted a struggle between espionage networks matching anything seen in Cold War Berlin." Publ Wkly

Includes bibliographical references

Horn, James P. P.

A **land** as God made it; Jamestown and the birth of America. [by] James Horn. Basic Books 2005 337p il maps $26   **975.5**

1. Jamestown (Va.) -- History
ISBN 0-465-03094-7

LC 2005-13054

"Possessing Jamestown's inherent drama, this is a solid rendition of the saga." Booklist

Includes bibliographical references

Noel Hume, Ivor

The **Virginia** adventure; Roanoke to James Towne: an archaeological and historical odyssey. University Press of Va. 1997 xxviii, 491p il map pa $19.95   **975.5**

1. Jamestown (Va.) -- History 2. Roanoke Island (N.C.) -- History 3. United States -- History -- 1600-1775, Colonial period
ISBN 0-8139-1758-1

LC 97-16651

First published 1994 by Knopf

The author discusses "the historical archaeology of the Roanoke and James Fort (later James Towne) settlements. Drawing extensively on firsthand accounts and other textual sources, he conjures up the feel of the Elizabethan experience that gave life to these settlements. . . . Hume also includes masterly and generous accounts of the history of the excavation of these sites and offers his well-informed views on where future work needs to be done. Written with wit, compassion, and tremendous attention to detail, this is historical archaeology at its best." Libr J

Price, David

★ **Love** and hate in Jamestown; John Smith, Pocahontas, and the heart of a new nation. {by} David A. Price. Knopf 2003 305p maps $25.95; pa $14.95   **975.5**

1. Princesses 2. Colonists 3. Indian leaders 4. Travel writers 5. Jamestown (Va.) -- History
ISBN 0-375-41541-6; 1-4000-3172-9 pa

LC 2002-43437

"For those general readers who wish to move beyond the myths and obtain a better understanding of them and the early years of the colony, this book will be an enjoyable and valuable tool." Booklist

Includes bibliographical references

Taylor, Alan

★ The **internal** enemy; slavery and war in Virginia, 1772-1832. Alan Taylor. W.W. Norton & Co. Inc. 2013 624 p. (hardcover) $35   **975.5**

1. Virginia -- History 2. Slavery -- United States -- History 3. United States -- History -- 1783-1815 4. Virginia -- History -- War of 1812 5. Slaves -- Virginia -- Tidewater (Region) -- History 6. Slavery -- Virginia -- Tidewater (Region) -- History 7. Plantation life -- Virginia -- Tidewater (Region) -- History 8. United States -- History -- War of 1812 -- Naval operations, British 9. United States -- History -- War of 1812 -- Participation, African American
ISBN 0393073718; 9780393073713

LC 2013009643

Pulitzer Prize: History (2014)

Author Alan Taylor "illustrates that a great factor in the liberation of thousands of slaves was the policy and intervention of the British government and military. Taylor concentrates on the six decades between the American Revolution and the slave revolt of Nat Turner, and he focuses on the Chesapeake region of Virginia. The area is dotted with numerous rivers flowing to the bay, and here hundreds of slaves paddled out to British warships, especially during the War of 1812." (Booklist)

"Exemplary work of history by Pulitzer and Bancroft winner Taylor (History/Univ. of Virginia; Colonial America: A Very Short Introduction, 2012, etc.), who continues his deep-searching studies of American society on either side of the Revolution. The world the slaves made was one of fear and loathing—on the part of the masters, that is, who indeed waited in a "cocoon of dread" for the day when their "internal enemy" would finally pounce. That day first came with a series of events that form the heart of the book: namely, the arrival of the War of 1812 in Virginia...One of the ironies of the war, which would eventually produce just the uprising of the internal enemy the Virginians dreaded, was that, so inept was the federal response, it advanced the cause of states' rights, which would lead to the broader Civil War two decades after Nat Turner's revolt. Full of implication, an expertly woven narrative that forces a new look at "the peculiar institution" in a particular time and place." (Kirkus)

Includes bibliographical references and index

975.6   North Carolina

Horn, James

A **kingdom** strange; the brief and tragic history of the lost colony of Roanoke. [by] James Horn. Basic Books 2010 296p il map $26   **975.6**

1. Roanoke Island (N.C.) -- History
ISBN 978-0-465-00485-0

LC 2010-563

"The author creates an engaging, you-are-there feel to the narrative, with rich descriptions of European politics, colonists' daily struggles and the vagaries of relations between Native American tribes. . . . A satisfying recounting of some of the earliest American history." Kirkus

Includes bibliographical references

975.7 South Carolina

Ball, Edward

Slaves in the family. Ballantine Books 1999 505p il map pa $17.95   **975.7**
> 1. Plantation life 2. Slaveholders 3. South Carolina 4. Plantation owners 5. Slavery -- United States 6. United States -- Race relations
> ISBN 978-0-345-43105-9; 0-345-43105-7
> First published 1998 by Farrar, Straus & Giroux

"For nearly a hundred and seventy years before the Civil War, members of the Ball family owned a string of plantations worked by slaves along South Carolina's Cooper River. After the war, the author's ancestors lost or sold their land and scattered to make new lives, but he wondered what happened to the slaves. This book, a brilliant blend of archival research and oral history, tells what he found." New Yorker

Includes bibliographical references

975.8 Georgia

Berendt, John

Midnight in the garden of good and evil; a story of Savannah. Random House 1994 388p $25; pa $14   **975.8**
> 1. Savannah (Ga.)
> ISBN 0-679-42922-0; 0-679-75152-1 pa
> > LC 93-3955

"Berendt has fashioned a Baedeker to Savannah that, while it flirts with condescension, is always contagiously affectionate. Few cities have been introduced more seductively." Newsweek

★ **Foxfire** 40th anniversary book; faith, family, and the land. edited by Angie Cheek, Lacy Hunter Nix, and Foxfire students. Anchor Books 2006 xxxix, 512p il pa $17.95   **975.8**
> 1. Handicraft 2. Country life -- Georgia 3. Appalachian region -- Social life and customs
> ISBN 0-307-27551-5; 978-0-307-27551-6
> > LC 2006-45311

"Drawing on the magazine's published talks by local high school students with elderly rural inhabitants, the books have explored the crafts, cooking, music, gardening and stories that have been passed down through the generations. The focus in this anniversary volume is on devotion to religion, family and the land. Collecting pieces from 40 years' worth of the magazine, the book inevitably covers topics covered in previous Foxfire collections, including snake handling, childhood toys and recipes. But the spoken words remain captivating, eloquent if plainspoken." Publ Wkly

Jones, Jacqueline

Saving Savannah; the city and the Civil War. Alfred A. Knopf 2008 510p il map $30   **975.8**
> 1. Savannah (Ga.) 2. United States -- History -- 1861-1865, Civil War
> ISBN 978-1-4000-4293-7; 1-4000-4293-3
> > LC 2008-11508

"Synthesizing the perspectives of the mercantile elite, the aristocratic upper crust and the downtrodden, . . . [the author has] fashioned a compelling social and political history." Washington Post Book World

Includes bibliographical references

Pressly, Paul M.

★ **On** the rim of the Caribbean; colonial Georgia and the British Atlantic world. Paul M. Pressly. University of Georgia Press 2013 xii, 354 p.p (hardcover : alk. paper) $69.95   **975.8**
> 1. Georgia -- History 2. International trade 3. United States -- History -- 1600-1775, Colonial period 4. Georgia -- Economic conditions -- 18th century 5. Plantations -- Georgia -- History -- 18th century 6. Georgia -- History -- Colonial period, ca. 1600-1775 7. Georgia -- Commerce -- West Indies, British -- History -- 18th century 8. West Indies, British -- Commerce -- Georgia -- History -- 18th century
> ISBN 0820335673; 0820345032; 9780820335674; 9780820345031
> > LC 2012033964

In this book, "Paul M. Pressly interprets Georgia's place in the Atlantic world in light of recent work in transnational and economic history." He "examines the ways in which Georgia came to share many of the characteristics of the sugar islands, how Savannah developed as a 'Caribbean' town, the dynamics of an emerging slave market, and the role of merchant-planters as leaders in forging a highly adaptive economic culture open to innovation." (Publisher's note)

"This richly documented, analytically complex, and well-written book is a major contribution to the study of Colonial Georgia and the 18th-century Atlantic world." Choice

Includes bibliographical references (p. [301]-335) and index

Sherrod, Shirley

The **courage** to hope; how I stood up to the right wing media, the Obama administration, and the forces of fear. Shirley Sherrod ; with Catherine Whitney. 1st Atria Books hardcover ed. Atria Books 2012 240 p., [8] p. of plates p col. ill. (hardcover : alk. paper) $24.99; (trade paper : alk. paper) $15.00   **975.8**
> 1. Rural development 2. Sherrod, Shirley, 1948- 3. United States -- Race relations 4. Rural poor -- Georgia 5. Georgia -- Rural conditions 6. Rural development -- Georgia 7. Farmers -- Georgia -- Economic conditions 8. Mass media -- Objectivity -- United States 9. African American farmers -- Georgia -- Economic conditions 10. United States. Dept. of Agriculture -- Officials and employees -- Biography
> ISBN 1451650949; 9781451650945; 9781451651010; 9781451651027
> > LC 2011050718

In this memoir, "[Shirley] Sherrod sets the record straight on her forced resignation from the Department of Agriculture in 2010. The author . . . was director for the USDA's Rural Development in Georgia when conservative political blogger Andrew Breitbart attacked her for allegedly reverse racist comments she made at an NAACP event. The threat of exposure on national TV was enough to send the USDA running for cover, and she was dismissed. Sherrod decided she had to fight back." (Kirkus Reviews)

Includes bibliographical references and index.

975.9 Florida

Allman, T. D.

Finding Florida. Pgw 2013 528 p. (hardcover)
$27.50 **975.9**
1. Florida -- History 2. Political corruption
ISBN 0802120768; 9780802120762

This book by T. D. Allman offers a history of Florida
that "spans half a millennium, from the myth of Ponce de
León's Fountain of Youth to the 2012 shooting of 17-year-
old Trayvon Martin, and it is a . . . cavalcade of would-be
'conquistadors,' epically corrupt and racist politicians, and
oligarch-wannabes. Allman argues that these individuals'
ideas about Florida were wildly wrong." (Booklist)

Gaines, Steven S.

Fool's paradise; players, poseurs, and the culture
of excess in South Beach. Crown Publishers 2009
274p il $25.95 **975.9**
1. South Beach (Miami Beach, Fla.) -- Social life and
customs
ISBN 978-0-307-34627-8; 0-307-34627-7
LC 2008-36067

This is a "terrific social history buffet. . . . [Gaines is] a
gifted storyteller. He fills the book with telling anecdotes and
bons mots, but the narrative never gets off track. It would be
easy to focus on the drug-and-sleaze aspect of South Beach.
But Gaines lets a little bit go a long way. He could fill the
book with stupid celebrity tricks. But again, less is more.
This book succeeds not because of star power but because
of story power. The centerpiece of the book is a war of
dueling architects and builders fighting to build the iconic
Fontainebleau hotel and then to destroy it out of spite." St.
Petersburg Times

Includes bibliographical references

Grunwald, Michael

The **swamp**; the Everglades, Florida, and the
politics of paradise. Simon & Schuster 2005 450p il
map hardcover o.p. pa $15 **975.9**
1. Everglades (Fla.)
ISBN 0-7432-5105-9; 978-0-7432-5105-1; 978-0-
7432-5107-5 pa; 0-7432-5107-5 pa
LC 2005-56329

This is a "chronicle of the history of the Everglades. . .
. [This] is a riveting tale of ambition versus ecological reality, politics versus science, and, on the upside, our gradual
awakening to the true nature of nature." Booklist

Includes bibliographical references

Roberts, Diane

Dream state; eight generations of swamp lawyers, conquistadors, Confederate daughters, banana
Republicans, and other Florida wildlife. Free Press
2004 355p il $25 **975.9**
1. Florida
ISBN 0-7432-5206-3
LC 2004-56276

"With hurricane-force prose, . . . Roberts hits the land of
orange groves, theme parks and mobile homes with a tor-
rential outpouring of love and hate, affection and disgust."
Publ Wkly

Includes bibliographical references

976.1 Alabama

Agee, James

Let us now praise famous men; [by] James Agee,
Walker Evans; with an introduction to the new edition
by John Hersey. Houghton Mifflin 2000 il $30; pa
$18 **976.1**
1. Farm tenancy 2. Alabama -- Social conditions
ISBN 978-0-395-95771-4; 0-395-95771-0; 978-0-618-
12749-8 pa; 0-618-12749-6 pa
First published 1941

This work documents "the ways of life of three Alabama
tenant-farming families. . . . It is a unique and complex book,
deeply honest and compassionate, and remarkable for its extraordinary descriptive, lyric, and meditative prose." Benet's
Reader's Ency of Am Lit

Agee, James, 1909-1955

★ **Cotton** Tenants; Three Families. Random
House Inc 2013 224 p. $24.95 **976.1**
1. Farm family -- Alabama -- History -- 20th century
2. Farm tenancy -- Alabama -- History -- 20th century
ISBN 1612192122; 9781612192123

This book, written during the Great Depression, was
"commissioned by Fortune magazine' as a 'report on working conditions of poor white farmers in the deep south.' The
report itself was never published. . . . It follows the lives of
three impoverished tenant farmers--Floyd Burroughs, Bud
Fields, and Frank Tingle--and their families". Topics include
"diet, shelter, and labor". (Publishers Weekly)

McWhorter, Diane

Carry me home; Birmingham, Alabama: the cli-
mactic battle of the civil rights revolution. Simon &
Schuster 2001 701p il hardcover o.p. pa $17 **976.1**
1. African Americans -- Civil rights 2. Birmingham
(Ala.) -- Race relations
ISBN 0-684-80747-5; 0-7432-1772-1 pa
LC 00-53827

McWhorter presents an account of the struggle for
civil rights in Birmingham, Ala., both from a personal and
societal perspective

"A daughter of Birmingham's privileged elite, Mc-
Whorter weaves a personal narrative through this startling
account of the history, events, and major players on both
sides of the civil rights battle in that city." Booklist

Includes bibliographical references

976.2   Mississippi

Welty, Eudora

One time, one place; Mississippi in the Depression : a snapshot album. rev ed; University Press of Miss. 1996 115p il $35   **976.2**

1. Mississippi -- Pictorial works
ISBN 0-87805-866-4

LC 95-46057

First published 1971 by Random House

This is a "collection of photographs of Mississippians that Welty took in the 1930s, when she worked for the Works Progress Administration (WPA). This Silver Anniversary Edition contains a great foreword by William Maxwell that absolutely nails the importance of the book for many readers." Booklist

976.3   Louisiana

Baum, Dan

Nine lives; death and life in New Orleans. Spiegel & Grau 2009 335p $26   **976.3**

1. New Orleans (La.) -- Social life and customs
ISBN 978-0-385-52319-6; 0-385-52319-X

LC 2008-31483

"Baum's in-depth reporting (he was on scene during Katrina, even turning himself in at the Convention Center to chronicle the out-of-sight outrages) is evident on every page." Booklist

Includes bibliographical references

Brinkley, Douglas

The great deluge; Hurricane Katrina, New Orleans, and the Mississippi Gulf Coast. Morrow 2006 716p il hardcover o.p. pa $17.95   **976.3**

1. Disaster relief 2. Hurricane Katrina, 2005
ISBN 0-06-112423-0; 0-06-114849-0 pa

LC 2006-43338

This is an account of Hurricane Katrina, which ravaged the Gulf Coast in late summer 2005.

The author "captures the human toll of Katrina as graphically as the most vivid newspaper and television accounts did, and by pulling together a huge, choral portrait of what happened during that first week of havoc and distress (from Saturday, Aug. 27, through Saturday, Sept. 3), he gives the reader a richly detailed timeline of disaster—a timeline in which the sheer cumulative power of details impresses upon us, again, just how abysmally inept relief efforts were on every level, from FEMA to the Red Cross to the New Orleans police department, from the federal government to state and local authorities." N Y Times (Late N Y Ed)

Clark, Joshua

Heart like water; surviving Katrina and life in its disaster zone. Free Press 2007 356p map $25 **976.3**

1. Hurricane Katrina, 2005
ISBN 978-1-4165-3763-2; 1-4165-3763-5

LC 2007-5157

"Clark was among the few hearty or hapless souls who remained in New Orleans during Hurricane Katrina. . . . In this riveting first-person account, Clark recalls the static in the air as the hurricane approached; the unnerving silence afterwards without even the sound of birds; and 'shopping' for supplies at a local store where the owner had apparently given permission before fleeing. . . . This is a raw, revealing, and highly personal look at surviving Hurricane Katrina." Booklist

Dyson, Michael Eric

Come hell or high water; Hurricane Katrina and the color of disaster. Basic Civitas 2006 258p $23; pa $14.95   **976.3**

1. Disaster relief 2. Hurricane Katrina, 2005 3. African Americans -- Social conditions
ISBN 978-0-465-01761-4; 0-465-01761-4; 978-0-465-01772-0 pa; 0-465-01772-X pa

LC 2007-310210

This book on Hurrican Katrina "not only chronicles what happened when, it also argues that the nation's failure to offer timely aid to Katrina's victims indicates deeper problems in race and class relations. . . . [The author's] contention that Katrina exposed a dominant culture pervaded not only by 'active malice' toward poor blacks but also by a long history of 'passive indifference' to their problems is both powerful and unsettling." Publ Wkly

Includes bibliographical references

Horne, Jed

★ Breach of faith; Hurricane Katrina and the near death of a great American city. Random House 2006 412p map hardcover o.p. pa $16 **976.3**

1. Disaster relief 2. Hurricane Katrina, 2005 3. New Orleans (La.) -- Description and travel
ISBN 978-1-4000-6552-3; 1-4000-6552-6; 978-0-8129-7650-2 pa; 0-8129-7650-9 pa

LC 2006-46468

This book does "an admirable job of detailing the design flaws that left New Orleans underwater." New Repub

Includes bibliographical references

Lane, Charles

The day freedom died; the Colfax massacre, the Supreme Court, and the betrayal of Reconstruction. Henry Holt and Co. 2008 326p il map $27 **976.3**

1. Massacres 2. Trials (Homicide) 3. Reconstruction (1865-1876) 4. Louisiana -- Race relations 5. African Americans -- History 6. United States -- Supreme Court
ISBN 978-0-8050-8342-2; 0-8050-8342-1

LC 2007-37514

"The Colfax Massacre . . . took place on an Easter Sunday afternoon in 1873. Within four hours, at least eighty black American men had been brutally murdered by white vigilantes in Colfax, La. Journalist Lane's groundbreaking and persuasive work illustrates this 'pivotal event in the political and constitutional history of post-Civil War America' and its social, political and judicial aftermath. . . . Students of American and African-American history will find it particularly valuable; fans of American history will find it a moving and instructive drama." Publ Wkly

Includes bibliographical references

Rasmussen, Daniel

American uprising; the untold story of America's largest slave revolt. Harper 2011 276p map **976.3**

1. Slavery -- United States 2. New Orleans (La.) -- History 3. African Americans -- Louisiana 4. New Orleans (La.) -- Race relations 5. Slavery -- Louisiana -- New Orleans 6. African Americans -- Louisiana -- New Orleans 7. Slave insurrections -- Louisiana -- New Orleans

ISBN 0061995215; 0062084356; 9780061995217; 9780062084354

LC 2010017855

This is a history of the 1811 slave rebellion in New Orleans. Bibliography. Index.

This is an "account of a large-scale, three-day slave revolt on the sugar plantations near New Orleans during the 1811 Carnival (Mardi Gras) season. The author argues that the slave-rebels, who had learned warfare tactics in their native Africa, were inspired by the successful Haitian revolution. . . . This is a welcome addition to popular history and an engaging read for anyone interested in this important chapter in the tragic story of American slavery." Libr J

Includes bibliographical references

Van Heerden, Ivor Ll.

The **storm**; what went wrong and why during Hurricane Katrina. [by] Ivor van Heerden and Mike Bryan. Viking 2006 308p il map hardcover o.p. pa $15 **976.3**

1. Disaster relief 2. Hurricane Katrina, 2005

ISBN 0-670-03781-8; 0-14-311213-9 pa

LC 2006-44727

This book focuses on public mismanagement relating to Hurricane Katrina.

"This serious, scientific explanation of what exactly happened in the hours—and years—leading up to Hurricane Katrina's devestation of New Orleans brings a fresh perspective to a tragedy that has generated remarkably similar news accounts over the past eight months." Publ Wkly

Includes bibliographical references

★ **Voices** rising; stories from the Katrina Narrative Project. edited by Rebeca Antoine; [afterword by Fredrick Barton] UNO Press 2008 244p pa $12.95 **976.3**

1. Hurricane Katrina, 2005 -- Personal narratives

ISBN 978-0-9728143-6-2; 0-9728143-6-1

In this "collection of personal narratives, readers come face-to-face with the stark reality wrought by Hurricane Katrina and the failure of the federal levees. . . . Every aspect of the post-Katrina New Orleans experience is present here, from areas as divergent as the I10 overpass, the French Quarter, and shelters across the South. The rescuers and rescued have equal voices and share memories poignant and startling. . . . Miles away from academic analysis, this is American social history from the ground up and staggering in its significance." Booklist

976.4   Texas

Davis, William C.

Three roads to the Alamo; the lives and fortunes of David Crockett, James Bowie and William Barret Travis. HarperCollins Pubs. 1998 791p il hardcover o.p. pa $20 **976.4**

1. Lawyers 2. Soldiers 3. Pioneers 4. Army officers 5. Texas -- History 6. Members of Congress 7. Alamo (San Antonio, Tex.)

ISBN 0-06-093094-2 pa

LC 97-43815

Davis provides portraits of the three frontiersmen "showing both the differences and similarities that propelled them into a remote Spanish mission in Mexican Texas for a fatal confrontation with the Mexican President, Santa Anna and his troops in March 1836." N Y Times Book Rev

This "is a readable, stimulating, and exceptionally well-researched narrative history." Libr J

Includes bibliographical references

Donovan, James

The **blood** of heroes; the 13-day struggle for the Alamo-- and the sacrifice that forged a nation. James Donovan. 1st ed. Little, Brown and Co. 2012 x, 500 p.p ill., maps $29.99 **976.4**

1. Texas -- History 2. Alamo (San Antonio, Tex.) -- Siege, 1836

ISBN 0316053740; 9780316053747

LC 2011050067

This book chronicles "the Battle of the Alamo" which the author characterizes as "the signal event of the Texas struggle for independence. . . . [James] Donovan's . . . story focuses on the 13-day standoff, but he also supplies . . . context, helping us to understand the history of the breakaway province and notable characters in the revolution like [Sam] Houston, Stephen Austin, Ben Milam and James C. Neill." (Kirkus Reviews)

Includes bibliographical references (p. [467]-488) and index.

Reid, Jan

Let the people in; the life and times of Ann Richards. by Jan Reid ; research assistance by Shawn Morris. University of Texas Press 2012 495 p. ill. **976.4**

1. Governors -- Texas -- Biography 2. Democratic Party (U.S.) -- Biography 3. Politicians -- United States -- Biography 4. Texas -- Politics and government -- 1951-

ISBN 0292719647; 9780292719644; 9780292744523

LC 2012016118

This biography by Jan Reid "tell[s] a very personal, human story of Ann Richards's remarkable rise to power as a liberal Democrat in a conservative Republican state. Reid traces the whole arc of Richards's life . . . [and] her rise and fall as governor of Texas. . . . He tells the full, inside story of Richards's rise from county office and the state treasurer's office to the governorship . . . [and] describes Richards's final years as a world traveler, lobbyist, public speaker, and mentor." (Publisher's note)

Includes bibliographical references and index

Valby, Karen

Welcome to Utopia; notes from a small town. Spiegel & Grau 2010 238p il $25   **976.4**

1. City and town life 2. Utopia (Tex.)
ISBN 978-0-385-52286-1; 0-385-52286-X

LC 2009-37970

"Entertainment Weekly magazine sent intrepid reporter Karen Valby into the great flyover zone in 2006 in search of a 'small town somewhere in America without popular culture.' She found Utopia, a town of a few hundred souls 90 miles west of the nation's seventh-largest city, San Antonio. Utopia is not exactly off the grid, and one suspects that its name appealed to Valby more than its isolation. Her book . . . is a pleasant moment-in-time postcard of a typical U.S. town." Minneapolis Star Tribune

Includes bibliographical references

976.6   Oklahoma

Hirsch, James S.

Riot and remembrance; the Tulsa race war and its legacy. Houghton Mifflin 2002 358p il $25; pa $14   **976.6**

1. Riots 2. Tulsa (Okla.) -- Race relations 3. African Americans -- Tulsa (Okla.)
ISBN 0-618-10813-0; 0-618-34076-9 pa

LC 2001-51615

"James S. Hirsch's history of the Tulsa, Okla., race riot in 1921 places the incident in a national debate on race and reparations." N Y Times Book Rev

"Hirsch unearths an important episode in U.S. history with verve, intelligence and compassion." Publ Wkly

Includes bibliographical references

976.8   Tennessee

Kiernan, Denise

The girls of atomic city; the secret history of the women who built WWII's most powerful weapon. by Denise Kiernan. Simon & Schuster 2013 400 p. $26   **976.8**

1. Atomic bomb 2. Women -- Tennessee -- Oak Ridge -- History 3. World War, 1939-1945 -- Tennessee -- Oak Ridge 4. Oak Ridge (Tenn.) -- History -- 20th century
ISBN 1451617526; 9781451617528

LC 2012045467

This book by Denise Kiernan tells the "story of the young women of Oak ridge, Tennessee, who unwittingly played a crucial role in . . . enriching uranium for the atomic bomb. . . . Few could piece together the true nature of their work until the bomb 'Little Boy' was dropped over Hiroshima, Japan, and the secret was out. Kiernan traces the astonishing story of these unsung WWII workers through interviews with dozens of surviving women and other Oak Ridge residents." (Publisher's note)

Includes bibliographical references

977   North central United States

Barry, John M.

Rising tide; the great Mississippi flood of 1927 and how it changed America. Simon & Schuster 1997 524p il maps hardcover o.p. pa $16   **977**

1. Generals 2. Bridge engineers 3. Military engineers 4. Floods -- Mississippi River 5. Mississippi River valley -- History
ISBN 0-684-84002-2 pa

LC 96-40077

This is the "story of human defeat by a savage, unpredictable river. . . . The flood of 1927, three times greater than the flood of 1993, was an unprecedented disaster that spurred a political innovation. Congress's agreement to rebuild the Mississippi's shattered flood-control system marked the federal government's first assumption of full financial responsibility for a regional calamity. Much of the book recounts how the greed of New Orleans bankers and Delta planters increased the sufferings of the rural poor. . . . Barry's book is a virtuoso piece of exposition." New Yorker

Includes bibliographical references

Dennis, Jerry

The living Great Lakes; searching for the heart of the inland seas. Thomas Dunne Bks. 2003 296p il maps hardcover o.p. pa $14.95   **977**

1. Great Lakes
ISBN 0-312-25193-9; 0-312-33103-7 pa

LC 2002-32500

The author offers a "description of being a crew member on the schooner Malabar on a six-week trip through the waters of Lakes Huron, Ontario, Michigan, Erie and Superior. . . . Dennis weaves anecdotes from his childhood, such as a family-fishing trip on Lake Michigan, together with informed commentary on the natural history of the lakes and the people who live there." Publ Wkly

Includes bibliographical references

Eckert, Allan W.

A sorrow in our heart: the life of Tecumseh. Bantam Bks. 1992 862p maps hardcover o.p. pa $7.99   **977**

1. Shawnee Indians
ISBN 0-553-56174-X pa

LC 91-31858

This is a "narrative biography of Tecumseh, the remarkable Shawnee warrior and statesman who succeeded in organizing a group of disparate tribes into a cohesive confederacy of nations. . . . Eckert places his subject firmly within his proper social and historical context by providing a tremendous amount of meticulously researched and authenticated background information, including illuminating details of tribal life and Shawnee culture." Booklist

Includes bibliographical references

Laskin, David

The children's blizzard; . HarperCollins 2004 307p map $24.95; pa $13.95   **977**

1. Blizzards
ISBN 0-06-052075-2; 0-06-052076-0 pa

LC 2005-295018

The author describes the events of the School Children's Blizzard, when "in 1888, a sudden, violent blizzard swept across the American plains, killing hundreds of people, many of them children on their way home from school." Publ Wkly

"An adroit, sensitive drama and a skillful addition to a popular genre." Booklist

Includes bibliographical references

977.1　Ohio

Frazier, Ian

Family. Farrar, Straus & Giroux 1994 386p il maps hardcover o.p.　pa $16　　　　**977.1**
1. City and town life 2. Ohio -- Social life and customs
ISBN 0-312-42059-5 pa

LC 94-14730

"An extraordinary history of an ordinary family, in which the author plays the roles of gossip, pedant and loyal member, yielding a reunion strangers are welcome—and fortunate—to attend." N Y Times Book Rev

Gup, Ted

A **secret** gift; how one man's kindness--and a trove of letters--revealed the hidden history of the Great Depression. Penguin Press 2010 365p il $25.95　　　　**977.1**
1. Charity 2. Businesspeople 3. Philanthropists 4. Great Depression, 1929-1939 5. Canton (Ohio)
ISBN 978-1-59420-270-4; 1-59420-270-2

LC 2010-17302

"As Gup interweaves the sagas of recipient families with the life of their anonymous benefactor, 'A Secret Gift' never fails to entertain, inform and sometimes astound." Cleveland Plain Dealer

Ryan, Terry

The **prize** winner of Defiance, Ohio; how my mother raised 10 kids on 25 words or less. foreword by Suze Orman. Simon & Schuster 2001 351p il $24; pa $13　　　　**977.1**
1. Homemakers 2. Prizewinners 3. Defiance (Ohio) -- Biography 4. Prize contests in advertising
ISBN 0-7432-1122-7; 0-7432-1123-5 pa

LC 2001-18379

"Although Terry Ryan's father, Kelly Ryan, drank away most of his weekly machinist's paycheck, her mother responded by finding a use for her skill with words {by entering and winning contests}." (Women's Rev Books)

The author recounts the life of her mother, "a small-town Ohio housewife in the nineteen-fifties who lived on the brink of dire poverty, thanks to a brood of ten kids and an ineffectual drunk of a husband. Since Evelyn couldn't work outside her home, she worked inside it, penning hundreds of product jingles and entering them in the national contests that drove the advertising industry of the day." New Yorker

977.3　Illinois

Abbott, Karen

Sin in the Second City; madams, ministers, playboys, and the battle for America's soul. Random House 2007 xxiv, 356p il $25.95　　　　**977.3**
1. Prostitution 2. Madams 3. Everleigh Club (Chicago, Ill.) 4. Chicago (Ill.) -- Social life and customs
ISBN 978-1-4000-6530-1; 1-4000-6530-5

LC 2006-51878

"Lavish in her details, nicely detached in her point of view, [and with] scrupulous concern for historical accuracy, Ms. Abbott has written an immensely readable book. Sin in the Second City offers much in the way of reflection for those interested in the unending puzzle that goes by the name of human nature." Wall Street Journal

Includes bibliographical references

Chase, John

Golden; how Rod Blagojevich talked himself out of the governor's office and into prison. Jeff Coen and John Chase. Chicago Review Press 2012 x, 486 p.p (hbk.) $27.95　　　　**977.3**
1. Trials 2. Biography 3. United States -- Politics and government 4. Political corruption -- Illinois 5. Governors -- Illinois -- Biography 6. Illinois -- Politics and government -- 1951-
ISBN 1569763399; 9781569763391

LC 2012017760

Author Jeff Coen presents a "complete telling of the [Rod] Blagojevich story . . . about one of the nation's most notorious politicians" by "detailing the mechanics of the corruption that brought him down. . . Sentenced to 14 years in prison in December 2011, this is the final word on who the governor was, how he was elected, how he got himself into trouble, and how the feds took him down." (Publisher's note)

Cohen, Adam

American pharaoh: Mayor Richard J. Daley: his battle for Chicago and the nation; {by} Adam Cohen and Elizabeth Taylor. Little, Brown 2000 614p map hardcover o.p.　pa $16.95　　　　**977.3**
1. Mayors 2. Political party leaders 3. Chicago (Ill.) -- Politics and government
ISBN 0-316-83489-0 pa

LC 99-42157

This is a biography of the man who was "mayor of Chicago from 1955 until his death in 1976. His command extended far beyond the boundaries of Cook County, where he greatly influenced such decisive events of the Sixties as Kennedy's election in 1960, Martin Luther King's ill-fated Chicago campaign for civil rights, and the notorious '68 Democratic Convention." Libr J

"Penetrating, nonsensationalistic and exhaustive, this is an impressive and important biography." Publ Wkly

Includes bibliographical references

Dyja, Thomas

The **third** coast; when Chicago built the American dream. Thomas Dyja. The Penguin Press 2013 xxxiv, 544 p.p ill. (hardcover) $29.95   **977.3**

    1. Chicago (Ill.) -- History -- 20th century 2. Chicago (Ill.) -- Social conditions -- 20th century 3. Chicago (Ill.) -- Relations -- United States 4. Chicago (Ill.) -- Intellectual life -- 20th century

    ISBN 1594204322; 9781594204326

LC 2012039710

This book, by Thomas Dyja, explores the industrial and cultural history of Chicago, Illinois in the mid-20th century. "Much of what defined the nation as it grew into a superpower was produced in Chicago. . . . Yet even as Chicago led the way in creating mass-market culture, its artists pushed back in their own distinct voices. . . . Thomas Dyja re-creates the story of the city in its postwar prime and explains its profound impact on modern America." (Publisher's note)

"A readable, richly detailed history of America's second city." Kirkus

Includes bibliographical references and index

Miller, Donald L.

City of the century; the epic of Chicago and the making of America. {by} Donald Miller. Simon & Schuster 1996 704p il maps hardcover o.p. pa $18   **977.3**

    1. Chicago (Ill.) -- History

    ISBN 0-684-83138-4 pa

LC 96-4018

In this account of Chicago's history in the nineteenth century "Miller tells of Chicago's historical and literary figures, reform leaders, architects, industrialists, and entrepreneurs." Libr J

Newberry Library

The **Encyclopedia** of Chicago; edited by James R. Grossman, Ann Durkin Keating, Janice L. Reiff; cartographic editor, Michael P. Conzen. University of Chicago Press 2004 xxix, 1117p il map $65 **977.3**

    1. Reference books 2. Chicago (Ill.) -- Encyclopedias

    ISBN 0-226-31015-9

LC 2004-3487

"The main alphabetical section of the Encyclopedia, comprising more than 1,400 entries, covers . . . Chicago's neighborhoods, suburbs, and ethnic groups, as well as the city's cultural institutions, technology and science, architecture, religions, immigration, transportation, business history, labor, music, health and medicine, and hundreds of other topics." Publisher's note

Pacyga, Dominic A.

Chicago; a biography. University of Chicago Press 2009 462p il map $35   **977.3**

    1. Chicago (Ill.) -- History

    ISBN 9780226644318; 0-226-64431-6

LC 2009-1192

The author "has written an urban biography that captures the spirit of Chicago. . . . Pacyga portrays Chicago with time-lapse velocity as it morphs from a swampy portage to a city of skyscrapers. Concentrating on Chicago's ever-changing cultural diversity, notorious politics, and the crucial role technology played in the city's rapid rise, Pacyga seeds the big picture with cameos of fascinating individuals. . . . A vivid, streamlined, and superbly well-illustrated portrait of an essential American city." Booklist

Includes bibliographical references

Preib, Martin

The **wagon** and other stories from the city. University of Chicago Press 2010 167p $20   **977.3**

    1. Police -- Chicago (Ill.) 2. Chicago (Ill.) -- Social conditions

    ISBN 978-0-226-67980-8; 0-226-67980-2

LC 2009-36010

"The book is anchored by 'The Wagon.' . . . In it, Preib details his work on the vehicle the CPD uses to pick up dead bodies. It seems incongruous to describe such a gut-wrenching story as gorgeous, but gorgeous it is; Preib's musings on the recently, often ignominiously departed are particularly affecting, with flashes of morbid humor for relief. Other trenchant essays touch on the trials of police work, his years as a doorman and a union organizer, his hitchhiking escapades as a young man, and his observations of Chicago. One thing's for sure: Preib isn't a cop moonlighting as a writer. He's a writer who happens to work as a cop." Chicago Reader

977.4   Michigan

LeDuff, Charlie

Detroit; an American autopsy. Charlie LeDuff. Penguin Press 2013 xvi, 286 p.p ill. (hardcover) $27.95   **977.4**

    1. Detroit (Mich.) -- History 2. Detroit (Mich.) -- Economic conditions 3. Detroit (Mich.) -- Social conditions 4. Detroit (Mich.) -- Politics and government 5. Journalists -- Michigan -- Detroit -- Biography

    ISBN 1594205345; 9781594205347

LC 2012030924

In this book, Charlie LeDuff profiles Detroit, Michigan. "Having led us on the way up, Detroit now seems to be leading us on the way down. Once the richest city in America, Detroit is now the nation's poorest. Once the vanguard of America's machine age . . . , Detroit is now America's capital for unemployment, illiteracy, dropouts, and foreclosures. . . . LeDuff sets out to uncover what destroyed his city." (Publisher's note)

Martelle, Scott

Detroit; a biography. Scott Martelle. Chicago Review Press 2012 xvi, 288 p.p   **977.4**

    1. Detroit (Mich.) -- History 2. Detroit (Mich.) -- Population 3. Detroit (Mich.) -- Economic conditions 4. African Americans -- Detroit (Mich.) -- History 5. African Americans -- Michigan -- Detroit -- History

    ISBN 156976526X; 9781569765265

LC 2011041173

This book on Detroit, Michigan "recounts the rise and downfall of a once-great city, from its origins as a French military outpost to protect fur traders and tame local Indian tribes, to the industrial giant, known colloquially as Motown, and now when its "economy seized up like an engine run dry." Founded by a French naval officer named Cadillac, the city became a vibrant river town with the Erie Canal's opening, exporting both to the east and westward to Chicago. The 1855 opening of Lake Superior later expanded its postbellum shipping capacity and brought heavy industry. . . . But a series of downturns ravaged the city: the 1973 OPEC oil embargo helped destroy the city's auto-industry dominance, and drug-dealing gangs caused a murder rate that far out-stripped New York's." (Publishers Wkly)

Includes bibliographical references (p. 261-280) and index

977.7 Iowa

Blair, Joe

By the Iowa Sea; a memoir. Joe Blair. Scribner 2012 280 p. **977.7**

1. Adultery 2. Midlife crisis 3. Marriage problems 4. Middle aged men -- Biography 5. Iowa -- Biography
ISBN 1451636059; 9781451636055

LC 2011038073

This memoir describes "[o]ne man's midlife crisis surrounding love, marriage and parenthood. As a child, [Joe] Blair imagined his adulthood including motorcycles and the freedom to come and go as he pleased. Years later, he was tied down with a heating-and-air-conditioning repair job, a wife, four children (one of them severely autistic), a mortgage and no motorcycle. . . . The author's need for a change became more urgent. Excessive drinking and sexual fantasies of his wife with another man were not enough, and Blair, desperate for an escape route, turned to another woman, finding passion and excitement in her arms. Internal confusion over his infidelity collided with the outer reality of his wife's anger, and the resulting changes surprised even the author." (Kirkus)

Includes bibliographical references and index

978 Western United States

Brown, Dee Alexander

The **American** West; photos edited by Martin F. Schmitt. Scribner 1994 461p il maps hardcover o.p. pa $17 **978**

1. Rodeos 2. Cowhands 3. Kiowa Indians 4. Apache Indians 5. Dakota Indians 6. Cheyenne Indians 7. Little Bighorn, Battle of the, 1876 8. Outlaws 9. Nez Percé Indians 10. West (U.S.) -- History 11. Frontier and pioneer life -- West (U.S.)
ISBN 0-684-80441-7 pa

LC 94-37444

"This narrative history of westward expansion paints a vivid portrait of the settlers, pioneers, entrepreneurs, and Native Americans of the old West. Useful as collateral research material and for recreational reading." Booklist

Includes bibliographical references

Calloway, Colin G.

One vast winter count; the Native American West before Lewis and Clark. University of Nebraska Press 2003 631p il (History of the American West) $39.95 **978**

1. West (U.S.) -- History 2. Native Americans -- West (U.S.)
ISBN 0-8032-1530-4

LC 2003-44757

"Calloway concentrates on the Indian experience from the Appalachians to the Pacific, in a time frame from prehistory to the 18th century. The scope is staggering, but Calloway masters it, demonstrating a remarkable command of a broad spectrum of historical, ethnographic and archeological sources including printed material and oral traditions." Publ Wkly

Includes bibliographical references

Carter, Robert A.

Buffalo Bill Cody; the man behind the legend. Wiley 2000 496p il hardcover o.p. pa $18.95 **978**

1. Entertainers 2. Scouts 3. Hunters 4. Circus executives 5. Circus performers 6. Frontier and pioneer life -- West (U.S.)
ISBN 0-471-31996-1; 0-471-07780-1 pa

LC 00-20368

The author "explores Buffalo Bill's life, moving from his childhood to his marriage to his years as a scout, expert marksman, peerless Buffalo hunter, and, finally, entrepreneur-entertainer to the world." Libr J

This is "a stolid sifting of facts from fiction." Booklist
Includes bibliographical references

Dary, David

★ The **Oregon** Trail; an American saga. Knopf 2004 414p il map $35 **978**

1. Oregon Trail 2. Frontier and pioneer life -- West (U.S.)
ISBN 0-375-41399-5

LC 2004-46512

The author "looks at the men and women who trekked the trouble-strewn paths to the nation's northwest coast. . . . Dary opens with 18th-century maritime explorers and carries us into the late 19th century, when the trail west from Independence, Mo., had ceded its importance to the railroads. . . . His closing chapter on the Oregon Trail's rebirth as a tourist draw in the 20th century is a real contribution to modern western lore. It's hard to imagine a more informative introduction to the westering itch along the Oregon Trail and to those who responded to it." Publ Wkly

Includes bibliographical references

Egan, Timothy

The **worst** hard time; the untold story of those who survived the great American dust bowl. Timothy Egan. Houghton Mifflin Co. 2006 340p ill., map $28; $28 **978**

1. Dust storms 2. Great Depression, 1929-1939 3. United States -- History -- 20th century 4. Great Plains -- History 5. Great Plains -- Social conditions -- 20th century
ISBN 061834697X; 9780618346974

LC 2005-08057

National Book Awards: Nonfiction (2006), Oklahoma Book Awards: Nonfiction Category (2006), Western Heritage Award: Outstanding Nonfiction (2007)

This book presents an "account of how America's . . . plains turned to dust, and how the ferocious plains winds stirred up an endless series of 'black blizzards' . . . in what became known as the Dust Bowl. But the plague was manmade, as Egan shows: the plains weren't suited to farming, and plowing up the grass to plant wheat, along with a confluence of economic disaster—the Depression—and natural disaster—eight years of drought—resulted in an ecological and human catastrophe. . . . [The author] grounds his tale in portraits of the people who settled the plains: hardy Americans and immigrants desperate for a piece of land to call their own and lured by the lies of promoters who said the ground was arable." (Publishers Weekly)

"With characters who seem to have sprung from a novel by Sinclair Lewis or Steinbeck, and Egan's powerful writing, this account will long remain in readers' minds." Publ Wkly

Includes bibliographical references (p. 315-327) and index

Encyclopedia of the Great Plains; David J. Wishart, editor. University of Nebraska Press 2004 919p il map $75 **978**
1. Reference books 2. Great Plains -- Encyclopedias
ISBN 0-8032-4787-7

LC 2003-21037
The author "presents 1,316 signed entries, written by some 1000 scholars and divided according to 27 topics that range from the Paleo-Indians to the 2000 census. The contents of each topic are outlined with an introductory essay, followed by specific articles arranged alphabetically within the topic. Historical figures are listed under their common names rather than their formal names." Libr J

"Here is a unique reference book that cuts a broad swath through parts of the U.S. and Canada, the region known as the heartland. The book's topical arrangement perfectly suits the cross-boundary approach." Booklist

Luchetti, Cathy
★ **Children** of the West; family life on the frontier. Norton 2001 253p il $39.95 **978**
1. Children -- West (U.S.) 2. West (U.S.) -- Social life and customs 3. Frontier and pioneer life -- West (U.S.)
ISBN 0-393-04913-2

LC 00-53287
"In the nineteenth and early twentieth centuries, the children who resided in the sparsely populated plains and prairies of the western U.S. were subject to a unique variety of hardships and joys. . . . Utilizing more than 100 vintage photographs and excerpts from letters, diaries, and journals, Luchetti examines aspects of childbearing, child rearing, childhood, and adolescence on the American frontier." Booklist
Includes bibliographical references

McLynn, Frank
Wagons west; the epic story of America's overland trails. Grove Press 2002 509p il maps $32.50; pa $16.50 **978**
1. Overland journeys to the Pacific 2. Frontier and

pioneer life -- West (U.S.)
ISBN 0-8021-1731-7; 0-8021-4063-7 pa

LC 2002-33859
This "account of the westward migration covers the years 1840-49, spanning the time between the eclipse of the mountain men and the beginning of the gold rush. . . . Relying on original diaries and memoirs, McLynn eloquently illustrates how diverse groups of people, including midwestern farmers, Native Americans, Mormons, and missionaries, played their parts in transforming the West while being transformed by it. This work will be a valuable addition to western history collections." Booklist
Includes bibliographical references

Morgan, Ted
A **shovel** of stars; the making of the American West, 1800 to the present. Simon & Schuster 1995 559p il maps hardcover o.p. pa $25 **978**
1. West (U.S.) -- History 2. Frontier and pioneer life -- West (U.S.)
ISBN 0-684-81492-7 pa

LC 94-43838
Companion volume Wilderness at dawn
"This grandly inspired work—a completely satisfying read—embraces the texture and the drama of the West in all its heartbreak and heroism." Booklist
Includes bibliographical references

The **New** encyclopedia of the American West; edited by Howard R. Lamar. Yale Univ. Press 1998 1324p il maps $60 **978**
1. Reference books 2. Frontier and pioneer life -- West (U.S.) -- Encyclopedias
ISBN 0-300-07088-8

LC 98-6231
First published 1977 by Crowell with title: The Reader's encyclopedia of the American West
This reference work covers "the history, geography, culture, literature, art, and natural history of both the real and the imaginary West. . . . {Coverage spans} prehistory to the present, and . . . {includes} events in the history of the trans-Mississippi West . . . {as well as} the frontier or 'western' stage of all 50 American states. Entries range from important events in the expansion of the U.S. . . . to the first European and American discoverers, among them Coronado, LaSalle, and Lewis and Clark." Publisher's note
Includes bibliographical references

Raban, Jonathan, 1942-
Bad land; an American romance. Pantheon Bks. 1996 324p hardcover o.p. **978**
1. West (U.S.) -- History 2. West (U.S.) -- Description 3. Frontier and pioneer life -- West (U.S.)
ISBN 0-679-75906-9 pa

LC 96-13432
This "book about Montana examines the present remains and historical origins of the last great wave of American western settlement, the migration of homesteaders to eastern Montana in the first decade of this century." (London Rev Books)

Raban "turns Montana into a profound symbol for America's sense of displacement; for its tragic romance with rootlessness, its search for identity under that big blue sky." New Statesman (1913)

Schlissel, Lillian

Far from home; families of the westward journey. [by] Lillian Schlissel, Byrd Gibbens, Elizabeth Hampsten; foreword by Robert Coles. University of Nebraska Press 2002 264p il pa $14.95 **978**

1. West (U.S.) -- Social life and customs 2. Frontier and pioneer life -- West (U.S.)

ISBN 0-8032-9295-3

First published 1989 by Schocken Bks.

"The authors relate the story of three pioneering families—largely through the words of mothers and daughters preserved in old correspondence and later autobiographical writings." Christ Sci Monit

"An immensely readable book that peers closely into the lives of ordinary American frontier families." Booklist

Includes bibliographical references

Schmidt, Thomas

The **Lewis** & Clark Trail; foreword by Stephen E. Ambrose. Bicentennial ed completely rev; National Geographic Soc. 2002 192p il maps pa $16 **978**

1. Lewis and Clark Expedition (1804-1806) 2. West (U.S.) -- Description and travel

ISBN 0-7922-6471-1

LC 2001-7003

First published 1998

Color photographs and maps provide a guide to the Lewis and Clark National Historic Trail

Sides, Hampton

Blood and thunder; an epic of the American West. Doubleday 2006 460p il $26.95 **978**

1. Navajo Indians 2. Scouts 3. Pioneers 4. West (U.S.) -- History 5. United States -- Territorial expansion 6. Frontier and pioneer life -- West (U.S.)

ISBN 978-0-385-50777-6; 0-385-50777-1

LC 2006-16579

This book "will surely capture readers, and it ought to. It's a riveting account of a vast swath of history with which few Americans are familiar." New Yorker

Includes bibliographical references

Slatta, Richard W.

The **cowboy** encyclopedia. Norton 1996 474p il pa $17 **978**

1. Reference books 2. Cowhands -- Encyclopedias

ISBN 0-393-31473-1

LC 94-19824

First published 1994 by ABC-CLIO

"Focusing on the cowboy experience in North and South America, The Cowboy Encyclopedia provides history, definitions, and commentary in an A-to-Z arrangement with major topics such as saddles and cowboy films receiving longer topical entries. Excellent cross-references and an extensive index provide easy access to all aspects of a topic. Appendixes cover cowboy films and videotape sources, museums, periodicals, and western cultural happenings." Am Libr

Slaughter, Thomas P.

Exploring Lewis and Clark; reflections on men and wilderness. Knopf 2003 231p il maps $24; pa $14 **978**

1. Slaves 2. Explorers 3. Lewis and Clark Expedition (1804-1806) 4. Interpreters 5. Guides (Persons) 6. Territorial governors 7. West (U.S.) -- Exploration

ISBN 0-375-40078-8; 0-375-70071-4 pa

LC 2002-69376

"It may be easy to dismiss as a nitpicking revisionist potshot at our beloved heroes, but as the expedition's bicentennial approaches, this book's perspective will help keep our understanding well nuanced and grounded in fact." Booklist

Includes bibliographical references

Stark, Peter

Astoria; John Jacob Astor and Thomas Jefferson's lost Pacific empire : a story of wealth, ambition, and survival. by Peter Stark. HarperCollins Publishers 2014 366 p. ill. (some col.), maps, port $27.99 **978**

1. Scientific expeditions 2. United States -- Exploring expeditions

ISBN 0062218298; 9780062218292

The launch -- The journey -- Pacific Empire and war -- Fate of the Astorians

This book, by Peter Stark, relates how "in 1810, entrepreneur John Jacob Astor proposed to Thomas Jefferson that Astor start a trading colony in what is now Oregon. . . . [Peter] Stark . . . chronicles Astor's mad dash to establish a fur-trading company, Astoria, which would capture the territory's wealth and allow Jefferson to inaugurate his vision of a democracy from sea to shining sea." (Publishers Weekly)

"A fast-paced, riveting account of exploration and settlement, suffering and survival, treachery and death." Kirkus

Includes bibliographical references and index

Ward, Geoffrey C.

The **West**; an illustrated history. narrative by Geoffrey C. Ward; based on a documentary film script by Geoffrey C. Ward and Dayton Duncan; with a preface by Stephen Ives and Ken Burns; and contributions by Dayton Duncan {et al.} Little, Brown 1996 445p il hardcover o.p. pa $24.95 **978**

1. West (U.S.) -- History

ISBN 0-316-73589-2 pa

LC 96-4323

"The book's eight chapters, each written by a different historian, are arranged according to the corresponding PBS series. Beginning with Western America in the 1500s, the work presents all aspects of Western culture from the reality to the myth, moving chronologically from the Spanish exploration of the West, Native Americans, Hispanic Westerners, women in the West, and the Gold Rush, and ending with Buffalo Bill's Wild West Show. If one is looking for an in-depth, comprehensive history of the westward movement, this is not it, but as an introduction, this work is an enjoyable and interesting place to start." Libr J

978.02   Western United States -- 1800-1899

Hyde, Anne F.

Empires, nations, and families; a history of the North American West, 1800-1860. Anne F. Hyde. University of Nebraska Press 2011 xv, 628 p.p   **978.02**
1. Frontier and pioneer life -- West (U.S.) 2. West (U.S.) -- Social conditions -- 19th century 3. Families -- West (U.S.) -- History -- 19th century 4. West (U.S.) -- Commerce -- History -- 19th century 5. Fur trade -- Social aspects -- West (U.S.) -- History -- 19th century 6. Indians of North America -- West (U.S.) -- Social conditions -- History -- 19th century
ISBN 0803224052; 9780803224056

LC 2011000174

Winner of the 2012 Bancroft Prize.
Nominated for the 2012 Pulitzer Prize.
Includes bibliographical references and index.

978.1   Kansas

Frank, Thomas

What's the matter with Kansas? how conservatives won the heart of America. Metropolitan Books 2004 306p map $24; pa $14   **978.1**
1. Conservatism 2. Kansas
ISBN 0-8050-7339-6; 0-8050-7774-X pa

LC 2004-44824

The author "turns his eye on what he calls the 'thirty-year backlash'—the populist revolt against a supposedly liberal establishment. . . . [Frank asks] 'what's the matter with Kansas?'—how a place famous for its radicalism became one of the most conservative states in the union." Publisher's note
This is "a brilliant book, one of the best so far this decade on American politics." Nation
Includes bibliographical references

Stratton, Joanna L.

Pioneer women; voices from the Kansas frontier. introduction by Arthur M. Schlesinger, Jr. Simon & Schuster 1981 319p il hardcover o.p. $15   **978.1**
1. Women -- Kansas 2. Kansas -- History 3. Frontier and pioneer life -- Kansas
ISBN 0-671-44748-3 pa

LC 80-15960

"A unique book based on the memoirs of nearly 800 pioneer women who lived in Kansas between 1854 and 1890. . . . The book presents personal and detailed accounts of life inside homes, the schools, and the social organizations of early Kansas." Choice
Includes bibliographical references

978.7   Wyoming

Black, George

Empire of shadows; the epic story of Yellowstone. George Black. St. Martin's Press 2012 548 p   **978.7**
1. West (U.S.) -- Exploration 2. Yellowstone National Park -- History 3. United States -- History -- 19th century 4. Native Americans -- West (U.S.) -- History 5. Yellowstone National Park -- Discovery and exploration
ISBN 9780312383190; 9781429989749

LC 2011041351

This book is an "account of the discovery and imaginative creation of Yellowstone National Park is told through the lives of the park's colorful and often tragically egotistic explorers and promoters. . . . Waging an irreverent battle against now traditional fakelore, [George] Black particularly emphasizes Native American presence in the region of geysers, hot springs, and the headwaters of the Yellowstone River and the role of Lt. Gustavus Doane's military exploration, which opened the wonderland to international attention." (Libr J) "Divided into five sections and beginning with the familiar expedition of Lewis and Clark, the book spans nearly the entire 19th century. . . . As the book continues, the government enters with paleontologists, entomologists, botanists, and mineralogists, among others." (Kirkus)
Includes bibliographical references

Meyer, Judith L.

The **spirit** of Yellowstone; the cultural evolution of a national park. photographs by Vance Howard. Roberts Rinehart 2003 145p il pa $19.95   **978.7**
1. Human influence on nature 2. Yellowstone National Park
ISBN 1-570-98395-X

LC 2002-156320

First published 1996 by Rowman & Littlefield
The author "pays tribute to the park and all its glories, covering the park's history, its prime landmarks, and its prominence in art. The photographs are truly striking and not the typical landscape fare. Howard plays with light and texture to capture images that will amaze even those already familiar with the park's unprecedented beauty." Libr J
Includes bibliographical references

978.9   New Mexico

Childs, Craig Leland

House of rain; tracking a vanished civilization across the American Southwest. [by] Craig Childs. Little, Brown and Co. 2006 496p il map $24.99   **978.9**
1. Pueblo Indians 2. Southwestern States -- Antiquities 3. Chaco Culture National Historical Park (N.M.)
ISBN 978-0-316-60817-6; 0-316-60817-3

LC 2006-19112

"Beginning at the monumental cultural center of Chaco Canyon, where the Anasazi flourished, Childs's quest to understand their apparent disappearance leads him to the numerous great houses of New Mexico, such as Pueblo Bonito, to the Four Corners area of northeastern Arizona, southern

Colorado and Utah, and beyond to northern Mexico. In these places, he identifies features that had not appeared prior to the apparent abandonment of Chaco (thus implying that the Anasazi migrated to these areas). Childs vividly weaves his personal narrative, imbued with a deep respect for the geography and cultural landscape, with scientific research and numerous interactions with foremost scholars." Libr J

979   Great Basin and Pacific Slope region of United States

Durham, Michael S.

Desert between the mountains; Mormons, miners, padres, mountain men, and the opening of the Great Basin, 1772-1869. University of Oklahoma Press 1999 336p il map pa $19.95   **979**
1. Mormons 2. Great Basin 3. Frontier and pioneer life -- West (U.S.)
ISBN 0-8061-3186-1; 978-0-8061-3186-3
LC 99-23572
First published 1997 by Holt & Co.
This is a history of the settlement of the Great Basin area in what is now Utah and Nevada.
"This is well-written history at its most easygoing." Publ Wkly
Includes bibliographical references

Groom, Winston

Kearny's march; the epic journey that created the American southwest, 1846-1847. Alfred A. Knopf 2011 310p il map $27.95; ebook $13.99   **979**
1. Generals 2. West (U.S.) -- History
ISBN 978-0-307-27096-2; 978-0-307-70141-1 ebook
LC 2011013889
"Groom brings to life the events of 1846–47 that transformed northern Mexico into the American Southwest during the Mexican War. He highlights General Stephen Kearny's Army of the West and the taking of New Mexico and California, Captain John Charles Fremont's expedition to California and his administrative battle with Kearny, the Mormon Battalion attached to Kearny's army, Colonel Alexander Doniphan's capture of Chihuahua, and the civilian emigration horror of the Reed-Donner overland wagon train disaster. Groom's narrative of national political scheming and the constant threat of British involvement in the Mexican War creates an intriguing international drama." Libr J
Includes bibliographical references

979.004   American native peoples--Great Basin and Pacific Slope

Utley, Robert Marshall, 1929-

★ **Geronimo**; Robert M. Utley. Yale University Press 2012 348 p. (clothbound : alk. paper) $30   **979.004**
1. Apache Indians -- History 2. Apache Indians -- Wars, 1883-1886 3. Apache Indians -- Kings and rulers

-- Biography
ISBN 9780300126389; 0300126387
LC 2012019521
This book by Robert M. Utley is a biography of "the Apache fighter Geronimo. . . . Utley unfolds the story through the alternating perspectives of whites and Apaches. . . . What it was like to be an Apache fighter-in-training, why Indians as well as whites feared Geronimo, how Geronimo maintained his freedom, and why he finally surrendered--the answers to these questions and many more fill the pages of this . . . volume." (Publisher's note)
Includes bibliographical references and index

979.1   Arizona

Dolnick, Edward

Down the great unknown; John Wesley Powell's 1869 journey of discovery and tragedy through the Grand Canyon. HarperCollins Pubs. 2001 367p il maps $27.50; pa $13.95   **979.1**
1. Explorers 2. Geologists 3. Large print books 4. Grand Canyon (Ariz.) 5. Colorado River (Colo.-Mexico) 6. Explorers -- United States -- Biography 7. Grand Canyon (Ariz.) -- Description and travel 8. Grand Canyon (Ariz.) -- Discovery and exploration 9. Colorado River (Colo.-Mexico) -- Discovery and exploration
ISBN 006019619X; 0060955864
LC 2001-24819
This is an account of Major John Wesley Powell's survey of the Grand Canyon. "Powell (one-armed since Shiloh) and nine men, six of them Civil War veterans, set out on May 24, 1869, at Green River Station on the Union Pacific Railroad in what was then Wyoming Territory. . . . One day before they reached the end of the canyon, three deserted, thinking that a rapids they could see ahead was certain death. These three climbed the walls of the canyon and were never seen again. The survivors came out into the flat country at the mouth of the Virgin River, ninety-nine days after they had set out." (Harpers)
"Dolnick, a science journalist who has rafted down the Grand, turns in a most estimable rendition of that storied expedition. It skillfully integrates the notes and journals of expedition members with technical insight about the perils of roiling whitewater." Booklist
Includes bibliographical references

Nasdijj

The blood runs like a river through my dreams; a memoir. Houghton Mifflin 2000 216p $23; pa $13   **979.1**
1. Authors 2. Memoirists 3. Navajo Indians -- Social conditions
ISBN 0-618-04892-8; 0-618-15448-5 pa
LC 00-38916
"Born on the Navajo reservation in 1950 to migrant workers (a Navajo storytelling mother and a white cowboy father) . . . Nasdijj writes about the life and death of his son, Tommy Nothing Fancy, their fishing trips, his travails as a committed but unpublished writer, life on the reservation, homelessness, ethnic cleansing in America, love, survival,

hope. Illuminating both the comic and the tragic, his writing is a striking blend of 'tell it like it is' truths that hit right between the eyes and sensuous, expressive, poetic passages that urgently bid the reader to reread, linger, share, and appreciate. The stories and their implications are heartbreaking; but more importantly, they are heart expanding." Booklist

Pasternak, Judy

Yellow dirt; an American story of a poisoned land and a people betrayed. Free Press 2010 317p il map $26; ebook $12.99 **979.1**
1. Navajo Indians 2. Uranium mines and mining
ISBN 1416594825; 1439100462; 9781416594826; 9781439100462

LC 2010-5546

"In the 1940s, when the U.S. government was embarking on developing atomic weapons, it discovered huge uranium deposits in Navajo territory covering parts of Utah, New Mexico, and Arizona. . . . The Navajo themselves saw little of the huge profits from uranium but as workers and land dwellers would suffer radiation exposure four times that of the Japanese targeted by the A-bomb. . . . Pasternak follows four generations of Navajo families, from the patriarch who warned against violating the land to those tempted by the prospects of jobs and money. . . . A stunning look at a shameful chapter in American history with long-lasting implications for all Americans concerned with environmental justice." Booklist

Includes bibliographical references

979.2 Utah

Walker, Ronald W.

★ Massacre at Mountain Meadows; an American tragedy. by Ronald W. Walker, Richard E. Turley, Jr., [and] Glen M. Leonard. Oxford University Press 2008 430p il map $29.95 **979.2**
1. Mountain Meadows Massacre, 1857
ISBN 978-0-19-516034-5

LC 2008-14451

The authors tell the story of "the titular 1857 tragedy in which 157 emigrants traveling to California were killed by local Mormons. With its understated prose, an essential purchase." Libr J

Includes bibliographical references

979.3 Nevada

D'Agata, John

About a mountain. W. W. Norton 2010 236p $23.95 **979.3**
1. Yucca Mountain Repository (Nev.) 2. Las Vegas metropolitan area (Nev.) -- Social life and customs
ISBN 978-0-393-06818-4; 0-393-06818-8

LC 2009-39295

D'Agata "uses the federal government's highly controversial (and recently rejected) proposal to entomb the U.S.'s nuclear waste located in Yucca Mountain, near Las Vegas, as his way into a spiraling and subtle examination of the modern city, suicide, linguistics, Edvard Munch's The Scream,

ecological and psychic degradation, and the gulf between information and knowledge. Acting as a counterpoint to Yucca is the story of a teenager named Levi who leapt to his death off Las Vegas' Stratosphere Motel. . . . A sublime reading experience, aesthetically rewarding and marked by moral courage and humility." Publ Wkly

Denton, Sally

The money and the power; the making of Las Vegas and its hold on America, 1947-2000. by Sally Denton and Roger Morris. Knopf 2001 479p hardcover o.p. pa $15 **979.3**
1. Gambling 2. Organized crime 3. Political corruption 4. Las Vegas (Nev.)
ISBN 0-375-70126-5 pa

LC 00-62011

"The idea of Las Vegas as the epitome of crass American pop culture has become at least a surface truism in most circles. But Denton and Morris . . . go much deeper than the surface in this sobering account of the famous Nevada resort town." Booklist

Includes bibliographical references

979.4 California

Didion, Joan

Where I was from. Knopf 2003 226p $23; pa $13.95 **979.4**
1. American national characteristics 2. California -- History 3. California -- Social conditions
ISBN 0-679-43332-5; 0-679-75286-2 pa

LC 2002-43325

This "is a complex and challenging memoir, difficult to enter into but just as difficult to put down. . . . Those who have long admired the clarity and precision of her prose will not be disappointed with this partly autobiographical, partly historical, but fully engrossing account." Libr J

Lee, Helie

In the absence of sun; a Korean American woman's promise to reunite three lost generations of her family. Harmony Bks. 2002 342p il maps hardcover o.p. pa $18.95 **979.4**
1. Korean Americans 2. Korea (North)
ISBN 0-449-91171-3 pa

LC 2002-1680

"Lee's Still Life with Rice (1996) was a novelized account of her grandmother's life and escape from what would become North Korea. As she now recounts her and her father's struggles to get other people out of the North, she continues to wrestle with her own Korean heritage—in particular, the paternalistic and patronizing attitudes toward women." Booklist

Menuez, Doug

Fearless genius; the digital revolution in Silicon Valley, 1985-2000. by Doug Menuez ; foreword by Elliott Erwitt ; introduction by Kurt Andersen. Atria

Books 2014 192 p. illustrations (hardcover : alk. paper) $39.99   **979.4**
1. Microelectronics 2. High technology industry 3. Computer industry -- United States 4. Santa Clara Valley (Santa Clara County, Calif.) 5. Santa Clara Valley (Santa Clara County, Calif.) -- Pictorial works 6. Documentary photography -- California -- Santa Clara Valley (Santa Clara County) 7. High technology -- California -- Santa Clara Valley (Santa Clara County) -- History 8. Microelectronics industry -- California -- Santa Clara Valley (Santa Clara County) -- History
ISBN 1476752699; 9781476752693

LC 2013045228

This book, by Doug Menuez, is a "chronicle of the Silicon Valley technology boom, capturing key moments in the careers of Steve Jobs and more than seventy other leading innovators . . . [including] John Warnock at Adobe, John Sculley at Apple, Bill Gates at Microsoft, John Doerr at Kleiner Perkins, Bill Joy at Sun Microsystems, Gordon Moore and Andy Grove at Intel, Marc Andreessen at Netscape." (Publisher's note)

"Menuez even makes the innovators' solitude--sequestered behind drawn blinds for days or cordoned off from the rest of the pack in lonely cubicles--surprisingly compelling. The accompanying text is both complementary and instructive." Kirkus

Includes bibliographical references and index

Muir, John
The **Yosemite**; the original John Muir text. illustrated with photographs by Galen Rowell; each photograph accompanied by an excerpt from the works of John Muir and an annotation by Galen Rowell; introduction by the photographer. Sierra Club Bks. 1989 218p il hardcover o.p. pa $14.95   **979.4**
1. Yosemite National Park (Calif.)
ISBN 0-87156-782-2 pa

LC 88-34919

New photographs complement Muir's classic 1912 natural history of the national park
Includes bibliographical references

Williams, Mary, 1967-
The **lost** daughter; Mary Williams. Blue Rider Press, A member of Penguin Group (USA) Inc 2013 320 p. $26.95   **979.4**
1. Abandoned children 2. Oakland (Calif.) -- Biography 3. Black Panther Party -- History 4. Adoptees -- California -- Biography 5. Mothers and daughters -- California -- Biography 6. Oakland (Calif.) -- Social conditions -- 20th century 7. African Americans -- California -- Oakland -- Biography 8. African Americans -- California -- Oakland -- Social conditions -- 20th century
ISBN 0399160868; 9780399160868

LC 2013001245

This book is a memoir by Mary Williams. Her "father was a [Black] Panther who served time in prison, her mother eventually succumbed to drinking and withdrew from family life, and her sister died a violent death. Traumatized by poverty and neglect at 16, Williams took the opportunity to flee to Santa Monica to live with Jane Fonda. . . . What fol-

lowed was an extraordinary life of wealth and privilege." She discusses her achievements and her attempts to reconcile with her biological family. (Booklist)

Winchester, Simon
A **crack** in the edge of the world; America and the great California earthquake of 1906. HarperCollins 2005 462p il maps $27.95   **979.4**
1. Earthquakes -- California
ISBN 0-06-057199-3

LC 2005-46009

The author "writes about the earthquake and fire that destroyed San Francisco almost 100 years ago." N Y Times Book Rev

"In this brawny page-turner, . . . [the author] has crafted a magnificent testament to the power of planet Earth and the efforts of humankind to understand her." Publ Wkly

Includes bibliographical references

979.7   Washington

Kluger, Richard
The **bitter** waters of Medicine Creek; a tragic clash between white and native America. Alfred A. Knopf 2011 330p il map $28.95   **979.7**
1. Generals 2. Territorial governors 3. Territorial legislators 4. Puget Sound region (Wash.) 5. Nisqualli Indians -- History 6. Puget Sound (Wash.) -- History 7. Native Americans -- Washington (State) 8. Nisqualli Indians -- Government relations
ISBN 978-0-307-26889-1; 0-307-26889-6

LC 2010-34249

"When Isaac Stevens, territorial governor of Washington, implemented plans to move the Nisquallies from their ancestral lands to reservations in 1853, Chief Leschi turned from 'good Indian' to incendiary. Implacably opposed to removal to a place 'where the sting of an insect killed like the stroke of a spear, and the streams were foul and muddy,' he organized armed resistance to the whites in Washington. Gov. Stevens' resolve to punish him became an obsession. . . . [Kluger] recounts the confrontation between the two men. Meticulously researched, elegantly written and sophisticated, the book uses this all but forgotten episode in American history to give a human face to the injustices visited on Indians in treaty-making, on the battlefield and, surprisingly, in the courtroom." Minneapolis Star Tribune

Krist, Gary
The **white** cascade; the Great Northern Railway disaster and America's deadliest avalanche. Henry Holt and Company 2007 315p il map $26   **979.7**
1. Avalanches 2. Railroad accidents
ISBN 978-0-8050-7705-6; 0-8050-7705-7

LC 2006-49047

"This is a tale in which snow falls, a mountain looms, and most of the protagonists simply sit. The outcome is predetermined. Mr. Krist does wonders with this unpromising material, however. Adopting a restrained, documentary tone, he slowly builds a picture of massing natural forces and helpless humanity, brought closer and closer to catastrophe with each tick of the clock. The pacing is expertly judged, and the potentially confusing narrative threads, involving multiple actors in scattered locations, are tied together neatly." N Y Times (Late N Y Ed)

Includes bibliographical references

979.8 Alaska

Borneman, Walter R.

★ **Alaska** : saga of a bold land. HarperCollins Pubs. 2003 608p il maps $34.95; pa $16.95 **979.8**

1. Alaska -- History

ISBN 0-06-050306-8; 0-06-050307-6 pa

LC 2002-27271

"Separated into nine chronologically based chapters, the text explores a recurring theme in Alaska's development: conflict among disparate groups over how the land would be used for personal enrichment. . . . Engaging chapters detail the important events and those who helped shape Alaska's history. . . . This expansive, comprehensive history is recommended for all libraries." Libr J

Includes bibliographical references

Jenkins, Peter

Looking for Alaska. St. Martin's Press 2002 434p il $25.95; pa $14.95 **979.8**

1. Alaska -- Description and travel 2. Alaska -- Social life and customs

ISBN 0-312-26178-0; 0-312-30289-4 pa

LC 2001-48871

This book "sparkles with adventure, quirky characters, unbelievable hardships, and indescribable beauty." Libr J

McPhee, John A.

Coming into the country; {by} John McPhee. Farrar, Straus & Giroux 1977 438p maps hardcover o.p. pa $15 **979.8**

1. Alaska -- Description and travel

ISBN 0-374-52287-1 pa

LC 77-12249

This book "is actually three lengthy bulletins about Alaska. . . . The first describes a canoe trip that McPhee and four companions took. . . . Second, McPhee tells of a helicopter ride with a committee looking for a site on which to build a new state capital. The last and longest section covers some wintry months spent in Eagle, a tiny settlement on the Yukon River." Time

Raban, Jonathan, 1942-

Passage to Juneau; a sea and its meanings. Pantheon Bks. 1999 435p $26.50; pa $15 **979.8**

1. Alaska -- Description and travel 2. Romanticism -- History -- 18th century 3. Inside Passage -- Description and travel 4. Northwest, Pacific -- Description and travel 5. Northwest Coast of North America -- Description 6. Indians of North America -- Northwest, Pacific -- Art 7. Indians of North America -- Northwest, Pacific -- Folklore 8. Northwest Coast of North America -- Description and travel

ISBN 0-679-44262-6; 0-679-77614-1 pa

LC 99-28777

"Sailing from Seattle to Alaska, {Raban} aims to replicate the 1792 explorations of English Capt. George Vancouver. . . . Then, suddenly, in the middle of his trip, Raban's father dies. . . . In the last half of the book, Raban finishes out his itinerary while reckoning with his father's memory." (Newsweek)

"Long fascinated by the Inside Passage (the protected waterway that runs from Washington State up to Alaska), Raban casts off in his 35'ketch from his home port in Seattle to follow in the wake of generations of salmon fishermen. He draws a rather dark portrait of the region as he fills out its history, through the cranky journals of Captain Vancouver and others, and meditates on the beautiful but threatening and lonesome landscape, with its struggling communities, submerged mountains, tricky waters, and names like Deception Pass and Desolation Sound." Libr J

980 History of South America

The **Cambridge** history of Latin America; edited by Leslie Bethell. Cambridge Univ. Press 1984 10v in 11 v1 $205; v2 $236; v3 $225; v4 $205; v5 $236; v6 pt. 1 $162; v6 pt. 2 $162; v7 $205; v8 $205; v10 $162; v11 $178 **980**

1. Latin America -- History

ISBN 0-521-23223-6 v1; 0-521-24516-8 v2; 0-521-23224-4 v3; 0-521-23225-2 v4; 0-521-24517-6 v5; 0-521-23226-0 v6 pt. 1; 0-521-46556-7 v6 pt. 2; 0-521-24518-4 v7; 0-521-26652-1 v8; 0-521-49594-6 v10; 0-521-39525-9 v11

LC 83-19036

"History of the areas south of the United States from just prior to the European invasions to the present. . . . Covers general themes in Latin American history with chronological accounts of the individual countries. Bibliographical essays are appended to each chapter." NY Public Libr Book of How & Where to Look It Up

Casey, Michael

Che's afterlife; the legacy of an image. Vintage Books 2009 388p il pa $15.95 **980**

1. Physicians 2. Photographers 3. Revolutionaries

ISBN 978-0-307-27930-9; 0-307-27930-8

LC 2008-32186

Casey "has written a book that is not only a cultural history of an image, but also a sociopolitical study of the mechanisms of fame. It is a book about how ideas travel and mutate in this age of globalization, how concepts of political ideology have increasingly come to be trumped by notions of commerce and cool and chic, and how the historical Che Guevara gave way, postmortem, to a host of other Ches." N Y Times (Late N Y Ed)

Includes bibliographical references.

Chasteen, John Charles

Born in blood and fire; a concise history of Latin America. 2nd ed; W.W. Norton 2006 372p il map pa $43.25 **980**

1. Latin America -- History

ISBN 978-0-393-92769-6; 0-393-92769-5

LC 2005-48248

First published 2000

"Chasteen focuses on major political, social and economic topics and trends that helped shape Latin America, including liberalism, the caste system, the mixing of races, nationalism and the Western notion of 'Progress'; he also examines the role that Europe and the United States played in the development of these phenomena. Also refreshing is Chasteen's examination of the periods he covers from the perspective of women." Publ Wkly [review of 2000 edition]

Includes bibliographical references

★ **Encyclopedia** of Latin American history and culture; Jay Kinsbruner, editor in chief; Erick D. Langer, senior editor. 2nd ed.; Gale 2008 6v il map set $695 **980**

1. Reference books 2. Latin America -- Encyclopedias
ISBN 978-0-684-31270-5

LC 2008-3461

First published 1996

"This reference set covers the Western Hemisphere from Mexico to the tip of South America. . . . [This is] an outstanding encyclopedia that will serve a wide range of users from high school students to Latin American scholars." Libr J

Includes bibliographical references

Thomas, Hugh

Rivers of gold; the rise of the Spanish Empire, from Columbus to Magellan. Random House 2003 xxi, 696p il map $35 **980**

1. Spain -- Colonies 2. America -- Exploration
ISBN 0-375-50204-1

LC 2003-69316

"Engagingly presented, this book clearly shows the author's passion for his subject." Booklist

Includes bibliographical references

Williamson, Edwin

The **Penguin** history of Latin America. Penguin Books 1992 631p map pa $18 **980**

1. Latin America -- History
ISBN 0-14-012559-0

LC 2005-412242

"The book is organized topically, rather than by country, and the author wisely selected regional examples of his major themes, rather than attempting a detailed analysis of each country. The work ends with an unusual exploration of literature and culture in relation to identity and modernization, followed by a helpful bibliographic essay." Libr J

Includes bibliographical references

981 Brazil

Meade, Teresa

A **brief** history of Brazil; [by] Teresa A. Meade. 2nd ed; Facts On File 2009 280p il (Brief history) $49.50; pa $19.95 **981**

1. Brazil -- History
ISBN 978-0-8160-7788-5; 0-8160-7788-6; 978-0-8160-7789-2 pa; 0-8160-7789-4 pa; 978-1-4381-

2736-1 ebook

LC 2009-33853

First published 2003

An account of Brazil's political, economic, and cultural landscape.

Includes bibliographical references

Reel, Monte

The **last** of the tribe; the epic quest to save a lone man in the Amazon. Scribner 2010 273p il map $26 **981**

1. Native Americans -- Brazil 2. Guapore River valley (Brazil and Bolivia)
ISBN 978-1-4165-9474-1; 1-4165-9474-4

LC 2009-37974

"In the opening scene of Monte Reel's 'The Last of the Tribe,' Brazilian government workers approach the deep jungle hideout of an Amazonian Indian they suspect to be the last living member of his tribe. The Indian sits in his hut, cornered, an arrow drawn on his bow, and waits. After two hours, the standoff ends. The government workers leave; the Indian disappears into the jungle. Again. 'The Last of the Tribe' is the story of the 20-year pursuit of that solitary Indian by aid workers who want to contact and protect him, and by loggers and miners who want him dead or moved before he gives the government a reason to protect more land from resource extraction. . . . Reel's tale is expertly told: perfectly timed, thoroughly researched and descriptively written." San Francisco Chron

Includes bibliographical references

Skidmore, Thomas E.

Brazil; five centuries of change. Oxford Univ. Press 1999 254p maps hardcover o.p. pa $28.95 **981**

1. Brazil
ISBN 0-19-505810-0 pa

LC 98-23122

Skidmore explores the country's "history, its political and economic development, and social and racial relationships. . . . This is a well-researched look at a fascinating country." Booklist

Includes bibliographical references

Whitaker, Robert

The **mapmaker's** wife; a true tale of love, murder, and survival in the Amazon. Basic Books 2004 352p il maps $25 **981**

1. Travelers 2. Scientific expeditions 3. Amazon River valley
ISBN 0-7382-0808-6; 978-0-7382-0808-4

LC 2003-26902

"The harrowing journey of Isabel Godin across the Andes and down the Amazon to rejoin her husband after a 20-year separation is only a small part of the extended history of the Charles-Marie de la Condamine expedition, which in turn is set within its context of the history of Enlightenment science, 18th-century mapping methods, the debate over the shape of the earth, and the sorry history of the Spanish and Portuguese conquest of South America." Sci Books Films

Includes bibliographical references

982 Argentina

Brown, Jonathan C.

A **brief** history of Argentina; 2nd ed; Facts On File 2010 354p il map (Brief history) $49.50; pa $19.95 **982**

1. Argentina -- History

ISBN 978-0-8160-7796-0; 978-0-8160-8361-9 pa; 978-1-4381-3111-5 ebook

LC 2010004887

First published 2002

This book covers "Argentina's diverse geography and its varied natural resources; the origins of the deep-seated practices of discrimination, which continue today; the effects of neoliberalism on Argentina's large working class and urban poor, culminating in the caserola movement, the piqueteros movement, and the birth of the cartoneros; the impact a changing global economy has had within Argentina's borders; [and] the rich culture of Argentina, which has created five Nobel laureates, vibrant cities that draw millions of tourists annually, and sports teams that have won multiple world championships." Publisher's note

Includes bibliographical references

Parrado, Nando

★ **Miracle** in the Andes; 72 days on the mountain and my long trek home. [by] Nando Parrado with Vince Rause. Crown Publishers 2006 291p il map hardcover o.p. pa $13.95 **982**

1. Survival after airplane accidents, shipwrecks, etc. 2. Andes

ISBN 1-4000-9767-3; 978-1-4000-9767-8; 1-4000-9769-X pa; 978-1-4000-9769-2 pa

LC 2005-21629

"In October 1972, a plane carrying an Uruguayan rugby team crashed in the Andes. Not immediately rescued, the survivors turned to cannibalism to survive and after 72 days were saved. Rugby team member Parrado has written a beautiful story of friendship, tragedy and perseverance." Publ Wkly

985 Peru

Adams, Mark

Turn right at Machu Picchu. Dutton 2011 333p il map $26.95 **985**

1. Explorers 2. Governors 3. Historians 4. Senators 5. Machu Picchu (Peru) 6. Peru -- Antiquities

ISBN 978-0-525-95224-4; 0-525-95224-1

LC 2011-10211

Traces the author's recreation of Hiram Bingham III's discovery of the ancient citadel, Machu Picchu, in the Andes Mountains of Peru, describing his struggles with rudimentary survival tools and his experiences at the sides of local guides.

"While some readers may prefer a more straightforward version of Bingham's exploits . . . , those favoring a quirkier retelling will relish Mr. Adams's wry, revealing romp through the Andes." Wall Street J

Bingham, Hiram

★ **Lost** city of the Incas; the story of Machu Picchu and its builders. with an introduction by Hugh Thomson; photographs by Hugh Thomson. Sterling 2002 274p il hardcover o.p. pa $12.95 **985**

1. Incas 2. Machu Picchu (Peru) 3. Peru -- Antiquities

ISBN 0-2976-0759-6; 1-84212-585-0 pa

LC 2002-483039

A reissue of the title first published 1948 by Duell

"In 1911 Bingham, an American explorer, found the Inca city of Machu Picchu, which had been lost for 300 years. In this volume he tells of its origin, how it came to be lost and how it was finally discovered." Libr J

Includes bibliographical references

Hunefeldt, Christine

A **brief** history of Peru; 2nd ed; Facts On File 2010 xx, 332p il map (Brief history) $49.50 **985**

1. Peru -- History

ISBN 978-0-8160-8144-8; 978-1-4381-0828-5 ebook

LC 2010-20748

First published 2004

This is a history of Peru ranging "from its ancient peoples and the Inca Empire through . . . recent political, social, and economic developments." Publisher's note

Includes bibliographical references

MacQuarrie, Kim

The **last** days of the Incas. Simon & Schuster 2007 522p il map $30; pa $16.95 **985**

1. Incas 2. Peru -- History

ISBN 978-0-7432-6049-7; 0-7432-6049-X; 978-0-7432-6050-3 pa; 0-7432-6050-3 pa

LC 2007-61700

This "is a first-rate reference work of ambitious scope that will most likely stand as the definitive account of these people." Booklist

Includes bibliographical references

Moseley, Michael Edward

★ The **Incas** and their ancestors; the archaeology of Peru. rev ed; Thames & Hudson 2001 288p il maps $27.50 **985**

1. Incas 2. Peru -- Antiquities

ISBN 0-500-28277-3

LC 00-108866

First published 1992

This account of Andean prehistory and archaeology takes us from the first settlement of 10,000 years ago to the Spanish conquest

"Clearly presented, with a generous ration of maps and illustrations, {the volume} is thoughtful and welcome." Times Lit Suppl {review of 1992 edition}

Includes bibliographical references

Thomson, Hugh

The **white** rock; an exploration of the Inca heartland. Overlook Press 2003 316p il map $27.95; pa $16.95   **985**

1. Incas
ISBN 1-585-67355-2; 1-585-67503-2 pa
LC 2002-34606

First published 2001 in the United Kingdom

"So entertaining and appealing is Thomson's story of his exploration of the Inca empire that readers will wish they could take off and follow in his footsteps. . . . Thomson's wit, eye for detail and reverence for humanity set him apart from the average travel-adventure writer—he is as good a companion as a traveler could hope for." Publ Wkly

Includes bibliographical references

990   History of Australasia, Pacific Ocean islands, Atlantic Ocean islands, Arctic islands, Antarctica, extraterrestrial worlds

Michener, James A.

Return to paradise. Random House 1951 437p hardcover o.p. pa $7.99   **990**

1. Islands of the Pacific
ISBN 0-449-20650-5 pa

"Alternate chapters describe each island followed by a short story set against the region described." Ont Libr Rev

Treister, Kenneth

Easter Island's silent sentinels; the sculpture and architecture of Rapa Nui. Kenneth Treister, Patricia Vargas Casanova, and Claudio Cristino ; foreword by Daniel Libeskind ; maps and illustrations by Roberto Izaurieta and Kenneth Treister. University of New Mexico Press 2013 xv, 144 p.p color illustrations (cloth : alk. paper) $45   **990**

1. Sculpture 2. Architecture 3. Easter Island
ISBN 0826352642; 9780826352644
LC 2013013728

Written by Kenneth Treister, Patricia Vargas Casanova, and Claudio Cristino, "this richly illustrated book of the history, culture, and art of Easter Island is the first to examine in detail the island's vernacular architecture, often overshadowed by its giant stone statues. It shows the conjecturally reconstructed prehistoric pole houses . . . and the Easter Island Statue Project's inventory of the colossal moai sculptures." (Publisher's note)

Includes bibliographical references (pages 123-132) and index

994   Australia

The **Australian** people; an encyclopedia of the nation, its people and their origins. edited by James Jupp. Cambridge Univ. Press 2001 xx, 940p il maps $150   **994**

1. Reference books 2. Australia -- Encyclopedias 3.

Australia -- Race relations
ISBN 0-521-80789-1
LC 2001-37896

First published 1988 in Australia

This "documents the dramatic history of Australian settlement and describes the rich ethnic and cultural inheritance of the nation through the contributions of its people." Publisher's note

Includes bibliographical references and index

Clarke, F. G.

The **history** of Australia. Greenwood Press 2002 236p (Greenwood histories of the modern nations) $45   **994**

1. Australia -- History
ISBN 0-313-31498-5
LC 2001-54704

This volume "begins with a timeline of historical events. The first chapter is a very short overview of Australia (geography, climate, culture, and so on). The rest of the text is a chronological study in short, concise chapters beginning 60,000 years ago with Aboriginal Australia and ending with 2001 and beyond. Each chapter is broken down into smaller sections, with headings, covering such essential topics as colonization, war, government, and politics. The work ends with smaller sections for notable people, notes, a bibliographic essay, and an index." Recomm Ref Books for Small & Medium-sized Libr & Media Cent, 2003

Includes bibliographical references (p. {225}-227) and index

Clendinnen, Inga

Dancing with strangers; Europeans and Australians at first contact. Inga Clendinnen. Cambridge University Press 2005 324p il map $60; pa $21.99   **994**

1. Aboriginal Australians 2. Australian national characteristics 3. Australia -- Race relations 4. Great Britain -- Colonies -- Australia
ISBN 0-5218-5137-8; 0-5216-1681-6 pa
LC 2005-11523

First published 2003 in Australia

"In January 1788, the First Fleet arrived in New South Wales, Australia and a thousand British men and women encountered the people who would be their new neighbors. . . . [This book] tells the story of what happened between the first British settlers of Australia and these Aborigines." Publisher's note

Includes bibliographical references

Hughes, Robert

The **fatal** shore. Knopf 1987 688p il maps hardcover o.p. pa $18   **994**

1. Penal colonies 2. Australia -- History
ISBN 0-394-75366-6 pa
LC 86-45272

"This epic account chronicles the history of Australia during the 80 years (1788-1868) of England's convict transportation system, when some 160,000 convicts reached 'the fatal shore.' Interweaving his own lucid narrative with untapped original sources—including the diaries and letters of the prisoners themselves—Hughes shows the evolution of the system and of the fledgling nation that emerged from the brutal penal colony." Libr J

Includes bibliographical references

Keneally, Thomas

A **commonwealth** of thieves; the improbable birth of Australia. Nan A. Talese/Doubleday 2006 385p map hardcover o.p. pa $15.95 **994**
1. Admirals 2. Penal colonies 3. Australia -- History 4. Colonial administrators 5. Frontier and pioneer life -- Australia
ISBN 0-385-51459-X; 978-0-385-51459-0; 1-4000-7956-X pa; 978-1-4000-7956-8 pa

LC 2006-44470

First published 2005 in Australia

This "book offers an engaging treatment of a subject which over the years has provoked a long and sometimes heated debate." Times Lit Suppl

Includes bibliographical references

995 New Guinea and neighboring countries of Melanesia

Hoffman, Carl

★ A **Savage** Harvest; A Tale of Cannibals, Colonialism, and Michael Rockefeller's Tragic Quest for Primitive Art. by Carl Hoffman. HarperCollins 2014 304 p. illustrations $26.99 **995**
1. New Guinea 2. Cannibalism 3. Missing persons
ISBN 0062116150; 9780062116154

This book, by Carl Hoffman, focuses on "the mysterious disappearance of Michael Rockefeller in New Guinea in 1961. . . . Soon after his disappearance, rumors surfaced that he'd been killed and ceremonially eaten by the local Asmat--a native tribe of warriors whose complex culture was built around sacred, reciprocal violence, head hunting, and ritual cannibalism. The Dutch government and the Rockefeller family denied the story, and Michael's death was officially ruled a drowning." (Publisher's note)

"[An] unforgettable story of a soothing and politically expedient cover-up and a brutal and tragic collision of cultures." Booklist

Includes bibliographical references (pages 310-312) and index.

995.3 Papua New Guinea

Flannery, Tim F.

Throwim way leg; tree-kangaroos, possums, and penis gourds--on the track of unknown mammals in wildest New Guinea. [by] Tim Flannery. Atlantic Monthly Press 1998 326p il map hardcover o.p. pa $14 **995.3**
1. Ethnology -- New Guinea 2. New Guinea -- Description
ISBN 0-8021-3665-6 pa

LC 98-38435

Flannery chronicles "his scientific and cross-cultural adventures during 15 expeditions of New Guinea—undertaken in order to research the many species of mammals that exist on this large island, which he refers to as 'one of the world's last frontiers.'" Publ Wkly

This "is more than an account of [the author's] fieldwork. It is an enthralling introduction to the mountain people of New Guinea." N Y Times Book Rev

996 Polynesia and other Pacific Ocean islands

Alexander, Caroline

The **Bounty** : the true story of the mutiny on the Bounty. Viking 2003 491p il hardcover o.p. pa $17 **996**
1. Admirals 2. Explorers 3. Oceania 4. Mutineers 5. Bounty (Ship) 6. Naval officers 7. Government officials 8. Colonial administrators
ISBN 978-0-670-03133-7; 0-670-03133-X; 978-0-14-200469-2 pa; 0-14-200469-3 pa

LC 2003-50158

Alexander reexamines the story of the 1789 mutiny on the Bounty during a voyage to the South Pacific. She explores "the Royal Navy's efforts to bring the mutineers who did not escape to Pitcairn [Island with Fletcher Christian] to justice, a proceeding complicated by the political, legal and social influence exerted to defend Christian's reputation in absentia and that of one of his well-born colleagues in mutiny. This was Peter Heywood." N Y Times Book Rev

"A rollicking sea adventure told with enormous confidence and style." Booklist

Includes bibliographical references

Severin, Timothy

In search of Robinson Crusoe. Basic Bks. 2002 333p il hardcover o.p. pa $16.95 **996**
1. Authors 2. Sailors 3. Novelists 4. Historians 5. Survival after airplane accidents, shipwrecks, etc. 6. Essayists 7. Pamphleteers 8. Writers on politics
ISBN 0-465-07699-8 pa

LC 2002-71661

The author examines "the fictional Crusoe alongside the historic realities of colonization and human ingenuity. . . . Readers learn about the history of marooning among plunderers, blockade navies and other piratical sailors, as well as the ethnography of the so-called 'Moskito Man' (aka Man Friday) and all the ways to provide for oneself on a deserted island. . . . The work is energetic and Severin is an ideal guide to the world behind the word. This will surely appeal to the lovers of maritime history." Publ Wkly

996.9 Hawaii and neighboring north central Pacific Ocean islands

Vowell, Sarah, 1969-

Unfamiliar fishes. Riverhead Books 2011 238p il map $25.95 **996.9**
1. Hawaii -- History 2. United States -- Territorial expansion 3. Hawaii -- Annexation to the United States
ISBN 978-1-59448-787-3

LC 2010-47943

"While Vowell's take on Hawaii's Americanization is abbreviated, it's never bereft of substance—her repartee manages to be filling, her insights astute and comprehensive." N Y Times Book Rev

Includes bibliographical references

998 Arctic islands and Antarctica

Alexander, Caroline

The **Endurance**; Shackleton's legendary Antarctic expedition. Knopf 1998 211p il $29.95   **998**
1. Explorers 2. Endurance (Ship) 3. Antarctica -- Exploration 4. Imperial Trans-Antarctic Expedition (1914-1917)
ISBN 0-375-40403-1

In 1914, Sir Ernest Shackleton "sailed to Antarctica with 27 men in hopes of being the first human to transverse the continent. But his ship, the Endurance, was trapped, then crushed, by ice in the Weddell Sea, propelling the party into a nightmare of cold and near starvation. Alexander, relying extensively on journals by crew members, some never published, as well as on myriad other sources, delivers a spellbinding story of human courage. . . . What makes this book especially exciting, however, are the 170 previously unpublished photos by the expedition's photographer, Frank Hurley." Publ Wkly

Avery, Tom

To the end of the earth; our epic journey to the North Pole and the legend of Peary and Henson. St. Martin's Press 2009 321p il map $26.95   **998**
1. Admirals 2. Explorers 3. North Pole 4. Arctic regions -- Exploration
ISBN 978-0-312-55186-5; 0-312-55186-X

LC 2008-44069

"To vindicate a controversial claim in Arctic annals (whether or not Robert Peary attained the . . . [North Pole] in 1909), Avery and his companions brave the unforgiving ice cap, confront numerous deadly situations, and return to Britain in triumph—only to weather heavy criticism about the exact significance of their feat. . . . A highly enjoyable chronicle of contemporary exploration." Booklist

Ehrlich, Gretel

This cold heaven; seven seasons in Greenland. Pantheon Bks. 2001 377p il maps hardcover o.p. pa $14   **998**
1. Inuit 2. Greenland
ISBN 0-679-44200-6; 0-679-75852-6 pa

LC 00-69277

"Ehrlich began traveling to Greenland during her recovery from a nearly fatal lightning strike, and her keen, often poetic responses to the beauty of the frigid landscape and the warmth of Inuit families, combined with a profound immersion in Greenland history, infuse her captivating account with both drama and reflection." Booklist

Includes bibliographical references

Emmerson, Charles

The **future** history of the Arctic. PublicAffairs 2010 405p il map   **998**
1. Geopolitics 2. Arctic regions
ISBN 978-1-58648-636-5

LC 2009-35094

"It's easy to romanticise the Arctic, and over the years plenty of authors have. Oddly though, given the region's increasing geopolitical significance, it's rare to find books that treat it as something other than a chilly adventure playground or an excuse for reams of purple prose. Thank goodness, then, for Charles Emmerson. In this book he looks at how the frozen north has played a key role in world affairs in the past and how it could prove more important in the years to come." Scotsman

Includes bibliographical references

Encyclopedia of the Arctic; Mark Nuttall, editor. Routledge 2005 3v il map set $525   **998**
1. Reference books 2. Arctic regions -- Encyclopedias
ISBN 1-57958-436-5

LC 2004-16694

For a fuller review see: Booklist, Jan. 1 & 15, 2005

Nuttall "has put together a multidisciplinary work that covers indigenous peoples, explorers, scientists, history, environment, climate, plants and animals, geography, current research concerns, and more. The 1200 alphabetically arranged entries, all written by experts from 20 countries (a number of them native to the Arctic), range in length from 500 to 5000 words." Libr J

The **ends** of the earth; an anthology of the finest writing on the Arctic and the Antarctic. Bloomsbury 2007 2v in 1 map $29.95   **998**
1. Antarctica 2. Polar regions 3. Arctic regions
ISBN 1-59691-443-2; 978-1-59691-443-8

The editors "present an anthology of writings about the Arctic and Antarctic, which is actually two books in one. Halfway through, readers can turn the book upside down for writings about the opposite end of the earth. . . . Included are primary-source accounts by early explorers such as Ernest Shackleton, John Franklin, and Kund Rasmussen, nature writings by Barry Lopez and Gretel Ehrlich, excerpts from novels by Jules Verne, Jack London, and H.P. Lovecraft, and essays by journalists and scientists. Each excerpt is just long enough to whet the reader's appetite. Great reading for the armchair adventurer." Libr J

Griffiths, Tom

Slicing the silence; voyaging to Antarctica. Harvard University Press 2007 399p map $29.95 **998**
1. Antarctica -- Description and travel
ISBN 978-0-674-02633-9; 0-674-02633-0

LC 2007-06549

Simultaneously published in Australia

"Believing that to understand the experiences of explorers and the history of Antarctica one must experience its mighty winds, cold, danger, and silence, the author, in 2002, joined a ship delivering scientists and supplies to Casey Station. This book is part diary of that voyage and part history of that most southerly land. . . . This enjoyable and highly readable book would be an excellent addition to any natural history, polar history, or adventure travel collection." Libr J

Includes bibliographical references

Kavenna, Joanna

The **ice** museum; in search of the lost land of Thule. Viking 2006 294p il map $24.95; pa $15 **998**

1. Arctic regions -- Exploration

ISBN 0-670-03473-8; 0-14-303846-X pa

First published 2005 in the United Kingdom

The author "chronicles her personal journey into the myth and reality of the legendary Arctic land of Thule. . . . [This book] transcends all genre description, and holds its own as a journey into a world that somehow vibrantly exists on paper and nowhere else." Booklist

McGonigal, David

Antarctica; secrets of the southern continent. chief consultant, David McGonigal. Firefly Books 2008 400p il map $59.95 **998**

1. Antarctica

ISBN 978-1-55407-398-6; 1-55407-398-7

This "book covers all aspects of the continent, including ecology, geography, wildlife, and exploration. . . . Sumptuously illustrated with photos, maps, and paintings, this will be the go-to reference on Antarctica for years to come. A truly superb production." Booklist

Riffenburgh, Beau

Shackleton's forgotten expedition; the voyage of the Nimrod. by Beau Riffenburgh. Bloomsbury, Distributed to the trade by Holtzbrinck Publishers 2004 xxiv, 358p il map $25.95; pa $15.95 **998**

1. Explorers 2. Antarctica -- Exploration

ISBN 1-58234-488-4; 1-58234-611-9 pa

LC 2004-11999

The author recounts Shackleton's "voyage to the Antarctic from 1907 to 1909, during which he led a small group of men to within 97 miles of the South Pole. . . . For those who thrilled to the Endurance saga, Riffenburgh offers an equally gripping adventure, which laid the foundations of Shackleton's capacity for brilliant leadership under pressure." Publ Wkly

Includes bibliographical references

Smith, Roff

Life on the ice; no one goes to Antarctica alone. National Geographic 2005 208p pa $16 **998**

1. Antarctica -- Description and travel

ISBN 0-7922-9345-2

LC 2005-298454

First published 2002 in Australia

"Smith is the most exceptional of travel writers: his portraits of people are deeply sympathetic, while his language is at once lyrical and knowledgeable. Not to be missed." Booklist

Streever, Bill

Cold; adventures in the world's frozen places. Little, Brown and Co. 2009 292p $24.99; pa $14.99 **998**

1. Cold 2. Arctic regions -- Description and travel

ISBN 978-0-316-04291-8; 0-316-04291-9; 978-0-316-04292-5 pa; 0-316-04292-7 pa

LC 2008-45350

Strever "delivers a poetic, anecdotal narrative complete with polar expeditions, Ice Age mysteries, igloos, permafrost and hailstorms. . . . This is a wonderful collection of one man's first-rate observations and commentary about the history and importance of cold to the earth and its occupants." Publ Wkly

Includes bibliographical references

Turney, Chris

1912; the year the world discovered Antarctica. Pgw 2012 358 p. $27 **998**

1. Explorers 2. Antarctica -- Exploration

ISBN 1582437890; 9781582437897

This book by Chris Turney presents "an in-depth look at a year in which five different expeditions set out to explore Antarctica. . . . The continent would see no fewer than five different national exploration teams during that year, and geologist Turney . . . examines each expedition in turn, after outlining some of the earliest attempts at exploring Antarctica, including Ernest Shackleton's 1907-1909 expedition." (Kirkus Reviews)

Includes bibliographical references and index.

AUTHOR, TITLE, AND SUBJECT INDEX

This index to the books in the Classified Collection includes author, title, and subject entries; added entries for publishers' series, joint authors, and editors of works entered under title; and name and subject cross-references; all arranged in one alphabet.

The number or symbol in boldface type at the end of each entry refers to the Dewey Decimal Classification section where the main entry for the book will be found. Works classed in 92 will be found under the headings for the biographies' subject.

ACTORS -- DICTIONARIES

ACTORS -- UNITED STATES

McMahon, S. Brewer's dictionary of Irish phrase & fable **427**

Oxford dictionary of phrase and fable **803**

Allyn, Pam

What to read when **028.5**

The **almanac** of American politics 2012. Barone, M. **328**

Almanac of Famous People. **920**

Almanac of World War I. Burg, D. F. **940.3**

ALMANACS

2013 Our Sunday Visitor Catholic almanac **282**

Barone, M. The almanac of American politics 2012 **328**

Bracks, L. African American almanac **973**

The CIA World Factbook 2014 **028**

Proquest Statistical Abstract of the United States 2013 **317**

The Statesman's Yearbook 2014 **330**

Woodward, D. R. World War I almanac **940.3**

The World Almanac and Book of Facts 2015 **030**

Almanacs of American life [series]

Gregory, R. Cold War America, 1946 to 1990 **973.92**

Almanacs of American wars [series]

Edwards, P. M. Korean War almanac **951.9**

Fredriksen, J. C. Civil War almanac **973.7**

Willbanks, J. H. Vietnam War almanac **959.704**

Woodward, D. R. World War I almanac **940.3**

Almereyda, Michael

(ed) Night wraps the sky **92**

Almond, Gabriel Abraham

Strong religion **200.9**

Almond, Steve

Candyfreak: a journey through the chocolate underbelly of America **338.4**

Rock and roll will save your life **781.66**

Almond, Steve

About

Almond, S. Candyfreak: a journey through the chocolate underbelly of America **338.4**

Almond, S. Rock and roll will save your life **781.66**

Almost a family. Darnton, J. **92**

Almost everyone's guide to science. Gribbin, J. R. **500**

Almost president. Farris, S. **920**

Almost there. O'Faolain, N. **070.92**

Alone in the universe. Gribbin, J. **525**

Alone on the ice. Roberts, D. **919.890**

Alone together. Turkle, S. **303.4**

Alone! alone!: lives of some outsider women. Dinnage, R. **920**

Alperovitz, Gar

The decision to use the atomic bomb and the architecture of an American myth **940.54**

Alpha dogs. Harding, J. **324.7**

Alpha dogs. Fenn, D. **658**

ALPHABET

Van Niekerk, D. Embroidered alphabets **746.44**

See also Writing

ALPHABET BOOKS *See* Alphabet

Alphabet juice. Blount, R. **817**

Alphabetter juice, or, The joy of text. Blount, R. **818**

Als, Hilton, 1960-

White Girls **814**

Alson, Peter

Atlas, T. Atlas **92**

ALTAMONT FESTIVAL

Russell, E. A. Let it bleed **781.66**

An **altar** in the world. Taylor, B. B. **92**

Alter, Jonathan

The promise **92**

Alter, Linda Lee

About

The female gaze **704**

Alter, Robert

(tr) Bible.O.T. Genesis The book of Genesis **222**

Bible.O.T. Pentateuch The five books of Moses **222**

Altered art. Taylor, T. **745.5**

ALTERNATE ENERGY RESOURCES *See* Renewable energy resources

ALTERNATIVE EDUCATION

See also Education

ALTERNATIVE FUEL VEHICLES

Sperling, D. Two billion cars **388.3**

ALTERNATIVE GRAINS

Ancient grains for modern meals **641.59**

Robertson, C. Tartine Book No. 3 **641.81**

ALTERNATIVE HISTORIES

See also Fantasy fiction

ALTERNATIVE LIFESTYLES

See also Lifestyles

ALTERNATIVE MEDICINE

Bausell, R. B. Snake oil science **615.5**

Bruce, D. F. Miracle touch **615.5**

Weil, A. Eight weeks to optimum health **613**

See also Medicine

ALTERNATIVE MEDICINE PRACTITIONERS

Lattin, D. The Harvard Psychedelic Club **920**

ALTERNATIVE PRESS

McMillian, J. Smoking typewriters **071**

Ostertag, B. People's movements, people's press **071**

See also Press

ALTITUDE, INFLUENCE OF *See* Environmental influence on humans

Altman, Adelaide

Elderhouse: planning your best home ever **720**

Altman, Ellen

Hernon, P. Assessing service quality **025.5**

Altman, Howard

western tradition 201

Amundsen, Roald, 1872-1928

About

Bown, S. R. The last Viking 92

Connell, E. S. The Aztec treasure house 814

Larson, E. J. An empire of ice 919.8

AMUSEMENT PARKS

Kirby, D. Death at SeaWorld 599.53

See also Parks

AMUSEMENTS

Denmead, K. Geek dad 790

Lithgow, J. A Lithgow palooza! 793

Amusing ourselves to death. Postman, N. 302.23

AMYOTROPHIC LATERAL SCLEROSIS

Albom, M. Tuesdays with Morrie 378.1

An Deming

Yang Lihui Handbook of Chinese mythology 299.5

ANABOLIC STEROIDS *See* Steroids

ANACONDAS

Murphy, J. C. Tales of giant snakes 597.96

The **Analects.** Confucius 181

ANALOGY

Hofstadter, D. Surfaces and essences 169

ANALYSIS (MATHEMATICS) *See* Calculus; Functions; Mathematical analysis

ANALYSIS OF FOOD *See* Food -- Analysis; Food adulteration and inspection

ANALYTIC GEOMETRY

See also Geometry

ANALYTICAL CHEMISTRY

See also Chemistry

Ananthaswamy, Anil

The edge of physics 530

ANARCHISM -- HISTORY

Butterworth, A. The world that never was 335

ANARCHISM -- UNITED STATES -- HISTORY

Avrich, K. Sasha and Emma 335

Miller, S. The President and the assassin 973.8

ANARCHISM AND ANARCHISTS

Avrich, K. Sasha and Emma 335

Butterworth, A. The world that never was 335

Merriman, J. M. The dynamite club 363.32

Miller, S. The President and the assassin 973.8

Strang, D. A. Worse than the devil 345.73

Tuchman, B. W. The proud tower 909.82

See also Freedom; Political crimes and offenses; Political science

ANARCHISM AND ANARCHISTS -- GRAPHIC NOVELS

Rudahl, S. A dangerous woman 335

ANARCHISTS

Merriman, J. M. The dynamite club 363.32

Miller, S. The President and the assassin 973.8

Rauchway, E. Murdering McKinley 973.8

Rudahl, S. A dangerous woman 335

Watson, B. Sacco and Vanzetti 345

ANARCHISTS -- UNITED STATES -- BIOGRAPHY

Avrich, K. Sasha and Emma 335

ANARCHISTS -- WISCONSIN -- MILWAUKEE -- HISTORY -- 20TH CENTURY

Strang, D. A. Worse than the devil 345.73

Anasi, Robert

The gloves 796.83

Anasi, Robert, 1966-

About

Anasi, R. The last bohemia 974.7

Anatomies. Aldersey-Williams, H. 612

ANATOMY

See also Biology; Medicine

Anatomy of a business plan. Pinson, L. 658.4

Anatomy of a miracle. Waldmeir, P. 968.06

Anatomy of an epidemic. Whitaker, R. 616.89

The **anatomy** of fascism. Paxton, R. O. 321.9

The **anatomy** of hope. Groopman, J. E. 616

The **anatomy** of influence. Bloom, H. 801

The **anatomy** of racial inequality. Loury, G. C. 305.896

The **anatomy** of violence. Raine, A. 616.85

ANATOMY, ARTISTIC *See* Artistic anatomy

Ancell, R. Manning

The biographical dictionary of World War II generals and flag officers 920.003

ANCESTOR WORSHIP

See also Religion

The **ancestor's** tale. Dawkins, R. 576.8

ANCESTRY *See* Genealogy; Heredity

Anchee Min

The Cooked Seed 92

ANCHOR & HOPE (RESTAURANT)

Cooking my way back home 641.5

Anchor Bible reference library [series]

Brown, R. E. An introduction to the New Testament 225

Meier, J. P. A marginal Jew 232.9

The **ancient** Americans. Schobinger, J. 970.01

ANCIENT ARCHITECTURE

See also Archeology; Architecture

ANCIENT ART

Frankfort, H. The art and architecture of the ancient Orient 709.3

See also Art

The **ancient** Celts. Cunliffe, B. 936

ANCIENT CIVILIZATION

Cantor, N. F. Antiquity: the civilization of the ancient world 930

Hancock, G. Underworld: the mysterious origins of civilization 551.7

Hunt, P. Ten discoveries that rewrote history 930.1

Kriwaczek, P. Babylon 935

The Oxford history of the biblical world 220.9

Teresi, D. Lost discoveries 509

Goldhagen, D. J. The Devil That Never Dies **305.892**

ANTISEMITISM -- HISTORY -- 21ST CENTURY

Goldhagen, D. J. The Devil That Never Dies **305.892**

ANTISEPTICS

See also Therapeutics

ANTISLAVERY *See* Abolitionists; Slavery; Slaves -- Emancipation

ANTISLAVERY MOVEMENTS -- UNITED STATES

Colaiaco, J. A. Frederick Douglass and the Fourth of July **973.7**

Rediker, M. The Amistad rebellion **326**

ANTISLAVERY MOVEMENTS -- UNITED STATES -- HISTORY

Oakes, J. Freedom national **973.7**

ANTISLAVERY MOVEMENTS -- UNITED STATES -- HISTORY -- 19TH CENTURY

Clinton, C. Harriet Tubman: the road to freedom **973.7**

Douglass, F. Frederick Douglass: selected speeches and writings **326**

Douglass, F. My bondage and my freedom **973.8**

Walters, K. The Underground Railroad **973.7**

Wineapple, B. Ecstatic nation **973.6**

ANTITRUST LAW

See also Commercial law

ANTIVIVISECTION MOVEMENT *See* Animal rights movement

Antoine, Rebeca

(ed) Voices rising **976.3**

Anton Chekhov's life and thought. Chekhov, A. P. **92**

Antonia, Mother

About

Jordan, M. The prison angel **92**

Antonius, Marcus, ca. 83-30 B.C.

About

Goldsworthy, A. K. Antony and Cleopatra **92**

Antony and Cleopatra. Goldsworthy, A. K. **92**

The **ants.** Holldobler, B. **595.79**

ANTS

See also Insects

Holldobler, B. The ants **595.79**

Holldobler, B. Journey to the ants **595.79**

Holldobler, B. The leafcutter ants **595.7**

Keller, L. The lives of ants **595.7**

Moffett, M. W. Adventures among ants **595.7**

ANTS -- BEHAVIOR

Moffett, M. W. Adventures among ants **595.7**

Ants on the melon. Adair, V. H. **811**

Antunes, Antonio Lobo

The fat man and infinity **869**

ANXIETY

Alcabes, P. Dread **614.4**

Clark, T. Nerve **152.4**

Kierkegaard, S. The concept of anxiety **233**

Smith, D. Monkey mind **616.85**

Stossel, S. My age of anxiety **616.85**

Tillich, P. The courage to be **179**

See also Emotions; Neuroses; Stress (Psychology)

ANXIETY -- CHEMOTHERAPY

Stossel, S. My age of anxiety **616.85**

ANXIETY -- RELIGIOUS ASPECTS -- CHRISTIANITY

Kierkegaard, S. The concept of anxiety **233**

ANXIETY DISORDERS

Smith, D. Monkey mind **616.85**

Anything goes. Moore, L. **973.91**

Anything goes. Mordden, E. **782.1**

Anzovin, Steven

(ed) Famous first facts, international edition **031.02**

Kane, J. N. Famous first facts **031.02**

APACHE INDIANS

Brown, D. A. The American West **978**

Debo, A. Geronimo **92**

Roberts, D. Once they moved like the wind **970.004**

Utley, R. M. Geronimo **979.004**

Apache: inside the cockpit of the world's most deadly fighting machine. Macy, E. **623.7**

Apana, Chang, 1871-1933

About

Yunte Huang Charlie Chan **92**

APARTHEID

Houze, D. Twilight people **92**

Mandela, N. Conversations with myself **92**

Smith, D. J. Young Mandela **92**

See also Segregation; South Africa -- Race relations

APARTMENT HOUSES

Gillingham-Ryan, M. Apartment Therapy presents real homes, real people, hundreds of real design solutions **747**

See also Buildings; Domestic architecture; Houses; Housing

Apartment Therapy presents real homes, real people, hundreds of real design solutions. Gillingham-Ryan, M. **747**

APATHY

Norris, K. Acedia & me **92**

APERTURE (PERIODICAL)

Photography past forward: Aperture at 50 **770.9**

APES

Among African apes **599.8**

Bearzi, M. Beautiful minds **599.8**

Morris, D. Planet ape **599.8**

Stanford, C. B. Planet without apes **599.88**

Waal, F. d. Bonobo **599.88**

World atlas of great apes and their conservation   **599.8**

   See also Primates

Apfelbaum, Steven I.

Nature's second chance   **639.9**

APHASIA

   See also Brain -- Diseases; Language disorders; Speech disorders

APHRODITE (GREEK DEITY)

   See also Gods and goddesses

APICULTURE *See* Beekeeping

Apocalypses. Weber, E.   **200**

APOCALYPTIC FICTION

   See also Fiction

APOCALYPTIC FILMS

   See also Motion pictures

Apocalyptic planet. Childs, C.   **550**

The **Apocrypha.** Bible O.T. Apocrypha   **229**

APOLLO (GREEK DEITY)

   See also Gods and goddesses

APOLLO 15 (SPACECRAFT)

French, F. Falling to Earth   **92**

APOLLO PROJECT

Bizony, P. The man who ran the moon   **629**

Chaikin, A. A man on the moon   **629.45**

French, F. Falling to Earth   **92**

French, F. In the shadow of the moon   **629.45**

Nelson, C. Rocket men   **629.45**

Pyle, R. Destination moon   **629.45**

Schefter, J. L. The race   **629.45**

Smith, A. Moondust   **920**

Zimmerman, R. Genesis: the story of Apollo 8   **629.45**

   See also Life support systems (Space environment); Orbital rendezvous (Space flight); Space flight to the moon

Apollo's angels. Homans, J.   **792.8**

Apollo's fire. Sims, M.   **529**

Apollonius

The voyage of Argo: the Argonautica   **881**

APOLOGETICS

Armstrong, K. The case for God   **211**

Concerning the city of God against the pagans **239**

John Paul Crossing the threshold of hope   **282**

Keller, T. J. The reason for God   **239**

   See also Theology

APOLOGIZING

Lazare, A. On apology   **155.9**

APOSTLES

Borg, M. J. The first Paul   **227**

Gubar, S. Judas   **92**

Kung, H. Great Christian thinkers   **230**

Murphy-O'Connor, J. Paul   **225.9**

Ruden, S. Paul among the people   **225.9**

Wilson, A. N. Paul: the mind of the Apostle   **225**

   See also Christian saints; Church history -- 30-600, Early church

Apostol, Tom M.

New Horizons in Geometry   **516**

APOSTOLIC CHURCH *See* Church history -- 30-600, Early church

Appalachia. Wright, C.   **811**

APPALACHIAN REGION

Animal, vegetable, miracle   **641**

Reece, E. Lost mountain   **622**

Ritchie, J. Singing family of the Cumberlands **784.4**

   See also United States

APPALACHIAN REGION -- DESCRIPTION AND TRAVEL

Bryson, B. A walk in the woods   **917**

APPALACHIAN REGION -- SOCIAL LIFE AND CUSTOMS

Foxfire 40th anniversary book   **975.8**

APPALACHIAN REGION, SOUTHERN -- ENVIRONMENTAL CONDITIONS

House, S. Something's rising   **338.2**

APPARATUS, ELECTRONIC *See* Electronic apparatus and appliances

APPARITIONS

   See also Parapsychology; Spirits

APPEARANCE, PERSONAL *See* Personal appearance

Appelfeld, Aron

    About

Langer, L. L. Admitting the Holocaust   **940.53**

APPERCEPTION

   See also Educational psychology; Psychology

APPETITE -- PSYCHOLOGICAL ASPECTS

Christensen, K. Blue plate special   **92**

Appetite for America. Fried, S.   **92**

Appetite for life. Fitch, N. R.   **92**

Appetite for life. Antine, S.   **641.5**

An **appetite** for poetry. Kermode, F.   **801**

Appetite for self-destruction. Knopper, S.   **384**

An **Appetite** for Wonder. Dawkins, R.   **92**

APPETIZERS

Andres, J. Tapas   **641.8**

Fine cooking appetizers   **641.8**

   See also Cooking

Appiah, Anthony

(ed) Africana: the encyclopedia of the African and African American experience   **909**

APPLE COMPUTER, INC

Lashinsky, A. Inside Apple   **338.7**

APPLE COMPUTER, INC. -- HISTORY

Isaacson, W. Steve Jobs   **92**

The **apple** trees at Olema. Hass, R.   **811**

Applebaum, Anne

Iron curtain   **947.0009**

Gulag   **365**

Applebaum, Wilbur

(ed) Encyclopedia of the scientific revolution   **509**

Applebome, Peter

See also Commercial law; Courts

ARBORICULTURE *See* Forests and forestry; Fruit culture; Trees

ARC LIGHT *See* Electric lighting

Arc of justice. Boyle, K.   345

Arcadia. Stoppard, T.   822

ARCHAEOLOGICAL THEFTS
    Atwood, R. Stealing history   364.1
    Felch, J. Chasing Aphrodite   930

ARCHAEOLOGISTS -- EGYPT -- BIOGRAPHY
    Noël Hume, I. Belzoni   932.0072

ARCHAEOLOGISTS -- ITALY -- BIOGRAPHY
    Noël Hume, I. Belzoni   932.0072

ARCHAEOLOGY -- POLITICAL ASPECTS -- UNITED STATES
    Kersel, M. M. U.S. cultural diplomacy and archaeology   930.1

Archaeology of prehistoric native America.   970.01

ARCHAEOLOGY, MEDIEVAL
    MacGregor, N. A history of the world in 100 objects   930.1

ARCHAEOPTERYX
    See also Dinosaurs

ARCHBISHOPS *See* Bishops

Archbold, Rick
    Ballard, R. D. Return to Midway   940.54

ARCHEOLOGICAL SPECIMENS *See* Antiquities

ARCHEOLOGISTS
    Brown, M. T.E. Lawrence   92
    Howell, G. Gertrude Bell   92
    Korda, M. Hero   92
    Ryan, D. P. Beneath the sands of Egypt   92
    Van Tilburg, J. Among stone giants   930.1
    Wallach, J. Desert queen   956
    See also Historians

ARCHEOLOGISTS -- BIOGRAPHY
    Noël Hume, I. Belzoni   932.0072

ARCHEOLOGISTS -- ETHICS
    Childs, C. L. Finders keepers   930.1

ARCHEOLOGY
    Ancient Nubia   932
    Beneath the seven seas   930.1
    Ceram, C. W. Gods, graves, and scholars   930.1
    Romer, J. A history of ancient Egypt   932
    See also History

ARCHEOLOGY -- DICTIONARIES
    The Oxford companion to archaeology   930.1

ARCHEOLOGY -- HISTORY
    Hunt, P. Ten discoveries that rewrote history   930.1

Archer, J. Clark
    Lavin, S. J. Atlas of the great plains   912

Archer, Richard
    As if an enemy's country   973.3

ARCHERY
    See also Martial arts; Shooting

Archibald MacLeish: reflections.   92

Archimedes, ca. 287-212 B.C.
About
    Bell, E. T. Men of mathematics   920
    Hirshfeld, A. Eureka man   92

The **architect** of genocide. Breitman, R.   92

ARCHITECTS
    Albrecht, D. The Work of Charles and Ray Eames   745.4
    Becker, C. The Declaration of Independence 973.3
    Bernstein, R. B. Thomas Jefferson   92
    Boucher, B. Andrea Palladio   720.9
    Burstein, A. Madison and Jefferson   973.4
    Cerami, C. A. Jefferson's great gamble   973.4
    Cohen, I. B. Science and the founding fathers 973.3
    De Vecchi, P. Raphael   759
    Ellis, J. J. American sphinx: the character of Thomas Jefferson   973.4
    Ferling, J. E. Setting the world ablaze   973.3
    Fest, J. C. Speer: the final verdict   92
    Galbraith, J. K. Name-dropping   973.9
    Hollis, L. London rising   942
    Huxtable, A. L. Frank Lloyd Wright   92
    Isenberg, B. Conversations with Frank Gehry   92
    King, R. Brunelleschi's dome   726
    King, R. Michelangelo & the Pope's ceiling   759
    Larson, E. J. A magnificent catastrophe   324
    Lepore, J. A is for American   306.44
    Lind, C. The Wright style   728
    Lorance, L. Becoming Bucky Fuller   92
    Malone, J. W. It doesn't take a rocket scientist 920
    Mathewson, C. C. M. Frank O. Gehry: selected works   720.9
    Miller, J. C. The Federalist era, 1789-1801   973.4
    Mormando, F. Bernini   92
    Pick, H. Simon Wiesenthal   940.53
    Rybczynski, W. The perfect house: a journey with the Renaissance architect Andrea Palladio   720.9
    Secrest, M. Frank Lloyd Wright   92
    Segev, T. Simon Wiesenthal   92
    Sereny, G. Albert Speer   92
    Simon, J. F. What kind of nation   342
    Staloff, D. Hamilton, Adams, Jefferson   973.4
    Storrer, W. A. The Frank Lloyd Wright companion   720.9
    Unger, H. G. The last founding father   92
    Vidal, G. Inventing a nation: Washington, Adams, Jefferson   973.4
    Walker, C. E. Mongrel nation   305.8
    Weber, N. F. The Bauhaus group   920
    Wiseman, C. Shaping a nation   720.9
    Zacks, R. The pirate coast   973.4
    See also Artists

ARCHITECTURAL ACOUSTICS
    See also Sound

ARCHITECTURAL DECORATION AND OR-

Avallone, Eugene A.
(ed) Marks' standard handbook for mechanical engineers 621
AVANT-GARDE (AESTHETICS)
Indiana, G. Andy Warhol and the can that sold the world 759.13
Weber, N. F. The Bauhaus group 920
See also Aesthetics; Modernism (Aesthetics)
AVARICE
See also Sin
The **avengers.** Cohen, R. 940.53
AVERAGE
See also Arithmetic; Probabilities; Statistics
Averno. Gluck, L. 811
Avery, Christine
(ed) Rethinking collection development and management 025.2
Avery, Kevin
Everything is an afterthought 92
Avery, Tom
To the end of the earth 998
AVIATION *See* Aeronautics
AVIATION ACCIDENTS *See* Aircraft accidents
AVIATION MEDICINE
See also Medicine
The **aviators.** Groom, W. 920
AVIATORS *See* Air pilots
AVOCATIONS *See* Hobbies
Avoid boring people. Watson, J. D. 92
Avonmore, William Charles Yelverton, Viscount, 1824-1883
About
Schama, C. Wild romance 92
Avorn, Jerry
Powerful medicines 338.4
Avrich, Karen
Sasha and Emma 335
Avrich, Paul
(jt. auth) Avrich, K. Sasha and Emma 335
Axelrod, Alan
Whiskey tango foxtrot 427
Axelrod, Alan
The encyclopedia of the American armed forces 355
Phillips, C. Encyclopedia of wars 355
Axelrod, Matt
Your guide to the Jewish holidays 296.4
AXIOLOGY *See* Values
Ayala, Don
About
Gezari, V. M. The tender soldier 958.104
Ayala, Francisco J.
Darwin's gift to science and religion 576.8
The **Ayatollah** begs to differ. Majd, H. 955
Aycoberry, Pierre
The social history of the Third Reich 943.086

Aydin, Andrew
(jt. auth) Lewis, J. R. March 741.5
Ayers, Amanda Conley
(ed) The Oxford handbook of happiness 158
Ayers, Edward L.
(ed) The Oxford book of the American South 810
Ayers, Nathaniel Anthony
About
Lopez, S. The soloist 92
Ayn Rand and the world she made. Heller, A. C. 92
Ayres, Alex
(ed) Twain, M. The wit and wisdom of Mark Twain 818
Ayres, Chris
Osbourne, O. I am Ozzy 92
Ayto, John
Brewer's dictionary of modern phrase & fable 803
The Oxford dictionary of slang 427
(ed) Oxford dictionary of English idioms 423
Azam Zanganeh, Lila
My sister, guard your veil; my brother guard, your eyes 305
The **Aztec** treasure house. Connell, E. S. 814
The **Aztecs.** Townsend, R. F. 972
The **Aztecs.** Smith, M. E. 972
AZTECS
Ceram, C. W. Gods, graves, and scholars 930.1
Prescott, W. H. History of the conquest of Mexico 972
Smith, M. E. The Aztecs 972
Townsend, R. F. The Aztecs 972

B

The **B** word. San Filippo, M. 791.4
B+ grades, A+ college application. Jager-Hyman, J. 378.1
B-24 BOMBER
Ambrose, S. E. The wild blue 940.54
B., David. B., D.Epileptic 616.8

B.F. Skinner. Bjork, D. W. 92
Baader-Meinhof. Aust, S. 363.32
Baars, Bernard J.
In the theater of consciousness 153
Baartman, Saartjie
About
Crais, C. C. Sara Baartman and the Hottentot Venus 92
Holmes, R. African queen 92
Babbage, Charles, 1791-1871
About
Snyder, L. J. The philosophical breakfast club 509
Babe. Creamer, R. W. 92
BABEL, TOWER OF
Ceram, C. W. Gods, graves, and scholars 930.1
BABIES *See* Infants

Imagination in place   **814**
New collected poems   **811**
A timbered choir   **811**
Berryman, John
Collected poems, 1937-1971   **811**
The dream songs   **811**
Bertholf, Robert J.
(ed) Duncan, R. E. Selected poems   **811**
Bertholle, Louisette
Child, J. Mastering the art of French cooking **641.5**
Berthon, Simon
Warlords   **940.53**
Beschloss, Michael R., 1955-
The conquerors: Roosevelt, Truman, and the destruction of Hitler's Germany, 1941-1945 **940.53**
(ed) Jacqueline Kennedy   **973.922**
(ed) Taking charge   **973.923**
Besh, John
Cooking from the heart   **641.5**
My family table   **641.59**
My New Orleans   **641.59**
Bessel, Richard
Germany 1945   **943.087**
The **best** American essays 2010.   **814**
The **best** American essays 2012.   **808**
The **Best** American essays 2013.   **814**
The **Best** American essays of the century.   **814**
The **best** American poetry.   **811.008**
The **best** American recipes 2005-2006.   **641.5**
The **best** American science and nature writing 2012.   **810.8**
The best American series
The best American essays 2010   **814**
The Best American series
The best American recipes 2005-2006   **641.5**
The **Best** American short plays.   **812**
The **Best** American sports writing of the century. **796**
The **best** American travel writing 2012.   **808**
The **best** and the brightest. Halberstam, D. **973.922**
BEST BOOKS
Alabaster, C. Developing an outstanding core collection   **025.2**
Basbanes, N. A. Every book its reader   **028**
Covert, J. The 100 best business books of all time   **016.6**
Dirda, M. Book by book   **028**
Ellington, E. A year of reading   **011**
Helbig, A. Dictionary of American young adult fiction, 1997-2001   **028.5**
Horror: another 100 best books   **823**
Isabella, T. 1,000 comic books you must read **741.5**
Moyer, J. E. The readers' advisory handbook **025.5**
Pearl, N. Book lust   **011**
Pearl, N. More book lust   **025**
Pearl, N. Now read this   **016**
Pearl, N. Now read this II   **016**

Pearl, N. Now read this III   **016**
Required reading   **301**
Rosow, L. V. Accessing the classics   **011.6**
Saricks, J. G. The readers' advisory guide to genre fiction   **025.5**
Saricks, J. G. Readers' advisory service in the public library   **025.5**
Wyatt, N. The readers' advisory guide to nonfiction   **025.5**
    See also Books
The **best** business writing 2012.   **070.449**
The **best** business writing 2013.   **330.9**
The **Best** Casserole cookbook ever.   **641.8**
The **best** chicken recipes. Cook's illustrated (Periodical)   **641.6**
The **best** game ever. Bowden, M.   **796.332**
The **best** homemade kids' lunches on the planet. Fuentes, L.   **641.5**
The **best** International recipe. Cook's illustrated (Periodical)   **641.5**
The **best** of Abbie Hoffman. Hoffman, A. **303.4**
The **best** of all possible worlds. Nadler, S. M. **190**
The **best** of it. Ryan, K.   **811**
Best of the Best American Poetry.   **811**
The **best** one-dish suppers.   **641.8**
The **best** plays of 2006-2007.   **808.82**
Best plays theater yearbook [series]
The best plays of 2006-2007   **808.82**
The **Best** poems of the English language.   **821**
The **best** quick breads. Hensperger, B.   **641.8**
BEST SELLERS (BOOKS)
    See also Books and reading
Best skillet recipes. Cook's illustrated (Periodical)   **641.7**
The **best** stage scenes of 2007.   **808.82**
The **best** within us.   **158**
The **best** year of their lives. Morrow, L.   **920**
Best, Joel
Stat-spotting   **301**
Bestor, Leslie Ann
Cast on, bind off   **746.43**
Bethell, Leslie
(ed) The Cambridge history of Latin America **980**
Betjeman. Wilson, A. N.   **92**
Betjeman, John Sir, 1906-1984
About
Wilson, A. N. Betjeman   **92**
BETRAYAL
Macintyre, B. A Spy Among Friends   **327.12**
The **betrayal** of the American dream. Barlett, D. L.   **330.973**
Betrayal of trust. Garrett, L.   **362.1**
The **betrayal** of work. Shulman, B.   **331.2**
BETROTHAL
    See also Courtship; Marriage
Betsy Ross and the making of America. Miller, M.

Biel, Steven
American Gothic   **759.13**
Bierce, Ambrose, 1842-1914?
About
Drabelle, D. The great American railroad war **385**
Morris, R. Ambrose Bierce **92**
Wilson, E. Patriotic gore **810**
Biever, John A.
The wandering mind **612.8**
BIG BANG THEORY
Frank, A. About time **523.1**
Halpern, P. Edge of the universe **523.1**
Kaku, M. Parallel worlds **523.1**
Rees, M. J. Just six numbers **523.1**
Singh, S. Big bang: the origins of the universe **523.1**
    See also Cosmology
Big bang: the origins of the universe. Singh, S. **523.1**
The **big** book of cross-stitch designs. Reader's Digest Association **746.44**
The **big** book of outdoor cooking and entertaining.
Jamison, C. A. **641.5**
The **big** book of preserving the harvest. Costenbader, C. W. **641.4**
BIG BOOKS
    See also Children's literature; Reading materials
The **big** burn. Egan, T. **973.91**
BIG BUSINESS
Power, Inc. **322**
BIG BUSINESS -- UNITED STATES
Coll, S. Private empire **338.7**
Big Chief Elizabeth. Milton, G. **970.004**
Big data. Cukier, K. **306.46**
BIG DATA -- SOCIAL ASPECTS
Cukier, K. Big data **306.46**
The **Big** Disconnect. Steiner-Adair, C. **303.48**
Big enough to be inconsistent. Fredrickson, G. M. **973.7**
BIG GAME HUNTING
    See also Hunting
Big game, small world. Wolff, A. **796.323**
Big Gipp (Performer)
(jt. auth) Wild, D. Everybody's brother **92**
Big girls don't cry. Traister, R. **324**
A **big** history. Brown, C. S. **909**
BIG HOLE, BATTLE OF THE, 1877
West, E. The last Indian war **973.8**
Big Ideas Simply Explained [series]
The business book **650**
The politics book **320.01**
Big ideas/small books [series]
Diski, J. The Sixties **92**
Orbach, S. Bodies **362.1**
Big in China. Paul, A. **92**
The **big** miss. Haney, H. **796.352**
The **big** necessity. George, R. **363.7**

The **big** payback. Charnas, D. **781.64**
The **big** picture. Reilly, T. A. **791.43**
The **big** policeman. Conway, J. N. **92**
The **big** rich. Burrough, B. **338.2**
The **big** screen. Thomson, D. **791.43**
The **big** scrum. Miller, J. J. **796.332**
The **big** short. Lewis, M. **330.9**
The **big** sort. Bishop, B. **305.8**
The **big** splat; or, How our moon came to be. Mackenzie, D. **523.3**
The **big** switch. Carr, N. **303.4**
The **big** thirst. Fishman, C. **333.91**
The **big** truck that went by. Katz, J. M. **363.34**
The **big-ass** book of home decor. Montano, M. **645**
Big-box swindle. Mitchell, S. **381**
Big-time sports in American universities. Clotfelter, C. T. **796**
Biggers, Jeff
Reckoning at Eagle Creek **333.73**
Biggest brother. Alexander, L. **92**
BIGOTRY *See* Prejudices; Toleration
BIGOTRY-MOTIVATED CRIMES *See* Hate crimes
Bigsby, Christopher
Arthur Miller **92**
Bike Snob
The enlightened cyclist **796.6**
Bilal, Wafaa, 1966-
About
Bilal, W. Shoot an Iraqi **92**
BILDUNGSROMANS
Mayes, F. Under magnolia **92**
    See also Fiction
BILINGUAL BOOKS
    See also Books; Editions
BILINGUAL EDUCATION
    See also Bilingualism; Multicultural education
BILINGUALISM
    See also Language and languages
Bill and Hillary. Chafe, W. H. **973.929**
Bill Mauldin. DePastino, T. **92**
The **Bill** McKibben reader. McKibben, B. **333.72**
The **bill** of the century. Risen, C. **342.73**
BILLIARDS
Byrne, R. Byrne's new standard book of pool and billiards **794.7**
    See also Ball games
Billick, Brian
More than a game **796.332**
Billie Holiday. Nicholson, S. **782.421**
Billie Holiday. Clarke, D. **92**
Billings, Lee
Five billion years of solitude **576.8**
The **billionaire's** vinegar. Wallace, B. **641.2**
Billions and billions. Sagan, C. **500**

Birkhead, Tim
Bird sense	**598**
Ten thousand birds	**598.09**

BIRMINGHAM (ALA.)
Barra, A. Rickwood Field	**796.357**

BIRMINGHAM (ALA.) -- RACE RELATIONS
Colton, L. Southern League	**796.357**
Rieder, J. Gospel of freedom	**323.11**

BIRMINGHAM BARONS (BASEBALL TEAM)
Barra, A. Rickwood Field	**796.357**
Colton, L. Southern League	**796.357**

Biron, Rebecca E.
Elena Garro and Mexico's modern dreams	**868**

BIRTH *See* Childbirth

The **birth** (and death) of the cool. Gioia, T. **306**

BIRTH ATTENDANTS *See* Midwives

BIRTH CONTROL
Baker, J. H. Margaret Sanger	**92**
May, E. T. America and the pill	**363.9**
Tone, A. Devices and desires	**363.9**
See also Population; Sexual hygiene	

BIRTH CONTROL -- ETHICAL ASPECTS
See also Ethics

BIRTH CONTROL -- UNITED STATES -- HISTORY
May, E. T. America and the pill	**363.9**
Tone, A. Devices and desires	**363.9**

BIRTH CUSTOMS *See* Childbirth

BIRTH DEFECTS
See also Medical genetics; Pathology
The **birth** of an opera. Rose, M.	**782.1**
The **birth** of pleasure. Gilligan, C.	**152.4**
The **birth** of plenty. Bernstein, W.	**339.2**
The **birth** of Satan. Wray, T. J.	**235**
The **birth** of the past. Schiffman, Z. S.	**901**
The **birth** of the pill. Eig, J.	**618.1**
The **birth** of the Republic, 1763-89. Morgan, E. S.	**973.3**

BIRTH ORDER
See also Children; Family

BIRTH RECORDS *See* Registers of births, etc.

BIRTH WEIGHT, LOW -- COMPLICATIONS
Preemies	**618.92**

Birth without violence. **618.4**

BIRTHDAY BOOKS
See also Birthdays; Calendars

BIRTHDAYS
Nowlan, R. A. Born this day	**808.88**
See also Anniversaries; Days	

BIRTHPARENTS
See also Parents

BIRTHPARENTS -- UNITED STATES -- IDENTIFICATION -- CASE STUDIES
Marshall, S. Reunited	**362.82**

BIRTHS, REGISTERS OF *See* Registers of births, etc.

BISEXUAL STUDENTS -- UNITED STATES
Cahill, S. LGBT youth in America's schools	**371.82**

BISEXUALITY
Bronski, M. You can tell just by looking	**306.76**
Eisner, S. Bi	**306.76**
San Filippo, M. The B word	**791.4**
See also Sex	

BISEXUALITY IN MOTION PICTURES
San Filippo, M. The B word	**791.4**

BISEXUALITY ON TELEVISION
San Filippo, M. The B word	**791.4**

BISEXUALS
Gambone, P. Travels in a gay nation	**306.76**

BISEXUALS -- UNITED STATES
Bronski, M. You can tell just by looking	**306.76**

Bishara, Rawia
Olives, lemons & za'atar	**641.59**

The **bishop's** daughter. Moore, H. **92**

Bishop, Bill
The big sort	**305.8**

Bishop, Elizabeth, 1911-1979
The collected prose	**818**
Edgar Allan Poe & the juke-box	**811**
Poems, prose, and letters	**818**

About
Heaney, S. Finders keepers	**821**

Bishop, Patrick
The Hunt for Hitler's Warship	**940.54**

BISHOPS
Burstein, A. Madison and Jefferson	**973.4**
Goldman, F. The art of political murder	**972.81**
Kung, H. Great Christian thinkers	**230**
Moore, H. The bishop's daughter	**92**
Newman, R. S. Freedom's prophet	**92**
Russell, B. A history of Western philosophy	**109**
Wills, G. Saint Augustine	**270.2**
See also Clergy	

Biskind, Peter
Easy riders, raging bulls	**791.43**
My Lunches With Orson	**791.430**
Star	**92**

Biskupic, Joan
Sandra Day O'Connor	**92**

Bismarck. Steinberg, J. **92**

Bismarck, Otto, Furst von, 1815-1898
Fulbrook, M. A concise history of Germany	**943**
Kissinger, H. Diplomacy	**327.2**
Steinberg, J. Bismarck	**92**

BISON
Rinella, S. American buffalo	**599.64**
See also Mammals	

Biss, Eula, 1977-
On immunity	**616.07**

About
Biss, E. Notes from no man's land	**305.8**

Bissell, John

Braving home. Halpern, J.   363
Brawley, Otis Webb
  How we do harm   362.109
Bray, Hiawatha
  You are here   910.285
Bray, Ilona M.
  How to get a green card   342
  Nolo's essential guide to buying your first home 643
  U.S. immigration made easy   342
Bray, Willie Reginald, 1879-1939
                About
  Tingey, J. The Englishman who posted himself and
    other curious objects   92
Brazelton, T. Berry
  The irreducible needs of children   155.4
  To listen to a child   155.4
  Touchpoints birth to 3   649
Brazil. Skidmore, T. E.   981
BRAZIL -- HISTORY
  Meade, T. A brief history of Brazil   981
  Skidmore, T. E. Brazil   981
BRAZILIAN LITERATURE
    See also Latin American literature; Literature
BRČKO (BOSNIA AND HERCEGOVINA) -- BI-
  OGRAPHY
  Shapiro, S. The Bosnia list   92
Breach of faith. Horne, J.   976.3
BREAD
  Alexander, W. 52 loaves   641.8
  Alford, J. Flatbreads and flavors   641.8
  Beard, J. Beard on bread   641.8
  Forkish, K. Flour water salt yeast   641.81
  Hensperger, B. The best quick breads   641.8
  Robertson, C. Tartine bread   641.8
    See also Baking; Cooking; Food
The **bread** of angels. Saldana, S.   92
BREAK DANCING
    See also Dance
Break on through: the life and death of Jim Mor-
  rison. Riordan, J.   782.421
Break, blow, burn. Paglia, C.   809.1
BREAKERS *See* Ocean waves
Breakfast at Sally's. LeMieux, R.   92
BREAKFAST AT TIFFANY'S (MOTION PIC-
TURE)
  Wasson, S. Fifth Avenue, 5 AM   791.43
BREAKFASTS
    See also Cooking; Menus
Breaking clean. Blunt, J.   92
Breaking free, starting over. Dalpiaz, C. M. 362.82
Breaking night. Murray, L.   92
Breaking the spell. Dennett, D. C.   200
Breaking through concrete. Hanson, D.   630
Breaking trail. Blum, A.   796.522
Breakout nations. Sharma, R.   330.91
Breakthrough branding. Kaputa, C.   658.8

BREAKTHROUGHS, SCIENTIFIC *See* Discov-
  eries in science
BREAST
  Love, S. M. Dr. Susan Love's breast book   618.1
  Williams, F. Breasts   612.6
BREAST CANCER
  Corrigan, K. The middle place   92
  Fertig, J. The back in the swing cookbook   641.5
  Gabriel, S. Eating pomegranates   92
  Jacobs, H. The Silver Lining   616.99
  Prijatel, P. Surviving triple negative breast can-
    cer   616.99
  Queller, J. Pretty is what changes   92
  Sikka, M. A breast cancer alphabet   616.99
  Silver, M. Breast cancer husband   616.99
  Straight Talk about Breast Cancer   616.99
  Wheelwright, J. The wandering gene and the In-
    dian princess   616.99
  Williams, F. Breasts   612.6
    See also Cancer; Women -- Diseases
BREAST CANCER -- TREATMENT
  Prijatel, P. Surviving triple negative breast can-
    cer   616.99
A **breast** cancer alphabet. Sikka, M.   616.99
Breast cancer husband. Silver, M.   616.99
BREAST FEEDING
  Huggins, K. The nursing mother's companion 649
  Neifert, M. R. Great expectations   649
  Pitman, T. Sweet sleep   649
  Rope, K. The Complete Guide to Medications Dur-
    ing Pregnancy and Breastfeeding   618.3
  The Womanly art of breastfeeding   649
BREAST NEOPLASMS -- GENETICS
  Wheelwright, J. The wandering gene and the In-
    dian princess   616.99
Breasts. Williams, F.   612.6
Breath. Levine, P.   811
The **breath** of a wok. Richardson, A.   641.59
Breathless homicidal slime mutants. Brower,
  S.   741.6
Brecht and company. Fuegi, J.   92
Brecht, Bertolt, 1898-1956
                About
  Fuegi, J. Brecht and company   92
Breckinridge, John Cabell, 1821-1875
                About
  Davis, W. C. An honorable defeat   973.7
Bredin, Jean-Denis
  The affair   944.081
BREEDING
  Hubbell, S. Shrinking the cat   660.6
  Palumbi, S. R. The evolution explosion   576.8
    See also Reproduction
BREEDING BEHAVIOR *See* Sexual behavior in
  animals
Breedlove, Craig, 1938-

CHILDREN -- MOLESTING *See* Child sexual abuse

CHILDREN -- NUTRITION

Antine, S. Appetite for life   **641.5**

     See also Children -- Health and hygiene; Nutrition

CHILDREN -- PHYSICAL FITNESS

     See also Children -- Health and hygiene; Physical fitness

CHILDREN -- PICTORIAL WORKS

Coles, R. When they were young   **779**

CHILDREN -- PLACING OUT *See* Adoption; Foster home care

CHILDREN -- PROTECTION

Bailey, E. Safe kids, smart parents   **613.6**

CHILDREN -- PSYCHOLOGY *See* Child psychology

CHILDREN -- RELIGIOUS LIFE

Barrett, J. L. Born believers   **200.1**

CHILDREN -- SOCIALIZATION *See* Socialization

CHILDREN -- SURGERY

     See also Surgery

CHILDREN -- TRAINING *See* Child rearing

CHILDREN -- TRAVEL

Maraniss, D. Barack Obama   **973.932**

CHILDREN -- UNITED STATES

Tough, P. How children succeed   **372.210**

CHILDREN -- UNITED STATES -- SOCIAL CONDITIONS

Kozol, J. Fire in the ashes   **362.7**

CHILDREN -- WEST (U.S.)

Luchetti, C. Children of the West   **978**

CHILDREN AND ADVERTISING *See* Advertising and children

CHILDREN AND DEATH

     See also Death

CHILDREN AND THE INTERNET *See* Internet and children

CHILDREN AND WAR

Beah, I. A long way gone   **92**

Nicholas, L. H. Cruel world   **940.53**

Stolen voices   **920**

     See also Children; War

Children for hire. Levine, M. J.   **331.3**

CHILDREN IN ART

Hirshler, E. E. Sargent's daughters   **759.13**

CHILDREN OF ALCOHOLICS

     See also Children

CHILDREN OF CANCER PATIENTS

     See also Cancer -- Patients

CHILDREN OF CANCER PATIENTS -- UNITED STATES -- BIOGRAPHY

Smith, C. B. The rules of inheritance   **616.99**

CHILDREN OF CLERGY -- NEW YORK (STATE) -- BIOGRAPHY

Ward, G. C. A disposition to be rich   **974.7**

Children of crisis. Coles, R.   **305.23**

CHILDREN OF DEAF PARENTS -- BIOGRAPHY

Crews, K. Burn down the ground   **306.874**

CHILDREN OF DIVORCED PARENTS

Wallerstein, J. S. Second chances   **306.89**

     See also Children; Divorce; Parent-child relationship

CHILDREN OF DRUG ADDICTS

Murray, L. Breaking night   **92**

Ruta, D. With or without you   **362.29**

     See also Children; Drug addicts

Children of dust. Eteraz, A.   **92**

CHILDREN OF GAY PARENTS

Abbott, A. Fairyland   **813**

Garner, A. Families like mine   **306.8**

     See also Children

The **Children** of Henry VIII. Guy, J.   **941**

CHILDREN OF IMMIGRANTS

Hajratwala, M. Leaving India   **92**

     See also Children; Immigration and emigration

CHILDREN OF MILITARY PERSONNEL

Scott, J. Raising children in the military   **355.1**

CHILDREN OF MINORITIES -- EDUCATION -- UNITED STATES -- CASE STUDIES

Abani, A. Teaching matters   **370.917**

CHILDREN OF NARCOTIC ADDICTS *See* Children of drug addicts

CHILDREN OF PRESIDENTS

Bruni, F. Ambling into history: the unlikely odyssey of George W. Bush   **973.931**

Bush, G. W. Decision points   **92**

Clarke, R. A. Against all enemies   **973.931**

Cordery, S. A. Alice   **92**

Corn, D. The lies of George W. Bush   **973.931**

Dershowitz, A. M. Supreme injustice   **324.9**

Dowd, M. Bushworld   **973.931**

Draper, R. Dead certain   **973.931**

Farmer, J. J. The ground truth   **973.931**

Hersh, S. M. Chain of command   **973.931**

Korda, M. Ulysses S. Grant: the unlikely hero   **92**

Millard, C. The river of doubt   **973.91**

Miller, T. C. Blood money   **956.7**

Minutaglio, B. First son: George W. Bush and the Bush family dynasty   **92**

Schlesinger, A. M. War and the American presidency   **327.1**

Woodward, B. Plan of attack   **956.7**

Woodward, B. State of denial   **973.931**

CHILDREN OF PROMINENT PERSONS

Ali, K. Fighting weight   **92**

Gimbel, W. Havana dreams   **972.910**

Heller, E. Yossarian slept here   **92**

Lindbergh, R. Under a wing   **92**

CHURCH OF JESUS CHRIST OF LATTER-DAY SAINTS -- PRESIDENTS -- BIOGRAPHY

Turner, J. G.   Brigham Young, pioneer prophet   **289.309**

CHURCH WORK

Boyle, G. J. Tattoos on the heart   **277**

CHURCH WORK WITH THE SICK

See also Church work; Sick

CHURCH WORK WITH YOUTH

See also Church work; Youth

CHURCH YEAR

See also Calendars; Religious holidays; Worship

CHURCHES *See* Church buildings; Religious institutions

Churchill. Johnson, P.   **92**

Churchill's empire. Toye, R.   **92**

Churchill, Buntzie Ellis

Notes on a century   **956**

Churchill, Caryl

Mad forest   **822**

Churchill, Winston, 1874-1965

Closing the ring   **940.53**
The gathering storm   **940.53**
The grand alliance   **940.53**
The great republic   **973**
The hinge of fate   **940.53**
Their finest hour   **940.53**
Triumph and tragedy   **940.53**

About

Clarke, P. Mr. Churchill's profession   **941.084**
Dobbs, M. Six months in 1945   **940.53**
Manchester, W. The last lion, Winston Spencer Churchill   **92**

Churchland, Patricia S.

Braintrust   **612.8**
The **CIA** at war. Kessler, R.   **973.931**
The **CIA** World Factbook 2014.   **028**

Cialdini, Robert B.

Influence: the psychology of persuasion   **153.8**

Cianciotto, Jason

(jt. auth) Cahill, S. LGBT youth in America's schools   **371.82**

Ciardi, John

The collected poems of John Ciardi   **811**

Cicero. Everitt, A.   **92**

Cicero, Marcus Tullius, 106-43 B.C.

On the good life   **878**
Political speeches   **875**
The republic; and, The laws   **320.1**

About

Everitt, A. Cicero   **92**

Cid

The poem of the Cid   **861**

Ciezadlo, Annia

Day of honey   **92**

Cifelli, Edward M.

(ed) Ciardi, J. The collected poems of John Ciardi   **811**

CIGARETTES

Proctor, R. N. Golden holocaust   **362.29**

Cikovsky, Nicolai

Winslow Homer   **759.13**

Ciment, James

(ed) Encyclopedia of conflicts since World War II   **909.82**
(ed) Postwar America   **973.92**

CINCINNATI REDS (BASEBALL TEAM)

Frost, M. Game six   **796.357**

CINCO DE MAYO (HOLIDAY)

See also Holidays

Cinderella ate my daughter. Orenstein, P.   **305.23**

Cinderella Man. Schaap, J.   **92**

CINEMA *See* Motion pictures

The **Cinema** of Terry Gilliam.   **791**

CINEMATOGRAPHERS -- CALIFORNIA -- BIOGRAPHY

Ball, E. The inventor and the tycoon   **777**

CINEMATOGRAPHY

Harryhausen, R. The art of Ray Harryhausen **778.5**
Netzley, P. D. The encyclopedia of movie special effects   **778.5**
Reilly, T. A. The big picture   **791.43**

See also Photography

CINEMATOGRAPHY -- UNITED STATES -- HISTORY

Ball, E. The inventor and the tycoon   **777**

CINESIOLOGY *See* Kinesiology

Cinque, 1811?-1879

About

Abdul-Jabbar, K. Black profiles in courage   **920**

Cioran, E. M. (Emile M.), 1911-1995

About

Sontag, S. Styles of radical will   **814**

CIPHER AND TELEGRAPH CODES

Silverman, K. Lightning man   **621.383**

See also Ciphers; Telegraph

CIPHERS

The book of codes   **652**
Fox, M. The Riddle of the Labyrinth   **487**
Tobin, J. Hidden in plain view   **973.7**

See also Signs and symbols

CIRCLE

See also Geometry; Shape

A **circle** of sisters. Flanders, J.   **920**

Circling faith.   **200.8**

Circling my mother. Gordon, M.   **92**

CIRCULATION OF LIBRARY MATERIALS

See Library circulation

Circumcision. Gollaher, D.   **392**

CIRCUMCISION

Gollaher, D. Circumcision   **392**

jah Muhammad 297.8

Evers, M. W. The autobiography of Medgar Evers: a hero's life and legacy revealed through his writings, letters, and speeches 92

Gardell, M. In the name of Elijah Muhammad 297

Gates, H. L. The future of the race 305.896

Giddings, P. Ida: a sword among lions 92

Halberstam, D. The children 323.1

Harlan, L. R. Booker T. Washington: the making of a black leader, 1856-1901 92

Harlan, L. R. Booker T. Washington: the wizard of Tuskegee, 1901-1915 92

I see the promised land 92

Jackson, T. Becoming King 92

Joseph, P. E. Dark days, bright nights 323.1

Joseph, P. E. Waiting 'til the midnight hour 323.1

King, M. L. The autobiography of Martin Luther King, Jr 323

Kotz, N. Judgment days 323

Lewis, D. L. W.E.B. Du Bois 92

Malcolm X The autobiography of Malcolm X 92

Marable, M. Malcolm X 92

Marshall, T. Thurgood Marshall 347

Norrell, R. J. Up from history 92

Pepper, W. F. An act of state 364.1

Perry, B. Malcolm 92

Rickford, R. J. Betty Shabazz: a remarkable story of survival and faith before and after Malcolm X 92

Risen, C. A nation on fire 973.923

Robeson, P. Here I stand 92

Robeson, P. The undiscovered Paul Robeson 782

Rowan, C. T. Dream makers, dream breakers 92

Sides, H. Hellhound on his trail 364.152

Smock, R. W. Booker T. Washington 92

Spagna, A. M. Test ride on the Sunnyland bus 323.1

Uncle Tom or new Negro 370

Washington, B. T. Up from slavery 92

Williams, J. Thurgood Marshall 347

Wilson, E. Patriotic gore 810

Young, A. An easy burden 92

Zellner, R. The wrong side of Murder Creek 92

CIVIL RIGHTS ACTIVISTS -- SOUTHERN STATES -- HISTORY

Arsenault, R. Freedom riders 323

Civil rights and the struggle for Black equality in the twentieth century [series]

Jackson, T. Becoming King 92

CIVIL RIGHTS DEMONSTRATIONS

Campbell, J. Setting the truth free 941.6

Euchner, C. C. Nobody turn me around 323.1

Zellner, R. The wrong side of Murder Creek 92

See also Demonstrations

CIVIL RIGHTS DEMONSTRATIONS -- UNITED STATES -- PICTORIAL WORKS

Kelley, K. Let Freedom Ring 323.1196

CIVIL RIGHTS MOVEMENTS

Branch, T. At Canaan's edge 973.923

Joseph, P. E. Waiting 'til the midnight hour 323.1

CIVIL RIGHTS MOVEMENTS -- ALABAMA -- BIRMINGHAM -- HISTORY -- 20TH CENTURY

McWhorter, D. Carry me home 976.1

Rieder, J. Gospel of freedom 323.11

CIVIL RIGHTS MOVEMENTS -- MISSISSIPPI -- HISTORY -- 20TH CENTURY

Marshall, J. P. Student activism and civil rights in Mississippi 323.1196

CIVIL RIGHTS MOVEMENTS -- PENNSYLVANIA -- PHILADELPHIA

Biddle, D. R. Tasting freedom 92

CIVIL RIGHTS MOVEMENTS -- SOUTHERN STATES

Arsenault, R. Freedom riders 323

CIVIL RIGHTS MOVEMENTS -- SOUTHERN STATES -- HISTORY -- 20TH CENTURY

Crespino, J. Strom Thurmond's America 328

McGuire, D. L. At the dark end of the street 323.1

Sokol, J. There goes my everything 305.8

CIVIL RIGHTS MOVEMENTS -- UNITED STATES

Dove, R. On the bus with Rosa Parks 811

The economic civil rights movement 323.1

CIVIL RIGHTS MOVEMENTS -- UNITED STATES -- COMIC BOOKS, STRIPS, ETC

Lewis, J. R. March 741.5

CIVIL RIGHTS MOVEMENTS -- UNITED STATES -- HISTORY -- 20TH CENTURY

Branch, T. At Canaan's edge 973.923

Cotton, D. If your back's not bent 323

Dyson, M. E. I may not get there with you: the true Martin Luther King, Jr 323

Lewis, A. B. The shadows of youth 323.1

Sugrue, T. J. Sweet land of liberty 323

CIVIL RIGHTS WORKERS -- ALABAMA -- MONTGOMERY -- BIOGRAPHY

Brinkley, D. Rosa Parks 323

Theoharis, J. The rebellious life of Mrs. Rosa Parks 323.092

CIVIL RIGHTS WORKERS -- SOUTHERN STATES -- HISTORY

Arsenault, R. Freedom riders 323

CIVIL RIGHTS WORKERS -- UNITED STATES -- HISTORY -- 20TH CENTURY

Arsenault, R. Freedom riders 323

Sugrue, T. J. Sweet land of liberty 323

CIVIL SERVICE

See also Administrative law; Political science; Public administration

CIVIL SERVICE -- EXAMINATIONS

Civil service arithmetic and vocabulary 351.076

CIVIL SERVICE -- UNITED STATES

COMMUNITY ORGANIZATION
See also Community life; Social work

COMMUNITY POLICING
Hanhardt, C. B. Safe space   **306.76**

Community quilts. Kavaya, K.   **746.46**

A community resilience guide [series]
Ackerman-Leist, P. Rebuilding the foodshed **338.1**

COMMUNITY SERVICES
See also Social work

COMMUTING
See also Transportation

COMPACT CARS
See also Automobiles

COMPACT DISC READ-ONLY MEMORY *See* CD-ROMs

COMPACT DISCS
See also Optical storage devices; Sound recordings

Compagno, Leonard J. V.
Sharks of the world   **597**

COMPANIES *See* Business enterprises; Corporations; Partnership

Companies we keep. Abrams, J.   **338.7**

Companion to Asian studies [series]
Keene, D. The pleasures of Japanese literature   **895.6**

Companion to Narnia. Ford, P. F.   **823**

The **Companion** to southern literature.   **810**

The **company.** Micklethwait, J.   **338.7**

Company of moths. Palmer, M.   **811**

COMPANY SYMBOLS *See* Trademarks

The **company** town. Green, H.   **307.7**

COMPANY TOWNS -- UNITED STATES -- HISTORY
Green, H. The company town   **307.7**

The **company** we keep. Chadwick, D. H.   **333.95**

COMPAQ COMPUTER CORPORATION
Burrows, P. Backfire: Carly Fiorina's high-stakes battle for the soul of Hewlett-Packard   **338.7**

COMPARATIVE ANATOMY
See also Anatomy; Zoology

COMPARATIVE CIVILIZATION
Morris, I. Why the West rules--for now   **909**

COMPARATIVE EDUCATION
Ripley, A. The smartest kids in the world   **370.9**

COMPARATIVE GOVERNMENT
Fukuyama, F. The origins of political order   **320**
See also Political science

COMPARATIVE LINGUISTICS *See* Linguistics

COMPARATIVE LITERATURE
See also Literature

COMPARATIVE PHILOSOPHY
See also Philosophy

COMPARATIVE PHYSIOLOGY
Hughes, H. C. Sensory exotica   **573.8**
See also Physiology

COMPARATIVE PSYCHOLOGY
Bearzi, M. Beautiful minds   **599.8**
Bowers, K. Zoobiquity   **636.089**
Braitman, L. Animal madness   **591.5**
Masson, J. M. When elephants weep   **591.5**
Suddendorf, T. The gap   **156**
Waal, F. d. Our inner ape   **156**
See also Zoology

COMPARATIVE RELIGION *See* Christianity and other religions; Religions

COMPARISON OF CULTURES *See* Cross-cultural studies

COMPASS
Aczel, A. D. The riddle of the compass   **912**
See also Magnetism; Navigation

The **compass** of pleasure. Linden, D. J.   **612.8**

COMPASSION
Armstrong, K. Twelve steps to a compassionate life   **177**
Bstan-'dzin-rgya-mtsho, D. L. X. How to be compassionate   **294.3**
See also Emotions

COMPENSATION *See* Pensions; Salaries, wages, etc.; Workers' compensation

COMPETENCE *See* Performance

Competing voices from the Russian Revolution.   **947.084**

COMPETITION
See also Business; Business ethics; Commerce

COMPETITION (PSYCHOLOGY)
Rosenbaum, D. A. It's a jungle in there   **153**
See also Interpersonal relations; Motivation (Psychology); Psychology

COMPETITION, INTERNATIONAL
Newman, K. S. The accordion family   **306.874**
See also International competition

COMPETITIVE BEHAVIOR *See* Competition (Psychology)

Competitive elections and the American voter. Lipsitz, K.   **324.9**

COMPLEMENTARY THERAPIES -- ENCYCLOPEDIAS -- ENGLISH
The Gale encyclopedia of alternative medicine   **615.5**

The **complete** artist's manual. Jennings, S.   **751**

The **complete** bedside companion. McFarlane, R.   **649.8**

The **complete** Bible handbook. Bowker, J.   **220.6**

The **complete** book of cacti & succulents. Hewitt, T.   **635.9**

The **complete** book of home crafts.   **745.5**

The **complete** book of home inspection. Becker, N.   **643**

The **complete** book of jewelry making. Codina, C.   **739.27**

Jamison, B. The border cookbook   **641.59**

COOKING -- SPICES
Duguid, N. Burma   **641.59**

COOKING -- STUDY AND TEACHING
Flinn, K. The kitchen counter cooking school **641.5**

COOKING -- VEGETABLES
Jacoby, K. Vedge   **641.6**
La Place, V. Verdura   **641.6**
Madison, D. Vegetable literacy   **641.6**
Moosewood restaurant favorites   **641.5**
Ottolenghi, Y. Plenty more   **641.6**
Wilkinson, M. Mr. Wilkinson's vegetables **641.65**
    See also Vegetables

COOKING -- YUCATAN PENINSULA
Sterling, D. Yucatán   **641.59**
Cooking dirty. Sheehan, J.   **92**

COOKING FOR ONE
    See also Cooking

COOKING FOR THE SICK
Katz, R. The cancer-fighting kitchen   **641.5**
    See also Cooking; Diet in disease; Nursing; Sick

COOKING FOR TWO
    See also Cooking
Cooking from the heart. Besh, J.   **641.5**
Cooking know-how. Weinstein, B.   **641.5**
Cooking my way back home.   **641.5**

COOKING TEACHERS
Hazan, M. Amarcord, Marcella remembers   **92**
Cooking with Italian grandmothers. Theroux, J.   **641.5**

COOKING, AFRICAN
Afro-vegan   **641.59**

COOKING, AMERICAN
The America's test kitchen do-it-yourself cookbook   **641.597**
The America's Test Kitchen healthy family cookbook   **641.5**
The America's Test Kitchen new family cookbook   **641.5**
Anthony, M. The Gramercy Tavern cookbook **641.5**
Bastianich, L. Lidia's Italian-American kitchen   **641.59**
Besh, J. My family table   **641.59**
Brennan, K. Keepers   **641.5**
Fried, S. Appetite for America   **92**
Goin, S. The A.O.C. cookbook   **641.5**
Hesser, A. The essential New York Times cookbook   **641.5**
Humm, D. I love New York   **641.59**
Kamp, D. The United States of Arugula   **641**
McMillan, T. The American way of eating   **338.4**
O'Neill, M. One big table   **641.5**
Phillips, M. The Chelsea Market cookbook **641.59**
Ridge, B. The Beekman 1802 heirloom dessert cookbook   **641.5**

Schlosser, E. Fast food nation   **394.1**
The Oxford encyclopedia of food and drink in America   **641.3**

COOKING, AMERICAN -- CALIFORNIA STYLE
Cooking my way back home   **641.5**

COOKING, AMERICAN -- HISTORY -- 20TH CENTURY
Barr, L. Provence, 1970   **641.59**

COOKING, AMERICAN -- MIDWESTERN STYLE
Thielen, A. The New Midwestern table   **641.59**

COOKING, AMERICAN -- SOUTHERN STYLE
Acheson, H. A New Turn in the South   **641.59**
Afro-vegan   **641.59**
Cooking my way back home   **641.5**
Dupree, N. Mastering the art of Southern cooking   **641.59**
Foose, M. H. A southerly course   **641.59**
Lee, E. Smoke and pickles   **641.59**
Lee, M. The Lee Bros. Charleston kitchen **641.59**
Lewis, E. The gift of Southern cooking   **641.59**
Miller, A. Soul food   **641.59**

COOKING, ASIAN
Asian dumplings   **641.59**

COOKING, BURMESE
Duguid, N. Burma   **641.59**

COOKING, CAJUN
Besh, J. My New Orleans   **641.59**

COOKING, CARIBBEAN
Afro-vegan   **641.59**
Gran cocina latina   **641.597**
New World kitchen   **641.59**

COOKING, CHINESE
Dunlop, F. Every grain of rice   **641.59**
Mastering the art of Chinese cooking   **641.59**
Richardson, A. The breath of a wok   **641.59**

COOKING, CREOLE
Besh, J. My New Orleans   **641.59**

COOKING, FRENCH
Baxter, J. The perfect meal   **641.59**
The country cooking of France   **641.59**
Dusoulier, C. The French market cookbook **641.5**
Friedman, A. One souffle at a time   **92**
Greenspan, D. Baking chez moi   **641.86**
Grigson, J. Charcuterie and French pork cookery   **641.6**
My Paris kitchen   **641.59**
Olney, R. Simple French food   **641.59**
Shulman, M. R. The art of French pastry **641.86**
Spitz, B. Dearie   **641.509**

COOKING, FRENCH -- PROVENCAL STYLE
Olney, R. Lulu's Provencal table   **641.59**
Olney, R. Simple French food   **641.59**

COOKING, INDIC
Iyer, R. Indian cooking unfolded   **641.59**

ics

COOPERATIVE AGRICULTURE
> *See also* Agriculture; Cooperation

COOPERATIVE BANKS
Friedman, J. Engineering the financial crisis **330.9**
> *See also* Banks and banking; Cooperation; Cooperative societies; Personal loans

COOPERATIVE DISTRIBUTION *See* Cooperation; Cooperative societies

COOPERATIVE HOUSING
> *See also* Cooperation; Housing

COOPERATIVE LEARNING
> *See also* Education; Teaching

COOPERATIVE LIVING *See* Collective settlements; Communal living

COOPERATIVE ORGANIZATION ADMINISTRATORS
O'Shea, J. The deal from hell **92**

COOPERATIVE SOCIETIES
Highfield, R. Supercooperators **519.3**
> *See also* Cooperation; Corporations; Societies

COOPERATIVE STORES *See* Cooperative societies

COOPERATIVENESS
> *See also* Social psychology

COOPERATIVES *See* Cooperative societies

Coote, Stephen
Napoleon and the Hundred Days **940.2**

Cope, Alan Ingram, 1925-1999
About
Guibert, E. Alan's war **741.5**

Cope, E. D. (Edward Drinker), 1840-1897
About
Wallace, D. R. The bonehunters' revenge **560**

Copeland, B. Jack
Turing **92**

Copeland, David A.
(ed) The Greenwood library of American war reporting **973**

Copeland, Edward
(ed) The Cambridge companion to Jane Austen **823**

Copeland, Lewis
(ed) The World's great speeches **808.85**

Copeland, Peter
Hamer, D. H. Living with our genes **155.2**

Copernicus' secret. Repcheck, J. **92**

Copernicus, Nicolaus, 1473-1543
About
Repcheck, J. Copernicus' secret **92**
Sobel, D. A more perfect heaven **520**
Vollmann, W. T. Uncentering the Earth **92**

Copi, Irving M.
Introduction to logic **160**

COPING BEHAVIOR *See* Adjustment (Psychology)

COPING SKILLS *See* Life skills

Coping with concussion and mild traumatic brain injury. Stoler, D. R. **617.4**

COPPER
Carter, B. Boom, Bust, Boom **622.434**

COPPER INDUSTRY AND TRADE -- HISTORY
LeCain, T. J. Mass destruction **338.2**

COPPER MINES AND MINING
Carter, B. Boom, Bust, Boom **622.434**
LeCain, T. J. Mass destruction **338.2**
Tobar, H. Deep down dark **363.11**

COPPER MINES AND MINING -- ACCIDENTS
Tobar, H. Deep down dark **363.11**

COPPER MINES AND MINING -- ENVIRONMENTAL ASPECTS
LeCain, T. J. Mass destruction **338.2**

COPPER MINES AND MINING -- WESTERN STATES
LeCain, T. J. Mass destruction **338.2**

Copper, John F.
Taiwan **951.249**

COPPERWORK
> *See also* Metalwork

Coppinger, Lorna
Coppinger, R. Dogs **636.7**

Coppinger, Raymond
Dogs **636.7**

COPY ART
> *See also* Art

COPYRIGHT
Butler, R. P. Copyright for teachers & librarians in the 21st century **346**
Decherney, P. Hollywood's copyright wars **346.04**
Fishman, S. Copyright handbook **346.04**
Fishman, S. The public domain **346**
Gasaway, L. N. Copyright questions and answers for information professionals **346.730**
Hyde, L. Common as air **346.04**
Hylton, K. N. Laws of creation **346.04**
Lessig, L. The future of ideas **004.67**
Lessig, L. Remix **346**
Stim, R. Patent, copyright & trademark **346**
Wherry, T. L. Intellectual property **346.04**

COPYRIGHT -- BROADCASTING RIGHTS -- UNITED STATES -- HISTORY
Decherney, P. Hollywood's copyright wars **346.04**

COPYRIGHT -- MOTION PICTURES -- UNITED STATES -- HISTORY
Decherney, P. Hollywood's copyright wars **346.04**

COPYRIGHT -- UNITED STATES
Crews, K. D. Copyright law for librarians and educators **346.04**
Gasaway, L. N. Copyright questions and answers for information professionals **346.730**
Russell, C. Complete copyright for K-12 librarians and educators **346.04**

CUBA -- HISTORY -- 1990- -- BIOGRAPHY
Cooke, J. The other side of paradise   **972.91**

CUBA -- POLITICS AND GOVERNMENT
Castro, F. Fidel Castro: my life   **92**
Coltman, L. The real Fidel Castro   **92**
Quirk, R. E. Fidel Castro   **972.910**
Szulc, T. Fidel   **92**

CUBA -- POLITICS AND GOVERNMENT -- 1959-
Coltman, L. The real Fidel Castro   **92**
Schoultz, L. That infernal little Cuban republic **327**

CUBA -- POLITICS AND GOVERNMENT -- 1990-
Cooke, J. The other side of paradise   **972.91**

CUBA -- SOCIAL LIFE AND CUSTOMS
Cooke, J. The other side of paradise   **972.91**
Cuba: art and history, from 1868 to today.   **709**

CUBAN AMERICANS
Eire, C. M. N. Learning to die in Miami   **92**

CUBAN ART
Cuba: art and history, from 1868 to today   **709**

CUBAN MISSILE CRISIS, 1962
Dobbs, M. One minute to midnight   **973.922**
Freedman, L. Kennedy's wars   **973.922**
Fursenko, A. V. One hell of a gamble   **973.922**
Kennedy, R. F. Thirteen days   **973.922**

CUBAN REFUGEES
Eire, C. M. N. Learning to die in Miami   **92**

CUBIC EQUATIONS
Ash, A. Elliptic tales   **515**
    See also Equations

CUBISM
    See also Art

Cuddon, J. A.
The Penguin dictionary of literary terms and literary theory   **803**

Cuhaj, George S.
2012 standard catalog of world coins, 1901-2000   **737.4**

Cukier, Kenneth
Big data   **306.46**

Culinary birds. Fraioli, J. O.   **641.6**

Culinary Institute of America
Vegetables   **641.6**

Culkin, Jennifer
A final arc of sky   **92**

Cullen, Charles, 1960-
    About
Graeber, C. The good nurse   **364.152**

Cullen, Dave
Columbine   **364.152**

Cullen, Heidi
The weather of the future   **551.63**

Cullen, Kevin
Whitey Bulger   **364.109**

Cullin, Robert

Bolan, K. Technology made simple   **025**

Cullina, William
Understanding perennials   **635.9**

Cullinane, Jan
The new retirement   **646.7**

The **cult** of the leader. Bones, C.   **658.4**

Cult pop culture.   **306**

CULTIVATED PLANTS
    See also Agriculture; Gardening; Plants

Cultivating delight. Ackerman, D.   **508**

CULTS
Belief beyond boundaries   **209**
Controversial New Religions   **200.9**
The encyclopedia of cults, sects, and new religions   **200**
Wright, L. Going Clear   **299**

CULTS
    See also Religions

Cultural amnesia. James, C.   **920**

CULTURAL ANTHROPOLOGY *See* Ethnology

CULTURAL CHANGE *See* Social change

CULTURAL CRITIQUE
Bissell, T. Magic hours   **153.35**
Deb, S. The beautiful and the damned   **954.05**
Fitzgerald, K. Volume   **700.9**
Gill, A. A. To America with love   **917.3**
Nelson, M. The art of cruelty   **700**
Yalom, M. How the French invented love   **944**
The **cultural** encyclopedia of baseball. Light, J. F.   **796.357**

CULTURAL HERITAGE *See* Cultural property

A **cultural** history of physics.   **530**

CULTURAL LIFE *See* Intellectual life

CULTURAL PATRIMONY *See* Cultural property

CULTURAL PLURALISM
Brysac, S. B. Pax ethnica   **323.11**

CULTURAL POLICY
    See also Culture; Intellectual life

CULTURAL POLICY -- UNITED STATES
Kersel, M. M. U.S. cultural diplomacy and archaeology   **930.1**

CULTURAL PROGRAMS
Librarians as community partners   **021.2**

CULTURAL PROPERTY
Cole, P. Sacred trash   **296.09**
Felch, J. Chasing Aphrodite   **930**

CULTURAL PROPERTY -- PROTECTION -- POLITICAL ASPECTS
Kersel, M. M. U.S. cultural diplomacy and archaeology   **930.1**

CULTURAL PROPERTY -- REPATRIATION -- ITALY
Felch, J. Chasing Aphrodite   **930**

CULTURAL RELATIONS
    See also Intellectual cooperation; International cooperation; International relations

See also Statistics

EDUCATION -- UNITED STATES

Mettler, S. Degrees of inequality 378.73

Rhee, M. A. Radical 371.010

Ripley, A. The smartest kids in the world 370.9

EDUCATION -- UNITED STATES -- HISTORY

Wolff, D. How Lincoln learned to read 920

EDUCATION FOR LIBRARIANSHIP *See* Library education

The **education** of a British-protected child. Achebe, C. 92

The **education** of a woman. Heilbrun, C. G. 92

EDUCATION OF ADULTS *See* Adult education

EDUCATION OF CHILDREN *See* Elementary education

The **education** of Henry Adams. Adams, H. 92

EDUCATION, ELEMENTARY *See* Elementary education

EDUCATION, HIGHER *See* Higher education

EDUCATION, HIGHER -- AIMS AND OBJECTIVES -- UNITED STATES

Delbanco, A. College 378.73

Selingo, J. J. College (un)bound 378

EDUCATION, HIGHER -- UNITED STATES

Martin, R. H. Racing Odysseus 92

EDUCATION, HIGHER -- UNITED STATES -- FINANCE

Dreifus, C. Higher education? 378

EDUCATION, PRIMARY *See* Elementary education

EDUCATION, SECONDARY *See* Secondary education

EDUCATION, URBAN -- UNITED STATES -- CASE STUDIES

Abani, A. Teaching matters 370.917

EDUCATIONAL ACCOUNTABILITY -- UNITED STATES

Ravitch, D. The death and life of the great American school system 379

EDUCATIONAL ACHIEVEMENT *See* Academic achievement

EDUCATIONAL ADMINISTRATION *See* Schools -- Administration

EDUCATIONAL CHANGE -- UNITED STATES

Mettler, S. Degrees of inequality 378.73

Rhee, M. A. Radical 371.010

EDUCATIONAL COUNSELING

See also Counseling

EDUCATIONAL EVALUATION

See also Education

EDUCATIONAL GAMES

McGonigal, J. Reality is broken 306.4

EDUCATIONAL GAMES

See also Education; Games

EDUCATIONAL MEASUREMENTS *See* Educational tests and measurements

EDUCATIONAL MEDIA CENTERS *See* Instructional materials centers

EDUCATIONAL PLANNING -- UNITED STATES

Selingo, J. J. College (un)bound 378

EDUCATIONAL PSYCHOLOGY

Levine, M. D. A mind at a time 370.15

See also Psychology; Teaching

EDUCATIONAL SOCIOLOGY

Hirsch, E. D. The schools we need and why we don't have them 370.9

See also Sociology

EDUCATIONAL TECHNOLOGY

Grover, S. Listening to learn 372.4

See also Education

EDUCATIONAL TESTS AND MEASUREMENTS

Fuhrken, C. What every middle school teacher needs to know about reading tests (from someone who has written them) 428

Ravitch, D. The death and life of the great American school system 379

Reese, W. J. Testing wars in the public schools 371.26

See also Education

EDUCATIONAL VOUCHERS

See also Education -- Finance

EDUCATORS

Art and social justice education 372.5

Ellison, R. The collected essays of Ralph Ellison 814

Francis, R. Fruitlands 974.4

Halberstam, D. The best and the brightest 973.922

Halberstam, D. The children 323.1

Harlan, L. R. Booker T. Washington: the making of a black leader, 1856-1901 92

Harlan, L. R. Booker T. Washington: the wizard of Tuskegee, 1901-1915 92

Hendricks, S. The unquiet grave 970.004

Kozol, J. Letters to a young teacher 371.1

Leibovitz, L. Fortunate sons 951.05

Matteson, J. Eden's outcasts 92

Menand, L. The Metaphysical Club 973.9

Norrell, R. J. Up from history 92

Singer, M. Character studies 920

Smock, R. W. Booker T. Washington 92

Taylor, A. The divided ground 974.7

Torres, A. American widow 741.5

Uncle Tom or new Negro 370

Washington, B. T. Up from slavery 92

Wilson, E. Patriotic gore 810

See also Education

Edvard Munch. Prideaux, S. 92

Edward Albee. Gussow, M. 92

Edward III. Ormrod, W. M. 942.03

Edward III, King of England, 1312-1377

Ackerman, D. The rarest of the rare   **578.68**

Barrow, M. V. Nature's ghosts   **333.95**

Chadwick, D. H. The company we keep   **333.95**

Ellis, R. The empty ocean   **577.7**

Ellis, R. Tuna   **333.95**

Fraser, C. Rewilding the world   **333.95**

Matthiessen, P. Tigers in the snow   **599.756**

McNamee, T. The return of the wolf to Yellowstone   **333.95**

Montaigne, F. Fraser's penguins   **577.2**

Owens, D. The eye of the elephant   **333.95**

Quammen, D. Monster of God   **591.6**

Smith, D. W. Decade of the wolf   **599.77**

Stanford, C. B. Planet without apes   **599.88**

Stolzenberg, W. Where the wild things were   **577**

Wilson, E. O. The future of life   **333.95**

> See also Environmental protection; Nature conservation

ENDANGERED SPECIES -- HAWAII

Williams, T. M. The odyssey of KP2   **599.79**

ENDANGERED SPECIES -- LAW AND LEGISLATION

Barrow, M. V. Nature's ghosts   **333.95**

ENDANGERED SPECIES -- RESEARCH

Rigney, M. In pursuit of giants   **597**

ENDANGERED SPECIES -- UNITED STATES

Mooallem, J. Wild ones   **333.95**

Neme, L. A. Animal investigators   **363.2**

The **endangered** species road trip. Macdonald, C.   **974**

Ende, Werner

(ed) Islam in der Gegenwart./English. Islam in the world today   **297**

Endersby, Jim

A guinea pig's history of biology   **576.5**

Endgame. Rohde, D.   **949.7**

The **endgame.** Gordon, M. R.   **956.7**

Endgame. Brady, F.   **92**

Ending the Vietnam War. Kissinger, H.   **959.704**

Endless forms most beautiful. Carroll, S. B.   **571.8**

Endless universe. Steinhardt, P. J.   **523.1**

ENDOCRINOLOGY

> See also Medicine

ENDOWED CHARITIES See Charities; Endowments

ENDOWMENTS

> See also Finance

ENDOWMENTS -- DIRECTORIES

The Foundation Directory 2014   **061**

ENDOWMENTS -- UNITED STATES -- HISTORY

Zunz, O. Philanthropy in America   **361.7**

Endpoint and other poems. Updike, J.   **811**

The **ends** of the earth.   **998**

The **Endurance.** Alexander, C.   **998**

ENDURANCE (SHIP)

Alexander, C. The Endurance   **998**

ENDURANCE, PHYSICAL See Physical fitness

Enelow, Wendy S.

Cover letter magic   **650.14**

Enemies. Weiner, T.   **363.25**

Enemies of the people. Marton, K.   **92**

Enemy of the state. Newton, M. A.   **345**

ENERGY See Energy resources; Force and energy

ENERGY AND STATE See Energy policy

ENERGY CONSERVATION

Feynman, R. P. Six easy pieces   **530**

Newton, D. E. World energy crisis   **333.79**

> See also Conservation of natural resources; Energy resources

ENERGY CONSERVATION -- UNITED STATES

Koerth-Baker, M. Before the lights go out **333.79**

ENERGY CONSUMPTION

Newton, D. E. World energy crisis   **333.79**

> See also Energy resources

ENERGY CONSUMPTION -- UNITED STATES

Koerth-Baker, M. Before the lights go out **333.79**

ENERGY CONVERSION, MICROBIAL See Biomass energy

ENERGY DEVELOPMENT

Alley, R. B. Earth   **621**

Muller, R. A. Energy for future presidents **333.79**

Renewable energy   **333**

> See also Energy resources

Energy for future presidents. Muller, R. A.   **333.79**

ENERGY INDUSTRIES

Newton, D. E. World energy crisis   **333.79**

ENERGY INDUSTRIES -- UNITED STATES

Levi, M. Power surge   **333.79**

ENERGY INDUSTRIES -- UNITED STATES -- BIOGRAPHY

Zuckerman, G. The frackers   **338.2**

ENERGY INDUSTRY EXECUTIVES

Bruni, F. Ambling into history: the unlikely odyssey of George W. Bush   **973.931**

Burrough, B. The big rich   **338.2**

Bush, G. W. Decision points   **92**

Chernow, R. Titan: the life of John D. Rockefeller, Sr.   **92**

Clarke, R. A. Against all enemies   **973.931**

Corn, D. The lies of George W. Bush   **973.931**

Dershowitz, A. M. Supreme injustice   **324.9**

Dowd, M. Bushworld   **973.931**

Draper, R. Dead certain   **973.931**

Epstein, E. J. Dossier   **92**

Farmer, J. J. The ground truth   **973.931**

Hersh, S. M. Chain of command   **973.931**

Miller, T. C. Blood money   **956.7**

Minutaglio, B. First son: George W. Bush and the Bush family dynasty   **92**

Schlesinger, A. M. War and the American presidency   **327.1**

Ramsey, D. Entreleadership   **658.4**

Sarillo, N. A slice of the pie   **658.02**

Slim, P. Escape from cubicle nation   **658.1**

Wasserman, N. The founder's dilemmas   **658.1**

   See also Business; Capitalism; Small business

ENTREPRENEURSHIP -- UNITED STATES

Casnocha, B. My start-up life   **338.7**

ENTREPRENEURSHIP -- UNITED STATES -- ANECDOTES

Stone, B. Things a little bird told me   **006.7**

ENTREPRENEURSHIP -- UNITED STATES -- BIOGRAPHY

Fox, M. Bend, not break   **004.092**

Entrepreneurship and small business management collection [series]

Barringer, B. Launching a Business   **658.11**

ENTROPY

   See also Thermodynamics

Entwined lives. Segal, N. L.   **155.4**

ENVIRONMENT

Park, C. A dictionary of environment and conservation   **333.7**

ENVIRONMENT -- GOVERNMENT POLICY

See Environmental policy

ENVIRONMENT AND STATE *See* Environmental policy

ENVIRONMENTAL DEGRADATION

Blackwell, A. Visit sunny Chernobyl   **363.73**

Kolbert, E. The sixth extinction   **576.8**

Ladd, B. Autophobia   **303.4**

McKibben, B. Eaarth   **253**

Novacek, M. J. Terra   **576.8**

Safina, C. The view from Lazy Point   **508**

Wilcove, D. S. No way home   **591.56**

Wilson, E. O. The future of life   **333.95**

   See also Environment; Natural disasters

ENVIRONMENTAL DESTRUCTION *See* Environmental degradation

ENVIRONMENTAL DETERIORATION *See* Environmental degradation

ENVIRONMENTAL DISASTERS

Kolbert, E. The sixth extinction   **576.8**

ENVIRONMENTAL ENGINEERING -- UNITED STATES

Humes, E. Garbology   **628.4**

ENVIRONMENTAL ETHICS

   See also Ethics

ENVIRONMENTAL ETHICS -- UNITED STATES -- HISTORY

Souder, W. On a farther shore   **92**

ENVIRONMENTAL HEALTH

Shulman, S. Cooler smarter   **363.7**

Smith, R. Slow death by rubber duck   **615.9**

Smith, R. Toxin toxout   **613**

Sustaining life   **333.95**

Terry, B. Plastic-free   **363.738**

   See also Environmental influence on humans; Public health

ENVIRONMENTAL INFLUENCE ON HUMANS

Ackerman, D. Dawn light   **508.2**

Diamond, J. M. Guns, germs, and steel   **303.4**

Hansen, J. E. Storms of my grandchildren   **363.7**

Louv, R. The nature principle   **128**

Louv, R. Last child in the woods   **155.4**

Lynas, M. Six degrees   **551.6**

McPhee, J. A. The control of nature   **304.2**

   See also Adaptation (Biology); Human ecology; Human geography

ENVIRONMENTAL LAW

   See also Environmental policy; Environmental protection; Law

ENVIRONMENTAL LOBBY *See* Environmental movement

ENVIRONMENTAL MONITORING -- HUDSON RIVER VALLEY (N.Y. AND N.J.)

Busch, A. The incidental steward   **363.7**

ENVIRONMENTAL MOVEMENT

American earth   **333.72**

Friedman, T. L. Hot, flat, and crowded   **363.7**

Gessner, D. My green manifesto   **304.2**

Kostigen, T. M. The green book   **333.72**

Lytle, M. H. The gentle subversive   **92**

McKibben, B. Oil and Honey   **363.7**

Nelson, G. Beyond Earth Day   **333.72**

Pipher, M. The green boat   **303.4**

Potter, W. Green is the new red   **320.5**

   See also Environment; Social movements

ENVIRONMENTAL POLICY

Diamond, J. M. Collapse: how societies choose to fail or succeed   **304.2**

Gore, A. Our choice   **363.7**

Pooley, E. The climate war   **363.7**

Speth, J. G. The bridge at the end of the world   **333.7**

   See also Environment

ENVIRONMENTAL POLICY -- CHINA

Watts, J. When a billion Chinese jump   **363.7**

ENVIRONMENTAL POLICY -- UNITED STATES

Chadwick, D. H. The company we keep   **333.95**

Friedman, T. L. Hot, flat, and crowded   **363.7**

Gore, A. An inconvenient truth   **363.7**

Jones, V. The green-collar economy   **363.7**

Speth, J. G. America the possible   **338.973**

ENVIRONMENTAL POLLUTION *See* Pollution

ENVIRONMENTAL PROTECTION

American earth   **333.72**

Beavan, C. No impact man   **333.72**

Brinkley, D. The quiet world   **333.72**

Busch, A. The incidental steward   **363.7**

Challenger, M. On extinction   **576.8**

Federico, Meg

About

Federico, M. Welcome to the departure lounge 92

The **feed** zone cookbook. Lim, A.   **641.5**

Feed zone portables. Lim, A.   **641.5**

FEEDBACK (PSYCHOLOGY)

See also Psychology of learning

Feel the fear--and do it anyway. Jeffers, S. J. **152.4**

FEELING *See* Perception; Touch

Feeling good. Burns, D. D.   **158**

The **feeling** of what happens. Damasio, A. R. **153**

FEES *See* Salaries, wages, etc.

Feifer, Gregory

The great gamble   **958.1**

Feiffer, Jules

Backing into forward   **92**

Feiffer, Jules

About

Feiffer, J. Backing into forward   **92**

Feige, David

Indefensible   **345**

Feige, David

About

Feige, D. Indefensible   **345**

Feiler, Bruce S.

Abraham   **222**

America's prophet   **973**

Walking the Bible   **915**

Feiling, Tom

Cocaine nation   **362.29**

Feinberg, Andrew

(jt. auth) Clark, M. Franny's   **641.594**

Feinberg, Kenneth R.

What is life worth?   **362.88**

Feingold, Henry L.

A time for searching   **305.8**

Feingold, Russ, 1953-

While America sleeps   **327**

Feinman, Jay M.

Law 101   **340**

Feinstein, Adam

Pablo Neruda   **92**

Feinstein, Elaine

Anna of all the Russias   **92**

Ted Hughes   **821**

(tr) Tsvetaeva, M. I. Selected poems   **891.7**

Feinstein, John

Where nobody knows your name   **796.357**

Feinstein, John

A good walk spoiled   **796.352**

Last dance   **796.323**

Living on the black   **92**

A march to madness   **796.323**

Next man up   **796.332**

Feinstein, Michael

About

Feinstein, M. The Gershwins and me   **782.421**

Feinstein, Michael, 1956-

The Gershwins and me   **782.421**

Feintuch, Burt

(ed) The Encyclopedia of New England   **974**

The **feisty** stitcher. Wasinger, S.   **746**

Felch, Jason

Chasing Aphrodite   **930**

Feldman, Burton

112 Mercer Street   **920**

The Nobel Prize   **001.4**

Feldman, Jay

When the Mississippi ran backwards   **551.2**

Feldman, Noah

Scorpions   **920**

Feldman, Paula R.

(ed) British women poets of the Romantic era **821**

Feldstein, Mark

Poisoning the press   **973.924**

FELINES *See* Cats

Felisbret, Eric

Graffiti New York   **751.7**

Fell, Derek

Encyclopedia of hardy plants   **635.9**

Fellman, Michael

Citizen Sherman   **92**

The making of Robert E. Lee   **973.7**

Fellow citizens.   **352.23**

Fellows, Will

Gay bar   **306.76**

The **fellowship.** Gribbin, J. R.   **509**

Fellowship in a ring. Hollands, N.   **809**

FELONY *See* Crime

Felsenthal, Carol

Clinton in exile   **92**

Felt jewelry. Searle, T.   **746**

Felt, Hali

Soundings   **526**

FEMALE ACTORS *See* Actresses

FEMALE CLIMACTERIC *See* Menopause

FEMALE FRIENDSHIP

Donoghue, E. Inseparable   **809**

Goodman, E. I know just what you mean **158.2**

FEMALE FRIENDSHIP

See also Friendship

FEMALE FRIENDSHIP -- FICTION

Count on me   **177**

FEMALE FRIENDSHIP --FRANCE.

Moorehead, C. A train in winter

The **female** gaze.   **704**

FEMALE IMPERSONATORS

See also Impostors and imposture

FEMALE ROLE *See* Gender role

FEMALE SUPERHERO GRAPHIC NOVELS

See also Female superhero graphic novels;
Graphic novels

A **fighting** chance. Warren, E.   92
Fighting chance. Dudden, F. E.   324.6
Fighting for common ground. Snowe, O. J.   328.73
Fighting the devil in Dixie. Greenhaw, W.   323.1
Fighting the Great War. Neiberg, M.   940.4
Fighting to serve. Nicholson, A.   355
Fighting weight. Ali, K.   92
Figone, Albert J.
   Cheating the spread   796.04
FIGURE DRAWING
   Barnet, W. Will Barnet   741
   Hart, C. Human anatomy made amazingly easy   743.4
   Lester, T. Da Vinci's ghost   741.092
   Robins, C. The art of figure drawing   743
   Watson, L. Life drawing class   743
FIGURE DRAWING
   See also Artistic anatomy; Drawing
FIGURE PAINTING
   See also Artistic anatomy; Painting
The **figured** wheel. Pinsky, R.   811
Figurehead & other poems. Hollander, J.   811
FIGURES OF SPEECH
   See also Rhetoric; Symbolism
The **file**. Garton-Ash, T.   327.12
Filene, Peter G.
   In the arms of others   179.7
FILIBUSTERING
   Arenberg, R. A. Defending the filibuster   328.73
FILIBUSTERS (POLITICAL SCIENCE) -- UNITED STATES
   Arenberg, R. A. Defending the filibuster   328.73
Filipovic, Zlata
   (ed) Stolen voices   920
Filkins, Dexter
   The forever war   956.7
Fillmore, Millard, 1800-1874
       About
   Finkelman, P. Millard Fillmore   92
FILM ADAPTATIONS
   See also Motion pictures
FILM CRITICISM
   Dyer, G. Zona   791.43
   O'Brien, G. Stolen glimpses, captive shadows   791.43
   Rich, B. R. New queer cinema   791.43
   San Filippo, M. The B word   791.4
   See also Criticism
FILM DIRECTORS *See* Motion picture producers and directors
FILM EPICS *See* Epic films
FILM FESTIVALS
   See also Festivals
FILM HISTORIANS
   Schiavi, M. Celluloid activist   92
   Thomson, D. Try to tell the story   92

FILM INDUSTRY (MOTION PICTURES) *See* Motion picture industry
Film noir.   791.43
FILM NOIR
   See also Motion pictures
FILM NOIR -- SOCIAL ASPECTS -- UNITED STATES -- HISTORY -- 20TH CENTURY
   Lingeman, R. The noir forties   973.91
FILM POSTERS
   See also Posters
FILM PRODUCERS *See* Motion picture producers and directors
FILMS *See* Filmstrips; Motion pictures
FILMSTRIPS
   See also Audiovisual materials; Photography
The **filter** bubble. Pariser, E.   025.04
A **final** arc of sky. Culkin, J.   92
The **final** days. Woodward, B.   973.924
Final exam. Chen, P. W.   92
Final exit. Humphry, D.   179.7
Final Jeopardy. Baker, S.   006.3
Final salute. Sheeler, J.   956.7
Finamore, Roy
   Moonen, R. Fish without a doubt   641.6
Finan, Christopher M.
   Alfred E. Smith, the happy warrior   92
FINANCE
   Smith, G. S. Cost control for nonprofits in crisis   025.1
   Weatherall, J. O. The physics of Wall Street 332.63
   Wheelan, C. J. Naked economics   330
   See also Economics
FINANCE -- UNITED STATES
   Guyer, C. S. On the Money Journal   332
   Stiglitz, J. E. The price of inequality   305.5
FINANCE -- UNITED STATES -- HISTORY -- 21ST CENTURY
   Lewis, M. Flash boys   332.6
Finance and investment handbook. Downes, J. 332.6
FINANCE, HOUSEHOLD *See* Household budgets
FINANCE, PERSONAL
   Economides, A. The moneysmart family system   332.024
   Glink, I. R. 50 simple things you can do to improve your personal finances   332.024
   Kobliner, B. Get a financial life   332.024
   Romans, C. How to speak money   332.024
   Schwab-Pomerantz, C. It pays to talk   332.024
   Yeager, J. The cheapskate next door   332.024
FINANCE, PUBLIC *See* Public finance
FINANCE, PUBLIC -- UNITED STATES -- HISTORY
   McCraw, T. K. The founders and finance 330.973
FINANCIAL ACCOUNTING *See* Accounting
FINANCIAL AID TO STUDENTS *See* Student aid

My Paris kitchen   **641.59**

FOOD HABITS -- HISTORY -- 20TH CENTURY
Collingham, L. The taste of war   **940.53**

FOOD HABITS -- RUSSIA (FEDERATION)
Jones, C. C. A year of Russian feasts   **641.59**

FOOD HABITS -- SOVIET UNION
Von Bremzen, A. Mastering the art of Soviet cooking   **641.59**

FOOD HABITS -- UNITED STATES
Obama, M. American grown   **635.09**

FOOD INDUSTRY
Bittman, M. Food matters   **613.2**
Bloom, J. American wasteland   **363.7**
Booth, M. Eating dangerously   **615.9**
Hesterman, O. B. Fair food   **338.1**
Hewitt, B. The town that food saved   **338.1**
Lappé, A. Diet for a hot planet   **641**
McWilliams, J. E. Just food   **394.1**
Schlosser, E. Fast food nation   **394.1**
Spurlock, M. Don't eat this book   **614.5**
Stuart, T. Waste   **363.8**
Wilson, B. Swindled   **363.1**

FOOD INDUSTRY
Nesheim, M. Why calories count   **613.2**

FOOD INDUSTRY -- UNITED STATES
Kurlansky, M. Birdseye   **338.7**
McMillan, T. The American way of eating   **338.4**
Moss, M. Salt, sugar, fat   **613.2**
Pollan, M. Cooked   **641.5**

FOOD INDUSTRY AND TRADE
Bittman, M. Food matters   **613.2**
Cowen, T. An economist gets lunch   **394.1**
Foer, J. S. Eating animals   **641.3**

FOOD INDUSTRY AND TRADE -- UNITED STATES
McMillan, T. The American way of eating   **338.4**
Moss, M. Salt, sugar, fat   **613.2**

FOOD INDUSTRY EXECUTIVES
Brenner, J. G. The emperors of chocolate   **338.7**
Cohen, R. Sweet and low   **920**
D'Antonio, M. Hershey   **92**

FOOD INSPECTION *See* Food adulteration and inspection
The **Food** Lover's Guide to Paris.   **914.4**
Food matters. Bittman, M.   **613.2**
The **food** matters cookbook. Bittman, M.   **641.3**
The **food** of a younger land.   **394.1**

FOOD OF ANIMAL ORIGIN
Masson, J. M. The face on your plate   **641.3**
Rinella, S. Meat eater   **799.29**
    See also Food
The **food** of Morocco.   **641.59**
The **food** of Portugal. Anderson, J.   **641.5**
The **food** of Spain. Roden, C.   **641.5**
The **food** of Vietnam. Nguyen, L.   **641.59**

FOOD PLANTS *See* Edible plants

Food plants of the world. Van Wyk   **581.6**

FOOD POISONING
Booth, M. Eating dangerously   **615.9**
    See also Poisons and poisoning

FOOD PREFERENCES -- ECONOMIC ASPECTS
Cowen, T. An economist gets lunch   **394.1**

FOOD PREPARATION *See* Cooking; Food industry

FOOD RELIEF
Astyk, S. A nation of farmers   **338.1**
    See also Charities; Disaster relief; Public welfare; Unemployed
Food security. Peacock, K. W.   **338.1**

FOOD SECURITY
Ackerman-Leist, P. Rebuilding the foodshed **338.1**

FOOD SECURITY -- HISTORY -- 20TH CENTURY
Collingham, L. The taste of war   **940.53**

FOOD SECURITY -- JUVENILE LITERATURE
Peacock, K. W. Food security   **338.1**

FOOD SERVICE
    See also Food industry; Service industries

FOOD STAMPS
    See also Food relief

FOOD SUPPLY
Astyk, S. A nation of farmers   **338.1**
Bloom, J. American wasteland   **363.7**
Booth, M. Eating dangerously   **615.9**
Diamandis, P. Abundance   **303.48**
Diamond, J. M. Guns, germs, and steel   **303.4**
Dikötter, F. Mao's great famine   **951.05**
Hesterman, O. B. Fair food   **338.1**
Hewitt, B. The town that food saved   **338.1**
Lappé, A. Diet for a hot planet   **641**
Peacock, K. W. Food security   **338.1**

FOOD SUPPLY -- CHINA
Dikötter, F. Mao's great famine   **951.05**

FOOD SUPPLY -- HISTORY -- 20TH CENTURY
Collingham, L. The taste of war   **940.53**

FOOD SUPPLY -- JUVENILE LITERATURE
Peacock, K. W. Food security   **338.1**

FOOD SUPPLY -- UNITED STATES
McMillan, T. The American way of eating   **338.4**
Pollan, M. The omnivore's dilemma   **394.1**

FOOD TRADE *See* Food industry

FOOD WRITERS -- UNITED STATES -- BIOGRAPHY
Von Bremzen, A. Mastering the art of Soviet cooking   **641.59**
Wizenberg, M. Delancey   **647.95**

FOOD WRITING
Consider the fork   **643**
Jacob, D. Will write for food   **808**

FOOD, CANNED *See* Canning and preserving
FOOD, COST OF *See* Cost and standard of living

See also Gifts

FREE PRESS *See* Freedom of the press

FREE SPEECH *See* Freedom of speech

Free speech in its forgotten years. Rabban, D.
M.   **342**

FREE TRADE

  Friedman, T. L. The Lexus and the olive tree   **337**

  Goldstein, N. Globalization and free trade   **382**

    See also Commercial policy; International
trade

FREE UNIVERSITIES

  See also Colleges and universities

FREE VERSE

  Glück, L. Poems 1962-2012   **811**

  See also Poetry

FREE WILL AND DETERMINISM

  Dennett, D. C. Freedom evolves   **153.8**

  May, R. Freedom and destiny   **158**

  See also Philosophy

Free world. Garton Ash, T.   **909.08**

Freeberg, Ernest

  The Age of Edison   **303.48**

FreeDarko presents the macrophenomenal pro basketball almanac.   **796.323**

Freedman, David Noel

  (ed) Eerdmans dictionary of the Bible   **220.3**

Freedman, Eric

  Presidents and Black America   **973.09**

Freedman, Estelle B.

  (ed) The essential feminist reader   **305.4**

Freedman, Lawrence

  Kennedy's wars   **973.922**

Freedman, Samuel G.

  Jew vs. Jew   **296**

FREEDMEN -- UNITED STATES

  Ward, A. The slaves' war   **973.7**

FREEDOM

  Allen, D. Our Declaration   **973.3**

  Fischer, D. H. Liberty and freedom   **323.44**

  Foner, E. The story of American freedom   **323.44**

  Hébrard, J. M. Freedom papers   **305.896**

  Lampo, D. A fundamental freedom   **323.3**

  Purdy, J. A tolerable anarchy   **320**

  See also Democracy; Political science

FREEDOM (PSYCHOLOGY) *See* Autonomy
(Psychology)

Freedom and destiny. May, R.   **158**

Freedom evolves. Dennett, D. C.   **153.8**

Freedom from fear. Kennedy, D. M.   **973.91**

Freedom from fear, and other writings. Aung San
Suu Kyi   **959.1**

Freedom in exile. Bstan-'dzin-rgya-mtsho, D. L.
X.   **92**

FREEDOM MARCHES FOR CIVIL RIGHTS

  See Civil rights demonstrations

Freedom national. Oakes, J.   **973.7**

FREEDOM OF ASSEMBLY

  See also Civil rights; Freedom

FREEDOM OF ASSOCIATION

  See also Civil rights; Freedom

FREEDOM OF CHOICE *See* Free will and determinism

FREEDOM OF CONSCIENCE

  See also Conscience; Freedom; Toleration

FREEDOM OF INFORMATION

  Morozov, E. The net delusion   **303.48**

  See also Civil rights; Intellectual freedom

FREEDOM OF MOVEMENT

  See also Civil rights; Freedom

FREEDOM OF RELIGION

  Berlinerblau, J. How to be secular   **211**

  Nussbaum, M. C. The new religious intolerance   **201**

  Nussbaum, M. C. Liberty of conscience   **342**

  Waldman, S. Founding faith   **342**

  Wexler, J. Holy hullabaloos   **342**

FREEDOM OF RELIGION

  See also Civil rights; Freedom; Toleration

FREEDOM OF RELIGION -- UNITED STATES

  Berlinerblau, J. How to be secular   **211**

  Nussbaum, M. C. Liberty of conscience   **342**

  Waldman, S. Founding faith   **342**

FREEDOM OF SPEECH

  Bawer, B. Surrender   **297**

  Bezanson, R. P. How free can the press be?   **342**

  Burn this book   **814**

  Healy, T. The great dissent   **342.73**

  Mersky, R. M. Landmark Supreme Court cases   **347.73**

  Rabban, D. M. Free speech in its forgotten
years   **342**

  Stone, G. R. Perilous times   **323.44**

  See also Censorship; Civil rights; Freedom;
Intellectual freedom

FREEDOM OF SPEECH -- UNITED STATES

  Healy, T. The great dissent   **342.73**

FREEDOM OF THE PRESS

  Mersky, R. M. Landmark Supreme Court cases   **347.73**

  See also Civil rights; Freedom; Intellectual
freedom; Press

**FREEDOM OF THE PRESS -- HISTORY -- 20TH
CENTURY**

  Rushdie, S. Joseph Anton   **92**

FREEDOM OF THE PRESS AND FAIR TRIAL

  See also Fair trial; Freedom of the press;
Press

FREEDOM OF THE WILL *See* Free will and determinism

FREEDOM OF WORSHIP *See* Freedom of religion

Freedom on my mind.   **305.8**

FRENCH POETRY
   See also French literature; Poetry
FRENCH POETRY -- COLLECTIONS
   French poetry, 1820-1950, with prose transla-
   tions   **841**
   The Random House book of twentieth-century
   French poetry   **841**
French poetry, 1820-1950, with prose transla-
   tions.   **841**
French provincial cooking. David, E.   **641.5**
The **French** Revolution. Lefebvre, G.   **944.04**
French women don't get facelifts. Guiliano, M. **613**
French, Francis
   Falling to Earth   **92**
   In the shadow of the moon   **629.45**
French, Howard W.
   A continent for the taking   **967**
French, Patrick
   India   **954.04**
   The world is what it is   **92**
French, Thomas
   Zoo story   **590.73**
FRESCO PAINTING *See* Mural painting and dec-
   oration
Fresh & fabulous painted furniture.   **745.7**
Fresh water. Pielou, E. C.   **551.48**
FRESHWATER BIOLOGY
   See also Biology
FRESHWATER ECOLOGY
   See also Ecology
FRESHWATER PLANTS
   Speichert, C. G. Encyclopedia of water garden
   plants   **635**
   See also Freshwater biology; Plants
FRESNO (CALIF.) -- PICTORIAL WORKS
   Stamolis, T. Frezno   **779**
Freud. Gay, P.   **92**
Freud and man's soul. Bettelheim, B.   **150.19**
The **Freud** reader.   **150.19**
Freud, Sigmund, 1856-1939
   The basic writings of Sigmund Freud   **150.19**
   The Freud reader   **150.19**
   Interpretation of dreams   **154.6**
      About
   Bettelheim, B. Freud and man's soul   **150.19**
   Bloom, H. The Western canon   **809**
   Flowers, C. Instability rules   **509**
   Gay, P. Freud   **92**
   Gay, P. A Godless Jew   **150.19**
   Thurschwell, P. Sigmund Freud   **150.19**
Freudenburg, William R.
   Blowout in the Gulf   **363.7**
Freund, Richard A.
   Digging through the Bible   **220.9**
Frey, Julia
   Toulouse-Lautrec   **92**

Frezno. Stamolis, T.   **779**
Frida Kahlo. Lozano   **759.9**
Frida: a biography of Frida Kahlo. Herrera, H. **709**
Friday night lights. Bissinger, H. G.   **796.332**
Friday, Nancy
   My mother/my self   **155.6**
Fried twinkies, buckle bunnies & bull riders. Peter,
   J.   **791.8**
Fried, Albert
   F.D.R. and his enemies   **92**
Fried, Stephen
   Appetite for America   **92**
Frieda, Leonie
   The Deadly Sisterhood   **945**
Friedan, Betty, 1921-2006
   The feminine mystique   **305.4**
   The fountain of age   **305.26**
   Life so far   **92**
Friedan, Betty. Feminine mystique
      About
   Coontz, S. A strange stirring   **305.42**
Friedlander, Edward Jay
   Feature writing for newspapers and maga-
   zines   **070.4**
Friedlander, Saul
   Nazi Germany and the Jews   **940.53**
   The years of extermination   **940.53**
Friedman, Amy
   One souffle at a time   **92**
Friedman, Andrew
   Knives at dawn   **641.5**
Friedman, Andrew, 1967-
   Classico e moderno   **641.59**
Friedman, Avi
   The adaptable house   **728**
Friedman, Barry
   The will of the people   **347**
Friedman, David M.
   The immortalists   **610.28**
   A mind of its own   **573.6**
Friedman, Howard S.
   The longevity project   **613.2**
Friedman, Ian C.
   Carey, C. W. American inventors, entrepreneurs &
   business visionaries   **920**
   Latino athletes   **920.003**
   Hamilton, N. A. Presidents   **920.003**
Friedman, Jaclyn
   (ed) Yes means yes!   **306.7**
Friedman, Jeffrey
   Engineering the financial crisis   **330.9**
Friedman, Lawrence Jacob
   Identity's architect   **92**
Friedman, Lawrence Meir
   American law in the 20th century   **349**
Friedman, Leon

Fleming, T. J. Washington's secret war   973.3

Flexner, J. T. George Washington and the new nation, 1783-1793   92

Flexner, J. T. George Washington: anguish and farewell 1793-1799   92

Flexner, J. T. George Washington: the forge of experience, 1732-1775   92

Flood, C. B. Grant and Sherman   92

Flood, C. B. Grant's final victory   92

Fowler, W. M. American crisis   973.3

Frank, R. B. MacArthur   92

Franks, T. American soldier   973.931

Freeman, D. S. Lee   973.7

Friedman, D. M. The immortalists   610.28

Gaines, J. R. For liberty and glory   92

Gates, H. L. Thirteen ways of looking at a black man   920.71

Geary, R. The Lindbergh child   364.1

Glines, C. V. I could never be so lucky again   92

Goldsworthy, A. K. Antony and Cleopatra   92

Grant, U. S. Memoirs and selected letters   973.8

Greenberg, S. B. Dispatches from the war room   324.7

Groom, W. Kearny's march   979

Groom, W. Patriotic fire   973.5

Groom, W. Vicksburg, 1863   973.7

Halberstam, D. The best and the brightest 973.922

Hanson, V. D. The soul of battle   355

Hefez, N. Ariel Sharon   92

Hibbert, C. Wellington   92

Hirshson, S. P. General Patton: a soldier's life 355

Hofstadter, R. The American political tradition, and the men who made it   973

Johnson, P. George Washington: the Founding Father   92

Jordan, J. W. Brothers, rivals, victors   940.54

Keneally, T. American scoundrel: the life of the notorious Civil War General Dan Sickles   92

Kennett, L. B. Sherman   355

Kessner, T. The flight of the century   92

Kissinger, H. Diplomacy   327.2

Kluger, R. The bitter waters of Medicine Creek   979.7

Korda, M. Ike   92

Korda, M. Ulysses S. Grant: the unlikely hero 92

Langguth, A. J. Driven West   973.5

Lemann, N. Redemption: the last battle of the Civil War   975

Lindbergh, C. The spirit of St. Louis   629.13

Lindbergh, R. Under a wing   92

Linklater, A. An artist in treason   92

Lockhart, P. D. The whites of their eyes   973.3

McPherson, J. M. Drawn with the sword   973.7

Meacham, J. American lion   92

Moore, H. G. We are soldiers still   959.704

Morris, R. Fraud of the century   324.9

Nelson, C. The first heroes   940.54

Nolan, A. T. Lee considered   973.7

Norris, R. S. Racing for the bomb: General Leslie R. Groves, the Manhattan Project's indispensable man   92

O'Connell, R. L. The ghosts of Cannae   937

Pakula, H. The last empress   92

Palmer, J. The bloody white baron   92

Parssinen, T. M. The Oster conspiracy of 1938   943.086

Perry, J. M. Touched with fire   973.7

Perry, M. The most dangerous man in America 92

Philbrick, N. The last stand   973.8

Powell, C. L. My American journey   92

Randall, W. S. George Washington   973.4

Remini, R. V. Andrew Jackson   92

Reynolds, D. S. Waking giant   973.5

Rhodes, R. Dark sun   623.4

Rice, A. The teeth may smile but the heart does not forget   967.6

Roberts, A. Masters and commanders   940.54

Sandoz, M. The Battle of the Little Bighorn 973.8

Schama, S. Dead certainties   974.4

Schwartz, R. A. Encyclopedia of the Persian Gulf War   956.704

Sears, S. W. Chancellorsville   973.7

Sears, S. W. George B. McClellan   92

Sheehan, N. A fiery peace in a cold war   92

Showalter, D. E. Patton and Rommel   92

Smith, J. E. Grant   973.8

Spencer, C. E. M. S. Prince Rupert   92

Steavenson, W. The weight of a mustard seed 92

Strachey, L. Elizabeth and Essex   92

Tacitus, C. Complete works of Tacitus   878

Taylor, J. The generalissimo   92

Thomas, E. M. Robert E. Lee   973.7

Thomas, E. Ike's bluff   973.921

Tuchman, B. W. Stilwell and the American experience in China, 1911-45   327

Unger, H. G. The last founding father   92

Utley, R. M. Custer: cavalier in buckskin   973.8

Vidal, G. Inventing a nation: Washington, Adams, Jefferson   973.4

Von Tunzelmann, A. Red heat   972.9

Wallace, A. F. C. The long bitter trail   323.1

Warner, E. J. Generals in blue   920

Warner, E. J. Generals in gray   920

Washington, G. George Washington's diaries 973.4

Weintraub, S. 15 stars   920

Wert, J. D. Cavalryman of the lost cause   92

Wert, J. D. Custer   973.8

Wicker, T. Dwight D. Eisenhower   973.921

Wiencek, H. An imperfect god   973.4

Wilentz, S. Andrew Jackson   92

Williams, C. The last great Frenchman   944

Wilson, E. Patriotic gore   810

Woodward, B. The commanders   **973.928**
Woodworth, S. E. Sherman   **92**
    See also Military personnel
GENERALS -- FRANCE -- BIOGRAPHY
The Black Count   **944.04092**
GENERALS -- ISRAEL -- BIOGRAPHY
Bar-On, M. Moshe Dayan   **956.940**
GENERALS -- UNITED STATES -- BIOGRA-PHY
Brands, H. W. The man who saved the union **355.009**
Kennett, L. B. Sherman   **355**
McMurtry, L. Custer   **973.8**
Perry, M. The most dangerous man in America **92**
Smith, J. E. Grant   **973.8**
Wheelan, J. Terrible swift sword   **355.009**
GENERALS -- UNITED STATES -- HISTORY -- 20TH CENTURY
Ricks, T. E. The generals   **355.009**
Generals in blue. Warner, E. J.   **920**
Generals in gray. Warner, E. J.   **920**
The **generals'** war. Gordon, M. R.   **956.7**
Generation kill. Wright, E.   **956.7**
Generations of captivity. Berlin, I.   **326**
GENERATIVE ORGANS *See* Reproductive system
GENERIC DRUGS
    See also Drugs; Generic products
GENERIC PRODUCTS
    See also Commercial products; Manufactures
GENES *See* Heredity
GENES, BRCA1
Wheelwright, J. The wandering gene and the Indian princess   **616.99**
Genes, girls, and Gamow. Watson, J. D.   **92**
The **Genesis** of justice. Dershowitz, A. M.   **222**
Genesis: a living conversation. Moyers, B.   **222**
Genesis: the story of Apollo 8. Zimmerman, R.   **629.45**
Genet, Jean
The blacks: a clown show   **842**
The maids [and] Deathwatch   **842**
GENETIC CODE
The annotated and illustrated double helix   **572.8**
Lewontin, R. C. The triple helix   **572.8**
    See also Molecular biology
GENETIC COUNSELING
    See also Medical genetics; Prenatal diagnosis
GENETIC ENGINEERING
Adamchak, R. W. Tomorrow's table   **664**
Fox, M. W. Beyond evolution   **174**
Green, R. M. Babies by design   **176**
Hubbell, S. Shrinking the cat   **660.6**
Rutherford, A. Creation   **576.8**
Stock, G. Redesigning humans   **176**
    See also Engineering; Genetic recombination
GENETIC FINGERPRINTING *See* DNA finger-

printing
GENETIC MAPPING *See* Gene mapping
GENETIC PREDISPOSITION TO DISEASE
Wheelwright, J. The wandering gene and the Indian princess   **616.99**
GENETIC RECOMBINATION
    See also Chromosomes
Genetic rounds. Marion, R.   **92**
GENETIC SCREENING
Collins, F. S. The language of life   **616**
GENETIC SURGERY *See* Genetic engineering
Genetically engineered food. Cummins, R.   **363.1**
Genetically modified foods.   **363.1**
GENETICALLY MODIFIED FOODS
Adamchak, R. W. Tomorrow's table   **664**
Genetically modified foods   **363.1**
Pringle, P. Food, inc   **363.1**
GENETICISTS
Flowers, C. Instability rules   **509**
Harman, O. S. The price of altruism   **92**
Henig, R. M. The monk in the garden: how Gregor Mendel and his pea plants solved the mystery of inheritance   **576.5**
Malone, J. W. It doesn't take a rocket scientist **920**
GENETICS
Beckwith, J. R. Making genes, making waves **576.5**
Dawkins, R. River out of Eden   **575**
Dawkins, R. The selfish gene   **576**
Endersby, J. A guinea pig's history of biology **576.5**
Epstein, D. The sports gene   **613.7**
Francis, R. C. Epigenetics   **572.8**
Harman, O. S. The price of altruism   **92**
Henderson, M. 100 most important science ideas   **500**
Kean, S. The violinist's thumb   **572.8**
Keller, E. F. The century of the gene   **576.5**
Kurzweil, R. The singularity is near   **153.9**
Marks, J. What it means to be 98[percent] chimpanzee   **599.93**
Moalem, S. Survival of the sickest   **616**
Raine, A. The anatomy of violence   **616.85**
Ridley, M. The agile gene   **155.7**
Ridley, M. Francis Crick   **92**
Ridley, M. Genome   **599.93**
Sagan, C. The dragons of Eden   **153**
Stock, G. Redesigning humans   **176**
Sykes, B. Adam's curse   **599.93**
Sykes, B. DNA USA   **559.9**
Sykes, B. The seven daughters of Eve   **599.93**
Wheelwright, J. The wandering gene and the Indian princess   **616.99**
    See also Biology; Embryology; Life (Biology); Mendel's law; Reproduction
Genetics & inherited conditions. Knight, J. A. **576.5**
GENETICS -- ENCYCLOPEDIAS
Knight, J. A. Genetics & inherited conditions **576.5**

Tillyard, S. K. A royal affair **920**

GEORGE INN (ENFIELD, LONDON, ENGLAND) -- HISTORY

Brown, P. Shakespeare's Pub **647.954**

George Mason, forgotten founder. Broadwater, J. **92**

George Sand. Harlan, E. **92**

George Sand. Jack, B. E. **843**

George V, King of Great Britain, 1865-1936
About

Carter, M. George, Nicholas, and Wilhelm **940.3**

Clay, C. King, Kaiser, Tsar **920**

George Washington. Randall, W. S. **973.4**

George Washington and the new nation, 1783-1793. Flexner, J. T. **92**

George Washington's diaries. Washington, G. **973.4**

George Washington: anguish and farewell 1793-1799. Flexner, J. T. **92**

George Washington: the forge of experience, 1732-1775. Flexner, J. T. **92**

George Washington: the Founding Father. Johnson, P. **92**

George, being George. **92**

George, Henry, 1839-1897
About

Heilbroner, R. L. The worldly philosophers **330.1**

George, John H.

Boller, P. F. They never said it **808.88**

George, Nicholas, and Wilhelm. Carter, M. **940.3**

George, Rose

The big necessity **363.7**

George-Warren, Holly

Public cowboy no. 1 **92**

Lang, M. The road to Woodstock **781.66**

Georges-Picot, Charles François, b. 1870
About

Barr, J. A line in the sand **956**

GEORGIA

Brown, A. Haunted Georgia **133.1**

GEORGIA -- COMMERCE -- WEST INDIES, BRITISH -- HISTORY -- 18TH CENTURY

Pressly, P. M. On the rim of the Caribbean **975.8**

GEORGIA -- RURAL CONDITIONS

Sherrod, S. The courage to hope **975.8**

GEORGIA -- SOCIAL LIFE AND CUSTOMS

Carter, J. An hour before daylight **973.926**

Georgia O'Keeffe: a life. Robinson, R. **709**

The Georgian star. Lemonick, M. D. **92**

Georgiana, Duchess of Devonshire. Foreman, A. **941.07**

The Georgics of Virgil. Virgil **872**

GEOSCIENCE *See* Earth sciences; Geology

GEOSPATIAL DATA

Bray, H. You are here **910.285**

GEOTHERMAL RESOURCES

See also Geochemistry; Ocean energy resources; Renewable energy resources

Geraghty, Tony

Soldiers of fortune **355.3**

Gerald Durrell. Botting, D. **92**

Gerardi, Juan, 1922-1998
About

Goldman, F. The art of political murder **972.81**

Gerber, Michael E.

The most successful small business in the world **658**

Gerding, Stephanie K.

Winning grants **025.1**

Gerdts, William H.

American impressionism **759.13**

Gerges, Fawaz

Obama and the Middle East **327**

Gerges, Fawaz A.

(jt. auth) Gerges, F. Obama and the Middle East **327**

Gerhartsreiter, Christian, 1961-
About

Kirn, W. Blood will out **364.152**

GERM THEORY *See* Life -- Origin

GERM THEORY OF DISEASE

Biddle, W. A field guide to germs **616**

See also Communicable diseases

GERM WARFARE *See* Biological warfare

German colonialism. Conrad, S. **325**

GERMAN ESPIONAGE

Vaughan, H. Sleeping with the enemy **92**

The German genius. Watson, P. **943**

GERMAN LANGUAGE

See also Language and languages

GERMAN LANGUAGE -- DICTIONARIES

Random House Webster's German-English, English-German dictionary **433**

German library [series]

Lessing, G. E. Nathan the Wise, Minna von Barnhelm, and other plays and writings **832**

GERMAN LITERATURE

Encyclopedia of German literature **830**

See also Literature

GERMAN LITERATURE -- BIO-BIBLIOGRAPHY

Encyclopedia of German literature **830**

GERMAN LITERATURE -- ENCYCLOPEDIAS

Encyclopedia of German literature **830**

GERMAN LITERATURE -- HISTORY AND CRITICISM

Sebald, W. G. On the natural history of destruction **833**

GERMAN OCCUPATION OF FRANCE, 1940-1945 *See* France -- History -- 1940-1945, German occupation

GERMAN POETRY -- COLLECTIONS

Across the land and the water **831**

German voices. Tubach, F. C. **943.086**

German, Bill

The history of jazz 781.65
Work songs 782.42
Giovanni, Nikki, 1943-
Bicycles 811
Blues 811
Chasing Utopia 811
The collected poetry of Nikki Giovanni, 1968-1998 811
Quilting the black-eyed pea 811
About
Black women writers (1950-1980) 810
GIRAFFE
Giraffe reflections 599.638
Giraffe reflections. 599.638
Girardet, Edward
Killing the cranes 958.4
Giridharadas, Anand
India calling 954.05
The **girl** from foreign. Shepard, S. 92
The **girl** in the green sweater. Chiger, K. 92
Girl land. Flanagan, C. 305.235
Girl power. Meltzer, M. 781.64
Girl sleuth. Rehak, M. 813
The **Girl** Who Fell to Earth. Al-Maria, S. 92
The **girl's** guide to absolutely everything. Kirsch, M. 646.7
The **girl's** guide to homelessness. Karp, B. 92
GIRLS
Deak, J. Girls will be girls 649
Flanagan, C. Girl land 305.235
Simmons, R. Odd girl out 305.23
See also Children
GIRLS -- EDUCATION
Lamb, C. I am Malala 92
See also Education
GIRLS -- EMPLOYMENT *See* Women -- Employment; Youth -- Employment
GIRLS -- HEALTH AND HYGIENE
Livingston, P. But dad! 306.874
GIRLS -- PSYCHOLOGY
Orenstein, P. Cinderella ate my daughter 305.23
Simmons, R. Odd girl out 305.23
GIRLS -- SEXUAL BEHAVIOR
Durham, M. G. The Lolita effect 302.23
Wolf, N. Promiscuities 306.7
Girls like us. Weller, S. 920
The **girls** of atomic city. Kiernan, D. 976.8
Girls of tender age. Tirone Smith 92
Girls to the front. Marcus, S. 781.66
The **girls** who went away. Fessler, A. 362.82
Girls will be girls. Deak, J. 649
Giroux, Robert
(ed) Bishop, E. The collected prose 818
Bishop, E. Poems, prose, and letters 818
Girzone, Joseph F.
Never alone 248.4

A portrait of Jesus 232.9
GIS *See* Soldiers -- United States
Gitler, Ira
Feather, L. The biographical encyclopedia of jazz 781.65
Gitlin, Todd
The sixties 973.922
Gitlitz, David M.
Davidson, L. K. Pilgrimage: from the Ganges to Graceland: an encyclopedia 203
Giuliani, Rudolph W.
Leadership 658.4
About
Kirtzman, A. Rudy Giuliani 92
Siegel, F. F. The prince of the city 92
Giunta, Salvatore A. (Salvatore Augustine), 1985-
About
Giunta, S. A. Living with honor 958.104
Give and take. Grant, A. 158.2
Give my poor heart ease. Ferris, W. 781.643
Given. Berry, W. 811
Givens, Terryl
By the hand of Mormon 289.3
Giving voice to values. Gentile, M. C. 174
Gizzi, Peter
(ed) Spicer, J. My vocabulary did this to me 811
GLACIERS
Heacox, K. John Muir and the ice that started a fire 92
Pollack, H. N. A world without ice 551.3
See also Geology; Ice; Physical geography
GLACIERS -- ALASKA
Heacox, K. John Muir and the ice that started a fire 92
GLADIATORS
Amidon, S. Something like the gods 306.4
GLADNESS *See* Happiness
Gladstone. Jenkins, R. 941.081
Gladstone, Brooke
The influencing machine 302.23
Gladstone, Brooke
About
Gladstone, B. The influencing machine 302.23
Gladstone, W. E. (William Ewart), 1809-1898
About
Jenkins, R. Gladstone 941.081
Gladwell, Malcolm
Gladwell, M. The tipping point 302
Blink: the power of thinking without thinking 153.4
Outliers 302
What the dog saw and other adventures 814
Gladwell, Malcolm, 1963-
David and Goliath 155.2
The tipping point 302
Glancey, Jonathan
The story of architecture 720.9

Gonzalez Echevarria, Roberto
The Cambridge history of Latin American literature   **860**

Gonzalez, Juan, 1969-
News for all the people   **302.23**

Gonzo. Wenner, J. S.   **92**

Gooch, Brad
Flannery   **92**

GOOD AND EVIL
Bloom, H. The Lucifer principle   **128**
Kushner, H. S. How good do we have to be? **296.7**
Made for goodness   **170**
Nadler, S. M. The best of all possible worlds **190**
Watson, L. Dark nature   **111**
Zimbardo, P. The Lucifer effect   **155.9**
     See also Ethics; Philosophy; Theology

Good boss, bad boss. Sutton, R. I.   **658.4**

GOOD FRIDAY
     See also Christian holidays; Holy Week; Lent

The **good** girls revolt. Povich, L.   **331.4**

The **good** good pig. Montgomery, S.   **636.4**

Good housekeeping (Periodical)
The Good Housekeeping cookbook   **641.5**

The **Good** Housekeeping cookbook. Good housekeeping (Periodical)   **641.5**

Good housekeeping drop 5 lbs. Jones, H. K. **613.2**

Good Housekeeping Institute (New York, N.Y.)
Jones, H. K. Good housekeeping drop 5 lbs **613.2**

The **Good** Housekeeping step-by-step cookbook.   **641.4**

A **good** man. Shriver, M. K.   **973.924**

Good morning blues: the autobiography of Count Basie. Basie, C.   **92**

The **good** neighbor cookbook. Quessenberry, S.   **641.5**

The **good** nurse. Graeber, C.   **364.152**

Good poems.   **811**

Good prose. Kidder, T.   **808.02**

The **good** rat. Breslin, J.   **364.1**

The **good** soldiers. Finkel, D.   **956.7**

The **Good** Spy. Bird, K.   **92**

Good to great. Collins, J. C.   **658**

A **good** walk spoiled. Feinstein, J.   **796.352**

The **good** war.   **940.54**

The **good,** the bad, and me. Wallach, E.   **92**

Goodall, Jane, 1934-
Beyond innocence   **92**
In the shadow of man   **599.8**
Reason for hope   **92**
The ten trusts   **333.95**
Through a window   **599.8**
     About
Goodall, J. Seeds of Hope   **580**
Peterson, D. Jane Goodall: the woman who redefined man   **92**

Goodall, Tiffany

The ultimate student cookbook   **641.5**

Goodbody, Mary
Barrenechea, T. The Basque table   **641.59**
Lobel, S. The meat bible   **641.6**

Goodbye, darkness. Manchester, W.   **940.54**

Goodbye, Descartes. Devlin, K. J.   **128**

Goodchild, Peter
Edward Teller, the real Dr Strangelove   **92**

Goode, J. J.
Lang, A. P. Serious barbecue   **641.5**
(jt. auth) Santibañez, R. Truly Mexican   **641.59**

Goodell, Jeff
How to cool the planet   **551.6**

Goodheart, Adam
1861   **973.7**

Goodman, Ellen
I know just what you mean   **158.2**

Goodman, Jordan
The devil and Mr. Casement   **305.8**

Goodman, Jordan Elliot
Downes, J. Finance and investment handbook **332.6**

Goodman, Linda
Linda Goodman's star signs   **130**
Linda Goodman's sun signs   **133.5**

Goodman, Martin
Rome and Jerusalem   **933**

Goodman, Matthew
The Sun and the moon   **974.7**

Goodrich, Frances
The diary of Anne Frank   **812**

Goodrich, Norma Lorre
King Arthur   **942.01**

Goodstein, David L.
Feynman's lost lecture   **521**
Out of gas   **333.8**

Goodstein, Judith R.
Goodstein, D. L. Feynman's lost lecture   **521**

Goodwin, Doris Kearns, 1943-
The Bully Pulpit   **973.91**
No ordinary time   **92**
Team of rivals   **92**
     About
Goodwin, D. K. Wait till next year   **796.357**

Goodwin, Jason
Lords of the horizons   **956.1**

Goodwin, Nancy
Montrose   **712**

The **Goodyear** story. Korman, R.   **678**

GOODYEAR TIRE & RUBBER COMPANY
Korman, R. The Goodyear story   **678**
Slack, C. Noble obsession   **678**

Goodyear, Charles, 1800-1860
     About
Korman, R. The Goodyear story   **678**
Slack, C. Noble obsession   **678**

Google hacks. Dornfest, R.   **025.04**

Schama, C. Wild romance   92
Sheridan, R. B. The school for scandal and other
   plays   822
Taylor, D. J. Bright young people   305.24
Tomalin, C. Samuel Pepys   941.06
Vickery, A. Behind closed doors   306.8
Victorian house Inside the Victorian home   306

GREAT BRITAIN -- SPECIAL OPERATIONS
   EXECUTIVE
Helm, S. A life in secrets   92

GREAT BRITAIN -- WAR CABINET
Roberts, A. Masters and commanders   940.54

GREAT BRITAIN. ARMY -- BIOGRAPHY
Anderson, S. Lawrence in Arabia   940.4

GREAT BRITAIN. GOVERNMENT COMMU-
   NICATIONS HEADQUARTERS -- HISTORY
McKay, S. The secret lives of codebreakers 940.54

GREAT BRITAIN. ROYAL NAVY. OFFICERS --
   BIOGRAPHY
Taylor, S. Commander   359.009

Great Britain: a reference guide from the Renais-
   sance to the present. Tompson, R. S.   941
Great Catherine. Erickson, C.   947
The **great** Chinese revolution: 1800-1985. Fair-
   bank, J. K.   951
Great Christian thinkers. Kung, H.   230
The **great** circle. Philip, N.   970.004
Great cookies. Walter, C.   641.8
The **great** crash, 1929. Galbraith, J. K.   338.5
The **great** deluge. Brinkley, D.   976.3

GREAT DEPRESSION, 1929-1939
Dickstein, M. Dancing in the dark   973.91
Egan, T. The worst hard time   978
The forgotten man   973.91
Galbraith, J. K. The great crash, 1929   338.5
Golay, M. America 1933   973.917
Gup, T. A secret gift   977.1
Snyder, J. Hill of Beans   92
Terkel, S. Hard times   973.91
   See also Depressions; Economic conditions

GREAT DEPRESSION, 1929-1939 -- GRAPHIC
   NOVELS
The forgotten man   973.91

Great discoveries [series]
Goldstein, R. Incompleteness   92
Johnson, G. Miss Leavitt's stars   92
Krauss, L. M. Quantum man   92
Leavitt, D. The man who knew too much   92
Lemonick, M. D. The Georgian star   92
Nuland, S. B. The doctors' plague   92
Quammen, D. The reluctant Mr. Darwin   92
Reeves, R. A force of nature   92
Vollmann, W. T. Uncentering the Earth   92
The **great** disruption. Gilding, P.   304.2
The **great** dissent. Healy, T.   342.73
The **great** divergence.   339.2

The **great** divide. Watson, P.   909
The **great** divorce. Woo, I.   92
The **great** emergence. Tickle, P.   270
The **great** enigma.   839.7
The **great** equations. Crease, R. P.   509
The **great** escape. Marton, K.   920
Great events from history, The 17th century, 1601-
   1700.   909
Great events from history, The 18th century, 1701-
   1800.   909.7
Great events from history, The 19th century, 1801-
   1900.   909.81
Great events from history, The ancient world, prehis-
   tory-476 C.E.   930
Great events from history, The Middle Ages, 477-
   1453.   909.07
Great events from history, The Renaissance & early
   modern era, 1454-1600.   909
Great events from history: The 20th century, 1901-
   1940.   909.82
Great events from history: The 20th century, 1941-
   1970.   909.82
Great events from history: The 20th century, 1971-
   2000.   909.82
Great expectations. Neifert, M. R.   649
The **great** father. Prucha, F. P.   323.1
The **great** gamble. Feifer, G.   958.1

Great generals series
Frank, R. B. MacArthur   92
Remini, R. V. Andrew Jackson   92
Woodworth, S. E. Sherman   92
The **great** hurricane-1938. Burns, C.   974.7
A **great** idea at the time. Beam, A.   973.91
The **great** influenza. Barry, J. M.   614.5

GREAT LAKES
Dennis, J. The living Great Lakes   977
The **great** lakes of Africa. Chretien   967.6
The **Great** Law and the Longhouse. Fenton, W.
   N.   970.004
Great lives from history.   920.009

Great lives from history
Great lives from history, The 18th century, 1701-
   1800   920.003
Great lives from history, The 17th century, 1601-
   1700.   920.003
Great lives from history, The 18th century, 1701-
   1800. Great lives from history   920.003
Great lives from history, The 19th century, 1801-
   1900.   920.003
Great lives from history, The ancient world, prehis-
   tory-476 C.E.   920.003
Great lives from history, the Middle Ages, 477-
   1453.   920.003
Great lives from history, the Renaissance & early
   modern era, 1454-1600.   920.003
Great lives from history: Notorious lives. 920.003

GUIDANCE *See* Counseling

GUIDANCE, VOCATIONAL *See* Vocational guidance

Guidara, Will, 1980-
(jt. auth) Humm, D. I love New York   **641.59**

A **guide** book of United States coins. Yeoman, R. S.   **737.4**

GUIDE DOGS
> *See also* Animals and people with disabilities; Working dogs

A **guide** to amphibians and reptiles.   **597.9**

Guide to Congress. Congressional Quarterly, I. **328**

The **guide** to good health for teens & adults with Down syndrome. Chicoine, B.   **618.92**

Guide to machine quilting. Gaudynski, D.   **746.46**

Guide to reference books.   **011**

Guide to reference materials for school library media centers. Safford, B. R.   **011.6**

Guide to summer camps and summer schools 2008/2009.   **796.54**

A **guide** to the ancient world. Grant, M.   **913**

Guide to the presidency and the executive branch.   **352.23**

Guide to U.S. elections. Congressional Quarterly, I.   **324.6**

GUIDED MISSILES
> *See also* Bombs; Projectiles; Rocketry; Rockets (Aeronautics)

GUIDES (PERSONS)
Clark, E. E. Sacagawea of the Lewis and Clark expedition   **92**
Hari, D. The translator   **92**
Slaughter, T. P. Exploring Lewis and Clark   **978**

Guiding your child through grief. Emswiler, M. A.   **155.9**

Guiley, Rosemary Ellen
The encyclopedia of demons and demonology **133.4**
The encyclopedia of ghosts and spirits   **133.1**
The encyclopedia of saints   **282**
The encyclopedia of vampires & werewolves   **398**
The encyclopedia of witches, witchcraft, and Wicca   **133.4**

Guiliano, Mireille
French women don't get facelifts   **613**

GUILLAIN-BARRÉ SYNDROME
Manguso, S. The two kinds of decay   **362**

Guillemin, Jeanne
Biological weapons   **358**

Guillen, Michael
Five equations that changed the world   **530.1**

Guillermoprieto, Alma
Dancing with Cuba   **972.91**

Guilloux, Louis, 1899-1980
> *About*

Kaplan, A. Y. The interpreter   **940.54**

GUILT

Kushner, H. S. How good do we have to be? **296.7**
> *See also* Conscience; Emotions; Ethics; Good and evil; Sin

A **guinea** pig's history of biology. Endersby, J. **576.5**

Guinier, Lani
The miner's canary   **323.1**

Guinn, Jeff
Go down together   **364.1**
Manson   **364.152**

GUITAR -- METHODS -- SELF INSTRUCTION
Chappell, J. Guitar All-in-one for Dummies **787.87**

Guitar All-in-one for Dummies. Chappell, J. **787.87**

GUITARISTS
The Beatles anthology   **782.421**
Brightman, C. Sweet chaos   **920**
Clapton, E. Clapton   **92**
Cross, C. R. Heavier than heaven: a biography of Kurt Cobain   **92**
Cross, C. R. Room full of mirrors   **92**
Dance, S. The world of Count Basie   **920**
Dregni, M. Django: the life and music of a Gypsy legend   **92**
Gordon, R. Can't be satisfied: the life and times of Muddy Waters   **782.421**
Govenar, A. B. Lightnin' Hopkins   **92**
Gray, M. Hand me my travelin' shoes   **92**
Jackson, B. Garcia   **92**
King, B. B. Blues all around me   **781.643**
Kruth, J. To live's to fly   **92**
McDermott, J. Ultimate Hendrix   **781.66**
McDonough, J. Shakey: Neil Young's biography   **782.421**
Murray, C. S. Crosstown traffic: Jimi Hendrix and the post-war rock'n'roll revolution   **787.87**
Richards, K. Life   **92**
Schumacher, M. Crossroads   **92**
Spitz, B. The Beatles: the biography   **920**
Wald, E. Escaping the delta   **92**
Wareham, D. Black postcards   **92**
Wolfe, C. K. The life and legend of Leadbelly   **92**
Zappa, F. The real Frank Zappa book   **92**

GUITARS
Chapman, R. The new complete guitarist   **787.87**
Chappell, J. Guitar All-in-one for Dummies **787.87**

Guiteau, Charles Julius, 1841-1882
> *About*

Millard, C. The destiny of the republic   **973.8**

GUJARATI AMERICANS
Hajratwala, M. Leaving India   **92**

Gulag. Applebaum, A.   **365**

Gulag. Kizny, T.   **365**

The **Gulag** Archipelago, 1918-1956 v1. Solzhenitsyn, A.   **365**

The **Gulag** Archipelago, 1918-1956 v2. Solzhenitsyn, A.   **365**

The **Gulag** Archipelago, 1918-1956 v3. Solzhenit-

Titian   **759.5**

Halevi, Yossi Klein

Like dreamers   **356**

Haley family

About

Haley, A. Roots   **920**

Haley, Alex

Roots   **920**

Malcolm X The autobiography of Malcolm X **92**

Half the sky. Kristof, N. D.   **362.83**

The **half-life** of facts. Arbesman, S.   **501**

Halfway to Hollywood. Palin, M.   **92**

HALIFAX (N.S.)

MacDonald, L. M. Curse of the Narrows   **971**

Halifax, Edward Frederick Lindley Wood, 1st Earl of, 1881-1959

About

Lukacs, J. Five days in London, May 1940 **940.53**

Hall, Donald

The back chamber   **811**

White apples and the taste of stone   **811**

Hall, James, III

About

Herrington, S. A. Traitors among us   **327.12**

Hall, Jean-Blaise

Spieler, M. Paris   **641.5**

Hall, Kermit

(ed) The Oxford companion to American law **349**

(ed) The Oxford companion to the Supreme Court of the United States   **347**

(ed) The Oxford guide to United States Supreme Court decisions   **342**

Hall, Meredith

Without a map   **92**

Hall, Stephen S.

Wisdom   **179**

Hall, Timothy L.

American religious leaders   **200**

(ed) U.S. laws, acts, and treaties   **348**

Hall, Trevor

(ed) Coles, R. Handing one another along **820**

Hallelujah junction. Adams, J.   **92**

HALLEY'S COMET

Sagan, C. Comet   **523.6**

    See also Comets

HALLIBURTON CO. -- HISTORY

Chatterjee, P. Halliburton's army   **956.7**

Halliburton's army. Chatterjee, P.   **956.7**

Halliday, Jon

Chang, J. Mao: the unknown story   **92**

Halligan, Karen

Doc Halligan's What every pet owner should know   **636**

Hallinan, Joseph T.

Why we make mistakes   **153**

Hallman, J. C.

The chess artist   **794.1**

(ed) The story about the story   **809**

Halloran, Andrew R.

The song of the ape   **599.885**

Halloran, Andrew R.

About

Halloran, A. R. The song of the ape   **599.885**

Hallowed ground. McPherson, J. M.   **973.7**

HALLOWEEN

Morton, L. Trick or Treat   **394.264**

    See also Holidays

Hallowell, Edward M.

Connect   **158.2**

Driven to Distraction   **616.85**

Shine   **658.3**

HALLUCINATIONS AND ILLUSIONS

Hustvedt, S. Living, thinking, looking   **814**

    See also Abnormal psychology; Parapsychology; Subconsciousness; Visions

HALLUCINOGENS

Davis, W. One river   **581.6**

Lattin, D. The Harvard Psychedelic Club   **920**

    See also Drugs; Psychotropic drugs; Stimulants

Halperin, Daniel

Tinderbox   **614.5**

Halperin, Mark

Double Down   **324.973**

Halpern, Jake

Braving home   **363**

Halpern, Paul

Edge of the universe   **523.1**

Halsey, William Frederick, 1882-1959

About

Borneman, W. R. The admirals   **920**

Halsted, Deborah D.

Disaster planning   **025.8**

Halsted, William Stewart, 1852-1922

About

Imber, G. Genius on the edge   **92**

Halverson, Anders

An entirely synthetic fish   **639.3**

Ham, Paul

Hiroshima Nagasaki   **940.54**

HAMAS

Remnick, D. Reporting   **814**

Hamberger, Lars

Nilsson, L. A child is born   **612.6**

Hamblin, Robert W.

Fargnoli, A. N. Critical companion to William Faulkner   **813**

Hamblyn, Richard

The invention of clouds   **551.57**

Hamer, Dean H.

Living with our genes   **155.2**

Hamer, Frank

Stevenson, N. J. Fashion   **391.009**
    See also Clothing and dress; Costume

Hatshepsut, Queen of Egypt
    About
Hatshepsut: from queen to Pharaoh   **932**
Mertz, B. Temples, tombs, & hieroglyphs   **932**
Ryan, D. P. Beneath the sands of Egypt   **92**
Hatshepsut: from queen to Pharaoh.   **932**
Hattie McDaniel. Watts, J.   **92**
Hattie: the life of Hattie McDaniel. Jackson, C.   **92**

Hattis, Shana Hertz
(ed) The United States government internet directory   **320**

Hatzfeld, Jean
The antelope's strategy   **967.571**
Machete season   **967.571**

Haubner, Shozan Jack
Zen confidential   **92**

Hauerwas, Stanley, 1940-
Hannah's child   **92**

Hauerwas, Stanley, 1940-
    About
Hauerwas, S. Hannah's child   **92**

Hauge, Michael
Writing screenplays that sell   **808.2**

Haunted America. Norman, M.   **133.1**
Haunted Arizona. Stansfield, C. A.   **133.1**
Haunted Connecticut. Farnsworth, C.   **133.1**
Haunted Delaware. Martinelli, P. A.   **133.1**
Haunted Florida. Thuma, C.   **133.1**
Haunted Georgia. Brown, A.   **133.1**

HAUNTED HOUSES
    See also Houses

Haunted Hudson Valley. Farnsworth, C.   **133.1**
Haunted Illinois. Taylor, T.   **133.1**
Haunted Jersey shore. Stansfield, C. A.   **133.1**
Haunted Kentucky. Brown, A.   **133.1**
Haunted Maine. Stansfield, C. A.   **133.1**
Haunted Maryland. Okonowicz, E.   **133.1**
Haunted Massachusetts. Farnsworth, C.   **133.1**
Haunted New Jersey. Martinelli, P. A.   **133.1**
Haunted New York. Farnsworth, C.   **133.1**
Haunted New York City. Farnsworth, C.   **133.1**
Haunted North Carolina. Wilson, P. A.   **133.1**
Haunted northern California. Stansfield, C. A. **133.1**
Haunted Ohio. Stansfield, C. A.   **133.1**
Haunted Pennsylvania. Nesbitt, M.   **133.1**
Haunted South Carolina. Brown, A.   **133.1**
Haunted Southern California. Stansfield, C. A.   **133.1**
Haunted Tennessee. Brown, A.   **133.1**
Haunted Texas. Brown, A.   **133.1**
Haunted Vermont. Stansfield, C. A.   **133.1**
Haunted Virginia. Taylor, L. B.   **133.1**
Haunted West Virginia. Wilson, P. A.   **133.1**
Haunted Wisconsin. Godfrey, L. S.   **133.1**

The **haunted** wood. Weinstein, A.   **327.12**

Hauser, Barbara
(ed) Women's legal guide   **346.01**

Hauser, Marc D.
Moral minds   **170**

Hauser, Peter C.
How deaf children learn   **371.91**

Hauser, Thomas
Boxing is--   **796.8**

HAVANA (CUBA)
Cooke, J. The other side of paradise   **972.91**

HAVANA (CUBA) -- BIOGRAPHY
Cooke, J. The other side of paradise   **972.91**
Eire, C. M. N. Waiting for snow in Havana   **92**
Havana dreams. Gimbel, W.   **972.910**

Havel, Václav, 1936-2011
To the castle and back   **92**
The garden party and other plays   **891.8**
Spontaneous mind   **811**
    About
Remnick, D. Reporting   **814**

The **haves** and the have-nots. Milanović, B.   **339.2**

Havil, Julian
The irrationals   **512**

Having been an accomplice. Cronk, L.   **811**
Having our say. Delany, S.   **92**

Havlice, Patricia Pate
Index to artistic biography   **920.003**

Hawa Abdi, 1947-
    About
Abdi, H. Keeping hope alive   **92**

HAWAII -- ANNEXATION TO THE UNITED STATES
Vowell, S. Unfamiliar fishes   **996.9**

HAWAII -- BIOGRAPHY
Maraniss, D. Barack Obama   **973.932**

HAWAII -- HISTORY
Tayman, J. The Colony   **614.5**
Vowell, S. Unfamiliar fishes   **996.9**
Hawaiian dictionary. Pukui, M. K.   **499**

HAWAIIAN LANGUAGE -- DICTIONARIES
Pukui, M. K. Hawaiian dictionary   **499**

HAWAIIAN MONK SEAL -- CONSERVATION
Williams, T. M. The odyssey of KP2   **599.79**

Hawass, Zahi A.
Hidden treasures of ancient Egypt   **932**
Tutankhamun and the golden age of the pharaohs   **932**

The **hawk** and the dove. Thompson, N.   **92**

Hawke, David Freeman
Everyday life in early America   **973.2**

Hawkes, David
John Milton   **92**

Hawking, S. W. (Stephen W.), 1942-
(ed) Einstein, A. A stubbornly persistent illusion   **530.1**

RAPHY

Montefiore, S. Stalin: the court of the red tsar **92**

Service, R. Lenin--a biography **947.084**

Taubman, W. Khrushchev **92**

Healey, Steve

10 Mississippi **811**

HEALING

See also Therapeutics

The **healing** of America. Reid, T. R. **362.1**

HEALING, MENTAL *See* Mental healing

HEALING, SPIRITUAL *See* Spiritual healing

HEALTH

Bittman, M. The food matters cookbook **641.3**

Complete guide to fitness & health **613.7**

Health and social relationships **613**

Iweala, U. Our kind of people **362.196**

Nestle, M. What to eat **613.2**

Reynolds, G. The first 20 minutes **613.7**

Velasquez-Manoff, M. An Epidemic of Absence **616.971**

> *See also* Medicine; Physiology; Preventive medicine

HEALTH & FITNESS -- GENERAL

Baroni, B. Fat kid got fit **362.196**

Broad, W. J. The science of yoga **613.7**

HEALTH & FITNESS -- WEIGHT LOSS

Baroni, B. Fat kid got fit **362.196**

HEALTH & FITNESS -- YOGA

Broad, W. J. The science of yoga **613.7**

HEALTH -- ENVIRONMENTAL ASPECTS *See* Environmental health

HEALTH -- PSYCHOLOGICAL ASPECTS

Scott, R. A. Miracle cures **231.7**

HEALTH -- SOCIAL ASPECTS

Health and social relationships **613**

Health and social relationships. **613**

HEALTH BEHAVIOR IN ADOLESCENCE

Levkoff, L. Got teens? **613**

HEALTH BOARDS

See also Public health

HEALTH CARE *See* Medical care

Health care for some. Hoffman, B. **362.1**

HEALTH CARE PERSONNEL

Foner, M. Not for bread alone **92**

HEALTH CARE POLICY *See* Medical policy

HEALTH CARE RATIONING -- UNITED STATES -- HISTORY

Hoffman, B. Health care for some **362.1**

Health care reform. Gruber, J. **362.1**

HEALTH CARE REFORM -- UNITED STATES

Gruber, J. Health care reform **362.1**

Hoffman, B. Health care for some **362.1**

Makary, M. Unaccountable **610.730**

HEALTH CARE, SELF *See* Health self-care

HEALTH COMMUNICATION

Topol, E. The creative destruction of medicine **610.28**

HEALTH COUNSELING

See also Counseling; Health education

HEALTH EDUCATION

See also Education; Health

HEALTH FACILITIES

See also Medical care; Public health

HEALTH FACILITIES -- LOUISIANA -- ADMINISTRATION -- CASE STUDIES

Fink, S. Five days at memorial **362.11**

HEALTH FACILITIES -- PUBLIC RELATIONS

Makary, M. Unaccountable **610.730**

HEALTH FOODS *See* Natural foods

HEALTH INSURANCE

Nather, D. The new health care system **344**

Starr, P. Remedy and reaction **362.1**

See also Insurance

HEALTH INSURANCE -- UNITED STATES

Atlas, S. W. In excellent health **362.109**

HEALTH MAINTENANCE ORGANIZATIONS

See also Health insurance; Medical practice

HEALTH POLICY *See* Medical policy

HEALTH RECORDS *See* Medical records

Health reference series

Domestic violence sourcebook **362.82**

Fitness and exercise sourcebook **613.7**

HEALTH RESORTS

See also Resorts

HEALTH SELF-CARE

Beattie, M. Codependent no more **616.86**

Hay, L. L. You can heal your life **158**

Weil, A. Eight weeks to optimum health **613**

See also Alternative medicine; Health; Medical care

HEALTH SERVICES ACCESSIBILITY *See* Access to health care

HEALTH SERVICES ADMINISTRATION -- UNITED STATES

101 careers in healthcare management **362.106**

HEALTHS, DRINKING OF *See* Toasts

Healthy aging. Weil, A. **612.6**

The **healthy** kitchen. Weil, A. **641.5**

Healthy women, healthy lives. **613**

Healy, Thomas

The great dissent **342.73**

Healy, Thomas, 1944-

I have heard you calling in the night **636.7**

Heaney, Christopher

Cradle of gold **92**

Heaney, Seamus

The burial at Thebes **822**

District and circle **821**

Electric light **821**

Finders keepers **821**

Human chain **821**

Opened ground **821**

Stafford, E. Walking the Amazon 918.11
Tilton, B. Hiking & backpacking 796.51
Wild 813
    See also Outdoor life
Hiking & backpacking. Tilton, B. 796.51
HIKING -- AMAZON RIVER REGION
Stafford, E. Walking the Amazon 918.11
HIKING -- RUSSIA (FEDERATION) -- URAL MOUNTAINS REGION
Eichar, D. Dead Mountain 914.743
Hilborn, Ray
Overfishing 338.3
Hilborn, Ulrike
(jt. auth) Hilborn, R. Overfishing 338.3
Hilburn, Robert
Johnny Cash 92
Hilburn, Robert
Cornflakes with John Lennon 92
Hilburn, Robert
    About
Hilburn, R. Cornflakes with John Lennon 92
Hilden, Joanne M.
Shelter from the storm 618.92
Hildy, Franklin J.
Brockett, O. G. History of the theatre 792.09
HILL DISTRICT (PITTSBURGH, PA.) -- DRAMA.
Wilson, A. Gem of the ocean 812
Wilson, A. Radio golf 812
Wilson, A. Two trains running 812
Hill of Beans. Snyder, J. 92
Hill, Anita, 1956-
Reimagining equality 305.8
Hill, Barbara Albers
(jt. auth) Stoler, D. R. Coping with concussion and mild traumatic brain injury 617.4
Hill, Christopher T.
Hall, C. Beyond the god particle 539.7
Hill, Chrystie
Inside, outside, and online 021.2
Hill, Clint
Five days in November 973.922
Mrs. Kennedy and me 973.922
Hill, Clint
    About
Hill, C. Mrs. Kennedy and me 973.922
Hill, Fionna
Microgreens 635
Hill, Geoffrey
The orchards of Syon 821
Selected poems 821
The triumph of love 821
Without title 821
Hill, Joe, 1879-1915
    About
Adler, W. M. The man who never died 92

Hill, Napoleon
Think and grow rich 650.1
Hill, Rosemary
Stonehenge 936
Hill, Samuel S.
Atwood, C. D. Handbook of denominations in the United States 280
HILLBILLY MUSIC *See* Country music
Hilleman, Maurice R., 1919-2005
    About
Offit, P. A. Vaccinated 92
Hillenbrand, Laura
Hillenbrand, L. Unbroken 940.54
Seabiscuit 798.4
Hillenbrand, Laura, 1967-
Unbroken 940.54
Hillerbrand, Hans J.
(ed) The encyclopedia of Protestantism 280
Hillerman, Tony
Seldom disappointed 813
Hillerman, Tony
    About
Hillerman, T. Seldom disappointed 813
The **Hillier** gardener's guide to trees & shrubs. 635.9
Hillier, Malcolm
Container gardening through the year 635.9
Flowers 745.92
Hillman, Brenda
Seasonal works with letters on fire 811
Hillman, Brenda
Cascadia 811
Pieces of air in the epic 811
Hillman, Robert
Ghahramani, Z. My life as a traitor 92
Hillstrom, Kevin
(ed) Contemporary women artists 920.003
The Cold War 909.82
Hillstrom, Laurie
(ed) Contemporary women artists 920.003
The Thanksgiving book 394.26
Hilton, Walter, 1340-1396
    About
Armstrong, K. Visions of God 248.2
Hilts, Philip J.
Protecting America's health 353.9
Hiltzik, Michael A.
Colossus 627
Him, Chanrithy
When broken glass floats 959.604
Him, Chanrithy
    About
Him, C. When broken glass floats 959.604
Him, Chanrithy, 1965-
    About
Him, C. When broken glass floats 959.604
HIMALAYA MOUNTAINS -- DESCRIPTION

Bastianich, L. M. Lidia's family table   **641.5**
Canal house cooks every day   **641.5**
Hirshey, David
The ESPN World Cup companion   **796.334**
Hirshfeld, Alan
The electric life of Michael Faraday   **92**
Eureka man   **92**
Hirshfield, Jane
After   **811**
Hirshler, Erica E.
Sargent's daughters   **759.13**
Hirshman, Linda
Victory   **306.76**
Hirshman, Susan L.
Does this make my assets look fat?   **332.024**
Hirshson, Stanley P.
General Patton: a soldier's life   **355**
Hirsi Ali, Ayaan, 1969-
Infidel   **92**
About
Hirsi Ali, A. Infidel   **92**
Scroggins, D. Wanted women   **305.48**
Hirst, Michael
Michelangelo   **709.2**
Hirtle, Sheila
De Villiers, M. Sahara: a natural history   **508**
His Excellency. Ellis, J. J.   **92**
His George Washington [series]
Flexner, J. T. George Washington and the new nation, 1783-1793   **92**
Flexner, J. T. George Washington: anguish and farewell 1793-1799   **92**
Flexner, J. T. George Washington: the forge of experience, 1732-1775   **92**
Hischak, Thomas
The Oxford companion to the American musical   **792.6**
The Tin Pan Alley song encyclopedia   **782.42**
HISPANIC AMERICAN ART
St. James guide to Hispanic artists   **920.003**
HISPANIC AMERICAN ATHLETES
Ruck, R. Raceball   **796.357**
HISPANIC AMERICAN WOMEN
Count on me   **177**
Sotomayor, S. My beloved world   **347.73**
Thorpe, H. Just like us   **305.8**
HISPANIC AMERICAN WOMEN -- HEALTH AND HYGIENE
Delgado, J. L. The Latina guide to health   **613**
HISPANIC AMERICANS
Monterrey, M. Americanos   **305.8**
Morales, E. Living in Spanglish   **305.868**
See also Latinos (U.S.)
HISPANIC AMERICANS -- BIOGRAPHY
Pawel, M. The Crusades of Cesar Chavez   **92**
HISPANIC AMERICANS -- BIOGRAPHY -- EN-

CYCLOPEDIAS
Great lives from history   **920.009**
HISPANIC AMERICANS -- DICTIONARIES
Friedman, I. C. Latino athletes   **920.003**
Martinez Wood, J. Latino writers and journalists   **920.003**
Newton, D. E. Latinos in science, math, and professions   **920.003**
Otfinoski, S. Latinos in the arts   **920.003**
HISPANIC AMERICANS -- EDUCATION (HIGHER) -- HANDBOOKS, MANUALS, ETC
The Latino student's guide to college success **378.1**
HISPANIC AMERICANS -- ENCYCLOPEDIAS
The Hispanic databook   **305.868**
HISPANIC AMERICANS -- HISTORY
Pawel, M. The Crusades of Cesar Chavez   **92**
HISPANIC AMERICANS -- POPULATION -- STATISTICS
The Hispanic databook   **305.868**
HISPANIC AMERICANS AND LIBRARIES
Moller, S. C. Library service to Spanish speaking patrons   **027.6**
HISPANIC AMERICANS IN LITERATURE
Latino and Latina writers   **810**
The **Hispanic** databook.   **305.868**
Hiss, Alger
About
Haynes, J. E. Venona   **327.12**
HISTORIANS
See also Authors
HISTORIANS -- FRANCE -- BIOGRAPHY
Tocqueville   **320.092**
HISTORIANS -- UNITED STATES
Schlesinger, A. M. Journals: 1952-2000   **92**
Schlesinger, A. M. A life in the twentieth century   **973.91**
HISTORIANS -- UNITED STATES -- BIOGRAPHY
Brookhiser, R. America's first dynasty   **973.4**
Crais, C. History lessons   **92**
Duberman, M. Howard Zinn   **973**
HISTORIC BUILDINGS
Unesco World heritage sites   **910.2**
See also Buildings; Historic sites; Monuments
HISTORIC BUILDINGS -- NEW YORK (N.Y.)
Freeland, D. Automats, taxi dances, and vaudeville
HISTORIC BUILDINGS -- UNITED STATES
Gugliotta, G. Freedom's cap   **975.3**
Historic lives [series]
Brown, M. T.E. Lawrence   **92**
HISTORIC PRESERVATION
Amery, C. Vanishing histories   **363.6**
Kersel, M. M. U.S. cultural diplomacy and archaeology   **930.1**

Schama, S. Dead certainties 974.4

Tuchman, B. W. Practicing history 907

    See also Authorship; History

HISTORIOGRAPHY -- PHILOSOPHY

Schiffman, Z. S. The birth of the past 901

HISTORIOGRAPHY -- WESTERN COUNTRIES

Schiffman, Z. S. The birth of the past 901

HISTORIOGRAPHY AND PHOTOGRAPHY -- UNITED STATES

Krauthamer, B. Envisioning emancipation 973.7

HISTORY

Crapol, E. P. John Tyler 92

Galeano, E. H. Mirrors 909

    See also Humanities; Social sciences

HISTORY -- ATLASES *See* Historical atlases

HISTORY -- CHRONOLOGY *See* Historical chronology

HISTORY -- CRITICISM *See* Historiography

HISTORY -- DICTIONARIES

    See also Encyclopedias and dictionaries

HISTORY -- HISTORIOGRAPHY *See* Historiography

HISTORY -- MISCELLANEA

Galeano, E. H. Mirrors 909

HISTORY -- PHILOSOPHY

Kreeft, P. Philosophy 101 by Socrates 183

    See also Philosophy

HISTORY -- POETRY

Schutt, W. Westerly 811

HISTORY -- RESEARCH

Mills, E. S. Evidence explained 907

HISTORY -- SOURCES

Competing voices from the Russian Revolution 947.084

    See also Historiography

HISTORY -- STUDY AND TEACHING

Lefkowitz, M. R. Not out of Africa 960

The **history** boys. Bennett, A. 822

History lessons. Crais, C. 92

A **history** of ancient Egypt. Romer, J. 932

A **history** of art in Africa. Visona, M. B. 709

The **history** of astronomy. Couper, H. 520

The **history** of Australia. Clarke, F. G. 994

History of beauty. Eco, U. 111

A **history** of Britain. Schama, S. 941

The **history** of British women's writing. 820.9

History of communication [series]

Bezanson, R. P. How free can the press be? 342

History of computing [series]

Campbell-Kelly, M. From airline reservations to Sonic the Hedgehog 005

History of disability series

Keller, H. Helen Keller: selected writings 92

History of East Central Europe [series]

Magocsi, P. R. Historical atlas of Central Europe 911

A **history** of Egypt. Thompson, J. 962

History of England [series]

Ackroyd, P. Tudors 942.05

A **history** of ghosts. Aykroyd, P. 133.1

A **history** of God. Armstrong, K. 200

The **history** of hell. Turner, A. K. 200

The **history** of Iceland. Johanneson, G. T. 949.12

The **history** of India. McLeod, J. 954

A **history** of Iraq. Tripp, C. 956.7

A **history** of Israel. Sachar, H. M. 956.94

A **history** of Israel. Bregman, A. 956.94

The **history** of Japan. Perez, L. G. 952

History of Japanese literature [series]

Keene, D. Seeds in the heart 895.6

The **history** of jazz. Gioia, T. 781.65

A **history** of mathematics. Boyer, C. B. 510

HISTORY OF MEDICINE

Kore 610.1

Mattern, S. P. Prince of medicine 610.9

Wheelwright, J. The wandering gene and the Indian princess 616.99

The **history** of Mexico. Kirkwood, B. 972

History of modern art. Arnason, H. H. 709.04

History of modern science and mathematics. 500

The **history** of pirates. Konstam, A. 910.4

A **History** of private life. Aries, P. 909

A **History** of private life. Aries, P. 909

A **history** of psychiatry. Shorter, E. 616.89

A **history** of Russia. Riasanovsky, N. V. 947

A **history** of Russian literature. Terras, V. 891.7

The **History** of science and religion in the western tradition. 201

A **history** of South Africa. Thompson, L. M. 968

The **history** of television, 1942 to 2000. Abramson, A. 621.388

History of the American West [series]

Calloway, C. G. One vast winter count 978

A **history** of the Arab peoples. Hourani, A. H. 909

History of the conquest of Mexico. Prescott, W. H. 972

A **history** of the devil. Messadie, G. 200

A **history** of the Federal Reserve. Meltzer, A. H. 332.1

A **history** of the French new wave cinema. Neupert, R. 791.43

A **history** of the Jews. Johnson, P. 909

A **history** of the Jews in the modern world. Sachar, H. M. 909

A **history** of the Ostrogoths. Burns, T. S. 909.07

The **history** of the Peloponnesian War. Thucydides 938

History of the theatre. Brockett, O. G. 792.09

History of the twentieth century. Gilbert, M. 909.82

A **history** of the wife. Yalom, M. 306.872

A **history** of the world in 100 objects. MacGregor,

Holbrook, Kate
(ed) Global values 101 — 170
Hold tight gently. Duberman, M. B. — 920
Holden, Alan
Crystals and crystal growing — 548
Holden, Andrew
Jehovah's Witnesses — 289.9
Holder, R. W.
How not to say what you mean — 427
Holding company. Jackson, M. — 811
The **hole** in the universe. Cole, K. C. — 530.01
Hole in the wall. Pickard, T. — 821
HOLIDAY COOKING
    See also Cooking
HOLIDAY DECORATIONS
    See also Decoration and ornament
Holiday symbols and customs. — 394.26
Holiday, Billie, 1915-1959
    About
Blackburn, J. With Billie — 92
Clarke, D. Billie Holiday — 92
Feather, L. From Satchmo to Miles — 920
Griffin, F. J. If you can't be free, be a mystery — 92
Holiday, B. Lady sings the blues — 92
Nicholson, S. Billie Holiday — 782.421
O'Meally, R. G. Lady Day — 92
HOLIDAYS
Holiday symbols and customs — 394.26
Rajtar, S. United States holidays and observances — 394.26
    See also Days; Manners and customs
HOLIDAYS -- DICTIONARIES
Holidays, festivals, and celebrations of the world dictionary — 394.26
Holidays, festivals, and celebrations of the world dictionary. — 394.26
HOLIDAYS, JEWISH *See* Jewish holidays
Holifield, E. Brooks
Theology in America — 230
HOLISTIC MEDICINE
Hay, L. L. You can heal your life — 158
    See also Alternative medicine; Medicine
Holladay, Wilhelmina Cole
A museum of their own — 704
Holland, James
Battle of Britain — 940.54
Hollander, John
(ed) American wits — 811
(ed) Christmas poems — 821
A draft of light — 811
Figurehead & other poems — 811
(ed) Lazarus, E. Emma Lazarus — 811
Hollands, Neil
Fellowship in a ring — 809
Read on . . . fantasy fiction — 016
Holldobler, Bert

The ants — 595.79
Journey to the ants — 595.79
The leafcutter ants — 595.7
The superorganism — 595.7
Hollenbeck, Don, 1905-1954
    About
Ghiglione, L. CBS's Don Hollenbeck — 92
Holler if you hear me: searching for Tupac Shakur. Dyson, M. E. — 782.421
Hollingsworth, Dennis, 1967-
    About
Becker, J. Forcing the spring — 346.0168
Hollis, Edward
The secret lives of buildings — 720.9
Hollis, Leo
London rising — 942
Hollis, Matthew
Now all roads lead to France — 821.912
Hollowing out the middle. Carr, P. J. — 307.7
HOLLYWOOD (LOS ANGELES, CALIF.)--HISTORY.
Goldman, W. Adventures in the screen trade — 791.43
Hollywood's ancient worlds. Richards, J. — 791.43
Hollywood's copyright wars. Decherney, P. — 346.04
Holman, James, 1786-1857
    About
Roberts, J. A sense of the world — 92
Holmes, David L.
The faiths of the postwar presidents — 973.92
Holmes, George
(ed) The Oxford history of medieval Europe — 940.1
Holmes, Martha
(jt. auth) Barrington, R. Life — 578.4
Holmes, Oliver Wendell, 1841-1935
    About
Commager, H. S. The American mind — 973
Healy, T. The great dissent — 342.73
Menand, L. The Metaphysical Club — 973.9
Wilson, E. Patriotic gore — 810
Holmes, Rachel
African queen — 92
Holmes, Richard, 1945-
The age of wonder — 509
Falling upwards — 387.7
Holmes, Roger
(ed) Taylor's master guide to gardening — 635.9
HOLMES, SHERLOCK (FICTIONAL CHARACTER)
Konnikova, M. Mastermind — 153.4
Wagner, E. J. The science of Sherlock Holmes — 363.2
    See also Fictional characters
Holocaust. Reznikoff, C. — 811
The **Holocaust** and history. — 940.53
HOLOCAUST DENIAL
    See also Holocaust, 1939-1945
The **Holocaust** encyclopedia. — 940.53

Frankl, V. E. Man's search for meaning   92
Kramer, C. Clara's war   92
Prose, F. Anne Frank   839.3
Rosenfeld, O. In the beginning was the ghetto   940.53
Smith, L. Remembering, voices of the holocaust   940.53
Wiesel, E. All rivers run to the sea   813
Wiesel, E. And the sea is never full   813
Wiesenthal, S. The sunflower   179.7
Witness   940.53

HOLOCAUST, 1939-1945 -- POETRY
Holocaust poetry   808.81

HOLOCAUST, 1939-1945, IN LITERATURE
Langer, L. L. Admitting the Holocaust   940.53
Nothing makes you free   808.8

HOLOCAUST, 1939-1945
Eisner, P. The Pope's Last Crusade   940.53
Pivnik, S. Survivor   940.53
Szegedy-Maszák, M. I kiss your hands many times   920
> *See also* Antisemitism; Germany -- History -- 1939-1945; Jews -- Persecutions

HOLOCAUST, 1939-1945 -- ENCYCLOPEDIAS
The United States Holocaust Memorial Museum encyclopedia of camps and ghettos, 1933-1945   940.53

HOLOCAUST, 1939-1945 -- PERSONAL NARRATIVES
> *See also* Autobiographies

HOLOCAUST, JEWISH (1939-1945)
Berenbaum, M. The world must know   940.53
Breitman, R. Official secrets   940.54
Encyclopedia of the Holocaust   940.53
Friedlander, S. The years of extermination   940.53
Fritzsche, P. Life and death in the Third Reich   943.086
Goldhagen, D. A moral reckoning   940.53
Goldsmith, M. The inextinguishable symphony   940.53
The Holocaust encyclopedia   940.53
Kershaw, I. Hitler, the Germans, and the final solution   940.53
Lipstadt, D. E. The Eichmann trial   345
Nothing makes you free   808.8
Snyder, T. Bloodlands   940.54
> *See also* Holocaust, 1939-1945

HOLOCAUST, JEWISH -- CZECH REPUBLIC -- PRAGUE -- PERSONAL NARRATIVES -- JUVENILE LITERATURE
Helga's diary   940.53

HOLOCAUST, JEWISH (1939-1945) -- FRANCE -- MARSEILLE
Zuccotti, S. Père Marie-Benoît and Jewish rescue   940.53

HOLOCAUST, JEWISH (1939-1945) -- GER-MANY
Fritzsche, P. Life and death in the Third Reich   943.086

HOLOCAUST, JEWISH (1939-1945) -- HUNGARY
Szegedy-Maszák, M. I kiss your hands many times   920

HOLOCAUST, JEWISH (1939-1945) -- NETHERLANDS -- AMSTERDAM -- BIOGRAPHY
Anne Frank   92

HOLOCAUST, JEWISH (1939-1945) -- POLAND
Horwitz, G. J. Ghettostadt   940.53
Holocaust: a history. Dwork, D.   940.53

HOLOGRAPHY
> *See also* Laser recording; Photography

Holoman, D. Kern
Berlioz   780

Holroyd, Michael
A book of secrets   306.874
A strange eventful history   92

Holt, Jim
Why does the world exist?   113

Holt, Nathalia
Cured   614.5

Holt, Saxon
Greenlee, J. The American meadow garden   635.9

Holton, Woody
Abigail Adams   92

Holtz, Allan
American newspaper comics   741.5

Holway, Tatiana
The flower of empire   727

HOLY DAYS *See* Religious holidays

HOLY GHOST *See* Holy Spirit

Holy hullabaloos. Wexler, J.   342

HOLY LAND *See* Palestine

HOLY OFFICE *See* Inquisition

Holy people of the world.   920.003
Holy roller. Wilson, D.   92

HOLY ROMAN EMPIRE
Reston, J. Defenders of the faith   940.2

HOLY SEE *See* Papacy; Popes

HOLY SPIRIT
Cox, H. G. The future of faith   270
> *See also* God -- Christianity; Trinity

Holy war. Cliff, N.   909

HOLY WAR (ISLAM) *See* Jihad

Holy warriors. Phillips, J.   909.07

HOLY WEEK
Benedict XVI, P. Jesus of Nazareth. part two   232.9

Holzer, Harold
The Civil War in 50 objects   973.707
(ed) Lincoln on war   973.7

Holzer, Harold
(ed) Hearts touched by fire   973.7
Lincoln president-elect   92

See also Alternative medicine; Pharmacy

The **homeowner's** complete tree & shrub handbook. O'Sullivan, P.   **635.9**

The **homeowner's** guide to managing a renovation. Solakian, S. E.   **643**

Homer

About

Alexander, C. The war that killed Achilles   **883**

Manguel, A. Homer's The Iliad and The Odyssey   **883**

Homer's odyssey. Cooper, G.   **636.8**

Homer's The Iliad and The Odyssey. Manguel, A.   **883**

Homer, Winslow, 1836-1910

About

Cikovsky, N. Winslow Homer   **759.13**

HOMES *See* Houses

HOMES (INSTITUTIONS) *See* Charities; Institutional care; Orphanages

Homes, A. M.

The mistress's daughter   **92**

HOMESTEAD GRAYS (BASEBALL TEAM)

Snyder, B. Beyond the shadow of the Senators   **796.357**

Hometown appetites. Alexander, K.   **92**

HOMEWORK

Jackson, R. The learning habit   **371.3**

HOMICIDE

Bowden, C. Murder city   **364.152**

Braude, J. The honored dead   **364.152**

Brown, E. Shake the devil off   **364.152**

Bugliosi, V. Helter skelter   **364.1**

Burke, T. M. The Paradiso files   **364.152**

Capote, T. In cold blood   **364.1**

Carrere, E. The adversary   **364.1**

Collins, P. The murder of the century   **364.152**

Douglas, J. E. The cases that haunt us   **364.1**

Flanders, J. The invention of murder   **364.152**

James, B. Popular crime   **364.1**

Jimenez, S. The Book of Matt   **364.1**

Junger, S. A death in Belmont   **364.152**

King, J. Hate crime: the story of a dragging in Jasper, Texas   **364.15**

Larson, E. Thunderstruck   **364.152**

Leake, J. Entering Hades   **364.152**

Levy, B. H. Who killed Daniel Pearl?   **070.92**

Matthews, J. Bringing Adam home   **364.1**

McConnell, D. American honor killings   **364.15**

McGinniss, J. Fatal vision   **364.1**

O'Brien, G. The fall of the house of Walworth   **920**

Olsen, J. I: the creation of a serial killer   **364.1**

Parry, R. L. People who eat darkness   **364.152**

Robisheaux, T. The last witch of Langenburg   **133.4**

Rule, A. --and never let her go   **364.1**

Rule, A. Bitter harvest   **364.1**

Rule, A. Dead by sunset   **364.1**

Rule, A. Everything she ever wanted   **364.1**

Rule, A. Too late to say goodbye   **364.152**

Salamon, J. Facing the wind   **364.15**

Schechter, H. Psycho USA   **364.152**

Schiller, L. Perfect murder, perfect town   **364.15**

Smith, H. W. The butcher's tale   **305.892**

Starr, D. The killer of little shepherds   **364.152**

Stashower, D. The beautiful cigar girl   **364.152**

Stewart, J. B. Blind eye   **364.1**

Summerscale, K. The suspicions of Mr. Whicher   **364.152**

Tucker, H. Blood work   **615**

The Ultimate Jack the Ripper companion   **364.15**

Worrall, S. The poet and the murderer   **364.15**

Zacharias, K. S. A silence of mockingbirds   **364.152**

See also Crime; Criminal law; Offenses against the person

HOMICIDE -- GRAPHIC NOVELS

Geary, R. The Lindbergh child   **364.1**

HOMICIDE TRIALS *See* Trials (Homicide)

HOMINIDS *See* Human origins

HOMINIDS, FOSSIL *See* Fossil hominids

Homo mysterious. Barash, D. P.   **303.4**

HOMO SAPIENS *See* Human beings

HOMOPHOBIA -- UNITED STATES

Lampo, D. A fundamental freedom   **323.3**

HOMOSEXUAL MARRIAGE *See* Same-sex marriage

HOMOSEXUAL PARENTS *See* Gay parents

HOMOSEXUALITY

Bagemihl, B. Biological exuberance   **591.56**

Bronski, M. You can tell just by looking   **306.76**

Faderman, L. Gay L.A.   **306.76**

Garner, A. Families like mine   **306.8**

Riggle, E. D. B. A positive view of LGBTQ   **155.3**

Robb, G. Strangers: homosexual love in the nineteenth century   **306.76**

See also Sex

HOMOSEXUALITY -- HISTORY

Blank, H. Straight   **306.76**

Parkinson, R. B. A little gay history   **306.76**

HOMOSEXUALITY -- LAW AND LEGISLATION -- TEXAS

Carpenter, D. Flagrant conduct   **342.7308**

HOMOSEXUALITY -- MORAL AND ETHICAL ASPECTS

Corvino, J. What's wrong with homosexuality?   **176**

HOMOSEXUALITY -- POETRY

Yeros, D. Shades of love   **778**

HOMOSEXUALITY -- POLITICAL ASPECTS -- UNITED STATES -- HISTORY -- 21ST CENTURY

Nicholson, A. Fighting to serve   **355**

HOMOSEXUALITY -- RELIGIOUS ASPECTS -- CHRISTIANITY

Chu, J. Does Jesus Really Love Me?   **261.8**

deficit disorder

HYPERLINKS

> *See also* Multimedia

Hyperspace. Kaku, M.   **530.1**

HYPERSPACE

Nadis, S. The shape of inner space   **530.1**
> *See also* Fourth dimension

**HYPERTENSION -- DIET THERAPY -- RECI-
PES**

Heller, M. The everyday DASH diet cook-
book   **613.2**

HYPERTENSION -- PREVENTION

Heller, M. The everyday DASH diet cook-
book   **613.2**

HYPNOTISM

> *See also* Mental healing; Psychophysiology

HYPNOTISTS

O'Dell, C. Miss O'Dell   **92**

The **Hypo.** Van Sciver, N.   **92**

Hysell, Shannon Graff

(ed) American reference books annual 2014, volume 45   **011**

(ed) Recommended reference books for small and
medium-sized libraries and media centers, Vol.
34   **011**

Hyslop, Stephen G.

Atlas of the Civil War   **973.7**

Currie, R. The letter and the scroll   **220.9**

I

I am a strange loop. Hofstadter, D. R.   **153**

I am Malala. Lamb, C.   **92**

I am Nujood, age 10 and divorced. Ali, N.   **92**

I am Ozzy. Osbourne, O.   **92**

I am the beggar of the world.   **891**

I and thou. Buber, M.   **181**

I celebrate myself. Morgan, B.   **92**

I ching

The classic of changes   **299.5**

I could never be so lucky again. Glines, C. V. **92**

I don't wish nobody to have a life like mine. Chura,
D.   **371.9**

I Dreamed I Was a Very Clean Tramp. Hell, R.   **92**

I feel bad about my neck. Ephron, N.   **814**

I fired God. Zichterman, J. R.   **286**

I had brain surgery, what's your excuse? Becker,
S.   **92**

I hate new music. Thompson, D.   **781.66**

The **I** hate to cook book. Bracken, P.   **641.5**

I hate to leave this beautiful place. Norman, H. **813**

I have a name. Ignatow, D.   **811**

I have heard you calling in the night. Healy, T. **636.7**

I heart design.   **741.6**

I kiss your hands many times. Szegedy-Maszák,
M.   **920**

I know just what you mean. Goodman, E.   **158.2**

I know why the caged bird sings. Angelou, M. **92**

I like you. Sedaris, A.   **793.2**

. . . i listen to the wind that obliterates my traces.
Roden, S.   **781.64**

I love a man in uniform. Burana, L.   **92**

I love New York. Humm, D.   **641.59**

I may be wrong but I doubt it. Barkley, C. **796.323**

I may not get there with you: the true Martin Luther
King, Jr. Dyson, M. E.   **323**

I only say this because I love you. Tannen, D. **306.87**

I Said Yes to Everything. Grant, L.   **92**

I see the promised land.   **92**

I shall not be moved. Angelou, M.   **811**

I shouldn't be telling you this. White, K. **650.108**

I shudder. Rudnick, P.   **92**

I swear I saw this. Taussig, M.   **301**

I thought my father was God and other true tales
from the National Story Project.   **810**

I want to thank my brain for remembering me. Breslin, J.   **92**

I will bear witness. Klemperer, V.   **943.086**

I wonder as I wander. Hughes, L.   **818**

I wore the ocean in the shape of a girl. Groom, K. **92**

I wouldn't start from here. Mueller, A.   **909.83**

I'd hate myself in the morning. Lardner, R.   **813**

I'll find a way or make one. Williams, J.   **378**

I'll sleep when I'm dead. Zevon, C.   **92**

I'll take you there. Kot, G.   **92**

I'm a stranger here myself. Bryson, B.   **818**

I'm looking through you. Boylan, J. F.   **92**

I'm off then.   **914**

I'm your man. Simmons, S.   **780**

I've got a home in glory land. Smardz Frost, K. **92**

I, Tina. Turner, T.   **92**

I.O.U. Lanchester, J.   **330.9**

I: the creation of a serial killer. Olsen, J. **364.1**

Iacoboni, Marco

Mirroring people   **573.8**

Ian, Janis

Society's child   **92**

Ibrahima, Abd al-Rahman, 1762-1829

About

Lepore, J. A is for American   **306.44**

Ibsen, Henrik, 1828-1906

The complete major prose plays   **839.8**

About

Bloom, H. The Western canon   **809**

ICBM *See* Intercontinental ballistic missiles

Ice. Ice-T   **92**

ICE

Gosnell, M. Ice   **551.3**

Pollack, H. N. A world without ice   **551.3**
> *See also* Cold; Frost; Physical geography;
> Water

Ice. Gosnell, M.   **551.3**

ICE AGE

Tribble, S. A colossal hoax **974.7**
    See also Crime; Criminals

IMPOSTORS AND IMPOSTURE -- UNITED STATES -- CASE STUDIES
    Kirn, W. Blood will out **364.152**

IMPOTENCE
    See also Diseases

Impresario. Maguire, J. **92**

IMPRESSIONISM (ART)
    Baillio, J. Claude Monet, 1840-1926 **759**
    Gerdts, W. H. American impressionism **759.13**
    Impressionism and post-impressionism in the Art Institute of Chicago **759.05**
    Kelder, D. The great book of French impressionism **759**
    King, R. The judgment of Paris **759**
    Roe, S. The private lives of the impressionists **759**
    See also Art

Impressionism and post-impressionism in the Art Institute of Chicago. **759.05**

IMPRISONMENT *See* Prisons

IMPRISONMENT -- SOVIET UNION
    Figes, O. Just send me word **365**

An **improvised** life. Arkin, A. **92**

IMPULSE RECORDS (FIRM)
    Kahn, A. The house that Trane built **781.65**

In a cardboard belt! Epstein, J. **814**
In a desert garden. Alcock, J. **595.7**
In a sunburned country. Bryson, B. **919**
In America's court. Geoghegan, T. **345**
In cold blood. Capote, T. **364.1**
In command of history. Reynolds, D. **940.53**
In defense of food. Pollan, M. **613**
In Europe. Mak, G. **940.5**
In excellent health. Atlas, S. W. **362.109**
In Fed we trust. Wessel, D. **332.1**
In focus. National Geographic Society (U.S.) **779**
In Hanuman's hands. Rao, C. **92**
In harmony. **704**
In heaven as it is on earth. Brown, S. M. **236**
In heaven everything is fine. Frank, J. **92**
In his own words. **92**
In Montgomery, and other poems. Brooks, G. **811**
In my father's country. Wahab, S. **958.104**
In other worlds. Atwood, M. **809**
In our image. Karnow, S. **959.9**
In our own best interest. Schulz, W. F. **323**
In our time. Brownmiller, S. **305.42**
In Patagonia. Chatwin, B. **918**
In praise of science. Bais, S. **500**
In pursuit of giants. Rigney, M. **597**
In pursuit of silence. Prochnik, G. **155.9**
In reckless hands. Nourse, V. F. **344**
In retrospect. McNamara, R. S. **959.704**
In rough country. Oates, J. C. **814**
In search of King Solomon's mines. Shah, T. **963**

In search of memory. Kandel, E. R. **153**
In search of nature. Wilson, E. O. **113**
In search of Nella Larsen. Hutchinson, G. **92**
In search of our roots. Gates, H. L. **305.8**
In search of Robinson Crusoe. Severin, T. **996**
In search of Schrodinger's cat. Gribbin, J. R. **530.1**
In search of small gods. Harrison, J. **811**
In search of the blues. Minutaglio, B. **305.8**
In search of the promised land. Franklin, J. H. **929**
In search of the Trojan War. Wood, M. **939**
In search of Tiger. Callahan, T. **92**
In search of time. Falk, D. **529**
In search of your European roots. Baxter, A. **929**
In Siberia. Thubron, C. **957**
In spite of myself. Plummer, C. **92**
In the absence of sun. Lee, H. **979.4**
In the American grain. Williams, W. C. **814**
In the arms of others. Filene, P. G. **179.7**
In the balance. Tushnet, M. **347.73**
In the beginning. Armstrong, K. **222**
In the beginning was the ghetto. Rosenfeld, O. **940.53**
In the belly of the beast. Abbott, J. H. **365**
In the blink of an eye. Waltrip, M. **796.72**
In the body of the world. Ensler, E. **812**
In the company of soldiers. Atkinson, R. **956.7**
In the crevice of time. Jacobsen, J. **811**
In the dark. Stone, R. **811**
In the dark before dawn. Merton, T. **811**
In the footsteps of Marco Polo. Belliveau, D. **915**
In the garden of beasts. Larson, E. **92**
In the green kitchen. Waters, A. **641.5**
In the house of the interpreter. Ngugi wa Thiong'o **823**
In the kingdom of ice. Sides, H. **910.4**
In the kitchen with a good appetite. Clark, M. **641.5**
In the land of invented languages. Okrent, A. **499**
In the name of Elijah Muhammad. Gardell, M. **297**
In the next galaxy. Stone, R. **811**
In the past lane. Kammen, M. G. **973**
In the pines. Notley, A. **811**
In the place of justice. Rideau, W. **92**
In the plex. Levy, S. **338.7**
In the room of never grieve. Waldman, A. **811**
In the shadow of man. Goodall, J. **599.8**
In the shadow of no towers. Spiegelman, A. **973.931**
In the shadow of the moon. French, F. **629.45**
In the shadow of the Oval Office. Daalder, I. H. **355**
In the sweet kitchen. Daley, R. **641.8**
In the theater of consciousness. Baars, B. J. **153**
In the time of Bobby Cox. Whitaker, L. **796.357**
In the valley of mist. Hardy, J. **954**
In the valley of the shadow. Kugel, J. L. **200.9**
In the wake of the plague. Cantor, N. F. **614.5**
In the water they can't see you cry. Beard, A. **797.2**
In these girls, hope is a muscle. Blais, M. **796.323**

Jetton, Tamara L.
(ed) Adolescent literacy in the academic disciplines **428**

Jew vs. Jew. Freedman, S. G. **296**

JEWELERS
Faber, T. Faberge's eggs **739.2**

Jewell, Andrew
(ed) Cather, W. The selected letters of Willa Cather **813**

JEWELRY
Codina, C. The complete book of jewelry making **739.27**
DeCoster, M. Marcia DeCoster's beaded opulence **739.27**
Deeb, M. The beader's color palette **745.594**
Gollberg, J. The art & craft of making jewelry **739.27**
Haab, S. The art of metal clay **739.27**
Heynen, J. Ceramic bead jewelry **745.59**
Michaels, C. F. Teach yourself visually jewelry making & beading **745.59**
Miller, J. Miller's costume jewelry **739.27**
Searle, T. Felt jewelry **746**
Wells, C. W. The art & elegance of beadweaving **745.58**
Wire, C. Creative metal clay jewelry **745.59**
Young, A. The workbench guide to jewelry techniques **739.27**
See also Clothing and dress; Costume; Decorative arts

JEWELRY THEFT -- ENGLAND -- LONDON -- CASE STUDIES
Crosby, M. C. The great pearl heist **364.16**

JEWELRY THEFT -- HISTORY
Crosby, M. C. The great pearl heist **364.16**

JEWELS See Gems; Jewelry; Precious stones

Jewish American literature. **810**

JEWISH ART AND SYMBOLISM
Levine, L. I. Visual Judaism in late antiquity **704.9**
The **Jewish** Bible. **221**

JEWISH BUSINESSPEOPLE -- LOUISIANA -- NEW ORLEANS -- BIOGRAPHY
Cohen, R. The fish that ate the whale **338.7**

JEWISH CHILDREN IN THE HOLOCAUST
Nicholas, L. H. Cruel world **940.53**
See also Holocaust, 1939-1945

JEWISH CHILDREN IN THE HOLOCAUST -- BIOGRAPHY
Anne Frank **92**

JEWISH CHILDREN IN THE HOLOCAUST -- CZECH REPUBLIC -- BIOGRAPHY -- JUVENILE LITERATURE
Helga's diary **940.53**

JEWISH CIVILIZATION
Cultures of the Jews **909**
Nirenberg, D. Anti-Judaism **305.892**

Roden, C. The book of Jewish food **641.5**
See also Civilization

JEWISH COOKING
Marks, G. The world of Jewish cooking **641.5**
Nathan, J. Jewish cooking in America **641.5**
Nathan, J. Quiches, kugels, and couscous **641.5**
The New York Times Jewish cookbook **641.5**
The New York Times Passover cookbook **641.5**
Ottolenghi, Y. Jerusalem **641.5**
Roden, C. The book of Jewish food **641.5**
Jewish cooking in America. Nathan, J. **641.5**

JEWISH CUSTOMS See Jews -- Social life and customs; Judaism -- Customs and practices

JEWISH DIASPORA
Brenner, F. Diaspora: homelands in exile **909**
See also Human geography; Jews

Jewish encounters [series]
Century, D. Barney Ross **92**
Lehman, D. A fine romance **782.42**
Lipstadt, D. E. The Eichmann trial **345**
Pinsky, R. The life of David **92**

JEWISH ETHICS
Telushkin, J. Biblical literacy **221**
Telushkin, J. Jewish wisdom **296.3**
See also Ethics

JEWISH FAMILIES -- CZECH REPUBLIC -- PRAGUE -- BIOGRAPHY
Albright, M. K. Prague winter **943.71**

JEWISH FOLK LITERATURE
Encyclopedia of Jewish folklore and traditions **398.208**

JEWISH GHETTOS -- EUROPE, EASTERN -- ENCYCLOPEDIAS
The United States Holocaust Memorial Museum encyclopedia of camps and ghettos, 1933-1945 **940.53**

JEWISH HOLIDAYS
Axelrod, M. Your guide to the Jewish holidays **296.4**
Goldman, A. L. Being Jewish **296.4**
See also Judaism; Religious holidays

JEWISH HOLOCAUST (1933-1945) See Holocaust, 1939-1945

JEWISH ILLUMINATION OF BOOKS AND MANUSCRIPTS
Bolsta, H. S. The illuminated Kaddish **296.4**

JEWISH LANGUAGE See Hebrew language; Yiddish language

JEWISH LEADERS
Pick, H. Simon Wiesenthal **940.53**
Segev, T. Simon Wiesenthal **92**

JEWISH LIFE See Jews -- Social life and customs; Judaism -- Customs and practices

JEWISH LITERATURE
See also Literature; Religious literature

JEWISH MEN

John Brown's spy. Lubet, S.   973.7

John Brown, abolitionist. Reynolds, D. S.   92

John Clare: a biography. Bate, J.   92

John Dryden. Selections.   821

John F. Kennedy. Brinkley, A.   973.922

John Glenn. Glenn, J.   973.927

John Gutmann. Stein, S.   779

JOHN H. REAGAN HIGH SCHOOL (AUSTIN, TEX.)

   Brick, M. Saving the school   373.22

John Huston. Meyers, J.   92

John James Audubon. Rhodes, R.   92

John Lennon. Norman, P.   92

John Marshall. Smith, J. E.   347

John Milton. Hawkes, D.   92

John Milton. Campbell, G.   92

John Muir. Wilkins, T.   333.7

John Muir and the ice that started a fire. Heacox, K.   92

John Osborne. Heilpern, J.   92

John Paul II. Flynn, R.   92

John Paul II, Pope, 1920-2005

   Crossing the threshold of hope   282

         About

   Buttiglione, R. Karol Wojtyla   282

   Cornwell, J. The pontiff in winter   92

   Flynn, R. John Paul II   92

   O'Connor, G. Universal Father: a life of John Paul II   92

   Reese, T. J. Inside the Vatican   262

   Weigel, G. Witness to hope: the biography of Pope John Paul II   92

John Paul Jones. Thomas, E.   973.3

John Paul Jones. Morison, S. E.   92

John Quincy Adams. Nagel, P. C.   92

John Quincy Adams. Remini, R. V.   973.5

John Quincy Adams. Giles Unger, H.   973.5

John Quincy Adams. Kaplan, F.   92

John Steinbeck.   813

John Tyler. Crapol, E. P.   92

John Tyler. May, G.   92

John Wayne: the life and legend. Eyman, S.   92

John Wesley. Tomkins, S.   287

John Winthrop. Bremer, F. J.   974.4

John, Catherine Rachel

   Attwater, D. The Penguin dictionary of saints   920.003

John, Lauren Z.

   Running book discussion groups   374

Johnny Appleseed. Means, H. B.   92

Johnny Cash. Kleist, R.   741.5

Johnny Cash. Streissguth, M.   92

Johnny Cash. Hilburn, R.   92

Johns Hopkins Press health book [series]

   Mace, N. L. The 36-hour day   618.97

A Johns Hopkins Press health book [series]

Kaye, L. W. A man's guide to healthy aging   613

Johns Hopkins, poetry and fiction [series]

   Jacobsen, J. In the crevice of time   811

Johnsen, Gregory D.

   The last refuge   363.325

Johnsen, Ole

   Minerals of the world   549

Johnson, Andrew, 1808-1875

         About

   Gordon-Reed, A. Andrew Johnson   92

Johnson, Catherine

   Grandin, T. Animals in translation   591.5

   Grandin, T. Animals make us human   636

Johnson, Charles Richard

   Turning the wheel   814

Johnson, Charles Richard, 1948-

         About

   Johnson, C. R. Turning the wheel   814

Johnson, Clay

   The information diet   303.483

Johnson, Dave

   How to do everything: digital camera   775

Johnson, Doug

   The indispensable librarian   025.1

Johnson, Eric A.

   What we knew   943.086

Johnson, George

   The cancer chronicles   616.99

Johnson, George

   Miss Leavitt's stars   92

   A shortcut through time   004.1

   Strange beauty: Murray Gell-Mann and the revolution in twentieth-century physics   92

   The ten most beautiful experiments   507.8

Johnson, Greg

   (ed) Oates, J. C. The journal of Joyce Carol Oates: 1973-1982   92

Johnson, Gus, 1913-2000

         About

   Dance, S. The world of Count Basie   920

Johnson, Harriet McBryde

   Too late to die young   92

Johnson, Haynes Bonner

   Balz, D. J. The battle for America, 2008   973.932

   The age of anxiety   973.921

   Sleepwalking through history   973.927

Johnson, Hugh

   The world of trees   582.16

Johnson, Ian

   A mosque in Munich   297

Johnson, Jack, 1878-1946

         About

   Runstedtler, T. Jack Johnson, rebel sojourner   796.83

   Ward, G. C. Unforgivable blackness   92

Johnson, James Weldon

LEFT (POLITICAL SCIENCE) *See* Liberalism; Right and left (Political science)

Left out. Stepan-Norris, J.   **331.8**

LEFT- AND RIGHT-HANDEDNESS
     See also Psychophysiology

LEGACIES *See* Inheritance and succession; Wills

Legacies: a Chinese mosaic. Lord, B. B.   **951.05**

A **legacy** of liberation. Gevisser, M.   **92**

LEGAL AID
     Houppert, K. Chasing Gideon   **345.73**

LEGAL ASSISTANCE TO THE POOR -- UNIT-ED STATES
     Houppert, K. Chasing Gideon   **345.73**

LEGAL DRAMA (FILMS)
     See also Motion pictures

LEGAL DRAMA (TELEVISION PROGRAMS)
     See also Television programs

LEGAL ETHICS
     See also Professional ethics

A **legal** guide for lesbian and gay couples. Clifford, D.   **346.01**

Legal history of North America [series]
     Documents of American Indian diplomacy **970.004**

LEGAL HOLIDAYS *See* Holidays

LEGAL MEDICINE *See* Medical jurisprudence

LEGAL PROFESSION *See* Lawyers

LEGAL SECRETARIES
     Gordon, M. Circling my mother   **92**

LEGAL STORIES
     See also Fiction

Legal systems of the world.   **340**

LEGAL TENDER *See* Money

LEGALIZATION OF DRUGS *See* Drug legalization

A **legend** in the making. Tofel, R. J.   **796.357**

LEGENDARY CHARACTERS
     See also Legends; Mythology

LEGENDS
     See also Fiction; Literature

LEGENDS -- UNITED STATES
     Brunvand, J. H. The vanishing hitchhiker   **398.2**
     Shenkman, R. Legends, lies & cherished myths of American history   **973**

Legends of modernity. Milosz, C.   **891.8**

Legends, lies & cherished myths of American history. Shenkman, R.   **973**

LEGERDEMAIN *See* Juggling; Magic tricks

LEGIBILITY OF HANDWRITING *See* Handwriting

LEGISLATION
     Congressional Quarterly, I. Congress and the Nation   **328**
     Stathis, S. W. Landmark legislation, 1774-2002 **348**
     See also Political science

LEGISLATION, DIRECT *See* Referendum

LEGISLATIVE BODIES

     See also Constitutional law; Legislation; Representative government and representation

LEGISLATORS
     Stahr, W. Seward   **973.709**
     See also Statesmen

LEGISLATORS -- UNITED STATES -- BIOG-RAPHY
     Clinton, H. R. Living history   **973.929**
     Crespino, J. Strom Thurmond's America   **328**
     Glenn, J. John Glenn   **973.927**
     Kennedy, J. F. Profiles in courage   **920**
     Snowe, O. J. Fighting for common ground **328.73**
     Thomas, E. Robert Kennedy   **973.922**
     Warren, E. A fighting chance   **92**

LEGITIMACY (LAW) *See* Illegitimacy

LEGO KONCERNEN (DENMARK)
     Breen, B. Brick by brick   **338.7**

LEGO TOYS -- HISTORY
     Breen, B. Brick by brick   **338.7**

The **legs** are the last to go. Carroll, D.   **92**

LeHand, Missy, 1898-1944
         About
     Persico, J. E. Franklin and Lucy   **920**

Lehman, David, 1948-
     A fine romance   **782.42**
     (ed) The best American poetry   **811.008**
     (ed) Best of the Best American Poetry   **811**
     (ed) The Oxford book of American poetry   **811**
     (ed) Selections. Selected poems   **811**

Lehmann, Ingmar
     The secrets of triangles   **516**
     (jt. auth) Posamentier, A. S. Magnificent mistakes in mathematics   **510**

Lehr, Dick
     The fence   **364.1**

Lehrer, Jonah
     How we decide   **153.8**

Leiber, Jerry, 1933-2011
         About
     Leiber, J. Hound dog   **92**

Leibniz, Gottfried Wilhelm, Freiherr von, 1646-1716
         About
     Bell, E. T. Men of mathematics   **920**
     Nadler, S. M. The best of all possible worlds **190**
     Russell, B. A history of Western philosophy **109**

Leibovich, Lori
     (ed) Maybe baby   **306.8**

Leibovitz, Annie
     Annie Leibovitz at work   **779**
     A photographer's life, 1990-2005   **779**
     Women   **779**

Leibovitz, Liel
     Fortunate sons   **951.05**

Leibowitz, Herbert A.
     Something urgent I have to say to you: the life and

LIE DETECTORS AND DETECTION

See also Criminal investigation; Medical jurisprudence; Truthfulness and falsehood

Lieberman, Daniel, 1964-

The story of the human body — 612

Lieberman, Ruby

Bray, I. M. How to get a green card — 342

Liebling, A. J.

Just enough Liebling — 814

The sweet science and other writings — 818

World War II writings — 940.54

Liebman, James S.

The wrong Carlos — 364.152

Liedtke, Walter A.

Vermeer and the Delft school — 759.9

Lies across America. Loewen, J. W. — 973

The **lies** of George W. Bush. Corn, D. — 973.931

Lieven, Anatol

Pakistan — 954.91

Lieven, Anatol

Chechnya — 947.086

Pakistan — 954.91

Lieven, D. C. B.

Russia against Napoleon — 940.2

Life. Richards, K. — 92

Life. Barrington, R. — 578.4

Life. Fortey, R. A. — 576.8

LIFE

Auster, P. Winter journal — 818

Deutsch, D. The fabric of reality — 530

Lepore, J. The mansion of happiness — 973

Toomey, D. Weird Life — 571

We Have Only This Life to Live — 848

Life & times [series]

Dry, S. Curie — 92

LIFE (BIOLOGY)

Capra, F. The web of life — 570.1

Gribbin, J. R. Stardust — 523

Lovelock, J. The ages of Gaia — 570.1

Margulis, L. What is life? — 570.1

Ward, P. D. Life as we do not know it — 576.8

See also Biology

LIFE (BIOLOGY) -- SOCIAL ASPECTS -- UNITED STATES -- HISTORY

Lepore, J. The mansion of happiness — 973

LIFE -- ORIGIN

Billings, L. Five billion years of solitude — 576.8

Gribbin, J. Alone in the universe — 525

Rutherford, A. Creation — 576.8

See also Evolution

LIFE -- SOCIAL ASPECTS -- UNITED STATES -- HISTORY

Lepore, J. The mansion of happiness — 973

Life after college. Blake, J. — 646.700

Life after death. Echols, D. — 364.66

LIFE AFTER DEATH *See* Future life; Immortality

Life after life. Moody, R. A. — 133.9

Life and death in Shanghai. Cheng, N. — 92

Life and death in the Third Reich. Fritzsche, P. — 943.086

The **life** and legacy of Annie Oakley. Riley, G. — 796.3

The **life** and legend of Leadbelly. Wolfe, C. K. — 92

The **life** and many deaths of Harry Houdini. Brandon, R. — 793.8

The **life** and times of Little Richard. White, C. — 782.421

The **life** and times of Pancho Villa. Katz, F. — 972.08

The **life** and times of the thunderbolt kid. Bryson, B. — 92

Life as we do not know it. Ward, P. D. — 576.8

Life at the Speed of Light. Venter, J. C. — 303.48

Life at the zoo: behind the scenes with the animal doctors. Robinson, P. T. — 590.73

LIFE CHANGE EVENTS

James, E. Paris in love — 92

LIFE CYCLE, HUMAN

Pepper, C. The seven pearls of financial wisdom — 332.024

LIFE CYCLE, HUMAN -- SOCIAL ASPECTS -- UNITED STATES -- HISTORY

Lepore, J. The mansion of happiness — 973

LIFE CYCLES (BIOLOGY)

Heinrich, B. Life everlasting — 591.7

See also Biology; Cycles; Life (Biology)

Life disrupted. Edwards, L. — 618.92

Life drawing class. Watson, L. — 743

Life everlasting. Heinrich, B. — 591.7

LIFE EXPECTANCY

See also Age; Life; Vital statistics

LIFE HISTORIES *See* Biography

Life in a medieval castle. Gies, J. — 940.2

Life in a medieval city. Gies, J. — 940.1

Life in a medieval village. Gies, F. — 940.1

Life in cold blood. Attenborough, D. — 597.9

A **life** in letters. Fitzgerald, F. S. — 813

Life in photographs. McCartney, L. — 779

Life in rewind. Murphy, T. W. — 92

A **life** in secrets. Helm, S. — 92

Life in the treetops. Lowman, M. — 577.34

A **life** in the twentieth century. Schlesinger, A. M. — 973.91

Life in the undergrowth. Attenborough, D. — 592

Life in year one. Korb, S. — 933

LIFE INSURANCE

Schultz, E. Retirement heist — 331.2

LIFE INSURANCE

See also Insurance

Life itself. Ebert, R. — 92

Life lessons. Kubler-Ross, E. — 170

Life list. Gentile, O. — 92

The **life** of a leaf. Vogel, S. — 575.5

The **making** of Robert E. Lee. Fellman, M. **973.7**

The **making** of the atomic bomb. Rhodes, R. **623.4**

The **making** of the fittest. Carroll, S. B. **572.8**

Making our democracy work. Breyer, S. G. **347**

Making peace with your past. Bloomfield, H. H. **158**

Making saints. Woodward, K. L. **235**

Making the most of your money now. Quinn, J. B. **332.024**

Making toast. Rosenblatt, R. **92**

Making your own days. Koch, K. **809.1**

MALADJUSTED CHILDREN *See* Emotionally disturbed children

MALADJUSTMENT (PSYCHOLOGY) *See* Adjustment (Psychology)

Malakov, Daniel, d. 2007

About

Malcolm, J. Iphigenia in Forest Hills **345**

Malamud, Bernard, 1914-1986

About

Langer, L. L. Admitting the Holocaust **940.53**

Smith, J. M. My father is a book **92**

MALARIA

Shah, S. The fever **614.5**

See also Diseases

MALAWI -- RURAL CONDITIONS

Kamkwamba, W. The boy who harnessed the wind **92**

Malcolm. Perry, B. **92**

Malcolm X. Marable, M. **92**

Malcolm X

The autobiography of Malcolm X **92**

Malcolm X, 1925-1965

About

Carson, C. Malcolm X: the FBI file **92**

Joseph, P. E. Dark days, bright nights **323.1**

Malcolm X The autobiography of Malcolm X **92**

Marable, M. Malcolm X **92**

Perry, B. Malcolm **92**

Malcolm X: the FBI file. Carson, C. **92**

Malcolm, Janet

Forty-one false starts **808.02**

Iphigenia in Forest Hills **345**

Reading Chekhov **891.7**

Two lives **92**

MALE ACTORS

See also Actors

The **male** body. Bordo, S. **305.31**

MALE CIRCUMCISION *See* Circumcision

MALE CLIMACTERIC

See also Aging

MALE FRIENDSHIP -- UNITED STATES

Kashatus, W. C. Jackie and Campy **92**

MALE IMPERSONATORS

See also Impostors and imposture

MALE ROLE *See* Gender role

MALE-FEMALE RELATIONSHIP *See* Man-woman relationship

Malebranche, Nicolas, 1638-1715

About

Nadler, S. M. The best of all possible worlds **190**

Malek, Alia

A country called Amreeka **305.8**

MALFEASANCE IN OFFICE *See* Misconduct in office

MALICIOUS ACCUSATION -- NORTH CAROLINA -- DURHAM

Cohan, W. D. The price of silence **364.15**

MALIGNANT TUMORS *See* Cancer

Malin, Jo

(ed) Encyclopedia of women's autobiography **920.003**

Malinowski, Sharon

(ed) Notable native Americans **920.003**

Maliszewski-Pickart, Margaret

Architecture and ornament **721**

Malkiel, Burton Gordon, 1932-

A random walk down Wall Street **332.6**

Mallarme, Stephane

Collected poems and other verse **841**

Mallayev, Mikhail

About

Malcolm, J. Iphigenia in Forest Hills **345**

Mallegg, Kristin

(ed) Almanac of Famous People **920**

Malley, Marjorie Caroline

Radioactivity **539.7**

Mallmann, Francis

Seven fires **641.5**

Mallon, Thomas

Mrs. Paine's garage and the murder of John F. Kennedy **364.1**

Yours ever **808.86**

MALLS, SHOPPING *See* Shopping centers and malls

MALNUTRITION

See also Nutrition

Malone, John Williams

It doesn't take a rocket scientist **920**

Malone, Michael S.

The guardian of all things **153.1**

Malory, Thomas Sir, 15th cent.

Ackroyd, P. The death of King Arthur **398.2**

Le morte Darthur, or, The hoole book of Kyng Arthur and of his noble knyghtes of the Rounde Table **398.2**

MALPRACTICE INSURANCE

See also Insurance

Malseed, Mark

Vise, D. A. The Google story **338.7**

Malthus, T. R. (Thomas Robert), 1766-1834

About

Heilbroner, R. L. The worldly philosophers **330.1**

Ferguson, K. Measuring the universe   **523.1**

Nicastro, N. Circumference   **526**

Robinson, A. The story of measurement   **530.8**

   See also Mathematics

MEASURES *See* Weights and measures

Measuring eternity. Gorst, M.   **115**

MEASURING INSTRUMENTS

   See also Measurement; Weights and measures

Measuring the universe. Ferguson, K.   **523.1**

Meat. Peterson, J.   **641.6**

MEAT

   See also Food

The **meat** bible. Lobel, S.   **641.6**

Meat eater. Rinella, S.   **799.29**

MEAT INDUSTRY

   See also Food industry

MEAT INSPECTION

   See also Food adulteration and inspection; Meat industry; Public health

MEATCUTTING -- UNITED STATES

   Guggiana, M. Primal cuts   **641.6**

Méchain, Pierre-Fran¿cois-André, 1744-1804

     About

   Alder, K. The measure of all things   **526**

MECHANICAL DRAWING

   See also Drawing; Engineering; Machinery; Patternmaking

MECHANICAL ENGINEERING

   See also Civil engineering

MECHANICAL ENGINEERING -- HAND-BOOKS, MANUALS, ETC.

   Marks' standard handbook for mechanical engineers   **621**

MECHANICAL ENGINEERS

   Lorance, L. Becoming Bucky Fuller   **92**

   Sobel, D. Longitude   **526**

MECHANICAL ENGINEERS -- MALAWI -- BIOGRAPHY

   Kamkwamba, W. The boy who harnessed the wind   **92**

MECHANICAL MUSICAL INSTRUMENTS

   See also Musical instruments

MECHANICS

   See also Physics

MECHANICS (PERSONS)

   Crawford, M. B. Shop class as soulcraft   **331**

   Robison, J. E. Look me in the eye   **92**

Mecom, Jane, 1712-1794

     About

   Lepore, J. Book of ages   **92**

MEDAL OF HONOR -- BIOGRAPHY

   Giunta, S. A. Living with honor   **958.104**

MÉDECINS SANS FRONTIÈRES (ORGANIZATION)

   Bortolotti, D. Hope in hell   **610**

   Orbinski, J. An imperfect offering   **610**

MÉDECINS SANS FRONTIÈRES (ORGANIZATION) -- GRAPHIC NOVELS

   Guibert, E. The photographer   **741.5**

MEDIA *See* Mass media

MEDIA CENTERS (EDUCATION) *See* Instructional materials centers

MEDIA LITERACY

   See also Literacy

Media man. Auletta, K.   **92**

The **media** relations department of Hizbollah wishes you a happy birthday. MacFarquhar, N.   **956.04**

MEDICAID

   Nather, D. The new health care system   **344**

MEDICAL -- NEUROLOGY

   Mukand, J. The man with the bionic brain   **617.4**

Medical apartheid. Washington, H. A.   **174.2**

MEDICAL ASSISTANCE

   Orbinski, J. An imperfect offering   **610**

MEDICAL BOTANY

   Davis, W. One river   **581.6**

   Peterson field guide to medicinal plants and herbs of eastern and central North America   **581.6**

   Sumner, J. The natural history of medicinal plants   **581.6**

     See also Botany; Medicine; Pharmacy

MEDICAL CARE

   Brawley, O. W. How we do harm   **362.109**

   Fadiman, A. The spirit catches you and you fall down   **306.4**

   Garrett, L. Betrayal of trust   **362.1**

   Gruber, J. Health care reform   **362.1**

   Lake, N. The caregivers   **610.73**

     See also Public health

MEDICAL CARE -- ACCESS *See* Access to health care

MEDICAL CARE -- COSTS

   Gruber, J. Health care reform   **362.1**

   Hoffman, B. Health care for some   **362.1**

MEDICAL CARE -- ETHICAL ASPECTS *See* Medical ethics

MEDICAL CARE -- GOVERNMENT POLICY

   Blumenthal, D. The heart of power   **362.1**

   Nather, D. The new health care system   **344**

   Reid, T. R. The healing of America   **362.1**

   Sommer, A. Getting what we deserve   **362.1**

   Starr, P. Remedy and reaction   **362.1**

     See also Medical policy

MEDICAL CARE -- QUALITY CONTROL

   Gawande, A. The checklist manifesto   **610.28**

   Makary, M. Unaccountable   **610.730**

MEDICAL CARE -- SOCIAL ASPECTS *See* Social medicine

MEDICAL CARE -- UNITED STATES

   Atlas, S. W. In excellent health   **362.109**

MEDICAL CARE FOR THE ELDERLY *See* Elderly -- Medical care; Medicare

MEDICAL CARE FOR THE POOR *See* Medicaid; Poor -- Medical care

MEDICAL CHARITIES
> *See also* Charities; Medical care; Public health

MEDICAL COLLEGES
> *See also* Colleges and universities

MEDICAL DIAGNOSIS *See* Diagnosis

MEDICAL DRAMA (FILMS)
> *See also* Motion pictures

MEDICAL DRAMA (TELEVISION PROGRAMS)
> *See also* Television programs

MEDICAL ECONOMICS
> *See also* Economics

MEDICAL ERRORS
Makary, M. Unaccountable   **610.730**
> *See also* Errors; Medical personnel -- Malpractice; Physicians -- Malpractice

MEDICAL ETHICS
Caplan, A. L. Smart mice, not-so-smart people   **174.2**
Elliott, C. White coat, black hat   **174.2**
The Ethics of organ transplants   **174**
Gawande, A. Better   **616**
Munson, R. Raising the dead   **174**
Peck, M. S. Denial of the soul   **179.7**
Shah, S. The body hunters   **362.1**
Teresi, D. The undead   **610**
Washington, H. A. Deadly monopolies   **338.4**
> *See also* Bioethics; Ethics; Professional ethics

MEDICAL ETHICS -- ENCYCLOPEDIAS
Encyclopedia of bioethics   **174**

MEDICAL ETHICS -- UNITED STATES
Elliott, C. White coat, black hat   **174.2**

MEDICAL EXAMINERS (LAW) -- NEW YORK (STATE) -- NEW YORK -- BIOGRAPHY
Mitchell, T. J. Working stiff   **92**

MEDICAL EXPERIMENTATION ON HUMANS
See Human experimentation in medicine

Medical firsts. Adler, R. E.   **610**

MEDICAL GENETICS
Collins, F. S. The language of life   **616**
Green, R. M. Babies by design   **176**
Marion, R. Genetic rounds   **92**
> *See also* Genetics; Pathology

MEDICAL GENETICS -- ENCYCLOPEDIAS
Knight, J. A. Genetics & inherited conditions **576.5**

Medical humanities [series]
Twelve breaths a minute   **616**

MEDICAL ILLUSTRATION
Anderson, J. The art of medicine   **610.22**

MEDICAL INFORMATICS APPLICATIONS
Topol, E. The creative destruction of medicine   **610.28**

MEDICAL INSTRUMENTS AND APPARATUS -- UNITED STATES -- HISTORY -- 19TH CENTURY
Millard, C. The destiny of the republic   **973.8**

MEDICAL INSURANCE *See* Health insurance

MEDICAL JURISPRUDENCE
Mitchell, T. J. Working stiff   **92**
> *See also* Forensic sciences

MEDICAL MISCONCEPTIONS
Goldacre, B. Bad science   **500**

MEDICAL MISSIONS
> *See also* Medicine

MEDICAL NOVELS
> *See also* Fiction

MEDICAL PERSONNEL
> *See also* Employees

MEDICAL PERSONNEL -- EMPLOYMENT
101 careers in healthcare management   **362.106**

MEDICAL PERSONNEL AND PATIENT
Makary, M. Unaccountable   **610.730**

MEDICAL PHOTOGRAPHY
> *See also* Photography; Photography -- Scientific applications

MEDICAL POLICY
Garrett, L. Betrayal of trust   **362.1**
> *See also* Social policy

MEDICAL POLICY -- UNITED STATES
Brawley, O. W. How we do harm   **362.109**
The economists' voice 2.0   **330.9**
Gruber, J. Health care reform   **362.1**

MEDICAL PRACTICE
> *See also* Medicine

MEDICAL PROFESSION *See* Medical personnel; Medical practice; Medicine

MEDICAL RECORDS
Makary, M. Unaccountable   **610.730**

MEDICAL RESEARCH *See* Medicine -- Research

MEDICAL SCIENCES *See* Medicine

MEDICAL SELF-CARE *See* Health self-care

MEDICAL SERVICE, COST OF *See* Medical care -- Costs

MEDICAL SERVICES *See* Medical care

MEDICAL SOCIOLOGY *See* Social medicine

MEDICAL TECHNOLOGY
Callahan, D. Taming the beloved beast   **338.4**
Finkel, E. The Genome Generation   **572**
Topol, E. The creative destruction of medicine   **610.28**
> *See also* Medicine

MEDICAL TRANSPLANTATION *See* Transplantation of organs, tissues, etc.

MEDICAL WASTES
> *See also* Refuse and refuse disposal

MEDICAL ZOOLOGY
> *See also* Medicine; Zoology

MEDICARE

Matthews, J. L. Social security, Medicare & government pensions **344**

Nather, D. The new health care system **344**

See also Elderly -- Medical care; National health insurance; State medicine

MEDICATION ABUSE

See also Drug abuse; Substance abuse

The **Medici** giraffe. Belozerskaya, M. **636**

Medici money. Parks, T. **332.1**

MEDICINAL HERBS *See* Herbs -- Therapeutic use; Medical botany

MEDICINAL PLANTS *See* Medical botany

MEDICINE

Bowers, K. Zoobiquity **636.089**

Gawande, A. Better **616**

Goleman, D. Emotional intelligence **152.4**

Groopman, J. E. How doctors think **610**

Groopman, J. E. Second opinions **610**

Groopman, J. E. Your medical mind **610**

Kore **610.1**

Preston, R. Panic in level 4 **616.02**

Sweet, V. God's hotel **610.92**

See also Life sciences; Therapeutics

MEDICINE -- BIOGRAPHY

See also Biography

MEDICINE -- COST OF MEDICAL CARE *See* Medical care -- Costs

MEDICINE -- DICTIONARIES

Mosby's medical dictionary **610**

Taber's cyclopedic medical dictionary **610.3**

MEDICINE -- ENCYCLOPEDIAS

Mosby's diagnostic and laboratory test reference **616.07**

MEDICINE -- ETHICAL ASPECTS *See* Medical ethics

MEDICINE -- HANDBOOKS, MANUALS, ETC.

Current Medical Diagnosis & Treatment 2015 **616**

MEDICINE -- HISTORY

Anderson, J. The art of medicine **610.22**

Burns, T. Our Necessary Shadow **616.89**

Hoffman, B. B. Adrenaline **616.4**

Johnson, G. The cancer chronicles **616.99**

Mattern, S. P. Prince of medicine **610.9**

MEDICINE -- LAW AND LEGISLATION

James, V. E. The Alzheimer's advisor **344**

See also Law; Legislation

MEDICINE -- MISCELLANEA

See also Curiosities and wonders

MEDICINE -- PHILOSOPHY

Haycock, D. B. Mortal coil **571.8**

Pollack, R. The missing moment **610**

MEDICINE -- PHYSIOLOGICAL EFFECT *See* Pharmacology

MEDICINE -- RESEARCH

Leaf, C. The truth in small doses **616.99**

See also Research

MEDICINE -- SOCIAL ASPECTS *See* Social medicine

MEDICINE -- UNITED STATES

Elliott, C. White coat, black hat **174.2**

MEDICINE -- UNITED STATES -- HISTORY

Cassedy, J. H. Medicine in America: a short history **610**

Finger, S. Doctor Franklin's medicine **610**

MEDICINE -- UNITED STATES -- HISTORY -- 19TH CENTURY

Millard, C. The destiny of the republic **973.8**

MEDICINE AND STATE *See* Medical policy

Medicine in America: a short history. Cassedy, J. H. **610**

MEDICINE IN ART

Anderson, J. The art of medicine **610.22**

MEDICINE MEN *See* Shamans

MEDICINE, PEDIATRIC *See* Children -- Diseases

MEDICINE, POPULAR *See* Popular medicine

MEDICINE, PSYCHOSOMATIC *See* Psychosomatic medicine

Medicine, science, and religion in historical context [series]

Schoepflin, R. B. Christian Science on trial **289.5**

MEDIEVAL ARCHITECTURE

Snyder, J. Art of the Middle Ages **709.02**

See also Architecture; Medieval civilization

MEDIEVAL ART

Lowden, J. Early Christian & Byzantine art **709.02**

Snyder, J. Art of the Middle Ages **709.02**

See also Art; Medieval civilization

Medieval children. Orme, N. **305.23**

MEDIEVAL CIVILIZATION

Al-Khalili, J. The house of wisdom **509**

Aries, P. A History of private life **909**

Asbridge, T. The crusades **909.07**

Burns, T. S. A history of the Ostrogoths **909.07**

Cahill, T. How the Irish saved civilization **941.501**

Crowley, R. City of fortune **945**

Gies, F. Life in a medieval village **940.1**

Gies, J. Life in a medieval city **940.1**

Great events from history, The Middle Ages, 477-1453 **909.07**

Herlihy, D. The black death and the transformation of the west **940.1**

The New Cambridge medieval history **940.1**

Tuchman, B. W. A distant mirror **944**

Wickham, C. The inheritance of Rome **940.1**

See also Civilization

MEDIEVAL CIVILIZATION -- ENCYCLOPEDIAS

Medieval England **942**

Medieval England. **942**

MEDIEVAL LITERATURE

See also Literature; Medieval civilization

MENSTRUATION

Kim, S. Flow   **612.6**

    See also Reproduction

MENSURATION

Ferguson, K. Measuring the universe   **523.1**

MENTAL CALCULATORS

Tammet, D. Born on a blue day   **92**

MENTAL DEPRESSION *See* Depression (Psychology)

MENTAL DISEASES *See* Abnormal psychology; Mental illness

MENTAL HEALING

Harrington, A. The cure within   **616**

    See also Alternative medicine

MENTAL HEALTH

Frances, A. Saving Normal   **616.89**

Saul, R. ADHD does not exist   **618.92**

Slone, L. B. After the war zone   **616.85**

    See also Happiness; Health

MENTAL HEALTH -- RELIGIOUS ASPECTS

Rennebohm, C. Souls in the hands of a tender God   **242**

MENTAL HEALTH SERVICES

Lawhorne-Scott, C. Military mental health care   **355.3**

Sederer, L. I. The family guide to mental health care   **616.89**

    See also Medical care

MENTAL ILLNESS

Adamec, C. When your adult child breaks your heart   **616.89**

Bailey, B. The Splendid Things We Planned   **92**

Biever, J. A. The wandering mind   **612.8**

Braitman, L. Animal madness   **591.5**

Frances, A. Saving Normal   **616.89**

Naifeh, S. Van Gogh   **759.9**

O'Brien, G. The fall of the house of Walworth   **920**

Porter, R. Madness   **616.89**

Rennebohm, C. Souls in the hands of a tender God   **242**

Slater, L. Prozac diary   **616.89**

Smoller, J. The other side of normal   **591.5**

Whitaker, R. Anatomy of an epidemic   **616.89**

    See also Abnormal psychology; Diseases

MENTAL ILLNESS -- PHYSIOLOGICAL ASPECTS

    See also Physiology

MENTAL ILLNESS -- UNITED STATES

Sederer, L. I. The family guide to mental health care   **616.89**

Whitaker, R. Anatomy of an epidemic   **616.89**

MENTAL INSTITUTIONS *See* Mentally ill -- Institutional care

MENTAL PATIENTS *See* Mentally ill

MENTAL RETARDATION

    See also Abnormal psychology

MENTAL STEREOTYPE *See* Stereotype (Social psychology)

MENTAL STRESS *See* Stress (Psychology)

MENTAL SUGGESTION

    See also Mind and body; Parapsychology; Subconsciousness

MENTAL TELEPATHY *See* Telepathy

MENTAL TESTS *See* Intelligence tests; Psychological tests

MENTALLY DEPRESSED *See* Depression (Psychology)

MENTALLY DERANGED *See* Mentally ill

MENTALLY HANDICAPPED

Lombardo, P. A. Three generations, no imbeciles   **344**

    See also People with mental disabilities

MENTALLY ILL

Bartok, M. The memory palace   **92**

Greenberg, M. Hurry down sunshine   **92**

Murphy, T. W. Life in rewind   **92**

Nathan, D. Sybil exposed   **616.85**

Smith, T. A balanced life   **362.1**

Von Ziegesar, P. The looking glass brother   **92**

Winchester, S. The professor and the madman   **423**

    See also Sick

MENTALLY ILL -- INSTITUTIONAL CARE

Ronson, J. The psychopath test   **616.85**

MENTALLY ILL -- UNITED STATES -- BIOGRAPHY

Smith, D. Monkey mind   **616.85**

MENTALLY ILL CHILDREN *See* Emotionally disturbed children

MENTALLY RETARDED *See* People with mental disabilities

Mentor. Grimes, T.   **92**

MENTORING

Chertavian, G. A Year Up   **331.25**

Edelman, M. W. Lanterns   **92**

Grimes, T. Mentor   **92**

    See also Counseling

Menuez, Doug

Fearless genius   **979.4**

MENUS

Bayless, R. Fiesta at Rick's   **641.5**

Brennan, K. Keepers   **641.5**

Garten, I. Barefoot Contessa at home   **641.5**

Tanis, D. Heart of the artichoke and other kitchen journeys   **641.5**

Tanis, D. A platter of figs and other recipes   **641.5**

    See also Cooking; Diet

Menzer, Joe

The wildest ride   **796.72**

MERCANTILE LAW *See* Commercial law

Mercatante, Anthony S.

The Facts on File encyclopedia of world mythology and legend   **201**

Min, A. Red Azalea   **92**

Minahan, James

The complete guide to national symbols and emblems   **929.9**

MIND *See* Intellect; Psychology

MIND AND BODY

Abram, D. The spell of the sensuous   **128**

Berdik, C. Mind over mind   **153.4**

Bor, D. The ravenous brain   **612.8**

Devlin, K. J. Goodbye, Descartes   **128**

Harrington, A. The cure within   **616**

Hay, L. L. You can heal your life   **158**

Horstman, J. The Scientific American day in the life of your brain   **616.8**

Kaku, M. The future of the mind   **612.8**

Lilienfeld, S. O. Brainwashed   **612.8**

Parks, T. Teach us to sit still   **616**

Raine, A. The anatomy of violence   **616.85**

    See also Brain; Medicine; Parapsychology; Philosophy

A **mind** at a time. Levine, M. D.   **370.15**

MIND CONTROL *See* Brainwashing

MIND CURE *See* Mental healing

A **mind** of its own. Friedman, D. M.   **573.6**

Mind of the raven. Heinrich, B.   **598**

The **mind** of the South. Cash, W. J.   **975**

Mind over matter. Cole, K. C.   **500**

Mind over mind. Berdik, C.   **153.4**

MIND READING *See* Telepathy

Mind wide open. Johnson, S.   **612.8**

The **mind's** eye. Sacks, O.   **616.85**

MIND-BODY RELATIONS, METAPHYSICAL

Edelman, S. The happiness of pursuit   **153**

Minders of make-believe. Neuburger, E. K.   **070.5**

Mindless eating. Wansink, B.   **616.85**

MINE SURVEYING

    See also Mining engineering; Prospecting; Surveying

The **miner's** canary. Guinier, L.   **323.1**

MINERAL LANDS *See* Mines and mineral resources

MINERALS

Chaline, E. Fifty minerals that changed the course of history   **549**

Chesterman, C. W. The Audubon Society field guide to North American rocks and minerals   **549**

Coenraads, R. R. Rocks and fossils   **552**

Johnsen, O. Minerals of the world   **549**

Klein, C. Manual of mineral science   **549**

Pough, F. H. A field guide to rocks and minerals   **549**

Rocks and minerals   **549**

    See also Geology

MINERALS IN HUMAN NUTRITION

    See also Food; Minerals; Nutrition

MINERALS IN THE BODY

    See also Metabolism; Minerals; Minerals in the body

Minerals of the world. Johnsen, O.   **549**

MINERS

Milner, C. A. As big as the West   **92**

    See also Labor

Minerva and the muse: a life of Margaret Fuller. Von Mehren, J.   **818**

MINES AND MINERAL RESOURCES

Chaline, E. Fifty minerals that changed the course of history   **549**

    See also Economic geology; Natural resources; Raw materials

MINES AND MINERAL RESOURCES -- UNITED STATES

Hedges, C. Days of destruction, days of revolt   **305.5**

Mingus, Charles, 1922-1979

About

Santoro, G. Myself when I am real: the life and music of Charles Mingus   **781.65**

Mini farming. Markham, B. L.   **635**

MINIATURE GARDENS

    See also Gardens; Miniature objects

MINIATURE OBJECTS

    See also Art objects

MINIATURE PAINTING

    See also Miniature objects; Painting

MINIATURES (ILLUMINATION OF BOOKS AND MANUSCRIPTS) *See* Illumination of books and manuscripts

MINIBIKES

    See also Bicycles; Motorcycles

MINIMUM WAGE

Ehrenreich, B. Nickel and dimed   **305.5**

Shulman, B. The betrayal of work   **331.2**

    See also Salaries, wages, etc.

MINING *See* Mines and mineral resources; Mining engineering

MINING ENGINEERING

LeCain, T. J. Mass destruction   **338.2**

    See also Civil engineering; Coal mines and mining; Engineering; Mines and mineral resources

MINING, OCEAN *See* Ocean mining

MINISTERS (DIPLOMATIC AGENTS) *See* Diplomats

MINISTERS OF STATE *See* Cabinet officers

MINISTERS OF THE GOSPEL *See* Clergy

MINISTRY

    See also Church work; Pastoral theology

Minnelli, Vincente, 1910-1986

About

Levy, E. Vincente Minnelli   **92**

MINNESOTA

Borich, B. J. Body geographic   **818**

Minois, Georges
The atheist's Bible   **200**
MINOR LEAGUE BASEBALL
Feinstein, J.   Where nobody knows your
name   **796.357**
Mann, L. Class A   **796.357**
  See also Baseball
**MINOR LEAGUE BASEBALL -- ALABAMA --
  BIRMINGHAM**
Colton, L. Southern League   **796.357**
**MINOR LEAGUE BASEBALL -- IOWA -- CLIN-
  TON -- HISTORY**
Mann, L. Class A   **796.357**
**MINOR LEAGUE BASEBALL -- UNITED
  STATES -- HISTORY**
Barry, D. Bottom of the 33rd   **796.357**
Feinstein, J.   Where nobody knows your
name   **796.357**
Minor, William C., d. 1920
          About
Winchester, S. The professor and the madman **423**
MINORITIES
Daniels, R. Coming to America   **325**
Gross, A. J. What blood won't tell   **305.8**
Guinier, L. The miner's canary   **323.1**
Peake, R. Mapping Census 2010   **304.6**
**MINORITIES -- CIVIL RIGHTS -- INDIA -- HIS-
  TORY**
Slate, N. Colored cosmopolitanism   **305.8**
**MINORITIES -- EDUCATION (HIGHER) --
  UNITED STATES -- HISTORY**
Wilder, C. S. Ebony and Ivy   **379.26**
MINORITIES -- ENCYCLOPEDIAS
The Greenwood encyclopedia of multiethnic Amer-
ican literature   **810**
**MINORITIES -- LEGAL STATUS, LAWS, ETC.
  -- UNITED STATES**
Gross, A. J. What blood won't tell   **305.8**
MINORITIES -- UNITED STATES
Bishop, B. The big sort   **305.8**
Slotkin, R. Lost battalions   **940.3**
**MINORITIES -- UNITED STATES -- POPULA-
  TION -- STATISTICS -- MAPS**
Peake, R. Mapping Census 2010   **304.6**
MINORITY GROUPS *See* Minorities
The **minority** quarterback, and other lives in sports.
Berkow, I.   **796**
MINORITY WOMEN
  See also Minorities; Women
MINORITY YOUTH
  See also Minorities; Youth
Minoui, Delphine
Ali, N. I am Nujood, age 10 and divorced   **92**
**MINSTREL SHOWS -- UNITED STATES -- HIS-
  TORY**
Austen, J. Darkest America   **791**

McAllister, M. Whiting up   **791.43**
MINSTRELS
  See also Poets
Mint condition. Jamieson, D.   **796.357**
MINTS
  See also Money
Mintz, Steven
Huck's raft   **305.23**
Mintzberg, Henry
Managing   **658**
Mintzer, Richard
Stephenson, J. Ultimate homebased business hand-
book   **658**
Minutaglio, Bill
Dallas 1963   **973.922**
First son: George W. Bush and the Bush family dy-
nasty   **92**
In search of the blues   **305.8**
Miracle cures. Scott, R. A.   **231.7**
Miracle in the Andes. Parrado, N.   **982**
MIRACLE PLAYS *See* Mysteries and miracle
plays
Miracle touch. Bruce, D. F.   **615.5**
The **miracle** worker. Gibson, W.   **812**
Miracles. Lewis, C. S.   **231.7**
MIRACLES
Lewis, C. S. Miracles   **231.7**
Woodward, K. L. The book of miracles   **231.7**
MIRACLES -- CHRISTIANITY
Scott, R. A. Miracle cures   **231.7**
Miracles of life. Ballard, J. G.   **823**
The **mirage** man. Willman, D.   **363.325**
Miraldi, Robert
  (ed) Kahn, R. Beyond the boys of summer **796.357**
Seymour Hersh   **92**
Mirarchi, Carlo
  (jt. auth) Parachini, C. Roberta's   **641.82**
Mires, Charlene
Capital of the world   **341.23**
Miró, Joan, 1893-1983
          About
Joan Miro   **759**
Mirror Earth. Lemonick, M. D.   **523.2**
Mirror mirror. Pendergrast, M.   **535**
Mirroring people. Iacoboni, M.   **573.8**
Mirrors. Galeano, E. H.   **909**
MIRRORS
  See also Furniture
Pendergrast, M. Mirror mirror   **535**
Mirrors of the unseen. Elliot, J.   **915**
Mirth of a nation.   **817**
Misalliance. Miller, E.   **959.704**
The **misanthrope** and other plays. Moliere   **842**
MISCARRIAGE
Kohn, I. A silent sorrow   **618.3**
Lerner, H. M. Miscarriage: a doctor's guide to the

Dancing to the precipice: Lucie de la Tour du Pin and the French Revolution **92**

A train in winter

Moorhouse, Roger

Berlin at war **943**

MOORPARK COLLEGE -- EXOTIC ANIMAL TRAINING AND MANAGEMENT PROGRAM

Sutherland, A. Kicked, bitten, and scratched **636.088**

MOORS See Muslims

Moose, Christina J.

(ed) Great events from history, The Renaissance & early modern era, 1454-1600 **909**

(ed) Great lives from history, the Renaissance & early modern era, 1454-1600 **920.003**

Moosewood Collective

Moosewood restaurant favorites **641.5**

Moosewood Foods (Company)

(comp) Moosewood Restaurant cooks at home **641.5**

(comp) Moosewood restaurant favorites **641.5**

MOOSEWOOD RESTAURANT

Moosewood Restaurant cooks at home **641.5**

Moosewood restaurant favorites **641.5**

Moosewood Restaurant cooks at home. **641.5**

Moosewood restaurant favorites. **641.5**

Moral combat. Burleigh, M. **940.54**

MORAL CONDITIONS

Moeller The moral fool **171**

MORAL DEVELOPMENT

See also Child psychology; Moral education

MORAL EDUCATION

See also Education; Ethics

The **moral** fool. Moeller **171**

Moral freedom. Wolfe, A. **170**

The **moral** imagination. Himmelfarb, G. **190**

The **moral** judgment of the child. Piaget, J. **155.4**

The **moral** lives of animals. Peterson, D. **156**

MORAL MAJORITY, INC

Winters, M. S. God's right hand **322**

Moral minds. Hauser, M. D. **170**

MORAL MOTIVATION

Peterson, D. The moral lives of animals **156**

MORAL PHILOSOPHY See Ethics

A **moral** reckoning. Goldhagen, D. **940.53**

MORAL THEOLOGY, CHRISTIAN See Christian ethics

Moral tribes. Greene, J. **170**

MORALE

See also Courage

Morales, Ed

Living in Spanglish **305.868**

MORALITY See Ethics

The **morality** of everyday life. Fleming, T. **170**

MORALITY PLAYS

See also Drama; English drama; Religious drama; Theater

MORALS See Conduct of life; Ethics; Human behavior; Moral conditions

Moran, Caitlin

How to be a woman **305.420**

Morante, Elsa, d. 1985

About

Tuck, L. Woman of Rome: a life of Elsa Morante **92**

MORAVIANS

See also Christian sects

Mordden, Ethan

Anything goes **782.1**

Love song **920**

Ziegfeld **92**

Mordock, John B.

Korach, M. Common phrases and where they come from **422**

More book lust. Pearl, N. **025**

More home cooking. Colwin, L. **642**

A **more** perfect heaven. Sobel, D. **520**

More stories from my father's court. Singer, I. B. **839**

More technology for the rest of us. **025**

More than a game. Billick, B. **796.332**

More than freedom. Kantrowitz, S. **323.1196**

More word histories and mysteries. **422**

More, Thomas Sir, Saint, 1478-1535

About

Bolt, R. A man for all seasons **822**

Russell, B. A history of Western philosophy **109**

Morehead, Albert H.

(ed) Hoyle, E. Hoyle's rules of games **795.4**

Morehead, Philip D.

(ed) Hoyle, E. Hoyle's rules of games **795.4**

Morell, Virginia

Animal wise **591.5**

Morello, Giuseppe, 1870-1930

About

Dash, M. The first family **364.1**

Moreno, Jonathan D.

The body politic **303.48**

Moreno, Megan

Sex, drugs 'n Facebook **004.67**

Moretzsohn, Fabio

Harasewych, M. G. The book of shells **594**

Morgan. Strouse, J. **92**

MORGAN LIBRARY & MUSEUM (NEW YORK, N.Y.)

Ardizzone, H. An illuminated life **92**

Morgan, Bill

(ed) Burroughs, W. S. Rub out the words **813**

(ed) Ginsberg, A. The letters of Allen Ginsberg **92**

(ed) Jack Kerouac and Allen Ginsberg **92**

I celebrate myself **92**

The typewriter is holy **810**

Muller, Richard A., 1944-
Dauber, P. M. The three big bangs   **523.1**
Energy for future presidents   **333.79**
Mulley, Clare
The Spy Who Loved   **940.54**
Mullin, Glenn H.
The second Dalai Lama   **92**
MULTICULTURAL EDUCATION
Schlesinger, A. M. The disuniting of America   **973**
See also Acculturation; Education; Multiculturalism
MULTICULTURAL LITERATURE
See also Literature; Multiculturalism
Multicultural manners. Dresser, N.   **395**
MULTICULTURALISM
Brysac, S. B. Pax ethnica   **323.11**
Levine, L. W. The opening of the American mind   **001.1**
Patel, E. Acts of faith   **92**
Postman, N. The end of education   **370.9**
Schlesinger, A. M. The disuniting of America   **973**
Woodard, C. American nations   **970.004**
See also Culture; Social policy
MULTILINGUALISM
See also Language and languages
MULTIMEDIA
Pattee, A. S. Developing library collections for to-day's young adults   **027.62**
See also Computer software; Information systems
MULTIMEDIA CENTERS *See* Instructional materials centers
MULTIMEDIA LIBRARY SERVICES
Gallaway, B. Game on!   **025.2**
MULTIMEDIA LIBRARY SERVICES -- UNITED STATES
Pattee, A. S. Developing library collections for to-day's young adults   **027.62**
MULTINATIONAL CORPORATIONS
Bown, S. R. Merchant kings   **338.8**
See also Business enterprises; Commerce; Corporations; International economic relations
MULTIPLE BIRTH
See also Childbirth
MULTIPLE PERSONALITY
Nathan, D. Sybil exposed   **616.85**
Schreiber, F. R. Sybil   **616.85**
See also Abnormal psychology; Mental illness; Personality disorders; Psychology
MULTIPLE PREGNANCY
See also Pregnancy
MULTIRACIAL PEOPLE *See* Racially mixed people
Mumford, Lewis
The city in history   **307.7**

The culture of cities   **307.7**
MUMMIES
Fowler, B. Iceman   **937**
Pringle, H. A. The mummy congress   **393**
See also Archeology; Burial; Human remains (Archeology)
The **mummy** congress. Pringle, H. A.   **393**
Munch, Edvard, 1863-1944
About
Dolnick, E. The rescue artist   **364.1**
Prideaux, S. Edvard Munch   **92**
MUNDANEUM -- HISTORY
Wright, A. Cataloging the world   **020.9**
Mundy, Liza
Everything conceivable   **176**
MUNICH (GERMANY)
Johnson, I. A mosque in Munich   **297**
MUNICH FOUR-POWER AGREEMENT (1938)
Faber, D. Munich, 1938   **940.53**
Munich, 1938. Faber, D.   **940.53**
MUNICIPAL ART
See also Art; Cities and towns
MUNICIPAL EMPLOYEES *See* Municipal officials and employees
MUNICIPAL ENGINEERING
See also Engineering; Public works
MUNICIPAL GOVERNMENT
See also Local government; Political science
MUNICIPAL OFFICIALS AND EMPLOYEES
Nagle, R. Picking up   **331.7**
MUNICIPAL OWNERSHIP
See also Corporations; Economic policy; Government ownership
MUNICIPAL PLANNING *See* City planning
MUNICIPALITIES *See* Cities and towns; Municipal government
MUNITIONS *See* Defense industry; Military weapons
Munro, Nell
Ives, M. Caring for a child with autism   **618.92**
Munson, Ronald
Raising the dead   **174**
MUPPET SHOW (TELEVISION PROGRAM)
Jones, B. J. Jim Henson   **92**
Murakami, Haruki
Underground   **364.1**
MURAL PAINTING AND DECORATION
Felisbret, E. Graffiti New York   **751.7**
Ganz, N. Graffiti world   **751**
Hirst, M. Michelangelo   **709.2**
King, R. Michelangelo & the Pope's ceiling   **759**
See also Decoration and ornament; Interior design; Painting
MURDER *See* Homicide
MURDER -- CONNECTICUT -- HISTORY -- 17TH CENTURY

My age of anxiety. Stossel, S. 616.85
My almost certainly real imaginary Jesus. Barth, K. 277
My American century. Terkel, S. 920
My American journey. Powell, C. L. 92
My Backyard Jungle. Barilla, J. 577.5
My battle of Algiers. Morgan, T. 965
My beloved world. Sotomayor, S. 347.73
My bondage and my freedom. Douglass, F. 973.8
My brief history. Hawking, S. W. 92
My bright abyss. Wiman, C. 814
My brother's book. Sendak, M. 811
My cross to bear. Allman, G. 780
My dearest friend. Adams, J. 92
My dog Skip. Morris, W. 813
My double life: the memoirs of Sarah Bernhardt. Bernhardt, S. 792
My dyslexia. Schultz, P. 92
My extraordinary ordinary life. Spacek, S. 791.43
My face is black is true. Berry, M. F. 323
My family table. Besh, J. 641.59
My father at 100. Reagan, R. 92
My father is a book. Smith, J. M. 92
My father's paradise. Sabar, A. 305.8
My father's people. Rubin, L. D. 920
My fellow citizens. 352.23
My first coup d'etat and other true stories from the lost decades of Africa. Mahama, J. D. 966.705
My friend Dahmer. 741.5
My German question. Gay, P. 943
My green manifesto. Gessner, D. 304.2
My Guantanamo diary. Khan, M. R. 909.83
My happiness bears no relation to happiness. Hoffman, A. 92
My heart is an idiot. Rothbart, D. 818
My hope for peace. Sadat, J. 956.05
My invented country. Allende, I. 863
My Isl@m. Nasr, A. A. 297.09
My Korean deli. Howe, B. R. 92
My life. Duncan, I. 792.802
My life. Clinton, B. 92
My life as a traitor. Ghahramani, Z. 92
My life as author and editor. 818
My life in France. Child, J. 92
My life in Middlemarch. Mead, R. 823.8
My life in politics. Chirac, J. 944.084
My life with Pablo Neruda. Urrutia, M. 92
My life with the saints. Martin, J. 270
My lives. White, E. 813
My losing season. Conroy, P. 796.323
My Lunches With Orson. Biskind, P. 791.43
My mother/my self. Friday, N. 155.6
My name on his tongue. Halaby, L. 811
My New Orleans. Besh, J. 641.59
My nuclear family. Brownfield, C. J. 92
My paper chase. Evans, H. 92

My Paris kitchen. 641.59
My poets. McLane, M. N. 811
My prison, my home. Esfandiari, H. 92
My promised land. Shavit, A. 956.05
My Russian grandmother and her American vacuum cleaner. Shalev, M. 92
My sister, guard your veil; my brother guard, your eyes. Azam Zanganeh, L. 305
My song. Belafonte, H. 92
My start-up life. Casnocha, B. 338.7
My stroke of luck. Douglas, K. 362.1
My sweet Mexico. Gerson, F. 641.5
My Tibet. Bstan-'dzin-rgya-mtsho, D. L. X. 951
My Times in black and white. Boyd, G. M. 92
My Venice and Other Essays. Leon, D. 945
My vocabulary did this to me. Spicer, J. 811
My war. Rooney, A. A. 940.54
My wars are laid away in books. Habegger, A. 92
My year of flops. Rabin, N. 791.43
MYANMAR
Duguid, N. Burma 641.59
MYANMAR -- DESCRIPTION AND TRAVEL
Kress, W. J. The weeping goldsmith 508
Thant Myint-U Where China meets India 959.1
MYANMAR -- FOREIGN RELATIONS -- CHINA
Thant Myint-U Where China meets India 959.1
MYANMAR -- FOREIGN RELATIONS -- INDIA
Thant Myint-U Where China meets India 959.1
MYANMAR -- POLITICS AND GOVERNMENT
Aung San Suu Kyi Freedom from fear, and other writings 959.1
Wintle, J. Perfect hostage 92
Myatt, John
About
Salisbury, L. Provenance 92
MYCOLOGY *See* Fungi
Myer, Valerie Grosvenor
(ed) The Continuum encyclopedia of British literature 810
Myers, Allen C.
(ed) Eerdmans dictionary of the Bible 220.3
Myers, Betsy
Take the lead 158
Myers, Isabel Briggs
Gifts differing 155.2
Myers, Marc
Why jazz happened 781.65
Myers, Peter B.
Myers, I. B. Gifts differing 155.2
Myerson, Joel
(ed) Transcendentalism 810
Myne. Presley, F. 821
Myrdal, Gunnar, 1898-1987
About
Ellison, R. The collected essays of Ralph Elli-

National Audubon Society guide to marine mammals of the world. Folkens, P. A. **599.5**

National Audubon Society guide to nature photography. National Audubon Society **778.9**

NATIONAL BASEBALL HALL OF FAME AND MUSEUM

Stanton, T. Road to Cooperstown **92**

NATIONAL BASKETBALL ASSOCIATION

Bradley, B. Values of the game **796.323**

FreeDarko presents the macrophenomenal pro basketball almanac **796.323**

Simmons, B. The book of basketball **796.323**

NATIONAL BASKETBALL ASSOCIATION

See also Basketball

NATIONAL BOOK WEEK

See also Books and reading

NATIONAL CHARACTERISTICS

See also Anthropology; Nationalism; Social psychology

NATIONAL CHARACTERISTICS -- ENCYCLOPEDIAS

Minahan, J. The complete guide to national symbols and emblems **929.9**

NATIONAL CHARACTERISTICS, AMERICAN

Brokaw, T. A long way from home **070**

Caputo, P. The longest road **973.93**

Commager, H. S. The American mind **973**

Cult pop culture **306**

Elliott, C. Better than well **306.4**

Ellis, J. J. American creation **973.3**

Fischer, D. H. Liberty and freedom **323.44**

Kalman, M. And the pursuit of happiness **170**

Levy, B. H. American vertigo **917**

Marcus, G. The shape of things to come **973**

Menand, L. The Metaphysical Club **973.9**

Noonan, P. A heart, a cross & a flag **973.931**

Prothero, S. The American Bible **973**

Purdy, J. A tolerable anarchy **320**

Rinella, S. American buffalo **599.64**

Walker, J. The United States of paranoia **973**

Well, F. Family trees **929.20973**

White, R. Railroaded **385**

Wood, G. S. Empire of liberty **973.4**

See also American national characteristics

NATIONAL CHARACTERISTICS, AMERICAN, IN LITERATURE

Parini, J. Promised land **810**

Prothero, S. The American Bible **973**

NATIONAL CHARACTERISTICS, EAST INDIAN

Giridharadas, A. India calling **954.05**

NATIONAL CHARACTERISTICS, MEXICAN, IN LITERATURE

Biron, R. E. Elena Garro and Mexico's modern dreams **868**

National Commission on Terrorist Attacks Upon the United States

Jacobson, S. The 9/11 report **741.5**

The 9/11 Commission report **973.931**

NATIONAL CONSCIOUSNESS *See* Nationalism

National electrical code handbook 2014. **621.3**

NATIONAL EMBLEMS

See also Signs and symbols

NATIONAL EMBLEMS -- ENCYCLOPEDIAS

Minahan, J. The complete guide to national symbols and emblems **929.9**

National Film Preservation Board (U.S.)

Eagan, D. America's film legacy **791.43**

National Fire Protection Association

Fire protection handbook **628.9**

National five digit zip code and post office directory. **383**

NATIONAL FOOTBALL LEAGUE

Dawidoff, N. Collision Low Crossers **796.3**

Fainaru, S. League of Denial **617.1**

See also Football

National Gallery (Great Britain)

Liedtke, W. A. Vermeer and the Delft school **759.9**

National Gallery of Art. National Gallery of Art (U.S.) **708**

National Gallery of Art (U.S.)

Cikovsky, N. Winslow Homer **759.13**

Dickerman, L. Dada **709.04**

Edouard Vuillard **759**

National Gallery of Art **708**

Stieglitz, A. Alfred Stieglitz: the key set **770**

National geographic (Periodical)

National Geographic Society (U.S.) Through the lens **779**

National Geographic atlas of the world. **912**

National Geographic birding essentials. Alderfer, J. **598**

National Geographic concise history of the world. **902**

National Geographic concise history of world religions. **200**

National Geographic directions [series]

Erdrich, L. Books and islands in Ojibwe country **92**

Morris, J. A writer's house in Wales **942.9**

National Geographic encyclopedia of space. **629.4**

National Geographic eyewitness to the 20th century. National Geographic Society (U.S.) **909.82**

National Geographic guide to America's great houses. Wiencek, H. **728.8**

National Geographic guide to the national parks of the United States. National Geographic Society (U.S.) **917**

National Geographic guide to the state parks of the United States. National Geographic Society (U.S.) **917**

National Geographic Society (U.S.)

Alderfer, J. National Geographic birding essen-

life and customs

NATIVE AMERICAN LANGUAGES
See also Language and languages

NATIVE AMERICAN LITERATURE
See also Literature

NATIVE AMERICAN LITERATURE -- ENCY-CLOPEDIAS
Encyclopedia of American Indian literature   810

NATIVE AMERICAN LITERATURE -- HISTO-RY AND CRITICISM
The Cambridge companion to Native American literature   897

NATIVE AMERICAN POLITICAL ACTIVISTS
Hoxie, F. E. This Indian country   323.11

NATIVE AMERICAN SIGN LANGUAGE
See also Sign language
Native American son. Buford, K.   92
Native American testimony.   970.004

NATIVE AMERICAN WOMEN
Sifters: Native American women's lives   920
See also Women

NATIVE AMERICANS
Bragdon, K. J. The Columbia guide to American Indians of the Northeast   970.004
Deloria, V. Custer died for your sins   970.004
Dorris, M. The broken cord   362.292
Hogan, L. The woman who watches over the world   818
Iverson, P. We are still here   970.004
Milton, G. Big Chief Elizabeth   970.004
Nagel, J. American Indian ethnic renewal   305.8
Philip, N. The great circle   970.004
Richter, D. K. Facing east from Indian country   970.004
Treuer, A. Everything you wanted to know about Indians but were afraid to ask   909
Waldman, C. Atlas of the North American Indian   970.004
Weatherford, J. M. Native roots   970.004
Wilson, J. The earth shall weep   970.004

NATIVE AMERICANS -- AGRICULTURE
See also Agriculture

NATIVE AMERICANS -- ANTIQUITIES
America in 1492   970.004
Schobinger, J. The ancient Americans   970.01
See also Antiquities

NATIVE AMERICANS -- ANTIQUITIES -- EN-CYCLOPEDIAS
Archaeology of prehistoric native America   970.01

NATIVE AMERICANS -- BIOGRAPHY
Black Elk   Black Elk speaks   92
Buford, K. Native American son   92
Crawford, B. All American   92
McMurtry, L. Crazy Horse   92

NATIVE AMERICANS -- BRAZIL
Reel, M. The last of the tribe   981

NATIVE AMERICANS -- CAPTIVITIES
Frankel, G. The searchers   791.43

NATIVE AMERICANS -- CAPTIVITIES
See also Frontier and pioneer life

NATIVE AMERICANS -- DICTIONARIES
Notable native Americans   920.003

NATIVE AMERICANS -- ECONOMIC CONDI-TIONS
See also Economic conditions

NATIVE AMERICANS -- EDUCATION
See also Education

NATIVE AMERICANS -- ENCYCLOPEDIAS
American Indians   970.004
Johnson, M. Encyclopedia of native tribes of North America   970.004
Native America in the twentieth century   970.004
Pritzker, B. A Native American encyclopedia   970.004
Waldman, C. Encyclopedia of Native American tribes   970.004

NATIVE AMERICANS -- ETHNOBOTANY
See also Ethnobotany

NATIVE AMERICANS -- FIRST CONTACT WITH EUROPEANS
See also Native Americans -- History

NATIVE AMERICANS -- FOLKLORE
See also Folklore

NATIVE AMERICANS -- GOVERNMENT RE-LATIONS
Documents of American Indian diplomacy   970.004
Hendricks, S. The unquiet grave   970.004
Native American testimony   970.004
Osborn, W. M. The wild frontier   970.004
Prucha, F. P. The great father   323.1
Schultz, E. B. King Philip's War   973.2
Wallace, A. F. C. The long bitter trail   323.1

NATIVE AMERICANS -- GOVERNMENT RE-LATIONS -- HISTORY
Berg, S. W. 38 nooses   973.7

NATIVE AMERICANS -- GREAT PLAINS
Fowler, L. The Columbia guide to American Indians of the Great Plains   970.004

NATIVE AMERICANS -- HISTORY
America in 1492   970.004
Egan, T. Short nights of the Shadow Catcher   770.92
Fenn, E. A. Encounters at the heart of the world   305.897
Hoxie, F. E. This Indian country   323.11
Mann, C. C. 1491   970.01
Wheelan, J. Terrible swift sword   355.009

NATIVE AMERICANS -- HISTORY -- SOURC-ES
Native American testimony   970.004

NATIVE AMERICANS -- HOUSING
See also Housing

NATIVE AMERICANS -- MEXICO -- ENCY-

The **new** solar system. Daniels, P.   **523.2**

The **new** stokes field guide to birds. Stokes, D. **598**

The **new** stokes field guide to birds. Stokes, D. **598**

The **new** terrarium. Martin, T.   **635.9**

NEW THOUGHT

   James, W. The varieties of religious experience **210**

A **new** time for Mexico. Fuentes, C.   **972.08**

The **new** time travelers. Toomey, D. M.   **530.1**

A **New** Turn in the South. Acheson, H.   **641.59**

The **new** vegetarian cooking for everyone. Madison, D.   **641.5**

NEW WAVE FILMS -- FRANCE

   Neupert, R. A history of the French new wave cinema   **791.43**

NEW WAVE MUSIC

   Bukszpan, D. The encyclopedia of new wave **781.66**

The **new** way things work. Macaulay, D.   **600**

NEW WORDS

   Metcalf, A. A. Predicting new words   **420**

   See also Vocabulary

The **new** work of dogs. Katz, J.   **636.7**

New world coming. Miller, N.   **973.91**

New World kitchen.   **641.59**

NEW YEAR

   See also Holidays

NEW YORK (N.Y.)

   Ninety days   **362.290**

   Winder, E. Pain, Parties, Work   **811**

NEW YORK (N.Y.) -- 20TH CENTURY

   McCourt, J. Lasting City   **92**

NEW YORK (N.Y.) -- BIOGRAPHY

   Mariani, P. L. The broken tower: a life of Hart Crane   **811**

   McCourt, M. A monk swimming   **974.7**

   McCourt, M. Singing my him song   **974.7**

   Napoli, P. F. Bringing it all back home   **959.704**

   Ward, G. C. A disposition to be rich   **974.7**

NEW YORK (N.Y.) -- BOARD OF EDUCATION

   Fertig, B. Why cant U teach me 2 read?   **372.4**

NEW YORK (N.Y.) -- BUILDINGS, STRUCTURES, ETC

   Mires, C. Capital of the world   **341.23**

NEW YORK (N.Y.) -- DESCRIPTION AND TRAVEL

   Anasi, R. The last bohemia   **974.7**

   Gopnik, A. Through the children's gate   **974.71**

   Greenberg, M. Beg, borrow, steal   **92**

   White, E. B. Essays of E.B. White   **814**

NEW YORK (N.Y.) -- ENCYCLOPEDIAS

   The encyclopedia of New York City   **974.7**

NEW YORK (N.Y.) -- ETHNIC RELATIONS

   Berger, J. The pious ones   **973**

   City of promises   **305.892**

NEW YORK (N.Y.) -- FIRE DEPT.

   Downey, T. The last men out   **363.34**

   Halberstam, D. Firehouse   **363.34**

   Smith, D. Report from ground zero   **363.34**

NEW YORK (N.Y.) -- HARLEM

   Gill, J. Harlem   **974.7**

NEW YORK (N.Y.) -- HISTORY

   Miller, D. L. Supreme city   **974.7**

NEW YORK (N.Y.) -- HISTORY -- 20TH CENTURY

   Miller, D. L. Supreme city   **974.7**

NEW YORK (N.Y.) -- HISTORY, MILITARY

   New York at war   **355.009**

NEW YORK (N.Y.) -- INTELLECTUAL LIFE

   The 40s   **973.917**

NEW YORK (N.Y.) -- PICTORIAL WORKS

   Smith, W. E. The jazz loft project   **779**

NEW YORK (N.Y.) -- POETRY

   Garcia Lorca, F. Poet in New York   **861**

NEW YORK (N.Y.) -- POLICE DEPT.

   Dickey, C. Securing the city   **363.32**

   Levitt, L. NYPD confidential   **364.1**

NEW YORK (N.Y.) -- POLITICS AND GOVERNMENT

   Kirtzman, A. Rudy Giuliani   **92**

   Siegel, F. F. The prince of the city   **92**

NEW YORK (N.Y.) -- POLITICS AND GOVERNMENT -- 1898-1951

   Miller, D. L. Supreme city   **974.7**

NEW YORK (N.Y.) -- RACE RELATIONS

   Lepore, J. New York burning   **974.7**

   White, S. Stories of freedom in Black New York   **974.7**

NEW YORK (N.Y.) -- SOCIAL CONDITIONS

   Anasi, R. The last bohemia   **974.7**

   Canada, G. Fist, stick, knife, gun   **305.23**

   Freeman, J. B. Working-class New York   **305.5**

   LeBlanc, A. N. Random family   **305.5**

NEW YORK (N.Y.) -- SOCIAL LIFE AND CUSTOMS

   Anasi, R. The last bohemia   **974.7**

   Cliff, N. The Shakespeare riots   **974.4**

   Fletcher, T. All hopped up and ready to go **781.64**

   Freeland, D. Automats, taxi dances, and vaudeville

   Gopnik, A. Through the children's gate   **974.71**

   Heap, C. Slumming   **305.8**

   Roiphe, A. R. 1185 Park Avenue   **813**

   Rudnick, P. I shudder   **92**

NEW YORK (N.Y.) -- SOCIAL LIFE AND CUSTOMS -- 20TH CENTURY

   Fletcher, T. All hopped up and ready to go **781.64**

   The Fun of it   **814**

   Miller, D. L. Supreme city   **974.7**

NEW YORK (STATE)

   Humm, D. I love New York   **641.59**

NEW YORK (STATE) -- ENCYCLOPEDIAS

   The encyclopedia of New York State   **974.7**

NEW YORK (STATE) -- HISTORY

   Cohen, E. A. Conquered into liberty   **355**

Achebe, C.   The education of a British-protected
 child   **92**
NIGERIA -- HISTORY -- CIVIL WAR, 1967-1970
 -- PERSONAL NARRATIVES
 Achebe, C.   There was a country   **823**
NIGERIA -- POLITICS AND GOVERNMENT
 Maier, K.   This house has fallen   **966.905**
Nigge, Klaus
 Whooping crane   **598**
NIGHT
 Bogard, P.   The end of night   **551.56**
 Ekirch, A. R.   At day's close   **306.4**
  See also Chronology; Time
NIGHT -- PSYCHOLOGICAL ASPECTS
 Bogard, P.   The end of night   **551.56**
The **night** Abraham called to the stars. Bly, R. **811**
Night and horses and the desert.   **892.7**
The **night** country. Eiseley, L. C.   **818**
Night draws near. Shadid, A.   **956.7**
The **night** of the gun. Carr, D.   **92**
Night of the republic. Shapiro, A.   **811**
A **night** to remember. Lord, W.   **910.4**
Night wraps the sky.   **92**
Nightcap at dawn. Walker, J. B.   **956.704**
Nightingale, Florence, 1820-1910
             About
 Bostridge, M.   Florence Nightingale   **92**
NIGHTINGALES
 Birkhead, T.   Bird sense   **598**
NIHILISM
 Camus, A.   The rebel   **303.6**
Nikita Khrushchev.   **92**
NILE RIVER -- DESCRIPTION AND TRAVEL
 Morrison, D.   The black Nile   **962**
NILE RIVER -- EXPLORATION
 Jeal, T.   Explorers of the Nile   **962**
NILE RIVER -- SOCIAL CONDITIONS
 Morrison, D.   The black Nile   **962**
Nilsen, Alleen Pace
 Encyclopedia of 20th century American humor **817**
Nilsen, Don L. F.
 Nilsen, A. P. Encyclopedia of 20th century Ameri-
  can humor   **817**
Nilsen, Kirsti
 Conducting the reference interview   **025.5**
Nilsson, Lennart
 A child is born   **612.6**
Nimitz, Chester W. (Chester William), 1885-1966
             About
 Borneman, W. R.   The admirals   **920**
Nims, John Frederick
 The powers of heaven and earth   **811**
Nin, Anaïs, 1903-1977
             About
 Pierpont, C. R. Passionate minds   **810**
The **nine.** Toobin, J. R.   **347**

Nine hills to Nambonkaha. Erdman, S.   **966.68**
Nine horses. Collins, B.   **811**
Nine lives. Dalrymple, W.   **294**
Nine lives. Baum, D.   **976.3**
Nine plays of the modern theater.   **808.82**
NINETEEN EIGHTIES
 Sirota, D.   Back to our future   **973.92**
  See also World history -- 20th century
NINETEEN FIFTIES
  See also World history -- 20th century
NINETEEN FORTIES
 The 40s   **973.917**
  See also World history -- 20th century
NINETEEN NINETIES
  See also World history -- 20th century
NINETEEN NINETIES -- DRAMA.
 Wilson, A.   Radio golf   **812**
NINETEEN SEVENTIES
 Frum, D.   How we got here   **973.92**
 Killen, A.   1973 nervous breakdown   **973.924**
 Wheen, F.   Strange days indeed   **973.92**
  See also World history -- 20th century
NINETEEN SIXTIES
 Diski, J.   The Sixties   **92**
 Huntington, C.   Heavenly bodies   **811**
 Markoff, J.   What the dormouse said--   **004**
 Stone, R.   Prime green   **92**
  See also World history -- 20th century
NINETEEN SIXTIES -- DRAMA.
 Wilson, A.   Two trains running   **812**
NINETEEN THIRTEEN, A.D
 Emmerson, C.   1913   **909.82**
NINETEEN THIRTIES
  See also World history -- 20th century
NINETEEN TWENTIES
 Mackrell, J.   Flappers   **920**
  See also World history -- 20th century
NINETEENTH CENTURY *See* World history --
 19th century
Ninety days.   **362.290**
Ninety degrees North. Fleming, F.   **919**
Ninja. Man, J.   **355.5**
NINJA
 Man, J.   Ninja   **355.5**
The **Ninth.** Sachs, H.   **785**
Niose, David
 Nonbeliever nation   **211**
Nirenberg, David
 Anti-Judaism   **305.892**
NIRVANA (MUSICAL GROUP)
 Cross, C. R.   Heavier than heaven: a biography of
  Kurt Cobain   **92**
 Cross, C. R.   Here we are now   **92**
NISQUALLI INDIANS -- HISTORY
 Kluger, R.   The bitter waters of Medicine
  Creek   **979.7**

Branch, T. Parting the waters: America in the King years, 1954-63 **973.921**

Brands, H. W. Woodrow Wilson **973.91**

Bstan-'dzin-rgya-mtsho, D. L. X. Freedom in exile **92**

Burns, J. M. The three Roosevelts **973.91**

Burns, R. Burial for a King **92**

Carlin, J. Playing the enemy **968.06**

Carter, J. Everything to gain **92**

Carter, J. An hour before daylight **973.926**

Carter, J. Keeping faith: memoirs of a president **92**

Carter, J. Living faith **248.4**

Carter, J. Sharing good times **92**

Cooper, J. M. The warrior and the priest: Woodrow Wilson and Theodore Roosevelt **92**

Cooper, J. M. Woodrow Wilson **92**

Cordery, S. A. Alice **92**

Dallek, R. Nixon and Kissinger **92**

Dershowitz, A. M. Supreme injustice **324.9**

DiSilvestro, R. L. Theodore Roosevelt in the Badlands **92**

Duke, L. Mandela, Mobutu, and me **968.06**

Dyson, M. E. I may not get there with you: the true Martin Luther King, Jr **323**

Ebadi, S. Iran awakening **92**

Egan, T. The big burn **973.91**

Feinstein, A. Pablo Neruda **92**

Frank, J. A. Obama on the couch **973.932**

Greenberg, S. B. Dispatches from the war room **324.7**

Halberstam, D. The best and the brightest **973.922**

Hayden, T. The long sixties **973.92**

Hofstadter, R. The American political tradition, and the men who made it **973**

I see the promised land **92**

In his own words **92**

Iyer, P. The open road **92**

Jackson, T. Becoming King **92**

Johnson, T. Tragedy in crimson **294.3**

Johnson-Sirleaf, E. This child will be great **92**

Joseph, P. E. Dark days, bright nights **323.1**

King, M. L. The autobiography of Martin Luther King, Jr **323**

Kissinger, H. Diplomacy **327.2**

Kissinger, H. Years of renewal **973.924**

Knight, L. W. Jane Addams **92**

Kotz, N. Judgment days **323**

Lourie, R. Sakharov **323**

Maathai, W. Unbowed **92**

MacMillan, M. Paris 1919 **940.3**

Mandela, N. Conversations with myself **92**

Mandela, N. Long walk to freedom: the autobiography of Nelson Mandela **92**

Mandela, N. Mandela **968.06**

Mann, J. The rebellion of Ronald Reagan **973.927**

Mann, J. About face **327**

McCullough, D. G. Mornings on horseback **92**

McCullough, D. G. The path between the seas **972.87**

Mendell, D. Obama **92**

Millard, C. The river of doubt **973.91**

Miller, J. J. The big scrum **796.332**

Morris, E. The rise of Theodore Roosevelt **92**

Morris, E. Theodore Rex **973.91**

Morris, K. E. Jimmy Carter, American moralist **973.926**

Neruda, P. The poetry of Pablo Neruda **861**

Obama, B. Dreams from my father **92**

O'Toole, P. When trumpets call **92**

Pauling, L. C. Linus Pauling in his own words **081**

Pepper, W. F. An act of state **364.1**

Pooley, E. The climate war **363.7**

Ratnesar, R. Tear down this wall **973.927**

Rauchway, E. Murdering McKinley **973.8**

Remnick, D. The bridge **92**

Remnick, D. Reporting **814**

Risen, C. A nation on fire **973.923**

Roberts, A. Masters and commanders **940.54**

Sadat, J. My hope for peace **956.05**

Sampson, A. Nelson Mandela **92**

Shalom, friend: the life and legacy of Yitzhak Rabin **92**

Sides, H. Hellhound on his trail **364.152**

Smith, D. J. Young Mandela **92**

Spink, K. Mother Teresa **271**

Talty, S. Escape from the land of snows **92**

Thomas, E. The war lovers **973.8**

Thurman, R. A. F. Why the Dalai Lama matters **294.3**

Tolstaia, T. Pushkin's children **891.7**

Tuchman, B. W. Practicing history **907**

Urrutia, M. My life with Pablo Neruda **92**

Weintraub, S. 15 stars **920**

Wiesel, E. All rivers run to the sea **813**

Wiesel, E. And the sea is never full **813**

Wintle, J. Perfect hostage **92**

Woodward, B. Shadow **973.92**

Young, A. An easy burden **92**

Zelizer, J. E. Jimmy Carter **92**

Zelnick, B. Gore: a political life **92**

Zimmermann, W. First great triumph **973**

NOBEL LAUREATES FOR PHYSICS

Aczel, A. D. God's equation **523.1**

Bodanis, D. E **530.1**

Bolles, E. B. Einstein defiant **530.1**

Brian, D. The Curies **92**

Cassidy, D. C. Beyond uncertainty **92**

Dry, S. Curie **92**

Einstein, A. Einstein on politics **92**

Einstein, A. A stubbornly persistent illusion **530.1**

Farmelo, G. The strangest man **92**

Feldman, B. 112 Mercer Street **920**

Browning, R. Robert Browning's poetry   **821**

Malory, T. Le morte Darthur, or, The hoole book of Kyng Arthur and of his noble knyghtes of the Rounde Table   **398.2**

Norton, Richard

(jt. auth) Bordman, G. American musical theatre   **782.1**

Norton, Trevor

Smoking ears and screaming teeth   **616.02**

The **Norton/Grove** dictionary of women composers.   **780.92**

NORWEGIAN LANGUAGE

See also Language and languages; Scandinavian languages

NORWEGIAN LITERATURE

See also Literature; Scandinavian literature

Norwich, John Julius

Byzantium: the apogee   **949.5**

Byzantium: the decline and fall   **949.5**

Byzantium: the early centuries   **949.5**

Shakespeare's kings   **822.3**

Nosakhere, Akilah S.

(ed) The 21st-century black librarian in America   **020.899**

Nossiter, Adam

The Algeria Hotel   **940.53**

NOSTALGIA -- POETRY

pH neutral history   **891.8**

Nostradamus. Gerson, S.   **133.3092**

Nostradamus, 1503-1566

About

Gerson, S. Nostradamus   **133.3092**

Not buying it. Levine, J.   **640.73**

Not for bread alone. Foner, M.   **92**

Not for specialists. Snodgrass, W. D.   **811**

Not out of Africa. Lefkowitz, M. R.   **960**

Not quite adults. Ray, B. E.   **306.8**

Not so big solutions for your home. Susanka, S. **728**

Not till the fat lady sings. Krantz, L.   **796**

Not war but murder. Furgurson, E. B.   **973.7**

Not your mother's divorce. Moffett, K.   **306.89**

Not your usual founding father. Franklin, B.   **92**

NOT-FOR-PROFIT ORGANIZATIONS   *See* Nonprofit organizations

Notable American women.   **920.003**

Notable American women: the modern period.   **920.003**

Notable black American men, book I.   **920.003**

Notable black American men, book II.   **920.003**

Notable black American scientists.   **509**

Notable black American women, book I.   **920.003**

Notable black American women, Book III. **920.003**

Notable Latino writers. Salem Press Inc.   **810**

Notable native Americans.   **920.003**

Notable scientists [series]

Gates, A. E. A to Z of earth scientists   **920.003**

Yount, L. A to Z of biologists   **920.003**

Notable voices [series]

Cording, R. Walking with Ruskin   **811**

Notable women in American history. Adamson, L. G.   **016**

Notable women in world history. Adamson, L. G.   **016**

NOTE-TAKING

See also Reporters and reporting; Study skills

NOTEBOOKS

See also Books

Notes from a small island. Bryson, B.   **914**

Notes from no man's land. Biss, E.   **305.8**

Notes from the air. Ashbery, J.   **811**

Notes on a century. Churchill, B. E.   **956**

Notes to an actor. Marasco, R.   **792**

Nothdurft, William E.

The lost dinosaurs of Egypt   **567.9**

Nothing. Close, F. E.   **530**

Nothing but the blues.   **781.643**

Nothing like it in the world. Ambrose, S. E.   **385**

Nothing makes you free.   **808.8**

The **nothing** that is. Kaplan, R.   **511**

Nothing to be frightened of. Barnes, J.   **92**

Nothing to envy. Demick, B.   **951.93**

Nothing was the same. Jamison, K. R.   **92**

Notley, Alice

Grave of light   **811**

In the pines   **811**

(ed) Poems/Selections The collected poems of Ted Berrigan   **811**

Notorious. Spoto, D.   **92**

The **notorious** Elizabeth Tuttle. Chamberlain, A. **92**

NOTRE DAME FIGHTING IRISH (FOOTBALL TEAM)

Dent, J. Resurrection   **796.332**

Robinson, R. Rockne of Notre Dame   **92**

NOTRE-DAME (CATHEDRAL: CHARTRES, FRANCE)

Adams, H. Mont-Saint-Michel and Chartres   **726**

Nourse, Victoria F.

In reckless hands   **344**

Nouwen, Henri

Discernment   **248.4**

Novacek, Michael J.

Terra   **576.8**

Time traveler   **92**

The **novel.** Moore, S.   **809**

NOVELISTS, AMERICAN

Darst, J. Fiction ruined my family   **92**

Didion, J. Blue nights   **92**

Heller, E. Yossarian slept here   **92**

Wilson, E. Patriotic gore   **810**

See also American novelists

NOVELISTS, AMERICAN -- 20TH CENTURY -- BIOGRAPHY

no, S.   **791.43**

OBSCENITY (LAW)

   See also Criminal law

OBSERVATION (SCIENTIFIC METHOD)

   Wilson, E. O. Letters to a Young Scientist   **570**

Obsessed. Brzezinski, M.   **362.196**

OBSESSION (PSYCHOLOGY) *See* Obsessive-compulsive disorder

OBSESSIVE-COMPULSIVE DISORDER

   Frost, R. O. Stuff   **616.85**

   Murphy, T. W. Life in rewind   **92**

Obst, Lynda

   Sleepless in Hollywood   **791.43**

OBSTETRICS *See* Childbirth

Obstfeld, Raymond

   Abdul-Jabbar, K. On the shoulders of giants   **92**

Occhiogrosso, Peter

   Zappa, F. The real Frank Zappa book   **92**

OCCIDENTAL CIVILIZATION *See* Western civilization

Occidental mythology. Campbell, J.   **201**

OCCULT FICTION

   See also Fiction

OCCULTISM

   Goodman, L. Linda Goodman's star signs   **130**

   See also Religions; Supernatural

OCCULTISTS

   Schmidt, L. E. Heaven's bride   **92**

The **occupation.** Cockburn, P.   **956.7**

The **occupation** of Iraq. Allawi, A. A.   **956.7**

OCCUPATION, MILITARY *See* Military occupation

OCCUPATIONAL ACCIDENTS *See* Industrial accidents

OCCUPATIONAL DISEASES

   See also Diseases

OCCUPATIONAL GUIDANCE *See* Vocational guidance

OCCUPATIONAL HEALTH AND SAFETY

   See also Environmental health; Management; Public health; Medical care

OCCUPATIONAL INJURIES *See* Industrial accidents

Occupational outlook handbook 2013-2014. **331.12**

OCCUPATIONAL RETRAINING

   See also Employees -- Training; Labor supply; Occupational training; Technical education; Unemployed; Vocational education

OCCUPATIONAL THERAPY

   See also Mental health; People with physical disabilities -- Rehabilitation; Physical therapy; Therapeutics

OCCUPATIONAL TRAINING -- UNITED STATES

   Chertavian, G. A Year Up   **331.25**

OCCUPATIONS

Farr, J. M. 100 fastest-growing careers   **331.7**

Ferguson Publishing The top 100   **331.7**

Lore, N. The pathfinder   **650.14**

McKenna, A. Nontraditional careers for women and men   **331.702**

Occupational outlook handbook 2013-2014 **331.12**

OCCUPATIONS -- ENCYCLOPEDIAS

   J.G. Ferguson Publishing Company Encyclopedia of careers and vocational guidance   **331.7**

OCCUPIED TERRITORY *See* Military occupation

OCCUPY PROTEST MOVEMENTS

   See also Demonstrations; Protest movements

OCEAN

   Carson, R. The sea around us   **551.46**

   Cramer, D. Smithsonian ocean   **578.7**

   Day, T. Oceans   **551.46**

   Nestor, J. Deep   **797.2**

   Pilkey, O. H. The rising sea   **363.34**

   Prager, E. J. Chasing science at sea   **551.46**

   Roberts, C. The unnatural history of the sea   **909**

   Stow, D. A. V. Oceans: an illustrated reference   **551.46**

   See also Earth; Physical geography; Water

OCEAN -- ECONOMIC ASPECTS *See* Marine resources; Shipping

OCEAN -- HISTORY

   Roberts, C. The ocean of life   **551.46**

OCEAN AND CIVILIZATION

   Roberts, C. The ocean of life   **551.46**

   Winchester, S. Atlantic   **551.46**

OCEAN BOTTOM

   See also Ocean; Submarine geology

OCEAN CABLES *See* Submarine cables

OCEAN CURRENTS

   Ebbesmeyer, C. Flotsametrics and the floating world   **551.46**

   See also Navigation; Ocean

Ocean drifters. Kirby, R. R.   **578.7**

OCEAN DRILLING PLATFORMS *See* Drilling platforms

OCEAN ENERGY RESOURCES

   See also Energy resources; Marine resources; Ocean engineering

OCEAN ENGINEERING

   See also Engineering; Marine resources; Oceanography

OCEAN LIFE *See* Marine biology

OCEAN LINERS

   Ujifusa, S. A man and his ship   **623.8**

OCEAN MINING

   Roberts, C. The ocean of life   **551.46**

   See also Marine mineral resources; Mining engineering; Ocean engineering

An **ocean** of air. Walker, G.   **551.5**

The **ocean** of life. Roberts, C.   **551.46**

OFFSHORE OIL INDUSTRY
   See also Petroleum industry
OFFSHORE OIL WELL DRILLING
   Freudenburg, W. R. Blowout in the Gulf   **363.7**
OFFSHORE OIL WELL DRILLING -- SAFETY MEASURES
   Magner, M. Poisoned legacy   **338.7**
OFFSHORE WATER POLLUTION *See* Marine pollution
Ofri, Danielle
   What doctors feel   **610.69**
Ogden Nash. Parker, D. M.   **92**
OGLALA INDIANS
   Black Elk Black Elk speaks   **92**
   McMurtry, L. Crazy Horse   **92**
   Powers, T. The killing of Crazy Horse   **92**
   Steltenkamp, M. F. Black Elk, holy man of the Oglala   **973**
The **ogre's** wife. Koertge, R.   **811**
The **oh** she glows cookbook. Liddon, A.   **641.5**
Ohanian, Hans C.
   Einstein's mistakes   **530**
Oher, Michael, 1986-
About
   Lewis, M. The blind side   **92**
OHIO
   Stansfield, C. A. Haunted Ohio   **133.1**
OHIO -- SOCIAL LIFE AND CUSTOMS
   Frazier, I. Family   **977.1**
   See also Manners and customs
OHIO -- STATISTICS
   See also Statistics
Oil. Sanmiguel, D.   **751.45**
OIL *See* Oils and fats; Petroleum
Oil and Honey. McKibben, B.   **363.7**
OIL DRILLING PLATFORMS *See* Drilling platforms
OIL INDUSTRY *See* Petroleum industry
Oil on the brain. Margonelli, L.   **338.2**
OIL PAINTING
   See also Painting
Oil painting for the absolute beginner. Willenbrink, M.   **751.45**
OIL POLLUTION OF WATER
   See also Water pollution
OIL SPILLS
   DeNapoli, D. The great penguin rescue   **639.9**
   Freudenburg, W. R. Blowout in the Gulf   **363.7**
OIL SPILLS -- ENVIRONMENTAL ASPECTS
   Magner, M. Poisoned legacy   **338.7**
OIL WELL DRILLING
   See also Drilling and boring (Earth and rocks); Petroleum industry
OIL WELL DRILLING, OFFSHORE *See* Offshore oil well drilling
OIL WELLS

   See also Petroleum industry
OIL WELLS -- BLOWOUTS
   Magner, M. Poisoned legacy   **338.7**
OIL WELLS -- HYDRAULIC FRACTURING -- POPULAR WORKS
   Prud'homme, A. Hydrofracking   **622**
Ojakangas, Beatrice
   The Best Casserole cookbook ever   **641.8**
OJIBWA INDIANS
   Erdrich, L. Books and islands in Ojibwe country **92**
Okinawa. Leckie, R.   **940.54**
OKLAHOMA SOONERS (FOOTBALL TEAM)
   Dent, J. The undefeated   **796.332**
Oklahoma western biographies [series]
   Riley, G. The life and legacy of Annie Oakley **796.3**
   Wilkins, T. John Muir   **333.7**
Okonowicz, Ed
   Haunted Maryland   **133.1**
Okrent, Arika
   In the land of invented languages   **499**
Okrent, Daniel, 1948-
   Last call   **363.4**
Ol' Dirty Bastard, 1969-2004
About
   Lowe, J. Digging for dirt   **92**
OLD AGE
   Athill, D. Somewhere towards the end   **92**
   Friedan, B. The fountain of age   **305.26**
   Jacoby, S. Never say die   **305.26**
   Lawrence-Lightfoot, S. The third chapter   **305.26**
   Pillemer, K. A. 30 lessons for living   **305.26**
OLD AGE PENSIONS
   See also Pensions; Retirement income
OLD GROWTH FOREST ECOLOGY -- TENNESSEE
   Haskell, D. G. The forest unseen   **577.3**
OLD GROWTH FORESTS -- TENNESSEE
   Haskell, D. G. The forest unseen   **577.3**
Old man Goya. Blackburn, J.   **92**
Old masters, new world. Saltzman, C.   **759.9**
OLD NORSE LANGUAGE
   See also Language and languages; Scandinavian languages
OLD NORSE LITERATURE
   The Sagas of Icelanders   **839**
   See also Literature; Medieval literature
OLD NORTHWEST
   See also United States
The **old** Patagonian express. Theroux, P.   **918**
OLD SOUTHWEST
   See also United States
The **old** ways. Macfarlane, R.   **914.2**
Old world, new world. Burk, K.   **327**
OLDER MEN -- EMPLOYMENT -- UNITED STATES
   Fideler, E. F. Men still at work   **331.3**

Wallechinsky, D. The complete book of the Winter Olympics **796.98**

See also Athletics; Contests; Games; Sports

OLYMPIC GAMES, 1936 (BERLIN, GER.)

Brown, D. J. The Boys in the Boat **797.12**

Schaap, J. Triumph **92**

OLYMPIC GAMES, 1968 (MEXICO CITY, MEX.)

Hoffer, R. Something in the air **796.4**

OLYMPIC GAMES, 2000 (SYDNEY, AUSTRALIA)

Mullen, P. H. Gold in the water **797.2**

OLYMPICS -- HISTORY

Davis, D. Showdown at Shepherd's Bush **796.42**

Guttmann, A. The Olympics, a history of the modern games **796.48**

The **Olympics,** a history of the modern games. Guttmann, A. **796.48**

Omaha blues. Lelyveld, J. **92**

Omar, Qais Akbar

A fort of nine towers **958.104**

An **omelette** and a glass of wine. David, E. **641**

Omeros. Walcott, D. **811**

The **omnivore's** dilemma. Pollan, M. **394.1**

On a farther shore. Souder, W. **92**

On apology. Lazare, A. **155.9**

On architecture. Huxtable, A. L. **724**

On Becoming a Mother. McConville, B. **306.874**

On becoming a novelist. Gardner, J. **808.3**

On being human. Fromm, E. **150.19**

On celestial music. Moody, R. **780.9**

On children and death. Kubler-Ross, E. **155.9**

On Conan Doyle; or, The whole art of storytelling. Dirda, M. **823**

On death and dying. Kubler-Ross, E. **155.9**

On desire. Irvine, W. B. **128**

On directing film. Mamet, D. **791.43**

On extinction. Challenger, M. **576.8**

On Hinduism. Doniger, W. **294.5**

On history. Hobsbawm, E. J. **901**

On immunity. Biss, E. **616.07**

On love. Hirsch, E. **811**

On monsters. Asma, S. T. **398.2**

On moral fiction. Gardner, J. **801**

On my country and the world. Gorbachev, M. **947.085**

On paper. Basbanes, N. A. **676.092**

On politics. Ryan, A. **320.01**

On Saudi Arabia. House, K. E. **953.8**

On second thought. Herbert, W. **153.4**

On Sunset Boulevard: the life and times of Billy Wilder. Sikov, E. **92**

On the backroad to heaven. Kraybill, D. B. **289.7**

On the brink. Paulson, H. M. **330.9**

On the bus with Rosa Parks. Dove, R. **811**

On the courthouse lawn. Ifill, S. A. **364.1**

On the edge. Koch, K. **811**

On the eve. Wasserstein, B. **305.892**

On the Front Line. Colvin, M. **070.4**

On the good life. Cicero, M. T. **878**

On the Irish waterfront. Fisher, J. T. **331.7**

On the law of nations. Moynihan, D. P. **327**

On the line. Ripert, E. **647**

On the Money Journal. Guyer, C. S. **332**

On the natural history of destruction. Sebald, W. G. **833**

On the nature of things: De rerum natura. Lucretius Carus, T. **187**

On the origin of species. Darwin, C. **576.8**

On the origin of stories. Boyd, B. **809**

On the rim of the Caribbean. Pressly, P. M. **975.8**

On the road with Charles Kuralt. Kuralt, C. **973.92**

On the shoulders of giants. Abdul-Jabbar, K. **92**

On the spectrum of possible deaths. Perillo, L. **811**

On the surface of things. Frankel, F. **530.4**

On the water. Stone, N. **917**

ON THE WATERFRONT (MOTION PICTURE)

Fisher, J. T. On the Irish waterfront **331.7**

On thin ice. Ellis, R. **599.78**

On top of the world. Lutnick, H. **332.6**

On ugliness. **111**

On war. Clausewitz, C. v. **355**

On Whitman. Williams, C. K. **811**

On wings of eagles. Follett, K. **955**

On writing. King, S. **813**

ON-DEMAND PUBLICATIONS

Crawford, W. The librarian's guide to micropublishing **070.5**

Onassis, Aristotle Socrates, 1906-1975

About

Gage, N. Greek fire **782.1**

Onassis, Jacqueline Kennedy, 1929-1994

About

Bowles, H. Jacqueline Kennedy **92**

Davis, J. H. Jacqueline Bouvier **92**

Galbraith, J. K. Name-dropping **973.9**

Hill, C. Five days in November **973.922**

Hill, C. Mrs. Kennedy and me **973.922**

Jacqueline Kennedy **973.922**

Kaplan, A. Dreaming in French **944**

Leaming, B. Mrs. Kennedy **973.922**

Once. O'Rourke, M. **811**

Once before time. Bojowald, M. **523.1**

Once more around the park. Angell, R. **796.357**

Once they moved like the wind. Roberts, D. **970.004**

Once upon a car. Vlasic, B. **338.4**

Once upon a country. David, A. **92**

Ondra, Nancy J.

Taylor's guide to roses **635.9**

The **one.** Smith, R. J. **782.421**

ONE ACT PLAYS

The Best American short plays **812**

See also Philosophy; Religion

PANTOMIMES

See also Acting; Amateur theater; Drama; Theater

Pantsov, Alexander V.

(jt. auth) Levine, S. I. Mao   951.05

Panzer, Mary

Mathew Brady and the image of history   770.92

PAPACY

Duffy, E. Saints & sinners   282

Maxwell-Stuart, P. G. Chronicle of the popes 282

McBrien, R. P. Lives of the popes   920

Reese, T. J. Inside the Vatican   262

Wills, G. Papal sin   262

Wills, G. Why I am a Catholic   282

See also Catholic Church; Church history

Papadaddy's book for new fathers. Edgerton, C.   649

Papadakis, Maxine A.

Current Medical Diagnosis & Treatment 2015 616

PAPAL ENCYCLICALS

See also Christian literature

Papal sin. Wills, G.   262

PAPAL VISITS

See also Voyages and travels

PAPER

Baker, N. Double fold   025.2

Basbanes, N. A. On paper   676.092

Grummer, A. E. Trash-to-treasure papermaking   676

PAPER -- HISTORY

Basbanes, N. A. On paper   676.092

PAPER BOUND BOOKS See Paperback books

PAPER CRAFTS

Beaman, S. Ultimate cardmaking   745.594

Hayakawa, H. Kirigami menagerie   736

Helfand, J. Scrapbooks: an American history   745.54

Melichson, H. The art of paper cutting   745.54

Reeder, D. Papier-mache monsters   745.54

See also Handicraft

PAPER FOLDING See Origami; Paper crafts

The **paper** garden. Peacock, M.   92

PAPER INDUSTRY

Basbanes, N. A. On paper   676.092

See also Industries

PAPER MAKING See Papermaking

PAPER MONEY

See also Money

PAPER, HANDMADE

Hiebert, H. The papermaker's companion   676

PAPERBACK BOOKS

Brower, S. Breathless homicidal slime mutants   741.6

Lavender, K. Book repair   025.7

See also Books; Editions

PAPERHANGING

Santos, B. Painting and wallpapering secrets from Brian Santos, the Wall Wizard   698

See also Interior design

The **papermaker's** companion. Hiebert, H.   676

PAPERMAKING

Grummer, A. E. Trash-to-treasure papermaking   676

Hiebert, H. The papermaker's companion   676

See also Manufactures; Paper

PAPERMAKING -- HISTORY

Basbanes, N. A. On paper   676.092

The papers of William F. "Buffalo Bill" Cody [series]

Buffalo Bill The Wild West in England   791.8

PAPIER-MÂCHÉ See Paper crafts

Papier-mache monsters. Reeder, D.   745.54

Papolos, Janice

The virgin homeowner   643

Papp, Joseph

Turan, K. Free for all   92

Pappalardo, Joe

Sunflowers   583

Paracelsus. Webster, C.   92

Paracelsus, 1493-1541

About

Ball, P. The devil's doctor   610

Webster, C. Paracelsus   92

Parachini, Chris

Roberta's   641.82

PARACHUTES

See also Aeronautics

PARADES

See also Festivals; Pageants

Paradis, Cheryl

The measure of madness   364.3

Paradis, Thomas W.

(ed) The Greenwood encyclopedia of homes through American history   728

PARADISE

See also Future life

A **paradise** built in hell. Solnit, R.   303.4

Paradise found. Nicholls, S.   508

Paradiso. Dante Alighieri   851

The **Paradiso** files. Burke, T. M.   364.152

Paradiso, Leonard J., 1942-2008

About

Burke, T. M. The Paradiso files   364.152

The **paradox** of gender equality. Goss, K. A. 323.3

Parallel worlds. Kaku, M.   523.1

PARALYTICS -- REHABILITATION

Mukand, J. The man with the bionic brain 617.4

PARANOIA

Walker, J. The United States of paranoia   973

Wheen, F. Strange days indeed   973.92

PARANOIA -- POLITICAL ASPECTS -- UNIT-

-- 19TH CENTURY

Hempel, S. The inheritor's powder   **364.152**

Poisoning the press. Feldstein, M.   **973.924**

POISONOUS ANIMALS

Campbell, J. The venomous reptiles of the Western Hemisphere   **597.96**

Ernst, C. H. Venomous reptiles of the United States, Canada, and northern Mexico   **597.9**

O'Shea, M. Venomous snakes of the world **597.96**

   See also Animals; Dangerous animals; Economic zoology; Poisons and poisoning

POISONOUS GASES

   See also Gases; Poisons and poisoning

POISONOUS GASES -- WAR USE *See* Chemical warfare

POISONOUS PLANTS

Turner, N. J. The North American guide to common poisonous plants and mushrooms   **581.6**

   See also Economic botany; Plants; Poisons and poisoning

POISONOUS SNAKES -- NORTH AMERICA

Ernst, C. H. Venomous reptiles of the United States, Canada, and northern Mexico   **597.9**

POISONS AND POISONING

Blum, D. The poisoner's handbook   **614**

Hempel, S. The inheritor's powder   **364.152**

   See also Accidents; Hazardous substances; Homicide; Medical jurisprudence

Poitier, Sidney

About

Goudsouzian, A. Sidney Poitier   **92**

Poitier, S. The measure of a man   **92**

POKER

McManus, J. Cowboys full   **795.4**

McManus, J. Positively Fifth Street   **795.4**

   See also Card games

Poker bride. Corbett, C.   **974.4**

Poker nation. Bellin, A.   **795.4**

Pol Pot

About

Brinkley, J. Cambodia's curse   **959.6**

The **Pol** Pot regime. Kiernan, B.   **959.6**

POLAND -- HISTORY -- 1918-1945

Kochanski, H. The Eagle Unbowed   **940.53**

POLAND -- HISTORY -- OCCUPATION, 1939-1945

Karski, J. Story of a secret state   **940.53**

POLAND -- POLITICS AND GOVERNMENT

Pleshakov, K. There is no freedom without bread!   **947**

POLAND -- POLITICS AND GOVERNMENT -- 1918-1945

Kochanski, H. The Eagle Unbowed   **940.53**

POLAND -- SOCIAL CONDITIONS -- 1918-1945

Kochanski, H. The Eagle Unbowed   **940.53**

Polanka, Sue

(ed) No shelf required   **025.17**

(ed) No shelf required 2   **070.5**

POLAR BEAR

Ellis, R. On thin ice   **599.78**

POLAR EXPEDITIONS *See* Antarctica -- Exploration; Arctic regions -- Exploration; Scientific expeditions

POLAR REGIONS -- DESCRIPTION AND TRAVEL

Challenger, M. On extinction   **576.8**

POLAR REGIONS -- DISCOVERY AND EXPLORATION

Wilkinson, A. The ice balloon   **910.91**

POLARIZATION (SOCIAL SCIENCES) -- UNITED STATES

Edwards, M. The parties versus the people **320.973**

Smith, H. Who stole the American dream? **973.91**

POLICE

Queen, W. Under and alone   **364.1**

   See also Administration of criminal justice; Law enforcement

POLICE -- CHICAGO (ILL.)

Preib, M. The wagon and other stories from the city   **977.3**

POLICE -- COMPLAINTS AGAINST *See* Police brutality; Police corruption

POLICE -- CORRUPT PRACTICES *See* Police corruption

POLICE -- NEW YORK (N.Y.)

Conway, J. N. The big policeman   **92**

Dickey, C. Securing the city   **363.32**

Levitt, L. NYPD confidential   **364.1**

POLICE BRUTALITY

Conroy, J. Unspeakable acts, ordinary people **323.4**

Hendrickson, P. Sons of Mississippi   **305.8**

Lehr, D. The fence   **364.1**

   See also Police

POLICE CORRUPTION

Lehr, D. The fence   **364.1**

Levitt, L. NYPD confidential   **364.1**

   See also Misconduct in office; Police

POLICE OFFICIALS

Conway, J. N. The big policeman   **92**

Dickey, C. Securing the city   **363.32**

POLICEWOMEN

   See also Police; Women

Polio. Oshinsky, D. M.   **614.5**

POLIO *See* Poliomyelitis

POLIOMYELITIS

Kluger, J. Splendid solution: Jonas Salk and the conquest of polio   **92**

   See also Diseases

POLIOMYELITIS VACCINE

Oshinsky, D. M. Polio   **614.5**

   See also Vaccination

POLISH LITERATURE

Prester John
About
Connell, E. S. The Aztec treasure house   814
PRESTIDIGITATION *See* Magic tricks
Preston, Andrew
Sword of the spirit, shield of faith   322
Preston, Katherine, 1984-
About
Preston, K. Out with it   92
Preston, Paul
Juan Carlos   92
Preston, Richard
The demon in the freezer   616.9
The hot zone   614.5
Panic in level 4   616.02
The wild trees   577.3
PRETENDERS *See* Impostors and imposture
Pretty is what changes. Queller, J.   92
Pretty little pincushions.   745.5
Prevallet, Kristin
(ed) Adam, H. A Helen Adam reader   811
PREVENTION OF CRIME *See* Crime prevention
PREVENTION OF CRUELTY TO ANIMALS
   See Animal welfare
PREVENTION OF FIRE *See* Fire prevention
PREVENTIVE MEDICINE
   See also Medicine
Prial, Dunstan
The producer   92
The **price** of altruism. Harman, O. S.   92
The **price** of civilization. Sachs, J.   330.9
The **price** of inequality. Stiglitz, J. E.   305.5
The **price** of justice. Leamer, L.   346.730
The **price** of silence. Cohan, W. D.   364.15
Price, David
Love and hate in Jamestown   975.5
Price, George
About
Harman, O. S. The price of altruism   92
Price, Maggie
Painting with pastels   741.2
Price, Reynolds
Bible/N.T./Gospels The three Gospels   226.3
Ardent spirits   92
A serious way of wondering   241
A whole new life   362.1
Price, Simon
(ed) The Oxford dictionary of classical myth and religion   292
Priceless. Wittman, R.   364.1
PRICES
The value of a dollar   338.5
The value of a dollar: colonial era to the Civil War, 1600-1865   338.5
   See also Commerce; Consumption (Economics); Economics; Finance; Manufactures

PRIDE AND VANITY
   See also Conduct of life; Sin
Pride of October. Madden, B.   796.357
Prideaux, Sue
Edvard Munch   92
Strindberg   839.7
Priestland, David
The red flag   335.4
Priestley, Joseph, 1733-1804
About
Horvitz, L. A. Eureka!: scientific breakthroughs that changed the world   509
Johnson, S. The invention of air   92
Malone, J. W. It doesn't take a rocket scientist   920
PRIESTS
Armenian Golgotha   956
Boyle, G. J. Tattoos on the heart   277
Carroll, J. Practicing Catholic   92
Fisher, J. T. On the Irish waterfront   331.7
Martin, J. The Jesuit guide to almost everything   248.4
Martin, J. My life with the saints   270
Schroth, R. A. Bob Drinan   92
   See also Clergy
PRIESTS -- FRANCE -- MARSEILLE -- BIOGRAPHY
Zuccotti, S. Père Marie-Benoît and Jewish rescue   940.53
Prijatel, Patricia
Surviving triple negative breast cancer   616.99
Primal cuts. Guggiana, M.   641.6
Primal leadership. Goleman, D.   658.4
PRIMARIES
   See also Elections; Political conventions; Politics
PRIMARY EDUCATION *See* Elementary education
Primary sourcebook series
Hillstrom, K. The Cold War   909.82
The **primate** family tree. Redmond, I.   599.8
A **primate's** memoir. Sapolsky, R. M.   599.8
PRIMATES
Redmond, I. The primate family tree   599.8
   See also Mammals
PRIMATES -- BEHAVIOR
De Waal, F. The Bonobo and the Atheist   205
   See also Animal behavior
PRIMATES -- EVOLUTION
Walter, C. Last ape standing   569.9
PRIMATES -- HABITS AND BEHAVIOR *See* Primates -- Behavior
PRIMATOLOGISTS
Goodall, J. Beyond innocence   92
Goodall, J. Reason for hope   92
Halloran, A. R. The song of the ape   599.885
Peterson, D. Jane Goodall: the woman who rede-

Pro secrets to dramatic digital photos. Zuckerman, J.   **775**

PRO-CHOICE ACTIVISTS
  Hull, N. E. H. Roe v. Wade   **344**

PRO-CHOICE MOVEMENT
  See also Social movements

PRO-LIFE MOVEMENT
  Press, E. Absolute convictions   **363.46**
  See also Social movements

PROBABILITIES
  Aczel, A. D. Chance: a guide to gambling, love, the stock market & just about everything else   **519.2**
  Arbesman, S. The half-life of facts   **501**
  Devlin, K. J. The unfinished game   **519.2**
  Mlodinow, L. The Drunkard's walk   **519.2**
  Rosenthal, J. Struck by lightning   **519.2**
  Santos, A. How many licks?   **519.2**
  See also Algebra; Logic; Mathematics; Statistics

PROBATE LAW AND PRACTICE
  See also Civil procedure; Inheritance and succession

PROBATION
  See also Corrections; Criminal law; Prisons; Punishment; Reformatories; Social case work

PROBIOTICS
  See also Dietary supplements; Microorganisms

PROBLEM CHILDREN *See* Emotionally disturbed children

PROBLEM DRINKING *See* Alcoholism

PROBLEM SOLVING
  Costa, R. D. The watchman's rattle   **501**
  Huber, M. R. Mythematics   **510**
  Mahajan, S. Street-fighting mathematics   **510**
  Penenberg, A. L. Play at work   **658.4**
  See also Psychology

PROBLEM YOUTH -- BOOKS AND READING -- UNITED STATES
  Sweeney, J. Literacy   **027.62**
The **problems** of philosophy. Russell, B.   **100**
Process and reality.   **113**

PROCESSED FOODS -- COSTS
  Reese, J. Make the bread, buy the butter   **641.3**
Prochnicky, Jerry
  Riordan, J. Break on through: the life and death of Jim Morrison   **782.421**
Prochnik, George
  In pursuit of silence   **155.9**
PROCRASTINATION
  Partnoy, F. Wait   **153.8**
Proctor, Rob
  Springer, L. Passionate gardening   **635**
Proctor, Robert N.
  Golden holocaust   **362.29**
PROCUREMENT OF ORGANS, TISSUES, ETC.

Carney, S. The red market   **364.1**
Cheney, A. Body brokers   **617.9**
Whitehouse, B. The match   **92**
The **prodigal.** Walcott, D.   **811**
The **producer.** Prial, D.   **92**

PRODUCT DEVELOPMENT *See* New products

PRODUCT RECALL
  Nestle, M. Pet food politics   **363.1**
  See also Consumer protection

PRODUCT SAFETY
  See also Consumer protection

PRODUCTION *See* Economics; Industries

PRODUCTION STANDARDS
  See also Labor productivity; Management

PRODUCTS, AGRICULTURAL *See* Farm produce

PRODUCTS, DAIRY *See* Dairy products

PROFESSIONAL BULL RIDERS, INC.
  Peter, J. Fried twinkies, buckle bunnies & bull riders   **791.8**
The **professional** chef.   **641.5**

PROFESSIONAL DEVELOPMEN -- HANDBOOKS, MANUALS, ETC.
  Blake, J. Life after college   **646.700**

PROFESSIONAL EDUCATION
  See also Education; Higher education; Learning and scholarship

PROFESSIONAL EMPLOYEES -- UNITED STATES
  Fideler, E. F. Men still at work   **331.3**

PROFESSIONAL ETHICS
  Defending professionalism   **020.92**
  See also Ethics

PROFESSIONAL SPORTS
  See also Sports

PROFESSIONS
  McKenna, A. Nontraditional careers for women and men   **331.702**
  See also Occupations; Self-employed
The **professor** and the madman. Winchester, S. **423**

PROFESSORS *See* Educators; Teachers

Profiles in courage. Kennedy, J. F.   **920**

PROFIT
  Dreman, D. Contrarian investment strategies   **332.601**
  See also Business; Capital; Economics; Wealth

PROFIT SHARING
  See also Commerce; Salaries, wages, etc.

PROGNOSIS
  Gawande, A. Being mortal   **362.17**

PROGRAMMING (COMPUTERS) *See* Computer programming

PROGRAMMING LANGUAGES
  See also Computer software; Language and languages

RACIALLY MIXED PEOPLE -- RACE IDEN-TITY

Sandweiss, M. A. Passing strange   **92**

RACIALLY MIXED PEOPLE -- UNITED STATES

Sharfstein, D. J. The invisible line   **305.8**

Walker, C. E. Mongrel nation   **305.8**

RACIALLY MIXED PEOPLE -- UNITED STATES -- BIOGRAPHY

Swarns, R. L. American tapestry   **973.932**

RACING

See also Sports

Racing for the bomb: General Leslie R. Groves, the Manhattan Project's indispensable man. Norris, R. S.   **92**

Racing Odysseus. Martin, R. H.   **92**

RACISM

Achebe, C. The education of a British-protected child   **92**

Blum, E. J. The color of Christ   **232**

Ezekiel, R. S. The racist mind   **320.5**

Ford, R. T. Rights gone wrong   **342**

Goldhagen, D. J. Worse than war   **364.1**

King, M. L. Where do we go from here   **323.1**

Reed, I. Another day at the front   **305.8**

Touré Who's afraid of post-blackness?

Zeskind, L. Blood and politics   **305.8**

See also Attitude (Psychology); Prejudices; Race awareness; Race relations

RACISM -- INDIA -- HISTORY

Slate, N. Colored cosmopolitanism   **305.8**

RACISM -- PSYCHOLOGICAL ASPECTS

Goldhagen, D. J. Worse than war   **364.1**

RACISM -- RELIGIOUS ASPECTS -- CHRISTI-ANITY

Blum, E. J. The color of Christ   **232**

RACISM -- UNITED STATES

Blum, E. J. The color of Christ   **232**

Loewen, J. W. Sundown towns   **363.5**

Reed, I. Another day at the front   **305.8**

Takaki, R. T. Double victory   **940.53**

RACISM -- UNITED STATES -- HISTORY

Bruinius, H. Better for all the world   **363.9**

Fredrickson, G. M. Big enough to be inconsis-tent   **973.7**

Slate, N. Colored cosmopolitanism   **305.8**

RACISM IN EDUCATION -- UNITED STATES

Wilder, C. S. Ebony and Ivy   **379.26**

RACISM IN MUSEUM EXHIBITS

Crais, C. C. Sara Baartman and the Hottentot Ve-nus   **92**

RACISM IN SPORTS

Runstedtler, T. Jack Johnson, rebel sojourn-er   **796.83**

RACISM IN SPORTS -- UNITED STATES

Kashatus, W. C. Jackie and Campy   **92**

The **racist** mind. Ezekiel, R. S.   **320.5**

RACKETEERING

See also Crime; Organized crime

RACQUETBALL

See also Ball games; Sports

RADAR

See also Navigation; Radio; Remote sensing

Radbourn, Charles, 1853-1897

About

Achorn, E. Fifty-nine in '84   **796.357**

Radcliffe Institute for Advanced Study

Notable American women   **920.003**

Radcliffe, Margaret

The knowledgeable knitter   **746.43**

Raddatz, Martha

The long road home   **956.7**

Radford, Marie L., 1951-

(jt. auth) Nilsen, K. Conducting the reference in-terview   **025.5**

A **radiant** life. O'Faolain, N.   **824**

RADIATION

Nelson, C. The age of radiance   **539.7**

See also Optics; Physics; Waves

RADIATION -- PHYSIOLOGICAL EFFECT

Biddle, W. A field guide to radiation   **539.2**

Radical. Rhee, M. A.   **371.010**

The **Radical** reader.   **303.4**

RADICALISM

Duberman, M. B. A saving remnant   **92**

Eteraz, A. Children of dust   **92**

Hamilton, N. A. Rebels and renegades   **322.4**

Hoffman, A. The best of Abbie Hoffman   **303.4**

Kurlansky, M. 1968   **909.82**

McMillian, J. Smoking typewriters   **071**

The Radical reader   **303.4**

Ronson, J. Them: adventures with extremists **322.4**

Rudd, M. Underground   **92**

See also Political science; Revolutions; Right and left (Political science)

RADICALISM -- UNITED STATES

Goldwag, A. The new hate   **306.2**

The **radicalism** of the American Revolution. Wood, G. S.   **973.3**

RADIO

Larson, E. Thunderstruck   **364.152**

See also Telecommunication

RADIO -- HANDBOOKS, MANUALS, ETC.

The ARRL handbook for radio communication 2014

RADIO ADDRESSES, DEBATES, ETC.

See also Debates and debating; Lectures and lecturing; Radio broadcasting; Radio scripts

RADIO BROADCASTING

Fisher, M. Something in the air   **384.54**

Heil, A. L. Voice of America   **384.54**

See also Broadcasting; Mass media

RADIO DIRECTORS

RATIONAL EXPECTATIONS (ECONOMIC THEORY)
Fox, J. The myth of the rational market   **332.6**
The **rational** optimist. Ridley, M.   **339.2**
RATIONALISM
     See also Philosophy; Religion; Secularism; Theory of knowledge
RATIONALISM -- HISTORY
   Minois, G. The atheist's Bible   **200**
Ratliff, Ben
   Coltrane   **92**
   The jazz ear   **781.65**
Ratner-Rosenhagen, Jennifer
   American Nietzsche   **193**
Ratnesar, Romesh
   Tear down this wall   **973.927**
Rattlesnake. Rubio, M.   **597.96**
RATTLESNAKES
   Rubio, M. Rattlesnake   **597.96**
     See also Poisonous animals; Snakes
Rauchway, Eric
   Murdering McKinley   **973.8**
Rause, Vince
   Parrado, N. Miracle in the Andes   **982**
Ravago, Miguel
   Tausend, M. Cocina de la familia   **641.5**
The **ravenous** brain. Bor, D.   **612.8**
RAVENS
   Heinrich, B. Mind of the raven   **598**
Ravitch, Diane, 1938-
   The death and life of the great American school system   **379**
Raw energy. Tourles, S. L.   **641.5**
Rawhide down. Wilber, D. Q.   **973.927**
Ray, Barbara E.
   Not quite adults   **306.8**
Ray, C. Claiborne
   The New York Times second book of science questions and answers   **500**
Ray, James Earl, 1928-1998
     About
   Sides, H. Hellhound on his trail   **364.152**
Ray, Man, 1890-1976
     About
   Lottman, H. R. Man Ray's Montparnasse   **709**
Raymo, Chet
   An intimate look at the night sky   **520**
   Walking zero   **526**
Raymond Carver. Sklenicka, C.   **92**
Raymond Chandler. Hiney, T.   **813**
Raynor, Michael E.
   (jt. auth) Ahmed, M. The three rules   **658**
RÉSUMÉS (EMPLOYMENT)
   Ghilani, M. E. Working in your major   **650.14**
Rea, Tom
   Bone wars   **560**

Reach for the skies. Branson, R.   **629.1**
Reaching down the rabbit hole. Ropper, A. H. **616.8**
REACTION (POLITICAL SCIENCE) *See* Conservatism
Reactions. Atkins, P. W.   **541**
REACTIONS, CHEMICAL *See* Chemical reactions
Read on . . . crime fiction. Trott, B.   **016**
Read on . . . fantasy fiction. Hollands, N.   **016**
Read on . . . horror fiction. Pulliam, J. M.   **025**
Read on series
   Hollands, N. Read on . . . fantasy fiction   **016**
   Pulliam, J. M. Read on . . . horror fiction   **025**
   Saricks, J. G. Read on--audiobooks   **011**
   Trott, B. Read on . . . crime fiction   **016**
Read on-- biography. Roche, R.   **016**
Read on--audiobooks. Saricks, J. G.   **011**
Read, Anthony
   The fall of Berlin   **940.54**
Read, J. Leighton
   Reeves, B. Total engagement   **303.4**
Read, Piers Paul
   Alive   **910.4**
Read, Piers Paul, 1941-
   The Dreyfus affair   **944.081**
A **reader** on reading. Manguel, A.   **818**
READER SERVICES (LIBRARIES) *See* Library services
A **reader's** book of days.   **809**
A **Reader's** companion to the short story in English. Society for the Study of the Short Story   **809**
Reader's Digest Association
   The big book of cross-stitch designs   **746.44**
   Everyday greatness   **170**
Reader's Digest Association (Canada) Ltd.
   Reader's Digest Association, I. New complete guide to sewing   **646.2**
Reader's Digest Association, Inc.
   Complete do-it-yourself manual   **643**
   New complete guide to sewing   **646.2**
Reader's guide [series]
   Reader's guide to Judaism   **296**
Reader's guide to Judaism.   **296**
Reader's guide to military history.   **355.009**
Reader's guide to the history of science.   **509**
READERS AND LIBRARIES *See* Library services
Readers on American musicians [series]
   The Richard Rodgers reader   **782.1**
The **readers'** advisory guide to genre fiction. Saricks, J. G.   **025.5**
The **readers'** advisory guide to genre fiction. Saricks, J. G.   **025.5**
The **readers'** advisory guide to graphic novels. Goldsmith, F.   **025.2**
The **readers'** advisory guide to nonfiction. Wyatt,

Woodward, B. Shadow   **973.92**

Real beauty. Kashuk, S.   **646.7**

Real Cajun. Link, D.   **641.5**

REAL ESTATE

  Andrews, E. L. Busted   **332.7**

REAL ESTATE -- DICTIONARIES

  Haden, J. The complete dictionary of real estate terms explained simply   **333.3**

REAL ESTATE BUSINESS

  Irwin, R. Tips & traps for negotiating real estate   **333.3**

      See also Business; Real estate

REAL ESTATE DEVELOPERS

  Korda, M. Ulysses S. Grant: the unlikely hero **92**

  McDougal, S. The woman who wouldn't talk   **973.929**

  Singer, M. Character studies   **920**

  Slater, R. No such thing as over-exposure **92**

REAL ESTATE DEVELOPMENT -- DRAMA.

  Wilson, A. Radio golf   **812**

REAL ESTATE INVESTMENT

  Corbett, M. Before you buy!   **643**

  Crook, D. The Wall Street Journal complete home owner's guidebook   **643**

  Irwin, R. Tips & traps for negotiating real estate   **333.3**

      See also Investments; Real estate; Speculation

REAL ESTATE INVESTMENT -- TAXATION

      See also Taxation

The **real** Fidel Castro. Coltman, L.   **92**

The **Real** Food Daily cookbook. Gentry, A. **641.5**

The **real** Frank Zappa book. Zappa, F.   **92**

Real happiness. Salzberg, S.   **158**

Real life journals: designing & using handmade books. Diehn, G.   **686.3**

The **real** life of Laurence Olivier. Lewis, R. **792**

The **real** North Korea. Lankov, A.   **951.9304**

The **real** story. Cords, S. S.   **025.5**

The **real** war, 1914-1918. Liddell Hart, B. H. **940.4**

Real-life math. Glazer, E.   **510**

REALISM

    See also Philosophy

REALISM IN ART

    See also Art

REALISM IN LITERATURE

    See also Literature

REALITY

  Dawkins, R. The magic of reality   **501**

  Deutsch, D. The fabric of reality   **530**

  Gribbin, J. R. In search of Schrodinger's cat **530.1**

  Gribbin, J. R. Schrodinger's kittens and the search for reality   **530.1**

      See also Philosophy; Truth

Reality is broken. McGonigal, J.   **306.4**

Reality is broken. McGonigal, J.   **306.4**

REALITY TELEVISION PROGRAMS

    See also Television programs

Ream, Anne K.

  Lived through this   **362.883**

Reappraisals. Judt, T.   **909.82**

Reardon, Joan

  (ed) As always, Julia   **92**

  (ed) Fisher, M. F. K. A stew or a story **641**

REASON

  Kant, I. Critique of pure reason   **193**

  Ridley, M. The rational optimist   **339.2**

      See also Intellect; Rationalism

The **reason** for God. Keller, T. J.   **239**

Reason for hope. Goodall, J.   **92**

The **reason** I jump.   **92**

REASONING

  Kahneman, D. Thinking, fast and slow **153.4**

  Pinker, S. How the mind works   **153**

  Watts, D. J. Everything is obvious   **153.4**

      See also Psychology; Reason; Thought and thinking

REASONING (PSYCHOLOGY)

  Dobelli, R. The art of thinking clearly **153.4**

Reaves, Wendy Wick

  Ballyhoo!   **741.6**

Reavill, Gil

  Mafia summit   **364.106**

The **rebel.** Camus, A.   **303.6**

Rebel land. de Bellaigue, C.   **956**

Rebel visions: the underground comix revolution, 1963-1975. Rosenkranz, P.   **741.5**

Rebel Yell. Gwynne, S. C.   **92**

The **rebellion** of Ronald Reagan. Mann, J. **973.927**

REBELLIONS *See* Insurgency; Revolutions

The **rebellious** life of Mrs. Rosa Parks. Theoharis, J.   **323.092**

Rebels and renegades. Hamilton, N. A. **322.4**

Rebels on the backlot. Waxman, S.   **920**

Rebels wit attitude. Ellis, I.   **781.66**

Reber, Grote, 1911-2002

      About

  Malone, J. W. It doesn't take a rocket scientist **920**

Rebirth of a nation. Lears, T. J. J.   **973.8**

Reborn. Sontag, S.   **92**

Rebuilding the foodshed. Ackerman-Leist, P. **338.1**

REBUSES

    See also Literary recreations; Puzzles; Riddles

RECALL OF PRODUCTS *See* Product recall

RECEIVING STOLEN GOODS -- ENGLAND -- LONDON -- CASE STUDIES

  Crosby, M. C. The great pearl heist   **364.16**

RECESSIONS

  Krugman, P. R. End this depression now! **330.9**

      See also Business cycles

Recipes.   **641.5**

ture **810**

Famous first facts, international edition **031.02**

Farmer, D. H. The Oxford dictionary of saints **920.003**

Fell, D. Encyclopedia of hardy plants **635.9**

Flora: a gardener's encyclopedia **635.9**

Fogle, B. The new encyclopedia of the dog **636.7**

Fonseca, A. J. Hooked on horror III **016**

Ford, C. Crash course in reference **025.5**

The Foundation Directory 2014 **061**

Fowler, H. W. Fowler's modern English usage **428**

Frazier, N. The Penguin concise dictionary of art history **703**

Friedman, I. C. Latino athletes **920.003**

Friedwald, W. A biographical guide to the great jazz and pop singers **920.003**

Frolund, T. Genrefied classics **016**

From bonbon to cha-cha **422**

Fry, J. L. The encyclopedia of weather and climate change **551.6**

Gale directory of databases **025.04**

The Gale encyclopedia of alternative medicine **615.5**

Gale encyclopedia of American law **349**

The Gale encyclopedia of psychology **150**

The Gallaudet dictionary of American Sign Language **419**

Garden perennials Armitage's garden perennials **635.9**

Garner, B. A. Garner's modern American usage **423**

Garraty, J. A. American national biography **920.003**

Gates, A. E. Encyclopedia of earthquakes and volcanoes **551.2**

Gates, A. E. Encyclopedia of pollution **363.7**

Gates, A. E. A to Z of earth scientists **920.003**

Gilbert, M. The Routledge atlas of the Holocaust **940.53**

Grant, M. A guide to the ancient world **913**

Gray's anatomy **611**

Great events from history, The 17th century, 1601-1700 **909**

Great events from history, The 18th century, 1701-1800 **909.7**

Great events from history, The 19th century, 1801-1900 **909.81**

Great events from history, The ancient world, pre-history-476 C.E. **930**

Great events from history, The Middle Ages, 477-1453 **909.07**

Great events from history, The Renaissance & early modern era, 1454-1600 **909**

Great events from history: The 20th century, 1901-1940 **909.82**

Great events from history: The 20th century, 1941-1970 **909.82**

Great events from history: The 20th century, 1971-2000 **909.82**

Great lives from history, The 17th century, 1601-1700 **920.003**

Great lives from history, The 19th century, 1801-1900 **920.003**

Great lives from history, The ancient world, prehistory-476 C.E **920.003**

Great lives from history, the Middle Ages, 477-1453 **920.003**

Great lives from history, the Renaissance & early modern era, 1454-1600 **920.003**

Great lives from history: Notorious lives **920.003**

Great lives from history: the 20th century, 1901-2000 **920.003**

Great lives from history Great lives from history, The 18th century, 1701-1800 **920.003**

Green volunteers **333.72**

Green, J. The encyclopedia of censorship **363.31**

The Greenwood encyclopedia of African American literature **810**

The Greenwood encyclopedia of American regional cultures **973**

The Greenwood encyclopedia of folktales and fairy tales **398.2**

The Greenwood encyclopedia of homes through American history **728**

The Greenwood encyclopedia of multiethnic American literature **810**

The Grove encyclopedia of materials and techniques in art **702.8**

Guide to reference books **011**

Guide to summer camps and summer schools 2008/2009 **796.54**

Guiley, R. E. The encyclopedia of demons and demonology **133.4**

Guiley, R. E. The encyclopedia of ghosts and spirits **133.1**

Guiley, R. E. The encyclopedia of saints **282**

Guiley, R. E. The encyclopedia of vampires & werewolves **398**

Guiley, R. E. The encyclopedia of witches, witchcraft, and Wicca **133.4**

Haden, J. The complete dictionary of real estate terms explained simply **333.3**

Hamer, F. The potter's dictionary of materials and techniques **738.1**

Hamilton, N. A. Presidents **920.003**

Harasewych, M. G. The book of shells **594**

Harper, J. E. Women during the Civil War **973.7**

The HarperCollins Bible dictionary **220.3**

The HarperCollins encyclopedia of Catholicism **282**

Hart, J. D. The Oxford companion to American literature **810**

The Harvard biographical dictionary of music **780**

REFERENCE BOOKS -- BIBLIOGRAPHY

REFERENCE BOOKS -- REVIEWS

REFERENCE BOOKS -- UNITED STATES

REFERENCE INTERVIEW

REFERENCE SERVICES (LIBRARIES)

REFERENCE SERVICES (LIBRARIES) -- UNITED STATES

Richardson, Robert D.
Emerson   **814**
William James   **92**
Richardson, Sarah
The political worlds of women   **305.42**
Richelson, Jeffrey
The wizards of Langley   **327.12**
RICHES *See* Wealth
Richet, Pascal
A natural history of time   **551.7**
Richetti, John J.
(ed) The Columbia history of the British novel **823**
Richie, Donald
The Japan journals, 1947-2004   **952.04**
RICHLAND (WASH.) -- HISTORY -- 20TH CENTURY
Brown, K. Plutopia   **363.17**
Richman, Shira
Raising a child with autism   **618.92**
RICHMOND (VA.) -- HISTORY
Furgurson, E. B. Ashes of glory   **975.5**
The **richness** of life. Gould, S. J.   **508**
Richter's scale. Hough, S. E.   **92**
Richter, Charles F., 1900-1985
About
Hough, S. E. Richter's scale   **92**
Richter, Daniel K.
Facing east from Indian country   **970.004**
Richter, Sviatoslav, 1915-1997
About
Schonberg, H. C. The great pianists   **920**
Rick Bayless's Mexican kitchen. Bayless, R. **641.59**
Rick Stein's complete seafood.   **641.6**
Rickards, James
Currency wars   **332.4**
Rickenbacker, Eddie, 1890-1973
About
Groom, W. The aviators   **920**
Ricketts, Harry
Rudyard Kipling   **92**
Rickey, Branch, 1881-1965
About
Breslin, J. Branch Rickey   **92**
Shapiro, M. Bottom of the ninth   **796.357**
Rickford, Russell John
Betty Shabazz: a remarkable story of survival and faith before and after Malcolm X   **92**
Ricks, Christopher
(ed) Inventions of the March Hare   **811**
(ed) Menashe, S. New and selected poems   **811**
Ricks, Thomas E.
Fiasco: the American military adventure in Iraq   **956.7**
The generals   **355.009**
Rickwood Field. Barra, A.   **796.357**
RICKWOOD FIELD (BIRMINGHAM, ALA.)

Barra, A. Rickwood Field   **796.357**
The **riddle** of Amish culture. Kraybill, D. B. **289.7**
The **riddle** of the compass. Aczel, A. D.   **912**
The **Riddle** of the Labyrinth. Fox, M.   **487**
Riddled with life. Zuk, M.   **616.07**
RIDDLES
    See also Amusements; Literary recreations
Ride, Sally
About
Sherr, L. Sally Ride   **92**
Rideau, Wilbert
In the place of justice   **92**
Ridge, Brent
The Beekman 1802 heirloom dessert cookbook   **641.5**
RIDING *See* Horsemanship
Riding rockets. Mullane, R. M.   **629**
Riding the iron rooster. Theroux, P.   **915**
Riding, Alan
And the show went on   **944**
Ridinger, Robert B. Marks
Bosman, E. Gay, lesbian, bisexual, and transgendered literature   **016**
Ridley, Glynis
The discovery of Jeanne Baret   **92**
Ridley, Jane
The heir apparent   **92**
Ridley, Jasper Godwin
The Freemasons   **366**
Ridley, Mark
(ed) Darwin, C. The Darwin reader   **576.8**
Ridley, Matt
The agile gene   **155.7**
Francis Crick   **92**
Genome   **599.93**
The rational optimist   **339.2**
Ridpath, Ian
The monthly sky guide   **523.8**
Stars and planets   **520**
Riechel, Rosemarie
Easy information sources for ESL, adult learners, & new readers   **016**
Rieder, Jonathan
Gospel of freedom   **323.11**
Riefenstahl, Leni, 1902-2003
About
Bach, S. Leni: the life and work of Leni Riefenstahl   **92**
Trimborn, J. Leni Riefenstahl   **92**
Rieff, David
(ed) As consciousness is harnessed to flesh   **818**
A bed for the night   **361.2**
Slaughterhouse   **949.7**
(ed) Sontag, S. Reborn   **92**
Rielly, Edward J.
Football   **796.332**

Buk-Swienty, T. The other half — 92

RIJEKA (CROATIA) -- HISTORY -- 20TH CENTURY

Hughes-Hallett, L. Gabriele d'Annunzio — 858

Riley, Charles A.

The art of Peter Max — 760

Riley, Glenda

The life and legacy of Annie Oakley — 796.3

Riley, Gregory J.

The river of God — 270.1

Riley, Kathleen, 1974-

The Astaires — 792.802

Riley, Tim

Lennon — 92

Riley-Smith, Jonathan

(ed) The Oxford illustrated history of the Crusades — 909.07

Rilke, Rainer Maria

Duino elegies — 831

New poems — 831

Sonnets to Orpheus — 831

Uncollected poems — 831

Rimbaud. White, E. — 92

Rimbaud. Rimbaud, A. — 848

Rimbaud, Arthur, 1854-1891

Poems — 841

About

White, E. Rimbaud — 92

Rin Tin Tin. Orlean, S. — 636.7

RIN-TIN-TIN (DOG)

Orlean, S. Rin Tin Tin — 636.7

Rinella, Steven

American buffalo — 599.64

Meat eater — 799.29

Rinella, Steven

About

Rinella, S. Meat eater — 799.29

Riordan, James

Break on through: the life and death of Jim Morrison — 782.421

Riot and remembrance. Hirsch, J. S. — 976.6

RIOT CONTROL

See also Crowds; Riots

The **riot** grrrl collection. — 781.64

RIOT GRRRL MOVEMENT

Marcus, S. Girls to the front — 781.66

Meltzer, M. Girl power — 781.64

The riot grrrl collection — 781.64

RIOTS

Hirsch, J. S. Riot and remembrance — 976.6

Risen, C. A nation on fire — 973.923

Schecter, B. The devil's own work — 974.7

See also Crime; Freedom of assembly; Offenses against public safety

RIOTS -- NEW YORK (N.Y.)

Cliff, N. The Shakespeare riots — 974.4

RIOTS -- UNITED STATES

Morley, J. Snow-storm in August — 305.8

Ripe. — 641.6

Ripert, Eric

On the line — 647

Ripken, Billy

Ripken, C. Play baseball the Ripken way — 796.357

Ripken, Cal, Jr.

Play baseball the Ripken way — 796.357

About

Ripken, C. The only way I know — 92

Will, G. F. Men at work — 796.35

Ripley, Amanda

The smartest kids in the world — 370.9

The unthinkable — 155.9

RIPOFFS *See* Fraud

Ripped. Kot, G. — 780.2

The **rise.** Schullery, P. — 799.1

The **rise** and fall of ancient Egypt. Wilkinson, T. — 932

The **rise** and fall of Arab presidents for life. Owen, R. — 352.230

The **rise** and fall of communism. Brown, A. — 320.5

The **rise** and fall of the American teenager. Hine, T. — 305.235

The **rise** and fall of the Bible. Beal, T. — 220.6

The **rise** and fall of the great powers. Kennedy, P. M. — 909.08

The **rise** and fall of the Third Reich. Shirer, W. L. — 943.086

The **rise** of American democracy. Wilentz, S. — 973.5

The **rise** of modern paganism. Gay, P. — 190

The **rise** of Rome. Everitt, A. — 937

The **rise** of Theodore Roosevelt. Morris, E. — 92

Rise to greatness. Von Drehle, D. — 973.7

Risen, Clay

American Whiskey, Bourbon & Rye — 641.2

The bill of the century — 342.73

Risen, Clay

A nation on fire — 973.923

Rising fire: volcanoes and our inner lives. Calderazzo, J. — 551.2

The **rising** sea. Pilkey, O. H. — 363.34

Rising tide. Barry, J. M. — 977

RISK

See also Economics

RISK FACTORS

Bracken, M. B. Risk, chance, and causation — 616.07

Risk, chance, and causation. Bracken, M. B. — 616.07

RISK-TAKING (PSYCHOLOGY)

See also Psychology

Riskin, Jessica

(ed) Nature engaged — 303.483

Ritchie, David

Gates, A. E. Encyclopedia of earthquakes and volcanoes — 551.2

Ritchie, Donald A.

Reporting from Washington 071
Ritchie, Jean, 1922-
About
Ritchie, J. Singing family of the Cumberlands **784.4**
Ritchin, Fred
After photography 775
RITES AND CEREMONIES
Encyclopedia of religious rites, rituals, and festivals 200
How to be a perfect stranger 203
New American Haggadah **296.4**
Rites of peace. Zamoyski, A. **940.2**
Ritter, Charles F.
(ed) Leaders of the American Civil War **973.709**
Ritter, Lawrence S.
The glory of their times 920
RITUAL See Liturgies; Rites and ceremonies
Ritz, David
Grandmaster Flash The adventures of Grandmaster Flash 92
James, E. Rage to survive 92
King, B. B. Blues all around me **781.643**
Lang, L. Journey of a thousand miles 92
Leiber, J. Hound dog 92
The **rivals.** Howard, J. 92
Rivals. Emmott, B. **327.1**
Rivas, Mim Eichler
Gardner, C. The pursuit of happyness 92
(jt. auth) Quiñones-Hinojosa, A. Becoming Dr. Q 92
The **river** at the center of the world. Winchester, S. 915
The **River** Cottage cookbook. Fearnley-Whittingstall, H. **641.5**
River Cottage every day. Fearnley-Whittingstall, H. **641.5**
River Cottage Veg. Fearnley-Whittingstall, H. **641.5**
RIVER ECOLOGY
See also Ecology
River house. Lawrence, S. 92
A **river** lost. Harden, B. **333.91**
River of dark dreams. Johnson, W. **305.8**
The **river** of doubt. Millard, C. **973.91**
The **river** of God. Riley, G. J. **270.1**
The **river** of lost footsteps. Thant Myint-U **959.1**
River out of Eden. Dawkins, R. 575
RIVER POLLUTION See Water pollution
River teeth literary nonfiction prize [series]
Spagna, A. M. Test ride on the Sunnyland bus **323.1**
A **river's** tale. Gargan, E. A. 915
Rivera, Diego, 1886-1957
About
Hamill, P. Diego Rivera **759.9**
Marnham, P. Dreaming with his eyes open 92
Rivera, Mariano, 1969-
The closer 92

RIVERS
Fagin, D. Toms River **363.72**
Mary, B. An American River
See also Physical geography; Water; Waterways
Rivers of gold. Thomas, H. 980
Rivlin, Gary
Broke, USA **339.4**
Roach, Mary, 1959-
Bonk **612.6**
Gulp **612.3**
Packing for Mars 571
Spook **133.9**
Stiff 611
ROAD BICYCLES -- MAINTENANCE AND REPAIR
Zinn & the art of road bike maintenance
ROAD CONSTRUCTION See Roads
The **road** less traveled. Peck, M. S. 158
The **road** less traveled and beyond. Peck, M. S. 158
ROAD MAPS
See also Maps
Road to Cooperstown. Stanton, T. 92
The **road** to Dallas. Kaiser, D. E. **973.922**
The **road** to home. Gregorian, V. 973
The **road** to Verdun. Ousby, I. **940.4**
The **road** to Woodstock. Lang, M. **781.66**
Roads. McMurtry, L. 917
ROADS
See also Civil engineering; Transportation
Conover, T. The routes of man **388.1**
McMurtry, L. Roads 917
The **roads** have come to an end now. Jacobsen, R. **839.8**
Roads to infinity. Stillwell, J. **511.3**
The **roads** to modernity. Himmelfarb, G. 190
Roads to Quoz. Heat Moon, W. L. 917
A **roadside** dog. Milosz, C. **891.8**
ROADSIDE IMPROVEMENT
See also Grounds maintenance; Landscape architecture; Roads
Roaf, Michael
Frankfort, H. The art and architecture of the ancient Orient **709.3**
ROANOKE ISLAND (N.C.) -- HISTORY
Horn, J. A kingdom strange **975.6**
Noel Hume, I. The Virginia adventure **975.5**
Roast figs, sugar snow. Henry, D. **641.5**
ROASTING (COOKING)
All about roasting **641.7**
Robb, Graham
Balzac 92
Parisians 944
Strangers: homosexual love in the nineteenth century **306.76**
Robb, John

Punk rock **781.66**

Robb, Peter

M: the man who became Caravaggio **759**

ROBBERS *See* Thieves

The **robbers** [and] Wallenstein. Schiller, F. **832**

ROBBERY INVESTIGATION -- ENGLAND --
 LONDON -- CASE STUDIES

Crosby, M. C. The great pearl heist **364.16**

Robbins, Alexandra

The geeks shall inherit the Earth

Robbins, Catherine C.

All Indians do not live in teepees (or casinos) **970.004**

Robbins, Christopher

Apples are from Kazakhstan **958.4**

Robbins, Jeffrey

(ed) Feynman, R. P. The pleasure of finding things
out **500**

Robbins, Jerome

About

Vaill, A. Somewhere **92**

Robbins, Liz

A race like no other **796.42**

Robbins, Martha M.

(ed) Among African apes **599.8**

Robbins, Tom, 1932-

Tibetan Peach Pie **92**

Robbins, Tony

Unlimited power **158**

Roberson, Ed

To see the earth before the end of the world **811**

Robert Altman. Zuckoff, M. **92**

Robert Browning. Browning, R. **821**

Robert Browning's poetry. Browning, R. **821**

Robert C. Byrd Center for Legislative Studies

Congress investigates **328**

Robert E. Lee. Thomas, E. M. **973.7**

Robert E. Lee. Blount, R. **973.7**

Robert Frost. Parini, J. **811**

Robert Kennedy. Thomas, E. **973.922**

Robert Kennedy and his times. Schlesinger, A.
M. **92**

Robert McConnell Productions

Webster's New World Robert's rules of order **060.4**

Robert Oppenheimer. Monk, R. **92**

Robert Schumann. Geck, M. **780.92**

Robert's rules of order newly revised. Robert, H.
M. **060.4**

Robert, Henry M.

Robert's rules of order newly revised **060.4**

Webster's New World Robert's rules of order **060.4**

Roberta's. Parachini, C. **641.82**

ROBERTA'S (RESTAURANT)

Parachini, C. Roberta's **641.82**

The **Roberts** court. Coyle, M. **347.73**

Roberts, Adam

(ed) Browning, R. Robert Browning **821**

Roberts, Andrew

Roberts, A. Masters and commanders **940.54**

The storm of war **940.54**

Waterloo: June 18, 1815 **940.2**

Roberts, Ann

Crash course in library services to people with disabilities **027.6**

Roberts, Callum

The ocean of life **551.46**

The unnatural history of the sea **909**

Roberts, Cokie

Founding mothers **920**

Ladies of liberty **920**

Roberts, David

(ed) Points unknown **910**

Once they moved like the wind **970.004**

Roberts, David, 1943-

Alone on the ice **919.890**

Roberts, Diane

Dream state **975.9**

Roberts, Dorothy

Fatal invention **305.8**

Roberts, Geoffrey

Stalin's general **940.54**

Roberts, Gillian

You can write a mystery **808.3**

Roberts, J. M.

The new history of the world **909**

Roberts, James A.

Shiny objects **339.4**

Roberts, Jason

A sense of the world **92**

Roberts, John G., 1955-

About

Coyle, M. The Roberts court **347.73**

Toobin, J. The oath **347.73**

Tribe, L. H. Uncertain justice **342.73**

Tushnet, M. In the balance **347.73**

Roberts, Nicole A.

(ed) Health and social relationships **613**

Roberts, Priscilla Mary

(ed) The encyclopedia of Middle East wars **355**

(ed) Encyclopedia of World War II **940.53**

Roberts, Ralph

Genealogy via the Internet **929**

Roberts, Randy

Joe Louis **92**

Roberts, Siobhan

King of infinite space **92**

Robertson, Chad

Tartine **641.8**

Tartine Book No. 3 **641.81**

Tartine bread **641.8**

Robertson, David

W.C. Handy **92**

Barry, D. Bottom of the 33rd   **796.357**

ROCK AND ROLL MUSIC *See* Rock music

Rock and roll will save your life. Almond, S. **781.66**

Rock climbing. Robinson, V.   **796.522**

Rock climbing. Trailside (Television program)   **796.522**

ROCK CLIMBING *See* Mountaineering

ROCK CLIMBING

Robinson, V. Rock climbing   **796.522**

ROCK DRAWINGS, PAINTINGS, AND ENGRAVINGS

Schobinger, J. The ancient Americans   **970.01**

    See also Archeology; Prehistoric art

ROCK GARDENS

    See also Gardens

Rock Harbor. Phillips, C.   **811**

ROCK MUSIC

Almond, S. Rock and roll will save your life **781.66**

Aronowitz, N. W. Out of the vinyl deeps   **781.66**

Bangs, L. Mainlines, blood feasts and bad taste   **781.66**

Blecha, P. Sonic boom   **781.66**

Browne, D. Fire and rain   **781.66**

Buckland, G. Who shot rock & roll   **781.66**

Cutler, S. You can't always get what you want   **781.66**

DeRogatis, J. The Beatles vs. the Rolling Stones   **781.66**

Ellis, I. Rebels wit attitude   **781.66**

Epting, C. Led Zeppelin crashed here   **781.66**

Hampton, H. Born in flames   **814**

Hayes, C. Gig posters volume 1   **741.6**

McDermott, J. Ultimate Hendrix   **781.66**

Reynolds, S. Retromania   **781.64**

Thompson, D. I hate new music   **781.66**

Thompson, G. Please please me   **781.64**

    See also Music; Popular music

ROCK MUSIC -- 1991-2000 -- HISTORY AND CRITICISM

Cross, C. R. Here we are now   **92**

ROCK MUSIC -- HISTORY AND CRITICISM

Almond, S. Rock and roll will save your life **781.66**

Aronowitz, N. W. Out of the vinyl deeps   **781.66**

Avery, K. Everything is an afterthought   **92**

Bangs, L. Mainlines, blood feasts and bad taste   **781.66**

Bangs, L. Psychotic reactions and carburetor dung   **781.66**

Browne, D. Fire and rain   **781.66**

Christgau, R. Grown up all wrong   **781.66**

Cook, J. Our noise   **338**

Klosterman, C. Killing yourself to live   **781.66**

Lauterbach, P. The chitlin' circuit   **781.64**

Leiber, J. Hound dog   **92**

Marcus, G. When that rough god goes riding **782.42**

Norman, P. John Lennon   **92**

Wald, E. How the Beatles destroyed rock 'n' roll   **781.64**

Yarm, M. Everybody loves our town   **781.66**

Zevon, C. I'll sleep when I'm dead   **92**

ROCK MUSIC -- PICTORIAL WORKS

Buckland, G. Who shot rock & roll   **781.66**

Marshall, J. Trust   **781.66**

ROCK MUSIC -- UNITED STATES -- HISTORY AND CRITICISM

Davis, C. The soundtrack of my life   **92**

ROCK MUSICIANS

Allman, G. My cross to bear   **780**

Bangs, L. Mainlines, blood feasts and bad taste   **781.66**

The Beatles anthology   **782.421**

Brightman, C. Sweet chaos   **920**

Buckland, G. Who shot rock & roll   **781.66**

Byrne, D. Bicycle diaries   **796.6**

Christgau, R. Grown up all wrong   **781.66**

Clapton, E. Clapton   **92**

Coleman, R. Blue Monday   **92**

Cross, C. R. Heavier than heaven: a biography of Kurt Cobain   **92**

Cross, C. R. Room full of mirrors   **92**

Dylan, B. Chronicles   **92**

Englehart, M. AC/DC   **920**

Frank, J. In heaven everything is fine   **92**

Gould, J. Can't buy me love   **920**

Greenberg, K. E. December 8, 1980   **92**

Gruen, B. New York Dolls   **781.66**

Guralnick, P. Careless love: the unmaking of Elvis Presley   **92**

Guralnick, P. Last train to Memphis: the rise of Elvis Presley   **782.421**

Hopkins, J. No one here gets out alive   **92**

Hoskyns, B. Lowside of the road   **92**

Jackson, B. Garcia   **92**

Johnston, D. Daniel Johnston   **741**

Klosterman, C. Killing yourself to live   **781.66**

Marcus, G. When that rough god goes riding **782.42**

Mason, B. A. Elvis Presley   **782.421**

McDermott, J. Ultimate Hendrix   **781.66**

McDonough, J. Shakey: Neil Young's biography   **782.421**

Murray, C. S. Crosstown traffic: Jimi Hendrix and the post-war rock'n'roll revolution   **787.87**

Norman, P. John Lennon   **92**

O'Dell, C. Miss O'Dell   **92**

Osbourne, O. I am Ozzy   **92**

Povey, G. Echoes: the complete history of Pink Floyd   **920**

Richards, K. Life   **92**

Riley, T. Lennon   **92**

Riordan, J. Break on through: the life and death of Jim Morrison   **782.421**

Rogovoy, S. Bob Dylan   **92**

Rusk, Dean, 1909-1994

About

Halberstam, D. The best and the brightest **973.922**

Russell Lee photographs. Lee, R. **779**

Russell, Bertrand, 1872-1970

A history of Western philosophy **109**

The problems of philosophy **100**

About

Durant, W. J. The story of philosophy **109**

Feldman, B. 112 Mercer Street **920**

Russell, Carrie

Complete copyright for K-12 librarians and educators **346.04**

Russell, David O.

About

Waxman, S. Rebels on the backlot **920**

Russell, Ethan A.

Let it bleed **781.66**

Russell, Jenna

Long mile home **363.325**

Russell, Karen Kramer

Shapeshifting **704.039**

Russell, Sharman Apt, 1954-

Standing in the light **211**

Russell, Thaddeus

Out of the jungle **92**

Russell, Tony

Country music originals **781.642**

Russell-Revesz, Heather

De Vito, D. World atlas of dog breeds **636.7**

RUSSIA (FEDERATION)

Brent, J. Inside the Stalin archives **947.086**

Meier, A. Black earth **947.086**

RUSSIA (FEDERATION) -- DESCRIPTION AND TRAVEL

Meier, A. Black earth **947.086**

Polonsky, R. Molotov's magic lantern **947**

Richards, S. Lost and found in Russia **947.086**

RUSSIA (FEDERATION) -- HISTORY

Riasanovsky, N. V. A history of Russia **947**

Service, R. A history of twentieth-century Russia **947.084**

RUSSIA (FEDERATION) -- POLITICS AND GOVERNMENT

Baker, P. Kremlin rising **947.086**

Gorbachev, M.   On my country and the world **947.085**

Politkovskaya, A. A Russian diary **947.086**

Remnick, D. Resurrection **947.086**

Treisman, D. The return **947.086**

RUSSIA (FEDERATION) -- POLITICS AND GOVERNMENT -- 1991-

Baker, P. Kremlin rising **947.086**

Brent, J. Inside the Stalin archives **947.086**

Politkovskaya, A.   Is journalism worth dying for? **070.92**

Politkovskaya, A. A Russian diary **947.086**

RUSSIA (FEDERATION) -- SOCIAL CONDITIONS -- 1991-

Baker, P. Kremlin rising **947.086**

Brent, J. Inside the Stalin archives **947.086**

Politkovskaya, A. A Russian diary **947.086**

Von Bremzen, A. Mastering the art of Soviet cooking **641.59**

RUSSIA (FEDERATION) -- SOCIAL LIFE AND CUSTOMS

Jones, C. C. A year of Russian feasts **641.59**

Richards, S. Lost and found in Russia **947.086**

RUSSIA -- CIVILIZATION

Massie, S. Land of the firebird **947**

RUSSIA -- COMMUNISM *See* Communism -- Russia

RUSSIA -- FOREIGN RELATIONS -- UNITED STATES

Cook, J. H. American phoenix **973.5**

Talbott, S. The Russia hand **327**

RUSSIA -- HISTORY

Smith, D. Former people **305.5**

RUSSIA -- HISTORY -- 1917-1921, REVOLUTION

Competing voices from the Russian Revolution **947.084**

See also Revolutions

RUSSIA -- HISTORY -- 1917-1991, SOVIET UNION

Figes, O.   Just send me word **365**

Von Bremzen, A. Mastering the art of Soviet cooking **641.59**

RUSSIA -- HISTORY -- DICTIONARIES

Borrero, M. Russia: a reference guide from the Renaissance to the present **947**

RUSSIA -- KINGS AND RULERS

Catherine   The memoirs of Catherine the Great **92**

Erickson, C. Great Catherine **947**

Ferro, M. Nicholas II **92**

Massie, R. K.   Catherine the Great **947**

Massie, R. K.   Nicholas and Alexandra **92**

Massie, R. K.   The Romanovs **947.08**

Romanov riches **891.7**

Rounding, V. Catherine the Great **92**

Troyat, H. Catherine the Great **92**

Warnes, D. Chronicle of the Russian tsars **947**

RUSSIA -- POLITICS AND GOVERNMENT

Tolstaia, T. Pushkin's children **891.7**

Russia against Napoleon. Lieven, D. C. B. **940.2**

Russia and the Russians. Hosking, G. A. **947**

The **Russia** hand. Talbott, S. **327**

Russia   under the Bolshevik regime.   Pipes, R. **947.084**

Russia: a reference guide from the Renaissance to the present. Borrero, M. **947**

Russia: people and empire, 1552-1917. Hosking, G.

Johnson, L. K. National Security Intelligence
    See also Police

SECRET SERVICE -- GERMANY (EAST)
Garton-Ash, T. The file   **327.12**

SECRET SERVICE -- ISRAEL
Bascomb, N. Hunting Eichmann   **943.086**
Pedahzur, A. The Israeli secret services and the struggle against terrorism   **363.32**

SECRET SERVICE -- UNITED STATES
Hill, C. Mrs. Kennedy and me   **973.922**

SECRET SOCIETIES
    See also Rites and ceremonies; Societies
The **secret** war against Hanoi. Shultz, R. H. **959.704**
Secret weapons. Eisner, T.   **595.7**
The **secret** wife of Louis XIV. Buckley, V.   **944**

SECRET WRITING *See* Cryptography

SECRETARIES
Rule, A. --and never let her go   **364.1**

SECRETARIES OF COMMERCE
Hofstadter, R. The American political tradition, and the men who made it   **973**
Leuchtenburg, W. E. Herbert Hoover   **92**

SECRETARIES OF DEFENSE
Halberstam, D. The best and the brightest **973.922**
Hendrickson, P. The living and the dead **959.704**
Roberts, A. Masters and commanders   **940.54**
Schwartz, R. A. Encyclopedia of the Persian Gulf War   **956.704**
Weintraub, S. 15 stars   **920**
Woodward, B. The commanders   **973.928**

SECRETARIES OF LABOR
Downey, K. The woman behind the New Deal **92**

SECRETARIES OF STATE
Balz, D. J. The battle for America, 2008 **973.932**
Berman, L. No peace, no honor   **959.704**
Bernstein, C. A woman in charge   **92**
Brookhiser, R. America's first dynasty   **973.4**
Burstein, A. Madison and Jefferson   **973.4**
Chace, J. Acheson   **92**
Clinton, H. R. Living history   **973.929**
Cohen, I. B. Science and the founding fathers **973.3**
Dallek, R. Nixon and Kissinger   **92**
De Young, K. Soldier: the life of Colin Powell **92**
Ellis, J. J. Founding brothers   **973.4**
Gates, H. L. Thirteen ways of looking at a black man   **920.71**
Goodwin, D. K. Team of rivals   **92**
Gormley, K. The death of American virtue **973.929**
Halberstam, D. The best and the brightest **973.922**
Heidler, D. S. Henry Clay   **92**
Hofstadter, R. The American political tradition, and the men who made it   **973**
Kazin, M. A godly hero   **92**
Kennedy, J. F. Profiles in courage   **920**
Kissinger, H. Years of renewal   **973.924**
Mann, J. About face   **327**

McPherson, J. M. Drawn with the sword   **973.7**
Meyerson, M. Liberty's blueprint   **342**
Miller, W. L. Arguing about slavery   **973.5**
Nagel, P. C. John Quincy Adams   **92**
O'Brien, M. Mrs. Adams in winter   **940.2**
Powell, C. L. My American journey   **92**
Remini, R. V. Daniel Webster   **328**
Remini, R. V. John Quincy Adams   **973.5**
Rice, C. Extraordinary, ordinary people   **92**
Roberts, A. Masters and commanders   **940.54**
Schwartz, R. A. Encyclopedia of the Persian Gulf War   **956.704**
Simon, J. F. What kind of nation   **342**
Smith, J. E. John Marshall   **347**
Traister, R. Big girls don't cry   **324**
Unger, H. G. The last founding father   **92**
Weintraub, S. 15 stars   **920**
Widmer, E. L. Martin Van Buren   **92**
Wills, G. James Madison   **973.5**
Woodward, B. The commanders   **973.928**
Zimmermann, W. First great triumph   **973**

SECRETARIES OF THE INTERIOR
Kennedy, J. F. Profiles in courage   **920**

SECRETARIES OF THE NAVY
Symonds, C. L. Lincoln and his admirals   **92**
Thompson, N. The hawk and the dove   **92**

SECRETARIES OF THE TREASURY
Beschloss, M. R. The conquerors: Roosevelt, Truman, and the destruction of Hitler's Germany, 1941-1945   **940.53**
Brookhiser, R. Alexander Hamilton, American **92**
Cannadine, D. Mellon   **92**
Chernow, R. Alexander Hamilton   **92**
Ellis, J. J. Founding brothers   **973.4**
Goodwin, D. K. Team of rivals   **92**
Hamilton, A. Writings   **973.4**
Larson, E. J. A magnificent catastrophe   **324**
Meyerson, M. Liberty's blueprint   **342**
Miller, J. C. The Federalist era, 1789-1801 **973.4**
Paulson, H. M. On the brink   **330.9**
Randall, W. S. Alexander Hamilton   **92**
Staloff, D. Hamilton, Adams, Jefferson   **973.4**

SECRETARIES OF WAR
Cooper, W. J. Jefferson Davis, American   **973.7**
Davis, B. Sherman's march   **973.7**
Davis, W. C. An honorable defeat   **973.7**
Fellman, M. Citizen Sherman   **92**
Flood, C. B. Grant and Sherman   **92**
Hanson, V. D. The soul of battle   **355**
Hofstadter, R. The American political tradition, and the men who made it   **973**
Kennett, L. B. Sherman   **355**
McPherson, J. M. Drawn with the sword   **973.7**
Moody, W. Demon of the lost cause   **973.709**
Wilson, E. Patriotic gore   **810**
Woodworth, S. E. Sherman   **92**

King, D. Death in the city of light
    See also Criminals; Homicide

SERIAL KILLERS -- HISTORY
  Schechter, H. Psycho USA   **364.152**

SERIAL MURDERERS -- UNITED STATES --
    BIOGRAPHY
  Graeber, C. The good nurse   **364.152**
  Stewart, J. B. Blind eye   **364.1**

SERIAL MURDERS -- NEW YORK (STATE) --
    LONG ISLAND
  Kolker, R. Lost Girls   **364.152**

SERIAL PUBLICATIONS
    See also Bibliography; Publishers and publishing

Serious barbecue. Lang, A. P.   **641.5**
Serious business. Kanfer, S.   **741.5**
A **serious** way of wondering. Price, R.   **241**
Seriously funny. Nachman, G.   **792.7**

SERMON ON THE MOUNT
  Bonhoeffer, D. The cost of discipleship   **226**

SERMONS
  American sermons   **252**
  King, M. L. Strength to love   **252**
  Tutu, D. The rainbow people of God   **968.06**
    See also Christian literature

SERPENTS *See* Snakes

Servadio, Gaia
  Rossini   **92**

Server, Lee
  Ava Gardner   **791**

Service. Hornfischer, J. D.   **956.704**

SERVICE (IN INDUSTRY) *See* Customer services
Service and style. Whitaker, J.   **381**

SERVICE DOGS
    See also Working dogs

SERVICE INDUSTRIES
    See also Industries

SERVICE STATIONS
    See also Automobile industry; Petroleum industry

SERVICE, CUSTOMER *See* Customer services

Service, Robert
  Service, R. Trotsky   **92**
  A history of twentieth-century Russia   **947.084**
  Lenin--a biography   **947.084**
  Stalin   **92**

Service, Robert, 1947-
  Trotsky   **92**

SERVICEMEMBERS UNITED (UNITED
    STATES)
  Nicholson, A. Fighting to serve   **355**

SERVICEMEN *See* Military personnel
SERVICES, CUSTOMER *See* Customer services
SERVICEWOMEN *See* Military personnel
SERVITUDE *See* Peonage; Slavery
SESAME STREET (TELEVISION PROGRAM)

Davis, M. Street gang   **791.45**
Jones, B. J. Jim Henson   **92**
Sestets. Wright, C.   **811**

SET DESIGNERS
  Brainard, J. The Nancy book   **759**
  Holroyd, M. A strange eventful history   **92**
  Ross, C. The world of Edward Gorey   **700.92**

SET THEORY
  Stillwell, J. Roads to infinity   **511.3**
    See also Mathematics

Seth, Vikram, 1952-
  Two lives   **92**

Seton, Elizabeth Ann, Saint, 1774-1821
    About
  Barthel, J. American saint   **92**

SETS (MATHEMATICS) *See* Set theory

Settersten, Richard
  (jt. auth) Ray, B. E. Not quite adults   **306.8**

The **setting** of the pearl. Weyr, T.   **940.53**
Setting the truth free. Campbell, J.   **941.6**
Setting the world ablaze. Ferling, J. E.   **973.3**
Settled in the wild. Shetterly, S. H.   **508**
The **settlement** of the Americas. Dillehay, T.
D.   **970.01**

Seuling, Barbara
  How to write a children's book and get it published   **808.06**

Seuss, Dr.
    About
  Morgan, J. Dr. Seuss & Mr. Geisel   **92**

Seven ages of Paris. Horne, A.   **944**
The **seven** daughters of Eve. Sykes, B.   **599.93**
Seven days in the art world. Thornton, S.   **709.05**
Seven experiments that could change the world.
  Sheldrake, R.   **507.8**
Seven fires. Mallmann, F.   **641.5**
Seven guitars. Wilson, A.   **812**
The **seven** pearls of financial wisdom. Pepper,
C.   **332.024**
Seven pillars of wisdom. Lawrence, T. E.   **940.4**
Seven pleasures. Spiegelman, W.   **814**
The **seven** sins of memory. Schacter, D. L.   **153.1**
The **seven** storey mountain. Merton, T.   **92**

SEVEN WONDERS OF THE WORLD
    See also Ancient architecture; Ancient art

SEVEN YEARS' WAR, 1756-1763
  Anderson, F. The crucible of war   **973.2**
  McLynn, F. 1759: the year Britain became master
  of the world   **941.07**

SEVENTEENTH CENTURY *See* World history
  -- 17th century

The **seventies.** Schulman, B. J.   **973.925**
The **Seventy** wonders of the modern world.   **720.9**

Severin, Timothy
  In search of Robinson Crusoe   **996**

Severson, Marilyn S.

About

Nolan, T. Three chords for beauty's sake: the life of Artie Shaw   **92**

Shaw, Bernard, 1856-1950

Arms and the man	**822**
Heartbreak House	**822**
Major Barbara	**822**
Man and Superman	**822**
Pygmalion . . . and My fair lady	**822**
Saint Joan	**822**

About

Peters, S. Bernard Shaw   **822**

Shaw, David, d. 2005

About

Finch, P. Diving into darkness   **627**

Shaw, Randy

Beyond the fields   **331.8**

Shawn, Allen

Wish I could be there   **92**

Shawn, William, 1907-1992

About

Fraser, K. Ornament and silence	**809**
Ross, L. Here but not here	**070**

SHAWNEE INDIANS

Eckert, A. W. A sorrow in our heart: the life of Tecumseh   **977**

SHAWNEE NATIONAL FOREST REGION (ILL.)

Biggers, J. Reckoning at Eagle Creek   **333.73**

Shay, Bee

Collage lab   **702.8**

She-wolves. Castor, H.   **920**

Shea, William R.

Galileo in Rome   **92**

Shearer, Barbara Smith

Shearer, B. F. State names, seals, flags, and symbols   **929.9**

Shearer, Benjamin F.

State names, seals, flags, and symbols   **929.9**

Shearer, Stephen Michael

Beautiful   **92**

Sheedy, Chris

Bond, J. Who the hell is Pansy O'Hara?   **920**

Sheehan, Jason

Cooking dirty   **92**

Sheehan, Neil

A bright shining lie: John Paul Vann and America in Vietnam	**959.704**
A fiery peace in a cold war	**92**

Sheehan, William

The transits of Venus   **523.9**

Sheehan-Dean, Aaron

(ed) The Civil War   **973.7**

Sheehy, Gail

Daring	**92**
New passages	**305.24**

The silent passage: menopause   **618.1**

Sheeler, Jim

Final salute   **956.7**

SHEEP

    See also Domestic animals; Mammals

SHEET METALWORK

    See also Metalwork

Sheftall, Mordecai G.

Blossoms in the wind   **940.54**

Shehadeh, Raja

Palestinian walks   **956.95**

Sheinkin, Steve

Bomb   **623.4**

SHELBY (MONT.)

Kelly, J. Shelby's folly	**796.8**
Shelby's folly. Kelly, J.	**796.8**

Shelden, Michael

Mark Twain   **92**

Sheldrake, Rupert

Dogs that know when their owners are coming home	**133.8**
The sense of being stared at	**133.8**
Seven experiments that could change the world	**507.8**

Shell chic. Marshall, M. H.   **745.55**

Shell games. Welch, C.   **364.1**

Shell, G. Richard

Springboard   **650.1**

Shelley's poetry and prose.   **821**

Shelley, Fred M.

Lavin, S. J. Atlas of the great plains	**912**
Atlas of American politics, 1960-2000	**973.92**

Shelley, Mary Wollstonecraft, 1797-1851

About

Montillo, R. The lady and her monsters	**823**
Seymour, M. Mary Shelley	**92**

Shelley, Percy Bysshe, 1792-1822

Poems Poems	**821**
Shelley's poetry and prose	**821**

About

Lee, H. Virginia Woolf's nose   **820**

SHELLS

Harasewych, M. G. The book of shells	**594**
Marshall, M. H. Shell chic	**745.55**

Shelter from the storm. Hilden, J. M.   **618.92**

SHELTER ISLAND (N.Y.) -- HISTORY

Griswold, M. The Manor   **974.7**

Shen, Aisling Juanjuan

A tiger's heart   **92**

Shenk, David

The forgetting: Alzheimer's, portrait of an epidemic	**616.8**
The genius in all of us	**155.2**

Shenk, Joshua Wolf

Lincoln's melancholy   **92**

Shenkman, Richard

(ed) Encyclopedia of African history   960

SHILOH (TENN.), BATTLE OF, 1862
Daniel, L. J. Shiloh   973.7
Groom, W. Shiloh, 1862   973.7
Shiloh, 1862. Groom, W.   973.7
Shilon, Avi
Menachem Begin   956.940
Shilts, Randy
And the band played on   362.1
Shim, Jae K.
Siegel, J. G. Accounting handbook   657
Shine. Hallowell, E. M.   658.3
Shing-Tung Yau
(jt. auth) Nadis, S. The shape of inner space 530.1
SHINTO
Eastern religions   200.9
    See also Religions
Shiny objects. Roberts, J. A.   339.4
SHIP CAPTAINS
Blainey, G. Sea of dangers   92
Harris, J. W. The hanging of Thomas Jeremiah 92
Ship of ghosts. Hornfischer, J. D.   940.54
SHIP PILOTS
    See also Sailors
A **ship** without a sail. Marmorstein, G.   782.1
SHIPBUILDING EXECUTIVES
Kahn, R. October men   796.357
Shipler, David K.
Arab and Jew   956.94
The rights of the people   323
Shipley, David
Send   658
Shipley, Graham
(ed) The Cambridge dictionary of classical civiliza-
tion   938
Shipman, Pat
Walker, A. The wisdom of the bones   599.93
Shipp, Steve
Latin American and Caribbean artists of the modern
era   920.003
SHIPPING
    See also Transportation
SHIPPING EXECUTIVES
Gage, N. Greek fire   782.1
Millard, C. The river of doubt   973.91
Renehan, E. J. Commodore   92
SHIPWRECKS
Ballard, R. D. Return to Midway   940.54
Bathurst, B. The wreckers   910.4
Beneath the seven seas   930.1
Junger, S. The perfect storm   910.4
Lord, W. A night to remember   910.4
Tougias, M. Ten hours until dawn   363.34
Woodward, H. A brave vessel   973.2
    See also Accidents; Adventure and adven-
turers; Disasters; Navigation; Voyages and

travels

**SHIPWRECKS -- ARCTIC OCEAN -- HISTORY
-- 19TH CENTURY**
Sides, H. In the kingdom of ice   910.4
SHIPWRECKS -- FICTION
Philbrick, N. Why read Moby-Dick?   813
SHIPWRECKS -- SCOTLAND -- ISLAY
Scott, R. N. Many were held by the sea   940.4
Shirer, William L.
The rise and fall of the Third Reich   943.086
Shirky, Clay
Cognitive surplus   303.4
Shirley, Don, 1958-
       About
Finch, P. Diving into darkness   627
Shlaes, Amity
The forgotten man   973.91
Coolidge   973.91
Shlaim, Avi
The iron wall   956.04
Israel and Palestine   956.04
Shlain, Leonard
Sex, time, and power   306.7
Shnayerson, Michael
Belafonte, H. My song   92
The **shock** of the old. Edgerton, D.   600
Shock value. Zinoman, J.   791.43
Shocked. Volk, P.   92
Shockley, Evie
The new black   811
SHOE INDUSTRY
    See also Clothing industry; Leather industry
Shoeless. Fleitz, D. L.   796.357
SHOES
Crowe, L. G. The towering world of Jimmy
Choo   391
    See also Clothing and dress
Shoolery, Judith
Teller, E. Memoirs   92
Shoot an Iraqi. Bilal, W.   92
Shooting star: the brief arc of Joe McCarthy. Wick-
er, T.   973.921
Shooting Victoria. Murphy, P. T.   941.081
SHOOTINGS IN SCHOOLS *See* School shoot-
ings
Shop class as soulcraft. Crawford, M. B.   331
Shop talk. Roth, P.   809
SHOPLIFTING
    See also Theft
SHOPPERS' GUIDES *See* Consumer education;
Shopping
SHOPPING
Levine, J. Not buying it   640.73
Underhill, P. Why we buy   658.8
    See also Home economics; Purchasing
SHOPPING CENTERS AND MALLS

O'Sullivan, P. The homeowner's complete tree & shrub handbook **635.9**

Symonds, G. W. D. The shrub identification book **582.1**

SHRUBS
> *See also* Plants; Trees

Shubin, Neil H., 1960-
The universe within **550**
Your inner fish **611**

Shulevitz, Judith
The Sabbath world **296.4**

Shulevitz, Uri
Writing with pictures **808.06**

Shulman, Alix Kates
To love what is **92**

Shulman, Beth
The betrayal of work **331.2**

Shulman, Lisa M.
Lang, A. E. Parkinson's disease **616.8**

Shulman, Martha Rose
The art of French pastry **641.86**
Mediterranean harvest **641.5**
The simple art of vegetarian cooking **641.5**
The very best of recipes for health **641.5**

Shulman, Seth
Cooler smarter **363.7**
The telephone gambit **621.3**

Shultz, George Pratt, 1920-
> **About**
Taubman, P. The partnership **327.1**

Shultz, Richard H.
The secret war against Hanoi **959.704**

Shuster, Joe
> **About**
Ricca, B. Super boys **92**

Shut out. Bryant, H. **796.357**

SHYNESS
> *See also* Emotions

SIBERIA (RUSSIA) -- DESCRIPTION AND TRAVEL
Frazier, I. Travels in Siberia **957**
Thubron, C. In Siberia **957**
Vaillant, J. The tiger **599.75**

The **Sibley** field guide to birds of Eastern North America. Sibley, D. **598**

The **Sibley** field guide to birds of Western North America. Sibley, D. **598**

The **Sibley** guide to bird life & behavior. Sibley, D. **598**

The **Sibley** guide to birds. Sibley, D. **598**

The **Sibley** guide to trees. Sibley, D. **582.16**

Sibley's birding basics. Sibley, D. **598**

Sibley, David
The Sibley field guide to birds of Eastern North America **598**
The Sibley field guide to birds of Western North

America **598**
The Sibley guide to bird life & behavior **598**
The Sibley guide to birds **598**
The Sibley guide to trees **582.16**
Sibley's birding basics **598**

Siblin, Eric
The cello suites **787.3**

SIBLING RIVALRY
> *See also* Child psychology; Siblings

SIBLINGS
Scheeres, J. Jesus land **92**
> *See also* Family

SIBLINGS -- INDIA
Chopra, D. Brotherhood **610.92**

SIBLINGS -- UNITED STATES
Chopra, D. Brotherhood **610.92**

SIBLINGS OF PRESIDENTS
Clarke, T. The last campaign **92**
English, B. Last lion **92**
Kennedy, E. M. True compass **92**
Mahoney, R. D. Sons and brothers: the days of Jack and Bobby Kennedy **92**
Schlesinger, A. M. Robert Kennedy and his times **92**
Thomas, E. Robert Kennedy **973.922**

Sicherer, Scott H.
Food allergies **616.97**

Sicherer, Scott H.
Understanding and managing your child's food allergies **618.92**

Sicherman, Barbara
(ed) Notable American women: the modern period **920.003**

SICILY (ITALY) -- DESCRIPTION AND TRAVEL
Keahey, J. Seeking Sicily **945**

SICILY (ITALY) -- SOCIAL LIFE AND CUSTOMS
Keahey, J. Seeking Sicily **945**

SICK
Filene, P. G. In the arms of others **179.7**
Gunther, J. Death be not proud **92**
Kore **610.1**
Reiner, J. The man who couldn't eat **92**
Whitehouse, B. The match **92**
> *See also* People with disabilities

SICK -- PRAYERS
> *See also* Prayers

Sickles, Daniel E., 1825-1914
> **About**
Keneally, T. American scoundrel: the life of the notorious Civil War General Dan Sickles **92**

SICKNESS *See* Diseases

Siddiqī, Afiyah, 1972-
> **About**
Scroggins, D. Wanted women **305.48**

Anderson, C. The numbers game   796.334

SOCCER COACHES

St. John, W. Outcasts united   796.334

Soccer empire. Dubois, L.   796.334

SOCCER EXECUTIVES

Greenfield, R. The last sultan   92

Soccer in sun and shadow.   796.334

SOCCER PLAYERS

Dubois, L. Soccer empire   796.334

Soccernomics. Kuper, S.   796.334

SOCIAL ACTION

Budd, K. The voluntourist   361.7

Shaw, R. Beyond the fields   331.8

    See also Social policy

SOCIAL ACTION -- UNITED STATES -- HISTORY -- 20TH CENTURY

Shaw, R. Beyond the fields   331.8

SOCIAL ADJUSTMENT

    See also Human behavior; Interpersonal relations; Social psychology

SOCIAL ADVOCACY

    See also Social work

The **social** animal. Brooks, D.   305.5

SOCIAL ANTHROPOLOGY *See* Ethnology

SOCIAL BEHAVIOR *See* Human behavior

SOCIAL BEHAVIOR IN ANIMALS

Balcombe, J. Second nature   591.5

Bekoff, M. Wild justice   591.5

Waldbauer, G. Millions of monarchs, bunches of beetles   595.7

SOCIAL CASE WORK

    See also Social work

SOCIAL CHANGE

Bram, C. Eminent outlaws   810.9

Diamond, J. M. Collapse: how societies choose to fail or succeed   304.2

Diamond, J. M. Guns, germs, and steel   303.4

Diamond, J. The third chimpanzee   599.93

Gilding, P. The great disruption   304.2

Hayden, T. The long sixties   973.92

Johnson, S. Future perfect   303.48

Kellerman, B. The end of leadership   303.34

King, B. J. Evolving God   200

Linden, E. The winds of change   551.6

Mainwaring, S. We first   658.8

Pagel, M. Wired for culture   303.4

Rosenberg, T. Join the club   303.3

Toffler, A. Future shock   303.4

Wade, N. Before the dawn   599.93

    See also Anthropology; Social sciences; Sociology

SOCIAL CHANGE -- CALIFORNIA -- SAN FRANCISCO -- HISTORY -- 20TH CENTURY

Talbot, D. Season of the witch   306

SOCIAL CHANGE -- CHINA -- SHANGHAI --

HISTORY

Qin Shao Shanghai gone   307.1

SOCIAL CHANGE -- CUBA -- HAVANA -- HISTORY -- 21ST CENTURY

Cooke, J. The other side of paradise   972.91

SOCIAL CHANGE -- INDIA

Giridharadas, A. India calling   954.05

SOCIAL CHANGE -- JAPAN -- HISTORY -- 20TH CENTURY

Dower, J. W. Ways of forgetting, ways of remembering   940.53

SOCIAL CHANGE -- NEW YORK (STATE) -- NEW YORK

Anasi, R. The last bohemia   974.7

SOCIAL CHANGE -- PSYCHOLOGICAL ASPECTS

Pipher, M. The green boat   303.4

SOCIAL CHANGE -- UNITED STATES

Howe, D. W. What hath God wrought   973.5

SOCIAL CHANGE -- UNITED STATES -- HISTORY -- 20TH CENTURY

Lingeman, R. The noir forties   973.91

SOCIAL CLASSES

Pickett, K. The spirit level   306.01

Tough, P. How children succeed   372.210

Veblen, T. The theory of the leisure class   305.5

    See also Caste; Sociology

SOCIAL CLASSES -- UNITED STATES

Hedges, C. Days of destruction, days of revolt   305.5

Murray, C. Coming apart   305.8

SOCIAL CONDITIONS

    See also Sociology

SOCIAL CONFLICT

Hedges, C. Days of destruction, days of revolt   305.5

Mueller, A. I wouldn't start from here   909.83

Murray, C. Coming apart   305.8

Roy, A. Walking with the comrades   954

Williams, D. Bitterly divided   973.7

    See also Social psychology; Sociology

SOCIAL CONFLICT -- SOUTHERN STATES -- HISTORY -- 19TH CENTURY

Williams, D. Bitterly divided   973.7

SOCIAL CONFLICT -- SOVIET UNION -- HISTORY -- SOURCES

Competing voices from the Russian Revolution   947.084

SOCIAL CONFLICT -- UNITED STATES

Bishop, B. The big sort   305.8

SOCIAL CONFORMITY *See* Conformity

The **social** conquest of earth. Wilson, E. O.   599.93

The **social** contract. Rousseau   320.1

SOCIAL CONTRACT

Corning, P. The fair society   303.3

    See also Political science; Sociology

Sowell, Thomas
  Basic economics **330**
Sowing seeds in the desert. Fukuoka, M. **631.6**
Soyinka, Wole
  Of Africa **960**
  You must set forth at dawn **92**
SPACE AND TIME
  Bodanis, D. E **530.1**
  Bojowald, M. Once before time **523.1**
  Carroll, S. M. From eternity to here **530.1**
  Frank, A. About time **523.1**
  Gott, J. R. Time travel in Einstein's universe **530.11**
  Hawking, S. W. The nature of space and time **530.1**
  Impey, C. How it began **523.1**
  Kaku, M. Hyperspace **530.1**
  Susskind, L. The black hole war **530.1**
  Toomey, D. M. The new time travelers **530.1**
    See also Fourth dimension; Metaphysics; Space sciences; Time
SPACE AND TIME -- POPULAR WORKS
  Impey, C. How it began **523.1**
Space atlas. Trefil, J. **520**
SPACE BIOLOGY
  Roach, M. Packing for Mars **571**
  Tyson, N. D. G. Death by black hole **523.8**
    See also Biology; Space sciences
SPACE CHEMISTRY
    See also Chemistry
Space chronicles. **629.4**
SPACE COLONIES
  McCray, W. P. The visioneers **509**
SPACE DEBRIS
    See also Pollution; Space environment
SPACE ENVIRONMENT
    See also Astronomy; Outer space
SPACE EXPLORATION (ASTRONAUTICS)
    See Outer space -- Exploration
SPACE FLIGHT
  Kranz, E. F. Failure is not an option **629.45**
    See also Aeronautics -- Flights; Astronautics
SPACE FLIGHT (FICTION) *See* Imaginary voyages; Science fiction
SPACE FLIGHT -- FORECASTING
  Space chronicles **629.4**
SPACE FLIGHT TO MARS
  Hubbard, S. Exploring Mars **523.430**
  Kessler, A. Martian summer **523.4**
SPACE FLIGHT TO MARS -- HISTORY
  Hubbard, S. Exploring Mars **523.430**
SPACE FLIGHT TO THE MOON
  Chaikin, A. A man on the moon **629.45**
  French, F. Falling to Earth **92**
  French, F. In the shadow of the moon **629.45**
  Nelson, C. Rocket men **629.45**
  Pyle, R. Destination moon **629.45**
  Schefter, J. L. The race **629.45**

Zimmerman, R. Genesis: the story of Apollo 8 **629.45**
    See also Astronautics; Space flight
SPACE FLIGHT TO THE MOON -- HISTORY
  Barbree, J. Neil Armstrong **92**
  Pyle, R. Destination moon **629.45**
SPACE INDUSTRIALIZATION
    See also Industrialization
SPACE LAW
    See also Astronautics and civilization; International law; Law
SPACE MEDICINE
    See also Medicine; Space biology; Space sciences
SPACE OPTICS
    See also Optics; Space sciences
SPACE PERCEPTION
  Ellard, C. You are here **153.7**
SPACE PHOTOGRAPHY
  Benson, M. Far out **778.3**
    See also Photography; Photography -- Scientific applications
SPACE PROBES
    See also Outer space -- Exploration; Space vehicles
Space race. Cadbury, D. **629.4**
SPACE RESCUE OPERATIONS
    See also Rescue work
SPACE RESEARCH *See* Outer space -- Exploration; Space sciences
SPACE SCIENCES
  Cole, K. C. The hole in the universe **530.01**
    See also Science
SPACE STATIONS
    See also Artificial satellites; Astronautics; Space vehicles
SPACE TRAVEL *See* Interplanetary voyages; Space flight
SPACE VEHICLES
    See also Rocketry
SPACE VEHICLES -- PILOTING
    See also Astronauts; Navigation (Astronautics)
SPACE VEHICLES -- THERMODYNAMICS
    See also Thermodynamics
SPACE WARFARE
    See also Outer space; War
SPACE WEAPONS
    See also Military weapons; Space warfare
Space, in chains. Kasischke, L. **811**
Spacek, Sissy
  My extraordinary ordinary life **791.43**
Spaeth, Paul J.
  (ed) A thing that is **811**
Spaethling, Robert
  (ed) Mozart, W. A. Mozart's letters, Mozart's

relations

TECHNICAL EDUCATION

See also Education; Higher education; Technology

TECHNICAL SERVICE *See* Customer services

TECHNICAL WRITING

Van Wicklen, J. The tech writer's survival guide   **808**

  See also Authorship; Technology -- Language

Techniques of the selling writer. Swain, D. V. **808.3**

TECHNOLOGICAL FORECASTING

Diamandis, P. Abundance   **303.48**

Kotler, S. Abundance   **303.48**

Long, J. Darwin's devices   **629.8**

TECHNOLOGICAL INNOVATIONS

Atlas, S. W. In excellent health   **362.109**

Burke, J. J. Neal-Schuman library technology companion   **025**

Carr, N. The big switch   **303.4**

Core technology competencies for librarians and library staff   **020**

Kunstler, J. H. Too much magic   **303.48**

Lanier, J. You are not a gadget   **303.4**

Pernick, R. Clean Tech Nation   **333.794**

Petroski, H. The essential engineer   **620**

Popular mechanics magazine. The wonderful future that never was   **609**

Tapscott, D. Macrowikinomics   **303.4**

Tenner, E. Our own devices   **303.48**

Terra Maxima   **902.2**

Topol, E. The creative destruction of medicine   **610.28**

Woodward, J. The transformed library   **020**

  See also Inventions; Technology

TECHNOLOGICAL INNOVATIONS -- CALIFORNIA -- SANTA CLARA COUNTY

Piscione, D. P. Secrets of Silicon Valley   **330.9**

TECHNOLOGICAL INNOVATIONS -- FORECASTING

Kotler, S. Abundance   **303.48**

Long, J. Darwin's devices   **629.8**

TECHNOLOGICAL INNOVATIONS -- HISTORY

Freeberg, E. The Age of Edison   **303.48**

Gertner, J. The idea factory   **384**

Lind, M. Land of promise   **330.973**

TECHNOLOGICAL INNOVATIONS -- SOCIAL ASPECTS

Bray, H. You are here   **910.285**

Thompson, C. Smarter Than You Think   **303.48**

TECHNOLOGICAL INNOVATIONS -- UNITED STATES -- HISTORY

Freeberg, E. The Age of Edison   **303.48**

TECHNOLOGICAL INNOVATIONS -- UNITED STATES -- HISTORY -- 20TH CENTURY

Gertner, J. The idea factory   **384**

The idea factory

TECHNOLOGICAL LITERACY

  See also Literacy

TECHNOLOGICAL LITERACY -- STUDY AND TEACHING

Braafladt, K. Technology and literacy   **027.62**

TECHNOLOGY

The Encyclopedia of science and technology   **503**

The handy science answer book   **500**

Macaulay, D. The new way things work   **600**

McGraw-Hill dictionary of scientific and technical terms   **503**

Tenner, E. Our own devices   **303.48**

TECHNOLOGY -- DICTIONARIES

McGraw-Hill dictionary of scientific and technical terms   **503**

  See also Encyclopedias and dictionaries

TECHNOLOGY -- ENCYCLOPEDIAS

The Encyclopedia of science and technology   **503**

Encyclopedia of science, technology, and ethics   **503**

McGraw-Hill Publishing Company McGraw-Hill concise encyclopedia of science & technology   **503**

TECHNOLOGY -- HISTORY

Denny, M. Ingenium   **609**

Edgerton, D. The shock of the old   **600**

Marchant, J. Decoding the heavens   **681.1**

TECHNOLOGY -- PHILOSOPHY

Arthur, W. B. The nature of technology   **600**

Rushkoff, D. Present Shock   **303.48**

TECHNOLOGY -- SOCIAL ASPECTS

Arthur, W. B. The nature of technology   **600**

Diamandis, P. Abundance   **303.48**

Kotler, S. Abundance   **303.48**

McLuhan, M. The global village   **302.2**

Noble, D. F. The religion of technology   **261.5**

Rushkoff, D. Present Shock   **303.48**

Tenner, E. Our own devices   **303.48**

TECHNOLOGY AND CIVILIZATION

Diamond, J. M. Guns, germs, and steel   **303.4**

Dick, P. K. The exegesis of Philip K. Dick   **818**

Johnson, S. Future perfect   **303.48**

Kotler, S. Abundance   **303.48**

Kunstler, J. H. Too much magic   **303.48**

Lanier, J. You are not a gadget   **303.4**

Malone, M. S. The guardian of all things   **153.1**

McLuhan, M. The global village   **302.2**

Noble, D. F. The religion of technology   **261.5**

Petroski, H. The essential engineer   **620**

Postman, N. The end of education   **370.9**

Tenner, E. Our own devices   **303.48**

Toffler, A. Future shock   **303.4**

  See also Civilization; Technology

Technology and literacy. Braafladt, K.   **027.62**

TECHNOLOGY AND STATE

Muller, R. A. Energy for future presidents   **333.79**

The **travels** of Marco Polo. Polo, M.   915.04
Travels with Charley. Steinbeck, J.   973
Travels with Herodotus. Kapuscinski, R.   930
Travels with the fossil hunters.   560
Travesties. Stoppard, T.   822
Travis, Joseph
   (ed) Evolution   576.8
Travis, William Barret, 1809-1836
         About
   Davis, W. C. Three roads to the Alamo   976.4
TREASON
   Read, P. P. The Dreyfus affair   944.081
     See also Crime; Political crimes and offenses;
     Subversive activities
Treason by the book. Spence, J. D.   951
Treasure, G. R. R.
   (ed) Who's who in British history   920.003
Treasures of Islam. O'Kane, B.   709.1
Treasury of XXth century murder [series]
   Geary, R. The Lindbergh child   364.1
Treat me, not my age. Lachs, M.   612.6
TREATIES
   Documents of American Indian diplomacy 970.004
     See also Diplomacy; International law; Inter-
     national relations
TREATMENT OF DISEASES *See* Therapeutics
TREATY OF VERSAILLES
   MacMillan, M. Paris 1919   940.3
Trebincevic, Kenan
   (jt. auth) Shapiro, S. The Bosnia list   92
Trebincevic, Kenan, 1980-
         About
   Shapiro, S. The Bosnia list   92
Trebing, Katie, 2002-
         About
   Whitehouse, B. The match   92
TREE HOUSES
     See also Buildings
TREES
   Dirr, M. A. Dirr's encyclopedia of trees and
   shrubs   635.9
   Dirr, M. Dirr's Hardy trees and shrubs   635.9
   Dirr, M. Dirr's trees and shrubs for warm cli-
   mates   635.9
   The Hillier gardener's guide to trees & shrubs 635.9
   Hugo, N. R. Seeing trees   582.16
   Johnson, H. The world of trees   582.16
   Nadkarni, N. Between earth and sky   582.16
   O'Sullivan, P. The homeowner's complete tree &
   shrub handbook   635.9
   Pakenham, T. Remarkable trees of the world 582.16
   Wells, D. Lives of the trees   582.16
     See also Plants
TREES -- NOMENCLATURE (POPULAR)
     See also Popular plant names
TREES -- NORTH AMERICA

Little, E. L. The Audubon Society field guide to
   North American trees   582.16
Sibley, D. The Sibley guide to trees   582.16
Treese, Joel D.
   Biographical directory of the American Congress,
   1774-1996   328
Trefil, James S.
   (ed) The Encyclopedia of science and technol-
   ogy   503
   Space atlas   520
Tregear, Mary
   Chinese art   709
Treglown, Jeremy
   V.S. Pritchett: a working life   92
Treisman, Daniel
   The return   947.086
Treister, Kenneth
   Easter Island's silent sentinels   990
Tremlett, Giles
   Ghosts of Spain   946
TRENT AFFAIR, 1861
     See also United States -- History -- 1861-
     1865, Civil War
Trethewey, Natasha D., 1966-
   Beyond Katrina   818
Tretick, Stanley
         About
   Kelley, K. Let Freedom Ring   323.1196
Treuer, Anton
   Everything you wanted to know about Indians but
   were afraid to ask   909
Trevelyan, George Macaulay
   The English Revolution, 1688-1689   942.06
The **trial.** Kadri, S.   345
The **trial** of Socrates. Stone, I. F.   183
TRIALS
   Bredin The affair   944.081
   Chase, J. Golden   977.3
   Dunne, D. Justice   345
   Evans, R. J. Lying about Hitler   940.53
   Great American trials   347
   Guttenplan, D. D. The Holocaust on trial   940.53
   Heard, A. The eyes of Willie McGee   364.66
   Hoffer, P. C. The Salem witchcraft trials   345
   Kadri, S. The trial   345
   Lipstadt, D. E. History on trial   940.53
   Long, J. The plot against Pepys   941.06
   Newton, M. A. Enemy of the state   345
   Rabinowitz, D. No crueler tyrannies   345
   Rule, A. Dead by sunset   364.1
   Strang, D. A. Worse than the devil   345.73
   Strebeigh, F. Equal   342
   Walsh, J. E. Moonlight   345
   Waterfield, R. Why Socrates died   183
   Weiner, M. S. Black trials   342
   Wise, S. M. Though the heavens may fall   342

TYPE AND TYPE-FOUNDING

Spiekermann, E. Stop Stealing Sheep and Find out How Type Works **686.2**

See also Founding; Printing

TYPE AND TYPE-FOUNDING -- HISTORY

Garfield, S. Just my type **686.2**

Houston, K. Shady characters **411**

TYPESETTING

See also Printing

The **typewriter** is holy. Morgan, B. **810**

TYPEWRITING

See also Business education; Office practice; Writing

TYPHOID FEVER

See also Diseases

TYPHOONS

See also Cyclones; Storms; Winds

TYPHUS

Allen, A. The fantastic laboratory of Dr. Weigl **614.5**

Talty, S. The illustrious dead **940.2**

TYPOGRAPHY

Houston, K. Shady characters **411**

Spiekermann, E. Stop Stealing Sheep and Find out How Type Works **686.2**

See also Graphic arts; Printing

TYPOLOGY (PSYCHOLOGY)

See also Personality; Psychology; Temperament

TYRANNOSAURUS REX

See also Dinosaurs

Tyrannosaurus Sue. Fiffer, S. **567.9**

Tyson, Mike, 1966-

About

Remnick, D. Reporting **814**

Tyson, Neil deGrasse, 1958-

Death by black hole **523.8**

Origins: fourteen billion years of cosmic evolution **523.1**

The Pluto files **523.4**

Space chronicles **629.4**

Universe down to Earth **523.1**

Tytell, John

Ezra Pound **92**

U

U-X-L graphic novelists. Pendergast, T. **920.003**

U.S. Chess Federation's official rules of chess. United States Chess Federation **794.1**

The U.S. Constitution A to Z. Maddex, R. L. **342**

U.S. cultural diplomacy and archaeology. Kersel, M. M. **930.1**

U.S. Department of Labor

(comp) Occupational outlook handbook 2013-2014 **331.12**

U.S. FISH AND WILDLIFE SERVICE -- FO-

RENSICS LABORATORY

Neme, L. A. Animal investigators **363.2**

U.S. immigration made easy. Bray, I. M. **342**

U.S. laws, acts, and treaties. **348**

UCHI (AUSTIN, TEX.: RESTAURANT)

Cole, T. Uchi: the cookbook **641.6**

Uchi: the cookbook. Cole, T. **641.6**

Udvardy, Miklos D. F.

National Audubon Society field guide to North American birds, Western region **598**

Uebbing, James J.

(ed) Love had a compass **811**

UFOS *See* Unidentified flying objects

UGANDA

Chretien The great lakes of Africa **967.6**

Rice, A. The teeth may smile but the heart does not forget **967.6**

Uglow, Jennifer S.

A gambling man **92**

Nature's engraver **92**

Ugly beauty. Brandon, R. **646.7**

Uhlberg, Myron

Hands of my father **92**

Uhlenbroek, Charlotte

(ed) Animal life **591.5**

Ujifusa, Steven

A man and his ship **623.8**

Ulanski, Stan L.

The Gulf Stream **551.46**

Ulianov, Aleksandr, 1886-1887

About

Pomper, P. Lenin's brother **92**

Ulrich, Laurel

Well-behaved women seldom make history **305.4**

The **Ultimate** audition book. **808.82**

Ultimate bar book. Hellmich, M. **641.8**

Ultimate cardmaking. Beaman, S. **745.594**

The **ultimate** cheapskate's road map to true riches. Yeager, J. **332.024**

Ultimate crochet bible. Crowfoot, J. **746.43**

Ultimate curry bible

Madhur Jaffrey's ultimate curry bible **641.5**

ULTIMATE FIGHTING CHAMPIONSHIP (ORGANIZATION)

Wertheim, L. J. Blood in the cage **92**

Ultimate fitness. Kolata, G. **613.7**

The **ultimate** garden designer. Newbury, T. **712**

Ultimate guide: home repair and improvement. **643**

Ultimate guide: porches. Cory, S. **690**

Ultimate Hendrix. McDermott, J. **781.66**

Ultimate homebased business handbook. Stephenson, J. **658**

The **Ultimate** Jack the Ripper companion. **364.15**

Ultimate journey. Bernstein, R. **294.3**

The **ultimate** Picasso. Leal, B. **759**

Ultimate punishment. Turow, S. **345**

Holzer, H. The Civil War in 50 objects   973.7075

UNITED STATES -- HISTORY -- CIVIL WAR, 1861-1865 -- NAVAL OPERATIONS, CONFEDERATE

Smith, M. J. The CSS Arkansas   973.5

UNITED STATES -- HISTORY -- CIVIL WAR, 1861-1865 -- PARTICIPATION, BRITISH

Foreman, A. A world on fire   973.7

UNITED STATES -- HISTORY -- CIVIL WAR, 1861-1865 -- PERSONAL NARRATIVES

Roper, R. Now the drum of war   973.7
Ward, A. The slaves' war   973.7

UNITED STATES -- HISTORY -- CIVIL WAR, 1861-1865 -- PHOTOGRAPHY

Wilson, R. Mathew Brady   770.92

UNITED STATES -- HISTORY -- CIVIL WAR, 1861-1865 -- PICTORIAL WORKS

Katz, H. L. Civil War sketch book   973.7

UNITED STATES -- HISTORY -- CIVIL WAR, 1861-1865 -- SECRET SERVICE

Sulick, M. J. Spying in America   327.120

UNITED STATES -- HISTORY -- CIVIL WAR, 1861-1865 -- SOCIAL ASPECTS

Faust, D. G. This republic of suffering   973.7
Furgurson, E. B. Freedom rising   973.7
Goldfield, D. R. America aflame   973.7
Harper, J. E. Women during the Civil War   973.7
Levine, B. The fall of the house of Dixie   973.7
Ward, A. The slaves' war   973.7
Williams, D. Bitterly divided   973.7

UNITED STATES -- HISTORY -- CIVIL WAR, 1861-1865 -- SOURCES

The Civil War   973.7

UNITED STATES -- HISTORY -- CIVIL WAR, 1861-1865 -- VETERANS -- BIOGRAPHY

Winchester, S. The professor and the madman   423

UNITED STATES -- HISTORY -- COLONIAL PERIOD, CA. 1600-1775

Bailyn, B. The barbarous years   973.2
Encyclopedia of the new American nation   973
Jordan, D. White cargo   326

UNITED STATES -- HISTORY -- DICTIONARIES

Cornelison, P. The great American history factfinder   973
Kane, J. N. Famous first facts   031.02
New York Public Library   The New York Public Library American history desk reference   973
The Oxford companion to United States history 973

UNITED STATES -- HISTORY -- ENCYCLOPEDIAS

Encyclopedia of American history   973

UNITED STATES -- HISTORY -- MISCELLANEA

The New encyclopedia of American scandal   973

UNITED STATES -- HISTORY -- PICTORIAL

WORKS

Virga, V. Eyes of the nation   973

UNITED STATES -- HISTORY -- REVOLUTION, 1775-1783

Archer, R. As if an enemy's country   973.3
Beeman, R. R. Our lives, our fortunes and our sacred honor   973.3
Brookhiser, R. What would the Founders do? 320
Ellis, J. J. American creation   973.3
Ellis, J. J. Revolutionary summer   973.3
Encyclopedia of the new American nation   973
Fenn, E. A. Pox Americana   614.5
Ferling, J. E. Setting the world ablaze   973.3
Fischer, D. H. Washington's crossing   973.3
Gaines, J. R. For liberty and glory   92
Jasanoff, M. Liberty's exiles   973.3
McCraw, T. K. The founders and finance 330.973
Paul, J. R. Unlikely allies   973.3
Phillips, K. 1775   973.3
Rakove, J. Revolutionaries   973.3

UNITED STATES -- HISTORY -- REVOLUTION, 1775-1783 -- BIOGRAPHY

Beeman, R. R. Our lives, our fortunes and our sacred honor   973.3
Morgan, E. S. American heroes   920

UNITED STATES -- HISTORY -- REVOLUTION, 1775-1783 -- COMMITTEES OF SAFETY

Breen, T. H. American insurgents, American patriots   973.3

UNITED STATES -- HISTORY -- REVOLUTION, 1775-1783 -- INFLUENCE

Gould, E. H. Among the powers of the earth 973.3

UNITED STATES -- HISTORY -- REVOLUTION, 1775-1783 -- SOCIAL ASPECTS

Breen, T. H. American insurgents, American patriots   973.3

UNITED STATES -- HISTORY -- SOCIETIES -- DIRECTORIES

American Association for State and Local History Directory of historical organizations in the United States and Canada   973

UNITED STATES -- HISTORY -- SOURCES

The American experience   973
Ashby, R. The great american documents   973
Daily life through American history in primary documents   973

UNITED STATES -- HISTORY -- WAR OF 1812

Taylor, A. The civil war of 1812   973.5

UNITED STATES -- HISTORY -- WAR OF 1812 -- BIOGRAPHY

Cook, J. H. American phoenix   973.5

UNITED STATES -- HISTORY -- WAR OF 1812 -- CAMPAIGNS

Vogel, S. Through the perilous fight   973.5

UNITED STATES -- HISTORY -- WAR OF 1812 -- DIPLOMATIC HISTORY

VENTRILOQUISM
 See also Amusements; Voice
VENTRILOQUISTS -- POETRY
 Fay-LeBlanc, G. Death of a ventriloquist **811**
VENTURE CAPITAL
 See also Capital
VENUS (PLANET)
 Wulf, A. Chasing Venus **523.9**
  See also Planets
VENUS (PLANET) -- EXPLORATION -- HISTORY -- 18TH CENTURY
 Anderson, M. The day the world discovered the sun
VENUS (PLANET) -- TRANSIT
 Sheehan, W. The transits of Venus **523.9**
 Wulf, A. Chasing Venus **523.9**
Venzon, Anne Cipriano
 (ed) The United States in the First World War **940.3**
VERBAL LEARNING
  See also Language and languages; Psychology of learning
Verdi with a vengeance. Berger, W. **782.1**
Verdi's Shakespeare. Wills, G. **822.3**
Verdi, Giuseppe, 1813-1901
   About
 Berger, W. Verdi with a vengeance **782.1**
 Wills, G. Verdi's Shakespeare **822.3**
Verducci, Tom
 Torre, J. The Yankee years **92**
Verdura. La Place, V. **641.6**
Veregin, Howard
 (ed) Rand McNally Goodes World Atlas **912**
Verkerk, Dorothy
 Snyder, J. Art of the Middle Ages **709.02**
Verlaine, Paul
 Selected poems **841**
Verlorene Bilder, Verlorene Leben./English
 Lost lives, lost art **709**
Vermeer and the Delft school. Liedtke, W. A. **759.9**
Vermeer, Johannes, 1632-1675
   About
 Dolnick, E. The forger's spell **759**
 Fraser, K. Ornament and silence **809**
 Liedtke, W. A. Vermeer and the Delft school **759.9**
Vermès, Géza, 1924-2013
 The changing faces of Jesus **232**
 The True Herod **92**
VERMONT
 Stansfield, C. A. Haunted Vermont **133.1**
Vernacchio, Al
 For goodness sex **613.9**
Verner, Miroslav
 The pyramids **932**
Verney family
   About
 Tinniswood, A. The Verneys **920**
The Verneys. Tinniswood, A. **920**

VERS LIBRE *See* Free verse
VERSE SATIRE, ENGLISH.
 Poems./Selections Selected poetry **821**
Versed. Armantrout, R. **811**
VERSIFICATION
  See also Authorship; Poetics; Rhythm
VERTEBRATES
  See also Animals
VERTICAL GARDENING
 Bartholomew, M. All new square foot gardening **635**
Vertigo. Auiler, D. **791.43**
VERTIGO (MOTION PICTURE)
 Auiler, D. Vertigo **791.43**
The vertigo years. Blom, P. **940.2**
The very best of recipes for health. **641.5**
A very brief history of eternity. Eire, C. M. N. **236**
A very different age. Diner, S. J. **973.8**
Very short introductions [series]
 Bushman, R. L. Mormonism **289.3**
 Catling, D. C. Astrobiology **576.8**
 Close, F. E. Nothing **530**
Vespasian, Emperor of Rome, 9-79
   About
 The twelve Caesars **878**
Vespucci, Amerigo, 1451-1512
   About
 Fernandez-Armesto, F. Amerigo **92**
VESTA (ROMAN DEITY)
  See also Gods and goddesses
VESUVIUS (ITALY)
 Scarth, A. Vesuvius: a biography **551.2**
Vesuvius: a biography. Scarth, A. **551.2**
VETERANS
 Alexander, L. Biggest brother **92**
 Bissell, T. The father of all things **959.704**
 Burgin, R. V. Islands of the damned **940.54**
 Cadillac Man Land of the lost souls **92**
 Cleland, M. Heart of a patriot **92**
 Dyer, G. The missing of the Somme **940.4**
 Guibert, E. Alan's war **741.5**
 Heard, A. The eyes of Willie McGee **364.66**
 Hillenbrand, L. Unbroken **940.54**
 Kaplan, A. Y. The interpreter **940.54**
 Nelson, J. C. The remains of Company D **920**
 Slone, L. B. After the war zone **616.85**
 Voices of war **355**
 Witter, B. Until Tuesday **362.4**
  See also Military art and science; Veterans
VETERANS -- EDUCATION
  See also Education
VETERANS -- EMPLOYMENT
 Finkel, D. Thank You for Your Service **362.86**
  See also Employment
VETERANS -- MENTAL HEALTH -- UNITED STATES -- HANDBOOKS, MANUALS, ETC

Wish I could be there. Shawn, A. 92
Wishart, David J.
  (ed) Encyclopedia of the Great Plains 978
WISHES
    See also Motivation (Psychology)
Wishful drinking. Fisher, C. 92
Wit. Edson, M. 812
WIT AND HUMOR
  Barry, D. You can date boys when you're for-
  ty 306.85
  Carlin, G. Napalm & silly putty 817
  Haubner, S. J. Zen confidential 92
  Nachman, G. Seriously funny 792.7
  Oxford dictionary of humorous quotations 808.88
  Pratchett, T. A slip of the keyboard 824
  Rothbart, D. My heart is an idiot 818
  Toasts 808.88
    See also Literature
The **wit** and wisdom of Mark Twain. Twain, M. 818
WITCHCRAFT
  Adler, M. Drawing down the moon 133.4
  Carlson, L. M. A fever in Salem 133.4
  Guiley, R. E. The encyclopedia of demons and de-
  monology 133.4
  Hoffer, P. C. The Salem witchcraft trials 345
  Hutton, R. The triumph of the moon 133.4
  Karlsen, C. F. The devil in the shape of a wom-
  an 133.4
  Robisheaux, T. The last witch of Langenburg 133.4
  Stark, R. For the glory of God 201
    See also Folklore; Occultism
WITCHCRAFT -- ENCYCLOPEDIAS
  Guiley, R. E. The encyclopedia of witches, witch-
  craft, and Wicca 133.4
WITCHCRAFT -- GERMANY -- HISTORY
  Robisheaux, T. The last witch of Langenburg 133.4
WITCHES
  Guiley, R. E. The encyclopedia of witches, witch-
  craft, and Wicca 133.4
  Ward, M. C. Voodoo queen 92
    See also Witchcraft
Witcover, Jules
  The year the dream died 973.923
With Billie. Blackburn, J. 92
With fire & sword. Nelson, J. L. 973.3
With God on our side. Martin, W. C. 261.8
With or without you. Ruta, D. 362.29
With speed and violence. Pearce, F. 551.6
With wings like eagles. Korda, M. 940.54
Without a map. Hall, M. 92
Without end. Zagajewski, A. 891.8
Without feathers. Allen, W. 817
Without saying. Howard, R. 811
Without title. Hill, G. 821
Witkowski, Jan
  (ed) The annotated and illustrated double he-

lix 572.8
Witness. Chambers, W. 92
Witness to an extreme century. Lifton, R. J. 973.92
Witness to hope: the biography of Pope John Paul II.
  Weigel, G. 92
WITNESSES
    See also Litigation; Trials
Witnesses of war. Stargardt, N. 940.53
Witt, John Fabian
  Lincoln's code 343
Witten, Edward
      About
  Mlodinow, L. Euclid's window 516
Witter, Bret
  Myron, V. Dewey 636.8
  Until Tuesday 362.4
Wittes, Tamara Cofman
  (ed) How Israelis and Palestinians negotiate 956.94
Wittgenstein family
      About
  Waugh, A. The House of Wittgenstein 920
Wittgenstein's poker. Edmonds, D. 192
Wittgenstein, Ludwig, 1889-1951
      About
  Edmonds, D. Wittgenstein's poker 192
  Gass, W. H. Finding a form: essays 814
Wittkower, Rudolf
  Art and architecture in Italy, 1600-1750 709
Wittman, Robert
  Priceless 364.1
The **wives.** Popoff, A. 891.709
WIVES
  Moore, W. How to create the perfect wife 823
  Popoff, A. The wives 891.709
    See also Family; Marriage; Married people;
  Women
The **wives** of Henry VIII. Fraser, A. 920
WIVES OF PRESIDENTS -- UNITED STATES
    See Presidents' spouses -- United States
The **wizards** of Langley. Richelson, J. 327.12
Wizenberg, Molly
  A homemade life 92
  Delancey 647.95
  Wizenberg, M. Delancey 647.95
Wodehouse. McCrum, R. 92
Wodehouse, P. G. (Pelham Grenville), 1881-1975
      About
  McCrum, R. Wodehouse 92
Woe is I. O'Conner, P. T. 428
Woestendiek, John
  Dog, Inc. 636.7
Wohlforth, Charles
  The fate of nature 304.2
  The whale and the supercomputer 305.897
WOK COOKING
  Richardson, A. The breath of a wok 641.59

Slaughter, T. P. The beautiful soul of John Woolman, apostle of abolition **92**

Wooster, Robert

(ed) Encyclopedia of Native American wars and
warfare **970.004**

The **Word** according to Eve. Murphy, C. **220.8**

WORD BOOKS *See* Picture dictionaries

WORD GAMES

See also Games; Literary recreations

Word histories and mysteries. **422**

WORD PROBLEMS (MATHEMATICS)

See also Mathematics

WORD RECOGNITION

See also Reading; Vocabulary

WORD SKILLS

See also Reading

Worden, Al

(jt. auth) French, F. Falling to Earth **92**

Worden, Alfred M., 1932-
About
French, F. Falling to Earth **92**

Worden, Minky

(ed) The unfinished revolution **305.42**

The **words.** Sartre, J. P. **92**

WORDS *See* Vocabulary; Word skills

Words and rules. Pinker, S. **401**

Words for the hour. **811**

Words to rhyme with. Espy, W. R. **423**

WORDS, NEW *See* New words

WORDS, OBSCENE

Nunberg, G. The ascent of the A-word **427**

Wordsworth, Dorothy, 1771-1855
About
Wilson, F. The ballad of Dorothy Wordsworth **92**

Wordsworth, William, 1770-1850

Selected poetry of William Wordsworth **821**
About
Bloom, H. The Western canon **809**

Johnston, K. R. The hidden Wordsworth **821**

Wilson, F. The ballad of Dorothy Wordsworth **92**

The **wordy** shipmates. Vowell, S. **974**

WORK

Crawford, M. B. Shop class as soulcraft **331**

Reeves, B. Total engagement **303.4**

Shulman, B. The betrayal of work **331.2**

Terkel, S. Working **331.2**

WORK -- SOCIAL ASPECTS

De Botton, A.   The pleasures and sorrows of
work **331**

WORK AND FAMILY

See also Family; Work

WORK AT HOME *See* Home-based business;
Telecommuting

WORK ENVIRONMENT

Annis, B. Work with me **306.3**

Penenberg, A. L. Play at work **658.4**

Williams, J. What works for women at work **650.1**

See also Environment; Work

WORK ETHIC

See also Ethics; Work

WORK GROUPS *See* Teams in the workplace

The **Work** of Charles and Ray Eames. Albrecht,
D. **745.4**

The **work** of Joe Webb. Cox, R. **728**

WORK PLACES *See* Work environment

WORK SATISFACTION *See* Job satisfaction

Work songs. Gioia, T. **782.42**

WORK TEAMS *See* Teams in the workplace

Work with me. Annis, B. **306.3**

The **work-at-home** sourcebook. Arden, L. **338.7**

WORKAHOLISM

See also Compulsive behavior

The **workbench** guide to jewelry techniques. Young,
A. **739.27**

WORKERS *See* Employees; Labor; Working class

WORKERS' COMPENSATION

See also Accident insurance; Health insurance; Social security

Working. Terkel, S. **331.2**

WORKING ANIMALS

See also Animals; Domestic animals; Economic zoology

WORKING AT HOME *See* Home-based business;
Telecommuting

WORKING CHILDREN *See* Child labor

WORKING CLASS

Dubofsky, M. Labor in America **331.8**

Freeman, J. B. Working-class New York **305.5**

Labor rising **331.880973**

Maharidge, D. Someplace like America **305.5**

Murolo, P. From the folks who brought you the
weekend **331**

Murray, C. Coming apart **305.8**

See also Social classes

**WORKING CLASS -- UNITED STATES -- BI-
OGRAPHY**

Laskas, J. M. Hidden America **305.5**

**WORKING CLASS -- UNITED STATES -- ECO-
NOMIC CONDITIONS -- 21ST CENTURY**

Barlett, D. L.   The betrayal of the American
dream **330.973**

**WORKING CLASS -- UNITED STATES -- HIS-
TORY**

Labor rising **331.880973**

Murolo, P. From the folks who brought you the
weekend **331**

**WORKING CLASS -- UNITED STATES -- SO-
CIAL CONDITIONS**

Laskas, J. M. Hidden America **305.5**

**WORKING CLASS FAMILIES -- RUSSIA (FED-
ERATION) -- OZËRSK (CHELIABINSKAIA
OBLAST) -- HISTORY -- 20TH CENTURY**

WORLD WAR, 1939-1945

Album of the damned	943.086
Alexander, L. Biggest brother	92
Atkinson, R. The guns at last light	940.54
Beevor, A. The Second World War	940.54
Brokaw, T. An album of memories	940.54
Churchill, W. Closing the ring	940.53
Churchill, W. The gathering storm	940.53
Churchill, W. The grand alliance	940.53
Churchill, W. The hinge of fate	940.53
Churchill, W. Their finest hour	940.53
Churchill, W. Triumph and tragedy	940.53
Dallas, G. 1945	940.53
Dower, J. W. Cultures of war	355
Encyclopedia of World War II	940.53
Gilbert, M. The Second World War	940.53
Glass, C. The deserters	940.54
Groom, W. 1942	940.53
Hastings, M. Armageddon: the battle for Germany, 1944-45	940.54
Hastings, M. Inferno	940.54
Hersey, J. Hiroshima	940.54
Keegan, J. The Second World War	940.53
Klein, M. A call to arms	940.53
Korda, M. Ike	92
Lineberry, C. The secret rescue	940.54
Lukacs, J. A short history of the twentieth century	909.82
Macintyre, B. Double cross	940.54
The New York Times complete World War II, 1939-1945	940.53
Overy, R. J. Why the Allies won	940.53
Rehnquist, W. H. All the laws but one	342
Reporting World War II	940.53
Roberts, A. The storm of war	940.54
Rooney, A. A. My war	940.54
Showalter, D. E. Patton and Rommel	92
Steil, B. The battle of Bretton Woods	339.5
Tobin, J. E. Ernie Pyle's war	070.4
Weinberg, G. L. A world at arms	940.53
World War II	940.53

See also Europe -- History -- 1918-1945; World history -- 20th century; World politics

WORLD WAR, 1939-1945 -- AERIAL OPERATIONS

Groom, W. The aviators	920
Lewis, D. The Dog Who Could Fly	940.54

WORLD WAR, 1939-1945 -- AERIAL OPERATIONS, AMERICAN

Ambrose, S. E. The wild blue	940.54
Cronkite, W. Cronkite's war	070.4
Grayling, A. C. Among the dead cities	940.54
Nelson, C. The first heroes	940.54
Zuckoff, M. Lost in Shangri-la	940.54

WORLD WAR, 1939-1945 -- AFRICAN AMERICANS

Kaplan, A. Y. The interpreter	940.54

See also African Americans

WORLD WAR, 1939-1945 -- AMPHIBIOUS OPERATIONS

Kennedy, P. M. Engineers of victory	940.54

See also World War, 1939-1945 -- Naval operations

WORLD WAR, 1939-1945 -- ANECDOTES

Soldaten	940.54

WORLD WAR, 1939-1945 -- ART AND THE WAR

Dolnick, E. The forger's spell	759
Scott-Clark, C. The Amber Room	940.54

See also Art

WORLD WAR, 1939-1945 -- ASIA

Bayly, C. A. Forgotten armies	940.54

WORLD WAR, 1939-1945 -- ATLANTIC OCEAN

Blair, C. Hitler's U-boat war	940.54

WORLD WAR, 1939-1945 -- ATROCITIES

Breitman, R. Official secrets	940.54
Hicks, G. The comfort women	940.54
Lewy, G. The Nazi persecution of the gypsies	940.53
Lifton, R. J. The Nazi doctors	940.53
Norman, E. M. Tears in the darkness	940.54
Snyder, T. Bloodlands	940.54
A woman in Berlin	940.53

See also Atrocities

WORLD WAR, 1939-1945 -- AUSTRIA

Weyr, T. The setting of the pearl	940.53

WORLD WAR, 1939-1945 -- BATTLES, SIEGES, ETC. *See* World War, 1939-1945 -- Aerial operations; World War, 1939-1945 -- Campaigns; World War, 1939-1945 -- Naval operations

WORLD WAR, 1939-1945 -- BIOGRAPHY

Ancell, R. M. The biographical dictionary of World War II generals and flag officers	920.003
Borneman, W. R. The admirals	920
Brighton, T. Patton, Montgomery, Rommel	920

See also Biography

WORLD WAR, 1939-1945 -- CAMPAIGNS

Ambrose, S. E. The victors	940.54
D'Este, C. Warlord	92
Hamilton, N. The mantle of command	940.54
Kennedy, P. M. Engineers of victory	940.54
Liebling, A. J. World War II writings	940.54
Megellas, J. All the way to Berlin	940.54
Patton, G. S. War as I knew it	940.54
Roberts, A. Masters and commanders	940.54
Weintraub, S. 15 stars	920
Weller, G. Weller's war	940.53

WORLD WAR, 1939-1945 -- CAMPAIGNS -- AFRICA, NORTH

Atkinson, R. An army at dawn	940.54

WORLD WAR, 1939-1945 -- CAMPAIGNS -- EASTERN FRONT

Merridale, C. Ivan's war	940.54

WORLD WAR, 1939-1945 -- DESERTIONS

Glass, C. The deserters   **940.54**

See also Military desertion

WORLD WAR, 1939-1945 -- DESTRUCTION AND PILLAGE

Harclerode, P. The lost masters   **709**

Petropoulos, J. The Faustian bargain   **709**

Pool, J. Hitler and his secret partners   **943.086**

Scott-Clark, C. The Amber Room   **940.54**

Verlorene Bilder, V. L. Lost lives, lost art   **709**

WORLD WAR, 1939-1945 -- DIPLOMATIC HISTORY

Dobbs, M. Six months in 1945   **940.53**

WORLD WAR, 1939-1945 -- ECONOMIC ASPECTS -- UNITED STATES

Herman, A. Freedom's forge   **940.53**

WORLD WAR, 1939-1945 -- EDUCATION AND THE WAR

See also Education

WORLD WAR, 1939-1945 -- ELECTRONIC INTELLIGENCE -- GREAT BRITAIN

McKay, S. The secret lives of codebreakers **940.54**

WORLD WAR, 1939-1945 -- ENCYCLOPEDIAS

Dunnigan, J. F. The Pacific War encyclopedia   **940.54**

Encyclopedia of World War II   **940.53**

WORLD WAR, 1939-1945 -- ENGLAND -- LONDON -- ANECDOTES

Cronkite, W. Cronkite's war   **070.4**

WORLD WAR, 1939-1945 -- EQUIPMENT AND SUPPLIES

See also Military weapons

WORLD WAR, 1939-1945 -- ETHICAL ASPECTS

Burleigh, M. Moral combat   **940.54**

Grayling, A. C. Among the dead cities   **940.54**

See also Ethics

WORLD WAR, 1939-1945 -- EUROPE

Ambrose, S. E. Band of brothers   **940.54**

Jordan, J. W. Brothers, rivals, victors   **940.54**

Megellas, J. All the way to Berlin   **940.54**

Pleshakov, K. Stalin's folly   **940.54**

WORLD WAR, 1939-1945 -- FINLAND

Edwards, R. The Winter War   **948.97**

WORLD WAR, 1939-1945 -- FOOD SUPPLY

Collingham, L. The taste of war   **940.53**

See also Food relief

WORLD WAR, 1939-1945 -- FORCED REPATRIATION

Shephard, B. The long road home   **940.53**

WORLD WAR, 1939-1945 -- FRANCE

Carroll, S. B. Brave genius   **920**

WORLD WAR, 1939-1945 -- FRANCE -- PARIS

Neiberg, M. The blood of free men   **940.54**

WORLD WAR, 1939-1945 -- GERMANY

Weale, A. Army of evil   **940.54**

WORLD WAR, 1939-1945 -- GERMANY -- POETRY

Across the land and the water   **831**

WORLD WAR, 1939-1945 -- GOVERNMENTS IN EXILE

See also World War, 1939-1945 -- Diplomatic history

WORLD WAR, 1939-1945 -- GRAPHIC NOVELS

Guibert, E. Alan's war   **741.5**

WORLD WAR, 1939-1945 -- GREAT BRITAIN

Manchester, W. The last lion, Winston Spencer Churchill   **92**

McKay, S. The secret lives of codebreakers **940.54**

WORLD WAR, 1939-1945 -- GREAT BRITAIN -- LITERATURE AND THE WAR

Swift, D. Bomber County   **821**

WORLD WAR, 1939-1945 -- GUERRILLAS *See* World War, 1939-1945 -- Underground movements

WORLD WAR, 1939-1945 -- HISTORIOGRAPHY

Reynolds, D. In command of history   **940.53**

WORLD WAR, 1939-1945 -- HUMOR

See also Wit and humor

WORLD WAR, 1939-1945 -- HUNGARY

Szegedy-Maszák, M. I kiss your hands many times   **920**

WORLD WAR, 1939-1945 -- INFLUENCE

Ballard, J. G. Miracles of life   **823**

Buruma, I. Year zero   **940.53**

WORLD WAR, 1939-1945 -- ITALY

Caddick-Adams, P. Monte Cassino   **940.54**

Mussolini's death march   **940.54**

WORLD WAR, 1939-1945 -- JAPAN

Hotta, E. Japan 1941   **940.54**

WORLD WAR, 1939-1945 -- JAPAN -- HIROSHIMA-SHI

Ham, P. Hiroshima Nagasaki   **940.54**

WORLD WAR, 1939-1945 -- JAPAN -- HISTORIOGRAPHY

Dower, J. W. Ways of forgetting, ways of remembering   **940.53**

WORLD WAR, 1939-1945 -- JAPAN -- NAGASAKI-SHI

Ham, P. Hiroshima Nagasaki   **940.54**

WORLD WAR, 1939-1945 -- JEWS

Maitland, L. Crossing the borders of time   **940.53**

See also Jews

WORLD WAR, 1939-1945 -- JEWS -- DRAMA

Goodrich, F. The diary of Anne Frank   **812**

WORLD WAR, 1939-1945 -- JEWS -- EUROPE -- ENCYCLOPEDIAS

The United States Holocaust Memorial Museum encyclopedia of camps and ghettos, 1933-1945   **940.53**

WORLD WAR, 1939-1945 -- JEWS -- FRANCE

gl   **614.5**

Karski, J. Story of a secret state   **940.53**

Kochanski, H. The Eagle Unbowed   **940.53**

WORLD WAR, 1939-1945 -- PRISONERS AND PRISONS

At the edge of the abyss   **940.53**

Mussolini's death march   **940.54**

The United States Holocaust Memorial Museum encyclopedia of camps and ghettos, 1933-1945   **940.53**

See also Concentration camps; Prisoners of war; Prisons

WORLD WAR, 1939-1945 -- PRISONERS AND PRISONS, AMERICAN

Colors of confinement   **940.53**

WORLD WAR, 1939-1945 -- PRISONERS AND PRISONS, BRITISH

Soldaten   **940.54**

WORLD WAR, 1939-1945 -- PRISONERS AND PRISONS, GERMAN

Soldaten   **940.54**

WORLD WAR, 1939-1945 -- PRISONERS AND PRISONS, JAPANESE

Norman, E. M. Tears in the darkness   **940.54**

WORLD WAR, 1939-1945 -- PROPAGANDA

Conant, J. The irregulars   **940.54**

Fussell, P. Wartime: understanding and behavior in the Second World War   **940.54**

See also Propaganda

WORLD WAR, 1939-1945 -- PSYCHOLOGICAL ASPECTS

Glass, C. The deserters   **940.54**

WORLD WAR, 1939-1945 -- PUBLIC OPINION

See also Public opinion

WORLD WAR, 1939-1945 -- QUOTATIONS

World War II   **940.53**

WORLD WAR, 1939-1945 -- RECONSTRUCTION *See* Reconstruction (1939-1951)

WORLD WAR, 1939-1945 -- REFUGEES

Shephard, B. The long road home   **940.53**

See also Political refugees

WORLD WAR, 1939-1945 -- REFUGEES -- FRANCE -- BIOGRAPHY

Maitland, L. Crossing the borders of time   **940.53**

WORLD WAR, 1939-1945 -- REPARATIONS

Japanese Americans, from relocation to redress   **940.53**

See also Reconstruction (1939-1951); World War, 1939-1945 -- Economic aspects

WORLD WAR, 1939-1945 -- RESISTANCE MOVEMENTS *See* World War, 1939-1945 -- Underground movements

WORLD WAR, 1939-1945 -- SCIENCE -- GERMANY

Biddle, W. Dark side of the moon   **92**

Cassidy, D. C. Beyond uncertainty   **92**

WORLD WAR, 1939-1945 -- SEARCH AND RESCUE OPERATIONS

Zuckoff, M. Lost in Shangri-la   **940.54**

WORLD WAR, 1939-1945 -- SECRET SERVICE

Talty, S. Agent Garbo   **940.5**

See also Secret service

WORLD WAR, 1939-1945 -- SECRET SERVICE -- SOVIET UNION

Sheinkin, S. Bomb   **623.4**

WORLD WAR, 1939-1945 -- SECRET SERVICE -- UNITED STATES

Conant, J. A covert affair   **940.54**

Conant, J. The irregulars   **940.54**

Woods, R. B. Shadow warrior   **327.127**

WORLD WAR, 1939-1945 -- SOCIAL ASPECTS -- JAPAN

Dower, J. W. Ways of forgetting, ways of remembering   **940.53**

WORLD WAR, 1939-1945 -- SOCIAL ASPECTS -- POLAND

Kochanski, H. The Eagle Unbowed   **940.53**

WORLD WAR, 1939-1945 -- SOVIET UNION

Merridale, C. Ivan's war   **940.54**

Roberts, G. Stalin's general   **940.54**

WORLD WAR, 1939-1945 -- TENNESSEE -- OAK RIDGE

Kiernan, D. The girls of atomic city   **976.8**

WORLD WAR, 1939-1945 -- THEATER AND THE WAR

See also Theater

WORLD WAR, 1939-1945 -- TRANSPORTATION

See also Transportation

WORLD WAR, 1939-1945 -- TREATIES

See also Treaties

WORLD WAR, 1939-1945 -- UNDERGROUND MOVEMENTS

The lone assassin   **943.086**

WORLD WAR, 1939-1945 -- UNDERGROUND MOVEMENTS -- FRANCE

Carroll, S. B. Brave genius   **920**

WORLD WAR, 1939-1945 -- UNDERGROUND MOVEMENTS -- POLAND

Allen, A. The fantastic laboratory of Dr. Weigl   **614.5**

WORLD WAR, 1939-1945 -- UNITED STATES

Fullilove, M. Rendezvous with destiny   **973.917**

Hamilton, N. The mantle of command   **940.54**

Moe, R. Roosevelt's second act   **973.917**

Olson, L. Those angry days   **940.53**

WORLD WAR, 1939-1945 -- UNITED STATES -- BIOGRAPHY

Hamilton, N. The mantle of command   **940.54**

WORLD WAR, 1939-1945 -- VETERANS

See also Veterans

WORLD WAR, 1939-1945 -- WAR CORRESPON-